Directory of Business Information Resources

2007

Fourteenth Edition

Directory of Business Information Resources

- Associations
- Newsletters
- Magazines & Journals
- Trade Shows
- Directories & Databases
- Web Sites

MILLERTON, NY 12546

PUBLISHER: Leslie Mackenzie
EDITOR: Richard Gottlieb
EDITORIAL DIRECTOR: Laura Mars-Proietti

PRODUCTION MANAGER: Karen Stevens
PRODUCTION ASSISTANTS: Kayla Mathers, Heather Stuermer

MARKETING DIRECTOR: Jessica Moody

Grey House Publishing, Inc.
185 Millerton Road
Millerton, NY 12546
518.789.8700
FAX 518.789.0545
www.greyhouse.com
e-mail: books @greyhouse.com

First edition published 1992
Fourteenth edition published 2007
Printed in the USA

The directory of business information resources. – 1992-2007

v. ; 27.5 cm.
Annual
Other title: Business information resources

1. Business information services – United States – Directories. 2. Reference books – Business – Bibliography – Periodicals. 3. Association, institutions, etc. – United States – Directories. 4. Business – Databases – Directories. 5. Trade shows – Directories. I. Title: Business information resources.
HF54.52.U5 D56
016.65
ISBN: 978-1-59237-146-4 softcover

Table of Contents

Chapters in this directory often include a wide range of topics, many of which appear in more than one chapter. A list of the subjects covered in each chapter follows this Table of Contents.

Introduction

This is the fourteenth edition of *The Directory of Business Information Resources*. It continues to be recognized as the premier reference book for business researchers covering 98 industries, from *Accounting* to *Wholesale Services*. Each chapter includes a wide variety of valuable industry-specific resources, including Associations, Magazines, Journals, Newsletters, Trade Shows, Directories, Databases and Web Sites. With over 22,000 listings, including 924 brand new listings and thousands of updates, the 2007 edition is the most comprehensive guide to business information on the market today. It is also available in a fully searchable Online Database.

Recent surveys, both private and from the Department of Labor, on the top high-growth industries -- those expected to average 30% growth over the next five years -- show a shift from goods-producing to **Service Providing**, as US firms continue to outsource manufacturing jobs offshore, where labor is less-expensive. **Educational & Health Services** continue to grow, due to rising student enrollments and an aging population. **Professional & Business Services**, especially **Employment Services,** are on the rise**. Leisure & Hospitality** will see an increase, specifically **Physical Fitness & Exercise.** And significant growth is anticipated for both **Information** and **Financial Services.** Following this Introduction is a report from the Bureau of Labor Statistics -- *Tomorrow's Jobs* – which details the how and why of business and job growth.

A quick look at the Table of Contents shows this 2007 edition of *The Directory of Business Information Resources* covers all the largest industries, including Healthcare, Drugs & Pharmaceutical, Computers & Data Processing, Banking, Financial Services, Credit & Lending Services, Internet, Broadcasting, Communications & Media, Environment & Conservation, Safety & Security, Management, Marketing, Hotels & Motels, Performing Arts, Restaurants, Sports & Recreation, and Travel.

Business researchers will find the resources they need for 98 industries. All chapters include industry-specific Associations, Newsletters, Magazines, Journals, Trade Shows, Directories, Databases and Web Sites.

When the first edition of *The Directory of Business Information Resources* was published in 1992, the wide range of information included was scattered over a dozen expensive directories, often available only at the largest libraries. Even then, chances of finding the most current editions of appropriate resources were slim. Now, as many sources for information shift from print to electronic formats, they are sometimes even more scattered and less reliable. Thus, the value of the current, comprehensive data found in this latest edition has never been more valuable.

The Directory of Business Information Resources answers the need for well-organized, accessible business information for market researchers, advertising agencies, job placement and career planning offices, public relations personnel, and business schools and colleges – a need well-documented by one of the identified high-growth sectors: **Information!**

Numbers for this edition: 5,484 associations, 2,784 newsletters, 4,886 magazines and journals, 3,056 trade shows, 2,624 directories and databases, and 247 international resources. Further details show 17,045 contact names, 17,106 fax numbers, 15,853 web sites, and 13,799 e-mail addresses.

Important features of this edition:

1. The **Table of Contents** is an alphabetical list of the 98 industries covered.

2. The **Content Summary of Chapter Listings** helps users see the wide range of topics included in each chapter, many of which appear in more than one chapter. It is designed to show exactly what is covered in each chapter.

3. The **Standard Industrial Code (SIC) Cross Reference Table** is included for users who wish to approach their topic based on the Department of Labor's standardized list of business codes. This recently expanded table links the SIC to appropriate chapters in the Directory.

4. Each of the 22,111 entries include name, address, phone, fax, web site, e-mail, and a brief description. Associations may include number of members, dues, and founding year. Publications may include cost and frequency. Trade shows may include time, place, number of exhibitors and attendees. Entries are numbered sequentially. See the **Users Guide** on the following pages for a detailed look at each field of data.

5. This edition has two indexes.

   Entry Index – an alphabetical list of all entries, identified by entry number.

   Publisher Index – an alphabetical list of publishers of industry literature. The entry number listed in the index identifies the title of the published material listed in this directory. It's important to note, however, that these publishers often offer additional material not included in these pages.

As always, we welcome comments and suggestions for continuous improvement, and encourage users of both the print and online versions of *The Directory of Business Information Resources* to bring new and unlisted business resources to our attention.

Tomorrow's Jobs

Making informed career decisions requires reliable information about opportunities in the future. Opportunities result from the relationships between the population, labor force, and the demand for goods and services.

Population ultimately limits the size of the labor force—individuals working or looking for work—which constrains how much can be produced. Demand for various goods and services determines employment in the industries providing them. Occupational employment opportunities, in turn, result from demand for skills needed within specific industries. Opportunities for medical assistants and other healthcare occupations, for example, have surged in response to rapid growth in demand for health services.

Examining the past and projecting changes in these relationships is the foundation of the Occupational Outlook Program. This chapter presents highlights of Bureau of Labor Statistics projections of the labor force and occupational and industry employment that can help to guide your career plans.

Population

Population trends affect employment opportunities in a number of ways. Changes in population influence the demand for goods and services. For example, a growing and aging population has increased the demand for health services. Equally important, population changes produce corresponding changes in the size and demographic composition of the labor force.

The U.S. civilian noninstitutional population is expected to increase by 23.9 million over the 2004-14 period, at a slower rate of growth than during both the 1994-2004 and 1984-94 periods (chart 1). Continued growth will mean more consumers of goods and services, spurring demand for workers in a wide range of occupations and industries. The effects of population growth on various occupations will differ. The differences are partially accounted for by the age distribution of the future population.

Chart 1. **Percent change in the population and labor force, 1984-1994, 1994-2004, and projected 2004-2014**

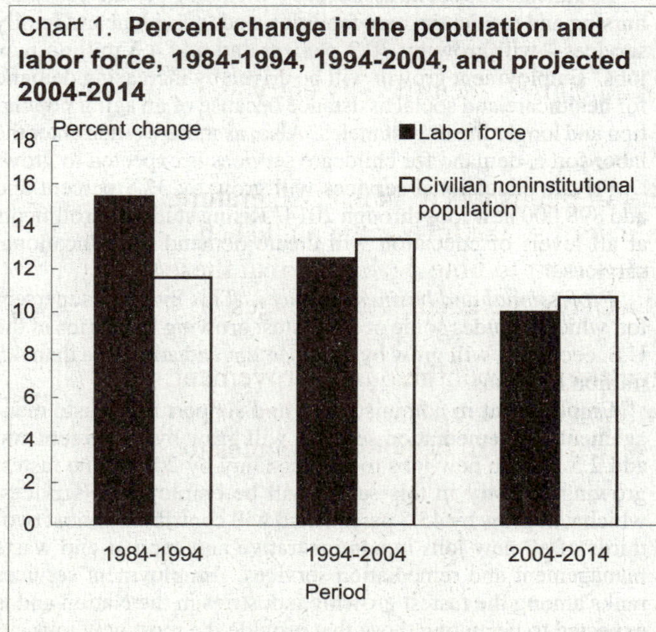

The youth population, aged 16 to 24, will grow 2.9 percent over the 2004-14 period. As the baby boomers continue to age, the group aged 55 to 64 will increase by 36 percent or 10.4 million persons, more than any other group. The group aged 35 to 44 will decrease in size, reflecting the birth dearth following the baby boom generation.

Minorities and immigrants will constitute a larger share of the U.S. population in 2014. The number of Hispanics is projected to continue to grow much faster than those of all other racial and ethnic groups.

Labor force

Population is the single most important factor in determining the size and composition of the labor force—that is, people who are either working or looking for work. The civilian labor force is projected to increase by 14.7 million, or 10 percent, to 162.1 million over the 2004-14 period.

The U.S. workforce will become more diverse by 2014. White, non-Hispanic persons will continue to make up a decreasing share of the labor force, falling from 70 percent in 2004 to 65.6 percent in 2014 (chart 2). However, despite relatively slow growth, white, non-Hispanics will remain the largest group in the labor force in 2014. Asians are projected to account for an increasing share of the labor force by 2014, growing from 4.3 to 5.1 percent. Hispanics are projected be the fastest growing of the four labor force groups, growing by 33.7 percent. By 2014, Hispanics will continue to constitute a larger proportion of the labor force than will blacks, whose share will grow from 11.3 percent to 12.0 percent.

The numbers of men and women in the labor force will grow, but the number of women will grow at a faster rate than the number of men. The male labor force is projected to grow by 9.1 percent from 2004 to 2014, compared with 10.9 percent for

Chart 2. **Percent of labor force by race and ethnic origin, 2004 and projected 2014**

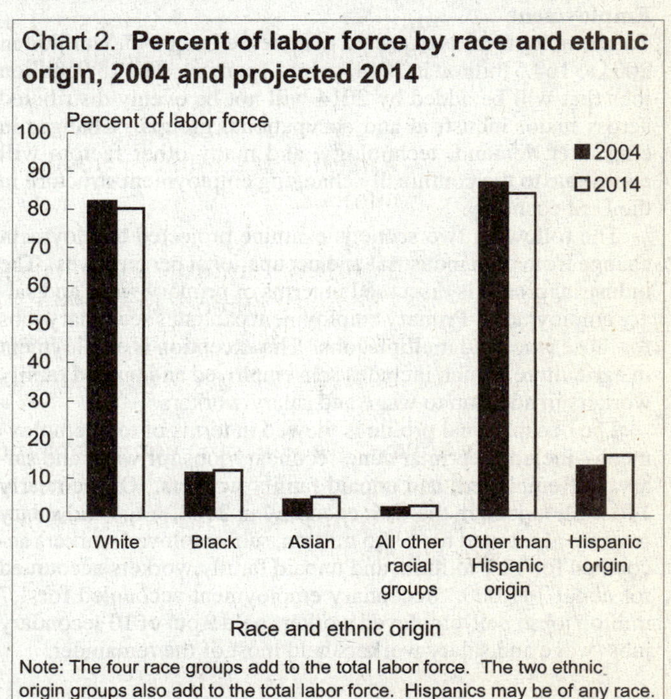

Note: The four race groups add to the total labor force. The two ethnic origin groups also add to the total labor force. Hispanics may be of any race.

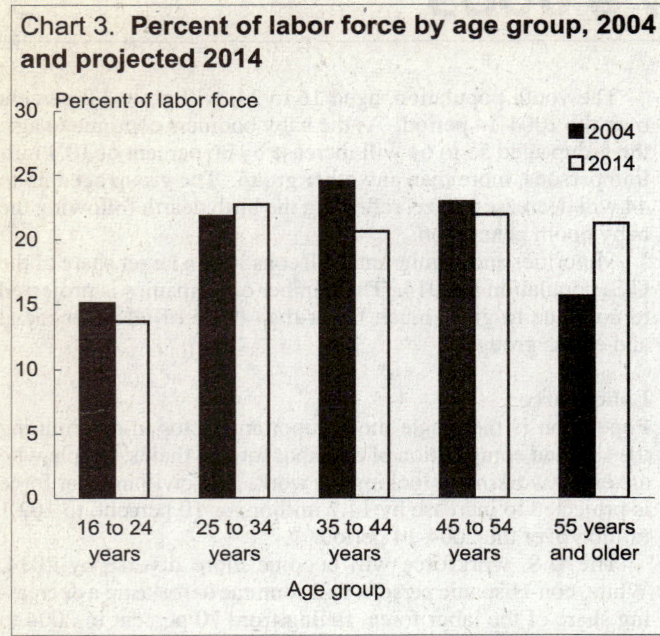

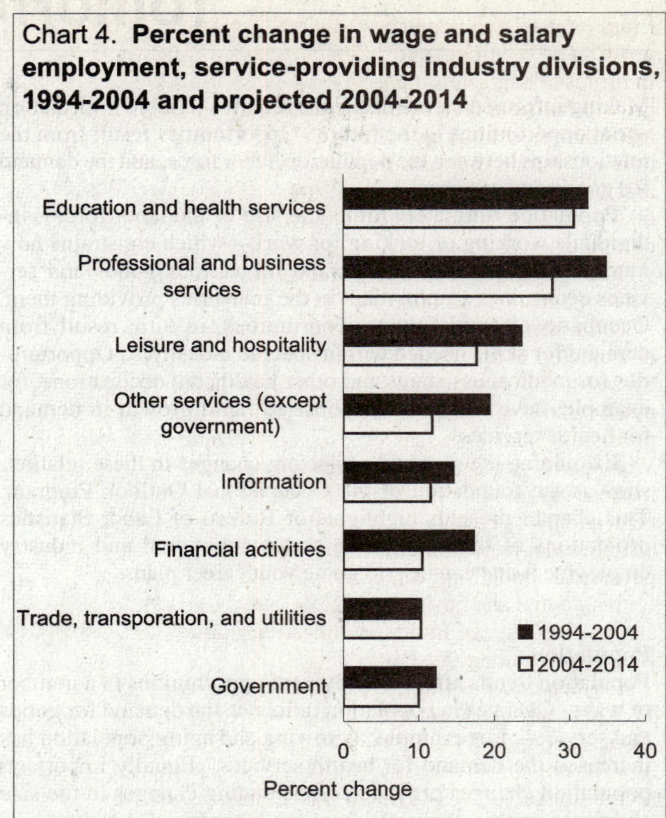

women. As a result, men's share of the labor force is expected to decrease from 53.6 to 53.2 percent, while women's share is expected to increase from 46.4 to 46.8 percent.

The youth labor force, aged 16 to 24, is expected to slightly decrease its share of the labor force to 13.7 percent by 2014. The primary working age group, between 25 and 54 years old, is projected to decline from 69.3 percent of the labor force in 2004 to 65.2 percent by 2014. Workers 55 and older, on the other hand, are projected to increase from 15.6 percent to 21.2 percent of the labor force between 2004 and 2014, due to the aging of the baby-boom generation (chart 3).

Employment

Total employment is expected to increase from 145.6 million in 2004 to 164.5 million in 2014, or by 13 percent. The 18.9 million jobs that will be added by 2014 will not be evenly distributed across major industrial and occupational groups. Changes in consumer demand, technology, and many other factors will contribute to the continually changing employment structure in the U.S. economy.

The following two sections examine projected employment change from both industrial and occupational perspectives. The industrial profile is discussed in terms of primary wage and salary employment. Primary employment excludes secondary jobs for those who hold multiple jobs. The exception is employment in agriculture, which includes self-employed and unpaid family workers in addition to wage and salary workers.

The occupational profile is viewed in terms of total employment—including primary and secondary jobs for wage and salary, self-employed, and unpaid family workers. Of the nearly 146 million jobs in the U.S. economy in 2004, wage and salary workers accounted for 133.5 million; self-employed workers accounted for 12.1 million; and unpaid family workers accounted for about 141,000. Secondary employment accounted for 1.7 million jobs. Self-employed workers held 9 out of 10 secondary jobs; wage and salary workers held most of the remainder.

Industry

Service-providing industries. The long-term shift from goods-producing to service-providing employment is expected to continue. Service-providing industries are expected to account for approximately 18.7 million of the 18.9 million new wage and salary jobs generated over the 2004-14 period (chart 4).

Education and health services. This industry supersector is projected to grow faster, 30.6 percent, and add more jobs than any other industry supersector. About 3 out of every 10 new jobs created in the U.S. economy will be in either the healthcare and social assistance or private educational services sectors.

Healthcare and social assistance—including private hospitals, nursing and residential care facilities, and individual and family services—will grow by 30.3 percent and add 4.3 million new jobs. Employment growth will be driven by increasing demand for healthcare and social assistance because of an aging population and longer life expectancies. Also, as more women enter the labor force, demand for childcare services is expected to grow.

Private educational services will grow by 32.5 percent and add 898,000 new jobs through 2014. Rising student enrollments at all levels of education will create demand for educational services.

Professional and business services. This industry supersector, which includes some of the fastest growing industries in the U.S. economy, will grow by 27.8 percent and add more than 4.5 million new jobs.

Employment in administrative and support and waste management and remediation services will grow by 31 percent and add 2.5 million new jobs to the economy by 2014. The fastest growing industry in this sector will be employment services, which will grow by 45.5 percent and will contribute almost two-thirds of all new jobs in administrative and support and waste management and remediation services. Employment services ranks among the fastest growing industries in the Nation and is expected to be among those that provide the most new jobs.

Employment in professional, scientific, and technical services will grow by 28.4 percent and add 1.9 million new jobs by 2014.

Employment in computer systems design and related services will grow by 39.5 percent and add almost one-fourth of all new jobs in professional, scientific, and technical services. Employment growth will be driven by the increasing reliance of businesses on information technology and the continuing importance of maintaining system and network security. Management, scientific, and technical consulting services also will grow very rapidly, by 60.5 percent, spurred by the increased use of new technology and computer software and the growing complexity of business.

Management of companies and enterprises will grow by 10.6 percent and add 182,000 new jobs.

Information. Employment in the information supersector is expected to increase by 11.6 percent, adding 364,000 jobs by 2014. Information contains some of the fast-growing computer-related industries such as software publishers; Internet publishing and broadcasting; and Internet service providers, Web search portals, and data processing services. Employment in these industries is expected to grow by 67.6 percent, 43.5 percent, and 27.8 percent, respectively. The information supersector also includes telecommunications, broadcasting, and newspaper, periodical, book, and directory publishers. Increased demand for residential and business land-line and wireless services, cable service, high-speed Internet connections, and software will fuel job growth among these industries.

Leisure and hospitality. Overall employment will grow by 17.7 percent. Arts, entertainment, and recreation will grow by 25 percent and add 460,000 new jobs by 2014. Most of these new job openings will come from the amusement, gambling, and recreation sector. Job growth will stem from public participation in arts, entertainment, and recreation activities—reflecting increasing incomes, leisure time, and awareness of the health benefits of physical fitness.

Accommodation and food services is expected to grow by 16.5 percent and add 1.8 million new jobs through 2014. Job growth will be concentrated in food services and drinking places, reflecting increases in population, dual-income families, and dining sophistication.

Trade, transportation, and utilities. Overall employment in this industry supersector will grow by 10.3 percent between 2004 and 2014. Transportation and warehousing is expected to increase by 506,000 jobs, or by 11.9 percent through 2014. Truck transportation will grow by 9.6 percent, adding 129,000 new jobs, while rail transportation is projected to decline. The warehousing and storage sector is projected to grow rapidly at 24.8 percent, adding 138,000 jobs. Demand for truck transportation and warehousing services will expand as many manufacturers concentrate on their core competencies and contract out their product transportation and storage functions.

Employment in retail trade is expected to increase by 11 percent, from 15 million to 16.7 million. Increases in population, personal income, and leisure time will contribute to employment growth in this industry, as consumers demand more goods. Wholesale trade is expected to increase by 8.4 percent, growing from 5.7 million to 6.1 million jobs.

Employment in utilities is projected to decrease by 1.3 percent through 2014. Despite increased output, employment in electric power generation, transmission, and distribution and natural gas distribution is expected to decline through 2014 due to improved technology that increases worker productivity. However, employment in water, sewage, and other systems is expected to increase 21 percent by 2014. Jobs are not easily eliminated by technological gains in this industry because water treatment and waste disposal are very labor-intensive activities.

Financial activities. Employment is projected to grow 10.5 percent over the 2004-14 period. Real estate and rental and leasing is expected to grow by 16.9 percent and add 353,000 jobs by 2014. Growth will be due, in part, to increased demand for housing as the population grows. The fastest growing industry in the financial activities supersector will be activities related to real estate, which will grow by 32.1 percent, reflecting the housing boom that persists throughout most of the Nation.

Finance and insurance is expected to increase by 496,000 jobs, or 8.3 percent, by 2014. Employment in securities, commodity contracts, and other financial investments and related activities is expected to grow 15.8 percent by 2014, reflecting the increased number of baby boomers in their peak savings years, the growth of tax-favorable retirement plans, and the globalization of the securities markets. Employment in credit intermediation and related services, including banks, will grow by 5.4 percent and add about one-third of all new jobs within finance and insurance. Insurance carriers and related activities is expected to grow by 9.5 percent and add 215,000 new jobs by 2014. The number of jobs within agencies, brokerages, and other insurance related activities is expected to grow about 19.4 percent, as many insurance carriers downsize their sales staffs and as agents set up their own businesses.

Government. Between 2004 and 2014, government employment, including that in public education and hospitals, is expected to increase by 10 percent, from 21.6 million to 23.8 million jobs. Growth in government employment will be fueled by growth in State and local educational services and the shift of responsibilities from the Federal Government to the State and local governments. Local government educational services is projected to increase 10 percent, adding 783,000 jobs. State government educational services is projected to grow by 19.6 percent, adding 442,000 jobs. Federal Government employment, including the Postal Service, is expected to increase by only 1.6 percent as the Federal Government continues to contract out many government jobs to private companies.

Other services (except government). Employment will grow by 14 percent. More than 1 out of every 4 new jobs in this supersector will be in religious organizations, which is expected to grow by 11.9 percent. Other automotive repair and maintenance will be the fastest growing industry at 30.7 percent. Also included among other services is personal care services, which is expected to increase by 19.5 percent

Goods-producing industries. Employment in the goods-producing industries has been relatively stagnant since the early 1980s. Overall, this sector is expected to decline 0.4 percent over the 2004-14 period. Although employment is expected to decline or increase more slowly than in the service-providing industries, projected growth among goods-producing industries varies considerably (chart 5).

Construction. Employment in construction is expected to increase by 11.4 percent, from 7 million to 7.8 million. Demand for new housing and an increase in road, bridge, and tunnel construction will account for the bulk of job growth in this supersector.

Manufacturing. Employment change in manufacturing will vary by individual industry, but overall employment in this supersector will decline by 5.4 percent or 777,000 jobs. For example, employment in transportation equipment manufacturing is expected to grow by 95,000 jobs. Due to an aging population and increasing life expectancies, pharmaceutical and medicine manufacturing is expected to grow by 26.1 percent and add 76,000 jobs through 2014. However, productivity gains, job automation, and international competition will adversely affect

Chart 5. **Percent change in wage and salary employment, goods-producing industry divisions, 1994-2004 and projected 2004-2014**

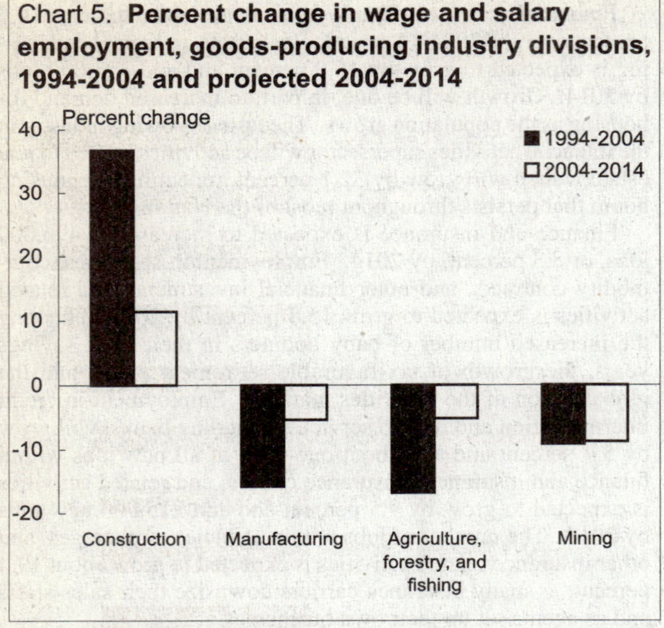

Chart 6. **Percent change in total employment by major occupational group, projected 2004-2014**

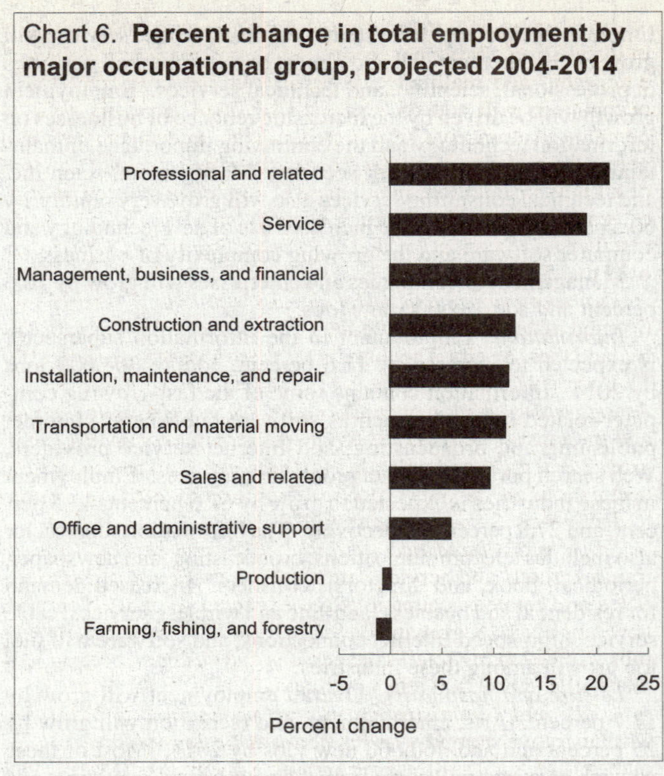

employment in many other manufacturing industries. Employment in textile mills and apparel manufacturing will decline by 119,000 and 170,000 jobs, respectively. Employment in computer and electronic product manufacturing also will decline by 94,000 jobs through 2014.

Agriculture, forestry, fishing, and hunting. Overall employment in agriculture, forestry, fishing, and hunting is expected to decrease by 5.2 percent. Employment is expected to continue to decline due to advancements in technology. The only industry within this supersector expected to grow is support activities for agriculture and forestry, which includes farm labor contractors and farm management services. This industry is expected to grow by 18.2 percent and add 19,000 new jobs.

Mining. Employment in mining is expected to decrease 8.8 percent, or by some 46,000 jobs, by 2014. Employment in coal mining and metal ore mining is expected to decline by 23.3 percent and 29.3 percent, respectively. Employment in oil and gas extraction also is projected to decline by 13.1 percent through 2014. Employment decreases in these industries are attributable mainly to technology gains that boost worker productivity, growing international competition, restricted access to Federal lands, and strict environmental regulations that require cleaning of burning fuels.

Occupation

Expansion of service-providing industries is expected to continue, creating demand for many occupations. However, projected job growth varies among major occupational groups (chart 6).

Professional and related occupations. Professional and related occupations will grow the fastest and add more new jobs than any other major occupational group. Over the 2004-14 period, a 21.2 percent increase in the number of professional and related jobs is projected, which translates into 6 million new jobs. Professional and related workers perform a wide variety of duties, and are employed throughout private industry and government. About three-quarters of the job growth will come from three groups of professional occupations—computer and mathematical occupations, healthcare practitioners and technical occupations, and education, training, and library occupations—which will add 4.5 million jobs combined.

Service occupations. Service workers perform services for the public. Employment in service occupations is projected to increase by 5.3 million, or 19 percent, the second largest numerical gain and second highest rate of growth among the major occupational groups. Food preparation and serving related occupations are expected to add the most jobs among the service occupations, 1.7 million by 2014. However, healthcare support occupations are expected to grow the fastest, 33.3 percent, adding 1.2 million new jobs.

Management, business, and financial occupations. Workers in management, business, and financial occupations plan and direct the activities of business, government, and other organizations. Their employment is expected to increase by 2.2 million, or 14.4 percent, by 2014. Among managers, the numbers of preschool and childcare center/program educational administrators and of computer and information systems managers will grow the fastest, by 27.9 percent and 25.9 percent, respectively. General and operations managers will add the most new jobs, 308,000, by 2014. Farmers and ranchers are the only workers in this major occupational group whose numbers are expected to decline, losing 155,000 jobs. Among business and financial occupations, accountants and auditors and management analysts will add the most jobs, 386,000 combined. Employment, recruitment, and placement specialists and personal financial advisors will be the fastest growing occupations in this group, with job increases of 30.5 percent and 25.9 percent, respectively.

Construction and extraction occupations. Construction and extraction workers construct new residential and commercial buildings, and also work in mines, quarries, and oil and gas fields. Employment of these workers is expected to grow 12 percent, adding 931,000 new jobs. Construction trades and related workers will account for more than three-fourths of these new jobs, 699,000, by 2014. Many extraction occupations will decline, reflecting overall employment losses in the mining and oil and gas extraction industries.

Installation, maintenance, and repair occupations. Workers in installation, maintenance, and repair occupations install new equipment and maintain and repair older equipment. These occupations will add 657,000 jobs by 2014, growing by 11.4 percent. Automotive service technicians and mechanics and general maintenance and repair workers will account for half of all new installation, maintenance, and repair jobs. The fastest growth rate will be among security and fire alarm systems installers, an occupation that is expected to grow 21.7 percent over the 2004-14 period.

Transportation and material moving occupations. Transportation and material moving workers transport people and materials by land, sea, or air. The number of these workers should grow 11.1 percent, accounting for 1.1 million additional jobs by 2014. Among transportation occupations, motor vehicle operators will add the most jobs, 629,000. Material moving occupations will grow 8.3 percent and will add 405,000 jobs. Rail transportation occupations are the only group in which employment is projected to decline, by 1.1 percent, through 2014.

Sales and related occupations. Sales and related workers transfer goods and services among businesses and consumers. Sales and related occupations are expected to add 1.5 million new jobs by 2014, growing by 9.6 percent. The majority of these jobs will be among retail salespersons and cashiers, occupations that will add 849,000 jobs combined.

Office and administrative support occupations. Office and administrative support workers perform the day-to-day activities of the office, such as preparing and filing documents, dealing with the public, and distributing information. Employment in these occupations is expected to grow by 5.8 percent, adding 1.4 million new jobs by 2014. Customer service representatives will add the most new jobs, 471,000. Desktop publishers will be among the fastest growing occupations in this group, increasing by 23.2 percent over the decade. However, due to rising productivity and increased automation, office and administrative support occupations also account for 11 of the 20 occupations with the largest employment declines.

Farming, fishing, and forestry occupations. Farming, fishing, and forestry workers cultivate plants, breed and raise livestock, and catch animals. These occupations will decline 1.3 percent and lose 13,000 jobs by 2014. Agricultural workers, including farmworkers and laborers, accounted for the overwhelming majority of new jobs in this group. The number of fishing and hunting workers is expected to decline, by 16.6, percent, while the number of logging workers is expected to increase by less than 1 percent.

Production occupations. Production workers are employed mainly in manufacturing, where they assemble goods and operate plants. Production occupations are expected to decline less than 1 percent, losing 79,000 jobs by 2014. Jobs will be created for many production occupations, including food processing workers, machinists, and welders, cutters, solderers, and brazers. Textile, apparel, and furnishings occupations, as well as assemblers and fabricators, will account for much of the job losses among production occupations.

Among all occupations in the economy, computer and healthcare occupations are expected to grow the fastest over the projection period (chart 7). In fact, healthcare occupations make up 12 of the 20 fastest growing occupations, while computer occupations account for 5 out of the 20 fastest growing occupations in the economy. In addition to high growth rates, these 17 computer and healthcare occupations combined will add more than 1.8 million new jobs. High growth rates among computer and healthcare occupations reflect projected rapid growth in the computer and data processing and health services industries.

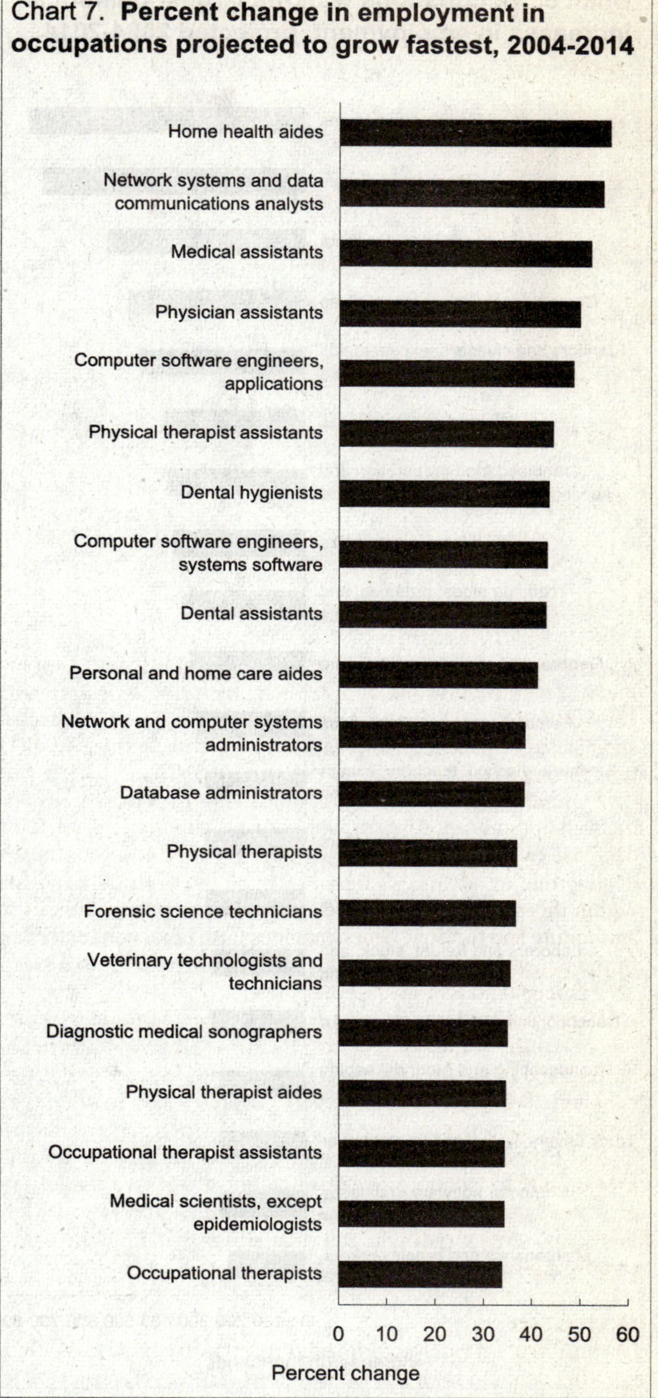

The 20 occupations listed in chart 8 will account for more than one-third of all new jobs, 7.1 million combined, over the 2004-14 period. The occupations with the largest numerical increases cover a wider range of occupational categories than do those occupations with the fastest growth rates. Health occupations will account for some of these increases in employment, as well as occupations in education, sales, transportation, office and administrative support, and food service. Many of these occupations are very large, and will create more new jobs than will those with high growth rates. Only 3 out of the 20 fastest

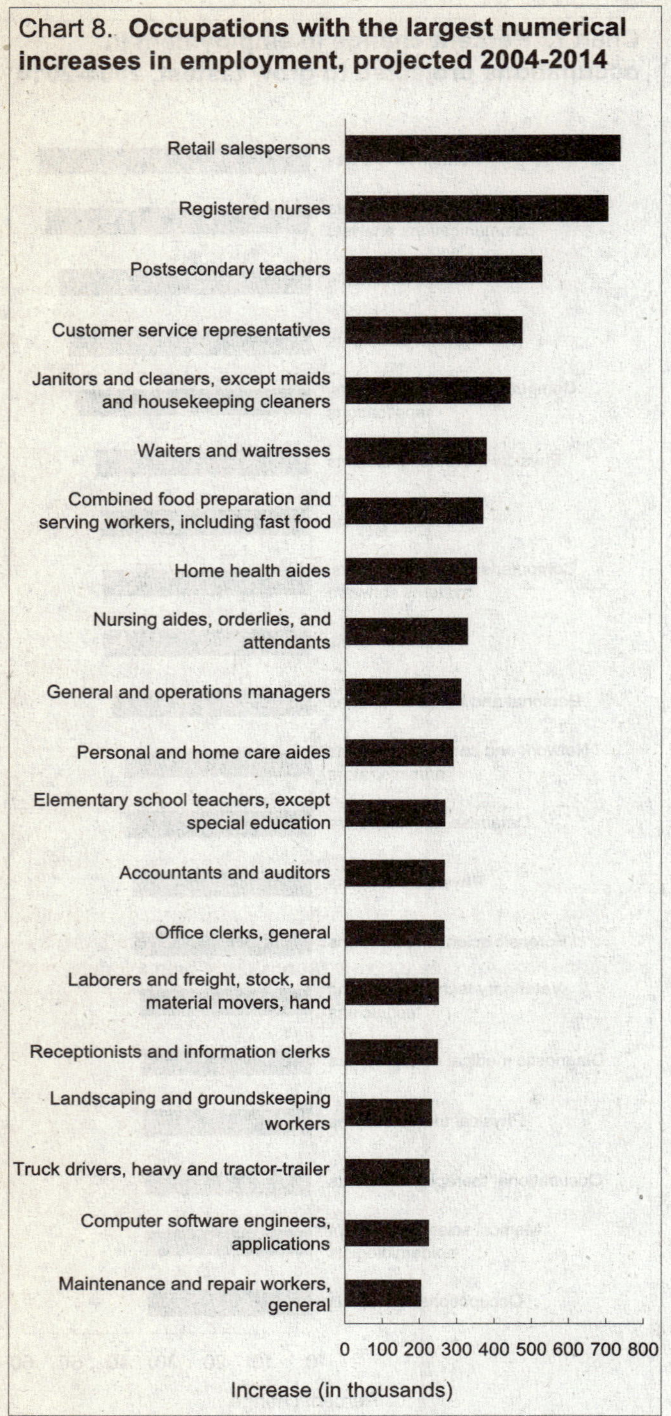

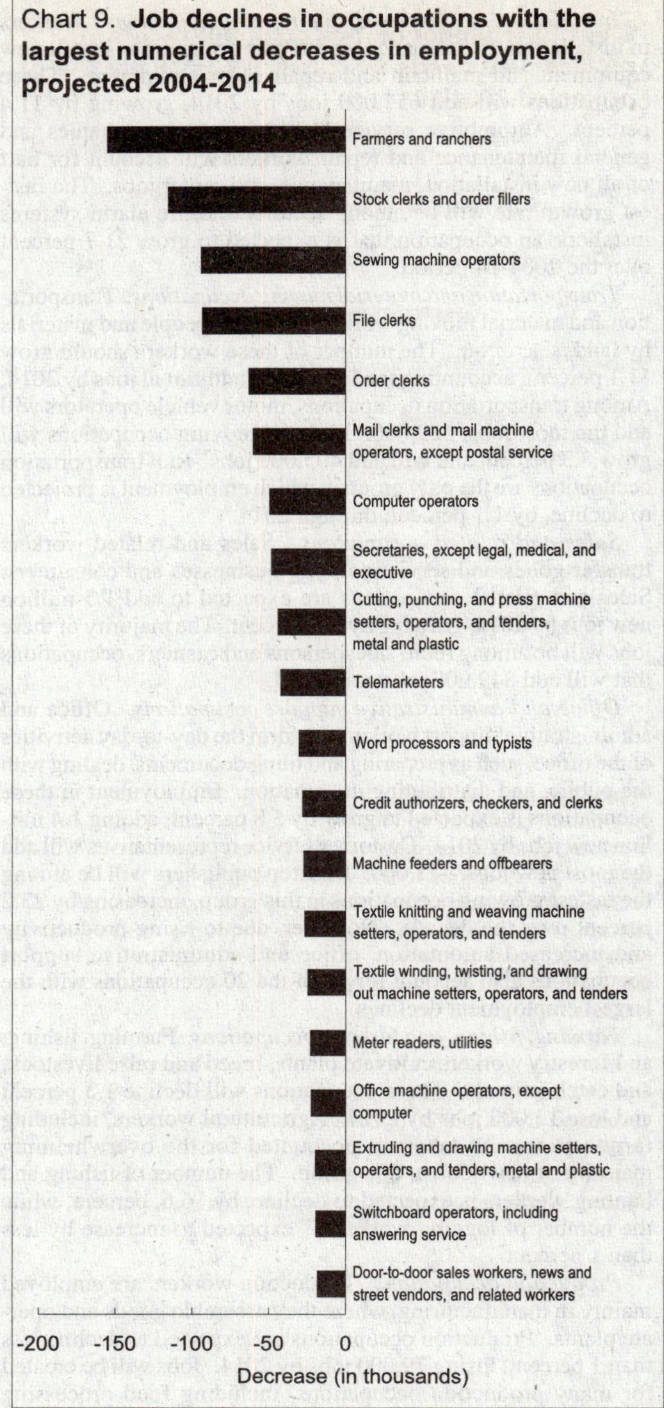

growing occupations—home health aides, personal and home care aides, and computer software application engineers—also are projected to be among the 20 occupations with the largest numerical increases in employment.

Declining occupational employment stems from declining industry employment, technological advancements, changes in business practices, and other factors. For example, increased productivity and farm consolidations are expected to result in a decline of 155,000 farmers and ranchers over the 2004-14 period (chart 9). The majority of the 20 occupations with the largest numerical decreases are office and administrative support and production occupations, which are affected by increasing plant and factory automation and the implementation of office technology that reduces the needs for these workers. For example, employment of word processors and typists is expected to decline due to the proliferation of personal computers, which allows other workers to perform duties formerly assigned to word processors and typists.

Education and training

Among the 20 fastest growing occupations, a bachelor's or associate degree is the most significant source of postsecondary education or training for 12 of them—network systems and data communications analysts; physician assistants; computer soft-

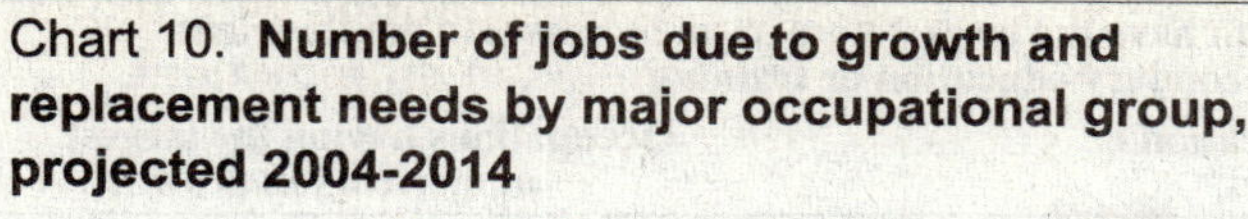
Chart 10. **Number of jobs due to growth and replacement needs by major occupational group, projected 2004-2014**

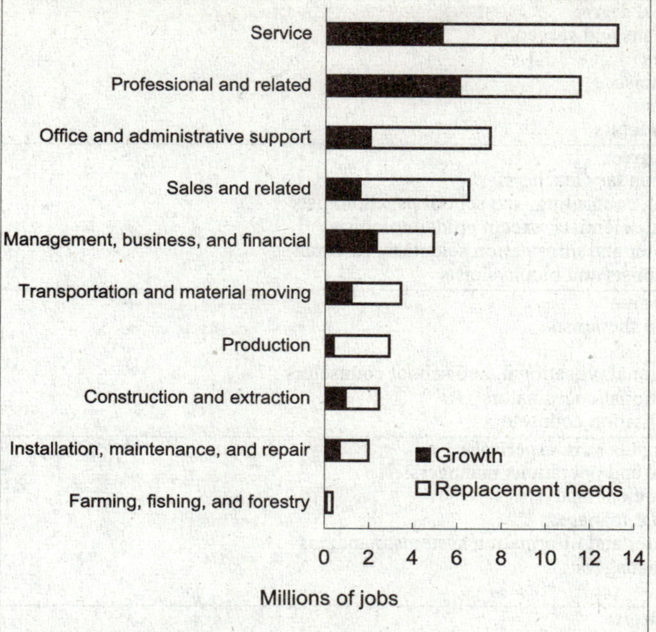

ware engineers, applications; physical therapist assistants; dental hygienists; computer software engineers, systems software; network and computer systems administrators; database administrators; forensic science technicians; veterinary technologists and technicians; diagnostic medical sonographers; and occupational therapists assistants. On-the-job training is the most significant source of postsecondary education or training for another 5 of the 20 fastest growing occupations—physical therapist aides, medical assistants, home health aides, dental assistants, and personal and home care aides. In contrast, on-the-job training is the most significant source of postsecondary education or training for 13 of the 20 occupations with the largest numerical increases; 6 of these 20 occupations have an associate or higher degree as the most significant source of postsecondary education or training. On-the-job training also is the most significant source of postsecondary education or training for all 20 of the occupations with the largest numerical decreases. Table 1 lists the fastest growing occupations and occupations projected to have the largest numerical increases in employment between 2004 and 2014, by level of postsecondary education or training.

Total job openings

Job openings stem from both employment growth and replacement needs (chart 10). Replacement needs arise as workers leave occupations. Some transfer to other occupations while others retire, return to school, or quit to assume household responsibilities. Replacement needs are projected to account for more than 60 percent of the approximately 55 million job openings between 2004 and 2014. Thus, even occupations projected to experience slower than average growth or to decline in employment still may offer many job openings.

Professional and related occupations are projected to grow faster and add more jobs than any other major occupational group, with 6 million new jobs by 2014. Three-fourths of the job growth in professional and related occupations is expected among computer and mathematical occupations; healthcare practitioners and technical occupations; and education, training, and library occupations. With 5.5 million job openings due to replacement needs, professional and related occupations are the only major group projected to generate more openings from job growth than from replacement needs.

Service occupations are projected to have the largest number of total job openings, 13.2 million, reflecting high replacement needs. A large number of replacements will be necessary as young workers leave food preparation and service occupations. Replacement needs generally are greatest in the largest occupations and in those with relatively low pay or limited training requirements.

Office automation will significantly affect many individual office and administrative support occupations. Overall, these occupations are projected to grow more slowly than average, while some are projected to decline. Office and administrative support occupations are projected to create 7.5 million job openings over the 2004-14 period, ranking third behind service and professional and related occupations.

Farming, fishing, and forestry occupations are projected to have the fewest job openings, approximately 286,000. Because job growth is expected to be slow, and levels of retirement and job turnover high, more than 95 percent of these projected job openings are due to replacement needs.

Table 1. Fastest growing occupations and occupations projected to have the largest numerical increases in employment between 2004 and 2014, by level of postsecondary education or training

Fastest growing occupations	Postsecondary education or training level	Occupations having the largest numerical job growth
	First-professional degree	
Pharmacists		Physicians and surgeons
Physicians and surgeons		Lawyers
Chiropractors		Pharmacists
Optometrists		Dentists
Veterinarians		Chiropractors
	Doctoral degree	
Medical scientists, except epidemiologists		Postsecondary teachers
Postsecondary teachers		Clinical, counseling, and school psychologists
Computer and information scientists, research		Medical scientists, except epidemiologists
Biochemists and biophysicists		Computer and information scientists, research
Clinical, counseling, and school psychologists		Biochemists and biophysicists
	Master's degree	
Physical therapists		Physical therapists
Occupational therapists		Clergy
Hydrologists		Educational, vocational, and school counselors
Substance abuse and behavioral disorder counselors		Instructional coordinators
Instructional coordinators		Rehabilitation counselors
	Bachelor's or higher degree, plus work experience	
Education administrators, preschool and child care center/program		General and operations managers
		Management analysts
Computer and information systems managers		Financial managers
Training and development managers		Computer and information systems managers
Actuaries		Sales managers
Medical and health services managers		
	Bachelor's degree	
Network systems and data communications analysts		Elementary school teachers, except special education
Physician assistants		Accountants and auditors
Computer software engineers, applications		Computer software engineers, applications
Computer software engineers, systems software		Computer systems analysts
Network and computer systems administrators		Secondary school teachers, except special and vocational education
	Associate degree	
Physical therapist assistant		Registered nurses
Dental hygienists		Computer support specialists
Forensic science technicians		Dental hygienists
Veterinary technologists and technicians		Paralegals and legal assistants
Diagnostic medical sonographers		Medical records and health information technicians
	Postsecondary vocational award	
Preschool teachers, except special education		Nursing aides, orderlies, and attendants
Surgical technologists		Preschool teachers, except special education
Gaming dealers		Automotive service technicians and mechanics
Emergency medical technicians and paramedics		Licensed practical and licensed vocational nurses
Fitness trainers and aerobics instructors		Hairdressers, hairstylists, and cosmetologists
	Work experience in a related occupation	
Self-enrichment education teachers		First-line supervisors/managers of food preparation and serving workers
Emergency management specialists		First-line supervisors/managers of office and administrative support workers
Gaming managers		First-line supervisors/managers of construction trades and extraction workers
Construction and building inspectors		Self-enrichment education teachers
First-line supervisors/managers of fire fighting and prevention workers		First-line supervisors/managers of retail sales workers
	Long-term on-the-job training	
Fire fighters		Carpenters
Tile and marble setters		Cooks, restaurant
Athletes and sports competitors		Police and sheriff's patrol officers
Coaches and scouts		Plumbers, pipefitters, and steamfitters
Interpreters and translators		Electricians
	Moderate-term on-the-job training	
Medical assistants		Customer service representatives
Dental assistants		Truck drivers, heavy and tractor-trailer
Hazardous materials removal workers		Maintenance and repair workers, general
Social and human service assistants		Medical assistants
Residential advisors		Executive secretaries and administrative assistants
	Short-term on-the-job training	
Home health aides		Retail salespersons
Personal and home care aides		Janitors and cleaners, except maids and housekeeping cleaners
Physical therapist aides		Waiters and waitresses
Amusement and recreation attendants		Combined food preparation and serving workers, including fast food
Occupational therapist aides		Home health aides

Content Summary of Chapter Listings

Chapters in this directory often include a wide range of topics. The following list of keywords from the Association listings shows the subjects covered in each chapter.

Accounting

Accounting Historians
Accounting Standards
Accreditation
Auditors
Black Accountants
Bookkeepers
Broadcast Cable Financial Management
Budget & Program Analysis
Computerized Accounting
Construction Financial Management
Cost Estimating
Government Accountability
Government Financial Officers
Healthcare Financial Management
Hospitality Financial Management
Insolvency
Insurance
Latino Accountants
Military Comptrollers
Newspapers Financial Management
Payroll
Public Accountants
Taxes
Trucking Financial Management
Valuation
Women Accountants

Advertising

Advertising Agencies
Advertising Research
Cable TV Advertising
Children's Advertising
Commercials
Communications
E Marketing
Educational Advertising
Exhibition Management
Newspaper Advertising
Outdoor Advertising
Photographers
Point of Purchase
Public Opinion
Railroad Advertising
Signs
Transportation Advertising
Women in Advertising

Agriculture

4-H
Agricultural Aviation
Agricultural Communications
Agricultural Consultants
Agricultural County Agents
Agricultural Economics
Agricultural Education
Agricultural Engineers
Agricultural Fairs
Agricultural History
Agricultural Law
Agricultural Management
Agricultural Manufacturers
Agricultural Marketing
Agricultural Research
Agricultural Retail
Agricultural Teachers
Agronomy
Alfalfa
Angus
Animal Health
Animal Hides
Animal Science
Aquatics
Arid Lands
Bedding Plants
Bee Keeping
Beef
Bio-Dynamic Farming
Biomolecular Study
Blacksmiths
Blueberries
Brahman Beef
Canola
Cereal
Christmas Trees
Conservation
Corn
Cotton
Cottonseed
Cranberries
Crops
Dairy
Ecological Farming
Eggs
Enology
Entomology
Family Farming
Feed
Fertilizer
Fisheries
Florals
Foresters
Gardening
Grain
Grapes
Grasslands
Guernsey
Hay
Herbs
Hereford
Holstein
Horticulture
Irrigation
Jersey Cattle
Livestock
Maple Syrup
Millers
Oil Seed
Onions
Organic
Pesticides
Phytopathology
Pork
Potato
Poultry
Produce
Santa Gertrudis
Seeds
Sheep
Soil
Soybean
Sugar
Sunflowers
Veal
Walnuts
Weeds
Wheat

Amusement & Entertainment

Amusement Equipment Manufacturers
Amusement Equipment Rentals
Amusement Industry Marketing
Amusement Parks
Amusement Safety
Aquariums
Caves
Circus
Coin Operated
Concessions
Game Developers
Go-Karts
Haunted Attractions
Jugglers
Kiddie Rides
Laser Attractions
Motor Sports
Roller Coasters
Theaters
Themed Amusements
Ticketing
Water Parks
Zoos

Content Summary of Chapter Listings

Apparel & Accessories

Cashmere & Camel Hair Manufacturers
Clothing Contractors
Clothing Manufacturers
Costume Designers
Cotton
Cotton Shippers
Fashion Designers
Footwear
Fur Manufacturers
Fur Merchants
Headwear
Home Sewing/Crafts
Hosiery
Infant & Children Wear
Intimate Apparel
Knitting
Leather
Millners, Dressmakers & Tailors
Neckwear
Needlework
Sportswear
Sunglasses
Uniform Manufacturers
Union Manufacturers & Distributors
Western & English Tack Apparel

Appliances

Manufacturers
Parts Suppliers
Repair
Retail Dealers
Service

Architecture

Accessibility for the Disabled
Architectural Historians
Building Officials
Cast Stone
Code Administrators
Concrete
Conservation
Design Drafting
Education
Environmental Design
Impact Assessment
Insulated Cable Engineers
Intelligent Buildings
Landscape Architects
Livable Communities
Marine Engineers
Naval Architects
Precasts
Preservation
Schools of Architecture
Sustainable Buildings
Urban Design

Art & Antiques

Aesthetics
American History
Animal Artists
Antique Dealers
Appraisal
Art Dealers
Art Education
Art Libraries
Art Materials
Art Museums
Art Placement
Art Research
Art Therapy
Auctioneers
Blacksmiths
College Art
Collectors
Conservation
Fine Arts
Fine Print Dealers
Illustrators
Library Art
Limited Edition Dealers
Photography
Picture Framers
Preservation Technology
School Programs
State Art Agencies

Automotive

Aftermarkets
Air Conditioning
Antique Trucks
Auto Auctions
Autobody Work
Automatic Transmission Rebuilders
Battery Manufacturers
Bearing Specialists
Body Engineers
Body Parts
Brake Manufacturers
Buses
Chemical Products
Collision Repair
Dealers
Diesel
Driving School
Emission Controls
Engine Rebuilders
Engineering
Filter Manufacturers
Fleet Administrators
Gasoline Marketers
Glass
Highway Users
Law Enforcement
Lifts
Maintenance
Mobile Air Conditioning
Motor & Equipment Manufacturers
Motoring & Leisure Travel
Motor Sports
Original Equipment
Overseas Market
Parking
Parts & Suppliers
Public Relations
Public Transit
Radiators
Recreation Vehicle Dealers
Recreational Vehicle Aftermarket
Recycling
Remanufacturing
Repair
Replacement Parts
Rubber
Safety
Service
Show Cars
Specialty Equipment Market
Stock Car Auto Racing
Teachers
Technicians
Theft Investigators
Tires & Rims
Tire Retread
Trucks
Used Cars
Warehouse Distributors
Wheels & Rims

Aviation & Aerospace

Aerospace Workers
Air Cargo
Air Medical Services
Air Traffic Controllers
Air Transportation
Aircraft Owners & Pilots
Historical Airlines
Airport Executives
Army Aviation
Astronautics
Beech Aircraft
Bonanza Aircraft
Buoyant Flight
Careers
Cessna Aircraft
Commercial Airports
Commercial Pilots
Consultants
Distributors
Electrical Equipment
Electronic Instrumentation
Flight Attendants
Flight Engineers
Flight Instructors
Flight Safety
Flight Test Engineers
Food
Gliding & Soaring
Helicopters
Insurance
Light Aircraft Manufacturers

Machinists
Maintenance
Management
Manufacturers
Medical Care
Medical Transport
Naval Aircraft
Noise
Nonflying Pilots
Owners & Pilots
Parachutes
Piper Aircraft
Public Airport Facilities
Safety
Seaplane Pilots
Small Satellites
Space Science
Survival & Flight Equipment
Technical Education
Test Pilots
Traffic Control
Transportation Communication
Ultralight
Vintage Aircraft
Women Pilots

Banking

ABA Endorsement
Affordable Housing Lenders
Bank Directors
Bankers Insurance
Bankruptcy
Certified Bankers
Certified Professionals
Community Bankers
Consumer Banks
Education & Training
Electronic Payments
Federal Credit Unions
Finance & Trade
Financial Management
Government Lenders
Independent Bankers
Interbank Marketing
Investment Management
Marine Bankers
Marketing
Military Banks
Minority & Women Banking
Mortgage Bankers
Mortgage Lenders
Credit Unions
Risk Management
Safe Deposit
State Savings
Women in Finance

Barbers & Beauty Shops

Aesthetics
Barber Styling
Barber Supply
Cosmetology
Electrology
Nail Technicians

Biotechnology

Biomaterials
Biomolecular Screening
Chemical
Chronobiology
Electrophoresis
Magnetic Resonance
Molecular Biology
Protein
Reproductive Medicine
Soil & Plant Analysis
Women in Science

Boating

Antique & Classic Boats
Boat Builders
Boat Owners
Canoes
Industrial Fabrics
Marine Operators
Marine Accessories
Marine Bankers
Marine Distributors
Marine Manufacturers
Marine Retailers
Marine Safety
Marine Trade
Merchant Marines
Personal Watercraft
Power Boats
Power Squadrons
Propellers
Sailing
State Boating Laws
Tides
Traditional Small Craft
Yacht Brokers
Yachting

Broadcasting

Antenna Television
Auto Racing Writers
Broadcast Designers
Broadcast Education
Broadcast Engineers
Broadcasting History
Cable & Telecommunications Marketing
Cable Television
College Radio/TV
Commercial Producers
Community Media
Correspondents
Country Radio
Educational Broadcasting
Electronic News Professionals
Emmy Awards
Families & TV
Farm Broadcasters
Geospatial Information & Technology
Industrial Radio
International Television
Local Cable Programmers
Local Television
Media Communications
Monitors
News Analysts
News Monitoring
Press Broadcasters
Private Radio
Public Service Radio
Public Television
Radio Communications
Radio Advertising
Radio Frequency Advisory
Religious Broadcasting
Reporters
Satellite Communications
Signal Theft
Speakers
Sportscasters
Sportswriters
Television Engineers
Television Producers
Television & Radio Artists
Television Arts & Sciences
Television Program Executives
Women In Radio & Television

Building & Construction

Acoustical Consultants
Apartment Management
Metal Architecture
Asbestos
Asphalt Manufacturers
Asphalt Pavement
Brick
Bridge Grid Flooring Manufacturers
Building Codes & Standards
Building Materials
Building Stone
Ceramic Tile & Dimensional Stones
Code Administrators
Concrete
Concrete Pipe
Concrete Pumping
Construction Estimators
Deep Foundations
Demolition Contractors
Distribution & Retail
Ducts, Pipes & Fittings
Education
Electrical Contractors
Elevator Contractors
Estimators
Facing Tile
Factory Built Housing

Content Summary of Chapter Listings

Fences
Floor Covering
Foundation Drilling
Garage Doors
Granite
Granite Quarriers
Hollow Metal Doors
Housing Endowment
Independent Contractors
Insulation Manufacturers
Interlocking Concrete
Laminating Materials
Lath & Plaster
Log & Dome Homes
Manufactured Housing
Masonry
Membrane Roofing
Metal Contractors
Metal Framing Manufacturers
Modular Building
Painting & Decorating Contractors
Panelized Systems
Perlite
Pile Driving
Pipe Fabrication
Pipe Fittings
Plasterers
Portable Sanitation
Power Equipment
Precast Prestressed Concrete
Public Works
Quartz Producers
Railroad Construction
Resilient Floors
Retail Lumber
Roof Coatings
Roof Tile
Rubber Pavements
Safety Glazing
Scaffolds
Screen Manufacturers
Senior Housing
Slag
Slurry Surfacing
Steel Joists
Steel Windows
Stone, Sand & Gravel
Structural Insulated Panel
Stucco Manufacturers
Subcontractors
Tech Home
Terrazzo & Mosaic
Tile Contractors
Tilt-Up Concrete
Timber Framers
Tools & Fasteners
Truck Mixer
Underground Construction
Unions
Utility Contractors
Wall & Ceiling Industries
Western Building Material
Women In Construction
Woodwork

Chemicals

Acrylonitrile
Adhesion
Aerosol
Agricultural Chemicals
Alkyl Amines
Analytical & Life Science Systems
Analytical Chemists
Analytical Communities
Bioanalysts
Biochemistry & Molecular Biology
Brewing Chemists
Cadmium
Catalysis
Chemical Engineers
Chemical Heritage
Chemical Manufacturers
Chemical Marketing Research
Chemical Recyclers
Chemical Strategies
Chlorine
Chlorine Chemistry
Chlorine Free
Chlorobenzene Producers
Clinical Chemistry
Coatings Technology
Coke & Coal Chemicals
Consumer Specialty Chemicals
Cosmetic Chemists
Crystal Growth
Drug, Chemical & Allied Trades
Electrochemical
Embalming Chemical Manufacturers
Fiber Manufacturers
Hydrogen
Leather Chemists
Liquid Terminals
Lubricant Manufacturers
Mass Spectrometry
Materials Technology
Methanol
Oil Chemists
Oxygenated Fuels
Ozone
Pest Management
Pesticide Applicators
Phosphate Chemicals
Pine Chemicals
Polyisocyanurate Insulation
Polyurethane Foam
Powder Coating
Process Equipment Manufacturers
Spectroscopy
Synthetic Organic Chemicals
Textile Chemists
Colorists
Toxicology

Cleaners & Laundries

Building Service Contractors
Diaper Services
Drycleaners
Environmental Management
Fabricare
Halogenated Solvents
Kitchen Exhaust
Linens
Power Washers
Uniform & Textile Service

Communications & Media

Abstracting & Information Services
Freedom Information Center
Information & Image Management
Information Systems
Information Technology
Medical Illustrators
Newspapers
Personal Achievement
Postal Commerce
Regional Magazines
Speakers
Technology in Education
Telecommunications Industry
Toastmasters
Translators
Writers

Computers & Data Processing

Alpha Micro Users
Artificial Intelligence
Audiovisual Catalogers
Automated Reasoning
Data Interchange Standards
Digital Dealers
Educational Communications & Technology
Electronic Engineers
Event Marketing
Identification Manufacturers
Imaging Science
Image Management
Information Display
Information Networking
Information Processing
Information Science
Information Systems Management
Intelligence
Interactive Multimedia
Knowledge Engineers
Language Instruction
Managing Human Resource Information
Medical Imaging
Medical Information
Open Applications
Optical Engineering
Precision Engineering
Recognition Technologies

Regional Sciences
Reprographic
Science Association
Security
Serial Storage Architecture
Software Users
Systems Management Technology
Technology in Education

Cosmetics, Perfumes & Personal Care

Aesthetics Manufacturers & Distributors
Aloe Science
Aromatics
Color
Consumer Healthcare Manufacturers
Cosmetology
Drug, Chemical & Allied Trades
Fragrance Research
Fragrances
Nail & Beauty
Nail Manufacturers
Tanning Manufacturers

Credit & Lending Services

Bankruptcy
Business Producers Credit
Commercial Collectors
Commercial Finance
Consumer Data
Consumer Debt Counseling
Credit Union Research & Consulting
Electronic Transactions
Financial Services
Fraud & Theft
Mortgage Brokers
Recovery Association
Risk Management

Direct Marketing

Art Directors
Digital Concepts
E-Marketing
Hispanic Marketing
Mail Marketing
Mobile Telecommunications
Publication Designers
Teleservices
Third Party Mailing
Writers

Drugs & Pharmaceuticals

Clinical
Clinical Laboratory
Distribution
Education
Efficient Operation
Ethical Pharmacies
Excipients
Generic
Health System
History of Pharmacy
Hospitals
Managed Care
Oil Chemists
Outsourcing Research
Parenteral & Enteral Nutrition
Pharmacy Law
Pharmaceutical Alliance
Pharmacy Cooperative
Senior Care
Standardization
Wholesale Druggists

Electrical

Apparatus Service
Bioelectrmagnetics
Contractors
Electrical Instruments
Electrochemical
Electronic Assembly
Electronic Measuring Instruments
Engineers
Generating Systems
Insulated Cable
Intercommunications Applications
Laser and Electro-Optic
Magnetic
Microelectronics
Microwave
Overstress/Electrostatic
Public Owned Utilities
Relay Electronics
Research
Rural Electric Cooperative
Safety
Sound Systems
Technical Certifications
Testing
Variable Resistive Products

Electronics

Agricultural
Aircraft
Armed Forces
Assembly
Certified Technicians
Commercialization Research
Consumer Electronics
Environmental
Instrumentation & Measurement
Interactive Services
Marine Electronics
Metals
Microchip Industry
Microelectronics
Minerals
Optics and Photonics
Power Electronics
Progressive Rental Merchandise
Relay Manufacturers
Rural Electric
Service Dealers

Engineering

Abrasive Engineering
Acoustical
Adhesive & Sealant
Aerospace
Applied Technology
Automated Procedures
Biomedical
Black Engineers
Boiler and Pressure Inspectors
Cable
Chemical
Civil
Code Administrators
Cold Regions Research
Corrosion
Cost Engineers
Crystallographic
Design
Die Casting
Education
Energy
Environmental Engineering
Ergosyst
Evaluation
Examiners
Foundation
Gas
Gas Turbine
Geologists
Geoprofessional
Heating, Refrigeration & Air-Conditioning
Illuminating Engineering
Industrial Designers
Industrial Fabrics
Industrial Research
Information Networking
Instrumentation & Measurement
Maintenance Professionals
Management
Materials
Mechanical
Minority Engineers
Naval
Noise Control
Nondestructive Testing
Oil Chemists
Petroleum Operations
Physics
Plumbing
Potash and Phosphate
Precision Engineering
Railway Engineering
Refrigerating
Reliability Engineering
Reprographic
Robotics

Safety
Sanitary
Structural Connections
Tribologists
Vacuum
Voluntary Consensus Standards

Environment & Conservation

Adirondack Region
Aerosol Research
Agriculture
Agronomy
Air & Waste Management
Appropriate Technology
Aquatic Plant Management
Assessment of the Environment
Audobon Society
Balancing Bureau
Biological Sciences
Bison Control
Compliance
Education
Energy Economics
Family Planning
Fire Chiefs
Fisheries
Floodplan Managers
Food Protection
Forest History
Gas
Geologists
Great Lakes
Greenpeace
Hazardous Materials Control
Historic Preservation
Imaging and Geospacial Information
Indoor Air
Lake Ecology
Law
Marine Technology
Methanol Institute
Noise Control
Nuclear Society
Packaging
Pesticide Toxicity
Phytopathological
Renewable Energy & Fuels
River Ecosystems
Safe Buildings
Scrap Recycling
Seeding
Senior Involvement
Shore and Beach Preservation
Silicone Health
Soil and Foundation Engineers
Soil and Plant Analysis
Solar Energy
Solid Waste Management
Steel Recycling
Treaty Support
Used Oil Services
Wildlife Federation
Woodland Owners
Zoo & Aquarium

Exhibits & Meeting Planners

Assembly Management
Business Media
Business-To-Business Information
Collegiate Conferences
Contractors
Cost Management Professionals
Healthcare Meetings
Hospitality
Information Technology
Museums
Religious Conferences
Science-Technology Centers

Financial Services

Aircraft Finance
Appraisers
Bankruptcy Institute
Broadcast Cable
Certified Divorce Planners
Collectors
Community Capital
Construction Financial Management
Consumer Data
Cost Engineering
Credit Union
Entrepreneurial Growth
Foreign Sales
Fraud & Theft Information
Individual Investors
Industrial Engineering
Internal Auditors
International Sales
Investor Responsibility Research
Life Insurance
Local Housing
Mutual Fund Investors
Neighborhood Reinvestment
Pension Plans
Tax Education
Urban Homesteading
Vehicle Leasing

Fishing

Atlantic States
Benthological Society
Great Lakes
Gulf and Caribbean
Middle Atlantic Fisheries
Inland
Pacific Coast
Pacific Seafood Processors
Southeastern
Women's Fisheries

Food & Beverage

African-American Natural Foods
Agricultural Research
Agronomy
Alfalfa Processors
Allergy & Anaphylaxis
Allied Purchasing
Aluminum Foil Container Manufacturers
Arborists
Association for Color
Association of Conservation
Automatic Merchandising
Bar and Restaurant Association
Beekeeping
Beverage Lincesees
Biodynamics Farming
Bio-Integrity
Biomolecular Screening
Biotechnology
Brewing Chemists
Cancer Research
Cereal Chemists
Chewing Gum
Club Management
Composite Cans and Tubes
Convenience Store Advisory
Cooperative Business
Correctional Food Service
Council on Science & Health
Crop Insurers
Deer Farmers
Distilled Spirits
Emu Associations
Enology and Viticulture
Enternal Nutrition
Entomological Society
Exporters and Importers
Extension 4-H Agents
Farm Managers
Feed Control
Fertilizer Institute
Food Information Council
Forage and Grassland
Fresh Produce and Floral
Ginseng Research
Glass Packaging
Grange Association
Healthy Water
Herbal Products
Horticulture Science
Hotel and Restaurant Industries
Hydroponic Society
Industrial Caterers
Inflight Food Service
Institute of Ammonia
Italian Trade Commission
Label Printin
Livestock Breeds
Mexican Restaurants & Cantinas
Nutritional Consultants
Ohytopathological Society

Organic Alliance
Ostrich Association
Packaging Education Forum
Pecan Shellers
Pomological Society
Poultry Association
Refrigeration
Roundtable of Food Professionals
Seed Trade
Sheep Industry
Special Supplement Nutrition
Spice Trade
Vegetarian Awareness
Women in Flavor & Fragrance

Foundations & Fund Raising

Black Foundation Executives
Campus Fund Raising
Catholic Development Conference
Center for Effective Philanthropy
Christopher Reeve Paralysis Center
Healthcare Philanthropy
Learning Institute
Music Performance Trust Funds
Nonprofit Organization
State and Provincial Lotteries

Freight & Packaging

Customs Brokers and Forwarders
Foodservice & Packaging
Glass Packaging
Healthcare Compliance Packaging
International Container Leasing
Petroleum Packaging
Transportation Intermediaries

Furnishings & Fixtures

Cotton Batting
Floorcovering
Futon Association
Glass & Ceramic Decorators
Housewares Manufacturers
Illuminating Engineering Society
Innerspring Manufacturers
Rental Dealers
Store Fixtures
Waterbed Retailers
Woodworking & Furnishings

Garden & Lawn

Consulting Arborists
Farm Equipment
Garden Writers
Grounds Management
Horticultural Therapy
Irrigation Consultants
Landscape Architects
Mailorder
Pest Management
Plants fr Clean Air

Society of Arboriculture

Glass & Ceramics

China Clay Producers
Flint Glass Workers Union
Glazing Industry Code Committee
Industrial Sand Association
Insulating Glass
Porcelain Enamel Institute
Refractory Ceramic Fiber

Government

Access Professionals
Board of National Labor Relations
Border Patrol Council
Center for Neighborhood
Chiefs of Police
Citizens Against Government Waste
Community Development
Conference of Mayors
Council of State Housing
Council on the Homeless
Council on Water Policy
County and City Health Officials
Emergency Management
Fire Chiefs
Governmental Purchasing
Housing Law Project
Interstate Oil and Gas
League of Cities
Local Air Pollution
Milk Control Agencies
Procurement Round Table
Rural Housing Coalition
Search and Rescue
State Community Service Programs
Study of the Presidency
Trust for Public Land
Urban and Regional Information
Urban Economic Development
Weatherization Assistance
World Federalist Association

Hardware

Doors
Equipment Lessors
Hand Tools
Locksmiths
Lumbermen
Metal Detectors

Healthcare

Applied Psychophysiology
Association for Worksite Health Promotion
Athletic Trainers
Blood Banks
Bone and Mineral Research
Breast Cancer
Cataract & Refractive Medicine
Cell Biology
Chiropractics
Cleft Palate Craniofacial
Clinical Nutrition
Compliance Packaging
Continuity of Care
Council on the Aging
County Health Facility Administration
Crematin
Dental
Gerantological Society
Headaches
Health Plans
Healthcare Recruitment
Home Care
Human Genetics
Human Services
Laser Medicine
Medical Imaging
Medical Instrumentation
Medical Libraries
Mental Retardation
Nonprescription Medicines
Nuclear Medicine
Pain
Pharmacology
Postgraduate Medicine
Psychiatry
Psychologyl
Radiology
Sleep Products
Speech-Language-Hearing
State Medicaid Directors
Suicidology
Textile Rental Services
Tissue Banks
Worksite Health

Heating & Air Conditioning

Air Balance Consultants
Flexible Air Duct
Gas Appliance Manufacturers
Masonry Heater
Microwave Power Institute
Mobile Air Conditioning
Power Engineers
Refrigeration
Solar Energy
Wholesalers

Hobbies & Games

American Craft Council
American Quilts
Archery
Camping
Home Sewing
Hooking Artists
Miniatures
Model Railroad
Philatelic Society

Society of Craft Designers

Hotels & Motels

Asian/American Hotel Owners
Executive Housekeepers
Facility Management
Hospitality Financial & Technology
Hotel and Motel Brokers
Hotel and Restaurant Employees
Resort Development
Small Luxury Hotels

Industrial Equipment

Abrasive Manufacturers
Asphalt Recycling and Reclaiming
Casting Industry Suppliers
Coatings
Composite Can and Tube Institute
Composite Fabricators
Corrugated Steel Pipe
Electroplaters Surface Finishers
Fluid Controls
Hack and Band Saw Manufacturers
Heat Processing Equipment
Hoist Manufacturers
Industrial Diamonds
Industrial Engineers
Industrial Security
Spray Equipment
Tribologists & Lubrication

Insurance

American Prepaid Legal Services
Arbitration Forums
Association of Retired Persons
Cargo War Risk Reinsurance
Certified Insurance Counselors
Committee for Arson Control
Crop Insurers
Defense & Corporate Counsel
Fire Investigators
Highway Loss Data Institute
Insurance Law
National Viatical Association
Property Insurance Loss Register
Registered Mail Insurance
Self Insurance Institute
Shipowners Claim
Transportation Consumer Protection
Underwriters Laboratories
Workers Compensation Reinsurance

Interior Design & Decorating

Can Manufacturers
Carpets and Rugs
Decorative Fabric Distributors
Floor Covering
Florists
Home Furnishings
Illuminating Engineering
Kitchen and Bath
Lighting Association
Paint and Decorating
Picture Framers
Upholstery
Window Coverings

International Trade

Academy of International Business
American League for Exports
Security Assistance
Hong Kong Trade Development
International Chambers of Commerce
Latin American Studies
Oil and Gas of Russian Far East
US China Business Council

Internet

Computing in Education
Public Technology
Security

Jewelry & Watches

Appraisers Association
Cultured Pearl Information
Diamond Council
Estate Jewelry
Gemological Institute
Gold Prospectors
Goldsmiths
Indian Arts & Crafts
Jewelers Vigilance Committee
Silversmiths
Traveling Jewelers
World Gold Council

Journalism

Collegiate Press
Environmental Journalists
Gay and Lesbian Press
Hollywood Foreign Press
Investigative Reporters and Editors
Overseas Press Club of America
Society for News Design
Society of American Travel Writers

Law Enforcement & Public Safety

Academy of Criminal Justice Science
American Jail Association
American Polygraph Association
Arson Investigators
Bloodhounds
Bombs
Drug Enforcement Officers
Footprint Association
Forensic Dentists
Livestock Theft
National Constables Association
Society of Criminology

Leather Products

Pedorthic Footwear Association
Restorers
Saddle Markers
Sponge and Chamois Institute

Legal Services

American Bar Foundation
American Institute of Parliamentarians
American Society of Family & Conciliation
American Society for Legal History
American Society for Trial Consultants
Arbitration Association
Center on Children and the Law
Commission on Mental Retardation & Physical Disability Law
Council on Legal Education Opportunity
Council on State Government
Equal Justice Works
Family Mediators
First Amendment Lawyers Association
Japanese American Society for Legal Studies
Legal Investigators
Mineral Law
Native American Rights Fund
People Against Racist Terror
Psychiatry and the Law

Libraries

American Archivists
American Indian Library
Art Libraries Society
Asian/Pacific American Librarians
Center for Children's Books
Library Blinding Institute
Library Needs of Nurses
Population/Family Planning
Recorded Sound
Society of Indexers
Special Libraries Association
Substance Abuse Librarians

Literary Services

Before Columbus Foundation
Dramatists Guild of America
Self-Employed Writers &Artists Network
Translators Association

Liquor

Enology & Vinticulture
Home Wine and Beer Trade Association
Society of Brewing Chemists
Wine and Spirits Shippers Association

Lumber & Wood

Arborist

Forest Landowners
Helicopter Loggers
Kiln Drying
National Wood Tank
Railway Ties
Truss Plate
Wood and Synthetic Flooring

Machinery

Abrasive Grain
Fluid Power Society
Mechanical Engineers
Polycrystalline Products
Powder Actuated Tool Manufacturers
Robotic Industries

Management

Best Employers Association
Center for Creative Leadership
Decision Sciences Institute
Floodplain Management Association
Executive Secretaries /Admin Assistants
Third World Resources
Work in America Institute
Young Presidents Organization

Metals & Metalworking

American Farriers Association
American Foundrymens' Society
Electrical Manufacturing & Coil
Winding Association
Gold Prospectors
Magnet Distributors and Fabricators
National Blacksmiths and Welders
Silver Institute
Society of American Silversmiths
Systems Builders Association
Welding Research Council

Mining

American Coal Ash Association
American Geological Institute
Bureau of Land Management
Crystal Growth
Desert Research Institute
Mineral Information Institute
Ocean Industries
Stone, Sand & Gravel Association

Motion Pictures

Assistant Directors Training Program
Casting Society of America
Film Society of Lincoln Center
International Documentary Association
International Stunt Association
Studio Teachers Association
Sundance Institute
University Film and Video Association

Music

Academy of Songwriters
American Kodaly Educators
American Music Scholarships
American Music Therapy Association
International Polka
Music Performance Trust Funds
Musical Box Society
Pitch Pipes

Office Supplies & Services

Business Forms
Copier Dealers
Express Carriers
Florists
Label Printing
Office Planners
Printing

Paper & Allied Products

Corrugated Container
Gummed Industries
International Union

Performing Arts

American Luthiers
Box Office Management
Composers, Authors
Conductors Guild
Costumers
Dance Critics
Disc Jockey
Drama Therapy
Jazz Education
Music Copyists
Music Publishers
Piano Manufacturers
Pipe Organ Builders
Square Dance
Theatre Equipment
Theatrical Mutual Association
Thespians
Ventriloquists

Petroleum & Allied Products

Drilling
Geologists
Nuclear Energy
Ocean Industries
Oil Scouts
Propane Gas
Royalty Owners
Spill Control
Stripper Well
Well Log Analysis

Pets & Pet Supplies

American Farriers
Animal Legal Defense
Delta Society
Pet Food Institute
Pet Sitters

Photography

Photogrammetry & Remote Sensing
Picture Archives
Picture Framers
Travelogue Sponsors
White House Press Photographers

Plastics

Composites Fabricators
Electrical Overstress/Electrostatic
Polyolefins Fire Performance
Rotational Molders
Thermoforming

Printing

Binding Industries
Die Stampers
Engravers Union
Flexographic Technical
Foil Stamping and Embossing
Lithographics
Metal Decorators
Plate Printers
Screen Printing & Graphic Imaging
Web Offset

Public Relations

Career Skills Press
Consumer Affairs
Public Affairs

Publishing

Antiquarian Booksellers
Audit Bureau of Circulation
Book Dealers Exchange
Business Publications
Copyright Society
Desktop Publishing
Digital Imaging
Flexographic Technical
Free Community Papers
Free Papers
Independent Publishers
Rare Books
Study Groups

Real Estate

Affordable Housing
American Rental
Appraisers
Building Owners and Managers
Council of Shopping
Farm Managers

Homeowners Foundation
Housing Cooperatives
International Exchangers Association
Land Title Association
Lobbies for the Industry
Low Income Housing
Mortgage Bankers
Neighborhood Reinvestment
Resort Development
Surveying & Mapping

Restaurants

American Bakers
Chef & Child Foundation
Cookware Manufacturers
Culinary Professionals
Educational Training
Mobile Industrial Caterers

Retailing

Business Practices
Franchises
Map Trades
Pawnbrokers
Store Planners
Surplus Dealers

Safety & Security

Aerosol Research
Biological Safety
Biometrics
Bomb Technicians
Conveyor Equipment
Cotton Ginners
Counterterroism
Dive Rescue Specialists
Fire Protection
Floodplain Managers
Holograms
Industrial Hygiene
Insurance Investigators
Lasers
Legal Investigators
National Standards Institute
Photoluminescent
Poison Control
Polygraphs
Prevention of Crime
Scaffold Industry
Society for Testing & Materials
Welding

Sports & Recreation

Aeronautics
Camping
Canoes
Cutting Horses
Football Writers Association
Golf Car Manufacturers
Greyhound Track Operators
Orthopaedic Society for Sports Medicine
Sports Dentistry
Tennis Computer Ranking System
Turf Managers
YMCA

Stone & Concrete

Expanded Shale Clay and Slate
Flexicore Manufacturers
Lime
Marble
Monuments
Natural Soda Ash
Post-Tensioning
Refractories Institute
Reinforcing Steel
Specialty Minerals

Telecommunications

Antenna Measurement Techniques
Exchange Carriers
Facsimiles
Insulated Cable
Micro Channels
Speech

Textiles

Carpet & Rug
Cleaning and Restoration
Cotton
Craft Yarn
Electrical Overstress & Electrostatic Discharge
Flock Association
Home Sewing & Craft Association
Hard Fibers
Knitting Guild of America
Lace & Embroidery Manufacturers
Knitwear & Sportswear Association
Recycled Textiles
Sheep Industry
Silk Association
Surface Design
Textile Care Allied Trades Association

Transportation

American Space Transportation
Brotherhood of Teamsters
Child Transport
Customs Brokers and Forwarders
Driving School Association of America
Movers Conference
Organization of Dredging
Parking
Railway Museums
Regional Airline Association
Renting and Leasing
Small Shipments
Space Transportation
Transport Workers Union
Warehouse Companies
Waterways Operators

Travel

Association of Convention and Visitors Bureaus
Caribbean Hotel Association
International Family Recreation
Travel Writers
International Workcamps

Trucking

Driver Employee Council
Transportation Loss, Claim Security
Travel Plaza and Truckstop Industry

Utilities

Energy Information Administration
International Right of Way
Municipal Waste Management
Rural Electric Cooperative Association
North American Electric Reliability
Solar Energy Society
US Energy Information Administration
Water Works Association

Warehousing & Storage

Internal Combustion Engines
Liquid Terminals
Refrigeration Research
Self Storage

Water Supply

Drilling
Irrigation Consultants
Onsite Wastewater Recycling
Recreation
Waste Water Pump Association
Waterjet Technology

Standard Industrial Codes: Cross Reference Table

The US Department of Labor identifies various industries according to a series of standard industry codes -- SICs. Below are the major SIC divisions and the relevant chapter in this directory. For a more detailed explanation of the SIC Division Structure, visit www.osha.gov/pls/imis/sic

SIC		
01-09	**Agriculture, Forestry, Fishing**	
	Agriculture	Chapter 59
	Environment & Conservation	Chapter 28
	Fishing	Chapter 31
	Lumber & Wood	Chapter 59
10-14	**Mining**	
	Mining	Chapter 65
	Metals & Metalworking	Chapter 64
	Petroleum & Allied Products	Chapter 70
15-17	**Construction**	
	Building & Construction	Chapter 16
	Heating & Air Conditioning	Chapter 43
	Plumbing	Chapter 76
20-39	**Manufacturing**	
	Apparel & Accessories	Chapter 6
	Chemicals	Chapter 17
	Electrical	Chapter 25
	Electronics	Chapter 26
	Food & Beverage	Chapter 32
	Furnishings & Fixtures	Chapter 35
	Glass & Ceramics	Chapter 38
	Healthcare	Chapter 42
	Industrial Equipment	Chapter 46
	Jewelry & Watches	Chapter 51
	Leather Products	Chapter 54
	Lumber & Wood	Chapter 59
	Manufacturing, Miscellaneous	Chapter 62
	Metals & Woodworking	Chapter 64
	Paper & Allied Products	Chapter 70
	Petroleum & Allied Products	Chapter 72
	Photography	Chapter 74
	Plastics	Chapter 75
	Printing	Chapter 77
	Publishing	Chapter 79
	Rubber	Chapter 83
	Stone & Concrete	Chapter 87
	Textiles	Chapter 89
	Tobacco	Chapter 90
	Transportation	Chapter 91
40-49	**Transportation, Communications, Utilities**	
	Aviation & Aerospace	Chapter 10
	Boating	Chapter 14
	Broadcasting	Chapter 15
	Communications & Media	Chapter 19
	Electrical	Chapter 25
	Electronics	Chapter 26
	Internet	Chapter 50
	Journalism	Chapter 52
	Public Relations	Chapter 78
	Retailing	Chapter 82
	Telecommunications	Chapter 88
	Transportation	Chapter 91
	Wholesale Services	Chapter 98
	Trucking	Chapter 93
	Utilities	Chapter 94
	Warehousing & Storage	Chapter 96

SIC	Industry	Chapter
	Water Supply	Chapter 97
50-51	**Wholesale Trade**	
	Automotive	Chapter 9
	Cosmetics, Perfumes & Personal Care	Chapter 21
	Drugs & Pharmaceuticals	Chapter 24
	Hardware	Chapter 41
	Jewelry & Watches	Chapter 51
	Liquor	Chapter 58
	Retailing	Chapter 82
	Wholesale Services	Chapter 98
52-59	**Retail Trade**	
	Apparel & Accessories	Chapter 5
	Automotive	Chapter 9
	Direct Marketing	Chapter 23
	Food & Beverage	Chapter 32
	Furnishings & Fixtures	Chapter 35
	Hobbies & Games	Chapter 44
	Liquor	Chapter 58
	Machinery	Chapter 60
	Marketing	Chapter 63
	Motorcycles	Chapter 67
	Office Supplies & Services	Chapter 69
	Photography	Chapter 74
	Restaurants	Chapter 81
60-67	**Finance, Insurance, Real Estate**	
	Banking	Chapter 11
	Credit & Lending Services	Chapter 22
	Financial Services	Chapter 30
	Insurance	Chapter 47
	Real Estate	Chapter 80
70-79	**Business Services**	
	Advertising	Chapter 2
	Agriculture	Chapter 3
	Amusement & Entertainment	Chapter 4
	Barbers & Beauty Shops	Chapter 12
	Cleaners & Laundries	Chapter 18
	Computers & Data Processing	Chapter 20
	Hotels & Motels	Chapter 45
	Interior Design & Decoration	Chapter 48
	Performing Arts	Chapter 71
	Safety & Security	Chapter 84
	Shoes	Chapter 85
	Sports & Recreation	Chapter 86
80	**Health Services**	
	Healthcare	Chapter 42
81	**Legal Services**	
	Law Enforcement & Public Safety	Chapter 53
	Legal Services	Chapter 55
84	**Museums, Art Galleries, Botanical and Zoological Gardens**	
	Art & Antiques	Chapter 8
	Garden & Lawn	Chapter 36
	Gifts	Chapter 37
87	**Engineering, Accounting, Management**	
	Accounting	Chapter 1
	Foundations & Fund Raising	Chapter 33
	Management	Chapter 61
	Public Relations	Chapter 78
91-97	**Public Administration**	
	Government	Chapter 39
	Law Enforcement & Public Safety	Chapter 53
	International Trade	Chapter 49

User Guide

Descriptive listings in *The Directory of Business Information Resources* are organized into 98 industry chapters. You will find the following types of listings throughout the book: Associations; Newsletters; Magazines & Journals; Trade Shows; Directories & Databases; and Web Sites.

Below is a sample listing illustrating the kind of information that is or might be included in an Association entry, with additional fields that apply to publication and trade show listings. Each numbered item of information is described in the paragraphs on the following page.

---

(1) **12345**

(2) **National Association of Big Band Musicians**

(3) 2061 Ryders Avenue
Westerville, OH 43081

(4) 002-208-0843

(5) 800-208-0845

(6) 002-208-0844

(7) info@bigb.com

(8) www.bigb.com

(9) Linda Whare, Executive Director
Keith Fallon, Secretary
Bill Jenkins, Editor

(10) A national organization that supports those musicians and instructors whose main interest is big band music. Committed to furthering the art of big bands through teaching, performance, compositions and scholarly research. Also promotes the growth and establishment of big band literature and libraries, and offers musicians and teachers guidance in instrument maintenance and performing venues.

(11) 1M *Members*

(12) *Founded*: 1984

(13) Bi Monthly

(14) $59.00

(15) 110,000

(16) **Special Issues:**
Top 100 Music Dealers
January

(17) 3,000 Attendees

(18) April

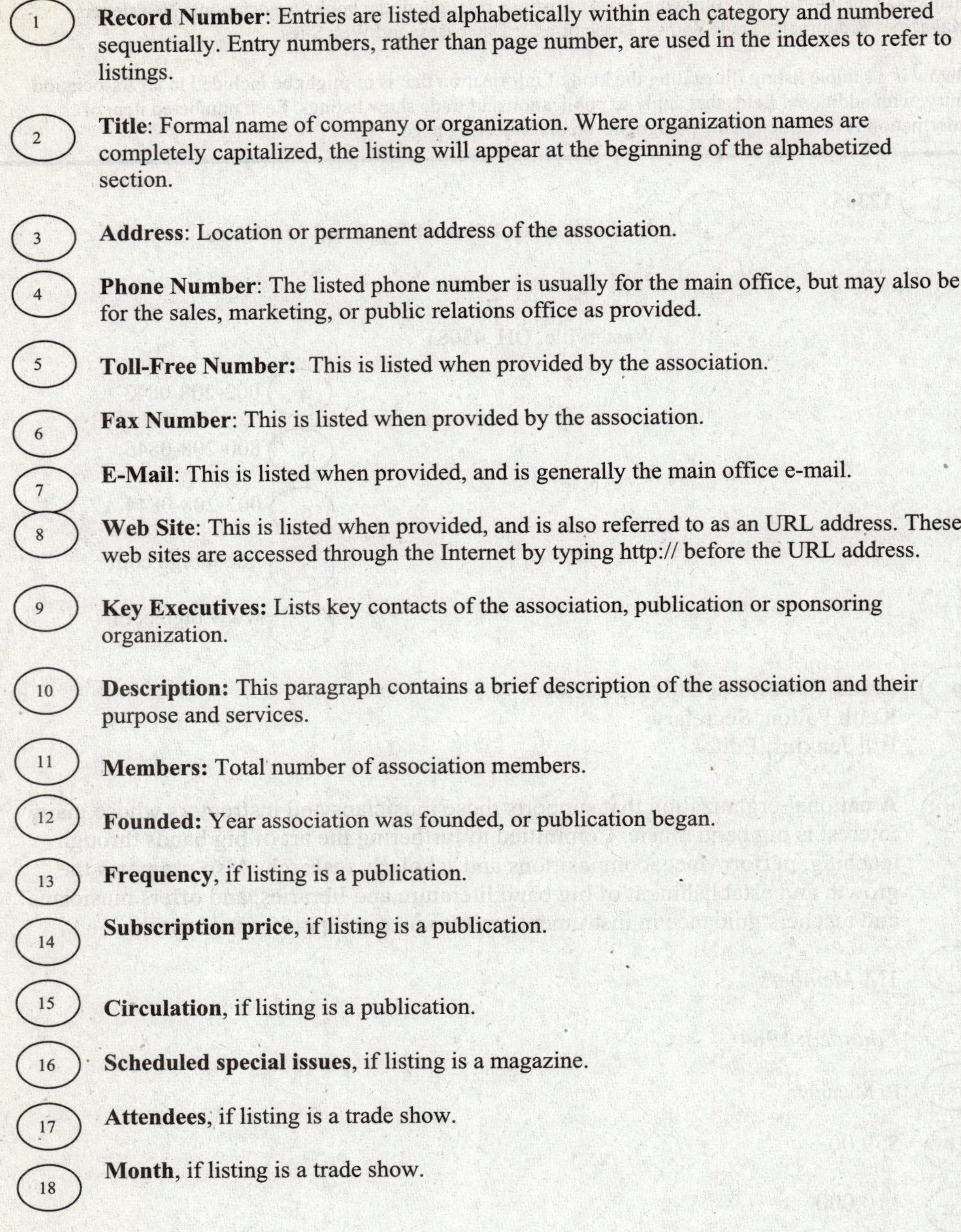

Resources User Key

1 **Record Number**: Entries are listed alphabetically within each category and numbered sequentially. Entry numbers, rather than page number, are used in the indexes to refer to listings.

2 **Title**: Formal name of company or organization. Where organization names are completely capitalized, the listing will appear at the beginning of the alphabetized section.

3 **Address**: Location or permanent address of the association.

4 **Phone Number**: The listed phone number is usually for the main office, but may also be for the sales, marketing, or public relations office as provided.

5 **Toll-Free Number:** This is listed when provided by the association.

6 **Fax Number**: This is listed when provided by the association.

7 **E-Mail**: This is listed when provided, and is generally the main office e-mail.

8 **Web Site**: This is listed when provided, and is also referred to as an URL address. These web sites are accessed through the Internet by typing http:// before the URL address.

9 **Key Executives:** Lists key contacts of the association, publication or sponsoring organization.

10 **Description:** This paragraph contains a brief description of the association and their purpose and services.

11 **Members:** Total number of association members.

12 **Founded:** Year association was founded, or publication began.

13 **Frequency**, if listing is a publication.

14 **Subscription price**, if listing is a publication.

15 **Circulation**, if listing is a publication.

16 **Scheduled special issues**, if listing is a magazine.

17 **Attendees**, if listing is a trade show.

18 **Month**, if listing is a trade show.

Associations

1 **AGN International - North America**
2851 S Parker Road
Suite 850
Aurora, CO 80014
303-743-7880
FAX: 303-743-7660
rhood@agn.org www.agn.org
Larry Kuechler, Chair
Rita J Hood, Executive Director
Worldwide association of separate and independent accounting and consulting firms. Composed of CPA consulting firms who share information and resources via the association programs.
200 Members Founded: 1978

2 **Academy of Accounting Historians**
University of Alabama
Box 870220
Tuscaloosa, AL 35487
205-587-7736
FAX: 205-348-8453
krice@cba.ua.edu
www.weatherhead.cwru.edu
Edward N Coffman, Chairman
Salvador Carmona, President
Jennifer Reynolds-Moerhrle, Treasurer
Michael Gaffikin, VP Communications
Kathy Rice, Academy Administrator
Encourages research, publication, teaching and personal interchanges in all phases of accounting history and its inter relation with business and economic history. Members are individuals and institutional affiliates with business and economic history.
875 Members Founded: 1973

3 **Accreditation Council for Accountancy**
1010 N Fairfax Street
Alexandria, VA 22314-1574
703-492-2228
FAX: 703-549-2984 888-289-7763
info@acatcredentials.org
www.acatcredentials.org
John W. Schabow, ABA, ATA, President
Wanda Samek, EA, ABA, First VP
Linda Trent, VP Taxation
Lanny Nelms, VP Accounting
Nonprofit independent testing, accrediting and monitoring organization. The council seeks to identify professionals in independent practice who specialize in providing financial, accounting and taxation services to individuals and small to mid-size businesses.
Founded: 1973

4 **Advancing Government Accountability**
2208 Mount Vernon Avenue
Alexandria, VA 22301-1314
703-684-6931
FAX: 703-548-9367 800-ABA-7211
Sam M. McCall, President
Deborah Loveless, CGFM, SVP at Large
Lealan Miller, SVP Regional Services
Relmond Van Daniker, Executive Director
Cristina Barbudo, Director Finance/Administration
Educational organization dedicated to the enhancement of public financial management. TOPICS Newsletter designed to give national exposure to chapter events, community service projects and member accomplishments while offering the most up-to-date Association news, released every other Monday morning by e-mail to members.
20000 Members Founded: 1950
Mailing list available for rent 18,000 names

5 **Affordable Housing Associations of Certified Public Accountants**
459 N 300 W #11
Kaysville, UT 84037
801-547-0809
FAX: 801-547-5070 800-532-0809
info@ahacpa.org www.ahacpa.org
Les Sparks, President
Mike Olsen, CFO
AHACP is a national association of CPAs and financial professionals providing financial service, support and education for the affordable housing and HUD-approved lender communities.

6 **American Accounting Association**
5717 Bessie Drive
Sarasota, FL 34233-2399
941-921-7747
FAX: 941-923-4093
office@aaahq.org http://aaahq.org
Judy D. Rayburn, President
James Hunton, VP
Tracey Sutherland, Executive Director
Promotes worldwide excellence in accounting education, research and practice. The association is a voluntary organization of people interested in accounting education and research and practice. Publications can be found online.
9000 Members Founded: 1916
Mailing list available for rent

7 **American Association for Budget and Program Analysis**
6425 Lakeview Drive
Falls Church, VA 22041
703-941-4300
FAX: 703-941-1535
aabpa@aol.com www.aabpa.org
Shelly McAllister, President
Bob Henke, VP
Keesha Pendergrast, VP Communications
Joe Byrns, VP Programs
Chris Lawson, Manager
Helps federal, state, and local government managers and analysts, corporate executives and academic specialists meet the unique challenges of their careers. By helping members keep up with the latest developments in their fields, establish and maintain contacts with colleagues, represent their interests and share opportunities, AABPA serves the key difference between simply having a job and being part of a highly respected and well trained profession.
400 Members Founded: 1976

8 **American Association of Attorney-Certified Public Accountants**
24196 Alicia Parkway
Suite K
Mission Viejo, CA 92691
949-768-0336
FAX: 949-768-7062 800-272-2889
aaacpa@attorney-cpa.com
www.attorney-cpa.com
Bernard Eizen, President
Cynthia M. Strouss, VP
Clark Mulligan, CAE, Executive Director
Kenneth D. Goodman, Treasurer
Seeks to safeguard the professional and legal rights of CPA attorneys.
1370 Members Founded: 1964

9 **American Institute of Professional Bookkeepers**
6001 Montrose Road
Suite 500
Rockville, MD 20852
301-770-7300
FAX: 800-541-0066 800-622-0121
info@aipb.org www.aipb.org
Stanley I Hartman, Executive Director/Co-President
Stephen Sahlein, Co-President
Barbara Regotti, Manager Education Support Services
To achieve recognition of bookkeepers as accounting professionals, to keep bookkeepers up to date on changes in bookkeeping, accounting and tax, to answer bookkeepers' everday bookkeeping and accounting questions, and to certify bookkeepers who meet high, national standards.
31000 Members Founded: 1987
Mailing list available for rent $110 per M.

10 **American Payroll Association**
American Payroll Association
660 N Main Avenue, Site 100
San Antonio, TX 78205-1217
210-226-4600
FAX: 210-226-4027
info@americanpayroll.org
www.americanpayroll.org
Dan Maddux, Executive Director
Professional society for payroll professional.
21000 Members

11 **American Society of Military Comptrollers**
2034 Eisenhower Avenue
Alexandria, VA 22314-4650
703-549-0360
FAX: 703-549-3181 800-462-5637
Sandra Gregory, National President
John Bunnell, Associate Director of Certification
Jennifer Sizemore, Chapter Management
Successor to the Society of Military Accountants and Statisticians. Nonprofit educational and professional organization for persons, military and civilian, involved in the overall field of military comptollership.
18000 Members Founded: 1948

12 **American Society of Tax Professionals**
PO Box 1213
Lynnwood, WA 98046
425-741-1996
kraemerc@juno.com
www.taxbeacon.com
Carol Kraemer, Executive Director
Strives to promote competence in tax preparation through continuing education, high ethics and a network of support.

13 **American Society of Women Accountants**
8405 Greensboro Drive
Suite 800
McLean, VA 22102
703-506-3265
FAX: 703-506-3266 800-326-2163
aswa@aswa.org www.aswa.org
Christi Olsen, President
Shelly L. Selby, CPA, VP

Joy N. Barron, VP
Karen J. Gunther, Treasurer

Organization for networking and information exchange in pursuit of professional development.

6000 Members Founded: 1938

14 **American Woman's Society of Certified Public Accountants**
236 S Keowee Street
Dayton, OH 45402
937-222-1872
FAX: 937-222-5794 800-297-2721
info@awscpa.org www.awscpa.org

Jennifer Goforth, President
Kimberly Fantaci, Executive Director
Jennifer Laudermilch, VP Marketing
Mary B. Riley, Treasurer
Mary Cheaney, Secretary

Provides supportive environment that promotes equity and provides opportunities for the achievement of career goals in a competitive and rapidly changing profession.

2000 Members Founded: 1933

15 **Association for Accounting Administration**
136 S Keowee Street
Dayton, OH 45402
937-222-0030
FAX: 937-222-5794
aaainfo@cpaadmin.org
www.cpaadmin.org

Fred Dillion, President
Kimberly Fantaci, Executive Director
Connie Harmsen, VP
Dawn Hanna Bell, Treasurer
Arlis Esnough, Secretary

Professional organization to further networking and the careers of those managing accounting practices.

600 Members Founded: 1984

16 **Association for Accounting Marketing/ Executives**
14 W 3rd Street
Suite 200
Kansas City, MO 64105
816-221-1296
FAX: 816-472-7765
info@accountingmarketing.org
www.accountingmarketing.org

Sally Glick, President
Jayne Bates, VP
Granville Loar, Executive Director
Debra Skolnick, Treasurer
Neil Fauerbach, Secretary

Professional association serving individuals actively engaged in developing and implementing marketing programs for accounting firms.

566 Members Founded: 1988

17 **Association of Chartered Accountants in the United States**
341 Lafayette Street
Suite 4262
New York, NY 10012-2417
212-334-2078

admin@acaus.org www.acaus.org

Ross Brown, President
Chris Gill, VP
Guy Langford, Treasurer
Sandy Needham, Secretary

ACAUS is a nonprofit professional and educational organization representing interests of over 6,000 US based chartered accountants from the institutes of Chartered Accountants across the globe.

Founded: 1980

18 **Association of College and University Auditors**
342 North Main Street
Suite 301
West Hartford, CT 06117-2507
860-586-7561
FAX: 860-586-7550
acua@acua.org
www.acua.org/organization

Ray Cochran, President

Provides an arena to discuss mutual professional problems and to generate new ideas and methods concerning the profession.

Founded: 1958

19 **Association of Credit Union Internal Auditors**
PO Box 1926
Columbus, OH 43216-1926
614-219-9702
FAX: 614-221-2335 866-254-8128

Terry McEachern, Founder
Barbara Netter, Chairman
Cathy Smoyer, Vice Chairman
Barry Lucas, Director
Brad L Feldman, MPA, Executive Director

Is committed to being a quality provider of credit union internal audit resources. Internal Audit Guide is available to its members and non-members electronically.

600 Members Founded: 1991

20 **Association of Healthcare Internal Auditors**
10200 W 44th Avenue
Suite 304
Wheat Ridge, CO 80003
303-327-7546
FAX: 303-422-8894
ahia@ahia.org www.ahia.org

Debi Weatherford, Chairman
Karen Young, Vice Chairman
Linda S. McKee, Director
Pat Bogusz, Executive Director
Randolph Just, Treasurer/Secretary

The Association of Healthcare Internal Auditors (AHIA) is an international organization dedicated to advancement of the healthcare internal auditing profession, which includes operational, compliance, clinical/medical, financial and information technology. AHIA is committed to providing for the continuing and specific professional education needs of healthcare auditors.

885 Members Founded: 1981

21 **Association of Insolvency Advisors and Restructuring Advisors**
221 Stewart Avenue
Suite 207
Medford, OR 97501
541-858-1665
FAX: 541-858-9187
aira@airacira.org www.airacira.org

James L Lukenda, Chairman
Soneet Kapila, President
Grant Newton, Executive Director
Nancy A. Ross, VP Development
Matthew Schwartz, Treasurer

Disseminates judicial and financial information relating to insolvency proceedings as well as offering methods to increase skills needed in these cases. Also administers the (CIRA) Certified Insolvency and Reorganization Account Program.

2000+ Members Founded: 1984

22 **Association of Latino Professionals in Finance and Accounting**
510 W 6th Street
Suite 400
Los Angeles, CA 90014
213-243-0004
FAX: 213-243-0006
info@national.alpfa.org
www.alpfa.org

Alfred Cepero, CPA, President
Manuel Espinoza, CPA, CEO
Hector Perez, CPA, VP
Habibe Ramirez, Treasurer
Maria Villanueva, Secretary

ALPFA is the leading professsional association dedicated to enhancing opportunities for Latinos in the accounting, finance and related professions. ALPFA is a nonprofit entity registered with the IRS.

Founded: 1972

23 **Broadcast Cable Credit Association**
550 Frontage Road
Suite 3600
Northfield, IL 60093
847-960-0200
FAX: 847-784-8059
info@bccacredit.com
www.bccacredit.com

Mary Collins, President/CEO
Jamie Smith, Operations Director
Doreen Colleti-Muhs, Marketing/Sales Manager

Subsidiary of the Broadcast Cable Financial Management Association. BCAA provides credit information, education, and networking opportunities which enables members to efficiently manage credit risk and increase profitability.

425 Members Founded: 1972

24 **CPA Network**
1320 Stony Brook Road
Suite 209
Stony Brook, NY 11790
631-751-6400
FAX: 631-751-6449
mmeyer@cpanetwork.org
www.cpanetwork.org

Neil Guilmette, Member Services
Matt Silvester, Member Services

CPA Network is an association for CPA firms who believe that their true value is their combined intellectual capital, business acumen, resources and understanding, applied in a unique partnering relationship with select clients.

25 **Construction Financial Management Association**
29 Emmons Drive
Suite F-50
Princeton, NJ 08540
609-452-8000
FAX: 609-452-0474
info@cfma.org www.cfma.org

William Schwab, President
Jeff Zogg, Executive Director
Herbert Brownett, SVP Finance
Henry R Waggoner, Treasurer

Non-profit organization dedicated to serving the financial professional in the construction industry.

7000 Members Founded: 1981

26 **Construction Industry CPA Consultants Association**
15011 E Twilight View Drive
Fountain Hills, AZ 85268
480-836-0300
FAX: 480-836-0400 800-864-0491
CICPAC is a nationwide network of accomplished CPA firms specifically selected for their experience in and commitment to serving the construction industry.
93 Members

27 **Financial Accounting Standards Board**
401 Merritt Boulevard
PO Box 5116
Norwalk, CT 06856-5116
203-847-0700
FAX: 203-849-9714
tallen@gasb.org www.fasb.org
Tom L Allen, Chairman
William B Holder, Board Member
David R Bean, Director Research
James R Fountain, Jr, Assistant Director Research
Establish and improve standards of state and local governmental accounting and financial reporting that will result in useful information for users of financial reports and guide and educate the public, including issuers, auditors and users of those financial institutions.
Founded: 1984

28 **Financial Executives International**
200 Campus Drive
PO Box 674
Florham Park, NJ 07932
973-360-0177
FAX: 973-898-4649 www.fei.org
Colleen S Cunningham, President/CEO
Barbara Chanes, Executive Assistant
Peter Montllor, Materials Production Supervisor
Paul Chase, VP/Chief Financial Officer
Christopher Allen, VP/Chief Marketing Officer
A professional organization of individuals performing the duties of CFO, Controller, Treasurer or VP of Finance. Has an annual budget of $5.5 million.
15M Members Founded: 1931

29 **Government Officers Finance Association**
203 N LaSalle Street
Suite 2700
Chicago, IL 60601-1210
312-977-9700
FAX: 312-977-4806 www.gfoa.org
Nancy L. Zielke, President
Jeffrey Esser, Executive Director/CEO
John Jurkash, Chief Financial Officer
Rob Roque, Senior Manager
Dennis Podgorski, IT Manager
GFOA is the professional association of state/provincial and local finance officers in the United States and Canada.
16000 Members Founded: 1906

30 **Healthcare Financial Management Association**
2 Westbrook Corporate Financial Center
Suite 701
Westchester, IL 60154-5700
708-531-9600
FAX: 708-531-0032 800-252-4362
taarya@hfma.org www.hfma.org
Joyce A Zimowski, Chairman
Richard L Clarke, President/CEO
Joseph J Fifer, National Secretary/Treasurer
Mary Ann Genellie, VP Marketing/Business Development
Brings perspective and clarity to the industry's complex issues for the purpose of preparing our members to succeed. Through our programs, publications and partnerships we enhance the capabilities that strengthen not only individual careers, but also the organizations from which our members come.
32000 Members

31 **Hospitality Financial & Technology Professionals**
11709 Boulder Lane
Suite 110
Austin, TX 78726
512-249-5333
FAX: 512-249-1533 800-646-4387
Frank I Wolfe, Executive VP/CEO
Shelley Brand, Director of Membership
Eliza Selig, Communications Manager
Thomas Atzebgifer, CPA, Controller
HFTP is an international, professional association providing a global network, continuing education and resources to the hospitality finance and technology communities.
4600 Members Founded: 1952

32 **Information Systems Audit & Control Association**
3701 Algonquin Road
Suite 1010
Rolling Meadows, IL 60008
847-253-1545
FAX: 847-253-1443
news@isaca.org www.isaca.org
Tim Winslow, CISA, President
Jason McKitrick, CISA, VP
Susan M Caldwell, Chief Executive Officer
Scott R Artman, Chief Financial Officer
Mike Brady, Treasurer
Formed to help auditors, managers and systems specialists address electronic data processing system control problems.
35000 Members Founded: 1967

33 **Institute of Certified Management Accountants**
10 Paragon Drive
Montvale, NJ 07645-1718
800-638-4427
FAX: 201-573-9000 800-638-4427
ima@imanet.org www.imanet.org
Carl S Smith, Chairman
Paul Sharman, President/CEO
Margaret Butler, Director
David Schweitz, Executive Director
Professional organization devoted exclusively to management accounting and financial management. Goals are to help members develop both personally and professionally, by means of education, certifacation and association with other business professionals.
67000 Members Founded: 1919

34 **Institute of Internal Auditors**
247 Maitland Avenue
Altamonte Springs, FL 32701-4201
407-937-1100
FAX: 407-937-1101
iia@theiia.org www.theiia.org
David A Richards, President
Betty L McPhilimy, Chair
Eugene O'Neill, CIA, Director Finance
Charity A. Prentice, CIA, Assistant VP Research/Education
Bonnie L. Ulmer, Assistant VP Educational Products
Independent, objective assurance and consulting activity designed to add value and improve an organization's operations. It helps an organization accomplish its objectives by bringing a systematic, disciplined approach to evaluate and improve the effectiveness of risk management, control and governance processes. Representation from more than 100 countries. *$60.00*
100M Members Founded: 1941

35 **Institute of Management and Administration**
3 Park Avenue, 30th floor
New York, NY 10016-5902
212-244-0360
FAX: 212-564-0465
subserve@ioma.com www.ioma.com
David Foster, President
Assists members in managenment of corporate accounting, boost staff productivity, reduce operation costs, adopt new technology, take charge of your dealing with auditors and lenders and more.
18000 Members

36 **Insurance Accounting Systems Association**
4705 University Drive, Suite 280
PO Box 51340
Durham, NC 27717-1340
919-489-0991
FAX: 919-489-1994
tstillman@iasa.org www.iasa.org
Cathy Ellwood, Director
Joseph Pomilia, Executive Director
Douglas Yenzer, VP Finance
Facilitates the exchange of ideas among insurance industry professionals and their industry-related associates.
1200 Members Founded: 1928

37 **International Accounting Firms**
9200 S Dadeland Boulevard
Suite 510
Miami, FL 33156-2713
305-670-0580
FAX: 305-670-3818
info@accountants.org
www.accountants.org
Art Goessel, Executive Director
Julio Gabay, Director Communications/Membership
Lourdes M Gomez, Administrative Director
Alba Granados, Accounting
Independent accounting firms in 70 countries promoting the profession through group affiliation.
135 Members Founded: 1978

38 **International Newspaper Financial Executives**
21525 Ridgetop Circle
Sterling, VA 20166
703-421-4060
FAX: 703-421-4068
infehg@infe.org www.infe.org
Jayne Hermiston, President
Robert Kasabian, VP/Executive Director
William Mickey, VP
Greg Robinson, Treasurer
Ralph Bender, Secretary
Controllers, chief accountants, auditors, business managers, treasurers, secretaries and related newspaper executives, educators and public accountants.
800 Members Founded: 1947

39 **National Accounting and Finance Council**
2200 Mill Road
Alexandria, VA 22314-4677
703-838-1915
FAX: 703-836-0751
nafc@trucking.org
www.truckline.com
Steve Dill, Chairman
David Hershey, Executive Director
Member organization of chief financial officers within the American Trucking Association.
1000 Members Founded: 1954

40 **National Association of Black Accountants**
7249-A Hanover Parkway
Greenbelt, MD 20770
301-746-6222
FAX: 301-474-3114 www.nabainc.org
Norman K Jenkins, CPA, President
Barry Winters, Executive VP
Darryl R Matthews, Sr, Executive Director
Wayne Lee, Director
Yolanda McBride, Secretary
Nationwide professional association with the primary purpose of developing, encouraging and serving as a resource for greater participation by African-Americans and other minorities in the accounting and finance professions.
Founded: 1969

41 **National Association of Certified Valuation Analysts**
1111 Brickyard Road
Salt Lake City, UT 84106-5401
801-486-0600
FAX: 801-486-7500 800-677-2009
nacva@nacva.com www.nacva.com
Parnell Black, President/CEO
Global, professional association that supports the business valuation and litigation consulting disciplines within the CPA and professional communities. Along with its training and certification progams, NACVA offers a range of professional capabilities and capacities of its members.
6000 Members Founded: 1990

42 **National Association of Computerized Tax Processors**
H&R Block
4400 Main Street
Kansas City, MO 64111
816-328-8485
FAX: 800-996-3526
mnolan@hrblock.com www.nactp.org

Mimi Nolan, President
Phil Kirchner, VP
Mark Castro, Treasurer
Sharon Hartman, Secretary
Nonprofit association that represents tax processing software and hardware developers, electronic filing processors, tax form publishers and tax processing service bureaus. The association promotes standards in tax processing and works closely with the Internal Revenue Service and state governments to promote efficient and effective tax filing.
14100 Members

43 **National Association of Enrolled Agents**
1120 Connecticut Avenue, NW
Suite 460
Washington, DC 20036-3922
202-822-6232
FAX: 202-822-6270
info@naeahq.org www.naea.org
Faye Touchet, EA, President
Susan Zuber, Executive VP
Lois Manning, Treasurer/Secretary
Sharon Cranford, Director Public Policy
Sarah Downey, Technical Manager
Members are individuals who are enrolled to represent taxpayers before the Internal Revenue Service. We advise, represent and prepare tax returns for individuals, partnerships, corporations, estates, trusts and any entities with tax reporting requirements.
Founded: 1972

44 **National CPA Healthcare Advisors Association**
One Valmont Plaza, 4th Floor
Omaha, NE 68154
888-475-4476
FAX: 402-964-3811 800-869-0491
nancyd@hcaa.com www.hcaa.com
Nancy Drennen, Executive Director
HCAA is an association of CPA firms that provide services to health care providers beyond traditional compliance work. Members are admitted on a territorial exclusive basis, one member in each territory.

45 **National Society of Accountants**
1010 N Fairfax Street
Alexandria, VA 22314-1504
703-549-6400
FAX: 703-549-2984 800-966-6679
members@nsacct.org www.nsacct.org

John G Ams, Executive VP
Susan Noell, Director Education
Arlene Richman, Communications Manager
Jodi Goldberg, Director Marketing
Sandra Herring, Sr Manager Member Services
Professional society of practicing accountants and tax practitioners that sponsors the Accreditation Council for Accountancy and Taxation and supports the National Society of Public Accountants Political Action Committee and NSPA Scholarship Foundation.
30000 Members Founded: 1945

46 **Society of Actuaries**
475 N Martingale Road
Schaumburg, IL 60173-2252
847-706-3500
FAX: 847-706-3599
webmaster@soa.org www.soa.org
Stephen G Kellison, President
Sarah Sanford, Executive Director
Christian J DesRochers, Treasurer/Secrtary
Nonprofit professional society involved in the modeling and management of financial risk and contingent events. The mission of the SOA is to advance actuarial knowledge and to enhance the ability of actuaries to provide expert advice and relevant solutions for financial, business and societal problems involving uncertain future events.
17000 Members Founded: 1949
Mailing list available for rent 17000 names $300 per M.

47 **Society of Cost Estimating and Analysis**
101 S Whiting Street
Alexandria, VA 22304-3416
703-751-8069
FAX: 703-461-7328
scea@sceaonline.net
www.sceaonline.net
Daniel Nussbaum, President
Richard Coleman, VP
Leonard Cheshire, Manager
Dedicated to improving cost estimating and analysis in government and industry and enhancing the competence and achievements of its members. The Society offers a unique collection of educational and training materials on cost estimating, cost analysis, earned value management and related disciplines through its professional development program.

48 **Society of Financial Examiners**
174 Grace Boulevard
Altamonte Springs, FL 32714
407-682-4930
FAX: 407-682-3175 www.sofe.org
Denise D Brignac, CFE, President
Stephen J Szypula, CFE, VP Management
Paula Keyes, CPCU, Executive Director
Richard Ford, CFE, VP Marketing/Nominations
Lester C Schott, CFE, Treasurer/Secretary
Is a professional society for examiners of insurance companies, banks, savings and loans, and credit unions.
1600 Members Founded: 1973

Newsletters

49 **AAA Report**
Association for Accounting Administration
136 S Keowee Street
Dayton, OH 45402
937-222-0030
FAX: 937-222-5794
aaainfo@cpaadmin.org
www.cpaadmin.org
Fred Dillon, President
Mary Ellen Meador, Director Information/Communications
Connie Harmsen, VP
Available electronically.
12 pages Founded: 1984
Circulation: 600
Printed in 4 colors

50 **AGA Today**
Advancing Government Accountability
2208 Mount Vernon Avenue
Alexandria, VA 22301-1314
703-684-6931
FAX: 703-548-9367 800-ABA-7211
Relmond Van Daniker, Executive Director
Christina M Camara, Publications Manager
This publication acts a a clearinghouse for current government financial management information. The information is pooled from a dozen or more reputable sources in the industry.

Bi-Weekly

51 **AIRA News**
Association of Insolvency Advisors and Restructing
221 Stewart Avenue
Suite 207
Medford, OR 97501
541-858-1665
FAX: 541-858-9187
aira@airacira.org www.aircira.org
James L. Lukenda, Chairman
Soneet Kapila, President
To provide accurate and authoritative information in regard to the subject matter covered. It is sold with the understanding that the publisher is not engaged in rendering legal, accounting or other professional service.
Six/Year

52 **ARCH**
Society of Actuaries
475 N Martingale Road
Schaumburg, IL 60173-2252
847-706-3500
FAX: 847-706-3599
webmaster@soa.org www.soa.org
Clay Baznik, Publishing Director
Glenda Maki, Senior Editor
Jill Acre, Managing Editor
Dennis Sjodin, President
Is an informal communication providing current actuarial research t friends and members of teh actuarial community. Its primary goal is the speedy dissemination of current thinking and aids to research.

53 **AWSCPA News**
American Woman's Society of CPAs
136 South Keowee Street
Dayton, OH 45402
937-222-1872
FAX: 937-222-5794 800-297-2721
info@awscpa.org www.awscpa.org
Jenifer Goforth, President
Lynne Himmer, VP Publications
Available electronically.
Quarterly Founded: 1933
Circulation: 1500
Printed in 4 colors

54 **Accounting Education News**
American Accounting Association
5717 Bessie Drive
Sarasota, FL 34233-2399
941-921-7747
FAX: 941-923-4093
office@aaahq.org www.aaahq.org
Tracey Sutherland, Executive Director
Helen Griffith, Publications Specialist
Information on industry development and associations.
8 pages Founded: 1916
Circulation: 9000
Printed in 3 colors on matte stock

55 **Accounting Office Management & Administration**
Institute of Management & Administration

3 Park Avenue
30th Floor
New York, NY 10016-2299
212-244-0360
FAX: 212-564-0465
subserve@ioma.com www.ioma.com
Sue Sandler, Editor
Information on operating your CPA firm at peak efficiency, improve firm profitability, cut costs, update staffing ratios, market and complete more effectively. Offers practical guidance on fees and billing rates, compensation levels and benefits for CPAs and staff, firm performance, benchmarks and more. *$279.00*
Monthly Founded: 1755
Circulation: 180000

56 **Accounting and Auditing Update Service**
RIA Group
395 Hudson Street
New York, NY 10014
212-367-6300
FAX: 212-367-6305 www.riahome.com
Analayzes FASB and AICPA pronouncements. *$465.00*
Bi-Weekly

57 **Action Letter**
Accreditation Council for Accountancy
1010 N Fairfax Street
Alexandria, VA 22314-1574
703-492-2228
FAX: 703-549-2984 888-289-7763
info@acatcredentials.org
www.acatcredentials.org
Cassandra Newby, Director
Marc Saluk, Program Coordinator
Accreditation Council for Accountancy and Taxation publishes this newsletter for its credential holders.
Semi-Annual

58 **Attorney/CPA**
American Association of Attorney-CPAs
3921 Old Lee Highway
Suite 71 A
Fairfax, CA 22030
703-528-8064
FAX: 703-352-8064 800-272-2889
aaacpa@attorney-cpa.com
www.attorney-cpa.com
Clark Mulligan, Executive Director
Bernard Eizen, President
To promote the study and understanding of the fields of Law and Accounting and those related professions.
Quarterly Founded: 1964

59 **Auditwire**
Institute of Internal Auditors
247 Maitland Avenue
Altamonte Springs, FL 32701-4201
407-937-1100
FAX: 407-937-1101
iia@theiia.org www.theiia.org
Stephanie Doyle, Editor
Provides IIA members' news and perspectives on current and emerging issues and delivers news abouth The IIA and the people, events, and issues that shpe the profession. *$60.00*
6x/per year
Circulation: 50,000

60 **Behavioral Research in Accounting**
American Accounting Association
5717 Bessie Drive
Sarasota, FL 34233-2399
941-921-7747
FAX: 949-923-4093
office@aaahq.org
www.aaahq.org/index.cfm
Stephen E. Kaplan, Editor
To promote the wide dissemination of the results of systematic scholarly inquiries into the broad field of accounting. *$20.00*
Year

61 **CFMA Building Profits**
Construction Financial Management Association
29 Emmons Drive
Suite F50
Princeton, NJ 08540
609-452-8000
FAX: 609-452-0474
info@cfma.org www.cfma.org
William M Schwab, President/CEO
Ronald C Kress, Director Sales/Advertising
James Bartsch, Director Marketing
Paula A Wristen, Editor
Information for financial managers and CPAs concerned with financial management.
Bi-Monthly
Circulation: 7,000

62 **CPA Managing Partner Report**
Aspen Publishers
1185 Avenue of the Americas
New York, NY 10036
212-597-0200
FAX: 212-597-0338 800-234-1660
Richard H Kravitz, Exec VP/Group Publisher
Gerry Centrowitz, VP Marketing/Communications
Provides managing partners of CPA firms with problem-solving tactics and managing methods that can help the firm maintain stability and enhance profitability for short term as well as long range goals. *$457.00*
Monthly

63 **CPA Marketing Report**
Aspen Publishers
1185 Avenue of the Americas
New York, NY 10036
212-597-0200
FAX: 212-597-0338 800-234-1660
Richard H Kravitz, Exec VP/Group Publisher
Gerry Centrowitz, VP Marketing/Communication
Helps public accounting firms design, implement and evaluate effective programs to attract new clients, enhance the firms' image, improve client relations and build sound practices. *$369.00*
8 pages Monthly

64 **CPA Personnel Report**
Aspen Publishers
1185 Avenue of the Americas
Manhattan, NY 10036
212-597-0200
FAX: 212-597-0338 800-234-1660
Richard H Kravitz, Exec VP/Group Publisher
Marc Jennings, Publisher
Gerry Centrowitz, VP Marketing and Communications
Mark Fried, Associate Publisher
Aids partners and human resources directors in taking a strategic role in recruiting, retention and compensation in a competitive staffing environment through case studies and the best practices at other CPA firms. *$400.00*
8 pages Monthly

65 **Client Information Bulletin**
WPI Communications
55 Morris Avenue
Springfield, NJ 07081
973-678-8700
FAX: 800-677-9742 800-323-4995
info@wpicomm.com
www.wpicomm.com

Steven Klinghoffer, Publisher
Marilyn Lang, Circulation Manager

Bulletin for lawyers and CPAs to distribute to clients to keep them informed on tax matters. This original publication which has been helping accountants build their practices since 1952, has been redesigned. Covers important new tax developments, general business principals, finanicial planning, estate planning and other related topics.

4 pages Monthly Founded: 1952
Printed in 2 colors

66 **Controller's Report**
Institute of Management & Administration
29 W 35th Street
5th Floor
New York, NY 10001-2299
212-244-0360
FAX: 212-564-0465
subserve@ioma.com www.ioma.com

Tim Harris, Editor

Aimed at corporate controllers in companies of all sizes. Provides benchmarks on virtually every cost area controllers are responsible for, along with articles on financial leadership and keeping control which show by interview or case study how controllers are contributing to the financial stability and growth of their companies. *$269.00*

16 pages Monthly

67 **Controller's Tax Letter**
Institute of Management & Administration
29 W 35th Street
5th Floor
New York, NY 10001-2299
212-244-0360
FAX: 212-564-0465
subserve@ioma.com www.ioma.com

Perry Patterson, VP/Publisher

Focuses on the tax implications of business decisions and provides readers in corporate finance/accounting details on recently settled cases from US Tax Court, with full citations for those who want to know more. CTL also shows controllers, accounting managers and tax managers the effects of business decisions as they relate to a company's strategic planning for new sales efforts, expanding their overseas or foreign presence, and exemptions and deductions available where laws have changed. *$259.00*

Monthly

68 **Controllers Council**
Institute of Certified Management Accountants
10 Paragon Drive
Montvale, NJ 07645-1718

FAX: 201-474-1603 800-638-4427
ima@imanet.org www.imanet.org

Monthly newsletter with useful information for chief financial officers, plant controllers and financial management personnel.

Monthly
Circulation: 2,200

69 **General Ledger**
American Institute of Professional Bookkeepers
6001 Montrose Road
Suite 500
Rockville, MD 20852
301-770-7300
FAX: 800-541-0066 800-622-0121
info@aipb.org www.aipb.org

Stanley I Hartman, Executive Director
Stephen Sahlein, Co-President

Monthly Founded: 1987
Circulation: 30000
Mailing list available for rent $110 per M.

70 **Government Accounting and Auditing Update**
Warren, Gorham & Lamont
395 Hudson Street
New York, NY 10014
212-367-6300
FAX: 212-367-6718 800-742-3348
vincentcecolini@riag.com
www.riahome.com

Vincent Cecolini, Editor

Includes changes taking place in government accounting and financial reporting; analysis of the latest developments, explanations of how they affect work and practical guidance on adapting to these changes. *$335.00*

8 pages Monthly Founded: 1935
Circulation: 5000
Mailing list available for rent 5000 names
Printed in 2 colors on glossy stock

71 **Governmental Accounting Standards Board Action Report**
401 Merritt 7
PO Box 5116
Norwalk, CT 06856-5116
203-847-0700
FAX: 203-849-9714
webmaster@gasb.org www.gasb.org

Attmore Robert, Chairman
Sheryl L Thompson, Media Contact

Action Report newsletter. *$155.00*

Monthly

72 **IOMA's Report on Salary Surveys**
Institute of Management & Administration
3 Park Avenue
30th Floor
New York, NY 10016-2221
212-244-0360
FAX: 212-564-0465
subserve@ioma.com www.ioma.com

Laime Vaitkus, Editor
Perry Patterson, VP/Publisher
Taul Morris, Circulation Manager
David Foster, President
Jim Bell, Marketing Manager

Provides information on setting and managing compensation. *$269.00*

16 pages Monthly Founded: 1984

73 **Information Management**
Information Resources Management Association
701 E Chocolate Avenue
Suite 200
Hershey, PA 17033
717-533-8879
717-533-8861
members@irma-international.org
www.irma-international.org

Mehdi Khosrow-Pour, Editor

This practical, informative newsletter is a leading publication of information technology resources management. Short, concise articles give you objective, professional views of newly emerging technologies and trends designed to help you be more competitive in your field. *$50.00*

Semi-Annually

74 **Internal Auditing Report**
Warren, Gorham & Lamont
395 Hudson Street
New York, NY 10014
212-367-6300
FAX: 212-367-6718 800-742-3348
vincentcecolini@riag.com
www.riahome.com

Andrea Kingston, Editor

Perfect for keeping up to date on new auditing standards and developments. Offers guidance on managing internal auditing departments, covers new audit technology, offers new audit techniques used by successful audit management practices, and provides practicioner level feedback on current Institute of Internal Auditors standards. *$325.00*

12 pages six times a yea Founded: 1980
Circulation: 5000
Mailing list available for rent 5000 names
Printed in 2 colors on glossy stock

75 **Internal Auditor**
Institute of Internal Auditors
247 Maitland Avenue
Altamonte Springs, FL 32701-4201
407-937-1100
FAX: 407-937-1101
iia@theiia.org www.theiia.org

Joanne Hodges, Asst VP/Editor-in-Chief
Anne Scott, Managing Editor
Dave Richards, Chief Executive Officer

Published to communicate with and inform members about news and events affecting the Institute and profession of internal auditing. *$60.00*

20 pages Founded: 1941
Circulation: 270000 Audited
Mailing list available for rent 36000 names
Printed in 4 colors on glossy stock

76 **Interpreter**
Insurance Accounting Systems Association
3511 Shannon Road
Suite 160
Durham, NC 27707
919-489-0991
FAX: 919-489-1994
info@iasa.org www.iasa.org

Douglas Yenzer, VP
Cathy Ellwood, President

Offers information to accountants specializing in insurance and real estate markets. *$35.00*

12 pages Quarterly Founded: 1928

77 **Letter Ruling Review**
Tax Analysts
6830 N Fairfax Drive
Arlington, VA 22213
703-533-4400
FAX: 703-533-4440 800-955-3444
cservice@tax.org www.tax.org

Christopher Bergin, CEO
David Brunori, Executive VP Editor

Publication analyzes significant private letter rulings issued by the Internal Revenue Service during the month.

4 pages Monthly Founded: 1970
Printed in 1 color on matte stock

78 **Management & Administration Report (ADMAR)**
Institute of Management & Administration

29 W 35th Street
5th Floor
New York, NY 10001-2299
212-244-0360
FAX: 212-564-0465
subserve@ioma.com www.ioma.com

Perry Patterson, VP/Publisher
Tim Harris, Editor

How to manage corporate accounting departments more effectively, boost staff productivity, reduce operation costs and adopt new systems and technology, take charge of your dealings with auditors and lenders and get results senior management is sure to notice.

79 **Managing Accounts Payable**
Institute of Management & Administration

29 W 35th Street
5th Floor
New York, NY 10001-2299
212-244-0360
FAX: 212-564-0465
subserve@ioma.com www.ioma.com

Mary S Schaeffer, Editor
Perry Patterson, VP/Publisher
Paul Mauris, Circulation Manager
David Foster, President

Topics covered in the newsletter include: invoice handling, check preparation, printing and filing exception and rush check processing; techniques for reducing duplicate payments, staff and career management working with other departments, master vendor files, terms and discounts and T&E, VAT reclaim, EDI, XML, technology, imaging p-cards, post audit firms, benchmarking, 1099s, check fraud, case studies, escheat or unclaimed property, sales and use tax. *$269.00*
Monthly Founded: 1984

80 **Managing the General Ledger**
Institute of Management & Administration

29 W 35th Street
5th Floor
New York, NY 10001-2299
212-244-0360
FAX: 212-564-0465
subserve@ioma.com www.ioma.com

Perry Patterson, VP/Publisher

Aimed at controllers and corporate accounting managers and shows the most current techniques for efficient monthly closings and AICPA approved methods for general ledger entries. *$308.14*
Monthly

81 **NCAC Newsletter**
National Council of Accountant Consultants
PO Box 359
Springfield, NJ 07081-0359
973-379-1090
FAX: 973-379-6507

Deborah Hart, Publisher

Council news offering information on the accounting community.
Quarterly

82 **NSPA Washington Reporter**
National Society of Public Accountants
1010 N Fairfax Street
Alexandria, VA 22314
703-549-6400
FAX: 703-549-2984 800-966-6679
members@nsacct.org www.nsacct.org

John G Ams, Exec VP
Mike Chakerman, Director
Jodie Munler, Marketing Manager
Susan Heisler, Editor

Coverage of NSPA activity with the government, and news on members in various states.
Monthly Founded: 1955

83 **National Association of Certified Valuation Analysts**
1111 Brickyard Road
Suite 200
Salt Lake City, UT 84106-5401
801-486-0600
FAX: 801-486-7500 800-677-2009
nacva@macva.com www.nacva.com

Parnell Black, CEO

Global, professional association that supports the business valuation and litigation consulting disciplines within the CPA and professional communities. Along with its training and certification programs, NACVA offers a range of support services, marketing tools, software programs, reference materials and customized databases to enhance the professional capabilities and capacities of its members.
Founded: 1990
Circulation: 10000
Printed in 4 colors

84 **National Estimator**
Society of Cost Estimating and Analysis
101 S Whiting Street
Alexandria, VA 22304-3416
703-751-8069
FAX: 703-461-7328
scea@sceaonline.net
www.sceonline.net

Daniel Nussbaum, President
Bill Stacy, Manager

The National Estimator contains articles, members highlights, and other items of interest to the membership.
Twice/year

85 **News Plus**
National Association of Black Accountants

7249-A Hanover Parkway
Greenbelt, MD 20770
301-474-6222
FAX: 301-474-3114 www.nabainc.org

Darryl R Matthews Sr., Executive Director
Barry Winters, Executive VP
Norman Jenkins, President

Updates on accounting proposals and regulations. *$20.00*
Quarterly Founded: 1969

86 **Nonprofit Report: Accounting, Taxation Management**
Warren, Gorham & Lamont
395 Hudson Street
New York, NY 10014
212-367-6300
FAX: 212-367-6314 800-742-3348
Offers CPA's with nonprofit clients, and professionals working in the nonprofit sector, a practical, timely look at today's key nonprofit issues, including IRS rulings and pronouncements, AICPA changes and legislation governing the financial management of most nonprofit organizations. *$215.00*
8 pages Monthly
Circulation: 46000
Mailing list available for rent
Printed in 2 colors on glossy stock

87 **Partner's Report for CPA Firm Owners**
Institute of Management & Administration

3 Park Ave
30th Floor
New York, NY 10016
212-244-0360
FAX: 212-564-0465
subserve@ioma.com www.ioma.com

Sue Sandler, Editor
David Foster, CEO

Management advice for partners, shareholders and owners of CPA firms to help them improve partner distribution, increase firm margins, and improve their stewardship of the firm. Includes practical guidance on partner and all compensation and benefits, retirement plan alternatives, professional liability coverage, rainmaking and more. *$279.00*
Monthly

88 **Payroll Manager's Report**
Institute of Management & Administration

29 W 35th Street
5th Floor
New York, NY 10001-2299
212-244-0360
FAX: 212-564-0465
subserve@ioma.com www.ioma.com

Donis Ford, Editor
Dave Foster, CEO/President
Tim Eelo, Marketing
Paul Moriss, Circulation Manager

Written for payroll practitioners working with small and large employers. Provides how to information on managing a payroll department cost effectively and service efficiently. Analysis includes the latest benchmarks on payroll metrics, technology updates and softwatre evaluations, latest trends in training staff and cutting edge counsel on developing leadership skills. *$249.00*
Monthly

89 **Payroll Practitioner's Monthly**
Institute of Management & Administration

29 W 35th Street
5th Floor
New York, NY 10001-2299
212-244-0360
FAX: 212-564-0465
subserve@ioma.com www.ioma.com

Perry Patterson, VP/Publisher

Shows payroll professionals what they need to do and how to do it when it comes to the many rules, regulations and laws they must follow to prepare and distribute a corporate payroll. In general terms, it is a step by step newsletter, focusing on the administrative details of payroll in plain English with proven suggestions on how to get the job done right and done once. *$239.00*
Monthly

90 **Payroll Tax Alert**
Institute of Management & Administration
3 Park Avenue
30th Floor
New York, NY 10016
212-244-0360
FAX: 212-564-0465
subserve@ioma.com www.ioma.com

Perry Patterson, VP/Publisher
David Sosters, CEO
Stephanie Mannino, Editor
Jim Bell, Marketing
Paul Morris, Circulation Manager

Used by payroll managers, professionals in accounting or human resources and provides quick, hard hitting updates on changes to federal and state payroll policy (wage-hour rules, industrial orders, new posting requirements and tax issues) from every agency that has a hand in corporate payroll & benefits administration. *$240.00*

Monthly Founded: 1984
Circulation: 2000

91 **Pocket MBA**
Practising Law Institute
810 7th Avenue
New York, NY 10019-5818
212-824-5700
FAX: 212-262-8180 800-260-4754
info@pli.edu www.pli.edu

Stephen Freeman, President
Victor J Rubino, Executive Director
Nickola Francis, Subscription Manager

Provides knowledge every lawyer needs about business and finance. *$1295.00*
Weekly Founded: 1933

92 **Public Accounting Desk Book**
Strafford Publications
590 Dutch Valley Road NE
Postal Drawer 13729
Atlanta, GA 30324-0729
404-881-1141
FAX: 404-881-0074 800-926-7926
custserv@straffordpub.com
www.straffordpub.com

Richard Ossoff, President
Jon McKenna, Executive Editor

Provides public accounting firms with authoritative news and analysis of developments in the accounting profession today and emerging trends for the future. Also reports SEC auditor changes, mergers, acquisitions, personnel changes and related events. *$39.00*
Annual Founded: 1984

93 **SEC Accounting Report**
Warren, Gorham & Lamont
395 Hudson Street
New York, NY 10014
212-367-6300
FAX: 212-367-6314 800-742-3348
ria@Thomson.com www.riahome.com

Kurt Horning, Securities Editor
Paul Wendell, Author

For senior executives for monthly news and insights on emerging SEC issues. The SEC Accounting Report can help you to understand SEC changes and their susbsequent compliance requirements. *$365.00*
8 pages Monthly
Circulation: 5000
Mailing list available for rent 5000 names
Printed in 2 colors on glossy stock

94 **TOPICS Newsletter**
Advancing Government Accountability
2208 Mount Vernon Avenue
Alexandria, VA 22301-1314
706-684-6931
FAX: 703-548-9367 800-ABA-7211

Sam M McCall, President
Deborah Loveless, CGFM, SVP at Large
Lealan Miller, SVP Regional Services
Relmond Van Daniker, Executive Director
Cristina Barbudo, Director Finance/Administration

Designed to give national exposure to chapter events, community service projects and member accomplishments while offering the most-up-to-date Association news, released every other Monday morning by e-mail to members.

95 **Tax Letter and Social Security Report**
Peyron Associates
350 N 9th Street
Suite 305
Boise, ID 83702
208-388-3800
FAX: 208-388-8898 info@peyron.com

Dan Peyron, Editor

Covers taxes, social security tax, benefit tips, information for middle income individuals and professionals. *$56.00*
4 pages Monthly
Circulation: 2000 Audited
Printed in 1 color on matte stock

Magazines & Journals

96 **Academy of Accounting Historians**
Culverhouse School of Accountancy
University of Alabama
Box 870223
Tuscaloosa, AL 35487-223
205-348-7443
FAX: 205-348-5308
krice@cba.ua.edu
www.cba.ua.edu/accounting

Stephen Walker, Editor
Kathy Rice, Administrative Coordinator
Ronald Dulek, Manager Marketing
Mary Stone, Director

Encourages research, publication, teaching and personal interchanges in all phases of accounting history and its interrelation with business and economic history.
Quarterly Founded: 1978
Printed in on matte stock

97 **Accountants SEC Practice Manual**
CCH
2700 Lake Cook Road
Riverwoods, IL 60015
847-267-7000
FAX: 773-866-3095 800-525-3335

Kevin Robert, President/CEO
James Rooney, Editor

Offers guidance for preparing and filing financial statements with the SEC, including regulations, forms and helpful summaries and checklists. *$819.00*
Annual+ Founded: 1913

98 **Accounting Horizons**
American Accounting Association
5717 Bessie Drive
Sarasota, FL 34233-2399
941-921-7747
FAX: 941-923-4093
office@aaahq.org www.aaahq.org

Tracey Sutherland, Executive Director
Diane Hazard, Assistant Director Publishing
Terry Shevlin, Senior Editor
Judy Cothern, Office Administrator
Helen Griffith, Publications Specialist

Accounting and business information. *$200.00*
Quarterly Founded: 1916
Circulation: 9000
Printed in 3 colors on matte stock

99 **Accounting Review**
American Accounting Association
5717 Bessie Drive
Sarasota, FL 34233-2399
941-921-7747
FAX: 941-923-4093
Office@aaahq.org www.aaahq.org

Tracey Sutherland, Executive Director
Terry Shevlin, Senior Editor
Diane Hazard, Assistant Director

Offers a review of topics and tips for the industry. *$275.00*
Quarterly Founded: 1916

100 **Accounting Today**
Thomson Media
1 State Street Plaza
25th Floor
New York, NY 10004
212-258-8445
FAX: 212-292-5216 800-221-1809
william.carlino@sourcemedia.com
www.webcpa.com

Bill Carlino, Editor-in-Chief
Daniel Hood, Managing Editor
Robert Whitaker, Publisher
Sue Korcynski, Marketing

Covers accounting and auditing standards, taxation and practice management. *$99.00*

48 pages Founded: 1987
Circulation: 34991 1000 names $130 per M.
Printed in 4 colors on glossy stock

101 **Accounting and Business Review**
World Scientific Publishing
27 Warren Street
Suite 401-402
Hackensack, NJ 07601
201-487-9655
FAX: 201-487-9656 800-227-7562
wspc@wspc.com www.wspc.com

Yang-Hoong Pang, Editor

Aims to provide a forum for the publication of accounting and business research papers which are of interest to educators, students and practititioners. *$60.00*
Founded: 1981

102 **Accounting and Tax Highlights**
Warren, Gorham & Lamont
395 Hudson Street
New York, NY 10014
212-645-4800
FAX: 212-367-6305 800-742-3348

Barry Brinker, Editor
Phil Brady, Advertising Manager

Covers current news and developments in the field. Audiocassette program for CPAs for continuing professional education. Accepts advertising. *$112.00*

28 pages Monthly

103 **Actuary Magazine**
Society of Actuaries
475 N Martingale Road
Schaumburg, IL 60173-2252
847-706-3500
FAX: 847-706-3599
webmaster@soa.org www.soa.org
Robert D Shapiro, Editor
Provides informative feature articles that will focus on a variety of actuarial topics. The Actuary magazine will include other articles of interest including career information, SOA education initiatives and trends in international business.
Bimonthly
Printed in 4 colors on glossy stock

104 **Audit Report**
Association of Credit Union Internal Auditors
PO Box 1926
Columbus, OH 43216-1926
614-219-9702
FAX: 614-221-2335 866-254-8128
Betty Cramer, Editor
Kelsey Hall, Managing Editor
Quarterly
Circulation: 800
Printed in 4 colors

105 **Auditing Journal of Practice and Theory**
American Accounting Association
5717 Bessie Drive
Sarasota, FL 34233-2399
941-921-7747
FAX: 941-923-4093
office@aaahq.org
www.aaahq.org/index.cfm
William F. Messier, Jr., Editor
Mark L. DeFord, Associate Editor
Twice/Year

106 **CPA Software News**
Cygnus Publishing
1233 Janesville Avenue
Fort Atkinson, WI 53538
920-563-6388
FAX: 920-563-1699 800-456-0864
shari.dodgen@cygnuspub.com
www.cpatechadvisor.com
Shari Dodgen, Publisher
Melody Wrinkle, Managing Editor
Sandra Burnett, Production Manager
Gregory LaFollette, Executive Editor
The independent voice for accountants' software. *$48.00*
Founded: 1991
Circulation: 50,000+
Printed in 4 colors on glossy stock

107 **Computers in Accounting**
Warren, Gorham & Lamont
395 Hudson Street
New York, NY 10014
212-367-6300
FAX: 212-367-6718 800-742-3348
RIA@Thomson.com
www.riahome.com
Rick Kravitz, Publisher
Ted Needleman, Editor
Contains the latest information on accounting, tax and business software, electronic spreadsheets, and available hardware. *$58.00*
40 pages Founded: 1935

108 **Controller's Cost & Profit Report**
Warren, Gorham & Lamont
395 Hudson Street
New York, NY 10014-3669
212-367-6324
FAX: 212-367-6718 800-742-3348
Dorothy Cummings, Publisher
Targets cash flow issues, risk/reward decisions, personnel trends, ways to increase productivity while reducing overhead costs, and technology updates for the new millennium. *$195.50*
SemiMonthly

109 **Disburse**
American Payroll Association
660 N Main Avenue
Suite 100
San Antonio, TX 78205-1217
210-226-4600
FAX: 210-226-4027
apamail@mindspring.com
www.americanpayroll.org
Daniel J Maddux, Publisher
Provides readers with a wealth of information on new products, banking solutions, educational events and opportunities, as well as a variety of other topics related to accounts payable business functions.
Quarterly
Circulation: 14000

110 **Employer Practices**
American Payroll Association
660 N Main Avenue
Suite 100
San Antonio, TX 78205
210-226-4600
FAX: 210-226-4027
apamail@mindspring.com
www.americanpayroll.org
Human resources information and trends.

111 **Financial Executive**
Financial Executives International
200 Campus Drive
PO Box 674
Florham Park, NJ 07932-674
973-360-0177
FAX: 973-765-1023
ccunningham@fei.org www.fei.org
Jeffrey Marshall, Editor-in-Chief
Laura Avello, Art Director
Brenda Newkirk, Advertising Sales
Colleen S Cunningham, President/CEO
Addresses accounting and treasury subjects, as well as overall strategies in corporate financial management. *$59.00*
72 pages 10x/yr Founded: 1931
Circulation: 17000
Printed in 4 colors on glossy stock

112 **Government Accountants Journal**
Association of Government Accountants
2208 Mount Vernon Avenue
Alexandria, VA 22301-1314
703-684-6931
FAX: 703-548-9367 800-ABA-7211
Relmond P Van Daniker, Executive Director
Charles W Culkin Jr, Publisher
Marie M Force MA, Editor
Since 1950 we have been providing valuable, in depth information to decision makers at all levels of government. Examines budgeting, accounting, auditing and data process developments and govermental regulations and legislation. *$60.00*

Quarterly
Circulation: 16,000
Mailing list available for rent 18,000 names

113 **Infoline**
Hospitality Financial & Technology Professionals
11709 Boulder Lane
Suite 110
Austin, TX 78726-1832
512-249-5333
FAX: 512-249-1533 800-646-4387
eliza.selig@hftp.org www.hftp.org
Frank Wolfe, Executive VP/CEO
Lance Peterson, Director Marketing
Thomas Atzenhofer, Controller
Chapter and officer activities.
Monthly Founded: 1952

114 **Information Systems Control Journal**
Information Systems Audit & Control Association
3701 Algonquin Road
Suite 1010
Rolling Meadows, IL 60008
847-253-1545
FAX: 847-253-1443
news@isaca.org www.isaca.org
Tim Winslow, CISA, President
Jason McKitrick, CISA, VP
Susan M Caldwell, Chief Executive Officer
Scott R Artman, Chief Financial Officer
Mike Brady, Treasurer
Provides professional standards, guidelines and procedures for the IS audit and control professions.
Bimonthly

115 **Insight**
Illinois CPA Society
550 W Jackson
Suite 900
Chicago, IL 60661-5716
312-993-0407
FAX: 312-993-9954 800-993-0407
jwinn@stametine.com www.icpas.org
Julia Winn, Publisher
Judy Gianetto Adams, Director
Elaine Weiss, CEO
Editorial content focuses on practical issues affecting professional development.
$30.00
Founded: 1980
Circulation: 23000

116 **Internal Auditing**
Warren, Gorham & Lamont
395 Hudson Street
New York, NY 10014
212-367-6300
FAX: 212-367-6718 800-742-3348
Rick Kravitz, Publisher
Ted Needleman, Editor
Provides solutions to internal auditing problems. Only professional resource written exclusively by leading practitioners.
$275.00
Annual+ Founded: 1935

117 **Internal Auditing (RIA Group)**
RIA Group
395 Hudson Street
New York, NY 10014-3669
212-367-6300
FAX: 212-367-6305 800-431-9025
RIA.EditorialQuestions@Thomson.com
www.riahome.com
Andrea Kingston, Editor
Dominick Rao, President

Provides auditors, corporate executives, and board members with current developments in theory and practice of interal auditing. $220.00
Founded: 1935
Circulation: 5000

118 Internal Auditor
Institute of Internal Auditors
247 Maitland Avenue
Altamonte Springs, FL 32701-4201
407-937-1100
FAX: 407-937-1101
editor@theiia.org www.theiia.org/
Joanne Hodges, Director/Editor-in-Chief
Anne Scott, Managing Editor
Dave Richards, Chief Executive Officer
International journal for internal auditors, corporate executives and board members; current developments in theory and practice of controls and internal auditing. Accepts advertising.
84 pages Founded: 1944
Circulation: 55000
Printed in 4 colors on matte stock

119 International Journal of Business Data Communications and Networking
Information Resources Management Association
701 E Chocolate Avenue
Suite 200
Hershey, PA 17033
717-533-8879
FAX: 717-533-8661
member@irma-international.org
www.irm-international.org
Jairo Gutierrez, Editor
This journal aims to disseminate practical and theoretical information, which will enable readers to understand, manage, use and maintain business data communication networks more effectively. $85.00
Annually

120 Jacobs Report
Offshore Press
PO Box 8194
4500 W 72nd Terrace
Prairie Village, KS 66208-2824
913-362-9667
FAX: 913-432-7174 888-516-3177
jacobs@offshorepress.com
www.offshorepress.com
Vernon K Jacobs, President
International tax news.
10 pages Daily Founded: 1981 400 names

121 Journal of Accounting Research
University of Chicago/Graduate School of Business
5807 South Woodlawn Avenue
Chicago, IL 60637
773-702-7743
FAX: 773-834-4585
webhelp@chicagogsb.edu
www.gsb.uchicago.edu
Allan Friedman, Executive Director of Communication
Jessamine Chan, Executive Editor
Offers research and information in the fields of empirical and experimental accounting. $86.00
Monthly
Circulation: 2800

122 Journal of Accounting and Public Policy
Elsevier Science
655 Avenue of the Americas
PO Box 945
New York, NY 10010
212-989-5800
FAX: 212-633-3680
usinfo-f@elsvevier.com
www.sciencedirect.com
Lawrence A Gordon, Editor-in-Chief
Martin P Loeb, Editor
Publishes research papers that focus on the intersection between accounting and public policy. It offers articles on accounting including public administration, political science and the law. $225.00
Annual+ Founded: 1997

123 Journal of Construction Accounting & Taxation
Warren, Gorham & Lamont
395 Hudson Street
New York, NY 10014-3669
212-367-6300
FAX: 212-367-6718 800-742-3348
aboden@riag.com www.wgl.com
Susan Weisenfeld, Managing Editor
Douglas McPherson, President
Articles are written by and for accountants, auditors, manager, controllers, sureties, attorneys, consultants, and others involved in the construction industry. $230.00
Founded: 1980
Circulation: 3400

124 Journal of Cost Analysis and Management
Society of Cost Estimating and Analysis
101 S Whiting Street
Alexandria, VA 22304-3416
703-751-8069
FAX: 703-461-7328
scea@sceaonline.net
www.sceaonline.net
Daniel Nussbaum, President
Is a forum by which these individuals may submit papers for publication and represent the Society in areas of research, analysis and education.
Twice/Year

125 Journal of Cost Management
Warren, Gorham & Lamont
395 Hudson Street
New York, NY 10014-3669
212-367-6300
FAX: 212-367-6718 800-742-3348
Catherine Stenzel, Editor-in-Chief
Joe Stenzel, Editor-in-Chief
Journal of modern cost management (including cost and managerial accounting topics), especially activity-based costing, activity-based management, performance measurement, target costing, investment justification. Accepts advertising. $230.00
64 pages

126 Journal of Information Systems
American Accounting Association
5717 Bessie Drive
Sarasota, FL 34233-2399
941-921-7747
FAX: 941-923-4093
Office@aaahq.org www.aaahq.org
Tracey Sutherland, Executive Director
James Szelminski, Assistant Director
Dan Stone, Editor
Helen Griffith, Publications Specialist
Covers developments relating to information systems in use in the accounting industry. $35.00
Monthly Founded: 1916

127 Journal of International Accounting Research
American Accounting Association
5717 Bessie Drive
Sarasota, FL 34233-2399
941-921-7747
FAX: 941-923-4093
office@aaahq.org
www.aaahq.org/index.cfm
Dr. Lee Radebaugh, Editor

128 Journal of Organizational and End User Computing
Information Resources Management Association
701 E Chocolate Avenue
Suite 200
Hershey, PA 17033
717-533-8879
FAX: 717-533-8661
members@irma-international.org
www.irm-international.org
M Adam Mahmood, Editor
The journal features a major emphasis on how to increase organizational and end user productivity and performance, and how to achieve organizational strategic and competitive advantage. $95.00
Quarterly

129 Journal of the America Taxation Association
American Accounting Association
5717 Bessie Drive
Sarasota, FL 34233-2399
941-921-7747
FAX: 941-923-4093
office@aaahq.org
www.aaahq.org/index.cfm
John R. Robinson, Editor

130 National Public Accountant
National Society of Accountants
1010 N Fairfax Street
Alexandria, VA 22314
703-549-6400
FAX: 703-549-2984 800-966-6679
members@nsacct.org www.nsacct.org
Kimberlee Lippencott, Editor
John G. Ams, Executive VP
News for practicing accountants and tax practitioners.
48 pages Founded: 1945
Circulation: 20000

131 New Accountant
REN Publishing
3550 W Peterson Avenue
Suite 100
Chicago, IL 60659
773-674-4069
FAX: 773-866-9881 888-641-3169
inquiries@RenPublishing.com
www.renpublishing.com/
Steven N Polydoris, President/Publisher/Editor
Offers news with special focus on careers, issues and developments in the field of accounting. $85.00
17 pages Monthly Founded: 1883
Circulation: 68000

132 **North American Journal**
Society of Actuaries
475 North Martingale Road
Suite 600
Schaumburg, IL 60173
847-706-3500
FAX: 847-706-3599 www.soa.org
Steve Callison, President
Robert Brueline, VP
Harry H Panjer, Editor
Coverage of the acutarial developments throughout the country.
Quarterly Founded: 1997
Circulation: 17000
Mailing list available for rent 17000 names $300 per M.

133 **Partner-To-Partner Advisory**
Harcourt Brace Professional Publishing
525 B Street
Suite 1900
San Diego, CA 92101-4495
619-231-6616
FAX: 619-699-6542 800-831-7799
propub@harcourtbrace.com
www.hbpp.com
News and reports focus on practice management techniques, partners advice, and other business topics of interest to CPA firms.
Founded: 1919

134 **Payroll Administration Guide**
Bureau of National Affairs
1231 25th Street NW
Washington, DC 20037-1157
202-452-4200
800-372-1033
customercare@bna.com www.bna.com
Gregory C McCaffery, Publisher
Michael Baer, Managing Editor
Sandra C. Degler, Chairman
A notification and reference service for payroll professionals. Covers federal and state employment tax, wage-hour and wage-payment laws. *$896.00*
Bi-Weekly Founded: 1929

135 **Paytech**
American Payroll Association
660 N Main Avenue
Suite 100
San Antonio, TX 78205-1217
212-686-2030
FAX: 212-686-4080
info@americanpayroll.org
www.americanpayroll.org
Monty Montgomery, Editorial Contact
maddus, CEO
Information and resources for payroll managers. *$200.00*
20 pages Annual+
Circulation: 40000

136 **Physicians Market Place**
MarketPlace Group
89 Access Road
Norwood, MA 02062-5212
781-762-6000
FAX: 781-762-1300
kmcurran@marketplace.group.com
www.physiciansmarketplace.com
Kevin M Curran, Marketing
Andy Nimmo, Advertising
Accounting news specific to medical practices.
32 pages Monthly Founded: 1966
Circulation: 113563

137 **Practical Accountant**
Thomson Media
One State Street Plaza
25th Floor
New York, NY 10004
212-258-8445
FAX: 212-292-5216 800-221-1809
howard.wolosky@sourcemedia.com
www.webcpa.com
Howard W Wolosky, Associate Publisher/Executive Edito
Robert Whitaker, Publisher
Jack Lynch, Sales Manager
The technical How-To Magazine for the growth-minded local and regional accounting firm. *$79.00*
52 pages Founded: 1968
Circulation: 36991 1000 names $130 per M.
Printed in 4 colors on glossy stock

138 **Practical Tax Strategies**
RIA Group
395 Hudson Street
New York, NY 10014
212-367-6300
FAX: 212-367-6305
bscharin@riag.com www.riahome.com
Bob D Scharin, Editor
Bob Trinz, Senior Tax Analyst
Features offer in-depth articles and technical notes on taxation. *$185.00*
64 pages Monthly Founded: 1935
Circulation: 12000

139 **Practicing CPA**
American Institute of CPAs
Harborside Financial Center
201 Plaza Three
Jersey City, NJ 07311-3881
201-383-3919
FAX: 727-376-2115
lcohen@aicpa.org www.aicpa.org/
William Moran, Editor
Adele Brady Bolson, Editorial Advisor
Barry Melancon, President
Linda Cohen, Publisher
Articles on development and management of firms.
Monthly Founded: 1887
Circulation: 6000

140 **Public Budgeting and Finance**
American Association for Budget and Program
6425 Lakeview Drive
Falls Church, VA 22041
703-941-4300
FAX: 703-941-1535
aabpa@aol.com www.aabpa.org
Judy D. Rayburn, President
Budget and program analysis professionals.
Quarterly

141 **Real Estate Taxation**
Warren, Gorham & Lamont
395 Hudson Street
New York, NY 10014-3669
212-367-6300
FAX: 212-367-6718 800-742-3348
John McHugh, Editor
Robert J Murdich JD, Managing Editor
Timely source of new ideas, trends and legal developments in real estate taxation. This journal gives you complete, ongoing coverage of all aspects of real estate tax planning. *$350.00*
Quarterly Founded: 1945

142 **Review of Taxation of Individuals**
Warren, Gorham & Lamont
395 Hudson Street
New York, NY 10014-3669
212-367-6300
FAX: 212-367-6345 800-742-3348
ria@thomson.com www.riahome.com
Roy Martin, President
Adam Schair, Marketing Manager
Offers information on the taxation of individuals, legislation, etc. *$58.00*
Monthly

143 **Spectrum Magazine**
International Newspaper Financial Executives
21525 Ridgetop Circle
Sterling, VA 20166
703-421-4060
FAX: 703-421-4068
bkasabian@infe.org www.infe.org
Greg Robinson, President
Ralph Bender, VP
William Mickey, VP
Greg Robinson, Treasurer
Ralph Bender, Secretary
Provides a communication mechanism whereby readers are kept abreast of key topics of interest within the accounting, finance, and business professions. Free with Membership. Non-member fee is $20.00. *$20.00*
Annual

144 **Strategic Finance**
Institute of Management Accountants
10 Paragon Drive
Montvale, NJ 07645-1718
201-573-9000
FAX: 201-573-0559 800-638-4427
ima@imanet.org www.imanet.org
Robert F Randall, Assistant Publisher
Kathy Williams, Editor
Michael Castellucio, Technology and Product In
Paul Sharman, President & CEO
Offers the latest financial and accounting techniques to help companies reduce costs and increase profits. *$130.00*
80 pages
Circulation: 80000
Printed in 4 colors on glossy stock

145 **Systematic Magazine**
American Payroll Association
660 N Main Avenue
Suite 100
San Antonio, TX 78205-1217
210-226-4600
FAX: 210-226-4027
apa@apa-ed.com
www.americanpayroll.org
Daniel J Maddux, Publisher
Covers new systems and implementation, the latest technology and its relation to human resources, payroll and accounting for CFOs, MIS department heads and top management in companies that use information technology for communication.
Quarterly
Circulation: 14M

146 **Tax Management Estates, Gifts and Trusts Journal**
Tax Management
1250 23rd Street NW
Washington, DC 20037-1166
202-833-7240
FAX: 202-496-6013 800-223-7270
tm@bna.com www.bnatax.com

Byrle M Abbin, Board Member
David P McFarland, President

Provides articles by leading tax practitioners and proven techniques for estate planning and planning opportunities. It also features reviews of legislative, administrative and judicial developments.

147 **Tax and Business Adviser**
Grant Thornton
175 W Jackson Boulevard
Chicago, IL 60604
312-856-0200
FAX: 312-602-8099
www.grantthornton.com

Mary Jaspers, Editor

Current tax and general business issues.
Founded: 1926
Circulation: 60000

148 **Today's CPA**
Texas Society of CPA's
14860 Montfort Drive
Suite 150
Dallas, TX 75254
972-878-8500
FAX: 972-687-8646 800-428-0272

Nita Clyde, Chairman
John Sharbaugh, Executive Director
Kathleen Klein, Editor

Includes articles, news and professional tips. *$28.00*
6 per year
Circulation: 11,600

Trade Shows

149 **ACUIA Teleseminar**
Association of Credit Union Internal Auditors
PO Box 1926
Columbus, OH 43216-1926
614-219-9702
FAX: 614-221-2335 866-254-8128

Barbara Netter, Chairman
Cathy Smoyer, Vice Chairman
Barry Lucas, Director
Brad L Feldman, Executive Director

The objective, procedures, and transaction testing for BSA areas will be reviewed. Handouts of the latest FFIEC BSA manual, as well as the NCUA BSA checklist will be available for participants.

150 **AIRA Annual Bankruptcy & Restructuring Conference**
Association of Insolvency & Restructuring Advisors
221 Stewart Avenue
Suite 207
Medford, OR 97501
541-858-1665
FAX: 541-858-9187
aira@airacira.org www.airacira.org

Beverly Huard, Public Relations Director
Grant Newton, Executive Director

Exhibits for professionals involved in insolvency and restructuring.
Annual/June 6-9 Founded: 1984

151 **AMAA Summer Conference**
Alliance of Merger and Acquistion Advisors
150 N Michigan Avenue
Chicago, IL 60601
312-856-9590
FAX: 312-729-9800 877-844-2535

Kevin Carlie, President

Hosts many of the world's leading mid-market M&A executives, top tier speakers, as well as an invaluable networking opportunity.

152 **Academy of Accounting Historians Research Conference**
University of Alabama
Box 870220
Tuscaloosa, AL 35487
205-348-9784
FAX: 205-348-8453
krice@eba.ua.edu
www.weatherhead.cwru.edu

Salvador Carmona, President

October

153 **Affiliated Conference of Practicing Accountants (ACPA)**
30 Massachusetts Avenue
Suite 2
North Andover, MA 01845
978-689-9420
FAX: 978-689-9404
kc@acpaint1.org www.acpaint1.org

Barry Sattel, President
Dawna G Burrus, Executive Director

Provides a forum for member communication by introducing new association members, highlighting news from member firms and exploring topics of international interest within the accounting profession. 80 member firms in 40 countries
80 Attendees Founded: 1978
Circulation: 800,000

154 **American Accounting Association Annual Meeting**
5717 Bessie Drive
Sarasota, FL 34233-2399
941-921-7747
FAX: 941-923-4093
office@aaahq.org http://aahq.org

Debbie Gardner, Asst. Director of Logistics

70 booths of accounting equipment, supplies and services. Accounting-educated related, textbooks, publishers, software, etc.
2500 Attendees August Annual

155 **American Association of Attorney-Certified Public Accountants Convention**
American Association of Attorney-CPAs
24196 Alicia Parkway
Suite K
Mission Viejo, CA 92691
949-768-0336
FAX: 949-768-7062 800-272-2889
aaacpa@attorney-cpa.com
www.attorney-cpa.com

Clarke Mulligan, Executive Director

Exhibits for persons licensed both as attorneys and CPAs.
July Annual

156 **American Payroll Association Annual Congress**
30 E 33rd Street
5th Floor
New York, NY 10016-5386
212-686-2030
FAX: 212-686-4080
apamail@mindspring.org
www.americanpayroll.org

Dave Maddux, Executive Director

Over 75 exhibits of software, hardware, and products related to payroll and human resources.
1500 Attendees Annual Founded: 1982

157 **American Society of Women Accountants Annual Conference**
8405 Greensboro Drive
Suite 800
McLean, VA 22102
703-506-3260
FAX: 703-506-3266 www.aswa.org

Banquet, luncheon, tours and over 30 exhibits of accounting, business and employment opportunities.
400 Attendees September

158 **American Woman's Society of Certified Public Accountants Conference**
136 S Keowee Street
Dayton, OH 45402
937-222-1872
FAX: 937-222-5794 800-297-2721
info@awscpa.org www.awscpa.org

Dedicated solely to women in accounting and related fields.
September Annual Founded: 2001

159 **Association for Accounting Administration National Practice Management**
Association for Accounting Administration
136 S Keowee Street
Dayton, OH 45402
937-222-0030
FAX: 937-222-5794
aaainfo@cpaadmin.org
www.cpaadmin.org

Kim Fantaci, Executive Director

Information and displays of accounting administration equipment and products.
200 Attendees June

160 **Association of College and University Audi tors Annual Conference**
Association of College and University Auditors
342 North Main Street
Suite 301
West Hartford, CT 06117-2507
860-586-7561
FAX: 860-586-8550
acua@acua.org
www.acua.org/organization

Ray Cochran, President

September

161 **Association of Credit Union Internal Auditors Annual Conference**
Association of Credit Union Internal Auditors
PO Box 1926
Columbus, OH 43216-1926
614-219-9702
FAX: 614-221-2335 866-254-8128

Barbara Netter, Chairman
Cathy Smoyer, Vice Chairman

Barry Lucas, Director
Brad L Feldman, MPA, Executive Director

Is strategically planned to include education skills training for credit union internal auditors and managers at every stage of their careers.
June

162 Association of Healthcare Internal Auditors Conference
PO Box 449
Onstead, MI 49265-0449
517-467-7729
FAX: 517-467-6104
ahia@ahia.org www.ahia.org

Mark Eddy, Director
Pat Bogusz, Executive Director

Exhibits concerning cost containment and increased productivity in health care institutions through internal auditing.
1000 Attendees Founded: 1981

163 IASA Annual Conference
Insurance, Accounting & Systems Association
3511 Shannon Road
Suite 160
Durham, NC 27707
919-489-0991
FAX: 919-489-1994
info@iasa.org www.iasa.org

Thom Hoffman, Exhibit Manager
R Iovino, Account Manager

Providing the most comprehensive education program and business show targeted for financial and technology professionals in the industry.
1800 Attendees June

164 Information Resources Management Associati on Conference
701 E Chocolate Avenue
Suite 200
Hershey, PA 17033
717-533-8879
FAX: 717-533-8861
members@irma-international.org
www.irma-international.org

Felix B Tan, Editor

Provides a forum for researchers and practitioners to share leading-edge knowledge in the global information resource management area. *$95.00*
Quarterly

165 Institute of Internal Auditors International Conference
247 Maitland Avenue
Altamonte Springs, FL 32701-4201
407-371-1100
FAX: 407-937-1101
iia@theiia.org www.theiia.org

John Covell, Chairman
Dave Richards, Chief Executive Officer

Annual conference and exhibits of internal auditing equipment, supplies and services. 30 booths.
84000 Attendees July Founded: 1941

166 National Leadership Conference
Advancing Government Accountability
2208 Mount Vernon Avenue
Alexandria, VA 22301-1314
703-684-6931
FAX: 703-548-9367 800-ABA-7211

Sam M. McCall, President
February

167 National Performance Management Conference
Advancing Government Accountability
2208 Mount Vernon Avenue
Alexandria, VA 22301-1314
703-684-6931
FAX: 703-548-9367 800-ABA-7211

Sam M. McCall, President
November

168 Professional Development Conference
Advancing Government Accountability
2208 Mount Vernon Avenue
Alexandria, VA 22301-1314
703-684-6931
FAX: 703-548-9367 800-ABA-7211

Sam M. McCall, President
July

169 Professional Development Conference & Exposition
Advancing Government Accountability
2208 Mount Vernon Avenue
Alexandria, VA 22301-1314
703-684-6931
FAX: 703-548-9367 800-ABA-7211

Sam M. McCall, President
July

170 Society of Actuaries Annual Meeting and Exhibit
Society of Actuaries
475 N Martingale Road
Suite 600
Schaumburg, IL 60173
847-706-3500
FAX: 847-706-3599
webmaster@soa.org www.soa.org

Stephen G Kellison, President
Sarah Sanford, Executive Director

An opportunity to go face-to-face with the decision-makers who use your products and services. Your prospective buyers and clients are amoung the 1700 delegates that will attend this year's annual meeting. More than half of the delegates hold high-level management positions in their companies and are the major buying influence.
1,700 Attendees November

171 Society of Cost Estimating and Analysis National Workshop
101 S Whiting Street
Suite 201
Alexandria, VA 20190
703-751-8069
FAX: 703-461-7328
scea@erols.com www.sceaonline.net

Frank R Flett, Executive Director Training
Leonard Cheshire, Manager

The training track is primarily designed as a refresher for individuals with academic and job experience in, or related to, cost estimating and analysis. It is also an excellent introduction for those new to the profession. It will provide a firm basis for further study and on the job training. 20 exhibits with 20 booths.
400 Attendees June

172 Wall Street Technology Show
Flagg Management
353 Lexington Avenue
New York, NY 10016
212-286-0333
FAX: 212-286-0086
flaggmgmnt@msn.com
www.flaggmgmt.com

Russell Flagg, President

Annual show of 150 exhibitors of accounting equipment, supplies and services, including information and technology solutions for the accounting, finance and business industries.
3000 Attendees

Directories & Databases

173 Accountancy: A Professional Reference Guide
Georgia State University
Robinson College of Business
35 Broad Street NW
Atlanta, GA 30303
404-651-2740

admissions@gsu.edu www.cba.gsu.edu

Elliot L Slocum, Editor
Alfred R Roberts, Editor

Listings of accounting firms, associations, regulatory agencies and schools offering accredited accounting programs. *$99.95*
450 pages Hardcover

174 Accounting Research Directory
Markus Wiener Publishing
231 Nassau Street
Princeton, NJ 08542
609-921-1141
FAX: 609-921-1140
info@markusweiner.com
www.markusweiner.com

John Gardner, Editor
Lawrence D Brown, Editor
Markus Wiener, President

Quick guide for those who can remember any of the author's names for a key article, but need more exact information for location or reference. It can enable those interested in quantitative literature analysis to test and verify much of the work in this area by the authors in this book. *$69.95*
Hardcover ISBN 1-558760-68-7

175 Accounting Software Guide
Anderson McLean
5 Town and Country Village
#508
San Jose, CA 95128-2026

Robert Pfahnl, President
Ray London, Senior Editor

Offers information on the developers and distributors of specialized microcomputer accounting software. *$29.95*
170 pages Annual

176 Accounting and Tax Database
Pro Quest Information and Learning
300 N Zeeb Road
Ann Arbor, MI 48103
734-761-4700
FAX: 800-864-0019 800-889-3358
support@il.proquest.com
www.il.proquest.com
Offers comprehensive indexing and informative abstracts of articles in prominent accounting, taxation and financial management publications from the US and other countries. Over 260,000 citations.
Bibliographic

177 **American Association of Attorney-Certified Public Accountants Directory**
24196 Alicia Parkway
Suite K
Mission Viejo, CA 92691-3926
949-768-0336
FAX: 949-768-7062 800-272-2889
aaacpa@attorney-cpa.com
www.attorney-cpa.com
Clark Mulligan, Executive Director
Offers names, addresses and biographical data on 1,400 individuals licensed as both attorneys and CPAs.
100 pages Annual
Printed in 1 color

178 **Directory of Actuarial Memberships**
Society of Actuaries
475 N Martingale Road
Suite 600
Schaumburg, IL 60173
847-706-3500
FAX: 847-706-3599 www.soa.org
Adam Fiedorowicz, Owner
Sarah Sanford, Executive Director
Bill Breedlove,
Marketing/Communications Specialist
Lists member names, affiliations and contact information for major US and international actuarial professional associations.
$ 150.00

Mailing list available for rent 17000 names
$300 per M.

179 **Federal Tax Coordinator 2D**
Research Institute of America
395 Hudson Street
New York, NY 10014-7696
212-367-6300
800-431-9025
customer_services@riag.com
www.riag.com
Provides verbatim text of the Internal Revenue Code and IRS Regulations. Information is arranged by subject rather than in Code order. Professional tax preparers are heavy users of this service because of the thorough authoritative analysis it provides.
$2460.00

180 **Future Actuary**
Society of Actuaries
475 N Martingale
Suite 600
Schaumburg, IL 60173
847-706-3500
FAX: 847-706-3599 www.soa.org
Sarah Sandford, Executive Director
Full coverage on topics like career development, nontraditional careers, grading systems, study tips, professional conduct and ethics and the structure of actuarial organizations.

Mailing list available for rent 17000 names
$300 per M.

181 **International Guide to Accounting Journals**
Wiener Markus Publication
231 Nassau Street
Princeton, NJ 08542-4600
609-921-1141
FAX: 609-921-1140
info@markuswiener.com
www.markuswiener.com
J David Spiceland, Editor
Surendra Agrawal, Editor
Approximately 300 journals in accounting and related areas, including about 150 published in the US and 150 from 33 other countries that are published in English.
$49.95
ISBN 1-558760-67-9

182 **Lexis Federal Tax Library**
LexisNexis
PO Box 933
Dayton, OH 45401-0933

FAX: 518-487-3584 800-227-4908
Database contains the current version of the Internal Revenue code, regulations and other useful tax information.

183 **Minority CPA's**
San Francisco Redevelopment Agency
770 Golden Gate Avenue
San Francisco, CA 94102
415-749-2400
FAX: 415-749-2525 www.ci.sf.ca.us
Over 80 Spanish speaking, Asian, Black or native American certified public accounting firms in Northern California; minority CPA associations.

184 **National Society of Public Accountants Yearbook**
National Society of Public Accountants
1010 N Fairfax Street
Alexandria, VA 22314
703-549-6400
FAX: 703-549-2984 800-966-6679
nsamrkt@wizard.net www.nsacct.org
John G Ams, Executive VP
Arleen Richman, Manager Communications
Association members and committees, lists of affiliated state organizations and members of governing board.
Annual

Industry Web Sites

185 **www.acatcredentials.org**
Accreditation Council for Accountancy

Identifies and accredits specialists in accountancy and federal taxation who serve the financial needs of individuals and small to mid-sized business entities. Offers 3 credentials: Accreditation in Accountancy/Accredited Business Accountant, Accredited Tax Preparer and Accredited Tax Advisor.

186 **www.accountants.org**
IA International Accounting Firms

Association of over 136 independent accounting firms located throughout the world. We developed this comprehensive search site as a means of helping people locate an accounting or consulting firm anywhere in the world.

187 **www.acpaint1.org**
Affiliated Conference of Practicing Accountants

Provides a forum for member communication by introducing new association members, highlighting news from member firms and exploring topics of international interest within the accounting profession.

188 **www.agacgfm.org**
Advancing Government Accountability

Educational organization dedicated to the enhancement of public financial management.

189 **www.agn.org**
Accountants Global Network International

Composed of CPA consulting firms who share information and resources via the associated programs.

190 **www.ahia.org**
Association of Healthcare Internal Auditors

Promotes cost containment and increased productivity in health care institutions through internal auditing. Serves as a forum for the exchange of experience, ideas, and information among members; provides continuing professional education courses and informs members of developments in health care internal auditing. Offers employment clearinghouse services.

191 **www.aipb.org**
American Institute of Professional Bookkeepers

Achieve recognition of bookkeepers as accounting professionals, to keep bookkeepers up-to-date on changes in bookkeeping, accounting and tax, to answer bookkeepers everyday bookkeeping and accounting questions, and to certify bookkeepers who meet high national standards.

192 **www.aswa.org**
American Society of Women Accountants

Organization for networking and information exchange in pursuit of professional development.

193 **www.attorney-cpa.com**
American Association of Attorney-CPAs

Seeks to safeguard the professional and legal rights of CPA attorneys.

194 **www.awscpa.org**
American Woman's Society of CPAs

Provides supportive environment that promotes equity and provides opportunities for the achievement of career goals in a competitive and rapidly changing profession.

195 **www.bccacredit.com**
Broadcast Cable Credit Association

Information on Credit Inquiry Service, credit and collection seminars yearly, credit personnel directories, surveys and on-line services.

196 **www.bna.com**

A national organization that has a broad range of employment topics, designed for the small to medium-sized organization.

197 **www.computercpa.com**
Accountant's Home Page

Provides information on general accounting for manufacturing, contstruction, service, not-for-profit, e-commerce and more.

198 **www.cpa.net**
Dietrich & Wilson, PC

Includes information on social security and alternatives, bill presentation and payment.

199 **www.cpaadmin.org**
Association for Accounting Administration

Enables accounting firm administrators to communicate with one another abd provide each other with the benefits of everyone's experiences in what was a new and emerging profession.

200 **www.expresscarriers.com**
Express Carriers Association

A member organization of chief financial officers within the American Trucking Association.

201 **www.gasb.org**
Governmental Accounting Standards Board

Establishes and improves standards of state and local governmental accounting and financial reporting that will result in useful information for users of financial reports and guide and educate the public, including issuers, auditors and users of those financial institutions.

202 **www.greyhouse.com**
Grey House Publishing

Selected Grey House directories in the fields of business, health and education are available online. Users can search our online databases by several different search criteria, such as product categories, geographic area, sales volume and much, much more. Full Grey House catalog and online ordering also available.

203 **www.imanet.org**
Institute of Certified Management Accountants

Professional organization devoted exclusively to management accounting and financial management. Goals are to help members develop both personally and professionally, by means of education, certification, and association with other business professionals.

204 **www.infe.org**
International Newspaper Financial Executives

Controllers, chief accountants, auditors, business managers, treasurers, secretaries and related newspaper executives, educators and public accountants.

205 **www.nabainc.org**
National Association of Black Accountants

Nationwide professional association with the primary purpose of developing, encouraging and serving as a resource for greater participation by African-Americans and other minorities in the accounting and finance professions.

206 **www.nactp.org**
Nat'l Association of Computerized Tax Processors

Nonprofit association that represents tax processing software and hardware developers, electronic filing processors, tax form publishers and tax processing service bureaus. The association promotes standards in tax processing and works closely with the Internal Revenue Service and state governments to promote efficient and effective tax filing.

207 **www.nacva.com**
National Association of Certified Valuation Analysts

Global, professional association that supports the business valuation and litigation consulting disciplines within the CPA and professional communities. Along with its training and certification programs, NACVA offers a range of support services, marketing tools, software programs, reference materials and customized databases to enhance the professional capabilities of its members.

208 **www.naea.org**
National Association of Enrolled Agents

Members are enrolled to represent taxpayers before the Internal Revenue Service. We advise, represent and prepare tax returns for individuals, partnerships, corporations, estates, trusts and any entities with tax reporting requirements.

209 **www.nsacct.org**
National Society of Accountants

Professional society of practicing accountants and tax practitioners that sponsors the Acceditation Council for Accountancy and Taxation and supports the National Society of Public Accountants Political Action Committee and NSPA Scholarship Foundation.

210 **www.sceaonline.net**
Society of Cost Estimating and Analysis

Dedicated to improving cost estimating and analysis in government and industry. Offers a unique collection of educational and training materials on cost estimating, cost analysis, earned value management and related disciplines through its professional development program.

211 **www.taxsites.com**
Tax and Accounting Sites Directory

A comprehensive index of internet resources, designed to be a starting point for people who are searching for tax and accounting information and services.

212 **www.theiia.org**
Institute of Internal Auditors

International organization of internal auditors, corporate executives and board members. Contact and current development information.

213 **www.weatherhead.cwru.edu/**
Academy of Accounting Historians

Members are individuals and institutional affiliates with an interest in accounting and economic history.

Associations

214 **Advertising Council**
261 Madison Avenue
11th Floor
New York, NY 10016-2301
212-922-1500
FAX: 212-962-1676
info@adcouncil.org
www.adcouncil.org

Peggy Conlon, President/CEO
Paula Veale, Executive VP
Jerry Judge, Chief Executive Officer

Private, non-profit organization that produces, distributes and promotes thousands of public service campaigns on behalf of non-profit organizations and government agencies in issue areas such as improving the quality of life for children, preventative health, education, community well being, environmental preservation and strengthening families.
100 Members Founded: 1942

215 **Advertising Educational Foundation**
220 E 42nd Street
Suite 3300
New York, NY 10017-5806
212-986-8060
FAX: 212-986-8061 www.aef.com

Paula Alex, CEO
Kathy Grantham, Deputy Director
Sharon Hudson, VP

Serves as the industry's clearinghouse, repository and distribution force for educational information and materials to improve the perception and understanding of the social, historical, cultural and economic role of advertising.
48 Members Founded: 1983

216 **Advertising Photographers of America**
27 W 20th Street #601
New York, NY 10011-3707
212-807-0399
FAX: 212-727-8120 800-817-2244
info@apany.com www.apany.com

Joe Pritchard, CEO
Holly King, Office Administrator

Promotes standards of business practices and awareness of the role of advertising photographers.
570 Members Founded: 1981

217 **Advertising Research Foundation**
432 Park Avenue South
New York, NY 10016-4503
212-751-5656
FAX: 212-319-5265 800-765-7514
info@thearf.org www.thearf.org

Robert Barocci, President/CEO
Cassandra Bates, VP Marketing
Diane Streckfuss, VP /Director Member Services
Bill Cook, SVP, Research and Standards
Felix Yang, Vice President/Director/Operations

The ARF is the premiere advertising industry association for creating, aggregating, synthesizing and sharing the knowledge required by decision makers in the field. The mission of the ARF is to improve the practice of avertising, marketing and media research in pursuit of more effective marketing and advertising communications.
400 Members Founded: 1936

218 **Advertising Specialty Institute**
4800 Street Road
Trevose, PA 19053
215-953-4000
FAX: 800-546-1399 800-546-1350
info@asicentral.com
www.asicentral.com

Rich Fairfield, Publisher
Tim Andrews, President
Carol Albright, VP Human Resources
Norman Unger Cohn, Chairman

Supports those involved in all areas of the advertising field. Publishes monthly magazine.
20000 Members Founded: 1950

219 **Advertising Women of New York**
25 W 45th Street
Suite 1001
New York, NY 10036
212-221-7969
FAX: 212-221-8296
awny@awny.org www.awny.org

Liz Schroeder, Executive Director
Carol Evans, President/CEO
Arlene Manos, First VP
Caroline McCurdy, Treasurer

Conducts professional development services and career clinic to provide personal job counseling.
1200 Members Founded: 1912

220 **American Academy of Advertising**
Brigham Young University
Department of Communications
Provo, UT 84602-6403

raymond.taylor@villanova.edu
www.advertising.utxas.edu/aaa/

Patricia Rose, President
Carrie LaFerle, VP
Hong Cheng, Secretary
Les Carlson, Treasurer

Organization of advertising scholars and professionals with an interest in advertising and advertising education. Also fosters research which is relevant to the field and provides a forum for the exchange of ideas among its academic and professional members.
600 Members Founded: 1957

221 **American Advertising Federation**
1101 Vermont Avenue NW
Suite 500
Washington, DC 20005-6306
202-898-0089
FAX: 202-898-0159 800-999-2231
aaf@aaf.org www.aaf.org

Wally S Snyder, President/CEO
Jack Griffin, Chair
Judy Hu, Secretary
Alan Schultz, Treasurer
Andrew Jung, Vice Chair

Educates policymakers, media and the public on the value of advertising. Includes a unique, nationally coordinated grassroots network of advertisers, advertising agencies, media companies, local advertising associations and college chapters.
50000 Members Founded: 1967

222 **American Association for Public Opinion Research**
PO Box 14263
Lenexa, KS 66285-4263
913-310-0118
FAX: 913-599-5340
AAPOR-info@goAMP.com
www.aapor.org

Rom Daves, President
Nancy Mathiowetz, VP
Paul Beatty, Secretary/Treasurer

Furthers the research of public opinion by conducting surveys, holding seminars and more.
1700 Members Founded: 1947
Mailing list available for rent 1000 names $400 per M.

223 **American Association of Advertising Agencies (AAAA)**
405 Lexington Avenue
18th Floor
New York, NY 10174-1801
212-682-2500
FAX: 212-682-8391
obd@aaaa.org www.aaaa.org

O Burtch Drake, President
Michael Donahue, Executive VP of Member Services
Ron Berger, Chair
Victor Ornelas, Secretary/Treasurer

The national trade association representing the advertising agencies in the US. Offers its members the broadest possible services, expertise and information regarding the advertising agency business with industry publications, conferences, trade shows and a variety of other supportive measures. The average AAAA agency has been a member for 20 years.
500 Members Founded: 1917

224 **American Marketing Association**
311 S Wacker Drive
Suite 5800
Chicago, IL 60606-6301
312-542-9000
FAX: 312-542-9001 800-262-1150
info@ama.org www.ama.org

Dennis Dunlap, CEO
Dr. Paul Root, Chairman
Jack Weekes, Chairperson
Dr. Thomas Kinnear, Foundation Chairperson
Debra Ringold, VP Secretary/Treasurer

Supports all those marketing executives and teachers involved with marketing techniques, trends and new ideas. Publishes quarterly magazine.
38000 Members Founded: 1937

225 **Association of Hispanic Advertising Agencies**
8201 Greensboro Drive
3rd Floor
McLean, VA 22102
703-610-9014
FAX: 703-610-9005
info@ahaa.org www.ahaa.org

Jackie Bird, Chairman-Elect
Carl Kravetz, Chairman
Jose Lopez Varela, Treasurer
Jackie Bird, Secretary

To grow, strengthen, and protect the Hispanic marketing and advertising industry by providing leadership in raising awareness of the value of the Hispanic market opportunitites and enhancing the professionalism of the industry.

226 **Association of Independent Commercial Producers**
3 W 18th Street
5th Floor
New York, NY 10011
212-929-3000
FAX: 212-929-3359
info@aicp.com www.aicp.com

Matt Miller, CEO
Christine Allen, Events Regional Manager
Steve Caplan, Executive VP

Represents the interests of United States companies that specialize in producing commercials on various media-film, video, computer-for advertisers and agencies.

500 Members Founded: 1972

227 Association of National Advertisers
708 3rd Avenue
New York, NY 10017-4270
212-697-5950
FAX: 212-661-8057 www.ana.net

Robert Liodice, President/CEO
Barbara Bacci-Mirque, Senior VP
James Stengel, Chairman
Keith Scarborough, VP

To provide industry leadership and proprietary resources that enable members to build brands, improve marketing productivity and drive business results.

562 Members Founded: 1910

228 Business Marketing Association
400 N Michigan Avenue
15th Floor
Chicago, IL 60611
312-822-0005
FAX: 312-822-0054 800-664-4262
bma@marketing.org
www.marketing.org

Rick Kean, Executive Director
Michelle Coughlin, Member Services

A service organization for professionals in this industry. A three part strategic vision. Also business to business marketing and communication.

3000 Members Founded: 1922

229 Cable TV Advertising Bureau
830 3rd Avenue
2nd Floor
New York, NY 10022-7521
212-508-1200
FAX: 212-832-3268
www.onetvworld.org

Joseph Ostrow, President/CEO
Robert Alter, Vice Chair

Supports all those involved with advertising-supported cable television networks and offers services to support local advertising sales. Hosts annual trade show.

200 Members Founded: 1981

230 Children's Advertising Review Unit

70 West 36th Street
13th Floor
New York, NY 10018-6601
212-396-6800
FAX: 212-705-0132
caru@caru.bbb.org www.caru.org

Paul Colleran, VP
Elizabeth le Lascoutx, Director
Phyllis Spaeth, Assistant Director

Promotes truthful and accurate advertising directed toward children under age 12 on network and cable TV and in printed media.

5 Members Founded: 1974

231 Communications Roundtable Association
1250 24th Street NW
Suite 250
Washington, DC 20037
202-755-5180
FAX: 202-466-0544
michael@SolutionsWebDesign.net
www.roundtable.org

Michael Reichgut, Chairman
Shawn Dolley, Chief Executive Officer

Association of more than 24 public relations, marketing, graphics, advertising, training and other communications organizations with more than 12,00 professional members. The goals include furthering professionalism and cooperation between member organizations, career and employment support, and employer assistance.

12000 Members Founded: 1991

232 Council of Better Business Bureaus
4200 Wilson Boulevard
Suite 800
Arlington, VA 22203-1838
703-276-0100
FAX: 703-525-8277 800-537-4600
webmaster@bbb.org www.bbb.org

Peter D Ryan, Chair
Deborah I Dingell, Vice Chair
Steven Cole, Chief Executive Officer
Anne Crichton Crews, Senior VP
Olivia Cohen-Cutler, Vice President

Helps all businesses understand and follow business laws and regulations, and acts as an advocate to consumers. Publishes monthly newsetter.

300,0 Members Founded: 1912

233 EMarketing Association
243 Post Road
Suite 129
Westerly, RI 02819
401-884-0614
FAX: 408-884-2461
admin@emarketingassociation.com
www.emarketingassociation.com

Robert Fleming, Executive Director

An international association of emarketing professionals. Members include governments, professionals and students involved with the emarketing arena. The eMA provides marketing resources, services, research, certifications, educational programs and events to its members and the marketing community.

2500 Members Founded: 1997

234 Eight-Sheet Outdoor Advertising Association
PO Box 2680
Bremerton, WA 98310

FAX: 916-646-4548 800-874-3387
davidjacobs@esoaa.com
www.esoaa.com

David Jacobs, Executive Director

Supports all those involved in the outdoor advertising field.

150 Members Founded: 1953

235 Insurance and Financial Communications Association
4311 E Locust Street
Des Moines, IA 50309

www.ifaconline.org

Gregg Cromeans, President,Director of Marketing
Virginia Alderman, VP,Communications Director
Cynthia Wujek, Marketing Manager

To encourage and promote the exchange of experience and ideas among its members through an extensive program of formal schools, workshops, seminars, Newsletters, research studies, networking, international awards competition and IFCAs showcase event: the three-day annual meeting.

650 Members Founded: 1933

236 Intermarket Advertising Network
3904 E Garfield Street
Milwaukee, WI 53233
414-425-8800
FAX: 414-425-0021

William Eisner, President

Strives to learn, prosper and serve their clients better and works for the betterment of the advertising industry in general.

19 Members Founded: 1967

237 International Advertising Association
521 5th Avenue
Suite 1807
New York, NY 10175-1899
212-557-1133
FAX: 212-983-0455
iaa@global.org www.iaaglobal.org

Michael Lee, President
Joseph Ghossoub, Sr. VP
Pinar Kilic, World Secretary
Heather Leembruggen, Treasurer

Global association of marketing communications. Professionals in 96 countries.

5400 Members Founded: 1938 $. per M.

238 International Communications Agency Network
1649 Lump Gulch Road
PO Box 490
Rollinsville, CO 80474-0490
303-258-9511
FAX: 303-484-4087
info@icomagencies.com
www.icomagencies.com

Gary Burandt, Executive Director
DeAnna Marcotte, Administrator

In today's global marketplace competition is fierce. To succeed globally you must succeed locally. Those most familiar with their customers and prospects market by market are the most likely to succeed. Local ICOM agencies help companies position their products for success in all the important markets of the world.

75 Members Founded: 1950

239 International Sign Association
707 N Saint Asaph Street
Alexandria, VA 22314
703-368-8353
FAX: 703-836-8353
webmaster@signs.org www.signs.org

Lori Anderson, President/CEO
Johnathan Kaupanger, Executive Assistant

Representing manufacturers, users and suppliers of on-premise signs and sign products. Our members represent the industry at all levels, across the world. ISA exists to support, promote and improve the sign industry.

2100 Members Founded: 1944

240 League of Advertising Agencies
65 Reade Street
New York, NY 10007
212-528-0364
wendell@clark-pope.com

An association of principals of small advertising agencies in the metropolitan New York area that conducts seminars, educational and research projects, offers counseling, networking, and access to legal, financial and PR advisors.

85 Members Founded: 1952

241 **MAGNET: Marketing & Advertising Global Network**
464 Walnut Street
Pittsburgh, PA 15238
412-284-4031

mxdirector@verizon.net
www.magnetglobal.org

Al Dudreck, Executive Director

Works to increase management efficiency, raise standards of advertising service and exchange information among members in North America and members of EMCO (European Marketing Communications Organization) in 14 European countries.

40 Members Founded: 1946

242 **Newspaper Association of America**
1921 Gallows Road
Suite 600
Vienna, VA 22182-3900
703-902-1600
FAX: 703-917-0636
webmaster@naa.org www.naa.org

Jay R Smith, Chair
John Sturm, President/CEO
Boisfeuillet Jones Jr, Vice Chair
James Abbott, VP
Susan Clark-Johnson, Secretary

Founded by the merger of seven associations serving the newspaper industry. Focuses on six key strategic priorities that collectively affect the newspaper industry. These include marketing, public policy, diversity, industry development, newspaper operations and readership.

Founded: 1992

243 **Outdoor Advertising Association of America**
1850 M Street NW
Suite 1040
Washington, DC 20036
202-833-5566
FAX: 202-833-1522
nfletcher@oaaa.org www.oaaa.org

Nancy J Fletcher, President
Stephen Freitas, Chief Marketing Officer
Ken Klein, Executive VP, Government Relations
Marci Werlinich, VP Membership
Kim Ramser, Director Marketing/Research

Promotes protects and advances outdoor advertising interests in the US with nearly 1,100 member companies. The OAAA represents more than 90% of industry revenues.

1100 Members Founded: 1891

244 **Point of Purchase Advertising International**
1660 L Street NW, 10th Floor
Suite 100
Washington, DC 20036
202-530-3000
FAX: 202-530-3030
info@popai.com www.popai.com

Richard Blatt, President/CEO
Jack Wuensch, Chairman
Tim Bucholz, VP

Promotes point of purchase advertising, administors trade forums, research, education and public affairs programs to facilitate the continued growth of the $12.7 billion point of purchase advertising industry.

1700 Members Founded: 1940

245 **Promotional Products Association International**
3125 Skyway Circle N
Irving, TX 75038-3526
972-520-0404
FAX: 972-258-3004
Steves@ppa.org www.ppa.org

Stephen Slagle, President

Represents the $8 billion specialty advertising, premium, incentive and gift industry. Members are suppliers or distributors of imprinted promotional advertising products.

6700 Members Founded: 1903

246 **Retail Advertising and Marketing Association**
325 7th Street NW
Suite 1100
Washington, DC 20004
202-268-8183
FAX: 202-661-3049
PerweilerP@rama-nrf.com
www.rama-nrf.org

Todd Alexander, Executive VP
Maureen Bausch, Senior VP
Kevin Barry, VP, Local Sales & Marketing
Ken Banks, EVP, Management

Trade association of retail marketing and advertising professionals, plus their counterparts on the agency, media and service-provider sides of business. Also hosts the Retail Advertising Conference.

1600 Members Founded: 1952

247 **Trade Promotion Management Association**
#174 13771 N Fountain Hills Boulevard
Suite 114
Fountain Hills, AZ 85268
480-837-9704
FAX: 602-296-0277
headquarters@tradepromo.org
www.tradepromo.org

Al DeMaranville, Chairman
Meredith Simpson, Vice Chair
Barry Haupt, Secretary
Gina Arch, Treasurer

Non-profit trade association that focuses on the development and adminstration of co-op advertising, market development funds and other program allowances provided by manufacturers' suppliers to their retail and wholesale or distributor clients.

90 Members Founded: 1989

248 **Traffic Audit Bureau for Media Measurement**
271 Madison Avenue
Suite 1504
New York, NY 10016
212-972-8075
FAX: 212-972-8928
inquiry@tabonline.com
www.tabonline.com

Joseph C Philport, President

Non-profit organization to lead and/or support other major out of home industry research initiatives.

450 Members Founded: 1933

249 **Transportation Marketing Communications**
380 Industrial Boulevard
Waconia, MN 55387
952-442-5638
FAX: 952-442-3941
winslow@utlx.com
www.tmcatoday.org

Bruce Winslow, President
John Ferguson, VP
Tracy Robinson, Treasurer
Edward Moritz, Secretary
Brian Everett, Executive Director

Only association to serve the professional development, networking, and information needs of marketing, sales, and communications professionals in all market segments in North American transportation. Members include motor carriers, railroads, air carriers, ocean lines, 3PLs, equipment manufacturers, passenger transit organizations, media, and suppliers.

225 Members Founded: 1924

250 **Transworld Advertising Agency Network: TAAN**
7920 Summer Lake Court
Fort Myers, FL 33907
239-433-0669
FAX: 239-433-1366
taan@taan.org www.taan.org

Gary Lessner, President

A network of independently owned advertising agencies that work closely together in the exchange of management information, reciprocal services and personal local contact.

45+ Members Founded: 1936

251 **Women in Advertising and Marketing**
4200 Wisconsin Avenue NW
Suite 106-238
Washington, DC 20016
301-369-7400
www.wamdc.org

Linda Hagopian, President

Serves as a network for women in advertising and marketing fields. Accepts advertising.

100 Members Founded: 1980

Newsletters

252 **AD Business Report**
Executive Communications
570 Group Grand Avenue
Englewood, NJ 07631
201-894-8200
FAX: 201-871-0471 800-874-8278
ecjteam@ecglink.com
www.ecglink.com

Sue Fulton, Publisher

Covers advertising agency business development, management and creative issues, marketing studies of opportunity areas with interviews nationwide.

10 pages Monthly Founded: 1980

253 **Admetrics**
C Systems Ltd
PO Box 708
Winnsboro, TX 75494-0708
903-342-5284

James Callan, Publisher
D Bailey, Editor

Analysis of high tech advertising.

254 Advertising Communications Times

Advertising Communications Times
123 Chestnut Street
Suite 202
Philadelphia, PA 19106
215-629-1666
FAX: 215-923-8358
info@adcommtimes.com
www.adcommtimes.com

Business-to-business newsletter in Philadelphia, Eastern Pennsylvania, New Jersey and Delaware. Accepts advertising, inserts, sells mailing list and produces the Philadelphia Advertising and Business Show. Also produces one-hour trade interview. Rodeo shows, Philadephia Advertising report.
$39.00
36 pages Monthly
Circulation: 40000

255 Advertising Media Credit Executives Association

8840 Columbia 100 Parkway
Columbia, MD 21045-2158
410-992-7609
FAX: 410-740-5574
amcea@amcea.org www.amcea.org

Mark Lee, VP
Mark Stepuszek, President
Marvina Dail, Secretary/Treasurer

Supports media credit managers, editors, business mangers and other professionals in the advertising industry.
Founded: 1953

256 Advertising Via Telemarketing Script Presentations Newsletter

Prosperity Partners of Co
303-573-5564

Telemarketing script presentations for various types of businesses and enterprises.
$49.95
4 pages
Circulation: 1000 Audited
Printed in 1 color on matte stock

257 Advisor

American Advertising Federation
1101 Vermont Avenue NW
Suite 500
Washington, DC 20005-6306
202-898-0089
FAX: 202-898-0159
aaf@aaf.org www.aaf.org

Wally Snyder, President/CEO
Peter Shih, Executive VP Marketing
Amber Jones, Editor

For college advertising professors at AAF-affiliated schools.
Founded: 1905
Circulation: 50,000

258 American Academy of Advertising Newsletter

Michigan State University
E. Lansing, MI 48824
517-355-1855
www.msu.edu

Jane Reid, Publisher

Offers articles regarding trends in advertising, the latest technology and campaign marketing ideas and Academy news and reports.
Quarterly Founded: 1955

259 Associated Spring Newsletter

Associated Spring Headquarters
18 Main Street
Bristol, CT 06010
860-582-9581
FAX: 860-589-3122 800-528-3795
springs@asbg.com
www.associatedspring.com

Richard P McCorry, President

Offers news, conferences and seminars.
Quarterly

260 BPAA Marketing, Advertising, Research Newsletter

Manville Consulting Group
84 Bayberry Lane
Westport, CT 06880-4030

Ron Coleman, Publisher

Trends and techniques in advertising/marketing research and sales.

261 Briefings

Marvin Spike
1120 Wheeler Way
Langhorne, PA 19047-1711
215-752-4200
FAX: 800-829-9240

Dan Cartledge, Editor

Address changes and other information for the advertising business. *$36.00*
Bi-Monthly

262 Classified Communications

A Franz Advertising
PO Box 4242
Prescott, AZ 86302-4242

FAX: 928-445-0517

Agnes Franz, Editor/Publisher

Brief articles address small budget advertising. *$29.00*
Monthly Founded: 1990

263 Communicator

American Advertising Federation
1101 Vermont Avenue NW
Suite 500
Washington, DC 20005-6306
202-898-0089
FAX: 202-898-0159
aaf@aaf.org www.aaf.org

Wally Snyder, President/CEO
Mary Hilton, Director Public Affairs

Newsletter featuring scholarship, career guidance information, and AAF student news, for advertising students and their academic advisors at AAF-affiliated college chapters.
Monthly

264 Direct Hit

4248 Park Glen Road
Minneapolis, MN 55416-4758
952-928-4643
FAX: 952-929-1318
mdma@mdma.org www.mdma.org

Dennis Bell, Editor
Linda Cummings, President
Alan Brown, Advertising Manager
Regina Cannon, Events Manager

News and events in the advertising industry.

Monthly Founded: 1960
Mailing list available for rent 1.1 M names

265 Dos and Don'ts in Advertising

Council of Better Business Bureaus
4200 Wilson Boulevard
Suite 800
Arlington, VA 22203-1838
703-276-0100
FAX: 703-525-8277
webmaster@bbb.org www.bbb.orgrg

Andrea C Levine, VP/Director National Advertising

Provides in depth coverage of the laws and regulations governing the advertising industry. Helps you to write, place and manage ads that foster consumer trust and confidence, follow federal and state ad rules, regulations and laws and keep up on the latest 50 years, it has helped legal and advertising professionals produce advertising that is ethical and correct.
4000 pages Monthly Founded: 1970

266 Eight-Sheet Outdoor Report

Eight-Sheet Outdoor Advertising Association
PO Box 2680
Bremerton, WA 98310-3616
360-377-9867
FAX: 360-377-9870 800-874-3387
davidjacobs@esoaa.com
www.esoaa.com

David Jacobs, Publisher
David Dean Jacobs, Executive Director
Rebecca Lambert, Editor

Information on the outdoor advertising field. *$250.00*
Monthly Founded: 1953
Circulation: 500 Audited
Printed in 2 colors on matte stock

267 Financial Advertising Review

Business Word
11211 E Arapahoe Road
Suite 101
Centennial, CO 80112-3851
303-290-8500
FAX: 303-290-9025 800-328-3211
customer.service@businessword.com
www.businessword.com

Donald El Johnson, Chairman/CEO/Publisher
Susan J Alt, President

Review of financial institution advertising print ads, radio, TV, outdoor, direct mail.
$294.00
24 pages
Circulation: 1000 500 names $375 per M.
Printed in 2 colors on matte stock

268 Healthcare Advertising Review

Business Word
11211 E Arapahoe Road
Suite 101
Centennial, CO 80112-3851
303-290-8500
FAX: 303-290-9025 800-328-3211
customer.service@businessword.com
www.businessword.com

Donald Johnson, Chairman/CEO/Publish
Susan J Alt, President
Tom Rees, Editor
Judy Botbin, Editor

Latest trends in health care advertising.
$314.00
40 pages 6 issues per ye Founded: 1983
Circulation: 450 1000 names $375 per M.
Printed in on matte stock

269 **Shopping Center Ad Trends**
National Research Bureau
320 Valley Street
Burlington, IA 52601-5513
319-752-5415
800-347-5291
webmaster@spatialinsights.com
www.spatialinsights.com

Diane Darnall, Publisher
Nancy Heinzel, Editor

Advertising and marketing information for the clothing and furniture industry.
Monthly Founded: 1993

270 **Who's Who: MASA Buyer's Guide to Blue Ribbon Mailing Services**
Mail Advertising Service Association International
1421 Prince Street
Suite 410
Alexandria, VA 22314-2806
703-836-9200
FAX: 703-548-8204 800-333-6272
mfsa-mail@mfsanet.org
www.mfsanet.org/

David A Weaver, President
Eric Casey, Marketing Director
Tyler Keeney, Circulation
Kimberly Kight, Communications Manager
Tyler Keeney, Director of Membership

One-stop reference to MFSA members, the products and services of members and suppliers to the industry, as well a directory of companies who maintain and/or broker resident list throghout the country.
Founded: 1923

Magazines & Journals

271 **Advertiser**
Decker & Decker Associates
120 East 38th Street
New York, NY 10016
212-683-1345
FAX: 212-683-1296 www.ana.net

Elizabeth Decker, Editor
Dave Decker, Production Manager
John L. Decker, President

Reports on today's most critical marketing issues such as measuring brand equity, using emerging technologies and global marketing. It also contains articles on key benchmarks and industry trends. Offers news and events in the advertising industry. *$595.00*
Bi-annually Founded: 1983
Circulation: 25000

272 **Advertising Age**
Ad Age Group/Division of Crain Communications
711 3rd Avenue
New York, NY 10017-4036
212-210-0100
FAX: 212-210-0465 800-678-9595
editor@adage.com www.adage.com

David Klein, Publishing/Editorial
Scott Donaton, Editor
Paul Audino, Advertising Director
Allison Arden, General Manager

For 73 years, the recognized source for the latest information to over 334,000 advertising, marketing and media professionals. Offers in-depth news analysis, extended media coverage and creative works. Provides the latest breaking news, e-mail alerts, extra regional news and new commercials each day. Supported by global and regional editions. *$178.50*
Weekly Founded: 1931
Circulation: 198000

273 **Advertising-Communications Times**
123 Chestnut Street
Suite 202
Philadelphia, PA 19106-1666
215-629-1666
FAX: 215-923-8358
info@adcommtimes.com
www.adcommtimes.com

Joseph Ball, Publisher

Offers news and information on the local communications industry. *$39.00*
Monthly Founded: 1976
Circulation: 40000

274 **Adweek**
VNU Business Publications
770 Broadway
New York, NY 10003
646-654-5100
FAX: 646-654-5365 800-562-2706
bmcomm@vnuinc.com
www.vnubusinessmedia.com

Tim Nudd, Editor-in-Chief
Allan Fahey, Editor
Susan Lilley, Marketing

Edited for ad agency executives, features the inside stories on creativity, client/agency relationships and successful global advertising strategies and also includes news of accounts in review, the best creative work and new campaigns. Adweek gives readers in the advertising community the global and national news they need, plus the local and metro news. *$189.60*
80 pages Weekly Founded: 1998
Circulation: 36032
Printed in 4 colors on glossy stock

275 **American Advertising**
American Advertising Federation
1101 Vermont Avenue NW
Suite 500
Washington, DC 20005-6306
202-898-0089
FAX: 202-898-0159
aaf@aaf.org www.aaf.org

Wally Snyder, President/CEO
Peter Lefkin, Senior VP
Peter Shih, Executive VP Marketing
Lauri Reese, Marketing Manager

Magazine promoting advertising. *$18.00*
28 pages Quarterly Founded: 1905

276 **American Speaker**
Briefings Publishing Group
1101 King Street
Suite 110
Alexandria, VA 22314
703-548-3800
FAX: 703-684-2136 800-722-9221
customerservice@briefings.com
www.briefings.com

Aram Bakshian Jr, Editor-in-Chief
Alan Douglas, President

An updateable loose leaf product geared to amateur and polished public speakers. The product has tips on speaking, model speeches, and filler material for all speaking needs. *$395.00*
Monthly Founded: 1992
Mailing list available for rent 14000 names $125 per M.
Printed in 2 colors on matte stock

277 **B-to-B**
Crain Communications
711 3rd Avenue
New York, NY 10017
212-210-0100
FAX: 212-210-0465
info@crain.com www.btobonline.com

Bob Felsenthal, Publisher
Ellis Booker, Editor
David Bernstein, Advertising Director

Features new developments, trends, case studies, proprietary research and industry rankings. *$59.00*
Monthly Founded: 1916
Circulation: 100000

278 **Body Copy**
Breznan Publishing
11190 Carpenter Road
Flushing, MI 48433-9746

David Breznan, Publisher

Covers the people behind ad campaigns. *$20.00*
Bi-Monthly

279 **Business Marketing Association**
Crain Communications
711 3rd Avenue
New York, NY 10017
212-210-0100
FAX: 212-210-0465
www.aamedia.chaffee.com

Rick Kean, Publisher
Bob Donath, Editor

Techniques and methods of advertising and selling to business and industry. *$30.00*
150 pages Monthly

280 **Corporate Logo Magazine**
Virgo Publishing
3300 N Central Avenue
Suite 2500
Phoenix, AZ 85012
480-990-1101
FAX: 480-675-8119
cs@vpico.com
www.corporatelogo.com

Mike Saxby, Publisher
Karen Butler, Editor
Steve Dietrich, Owner

Gives the promotional products distributor the power to grow their business in competitive marketplace.
Founded: 1986
Circulation: 20000
Printed in on glossy stock

281 **Counselor**
Advertising Specialty Institute
4800 Street Road
Trevose, PA 19053
215-953-4000
FAX: 800-546-1399 800-546-1350
info@asicentral.com
www.asicentral.com

Marvin Spike, Chairman/Publisher
Tim Andrews, President

Covers all areas of the advertising field. *$75.00*
Monthly Founded: 1950
Circulation: 20000

282 **Creativity**
Ad Age Group/Division of Crain Communications
711 3rd Avenue
New York, NY 10017
212-210-0100
FAX: 212-210-0465
info@crain.com www.crain.com
David Kleinman, Publishing/Editorial
Jill Manee, Publisher
Dedicated to the cutting edge creative in film, radio, print, graphic and Web design. All issues identify and evaluate new trends, highlight late-breaking campaigns and honor the latest work and its creators. See AdCritic.com for news and catch the buzz on the best creative work and top talent in the industry. *$99.95*
Monthly Founded: 1916
Circulation: 32,414

283 **DECA Dimensions**
Distributive Education Clubs of America
1908 Association Drive
Reston, VA 20191
703-860-5000
FAX: 703-860-4013
decainc@aol.com www.deca.org
Traci Vares, Editor
Cindy Allen, Advertising Director
Edward Davis, Executive Director
For student members interested in marketing, management, and entrepreneurial careers. Delivered to members in the classroom and integrated into the curriculum. Exhibitors welcome to our national and regional conferences. *$5.00*
Founded: 1948
Circulation: 185,000
Printed in 4 colors

284 **Executive Review**
Association of National Advertisers
708 3rd Avenue
New York, NY 10017-4270
212-697-5950
FAX: 212-661-8057 www.ana.net
Robert Liodice, President/CEO
Michelle Hunter, Publication Director
Association news for advertising management.
Monthly Founded: 1910

285 **Hispanic Business Magazine**
425 Pine Avenue
Santa Barbara, CA 93117-3709
805-964-4554
FAX: 805-964-5539
info@hispanstar.com
www.hispanstar.com
Jesus Chavarria, President
Reaches the most educated, affluent Hispanic business and community leaders. Also the market leader at delivering the Hispanic market. *$10.00*
Founded: 1981

286 **IQ News**
ADWEEK
770 Broadway
7th Floor
New York, NY 10003
646-545-5220
FAX: 646-654-5351
info@adweek.com www.adweek.com
Sid Holt, Editor-in-Chief
Alison Fahey, Editor
Weekly magazine about new media and Internet marketing.
Weekly

287 **International Archive Magazine**
Showcase Archive
200 Park Avenue South
Suite 1703
New York, NY 10003
212-941-2496
FAX: 212-941-5490 800-894-7469
Walter Lurzer, Publisher
Erica Sturdevant, Director Marketing/Sales
Presents new and innovative TV, magazine, poster and newspaper ads from 20 countries. Devoted to presentation of ads. Translations are provided. *$44.00*

90 pages Bi-Monthly

288 **Journal of Advertising**
Iowa State University
College of Business
2350 Gerdin Business Building
Ames, IA 50011-1350
515-969-9900
FAX: 515-294-7112
journalofadvertising@bus.iastate.edu
www.bus.iastate.edu
Russell Laczniak, Editor
Larisa Vereshchagina, Editorial Assistant
Publishes articles on the development of advertising theory and research. *$69.00*
Quarterly
Circulation: 1,850

289 **Journal of Advertising Research**
Advertising Research Foundation
College of Business
2200 Gerdin Business Building
Ames, IA 50011-1350
515-294-2422
FAX: 515-294-6060
journalofadvertising@bus.iastate.ed
www.bus.iastate.edu
Russell Laczniak, Editor
Larisa Vereshchagina, Editorial Assistant
Offers information on advertising, marketing and media research. *$69.00*
Quarterly Founded: 1984
Circulation: 1850

290 **Journal of Current Issues and Research in Advertising**
CTC Press
PO Box 290159
Columbia, SC 29229-159
803-754-3112
FAX: 803-754-3013 800-382-8856
info@ctcpress.com www.ctcpress.com
Claude Martin, Editor
Charles Barnett, Operations Manager
Educates advertising students, professionals and all others interested in advertising. *$45.00*

Circulation: 850

291 **Journal of Euromarketing**
Haworth Press
10 Alice Street
Binghamton, NY 13904
607-722-5857
FAX: 607-722-4583 800-429-6784
getinfo@haworthpress.com
www.haworthpress.com
Bill Cohen, Owner/Publisher
Erdener Kaynak, Editor
Aims to meet the needs of academicians, practitioners, and public policymakers in the discussion of marketing issues pertaining to Europe. *$75.00*

Quarterly Founded: 1978

292 **Journal of Marketing**
American Marketing Association
311 S Wacker Drive
Suite 5800
Chicago, IL 60606
312-542-9000
FAX: 312-542-9001 800-262-1150
info@ama.org www.ama.org
Ronald T Rust, Editor
Jack Hollfelder, Publisher
Publishes articles concerning marketing discoveries, techniques, trends and new ideas. Serves marketing executives and teachers. *$53.00*
140 pages Quarterly Founded: 1936
Circulation: 42000
Printed in 1 color on matte stock

293 **MC Magazine**
ADWEEK
770 Broadway
7th Floor
New York, NY 10003
646-545-5220
FAX: 646-654-5351 800-641-2030
info@adweek.com www.adweek.com
Sid Holt, Editor-in-Chief
Laura Martinez, Editor
Specifically written and edited for the highest ranking marketer at a given technology organization. Readers are directly responsible for corporate marketing and positioning. The magazine's content profiles marketing innovation in all areas of the technology industry including: telecommunications, Internet services, professional services, e-commerce, information technology, consumer electronics, networking, e-business and semiconductors. *$55.00*
Monthly

294 **Marketing Computers**
VNU
770 Broadway
5th Floor
New York, NY 10003-9595
646-547-7680
FAX: 646-654-5003
info@brandweek.com
www.brandweek.com
Jeffrey O'Brien, Editor
Lou Seager, Production Manager
Edited for advertising and marketing executives in the high-tech industries. The publication covers interpretive news, timely big picture features, departments, and analysis by staff editors and industry experts. *$5.00*
Monthly Founded: 1964
Circulation: 15484

295 **Marketing Science: INFORMS**
INFORMS
7240 Parkway Drive
Suite 310
Hanover, MD 21076
443-757-3500
FAX: 443-757-3515 800-446-3676
mktgsci@cba.ufl.edu
www.informs.org
Steven M. Shugan, Editor-in-Chief
Barry List, Director Marketing
Patricia Shaffer, Director Publications
Richard C. Larson, President
Mark Doherty, Executive Director
Marketing journal offering marketing and advertising articles. Provides help for marketing decision makers and deeper understanding of marketing phenomena. *$172.00*

Quarterly Founded: 1982
Circulation: 1800

296 Media
Media Index Publishing
1201 1st Avenue S Suite 309
PO Box 24365
Seattle, WA 98124-365
206-382-9220
FAX: 206-382-9437 800-332-1736
media@media-inc.com
www.media-inc.com

James Baker, President
Audra Higgins, Editor

News and information monthly for ad agency, marketing and creative service professionals. Accepts advertising. *$25.00*
32 pages
Circulation: 10,000
Mailing list available for rent 35M names
Printed in 4 colors on newsprint stock

297 Mediaweek
ASM Communications
770 Broadway
7th Floor
New York, NY 10003
646-654-5259
FAX: 646-654-5254
info@mediaweek.com
www.mediaweek.com

Michael Bürgi, Editor
Geri Fitzgerald, Publisher
Jim Cooper, Managing Editor

Highly targeted circulation covers media decision makers at the top 350 ad agencies in America, all top buying services and client media departments. *$149.00*
60 pages Weekly Founded: 1964
Circulation: 21208
Printed in 4 colors on glossy stock

298 Outdoor Advertising Magazine
OAM Publications
7040 Gadsen Highway
Suite 104
Trussville, AL 35173
205-655-9339
FAX: 205-655-9399 877-688-6346
sbarber@oam.net www.oam.net

Barbara Grahn, Editor

Companies offering out-of-home advertising opportunities, such as aerial or inflatable display, airports, bus benches, bus shelters, hotels, in-flight, in-store, transit, outdoor and event marketing. *$24.95*
Founded: 1920

299 POP Design
Hoyt Publishing
7400 Skokie Boulevard
Skokie, IL 60077
847-675-7400
FAX: 847-675-7494
info@instoremarketer.org
www.hoytpub.com

Peter W Hoyt, President
Harold Fischer, Publisher
Anne Clark, Managing Editor
Karen Ebbesmeyer, Circulation Associate

Provides designers, builders and vendors of displays, signs and fixtures with current developments in materials, components, processes, systems and services used in production. Includes updates on products, industry literature, patents and legal matters affecting designers and manufacturers. *$59.00*
Founded: 1959
Circulation: 18000
Printed in 4 colors on glossy stock

300 PSMJ Marketing Tactics
PSMJ Resources
10 Midland Avenue
Newton, MA 02458
617-965-0055
FAX: 617-965-5152 800-537-7765
info@psmj.com www.psmj.com

Frank Stasiowski, Production Manager
Judy Clausen, Marketing

Provides marketing tactics and techniques for the design industry. *$628.20*
8 pages Monthly Founded: 1976
Mailing list available for rent $125 per M.
Printed in 2 colors on matte stock

301 Promotional Products Business
Promotional Products Association International
3125 Skyway Circle N
Irving, TX 75038-3526
972-252-0404
FAX: 972-258-3004
LisaH@ppa.org www.ppa.org

Lisa Horn, Publisher
Mellisa Klusmeyer, Editor
Steve Slagle, President
Lisa Horn, Circulation Manager

Coverage concentrates on news activities and events of the promotional products industry. *$62.00*
140 pages Monthly Founded: 1903
Circulation: 8000

302 Response
Advanstar Communications
1 Park Avenue
New York, NY 10016
212-797-7631
FAX: 212-951-6793
info@advanstar.com
www.advanstar.com

Thomas Haire, Editor
Dan Kern, President

Magazine of direct response television reporting. Educates marketers and advertising executives on how to sell products, generate leads and drive store sales through infomercials, short-form commercials, televised shopping and multi-media retailing.
Monthly Founded: 1987
Circulation: 12000

303 Retail Advertising & Marketing Association Magazine
Retail Advertising & Marketing International
325 7th Street NW
Suite 1100
Washington, DC 20004-2802
202-268-8183
FAX: 202-661-3049
perweilerp@nrf.com
www.rama-nrf.org

Tom Holliday, President
Mike Gatti, Executive VP

National magazine devoted exclusively to retail advertising and marketing professionals. Accepts advertising. *$125.00*
Monthly

304 Select
841 Nineteenth Street
Miami Beach, FL 33139
305-299-9473
FAX: 305-532-3905
David.Colby@selct-magazine.com
www.selectonline.com

Joe Carbonara, Managing Editor

Geared toward creative decision makers and photographers, emphasis is placed on the imagination, favorite images and emotions induced by photos. Includes detailed photography location information. *$90.00*

Founded: 1982
Circulation: 35,000

305 Senior Business Digest
Vital Information
321 Carrera Drive
Mill Valley, CA 94941

FAX: 650-345-7018

306 Shoot Magazine
ADWEEK
770 Broadway
7th Floor
New York, NY 10003
646-545-5220
FAX: 646-654-5351 800-641-2030
publisher@adweek.com
www.adweek.com

Gina Keena, Publisher

For those involved in production and post-production work on TV commercials. *$187.00*

Circulation: 14170

307 Sign Builder Illustrated
Simmons-Boardman Publishing Corporation
345 Hudson Street
12th Floor
New York, NY 10014
212-379-9300
FAX: 212-633-1863
rdemarco@sbpub.com
www.signshop.com

Robert DeMarco, Publisher
Jeff Wooten, Editor
Arthur J McGinnis, Jr., President
Tom Leader, Circulation Manager

How-to sign magazine with articles on fabricating, installation and service and highlight neon and computer-aided signmaking. Features step-by-step guides.
Monthly
Circulation: 1800
Printed in 4 colors on glossy stock

308 Sign Business
National Business Media
2800 W Midway Boulevard
PO Box 1416
Broomfield, CO 80020-1416
303-469-0424
FAX: 303-469-5730 800-669-0424
sbpublisher@nbm.com
www.nbm.com/signbusiness

Robert H Wieber, President
Eddie Wieber, Editor
Mary Tohill, Group Publisher

Contains information on electrical illuminated signage, outdoor advertising and commercial sign shops. *$38.00*
120 pages Monthly Founded: 1986
Circulation: 18348
Mailing list available for rent 1000 names $225 per M.
Printed in 4 colors

309 **SignCraft Magazine**
Signcraft Publishing Company
PO Box 60031
Fort Myers, FL 33906
239-939-4644
FAX: 239-939-0607 800-204-0204
signcraft@signcraft.com
www.signcraft.com

William McIltrot, President
Tom McIltrot, Editor
Dennis McIltrot, Circulation Manager

Helps sign makers get their work done more easily, run their shops more efficiently, market their work more effectively and increase their profits. *$35.00*
108 pages Founded: 1980
Circulation: 14000
Mailing list available for rent 25M names
Printed in 4 colors on matte stock

310 **Signs of the Times Magazine**
ST Publications
407 Gilbert Avenue
Cincinnati, OH 45202
513-421-2050
FAX: 513-421-5144 800-925-1110
customer@stmediagroup.com
www.signweb.com

Tedd Swormstedt, President/CEO
Brian Foos, CFO
Wade Swormstedt, Editor/Publisher
Lise Gillen, VP Circulation

Includes the latest technological information, product news, in-depth analysis and regular columns by top industry experts. *$39.00*
200 pages Founded: 1906
Circulation: 17000 17,000 names $200 per M.
Printed in 4 colors

Trade Shows

311 **Advertising Media Credit Executives Association Annual Conference**
Advertising Media Credit Executives Association
8840 Columbia 100 Parkway
Columbia, MD 21045-2158
410-740-5560
FAX: 410-740-5574
nacmainfo@nacm.org www.nacm.org

Norma Heim, Director Communications

Media credit managers, editors, business mangers and other professionals gather for exhibits of advertising media such as newspapers, magazines, radio and television.
400 Attendees October Founded: 1896

312 **American Advertising Federation: National Advertising Conference**
American Advertising Federation
1101 Vermont Avenue NW
Suite 500
Washington, DC 20005-6306
202-898-0089
FAX: 202-898-0159 800-999-2231
aaf@aaf.org www.aaf.org

Wally Snyder, President
Karen Cohn, Conference Services

50 booths related to advertising.
807 Attendees Annual
Circulation: 50,000

313 **Cable TV Advertising Bureau: Cable Advertising Conference**
830 3rd Avenue
2nd Floor
New York, NY 10022
212-508-1200
FAX: 212-832-3268
www.onetvworld.org

Joseph Ostrow, President/CEO

Annual conference and exhibits of advertising-supported cable television networks; services to support local advertising sales.
2000 Attendees February Founded: 1981

314 **DECA International Career Development Conference**
New Dimensions
1908 Association Drive
Reston, VA 20191
703-860-5000
FAX: 703-860-4013
deacinc@aol.com www.deca.org

Ed Davis, Executive Director
Larry Lorenzi, Conference/Meeting Planning

Gathering of 13,000 students, advisors, businesspersons and alumni. Winners of local, state and regional competitions, national elections, workshops and leadership academies. Over 60 booths and exhibits.
12M Attendees April/May
Circulation: 188,500

315 **Exhibitor Conference**
Exhibitor Magazine Group
98 E Naperville Road
Westmont, IL 60559
630-434-7779
FAX: 630-434-1216 800-752-6312
exhibitorshow@heiexpo.com
www.exhibitorshow.com

Carol Fojtik, Managing Director/Sr Vice President

Conference program combined with exhibit hall featuring latest products and resources shaping the future of exhibiting and corporate event programs. Anyone responsible for planning, managing or implementing trade show or corporate event marketing functions should attend. Conference is held annually in Las Vegas, NV.
5M Attendees March Founded: 1989

316 **Global Shop**
VNU Expositions
1145 Sanctuuary Parkway
Suite 355
Alpharetta, GA 30074
770-569-1540
FAX: 770-569-5105 800-933-8735
kkobrzycki@vnuexpo.com
www.globalshop.org

Kara Kobrzycki, Conference Manager
Maddie Oelkers, Operations Manager

The show for manufacturers and representatives of equipment for visual merchandising exhibiting the current trends related to the interior store displays.
20M Attendees March Founded: 1982

317 **International Licensing and Merchandising Conference and Expo**
Expocon Management Associates
363 Reef Road
PO Box 915
Fairfield, CT 06430-0915
203-256-4700
FAX: 203-256-4730
abilities@expocon.com
www.expocon.com

Annual show of 220 exhibitors of logos, corporate trademarks, characters, designs and other advertising techniques that require licensing.
7000 Attendees May

318 **National Advertising Service Association Annual Conference and Expo**
1421 Prince Street
Suite 200
Alexandria, VA 22314-2805

Susan Groff, Director Conference

45 booths.
250 Attendees June

319 **National Hispanic Market Trade Show and Media Expo**
Hispanic Business
425 Pine Avenue
Santa Barbara, CA 93117-3709
805-964-4554
FAX: 805-964-5539
info@hispanstar.com
www.hispanstar.com

Jesus Chavarria, President
Luisa Donis, Corporate Communications

Annual show of 100 exhibitors of market/research, media, advertising, public relations, information services and recruitment. Se habla espanol.
1500 Attendees Founded: 1979
Circulation: 200,000

320 **Point-of-Purchase Advertising Institute Marketplace**
66 N Van Brunt Street
Englewood, NJ 07631
201-894-8899
FAX: 201-894-0529

Richard K Blatt, Executive Director
Rick Walsh, Trade Show Manager

Brings together thousands of point-of-purchase advertising buyers and users with nearly 400 exhibitors, featuring their instore displays and merchandising programs. The show also features a seminar series and display competition.
October
Circulation: 9,000

Directories & Databases

321 **AAF Internship Directory**
American Advertising Federation
1101 Vermont Avenue NW
Suite 500
Washington, DC 20005
202-898-0089
FAX: 202-898-0159 800-999-2231
aaf@aaf.org www.aaf.org

Wally Snyder, President/CEO

Contains over 1,500 internships available at businesses and organizations affiliated with the American Advertising Federation. Also included is a special section listing internship opportunities for minority students.
February
Circulation: 50,000

322 AAF Speakers Directory
American Advertising Federation
1101 Vermont Avenue NW
Suite 500
Washington, DC 20005
202-898-0089
FAX: 202-898-0159 800-999-2231
aaf@aaf.org www.aaf.org
Wally Snyder, President/CEO
Sean Sullivan, Director Information Services

Compiled by the American Advertising Federation for locally affiliated associations' use in programming. Speakers are listed by topics of expertise. Specific topics, speech titles, and fees are listed after each speaker.
140 pages

323 ADWEEK Directory
770 Broadway
7th Floor
New York, NY 10003
646-545-5220
FAX: 646-654-5365 800-064-2030
publisher@adweek.com
www.adweek.com
Sid Holt, Editor-in-Chief
Moses Frenck, Managing Editor

For anyone seeking agency-specific information. Over 26,000 personnel listings, more than 6,400 full service advertising agencies and networks, public relations firms, media buying services, recruitment, entertainment marketing, yellow pages, health care, interactive, sports marketing, infomercials, direct marketing, creative design, marketing communications and research, consultancies and many more media related listing. *$699.00*
Annual Founded: 1981

324 Advertisers and Agency Red Book Plus
Engel Publishing Partners
828A Newtown-Yardley
Newtown, PA 18940
215-867-0044
FAX: 215-867-0053
www.engelpub.com
Karl Engel, President
Styli Engel, Executive VP/Editor-in-Chief
James Hannan, CEO/Group Publisher
Lisa Aberman, CFO/COO

Advertising information. *$1788.00*
Quarterly Founded: 1982

325 Advertising Age: Leading National Advertisers Issue
Crain Communications
1155 Gratiot Avenue
Detroit, MI 48207-2997
313-446-6000
www.crain.com
Keith E. Crain, Chairman/Publisher
Rance E. Crain, President/Editor-In-Chief
David S. Klein, VP Publishing/Editorial Director

List of 100 leading US advertisers in terms of amount spent in national media advertising and below-the-line forms of spending. *$ 5.00*
Annual Founded: 1930
Circulation: 59,000

326 Advertising Career Directory
Gale Research
27500 Drake Road
Farmington Hills, MI 48331-3535
248-699-4253
FAX: 248-699-8214 800-877-4253
gale.contentQA@thomson.com
www.gale.com
Gordon T Macomber, President
Dennis Stepaniak, Executive VP/CFO
Dennis Poupard, Executive VP Editorial/Production

Lists more than 150 companies and organizations offering job opportunities and training possibilities in advertising account management. *$34.95*
255 pages Cloth

327 Advertising and Marketing Intelligence
New York Times
1719 State Route 10
#A
Parsippany, NJ 07054-4507

Contains abstracts of articles from over 75 publications on advertising, marketing and the media.
Bibliographic

328 Agri-Marketing Top 50: Ag's Biggest Agencies Issue
Doane Agricultural Services
11701 Borman Drive
Suite 300
Saint Louis, MO 63146-4139
314-569-2700
FAX: 314-569-1083
info@agrimarketing.com
www.agrimarketing.com
Bill Schuermann, Publisher/Editorial Director
Judy Knoll, Advertising Sales/Customer Service

List of the top 50 US and Canadian advertising agencies and public relations firms, chosen on the basis of agricultural business income. Reaches key corporate executives, sales and marketing officers, marketing communications and advertising/PR professionals, agri-media and others allied to this industry. Primary source of agribusiness news and discussion for the North American agribusiness community. *$30.00*
10 per year Founded: 1969
Circulation: 9,000 $105 per M.
Printed in 4 colors on glossy stock

329 BRANDWEEK Directory
ADWEEK
770 Broadway
7th Floor
New York, NY 10003
646-545-5220
FAX: 646-654-5365 800-641-2030
info@adweek.com www.adweek.com
Sid Holt, Editor-in-Chief
Charlotte Erwin, Publisher

Featuring in depth information in a clear and easy-to-use format,organized by brand name with marketer,personnel,lead agency and media expenditure data. Contains stand alone listings for over 6,900 brands, including 18,000 personnel at both corporate and brand level. *$699.00*
Annual Founded: 1981

330 Brands and Their Companies
Gale Research
27500 Drake Road
Farmington Hills, MI 48331-3535
248-699-4253
FAX: 248-699-8214 800-877-4253
gale.contentQA@thomson.com
www.gale.com
Gordon T Macomber, President
Dennis Stepaniak, Executive VP/CFO
Dennis Poupard, Executive VP Editorial/Production

Approximately 430,000 trade names' trademarks and brand names of consumer oriented products and their 73,000 manufacturers, importers, marketers, or distributors. Provides a current and accurate source of information for people seeking answers to questions about companies and brands. *$995.00*
Annual

331 Broadcasting & Cable Yearbook
R.R. Bowker LLC
630 Central Avenue
New Providence, NJ 07974
908-286-1090
FAX: 908-464-3553 800-526-9537
info@bowker.com www.bowker.com
Andrew Grabois, Managing Director

Single source for unbiased media information. Includes profiles of 4,825 AM radio stations, 9,000 FM radio stations and 2,180 television stations in the United States. A station's call letters,frequency or channel,address,telephone,fax,Internet address,ownership, and programming format are all provided. Also 1,100 Canadian radio and television stations are profiled, along with more than 5,100 industry service providers from law firms to engineers to industry associations, and more. *$199.95*
1277 pages Annual Founded: 1948 ISBN 1-560560-24-X
Circulation: 9000 : cd-rom/web

332 Buyers Guide to Outdoor Advertising
Interactive Market Systems(IMS)
1200 Bay Street
Suite 301
Toronto, Canada M5S-2Z7
416-961-2840
FAX: 416-961-2874
imscan@interlog.com
www.imscan.com
FC Miller, Publisher
Robert Gainey, Circulation Manager

Offers valuable information on outdoor advertising companies and their markets. *$300.00*

333 Circulation
Standard Rate & Data Services
1700 Higgins Road
Des Plaines, IL 60018-5605
847-375-5000
FAX: 847-375-5001 800-851-7737
contact@srds.com www.srds.com
Annual directory of major print media including daily and Sunday newspapers. *$312.00*
Annual Founded: 1920
Circulation: 2,000

334 **Co-op Advertising Programs Sourcebook**
National Register Publishing
562 Central Avenue
New Providence, NJ 07974

FAX: 908-673-1179 800-473-7020
alison.perruso@marquiswhoswho.com
www.co-opsourcebook.com
Alison Perruso, Contact
Nearly 6,300 cooperative advertising programs offered by manufacturers. Lists nearly 4,500 available co-op programs in 52 different product classifacations from agricultural products to toys. *$637.00*
Semi-Annual

335 **Consumer Magazine Advertising Source**
Standard Rate & Data Services
1700 Higgins Road
Des Plaines, IL 60018-5605
847-375-5000
FAX: 847-375-5001 800-851-7737
contact@srds.com www.srds.com
Joseph Hayes, Publisher
Over 2,700 comprehensive listings to identify ideal publications easily from more than 80 markets covering consumer and farm titles. Over 15,000 updates every year, continuously incorporated online to make decisions with the latest data. *$748.00*
Annual

336 **Creative Black Book**
Black Book Marketing Group
740 Broadway
2nd Floor
New York, NY 10003
212-979-6700
FAX: 212-673-4321 800-841-1246
info@blackbook.com
www.blackbook.com
Ted Rubin, President
Josephine Hu, Multimedia Coordinator
Photographers and photographic services, design firms, advertising agencies and other firms whose products or services are used in advertising. *$20.00*
Annual

337 **Creative's Illustrated Guide to P-O-P Exhibits and Promotion**
Magazines Creative
37 W 39th Street
New York, NY 10018-3886

FAX: 212-819-0945
David Flasterstein, Editor
List of more than 400 manufacturers and producers of point-of-purchase displays, signs, and other promotional materials and equipment. *$20.00*
Annual

338 **Directory of Advertising & Marketing Services**
Towne Silverstein Rotter
411 Lafayette Street
Suite 300
New York, NY 10003-7032
212-260-3736

Over 450 services are profiled that use advertisers and agencies in marketing a product. *$75.00*
180 pages

339 **IQ Directory**
ADWEEK
770 Broadway
7th Floor
New York, NY 10003
646-545-5220
FAX: 646-654-5351
publisher@adweek.com
www.adweek.com
Mitch Tebo, Publishing Director
David Maddux, Editor
Profile of companies at the leading edge of digital marketing, has the specifics you'll need to investigate, launch and/or expand your digital presence. Profiles over 2,200 interactive agencies, web developers, brand marketers, online media, CD-ROM developers, POP/Kiosk designers and multimedia creative companies *$399.00*
Founded: 1981

340 **Infomercial Marketing Sourcebook**
ADWEEK
770 Broadway
7th Floor
New York, NY 10003
646-545-5220
FAX: 646-654-5351
publisher@adweek.com
www.adweek.com
Wright Ferguson Jr, VP/Magazine Publisher
A complete resource guide for everyone involved in the infomercial industry.

341 **Madison Avenue Handbook**
Peter Glenn Publications
6040 NW 43rd Terrace
Boca Raton, FL 33496
561-999-8930
FAX: 561-999-8931 888-332-6700
gjames@pgdirect.com
www.pgdirect.com
Gregory James, CEO/Publisher
Tricia Mazzilli-Blout, VP
L Chip Brill, Director
Umberto Guido III, Editor
Advertising agencies and related services in the US and Canada for television, film and music producers. *$59.95*
400 pages Annual Founded: 1956

342 **Marketing Resources Directory**
Gale Research
27500 Drake Road
Farmington Hills, MI 48331-3535
248-699-4253
FAX: 248-699-8214 800-877-4253
galeord@gale.com www.gale.com
Dennis Poupard, Executive VP
Allen W Paschal, President
27,000 marketing consultants, advertising and PR agencies, business and trade associations, business libraries and publications, and marketing experts. *$275.00*

343 **Mediaweek Multimedia Directory**
ADWEEK
770 Broadway
7th Floor
New York, NY 10003
646-545-5220
FAX: 646-654-5351
publisher@adweek.com
www.adweek.com
Mitch Tebo, Publishing Director
Focuses on the most powerful segments covering 9,000 media companies from the top 100 media markets for radio, broadcast TV, cable TV and daily newspapers. Also includes the top 300 consumer magazines, the top 150 trade magazines, networks, syndicators, sales representatives, multi-media holding companies, trade associations and rating organizations. *$700.00*

344 **Medical Marketing and Media**
Haymarket Media
PO Box 5015
Brentwood, TN 37024-5015
561-368-9301
FAX: 561-368-7870
mmm@haymarketmedia.com
www.cpsnet.com
Suzanne Besse, Advertising Sales Contact
James Chase, Managing Editor
For the pharmaceutical and medical marketing industry. Accepts advertising.
96 pages Monthly Founded: 1976 $5 per M.
Printed in 4 colors on glossy stock

345 **Minority Student Guide to Employers**
American Advertising Federation
1101 Vermont Avenue NW
Suite 500
Washington, DC 20005-6306
202-898-0089
FAX: 202-898-0159
aaf@aaf.org www.aaf.org
Wally Snyder, President/CEO
Offers information on hiring minorities.

Circulation: 50,000

346 **National Directory of Clubs and Federations**
1101 Vermont Avenue NW
Suite 500
Washington, DC 20005-6303
202-898-0089
FAX: 202-898-0159 800-999-2231
aaf@aaf.org www.aaf.org
Wally Snyder, President
Laurie Reese, Manager Marketing
This directory includes contact information for each of 204 local advertising clubs and federations which comprise the AAF's grass roots networks, the industry's most valuable resource in advancing and protecting advertising interests. It is a valuable networking tool to gain invaluable information about clubs and fererations nationwide. It lists clubs and federations alphabetically by state and includes the president of the federation, and if on record with the AFFA, the executive director.

347 **Print Media Production Source**
Standard Rate & Data Services
1700 Higgins Road
Des Plaines, IL 60018-5605
847-375-5000
FAX: 847-375-5001 800-851-7737
This print service provides complete data on all critical ad production specifications for business and consumer magazines and newspapers. Production, traffic and graphic design personnel use this current, accurate resource to confirm essential production information so they can control production deadlines and budgets. *$844.00*
Quarterly Founded: 1968
Circulation: 2,403

348 **Radio Co-op Directory**
Radio Advertising Bureau
1320 Greenway Drive
Suite 500
Irving, TX 75038
972-536-6700
FAX: 972-753-6727 800-232-3131
gfries@rab.com www.RAB.com
Gary Fries, President/CEO
Van Allen, Executive VP/CFO
Over 5,000 manufacturers that provide co-operative allowances for radio advertising.
$125.00
Annual

349 **Recruitment Solution**
Standard Rate & Data Services
1700 Higgins Road
Des Plaines, IL 60018-5605
847-375-5000
FAX: 847-375-5001 www.srds.com
Wenda Harris-Millard, President
Tom Drouillard, VP Circulation
Approximately 4,800 media options for placing recruitment advertising, including business publications, daily newspapers, health care publications, and weekly community publications. *$95.00*
Annual

350 **Student Guide to Mass Media Internships**
Intern Research Group
PO Box 52
Boulder, CO 80309-0052
Ronald H Claxton, Editor
About 10,000 internships offered by 2,700 newspapers, radio and television stations, cable television companies, magazines, publishing houses, advertising agencies and other firms. *$45.00*
Annual

351 **Tie-In Promotion Service**
Association of National Advertisers
708 3rd Avenue
New York, NY 10017-4270
212-697-5950
FAX: 212-661-8057 www.ana.net
Robert Liodice, President/CEO
Michelle Hunter, Assistant Communications Manager
Christina Ricci, Database Manager
Brand names listed by their companies as available for possible tie-in promotions with other companies. *$189.95*
Annual, December Founded: 1910

352 **US Source Book of Advertisers**
Schonfeld & Associates
2830 Blackthorn Road
Riverwoods, IL 60015
847-948-8080
FAX: 847-948-8096 800-205-0030
saiinfo@saibooks.com
www.saibooks.com
Carol J Greenhut, Publisher
A list of over 5,700 public companies in the United States that advertise. Includes names and titles of their executives along with ad budget and sales. Ideal reference for media, sales, ad agency new business development. *$395.00*
230 pages Annual Founded: 1989 ISBN 1-932024-18-2 : cisk

353 **Workbook**
Scott & Daughters Publishing
940 N Highland Avenue
Suite A
Los Angeles, CA 90038
323-856-0008
FAX: 323-856-4368 800-547-2688
Alexis Scott, Publisher
Susan Haller, Managing Editor
This directory, offered in four volumes, lists over 25,000 advertising agencies, art directors and freelance illustrators in the United States.
2800 pages Annual
Circulation: 35,000

Industry Web Sites

354 **www.aaf.org**
American Advertising Federation
Educates policymakers, media and the public on the value of advertising. Includes a unique, nationally coordinated grassroots network of advertisers, advertising agencies, media companies, local advertising associations and college chapters.

355 **www.aapor.org**
American Association for Public Opinion Research
Furthers the research of public opinion by conducting surveys, holding seminars and more.

356 **www.adweek.com**
Adweek
Leading descision makers in the advertising and marketing field go to Adweek.Com every day for breaking news, insight, buzz, opinion and classifieds. The resources of all six regional editions of Adweek, as well as the national edition of Brandweek are combined with the knowledge of our online editors and the mulimedia-interactive capabilities of the Web to deliver vital information quickly and effectively to our target audience.

357 **www.ahaa.org**
Association of Hispanic Advertising Agenices
The first trade association of its kind to be established specifically for agencies working within the US Hispanic advertising industry.

358 **www.ana.net**
Association of National Advertisers
Conducts surveys, studies, workshops and seminars, disseminates information.

359 **www.apanational.com**
Advertising Photographers of America
Promotes standards of business practices and awareness of the role of advertising photographers.

360 **www.awny.org**
Advertising Women of New York
The first women's association in the communications industry.

361 **www.getbiz.com**
BizNet Internet Solutions
Literature and information sources useful to international advertising researchers and practitioners.

362 **www.greyhouse.com**
Grey House Publishing
Selected Grey House directories in the fields of business, health and education are available online. Users can search our online databases by several different search criteria, such as product categories, geographic area, sales volume and much, much more. Full Grey House catalog and online ordering also available.

363 **www.icomagencies.com**
International Communications Agency Network
In today's global marketplace competition is fierce. To succeed globally you must succeed locally. Those most familiar with their customers and prospects market by market are the most likely to suceed. Local ICOM agencies help companies position their products for success in all the important markets of the world.

364 **www.ifcaonline.org**
Insurance And Financial Communicators Association
International organization dedicated to the ongoing professional development of its members in life insurance and related financial services communications.

365 **www.kcadclub.com**
Advertising Club of Kansas City
To enhance the professional development of the club's diverse membership, while increasing local and national recognition for the advertising industry.

366 **www.naa.org**
Newspaper Association of America

367 **www.oaaa.org**
Outdoor Advertising Association of America

Promotes protects, and advances outdoor advertising interests in the US with nearly 1,100 member companies. The OAAA represents more than 90% of industry revenues and guides itself by the needs of advertisers and communities in its development of responsible controls, policies and better product and service standards.

368 **www.onetvworld.org**
Cable TV Advertising Bureau

Promotes cable TV as an advertising medium.

369 **www.popai.com**
Point-Of-Purchase Advertising International

Promotes point of puchase advertising.

370 **www.ppa.org**
Promotional Products Association International

Represents the $8 billion specialty advertising, premium, incentive and gift industry. Members are suppliers or distributors of imprinted promotional advertising products.

371 **www.rama-nrf.com**
Retail Advertising & Marketing International

Devoted exclusively to the needs of retail advertising and marketing professionals.

372 **www.signs.org**
International Sign Association

Members represent manufacturing of all types of on premesis sign, materials and supplies. 1,500 members, founded in 1944.

373 **www.taan.org**
Transworld Advertising Agency Network

A network of independently owned advertising agencies that work closely together in the exchange of management information, reciprocal services and personal local contact.

374 **www.tradepromo.org**
Trade Promotion Management Association

Non-profit trade association for professionals and organizations involved with trade promotion. Membership is open to any organization dealing with trade promotion, whether manufacturer, retailer, media representative, or serivce provider.

375 **www.wamdc.org**
Women in Advertising and Marketing

Serves as a network for women in advertising and marketing fields. Accepts advertising.

Associations

376 Abundant Life Seed Foundation
PO Box 157
saginaw, OR 97472
541-767-9606
866-514-7333
als@abundantlifeseeds.com
www.abundantlifeseed.org
Our goal is to offer true-to-type open pollinated varieties grown using only certified organic or biodynamic farming methods. Our research staff grows and evaluated thousands of open pollinated varieties so you can trust that every variety has been grown at our trail grounds and has passed our stringent equirements. We offer a seed catalog with varieties of vegetables, flowers, herb seeds, garlic, seed potatoes and live plants all 100% certified organic.
Founded: 1975

377 Agribusiness Council
1312 Eighteenth Street NW
Suite 300
Washington, DC 20036

FAX: 202-887-9178
info@agribusinesscouncil.org
www.agribusinesscouncil.org
Private, nonprofit/tax-exempt, membership organization dedicated to strengthening U.S. agro-industrial competitiveness through programs which highlight international trade and development potentials.
Founded: 1967

378 Agricultural Communications in Excellence
Mowry Road, Building 116
PO Box 110811
Gainesville, FL 32611-0811
352-392-9588
FAX: 358-392-7902
ace@ifas.ufl.edu www.aceweb.org
Judy Winn, President
Bob Sams, VP
Judy Rude, DC Region Director
Owens Roberts, International Director
Laura Miller, North Central Director
Members are writers, editors, broadcasters and communicators who are involved in the dissemination of agricultural, food sciences and natural resource information in land-grant colleges, federal and state agencies, international agencies and other private communications work.
Founded: 1970

379 Agricultural Communicators of Tomorrow
Kansas State University
220 Rolfs Hall
Gainesville, FL 32611
352-392-0502
FAX: 352-392-9589
rtelg@ifas.ufl.edu www.ifas.ufl.edu
Ricky Telg, Advisor
A national organization of college students professionally interested in communications related to agriculture, food, natural resources and allied fields.
Founded: 1970

380 Agricultural History Society
University of Arkansas at Little Rock
Department of History
2801 South University Avenue
Little Rock, AR 72204-1099
501-693-3000
FAX: 501-569-6059
cfwilliams@ualr.edu
www.agriculturalhistory.ualr.edu
Larry Poldrack, Executive Director
C Fred Williams, Executive Secretary/Treasurer
Organized to stimulate the interest in and promote the study of the history of agriculture, and rural life.
915 Members Founded: 1919

381 Agricultural Relations Council
11020 King Street
Suite 205
Overland Park, KS 66210-1201
913-491-6500
FAX: 913-491-6502
agrimktg@nama.org www.nama.org
Tom Taylor, President
Eldon White, Executive Director
A national association with members involved in agricultural public relations. Electronic newsletter of interest to association members.
1500 Members

382 Agricultural Research Society
1301 New York Avenue NW
#928
Washington, DC 20005-4701
202-479-3872
FAX: 202-219-0391
Organized to stimulate the interest in and promote the study of the history of agriculture.
1.5M Members Founded: 1919

383 Agricultural Retailers Association
11701 Borman Drive
Saint Louis, MO 63146-4193
314-567-6655
800-844-4900
ara@agretailerassn.org
www.agretailerassn.org
Annual Founded: 1993

384 Agricultural and Industrial Manufacturers' Representatives Association
7500 Flying Cloud Drive
Suite 900
Eden Prairie, MN 55344
952-253-6230
FAX: 952-835-4774 800-759-2467
jrmanke@aol.com www.aimrareps.org

Mike Kowalczyk, President
Ron Reed, VP
Ries Morrissey, Chairman
Jim Manke, Chief Administrator Executive
Miller Hadskey, Director
Association of industrial manufacturers who sell equipment into light industrial, agricultural, lawn and garden markets.
125 Members Founded: 1961

385 Agriculture Council of America
11020 King Street
Suite 205
Overland Park, KS 66210-1201
913-491-1895
FAX: 913-491-6502
info@agday.org www.agday.org
Eldon White, President
A nonprofit umbrella organization uniquely composed of leaders in the agriculture, food and fiber communities dedicated to increasing the public awareness of agriculture's vital role in our society.
75 Members Founded: 1973

386 American Agricultural Economics Association
415 S Duff Avenue
Suite C
Ames, IA 50010-6600
515-233-3202
FAX: 515-233-3101
info@aaea.org www.aaea.org
Laurian Unnevehr, President
Yvonne C Bennett, Executive Director
The professional association for agricultural economists and related fields.
3000 Members Founded: 1910
Mailing list available for rent

387 American Agricultural Law Association
American Agricultural Economics Association
2585 Bowmont Drive
PO Box 2025
Eugene, OR 97402-2025
541-021-1958
FAX: 541-302-1958
roberta@aglaw-assn.org
www.aglaw-assn.org
Robert Achenbach, Executive Director
Don Uchtmann, President
Non-profit association devoted to education about agricultural law.
600 Members Founded: 1980

388 American Agriculture Movement
PO Box 703
Spearman, TX 79081-0703
517-568-2203
FAX: 517-568-4090
cemiller@dmci.net www.aaminc.org
Larry Matlack, President
Arthur Chaney, Executive VP
Wayne Allen, VP
Anna Kirkpatrick, Secretary
Lynn Kirkpatrick, Vice President Marketing
The American Agriculture Movement was founded in 1977 after Congress enacted another farm bill that insured four more years of prices paid to farmers below their cost of production.
Founded: 1977

389 American Alfalfa Processors Association
8810 Craig Drive
Overland Park, KS 66212-4768
913-648-6800
FAX: 913-648-2648
aapa@cysource.com
www.aapausa.org
Wanda L Cobb, Executive VP
For operators and suppliers of alfalfa processing farms.
Founded: 1941

390 American Angus Association
3201 Frederick Avenue
Saint Joseph, MO 64506-2997
816-383-5100
FAX: 816-233-9703
angus@angus.org www.angus.org
Minnie Lou Bradley, President
John R Crouch, Executive VP
Beef breed organization.

36000 Members Founded: 1873

391 **American Association of Cereal Chemists**
3340 Pilot Knob Road
Saint Paul, MN 55121-2097
651-454-7250
FAX: 651-454-0766
skohn@scisoc.org www.aaccnet.org
James Dexter, Chair
George L Lookhart, President
Steven Nelson, VP
Elizabeth A Knight, Treasurer
Virgil W Smail, Director

An international organization of scientists and other professionals studying the chemistry of cereal grains and their products or working in related fields.
4000 Members

392 **American Association of Crop Insurers**
1 Massachusetts Avenue NW
Suite 800
Washington, DC 20001-1401
202-789-4100
FAX: 202-408-7763
aaci@mwmlaw.com
www.aginsurance.org
Michael R McLeod, General Counsel/Executive Director

A nonprofit industry service organization representing the interests of insurance companies, agents, and adjusters involved in the Federal crop insurance program.
25 Members

393 **American BeeKeeping Federation**
115 Morning Glory Circle
Jesup, GA 31546-1337
912-427-4233
FAX: 912-427-8447
info@abfnet.org www.abfnet.org
Daniel Weaver, President
Troy Fore, Executive Director
George Hansen, Director
Gus Rouse, Director
Zac Browning, Director

Members include honey producers, packers, suppliers and shippers of honey products.
1200 Members Founded: 1943

394 **American Brahman Breeders Association**
3003 South Loop W
Suite 140
Houston, TX 77054-1301
713-349-0854
FAX: 713-349-9795
abba@brahman.org www.brahman.org
James C Chapman, President
Carl McKenney, VP
Chris Shivers, Executive VP
Bill Dan Lindley, Secretary/Treasurer

The first beef breed developed in the US, has played an important role not only in crossbreeding programs throughout the US and beyond, but also has become a common thread connecting other american breeds developed in the last century.
Founded: 1924

395 **American Cranberry Growers Association**
126 Forrest Meadows Road
Tabernacle, NJ 08088
609-268-0641
FAX: 609-268-9232
Neva Moore, Secretary/Treasurer

Members include cranberry growers, packers, suppliers and shippers of cranberry products.

396 **American Dairy Science Association**
1111 N Dunlap Avenue
Savoy, IL 61874-9604
217-565-5146
FAX: 217-398-4119
adsa@assochq.org www.adsa.org
Mike Hutjens, President
Dave Barbano, VP
Brenda Carlson, Executive Director
Don Beitz, Director
Steve Nickerson, Director/Editor

Organization of professional researchers. Publishes journals and holds annual member meetings.
3000 Members Founded: 1898
Mailing list available for rent

397 **American Farm Bureau Federation**
600 Maryland Avenue SW
Washington, DC 20024
202-406-3600
FAX: 202-406-3604
bstallman@fb.org www.fb.com
Bob Stallman, President
Steven Appel, VP
Richard W Newpher, Secretary/Treasurer
Julie Anna Potts, General Counsel
Don Lipton, Public Relations

Members are the state Farm Bureaus in the 50 states and Puerto Rico.
3M Members Founded: 1919

398 **American Feed Industry Association**
1501 Wilson Boulevard
Suite 1100
Arlington, VA 22209-2403
703-524-0810
FAX: 703-524-1921
afia@afia.org www.afia.org
Joel Newman, President
Rex Runyon, VP
Judy Pilgrim, Assistant to the President
Jim Rydell, Director
Betty Pendleton, Regulatory Affairs

Provides the following member services concerning federal and state legislation and regulation: information on industry developments; assistance in efficient operations; and cooperation on projects of mutual interest with other organizations.
690 Members Founded: 1909

399 **American Forage and Grassland Council**
350 Poplar Avenue
Elmhurst, IL 60126
630-941-3240
FAX: 630-359-4274 800-944-2342
dtucker@io.com www.afgc.org
Bill Talley, President
Gary A Pederson, VP
Ray Smith, Secretary

Its mission is to be recognized as the leader and voice of economically and environmentally sound forage agriculture. The American Forage and Grassland Council (AFGC) is an international organization made up of 24 affiliate councils in the United States and Canada.
2700 Members

400 **American Guernsey Association**
7614 Slate Ridge Boulevard
Reynoldsburg, OH 43068-3126
614-864-2409
FAX: 614-864-5614
sjohnson@usguernsey.com
www.usguernsey.com
Seth Johnson, Executive Secretary/Treasurer
Josey Morris, Programs Coordinator
Ida Albert, Records Director
Lynnett Wright, Editor
Mary Ann D'Ippolito, Finance Manager

Provides and promote programs and services to enhance the value and profitability of the Guernsey breed for members, owners and the dairy industry worldwide. Registers and delivers guernsey cattle throughout the US.
900 Members Founded: 1877

401 **American Herbal Products Association**
8484 Georgia Avenue
Suite 370
Silver Spring, MD 20910-5606
301-588-1171
FAX: 301-588-1174
ahpa@ahpa.com www.ahpa.org
Michael McGuffin, President
Steven Dentali, PhD, VP
Devon Powell, Director of Administration

The national trade association which represents manufacturers, importers and distributors of herbs and herbal products. AHPA seeks self-regulation, establishment of standards and rules of ethical conduct, member enrichment and public outreach.
200 Members Founded: 1983
Mailing list available for rent 200 names $350 per M.

402 **American Hereford Association**
PO Box 014059
Kansas City, MO 64101
816-182-2250
FAX: 816-842-6931
chuffhin@hereford.org
www.hereford.org
Jack Holden, Chairman
Dale Spencer, Vice Chair
Richard Hudson, Executive VP
Huff Hines, Chief Executive Officer

Association for people in the Hereford cattle industry.

403 **American Jersey Cattle Association**
6486 E Main Street
Reynoldsburg, OH 43068-2349
614-861-3636
FAX: 614-861-8040
nsmith@usjersey.com
www.usjersey.com
Neal Smith, Executive Secretary/CEO
Cherie L Bayer, Director of Development

The most profitable, adaptable and responsive dairy producers in the world.
540 Members Founded: 1868

404 **American Meat Science Association**
1111 N Dunlap Avenue
Savoy, IL 61874
217-356-5368
FAX: 217-398-4119
information@meatscience.org
www.meatscience.org

Dennis R Buege, President
C Ann Hollingsworth, Secretary/Treasurer
Thomas Powell, Executive Director
Rachel Hamilton, Project Director

A broad-reaching organization of individuals that develops and disseminates its collective food and animal science knowledge to provide meat science education and professional development.

405 American Oilseed Coalition
1255 23rd Street NW
Suite 220
Washington, DC 20037-1125
202-842-0463

Thomas A Hammer, Coordinator

Successor to the Oilseed Council of America. AOC consists of oilseed growers, processors, handlers, exporters and end users. The council promotes economically sound long range government policies that ensure an adequate supply of oilseeds.

406 American Phytopathological Society
3340 Pilot Knob Road
Saint Paul, MN 55121-2097
651-454-7250
FAX: 651-454-0766 800-328-7560
aps@scisoc.org www.apsnet.org

Don E Mathre, Chair
Ann R Chase, Vice Chair
Steven Nelson, VP
William E Fry, Secretary
Erik L Stromberg, Treasurer

A non-profit, professional scientific organization dedicated to the study and control of plant diseases.
5000 Members Founded: 1908

407 American Seed Trade Association
225 Reinekers Lane
Suite 650
Alexandria, VA 22314-2875
703-837-8140
FAX: 703-837-9365 www.amseed.com

Richard Crowder, Executive VP

Producers of seeds for planting purposes. Consists of companies involved in seed production and distribution, plant breeding and related industries in North America.
850 Members Founded: 1883

408 American Sheep Industry Association
9785 Maroon Circle
Suite 360
Englewood, CO 80112
303-771-3500
FAX: 303-771-8200
info@sheepusa.org
www.sheepusa.org

Paul Frischknecht, President
Peter Orwick, Executive Director
Rita Kourlis Samuelson, Wool Marketing Director

A federation of state associations dedicated to the welfare and profitability of the sheep industry. *$25.00*
40+ Members Monthly Founded: 1865
Circulation: Mbrshp

409 American Society for Enology and Viniculture
PO Box 1855
Davis, CA 95617-1855
530-753-3142
FAX: 530-753-3318
society@asev.org www.asev.org

Thomas Smith, President
Dr Robert Wample, First VP
Patricia Howe, Second VP
Lyndie Boulton, Executive Director
Dr Linda Bisson, AJEV Science Editor

A non-profit scientific society dedicated to the interests of enologists, viticultures and others in the fields of wine and grape research and production throughout the world. Membership includes professionals from wineries, vineyards, academic institutions and organizations.
2400+ Members Founded: 1950 1500 names

410 American Society for Horticultural Science
ASHS 113 South West Street
Suite 200
Alexandria, VA 22314-2851
703-360-0774
FAX: 703-836-2024
webmaster@ashs.org www.ashs.org

Cary Mitchell, Chair
Frederick S Davies, President
Elizabeth Lamb, Education Division
Charles Amorosino, Executive Director

Is a cornerstone of research and education in horticulture and an agent for active promotion of horticultural science.
1200 Members Founded: 1903

411 American Society of Agricultural Consultants
950 S Cherry Street
Suite 508
Denver, CO 80246-2664
303-583-3513
FAX: 303-758-0190
asac@agri-associations.org
www.agconsultants.org

Fred L Hepler, President
Sam N Bartee, VP/Secretary

An association representing the full range of agricultural consultants which serves as an information, resource, and networking base for its members.
181 Members Founded: 1963

412 American Society of Agricultural and Biological Engineers
2950 Niles Road
Saint Joseph, MI 49085-9659
269-429-0300
FAX: 269-429-3852 800-371-2723
hq@asabe.org www.asabe.org

Melissa Moore, Executive VP
Donna Hull, Publication Director
Michael Chesser, Director Meetings/Conferences
Scott Cedarqurst, Standards Director
Mark Crossley, Membership Director

Holds annual meetings and conferences and publishes journals related to agricultural engineering, biological engineering and food process engineering.
9000 Members Founded: 1907 10000 names $120 per M.

413 American Society of Agronomy
677 S Segoe Road
Madison, WI 53711-1048
608-273-8080
FAX: 608-273-2021
headquarters@agronomy.org
www.agronomy.org

Ellen Bergfeld, Executive VP
Luther Smith, Executive Director
Michela Cobb, Director Financial Services
Audrey Jankowski, Analyst/Programmer
Ian Popkewitz, Director IT/Operations

Promote human welfare through advancing the acquisition and dissemination of scientific knowledge concerning the nature, use improvement and interrelationships of plants, soils, water and environment. The society shall promote effective research, disseminate scientific information, facilitate technology transfer, foster high standards of education, strive to maintain high standards of ethics, promote advancements in this profession and cooperate with other organizations of similar objectives.
11000 Members Founded: 1907

414 American Society of Animal Science
1111 N Dunlap Avenue
Savoy, IL 61874
217-356-9050
FAX: 217-398-4119
web@assochq.org www.asas.org

Dr Jerome Baker, Executive Director
Louise Adams, Managing Editor
Lorena Nicholas, Communications Director
Jean Rice, Managing Editor

A professional organization for animal scientists designed to help members provide effective leadership through research, extension, teaching and service for the dynamic and rapidly changing livestock and meat industries.
Founded: 1908

415 American Society of Consulting Arborists
15245 Shady Grove Road
Suite 130
Rockville, MD 20850-3222
301-947-0483
FAX: 301-990-9771
asca@mgmtsol.com
www.asca-consultants.org

Steven Geist, President
Beth Palys, Executive Director
John Lichter, Treasurer
James Allen, Director
David Hucker, Director

About 270 persons specializing in the growth and care of urban shade and ornamental trees.

416 American Society of Farm Managers and Rural Appraisers
950 S Cherry Street
Suite 508
Denver, CO 80246
303-758-3513
FAX: 303-758-0190
nhardiman@agri-associations.org
www.asfmra.org

Nancy Hardiman, Director Education
Henry Long, Executive VP
Debe L. Alvarez, Manager Education/Faculty

The general object of the society is to promote, without profit to itself, the profes-

sions of rural appraisal, real property review appraisal and farm management.
2300 Members Founded: 1929
Mailing list available for rent

417 American Soybean Association
12125 Woodcrest Executive Drive
Suite 100
Saint Louis, MO 63141-5009
314-576-1770
FAX: 314-576-2786 800-688-7692
scensky@asaim.soy.org
www.soygrowers.com

Ron Heck, Chair
Neal Bredehoeft, President
Bob Metz, First VP
John Dodson, VP
Steve Censky, Chief Executive Officer

Leading a dynamic industry supplying the preferred soy products to the world, improving the quality of life and the environment to improve the soybean farmer profitability.
30000 Members Founded: 1920

418 American Sugar Alliance
2111 Wilson Boulevard
Suite 600
Arlington, VA 22201
703-351-5055
FAX: 703-351-6698
asainfo@aol.com
www.sugaralliance.org

Vickie Myers, Executive Director
Jack Roney, Director Economics/Policy Analysis
Phillip W Hayes, Director Media Relationsy Analysis
Kendra Lockhart, Staff Assistant

National coalition of cane, beet and corn farmers, processors, suppliers, workers and others dedicated to preserving a strong domestic sweetener industry.
Founded: 1983

419 American Veal Association
1500 Fulling Mill Road
Middletown, PA 17057-3116
717-985-9125
FAX: 717-985-9127
info@vealfarm.com
www.vealfarm.com

Paul Slayton, Executive Director

Members include veal producers and processors.
1300 Members Founded: 1984

420 Animal Agricultural Alliance
PO Box 9522
Arlington, VA 22209
703-562-5160
FAX: 703-524-1921
info@animalagalliance.org
www.animalagalliance.org

Bruce Andrews, President
Kay Johnson, Executive VP

The Animal Agricultural Alliance is a 501 (c)(3) education foundation. The alliance's mission is to support and promote animal agricultural practices that provide for farm animal well-being through sound science and public education.
3000 Members Founded: 1987

421 Aquatic Plant Management Society
PO Box 821265
Vicksburg, MS 39182-1477
239-694-1129
doggett@lchcd.org www.apms.org

Jim Petta, President
Steve Cockrehaw, Director
Greg McDonald, Director

Individuals and companies interested in the control of water plants that hinder recreation or navigation.
Founded: 1961

422 Association for Arid Lands Studies
Texas Tech University
601 Indiana Avenue
Lubbock, TX 79409-1036
806-742-2974
FAX: 806-742-1954
gay.riggan@ttu.edu www.iaff.ttu.edu

Ambas Tibor Nagy, Executive Director
Dr. A C Correa, International Director/ICASALS

To promote the university's special mission of the interdisciplinary study of arid and semi-arid environments and the human relationship to these environments from an international perspective.
200 Members Founded: 1966

423 Association for Communications Excellence
Mowry Road, Building 116
PO Box 110811
Gainesville, FL 32611
352-392-9588
FAX: 352-392-7902
ace@mail.ifas.ufl.edu
www.aceweb.org
International association of communicators and information technologists. Develops professional skills of its members to extend knowledge about agriculture, natural resources and life and human sciences to people worldwide.
600 Members Founded: 1970

424 Association of American Feed Control Officials
Office of the Indiana State Chemist Building
175 South University Street
West Lafayette, IN 47907-2063
765-494-1561
FAX: 765-496-6349
noelr@purdue.edu
www.isco.perdue.edu

Phil Petry, President
Eric Nelson, Director
Judy Thompson, Director
Dr Allan Hanks, Indiana State Chemist

Officials of government agencies at the state and federal levels engaged in the regulation and distribution of products, animal feeds and livestock remedies.

425 Association of American Seed Control Officials
Utah Department of Agriculture
350 N Redwood Road
PO Box 146500
Salt Lake City, UT 84114-6500
801-848-8543
FAX: 801-538-7189
stburningham@utah.gov
www.seedcontrol.org/utah

G Richard Wilson, Director
Gary G Peterson, Commissioner
Dr. Stanford Young, Secretary/Treasurer
Founded: 1949

426 Association of Equipment Manufacturers
6737 W Washington St
Milwaukee, WI 53214-5647
414-272-0943
FAX: 414-272-1170
info@aem.org www.aem.org

Dennis Slater, President
Darrin Drollinger, VP
Patricia Monroe, Director Public Relations
John Nowak, Chief Financial Officer
Nick Yaksich, Vice President/Government Affairs

International trade and business development resource for companies that manufacture equipment, products and services used worldwide in the construction, agriculture, mining, forestry and utility industries.
750 Members Founded: 1946

427 Bedding Plants International
206 6th Avenue
Suite 900
Des Moines, IA 50309
800-647-7742
FAX: 515-282-9117
www.floriculture.com
Offers the gardeners or other plant enthusiast a resource to learn about and use new and exciting floriculture products and services.
Founded: 1969

428 Bio-Dynamic Farming and Gardening
25844 Butler Road
Junction City, OR 97448
541-998-0105
FAX: 541-998-0106 888-516-7797
biodynamics@aol.com
www.biodynamics.com
Restoring to the soil a balanced living condition through the application and use of the completely digested form of crude organic matter known as stabilized humus. Crop rotation, correct composting and proper intercropping can all contribute to a healthier biodynamic yield.

429 Communicating for Agriculture
112 E Lincoln Avenue
Fergus Falls, MN 56537-2217
218-739-3241
FAX: 218-739-3832
caep@cainc.org www.ca.cainc.org

M Smedsrud, CEO

Strives to promote health, well-being and advancement of people in agriculture and agribusiness.
40M Members Founded: 1972

430 Community Alliance with Family Farmers
36355 Russell Boulevard
Davis, CA 95617
530-756-8518
FAX: 530-756-7857 800-892-3832
judith@fullbellyfarm.com
www.caff.org

Judith Redmond, President
George Davisor, VP
Pete Price, Secretary
Poppy Davis, Treasurer

Mission is to build a movement of rural and urban people to foster family-scale agriculture that cares for the land, sustains local economies and romotes social justice.
$47.95
Founded: 1978 ISBN 1-891894-04-8

431 **Concept Marketing Group Incorporated**
8655 East Via de Ventura
Suite G-200
Scottsdale, AZ 85258

FAX: 866-858-7488 800-575-5369
concept@marketingsource.com
www.marketingsource.com

Barbara Spagnola, CEO

Our goal is to create a positive awareness of your company whether it is locally, regionally or in the worldwide marketplace. We work to enhance profitability, improve corporate image, grow your customerbase and maximize sales through effective marketing strategies.

432 **Corn Refiners Association**
1701 Pennsylvania Avenue
Suite 950
Washington, DC 22203-5805
202-331-1634
FAX: 202-331-2054
aerickson@corn.org www.corn.org

Patrick E Bowe, Chairman of the Board
Jack Fortum, Vice Chairman of the Board
Audrae Erickson, President
J Patrick Mohan, Treasurer

Supports carbohydrate research programs through grants to colleges, government laboratories and private research centers.
8 Members Founded: 1913

433 **Council for Agricultural Science and Technology**
4420 West Lincoln Way
Ames, IA 50014-3447
515-292-2125
FAX: 515-292-4512
cast@cast-science.org
www.cast-science.org

John M Bonner, Executive Vice President
Donna Freeman, Director Membership/Marketing

Assembles, interpets and communicates science based information regionally, nationally and internationalally on food, fiber, agriculture, natural resources, and related societal and environmental issues.
2000+ Members Founded: 1972

434 **Cranberry Institute**
3203-B Cranberry Highway
East Wareham, MA 02538
508-954-4132
FAX: 508-759-6294 800-295-4132
cinews@earthlink.net
www.cranberryinstitute.org

Bill Cutts, Chairman
Jeff Kapell, Vice Chair
David McCarthy, Secretary/Treasurer
Jere Downing, Executive Director
Mark Fields, Manager/Research & Communications

A nonprofit organization founded to further the success of US and Canadian cranberry growers through health, agricultural and environmental stewardship research as well as cranberry promotion and education.
Founded: 1951

435 **Crop Insurance Research Bureau**
10800 Farly
Suite 330
Overland Park, KS 66210-2008
913-338-0470
FAX: 913-339-9336 888-274-2472
paulh@cropinsurance.org
www.cropinsurance.org

Paul L Horel, President
Steve Rutledge, Vice Chairman
David Johnson, Treasurer

The Crop Insurance Research Bureau (CIRNB) is a national trade association made up of insurance providers and related organizations that provide a variety of insurance products to farmers. CIRB companies are big and small and offer private hail/fire coverage on growing crops, as well as participate in the federal crop insurance program which offers a greater variety of subsidized insurance products from yield based coverages to revenue products.

Founded: 1964

436 **Crop Science Society of America**
677 S Segoe Road
Madison, WI 53711-1048
608-273-8086
FAX: 608-273-2021
headquarters@crops.org
www.crops.org

Ellen Bergfeld, Executive Vice President
Susan G Chapman, Director/Member Services
Paul Kamps, Development Officer
Ian Popkewitz, Director IT & Operations
Luther Smith, Exec VP/Executive Dir Certification

Seeks to advance research, extension, and teaching of all basic and applied phases of the crop sciences.
4700 Members Founded: 1955 4000 names $110 per M.

437 **Croplife America**
1156 15th Street NW
Suite 400
Washington, DC 20005-1752
202-296-1585
FAX: 202-463-0474
webmaster@croplifeamerica.org
www.croplifeamerica.org

Jay Vroom, President

Members are interested in protecting crops and environmentally fragile agriculture.
Founded: 1933

438 **Eastern Milk Producers Cooperative**
1985 Isaac Newton Square West
Reston, VA 20190-5094
703-742-6800
FAX: 703-742-7459
www.mdvamilk.com
Known for being a leader in the dairy industry, the Eastern Milk Producers Cooperative has an 85-plus year reputation for integrity, service and high quality products.

439 **Ecological Farming Association**
406 Main Street
Suite 313
Watsonville, CA 95076
831-763-2111
FAX: 831-763-2112
info@eco-farm.org
www.eco-farm.org

Kristin Rosenow, Executive Director

A nonprofit educational organization that promotes ecologically sound agriculture. Seeks to promote agricultural practices that are ecologically sound, economically viable and socially just.
2M Members Founded: 1980

440 **Entomological Society of America**
10001 Derekwood Lane
Suite 100
Lanham, MD 20706-4876
301-731-4535
FAX: 301-731-4538
esa@entsoc.org www.entsoc.org

Michael A Ivic, President
Frank E Gilstrap, VP
Scott H Hutchens, VP
Marlin E Rice, Secretary/Treasurer
Paula G Lettice, Executive Director

Serves the professional and scientific needs of entomologists and people in related disciplines.
6000+ Members Founded: 1889

441 **Farm Equipment Manufacturers Association**
1000 Executive Parkway
Suite 100
Saint Louis, MO 63141-6369
314-878-2304
FAX: 314-878-1742
info@farmequip.org
www.farmequip.org

Timothy Perkins, President
Jim Wesseng, First VP
Richard W Heiniger, Second VP
Robert Schnell, Executive Vice President
Paula Kaster-Purvis, Secretary

An information gathering and distributing organization for farm equipment manufacturers and suppliers.
730+ Members Founded: 1950

442 **Farm Foundation**
1211 W 22nd Street
Suite 216
Oak Brook, IL 60523-2197
630-571-9393
FAX: 630-571-9580
www.farmfoundation.org

Walter Armbruster, President
Steve Halbrook, VP

A publicly supported nonprofit organization working to improve the economic health and social well being of US agriculture, the food system and rural people by helping private and public sector decision makers identify and understand forces that will shape the future.

443 **Fertilizer Institute**
Union Center Plaza, 820 1st Street NE
Washington, DC 20002
202-623-3956
FAX: 202-962-0577
information@tfi.org www.tfi.org

Kraig R Naasz, President
Ford B West, Senior VP
Harry L Vroomen, PhD, VP
Kathy Mathers, VP
Pamela D Guffain, Director/Government Relations

Members include brokers, producers, importers, dealers and manufacturers of fertilizer and fertilizer-related equipment.
325 Members Founded: 1970

444 **Fresh Produce Association of the Americas**
30 N Hudgins Street
PO Box 848
Nogales, AZ 85628
520-287-2707
FAX: 520-287-2948
info@fpaota.org www.fpaota.org

William Sykes, Chair
Alicia Bon Martin, Vice Chair

Lee Frankel, President
Jose Luis Obregon, Deputy Director
Martha Rascon, Public Affairs Director

Represents more than 125 member companies involved in growing, harvesting, marketing and importing of mexican produce entering the US at Nogales, Arizona.

125+ Members Founded: 1944

445 **Fresh Produce and Floral Council**
16700 Valley View Ave
Ste 130
La Mirada, CA 90638-5844
714-739-0177
FAX: 714-739-0226
fpfc@aol.com www.fpfc.org

Jack Gyben, Chairman
Linda Stine, President
Raul Gallgos, Treasurer
Pauleen Yoshikane, Director Operations

Promotes through communication and education, fresh fruit, vegetable and floral products. Acts as a trade organization providing an environment for better communication within the industry.

600+ Members Founded: 1965

446 **Herb Growing and Marketing Network**
529 North Mary Street
Lancaster, PA 17603
717-393-3295
FAX: 717-393-9261
herbworld@aol.com
www.herbworld.com/about_us.htm

Maureen Rogers, Director

Trade association for the herb industry

$48.00
2000 Members Founded: 1990

447 **Holstein Association USA**
1 Holstein Place
Brattleboro, VT 05302
802-254-4551
FAX: 802-254-8251 800-965-5200
info@holstein.com
www.holsteinusa.com

John Meyer, CEO
Lisa Perrin, Marketing

Dairy cattle breed association with a membership base of people with strong interests in breeding, raising and milking Holstein cattle.

30000 Members Founded: 1885

448 **Horticultural Crop and Sciences Center**
Ohio State University
1680 Madison Avenue
Wooster, OH 44691-4114
330-263-3700
FAX: 330-263-3658

More than 750 individuals and institutions in 72 countries involved in the research or application of soil tilage and related subjects.

449 **International Agricultural Aviation Associ ation**
PO Box 1607
Mount Vernon, WA 98273-1607
360-734-9757
FAX: 360-336-2506

Members are pilots and aircraft owners licensed by the FAA as agricultural aviators (crop dusters).

4859 Members Founded: 1978

450 **International Association of Fairs and Expositions**
3043 East Cairo
PO Box 985
Springfield, MO 65802
417-862-5771
FAX: 417-862-0156
jimt@fairsandexpos.com
www.iafenet.org

Jim Tucker, President/CEO
Max Willis, COO/CFO
Steve Siever, Assistant Manager
Gary Goodman, Chair
Gary McRae, First Vice Chair

Membership consists of individual agricultural fairs and regional associations of agricultural fairs.

1500+ Members Founded: 1885

451 **International Association of Operative Millers**
5001 College Boulevard
Suite 104
Leawood, KS 66211-1618
913-338-3377
FAX: 913-338-3553
info@iaom.info www.aomillers.org

Steve Curran, President
Gary A Anderson, Executive VP
Keith Horton, VP

An international organization, comprised of flour millers, cereal grain and seed processors and allied trades representatives and companies devoted to the advancement of technology in the flour milling, cereal grain processing industries.

1500 Members Founded: 1896

452 **International Maple Syrup Institute**

10010 West Givens Road
Hortonville, WI 54944
802-524-4966

Lynn Reynolds, Executive Manager
Luc Lussier, General Manager/CEO
Robert Montambault, Director Quality
Yves Gosselin, Director Human Ressources
Lise Belleville, Executive Secretary

Members are producers, processors, industry suppliers and others interested in promoting the industry.

15M Members Founded: 1975

453 **International Professional Applicators Ass ociation**
International Pesticide Applicators Association
PO Box 1420
Milton, WA 98354
253-922-9437
www.ipaa.net

Provides education and information for the professional horticultural applicator. Legislative work involves the states of Washington, Oregon, Idaho in the area of laws and regulations.

454 **International Weed Science Society**
Oregon State University
Corvallis, OR 97331-3002
541-737-6145
FAX: 541-737-3407
www.css.orst.edu/weeds/iwss

Members are institutions and individuals concerned with the study of weeds and their control.

455 **Irrigation Association**
6540 Arlington Boulevard
Falls Church, VA 22042-6638
703-536-7080
FAX: 703-536-7019
webmaster@irrigation.org
www.irrigation.org

John Roberts, President
Doug York, VP
Cynthia Amos, Marketing Director
Rebecca Beverly, Finance Manager
Beth Casteel, Communincaiton Manager

Promotes education and use of irrigation in many areas of agriculture.

1600 Members Founded: 1949

456 **Livestock Marketing Association**
10510 NW Ambassador Drive
Kansas City, MO 64153
816-891-0502
FAX: 816-891-7926 800-821-2048
lmainfo@lmaweb.com
www.lmaweb.com

Ivan Harder, President
Mark Mackey, CEO
Nancy Robinson, VP/Government & Industrial Affairs
Vincent Nowak, CFO
John J McBride, Director, Information

Providing members the industry information, insurance and legislative/regulatory services which they need to remain viable businesses.

630 Members

457 **Mailorder Gardening Association**
5836 Rockburn Woods Way
Elkridge, MD 21075
410-540-9830
FAX: 410-540-9827
info@mailordergardening.com
www.mailordergardening.com

Camille Cimino, Executive Director
Jim Bryant, First VP/Program Chair
Roberta Simpson, Second VP
Tina Pipitone, Executive Assistant

Mail-order suppliers of gardening and nursery stock and supplies.

210 Members Founded: 1934

458 **Mid-South Grain Inspection**
1390 Channel Avenue
Memphis, TN 38114
901-942-3216
FAX: 901-774-9651
mphsgrain@aol.com

Tim Adams, Agency Manager

Established to provide a liaison between the Federal Grain Inspection Service and designated agencies. Annual meeting held in January.

60 Members Founded: 1980

459 **Midwest Equipment Dealers Association**
5330 Wall Street
Suite 100
Madison, WI 53718-1109
608-240-4700
FAX: 608-240-2069
midwestequ@aol.com
www.meda-online.com

Gary Manke, CAE, Executive VP
Dale Gaugert, Membership Service Representative
Sandy Glaeve, Business Farms Director
Laurie Hansen, Administrator Assistant

Our mission is to promote the farm, industrial, outdoor power equipment, dairy and farmstead mechanization industry and to provide services that will assist Association

members in becoming more profitable and better equipped to operate in today's business environment.
Founded: 1991

460 Milking Machine Manufacturers Council
111 E wisconsin Avenue
Suite 1000
Newark, WI 53202-3710
414-272-0943
FAX: 414-272-1170
aem@aem.org www.aem.org

John Smylie, VP
Jim Parker, Chairman
Joe Horkan, Vice Chairman

Representing manufacturers of architectural, construction, forestry, materials handling and liabilty equipment.
5 Members Founded: 1946

461 National 4-H Council
7100 Connecticut Avenue
Chevy Chase, MD 20815-4934
301-961-2800
FAX: 301-961-2894
info@fourcouncil.edu
www.fourhcouncil.edu

Donald T Floyd Jr, President/CEO

Works to advance the 4-H youth development movement, building a world in which youth and adults learn, grow, and work together as catalysts for positive change. National 4-H Council partners with the Cooperative Extension System and other organizations to provide technical support and training, develop curricula, create model programs and promote positive youth development to fulfill its mission. National 4-H Council also manages the National 4-H Conference.
7M Members Founded: 1902

462 National Agri-Marketing Association
11020 King Street
Suite 205
Overland Park, KS 66210-1201
913-491-6500
FAX: 913-491-6502
agrimktg@nama.org www.nama.org

Tom Smull, President
Susie Decker, VP/Farm Progress
Monte Reese, VP/Cattlemen Beef Promotion
Eldon White, Chief Executive Officer

Marketing and communication suppliers, including trade publications, radio and television broadcast sales organizations, premium/incentive manufacturers, printers, marketing research firms, photographers and related professionals.
3500 Members Founded: 1957

463 National Alliance of Independent Crop Consultants
349 East Nolley Drive
Collierville, TN 38017-1544
901-861-0511
FAX: 901-861-0512 www.aaicc.org

Allison Jones, Executive VP

Represents individual crop consultants and contract researchers.
500+ Members Founded: 1978

464 National Association Extension 4-H Agents
University of Georgia
1235-E East Boulevard
Suite 213
Charlotte, NC 28203
704-333-3234
FAX: 706-542-2115
4th@the managementoffices.com
www.nae4ha.org

Lisa Lauxman, President
Allen Auch, VP Finance/Operations
David Sorrell, VP Marketing/Outreach
Janet Fox, VP Professional Development

Our members, committees, and board developed an adopted the following strategic goals: meet the needs of youth development progessionals by maximizing the use of technology, provide progressive levels of professional development, elevate the quality of youth development work through scholarship, research and practice, advocate for the 4-H youth development profession.
3600 Members Founded: 1946

465 National Association of Agricultural Fairs
Michigan State Department of Agriculture

440 Hogan Road
PO Box 40627
Nashville, TN 37220
615-837-5160
FAX: 615-837-5194 800-342-8206
marketingstaff@state.tn.us
www.picktnproducts.org

Joe Gaines, Assistant Commissioner
Paul Nordstrom, Chief Marketing Service
Lynne Williams, Fair Administrator
Anne Dale, Manager
Nelson Baker, Livestock Grading/Market

US and Canadian representatives of state/provincial agencies that are responsible for the support of educational and agricultural fairs.
35 Members Founded: 1966

466 National Association of Animal Breeders
PO Box 1033
Columbia, MO 65205-1033
573-445-4406
FAX: 573-446-2279
naab-css@naab-css.org
www.naab-css.org

Denny Funk, PhD, Chairman
Al Kuck, Vice Chairman
Gordon A Doak, PhD, President
Donna Craig, Office Manager

Members are farmer co-ops and others interested in livestock improvement.
20 Members Founded: 1946

467 National Association of Conservation Districts (NACD)
509 Capitol Court Northeast
Washington, DC 20002-4937
202-547-6223
FAX: 202-547-6450
Bill-Wilson@nacdnet.org
www.nacdnet.org/

Bill Wilson, President
Krysta Harden, Chief Executive Officer
John Redding, Secretary/Treasurer
Arthur Ganta, Director Finance & Administration
Keira Franz, Director Government Affairs

NACD develops national conservation policies, influences lawmakers and builds partnerships with other agencies and organizations. NACD also provides services to its districts to help them share ideas in order to better serve their local communities.
17000 Members Founded: 1946

468 National Association of County Agricultural Agents
252 N Park Street
Decatur, IL 62523
217-876-1220
FAX: 217-877-5382
nacaaemail@aol.com www.nacaa.com

Glenn Rogers, President
Scott Hawbaker, Executive Director
Chuck Otte, VP
Fred Miller, Secretary
Chuck Schwartau, Treasurer

3850 Members Founded: 1917
Mailing list available for rent 3500 names $500 per M.

469 National Association of State Department of Agriculture
1156 15th Street NW
Suite 1020
Washington, DC 20005
202-235-5454
FAX: 296-296-9686
nasda@nasda.org www.nasda-hq.org

Richard Kirchhoff, Executive VP/CEO
Stephen R Cox, COO
Carlton Courter, President
Valoria Loveland, Vice President

Represents the state departments of agriculture in the development, implementation and communication of sound public policy and programs which support and promote the American agricultural industry.

470 National Association of Wheat Growers
415 2nd Street NE
Washington, DC 20002-4993
202-547-7800
FAX: 202-546-2638
wheatworld@whearworld.org
www.wheatworld.org

Darren Coppock, CEO
Reese Sherman, President
Dale Schuler, First VP
David Cleavinger, Secretary/Treasurer
Mark Gaede, Director Government Affairs

Nonprofit partnership of US wheat growers, by combining their strengths, voices and ideas are working to ensure a better future for themselves, their industry and the general public.
35000 Members Founded: 1950

471 National Bison Association
1400 W 122nd Avenue
Suite 106
Westminster, CO 80234
303-292-2833
FAX: 303-292-2564
info@bisoncentral.com
www.bisoncentral.com

Dave Carter, Executive Director

Formed to promote the production, marketing and preservation of bison.
2400 Members Founded: 1995

472 **National Cattlemen's Beef Association**
444 N Michigan Avenue
Suite 1800
Chicago, IL 60611-3903
312-467-5520
FAX: 312-670-9414 800-368-3138

Terry Stokes, CEO

Membership organization of 35,000 cattlemen.

23000 Members Founded: 1898

473 **National Christmas Tree Association**
16020 Swingley Ridge Road
Suite 300
Chesterfield, MO 63017-6372
636-449-5070
FAX: 636-449-5051
info@realchristmastrees.org
www.realchristmastrees.org

Steve Drake, President
Pam Helmsing, Executive Director
Rick Dungey, Public Relations Manager

NCTA is a professional organization that exists to promote the use of real Christmas Trees and support the industry that provides them.

5100+ Members Founded: 1955
Mailing list available for rent 5100 names $100 per M.

474 **National Cooperative Business Association**
1401 New York Avenue NW
Suite 1100
Washington, DC 20005-2102
202-638-6222
FAX: 202-638-1374
ncba@ncba.org www.ncba.org

Jack Bailey, President/CEO
Fred Becker, President/CEO
Wilson Beebe, President
Larry Blanchard, Senior VP
Kathy Brick, Senior VP/Secretary Treasurer

Leading US organization strengthening the cooperative form of business to empower people and improve quality of life worldwide. To make cooperatives a strong, distinct and unified sector, recognized by the American public. Our member co-ops operate in the areas including, agricultural supply and marketing, children, energy, food distribution, healthcare, housing and many more.

1800 Members Founded: 1916

475 **National Cotton Council of America**
1918 N Parkway
Memphis, TN 38112-5000
901-274-9030
FAX: 901-725-0510 www.cotton.org

Woods E Eastland, Chairman
Allen B Helms, Jr, Vice Chairman
Mark D Lange, President/CEO
G Stephen Felker, VP
Gail Kring, VP

Membership consists of approximately 300 delegates named by cotton interests in the cotton-producing states.

35 Members

476 **National Cottonseed Products Association**
104 Timber Creek Drive
Suite 200
Cordova, TN 38018-2267
901-682-0800
FAX: 901-682-2856
info@cottonseed.com
www.cottonseed.com

Ben Morgan, Publisher

National association of cottonseed products.

200 Members Founded: 1929

477 **National Council of Agricultural Employers**
1112 16th Street NW
Suite 920
Washington, DC 20036
202-728-0300
FAX: 202-728-0303
hughes@ncaeonline.org
www.ncaeonline.org

Sharon M Hughes, Executive Vice President
Tiffany Georg, Administration Manager
Michael Gempler, Western VP
Jodie L Stearns, Eastern Vice President
John S Arnold, Treasurer

Members are growers and producers who employ agricultural laborers, as well as processors and organizations related to the agriculture business.

250 Members Founded: 1964

478 **National Crop Insurance Services**
8900 Indian Creek Parkway
Suite 600
Overland Park, KS 66210-2628
913-685-2767
FAX: 913-685-3080 www.ag-risk.org

Robert W Parkerson, President
Laurie Langstraat, Public Relations

Formed in 1989 by the merger of the Crop Hail Insurance Actuarial Association and the National Crop Insurance Association. NCIS is an association of insurance companies writing insurance for damage by hail, fire and other weather perils to growing crops.

60+ Members

479 **National Dairy Herd Improvement Association**
PO Box 930399
421 S Nine Mound Rd
Verona, WI 53593-0399
608-848-6455
FAX: 608-848-7675 www.dhia.org

Jamie Zimmerman, Chair
Neil Hoffman, Vice Chair
Susan Lee, President
Mark Adam, VP
Jay Mylin, Secretary

Sets policies, holds meetings and offers seminars for dairymen.

24 Members Founded: 1965

480 **National Farmers Organization**
528 Billy Sunday Road
Suite 100
Ames, IA 50010-8087
515-922-2000
FAX: 515-292-7106
nfo@nfo.org www.nfo.org

Paul Olson, Executive Director
Pete Lorenz, Regional Director
Perry Gainer, Communications Director

Advocates collective bargaining through contract marketing by farmers.

30M Members Founded: 1955

481 **National Farmers Union**
5619 DTC Pkwy
Ste 300
Greenwood Village, CO 80111-3136
303-337-5500
FAX: 303-368-1390 800-347-1961
dave.frederickson@nfu.org
www.nfu.org

Dave Frederickson, President
Clay Pederson, VP
Tom Buis, VP Government Relations
Jennifer Luitjens Bahr, Director Member Services
Emily Eisenberg, Communications Director

Promotes educational, cooperative and legislative activities of farm families in 26 states.

25000 Members Founded: 1902

482 **National Fisheries Institute**
7918 James Branch Drive
Suite 700
McLean, VA 22102-1609
703-524-8880
FAX: 703-524-4619 www.nfi.org

Wally Pereyra, Chairman of Board
David Weber, Vice Chair
John Connelly, President
Rick Martin, Secretary
Eric Bloom, Treasurer

Members are farmers, food processors and food distributors with an interest in aquaculture.

483 **National Grain and Feed Association**
1250 I Street NW
Suite 1003
Washington, DC 20005-3922
202-289-0873
FAX: 202-289-5388
ngfa@ngfa.org www.ngfa.org

Steve Nail, Chairman
Ronald D Olson, First Vice Chair
Tom Coyle, Second Vice Chair
Kendall W Keith, President
Randall Gordon, Vice President

A broad based nonprofit trade association that represents and provides services for grain, feed and grain-related commercial businesses.

Founded: 1896

484 **National Grange**
1616 H Street NW
Washington, DC 20006-4999
202-628-3507
FAX: 202-347-1091 888-447-2643
bsteel@nationalgrange.org
www.nationalgrange.org

William Steel, President
Richard Weiss, COO
Leroy Watson, Legislative Director
Cindy Greer, Director Youth\Young Adult
DoriAnn Gedris, Marketing Director

Promotes general welfare and agriculture through local organizations. Presides over the advancement and promotion of the farming and agriculture industry.

300k Members Founded: 1960

485 **National Grape Co-operative**
1223 Potomac Street NW
Washington, DC 20007-3212
202-333-8190
FAX: 202-337-3810

Nicholas Pyle, Manager

10 Members

486 National Hay Association
102 Treasure Island Causeway
St Petersburg, FL 33706
727-367-9702
FAX: 727-367-9608 800-707-0014
haynha@aol.com
www.nationalhay.org

Raymond J Bricker, President
Tom Creech, First VP
Richard Larsen, Second VP
Rollie Bernth, Director
Don Kieffer, Executive Director

NHA is the trade group that represents the interests of the hay industry throughout the United States and internationally.
750 Members Founded: 1895

487 National Onion Association
822 7th Street
Suite 510
Greeley, CO 80631-3941
970-353-5895
FAX: 970-353-5897
kreddin@onions-usa.org
www.onions-usa.org

Wayne Mininger, Executive VP

Represents interests of US onion producers. Informational lobbying and generic promotional headquarters for fresh dry bulb onion growers. Provides connections for networking and education exchange. Membership fees are from $150-750 per year based upon size and classification of business.
550 Members Founded: 1913
Mailing list available for rent 600 names

488 National Organic Program
1400 Independence Avenue SW
Room 4008, South Building
Washington, DC 20250-0020
202-720-3252
FAX: 202-205-7808
www.ams.usda.gov/nop

Richard Mathews, Program Manager

NOP is a marketing program housed within the USDA Agricultural Marketing Service.

489 National Plant Board
1220 N Street, Room A-316
Sacramento, CA 95814
916-654-0317
FAX: 916-654-1018
bill.dickerson@ncmail.net
www.cdfa.ca.gov

Bill Dickerson, President
Kenneth Rauscher, VP
Scott Pfister, Secretary/Treasurer
David Nelson, Board President
Ken Rauscher, VP

Representatives from each state and Puerto Rico interested in protecting agriculture, forestry and horticulture throughout the US.
51 Members Founded: 1925
Mailing list available for rent

490 National Pork Producers Council
10664 Justine Drive
Urbandale, IA 50322
515-278-8012
FAX: 515-278-8011 800-937-7675
mcgonegp@nppc.org www.nppc.org

Keith Berry, President
Neil Dierks, Chief Executive Officer
Pat McGonegle, VP
John Wrigley, Director Resource Development
Craig Boelling, Director Producer Services

Established as the National Swine Growers Council, NPPC assumed its present name in 1967 and is now a federation of 45 state associations.
44 Members

491 National Potato Council
1300 L Street NW
Suite 910
Washington, DC 20005
202-682-9456
FAX: 202-682-0333
spudinfo@nationalpotatocouncil.org
www.nationalpotatocouncil.org

John Keeling, Executive VP/CEO
Hollee Stubblebine, Director Industry Communications
Keith Masser, President
Jim Wysocki, VP Finance
Dan Elmore, VP Grower/Public Relations

Represents US potato growers on federal legislative and regulatory issues.
45000 Members Founded: 1948

492 National Potato Promotion Board
7555 E Hampden Avenue
Suite 412
Denver, CO 80231-4835
303-696-6420
FAX: 303-369-7718
info@uspotatoes.com
www.uspotatoes.com

Tim OConnor, President/CEO
Linda McCashion, VP Public Relations
Mac Johnson, VP Marketing (Domestic)
Diane LeDoux, VP Finance/Information Technology
Carroll Little, Marketing/Sales Manager

Also known as the US Potato Board. Organized to operate a national marketing program to position potatoes as low calorie, nutritious vegetables and to facilitate market expansion into domestic and export sales.
109 Members Founded: 1971

493 National Poultry Improvement Plan
1500 Klondike Road
Suite A-102
Conyers, GA
404-646-6539
Andrew.R.Rhorer@usda.gov

On the federal level, administers any problems relating to poultry.

494 National Sunflower Association
4023 State Street
Bismarck, ND 58503
701-328-5100
FAX: 701-328-5101 888-718-7033
klgrtnr@sunflowernsa.com
www.sunflowernsa.com

Larry Kleingartner, Executive Director
John Sandbakken, International Marketing Director

Trade association for the sunflower industry.
200 Members Founded: 1981
Printed in 4 colors on glossy stock

495 National Vocational Agricultural Teachers Association
300 Garrigus Building
University of Kentucky
Lexington, KY 40545
859-257-2284
FAX: 859-323-3919
jay_jackman@ffa.org

William Jay Jackman, Executive Director
Jeff Maierhofer, President
Allan Sulser, Regional VP
Dr. Bill Hunter, Region II VP

A federation of 50 affiliated state vocational agricultural teacher associations.
7600 Members Founded: 1948

496 National Young Farmer Educational Association
PO Box 203326
Montgomery, AL 36120
334-213-3276
FAX: 334-213-3276 888-332-2668
natloffice@nyfea.org www.nyfea.org

Gordon Stone, Executive Vice President
Mary Patterson, Manager

To promote the personal and professional growth of all people involved in agriculture.

497 North American Agricultural Marketing Officials
CA Department of Food & Agriculture
1220 North Street, Room A270
Sacramento, CA
902-424-8870
FAX: 902-424-4671
joe.gaines@state.tn.us
www.naamo.org

Kellly Krug, President
Linda MacDonald, First VP
Tom Slade, Second VP
Cindy Garretson-Weibel, Secretary/Treasurer

Members are state and provincial officials responsible for agricultural products marketing programs in the US, Canada and ultimately Mexico.

498 North American Farm Show Council
Info@
590 Woody Hayes Drive
Room 232
Columbus, OH 43210-1058
614-292-4278
FAX: 614-292-9448
fendrick.1@osu.edu
www.farmshows.org

Robert Oberheim, President
Scott Grigor, First VP
Patrick Kennedy, Second VP

Members are agriculture trade show sponsors and suppliers of services to these shows. Provides members with education, communication and evaluation. Provides the best possible marketing showcase for exhibitors and related products to the farmer/rancher/producer customer.
29 Members Founded: 1972

499 Northeastern Weed Science Society

67 Pinewood Road
Hudson, NY 12534-1115
518-851-2122
FAX: 518-851-9790
dg11@umail.umd.edu www.newss.org

William S Curran, President
Renee J Keese, VP
Brian S Manley, Secretary/Treasurer
Brent A Lockey, Public Relations Representative

Serves the Northeastern US by bringing together those who are concerned with the knowledge of weeds and their control, cooperates with other scientific societies to promote research, education and outreach activities and publishes scientific and practical information of value concerning weed sciences and other fields.

Founded: 1946

500 **Northwest Agricultural Congress**
4672 Drift Creek Road SE
Sublimity, OR 97385-9764
503-769-7120
FAX: 503-769-3549
Jim@NWAgShow.com
www.northwestagshow.com

Jim Heater, Show Manager

Second largest agricultural show on the west coast. show is produced by the Northwest Horticultural Congress which is a partnership between Oregon Horticultural Society, the Oregon Association of Nurseries and Northwest Nut Growers Association. Show held in conjunction with annual meetings and seminars by all three of the horticultural groups.

21000 Members

501 **Organic Crop Improvement Association**
6400 Cornhusker Highway
Suite 125
Lincoln, NE 68507-3160
402-477-2323
FAX: 402-477-4325
info@ocia.org www.ocia.org

Jeff See, Executive Director

OCIA International is a farmer owned international program of certification, which adheres to strict organic standards. It currently certifies thousands of farmers and processors in North, Central and South America and Asia. OCIA International is IFOAM accredited and adheres to the USDA ISO Guide 65, Japan Agriculture Standards and the Quebec Accreditation Council. OCIA has also been accredited from the USDA National Organic Program and Costa Rica Ministry of Agriculture.

3500 Members Founded: 1985
Mailing list available for rent 3500 names $50 per M.

502 **Organic Trade Association**
60 Wells Street
PO Box 547
Greenfield, MA 01302
413-774-7511
FAX: 413-774-6432
info@ota.com www.ota.com

Katherine DiMatteo, Executive Director
Holly Givens, Communications Director
David Gagnon, Director/Operations
Lisa Murray, Sales Manager
Dan Pratt, Directory Coordinator

Members are businesses involved in the organic agriculture and products industry. Seeks to promote the industry and establish production and marketing standards.

1200 Members Founded: 1985

503 **Produce Marketing Association**
1500 Casho Mill Road
Newark, DE 19711-6036
302-738-7100
FAX: 302-731-2409
pma@mail.pma.com www.pma.com

Bryan E Silbermann, President
Lorna Christie, VP/Industry Products & Services
Julie Stewart, Director Communications
Nancy Tucker, VP Global Business Development
Rayne Yori, VP Finance

The Produce Marketing Association, founded in 1949, is a not-for-profit trade association serving over 2,500 members who market fresh fruits, vegetables, and floral products worldwide. Its members are involved in the production, distribution, retail, and foodservice sectors of the industry.

2400+ Members Founded: 1949

504 **Professional Farmers of America**
1818 Market Street, 31st Floor
Philadelphia, PA 19103
319-827-1792
800-772-0023

Provides farmers with marketing strategies and market-trend data, as well as seminars and home study courses.

25M Members Founded: 1973

505 **Santa Gertrudis Breeders International**
PO Box 1257
Kingsville, TX 78364-1257
361-592-9357
FAX: 361-592-8572
www.strangertrudis.ws

Ervin Kaatz, Executive Director

America's First Beef Breed developed in 1918 at the famous King Ranch in Texas. Recognized in 1940 by the USDA. Famous for raid and efficient growth, solid red color, hardiness and good disposition. They are adaptable to many environments and are present throughout the US and in other countries.

506 **Society for Biomolecular Screening**
36 Tamarack Avenue
Suite 348
Danbury, CT 06811
203-788-8828
FAX: 203-748-7557
email@aol.com www.sbsonline.org

Al Kalb, President
Christine Giordano, Executive Director
Larry Walker, Editor-in-Chief
Betty Soltesz, Board Secretary

Supports research and discovery in pharmaceutical biotechnology and the agrichemical industry that utilize biomolecular screening procedures.

2000+ Members Founded: 1994

507 **Society of American Foresters**
5400 Grosvenor Lane
Bethesda, MD 20814-2198
301-897-8720
FAX: 301-897-3690
goergenm@safnet.org www.safnet.org

Michael T Goergen Jr, Executive VP/CEO
Larry D Burner, Senior Director Finance
Amy Ziadi, Information Technology Manager
Lori Gardner, Senior Director
Delisa Barron, Public Project Manager

Supports all those involved in forestry research and technology. Publishes monthly newsletter.

Founded: 1900

508 **Society of Commercial Seed Technologists**
101 E State Street
Suite 214
Ithaca, NY 14850-1257
607-256-3313
FAX: 607-256-3313
scst@twcny.rr.com
www.seedtechnology.net

Professionals involved in the testing and analysis of seeds, including research, production and handling based on botanical and agricultural sciences.

250 Members Founded: 1922

509 **Soil and Plant Analysis Council**
621 Rose Street
Lincoln, NE 68502-2040
402-437-4944
FAX: 402-476-7598
bvaug12345@aol.com
www.spcouncil.com

Mark Flock, President
Don Horneck, VP
Byron Vaughan, Secretary/Treasurer

Promotes uniform soil test and plant analysis methods, use, interpretation and terminology.

250 Members Founded: 1969

510 **Southern Cotton Ginners Association**
874 Cotton Gin Place
Memphis, TN 38106-2543
901-947-3104
FAX: 901-947-3103
carmen.griffin@southerncottonginners.org www.southerncottonginners.org

Chris Clegg, Chairman of Board
Will Wade, President/Tennessee
Richard Kelly, VP
Allen Espey, VP/Tennessee
Tim Price, Executive Vice President

Operates in a five state area as an information center covering safety and governmental regulations. Serves its members by providing safety, training and regulatory representation. Sponsors certification programs and hosts the industry's leading trade show, The Mid-South Farm & Gin Show.

700 Members Founded: 1950

511 **Southwestern Association**
638 West 39th Street
PO Box 419265
Kansas City, MO 64141-6264
816-561-5323
FAX: 816-561-1249 800-762-5616

Jeffrey H Flora, Chief Executive Officer

National association of manufacturers, suppliers and distributors of equipment, supplies and services relating to the agricultural industry.

Founded: 1889

512 **Texas Agribusiness Market Research Center**
Dept of Agricultural Economics
Suite 321 Blocker
College Station, TX 77843
979-845-5911
FAX: 979-845-6378 agrinet.tamu.edu

Gary W Williams, Coordinator
Oral Caps, Jr, Chair/Dept of Agri Economics
Stephen W Fuller, Dept of Agri Economics

Eluened Jones, Dir Master Agribusiness
George Davis, Dept of Agri Economics

Provide a single point to all agricultural resources on the internet. Objective is to promote agribusiness and to enhance agricultural produc t marketing and research.

513 **United Fresh Fruit and Vegetable Association**
1901 Pennsylvania Avenue NW
Suite 1100
Washington, DC 20006
202-624-4989
FAX: 202-303-3433
tstenzel@uffva.org www.uffva.org

Tom Stenzel, President/CEO
Nicholas J Tompkins, Chair
Robert A Grimm, Executive Committee
Daniel G Vache, Secretary/Treasurer

Equipment, supplies, cartons, packaging machinery, computers, sorting and sizing equipment, harvesting equipment, film wrap manufacturing and commodity organizations.

1000+ Members Founded: 1904

514 **United Producers**
5909 Cleveland Avenue
PO Box 29800
Columbus, OH 43229
614-890-6666
FAX: 614-890-4776 800-456-3276

Dennis Bolling, President/CEO

A cooperative marketing organization owned by farmers and ranchers in the United States' corn belt, midwest and southeast.

36000 Members Annual Meetings Founded: 1962

515 **United States Animal Health Association**
8100 Three Chopt Road, Suite 203
PO Box K227
Richmond, VA 23288
804-285-3210
FAX: 804-285-3367
usaha@usaha.org www.usaha.org

Dr Lee Myers, President
James Leafstedt, Second VP
Linda Ragland, Manager

Seeks to prevent, control and eliminate livestock diseases.

1000 Members Founded: 1897

516 **United States Canola Association**
600 Pennsylvania Avenue SE
Suite 320
Washington, DC 20003
202-697-7040
www.uscanola.com

John Haas, President
Steve Kakela, First VP
Doug Scoville, Second VP
John Gordley, Executive Director
Dale Thorenson, Assistant Director

USCA members are producers and processors of canola and rapeseed.

517 **United States Egg Marketers**
4500 Hugh Howell Road
Suite 270
Tucker, GA 30084
770-360-9220
FAX: 770-360-7058
info@unitedegg.org
www.unitedegg.org

Al Pope, President & CEO
Gene Gregory, Sr. VP

A producer cooperative established specifically for the purpose of exporting large quantities of U.S. Shell Eggs.

518 **United States Grains Council**
1400 K Street NW
Suite 1200
Washington, DC 20005-2403
202-789-0789
FAX: 202-898-0522
grains@grains.org www.grains.org

Kenneth Hobbie, President/CEO
Michael T Callahan, Director International Operations
Cheri Johnson, Manager Communications
Valerie Smiley, Manager Membership
Andrew Pepito, Director Finance/Administration

Motivated by the grain sorghum, barley and corn producer associations and representatives of the agricultural community. Provides commodity export market development.

175 Members Founded: 1960

519 **United States Hide, Skin & Leather**

3369 Fiddlers Green Road
Cincinnati, OH 45248
513-574-7692
FAX: 513-574-7692 www.meatami.com

Exclusive representative of the hide and skin industry in the United States. Member companies include meat packers, hide processors, brokers, dealers, and exporters. Associate members represent suppliers and trade associated with the industry, such as tanners, chemical and equipment manufacturers, and transporters. Operates testing laboratory.

520 **Walnut Council**
Wright Forestry Center
1011 N 725 West
West Lafayette, IN 47906-9431
765-583-3501
FAX: 765-583-3512
walnutcouncil@walnutcouncil.org
www.walnutcouncil.org

R Daniel Schmaker, President
Larry R Frye, VP
Liz Jackson, Executive Director
William L Hoover, PhD, Treasurer
Hugh Pence, Finance & Audit

1000 Members Founded: 1970

521 **Weed Science Society of America**
810 E 10th Street
PO Box 7050
Lawrence, KS 66044-7050
785-429-9622
FAX: 785-843-1274 800-627-0629
wssa@allenpress.com www.wssa.net

Dale Shaner, President
Jeff Derr, VP
Tom Mueller, Secretary
Dave Gealy, Treasurer
Michael Foley, Director Publications

Promotes research, education and extension outreach activities related to weeds, provides science-based information to the public and policy makers; and fosters awarenes of weeds and their impacts on managed and natural ecosystems.

2000 Members Founded: 1956

522 **Western Fairs Association**
1776 Tribute Road
Suite 210
Sacramento, CA 95815-4495
916-927-3100
FAX: 916-927-6397
wfa@fairsnet.org
www.westernfairs.org

Stephen J Chambers, Executive Director
Laura C Trout, Assistant Executive Manager
Stephanie Azores, Program Manager

National association for fairground owners, managers and workers. Also includes government regulations, fair vendors and service providers.

2200 Members Founded: 1922

523 **Western United States Agriculture Association**
4601 North East 77th Avenue
Suite 200
Vancouver, WA 98662-2697
360-693-3373
FAX: 360-693-3464 www.wusata.org

Andy Anderson, Executive Director
Eliza Lane, Outreach Coordinator

A nonprofit organization that promotes the export of food and agricultural products from the Western region of the US Comprised of 13 state funded agricultural promotion agencies.

524 **Wild Blueberry Association of North America**
PO Box 1130
Kennebunkport, ME 04046-1130
207-967-5024
FAX: 207-967-5023 800-ADD-WILD
inquiries@wildblueberries.com
www.wildblueberries.com

John M Sauve, Executive Director

Represents processors and growers of wild blueberries in Eastern Canada and Maine. The Association is focused on the generic promotion of wild blueberries around the world. It offers promotional materials, joint funding, product development, assistance, seminars, newsletters, supplier lists and ongoing support to users of wild blueberries in all retail, manufacturing, foodservice and bakery trade segments.

50+ Members Founded: 1981

Newsletters

525 **5-State Farmer-Rancher**
PO Box 889
Liberal, KS 67905-0889

James Head, Publisher

Farm news.

Monthly

526 **ALBC News**
American Livestock Breeds Conservancy
16 Hillsboro Street
PO Box 477
Pittsboro, NC 27312
919-542-5704
FAX: 919-545-0022
albc@albc-usa.org www.albc-usa.org

Charles Bassett, Executive Director

Breeders directory; annual conference; catalog of publications available. *$30.00*

20 pages
Circulation: 4000
Printed in 1 color on matte stock

527 **APIS**
CITA International
3464 W Earll Drive
Suites E&F
Phoenix, AZ 85017
602-447-0480
FAX: 602-447-0305
esam@citainternational.com
www.citainternational.com

E M Morsy, Editor
P E Pederson, Advertising/Sales Manager

The international bulletin for specialty livestock, pet animal and ag-chem product developments.
Quarterly

528 **ARClight**
National Agri-Marketing Association
11020 King Street
Suite 205
Overland Park, KS 66210-1201
913-491-6500
FAX: 913-491-6502
arc@nama.org www.nama.org/arc

Kathleen Montgomery, Editor

Agricultural Relations Council - a national association with members involved in agricultural public relations. Electronic newsletter of interest to association members.

529 **ASAC News**
American Society of Agricultural Consultants
950 S Cherry Street
Suite 508
Denver, CO 80246-2664
303-759-5091
FAX: 303-758-0190
info@agri-associations.org
www.agconsultants.org

Douglas W Slothower, Executive VP
Cheryl L Cooley, PR/Communications Manager
Sally Quinn, Business Director / Contr
David J. Harms, President
Robert K. Mehrle, CFO

Informs ASAC members of news regarding members, events, education and government issues.
8 pages Quarterly Founded: 1963
Circulation: 300 200 names
Printed in 2 colors

530 **Agri Times Northwest**
Sterling Ag, lLC
146 S Main Street
Suite 204
Pendleton, OR 97801
541-276-6202
FAX: 541-278-4778
info@agritimes.com
www.agritimes.com

Sterling Allen, Publisher
Virgil Rupp, Editor
Beth Mills, Field Editor
Jim Eardley, Associate Editor

Agri- Times NW, The Region Agricultural Newspaper, is a subscription publis semi-monthly. *$20.00*
16 pages Founded: 1984
Circulation: 3700
Printed in 4 colors on newsprint stock

531 **Agweek**
Grand Forks Herald
375 2nd Avenue N
PO Box 6008
Grand Forks, ND 58206-6008
701-780-1100
FAX: 701-780-1211 800-477-6572
feedback@gfherald.com
www.gfherald.com

Kim Deats, Editor
Michael Jacobs, Publisher

Offers information to professionals working in the field of agriculture, from farmers to equipment manufacturers. *$32.00*
80 pages Weekly
Circulation: 26000
Printed in on newsprint stock

532 **American Agriculturist**
Rural Press
5318 Fox Road
Ithaca, NY 14425
315-986-9320
FAX: 315-986-8534

John Vogel, Editor
Judy Brent, Production Manager
Steve Joss, VP Marketing
Sarah Hess, Circulation Director

Agricultural magazine serving New York farmers and agri-businesses. *$21.95*
Monthly
Circulation: 20,000

533 **American Alfalfa Processors Bulletin**
American Alfalfa Processors Association
8810 Craig Drive
Overland Park, KS 66212
913-648-6800
FAX: 913-648-2648
aapa@cysource.com www.aapausa.org

Wanda L Cobb, APC Contact

Information for the processors and suppliers in the alfalfa industry.
Weekly

534 **American Beekeeping Federation Newsletter**
American Beekeeping Federation
115 Morning Glory Circle
PO Box 1337
Jesup, GA 31598-1038
912-427-4233
FAX: 912-427-8447
info@abfnet.org www.abfnet.org

David Ellingson, President
Danny Weaver, VP
Troy Fore, Editor

Newsletter for members of the American Beekeeping Federation. *$35.00*
24 pages Founded: 1943
Circulation: 1750 Audited
Printed in on newsprint stock

535 **American Feed Industry Newsletter**

American Feed Industry Association
1501 Wilson Boulevard
Suite 1100
Arlington, VA 22209
703-524-0810
FAX: 703-524-1921
afia@afia.org www.afia.org

Joel Newman, President/CEO
Rex Runyon, Editor
Jeff Haaf, Marketing Manager

Newsletter published by the American Feed Industry for members only.

Monthly Founded: 1909
Circulation: 700

536 **American Soybean Association Newsletter**
12125 Woodcrest Executive Drive
Suite 100
Saint Louis, MO 63141-5009
314-576-1770
FAX: 314-576-2786 800-688-7692
scensky@asaim.soy.org
www.soygrowers.com

Steve Censky, CEO
Ron Heck, Chairman
Bridget Owen, Marketing Manager

To improve US soybean farmer profitability.
Monthly Founded: 1920
Printed in 4 colors on glossy stock

537 **Association of American Seed Control Officials Bulletin**
Utah Department of Agriculture
350 N Redwood Road
PO Box 146500
Salt Lake City, UT 84114-6500
801-848-8543
FAX: 801-538-7189
stburningham@utah.gov
www.ag.utah.gov

Stephen T Burningham, Control Officer
Leonard Blachham, Commissioner
Jed Christenson, Marketing

Seed laws in the United States and Canada.
Annual+
Circulation: 5000

538 **Chaff Newsletter**
American Association of Grain Inspection
1390 Channel Avenue
Memphis, TN 38113-1640
901-942-3216
FAX: 901-774-9651 www.aagiwa.org

Tom Meyer, President
Tom Dahl, VP

Offers information and news of the Association.
BiWeekly

539 **Council for Agricultural Science and Technology Newsletter**
4420 West Lincoln Way
Ames, IA 50014-3447
515-292-2125
FAX: 515-292-4512
cast@cast-science.org
www.cast-science.org

Linda Chimenti, Managing Scientific
John M Bonner, Executive VP

Identifies food, fiber, environmental and other agricultural issues for all stake holders, including legislators, policy makers and the public.
Quarterly Founded: 1972
Circulation: 4000
Printed in 2 colors

540 **Country World Newspaper**
Echo Publishing Company
401 Church Street
PO Box 596
Sulphur Springs, TX 75483
903-885-8663
FAX: 903-885-8768 800-245-2149
jim@countryworldnews.com
www.countryworldnews.com

Scott Keys, Publisher
Jim Horton, Advertisting Manager
Lori Cope, Editor
Kristi Hayes, Circulation Manager
Jim Horton, Marketing

A newspaper offering agricultural information to farmers, ranchers, dairyfarmers, and agribusinesses. *$24.00*
36 pages Weekly Founded: 1981
Circulation: 16200
Printed in 4 colors on n stock

541 **Crop Protection Management**
2892 Crescent Avenue
Eugene, OR 97408
541-343-5641
FAX: 541-335-2136 800-972-1635
rdyke@professionalcredit.com
www.professionalcredit.com
Jeff Powell, Publisher
Joe Hawes, CEO
Rob Dyke, VP
This newsletter covers all aspects of crop management and protection, including pesticides, agricultural chemicals and legislation.
Founded: 1933

542 **Daily Advocate**
Brown Publishing
428 S Broadway St
Greenville, OH 45331-220
937-548-3151
FAX: 937-548-3913
info@brownpublishing.com
www.brownpublishing.com
Gary Lamberg, Publisher
Bob Robinson, Editor
Roy Brown, President/CEO
Carol Hahn, Marketing Director
Farming interests, grain, livestock. Sections on senior citizens, farmers, builders, religion, sports, as well as special sections on agriculture and home improvement. *$42.00*
Daily Founded: 1920
Circulation: 110,053

543 **Dairy Profit Weekly**
DairyBusiness Communications
6437 Collamer Road
East Syracuse, NY 13057-1031
315-703-7979
FAX: 630-654-4470 866-239-5448
dgarno@dairybusiness.com
www.dairyprofit.com/
Eleanor Jacobs, Regional Editor
Dave Natzke, Editorial Director
Susan Harlow, Associate Editor
Latest information, tips, and trends. *$179.00*
4 pages Weekly
Printed in 2 colors on newsprint stock

544 **Decision Support Systems for Agrotechnology Transfer**
ICASA
2440 Campus Road
PO Box 527
Honolulu, HI 96822
808-956-7531
FAX: 808-956-2711
icasa@icasanet.org www.icasa.net
Systems analysis and crop simulation models for agrotechnology transfers and risk assessment. Reference guides and models for maize, wheat, rice, sorghum, millet, barley, soybean, peanut and potato are included. Linked to GIS sofeware. *$495.00*
Annual ISBN 1-886684-00-6
Circulation: 2,500 Audited
Printed in 2 colors on matte stock

545 **Doane's Agricultural Report**
Doane Agricultural Services
11701 Borman Drive
Suite 300
Saint Louis, MO 63146-4193
314-569-2700
FAX: 314-569-1083
doaneag@aol.com www.doane.com
Dan Mantemach, Publisher/Editor
Kathy Topping, Managing Editor
Lynn Henderson, CEO/President
Michael Stanly, Marketing
Marketing and management information for farmers and agribusiness professionals. *$126.00*
6 pages Weekly Founded: 1925

546 **Farm Managers & Rural Appraisers News**
Amer. Society of Farm Managers & Rural Appraisers
950 S Cherry Street
Suite 508
Denver, CO 80246-2664
303-758-3513
FAX: 303-758-0190
asfmra@agri-associations.org
www.asfmra.org
Douglas W Slothower, Executive VP
Hope S. Evans, Membership Coordinator
Tamela White, Meetings Manager
Cheryl L. Cooley, Public Relations/Communications
Sally Quinn, Administration/Finance
Published by the American Society of Farm Managers and Rural Appraisers. *$24.00*
Founded: 1929
Mailing list available for rent 2500 names $1M per M.
Printed in 3 colors on glossy stock

547 **Farm and Ranch Guide**
4023 State Street
PO Box 1977
Bismarck, ND 58502-1977
701-255-4905
FAX: 701-255-2312 800-594-8433
office@farmandranchguide.com
www.farmandranchguide.com
Mark Conlon, Editor
Brian Kroshus, Group Publisher
Margeret Kiefer, Marketing Manager
Becky Lensegrav, Circulation Manager
A leading agriculture publication in the upper Midwest, distributed to 38,000 qualified farmers and ranchers in North Dakota, Minnesota, northern South Dakota and eastern Montana. Our readers re-qualify every year so our database is up to date with their farming information. *$32.95*
Monthly
Circulation: 38,000
Printed in 4 colors on newsprint stock : online

548 **Farm and Ranch Living**
Reiman Publications
5400 South 60th Street
Greendale, WI 53129
414-423-0100
FAX: 414-423-8463
editors@farmandranchliving.com
www.reimanpub.com
Roy Reiman, Publisher
Barbara Newton, President
Nick Pabst, Editor
Lisa Karpinski, Marketing
Lisa Karpinski, Circulation Manager
Newspaper for farmers. *$19.98*
68 pages Fortnightly

549 **Farmers Friend**
116 Main Street
Suite 503
Towanda, PA 18848-1832
570-265-2151
FAX: 570-265-1647
review@epix.net www.
James Towner, President/Publisher
Jennifer Hutchinson, Editor
Farming news.
Weekly
Circulation: 10300

550 **Feedstuffs**
Miller Publishing Group
12400 Whitewater Drive
Suite 160
Minnetonka, MN 55343
952-931-0211
FAX: 952-938-1832 800-441-1410
mwolske@feedstuffs.com
www.feedstuffs.com
Sarah Muirhead, Publisher/Editor
Michael Howie, Managing Editor
Jess Latin, CEO/President
Susan Dahtgrem, Circulation Manager
Mike Miller, Manager
A weekly newspaper for agribusiness, each week of the month focuses on a different animal species. Topics include nutrition, health, marketing issues and the popular Bottom Line of Nutrition section. *$144.00*
24 pages Weekly Founded: 1895
Circulation: 16590

551 **Fencepost**
The Fencepost
423 Main Street
Windsor, CO 80550-5129
970-686-5691
FAX: 970-686-5694
www.thefencepost.com
Gary Sweeney, Publisher
Chuk Baloou, Editor
Dave Moore, Marketing
Joe Luetgrs, Circulation Manager
Farming news and reports. *$39.00*
Weekly Founded: 1980

552 **Food & Fiber Letter**
Sparks Companies
6862 Elm Street
Suite 350
Mc Lean, VA 22101
703-848-4700
FAX: 703-893-1065
editor@scipubs.com
www.sparksco.com
Barry Jenkins, Editor
Legislative updates, news and information on agricultural policy, environment and conservation industry. *$473.90*
Weekly
Printed in 2 colors on matte stock
Computerized version available

553 **Forestry Source**
Society of American Foresters
5400 Grosvenor Lane
Bethesda, MD 20814-2198
301-897-8720
FAX: 301-897-3690
goergenm@safnet.org www.safnet.org
Michael T Goergen, Executive VP/CEO
Joe Smith, Editor
Delisa Barrons, Publication Manager
A tabloid newsletter covering important information regarding critical issues in forestry research and technology, legislative updates and news about SAF programs and

activities on a national and local level. *$30.00*
20 pages Monthly Founded: 1990
Printed in 4 colors on newsprint stock

554 **Global Dairy Update**
6437 Collamer Road
East Syracuse, NY 13057-1031
315-703-7979
FAX: 315-703-7988 800-334-1904
dgarno@dairybusiness.com
www.dairybusiness.com
Focuses on dairy developments throughout the world. *$197.00*
4 pages Monthly Founded: 1904
Printed in 2 colors on newsprint stock

555 **Greenhouse Grower**
Meister Media Worldwide
37733 Euclid Avenue
Willoughby, OH 44094
440-942-2000
FAX: 440-942-0662 800-572-7740
info@meistermedia.com
www.meistermedia.com
Gary Fitzgerald, President
Elliott Nowels, VP
Laura Henne-Drotleff, Editor
Joseph Monahan, Publisher
Dan Keating, Circulation Manager
Association news offering articles of information on crops, farming, and nursery news. *$36.00*
Monthly Founded: 1932

556 **Greenhouse Product News**
Scranton Gillette Communications
380 E NW Highway
Suite 200
Des Plaines, IL 60016-2282
847-298-6622
FAX: 847-390-0408 www.onhort.com
Kim Candle, Managing Editor
Tim Campbell, Publisher, Marketing
Lynda Landell, Circulation Manager
For owners and managers of commercial floricultural growing facilities.
Monthly
Circulation: 20000
Mailing list available for rent 19,000 names

557 **Hay There**
National Hay Association
102 Treasure Island Causeway
St Petersburg, FL 33706
727-367-9702
FAX: 727-367-9608 800-707-0014
haynha@aol.com
www.nationalhay.org/
Raymond J Bricker, President
Don Kieffer, Executive Director
Production and marketing information for members. Accepts advertising.
Monthly Founded: 1895
Circulation: 700 Audited
Printed in 1 color on glossy stock

558 **Holstein Association USA**
1 Holstein Place
Brattleboro, VT 05302
802-254-4551
FAX: 802-254-8251 800-052-5200
info@holstein.com
www.holsteinusa.com/
John M Meyer, CEO
Connie Andrews, Customer Relations
To provide the information dairy producers will use to breed, manage and market higher producing more durable cows.
8 pages
Circulation: 35000
Printed in 4 colors on glossy stock

559 **Irrigation News**
Irrigation Association
6540 Arlington Boulevard
Falls Church, VA 22042-6638
703-536-7080
FAX: 703-536-7019 www.irrigation.org
Thomas H Kimmell, Executive Director
Industry news and information.

560 **Kiplinger Agricultural Letter**
Kiplinger Washington Editors
1729 H Street NW
Washington, DC 20006
202-887-6400
FAX: 202-785-3648 800-544-0155
Austin Kiplinger, Publisher
David Harrison, Manager
Forecasts and judgments on wages, income, food packaging, processing and marketing techniques. *$56.00*

561 **National Bison Association Newsletter**
National Bison Association
4701 Marion Street
Suite 100
Denver, CO 80216-2140
303-292-2833
FAX: 303-292-2564
info@bisoncentral.com
www.bisoncentral.com
Dave Carter, Editor
Formed to promote the production, marketing and preservation of bison. *$12.00*
Monthly Founded: 1995
Circulation: 1500

562 **National Cottonseed Products Association Newsletter**
National Cottonseed Products Association
104 Timber Creek Drive
Suite 200
Cordova, TN 38018
901-682-0800
FAX: 901-682-2856
info@cottonseed.com
www.cottonseed.com
Ben Morgan, Publisher
Current events.
Founded: 1897

563 **National Fertilizer Solutions Association**
339 Consort Drive
Manchester, MO 63011
636-256-6650
FAX: 636-256-4901
Kelly O'Brien-Wray, Publisher
Fred Speckmann, Editor
Accepts advertising.
90 pages Bi-Monthly

564 **National Honey Market News**
US Department of Agriculture
21 N 1st Avenue
Suite 224
Yakima, WA 98902-2663
509-454-6550
FAX: 509-454-5646
Linda Verstrate, Publisher
Current honey market information and colony conditions in the United States. *$50.58*
10-12 pages Monthly

565 **National Onion Association Newsletter**
National Onion Association
822 7th Street
Suite 510
Greeley, CO 80631
970-353-5895
FAX: 970-353-5897
wmininger@onions-usa.org
www.onions-usa.org
Dave Rietveld, President
Wyane Mininger, Executive VP
Kim Redtin, Publisher
Newsletter published by and only for the National Onion Association.
Monthly Founded: 1913
Circulation: 600
Mailing list available for rent 600 names

566 **National Young Farmer Educational News**
PO Box 15160
Alexandria, VA 22309-0160

FAX: 800-366-6556 888-332-2668
Wayne Sprick, Publisher
Tabloid which receives articles and information from state associations, as well as information from the National Association.

12 pages TriAnnual Founded: 1928
Circulation: 45,000

567 **New England Farm Bulletin and Garden Gazette**
Jacob's Meadow
PO Box 67
Townton, MA 02780

Ed Comstock, Editor
Pam Comstock, Editor
Features articles with tongue-in-cheek humor, classified pages for agriculture, gardening tips and more. *$17.00*
8 pages Annual Founded: 1970
Circulation: 17,000
Printed in 1 color on matte stock

568 **News of the Association of Official Seed Analysts**
201 N 8th Street
Suite 400
Lincoln, NE 68508-1360
402-476-1677
FAX: 402-476-6547
aosaoffice@earthlink.net
www.aosaseed.com
Lee Daughtry, President
Ellen Chirco, VP
News items, technical reports, rules changes for testing seeds, surveys, identification and tax news, legislative updates and updates on the Association and publications in progress. *$20.00*
TriAnnual
Circulation: 500
Printed in 1 color on matte stock

569 **No-Till Farmer**
Lessiter Publications
225 Regency Court
Suite 200 PO Box 624
Brookfield, WI 53045
262-782-4480
FAX: 262-782-1252 800-645-8455
info@lesspub.com
www.no-tillfarmer.com
Frank Lessiter, Editor/Publisher
Mike Lessiter, Executive VP

Erin Weileber, Marketing
Stacy Johnson, Circulation Manager

Management information for farmers interested in conservation tillage. *$37.95*

Monthly Founded: 1972
Circulation: 8000 5,000 names $90m per M.
Printed in 2 colors on glossy stock

570 OCIA Communicator Newletter
6400 Cornhusker Highway
Suite 125
Lincoln, NE 68507
402-477-2323
FAX: 402-477-4325
info@ocia.org www.ocia.org

Jeff See, Executive Director
Patricia Saldania, Marketing/Communications

A quarterly newsletter published by the Organic Crop Improvement Association International (OCIA). *$50.00*

Quarterly
Circulation: 300
Mailing list available for rent 3500 names $50 per M.

571 Organic Report
Organic Trade Association
60 Wells Street
PO Box 547
Greenfield, MA 01301
413-774-7511
FAX: 413-774-6432
info@ota.com www.ota.com

Dan Pratt, Directory Coordinator
Phil Margolis, CEO/President

Targets an audience of manufacturers, growers, retailers, importers, distributors, and consultants in the organic food and fiber industry.

Monthly
Circulation: 2500
Printed in 2 colors on matte stock

572 Peterson Patriot
Peterson Patriot Printers-Publishers
202 Main Street
PO Box 126
Peterson, IA 51047-126
712-295-7711
FAX: 712-295-7711
patriot@iowatelecom.net

Roger Stoner, Publisher
Jane Stoner, Editor/Circulation Manager

Agricultural news. *$18.00*

12 pages Weekly
Circulation: 549

573 Pro Farmer
Farm Journal Media
1818 Market Street
31st Floor
Philadelphia, PA 19103
215-578-8900
FAX: 215-568-6782 800-320-7992
cflory@profarmer.com
www.farmjournalmedia.com

Chip Flory, Publisher
Roger Bernard, Editor
Andrew J Weber, CEO

Farm market news, analysis and management advice. *$159.00*

8 pages Annual+ Founded: 1973

574 SI Report
Salt Institute
700 N Fairfax Street
Suite 600
Alexandria, VA 22314-2040
703-549-4648
FAX: 703-548-2194
info@saltinstitute.org
www.saltinstitute.org

Dick Hanneman, President

A quarterly e-newsletter published by the Salt Institute.

Monthly Founded: 1914
Printed in on glossy stock

575 Salt & Trace Mineral Newsletter
Salt Institute
700 N Fairfax Street
Suite 600
Alexandria, VA 22314-2040
703-549-4648
FAX: 703-548-2194
info@saltinstitute.org
www.saltinstitute.org

Dick Hanneman, President

Information on animal nutrition.

Quarterly Founded: 1914
Printed in on glossy stock

576 Seed Midden
Abundant Life Seed Foundation
930 Lawrence Street
PO Box 772
Port Townsend, WA 98368
360-385-5660
FAX: 360-385-7455
abundant@olypen.com
www.abundantlifeseed.org

Elsa Golts, President
Matthew Dillon, Executive Director

Information covering events, seminars and meetings. *$8.00*

8 pages

577 Signals Newsletter
Agricultural Communicators in Education

PO Box 110810
Gainesville, FL 32611-0810
352-392-1582
FAX: 352-392-7902

Offers news and information to communications professionals in the agricultural and farming industry. *$75.00*

BiWeekly

578 TecAgri News
Clark Consulting International
442 Edwards Avenue Suite 100
PO Box 600
Dundee, IL 60118-600
847-836-5100
FAX: 847-836-5140
warren.clark@ccimarketing.com
www.ccimarketing.com

Warren E Clark, President

News on new technology in agriculture reaching large computerized family farmers.

Weekly Founded: 1986
Circulation: 100000 Audited
Mailing list available for rent 155M names $120 per M.
Printed in 2 colors on glossy stock
Computerized version available

579 Vegetarian Journal
Vegetarian Resource Group
PO Box 1463
Baltimore, MD 21203
410-366-8343
FAX: 410-366-8804
vrg@vrg.org www.vrg.org

Debra Wasserman, Circulation Manager
Keryl Cryer, Senior Editor
Charles Stahler, CEO

Informative articles, recipes, book reviews, notices about vegetarian events, product evaluations, where to find vegetarian products and services. All nutrition information based on scientific studies. *$20.00*

36 pages Quarterly Founded: 1982
Circulation: 20000 $85 per M.
Printed in 4 colors
Computerized version available

580 Voice of the Fields
Farm Labor Information Bulletin
7801 Folson Blvd
Sacramento, CA 95816
916-388-2228
FAX: 916-388-2425

Jazier Juarez, Outreach

Provides informtion in English and Spanish about farm labor issues and resources.

Monthly

581 Webster Agricultural Letter
Webster Communications Corporation
3835 N 9th Street
Suite 401W
Arlington, VA 22203-5812
703-525-4512
FAX: 703-852-3534
editor@agletter.com
www.agletter.com

James C Webster, CEO

Agricultural politics and policy issues. *$397.00*

6 pages Fortnightly Founded: 1980
Printed in 1 color on matte stock

582 Weekly Livestock Reporter
PO Box 7655
Fort Worth, TX 76111-655
817-838-0106
FAX: 817-831-3117
service@weeklylivestock.com
www.weeklylivestock.com

Ted Gouldy, Publisher
Phil Stoll, CEO/President
Mickey Schwarz, Circulation Manager

Offers comprehensive weekly information for cattle farmers and livestock agricultural professionals. *$18.00*

Weekly Founded: 1897
Circulation: 10000

583 Weekly Weather and Crop Bulletin

NOAA/USDA Joint Agricultural Weather Facility
Room 112-A
US Department Of Agriculture
Washington, DC 20250-3810
202-720-4722
FAX: 202-690-4915
jawfweb@oce.gov www.usda.gov

Douglas LeComte, Publisher
Annette Holmes, Secretary

Text and tables describing the weekly weather over the US and other major crop producing countries. *$60.00*

Weekly Founded: 1862
Circulation: 1,500

Magazines & Journals

584 **Acreage Magazine**
Malheur Publishing Company
PO Box 130
Ontario, OR 97914-0130
541-889-5387
FAX: 541-889-3347
Francis McLean, Publisher
Cultural news and features edited for rural farm producers magazine. *$5.00*
40 pages Monthly

585 **Acres USA**
5321 Industrial Oaks Boulevard
Suite 128
Austin, TX 78735
512-892-4446
FAX: 512-892-4448 800-355-5315
info@acresusa.com
www.acresusa.com
Fred C Walters, CEO/President
Articles of exposition and analysis in biologically sound farming. *$27.00*
50 pages Monthly Founded: 1970
Circulation: 12500

586 **Ag Retailer**
Doane Agricultural Services
11701 Borman Drive
#300
Saint Louis, MO 63146-4193
314-569-2700
FAX: 314-569-1083
agretailer@doane.com
www.agretailer.com
Lynn Henderson, President
Joe Michaelree, Market Research Manager
Rich Jarrett, Circulation Manager
Serves retailers/dealers and distributors of fertilizers and pesticides. *$40.00*
80 pages Founded: 1938
Circulation: 28,500
Printed in 4 colors

587 **Agri Marketing Magazine**
Doane Agricultural Services
11701 Borman Drive
Suite 300
Saint Louis, MO 63146
314-569-2700
FAX: 314-569-1083
info@agrimarketing.com
www.agrimarketing.com
Bill Schuermann, Publisher/Editorial
Bekah Reddick, Assistant Editor
Agri Marketing Magazine is the premier publication of the agriculture industry, reaching over 9,000 sales, marketing, and advertising executives in the US and Canada. The Marketing Services Guide is published in December; it lists companies, advertising agencies, direct marketing, market research, print media, broadcast media, e-business, and associations. *$40.00*
88 pages Founded: 1963
Circulation: 9000 9,227 names $105 per M.
Printed in on matte stock : Web

588 **Agribusiness Council Magazine**
1312 18th Street NW
Suite 300
Washington, DC 20036
202-296-4563
FAX: 202-887-9178
info@agribusinesscouncil.org
www.agribusinesscouncil.org
Nicholas E Hollis, President
Council news, information and calendar.
Monthly Founded: 1967

589 **Agribusiness Fieldman**
Western Agricultural Publishing Company

4969 E Clinton Way
Suite 104
Fresno, CA 93727-1549
559-252-7000

westag@psnw.com
www.westagpubco.com
For the professional agricultural consultant, featuring the latest information on chemical regulation, pest control techniques and feature stories on PCA and PCO community. *$23.00*
Monthly

590 **Agribusiness Fresh Fruit and Raisin News**
Agribusiness Publications
612 N Street
PO Box 669
Sanger, CA 93657-669
559-875-4585
FAX: 559-875-4587 800-364-4894
editor@agribusinesspublisher.com
www.agribusinesspublisher.com
John Van Nortwick, Sole Proprietor Editor
Keeps subscribers abreast of business news for the fruit growing and producing industry. *$35.00*
Monthly
Circulation: 10,000

591 **Agrichemical Age**
Farm Progress Publishers
191 S Gary Avenue
Carol Stream, IL 60188-2095
630-690-5600
FAX: 630-462-2869
www.farmprogress.com
Bill Edy, Editor
Information for fertilizer/pesticide dealers, distributors, commercial applicators and crop consultants. *$20.00*
Monthly Founded: 1841

592 **Agricultural History**
Agricultural History Society
Department of History
2801 University Avenue
Little Rock, AR 72204-1099
501-712-2200
FAX: 501-569-3059
cfwilliams@ualr.edu www.ualr.edu
Larry Poldrack, Executive Director
R Douglas Hurt, Editor
Traces historical lineage of agriculture in the US. *$47.00*
Quarterly Founded: 1919
Circulation: 900

593 **Agriculture Research Magazine**
Agricultural Research Service
5601 Sunnyside Avenue
Beltsville, MD 20705-5130
301-504-1651
FAX: 301-504-1641
rsowers@ars.usda.gov
www.ars.usda.gov/is/ar
Robert Sowers, Editor
Sue Kendall, Associate Editor *$50.00*
27 pages Monthly Founded: 1954
Circulation: 44000

594 **Agweek**
Grand Forks Herald
375 2nd Avenue
PO Box 6008
Grand Forks, ND 58206
701-780-1100
FAX: 701-780-1211 800-477-6572
tdennis@gfherald.com
www.gfherald.com
Michael Jacobs, Publisher
Kim Deats, Editor
Beth Bohlman, Circulation Manager
Weekly magazine of agriculture which emphasizes market trends and the people making them happen. *$32.00*
80 pages Weekly Founded: 1879
Circulation: 25,000
Printed in 4 colors

595 **Alimentos Balanceados Para Animales**
WATT Publishing Company
122 S Wesley Avenue
Mount Morris, IL 61054
815-734-4171
FAX: 815-734-4201
gill@wattmm.com www.wattnet.com
Jim Watt, Chairman/CEO
Clayton Gill, Editorial Director
For feed industry professionals in Latin America. *$42.00*
Monthly Founded: 1994
Circulation: 7021
Printed in 4 colors on glossy stock

596 **American Bee Journal**
Dadant and Sons
51 South 2nd Street
Hamilton, IL 62341
217-847-3324
FAX: 217-847-3660
dadant@dadant.com www.dadant.com
Joe Graham, Editor
Marta Menn, Advertising
Dianne Behnke, Publisher
Timothy Dadant, Owner
Read by commercial and hobby beekeepers and entymologists. *$22.95*
80 pages Monthly Founded: 1861
Circulation: 11000
Printed in 4 colors on glossy stock

597 **American Christmas Tree Journal**
National Christmas Tree Association
16020 Swingley Ridge Road
Suite 300
Chesterfield, MO 63017-6372
636-449-5070
FAX: 636-449-5051
info@realchristmastrees.org
www.realchristmastrees.org
Steve Drake, President
Pam Helmsing, Executive Director
Each issue contains feature stories, production and management advice, the latest NCTA news, state association updates, marketing tips, industry trends and much more. *$50.00*
Quarterly
Circulation: 1500+

598 **American Fruit Grower**
Meister Media Worldwide
37733 Euclid Avenue
Willoughby, OH 44094-5992
440-942-2000
FAX: 440-942-0662 800-572-7740
joe_monahan@meisternet.com
www.meisterpro.com
Richard T Meister, Chairman
Gary T Fitzgerald, President

Frank Giles, Editor
Frank Maxcy, Publisher

Specialized production and marketing information and industry-wide support for fruit growers. *$19.95*

66 pages Monthly Founded: 1932
Circulation: 35143

599 American Small Farm Magazine
560 Sunbury Rd
Ste 6
Delaware, OH 43015-8692
740-363-2395
FAX: 740-369-9526
sales@smallfarm.com
www.smallfarm.com

Marti Smith, Information and Production
Andy Stevens, Editor

Published for the owner/operator of farms from 5 to 300 acres. Focuses on production agriculture including alternative and sustainable farming ideas and technology, case studies, small farm lifestyle and tradition. *$18.00*

Monthly Founded: 1992
Circulation: 62,444 71M names

600 American Vegetable Grower
Meister Media Worldwide
37733 Euclid Avenue
Willoughby, OH 44094-5925
440-942-2000
FAX: 440-942-0662 800-572-7740

Richard T Meister, Chairman
Gary T Fitzgerald, President
Rosemary Gordon, Editor
Jo Monahan, Publisher

Information source for commercial vegetable growers. *$19.95*

Monthly Founded: 1932
Circulation: 34772

601 Animal Therapy Journal
Mt Adams Publishing and Design
14161 Fort Road
White Swan, DC 98952-9786
509-848-2706
FAX: 509-848-3896 800-554-0860
hortexponw@aol.com
www.hortexponw.com

Vee Graves, Editor
Julie LaForge, Advertising Manager

602 Arbor Age
Adams Business Media
250 S Wacker Drive
Suite 1150
Chicago, IL 60606
773-932-2774
FAX: 312-846-4634
jkmitta@aip.com
http://greenmediaonline.com/

John Kmitta, Editor
Joanne Juda, Circulation Manager

Serves the urban industry including tree service companies/arborists, railroads, utilities, etc. *$50.00*

43 pages Monthly Founded: 1981
Circulation: 18590
Printed in 4 colors on glossy stock

603 Bee Culture
AI Root Company
623 W Liberty Street
Medina, OH 44256
330-725-6677
FAX: 330-725-5624 800-289-7668
kim@beeculture.com
www.beeculture.com

John A Root, President
Kim Flottum, Editor

Honey bees and their keeping for beginners and experienced agriculturists. Accepts advertising, press releases, new products, and book reviews. *$21.50*

64 pages Monthly Founded: 1879
Circulation: 12000
Mailing list available for rent 20,000 names $45 per M.
Printed in 4 colors on matte stock

604 CALF New Magazine Ltd.
1531 Kensington Blvd
Garden city, KS 67846
620-276-7844
FAX: 719-495-9204 800-888-0368
wilsoncattle@cornhusker.net
www.calfnews.com

Betty Jo Gigot, Editor/Publisher
Patti Wilson, Sales Manager
Larisa Willrett, Circulation Manager

This magazine offers the latest information to cattle breeders and feeders 1,000 heard+ *$33.00*

Founded: 1963
Circulation: 7000

605 Capital Press
Press Publishing Company
1400 Broadway NE
PO Box 2048
Salem, OR 97308-2048
503-644-4431
FAX: 503-370-4383 800-882-6789
news@capitalpress.com
www.capitalpress.info

Carl Sampson, Managing Editor
Elaine Shein, Executive Editor
Michael O'Brien, General Manager

For the agricultural and forest community of the Pacific Northwest. *$44.00*

60 pages Weekly Founded: 1928
Circulation: 37000
Printed in 4 colors on newsprint stock

606 Carrot Country
Columbia Publishing
417 North 20th Avenue
Yakima, WA 98902
509-248-2452
FAX: 509-248-4056 800-900-2452
dbrent@columbiapublications.com
www.carrotcountry.com

Brent Clement, Editor/Publisher
Mike Stolker, Publisher/Advertising Sales Manager

Includes information on carrot production, grower and shipper feature stories, carrot research, new varieties, market reports, spot reports on overseas production and marketing and other key issues and trends of interest to US and Canadian carrot growers. *$8.00*

Quarterly Founded: 1993
Circulation: 2500 2400 names $200 per M.
Printed in 4 colors on glossy stock

607 Cattleman
Texas & Southwestern Cattle Raisers Association
1301 W 7th Street
Fort Worth, TX 76102
817-332-7064
FAX: 817-332-5446 800-242-7820
lionel@thecattlemanmagazine.com
www.texascattleraisers.org

Bob McCan, President
Lionel Chambers, Editor
Anita Braddock, Marketing
Sherrie Caraway, Circulation Manager
Matt Brockman, Manager

Full overview of information for the cattle producer in Texas and Oklahoma. *$25.00*

130 pages Monthly Founded: 1877
Circulation: 16000
Printed in 4 colors on glossy stock

608 Cereal Foods World
American Association of Cereal Chemists

3340 Pilot Knob Road
Saint Paul, MN 55121-2097
651-454-7250
FAX: 651-454-0766
aacc@scisoc.org www.aaccnet.org

Steven Nelson, Publisher
Jody Grider, Executive Editor
Dawn Wuest, Circulation Coordinator
Rhonda Wilkie, Advertising

This publicatioin is a leading source of information on grain-based food science, technology, and new product development. Cereal Foods World includes scientific research papers that focus on advances in grain-based food science and the application of these advances to product development and current food production practices. Food industry professionals rely on this publication. *$224.00*

Founded: 1956
Circulation: 4500
Printed in 4 colors on glossy stock

609 Chemical and Pharmaceutical Press
Vance Communication Corporation
90 William Street
Suite 504
New York, NY 10038-4703
212-851-1366
FAX: 646-733-6020 800-544-7377
customerservice@greenbook.net
www.greenbook.net

Greg Vincent, Associate Publisher
Dave Furbeck, Sales Manager

Supplies chemical information to professionals involved with the sale, application, storage or regulations of agricultural or ornamental and turf pesticides. Information is available in either reference book form, or on computer disc. Complete product labels, MSDS's and indexes are included. *$200.00*

Annual+ Founded: 1984
Circulation: 20000

610 Chemistry of Crop Protection: Progress and Prospects in Science/Regulation
John Wiley & Sons
111 River Street
Hoboken, NJ 07030-5774
201-748-6000
FAX: 201-748-6088 800-225-5945
customer@wiley.com
www.wiley.com

Gunther Voss, Editor
Gerardo Ramos, Editor

This guide offers information on chemicals and hazardous materials used in crop protection. *$225.00*

406 pages Monthly Founded: 1807

611 Choices
American Agricultural Economics Association
415 South Duff Avenue
Suite C
Ames, IA 50010-6600
515-233-3202
FAX: 515-233-3101
choices@ag.tamu.edu
www.choicesmagazine.org

Laurian Unnevehr, President
Yvonne Bennett, Executive Director
Bruce McCarl, Coordinating Editor

The magazine of food, farm and resource issues.

Quarterly Founded: 1910 600 names
Printed in 4 colors on glossy stock

612 Christmas Tree Lookout
Pacific Northwest Christmas Tree Association
4093 12th Street SE
PO Box 3366
Salem, OR 97302
503-364-2942
FAX: 503-581-6819
info@christmas-tree.com
www.nwtrees.com

Chuck Wright, Editor
Bryan Ostlund, Executive Secretary

Marketing research and industry information for Christmas tree growers. Mailing list available. *$25.00*

80 pages Quarterly Founded: 1955
Circulation: 1500 800 names
Printed in 4 colors on glossy stock

613 Christmas Trees
Tree Publishers
PO Box 107
Lecompton, KS 66050-107
785-887-6324
FAX: 785-887-6324
Ctreesmag@aol.com
www.christmastreesmagazine.com

Cathrine Howard, Editor
Chuck Wright, Publisher
Sally Wright, Circulation Manager

Magazine of plantation management for Christmas tree growers, shearing, shaping and marketing. Accepts advertising. *$16.00*

44 pages Quarterly Founded: 1973
Circulation: 3200
Printed in 4 colors on glossy stock

614 Citograph
Western Agricultural Publishing Company

4969 E Clinton Way
#104
Fresno, CA 93727-1549
559-252-7000
FAX: 559-252-7387 800-382-9772
westag@psnw.com
www.westagpubco.com

Paul Baltimore, Publisher
Jim Baltimore, Publisher
Randy Bailey, Editor
Robert Fujimoto, Assistant Director

The oldest continuous citrus-specific publication in the world. Stories centering on all aspects of citrus production from planting to harvest and all maintenance in between. Lemons, limes, oranges, avocados - all citrus is included.

Monthly

615 Citrus & Vegetable Magazine
Vance Publishing
10901 W 84th Terrace
200 street
Lenexa, KS 66214
913-388-8700
FAX: 847-634-4379 800-255-5113

Scott Emerson, Editor
Jina Martin, Associate Editor
William C. Vance, Chairman *$45.00*

Monthly Founded: 1937
Circulation: 12003 $125 per M.
Printed in 4 colors on glossy stock

616 Citrus Industry
Associated Publications Corporation
495 E Summerlin Street
Bartow, FL 33830
863-533-4114
FAX: 863-534-1758
tkelly@barpr.com
www.citrusindustry.net

Gary Cooper, Publisher
Ernie Neff, Editor
Robin Loftin, Marketing

News, facts and data of interest to citrus growers, processors and shippers. *$24.00*

64 pages 6 issues per ye Founded: 1920
Circulation: 9851
Printed in 4 colors on glossy stock

617 Communications in Soil Science and Plant Analysis
Marcel Dekker
270 Madison Avenue
New York, NY 10016-602
212-696-9000
FAX: 212-685-4540 800-797-3803
journals@dekker.com
www.dekker.com

Harry A Mills, Editor-in-Chief
Eric H Simonne, Associate Executive Editor
Marcel Dekker, President

All aspects of soil science and crop production in all climates. *$567.00*

120 pages Founded: 1963

618 Cotton Farming
Vance Publishing
5118 Park Ave
Ste 111
Memphis, TN 38117-5710
901-767-4020
FAX: 901-767-4026 800-888-9784

Mike Rolfs, President
Tommy Horton, Editor
Cheri Knoy, Sales Director

For commercial cotton growers across the United States Cotton Belt.

52 pages Monthly Founded: 1993
Circulation: 36,297 35 names $125 per M.
Printed in 4 colors on glossy stock

619 Country Folks
Lee Publications
6113 State Highway 5
PO Box 121
Palatine Bridge, NY 13428
518-673-2269
FAX: 518-673-3245 800-218-5586
CFeditor@leepub.com
www.leepub.com

Frederick Lee, Publisher
Scott Duffy, Sales Manager

Agricultural news from national, state and local levels. Some features on farm and agricultural industry, rural interest, etc. *$ 35.00*

75 pages Weekly Founded: 1973
Circulation: 27000

620 Country Living
Arens Corporation
395 S High Street
Covington, OH 45318-1121
937-473-2028
FAX: 937-473-2500
garyg@arnespub.com
www.arenspub.com

Gary Godfrey, Editor

Current news and features devoted to the agricultural industry. *$13.95*

Monthly Founded: 1947
Circulation: 17000

621 Country Woman
Reiman Publications
5400 S 60th Street
Greendale, WI 53129
414-423-0100
FAX: 414-423-8463 800-344-6913
editors@countrywomenmagazine.com
www.reimanpub.com

Ann Kaiser, Managing Editor
Marylin Kruse, Editor

Offers recipes, stories, profiles and articles pertaining to the country woman. *$14.98*

68 pages 6 issues in a y Founded: 1970
Circulation: 50,000 +

622 Countryside and Small Stock Journal
Countryside Publications
145 Industrial drive
Winter Sports Road
Medford, WI 54451
715-785-7979
FAX: 715-785-7414 800-551-5691
csymag@midway.tds.net
www.countrysidemag.com

Anne-Marie Tucker, Owner
Dave Belanger, Publisher

Offers information for homesteaders seeking a self-reliant lifestyle. *$18.00*

132 pages Founded: 1917
Circulation: 115000
Printed in on newsprint stock

623 County Agents
National Association of County Agricultural Agents
252 N Park Street
Decatur, IL 62523
217-876-1220
FAX: 217-877-5382
nacaaemail@aol.com www.nacaa.com

Glenn Rogers, President
Scott Hawbaker, Executive Director

Members receive professional improvement, news of association activities, shared education efforts from other states and reports from NACAA leadership and member states. *$10.00*

Founded: 1916
Circulation: 5000
Mailing list available for rent 3850 names
$125 per M.
Printed in 4 colors on matte stock

624 Cranberries Magazine
Cranberries Magazine
PO Box 190
Rochester, MA 02770-190
508-763-8080
FAX: 508-763-4141
cranberries@comcast.net
www.cranberriesmagazine.com

Carolyn Gilmore, Editor/Publisher

Containing up-to-date news, technical articles, new product information, grower profiles, economic data and other related features regarding the cranberry industry. Accepts advertising. *$25.00*

28 pages Monthly Founded: 1936
Circulation: 850

625 **Crop Decisions**
Doane Agricultural Services
11701 Borman Drive
Suite 100
Saint Louis, MO 63146-4199
314-569-2700
FAX: 314-569-1083
cropdecisions@doane.com
www.cropdecisions.com

Lynn Henderson, President/CEO

Published to serve employees of professional farm management firms, crop consulting firms, farm suppliers, contract research firms, financial institutions and other agricultural related businesses. *$35.00*
48 pages Monthly Founded: 1997
Circulation: 16500
Printed in 4 colors

626 **DVM Magazine**
Advanstar Communications
1 Park Avenue
Newyork, NY 10016
212-797-7631
FAX: 212-951-6793 800-225-4569
info@advanstar.com
www.advanstar.com

Maureen Hrehocik, Editor
Joseph Loggia, Chief Executive Officer
Francis Heid, VP

The leading news in veterinary medicine covering news, features, practice management and new products and services. *$48.00*
Monthly Founded: 1992
Circulation: 20000+

627 **Dairy Herd Management**
Vance Publishing
10901 W 84th Terrace
Suite 200
Lenexa, KS 66214
913-438-8700
FAX: 913-438-0695 800-255-5113
jarnold@vancepublishing.com
www.dairyherd.com

Tom Quaife, Editor
Shirley Roenfeldt, Managing Editor
Bill Newham, Senior VP

Magazine for dairy farmers that offers the latest information and updates on the industry.
Monthly

628 **Dairy Producer**
191 S Gary Avenue
Carol Stream, IL 60188
630-690-5600
FAX: 913-438-0695 http://

Allen Johnson, Publisher
Sevie Kenym, Editor

Management publication to help dairy producers in the production, marketing and financial planning of their milk.

629 **Dairy Today**
Farm Journal
1818 Market Street 31st Floor
Philadelphia, PA 19102
215-578-8900
800-320-7992
dcrisafulli@farmjournal.com
www.farmjournal.com

Allen Moczygemba, Publisher
Wayne Bollum, National Sales Manager
Sue Lee, Regional Sales Manager
Jim Dickrell, Editor

Award-winning editorial covers the broad spectrum of production, nutrition and marketing information. It serves dairy producers who milk 40+ cows or are members of the Dairy Herd Improvement Association.
Monthly Founded: 1989
Circulation: 124421

630 **Dealer & Applicator**
Vance Publishing
400 Knightsbridge Parkway
Lincolnshire, IL 60069
847-634-2600
FAX: 847-634-4373
www.dealerandapplicator.com

Peggy Walker, Group Publisher
Greg Vincent, Editor
Angie Skochdopole, Marketing Manager
William C. Vance, CEO

Serves as the reader's business partner to provide full-service dealers and custom applicators with management and business strategies to increase profitability.
11 issues per y Founded: 1937
Circulation: 22002

631 **Down to Earth**
DowElanco/Dow AgroSciences
9330 Zionsville Road
Indianapolis, IN 46268-1054
317-373-3000
FAX: 800-905-7326 www.drovers.com

Steve Gehrls, Editor

Offers international reviews of agricultural research and practice.
32 pages Quarterly

632 **Drovers Journal**
Vance Publishing
10901 W 84th Terrace
Suite 200
Lenexa, KS 66214-1631
913-438-8700
FAX: 913-438-0695 800-255-5113
ghenderson@vancepublishing.com
www.drovers.com

Stan Erwine, Publisher
Greg Henderson, Editor

Farming news.
Monthly Founded: 1873
Circulation: 98968

633 **Egg Industry**
WATT Publishing Company
122 S Wesley Avenue
Mount Morris, IL 61054-1497
815-734-4171
FAX: 815-734-4201
olentine@wattmm.com
www.wattnet.com

Clay Schreiber, Publisher
Roy Leidahl, Editorial Director
Pam Ballard, US Regional Sales Manager
Jeff Swanson, Production Director
James Watt, CEO

For executives and managers of egg operations. *$36.00*
Monthly
Circulation: 2500

634 **Executive Guide**
WATT Publishing Company
122 S Wesley Avenue
Mount Morris, IL 61054-1497
815-734-4171
FAX: 815-734-4201
olentine@wattmm.com
www.wattnet.com

James Watt, CEO

635 **Farm Chemicals International**
Meister Media Worldwide
37733 Euclid Avenue
Willoughby, OH 44094-5992
440-942-2000
FAX: 440-942-0662 800-572-7740
fci.circ@meistermedia.com
www.meistermedia.com

Richard T Meister, Chairman
Gary T Fitzgerald, President
Frank Giles, Editor

Information on production, marketing and application of crop protection chemicals and fertilizers.
Founded: 1932
Circulation: 9334

636 **Farm Equipment**
Cygnus Publishing
1233 Janesville Avenue
Fort Atkinson, WI 53538
920-563-6388
FAX: 920-563-1699 800-456-0864
editor@cpasn.com
www.cygnusb2b.com

Dan Newman, Publisher
Grant Bunham, Editor

An industry-wide information and product news curriculum for farm equipment dealers that enhances their knowledge of business management principles. *$48.00*
Monthly Founded: 1937
Circulation: 10000
Printed in 4 colors on glossy stock

637 **Farm Equipment Guide**
Heartland Communications
1003 Central Avenue
PO Box 1115
Fort Dodge, IA 50501-1115
515-551-1600
FAX: 515-574-2182 800-673-4763
feg@farmequipmentguide.com
www.agdeal.com

Sandra J Simonson, Group Publisher
Tracy Roper, Production Manager
Tammy Sweeney, Operational Manager

A subscription that includes an annual blue book of specifications, serial numbers and average pricing on farm machinery with monthly updates that list thousands of pieces for sale and thousands of actual auction values.
120 pages Monthly Founded: 1981
Circulation: 20,000 1.5MM names
Printed in 4 colors on glossy stock : internet

638 **Farm Impact**
314 E Church Street
Mascoutah, IL 62258-2100

FAX: 618-566-8283

Greg Hoskins, Publisher
Michael King, Advertising Manager

Offers information to farmers.
Monthly

639 **Farm Journal**
1818 Market Street
31st Floor
Philadelphia, PA 19103
215-557-8900
FAX: 215-568-4436 800-523-1538
scuster@farmjournal.com
www.farmjournalmedia.com

Andrew J Weber, Jr, CEO/President
Crain Freiberg, Editor
Steve Custer, Publisher

Published for operators and owners of commercial farms and ranches. Provides

timely, useful marketing and management information to help them produce more efficiently, buy more wisely, sell their products at the highest possible prices, and retain as much of their income as possible. *$24.75*
182 pages Monthly Founded: 1878
Circulation: 443,529

640 Farm Reporter
Meridian Star
814 22nd Avenue
PO Box 1591
Meridian, MS 39302
601-693-1551
FAX: 601-485-1210
Reports on every phase of farming including timber, cattle, poultry and all growing crops. *$2.00*
Monthly

641 Farm Review
Lewis Publishing Company
113 N 6th Street
Lynden, WA 98264-153
360-354-4444
FAX: 360-354-4445
tribune@lyndentribune.com
www.lyndentrib.com
Michael Lewis, Publisher
Calvin Bratt, Editor
Diane Partlow, Circulation Manager
Offers a review of farming techniques and trends nationwide. *$30.00*
Quarterly Founded: 1888
Circulation: 7000

642 Farm Show Magazine
Farm Show Publishing
20088 Kenwood Trail
PO Box 1029
Lakeville, MN 55044
952-469-5572
FAX: 952-469-5579
www.farmshow.com/
Mark Newhall, Editor/Publisher
Bill Gergen, Associate Editor
Focuses on latest agricultural products, and product evaluation. Contains no advertising. *$17.95*
Founded: 1977

643 Farm Talk
Farm Talk
S Highway 59
PO BOX 601
Parsons, KS 67357-4900
620-421-9450
FAX: 620-421-9473 800-356-8255
farmtalk@terraworld.net
www.farmtalknewspaper.com
Mark Parker, Publisher
Ted Gum, Manager
Agriculture for Eastern Kansas, Western Missouri, Northeast Oklahoma and Northwest Arkansas. *$30.00*
60 pages Weekly Founded: 1974
Circulation: 10000

644 Farm World (Farm Week)
Mayhill Publications
27 N Jefferson Street
PO Box 90
Knightstown, IN 46148-1242
317-326-2235
FAX: 765-345-3398 800-876-5133
webmaster@mayhill-publications.com
www.mayhill-publications.com/
Dave Blower Jr, Editor
Richard Lewis, Publisher
Diana Scott, Marketing Manager
Agriculture, farming, and related areas in Indiana, Ohio and Kentucky. Accepts advertising. *$28.50*
84 pages Monthly

645 Farm and Dairy
Lyle Printing and Publishing Company
185 E State Street
PO Box 38
Salem, OH 44460
330-337-3419
FAX: 330-337-9550 800-837-3419
farmanddairy@aol.com
www.farmanddairy.com
Scot Darling, Publisher
Susan Crowell, Editor
Scot Darling, CEO
Billie Sekely, Advertising Manager
Howard Marsh, Circulation Manager
Briefs of research reports from experiment stations in agriculture, success stories concerning farmers of Ohio, Pennsylvania and West Virginia, sale and livestock market reports, auctions and more. Accepts advertising. *$28.00*
132 pages Founded: 1914
Circulation: 33500
Printed in 4 colors on n stock

646 Farmer's Friend
116 Main Street
Suite 503
Towanda, PA 18848-1832
570-265-2151
FAX: 570-265-1647 800-253-3662
towner@epix.net www.zwire.com
Jim Towner, Publisher
Ronald W Hosie, Editor
Debbie Fero, Circulation Manager
Kathy Thomas, Managing Editor
Farming news.
Founded: 1977

647 Farmers Digest
Heartland Communications
1003 Central Avenue
PO Box 1115
Fort Dodge, IA 50501-1115
515-955-1600
FAX: 515-574-2182 800-247-2000
fd@farmersdigest.com
www.agdeal.com
Sandra J Simonsoa, Group Publisher
Melanie Filloon, Subscription Coordinator
Straightforwarded, commonsense articles on every aspect of farming and ranching edited with one goal in mind - to make you a better farmer or rancher. *$19.95*
100 pages 10 per year Founded: 1941 61m names $75 per M.
Printed in 4 colors on matte stock

648 Farmers Hot Line
Heartland Communications
1003 Central Avenue
Fort Dodge, IA 50501
515-955-1600
FAX: 515-574-2182 800-247-2000
fhl@farmershotline.com
http://agdeal.com
Joseph W Peed, Chairman
Gale W McKinney II, President/CEO
Tony Smith, Publisher
Distributed to manufacturers, farmers, auctioneers and service companies nationwide. Designed to help buyers and sellers of new and used farm machinery, auctions, farm real estate, services and supplies. *$9.95*
Founded: 1988
Circulation: 50000

649 Farmers' Advance
Camden Publications
331 E Bell Street
PO Box 130
Camden, MI 49232
517-368-0365
FAX: 517-368-5131 800-222-6336
transfer@ca.homecomm.net
www.farmersadvance.com/
Deb Fink, Circulation Coordinator
Julia Hite, Printing & Production Manager
Kurt Greenhoe, Sales Manager
Farming technology magazine. *$25.00*
Weekly
Circulation: 17500

650 Farmers' Exchange
Exchange
404 Main Avenue S
PO Box 490
Fayetteville, TN 37334-3446
931-433-9737
FAX: 931-433-0053
exchange@vallnet.com
www.exchangeonline.com
William F Thomas, Publisher
Judy Flynt, Operations Manager
Jim Bowers, Sales Manager
Greta Painter, Distribution Manager
Magazine offers a forum for the exchange of farming ideas and information country-wide.
56 pages Monthly Founded: 1987
Circulation: 20,800

651 Farmshine
Dieter Krieg
State and Main Streets
PO Box 219
Brownstown, PA 17508
717-656-8050
FAX: 717-656-8188 866-724-6455
advertise@farmshine.com
www.farmshine.com
Dieter Krieg, Editor/Publisher
Information pertaining to the farming community. *$30.00*
Weekly Founded: 1979
Printed in on newsprint stock

652 Fastline Productions
Fastline Publications
4900 Fox Run Road
PO Box 248
Buckner, KY 40010
502-222-0146
FAX: 502-222-0615 800-626-6409
custcare@fastline.com
www.fastline.com
William G Howard, President/Editor
Nationwide and regional picture buying guides for the farming industry. *$12.00*
Monthly Founded: 1978

653 Feed Additive Compendium
12400 Whitewater Drive
Suite 160
Minnetonka, MN 55343-2524
952-931-0211
FAX: 952-938-1832 800-441-1410
circhelp@feedstuffs.com
www.feedstuffs.com
Sarah Muirhead, Publisher/Editor
Daniel Little, Production Manager
This magazine takes a closer look at the food additives and agriculture industries. *$260.00*
Weekly Founded: 1935

654 **Feed International**
WATT Publishing Company
122 S Wesley Avenue
Mount Morris, IL 61054-1497
815-734-4171
FAX: 815-734-7727
olentine@wattmm.com
www.wattnet.com

Jim Watt, Chairman/CEO
Clay Schreiber, Publisher

A magazine for feed manufacturers outside North America, provides vital information on the efficient, profitable and safe manufacture and distribution of animal feed products. *$48.00*

Monthly Founded: 1980
Circulation: 19191
Mailing list available for rent 19,191 names $225 per M.
Printed in 4 colors

655 **Feed Management**
WATT Publishing Company
122 S Wesley Avenue
Mount Morris, IL 61054-1497
815-734-4171
FAX: 815-734-7727
olentine@wattmm.com
www.wattnet.com

Jim Watt, Chairman/CEO
Clay Schreiber, Publisher

A magazine for feed manufacturers in North America providing vital information on the efficient, profitable and safe manufacture and distribution of animal feed products and helps identify and develop market opportunities for the feed manufacturer. *$48.00*

Founded: 1950
Circulation: 20249
Mailing list available for rent 20,249 names $155 per M.
Printed in 4 colors on glossy stock

656 **Feed and Grain**
Cygnus Publishing
1233 Janesville Avenue
Fort Atkinson, WI 53538
920-563-6388
FAX: 920-563-1699 800-547-7377
arlette.sambs@cygnuspub.com
www.cygnusb2b.com

Arlette Sambs, Publisher
Jean Van Dyke, Editor

Trade magazine serving feed manufacturers and firms involved in handling and processing grain commodities including feed mixers/dealers, country and terminal elevators and allied grain processors. *$48.00*

Founded: 1986
Circulation: 16831
Mailing list available for rent 16,831 names $125 per M.
Printed in 4 colors

657 **Flue Cured Tobacco Farmer**
Tabacco Farmer.Com
5808 Faringdon Place
Suite 200
Raleigh, NC 27609
919-872-5040
FAX: 919-876-6531
publisher@tobaccofarmer.com
www.tobaccofarmer.com

Dayton Matlick, Chairman
Mary Evans, Publisher/Sales Director
Arnold Hamm, Manager

Business of farming publication for commercial tobacco producers. Feature articles deal with the research-backed production, harvesting and marketing aspects of the flue cured tobacco. *$25.00*

Founded: 1964
Circulation: 14000 17000 names $80 per M.
Printed in 4 colors on glossy stock

658 **Food Aid Needs Assessment**
US Department of Agriculture
1400 Independence Ave SW
Washington, DC 20250-4701
202-907-7650
FAX: 202-720-2030 800-999-6779

Gene Mathia, Branch Chief

This annual report assesses the food situation in 60 developing countries. Most of the data are presented by region; crisis countries are covered individually. *$30.00*

Founded: 1862

659 **Fresh Cut Magazine**
Columbia Publishing
417 N 20th Avenue
Suite 2
Yakima, WA 98902-7008
509-248-2452
FAX: 509-248-4056 800-900-2452
dede@freshcut.com
www.freshcut.com

Carrie Kennington, Editor
Kimberly Warren, Managing Editor
Matt McCallum, Publisher
Erica Bernard, Circulation Manager

Features all aspects of fresh-cut fruits and vegetables, from processors who cut, package and handle them to retail and foodservice outlets where consumers buy or consume them. Readership includes processors, wholesalers, distributors, brokers, retailers, foodservice operators and chains. *$25.00*

40 pages Monthly Founded: 1993 18,464 names $200 per M.
Printed in 4 colors on glossy stock

660 **Fruit Country**
Clintron Publishing
PO Box 547
Yakima, WA 98907-0547
509-248-2452
FAX: 509-248-4056 800-869-7923

Clintke Withers, Publisher
John M Dahlin, Editor

Written for and about growers, their operations and their needs. Stories on growers and shippers, developments and trends in the fruit industry, human interest stories and politics, new products, chemicals and supplies, avant garde management techniques, cultural practices and tips on profitability. Advertising equipment and services to the fruit industry and distribution system. *$12.00*

Monthly
Circulation: 11,500

661 **Future Farmers of America New Horizons**
191 S Gary Avenue
Carol Stream, IL 60188-2095
217-877-9070
FAX: 630-462-2202 http://

Mike Wilson, Editor
Lawinna McGary, Managing Editor

Contains articles on agricultural education and vocations, targeted at high school age students. *$5.00*

Circulation: 410000

662 **Futures Magazine**
Futures Magazine
833 W Jackson
7th Floor
Chicago, IL 60607
312-770-0999
FAX: 312-846-4638
www.futuresmag.com

Ginger Szala, Group Publisher
James T Holter, Editor
Steve Lown, Manager

Agriculture commodities charted by various technical studies, plus analysis. *$39.00*

24 pages Monthly Founded: 1972

663 **Game Bird Breeders, Agiculturists, Zoologists and Conservationists**
Game Bird Breeders
1155 W 4700 S
Salt Lake City, UT 84123

George Allen, Editor

Articles on how to keep and breed all types of game birds. *$18.00*

45 pages Monthly Founded: 1974

664 **Grape Grower**
Western Agricultural Publishing Company
4969 E Clinton Way
Suite 104
Fresno, CA 93727
559-252-7000
FAX: 559-252-7387
westag@psnw.com
www.westagpubco.com

Paul Baltimore, Publisher
Jim Baltimore, Publisher
Randy Bailey, Editor
Robert Fujimoto, Assistant Editor

The West's most widely read authority on the cultivation of table grapes, raising grapes and wine grapes. All aspects of production are covered with the most current university, government and private research. *$19.95*

Monthly
Circulation: 11,276

665 **Grower**
Vance Publishing
10901 W 84th Terrace
Lenexa, KS 66214
913-438-8700
FAX: 913-438-0697
thegrower_editor@compuserve.com
www.grower.com

William C Vance, Chairman
Peggy Walker, President
Vicky Boyd, Publisher/Editor
Kevin Murphy, Marketing Manager
Al Fagen, Circulation Manager

Food safety, new technology, growing equipment, legislation. *$20.00*

Monthly Founded: 1937
Circulation: 22,004

666 **Growertalks Magazine**
Ball Publishing
335 N River Street
PO Box 9
Batavia, IL 60510
630-208-9080
FAX: 630-208-9350 800-456-5380
info@ballpublishing.com
www.growertalks.com

Chris Beytes, Editor
Jennifer White, Managing Editor

Specializes in the publishing of horticulture information, primarily related to floriculture production and marketing. *$29.00*
Monthly Founded: 1937
Circulation: 12000

667 Guernsey Breeders' Journal
American Guernsey Association
7614 Slate Ridge Boulevard
Reynoldsburg, OH 43068
614-864-2409
FAX: 614-864-5614
info@usguernsey.com
www.usguernsey.com
Lynnette White, Editor
Seth Johnson, Manager *$20.00*

668 Gulf Coast Cattleman
EC Larkin
11201 Morning Center
San Antonio, TX 78213
210-448-8300
FAX: 210-344-4258
info@gulfcoastcattleman.com
www.gulfcoastpub.com
Eys Larkin Jr, President/Publisher
Joan Dover, Circulation
M'Lys Lloyd, Managing Editor
Services commercial cattlemen along the Gulf Coast states with industry news, management and herd health related articles. *$15.00*
64 pages Monthly Founded: 1935
Circulation: 16000 16M names
Printed in 4 colors on glossy stock

669 Hereford World
American Hereford Association
PO Box 014059
Kansas City, MO 64101-59
816-218-2250
FAX: 816-842-6931
hworld@hereford.org
www.hereford.org
Craig Huffhines, Executive VP
Mary Ellen Hummel, Executive Assistant
Trade magazine for breeders of registered Polled Hereford cattle.
Monthly Founded: 1742
Circulation: 9500

670 High Country News
High Country Foundation
119 Grand Avenue
PO Box 1090
Paonia, CO 81428
970-527-4898
FAX: 970-527-4897 1 8-0 9-5 11
circulation@hcn.org www.hcn.org
Paul Larmer, Executive Director
Greg Hanscom, Editor
Gretchen Nicholoff, Circulation Manager
Covers environmental and public lands issues. *$32.00*
Founded: 1970
Circulation: 23000 22,000 names

671 High Plains Journal/Midwest Ag Journal
High Plains Publishing Company
1500 E Wyatt Earp Boulevard
PO Box 760
Dodge City, KS 67801
620-227-1834
FAX: 620-227-7173 800-452-7171
journal@hpj.com www.hpj.com
Duane Ross, Publisher
Holly Martin, Editor
Todd Fuller, Director of Consumer Mark
Jeff Keeten, Circulation Manager
Farming news for the central states. *$46.00*
Weekly
Circulation: 50000
Printed in 4 colors on glossy stock

672 Hog Producer
Farm Progress
6200 Aurora Avenue
Suite 609 E
Urbandale, IA 50322-2838
515-278-6693
FAX: 515-278-7797
jotte@farmprogress.com
www.farmprogress.com
Sara Wyant, Publisher
John Otte, Editor
Management publication to help pork producers in the production, housing, genetics, health care and marketing of hogs.
Bi-Monthly
Circulation: 119,700

673 Holstein Pulse
Holstein Association USA
1 Holstein Place
Brattleboro, VT 05302
802-254-4551
FAX: 802-254-8251 800-965-5200
info@holstein.com
www.holsteinusa.com
John Meyer, CEO
Lisa Perrin, Marketing
Quarterly
Circulation: 19000

674 Holstein World
Dairy Business Communications
6437 Collamer Road
East Syracuse, NY 13057
315-703-7979
FAX: 315-703-7988 800-334-1904
Joel P Hastings, Publisher/Editor
Janice Barrett, Associate Editor
Showcases breeders who own America's genetically superior cattle. Elite group of progressive dairymen who have income, herd size, and milk production considerably above the national averages. *$38.95*
123 pages Monthly Founded: 1904
Circulation: 12000
Printed in 4 colors on glossy stock

675 HortScience
American Society for Horticultural Science
113 SW Street
Suite 200
Alexandria, VA 22314-2851
703-836-4606
FAX: 703-836-2024
webmaster@ashs.org www.ashs.org
Michael W Neff, Publisher/Publicatio
Nancy Hubbell, Managing Editor
HortScience is a bimonthly journal concentrating on significant research, education, extension findings, and methods. *$55.00*
160 pages Monthly Founded: 1903
Circulation: 2500
Mailing list available for rent 2500 names $100 per M.

676 International Poultry Exposition Guide
WATT Publishing Company
122 S Wesley Avenue
Mount Morris, IL 61054-1497
815-734-4171
FAX: 815-734-4201
olentine@wattmm.com
www.wattnet.com
Jim Watt, Chairman/CEO
Lisa Thornton, Managing Editor
Clay Schreiber, Publisher
Annual+
Circulation: 22000

677 Jojoba Happenings
John S Turner Public Relations
805 N 4th Avenue
Unit 404
Phoenix, AZ 85003-1304
FAX: 602-252-5722
John Turner, Publisher
Ken Lucas, Editor
Jojoba farming. Accepts advertising.
8 pages Bi-Monthly

678 Journal of Agricultural & Food Chemistry
American Chemical Society
1155 16th Street NW
Washington, DC 20036
202-724-4600
FAX: 202-872-6325 800-227-9919
jafc@ucdavis.edu www.pubs.acs.org
James N Seiber, Editor
John W Finley, Associate Editor
Elizabeth Waters, Associate Editor
Research results in pesticides, fertilizers, agricultural and food processing chemistry. *$146.00*
Monthly Founded: 1856
Circulation: 159000

679 Journal of Animal Science
American Society of Animal Science
1111 North Dunlap Avenue
Savoy, IL 61874
217-356-9050
FAX: 217-398-4119
asas@assochq.org www.asas.org
Jerry Baker, Executive Director
Amy Kemp, Editorial Manager
Judy McClughen, Administrator Assistant
Mike Galyean, Editor-in-Chief
For professional researchers in the Animal Science field. *$110.00*
Monthly Founded: 1908
Circulation: 3000 3000 names $100 per M.
Printed in on glossy stock

680 Journal of Forestry
Society of American Foresters
5400 Grosvenor Lane
Bethesda, MD 20814-2198
301-897-8720
FAX: 301-897-3690
safweb@safnet.org www.safnet.org
Michael T Goergen Jr, Executive VP/CEO
Matt Vallf, Editor
lori Gardner, Marketing
For the forestry profession, both nationally and internationally. Delivers practical information to help forestry professionals meet the challenges of a rapidly changing and increasingly technical environment. *$85.00*
50 pages Monthly Founded: 1900
Circulation: 18000 18000 names $50 per M.
Printed in 4 colors on glossy stock

681 Journal of Sustainable Agriculture
Haworth Press
10 Alice Street
Binghamton, NY 13904-1580
607-722-5857
FAX: 607-722-4583 800-429-6784
getinfo@haworthpress.com
www.haworthpress.com/web/jsa

Bill Cohen, Owner/Publisher
Bill Palmer, VP/Publications Director
Raymond P. Poincelot, Editor

This professional journal is specifically devoted to the rapidly growing field of sustainable agriculture, and is aimed at increasing professional and public awareness and gaining support for necessary changes in agricultural industry. *$60.00*
Quarterly Founded: 1978

682 Journal of Vegetable Crop Production
Haworth Press
10 Alice Street
Binghamton, NY 13904-1580
607-722-5857
FAX: 607-722-6362 800-429-6784
getinfo@haworthpress.com
www.haworthpress.com

Bill Cohen, Owner/Publisher
Bill Palmer, VP/Publications Director
Vincent M. Russo, Editor

Journal aimed at those specialists and professionals who labor with the problems of vegetable crop management from land preparation to seeding and consumption. *$48.00*
Quarterly Founded: 1978

683 Land
Free Press Company
418 S 2nd Street
PO Box 3169
Mankato, MN 56001
507-344-6395
800-657-4665
theland@the-land.com
www.the-land.com

Kevin Schulz, Editor
Lynnae Schrader, Assistant Editor
Kim Henrickson, Advertising Manager
Ken Lingen, Manager

Agricultural news *$20.00*
48 pages Weekly Founded: 1976
Circulation: 40000 39000 names
Printed in 4 colors on newsprint stock

684 Landscape Management
Advanstar Landscape Group
7500 Old Oak Boulevard
Cleveland, OH 44130
440-243-8100
FAX: 440-891-2675 800-225-4569
info@landscapegroup.com
www.landscapegroup.com

Ron Hall, Editor-in-Chief
Jason Stahl, Managing Editor

Covers news, market trends, business and operations management, technical information on horticulture and agronomy for 51,000 professional landscape contractors, lawncare operators and inhouse grounds managers. *$3.83*
Founded: 1962
Circulation: 60014
Printed in 4 colors on glossy stock

685 MidAmerican Farmer Grower
MidAmerica Farm Publications
19 N Main Street
PO Box 323
Perryville, MO 63775
573-547-2244
FAX: 573-547-5663 877-486-6997
publisher@mafg.net www.mafg.net

John M. LaRose, CEO
John M. LaRose, Publisher
Barbara Galeski, Editor
Jack R. Thompson II, Marketing

Offers farming news for the middle states. *$19.00*
Weekly

686 Midwest DairyBusiness
DairyBusiness Communications
6437 Collamer Road
East Syracuse, NY 13057-1031
315-703-7979
FAX: 315-703-7988 1 8-0 3-4 19
cbryant@dairybusiness.com
www.dairybusiness.com/midwest

Dave Natzke, Editorial Director
Joel P Hastings, Publisher
JoDee Sattler, Associate Editor

Business resource for successful milk producers. Only business-oriented dairy publication exclusively for the large herd, Midwest milk producer. *$45.00*
43 pages Monthly Founded: 1904
Circulation: 27500
Printed in 4 colors on glossy stock

687 Milling Journal
3065 Pershing Court
Decatur, IL 62526
217-877-9660
FAX: 217-877-6647 800-728-7511
ed@grainnet.com www.grainnet.com

Mark Avery, Publisher
Arvin Donley, Editor
Jody Sexton, Production Manager

Mailed to all active AOM members in the US, Canada, and internationally, including wheat flour/corn mills and corn/oilseed processors in US and Canada.
Quarterly
Circulation: 1224

688 Mushroom News
American Mushroom Institute
1284 Gap Newport Pike
Suite 2
Avondale, PA 19311-1030
610-268-7483
FAX: 610-268-8015
ami@mwmlaw.com
www.americanmushroom.org

Mark Wach, Chairman
Sara Manning, Editor
Bill Barber, Publisher

For growers and scientists in the mushroom production. *$275.00*
Monthly Founded: 1955

689 NWAC News: Thad Cochran National Warmwater Aquaculture Center
127 Experiment Station Road
PO Box 197
Stoneville, MS 38776
662-686-3302
FAX: 662-686-3568
sharris@drec.msstate.edu
www.msstate.edu/dept/tcnwac

Jammy Avery, Publisher
J Charles Lee, President

Bi-annually Founded: 1993
Circulation: 1000
Printed in 3 colors on matte stock

690 National Farmers Union News
National Farmers Union
11900 E Cornell Avenue
Aurora, CO 80014-3194
303-338-2300
FAX: 303-368-1390 800-347-1961
info@nfu.org www.nfu.org

Dave Frederickson, President
Rae Price, Editor

Grass roots structure in which policy positions are initiated locally. The goal is to sustain and strengthen family farm and ranch agriculture. *$10.00*
Monthly Founded: 1902
Circulation: 250000

691 National Hog Farmer
7900 International Drive
Suite 300
Minneapolis, MN 55425-1510
952-514-4710
FAX: 952-851-4601
dpmiller@primediabusiness.com
www.nationalhogfarmer.com

Dale Miller, Editor
Steve May, Publisher
John Frinch, President
Robert Moraczewski, Senior Vice President
Susan Rowland, Marketing Manager

Offers production information for hog farming business managers. *$35.00*
Monthly Founded: 1956
Circulation: 31000
Mailing list available for rent 84M names
Printed in 4 colors on glossy stock

692 National Wheat Growers Journal
National Association of Wheat Growers
415 2nd Street NE
Suite 300
Washington, DC 20002-4993
202-547-7800
FAX: 202-546-2638
wheatworld@wheatworld.org
www.wheatworld.org

Daren Coppock, CEO
June Silverberg, Director Corporate Relations

Accepts advertising.
Founded: 1950

693 North Africa and Middle East Int'l Agricultural and Trade Report
US Department of Agriculture
1400 Independence Ave
S.W
Washington, DC 20250
202-907-7650
FAX: 202-512-2250 800-999-6779

Michael Kurrzig, Editor

Information on current and projected agriculture production and trade in North Africa and the Middle East. Reports include trade and production data, highlights United States and European trade with the region.
Annual+ Founded: 1862

694 North American Deer Farmers Magazine
North American Deer Farmers Association
1215 N 7th St
Ste 104
Lake City, MN 55041-1266
651-345-5600
FAX: 651-345-5603
info@nadefa.org www.nadefa.org

Dave Griffith, President
Phyllis Menden, Executive Director

National association of deer farming and ranching. Membership dues include this quarterly magazine. *$15.00*
32 pages Quarterly Founded: 1983
Circulation: 1000
Printed in 4 colors on glossy stock

695 **Northeast DairyBusiness**
DairyBusiness Communications
6437 Collamer Road
East Syracuse, NY 13057-1031
315-703-7979
FAX: 315-703-7988 800-334-1904
webmastr@dairybusiness.com
www.dairybusiness.com/northeast

Eleanor Jacobs, Editor
Susan Harlow, Managing Editor
Joel Hasting, CEO
Joel Hasting, Publisher
Sue Miller, Circulation Manager

Business resource for successful milk producers. Devoted exclusively to the business and dairy management needs of milk producers in the 12 northeastern states. *$3.00*
51 pages Monthly Founded: 1904
Circulation: 17500
Printed in 4 colors on glossy stock

696 **Nut Grower**
Western Agricultural Publishing Company

4969 E Clinton Way
Suite 119
Fresno, CA 93727-1549
559-252-7000
FAX: 559-252-7387
westag@psnw.com
www.westagpubco.com

Paul Baltimore, Publisher
Jim Baltimore, Publisher
Randy Bailey, Editor
Robert Fujimoto, Assistant Editor

Covers production topics, the latest in research developments, and crop news on almonds, walnuts, pistachios, pecans and chestnuts. *$19.95*
Monthly
Circulation: 11,993

697 **OEM Off-Highway**
1233 Janesville Avenue
Fort Atkinson, WI 53538-2738
920-563-6388
FAX: 920-563-1701 800-547-7377
Leslie.Shalabi@cygnuspub.com
www.cygnusb2b.com

Richard Reiff, President
Leslie Shalabi, Publisher
Chad Elmore, Associate Editor
James S. Rank, VP

Offers information on off-road machinery and farm equipment.
Founded: 1966

698 **Onion World**
Columbia Publishing
417 N 20th Avenue
Suite 2
Yakima, WA 98902
509-248-2452
FAX: 509-248-4056 800-900-2452
mike@freshcut.com
www.freshcut.com

D Brent Clement, Editor
J Mike Stoker, Publisher/Manager

Includes information on onion production and marketing, grower and shipper feature stories, onion research, from herbicide and pesticide studies to promising new varieties, martket reports, feedback from major onion meetings and conventions, spot reports on overseas production and marketing, and other key issues and trends of interest to US and Canadian onion growers. *$15.00*
32 pages Founded: 1984
Circulation: 6500 6300 names $200 per M.
Printed in 4 colors on glossy stock

699 **Organic WORLD**
Loft Publishing
3939 Leary Way NW
Seattle, WA 98107-5043
206-632-2767
FAX: 206-632-7055
Covers the news of organic gardening. *$15.00*
Quarterly

700 **Pacific Farmer-Stockman**
999 W Riverside
PO Box 2160
Spokane, WA 99201
509-595-5385
FAX: 509-459-5102 800-624-6618

Michael R Craigen, General Manager
Tracy Sikes, Sales Manager

Offers farming news and information for farmers and herdsmen located in the Pacific states.

701 **Peanut Farmer**
Specialized Agricultural Publications
5808 Faringdon Place
Suite 200
Raleigh, NC 27609
919-872-5040
FAX: 919-876-6531
publisher@peanutfarmer.com
www.peanutfarmer.com

Dayton H Matlick, Chairman
Mary Evans, Publisher/Sales Director
Mary Ann Rood, Editor

Offers peanut farmers profitable methods of raising, marketing and promoting peanuts, plus key related issues. *$15.00*
24 pages Monthly January-July Founded: 1965
Circulation: 18,500 18,500 names $80 per M.
Printed in 4 colors on glossy stock

702 **Peanut Grower**
Vance Publishing
10901 W 84th Terrace
Lenexa, KS 66214
913-438-8700
FAX: 913-438-0697
mweeks@vancepublishing.com
www.peanutgrower.com/home/main.ihtml

Amanda Huber, Editor
William C Vance, Ceo

Written for the largest 17,000 US peanut farmers. Covers disease, weed and insect control, legislation, farm equipment, marketing and new research.

Circulation: 17700

703 **Pesticide Chemical News Guide**
Food Chemical News
1725 K Street NW
Suite 506
Washington, DC 20006-1401
202-887-6320
FAX: 202-887-6335
newsdiv@crcpress.com
www.foodchem.crcpress.com

Rich O'Hanley, Editor

Tracks changes to existing and pending regulations for the use of over 1,100 chemicals on approximately 360 crops and foodstuffs. Compiled from the CFR and the Federal Register, the guide is conveniently organized. *$742.00*
Monthly

704 **Pig International**
WATT Publishing Company
122 S Wesley Avenue
Mount Morris, IL 61054
815-734-4171
FAX: 815-734-4201
schreiber@wattmm.com
www.wattnet.com

Jim Watt, Chairman/CEO
Clay Schreiber, Publisher

Edited for pig producers and others allied to the field in Asia, Europe, Africa and the United States. Provides information to the commercial pig industry on the efficient and profitable production and processing of pig meat.
Monthly Founded: 1971
Circulation: 17604
Mailing list available for rent
Printed in 4 colors on glossy stock

705 **Plant Disease**
American Phytopathological Society
3340 Pilot Knob Road
Saint Paul, MN 55121-2097
651-454-7250
FAX: 651-454-0766 800-328-7560
aps@scisoc.org www.apsnet.org

Kira Bowen, Editor
Michelle B Jerkness, Marketing Director
Steve Nelson, Executive VP
Diana Roeder, Publisher

The respected international journal of plant pathology for rapid reporting of research, new diseases and epidemics, fungicides and nematicides and new products and equipment, all with emphasis on the applied or practical aspects of diagnosing and treating plant diseases. *$ 531.00*
Monthly Founded: 1908
Circulation: 4283

706 **Pork**
Vance Publishing
10901 W 84th Terrace
Lenexa, KS 66214
913-438-8700
FAX: 913-438-0695 800-255-5113
bnpork@aol.com www.porkmag.com

Cliff Becker, Publisher
Marlys Miller, Editor

A magazine specifically designed for the professional pork producer. *$25.00*
Monthly Founded: 1869
Circulation: 75261
Mailing list available for rent

707 **Pork Report**
PO Box 10383
Clive, IA 50325
515-223-6186
FAX: 515-223-2646 http://

Charles Harness, Publisher

Hog farming news and information.

708 **Potato Country**
Columbia Publishing
417 N 20th Avenue
Suite 2
Yakima, WA 98902
509-248-2452
FAX: 509-248-4056 800-900-2452
mike@freshcut.com
www.freshcut.com

D Brent Clement, Editor
J Mike Stoker, Publisher/Manager

Edited for potato growers and allied industry people throughout the Western fall-production states. Editorial material covers production, seed, disease forecast, equip-

ment, fertilizer, irrigation, pest/weed management, crop reports and annual buyers guide. *$15.00*
32 pages Daily Founded: 1993
Circulation: 7500
Printed in 4 colors on glossy stock

709 **Potato Grower**
Harris Publishing Company
360 B Street
Idaho Falls, ID 83402
208-524-4217
FAX: 208-522-5241
jason@potatogrower.com
www.potatogrower.com
Jason Harris, Publisher
Gary Rawlings, Editor
Current news on growing potatoes, market trends, technology. *$20.95*
48 pages Monthly Founded: 1971
Printed in on glossy stock

710 **Poultry Digest**
WATT Publishing Company
122 S Wesley Avenue
Mount Morris, IL 61054
815-734-4171
FAX: 815-734-4201
olentine@wattmm.com
www.wattnet.com
Jim W Watt, Chairman/CEO
Charles G Olentine Jr, PhD, VP/Publisher
Clay Schreiber, Publisher
Jim Wessel, Circulation Director
A magazine serving the production side of the entire poultry industry. *$15.00*
Monthly
Circulation: 19000

711 **Poultry International**
WATT Publishing Company
122 S Wesley Avenue
Mount Morris, IL 61054-1497
815-734-4171
FAX: 815-734-4201
olentine@wattnet.com
www.wattnet.com
Jim Watt, Chairman/CEO
Jackie Linden, Editor
Poultry International serves the poultry industry worldwide.
68 pages Monthly Founded: 1962
Circulation: 23427
Printed in 4 colors

712 **Poultry Times**
Poultry & Egg News
345 Green Street NW
PO Box 1338
Gainesville, GA 30503
770-536-2476
FAX: 770-532-4894
business@poultryandeggnews.com
www.poultryandeggnews.com
Christopher Hill, Publisher/Editor
Randall Smallwood, President
Barbara Olejnik, Production Coordinator
Forum for poultry industry news. *$22.00*
Monthly Founded: 1970
Circulation: 13017+

713 **Practical Winery & Vineyard**
58-D Paul Drive
San Rafael, CA 94903-1534
415-479-5819
FAX: 415-492-9325
officepwv@aol.com
www.practicalwinery.com
Don Neel, CEO
Don Neel, Publisher
Carol Caldwell Ewart, Senior Editor
Don Neel, Publisher Editor
A bi-monthly magazine of winegrowing, winemaking news and reviews. *$31.00*
Founded: 1985
Circulation: 7500

714 **Prairie Farmer**
Prairie Farm Dairy
1301 E Mound Road
PO Box 348
Pana, IL 62557
217-562-3956
FAX: 217-877-9695
Tom Budd, Publisher
Mike Wilson, Editor
Agricultural news.

715 **Progressive Farmer**
2100 Lakeshore Drive
Birmingham, AL 35209-6721
205-445-6000
FAX: 205-445-6422
bruce_thomas@timeinc.com
www.progressivefarmer.com
Bruce Thomas, Publisher
Jack Odle, Editor
Allen Vaughan, Business Manager
Farming news with regional focus on the midwest, midsouth and southwest. *$18.00*
106 pages 6 issues/Year Founded: 1886
Circulation: 610000

716 **RF Design**
RFD News
131 E Main Street
Bellevue, OH 44811-1449
419-483-7410
FAX: 419-483-3737 http://
Barry LeCerf, Publisher
Comprehensive source of rural agricultural news and information for farmers and the general public.
Weekly

717 **Rice Farming**
Vance Publishing
400 Knightsbridge Parkway
Lincolnshire, IL 60069
847-634-2600
800-888-9784
vlboyd@worldnet.att.net
www.vancepublishing.com
Sonia M Tighe, Group Publishing Director
William Vance, Chairman
Judy Riggs, Director
Vicky Boyd., Editor
Profitable production strategies for commercial rice growers. *$25.00*
Monthly Founded: 1937
Circulation: 13000
Printed in 4 colors on glossy stock

718 **Rice Journal**
Specialized Agricultural Publications
3000 Highwoods Boulevard
Suite 300
Raleigh, NC 27604-1029
919-878-0540
FAX: 919-876-6531
publisher@ricejournal.com
www.ricejournal.com
Dayton H Matlick, President
Mary Evans, Publisher
Offers rice growers profitable methods of producing, marketing and promoting rice, plus key related issues. *$15.00*
24 pages Founded: 1897
Circulation: 11600 $80 per M.
Printed in 4 colors on glossy stock

719 **RuraLife**
William Johnston
300 N Washington Avenue
Mason City, IA 50401-3222
Jerry Moriarity, Publisher
Gary Grimmond, Editor
Farm and agricultural news.

720 **Rural Heritage**
Allan Damerow
281 Dean Ridge Lane
Gainesboro, TN 38562-5039
931-268-0655
editor@ruralheritage.com
www.ruralheritage.com
Gail Damerow, Editor
Publication for people who farm and log with horses and other draft animals. *$26.00*
100 pages Bi-Monthly Founded: 1976
Circulation: 8500
Printed in 4 colors on matte stock

721 **Rural Living**
Michigan Farm Bureau
7373 W Saginaw Highway
PO Box 30960
Lansing, MI 48909-8460
517-323-7000
FAX: 517-323-6793
mifarmnews@michfb.com
www.michiganfarmbureau.com
Dennis Rudat, Editor
Paul W. Jackson, Editor
Editorial emphasis on consumer food news, travel information and issue analysis.
24 pages Quarterly
Circulation: 200000

722 **Seed Industry Journal**
Freiberg Publishing Company
2302 W 1st Street
PO Box 7
Cedar Falls, IA 50613-0007
319-530-0642
FAX: 319-277-3783
Bill Freiberg, Publisher
Carol Cutler, Editor
International seed industry news.

723 **Seed Today**
Grain Journal Publishing Company
3065 Pershing Court
Decatur, IL 62526
217-877-9660
FAX: 217-877-6647 800-728-7511
ed@grainnet.com www.grainnet.com
Deb Coontz, Publisher
Joe Funk, Editor
Kay Merryfield, Circulation Administrator
Ayanna Green, Manager
Quarterly Founded: 1978
Circulation: 4000

724 **Seed World**
Scranton Gillette Communications
380 E Northwest Highway
Suite 200
Des Plaines, IL 60016-2282
847-298-6622
FAX: 847-390-0408
sweditor@sgcmail.com
www.seedworld.com

E S Gillette, Publisher
Angela Dansby, Editor

Seed marketers. *$30.00*
48 pages Monthly Founded: 1915
Circulation: 5000

725 **Self Employed Country**
Communicating for Agriculture & The Self Employed
112 E Lincoln Avenue
Fergus Falls, MN 56537-2216
218-739-4950
FAX: 218-739-3832 800-432-3276

Milt Smedsrud, Publisher
Jerry Barney, Production Manager

For members of Communicating for Agriculture, including legislation relating to CA activities, exchange program activities, rural seniors news, health and insurance material, feature stories and columns. *$6.00*
Quarterly Founded: 1985

726 **Shorthorn Country**
Durham Management Company
8288 Hascall Street
Omaha, NE 68124-3234
402-393-7200
FAX: 402-393-7203
durham@beefshorthornusa.com
www.beefshorthornusa.com

Don Cagwin, Publisher
Tracy Duncan, Editor
Peggy Gilliland, Circulation Manager

Magazine published for cattle producers who breed and sell registered Shorthorn and Polled Shorthorn cattle. *$24.00*
Founded: 1956
Circulation: 3000

727 **Society of American Foresters**
5400 Grosvenor Lane
Bethesda, MD 20814-2198
301-897-8720
FAX: 301-897-3690 www.safnet.org

Michael Goergen, Executive Vice President
William Banzhaf, Production Manager
Jeff Glannam, VP Marketing

Monthly newsletter for all those involved in forestry research and technology. Regular editorial features.

728 **Soil Science**
Lippincott Williams & Wilkins
351 W Camden Street
Baltimore, MD 21201-2436
410-528-4000
FAX: 410-361-8040 800-638-6423
soilscience@rutgers.edu
www.lww.com

Robert Tate III, Editor

Covers investigations in environmental soils. *$205.00*
Monthly
Circulation: 2800

729 **Soil Science of America Journal**
Soil Science Society of America
677 S Segoe Road
Madison, WI 53711
608-273-8095
FAX: 608-273-2021
headquarters@soils.org www.soils.org

Francis Katz, Director Publications
Ellen Bergfeld, Executive VP

For those involved in research, teaching and extension activities in physics, chemistry, mineralogy, microbiology, soil fertility and plant nutrition *$600.00*
Founded: 1961
Circulation: 4000

730 **Southeast Farm Press**
Primedia Business
745 Fifth Avenue
New York, NY 10151
212-745-0100
FAX: 212-745-0121
information@primedia.com
www.primediabusiness.com

Greg Frey, Publisher
Paul Hollis, Editor
Darrah Parker, Director of Marketing

Offers farming news for the southeastern states.
Weekly Founded: 1989
Circulation: 47,700

731 **Southeastern Peanut Farmer**
Southern Peanut Farmer's Federation
110 E 4th Street
Tifton, GA 31794
229-386-3470
FAX: 229-386-3501 800-346-4993
info@gapeanuts.com
www.gapeanuts.com

Don Koehlr, Executive Director
Emory Murphy, Assistant Executive
Joan Underwood, Production Manager

Offers information to peanut farmers. *$25.00*
20 pages Monthly Founded: 1961
Circulation: 8400
Printed in 4 colors on glossy stock

732 **Southwest Farm Press**
Farm Press Publications
2104 Harvell Circle
Bellevue, NE 68005
402-505-7173
FAX: 402-293-0741 866-505-7173
sscs@pbsub.com
http://southwestfarmpress.com

Greg Frey, Publisher
Ron Smith, Editor
Hembree Brandon, Editorial Director
Forrest Laws, Executive Editor
Darrah Parker, Marketing Manager

Farming news. *$40.00*
Fortnightly Founded: 1974
Circulation: 33,100

733 **Soybean South**
6263 Poplar Avenue
Suite 540
Memphis, TN 38119-4736
901-385-0595
FAX: 901-767-4026

John Sowell, Publisher
Jeff Kehl, Circulation Director

Profitable prediction strategies for soybean farmers.
5 per year
Printed in 4 colors on glossy stock

734 **Speedy Bee**
Fore's Honey Farms
115 Morning Glory Circle
PO Box1317
Jesup, GA 31598
912-427-4018
FAX: 912-427-8447
info@abfnet.org www.abfnet.org

Troy Fore, Editor
Troy Fore, Marketing Representative
Troy Fore, Publisher

Honey and beekeeping industry news. *$17.95*
16 pages Monthly Founded: 1972
Circulation: 1500
Printed in on newsprint stock

735 **Spudman Magazine**
Great American Publishing
75 Applewood Drive
Suite A
Sparta, MI 49435
616-887-9008
FAX: 616-887-2666 www.spudman.com

Matt McCallum, Publisher
Kimberly Warren, Managing Editor
Erica Bernard, Circulation Manager
Matt McCallum, CEO

Information for potato farming and marketing.

Circulation: 15500 14,000 names
Printed in on glossy stock

736 **Successful Farming**
Meredith Corporation
1716 Locust Street
Des Moines, IA 50309-3023
515-284-3000
FAX: 515-284-3563 800-678-2659
tom.davis@meredith.com
www.agriculture.com

Lorrane Kruse, Editor-in-Chief
Sandy Williams, Production Manager
William Kerr, CEO
Tom Davis, Publisher

U.S. commerical farmers, ranchers and those employed in those operations or a directly related occupation. *$15.95*
Monthly Founded: 1902
Circulation: 442000
Mailing list available for rent 500M names $75 per M.
Printed in 4 colors on glossy stock

737 **Sugar: The Sugar Producer Magazine**
Harris Publishing Company
360 B Street
Idaho Falls, ID 83402
208-524-4217
FAX: 208-522-5241 800-638-0135
customerservice@harrypublishing.com
www.sugarproducer.com

Jason Harris, Publisher
David FairBourn, Editor
Rob Erickson, Marketing
Eula Endecott, Circulation Manager

Sugar beet industry information. *$15.95*
Monthly Founded: 1975
Circulation: 16000

738 **Sugarbeet Grower**
Sugar Publications
503 Broadway
Fargo, ND 58102-4416
701-476-2111
FAX: 701-476-2182
sugar@kayesprinting.com
www.sugarpub.com

Don Lilleboe, Manager
Don Lilleboe, Editor
Heidi Wieland, Advertising Manager

Provides news and feature articles pertaining to sugarbeet production practices, research, legislation and marketing, along with profiles of industry leaders and outstanding producers. Primary audience is United States and Canadian sugarbeet growers. *$12.00*

Founded: 1963
Circulation: 11,336

739 Sunflower Magazine
National Sunflower Association
4023 State Street
Bismarck, ND 58503
701-328-5100
FAX: 701-328-5101 888-718-7033
tinam@sunflowernsa.com
www.sunflowernsa.com

Larry Kleingartner, Executive Director
Tracy Sayler, Editor

Magazine geared to sunflower products. *$9.00*

Founded: 1981
Circulation: 29300 $150 per M.
Printed in 4 colors

740 Sunflower and Grain Marketing Magazine
Sunflower World Publishers
3307 Northland Drive
Suite 130
Austin, TX 78731-4964
512-407-3434
FAX: 512-323-5118

Ed Randall Allen

Offers news and information on the sunflower and grain industries. *$1.00*

Circulation: 15,000

741 Super Hay Today Magazine
Mt Adams Publishing and Design
14161 Fort Road
White Swan, DC 98552-9786
509-848-2706
FAX: 509-848-3896 800-554-0860
hortexponw@aol.com
www.hortexponw.com

Vee Graves, Editor
Julie LaForge, Advertising Manager

742 Swine Practitioner
10901 W 84th Terrace
Suite 200
Lenexa, KS 66214-1649
913-438-8700
FAX: 913-438-0695 800-255-5113
bnewham@vancepublishing.com
www.vancepublishing.com

Kristal Arnold, Editor
Kevin Murphy, Sales/Marketing Manager
Bill Newham, Publishing Director
Cliff Becker, Group Publisher

Offers technical information, primarily on swine health and related production areas, to veterinarians and related industry professionals.

Monthly
Circulation: 4800
Mailing list available for rent

743 Today's Farmer
MFA
201 Ray Young Drive
Columbia, MO 65201
573-874-5111
FAX: 573-876-5505
hr@mfa-inc.com
www.mfaincorporated.com

Don Copenhaver, President
J Brian Griffith, VP

Management and marketing news. *$12.00*

Founded: 1914

744 Tomato Country
Columbia Publishing
417 N 20th Avenue
PO Box 9036
Yakima, WA 98902
509-248-2452
FAX: 509-248-4056 800-900-2452

J Stoker, Publisher

Includes information on tomato production and marketing, grower and shipper feature stories, tomato research, from herbicide and pesticide studies to new varieties, market reports, feedback from major tomato meetings and conventions, along with other key issues and points of interest for USA and Canada tomato growers.

745 Tree Farmer Magazine
American Forest Foundation
1111 19th Street NW
Suite 780
Washington, DC 20036
202-632-2455
FAX: 202-463-2461
info@treefarmsystem.org
www.treefarmsystem.org

Laurence Wiseman, President
Brigitte Johnson, Editor

Practical information on a number of tree farming-related topics, including sustainable forestry, private landowners, professional forests, wildlife, recreation, as well as water and soil conservation. *$18.00*

Founded: 1941
Circulation: 65000
Printed in on glossy stock

746 Tree Fruit
Western Agricultural Publishing Company
4969 E Clinton Way
Suite 104
Fresno, CA 93727-1546
559-252-7000
FAX: 559-252-7387
westag@psnw.com
www.westagpubco.com

Paul Baltimore, Publisher
Jim Baltimore, Publisher
Randy Bailey, Editor
Robert Fujimoto, Assistant Editor

For tree fruit growers in California. *$19.95*

8 per year
Circulation: 7,470

747 Valley Potato Grower
420 Business Highway 2
PO Box 301
East Grand Forks, MN 56721
218-773-7783
FAX: 218-773-6227
vpgsales@nppga.org www.nppga.org

Todd Phelph, CEO
Duane Maatz, Executive Director

Information on potato farming.

Founded: 1946
Circulation: 10616

748 Vegetable Growers News
Great American Publishing
75 Applewood Drive Suite A
PO Box 128
Sparta, MI 49345
616-887-9008
FAX: 616-887-2666
www.vegetablegrowersnews.com

Matt McCallum, Executive Publisher
Brenda Bradford, Advertising
Kimberly Warren, Managing Editor
Erica Bernard, Circulation Department

Market and marketing news. *$12.00*

Monthly

749 Vegetables
Western Agricultural Publishing Company
4969 E Clinton Way
#104
Fresno, CA 93727-1549
559-252-7000
FAX: 559-252-7387
westag@psnw.com
www.westagpubco.com

Paul Baltimore, Publisher
Jim Baltimore, Publisher
Randy Bailey, Editor
Robert Fujimoto, Assistant Editor

The definitive source for information on all aspects of western vegetable production.

Monthly

750 Vineyard and Winery Management

PO Box 2358
Winsdor, CA 95492
707-366-6820
FAX: 607-535-2998 800-535-5670

Robert Merletti, President
Tom Loid, Executive Editor
Robert Merletti, Publisher

To be the bottom line resource for growers and vintners; to keep our readers tuned and primed for profit. *$37.00*

100 pages Founded: 1975
Circulation: 6000
Printed in 4 colors on glossy stock

751 WATT Poultry Magazine
WATT Publishing Company
122 S Wesley Avenue
Mount Morris, IL 61054-1451
815-734-4171
FAX: 815-734-4201
wright@wattmm.com
www.wattpoultry.com

Jim Watt, Chairman/CEO
Clay Schreiber, Publisher
Gary Thornton, Editor
Jim Wessel, Circulation Director

Dedicated to supporting every phase of the turkey industry by providing information for decision-makers on breeding, production, management, processing and marketing.

Monthly
Circulation: 15,092

752 WD Hoard and Sons Company
28 Milwaukee Avenue W
Fort Atkinson, WI 53538
920-563-5551
FAX: 920-563-7298
hoards@hoards.com www.hoards.com

W D Knox, Publisher
Gary L Vorpahl, Director Marketing

News aimed at the dairy farmer. *$16.00*
Founded: 1885
Circulation: 85564
Printed in 4 colors on glossy stock

753 **Wallaces Farmer**
Farm Progress Publishers
191 S Gary Avenue
Carol Stream, IL 60188-2095
630-690-5600
FAX: 630-462-2885
jtennant@farmprogress.com
www.farmprogress.com
Thomas Budd, Publisher
Monte Sesker, Editor
Farm management and agricultural news serving midwest farmers. *$23.95*
Founded: 1850

754 **Western DairyBusiness**
DairyBusiness Communications
6437 Collamer Road
East Syracuse, NY 13057-1031
315-703-7979
FAX: 315-703-7988 800-334-1904
bbaker@dairyline.com
www.dairybusiness.com
Joel P Hastings, Editor
John Montandon, President & Co-CEO
Debbie Morneau, Marketing Coordinator
Business resource for successful milk producers. Covers 13 Western states. Provides information and news that is helpful in the daily operations of dairymen. *$49.95*
67 pages Monthly Founded: 1904
Circulation: 14000
Printed in 4 colors on glossy stock

755 **Western Farm Press**
Primedia
9800 Metcalf Avenue
Overland Park, KS 66212
913-341-1300
FAX: 913-967-1898
hbrandon@primediabusiness.com
www.westernfarmpress.com
Harry Cline, Editor
Robert Frazer, Managing

756 **Western Fruit Grower**
Meister Media Worldwide
37733 Euclid Avenue
Willoughby, OH 44094-5925
440-942-2000
FAX: 440-942-0662 800-572-7740
rljones@meistermedia.com
www.meistermedia.com
Richard T Meister, Chairman
Gary T Fitzgerald, President
John Monahan, Publisher
Richard Jones, Editor
Edited for commercial growers of deciduous crops, citrus fruit and nut grape crops in the Western US. *$19.95*
66 pages Monthly Founded: 1933
Circulation: 36000

757 **Western Livestock Journal**
Crow Publications
650 S Lipan Street
Denver, CO 80223-2307
303-722-7600
FAX: 303-722-0155 800-850-2769
pete@wlj.net www.wlj.net
Richard Crow, Publisher
Michele McRae, Circulation Manager
Valuable information to cattle breeders and farmers. *$35.00*
Weekly Founded: 1922
Circulation: 30000+

758 **Wheat Grower**
National Association of Wheat Growers
415 2nd Street NE
Suite 300
Washington, DC 20002-4993
202-547-7800
FAX: 202-546-2638
wheatworld@wheatworld.org
www.wheatworld.org
Mark Gage, President
Daren Coppock, CEO
Offers valuable information aimed at the farmer of wheat. *$100.00*
Weekly Founded: 1950
Circulation: 30000

Trade Shows

759 **AAEA Annual Meeting**
American Agricultural Economics Association
415 S Duff Avenue
Suite C
Ames, IA 50010-6600
515-233-3202
FAX: 515-233-3101
nknight@iastate.edu www.aaea.org
Per Pinstrup-Anderson, President
Yvonne C Bennett, Executive Director
Nancy Knight, Manager Meetings
Joan Greiner, Events Coordinator
Annual meeting and trade show of 25 exhibitors.
1700 Attendees August Founded: 1985

760 **AFIA Expo**
American Feed Industry Association
1501 Wilson Boulevard
Suite 1100
Arlington, VA 22209
703-524-0810
FAX: 703-524-1921
afia@afia.org www.afia.org
Joel Newmann, President
Rex Runyon, VP Public Relations
Richard Sellers, VP/Feed, Control & Nutrition
Jim Rydell, Director/Quality & International
Jeff Haas, Director/Sales & Marketing
250 exhibits of feed equipment, ingedients and services. Containing 500+ booths.
3000 Attendees September Founded: 1949

761 **AOSA/SCST Annual Meeting-Association of Official Seed Analysts**
PMB #411
1763 East University Bouldevard
Suite A
Las Cruces, NM 88001
505-522-1437
FAX: 505-522-1437
aosaoffice@earthlink.net
www.aosaseed.com
Ellen Chirco, President
Wayne Guerke, VP
Dan Curry, Secretary/Treasurer
Aaron Palmer, Certificate/Analysist
Larry Nees, Membership
Seed testing and laboratory equipment, supplies and services.
June

762 **ASAS-ADSA-PSA Joint Annual Meeting**
American Society of Animal Science
1111 N Dunlap Avenue
Savoy, IL 61874
217-356-9050
FAX: 217-398-4119
asas@assochq.org www.asas.org
Terry D Etherton, President
Normand St Pierre, Treasurer
Mary M Beck, Director
Lorena K Nicholas, Conventions/Communications
Professional organization for animal scientists designed to help members provide effective leadership through research, extension, teaching and service for the dynamic and rapidly changing livestock and meat industries. Containing 45 booths.
2000 Attendees July Founded: 1908

763 **Ag Progress Days**
Penn State University Agricultural Sciences
420 Agricultural Administration Building
University Park, PA 16802
814-865-2081
FAX: 814-865-1677
agprogressdays@psu.edu
www.apd.cas.psu.edu
Bob Oberheim, Manager
Agricultural trade show focusing on the innovations and progress made in the agricultural industry.
50M Attendees August 15-17, 2006
Founded: 1976

764 **Agri News Farm Show**
Agri News
18 1st Avenue SE
Rochester, MN 55904-6118
507-857-7707
FAX: 507-281-7436 800-533-1727
rallen@agrinew.com
www.agrinew.com
John Losness, Publisher
Rosie Allen, Advertsising Manager
Annual show of 123 exhibitors of farming equipment, supplies and services.
7,500 Attendees March

765 **Agricultural Retailers Association Convention and Expo**
Agricultural Retailers Association
1156 15th Street
Suite 302
Washington, DC 20005
202-570-0825
FAX: 314-567-6808 800-535-6272
Jack Eberstacher, CEO/President
Annual show of 120 manufacturers, suppliers and distributors of agricultural chemicals and fertilizers. Seminar, conference and banquet.
1200 Attendees December Founded: 1993

766 **Agro-International Trade Fair for Agricultural Machinery & Equipment**
Glahe International
118 Water Street
PO Box 2460
Germantown, MD 20877
301-515-0012
FAX: 301-515-0012 glahe@glahe.com
Biennial show of agricultural machinery and equipment.

767 **American Agri-Women**
1005 Highway 92
Keota, IA 52248-9110
641-636-2293

info@americanangriwomen.org
www.americanagriwomen.org

Carol Marx, President
Yvonne Erickson, VP/Resoultions & Vital Issues
Dana Hoffman, VP/Communications
Doris Mold, VP/Education
Katie Edwards, Secretary

Tradeshow consisting of products of interest to women in agriculture.

350 Attendees November Founded: 1974

768 **American Agricultural Economics Association Annual Meeting**
American Agricultural Economics Association
415 S Duff Avenue
Suite C
Ames, IA 50010-6600
515-233-3202
FAX: 515-233-3101
meetings@aaea.org www.aaea.org

James Novak, President
Yvonne Bennett, Executive Director
Michael Bochlje, Agribusiness Economics/Management
Keith Coble, Food/Agricultural Marketing Policy
Joan Greiner, Meeting Coordinator

Agricultural economics hardware, software, teaching texts, tools, equipment and supplies. Banquet and conference.

1600 Attendees January Founded: 1910 3500 names $140 per M.

769 **American Association of Bovine Practicioners Annual Conference**
American Association of Bovine Practicioners
Box 1755
Rome, GA 30162-1755
706-232-2220
FAX: 706-232-2232
aabphq@aabp.org www.aabp.org

John Ferry, President
Charlie Hatcher, VP
Gatz Riddell, Executive Vice President
Sam Hutchins, Exhibits Chairman

130 exhibits of parmaceutical and biological manufacturers, equipment and agricultural companies, computer programs and supplies.

1905 Attendees Annual/September Founded: 1967

770 **American Association of Cereal Chemists**
3340 Pilot Knob Road
Saint Paul, MN 55121-2097
651-454-7250
FAX: 651-454-0766
aacc@scisoc.org www.aaccnet.org

Stuart Craig, President
James Dexter, Chairman/Board
Steven Nelson, VP
Betty Ford, Director Meetings

The AACC Annual Meeting is the primary education and networking event for close to 5,000 member professionals working in the grain based foods industry, including product developers, researchers, managers, quality control specialists, marketers, engineers, nutritionists, teachers, and students. It offers the opportunity for members and other attendees to stay on top of industry issues and trends by delivering the most up to date information regarding scientific developments and new technology.

1,700 Attendees September Founded: 1915

771 **American Beekeeping Federation Convention**
American Beekeeping Federation
115 Morning Glory Circle
PO Box 1337
Jesup, GA 31546
912-427-4233
FAX: 912-427-8447
info@abfnet.org www.abfnet.org

Daniel Weaver, President
Troy Fore, Executive Director
Bob Miller, Director/Commercial Beekeepers
Reg Wilbanks, Director/Queen Breeders

Has been serving the needs of the US beekeeper for over 50 years. 40+ booths.

1500 Attendees January Founded: 1943

772 **American Farriers Association Annual Convention Marketplace**
American Farriers Association
4059 Iron Works Parkway
Suite 1
Lexington, KY 40511
859-233-7411
FAX: 859-231-7862
farriers@americanfarriers.org
www.americanfarriers.org

Craig Trnka, President
Bob Earle, VP
Walt Taylor, Secretary
Jeff Ridley, Representative/Board of Directors
Bryan J Quinsey, Executive Director

One-hundred and seventy exhibits of equipment and supplies for farriers, seminar, banquet, luncheon and tours.

1500 Attendees Annual/February Founded: 1971

773 **American Rabbit Breeders Association National Convention**
8 Westport Court
Bloomington, IL 61704
309-664-7500
FAX: 309-664-0941
arbamail@aol.com www.arba.net

Glen Carr, Executive Director

Seminar, banquet, luncheon and 1500 rabbit breeders exhibits.

3000 Attendees Annual/April Founded: 1910

774 **American Royal Livestock Horse Show and Rodeo**
1701 American Royal Court
Kansas City, MO 64102
816-221-9800
FAX: 816-221-8189
info@americanroyal.com
www.americanroyal.com

Neal Patterson, Chair Board/Directors
Malcolm M Aslin, First VP
George M Guastello, President/CEO
Flo Coffey, Show Manager
Pat Meads, Commercial Exhibits

Livestock show, horse show and rodeo, and 200 exhibits of gift items, clothing and jewelry. Also equipment, supplies and services related to livestock and horses.

50k Attendees October/November

775 **American Society Agricultural Engineers**
2950 Niles Road
Saint Joseph, MI 49085
269-429-0300
FAX: 269-429-3852 800-371-2723
hq@asae.org www.asae.org

Melissa Moore, Executive Vice President
Barbara Sowden, Director Meetings & Conferences

100 booths.

10M Attendees July Founded: 1907 10000 names $120 per M.

776 **American Society for Enology and Vinticulture Annual Meeting**
American Society for Enology and Vinticulture
PO Box 1855
Davis, CA 95617-1855
530-753-3142
FAX: 530-753-3318
society@asev.org www.asev.org

Thomas Smith, President
Dr. Robert Wample, First VP
Craig Rous, Director Operations
Lyndie Boulton, Executive Dircetor
Mike Vail, Director Viticulture

250 exhibits of equipment, supplies and services to the wine and grape industries, as well as a seminar.

2300 Attendees June Founded: 1951 1500 names

777 **American Society for Horticultural Science Annual Conference**
American Society for Horticultural Science
113 SW Street
Suite 200
Alexandria, VA 22314-2851
703-836-4606
FAX: 703-836-2024
webmaster@ashs.org www.ashs.org

Cary Mitchell, Chair
Paul E Read, President
Elizabeth Lamb, Education Division
Michael Neff, Executive Director

August

778 **American Society of Agronomy Meeting and Exhibits**
American Society of Agronomy
677 S Segoe Road
Madison, WI 53711-1086
608-273-8080
FAX: 608-273-2021
pscullion@agronomy.org
www.agronomy.org

Lee E Sommers, President
Ellen G M Bergfeld, Executive VP
Patricia Scullion, Exhibits Manager

Society members are dedicated to the conservation and wise use of natural resources to produce food, feed and fiber crops while maintaining and improving the environment. Annual meeting and exhibits of agricultural equipment, supplies and services.

October/November

779 **American Society of Farm Managers and Rural Appraisers Convention**
950 S Cherry Street
Suite 508
Denver, CO 80246-2664
303-758-3513
FAX: 303-758-0190
meetings@asfmra.org
www.asfmra.org

Cheryl L Cooley, IT Manager
Brain Stockman, Executive VP
Sally Quinn, Director Finance/Administration
Debe L Alvarez, Education Manager

Fifty-five exhibits of agricultural equipment, supplies and services, conference.
$1.00
500 Attendees November

780 American Veterinary Medical Association Annual Convention
American Veterinary Medical Association
1931 N Meacham Road
Suite 100
Schaumburg, IL 60173
847-036-6142
FAX: 847-925-1329
avmaininfo@avma.org www.avma.org

Bonnie V Beaver,DVM, President
David Little, Director Conventions/Meerings

Seminar and 310 exhibits of products, materials, equipment, data, and services for veterinary medicine.
10000 Attendees Annual/July

781 Animal Transportation Association
111 E Loop North
PO Box 797095
Dallas, TX 77029
713-532-2177
FAX: 713-532-2166
info@aata-animaltransport.org
www.aata-animaltransport.org

Cherie Derouin, Publications/Meetings Coordinator

An international association promoting the humane handling and transportation of animals. 10-15 booths.
150 Attendees April

782 Beltwide Cotton Conference
National Cotton Council of America
1918 North Parkway
Memphis, TN 38182-5000
901-274-9030
FAX: 901-725-0510
info@natbat.com www.cotton.org

Ward E Eastland, Chair
Allen B Helms Jr, Vice Chair
Mark D Lange, President/CEO
G Stephen Felker, VP
Gail Kreng, Vice President

Offers a forum for agricultural professionals.
January

783 Big Iron Farm Show and Exhibition

Red River Valley Fair Association
1201 West Main Avenue
PO Box 797
West Fargo, ND 58078-0797
701-282-2200
FAX: 701-282-6909 800-456-6408
info@redrivervalleyfair.com
www.bigironfarmshow.com

Bruce A Olson, Manager

Annual show of 500 manufacturers of agricultural machinery and related products.
70M Attendees September, West Fargo

784 Citrus Expo
Associated Publishing Corporation
495 E Summerlin Street
Bartow, FL 33830
863-533-4114
FAX: 863-534-1758
lbrickey@barpr.com
www.citrusindustry.net

Maryann Holland, Show Manager

Citrus Trade Show with seminars, containing 150 exhibits.
1500 Attendees August

785 Crop Science Society of America Meeting and Exhibits
Crop Science Society of America
677 S Segoe Road
Madison, WI 53711-1048
608-273-8086
FAX: 608-273-2021
tmoeller@agronomy.org
www.crops.org

Ellen Bergfeld, Executive Vice President
Sisan G Champan, Director/Member Services
Pauln G M Kampseld, Development Officer
Ian Popkewitz, Director/IT /Operations
Keith Schlesinger, Director/Meeting

Annual exhibits of agricultural equipment, supplies and services.
October

786 Delmarva Ag Show
Lee Publications
6113 State Highway 5
PO Box 121
Palatine Bridge, NY 13428-0121
518-732-2269
FAX: 518-673-3245 800-218-5586
kmaring@leepub.com
www.leepub.com

Bruce Button, VP
Janet Button, VP/Sales/Marketing
Tom Mahoney, Sales Manager
Richard Brown, Production Coordinator
Ken Maring, Show Manager

Agriculture and construction eqipment expostion with hundreds of exhibits, and a skid steer rodeo. Located at the Wicomico Youth and Civic Center in Maryland.
December

787 El Foro
WATT Publishing Company
122 S Wesley Avenue
Mount Morris, IL 61054
815-734-4171
FAX: 815-734-4201
olentine@wattmm.com
www.wattnet.com

Jim Watt, Chairman/CEO

A trade show and technical symposium for the Latin American poultry, pig and feed industries. Containing 50 booths and 150 exhibits.
275 Attendees July

788 Entomological Society of America
10001 Derekwood Lane
Suite 100
Lanham, MD 20706-4876
301-731-4535
FAX: 301-731-4538
esa@entsoc.org www.entsoc.org

Frank E Gilstrap, VP
Scott Hutchins, VP
Lisa Spurlock, Society Relations Officer
Paula Lettice, Executive Director

50 booths of scientific equipment, supplies and services relevant to entomology.
3M Attendees November 3k names $125 per M.

789 FEWA's Industry Showcase
FEWA
PO Box 1347
Iowa City, IA 52244
319-354-5156
FAX: 319-354-5157
info@fewa.org www.fewa.org

Patricia A Collins, Executive VP

Annual convention and 130 exhibits of equipment, supplies and services for independent wholesalers of shortline and specialty farm equipment, light industrial tractors, lawn and garden tractors, turf care equipment, estate and park maintenance equipment and power vehicles for outdoor recreation and sports.
800 Attendees October

790 FFA National Agricultural Career Show
5632 Mount Vernon Memorial Highway
Alexandria, VA 22309-1502

FAX: 800-366-6556 888-332-2668
jack-pitzer@ffa.org www.ffa.org

Jack Pitzer, Show Manager

850 booths encouraging high school youth to select careers in the agricultural industry.

45M Attendees November

791 Farm Bureau Showcase
American Farm Bureau Federation
1850 Howard Avenue
Suite C
Elk Grove, IL 60007
224-656-6600
FAX: 847-685-8696 www.fb.org

Bob Stallman, President

Two-hundred plus booths featuring exhibits of agricultural equipment, supplies and services.
6-8M Attendees January

792 Farm Progress Show
Farm Progress Companies
191 South Gary Avenue
Carol Stream, IL 60188-2095
630-905-5600
FAX: 630-462-2869 866-264-7469
info@farmprogress.com
www.farmprogressshow.com

Dottie Rovner, National Sales/Shows Coordinator

Annual farm show of 400 exhibitors representing various types of agricultural products and services for farmers and agribusiness, including small operations to top producers. The show for 2006 is scheduled for September 29th toSeptember 30th.
August/September

793 Farm Science Review
Ohio State University
590 Woody Hayes Drive
232 Ag Engineering Building
Columbus, OH 43210-1057
614-926-6691
FAX: 614-292-9448 800-644-6377
gamble.18@osu.edu fsr.osu.edu

Chuck Gamble, Manager
Mattk Sullivan, Assistant Manager
Suzanne Steel, Media Coordinator

Annual show of 600 exhibitors of agricultural equipment, supplies and services.
140M Attendees September

794 **Farm/Ranch Expo**
Bacon Hedland Management
475 S Frontage Road
Suite 101
Burr Ridge, IL 60527
630-323-6880
FAX: 630-898-3550
Gene Bacon, Show Manager
160 booths
7M Attendees January

795 **Farmfest**
Farm Fairs
Highway 60 West
PO Box 731
Lake Crystal, MN 56055
507-726-6863
FAX: 507-726-6750
Annual show of 450 manufacturers, suppliers and distributors of farm equipment and machinery, computers and software products, chemicals, seeds and crops, and techniques of planting, tillage and harvesting.
50M Attendees

796 **Grain Elevator Processing Society International Technical Conference**
301 4th Avenue S, Suite 365
PO Box 15026
Minneapolis, MN 55415-0026
612-339-4625
FAX: 612-339-4644
info@geaps.com www.geaps.com
David Krejci, Executive Vice President/Secretary
Darren Grahsl, Manager/Member & Chapter Services
Chuck House, Manager/Comm & Professional Dev
Amy McGarrigle, Manager/Member Ser & Information
Jason Stones, Manager/Member Ser & Publications
250 booths of equipment, supplies and services for the grain farming industry.
2,000 Attendees March Founded: 1937

797 **Grain Feed Association Trade Show**
National Grain and Feed Association
1250 Eye Street NW
Suite 1003
Washington, DC 20005-3922
202-289-0873
FAX: 202-289-5388 ngfa@ngfa.org
Kendall Keith, President
One hundred and thirty booths exhibiting agribusiness products, supplies and services.
1.3M Attendees March

798 **Grape Grower Magazine Farm Show**
Western Agricultural Publishing Company
4974 E Clinton Way
Suite 123
Fresno, CA 93727-1520
559-261-0396
FAX: 559-252-7387
www.westagpubco.com
Phill Rhoads, Manager
Seminars, exhibits and prizes for grape growers. Contianing 80 booths and exhibits.
1000 Attendees March/November

799 **GrowerExpo**
Ball Publishing
335 N River Street
PO Box 9
Batavia, IL 60510-0009
630-208-9080
FAX: 630-208-9350 800-456-5380
Diane Blazek, President
A trade show devoted to horticulture and floriculture production and marketing. 200 booths.
2M Attendees January

800 **Hawkeye Farm Show**
Midwest Shows
PO Box 737
Austin, MN 55912
507-437-7969
FAX: 507-437-7752
www.farmshowsusa.com
Penny Swank, Show Manager
18000 Attendees March

801 **Hydroponic Society of America**
PO Box 1183
El Cerrito, CA 94583
510-232-2323
FAX: 510-232-2384
www.aquamist.com
Gene Brisbon, Executive Director
Bill Graham, VP
35 booths featuring the latest in hydroponic equipment.
500 Attendees April

802 **International Hoof-Care Summit**
American Farriers Journsl
223 Regency Court, PO Box 624
Suite 200
Brookfield, WI 53008-0624
262-782-4480
FAX: 262-782-1252 800-645-8455
info@lesspub.com
www.americanfarriers.com
Alice Musser, Conference Manager
Conference held for America's leading most innovative hoof-care professionals.
800 Attendees January

803 **International Off-Highway and Power Plant Meeting and Exposition**
Society of Automotive Engineers
400 Commonwealth Drive
Warrendale, PA 15096-0001
724-776-4841
FAX: 724-776-4026
advertising@sae.org www.sae.org
Diane Rogne, Show Manager
Sam Barill, Student Design Competition
Annual show of 270 suppliers of parts, components, materials and systems utilized in farm and industrial machinery and off-road and recreational vehicles.
5000 Attendees
Circulation: 84,000

804 **Irrigation Association Annual Meeting**
6260 Willow Oaks Corporate Drive, #120
Fairfax, VA 22031
703-573-3551
FAX: 800-937-8477
Bob Sears, Executive VP
425 booths of the newest in irrigation equipment for the agricultural industry.
3.5M Attendees November

805 **KFYR Radio Agri International Stock & Trade Show**
KFYR Radio
3500 East Rosser Avenue
PO Box 1658
Bismarck, ND 58501
701-580-0550
FAX: 701-255-8155 800-472-2170
mwall@clearchannel.com
www.kfyr.com
Syd Stewart, General Manager
Neil Cary, Contact
Annual show of 400 exhibitors of agricultural equipment, livestock and services.
15M Attendees February

806 **Mid South Farm Gin Supply Exhibit**
Southern Cotton Ginners Association
874 Cotton Gin Place
Memphis, TN 38106
901-947-3104
FAX: 901-947-3103
scga@netten.net
www.southerncottonginners.org
Chris Clegg, Chairman of Board
Will Wade, President/Tennessee
Tim Price, Executive VP
Richard Kelly, VP/Tennessee
Allen Espey, Vice President/Tenessee
Exhibits new technology and practices for those in the cotton industry.
February

807 **Mid-America Farm Show**
Salina Area Chamber of Commerce
120 W Ash Street
PO Box 586
Salina, KS 67401
785-827-9301
FAX: 785-827-9758
chamber@informatics.net
www.salinakansas.org
Don Weiser, Show Manager
Annual show of 325 exhibitors of agricultural equipment, supplies and services, including irrigation equipment, fertilizer, farm implements, hybrid seed, agricultural chemicals, tractors, feed, farrowing crates and equipment, silos and bins, storage equipment and farm buildings.
13M Attendees March 20, 21, 22 Founded: 1911

808 **Mid-America Horticulture Trade Show**
1000 N Rand Road
Suite 214
Wauconda, IL 60084-1188
847-526-2010
FAX: 847-526-3993 www.midam.org
Rand A Baldwin CAE, Managing Director
Suzanne Spohr, Show Manager
Mid-Am is the premier event featuring more than 650 leading suppliers offering countless products, equipment, and services for the horticulture industry. Mid-Am also offers a variety of educational seminars featuring the best and the brightest in the horticultural and business communities to help keep you informed of the latest trends.
January 17-19, 2007

809 **Mid-West Ag Expo**
Midwest Equipment Dealers Association
5330 Wall Street
Suite 100
Madison, WI 53718
608-240-4700
FAX: 608-240-2069

Gary Manke, Executive VP

Annual show of 300 exhibitors of farm machinery, including tractors, field equipment, minimum tillage, no-till harvesting equipment and farm supplies, lawn, garden and outdoor power equipment, irrigation equipment, farmstead mechanization equipment and dairy equipment.
18M Attendees March

810 **Midwest Agri Industries Expo**
Illinois Fertilizer & Chemical Association
130 W Dixie Highway
PO Box 186
Saint Anne, IL 60964-0186
815-939-1566
FAX: 815-427-6573 800-892-7122

Jean Trobec, President

Annual show of 130 manufacturers, suppliers and distributors of agricultural chemical and fertilizer application equipment, supplies and services.
2500 Attendees August, Danville

811 **Midwest Farm Show**
North Country Enterprises
5322 200 50th Street
Cadott, WI 54727-0001
715-894-4632

Bill Henry, President

250 booths. Top farm show exhibiting dairy and Wisconsin's tillage equipment, feed and seed.
11M+ Attendees January

812 **NHA Annual Convention**
National Hay Association
102 Treasurer Island Causeway
St Petersburg, FL 33706
727-367-9702
FAX: 727-367-9608 800-707-0014
haynha@aol.com
www.nationalhay.org

Raymond J Bricker, President
Tom Creech, First VP
Richard Larsen, Second VP
Rollie Bernth, Director
Don Kieffer, Executive Director

813 **National Agri-Marketing Association Conference**
National Agri-Marketing Association
11020 King Street
Suite 205
Overland Park, KS 66210
913-491-6500
FAX: 913-491-6502
info@nama.org www.nama.org

Blydon White, Executive Director

Annual show of 60 exhibitors of marketing and communication suppliers, including trade publications, radio and television broadcast sales organizations, premium/incentive manufacturers, printers, marketing research firms and photographers.
1400 Attendees April

814 **National Agricultural Plastics Congress**
American Society for Plasticulture
526 Brittany Drive
State College, PA 16803
814-238-7045
FAX: 814-238-7051
info@plasticulture.org
www.plasticulture.org

William Tietjen, President
Jodi Fleck-Arnold, VP
Edward Cary, Secretary/Treasurer
Patricia Heuser, Executive Director

Congress of research presentations, with exhibit area of equipment, supplies and services relating to greenhouse production and mulch film production of agricultural and horticultural crops.
225 Attendees March

815 **National Association Extension 4-H Agents Convention**
University of Georgia
Hoke Smith Annex
Athens, GA 30602
706-542-8804
freemand@vt.edu

Bo Ryles, State 4-H Leader
Heather Schultz, Live Stock Coordinator

50 booths for young people, youth staff and volunteers involved in 4-H.
1.2M Attendees November

816 **National Association of County Agricultural Agents Conference**
National Association of County Agricultural Agents
252 North Park Street
Decatur, IL 62523
217-876-1220
FAX: 217-877-5382
nacademail@aol.com www.nacad.com
Annual conference and exhibits for county agricultural agents and extension workers.

817 **National Association of Wheat Growers Convention**
415 2nd Street NE
Suite 300
Washington, DC 20002-4993
202-547-7800
FAX: 202-546-2638
wheatworld@wheatworld.org
www.wheatworld.org

Daren Coppock, CEO
Reese Sherman, President
Dale Schuler, First VP
Mark Gaede, Director/Government Affairs
June Silverberg, Director/Business Development

100 booths of major agri business exhibits including farm equipment and services.
February

818 **National Conservation Association District Annual Convention**
NACD Headquarters
509 Capitol Court NE
Washington, DC 20002-4946
202-547-6223
FAX: 202-547-6450
washington@nacdnet.org
www.nacdnet.org

Krysta Harden, CEO
Bill Wilson, President
Tim Reich, First VP
Olin Sims, Second Vice President
Beverly Russell, Executive Director

80 booths including companies who manufacture, service or who are otherwise involved with equipment used in agricultural production.
2M Attendees February

819 **National Corn Growers Association**

632 Cepi Drive
Chesterfield, MO 63005-6397
636-733-9004
FAX: 636-733-9005
corninfo@ncga.com www.ncga.com

Rick Tolman, CEO
Fred Stemme, VP/Marketing
Richard Glass,PhD, Research/Business Development
Mimie Ricketts, Director of Marketing
Peggy Findley, Direcetor of Conventions

550 booths of equipment, seed and chemicals.
4000 Attendees February

820 **National Custom Applicator Exposition**
Agribusiness Association of Iowa
900 Des Moines Street
Suite 150
Des Moines, IA 50309-5549
515-262-8323
FAX: 515-262-8960
info@agribiz.org www.agribiz.org

Ed Beaman, President/CEO

Annual show of 70 manufacturers, suppliers and distributors of agrichemicals, fertilizers, spray equipment, tanks, agriplanes and agricomputer and flotation equipment.
2500 Attendees August

821 **National Farm Machinery Show and Championship Tractor Pull**
Kentucky Fair and Exposition Center
937 Phillips Lane
PO Box 37130
Louisville, KY 40233-7130
502-367-5000
FAX: 502-367-5299
harold.workman@mail.state.ky.us
www.farmmachineryshow.org

Harold Workman, President/CEO

Annual show of 800 plus exhibitors of agricultural products, equipment, supplies and services.
293M Attendees February

822 **National Fertilizer Solutions Association Annual Meeting**
339 Consort Drive
Manchester, MO 63011-4439
636-256-6650
FAX: 636-256-4901

Kelly O'Brien-Wray, Editor
Fred Speckmann, Sales Director

120 booths. Largest fertilizer trade show in the country.
1.5M Attendees December

823 **National Grain Feed Association Annual Meeting**
1250 Eye Street NW
Suite 1003
Washington, DC 20005
202-289-0873
FAX: 202-289-5388
ngfa@ngfa.org www.ngfa.org

Steve Nail, Chairman
Tom Coyle, Second Vice Chair
Kendall Keith, President
Ronald D Olson, First Vice President
Stacey Jacobs, Meetings Mgr/Executive Assistant

For grain, feed and related commercial businesses.
1.3M Attendees March/April Founded: 1896

824 National Grange Annual Meeting
1616 H Street NW
Washington, DC 20006
202-628-3507
FAX: 202-347-1091 888-447-2643
William Steel, President
Agricultural forum.
3M Attendees November

825 National No-Tillage Conference
No-Till Farmer
225 Regency Court, PO Box 624
Suite 200
Brookfield, WI 53008-0624
262-782-4480
FAX: 262-782-1252 800-645-8455
info@lesspub.com
www.no-tillfarmer.com
Mike Lessitor, Executive Vice President
Alice Musser, Conference Manager
Conference held for America's leading most innovative no-till farmers.
January

826 National Orange Show
689 E Street
PO Box 5749
San Bernardino, CA 92408
909-888-6788
FAX: 909-889-7666
nationalorangeshow.com
Esther Armstrong, Executive Director
Brad Randall, Manager
Agricultural forum.
262M Attendees May Founded: 1911

827 National Potato Council's Annual Meeting
National Potato Council
1300 L Street
Suite 910
Washington, DC 20005
202-682-9456
spudinfo@nationalpotatocouncil.org
www.nationalpotatocouncil.org
John Keeling, Chief Executive Officer
Holly Stubblebine, Communications Director
Annual meeting and exhibits of potato growing equipment, supplies and services.

828 New England Equipment Dealers Association
PO Box 895
Concord, NH 03302-0895
603-225-5510
FAX: 603-225-5510
George M Becker, Managing Director
Annual convention and trade show held the first weekend in December for farm, industrial and outdoor equipment dealers in the six New England states. 95 booths.
300 Attendees December

829 New England Grows
Hynes Convention Center
415 Summer Street
Boston, MA 07115
617-954-2000
FAX: 617-954-2125
info@mccahome.com
www.negrows.org
M Virginia Wood, Executive Director
Dianne B McCulley, Director Exhibits
Diane Zinck, Exhibits Coordinator
Annual show of 620 exhibitors of the latest plant material, products, equipment and services for green industry professionals.
13000 Attendees February

830 North American Deer Farmers Association Annual Conference & Exhibit
North American Deer Farmers Association
1215 N 7th St
Ste 104
Lake City, MN 55041-1266
651-345-5600
FAX: 651-345-5603
info@nadefa.org www.nadefa.org
Phyllis Menden, Executive Director
Annual show of 30+ exhibitors of deer farming equipment, supplies and services.
300 Attendees February Founded: 1983

831 North American Farm and Power Show
Tradexpos
811 W Oakland Avenue
PO Box 1067
Austin, MN 55912
507-437-4697
FAX: 507-437-8917 800-949-3976
steve@tradexpos.com
www.tradexpos.com
Steve Guenthner, Show Director
Agri-business farm show for the 5-state region. Free admission and parking.
28M Attendees March

832 North American International Livestock Exposition
Kentucky Fair and Exposition Center
937 Phillips Lane
PO Box 37130
Louisville, KY 40209-7130
502-367-5000
FAX: 502-367-5139
ellenaderson@mail.state.ky.us
www.livestockexpo.org
Debbie Burda, Booking/Events
Ellen Anderson, Event Contact
Purebred livestock show with more than 20,000 entries in eight major divisions: dairy cattle, dairy goats, llamas, quarter horses, draft horses, market swine, beef cattle, sheep. Held at Kentucky Fair and Exposition Center in Louisville, Kentucky.
November

833 Northwest Agricultural Show
4672 Drift Creek Road SE
Sublimity, OR 97385-9764
503-769-7120
FAX: 503-769-3549
www.nwagshow.com
James Heater, Show Manager
Amy Patrick, Exhibits Director
Features educational meetings, seminars and exhibits of agricultural equipment.
15M Attendees January Founded: 1979

834 Nut Grower Magazine Farm Show
Western Agricultural Publishing Company
4974 E Clinton Way
Suite 123
Fresno, CA 93727-1520
559-252-7000
FAX: 559-252-7387
Phill Rhoads, Manager
Productions seminars, guest speakers, prizes and exhibits for nut growers. Containing 80 booths and exhibits.
1000 Attendees March

835 Nut Grower Magazine Harvest Show
Western Agricultural Publishing Company
4974 E Clinton Way
Suite 123
Fresno, CA 93727-1520
559-261-0396
FAX: 559-252-7387
Phill Rhoads, Manager
Productions seminars, guest speakers, prizes and exhibits for nut growers. Containing 80 booths and exhibits.
1000 Attendees November

836 Ozark Fall Farmfest
Ozark Empire Fair
3001 North Grant Street
PO Box 630
Springfield, MO 65308
417-833-2660
FAX: 417-833-3769
www.ozarkempirefair.com
Pat Lloyd, Manager
Annual show of 700 exhibitors with about 600 booths of agricultural products and services, including livestock.
40M Attendees October

837 PMA Convention & Exposition
Produce Marketing Association
1500 Casho Mill Road
PO Box 6036
Newark, DE 19711-3547
302-738-7100
FAX: 302-731-2409
pma@pma.com www.pma.com
Janet Erickson, Chairman
Bryan Silbermann, President
Dave Corsi, Retail Chairman
Gene Harris, Food Service Chairman
A trade association of companies engaged in the marketing of fresh and safe produce and floral products. Show will inlcude 600 exhibitors with 1,600 booths.
16000 Attendees October Founded: 1949

838 Pest World
National Pest Management Association
9300 Lee Highway
Suite 301
Fairfax, VA 22031
703-738-8330
FAX: 703-352-3031
www.pestworld.org
Robert Lederer, Executive VP
Dominique Broyles, Director Conventions/Meetings
240 booths.
4000 Attendees October

839 Prairie Farmer Farm Progress Show
Farm Progress Publishers
1301 E Mound Road
Decatur, IL 62526-9394
217-877-9070
FAX: 217-877-9695
Sherry Stout, Editor
Jeffrey Smith, Advertising
One of the largest farm shows in the country.

840 Society for Biomolecular Screening Trade Show
Society for Biomolecular Screening
36 Tamarack Avenue
Suite 348
Danbury, CT 06810
203-788-8828
FAX: 203-748-7557
sbsemail@aol.com www.sbsonline.org

Al Kolbh, President
Christine Giordano, Executive Director
Larry Walker, Editor-in-Chief
Marietta Manono, Manager Meetings/Exhibitions

Technical sessions, exhibits, exhibitor tutorials, short courses, discussion groups related to discovery in the pharmaceutical and agrochemical industry. Containing 74 booths and 181 exhibits.
700 Attendees September

841 Soil and Water Conservation Society Convention
Soil and Water Conservation Society
945 SW Ankeny Road
Ankeny, IA 50021-9764
515-289-2331
FAX: 515-289-1227 800-843-7645
swsc@swsc.org www.swsc.org

Craig A Cox, Executive VP

60 exhibitors
1200 Attendees Summer

842 St. Louis All Equipment Expo
Mississippi Valley Equipment Association
10805 Sunset Office Drive
Suite 405
Saint Louis, MO 63127
314-966-5757
FAX: 314-966-8438 800-430-6334
stLfarmshow@mvea.com
www.mvea.com

Joyce Wright, Show Manager

Manufacturers, suppliers and distributors of farm equipment, outdoor power equipment, supplies and agriculture products. Containing 350 booths.
15M Attendees December

843 Sunbelt Agricultural Exposition
290-G Harper Boulevard
PO Box 28
Moultrie, GA 31788
229-985-1968
FAX: 229-890-8518
info@sunbeltexpo.com
www.sunbeltexpo.com

Chip Blalock, Director
Dian Causey, Exhibitor Coordinator

Over 1,200 exhibitors showing the latest agricultural technology in products and equipment plus harvesting and tillage demonstrations in the field. Largest farm show in North America's premier farm show.
200M Attendees Oct 17-19

844 Tree Fruit Expo
Western Agricultural Publishing Company

4974 E Clinton Way
Suite 123
Fresno, CA 93727-1520
559-252-7000
FAX: 559-252-7387

Phill Rhoads, Manager

Productions seminars, dessert contest, guest speakers, prizes and exhibits for tree fruit growers. Containing 80 booths and exhibits.
1000 Attendees October

845 United Fresh Fruit and Vegetable Association Annual Convention
United Fresh Fruit & Vegetable Association
1901 Pennsylvania Avenue NW
Suite 1100
Washington, DC 20006
202-624-4989
FAX: 202-303-3433
united@uffva.org www.uffva.org

Thomas Stenzel, Chief Executive Officer
Mark Overbay, Manager Communications
30000 Attendees

846 Virginia Farm Show
Lee Publications
6113 State Highway 5
PO Box 121
Palatine Bridge, NY 13428-0121
518-673-2269
FAX: 518-673-3245 800-218-5586

Ken Maring, Trade Show Manager

This show caters to the full-time farmer. In addition to exhibits of all the major lines of equipment and services, there are seminars presented by industry experts in dairy, beef and crop production.
January Founded: 1982

847 Walnut Council Conference
Walnut Council
1011 North 725 West
West Lafayette, IN 47906-9431
765-583-3501
FAX: 765-583-3512
www.walnutcouncil.org

R Daniel Schmokey, President
Larry R Frye, VP
Liz Jackson, Executive Director
Robert D Burke, Legislative Committee
Keith Wolste, Nut Culture Committee

Annual conference and exhibits of equipment, supplies and services for walnut growing.
July Founded: 1970

848 Western Farm Show
Southwestern Association
638 W 39th Street
PO Box 419264-64141
Kansas City, MO 64141-6264
816-561-5323
FAX: 816-561-1249 800-762-5616
donnah@swassn.com
www.westernfarmshow.com

Jeff Flora, CEO
Curtis Kleappel, Show Manager
Donna Haughenberry, Exhibition Relations Manager

Annual show of 700 manufacturers, suppliers and distributors of equipment, supplies and services relating to the agricultural industry.
35M Attendees February Founded: 1962

Directories & Databases

849 AGRICOLA
US National Agricultural Library
10301 Baltimore Avenue
Beltsville, MD 20705
301-504-5755
FAX: 301-504-7473
director@nalusda.gov
www.nalusda.gov

Peter Young, Director
Eleanor Freerson, Deputy Director
Gary K McCone, Associate Director
Len Cary, Public Affairs Specialist
Deborah Richardson, Tours/Exhibits

A database containing more than 3.3 million citations to journal literature, government reports, proceedings, books, periodicals, theses, patents, audiovisuals, electronic information, and other materials related to agriculture and its allied sciences.

Bibliographic Founded: 1962

850 ARI Network
Ari Network Services
11425 W Lake Park Drive
Suite 900
Milwaukee, WI 53224-3025
414-787-7676
FAX: 414-283-4357 800-558-9044
info@airnet.com www.arinet.com

Brian E Dearing, President/CEO
Timothy Sherlock, VP/Finance/CFO/Secretary/Treasurer
John C Bray, VP/New Market Division
Jeffrey E Horn, VP/North American Sales
Michael E McGurk, VP/Technology Operations

Offers current information on agricultural business, financial and weather information as well as statistical information for farmers.
Numeric

851 Ag Ed Network
ARI Network Services
11425 W Lake Park Drive
Suite 900
Milwaukee, WI 53224
414-787-7676
FAX: 414-973-4357 800-558-9044

Brian E Dearing, President/CEO
John C Bray, New Market Development

Offers access to more than 1500 educational agriculture lessons covering farm business management and farm production.
Full-text

852 Agri Marketing: Marketing Services Guide Issue
Doane Agricultural Services
11701 Borman Drive
Suite 300
Saint Louis, MO 63146-4139
314-569-2700
FAX: 314-569-1083
info@agrimarketing.com
www.agrimarketing.com

Bill Schuermann, Editorial Director/Publisher
Judy Knoll, Group Manager/Sales & Services

Offers lists of top agricultural companies in the United States, top agricultural advertisers and marketing services firms, as well as network programmers related to the agriculture industry. *$30.00*
10 per year Founded: 1969
Circulation: 9,000

853 Agricultural Research Institute: Membership Directory
Agricultural Research Institute
9650 Rockville Pike
Bethesda, MD 20814-3998
301-530-7122
FAX: 301-571-1816 ari@nal.usda.gov

Richard A Herrett, Executive Director

125 member institutions; also lists study panels and committees interested in envi-

ronmental issues, pest control, agricultural meteorology, biotechnology, food irradiation, agricultural policy, research and development, food safety, technology transfer and remote sensing. *$50.00*
Annual

854 American Feed Industry Association: Software Directory
American Feed Industry Association
1501 Wilson Boulevard
Suite 1100
Arlington, VA 22209
703-524-0810
FAX: 703-524-1921
afia@afia.org www.afia.org
Robert Galloway, Chairman
Joel Newman, President/CEO/Corporate Treasurer
Rex Runyon, VP/Public Relations
Jeff Haas, Director/Sales/Marketing
Richard Sellers, VP/Feed & Control
About 20 companies that design software programs applicable to the feed industry. *$25.00*

855 American Fruit Grower: Source Book Issue
Meister Media Worldwide
37733 Euclid Avenue
Willoughby, OH 44094-5992
440-942-2000
FAX: 440-942-0662 800-572-7740
joe_monahan@meisternet.com
www.meisterpro.com
Richard T Meister, Chairman
Gary T Fitzgerald, President
Joe Monahan, Group Publisher
Offers a list of manufacturers and distributors of equipment and supplies for the commercial fruit growing industry. *$19.95*
66 pages
Circulation: 35,143

856 American Meat Science Association Directory of Members
American Meat Science Association
1111 N Dunlap Avenue
Savoy, IL 61874
217-356-5368
FAX: 217-398-4119
information@meatscience.org
www.meatscience.org
Dennis R Buege, President
C Ann Hollingsworth, Secretary/Treasurer
Thomas Powell, Executive Director
Rachel Hamilton, Project Director
Offers information on over 900 persons that are engaged in meat research, extension and education in industry, government and other organizations. *$20.00*
230 pages Biennial Founded: 1964

857 American Society of Consulting Arborists: Membership Directory
American Society of Consulting Arborists
15245 Shady Grove Road
Suite 130
Rockville, MD 20850
301-947-0483
FAX: 301-990-9771
asca@mgmtsol.com
www.asca-consultants.org
Steven Geist, President
Beth Palys, Executive Director
About 270 persons specializing in the growth and care of urban shade and ornamental trees; includes expert witnesses and monetary appraisals.
Annual March

858 Aquaria and Fish Forum
CompuServe Information Service
5000 Arlington Centre Boulevard
Columbus, OH 43220-5439
614-457-8600
FAX: 614-538-3383
www.compuserve.com
John Benn, Forum Administrator
Offers trade and hobby information on fish, aquaria and aquatic sciences.
Bulletin Board

859 Biological & Agricultural Index
HW Wilson Company
950 University Avenue
Bronx, NY 10452-4224
718-888-8405
FAX: 800-590-1617 800-367-6770
custserv@hwwilson.com
www.hwwilson.com
Harold Regan, President/CEO
Ann Case, VP Editorial
Phillip Taylor, Director Customer Service
Amy Rosenbaum, Senior Manager/International
Provides fast access to core literature. In addition to citations to research and feature articles, users finding indexing of reports of symposia and conferences, and citations to current book reviews. Available on Web and disc.
359 pages Founded: 1898

860 Citrus & Vegetable Magazine: Farm Equipment Directory Issue
Vance Publishing
1901 W 84th Terrace
Suite 200
Lenexa, KS 66214
913-438-8700
FAX: 913-438-0695
cvmscott@compuserve.com
www.vancepublishing.com
William C Vance, Chairman/CEO
Michael H Ross, President/COO
Judy Riggs, Director/Research Marketing
Offers information on a list of manufacturers of produce and citrus growing, handling, picking and packaging equipment. *$25.00*
48 pages Annual Founded: 1938
Circulation: 12,000

861 Complete Guide to Gardening and Landscaping by Mail
Mailorder Gardening Association
5836 Rockburn Woods Way
Elkridge, MD 21075
410-409-9830
FAX: 410-540-9827
www.mailordergardening.com
Bruce Frasier, President
Jim Bryant, First VP
Roberta Simpson, Second VP
Jean Vivlamore Norton, Treasurer
Camille Cimino, Executive Director
Member catalogers who sell gardening and nursery stock and supplies to consumers. *$2.00*
Annual Founded: 1934

862 Contemporary World Issues: Agricultural Crisis in America
ABC-CLIO
130 Cremona Drive
PO Box 1911
Santa Barbara, CA 93117-1911
805-681-1911
FAX: 805-685-9685 800-422-2546
Ron Boehm, President/CEO
List of agencies and organizations in the US concerned with agricultural issues. *$50.00*
Founded: 1953

863 Crop Protection Reference
Vance Communications Corporation
90 Williams Street
Suite 504
New York, NY 10038
212-851-1366
FAX: 646-733-6010 800-839-2420
cpp@cppress.com
www.greenbook.net
Hilda Vazquez, Director Marketing/Sales
A single comprehensive source of up-to-date label information of crop protection products marketed in the United States by basic manufacturers and formulators. Extensive product indexing helps to locate products by: brand name, manufacturer crop site, mode of action, disease, insect, week, product category, common name, tank mix. *$50.00*
Annual

864 Directory for Small-Scale Agriculture
US Department of Agriculture
Secretary oF Agriculture
Whitten Building/Room 200A
Washington, DC 20250-0001
202-012-2000
Offers information on persons involved with projects and activities relating to small-scale agriculture. *$5.50*
119 pages

865 Directory of American Agriculture
Agricultural Resources & Communications
4210 Wam-Teau Drive
Wamego, KS 66547
785-456-9705
FAX: 785-456-1654 800-404-7940
chris@agresources.com
www.agresources.com
Christina Wilson, President
This directory lists over 7,000 state and national associations involved in providing products and services related to food and fiber industries, in 27 categories. There are categorical indexes as well. Includes guide to Washington, D.C. offices, USDA listings, and guide to ag commodity commissions. Available on CD for $99. *$64.95*
350 pages Founded: 1988
Printed in on matte stock : CD

866 Directory of State Departments of Agriculture
US Department of Agriculture
1400 Independence Avenue SW
Whitten Building/Room 200A
Washington, DC 20250-0001
202-690-7650
Honor Mike Johanns, Secretary of Agriculture

Offer valuable information on all the state departments of agriculture, including their officials.

73 pages Biennial Founded: 1862

867 Electronic Pesticide Reference: EPR II

Vance Communications Corporation
90 Williams Street
Suite 504
New York, NY 10038
212-851-1366
FAX: 646-733-6020
cpp@cppress.com www.greenbook.net

Hilda Vazquez, Director Marketing/Sales

Complete electronic reference to our 1,500 crop protection products; a full range of product information: full text labels and supplemental labels, full text MSDS's, product summaries, list of labeled tank mixes, worker protection information, DOT shipping information, SARA Title III reporting information. Search by brand name, manufacturer, common name crop, plant, site, weed, disease, insect plus much more. All versions of EPR II are provided on CD-ROM for windows.

868 Food and Agricultural Export Directory

National Technical Information Service
5285 Port Royal Road
Springfield, VA 22161
703-874-4650
FAX: 703-605-6900 800-553-6847
orders@ntis.gov
www.ntis.gov/products

Includes up to date listings of federal and state agencies, trade associations and a host of other organizations that can help you penetrate foreign markets. Includes phone and fax numbers.

100 pages Annual

869 Food, Hunger, Agribusiness: A Directory of Resources

Center For Third World Organizing
1218 E 21st Street
Oakland, CA 94606
510-533-7583
FAX: 510-533-0923

Lian Cheun, MAAP Director

Offers information on organizations and publishers of books and other materials on food, hunger and agribusiness overseas. *$12.95*

160 pages

870 Grain & Milling Annual

Sosland Publishing Company
4800 Main Street
Suite 100
Kansas City, MO 64112-2513
816-756-1000
FAX: 816-756-0494
web@sosland.com www.sosland.com

Morton Sosland, Chairman

Offers a list of milling companies, mills, grain companies and cooperatives. *$115.00*

Annual
Circulation: 6,000

871 Grain Journal

Country Journal Publishing Company
3065 Pershing Court
Decatur, IL 62526
217-877-9660
FAX: 217-877-6647 800-728-7511
mark@grainnet.com
www.grainnet.com

Mark Avery, Publisher
Ed Zdrojewski, Editor
Deb Coontz, Advertising Sales
Jeff Miller, Advertising Sales
Jody Sexton, Production Manager

Provides a list of over 700 equipment manufacturers, suppliers and system designers, as well as offering useful information on governmental agencies relevant to the grain industry. *$40.00*

254 pages Bi-Monthly Founded: 1972
Circulation: 13,000
Mailing list available for rent 10,000 names $600 per M.
Printed in 4 colors on glossy stock

872 Guernsey Breeders' Journal: Convention Directory Issue

American Guernsey Association
7614 Slate Ridge Boulevard
Reynoldsburg, OH 43068
614-864-2409
FAX: 614-864-5614
info@usguernsey.com
www.usguernsey.com

Lynnette Wright, Editor
Seth Johnson, Executive Secretary/Treasurer
Mary Ann D'Ippolito, Director/Finance
Josey Morris, Programs Coordinator
Ida Albert, Records Director

A convention directory offering a list of officers and national members of the American Guernsey Cattle Association. *$20.00*

10 per year

873 Healthy Harvest: A Global Directory of Sustainable Agriculture

AgAccess
424 2nd Street
Suite B
Davis, CA 95616
530-756-0778
FAX: 530-756-0484

Chris Fisher, President

This directory offers a list of over 1,800 agriculture and horticulture training institutions, research institutions and development programs. *$24.95*

175 pages Annual
Circulation: 3,000

874 Holstein Association News

Holstein Association
1 Holstien Place
Brattleboro, VT 05302-0808
802-254-4551
FAX: 802-254-8251 800-952-5200
info@holstein.com
www.holsteinusa.com

John M Meyer, CEO
Tom A Nunes, President
Beth Patchen, Communication Specialist

Bimonthly newsletter provides active customers with information on the association programs and services and how to intergrate them into their dairy operations.

15 pages Founded: 1953
Printed in 4 colors on glossy stock

875 Hort Expo Northwest

Mt Adams Publishing and Design
14161 Fort Road
White Swan, WA 98952-9786
509-848-2706
FAX: 509-848-3896 800-554-0860
hortexponw@aol.com
www.hortexponw.com

Vee Graves, Editor
Julie LaForge, Advertising Manager

Besides being mailed to it's family of subscribers it is alson available complimentary at horticulture shows in the Northwest.

32 pages Annually Founded: 1989
Circulation: 8,700 10,200 names $200 per M.
Printed in 4 colors on glossy stock

876 Industrial Economic Information

Global Insight
800 Baldwin Tower
Eddystone, PA 19022
610-490-4000
FAX: 610-490-2557 800-933-3374
info@globalinsight.com
www.globalinsight.com

Joseph E Kasputys, Chair/President/CEO
Pricella Trumbull, Chief Operations Officer
Vicki Van Mater, VP
Kenneth J McGill, Product Management

Global Insight's unique perspective provides the most comprehensive economic and financial coverage of countries, regions and industries from any source.

877 International Green Front Report

Friends of the Trees Society
PO Bo 253
Twisp, WA 98856
509-997-9200
FAX: 509-997-4812
friendsofthetree@yahoo.com
www.friendsofthetrees.net

Michael Pilarski, Director

Organizations and periodicals concerned with sustainable forestry and agriculture and related fields. *$7.00*

192 pages Irregular Founded: 1978
Circulation: 8,000

878 International Soil Tillage Research Organization

International Soil Tillage Research
1680 Madison Avenue
Wooster, OH 44691-4114
330-263-3700
FAX: 330-263-3658

A Franzluebbers, Editor-in-Chief

More than 750 individuals and institutions in 72 countries involved in the research or application of soil tilage and related subjects. *$100.00*

10 per year

879 Journal of the American Society of Farm Managers and Rural Appraisers

ASFMRA
950 S Cherry Street
Suite 508
Denver, CO 80246
303-758-3513
FAX: 303-758-0190
asfmra@agri-associations.org
www.asfmra.org

Cheryl L Cooley, Manager Communications/PR

Annually
Mailing list available for rent 2500 names
$1M per M.

880 **Landscape & Irrigation: Product Source Guide**
Adams Business Media
675 3rd Street
New York, NY 10017-5704
212-661-6360
FAX: 212-370-0736
info@admmail.com
www.americanbusinessmedia.com
Gordon T Hughes, President/CEO
Jean M Maddalon, Chief Financial Officer
John Holden, Senior VP
Claudia Flowers, VP/Business Development
Steve Ennen, Director Communications

Offers information on suppliers, distributors and manufacturers serving the professional agriculture and landscaping community. *$ 6.00*

Circulation: 37,000

881 **Material Safety Data Sheet Reference**
Vance Communications Corporation
90 Williams Street
Suite 504
New York, NY 10038
212-851-1366
FAX: 646-733-6020
cpp@cppress.com
www.greenbook.net
Hilda Vazquez, Director Marketing Sales
Regulatory and product safety requirements. Contains full text MSDS's for products listed in the 1999 15th Edition Crop Protection Reference plus additional safety information such as DOT shipping information, SARA Title III regulations, Hazardous Chemical inventory reporting information plus much more.

882 **Meat and Poultry Inspection Directory**
US Department of Agriculture
Administration Building
Room 344
Washington, DC 20250-0001
202-690-7650
FAX: 202-512-2250
www.access.gpo.gov
Offers valuable information on all meat and poultry plants that ship meat interstate and therefore come under the US Department of Agriculture inspection. *$16.00*
600 pages SemiAnnual

883 **NASDA Directory**
National Association of State Dept of Agriculture
1156 15th Street NW
Suite 1020
Washington, DC 20005-1711
202-235-5454
FAX: 202-296-9686
nasda@nasda.org www.nasda.org
J Carlton Courter, President
Richard Kirchoff, Executive VP/CEO
Valoria Loveland, VP
Patty Judge, Secretary/Treasurer
Top agricultural officials in 50 states and four territories. *$100.00*
Annual

884 **National Agri-Marketing Association Directory**
11020 King Street
Suite 205
Overland Park, KS 66210-1201
913-491-6500
FAX: 913-491-6502
agrimktg@nama.org www.nama.org
Tom Taylor, President
Eldon White, Executive VP/CEO
Jenny White, Director/Communications/Operations
Orginated as the Chicago Area Agricultural Advertising Association with 39 charter members. In 1963 the name was changed to the National Agricultural Advertising and Marketing Association and the present name was assumed in 1973. *$150.00*
2500 pages Annual Spring Founded: 1956

885 **National Organic Directory**
Community Alliance with Family Farmers

36355 Russell Boulevard
PO Box 363
Davis, CA 95617-0363
530-756-8518
FAX: 530-756-7857 800-892-3832
nod@caff.org www.caff.org
Judith Redmond, President
George Davis, VP
Pete Price, Secretary
Poppy Davis, Treasurer
Leland Swendon, Executive Director
Wriiten for all sectors of the booming organic food and fiber industry. Offers international listing with full contact information and extensive, cross-referenced index. Also provides regulatory updates, essays by industry leaders and other ressources. *$47.95*
400 pages Annual Founded: 1983 ISBN 1-891894-04-8
Circulation: 2,500

886 **Organic Pages Online North American Resource Directory**
Organic Trade Association
60 Wells Street
PO Box 547
Greenfield, MA 01301
413-774-7511
FAX: 413-774-6432
info@ota.com www.ota.com
Katherine DiMatteo, Executive Director
Holly Givens, Communications Director
David Gagnon, Director Operations
Lisa Murray, Sales Manager
Linda Lutz, Membership Manager
Provides over 1,300 listings by company name, brand name, business type, supply chain, product and service.

Printed in 2 colors

887 **Produce Marketing Association Membership Directory and Buyer's Guide**
Produce Marketing Association
1500 Casho Mill Road
PO Box 6036
Newark, DE 19711-3547
302-738-7100
FAX: 302-731-2409
bsilbermann@mail.pma.com
www.pma.com
Bryan Silbermann, President
Julie Koch, Production Manager
A list of over 2,000 members that are involved in retail grocery and foodservice marketing businesses, including international companies. *$70.00*
280 pages Annual

888 **Professional Workers in State Agricultural Experiment Stations**
US Department of Agriculture
1400 Independence Avenue SW
Whitten Bldg/Room 200A
Washington, DC 20250-0001
202-690-7650
FAX: 202-512-2250
www.access.gpo.gov
Honor Mike Johanns, Secretary of Agriculture
This directory offers information on academic and research personnel in all agricultural, forestry, aquaculture and home economics industries. *$15.00*
289 pages Annual Founded: 1963

889 **Turf & Ornamental Reference**
Vance Communications Corporatión
90 Williams Street
Suite 504
New York, NY 10038
212-851-1366
FAX: 646-733-6020
cpp@cppress.com
www.greenbook.net
Hilda Vazquez, Director Marketing/Sales
Professional guide to plant protection problems. Provides the turf and ornamental industry with a single comprehensive source of up to date label and MSDS information of plant protection products marketed in the United States by basic manufacturers and formulators. Extensive product indexing helps to locate products by: brand name; manufacturer; plant site; mode of action; disease, insect, weed; product category; common name; tank mix. *$159.00*

890 **US Agriculture**
Global Insight
800 Baldwin Tower Boulevard
Eddystone, PA 19022-1368
610-490-4000
FAX: 610-490-2770
info@globalinsight.com
www.globalinsight.com
Harry Baumes, Manager
This large database offers information on US macroeconomic farm crop and related agricultural data.

891 **Warehouses Licensed Under US Warehouse Act**
Farm Service Agency-US Dept. of Agriculture
1400 Independence Avenue SW
Stop Code 0506
Washington, DC 20013-2415
202-720-7809
FAX: 202-690-0014
Eric Parsons, Chief Public Affairs
Agricultural warehouses voluntarily licensed under the US Warehouse Act governing public storage facilities.
Annual

892 **Who is Who: A Directory of Agricultural Engineers Available for Work**
American Society of Agricultural Engineers
2950 Niles Road
Saint Joseph, MI 49085-8607
269-429-0300
FAX: 269-429-3852
hq@asae.org www.asae.org

Melissa Moore, Executive VP
Donna Hull, Publications

This directory pertains to the availability of agricultural engineers to work in developing countries. The directory lists over 650 individuals from 60 countries, primarily engineers, available for work in land or water management, farm structures and other aspects of the field. *$25.00*
210 pages

893 **Who's Who in the Egg & Poultry Industry in the US and Canada**
WATT Publishing Company
122 S Wesley Avenue
Mount Morris, IL 61054
815-734-4171
FAX: 815-734-4201
olentine@wattmm.com
www.wattnet.com

Jim Watt, Chairman/CEO

Contains a detailed statistical section of key contacts in the industry. Includes industry phone book, genetic hatcheries and products, company directories, poultry marketers by city and state, refrigerated warehouses and federal agencies and associations. *$105.00*
Annual

894 **Who's Who in the Egg & Poultry Industry: International**
WATT Publishing Company
122 S Wesley Avenue
Mount Morris, IL 61054-1497
815-734-4171
FAX: 815-734-7727
olentine@wattmm.com
www.wattnet.com

Jim Watt, Chairman/CEO

Contains a detailed statistical section of key contacts in the industry. Includes industry phone book, genetic hatcheries and products, company directories, poultry marketers by city and state, refrigerated warehouses and federal agencies and associations.
310 pages

895 **World Databases in Agriculture**
National Register Publishing
562 Central Avenue
New Providence, NJ 07974

FAX: 908-673-1189 800-473-7020

Eileen Fanning, Managing Editor

Agricultural information on databases, including CD-ROM, magnetic tape, diskette, online, fax or databroadcast worldwide. *$165.00*

Industry Web Sites

896 **www.aaccnet.org**
American Association of Cereal Chemists

Nonprofit, international organization of nearly 4,000 members who are specialists in the use of cereal grains in foods. AACC has been an innovative leader in gathering and disseminating scientific and technical information to professionals in the grain based foods industry worldwide for over 85 years. We know it's not easy to keep up with the latest technology, that's why AACC is here to help you. We're a tool unlike any other in your lab or office. Industry leaders turn to and trust AACC.

897 **www.aaea.org**
American Agricultural Economics Association

The professional association for agricultural economists and related fields.

898 **www.aafco.org**
Association of American Feed Control Officials

Officials of government agencies at the state and federal levels engaged in the regulation and distribution of products, animal feeds and livestock remedies.

899 **www.aagiwa.org**
American Assoc Grain Inspection & Weighing

Established to provide a liaison between the Federal Grain Inspection Service and designated agencies.

900 **www.aaminc.org**
American Agriculture Movement

An umbrella organization composed of state organizations representing family farm producers.

901 **www.aapausa.org**
AFIA Alfalfa Processors Council

Information for the processors and suppliers in the alfalfa industry.

902 **www.abfnet.org**
American Beekeeping Federation

For honey producers, packers, suppliers and shippers of honey products.

903 **www.aceweb.org**
Agricultural Communicators in Education

For writers, editors, broadcasters and communicators who are involved in the dissemination of agricultural, food sciences and natural resource information in land-grant colleges, federal and state agencies, international agencies and other private communications work.

904 **www.adsa.org**
American Dairy Science Association

Organization of professional researchers. Publishes journals and holds annual member meetings. Provides leadership in scientific and technical support to sustain and grow the global dairy industry through generation, dissemination and exchange of information and services.

905 **www.afgc.org**
American Forage and Grassland Council

To promote the use of forages as economically and environmentally sound agriculture through education, communication, and professional development of producers, scientists, educators and commercial representatives and through communication with policy makers and consumers in North America.

906 **www.afia.org**
American Feed Industry Association

Works to improve animal production practices in the United States, works to dispel misconceptions that a diet containing meat, milk and eggs is unhealthy and dispel that animals raised for foods in the United States are mistreated.

907 **www.ag.ohio-state.edu/~farmshow**
North American Farm Show Council/Ohio State Univ

Agriculture trade shows and suppliers of services to these shows. Strives to improve education, communication and evaluation and provide the best possible marketing showcase for exhibitors and related products to the farmer/rancher/producer customer.

908 **www.agconsultants.org**
American Society of Agricultural Consultants

For agricultural consultants acting as an information base for members. Specific purpose is to foster the science of agricultural consulting in all its varied fields; promote the profession and maintain high standards under which the members conduct their service to the public, hold meeting for the exchange of ideas and the study of the profession of agricultural consulting.

909 **www.agday.org**
Agriculture Council of America

Celebrating American agriculture by educating consumers about agriculture's role in daily life.

910 **www.agnic.org/**
Agriculture Network Information Center

Access to experts in various fields of agriculture as well as links to agricultural databases. Find out about conferences, meetings and seminars in your area.

911 **www.agribusiness.com**
National Agri-Marketing Association

Industry information, member directory and links to member sites.

912 **www.agview.com/**

All aspects of agriculture: Usenet groups, Web resources, archives, mailing lists, etc.

913 **www.amseed.com**
American Seed Trade Association

Producers of seeds for planting purposes.

914 **www.amsoy.org**
American Soybean Association

A membership-driven grassroots policy organization that represents US soybean farmers. Offers a variety of programs in leadership, education, marketing trade, conservation best management practices and profitability. Promotes market access for US soybean exorts working in cooperation with other commodity groups and international organizations.

915 **www.angus.org**
American Angus Association

The largest angus breed registry association in the world.

916 **www.animalalliance.org**
Animal Agricultural Alliance

The Animal Agricultural Alliance is a 501 (c)(3) education foundation. The alliance's mission is to support and promote animal agricultural practices that provide for farm animal well-being through sound science and public education.

917 **www.aphis.usda.gov/npb**
National Plant Board

Representatives from each state and Puerto Rico interested in protecting agriculture, forestry and horticulture throughout the US.

918 **www.apms.org**
Aquatic Plant Management Society

Individuals and companies interested in the control of water plants that hinder recreation or navigation.

919 **www.asae.org**
American Society of Agricultural Engineers

The Society is a professional and technical organization dedicated to the advancement of engineering applicable to agricultural, food and biological systems.

920 **www.asas.org**
American Society of Animal Science

The Society is a professional organization for animal scientists designed to help members provide effective leadership through research, extension, teaching and service for the rapidly changing livestock and meat industries.

921 **www.biodynamics.com**
Bio-Dynamic Farming and Gardening Association

Restoring to the soil a balanced living condition through the application and use of the completely digested form of crude organic matter known as stabilized humus. Crop rotation, correct composting and proper intercropping can all contribute to a healthier biodynamic yield.

922 **www.cast-science.org**
Council for Agricultural Science and Technology

Idenitfy food, fiber, environmental and other agricultural issues for all stake holders.

923 **www.christree.org**
National Christmas Tree Association

Provides industry leaders a chance to work directly with their suppliers and distributors.

924 **www.corn.org**
Corn Refiners Association

Supports carbohydrate research programs through grants to colleges, government laboratories and private research centers.

925 **www.cottonseed.com**
National Cottonseed Products Association

National association of cottonseed products. Products include cottonseed vegetable oil for cooking, cottonseed meal, a high protein supplement for livestock and poultry, hulls, a roughage for cattle feed and linter a cellulose feed for many industrial and consumer products.

926 **www.cropinsurance.org**
Crop Insurance Research Bureau

Crop insurance trade organization.

927 **www.croplifeamerica.org**
CropLife America

Information on protecting crops and environmentally fragile agriculture.

928 **www.crops.org**
Crop Science Society of America

Seeks to advance research, extension, and teaching of all basic and applied phases of the crop sciences.

929 **www.dhia.org**
National Dairy Herd Improvement Association

Sets policies, holds meetings and offers seminars for dairymen.

930 **www.eap.mcgill.ca/cfbmc.htm**
Canadian Farm Business Management Council

Developing and sharing business ideas for successful agriculture.

931 **www.fairsandexpos.com**
International Association of Fairs & Expositions

Membership consists of individual agricultural fairs and regional associations of agricultural fairs.

932 **www.fb.com**
American Farm Bureau Federation

For state Farm Bureaus in the 50 states and Puerto Rico.

933 **www.fewa.org**
Farm Equipment Wholesalers Association

For wholesale/distributors of ag equipment and related products.

934 **www.fourhcouncil.edu**
National 4-H Council

Focuses on diverse groups of young people in a variety of urban and suburban locales while continuing to serve youth in rural areas. Helps provide hands-on co-educational programs and activities to young people nationwide.

935 **www.fpaota.org**
Fresh Produce Association of the Americas

Trade association for Mexican produce. Formerly known as West Mexico Vegetable Distributors Association.

936 **www.fpfc.org**
Fresh Produce and Floral Council

Promotes through communication and education, fresh fruit, vegetable and floral products.

937 **www.freshcut.com**
Great American Publishing

Information on carrot production, growers and shippers.

938 **www.grains.org**
US Grains Council

For grain sorghum, barley and corn producer associations and representatives of the agricultural community. Provides commodity export market development.

939 **www.greyhouse.com**
Grey House Publishing

Selected Grey House directories in the fields of business, health and education are available online. Users can search our online databases by several different search criteria, such as product categories, geographic area, sales volume and much, much more. Full Grey House catalog and online ordering also available.

940 **www.hereford.org**
American Hereford Association

For the raising and breeding of stock in the hereford cattle industry.

941 **www.holsteinusa.com**
Holstein Association

For people with strong interests in breeding, raising and milking Holstein cattle.

942 **www.iaff.ttu.edu/aals**
Association for Arid Land Studies

943 **www.ifas.ufl.edu**
Institute of Food & Agriculture/Univ of Florida

For college students professionally interested in communications related to agriculture, food, natural resources and allied fields.

944 **www.ipaa.net**
International Pesticide Applicators Association

Provides education and information for the professional horticultural applicator. Legislative work involves the states of Washington, Oregon, Idaho in the area of laws and regulations.

945 **www.irrigation.org**
Irrigation Association

Members worldwide have worked toward a shared vision - water conservation through efficient irrigation. Provides modern water management skills and techniques for irrigated agriculture, turf, landscape and golf.

946 **www.mailordergardening.com**
Mailorder Gardening Association

Mail-order suppliers of gardening and nursery stock and supplies.

947 **www.meatami.org**
American Meat Institute

Oldest and largest meat and poultry trade association dedicated to increasing the efficiency, profitability and safety of meat and poultry trade worldwide.

948 **www.naab-css.org**
National Association of Animal Breeders

For farmer co-ops and others interested in livestock improvement.

949 **www.nacaa.com**
National Association County Agricultural Agents

For agents focusing on educational programs for the youth of the community.

950 **www.naicc.org**
National Alliance of Independent Crop Consultants

Represents individual crop consultants and contract researchers.

951 **www.nama.org**
National Agri-Marketing Association

Marketing and communication suppliers, including trade publications, radio and television broadcast sales organizations, premium/incentive manufacturers, printers, marketing research firms, photographers and related professionals.

952 **www.nationalgrange.org**
National Grange of the Patrons of Husbandry

Promotes general welfare and agriculture through local organizations. Presides over the advancement and promotion of the farming and agriculture industry.

953 **www.nationalpotatocouncil.Org**
National Potato Council

Represents US potato growers on federal legislative and regulatory issues.

954 **www.nfu.org**
National Farmers Union

Promotes educational, cooperative and legislative activities of farm families in 44 states.

955 **www.nppc.org**
National Pork Producers Council

Established as the National Swine Growers Council. Enhancing opportunities for the success of US pork producers and other industry stakeholders by establishing the US pork industry as a consistent and responsible supplier of high quality pork to the domestic and world market.

956 **www.ocia.org**
Organic Crop Improvement Association International

For farmers, processors, manufacturers and traders of organic crops.

957 **www.onions-usa.org**
National Onion Association

Represents interests of US onion producers. Informational lobbying and generic promotional headquarters for fresh dry bulb onion growers. Provides connections for networking and education exchange.

958 **www.ota.com**
Organic Trade Association

For businesses involved in the organic agriculture and products industry. Seeks to promote the industry and establish production and marketing standards.

959 **www.pma.com**
Produce Marketing Association

For those who market fresh fruits, vegetables, and floral products worldwide; involved in the production, distribution, retail, and foodservice sectors of the industry.

960 **www.profarmer.com**
Professional Farmers of America

danman@profarmer.com
Provides farmers with marketing strategies and market-trend data, as well as seminars and home study courses.

961 **www.sbsonline.org**
Society for Biomolecular Screening

Supports research and discovery in pharmaceutical biotechnology and the agrichemical industry that utilize biomolecular screening procedures.

962 **www.seedtechnology.net**
Society Commercial Seed Technologists

Professionals involved in the testing and analysis of seeds, including research, production and handling based on botanical and agricultural sciences.

963 **www.sheepusa.org**
American Sheep Industry Association

For state associations dedicated to the welfare and profitability of the sheep industry.

964 **www.southerncottonginners.org**
Southern Cotton Ginners Association

Operates in a five state area as an information center covering safety and governmental regulations.

965 **www.southwesternassn.com**
SouthWestern Association

For manufacturers, suppliers and distributors of equipment, supplies and services relating to the agricultural industry.

966 **www.soygrowers.com**
American Soybean Association

To improve US soybean farmer profitability.

967 **www.sugaralliance.org**
American Sugar Alliance

For domestic producers, processors, suppliers and labor organizations in the sugar and sugarcane industry.

968 **www.sunflowernsa.com**
National Sunflower Association

For companies associated with sunflower products. Helps with market development and promotion, production research, education and policy issues.

969 **www.tfi.org**
Fertilizer Institute

For brokers, producers, importers, dealers and manufacturers of fertilizer and fertilizer-related equipment.

970 **www.turfweeds.net**
Turfgrass Weed Science/Virginia Polytech Institute

Provides weed management information and research reports to turfgrass managers.

971 **www.uffva.org**
United Fresh Fruit & Vegetable Association

Equipment, supplies, cartons, packaging machinery, computers, sorting and sizing equipment, harvesting equipment, film wrap manufacturing and commodity organizations.

972 **www.usguernsey.com**
American Guernsey Association

Register and deliver guernsey cattle throughout the United States.

973 **www.uspotatoes.com**
United States Potato Board

Also known as the potato board. Organized to operate a national promotion plan to position potatoes as low calorie, nutritious vegetables and to facilitate market expansion into domestic and export sales.

974 **www.vealfarm.com**
Veal Quality Association Program

For veal producers and processors.

975 **www.wawgg.org**
Washington Association of Wine Grape Growers

Guidance in research and education, and maintaining leadership in local, state and national wine grape issues.

976 **www.wildblueberries.com**
Wild Blueberry Association of North America

For processors and growers of wild blueberries in Eastern Canada and Maine.

Associations

977 **Academy of Science Fiction Fantasy and Horror Films**
334 West 54th Street
Los Angeles, CA 90037
323-752-5811
FAX: 323-752-5811
scifiacademy@comcast.net
www.saturnawards.org

Roger Fenton, VP
Jack B Delpit, Vice Chairman
Michael Laster, Director Operations
Robert Holguin, Awards Manager

Annually vote for awards in this genre and once a month a 'Golden Scroll' is given to a book, movie, etc.
Founded: 1972

978 **American Alliance for Health, Physical Education**
1900 Association Drive
Reston, VA 20191-1598
703-476-3400
FAX: 703-476-9527 800-213-7193
membership@aahperd.org
www.aahperd.org

Shirley Holt-Hale, President
Harvey Mark, Chairman
Michael G Davis, CEO
Danny Ballard, Board Member
Rick LaRue, Board Member

Organization of professionals supporting and assisting those involved in physical education, leisure, fitness, dance, health promotion and education and all specialties related to achieving a healthy lifestyle.
26000 Members Founded: 1885

979 **American Amusement Machine Association**
450 E Higgins Road
Suite 201
Elk Grove Village, IL 60007
847-290-9088
FAX: 847-290-9121
information@coin-op.org
www.coin-op.org

Mike Rudowicz, President
Tina Schwartz, Business/Finance Manager
Vanessa Cabrera, Marketing/Communications Manager

AAMA is an international nonprofit trade organization representing the manufacturers, distributors and suppliers of the coin-operated amusement industry.
Founded: 1981

980 **American Association of Cheerleading Coaches and Advisors**

6745 Lenox Center Court
Suite 318
Memphis, TN 38115

FAX: 901-251-5851 800-533-6583

Monti Hillis, President
Terry Blocker, Membership

A non-profit educational association for the over 50,000 cheerleading coaches across the United States.
50000 Members Founded: 1988

981 **American Coaster Enthusiasts**
3650 Annapolis Ln N
Ste 107
Minneapolis, MN 55447-5434
763-765-2322
FAX: 763-765-2329
sgzesh@aceonline.org
www.aceonline.org

Carole Sanderson, President
Mark Cole, VP
Jeffrey Seifert, Secretary
David Altman, Treasurer
Brian Peters, Membership Director

Non-profit, all volunteer club founded to foster and promote the conservation, appreciation, knowledge and enjoyment of the art of the classic wooden roller coaster and the contemporary steel coaster.
8000 Members Founded: 1978

982 **American Disc Jockey Association**
20118 N 67th Avenue
Suite 300-605
Glendale, CA 85308

888-723-5776
office@adja.org www.adja.org

Peter Merry, President

A national, non-profit association for professional mobile and night club entertainers.

983 **American Kiddie Ride Association**
2335 Nevada Avenue North
Golden Valley, MN 55427-1304
612-827-5588
FAX: 612-827-7543 800-633-3436
tom@theisenvending.com
www.theisenvending.com

Thomas Theisen, President
Daniel Wright, Controller
Anita Bennett, General Manager

Largest provider of kiddie rides in the world, national provider of bulk vending equipment and product.
30000 Members Founded: 1960

984 **American Zoo & Aquarium Association**
8403 Colesville Road
Suite 710
Silver Spring, MD 20910-3314
301-562-0777
FAX: 301-562-0888
generalinquiry@aza.org www.aza.org

Elizabeth Stevens PhD, President
Paula Schaedlich, Chairperson
Syd Butler, Executive Director

Formerly the American Association of Zoological Parks and Aquariums, this nonprofit organization dedicated to the advancement of zoos and aqariums in the areas of conservation, education, science and recreation. AZA's vision is to work cooperatively to save and protect the wonders of the living natural world.
5,500 Members Founded: 1924

985 **Amusement Industry Manufacturers & Suppliers International: AIMS**
1250 SE Port Street Lucie Boulevard
Suite C
Port St. Lucie, FL 34952
772-398-6701
FAX: 772-398-6702
info@aimsintl.org www.aimsintl.org

Thomas Sheehan, President

Evolved from the American Recreational Equipment Association. Like its predecessor, this group is dedicated to continuing safety in the amusement industry. The association's purpose is to establish communications and foster working relations using the highest degree of professionalism with other amusement industry trade associations, local, state and federal government entities in order to promote and preserve the prosperity of the amusement industry.
Founded: 1994

986 **Amusement and Music Operators Association**
33 W Higgins Road
Suite 830
South Barrington, IL 60010
847-428-7699
FAX: 847-428-7719 800-937-2662
amoa@amoa.com www.amoa.com

Jack Kelleher, VP
Nancy Gigac, Event Coordinator

Provided leadership for the amusement, music, entertainment and vending industry. AMOA works vigorously to protect and promote industry interests.
Founded: 1948

987 **Association of College Unions International**
120 W Seventh Street
One City Centre, Suite 200
Bloomington, IN 47404-3925
812-558-8550
FAX: 812-855-0163
acui@indiana.edu www.acui.org

Maxwell Daniel, President
Marsha Herman-Betzen, Executive Director

Non-profit organization. The association has member institutions in a number of countries. ACUI members work at and attend urban and rural campuses, in two-year and four-year institutions, in large universities and small colleges. Dedicated to building community on campus through programs, services and publications with the common goal unifying the union and activities fields. *$55.00*
1000 Members Founded: 1914

988 **Casino Management Association**
PO Box 14610
Detroit, MI 48214
313-965-9038
FAX: 313-961-1651
info@cmaweb.org www.cmaweb.org

Robert Russell, President
Debra Kent, Secretary

National non-profit professional trade association of and for casino professionals. Our goal is to develop and expand concrete educational programs and certification standards for our members and the gaming industry.

989 **Circus Fans Association of America**

2704 Marshall Avenue
Lorain, OH 44052-4315

deptulascircus@centurytel.net
www.circusfans.org

Mary-Jane Foote, President
Cheryl Depula, Executive Secretary/Treasurer

Established to enjoy and preserve the circus as an institution. This original goal is still the cornerstone of our organization.

Founded: 1926

990 **Circus Historical Society**
600 Kings Peak Drive
Alpharetta, GA 30022-7844
615-373-0946
FAX: 615-373-0946
www.circusmodelbuilders.org

Al Stencell, President

A tax-exempt, not for profit educational organization dedicated to recording the history of the American circus from the first one in Philadelphia during 1793 to today.
1000 Members Founded: 1939

991 **Clowns of America International**
PO Box C
Richeyville, PA 15358-0532
724-938-8765
888-522-5696

Cheri Venturi, President
Paul Kleinberger, Executive VP
Teresa Gretton, Secretary
Claudia Keener, Treasurer
Shirley Long, Business Manager

To share, educate, and act as a gathering place for serious minded amateurs, semiprofessionals, and professional clowns
Founded: 1926

992 **Council for Amusement & Recreational Equipment Safety: CARES**
101 S Broad Street
PO Box 816
Trenton, NJ 08625
609-984-7974
FAX: 225-925-3699 800-256-5452
bcate@dps.state.la.us
www.uscancares.org

Don Hankins, President
Jonathan Brooks, VP
Terry Hennessee, Chairperson
Jonathan Brooks, Information Management
Mike Rinehart, Chairperson

Voluntary organization of U.S. state and Canadian province government official who are responsible for the enforcement of amusement ride and recreational equipment regulations within their jurisdictions.

Founded: 1996

993 **Entertainment Services and Technology Association**
875 Sixth Avenue
Suite 1005
New York, NY 10001
212-244-1505
FAX: 212-244-1502
info@esta.org www.esta.org

Lori Rubinstein, Executive Director
Karl Ruling, Technical Standards Manager
Katie Geraghty, Certification Director

Non-profit trade association representing the North American entertainment technology industry.
480 Members Founded: 1987

994 **Game Manufacturers Association**
280 North High Street
Suite 230
Columbus, OH 43215
614-255-4500
FAX: 614-255-4499
ed@gama.org www.gama.org

Anthony J Gallela, Executive Director
Richard Loomis, President

A non-profit trade association dedicated to the advancement of the hobby game business.
Founded: 1977

995 **International Amusement & Leisure Defense Association**
285 Summer Street
Boston, MA 02210
617-951-0015
FAX: 617-951-0053
info@ialda.org www.ialda.org

Joseph Brownlee, President
David Daly, VP
Sean Hannon, Treasurer
Gaylee Gillim, Secretary

Nonprofit association of lawyers and other professionals who are actively engaged in representing the interests of the amusement and leisure industries. IALDA is an independent organization and not affiliated with any insurance company, brokerage or law firm. Our mission is to promote and protect the legal interests of the amusement and leisure industry.

996 **International Association for the Leisure & Entertainment Industry: IALEI**
33 Henniker Street
Hillsboro, NH 03244
603-464-6498
FAX: 603-464-6497 888-464-6498
carole@ialei.com www.ialei.org

Laurien Henry, President
Carole Sjolander, Executive Director
Ed Stone, Marketing/Communications Director

Where fun is serious business. Our members comprise every type of interactive entertainment venue — almost all of them have multiple attractions. Our mission is to assist owners and managers of entertainment centers to be more sucessful and profitable. We focus on practical, bottom line impacting services and information.

997 **International Association of Amusement Parks and Attractions**
1448 Duke Street
Alexandria, VA 22314-3403
703-836-4800
FAX: 703-836-9678 www.iaapa.org

Clark Robinson, President
Jane Cooper, Chairperson
Charlie Bray, Chief Financial Officer
Susan Mosedale, Executive Vice President

A non-profit organization with a membership consisting of fixed-site facilities and suppliers. The association is dedicated to the preservation and prosperity of the amusement industry worldwide.
5000 Members Founded: 1918

998 **International Association of Fairs Expositions**
3043 E Cairo
PO Box 985
Springfield, MO 65801
417-862-5771
FAX: 417-862-0156 800-516-0313
iafe@fairsandexpos.com
www.fairsandexpos.com

Jim Tucker, President/CEO
Max Willis, CFO
Steve Siever, Assistant Manager
Rebekah Lee, Managing Editor

Voluntary, non-profit corporation, organizing state, district, and county agricultural fairs, expositions, associations, corporations and individuals into one large association interested in the improvement of fairs and allied fields.
1500 Members Founded: 1885

999 **International Association of Haunted Attractions**
PO Box 1310
Pilot Mountain, NC 27041
866-462-4242
FAX: 402-597-6140 866-462-4242
info@iahaweb.com
www.iahaweb.com

Liz Foral, President
Jim Upchurch, VP
Cliff Martin, Treasurer
Karen Murphy, Secretary

Established to assist and advance the haunted attraction industry through communication, education and information.
400 Members Founded: 1998

1000 **International Brotherhood of Magicians**
11155 S Towne Square
Suite C
St Louis, MO 63123
314-845-9200

office@magician.org
www.magician.org

Roger Miller, President
Fred Casto, VP
Don Wiberg, Secretary
Sindie Richison, International Executive Secretary

The world's largest and the most respected organization for amateur and professional magicians in the world.
15000 Members

1001 **International Festivals & Events Association (IFEA)**
2601 Eastover Terrace
Boise, ID 83706
208-433-0950
FAX: 208-433-9812
schmader@ifea.com www.ifea.com

Steven Wood Schmader, President/CEO
Kaye Campbell, Senior VP
Irene Castillo, Director Finance/Human Resources
Julie Parke, Director Operations
Beth Petersen, Director Member Services

A voluntary association of events, event producers, event suppliers, and related professionals and organizations whose common purpose is the production and presentation of festivals, events, and civic and private celebrations.
2000 Members Founded: 1956
Mailing list available for rent

1002 **International Game Developers Association**
870 Market Street
Suite 1181
San Francisco, CA 94102-3002
415-991-1151
FAX: 415-738-2178
info@igda.org www.igda.org

Jesse Schell, Chairperson
Jason Della Rocca, Executive Director
Brian Reynolds, Treasurer
Mitzi McGlivray, Treasurer
Sora Bai, Operations Coordinator

IGDA is an independent non-profit professional organization for developers of entertainment software, helping the game development community achieve its common goals.

1003 International Jugglers' Association
PO Box 112550
Carrollton, TX 75011-2550
415-596-3307
FAX: 302-397-2345
memberships@juggle.org
www.juggle.org

Todd Strong, Chairman
Jack McMichael, Treasurer
Martin Frost, Communications Director

A nonprofit 501(c)(3) tax-exempt organization uniquely dedicated to the advancement and promotion of juggling worldwide.
Founded: 1947

1004 International Laser Display Association
3721 SE Henry Street
Portland, OR 97202-2700
503-407-0289
FAX: 503-775-9358
info@laserist.org www.laserist.org

David Lytle, Executive Director
Alberto Kellner, President
Melissa Chisolm, Secretary

The world's leading organization dedicated to advancing the use of laser displays in the fields of art, entertainment and education.
Founded: 1986

1005 International Laser Tag Association: ILTA
5351 E Thompson Road
Suite 236
Indianapolis, IN 46237
317-786-9755
FAX: 317-786-9757
info@lasertag.org www.lasertag.org

Shane Zimmerman, Executive Director

The ILTA has been in existence for several years with the purpose of helping individuals and companies start or add a lasertag facility.
350 Members Founded: 1996

1006 International Magicians Society
581 Ellison Avenue
Westbury, NY 11590
516-333-2377
FAX: 516-333-6328
info@learnmagic.com
www.learnmagic.com

Tony Hassini, Chairman/CEO

For illusionists and magicians.
37000 Members Founded: 1968

1007 International Ticketing Association
330 W 38th Street
Suite 605
New York, NY 10018
212-629-4036
FAX: 212-629-8532
info@intix.org www.intix.org

Jeffrey Larris, President
Kathleen O'Donnell, Deputy Director
Cindy Wong, Controller
Robert M Carr, Treasurer

Not-for-Profit association representing 33 countries worldwide. Commited to the improvement, progress and advancement of ticket management, and to reach this goal, provides educational programs, trade shows, conduct surveys, conference proceedings manuals, and its valuable membership directory.
1400 Members Founded: 1980

1008 Marcel Marceau Foundation for the Advancement of the Art of Mime
253 W 73rd Street
Suite 8G
New York, NY 10023
212-874-2030
FAX: 212-874-1175
staff@marceau.org www.marceau.org

Marcel Marceau, Honorary Chairman
Peter C Wiese, Chairman
John Gula, Treasurer
Tony Micocci, Secretary/Director

Purpose of promoting, fostering and encouraging the art of mime and mime-drama in the United States and abroad and preserving and perpetuating the work of Marcel Marceau.
Founded: 1996

1009 Micro-Reality Motorsports
1500 SW 7th Street
Atlantic, IA 50022
712-243-9035
FAX: 712-243-8552
nsei@metc.net www.microreality.org

Keith Namanny, Executive Director

Manufactures and promotes NASCAR micro-reality racing centers and speedshops, plus several other sports and entertainment/promotions.
321 Members Founded: 1986

1010 National Association of Amusement Ride Safety Officials
PO Box 638
Brandon, FL 33509-0608
813-661-2779
FAX: 813-685-5117 800-669-9053
naarsoinfo@aol.com www.naarso.com

Joe Gallagher, President
Clyde Wagner, VP
Leonard Cavalier, Executive Director
Joseph D Gallagher, Treasurer
Clyde D Wagner, Secretary

We are amusement ride inspectors representing jurisdictional agencies, insurance companies, private consultants, safety professionals and federal government agencies. Benefits of membership include quarterly newsletters, a membership directory and seminars. Level I, Level II and Level III inspector certifacation, instructor and supervisor endorsements are offered. Membership is available to anyone interested in amusement ride safety.
668 Members Founded: 1987

1011 National Association of Teachers of Singing
4745 Sutton Park Court
Suite 201
Jacksonville, FL 32224
904-992-9101
FAX: 904-992-9326
info@nats.org www.nats.org

Martha Randall, President
William Vessels, Executive Director

The largest association of teachers of singing in the world.
6000 Members Founded: 1944

1012 National Association of Theatre Owners
PO Box 77318
Washington, DC 20013-8318
202-962-0054
FAX: 202-962-0370
nato@natodc.com www.natoonline.org

John Fithian, President
Mary Ann Anderson, VP
Kurt Hall, Treasurer
Mark O'Meara, Secretary
Jim Kozak, Communications Director

Professional trade association serving the business intervals of theatre owners domestically and around the world. Assist theatre owners, work with picture distribution and issues such as new technologies, legislation, marketing and first amendment. Publishes monthly magazine and annual encyclopedias.
26000 Members Founded: 1948
Printed in on glossy stock

1013 National Caves Association
PO Box 280
Park City, KY 42160
270-492-2228
FAX: 931-688-3988
info@cavern.com www.cavern.com

Susan Berdeaux, Executive Director

Nonprofit organization of publicly and privately owned show caves and caverns - caves developed for public visitation.
Founded: 1965

1014 National Independent Concessionaires
6671 13th Avenue N
Suite 1B
St. Petersburg, FL 33710
727-346-9302
FAX: 727-346-9312
cgnica@nicainc.org www.nicainc.org

Adam McKinney, President
Ron Smith, VP
Mike Pence, Secretary
Larry Lee, Treasurer
Dave Schlabha, Executive Director

Striving towards better communication between fairs, festivals and independent concessionaires nationwide.
1,300 Members

1015 National Recreation & Park Association
22377 Belmont Ridge Road
Ashburn, VA 20148-4501
703-584-4635
FAX: 703-858-0794
info@nrpa.org www.nrpa.org

Ronald Lehman, Chairman
Steven Neu, President
Penny Randel, Secretary
Robert Farnsworth, Treasurer

Advancing parks, recreation and environmental conservation efforts that enhance the quality of life for all people.
19000 Members Founded: 1905

1016 Outdoor Amusement Business Association
1035 S Semoran Boulevard
Suite 1045A
Winter Park, FL 32792
407-681-9444
FAX: 407-681-9445 800-517-6222
oaba@aol.com www.oaba.org

Robert W Johnson, President
Ronald Burback, Chairman
Don Deggeller, Trustee

Guy Leavitt, First Vice Chairman
Dominic Vivona, Jr., Treasurer

The OABA manages and influences concerns for its members. OABA believes that all business owners and members of the trade association should continue to raise the level of safety and quality in the mobile amusement industry.
4000 Members Founded: 1964

1017 Production Equipment Rental Association
PO Box 77327
San Francisco, CA 94107-0327
415-552-2094

eclare@pera.ws www.pera.ws

Ed Clare, President/Executive Director
Kay Baker, VP
Lee Utterman, Secretary
Archie Fletcher, Treasurer

A worldwide trade organization that supplies production equipment to the entertainment industry. PERA promotes the commercial advancement of new technologies available from member companies to meet the ever-changing requirements of their client's artistic challenges.
180+ Members Founded: 1992

1018 Roller Skating Association International
6905 Corporate Drive
Indianapolis, IN 46278
317-347-2626
FAX: 317-347-2636
rsa@rollerskating.com
www.rollerskating.com

Dan Brown, President
Joe Champa, VP
Budd Eversman, Treasurer
Robin Brown, Executive Director

Established by a group of skating center owners to promote roller skating and establish good business practices for skating rinks.
Founded: 1937

1019 Showmen's League of America
300 W Randolph
Chicago, IL 60609
312-332-6236
FAX: 312-332-6237 800-350-9906
rick@showmensleague.org
www.showmensleague.org

Claire Morton, President
Donnie Massie III, Treasurer
Rick Haney, Executive Secretary

Promotes friendship and fellowship between its members and the outdoor amusement industry, and pledges to help those in need through one of its many programs.
Founded: 1913

1020 Society of Broadcast Engineers
9102 N Meridian St
Ste 150
Indianapolis, IN 46260-1896
317-846-9000
FAX: 317-846-9120
lbaun@sbe.org www.sbe.org

Raymond Benedict, President
Chriss Scherer, VP
Ralph R Hogan, Secretary
Barry Thomas, Treasurer
John Poray, Executive Director

Offers a range of services to members including technology updates, idea exchanges, training, examinations and certification. Includes membership and contact details, technical papers and events.
Founded: 1963
Mailing list available for rent 5700 names $170 per M.

1021 Society of Camera Operators
PO Box 2006
Toluca Lake, CA 91610

818-382-7070
info@soc.org www.soc.org

Non-profit organization representing camera operators, camera assistants, DPs and other crew members worldwide.
Founded: 1978

1022 Themed Entertainment Association

175 E Olive Avenue
Suite 100
Burbank, CA 91502
818-843-8497
FAX: 818-843-8477
info@themeit.com www.themeit.com

Pat Gallegos, President
Nick Farmer, VP
Marc Rosenthal, Secretary
Nick Winslow, Treasurer
Gene Jeffers, Executive Director

International alliance of talented and experienced professionals in the location-based entertainment industry.

1023 Western Fairs Association
1776 Tribute Road
Suite 210
Sacramento, CA 95815-4495
916-927-3100
FAX: 916-927-6397
wfa@fairsnet.org
www.westernfairs.org

Stephen J Chambers, Executive Director
Laura C Trout, Assistant Executive Director
Sarah Ruzanov, Marketing Assistant

Non-profit trade association serving the fair industry throughout the Western United States and Canada. The association's primary purpose is to assist in maintaining the highest professional standards within the fair industry through a voluntary network of individuals and organizations.
2000 Members Founded: 1922

1024 World Waterpark Association
8826 Santa Fe Drive
Suite 310
Overland Park, KS 66212
913-599-0300
FAX: 913-599-0520
memberservices@waterparks.org
www.waterparks.org

Rick Root, President
Patty Miller, Director Tradeshows
Gina Kellogg, Director Communications
Kelly Harris, Director Operations/Member Services

Provides forum for exchange of ideas related to water amusement park industry.
800 Members Founded: 1981

Newsletters

1025 Casino Chronicle
Casino Chronicle
PO Box 740465
Boynton Beach, FL 33474-465
561-732-6117
FAX: 561-732-6117
casinochronicle@aol.com
www.casinovendors.com

Ben A Borowsky, CEO

Focuses on the gaming industry; emphasis is on Atlantic City, although includes nationwide coverage. *$175.00*
Weekly Founded: 1983
Circulation: 1500

1026 Celebrity Bulletin
Celebrity Service
250 W 57th Street
Suite 819
New York, NY 10107
212-757-7979
FAX: 212-582-7701
www.celebrityservice.com

Mark Kerrigan, Contact

A daily guide on the whereabouts and vital information of the famous. Includes celebrity contacts including agents, business managers, publicists, and record companies. Gives advanced notice of who's coming to town, what projects they're working on and how to get in touch with them. Features an International Page noting arrivals in cities worldwide. *$2336.90*
4 pages Daily Founded: 1939

1027 Entertainment Marketing Letter
EPM Communications
160 Mercer Street
3rd Floor
New York, NY 10012-3212
212-941-0099
FAX: 212-941-1622
imayer@epmcom.com
www.epmcom.com

Ira Mayer, Publisher
Susan Nunziata, Executive Editor
Loretta Netzer, Circulation Manager
Michelle Jenson, Marketing
Ira Mayer, President

Covers marketing techniques used in the entertainment industry, and by others who link their goods and services marketing through entertainment properties. *$449.00*

Founded: 1985
Printed in on matte stock

1028 INTIX Newsletter
INTIX
330 W 38th Street
Suite 605
New York, NY 10018
212-719-0220
FAX: 212-629-8532
info@intix.org www.intix.org

Jeffrey Laris, President
Ann Marie Gennardo, Special Projects Director

Provides success of the admission service industry and its membership.

1029 International Festivals & Events Association: Chapter Newsletter
International Festivals and Events Association
2601 Eastover Terrace
Boise, ID 83706
208-433-0950
FAX: 208-433-9812
craig@ifea.com www.ifea.com
Steven Schmader, President/CEO
Beth Petersen, Director Member Services
Kay Campbell, Senior VP
A quarterly newsletter published by the International Festivals & Events Association.

Quarterly Founded: 1957
Circulation: 2,700
Mailing list available for rent 20000 names $235 per M.

1030 Laughter Works
Laughter Works Seminars
PO Box 1220
Folsom, CA 95763-1220
916-985-6570

info@laughterworks.com
www.laughterworks.com
Jim Pelley, CEO/President
Seminars and keynote speeches on humor, create positive team environment, unleash creativity and enhance productivity in the workplace. *$18.00*
Quarterly
Circulation: 10000
Printed in on matte stock

1031 Managing Travel & Entertainment
Institute of Management & Administration

3 Park Avenue
30th Floor
New York, NY 10016
212-244-0360
FAX: 212-564-0465
subserve@ioma.com www.ioma.com
Randy Cochran, Director Business Development
The report covers new technologies, T and E processing strategies, techniques and software, legal issues, how to get the most from third party service providers, gives readers sample company T and E policies they can use in their operations, and current methods for finding fraud in T and E reports. *$249.00*
Annual
Circulation: 185,000

Magazines & Journals

1032 Amusement Business
VNU Business Media
49 Music Square W
Suite 300
Nashville, TN 37203
615-321-4240
FAX: 615-327-1575 888-900-3782
mshear@amusementbusiness.com
www.amusementbusiness.com
Michael Marchesano, President/CEO
Karen Oertley, Publisher
James Zoltak, Editor
Lisa Krugel, Classified Ad Manager
Serves the management of more than 10,000 mass entertainment and amusement facilities. *$129.00*
Monthly Founded: 1894 : online

1033 Amusement Today
Amusement Today
2012 E Randol Mill Road
PO Box 5427
Arlington, TX 76011
817-460-7220
FAX: 817-265-6397
spiccola@amusementtoday.com
www.amusementtoday.com
Gary Slade, Editor/Publisher
Sammy Piccola, Circulation
Keeps decision makers in the amusement industry up-to-date with current events, business, international developments and new attractions at amusement parks and waterparks. *$40.00*
Monthly
Circulation: 16000
Mailing list available for rent 3000 names

1034 Balloons & Parties
PartiLife Publications
65 Sussex Street
Hackensack, NJ 07601
201-441-4224
FAX: 201-342-8118
info@balloonsandparties.com
www.balloonsandparties.com
Mark Zettler, Publisher
Andrea P. Zettler, Managing Editor
Carolyn Cardaci, Director of Sales
Targeted, informative and practical ideas for the event decorating industry. Motivates readers to produce professional, innovative party services. *$34.95*
Quarterly Founded: 1986
Circulation: 8000
Printed in 4 colors on glossy stock

1035 Bandwagon
Circus Historical Society
600 Kings Peak Drive
Alpharetta, GA 30022-7844
615-373-0946
FAX: 615-373-0946
www.circusmodelbuilders.org
Al Stencell, President
Publishes captivating articles relating to circus history. *$5.00*
Bimonthly Founded: 1939

1036 Carnival Magazine
PO Box 4138
Salisbury, NC 28145-4138
704-638-0878
FAX: 704-636-1051
info@carnivalmag.com
www.carnivalmag.com
Charles Dabbs, Publisher
Vicky Goga, Editor
Chronicles contemporary outdoor amusement history. *$35.00*
Monthly Founded: 1965

1037 Carousel News & Trader
87 Park Avenue W
Suite 206
Mansfield, OH 44902-1612
419-529-4999
FAX: 419-529-2321
carouselnews@neo.rr.com
www.carouseltrader.com
Walter L Loucks, Publisher/Editor
Noreene Sweeney, Associate Editor
Articles devoted to the collecting, restoration and selling of carousel art. *$35.00*
Founded: 1985

1038 Casino Journal
Ascend Media Gaming Group
1771 E Flamingo Road
Suite 208A
Las Vegas, NV 89119
702-794-0718
FAX: 702-794-0799
casino@mail.idt.net
www.ascendgaming.com
Paul Doocey, Editor
Andy Holtmann, Managing Editor
GEM's mission is to be the primary information source for the key decision makers in the worldwide casino, lottery, parimutuel, bingo and emerging internet wagering markets.
Monthly
Circulation: 13034

1039 Daily Variety
Reed Business Information
5700 Wilshire Boulevard
Suite 120
Los Angeles, CA 90036
323-576-6600
FAX: 323-857-0494 866-698-743
news@variety.cahners.com
www.variety.com
Charlie Koones, Group VP/Publisher
Peter Bart, VP/Editor-in-Chief
Focuses on film, television, video, cable, music and theater. Includes coverage of financial, regulatory and legal matters pertaining to the entertainment industry. *$299.00*
24 pages Daily Founded: 1933
Circulation: 38248

1040 Entertainment, Publishing and the Arts Handbook
Thomson West Publishing
610 Opperman Drive
Eagan, MN 55123
651-687-7000
west.thomson.com
Robert Thorne, Editor
Peter Warwick, President
Howard Zack, Senior VP Sales & Account

Provides information on the latest development in the expanding legal field of entertainment, publishing, and the arts. The articles focus on such issues as books, copyrights, right-of-publicity and more. *$324.00*
Annual

1041 FUNWORLD
International Association of Amusement Parks
1448 Duke Street
Alexandria, VA 22314-3403
703-836-4800
FAX: 703-836-4801
iaapa@iaapa.org www.iaapa.org
J Clark Robinson, President
Susan Mosedale, Executive VP
Amanda Kazdoy, Editor
For the amusement park and attraction industry. Published by the International Association of Amusement Parks and Attractions. *$ 5.00*
Founded: 1918
Circulation: 8500

1042 Fair Dealer
Western Fairs Association
1776 Tribute Road
Suite 210
Sacramento, CA 95815-4495
916-927-3100
FAX: 916-927-6397
wfa@fairsnet.org
www.westernfairs.org

Laura Troat, Publisher
Stephanie Azores, Managing Editor
Stephen Chambers, Executive Director

Offers information for fairground owners, managers and workers, fair related businesses. *$35.00*

Quarterly Founded: 1922
Circulation: 1500
Printed in on glossy stock

1043 Fairs & Expos
International Association of Fairs & Expositions
PO Box 985
Springfield, MO 65801-985
417-862-5771
FAX: 417-862-0156 800-516-0313
iafe@fairsandexpos.com
www.fairsandexpos.com

Jim Tucker, President/CEO
Gary Goodman, Chairman
Max Willis, Editor
Steve Siever, Associate Editor
Rebekah Lee, Managing Editor

The source for information on fair trends, innovative ideas, and association activities. *$30.00*

Founded: 1885
Circulation: 3250
Printed in 4 colors on glossy stock

1044 Hollywood Reporter
Hollywood Reporter
5055 Wilshire Boulevard
Los Angeles, CA 90036-4396
323-525-2000
FAX: 323-525-2377 888-900-3782
subscriptions@hollywoodreporter.com
www.hollywoodreporter.com

Robert J Dowling, Editor-in-Chief/Publisher
Glenn Abel, Editor

Gives fresh ideas for film and TV. Covers the full spectrum of craft and commerce in the entertainment industry. *$265.00*

Daily Founded: 1930

1045 In Focus
National Association of Theatre Owners
750 First St. NE
Suite 1130
Washington, DC 20002
202-962-0054
FAX: 202-962-0370
nato@mindspring.com
www.natoonline.org

John Fithian, President
Robert Cane, Executive Director
Jim Kozak, Editor

Keeps readers apprised of current events within the cinema industry, with a range of departments and recurring features designed to interest those who make exhibition their business. *$70.00*

75 pages
Circulation: 4000
Printed in on glossy stock

1046 International Gaming and Wagering Business
Ascend Media Gaming Group
530 5th Avenue
24th Floor
New York, NY 10036-5101
212-302-4200
FAX: 212-302-0007
bmt@bmktny.com www.bmtny.com

Paul Dworin, Publisher

Focuses on business strategy, legislative information, food service and promotional concerns.

Monthly Founded: 1922
Circulation: 25000

1047 International Magicians Society Magic Magazine
581 Ellison Avenue
Westbury, NY 11590
516-333-2377
FAX: 516-333-6328
info@learnmagic.com
www.learnmagic.com

Tony Hassini, Chairman/CEO

Provides excellent tricks, hints, tips and ideas that we present to you that will be useful and practical.

Monthly/Member

1048 JUGGLE
International Jugglers Association
PO Box 112550
Carrollton, TX 75011-2550
415-596-3307
FAX: 302-397-2345
memberships@juggle.org
www.juggle.org

Steve Allen, Publisher
Alan Howard, Editor

Contains reviews of videos, books and props; descriptions of some of history's great juggling acts; interviews with the juggling world's most fascinating personalities; juggling instructions for various props; lists of juggling clubs; dates of upcoming juggling events; and more.

6 Times a Year Founded: 1998

1049 Journal of Singing
National Association of Teachers of Singing
4745 Sutton Park Court
Suite 201
Jacksonville, FL 32224
904-992-9101
FAX: 904-992-9326
info@nats.org www.nats.org

Richard Sjoerdsma, Editor
William Vessels, Executive Director

The only nationally distributed magazine devoted exclusively to the art of singing, vocal function, vocal literature, care of the professional voice and the teaching of singing. *$45.00*

5x times/year

1050 Laserist
International Laser Display Association
3721 SE Henry Street
Portland, OR 97202
503-407-0289
FAX: 503-775-9358
david@laserist.org www.laserist.org

Jim Hardaway, President
David Lytle, Executive Director

Providing the latest news about the art and technology of laser displays.

Quarterly Founded: 1986
Circulation: 2000
Printed in 4 colors

1051 Magic-Unity-Might: MUM Magazine
Society of American Magicians
7566 John Avenue
PO Box 510260
Saint Louis, MO 63129
314-846-5659
FAX: 314-846-5659
ed@hjta.org www.magicsam.com

John Apperson, President
David Goodsell, Editor

You will find articles dealing with the business of magic, publicity, showmanship and the history of magic and the lives of famous magicians. Many of the creative minds in the business are regular contributors.

60 pages Monthly Founded: 1902
Circulation: 30,000

1052 Park & Rec Trades
Trades Publications
20 Our Way Drive
Crossville, TN 38555
931-484-8819
FAX: 931-484-8825
park@thetrades.com
www.thetrades.com

Tim Wilson, Publisher
Randy Guidry, Editor

Event calendar and buying guides for amusement and recreation park professionals.

Monthly Founded: 1990
Circulation: 3000
Printed in 4 colors on newsprint stock

1053 Play Meter
Skybird Publishing Company
PO Box 337
Metairie, LA 70004-0337
504-488-7003
FAX: 504-488-7083 888-473-2376
news@playmeter.com
www.playmeter.com

Valerie Cognevich, Editor

Covers the industry every month with the new product descriptions, interviews with the movers and shakers in the coin - operated entertainment industry, news, company profiles, trends, family entertainment center information, tax tips, game reviews from players, tournament and leauge updates, international news and more. *$60.00*

Monthly Founded: 1974

1054 Pollstar: Concert Hotwire
Pollstar USA
4697 W Jacquelyn Avenue
Fresno, CA 93722-6413
559-271-7900
FAX: 559-271-7979
info@pollstar.com www.pollstar.com

Gary Bongiovanni, President/Editor
Jay Smith, Managing Editor
Lowry Mays, CEO

For 23 years, Pollstar has provided music business professionals with the most reliable and accurate source of worldwide concert tour schedules, ticket sales results, music industry contact directories, trade news and unique specialized data services. *$339.00*

Weekly Founded: 1985
Printed in 4 colors

1055 **Protocol**
Entertainment Services and Technology Association
875 Sixth Avenue
Suite 1005
New York, NY 10001
212-244-1505
FAX: 212-244-1502
info@esta.org www.esta.org
Beverly Inglesby, Editor
Lori Rubinstein, Executive Director
Featuring columns and articles of interest to professionals in the entertainment technology industry on business and technical topics, current standards issues, certification developments, and trade shows.
Quarterly Founded: 1994
Printed in 4 colors

1056 **RePlay Magazine**
PO Box 7004
Tarzana, CA 91357
818-776-2880
FAX: 818-776-2888
editor@replaymag.com
www.replaymag.com
Steve White, Editor
Edward Adlum, Publisher
Trade journal for the coin-operated amusement route, arcade and park owner. *$65.00*
Monthly Founded: 1975
Circulation: 4000
Printed in 4 colors on glossy stock

1057 **Rollercoaster Magazine**
American Coaster Enthusiasts
13355 10th Avenue N
Suite 108
Minneapolis, MN 55441-5554
763-765-2322
FAX: 763-765-2329
info@aceonline.org
www.aceonline.org
Carole Sanderson, President
Tim Baldwin, Publications Director
Tom Rhodes, Editor
Features news about roller coasters all over the world, roller coaster openings and preservation of coasters and all news associated with roller coasters. *$50.00*
Quarterly Founded: 1978
Circulation: 8000
Printed in 4 colors on glossy stock

1058 **Souvenirs, Gifts & Novelties Magazine**
10 E Athens Avenue
Suite 208
Ardmore, PA 19003
610-645-6940
FAX: 610-645-6943
sgnmag@kanec.com
www.sgnmag.com
Tony DeMasi, Editor
Scot C Borowsky, Executive Editor
Trade magazine for the resort-gift, souvenir industry. Articles cover merchandising trends, profile successful operations, new products, trade show calendar, plus buyer's guide issue. *$40.00*
Founded: 1962
Circulation: 42,362
Printed in 4 colors on glossy stock

1059 **Tourist Attractions & Parks**
10 E Athens Avenue
Ste. 208
Ardmore, PA 19003
610-645-6940
FAX: 610-645-6943
tapmag@aol.com www.tapmag.com
Scott C Borosky, President/Executive
Caroline Burns, Editor
Janice Weiss, Publisher
Trade magazine for the attraction owner and manager. *$30.00*
Founded: 1977
Circulation: 31,388

1060 **White Tops**
Circus Fans Association of America
2704 Marshall Avenue
Lorain, OH 44052-4315
440-520-4315
circus@inficad.com
www.circusfans.org
Colleen Stewart, President
Joe DeMike, Senior Editor
Robert J. Goldsack, Editor
Contains columns about current circus acts, show locations, management shifts, marketing strategies, births and deaths. It is resplendent with articles about the illustrious history of circus, including the greatest performers, famous acts and feats, logistical facts and figures, management and marketing, and the shows of yesteryear.
Founded: 1926
Circulation: 2000

Trade Shows

1061 **American Coaster Enthusiasts Convention**
3650 Annapolis Ln N
Ste 107
Minneapolis, MN 55447-5434
763-513-9292
FAX: 763-765-2329
info@ConveneMachine.com
www.ConveneMachine.com
Yvonne Janik, Events Director
Dave Bird, Registration Director
An annual convention, a great opportunity for fellow ACEers to gather together to ride coasters.
8000 Attendees Annual Founded: 1978

1062 **Amusement Industry Expo**
I-X Center
One I-X Center Drive
Cleveland, OH 44135
216-621-1500
FAX: 216-265-2621 800-870-3976
events@i-xcenter.com
www.i-xcenter.com
Brian Hopkins, Show Manager
Supplies and products for the amusement industry.
4100 Attendees Annual/October Founded: 1995

1063 **Amusement Industry Manufacturers & Suppliers: Safety Seminar**
AIMS International
1250 SE Port Street Lucie Boulevard
Suite C
Port St. Lucie, FL 34952
772-398-6701
FAX: 772-398-6702
info@aimsintl.org www.aimsintl.org
Thomas Sheehan, President
This AIMS event is a comprehensive week of hands-on instruction taught by today's top industry professionals. *$650.00*
January

1064 **Amusement Showcase International: ASI**
10729 W 163rd Place
Orland Park, IL 60467
708-226-1300
FAX: 708-226-1310
info@asi-show.com
www.asi-show.com
Brian Glasgow, Show Manager
Vanessa Cabrera, Contact Person
Sponsored and produced by the American Amusement Machine Association. Spring show that features exhibits and seminars for the coin-operated amusement industry. Formerly known as the American Coin Machine Exposition.
4000 Attendees Annual/March Founded: 1981

1065 **Amusement and Music Operators Association International Expo**
Amusement & Music Operators Association
33 W Higgins Road
Suite 830
South Barrington, IL 60010
847-428-7699
FAX: 847-428-7719 800-937-2662
amoa@amoa.com www.amoa.com
Nancy Gigac, Event Coordinator
Jack Kelleher, Executive VP
8000 Attendees Annual/September Founded: 1948

1066 **Association of College Unions International Conference**
120 W Seventh Street
One City Centre, Suite 200
Bloomington, IN 47404-3925
812-855-8550
FAX: 812-855-0162
acui@indiana.edu www.acui.org
Kim Keller, Exhibit/Member Services Manager
Marsha Herman-Betzen, Executive Director
Brett Perozzi, Associate Executive Director
One hundred exhibits of graphic supplies, recreation equipment, computer hardware and software, furnishings, entertainment and speaker bureau information, food service equipment, and more related information and supplies.
1000 Attendees Annual, Feb & April
Founded: 1922

1067 **Association of Performing Arts Presenters Annual Members Conference**
Association of Performing Arts Presenters
1112 16th Street NW
Suite 400
Washington, DC 20036-4820
202-833-2787
FAX: 202-833-1543
info@artspresenters.org
www.artspresenters.org
Sandra Gibson, President
Karen Spellman, Conference Consultant Specialist
Margaret Stevens, Executive Associate
Providing valuable networking resources and opportunities for performing arts presenters, artists and artist managers throughout the world.
3500 Attendees January Founded: 1957

1068 Fun Expo
William T. Glasgow
10729 W 163rd Place
Orland Park, IL 60467
708-226-1300
FAX: 708-226-1310 888-386-3976
info@wtglasgow.com
www.funexpo.com

Mike Rudowicz, Co-Owner
William Glasgow Sr, President

Devoted to the family and location based entertainment industry and the trends that drive it. It's a focused and efficient event bringing buyers and sellers together in an atmosphere that allows industry professionals to conduct business.
Annual/September

1069 GAMA Trade Show
Game Manufacturers Association
280 N High Street
Suite 230
Columbus, OH 43215
614-255-4500
FAX: 614-255-4499 www.gama.org

Anthony Gallela, Executive Director
Sean Patrick Fannon, Events Coordinator

For retailers, manufacturers, and industry professionals to network, see the newest products, and learn from others about ways to make their stores and businesses successful.
2175 Attendees

1070 Great Lakes Broadcasting Conference & Expo
Society of Broadcast Engineers
9247 N Meridian Street
Suite 305
Indianapolis, IN 46260-2454
317-846-9000
FAX: 317-846-9120 800-968-7622
lbaun@sbe.org
www.michmab.com/conferences/glbcmain.html

Raymond Benedict, President
John Poray, Executive Director

Offers broadcast engineers the opportunity to attend educational sessions, see the latest equipment and supplies, and meet with peers. *$249.00*
Annual
Mailing list available for rent 5700 names $170 per M.

1071 IFEA's Annual Convention & Expo
International Festivals & Events Association
2603 Eastover Terrace
Boise, ID 83706
208-433-0950
FAX: 208-433-9812
schmader@ifea.com www.ifea.com

Steve Wood Schmader, CFEE, President/CEO

Unites hundreds of the world's leading festivals and events, suppliers, media, sponsors and related industry professionals to share information on every aspect of event production through in depth workshops, round table discussions and networking.
Annual/Sept Founded: 1955
Mailing list available for rent 20000 names $235 per M.

1072 International Association of Amusement Parks & Attractions Convention
Int'l Association of Amusement Parks & Attractions
1448 Duke Street
Alexandria, VA 22314
703-836-4800
FAX: 703-836-9678
convention@iaapa.org
www.iaapaorlando.com

David Lee, Exhibit, Convention & Meetings VP
Alicia Cronin Dimaio, Meetings & Events Manager

Geared to the amusement park and attraction industry, running the gamut of exhibitions from high tech, to games, rides, food and beverage and much more. IAAPA showcases products and services for amusement parks, water parks, family entertainment centers, zoos, aquariums, museums — any company in the business of entertainment.
30M Attendees Annual/Nov Founded: 1918

1073 International Association of Fairs Expositions Annual Convention
International Association of Fairs & Expositions
3043 E Cairo
PO Box 985
Springfield, MO 65801
417-862-5771
FAX: 417-862-0156 800-516-0313
iafe@fairsandexpos.com
www.fairsandexpos.com

Jim Tucker, President/CEO
Kate Turner, Meeting Planner/Office Manager
Steve Siever, Assistant Manager

Largest event serving fairs and expositions. Convention attendees are able to network and learn from each other during the intensive four days of workshops, special seminars, and round table discussions. The Trade Show allows companies to showcase themselves while serving as a one-stop shop for all of a fair's booking, product, and service needs.
5000 Attendees Nov 28-30th

1074 International Laser Display Association Annual Conference
3721 SE Henry Street
Portland, OR 97202-2700
503-407-0289
FAX: 503-775-9358
info@laserist.org www.laserist.org

David Lytle, Executive Director
Alberto Kellner, President
Melissa Chisolm, Secretary

One of the world's largest exhibitions of entertainment technology. Held every two years, features international exhibitors form the fields of lighting, lasers, audio, video and staging.
70000 Attendees March

1075 International Ticketing Association Annual Conference
INTIX
330 W 38th Street
Suite 605
New York, NY 10018
212-629-4036
FAX: 212-629-8532
info@intix.org www.intix.org

Jeffrey Larris, President

For ticket management groups and organizations.
2000 Attendees January Founded: 1980

1076 National Recreation & Park Association's Congress & Exposition
National Recreation & Park Association
22377 Belmont Ridge Road
Ashburn, VA 20148-4501
703-584-4635
FAX: 703-858-0794
info@nrpa.org www.nrpa.org

Cynthia Davis, Exposition Manger
Matt Danzig, Exhibit Coordinator
Meredith Thomas, Meeting & Events Manager

Education and training opportunity plus a tradeshow for the park and recreation industry.
4000 Attendees October

1077 Pinball Expo
Pinball Expo
3869 Niles Road SE
Warren, OH 44484
330-369-1192
FAX: 330-369-6279 800-323-3547
brkpinball@aol.com
www.pinballexpo.org

Robert Berk, Expo Chairman
Mike Pacak, Co-Expo Chairman

Annual show of 25 manufacturers and related suppliers of pinball machines and supplies. Containing 70 booths and 25 exhibits.
1,000 Attendees November Founded: 1984

1078 RSA Convention and Trade Show
Roller Skating Association
6905 Corporate Drive
Indianapolis, IN 46278
317-347-2626
FAX: 317-347-2636
rsa@rollerskating.com
www.rollerskating.com

Dan Brown, President
Cindy Anderson, Convention Planning Chairperson
Ingrid Thorson, Trade Show Coordinator
Robin Brown, Executive Director

Helping roller skating industry professionals discover ways to build strong foundations for their businesses.
Annual/May

1079 World Waterpark Association Annual Tradeshow
World Waterpark Association
8826 Santa Fe Drive
Suite 310
Overland Park, KS 66212
913-599-0300
FAX: 913-599-0520
www.waterparks.org

Patty Miller, Director Tradeshow Relations
Anthony Frisbie, Coordinator Tradeshow
Rick Root, President

Three hundred and twenty booths: exhibits include waterpark attractions, water quality equipment and apparel.
2600 Attendees October

Directories & Databases

1080 American Casino Guide
Casino Vacations
PO Box 703
Dania, FL 33004-0703
954-989-2766
FAX: 954-966-7048 800-741-1596
questions@americancasinoguide.com
www.americancasinoguide.com
Steve Bourie, Author
A guide to every casino/resort, riverboat and Indian casino in the United States. *$16.95*
448 pages Annually Founded: 1992 ISBN 1-883768-11-X
Printed in 1 color

1081 Association of Performing Arts Presenters Membership Directory
1112 16th Street NW
Suite 400
Washington, DC 20036-4820
202-833-2787
FAX: 202-833-1543
info@artspresenters.org
www.artspresenters.org
Sandra Gibson, President/CEO
A national membership and advocacy organization dedicated to bringing performing artists and audiences together. *$122.00*
1600 pages Annual Founded: 1957

1082 BASELINE
BaselineFT
520 Broadway Street
Suite 230
Santa Monica, CA 90401
310-239-3999
FAX: 310-393-7799 800-858-3669
info@baseline.hollywood.com
www.pkbaseline.com
Rafi Gordon, President
Alex Amin, Executive VP
Gary Miller, Chief Executive Officer
This large database offers access to information on the US entertainment industry, with an emphasis on films, television and theater. Files included in this database range from Names, Titles and Rights to Polls, Mail and Video Sales/Rentals.
1500 pages Full-Text Founded: 1982

1083 Cavalcade of Acts and Attractions
Amusement Business
49 Music Square W
Nashville, TN 37203-3213
615-321-4250
FAX: 615-327-1575
info@amusementbusiness.com
www.amusementbusiness.com
James Zoltak, Editor
Tom Powell, Senior Editor
Julie Wood, Managing Editor
Directory of personal appearance artist (musical and theatrical), touring shows, carnivals and other specialized entertainment such as fireworks firms, rodeos, etc. Also contains listings of booking agents, personal managers, promoters and producers. *$89.00*
350 pages Annual/December
Circulation: 7,000

1084 Celebrity Access Directory: How and Where to Write the Rich & Famous
Celebrity Access
PO Box 429
East Lyme, CT 06333
860-691-5000
FAX: 860-739-0417
sales@celebrityaccess.com
www.celebrityaccess.com
Catherine Burford, Editor
Directory of Hollywood's finest. *$21.95*
327 pages Annual Founded: 1997 ISBN 0-961975-85-7

1085 Data List & Membership Directory
Western Fairs Association
1776 Tribute Road
Suite 210
Sacramento, CA 95815-4495
916-927-3100
FAX: 916-927-6397
wfa@fairsnet.org
www.westernfairs.org
Stephen Chambers, Executive Director
Laura Trout, Assistant Executive Director
A premier source of fair industry information for the Western United States and Canada. Referred to as the Bible of the fair industry, this annual directory contains a complete listing of every member fair, festival, special event, fair-related business, fair association, and agriculture-related organization.
Printed in on glossy stock

1086 Dinner Theatre: A Survey and Directory
Greenwood Publishing Group
88 Post Road W
PO Box 5007
Westport, CT 06881-5007
203-226-3571
FAX: 203-750-9790 800-225-5800
William Lynk, Author
Wayne Smith, President/CEO
Listings of dinner theaters, including in-depth profiles are offered in this comprehensive directory. *$67.95*
160 pages Hardcover Founded: 1967 ISBN 0-313284-42-3

1087 Directory of Fairs, Festivals & Expositions
Amusement Business
49 Music Square W
Nashville, TN 37203-3213
615-321-4250
FAX: 615-327-1575
www.amusementbusiness.com
James Zoltak, Editor
Tom Powell, Senior Editor
Mike Barnes, Executive Editor
Julie Wood, Managing Editor
Directory of over 5,000 state and county fairs, festivals and public expositions in the U.S. and Canada which run for three days or more. Contains dates, booking information, demographics, and other details. *$79.00*
350 pages Annual/January
Circulation: 7,000

1088 Directory of Funparks & Attractions
Amusement Business
49 Music Square W
Nashville, TN 37203-3213
615-321-4250
FAX: 615-327-1575
www.amusementbusiness.com
James Zoltak, Editor
Tom Powell, Senior Editor
Mike Barnes, Executive Editor
Julie Wood, Managing Editor
Guide to over 2,800 amusement/theme parks, water parks, tourist attractions, zoos, kiddielands and family entertainment centers worldwide. *$69.00*
130 pages Annual/March
Circulation: 8,000

1089 Directory of Historic American Theatres
Greenwood Publishing Group
88 Post Road W
PO Box 5007
Westport, CT 06880-4208
203-226-3571
FAX: 203-750-9790 800-225-5800
John Frick, Author
Carlton Ward, Author
Directory of theaters built between 1800 and 1915. *$75.00*
367 pages Hardcover ISBN 0-313248-68-0

1090 EPM Entertainment Marketing Sourcebook
EPM Communications
160 Mercer Street
3rd Floor
New York, NY 10012-3208
212-941-0099
FAX: 212-941-1622 888-852-9467
info@epmcom.com
www.epmcom.com
Ben Jurin, Managing Editor
Loretta Netzer, Circulation Manager
Ira Mayer, Founder/President/Publisher
Over 4,600 media companies, sponsors and retailers that provide products and services to entertainment marketers. *$345.00*
Also available on CD-ROM
Annual/November
Printed in on matte stock

1091 Entertainment Marketing Letter
EPM Communications
160 Mercer Street
3rd Floor
New York, NY 10012-3208
212-941-0099
FAX: 212-941-1622 888-852-9467
Ira Mayer, President/Publisher
Susan Nunziata, Executive Editor
Database covering marketing techniques used in the entertainment industry. *$449.00*
24 Issues/Year

1092 Grey House Performing Arts Directory
Grey House Publishing
185 Millerton Road
PO Box 860
Millerton, NY 12546
518-890-0526
FAX: 518-789-0545 800-562-2139
books@greyhouse.com
www.greyhouse.com
Leslie Mackenzie, Publisher
Richard Gottlieb, Editor

The most comprehensive resource covering the Performing Arts. This directory provides current information on over 9,000 Dance Companies, Instrumental Music Programs, Opera Companies, Choral Groups, Theater Companies, Performing Arts Series and Performing Arts Facilities.
$185.00
1500 pages Annual ISBN 1-592370-23-3

1093 Inside Arts
Association of Performing Arts Presenters

1112 16th Street NW
Suite 400
Washington, DC 20036-4820
202-833-2787
FAX: 202-833-1543 888-820-2787
doleary@artspresenters.org
www.artspresenters.org
Alicia Anstead, Editor
Patrick Madden, Publisher, VP External Affairs
Brian Noyes, Art Director
David O'Leary, Advertising Director
Sandra Gibson, President
This publication explores issues critical to the performing arts, presenting and touring field. *$36.00*
Bi-Monthly
Printed in 4 colors

1094 International Amusement Industry Buyers Guide
Amusement Business
49 Music Square W
Nashville, TN 37203-3213
615-321-4250
FAX: 615-327-1575
www.amusementbusiness.com
James Zoltak, Editor
Tom Powell, Senior Editor
Mike Barnes, Executive Editor
Julie Wood, Managing Editor
Complete source book containing comprehensive listings of manufacturers, importers and suppliers of all types of rides, games and merchandise, plus food and drink equipment and suppliers. *$69.00*
130 pages Annual/October
Circulation: 8,000

1095 International Directory & Buyers Guide
Int'l Association of Amusement Parks & Attractions
1448 Duke Street
Alexandria, VA 22314-3403
703-836-4800
FAX: 703-836-9678
iaapa@iaapa.org www.iaapa.org
Clark Robinson, President
William Stevenson, Publisher
Directory of amusement parks, the attraction industry and related topics.

1096 Vending Times Buyers Guide
Vending Times
1375 Broadway
6th Floor
New York, NY 10018-7001
212-302-4700
FAX: 212-221-3311
info@vendingtimes.com
www.vendingtimes.com
Alicia Lavay-Kertes, President/Publisher
Tim Sanford, Editor-in-Chief
Emily Jed, Senior Editor
Randy Parnell, Production Manager
Lists of manufacturers and suppliers of equipment and products used by vending machine industry operators, including product venders, juke boxes, pinball and other games; industry trade associations.
$41.00
Annual/June
Circulation: 18,000

1097 Who's Who in Entertainment
Marquis Who's Who
121 Chanlon Road
New Providence, NJ 07974-1544
908-731-1000
FAX: 908-673-1189 800-473-7020
marquisinfo@marquiswhoswho.com
www.marquiswhoswho.com
Gene McGovern, Publisher
A list of the industry's finest. *$235.00*
702 pages 3rd Edition

1098 Who's Who in Festivals
International Festivals and Events Association
2601 Eastover Terrace
Boise, ID 83706
208-433-0950
FAX: 208-433-9812
nia@ifea.com www.ifea.com
Steve Schmader, President/CEO
Membership directory list hundreds of festivals and vendor members.
2000 pages
Mailing list available for rent 2000 names
$235 per M.

Industry Web Sites

1099 www.acui.org
Association of College Unions International

Nonprofit organization. The association has member institutions in a number of countries. ACUI members work at and attend urban and rural campuses, in two-year and four-year institutions, in large universities and small colleges. Dedicated to building community on campus through programs, services and publications with the common goal unifying the union and activities fields.

1100 www.amoa.com
Amusement and Music Operators Association

Providing leadership for the amusement, music, entertainment and vending industry. AMOA works vigorously to protect and promote industry interests.

1101 www.cavern.com
National Caves Association

Nonprofit organization of publicly and privately owned show caves and caverns — caves developed for public visitation.

1102 www.circushistory.org
Circus Historical Society

Information on the historical applications of the circus.

1103 www.fairsnet.org
Western Fairs Association

For fairground owners, managers and workers.

1104 www.greyhouse.com
Grey House Publishing

Selected Grey House directories in the fields of business, health and education are available online. Users can search our online databases by several different search criteria, such as product categories, geographic area, sales volume and much, much more. Full Grey House catalog and online ordering also available.

1105 www.iaapa.org
Int'l Association of Amusement Parks & Attractions

For permanently situated amusement facilities worldwide.

1106 www.ifea.com
International Festivals and Events Association

Cutting-edge professional development and fund-raising ideas to the special events industry.

1107 www.intix.org
International Ticket Association

Not-for-profit association representing 33 countries worldwide. Commited to the improvement, progress and advancement of ticket management, and to reach this goal, provides educational programs, trade shows, conduct surveys, conference proceedings manuals, and its valuable membership directory.

1108 www.laserist.org
International Laser Display Association

Dedicated to advancing the use of laser displays, in the art, entertainment and education.

1109 www.magicsam.com
Society of American Magicians

To promote and maintain harmonious fellowship among those interested in magic as an art, to improve ethics of the magical profession, and to foster, promote and improve the advancement of magical arts in the field of amusement and entertainment. Membership includes professional and amateur magicians, manufacturers of magical apparatus and collectors.

1110 www.merchandisegroup.com
ASD/AMD Merchandise Group

Leading producer of trade shows and publications in the variety and general merchandise industry.

1111 www.music-rights.com
Ad Producer.com

Dedicated to providing music rights providers with the highest quality platform to leverage the Web to market your services around the world around the clock.

1112 www.oaba.org
Outdoor Amusement Business Association

Promotes interest of the outdoor amusement industry.

1113 www.toy-tia.org
Toy Industry Association

National organization for U.S. producers and importers of toys, games and children's entertainment products.

1114 www.waterparks.com
World Waterpark Association

Official Web site for the waterpark and water-leisure industries. It is the most comprehensive listing of waterparks in the world! It was developed and is maintained by the World Waterpark Association, the international organization created to further safety and business effectiveness in the waterpark industry.

Associations

1115 Allied Underwear Association
100 E 42nd Street
New York, NY 10017-5613
212-867-5720

Sidney Orenstein, Executive Director

Manufacturers of women's and children's sleepwear.

20 Members Founded: 1913

1116 American Apparel & Footwear Association
1601 N Kent Street
Suite 1200
Arlington, VA 22209
703-241-1864
FAX: 703-522-6741 800-520-2262
mrust@apparelandfootwear.org
www.apparelandfootwear.org

Kevin M Burke, President/CEO
Ralph Reinecke, Finance Manager
Rachel E Subler, Manager Government Contracts
Marti Rust, Executive Administrator

Formed through the merger of two highly regarded trade associations: the American Apparel and Manufacturers Association and Footwear Industries of America. AAFA is the national trade association representing apparel, footwear, and other sewn products companies, which compete in the global marketplace.

600 Members Founded: 2000

1117 American Cotton Shippers Association
88 Union Avenue
Suite 1204
Memphis, TN 38103
901-525-2272
FAX: 901-527-8303
www.acsa-cotton.org

Manfred Schiefer, President
Adolph Weil, III, First VP
Neal Gillen, Executive VP/General Counsel
William May, Senior VP/Foreign & Domestic Ops
Thomas Hayden, Treasurer

Provides a united voice for the cotton merchandising trade of the United States. ACSA is comprised of merchants, primary buyers and mill service agents who are members of four federal associations located throughout the cotton belt.

Founded: 1924

1118 American Flock Association
6 Beacon Street
Suite 1125
Boston, MA 02108
617-428-8220
FAX: 617-542-2199
info@flocing.org www.flocking.org

Thomas Witham, Chairman
Todd Der Manouelian, Vice Chairman
Barrett F Ripley, Executive Director

Provides positive leadership to foster a strong flock industry in north America. It proactively and effectively provides members with relevant services and information, thereby enabling our members to achieve their desired results.

1119 American Fur Merchants Association
363 7th Avenue
New York, NY 10001-3904
212-563-1143
FAX: 212-290-8298

Sandy Blye, Executive Director

Acts as a credit agency for members in the fur industry. Members include dealers, brokers and suppliers in the New York area.

80 Members Founded: 1996

1120 American Home Sewing and Craft Association
494 8th Avenue
Suite 802
New York, NY 10018-7716
212-714-1633
FAX: 212-714-1655 www.sewing.org

Leonard Ennis, Executive VP
Cathleen Campbell, VP

Handicraft and collectibles forum.

1121 American Sewing Guild
9660 Hillcroft
Suite 510
Houston, TX 77096
713-729-3000
FAX: 713-721-9230
info@asg.org www.asg.org

Joanna Crenshaw, President
Margo Martin, Executive Director

Advancing sewing as an art and life skill.

Founded: 1993

1122 Associated Fur Manufacturers
132 W 31st Stree,t 16th floor
New York, NY 10001-3904
212-563-1144
FAX: 212-290-8299
www.kumquatsystems.com

Charles Andrews, Executive Director

Seeks to promote understanding and improve public relations for manufacturers of fur apparel.

5 Members Founded: 1992

1123 Atlanta Apparel Association
107 E Main Street
Suite 202
Bath, PA 18014-1519
610-837-4220
FAX: 610-837-4224
arnold@atlanticapparel.com
www.atlanticapparel.com
Represents lady apparel manufacturers in Pennsylvania and South Jersey.

Founded: 1948

1124 Belt Association
225 West 39th Street
New York, NY 10018
212-398-5400
FAX: 212-398-7818
joey5400@aol.com

Sheldon M Edelman, Executive Director

Membership originally consisted of manufacturers of ladies' belts.

Founded: 1934

1125 Cashmere and Camel Hair Manufacturers Institute
6 Beacon Street
Suite 1125
Boston, MA 02108-3812
617-542-7481
FAX: 617-542-2199
info@cashmere.org
www.cashmere.org

Karl H Spilhaus, President

Trade association of cashmere and camel hair products.

25 Members Founded: 1984

1126 Color Association of the US
315 W 39th Street
Studio 507
New York, NY 10018
212-947-7774
FAX: 212-594-6987
caus@colorassociation.com
www.colorassociation.com

Margaret Walch, Director
Sherri Donghia, Chair
William P Baccini, Chairman
Roseann Forde, Chairperson

Association devoted to color/design issues. The association issues color charts two years in advance of selling seasons in order to profile popular American colors. Forecasts are issued in women's fashions and men's and children's clothing.

Founded: 1915

1127 Costume Designers Guild
4730 Woodman Avenue
Suite 430
Sherman Oaks, CA 91423-3570
818-905-1557
FAX: 818-905-1560
www.costumedesignersguild.com

Deborah Nadoolman-Landis, President
Cheryl Downey, Executive Director

Works to promote employment and to create improved working conditions for costume designers.

594 Members Founded: 1953

1128 Cotton Incorporated
6399 Weston Parkway
Cary, NC 27513
919-678-2220
FAX: 919-678-2230
www.cottoninc.com

J Berrye Worsham III, President/CEO
High Malone, VP
David Byrd, VP/CFO
Ira Livingston, Senior VP

To ensure that cotton remains the first choice among consumers in apparel and home products.

1129 Council of Fashion Designers of America
1412 Broadway
Suite 2006
New York, NY 10018-3320
212-302-1821
FAX: 212-768-0515 www.cfda.com

Peter D Arnold, Executive Director
Lisa Smillor, Associate Director
Tina Sibulkin, Director Special Events

Works to further the position of fashion design as a recognized branch of art and culture.

250 Members Founded: 1962

1130 **Custom Tailors and Designers Association of America**
19 Mantua Rd
Mount Royal, NJ 08061-1006
856-423-1621
FAX: 856-423-3420 www.ctda.com

Susanne Kilgore, Executive Director

Seeks to promote awareness of designers and makers of men's custom tailored clothing.

300 Members Founded: 1880

1131 **Embroidery Trade Association**
12300 Ford Road
Suite 135
Dallas, TX 75234
972-470-0415
FAX: 972-755-2561 888-628-2545
info@embroiderytrade.org
www.embroiderytrade.org

Lance Sabo, Founder
John Swinburn, CAE, Executive Director
Dick Williams, Account Executive

Our mission is to strengthen the commercial embroidery business through member education, business support, representation, networking, research, and consumer outreach. UpFront Newsletter delivers current information to members' email boxes every month.

1132 **Fashion Footwear Association of New York**
1414 6th Avenue
New York, NY 10019
212-751-6422
FAX: 212-751-6404

Joseph Moore, President

A nonprofit organization that promotes and improves the general awareness and demand for fashion footwear and related products and to serve as advocate of the multi-billion dollar footwear industry globally. FFANY represents 300 corporations and 800 of the most prestigious brand names worldwide.

1133 **Greater Blouse, Skirt and Undergarment Ass ociation**
1359 Broadway
Suite 1814
New York, NY 10018
212-634-4344
FAX: 212-563-5373
info@greaterblouse.org
www.greaterblouse.org
The Greater Blouse, Skirt and Undergarment Association (GBSUA) is a membership organization of apparel contractors.

200 Members Founded: 1932

1134 **Headwear Information Bureau**
302 W 12th Street
New York, NY 10014-6025
212-627-8333
FAX: 212-627-0067
milicase@aol.com
www.hatsworldwide.com

Casey Bush, Founder/Executive Director
Ann Marie Morris, Public Relations Executive

Promotes the wearing of hats by men and women of all ages.

85 Members Founded: 1989

1135 **Home Sewing Association**
105 Mall Boulevard
PO Box 1312
Monroeville, PA 15146
412-372-5950
FAX: 412-372-5953 www.sewing.org

Dotty Grexa, President
Joyce Perhac, Executive Director
Jenna Sheldon, Director Trade Show/Meetings
Jenny Prevatte, Director Information Services
Dale Sutherland, Treasurer

A nonprofit organization comprised of members who support and promote the home sewing industry. This includes manufacturers, suppliers and retailers of sewing machines, fabrics, notions and sewing related craft products.

1136 **Hosiery Association**
3623 Latrobe Drive
Suite 130
Charlotte, NC 28211-3004
704-365-0913
FAX: 704-362-2056
hosierytha@aol.com
www.hosieryassociation.com

Sally Kay, President
Sheila Simpson, VP
Jeanna Sheldon, Executive Assistant
Vicki Camp, Office Manager
Mike Austell, Sales Director

Trade association that develops standards for hosiery measurement.

215 Members Founded: 1905

1137 **International Association of Clothing Designers & Executives**
34 Thorton Ferry Road
#1
Amherst, NH 03031
603-672-4065
FAX: 603-672-4064
dnschmida@aol.com www.iacde.com

Udo Maelzer, President
David Schmida, Executive Director

Sponsors competitions, presents awards, maintains archives, conducts research for clothing designers; provides a network for apparel executives to network information on RED, style trends and workshop procedures.

300 Members Founded: 1911

1138 **International Glove Association**
PO Box 146
Brookville, PA 15825
814-328-5208

gloves@alltel.net www.iga-online.com

Members are manufacturers of workman's gloves and related workplace safety material.

1139 **Intimate Apparel Council**
220 W 19th Street
Floor 6
New York, NY 10011
212-807-0878
FAX: 212-807-0878
www.bromley-group.com

Stuart Greenberg, Chair/President/CEO
Mary R Howell, Staff Liaison

Promotes interests of buyers of intimate apparel and accessories.

1140 **Knitting Guild of America**
1100-H Brandywine Blvd
Zanesvill, OH 43701-7303
865-524-8677
FAX: 865-521-6034 800-274-6034
tkga@tkga.com www.tkga.com

Debby Johnston, Program Coordinator

The Knitting Guild Association (TKGA) is a non-profit organization dedicated the hand and machine knitting industry.

11600 Members

1141 **Ladies' Apparel Contractors Association**
450 Fashion Avenue
Suite 1009
New York, NY 10123-1090
212-564-6161
FAX: 212-564-6166

Sidney Reiff, Executive Director

Conducts labor negotiations and monitors legislation.

50 Members Founded: 1964

1142 **Leather Apparel Association**
19 W 21st Street
Suite 403
New York, NY 10010
212-727-1210
FAX: 212-727-1218
info@leatherassociation.com
www.leatherassociation.com

Morrisd Goldfarb, President
Richard Harrow, Executive Director
Sandy Blye, Director/Public Relations

Founded by retailers, manufacturers, tanners, cleaners and suppliers from across the US to unify the industry. Promotes the sale of leather garments through publicity, education and business support services.

Founded: 1990

1143 **National Association of Blouse Manufacture rs**
450 7th Avenue
Suite 2304
New York, NY 10016
212-563-6390
www.latinotalentnetwork.com
Membership concentrated in the New York Area. Major purpose is labor negotiations with the International Ladies Garment Workers Union.

170 Members Founded: 1933

1144 **National Association of Mens' Sportswear Buyers**
PO Box 227
Millwood, NY 10546-0227

tochs@namsb.org www.namsb.org

Theresa Ochs, Executive Director
Jeff Campbell, Information Director

A membership association of men's wear retailers serving the fashion industry. Monthly membership newsletter on men's fashion.

1M Members Founded: 1954

1145 **National Association of Uniform Manufacturers and Distributors**
16 E 41st Street
Suite 700
New York, NY 10017
212-869-0670
FAX: 212-575-2847
Rjlerman@naumd.com
www.naumd.com

Richard Lerman, Executive Director
Anne Marie McCann, Accounting Manager

Represents and provides public relations activities for suppliers, manufacturers and retailers of career apparel.

450+ Members Founded: 1933

1146 National Luggage Dealers Association
1817 Elmdale Avenue
Glenview, IL 60025
847-988-8198
FAX: 847-998-6884
inquiry@nlda.com www.nlda.com

Marilyn Murray, Executive Administrator

Members are retailers of luggage, leather goods, gifts and handbags with over 300 stores nationally. NLDA acts as a purchasing office for membership.

1147 National NeedleArts Association
1100-H Brandywine Boulevard
PO Box 3388
Zanesville, OH 43701-7303
740-455-6773
FAX: 740-452-2552 800-889-8662
tnna.info@offinger.com
www.tnna.org

Stacy Charles, President
Marilyn Murphy, VP
Jim Bryson, Secretary/Treasurer
Patty Parrish, Executive Director

An international trade organization representing retailers, manufacturers, distributors, professional designers, manufacturer's representatives, publishers and wholesalers of upscale needleart products and supplies.

2500 Members Founded: 1975

1148 Neckwear Association of America
151 Lexington Avenue
Suite 2F
New York, NY 10016
212-683-8454
FAX: 212-686-7382
geralda476@aol.com
www.nysaenet.org

Gerald Anderson, President

Serves the manufacturers of men's and boys' neckwear and the suppliers to the field.

100 Members Founded: 1946

1149 Professional Apparel Association
994 Old Eagle School Road
Suite 1019
Wayne, PA 19087-1866
610-971-4850
FAX: 610-971-4859 800-722-7712
info@proapparel.com
www.proapparel.com

Sharon Tannahill, Executive Director
Hope Silverman, Administrative Director

Members are manufacturers of health care and hospitality uniforms, shoes and accessories, as well as career apparel.

1200+ Members Founded: 1984

1150 San Francisco Fashion Industries
1000 Brannan Street
Suite 206
San Francisco, CA 94103-4831
415-621-6100
FAX: 415-621-6384 www.sffi.org

David Zeimer, President
Jeff Graff, VP
Steve Pinsky, VP
Kathy Liu, VP
Randall Harris, Executive Director

Promotes the health of the local apparel industry by providing valuable business services such as consulting, legislative advocacy, group health, employment referrals, educational seminars and more.

Founded: 1920

1151 Sunglass Association of America
390 North Bridge Street
LaBelle, FL 33935
863-612-0085
FAX: 863-612-0250
info@sunglassassociation.com
www.sunglassassociation.com

Tibor Gross, President
Swea Nightingale, Executive Director
Alvin Hutzler, II, VP
Bruce Bartley, VP/Secretary
Henry Lane, VP/Chair Market Research

A nonprofit trade association of manufacturers and import wholesale sunglasses, sunglass parts, components, materials and reading glasses.

Founded: 1971

1152 Textile Rental Services Association
1800 Diagonal Road
Suite 200
Alexandria, VA 22314
703-190-0029
FAX: 703-519-0026
trsa@trsa.org www.trsa.org

David Rawlinson, Chairman
Roger F Cocivera, President/CEO
George Ferencz, Jr, VP
Debbie Smith, Advertising Director

Covers the uniform, linen supply, health care and dust control service markets.

25 Members Founded: 1913

1153 Uniform Code Council
7887 Washington Village Drive
Suite 300
Dayton, OH 45459
937-435-3870
FAX: 937-435-7317
info@uc-council.org
www.uc-council.org

Danny Wegman, Chairman
Stephen Demeritt, Vice Chair
Miguel Lopera, Chief Executive Officer

A nonprofit standards organization and one of the most respected leaders in global commerce.

Members 280,000 Founded: 1974

1154 Unite Here International Union
275 7th Avenue
New York, NY 10001-6708
212-265-7000
FAX: 212-265-3415 www.unitehere.org

Bruce Raynor, General President
John Wilhelm, President/Hospitality Industries
Dave Sanders, Director Communications

Boasts a diverse membership, comprised largely of immigrants and including high percentages of African-American, Latino, and Asian-American workers. The majority of Unite Here members are women.

440M Members Founded: 2004

1155 United Infants' and Children's Wear Association
1430 Broadway
New York, NY 10018
212-244-2953
FAX: 212-221-3540

Alan Lubell, President
Alex Glauberman, Executive Director

Promotes interests of manufacturers, jobbers and distributors of infants' and children's clothing.

50 Members Founded: 1933

1156 Vows Bridal and Wedding Business

Grimes and Associations Inc.
24 Daisy Street
Ladera Ranch, CA 92694
949-388-4848
FAX: 949-388-8448
petergrimes@vowsmagazine.com
www.vowsmag.com

Peter Grimes, Publisher
Shannon Hurd, Editor in Chief

Association concentrating on the business specifics necessary for today's wedding professional.

1157 Western and English Sales Association
451 E 58th Avenue
Suite 4128
Denver, CO 80216
303-295-1040
FAX: 303-295-0941 800-295-1041
info@denver-wesa.com
www.denver-wesa.com

Toni High, Executive Director

Association members are from the Western and English tack and apparel industry.

1100 Members Founded: 1922

1158 Young Menswear Association
47 W 34th street
New York, NY 10001-2121
212-594-6422
FAX: 212-594-9349

Eric Hertz, CAE, Director
Joe Rivers, Manager

Seeks to further interests of young people involved with the men's apparel industry to encourage talent interested in the textile/apparel economy through scholarships and endowments at selected colleges offering degrees in textile and apparel productions and marketing.

800+ Members Founded: 1941

Newsletters

1159 AAFA Newsletter
American Apparel & Footwear Association
1601 N Kent Street
Suite 1200
Arlington, VA 22209
703-524-1864
FAX: 703-522-6741 800-520-2262

Jock Morgan, Publisher
Kevin Burke, President/CEO
Marti Rust, Executive Administrator

Information providing members with the developments and changes in the apparel industry.

1160 **Barbara's View/Shopping Guides**
Barbara's View
PO Box 531006
Miami, FL 33153-1006
305-757-7638
FAX: 305-756-5353
barbarasview@webtv.net
www.barbarasview.com

Barbara Wexner Levy, Publisher
Barbara Wexner Levy, CEO/President

30th year of shopping guides. *$14.00*
Monthly Founded: 1976 ISBN 1-882340-96-5

1161 **Clothing Manufacturers Association of the USA**
730 Broadway
10th Floor
New York, NY 10003
212-774-4727
FAX: 212-529-1739

Robert A Kaplan, Editor
Tanya Brown, Assistant
Y Chang, Manager

The annual statistical report offers data on sales, production, imports and exports of men's and boys' tailored clothing. *$30.00*
Daily Founded: 1968
Circulation: 300
Mailing list available for rent 100 names $200 per M.

1162 **DNR-Daily News Record**
Fairchild Publications
7 W 34th Street
New York, NY 10001-8191
212-630-3880
FAX: 212-630-4707 800-360-1700
info@dnrnews.com www.dnrnews.com

Samuel Farrel, President/CEO
John Birmingham, Editor-in-Chief
Jim Rossi, Marketing
Don Miller, Circulation Manager
Tom Beebe, Creative Director

Supplies retail fashion, product merchandising and marketing news for men's and boys' fashion. *$85.00*
Weekly
Circulation: 15755

1163 **Fashion Newsletter**
Omniprint
9700 Philadelphia Court
Lanham, MD 20706-4405
301-731-7000
FAX: 301-731-7001 800-774-6809
info@omniprint.net
www.omniprint.net

Alice Meyer, Editor
Michael Nagan, Publisher

Accurate forecasts of the hottest styles, colors and fabrics. Fashion news for buyers, apparel merchandisers, retailers and apparel and textile manufacturers. *$179.00*
8 pages Monthly Founded: 1963
Circulation: 817 Controlled
Printed in 2 colors on matte stock

1164 **Notions**
American Sewing Guild
9660 Hillcroft
Suite 510
Houston, TX 77096
713-729-3000
FAX: 713-729-9230
info@asg.org www.asg.org

Joanna Crenshaw, President

Contains articles written exclusively for us by sewing experts, messages from the ASG Board of Directors and ASG National Headquarters, news of recent guild activities from chapters around the country, information about the latest sewing products and books, and a Chapter Calendar where individual chapters list their upcoming events. Free to members.
Quarterly

1165 **Sunglass Association of America Newsletter**
390 North Bridge Street
LaBelle, FL 33935
863-612-0085
FAX: 863-612-0250
info@sunglassassociation.com
www.sunglassassociation.com

Swea Nightingale, Publisher/Executive Director
Tibor Gross, President

Newsletter for the membership of the Sunglass Association of America. A nonprofit association of manufacturers and distributors of sunglasses and sunglass parts.
12 pages

1166 **Uniformer**
Professional Apparel Association
994 Old Eagle School Road
Suite 1019
Wayne, PA 19087-1802
610-971-4850
FAX: 610-971-4859 800-722-7712
info@proapparel.com
www.proapparel.com
Distributed to 500 manufacturers, retailers and sales representatives in the health care and hospitality uniform industry.
16 pages Quarterly
Circulation: 500

Magazines & Journals

1167 **Accessories**
Business Journals
185 Madison Avenue
5th Floor
New York, NY 10016-4325
212-686-4412
FAX: 212-686-6821
lorrief@busjour.com
www.busjour.com

Helen Welsh, President
Lorrie L Frost, Publisher
Irenka Jakubiak, Editor-in-Chief

This magazine profiles the national fashion trade for women's accessories. *$35.00*
Monthly Founded: 1908
Circulation: 100000

1168 **Agent**
Halper Publishing Company
830 Moseley Rd
Highland Park, IL 60035-3256
847-780-2900
FAX: 847-780-2902
info@halper.com www.halper.com

William Halper, Publisher
Donna J Pierson, Director of Marketing

A reference source for fabrics, trimmings, supplies, services and equipment for the garment manufacturing industry and sewn products market. *$30.00*
Bi-annually Founded: 1930
Circulation: 25000

1169 **Apparel Industry International**
Dave Doucette
1115 Northmeadow Parkway
Roswell, GA 30076
770-569-1540
800-241-9034

Mercedes Cortazar, Editor
Eva Martinez, Associate Editor

Written for the management, technology, international commerce and economy of the Latin American apparel industry.
Monthly

1170 **Apparel Magazine**
801 Gervais Street
Suite 101
Columbia, SC 29201
803-771-7500
FAX: 803-799-1461 800-845-8820
cdeberry@apparelmag.com
www.apparelmag.com

Susan Black, Publisher
Kathleen DesMarteau, Editor in Chief
Jackie Ellen, Sales Director

Trade publication for apparel/sewn products, manufacturing executives. Accepts advertising. Covers topics ranging from new products and technology to production management, sourcing, fabrics and financial news. *$48.00*
180 pages Monthly
Circulation: 18752
Printed in 4 colors on matte stock

1171 **Children's Business**
Fairchild Publications
7 W 34th Street
New York, NY 10001-8100
212-630-3880
FAX: 212-630-4837
debra.goldberg@fairchildpub.com
www.fairchildmediakit.com

Debra Goldberg, Publisher
Tracy R Mitchell, Executive Editor
Ralph Erardy, Senior VP

Infants' and toddlers' wear, juvenile merchandise, footwear and toys. *$5.00*
45 pages Monthly Founded: 1985
Circulation: 30458

1172 **Clothing & Textile Research Journal**
International Textile & Apparel Association
PO Box 1360
Monument, CO 80132-1360
719-488-3716
FAX: 719-488-3716
info@itaaonline.org
www.itaaonline.org

Sandra Hutton, Executive Director
Kim Johnson, Editor

Offers the latest information on all areas of clothing and textiles. *$85.00*
64 pages Quarterly Founded: 1982
Circulation: 1300
Printed in 1 color on matte stock

1173 **Costume! Business**
Gift Basket Review
815 Haines Street
Jacksonville, FL 32206-6025
904-634-1902
FAX: 904-633-8764 800-729-6338
readermail@festivities-pub.com
www.festivities-pub.com

Debra Paulk, Publisher
Kathy Horak, Editor

News and current issues in the costume retailling business. *$29.95*

Quarterly
Circulation: 8,000

1174 Dress
Costume Society of America
PO Box 73
Earleville, MD 21919
410-275-1619
FAX: 410-275-8936 800-272-9447
national.office@costumesocietyamerica.co www.costumesocietyamerica.com/
Sally Halverston, Associate Editor
Rosalyn M Lester, President
Linda Welters, Editor-in-Chief
Margaret Ordonez, Managing Editor
Journal of the Costume Society of America. The Costume Society of America advances the global understanding of all aspects of dress and appearance.
Founded: 1973 1850 names
Printed in on matte stock

1175 EMB Magazine
1115 Northmeadow Parkway
Roswell, GA 30076
770-291-5534
FAX: 770-777-8733 800-241-9034
rlebovitz@embmag.com
www.embmag.com
Richard Lebovitz, Editor-In-Chief
Chris Casey, Publisher
Offers information on the apparel industry. *$18.00*
Monthly Founded: 1994

1176 Embroidery Business News
Virgo Publishing
3300 N Central Avenue, Suite 2500
PO Box 40079
Phoenix, AZ 85067-0079
480-990-1101
FAX: 480-675-8146
mgardner@vpico.com
www.ebnmag.com
Michelle Gardner, Editor
Complete business resource for commercial embroiderers.
Circulation: 18,937

1177 Fashion Accessories Magazine
SCM Publications
10 DeGraaf Court
PO Box 859
Mahwah, NJ 07430
201-684-9222
FAX: 201-684-9228
Samuel Mendelson, Publisher
Samuel Mendelson, CEO/President
Samuel Mendelson, Editor
Caroline Raftery, Marketing
Caroline Raftery, Circulation Manager
Offers information on the latest in fashion, jewelry and accessories. *$24.00*
Monthly Founded: 1951
Circulation: 9500
Printed in 4 colors on newsprint stock

1178 Fashion Market Magazine
Fashion Market Magazine Group
330 W 38th Street
Suite 1500
New York, NY 10018-2999
212-541-9350
fashionmmg@aol.com
www.fashionmarketmagazine.com
Victoria Monjo, Editor
News for the apparel industry in New York, with original pictures and news in fashion, technology, finance and real estate. *$84.74*
64 pages Monthly Founded: 1985
Circulation: 80000

1179 Footwear Plus
Symphony Publishing
8 W 38th St
Rm 201
New York, NY 10018-6271
646-278-1550
GDutter@footwearplus.net
www.footwearplus.net
Greg Dutter, Editor-in-Chief
Pauline Lee, Associate Editor
Focuses on fashion, merchandising, trends and ideas in the retail footwear industry. *$50.58*
Founded: 1989
Printed in on glossy stock

1180 Hosiery News
Home Sewing Association
105 Mall Boulevard
PO Box 1312
Monroeville, PA 15146
412-372-5950
FAX: 412-372-5953 www.sewing.org
Dotty Grexa, President
Dale Sutherland, Treasurer
Jenna Sheldon, Director Trade Show/Meetings
Jenny Prevatte, Director Information Services
It covers all THA activities, industry news, personnel changes, statistics, legislative and regulatory concerns, marketing, technology, financial reports and new product information.

1181 Impressions Magazine
1717 Main Street
Suite #3300
Dallas, TX 75201
800-527-0207
FAX: 214-290-9982 800-527-0207
impressions@bill.com
www.impressionsmag.com
Chris Casey, Publisher
Marcia Derryberry, Editor-in-Chief
Offers news and information on the development or imprintable and imprinted sportswear and textiles. *$69.00*
Circulation: 30000

1182 Industrial Fabric Products Review
Industrial Fabrics Association International
1801 County Road BW
Roseville, MN 55113-4061
651-222-2508
FAX: 651-631-9334 800-225-4324
generalifno@ifai.com www.ifai.com
Stephen M Warner CAE, President/CEO
Mary L Conner, Managing Editor
Published monthly, this magazine provides timely reports on emerging and traditional end markets for products made of industrial fabrics; new technical developments in fiber, fabrics, and treatments; general interest articles on growth-oriented products and companies; profiles on industry members; and the latest information on equipment. *$67.00*
Monthly Founded: 1915
Circulation: 10000 $250 per M.
Printed in 4 colors on glossy stock

1183 Juvenile Merchandising
EW Williams Publications
2125 Center Avenue
Suite 305
Fort Lee, NJ 07024-5898
201-592-7007
FAX: 201-592-7171
webeditor@ewwpi.com
www.williamspublications.com
Janys Kuznier, Circulation Director
Phillip Russo, Publisher
Peter Berlinski, Editor-in-Chief
Andrew Williams, President
Offers news on the juvenile clothing, accessories and furniture industry. *$85.00*
Founded: 1938
Circulation: 8000

1184 Knit Ovations Magazine
Woolknit Associates
267 5th Avenue
Suite 806-807
New York, NY 10016
212-683-7785
FAX: 212-683-2682
Eleanor Kairalla, Publisher
Fashions in knitwear for men and women trends in market; fashion color forcasts; guest features on knitwear by retail executives. *$10.00*
Circulation: 5,500

1185 Made to Measure
Halper Publishing Company
830 Moseley Road
Highland Park, IL 60035
847-780-2900
FAX: 847-780-2902
info@halper.com
www.madetomeasuremag.com
Rick Levine, Publisher
William Halper, President
Serves the uniform and career apparel industry.
Bi-annually Founded: 1930
Circulation: 25000
Printed in 4 colors on glossy stock

1186 Magazine of Menswear Retailing
American City Business Journals
120 W Morehead Street
Charlotte, NC 28202
704-731-1000
FAX: 704-973-1001
charlotte@amcity.com
www.bizjournals.com
Robert Morris, Editor
David Harris, Managing Editor
Features men's clothing, accessories and sportswear.

1187 Market Maker
Advanstar Communications
1 Park Avenue
New York, NY 10016
212-797-7631
FAX: 212-951-6793
info@advanstar.com
www.advanstar.com
Jill Gerson-Price, Publisher
Joseph Loggia, CEO
Body fashions, intimate apparel. *$2.00*
Founded: 1987
Circulation: 14900

1188 **Needle's Eye**
Union Special Corporation
1 Union Special Plaza
Huntley, IL 60142-7007
847-695-5101
FAX: 847-669-4535
dkanies@unionspecial.com
www.unionspecial.com

Doug Kanies, Editor-In-Chief
David Keisa, Executive Editor

Industry events, describes developments in machine-sewed products, informs about improved manufacturing methods, and promotes interest in Union Special machinery.
Monthly Founded: 1881
Circulation: 28595

1189 **Outerwear**
Creative Marketing Plus
19 W 21st Street
Room 403
New York, NY 10010-6805
212-727-1210
FAX: 212-727-1218
rharrow@cmponline.com
www.cmponline.com

Richard Harrow, Publisher
Rich Harrow, CEO/President
Olimka Brown, Manager

Focuses on outerwear buyers' needs, fashion trends, as well as leading buying offices and promotional plans. *$62.00*
30 pages Monthly Founded: 1986
Circulation: 16000 16,000 names $150 per M.
Printed in 4 colors on glossy stock

1190 **Printwear Magazine**
National Business Media
PO Box 1416
Broomfield, CO 80038
303-469-0424
FAX: 303-469-5730
aciesla@nbm.com www.nbm.com/

Alexis Ciesla, Publisher
Leah Smith, Managing Editor
Robert Wieber, President

Published for imprinted sportswear professionals.
Monthly
Circulation: 25000

1191 **Promotional Sportswear**
520 W Foothill Parkway
Corona, CA 92882
951-799-9327
FAX: 909-279-9327
sales@promowear.com
catalogsportwear.com

Ted Taylor, Owner

Commercial direct screen printing, embroidery and complete art services on the highest quality sportswear available.

1192 **Promowear**
Beacon Funding Corporation
3400 Dundee Road
Suite 180
Northbrook, IL 60062
847-291-6494
FAX: 847-291-3414 800-866-6396
sales@freeembroiderystuff.com
www.promowaermag.com

Ann McNeill, Marketing
Mark Buchanan, Editor
Alexis Ciesla, Publisher

6 Issues In a Y Founded: 1990

1193 **Stitches**
PRIMEDIA Intertec Publication
745 Fifth Avenue
New York, NY 10151-3903
212-745-0100
FAX: 212-745-0121 866-505-7173
information@primedia.com
www.primedia.com

Doug MacDonald, Publisher
Ken Parsons, Editor

Provides information and the latest technology for embroidery professionals.
Founded: 1986
Circulation: 17233

1194 **Sunday New York Times**
New York Times
229 W 43rd Street
6th Floor
New York, NY 10036
212-561-1958
FAX: 212-556-7787 800-458-5522
public@nytimes.com
www.nytimes.com

Russell T Lewis, President/CEO
Bill Keller, Executive Editor
Daniel McGlynn, Executive Director

Weekly Founded: 1851
Circulation: 1.7 mill

1195 **Tack N' Togs Merchandising**
12400 Whitewater Drive
Suite 160
Minnetonka, MN 55343-9466
952-931-0211
FAX: 952-930-4362
pwahl@tagntogs.com
www.tackntogs.com

Paul Wahl, Editor
Barb Kastens, Promotions/Production Manager

Serves the horse and rider supply industry.
Monthly Founded: 1970
Circulation: 20424

1196 **Textile Rental Magazine**
Textile Rental Services Association
1800 Diagonal Road
Suite 200
Alexandria, VA 22314
703-190-0029
FAX: 703-519-0026
tras@trsa.org www.trsa.org

Jack Morgan, Editor
Paul Taub, Art Director
Debbie Smith, Advertising Director
Roger Cocivera, President

Featuring articles and analysis of every aspect of textile rental operations.
Annual

1197 **Uniformer**
Professional Apparel Association
994 Old Eagle School Road
Suite 1019
Wayne, PA 19087-1866
610-971-4850
FAX: 771-261-4859 800-722-7712
info@proapparel.com
www.proapparel.com

Hope Silverman, Executive Director

Quarterly

1198 **Upper Midwest Men's, Women's & Children's Apparel Club**
Northstar Apparel
CaliforniaMart 110 E. 9th St.
Suite A-777
Los Angeles, CA 90079-1777
213-627-3737
213- 62- 570
webmaster@apparelnews.net
www.apparelnews.net

Alison A Nieder, Executive Editor
Martin Wernicke, Publisher/Chairman/CEO
Molly Rhodes, President

450 pages

1199 **Wearables Business**
5680 Greenwood Plaza Boulevard
Suite 100
Greenwood Village, CO 80111
303-741-2901
FAX: 720-489-3101 866-505-7173
wucs@pbsub.com www.pbsub.com

Doug MacDonald, Publisher
Jeff Rundles, Editor
Brian Anderson, Senior Managing Editor
Suzi Link, Circulation Manager

Serves the apparel category of the burgeoning promotional products industry. Resource for wearable products among promotional products distributors. *$1320.00*
Monthly Founded: 1987
Circulation: 13533

1200 **Women's Wear Daily**
Fairchild Publications
7 W 34th Street
New York, NY 10001-8100
212-630-3880
FAX: 212-630-4580
advertising@wwd.com
www.fairchildpub.com

Edward Menicheschi, President
Edward Nardoza, Editorial Director
Sarah Murphy, Publisher

WWD is dedicated to providing a balance of timely, credible business news and key women's fashion trends to a dedicated readership. This readership includes retailers, designers, manufacturers, marketers, financiers, Wall Street analysts, international moguls, media executives, ad agencies, socialities and trendmakers. *$195.00*
Daily Founded: 1892
Circulation: 43618

Trade Shows

1201 **ASD/AMD Las Vegas Trade Show**
VNU Expositions/ASD-AMD Group
2950 31st Street
Suite 100
Santa Monica, CA 90405
310-966-6006
FAX: 310-399-2662 800-421-4511

Sam Bundy, Group President

As the nation's largest variety and general merchandise show we attract top exhibitors in all categories. This cost effective one-stop mega-marketplace lets you source the latest products in 150 leading categories, from a roster of companies that is unequalled at any other variety and general merchandise trade show in the nation.
10000 Attendees Annual/August

1202 ASG Conference
American Sewing Guild
9660 Hillcroft
Suite 510
Houston, TX 77096
713-729-3000
FAX: 713-729-9230
info@asg.org www.asg.org
Joanna Crenshaw, President
Margo Martin, Executive Director
The annual Conference gives all Guild members the opportunity to meet sewing professionals, industry representatives, and other sewing enthusiasts from around the country, and to participate in sewing seminars and sewing related special events and tours.
July

1203 ASR: Action Sports Retailer Trade Exposition
VNU Expositions
310 Broadway
Laguna Beach, CA 92651
949-766-6161
FAX: 949-497-3932 www.asrbiz.com
Chris Fraser, Expo Coordinator
Lora Bodmer, Contact
Allison Singer, Senior Accuont Manager
Alicia Keith, Operations Director
1,500 booths, 500 brands and youth lifestyle market.
20000 Attendees Annual/September 7500 names $295 per M.

1204 AccessoriesTheShow
Conference Management Company
50 Day Street
Norwalk, CT 06854
203-853-6015
FAX: 203-838-5028
Steve Levine, Executive Director
America's most important trade event for women's fashion jewelry, accessories, leathergoods and collectibles.
7M Attendees

1205 Action Sports Retailer Trade Exposition
Miller Freeman Publications
PO Box 1899
Laguna Beach, CA 92652
847-296-6742
FAX: 847-391-9827 www.nsga.org
Kevin Flanagan, Show Director
Peter Devin, Group Show Director
Kristen Novick, Expo Services Coordinator
Alicia Keith, Director Operations
Manufacturers, suppliers, retailers, buyers, guides, outfitters, distributors, importers, exporters, press and industry influencers have converged at Fly-Fishing Retailer to chart the future of their business.
6000 Attendees Annual/September

1206 American Flock Association Annual Meeting
6 Beacon Street
Suite 1125
Boston, MA 02108
617-428-8220
FAX: 617-542-2199
info@flocking.org www.flocking.org
Thomas Witham, Chairman
Todd Der Manouelian, Vice Chairman
Barrett F Ripley, Executive Director
The program will be a one-day business meeting including: Flock Safety and Health Update, NIOSH Cleaning Equipment Project, Flock versus Microsuede: Upholstery Specification Comparison, Flock Automotive Industry.

1207 Annual Meeting and Conference
Sunglass Association of America
390 North Bridge Street
LaBelle, FL 33935
863-612-0085
FAX: 863-612-0250
info@sunglassassociation.com
www.sunglassassociation.com
Kenneth Frederick, President
Jim Pritts, VP
Alvin Hutzler, II, VP
Henry Lane, VP Market Research
Bruce Bartley, VP/Secretary
Learn about new market information, statistics, training and industry trends.
September

1208 Apparel Show of the Americas
Bobbin Publishing/Miller Freeman
PO Box 279
Euless, TX 76039
817-215-1600
FAX: 817-215-1666 800-693-1363
bobbin.expoinfo@mfi.com
wwwmfi.com
Betty Webb, Trade Show Director
Conference, seminar and 329 exhibits of equipment, fabrics, accessories and services for sewn products and apparel.
5790 Attendees Annual Founded: 1992

1209 Arnold Schwarzenegger Fitness Exposition
Arnold Fitness Exposition
1245 Worthington Woods Boulevard
Worthington, OH 43085
614-431-2600
FAX: 614-431-3493
jlorimer@arnoldexpo.com
arnoldclassic.com
Jim Lorimer, Event Producer
Lynn Arnold, Manager
Featuring 600 Booth exposition promoting muscle supplements, magazines, clothing and memorabilia commemorating Schwarzenegger.
100M Attendees March

1210 Bead and Button Show
Kalmbach Publishing Company
21027 Crossroads Circle
PO Box 1612
Waukesha, WI 53187-1612
262-968-8776
FAX: 262-796-1615 800-533-6644
Robin Carlson, Executive Director
Beads and buttons from around the world, classess and workshops offered.
3500 Attendees Annual/May Founded: 1985

1211 Big and Tall Men's Apparel Needs Show
Specialty Trade Show
3939 Hardie Road
Coconut Grove, FL 33133
305-663-6635
FAX: 305-661-8118
A gathering of buyers and vendors of apparel and accessories for tall and plus sized men. 200 Exhibitors.
1,500 Attendees February/August

1212 Chicago Men's Collective: Winter
Merchandise Mart Center
350 N Orleans
Room 904
Chicago, IL 60654
312-274-4141
FAX: 312-670-1250 800-677-6278
Bruce Schedler, Managing Director
This is the finest and most upscale men's show in the country attracting the best men's specialty stores from the greater Midwest area and from across the nation.
5000 Attendees August

1213 Convergence
2402 University Avenue W
#702
Saint Paul, MN 55114-1701
651-178-8805
FAX: 651-646-0806
www.weavespindye.org
Robert Wolf, President
Stephen Banks, Chief Executive Officer
Sandra Bowles, Editor
Conference for everyone who loves and works in fiber.
3M Attendees June, Biennial

1214 E-Sports & Business Services Show at the Super Show
Communications & Show Management
1450 NE 123rd Street
North Miami, FL 33161
305-893-8771
FAX: 305-893-8783 800-327-3736
thesupershow@csmipi.com
www.thesupershow.com
Hardy Katz, Show Director
Laurie Aronson, Exhibitor Services
Lizette Piedra, Exhibit Booth Sales
Retailers, distributors, wholesalers, importers/exporters and other buyers of sports related products come for 10,000 exhibits of sports apparel, footwear, accessories and e-commerce products and services.
80000 Attendees January

1215 Eastern Men's Market/Collective
AMC Trade Shows/DMC Expositions
240 Peachtree Street NW
Suite 2200
Atlanta, GA 30303
404-220-2000
FAX: 404-220-2442
Jessica Johnson, Executive Director
Jeff Portman, Chief Executive Officer
Sarah Adamson, Show Manager
An outlet for the latest trends and designs in products and services. Attendees include store buyers, interior designers, architects, museum buyers, sales reps and mail order catalog buyers.
500 Attendees

1216 Embroiders Guild of America
Brown Hotel
335 W Broadway
Suite 100
Louisville, KY 40202-2167
502-583-1234
FAX: 502-584-7900 www.egausa.org
Armida L Taylor, President
Adrienne Meyer, VP Operations
Karen Wohahn, Treasurer
Helena Dittmar, Secrtary
Barbara Kammerzell, Contact
Fostering the art of needlework and associated arts. 40 tables.
20000 Attendees

1217 **Embroidery Trade Association Convention**
12300 Ford Road
Suite 135
Dallas, TX 75234
972-470-0415
FAX: 972-755-2561 888-628-2545
info@embroiderytrade.org
www.embroiderytrade.org
Lance Sabo, Founder
John Swinburn, CAE, Executive Director
Dick Williams, Account Executive
Embroidery Business Management.

1218 **FFANY Collections**
Fashion Footwear Association of New York
1414 6th Avenue at 58th Street
Suite 203
New York, NY 10019
212-751-6422
FAX: 212-751-6404
jmoore@ffany.org www.ffany.org
Joseph C Moore, Chairman/President/CEO
Phyllis Rein, Senior VP
The essential venue for fashion footwear. Held at FFANY participating show rooms. 50 Exhibitors.
300 Attendees August

1219 **Fabric Exhibition**
Advanstar Communications
1 Park Avenue
New York, NY 10016
212-797-7631
FAX: 212-951-6793
info@advanstar.com
www.advanstar.com
Alexander S DeBarr, Executive Vice President
Josphe Loggia, Chief Executive Officer
David W Montgomery, VP Finance/CFO/Secretary
Conference and exhibition of interest to those in the fabric and garment industry.
7000 Attendees

1220 **Fitness Show at the Super Show**
Communications & Show Management
1450 NE 123rd Street
North Miami, FL 33161
305-893-8771
FAX: 305-893-8783 800-327-3736
thesupershow@csmipi.com
www.thesupershow.com
Hardy Katz, Show Director
Laurie Aronson, Exhibitor Services
Lizette Piedra, Exhibit Booth Sales
Retailers, distributors, wholesalers, importers/exporters and other buyers of sports related products come for 10,000 exhibits of sports apparel, footwear, accessories and e-commerce products and services.
80000 Attendees January

1221 **Gatlinburg Apparel & Jewelry Market**
Norton Shows
PO Box 265
Gatlinburg, TN 37738
865-436-6151
FAX: 865-436-6152
nortonshows@aol.com
www.nortonshows.com
Tom Norton, Show Manager/Owner
Linda Norton, Owner
Trade show that takes place 4 times per year and has wholesale, cash-and-carry, ladies, mens, and children's apparel, fashion jewelry, accessories, fine jewelry and gifts from around the world. There are 500-700 booths.
20000 Attendees March/June/Sept/Nov
Founded: 1987
Mailing list available for rent 70,000 names

1222 **Global Leather**
Footwear Industries of America
1601 N Kent Street
Suite 1200
Arlington, VA 22205
703-524-1864
FAX: 703-522-6741 800-520-2262
Fawn Evenson, President
Mary R Howell, Contact
Showcases the best in new leather materials and components for footwear leather, needle and allied trades of North America. Brings together hundreds of exhibitors from the major sourcing cities around the world, showcasing thousands of products.
1500 Attendees February/August

1223 **Holiday Sample Sale**
San Francisco Design Center
635 8th Street
San Francisco, CA 94103
415-490-5800
FAX: 415-490-5885
www.sfdesigncenter.com
Dianne Travalini, Show Director
Aruex Dalmacio, Show Manager
Open to the public and offers jewelry, accessories and leather items, gift items, home accessories, housewares, toys and apparel.
11000 Attendees November

1224 **Hospitality Design Expo**
American Flock Association
6 Beacon Street
Suite 1125
Boston, MA 02108
617-428-8220
FAX: 617-542-2199
info@flocking.org www.flocking.org
Thomas Witham, Chairman
Todd Der Manouelian, Vice Chairman
Barrett F Ripley, Executive Director
Will exhibit flocked products for the hospitality design industries. 1,000 Exhibitors.
May

1225 **ISAM: International Swimwear and Activewear Market**
California Market Center
110 E 9th Street
Los Angeles, CA 90079
213-303-3688
FAX: 213-630-3708 800-225-6278
Barbara Brady, Director
Serves the swimwear and resortwear industry.
August/September Founded: 1978

1226 **Imprinted Sportswear Shows**
650 S Griffin Street
Dallas, TX 75380
214-939-2700
FAX: 972-385-9003
Chris Brewer, Director
Richard Lebovitz, Editorial Director
Serves the imprinted sportswear/textile screen printing/embroidery/monogramming industry.
6-9M Attendees

1227 **International Association of Clothing Desi gners Convention**
34 Thornton Ferry Road
#1
Amherst, NH 03031
603-672-4065
FAX: 603-672-4064
dmschmida@aol.com www.iacde.com
Udo Maelzer, President
David Schmida, Executive Director
Focus is on the retail link in the apparel supply chain. The students and faculty of the Fashion Institute of Technology are involved in the planning and presentation of many of the convention programs.
April

1228 **International Fashion Boutique Show**
Advanstar Communications
757 3rd Ave
New York, NY 10017-2013
212-951-6600
FAX: 212-951-6793
info@advanstar.com
www.advanstar.com
Alexander S DeBarr, Executive Vice President
Joseph Loggia, Chief Executive Officer
David W Montgomery, VP Finance/CFO/Secretary
Offers a variety of fashion trade shows throughout each year at the Javitz Convention Center in New York.
25000 Attendees

1229 **International Fashion Fabric Exhibition**
Advanstar Communications
545 Boylston Street
Boston, MA 02116
617-514-4600
FAX: 617-267-6900
info@advanstar.com
www.advanstar.com
Alexander S DeBarr, Executive Vice President
Joseph Loggia, Chief Executive Officer
David W Montgomery, VP Finance/CFO/Secretary
Conference and exibits of interest to those in the fabric and garment industries.
15000 Attendees

1230 **International Hosiery Exposition**
Home Sewing Association
105 Mall Boulevard
PO Box 1312
Monroeville, PA 15146
412-372-5950
FAX: 412-372-5953 www.sewing.org
Dotty Grexa, President
Jenna Sheldon, Director Trade Show/Meetings
Jenny Prevatte, Director Information Services
Specialize in the latest hosiery and sewn products industries' supplies and services. 250 Exhibitors.
10000 Attendees

1231 **International Intimate Apparel Lingerie Show**
Specialty Trade Show
3939 Hardle Road
Coconut Grove, FL 33133
305-663-6635
FAX: 305-661-8118
Specializing in sexy lingerie and adult products.

2,000 Attendees October

1232 International Kids Fashion Show
Advanstar Communications
545 Boylston Street
Boston, MA 02116
617-514-4600
FAX: 617-267-6900
info@advanstar.com
www.advanstar.com

Denise Raeside, Show Manager

Children's fashions, accessories, gift items, and footwear.

3500 Attendees Jan/March/August/Octobet

1233 International Show at the Super Show
Communications & Show Management
1450 NE 123rd Street
North Miami, FL 33161
305-893-8771
FAX: 305-893-8783 800-327-3736
thesupershow@csmipi.com
www.thesupershow.com

Hardy Katz, Show Director
Laurie Aronson, Exhibitor Services
Lizette Piedra, Exhibit Booth Sales

Retailers, distributors, wholesalers, importers/exporters and other buyers of sports related products come for 10,000 exhibits of sports apparel, footwear, accessories and e-commerce products and services.

80000 Attendees January

1234 International Western Apparel and Accessories Market
Dallas Market Center
2100 Stemmons Freeway
Dallas, TX 75207
214-556-6100
FAX: 800-637-6833 800-325-6587

Bill Winsor, President/CEO
Pat Zajac, Contact Home Expo

Offers array of services geared toward helping retailers expand business and increase profits.

200M Attendees March/August Founded: 1957

1235 Licensed Sports Show at the Super Show
Communications & Show Management
1450 NE 123rd Street
North Miami, FL 33161
305-893-8771
FAX: 305-893-8783 800-327-3736
thesupershow@csmipi.com
www.thesupershow.com

Hardy Katz, Show Director
Laurie Aronson, Exhibitor Services
Lizette Piedra, Exhibit Booth Sales

Retailers, distributors, wholesalers, importers/exporters and other buyers of sports related products come for 10,000 exhibits of sports apparel, footwear, accessories and e-commerce products and services.

80000 Attendees January

1236 MAGIC International Show
MAGIC International
6320 Canoga Avenue
12th Floor
Woodland Hills, CA 91367
818-593-5000
FAX: 310-593-5020
www.magiconline.com

Joe Loggia, President/CEO

Fashion trade show in Las Vegas. 3,000 exhibitors.

75000 Attendees February/August
Founded: 1933

1237 MAGIC Kids
6320 Canoga Avenue
Suite 303
Woodland Hills, CA 91367
818-593-5000
FAX: 310-593-5020
www.magiconline.com

Joe Loggie, President/CEO
Laura McConnell, VP
Ted Farthing, Media Contact

The largest, most prestigious children's apparel show in the United States, and the undisputed marketplace for kids' fashions. MAGIC kids presents a full spectrum of products from layette and toddler to tween. Preview the newest offerings for both boys and girls from designers and manufacturers from around the worlds. The trade show is held annually in Las Vegas.

80000 Attendees February Founded: 1933

1238 Manufacturers Wholesalers Outerwear Sportswear Show
I. Spiewak & Sons
469 7th Avenue
10th Floor
New York, NY 10018-6505
212-695-1620
FAX: 212-629-4803 800-223-6850
jerry@spiewak.com
www.spiewak.com

Gerald Spiewak, Executive Director

180 booths for manufacturers and importers of outerwear and rainwear.

3M Attendees January

1239 Material World
Urban Expositions
1395 S Marietta Parkway
Building 400, Suite 210
Marietta, GA 30067
770-180-0972
FAX: 678-285-7469 800-318-2238

Doug Miller, President
Tim von Gal, Executive VP
Suzanne Pruitt, Contact

From design to delivery, Material World is the international full package, sourcing and fashion information event for the fabric related industries.

10600 Attendees May

1240 Men's and Boy's Apparel Show
Miami International Merchandise Mart
777 NW 72nd Avenue
Miami, FL 33126
305-665-5630
FAX: 305-261-3659
www.miamimart.net

Martiza Agudo, President
Glorys Covo, Administrator

This is a three-day show where wholesale buyers will find an extensive display of apparel lines including Calvin Klein, Perruzo, Supreme, just to name a few.

1000 Attendees April 29-May 2

1241 NSGA: National Sporting Goods Association World Sports Exposition
National Sporting Goods Association
1699 Wall Street
Suite 1
Mt. Prospect, IL 60056
847-439-4000
FAX: 847-391-9827 www.nsga.org

Ron Kruse, Chairman
Jim Sadek, President
Kevin Adams, Director

85000 Attendees Founded: 1929

1242 National Bridal Market: Fall
Merchandise Mart Properties
200 World Trade Center
Suite 470
Chicago, IL 60654
312-274-4141
FAX: 312-527-7782 800-677-6278

Bruce Schedler, Managing Director
Mary Beth Stewart, Public Relations

Features the most extensive selection of bridal resources in the country.

3000 Attendees October

1243 National Halloween & Costume & Party Show
Transworld Exhibits
18850 Oak Street
Northfield, IL 60093
847-784-6905
FAX: 847-446-3523 800-323-5462

Joe Thaler, CEO
Paul O'Connor, Executive Director

This once a year event is where over 10,000 attendees will converge on Chicago from all across the US and over 50 foreign countries to see what over 700 manufacturers and distributors are showcasing as new and exciting for parties, shops and haunted houses. Free educational seminars and workshops.

10000 Attendees February

1244 National NeedleArts Association Markets
PO Box 3388
Zanesville, OH 43702-3388
740-455-6773
FAX: 740-452-2552 800-889-8662
tnna.info@offinger.com
www.tnna.org

Stacy Charles, President
Marilyn Murphy, VP
Jim Bryson, Treasurer/Secretary

Five hundred booths representing the needlework industry, currently offering trade shows, including an extensive educational seminar program.

5M Attendees June

1245 National NeedleArts Association Trade Show
National Needlework Association
PO Box 3388
Zanesville, OH 43702-3388
740-452-4541
FAX: 740-452-2552 800-889-8662
tnna.info@offinger.com
www.tnna.org

Rise Fulmer, Trade Show Manager
Patty Parrish, Executive Director

January Founded: 1974

1246 National Sewing Show
Home Sewing Association
105 Mall Boulevard
PO Box 1312
Monroeville, PA 15146
412-372-5950
FAX: 412-372-5953 www.sewing.org

Dotty Grexa, President

September

1247 New England Apparel Club
New England Apparel Club
26 Dartmouth Street
Suite 130
Westwood, MA 02090
781-326-9223

neacrlg@aol.com www.neacshow.com
Richard Usherwood, President
2500 regional sales reps exhibiting clothing and related equipment, supplies and services.
2000 Attendees October, Boston

1248 Northstar Fashion Exhibitors
3001 Hyatt Merchandise Mart
Minneapolis, MN 55403
612-333-5219
FAX: 612-333-5226 800-272-6972
northstarfashion@aol.com
northstarfashion.com
Elyse Kroll, Executive Director
Stanley Kaye, Show Coordinator
Debi Higgins, Manager
Trade show collections for mens, womens, childrens apparel, accessories and textiles. 250 Booths.
1,260 Attendees August/October

1249 Northwest Shoe Traveler's Buying Shoe Market
Northwest Shoe Traveler's
12630 12th Street N
Lake Elmo, MN 55042
651-436-2709
FAX: 651-436-2028
Teri Tompkins, Show Manager
Trade show collections for mens, womens and childrens.
250 Attendees January

1250 Off-Price Specialist Show
Off Price Specialist Center
16985 W Bluemound Road
Suite 210
Brookfield, WI 53005
262-821-1900
FAX: 262-782-1601
info@offpriceshow.com
www.offpriceshow.com
Bill Jage, President/CEO
Carol FitzMaurice, Executive Show Director
Bob Milner, Buyers Contact
Carol Fitzmaurice, Exhibitors Contact
Premiere show for off-price apparel and accessories.
12000 Attendees May 8-10

1251 Outdoor Retailer Summer Market
VNU Expositions
310 Broadway
Laguna Beach, CA 92652
949-766-6161
FAX: 949-497-2093 800-486-2701
Peter Devin, Group Show Director
Kristen Novick, Attendee Information
David Lockner, Manager
Features the most comprehensive collection of outdoor apparel, gear, equipment, climbing technology, footwear, ski mountaineering, camping, backpacking, cycling and accessory companies from which to buy products.
16000 Attendees August

1252 Outdoor Retailer Winter Market
VNU Expositions
PO Box 1899
Laguna Beach, CA 92652
949-226-5722
FAX: 949-226-5625
Kristen Novick, Attendee Information
Megan Lara, Exposition Coordinator
Peter Devin, Group Show Director
David Lockner, Manager
Features the most comprehensive collection of outdoor apparel, gear, equipment, climbing technology, footwear, ski mountaineering, hunting, rescue outerwear and accessory companies from which to buy products.
13000 Attendees January

1253 PGA Merchandise Show
Reed Exhibition Companies
383 Main Avenue
Suite 3
Norwalk, CT 06851
203-840-4800
FAX: 203-840-9628 800-840-5628
inquiry@pga.reedexpo.com
www.pgaexpo.com
Stan Phelps, Director Marketing/Special Events
Fred Evanko, Group Sales Director
Joshua Crum, Media Contact
World's largest golf industry trade event. Open to retail buyers and golf industry professionals. Not open to the public
38500 Attendees January Founded: 1954

1254 Panamerican Leather Fair
CMP Princeton
125 Village Boulevard
Suite 220
Princeton, NJ 08540
609-452-2800
FAX: 609-452-2875
rbianchi@cmpprinceton.com
www.palfair.com
Raymond Bianchi, Show Manager
Panamerican Leather Fair is a premier event that brings together the entire leather market in the Western Hemisphere.
3,000 Attendees January

1255 Performance & Lifestyle Footwear Show at the Super Show
Communications & Show Management
1450 NE 123rd Street
North Miami, FL 33161
305-893-8771
FAX: 305-893-8783 800-327-3736
thesupershow@csmipi.com
www.thesupershow.com
Hardy Katz, Show Manager
Franc Boza, Exhibit Sales Manager
Retailers, distributors, wholesalers, importers/exporters and other buyers of sports related products come for 10,000 exhibits of sports apparel, footwear, accessories and e-commerce products and services.
80000 Attendees January

1256 Printwear Show
National Business Media
2800 W Midway Boulevard
PO Box 1416
Broomfield, CO 80020
303-469-0424
FAX: 303-469-5730
Robert H Wieber, Jr, President/CEO
Greg Hadden, Production/Technology Manager
Cory Gonzales, Controller
Features screen printing, embroidery, heat applied graphics, digital textile printing, sublimation and apparel.
August

1257 Professional Apparel Association Expo
994 Old Eagle School Road
Suite 1019
Wayne, PA 19087-1866
610-971-4850
FAX: 610-971-4859 800-722-7712
info@proapparel.com
www.proapparel.com
Sharon Tannahill, Executive Director
Exhibitors display health care and hospitality uniforms, shoes, and accessories, and career apparel. Workshops and seminars for uniform retailers are also available. 36 booths.
600 Attendees September

1258 Seattle Trend Show
Pacific Northwest Apparel Association
600 SW Kenyon Street
Suite T-201
Seattle, WA 98106
206-767-9200
FAX: 206-767-0707
pnaa@earthlink.com
Patricia Hodges, Executive Director
Cindy Steele, Associate Director
Show and exhibits of apparel and related accessories.
2000 Attendees Jan/Apr/Jun/Aug/Oct

1259 Shoe Market of America
Miami Merchandise Mart
777 NW 72nd Avenue
Miami, FL 33126
305-612-2900
FAX: 786-331-9955
info@smota.com www.smota.com
Dianne Travalini, Executive Director
Alex Meme, Manager
Conducts three trade shows a year. Features the entire spectrum of footwear companies.
2500 Attendees June

1260 Southeastern Shoe & Accessories Market
Southern Shoe Travelers Association
800 Old Rosewell Lakes Parkway
Rosewell, GA 30076
770-587-6702
FAX: 770-587-6704 www.sesta.org
Servicing those in the Southern United States engaged in the sale and distribution of footwear.
2000 Attendees February

1261 Southwestern Shoe Traveler's
Southwestern Shoe Traveler's Association
2300 Stemmons Freeway, Suite 4F03
PO Box 586118
Dallas, TX 72528
214-638-5770
FAX: 214-292-9691 swst@swbell.net
Dianne Travalini, Executive Director
Definitive footwear trade site for footwear retailers.
1800 Attendees June

1262 **Team Sports Show at the Super Show**
Communications & Show Management
1450 NE 123rd Street
North Miami, FL 33161
305-893-8771
FAX: 305-893-8783 800-327-3736
thesupershow@csmipi.com
www.thesupershow.com

Hardy Katz, Show Director
Laurie Aronson, Exhibitor Services
Lizette Piedra, Exhibit Booth Sales

Retailers, distributors, wholesalers, importers/exporters and other buyers of sports related products come for 10,000 exhibits of sports apparel, footwear, accessories and e-commerce products and services.
80000 Attendees January

1263 **Tennis & Golf Show at the Super Show**
Communications & Show Management
1450 NE 123rd Street
North Miami, FL 33161
305-893-8771
FAX: 305-893-8783 800-327-3736
thesupershow@csmipi.com
www.thesupershow.com

Hardy Katz, Show Manager
Laurie Aronson, Exhibitor Services
Lizette Piedra, Exhibit Booth Sales

Retailers, distributors, wholesalers, importers/exporters and other buyers of sports related products come for 10,000 exhibits of sports apparel, footwear, accessories and e-commerce products and services.
80000 Attendees January

1264 **Trimmings, Accessories, Fabrics Expo**
National Knitwear & Sportswear Association
386 Park Avenue S
Suite 5741
New York, NY 10016-8804
212-683-7520
FAX: 212-532-0766

Seth Bodner, Executive Director

The only all-inclusive trimmings show in the United States. 160 booths.
6M Attendees November

1265 **WAM: Western Apparel Manufacturers Show**
Dallas Market Center
2300 Stemmons Freeway
Dallas, TX 75258
214-556-6100
FAX: 214-638-7221
info@dmcmail.com
www.dallasmarketcenter.com
Apparel manufacturing equipment. Held to meet the needs of the TOLA retailers who take advantage of the early fall buying opportunities.
3.2M Attendees April

1266 **WSA: Western Shoe Associates**
Western Shoe Associates
20281 SW Birch Street
Newport Beach, CA 92660
949-851-8451
FAX: 949-851-8523

Mitch Fisherman, President
Steve Katz, VP
Marie Mussabini, Exhibitor Coordinator
Dave Darling, Treasurer

Trade show held twice a year and featuring footwear.
26000 Attendees

1267 **WWD Magic**
MAGIC International
6200 Canoga Avenue
Suite 303
Woodland Hills, CA 91367
818-593-5000
FAX: 310-593-5020
www.magiconline.com

Joe Loggia, President/CEO
Laura McConnell, VP

WWD Magic, a joint venture with Women's Wear Daily, is the recognized leader in women's apparel and accessories expositions in the world. WWD Magic offers the opportunity to discover new resources, network with industry peers, attend trend seminars and fashion shows, and meet with major manufacturers in an exciting and efficient forum. Containing over 1,000 exhibitors and 2,000 booths.
85000 Attendees August Founded: 1933

1268 **Western Shoe Associates International Buying Market**
Western Shoe Associates
20281 SW Birch Street
Suite 100
Newport Beach, CA 92660
949-851-8451
FAX: 949-851-8523

Mitch Fisherman, President
Marie Mussabini, Exhibitor Coordinator

Footwear trade market.
26000 Attendees

1269 **Western and English Sales Association Trade Shows**
Western and English Sales Association
451 E 58th Avenue
Suite 4128
Denver, CO 80216
303-295-1040
FAX: 303-295-0941 800-295-1041
info@denver-wesa.com
www.denver-wesa.com

Toni High, Executive Director

Featuring equestrain related apparel, tack, equipment, animal health, home decor, gifts, jewelry, art and leather goods.
8000 Attendees Sept/Jan

1270 **Women and Children's Market**
AMC Trade Shows/DMC Expositions
2140 Peachtree Street NW
Suite 2200
Atlanta, GA 30303
404-220-2000
FAX: 404-220-2442 800-285-6278

Sarah Adamson, Show Manager

Women and children's apparel.
9000 Attendees

1271 **Women's and Children's Apparel Market**
Dallas Market Center
2100 Stemmons Freeway
Dallas, TX 75207
214-556-6100
800-325-6587
ahood@dmcmail.com
www.dallasmarketcenter.com

Pat Zajac, Home Expo

Features the most comprehensive variety of apparel and accessories lines.
20000 Attendees October Founded: 1957

1272 **Women's and Children's Fall Market**
Merchandise Mart Properties
350 North Orleans
Chicago, IL 60654
312-274-4141
FAX: 312-527-7782
www.merchandisemart.com

H Brennen, III, Execuive Vice President
5000 Attendees Founded: 1950

1273 **Women's and Children's Summer/Fall Preview Market**
Merchandise Mart Properties
350 N Orleans
Chicago, IL 60654
312-527-4141
FAX: 312-527-7782 800-677-6278

H Brennen III, Executive VP

Women's and children's apparel.
5000 Attendees June

1274 **Wonderful World of Weddings and Occasions**
Expo Productions
510 Hartbrook Drive
Hartland, WI 53029
262-367-5500
FAX: 262-367-9956 800-367-5520
margegogin@sbcglobal.net
www.weddingshowepi.com

Marge Gogin, Show Contact

Wedding and other special occasion products, services, ideas including live and recorded music, still and video photography, cakes and catering, formal wear, gifts and much more.
6000 Attendees January

1275 **X-treme Sports Show at the Super Show**
Communications & Show Management
1450 NE 123rd Street
North Miami, FL 33161
305-893-8771
FAX: 305-893-8783 800-327-3736
thesupershow@csmipi.com
www.thesupershow.com

Hardy Katz, Show Manager
Laurie Aronson, Exhibitors Services
Lizette Piedra, Exhibit Booth Sales

Retailers, distributors, wholesalers, importers/exporters and other buyers of sports related products come for 10,000 exhibits of sports apparel, footwear, accessories and e-commerce products and services.
80000 Attendees January

Directories & Databases

1276 **Action Sports Retailer Buyer's Guide Issue**
Miller Freeman Publications
2655 Seely Avenue
San Jose, CA 95134
408-943-1234
FAX: 408-943-0513

Pat Cochran, Editor

Guide to 1,600 manufacturers and distributors of specialty watersports, beach, skateboarding, snowboarding, volleyball and bicycling equipment and clothing. *$25.00*

1277 American Apparel Contractors Association Directory - American Made Apparel
140 Maryanna Drive NE
PO Box 720693
Atlanta, GA 30342-1904
404-843-3171

Sue C Strickland, Executive Director
Over 300 listings are offered pertaining to contractors, manufacturers and suppliers to the apparel industry.
100 pages Annual Founded: 1981

1278 Apparel Specialty Stores Directory
Chain Store Guide
3922 Coconut Palm Drive
Tampa, FL 33619
813-276-6700
FAX: 813-627-6882 800-778-9794
info@csgis.com www.csgis.com
Jay Byin, Media General Contact
Chris Leedy, Advertising Sales
Shami Choon, Manager
The facts on more than 4,800 companies operating more than 70,700 stores all involved in the sale of women's, men's, family and children's wear. Also included are sporting goods stores that offer apparel and active wear as well as related merchandise. Includes more than 15,000 key buyers and executives. *$335.00*

1279 Bobbin-Suppliers Sourcing Issue
Bobbin Blenheim Media Corporation
1110 Shop Road
PO Box 1986
Columbia, SC 29201-4743

FAX: 803-799-1461 800-845-8820
Offers information on over 8,000 suppliers to the apparel/sewn products industry.
$35.00

Circulation: 2,000

1280 College Store Executive: Emblematics Directory Issue
Executive Business Media
825 Old Country Road
Westbury, NY 11590
516-334-3030
FAX: 516-334-3059
ebm-mail@ebmpubs.com
www.ebmpubs.com
Janice Costa, Editor
List of distributors of products with emblems or insignia; coverage includes Canada. *$5.00*
Annual, February

1281 Complete Directory of Apparel
Sutton Family Communications & Publishing Company
155 Sutton Lane
Fordsville, KY 42343
270-740-0870

jlsutton@apex.net
www.fleamarketeer.net
Theresa Sutton, Editor
Lee Sutton, General Manager
Print-out from database of wholesalers, manufacturers, distributors, importers and close-out houses. Database is updated daily to guarantee the most current sources available. *$77.65*
100+ pages

1282 Complete Directory of Apparel Close-Outs
Sutton Family Communications & Publishing Company
155 Sutton Lane
Fordsville, KY 42343
270-740-0870

jlsutton@apex.net
www.fleamarketeer.net
Theresa Sutton, Editor
Lee Sutton, General Manager
Print-out from database of wholesalers, manufacturers, distributors, importers and close-out houses. Database is updated daily to guarantee the most current sources available to the close-out apparel industry.
$55.20
100+ pages

1283 Complete Directory of Baby Goods and Gifts
Sutton Family Communications & Publishing Company
155 Sutton Lane
Fordsville, KY 42343
270-740-0870

jlsutton@apex.net
www.fleamarketeer.net
Theresa Sutton, Editor
Lee Sutton, General Manager
Print-out from database of wholesalers, manufacturers, distributors, importers and close-out houses for baby goods and gifts. Database is updated daily to guarantee the most current sources available. *$57.65*
100+ pages

1284 Complete Directory of Belts, Buckles & Boots
Sutton Family Communications & Publishing Company
155 Sutton Lane
Fordsville, KY 42343
270-740-0870

jlsutton@apex.net
www.fleamarketeer.net
Theresa Sutton, Editor
Lee Sutton, General Manager
Print-out from database of wholesalers, manufacturers, distributors, importers and close-out houses. Database is updated daily to guarantee the most current sources available. *$55.20*
100+ pages

1285 Complete Directory of Brand New Surplus Merchandise
Sutton Family Communications & Publishing Company
155 Sutton Lane
Fordsville, KY 42343
270-740-0870

jlsutton@apex.net
www.fleamarketeer.net
Theresa Sutton, Editor
Lee Sutton, General Manager
Print-out from database of wholesalers, manufacturers, distributors, importers and close-out houses. Database is updated daily to guarantee the most current sources available. *$92.70*
100+ pages

1286 Complete Directory of Caps & Hats
Sutton Family Communications & Publishing Company
155 Sutton Lane
Fordsville, KY 42343
270-740-0870

jlsutton@apex.net
www.fleamarketeer.net
Theresa Sutton, Editor
Lee Sutton, General Manager
Print-out from database of wholesalers, manufacturers, distributors, importers and close-out houses. Database is updated daily to guarantee the most current sources available. *$55.20*
100+ pages

1287 Complete Directory of Clothing & Uniforms
Sutton Family Communications & Publishing Company
155 Sutton Lane
Fordsville, KY 42343
270-740-0870

jlsutton@apex.net
www.fleamarketeer.net
Theresa Sutton, Editor
Lee Sutton, General Manager
Print-out from database of wholesalers, manufacturers, distributors, importers and close-out houses. Database is updated daily to guarantee the most current sources available. *$55.20*
100+ pages

1288 Complete Directory of Hat Pins, Feathers and Fads
Sutton Family Communications & Publishing Company
155 Sutton Lane
Fordsville, KY 42343
270-740-0870

jlsutton@apex.net
www.fleamarketeer.net
Theresa Sutton, Editor
Lee Sutton, General Manager
Print-out from database of wholesalers, manufacturers, distributors, importers and close-out houses. Database is updated daily to guarantee the most current sources available. *$67.70*
100+ pages

1289 Complete Directory of Purses & Handbags
Sutton Family Communications & Publishing Company
155 Sutton Lane
Fordsville, KY 42343
270-740-0870

jlsutton@apex.net
www.fleamarketeer.net
Theresa Sutton, Editor
Lee Sutton, General Manager
Print-out from database of wholesalers, manufacturers, distributors, importers and close-out houses. Database is updated daily to guarantee the most current sources available. *$55.20*
100+ pages

1290 **Complete Directory of Sunglasses & Eye Weather**
Sutton Family Communications & Publishing Company
155 Sutton Lane
Fordsville, KY 42343
270-740-0870

jlsutton@apex.net
www.fleamarketeer.net

Theresa Sutton, Editor
Lee Sutton, General Manager

Print-out from database of wholesalers, manufacturers, distributors, importers and close-out houses. Database is updated daily to guarantee the most current sources available. *$55.20*

100+ pages

1291 **Complete Directory of T-Shirts, Heat Transfers & Supplies**
Sutton Family Communications & Publishing Company
155 Sutton Lane
Fordsville, KY 42343
270-740-0870

jlsutton@apex.net
www.fleamarketeer.net

Theresa Sutton, Editor
Lee Sutton, General Manager

Print-out from database of wholesalers, manufacturers, distributors, importers and close-out houses. Database is updated daily to guarantee the most current sources available. *$55.20*

100+ pages

1292 **Complete Directory of Western Wear**
Sutton Family Communications & Publishing Company
155 Sutton Lane
Fordsville, KY 42343
270-740-0870

jlsutton@apex.net
www.fleamarketeer.net

Theresa Sutton, Editor
Lee Sutton, General Manager

Print-out from database of wholesalers, manufacturers, distributors, importers and close-out houses. Database is updated daily to guarantee the most current sources available. *$55.20*

100+ pages

1293 **Complete Directory of Women's Accessories**
Sutton Family Communications & Publishing Company
155 Sutton Lane
Fordsville, KY 42343
270-740-0870

jlsutton@apex.net
www.fleamarketeer.net

Theresa Sutton, Editor
Lee Sutton, General Manager

Print-out from database of wholesalers, manufacturers, distributors, importers and close-out houses. Database is updated daily to guarantee the most current sources available. *$55.20*

100+ pages

1294 **Directory of Active Sportswear**
Sutton Family Communications & Publishing Company
155 Sutton Lane
Fordsville, KY 42343
270-740-0870

jlsutton@apex.net
www.fleamarketeer.net

Theresa Sutton, Editor
Lee Sutton, General Manager

Print-out from database of wholesalers, manufacturers, distributors, importers and close-out houses. Database is updated daily to guarantee the most current sources available. Approximately 740 wholesale sources in a 3-ring binder. *$67.20*

100+ pages

1295 **Directory of Apparel Specialty Stores**
AKTRIN Textile Information Center
164 S Main Street
PO Box 898
High Point, NC 27261
336-418-8583
FAX: 336-841-5435
aktrin@aktrin.com
www.textile-info.com

Information resource for people seeking in-depth, up-to-date data on the apparel specialty stores marketplace. Fully searchable database, either in form of a CD-ROM or downloadable over the Internet. *$780.00*

Annual

1296 **Directory of Hosiery Manufacturers**
Hosiery Association
3623 Latrobe Drive
Suite 130
Charlotte, NC 28211
704-365-0913
FAX: 704-362-2056
hosierytha@aol.com
www.hosieryassociation.com

Sally Kay, President

Over 700 hosiery manufacturers and distributors. *$100.00*

Annual Founded: 1905 : Disc

1297 **Directory of Mail Order Catalogs**
Grey House Publishing
185 Millerton Road
PO Box 860
Millerton, NY 12546
518-890-0526
FAX: 518-789-0545 800-562-2139
books@greyhouse.com
www.greyhouse.com

Leslie Mackenzie, Publisher
Richard Gottlieb, Editor

The premier source of information on the mail order catalog industry. Covers over 12,000 consumer and business catalog companies with 44 different product chapters including clothing and sportswear. *$350.00*

1600 pages Annual Founded: 1980 ISBN 1-592370-66-7

1298 **Earnshaw's Buyer's Guide to the New York Market**
Earnshaw Publications
225 W 34th Street
Suite 1212
New York, NY 10122-1201
212-563-2742
FAX: 212-629-3249

A children's wear guide offering over 1,200 manufacturers and suppliers of clothing for infants, boys and girls apparel.

200 pages Annual
Circulation: 10,000

1299 **Earnshaw's Infants', Girls', Boys' Wear Review: Children's Wear Directory**
Earnshaw Publications
225 W 34th Street
Suite 1212
New York, NY 10122-1201
212-563-2742
FAX: 212-629-3249

A directory of over 1,500 children's apparel and accessory firms with offices or showrooms in the United States. *$10.00*

Annual
Circulation: 10,000

1300 **Financial Performance Profile of Public Apparel Companies**
Kurt Salmon Associates
1355 Peachtree Street NW
Suite 900
Atlanta, GA 30309-3257
404-892-0321
FAX: 404-898-9590
www.kurtsalmon.com

William B Pace, CEO

Information on over 60 publicly held apparel manufacturers are available. *$400.00*

300 pages Annual Founded: 1935

1301 **Garment Manufacturers Index**
Klevens Publications
411 S Main Street
Suite 209
Los Angeles, CA 90013
213-625-9000
FAX: 213-625-5002
editor@klevenspub.com
www.garmentindex.com

Herbert Schwartz, Editor

A list of over 5,000 manufacturers and suppliers of products and services such as fabrics, trimmings, factory equipment and sewing contractors used in the manufacture of apparel and other sewn products. *$105.00*

264 pages Annual Founded: 1938
Circulation: 29,495
Printed in 4 colors on matte stock

1302 **Hosiery and Bodywear: Buyer's Guide to Support and Control Top Pantyhose**
Advanstar Communications
545 Boylston Street
Boston, MA 02116
617-514-4600
FAX: 617-267-6900
info@advanstar.com
www.advanstar.com

Jill Gerson-Price, Executive Editor

List of about 50 hosiery manufacturers. *$3.00*

Annual September
Circulation: 10,500

1303 **Impressions: Directory Issue**
Miller Freeman Publications
1199 S Belt Line Road
Suite 100
Coppell, TX 75019
972-906-6500
FAX: 972-906-6671
www.impressionsmag.com

A list of more than 1,500 suppliers of products, services and equipment used in the imprinted sportswear industry including

textile screen print equipment, supplies, embroidery equipment and supplies, and all types of imprintables. *$18.00*
Annual
Circulation: 60,000

1304 **International Nonwovens Directory**
PO Box 1288
Cary, NC 27512-1288
919-233-1210
FAX: 919-233-1282 www.inda.org
Lori L Reynolds, Production Manager
A Who's Who directory of services and supplies to the nonwovens industry.
750 pages Biennial
Circulation: 2,000

1305 **Nationwide Directory of Men's & Boys' Wear Buyers**
Reed Reference Publishing RR Bowker
121 Chanlon Road
New Providence, NJ 07974-1544
908-665-2834
FAX: 908-464-3553 800-269-5372
info@bowker.com www.bowker.com
A who's who directory of services and supplies to the industry. *$147.00*
700 pages Annual
Circulation: 1,000

1306 **Outerwear Sourcebook: Directory Issue**
Fur Publishing Plus
19 W Street
Suite 403
New York, NY 10004-1006
212-727-1210
FAX: 212-727-1218
Richard Harrow, Editor
List of more than 3,500 outerwear manufacturers in the US and Canada; 1,000 companies providing products and services to the outerwear trade. *$40.00*
Annual

1307 **WWD Buyers Guide: Womens Apparel and Accessories Manufacturers**
Fairchild Publications
7 W 34th Street
New York, NY 10001-8100
212-630-3880
FAX: 212-630-4295 800-360-1700
Patrick McCarthy, Chairman/Editorial Director
Mary G Berner, President/CEO
Ed Nardoza, VP/Editor-in-Chief
Robert Sauerberg, Chief Operating Officer
Over 5,500 apparel and accesory manufacturers.
Founded: 1892

1308 **WWD Suppliers Guide**
Fairchild Books and Visuals
7 W 34th Street
New York, NY 10001-8100
212-630-3880
FAX: 212-630-3898 800-247-6622
Patrick McCarthy, Chairman/Editorial Director
Mary G Berner, President/CEO
Ed Nardoza, VP/Editor-in-Chief
Robert Sauerberg, Chief Operating Officer
Over 5,500 apparel and accessory manufacturers in the US. Supplement to WWD Magazine.

Industry Web Sites

1309 **www.americanapparel.org**
American Apparel & Footwear Association

For the apparel and footwear industries. Conducts seminars, compiles statistics and produces industry reports.

1310 **www.apparelandfootwear.org**
American Apparel & Footwear Association

The national trade association for the apparel and footwear industries. Conducts seminars, compiles statistics and produces industry reports.

1311 **www.cashmere.org**
Cashmere and Camel Hair Manufacturers Institute

For cashmere and camel hair product manufacturers.

1312 **www.colorassociation.com**
Color Association of the US

Information on color/design issues; issues color charts two years in advance of selling seasons in order to profile popular American colors. Forecasts are issued in women's fashions and men's and children's clothing.

1313 **www.costumedesignersguild.com**
Costume Designers Guild

Works to promote employment and to create improved working conditions for costume designers.

1314 **www.ctda.com**
Custom Tailors and Designers Assn of America

Seeks to promote awareness of designers and makers of men's custom tailored clothing.

1315 **www.formalwear.org**
International Formalwear Association

For the formal wear industry.

1316 **www.greyhouse.com**
Grey House Publishing

Selected Grey House directories in the fields of business, health and education are available online. Users can search our online databases by several different search criteria, such as product categories, geographic area, sales volume and much, much more. Full Grey House catalog and online ordering also available.

1317 **www.iacde.com**
Int'l Assn of Clothing Designers & Executives

Sponsors competitions, presents awards, maintains archives, conducts research for clothing designers; provides a network for apparel executives to network.

1318 **www.ifai.com**
Industrial Fabrics Association International

For geosynthetics, fabricators, installers, equipment manufacturers, suppliers, testing firms, consultants, and educators, who produce textiles, nets, mats, grids, and other products.

1319 **www.itaaonline.org**
Int'l Textile & Apparel Assn Membership Directory

For college professors of clothing and textile studies.

1320 **www.nahm.com**
Hosiery Association

Develops standards for hosiery measurement.

1321 **www.naumd.com**
National Association of Uniform Manufacturers

For manufacturers and distributors of uniforms and career wear.

1322 **www.proapparel.com**
Professional Apparel Association

For manufacturers of health care and hospitality uniforms, shoes, and accessories, as well as career apparel and school uniforms.

1323 **www.sewing.org**
American Home Sewing and Craft Association

Handicraft and collectibles forum.

1324 **www.uc-council.org**
GS1 US

Members rely on the standards and services of GS1 US for the effective management and control of their supply chains. Everyday we strive to keep a leader's pace in developing, maintaining, supporting and expanding the services we offer to fulfill our mission.

1325 **www.uniteunion.org**
Union of Needletrade Industrial Textile Employees

A union fighting for working people.

1326 **www.vowsmag.com**
Grimes & Associates

Information on the business specifics necessary for today's wedding professional.

Associations

1327 Air Conditioning & Refrigeration Institute
4100 N Fairfax Drive
Suite 200
Arlington, VA 22203
703-524-8800
FAX: 703-528-3816
ari@ari.org www.ari.org

Geraud Darnis, Chairman
William G. Sutton, President

National trade association representing manufacturers of more than 90 percent of North American produced central air-conditioning and commercial refrigeration equipment.
Founded: 1953

1328 Air Conditioning Contractors of America
2800 Shirlington Road
Suite 300
Arlington, VA 22206
703-575-4477
FAX: 703-575-4449
info@acca.org www.acca.org

Richard Dean, Senior Vice Chairman
Ray Isaac, Secretary
Phil Forner, Treasurer

Representing the HVACR contracting industry. We help our members acquire and satisfy customers while upholding the most stringent requirements for professional ethics, and advocating for improvements to the industry overall.
Founded: 1914

1329 American Boiler Manufacturers Association
8221 Old Courthouse Rd
Ste 207
Vienna, VA 22182-3839
703-356-7172
FAX: 703-356-4543
randy@abma.com www.abma.com

Blake McBurney, Chairman
W Randall Rawson, President
Diana McClung, Executive Assistant to President

Manufacturers' trade association representing companies involved in utility, industrial and commercial steam generation. Includes associate memberships for companies who sell to or work with these companies and those who own boilers. Holds technical and production conferences and publishes technical guideline publications.
115 Members Founded: 1888

1330 American Society of Heating, Refrigeration & Air-Conditioning Engineers
1791 Tullie Circle NE
Atlanta, GA 30329
404-636-8400
FAX: 404-321-5478 800-527-4723
ashrae@ashrae.org www.ashrae.org

Kent Peterson, President
William Harrison, Treasurer

ASHRAE will advance the arts and sciences of heating, ventilation, air-conditioning and refrigeration and related human factors to serve humanity and promote a sustainable world. *$59.00*
55000 Members Monthly Founded: 1894
Circulation: 55000

1331 American Society of Mechanical Engineers
3 Park Avenue
New York, NY 10016-5990
212-917-7740
FAX: 212-591-7739 800-843-2763
infocentral@asme.org www.asme.org

Richard E Feigel, President
Virgil R Carter, Executive Director

A professional organization focused on technical, educational and research issues of the engineering and technology community.
12000 Members Founded: 1880

1332 Association of Home Appliance Manufacturers
1111 19th Street NW
Suite 402
Washington, DC 20036
202-872-5955
FAX: 202-872-9354
jmcguire@aham.org www.aham.org

Liston P Durden, Chairman
Barbara F Garrett, First Vice Chairperson
Joseph McGuire, President

A not-for-profit trade association representing manufacturers of major and portable home appliance, floor care appliances and suppliers to the industry.
Founded: 1915

1333 Gas Appliance Manufacturers Association
2107 Wilson Boulevard
Suite 600
Arlington, VA 22201
703-525-7060
FAX: 703-525-6790
information@gamanet.org
www.gamanet.org

Jack Klimp, President
Thomas W Parker, VP/Chief of Staff
Joseph Mattingly, VP/Secretary/General Counsel

Represents manufacturers of residential, commercial and industrial gas and oil fired appliances, associated controls and accessories, as well as equipment used in the production, transmission and distribution of fuel gases.
300 Members Founded: 1935

1334 Industrial Heating Equipment Association
8595 Beechmont Ave
Ste 204
Cincinnati, OH 45255-4740
513-231-5613
FAX: 513-624-0601
ihea@ihea.org www.ihea.org

Jeffrey W Boswell, President
Steve W Furth, First VP
Brian Russell, Second VP
John B Clarke, Treasurer

A voluntary national trade association representing the major segments of the industrial heat processing equipment industry.
Membership Fee Founded: 1929

1335 International Housewares Association
6400 Shafer Court
Suite 650
Rosemont, IL 60018
847-292-4200

mkulik@housewares.org
www.housewares.org

Linda S Graebner, Vice Chairman/Chairman
Philip J Brandl, President
Jennier Lamberg, Executive Assistant

A full-service trade association dedicated to promoting the sales and marketing of housewares.
Founded: 1938

1336 International Microwave Power Institute
7076 Drinkard Way
Mechanicsville, VA 23111
804-596-6667
FAX: 804-559-4087
impi@impi.org www.impi.org

Neal S Cooper, President
Kimberly Thies, Executive Director

An organization that provides a forum for the exchange of information on all aspects of microwave and RF heating technologies.
$ 160.00
Membership Fee Founded: 1966

1337 National Appliance Parts Suppliers Association
PO Box 87907
Vancouver, WA 98687-7907
360-834-3805
FAX: 360-834-3507
info@napsaweb.org
www.napsaweb.org

Stan Fox, President
Ron Ellis, VP
Sherry Harrell, Treasurer
Jason Cunningham, Secretary
Suzanne Stilwill, Executive Director

Provides distributors of replacement parts for major home appliances with information and services.
100 Members Founded: 1966

1338 National Appliance Service Association
PO Box 2514
Kokomo, IN 46904
765-453-1820
FAX: 765-453-1895
nasahq@sbcglobal.net www.nasa1.org

Ralph Grimaldi, President
Mike Donovan, VP
Carrie Giannakos, Executive Director

Promotes interests of portable and commercial appliance service repair and sales to industry owners.
200 Members Founded: 1949

1339 National Kitchen & Bath Association
687 Willow Grove Street
Hackettstown, NJ 07840-1731
908-852-0033
FAX: 908-852-1695 800-843-6522

Larry Spangler, Chief Executive Officer
Paul A Kohmescher, Executive Director
Jessica Figlar, Media Contact

Protects the interests of members by fostering a better business climate. Awards certification. Conducts training schools and seminars.
25000 Members Founded: 1965

1340 North American Retail Dealers Association
10 E 22nd Street
Suite 310
Lombard, IL 60148-6191
630-953-8950
FAX: 630-953-8957 800-621-0298
jevans@narda.com www.narda.com

Michael Corder, Chairman
Tom Drake, President/CEO

Rosemary Jacobshagen, Executive VP
Timothy Seavey, Secretary
Robert Cremer, Treasurer

To enhance the ability of independent appliance retailers to build progressive, profitable businesses. NARDA members sell and serve kitchen and laundry appliances, consumer home and mobile electronics, computers and other home and small office products, furniture, sewing machines, vacuum cleaners, room air conditioners, and other cosumer home products.

3000 Members Founded: 1943 1800 names

1341 Professional Service Association
71 Columbia Street
Cohoes, NY 12047-2939
518-237-7777
FAX: 518-237-0418 888-777-8851
psaworld@aol.com
www.psaworld.com

Ralph Wolff, President
Carmine D'Alessandro, VP
Jeff Olson, Secretary/Treasurer
Ron Sawyer, Executive Director

Members are companies servicing and repairing electronics and appliances. *$150.00*

1105 Members Membership Fee

1342 Refrigerating Engineers & Technicians Association
PO Box 1819
Salinas, CA 93902
831-455-8783
FAX: 831-455-7856
info@reta.com www.reta.com

Dave Murphy, President
Doug Sweet, Chairman
Stephen L Shaub, Executive VP
Edward Seffens, VP
Jim Barron, Treasurer

Seeks to upgrade the skills and knowledge of experienced members. Offers home-study courses on refrigeration and air conditioning.

3000 Members Founded: 1910

1343 Refrigeration Service Engineers Society
1666 Rand Road
Des Plaines, IL 60016
847-759-4045
FAX: 847-297-5038
general@rses.org www.rses.org

Josh Flaim, Manager HR/Administrative Services

To provide opportunities for enhanced technical competence by offering comprehensive, cutting edge education and certification to our members and the HVAC/R industry. *$96.00*

20000 Members Annual Dues Founded: 1933

1344 Whirlpool
2000 N. M-63
Benton Harbor, MI 49022-2692
269-923-5000
800-253-1301

Jeff M Fettig, Chairman/President/CEO
Roy Templin, Executive VP/CFO
Daniel F. Hopp, Sr. VP Corporate Affairs
Robert T. Kenagy, Corporate Secretary

World's leading manufacturer and marketer of major home appliance and provides our operations with resources and capabilities no other manufacturer can match.

Founded: 1911

Newsletters

1345 ACCA Insider
2800 Shirlington Road
Suite 300
Arlington, VA 22206
703-575-4477
FAX: 703-575-4449
info@acca.org www.acca.org

Kimya Bailey Cajchun, Director of Member Relations
Vickie Ellis, Sr. Coordinator Membership

Each issue contains association and industry news, boiled down into a brief, easy to read format that will keep you up to date in just five minutes each Monday.

Weekly

Magazines & Journals

1346 ASHRAE Journal
American Society of Heating, Refrigeration & AC
1791 Tullie Circle NE
Atlanta, GA 30329
404-636-8400
FAX: 404-321-5478 800-527-4723
ashrae@ashrae.org www.ashrae.org

Fred P Turner, Editor
Barry Kurian, Publishing Services Manager

Explores topical technical issues, such as: indoor air quality, energy management, thermal storage, alternative refrigerants, fire and life safety and more. Dual units of measurement. *$59.00*

Monthly

1347 Appliance
Dana Chase Publications
1110 Jorie Boulevard
#CS90919
Oak Brook, IL 60522-9019
630-990-3484
FAX: 630-990-0078
lisa@appliance.com
www.appliancemagazine.com

George Shurtleff, Production Manager
Maria Nigro, Circulation Director
Dana Chase Jr, Chairman

Devoted to serving the appliance industry worldwide, producers of consumer, commercial, business and medical appliances. Editorial material serves product engineering and design, production management and supervision, purchasing, management, marketing, sales and service. Accepts advertising. *$75.00*

90 pages Monthly Founded: 1944
Circulation: 34500

1348 Appliance Design
Business News Publishing
2401 W Big Beaver Road
Suite 700
Troy, MI 48084
248-893-3500
FAX: 630-845-9483 877-747-1625
info@asnews.com www.appliance

Fern Sheinman, Publisher
Richard Babyak, Editor-in-Chief
Amy Alef, Production Manager
Mary Lowe, Associate Editor

Devoted to providing solutions for design and engineering teams in the global, commercial, and medical appliance/durable goods industry.

Founded: 1955
Circulation: 25,000 12 names $175 per M.
Printed in 4 colors on glossy stock

1349 Appliance Service News
Gamit Enterprises
1917 S Street
PO Box 808
St Charles, IL 60174
630-845-9481
FAX: 630-845-9483 877-747-1625
info@asnews.com www.asnews.com

William Wingstedt, Editor/Publisher
Peggy Wingstedt, Sales Representative

Published for owners, managers and technicians of appliance repair dealers. Accepts advertising. *$59.95*

36 pages Monthly Founded: 1950
Circulation: 33000 12 names $175 per M.
Printed in 4 colors on glossy stock

1350 Contractor Excellence
Air Conditioning Contractors of America
2800 Shirlington Road
Suite 300
Arlington, VA 22206
703-575-4477
FAX: 703-575-4449
info@acca.org www.acca.org

Jason White, Subscription Services
Craig Gotthardt, Director of Information Services

A reputation as a quality source of business information for the HVAC industry. Currently, Contractor Excellence is available only to members in good standing.

Quarterly Founded: 2002

1351 HVAC&R Research Journal
American Society of Heating, Refrigeration & AC
1791 Tullie Circle NE
Atlanta, GA 30329
404-636-8400
FAX: 404-321-5478 800-527-4723
ashrae@ashrae.org www.ashrae.org

Mildred Geshwiler, Special Publications Editor
Barry Kurian, Publishing Services Manager

Reporting significant research from ASHRAE and the international HVAC&R research communities. *$160.00*

Quarterly ISBN 1-883413-98-2

1352 Indoor Comfort News Magazine
Institute of Heating and Air Conditioning
454 W. Broadway
Glendale, CA 91204
818-551-1555
FAX: 818-551-1115
ihaci@ihaci.org www.ihaci.org

Susan Evans, Executive Director

A tool for attaining the trade association's goal of educating and promoting the HVAC/R/SM industry. Readers are top buyers and decision makers. They service and install new construction and replacement/retrofit projects.

Monthly Founded: 1955

1353 JSME International Journal
American Society of Mechanical Engineers
3 Park Avenue
New York, NY 10016-5990
212-917-7740
FAX: 212-591-7739 800-843-2763
infocentral@asme.org www.asme.org

Richard E Feigel, President
Virgil R Carter, Executive Director

Provides advanced scientific and technological information for the mechanical engineering industry to facilitate the international exchange and transfer of technology. *$375.00*
Monthly

1354 Journal of Microwave Power and Electromagnetic Energy
International Microwave Power Institute
1916 Sussex Road
Blacksburg, VA 24060
540-552-3070
FAX: 540-961-1463
impi@impi.org www.impi.org

Dr John A Pearace, Editor-in-Chief

Designed for the information needs of professionals specializing in the research and design of industrial systems and bio-medical applications, the Journal exemplifies the highest standards of scientific and technical information on the theory and application of electromagnetic power. *$250.00*
Quarterly/Fee Non-Members

Trade Shows

1355 ACCA Conference & Indoor Air Expo
Air Conditioning Contractors of America
2800 Shirlington Road
Suite 300
Arlington, VA 22206
703-575-4477
FAX: 703-575-4449
info@acca.org www.acca.org

Michael Honeycutt, Sr. VP
Sandra Kyles, Meetings Manager

Workshops and learning opportunities for HVAC contractors.
Annual/March

1356 AHAM Annual Meeting
Association of Home Appliance Manufacturers
1111 19th Street NW
Suite 402
Washington, DC 20036
202-872-5955
FAX: 202-872-9354 www.aham.org

Joseph McGuire, President
Jill A Notini, Communications/Marketing Director
Christy McGinty, Member Services Manager

Provides ideas for the solution of problems and concerns of the Cross Functional Design.
Annual/April

1357 ARI Annual Meeting
Air Conditioning & Refrigeration Institute
4100 N Fairfax Drive
Suite 200
Arlington, VA 22203
703-524-8800
FAX: 703-528-3816
ari@ari.org www.ari.org

Dana Durr, Contact
Gwen Horton, Contact

Representing manufacturers of US produced central air-conditioning and commercial refrigeration equipment.
November

1358 ASME International Mechanical Engineering Congress and Exposition
American Society of Mechanical Engineers
3 Park Avenue
New York, NY 10016-5990
212-917-7740
FAX: 212-591-7739 800-843-2763
infocentral@asme.org www.asme.org

Richard E Feigel, President
Virgil R Carter, Executive Director

Hundreds of sessions, forums, exhibits, tours and social events keep you current on the latest trends in technology and industry, and provide the opportunity to trade tips and share ideas with engineers in different industries and companies around the world.
November

1359 Clean Show
Riddle & Associates
1874 Piedmont Road NE
Suite 360-C
Atlanta, GA 30324
404-876-1988
FAX: 404-876-5121
info@cleanshow.com
www.cleanshow.com

John Riddle, Manager
Ann Howell, Communications

Among top 100 North American trade shows and largest industry show in the world. Features demonstrations of hundreds of products. Attracts all facets of the laundering, drycleaning and textile care industry.
17000 Attendees Biennial, Odd Years
Founded: 1977

1360 GAMA Annual Meeting
Gas Appliance Manufacturers Association
2107 Wilson Boulevard
Suite 600
Arlington, VA 22201
703-525-7060
FAX: 703-525-6790
events@gamanet.org
www.gamanet.org

Jack W Klimp, President/CEO
Sabrina Thomas, Executive Assistant to President
Joseph Mattingly, VP, Secretary & General Counsel

National trade association whose members manufacture space and water heating appliances, components and related products.
Annual Founded: 1935

1361 IMPI Annual Symposium
International Microwave Power Institute
1916 Sussex Road
Blacksburg, VA 24060
540-552-3070
FAX: 540-961-1463
impi@impi.org www.impi.org

Kimberly Thies, Executive Director

The major global technology exchange forum for microwave and radio frequency specialists.
Annual Founded: 1966

1362 International Air Conditioning, Heating & Refrigerating Expo
International Exposition Company
15 Franklin Street
Westport, CT 06880
203-221-9232
FAX: 203-221-9260
info@ahrexpo.com www.ahrexpo.com

Mark Stevens, VP
Jeff Stevens, Sales VP
Kelley Stevens, Sales Manager

Co-sponsored by Ameriacn Society of Heating, Refrigeration and Air Conditioning Engineers and the Air Conditioning and Refrigeration Institute. Featuring exhibits that include; equipment and services of industrial, commercial and residential heating, refrigeration, air conditioning and ventilation.
37292 Attendees January Founded: 1930

1363 International Housewares Show
International Housewares Associaton
6400 Shafer Court
Suite 650
Rosemont, IL 60018
847-292-4200

mkulik@housewares.org
www.housewares.org

Mia Rampersad, VP
Marie Kulik, Manager, Trade Show Operations

World's largest housewares marketplace, showcasing thousands of new products and designs.
18500 Attendees March

1364 Kitchen/Bath Industry Show and Conference
National Kitchen & Bath Association
687 Willow Grove Street
Hackettstown, NJ 07840-1731
908-852-0033
FAX: 908-852-1695 800-843-6522

Grayson Lutz, Conference Operations Manager
Cindy Stringer, Exhibit Concierge

Showcases the latest products and cutting-edge design ideas of the kitchen and bath industry.
40000 Attendees May

1365 NASA Convention & Trade Show
National Appliance Service Association
PO Box 2514
Kokomo, IN 46904
765-453-1820
FAX: 765-453-1895
carrienasa@aol.com www.nasa1.org

Carrie Giannakos, Executive Director

Classes on marketing, advertising, customer service, machine repair, all taught by experienced professionals in the industry. Keeping you informed about the industry and every product available. Attendees also have the opportunity to take advantage of show specials offered by exhibitors.
Annual

1366 NCCA Annual Meeting
National Coil Coaters Association
1300 Sumner Avenue
Cleveland, OH 44115-2851
216-241-7333
FAX: 216-241-0105
www.coilcoating.org

John Mitchell, President
Roger Sieja, VP
Dick Klein, Treasurer

Provide the coil coating service and are manufacturers and suppliers of metal, coatings, chemicals, and equipment.
May

1367 **National Appliance Parts Suppliers Association National Convention**
National Appliance Parts Suppliers Association
PO Box
Vancouver, WA 98683
360-834-3805
FAX: 360-834-3507
info@napsaweb.org
www.napsaweb.org
Suzanne M Stilwill CTC, Executive Director
Jody Terrell, Executive Assistant
Appliance parts replacement business. Containing 62 booths and 60 exhibits.
300+ Attendees Annual/Sept

1368 **RSES Annual Conference**
Refrigeration Service Engineers Society
1666 Rand Road
Des Plaines, IL 60016
847-976-6464
FAX: 847-297-5038 800-297-5660
jbirch@rses.org www.rses.org
Jean Birch, Conference/Seminar Manager
Kim Heselbarth, Marketing Director
Robb Isaacs, Executive VP
Feature the latest HVAC/R equipment, tools and services, with manufacturer representatives on hand to answer questions and explain their products' features.
October

Directories & Databases

1369 **A Portrait of the US Appliance Industry**
Chase Dana Publications
1110 Jorie Boulevard
Suite 203
Oak Brook, IL 60523-2259
630-990-3484
FAX: 630-990-0078
www.appliancemagazine.com
David J Chase, President
Susan Chase Korin, CEO
Appliance companies in the US. *$45.00*
Annual Founded: 1944

1370 **Complete Directory of Small Appliances**
Sutton Family Communications & Publishing Company
155 Sutton Lane
Fordsville, KY 42343
270-740-0870
jlsutton@apex.net www.pubdisco.com
Theresa Sutton, Publisher
Lee Sutton, Editor
Print-out from database of wholesalers, manufacturers, distributors, importers and close-out houses. Database is updated daily to guarantee the most current and up-to-date sources available. *$55.20*
100 pages

1371 **Directory of Certified Applied Air Conditioning Products**
Air Conditioning & Refrigeration Institute
4100 N Fairfax Drive
Suite 200
Arlington, VA 22203
703-524-8800
FAX: 703-528-3816
ari@ari.org www.ari.org
Geraud Darnis, Chairman
William G Sutton, President
Provides information on air cooling/heating coils, central station air handling units, room fan-coil air conditioners, packaged terminal air conditioners and heat pumps, water source and ground water source heat pumps, ground source closed-loop heat pumps, variable air volume terminals, unitary large equipment, positive displacement compressors, air-cooled rotary screw water-chilling packages and non-condensable gas purge equipment.
$99.00
Twice a year

Industry Web Sites

1372 **www.abma.com**
American Boiler Manufacturers Association
Represents companies involved in utility, industrial and commercial steam generation.

1373 **www.acca.org**
Air Conditioning Contractors of America
Representing the HVACR contracting industry. We help our members acquire and satisfy customers while upholding the most stringent requirements for professional ethics, and advocating for improvements to the industry overall.

1374 **www.aga.org**
American Gas Association
Represents local energy utility companies that deliver natural gas to more than 56 million homes, businesses and industries throughout the United States.
195 pages

1375 **www.aham.org**
Association of Home Appliance Manufacturers
Statistical information and summaries on appliances.

1376 **www.apda.com**
Appliance Parts Distributors Association
Promotes the sale of appliance parts through independent distributors.

1377 **www.appliancemagazine.com**
Dana Chase Publications
The premiere electronic industry information source, with content focused into 20 Industry Zones for targeted editorial coverage.

1378 **www.ari.org**
Air Conditioning & Refrigeration Institute
Representing manufacturers of central air-conditioning and commercial refrigeration equipment.

1379 **www.ashrae.org**
American Society of Heating, Refrigeration & A/C
Serving the heating, ventilation, air conditioning and refrigeration areas.

1380 **www.asme.org**
American Society of Mechanical Engineers
Focused on technical, educational and research issues of the engineering and technology community.

1381 **www.bema.org**
Bakery Equipment Manufacturers Association
Baking and snack food industries.

1382 **www.gamanet.org**
Gas Appliance Manufacturers Association
Residential, commercial and industrial gas and oil fired appliances.

1383 **www.ge.com**
General Electric
Home appliances, lighting, home solutions, corporate info and customer service.

1384 **www.greyhouse.com**
Grey House Publishing
Selected Grey House directories in the fields of business, health and education are available online. Users can search our online databases by several different search criteria, such as product categories, geographic area, sales volume and much, much more. Full Grey House catalog and online ordering also available.

1385 **www.housewares.org**
International Housewares Association
Provides a year round gateway to the International Home & Housewares Show, industry search tools, consumer purchase trend data, and offers International Housewares Association members access to global opportunities and discount business services.

1386 **www.ihea.org**
Industrial Heating Equipment Association

A voluntary national trade association representing the major segments of the industrial heat processing equipment industry.

1387 **www.impi.org**
International Microwave Power Institute

A forum for the exchange of information on all aspects of microwave and RF heating technologies.

1388 **www.napsaweb.org**
National Appliance Parts Suppliers Association

Provides distributors of replacement parts for major home appliances with information and services.

1389 **www.narda.com**
North American Retail Dealers Association

For independent retailers.

1390 **www.nasa1.org**
National Appliance Service Association

Promotes interests of portable and commercial appliance service repair and sales to industry owners.

1391 **www.nkba.com**
National Kitchen & Bath Association

Protects the interests of members by fostering a better business climate. Awards certification. Conducts training schools and seminars.

1392 **www.psaworld.com**
Professional Service Association

Information for companies that service and repair electronics and appliances.

1393 **www.repairclinic.com**
RepairClinic

Installation tips and how-to information on your appliances.

1394 **www.reta.com**
Refrigerating Engineers & Technicians Association

Seeks to upgrade the skills and knowledge of experienced members. Offers home-study courses on refrigeration and air conditioning.

1395 **www.rses.org**
Refrigeration Service Engineers Society

To provide opportunties for enhanced technical competence by offering comprehensive, cutting edge education and certification to our members and the HVAC/R industry.

1396 **www.supco.com**
Sealed Unit Parts

Manufacturer of precision electronic Test and Service Instruments and Refrigeration & Air Conditioning components. We are dedicated to producing high quality, innovative products at affordable prices to a wide range of customers.

Associations

1397 American Architectural Foundation
1799 New York Avenue NW
Washington, DC 20006
202-626-7318
FAX: 202-626-7420
info@archfoundation.org
www.archfoundation.org
Ronald E Bogle, President/CEO
Sherry Birk, Director
Carol Coletta, Executive Director
Education foundation/association. Architecture and design.
Founded: 1943

1398 American Design Drafting Association
105 East Main Street
Newbern, TN 38059
731-627-0802
FAX: 731-627-9321
corporate@adda.org www.adda.org
Luis F Aguirre, President
Terry Schultz, Executive VP
Gene Fosheim, Treasurer/Secretary
Floyd McWilliams, Education
Olen Parker, Manager
Membership organization exclusively for the professional designer/drafter in all disciplines including manufacturing, utilities, construction, engineering, government and education. We are pledged to professional growth and advancement of the individual working in the design drafting community.
2000 Members Founded: 1948

1399 American Institute of Architects (AIAA)
1735 New York Avenue NW
Washington, DC 20006-5209
202-626-7300
FAX: 202-626-7547 800-242-3837
infocentral@aia.org www.aia.org
Douglas L. Steidl, President
Kate Schwennsen, First VP
Norman L Koonce, CEO
James A Gatsch, Treasurer
John C. Senhauser, Secretary
Representing 74,000 architects, this professional society provides a variety of educational programs to its member architects as well as seeks to heighten the awareness among the general public of the contributions that architectural design makes to our daily lives.
70000 Members Founded: 1857

1400 American Society for Aesthetics
11935 Abercorn Street
Savannah, GA 31419
912-921-2124

asa@aesthetics-online.org
www.aesthetics-online.org
Carolyn Korsmeyer, President
Stephen Davies, VP
Curtis Carter, Secretary/Treasurer
Promotes study, research, discussion and publication in aesthetics, which includes all studies of the arts and related experiences from a philosophic, scientific or theoretical viewpoint.
Founded: 1942

1401 American Society of Landscape Architects
636 Eye Street NW
Washington, DC 20001-3736
202-898-2444
FAX: 202-898-1185 800-787-2752
nsomerville@asla.org www.asla.org
Nancy Somerville, Executive VP/CEO
Gerald Beaulieu, CFO/Director Business Operations
Susan Cahill-Aylward, Information Managing Director
Residential and commercial real estate developers, federal and state agencies, city planning commissions and individual property owners are all among the thousands of people and organizations in America and Canada that will retain the services of a landscape architect this year.
15000 Members Founded: 1899

1402 Architectural League
457 Madison Avenue
New York, NY 10022
212-753-1722
FAX: 212-486-9173
info@archleague.org
www.archleague.org
Rosalie Genevro, Executive Director
Anne Rieselbach, Program Director
Terri Chiao, Program Associate
Independent forum for the presentation and discussion of creative and intellectual work in architecture, urbanism, and related disciplines. Promotes the landscape architecture profession and advances the practice through advocacy, education, community and fellowship.
Founded: 1881

1403 Architectural Precast Association
6710 Winkler Road
Suite 8
Fort Myers, FL 33919
239-454-6989
FAX: 239-454-6787
info@archprecast.org
www.archprecast.org
Brad Thompson, President
Roger Teague, VP
Fred L McGee, Executive Director
Randy Daniel, Secretary/Treasurer
Tim Michael, Director
Nonprofit trade association organized to serve the informational, technical and business needs of architectural precast concrete manufacturers and their suppliers and to promote high standards of workmanship throughout the industry.
50 Members Founded: 1966

1404 Architectural and Transportation Barriers
Access Board
1331 F Street NW
Washington, DC 20004-1111
202-272-0080
FAX: 202-272-0081 800-872-2253
info@access-board.gov
www.access-board.gov
Jan Tuck, Chair
David L. Bibb, Vice Chair
Douglas Anderson, Member of the Board
Otto J Wolff, Member of the Board
Charles S Abell, Member of the Board
Independent federal agency devoted to accessibility for people with disabilities. Its key missions include developing and maintaining guidelines for the built environment, transit vehicles, telecommunications equipment and standards for electronic and information technology; providing technical assistance and training on these guidelines and standards and enforcing design standards for federally funded facilities.
Founded: 1968

1405 Association for Preservation Technology International (APT)
1224 Centre West
Suite 400B
Springfield, IL 62704
217-793-7874
FAX: 888-723-4242
info@apti.org www.apti.org
Barbara Campagna, President
Anne T. Sullivan, VP
Dan Worth, VP
Ron Staley, Secretary/Treasurer
Tim Seeden, Administrative Director
Cross-disciplinary organization dedicated to promoting the best technology for conserving historic structures and their settings. With members in 28 countries, APT connects a network of architects, conservators, tradespeople, consultants, planners, curators, landscape architects, engineers, developers, educators, historians, apprentices and students.
1600 Members Founded: 1968

1406 Association of Collegiate Schools of Architecture
1735 New York Avenue NW
Washington, DC 20006
202-785-2324
FAX: 202-628-0448
andrealeal@acsa-arch.org
www.acsa-arch.org
Michael J Monti, Executive Director
Kathy Hillegas, Assistant Executive Director
Chhayal Parikh, Project Manager
Kevin Mitchell, Administrative Associate

Nonprofit membership association founded to advance the quality of architectural education.
500 Members Founded: 1912 732 names

1407 Association of University Architects
17595 S Tamiami Trail
Fort Myers, FL 33908-4570

FAX: 239-590-1010 www.auaweb.net
Evie Asken, Director Campus Planning
Purpose is to achieve more effective planning in the field of higher education, improve the design and construction standards of university buildings and to develop common bonds and establish standards which will ensure clarity of communications and render effective the exchange of information.
Founded: 1955

1408 Building Officials & Code Administrators International Code Council
4051 W Flossmoor Road
Country Club Hills, IL 60478
708-992-2300
888-422-7233
James Lee Witt, CEO
A nonprofit membership association dedicated to preserving the public health, safety and welfare in the built environment through the promulgation of model codes suitable for adoption by governmental entities and assisting code enforcement officials, design professionals, builders, manufacturers and others involved in the

design, construction and regulatory processes.
16000 Members Founded: 1915

1409 Cast Stone Institute
850 Dogwood Road
Suite A-400636
Lawrenceville, GA 30044-7218
770-972-3011
FAX: 770-972-3012
staff@caststone.org
www.caststone.org

Tony Garcia, President
David Laird, VP
Tome Lepisto, Secretary/Treasurer
Mimi Harlan, Executive Director

An organization of cast stone manufacturers, associates, professional architects, engineers and concrete technologists formed for the purpose of improving the quality of cast stone and disseminating information regarding its use.
70 Members Founded: 1927

1410 Center for Environmental Design Research
University of California at Berkeley
390 Wurster Hall, #1839
Berkeley, CA 94720-1839
510-420-0460
FAX: 510-643-5571
earens@uclink.berkeley.edu
www.cedr.berkeley.edu

Ed Arens, Director
Kathleen Kunlman, Management Service Officer
Randy Schmidt, Manager

A research unit of the University of California at Berkeley. The center offers a wide range of projects undertaken in cooperation with government agencies, foundations and private industry. Documents reporting research results are distributed through the center's publications program.

1411 Council on Tall Buildings & Urban Habitat
3360 South State Street
Chicago, IL 60616-3793
312-909-0253
FAX: 610-419-0014
info@ctbuh.org www.ctbuh.org

David Scott, Chairman
Geri Kery, Manager Operations
David Maola, Executive Director

Nonprofit organization sponsored by architectural, engineering, planning and construction professionals established to facilitate professional exchanges among those involved in all aspects of the planning, design, construction and operation of tall buildings and the urban habitat.
1400 Members Founded: 1969

1412 Historic New England
Soc for Preservation of New England Antiquities
141 Cambridge Street
Boston, MA 02114
617-227-3956
FAX: 617-227-9204
www.historicnewengland.org

Nancy Curtis, Publisher

Focuses on buildings, landscapes and objects reflecting New England life from the 17th century to the present. Also publishes a magazine about the organizations objects, architectural holdings and activities.
6000 Members Founded: 1910
Printed in 4 colors on glossy stock

1413 Institute for Urban Design
4253 Karensue Avenue
San Diego, CA 92122-3731
858-455-1251

Ann Ferebee, President

Responsible for city planning.
1M Members Founded: 1979

1414 Intelligent Buildings Institute
2101 L Street NW
Washington, DC 20037-1526
202-457-8437

Marketing information, certification and training programs, guidelines and government advocacy programs are provided for members.
110 Members Founded: 1986

1415 International Association for Impact Assessment
1330 23rd Street S
Suite C
Fargo, ND 58103
701-297-7908
FAX: 701-297-7917
info@iaia.org www.iaia.org

Richard Fuggle, President
William Jones, Director
Jill Baker, Secretary
Marcel Ayite Baglo, Director

IAIA provides a forum for the exchange of the ideas and experiences to stimulate innovation in assessing, managing and mitigating the consequences of development.
2500 Members Founded: 1980

1416 National Council of Architectural Registration Boards
1801 K Street NW
Suite 1100K
Washington, DC 20006-1310
202-269-9200
FAX: 202-783-0290
customerservice@ncarb.org
www.ncarb.org

Frank M. Guillot, President
H. Carleton Godsey, First VP
Robert E. Luke, Second VP
Lenore Lucey, VP
Douglas K Engebretson, Secretary

Regulates the practice of architecture and is dedicated to assisting these member state registration boards in carrying out their duties and to providing a certification program for individual architects.
55 Members Founded: 1919

1417 Partners for Livable Communities
1429 21st Street NW
Washington, DC 20036-5976
202-887-5990
FAX: 202-466-4845
bmcnulty@livable.com
www.livable.com

Robert McNulty, President
Ruth Kelliher, VP
Penelope Cuff, Senior Program Officer
Irene Garnett, Director of Public Programs
Elli Dalrymple, Program Officer

A nonprofit organization working to improve the livability of communities by promoting quality of life, economic development and social equity. Helps communities set a common vision for the future, discover and use of new resources for community and economic development and build public/private coalitions to further their goals.
1200 Members Founded: 1977

1418 Society for Environmental Graphic Design
1000 Vermont Avenue
Suite 400
Washington, DC 20005
202-638-5555
FAX: 202-638-0891
segd@segd.org www.segd.org

Peter Dixon, President
Jonathan Alger, VP
Alan Jacobson, Treasurer
Ann Makowski, Director Membership/Communications

SEGD is an international nonprofit educational organization providing resources for design specialists in the field of environment graphic design, architecture and landscape, interior and industrial design.

1419 Society of American Registered Architects
305 E 46th Street
New York, NY
212-371-3132
www.sara-national.org

Gerald Gross, President
Sheldon Goldstone, VP

A professional society that includes the participation of all architects, regardless of their roles in the architectural community. Supports the concept of profitable professionalism for its members.
Founded: 1956

1420 Society of Architectural Historians
1365 N Astor Street
Chicago, IL 60610
312-573-1365
FAX: 312-573-1141
info@sah.org www.sah.org

Therese O'Malley, President
Pauline Saliga, Executive Director
Robert Craig, Secretary

A not-for-profit organization that provides an international forum for those who care about architecture and its related arts. The Society encourages scholarly research in the field and promotes the preservation of significant architectural monuments worldwide.
3500 Members Founded: 1940

1421 Society of Naval Architects and Marine Engineers
601 Pavonia Avenue
Jersey City, NJ 07306
201-798-4800
FAX: 201-798-4975 800-798-2188
pkimball@sname.org www.sname.org

Susan Giver, Director of Marketing
Philip B. Kimball, Executive Director
Martin Toyen, Chair Finance Committee
Edward M. Lewandowski, Chair/Marine Tech Committee
R. Keith Michel, Chair Investments Committee

Internationally recognized nonprofit technical, professional society of individual members serving the maritime and offshore industries and their suppliers. Dedicated to advancing the industry by recording information, sponsoring research, offering career guidance and supporting education.
10,00 Members Founded: 1893

1422 **Sustainable Buildings Industry Council**
1112 16th Street NW
Suite 240
Washington, DC 20036
202-628-7400
FAX: 202-393-5043
sbic@sbiccouncil.org
www.sbicouncil.org
Greg Franta, Chairman
Deane Evans, Vice Chair
Mike Weise, Treasurer
Gregg Ander, Secretary
Helen English, Executive Director
Independent, nonprofit organization whose mission is to advance the design, affordability, energy performance, and enviromental soundness of residential, institutional, and commercial buildings. Members include trade associations, architects, engineers, product manufacturers and suppliers interested in sustainable, energy and resource-efficient green buildings.
250 Members Founded: 1980

Newsletters

1423 **A/E Business Review**
6524 E Rockaway Hills Drive
PO Box 4808
Cave Creek, AZ 85331-7609
480-488-0311
FAX: 480-488-0311
Clare Ross, Publisher
The management and marketing newsletter of architects, engineers and planners.
7 pages Monthly

1424 **A1 Architect**
American Institute of Architects
1735 New York Avenue NW
Washington, DC 20006-5292
202-626-7300
FAX: 202-626-7547 800-242-3837
infocentral@aia.org www.aia.org
Stephani Stubbs, Editor
Douglas L Steidl, President
Membership news. *$100.00*
5 pages Monthly Founded: 1857
Circulation: 840
Printed in 2 colors on matte stock

1425 **APT Bulletin: Technology International**
Association for Preservation Technology Int'l
4513 Lincoln Avenue
Suite 213
Lisle, IL 60532-1290
630-968-6400
FAX: 888-723-4242
information@apti.org www.apti.org
Diana Waite, Editor
Tim Seeden, CEO/President
Educational-encompassing past and current technology for the conservation of historic cultures and artifacts.
Quarterly
Circulation: 2000

1426 **Access Currents**
Access Board
1331 F Street NW
Suite 1000
Washington, DC 20004-1111
202-272-0080
FAX: 202-272-0081 800-872-2253
info@access-board.gov
www.access-board.gov/
Lawrence W Roffee, Executive Director
Dave Yanchulis, Public Affairs
Jan Tuck, Chairman
A bi-monthly newsletter published by the Architectural and Transportation Barriers Compliance Board.
4 pages Monthly Founded: 1973
Circulation: 16,000

1427 **Certifier**
Nat'l Council of Architectural Registration Boards
1801 K Street NW
Washington, DC 20006
202-836-6500
FAX: 202-783-0290 www.ncarb.org
William Houseman, Publisher
State architectural registration boards.
Annual Founded: 1919

1428 **Design Drafting News**
American Design Drafting Association
PO Box 11937
Columbia, SC 29211
803-771-0008
FAX: 803-771-4272
national@adda.org www.adda.org
Rachel Howard, Publisher
Newsletter for the American Design Drafting Association. Accepts advertising.
8 pages Monthly
Printed in 1 color on matte stock

1429 **Design Firm Management & Administration Report**
Institute of Management & Administration
29 W 35th Street
5th Floor
New York, NY 10001-2299
212-244-0360
FAX: 212-564-0465
subserve@ioma.com www.ioma.com
Ned Godfrey, Publisher
Lee Rath, Editor
Provides information to manage design firms. *$245.00*
20 pages Monthly

1430 **Designline**
American Institute of Building Design
2505 Main Street
Suite 209B
Stratford, CT 06615
203-783-3480
FAX: 203-378-3568 800-366-2423
bobbi@aibd.org www.aibd.org
Bobbi Currie, Production Manager
Pam Palko, Circulation Director
Lyle Breeze, President
Steven Mickley, Interim Executive Director
Showcasing residential design.
24 pages Quarterly Founded: 1950

1431 **Direct Connection**
Nat'l Council of Architectural Registration Boards
1801 K Street NW
Washington, DC 20006-5209
202-783-6500
FAX: 202-783-0290
customerservice@ncarb.org
www.ncarb.org
Offers information and news on licensing, board certification, architectural trends and more for the professional architect and intern architect.
16 pages
Circulation: 50000
Printed in 2 colors on glossy stock

1432 **Energy Design Update**
Aspen Publishers
37 Broadway
Arlington, MA 02474-5552
781-641-2886
FAX: 301-698-7100 800-234-1660
Ned Nisson, Editor
For professionals concerned with residential load management and energy efficient design and construction in housing. *$297.00*
16 pages Monthly

1433 **Guidelines Letter: New Directions and Techniques in the Design Profession**
Guidelines
PO Box 2590
Alameda, CA 94501
510-235-5172
FAX: 510-523-5175 800-634-7779
sfia@aol.com www.sfia.net
Fred Stitt, Director
Chandler Vienneau, Circulation Director
Fred Stitt, Editor
Business and technical information for design professionals including comprehensive survey information regarding fees and client costs. The Guidelines Letter is in its 28th year of publication. *$70.00*
4 pages Monthly Founded: 1992

1434 **Landscape Architectural News Digest**
American Society of Landscape Architects
636 Eye Street NW
Washington, DC 20001-3736
202-898-2444
FAX: 202-898-1185 www.asla.org
Bill Thompson, Publisher
Seck Hardi, Editor
Susan Everett, Executive Director
Provides a comprehensive view of the latest developments in regional, residential and corporate architecture. *$42.00*
16 pages Monthly

1435 **Memo**
American Institute of Architects
1735 New York Avenue NW
Washington, DC 20006-5209
202-626-7300
FAX: 202-626-7547 800-242-3837
infocentral@aia.org www.aia.org
Peter McCall, Publisher
Stephny Stubbs, CEO/President
Norman Koonce, Editor
Phial Simmons, Marketing Manager
Architectural news and information.
Monthly
Circulation: 85000

1436 **Principal's Report**
Institute of Management & Administration

29 W 35th Street
5th Floor
New York, NY 10001-2299
212-244-0360
FAX: 212-564-0465
subserve@ioma.com www.ioma.com

Ned Godfrey, Publisher
Lee Rath, Editor

Provides information and guidance to design firm owners. *$245.00*
16 pages Monthly

1437 **SARAscope**
Society of American Registered Architects

1411 London Road
Duluth, MN 55805-5410
914-332-5430
FAX: 218-728-5361
bdpArch@cpinternet.com
www.sara-national.org

Raymond Blesener

Listing society conventions, meetings and other activities. Discusses news about the Society of interest to members.
BiWeekly Founded: 1956

1438 **SBIC Newsletter**
Sustainable Buildings Industry Council
1331 H Street NW
Suite 1000
Washington, DC 20005
202-628-7400
FAX: 202-393-5043
SBIC@SBIcouncil.org
www.sbicouncil.org

Helen English, Executive Director
Doug Schroeder, Associate Director
Will Zachmann, Director Communications

Published to inform the members of the mission to advance the design, affordability, energy performance and environmental soundness of residential, institutional and commercial buildings. Newsletter is free to members.
6-8 pages 2-3 per year Founded: 1995
Circulation: 400
Printed in 2 colors on matte stock

1439 **Society of Architectural Historians Newsletter**
Society of Architectural Historians
1365 N Astor Street
Chicago, IL 60610
312-573-1365
FAX: 312-573-1141
1-torrance@nwn.edu www.sah.org

Diane Greer, Editor
Pauline Saliga, Executive Director

Meetings, tours and publications dealing with architecture, available to members of the society only.
10 pages
Circulation: 4500

1440 **Times**
Council of Tall Buildings and Urban Habitat
Illinois Institute Of Technology S.R. Crown
3360 S State Street
Chicago, IL 60616-3793
312-909-0253
FAX: 610-419-0014
info@ctbuh.org www.ctbuh.org

Geri Kery, Operations Manager
David Maola, Executive Editor

Newsletter for members of CTBUH. *$75.00*
Monthly Founded: 1969
Circulation: 1200 4500 names $100 per M.
Printed in 2 colors on matte stock

Magazines & Journals

1441 **AI Communications**
AIAA
1735 New York Avenue NW
Washington, DC 20006-5292
202-626-7300
FAX: 202-626-7421
infocentral@aia.org www.aia.org

Catherine Miller, Editor
Douglas L Steidl, President
Norman L. Koonce, CEO

Student programs and issues dealing with architectural education.
Founded: 1857

1442 **Adobe Magazine**
Adobe Systems
345 Park Avenue
San Jose, CA 95110-2704
408-536-6000
FAX: 408-537-6000 www.adobe.com

Michael Moquin, Editor
Bruce Chizen, Chief Executive Officer

Devoted to adobe and earthen architecture. Showing both old and new traditions of building the earth. *$4.00*

Circulation: 4,500

1443 **American School & University**
PRIMEDIA Intertec Publication
9800 Metcalf Avenue
Overland Park, KS 66212-2216
913-341-1300
FAX: 913-967-1898
jagron@primediabusiness.com
www.asumag.com

Joe Agron, Editor-In-Chief
Gregg Herring, Publisher
Molly Roudebush, Marketing Manager

The industry's definitive educational facilities publication. *$50.00*
508 pages Monthly Founded: 1928
Circulation: 63540
Printed in 4 colors on glossy stock

1444 **Architectural Design**
John Wiley & Sons
111 River Street
Hoboken, NJ 07030-5774
201-748-6000
FAX: 201-748-6088
customer@wiley.com www.wiley.com

William J Pesce, President/CEO

Continues to publish a vigorous and wide range treatment of architectural trends of topical importance. *$145.00*
Founded: 1807

1445 **Architectural Digest**
4 Times Sq.
New York, NY 10036-8022
212-286-2860
FAX: 212-286-6867
www.condenast.com

Paige Rense, Editor-in-Chief
Amy R Churgin, Publisher

For the connoisseur of interior design. The purpose is to cultivate an appreciation of excellence in the luxury world of design and furnishing. *$39.95*
Monthly Founded: 1999
Circulation: 812,892

1446 **Architectural Record**
McGraw Hill
1221 Avenue of the Americas
New York, NY 10020-1095
212-512-2000
FAX: 212-512-2000
customer.service@mcgraw-hill.com
www.mcgraw-hill.com

Steve Weiss, President
Elaine Shusterman, Publisher

A magazine for architects and engineers which covers business topics, design, new products and trends in urban planning and engineering. *$49.00*
Monthly Founded: 1888
Circulation: 100000+

1447 **Architecture Magazine**
VNU eMedia
770 Broadway
New York, NY 10003
646-545-5100
FAX: 646-654-7318
info@architecturemag.com
www.architecturemag.com

Katie Gerfen, Assistant Editor
Suzanne Tron Haber, Publisher
Gary Gyss, Group Publisher

Evaluation of new and existing buildings and related news that affects the profession.

Monthly
Circulation: 63449

1448 **Assemblage**
MIT Press
Five Cambridge Center
Cambridge, MA 02142-1493
617-532-2864
FAX: 617-258-6779 800-405-1619
journals-orders@mit.edu
http://mitpress.mit.edu

Janet Fisher, Publisher
Michael Sims, Editor
Tom Clerkin, Marketing Manager
Abbie Hiscox, Circulation Manager
Rebecca McLeod, Journal Manager
$20.00

Founded: 1986
Circulation: 1600

1449 **Ballast Quarterly Review**
Ballast
2022 X Avenue
Dysart, IA 52224-9767

ballast@netins.net

Roy Behrens, Editor

Examines an eclectic assortment of publications with an emphasis on graphic design and architecture.
16 pages Magazine

1450 **Building Design & Construction**
Reed Business Information
360 Park Avenue S
New York, NY 10014
212-450-0067
FAX: 630-288-8686
subsmail@reedbusiness.com
www.reedbusiness.com

Robert Cassidy, Editor-in-Chief
James Reed, President
Gerard Van de Ast, CEO

Serves the needs of the design and construction professionals of commercial, industrial and institutional buildings that include new and retrofit projects. Geared towards the

building team that includes professionals from building firms, owning firms and design firms.
Monthly Founded: 1946

1451 CRIT: Journal of the American Institute of Architecture Students
Telesis
1735 New York Avenue NW
Washington, DC 20006-5292
202-626-7472
FAX: 202-626-7414
mail@aiasnatl.org www.aiasnatl.org
R Todd Gabbard, Editor-in-Chief
Jacob Day, President
Student oriented articles and news items on environmental issues, aspects of architecture education, and professional development. *$6.00*
Founded: 1956
Circulation: 10000

1452 CTBUH Review Journal
Council on Tall Buildings and Urban Habitat
Lehigh University
117 Atlss Drive
Bethlehem, PA 18015
610-758-3515
FAX: 610-758-4522
inctbuh@lehigh.edu
www.ctbuh.org/journal/index.htm
Mir M Ali, Editor
Paul J Armstrong, Co-Editor
Abbas Aminmansour, Managing Editor
Hwang MoonHoon, Publication Assistant
R Shankar Nair, Chairman
CTBUH Review is the Professional Journal of the Council on Tall Buildings and Urban Habitat. It includes refereed papers submitted by researchers, scholars, suppliers, and practicing professionals engaged in the planning, design, construction, and operation of tall buildings and the urban environment throughout the world. Membership benefits include monthly e-updates, access to on-line buildings database, discounts on selected publications and registration at Council-sponsored activities. *$150.00*
1400 pages Quarterly

1453 Church Business
Virgo Publishing
3300 N Central Avenue
Suite 2500
Phoenix, AZ 85012
480-990-1101
FAX: 480-990-0819
cs@vpico.com
www.churchbusiness.com
Kerry Layeux, Publisher
Mike Saxby, Group Publisher
RaeAnn R. Slaybaugh, Editor
For those planning a church, building a new facility, or expanding a current church. Provides vital ministry, product and service information. *$69.00*
Monthly Founded: 1996
Circulation: 20,000+

1454 Classicist
Transaction Publishing Rutgers
State University of New Jersey
35 Berrue Circle
Piscataway, NJ 08854-8042
732-445-2280
FAX: 732-445-3138
trans@transactionpub.com
Mary E Curtis, President
Donald M Rattner, Editor
Dedicated to the theory and practice of architecture and artistic classicism. *$39.95*
164 pages

1455 Computer-Aided Engineering
Penton Media
1300 E 9th Street
Cleveland, OH 44114
216-696-7000
FAX: 216-696-1752
information@penton.com
www.penton.com
William Tucker, Editor
Data base applications in design and manufacturing. *$50.00*
96 pages Founded: 1982

1456 Concrete Masonry Designs
13750 Sunrise Valley Drive
Herndon, VA 20171-4662
703-713-1900
FAX: 703-713-1910 877-343-6268
ncma@ncma.org www.ncma.org
Randi Hertzberg, Editor
Mark B. Hogan, President
Jerry R. Harke, VP
Highlights concrete masonry applications, best practice tips, specifications and details. Also showcases concrete masonry landscape products. *$2.50*
Monthly Founded: 1918
Circulation: 25000
Printed in 4 colors on glossy stock

1457 Contemporary Stone & Tile Design
Business News Publishing Company
210 Route 4 E
Suite 311
Paramus, NJ 07652
201-291-9001
FAX: 201-291-9002
cstd@stoneworld.com
www.stoneworld.com
Alex Bachrach, Publisher
Michael Reis, Editor/Associate Publisher
With technical information, high quality architectural photography and in depth international industry coverage, StoneWorld magazine is designed for and read by top buyers and decision-makers who specify, quarry, fabricate, export, import, distribute, design, sell and install stone and stone-related equipment and supplies.
Quarterly Founded: 1934
Circulation: 15225

1458 Design Issues
MIT Press
Five Cambridge Center
Cambridge, MA 02142-1493
617-532-2864
FAX: 617-258-6779 800-356-0343
journals-orders@mit.edu
www.mitpress.mit.edu/
Richard Buchanan, Editor
Dennis P Doordan, Editor
Victor Margolin, Editor
American journal that provides a scholarly forum for the history, theory and critisism of the design of performing arts facilities. *$48.00*
Quarterly Founded: 1984
Circulation: 1450

1459 Design Journal
Journal Communications Group
1431 7th Street
#205
Santa Monica, CA 90401-2637
310-394-4394
FAX: 310-394-0966
customer.services@benjamins.nl
www.benjamins.nl
Douglas G Kiel, President
Karin Plijnaar, Marketing Manager
Focuses on the design and architecture marketplace. Includes newsbites and a calendar, as well as designer and lighting resources.
Monthly Founded: 1982
Circulation: 34000

1460 Design Quarterly
MIT Press
Five Cambridge Center
Cambridge, MA 02142-1493
617-532-2864
FAX: 617-258-6779 1 8-0 4-5 16
customer.care@triliteral.org
http://mitpress.mit.edu
Janet Fisher, Publisher
Covers architecture, design and contemporary graphics for performing arts facilities. *$8.00*
Founded: 1926
Circulation: 9200

1461 Design Solutions Magazine
Architectural Woodwork Institute
1952 Isaac Newton Square W
Reston, VA 20190-5001
703-733-0600
FAX: 703-733-0584
adsales@awinet.org www.awinet.org
Jay Blankenship, President
Judith Durham, Executive VP
Featuring beautiful woodwork projects manufactured by members of the Architectural Woodwork Institute (AWI). Many other related publications, including woodworking quality standards used by woodwork manufacturers and design professionals. *$25.00*
Quarterly Founded: 1953
Circulation: 25000

1462 Design/Build Business
Cygnus Publishing
1233 Janesville Avenue
Fort Atkinson, WI 53538
920-563-6388
FAX: 920-563-1699 800-547-7377
krik.moen@cygnusb2b.com
www.designbuildbusiness.com
Kirk Moen, Publisher
Rob Heselbarth, Editor
Serves builders, architects and designing and remodeling firms, nationwide. Edited to these professions serving the residential and light commercial marketplaces. *$24.00*
72 pages Monthly Founded: 1935
Circulation: 60424 60,424 names

1463 Dodge Construction News
McGraw Hill
PO Box 182604
Columbus, OH 43272
614-866-5769
FAX: 614-759-3749 877-833-5524
customer.service@mcgraw-hill.com
www.mcgraw-hill.com
Jennifer Hayes, Editor
Harold McGraw III, President/CEO

Consists of program edition and proceedings and recap edition for the National Conventions of the American Institute of Architects and Construction Specifications Institute.
Founded: 1958
Circulation: 86400

1464 Fabrics Architecture
Industrial Fabrics Association International

1801 County Road BW
Roseville, MN 55113
651-222-2508
FAX: 651-631-9334 800-225-4324
fabarch@ifai.com www.ifai.com
Mary Hennessey, Publisher
Bruce Wright, Editor
Sarah Hyland, Advertising
This magazine strives to inform architects, designers, landscape architects, engineers and other specifiers about architectural fabric structures, the fibers and fabrics used to make them, their design possibilities, their construction, and issues regarding their applicability and acceptance. Fabric Architecture showcases indutrial-fabric applications to 13,000+ architects. Featured works include awnings, canopies, flags, banners, tension structures and other end products.
Fortnightly Founded: 1988
Circulation: 13000 $250 per M.
Printed in 4 colors on glossy stock

1465 Glass Magazine
National Glass Association
8200 Greensboro Drive
Suite 302
McLean, VA 22102-3881
703-424-4890
FAX: 703-442-0630
nga@glass.org www.glass.org
Charles Cumpston, Editor
Nancy Davis, Managing Editor
Nicole Harris, VP
Departments include new products, newsline, letters, management and financial tips, calendar and company news. $34.95
Monthly Founded: 1948
Circulation: 17313

1466 Harvard Design Magazine
Harvard University Graduate School of Design
48 Quincy Street
Cambridge, MA 02138-3000
617-954-4731
FAX: 617-496-3391
hdm@gsd.harvard.edu
www.gsd.harvard.edu
William S Saunders, Editor/Asst Dean External Relations
Meghan Ryan, Editorial & Business Coordinator
Alan Altshuler, Dean of Faculty Design School
Emphasizes ideas, insight, interpretation and improvement of the built environment. Includes interviews and profiles of well known designers. *$35.00*
100 pages Bi-annually Founded: 1978
Circulation: 16000

1467 Inland Architect
Real Estate News Corporation
3550 West Peterson Avenue
Suite 100
Chicago, IL 60659
773-674-4069
FAX: 773-866-9881 888-641-3169
info@inlandarchitectmag.com
www.inlandarchitectmag.com
Steven Polydoris, Publisher/Editor
Covers distinguished and historical buildings. *$27.00*
120 pages Founded: 1883
Printed in 4 colors on glossy stock

1468 Journal of Architectural Education
Association of Collegiate Schools of Architecture
1735 New York Avenue NW
Washington, DC 20006
202-785-2324
FAX: 202-628-0448
aleal@acsa-arch.org
www.acsa-arch.org
Andrea Leal, President
Referred architectural journal which addresses significant questions in architectural thought, practice, and education.
Quarterly Founded: 1974

1469 Journal of Architectural and Planning Research
Locke Science Publishing
1735 New York Avenue NW
3rd Floor
Washington, DC 20006
202-785-2324
FAX: 202-628-0448
info@acsa-arch.org
www.acsa-arch.org
Howard Smith, Editor
Barbara Allen, Editor
Research and practice of architectural urban planning interdisciplinary.
Quarterly Founded: 1974
Circulation: 4300

1470 Journal of Urban Technology
New York City Technical College
300 Jay Street
Brooklyn, NY 11201-1909
718-260-5000
FAX: 718-260-5524
connect@citytech.cuny.edu
www.citytech.cuny.edu/
Ricahrd Hanley, Editor
Russ Hotzler, President
Covers technological developments in the architecture and transporatation fields.
Founded: 1946
Circulation: 10000

1471 Journal of the Society of Architectural Historians
Society of Architectural Historians
1365 N Astor Street
Chicago, IL 60610-2144
312-573-1365
FAX: 312-573-1141
info@sah.org www.sah.org
Elizabeth Blau, Editor
Therese O'Malley, President
Articles on architectural history and critisism. *$115.00*
Quarterly Founded: 1940
Circulation: 4000

1472 Metal Architecture
Modern Trade Communications
7450 N Skokie Boulevard
Skokie, IL 60077-3395
847-674-2200
FAX: 847-674-3676
circulation@moderntrade.com
www.moderntrade.com
Jon Lawrence, President/Publisher
Bob Sictro, Editor
Low-rise construction involving architects, engineers and specifiers.
Monthly Founded: 1980
Circulation: 33000

1473 Metropolis Magazine
Bellerophon Publications
61 W 23rd Street
4th Floor
New York, NY 10010
212-627-9977
FAX: 212-627-9988
edit@metropolismag.com
www.metropolismag.com
Horace Havemeyer, Publisher
Susan Szenasy, Editor-in-Chief
The only magazine that covers all facets of design: architecture, interiors, furniture, preservation, urban design, graphics and crafts. *$27.95*
Founded: 1980
Circulation: 61000

1474 Old House Interiors
Gloucester Publishers Corporation
108 E Main Street
Gloucester, MA 01930
978-283-3200
FAX: 978-283-4629 800-356-9313
info@oldhouseinteriors.com
www.oldhouseinteriors.com
Patricia Poore, Editor-in-Chief
William J O'Donnell, Publisher
Covers restoration techniques for the pre-1939 home. *$26.00*
116 pages Founded: 1995
Circulation: 100000
Printed in 4 colors on glossy stock

1475 Places: A Forum of Environmental Design
Journal of Environmental Design
100 Higgans Hall
Brooklyn, NY 11205

FAX: 718-399-4332
James F Fulton, Publisher
Covers architecture, landscape architecture, urban design, with a multidisciplinary view of all aspects of public and private places. *$35.00*

1476 Preservation
National Trust for Historic Preservation
1785 Massachusetts Avenue NW
Washington, DC 20036-2189
202-886-6295
FAX: 202-588-6038 800-944-6847
preservation@nthp.org
www.nationaltrust.org
Bob Barron, Publisher
David Brown, Executive VP
James W Cooke, Sales Representative
Historic preservation. Sites and buildings in danger, and proposed for preservation. Legislation zoning and law affecting historic preservation. *$20.00*
Fortnightly Founded: 1949
Circulation: 500,000

1477 **Professional Builder**
Reed Business Information
360 Park Avenue South
New York, NY 10014
212-450-0067
FAX: 646-746-7583
corporatecommunications@reedbusiness.com www.reedbusiness.com

Dean Horowitz, Group Publisher
Heather McCune, Editor-in-Chief
James A. Casella, CEO
James Reed, President
Jane Aboyoun, Vice President

New residential construction magazine with a more than 63 year tradition of providing builders the solutions they need to maximize profits.
Monthly Founded: 1936

1478 **Residential Architect**
Hanley-Wood
1 Thomas Circle NW
Suite 600
Washington, DC 20005
202-452-0800
FAX: 202-785-1974 888-269-8410
res@omeda.com
www.hanleywood.com

Michael Boyle, Publisher
S Claire Conroy, Editor
Stephen Sheikhli, Managing Editor

It delivers substantive editorial on marketing, presentation, products, technology and business management to 22,000 - plus architects and designers. *$39.95*
Founded: 1976
Circulation: 22000

1479 **Society of Architectural Administrators News Journal**
Society of Architectural Administrators
15 E 7th Street NW
Cincinatti, OH 45202
513-684-3451

Patsy Frost, Publisher

Society news for professionals in the architectural community.

1480 **World Monuments Fund**
95 Madison Avenue
9th floor
New York, NY 10016-439
646-424-9594
FAX: 646-424-9593
wmf@wmf.org www.wmf.org

Bonnie Burnham, President
Irene Bareis, VP

This magazine offers information on the latest architectural trends, specifically landmarks, monuments, antiquities. 16 page quarterly newsletter. *$17.95*
Quarterly Founded: 1965 $var per M.
Printed in 4 colors on glossy stock

Trade Shows

1481 **American Institute of Architects Minn. Convention & Products Exhibition**
American Institute of Architects, Minnesota Chap.
275 Market Street
Suite 54
Minneapolis, MN 55405
612-339-6904
FAX: 612-338-7981
infocentral@aia.org www.aia.org

Jay Brand, Public Director

175 exhibits of windows, concrete, roofing, millwork, tile and more, plus conference, seminar and dinner.
2500 Attendees Annual Founded: 1934

1482 **American Institute of Architects National Convention**
American Institute of Architects
1735 New York Avenue NW
Washington, DC 20006
202-626-7300
FAX: 202-626-7547 800-242-3837
infocentral@aia.org www.aia.org

Christine McEntee, Executive VP/CEO
Christopher Gribbs, Convention Manager

Architect equipment, supplies and services. Check our website for details of the conference, online registration and much more. Premium event for building and designing industry profession and architectural innovation.
May

1483 **American Institute of Building Design Annual Convention**
2505 Main Street
Suite 209B
Stratford, CT 06615
203-783-3480
FAX: 203-378-3568 800-366-2423
aibdnat@aol.com www.aibd.org

Steven Mickley, Executive Director
Bobbi Currie, Manager

Annual convention and exhibition of 25 manufacturers, suppliers, distributors and plan publishers of building products including: roofing, windows, doors, floor covering, fire places, spas/jacuzzis, lumber, intercom systems, alarm systems and appliances; computer-aid design technology, computer hardware/software and plan publishers. Containing 30 booths and 30 exhibits.
300 Attendees Annual Founded: 1950

1484 **American Society for Aesthetics Annual Conference**
American Society for Aesthetics
11935 Abercorn Street
Savannah, GA 31419
912-921-2124

asastcar@vms.csd.mu
www.aestheticsonline.org

Carolyn Korsmeyer, President
Stephen Davies, VP

Seminar, conference, and exhibits related to the study of the arts, all disciplines.
500 Attendees Annual/October Founded: 1942

1485 **American Society of Landscape Architects Annual Meeting & Educational Expo**
636 Eye Street NW
Washington, DC 20001-3736
202-898-2444
FAX: 202-898-1185 800-787-2752

Nancy Somerville, Executive VP/CEO
Gerald Beaulieu, CFO/Director Business Operations

Landscape architect educational session and workshop plus 500 exhibits of outdoor lighting, playground and park equipment, landscape maintenance equipment, computer hardware and software and much more.
4700 Attendees

1486 **Association of Higher Education Facilities Officers Annual Meeting/Exhibition**
1643 Prince Street
Alexandria, VA 22314-2818
703-684-1446
FAX: 703-549-2772
diana@appa.org www.appa.org

E. Lander Medlin, Executive VP

Conference and 250 exhibits relating to consulting services and publications, equipment and supplies for physical site administrators.
750 Attendees Founded: 1914

1487 **Computers for Contractors and A/E/C Systems Fall**
AEC Systems International/Penton Media
1300 E 9th Street
Cleveland, OH 44114

FAX: 610-280-7106 800-451-1196
info@aecsystems.com
www.aecsystems.com

Philip McKay, Manager

Computers for construction is the only tradeshow and conference dedicated exclusively to computer use by contractors. A/E/C SYSTEMS Fall is the regional technology event for the entire design and construction industry.
7000 Attendees November

1488 **Council on Tall Buildings & Urban Habitat Congress**
Lehigh University
11 East Packer Avenue
Bethlehem, PA 18015
610-583-3000
FAX: 610-758-4522
inctbuh@lehigh.edu
www.construction.com

David Scott, Chairman
Geri Kery, Manager Operations

Brings the world's leading decision makers together. For additional information visit our website or email us.
600+ Attendees Feburary/March Founded: 1969
Mailing list available for rent 4500 names

1489 **EDM/PDM Expo**
AEC Systems International/Penton Media
1300 E 9th Street
Cleveland, OH 44114

FAX: 610-280-7106 800-451-1196
info@aecsystems.com
www.aecsystems.com

Philip McKay, Manager

Showcases ways to manage technical/engineering documents, product management, and drawing conversion. 500 exhibits.
20M Attendees May

1490 **International Manufacturing & Engineering Technology Congress**
AEC Systems International/Penton Media
1300 E 9th Street
Cleveland, OH 44114

FAX: 610-280-7106 800-451-1196
info@aecsystems.com
www.imetcongress.com
Loretta Savage, Manager
Automotive, aeronautics, and aerospace, electrical and electronics, consumer products, industrial, heavy equipment, and process industries. 1000 exhibits.
15M Attendees November

1491 **LightFair**
AMC
120 Wall Street
17th Floor
New York, NY 10005
212-843-8358
FAX: 212-248-5017 www.iesna.org
Pamela R Weess, Circulation Director
Nini Schwenk, Manager
A major lighting trade show in North America featuring architectural lighting products from all spectrons of the industry. Containing 600 booths and 400 exhibits.
17M Attendees June
Mailing list available for rent 10M names $100 per M.
Printed in 4 colors on glossy stock

1492 **Lightfair International**
Atlanta Market Center
240 Peachtree Street NW
Suite 2200
Atlanta, GA 30303-1340
404-220-3000
FAX: 404-220-3030
www.americasmart.com
Libby Morley, VP Trade Shows
Keri Arroll, Director Public Relations
April McAllister, Trade Show Manager
The world's largest annual architectural/commercial lighting trade show and conference program. Lightfair International features the latest technology, products, education, information, awards and industry association events. 600 booths.
20M Attendees April/May

1493 **M/Tech**
AEC Systems International/Penton Media
1300 E 9th Street
Cleveland, OH 44114

FAX: 610-280-7106 800-451-1196
info@aecsystems.com
www.imetcongress.com
Scott Merriman, Owner
Loretta Savage, Manager
Focuses on applications to improve every phase of the product development cycle including CAD/CAM/CAE, Internet/intra/extranct, rapid prototyping and tooling, project/financial management, simulation and analysis, EDM/PDM and much more. 300 exhibits.
15M Attendees November

1494 **M/Tech West**
AEC Systems International/Penton Media
1300 E 9th Street
Cleveland, OH 44114

FAX: 610-280-7106 800-451-1196
info@aecsystems.com
www.acesystems.com
Philip McKay, Manager
Explores concurrent engineering practices, computer integrated manufacturing, and mechanical engineering applications. 50 exhibits.
20M Attendees May

1495 **National Council of Architectural Registration Boards Annual Meeting**
Natl. Council of Architectural Registration Boards
1801 K Street NW
Suite 1100-K
Washington, DC 20006
202-783-6500
FAX: 202-783-0290
customerservice@ncarb.org
www.ncarb.org
Frank M. Guillot, President
H. Carleton Godsey, First VP
Robert E. Luke, Second VP
Douglas K. Engebretson, Secretary
Lenore Lucey, Vice President
Annual meeting and exhibits of architecture equipment, supplies and services.

1496 **Retail Design & Construction Conference & ExpoCRAMMM**
Primedia
9800 Metcalf Avenue
#12901
Overland Park, KS 66212
913-341-1300
FAX: 913-967-1898
mpederson@primediabusiness.com
www.primediabusiness.com
Margaret Pederson, VP
Annual show of 145 exhibitors of equipment, supplies and services for retail design, construction, development, operations and maintenance, including signage, building equipment and materials, fixtures, floor coverings, furnishings, lighting, landscaping, store fronts, roofing, HVAC, maintenance materials and contractor services.
1000 Attendees

1497 **Technology for Construction**
Hanley-Wood
8600 Freeport Parkway
Suite 200
Irving, TX 75063
972-366-6300
FAX: 972-536-6402 866-962-7469
tcindric@hanleywood.com
www.technologyforconstruction.com
Tom Cindric, Director
Jackie James, Show Manager
Annual forum that showcases the technology, tools and solutions for the design, construction, maintenance and modification of commercial buildings, institutions and other structures. These tools and education are essential for the seamless collaboration and communication between all those involved throughout the asset lifecycle.
72M Attendees Annual Founded: 1976

Directories & Databases

1498 **Dodge Building Stock**
DRI/McGraw-Hill
148 Princeton Heights Town Road
Height Town, NJ 08520
609-710-0295
800-393-6343
Norbert W. Young, President
Joseph A. Scott, National Marketing Director
This database contains more than 18,000 historical and forecast quarterly time series on US buildings, including total square footage, number of buildings, and roof area for groups of structures in the categories of commercial, institutionals, manufacturing and residential.

1499 **Encyclopedia of Associations: Sources for Architects, Deigners, & Engineers**
ME Sharpe
80 Business Park Drive
Suite 202
Armonk, NY 10504-1715
914-273-1800
FAX: 914-273-2106 800-541-6563
David Kent Ballast, Editor
Myron Sharpe, Publisher
Information sources for architects, designers and engineers. *$167.95*
832 pages ISBN 0-765600-35-8

1500 **Pro File/Official Directory of the American Institute of Architects**
1735 New York Avenue NW
Washington, DC 20006-5209
202-783-6500
FAX: 202-626-7364
Over 18,000 architectural firms are listed. These listings have one or more principals who is a member of the American Institute of Architects. *$225.00*
1800 pages Annual ISBN 1-929990-89-

1501 **Progressive Architecture: Information Sources Issue**
Penton Media
1300 E 9th Street
Cleveland, OH 44114
216-696-7000
FAX: 216-696-1309
information@pentonmedia.com
www.penton.com
List of trade and professional architecture associations. *$48.00*

1502 **Visual Merchandising and Store Design**
ST Publications
407 Gilbert Avenue
Cincinnati, OH 45202
513-421-2050
FAX: 513-421-5144 800-925-1110
cust_service@stpubs.com
www.visualstore.com
Carole Winters, Publisher
Tedd Swormstedt, President *$42.00*
Monthly Founded: 1922
Circulation: 27,500

Industry Web Sites

1503 **www.access-board.gov**
Architectural & Transportation Barriers Compliance

Devoted to accessibility for people with disabilities.

1504 **www.acsa-arch.org**
Association of Collegiate Schools of Architecture

Advancing the quality of architectural education.

1505 **www.adda.org**
American Design Drafting Association

For individuals and educational institutions seeking to promote improved quality in the drafting/design profession.

1506 **www.aecsystems.com**
A/E/C Systems International/Penton Media

Focuses on Internet/Intranet for the design, engineering and construction industries.

1507 **www.aia.org**
American Institute of Architects

For professional architects as well as the general public.

1508 **www.apti.org**
Association for Preservation Technology Int'l

Cross-disciplinary organization dedicated to promoting the best technology for conserving historic structures and their settings. With members in 28 countries, APT connects a network of architects, conservators, tradespeople, consultants, planners, curators, landscape architects, engineers, developers, educators, historians, apprentices and students.

1509 **www.archprecast.org**
Architectural Precast Association

Nonprofit trade association organized to serve the informational, technical and business needs of architectural precast concrete manufacturers and their suppliers and to promote high standards of workmanship throughout the industry.

1510 **www.asla.org**
American Society of Landscape Architects

National professional association representing landscape archtects.

1511 **www.builderspace.com**
BuilderSpace.com

An online directory of building industry businesses and resources created to help users find the services and information they need.

1512 **www.ctbuh.org**
Council on Tall Buildings and Urban Habitat

For architects, engineers, planners and designers who primarily disseminate information regarding tall buildings and the urban habitat. The primary goal of the council is to promote better urban environments by maximizing the international interaction of professionals, and by making the latest knowledge available to its members and to the public at large in useful form.

1513 **www.e-architect.com**
TeleBuild

For architects and the architectural profession.

1514 **www.firstsourceonl.com**
Architects First Source Online

Comprehensive building products information.

1515 **www.greyhouse.com**
Grey House Publishing

Selected Grey House directories in the fields of business, health and education are available online. Users can search our online databases by several different search criteria, such as product categories, geographic area, sales volume and much, much more. Full Grey House catalog and online ordering also available.

1516 **www.historicnewengland.org**
Soc. for Preservation of New England Antiquities

Focuses on buildings, landscapes and objects reflecting New England life from the 17th century to the present.

1517 **www.icea.net**
Insulated Cable Engineers Association

Professional organization dedicated to developing cable standards for the electric power, control and telecommunications industries. Ensures safe, economical and efficient cable systems utilizing proven state-of-the-art materials and concepts. ICEA documents are of interest to cable manufacturers, architects and engineers, utility and manufacturing plant personnel, telecommunication engineers, consultants and OEMs.

1518 **www.ihs.com**
International Code Council

Nonprofit membership association with more than 16,000 members who span the building community, from code enforcement officials to materials manufacturers. Dedicated to preserving the public health, safety and welfare in the built environment through the effective use and enforcement of model codes.

1519 **www.ncarb.org**
Nat'l Council of Architectural Registration Boards

For state registration boards in the United States regulating the practice of architecture.

1520 **www.sah.org**
Society of Architectural Historians

Provides an international forum for those who care about architecture and its related arts.

1521 **www.sbicouncil.org**
Sustainable Buildings Industry Council

Information on the design, affordability, energy performance, and enviromental soundness of residential, institutional and commercial buildings.

1522 **www.smalltown.sarc.msstate.edu**
Small Town Center

To maintain and improve the quality of life in American small towns.

1523 **www.sname.org**
Society of Naval Architects and Marine Engineers

Internationally recognized nonprofit, technical, professional society of individual members serving the maritime and offshore industries and their suppliers. Dedicated to advancing the industry by recording information, sponsoring research, offering career guidance and supporting education.

Associations

1524 **American Antiquarian Society**
185 Salisbury Street
Worcester, MA 01609-1634
508-755-5221
FAX: 508-754-9069
csloat@mwa.com
www.americanantiquarian.org

Ellen Dunlap, President
John B Hench, VP Collections/Programs
John M Keenum, VP Development
Jonathan Lane, Director Annual Fund

Maintains a research library in American history and publishes proceedings of the American Antiquarian Society.
800 Members Founded: 1812

1525 **American Art Therapy Association**
5999 Stevenson Ave
Ste 200
Alexandria, VA 22304-3302
703-212-2238
888-290-0878
info@arttherapy.org
www.arttherapy.org

Edward Stygar Jr, Executive Director
Mary Buckley, Assistant Executive Director & Conf

An organization of professionals dedicated to the belief that the creative process involved in art making is healing and life enhancing. Its mission is to serve its members and the general public by providing standards of professional competence, and developing and promoting knowledge in, and of, the field of art therapy.
4500 Members Founded: 1969

1526 **American Association of Museums**
1575 Eye Street NW
Suite 400
Washington, DC 20005
202-289-1818
FAX: 202-289-6578 www.aam-us.org

Edward Able, President/CEO
Mary Bowie, VP/Finance & Administration
Kim Igoe, VP Policy & Program

Dedicated to promoting excellence within the museum community. Through advocacy, professional education, information exchange, accreditation and guidance on current professional standards of performance, AAM assists museum staff, boards and volunteers across the country to better serve the public.
16000 Members Founded: 1906

1527 **American Fine Arts Society**
215 W 57th Street
New York, NY 10019
212-247-4510
FAX: 212-541-7024
www.theartstudentsleague.org

John Varriano, President

Educational organization that provides space, studios and offices to members.
Founded: 1875

1528 **American Institute for Conservation of Historic and Artistic Works**
1717 K Street NW
Suite 200
Washington, DC 20036-5346
202-452-9545
FAX: 202-452-9328
info@aic-faic.org www.aic-faic.org

Eryl P Wentworth, Executive Director
Eric Pourchot, Program Officer
Jean Arnold, Publications Manager
Sheila Paige, Meetings Manager

Conservators of artistic and cultural property.
3,000 Members Founded: 1961

1529 **American Society for Aesthetics**
11935 Abercorn Street
Savannahe, GA 31419
912-921-2124

asa@aesthetics-online.org
www.aesthetics-online.org

Carolyn Korsmeyer, President
Stephen Davies, VP
Curtis Carter, Secretary/Treasurer

Promotes study, research, discussion and publication in aesthetics, which includes all studies of the arts and related experience including philosophic, scientific and theoretical viewpoints.
Founded: 1942

1530 **American Society of Bookplate Collectors**
605 N Stoneman Avenue
Alhambra, CA 91801-1881
414-228-7831

exlibris@att.net www.bookplate.org
For designers, owners and collectors of bookplates.
Founded: 1942

1531 **Antique Appraisal Association of America**
11361 Garden Grove Boulevard
Garden Grove, CA 92843-1354
714-530-7090

Helen Nolan, Executive Director

Members are professional antique appraisers.

1532 **Antiques & Collectibles Association**

PO Box 4389
Davidson, NC 28036
704-895-9088
FAX: 704-895-0230 800-287-7127
info@antiqueandcollectible.com
www.antiqueandcollectible.com

Jim Tucker, President/Founder

Association open to all reputable dealers and mall owners. Providing newsletter, insurance programs and other benefit programs.
4300 Members Founded: 1991

1533 **Antiques Council**
PO Box 1508
Warren, MA 01083
413-436-7064
FAX: 413-436-7066
info@antiquescouncil.com
www.antiquescouncil.com

Charles Probst, President
Marty Shapiro, VP
Kathleen Haller, Secretary
Christine Vining, Treasurer

A nonprofit organization created by professional antique dealers to improve the confidence of the public in antiques and their dealers through education, service and example.
100 Members Founded: 1990

1534 **Art Dealers Association of America**
575 Madison Avenue
New York, NY 10022
212-940-8590
FAX: 212-940-6484
adaa@artdealers.org
www.artdealers.org

Dick Solomon, President
Gilbert Edelson, Administrative VP

Nonprofit organzation that works to improve the stature and standing of the art gallery business. Members deal primarily with paintings, sculpture, prints, drawings and photographs from the Renaissance to the present day. We have more than 160 member galleries in more than 25 US cities.
160 Members Founded: 1962

1535 **Art Libraries Society of North America**
329 March Road, Suite 232
PO Box 11
Kanata, On K2K 2-2E1
800-817-0621
FAX: 613-599-7027 800-892-7547
arlisna@igs.net www.arlisna.org

Ann Baird, President
Eumie Imm-Stroukoff, Secretary

Devoted to fostering excellence in art librarianship, visual resources and curatorship for the advancement of visual arts. See website for available publications.
1000 Members Founded: 1972
Mailing list available for rent $200 per M.

1536 **Art and Antique Dealers League of America**
1040 Madison Avenue
New York, NY 10021
212-879-7558
FAX: 212-772-7197
secretary@artantiquedealersleague.com
www.artantiquedealersleague.com

Robert Isaraet, President
Clinton Howell, VP
Susan Caplan Jacobson, Treasurer
James D Frankel, Secretary
Ira Spanierman, Vice Chairperson

Nonprofit organization promotes interests of retailers and wholesalers of antiques and art objects.
109 Members November/50 Attendees
Founded: 1926

1537 **Art and Creative Materials Institute/ACMI**
1280 Main Street, 2nd Floor
PO Box 479
Hanson, MA 02341-0479
781-293-4100
FAX: 781-294-0808
debbief@acminet.org
www.acminet.org

Deborah M Fanning, Executive VP
Deborah S Gustafson, Associate Director
Debbie Munroe, Certification Director
Sarah M Skarinka, Membership Director

A non-profit association of manufacturers of art, craft and other creative materials, ACMI sponsors a certification program for both children's and adult's art materials and products, certifying that these products are non-toxic and meet voluntary standards of quality and performance. ACMI seeks to create and maintain a positive environment for art, craft and other creative materials usage, promoting safety in the materials and providing information and service resources on such products.
210 Members Founded: 1940
Mailing list available for rent 199 names

1538 **Artist-Blacksmiths Association of North America, Incorporated**
PO Box 816
Farmington, GA 30638-0816
706-310-1030
FAX: 706-769-7147
abana@abana.org www.abana.org
Don Kemper, President
Clare Yellin, First VP
Dave Mudge, Second VP
Will Hightower, Secretary
Dorothy Stiegler, Treasurer
For the professional and amateur blacksmith and to perpetutate the noble art of blacksmithing.
4500 Members Quarterly Founded: 1973
Circulation: 2 Mag.

1539 **Association for Preservation Technology**
1224 Centre West
Suite 400B
Springfield, IL 62704
217-793-7874
FAX: 888-723-4242
info@apti.org www.apti.org
Barbara Campagna, President
Anne T. Sullivan, VP
Barbara A Campagna, VP
Ron Staley, Secretary/Treasurer
Tim Seeden, Administrative Director
Cross-disciplinary organization dedicated to promoting the best technology for conserving historic structures and their settings. With members in 28 countries, APT connects a network of architects, conservators, tradespeople, consultants, planners, curators, landscape architects, engineers, developers, educators, historians, apprentices and students.
1600 Members Founded: 1968

1540 **College Art Association**
TERRA Foundation
275 7th Avenue
New York, NY 10001
212-691-1051
FAX: 212-627-2381
nyoffice@collegeart.org
www.collegeart.org
Ellen K Levy, President
Catherine Asher, VP Publications
Susan Ball, Executive Director
John Hyland Jr, Treasurer
Andrea S Norris, VP Annual Conference
Promotes excellence in scholarship and technology in the criticisim of the visual arts and in the creativity and technical skill in the teaching and practices of art.
13000 Members Founded: 1911

1541 **International Fine Print Dealers Association (IFPDA)**
15 Gramercy Park S
Suite 7A
New York, NY 10003
212-674-6095
FAX: 212-674-6783
ifpda@printdealers.com
www.printdealers.com
Michele Senecal, Executive Director
Robert K Newman, President
Diane Villani, Executive VP
Tara K Reddi, Treasurer
Susan Teller, Secretary
A nonprofit organzation that aspires to create a greater awareness and appreciation of fine prints among collectors and the general public. Povides funding for a variety of print-related educational programs, including pubications, lectures and symposia.
160 Members Founded: 1987

1542 **International Foundation for Art Research**
500 5th Avenue
Suite 935
New York, NY 10110
212-391-6234
kferg@ifar.org www.ifar.org
Sharon Flescher, Executive Director
Nonprofit educational and research organization working for the interests of art scholarship, law and the public interest.
Founded: 1969

1543 **National Antique and Art Dealers Association of America**
220 E 57th Street
New York, NY 10022
212-826-9707
FAX: 212-832-9493 www.naadaa.org
Mark A Schaffer, President
Leon J Dalva, VP
Enrique Goytizolo, Second VP
Works to promote the best interests of the antique art exhibitions and to promote just, honorable and ethical trade practices.
38 Members Founded: 1954

1544 **National Art Education Association**
1916 Association Drive
Reston, VA 20191-1590
703-860-8000
FAX: 703-860-2960
thatfield@naea-reston.com
www.naea-reston.org
Thomas A Hatfield, Executive Director
Promote art education through professional development, service, advancment of knowledge and leadership.
22000 Members Founded: 1947
Mailing list available for rent 22,000 names $95 per M.

1545 **National Art Materials Trade Association**
1077 Bridgeport Avenue
Shelton, CT 06484-6486
203-929-9444
steve@namta.org www.arcat.com
Rick Jannott, President
Steve LeFebvre, Executive Director
Katharine Coffey, Manager
International association of manufacturers, importers, wholesalers and retailers of art materials.
2.1M Members

1546 **National Assembly of State Arts Agencies**
1029 Vermont Avenue NW
2nd Floor
Washington, DC 20005
202-347-6352
FAX: 202-737-0526
nasaa@nasaa-arts.org
www.nasaa-arts.org
Jonathan Katz, CEO
Dennis Dewey, Managing Director
Carmen Boston, Arts & Education Manager
Kelly J Barsdate, Director Policy/Research/Evaluation
NASAA's mission is to advance and promote a meaningful role for the arts in the lives of individuals, families and communities throughout the United States. We empower state art agencies through strategic assistance that fosters leadership, enhances planning and decision making, and increases resources. TDD 202-347-5948.
56 Members Founded: 1968

1547 **National Association of Artists' Organizations**
Intermedia Arts
2822 Lyndale Avenue South
Minneapolis, MN 55408
612-871-4444
info@naao.net www.naao.net
Edmund Cardini, President
Laurel Raczka, Executive Director
Strengthens artists' organizations by convening them, connecting them, and championing their work, and through them, serves the diverse artists, art and free expression that inspire and enrich American society.
600 Members Founded: 1982

1548 **National Association of Dealers in Arts & Antiques**
1525 Morrow Avenue
Waco, TX 76707-3062
254-752-5372
FAX: 254-752-9886
antiques@nadaweb.com
www.nadaweb.org

1549 **National Association of Fine Arts**
PO Box 1360
Nevada City, CA 95959
800-383-0677
FAX: 530-470-0256
info@artmarketing.com
www.nafa.com
Seeks to provide services and networking opportunities to individuals in the arts community.
100 Members Founded: 1986

1550 **National Association of Limited Edition Dealers**
332 Hurst Mill North
Bremen, GA 30110
770-537-1970
FAX: 770-824-5618 800-446-2533
naledoffice@ol.com www.naled.org
Helen Yanek, President
Members include manufactureres, producers, artists, manufacture sales representatives, and other industry related entitites, all of which are non-voting members.
500 Members Founded: 1976

1551 **National Auctioneers Association**
8880 Ballentine
Overland Park, KS 66214
913-541-8084
FAX: 913-894-5281
joyce@auctioneers.org
www.auctioneers.org
Mike A Jones, President
William L Sheridan, VP
NAA promotes the auction method of marketing and enhances the professionalism of its practitioners
6,000 Members Founded: 1948

1552 **National Guild of Community Schools of the Arts**
520 8th Avenue
3rd Floor, Suite 302
New York, NY 10018
212-268-3337
FAX: 212-268-3995
jonathanherman@nationalguild.org
www.nationalguild.org

Jonathan Herman, Executive Director
Kenneth Cole, Program Director
Andy Behrens, Membership Associate
Annie Walker, Bookkeeper/Operations Manager

Arts Management in Community Institutions (AMICI) Summer Institute trains administrators to meet needs of growing and emerging arts schools. Other programs, services, guildnotes newsletter, job opportunities listings, and publications catalog available upon request on online. Mailing list $25 for non-members, free for members.

300 Members Founded: 1892

1553 National Network for Art Placement
935 W 37th Street
Los Angeles, CA 90065
323-222-4035

info@artisplacement.com
www.artistplacement.com
An organization that helps any artist with start up capital and services for small businesses.

1554 Professional Picture Framers Association
3000 Picture Place
Jackson, MI 49201
517-788-8100
FAX: 517-788-8371
ppfa@ppfa.com www.ppfa.com

Mark Klostermeyer, President
John Pruitt, VP
Fran Gray, Treasurer
Ted Fox, Secretary/Executive Director

A trade association of manufacturers, wholesalers, print publishers, importers and retailers selling art, framing and related supplies.
3000 Members Founded: 1971

1555 Society of Animal Artists
47 5th Avenue
New York, NY 10003
212-741-2880
FAX: 212-741-2262
www.societyofanimalartists.com

Leslie Delgyer, President
Wayne Trimm, VP
Marilyn Newmark, VP
Joan Binney Ross, VP

Devoted to promoting excellence in the protrayal of the creatures sharing our planet and to the education of the public through informative art seminars, lectures and teaching demonstrations.
360 Members Founded: 1960

1556 Society of Illustrators
128 E 63rd Street
New York, NY 10021-7392
212-838-2560
FAX: 212-838-2561
www.societyillustrators.org

Terry Brown, Director

A professional society of illustrators and art directors.
950 Members Founded: 1901

1557 Society of Photographers and Artists Representatives (SPAR)
60 East 42nd Street
Suite 1166
New York, NY 10165
212-779-7464
FAX: 212-253-9996
info@spar.org www.spar.org

George Watson, President

The Society of Photographers and Artists Representatives (SPAR), encourages high standards of conduct from professional representatives across the country. It fosters an environment of shared information that includes the compilation, collection and distribution of equitable strategies and ethical guidelines concerning the effective marketing and sale of artists' work. Since it's founding in 1965, SPAR has sought to continuously improve the business of artist representation.
108 Members Founded: 1965

1558 Volunteer Committees of Art Museums
New Orleans Museum of Art
PO Box 19123
New Orleans, LA 70179
504-488-2631
FAX: 504-484-6662
robin@sfu.ca www.vcam.org

Grace Robin, President
Nancy Rosenbloom, Treasurer

An internationally recognized non-profit organization. VCAM is committed to provide a forum for information exchange, mutual education and enhancement of services to its art museum volunteer committee members through international conferences, regional meetings, published comprehensive conference reports, resource files and the VCAM NEWS publication.
19 Members Founded: 1952

Newsletters

1559 ARTnewsletter
ARTnews Associates
48 W 38th Street
New York, NY 10018-6211
212-398-1690
FAX: 212-819-0394 800-284-4625
info@artnewsonline.com
www.artnewsonline.com

Milton Esterow, Publisher/CEO
Eileen Kinsella, Editor
Debra Melson, Marketing
Elizabeth McNamara, Circulation Manager

Businesss report on the world art market. Targeted to private collectors, dealers, gallery owners, museum directors and curators, tax and estate buyers. *$279.00*
Bi-weekly Founded: 1902
Circulation: 83375

1560 Antique Appraisal Association of America Newsletter
Antique Appraisal Association of America
11361 Garden Grove Boulevard
Garden Grove, CA 92843-1354
714-530-7090

Marge Swenson, Publisher

Supplies members with additional knowledge of antiques from research.

1561 Art Hazards Newsletter
New York Foundation for the Arts
155 Avenue of the Americas
14th Floor
New York, NY 10013
212-366-6900
FAX: 212-366-1778 csa@tmn.com

Theodore Berger, Executive Director
Toni Lewis, Director Administration

Contains information on all hazardous materials; art materials and articles. *$24.00*
Quarterly Founded: 1977

1562 Arts & Culture Funding Report
Capitol City Publishers
4416 East West Hwy
Suite 400
Bethesda, MD 20814-4568
301-916-1800
FAX: 301-528-2497 800-637-9915
A monthly newsletter on federal, state, private and nonprofit sector funding and financial assistance to arts and cultural organizations. *$198.00*
Monthly

1563 Arts Management
Radius Group
110 Riverside Drive
New York, NY 10024
212-722-2929

Alvin H Reiss, Editor/Publisher

The national news service for those who finance, manage and communicate the arts.
$18.00
5 per year

1564 Artsfocus
Colorado Springs Fine Arts Center
30 W Dale Street
Colorado Springs, CO 80903-3210
719-634-5581
FAX: 719-634-0570
info@csfineartscenter.org
www.csfineartscenter.org

Michael De Marsche, President/CEO
Madeleine Mellini, Marketing and Public Relations
Jenny Schatz Stafford, Director of Development

Museum members publication. *$5.00*
24 pages Quarterly Founded: 1936
Printed in 2 colors on matte stock

1565 Association for Preservation Technology International Communique
Association for Preservation Technology Int'l
4513 Lincoln Avenue
Suite 213
Lisle, IL 60532-1290
630-968-6400
FAX: 888-723-4242 888-723-4242
information@apti.org www.apti.org

Susan Johnson, Publisher
Rosanne Dube, Editor

Information on job openings, advertising and meeting announcements.
Quarterly Founded: 1960
Circulation: 1500

1566 Aviso
American Association of Museums
1575 Eye Street NW
Suite 400
Washington, DC 20005-1113
202-289-1818
FAX: 202-289-6578
aviso@aam-us.org www.aam-us.org

Susan Bertots, Senior Editor
Edward Able, Chief Executive Officer

Monthly newletter providing information on the museum world, federal legislation, AAM activities and services and a job bank.
$ 40.00

Monthly Founded: 1906
Circulation: 18000
Mailing list available for rent

1567 **Bookplates in the News**
Amer. Society of Bookplate Collectors & Designers
605 N Stoneman Avenue
Suite F
Alhambra, CA 91801-1406
626-579-9147

exlibris@att.net
www.artisanale@hotmail.com
Audrey Spencer Arellanes, Publisher
Victor Amor, Owner
Collectors' news for designers, owners and collectors of bookplates. *$25.00*
200 pages Quarterly
Circulation: 250

1568 **Cotton & Quail Antique Gazette**
Krause Publications
700 E State Street
Iola, WI 54990-1
715-445-2214
FAX: 715-445-4087
info@krause.com www.krause.com
Greg Smith, Publisher
Linda Kunkel, Editor
Dave Paul, Marketing
The largest monthly antiques & collectibles trade newspaper in the South. Contains articles about various collecting topics, announcements of upcoming shows, reviews of shows and auctions (with prices realized), a Q&A column on antiques, 'how-to' articles, regular features about collecting and selling, an extensive show and auction calendar, classified advertising, and a large section of advertising containing photos of items that will appear in upcoming auctions. *$20.00*
Monthly Founded: 1965
Circulation: 25000

1569 **Encouraging Rejection**
Noforehead Press
Box 55
Kearsarge, NH 03847-0130

www.reuben.org
Mark Heath, Editor/Publisher
To inspire and encourage artists in the face of rejection. *$19.00*
Bi-Monthly Founded: 1994

1570 **Folk Art Finder**
Gallery Press
117 N Main Street
Essex, CT 06426-1302
860-767-0313

Florence Laffal, Editor/Publisher
Contains feature stories, a calendar of events, a readers exchange, news items, book reviews, and classified and display ads relating to 20th century American folk art. Other issues addressed are folk art preservation, laws affecting the arts and funding for the arts. *$14.00*
24 pages Quarterly
Mailing list available for rent
Printed in 1 color on matte stock

1571 **IFAR Journal**
International Foundation for Art Research

500 5th Avenue
Suite 935
New York, NY 10110
212-391-6234
FAX: 212-391-8794 www.ifar.org
Sharon Flescher PhD, CEO
Listings of stolen art and the legal developments of articles on art recovery, art law, cultural property and art authentication. *$65.00*
32 pages Quarterly Founded: 1969

1572 **International Association of Auctioneers Newsletter**
Butterfield & Butterfield Auctioneers
220 San Bruno Avenue
San Francisco, CA 94103-5018
415-861-7500
FAX: 415-861-8951
appraisals.us@bonhams.com
www.butterfields.com
John D Gallo, CEO
A news bulletin with descriptions of upcoming auctions around the world.
8 pages Quarterly Founded: 1865
Circulation: 6500

1573 **Kovels on Antiques and Collectibles**
Antiques
PO Box 22200
Cleveland, OH 44122

FAX: 216-752-3115 www.kovels.com
Terry Kovel, Co-Publisher
Ralph Kovel, Co-Publisher
Newsletter for dealers, investors and collectors. *$27.00*
12 pages Monthly Founded: 1995
Printed in 4 colors on matte stock

1574 **National Association of Antiques Bulletin**
National Association of Dealers in Antiques
PO Box 421
Barrington, IL 60011-0421
847-381-3101
FAX: 815-877-4282
Shirley Kowing, Publisher
Educational and association news.

1575 **Professional Picture Framers Association Newsletter**
4305 Sarellen Road
Richmond, VA 23231-4311
804-226-0430
FAX: 804-222-2175 framers@gnn.com

Rex P Boynton, Executive Director
Trade association news for manufacturers, wholesalers, print publishers, importers and retailers selling art, framing and related supplies.

1576 **Washington International Arts Letter**
Allied Business Consultants
265 Grove Street
Montclair, NJ 07042
973-783-8399
FAX: 973-783-0098
info@theabcgroup.com
www.theabcgroup.com/
Nancy Fandel, Publisher
Financial information. *$40.00*
10 pages Monthly

1577 **World Fine Art**
Art Baron Management Corporation
PO Box 5365
Scottsdale, AZ 85261-5365

Jeffrey Coffin, Publisher
Steve Shipp, Editor
Art history, values and projections regarding artists and movements. *$95.00*
10 pages 9 per year
Printed in 1 color

Magazines & Journals

1578 **Airbrush Action**
3209 Atlantic Avenue
PO Box 438
Allenwood, NJ 08720
732-223-7878
FAX: 732-223-2855 800-876-2472
customerservice@airbrushaction.com
www.airbrushaction.com
Clifford S Stieglitz, President/Publisher
Offers information on the art and graphic design community. Airbrush Action's editorial includes features/coverage on: automotive customizing, hobby applications, illustration, signs, t-shirts, body art, home decorative and more. *$26.95*

Circulation: 35000
Printed in 4 colors on glossy stock

1579 **Airbrush Art and Action**
Paisano Publishers
28210 Dorothy Drive
PO Box 3000
Agoura Hills, CA 91301
818-889-8740
FAX: 818-889-1252 800-247-6246
Joseph Teresi, Publisher
A look at new products, step by step instruction features, profiles of professionals in the airbrushing field, and examples of airbrushed artworks.
Bi-annually
Circulation: 68500

1580 **American Artist**
Billboard
770 Broadway
New York, NY 10003
646-544-4600
FAX: 646-654-5514 800-562-2706
billboard@espcomp.com
www.billboard.com
Barry A Jeckell, Managing Editor
John Kilcullen, Publisher
A magazine devoted to the best of the best in the art industry. *$43.45*
Monthly Founded: 1894
Circulation: 71,435

1581 **Antique Trader**
Krause Publications
700 E State Street
Iola, WI 54990
715-445-2214
FAX: 715-445-4087 800-531-0880
info@krause.com www.krause.com
Grey Smith, Publisher
Patricia DuChene, Editor
D'Ann Jackson, Circulation Manager

For the antiques and collectibles hobby industry. Accepts advertising. *$38.00*
100 pages Weekly Founded: 1957
Circulation: 27363

1582 Antique Week
Mayhill Publications
27 N Jefferson Street
PO Box 90
Knightstown, IN 46148
800-876-5133
FAX: 765-345-3398 800-876-5133
Gary Thoe, President
Richard Lewis, Publisher
Antique dealers. *$38.95*
Weekly Founded: 1968
Circulation: 65000

1583 Antiques & Collecting Magazine
Lightner Publishing Corporation
1006 S Michigan Avenue
Chicago, IL 60605-2254
312-939-4767
FAX: 312-939-0053
lightnerpb@aol.com
www.antiqueweek.com
Dale K Graham, Publisher
Therese Nolan, Editor
Frances Graham, President
Information for antique and limited edition collectors. *$32.00*
Monthly Founded: 1931
Circulation: 20000

1584 Aristos
Aristos Foundation
P. O. Box 20845
Park West Station
New York, NY 10025
212-678-8550
aristos@aristos.org www.aristos.org
Louis Torres, Editor
Michelle Marder Kamhi, Editor
Independent online journal advocating objective standards in arts scholarship and criticism. Our aim is to present well-reasoned commentary on the arts and on the philosophy of art, for a broad audience of general readers and scholars. *$25.00*
Monthly Founded: 1982

1585 Art & Antiques
Trans World Publishing
2100 Powers Ferry Road
Suite 300
Atlanta, GA 30339
770-955-5656
FAX: 770-952-0669
info@billian.com www.billian.com
Jacy C Perkins, Publisher
Barber Tapp, Editor-in-Chief
Douglas Billian, Owner
Magazine for high-end, affluent collectors. Both the site and elegance of the magazine capture the passion and elegance of the diverse world of art and antiques- from Old Master paintings to eighteenth century furniture; from contemporary art to antiquities; from modern photography to ancient hieroglyphics. Our mission is to entertain and inform our readers by bringing the world of art and antiques to their fingertips. *$24.95*
Monthly Founded: 1978
Circulation: 127393 100000 names $100 per M.
Printed in 4 colors on glossy stock

1586 Art & Auction
Art & Auction
111 8th Ave
Ste 302
New York, NY 10011-5204
212-447-9555
FAX: 212-447-5221 800-777-8718
info@artandauction.com
www.artandauction.com
Louise T Blouin, President/Owner
Bruce Wolmer, Editor-in-Chief
Editorial covers the art market from antiquities to contempory art, monthly calendar of gallery exhibitions and auction sales. *$ 80.00*
Monthly Founded: 1996
Circulation: 38500

1587 Art Business News
Advanstar Communications
275 Grove Street
Suite 2-130
Newton, MA 02466
617-219-8300
FAX: 617-219-8310 800-552-4346
info@advanstar.com
www.advanstar.com/
Julie MacDonald, Editor
Publication addressing the business aspect of art and framing. Edtitorial covers everything from trends and sales to new colors and the latest tax changes. *$43.00*
Monthly Founded: 1992

1588 Art Materials Retailer
Fahy-Williams Publishing
171 Reed Street
PO Box 1080
Geneva, NY 14456-2137
315-789-0458
FAX: 315-789-4263 800-344-0559
kfahy@fwpi.com www.fwpi.com
J Kevin Fahy, Publisher
Tina Manzer, Editorial Director
Bradley G. Gordner, Senior Editor
Quarterly
Circulation: 12000
Printed in 4 colors on glossy stock

1589 Art in America
Brant Publications
575 Broadway
5th Floor
New York, NY 10012-3230
212-941-2800
FAX: 212-941-2819
brantpbs@aol.com
www.artinamericamagazine.com
Sandra J Brant, CEO
Elizabeth Baker, Editor
Includes show reviews, event schedules, profiles of artists and genres and updates on literature and materials. *$24.95*
Monthly Founded: 1984
Circulation: 64,182

1590 Artist's Sketchbook
Krause Publications
700 E State Street
Iola, WI 54990-1
715-445-2214
FAX: 715-445-4087 800-942-0673
info@krause.com www.krause.com/
Colleen Cannon, Publisher
Ann Abbott, Editor
William R. Reed, President
Jim Gleim, Executive Vice President
Helps artists of every level and type discover and tap into their creative potential. Using a variety of art-making techniques and processes, from sketching in a journal to taking photographs and even such high-end crafting activities as making mosaic tiles and homemade stationery, Artist's Sketchbook inspires the reader to create. While this magazine does offer step-by-step painting and drawing exercises, its focus is more on enjoying the process of making art. *$6.00*
60 pages Monthly Founded: 2001
Circulation: 46226

1591 Arts and Activities
Publishers' Development Corporation
12345 World Trade Drive
San Diego, CA 92128
858-050-0200
FAX: 858-605-0214
promo@artsandactivities.com
www.artsandactivities.com
Tracy Brdicko, Advertising
Maryellen Bridge, Editor
Offers information and news on the latest in the visual arts. *$24.95*
Monthly Founded: 1932

1592 Artweek
PO Box 52100
Palo Alto, CA 94303-751
800-733-2916
FAX: 262-495-8703 800-733-2916
info@artweek.com www.artweek.com
Debra Koppman, Editor
Laura Richar Janku, Editor
Critical reviews of contemporary West Coast art as well as news, features, articles, interviews, special sections and opinion pieces. *$34.00*
Monthly Founded: 1968

1593 Breakthrough Magazine
Breakthrough Magazine
2271 Old Baton Rouge Highway
PO Box 2945
Hammond, LA 70404-2945
985-345-7266
FAX: 985-542-1831 800-783-7266
breakthrough@earthlink.net
www.breakthroughmagazine.com
Larry Blomquist, Publisher
Artist profiles, tips, previews, and a calendar of events. Incorporates similar techniques related to wildlife carvings, sculpture and photography, *$32.00*
Quarterly
Circulation: 8932

1594 CNA
Krause Publications
700 E State Street
Iola, WI 54990
715-445-2214
FAX: 715-445-4087
info@krause.com www.krause.com
Debbie Knauer, Publisher
Karen Ancona, Editor
A craft industry trade magazine reaching 20,000 retailers and industry leaders. Readers turn to CNA each month in search of trends, innovative products, partnerships, corporate accomplishments, and retail strategies that positively impact their businesses. Regular editorial includes timely product showcases and special sections that target arts, crafts, scrapbooking, children's activities, sewing and needlework products. The editorial team has much experience in the industry. *$30.00*
112 pages Founded: 1945
Circulation: 21777

1595 Christie's International Magazine
Christies Publications
2124 44th Avenue
Long Island City, NY 11101-5008
718-784-1480
FAX: 212-636-4940 800-395-6300
info@christies.com
www.christies.com

Mark Wrey, Publisher
Victoria Tremlett, Editor

Devoted to the promotion of Christie's fine art auctions worldwide. *$70.00*
Founded: 1766
Circulation: 60000

1596 Craft and Needlework Age
Krause Publications
700 E State St
Iola, WI 54990-2214
715-445-2214
FAX: 715-445-4087 800-942-0673
info@krause.com www.krause.com

Karen Ancona, Editor

Trade magazine serving the crafts and needlework industry. Accepts advertising. *$20.00*
Monthly Founded: 1952

1597 Decorative Artist's Workbook
Krause Publications
700 E State Street
Iola, WI 54990-1
715-445-2214
FAX: 715-445-4087
info@krause.com www.krause.com

Colleen Cannon, Publisher
Anne Hevener, Editor

The leading how-to magazine for decorative painters, because it offers detailed step-by-step instruction and illustrations for fabulous projects, plus problem-solving tips, and articles on new techniques, products and books. Readers find a full range of decorative painting subjects and styles painted in a whole range of skill levels and mediums and on a variety of surfaces...and all designed by the most well known artists and instructors in decorative painting! *$27.00*
72 pages Quarterly Founded: 1987
Circulation: 111573

1598 Donna Dewberry's One-Day Decorating
Krause Publications
700 E State Street
Iola, WI 54990-1
715-445-2214
FAX: 715-445-4087
info@Krause.com www.krause.com

Colleen Cannon, Publisher
Anne Hevener, Editor

A how-to magazine for decorative painters, crafters, and do-it-yourself home decorators. Its goal is to inspire anyone interested in embellishing their home, and it features easy-to-complete, step-by-step project ideas using decorative painting, stamping, faux finishing, stenciling, and other crafting techniques. *$27.00*
76 pages Monthly Founded: 1945
Circulation: 100000

1599 Folk Art
American Folk Art Museum
45 West 53rd Street
New York, NY 10019
212-265-1040
FAX: 212-265-2350
info@folkartmuseum.org
www.folkartmuseum.org

Maria Ann Conelli, Director

An award winning publication. The editorial content is geared toward collectors, scholars, and the museum community interested in traditional and contemporary American folk and decorative arts. A benefit of membership, and is delivered to a targeted national and international readership.

1600 HOW Magazine
F&W Publications
4700 E Galbraith Road
Cincinnati, OH 45236
513-312-2222
www.fwpublications.com

Jeffry M Lapin, Publisher
Bryn Mooth, Editor

The industry's leading creativity, business and technology magazine for graphic design professionals. Each issue provides a mix of essential business information, up-to-date technology tips, the creative whys and hows behind noteworthy projects, and profiles of professionals who are influencing design. *$27.73*
140 pages Monthly Founded: 1985
Circulation: 44883

1601 I.D. Magazine
Krause Publications
700 E. State Street
Iola, WI 54990-1
715-445-2214
FAX: 715-445-4087
idedit@fwpubs.com
www.fwpublications.com

Steve Pippin, Publisher
Julie Lasky, Editor
William R Reed, CEO/President
Nicole Martin, Circulation Manager
Andréa Pellegrino, Advertising Director

The international design magazine, showcases innovative products and technologies for sophisticated readers who are at the forefront of shaping the world through design. The multi-disciplinary coverage embraces design trends, theories, experiments and innovators. *$59.96*
96 pages 1 Year 8 Issues Founded: 1954
Circulation: 31,424

1602 Magazine Antiques
Brant Publications
575 Broadway
5th Floor
New York, NY 10012-3230
212-941-2800
FAX: 212-941-2927
jnorton@brantpub.com
www.magazineantiques.com

Sandra J Brant, CEO/Publisher
Allison Ledes, Editor
Donald Liebling, Circulation Manager
Jennifer Norton, Marketing Executive

Articles on American and European decorative and fine arts, architecture, historic preservation, and collecting. *$24.95*
Monthly Founded: 1969
Circulation: 64402

1603 Memory Makers
Krause Publications
700 E State Street
Iola, WI 54990-1
715-445-2214
FAX: 715-445-4087 800-258-0929
info@krause.com www.krause.com

Bob Kaslik, Publisher
Debbie Mock, Editor
Stephen Kent, CEO
D'ann Jackson, Marketing Manager
Buddy Redling, Editor in Chief

Entertains, informs, and inspires the burgeoning number of scrapbook enthusiasts. Features the ideas and stories of its readers - people who believe in keeping scrapbooks and the tradition of the family photo historian alive. Two special newsstand-only issues are dedicated to specific areas of interest including holidays, heritage albums, and more. *$45.00*
144 pages Bi-annually Founded: 1996
Circulation: 203287

1604 Michaels Create!
Krause Publications
700 E State Street
Iola, WI 54990
715-445-2214
FAX: 715-445-4087
info@krause.com www.krause.com

Debbie Knauer, Publisher
Jane Beard, Editor

Features contemporary designs reflecting the latest trends with clear instructions. The home decorating, fashion, and gift ideas will inspire experienced crafters as well as seasonal crafters to explore new possibilities. Step-by-step instructions, tips, and techniques will engage crafters of all ages - including kids - with the creative skills of crafting to be enjoyed as a year-round activity. *$21.97*
116 pages Monthly Founded: 1975
Circulation: 24991

1605 Military Trader
Krause Publications
700 E State Street
Iola, WI 54990-2214
715-452-2214
FAX: 563-588-0888 800-482-4150
info@krause.com www.krause.com

Roger Case, President

Monthly publication for collectors of military memorabilia. *$19.00*
Monthly Founded: 1952

1606 Museum News
American Association of Museums
1575 Eye Street NW
Suite 400
Washington, DC 20005-1113
202-289-1818
FAX: 202-289-6578 888-491-8833
infocenter@aam-us.org
www.aam-us.org

Susan Ciccotti, Senior Editor
Darryl Gale, Advertising Sales Associate
Edward H Able, President/CEO
John Strand, Publisher

Includes articles about museum management, curatorship, marketing, culture touring, funding, security, ethics and politics. Readers will find practical information as well as philosophical debate. *$38.00*
Founded: 1906
Mailing list available for rent

1607 Pastel Journal
Krause Publications
700 E State Street
Iola, WI 54990
715-445-2214
FAX: 715-445-4087
info@krause.com www.krause.com

Colleen Cannon, Publisher
Tom Zeit, Editor

Written by pastel artists for pastel artists. Content is geared toward artists, amateur & professional alike, who already work in pastels and who want to further develop

their skills through in-depth information on pastel painting processes and thought-provoking ideas from successful pastel artists. Also included is information on workshops and exhibitions, as well as articles providing details on the business aspects of art - creating prints, creating websites, framing prints, and shipping. *$27.00*
84 pages Founded: 1999
Circulation: 19167

1608 Picture Framing Magazine
Hobby Publications
PO Box 102
207 Commercial Court
Morganville, NJ 07751
732-536-5160
FAX: 732-536-5761 800-969-7176
pfm@hobbypub.com
www.pictureframingmagazine.com
Bruce Gherman, Publisher
Anne Vazquez, Editor
News and trends in the picture framing trade, marketing strategies, and economic developments. *$20.00*
Monthly Founded: 1955
Circulation: 25000

1609 Postcard Collector
Krause Publications
700 E State St
Iola, WI 54990
715-445-2214
FAX: 715-445-4087 800-942-0673
info@Krause.com www.krause.com
Julie Kernall, Editor
Steve Pippin, Publisher
Monthly publication for postcard collectors. *$29.98*
Monthly Founded: 1982

1610 Proceedings of the American Antiquarian Society
American Antiquarian Society
185 Salisbury Street
Worcester, MA 01609-1634
508-755-5221
FAX: 508-753-3311
www.americanantiquarian.org
Ellen S. Dunlap, President
Caroline Sloat, Editor
Presents research tools and monographic literature within the field of American culture and history to 1876 *$45.00*
Monthly Founded: 1876
Circulation: 1000
Mailing list available for rent 2800 names $150 per M.

1611 SchoolArts
Davis Publications
50 Portland Street
Worcester, MA 01608
508-754-7201
FAX: 508-753-3834 800-533-2847
contactus@davis-art.com
www.davis-art.com
Eldon Katter, Editor
John Carr, Marketing
For art educators. *$23.95*
60 pages Monthly Founded: 1901
Circulation: 23717 24000 names $95 per M.

Printed in 4 colors on matte stock

1612 Sotheby's Preview Magazine
Sotheby's
1334 York Avenue
New York, NY 10021
212-067-7000
FAX: 212-894-1116 541-312-5682
preview@sothebys.com
www.sothebys.com
Diana D Brooks, President/CEO
Auction schedule listings, exhibition dates and catalogue pricing. *$75.00*
48 pages Founded: 1976
Circulation: 80,000
Printed in 4 colors on newsprint stock

1613 Style: 1900
333 N Main Street
Lambertville, NJ 08530
609-397-4104
FAX: 609-397-4409
mfish@style1900.com
www.style1900.com
Marilyn Fish, Editor
Jennifer Strowss, Director Advertising
David Rago, Publisher
The only publication devoted solely to the works and thoughts of the arts and crafts movement. *$6.95*
88 pages Quarterly Founded: 1987
Circulation: 20000
Mailing list available for rent 7,000 names $250 per M.
Printed in 4 colors on glossy stock

1614 Visual Anthropology Review
American Anthropoligical Association
2200 Wilson Boulevard
Suite 600
Arlington, VA 22201-1620
703-528-1902
FAX: 703-528-3546
najwa@optonline.net www.aaanet.org
Najwa Adra, Editor
Marge Dean, Advertising Director
Elizabeth M Brumfiel, President
Bill Davis, Executive Director
Directed toward the study of visual aspects of human behavior including anthropology of art and museology and the use of media in anthropological research, representation, and teaching. *$25.00*
Founded: 1902
Circulation: 1000
Mailing list available for rent
Printed in 1 color on glossy stock

1615 Watercolor Magic
Krause Publications
700 E State Street
Iola, WI 54990-1
715-445-2214
FAX: 715-445-4087
info@Krause.com www.krause.com
Colleen Cannon, Publisher
Tom Zeit, Editor
Offers valuable how-to instruction and creative inspiration for artists who work in water-based media. From page after page of inspirational ideas, to illustrations of the best techniques, to must-have painting tools and materials, watercolorists will find everything they need to know to help them create art from the inside out. Plus, each issue includes special reports and tons of tips from the foremost experts in the field. The definitive source of creative inspiration and technical info. *$27.00*
72 pages Monthly Founded: 1993
Circulation: 94636

Trade Shows

1616 American Art Therapy Association Conference
American Art Therapy Association
5999 Stevenson Ave
Ste 200
Alexandria, VA 22304-3302
703-212-2238
888-290-0878
info@arttherapy.org
www.arttherapy.org
Lynn Kapitan, President
Edward J Styger Jr, Executive Director
Over 20 exhibitors of art supplies, books, therapeutic materials and schools.
800 Attendees Annual Founded: 1969

1617 American Institute for Conservation Annual Meeting
Amer Institute for Conservation of Historic Works
1717 K Street NW
#200
Washington, DC 20036-5346
202-452-9545
FAX: 202-452-9328
info.@aic-faic.org www.aic-faic.org
Eryl P Wentworth, Executive Director
Sheila Paige, Meeting Manager
Annual meeting of conservators of artistic and cultural property, which includes seminars and workshops with over 1,000 members attending yearly. 50 booths.
1000 Attendees June Founded: 1971

1618 American Society for Aesthetics Annual Conference
American Society for Aesthetics
11935 Abersorn Street
Savannah, GA 31419
912-921-2124

asastcar@vms.csd.mu
www.aestheticsonline.org
Carolyn Korsmeyer, President
Stephen Davies, VP
Seminar, conference, and exhibits related to the study of the arts, all disiplines.
500 Attendees Annual Founded: 1942

1619 Antique Arms Show
Beinfeld Productions
PO Box 2197
Cathdral City, CA 92235
760-202-4489
FAX: 760-202-4793
www.antiquearmsshow.com
Wallace Beinfeld, Show Manager
Public show with 1000 booths of antiques and collectibles.
5M/6M Attendees January

1620 Antique-A-Rama
Maven Company
PO Box 937
Plandome, NY 11020-0937
914-248-4646
FAX: 914-248-0800
www.mavencompany.com
N Chittenden, VP
Show with 240 booths.
5,000 Attendees January/Annual Founded: 1970

1621 Art Expo New York
Advanstar Communications
545 Boylston Street
Boston, MA 02116
617-514-4600
FAX: 617-267-6900
info@advanstar.com
www.advanstar.com
Eric Smith, Director of Sales
Five hundred and eighty exhibitors of artwork including: paintings, sculpture, prints and graphics.
15000 Attendees Annual Founded: 1985

1622 Art Libraries Society of North America Annual Conference
Art Libraries Society of North America
4101 Lake Boone Trail
Suite 201
Raleigh, NC 27607-7506
919-518-1919
FAX: 919-787-4916 800-892-7547
arlisna@mercury.interpath.com
www.arlisna.org
Margaret Webster, President
Sherman Clark, Conference Proceedings Editor
Annual conference and show of publishers, book dealers, library suppliers and visual resources suppliers.
500 Attendees April Founded: 1977

1623 Art Methods & Materials Meeting
VNU Expositions
PO Box 17413
Washington, DC 20041
646-654-5000
FAX: 703-318-8833 800-765-7616
Luellen Hoffmann, Show Director
Seminar and 80 suppliers, manufacturers and distributors of art materials and equipment.
4000 Attendees Annual

1624 Art Miami: International Art Fair
Advanstar Communications
545 Boylston Street
Boston, MA 02116
617-514-4600
FAX: 617-267-6900
info@advanstar.com
www.advanstar.com
99 exhibits of fine arts, attended by professionals.
44500 Attendees

1625 Art Supply Expo
Marketing Association Services
1516 Pontius Avenue
Floor 2
Los Angeles, CA 90025-3306
310-478-0074
Randy Bauler, Executive Director
Exhibits consist of art and drafting equipment and computer graphics supplies.
10M Attendees October

1626 Artist-Blacksmiths Association of North America Conference
PO Box 816
Farmington, GA 30638
706-310-0323
FAX: 706-769-7147
conference@abana.org
www.abana.org
Don Kemper, President
Marcus Vickery, Conference Coordinator
Meeting and exhibitions, workshops, demonstrations and artistic metalwork for the professional and amateur blacksmith. Show has 50+ vendors.
1000 Attendees Biennial Founded: 1975

1627 Conference of the Volunteer Committees of Art Museums of Canada and the US
Volunteer Committees of Art Museums
Philbrook Museum
2727 S Rockford
Tulsa, OK 74114
FAX: 918-743-4230
Grace Robin, VCAM President
Triennial conference and exhibits of art museum equipment, supplies and services.
Founded: 1952

1628 Craftsmen's Christmas Classic Arts and Crafts Festival
Gilmore Enterprises
1240 Oakland Avenue
Greensboro, NC 27403
336-274-5550
FAX: 336-274-1084
gilmoreshows@triad.rr.com
www.craftlister.comE5424
Jennifer Palmer, Show Manager
Features work from over 305 talented artists and craftspeople. All juried exhibitors work has been hand made by the exhibitors and must be original design and creation. Visit Christmas Tree Village to view the uniquely decorated Christmas Trees by some of our exhibitors. Something from every taste and budget with items from the most contemporary to the most traditional.
20000 Attendees October/November
Founded: 1982

1629 Craftsmen's Classic Arts and Crafts Festival
Gilmore Enterprises
1240 Oakland Avenue
Greensboro, NC 27403
336-274-5550
FAX: 336-274-1084
gilmoreshows@triad.rr.com
www.craftlister.com
Jennifer Palmer, Show Manager
Features work from over 305 talented artists and craftspeople. All work has been hand made by the juried exhibitors and must be original design and creation. See the creative process in action with several exhibitors demonstrating their craft in their booths. Something from every style, taste and budget with items from the most contemporary to the most traditional.
15000 Attendees March/April/Aug/Sept/Oct.
Founded: 1982

1630 Decor Expo
Pfingsten Publishing
6000 Lombardo Center Drive
Suite 420
Seven Hills, OH 44131
216-328-8926
FAX: 216-328-9452 888-772-8926
iafg-info@pfpublish.com
www.decor-expo.com
Hugh T Tobin, Group Show Director
Rob Spademan, Marketing Director
Five hundred booths exhibiting fine art, limited edition prints, graphics, oil paintings and reproductions. Three shows a year in Orlando (January), New York City (March), and Atlanta (September).
4M Attendees September

1631 Morristown Antiques Show
Wendy Management
PO Box 707
Rye, NY 10580
914-698-3442
FAX: 914-698-6273
www.wendyantiquesshows.com
Three day show of 85 important dealers from the Northeast. Covers the key periods of antiques for budget minded collectors.
November/Annual Founded: 1930

1632 MuseumExpo
American Association of Museums
1575 Eye Street NW
Suite 400
Washington, DC 20005
202-289-1818
FAX: 202-289-6578
museumexpo@aam-us.org
www.aam-us.org
Edward Able, Chief Executive Officer
Cultural exposition with more than 320 exhibitors and 5,000 decision-makers from every type of museum in attendance. This audience includes museum CEOs, directors, exhibit designers, curators, registrars, educators, marketing and public relations personnel, security directors, store managers and other professionals from art museums, history museums, science and technology centers, natural history museums, youth museums, aquariums, zoos and botanical gardens.
1,500 Attendees May

1633 National Art Education Association Convention
National Art Education Association
1916 Association Drive
Reston, VA 20191-1590
703-860-8000
FAX: 703-860-2960
kduse@naea-reston.com
www.naea-reston.org
Kathy Duse, Show Manager
Thomas Hatfield, Executive Director
Annual show of 140-200 exhibitor booths displaying manufacturers, suppliers, distributors, publishing companies and universities latest art textbooks and high-tech software. Show draws approximately 4,000 or more attendees.
April

1634 National Art Materials Trade Association Spectrum Int'l Convention & Show
10115 Kincey Avenue
Suite 260
Huntersville, NC 28078-6486
704-926-6244
FAX: 702-892-6247
Steve LeFebvre, Executive Director
Katharine Coffey, Manager
Seven hundred and fifty booths including educational programs to advance the welfare of the art materials and framing industry.
5M Attendees May

1635 National Guild of Community Schools of the Arts Conference
National Guild of Community Schools of the Arts
520 Eighth Avenue, 3rd Floor
Suite 302
New York, NY 10018-8018
212-268-3337
FAX: 212-268-3995
info@nationalguild.org
www.nationalguild.org

Jonathan Herman, Executive Director
Kenneth Cole, Director

Exhibits of equipment, supplies and services for the advancement of education in the performing and visual arts. Arts Management in Community Institutions (AMICI) Summer Institute trains administrators to meet needs of growing and emerging arts schools. Other programs, services, guildnotes newsletter, job opportunities listings, and publications catalog available upon request on online. Mailing list $25 for non-members, free for members.

350 Attendees Annual 300+ names

1636 New York Antiques Show
Wendy Management
PO Box 707
Rye, NY 10580
914-698-3442
FAX: 914-698-6273
www.wendyantiquesshows.com

This unique, sophisticated show is an important convenient source for trend setting decorators. There are quality antiques for new, young, collectors as well as seasoned pros. This show is filled with 17th, 18th, and 19th Century American, English, French, Oriental and Continental furniture and decorative accessories, including rare books, clocks, silver, brass, paintings, prints, maps, porcelain, rugs, glass, lighting devices, sconces, candlesticks, garden urns, and so much more. 80/90 Dealers

September Founded: 1930

1637 Professional Picture Framers Association Show
Professional Picture Framers Association
4305 Sarellen Road
Richmond, VA 23231
517-788-8100
FAX: 517-788-8100
ppfa@ppfa.com www.ppfa.com

Mark Klostermeyer, President

Source for manufacturers, wholesalers, print publishers, importers and retailers selling art, framing and related supplies.

Annual Founded: 1971

1638 Surtex
George Little Management
Ten Bank Street
Suite 1200
White Plains, NY 10606-1954
914-486-6070
FAX: 914-948-6180 800-272-7469

George(Jeff) Little II, President/COO
Penny Sikalis, VP
Rita Malek, Show Manager

In addition to providing the art and design component of this market we also include important home products.

5000 Attendees May/October

Directories & Databases

1639 AADA Membership Directory
Art Dealers Association of America
575 Madison Avenue
New York, NY 10022
212-940-8590
FAX: 212-940-6484
straussnatt.net www.artdealers.org

Dic Solomon, President

An annual directory listing the AADA members. Published by the Art Dealers Association of America.

77 pages Founded: 1962

1640 ARTWEEK Gallery Calendar Section
Spaulding Publishing
PO Box 52100
Palo Alto, CA 94303-0751

FAX: 262-495-8703 800-733-2916
info@artweek.com www.artweek.com

Richard J O'Brien, Chairman
John T Bourger, Vice Chairman

A screened list of galleries on the West coast and other Western states are profiled.
$34.00

Circulation: 14,500

1641 Art Index
HW Wilson Company
950 University Avenue
Bronx, NY 10452
718-888-8405
FAX: 718-590-1617 800-367-6770
custserv@hwwilson.com
www.hwwilson.com

Harold Regan, President/CEO

Offers more than 500,000 citations to articles and book reviews in over 300 periodicals, yearbooks and museum bulletins.

Bibliographic Founded: 1929

1642 Art Museums of the World
Greenwood Publishing Group
88 Post Road W
PO Box 5007
Westport, CT 06881-5007
203-226-3571
FAX: 203-750-9790 800-225-5800
sales@geenwood.com
www.greenwood.com

Wayne Smith, President/CEO

National and international art museum list.
$215.00
1696 pages 2 Volumes Founded: 1967

1643 Art in America: Guide to Galleries, Museums, and Artists
Brant Publications
575 Broadway
New York, NY 10012
212-941-2800
FAX: 212-941-2927

Sandra J Brant, Publisher

A list of over 4,000 museums, galleries and other display areas. *$15.00*

Annual Founded: 1969
Circulation: 70,000

1644 Arts and Humanities Search
Institute for Scientific Information
3501 Market Street
Philadelphia, PA 19104-3389
215-386-0100
FAX: 215-386-2911 800-386-4474

Offers data from more than 1100 arts and humanities journals.

Bibliographic

1645 Directory of MA and PhD Programs in Art and Art History
College Art Association
275 7th Avenue
Room 1800
New York, NY 10001
212-691-1051
FAX: 212-627-2381
caareviews@collegeart.org
www.caareviews.org

Larry Silver, Editor-in-Chief
Christopher Howard, Editor

Institutions are profiled that offer M.A. and Ph.D. programs in art and art history.
$12.50
152 pages Founded: 1911

1646 Films and Videos on Photography
Program for Art on Film
200 Willoughby Avenue
Brooklyn, NY 11205
718-399-4506
FAX: 718-399-4507
info@artfilm.org www.artfilm.org

Nadine Covert, Executive Director

An annotated directory of over 500 films and videos on photography, photographers, and photographic techniques. *$15.00*

132 pages Founded: 1990 ISBN 0-870995-75-1

1647 Illustrators Annual
Society of Illustrators
128 E 63rd Street
New York, NY 10021-7303
212-838-2560
FAX: 212-838-2561
info@societyillustrators.org
www.societyillustrators.org

Terrence Brown, Director
Jill Bossert, Editor

Published by the Society of Illustrators
$49.95
320 pages Founded: 1959
Circulation: 7000
Mailing list available for rent 1000 names $600 per M.
Printed in 4 colors

1648 Key Guide to Electronic Resources: Art and Art History
Information Today
143 Old Marlton Pike
Medford, NJ 08055-8750
609-654-6266
FAX: 609-654-4309
custserve@infotoday.com
www.infotoday.com

Martin Raish, Editor
Pat Ensor, Series Editor

An evaluative directory of electronic reference in the fields of art and art history.
$39.50
120 pages ISBN 1-573870-22-6

1649 NAMTA International Convention & Trade Show Directory
National Art Materials Trade Association
15806 Broadway Drive
Suite 300
Huntersville, NC 28078
704-892-6244
FAX: 704-892-6247
info@namta.org www.namta.org

Eileen Fanning, Editorial

National Art Materials Trade Association directory.

1650 National Directory of Arts Internships
National Network for Artist Placement
935 W Avenue 37
Suite 9
Los Angeles, CA 90065
323-222-4035

info@artisplacement.com
www.artistplacement.com

Warren Christensen, Director/Editor
Ron Clawges, Editor
Jennifer Hattam, Assistant Editor

Internship opportunities in dance, music, theatre, art and film. *$85.00*
375 pages Bi-Annual ISBN 0-945941-13-7

1651 Official Museum Directory
National Register Publishing
121 Chanlon Road
New Providence, NJ 07974-1541
908-464-6800
FAX: 908-464-3553 800-473-7020
Eileen Fanning, Editorial
Gene McGovern, Publisher
Comprehensive reference for those seeking information on the country's museums. Features profiles and statistics on more than 7,700 museums in the US.

1652 The Artful Home: Furniture, Sculpture and Objects
Kraus Sikes
931 E Main Street
Suite 106
Madison, WI 53703-2955
608-572-2590
FAX: 608-257-2690 877-344-8453
art-info@guild.com www.guild.com
Michael Baum, President
Toni Sikes, Editor
A wealth of information on craft artists working in furniture,wall decor and accessories are listed. *$29.95*
256 pages Annual
Circulation: 15,000

1653 What Museum Guides Need To Know:Access For Blind & Visually Impaired Visitors
American Foundation for the Blind
11 Penn Plaza
Suite 300
New York, NY 10001
212-502-7600
FAX: 212-502-7777
afbinfo@afb.net www.afb.org
Carl R Augusto, President/CEO
Provides practical, easy-to-use guidelines on how to greet blind and visually impaired museum goers. This handbook also covers aesthetics and visual impairment and a training outline for museum requirements for accessibility. *$16.95*
64 pages

1654 Who's Who in Art Materials
National Art Materials Trade Association
15806 Broadway Drive
Suite 300
Huntersville, NC 28078
704-892-6244
FAX: 704-892-6247
eileen.fanning@marquiswhoswho.com
www.namta.org
Eileen Fanning, Editorial
Membership directory of the National Art Materials Trade Association.

Industry Web Sites

1655 www.aam-us.org
American Association of Museums

For the museum community, enhances the ability of museums to serve the public interest, works on behalf of museums in educating federal legislators, assists museums in improving technical standards.

1656 www.acminet.org
Art and Creative Materials Institute

For art and craft product makers who encourage safe use of materials and proper labeling through certification.

1657 www.albemarle-nc.com/camden
Watermark Association of Artisans

Provides marketing assistance to craft producers.

1658 www.aristos.org/aristos2.htm
Aristos Foundation

The Foundation's purpose is to deepen public understanding of the nature of art as well as to foster the understanding and appreciation of humanistic values in the arts. Publishes an online journal.

1659 www.artantiquedealersleague.com
Art and Antique Dealers League of America

Nonprofit organization promotes interests of retailers and wholesalers of antiques and art objects.

1660 www.artdealers.org
Art Dealers Association of America

Works to improve the stature and standing of the art gallery business. Members deal primarily in paintings, sculpture, prints, drawings and photographs from the Renaissance to the present day. We have over 160 member galleries in more than 25 US cities.

1661 www.artnet.com
Art Net United States

The place to buy, sell and research fine art online.

1662 www.collegeart.org
College Art Association

Association for institutions that offer MA and PhD programs in art and art history.

1663 www.greyhouse.com
Grey House Publishing

Selected Grey House directories in the fields of business, health and education are available online. Users can search our online databases by several different search criteria, such as product categories, geographic area, sales volume and much, much more. Full Grey House catalog and online ordering also available.

1664 www.naadaaa.org
National Association of Dealers in Antiques

Nonprofit trade association of America's leading dealers mutually pledged to safeguard the interests of those who buy, sell or collect antiques and works of art.

1665 www.naao.net
National Association of Artist's Organizations

For artists within nonprofit organizations. Dedicated to the presentation of alternative visual arts, media, literature, new music and performing arts.

1666 www.naea-reston.org
National Art Education Association

Manufacturers, suppliers, distributors, publishing companies and universities.

1667 www.naled.com
National Association of Limited Edition Dealers

For dealers, vendors and publishers involved with collectibles and gifts.

1668 www.namta.org
National Art Materials Trade Association

For manufacturers, importers, wholesalers and retailers of art materials.

1669 www.nasaa-arts.org
National Assembly of State Arts Agencies

For those in the arts agency field in the US.

1670 www.societyillustrators.com
Society of Illustrators

For professional illustrators and art directors.

1671 www.sothebys.com
Sotheby's

Auction schedule listings, exhibition dates and catalogue pricing.

Associations

1672 Advocates for Highway and Auto Safety
750 1st Street, NE
Suite 901
Washington, DC 20002
202-408-1711
FAX: 202-408-1699
advocates@saferoads.org
www.saferoads.org

Judith Lee Stone, President
Jacqueline Gillan, VP

An alliance of consumer, health and safety groups and insurance companies and agents working together to make America's roads safer.

1673 Alliance of State Automotive Aftermarket Associations
5330 Wall Street
Suite 100
Madison, WI 53718
608-240-2066
FAX: 608-240-2069
info@asaaa.com www.asaaa.com

Gary Manke, Executive Director

Comprised of 20 regional and state associatons representing the automotive aftermarket.
10000 Members Founded: 1946

1674 American Association of Motor Vehicle Administrators
4301 Wilson Boulevard
Suite 400
Arlington, VA 22203
703-522-4200
FAX: 703-522-1553
info@aamva.org www.aamva.org

Linda Lewis-Pickett, President/CEO
Joy Mills, Executive Assistant
Jim Magruder, Chief of Staff

Nonprofit organization represents state and provincial officials in the US and Canada who administer and enforce motor vehicle laws. Strives to develop model programs in motor vehicle administration, police traffic services and highway safety.
198 Members Founded: 1933

1675 American Automobile Association
1000 AAA Drive
Heathrow, FL 32746-5062
407-444-7000
FAX: 407-444-7380 www.aaa.com

Robert Darbelnet, President
Jerry Cheske, Director Public Relations

Nation's largest motoring and leisure travel organization. AAA provides travel, insurance, financial and automotive related services. The not-for-profit, fully tax paying AAA has been a leader and advocate for the safety and security of all travelers.
45MM Members Founded: 1902

1676 American Highway Users Alliance
1101 14th Street, NW
Washington, DC 20005
202-857-1200
FAX: 202-857-1220
info@highways.org
www.highways.org

Greg Cohen, President
Norman Y Mineta, Chairman

Advocacy trade association promoting safe and uncongested highways and America's freedom of mobility.

1677 American International Automobile Dealers Association
211 N Union Street
Suite 300
Alexandria, VA 22314
703-519-7800
FAX: 703-519-7810 800-462-4232
GOAIADA@aiada.org www.aiada.org

Don Hicks, Chairman
Marianne McInerney, President
Don Beyer, Vice Chairman
I Bradley Hoffman, Secretary/Treasurer

Lobbying and communications organization for American automobile dealerships that sell and service intenational nameplate brands.
10000 Members Founded: 1970

1678 American Public Transit Association
1666 K Street NW
Suite 1100
Washington, DC 20006
202-496-4800
FAX: 202-996-4321
ptads@apta.com www.apta.com

William W Millar, President
Karol J Popkin, Chief of Staff
Nancy Steckel, Executive Assistant
Daniel Duff, Chief Counsel/VP
Government Affairs

Supports professionals in the public transportation industry with publications and seminars.
Founded: 1882

1679 American Society for Quality
600 N Plankinton Avenue
Milwaukee, WI 53203
414-988-8789
FAX: 414-272-1734 800-248-1946
help@asq.org www.asq.org

Kenneth E Case, Chairman
Jerry Mairani, President
Maryann Brennan, Treasurer

The world's leading authority on quality that creates better workplaces and communitites worldwide by advancing learning, quality improvement, and knowledge exchange to improve business results.
104M Members Founded: 1946

1680 American Society of Body Engineers
PO Box 80363
Rochester, MI 48308
248-219-4881
FAX: 586-268-2187
asbe@asbe.com www.asbe.com

Richard George, President
TB TB, VP
Rich Blue, Secretary
Dane Fourtney, Treasurer
Barbara Petoskey, Manager

The American Society of Body Engineers in a non-profit corporation,whose primary purpose is to keep its members abreast of the latest technical developments in the field of Automotive Body Engineering. The Society conducts meetings and events periodically for this purpose.
1000 Members

1681 Antique Truck Club of America
PO Box 91
Imgomar, PA 15127
412-366-0392

atcamanager@verizon.net
www.atca-inc.net

Jim Widmann, President
Douglas Maney, VP
Mark Woods, Secretary
Mike Caskinette, Treasurer
Stefanie Woods, Office Manager

Supports all those involved in the antique truck industry. *$30.00*
Membership Fee Founded: 1971

1682 Association for the Advancement of Automotive Medicine
PO Box 4176
Barrington, IL 60011-4176
847-844-3880
FAX: 847-844-3884
info@aaam.org www.aaam.org

A professional multidisciplinary organization dedicated entirely to motor vehicle crash prevention and control. *$260.00*
Annual Membership Dues Founded: 1957

1683 Association of Diesel Specialists
10 Laboratory Drive
PO Box 13966
Research Triangle Park, NC 27709-3966
919-406-8804
FAX: 919-406-1306
info@diesel.org www.diesel.org

Robert Breunig, President
Tom Folmar, VP
Ken O'Brien, Treasurer
Ben Seidel, Secretary

The worldwide diesel industry's leading trade association, dedicated to the highest level of service on diesel fuel injection and related systems.
700+ Members Founded: 1991

1684 Association of International Automobile Manufacturers
2111 Wilson Boulevard
Suite 1150
Arlington, VA 22201
703-525-7788
FAX: 703-525-8817
webmaster@aiam.org www.aiam.org

James C Morton Jr, Chairman
James E Press, Vice Chairman
Timothy C MacCarthy, President/CEO
Peter M Butterfield, Treasurer
Thomas G Elliot, Secretary

Monitors government regulations and provides information. Members are manufacturers of imported automobiles.
40 Members Founded: 1964

1685 Auto International Association
4600 E West Highway
Suite 300
Bethesda, MD 20814
301-654-6664
FAX: 301-654-3299
aaia@aftermarket.org
www.aiaglobal.org

W. Michael Brown, Chairman
Anthony Peticari, Vice Chairman
Mary DellaValle, Secretary
Roger Patkin, Treasurer
Henry P. Allessio, Board Member

The Auto International Association (AIA) segment of the Automotive Aftermarket Industry Association promotes global trade in automotive products by providing a bridge between the international automotive community and the North American aftermarket. AIA is organized, and functions, for the benefit and advancement of all branches of the industry engaged in the import into North America and export from foreign contries of accessories for imported vehicles sold in North America.

1686 Automatic Transmission Rebuilders Association
2400 Latigo Avenue
Oxnard, CA 93030
805-604-2000
FAX: 805-604-2027 866-GO4-ATRA
Jim Rodd, President
Gary Jennings, VP
Chuck Baker, Secretary/Treasurer
Not-for-profit professional organization dedicated to the improvement and welfare of the automatic transmission repair industry for the benefit of the motoring public. *$85.00*
2000 Members Membership Fee/Monthly
Founded: 1954

1687 Automotive Aftermarket Industry Association
4600 E West Highway
Suite 300
Bethesda, MD 20814
301-654-6664
FAX: 301-654-3299
aaia@aftermarket.org
www.aftermarket.org
Kathleen Schmatz, President/CEO
Susan Medick, CFO/COO
Jim Hilbert, Membership Director
An association whose member companies and affiliates manufacture, distribute and sell motor vehicle parts, accessories, service, tools, equipment, materials and supplies. Through its membership, AAIA represents more than 45,000 repair shops and parts stores.
4400 Members Founded: 1999

1688 Automotive Body Parts Association
Po Box 820689
Houston, TX 77282-0689
281-531-0809
FAX: 281-531-9411 800-323-5832
srodman1@sbcglobal.net
www.autobpa.com
Stanley A Rodman, Executive Director
Dolores Richardson, President
Members are companies that distribute, supply or manufacture automotive replacement body parts.
180 Members Founded: 1980

1689 Automotive Consulting Group
Automotive Consulting Group
3915 Research Park Drive
Suite A-13
Ann Arbor, MI 48108
734-827-1110
FAX: 734-827-9468
acg@autoconsulting.com
www.autoconsulting.com
Dennis Virag, Director
Management consulting firm providing top line and bottom line business performance improvement services to the worldwide automotive industry.

1690 Automotive Engine Rebuilders Association
330 Lexington Drive
Buffalo Grove, IL 60089-6998
847-541-6550
FAX: 847-541-5808
jan@aera.org www.aera.org
John Goodman, President
Jan Juhl, VP Operations
Provides services and support for the engine rebuilding industry.
Founded: 1922

1691 Automotive Fleet and Leasing Association
1000 Westgate Drive
St. Paul, MN 55114
651-037-7247

info@aflaonline.com
www.aflaonline.com
Richard Nicoletti, President
Patsy Brownson, Executive VP
Mark Conroy, VP
Charles Scharmen, Treasurer
Debra Watkins, Secretary
The best source of information and contacts for automotive fleet and leasing professionals. *$200.00*
300 Members Membership/Annual
Founded: 1975

1692 Automotive Industry Action Group

26200 Lahser Road
Suite 200
Southfield, MI 48034-7100
248-358-3003
FAX: 248-799-7995
memberinfo@aiag.org www.aiag.org
Scott Gray, Chairman
Edward T Sprock, Vice Chairman
Composed of major North American vehicle manufacturers and their suppliers. Provides an open forum where members cooperate to develop and promote solutions that enhance prosperity in the automotive industry. *$600.00*
1600 Members Membership Fee Founded: 1982

1693 Automotive Lift Institute
PO Box 85
Cortland, NY 13045
607-756-7775
FAX: 607-756-0888
info@autolift.org www.autolift.org
Bob O'Gorman, President
An association of manufacturers and distributors of automotive lifts used to raise motor vehicles for undercarriage work. Promotes awareness of safety measures used in operating lifts.
25 Members Founded: 1945

1694 Automotive Oil Change Association
12810 Hillcrest
Suite 221
Dallas, TX 75230
972-589-9468
FAX: 972-458-9539 800-331-0329
info@aoca.org www.aoca.org
Sue Ackley, President
Stephen Christie, Executive Director
Representing the convenient automotive service industry. Dedicated to enhancing the competency of fast lube owners, educating the public about services our members offer and maintaining a favorable business environment for the industry as a whole.
1200 Members Founded: 1987

1695 Automotive Parts Rebuilders Association
14160 Newbrook Drive
Suite 210
Chantilly, VA 20151-2223
703-968-2772
FAX: 703-968-2878
mail@apra.org www.apra.org
William C Gager, President
Jeanie Magathan, Senior VP
Phil Bolbach, Advertising Sales Director
Teresa Giroux, Financial Services Director
Association of more than 1,500 member companies engaged in the rebuilding of automotive related hard parts, including starters, alternators, clutches, transmissions, brakes, drive shafts and other parts for passenger cars, trucks, off road, equipment and industrial uses.
1800+ Members Founded: 1941
Mailing list available for rent

1696 Automotive Public Relations Council
10 Laboratory Drive
PO Box 13966
Research Triangle Park, NC 27709-3966

919-406-8811
FAX: 919-549-4824
nzipser@mema.org www.autopr.org
Neal Zipser, Director
Jobie Dowd, Assistant Director
A common-grounds professional organization for public relations practitioners in all segments of the automotive industry whether OE, aftermarket, performance, passenger car or heavy duty truck.
75 Members Founded: 1974

1697 Automotive Recyclers Association
3975 Fair Ridge Drive
Suite 20 N
Fairfax, VA 22033-2924
703-385-1001
FAX: 703-385-1494 888-385-1005
George Elidas, CAE, Executive VP
Representing an industry dedicated to the efficient removal and reuse of automotive parts, and the safe disposal of inoperable motor vehicles. *$300.00*
1000 Members Membership Fee Founded: 1943

1698 Automotive Service Association
PO Box 929
Bedford, TX 76095
817-283-6205
FAX: 817-685-0225 800-272-7467
asainfo@asashop.org
www.asashop.org
Denny Kahler, Chairman
Charlie Elder, Secretary/Treasurer
Ron Pyle, President
Leading organization for owners and managers of automotive service businesses that strive to deliver excellence in service and repairs to consumers. *$195.00*
12000 Members Membership Fee/Annual
Founded: 1951

1699 Automotive Specialty Products Alliance
900 17th Street NW
Suite 300
Washington, DC 20006
202-728-8110
FAX: 202-872-8114
ahackman@cspa.org
www.aspalliance.org

Christopher Cathcart, President

Provides a unified industry voice for its members engaged in the automotive chemical and vehicle appearance product markets before state, regional and federal legislators and regulators. *$1500.00*
Membership Fee/Annual Founded: 1966

1700 Automotive Warehouse Distributors Association
Automotive Aftermarket Industry Association
7101 Wisconsin Ave
Suite 1300
Bethesda, MD 20814-3415
301-654-6664
FAX: 301-654-3299
aaia@aftermarket.org
www.aftermarket.org

Richard Morgan, Chairman
David Bell, Vice Chairman
Tim Sturdevant, Secretary
Timothy A Lee, Treasurer

Oldest organized group of warehouse distributors and their respective suppliers of parts, accessories tools and other supplies for the automotive aftermarket. On January 1, 2004, AWDA joined forces with the Automotive Aftermarket Industry Association (AAIA).
400 Members Founded: 1947
Mailing list available for rent 1800 names $200 per M.

1701 Battery Council International
401 North Michigan Avenue
24th Floor
Chicago, IL 60611-4267
312-644-6610
FAX: 312-527-6640
www.batterycouncil.org

Maurice A Desmarais, Executive Vice President
Alison Davis, Senior Association Assistant

A not-for-profit trade association formed to promote the interests of an international battery industry.
190 Members Founded: 1924

1702 Bearing Specialists Association
800 Roosevelt Road, Building C
Suite 20
Glen Ellyn, IL 60137
630-858-3838
FAX: 630-790-3095
info@bsahome.org www.bsahome.org

Craig A Gipson, President
Douglas Savage, First VP
Thomas L Miller, Second VP
Cam Lawrence, Treasurer
Richard Church, Executive Director

International service and educational organization distributing factory-warranted ball, roller, and antifriction bearings and 60 participating, nonmember manufacturers of bearings and related products.Distributors of antifriction bearings.
142 Members Founded: 1966

1703 Brake Manufacturers Council
10 Laboratory Drive
PO Box 13966
Research Triangle Park, NC 27709-3966
919-406-8841
FAX: 919-406-1306
bmc@mema.org
www.brakecouncil.org

Don Betts, Chairman

Obtaining and disseminating to members information on topics of interest to the brake parts industry.
Founded: 1973

1704 Buses International Association
PO Box 9337
Spokane, WA 99209
509-328-2494
FAX: 509-325-5396
billluke@ztc.net www.busesintl.com

William A Luke, Executive Director

An organization of persons throughout the world who are professionally involved in the management of companies or organizations which operate or manufacture buses.
$25.00
Membership Fee
Printed in 4 colors on glossy stock

1705 California Autobody Association
555 University Avenue
Suite 236
Sacramento, CA 95825
916-646-8111
FAX: 916-646-8113
feedback@calautobody.com
www.calautobody.com

David McClune, Executive Director
Jackie Smith, VP

A nonprofit trade association comprised of over 1000 individual and independent businesses within the automobile collision repair industry.
1000+ Members Founded: 1967

1706 Car Care Council
7101 Wisconsin Ave
Ste 1300
Bethesda, MD 20814-4866
301-610-0100
FAX: 240-333-1088
info@carcare.org www.carcare.org

Jay Burkhart, Chairman
Greg Lancour, Director
Bob Carr, Manager

A nonprofit 501 (c) (3) educational foundation whose purpose is to educate motorists about the importance of maintenance repairs and entertainment for safer, cleaner better performing vehicles. Provides editorial and public service material for media use.
2000 Members Founded: 1968

1707 Center for Auto Safety
1825 Connecticut Avenue NW
Suite 330
Washington, DC 20009-5708
202-328-7700
www.autosafety.org

Ralph Nader, Founder
Clarence Ditlow III, Executive Director

To provide consumers a voice for auto safety and quality in Washington and to help lemon owners fight back across the country. CAS has a small budget but a big impact on the auto industry.
15000 Members Founded: 1970

1708 Division of Dealers Alliance
Continental Plaza
401 Hackensack Avenue
Hackensack, NJ 07601
201-342-4542
FAX: 201-342-3997
FDA@dealersalliance.org
www.dealersalliance.org

John B Darling, VP
Lawrence T Fette, VP
Timothy J Guinee, VP
Robert X Robertazzi, VP
A Mitchell Van Vorst, Executive Director

Attempts to protect dealers against factory encroachment into retail.
Founded: 1969

1709 Driving School Association of the Americas
3090 E Gause Boulevard
Suite 425
Slidell, LA 70461

FAX: 985-649-9877 800-270-3722
dsaa@charter.net www.thedsaa.org

Bradley Huspek, President
Charles Chauncy, Administrative VP
Tim Cooney, Executive VP
Robert Cole, Treasurer
Sharon Pastigo, Secretary

A nonprofit organization for the purpose of raising the standards of educational methods in teaching drivers education, to promote traffic safety on the highways and streets, to publicize, inform and educate the general public to the need for more intensive driver training, safer roadways and all things relating there to.
58000 Members Founded: 1973

1710 Filter Manufacturers Council
10 Laboratory Drive
PO Box 13966
Research Triangle Park, NC 27709-3966
919-406-8809
FAX: 919-549-4824 800-993-4583
bhazelett@mema.org
www.filtercouncil.org

Brent A Hazelett, Executive Director

For manufacturers of vehicular and industrial filtration products in North America. Active in efforts to educate people on proper disposal of used oil filters.
Founded: 1971

1711 International Association of Auto Theft Investigators
PO Box 223
Clinton, NY 13323-0223
315-853-1913
FAX: 315-793-0048
jvabounader@iaati.org www.iaati.org

Karen Metz, President
Kevin P McHugh, First VP
John V Abounader, Executive Director

To improve communication and coordination among the growing family of professional auto theft investigators. *$25.00*
3369 Members Annual Dues Founded: 1952

1712 International Automotive Technician's Network
411 W Lambert Road
Suite 409
Brea, CA 92821
714-257-1335

support@iatn.net www.iatn.net
A group of professional automotive technicians from 139 countries who exchange

technical knowledge and information with other members from around the globe.
46980 Members

1713 International Motor Press Association
4 Park Street
Harrington Park, NJ 07640
201-750-3533
FAX: 201-750-2010 www.impa.org
Dave Kiley, President
Kate McLeod, First VP
Rick Newman, Second VP
Michelle Murad, Secretary
Mike Geylin, Treasurer
Professional group of writers and editors producing auto articles for the press, radio or TV. *$60.00*
Annual Membership Dues

1714 International Show Car Association
1092 Centre Road
Auburn Hills, MI 48326
248-731-1700

ccarshowbob@aol.com
www.theisca.com
Bob Larivee, Owner
Bob Millard, General Manager
An organization of automotive enthusiasts who enjoy building, showing and viewing customs (cars, bikes and trucks), hot rods, competition cars, street machines and antique/restored vehicles. *$35.00*
Membership Fee/Annual

1715 Manufacturers of Emission Controls Association
1730 M St Nw
Ste 206
Washington, DC 20036-4535
202-570-0911
FAX: 202-331-1388
info@meca.org www.meca.org
Dale McKinnon, Executive Director
Joseph Kubsh, Deputy Director
Nonprofit association of the world is leading manufacturers of mobile source emission control manufacturers. Serves as a source of technical information on motor vehicle emission control technology.
Founded: 1976

1716 Metropolitan Parking Association
1112 16th Street NW
Suite 300
Washington, DC 20036-1901
202-296-4336
FAX: 202-331-8523 www.npapark.org
Robert Chaplinske, President
Joel Stahl, Executive Director
To promote and encourage ethical business practices among the operators of parking facilities, and to instill in public and non-public users of parking services confidence in the integrity and skills of parking operators.
400 Members

1717 Mobile Air Conditioning Society Worldwide
225 S Broad Street
PO Box 88
Lansdale, PA 19446
215-631-7020
FAX: 215-631-7017
info@macsw.org www.macsw.org
Elvis Hoffpauir, President/COO
Marion Posen, VP Marketing/Sales
Provides technical training, information and communication for the professionals in the automotive air conditioning industry.
1700 Members Founded: 1981

1718 Motor & Equipment Manufacturers Association
10 Laboratory Drive
PO Box 13966
Research Triangle Park, NC 27709-3966

919-549-4800
FAX: 919-549-4824
info@mema.org www.mema.org
Robert McKenna, President/CEO
Ann Wilson, VP, Government Relations
Serves manufacturers of all types of automotive and truck products through market research, legislative and regulatory representation and reporting, information services, EDI network and credit reporting.
2000 Members Founded: 1904

1719 National Association of Fleet Administrators
125 Village Blvd
Suite 200
Princeton, NJ 08540
609-720-0882
FAX: 609-452-8004
info@nafa.org www.nafa.org
Gayle Pratt, President
Christopher Amos, Senior VP
Christopher D Amos, VP
Walter J Burnett, VP
Joanne Marsh, Director Membership & Marketing
Serving the needs of those managing fleets of automobiles, light duty trucks and/or vans for US and Canadian organizations. Offers statistical research, publications, including NAFA's Fleet Executive monthly magazine, regional meetings, government representation, conferences, trade shows and seminars. *$415.00*
2600+ Members Membership Fee 4000 names
Printed in on glossy stock

1720 National Auto Auction Association
5320-D Spectrum Drive
Frederick, MD 21703-7337
301-696-0400
FAX: 301-631-1359
naaa@naaa.com www.naaa.com
Gregg Kobel, President
John Rea, VP
Laurie Oakman, Communications
Frank Hackett, Manager
NAAA represents dealer wholesale auto auctions. Promotes exchange of ideas and public relations in the used car merchandising industry.
360 Members Founded: 1948 1500 names

1721 National Automobile Dealers Association
8400 Westpark Drive
McLean, VA 22102
703-821-7000
FAX: 800-252-6232 800-252-6232
nadainfo@nada.org www.nada.org
Jack Kain, Chairman
Phillip D Brady, President
Joseph L Cowden, CFO
Bruce Kelleher, Chief Administrative Officer
Richard E Malaise, Chief Information Officer
Provides representation for franchised new car and truck dealers in government, industry and public affairs. Provides counsel on legal and regulatory matters and political representation on Capitol Hill.
400+ Members Founded: 1917

1722 National Automotive Radiator Service Association
15000 Commerce Parkway
Suite C
Mt Laurel, NJ 08054
856-439-1575
FAX: 856-439-9596 800-551-3232
info@narsa.org www.narsa.org
Mike Dwyer, Executive Director
Jen Jones, Assistant Executive Director
Amy Chezem, Director of Communications
Lia Moore, Administrative Assistant
Trade association serving the cooling system service industry and the public.
1500 Members Founded: 1953

1723 National Glass Association
8200 Greensboro Drive
Suite 302
McLean, VA 22102-3881
703-424-4890
FAX: 703-442-0630
customersvc@glass.org
www.glass.org
Thomas D Lee III, Chairman
Philip J James, President/CEO
Joe N Mesko, Treasurer
Supports professionals in the glass industry, including automotive glass. Publishes bi-monthly magazine.
4000 Members Founded: 1948

1724 National Independent Automobile Dealers Association
2521 Brown Boulevard
Arlington, TX 76006-5203
817-492-2377
FAX: 817-649-5866 800-682-3837
mike@naida.com www.niada.com
Karen Barbee, President
Michael R Linn, Executive VP/CEO
Mike Linn, Executive Vice President
Sandra Moss, Senior Vice President
Representing quality independent automobile dealers for almost 60 years. NIADA is here to assist members in becoming more successful within the used motor vehicle industry.
19000 Members Founded: 1946

1725 National Motorists Association
402 W 2nd Street
Waunakee, WI 53597
608-849-6000
FAX: 608-849-8697
nma@motorists.org
www.motorists.com
James J Baxter, President
Eric Skrum, Communications Director
Advocates, represents and protects the interests of North American motorists. *$35.00*
Annual Membership Dues Founded: 1982

1726 National Parking Association
1112 16th Street NW
Suite 300
Washington, DC 20036
202-296-4336
FAX: 202-331-8523 800-647-7275
info@npapark.org www.npapark.org
Martin L Stein, Executive Director
Barbara Kronee, Director of Finance
Patricia Langfelp, Dir Marketing/Business Development

Kimberley Morgan, Director of Communications

Our members are comprised of parking professionals in both the public and private sectors from across the country and around the world. NPA members are private operators, parking consultants, colleges and universities, municipalities, parking authorities, hospitals and medical centers and industry vendors. *$370.00*

1200 Members Membership Fee Founded: 1951

Mailing list available for rent 1700 names $250 per M.

1727 National Truck Equipment Association

37400 Hills Tech Drive
Farmington Hills, MI 48331-3414
248-489-7090
FAX: 248-489-8590 800-441-6832
info@ntea.com www.ntea.com

Robert S Green, President
Jim Carney, Executive Director
Sheree Campbell, Executive Assistant

Represents small to mid-sized companies that manufacture, distribute, install, buy, sell and repair commercial trucks, truck bodies, truck equipment, trailers and accessories.

1600 Members Founded: 1964 1600 names $400 per M.

1728 National Wheel and Rim Association

5121 Bowden Road
Suite 303
Jacksonville, FL 32216-5950
904-737-2900
FAX: 904-636-9881
nwra@bellsouth.net
www.nationalwheelandrim.org

Angelo Volpe, Executive Vice President
Ken Duval, Treasurer
Angelo Volpe, Executive VP
Richard Taylor, Member Board of Trustees

Represents warehouse distributors of wheels, rims and related parts.

230 Members Founded: 1924

1729 North American Council of Automotive Teachers (NACAT)

PO Box 80010
Charleston, SC 29416
843-556-7068
FAX: 843-556-7068
office@nacat.com www.nacat.com

Dan Perrin, Executive Manager

Supports all educators in the automotive industry, with training and education, publications and seminars. *$40.00*

750 Members Annual Membership Dues Founded: 1974

1730 Original Equipment Suppliers Association

1301 Long Lake Road
Suite 225
Troy, MI 48098
248-952-6401
FAX: 248-952-6404
info@oesa.org www.oesa.org

Neil De Koker, President
Karen Bohannon, Executive Assistant
Noelle Schiffer, VP Sales & Marketing
Dawn M Geiger, Director of Member Services

Dedicated to advancing the business interests of companies supplying components, systems, modules, equipment, materials and services used in and by the original equipment automotive industry and to engage in activities in support fo the welfare of the association membership. OESA is an affiliate of the Motor and Equipment Manufacturers Association.

340 Members Founded: 1998

1731 Overseas Automotive Council

10 Laboratory Drive
PO Box 13966
Research Triangle Park, NC 27709-3966
919-406-8810
FAX: 919-549-4824
oac@mema.org www.oac-intl.org

Anthony Cardez, Director

Members include US and foreign individuals who import and export.

700+ Members Founded: 1923

1732 Overseas Automotive Councils

Overseas Automotive Council
10 Laboratory Drive
PO Box 13966
Research Triangle Park, NC 27709-3966
919-406-8810
FAX: 919-549-4824
oac@mema.org www.oac-intl.org

Robert Smith, President
Rafaat N Kureshi, First VP
Richard Mezadurian, Second VP
Anthony C Cardez, Director of Business Development

One of the oldest and most unique organizations in the global automotive aftermarket. Members include US and foreign individuals who import and export, OE parts manufacturers, freight forwarders, importers, distributors, and manufacturer's sales representatives all are involved with the sales of automotive products and services beyond the U.S. borders. *$325.00*

500 Members Membership Fee Founded: 1923

1733 Performance Warehouse Association

41-701 Corporate Way
Suite 1
Palm Desert, CA 92260
760-346-5647
FAX: 760-346-5847
van@weathers.com www.pwa-par.org

Gary Light, President
John Towle, Executive Director
Anne Graves, Treasurer

For distributors of specialty automotive parts and supplies.

10000 Members Founded: 1971

1734 Production Engine Remanufacturers Association

14160 Newbrook Drive
Suite 210
Chantilly, VA 20151-2223
703-968-2772
FAX: 703-968-2878
gager@pera.org www.pera.org

William C Gager, President
Roy Berndt, Executive Director

Worldwide organization whose gives its members the information they need to produce remanufactured engines equal or superior to suppliers of the production line combustion engine industry.

Membership Fee Founded: 1946

1735 Recreation Vehicle Dealers Association

3930 University Drive
Fairfax, VA 22030-2515
703-591-7130
FAX: 703-591-0734
info@rvda.org www.rvda.org

Mike Molino, President
Ronnie Hepp, VP of Administration
Hank Fortune, Director of Finance
Susan Charter, Associate Services Manager

National association advances the best interests of RV retailers through education, services, leadership and programs of market expansion that promote increased use and sale of RVs while enhancing their image.

Annual Membership Dues

Mailing list available for rent 1500 names

1736 Recreational Vehicle Aftermarket Association

54 Westerly Road
Camp Hill, PA 17011
717-730-0300
FAX: 717-730-0544
ellenkietzmann@blueox.us
www.rvaftermarket.org

Ellen Kietzmann, President
Ron Dempster, VP
Jess Fowler, Secretary
Bill Fudale, Treasurer

An organization for the suppliers, distributors and agents that represent the aftermarket segment of the RV industry.

110 Members Founded: 1969

1737 Remanufacturing Industries Council

14160 Newbrook Drive
Suite 210
Chantilly, VA 20151-2223
703-968-2772
FAX: 703-968-2878
info@remancouncil.org
www.remancouncil.org

Nabil Nasr, Chairperson
Lester Cornelius, President
Bill Davies, Treasurer/Secretary

To promote, protect and advance the entire remanufacturing industry. Publishes monthly newsletter.

Founded: 2001

1738 Rubber Manufacturers Association

1400 K Street NW
Suite 900
Washington, DC 20005-2403
202-682-4800
FAX: 202-682-4854
info@rma.org www.rma.org

Donald B Shea, President/CEO

National trade association for makers of tires and other rubber products.

100 Members

1739 Service Specialists Association

4015 Marks Road
Apartment 2B
Medina, OH 44256-8316
330-725-7160
FAX: 330-722-5638 800-763-5717

Cara R Giebner, Executive VP

Members are persons, firms or corporations who have operated a full line heavy duty repair service shop for at least one year with sufficient inventory to service market area, having rebuilding department capable of making all necessary repairs.

140 Members Founded: 1981

1740 **Society of Automotive Engineers**
SAE Automotive Headquarters
755 W Big Beaver
Suite 1600
Troy, MI 48084
248-732-2455
FAX: 248-273-2494 877-606-7323
CustomerService@sae.org
www.sae.org

J E Robertson, President
Richard O Schaum, VP, Automotive
Greg Henderson, Treasurer
Raymond A Morris, Secretary
Jack Pokrzywa, Executive Director

Offers automotive engineers the technical information and expertise used in building, maintaining and operating self propelled vehicles for use on land, sea, air or space.
84000 Members Founded: 1905

1741 **Society of Collision Repair Specialists**
PO Box 909
Prosser, WA 99350

FAX: 877-851-0660 877-841-0660

Lou DiLisio Jr, Chairman
Tom Moreland, Vice Chairman
Gary Wano Jr, Treasurer
Barry Dorn, Secretary

For owners and managers of auto collision repair shops, suppliers, insurance and educational associates and suppliers in the US, Canada, Australia and New Zealand. Distributes technical, management, marketing and sales information. Works to promote professionalism within the collision repair industry. *$300.00*
Membership Fee Founded: 1983

1742 **Society of Independent Gasoline Marketers of America**
11495 Freedom Drive
Suite 215
Reston, VA 20190-5602
703-750-0478
FAX: 703-709-7007
sigma@sigma.org www.sigma.org

William S Shipley III, President
Paul D Reid, First VP
Carl Boyett, Second VP
Kenneth Doyle, Executive Vice President
Jack C Pester, Secretary/Treasurer

Supports independent fuel marketers and suppliers, providing training and education, publications and seminars.
250 Members Founded: 1958

1743 **Specialty Equipment Market Association**
PO Box 4910
Diamond Bar, CA 91765-0289
909-396-0289
FAX: 909-860-0184
sema@sema.org www.sema.org

Chris Kersting, President/CEO
Linda Czarkowski, VP Administration
Cher Borden, Membership Coordinator
Tom Myroniak, Marketing Director

This trade association consists of a diverse group of manufacturers, distributors, retailers, publishing companies, auto restorers, street rod builders, restylers, car clubs, race teams and more.
5700+ Members Founded: 1963

1744 **Tire Industry Association**
1532 Pointer Ridge Place
Suite G
Bowie, MD 20716-1883
301-430-7280
FAX: 301-430-7283
info@tireindustry.org
www.tireindustry.org

Roy Littlefield, Executive Vice President
Sandra Martinez, Director Operations

Representing all segments of the tire industry, including those that manufacture, repair, recycle, sell, service or use new or retreaded tires, and also those suppliers or individuals who furnish equipment, material or services to the industry.
5000 Members Founded: 2002

1745 **Tire Retread Information Bureau**
900 Weldon Grove
Pacific Grove, CA 93950
831-372-1917
FAX: 831-372-9210 888-473-8732
info@retread.org www.retread.org

Harvey Brodsky, Managing Director
Rachel Lewis, IT Manager

Serving as the public relations arm of the retread industry. Gathering and disseminating information on retread passenger and truck tires to members and the general public.
500 Members Founded: 1973

1746 **Tire and Rim Association**
175 Montrose W Avenue
Suite 150
Copley, OH 44321-2793
330-666-8121
FAX: 330-666-8340
tra@us-tra.org www.us-tra.org

JF Pacuit, Executive VP

Technical standardizing organization for tire, rim and valve manufacturers.
110 Members Founded: 1903

1747 **United States Auto Club**
USAC National Office
4910 W 16th Street
Speedway, IN 46224-5703
317-247-5151
FAX: 317-247-0123

Rollie Helmling, President

Supports all driving professionals and consumers with education, publications, driving and vacation tips. Publishes monthly magazine.

1748 **Womens Automotive Association International**
PO Box 2535
Birmingham, MI 48012
248-646-5250
FAX: 248-646-6721 www.waai.com

Lorraine H Schultz, Founder/CEO

Dedicated to the development and advancement of women as automotive industry leaders. Today, the organization continues to thrive throughout the United States and Canada as the leading women's global organization dedicated to this purpose. *$85.00*
600 Members Membership Fee Founded: 1995

Newsletters

1749 **AWDA Aftermarket Distribution**
Automotive Warehouse Distributors Association
7101 Wisconsin Ave
Suite 1300
Bethesda, MD 20814-3415
301-654-6664
FAX: 301-654-3299
info@awda.org www.awda.org

Margaret Beck, Publisher
David Caracci, Chairman
Kathleen Schmatz, President

Presents news of programs, benefits and services of the Automotive Warehouse Distributors Association.
10 pages Founded: 1947
Printed in 2 colors on matte stock

1750 **Automotive Cooling Journal**
15000 Commerce Parkway
Suite C
Mt Laurel, NJ 08054
856-439-1575
FAX: 856-439-9596 800-551-3232
info@narsa.org www.narsa.org

Mike Dwyer, Executive Director
Jen Jones, Assistant Executive Director
Lia Moore, Membership Coordinator
Anthony Celenza, Meeting Manager
Sarah Lerow, Associate Editor

Newsletter for manufacturers of auto cooling systems and covers of radiators.
$30.00
5 pages Monthly Founded: 1890
Circulation: 10000

1751 **Automotive Market Report**
Automotive Auction Publishing
607 Laurel Drive
Monroeville, PA 15146-4405
412-373-6383
FAX: 412-373-6388

Clyde K Hillwig, Publisher

News items pertinent to auto auctions and the auto industry.
BiWeekly
Circulation: 10000

1752 **Automotive Week: Greensheet**
Molinaro Communications
PO Box 355
Munroe Falls, OH 44262-0355
330-688-4960
FAX: 330-688-4908 877-694-6076
greensheet@auto-week.com
www.auto-week.com

Gary Molinaro, Publisher/Editor
Marc Vincent, Managing Editor

Intelligence concerning the $270 billion independent automotive aftermarked. Breaking news & analysis not available anywhere else in the industry. Key moves in the retail and wholesale distribution channels, mergers & acquisitions; financial analysis of publicly-traded entities. Classified, non-product advertising accepted. *$225.00*
4 pages 48 issues Founded: 1975 3000 names
Printed in on matte stock

1753 Buses International
Buses International Association
PO Box 9337
Spokane, WA 99209-9337
509-328-2494
FAX: 509-325-5396
billluke@ztc.net www.busesintl.com

William A Luke, Publisher

Articles about bus transportation in various countries. Also news of the world bus industry association news and list events.
4 pages Quarterly Founded: 1981
Circulation: 150

1754 Car Dealer Insider
United Communications Group
11300 Rockville Pike
Suite 1100
Rockville, MD 20852-3030
301-816-8950
FAX: 301-816-8945
webmaster@ucg.com www.ucg.com

Jill Gardner, Publisher
Donna Lawrence, Editor
Dan Brown, Reporter

Marketing intelligence for new car dealers includes dealer-tested tactics, best management practices and breaking news stories. *$ 285.00*
Weekly Founded: 1977
Printed in on matte stock

1755 Chek-Chart Service Bulletin
Motor Information Systems/Chek-Chart
5600 Crooks Road
Suite 200
Troy, MI 48098
248-828-0000
FAX: 248-828-0215 800-426-6867

James Reese, Managing Editor
Anthony Mattar, Owner

Up-to-date information on all the new automotive developments from the car manufacturers. Information bulletin for service station dealers, mechanics, and instructors. Chek/Chart is part of MotorInformation Systems.

1756 EngiNEWS
Production Engine Remanufacturers Association
4215 Lafayette Center Drive
Suite 3
Chantilly, VA 20151-1243
703-968-2772
FAX: 703-968-2878
kase@buyreman.com www.pera.org/

William Gager, Executive Vice President
Roy Berndt, Technical Director
Kirsten Case, Editor
Phil Bolbach, Adverstise and Sales Manager
Kirsten Berndt, Circulation Manager

Quarterly newsletter.
Monthly Founded: 1943
Circulation: 500
Printed in 2 colors

1757 Executive Directors Report
Society of Collision Repair Specialists
PO Box 4519
West Richland, WA 99353-4519
509-735-0607
FAX: 509-943-8942 877-841-0660
scrs1@aol.com www.scrs.com

Dan Risley, Editor
Lou DiLisio, Chairman

Newsletter for owners and managers of auto collision repair shops, suppliers, insurance and educational associates and suppliers in the US, Canada, Australia and New Zealand. Technical, management, marketing and sales information. Free to members. *$300.00*
Founded: 1982
Circulation: 6000

1758 Fleet Administration News
PO Box 159
Litchfield Park, AZ 85340
623-772-9096
FAX: 623-772-9098
ncsfa@qwest.net ncsfa.state.ut.us

Joe O'Neill, Executive Director

NCSFA members are state government administrators responsible for vehicle fleet management. *$50.00*
Quarterly 250 names
Printed in on matte stock

1759 Global Connection
Automotive Parts Rebuilders Association
4215 Lafayette Center Drive
Suite 3
Chantilly, VA 20151-1243
703-968-2772
FAX: 703-968-2878
mail@apra.org www.apra.org

William C Gager, President
Jeanie Magathan, Senior VP
Teresa Giroux, Financial Services Direct
Kirsten Kase, Editor
Phil Bolbach, Director of Advertising Sales

Association newsletter. *$35.00*
Monthly Founded: 1941 20000 names

1760 Highway & Vehicle/Safety Report
Stamler Publishing Company
178 Thimble Island Road
PO Box 3367
Branford, CT 06405-1967
203-488-9808
FAX: 203-488-3129
hvsrsafe@aol.com
www.trafficsafetynews.com

S Paul Stamler, Publisher
Suzanne Reutenauer, Circulation Manager

Business to business newsletter on the latest developments in transportation safety, regulations and new legislation, and new technology in the automotive industry. *$467.00*
Monthly Founded: 1973

1761 Hybrid & Electric Vehicle Progress
Alexander Communications Group
28 W 25th Street
8th Floor
New York, NY 10010
212-228-0246
FAX: 212-228-0376 800-232-4317
info@evprogress.com
www.evprogress.com

Margaret DeWitt, Publisher
Laurence Alexander, CEO

News of hybrid and electric vehicle commercialization. Worldwide coverage focuses on news and data on both the technical and business aspects of the hybrid or electric vehicle industry. *$477.00*
8 pages Fortnightly Founded: 1954
Circulation: 800
Printed in 2 colors on matte stock

1762 IMPACT
Center for Auto Safety
1825 Connecticut Avenue NW
Suite 330
Washington, DC 20009-5708
202-328-7700
www.autosafety.org

Ralph Nader, Founder
Irene Nagaraj, Editor
Clarence Ditlow III, Executive Director

Reports on the auto safety world of CAS, as well as covering safety litigation, secret warranties, crash tests, lemon laws, recalls, federal and state investigations. *$75.00*
Bi-Monthly

1763 Independent Gasoline Marketing (IGM)
Soc. of Independent Gasoline Marketers of America
11495 Sunset Hills Rd
Ste 215
Reston, VA 20190-5213
703-750-0478
FAX: 703- 70- 700
sigma@sigma.org www.sigma.org

Thomas L Osborne, Director Communications
Kenneth A Doyle, Executive VP
Marilyn Selvitelle, VP

Information for independent fuel marketers and suppliers on legislative issues, new market trends, equipment use and management techniques.
32 pages Founded: 1958
Circulation: 4000
Printed in 4 colors on glossy stock

1764 Motor
Hearst Business Communications
5600 Crooks Road
Suite 200
Troy, MI 48098
248-828-0000
FAX: 248-828-7004
jlypen@motor.com www.motor.com

John Lypen, Editor
Kevin Carr, President
Todd Ladson, Business Manager
Lori Aemiseqqer, Marketing
Richard Laimbeer, Publisher

Articles to keep readers up to date on the latest diagnostic techniques and service procedures. Management articles to help shop owners increase profitability, latest tools available, new products and industry news. *$48.00*
Monthly Founded: 1903
Circulation: 138941

1765 NACAT News
North American Council of Automotive Teachers
PO Box 80010
Charleston, SC 29416
843-556-7068
FAX: 843-556-7068
office@nacat.com www.nacat.com

Al Goodyear, Executive Manager
Jeff Hunt, President

Cutting edge automotive information for automotive educators. Also news of the organization and the automotive industry.
Founded: 1974
Circulation: 750

1766 NAFA Fleet Executive
National Association of Fleet Administrators
100 Wood Avenue S
Suite 310
Iselin, NJ 08830
732-494-8100
FAX: 732-494-6789
publicatons@nafa.org www.nafa.org

Jessica Sypniewski, Communications Director
Joanne Marsh, Director Membership & Marketing

Contains articles pertaining to car, van and light truck fleet management by United States and Canadian corporations and government agencies. Editorial emphasis is on legislation and regulation, alternate fuels, safety, interviews with prominent industry personalities, technology, association news, public service fleet management and light truck fleet management. *$48.00*
36 pages Monthly
Circulation: 4000
Printed in 4 colors on glossy stock : web

1767 NAFA Fleetfocus
National Association of Fleet Administrators
100 Wood Avenue S
Suite 310
Iselin, NJ 08830
732-494-8100
FAX: 732-494-6789
info@nafa.org www.nafa.org
Jean Fritzen, Communications Manager
Jean Fritzen, Editor
Joanne Marsh, Director Membership & Marketing
Electronic newsletter available to members on the web. Quick reading updates on legislative and industry news important to fleet administrators in the US and Canada.
Weekly Founded: 1946
Circulation: 3600
Printed in 1 color on matte stock : web

1768 OAC Global Report
Overseas Automotive Council
10 Laboratory Drive
Research Triangle Park, NC 27709-3966
919-406-8810
FAX: 919-549-4824 www.oac-intl.org
Anthony Cardez, Director Business Development
Robert B Smith, President
Free to members.
Monthly Founded: 1923

1769 Passenger Transport
American Public Transit Association
1666 K Street NW
Suite 1100
Washington, DC 20006
202-496-4800
FAX: 202-496-4321
ptsubscriptions@apta.com
www.apta.com
Rhonda Goldberg, Managing Editor
George F Dixon III, Chairman
William W Millar, President
Rosemary Sheridan, VP-Communications and M
Frances Hooper, Director-Member Services
Information on federal legislative, administrative and regulatory developments, management and operations, new technology, and state and local developments in public transit. *$65.00*
16 pages Weekly Founded: 1882
Circulation: 5000

1770 Power Report
JD Power and Associates Publications Division
2625 Townsgate Road
Westlake Village, CA 91361
805-418-8000
FAX: 805-418-8900 800- 27- 537
info@jdpower.com www.jdpa.com
Stephen C Goodall, President/CEO
Mary Ann Maskery, Editor
JD Power, Chairman
Focuses on what car buyers and owners feel about their current vehicles. *$299.00*
Monthly Founded: 1968

1771 Remanufacturing Institute Bulletin
Remanufacturing Institute International
14160 Newbrook Drive
Suite 210
Chantilly, VA 20151-2223
703-968-2772
FAX: 703-968-2878
gager@buyreman.com
www.reman.org
William G Gager, President
An electronic newsletter written for companies in the remanufacturing business. An estimated 73,000 in the USA and another 73,000 outside the USA.
Circulation: 10,000

1772 Service Executive
Automotive Week Publishing
PO Box 3495
Wayne, NJ 07474-3495
973-694-7792
laverty@auto-week.com
www.auto-week.com
Marketing information for the independent automotive aftermarket. Fast-breaking news of new market entries and strategies; key retail and wholesale developments; merger, acquisition, bankruptcy reports; regular charts of the Top 25 market leaders in various segments (parts, chains, tune-up specialists, brake specialists, tire, fast lube, etc.). The market's sole weekly. Classified non-product advertising accepted. *$130.00*
4 pages Monthly Founded: 1975
Printed in on matte stock

1773 Shop Talk
IMACA Education Foundation
6410 Southwest Boulevard
Suite 212
Fort Worth, TX 76109-3920
817-732-4600
FAX: 817-732-9610
info@imaca.org www.imaca.org
Joan M Jones, Circulation Director
Technical and industry information for the mobile air conditioning industry. *$20.00*
Founded: 1958

1774 Shoptalk
Automotive Engine Rebuilders Association
330 Lexington Drive
Buffalo Grove, IL 60089-6933
847-541-6550
FAX: 847-541-5808 888-326-2372
info@aera.org www.aera.org
Maryanne Ingratta, Editor
Jan Juhl, VP Operations
Provides technical and management information for members of the automotive aftermarket, especially engine rebuilders and remanufacturers.
8 pages Daily
Mailing list available for rent
Printed in 2 colors on matte stock

1775 Show Stopper
International Show Car Association
1092 Centre Road
Auburn Hills, MI 48326
248-731-1700
www.theisca.com
Bob Millard, Managing Director
Bob Larivee, Owner
Car association report about shows.

1776 Society of Collision Repair Specialists: All Member Mailing
PO Box 909
Prosser, WA 99350-0909
FAX: 877-851-0660 877-841-0660
scrs1@aol.com www.scrs.com
Dan Risley, Executive Director
Joel Lofton, Chairman
Makes promotions available to members of the society. Free to members.
500 pages Quarterly Founded: 1982

1777 Specialized Vehicles: E-mail News
Forecast International
22 Commerce Road
Newtown, CT 06470-1643
203-426-0800
FAX: 203-426-0223 800-451-4975
info@forecast1.com
www.forecast1.com
Douglas A Nebinger, President
An electronic information/data service sourced from thousands of worldwide publications, in 15 languages. Provides concise summaries, news, trends and contract information with hyper-links to the source or a related website. Delivered 100 times a year. *$425.00*
2 per year Founded: 1973

1778 Today's Tire Industry
Tire Industry Association
1532 Pointer Ridge Place
Suite E
Bowie, MD 20716-1883
301-430-7280
FAX: 301-430-7283 800-876-8372
Kevin Rohlwing, Editor
Features retail, management, personnel and industry related information. *$13.00*

1779 UPdate: Society of Automotive Engineers
Society of Automotive Engineers
400 Commonwealth Drive
Warrendale, PA 15096-1
724-776-4841
FAX: 248-273-2494 877-606-7323
update@sae.org www.sae.org
Jennifer Newton, Editor
Martha Schanno, Circulation Manager
Published to enhance communications with and among SAE members on such non-technical issues as society activities, meetings and members. Recruitment advertising is accepted.
Monthly Founded: 1905
Circulation: 65000 Audited
Printed in 2 colors on newsprint stock
Computerized version available

1780 USAC News
United States Auto Club
4910 W 16th Street
PO Box 24001
Speedway, IN 46224
317-247-5151
FAX: 317-247-0123
usacracing@iquest.net
www.usacracing.com
Richard King, President
Dick Jordan, Editor
Rollie Helmling, President

Contains schedules and news from USAC divisions.
8 pages Monthly Founded: 1982

1781 **Ward's Automotive Reports**
Ward's Communications
3000 Town Center
Suite 2750
Southfield, MI 48075-1245
248-357-0800
FAX: 248-357-0810 877-825-1815
wards@primediabusiness.com
www.wardsauto.com

Tom Duncan, Publisher
Alisa Priddle, Editor
Jim Bush, Business Manager
Chris Lamphear, Marketing Manager

Automotive sales, production and inventory statistics, news and analysis. *$1195.00*

8 pages Weekly Founded: 1924
Printed in 2 colors on matte stock

1782 **Ward's Dealer Business**
PRIMEDIA Intertec-Technology & Transportation
3000 Town Center
Suite 2750
Southfield, MI 48075-1245
248-357-0800
FAX: 248-357-0810 877-778-2512
information@primedia.com
www.wardsauto.com

Thomas Duncan, Group Publisher
Chris Lamphear, Marketing Manager
Steve Sindly, Editor
James Bush, Managing Director

Information for the management of US new car dealerships by covering profit building techniques and business expansions. Includes analysis of current automotive trends. *$36.00*
Monthly
Circulation: 32635

1783 **Ward's Engine and Vehicle Technology Update**
Ward's Communications
3000 Town Center
Suite 2750
Southfield, MI 48075-1245
248-357-0800
FAX: 248-357-0810
www.wardsauto.com

Thomas Duncan, Group Publisher
Chris Lamphear, Director Marketing
Barbara McClellan, Senior International Edit
James Bush, Managing Director
John Sousanis, Publication Manager

Review of the latest advances in engine and vehicle technology. *$935.00*
8 pages
Printed in 2 colors on ³ stock

Magazines & Journals

1784 **AGRR**
Key Communications
PO Box 569
Garrisonville, VA 22463
540-577-7174
FAX: 540-720-5687
agrr@glass.com www.agrrmag.com

Debra Levy, Publisher
Charles Cumpston, Editor

Source of unbiased, accurate information about the auto glass repair and replacement industry.
Monthly Founded: 2001
Circulation: 10,000

1785 **AIADA's Showroom**
American Int'l Automobile Dealers Association
211 N Union Street
Suite 300
Alexandria, VA 22314
703-519-7800
FAX: 703-519-7810 800-462-4232
showroom@aiada.org www.aiada.org

Virginia Sowers, Managing Editor
Mary Evans, Marketing Manager
Marianne McInerney, President

In-depth articles on trade issues, business regulations and pending legislation that affect the industry. Also features international automobile news, information on customer satisfaction and service, and automobile manufacturing and distribution. Learn how some of the nation's top dealers achieved their success. *$27.00*
40 pages Monthly Founded: 1984
Circulation: 11,400
Printed in 4 colors on glossy stock

1786 **Aftermarket Business Magazine**
Advanstar Communications
One Park Avenue
New York, NY 10016
212-797-7631
FAX: 212-951-6793 818-227-4465
info@advanstar.com
www.aftermarketbusiness.com

Douglas E Ferguson, Group Publisher
Larry Silvey, Editorial Director

Specializing in providing news, trends, research and anyalysis on all the newest retailing methods and products available in the marketplace. Articles include industry legislation, current retailing and merchandising trends, business management tecniques, environmental updates and product selling tips. *$5.00*
Monthly Founded: 1936
Circulation: 41,077
Printed in on glossy stock

1787 **Alt Fuels Advisor**
Alexander Communications Group
28 W 25th Street
8th Floor
New York, NY 10010
212-228-0246
FAX: 212-228-0376 800-232-4317
info@altfuels.com www.altfuels.com

Nadine Harris, Marketing Manager
Laurence Alexander, CEO

News and developments in alternative fuel vehicles, including natural gas, propane, CNG, ethanol, electric, hybrid and fuel cells. Alt Fuels brings together news of technical and business developments, usage, infrastructure and regulations for all types of alternative and clean fuel vehicles. *$367.00*
Monthly

1788 **American Rodder**
Buckaroo Communications
701 Arcturus Avenue
Oxnard, CA 93033
805-986-0400
FAX: 810-735-6765 866-515-5600

Gerry Burgel, Editor
Debby Wheeler, Customer Service

Covers the street-rod and custom-car industries. Accepts advertising. *$39.99*
100 pages

1789 **Auto**
Automotive Service Association
PO Box 929
Bedford, TX 76095-929
817-283-6205
FAX: 817-685-0225 800-272-7467
editor@asashop.org www.asashop.org

Angie Wilson, VP Communications
Leona Dalava Scott, Editor

Delivers technical, legislative and business management information to auto repair shop owners. *$35.00*
Monthly Founded: 1951
Circulation: 15000
Printed in 4 colors on glossy stock

1790 **Auto Laundry News**
EW Williams Publications
2125 Center Avenue
Suite 305
Fort Lee, NJ 07024-5898
201-592-7007
FAX: 201-592-7171
aealn@aol.com
www.williamspublications.com

Andrew Williams, Publisher
Stefan Budricks, Editor
Janys Kuznier, Circulation Director

Provides technical, operational, marketing, advertising, and managerial information for owners, operators, and investors in self services and automatic carwashes, as well as auto detailing information. *$56.00*
Monthly Founded: 1953
Circulation: 17292

1791 **Auto Remarketing**
Cherokee Publishing Company
Westview at Weston
301 Cascade Pointe Lane Suite 101
Cary, NC 27513
919-674-6020
FAX: 919-674-6027 800-608-7500
subscriptions@autoremarketing.com
www.autoremarketing.com

Ron Smith, Publisher/Editor
Richard Greene, News Magazine Editor

Reports on changes in the automotive industry and their effects on the buying and selling of cars. *$24.95*
Monthly Founded: 1990
Circulation: 22000

1792 **Auto Rental News**
Bobit Business Media
3520 Challenger Street
Torrance, CA 90503
310-533-2400
FAX: 310-533-2503
arn@bobit.com
www.autorentalnews.com

Sherb Brown, Group Publisher
Cathy Stephens, Executive Editor
Ed Bobit, CEO

For those involved in the renting of cars and trucks. *$30.00*
Monthly
Circulation: 16000

1793 **Auto Trim and Restyling News**
Bobit Publishing
3520 Challenger Street
Torrance, CA 90503
310-533-2400
FAX: 310-533-2504 800-241-9034
info@atrn.com www.atrn.com

John Jeffries, Editor
Travis Weeks, Group Publisher
Ed Bobit, CEO

Latest information on enhancing the appearance of cars with new upholstery, convertible tops and more. *$19.95*
Monthly Founded: 1955

1794 **AutoSmart**
Aegis Group-Publishers
30400 Van Dyke Avenue
Warren, MI 48093-2368
586-574-3400
FAX: 248-447-7566
jmorris@campbell-ewald.com
www.campbell-ewald.com
Jim Palmer, President
Tony Hopp, CEO
Jeremy Morris, Publisher
Published for Delco Electronics for car company decision makers who deal with such systems.
Monthly

1795 **Autoglass**
National Glass Association
8200 Greensboro Drive
#302
McLean, VA 22102
703-442-4890
FAX: 703-442-0630 186- 34- 564
nicole@glass.org www.glass.org
Nicole Harris, Publisher
Nancy Davis, Editor-in-Chief
Forum for owners, managers and distributors in glass replacement, repair, tinting, and also auto security fields. News and reports on insurance and legislative regulations. New product updates, news and technology information. *$24.95*
Founded: 1948
Circulation: 7000

1796 **Automotive Cooling Journal**
National Automotive Radiator Service Association
15000 Commerce Parkway
Suite C
Mt Laurel, NJ 08054
856-439-1575
FAX: 856-439-9596 800-551-3232
info@narsa.org www.narsa.org
Mike Dwyer, Editor
Joe Ettwein, Communications Manager
Auto cooling system service data. Free to members. *$30.00*
60 pages Monthly Founded: 1956
Circulation: 10000

1797 **Automotive Design & Production**
Gardner Publications
192 N Main Street
Plymouth, MI 48170
734-416-9705
FAX: 734-416-9707
daver@autofieldguide.com
www.gardnerweb.com
Gary Vasilash, Editor-In Chief
Lawrence S Gould, Contributing Editor
Rick Kline Jr, Publisher
Coverage of the automotive industry: suppliers, manufacturers from design through delivery. *$65.00*
Monthly Founded: 1928
Circulation: 60,404

1798 **Automotive Engineering International Magazine**
Society of Automotive Engineers
400 Commonwealth Drive
Warrendale, PA 15096-1
724-772-8548
FAX: 724-776-9765 877-606-7323
customerservice@sae.org
www.sae.org
Larry Schneider, Publisher
Kevin Jost, Editor
Cars, aircraft, trucks, off highway equipment, engines, materials, manufacuring and fuels have the Society of Engineers in common. The SAE is your one stop resource for technical information and expertise used in building, maintaining and operating self propelled vehicles for use on land, sea, air or space. *$120.00*
125 pages Monthly Founded: 1905
Circulation: 124451

1799 **Automotive Executive Magazine**
National Auto Dealers Association
8400 Westpark Drive
Mc Lean, VA 22102-3522
703-217-7000
FAX: 703-821-7234 800-252-6232
msaldana@nada.org www.aemag.com
Marc H Stertz, Publisher/Editor
Dianne Vance, Advertising Manager
Devoted exclusively to the automotive executive. Feautures that take on the new topics in the industry, and columns filled with practical, solid business advice for each dealership department. *$24.00*
40 pages Monthly Founded: 1917
Circulation: 23000

1800 **Automotive Fleet**
Bobit Publishing Company
3520 Challenger Street
Torrence, CA 90503-1711
310-533-2400
FAX: 310-533-2500 847-647-9780
Bobitpubs@halldata.com
www.automotive-fleet.com
Ed Bobit, Chairman/CEO
Ty Bobit, President
Improvements in operational, purchasing and management responsibilities. *$35.00*
Monthly Founded: 1961
Circulation: 21037

1801 **Automotive Industries**
Worldwide Purchasing Ltd
313-262-5702

jal@autoindustry.us
www.ai-online.com
John Larkin, Publisher
Ed Richardson, Editor
Ben Adler, Finance
Nick Palmen, Associate Publisher
Rob White, Advertising
Offers information for vehicle producers and suppliers worldwide. *$70.00*
Monthly Founded: 1895
Circulation: 85000
Printed in on glossy stock

1802 **Automotive Manufacturing & Production**
Gardner Publications
6915 Valley Avenue
Cincinnati, OH 45244
513-278-8977
FAX: 513-527-8801 800-950-8020
rkline2@autofieldguide.com
www.autofieldguide.com
Gary S Vasilash, Executive Editor
Rick Kline, Publisher
Richard G. Kline, VP
For engineers and managers who are concerned with improving manufacturing. *$89.00*
110 pages Monthly Founded: 1934

1803 **Automotive News**
Crain Communications
1155 Gratiot Avenue
Detroit, MI 48027-2997
313-446-6000
FAX: 313-446-0383 800-678-9595
info@craine.com www.crain.com
Keith Crain, Publisher/Editorial Director
Peter Brown, Assoc. Publisher
Keiph Crain, CEO
All facets of the automotive and truck industry. *$145.00*
Weekly Founded: 1925
Circulation: 80000

1804 **Automotive Recycling**
Automotive Recyclers Association
3975 Fair Ridge Drive
Suite 20 North
Fairfax, VA 22033-2924
703-385-1001
FAX: 703-385-1494 888-385-1005
george@a-r-a.org www.a-r-a.org
Kristin Patterson, Editor
George K Eliades, Publisher
Offers information on the recycling of automobiles and automotive parts. *$40.00*
Bi-Monthly Founded: 1943
Circulation: 1100
Printed in on glossy stock

1805 **Battery Man**
Independent Battery Manufacturers Association
401 N Michigan Avenue
24th Floor
Chicago, IL 60611
312-245-1074
FAX: 312-527-6640
info@thebatteryman.com
www.thebatteryman.com
George Ames, Editor
International journal for starting, lighting, ignition, and generating systems.
Monthly

1806 **Body Language**
Automotive Body Parts Association
PO Box 820689
Houston, TX 77282
281-531-0809
FAX: 281-531-9411 800-323-5832
srodman1@sbcglobal.net
www.autobpa.com
Published by the Automotive Body Parts Association. *$90.00*
167 pages Founded: 1980
Circulation: 400

1807 **BodyShop Business**
Babcox Publications
3550 Embassy Parkway
Akron, OH 44333
330-670-1234
FAX: 330-670-0874
ncope@babcox.com
www.bodyshopbusiness.com
Denise Lloyd, Publisher
Georgina Carson, Editor
Bob Bissler, Senior Editor
Devoted to helping collision-repair shop owners and managers run more profitable businesses. Editorially, BodyShop business covers all aspects of collision repair, with a focus on how-to topics include management, dimensioning, straightening, welding, refinishing, law and technology. *$64.00*
Monthly Founded: 1920
Circulation: 60145

1808 **Brake & Front End**
Babcox Publications
3550 Embassy Parkway
Akron, OH 44333
330-670-1234
FAX: 330-670-0874
amarkel@babcox.com
www.babcox.com

Tim Fritz, Managing Editor
Andrew Markel, Editor
Brad Mitchell, Circulation/IT Director

Has monthly service articles that feature the latest information on brake, chassis, exhaust, front end, front-wheel drive and wheel alignment. Each issue also profiles the newest product and service offerings from aftermarket suppliers. *$64.00*
Monthly Founded: 1920
Circulation: 40,310

1809 **Cars & Parts**
Amos Press
911 Vandemark Road
Sidney, OH 45365-482
937-982-2111
FAX: 937-498-0808 800-448-3611
editorial@carsandparts.com
www.carsandparts.com

Wes Peterson, Editor
Margie Bruns, Advertising Manager
Mark Kaufman, Associate Publisher

Focused to the serious collector car lobbyist. Each issue has an array of how-to articles, detailed coverage of feature cars and intriguing historical views of the auto companies and their most influential players. Additionally there are reports on major collector car shows and auctions including analysis of price trends on major categories of cars. Also included is a calendar of upcoming events: shows, auctions and swap meets. Finally, each issue has an extensive classified section. *$31.95*
124 pages Monthly Founded: 1957
Printed in 4 colors on glossy stock

1810 **Collision Parts Journal**
Automotive Body Parts Association
PO Box 820689
Houston, TX 77282-689
281-531-0809
FAX: 281-531-9411 800-323-5832
srodman1@sbcglobal.net
www.autobpa.com

Stanley Rodman, Editor

Covers the collision replacement parts industry. *$90.00*
64 pages Quarterly Founded: 1980
Circulation: 2300 2,300 names
Printed in 4 colors on glossy stock

1811 **Counterman**
Babcox Publications
3550 Embassy Parkway
Akron, OH 44333
330-670-1234
FAX: 330-670-0874
jowens@babcox.com
www.babcox.com

Brian Cruickshank, Editor
Jon Owens, Publisher
Bill Babcox, Owner

Targeted at the needs of the jobber sales team — those who buy and sell parts, services, equipment, build brand awareness, preference and loyalty by recommending parts to the DIY customer and professional technician. *$110.00*
Monthly Founded: 1920
Circulation: 50,000

1812 **Dealer**
Horizon Communications
5201 Great American Parkway
Suite 320
Santa Clara, CA 95054
408-969-4888
FAX: 408-969-4895
info@horizonpr.com
www.horizonpr.com

Mike Roscoe, Publisher

Information for automobile dealers on service, parts, used car merchandising, financing, body shop, planning and risk management. *$35.00*
Monthly Founded: 1995
Circulation: 21178

1813 **Diesel Progress: North American Edition**
Diesel & Gas Turbine Publications
20855 Watertown Road
Suite 220
Waukesha, WI 53186
262-832-5000
FAX: 262-832-5075
mosenga@dieselpub.com
www.dieselpub.com

Michael Osenga, Publisher
S Bollwahn, Circulation Manager

Geared towards readers interested in state-of-the-art systems technology. Features include new product listings, systems design, research and product testing as well as systems maintenance and rebuilding.
Monthly Founded: 1837
Circulation: 26,011

1814 **Double Clutch**
Antique Truck Club of America
P. O. Box 91
Imgomar, PA 15127
412-366-0392
FAX: 724-727-9768
atcamanager@verizon.net
www.atca-inc.net/

Bill Powell, Publisher
Greg Matecko, Publisher
Jim Widmann, President

Magazine for antique truck enthusiasts. *$50.00*
Founded: 1971

1815 **Engine Builder**
Babcox Publications
3550 Embassy Parkway
Akron, OH 44333-3550
330-670-1234
FAX: 330-670-0874
ncope@babcox.com
www.engine-builder.com

David Wooldridge, Publisher
Doug Kaufman, Editor
Bill Babcox, CEO

Business magazine serving the machine shop, custom engine, production engine and small parts rebuilding markets. It delivers editorial excellence that reflects the growing sophistication of the rebuilding industry and aids its readers in the profitable operation of their businesses. *$64.00*
72 pages Monthly Founded: 1920
Circulation: 19500
Printed in 4 colors on glossy stock

1816 **Family Motor Coaching Magazine**
8291 Clough Pike
Cincinnati, OH 45244-2756
513-474-3622
FAX: 513-474-2332

Pamela Kay, Editor
Don Eversman, Executive Director

Official publication of the Family Motor Coach Association, an organization for owners of self-contained motor homes. Publishes articles regarding motor home maintenance and repair, new products, travel destinations of interest to RV travelers and association news. *$24.00*
Monthly
Circulation: 98000

1817 **Fleet Financials**
Bobit Publishing Company
21061 S Western Avenue
Torrence, CA 90501-1711
310-533-2400
FAX: 310-533-2503
mike.antich@bobit.com
www.fleet-central.com

Ed Bobit, President/Publisher

Features profiles of successfully managed fleets and analysis of lease verses company ownership. *$28.00*
Monthly
Circulation: 15500

1818 **Global Insight**
MEMA-Motor & Equipment Manufacturers Association
10 Laboratory Drive
PO Box 13966
RTP, NC 27709-3966
919-549-4800
FAX: 919-549-4824
info@mema.org www.mema.org

Robert Bob McKenna, President/CEO
Neal Zipser, VP Marketing/Communications
Margaret Beck, Communications Manager

Member publication examines critical issues and challenges facing today's OE, aftermarket and heavy duty suppliers. Subscriptions and advertising available.
Quarterly Founded: 1904
Circulation: 2400

1819 **Hemmings Motor News**
PO Box 100
Bennington, VT 05201
802-477-7344
FAX: 802-447-9631 800-227-4373
hmnmail@hemmings.com
www.hemmings.com

Terry Ehrich, Publisher
Eileen Desmarais, Marketing

The bible of the car collector, this monthly magazine serves to enhance the experience of the car collector-enthusiast. Regular departments include vehicle and parts search, price checkers, dealers tips, hobby directory and more. *$31.95*
Monthly Founded: 1954
Circulation: 210000

1820 **ImportCar**
Babcox Publications
3050 Embassy Parkway
Akron, OH 44333
330-670-1234
FAX: 330-670-0874
mdellavalle@babcox.com
www.babcox.com

Mary Dellavalle, Editor
David Wooldridge, Publisher
Bill Babcox, CEO

Complete import service magazine. It is geared exclusively to the vehicle repair needs of import specialist technicians. The in-depth, technical nature of the magazine's editorial content helps technicians of all abilities do their jobs more efficiently and effectively. *$64.00*

Monthly Founded: 1979
Circulation: 29190 29,062 names $90 per M.

1821 **Independent Battery Manufacturers**
401 North Michigan Avenue
24th Floor
Chicago, IL 60611
312-245-1074
FAX: 312-527-6640
info@thebatteryman.com
www.thebatteryman.com
Founded: 1921

1822 **Journal of Quality Technology**
American Society for Quality
600 N Plankinton Avenue
Milwaukee, WI 53203
414-988-8789
FAX: 414-272-1734 800-248-1946
help@asq.org
www.qualitypress.asq.org
Paul E Borawski, Executive Director
Christopher Bauman, Managing Director
Brian J LeHouillier, Managing Director
Laurel E Nelson-Rowe, Managing Director
Steve R Wnuk, Managing Director
It contributes to the technical advancement of the quality sciences by publishing papers that emphasize the practical applicability of new statistical techniques on design of experiments, process monitoring, reliability, and applied statistics. Papers present new methods, case study examples, comparisons of existing methods, and reviews of the literature on topics of current interest. *$45.00*
Quarterly

1823 **LCT Magazine**
Bobit Publishing Company
3520 Challenger Street
Torrance, CA 90501
310-533-2400
FAX: 310-533-2500 800-380-8335
webmaster@bobit.com
www.bobit.com
Sara Eastwood, Publisher
Ed Bobit, CEO
Serves the limousine agency owner. *$28.00*
Monthly Founded: 1961
Circulation: 10000

1824 **Limousine Digest**
Digest Publications
29 Fostertown Road
Medford, NJ 08055
609-953-4900
FAX: 609-953-4905
info@limodigest.com
www.limodigest.com
Linda M Moore, Publisher
Susan Keehn, Assistant Publisher
Ric Cohen, President
Information for owners and operators of limousine, livery and transportation fleets, including day to day operational information, industry trends, product reviews, technical advances, as well as success stories. *$24.95*
100 pages Monthly Founded: 1990
Circulation: 12500 15000 names
Printed in 4 colors on glossy stock

1825 **Locator**
John Holmes Publishing Company
521 Main Street
PO Box 286
Whiting, IA 51063
712-458-2213
FAX: 712-458-2687 800-831-0820
sales@partslocator.com
www.partslocator.com
John Holmes, President
Charis Lloyd, VP
Wendy Lloyd, Marketing Director
Stacy Phillips, Editor
Nation's leading auto and truck parts magazine. *$29.00*
250 pages Monthly Founded: 1957
Circulation: 18500 $150 per M.
Printed in 4 colors on newsprint stock

1826 **Lubes-N-Greases**
LNG Publishing Company
6105 Arlington Boulevard
Suite G
Falls Church, VA 22044
703-536-0800
FAX: 703-536-0803
info@Lngpublishing.com
www.lngpublishing.com
Nancy J DeMarco, Publisher
Gloria Steinberg Briskin, Advertising Director
Deborah Wessmiller, Circulation Manager
The magazine of industry in motion.
Monthly Founded: 1995
Circulation: 17300 $225 per M.
Printed in 4 colors on glossy stock

1827 **Lubricants World**
4545 Post Oak Place
Suite 230
Houston, TX 77027
713-840-0378
FAX: 713-840-8585
Kathryn B Carnes, Editor
Professional journal for those in the oil and grease industry.

1828 **MEMA: Motor & Equipment Manufacturers Association Magazine**
Motor and Equipment Manufacturers Association
10 Laboratory Dr
PO Box 13966
Research Triangle Park, NC 27709-3966

919-549-4800
FAX: 919-549-4824
info@mema.org www.mema.org
Neal Zipser, Editor
Robert McKenna, CEO/President
Items of interest on the automotive products market: consumers, distribution channels, etcetera. Most taken from more extensive market studies.
Founded: 1904
Circulation: 1200

1829 **MOVE Magazine**
American Assn. of Motor Vehicle Administrators
Executive Plaza 1 Suite 900
11350 McCormick Road
Hunt Valley, MD 21031
410-584-1955
FAX: 410-584-1998
info@aama.org www.aamva.org
Linda Lewis-Pickett, President/CEO
Bonnie L Rutledge, First Vice Chair
Journal of the voluntary, nonprofit, educational organization. AAMVA represents the state and provincial officials in the US, Canada and Mexico, who are responsible for the administration and enforcement of laws pertaining to the motor vehicle and its use. *$26.00*
Quarterly Founded: 1996
Circulation: 32000
Printed in 4 colors on glossy stock

1830 **Mobility Matters**
Highway Users Federation
One Thomas Circle NW
10th Floor
Washington, DC 20036-1904
202-857-1200
FAX: 202-857-1220
Greg Cohen, Senior VP
National coalition of business, industries and associations promoting improved highway transportation, safety and mobility. *$30.00*
Monthly
Circulation: 2,000

1831 **Modern Car Care**
Virgo Publishing
3300 N Central Avenue Suite 2500
PO Box 40079
Phoenix, AZ 85012
480-990-1101
FAX: 480-990-0819
cs@vpico.com
www.moderncarcare.com/
Tracy Charuhas, Editor
Troy Bix, Group Publisher
Magazine for automotive professionals.
Monthly Founded: 1986
Circulation: 20000

1832 **Motor Age**
Chilton Company
One Park Avenue
New York, NY 10016-2345
212-513-3596
FAX: 212-951-6793 888-527-7008
info@advanstar.com
www.motorage.com
Bill Cannon, Editor-in-Chief
K Meyer, Circulation Manager
Features developments in the auto industry. *$14.00*
Monthly Founded: 1992
Circulation: 143,000

1833 **Motor Magazine**
Hearst Business Communications
5600 Crooks Road
Suite 200
Troy, MI 48098
248-828-0000
FAX: 248-879-8603
tnash@motor.com www.motor.com
Kevin Carr, President
John Lypen, Editor
Richard Laimbeer, Publisher
Emphasis on repair and service end of automobile business for owners and managers. *$63.00*
Monthly Founded: 1903
Circulation: 140000

1834 **Motor Trend**
Primedia
6420 Wilshire Boulevard
Los Angeles, CA 90048-5502
323-822-2201
FAX: 323-782-2467
mtletters@aol.com
www.motortrend.com

Tom Rogers, CEO
Eric Schwab, Advertising Manager
Peter Clancey, Marketing Executive

Comprehensive magazine offers the latest information and news on the automotive industry. *$47.88*

Monthly Founded: 1988
Circulation: 999999
Printed in 4 colors on glossy stock

1835 NADA'S Automotive Executive
National Automobile Dealers Association
8400 Westpark Drive
9th Floor
McLean, VA 2102-3522
703-217-7000
FAX: 703-821-7234 800-252-6232
help@nada.org www.nada.org

Marc H Stertz, Publisher
Rick Wagoner, CEO

Provides up to the minute legislative, regulatory and state association news, also includes product development and implementation, labor relations and the economic climate. *$24.00*

Monthly Founded: 1975
Circulation: 21850

1836 NAPA Outlook
National Auto Parts Association
2999 Circle 75 Parkway
Atlanta, GA 30339-3050
770-956-2200
FAX: 770-956-2201 1 8-7 8-5 62
customersupport@napaonline.com
www.napaonline.com

Don Kite, Editor

Ideas for business procedures for jobber store owners.

28 pages Monthly Founded: 1925

1837 NASCAR Performance
Babcox Publications
3550 Embassy Parkway
Akron, OH 44333-1398
330-670-1234
FAX: 330-670-0874
dkaufman@babcox.com
www.babcox.com

Becky Babcox, Group Publisher
Doug Kaufman, Editor
Bill Babcox, President

Focuses on what goes on behind the scenes in NASCAR racing, and how that advanced technology transfers to automotive aftermarket applications. Professional NASCAR Garage is a quarterly supplement to all Babcox publications.

Founded: 1920

1838 National Oil & Lube News
National Oil & Lube News
4418 74th St
Suite 66
Lubbock, TX 79424-2417
806-762-4464
FAX: 806-762-4023 800-796-2577
info@noln.net www.noln.net

Garrett Mckinnon, Editor
Steve Hurt, Publisher
Barbara Tinsley, Associate Publisher

Geared towards fast oil change and lubrication shop owners and managers. Information on the latest technology and environment concerns, also provides a link between shops and suppliers. *$29.00*

76 pages Monthly Founded: 1986
Circulation: 17000
Printed in 4 colors on glossy stock

1839 New England Automotive Report
Thomas Greco Publications
244 Chestnut Street
Suite 202
Nutley, NJ 07110-2312
973-667-6922
FAX: 973-235-1963
tgp1@earthlink.net www.aaspnj.org

Thomas Greco, Publisher
Alicia D'Aquila, Editor

Provides reports on ideas, products and services to enhance collision repair productivity, also identifies insurance issues. *$ 48.00*

85 pages Monthly Founded: 1996
Circulation: 4500 55 names
Printed in 4 colors on glossy stock

1840 Nozzle & Wrench
Service Station & Auto Repair Association

1532 Pointer Ridge Place
Suite G
Bowie, MD 20716
301-774-4956
FAX: 301-390-3161 800-492-0329
wmda@mindspring.com
www.wmda.net/newsadrates.html

Brenda Catlett, Publisher

Information for service station dealers problems, legislation and general news.

Founded: 1937
Circulation: 4000

1841 Old Cars Price Guide
Krause Publications
700 E State Street
Iola, WI 54990
715-445-2214
FAX: 715-445-4087 800-258-0929
info@krause.com www.krause.com

Rick Groth, Publisher
Ron Kowalke, Editor

The nation's most respected authority for pricing antique and collectible automobiles. The extensive price-guide section covers makes and models of domestic cars, from AMC to Willys, from model years 1901 to 1994. Also included are light-duty trucks and selected makes of imported cars. Cars are valued in six conditions - from 'Excellent' down to 'Parts Car.' Also includes columns and features on collectible cars. *$19.98*

148 pages Monthly Founded: 1978
Circulation: 61000

1842 Old Cars Weekly
Krause Publications
700 E State Street
Iola, WI 54990-1
715-445-2214
FAX: 715-445-4087
info@hrause.co www.krause.com

Rick Groth, Publisher
Keith Mathiowetz, Editor

Covers the entire field of collectible automobiles - from classic touring cars and roadsters of the early 1900s to the popular muscle cars of the 1960s and 1970s. Includes historical prespectives and facts on cars and their manufacturers, and reports on attractions at upcoming shows. Regular columns include 'New Products,' 'Questions & Answers,' 'Show Biz,' 'Bookmobile,' 'Restoration Basics,' and an extensive calssified word ad section. Hundreds of car show listings are included. *$41.98*

64 pages Weekly Founded: 1971
Circulation: 63104

1843 Pacific Automotive News
Automotive Counseling & Publishing
450 Lincoln Street
Suite 110
Denver, CO 80203
303-654-4650
FAX: 303-765-4650
kevin@partsandpeople.com
www.partsandpeople.com

Lance Buchner, Publisher
Kevin Loewen, Editor

Contains local auto news. *$36.00*

Monthly Founded: 1986
Circulation: 59000

1844 Parking Magazine
National Parking Association
1112 16th Street NW
Suite 300
Washington, DC 20036
202-296-4336
FAX: 202-331-8523 800-647-7275
info@npapark.org www.npapark.org

Martin L Stein, Executive Director
Logan Hunter-Thompson, Director Communication

Published by the National Parking Association. *$99.00*

Monthly Founded: 1952
Circulation: 4000
Mailing list available for rent 1700 names $250 per M.
Printed in 4 colors

1845 Parts & People
Automotive Counseling & Publishing
PO Box 300804
Denver, CO 80203
303-765-4664
FAX: 303-765-4650 800-530-8557
lance@partsandpeople.com
www.partsandpeople.com

Lance Buchner, President/Publisher
Kevin Loewen, VP

Five-edition publication for automotive parts and service industry in the western US.

32 pages Monthly Founded: 1986

1846 Parts Plus Magazine
5050 Popular Avenue
Suite 2020
Memphis, TN 38157-2001
901-766-4001
FAX: 901-682-9098 800-727-8112
info@partsplus.com
www.partsplus.com

Alan Bostwick, Executive VP

Published by the Association of Automotive Aftermarkets Distributors. *$29.95*

Monthly Founded: 1965
Circulation: 5000

1847 Professional Carwashing and Detailing
National Trade Publications
13 Century Hill Drive
Latham, NY 12110-2197
518-783-1281
FAX: 518-783-1386
dmarino@ntpinc.com
www.carwash.com

Michael Barry, Circulation Manager
Kevin Hart, Publisher

Provides technical and marketing information to professional vehicle washing owners, managers and investors. Accepts advertising. *$42.00*

76 pages Monthly Founded: 1976
Circulation: 19000
Mailing list available for rent 18M names

$125 per M.
Printed in 4 colors on matte stock

1848 **Professional Tool & Equipment News**
25401 Cabot Road
Suite 209
Laguna Hills, CA 92653-5514
949-830-7520
FAX: 920-563-1699 888-966-3976
sales@pten.com www.pten.com

Rudy Wolf, Managing Director
Jeff Reinke, Editor
Tom Lynch, Publisher

Information for personnel and owners of general and specialty repair shops, including buying tools and equipment, technological innovations, new systems, time saving ideas and product releases. *$32.00*
Monthly Founded: 1996
Circulation: 105044

1849 **Quality Engineering**
American Society for Quality
600 N Plankinton Avenue
Milwaukee, WI 53203
414-988-8789
FAX: 414-272-1734 800-248-1946
help@asq.org
www.qualitypress.asq.org

Paul E Borawski, Executive Director
Christopher Bauman, Managing Director
Brian J LeHouillier, Managing Director
Laurel E Nelson-Rowe, Managing Director
Steve R Wnuk, Managing Director

Co-published with Taylor and Francis, this journal is directed to professionals in all engineering and management fields interested in quality improvement. Providing the widest ranging coverage of how we did it accomplishments focusing on comprehensive quality science applications throughout the entire economy and society. *$34.75*
Quarterly/Members Price

1850 **Quality Management Journal**
American Society for Quality
600 N Plankinton Avenue
Milwaukee, WI 53203
414-988-8789
FAX: 414-272-1734 800-248-1946
help@asq.org
www.qualitypress.asq.org

Paul E Borawski, Executive Director
Christopher Bauman, Managing Director
Brian J LeHouillier, Managing Director
Laurel E Nelson-Rowe, Managing Director
Steve R Wnuk, Managing Director

Aims to link the efforts of academic researchers and quality management practitioners by publishing significant research relevant to quality management practice and provide a forum for discussion of such research by academics and practitioners. *$75.00*
Quarterly

1851 **RV Trade Digest**
Cygnus Publishing
1233 Janesville Avenue
Fort Atkinson, WI 53538
920-563-6388
FAX: 920-563-1699 800-308-6397
editor@rvtradedigest.com
www.rvtradedigest.com

John Spaulding, Publisher
Greg Gerber, Editor-in-Chief
Brett Apold, Production Manager
Marie Escobar, Circulation Manager

Offers in-depth information to a trade audience of business professionals actively engaged in the manufacture, distribution and sales of RVs, supplies and accessories. *$40.00*
9 issues (1year Founded: 1966
Circulation: 16055
Printed in 4 colors on glossy stock

1852 **Recyclers Power Source**
Wolf Advertising
PO Box 556
Spirit Lake, IA 51360-556
712-336-5614
FAX: 712-336-5617 800-336-5614
rps@rpowersource.com
www.rpowersource.com

Laura Kabele, General Manager
D J Harrington, Marketing Manager

Purchasing guide for automotive recycling. *$40.00*
Monthly Founded: 1993
Circulation: 16000

1853 **SAE Off-Highway Engineering**
Society of Automotive Engineers
400 Commonwealth Drive
Warrendale, PA 15086-7511
724-772-8544
FAX: 724-776-4026
sohe@sae.org www.sae.org

Carolyn Taylor, Editor
J.E. Robertson, President

Member services and news, as well as activities including meetings, professional development seminars, publication introductions and education programs. *$70.00*
Monthly Founded: 1905
Circulation: 58263

1854 **SEMA News**
Performance Aftermarket Publishers
1575 Valley Vista Drive
Diamond Bar, CA 91765-3914
909-860-2961
FAX: 909-860-1709
editors@semanews.com
www.semanews.com

Steve Campbell, Editorial Director
Peter MacGillivray, VP Communications
Christopher Kersting, President

Covers specialty and performance segment of autos with the Auto Aftermarket, Specialty Equipment and Marketing Association. *$39.95*
96 pages Monthly Founded: 1988
Circulation: 35000
Printed in 4 colors on matte stock

1855 **School Bus Fleet**
Bobit Publishing Company
3520 Challenger St.
Torrence, CA 90503-1711
310-533-2400
FAX: 310-533-2503
sbf@bobit.com
www.schoolbusfleet.com

Ed Bobit, CEO
Mark Hollenbeck, Sales Manager
Frank DiGiacomo, Publisher

Published for persons involved with the transportation of school children grades K-12, includes articles on lowering costs, improving fleet operations, scheduling techniques, vehicle maintenance and federal regulatory issues. *$25.00*
Monthly Founded: 1961
Circulation: 22000

1856 **Shop Talk**
Modine Manufacturing Company
1500 De Koven Avenue
Racine, WI 53403-2552
262-636-1200
FAX: 262-636-1424
d.a.prichard@na.modine.com
www.modine.com/

Ray Schaffart, Marketing Manager
David B Rayburn, CEO/President

Newsletter for radiator repair professionals who work in radiator shops or service stations. Car and truck radiator repair tips.
Founded: 1916
Circulation: 16000

1857 **Software Quality Professional**
American Society for Quality
600 N Plankinton Avenue
Milwaukee, WI 53203
414-988-8789
FAX: 414-272-1734 800-248-1946
help@asq.org
www.qualitypress.asq.org

Paul E Borawski, Executive Director
Christopher Bauman, Managing Director
Brian J LeHouillier, Managing Director
Laurel E Nelson-Rowe, Managing Director
Steve R Wnuk, Managing Director

The mission is to help software professionals apply quality principles to the development and use of software and software-based systems. SQP publishes case studies, experienced-based reports, and state-of-the-art reviews in order to provide practitioners with an understanding of those software quality practices that have proven effective in a wide range of industries, applications, and organizational settings. *$75.00*
Quarterly

1858 **Special Interest Autos**
Hemmings Motor News
PO Box 100
Bennington, VT 05201
802-442-3101
FAX: 802-447-9566 800-227-4373
hmnmail@hemmings.com
www.hemmings.com

Jim Menneto, Publisher
Richard Lentinallo, Editor

Offers information on collectible and older cars with developmental histories, restoration informaiton, engineering information and more. *$18.00*
Monthly Founded: 1954

1859 **Specialty Automotive Magazine**
Meyers Publishing
799 Camarillo Springs Road
Camarillo, CA 93012-8111
805-445-8881
FAX: 805-445-8882
len@meyerspublishing.com
www.meyerspublishing.com/

Steve Relyea, Editor
Len Meyers, Publisher
Andrew Meyers, Associate Publisher
Harriet Kaplan, Assistant Editor

For accesories and performance specialists, dedicated for car and truck product suppliers and installers. Various fatermaker segments are covered: street, track, van, truck, and off-road. Features cover: technology and trends, performance retailing, new product showcases, upgrade news, trade shows, legislation, advertising, OEM's industry news, and people on the move. *$10.00*

Monthly Founded: 1983
Circulation: 25000
Printed in 4 colors on glossy stock

1860 Sport Truck & SUV Accessory Business
Cygnus Publishing
1233 Janesville Avenue
Fort Atkinson, WI 53538
920-563-6388
FAX: 920-563-1699
paul.bowers@cygn.com
www.cygnuspub.com

Bob Spaulding, Publisher
Pat Walker, Editor
Paul Mackler, President/CEO

Founded: 1966

1861 Supercharger
Detroit Section Society of Automotive Engineers
28535 Orchard Lake Road
Suite 200
Farmington Hills, MI 48334
248-324-4445
FAX: 248-324-4449
info@sae-detroit.org
www.sae-detroit.org

Barb Bailey, Account Manager

Information on SAE events and news for engineers in the southeastern Michigan and northwestern Ohio area.

Founded: 1905
Circulation: 16687
Printed in on glossy stock

1862 Tire Business
Crain Communications
1725 Merriman Road
Suite 300
Akron, OH 44313-5283
330-836-9180
FAX: 330-836-2831 800-678-9595
editorial@tirebusiness.com
www.tirebusiness.com

David E Zielasko, Publisher
Robert S Simmons, VP

Newspaper edited for the independent tire dealer with emphasis on auto service. Accepts advertising. *$55.00*

32 pages Founded: 1983

1863 Tire Retread Information Packet & Buyers Guide
Tire Retread Information Bureau
900 Weldon Grove
Pacific Grove, CA 93950
831-372-1917
FAX: 831-372-9210 888-473-8732
info@retread.org www.retread.org

Harvey Brodsky, Managing Director
Rachel Lewis, Website Director

Published by the Tire Retread Information Bureau.

380 pages Weekly Founded: 1972

1864 Tire Review
Babcox Publications
3550 Embassy Parkway
Akron, OH 44333
330-670-1234
FAX: 330-670-0874
dmoniz@babcox.com
www.tirereview.com

Jim Smith, Editor
David Modiz, Group Publisher
Steve LaFerre, Senior Editor

Designed to assist the independent retail tire dealer in his number one concern — profitability. It focuses on pricing strategies, marketing and effective advertising to meet the challenges of today's industry. *$64.00*

84 pages Monthly Founded: 1902 : web

1865 Tow Times
TT Publications
203 W State Road 434
Winter Springs, FL 32708-2581
407-327-4817
FAX: 407-327-2603 1 8-0 3-8 37
cpowell@towtimes.com
www.towtimes.com/

Clarissa Powell, Publisher
Tim Jackson, Editor
Peter Aspesi, President

Edited to review various aspects of the towing and road services. Accepts advertising. *$34.00*

56 pages Monthly Founded: 1983

1866 Toy Cars & Models
Krause Publications
700 E State Street
Iola, WI 54990-1
715-445-2214
FAX: 715-445-4087 800-942-0673
info@krause.com www.krause.com

Mark Williams, Publisher
Merry Dudley, Editor

Provides comprehensive coverage of the model car hobby without bias toward scale, subject, manufacturer or material. Offers columns and news stories featuring models made of die-cast, white metal, plasic, resin and more while getting readers in touch with the manufacturers, distributors and retailers who sell these model cars. Monthly giveaways, reader polls and an active letters column give readers a chance to participate in their hobby. *$29.98*

88 pages Monthly Founded: 1998
Circulation: 17916

1867 Truck & SUV Performance
Bobit Publishing Company
3520 Challenger Street
Torrance, CA 90501
310-533-2400
FAX: 310-533-2504
travis.weeks@bobit.com
www.bobit.com

Travis Weeks, Publisher
John Jeffries, Editor
Ty Bobit, Chief Executive Officer

Founded: 1961
Circulation: 32,000 $200 per M.

1868 Underhood Service
Babcox Publications
3550 Embassy Parkway
Akron, OH 44333
330-670-1234
FAX: 330-670-0874
ncope@babcox.com www.babcox.com

Edward Sunkin, Editor
Bill Babcox, CEO
Jennifer McMullen, Managing Editor

Meets the special needs of those technicians where most of their jobs involve the service and repair of under-the-hood systems. Answers the challenge of a continuing expansion of automotive technology. *$64.00*

Monthly Founded: 1920
Circulation: 40500

1869 Used Car Dealer Magazine
Nat'l Independent Automobile Dealers Association
2521 Brown Boulevard
Arlington, TX 76006-5203
817-492-2377
FAX: 817-649-5866 800-682-3837
darrin@niada.com www.niada.com/

Michael R Linn, CEO/Publisher
Darrin Scheid, Editor
Angela Ledbetter, Executive Assistant
Adrianne Argumaniz, Publication Manager

Information on auctions, profit center opportunities, trends in used car market, and updates on legislation. Coverage on association membership and the entire used vehicle industry. *$36.00*

Founded: 1946
Circulation: 15000 15000 names
Printed in 4 colors on glossy stock

1870 Ward's Autoworld
Ward's Communications
3000 Town Center
Suite 2750
Southfield, MI 48075-1245
248-357-0800
FAX: 248-357-0810
dwinter@primediabusiness.com
www.wardsauto.com

Jim Bush, Publisher
Drew Winter, Editor

News and analysis for automotive OEM professionals. *$55.00*

130 pages Monthly Founded: 1924
Circulation: 102000
Mailing list available for rent 99,000 names
Printed in 4 colors on glossy stock
Computerized version available: On-line

1871 Ward's Dealer Business
Ward's Communications
3000 Town Center
Suite 2750
Southfield, MI 48075-1245
248-357-0800
FAX: 248-357-0810
sfinlay@primediabusiness.com
www.wardsdealer.com

Thomas Duncan, Group Publisher
Steve Finlay, Editor
Tony Noland, CEO
James Bush, Managing Director

News and analysis for auto dealership professionals.

80 pages Monthly Founded: 1924
Circulation: 27000
Mailing list available for rent 98,861 names
Printed in 4 colors
Computerized version available: On-line

Trade Shows

1872 AAIW: Automotive Aftermarket Industry Week Expo
Overseas Automotive Council
10 Laboratory Drive
Po Box 13966
Reserach Triangle, NC 27709-3966
919-406-8810
FAX: 919-549-4824
NovakJudyAnn@aol.com
www.oac-intl.org

Judy Novak, Show Management

Containing 2,500 exhibits.
100M+ Attendees November

1873 AAMVA Annual International Conference
American Assoc. of Motor Vehicle Administrators
4301 Wilson Boulevard
Suite 400
Arlington, VA 22203-1867
703-522-4200
FAX: 703-522-1553
dgraham@aamva.org www.aamva.org

Diane Graham, Member & Conference VP
Kim Sarkady, Member & Conference Sr Coordinator

Containing 40 plus exhibits.
800 Attendees August/September

1874 ABPA Trade Show Fair
Automotive Body Parts Association
2000 S Dairy Ashford Street, Suite 270
PO Box 820689
Houston, TX 77077
281-531-0809
FAX: 281-531-9411 800-323-5832
srodman1@sbcglobal.net
www.autobpa.com

Stan Rodman, Executive Director

Trade show with 35 exhibitors and over 43 booths.
September

1875 AFLA Annual Meeting & Conference
Automotive Fleet & Leasing Association
1000 Westgate Drive
St. Paul, MN 55114
651-037-7247

info@aflaonline.com
www.aflaonline.com

David Ewald, Executive Director
Paul Hanscom, Assistant Director

Providing the opportunity and a forum for the exchange of information and ideas between related segments of the fleet industry.
200 Attendees September

1876 AIAG AutoTech Conference
Automotive Industry Action Group
26200 Lahser Road
Suite 200
Southfield, MI 48034-7100
248-358-3003
FAX: 248-799-7995
memberinfo@aiag.org www.aiag.org

Scott Gray, Chairman
Edward T Sprock, Vice Chairman

It's a venue where the collaboration between OEMs and suppliers is showcased through educational sessions, product and service exhibits and demonstrations, and networking opportunities.
3000 Attendees Founded: 1988

1877 AOCA Annual Convention & Fast Lube Expo
Automotive Oil Change Association
12810 Hillcrest
Suite 221
Dallas, TX 75230
972-458-9468
FAX: 972-458-9539 800-331-0329
aoca@aoca.org www.aoca.org

Joyce Laurie, Director Conventions/Meetings
Sue Ackley, President
Stephen Christie, Executive Director

Brings hundreds of vendors offering thousands of products and services to the fast lube industry and ancillary profit centers.
2500 Attendees Annual/April-May

1878 APTA International Public Transportation Expo
American Public Transit Association
1666 K Street NW
Suite 1100
Washington, DC 20006
202-496-4800
FAX: 202-496-4321 www.apta.com

Jennifer Hoff, Show Director
Kellie Shevlin, Exhibit Sales
Karol Popkin, Chief Executive Officer

Industry leaders from around the globe attend to meet suppliers of the latest public transportation products, services, and technologies designed to enhance the passenger experience and make your transit system more efficient and profitable.
16000 Attendees Every 3 years

1879 ARA Annual Convention & Exposition
Automotive Recyclers Association
3975 Fair Ridge Drive
Suite 20-N
Fairfax, VA 22033-2924
703-851-1001
FAX: 703-385-1494 888-385-1005
mark@a-r-a.org www.a-r-a.org

Mark Mohay, Meetings/Communications Director
George Eliades, Executive VP

Automotive recycling trade show. Containing over 150 booths and more than 100 exhibits. The 2006 trade show is scheduled for September 27th to September 30th in Indianapolis, Indiana and the 2007 trade show is scheduled for September 26th to September 29th in Orlando, Florida.
800 Attendees Annual/September

1880 ARTA Powertrain Expo
Automatic Transmission Rebuilders Association
2400 Latigo Avenue
Oxnard, CA 93030-5776
805-604-2000
FAX: 805-604-2003 800-428-8489
expo@atra.com
www.atraonline.com/events/expo

Vivi Johansen, Expo Sponsorship

Speakers on many subjects, providing tips and tricks that'll start paying dividends your first day back. Learn the hottest tips and tricks for the problems showing up in your shop every day, and take a sneak peek at what's coming down the pike, from some of the top names in the automotive industry. *$315.00*
September

1881 ASA Annual Business Meeting Conference
Automotive Service Association
PO Box 929
Bedford, TX 76021-5732
817-283-6205
FAX: 817-685-0225
robbiet@asashop.org www.

Robbie Talley, Meetings & Travel Manager

Designed to bring members and industry professionals together to conduct association business, share knowledge and expertise, and renew friendships.
Annual Founded: 1951

1882 American Engine Rebuilders Association Expo
American Engine Rebuilders Association
330 Lexington Drive
Buffalo Grove, IL 60089
847-541-6550
FAX: 847-541-5808 www.aera.org

John Goodman, President

550 exhibits with automotive services equipment, parts, tools, supplies and services. Seminar and dinner also offered.
6000 Attendees Annual Founded: 1974

1883 Auto Remarketing Convention
Auto Remarketing
301 Cascade Pointe Lane
Suite 101
Cary, NC 27513
919-674-6020
FAX: 919-674-6027 800-608-7500
colby@autoremarketing.com
www.autoremarketing.com

Shannon Colby, Sales Manager
Ron Smith, Publisher

Executive conference focused on remarketing strategies for manufacturer, bank, finance, commercial and rental fleet/lease vehicles.
February Founded: 1996

1884 Automotive Aftermarket Products Expo
Automotive Aftermarket Industry Association
4600 E West Highway
Suite 300
Bethesda, MD 20814
301-654-6664
FAX: 301-654-3299
aaia@aftermarket.org
www.aftermarket.org

Arlene Davis, Trade Show Management
Kathleen Schmatz, President/CEO

Largest aftermarket trade show in North America, featuring over 1700 exhibitors of auto parts, accessories and services.
80000 Attendees November

1885 Automotive Engine Rebuilders Association Expo
330 Lexington Drive
Buffalo Grove, IL 60089-6933
847-541-6550
FAX: 847-541-5808 888-326-2372

Karen Tendering, Convention Contact
John Goodman, President

See and feel live operating demonstrations of the industry's latest technology in equipment, tools, supplies, parts, and services for automotive, heavy-duty, industrial, high-performance, marine, and specialty engines. Featuring the leading national and international companies showcasing the latest new products and services in the world of engine building, remanufacturing, and installation.
April

1886 BCI Annual Convention
Battery Council International
401 North Michigan Avenue
24th Floor
Chicago, IL 60611-4267
312-644-6610
FAX: 312-527-6640
icondon@sba.com
www.batterycouncil.org

Irene Condon, Convention Manager
Kris Delas Armas, Convention Assistant

Offers members the opportunity to exchange ideas and views with industry mem-

bers from around the world in a working meeting atmosphere.
Annual/April

1887 **Convergence Conference and Exhibition**
Society of Automotive Engineers
755 W Big Beaver
Suite 1600
Troy, MI 48084
248-273-2455
FAX: 248-273-2494
pkreh@sae.org
www.sae.org/convergence

Patti Kreh, Meetings, Exhibits Contact
Nori Fought, Meetings, Exhibits Contact

Serving the automotive and transportation electronics community by delivering relevant technology solutions and an electrifying line-up invited speakers and presenters.

8900+ Attendees October

1888 **Dayton Auto Show**
Hart Productions
3307 Clifton Avenue
Suite 4
Cincinnati, OH 45220
513-281-0022
FAX: 513-281-3322 877-281-0022

Chip Hart, Show Management
Doug Hart, Show Management
Vicki Diebold, Show Management

Annual auto show presented by the Dayton area Auto Dealers Association.
March

1889 **Fleet Management Institute & Law Enforcement Conference**
National Association of Fleet Administrators
100 Wood Avenue S
Suite 310
Iselin, NJ 08830-2709
732-494-8100
FAX: 732-494-6789
info@nafa.org www.nafa.org

Phillip E Russo, Executive Director
Patricia Murtaugh, Assistant Executive Director
Jennifer Buchanan, Project Assistant
Joanne Marsh, Director Membership & Marketing

To provide attendees and exhibitors alike with a more dynamic interaction on the exhibit hall floor and within concurrent sessions. An excellent opportunity to attend valuable education courses designed to benefit the veteran fleet professional as well as challenge first-time attendees!
April 4000 names
Printed in on glossy stock

1890 **International Autobody Congress and Exposition**
Hanley-Wood
8600 Freeport Parkway
Suite 200
Irving, TX 75063
972-366-6300
FAX: 972-536-6301 888-529-1641
dteague@hanleywood.com
www.naceexpo.com

Dana Teague, Senior Show Director
Ellen Pipkin, Associate Show Manager

Specifically created for professionals involved in all aspects of the collision repair industry.
15M Attendees November

1891 **International Big R Show**
Automotive Parts Remanufacturers Association
4215 Lafayette Center Drive
Suite 3
Chantilly, VA 20151-1243
703-968-2772
FAX: 703-968-2878
mail@apra.org
www.apra.org/www.bigrshow.com

Jeanie Magathan, Senior VP/Convention Information

Designed to attract rebuilders of a wide range of automotive and truck parts, exposing them to the key suppliers in this industry. Rebuilders specializing in electrical, c.v. joints, brake, clutch, transmissions, mechanical hydraulic, fuel systems, rack and pinion and air conditioning products will visit the show.

william c gager president

2500+ Attendees October 28-30 Founded: 1988

1892 **MACS Convention and Trade Show**

Mobile Air Conditioning Society Worldwide
225 S Broad Street
PO Box 88
Lansdale, PA 19446
215-631-7020
FAX: 215-631-7017
wendym@macsw.org www.macsw.org

Wendy Moyer, Events Manager
Marion Posen, VP

MACS 2006 Convention and Trade Show will be held in Orlando, Florida.
2000 Attendees January 26-28, 2006 2,000 names

1893 **NADA Convention & Expo**
National Automobile Dealers Association
8400 Westpark Drive
Mc Lean, VA 22102-3522
703-217-7000
FAX: 703-821-7075 800-252-6232
conven@nada.org www.nada.org

Gary Heimes, Convention Director
Stephen R Pitt, Executive Director, Convention
Phillip Brady, President

Providing automobile dealers with the latest in cutting edge technology, products and services they need to impact the future success of their businesses.
25000 Attendees January/February

1894 **NAFA Fleet Management Seminar**
National Association of Fleet Administrators
100 Wood Avenue S
Suite 310
Iselin, NJ 08830-2709
732-494-8100
FAX: 732-494-6789
info@nafa.org www.nafa.org

Phillip E Russo, Executive Director
Patricia Murtaugh, Assistant Executive Director
Jennifer Buchanan, Project Assistant
Joanne Marsh, Director Membership & Marketing

Designed to provide comprehensive education to fleet managers like you who seek the fundamental principles and practices of successful fleet management.
4000 names
Printed in on glossy stock

1895 **NARSA Annual Convention & Trade Show**
National Automotive Radiator Service Association
15000 Commerce Parkway
Suite C
Mt Laurel, NJ 08054
856-439-1575
FAX: 856-439-9596 800-551-3232
info@narsa.org www.narsa.org

Mike Dwyer, Executive Director
Jen Jones, Assistant Executive Director
Anthony Celenza, Meetings Manager
Kelly Calzaretta, Exhibit Manager

180 booths featuring seminars and workshops of parts, equipment and supplies.
1.8M Attendees Annual/November

1896 **NPA Annual Parking, Transportation and Services Convention & Expo**
National Parking Association
1112 16th Street NW
Suite 300
Washington, DC 20036
202-296-4336
FAX: 202-331-8523 800-647-7275
plangfeld@npapark.org
www.npapark.org

Patricia Langfeld, Director Mktg/Business Development
Marty Stein, Manager

Bringing together parking professionals from around the world with leading experts from business and industry to explore the latest trends and developments. The Convention also affords members an opportunity to share ideas and experiences and to explore the latest equipment and technologies at the Exposition.
Annual Founded: 1955
Mailing list available for rent 1700 names $250 per M.

1897 **National Auto Auction Association Annual Convention (NAAA)**
National Auto Auction Association
5320 Spectrum Drive
Suite D
Frederick, MD 21703-7303
301-696-0400
FAX: 301-631-1359
naaa@naaa.com www.naaa.com

Gregg Kobel, President
John Rea, VP
Laurie Oakman, Communications
Frank Hackett, Executive Director

Annual convention and exhibits of automobile and truck auction equipment, supplies and services.
Annual/September

1898 **National Auto Glass Conference & Expo**
National Glass Association
8200 Greensboro Drive
Suite 302
McLean, VA 22102-3881
703-442-4890
FAX: 703-442-0630
attend@glass.org www.glass.org

Philip J James, President/CEO
Joe N Mesko, Treasurer

Visit with over 50 companies and get informed about the latest technology and see products demonstrated live. Get answers to your technical questions and find out which solutions are right for your business.
800 Attendees Annual/May

1899 National Independent Automobile Dealers Association Convention & Expo
National Independent Automobile Dealers Assoc.
2521 Brown Boulevard
Arlington, TX 76006-5203
817-492-2377
FAX: 817-649-5866 800-682-3837
kimberly@niada.com www.niada.com

Kimberly Cook, Convention Director
Michael R Linn, Executive VP/CEO

75 booths including automobile aftermarkets and finance companies.

June

1900 New York International Auto Show

Jacob Javitz Center
New York, NY
718-746-5300
FAX: 718-746-9333 800-282-3336

This show showcases some of the hottest concept and production cars ever seen. Many of the vehicles will be cutting edge innovative design studies, others just a few steps away from production, but all provide a window on the future of automobile design and technology. In addition, more than 43 vehicle manufacturers will feature over 1000 new cars, trucks, minivans and SUVs.

1901 North American Council of Automotive Teachers International Conference
North American Council of Automotive Teachers
PO Box 80010
Charleston, SC 29416
843-556-7068
FAX: 843-556-7068
office@nacat.com www.nacat.com

Dan Perrin, Conference Vice President

Annual show of 70 exhibits and 50 seminars, suppliers, distributors, publishing companies and other trade organizations.

July
Mailing list available for rent 750 names $165 per M.

1902 North American International Auto Show
Detroit Auto Dealers Association
1900 W Big Beaver
Troy, MI 48084
248-643-0250
FAX: 248-637-0784
naiasmail@dada.org www.naias.com

Rod Alberts, Executive Director

Annual show and exhibits of new automobiles and trucks, concept cars and van conversions.

808M Attendees January Founded: 1907

1903 PWA Annual Conference
Performance Warehouse Association
41-701 Corporate Way
Suite 1
Palm Desert, CA 92260
760-346-5647
FAX: 760-346-5847
van@weathers.com www.pwa-par.org

Gary Light, President
Anne Graves, Treasurer
John Towle, Executive Director

This is an exclusive opportunity for manufacturers and distributors to meet in a private, businesslike environment to discuss sales and marketing policies and programs.

165 Attendees Annual/September Founded: 1974

1904 Performance Racing Industry Trade Show
31706 South Coast Highway
Laguna Beach, CA 92651
949-499-5413
FAX: 949-499-0410
mail@performanceracing.com
www.performanceracing.com

Karin Davidson, Trade Show Manager
Steven Lewis, Owner

Annual show. Features the latest in motorsports technology from 1400 companies with 4000 booths.

42000 Attendees Annual

1905 RV Dealers International Convention & Expo
Recreation Vehicle Dealers Association
3930 University Drive
Fairfax, VA 22030-2515
703-591-7130
FAX: 703-591-0734
info@rvda.org www.rvda.org

Susan Charter, Exhibit Sales

For RV retailers from across the U.S. and Canada.

September
Mailing list available for rent 1500 names

1906 RVAA Executive Conference
Recreational Vehicle Aftermarket Association
54 Westerly Road
Camp Hill, PA 17011
717-730-0300
FAX: 717-730-0544
karl@rvaahq.com
www.rvaftermarket.org

Ellen Kietzmann, President
Karl Etshied, Dues/Fees Contact Person

An event which allows members to meet with each other to develop strategies for the coming year. It's the perfect opportunity for you to make the contacts and have the important face to face meeting time, with the potential partners that will enhance your success.

October

1907 SAE International Truck & Bus Meeting and Exhibition
Society of Automotive Engineers
755 W Big Beaver
Suite 1600
Troy, MI 48084
248-273-2455
FAX: 248-273-2494 877-606-7323
pkreh@sae.org www.sae.org

Patti Kreh, Manager Automotive Meetings
Nori Fought, Conference Service Representative
John Miller, Program Developer
Jack Pokrzywa, Operations Director

100 booths featuring suppliers of parts and components.

2.5M Attendees November

1908 SEMA International Auto Salon Trade Show
Specialty Equipment Market Association
PO Box 4910
Diamond Bar, CA 91765
909-396-0289

showinfo@sema.org
www.semaias.com

Gary Vigil, Trade Show Director
Marel Del Rio, Trade Show Coordinator

When the sport-compact scene was just beginning, the show was launched to educate members about the growing market and to bring new buyers and opportunities to manufacturers.

May Founded: 1998

1909 SEMA Offroad Convention
Specialty Equipment Market Association
PO Box 4910
Diamond Bar, CA 91765-0910
909-396-0289

sor@sema.org www.semaoffroad.com

Gary Vigil, Trade Show Director
Marel Del Rio, Trade Show Coordinator
Cheryl Perry, Exhibitor Services

Designed as a companion event to the well established SEMA Spring Expo, and as an extension of the SEMA Show, will target companies serving the recreational and performance off-road segments and aims to create new opportunities for this growing market.

February

1910 SEMA Show
Specialty Equipment Market Association
PO Box 4910
Diamond Bar, CA 91765-0910
909-396-0289

showinfo@sema.org
www.semashow.com

Gary Vigil, Trade Show Director
Marel Del Rio, Trade Show Coordinator

The premier automotive specialty performance products trade event in the world featuring performance, accessories, restoration and motorsports products.

100M Attendees November

1911 SEMA Spring Expo
Specialty Equipment Market Association
PO Box 4910
Diamond Bar, CA 91765-0910
909-396-0289

sse@sema.org www.semashow.com

Gary Vigil, Trade Show Director
Marel Del Rio, Trade Show Coordinator
Cheryl Perry, Exhibitor Services

The only trade show delivering the SEMA Show experience to the doorsteps of regional auto and truck parts and accessory businesses. We feature the leading companies that produce truck caps and accessories, automotive trim and restyling products, wheels and tires, guages and instruments, performance parts and more.

February

1912 **SIGM Annual Meeting**
Society of Independent Gasoline Marketers
11911 Freedom Drive
Suite 590
Reston, VA 20190-5602
703-750-0478
FAX: 703-709-7007
sigma@sigma.org www.sigma.org

Mary Alice Kutyn, Meetings Director
Lisa Freedman, Sales & Development Manager
Kenneth Doyle, Executive VP

SIGMA meetings are valuable and varied, addressing topics of interest for branded or unbranded motor fuel marketers, those interested in alternative fuels, fuel suppliers, and of course administrative and financial discussions for all types of organizations.
October

1913 **SOUTHCON**
Wescon
1230 Rosecrans Avenue
Suite 100
Manhattan Beach, CA 90266
310-524-4100
FAX: 310-643-7328 800-877-2668
j.cruz@ecishow.com
www.southcon.org

Joey Quesada Cruz, Show Management
Rod Mann, Conference Management

Issues that concern design, manufacturing and test departments. Instructors are leading experts in the topics they present.
10M Attendees February

1914 **Supernationals Custom Auto Show**
TNT Promotions Inc
PO Box 50386
Albuquerque, NM 87181-0386
505-480-0056
800-300-9381

Held annually in New Mexico. Each year, the show attracts prominent street rods and customs from throughout the country. 3-day event.
25000 Attendees Annual Founded: 1992

1915 **TIA World Tire Expo**
Tire Industry Association
1532 Pointer Ridge Place
Suite G
Bowie, MD 20716-1883
301-430-7280
FAX: 301-430-7283 800-426-8835
info@tireindustry.org
www.WorldTireExpo.org

Lakisha Pindell, Meeting Planner Director
Vicky Strack, Office Administrator

Providing an ideal forum for diverse individuals to meet, network and advance new business and marketing opportunities. This world-class exhibition is the number one showcase dedicated to those who have an interest in tire, rubber and transportation services.
April

1916 **WMDA Mega Show Annual Convention**
WMDA Service Station & Automotive Repair Assoc.
1532 Pointer Ridge Place
Suite G
Bowie, MD 20716
301-390-0900
FAX: 301-390-3161 800-492-0329

Marta Gates, Operations Director
LaKisha Pindell, Marketing Director

Featuring Over 225 Exhibits for the service station, automotive repair, car wash, convenience store& tire industries.
1500 Attendees

Directories & Databases

1917 **Automotive Aftermarket Suppliers**
Automotive Aftermarket Suppliers Association
10 Laboratory Drive
PO Box 13966
Research Triangle Park, NC 27709-3966
919-549-4800
FAX: 919-549-4824
tspera@mema.org
www.aftermarketsupplier.org

Paul Foley, VP
Teresa Spera, Director

Directory of automotive supply chains and jobbers/retailers in North America. Also, warehouse distributors and major programmed distribution groups.

1918 **Automotive Parts Rebuilders Association Membership Directory**
14160 Newbrook Drive
Suite 210
Chantilly, VA 20151-2223
703-968-2772
FAX: 703-968-2878
mail@apra.org www.apra.org

William C Gager, President
Kathy Olson, Directory Contact

Lists member companies and their products, addresses, phone and fax numbers, key personnel and sometimes even internet information. Keep this directory, your network resource for the automotive parts rebuilding industry, on your desk throughout the year. *$35.00*
Annual

1919 **ELM Guide to Automakers in North America**
ELM International
PO Box 1740
East Lansing, MI 48826-1740
517-332-4900
FAX: 517-351-3032
contact_us@automotivesuppliers.com
www.automotivesuppliers.com
The third edition of this guide contains more than 400 profiles that highlight the North American manufacturing operations of Chrysler, Ford, GM and all of the foreign owned automakers. *$350.00*
Semiannual

1920 **ELM Guide to Japanese Affiliated Suppliers in North America**
ELM International
PO Box 1740
East Lansing, MI 48826-1740
517-332-4900
FAX: 517-351-3032
contact_us@automotivesuppliers.com
www.automotivesuppliers.com

Mark Santucci

Offers information on approximately 290 Japanese owned automotive original equipment components manufacturers that operate in North America. *$350.00*

1921 **ELM Guide to US Automotive Sourcing**
ELM International
PO Box 1740
East Lansing, MI 48826-1740
517-332-4900
FAX: 517-351-3032
contact_us@automotivesuppliers.com
www.automotivesuppliers.com

Mark Santucci, Executive Director

Two volumes offering information on automotive original equipment manufacturer parts and components suppliers and profiles of plants belonging to 576 companies.
$775.00
1200 pages

1922 **PXN Parts Exchange New**
ADP Corporate Headquarters
1 ADP Boulevard
Roseland, NJ 07068
973-994-5000
FAX: 973-994-5495 800-366-4237
web@marketing.ADPClaims.com
www.adpclaims.com

Carlos Rodriguez, Division President
Sergio Fernandez, Chief Financial Officer

Provides an electronic link from your ADP estimating system to comprehensive database of new replacement parts. Data on over three and a half million parts facilitates the writing of complete, cost-effective damage reports.

1923 **RV Trade Digest**
Cygnus Publishing
1233 Janesville Avenue
Fort Atkinson, WI 53538
920-563-6388
FAX: 920-563-1699 800-547-7377

John Spaulding, Publisher
Greg Gerber, Editor-in-Chief
Brett Apold, Production Manager
Marie Escobar, Circulation Manager

Edited for detailers/retailers of light truck, van conversion, sport utility vehicles, recreational vehicles, selling (caps, covers, liners) parts, supplies and accessories, manufacturers of van conversiosn, truck conversion, 4x4's and SUV's. *$40.00*
40 pages Bi-Monthly Founded: 1983
Circulation: 15,000
Printed in 4 colors on glossy stock

1924 **Transmission Digest Buyer's Guide Issue**
MD Publications
PO Box 2210
3057 E Cairo Street
Springfield, MO 65801-2210
417-866-3917
FAX: 417-866-2781 800-274-7890
bmace@mdpublications.com
mdpublications.com

Bobby Mace, Publisher
Gary Sifford, Editor

List of over 500 manufacturers and distributors of products and services for the motor vehicle transmission repair industry. *$ 15.00*
20000 names
Printed in 4 colors on glossy stock

1925 **Ward's Automotive Yearbook**
Ward's Communications
3000 Town Center
Suite 2750
Southfield, MI 48075-1245
248-357-0800
FAX: 248-357-0810
a_binder@intertec.com
www.wardsauto.com
Alan K Binder, Editor
Rich West, Publisher
James Bush, Managing Director
Directory of suppliers to the vehicle manufacturing industry. New vehicle sales, production and inventory data and new vehicle product information and statistics. *$475.00*
500 pages Annual Founded: 1938 ISBN 0-910589-15-1
Circulation: 26,000
Computerized version available: On-line

1926 **Who Makes It and Where Directory**
Tire Guides
1101 S Rogers Circle
Suite 6
Boca Raton, FL 33487-2748
561-997-9229
FAX: 561-997-9233
tireinfo@tireguides.com
www.tireguides.com
Nancy Garfield-Chychrun, Senior Publisher
James Garfield, Chief Editor
Al Snyder, Contributing Editor
Jeff Chychrun, Associate Editor
Brand listings with manufacturer & distributor information; worldwide listing of web site addresses, fax numbers & U.S. toll free numbers. *$7.00*
62 pages Annual : cd rom

1927 **Wholesale Source Directory of Auto Parts, Accessories & Batteries**
Jerry Sutton
155 Sutton Lane
Fordsville, KY 42343
270-276-9546
jlsutton@apex.net www.pubdisco.com
Theresa Sutton, Publisher
Lee Sutton, Editor
Wholesale sources for auto parts, auto accessories, auto tools, alkaline batteries, automotive batteries, button cell batteries, closed circuit batteries, diesel engine-starting batteries, emergency lighting batteries and flashlight batteries. *$55.20*

1928 **Worldwide Automotive Supplier Directory**
Society of Automotive Engineers
SAE Magazines
400 Commonwealth Drive
Warrendale, PA 15096-0001
734-446-4970
FAX: 724-776-0790 877-606-7323
customerservice@sae.org
www.sae.org
Daniel J Holt, Editor
Directory features 10,000+ supplier listings from every major vehicle-producing region. And, it is the ONLY directory to provide information on a company's technical capabilities. *$329.00*
Annual ISBN 0-768015-36-7
Circulation: 60,550

Industry Web Sites

1929 **www.aaam.org**
Assn for the Advancement of Automotive Medicine

A professional multidisciplinary organization dedicated entirely to motor vehicle crash prevention and control.

1930 **www.aamva.org**
American Assn. of Motor Vehicle Administrators

Nonprofit organization represents state and provincial officials in the US and Canada who administer and enforce motor vehicle laws. Strives to develop model programs in motor vehicle administration, police traffic services and highway safety.

1931 **www.aflaonline.com**
Automotive Fleet & Leasing Association

Designed to improve communications among buyers, sellers, fleet administrators, lending institutions, lessors, used vehicle marketers and allied automotive service companies.

1932 **www.aftermarket.org**
Automotive Aftermarket Industry Association

For those involved in the motor vehicle replacement parts industry.

1933 **www.aiada.org**
American Int'l Automobile Dealers Assocation

Lobbying and communications organization for American automobile dealerships that sell and service international nameplate brands.

1934 **www.aiag.org**
Automotive Industry Action Group

Composed of major North American vehicle manufacturers and their suppliers. Provides an open forum where members cooperate to develop and promote solutions that enhance prosperity in the automotive industry.

1935 **www.aoca.org**
Automotive Oil Change Association

Representing the convenient automotive service industry. Dedicated to enhancing the competency of fast lube owners, educating the public about services our members offer and maintaining a favorable business environment for the industry as a whole.

1936 **www.apra.org**
Automotive Parts Rebuilders Association

Association of more than 1,500 member companies engaged in the rebuilding of automotive related hard parts, including starters, alternators, clutches, transmissions, brakes, drive shafts and other parts for passenger cars, trucks, off road, equipment and industrial uses.

1937 **www.asq.org**
American Society for Quality

The world's leading authority on quality that creates better workplaces and communitites worldwide by advancing learning, quality improvement, and knowledge exchange to improve business results.

1938 **www.atra-gears.com**
Automatic Transmission Rebuilders Association

Not for profit professional organization dedicated to the improvement and welfare of the automatic transmission repair industry for the benefit of the motoring public.

1939 **www.autobpa.com**
Automotive Body Parts Association

Members are companies that distribute, supply or manufacture automotive replacement body parts.

1940 **www.autoconsulting.com**
Automotive Consulting Group

Management consulting firm providing top line and bottom line business performance improvement services to the worldwide automotive industry.

1941 **www.automotivefleetmgt.com**
Automotive Fleet Management Corporation

Formed in order that financial institutions such as banks, credit unions and finance companies could repossess and dispose of their automotive collateral in a manner that is quick, efficient and cost effective.

1942 **www.awda.org**
Automotive Warehouse Distributors Association

Oldest organized group of warehouse distributors and their respective suppliers of parts, accessories tools and other supplies for the automotive aftermarket. In January 2004, AWDA joined forces with the Automotive Aftermarket Industry Association.

1943 **www.busesintl.com**
Buses International Association

An organization of persons throughout the world who are professionally involved in the management of companies or organizations which operate or manufacture buses.

1944 **www.carcare.org**
Car Care Council

A nonprofit 501 (c) (3) educational foundation whose purpose is to educate motorists about the importance of maintenance repairs and entertainment for safer, cleaner better performing vehicles. Provides editorial and public service material for media use.

1945 **www.classiccar.com**
ClassicCar.Com

Offers classic car enthusiasts around the world an online community with chats, forums and discussion groups.

1946 **www.diesel.org**
Association of Diesel Specialists

The worldwide diesel industry's leading trade association, dedicated to the highest level of service on diesel fuel injection and related systems.

1947 **www.edmunds.com**
Edmunds.Com

Founded in 1966 for the purpose of publishing new and used automotive pricing guides for automobile buyers.

1948 **www.filtercouncil.org**
Filter Manufacturers Council

For manufacturers of vehicular and industrial filtration products in North America. Active in efforts to educate people on proper disposal of used oil filters.

1949 **www.forecast1.com**
Forecast International

An electronic information/data service sourced from thousands of worldwide publications, in 15 languages. Provides concise passenger vehicles e-mail news and analysis summaries, news, trends and contract information with hyper-links to the source or a related website. Delivered 100 times a year.

1950 **www.greyhouse.com**
Grey House Publishing

Selected Grey House directories in the fields of business, health and education are available online. Users can search our online databases by several different search criteria, such as product categories, geographic area, sales volume and much, much more. Full Grey House catalog and online ordering also available.

1951 **www.hemmings.com**
Hemmings Motor News

Hemmings Motor News for the car collector and enthusiast.

1952 **www.iaati.org**
Int'l Association of Auto Theft Investigators

To improve communication and coordination among the growing family of professional auto theft investigators.

1953 **www.impa.org**
International Motor Press Association

Professional group of writers and editors producing auto articles for the press, radio or TV.

1954 **www.macsw.org**
Mobile Air Conditioning Society Worldwide

Provides technical training, information and communication for the professionals in the automotive air conditioning industry.

1955 **www.mema.org**
Motor and Equipment Manufacturers Association

Serves manufacturers of all types of automotive and truck products through market research, legislative and regulatory representation and reporting, information services, EDI network and credit reporting.

1956 **www.naaa.com**
National Auto Auction Association

Represents dealer wholesale auto auctions. Promotes exchange of ideas and public relations in the used car merchandising industry.

1957 **www.nada.com**
National Automobile Dealers Association

Provides representation for franchised new car and truck dealers in government, industry and public affairs. Provides counsel on legal and regulatory and political representation on Capital Hill.

1958 **www.nafa.org**
National Association of Fleet Administrators

Serving the needs of those managing fleets of automobiles, light duty trucks and/or vans for US and Canadian organizations. Offers statistical research, publications, regional meetings, government representation, conferences, trade shows and seminars.

1959 **www.narsa.org**
National Automotive Radiator Service Association

Trade association serving the cooling system service industry and the public.

1960 **www.nascar.com**
Turner Sports Interactive

Providing up-to-the-minute coverage on a 24-hour basis, NASCAR.COM delivers news, statistics and information on races, drivers, teams and industry events.

1961 **www.nationalwheelandrim.org**
National Wheel and Rim Association

Represents warehouse distributors of wheels, rims and related parts in the US and Canada.

1962 **www.ncsfa.state.ut.us**
National Conference of State Fleet Administrators

For state government administrators responsible for vehicle fleet management.

1963 **www.ntea.com**
National Truck Equipment Association

Represents small to mid-sized companies that manufacture, distribute, install, buy, sell and repair commercial trucks, truck bodies, truck equipment, trailers and accessories.

1964 **www.partsplus.com**
Association of Automotive Aftermarkets

Purchases and markets automotive replacement parts. Headquarters office for Parts Plus program distributors.

1965 **www.pera.org**
Production Engine Remanufacturers Association

Worldwide organization whose gives its members the information theyneed to produce remanufactured engines equal or superior to suppliers of the production line combustion engine industry.

1966 **www.pwa-par.org**
Performance Warehouse Association

For distributors of specialty automotive parts and suppliers.

1967 www.retread.org
Tire Retread Information Bureau

Serving as the public relations arm of the retread industry. Gathering and disseminating information on retread passenger and truck tires to members and the general public.

1968 www.rma.org
Rubber Manufacturers Association

National trade association for makers of tires and other rubber products.

1969 www.rvda.org
National RV Dealers Association

National association advances the best interests of RV retailers through education, services, leadership and programs of market expansion that promote increased use and sale of RVs as well as enhancement of the RV's image.

1970 www.scrs.com
Society of Collision Repair Specialists

For owners and managers of auto collision repair shops, suppliers, insurance and educational associates and suppliers in the US, Canada, Australia and New Zealand. Distributes technical, management, marketing and sales information. Works to promote professionalism within the collision repair industry.

1971 www.theautochannel.com
Auto Channel

Auto news, commentary and other useful information.

1972 www.tireindusty.org
Tire Industry Association

Representing all segments of the tire industry, including those that manufacture, repair, recycle, sell, service or use new or retreaded tires and also those suppliers or individuals who furnish equipment, material or services to the industry.

Associations

1973 **Aero Safety & Maintenance Association**
1200 G Street NW
Suite 900
Washington, DC 20005
202-383-2361
FAX: 202-383-2437
www.mcgrawhill.com

Herald McGraw, President
Jim Mathews, Publisher

A nonprofit research organization that depends primarily upon tax-deductible contributions.

1974 **Aeronautical Radio & Research Incorporated**
2551 Riva Road
Annapolis, MD 21401

FAX: 410-266-2020 800-633-6882
flightops@arinc.com www.arinc.com

Frederic J Jacoby, Chairman
John M Belcher, Chairman/CEO
Richard F Jones, VP Business Operations/CFO
Linda Hartwig, Sr Dir Corporate Communications

Aeronautical Radio provides transportation communications and systems engineering solutions for five major industries: aviation, airports, defense, government, and transportation

Founded: 1929

1975 **Aeronautical Repair Station Association**
121 N Henry Street
Alexandria, VA 22314-2903
703-739-9543
FAX: 703-739-9488
arsa@arsa.org www.arsa.org

Gary H Garvens, President
Bernard E Rookey, Senior VP
Sarah MacLeod, Executive Director
Marshall S Filler, Managing Director/General Counsel
Ian Cheyne, Treasurer

Represents members in regulatory and legislative issues before the FAA and other government agencies. The owners and operators of the world's aircraft depend on certified aeronautical repair stations for essential engineering, maintenance, and modification services.

600 Members Founded: 1984

1976 **Aerospace Industries Association**
1000 Wilson Boulevard
Suite 1700
Arlington, VA 22209-3924
703-120-0600
FAX: 703-358-1011
aia-aerospace.org
www.aia-aerospace.org

Robert D Johnson, Chairman
Ronald D Sugar, Vice Chairman
John W Douglass, President/CEO
Alan R Mulally, Executive VP
Ginette C Colot, Secretary/Treasurer

Trade association representing the nation's manufacturers of commercial, military and business aircraft, helicopters, aircraft engineers, missiles, spacecraft, material and related components and equipment.

281 Members Founded: 1919

1977 **Aerospace Medical Association**
320 S Henry Street
Alexandria, VA 22314-3579
703-739-2240
FAX: 703-739-9652 www.asma.org

Melchor J Antunano, President
Russell B Rayman, Executive Director

Aerospace medical association offers valuable information on the technological advances in medicine, pertaining to the aviation and aerospace industry.

3500 Members Founded: 1929
Mailing list available for rent

1978 **Air Force Association**
1501 Lee Highway
Arlington, VA 22209-1109
703-247-5800
FAX: 703-247-5853
service@afa.org www.afa.org

John J Politi, Chairman
Stephen P Condon, National President
Thomas Kemp, National Secretary
Edward Grillo Jr, Memorial Foundation President
Donald L Peterson, Executive Director

Independent nonprofit, civilian organization promoting public understanding of aerospace power and the pivotal role it plays in the security of the nation.

1,400 Members Founded: 1946

1979 **Air Taxi and Commercial Pilots Association**
7940-2 Airpark Road
Gaithersburg, MD 20879
301-330-6750

Professionals in the aviation industry.

1980 **Air Traffic Control Association**
1101 King Street
Suite 300
Alexandria, VA 22314-3367
703-299-2430
FAX: 703-299-2437
info@atca.org www.atca.org

Lawrence C Fortier Jr, Chairman
Garland Castleberry, President
Gerald L Thompson, Treasurer
Ron Morgan, Secretary

Works to establish and maintain a safe and efficient air traffic control system.

2400+ Members Founded: 1956

1981 **Air Transport Association of America**
1301 Pennsylvania Avenue NW
Suite 1100
Washington, DC 20004-1707
202-626-4000
FAX: 301-206-9789 800-497-3326
ata@airlines.org www.airlines.org

James C May, President/CEO
John M Meenan, Executive VP/COO
Paul R Archambeault, VP/CFO/Treasurer
Basil J Barino, VP Operations/Safety
David A Berg, VP General Counsel/Secretary

Supports and assits its members by promoting the air transport industry and the safety, cost effectiveness, and technical advancement of its operators; advocating common industry positions before state and local governments; conducting designated industry-wide programs; and assuring governmental and public understanding of all aspects of air transport.

25 Members Founded: 1936

1982 **Aircraft Electronics Association**
4217 S Hocker Drive
Independence, MO 64055
816-373-6565
FAX: 816-478-3100
info@aea.net www.aea.net

Paula Derks, President
Debbie McFarland, VP
Mark Gibson, Information Services Director
Mike Adamson, Director Training/Education

Persons interested in aviation and avionics.

1200 Members

1983 **Aircraft Owners & Pilots Association**
421 Aviation Way
Frederick, MD 21701
301-695-2000
FAX: 301-695-2375 800-872-2672
phil.boyer@aopa.org www.aopa.org

Phil Boyer, President

AOPA has achieved its prominent position through effective advocacy, enlightened leadership, technical competence, and hard work. Providing member services that range from representation at the federal, state, and local levels to legal services, advice, and other assistance, we have built a service organization that far exceeds any other in the aviation community. AOPA ePilot and AOPA ePilot Flight Training Edition unique e-mail newsletters issued every Friday morning only to AOPA members.

405k Members Founded: 1939

1984 **Airline Employee Association International**
6520 S Cicero Avenue
Bedford Park, IL 60638-5804
708-563-9999
FAX: 708-563-9958

Offers information regarding the airline industry, union representation information and general news.

1985 **Airline Pilots Association International**
535 Herndon Parkway
Herndon, VA 22070
703-689-2270
FAX: 952-941-1017 www.alpa.org

Duane E Woerth, President
Dennis J Dolan, First VP
Paul Rice, VP Administration
Chris Beebe, VP Finance

Promotes airplane use and co-operates with government agencies and private and public flying organizations to increase general safety.

64000 Members Founded: 1931

1986 **Airport Consultants Council**
908 King Street
Suite 100
Alexandria, VA 22314-3121
703-683-5900
FAX: 703-683-2564
info@acconline.org
www.acconline.org

Paula P Hochstetler, President
Anthony N Mavrogiannis, VP
Stephen V Berardo, Institute Director
Cassandra Lamar, Director Programs/Marketing
Sharon D Brown, Operations Manager

Represents the majority of airport consulting firms in the United States.

200+ Members Founded: 1978

1987 Airports Association Council International
1775 K Street NW
Suite 500
Washington, DC 20036-2463
202-293-8500
FAX: 202-331-1362 www.aci-na.org

Gregory Principato, President
Nancy Zimini, Staff VP
Richard F Marchi, SVP Technical Affairs
Ian A Redhead, VP Airport Services
Patricia Hahn, EVP Operations/General Counsel

Members are boards, commissions, local governmental entities operating public airport facilities and more.
240 Members Founded: 1947

1988 Airports Council International: North
1775 K Street NW
Suite 500
Washington, DC 20006
202-293-8500
FAX: 202-331-1362 www.aci-na.org

Gregory Principato, President
Nancy Zimini, VP
Todd Hauptli, Senior VP
Patricia Hahn, EVP Operations/General Counsel

Represents local, regional and state governing bodies that own and operates commercial airports throught the United States and Canada.
180M Members Founded: 1947

1989 Allied Pilots Association
O'Connell Building
14600 Trinity Blvd, Suite 500
Fort Worth, TX 76155-2512
817-302-2272
www.alliedpilots.org

Ralph Hunter, President
Sam Bertling, VP
James Eaton, Secretary/Treasurer

Provides all the traditional union representation services for its members. This includes the lobbying of airline pilots views to Congress and government agencies. In addition, it devotes more than 20 percent of its dues income to support aviation safety.
11500 Members Founded: 1963

1990 American Association of Airport Executives
601 Madison Street
Suite 400
Alexandria, VA 22314
703-824-0500
FAX: 703-820-1395
felicia.rindon@airportnet.org
www.airportnet.org

Charles Barclay, President
Spencer Dickerson, Senior Executive VP
Joel Bacon, Staff VP
Brad Van Dam, Staff VP
Eryn Travis, Director Media Relations

Exchanges ideas on construction, management and operation of civil airports.
2.6M Members Founded: 1992

1991 American Astronautical Society
6352 Rolling Mill Place
Suite 102
Springfield, VA 22152-2354
703-866-0020
FAX: 703-866-3526
aas@astronautical.org
www.astronautical.org

Kathleen Howell, Chairman
Jonathan T Malay, President
Mark K Craig, Executive VP
James R Kirkpatrick, Director
Shannon Coffey, VP Finance

Independent scientific and technical group in the United States exclusively dedicated to the advancement of space science and exploration.
1400 Members Founded: 1954

1992 American Bonanza Society
Mid-Continent Airport
PO Box 12888
Wichita, KS 67277
316-856-6112
FAX: 316-945-1710
bonanza2@bonanza.org
www.bonanza.org

Nancy Johnson, Executive Director
Tom Turner, Technical Manager

We are nearly 10,000 owners and pilots of Bonanza, Baron and Travel Air type aircraft who have banded together to share information and experiences involving the operation and maintenance of the Beech produced aircraft. Together, we offer an underwriter recognized flight proficiency program, and service clinics scheduled throught the year at various locations. These clinics provide members the opportunity to have their aircraft evaluated by highly experienced ABS technical personnel.
10K Members Founded: 1967

1993 American Helicopter Society
217 N Washington Street
Alexandria, VA 22314-2538
703-684-6777
FAX: 703-739-9279
staff@vtol.org www.vtol.org

Paul W Martin, Chairman
William H Forster, President
ME Rhett Flater, Executive Director/Legal Counsel
Patrick M Shanahan, Secretary/Treasurer
Michael S Torok, Technical Director

Promotes the interests of designers, engineers and manufacturers of the vertical flight industry. Serving as a clearinghouse for technical information, the society publishes several periodicals, organizes the largest vertical flight technology display in the world, and maintains a comprehensive library.
6000 Members Founded: 1944

1994 American Institute of Aeronautics and Astronautics
1801 Alexander Bell Drive
Suite 500
Reston, VA 20191-4344
703-264-7500
FAX: 703-264-7551 800-639-2422
tammys@aiaa.org www.aiaa.org

Alan R Mulally, Chairman
Robert Dickman, President/Executive Director
Klaus D Dannenberg, VP Finance
John E LaGraff, VP Education
David S Dolling, VP Publications

Advancing the arts, sciences and technology of aeronautics and astronautics and promotes the professionalism of those engaged in these pursuits.
31,00 Members Founded: 1963

1995 Army Aviation Association of America
755 Main Street
Suite 4D
Monroe, CT 06468-2830
203-268-2450
FAX: 203-268-5870
aaaa@quad-a.org www.quad-a.org

BG Thomas J Konitzler, President
William R Harris, Executive Director
Richard A Cody, Vice Chief of Staff

A professional force that holds the aviation community, both military and industry together.

1996 Association of Air Medical Services

526 King Street
Suite 415
Alexandria, VA 22314-3143
703-836-8732
FAX: 703-836-8920
tjudge@ahs.emh.org www.aams.org

Tom Judge, President
Ed Eroe, VP
Dawn M Mancuso, Executive Director
Saverio Cimone, RN, Treasurer
Kevin Hutton, MD, Secretary

Voluntary nonprofit organization, encourages and supports its members in maintaining a standard of performance reflecting safe operations and efficient, high quality patient care. Built on the idea that representation from a variety of medical transport services and businesses can be brought together to share information, collectively resolve problems and provide leadership in the medical transport community. We provide a e-mail newsletter called Capitol Watch for AAMS Members.
581 Members Founded: 1980 350 names $250 per M.

1997 Association of Flight Attendants
501 Third Street NW
Washington, DC 20001
202-434-1300

webmaster@afacwa.org
www.afanet.org

Patricia A Friend, International President
George M Donahue, International VP
Paul G Mac Kinnon, International Secretary/Treasurer
Eliott Kindred, Manager

Represents over 50,000 flight attendants at 26 airlines, serving as a voice for flight attendants at their workplace, in the industry, the media and on Capitol Hill.
50000 Members Founded: 1930

1998 Association of Naval Aviation
2550 Huntington Avenue
Suite 201
Alexandria, VA 22303-1400
703-960-2490
FAX: 703-960-4490
ana@anahq.org www.anahq.org

Stanley R Arthur, Chairman
P D Smith, President
Robin Braun, Executive VP
Eric L Wheeler, Executive Director
Jacqueline M Hayes, Membership Coordinator

Professional, nonprofit, educational and fraternaL society of Naval Aviation, whose main purpose is to educte the public and our national leaders on the vital roles of the Navy, Marine Corp and Coast Guard Aviation as key elements of our national defense posture. ANA continuosly seeks to elucidate the key current issues impacting Naval Aviation through published writing, symposia, speeches and discussions with various interest groups.

1999 Aviation Development Council
14107 20th Avenue
Suite 404
Whitestone, NY 11357-3097
718-746-0212
FAX: 718-746-1006
shellyade@aol.com
www.aviationdevelopmentcouncil.org

Bill Huisman, Director

Addresses noise problems from air carriers in the New York - New Jersey region.
Founded: 1962

2000 Aviation Distributors and Manufacturers
1900 Arch Street
Philadelphia, PA 19103-1404
215-564-3484
FAX: 215-564-2175 www.adma.org

H George Maxwell, President
Mark Morrow, VP
Talbot H Gee, Executive Director
Patricia Lilly, Management Liaison
Vaughn E Wurst, Membership Director

Promotes interests of wholesalers and manufacturers of general aviation aircraft parts and supplies.
Founded: 1943

2001 Aviation Insurance Association
14 W 3rd Street
Suite 200
Kansas City, MO 64105-6301
816-221-8488
FAX: 816-472-7765
tfry@ameritech.net www.aiaweb.org

Tom Fry, President
Tom Thornton, VP
Gary Hicks, Executive Director
Todd McCredie, Treasurer
Mandie Bannwarth, Marketing Director

Is a not-for-profit association dedicated to expanding the knowledge of and promoting the general welfare of the aviation insurance industry through numerous educational programs and events. AIA welcomes members of all facets of the aviation insurance industry, including such professionals as: agents/brokers, cliams professionals, underwriters, attorneys, associates and college students interested in the business. Online version of AIA's member newsleter The Binder.
900 Members Founded: 1976

2002 Aviation Technician Education Council
2090 Wexford Court
Harrisburg, PA 17112-1579
717-540-7121
FAX: 717-540-7121
info@atec-amt.org www.atec-amt.org

Richard Dumaresq, Executive Director

Organization of Federal Aviation Administration approved Aviation Maintenance Technician schools and supporting industries.
Founded: 1961

2003 Cessna Owner Organization
N7 450 Aanstad Road
Iola, WI 54945-5000
715-445-5000
FAX: 715-445-4053 888-692-3776
help@cessnaowner.org
www.cessnaowner.com

Jennifer Julin, Executive Director

Independent group of Cessna owners, pilots, and enthusiasts, the POS is committed to the goal of safe, fun, and affordable flying. Membership benefits include: Pre-buy referral service; free STC summaries, free parts locating and a referral service. Cessna Owner Magazine, exclusively for COO members, is published monthy and includes pilot tips, owner/aircraft articles, alerts, maintenance tips, new product information, SDR summaries, AD's, insurance updates, and much more.
5000 Members Monthly

2004 Civil Aviation Medical Association
PO Box 23864
Oklahoma City, OK 73123-2864
405-840-0199
FAX: 405-848-1053
jimlharris@aol.com
www.civilavmed.com

David Bryman, President
James L Harris, Executive VP
Gordon L Ritter, DO, Secretary/Treasurer

Aviation medical equipment, supplies and services. Working on behalf of physicians engaged in the practice of aviation medicine and dedicated to civil aviation safety. *$5.00*

800+ Members Founded: 1948

2005 Experimental Aircraft Association
3000 Poberezny Road
PO Box 3086
Oshkosh, WI 54902-3086
920-426-4800
FAX: 920-232-7772 800-236-4800

Tom Poberezny, President
Roger Jaynes, VP Communications

Works to keep aviation history alive. Members are active restorers and enthusiasts working to keep vintage aircraft in the air and flying for the pleasure and education of themselves and the public at large. EAA;s weekly electronic newsletter e-Hot Line.
170M Members Founded: 1953

2006 Flight Safety Foundation
601 Madison Street
Suite 300
Alexandria, VA 22314-1756
703-396-6000
FAX: 703-739-6708
www.flightsafety.org

Jerry Lederer, Founder
Edward W Stimpson, Chairman
Stuart Matthews, President/CEO
Robert H Vandel, Executive VP

Supported by airlines, aerospace manufacturers, aviation professionals, corporate flight departments and others interested in flight safety.
900 Members Founded: 1947

2007 Future Aviation Professionals of America (FAPA)
4959 Massachusetts Boulevard
Atlanta, GA 30337
404-997-8097
FAX: 770-997-8111

Linda Nelson, Chairman

Provides career information for those seeking careers in aviation, publications, newsletter, interview briefings and Aviation Job Bank. Also provides personal financial planning for airline pilots.
15M Members Founded: 1974

2008 General Aviation Manufacturers Association
1400 K Street NW
Suite 801
Washington, DC 20005
202-393-1500
FAX: 202-842-4063
webmaster@gama.aero
www.gama.aero

Pete Bunce, President/CEO
Katie Pribyl, Director of Communications
Ronald L Swanda, SVP Operations
Brian Riley, VP Government Affairs
Aubree J Foran, Meeting/Office Coordinator

Manufacturers of general aviation aircraft and related equipment. Members also operate fleets of aircraft, fixed based operations and pilot training facilities.
50 Members Founded: 1970

2009 Helicopter Association International
1635 Prince Street
Alexandria, VA 22314-2818
703-683-4646
FAX: 703-683-4745 800-435-4976
webmanager@rotor.com
www.rotor.com

Timothy Wahlberg, Chairman
Ed Newtonrg, Vice Chairman
Matt Zuccaro, President

Nonprofit organization provides members with services that directly benefit their operations and advances the civil helicopter industry by providing programs to enhance safety, encourage professionalism and promote the unique societal contributions made by the rotary flight industry.
2500 Members Founded: 1948

2010 Helicopter Safety Advisory Conference
Marathon Oil Company
PO Box 60136
Houston, TX 77205
281-443-2905
www.hsac.org

Casey Lowery, Chairman
John Davis, Treasurer
Ted Winslow, Secretary

Promotes safety and seeks to improve operations through establishment of standards of practice.
115 Members Founded: 1978

2011 International Association of Machinists and Aerospace Workers
9000 Machinists Place
Upper Marlboro, MD 20772-2687
301-967-4500
FAX: 301-967-4584
websteward@goiam.org
www.iamaw.org

R Thomas Buffenbarger, President/CEO
Lee Pearson, VP
Dave Ritchie, General VP
Bill Trbovitch, Director Communications
Warren L Mart, General Secretary/Treasurer

Has an annual budget of approximately $101.3 million.
700K Members

2012 International Council of Aircraft Owner and Pilot Associations
421 Aviation Way
Frederick, MD 21701
301-695-2220
FAX: 301-695-2375
webmaster@iaopa.org www.iaopa.org

Phil Boyer, President
John J Sheehan, Secretary General

Nonprofit federation of 53 autonomous, nongovernmental, national general aviation organizations. Facilitates the movement of general aviation aircraft.
40000 Members Founded: 1962

2013 International Inflight Food Service Association
1100 Johnson Ferry Road
Suite 300
Atlanta, GA 30342
404-252-3663
FAX: 404-252-0774
ifsa@kellencompany.com
www.ifsanet.com

Sandra Pineau, VP
Michael J Currie, Chairman
Sandra Pineau, President
Ken Samara, VP

The International Inflight Food Services Association is a global professional association created to serve the needs and interests of airline and railway personnel, inflight and rail caterers and suppliers responsible for providining passenger foodservice on regularly scheduled travel routes.
Founded: 1966

2014 International Society of Women Airline Pilots
ISA + 21
2250 E Tropicana Avenue
Suite 19-395
Las Vegas, NV 89119-6594

TianaD777@aol.com www.iswap.org

Tiana Daugherty, Chair
Melissa Monahan, Membership Chair
Mary Ana Gilbert, Vice Chair Education
Laura Reeves, Treasurer
Jessica Sterns, Secretary

Fosters cooperation and exchange among women airline pilots employed as flight crew members (Captain, First Officer or Second Officer) and holding seniority numbers with an air carrier which operates at least one aircraft with a gross weight of 90,000 pounds or more.
4000 Members Founded: 1978

2015 Light Aircraft Manufacturers Association
22 Deer Oaks Ct
Pleasanton, CA 94588-8233
925-426-0771
FAX: 925-426-0771 866-303-6285
info@lama.bz www.lama.bz

Lawrence P Burke, President

Promotes interests of kit-built light aircraft. Membership dues are $125 for voting members and $25 for non-voting members.
50 Members Founded: 1984

2016 Lighter Than Air Society
Lighter Than Air Society
526 S Main Street
Suite 232
Akron, OH 44311-3311
330-535-5827

suggest@blimpinfo.com
www.blimpinfo.com

Joseph Huber, President
Ron Browning, Director Business Development

Nonprofit organization whose members are devoted to the study of the history, science and techniques of all forms of buoyant flight.
1000 Members Founded: 1952

2017 National Aeronautic Association
1737 King Street
Suite 220
Alexandria, VA 22314
703-527-0226
FAX: 703-527-0229 800-644-9777
naa@naa.aero www.naa.aero

David Ivey, President
Shannon Chambers, Director Membership/Marketing
David L Ivey, President
J Richard Brown, Treasurer
Elizabeth Matarese, Secretary

The advancement of the art, sport, and science of aviation and space flight by fostering opportunities to participate fully in aviation activities and by promoting public understanding of the importance of aviation and space flight to the United States. We are an aviation and aeospace membership organization and record keeper.
3000 Members Founded: 1905

2018 National Agricultural Aviation Association
1005 E Street SE
Washington, DC 20003
202-546-5722
FAX: 202-546-5726
information@agaviation.org
www.agaviation.org

Cary A Rucker, VP
Andrew Moore, Executive Director
Peggy I Knizner, Assistant Executive Director

Voice of the aerial application industry, we work to preserve aerial application's place in the protection and production of America's food and fiber supply. Aerial application is one of the safest, fastest, most efficient and economical ways to apply pesticides. It is also the most environmentally friendly tool of modern agriculture.
1,300 Members

2019 National Air Traffic Controllers Association
1325 Massachusetts Avenue
Washington, DC 20005
202-628-5451
FAX: 202-628-5767 www.natca.org

John Carr, President
Ruth Marlin, Executive VP
Ricky Thompson, Alaskan Region VP
John Tune, Central Regional VP
Phil Barbarello, Eastern Regional VP

Founded to ensure safety and longevity of air traffic controller positions around the nation. Represents over 15,000 air traffic controllers throughout the US, Puerto Rico and Guam, along with 2,508 other bargaining unit members that span all areas from engineers and architects to nurses and health care professionals to members of the accounting community.
15000 Members Founded: 1987

2020 National Air Transportation Association
4226 King Street
Alexandria, VA 22302-1507
703-845-9000
FAX: 703-845-8176 800-808-6282

James K Coyne, President
Eric R Byer, VP Government/Industry Affairs
Alan Darrow, VP/CFO
David Almy, VP Marketing

National association of aviation business service providers.
2000 Members Founded: 1944
Mailing list available for rent 2,000 names
Printed in r colors on glossy stock

2021 National Association of Flight Instructors
EAA Aviation Center
PO Box 3086
Oshkosh, WI 54903-3086
920-426-6801
FAX: 920-426-6865
nafi@eaa.org www.nafinet.org

Rusty Sachs, Executive Director

Dedicated exclusively to raising and maintaining the professional standing of the flight instructor in the aviation community. Maintains a benefits package available for everyone from the independent instructor to those teaching at flight schools. Every other week we'll send NAFI memebrs with access to e-mail and electronic eMentor.
Founded: 1967

2022 National Business Aviation Association
1200 18th Street NW
Suite 400
Washington, DC 20036-2527
202-783-9000
FAX: 202-331-8364
info@nbaa.org www.nbaa.org

Kenneth E Emerick, Chairman
Edward M Bolen, President/CEO
Jeffrey W Lee, Treasurer
Sandy Murdock, Corporate Secretary

Not-for-profit, nonpartisan corporation dedicated to the success of the business aviation community.
7700 Members

2023 Ninety-Nines
4300 Amelia Earhart Road
Oklahoma City, OK 73159-1140
405-685-7969
FAX: 405-685-7985 800-994-1929
99s@ninety-nines.org
www.ninety-nines.org

Ealine Morrow, President
Pat Prentiss, VP
Martha Dunbar, Director
Susan Larson, Treasurer
Donna Moore, Secretary

International organization of licensed women pilots from 35 countries. We are a nonprofit, charitable membership corporation holding 501(c)(3) US tax status. Members are professional pilots for airlines, industry and government; we are pilots who teach and pilots who fly for pleasure; we are pilots who are technicians and mechanics. First and foremost, we are women who love to fly.
5500 Members Founded: 1929

2024 Pipers Owner Society
PO Box 5000
Iola, WI 54945
715-445-5000
FAX: 715-445-4053 866-697-4737
piper@aircraftownergroup.com
www.piperowner.org

Skip Carden, Executive Director

To support private owners of all models of Piper light aircraft. Members receive a full color monthly magazine which includes flying experiences, aircraft parts explained and historical features.
Founded: 1987

2025 Popular Rotorcraft Association
PO Box 68
Mentone, IN 46539
574-353-7227
FAX: 574-353-7227
prahq@pra.org www.pra.org

Igor Bensen, Founder
Gary Goldsberry, President
Dave Prater, VP
Robert Rymer, Treasurer
Glenn Bundy, Secretary

We are a group of people who love homebuilt rotorcraft—gyroplanes and helicopters that they build and fly themselves. These rotorcraft enthusiasts get together to exchange ideas, information, help one another, promote safety and help with flight training.
Founded: 1962

2026 Professional Aeromedical Transport
PO Box 7519
Alexandria, VA 22307
800-541-7517
800-541-7517

Purpose is to standardize and upgrade services of aeromedical transport operations. Membership is open to companies and individuals active in the industry.
170 Members Founded: 1986

2027 Professional Aviation Maintenance Association
717 Princess Street
Alexandria, VA 22314
703-683-3171
FAX: 703-683-0018 866-865-7262
hq@pama.org www.pama.org

David Orcutt, Chairman
Clark Gordon, Vice Chairman
Brian Finnegan, President
Gerry Goguen, Director
Sal Agosta, Treasurer

Enhances professionalism and recognition of the Aviation Maintenance Technician through communication, education, representation and support for continuous improvement in aviation safety.
3300 Members Founded: 1972

2028 Regional Airline Association
2025 M Street NW
Suite 800
Washington, DC 20036
202-367-1170
FAX: 202-367-2170
raa@dc.sba.com www.raa.org

Peter Bowler, Chairman
Jeff Pinneo, Vice Chairman
Deborah C McElroy, President
Scott W Foose, VP
David Lotterer, VP Technical Services

Membership consists of more than 70 airlines, plus 350 Associate members provide goods and services.
510 Members Founded: 1975

2029 Seaplane Pilots Association
4315 Highland Park Boulevard
Suite C
Lakeland, FL 33813-1639
863-701-7979
FAX: 863-701-7588 888-772-8923
spa@seaplanes.org www.seaplanes.org

J J Frey, Chairman
Michael Volk, President
Walter Windus, VP
Roger C Myers, Jr, Treasurer
Jerry Potter, Secretary

Represents members in dozens of seaplane access issues annually and provides numerous exclusive benefits. Members who have provided SPA with a vaild email address recieve Water Flying Update, a bimonthly e-newsletter that provides recent news, advocacy updates, technical tips, upcoming events, and a tip for using SPA's web site.
375 Members Founded: 1972

2030 Soaring Society of America
5425 West Jack Gomez Blvd
PO Box 2100
Hobbs, NM 88241-2100
505-392-1177
FAX: 505-392-8154
feedback@ssa.org www.ssa.org

Larry Sanderson, President
Dennis Wright, Executive Director
Alan Gleason, CFO

Fosters and promote all phases of gliding ans soaring, nationally and internationally.
16K Members Founded: 1932

2031 Society of Experimental Test Pilots
44814 N Elm Avenue
Lancaster, CA 93534
661-942-9574
FAX: 661-940-0398
step@step.org www.step.org

Michael V Rabens, President
Paula S Smith, Executive Director
Ricardo Traven, Treasurer
Sarah Reeder, Membership Manager

International organization that seek to promote air safety and contributes to aeronautical advancement by promoting sound aeronautical design and development; interchanging ideas, thoughs and suggestions of the members, assisting in the professional development of experimental pilots, and providing scholarships and aid to members and the families of deceased members.
2000 Members Founded: 1955

2032 Society of Flight Test Engineers
44814 N Elm Avenue
Lancaster, CA 93534-4037
661-949-2095
FAX: 661-949-2096
sfte@sfte.org www.sfte.org

John L Minor, President
Harold E Weaver, VP
Margaret Drury, Executive Director
Joseph T Dagata, Jr, Treasurer
Robert N Burton, Secretary

Members are engineers whose principal professional interest is the flight testing of aircraft. Purpose is to improve communications in the fields of flight test operations, analysis, instrumentation and data systems. We offer an online newsletter called SFTE Flight Test News.
900 Members Founded: 1968

2033 Space Foundation
310 South 14th Street
Colorado Springs, CO 80904
719-576-8000
FAX: 719-576-8801 800-691-4000
web@spacefoundation.org
www.spacefoundation.org

Robert S Walker, Chairman
Elliot G Pulham, President/CEO
Chuck Zimkas, Chief Operating Officer
Holly Roberts, Chief Financial Officer

Nonprofit organization advancing the exploration, development and use of space and space education for the benefit of humankind.
- Members Founded: 1983

2034 Transportation-Communications International Union
3 Research Place
Rockville, MD 20850
301-948-4910
FAX: 301-948-1872 www.tcunion.org

Robert A Scardelletti, International President
Joseph P Condo, Internatinal VP

Members come from diverse transportation industries. In addition to bargaining and representation of its members, provides mortgage and bankcard programs and other services to its members.
Founded: 1899

2035 Tripoli Rocketry Association
PO Box 970010
Orem, UT 84097-0010
801-225-9306
801-225-9307

Ken Good, President
Pat Gordzelik, VP
Bruce Lee, Treasurer
Bob Schoner, Secretary

This is a non-profit organization dedicated to the advancement and operation of non-professional high power rocketry.

2036 United States Parachute Association
1440 Duke Street
Alexandria, VA 22314-3488
703-836-3495
FAX: 703-836-2843 800-371-8772
uspa@uspa.org www.uspa.org

B J Worth, Chairman
Glenn Bangs, President
Mike Perrry, VP
Lee Schlichtemeier, Treasurer
Madolyn Murdock, Secretary

A not-for-profit membership association dedicated to the promotion of safe skydiving and the support of those who enjoy it. Sponsors Instructor Rating Program to train and certify instructors, jump masters and examiners.
34000 Members 34000 names $250 per M.

2037 United States Pilots Association
483 S Kirkwood Road
Suite 10
Saint Louis, MO 63122
314-849-8772
FAX: 314-338-8626
zimjr@earthlink.net www.uspilots.org

Paul Hough, Chairman
Jan Hoynacki, Executive VP

Works to promote aviation safety and pilot education and also acts as a forum for exchange of ideas.
5000 Members

2038 **United States Ultralight Association**
104 Carlisle St
Gettysburg, PA 17325-1810
717-339-0200
FAX: 717-339-0063
usua@usua.org www.usua.org

Lewis S Clement, Chairman
Reginald E DeLoach, President
Dale Hooper, Executive VP
Carol Plotnick, Managing Editor/Financial Admin

Annual meeting and exhibits of ultralight and microlight aviation equipment, supplies and services. There will be 20 booths.

3000 Members Founded: 1985

2039 **University Aviation Association**
3410 Skyway Drive
Auburn, AL 36830-6444
334-844-2434
FAX: 334-844-2432 www.uaa.aero

Allan Skramstad, President
Carolyn Williamson, Executive Director
Steve Anderson, Treasurer
Raymond E Cain, Jr, Secretary

Is the voice of collegiate aviation education to its members, the industry, governments and the general public.
800 Members

2040 **University of Arizona Department of Aerospace & Mechanical Engineering**
1130 North Mountain Avenue
Building 119
Tucson, AZ 85721-0119
520-621-6120
FAX: 520-621-8191
dimitri@u.arizona.edu
www.u.arizona.edu/~dimitri

Dr Dimitri Kececioglu PE, Prof Aerospace/Mech Engineering

An aerospace institute devoted to providing a working knowledge of reliability engineering theory and practice; mechanical reliability prediction; reliability testing and demonstration; failure analysis techniques; failure modes, effects and cricality analysis; complete industry product assurance strategies; maitainability engineering and many more.

2041 **World Airline Historical Society**
13739 Picarsa Drive
Jacksonville, FL 32225
904-221-1446
FAX: 786-331-7024
Information@WAHSOnline.com
www.wahsonline.com

Duane Young, President
Craig Morris, VP
Jay Prall, Secretary/Treasurer
Bill Demarest, LOG Editor

Open to all persons and groups interested in collecting airline memorabilia and the study of the airline industry, past and current.
6000 Members Founded: 1977

Newsletters

2042 **ATCA Bulletin**
Air Traffic Control Association
1101 King Street
Suite 300
Alexandria, VA 22314
703-299-2430
FAX: 703-299-2437
info@atca.org www.atca.org

Paul Bollinger, President
Mark DePlasco, Senior VP
Kate Kolstad, Director of Communication
Anne Harlan, Chairman Publications
Judy M. Gibbons, Manager, Conference & Publications

Provides information on activities of the association, important developments in the air traffic control industry, member news, information from governments and providers of air navigation service providers worldwide. For members only.
Monthly Founded: 1956
Printed in on matte stock

2043 **Accident Prevention**
Flight Safety Foundation
601 Madison Street
Suite 300
Alexandria, VA 22314-1756
703-396-6000
FAX: 703-739-6708
www.flightsafety.org

Roger Rozelle, Director Publications
Mark Lacagnina, Senior Editor
Wayne Rosenkrans, Senior Editor
Linda Werfelman, Senior Editor
Rick Darby, Associate Editor

Focuses on the flight deck, including in-depth reviews of accident reports. Authors offer tips and descriptions on pilot incapacitation, outlines techniques to prevent runway overrun and addresses a wide variety of other subjects aimed at the experienced cockpit crew. Subscription included with FSF membership. Others will be $280.00/year.
4-16 pages Monthly Founded: 1948
Circulation: 3,000
Printed in 2 colors

2044 **AeroLine**
ARINC
2551 Riva Road
Annapolis, MD 21401
410-664-4000
FAX: 410-266-2020 800-633-6882
flightops@arinc.com www.arinc.com

Frederic J Jacoby, Chairman
John M Belcher, Chairman/CEO
Richard F Jones, VP Business Operations/CFO
Linda Hartwig, Sr Dir Corporate Communications

A round-up of the monthly activities of the Airlines Electronic Committee.
Monthly

2045 **Aerospace Daily**
AviationNow
1200 G Street NW
Suite 900
Washington, DC 20005
202-383-2350
FAX: 202-383-2438 800-525-5003
aviationdaily@aviationnow.com
www.aviationnow.com

Lee Ewing, Editor-in-Chief
Brett Davis, Managing Editor
Mark Lipowicz, Publisher

Daily intelligence on the defense and space industries. If you're a prime or subcontractor, an aviation, defense or space official, a consultant or analyst, or an engineering or research and development mananger, you'll benefit from our news on policy and programs.
8 pages Daily Founded: 1963

2046 **Aerospace Electronics Business**
Phillips Publishing
7811 Montrose Road
Suite 100
Potomac, MD 20854
301-208-6787
www.phillips.com

Thomas Phillips, Publisher

Business opportunities and technology in the aerospace electronics industry.

2047 **Aerospace Industries Association Newsletter**
Aerospace Industries Association
1000 Wilson Boulevard
Suite 1700
Arlingron, VA 22209-3901
703-120-0600
FAX: 703-358-1011
michelle.princi@aia-aerospace.org
www.aia-aerospace.org

Marshall O Larsen, Chairman
Vance D Coffman, Vice Chairman
Michelle Princi, Membership
Matt Grimison, Communications

Offers information on association activities and events.
Monthly Founded: 1919
Circulation: 6000

2048 **Air Safety Week**
Phillips Publishing
7811 Montrose Road
Potomac, MD 20854
703-522-8502
www.phillips.com

Dan Cook, Publisher

Weekly newsletter dealing with aviation safety, security, recreation, certification and accident investigation. *$695.00*
10 pages Monthly

2049 **Air Taxi and Commercial Pilots Association Newsletter**
Air Taxi and Commercial Pilots Association
7940 Airpark Road
#2
Gaithersburg, MD 20879-4176
301-306-6750

Offers information and association news for professionals in the aviation industry.
Annual

2050 **Airlines & Fleets: E-mail News & Analysis**
Forecast International
22 Commerce Road
Newtown, CT 06470-1643
203-426-0800
FAX: 203-426-1964
www.forecast1.com

Kathy Bertrand, Production Manager
Monty Nebinger, Circulation Director

An electronic information/data service sourced from thousands of worldwide publications, in 15 languages. Provides concise summaries, news, trends and contract information with hyper-links to the source or a related website. Delivered 100 times a year. *$425.00*

2051 Airport Consultants Council News
Airport Consultants Council
908 King Street
Suite 100
Alexandria, VA 22314-3121
703-683-5900
FAX: 703-683-2564
info@acconline.org
www.acconline.org

Cassandra Lamar, Programs Manager
Paula Hochstetoer, CEO
Anthony Mavrogiannis, Editor
Sharon Brown, Operations Manager
Cassandra Lamar, Marketing Manager

Council newsletter offering information on important and relevant issues for the aviation consulting community.
Quarterly Founded: 1978
Circulation: 300

2052 Airport Highlights
Airports Council International-North America
1775 K Street NW
Suite 500
Washington, DC 20006
202-293-8500
FAX: 202-331-1362
lwerner@aci-na.org www.aci-na.org

Juliet Wright, Editor
Gregory Principato, President
Kent George, Chairman

News for airport executives.
Monthly Founded: 1977
Circulation: 2500

2053 Airport Operations
Flight Safety Foundation
601 Madison Street
Suite 300
Alexandria, VA 22314-1756
703-396-6000
FAX: 703-739-6708
www.flightsafety.org

Roger Rozelle, Director Publications
Mark Lacagnina, Senior Editor
Wayne Rosenkrans, Senior Editor
Linda Werfelman, Senior Editor
Rick Darby, Associate Editor

Directs attention to ground operations that involve aircraft and other equipment, airport personnel and services, air traffic control and passengers. Subscription included with FSF membership. Others will be $280.00/year.
4-8 pages Bi-Monthly Founded: 1974
Printed in 2 colors on glossy stock

2054 Airport Report
American Association of Airport Executives
601 Madison Street
Alexandria, VA 22314
703-824-0500
FAX: 703-820-1395
barbara.cook@aaae.org
www.airportnet.org

Charles Barclay, Publisher
Susan Lausch, VP Sales/Marketing
Barbara Cook, Editor
Holly Ackerman, Director of Publications

Information on national, federal and regional issues facing airport managers. Accepts advertising.
12 pages Founded: 1928

2055 American Association Airport Executives Newsletter
601 Madison Street
Number 400
Alexandria, VA 22314
703-824-0500
FAX: 703-820-1395 www.aaae.org

Charles Barclay AAE, President
Sean Broderick, Editor
Susan Lausch, Marketing

Association news aimed at management executives in the airline industry. *$650.00*
72 pages Founded: 1929

2056 Annual Conference Proceedings
Air Traffic Control Association
1101 King Street
Suite 300
Alexandria, VA 22314-3367
703-299-2430
FAX: 703-299-2437
info@acta.org www.atca.org

Judy M Gibbons, Manager Conference/Publications

Is a compendium of fifty or more air traffic control technical papers, covering the entire range of ATC subjects, authored by ATC experts from the full spectrum of public and private organizations engaged in advancement of the science of air traffic control.

2057 Antique Airplane Association Newsletter
22001 Bluegrass Road
Ottumwa, IA 52501-8569
641-938-2773
FAX: 641-938-2093
antiqueairfield@sirisonline.com
www.aaa-amp.org

Robert Taylor, Publisher
Lucinda Reis, Editor

Air museums, US and abroad historical aviation societies, for AAA chapters, flying aircraft company histories, etc. - For AAA Digest: antique and classic aircraft restorations, mystery aircraft, etc.
Founded: 1953
Printed in 4 colors on glossy stock

2058 Aviation Accident Law & Practice
LexisNexis Matthew Bender & Company
PO Box 933
Dayton, OH 45401-0933
212-448-2000
FAX: 518-487-3584 800-253-5624

R Kaye Esq., Publisher

Domestic and international laws.

2059 Aviation Consumer
Belvoir Publishers
PO Box 2626
Greenwich, CT 06836-2626
203-422-7300
FAX: 203-661-4802

Robert Englander, Publisher
Richard Weeghman, Editor

Offers valuable information to the consumer regarding airports, airlines, safety and values.

2060 Aviation Daily
Aviation Week
1200 G Street NW
Suite 922
Washington, DC 20005
202-383-2374
FAX: 202-383-2346 800-525-5003
aviationdaily@aviationnow.com
www.aviationnow.com

Jim Mathews, Editor-in-Chief
Alfhild Winder, Managing Editor
Kenneth Gazzola, VP
Mark Lipowicz, Publisher

Daily intelligence information on the commercial aviation and air transportation industry worldwide. *$1985.00*
10 pages Daily Founded: 1939
Printed in on n stock

2061 Aviation Education News Bulletin
Aviation Distributors & Manufacturers Association
100 North 20th Street
4th-Floor
Philadelphia, PA 19103-1443
215-564-3484
FAX: 215-963-9784
adma@fernley.com www.adma.org

H George Maxwell, President
Mark Morrow, VP
Talbot H Gee, Executive Director
Vaughn E Wurst, Membership Director

Association news pertaining to suppliers, distributors and manufacturers of aviation materials.
Monthly Founded: 1943

2062 Aviation Law Reports
CCH
2700 Lake Cook Road
Riverwoods, IL 60015-3867
847-267-7000
FAX: 773-866-3895 800-835-5224

Bob Becker, President
Steven Rudolph, Editor
Linda lev Gunton, Marketing Manager

News covering aviation law and regulations. *$2495.00*
Weekly Founded: 1913

2063 Aviation Maintenance
Professional Aviation Maintenance Association
717 Princess Street
Alexandria, VA 22314
703-683-3171
FAX: 703-683-0018 866-865-7262
hq@pama.org www.pama.org

David Orcutt, Chairman
Clark Gordon, Vice Chairman
Brian Finnegan, President
Gerry Goguen, Director
Sal Agosta, Treasurer

Free annual subscription.

2064 Aviation Mechanics Bulletin
Flight Safety Foundation
601 Madison Street
Suite 300
Alexandria, VA 22314-1756
703-396-6000
FAX: 703-739-6708
www.flightsafety.org

Stuart Matthews, President/CEO
Roger Rozelle, Publisher

Directed to the aviation maintenance technician, with an emphasis on airline and corporate operations. Other regular sections include maintenance safety alerts, mechanical-incident reports and reviews of new

products of interest to maintenance technicians. *$24.00*
16 pages Bi-Monthly Founded: 1953

2065 Aviation Medical Bulletin
Aviation Insurance Agency
475 N Central Avenue
PO Box 20787
Atlanta, GA 30354
404-767-7501
FAX: 404-761-8326 800-241-6103
Harvey Watt, Publisher
Bill Maness, Editor
Health education for the professional airline pilot. *$13.95*
Monthly Founded: 1951

2066 Aviators Hot Line
Heartland Communications
1003 Central Avenue
Fort Dodge, IA 50501
515-955-1600
FAX: 515-574-2199 800-247-2000
Mr. Gale W McKinney II, President/CEO
Joseph W Peed, Chairman
Mary Gonnerman, VP
Airline Trade Magazine. *$24.95*
Monthly Founded: 1968

2067 Buoyant Flight
Lighter Than Air Society
526 S Main Street
Suite 232
Akron, OH 44311-3311
330-535-5827
suggest@blimpinfo.com
www.blimpinfo.com
AD Topping, Publisher
Vincent Rubino, President
Articles on the history, science and techniques of buoyant flight.
Founded: 1954

2068 Cabin Crew Safety
Flight Safety Foundation
601 Madison Street
Suite 300
Alexandria, VA 22314-1756
703-396-6000
FAX: 703-739-6708
www.flightsafety.org
Stuart Matthews, President/CEO
Roger Rozelle, Publisher
Rick Derby, Editor
Patzy Sepezy, Circulation Manager
Focuses attention on the cabin crew, especially in airline operations, but the special requirements of corporate operations are also presented. Explanations on how to deal with hijackers, advocates of child restraints, emergency action plans and tips to reduce stress. Subscription included with FSF membership. Others will be $280.00/year. *$240.00*
4 pages
Printed in 2 colors

2069 Captain's LOG
World Airline Historical Society
13739 Picarsa Drive
Jacksonville, FL 32225
904-221-1446
FAX: 786-331-7024
information@wahsonline.com
www.wahsonline.com
Bill Demarest, LOG Editor
Quarterly

2070 Civil & Commercial Aviation E-mail News & Analysis
Forecast International
22 Commerce Road
Newtown, CT 06470-1643
203-426-0800
FAX: 203-426-1964
www.forecast1.com
Kathy Bertrand, Production Manager
Monty Nebinger, Circulation Director
An electronic information/data service sourced from thousands of worldwide publications, in 15 languages. Provides concise summaries, news, trends and contract information with hyper-links to the source or a related website. Delivered 100 times a year. *$425.00*
2 per year

2071 Command, Control, Communications and Intelligence
American Defense Preparedness Association
22 Commerce Road
Newtown, CT 22201-3062
203-426-0800
FAX: 203-426-0223 800-451-4975
info@forecast1.com
www.forecast1.com
Edward M Do Hebinger, President
Andrew Briney, Editor
Programs and funding information. *$1640.00*
Founded: 1973

2072 Federal Air Surgeons Medical Bulletin
US Federal Aviation Administration
800 Independence Avenue SW
Washington, DC 20591-1
202-664-4000
FAX: 405-954-8016
mike.wayda@faa.gov www.faa.gov
Jon L Jordan, CEO/President
Michael Wayda, Editor
Offers the latest technology, legislation, and news to medical and health care professionals working in the aviation field.
Quarterly Founded: 1967
Circulation: 8000

2073 Flight Safety Foundation NEWS
Flight Safety Foundation
601 Madison Street
Suite 300
Alexandria, VA 22314-1756
703-396-6000
FAX: 703-739-6708
info@flightsafety.org
www.flightsafety.org
Stuart Matthews, President
Roger Rozelle, Publisher
Allen Smith, Marketing Manager
A primary tool for communicating the Foundation's activities through seminars, workshops, special projects, committee actions, awards to its members. *$480.00*
Monthly

2074 Flight Test News
Society of Flight Test Engineers
44814 N Elm Avenue
PO Box 4037
Lancaster, CA 93539-4037
661-949-2095
FAX: 661-949-2096
sfte@sfte.org www.sfte.org
Jack Strier, Publisher
Offers specific information for flight test engineers.

2075 Flightlog
Association of Flight Attendants
1275 K Street NW
Suite 500, 5th Floor
Washington, DC 20005
202-428-8181
FAX: 202-712-9792 www.afanet.org
Eliott Kindred, Manager
Offers updated information and news for flight attendants.
Monthly

2076 General Aviation Accident Report
Andrews Communications
175 Stafford Street Building 4
Suite 140
Wayne, PA 19087
610-225-0510
FAX: 610-225-0501 800-345-1101
editor@andrewspub.com
www.andrewspub.com
Robert Maroldo, Publisher
Nicholas Sullivan, Editor
General aviation laws.
20 pages Founded: 1972

2077 Global Link
ARINC
2551 Riva Road
Annapolis, MD 21401
410-664-4000
FAX: 410-266-2020 800-633-6882
flightops@arinc.com www.arinc.com
Frederic J Jacoby, Chairman
John M Belcher, Chairman/CEO
Richard F Jones, VP Business Operations/CFO
Linda Hartwig, Sr Dir Corporate Communications
Communications, navigation, surveillance, and air traffic management for the aviation.

2078 Helicopter News
Phillips Business Information
1201 Seven Locks Road
Potomac, MD 20854
301-354-1400
FAX: 301-309-3847
Thomas Phillips, Publisher
Holly Yeager, Editor
Information on the rapidly changing helicopter industry. *$797.00*
25 Issues

2079 Helicopter Safety
Flight Safety Foundation
601 Madison Street
Suite 300
Alexandria, VA 22314-1756
703-396-6000
FAX: 703-739-6708
www.flightsafety.org
Roger Rozelle, Director Publications
Mark Lacagnina, Senior Editor
Wayne Rosenkrans, Senior Editor
Linda Werfelman, Senior Editor
Rick Darby, Associate Editor
Highlights the broad spectrum of real-world helicopter operations. Subscription included with FSF membership. Others will be $280.00/year.
4-8 pages Bi-Monthly Founded: 1974
Printed in 2 colors

2080 **Hotline**
Aeronautical Repair Station Association
121 N Henry Street
Alexandria, VA 22314-2903
703-739-9543
FAX: 703-739-9488
arsa@arsa.org www.arsa.org
Bennett Kobb, Publication Services
Is the leading newsletter on aircraft maintenance regulation. Each month, the hotline reports on the latest FAA rules and guidance material, legislation and international aviation developments. The newsletter is available only to members and federal employees.
Monthly

2081 **Human Factors & Aviation Medicine**
Flight Safety Foundation
601 Madison Street
Suite 300
Alexandria, VA 22314-1756
703-396-6000
FAX: 703-739-6708
www.flightsafety.org
Roger Rozelle, Director Publications
Mark Lacagnina, Senior Editor
Wayne Rosenkrans, Senior Editor
Linda Werfelman, Senior Editor
Rick Darby, Associate Editor
Presents information important to the training and performance of all aviation professionals. Subscription included with FSF membership. Others will be $280.00/year.
4-8 pages Bi-Monthly Founded: 1953
Printed in 2 colors

2082 **IE News: Aerospace and Defense**
Institute of Industrial Engineers
25 Technology Parkway
Suite 200
Norcross, GA 30092-2928
770-494-4951
FAX: 770-263-8532 800-494-0460
boyeyemi@iienet.org www.iienet.org
Jane Gaboury, Editorial Director
Peggy Rubin, President
Tom Miller, Sales Associate
Offers information and updates for industrial engineers.

2083 **Inside the Air Force**
Inside Washington Publishers
PO Box 7167
Washington, DC 20044-7167
703-685-5009
FAX: 703-416-8543 800-424-9068
Donna Haseley, Editor
An executive weekly report on Air Force programs, procurement and policymaking.
$980.00
Weekly
Printed in 1 color on matte stock
Computerized version available

2084 **International Operations Bulletin**
National Business Aviation Association
1200 18th Street NW
Suite 400
Washington, DC 20036-2598
202-783-9000
FAX: 202-331-8364
info@nbaa.org www.nbaa.org
William Stine II, Publisher
Edward M Bolen, CEO/President
Flight information for international business flight crews.
Quarterly Founded: 1947
Circulation: 4000

2085 **Jet Fuel Intelligence**
Energy Intelligence Group
5 E 37th Street
New York, NY 10016-3230
212-321-1112
FAX: 212-941-5509
info@energyintel.com
www.energyintel.com
Thomas E Wallin, President
Cristina Haus, Executive Editor
Raja W Sidawi, Chairman
Peter Kemp, Editor
Sarah Miller, Editor-at-Large
Offers the latest information on jets, fuel, cargo, safety and legislation. *$2595.00*
Weekly Founded: 1951

2086 **Light Aircraft Manufacturers Association Newsletter**
Light Aircraft Manufacturers Association
22 Deer Oaks Center
Pleasanton, CA 94588-8233
925-426-0771
FAX: 925-426-0771
info@lama.bz www.lama.bz
Larry Burke, President
Dave Martin, Editor
Manufacturers, distributors and suppliers receive the latest information and news pertaining to light aircraft, including updated news from Washington, DC.
Quarterly Founded: 1984
Circulation: 66 400 names
Printed in 2 colors on glossy stock

2087 **Light Plane Maintenance**
Belvoir Publishers
PO Box 420235
Palm Coast, FL 32142-235
203-422-7300
FAX: 203-661-4802 800-829-9085
lightplane@palmcoastd.com
www.lightplane-maintenance.com
John Likakis, Publisher
Articles of interest for light aircraft owners.
$19.97
24 pages

2088 **Mx Newsletter**
Professional Aviation Maintenance Association
717 Princess Street
Alexandria, VA 22314
703-683-3171
FAX: 703-683-0018 866-865-7262
hq@pama.org www.pama.org
David Orcutt, Chairman
Clark Gordon, Vice Chairman
Brian Finnegan, President
Gerry Goguen, Director
Sal Agosta, Treasurer
Features news for and about members, relevant articles and hot legislative information. Distributed as a stand alone publication.
Six/Year
Printed in 1 color

2089 **NATA News**
National Air Transportation Association
4226 King Street
Alexandria, VA 22302
703-845-9000
FAX: 703-845-8176 800-808-6282
Jim Coyne, President
Alan Darrow, VP
Dan Kidder, Manager of Communications
Dan Dent, Director of Membership Services
Deborah Highsmith, Manager, Education and Training
Aviation and business news.
16 pages Monthly Founded: 1940
Circulation: 3000
Mailing list available for rent 2,000 names
Printed in r colors on glossy stock

2090 **NBAA Management Guide**
National Business Aviation Association
1200 18th Street NW
Suite 400
Washington, DC 20036-2527
202-783-9000
FAX: 202-331-8364
info@nbaa.org www.nbaa.org
Ed Bolen, President/CEO
Steve Brown, Senior VP Operations
This reference assists corporate aviation departments with operational, maintenance and administreive requirements and provides useful guidance for establishing and operating a flight department.
Computerized version available

2091 **National Aeronautics**
National Aeronautic Association
1737 King Street
Suite 220
Alexandria, VA 22314
703-527-0226
FAX: 703-527-0229 800-644-9777
Shannon Chambers, Editor
David L Ivey, President
Nancy Sack, Office Manager
Information on industry events for the aviation community, also opinion articles, records and awards, technology developments, education, and future events.
8 pages Founded: 1905
Circulation: 3500
Printed in 2 colors on glossy stock

2092 **National Transportation Safety Board Digest Service**
Hawkins Publishing Company
103 River Road
Edgewater, MD 21037
410-662-2551
FAX: 410-798-1098 www.ntsb.gov
Mark V Rosenker, Chairman
Loose-leafed indexed-digested-analysis of the decisions of the National Transportation Safety Board and its predecessor (the CAB), dealing with Aviation Safety Enforcement matters. *$390.00*
Monthly

2093 **News & Views**
Association of Air Medical Services
526 King Street
Suite 415
Alexandria, VA 22314-3143
703-836-8732
FAX: 703-836-8920
information@aams.org www.aams.org
Renee Holleran, Editor
David J Dries, Editor
Gloria Dow, Editor
This faxed/e-mailed newsletter contains information on association activity updates, community and member news, crew fitness and survival, member survey data, member profiles, editorials, and classifieds.
Monthly

2094 Ninety-Nines News
Ninety-Nines
4300 Amelia Earhart Road
Oklahoma City, OK 73159
405-685-7969
FAX: 405-685-7985 800-994-1929
ihq99s@cs.com
www.ninety-nines.org

Bobbi Roe, Publisher
Elaine Morrow, President
Pat Prentiss, VP
Donna Moore, Secretary
Liz Lundin, Headquarters Manager

News and events for licensed women pilots.
Founded: 1929

2095 Operations Update
Helicopter Association International
1635 Prince Street
Alexandria, VA 22314-2818
703-683-4646
FAX: 703-683-4745 www.rotor.com

Marty Lenehan, Publications

Provides useful information to helicopter owners and operators regarding issues, events and new technologies that may effect or enhance the operator's ability to conduct business with helicopters.
Monthly

2096 PAMA News
Professional Aviation Maintenance Association
717 Princess Street
Alexandria, VA 22314
703-683-3171
FAX: 703-683-0018 866-865-7262
hq@pama.org www.pama.org

Peter Rohrbach, Publisher
Brian Finnegan, President

Publication for aviation maintenance personnel.
Monthly Founded: 1972
Circulation: 2000

2097 Plane Talk
ARINC
2551 Riva Road
Annapolis, MD 21401
410-664-4000
FAX: 410-266-2020 800-633-6882
flightops@arinc.com www.arinc.com

Frederic J Jacoby, Chairman
John M Belcher, Chairman/CEO
Richard F Jones, VP Business Operations/CFO
Linda Hartwig, Sr Dir Corporate Communications

A publication for the Avionics Maintenance Conference, wrapping up their monthly activities.

2098 Preliminary Accident Reports
Helicopter Association International
1635 Prince Street
Alexandria, VA 22314-2818
703-683-4646
FAX: 703-683-4745 www.rotor.com

Marty Lenehan, Publications

PARs summarize civil helicopter accident reports as received from the National Transportation Safety Board and the Transportation Safety Board of Canada. One subscription included upon request in Regular and Associate member dues.
Quarterly

2099 Regional Horizons
Regional Airline Association
2025 M Street NW
Suite 800
Washington, DC 20036
202-367-1170
FAX: 202-367-2170
raa@dc.sha.com www.raa.org

Peter Bowler, Chairman
Jeff Pinneo, Vice Chairman
Deborah McElroy, President
Scott W Foose, VP
David Lotterer, VP Technical Services

Provided to members in print and electonic format. The launch issue was distributed in mid-March and includes information about the association and how its staff works for members in the areas of government relations, technical services and general industry issues.
Bi-Monthly

2100 Rotor Breeze
Bell Helicopter Textron
600 E Hurst Boulevard
PO Box 482
Hurst, TX 76053
817-280-3608
FAX: 817-280-2321
dlacroix@bellhelicopter.textron.com
www.bellhelicopter.com

Mike Redenbaugh, Chairman/CEO
Brandon Battles, Editor

Newsletter on Bell Helicopter products and customer support.
Quarterly Founded: 1935

2101 Space Calendar
Space Age Publishing Company
65-1230 Mamalahoa Highway
Suite D-20
Kamuela, HI 96743-1752
808-885-3473
FAX: 808-885-3475
news@spaceagepub.com
www.spaceagepub.com

Steve Durst, Publisher

Publication for the space industry. *$59.00*
Weekly

2102 Space Fax Daily
Space Age Publishing Company
65-1230 Mamalahoa Hwy
Suite D-20
Kamuela, HI 96743
808-885-3473
FAX: 808-885-3475
news@spaceagepub.com
www.spaceagepub.com

Steve Durst, Publisher
Charles Bohannan, Associate Editor
Michelle Gonella, Marketing Manager

Information covering the space industry.
$59.00
Weekly Founded: 1988

2103 Space Letter
Callahan Publications
6220 Nelway Drive
PO Box 1173
Mclean, VA 22101
703-356-1925

Vincent F Callahan Jr, Editor

Information from Washington on the US multi-billion dollar National Space Program. Legislation, budgets, marketing trends and contracting. *$190.00*
8 pages 24/Yr
Printed in 1 color

2104 Space Station News
Phillips Publishing
7811 Montrose Road
Potomac, MD 20854-3363
301-208-6787
FAX: 301-340-0877

Tom Phillips, President/CEO/Publisher

Information pertaining to the space station program.
Founded: 1974

2105 Space Watch Newsletter
Space Foundation
310 South 14th Street
Colorado Springs, CO 80904
719-576-8000
FAX: 719-576-8801 800-691-4000
web@spacefoundation.org
www.spacefoundation.org

Elliot G Pullman, President/CEO
Robert S Walker, Chairman
Stephanie Fibbs, Communications/Media Relations

Monthly free newsletter accessible through their Website that provides a vital link to readers on global space issues.

2106 SpaceWatch
Space Foundation
310 S 14th Street
Colorado Springs, CO 80904
719-576-8000
FAX: 719-576-8801 www.ussf.org

Beth Ann Lipskin, Publisher
Barry M Grossman, Editor
Patricia J Arnold, VP
Mary Ann Bobko, Director,Marketing

Provides a concise synopsis of current civil, military and commercial space activities and emerging policy. It also provides space information to educators and the public. Sent to Foundation members, government officials and aerospace professionals.
16 pages Monthly Founded: 1983
Circulation: 2000

2107 Speednews
Speednews
1801 Avenue of the Stars
Suite 210, Century City
Los Angeles, CA 90067-5904
310-203-9603
FAX: 310-203-9352
speednews@aol.com
www.speednews.com

Gilbert Speed, Publisher
Michael Ward, Editor
Joanna Speed, VP, Circulation & Confere
Stephen A. Costley, VP, Managing Editor
Pamela Leven, Subscription Sales

Market intelligence newsletter for the aviation industry. *$687.00*
Weekly Founded: 1979
Circulation: 50000

2108 World Aerospace and Defense Intelligence Report
Forecast International
22-25 Commerce Road
Newtown, CT 06470
203-426-0800
FAX: 203-426-0223 800-451-4975
sales@forecast1.com
www.forecast1.com

Douglas A Nebinger, President

A weekly look at world aircraft, space, defense and geo-political developments covered by an international research base. Intended for use by individuals who need

more analytical information regarding the defense (and related) industries. *$495.00*
24 pages Weekly Founded: 1973
Printed in 4 colors on matte stock

2109 World Airline News
Phillips Publishing
7811 Montrose Road
Potomac, MD 20854
301-354-1400
FAX: 301-340-0877 www.phillips.com
Tom Phillips, President/CEO/Publisher
Provides airline executives with news and analysis on route developments, codesharing agreements, and traffic statistics as well as aviation entertainment. *$697.00*
Weekly/Newsletter Founded: 1974
Circulation: 1,850

2110 World Airport Week
Phillips Publishing
7811 Montrose Road
Potomac, MD 20854
301-354-1400
FAX: 301-340-0877 www.phillips.com
Tom Phillips, CEO
Focuses on commercialization and privatization of airports around the world. *$597.00*
Weekly
Circulation: 1800

Magazines & Journals

2111 ABS Magazine
American Bonanza Society
PO Box 1288
Wichita, KS 67277
316-945-1700
FAX: 316-945-1710
bonanza2@bonanza.org
www.bonanza.org
Nancy Johnson, Executive Director
Peggy L Fuksa, Events Coordinator
Offers a treasury of practical information on such topics as maintenance, piloting techniques, aircraft restoration, aircraft insurance and ot her important subjects especially chosen for those with a specific interest in Bonanza, Baron, and Travel Air models of aircraft. This colorful magazine also features aircraft owned by an ABS members on its cover every month, as well as schedules of the numerous member activities which are conducted all around the nation.
Monthly

2112 AIAA Technical Reports
American Institute of Aeronautics and Astronautics
1801 Alexander Bell Drive
Suite 500
Reston, VA 20191-4344
703-264-7500
FAX: 703-264-7657 800-639-2422
custserv@aiaa.org www.aiaa.org
Don Richardson, President
Kathy Watkins, Maketing Manager
Dr David S Dolling, VP Publications
Cort Durocher, Executive Director
Each year AIAA sponsors approximately 25 national meetings where professionals present technical papers on subjects such as guidance and control Computers in Aerospace, etc. *$3.00*
Founded: 1963
Circulation: 1925

2113 AMT Magazine
Professional Aviation Maintenance Association
717 Princess Street
Alexandria, VA 22314
703-683-3171
FAX: 703-683-0018 866-865-7262
hq@pama.org www.pama.org
David Orcutt, Chairman
Clark Gordon, Vice Chairman
Brian Finnegan, President
Gerry Goguen, Director
Sal Agosta, Treasurer
Free annual subscription to qualified members. Free subscription to BCA Magazine. Business & Commerical Aviation is edited for the aviation professional in busines and corporate flight departments, helicopter operations and owner/pilots. Regular features include Washington Report, Observer a detailed evaulation of a particular new aircraft, Fit for Flight and maintenance problems.

2114 AOPA Flight Training Magazine
Aircraft Owners & Pilots Association
421 Aviation Way
Frederick, MD 21701
301-695-2000
FAX: 301-695-2375 800-872-2672
phil.boyer@aopa.org www.aopa.org
Mike Collins, Editor
Phil Boyer, President
Provides up-to-date aviation news and safety tips for student pilots and CFIs.

2115 AOPA Pilot Magazine
Aircraft Owners & Pilots Association
421 Aviation Way
Frederick, MD 21701
301-952-2000
FAX: 301-695-2180 800-872-2672
pilot@aopa.org www.aopa.org
Thomas B Haines, Editor-in-Chief
Phil Boyer, President
Will keep you up to date on all the hottest issues in general aviation from the newest technologies in avionics to the latest safety and techniques to enhance your flying. Available only to AOPA members. Membership costs only $39.00/annually.
Monthly
Circulation: 34,000

2116 AUSA News
Association of the United States Army
2425 Wilson Boulevard
Arlington, VA 22201-3326
703-841-4300
FAX: 703-525-9039 800-336-4570
ausa-info@ausa.org www.ausa.org
Peter Murphy, Editor
Gordon R Sullivan, President
AUSA represents every American soldier by: being the voice for all components of America's army; fostering public support of the Army's role in national security; providing professional education and information programs.
Monthly Founded: 1950
Circulation: 10000

2117 Aero Magazine
National Aeronautic Association
1815 Fort Myer Drive
Suite 700
Arlinton, VA 22209
703-527-0226
FAX: 703-527-0229
naa@naa.aero www.naa.aero
Wesley L McDonald, Chairman
E W Baragar, Vice Chairman
David L Ivey, President
J Richard Brown, Treasurer
Elizabeth Matarese, Secretary
Is is a benefit of membership with NAA, and it includes news and stories about the association and a variety of aviation subjects. In each issue there will be in-depth stories focusing on an important person or trend in aviation.
Bi-Monthly
Printed in 4 colors

2118 Aerospace Engineering
400 Commonwealth Drive
Warrendale, PA 15096-1
724-776-4841
FAX: 724-776-9765
magazines@sae.org www.sae.org
Rodica A Baranescu, President
Max E Rumbaugh Jr, Executive VP
Serves the international aerospace design and manufacturing field which consists of producers of airliners, helicopters, spacecraft, missles; their powerplants, propulsion systems, avionics, electronic/electrical systems, parts and components. *$75.00*
10 issues Founded: 1905
Circulation: 28440

2119 Agricultural Aviation
National Agricultural Aviation Association
1005 E Street SE
Washington, DC 20003-2847
202-546-5722
FAX: 202-546-5726
information@agaviation.org
www.agaviation.org
Andrew D Moore, Executive Director
Lindsay Barber, Manager Communications
Scott Schertz, President
Official publication of the National Agricultural Aviation Association. Typical subject matter includes information on agricultural aviation business, agricultural aircraft, legislative issues, pesticides, new products and services, safety, maintenance, people profiles. *$30.00*
Founded: 1921
Circulation: 5200

2120 Air Classics
Challenge Publications
9509 Vassar Ave
Unit A
Chatsworth, CA 91311-883
818-700-6868
FAX: 818-700-6282 800-562-9182
customerservice@challengeweb.com
www.challengeweb.com/
Edwin Schnepf, President/Publisher
Magazine of military aviations. *$36.95*
76 pages Monthly Founded: 1963

2121 Air Force Magazine
Air Force Association
1501 Lee Highway
Arlington, VA 22209-1198
703-247-5800
FAX: 703-247-5855 800-727-3337
letters@afa.org www.afa.org/

Donald L Peterson, Publisher
Robert S. Dudney, Editor in Chief
Stephen P. Condon, National President
Suzann Chapman, Editor
John A. Tirpak, Executive Editor

Analysis of all aspects of aerospace power, from military and scientific advances to political ramifications. Includes reports on new technology and studies missile management. *$36.00*

Monthly Founded: 1946
Circulation: 202718

2122 Air Line Pilot
Air Lines Pilot Association International
1625 Massachusetts Ave NW
Washington, DC 20036
202-974-4033
FAX: 703-689-4370 www.alpa.org

Gary DiNunno, Editor-in-Chief
Mary Jo McPherson, Associate Editor
Duane Woerth, President

Emphasizes advances in air safety, flight technology, industry developments and aviation history. *$32.00*

56 pages Monthly Founded: 1931
Circulation: 86,656

2123 Air Medical Journal
Elsevier, Health Sciences Division
11830 Westline Industrial Drive
Saint Louis, MO 63146
314-534-4100
FAX: 314-997-5080 800-401-9962
elspcs@elsevier.com
http://www2.us.elsevierhealth.com

Renee S Holleran RN, Editor
David J Dries, Editor

Is the industry's combined trade and research journal. Each issue contains research articles, abstracts and book reviews designed to keep you up-to-date on the latest discoveries. Membership benefits includes a complimentary subscription. *$82.00*

Founded: 1986

2124 Air Progress
Challenge Publications
9509 Vassar Ave
Unit A
Chatsworth, CA 91311-883
818-700-6868
FAX: 818-700-6282
customerservice@challengeweb.com
www.challengeweb.com

Edwin Schnepf, President/Publisher
Taccy Kruger, Editor

Covers all phases of aviation. *$36.95*

84 pages Monthly Founded: 1963

2125 Air Progress - Warbirds International
Challenge Publications
9509 Vassar Avenue
Unit A
Chatsworth, CA 91311
818-700-6868
FAX: 818-700-6282 800-562-9182
customerservice@challengeweb.com
www.challengeweb.com

Edwin Schnepf, Publisher
Michael O'Leary, Editor
Tim Baudler, Associate Publisher

The magazine of veteran and vintage military aircraft. *$22.00*

80 pages Quarterly Founded: 1963
Circulation: 3836

2126 Air Transport World
Penton Media
1350 Connecticut Avenue NW
Suite 902
Washington DC, MD 20036
202-659-8500
FAX: 202-223-1979
informatio@pentonmedia.com
www.atwonline.com

J.A. Donoghue, Editorial Director
William A Freeman III, Publisher

Lists nationwide and international information on airports, airlines and the latest technology in the aviation industry. *$65.00*

85 pages Monthly Founded: 1964
Circulation: 40000
Printed in 4 colors on glossy stock

2127 Air and Space/Smithsonian
National Air and Space Museum
Smithsonian Institution
PO Box 37012 ,Victor Bldg 7100 MRC
Washington, DC 20013-7012
202-275-1230
FAX: 202-275-1886 800-766-2149
editors@airspacemag.si.edu
www.airspacemag.com/

Joseph Bonsignore, Publisher
George C Larson, Editor

Smithsonian magazine offering information on the latest developments, technology, and historical news of the aviation industry. *$ 24.00*

124 pages Founded: 1986

2128 Aircraft Ground Service Guide
National Air Transportation Association
4226 King Street
Alexandria, VA 22302
703-845-9000
FAX: 703-845-8176 800-808-6282
csipes@nata-online.org
www.nata.aero

James K Coyne, President
Alan Darrow, VP
Eric R Byer, Dir Government/Industry Affairs

The AGSG includes updated information on all facets of safe ground-handling piston, jet and turboprop aircraft. 5x7 Spiral Bound Pocket Size version. *$24.95*

2129 Aircraft Handling Guidepost
National Air Transportation Association
4226 King Street
Alexandria, VA 22302
703-845-9000
FAX: 703-845-8176 800-808-6282
csipes@nata-online.org
www.nata.aero

James K Coyne, President
Alan Darrow, VP
Eric R Byer, Dir Government/Industry Affairs

Is your all inclusive guide to handling the many aircraft that frequent your ramp. *$195.00*

2130 Aircraft Maintenance Technology
Cygnus Publishing
1233 Janesville Avenue
Fort Atkinson, WI 53538-803
920-563-6388
FAX: 920-563-1704
jescobar@amtonline.com
www.amtonline.com

Joe Escobar, Editor
Greg Napert, Publisher
Richard Reiff, President

Editorially focused on the technical and professional needs of the aviation maintenance professional. *$90.00*

98 pages Monthly Founded: 1989
Circulation: 44000
Mailing list available for rent 41M names
Printed in 4 colors on glossy stock

2131 Airline Pilot Careers
Aviation Information Resources
3800 Camp Creek Parkway
Suite 18-100
Atlanta, GA 30331
404-592-6500
FAX: 404-592-6515 800-538-5627
webeditor:airinfo@airapps.com
www.jet-jobs.com

Kit Darby, President/Publisher

Information to assist pilots in their career development as a airline pilot. Includes feature airline news, personnel announcements, aviation medical information, classifieds and calendar events. *$29.95*

40 pages Monthly Founded: 1989

2132 Airliners
World Transport Press
2854 Sterling Road
Hollywood, FL 33020
954-923-4474
FAX: 954-923-4541 800-875-6711
airlinesonline@earthlink.net
www.airlinersonline.com

Jon Proctor, Editor

Dedicated solely to the exciting world of airlines and airliners, past, present, and future. Airline histories, travel adventures, color photos of the latest airlines, humorous articles and much more. Accepts advertising. *$26.95*

80 pages
Circulation: 80000

2133 Airport Business
Cygnus Publishing
1233 Janesville Avenue
Fort Atkinson, WI 53538
920-563-6388
FAX: 920-563-1699
john.infanger@cygnuspub.com
www.airportbusiness.com/

Holly Hoffer, Publisher
John Infanger, Editorial Director
Jodi Richards, Associate Editor
Paul Mackler, CEO/President

An ongoing source of how-to information for managers of airports and airport-based businesses. Management, finance and funding, regulations, community relations, sales and marketing, operations, maintenance, security, fuel and ground services are all presented in an innovative, case study format. Subscription is $49.50 per year *$60.00*

44 pages Founded: 1986
Circulation: 17500

2134 Airport Equipment & Technology
8380 Colesville Rd
Ste 700
Silver Spring, MD 20910-6257
301-650-2420
FAX: 301-650-2433
billfreeman@penton.com
www.atwonline.com

William A Freeman III, Publisher
Perry Flint, Editor-in-Chief

Related to airport and airport operations. *$65.00*

Quarterly Founded: 1965
Circulation: 40000

2135 Airport Journal
Airport Journal
551 Revere Avenue
PO Box 66001
Westmont, IL 60559
630-986-8132
FAX: 630-986-5010
www.airportjournal.com

John Andrews, Editor

This journal offers news, information, statistics and reviews pertaining to airports across the globe. *$13.00*
Monthly

2136 Airport Magazine
American Association of Airport Executives
601 Madison Street
Alexandria, VA 22314-1507
703-824-0500
FAX: 703-820-1395
sean.broderick@aaae.org
www.airportnet.org

Sean Broderick, Editor
Charles Barclay, President
Betsy Woods, Assistant Editor
Susan Lausch, Marketing Manager

Magazine offering information on airlines, technology, airports and aviation in general, focusing primarily on executives in the industry. *$18.00*
Monthly Founded: 1928

2137 Airport Press
PATI
PO Box 879 JFK Sta.
Jamaica, NY 11430
718-244-6788
FAX: 718-995-3432 800-982-5832
airprtpres@aol.com
www.airportpress.com

William Puckhaber, Publisher

Reports on international, national, and local events which impact on air cargo, airport, and passenger segments of the industry.
24 pages Monthly Founded: 1985
Circulation: 18000 100 names
Printed in 4 colors

2138 Airport Report
American Association of Airport Executives
601 Madison Street
Alexandria, VA 22314-1507
703-824-0500
FAX: 703-820-1395
barbara.cook@aaar.org
www.airportnet.org

Charles Barclay, President
Barbara Cook, Editor
Susan Lausch, Marketing Manager

Information on national, federal and regional issues facing airport managers.
Monthly Founded: 1928

2139 Airport Services Management Magazine
Lakewood Publications
50 S 9th Street
Minneapolis, MN 55402-3118
612-340-4903
FAX: 612-340-4869

James P Secord, President/CEO
Frank W Cooley, Editor

Edited for managers of airports and aircraft service facilities. It carries articles dealing with the management of general aviation centers, airline properties/facilities/ground service operations, corporate aviation dept commuter/charter businesses, and the general aviation/air carrier airports on which they are located. *$24.00*
36 pages Bi-Monthly

2140 Airports
Aviation Week
1200 G Street NW
Suite 900
Washington, DC 20005
202-383-2350
FAX: 202-383-2438 800-525-5003
aw_intelligence@aviationnow.com
www.aviationnow.com

Christopher Fotos, Editor
Kimberley Johnson, Associate Editor
Mark Lipowicz, Publisher

Airports, the weekly for airport managers, users and suppliers, gives you exclusive insider intelligence to meet business challenges with your eyes open. *$98.00*
Weekly Founded: 1920

2141 Airpower
Sentry Books
Republic Press
4426 Deseret Drive
Woodland Hills, CA 91364
818-368-2012

info@mikemachat.com
www.wingsairpower.com

Joseph Mizrahi, Publisher
Mike Machat, Editor/Publisher

Military and commercial aviation history, contains photos, drawings and interviews. *$44.00*
56 pages Monthly Founded: 1971
Circulation: 45000

2142 Airways
Airways International
120 McGhee Road
PO Box 1109
Sandpoint, ID 83864
208-263-2098
FAX: 208-263-5906 800-440-5166
airways@airwaysmag.com
www.airwaysmag.com

John Wegg, Editor-in-Chief
Seija Wegg, VP Marketing

Written for airline and air travel professionals, and the consumer. Focuses on the current air transport industry: the airliner, manufacturers, the people, technologies, the airports and the airways. Plus takes a nostalgic look at the past. *$39.95*
80 pages Monthly Founded: 1994
Circulation: 43000

2143 America's Flyways
United States Pilots Association
483 S Kirkwood Road
Suite 10
Saint Louis, MO 63122
314-849-8772
FAX: 314-338-8626
zimjr@earthlink.net www.uspilots.org

Paul Hough, Chairman
Jan Hoynacki, Executive VP

Memberships includes annual subscription.

Monthly

2144 Army Aviation
Army Aviation Publications
755 Main Street
Suite 4D
Monroe, CT 06468-2830
203-268-2450
FAX: 203-268-5870
aaaa@quad-a.org www.quad-a.org

William R Harris, Publisher
Maryann Stirling, Circulation Manager
Ronald K. Anderson, President

Is a professional military publication reporting on news and developments pertinent to the field of U.S. Army Aviation and is the official publication of the Army Aviation Association of America. Each issue offers in-depth coverage of a specific development or program within U.S. Army Aviation along with dynamic, easy-to-read feature articles from key offices, agencies, and operational units worldwide. *$30.00*
Monthly Founded: 1957
Printed in 4 colors on glossy stock

2145 Aviation Business Journal
National Air Transportation Association
4226 King Street
Alexandria, VA 22302
703-845-9000
FAX: 703-845-8176 800-808-6282
csipes@nata-online.org www.nata.aero

Kathy Bailey-Sumlin, Ordering Contact

This journal is authored by experienced aviation journalists and industry experts. In addition to feature articles, regular departments include President's Message, Inside Washington and Member News. This is mailed to all NATA members free of charge. Cost for non-members is listed below. *$50.00*
Quarterly
Printed in 4 colors

2146 Aviation Digest Associates
288 Christian Street
Oxford, CT 06478-1038
203-264-3727

Robert Dorr, Publisher
Sharon Simmons, Associate Publisher

Newsmagazine/shopper distributed to owners of general aviation (private and corporate) aircraft. *$20.00*
Monthly
Circulation: 12,000

2147 Aviation Equipment Maintenance
Phillips Business Information
7811 Montrose Road
Potomac, MD 20854
301-354-1400
FAX: 301-309-3847
information@phillips.com
www.phillips.com

Richard Koulbanis, Publisher
Clif Stroud, Editor
John J. Coyle, President

Produced monthly and is the leading publication for airline and general aviation maintenance managers. AEM provides information on maintenance techniques, management procedures, new products and ground support equipment.
Monthly Founded: 1974

2148 Aviation International News
Convention News Company
81 Kenosia Avenue
Danbury, CT 06810
203-798-2400
FAX: 203-798-2104
ckilmer@ainonline.com
www.ainonline.com

Perry E Bradley, Publisher
R Randall Padfield, Editor
Claire Kilmer, Circulation Manager
Wilson Leach, Executive Director

Update on aviation, equipment and services, and aviation news and events. *$74.98*
116 pages Monthly Founded: 1972
Circulation: 36,000
Printed in 4 colors on glossy stock

2149 Aviation Safety
Belvoir Publishers
800 Connecticut Avenue
PO Box 5656
Norwalk, CT 06856
203-857-3100
FAX: 203-857-3103
customer_service@belvoir.com
www.belvoir.com

Ken Ibold, Editor-in-Chief
Robert Englander, Chief Executive Officer
Tom Canfield, VP

Journal on risk management and accident prevention, includes interviews with officals of the FFA. *$65.00*
Monthly Founded: 1972

2150 Aviation Week & Space Technology
Aviation Week
1200 G Street NW
Suite 900
Washington, DC 20005
202-832-2377
FAX: 202-383-2438 800-525-5003
letters@aviationnow.com
www.aviationnow.com

Anthony L Velocci Jr, Editor-in-Chief
James R Asker, Manager Editor
Jim Mathews, Publisher

Articles and features on the aviation/aerospace industry, including aircraft rockets, missiles, space vehicles, powerplants, avionics and related components and equipment. *$5.00*
Weekly Founded: 1884
Circulation: 140000

2151 Aviation, Space and Environmental Medicine
Aerospace Medical Association
320 S Henry Street
Alexandria, VA 22314-3579
703-739-2240
FAX: 703-739-9652
ASEMJournal@worldnet.att.net
www.asma.org

Russell B Rayman, Executive VP
Melchor J Antunano., President
Sally Nunneley, Editor

Offers valuable information on the techological advances in medicine, pertaining to the aviation and aerospace industry. *$86.00*
Monthly Founded: 1929

2152 Aviation, Space, and Environmental Medicin e
Aerospace Medical Association
320 S Henry Street
Alexandria, VA 2314-3579
703-739-2240
FAX: 703-739-9652 www.asma.org

Sarah A Nuneley, MD, Editor-in-Chief
Sarah Pierce-Rubio, BA, Assistant to Editor
Pamela Day, BA, Managing Editor
Rachel Trigg, Editorial Assistant

The journal provides contact with physicians, life scientists, bioengineers, and medical specialists working in both basic medical research and in its clinical applications.
Monthly

2153 Avionics News
Aircraft Electronics Association
4217 S Hocker
Independence, MO 64055
816-373-6565
FAX: 816-478-3100
info@aea.net www.aea.net

Monte Mitchell, Editor
Paula Derks, Publisher
Debbie McFarland, VP

A magazine devoted exlusively to persons interested in aviation and avionics. Complimentary within North America. *$132.00*
Monthly Founded: 1975
Circulation: 8500

2154 Avionics: The Journal of Global Airspace
PBI Media
1201 Seven Locks Road
Potomac, MD 20854
301-354-1400
FAX: 301-340-0542 847-559-7314
djensen@accessintel.com
www.avionicsmagazine.com

Daniel E Comiskey, Publisher
Stuart Bonner, Circulation Manager
Don Pazour, CEO
David Jensen, Editor-In-Chief

Covers electronics carried aboard aircraft, ground navigational and systems for air traffic control. *$89.00*
Monthly Founded: 1999
Printed in 4 colors on glossy stock

2155 Balloon Life
Balloon Life Magazine
9 Madelaine Avenue
Westport, CT 06880
203-629-1241
FAX: 206-935-3326
bill_armstrong@balloonlife.com
www.balloonlife.com

Bill Armstrong, Publisher/Editor

Dedicated to the sport of hot air ballooning. Four-color magazine contains articles on major events, safety, education, news, calendar and special reports to bring alive the life of ballooning. *$21.00*
40 pages Bi-Monthly Founded: 1986
Circulation: 4000
Printed in 4 colors on glossy stock

2156 Business & Commercial Aviation
McGraw Hill
4 International Drive
Suite 260
Rye Brook, NY 10573
914-939-0300
FAX: 914-939-1184 800-257-9402
p02cs@mcgraw-hill.com
www.aviationnow.com

William Garvey, Editor-in-Chief
Mark Lipowicz, Publisher
Richard Aarons, Safety Editor

Information for the management and executive levels of aircraft companies on improvements in operations and news of todays general aviation industry. *$60.00*
Monthly
Circulation: 52329

2157 Business Aircraft Deicing Guide
National Air Transportation Association
4226 King Street
Alexandria, VA 22302
703-845-9000
FAX: 703-845-8176 800-808-6282
csipes@nata-online.org
www.nata.aero

James K Coyne, President
Alan Darrow, VP
Eric R Byer, Dir Government/Industry Affairs

Our guide will give you and your deicing crews the guidance necesary to deice with confidence. *$150.00*

2158 Civil Air Patrol News
105 S Hansell Street
Building 714
Maxwell AFB, AL 36112-6332
334-834-2236
FAX: 334-953-4262
capnews@cap.gov www.capnhq.gov

James F Tynan, Editor
Mary Nell Crowe, VP Marketing
Donna Sparks, Assistant Editor
Don Rowland, Executive Director

Aerial search and rescue, cadet activities, aerospace education, news of interest to Civil Air Patrol members, aviation news, local activities of CAP units. Accepts advertising. *$5.00*
20 pages Founded: 1941

2159 Controller
Sandhills Publishing
PO Box 82545
Lincoln, NE 68501-5310
402-479-2181
FAX: 402-479-2188 800-247-4890
human-resources@sandhills.com
www.sandhills.com

Tom Peed, Publisher

A magazine designed and edited to provide a means of communication between buyer and seller in today's general aviation marketplace. *$52.00*
60 pages Weekly Founded: 1978
Circulation: 20,000 +

2160 EAA Sport Aviation
Experimental Aircraft Association
3000 Poberezny Road
PO Box 3086
Oshkosh, WI 54903-3086
920-426-4800
FAX: 920-232-7772
editorial@eaa.org www.eaa.org

Tom Poberezny, Publisher
Scott Sangria, Managing Editor
Bob Warner, Marketing Manager

For pilots, designers, and enthusiasts of sport and homebuilt aircraft. *$40.00*
100 pages Monthly Founded: 1953
Circulation: 165000
Printed in 4 colors on glossy stock

2161 **EAA Sport Pilot Magazine**
Experimental Aircraft Association
3000 Poberezny Road
PO Box 3086
Oshkosh, WI 54903-3086
920-426-4800
FAX: 920-232-7772 800-236-4800
editorial@eaa.org www.eaa.org
Tom Poberezny, President
Roger Jaynes, VP Communications
Dedicated to those to fly, buy, build/assemble, maintain, and have fun with light-sport aircraft, sport pilot eligible aircraft, and ultralights, as well as the full spectrum of member activities that give people the opportunity to participate in recreational aviation.

2162 **FAA Aviation News**
Government Printing Office
AFS-805 Room 832
800 Independence Avenue, S.W.
Washington, DC 20591
202-512-0000
webmasteravnews@faa.gov
www.faa.gov/
Phyllis Duncan, Editor
Marion C Blakey, Administrator
Russel G Chew, CEO
Daniel J. Mehan, Chief Information Officer
Contains regulations and approved operational techniques, also in depth accident and incident reports. *$21.00*
Bi-monthly Founded: 1966
Circulation: 50,000

2163 **Flight Physician**
Civil Aviation Medical Association
PO Box 23864
Oklahoma City, OK 73123-2864
405-840-0199
FAX: 405-848-1053
jimlharris@aol.com
www.civilmed.com
David Brynam, President
James L Harris, Executive VP
Gordon L Ritter, Secretary/Treasurer
$5.00
Bi-Monthly

2164 **Flight Safety Digest**
Flight Safety Foundation
601 Madison Street
Suite 300
Arlington, VA 22314-1756
703-247-0700
FAX: 703-739-6708
wahdan@flightsafety.org
www.flightsafety.org
Stuart Matthews, President
Roger Rozelle, Publisher
Mark Lacagnina, Sen.Editor
Analyzes controversial industry issues; and authors have shared observations of important, but sometimes subtle influences that affect the airline industry. Authors have described the latest innovations in training, technology and management. Monthly sections present analyses of aviation statistics, brief accident reports and abstracts of information received at FSF Jerry Lederer Aviation Safety Library. Subscription included with FSF membership. Others will be $520.00. *$520.00*
Monthly Founded: 1982
Circulation: 1000
Printed in 1 color

2165 **Flight Training**
Aircraft Owners & Pilots Association
421 Aviation Way
Frederick, MD 21701
301-695-2000
FAX: 301-695-2375 800-872-2672
flighttraining@aopa.org
www.aopa.org
Phil Boyer, President/Publisher
Thomas B Haines, Editor-in-Chief
Offers information to new pilots and their instructors as well as flight school managers and owners. *$21.00*
Monthly Founded: 1939
Circulation: 40000+

2166 **Flightline Magazine**
Allied Pilots Association
O'Connell Building
14600 Trinity Blvd, Suite 500
Fort Worth, TX 76155-2512
817-302-2272
www.alliedpilots.org
Ralph Hunter, President
Sam Bertling, VP
James Eaton, Secretary/Treasurer

2167 **Flyer**
Flyer Media
5611 76th Street W
PO Box 39099
Lakewood, WA 98439
253-471-9888
FAX: 253-471-9911 800-426-8538
comments@generalaviationnews.com
www.generalaviationnews.com
Janice Wood, Editor
Dave Sclair, Publisher
Roy McGhee, Production Manager
Ron Boydston, Circulation Manager
For general and business aviation. *$35.00*
72 pages Monthly Founded: 1949
Circulation: 50000
Printed in 4 colors on newsprint stock

2168 **Flying**
1633 Broadway
45th Floor
New York, NY 10019
212-767-6000
FAX: 212-767-4932
flying@neodata.com
www.flyingmag.com
J Mac McClellan, Editor-in-Chief
Wayne Lincourt, Associate Publisher
Rachel Goldstein, Sales Development Manager
Dedicated to general aviation and includes industry news, products, reports on every aircraft category, the latest new products, technology and photography. *$54.00*
116 pages Monthly Founded: 1918
Circulation: 310321
Printed in 4 colors

2169 **Flying Magazine**
National Association of Flight Instructors
EAA Aviation Center
PO Box 3086
Oshkosh, WI 54903-3086
920-426-6801
FAX: 920-426-6865
nafi@eaa.org www.nafinet.org
Sean Elliot, President
Rusty Sachs, Executive Director
Provided to all NAFI members, this highly respected general aviation magazine is a great source of information. NAFI and Flying have entered into a partnership that directly benefits you - the NAFI member! Flying is the perfect compliment to the technical flight instruction how-to's contained in NAFI Mentor.

2170 **GPS World**
Advanstar Communications
1 Park Avenue
New York, NY 10016
212-797-7631
FAX: 212-951-6793 800-225-4569
info@advanstar.com
www.advanstar.com
Edward Aster, Publisher
Glen Gibbons, Editor
Elisoseu Nascimpo, Manager
Covers current news and developments in the area of GPS (global positioning system) technology. *$54.00*
Monthly Founded: 1987
Circulation: 35010

2171 **Helicopter Association International Magazine**
1635 Prince Street
Alexandria, VA 22314-2818
703-683-4646
FAX: 703-683-4745 800-435-4976
marty.lenehan@rotor.com
www.rotor.com
Matthew Zuccaro, President
Elizabeth Meade, Executive VP/Corporate Secretary
Dedicated exclusively to the civil helicopter industry. It covers pertinent helicopter operational safety and regulatory issues, including FAA question and answer column, legislative and lobbying issues, and HAI committee and member activities. Accepts advertising. *$15.00*
48 pages Quarterly Founded: 1988
Printed in 4 colors on matte stock

2172 **IAM Journal**
International Association of Machinists and
9000 Machinists Place
Upper Marlboro, MD 20772-2687
301-967-4500
FAX: 301-967-4584
websteward@goiam.org
www.iamaw.org
R Thomas Buffenbarger, President/CEO
Lee Pearson, VP
Dave Ritchie, General VP
Bill Trbovitch, Director Communicatins
Warren L Mart, General Secretary/Treasurer
This advocacy magazine addresses the trends and forces that affect us all. It covers stories provide an indepth analysis of today's hot issues and are meant to spark discussion among IAM members. Its feature stories provide a glimpse of the men and women who belong to the IAM. IAM represents works primarily in the air transport, aerospace, metalworking, machinery, manufacturing and automotive industries.

2173 **Journal of Aerospace Engineering**
American Society of Civil Engineers
1801 Alexander Bell Drive
Reston, VA 20191-4400
703-956-6000
FAX: 703-295-6211 800-548-2723
marketing@asce.org
www.pubs.asce.org
Firdaus Udwadia, Editor
Bill Henry, President
Johanna Reinhart, Managing Director

Covers lunar soil mechanics, aerospace structures, and materials, extraterrestrial construction, robotics, remote sensing, applications, and real time data collection systems. Defines the role of civil engineering in space and emphasizes the practical applications of civil engineering in space and on earth. *$140.00*

Quarterly Founded: 1852

2174 Journal of Air Traffic Control
Air Traffic Control Association
1101 King Street
Suite 300
Alexandria, VA 22314-2944
703-299-2430
FAX: 703-299-2347
info@atca.org www.atca.org

Paul Bollinger, President
Kate Kolstad, Director of Communication

Devoted to developments in air traffic control. It contains articles on current issues involving ATC operations, innovative concepts and applications of technology to ATC, public policy debates impacting ATC, commentary by noted aviation experts and policy makers, ATC historical material, and reviews of books and videos of interest to the aviation community. *$130.00*

60 pages Quarterly Founded: 1956
Circulation: 2900
Printed in 4 colors on matte stock

2175 Journal of Guidance, Control & Dynamics
American Institute of Aeronautics and Astronautics
1801 Alexander Bell Drive
Suite 500
Reston, VA 20191-4344
703-264-7500
FAX: 703-264-7551 800-639-2422
custserv@aiaa.org www.aiaa.org

Donald W Richardson, President
George T Schmidt, Editor-in-Chief

Offers information on guidance control, navigation, electronics and more related to astronautical and aeronautical systems. *$ 675.00*

Fortnightly Founded: 1930
Circulation: 3000

2176 Journal of Propulsion & Power
American Institute of Aeronautics and Astronautics
1801 Alexander Bell Drive
Suite 500
Reston, VA 20191-4344
703-264-7500
FAX: 703-264-7551 800-639-2422
custserv@aiaa.org www.aiaa.org

Donald W Richardson MD, President
Vigor Yang MD, Editor

Offers information on new advances and technology in airbreathing, propulsion systems, fuels, power generation and more. *$730.00*

Fortnightly Founded: 1930
Circulation: 1900

2177 Journal of Rocket Motor and Propellant Developers
California Rocketry Publishing
PO Box 1242
Claremont, CA 91711-1242
626-974-9417
FAX: 626-974-9407
01rocket@gte.net
www.v-serv.com/dpt

Jerry Irvine, Publisher

Technical journal covering propellant formulations, motor design, performance results and methods. Back issues available. *$499.00*

16 pages Annual Founded: 1994
Circulation: 500
Printed in on matte stock

2178 Journal of the American Helicopter Society
American Helicopter Society International

217 N Washington Street
Alexandria, VA 22314-2520
703-684-6777
FAX: 703-739-9279
ahs703@aol.com www.vtol.org

J Gordon Leishman, Editor-in-Chief
Ashis Bagai, Associate Editor

The scope of the Journal covers the full range of research, analysis, design, manufacturing, test, operations, and support. A constantly growing list of specialty areas is included within that scope. Is distributed to the AHS membership for $20.00 and is also available for subscription. *$95.00*

Quarterly

2179 KITPLANES
Light Aircraft Manufacturers Association
22 Deer Oaks Ct
Pleasanton, CA 94588-8233
925-426-0771
FAX: 925-426-0771
info@lama.bz www.lama.bz

Davie Martin, Editor

Experimental-category homebuilt aircraft.

Monthly

2180 Maintenance Update
Helicopter Association International
1635 Prince Street
Alexandria, VA 22314-2818
703-683-4646
FAX: 703-683-4745 www.rotor.com

Marty Lenehan, Publications

Provides a forum for mechanics and technicians to exchange information. It includes regulatory issues, airworthiness directives, aircraft alerts and items of special interest. *$50.00*

Quarterly

2181 Midwest Flyer Magazine
Flyer Publications
PO Box 199
Oregon, WI 53575-199
608-835-7063

weiman@mailbag.com
www.midwestflyer.com

Dave Weinman, Publisher
Dave Weinman, Editor

Reaches all aircraft owners in the Upper Midwest. Articles include flying travel destinations, fly-in restaurants and the issues affecting general aviation in the Midwest and nationwide. *$15.00*

32 pages Founded: 1978

2182 Mx Magazine
Professional Aviation Maintenance Association
717 Princess Street
Alexandria, VA 22314
703-683-3171
FAX: 703-683-0018
hq@pama.org www.pama.org

Peter Rohrbach, Publisher

Flagship publication of Professional Aviation Maintenance Association. Distributed to members and at trade shows across the country.

Quarterly
Printed in 4 colors

2183 NAFI Magazine
National Association of Flight Instructors
PO Box 3086
Oshkosh, WI 54903-3086
920-426-6801
FAX: 920-426-6865
nafi@eaa.org www.nafinet.org

Sean Elliot, President

A monthly magazine published by the National Association of Flight Instructors. *$39.00*

18 pages Monthly Founded: 1967
Circulation: 5400

2184 NAFI Mentor
National Association of Flight Instructors
EAA Aviation Center
PO Box 3086
Oshkosh, WI 54903-3086
920-426-6801
FAX: 920-426-6865
nafi@eaa.org www.nafinet.org

Sean Elliot, President
Rusty Sachs, Executive Director

Membership includes this magazine created exclusively for flight instructors.

20 pages Monthly

2185 NASA Tech Briefs
Associated Business Publications International
1466 Broadway Ste. 910
New York, NY 10036-5201
212-490-3999
FAX: 212-986-7864
cathleen@abpi.net www.nasatech.com

Linda L. Bell, Publisher
Cathleen Lambertson, Editor
Hugh Dowling, Circulation Manager
Domenic Mucchetti, CEO
Zoe Wai, Manager

Features exclusive reports of innovations developed by NASA and its partners that can be applied to develop new and improved products and solve engineering or manufacturing problems. *$49.00*

Monthly Founded: 1985
Circulation: 30000

2186 NBAA Digest
National Business Aviation Association
1200 18th Street NW
Suite 400
Washington, DC 20036-2527
202-783-9000
FAX: 202-331-8364
info@nbaa.org www.nbaa.org

Shelly A Longmuir, President
Edward M. Bolen, CEO/President

Publication covering business aviation news and issues.

8 pages Monthly Founded: 1947
Printed in 4 colors on glossy stock : web

2187 Naval Aviation News
Naval Historical Center
1242 10th Street SE
Washington Navy Yard
Washington, DC 20374-5060
202-433-4407
FAX: 202-433-2343
nanews@nhc.navy.mil
www.history.navy.mil

Wendy Lelend, Managing Editor

Professional magazine of naval aviation. *$21.00*

42 pages Monthly Founded: 1917
Circulation: 25,000
Printed in 4 colors on glossy stock

2188 Ninety-Nines News
Ninety-Nines
4300 Amelia Earhart Road
Oklahoma City, OK 73159-1140
405-685-7969
FAX: 405-685-7985 800-994-1929
99sPrez@ninety-nines.org
www.ninety-nines.org

Pat Prentiss, Vice-President
Elaine Morrow, President
Boby Row, Editor
Liz Lundin, Headquarters Manager

A bi-monthly magazine published by Ninety-Nines. *$20.00*

Founded: 1929
Circulation: 6500

2189 Northwest Airlifter
PO Box 98801
Tacoma, WA 98498
253-584-1212
FAX: 253-581-5962 800-293-1216

Tom Swarner, CEO

Features news, mission stories and entertainment for military personnel and families of McChord AFB.

Weekly

2190 Overhaul & Maintenance
McGraw Hill
1221 Avenue of the Americas
New York, NY 10020-1095
212-122-2000
800-525-5003
p18cs@mcgraw-hill.com
www.awgnet.com

Charles Hull, Publisher

Information for people in airlines, flight departments, maintenance bases, military logistics, issues on safety, quality, and compliance in the aviation aftermarket. *$54.00*

Monthly
Circulation: 35000

2191 Parachutist Magazine
United States Parachute Association
1440 Duke Street
Alexandria, VA 22314-3488
703-836-3495
FAX: 703-836-2843
uspa@uspa.org www.uspa.org

Glen Bangs, President
Jason Bell, Editor

Up-to-date comprehensive reports on the sport of parachuting (skydiving), including coming events, national, international competition championships and techniques. *$4.50*

112 pages Monthly Founded: 1957
Circulation: 35000

2192 Plane and Pilot
Werner Publishing
12121 Wilshire Boulevard 12th Floor
Suite 1220
Los Angeles, CA 90025-1176
310-820-1500
FAX: 310-826-5008
editors@planeandpilotmag.com
www.planeandpilotmag.com

Steve Werner, Editor
Abby Ventzke, Production Manager

Articles on general aviation from light single-engine planes to medium weight twins and related products. *$11.97*

92 pages Monthly Founded: 1965

2193 Professional Pilot
Queensmith Communications
30 S Quaker Lane
Suite 300
Alexandria, VA 22314
703-370-0606
FAX: 703-370-7082
editorial@propilotmag.com
www.propilotmag.com

Murray Smith, Editor/Publisher
Anthony Herrera, General Manager
Phil Rose, Managing Editor
David Stockett, Communications Manager

Offers information for career pilots. *$50.00*

Monthly Founded: 1966
Circulation: 35000
Printed in 4 colors on glossy stock

2194 ROTOR Magazine
Helicopter Association International
1635 Prince Street
Alexandria, VA 22314-2818
703-683-4646
FAX: 703-683-4745 www.rotor.com

Marty Lenehan, Publications

Dedicated to exclusively to the civil helicopter industry. It covers pertinent helicopter operations, safety and regulatory issues including an FAA question and answer column, legislative and lobbying issues, and HAI committee and member activities. Advertising space is available is this publication. Subscription included with membership. *$15.00*

Quarterly

2195 Rotor & Wing
Access Intelligence
4 Choke Cherry Rd
2nd Fl
Rockville, MD 20850-4024
301-354-1400
FAX: 301-340-0542
asteinebach@pbimedia.com
www.aviationtoday.com

Douglas Nelms, Editor
Julian Clover, Managing Editor
Jim McKenna, Manager

Semitechnical information for helicopter industry, both civil and military. Includes pilot reports, features, news and product section. *$90.99*

88 pages Monthly Founded: 1977
Circulation: 33,400

2196 Rotorcraft Magazine
Popular Rotorcraft Association
PO Box 68
Mentone, IN 46539
574-353-7227
FAX: 574-353-7227
prahq@pra.org www.pra.org

Igor Bensen, Founder
Gary Goldsberry, President
Dave Prater, VP
Robert Rymer, Treasurer
Glenn Bundy, Secretary

Devoted exclusively to homebuilt rotorcraft. Free to members. *$26.00*

60 pages Founded: 1963

2197 Russian Aeronautics
Allerton Press
18 W 27th Street
New York, NY 10011
646-249-9686
FAX: 646-424-9695
journals@allertonpress.com
www.allertonpress.com

W Shalof, Publisher
Vyacheslav A Firsov, Editor-in-Chief

English translation of Russian Journal of aerounautical science and engineering. *$1945.00*

Quarterly Founded: 1971

2198 Soaring Magazine
Soaring Society of America
5425 West Jack Gomez Blvd
PO Box 2100
Hobbs, NM 88241-2100
505-392-1177
FAX: 505-392-8154
feedback@ssa.org www.ssa.org

Susan Dew, Staff Writer
Amaris Bradford, Editorial Assistant
Denise Layton, Managing Editor
Dennis Wright, Executive Director

Each issue brings you the latest developments on safety issues, delightful accounts of individual soaring accomplishments, a sharing of ideas and experiences, tips from the great soaring pilots of our times, and much more. *$26.00*

60 pages Monthly Founded: 1932

2199 Space News
Army Times Publishing Company
6883 Commercial Drive
Springfield, VA 22159
703-750-9000
FAX: 703-750-8913 800-368-5718

Elaine Howard, President/CEO
Tobias Naegele, Editor-in-Chief
Alex Neill, Managing Editor
Judy McCoy, Publisher

For top level executives in government and industry worldwide. Devoted exclusively to issues for military government and commercial space. *$55.00*

Weekly Founded: 1990
Circulation: 360000

2200 Space Press
Vernuccio Publications
3148 Fairmount Avenue
Bronx, NY 10465-1415

FV Vernuccio Jr, Publisher
Frank Vernuccio, Editor

Comprehensive, authoritative, international coverage of outer space related news. *$15.00*

20 pages Monthly

2201 Space Times
American Astronautical Society
6352 Rolling Mill Place
Suite 102
Springfield, VA 22152-2354
703-866-0020
FAX: 703-866-3526
aas@astronautical.org
www.astronautical.org

Jonathan T Malay, President
Amy Kaminski, Editor

AAS magazine publishes timely articles for audiences of space professionals and enthusiasts on space technologies and exploration, policy and commercial and military space developments. *$80.00*

24 pages Founded: 1954
Circulation: 1200
Printed in 4 colors on glossy stock

2202 Trade-A-Plane
TAP Publishing Company
174 4th Street
Crossville, TN 38555-4303
931-484-5137
FAX: 931-484-2532 800-337-5263
info@trade-a-plane.com
www.trade-a-plane.com
Cosby Stone, Publisher
L Stone, Circulation Manager
World's largest advertising periodical for general aviation. *$14.95*
Monthly Founded: 1937
Circulation: 118000

2203 Ultralight Flying
Glider Rider
PO Box 6009
Chattanooga, TN 37401
423-629-5378
FAX: 423-629-5379
www.ultralightflying.com
Tracy Knauss, Publisher
Sharon Hill, Editor
Conventional and motorized ultralight flying. *$36.95*
48 pages Monthly Founded: 1973
Circulation: 50000+
Printed in on newsprint stock

2204 Vertiflite
American Helicopter Society International
217 N Washington Street
Alexandria, VA 22314-2520
703-684-6777
FAX: 703-739-9279
staff@vtol.org www.vtol.org
Rhett Flater, Publisher
Kim Smith, Editor
Mike Hirschberg, Managing Editor
Magazine published for the vertical flight industry, pursuing excellence within the business, stimulating research, debate and expert opinion. *$80.00*
72 pages Monthly Founded: 1943
Circulation: 12000
Printed in 4 colors on glossy stock

2205 Vintage Airplane
Experimental Aircraft Association
PO Box 3086
Oshkosh, WI 54903-3086
920-264-4800
FAX: 920-426-6865 888-322-4636
vintageaircraft@eaa.org
www.vintageaircraft.org
H G Fraupschy, Executive Director
Geoff Robinson, President
Devoted to all aspects of antique and classic aircraft. *$36.00*
32 pages Monthly Founded: 1971
Circulation: 10,000

2206 Water Flying
Seaplane Pilots Association
4315 Highland Park Boulevard
Suite C
Lakeland, FL 33813-1639
863-701-7979
FAX: 863-701-7588 888-772-8923
spa@seaplanes.org
www.seaplanes.org
Roger C Myers Jr, Publisher
Mark Twombly, Editor
Michael E. Volk, President
Features articles covering everything from pilot technique and safety to destinations and personalities. Each issue includes industry news and an update on regulatory issues across the country. The March/April issue is our Directory Special, with flight school and float directories. *$45.00*
32 pages Founded: 1972
Circulation: 7500
Printed in on glossy stock

2207 Western Flyer
Northwest Flyer
PO Box 98786
Tacoma, WA 98498-0786
253-968-3422
FAX: 253-588-4005
Dave Sinclair, Publisher
Kirk Gormley, Editor
Covering general aviation, including all aspects of business and sport aviation. *$24.00*
84 pages BiWeekly
Circulation: 38,000

2208 Wings
Sentry Books
4426 Deseret Drive
Woodland Hills, CA 91364-4699
818-368-2012
www.wingsairpower.com
Mike Machat, Publisher/Editor
Historic aviation, heavy on photos, artwork, drawings, interviews with aviation designers, pilots, engineers. *$44.00*
56 pages Monthly Founded: 1971
Circulation: 30000 4000 names $450 per M.

2209 Wings West
Wiesner Publishing
7009 S Potomac Street
Suite 200
Centennial, CO 80112
303-397-7600
FAX: 303-397-7619
www.wiesnerpublishing.com
Babette Andre, Editor
Becky Stairs, Advertising Executive
Information for the mountain aviation community on various facets of western flying, including travel and safety for active pilots. *$17.97*
72 pages Bi-Monthly

2210 Wings of Gold Magazine
Association of Naval Aviation
2550 Huntington Avenue
Suite 201
Alexandria, VA 22303-1400
703-960-2490
FAX: 703-960-4490
ana@anahq.org www.anahq.org
R M Rausa, Editor
Hal Andrews, Consulting Editor
Linda Bubien, Advertising Director
Jacqueline M Hayes, Editorial Assistant
Articles and commentary designed to inform the pubiic of the value of a strong maritime air posture to US national policy. Also, articles on subjects related to Navy, Marine Corps and Coast Guard aviation, such as personnel technology, history, readiness, aircraft and weapon systems and budgetary issues within DOD and before the Congress. *$25.00*

2211 World Airshow News
Flyer Publications
PO Box 199
Oregon, WI 53575-199
608-835-7063
migbird@aol.com
www.worldairshownews.com
Sandra Ruka, Business Administrator
Jeff Parnau, Editor/Publisher
Kyle Vaculik, Production Manager
Reaches all known airshows and military bases regardless of organization affiliation. *$19.95*
68 pages Monthly Founded: 1986
Circulation: 4000+

Trade Shows

2212 Aerofast SAE Aerospace Automated Fastening Conference & Exposition
Society of Automotive Engineers
400 Commonwealth Drive
Warrendale, PA 15096-0001
724-772-8548
FAX: 412-776-0210
meetings@sae.org www.sae.org
Diane Applegate, Meetings/Exhibits
Annual show of 45 manufacturers or suppliers of fasteners, assembly systems, CNC's, tooling and fixtures, fully automated systems.
400 Attendees September Founded: 1990

2213 Aeronautical Repair Staion Association Sym posium
121 N Henry Street
Alexandria, VA 22314-2903
703-739-9543
FAX: 703-739-9488
arsa@arsa.org www.arsa.org
Gary H Garvens, President
Bernard E Rookey, Senior VP
Sarah MacLeod, Executive Director
Marshall S Filler, Managing Director/General Counsel
Ian Cheyne, Treasurer
Helps you learn directly from industry experts and national aviation authorities, the National Transportation Safety Board and other agency representatives. The Symposium convenes each spring in the Washington, DC area. Members receive substantial registration discounts.

2214 Aerospace Atlantic
Society of Automotive Engineers
400 Commonwealth Drive
Warrendale, PA 15096-0001
724-772-8548
FAX: 724-776-4026
advertising@sae.org www.sae.org
Drew Kessler, President
Annual show of 30 exhibitors of aircraft systems and components, engineering services, electronics, power systems and computer services.
700 Attendees 84,000 Members

2215 Aerospace Medical Association Annual Scientific Meeting
Aerospace Medical Association
320 S Henry Street
Alexandria, VA 22314-3579
703-739-2240
FAX: 703-739-9652 www.asma.org

Russell B Rayman MD, Executive Director
Gloria Carter, Membership Director
Pamela Day, Managing Editor

Annual show of 50-90 exhibitors for aviation medical examiners, scientists and bioengineers engaged in biomedical research, physicians and nurses of Aerospace Medical Association.

3000 Attendees
Mailing list available for rent

2216 Aerospace Medical Association Meeting
320 S Henry Street
Alexandria, VA 22314-3579
703-392-2240
FAX: 703-739-9652 www.asma.org

Kristofer S Herlitz, Exhibit Services
Russell Rayman, Executive Director

Provides a multi-faceted forum for all aerospace medical disciplines and concurrently provides continuing education credits for those attending the meeting. Lectures, seminars, panels, poster presentations, workshops, film reports, and technical and scientific exhibits present data on the latest results of clinical and research studies.

May

2217 Aerospace Testing Expo
Society of Flight Test Engineers
44814 N Elm Avenue
Lancaster, CA 93534
661-949-2095
FAX: 661-949-2096
sfte@sfte.org www.sfte.org

John L Minor, President
Harold E Weaver, VP
Margaret Drury, Executive Director
Joseph T Dagata, Jr, Treasurer
Robert N Burton, Secretary

April

2218 Aerotech: Society of Automotive Engineers Aerospace Technology Congress
Society of Automotive Engineers
400 Commonwealth Drive
Warrendale, PA 15096-0001
724-772-8548
FAX: 724-776-4026
advertising@sae.org www.sae.org

Diane Applegate, Meetings/Exhibition

Annual show of 80 suppliers to aerospace engineers and designers.

2500 Attendees October

2219 Agricultural Aviation Convention
National Agricultural Aviation Association

1005 E Street SE
Washington, DC 20003
202-546-5722
FAX: 202-546-5267
information@agaviation.org
www.agaviation.org

Andrew Moore, Executive Dir./Government Relations

Information on agricultural aviation business, agricultural aircraft, legislative issues, pesticides, new products and services, safety, maintenance, people, state and regional association news. 135 booths.

1300 Attendees

2220 Air Cargo Forum and Exposition
The International Air Cargo Association
PO Box 661510
Miami, FL 33266-1510
786-265-7011
FAX: 786-265-7012
secgen@tiaca.org www.tiaca.org

Tom\ Davis, Deputy Director, Exhibits

This is the premier show for the Air Cargo Industry.

3000 Attendees September

2221 Air Medical Transport Conference
Association of Air Medical Services
526 King Street
Suite 415
Alexandria, VA 22314-3143
703-836-8732
FAX: 703-836-8920
information@aams.org www.aams.org

Natasha Ross, Education/Meetings Director
Blair Marie Beggan, Communications/Marketing Director
Natasha Ross, Education/Meetings Manager
Melissa Porter, Membership Manager

Attendees are emergency medical and critical care professionals from both hospital and independent providers of air and ground medical transport services. CEO's, program directors, medical directors, physicians, nurses, respiratory therapists, paramedics, pilots, communication specialists and mechanics. *$300.00*

1800 Attendees Annual/Fall Founded: 1980
Mailing list available for rent 1600 names

2222 Air Show Trade Expo International

Dayton International Airport
3600 Terminal Drive
Suite 300
Vandalia, OH 45377
937-454-8200
FAX: 937-898-5121 877-359-3291
info@daytonairshow.com
www.daytonairshow.com

Terry Greivous, Executive Director
Nan Holler-Potter, Air Show Coordinator

One hundred and thirty three booths that encompass all aspects of the global aerospace industry. Commercial and military aircraft and equipment, plus major suppliers' products and services display.

12M Attendees July

2223 Air Traffic Control Association Convention
Air Traffic Control Association
2300 Clarendon Boulevard
Suite 711
Arlington, VA 22201
703-522-5717
FAX: 703-527-7251
arca@worldnett.att.net www.atca.org

Carol Newmaster, Senior VP/Show Manager

Containing over 325 booths and exhibits of air traffic control products and services.

4,500 Attendees 3 times per year

2224 Aircraft Electronics Association Annual Convention & Trade Show
Aircraft Electronics Association
4217 S Hocker
Independence, MO 64055
816-373-6565
FAX: 816-478-3100
info@aea.net www.aea.net

Paula Derks, President
Debra McFarland, VP

Annual show of 131 exhibitors of industry related equipment and supplies.

1500 Attendees March/April Annual
Founded: 1957

2225 Aircraft Electronics Association Trade Sho w
4217 S Hocker Drive
Independence, MO 64055
816-373-6565
FAX: 816-478-310
info@aea.net www.aea.net

Paula Derks, President
Debbie McFarland, VP
Mark Gibson, Information Services Director
Mike Adamson, Director Training/Education

April

2226 Aircraft Owners & Pilots Association Expo
421 Aviation Way
Frederick, MD 21701
301-695-2000
FAX: 301-695-2375 800-872-2672
phil.boyer@aopa.org www.aopa.org

Phil Boyer, President

From the latest technology, to tools and flight gear, you'll find today's best products. 500 Exhibit Booths.

June

2227 Aircraft Owners Pilots Association Expo
Aircraft Owners & Pilots Association
421 Aviation Way
Frederick, MD 21701
301-695-2000
FAX: 301-695-2375 888-462-3976

Phil Boyer, President

Annual exhibits of single-engine and multi-engine aircraft, avionics, financing information and related equipment, supplies and services. Expo offers 75 seminar hours covering the latest safety, medical, proficiency, ownership, and technology issues. Over 500 booths.

November

2228 Airliners International Convention
World Airline Historical Society
13739 Picarsa Drive
Jacksonville, FL 32225
904-221-1446
FAX: 786-331-7024
information@wahsonline.com
www.wahsonline.com

Duane Young, President
Craig Morris, VP
Jay Prall, Secretary/Treasurer
Bill Demarest, LOG Editor

Attracts over 1,000 airline collectible enthusiasts from around the world.

July

2229 Airlines Electronic Engineering Committee Conference
Airlines Electronic Engineering Committee
2551 Riva Road
Annapolis, MD 21401-7435
410-266-4000
FAX: 410-266-2047 www.arinc.com

Daniel A Martinec, Chairman
Roger S Goldberg, Show Contact

Annual show and exhibit of air transport avionics equipment and systems.

October

2230 Airport Consultants Council Workshops
908 King Street
Suite 100
Alexandria, VA 22314-3121
703-683-5900
FAX: 703-583-2564
info@acconline.org
www.acconline.org

Paula P Hochstetler, President
Anthony N Mavrogiannis, VP
Stephen V Berardo, Institute Director
Cassandra Lamar, Director Programs/Marketing
Sharon D Brown, Operations Manager

July

2231 Airport Consultants Council's Institute Ai rport Essentials Expo
908 King Street
Suite 100
Alexandria, VA 22314-3121
703-683-5900
FAX: 703-683-2564
info@acconline.org
www.acconline.org

Paula P Hochstetler, President
Anthony N Mavrogiannis, VP
Stephen V Berardo, Institute Director
Cassandra Lamar, Director Programs/Marketing
Sharon D Brown, Operations Manager

June

2232 Airport Systems Action Planning Meeting
ARINC
2551 Riva Road
Annapolis, MD 21401
410-664-4000
FAX: 410-266-2020 800-633-6882
flightops@arinc.com www.arinc.com

Frederic J Jacoby, Chairman
John M Belcher, Chairman/CEO
Richard F Jones, VP Business Operations/CFO
Linda Hartwig, Sr Dir Corporate Communications

The meeting format will include organizational, technical, and project updates from the ARINC management team.

September

2233 Airports Association Council International Conference
1775 K Street NW
Suite 500
Washington, DC 20036-2463
202-293-8500
FAX: 202-331-1362 www.aci-na.org

Gregory Principato, President
Nancy Zimini, VP
Richard F Marchi, SVP Technical Affairs
Ian A Redhead, VP Airport Services
Patricia Hahn, EVP Operations/General Counsel

September

2234 Airports Consultants Council Conference
908 King Street
Suite 100
Alexandria, VA 22314-3121
703-683-5900
FAX: 703-683-2564
info@acconline.org
www.acconline.org

Paula P Hochstetler, President
Anthony N Mavrogiannis, VP
Stephen V Berardo, Institute Director
Cassandra Lamar, Director Programs/Marketing
Sharon D Brown, Operations Manager

November

2235 Airports Council International: North America Convention
Airports Council International-North America
1775 K Street NW
Suite 500
Washington, DC 20006
202-293-8500
FAX: 202-331-1362 www.aci-na.org

John Rodgers, Director
Amy Peters, Sr Director Conferences/Exhibitions
Juliet Wright, Senior Director Public Relations
Gregory Principato, President

Annual show and exhibit of air transportation equipment, supplies and services.

Annual

2236 American Association of Airport Executives Conference & Exposition
American Association of Airport Executives
601 Madison Street
Suite 400
Alexandria, VA 22314
703-824-0500
FAX: 703-820-1395
member.services@airportnet.org
www.airportnet.org

Charles Barclay, President
Spencer Dickerson, Senior VP
Todd Hauptli, Senior Executive VP
Susan Lausch, VP Sales/Marketing

Three exhibits from manufacturers, suppliers and distributors of aviation equipment and services. Seminar, workshop & conference.

3000 Attendees May Founded: 1928

2237 American Bonanza Society Convention
Midcontinent Airport
PO Box 12888
Wichita, KS 67277
316-945-1700
FAX: 316-945-1710
bonanza2@bonanza.org
www.bonanza.org

Nancy Johnson, Executive Director
Peggy L Fuksa, Events Coordinator

Annual convention featuring educational seminars and 75-100 exhibits of equipment, supplies and services for the aviation industry, including aftermarket products, safety items and computer weather services.

1200 Attendees September Founded: 1967

2238 American Helicopter Society International Annual Convention
217 N Washington Street
Alexandria, VA 22314-2520
703-684-6777
FAX: 703-739-9279
ahs703@aol.com www.vtol.org

ME Rhett Flater, Executive Director
L Kim Smith, Deputy Director/Production Mgr

Exhibits for technical professionals in aircraft design, engineering, government, operators and industry executives.

6M Attendees Founded: 1943

2239 American Institute of Aeronautics & Astron autics Meeting
1801 Alexander Bell Drive
Suite 500
Reston, VA 20191-4344
703-264-7500
FAX: 703-264-7551 800-639-2422
customerserv@aiaa.org www.aiaa.org

Cort Durocher, President

One hundred and fifty exhibitors displaying equipment supplies and services for the aerospace industry.

January/Annual Founded: 1930

2240 Annual Convention & Fly In
Pipers Owner Society
PO Box 5000
Iola, WI 54945
715-445-5000
FAX: 715-445-4053 866-687-4137

Skip Carden, Executive Director

July

2241 Annual European Business Aviation Convention & Exhibition
National Business Aviation Association
1200 18th Street NW
Suite 400
Washington, DC 20036-2527
202-783-9000
FAX: 202-331-8364
info@nbaa.org www.nbaa.org

Kenneth E Emerick, Chairman
Edward M Bolen, President/CEO
Jeffrey W Lee, Treasurer
Sandy Murdock, Corporate Secretary

The only European exhibition of its kind to focus totally on business aviation, EBACE is organized jointly by the European Business Aviation Association(EBAAA) and National Business Aviation Association (NBAA).

May

2242 Army Aviation Association of America Convention
Army Aviation Association of America
755 Main Street
Suite 4D
Monroe, CT 06468-2830
203-268-2450
FAX: 203-268-5870
bob@quard-a.org www.quad-a.org

William Harris, Publisher

A show of 275 or more exhibitors both military and industry displaying technology and material pertinent to the army aviation community.

6000 Attendees Annual/May, 2007
Founded: 1978

2243 Arnic Aviation Customer Meeting
British Telecommunications
2551 Riva Road
Annapolis, MD 21401

FAX: 410-266-2020 800-633-6882
flightops@arinc.com www.arinc.com

Frederic J Jacoby, Chairman
John M Belcher, Chairman/CEO
Richard F Jones, VP Business Operations/CFO
Linda Hartwig, Sr Dir Corporate Communications

Up to date information on the current and future products and services of Arnic and its strategic partners in Asia.

May

2244 **Arnic Global Communications Workshop**
British Telecommunications
2551 Riva Road
Annapolis, MD 21401

FAX: 410-266-2020 800-633-6882
flightops@arinc.com www.arinc.com
Frederic J Jacoby, Chairman
John M Belcher, Chairman/CEO
Richard F Jones, VP Business Operations/CFO
Linda Hartwig, Sr Dir Corporate Communications
Concentrates on the communications needs of the airlines serving the Latin America/Carribbean region, and provides information on the benefits of implementing a data link program and associated applications.
May

2245 **Asian Business Aviation Conference & Exhibition**
National Busness Aviation Association
1200 18th Street NW
Suite 400
Washington, DC 20036-2527
202-783-9000
FAX: 202-331-8364
info@nbaa.org www.nbaa.org
Kenneth E Emerick, Chairman
Edward M Bolen, President/CEO
Jeffrey W Lee, Treasurer
Sandy Murdock, Corporate Secretary
Globally, tens of thousands of companies, governments and organizations already use business aircraft daily to daramatically increase employee productivity, expand maekets, secure competitive advantages, induce operational efficiency, offset company expenses and improve risk management.
August

2246 **Association of Air Medical Services Confer ence**
526 King Street
Suite 415
Alexandria, VA 22314-3143
703-836-8732
FAX: 703-836-8920
information@aams.org www.aams.org
Dawn M Mancuso, CAE, Executive Director
Natasha Ross, Education/Meeetings Manager
Will be offering a unique education session with a focus on clinical training and readiness, with a special interest in trauma training.
March

2247 **Astrodynamics Specialist Conference**
American Astronautical Society
6352 Rolling Mill Place
Suite 102
Springfield, VA 22152-2354
703-866-0020
FAX: 703-866-3526
aas@astronautical.org
www.astronautical.org
Kathleen Howell, Chairman
Jonathan T Malay, President
Mark K Craig, Executive VP
James R Kirkpatrick, Director
Shannon Coffey, VP Finance
Summer

2248 **Aviation Distributors and Management Meeti ng**
1900 Arch Street
Philadelphia, PA 19103-1404
215-564-3484
FAX: 215-564-2175 www.adma.org
H George Maxwell, President
Mark Morrow, VP
Talbot H Gee, Executive Director
Patricia Lilly, Management Liaison
Vaughn E Wurst, Membership Director
May, November

2249 **Aviation Insurance Association Conference**
14 W 3rd Street
Suite 200
Kansas City, MO 64105-6301
816-221-8488
FAX: 816-472-7765
tfry@ameritech.net www.aiaweb.org
Shelby Diltz, Conference Director
550 Attendees April

2250 **Aviation Services and Suppliers Supershow**
National Air Transportation Association
4226 King Street
Alexandria, VA 22302
703-845-9000
FAX: 703-845-8176 800-808-6282
csipes@nata-online.org www.nata.aero

James K Coyne, President
Alan Darrow, VP
Diane Gleason, Manager Meetings/Conventions
Eric R Byer, Dir Government/Industry Affairs
Workshop, conference, seminar and 700 exhibits of aviation products & services for fixed base and air charter operators.
5000 Attendees May/Annual

2251 **Aviation Show South America**
American Aerospace & Defense Industries

212 Carengie Center
Suite 203
Princeton, NJ 08540
609-987-9050
FAX: 609-987-0277
info@aadi.net www.aadi.net
Marianne Ferrandi, Show Contact
One hundred and seven exhibitors of areospace information.
90000 Attendees July

2252 **Aviation Technician Education Council Conference**
Aviation Technician Education Council
2090 Wexford Court
Harrisburg, PA 17112-1579
717-540-7121
FAX: 717-540-7121
info@atec-amt.org www.atec-amt.org
Vince Jones, President
Richard Dumaresq, Executive Director
Annual conference and exhibits of aviation maintenance equipment, supplies and services.
150 Attendees April

2253 **Business Information Meeting of the Airpor ts Association Council**
1775 K Street NW
Suite 500
Washington, DC 20036-2463
202-293-8500
FAX: 202-331-1362 www.aci0na.org
Gregory Principato, President
We discuss the most recent trends and innovations in wireless technology as it applies to airports and aviation. Attendees include IT directors from US and Canadian airports.
May

2254 **Civil Air Patrol**
105 S Hansell Street
Building 714
Maxwell AFB, AL 36112-6332
334-834-2236
FAX: 334-953-4262 www.capnhq.gov
Don Rowland, Executive Director
Dwight Wheless, National Commander
Mark Richardson, Director Plans/Programs
Annual conference brings over 1,000 of the most dedicated Civil Air Patrol members from across the nation together to attend seminars and workshops, network with each other and the headquarters staff, and have fun.
1.2M Attendees August Founded: 1930

2255 **Civil Aviation Medical Association Conference**
Civil Aviation Medical Association
PO Box 23864
Oklahoma City, OK 73123-3864
405-840-0199
FAX: 405-848-1053
jimlharris@aol.com
www.civilavmed.com
David Bryman, President
James L Harris, Executive VP
Gordon Ritter, Secretary/Treasurer
Annual conference and exhibits of aviation medical equipment, supplies and services. Containing 15 booths.
250 Attendees October Founded: 1948

2256 **Defense & Security Symposium**
International Society for Optical Engineering
PO Box 10
Bellingham, WA 98227-0010
360-676-3290
FAX: 360-647-1445
spie@spie.org www.spie.org
Dr John C Carrano, Contact Person
Dr Larry B Stotts, Contact Person
Bonnie Peterson, Event Project Manager
A large, unclassified international symposium related to sensors and sensor networks.
5700 Attendees March

2257 **Economic Specialty Conference**
Airports Association Council International
1775 K Street NW
Suite 500
Washington, DC 20036-2463
202-293-8500
FAX: 202-331-1362 www.aci-na.org
Gregory Principato, President
Nancy Zimini, VP
Richard F Marchi, SVP Technical Affairs
Ian A Redhead, VP Airport Services
Patricia Hahn, EVP Operations/General Counsel
Provided with information on the latest economic trends for airports and the airport industry. Attendees include executive directors and CFOs from airports thoughout North America, plys representatives from insurance companies and airport concessionaires.
May

2258 **Experimental Aircraft Association AirVentu re**
Experimental Aircraft Association
EAA Aviation Center
PO Box 3086
Oshkosh, WI 54903
920-426-4800
FAX: 920-232-7772 800-236-4800
convention@eaa.org
www.airventure.org

Tom Poberezny, President
Earl Lawrence, VP Government/Indusry Affairs
John Tennyson, VP Corporate Sponsorship

Recreational aviation event, with more than 765,000 people and 10,000 airplanes attending. Containing 900 booths and 730 exhibits.

765M Attendees Founded: 1953

2259 **Florida Space**
Space Foundation
310 South 14th Street
Colorado Springs, CO 80904
719-768-8000
FAX: 719-576-8801 800-691-4000
web@spacefoundcation.org
www.spacefoundation.org

Elliot G Pulham, President/CEO
Robert S Walker, Chairman
Steve Eisanhart, SVP Policy & Public Affairs
Stephanie Fibbs, Communications/Media Relations

Florida Space serves Florida's diverse space community, including civil, commercial, national security and education sectors spread across the entire Sunshine State. This conference builds on the best features of Space Congress and the Cape Canaveral Spaceport Symposium, both long-time community space events now retired.

1000 Attendees December

2260 **Helicopter Association International**
1635 Prince Street
Alexandria, VA 22314-2818
703-683-4646
FAX: 703-683-4745 www.rotor.com

Matthew Zuccaro, President
Elizabeth W Meade, Executive VP/Corporate Secretary
Bill Wright, Administrative Services Manager

Regarded throughout the world as the voice of the civil helicopter industry, the HAI represents helicopter owners, operators, affiliated companies, and helicopter enthusiasts.

11M Attendees February

2261 **IFSA Global Leadership Conference - Asia Pacific**
International Inflight Food Service Association
5775 Peachtree-Dunwoody Road
Suite 500
Atlanta, GA 30342
404-252-3663
FAX: 404-252-0774
ifsa@kellencompany.com
www.ifsanet.com

Michael J Currie, Chairman
Sandra Pineau, President
Kenneth Samara, VP
Vicky Stennens, Secretary
Pam Chumley, Executive Administrator

September

2262 **IFSA Global Leadership Conference - Latin America**
International Inflight Food Service Association
575 Peachtree-Dunwoody Road
Suite 500
Atlanta, GA 30342
404-252-3663
FAX: 404-252-0774
ifsa@kellencompany.com
www.ifsanet.com

John G Long, Chairman
Michael J Currie, President
Sandra Pineau, VP
Jim Fowler, Executive Director
Bill Braun, Managing Director Operations

December

2263 **Inflight Food Service Association Show**
304 W Liberty Street
Suite 201
Louisville, KY 40202-3011
502-583-3783
FAX: 502-589-3602 www.ifsanet.com

Michael J Currie, President
Sharon Collins, Director of Meetings

Annual show and exhibits of airline catering equipment, supplies and services.

April

2264 **International Air Cargo Forum & Exposition**
International Air Cargo Association
5600 NW 36th Street
Suite 620
Miami, FL 33266-1510
786-265-7011
FAX: 786-265-7012
secgen@tiaca.org www.tiaca.org

Larry Coyne, Chairman
Dora Kay, President
George F Johnson, Treasurer
Daniel F Fernandez, Secretary General

Biennial trade show of the air cargo industry featuring services and products from aircraft manufacturers, airlines, airports, freight forwarders trade publications logistics consultants.

4,000 Attendees September Founded: 1960

2265 **International Society of Women Airline Pil ots Convention**
ISA + 21, 2250 E Tropicana Avenue
Suite 19-395
Las Vegas, NV 89119-6594

tianad777@aol.com www.iswap.org

Cammy McHenry, Show Contact

2266 **Joint Airports Environmental/Technical Com mittee Meeting**
Airports Association Council International
1775 K Street NW
Suite 500
Washington, DC 20036-2463
202-293-8500
202-331-1362

Gregory Principato, President
Nancy Zimini, VP
Richard F Marchi, SVP Technical Affairs
Ian A Redhead, VP Airport Services
Patricia Hahn, EVP Operations/General Counsel

May

2267 **Lighter Than Air Society Meeting**
526 S Main Street
Suite 232
Akron, OH 44311-3311
330-355-5827

suggest@blimpinfo.com
www.blimpinfo.com

Joseph Huber, President

April

2268 **National Air Transportation Association Meeting**
4226 King Street
Alexandria, VA 22302-1507
703-845-9000
FAX: 703-845-8176 800-808-6282
info@nata-online.org www.nata.aero

Diane Gleason, Manager Meetings/Conventions
James Coyne, President

Designed to promote a strong relationship with its members and to provide them with educational opportunities, including regular workshops, shows and seminars.

June

2269 **National Business Aviation Association Mee ting**
1200 18th Street NW
Suite 400
Washington, DC 20036-2527
202-783-9000
FAX: 702-331-8364
info@nbaa.org www.nbaa.org

Kenneth E Emerick, Chairman
Edward M Bolen, President/CEO
Jeffery W Lee, Treasurer
Sandy Murdock, Corporate Secretary

This annual event is the business aviation industry's largest and most efficient annual gathering of buyers and sellers.

31259 Attendees November

2270 **National Space Symposium**
Space Foundation
310 South 14th Street
Colorado Springs, CO 80904
719-768-8000
FAX: 719-576-8801 800-691-4000
web@spacefoundation.org
www.spacefoundation.org

Robert S Walker, Chairman
Elliot G Pulham, President/CEO
Stephanie Fibbs, Communications/Media Relations

The National Space Symposium is the premier U.S. policy and program forum, providing an opportunity for information and interaction on all sectors of space - civil, commercial, and national security. The conference is attended by industry leaders, military and government officials and general space enthusiasts, and covered locally and nationally by broadcast, print and industry trade media.

Annually/April

2271 **Ninety Nines International Conference**
International Organization of Women Pilots
4300 Amelia Earhart Road
Oklahoma City, OK 73159-1140
405-685-7969
FAX: 405-685-7985 800-994-1929
99s@ninety-nines.org
www.ninety-nines.org

Elaine Morrow, President
Pat Prentiss, VP
Martha Dunbar, Director

Liz Lundin, Headquarters Manager
Donna Moore, Secretary
August

2272 Popular Rotorcraft Association Convention
Popular Rotorcraft Association
PO Box 68
Mentone, IN 46539
574-353-7227
FAX: 574-353-7227
prahq@pra.org www.pra.org
Igor Bensen, Founder
Gary Goldsberry, President
Dave Prater, VP
Robert Rymer, Treasurer
Glenn Bundy, Secretary
The largest gathering of homebuilt rotorcraft in the world. It has exhibits, flight demonstrations, contests, commercial exhibits, great food, forums on rotorcraft topics, and unlimited fun!
July

2273 Professional Aviation Maintenance Symposium and Trade Show
Professional Aviation Maintenance Association
Ronald Regan Washington National Airport
Washington, DC 20001
202-300-0258
FAX: 202-367-2170 www.pama.org
Jill Hilgenberg, Show Director
Annual show of 200 exhibitors of aviation and aerospace products for the aviation maintenance industry.
2000 Attendees March

2274 Professional Aviation Maintenance Associat ion Symposium
717 Princess Street
Alexandria, VA 22314
703-683-3171
FAX: 703-683-0018 866-865-7262
hq@pama.org www.pama.org
David Orcutt, Chairman
Clark Gordon, Vice Chairman
Brian Finnegan, President
Gerry Goguen, Director
Sal Agosta, Treasurer
Offers you a full day and multi-hour sessions, taught by leading industry experts. In all, over 100 hours of technical training sessions! In order to receive IA/AMT Awards credit for attending qualified PAMA technical sessions, you must be registered for the PAMA Symposium.
March

2275 Regional Airline Association Convention
2025 M Street NW
Suite 800
Washington, DC 20036
202-367-1170
FAX: 202-367-2170
raa@dc.sba.com www.raa.org
David Corson, Convention Manager
Debbie McElroy, President
A forum for airport and airline professionals held twice a year in the spring and fall.
May 23-26

2276 Regional Airline Association Spring Meeting
Regional Airline Association
2025 M Street NW
Washington, DC 20036
202-367-1170

raa@dc.sba.com www.raa.org
Debbie McElroy, President
Forum for airport and airline professionals.
1.6M Attendees May

2277 Reliability Engineering & Management Institute
University Of Arizona
6801 South Tucson Boulevard
Tucson, AZ 85706
520-621-6120
FAX: 520-621-8191
dimitri@u.arizona.edu
Dr Dimitri Kececioglu PE, Prof Aerospace/Mech Engineering
An institute to help provide a working knowledge in reliabilty engineering.
November

2278 Reliability Engineering and Management Ins titute Conference
Univ of Arizona, Aerospace & Mechanical Engin Dept
Building 119
Tucson, AZ 85721-0119
520-621-6120
FAX: 520-621-8191
dimitri@u.arizona.edu
www.u.arizona.edu/~dimitri
Dr Dimitri B Kececioglu, Manager
Provides all engineers, and particularly Reliability Managers and Engineers, and Products Assurance Managers and Engineers in government and Industry, with a working knowledge of Reliability Engineering Theory and Practice; Mechanical Reliability Prediction; Reliability Testing and Demonstration; Failure Analysis (FAMECA); Complete Industry Product Assurance strategies; Maintainability Engineering; Reliability and Quality Management; Manufacturing Techniques, and more.
Nov Arizona

2279 Reliability Testing Institute
University Of Arizona
6801 South Tucson Boulevard
Tucson, AZ 85706
520-621-6120
FAX: 520-621-8191
dimitri@u.arizona.edu
Dr Dimitri Kececioglu PE, Prof Aerospace/Mech Engineering
An institute to help provide a working knowledge in reliabilty engineering.
May

2280 SAFE Symposium
SAFE Association
PO Box 130
Creswell, OR 97426-0130
541-895-3012
FAX: 514-895-3014
safe@peak.org
www.safeassociation.com
Joe Spinosa, Chairman
Ed McDonald, President
Christy Cornette, VP
Mark I Darrah, Executive Advisor
Robert Billings, Treasurer
The Symposium provides an internationally attended marketplace for the exchange of technical information, product and service exhibitions, and the showcasing of industry capabilities for meeting challenges in vehicular occupant protection and personnel worn safety equipment.
October

2281 Sea-Air-Space
Navy League of the United States
11208 Waples Mill Road
Fairfax, VA 22030
703-631-6200
FAX: 703-654-6931 800-564-4220
info@jspargo.com www.jspargo.com
Paul doCarmo, Assistant Director/Exhibit Sales
Connie Shaw, Exhibit Sales Account Manager
Annual event to help promote and develop a technologically advanced naval force.
6000 Attendees April

2282 Seaplane Pilots Association Conference
4315 Highland Park Boulevard
Suite C
Lakeland, FL 33813-1639
863-701-7979
FAX: 863-701-7588 888-772-8923
spa@seaplanes.org www.seaplanes.org

Mike Volk, President
Robert Murray, Executive Director
Thirty booths and conference.
1.5M Attendees September

2283 Soaring Society of America Convention
5425 West Jack Gomez Blvd
PO Box 2100
Hobbs, NM 88241-2100
505-392-1177
FAX: 505-392-8154
feedback@ssa.org www.ssa.org
Gaynell Temple, Convention/Events Coordinator
C Wright, Executive Director
February

2284 Society Automotive Engineers Aerospace Technology Conference and Expo
400 Commonwealth Drive
Warrendale, PA 15086-7511
724-772-8544
FAX: 724-776-5760 www.sae.org
Diane Applegate, Meetings/Conferences
One hundred booths of aerospace and related products.
3.5M Attendees September

2285 Society Automotive Engineers General Aviation Aircraft Marketing Expo
400 Commonwealth Drive
Warrendale, PA 15086-7511
724-772-8544
FAX: 724-776-5760 www.sae.org
Arthur Weldy, Show Manager
One hundred booths featuring parts and components for the aviation industry.
3M Attendees May

2286 Society for the Advancement of Material & Process Engineers Symposium
1161 Park View Drive
Covina, CA 91724-3748
626-331-0616
FAX: 626-332-8929 800-562-7360
sampeibo@aol.com www.sampe.org

Symposium topics on leading-edge advanced materials technology with a strong focus on diversification and technology transfer, customers from every type of material and process engineering application — from acrospace to sporting goods to biomedical. Over 45 technical educational sessions and tutorials.
May

2287 Society of Automotive Engineers: Aerotech Expo
Society of Automotive Engineers
400 Commonwealth Drive
Warrendale, PA 15096-0001
724-772-8548
FAX: 724-776-4026
advertising@sae.org www.sae.org
Diane Applegate, Meetings/Conventions
Exhibits of commercial, military, business and general aviation.

2288 Society of Experimental Test Pilots
Society of Experimental Test Pilots
44814 Elm Avenue
PO Box 986
Lancaster, CA 93584
661-942-9574
FAX: 661-940-0398 www.step.org
Amanda Seal, Events Manager
Anne Smith, Events/Publicity Coordinator
These conferences provide major forums for the discussion of aspects of tax, accounting, administration, statute and case law, which are of general concern to practitioners, as well as providing advance knowledge of developments affecting trusts, estates and subjects of allied subjects. Twenty Booths.
1.5M Attendees September

2289 Society of Flight Test Engineers Conferenc e
44814 N Elm Avenue
Lancaster, CA 93534
661-949-2095
FAX: 661-949-2096
sfte@sfte.org www.sfte.org
John L Minor, President
Harold E Weaver, VP
Margaret Drury, Executive Director
Joseph T Dagata, Jr, Treasurer
Robert N Burton, Secretary
October

2290 Space Flight Mechanics Meeting
American Astronautical Society
6352 Rolling Mill Place
Suite 102
Springfield, VA 22152-2354
703-866-0020
FAX: 703-866-3526
aas@astronautical.org
www.astronautical.org
Kathleen Howell, Chairman
Jonathan T Malay, President
Mark K Craig, Executive VP
James R Kirkpatrick, Director
Shannon Coffey, VP Finance
Winter

2291 Space at the Crossroads
Space Foundation
310 S 14th Street
Colorado Springs, CO 80904
719-576-8000
FAX: 719-576-8801
web@spacefoundation.org
www.ussf.org
John Higginbotham, Chairman
Robert S Walker, Vice Chairman
Elliot G Pulham, President
Holly Roberts, Chief Financial Officer
Chuck Zimkas, Chief Operating Officer
Is a highly focused one-day conference, organized to discuss critical issues affecting national security, commercial and civil space activities. Speakers and panelists include government officials, senior Congressional staff, leaders from throughout the military space community and industry executives.
May

2292 Strategic Space and Defense
Space Foundation
310 South 14th Street
Colorado Springs, CO 80904
719-768-8000
FAX: 719-576-8801 800-691-4000
web@spacefoundation.org
www.spacefoundation.org
Elliot G Pullman, President/CEO
Steve Eisanhart, SVP Policy & Public Affairs
The Strategic Space and Defense Conference addresses both the space-related and strategic missions of the Command amongst the senior leadership of U.S. Strategic Command, appropriate component and supported commands, the aerospace contractor community, federal officials and other leaders. The primary objective is to foster relationships and understanding among the Command and its constituencies in support of America's strategic forces.
October

2293 United States Pilots Association Meeting
483 S Kirkwood Road
Suite 10
Saint Louis, MO 63122
314-849-8772
FAX: 314-338-8626
zimjr@earthlink.net www.uspilots.org
Paul Hough, Chairman
Jan Hoynacki, Executive VP
Holds two meetings a year — in the spring and fall.
June/Septemter

2294 United States Ultralight Association
United States Ultralight Association
104 Carlisle St
Ste 1
Gettysburg, PA 17325-1810
717-339-0200
FAX: 717-339-0063
usua@usua.com www.usua.org
John Ballantyne, President
Dale Hooper, Executive VP
Annual meeting and exhibits of ultralight and microlight aviation equipment, supplies and services. There will be 20 booths.
3000 Attendees February Founded: 1998

2295 World Airline Historical Society Convention
PO Box 660583
Miami Springs, FL 33266
904-221-1446
Information@WAHSOnline.com
www.wahsonline.com
Bill Demarest, President
Convention and exhibits of airline memorabilia, including airplane models, airline schedules, postcards, posters, photos and publications from airlines.
Annual

Directories & Databases

2296 AAMS Resource Guide
Association of Air Medical Services
526 King Street
Suite 415
Alexandria, VA 22314-3143
703-836-8732
FAX: 703-836-8920
information@aams.org www.aams.org
Renee Holleran, Editor
David J Dries, Editor
Gloria Dow, Editor
Dawn Mancuso, Executive Director
The directory contains information on the association and its products and services; pertinent details on members, including demographc and historical information; and special crew listings that help community members perform their jobs better through enhanced networking opportunities. It also provides decision makers with a buyer's guide of community vendors and suppliers and the services they supply.

2297 ABD: Aviation Buyer's Directory
Air Service Directory
105 Calvert Street
Harrison, NY 10528-3143
914-835-3000
Manufacturers and dealers of aviation equipment and aircraft are the focus of this directory. *$25.00*
400 pages Quarterly
Circulation: 17,000

2298 AOPA's Airport Directory
Aircraft Owners & Pilots Association
421 Aviation Way
Frederick, MD 21701
301-695-2000
FAX: 301-695-2375 800-872-2672
aopahs@aopa.org www.aopa.org
Phil Boyer, President
Includes information on over 7,400 airports, seaplane bases and heliports may with a diagram. Also covers more than 2,200 private use airports. In addition to basic airport information such as runways, lighting, approaches, frequencies, identifiers and lat/long, you'll also find listings of nearby hotels, transportation, restaurants, etc. Paperback. *$29.95*
680 pages Annual Founded: 1962
Circulation: 300,000
Printed in 1 color on glossy stock
Computerized version available: Internet

2299 Address List for Regional Airports Divisions and Airport Districts
US Federal Aviation Administration
800 Independence Avenue SW
Washington, DC 20591-0001
202-366-4000
FAX: 202-493-5032
7-AWA-ARC@FOIA@faa.gov
www.faa.gov
Offers district offices and airports.
20 pages

2300 Aerospace Database
Cambridge Scientific Abstracts
Aerospace Access
59 John Street, 7th Floor
New York, NY 10038
212-349-1120
FAX: 212-349-1283 tlenti@csa.com

Tony Lenti, Managing Editor
Earl Spencer, Owner

Provides bibliographic coverage of basic and applied research in aeronautics, astronautics, and space sciences. The database also covers technology development and applications in complementary and supporting fields such as chemistry, geosciences, physics, communications, and electronics. In addition to periodic literature, the database also includes coverage of reports issued by NASA, other US government agencies, international institutions, universities, and private firms.
Bibliographic

2301 Airline Handbook
Air Transport Association
PO Box 511
Annapolis Junction, MD 20701
301-490-7951
FAX: 301-206-9789 800-497-3326
pubs@airlines.org www.airlines.org
Overview of the history, structure, economics and operations of the airline industry. Includes a glossary of commonly used airline terminology. *$10.00*
Hardcover Founded: 2001

2302 Airport Operators Council International
1775 K Street NW
Suite 500
Washington, DC 20006
202-293-8500
FAX: 202-331-1362

Randall H Walker, Director
John D Clark, III, Executive Director
Juliet Wright, Senior Director Public Affairs
Gregory Principato, President

Contains an annual time series of aviation and airport data for more than 580 airports from the Worldwide Airport Traffic Report.

Founded: 1948

2303 Airports
CTB/McGraw Hill
20 Ryan Ranch Road
Monterey, CA 93940
831-498-8400
FAX: 180-028-2026

Larry Fruth, Executive Director

Offers information on airport management issues, including funding. Congressional and regulatory activities, legal matters, noise and capacity problems are offered as well.
Full-text

2304 Aviation Businesses and the Service They Provide
National Air Transportation Association
4226 King Street
Alexandria, VA 22302
703-845-9000
FAX: 703-848-175 800-808-6282
csipes@nata-online.org www.nata.aero

James K Coyne, President
Alan Darrow, VP
Eric R Byer, Dir Government/Industry Affairs

A detailed fact book, complete with statistical data, on the aviation services industry.
$50.00

2305 Aviation Telephone Directory
Aviation Telephone Directory
6619 Tumbleweed Ridge Lane
Suite 102
Henderson, NV 89015

FAX: 702-943-8982 800-437-2962
Is the leading source for General Aviation information with more than 14,000 Companies and 10,000 airports. Yellow pages, White pages, and Blue pages(by airport). Thousands of phone numbers. *$19.95*
790 pages BiAnnually Founded: 1949
Circulation: 20000
Printed in 4 colors on newsprint stock : web

2306 Business Commercial Aviation Planning & Purchasing Handbook
Business & Commercial Aviation
Div./McGraw-Hill
4 International Drive
Rye Brook, NY 10573-1065
914-937-9009
www.aviationnow.com

Mark Lipowicz, Publisher
William Garvey, Editor-in-Chief
Matt Holdreith, Sales Director

Directory of services and supplies to the industry. *$52.00*
Annual
Circulation: 50,000

2307 Collegiate Aviation Guide
University Aviation Association
3410 Skyway Drive
Auburn, AL 36830-6444
334-844-2434
FAX: 334-844-2432 www.uaa.aero

Allan Skramstad, President
Carolyn Williamson, Executive Director
Steve Anderson, Treasurer
Raymond E Cain, Jr, Secretary

Is a directory of useful information on colleges and universities that offer non-engineering aviation programs in the United States, Puerto Rico, Canada and Brazil.
$24.95

2308 Commuter Flight Statistics and Online Origin & Destination Data
US Department of Transportation
Kendall Square
Cambridge, MA 02142-1093
617-494-5906

Robin A Caldwell, Director

Covers all areas of the commuter airline flight industry, including statistical information on flights by commuter airlines.
Statistical

2309 Flying Annual and Buyers Guide
Hachette Filipacchi Magazines
1633 Broadway
42nd Floor
New York, NY 10019
212-767-6000
www.hfmnewsstand.com/index

J Mac McClellan, Editor-in-Chief
Richard Collins, Editor at Large

This substantial guide lists manufacturers, dealers, suppliers and professionals in the aviation industry. *$18.00*

2310 General Aviation Statistical DataBook
General Aviation Manufacturers Association
1400 K Street NW
Suite 801
Washington, DC 20005
202-393-1500
FAX: 202-842-4063
www.generalaviation.org

Pete Bunce, President/CEO

Statistics on US general aviation shipments, aircraft fleet, international trade, safety and the most current data on airport statistics and pilot population. *$10.00*
Annual

2311 Guide to Selecting Airport Consultants and Membership Directory
Airport Consultants Council
908 King Street
Suite 100
Alexandria, VA 22314
703-683-5900
FAX: 703-683-2564
info@acconline.org
www.acconline.org

Paula P Hochstetler, President

A full nationwide listing of airport consultants and association news.
Annual

2312 Helicopter Annual
Helicopter Association International
1655 Prince Street
Alexandria, VA 22314-2818
703-683-4646
FAX: 703-683-4745 www.rotor.com

Marty Lenehan, Publications

A comprehensive reference guide for th civil helicopter industry. Includes specifications, industry statistics, HAI membership directories by class and geographic matrix, listings of international civil aviation contacts, key FAA personnel, association committees, and more. First copy included free with membership. *$50.00*
360 pages Annual
Circulation: 25,000

2313 High-Performance Composites
Ray Publishing
4891 Independence
Suite 270
Wheat Ridge, CO 80033
303-467-1776
FAX: 303-467-1777
www.compositesworld.com

Judith Hazen, Publisher
Mike Mussleman, Managing Editor

The publisher of High-Performance Composites and Composites Technology magazines and well as the Sourcebook Industry directory and special design and application guides.
60 pages Founded: 1993
Printed in 4 colors on glossy stock

2314 High-Performance Composites Directory
Ray Publishing
4891 Independence
Suite 270
Wheat Ridge, CO 80033
303-467-1776
FAX: 303-467-1777
www.compositesworld.com

Judith Hazen, Publisher
Mike Mussleman, Managing Editor

60 pages Founded: 1993
Printed in 4 colors on glossy stock

2315 **International Aerospace Abstracts**
American Institute of Aeronautics and Astronautics
1801 Alexander Bell Drive
Suite 500
Reston, VA 20191-4344
703-264-7500
FAX: 703-264-7551 800-639-2422
Donald W Richardson, President
This database contains more than 2 million references and abstracts of journal and monograph literature relating to aerospace science and technology.
Monthly

2316 **Light Aircraft Manufacturers Association Directory**
22 Deer Oaks Center
Pleasanton, CA 94588
925-426-0771
FAX: 925-426-0771
info@lama.bz www.lama.bz
Larry Burke, President
A list of over 400 member manufacturers of light and ultralight aircraft and suppliers of related products and services.

2317 **Living with Your Plane**
Flyer Media
5611 76th Street W
PO Box 39099
Lakewood, WA 98499-0099
253-471-9888
FAX: 253-471-9911 800-426-8538
dsclair@flyer.online.com
www.flyer-online.com/airparks
Dave Sclair, Editor
Janice Wood, Editorial Coordinator
Offers a large amount of information including 400 residential airports with phones, addresses and contact names.
$20.00
Annual
Circulation: 1,000

2318 **NBAA Directory of Member Companies, Aircraft & Personnel**
National Business Aviation Association
1200 18th Street NW
Suite 400
Washington, DC 20036-2527
202-783-9000
FAX: 202-331-8364
info@nbaa.org www.nbaa.org
Ed Bolen, President
Annual directory for business aviation professionals.
200 pages February/Annual
Circulation: 20,000

2319 **Space Law**
Oceana Publications
75 Main Street
Dobbs Ferry, NY 10522
914-938-8100
FAX: 914-693-0402
info@oceanalaw.com
www.oceanalaw.com
Paul Stephen Dempsey, Editor
Provides in-depth expert coverage by today's preeminent expoert of the most pressing issues currently being faced by international regulators in this dynamic and growing area of the law. *$625.00*
40 pages 5 Volume Set ISBN 0-379012-92-8

Circulation: 2,000
Printed in 4 colors

2320 **United States Civil Aircraft Registry**
Insured Aircraft Title Service
4848 SW 36th Street
PO Box 19257
Oklahoma City, OK 73179
405-681-6663
FAX: 405-681-9299 800-654-4882
iats@earthlink.net
www.insuredaircraft.com
This directory covers owners of over 275,000 aircraft. *$600.00*
190 pages Monthly Founded: 1963

2321 **Water Landing Directory**
Seaplane Pilots Association
4315 Highland Park Boulevard
Suite C
Lakeland, FL 33813-1639
863-701-7979
FAX: 863-701-7588 888-772-8923
spa@seaplanes.org
www.seaplanes.org
Roger C Myers Jr, Publisher
Mark Twombly, Editor
Michael E Volk, Executive Editor
Joe Cliber, Art Director
Is the only publication that combines federal, state, provincial and special agency regulations affecting seaplane operators. The directory includes waterway closures and restrictions, seaplane bases listed by state and city, informative seaplane base diagrams, customs information, flight planning charts and other miscellaneous quick reference materials.

2322 **World Aviation Directory and Aerospace Database**
McGraw Hill
1200 G Street NW
Suite 200
Washington, DC 20005-3815
202-383-2350
FAX: 202-383-2440
www.aviationnow.com/wad
Gert Shayte, Managing Editor
Aviation and the aerospace industry are covered in this global directory offering information on manufacturers, subcontractors, support services and associations.
2500 pages SemiAnnual

Industry Web Sites

2323 **www.aams.org**
Association of Air Medical Services

Air medical transport equipment, supplies and services.

2324 **www.aci-na.org**
Airports Council International-North America

Represents local, regional and state governing bodies that own and operate commercial airports throughtout the United States and Canada.

2325 **www.aeronet.com**
Aeronet Worldwide

Specializes in urgent shipping solutions. From computer and technical supplies, to medical equipment, to odd size, one of a kind machine parts, we have always been there for our clients, one shipment at a time.

2326 **www.afa.org**
Air Force Association

Independent nonprofit, civilian organization promoting public understanding of aerospace power and the pivotal role it plays in the security of the nation.

2327 **www.afanet.org**
Association of Flight Attendants

Represents over 50,000 flight attendants at 26 airlines, serving as a voice for flight attendants at their workplace, in the industry, the media and on Capitol Hill.

2328 **www.agaviation.org**
National Agricultural Aviation Association

Voice of the aerial application industry, we work to preserve aerial application's place in the protection and production of America's food and fiber supply. Aerial application is one of the safest, fastest, most efficient and economical ways to apply pesticides. It is also the most environmentally friendly tool of modern agriculture.

2329 **www.aia-aerospace.org**
Aerospace Industries Association

For manufacturers of commercial, military and business aircraft, helicopters, aircraft engineers, missiles, spacecraft, material and related components and equipment.

2330 **www.aiaa.org**
American Institute of Aeronautics and Astronautics

Advances the arts, sciences, and technology of aeronautics and astronautics and promotes the professionalism of those engaged in these pursuits.

2331 **www.airlines.org**
Air Transport Association

Supports and assits its members by promoting the air transport industry and the safety, cost effectiveness, and technical advancement of its operators; advocating common industry positions before state and local governments; conducting designated industry-wide programs; and assuring governmental and public understanding of all aspects of air transport.

2332 **www.airportnet.org**
American Association of Airport Executives

Exchanges ideas on construction, management and operation of civil airports.

2333 **www.airship-association.org**
Airship Association

Circulates information on all matters affecting airships.

2334 **www.anahq.org**
Association of Naval Aviation

Professional, nonprofit, educational and fraternaL society of Naval Aviation, whose main purpose is to educte the public and our national leaders on the vital roles of the Navy, Marine Corp and Coast Guard Aviation as key elements of our national defense posture. ANA continuosly seeks to elucidate the key current issues impacting Naval Aviation through published writing, symposia, speeches and discussions with various interest groups.

2335 **www.aopa.org**
Aircraft Owners & Pilots Association

Works to make flying safer, more economical and enjoyable for private aircraft owners.

2336 **www.arinc.com**
Aeronautical Radio

Aeronautical Radio provides transportation communications and systems engineering solution for five major industries: aviation, airports, defense, government, and transportation

2337 **www.arsa.org**
Aeronautical Repair Station Association

Information on regulatory and legislative issues before the FAA and other government agencies. The owners and operators of the world's aircraft depend on certified aeronautical repair stations for essential engineering, maintenance and modification services.

2338 **www.astronautical.org**
American Astronautical Society

Independent scientific and technical group in the United States exclusively dedicated to the advancement of space science and exploration.

2339 **www.atec-amt.org**
Aviation Technician Education Council

Organization of Federal Aviation Administration approved Aviation Maintenance Technician schools and supporting industries.

2340 **www.blimpinfo.com**
Lighter Than Air Society

Nonprofit organization whose members are devoted to the study of the history, science and techniques of all forms of buoyant flight.

2341 **www.bonanza.org**
American Bonanza Society

ABS is a group of members who own, fly or have a sincere interest in Bonanza, Baron, and Travel air type aircraft. Because of this common interest we share information and experiences involving the operation and maintenance of the Beech produced aircraft.

2342 **www.civilavmed.com**
Civil Aviation Medical Association

Aviation medical equipment, supplies and services. Working on behalf of physicians engaged in the practice of aviation medicine, dedicated to civil aviation safety.

2343 **www.eaa.org**
Experimental Aircraft Association

Equipment, supplies and services for sport and recreational flying.

2344 **www.generalaviation.org**
General Aviation Manufacturers Association

Manufacturers of general aviation aircraft, and related equipment.

2345 **www.greyhouse.com**
Grey House Publishing

Selected Grey House directories in the fields of business, health and education are available online. Users can search our online databases by several different search criteria, such as product categories, geographic area, sales volume and much, much more. Full Grey House catalog and online ordering also available.

2346 **www.iaopa.org**
Int'l Council of Aircraft Owner & Pilot Assns.

Nonprofit federation of 53 autonomous, nongovernmental, national general aviation organizations. Facilitates the movement of general aviation aircraft.

2347 **www.ifsanet.com**
International Inflight Food Service Association

For airline and railway personnel, caterers and suppliers responsible for providing passenger food service.

2348 **www.iswap.org**
International Society of Women Airline Pilots

Organization for all women pilots who are employed as flight crew members (Captain, First Officer, or Second Officer) and hold senority numbers with an airline carrier that operates at least one aircraft with a gross wieght of 90,000 pounds or more.

2349 **www.naa.usa.org**
National Aeronautic Association

For aerospace corporations, aero clubs, affiliates and major national sporting aviation organizations.

2350 **www.nafinet.org**
National Association of Flight Instructors

Dedicated to raising and maintaining the professional standing of the flight instructor in the aviation community. Maintains a benefits package available for everyone from the independent instructor to those teaching at flight schools.

2351 **www.nata.aero**
National Air Transportation Association

National association of aviation business service providers.

2352 **www.natca.org**
National Air Traffic Controllers Association

Founded to ensure the safety and longetivity of air traffic controller positions around the nation. Represents over 15,000 air traffic controllers throughout the US, Puerto Rico and Guam, along with 2,508 other bargaining unit members that span the areas of engineers and architects to nurses and health care professionals to members of the accounting community.

2353 **www.nbaa.org**
National Business Aviation Association

Not-for-profit, nonpartisan corporation dedicated to the success of the business aviation community.

2354 **www.ninety-nines.org**
Ninety-Nines

International organization of licensed women pilots from 35 countries. We are a nonprofit, charitable membership corporation holding 501(c)(3) US tax status. Members are professional pilots for airlines, industry, government; we are pilots who teach and pilots who fly for pleasure; we are pilots who are technicians and mechanics. First and foremost, we are women who love to fly.

2355 www.ofainc.com.
Organization of Flying Adjusters

Dedicated to the highest standard of professional ethics in handling aviation insurance claims, investigating causes of aircraft accidents objectively and promoting every aspect of air safety.

2356 www.piperowner.org
Pipers Owner Society

Independent group of Piper owners, pilots, and enthusiasts, the POS is committed to the goal of safe, fun, and affordable flying. Membership benefits include: pre-buy referral service; free STC summaries, free parts locating and a referral service. Pipers magazine is exclusively for POS members.

2357 www.quad-a.org
Army Aviation Association of America

Aerospace products, helicopters, rotor blades, engines, tires, helmets and related aviation equipment. Representing membership interests to the Army and the Legislative Branch.

2358 www.rotor.com
Helicopter Association International

Receives and disseminates information concerning the use, operation, hiring, contracting and leasing of helicopters.

2359 www.safeassociation.com
SAFE Association

Website of the nonprofit organization dedicated to the preservation of human life. It provides a common meeting ground for the sharing of problems, ideas and information.

2360 www.seaplanes.org
Seaplane Pilots Association

Represents our members in dozens of seaplane access issues annually and provides numerous exclusive benefits.

2361 www.ssa.org
Soaring Society of America

Fosters and promote all phases of gliding and soaring, nationally and internationally.

2362 www.tcunion.org
Transportation-Communications International Union

Members come from diverse transportation industries. In addition to bargaining and representation of its members, provides mortgage and bankcard programs and other services to its members.

2363 www.tiaca.org
International Air Cargo Association

For air cargo industry services and products from aircraft manufacturers, airlines, airports, freight forwarders trade publications logistics consultants, etc.

2364 www.ussf.org
Space Foundation

Nonprofit organization advancing the exploration, development and use of space and space education for the benefit of humankind.

2365 www.vtol.org
AHS International

For designers, engineers and manufacturers of the vertical flight industry.

2366 www.wahsonline.com
World Airline Historical Society

Open to all persons and groups interested in collecting airline memorabilia and the study of the airline industry, past and current.

Associations

2367 ABA Marketing Network
American Bankers Association
1120 Connecticut Avenue NW
Washington, DC 20036-3971
202-663-5000
FAX: 202-828-4540
marketingnetwork@aba.com
www.aba.com/marketingnetwork/

Edward L Yingling, President/CEO
Brenda Marlin, Associate Director
Howard Walseman, Group Director
Barbara Payne, Chapter Relations Manager
Larry Price, Publisher/Periodicals

Provider of marketing education and information, professional growth opportunities and networking resources.
Founded: 1915

2368 America's Community Bankers
900 Nineteenth Street NW
Suite 400
Washington, DC 20006
202-857-3100
FAX: 202-296-8716
info@acbankers.org
www.americascommunitybankers.com

William W Zuppe, Chairman
Mark E Macomber, First Vice Chairman
Edwin R Maus, Second Vice Chairman
Diane Casey-Landry, President/CEO
Monique Hanis, Marketing/Business Development

National banking association enhancing business opportunities, mortgage and payment programs. ACA also has a strong advocacy program in Washington, DC and supports financial literacy.

2369 American Association of Bank Directors
4701 Sangamore Road
Suite P15
Bethesda, MD 20816
301-263-9841
FAX: 301-229-2443
dbaris@aabd.org www.aabd.org

Keith Dalrymple, President/CEO
James I Lundy, VP
David Baris, Executive Director
Betty Pelton, Membership Director

Devoted to serving the information, education and advocacy needs of individual bank and savings institution directors. This nonprofit organization has members nationwide.
Founded: 1989

2370 American Bankers Association
1120 Connecticut Avenue NW
Washington, DC 20036-3902
202-663-5000
FAX: 202-828-4540
custserv@aba.com www.aba.com

Earl D McVicker, Chairman-Elect
Bradley E Rock, Vice Chairman
Edward Yingling, President/CEO
David S Hickman, Treasurer

Brings together all categories of banking institutions to best represent the interests of this rapidly changing industry. It's membership — which includes community, regional and money center banks and holding companies, as well as savings associations, trust companies and savings banks, makes ABA one of the largest banking trade associations in the country.
Founded: 1875

2371 American Bankers Insurance Association
American Bankers Association
1120 Connecticut Avenue NW
Washington, DC 20036
202-635-5000
FAX: 202-828-4546 800-226-5377
nbryant@aba.com www.theabia.com

Thomas J Cook, President/Chairman
Richard L Spickard, VP
John f Bruder, Secretary
Beth L Climo, Executive Director
J Kevin A McKechnie, Associate Director

Seperately chartered affiliate of the American Bankers Asssociation. Washington, DC based full service association for bank insurance interests, ABIA is dedicated to furthering the policy and business objectives of banks in insurance.
200 Members Founded: 2001

2372 American Council of State Savings Supervisors
PO Box 1904
Leesburg, VA 20177
703-669-5440
FAX: 703-669-5441
amfalz@acsss.org www.acsss.org

Sid Seymour, Chairman
Jonathan Smith, Vice Chairman
Danny Payne, Commissioner
Bill Waits, Assistant Director
Andrea Falzaranom, CAE, Executive Director

Provides professional supervisory information and insight in support of the state charter for savings institutions through Congressional testimony and FFIEC participation. ACSS also provides valuable information about legislative activity in Washington to state financial institution regulators. Provides training and a monthly newsletter.
30 Members Founded: 1939

2373 American Safe Deposit Association
PO Box 519
Franklin, IN 46131
317-738-4432
FAX: 317-738-5267
tasda1@aol.com
www.americansafedeposit.org

Thomas Cullinan, President
J Wayne Merrill, First VP
Winnifred Howard-Hammack, Second VP
Joyce A McLin, Executive Director
Kevin Fanning, Treasurer

Sets standards for those engaged in the safe deposit business.
2300 Members Founded: 1924

2374 Association of Independent Trust Companies
8 South Michigan Avenue
Suite 1000
Chicago, IL 60603
312-223-1611
FAX: 312-580-0165
aitco@gss.net www.aitco.net

Joe Alerding, President
Troy Kennedy, VP/Conference Chairman
Jeff Kanaly, Treasurer
Kathleen Lukasik, Executive Director

Founded to create a source for education,information and networking opportunities in order to have better resources to operate, manage and compete.
150 Members Founded: 1989

2375 Association of Military Banks of America (AMBA)
PO Box 3335
Warrenton, VA 20188
540-347-1044
FAX: 540-347-7964
info@ambahq.org www.ambahq.org

Robert H Croak, Chairman
Terry Tuggle, Vice Chairman
Andrew M Egeland, Jr, President/Treasurer/Secretary

Is a not for profit association of banks operating on military installations, banks not located on military installations but serving military customers, and military banking facilities designated by the US Treasury.
130 Members Founded: 1959

2376 Bank Administration Institute
One North Franklin Street
Suite 1000
Chicago, IL 60606-3421
312-534-4600
FAX: 312-683-2373 888-284-4078
info@bai.org www.bai.org

Douglas K Freeman, Chairman
Timothy P Moen, Vice Chairman
Deborah L Bianucci, President/CEO
Scott K Heitmann, Treasurer
Charles M Diggs, Secretary

Provides information for member bankers in areas such as human resources, finance, strategic planning and marketing, accounting, corporate services, audit, taxes, retail, operations and technology, through its series of emerging issues studies, professional conferences and education programs.
1500 Members Founded: 1985

2377 Bank Insurance and Securities Association
303 West Lancaster Avenue
Suite 2D
Wayne, PA 19087
610-989-9047
FAX: 610-989-9102
bisa@bisanet.org www.bisanet.org

John Vaughan, President
Heywood Sloane, Managing Director
Jordan Miller, VP
John Lewis, Treasurer

Works to foster the full integration of securities and insurance businesses with depository institutions' traditional banking businesses. BISA's goal is to advance profit wealth and risk management solutions through banks, thrifts and credit unions. Provides members with knowledge and support to help grow their businesses, and works to help create a legislative and regulatory environment healthy for members' future growth.
Founded: 2002

2378 Bankers' Association for Finance & Trade
1120 Connecticut Avenue NW
5th Floor
Washington, DC 20036-3902
202-635-5000
FAX: 202-663-5538
baft@aba.com www.baft.org

Madeleine L Champion, President
Harry G Haymann, III, VP
Rebecca Morter, Executive Director
Bruce Portillo, Director Communications/Membership
Robert Clements, Treasurer/Secretary

Financial trade association whose membership consists principally of the internationally active US banks, many non-US banks

with US operations and firms that provide services to such institutions.
160 Members Founded: 1921

2379 CFA Institute
560 Ray C Hunt Drive
Charlottesville, VA 22903
434-951-5499
FAX: 434-951-5262 800-247-8132
info@aimr.org www.cfainstitute.org
Frank R Reilly, Chairman
Jeffrey J Diermeir, President/CEO
Katrina F Sherrerd, Executive Director
Kathy Valentine, Media Contact, North America
Is the global, non-profit professional association that administers the Chartered Financial Analyst curriculum and examination program worldwide and sets voluntary, ethics-based professional and performance-reporting standards for the investment industry.
70000 Members Founded: 1990

2380 Check Payment Systems Association
2025 M Street NW
Suite 800
Washington, DC 20036-2422
202-671-1144
FAX: 202-223-4579
info@cpsa-check.org
www.cpsa-checks.org
Wade Delk, Executive Director
Non-profit membership organization dedicated to advancing and promoting the long-term value of the paper-based payment system.
60 Members Founded: 1952

2381 Commercial Mortgage Securities Association
30 Broad Street
28th Floor
New York, NY 10004-2304
212-509-1844
FAX: 212-509-1895
info1@cmbs.org www.cmbs.org
Kent Born, President
Christopher Hoeffel, VP
Dottie Cunningham, Chief Executive Officer
Annemarie DiCola, Treasurer
Represents and promotes an orderly and ethical global institutional secondary market for the sale of commercial mortgage loans and equity investments.
309 Members Founded: 1994

2382 Community Banking Advisory Network
10831 Old Mill Road
Suite 400
Omaha, NE 68154
402-778-7922
FAX: 402-778-7931 888-475-4476
info@bankingcpas.com
www.bankingcpas.com
Nancy Drennen, Executive Director
An association of CPA firms that concentrate a substantial portion of their business on providing financial and consulting services to community banks and financial institutions. Member firms are accepted on a territorial protected basis.
24 Members Founded: 1995

2383 Conference of State Bank Supervisors
1155 Connecticut Avenue NW
5th Floor
Washington, DC 20036-4306
202-296-2840
202-296-1928
rstromberg@csbs.org www.csbs.org
E Joseph Face, Jr, Chairman
Jeffrey C Vogel, Vice Chairman
Neil Milner, CAE, President/CEO
Roger Stromberg, Senior Vice President
The professional organization of the state bank regulators of the 50 States. Associate membership offered to state-chartered commercial and mutual savings bank.
Founded: 1902

2384 Corporation for American Banking
American Banking Association
1120 Connecticut Avenue NW
Washington, DC 20036
202-663-5000
FAX: 202-663-7540 800-226-5377
custserv@aba.com www.aba.com/cab
John Wolff, Executive Director
Monica Condon, Director Finance/Operations
Robin D Gordon, Director Marketing
Subsidiary of the American Banking Association, this group awards the ABA endorsement to products and services that help banks improve profitability and compete more effectively. Programs range from mission-critical insurance, capital management and technology services to income-enhancing financial marketing products.

2385 Eastern Finance Association
220 Holman Hall
PO Box 1848
University, MS 38677
404-498-8937
FAX: 404-498-8956
larry.wall@atl.frb.org
www.easternfinance.org
Stephen P Ferris, President
Walter J Reinhart, VP Finance
John D Finnerty, VP Planning
Mark Walker, Executive Director
Finance, including financial management, investments and banking.

2386 Electronic Funds Transfer Association
11350 Random Hills Road
Suite 800
Fairfax, VA 22030-.
703-359-9800
FAX: 703-934-6058
eftassoc@efta.org www.efta.org
Frank D'Angelo, Chairman
Scott Qualls, Vice Chairman
Jack Antonini, President/CEO
Kurt Helwig, Executive Director
Sandra Hartfield, Treasurer
Dedicated to the advancement of electronic payment systems and commerce. Members include financial institutions, EFT networks, bank card associations, retailers, information processors, equipment, card and software manufacturers and vendors, Internet providers, telecommunications companies, state governments, and federal agencies.
180 Members Founded: 1977

2387 Environmental Bankers Association
510 King Street
Suite 410
Alexandria, VA 22314
703-549-0977
FAX: 703-548-5945 800-966-7475
eba@envirobank.org
www.envirobank.org
DJ Telego, Executive Co-Director
Tacy Cook Telego, Executive Co-Director
EBA voting members are banks, trust companies, credit unions, savings and loan associations, and other financial services organizations with an interest in environmental risk management and related issues. Active participants are bankers from Trust or Credit offices with responsibility for environmental liability, and financial services officers with environmental interests. Affiliate members are from law firms, consulting and insurance organizations.
76 Members Founded: 1994

2388 Export-Import Bank of the United States
811 Vermont Avenue NW
Washington, DC 20571
202-565-3946
800-565-3946
info@exim.gov www.exim.gov
James H Lambright, President & Chairman
Brett M Decker, Senior VP of Communications
Mission is to assist in financing the export of U.S. goods and services to international markets.

2389 Financial & Security Products Association
Plaza Ladera, 5300 Sequoia NW
Suite 205
Albuquerque, NM 87120
505-839-7958
FAX: 505-839-0017 800-843-6082
info@fspa1.com www.fspa1.com
Pat Hughes, Chairman
Christen Womack, President
Mark Barclay, Director
Mark Thatcher, VP
John Vrabec, Executive Director
Independent dealers, manufacturers and associates whos outstanding products and services give financial institutions a crucial edge in performance.
265 Members Founded: 1973

2390 Financial Markets Association - USA
PO Box 156
Parlin, NJ 08859
732-316-0384
info@fma-usa.org www.fma-usa.org
Peter Wadkins, President
Geoffrey Gowey, VP
Robert J Tum-Suden, Treasurer
Carlene Crnkovich, Secretary
Not-for-Profit, membership corporation dedicated to enhancing professionalism in capital markets.
300 Members Founded: 1958

2391 Financial Services Roundtable
1001 Pennsylvania Avenue NW
Suite 500 South
Washington, DC 20004
202-289-4322
FAX: 202-628-2507
info@fsround.org www.fsround.org

James H Blanchard, Chairman
Steve Bartlett, President/CEO
Richard M Whiting, Executive Director/General Counsel
Jennifer Smith, VP Public Affairs

Originally founded as the Bankers Roundtable; the result of a merger in 1993 of the Association of Bank Holding Companies and the Association of Reserve City Bankers.
100 Members Founded: 1993

2392 Financial Women International
1027 West Roselawn Avenue
Roseville, MN 55113
651-487-7632
FAX: 651-489-1322 866-807-6081
info@fwi.org www.fwi.org

Cindy Bateman, President
Nancy Kinder, VP
Rilla Dath, Director
BJ Cary, Treasurer
Carol Crilly, Chairman Public Affairs

Serves nearly 10,000 female financial service professionals, helping them to attain their economic, professional and personal goals. *$100.00*
10000 Members Founded: 1921

2393 Freddie Mac
8200 Jones Branch Drive
McLean, VA 22102-3110
703-903-2000
FAX: 703-903-4270
www.freddiemac.com

Richard F Syron, Chairman/CEO
Eugene McQuade, President/COO
Martin F Baumann, EVP/CFO
John V Britti, VP Sales
Margaret A Colon, SVP/CAO

Freddie Mac is a stockholder owned corporation chartered by Congress to increase the supply of funds that mortgage lenders, such as commercial banks, mortgage bankers, saving institutions and credit unions, can make available to homebuyers and multifamily investors.
4000 Members Founded: 1970

2394 Global Association of Risk Professionals
111 Town Square Place
Suite 1215
Jersey City, NJ 07310
201-702-1500
FAX: 201-222-5022
info@garp.com www.garp.org

Richard Apostolik, President/CEO
Chris Donohue, Managing Director
Mark Wallace, Chief Operating Officer
Thomas Daula, Chief Risk Officer

To be the leading professional association for risk managers, managed by and for its members dedicated to the advancement of the risk profession through education, training and the promotion of best practices globally. Members come from over 100 countries.
52330 Members Founded: 2000

2395 Independent Community Bankers of America
518 Lincoln Road
PO Box 267
Sauk Centre, MN 56378
320-352-6546
FAX: 320-352-5766 800-422-7285
info@icba.org www.icba.org

James P Ghiglieri, Jr, Chairman
Cynthia Blankenship, Vice Chairman
Camden R Fine, President/CEO
Harold DeVries, SVP/CFO

23000 Members

2396 Institute of Certified Bankers
American Bankers Association
1120 Connecticut Avenue NW
Suite 600
Washington, DC 20036
202-635-5000
FAX: 202-828-4540
icb@aba.com
www.aba.com/icbcertifications

William J Foote, Chairman
Mark P Bensabat, President
Howard Walseman, Executive Director
Lisa Underwood, Associate Director
Mark Debaugh, Marketing/Communications Manager

National association of certified professionals in the financial services industry created to meet industry needs for programs that would help banking professionals improve proficiency.
7800 Members Founded: 1990

2397 Institute of International Bankers
299 Park Avenue
17th Floor
New York, NY 10171
212-421-1611
FAX: 212-421-1119
iib@iib.org www.iib.org

Everett Schenk, Chairman
Robert C O'Brien, Vice Chairman
Lawrence R Uhlick, Executive Director/General Counsel

The Institute is a trade association engaged in lobbying on behalf of foreign banks doing business in the United States.
230 Members Founded: 1966

2398 International Financial Services Association
9 Sylvan Way
First Floor
Parsippany, NJ 07054-3802
973-656-1900
FAX: 973-656-1915
info@intlbanking.org
www.ifsaonline.org

Dan Taylor, President

Members are banks involved in international operations.
250 Members Founded: 1924

2399 JPMorgan Chase
212-270-6000
www.jpmorganchase.com

James Dimon, Chief Executive Officer
Joseph Evangilesti, Global Media Relations

A leading global financial services firm with assets of $1.3 trillion and operations in more than 50 countries.

2400 MasterCard International
2000 Purchase Street
Purchase, NY 10577
914-249-2000
FAX: 914-249-4206
www.mastercardinternational.com

Robert W Selander, President/CEO
Sharon Gamsin, VP
Chris Harral, Director
Chris A McWilton, Chief Financial Offcier
Lawrence Flanagan, Chief Marketing Officer

Administers the MasterCard credit and other MasterCard products for 25,000 member financial institutions around the world.
25000 Members Founded: 1940

2401 Mortgage Bankers Association
1919 Pennsylvania Avenue NW
Washington, DC 20006-3404
202-557-2700
FAX: 202-721-0198 800-793-6222
membership@mortgagebankers.org
www.mortgagebankers.org

Regina M Lowrie, Chairman
Jonathan L Kempner, President/CEO
Mariangela Lazear, VP/Chief Financial Officer
Cheryl Crispen, SVP Communications/Marketing
Dan Thoms, VP Education/Business Development

Seeks to improve methods of originating, servicing and marketing loans.
2900 Members Founded: 1914

2402 NACHA: Electronic Payments Association
13665 Dulles Technology Drive
Suite 300
Herndon, VA 20171
703-561-1100
FAX: 703-787-0996
info@nacha.org www.nacha.org

Elliott McEntee, President/CEO
William B Nelson, Executive VP

Industry self regulatory organization for automated clearing house payment systems and other electronic payments.
12000 Members Founded: 1974

2403 National Association of Affordable Housing Lenders
1300 Connecticut Avenue NW
Washington, DC 20036
202-293-9850
FAX: 202-293-9852
info@naahl.org www.naahl.org

Judith Kennedy, President/CEO
Ellen Lazar, Executive Director
Paul Haaland, Director Communications

Leadership organization serving the full range of affordable housing and community development practitioners. Promotes private investment in affordable housing to create and preserve sustainable communities.
Founded: 1990

2404 National Association of Bankruptcy Trustees
One Windsor Cove
Suite 305
Columbia, SC 29223
803-252-5646
FAX: 803-765-0860
info@nabt.com www.nabt.com

Eugene Crane, President
Samuel K Crocker, VP

Robert Frr, VP
Christina Hicks, Executive Director

Is a non profit association formed to address the needs of the bankruptcy trustees throughout the country and to promote the effectiveness of the bankruptcy system as a whole.

1200 Members Founded: 1982

2405 National Association of Chapter 13 Trustees
1 Windsor Cove
Suite 305
Columbia, SC 29223
803-252-5646
FAX: 803-765-0860 800-445-8629
Info@NACTT.com www.nactt.com

Courtney Waldrup, Executive Director
Robin R Weiner, VP
Kevin R Anderson, Treasurer

Provides a forum within which Chapter 13 Trustees will act as an information and communication resource to advance education, leadership, and continuous improvement in the administration of bankruptcy. We will provide the means to establish and implement professional standards and participate in the national legislative and administrative processes while promoting the highest ethical principles.

1000 Members Founded: 1965

2406 National Association of Credit Union Supervisory and Auditing Committees
PO Box 160
Del Mar, CA 92014

FAX: 858-792-3884 800-287-5949
nacusac@nacusac.org
www.nacusac.org

Linda Treml, Chairman
Robert Butler, Vice Chairman
Bob Spindler, Associate Director
Celeste Shelton, Associate Director
Katherine E Clark, Executive Director

A unique organization of, by and for credit union supervisory committee members.

500 Members Founded: 1985

2407 National Association of Federal Credit Unions
3138 10th Street North
Arlington, VA 22201-2149
703-522-4770
FAX: 703-524-1082 800-336-4644
jbruce@nafcu.org www.nafcu.org

Michael S Vadala, Chairman
John W Milazzo, Jr, Vice Chairman
Fred R Becker, Jr, President/CEO
Joseph Boyle, Director
Diane Swenson, Executiv VP

Trade association exclusively represents the interests of federal credit unions before the federal government and the public. Provides members with representation, information, education and assistance to meet the challenges that cooperative financial institutions face in today's economic environment. Stands as a national forum for the federal credit union where new ideas, issues, concerns and trends can be identified, discussed and resolved.

6468 Members Founded: 1967

2408 National Association of Government Guaranteed Lenders
424 South Squires Street
Stillwater, OK 74074
405-377-4022
FAX: 405-377-3931
bfortune@naggl.com www.naggl.com

Tony Wilkinson, President/CEO
Karen High, EVP/COO
Jenifer Brake, Assistant VP Marketing
Jennifer Sterret-O'Neill, Assistant VP Communications

Promotes professional and governemntal affairs interests of financial institutions and small businesses who participate in Small Business Administration guaranteed lending and secondary market programs.

600 Members Founded: 1984

2409 National Association of Mortgage Brokers
7900 Westpark Drive
Suite T309
McLean, VA 22102
703-342-5900
FAX: 703-342-5905 www.namb.org

Mike Nizankiewicz, CEO
Harry H Dinham, CMC, President
George Hanzimanolis, CRMS, VP
Roy DeLoach, SVP/CFO
Allan Daniels, Treasurer

Mortgage brokers who seek to increase professionalism and to foster business relationships among members.

27000 Members Founded: 1973

2410 National Association of Professional Mortgage Women
PO Box 2016
Edmonds, WA 98026
425-775-6589
FAX: 425-771-9588 800-827-3034
info@napmw.org www.napmw.org

Katherine L Kosicki, President
Michelle F Swanson, Senior VP
Patricia Hull, Executive Director
Connie Tench, Treasurer

A net work of more than 80 local associations in 21 states. Members are individuals employed in mortgage banking and related fields.

4500 Members Founded: 1964

2411 National Bankers Association
1513 P Street NW
Washington, DC 20005-1909
202-588-5432
FAX: 202-588-5443
www.nationalbankers.org

James E Young, Chairman
Norma Alexander Hart, President
Tommy Brooks, Treasurer
Robert P Cooper, Secretary

Members are minority and womens banking institutions, minority individuals employed by majority banks and institutions.

16000 Members Founded: 1927

2412 National Credit Union Administration
1775 Duke Street
Alexandria, VA 22314-3428
703-518-6300
FAX: 703-518-6661
pacamail@ncua.gov www.ncua.gov

JoAnn Johnson, Chairman
Rodney E Hood, Vice Chairman
Robert Fenner, Director/General Counsel
Jane Walters, Deputy Executive Director
J Leonard Skiles, Executive Director

Governed by a three member board appointed by the President and confirmed by the US Senate, this independent federal agency charters and supervises federal credit unions. NCUA, with the backing of the full faith and credit of the US government, operates the National Credit Union Share Insurance Fund, insuring the savings of 80 million account holders in all federal credit unions and many state chartered credit unions.

700 Members Founded: 1909

2413 National Investment Banking Association
PO Box 6625
Athens, GA 30604
706-208-9620
FAX: 706-208-1033
conferences@nibanet.org
www.nibanet.org

Carlo Corzine, Chairman
Anthony B Petrelli, Director
Emily Foshee, Executive Director
D Scott Foshee, Chief Technology Officer
Vickitt Barone, Treasurer/Secretary

NIBA members are regional and independent broker-dealer and investment banking firms, and related capital market service providers.

250 Members Founded: 1994

2414 National Marine Bankers Association
200 East Randolph Street
Suite 5100
Chicago, IL 60601-6528
312-812-2777
FAX: 312-946-0388
bmcardle@nmma.org
www.marinebankers.org

Donald C Parkhurst, President
Bernice McArdle, Association Manager
Jim Coburn, Treasurer
James Y Stewart, Legal Counsel
Don Mattocks, Vice President

Seeks to provide a forum to exchange information useful to the development of sound recreational marine lending through education, surveys, conferences, and workshops.

70 Members Founded: 1980

2415 National Real Estate Forum
679 Baldwin Road
PO Box 598
Ticonderoga, NY 12883-2209
518-585-3546
FAX: 518-585-3206
eahowe@rosevilleco.com

Edwin A Howe, Jr, Executive Director

Membership consists of individuals who have achieved distinction in one or more areas of real estate/real estate finance.

70 Members Founded: 1978

2416 Risk Management Association
1801 Market Street
Suite 300
Philadelphia, PA 19103
215-635-5398
FAX: 215-446-4101 800-677-7621
customers@rmahq.org
www.rmahq.org

W Kendall Chalk, Chairman
Glenn L Wilson, Vice Chairman
Maurice H Hartigan, II, President/CEO
Dwight Overturf, Chief Financial Officer
Valerie Morris, Director Marketing

Topics relating to all aspects of commercial lending, financial statement analysis and

credit information exchange and managerial aspects of consumer lending.
19000 Members Founded: 1914

2417 Urban Financial Services Coalition
1212 New York Avenue
Suite 950
Washington, DC 20005
202-289-8335
FAX: 202-842-0567
ufsc@ufscnet.org www.ufscnet.org
Andrew T Carr, President
Carol A Hendrix, VP
Wayne R Young, Treasurer
The Urban Financial Service Coalition is a nonprofit organization of minority professionals in the financial services industry. Members are primarily from large institutions in the banking industry and related fields.
5000+ Members Founded: 1975

Newsletters

2418 A Comprehensive Business Reporting Model: Financial Reporting for Investors
CFA Institute
560 Ray C Hunt Drive
Charlottesville, VA 22903
434-951-5499
FAX: 434-951-5262 800-247-8132
info@amir.org www.cfainstitute.org
Frank K Reilly, Chairman
Jeffrey J Diermeier, President/CEO
Katrina F Sherrerd, Executive Director
Kathy Valentine, Media Contact, North America
Publishes codes and standards that lead the investment industry in setting the highest standards of ethics and professional conduct.

2419 AABD Survey of Bank and Savings Institutio n Boards of Directors
American Association of Bank Directors
4701 Sangamore Road
Suite P15
Bethesda, MD 20816
301-263-9841
FAX: 301-229-2443 www.aabd.org
Keith Dalrymple, President/CEO
James I Lundy, VP
David Baris, Executive Director
Betty Pelton, Membership Director
Provides critical data and analysis. *$125.00*

2420 ABA Bankers News
American Bankers Association
1120 Connecticut Avenue NW
Washington, DC 20036-3902
202-635-5000
FAX: 202-663-7543 www.aba.com
Donald C Ogilvie, President/CEO
Brian Nixon, Editor/Publisher
For everyone in the banking industry especially CEOs and compliance officers. Learn to use the internet effectively, retain your best customers, reduce risk, nurture a sales culture and more. *$96.00*
12 pages Bi-Weekly Founded: 1875

2421 ABA Marketing Edge
American Bankers Association
1120 Connecticut Avenue NW
Washington, DC 20036-3902
202-635-5000
FAX: 202-663-7597 800-226-5377
Larry Price, Publisher
Walt Albro, Senior Associate Editor
Keep up with professional development topics, hot ad campaigns and fresh ideas from your peers that will stimulate your own marketing efforts.

2422 ABA Trust Letter
American Bankers Association
1120 Connecticut Avenue NW
Washington, DC 20036-3902
202-635-5000
FAX: 202-663-7597 800-226-5377
Larry Price, Publisher
Sally Miller, Director/Regulatory Counsel
Delivers the most accurate, timely coverage of laws and regulations affecting all areas of trusts. *$270.00*
Monthly

2423 AITCO Advisor
Association of Independent Trust Companies
8 South Michigan Avenue
Suite 1000
Chicago, IL 60603
312-223-1611
FAX: 312-580-0165
atico@gss.net www.aitco.net
Joe Alerding, President
Troy Kennedy, VP/Conference Chairman
Jeff Kanaly, Treasurer
Features professionally written articles on marketing and legislative issues as well as association updates.
Quarterly

2424 Access
American Safe Deposit Association
PO Box 519
Franklin, IN 46131-519
317-738-4432
FAX: 317-738-5267
jmclin@aol.com www.tasda.com
Bill Lee, Publisher
Thomas Cullinan, President
J Wayne Merrill, First VP
Winnifred Howard-Hommack, Second Vice President
Kevin Fanning, Treasurer
A newsletter full of timely articles on safe deposit procedures, policies, problems and solutions. *$10.00*

2425 Actions of the Board
Federal Reserve Board Publishers
20th Street & Constitution Avenue NW
Washington, DC 20551
202-452-3000
FAX: 202-728-5886
www.federalreserve.gov
Alan Greenspan, Chairman
Roger W Ferguson, Jr, Vice Chairman
Deborah Lagomarsino, Media Contact
To provide the nation with a safer, more flexible, and more stable monetary and financial system.
Monthly Founded: 1913

2426 Advocacy Bulletins
CFA Institute
560 Ray C Hunt Drive
Charlottesville, VA 22903
434-951-5499
FAX: 434-951-5262 800-247-8132
info@amir.org www.cfainstitute.org
Frank K Reilly, Chairman
Jeffrey J Diermeier, President/CEO
Katrina F Sherrerd, Executive Director
Kathy Valentine, Media Contact, North America
To communicate time-sensitive information to interested AIMR/CFA Member Societies and members.
Periodically

2427 Allied News
Allied Finance Adjusters Conference
PO Box 20708
Chicago, IL 60620-708
800-621-3016
FAX: 800-782-2067 800-843-1232
fedauto@bellsouth.net
www.alliedfinanceadjusters.com
George Badeen, President
Offers important financial news to finance adjusters. *$200.00*
Founded: 1936

2428 BISA Enacted Report
Bank Insurance and Securities Association
303 West Lancaster Avenue
Suite 2D
Wayne, PA 19087
610-989-9047
FAX: 610-989-9102
bisa@bisanet.org www.bisanet.org
John Vaughan, President
Heywood Sloane, Managing Director
Jordan Miller, VP
John Lewis, Treasurer
A review of all legislation signed at the State and Federal levels.
Monthly

2429 BISA Regulatory Report
Bank Insurance and Securities Association
303 West Lancaster Avenue
Suite 2D
Wayne, PA 19087
610-989-9047
FAX: 610-989-9102
bisa@bisanet.org www.bisanet.org
John Vaughan, President
Heywood Sloane, Managing Director
Jordan Miller, VP
John Lewis, Treasurer
A review of all proposed and adopted regulations at the State and National levels.
Monthly

2430 BNA's Banking Report
Bureau of National Affairs
1231 25th Street NW
Washington, DC 20037
202-452-4200
800-372-1033
customercare@bna.com www.bna.com
Gregory C McCaffery, Publisher
Kirk A Swanson, Managing Editor
Legal and regulatory developments in the financial services industry. *$1780.00*
Weekly Founded: 1929

2431 Bank Fraud
Bank Administration Institute
One North Franklin Street
Suite 1000
Chicago, IL 60606-3421
312-534-4600
FAX: 312-683-2373 800-224-9889
Richard Kemmer, Editor
Douglas K Freeman, Chairman
Timothy P Moen, Vice Chairman
Deborah L Bianucci, President/CEO
Scott K Heitmann, Treasurer
Provides a foundation for institutions to prepare, prevent, detect and identify when fraud has occurred, as well as covering the interrogation, handling, prosecution, and retrieval stages. *$174.00*
Monthly
Circulation: 1500

2432 Bank Mergers & Acquisitions
SNL Securities
One SNL Plaza
PO Box 2124
Charlottesvle, VA 22902
434-977-1600
FAX: 434-977-4466
CustomerService@snl.com
www.snl.com
Ed Dillon, Editor
John Minor, Editor
Reports, analyzes and interprets the month's merger and acquisition activity. Includes the latest branch sales and purchases, merger conversions, legislative actions, shareholder rights plans and rumored M&A activity. Combines detailed terms of each deal with financial data for both the buyer and the seller. *$795.00*
40 pages Monthly Founded: 1987

2433 Bank Network News
SourceMedia
1 State Street Plaza
27th Floor
New York, NY 10004
212-803-8200
800-221-1809
virginia.wiese@sourcemedia.com
www.sourcemedia.com
Ann O'Brien, VP
William Johnson, Director Marketing/Communications
Highlights trade literature relating to new products, concepts, and oppurtunities in the field. Also special coverage of automated teller machines, debit cards, internet commerce and electronic funds transfer as it relates to retail banking. *$99.00*
Monthly Founded: 2005

2434 Bank Rate Monitor
Bank Rate
11760 US Highway 1
Suite 500
North Palm Beach, FL 33408-8888
561-630-2400
FAX: 561-625-4540 www.bankrate.com
Don Munsell, Production Director
Independent national source for the financial industry. *$499.00*
4 pages Weekly 750 names
Printed in 3 colors

2435 Bank Security Report
Warren, Gorham & Lamont
395 Hudson Street
New York, NY 10014-3669
212-367-6305
FAX: 212-367-6718 800-742-3348
Peter Knopp, Editor
Highlights the latest techniques in bank crime prevention, surveillance, and defense. *$375.00*
Monthly

2436 Bank Tellers Report
Warren, Gorham & Lamont
807 Las Cimas Pkwy
Suite 300
Austin, TX 78746
512-472-2244
FAX: 512-305-6575 800-456-2340
customercare.sis@sheshunoff.com
www.sheshunoff.com
Joe Tessitore, Publisher
Marge Simmons, Author
General interest publication for bank tellers. *$449.00*
Monthly Founded: 1975

2437 Bank and S&L Quarterly Rating Service
Sheshunoff Information Services
807 Las Cimas Parkway
Suite 300
Austin, TX 78764
512-472-2244
FAX: 512-305-6575 800-456-2340
Gabrielle Sheshunoff, Chief Executive Officer
Statistical reports and research on savings and loan institutions. *$580.00*
Quarterly
Circulation: 5000 5000 names

2438 Banks in Insurance Report
John Wiley & Sons
111 River Street
Hoboken, NJ 07030-5774
201-486-6000
FAX: 201-748-6021 800-225-5945
subinfo@wiley.com www.wiley.com
Edward J Stone, Editor
Sheck Cho, Managing Editor
Dan Payne, Publisher
William J Pesce, President/CEO
Highlights the steps necessary for expansion into insurance products and services through articles that report on legislative activities, regulatory concerns, business and strategies. *$745.00*
16 pages Monthly Founded: 1807
Printed in 1 color on matte stock

2439 Basic Guide for Audit Committee Members
American Association of Bank Directors
4701 Sangamore Road
Suite P15
Bethesda, MD 20816
301-263-9841
FAX: 301-229-2443 www.aabd.org
Keith Dalrymple, President/CEO
James I Lundy, VP
David Baris, Executive Director
Betty Pelton, Membership Director
Audit committee members, and directors in general, will have to make certain that the duties mandated by the 1991 law are carried out because federal penalties can be imposed for failure to do so. *$35.00*

2440 Bowne Review for CFO's and Investment Bankers
Brumberg Publications
124 Harvard Street
Brookline, MA 02446-6454
617-734-1979
FAX: 617-734-1989 www.bowne.com
Bruce Brumberg, Editor
Karen Axelrod, Managing Editor
Susan Koffman, Executive
Summaries of articles on corporate finance, mergers acquisitions, intial public offerings (IPOs) and restructuring. Selects articles from hundreds of publications focusing on articles trends, strategies and advice on deal sturturing.

2441 Business Owner
Financial & Security Products Association
Plaza Ladera, 5300 Sequoia NW
Suite 205
Albuquerque, NM 87120
505-839-7958
FAX: 505-839-0017 800-843-6082
info@fspa1.com www.fspa1.com
Pat Hughes, Chairman
Christen Womack, President
Mark Barclay, Director
Mark Thatcher, VP
John Vrabec, Executive Director
This electronic publication is a superb source of pertinent information for business owners and operators.
Bi-Monthly

2442 CBA Reports
Consumer Bankers Association
1000 Wilson Boulevard
Suite 2500
Arlington, VA 22209-3912
703-276-1750
FAX: 703-528-1290
research@cbanet.org www.cbanet.org
Joe Belew, President
Frtiz Elmendorf, Editor
New legislation new on retail banking for association members.
Monthly Founded: 1919
Circulation: 10,000
Printed in on newsprint stock

2443 CFA Institute Conference Proceedings
CFA Institute
560 Ray C Hunt Drive
Charlottesville, VA 22903
434-951-5499
FAX: 434-951-5262 800-247-8132
info@amir.org www.cfainstitute.org
Rodney N Sullivan, Editor
Jeff Diermeier, Chief Executive Officer
Brings you presentations in an edited, easy-to-read format that lets you experience the flavor of a conference without actually being there.
Quarterly

2444 CSBS Examiner
1155 Connecticut Avenue NW
Suite 500
Washington, DC 20036-4306
202-296-2840
FAX: 202-296-1928 800-886-2727
rstromberg@csbs.org www.csbs.org
Neal Milner, Chief Executive Officer
Roger Stromberg, Senior VP
54 pages Weekly Founded: 1902

2445 Cheklist
BKB Publications
98 Greenwich Avenue
1st Floor
New York, NY 10011-7743
212-807-7933
FAX: 212-807-1821
bkbpub1@ix.netcom.com
Brian Burkart, Publisher
Charlene Komar Storey, Editor
Features general news, feature articles, legislative updates, reports on trends, legal advice, marketing ideas, product information and news of state and national association activities. *$35.00*
Quarterly
Circulation: 16,000

2446 Client Quarterly
WPI Communications
55 Morris Avenue
Springfield, NJ 07081
973-678-8700
FAX: 800-677-9742 800-323-4995
info@wpicomm.com
www.wpicomm.com
Ken Barry, Editor
Steven Klinghoffer, Publisher/President
Information and advice on financial, business and tax matters.
Quarterly Founded: 1952

2447 Community Bank President
Siefer Consultants
525 Cayuga Street
PO Box 1384
Storm Lake, IA 50588-1384
712-732-7340
FAX: 712-732-7906
info@siefer.com www.siefer.com
Dan Siefer, Publisher
Profit making opportunities for financial institutions. *$297.00*
8 pages Monthly

2448 Compliance & Management Bulletin
America's Community Bankers
900 19th Street NW
Suite 400
Washington, DC 20006
202-857-3100
FAX: 202-296-8716 888-872-0275
info@acbankers.org
www.americascommunitybankers.com
Diane Casey-Landry, President/CEO
Micheal Shu, Editor
Includes the information you need to keep up with and respond to the latest in new and revised laws and regulations affecting your institution's management and operations. *$375.00*
Published, As Needed Founded: 1992
Circulation: 2000

2449 Consumer Bankers Association
1000 Wilson Boulevard
Suite 2500
Arlington, VA 22209-3912
703-276-1750
FAX: 703-528-1290
webmaster@cbanet.org
www.cbanet.org
Joe Belew, President
Fritz Elmendorf, Editor
Legislative newsletter on retail banking for association members.
Founded: 1919

2450 Credit Card Management
Thomson Financial Publishing
1 State Street Plaza Front
27th Floor
New York, NY 10004
212-825-8445
FAX: 212-292-5216 800-328-9378
general.info@thomson.com
www.tfn.com
James Daly, Editor
Richard J Harrington, President/CEO
Jose Thomas, Manager
Information on the major developments in the credit card industry. *$98.00*
74 pages Monthly
Circulation: 19000
Printed in 4 colors on glossy stock

2451 Current Issues in Bank Auditing
Bank Research Associates
5866 Kootenai Lane
PO Box 7812
Boise, ID 83707-1812
208-322-3508
www.bankresearchassociates.com
Don L Raymond CPA, Editor
Offers information and updates on auditing of financial institutions. *$98.00*
6 pages Monthly Founded: 1979

2452 DTCC Newsletter
Depository Trust Company
55 Water Street
New York, NY 10041
212-551-1200
FAX: 212-785-9681
info@dtcc.com www.dtcc.com
Stephen Letzler, Editor
Jill M Considine, Chairman/CEO
Janet Wynn, Managing Director
Information for the banking and securities industry.
Monthly Founded: 1999
Circulation: 7000

2453 Daily Treasury Statement
Financial Management Service
3700 E West Highway
Room 502A
Hysttaville, MD 20782
202-874-9790
FAX: 202-874-8447 800-826-9434
dts.Questions@fms.treas.gov
www.fms.treas.gov
Richard L Gregg, Commissioner
Melanie Rigney, Editor
This report offers the latest news of the Treasury Department.
Daily Founded: 1974

2454 Digest for Corporate & Securities Lawyers
Bowne & Company
345 Hudson Street
New York, NY 10014
212-924-5500
www.bowne.com
Bruce Brumberg, Editor-in-Chief
Johanna McKenzie, Editor
Susan Koffman, Editor
Karen Axelrod, Managing Editor
Philip E Kucera, Chairman/CEO
Summaries of articles on corporate finance, mergers acquisitions, intial public offerings (ipos) and restructuring. Selects articles from hundreds of publications focusing on articles trends, strategies and advice on deal structuring.
Monthly Founded: 1775

2455 Directors & Trustees Digest
America's Community Bankers
900 Nineteenth Street NW
Suite 400
Washington, DC 20006
202-857-3100
FAX: 202-296-8716
www.americascommunitybankers.com
Diane Casey-Landry, President/CEO
Nancy Feig, Senior Editor
James Swann, Associate Editor
Monique Hanis, Marketing/Business Development
Provides corporate governance guidance, outlines board legal and fiduciary responsibilities and offers resourceful information on board management relations.
Monthly

2456 E-News
Electronic Funds Transfer Association
11350 Random Hills Road
Suite 650
Fairfax, VA 22030
703-359-9800
FAX: 703-934-6058
eftassoc@efta.org www.efta.org
Kurt Helwig, Executive Director
An electronic newsletter for the banking industry.
180 pages Monthly Founded: 1977

2457 Examiner
Conference of State Bank Supervisors
1155 Connecticut Avenue NW
5th Floor
Washington, DC 20036-4306
202-296-2840
FAX: 202-296-1928
rstromberg@csbs.org www.csbs.org
E Joseph Face, III, Chairman
Jeffrey C Vogel, Vice Chairman
Neil Milner, President/CEO
Roger Stromberg, Senior Vice President
Provides news, analysis and commentary on the important events affecting the state banking system.
Weekly

2458 FSPA Newsletter
Financial & Security Products Association
Plaza Ladera, 5300 Sequoia NW
Suite 205
Albuquerque, NM 87120
505-839-7958
FAX: 505-839-0017 800-843-6082
info@fspa1.com www.fspa1.com
Pat Hughes, Chairman
Christen Womack, President
Mark Barclay, Director
Mark Thatcher, VP
John Vrabec, Executive Director
We offer timely ideas and techniques to help you compete and run your business more effectively.
Monthly

2459 Federal Reserve Bulletin
Board of Governors of the Federal Reserve System
20th Street and Constitution Avenue NW
Washington, DC 20551
202-452-3284
FAX: 202-452-3819
www.federalreserve.gov
Reports on analysis on economic developments, regulatory issues and new data. The quarterly version will no longer be published, however the Board will print an annual compendium.
Annual Founded: 1913

2460 Federal Reserve Regulatory Service
Federal Reserve Board Publishers
20th Street and Constitution Avenue
Washington, DC 20551
202-452-3000
FAX: 202-452-3819
publication-bog@frbog.frb.gov
www.federalreserve.gov
Consumer and community affairs. *$200.00*

Monthly

2461 Funds Transfer Report
Bankers Research
PO Box 431
Westport, CT 06881-0431

Ted Volckhausen Sr, Publisher/Co-Editor
Ted Volckhausen Jr, Editor
Offers banking and financial information to professionals and consumers. *$324.00*
Monthly

2462 Global Investment Technology
Global Investment Technology
820 2nd Avenue
4th Floor
New York, NY 10017
212-370-3700
FAX: 212-370-4606
info@globalinv.com
www.globalinv.com
Michael Horton, Publisher
Paven Saeghel, Editor-in-Chief
Focuses exclusively on strategic business trends, operations, and automation issues facing US and non-US investment institutions and banks. *$695.00*
Bi-Weekly Founded: 1991
Circulation: 1800

2463 Global Survey of Regulatory & Market Devel opments in Banking
Institute of International Bankers
299 Park Avenue
17th Floor
New York, NY 10171
212-421-1611
FAX: 212-421-1119
iib@iib.org www.iib.org
Everett Schenk, Chairman
Robert C O'Brien, Vice Chairman
Lawrence R Uhlick, Executive Director/General Counsel
The study documents the economic contributions that international banks make to the United States, and also addresses the benefits that other countries enjoy from the extensiv activities of United States and other non-domestic banks in their markets.

Annual

2464 IBES Monthly Comments
Lynch, Jones and Ryan
1633 Broadway
48th Floor
New York, NY 10019
212-310-9500
FAX: 646-223-9081 800-992-7526
ljrinfo@ljr.com www.ljr.com
Stanley Chamberlin, Publisher
Todd W Burns, President
Monitors changes in global earning estimates database.
Founded: 1966

2465 IFSA Newsletter
9 Sylvan Way
First Floor
Parsippany, NJ 07054-3802
973-656-1900
FAX: 973-656-1915
info@intlbanking.org
www.ifsaonline.org
Dan Taylor, President
250 pages Quarterly Founded: 1924

2466 In Focus
National Assn of Government Guaranteed Lenders
424 South Squires Street
Stillwater, OK 74074
405-377-4022
FAX: 405-377-3931
bfortune@naggl.com www.naggl.org
Tony Wilkinson, President/CEO
Karen High, EVP/COO
Jenifer Brake, Assistant VP Marketing
Jennifer Sterrett-O'Neill, Assistant VP Communications
Pratical tips that will help you build the little efficiencies that make a big difference.
Monthly

2467 Inside Mortgage Compliance
Inside Mortgage Finance Publishers
7910 Woodmont Avenue
Suite 1010
Bethesda, MD 20814
301-951-1240
FAX: 301-656-1709
imce@imfpubs.com
www.imfpubs.com
George Brooks, Editor
Guy Cecala, Publisher
Keeps executives on top of crucial and evolving legal and regulatory issues. Covers fair housing, predatory lending, consumer protection, RESPA, TILA, lawsuits. Features monthly CRA ratings. *$571.00*
14 pages Monthly Founded: 1990 750 names
Printed in 2 colors on matte stock

2468 Inside Strategy
Strategy Research Corporation
100 NW 37th Avenue
Miami, FL 33125
305-649-5400
FAX: 305-643-5584
strategy@canect.net
www.strategyresearch.com
Johanna Strouss, Editor
Richard Tobin, President
Inside Strategy is a newsletter that covers trends and developments in Latin America and the US Hispanic market mostly obtained from SRC, studies, products services and reports.
38511 pages Monthly Founded: 1998

2469 Inside The GSEs
Inside Mortgage Finance Publishers
7910 Woodmont Avenue
Suite 1010
Bethesda, MD 20814
301-951-1240
FAX: 301-656-1709
service@imfpubs.com
www.imfpubs.com
Guy Cecala, Publisher
Greg Johnson, Editor
John Bancroft, Managing Editor
Mary L Probka, Director Marketing/Circulation
Subscribers know the latest on GSE finance, products, political contributions, their critics and supporters, and news on potential reform, controversies and regulatory activities. *$763.00*
14 pages Bi-Weekly Founded: 1985 400 names
Printed in 2 colors on matte stock

2470 John Bollinger's Capital Growth Letter
Bollinger Capital Management
PO Box 3358
Manhattan Beach, CA 90266
310-798-8855
FAX: 310-798-8858 800-888-8400
bbands@bollingerbands.com
www.bollingerbands.com
John Bollinger, Author/CEO
Covers stocks, bonds, precious metals, commodities, the dollar and the international markets. Utilizes a technically driven asset allocation approach and investment recommendations. A free twice-a-week hotline is available to all subscribers. Online or by mail. *$300.00*
12 pages Monthly Founded: 1980
Circulation: 500
Printed in 2 colors : E-mail

2471 John Bollinger's Group Power
Bollinger Capital Management
PO Box 3358
Manhattan Beach, CA 90266
310-798-8855
FAX: 310-798-8855 800-888-8400
BBands@BollingerBands.com
www.BollingerBands.com
John Bollinger, Author
Dorit Kehr, Contact
Electronic daily newsletter available everyday via email or on Bollinger's home page. Provides group analysis using a group structure, provides a wide array of marketing statistics designed to assist the investor in making market timing and investment decisions.
Daily : E-mail

2472 MSRB Manual
Municipal Securities Rulemaking Board
1900 Duke Street
Suite 600
Alexandria, VA 22747
703-797-6600
FAX: 703-797-6700 www.msrb.org
Christopher Taylor, President/CEO
Phillip Smith, Managing Director
Rules of the Municipal Rule-Making Board. *$7.00*
Founded: 1975

2473 NACHA: Electronic Payments Association Newsletter
13665 Dulles Technology Drive
Suite 300
Herndon, VA 20171
703-561-1100
FAX: 703-787-0996
info@nacha.org www.nacha.org
Elliot McEntee, President/CEO
William B Nelson, Executive VP
Articles on industry self regulatory organizations for automated clearing house payment systems and other electronic payments. *$ 120.00*

Printed in 2 colors on matte stock

2474 NAGGL News Flash
National Assn of Government Guaranteed Lenders
424 South Squires Street
Stillwater, OK 74074
405-377-4022
FAX: 404-377-3931
bfortune@naggl.com www.naggl.com
Tony Wilkinson, President/CEO
Karen High, EVP/COO
Jenifer Brake, Assistant VP Marketing
Jennifer Sterrett-O'Neill, Assistant VP Communications
This email is an at-a-glance review of recent industry news.
Bi-Monthly

2475 Nilson Report
HSN Consultants
PO Box 49936
Los Angeles, CA 90049
310-396-0615
FAX: 805-983-0792
www.nilsonreport.com
H Spencer Nilson, Publisher
Credit card newsletter. *$945.00*
12 pages BiWeekly

2476 Opportunities for Banks in Life Insurance
American Association of Bank Directors
4701 Sangamore Road
Suite P15
Bethesda, MD 20816
301-263-9841
FAX: 301-229-2443 www.aabd.org
Kenneth Kehrer, MD, Author/Insurance Products Advisor
Keith Dalrymple, President/CEO
James I Lundy, VP
David Baris, Executive Director
Betty Pelton, Membership Director
The guide reviews best insurance sales practices, distribution strategies, selling through investment brokers, using licensed branch bankers, referrals from investment specialists, referrals from licensed branch bankers, stand alone life specialists, direct sales and more. *$ 12.50*

2477 Origination News
Thomson Financial
195 Broadway
New York, NY 10007
646-222-2000
FAX: 212-803-8760
www.originationnews.com
Mark Fogarty, Associate Editor
Richard J Harrington, President/CEO
Information for mortgage industry executives on mortgage brokers, mortgage bankers and mortgage executives in commercial banks, savings banks, savings and loan associations and credit unions. *$78.00*
Monthly

2478 Payments System Report
National Automated Clearing House Association
13665 Dulles Technology Drive
Suite 300
Herndon, VA 20171
703-561-1100
FAX: 703-787-0996 800-487-9180
info@nacha.org www.nacha.org
Michael Herd, Editor
Official source for Automated Clearing House (ACH) news and information. Contains reports on rule changes, legislative and regulatory developments, policy issues, market research, product developments and marketing solutions.
Monthly

2479 Peer News
American Bankers Association
1120 Connecticut Avenue NW
Suite 600
Washington, DC 20036
202-635-5000
FAX: 202-828-4540
icb@aba.com
www.aba.com/icbcertifications
William J Foote, Chairman
Mark P Bensabat, President
Howard Walseman, Executive Director
Lisa Underwood, Associate Director
Mark DeBaugh, Marketing/Communications Manager
ICB members receive a newsletter that shares program developments, member career notes, insights from ICB leadership, the latest continuing education opportunities, and more.
Quarterly

2480 RTC Suits Against Savings Institution Dire ctors and Officers
American Association of Bank Directors
4701 Sangamore Road
Suite P15
Bethesda, MD 20816
301-263-9841
FAX: 301-229-2443 www.aabd.org
Keith Dalrymple, President/CEO
James I Lundy, VP
David Baris, Executive Director
Betty Pelton, Membership Director
This study reviews all 90 of the cases in the RTC's public files that were filed by the RTC against directors and officers. *$85.00*

2481 Regional Mortgage Market Report
Mortgage Bankers Association
1919 Pennsylvania Avenue NW
Washington, DC 20006-3404
202-557-2700
FAX: 202-721-0198 800-793-6222
brian_carey@mbaa.org www.mbaa.org
Jonathan L Kempner, President/CEO
The Regional Mortgage Market Report for MSAs and/or states has been designed to provide mortgage professionals with a primary source of information to help identify mortgage lending opportunities and manage the risks associated with mortgage servicing. *$395.00*
Quarterly Founded: 1914
Computerized version available

2482 Report of Task Force on Asset Freezes of B ank Directors and Officers
American Association of Bank Directors
4701 Sangamore Road
Suite P15
Bethesda, MD 20816
301-263-9841
FAX: 301-229-2443 www.aabd.org
Keith Dalrymple, President/CEO
James I Lundy, VP
David Baris, Executive Director
Betty Pelton, Membership Director
$25.00

2483 SCOR Report
Stewart Gordon Associates
PO Box 781992
Dallas, TX 75378-1992
972-620-2489
FAX: 972-406-0213
tsg@scor-report.com
www.scor-report.com
Tom Stewart Gordon, Publisher
C Delton Simmons, Circulation Manager
Anne D Hall, Production Manager
Capital information alternatives for small business. Target audience: small business, their lawyers and accountants. *$280.00*
Founded: 1994

2484 SNL Bank & Thrift Daily
SNL Securities
One SNL Plaza
PO Box 2124
Charlottesville, VA 22902-2124
434-977-1600
FAX: 434-977-4466
subscriptions@snl.com www.snl.com
Reid Nagle, Publisher
John Minor, Editor
Mike Chinn, President
Summary of previous week's acquisition announcements, branch sales, merger conversions, FDIC transactions and deal updates and perspectives. *$1700.00*
Weekly Founded: 1987

2485 SNL REIT Weekly
SNL Securities
One SNL Plaza
PO Box 2124
Charlottesvle, VA 22902
434-977-1600
FAX: 434-977-4466
subscriptions@snl.com www.snl.com
Chandler Spears, Editor
Glenn Doggett, Director Data Analysis
Keven Lindemann, Director Real Estate
Fax newsletter that summarizes the previous week's activity involving REITs. Includes comprehensive articles on current industry trends, condensed news stories, recent capital offerings and the latest market information. *$496.00*
15 pages Weekly Founded: 1987

2486 Secondary Mortgage Markets
Federal Home Loan Mortgage Corporation
8200 Jones Branch Drive
McLean, VA 22102-3110
703-903-2000
FAX: 703-903-4045
smm@frediemac.com
www.freddiemac.com
Richard Syrom, President/CEO
Covers buying and selling residential and commercial mortgage-backed and asset-backed loans, marketing, and risk management.
Monthly Founded: 1970
Circulation: 15000

2487 Study of Leading Banks in Insurance
American Bankers Insurance Association
1120 Connecticut Avenue NW
Washington, DC 20036
202-635-5000
FAX: 202-828-4546 800-226-5377
nbryant@aba.com www.theabia.com
Valerie Barton, Associate Director
Thomas J Cook, Chairman/President
Richard L Spickard, VP

Beth L Climo, Executive Director
Paul G Petrylak, Treasurer

A comprehensive look at the broad trends of bank insrance participation, product strategies, distribution platforms and operating practices. The Study also analyzes recent agency acquisitions and results achieved by bank insurance leaders.
Annual

2488 Thrift Insider
Inside Mortgage Finance Publishers
7910 Woodmont Avenue
Suite 1010
Bethesda, MD 20814
301-951-1240
FAX: 301-656-1709
service@imfpubs.com
www.imfpubs.com

Guy D Cecala, Publisher

Complete coverage of regulatory, legislative, legal, accounting, and market issues in the thrift industry. *$485.00*
Bi-Weekly

2489 World Bank News
World Bank
1818 H Street NW
Room U11-147
Washington, DC 20433-2
202-473-1000
FAX: 202-477-6391
www.worldbank.org

Joelle Dehasse, Editor
Paul Wolfowitz, President
Cynthia Delgadillo, Production Manager

For journalists and the developing community
Fortnightly Founded: 1980
Circulation: 9000

Magazines & Journals

2490 A Bank Director's Guide to Avoiding Enforc ement Actions
American Association of Bank Directors
4701 Sangamore Road
Suite P15
Bethesda, MD 20816
301-263-9841
FAX: 301-229-2443 www.aabd.org

Keith Dalrymple, President/CEO
James I Lundy, VP
David Baris, Executive Director
Betty Pelton, Membership Director

Reviews various federal bank agency enforcement actions, and what you, as a bank director, can do to prevent them or, in the worst case, minimize their impact on your institution. *$12.50*

2491 A Bank Director's Guide to Codes of Conduc t
American Association of Bank Directors
4701 Sangamore Road
Suite P15
Bethesda, MD 20816
301-263-9841
FAX: 301-229-2443 www.aabd.org

Keith Dalrymple, President/CEO
James I Lundy, VP
David Baris, Executive Director
Betty Pelton, Membership Director

Will assist Boards in writing and adopting the codes of conduct which have become a necessary requirement since banking enforcement agencies have published new rules, regulations and policy statements they expect employees of financial institutions, particularly directors and officers, to adhere to in order to avoid administrative enforcement action, or a civil suit, if the institution fails. *$12.50*

2492 A Guide to Implementing Direct Payment Through the ACH
NACHA: Electronic Payments Association
13665 Dulles Technology Drive
Suite 300
Herndon, VA 20171
703-561-1100
FAX: 703-787-0996
info@nacha.org www.nacha.org

Elliott McEntee, President/CEO
William B Nelson, Executive VP

A complete overview of these popular ACH applications. Also discussed are benefits, costs, operational/implementation concerns and promotional efforts. Included are sample promotional materials and implementation checklists. *$10.00*

2493 A Profile of State Chartered Banking
1155 Connecticut Avenue NW
Suite 500
Washington, DC 20036-4306
202-296-2840
FAX: 202-296-1928 800-886-2727
rstromberg@csbs.org www.csbs.org

Roger Stromberg, Senior Vice President
54 pages Monthly Founded: 1902

2494 ABA Bank Compliance
American Bankers Association
1120 Connecticut Avenue NW
Washington, DC 20036-3971
202-635-5000
FAX: 202-828-4540 www.aba.com

Larry Price, Publisher
Joe Kelly, Senior Editor

Timely, authoritative analysis of the ever-changing regulatory environment. *$450.00*
Bi-Monthly Founded: 1875
Circulation: 3,000+

2495 ABA Bank Marketing
American Bankers Association
1120 Connecticut Avenue NW
Washington, DC 20036-3971
202-635-5000
FAX: 202-828-4540 800-226-5377
walbro@aba.com www.aba.com

Larry Price, Publisher
Walt Albro, Senior Associate Editor

A designed package of marketing intelligence, featuring essential industry news, in-depth articles, award-winning columnists and opinions, useful case studies and time-saving advice. *$120.00*
Monthly Founded: 1875

2496 ABA Banking Journal
Simmons Boardman Publishing Corporation
345 Hudson Street
New York, NY 10011
212-379-9300
FAX: 212-633-1165 800-895-4389
ababj@sbpub.com www.ababj.com

William Streeter, Editor-in-Chief
Art McGinnis, Associate Publisher

Features esssential industry news, in-depth articles, award-winning columnists and opinions, useful case studies and time-saving advice. *$40.00*
Monthly Founded: 1908
Circulation: 29,100
Printed in 4 colors

2497 ABA Consumer Banking Digest
American Bankers Association
1120 Connecticut Avenue NW
Washington, DC 20036-3902
202-635-5000
FAX: 202-828-4547
drhodes@aba.com www.aba.com

John Ginovsky, Editor
Doug Johnson, Editor
Mako Parker, Editor
Donald Rhodes, Editor
Aimee Van Zandt, Editor

Provides perspectives on the latest developments, shifts and changes in the e-commerce sector. The goal is to provide a comprehensive, yet concise, description of current events shaping the rapidly emerging world of e-commerce and banking. *$450.00*
Bi-Monthly Founded: 1875

2498 ABA Consumer Credit Delinquency Bulletin
American Bankers Association
1120 Connecticut Avenue NW
Washington, DC 20036-3200
202-635-5000
FAX: 202-663-7597 800-226-5377

Jane Yao, Managing Director

Compare your bank's loan portfolio delinquency rate to other banks in your area. Detailed data you need to evaluate where your bank stands in today's economic landscape. *$260.00*
Quarterly Founded: 1875

2499 ABA Reference Guide for Regulatory Complia nce
American Bankers Association
1120 Connecticut Avenue NW
Washington, DC 20036-3200
202-635-5000
FAX: 202-663-7597 800-226-5377

Kathlyn Farrell, Esq, Author
Janita Ponze, Contact

Reference guide for those preparing for the Certified Regulatory Compliance Manager Exam. *$350.00*
Annual

2500 ABA Trust & Investments
American Bankers Association
1120 Connecticut Avenue NW
Washington, DC 20036
202-635-5000
FAX: 202-828-4540 800-226-5377
lprice@aba.com www.aba.com

Larry Price, Publisher
Joe Kelly, Senior Editor

Articles written for bankers concerning client management, tax planning for various situations, distribution, private banking and financial planning services. *$120.00*
15 pages Bi-Monthly

2501 ACH Marketing Handbook: A Guide for Financial Institutions & Companies
NACHA: Electronic Payments Association

13665 Dulles Technology Drive
Suite 300
Herndon, VA 20171-4607
703-561-1100
FAX: 703-787-0996
info@nacha.org www.nacha.org

Elliott McEntee, President/CEO
William B Nelson, Executive VP

Offers step-by-step ACH marketing guidelines with separate sections for financial institutions and corporations. Details how to identify potential customers, develop and implement an effective marketing plan and sell ACH benefits to consumers and to your own organization. *$70.00*

Annual+

2502 ACH Operating Rules & Guidelines

NACHA: Electronic Payments Association

13665 Dulles Technology Drive
Suite 300
Herndon, VA 20171
703-561-1100
FAX: 703-787-0996
info@nacha.org www.nacha.org

Elliott McEntee, President/CEO
William B Nelson, Executive VP

Details current rule changes and how to comply with these changes. *$55.00*

2503 ACH Operating Rules, Corporate Edition
NACHA: Electronic Payments Association

13665 Dulles Technology Drive
Suite 300
Herndon, VA 20171
703-561-1100
FAX: 703-787-0996
info@nacha.org www.nacha.org

Elliott McEntee, President/CEO
William B Nelson, Executive VP

An overview of the ACH Network and how it works, plus sections on ACH system development and originators. *$37.00*

2504 ACH Settlement Guide
NACHA: Electronic Payments Association

13665 Dulles Technology Drive
Suite 300
Herndon, VA 20171
703-561-1100
FAX: 703-787-0996
info@nacha.org www.nacha.org/

Elliott McEntee, President/CEO
William B Nelson, Executive VP

Designed to provide a thorough working knowledge of how money flows through the ACH Network and to equip financial institutions with the necessary tools to reconcile the daily ACH. Included in this publication are examples of statements, ACH advices and a sample balancing worksheet that financial institutions can use as a model for daily reconciling. This document was written as a direct result of financial institutions losing money due to the mismanagement of the ACH settlement function. *$75.00*

2505 AFP Exchange
Association for Financial Professionals
7315 Wisconsin Avenue
Suite 600 W
Bethesda, MD 20814
301-907-2862
FAX: 301-907-2864
afp@afponline.org www.afponline.org

Leigh Marjamaga, Editor
Matt Mientka, Reporter
James Kaitz, President & CEO

AFP Exchange is published for financial professionals. Editorial highlights include case studies and practical business information. Regular departments include outlook, new products and services, calendar and book reviews. *$90.00*

80 pages Bi-Monthly Founded: 1979
Circulation: 12000
Printed in 4 colors on glossy stock : PDF

2506 AITCO Membership Directory
Association of Independent Trust Companies
8 South Michigan Avenue
Suite 1000
Chicago, IL 60603
312-223-1611
FAX: 312-580-0165
aitco@gss.net www.aitco.net

Joe Alerding, President
Troy Kennedy, VP/Conference Chairman
Jeff Kanaly, Treasurer

Provides members with contact information on peers as well as industry vendors. This reference tool also include a listing of key officers as well as detailed descriptions of the company's product line and specialty areas.

50+ pages

2507 American Banker
American Banker/SourceMedia
1 State Street Plaza
27th Floor
New York, NY 10004-1549
212-631-1271
FAX: 212-843-9600 800-221-1809
adam.silverstone@sourcemedia.com
www.americanbanker.com

Bruce Morris, Publisher
David Longobardi, Editor-in-Chief
John Crewe, Circulation Director

Focuses on the continuing changes in banking, including lending, money market shifts, developments in operations and technology, marketing, mortgages and mergers. *$945.00*

Founded: 1835
Circulation: 18754

2508 Bank Insurance & Securities Marketing
Bank Insurance and Securities Association
303 West Lancaster Avenue
Suite 2D
Wayne, PA 19087
610-989-9047
FAX: 610-989-9102
bisa@bisanet.org www.bisanet.org

John Vaughan, President
Heywood Sloane, Managing Director
Jordan Miller, VP
John Lewis, Treasurer

Offers readers expert advice, exemplary editorials, in-depth articles and timely news updates.

Online Founded: 1992

2509 Bank Insurance Compliance: Fundamentals
American Bankers Insurance Association
1120 Connecticut Avenue NW
Washington, DC 20036
202-635-5000
FAX: 202-828-4546 800-226-5377

Valerie Barton, Associate Director
Thomas J Cook, Chairman/President
Richard L Spickard, VP
Beth L Climo, Executive Director
Paul G Petrylak, Treasurer

The ABIA, in collaboration with the Life Office Management Association (LOMA), developed a workbook and on-line training course describing the applicable state and federal rules for banks selling insurance.

2510 Bank News
Bank News Publications
PO Box 29156
Shawnee Mission, KS 66205-9156
913-261-7000
FAX: 913-261-7010 800-336-1120
info@banknews.com
www.banknews.com

Bill Poquette, Editor
Pam Baker, Publisher
Rich Galloway, Advertising/Sales Manager

News and features for banks and bankers. *$79.00*

64 pages Monthly Founded: 1901
Circulation: 7000
Printed in 4 colors on glossy stock

2511 Bank Notes
510 King Street
Suite 410
Alexandria, VA 22314
703-549-0977
FAX: 703-548-5945 800-966-7475
eba@envirobank.org
www.envirobank.org

DJ Telego, Executive Co-Director
Tacy Cook Telego, Executive Co-Director

76 pages Bi-Monthly Founded: 1994

2512 Bank Systems & Technology
CMP Media
11 West 19th Street
3rd Floor
New York, NY 10011
212-928-8400
FAX: 212-600-3080
siannuz@cmp.com www.cmp.com

Peter McManus, Publisher
Katherine Burger, Editorial Director
Sophie Chan, Production Manager

In-depth look into the new age of banking where total integration of technology is the driving force of new product business growth. Features deliver critical information on the strategic use of technology for increased profitability and productivity, in turn providing bankers with the tools to gain the competitive advantage on today's changing financial services landscape. *$52.00*

Monthly
Circulation: 23753

2513 Bank Technology News
Thomson Media
1 State Street Plaza
27th Floor
New York, NY 10004
212-258-8445
FAX: 212-843-9635
www.banktechnews.com

Chris Costanzo, Editor
Jay Berfas, Group Publisher
David Cleworth, Associate Publisher

The leading source for financial services technology coverage, written for those individuals who are responsible for the front, middle and back office technology needs of their financial institutes.

52 pages Monthly Founded: 1987

2514 Bankers Digest
9550 Forest Lane
Suite 125
Dallas, TX 75243-5928
214-221-4544
FAX: 214-221-4546
bankersdigest@bankersdigest.com
http://bankersdigest.com

Bonnie J Blackman, Editor
R Blackman Jr, Managing Editor

A weekly news magazine devoted to the southwest banking news. Accepts advertising. *$29.00*

16 pages Weekly Founded: 1942
Circulation: 3100
Printed in 2 colors on glossy stock

2515 Bankers' Magazine
Warren, Gorham & Lamont
395 Hudson Street
New York, NY 10014-3669
212-367-6300
FAX: 212-367-6718 800-742-3348
ria@thomson.com www.riahome.com

Kenneth G Oehlkers, Editor

Written by bank professionals who offer urgent information about the banking industry to the banking community. *$115.00*

Bi-Monthly Founded: 1935

2516 Banking Strategies
Bank Administration Institute
One North Franklin Street
Suite 1000
Chicago, IL 60606-3421
312-553-4600
FAX: 800-375-5543 800-224-9889
info@bai.org www.bai.org

Steven C Klinkerman, Editor-in-Chief
Kenneth Cline, Senior Editor
Deborah L Bianucci, President & CEO

Includes information on finance, economics, planning, operations, regulations, retail, technology and human resources management. *$66.50*

66 pages Founded: 1945
Circulation: 42175

2517 Banking Strategies Magazine
Bank Administration Institute
One North Franklin Street
Suite 1000
Chicago, IL 60606-3421
312-534-4600
FAX: 312-683-2373 888-284-4078
info@bai.org www.bai.org

Thomas P Johnson, Jr, Editor
Deborah L Bianucci, President/CEO

To present the latest in best practices and thought leadership through high-quality, in-depth, unbiased editorial coverage of strategic and managerial issues in today's complex and dynamic financial services business. *$66.50*

Annual

2518 Broker Magazine
Thomson Media
One State Street Plaza
27th floor
New York, NY 10004
212-258-8445
FAX: 212-292-5216 888-501-8850
Custserv@thomsonmedia.com
www.brokermagazine.com

Mark Fogarty, Editorial Director
Brad Finkelstein, Editor
Timothy Reifschneider, Advertising Director

Features on training, motivation, technology, legislation and marketing *$60.00*

Bi-Monthly

2519 Business Credit
Assn of Executives in Finance, Credit & In'tl Bus
8840 Columbia 100 Parkway
Columbia, MD 21045-2158
410-423-1840
FAX: 410-423-1845 888-256-3242
fcib_info@fcibglobal.com
www.fcibglobal.com

For professionals responsible for extending credit and collecting receivables. Topics include business law, lein law, technology, credit management, collections, deductions, fraud, credit risk, credit scoring, outsourcing, information services, trade finance and more. *$54.00*

72 pages 10x/Year Founded: 1896
Circulation: 32000
Printed in 4 colors on matte stock

2520 CFA Digest
CFA Institute
560 Ray C Hunt Drive
Charlottesville, VA 22903
434-951-5499
FAX: 434-951-5262 800-247-8132
info@aimr.org www.cfainstitute.org

Robert D Arnott, Editor
Rodney N Sullivan, Associate Editor

Distills selected current industry research into short, easy-to-read summaries. For each issue, we review about 50 investment-related journals and create short abstracts of selected articles.

Quarterly Founded: 1971

2521 CFA Magazine
CFA Insitute
560 Ray C Hunt Drive
Charlottesville, VA 22903
434-951-5499
FAX: 434-951-5262 800-247-8132
info@amir.org www.cfainstitute.org

Derik Rice, Editor
Roger Mitchell, Associate Editor

Focus on behavioral finance, this issue investigates the questions that may be lurking in the psychological shadows of financial markets and the investment industry.

2522 CMBS World
30 Broad Street
28th Floor
New York, NY 10004-2304
212-509-1844
FAX: 212-509-1895
info@cmbs.org www.cmbs.org

Kent Born, President
Christopher Hoeffel, VP
Dottie Cunningham, Chief Executive Officer
Annemarie DiCola, Treasurer

To inform, educate and stimulate meaningful discussions and exchanges among CMBS members on the risks and benefits of commercial mortgage-backed securities.

309 pages Quarterly Founded: 1994

2523 Commercial Mortgage Insight
Zackin Publications
PO Box 2180
Waterbury, CT 06722-2180

FAX: 203-262-4680 800-325-6745
info@cmi-online.com
www.cmi-online.com/cmi

Paul Zackin, Publisher
Joe Caton, Editor

For decision-making executives in commercial mortgage banking and brokerage firms, commercial banks and community/savings institutions. Provides professionals with timely and comprehensive market news, trends and know-how needed to make informed decisions and choices. *$48.00*

32 pages Monthly Founded: 1997
Circulation: 16089 $100 per M.
Printed in 4 colors on glossy stock

2524 Community Bank President
Siefer Consultants
PO Box 1384
Storm Lake, IA 50588-1384
712-732-7340
FAX: 712-732-7906 siefer@ncn.net

Dan Siefer, Publisher

Analysis of trends, new ideas and implementation strategies, regulatory compliance, and bank profitability. Provides a glimpse at the latest deposit and loan statistics, marketing and new technology updates and bank management issues.

Monthly
Circulation: 1800

2525 Community Banker Magazine
America's Community Bankers
900 19th Street NW
Suite 400
Washington, DC 20006
202-857-3100
FAX: 202-296-8716 888-872-0275
info@acbankers.org
www.americascommunitybankers.org

Debra Cope, Senior VP/Publisher
Monique Hanis, Senior VP Marketing
Leann Shepp, Circulation Manager
Diane Casey-Landry, President

Community Banker presents engaging, practical and timely reporting and analysis on industry issues. Enhanced coverage of major interest to community bank leaders includes mortgages, management, technology and wealth. *$66.00*

Monthly
Circulation: 10500+ $.32 per M.
Printed in 4 colors on glossy stock

2526 Community Banking Advisor
10831 Old Mill Road
Suite 400
Omaha, NE 68154
402-778-7922
FAX: 402-778-7931 888-475-4476
info@bankingcpas.com
www.bankingcpas.com

Nancy Drennen, Executive Director

A publication for banking professionals that features articles on management, tax, operational, and other issues confronting community banks.

24 pages Quarterly Founded: 1995

2527 Compendium of the Constitional Rights Task Force
American Association of Bank Directors
4701 Sangamore Road
Suite P15
Bethesda, MD 20816
301-263-9841
FAX: 301-229-2443 www.aabd.org

Keith Dalrymple, President/CEO
James I Lundy, VP
David Baris, Executive Director
Betty Pelton, Membership Director

In-depth commentary on the dwindling constitutional rights of bank directors and officers by constitutional and banking law experts. *$134.00*
170 pages

2528 Compliance Manual
NACHA: Electronic Payments Association

13665 Dulles Technology Drive
Suite 300
Herndon, VA 20171
703-561-1100
FAX: 703-787-0996 800-487-9180
info@nacha.org www.nacha.org

Elliott McEntee, President/CEO
William B Nelson, Executive VP

Published by NACHA. *$250.00*

2529 Consumer Education Information
NACHA: Electronic Payments Association

13665 Dulles Technology Drive
Suite 300
Herndon, VA 20171
703-561-1100
FAX: 703-787-0996
info@nacha.org www.nacha.org

Elliott McEntee, President/CEO
William B Nelson, Executive VP

Developed to create a consumer education campaign.

2530 Consumer's Guide to Direct Deposit
NACHA: Electronic Payments Association

13665 Dulles Technology Drive
Suite 300
Herndon, VA 20171-4607
703-561-1100
FAX: 703-787-0996
info@nacha.org www.nacha.org/

Elliott McEntee, President/CEO
William B Nelson, Executive VP

Explains the benefits of and consumer protections of Direct Deposit. *$55.00*

2531 Credit Union Journal
Thomson Media
1 State Street Plaza
27th Floor
New York, NY 10004
212-258-8445
FAX: 800-235-5552 800-221-1809
Richard.Scalise@sourcemedia.com
www.cujournal.com

Frank J Diekmann, Editor/Co-Publisher
Tim O'Hara, Advertising Director/Co-Publisher

A surging economy, combined with competitive pricing policies and regulatory changes allowing credit unions to expand their field of membership. *$119.00*
Weekly

2532 Credit Union Management Magazine
Credit Union Executives Society
5510 Research Park Drive
PO Box 14167
Madison, WI 53708-167
608-271-2664
FAX: 608-271-2303 800-252-2664
cues@cues.org www.cues.org

Fred Johnson, President
Bryan Ochalla, Editor
Mary Arnold, VP Publications
Jessica Hrubes, Marketing Manager

Published for credit union CEOs and senior management, the magazine focuses each month on general management, operations, marketing and human resource functions. Includes in-depth coverage of technology, facilities, finance, lending, staffing and card services, among other topics. *$129.00*
Monthly Founded: 1962
Circulation: 8000

2533 Direct Deposit Authorization Forms
NACHA: Electronic Payments Association

13665 Dulles Technology Drive
Suite 300
Herndon, VA 20171
703-561-1100
FAX: 703-787-0996 800-487-9180
info@nacha.org www.nacha.org/

Elliott McEntee, President/CEO
William B Nelson, Executive VP

For companies looking for generic authorization forms that market ACH benefits to consumers. *$30.00*
Monthly

2534 Directors and Trustees Digest
America's Community Bankers
900 19th Street NW
Suite 400
Washington, DC 20006
202-857-3100
FAX: 202-296-8716 888-872-0275
info@acbankers.org
www.americascommunitybankers.com

Cope Debra, Publisher
Diane Casey-Landry, President/CEO

Offers resourceful information on board management relations for community bank board members. *$105.00*
Monthly Founded: 1992

2535 Documentary Credit World
International Financial Services Association
9 Sylvan Way
First Floor
Parsippany, NJ 07054-3802
973-656-1900
FAX: 973-656-1915
info@intlbanking.org
www.ifsaonline.org

James E Byrne, Editor-in-Chief

Published jointly by the Institute of International Banking Law and Practice and the IFSA. DCW is your source for information on LCs. *$595.00*
10x/Year

2536 Electronic Payments Buyers Guide
NACHA: Electronic Payments Association

13665 Dulles Technology Drive
Suite 300
Herndon, VA 20171
703-561-1100
FAX: 703-787-0996
info@nacha.org www.nacha.org

Elliott McEntee, President/CEO
William B Nelson, Executive VP
John S Stone, Editor

Offered as a convenient resource for ACH and electronic payments systems users of all types and is not intended as a definitive compendium of all industry vendors.

2537 Electronic Payments Journal
NACHA: Electronic Payments Association

13665 Dulles Technology Drive
Suite 300
Herndon, VA 20171
703-561-1100
FAX: 703-787-0996
info@nacha.org www.nacha.org

Elliott McEntee, President/CEO
William B Nelson, Executive VP
John S Stone, Editor

Helps industry professionals to track the latest developments in electronic payments and provides in-depth coverage of a broad array of payment issues. *$180.00*
Bi-Monthly Founded: 1978

2538 Federal Credit Union Magazine
National Association of Federal Credit Unions
3138 10th Street North
Arlington, VA 22201-2149
703-522-4770
FAX: 703-522-2734 800-336-4644
tfcu@nafcunet.org www.nafcunet.org

Fred R Becker Jr, President/CEO
Rebecca Somers, Public Relations Manager
Peter Taylor, Marketing Director

Written for CEOs, senior staff and volunteers of Federal Credit Unions. Offers legislative and regulatory news, as well as technology and operational issues. *$99.00*
80 pages Bi-Monthly Founded: 1967
Circulation: 11136
Printed in 4 colors on glossy stock

2539 Finance and Development
International Monetary Fund
700 19th Street NW
Washington, DC 20431
202-623-7000
FAX: 202-623-4661
publicaffairs@imf.org www.imf.org

Shuja Nawaz, Editor
Rodrigo de Rato y Figaredo, Managing Director

Analysis of financial and economic developments and explanation of the policies and work of the International Monetary Fund and the World Bank. *$10.00*
Quarterly Founded: 1945
Circulation: 130000
Mailing list available for rent 120M names
Printed in 4 colors

2540 Financial Analyst
Association for Investment Management & Research
560 Ray C Hunt Drive
PO Box 3668
Charlottesville, VA 22903-0668
434-951-5499
FAX: 434-951-5262 800-247-8132
info@aimr.org www.cfainstitute.org

Robert D Arnott, Editor
Rodney N Sullivan, Associate Editor

Is to advance the knowledge and understanding of the practice of investment management through the publication of high-quality, practitioner-relevant research.

2541 Financial Review
Eastern Finance Association
220 Holman Hall
PO Box 1848
University, MS 38677
404-498-8937
FAX: 404-498-8956
www.easternfinance.org

Cynthia J Campbell, Editor
Arnold R Cowan, Editor

Publishes original empirical, theoretical and methodological research providing new insights into issues of importance in financial economics. *$32.00*

2542 Financial Women Today Magazine
Financial Women International
1027 W Roselawn Avenue
Roseville, MN 55113
651-487-7632
FAX: 651-489-1322 866-236-2007
info@fwi.org www.fwi.org

Cindy Bateman, President
Nancy Kinder, VP
Rilla Dath, Director
BJ Cary, Treasurer
Carol Crilly, Chairman Public Affairs

Serves nearly 10,000 female financial service professionals, helping them to attain their economic, professional and personal goals. *$24.00*
Quarterly Founded: 1921
Circulation: 19000
Printed in 4 colors on matte stock

2543 Global Custodian
Asset International
125 Greenwich Avenue
Greenwich, CT 06830-5512
203-295-5015
FAX: 203-769-2846
education@globalcustodian.com
www.globalcustodian.com

Dominic Hobson, Editor-in-Chief
Charles Ruffel, Founder/CEO
Maredith Hughes, VP

Written for international institutional investors. Stories cover engineering markets, cross border investing, securities lending and more. *$185.00*
5x/Year Founded: 1989
Circulation: 20000

2544 Government Affairs Bulletin
Financial Services Roundtable
805 15th Street NW
Suite 600
Washington, DC 20005
202-289-4322
FAX: 202-289-1903
info@fsround.org www.fsround.org

Richard M Whiting, Executive Director/General Counsel

This bulletin keeps the members of the Roundtable informed on issues in the financial services industry and how the Roundtable views them.
100 pages Weekly Founded: 1993

2545 Guide to ACH Origination
NACHA: Electronic Payments Association
13665 Dulles Technology Drive
Suite 300
Herndon, VA 20171
703-561-1100
FAX: 703-787-0996 800-487-9180
info@nacha.org www.nacha.org

Elliott McEntee, President/CEO
William B Nelson, Executive VP

This guide covers preliminary requirements, fundamental operations and implementation concerns about specific ACH applications. Easy to use, this guide contains a section on ACH applications as well as ACH risk management, exposure limits, OFAC regulations and the amended ACH audit criteria. Our Fast Start to ACH origination provides checklists for getting started quickly, plus the Appendix has sample forms, agreements and a complete list of return, reject and NO codes. *$50.00*

2546 Guide to Collecting Lost or Destroyed Checks Through the ACH Network
NACHA: Electronic Payments Association
13665 Dulles Technology Drive
Suite 300
Herndon, VA 20171
703-561-1100
FAX: 703-787-0996
info@nacha.org www.nacha.org

Elliott McEntee, President/CEO
William B Nelson, Executive VP

Guide for originating and receiving financial institutions that want to use the ACH network for recovery of lost or destroyed checks. Defines XCK entries and eligible items. Reviews benefits, legal issues, implementation procedures and returns. *$28.00*

2547 Guide to Implementing Direct Deposit Through the ACH Network
NACHA: Electronic Payments Association
13665 Dulles Technology Drive
Suite 300
Herndon, VA 20171
703-561-1100
FAX: 703-787-0996
info@nacha.org www.nacha.org

Elliott McEntee, President/CEO
William B Nelson, Executive VP

This guide is written in a clear, easy to follow style which addresses benefits, costs, and operational and implementation issues. Also included are promotional suggestions, sample materials, and implementation checklists. *$10.00*

2548 Guideline to Enhanced Check Security
2025 M Street, N.W.
Suite 800
Washington, DC 20036-2422
202-367-1144
FAX: 202-223-4579
info@cpsa-check.org
www.cpsa-checks.org

Wade Delk, Executive Director

60 pages Founded: 1952

2549 ICBA Independent Banker Magazine
Independent Community Bankers of America
518 Lincoln Road
PO Box 267
Sauk Centre, MN 56378
320-526-6546
FAX: 320-352-5766 800-422-7285
info@icba.org www.icba.org

Camden R Fine, President/CEO
Rachael Solomon, Advertising Contact

ICBA members rely on for community banking news. *$60.00*
Monthly

2550 Indelible Check
2025 M Street NW
Suite 800
Washington, DC 20036-2422
202-367-1144
FAX: 202-223-4579
info@cpsa-check.org
www.cpsa-checks.org

Wade Delk, Executive Director

An Assessment of the Dominance of the Check in the United States Payment System at the Close of the 20th Century.
60 pages Founded: 1952

2551 Independent Banker
Inside Mortgage Finance Publishers
7910 Woodmont Avenue
Suite 1010
Bethesda, MD 20814
301-951-1240
FAX: 301-915-0143 800-422-8439
service@imfpubs.com
www.imfpubs.com

Ken Guenther, President/CEO

Features strategies for high-performance community banks. Also includes profiles of success stories in community banks and assesses developments in legislation and regulation.
Monthly
Circulation: 9,800

2552 International Banking Focus
299 Park Avenue
17th Floor
New York, NY 10171
212-421-1611
FAX: 212-421-1119
iib@iib.org www.iib.org

Lawrence R Uhlick, Executive Director/General Counsel

The Focus describes the latest legislative, regulatory and tax developments in Washington and various states, along with the Institute's efforts to address particular problems that affect international banks.
230 pages 11 X'S Year Founded: 1966

2553 Journal of Bank Cost and Management Accounting
Association for Management in Financial Services
3895 Fairfax Court
Atlanta, GA 30339
770-444-3557
FAX: 770-444-9084
ami@amifs.org www.amifs.org

Charles Stockton, President
Lori Oswald, Senior VP

The only publication dedicated solely to management accounting in the financial services industry. *$75.00*

Quarterly Founded: 1980
Circulation: 500

2554 Mortgage Banking
Mortgage Bankers Association
1919 Pennsylvania Avenue NW
Washington, DC 20006-3404
202-557-2700
FAX: 202-721-0198
janet_hewitt@mbaa.org
www.mortgagebankingmagazine.com

Janet Hewitt, Editor
Jonathan L Kempner, President/CEO

Provides in-depth coverage of the real estate finance industry. Itelligent analysis of news and the most important issues and trends affecting the industry. Association discount available. *$60.00*

120 pages 14x/Year Founded: 1914
Circulation: 6000 2800 names $100 per M. Printed in 4 colors on glossy stock

2555 Mortgage Servicing News
Thomson Media
One State Street Plaza
27th Floor
New York, NY 10004
212-258-8445
FAX: 212-803-1592 800-221-1809
custserv@thomsonmedia.com
www.mortgageservicingnews.com/

Ted Cornwell, Editor
James Malkin, Chairman/CEO
Timothy Reifschneider, Marketing Manager
Virginia Wiese, Custom Publishing

Information on cross serving techniques, legislative decisions, management strategies, and professional profiles. *$98.00*

Monthly
Circulation: 20,000

2556 NABTalk It
National Association of Bankruptcy Trustees
One Windsor Cove
Suite 305
Columbia, SC 29223
803-252-5646
FAX: 803-765-0860
info@nabt.com www.nabt.com

Nancy H Cooper, Staff Editor
David A Birdsell, President

Quarterly

2557 NACTT Quarterly
National Association of Chapter 13 Trustees
3008 Milwood Avenue
Columbia, SC 29205
803-252-5646
FAX: 803-765-0860 800-445-8629
info@nactt.com www.nactt.com

Paul R Chael, President
Robin R Weiner, VP
Kevin R Anderson, Treasurer

The Quarterly emphasizes current local and national developments in Chapter 13. Each Quarterly provides a summary of the most recent Chapter 13 Bankruptcy court decisions.

2558 NACUSAC News
National Association of Credit Union Supervisory
PO Box 160
Del Mar, CA 92014

FAX: 858-792-3884 800-287-5949
nacusac@nacusac.org
www.nacusac.org

Linda Treml, Chairman
Robert Butler, Vice Chairman
Bob Spindler, Associate Director
Celeste Shelton, Associate Director
Katherine E Clark, Executive Director

Keeps you up to date on the latest developments and events affecting supervisory/auditing committee members.

Quarterly

2559 NMB Magazine
National Association of Mortgage Brokers
7900 Westpark Drive
Suite T309
McLean, VA 22102
703-342-5900
FAX: 703-342-5905 www.namb.org

Jon Ruzan, Publisher/Editorial Director
Scott Hover, Editor
Debbie Maxwell, Production Manager
$59.95

Monthly

2560 National Mortgage Broker Magazine
Banat Communications
23425 N 39th Drive
104-193
Glendale, AZ 85310
623-516-2723
FAX: 623-516-7738
jon@banatcommunications.com
www.nationalmortgagebroker.com

Jon Ruzan, Publisher/Editorial Director
Scott Hover, Editor
Debbie Maxwell, Production Manager
$59.95

Monthly Founded: 1984

2561 New England Economic Indicators
Federal Reserve Bank of Boston
600 Atlantic Avenue
Suite 100
Boston, MA 02210-2204
617-973-3000
FAX: 617-973-3957
boston.library@bos.frb.org
www.bos.frb.org

Thomas A DeCoff, Editor
Cathy E Minehan, President/CEO

Contains current and historical economic data for the states of CT, ME, MA, NH, RI, and VT, as well as the US data include employment, unemployment, prices and construction activity.

80 pages Monthly Founded: 1914
Circulation: 7000

2562 North Western Financial Review
NFR Communications
7614 York Avenue South
Suite 3314
Edina, MN 55435-1439
612-929-8110
FAX: 612-831-1464 web@nfrcom.com

Tom Bengston, Publisher

Provides useful information and useful data regarding developments without trade association bias.

Annual+ Founded: 1989
Circulation: 9,000

2563 Practical Handbook for Bank Directors
American Association of Bank Directors
4701 Sangamore Road
Suite P15
Bethesda, MD 20816
301-263-9841
FAX: 301-229-2443 www.aabd.org

Keith Dalrymple, President/CEO
James I Lundy, VP
David Baris, Executive Director
Betty Pelton, Membership Director

An easy-to-read guide for directors which reviews all aspects of director duties and responsibilities. *$35.00*

162 pages Softboud

2564 Procedures Manual Guidelines
American Safe Deposit Association
PO Box 519
Franklin, IN 46131
317-738-4432
FAX: 317-738-5267
www.americansafedeposit.org

Thomas Cullinan, President
J Wayne Merrill, First VP
Winnifred Howard-Hammack, Second VP
Joyce A McLin, Executive Director
Kevin Fanning, Treasurer

Can be used as a guide in developing yoiur own-in-house policy and procedures manual to be used in day-to-day operation of your vault. *$40.00*

2565 RMA Annual Statement Studies
Risk Management Association
1 Liberty Place 1650 Market Street
Suite 2300
Philadelphia, PA 19103
215-446-4000
FAX: 215-446-4101
customers@rmahq.org
www.rmahq.org

Maurice H Hartigan, II, President/CEO
Valerie Morris, Director Marketing

Report offering information on balance sheets and income statements for more than 400 industries, including health foods and vitamin stores. *$400.00*

Annual+ Founded: 1914
Circulation: 40000

2566 RMA Journal
Risk Management Association
1801 Market Street
Suite 300
Philadelphia, PA 19103-1628
215-635-5398
FAX: 215-446-4101 800-677-7621
customers@rmahq.org
www.rmahq.org

Beverly Foster, Publisher
W Kendall Chalk, Chairman
Glenn L Wilson, Vice Chairman
Maurice H Hartigan, II, President/CEO
Dwight Overturf, Chief Financial Officer

Journal coverage spans the gamut of risk management issues from credit operations, problem loans and workouts, small business lending, loan training and loan management to analyzing customer profitability, risk management, loan pricing, lender compensation, and the effect of reengineering. Dis-

count on subscription with membership. *$95.00*
Monthly Founded: 1914
Circulation: 23000
Printed in 4 colors on glossy stock

2567 Reg/Ops
America's Community Bankers
900 19th Street NW
Suite 400
Washington, DC 20006
202-857-3100
FAX: 202-296-8716 888-872-0275
info@acbankers.org
www.americascommunitybankers.com
Diane Casey-Landry, President/CEO
Nancy Feig, Senior Editor
James Swann, Associate Editor
Monique Hanis, Marketing/Business Development
Offers detailed reporting and analysis of the latest banking legislation, regulations, and agency compliance guidance. *$405.00*
16 pages Monthly Founded: 1950

2568 Regional Review
Federal Reserve Bank of Boston
600 Atlantic Avenue
Boston, MA 02210-2076
617-973-3000
FAX: 617-973-3957 800-409-1333
bostonlibrary@bos.frb.org
www.bos.frb.org
Jane Katz, Editor
Magazine on economics, banking, business topics, designed for the busy professional.
Quarterly Founded: 1913
Circulation: 15000
Printed in 5 colors on glossy stock

2569 Regulatory Report
America's Community Bankers
900 19th Street NW
Suite 400
Washington, DC 20006
202-857-3100
FAX: 202-296-8716 888-872-0275
info@acbankers.org
www.americascommunitybankers.com
Diane Casey-Landary, President
Harry P. Doherty, Chairman
Dedicated to thoroughly analyzing regulations and laws of key importance to banks. *$680.00*
38702 pages Monthly

2570 SNL Quarterly Bank & Thrift Digest
SNL Securities
One SNL Plaza
PO Box 2124
Charlottesvle, VA 22902-2124
434-977-1600
FAX: 434-977-4466
customerservice@snl.com
www.snl.com
P Mark Outlaw, Publisher
John McCune, Director Research
Contains all relevant information on every publicly traded bank and thrift providing insight into each individual institution and allowing quick and accurate comparisons with both peer institutions and industry benchmarks. *$799.00*
600 pages Quarterly Founded: 1987

2571 SNL Real Estate Securities Quarterly
SNL Securities
One SNL Plaza
PO Box 2124
Charlottesville, VA 22902-2124
434-977-1600
FAX: 434-977-4466
subscriptions@snl.com www.snl.com
Amy Woolard, Editor
Keven Lindemann, Director Real Estate
Mike Chinn, President
This data digest provides comprehensive corporate, market, and financial information and portfolio level property data on more than 240 publicly traded and privately held real estate companies. SNL Real Estate Securities Quarterly is the industry's most comprehensive publication for evaluating real estate company performance at both a property and financial level. *$696.00*
Quarterly Founded: 1987

2572 Safe Deposit Policy and Procedures Handboo k
American Safe Deposit Association
PO Box 519
Franklin, IL 46131
317-738-4432
FAX: 317-738-5267
www.americansafedeposit.org
Thomas Cullinan, President
J Wayne Merrill, First VP
Winnifred Howard-Hammack, Second VP
Joyce A McLin, Executive Director
Kevin Fanning, Treasurer
Over 150 topics are covered in such topics as customer relation, surrending, renting, billing and collecting, insurance, lock charges and drilling, and more. *$224.97*
300+ pages

2573 Secondary Marketing Executive
Zackin Publications
70 Edwin Avenue
PO Box 2180
Waterbury, CT 06708
203-755-0158
FAX: 203-755-3480 800-325-6745
info@sme-online.com
www.sme-online.com/sme
Paul Zackin, Publisher
Mike Kling, Editor
June Han, Marketing
Offers how-to information for buyers and sellers of mortgage loans. *$48.00*
48 pages Monthly Founded: 1970
Circulation: 95000

2574 Servicing Management
LDJ Corporation
70 Edwin Avenue
PO Box 2180
Waterbury, CT 06722-2330
203-755-0158
FAX: 203-755-3480 800-325-6745
info@sm-online.com
www.sm-online.com
Paul Zackin, Publisher
Michael Bates, Editor
June Han, Marketing
Includes updates on industry and regulatory trends, and advise on operating their departments more profitably and efficiently. *$ 48.00*
Monthly Founded: 1989
Circulation: 22500

2575 US Banker
Thomson Media
1 State Street Plaza
27th Floor
New York, NY 10004
212-258-8445
FAX: 800-235-5552
ustserv@sourcemedia.com
www.thomasmedia.com
Holly Sraeel, Editor-in-Chief
David Cleworth, Publisher
James Malkin, Chairman/CEO
Features on news and technological developments in the banking industry. Includes reports on companies, personalities and industry trends. *$109.00*
Monthly Founded: 1955
Circulation: 80000

2576 Washington Perspective
America's Community Bankers
900 19th Street NW
Suite 400
Washington, DC 20006
202-857-3100
FAX: 202-296-8716 888-872-0275
info@acbankers.org
www.americascommunitybankers.com
Jim Eberle, Editor
Diane Casey-Landry, President/CEO
Debra Cope, SVP Publisher
Zeroes in on the issues developing on Capital Hill and at the regulatory agencies that affect community banking. *$595.00*
4 pages Weekly Founded: 1992
Circulation: 2200

2577 Your Financial Institution & the Environment
510 King Street
Suite 410
Alexandria, VA 22314
703-549-0977
FAX: 703-548-5945 800-966-7475
eba@envirobank.org
www.envirobank.org
DJ Telego, Executive Co-Director
Tacy Cook Telego, Executive Co-Director
76 pages Annual Founded: 1994

Trade Shows

2578 ABA National Conference for Community Bank ers
American Bankers Association
1120 Connecticut Avenue NW
Washington, DC 20036
202-635-5000
800-338-0626
lindas@aba.com www.abn.com
Linda Singleton, Contact
Joanne Buck, Contact
Traci Golightly, Exhibits Contact
One hundred and sixteen exhibits relating to products and services for investment management, customer service improvements advertising asset/liabilty management, plus conference meetings.
1500 Attendees Annual, February

2579 **ABA Sales Management Workshop**
American Bankers Association
1120 Connecticut Avenue NW
Washington, DC 20036
202-635-5000
800-338-0626
custserv@aba.com www.apa.com
Edward Yingling, President/CEO
Workshop on creating and keeping customers, over 13 exhibitors, visited by community bank executives, managers, sales and marketing staff.
Annual, September

2580 **ABA Wealth Management & Trust Conference**
American Bankers Association
1120 Connecticut Avenue NW
Washington, DC 20036
202-635-5000
FAX: 202-663-7540 800-338-0626
custserv@aba.com www.apa.com
John Capotosto, Contact
Krista Ketschek, Exhibits Contact
Senior executive trust officers, trust department managers, investment managers and others attend. 81 exhibits offering information and products relating to equipment, supplies and services for private banking and asset management.
Annual, May

2581 **ACH Participant Directory**
NACHA: Electronic Payments Association

13665 Dulles Technology Drive
Suite 300
Herndon, VA 20171
703-561-1100
FAX: 703-787-0996
info@nacha.org www.nacha.org
Elliott McEntee, President/CEO
William B Nelson, Executive VP
Provides quick access to routing numbers and contact information for financial institutions that participate in the ACH Network. Includes American Bankers Association routing numbers and, when applicable, ACH over-ride routing numbers, association memberships, EDI receipt/reporting capabilities, institution names, street and mailing addresses and telephone numbers for the ACH officer, coordinator or department.

2582 **American Bankers Insurance Association Ann ual Conference**
American Bankers Insurance Association
1120 Connecticut Avenue NW
Washington, DC 20036
202-635-5000
FAX: 202-828-4546 800-226-5377
Valerie Barton, Associate Director
Thomas J Cook, Chairman/President
Richard L Spickard, VP
Beth L Climo, Executive Director
Aaron Albright, Media Contact
The Conference highlights Best Practices Panel presentations as well as numerous break-out sessions with case studies by bankers and providers of insurance products and services.
September

2583 **American League of Financial Institutions Annual Conference**
America's Community Bankers
900 19th Street NW
Suite 400
Washington, DC 20006
202-857-3100
FAX: 202-296-8716
William W Zuppe, Chairman
Mark Macomber, First Vice Chairman
Edwin R Maus, Second Vice Chairman
Diane Casey-Landry, President/CEO
Monique Hanis, Marketing/Business Development
Exhibits for financial institutions, federal and state chartered minority savings and loan associations in 25 states and DC.
Annual

2584 **American Safe Deposit Association Conference**
American Safe Deposit Association
PO Box 519
Franklin, IN 46131-0519
317-738-4432
FAX: 317-738-5267 www.tasda.com
Thomas Cullinan, President
J Wayne Merrill, First VP
Winnifred Howard-Hammack, Second VP
Joyce A McLin, Executive Director
Kevin Fanning, Treasurer
Offers jam-packed sessions full of information and ideas that can be implemented immediately after conference.
200 Attendees June

2585 **Annual Asia Pacific Convention & Exhibitio n**
Global Association of Risk Professionals
100 Pavonia Avenue
Suite 405
Jersey City, NJ 07310
201-222-0054
FAX: 201-222-5022
rich.apostolik@garp.com
www.garp.com
Richard Apostolik, President/CEO
Kenneth Abbott, Managing Director
Mark Wallace, Chief Operating Officer
Thomas Daula, Chief Risk Officer
GARP's flagship event for Asia, with Keynote presentations, multi-track forum and separate workshops.

2586 **Annual Convention of Mortgage Bankers**
Mortgage Bankers Association
1919 Pennsylvania Avenue NW
Washington, DC 20006-3438
202-557-2700
FAX: 202-721-0198 800-793-6222
Edward Callahan, Show Manager
Annual convention and exhibits for all aspects of the mortgage banking industry.
October

2587 **Annual Global Investors Workshop**

CFA Institute
560 Ray C Hunt Drive
Charlottesville, VA 22903
434-951-5499
FAX: 434-951-5262 800-247-8132
info@amir.org www.cfainstitute.org
Frank K Reilly, Chairman
Jeffrey J Diermeier, President/CEO
Katrina F Sherrerd, Executive Director
Kathy Valentine, Media Contact, North America
The interactive curriculum examines practical investment decision-making processes and offers global perspectives from international participants.
June

2588 **Annual Legislative, Regulatory & Complianc e Conference**
Bank Insurance and Securities Association
303 West Lancaster Avenue
Suite 2D
Wayne, PA 19087
610-989-9047
FAX: 610-989-9102
bisa@bisanet.org www.bisanet.org
John Vaughan, President
Heywood Sloane, Managing Director
Jordan Miller, VP
John Lewis, Treasurer
Focus on the internal administration of the supervisory and compliance functions of the bank broker-dealer and its related activities.
June

2589 **Association for Financial Professionals Annual Conference**
Association for Financial Professionals
7315 Wisconsin Avenue
Suite 600W
Bethesda, MD 20814
301-907-2862
FAX: 301-907-2864
AFP@AFPonline.org
www.AFPonline.org
James A Kaitz, President/CEO
Workshop and 642 exhibits of lockboxes, check processing systems, computers, investments, pensions, foreign exchange, consulting, mergers, aquistions and more information of interest to finacial professionals.
6000 Attendees October Founded: 1979

2590 **Association for Management Information in Financial Services Conference**
Assn for Management Information in Financial Svcs
3895 Fairfax Court
Atlanta, GA 30339
770-444-3557
FAX: 770-444-9084
ami@amifs.org www.amifs.org
Charles Stockton, Chairman Conference/EVP
Jane Blake, Conference Committee
Kevin W Link, Executive Director
Exhibits for employees of companies that directly serve the financial services industy, commercial banks, savings and loan banks, credit unions, Federal Reserve or bank holding companies and other banking professionals.
April

2591 **Association of Independent Trust Companies Conference**
Association of Independent Trust Companies
8 South Michigan Avenue
Suite 1000
Chicago, IL 60603
312-223-1611
FAX: 312-580-0615
aitco@gss.net www.aitco.net
Joe Alerding, President
Troy Kennedy, VP/Conference Chairman
Jeff Kanaly, Treasurer
Kathleen Lukasik, Executive Director

Session topics include current legislative issues and the latest marketing strategies.
Annual

2592 Association of Military Banks of America Conference
Association of Military Banks of America(AMBA)
PO Box 3335
Warrenton, VA 20188
540-347-1044
FAX: 540-347-7964
info@ambahq.org www.ambahq.org
Robert H Croak, Chairman
Terry Tuggle, Vice Chairman
Andrew M Egeland, Jr, President/Treasurer/Secretary
September

2593 Bank Financial Executives Conference
Bank Administration Institute
One North Franklin Street
Suite 1000
Chicago, IL 60606-3421
312-534-4600
FAX: 312-683-2373 888-284-4078
info@bai.org www.bai.org
Timothy Moen, Chairman
Deborah L Bianucci, President/CEO
Scott K Heitmann, Treasurer
Charles M Diggs, Secretary
Developed specifically for community, mid-sized and large banks to provide the most up-to-date accounting, reporting and regulatory update information, along with other financial topics that affect the way you conduct business.
May

2594 Bankers' Association for Finance & Trade Annual Conference
Bankers' Association for Finance & Trade
1120 Connecticut Avenue NW
5th Floor
Washington, DC 20036-3902
202-635-5000
FAX: 202-663-5538
baft@aba.com www.baft.org
Madeleine L Champion, President
Harry G Haymann, III, VP
Rebecca Morter, Executive Director
Bruce Portillo, Director Communications/Membership
Michael D'Orazio, Planning Coordinator
Focused on the global environment and the impact of economic developments in specifications and markets including consecutive breakouts on compliance, risk mitigation and key issues.
April

2595 Boot Camp for BSA Professionals
Conference of State Bank Supervisors
1155 Connecticut Avenue NW
5th Floor
Washington, DC 20036-4306
202-296-2840
FAX: 202-296-1928
rstromberg@csbs.org www.csbs.org
E Joseph Face, Jr, Chairman
Jeffrey C Vogel, Vice Chairman
Robert Holleyman, President/CEO
Roger Stromberg, Senior Vice President
Will provide BSA Compliance knowledge and value to your regulatory agency, financial institution or money service business.
May

2596 CFA Institute Annual Conference
CFA Institute
560 Ray C Hunt Drive
Charlottesville, VA
434-951-5499
FAX: 434-951-5262 800-247-8132
info@amir.org www.cfainstitute.org
Frank K Reilly, Chairman
Jeffrey J Diermeier, President/CEO
Katrina F Sherrerd, Executive Director
Kathy Valentine, Media Contact, North America
Participants meet peers from around the world and hear leading industry figures share insights on today's most critical investment issues.
April

2597 CREF/Multifamily Housing Convention & Expo
Mortgage Bankers Association
1919 Pennsylvania NW
Washington, DC 20006-3438
202-557-2700
FAX: 202-721-0198 800-793-6222
Edward Callahan, Show Manager
Andrew Harris, Manager
Annual conference and exhibits for commercial real estate and multi-family housing professionals.
February

2598 CSBS Annual Meeting & Conference
Conference of State Bank Supervisors
1155 Connecticut Avenue NW
5th Floor
Washington, DC 20036-4306
202-296-2840
FAX: 202-296-1928
rstromberg@csbs.org www.csbs.org
E Joseph Face, III, Chairman
Jeffrey C Vogel, Vice Chairman
Neil Milner, President/CEO
Roger Stromberg, Senior Vice President
May

2599 Check Payment Systems Association Annual Conference
Check Payment Systems Association
2025 M Street NW
Suite 800
Washington, DC 20036-2422
202-671-1144
FAX: 202-223-4579
info@cpsa-check.org
www.cpsa-checks.org
Wade Delk, Executive Director
Ashley Robinson, Manager
May

2600 CheckImage Conference
Bank Administration Institute
One North Franklin Street
Suite 1000
Chicago, IL 60606-3421
312-534-4600
FAX: 312-683-2373 888-284-4078
info@bai.org www.bai.org
Timothy P Moen, Chairman
Deborah L Bianucci, President/CEO
Scott K Heitmann, Treasurer
Charles M Diggs, Secretary
Learn how to position and equip your organization to successfully address the impacts of electronification.
September

2601 Combating Payments & Check Fraud Conference
Bank Administration Institute
One North Franklin Street
Suite 1000
Chicago, IL 60606-3421
312-534-4600
FAX: 312-683-2373 888-284-4078
info@bai.org www.bai.org
Timothy P Moen, Chairman
Deborah L Bianucci, President/CEO
Scott K Heitmann, Treasurer/CEO
Charles M Diggs, Secretary
Provide the latest intelligence, legislation and critical solutions for the fight against payments and check fraud.
September

2602 Commercial Mortgage Securities Association Conference
Commercial Mortgage Securities Association
30 Broad Street
28th Floor
New York, NY 10004-2304
212-509-1844
FAX: 212-509-1895
info1@cmbs.org www.cmbs.org
Elisabeth Fermsgard, Director Meetings/Conferences
Dottie Cunningham, Chief Executive Officer
Intensive educational offerings and presentations on the CMBS industry's biggest challenges.
June

2603 Community & Regional Bank Forum
Bank Insurance and Securities Association
303 West Lancaster Avenue
Suite 2D
Wayne, PA 19087
610-989-9047
FAX: 610-989-9102
bisa@bisanet.org www.bisanet.org
John Vaughan, President
Heywood Sloane, Managing Director
Jordan Miller, VP
John Lewis, Treasurer
September

2604 Community Bank Asset/Liability Management Conference
Bank Administration Institute
One North Franklin Street
Suite 1000
Chicago, IL 60606-3421
312-534-4600
FAX: 312-683-2373 888-284-4078
info@bail.org www.bai.org
Timothy P Moen, Chairman
Deborah L Bianucci, President/CEO
Scott K Heitmann, Treasurer
Charles M Diggs, Secretary
Discover innovative ways to take on these challenges by attending this conference.
May

2605 Community Banking Advisory Network Super Conference
Community Banking Advisory Network
10831 Old Mill Road
Suite 400
Omaha, NE 68154
402-778-7922
FAX: 402-778-7931 888-475-4476
info@bankingcpas.com
www.bankingcpas.com
Nancy Drennen, Executive Director

Provides intense education and training to CPA's who serve community banks.
Semi-Annual, July

2606 Eastern Finance Association Meeting
220 Holman Hall
PO Box 1848
University, MS 38677
404-498-8937
FAX: 404-498-8956
admin@easternfinance.org
www.easternfinance.org
Stephen P Ferris, President
Jacqueline Garner, VP Local Arrangements
Annual meeting and exhibits relating to any aspect of finance, including financial management, investments and banking.
April

2607 Environmental Bankers Association Membersh ip Meeting
Environmental Bankers Association
510 King Street
Suite 410
Alexandria, VA 22314
703-549-0977
FAX: 703-548-5945 800-966-7475
cna@envirobank.org
www.envirobank.org
DJ Telego, Executive Co-Director
Tacy Cook Telego, Executive Co-Director
January/June

2608 Federal Reserve Board Conference
Federal Reserve Board Publishers
20th Street & Constitution Avenue NW
Washington, DC 20551
202-452-3000
FAX: 202-728-5886
www.federalreserve.gov
Lucrezia Reichlin, Conference Organizer
Dale Henderson, Conference Organizer
Deborah Lagomarsino, Media Contact
Organized by the International Research Forum on Monetary Policy. Its purpose is to encourage research on monetary policy issues that are relevant for monetary policy making in interdependent economies.
December

2609 Financial & Security Products Association Annual Conference
Financial & Security Products Association
Plaza Ladera, 5300 Sequoia NW
Suite 205
Albuquerque, NM 87120
505-839-7958
FAX: 505-839-0017 800-843-6082
fspa@fspa1.com www.fspa1.com
Pat Hughes, Chairman
Christen Womack, President
Mark Barclay, Director
Mark Thatcher, VP
John Vrabec, Executive Director
Annual convention containing 86 exhibit booths of equipment, supplies and services for banks and bankers.
200 Attendees May Founded: 1973

2610 Financial Women International Annual Confe rence
Financial Women International
1027 West Roselawn Avenue
Roseville, MN 55113
651-487-7632
FAX: 651-489-1322
info@fwi.org www.fwi.org
Cindy Bateman, President
Nancy Kinder, VP
Rilla Dath, Director
Bj Cary, Treasurer
Carol Crilly, Chairman Public Affairs
September

2611 GARP Annual Risk Management Convention & E xhibit
Global Association of Risk Professionals
100 Pavonia Avenue
Suite 405
Jersey City, NJ 07310
201-222-0054
FAX: 201-222-5022
rich.apostolik@garp.com
www.garp.com
Richard Apostolik, President/CEO
Kenneth Abbott, Managing Director
Mark Wallace, Chief Operating Officer
Thomas Daula, Chief Risk Officer
February

2612 Independent Community Bankers of America National Convention and Techworld
Independent Community Bankers of America
518 Lincoln Road
PO Box 267
Sauk Centre, MN 56378
320-526-6546
FAX: 320-352-5766 800-422-7285
mark_traeger@icba.org www.icba.org
Jan Meyer, Director Conferences
Mark Traeger, Associate Dir Conferences/Exhibits
Sandy Zehrer, Supervisor Conference/Exhibits
Greg Martinson, Executive Director
Only national trade show exclusively representing America's independent/community banks. Containing 200+ booths and 175+exhibitors.
3000 Attendees March

2613 Institute of International Bankers Annual Conference
Institute of International Bankers
299 Park Avenue
17th Floor
New York, NY 10171
212-421-1611
212-421-1119
iib@iib.org www.iib.org
Everett Schenk, Chairman
Robert C O'Brien, Vice Chairman
Lawrence R Uhlick, Executive Director/General Counsel
March

2614 International Financial Services Associati on Annual Conference
International Financial Services Association
9 Sylvan Way
First Floor
Parsippany, NJ 07054-3802
973-656-1900
973-656-1915
info@intlbaning.org
www.ifsaonline.org
Dan Taylor, President
September

2615 International Wealth & Tax Planning Semina r
CFA Institute
560 Ray C Hunt Drive
Charlottesville, VA 22903
434-951-5499
FAX: 434-951-5262 800-247-8132
info@amir.org www.cfainstitute.org
Frank K Reilly, Chairman
Jeffrey J Diermeier, President/CEO
Katrina F Sherrerd, Executive Director
Kathy Valentine, Media Contact, North America
Taught by renowned academics and practitioners recognized as leaders in their field, this seminar conveys a structured understanding of the international tax and estate planning issues affecting individuals.
May

2616 Legal Issues/Regulatory Compliance Confere nce
Mortgage Bankers Association
1919 Pennsylvania Avenue
Washington, DC 20006-3404
202-557-2700
FAX: 202-721-0198 800-793-6222
membership@mortgagebankers.org
www.mortgagebankers.org
Jonathan L Kemper, President/CEO
Laura Armstrong, VP Meetings/Conferences
April

2617 Microbanker
Microbanker
PO Box 708
Lake George, NY 12061
518-745-7071
FAX: 518-745-7071
webmaster@microbanker.com
www.microbanker.com
Annual show and exhibits of microcomputer software, hardware and services for banking, savings and loans, and credit unions.
200 Attendees

2618 Mid-Year Technical Conference
National Assn of Government Guaranteed Lenders
424 South Squires Street
Stillwater, OK 74074
405-377-4022
FAX: 405-377-3931
bfortune@naggl.com www.naggl.com
Tony Wilkinson, President/CEO
Karen High, EVP/COO
Jenifer Brake, Assistant VP Marketing
Jennifer Sterrett-O'Neill, Assistant VP Communications
Cheryl Stone, VP Conferences
May

2619 NACHA: Electronic Payments Association Ann ual Conference
NACHA: Electronic Payments Association
13665 Dulles Technology Drive
Suite 300
Herndon, AV 20171
703-561-1100
FAX: 703-787-0996
info@nacha.org www.nacha.org
Elliott McEntee, President/CEO
William B Nelson, Executive VP
May

2620 NACUSAC Annual Conference & Exposition
National Association of Credit Union Supervisory
PO Box 160
Del Mar, CA 92014

FAX: 858-792-3884 800-287-5949
nacusac@nacusac.org
www.nacusac.org

Linda Treml, Chairman
Robert Butler, Vice Chairman
Bob Spindler, Associate Director
Celeste Shelton, Associate Director
Katherine E Clark, Executive Director

These events offer second-to-none networking and educational opportunities for supervisory and auditing committees.
June

2621 National Association of Bankruptcy Trustee s Annual Convention
National Association of Bankruptcy Trustees
One Windsor Cove
Suite 305
Columbia, SC 29223
803-252-5646
FAX: 803-765-0860
info@nabt.com www.nabt.com

Eugene Crane, President
Samuel K Crocker, VP
Robert Furr, VP
Christina Hicks, Executive Director

September

2622 National Association of Chapter 13 Trustee s Annual Seminar
National Association of Chapter 13 Trustees
3008 Millwood Avenue
Columbia, SC 29205
803-252-5646
FAX: 803-765-0860 800-445-8629
info@nactt.com www.nactt.com

Paul R Chael, President
Robin R Weiner, VP
Kevin R Anderson, Treasurer

This seminar is NACTT's educational highlight. National experts discuss complex issues and recent developments in the Chapter 13 areas.

2623 National Association of Federal Credit Unions Conference
National Association of Federal Credit Unions
3138 10th Street N
Suite 300
Arlington, VA 22201-2149
703-522-4770
FAX: 703-524-1082 800-336-4644
jbruce@nafcu.org www.nafcu.org

Michael S Vadala, Chairman
John W Milazzo, Jr, Vice Chairman
Fred R Becker, Jr, President
Joseph Boyle, Director
Jerome Bruce, Exhibits/Special Projects

Stands as a national forum for the federal credit union community where new ideas, issues, concerns and trends can be identified, discussed and resolved.
July

2624 National Association of Mortgage Brokers A nnual Conference
National Association of Mortgage Brokers

7900 Westpark Drive
Suite T309
McLean, VA 22102
703-342-5900
FAX: 703-342-5905 www.namb.org

Harry H Dinham CMC, President
George Hanzimanolis CRMS, VP
Roy DeLoach, SVP/CFO
Allan Daniels, Treasurer

June

2625 National Association of Professional Mortg age Women Annual Conference
National Assn of Professional Mortgage Women
PO Box 2016
Edmonds, WA 98026
425-775-6589
FAX: 425-771-9588 800-827-3034
info@napmw.org www.napmw.org

Katherine L Kosicki, President
Michelle F Swanson, Senior VP
Patricia Hull, Executive Director
Connie Tench, Treasurer

May

2626 National Investment Banking Association An nual Conference
National Investment Banking Association
PO Box 6625
Athens, GA 30604
706-208-9620
FAX: 706-208-1033
conference@nibanet.org
www.nibanet.org

Carlo Corzine, Chairman
Anthony B Petrelli, Director
Emily Foshee, Executive Director
D Scott Foshee, Chief Technology Officer
Vicki Barone, Treasurer/Secretary

May

2627 National Marine Bankers Association Annual Conference
National Marine Bankers Association
200 East Randolph Street
Suite 5100
Chicago, IL 60601-6528
312-812-2777
FAX: 312-946-0388
bmcardle@nmma.org
www.marinebankers.org

Donald C Parkhurst, President
Bernice McArdle, Association Manager
Jim Coburn, Treasurer
James Y Stewart, Legal Counsel

Offers insights to boat building and the broader leisure sector, and took a look at government activities affecting lender business and profit.
180 Attendees September

2628 National Mortgage Servicing Conference
Mortgage Bankers Association
1919 Pennsylvania Avenue NW
Washington, DC 20006-3438
202-557-2700
FAX: 202-721-0198 800-793-6222

Edward Callahan, Show Manager

Annual conference and exhibits of equipment supplies and services for lending, pensions and mortgaging.
February

2629 National Policy Conference
Mortgage Bankers Association
1919 Pennsylvania Avenue NW
Washington, DC 20006-3404
202-557-2700
FAX: 202-721-0198 800-793-6222
membership@mortgagebankers.org
www.mortgagebankers.org

Jonathan L Kemper, President/CEO
Laura Armstrong, VP Meetings/Conferences

April

2630 National Secondary Market Conference
Mortgage Bankers Association
1919 Pennsylvania Avenue NW
Washington, DC 20006-3438
202-557-2700
FAX: 202-721-0198 800-793-6222

Edward Callahan, Show Manager
Elaine Howard, VP Meetings/Conferences

Annual conference and exhibits premiers and explores current business issues and future market opportunities in residential mortgage finance.
May

2631 National Technology in Mortgage Banking Conference
Mortgage Bankers Association
1919 Pennsylvania Avenue NW
Washington, DC 20006-3438
202-557-2700
FAX: 202-721-0198 800-793-6222

Edward Callahan, Show Manager

Annual conference and exhibits for those responsible for evaluating and implementing information systems for the mortgage banking industry.
March

2632 RMA Annual Conference of Lending & Credit Risk Management
Risk Management Association
1801 Market Street
Suite 2300
Philadelphia, PA 19103-1628
215-635-5398
FAX: 215-446-4101 800-677-7621
customers@rmahq.org
www.rmahq.org

Maurice H Hartigan II, President/CEO

Containing 31 booths and 28 exhibits.
600 Attendees October

2633 Retail Delivery Conference & Expo

Bank Administration Institute
One North Franklin Street
Suite 1000
Chicago, IL 60606-3421
312-534-4600
FAX: 312-683-2373 888-284-4078
info@bai.org www.bai.org

Timothy P Moen, Chairman
Deborah L Bianucci, President/CEO
Scott K Heitmann, Treasurer
Charles Diggs, Secretary

Three hundred and fifty booths of retail systems equipment and related accessories.
2M Attendees November

2634 Sales Management Workshop
Bank Insurance and Securities Association
303 West Lancaster Avenue
Suite 2D
Wayne, PA 19087
610-989-9047
FAX: 610-989-9102
bisa@bisanet.org www.bisanet.org
John Vaughan, President
Heywood Sloane, Managing Director
Jordan Miller, VP
John Lewis, Treasurer
October/December

2635 Senior Executives' Conference
Mortgage Bankers Association of America

1919 Pennsylvania Avenue NW
Washington, DC 20006-3438
202-557-2700
FAX: 202-721-0198 800-793-6222
Edward Callahan, Show Manager
Carol Bonosaro, President
This annual two-day conference is traditionally held the second week of January in New York City and brings together national known authorities and industry leaders to discuss forces shaping the economy.
January

2636 TransPay Conference & Expo
Bank Administration Institute
One North Franklin Street
Suite 1000
Chicago, IL 60606-3421
312-534-4600
FAX: 312-683-2373 888-284-4078
info@bai.org www.bai.org
Timothy P Moen, Chairman
Offers top solutions providers, innovators and your peers at BAI TransPay - focused on your financial institution profitability in payments.
May

2637 Treasury Management Conference
Bank Administration Institute
One North Franklin Street
Suite 1000
Chicago, IL 60606-3421
312-534-4600
FAX: 312-683-2373 888-284-4078
info@bai.org www.bai.org
Timothy P Moen, Chairman
Deborah L Bianucci, President/CEO
Scott K Heitmann, Treasurer
Charles M Diggs, Secretary
Provide advanced information on highly complex adn technical topics that treasury managers need to execute complicated responsibilities representing areas of high risk for their banks.
May

2638 US League Savings Association
111 E Wacker Drive
Chicago, IL 60601-3713
312-552-4102

Gene Barry, Show Manager
Financial forum.
5M Attendees October

2639 Urban Financial Services Coalition Annual Conference
Urban Financial Services Coalition
1300 L Street NW
Suite 285
Washington, DC 20005
202-289-8335
FAX: 202-842-0567
ufsc@ufscnet.org www.ufscnet.org
Andrew T Carr, President
Carol A Hendrix, VP
Wayne R Young, Treasurer
May

Directories & Databases

2640 ABA Directory of Trust Banking
TFP
4709 Golf Road
Suite 600
Skokie, IL 60076
847-676-9600
FAX: 847-933-8101 800-321-3373
customerservice@tfp.com
www.tfp.com
Marideth Johnson, Manager
Marketing/Communications
An official publication of the American Bankers Association. Listings include information such as national and state rankings, collective investment funds and corporate trusts. *$403.00*
ISBN 1-563103-53-2
Circulation: 2800 : Paperback

2641 ABA Financial Institutions Directory
TFP
4709 Golf Road
Suite 600
Skokie, IL 60076
847-676-9600
FAX: 847-933-8101 800-321-3373
customerservice@tfp.com
www.tfp.com
Marideth Johnson, Manager
Marketing/Communications
This two-volume Executive Desktop Edition includes a special ABA Resource Guide with a Quick Reference Guide to Banking Regulations. *$500.00*
January/July
Circulation: 31850 : Paperback

2642 ABA Key to Routing Numbers
TFP
4709 Golf Road
Suite 600
Skokie, IL 60076
847-676-9600
FAX: 847-933-8101 800-321-3373
customerservice@tfp.com
www.tfp.com
Marideth Johnson, Manager
Marketing/Communications
Jean McCord, Editor
David Loor, Editor *$184.00*
January/July Founded: 1911
Circulation: 83300 : Paperback

2643 ACH Participant Directory
TFP
4709 Golf Road
Suite 600
Skokie, IL 60076
847-676-9600
FAX: 847-933-8101 800-321-3373
customerservice@tfp.com
www.tfp.com
Marideth Johnson, Manager
Marketing/Communications *$207.00*
February/August
Circulation: 54600 : Paperback

2644 American Financial Directory
TFP
4709 Golf Road
Suite 600
Skokie, IL 60076
847-676-9600
FAX: 847-933-8101 800-321-3373
customerservice@tfp.com
www.tfp.com
Marideth Johnson, Manager
Marketing/Communication *$558.00*
January/July Founded: 1836 ISBN 1-563103-47-8
Circulation: 41300 : Hardcover

2645 Annual Membership Directory & Buyers' Guid e
Financial & Security Products Association
Plaza Ladera, 5300 Sequoia NW
Suite 205
Albuquerque, NM 87120
505-839-7958
FAX: 505-839-017 800-843-6082
info@fspa1.com www.fspa1.com
Pat Hughes, Chairman
Christen Womack, President
Mark Barclay, Director
Mark Thatcher, VP
John Vrabec, Executive Director
Our Who's Who of independent firms serving financial institutions hleps readers locate new dealers, products/service suppliers and strategic business partners.

2646 Annual Report of the Board of Governors of the Federal Reserve System
Board of Governors
20th Street & Constitution Avenue NW
Washington, DC 20551-0001
202-523-3284
www.federalreserve.gov
Rick McKinney, Manager
Listing of directors, advisory councils and officers of banks and branches involved in mergers and acquisitions.
Annual

2647 Annual Software Guide
Financial & Security Products Association
Plaza Ladera, 5300 Sequoia NW
Suite 205
Albuquerque, NM 87120
505-839-7958
FAX: 505-839-0017 800-843-6082
info@fspa1.com www.fspa1.com
Pat Hughes, Chairman
Christen Womack, President
Mark Barclay, Director
Mark Thatcher, VP
John Vrabec, Executive Director
This detailed evaluation of the latest software to enhance business performance is provided by Brown Smith Wallace (BSW) only to members of participating associations, including FSPA.

2648 **Anti-Money Laudering & Anti-Terrorism Fina ncing CD Rom**
International Financial Services Association
9 Sylvan Way
First Floor
Parsippany, NJ 07054-3802
973-656-1900
FAX: 973-656-1915
info@intlbanking.org
www.ifsaonline.org
Dan Taylor, President
This CD includes the entire contents of the 9/27 Forum including broadcast quality of the video of the speaker presentation with a fully synchronized PowerPoint presentation. *$175.00*

2649 **BAI Resource Directory**
Bank Administration Institute
One North Franklin Street
Suite 1000
Chicago, IL 60606-3421
312-534-4600
FAX: 312-683-2373 888-284-4078
info@bai.org www.bai.org
Timothy P Moen, Chairman
Deborah L Bianucci, President/CEO
Scott K Heitmann, Treasurer
Charles M Diggs, Secretary
A comprehensive and easy-to-use online guide to the industry's top solutions, providers, their products and services.

2650 **Bank Securities Monthly**
SNL Securities
PO Box 2124
Charlottesvle, VA 22902-2124
434-977-1600
FAX: 434-977-4466
subscriptions@snlnet.com
www.snlnet.com
Wendy Cholbi, Editor
Steve Tomasi, Editor
Reid Nagle, Publisher
Mark Outlaw, Senior Vice President
Provides current financial, market and merger information on publicly traded banks. News highlights of the past month and comprehensive industry articles addressing topics such as bank investment opportunities, capital structure and earnings prospects.
70 pages Monthly

2651 **BankNews Montain States Bank Directory**
BankNews Publications
PO Box 29156
Shawnee Mission, KS 66201-9156
913-261-7000
FAX: 913-261-7010 800-336-1120
Bill Baker, President
Bill Poquette, Publisher
Over 600 commercial banks, savings and loans, and holding companies are listed in this directory, state banking and regulatory agencies are also studied in the areas of Colorado, Wyoming, New Mexico, Montana and Utah. *$35.00*
350 pages Annual
Circulation: 3,500

2652 **BankRoll II**
US Federal Reserve System, Board of Governors
20th Street & Constitution Avenue NW
Washington, DC 20551-0001
This database contains descriptive information and financial information from the Financial Report Bank Holding Companies (Y9) submitted to the Federal Reserve Board.
Numeric

2653 **Bankcard Barometer**
RAM Research Corporation
1230 Avenue of the Americas
7th Floor, Rockefeller Center
New York, MD 21702-0700
301-954-4660
FAX: 301-695-0160
www.ramresearch.com
Robert B McKinley, Publisher/Editor
Database of nation's capital largest bank credit card issuers. *$1295.00*
600 pages Monthly Founded: 1986
Printed in 1 color on matte stock

2654 **Branch Deposit Reporting Software**
Sheshunoff Information Services
505 Barton Springs Road
Suite 1200
Austin, TX 78704
512-472-2244
FAX: 512-305-6575 800-456-2340
Sheshunoff Information Services provides banks a tool to prepare their annual summary of deposits report for the FDIC. The government extends the filing deadline for banks who submit their report electronically. $125.00 for Sheshunoff call report analyzer customers. *$145.00*
Annual

2655 **Branch Source CD**
Sheshunoff Information Services
505 Barton Springs Road
Suite 1200
Austin, TX 78704
512-472-2244
FAX: 512-305-6575 800-456-2340
Provides assistance in appointing the best market areas to locate a branch or market specific products; and to understand how the branches in your market area are doing. *$692.00*

2656 **Branches of Your State: Banks, Savings & Loans, Credit Unions & Savings**
Sheshunoff Information Services
505 Barton Springs Road
Suite 1200
Austin, TX 78704
512-472-2244
FAX: 512-305-6575 800-456-2340
State editions list banks, savings and loan branches and credit unions. Individual banks are listed for states without branch banking. *$345.00*
Annual

2657 **Call Report Analyzer**
Sheshunoff Information Services
505 Barton Springs Road
Suite 1200
Austin, TX 78704
512-472-2244
FAX: 512-305-6575 800-456-2340
Sheshunoff Information Services provides banks a tool to file quarterly regulatory data (call reports). Built in edit checks and ensure banks file the most accurate report possible. Price is based on the form filed.

2658 **Data Book**
FDIC Public Information Center
550 17th Street NW
Washington, DC 20429-9990
202-898-3652
FAX: 202-416-2076 877-275-3342
publicinfo@fdic.gov www.fdic.gov
Thomas J Curry, Director
Offers information on bank names, locations, bank numbers and branches for each banking office, in seven volumes, divided geographically and aggregate bank deposits also known as Summary of Deposits
Quarterly

2659 **Directory of Minority and Women-Owned Investment Bankers**
San Francisco Redevelopment Agency
One South Van Ness Avenue
San Francisco, CA 94103
415-749-2400
www.ci.sf.ca
Marcia Rosen, Executive Director
Erwin Tanjuaquio, Director Public Affairs
Lists 18 minority-owned investment banking firms.
Biennial

2660 **Directory of Venture Capital and Private Equity Firms**
Grey House Publishing
185 Millerton Road
PO Box 860
Millerton, NY 12546
518-890-0526
FAX: 518-789-0545 800-562-2139
books@greyhouse.com
www.greyhouse.com
Leslie Mackenzie, Publisher
Richard Gottlieb, Editor
Offers access to over 3,000 domestic and international venture capital and private equity firms, including detailed contact information and extensive data on investments and funds. *$450.00*
1,200 pages Annual ISBN 1-592370-62-4

2661 **Financial Institutions Directory of New England**
TFP
4709 Golf Road
Suite 600
Skokie, IL 60076
847-676-9600
FAX: 847-933-8101 800-321-3373
customerservice@tfp.com
www.tfp.com
Marideth Johnson, Manager Marketing/Communications *$114.00*
January/July : Paperback

2662 **Financial Management**
University of South Florida COBA
4202 East Fowler Avenue
Suite 3331
Tampa, FL 33620
813-326-6893
FAX: 813-974-3318 fma@coba.usf.edu
Douglas Emery, Editor
Jack Rader, Executive Director
Financial management of individual firm, governmental unit or nonprofit institution, as opposed to financial structure of whole

economy for practitioners and professors of financial management. *$20.00*
Founded: 1970
Circulation: 11,500

2663 Insider's Guide to Credit Cards
Todd Publications
PO Box 635
Nyack, NY 10960-0635
845-358-6213

Barry Klein, Editor

One hundred Mastercard, Visa and Amex programs in the US. *$35.00*
ISBN 0-915344-61-0

2664 National Credit Union Administration Directory
National Credit Union Administration
1775 Duke Street
Alexandria, VA 22314-3428
703-518-6300
FAX: 703-518-6661 www.ncua.gov

JoAnn Johnson, Chairman
Rodney E Hood, Vice Chairman
Robert Fenner, Director/General Counsel
Jane Walters, Deputy Executive Director
J Leonard Skiles, Executive Director

Directory of credit unions governed by a three member board appointed by the President and confirmed by the US Senate, by the independent federal agency that charters and supervises federal credit unions. NCUA, with the backing of the full faith and credit of the US government, operates the National Credit Union Share Insurance Fund, insuring the savings of 80 million account holders in all federal credit unions and many state chartered credit unions.

2665 North American Financial Institutions Directory
TFP
4709 Golf Road
Suite 600
Skokie, IL 60076
847-676-9600
FAX: 847-933-8101 800-321-3373
customerservice@tfp.com
www.tfp.com

Marideth Johnson, Manager, Marketing/Communications *$495.00*

January/July Founded: 1895
Circulation: 31850

2666 Ranking the Banks
American Banker
One State Street Plaza
27th Floor
New York, NY 10004
212-038-8350
FAX: 212-843-9600
www.americanbanker.com

Bruce Morris, Publisher
David Longobardi, Editor-in-Chief
Richard Melville, Managing Editor
Timothy Reifschneider, Advertising Director

A comprehensive database of banking and financial services rankings, league tables, and vital statistics. Includes all tables published in the print edition of American Banker, and more. Organized by category with historical data. *$945.00*
128 pages

2667 Sheshunoff Bank & S&L Quarterly

Sheshunoff Information Services
505 Barton Springs Road
Suite 1200
Austin, TX 78704
512-472-2244
FAX: 512-305-6575 800-456-2340

Gabrielle Sheshunoff, Chief Executive Officer

Overview of the financial health of the banking industry and of every bank and S&L in the nation. Information includes CAMEL, fachois, asset quality, earnings, and rotation. *$543.00*
Quarterly

2668 State and Local MBA Directory
Mortgage Bankers Association of America

1919 Pennsylvania Avenue NW
Washington, DC 20006-3438
202-557-2700
FAX: 202-721-0198 800-793-6222

Jonathan L Kempner, President/CEO
Janice Walls, Director

All state and local MBA officers and a calendar of significant meeting dates. *$50.00*
SemiAnnual

2669 Thomson Bank Directory
TFP
4709 Golf Road
Suite 600
Skokie, IL 60076
847-676-9600
FAX: 847-933-8101 800-321-3373
customerservice@tfp.com
www.tfp.com

Marideth Johnson, Manager Marketing/Communications
Glenn Gottfried, Chief Operating Officer
$684.00

June/December ISBN 1-563103-45-1
Circulation: 35000 : Hardcover

2670 Thomson Credit Union Directory
Thomson Financial Publishing
4709 Golf Road
Suite 600
Skokie, IL 60076-1231
847-778-8037
FAX: 847-933-8101 800-321-3373

Marideth Johnson, Manager Marketing/Communications
Sarah Frazer, Product Manager
Glenn Gottfried, Chief Operating Officer

Semi-annual directory that includes valuable industry statistics, a quick telephone lookup index of all credit unions and a resource guide featuring vendors within the credit union marketplace. Includes over 12,500 major credit unions and 5,500 branches, with asset rankings, membership totals and more. Published in partnership with the Credit Union National Association. *$247.00*

January/July ISBN 1-563103-24-9 : Paperback

2671 Thomson Regulation CC Directory
TFP
4709 Golf Road
Suite 600
Skokie, IL 60076
847-676-9600
FAX: 847-933-8101 800-321-3373
customerservice@tfp.com
www.tfp.com

Marideth Johnson, Manager Marketing/Communications
Glenn Gottfried, Chief Operating Officer
$144.00

January/July
Circulation: 30100

2672 Thomson Savings Directory
Thomson Financial Publishing
4709 Golf Road
Suite 600
Skokie, IL 60076-1231
847-778-8037
FAX: 847-933-8101 800-321-3373

Marideth Johnson, Manager Marketing/Communications
Glenn Gottfried, Chief Operating Officer

Semi-annual directory dedicated to the thrift industry. Listings include primary correspondent information, national indutry statistics and breakdowns of mortgage portfolios. *$316.00*
January/July : Paperback

2673 World Bank Directory
Thomson Financial Publishing
PO Box 668
Skokie, IL 60076-1231
847-778-8037
FAX: 847-933-8101 800-247-7376

Marideth Johnson, Manager Marketing/Communications

Contains detailed listings for 10,000 international banks and their branches worldwide plus the top 1,000 US banks. The information in this annual directory includes world and country rankings, international and correspondent contact information, principal correspondent institutions an standard settlement instructions. *$495.00*
September Founded: 1895

2674 Worldwide Correspondents & Resource Guide
Thomson Financial Publishing
4709 Golf Road
6th Floor
Skokie, IL 60076-1231
847-778-8037
FAX: 847-933-8101 800-321-3373

Marideth Johnson, Manager Marketing/Communications

A convenient one-volume directory listing the principal correspondent relationships for banks worldwide. *$184.00*
June/December : Paperback

2675 Y-9 Report Analyzer
Sheshunoff Information Services
505 Barton Springs Road
Suite 1200
Austin, TX 78704
512-472-2244
FAX: 512-305-6575 800-456-2340
Sheshunoff Information Services provides bank holding companies (BHC) a tool to prepare and electronically file the following government forms: Y-9C, Y9-LP, Y11Q, and Y11I. Built in edit checks ensure the BHC's file the most accurate report possible. *$495.00*
Annual w/Quarterly Update

Industry Web Sites

2676 www.aba.com
American Bankers Association

Brings together all categories of banking institutions to best represent the interests of this rapidly changing industry. It's membership — which includes community, regional and money center banks and holding companies, as well as savings associations, trust companies and savings banks makes ABA one of the largest banking trade associations in the country.

2677 www.baft.org
Bankers' Association for Finance & Trade

Financial trade association whose membership represents a broad range of internationally active financial institutions and companies that provide important services to the global financial community. BAFT serves as a forum for analysis, discussion and action among international financial professionals on a wide range of topics affecting international trade and finace, including legislative/regulatory issues.

2678 www.cbanet.org
Consumer Bankers Association

Recognized voice on retail banking issues in the nation's capital. Member institutions are the leaders in consumer financial services, including auto finance, home equity lending, card products, education loans, small business services, community development, investments, deposits, and delivery.

2679 www.ffhsj.com/fairlend/naahl.htm
National Association of Affordable Housing Lenders

For financial institutions and others with an interest in affordable housing and development lending.

2680 www.fitech.org
Association for Financial Technology

Association founded in 1972 to promote high standards of professionalism in the planning, development, inplemtation and application of technology to the financial services industry.

2681 www.freddiemac.com
Freddie Mac

Freddie Mac is a stockholder-owned corporation chartered by Congress to create a continuous flow of funds to mortgage lenders in support of homeownership and rental housing.

2682 www.fwi.org
Financial Women International

Formerly the National Association of Bank Women, the Association was founded in 1921 - one year after women won the right to vote, by a group of New York City women bankers. FWI serves women in the financial services industry that seeks to expand their personal and professional capabilities through self-directed growth in a supportive environment.

2683 www.greyhouse.com
Grey House Publishing

Selected Grey House directories in the fields of business, health and education are available online. Users can search our online databases by several different search criteria, such as product categories, geographic area, sales volume and much, much more. Full Grey House catalog and online ordering also available.

2684 www.icba.org
Independent Community Bankers of America

Dedicated exclusively to enhancing the franchise value of the nation's community banks for the benefit of their customers and the communities they serve.

2685 www.marinebankers.org
National Marine Bankers Association

Formed in 1980 in response to a request by the National Marine Manufacturers Association - NMMA - for additional sources of financing for it's members products. The purpose of the NMBA is to educate prospective lenders in marine finacing procedures, create new lenders to help finance the sales of the manufacturers products, and to create an information exchange for its members.

2686 www.mbaa.org
Mortgage Bankers Association of America

Representing the real estate finance industry, MBA serves its membership by representing their legislative and regulatory interests before the US Congress and federal agencies; by meeting their educational needs through programs and a range of periodicals and publications; and by supporting their business interests with a variety of research initiatives and other products and services.

2687 www.nabt.com
National Association of Bankruptcy Trustees

Nonprofit association formed in 1982 to address the needs of the bankruptcy trustees thoughout the country and to promote the effectiveness of the bankruptcy system as a whole. While the majority of trustees who are members of the NABT are Chapter 7 trustees who primarily liquidate nonexempt assets for the benifit of creditors, many Chapter 7 trustees also serve as Chapter 11 trustees, who operate and reorganize companies. Some of our memebers are also Chapter 12 or Chapter 13 trustees.

2688 www.nacha.org
NACHA: Electronic Payments Association

Organization developing electronic solutions to improve the payments system. Representing more than 12,000 financial institutions through direct memberships and a network of regional payments associations, and 650 organizations through its industry councils, NACHA develops operating rules and business practices for the Automated Clearing House network and for electronic payments in the areas of internet commerce, electronic bill and invoice presentment and payment and other electronic payments.

2689 www.rmahq.org
Risk Management Association

Topics relating to all aspects of commercial lending, financial statement analysis and credit information exchange and managerial aspects of consumer lending.

2690 www.snl.com
SNL Securities

News articles on banks and thrifts, insurance and other financial services. Also features vital company information.

2691 www.wiley.com
John Wiley & Sons

Wiley is a global publisher of print and electronic products, specializing in science, technical, and material books and journals, professional and consumer books and subscription services, textbooks and other educational materials for undergraduate and graduate students as well as lifelong learners. Wiley has approximately 22,700 active titles and about 400 journals, and publishes about 2000 new titles in a variety of print and electronic formats each year.

Associations

2692 **Aesthetics' International Association**
2611 N Beltline Road
Suite 140
Sunnyvale, TX 75182
972-203-8530
FAX: 972-226-2339 877-968-7539
AIAthekey@aol.com
www.beautyworks.com/aia

Julie Quire, Director

International professional organization for aestheticians that has over 25 years of professional experience and represents every facet of the aesthetics industry. We offer something for the student, aesthetician, make-up artist, reflexologist, aromatherapist, massage therapist, nutritionist, nurse, holistic practitioner and physician to the day spa and salon owner.
Founded: 1972

2693 **American Association of Cosmetology Schools**
15825 North 71st Street
Suite 100
Scottsdale, AZ 85254-1521
480-281-0431
FAX: 480-905-0993 800-831-1086
jim@beautyschools.org
www.beautyschools.org

Jim Cox, Executive Director
Krystal Hayes, Creative Manager

National non-profit association open to all privately owned schools of Cosmetology Arts and Sciences.
550 Members Founded: 1924

2694 **American Beauty Association**
15825 N 71 Street
Scottsdale, AZ 85254-9199
800-468-2274

info@probeautyassociation.org
www.abbies.org

Myriam Clifford, President
Bruce Selan, VP
George Schaeffer, Secretary/Treasurer

ABA members are manufacturers, manufacturer reps and consultants in the professional beauty industry. Associate members are made up of trade publications, distributors and salons. The ABA's mission is to expand, serve and protect the interests of the professional beauty industry.
250 Members Founded: 1985

2695 **American Electrology Association**
PO Box 687
Bodega Bay, CA 94923
707-875-9135
FAX: 707-875-3340
info@aea@electrology.com
www.electrology.com

Sharon Ortiz, President
Patsy Kirby, Executive Director

The largest international not for profit membership organization. Promotes the highest standards in Electrology education, practice and ethics and champions state licensing and regulation of the profession to protect public interest.
2000 Members Founded: 1958

2696 **American Hair Loss Council**
125 Seventh Street
Suite 625
Pittsburgh, PA 15222
412-765-3666
FAX: 412-765-3669
info@ahcl.org www.ahlc.org

Susan Kettering, President

The nation's only, unbiased, not for profit agency, dedicated to sorting through this information, discovering what works and what doesn't, and presenting our finding to the consumer.

2697 **American Society of Hair Restoration Surgery**
373 North Michigan Avenue
Suite 2100
Chicago, IL 60611
312-981-6760
FAX: 312-981-6787
info@cosmeticsurgery.org
www.cosmeticsurgery.org

Jeffrey P Knezovich, Executive Vice President

1600 Members

2698 **Association of Cosmetologists and Hairdressers**
402 N. Michigan Avenue
22nd Floor
Chicago, IL 60611
312-527-6765
FAX: 312-464-6118 www.ncacares.org

Mary Ann Neuman, President

Association of Cosmetologists membership includes more than 25,000 salon owners, hairdressers, nail technicians, estheticians, eduators, and students, and is the world's largest association of salon professionals.
3910 Members Founded: 1985

2699 **College of Hair Design**
304 S 11th Street
Lincoln, NE 68508
402-744-4244
800-798-4247
greg@collegeofhairdesign.com
www.collegeofhairdesign.com

Greg Howard, Owner/School Director
Alyce Howard, Owner/Financial Aid Director
Chris Hobbs, Admissions Representative

Helps people make their dream of having a career in cosmetology and barber styling come true.

2700 **Cosmetologists Chicago**
401 N Michigan Avenue
Suite 2200
Chicago, IL 60611
312-321-6809
FAX: 312-245-1080 800-648-2505
info@chicagomidwestbeautyshow.com
www.chicagomidwestbeautyshow.com

Jerry Gordon, President
Luz Segovia, First VP
Joseph Cartagena, Secretary
Paul Dykstra, Chief Executive Officer
Marsha Hagney, Associate Executive Director

Voice of the salon industry. For over eight decades, we have been a beauty authority and presenter of the Chicago Midwest Beauty Show. We are stylists, estheticians, color technicians, salon owners, educators and nail technicians.
35000 Members

2701 **Cosmoprof North America (CPNA)**
15825 N 71st Street
Suite 100
Scottsdale, AZ 85254

FAX: 480-905-0708 800-468-2274
info@probeautyassociation.org
www.cosmoprofnorthamerica.com

Meghan Samson
Melissa Coe, Events Manager
Stan Klet,Sr., Second VP
Jim Marshall, Treasurer
Jill Jensen, Marketing/Comm Coordinator

Supports all those involved with industry related equipment, supplies and services.
Annual Founded: 1892

2702 **Intercoiffure of America**
5151 Reed Road
Columbus, OH 43220-2543
614-457-7712
FAX: 614-457-7794 www.kenneths.com

Kenneth Anders, President

Sponsors semiannual hair fashion shows in New York City.
260 Members Founded: 1933

2703 **International Chain Salon Association**
2323 Georgetown Circle
Aurora, IL 60504-6712

866-444-4272
mmelaniphy@icsa.cc www.icsa.cc

Ron Provenzano, President
Margie Melaniphy, Director

Dedicated to helping its members grow their business, effect positive change politically, provide a forum for members to share their views and ideas and interface with the professional beauty industry on behalf of the chain salons and spas.
70 Members Founded: 1972

2704 **International Guild of Professional Elecrtologists**
803 North Main Street
Suite 3A
High Point, NC 27262-3921
336-841-6631
FAX: 336-841-5187 800-830-3247

Trudy Brown, President

Non profit organization dedicated to providing the latest information about permanent hair removal to the consumer.
2000 Members Founded: 1979

2705 **International Nail Technicians Association**
2035 Paysphere Circle
Chicago, IL 60674
312-321-5161
FAX: 312-245-1080
membership@isnow.com
www.isnow.com

Paul Dykstra, Executive Director
Kaathy Kafka, President

An international organization for nail professionals. In 2001 it was aquired by Cosmetologists Chicago with the purpose of providing an association 'home' to nail care professionals that is dedicated to the needs of technicians and the industry

2706 National Beauty Culturists' League
25 Logan Circle NW
Washington, DC 20005
202-332-2695
FAX: 202-332-0940
nbcl@bellsouth.net www.nbcl.org
Dr Katie B Catalon, President
Established as the National Hair System Culture League, members are black beauticians and cosmetologists who embrace diversity.
3000 Members Founded: 1919

2707 National Cosmetology Association
401 N Michigan Avenue
22nd Floor
Chicago, IL 60611
312-527-6765
FAX: 312-245-1080 www.ncacares.org
Gordon Miller, Executive Director
Kathy Broemmel, Manager
Membership includes more than 25,000 salon owners, hairdressers,nail technicians, estheticians, educators, and students. Is also the worlds largest association of salon professionals. Members live and work in all 50 states, and also have the option to participate in the state and local affiliate, along with national activities.
25000 Members Founded: 1921

2708 Professional Beauty Association
15825 North 71st Street
Suite 100
Scottsdale, AZ 85254
480-281-0424
FAX: 480-905-0708 800-468-2274
info@probeauty.org
www.probeauty.org
Steve Sleeper, Executive Director
Laura Hubbard, Director Member Services
Nick Capertina, Director Finance & Administration
Nathan Miner, Director Business Development
Sage Dillon, Director Marketing & Communication
The Professional Beauty Association (PBA) is a non-profit trade association that represents the interests of the professional beauty industry from manufacturers and distributors to salons and spas. PBA serves the industry through five core competencies: education, government advocacy, commerce opportunities, research/statistics and public relations/image building.
1400 Members Founded: 1904

2709 Society of Clinical and Medical Hair Removal
7600 Terrace Avenue
Suite 7
Middleton, WI 53562
608-831-8009
FAX: 608-831-5485
scmhr@reesgroupinc.com
www.scmhr.org
Lisa Nelson, Executive Secretary
An international non profit organization with members in the United States, Canada, Australia, Japan and beyond. Supports all methods of hair removal and is dedicated to the research of new technology that will keep its members at the pinnacle of their profession, offering safe, effective hair removal to their clients.
350 Members Founded: 1985

2710 The Salon Association
15825 North 71st Street
Suite 100
Scottsdale, AZ 85254
480-281-0429
FAX: 480-905-0708 800-211-4872
Sasha Rash, President
NeCole Cumberlander, First VP
Steve Sleeper, Executive Director
Members are owners of salons. Offers bankcard and insurance programs, information networking and opportunitites for continued professional business development.
50000 Members Founded: 1996

Newsletters

2711 ISNOW Cosmetologists Chicago
401 N Michigan Avenue
Suite 2200
Chicago, IL 60611-4255
312-321-6809
FAX: 312-245-1080 800-648-2505
home@isnow.com www.isnow.com
Kathy Kafka, President
Represents the industries various constituencies and salon owners. *$18.95*
Monthly Founded: 2004
Circulation: 5000

2712 National Beauty News
10405 E 55th Place
Suite B
Tulsa, OK 74146-6502
918-627-8000
FAX: 918-627-8660
Douglas Von Allmen, Owner
Offers news of shows, seminars, product information and columns for the professional beauty industry. *$12.00*
Monthly
Circulation: 35,500

2713 Rose Sheet
FDC Reports
5550 Friendship Boulevard
Suite 1
Chevy Chase, MD 20815-7278
301-657-9830
FAX: 301-664-7258 800-322-2181
roseeditor@elsevier.com
www.fdcreports.com/
Mike Squires, President
Cathy Kelly, Executive Editor
Brooke McManus, Managing Editor
Jim Chicca, Executive Director
Melissa Carlson, Editorial Operations Manager
Chronicles regulatory and legal news, major scientific developments and testing methodologies, and their effect on these industries. Product marketing news, new product launches, and promotions and advertising at the retail level, are also included. *$1050.00*
Weekly Founded: 1939

Magazines & Journals

2714 Beauty Store Business
Creative Age Publications
7628 Densmore Avenue
Van Nuys, CA 91406-2042
818-782-7328
FAX: 818-782-7450 800-442-5667
sverba@creativeage.com
www.beautystorebusiness.com/
Deborah Carver, Publisher/CEO
Steve Verba, Circulation/List Rental
Beverly Denice Sparks, Advertising/Marketing Dir
Linda L. Lewis, Editorial Director
Industry trends and valuable tips concerning real estate, banking, insurance, product liability, advertising, merchandising, and more.
Monthly Founded: 1971
Circulation: 15000

2715 Cosmetic World
Ledes Group
8 W 38th Street
Suite 200
New York, NY 10018
212-840-8800
FAX: 212-840-7246
vkelly@cosmeticworld.com
www.cosmeticworld.com
John G Ledes, Publisher
Dorene Kaplan, Managing Editor
Meghan Shaner, Director of Advertising
Current industry events, legislation, management changes and corporate activities, as well as marketing developments and financial analysis. *$175.00*

Circulation: 5397
Printed in on glossy stock

2716 Cosmetics & Toiletries Magazine
Allured Publishing Corporation
362 S Schmale Road
Carol Stream, IL 60188-2787
630-653-2155
FAX: 630-653-2192 www.allured.com
Nancy Allured, Publisher
Laurie Diberardino, Editor
Exclusively written by and edited for cosmetic chemists and research scientists in the personal-care industry who have key buying responsibilities for raw materials, instrumentation, testing and laboratory services. This specialized niche is served through scientific articles penned by the industry's leading experts. Includes new raw materials, product-development strategies, basic and applied research, formulation how-to's, new technology. *$114.75*
Monthly Founded: 1925
Circulation: 3430

2717 DaySpa Magazine
Creative Age Publications
7628 Densmore Avenue
Van Nuys, CA 91406-2042
818-782-7328
FAX: 818-782-7450
DandT@creativeage.com
www.eneph.com
Joseph G Herman, Executive Editor
Carlos Benskin, Circulation Manager
DaySpa is dedicated to helping premium salon and spa owners better serve their client enhance their bottom line. Presents the most accurate, up-to-date information available on trends, products, equipment,

services, and management and management tools in easy-to-read, entertaining articles.
$17.50
Annual+ Founded: 1972
Circulation: 24,000+

2718 **Dermascope Magazine**
Aesthetics International Association
2611 N Belt Line Road
Suite 101
Sunnyvale, TX 75182
972-038-8530
FAX: 972-226-2339 800-961-3777
dermascope@aol.com
www.dermascope.com
William Strunk, Publisher
Sandra S Brown, Editor-in-Chief
Patracia Strunk, Managing Editor
Provides education for skin care professionals. One of the oldest magazines in the industry. *$45.00*
148 pages Monthly Founded: 1972
Circulation: 16000

2719 **Looking Fit**
Virgo Publishing
3300 N Central Avenue
Suite 2500
Phoenix, AZ 85012
480-990-1101
FAX: 480-990-0819
lookfit@vpico.com
www.lookingfit.com
Jenny Bolton, Publisher
Judie Bizzozero, Editorial Director
Magazine for people with active lifestlyes.
$70.00
300 pages Monthly Founded: 1986

2720 **Modern Salon**
Vance Publishing
400 Knightsbridge Parkway
Lincolnshire, IL 60069-3628
847-634-2600
FAX: 847-634-4342
matherton@vancepublishing.com
www.modernsalon.com
Mary Atherton, Editor-in-Chief
Douglas Riemer, Circulation Director
Robert Bellew, Publisher
Diana Fitzgerald, Production Manager
The professional's choice for step-by-step education and your full-service connection to industry trends, news and ideas. *$20.00*
Monthly Founded: 1924
Circulation: 127000
Printed in 4 colors on glossy stock

2721 **NW Stylist and Salon**
Porter Publishing
1750 SW Skyline Boulevard
Suite 24
Portland, OR 97221
503-297-7010
FAX: 503-297-7022 888-297-7010
Linda Holland, Publisher
Lisa Kind, Managing Editor
Joel Holland, VP
Marcy Avenson, Advertising Director
Business trade journal mailed free to every salon school and practitioner in Oregon. Accepts advertising. *$20.00*
36 pages Monthly Founded: 1983
Circulation: 22000

2722 **NailPro**
Creative Age Publications
7628 Densmore Avenue
Van Nuys, CA 91406-2042
818-782-7328
FAX: 818-782-7450 800-442-5667
webmaster@creativeage.com
www.nailpro.com
Deborah Carver, Publisher/CEO
Linda W Lewis, Associate Publisher/Editorial Direc
Mindy Rosiejka, VP/COO
Barbara Shepherd, Circulation Director
Nail care how-to's, business related articles, information on nail anatomy and pathology, as well as new products, trends, profiles and a calendar of events. *$21.95*
Monthly Founded: 1971
Circulation: 50713

2723 **Nails Magazine**
Bobit Publishing Company
3520 Challenger Street
Torrance, CA 90503
310-533-2400
FAX: 310-533-2500
Hannah.Lee@bobit.com
www.bobit.com
Cyndy Drummey, Publisher/Editor
Hannah Lee, Executive Editor
Uyonna Beckham, Sales Assistant
Sarah Paredes, Senior Production Manager
Ty Bobit, Chief Executive Officer
Offers business information on products and application techniques for professional manicurists and salon owners. *$20.00*
Monthly Founded: 1961
Circulation: 62274

2724 **Salon News**
Fairchild Publications
7 W 34th Street
New York, NY 10001-8100
212-630-3880
FAX: 212-630-4295
www.fairchildpub.com
Robert Mugnai, Publisher
Profitability and stability, salon services and resale, and on motivation and education.
Monthly
Circulation: 77,603

2725 **Salon Today**
Vance Publishing
400 Knightsbridge Parkway
Lincolnshire, IL 60069-3613
847-634-2600
FAX: 847-634-4379
info@vancepublishing.com
www.salontoday.com
Laurel Smoke, Editor
Douglas Riemer, Circulation Manager
A monthly magazine on salon growth, written for and about the most successful salon owners in the industry. *$42.00*
Monthly
Circulation: 23000

2726 **Skin Magazine**
Allured Publishing Corporation
PO Box 506
Mt Morris, IL 60154-506
815-734-1147
FAX: 815-734-5880 800-469-7445
skni@kable.com www.skininc.com
Marian S Raney, Publisher
Melinda Taschetta-Millane, Editor
Janet Ludwig, CEO
The business magazine preferred by owners and managers of salons and spas and the official publication of the American Aestheticians Education Association. Recently awarded a Gold award for editorial from the American Business Publication editors association. *$49.00*
120 pages Monthly Founded: 1988
Circulation: 16000

2727 **WWD Beauty Biz**
Fairchild Publications
7 W 34th Street
New York, NY 10010
212-630-4000
FAX: 212-630-4295
summits@fairchildpub.com
www.fairchildpub.com
Mary Berner, President/CEO
Patrick McCarthy, Chairman/Editorial Director
Jenny B. Fine, Editor-in-Chief
Sarah Murphy, Publisher
The premier guide to the beauty industry. Provides in-depth coverage and analysis on all aspects of the industry, including trends, brands, retailers, and personalities driving both the general comsumer and insider sides of the business. *$60.00*
Monthly Founded: 1892
Circulation: 40,056

Trade Shows

2728 **ASWC**
Aestheticis' International Association
2611 N Belt Line Road
Suite 140
Sunnyvale, TX 75182-9357
972-203-8530
FAX: 972-203-8754 877-968-7539
Marlene Hays, Manager
Biennial show of skin care, makeup and body therapy products and equipment. Containing 250 booths and 250 exhibits.
3000 Attendees

2729 **Aesthetics' World Expositions**
Aesthetics' International Association
2611 N Belt Line Road
Suite 140
Sunnyvale, TX 75182-9357
972-203-8530
FAX: 972-226-2339 877-968-7539
Althekey@aol.com
www.beautyworks.com/aia
150-250 exhibits of skin care, body therapy products make up and equipment. Salon owners, body massage thearpists, and dermatologists attend.
3000 Attendees Biennial Founded: 1979

2730 **American Electrology Association Convention**
American Electrology Association
106 Oakridge Road
Trumbull, CT 06611-5213
203-374-6667
FAX: 203-372-7134
www.electrology.com
The conventions feature the largest number of exhibitors with the latest state of the art equipment and plenty of time for viewing and purchasing.
Annual

2731 Big Show Expo
Big Show Expo
1841 Broadway
Room 812
New York, NY 10023-7603
212-580-1407
FAX: 212-757-3611

Bernice Calvin, President
Maggie Smallwood, Conference Coordinator

Largest group of ethnic beauty shows. 200 booths updating the skills and expertise of hairdressers with ethnic clientele and spotlighting new trends in hair fashions, with all new styles for today's fashion looks.
15M Attendees August, September

2732 Cosmoprof North America
15825 North 71st Street
Suite 100
Scottsdale, AZ 85254

FAX: 480-905-0708 800-468-2274
jen@probeautyassociation.org
www.cosmoprofnorthamerica.com

Jen Ingalls, Trade Show Manager

The most comprehensive and international professional beauty industry show on the continent. Attendees include manufacturers to distributors , salon owners to spa professionals, importers to retail buyers with 760 exhibitors.
25000 Attendees July

2733 Hairworld
National Cosmetology Association
401 N Michigan Avenue
Chicago, IL 60611-4255
312-527-6765
FAX: 312-464-6118
nca@sba.com www.ncacares.org

Josephine Zeppieri, President
Gordon Miller, Executive Director

Annual show of 125 exhibitors of hair products, cosmetics and jewelry.
3000 Attendees July
Circulation: 30,000

2734 International Congress of Esthetics

Aesthetics' International Association
2611 N Belt Line Road
Suite 140
Sunnyvale, TX 75182-9301
972-203-8530
FAX: 972-226-2339 800-961-3777
asathekey@aol.com
www.dermascope.com

Marlene Hays, Show Coordiantor
Julie Quire, Membership Coordinator

Biennial show of skin care, makeup and body therapy products and equipment.
3000 Attendees February Founded: 1977

Directories & Databases

2735 Drug Store and HBC Chains Database
Chain Store Guide
3922 Coconut Palm Drive
Tampa, FL 33619
813-276-6700
FAX: 813-627-6882 800-778-9794
info@csgis.com www.csgis.com

Chris Leedy, Advertising Sales
Arthur Sciarrotta, Senior VP

Tap into the lucrative drug industry with profiles on more than 1,700 US and Canadian companies operating two or more retail drug stores, deep discount stores, health and beauty care (HBC) stores, cosmetic stores or vitamin stores that have industry sales of at least $250,000. This powerful database empowers you to sell and market your products successfully by reaching more than 8,300 key decision-makers. *$335.00*

Circulation: 8,300

2736 Hayes Chain Drug Store Directory
Hayes Directories
PO Box 3436
Mission Viejo, CA 92690
949-583-0537
FAX: 949-583-7419 www.hayesdir.com

James Edward Hayes, Editor

Comes in two volumes and contains information for 34,773 chain pharmacies in the United States, 8 stores or more. First volume lists the chain headquarters, and includes the total count of stores with pharmacies. The second volume groups the individual chain stores alphabetically by chain name followed by the name and address information for the headquarters of the parent company. *$250.00*
Annual,November

2737 Hayes Drug Store Directory
Hayes Directories
PO Box 3436
Mission Viejo, CA 92690
949-583-0537
FAX: 949-583-7419 www.hayesdir.com

Jay Douglas Hayes, Editor

Contains information for the 53,821 retail drug stores in the United States. *$335.00*
Annual,November

2738 Hayes Independent Drug Store Directory
Hayes Directories
PO Box 3436
Mission Viejo, CA 92690
949-583-0537
FAX: 949-583-7419
www.haynesdir.com

James Edward Hayes, Editor

Published annually and contains information for 19,048 independent retail pharmacies in the United States. Independent stores are 7 stores or less. *$300.00*
Annual,November

2739 Rauch Guide to the US Cosmetics & Toiletri es Industry
Grey House Publishing
PO Box 860
Millerton, NY 12546
518-789-8700
FAX: 518-789-0545 800-562-2139
books@greyhouse.com
www.greyhouse.com

Leslie Mackenzie, Publisher
Richard Gottlieb, President

Guide is organized into several information-packed chapters. Chapters consists of economics, technology & raw materials, products & markets, industry activities, organizations & sources of information, company directory and appendices. *$895.00*
Annual

Industry Web Sites

2740 www.bbsi.org
Beauty and Barber Supply Institute

Our members are wholesaler-distributors, manufacturers and manufacturers' representatives from around the world. Our mission is to maximize the potential of the professional salon industry.

2741 www.beautyschools.org
American Association of Cosmetology Schools

Non-profit association open to all privately owned schools of Cosmetology Arts & Sciences.

2742 www.dermascope.com
Aesthetics' International Association

International professional organization for aestheticians representing every facet of the aesthetics industry. From the student, aesthetician, make-up artist, reflexologist, aromatherapist, massage therapist, nutritionist, nurse, holistic practitioner and physician to the day spa/salon owner.

2743 www.electrology.com
American Electrology Association

Organization of professional hair removal practitioners promoting the highest standards of electrology education through our annual and state conventions with seminars following a prescribed learning standard.

2744 www.greyhouse.com
Grey House Publishing

Selected Grey House directories in the fields of business, health and education are available online. Users can search our online databases by several different search criteria, such as product categories, geographic area, sales volume and much, much more. Full Grey House catalog and online ordering also available.

2745 www.isnow.com
Cosmetologists Chicago

Voice of the salon industry. Presenter of the Chicago Midwest Beauty Show, we are stylists, estheticians, color technicians, salon owners, educators and nail technicians.

2746 www.oneroof.org
American Beauty Association

Mission is to expand, serve and protect the interests of the professional beauty industry.

2747 **www.salons.org**
The Salon Association

Non-profit organization representing 7,000 employment-based salons and spas across the United States and Canada

Associations

2748 **American Association of Bioanalysts**
906 Olive Street
Suite 1200
Saint Louis, MO 63101-1434
314-241-1445
FAX: 314-241-1449
aab@aab.org www.aab.org
Dedicated to serving the community clinical laboratory and the professionals involved in clinical laboratory operations.

2749 **American Association of Immunologists**
9650 Rockville Pike
Bethesda, MD 20814
301-634-7178
FAX: 301-530-7007
infoaai@aai.org www.aai.org
M. Michelle Hogan, Executive Director
Lauren G. Gross, Director of Public Policy
Michael W. Cuddy, Executive Assistant
One hundred and twenty-five member institutions concerned with environmental issues, pest control, agricultural meteorology, biotechnology, food irradiation, agricultural policy, research and development, food safety, technology transfer and remote sensing. *$50.00*
6500 Members Founded: 1913

2750 **American Chemical Society**
1155 16th Street NW
Washington, DC 20036
202-724-4600
FAX: 202-872-4615
help@acs.org www.chemistry.org
E Anne Nalley, President
James D Burke, Board Chairman
John Crum, Chief Executive Officer
Madeleine Jacobs, Executive Director
Self-governed individual membership that consists of more than 159,000 members, at all degree levels and fields in chemistry. Also provides a broad range of opportunities for peer interactiom and career development, regardless of professional or scientific interests.
15900 Members Founded: 1876

2751 **American Society for Biochemistry and Molecular Biology**
9650 Rockville Pike
Bethesda, MD 20814-3996
301-634-7145
FAX: 301-634-7126
asbmb@asbmb.org www.asbmb.org
Judith Bond, President
Peggy Farnum, Secretary
Kenneth Neet, Treasurer
A professional and educational association for biochemists and molecular biologists which seeks to extend and utilize the field of biochemistry and molecular biology. *$18.50*
11900 Members Founded: 1906 11000 names

2752 **Association for Women in Science**
1200 New York Avenue
Suite 650
Washington, DC 20005
202-326-8940
FAX: 202-326-8960
webadmin@awis.org www.awis.org
Donna Dean, President
Nancy Bakowski, Executive Director
Barbara Filner, President Educational Foundation
Provides support for female scientists and bioengineers. Also dedicated to achieving equity and full participation for women in science,mathematics,engineering and technology.
5000 Members Founded: 1971

2753 **Biotechnology Industry Organization**
1225 Eye Street NW
Suite 400
Washington, DC 20005
202-962-9200

info@bio.org www.bio.org
Jim Greenwood, President
Richard Props, Chair
James Mullen, Vice Chair Human Healthcare
Frederick Telling, Secretary
Frances Christian, Manager
Provides support for all those involved in biotechnology from a government, corporate, and trade viewpoint. Also represents more than 1,100 biotechnology companies,academic institutions, biotechnology centers and related organizations on all of 50 US states and 31 other nations. Researchers expand the boundaries of science to benefit mankind by providing better healthcare, enhanced agriculture,and a cleaner and safer environment.
1100+ Members Founded: 1993

2754 **Council for Biotechnology Information**
1225 Eye Street NW
Suite 400
Washington, DC 20043-0380
202-467-6565
FAX: 202-467-6565
www.whybiotech.com
Sean Darragh, Executive Director
Communicates science-based information about the benefits and safety of agricultural and food biotechnology. Members are leading biotechnology companies and trade associations. New technology in this arena aims to improve the food supply while protecting the enviroment.

2755 **Electrophoresis Society**
1202 Ann Street
Madison, WI 53713
608-258-1565
FAX: 608-258-1569
matt-aes@tds.net www.aesociety.org
Dave Garfin, President
Scott Rodkey, VP
Matt Hoelter, Executive Director
Unique international organization founded to improve and promote technologies necessary for biomolecular separation and detection.
200 Members Founded: 1954

2756 **International Society for Chronobiology**
University of Texas-Medical Branch
301 University Boulevard
Galveston, TX 77555
409-611-1011

hzengil@gazi.edu.tr
www.chronobiology.org.tr
Promotes studies on temporal parameters of biological variables and pursues related scientific and educational purposes. Encourages research centers and the establishment of chronobiology as an academic discipline in its own right.
300 Members Founded: 1937

2757 **International Society for Magnetic Resonance in Medicine**
2118 Milvia Street
Suite 201
Berkeley, CA 94704
510-841-1899
FAX: 510-841-2340
info@ismrm.org www.ismrm.org
Jane Tiemann, Executive Director
Jennifer Olson, Associate Executive Director
Roberta A Kravitz, Director of Meetings/Electronic Com
Anne Ornelas De Lemos, Membership Director
Robert Goldstein, Education Director
Nonprofit professional association devoted to furthering the development and application of magnetic resonance techniques in medicine and biology. Also holds annual scientific meeting and sponsors other major educational and scientific workshops.
5000 Members Founded: 1994

2758 **Massachusetts Biotechnology Council**
One Cambridge Center
9th Floor
Cambridge, MA 02142
617-778-8198
FAX: 617-577-7860
inforequest@massbio.org
www.massbio.org
Una Ryan, Chair
Garen Bohlin, Vice Chair
Thomas M Finneran, President
Mark Trusheim, Treasurer
Not for profit organization that provides services and support for the Massachusetts biotechnology industry. Committed to advancing the development of critical new science technology and medicines that benefit people worldwide.
400+ Members Founded: 1985

2759 **National Center for Biotechnology Information**
National Library of Medicine
Building 38A
Bethesda, MD 20894
301-654-4480
FAX: 301-480-9241
info@ncbi.nlm.nih.gov
www.ncbi.nlm.nih.gov
To develop new information technologies to aid in the understandingof fundamental molecular and genetic processes that control health and disease.
Founded: 1988

2760 **New York Biotechnology Association**
30 Rockefeller Plaza
27th Floor
New York, NY 10112
212-332-4395

info@nyba.org www.nyba.org
Karin Duncker, Executive Director
Tina Lopingco, Director Technology/Business Develo
A nonprofit trade association dedicated to the development and growth of New York State based biotechnology related industries and institutions. And to strengthening

the competiveness of NY State as a premier global location for biotechnology/biomedical research, education and industry.
260 Members

2761 North American Benthological Society
PO Box 7065
Lawrence, KS 66044-7065
785-843-1221
FAX: 785-843-1274
amorin@uottawa.ca www.benthos.org
Michael T Barbour, President
Lucinda B Johnson, President-Elect
Kim Haag, Treasurer
International Scientific organization with the purpose to promote better understanding of the biotic communitites of lake and stream bottoms and their role in aquatic ecosystems, by providing media and disseminating new investigation results , new interpretations and other benthological informatoin to aquatic biologists and the scientific community. Also publishes a journal.
Founded: 1953

2762 North Carolina Biotechnology Center
15 TW Alexander Drive
Research Triangle Park, NC 27709
919-541-9366

info@ncbiotech.org
www.ncbiotech.org
Leslie Alexandre, President/CEO
Ken Tindall, Senior VP
Kathleen Kennedy, VP, Education And Training
Lori Greenstein, VP,Corporate Administration And CFO
A private nonprofit corporation established by the state's General Assembly. The mission is to provide long term economic benefit to North Carolina through support of biotechnology research, development and commercialization statewide.
65 Members Founded: 1981

2763 Pennsylvania Biotechnology Association
7 Great Valley Pkwy
Ste 290
Malvern, PA 19355-1425
610-578-9220
FAX: 610-578-9219
info@pabiotech.org
www.pabiotech.org
Dennis M Flynn, President
Lisa Goldsborough, Director Business Development
Paul Kornblith, Director
Karla Beckner White, Director Communications
Laura Alexandre, Assistant to the President
To advance the life sciences in Pennsylvania by creating commercial opportunities and public policy strategies that lead to greater understanding, growth and community support of biotechnology.
2000+ Members Founded: 1989

2764 Protein Society
9650 Rockville Pike
Bethesda, MD 20814-3992
301-511-1527
FAX: 301-634-7271 800-992-2616
cyablonski@proteinsociety.org
www.proteinsociety.org
Purpose is to provide national and international forums to facilitate communication, cooperation, and collaboration with respects to all aspects of the study of proteins.

3000 Members Founded: 1986
Mailing list available for rent 3,000 names $200 per M.

2765 Society for Biomaterials
17000 Commerce Parkway
Suite C
Mt. Laurel, NJ 08054-5554
856-439-0826
FAX: 856-439-0525
info@biomaterials.org
www.biomaterials.org
Michael Sefton, President
C Mauli Agrawal, Secretary/Treasurer
To provide the leading forum to disseminate knowledge of biomaterials among researchers, educators, and developers of materials and biomedical device technology using coordinated educational programs, publications, prfessional services, and development of professional standards.
1550 Members Founded: 1974

2766 Society for Biomolecular Screening
36 Tamarack Avenue
Suite 348
Danbury, CT 06811
203-788-8828
FAX: 203-748-7557
email@sbsonline.org
www.sbsonline.org
Al Kolb, President
Christine Giordano, Executive Director
Betty Soltesz, Board Secretary
Provides a forum for education and information exchange among professionals within drug discovery and related disciplines.
2000+ Members Founded: 1994

2767 Strategic Information For The Life Sciences
3200 Chapel Hill Nelson Boulevard
Suite 201 POBox 14569
Research Triangle Park, NC 27709-4569
919-544-5111
FAX: 919-544-5401
info@bioability.com
www.bioability.com
Mark D Dibner, President/Founder
Tracey du Laney, Sr. Research Analyst
Kaye Webb, Information Specialist
Melanie Tull, Sr. Research Analyst
Provides support for all those involved with analyzing or using strategic business information in biotechnology.
14 Members Founded: 1986

2768 Virginia Biotechnology Association
800 E Leigh Street
Suite 14
Richmond, VA 23219-1534
804-285-5390
FAX: 804-643-6361
questions@vabio.org www.vabio.org
Mark Herzog, Executive Director
Dennis Fisher, Chairman
Donald McAfee, Vice Chair
S Brian Farmer, Secretary
Robert Skunda, Chief Executive Officer
Promote the biotechnology industry in Virginia, expand the knowledge and expertise of Virginia's business concerning biotechnology through seminars, educational publications and other means, to enhance, public awareness of the biotechnology industry in Virginia and the scientific, economic and other benefits it provides.
200 Members Founded: 1992

Newsletters

2769 BioPeople Magazine
PO Box 5778
Walnut Creek, CA 94596
925-932-6364

info@biotechmedia.com
www.biotechmedia.com
Lisa Wagner, Advertising Executive
Charlene Carpentier, Production Manager
Sukaini Virji-Jeganathan, Editor
Provides information and analysis of the international biotechnology industry, including corporate agreements, product status, financial transactions and new technologies. *$675.00*
Quarterly
Circulation: 10,000 Audited
Printed in on glossy stock
Computerized version available: Bulletin

2770 BioWorld Financial Watch
BioWorld
3525 Piedmont Road
Building 6, Suite 400
Atlanta, GA 30305-4031
650-696-9400
FAX: 404-814-0759 800-688-2421
bioworld.customerservice@thomson.com
www.bioworld.com
Donald R Johnston, Publisher
Brady Huggett, Managing Editor
Chris Walker, Marketing Manager
Tracks public financing and portfolio performance offering expert analysis. The weekly source for biotechnology financial news. *$1197.00*
Weekly

2771 Biotechnology News
CTB International Publishing
PO Box 218
Maplewood, NJ 07040-218
973-966-0997
FAX: 973-966-0242
info@ctnintl.com www.ctbintl.com
F G Racioppi, Marketing Director
A leading biotechnology publication for executives. Provides incisive intelligence on the ever-changing biotechnology industry and includes news on research, product development and corporate doings. *$634.00*
Founded: 1985
Printed in 1 color on newsprint stock

2772 Biotechnology Newswatch
McGraw Hill
1221 Avenue of the Americas
Suite C3A
New York, NY 10020-1095
212-123-3916
FAX: 212-512-2723
customer.service@mcgraw-hill.com
www.mcgraw-hill.com
Kevin Hamilton, Publisher
Mara Bovsun, Editor
Kenneth M Vittor, VP
Covers the business and technical news affecting companies engaged in serving the biotechnology sciences. *$737.00*
12 pages Monthly Founded: 1910

2773 **Genetic Technology News**
John Wiley & Sons
111 River Street
Hoboken, NJ 07030-5774
201-748-6000
FAX: 201-748-6088
service@wiley.com www.wiley.com

Albert Hester, Publisher
William J Pesce, CEO/President

Covers technical and business developments in every area of genetic engineering and related techniques, analyzing their applications in the chemical, pharmaceutical and energy industries as well as in agriculture, animal breeding and medicine. *$585.00*
18 pages Monthly Founded: 1807

2774 **Industrial Bioprocessing**
John Wiley & Sons
111 River St
Hoboken, NJ 07030-5774
201-748-6000
FAX: 201-748-6088
e-service@wiley.com www.wiley.com

Kenneth A Koyaly, Publisher
Karen L Dean, Editor
William J Pesce, CEO/President

Focuses on industrial processes involving biological routes to produce chemicals/energy; the conversion of biomaterials via fermentation, process monitoring and more. *$545.00*
10 pages Monthly Founded: 1807
Mailing list available for rent $180 per M.
Printed in 1 color on matte stock
Computerized version available

2775 **J Biomolecular Screening**
Society for Biomolecular Screening
36 Tamarack Avenue
Suite 348
Danbury, CT 06811-4822
203-788-8828
FAX: 203-748-7557
email@sbsonline.org
www.sbsonline.org

Larry Walker, Editor-in-Chief
Dejan Bojanic, President
David Roman, Publications Services Adm

Biomolecular industry news and information. *$478.00*
Founded: 1992

2776 **Technotrends Newsletter**
Burrus Research Associates
PO Box 47
Hartland, WI 53029
262-367-0949
FAX: 262-367-7163 800-827-6770
office@burrus.com www.burrus.com/

Daniel A Burrus, Publisher/CEO
Patti A Thomsen, Editor
Jennifer Metcalf, Marketing

This newsletter researches the latest innovations in science and technology. Provides access to information that can give an edge on tomorrow, today and shows how you might benefit from each innovation. *$39.95*
Monthly Founded: 1984
Circulation: 1000
Printed in 4 colors on matte stock

Magazines & Journals

2777 **American Biotechnology Laboratory**
International Scientific Communications
30 Controls Drive
PO Box 870
Shelton, CT 06484-870
203-926-9300
FAX: 203-926-9310
webmaster@iscpubs.com
www.iscpubs.com

Brian Howard, Editor
Danyelle Villagomez, Marketing
Patricia Ekbatani, Directing Editor

American Biotechnology Laboratory serves Industry, Universities, Government and others allied to the field with special interest in life science research. *$173.12*
64 pages Monthly
Circulation: 60058 60M names $170 per M.
Printed in 4 colors on glossy stock

2778 **Applied Biochemistry and Biotechnology**
Humana Press
999 Riverview Drive
Suite 208
Totowa, NJ 07512-1165
973-256-1699
FAX: 973-256-8341
humana@humanapr.com
www.humanapress.com

David Watt, Editor
Ashok Mulchandani, Editor-in-Chief
Paul Dolgert, Director
Fran Lipton, Production Manager

Reports on new techniques and original research in biotechnology and biochemistry with a focus on the application of new technologies. *$1505.00*
Monthly Founded: 1977
Circulation: 373

2779 **BioTechniques**
1 Research Drive
Suite 400A
Westborough, MA 01581-6070
508-614-1425
FAX: 508-616-2930
info@biotechniques.com
www.biotechniques.com

Jim Wagner, President
Mary McCarthy, Edito-in-Chief
Bill Moran, Director of Sales
John C. Yarosh, Production Manager

Serves the biotechnical and pharmaceutical industries. *$145.00*
254 pages Monthly Founded: 1983
Circulation: 85,000
Printed in 4 colors on glossy stock

2780 **Biomedical Products**
Reed Business Information
301 Gibraltar Drive
PO Box 650
Morris Plains, NJ 07950-650
973-920-7000
FAX: 973-920-7531
corporatecommunications@reedbusiness.com www.biomedicalproducts.com/

Steve Ernst, Senior Editor
Jim Casella, CEO

Delivers information on the newest products, technologies and services available to life scientists/biotechnologists. Its content is edited exclusively for bioresearchers in both commercial and public facilities.
Monthly
Circulation: 71012

2781 **Biotechnology Investment Opportunities**
High Tech Publishing Company
PO Box 1275
Amherst, MA 01004-1275
413-534-4500
FAX: 413-256-6378

Judy Wieland, Editor

Identifies and analyzes emerging investment opportunities in genetic engineering. Follows trends and conditions having significant impact on the development and commercial application of leading edge biotechnology research. *$325.00*
Monthly

2782 **Biotechnology Progress**
American Chemical Society
1155 16th Street NW
Suite 600
Washington, DC 20036-4892
202-872-4600
FAX: 202-872-4615 800-333-9511
help@acs.org www.chemistry.org

Jerome S Schultz, Editor
Madeleine Jacobs, Executive Director
William F. Carroll Jr., CEO

Information on new technology. *$924.00*
Founded: 1876

2783 **Biotechnology and Bioengineering**
John Wiley & Sons
111 River Street
Hoboken, NJ 07030-5774
201-748-6000
FAX: 201-748-6088
customer@wiley.com
www.wiley.com

Douglas S. Clark, Editor
William J Pesce, CEO/President

A scientific journal publishing new papers in the field of biotechnology and bioengineering. *$750.00*
1 Year 28 Issue Founded: 1807

2784 **CleanRooms Magazine**
PennWell Publishing Company
98 Spit Brook Road
Nashua, NH 03062
603-891-0123
FAX: 603-891-9200
mikel@pennwell.com
www.pennwell.com

Michael Levans, Chief Editor
Mark A Desorbo, Associate Editor
James Enos, Publisher

Serves the contamination control and ultrapure materials and process industries. Written for readers in the microelectronics, pharmaceutical, biotech, health care, food processing and other user industries. Provides technology and business news and new product listings.
Monthly Founded: 1987
Circulation: 35031

2785 **Engineering in Medicine and Biology**
10662 Los Vaqueros Circle
P. O. Box 3014
Los Alamitos, CA 90720-1264
714-821-8380
FAX: 714-821-4010 800-272-6657
jenderle@bme.uconn.edu
www.ieee.org

Dr. John D Enderle, Editor
Desirée de Myer, Managing Editor

Susan Schneiderman, Advertising Sales Manager

Focuses on up-to-date biomedical engineering applications for engineers who are at the forefront of electrotechnology innovation. *$300.00*

Founded: 1963
Circulation: 7983

2786 Industrial Biotech News
Biotechnology Industry Organization
1225 Eye Street NW
Suite 400
Washington, DC 20005
202-962-9200
FAX: 202-589-2545 www.bio.org

Morrie Ruffin, Publisher
Frances Christian, Manager

Publication includes news on government, corporate, and professional trade groups, conferences, and international activities with focus on the optimization of microbial activity for remediation of contaminated soil, water, air and sludge for pollution prevention and control, and for process industries, including the chemical, food, cleaning and textile industries. *$215.00*

Bi-Monthly
Circulation: 2,000

2787 Journal of Biomolecular Screening
Sage Publications
2455 Tell Road
Thousand Oaks, CA 91320-4822
805-990-0721
800-818-7243
journals@sagepub.com
www.sagepublications.com/www.sbsonline.org

Larry Walker, Editor
Mark Beggs, Associate Editor
Stein Roaldset, Advertising Editor
Steven Kahl, Associate Editor
Ricardo Macarron, Associate Editor

The official publication of the Society for Biomolecular Sciences. You will find timely information on novel detection technologies for characterizing chemical-biological interactions; profiling complex cellular responses to transmitters, hormones, cytokines, drugs or xenobotics; nanotechnologies for sample handling and assay developments and much more. *$86.00*

8x year/Price Varies Founded: 1994

2788 Journal of the North American Benthological Society
The North American Benthological Society
PO Box 7065
Lawrence, KS 66044-7065

www.benthos.org/jnabs

Ernest F Benfield, Book Review Editor
Jack Faminella, Co-Editor
David Rosenberg, Co-Editor
Michelle Baker, Associate Editor
Robert Baker, Associate Editor

Articles that will promote further understanding of benthic communitites and their role in aquatic ecosystems *$65.00*

Quarterly

2789 Lab Animal
Nature Publishing Group
345 Park Avenue South
6th Floor
New York, NY 10010
212-788-8600
FAX: 212-696-9638
info@labanimal.com
www.labanimal.com

Philip Campbell, Editor-in-chief
Rachel Burley, Publisher
Richard Charkin, CEO

A peer-reviewed journal for professionals in animal research, empasizing proper management and care. Offers the latest on animal models, breeds, breeding practices, in vitro and computer models, lab care, nutrition, and improved animal handling techniques. Offers timely and informative material, reaching both the academic research world and applied research industries, including genetic engineering, human therapeutics and pharmaceutical companies. *$159.00*

Founded: 1869

2790 Molecular Plant: Microbe Interactions
American Phytopatholgical Society
3340 Pilot Knob Road
Saint Paul, MN 55121-2097
651-454-7250
FAX: 651-454-0766 800-328-7560
aps@scisoc.org www.apsnet.org/

James Stougaard, Editor
Rhonda Wilkie, Circulation Manager
Michelle Bjerkness, Director of Marketing

MPMI is the groundbreaking journal for publication of original, referenced research on the molecular biology and molecular genetics of pathological, symbiotic and associative interactions of microbes with plants, including plant response. *$451.00*

Monthly Founded: 1908
Printed in 4 colors on glossy stock : online

2791 Nature
Nature Publishing Group
345 Park Avenue S
New York, NY 10010-1707
212-788-8600
FAX: 212-696-9006 800-221-2123
nature@natureny.com
www.nature.com

Phillip Campbell, Editor
Josie Natori, Chief Executive Officer

A reliable source of up-to-date scientific information. Publishes papers from any area of science with great potential impact. Also publishes a broad range of informal material in the form of opinion articles, news stories, briefings and recruitment features, and contributed material.

Monthly
Circulation: 60289

2792 Nature Biotechnology
Nature America
345 Park Avenue S
10th Floor
New York, NY 10010-1707
212-726-9200
FAX: 212-696-9635 800-221-2123
biotech@natureny.com
www.biotech.nature.com

Andrew Marshall, Editor
Richard Charkin, Chief Executive
Annette Thomas, Managing Director
Philip Campbell, Editor-in-Chief
Peter Collins, Publishing Director

A monthly magazine of biotechnology news and research. *$178.00*

550 pages Monthly Founded: 1983
Circulation: 18798
Printed in 4 colors on glossy stock

2793 Science Illustrated
Communications Solutions
8428 Holly Leaf Drive
McLean, VA 22102-2224
703-356-1688
FAX: 202-296-1857

Tod Herbers, Editor

Provides physicians with information on research and development in the fields of science related to medicine. *$18.00*

Circulation: 103200
Printed in 4 colors on glossy stock

Trade Shows

2794 American Association of Bioanalysts Annual Meeting & Conference
American Association of Bioanalysts
906 Olive Street
Suite 1200
Saint Louis, MO 63101
314-241-1445
FAX: 314-241-1449
aab@aab.org www.aab.org

Mark S Birenbaum PhD, Show Manager

Assembles clinical laboratory directors, managers, supervisors, medical laboratory technologists, technicians for technical and managerial educational sessions and workshops. 5-10 booths.

400 Attendees May

2795 Biometrics Technology Expo and Consortium Conference
J Spargo & Associates
11208 Waples Mill Road
Suite 112
Fairfax, VA 22030
703-631-6200
FAX: 703-654-6931 800-564-4220
biometrics@jspargo.com
www.biometrics.org

Paul doCarmo, Assistant Director/Exhibit Sales
Connie Shaw, Exhibit Sales Account Manager

Co-located with the Biometric Consortium Conference, this event offers unparalleled opportunities to reach top buyers, federal and state agencies and leading industry corporations.

2000 Attendees September

2796 Biophysical Society Annual Meeting

Biophysical Society
9650 Rockville Pike
Bethesda, MD 20814
301-634-7114
FAX: 301-634-7133
society@biophysics.org
www.biophysics.org

Melissa Pewett, Exhibit Coordinator

Includes 3,000 poster presentations, 200 exhibits, 20 symposias, workshops, platform sessions, and subgroup meetings. It is also the worlds largest meeting for biophysicists.

6M Attendees February/March

2797 **Biotechnology Investment Conference**
Massachusetts Biotechnology Council
One Cambridge Center
9th Floor
Cmabridge, MA 02142
617-778-8198
FAX: 617-577-7860
inforequest@massbio.org
www.massbio.org
Amy Goodman, Coordinator Events/Membership
Christine LeBlanc, Manager Sponsorship/Events
Mark Trusheim, President
New England's largest biotechnology investor forum. Allows more than 70 local public and private companies to showcase their technologies and products in front of portfolio managers, analysts, venture capitalists and other investment professionals.
700 Attendees November

2798 **Int'l Conference on Strategic Business Information in Biotechnology**
Institute for Biotechnology Information
3200 Chapel Hill/Nelson Blvd. Suite 201
POBox 14569
Research Triangle Park, NC 27709-4569

919-544-5111
FAX: 919-544-5401
info@bioability.com
www.biotechinfo.com
For strategists, company managers, information specialists, financial analysts or users of strategic business information in biotechnology.
150 Attendees October

Directories & Databases

2799 **Association for Women in Science Directory**
Association for Women in Science
1200 New York Avenue NW
Suite 650
Washington, DC 20005-3929
202-326-8940
FAX: 202-326-8960
ruby@awis.org www.awis.org
Kathy Ruby, Publications Manager
Nancy Bakowski, Executive Director
Over 5,000 female scientists and engineers.
Irregular

2800 **BioWorld Online**
217 S B Street
San Mateo, CA 94401-4031

FAX: 404-814-0759 800-879-8790
Randy Osborne
This database contains a variety of information on biotechnology companies, products, and services.
Full-text

2801 **Biosis/Thomson Scientific**
BIOSIS
3501 Market Street
Philadelphia, PA 19104
215-386-0100
FAX: 215-386-2911 800-336-4474
Vin Caraher, President/CEO
Keith MacGregor, Executive VP
Andrea Degutis, Senior VP/Communications
A bibliographic database covering worldwide research on all biological and biomedical topics. Records contain bibliographic data, indexing information, and abstracts for most references. Biosis joined with the Thomson Corporation in early 2006 to expand its global presence.
Updated Weekly

2802 **Biotechnology Directory**
Rich's Business Directories
2551 Casey Suite A
Mountain View, CA 94043
650-564-9464
FAX: 650-564-9465 800-696-7424
richsguides@yahoo.com
www.norcalcompanies.com
Kelly Hudson, Contact
Offers information on over 150 biotechnology companies in San Diego County, California.

2803 **Grey House Biometric Information Directory**
Grey House Publishing
185 Millerton Road
Millerton, NY 12546
518-890-0526
FAX: 518-789-0545 800-562-2139
books@greyhouse.com
www.greyhouse.com
Leslie Mackenzie, Publisher
Richard Gottlieb, Editor
The most comprehensive resource covering biometric technology. Contains hundreds of organizations providing biometric products and services. The directory encompasses emerging identification technology, such as fingerprint ID, facial recognition, key stroke scan, hand geometry, voice recognition, iris scan and many other methods. *$295.00*
360 pages Annual Founded: 2005

2804 **Multilingual Thesaurus of Geosciences**
Information Today
143 Old Marlton Pike
Medford, NJ 08055-8750
609-654-6266
FAX: 609-654-4309
custserv@infotoday.com
www.infotoday.com
J Gravesteijn, Editor
C Kortman, Editor
G N Rassam
Represents the state of the art use of geoscience terminology by informations centers around the world. *$99.00*
654 pages ISBN 1-573870-09-9

2805 **Research Services Directory**
Grey House Publishing
185 Millerton Road
PO Box 860
Millerton, NY 12546
518-890-0526
FAX: 518-789-0545 800-562-2139
books@greyhouse.com
www.greyhouse.com
Leslie Mackenzie, Publisher
Richard Gottlieb, Editor
This Ninth Edition provides access to well over 7,700 independent Commercial Research Firms, Corporate Research Centers and Laboratories offering contract services for hands-on, basic or applied research. *$550.00*
992 pages Annual ISBN 1-592370-03-9

Industry Web Sites

2806 **www.aesociety.org**
Electrophoresis Society

International organization founded to improve and promote technologies necessary for biomolecular separation and detection. The techniques of electrophoresis are numerous and include isoelectric focusing, 2-D/IEF/SDS PAGE, capilllary, free-flow, as well as classical gel systems.

2807 **www.asbmb.org**
American Society for Biochemistry and Molecular

Non-profit scientific and educational organization with over 11,900 members. Most members teach and conduct research at colleges and universities. Others conduct research in various government laboratories, nonprofit research institutions and industry. The Society's student members attend undergraduate or graduate institutions.

2808 **www.asrm.org**
American Society for Reproductive Medicine

Organization devoted to advancing knowledge and expertise in reproductive medicine and biology. Members of this voluntary nonprofit organization must demonstrate the high ethical principals of the medical profession, evince an interest in reproductive medicine and biology, and adhere to the objectives of the Society.

2809 **www.benthos.org**
North American Benthological Society

International scientific organization whose purpose is to promote better understanding of the biotic communities of lake and stream bottoms and their role in aquatic ecosystems, by providing media and disseminating new investigation results, new interpetations, and other benthological information to aquatic biologists and to the scientific community at large.

2810 **www.bio.org**
Biotechnology Industry Organization

For firms involved in the use of recombinant DNA, hybridoma and immulogical technologies in a wide range of applications including human health care, animal husbandry, agriculture and specialty chemical production.

2811 **www.greyhouse.com**
Grey House Publishing

Selected Grey House directories in the fields of business, health and education are available online. Users can search our online databases by several different search criteria, such as product categories, geographic area, sales volume and much, much more. Full Grey House catalog and online ordering also available.

2812 www.ismrm.org
Int'l Society for Magnetic Resonance in Medicine

For physicians and scientists promoting the applications of magnetic resonance techniques to medicine and biology. The Society holds annual scientific meetings and sponsors other major educational and scientific workshops.

2813 www.massbio.org
Massachusetts Biotechnology Council

Organization that provides services and support for the Massachusets biotechnology industry.

2814 www.proteinsociety.org
Protein Society

Formed in 1986 to promote international interactions among investigators in order to explore all aspects of the building blocks of life, protien molecules. Members come from universities, foundations, institutes and corporations to provide leadership in this broad field of research. The Society and its members are making a strong impact on the advancements of protien science.

2815 www.whybiotech.com
Council for Biotechnology Information

Our vision and mission is to improve understanding and acceptance of biotechnology by collecting balanced, credible and science based information, then communicating this information through a variety of channels. Plant biotechnology has the potential to provide more and better food for a growing world population while helping the enviroment.

Associations

2816 **American Boat Builders and Repairers Association**
50 Water Street
Warren, RI 2885
401-247-0318
FAX: 401-247-0074 www.abbra.org
Jonathan Jones Haven, President
Peter Sabo, VP
Mark Amaral, Managing Director
Charles Teran, Treasurer/Secretary
Trade association for marinas, boat builders and repairers. Also offers a monthly newsletter and training seminars.
300 Members Founded: 1943

2817 **American Boat and Yacht Council Association**
3069 Solomons Island Road
Edgewater, MD 21037
410-956-1050
FAX: 410-956-2737
info@abycinc.org www.abycinc.org
Dennis Graham, Chairman
Skip Burdon, President/CEO
Gerard Douglas, Treasurer
Is a not-for-profit membership organization that has been developing and updating the safety standards for boat building and repair.
3500 Members Founded: 1954

2818 **American Boating Association**
PO Box 417
Harwich Port, MA 02646
508-432-8846
FAX: 508-430-2049
admin@americanboating.org
www.americanboating.org
Bill Condon, Founder/President
ABA's mission is to promote boating safety, affordability, growth, and a clean environment. It provides exclusive services and benefits for boaters and boating enthusiasts. *$10.00*
30000 Members

2819 **American Power Boat Association**
17640 Nine Mile Road
Eastpointe, MI 48021
586-773-9700
FAX: 586-773-6490
apbahq@apba-racing.com
www.apba-boatracing.com
Fred Hauenstein, President/CEO
Chris Reindl, Director Marketing
Jean Reindl, Treasurer
Gloria Urbin, Finance/Insurance Committee Member
The nation's authority on power boat racing which sanctions over 200 races each year.
6000 Members Founded: 1903

2820 **American Sail Training Association**
240 Thames Street
PO Box 1459
Newport, RI 2840
401-846-1775
FAX: 401-849-5400
asta@sailtraining.org
www.tallships.sailtraining.org
Peter A Mello, Executive Director
Adria Lande, Education Coordinator
Robert Hofmann, Development Director
Jonathan Harley, Race Director
Lori A Aguiar, Program Manager
Supports all those involved with sail training ships and programs, as well as ships under construction or renovation.
300 Members Founded: 1974

2821 **American Society of Marine Artists**
Po Box 369
Ambler, PA 19002
215-283-0888
asma@icdc.com
www.americansocietyofmarineartists.com
Peter Rogers, VP
Nancy Stiles, Executive Director
Provides you with access to the society's network of members, local and national marine art news and information about art exhibitions and exhibition opportunities.
530 Members Founded: 1978

2822 **Antique & Classic Boat Society**
422 James Street
Clayton, NY 13624
315-686-2628
FAX: 315-686-2680
hqs@acbs.org www.acbs.org
Jeff Rogers, President
Bob Bush, First VP
Gene Porter, Second VP
Jim Mersman, Treasurer
Kathleen Snyder, Membership/Billing
Society devoted to disseminating information on building and restoring wooden and antique boats.
12000 Members Founded: 1975

2823 **Association of Marina Industries**
444 North Capitol Street NW
Suite 645
Washington, DC 20001
202-379-9768
FAX: 202-628-8679
info@imimarina.org
www.imimarina.org
Gregg Kenney, Chairman
Alex Laidlaw, Vice Chairman
James Frye, President/CEO
Maureen Healey, Executive Director
Brooke Fishel, Manager Communications
The Association of Marina Industries is the international trade marine association for the marina industry.
1500 Members Founded: 1986

2824 **Boat Owners Association of the US**
800 South Pickett Street
Alexandria, VA 22304
703-412-2770
FAX: 703-461-2847 800-395-2628
membership@boatus.com
www.boatus.com
Richard Schwartz, Chairman/Founder
Jim Ellis, President/CEO
Supports all who are involved with legislation, regulations and consumer aspects of the industry.
62500 Members Founded: 1966

2825 **Boating Writers International**
108 Ninth Street
Wilmette, IL 60091
847-736-4142
info@bwi.org www.bwi.org
Roger Marshall, President
Kim Kavin, First VP
Betsy Frawley Haggerty, Second VP
Greg Proteau, Executive Director
Non-profit professional organization consting of writers, broadcasters, editors, photographers, public relations specialists and others in the communications profession associated with the boating industry. Members include active marine journalists across the U.S., in Canada and Europe, supporting marine manufacturers and service entities, and associates in communication roles.
300 Members Founded: 1970

2826 **Coastal Yachting Academy**
PO Box 551733
Jacksonville, FL 32255
904-928-1617
www.boatingclasses.com
Don Harper, Captain/Owner
To provide the recreational boater reasonably priced training equal to the training of professional mariners.

2827 **Industrial Fabrics Association International**
1801 County Road B W
Roseville, MN 55413
651-222-2508
FAX: 651-631-9334 800-225-4324
generalinfo@ifai.com www.ifai.com
George K Ochs, Chairman
Jeffrey W Kirk, President
Stephen Warner, Chief Executive Officer

2828 **Marine Retailers Association of America**
PO Box 1127
Oak Park, IL 60304
708-763-9210
FAX: 708-763-9236
mraa@mraa.com www.mraa.com
Glenn Mazzella, Chairman
Phil Keeter, President/CEO
Larry Innis, Director Government Affairs
Marge Eckenroad, Director Conventions/Meetings
Manufacturers and dealers of boats, equipment, supplies and services.
3000 Members Founded: 1971

2829 **Marine Safety Foundation**
5050 Industrial Road
Farmingdale, NJ 07727
732-751-0295
FAX: 732-751-0508
msf@marinesafety.org
www.marinesafety.org
John P Harkrader, Jr, Chairman
Burt W Thompson, President
Richard C Hiscock, VP
Gregory Switlik, Treasurer
Promotes the development and implementation of the highest possible performance, manufacturing, maintenance, service and training standards, for all lifesaving, survival and emergency rescue equipment. Also acts as a centralized network for the collection and dissemination of useful information. Serves and educates the membership, general public, and governing agencies in a manner which exhibits a commitment to the highest degree of quality and integrity.
131 Members Founded: 1986

2830 National Association of Charterboat Operators
Po Box 2990
Orange Beach, AL 36561
251-981-5136
FAX: 251-981-8191 866-981-5136
info@nacocharters.org
www.nacocharters.org

Bobbi Walker, Executive Director

NACO members are operators of sportfishing, diving and small excursion vessels. NACO provides group charterboat insurance and a drug testing consortium. Quarterly publication for members only

3600+ Members Founded: 1991

2831 National Association of Sailing
15 Renier Court
Middletown, NJ 07748-1612
732-716-6190

Accredits sailing schools, certifies instructors and provides teaching and management information. Publishes a quarterly newsletter and directory of American sailing schools and charter operators. Provides free consulting services for start-ups of new schools.

100 Members Founded: 1980

2832 National Association of State Boating Law Administrators
1500 Leestown Road
Suite 330
Lexington, KY 40511
859-225-9487
FAX: 859-231-6403
george@nasbla.org www.nasbla.org/

Charles A Sledd, President
Jeff Johnson, VP
John Johnson, Chief Executive Officer
Ron Sarver, Deputy Director
Libby Osborne, Chief Financial Officer

Concerned with boating education, accident investigation and state-by-state regulations.

56 Members Founded: 1960
Mailing list available for rent 56 names

2833 National Marine Bankers Association
200 East Randolph
Suite 5100
Chicago, IL 60601
312-812-2777
FAX: 312-946-0388
bmcardle@nmma.org
www.marinebankers.org

Michael Bryant, Director
Donald Parkhurst, Senior VP
Jim Meere, VP
Bernice McArdle, Association Manager

The NMBA is an association dedicated to educating its current and prospective lenders in marine financing procedures, proactively seeking new marine lenders, maintaining alliances with industry partners, actively supporting a network-communication exchange for its members, and continuing the overall promotion of marine lending.

81 Members Founded: 1980

2834 National Marine Distributors Association
37 Pratt Street
Essex, CT 06426-1159
860-767-7898
FAX: 860-767-7932
info@nmdaonline.com
www.nmdaonline.com

Nancy Cueroni, Executive Director

Wholesale distributors of marine accessories and hardware.

200 Members

2835 National Marine Manufacturers Association
200 East Randolf Street
Suite 5100
Chicago, IL 60601-4255
312-946-6200
FAX: 312-946-0401 www.nmma.org

William Barrington, Chairman
Robert Selig, Vice Chairman
Thomas Dammrich, President
Ben Wold, Executive Vice President
Craig Boskey, VP Finance/CFO

Dedicated to creating, promoting and protecting an environment where members can achieve financial success through excellence in manufacturing, selling and service for their customers.

1400+ Members Founded: 1979

2836 National Marine Representative Association
PO Box 360
Gurnee, IL 60031
847-662-3167
FAX: 847-336-7126
info@nmraonline.org
www.nmraonline.org

Jim Hannan, President
Jay Sanders, VP
Norm MacLeod, Treasurer
Tim Luehmann, Secretary

The NMRA is a national organization serving marine industry independent representatives and the manufacturers who sell through representatives.

300 Members Founded: 1960

2837 National Safe Boating Council
PO Box 509
Bristow, VA 20136
703-361-4294
FAX: 703-361-5294
www.safeboatingcouncil.org

Ed Carter, Chairman
Ruth Wood, Vice Chairman
Virgil Chambers, Executive Officer
Sandy Smith, Chief Financial Officer
Veronica Floyd, Treasurer

NSBC has an interest in boating safety and education to reduce accidents and enhance the boating experience.

350 Members Founded: 1958

2838 Northwest Marine Trade Association
1900 North Northlake Way
Suite 233
Seattle, WA 98103-9087
206-634-0911
FAX: 206-632-0078
info@seattleboatshow.com
www.nmta.net

Michael Campbell, President
Tony Floor, Director Fishing Affairs
Jennifer Horn, Director Sales/Marketing
Liz Manning, Membership Director

Seeks to promote interest in boating, sponsors boat shows and acts as a legislative consultant and watchdog.

850 Members Founded: 1947

2839 Offshoreonly
PO Box 10868
St Petersburg, FL 33733
954-463-1101
FAX: 727-394-2451
offshoreonly@offshoreonly.com
www.offshoreonly.com

Kathe Walker, President
Scott Ryerson, VP

OPBA is a nonprofit organization catering to fun loving boaters in the Tampa/Clearwater/St. Petersburg areas of Florida.

2840 Personal Watercraft Industry Association
444 North Capitol Street NW
Suite 645
Washington, DC 20001
202-737-9768
FAX: 202-628-4716
info@pwia.org www.pwia.org

Maureen Healey, Executive Director
Jeff Ludwig, Manager Regulatory Affairs
Elinore Boeke, Manager Communications

Members are manufacturers of personal watercraft.

4 Members Founded: 1987

2841 Propeller Club of the United States
3927 Old Lee Highway
Suite 101A
Fairfax, VA 22030-2422
703-691-2777
FAX: 703-691-4173
info@propellerclubhq.com
www.propellerclubhq.com

Thomas Allegretti, President
John Angus, III, SVP/General Counsel
Bart A Goedhard, VP International Executive
Virgil R Allen, VP Development

Promotes and supports the American Merchant Marine and aids in the development of Great Lakes, inland waterway, and harbor improvement. Conventions are listed on web site.

10000 Members Founded: 1927

2842 Recreational Boaters of California
925 L Street, Suite 220
Sacramento, CA 95814

rboc@rboc.org www.rboc.org

Jerry Lounsbury, President
Bob White, Secretary/Treasurer

Monitors the proceedings in the State Capitol, reviewing each of the bills that are introduced and/or amended as to whether they would have an impact on boating.

Founded: 1968

2843 Shipbuilders Council of America
1455 F Street NW
Suite 225
Washington, DC 20005
202-383-3307
FAX: 202-347-5464
awalker@vesselalliance.com
www.shipbuilders.org

Donald T Bollinger, Chairman
Steve Welch, Vice Chairman
Allen Walker, President
Irene Ringwood, Manager

Private shipbuilding and repair companies and related firms such as manufacturers of marine equipment and supplies, many of which do work for the federal government. Representing more than 35,000 workers in

23 states. Sponsors a newsletter, annual meetings and educational sessions.
43 Members Founded: 1946

2844 **Society of Accredited Marine Surveyors**
4605 Cardinal Boulevard
Jacksonville, FL 32210
904-384-1494
FAX: 904-388-3958 800-344-9077
samshq@aol.com
www.marinesurvey.org
Norman L Leblanc, President
Geroge J Sepel, Executive VP
Mary Stahler, Executive Director
George A Gallup, Treasurer/Secretary
Stuart J McLea, VP Public Relations
SAMS is committed to enhancing the profession of marine surveying, avoiding prejudice, conflict of interest, and maintaining professional independence.
1000 Members Founded: 1986

2845 **Texas Dragon Boat Association**
4723 Waring Street
Houston, TX 77027
832-687-7208

info@houstondragonboat.com
www.texasdragonboat.com
Caroline Quan Long, President/Executive Director
Marla Massey, Associate Executive Director
Promotes the tradition and sport of dragon boating; increases the awareness of Asian and Asian-American culture; and enhances cross-cultural understanding.

2846 **Traditional Small Craft Association**
PO Box 350
Mystic, CT 06355

drathmarine@rockisland.com
www.tsca.net
David Cockey, Interim Chairman
Elizabeth Evans, President
Chauncy Rucker, VP
John Symons, Treasurer
Mike Wick, Secretary
Nonprofit, tax-exempt educational organization which works to preserve and continue the living traditions, skills, lore and legends surrounding working and pleasure watercraft. It encourages the design, construction and use of boats and it embraces contemporary variants and adaptions of traditional design. Publishes a quarterly journal called Ash Breeze.

2847 **United States Power Squadrons**
1504 Blue Ridge Road
Raleigh, NC 27622
919-210-0281
FAX: 888-304-0813 www.usps.org
Darrell Allison, Rear Commander
Dave Rickard, Director Marketing/PR
Mary Berube, Manager
Is a non-profit, educational organization dedicated to making boating safer and more enjoyable by teaching classes in seamanship, navigation and related subjects.
60000 Members Founded: 1914

2848 **United States Rowing Association**
2 Wall Street
Princeton, NJ 08540
609-751-0700
FAX: 609-924-1578 800-314-4769
members@usrowing.org
www.usrowing.org
Glenn Merry, Executive Director
Brian Klausner, Chief Financial Officer
Brett Johnson, Director Commuications
Non-profit membership organization, recognized by the U.S. Olympic Committee as the national governing body for the sport of rowing in the United States.
14000 Members Founded: 1982

2849 **United States Sailing Association**
15 Maritime Drive
PO Box 1260
Portsmouth, RI 02871-0907
401-683-0800
FAX: 401-683-0840 800-877-2451
info@ussailing.org www.ussailing.org

Janet C Baxter, President
Jim Capron, VP
Charlie Leighton, Executive Director
Bobbi Warren, Director Finance
Dan Cooney, Marketing Director
National governing body for the sport of sailing.
46000 Members Founded: 1897

2850 **United Tuna Cooperative**
2535 Kettner Boulevard
Suite 3C1
San Diego, CA 92101
619-238-1838
FAX: 619-238-1708 phf@pacbell.net
Paul Krampe, Executive Director
Established as the American Fisherman's Protective Association, ATA has also been known as American Fisherman's Tunaboat Association. Sponsors the American Tunaboat Association Political Action Committee.
18 Members Founded: 1921

2851 **Yacht Brokers Association of America**
105 Eastern Avenue
Suite 104
Annapolis, MD 21403-3300
410-263-1014
FAX: 410-263-1659
info@ybaa.com www.ybaa.com
Joe Thompson, Executive Director
Kristin Thompson, Dir Communications/Conference
Robb Fish, Program Development Manager
Exists to unite yacht brokers throughout North America in order to: establish, promote & enforce high standards of professional competance & ethical conduct; foster public recognition of, & support for, YBAA & its member brokers; facilitate cooperation among member brokers; & enhance each members success.
250 Members Founded: 1920

2852 **Yachting Club of America**
PO Box 1040
Marco Island, FL 34146
239-642-4448
FAX: 239-642-5284
ycaol@hotmail.com www.ycaol.com
David Martin, Owner
Supports all those involved with the sport of yaching.
30,00 Members Founded: 1963

Newsletters

2853 **ASMA News**
American Society of Marine Artists
PO Box 369
Ambler, PA 19002
215-283-0888

asma@icdc.com
www.americansocietyofmarineartists.com
Peter Rogers, VP
Nancy Stiles, Executive Director
Provides you access to the Society's network of members, local and national marine art news and information about art exhibitions and exhibition opportunities.
Quarterly

2854 **American Boat & Yacht Council News**
American Boat and Yacht Council
3069 Solomons Island Road
Edgewater, MD 21037
410-956-1050
FAX: 410-956-2737
info@abycinc.org www.abycinc.org
Judith Ramsey, Editor
Skip Burdon, President/CEO
Caroline Chetelat, Director Marketing/Communications
News and technical information of interest to ABYC members.
8 pages Quarterly Founded: 1988

2855 **American Boat Builders and Repairers Association Newsletter**
American Boat Builders and Repairers Association
50 Water Street
Warren, RI 2885
401-247-0318
FAX: 401-247-0074
mamaral@abbra.org www.abbra.org
Jonathan Jones Haven, President
Peter Sabo, VP
Mark Amaral, Managing Director
Charles Teran, Treasurer/Secretary
Accepts advertising.
4 pages Monthly Founded: 1943

2856 **Anchor Line Newsletter**
National Safe Boating Council
PO Box 509
Bristow, VA 20136
703-361-4294
FAX: 703-361-5294
www.safeboatingcouncil.org
Ed Carter, Chairman
Ruth Wood, Vice Chairman
Virgil Chambers, Executive Director
Sandy Smith, Chief Financial Officer
Veronica Floyd, Treasurer

2857 **Auto Parking in Marinas**
Association of Marina Industries
444 North Capitol Street NW
Suite 645
Washington, DC 20001
202-379-9768
FAX: 202-628-8679
info@imimarina.org
www.imimarina.org
Gregg Kenney, Chairman
Alex Laidlaw, Vice Chairman

Maureen Healey, Executive Director
Cris McSparen, Treasurer
Brooke Fishel, Manager Communications

A national survey of marinas that compares levels of boat use and number of autos parked in the facilities. *$45.00*

2858 Business of Pleasure Boats
National Marine Bankers Association
200 East Randolph Street
Suite 5100
Chicago, IL 60601
312-812-2777
FAX: 312-946-0388
bmcardle@nmma.org
www.marinebankers.org

Michael Bryant, Director
Donald Parkhurst, President
Jim Meere, VP
Jim Coburn, Treasurer
Bernice McArdle, Association Manager

Quarterly

2859 Fire Protection Standards for Marinas & Bo atyards
Association of Marina Industries
444 North Capitol Street NW
Suite 645
Washington, DC 20001
202-379-9768
FAX: 202-628-8679
infoWimimarina.org
www.imimarina.org

Gregg Kenney, Chairman
Alex Laidlaw, Vice Chairman
Maureen Healey, Executive Director
Cris McSparen, Treasurer
Brooke Fishel, Manager Communications

National Fire Protection Association standards for marinas, including: Management, Electrical wiring, Fire protection, Berthing & storgage, Operational hazards. *$45.00*

2860 Hurricane Risk Management Series

Association of Marina Industries
444 North Capitol Street NW
Suite 645
Washington, DC 20001
202-379-9768
FAX: 202-628-8679
info@imimarina.org
www.imimarina.org

Gregg Kenney, Chairman
Alex Laidlaw, Vice Chairman
Maureen Healey, Executive Director
Cris McSparen, Treasurer
Brooke Fishel, Manager Communications

New information has been added to this series of five (5) short papers intended to update marinas located in coastal hurricane threatened areas with the hurricane preparedness planning for boats and boating facilities. Also included is a Hurricane Manual and Hurricane Preparedness Plan. *$20.00*

2861 MRAA Bearings
Marine Retailers Association of America
PO Box 1127
Oak Park, IL 60300
708-763-9210
FAX: 708-763-9236
mraa@mraa.com www.mraa.com

Nicole Maiman, Editor
Glenn Mazzella, Chairman
Phil Keeter, President/CEO
Marge Eckenroad, Executive Administrator

A publication encompassing issues that you need to know about, issues such as legislation, environment and compliance, legal, association and industry news, and much more.

Monthly Founded: 1972
Circulation: 2000

2862 Mainsheet
Rhodes 19 Class Association
174 Walnut Street
Reading, MA 01867
781-944-2697

michael.carpenter@attbi.com
www.rhodes19.org

Wiley Crockett, President
Michael Carpenter, Marketing Contact

Newsletter concerning the Rhodes 19 design sailboat. Our mission is to promote Rhodes 19 racing by encouraging and supporting local fleet development nationally, and by working to maintain the one-design integrity of the boat.

2863 Marine Safety and Security Report
Stamler Publishing Company
PO Box 3367
Branford, CT 06405-1967
203-488-9808
FAX: 203-488-3129 800-422-4121

S Paul Stamler, President/CEO

Business-to-business newsletter providing information on boating and shipping safety and enforcement issues, including federal regulations and Coast Guard Actions, state safety programs, IMO activity, classification studies, vessel recalls, and safety equipment. Accepts no advertising and is solely supported by subscribers worldwide.
$77.00
4 pages
Printed in 2 colors on matte stock

2864 Maritime Reporter and Engineering News
118 East 25th Street
New York, NY 10010
212-238-8029
FAX: 212-254-6271
angie@maritimejobs.com
www.marinelink.com

John O'Malley, Publisher
Greg Trauthwein, Associate Publisher
Michael Martino, Owner
Lucia M Annunziata, VP
Jennifer Rabulan, Technical Editor

Provides unparalleled coverage of the maritime industry covering the inland, Coastal and Great Lakes region.
Monthly
Circulation: 50000

2865 NACO Report
National Association of Charterboat Operators
Po Box 2990
Orange Beach, AL 36561
251-981-5136
FAX: 251-981-8191 866-981-5136
info@nacocharters.com
www.nacocharters.org

Bobbi Walker, Executive Director

Keeps members informed and educated on crucial issues affecting the industry. It provides valuable information on trends and developments in the charter industry including updates on new and pending Federal regulations.

Quarterly
Circulation: 3600+

2866 Propeller Club Newsletter
Propeller Club of the United States
3927 Old Lee Highway
Suite 101A
Fairfax, VA 22030-2422
703-691-2777
FAX: 703-691-4173
info@propellerclubhq.com
www.propellerclubhq.com

Bart Goedhard, Editor/VP International Executive
Thomas Allegretti, President
John Angus, III, SVP/General Counsel
Virgil R Allen, VP Development

Features expanded coverage of Propeller Club activities, including legislative and regulatory reports, feature-length member profiles, regional news and expanded coverage of national maritime issues.
Quarterly

2867 Rudder
Antique & Classic Boat Society
422 James Street
Clayton, NY 13624
315-686-2628
FAX: 315-686-2680
hqs@acbs.org www.acbs.org

Chris Eden, Editor
Herb Anthony, Advertising
Jeff Rogers, President
Bob Bush, First Vice President
Gene Porter, Second Vice President

Historical news and how-to-restore wooden and antique boats.
Quarterly Founded: 1975
Printed in 4 colors

2868 Safety Guidelines for Tank Vessel Clearnin g Facilities Manual
Shipbuilders Council of America
1455 F Street NW
Suite 225
Washington, DC 20005
202-383-3307
FAX: 202-347-5464
awalker@vesselalliance.com
www.shipbuilders.org

Donald T Bollinger, Chairman
Steve Welch, Vice Chairman
Allen Walker, President
Irene Ringwood, Manager

This guide makes recommendations for tank vessel personnel on the sfe cleaning of tank vessels at shore based cleaning facilities of crude oil, petroleum products, and chemicals. *$15.00*

2869 Seamanship Training
American Boating Association
PO Box 417
Harwich Port, MA 02646
508-432-8846
FAX: 503-430-2049
admin@americanboating.org
www.americanboating.org
Free to all ABA (American Boating Association) members as well as all boaters. Informative content on boating skills and safety issues.
Bi-Monthly

2870 Shipyard Chronicle Newsletter
Shipbuilders Council of America
1455 F Street NW
Suite 225
Washington, DC 20005
202-383-3307
FAX: 202-347-5464
awalker@vesselalliance.com
www.shipbuilders.org
Donald T Bollinger, Chairman
Steve Welch, Vice Chairman
Allen Walker, President
Irene Ringwood, Manager
The publication is devoted to keeping members up to date on the latest legislative and regulatory developments. It also includes a schedule of upcoming association and industry related government meetings, as well as news regarding SCA member companies.

2871 Soundings Trade Only
Soundings Publications
10 Bokum Road
Essex, CT 06426
860-767-3200
FAX: 860-767-0642
www.tradeonlytoday.com
Tom Hubbard, Editor
Peter Mitchel, Publisher
Nation's boating business newspaper. Coverage of the recreational boating business; for marine dealers, marine operators, distributors and manufacturers. BPA audited.
$13.97
33 pages Monthly Founded: 1965
Circulation: 34,000

2872 Tank Barge Stripping and Cleaning Process Manual
Shipbuilders Council of America
1455 F Street NW
Suite 225
Washington, DC 20005
202-383-3307
FAX: 202-347-5464
awalker@vesselalliance.com
www.shipbuilders.org
Donald T Bollinger, Chairman
Steve Welch, Vice Chairman
Allen Walker, President
Irene Ringwood, Manager
This guide makes recommendations for compliance with federal regulations regarding tank barge stripping and cleaning processes. *$ 15.00*

2873 Tidings
National Marine Representatives Association
PO Box 360
Gurnee, IL 60031
847-662-3167
FAX: 847-336-7126
info@nmraonlne.org
www.nmraonline.org
Jim Hannan, President
Jay Sanders, VP
Norm MacLeod, Treasurer
Tim Luehmann, Secretary
Contains informative articles to help manufacturers develop sound and profitable relationships with independent sales representatives and keep informed about the marine market in general.
500+ pages Quarterly Founded: 1960

2874 Uniform System of Accounts for Marinas & B oatyards
Association of Marina Industries
444 North Capitol Street NW
Suite 645
Washington, DC 20001
202-379-9768
FAX: 202-628-8679
info@imimarina.org
www.imimarina.org
Gregg Kenney, Chairman
Alex Laidlaw, Vice Chairman
Maureen Healey, Executive Director
Cris McSparen, Treasurer
Brooke Fishel, Manager Communications

Provides standard financial organization and account structure for marinas and boatyards. Its purpose is to provide a mechanism to achieve comparable financial information throughout the industry, whereby owners, operators, investors and lenders can improve, value and compare operations of these facilities. *$30.00*

2875 Water Life
Northwest Marine Trade Association
1900 North Northlake Way
Suite 233
Seattle, WA 98103-9051
206-634-0911
FAX: 206-632-0078
info@seattleboatshow.com
www.nmta.net
Michael Campbell, President
Tony Floor, Director Fishing Affairs
Jennifer Horn, Director Sales/Marketing
Liz Manning, Membership Director
Provides industry information, member benefits, committee activity and new member announcements and anniversaries. Water Life continues to evolve into a valuable tool for Pacific Northwest marine leaders.

2876 Yacht Broker Newsletter
Yacht Brokers Association of America
105 Eastern Avenue
Suite 104
Annapolis, MD 21403-3300
410-263-1014
FAX: 410-263-1659
info@ybaa.com www.ybaa.com
Joe Thompson, Executive Director
Kristin Thompson, Dir Communications/Conference
Robb Fish, Program Development Manager
Reports on latest business issues, industry concerns, legislation, regulatory activities and includes a member-to-member section(WayPoints), where members can report on their own company news, personnel updates and business expansion.

Magazines & Journals

2877 ABBRA Boatyard & Marina Operator's Manual
American Boat Builders and Repairers Association
50 Warren Street
Warren, RI 02885
401-247-0318
FAX: 401-247-0074 www.abbra.org
Jonathan Jones Haven, President
Peter Sabo, VP
Mark Amaral, Managing Director
Charles Teran, Treasurer/Secretary
The primary reference for operators of modern boatyards and marinas. *$175.00*

2878 American Sailor
US Sailing Association
PO Box 209
Newport, RI 02840-0209
401-683-0800
FAX: 401-683-0840
info@ussailing.org www.ussailing.org

Boating news.
Monthly Founded: 1986

2879 Ash Breeze
Traditional Small Craft Association
PO Box 350
Mystic, CT 06355

drathmarine@rockisland.com
www.tsca.net
Dan Drath, Editor
Devoted to topics ranging from reports from the chapters to technical details and specific designs with lines and offsets. You may find anecdotal accounts of experiences in traditional boats, and tips on how to spile a plank.
Quarterly

2880 Boat & Motor Dealer
Preston Publications
6600 W Touhy Avenue
PO Box 48312
Niles, IL 60714-4588
847-647-2900
FAX: 847-647-1155
circulation@boatmotordealer.com
www.boatmotordealer.com
Janice Gordon, Publisher
Jerome Koncel, Editorial Director
Dedicated to providing businesses in the recreational marine industry with the information, commentary and analysis needed to expand their businesses and improve profitability. *$45.00*
52 pages Monthly Founded: 1959
Circulation: 30000 30000 names $100 per M.

2881 Boat Accident Investigator's Field Guide
National Association of State Boating Law
1500 Leestown Road
Suite 300
Lexington, KY 40511
859-225-9487
FAX: 859-231-6403
info@nasbla.org www.nasbla.org
Kim Hermes, Editor
George Stewart, Executive Director
John Johnson, Chief Executive Officer
Topics covered in this Field Guide include: Accidents, Fraud, B.A.R.D., Recalls & MOUs Investigative Procedures Sketching & Diagramming Stability, Capacity & Loading Collision Investigations Injury Assessment Personal Watercraft Basics of Electricity Lighting & Other High Voltage Accidents, and many more. *$49.00*

Mailing list available for rent 56 names

2882 Boat US Magazine
Boat Owners Association of the US
880 South Pickett Street
Alexandria, VA 22304-4606
703-412-2770
FAX: 703-461-2845
magazine@boatus.com
www.boatus.com

Michael Sciulla, Editor
Richard Schwartz, Chairman/Founder
Jim Ellis, President/CEO

Boating magazine includes political, legislative and consumer news of interest to recreational boat owners. *$19.00*
Bi-Monthly Founded: 1966

2883 Boatbuilder
Belvoir Publishers
800 Connecticut Avenue
Norwalk, CT 06854-1631
203-857-3100
FAX: 203-857-3103
customer_service@belvoir.com
www.belvoir.com

Keith Lawrence, Editor
Robert Englander, CEO

The magazine is for those who build, modify and repair boats. *$19.97*
6 Issues Founded: 1972

2884 Boating Industry
Ehlert Publishing Group
6420 Sycamore Lane
Suite 100
Maple Grove, MN 55369
763-383-4400
FAX: 763-383-4499 800-848-6247
acollins@ehlertpublishing.com
www.boating-industry.com

Liz Walz, Senior Editor
Sarah Karasch, Production Coordinator

Links together all sectors of the boating market from boat and motor dealers to marinas, boatyards, builders and suppliers. It also provides strategic analysis, in-depth coverage and proprietary research of the most critical issues.
8 Issues/2 Special Issues

2885 Boating Magazine
1633 Broadway
41st Floor
New York, NY 10019-6741
212-675-5525
FAX: 212-767-4831
fday@hfmmag.com
www.boatingmag.com

Wade Luce, Publisher
Natalie Rankin, Director Marketing

Offers up-to-date information on boats, manufacturers, suppliers, distributors related to the boating industry. *$17.95*
Monthly

2886 Boating Writers International Journal
Boating Writers International
108 Ninth Street
Wilmette, IL 60091
847-736-4142
www.bwi.org

Greg Proteau, Editor/Executive Director
Jim Hendricks, Associate Publisher
Roger Marshall, President
Kim Kavin, First Vice President
Betsy Fawley Haggerty, Second Vice President

Provides materials about boating and other legislation.
11x/Year Founded: 1970

2887 Canoe & Kayak Magazine
Canoe & Kayak
10526 NE 68th Street
Suite 3
Kirkland, WA 98083
425-827-6363
FAX: 425-827-1893 800-692-2663
letters@canoekayak.com
www.canoekayak.com

Ross Prather, Editor
Robin Stanton, Managing Editor
Chris Callahan, Director Sales/Marketing

Published by the Canoe American Associates. *$17.95*
7 Issues Founded: 1973
Circulation: 62000
Mailing list available for rent

2888 Dry Stack Marina Handbook
Association of Marina Industries
444 North Capitol Street NW
Suite 645
Washington, DC 20001
202-379-9768
FAX: 202-628-8679
info@imimarina.org
www.imimarina.org

Gregg Kenney, Chairman
Alex Laidlaw, Vice Chairman
Maureen Healey, Executive Director
Cris McSparen, Treasurer
Brooke Fishel, Manager Communications

This book covers: Dry stack buildings and racks, Boat handling equipment, Statistics, Site planning, Typical costs, Fire protection problems & solutions, Comparision of dry stack vs. wet slip demand, Marketing, Facility operations, Lease or purchase decision, Loss control considerations. *$90.00*
61 Illustrations

2889 Ensign
United States Power Squadrons
PO Box 31664
Raleigh, NC 27622-1664
919-210-0281
FAX: 888-304-0813 888-367-8777
hilly@hq.usps.org www.usps.org

Yvonne Hill, Editor
Kelly Anderson, Associate Editor
Mary Catherine Berube, Publisher

Ensign magazine is the official magazine of United States Power Squadrons. The mission is to promote recreational boating safety through education and civic activities while providing fellowship for our members. *$10.00*
48 pages Monthly Founded: 1914
Circulation: 35,000
Printed in 4 colors on glossy stock

2890 Financial Operational Benchmark Study for Marina Operators
Association of Marina Industries
444 North Capitol Street NW
Suite 645
Washington, DC 20001
202-379-9768
FAX: 202-628-8679
info@imimarina.org
www.imimarina.org

Gregg Kenney, Chairman
Alex Laidlaw, Vice Chairman
Maureen Healey, Executive Director
Cris McSparen, Treasurer
Brooke Fishel, Manager Communications

This comprehensive report contains the results of a current national survey of over 1,300 marina operators. The study benchmarks the following: Marina facility characteristics (number of slips, occupancy rates, waiting list size, average slip turnover rate, covered and uncovered dockage rates by length, amenties offered and services provided, dockage provided and dry storage data). *$195.00*
84 pages

2891 Marina Investment & Appraisal Notebook
Association of Marina Industries
444 North Capitol Street NW
Suite 645
Washington, DC 20001
202-379-9768
FAX: 202-628-8679
info@imimarina.org
www.imimarina.org

Gregg Kenney, Chairman
Alex Laidlaw, Vice Chairman
Maureen Healey, Executive Director
Cris McSparen, Treasurer
Brooke Fishel, Manager Communications

Marina site, design issues, buying and managing marinas, the marina appraisal process and Marina development. *$85.00*

2892 Marina/Dock Age
Preston Publications
6600 West Touhy Avenue
PO Box 48312
Niles, IL 60714-4516
847-647-2900
FAX: 847-647-1155
webadmin@prestonpub.com
www.prestonpub.com

Janice Gordon, Publisher
Jerome Koncel, Editorial Director

Provide marina/boatyard owners and managers with the information they need to meet ever-changing government regulations, operate more efficiently, expand their business, and improve their profitability. *$50.00*
Monthly
Circulation: 24000

2893 Marinas and Small Craft Harbors
Association of Marina Industries
444 North Capitol Street NW
Suite 645
Washington, DC 20001
202-379-9768
FAX: 202-628-8679
info@imimarina.org
www.imimarina.org

Gregg Kenney, Chairman
Alex Laidlaw, Vice Chairman
Maureen Healey, Executive Director
Cris McSparen, Treasurer
Brooke Fishel, Manager Communications

The new edition includes updated and redrawn tables, charts, figures and text editing and additions, as well as newly created information on marina design characteristics of megyachts and test data, design loads, and recommendations on design and performance of dock cleats. *$89.95*

2894 Marine Fabricator
Industrial Fabrics Association International

1801 County Road BW
Roseville, MN 55113-4061
651-222-2508
FAX: 651-631-9334 800-225-4324
generalinfo@ifai.com www.ifai.com

Mary Hennessey, Publisher/VP Communications
Melissa Kaudy, Editor
Mary J Moore, Circulation/Promotions Manager

Marine Fabricator provides reportage that reflects the innovations and trends of the industry. Features include fabrication techniques, fabricator profiles, case studies, business tips and solutions, a buyer's guide showcase, MFA news, and more. *$36.00*
Quarterly Founded: 1995
Circulation: 5000 $250 per M.
Printed in 4 colors on glossy stock

2895 Marine Log
345 Hudson Street
New York, NY 10014
212-620-7200
FAX: 212-633-1165
marinelog@sbpub.com
www.marinelog.com
Arthur J McGinnis Jr, Publisher
John Snyder, Editor
Tom Leader, Circulation Director
Dedicated to providing marine industry professionals with the information they need to enable them to design, build and operate vessels, rigs and offshore structures profitably, safely, legally and in an environmentally responsible manner. *$99.95*
Monthly Founded: 1878

2896 Marine News
Maritime Activity Reports
118 East 25th Street
New York, NY 10010
212-477-6700
FAX: 212-254-6271
info@marinelink.com
www.marinelink.com
John C O'Malley, Publisher
Greg Trauthwein, Associate Publisher
Jennifer Rabulan, Technical Editor
Lucia M Annunziata, VP
Mark O'Malley, Manager
Features marine industry news and issues effecting maritime activity. Includes updates on vessel building and acquisitions as well as regular columns on research and devleopment, equipment reports and an events calendar.
Monthly Founded: 1945
Circulation: 23000

2897 Motor Boating
Time4 Media Marine Group
18 Marshall Street
Suite 114
South Norwalk, CT 06854
203-299-5950
FAX: 203-299-5951
www.motorboating.com
Ed Baker, Associate Publisher
Helps its readers buy, maintain and get the most out of their powerboats. It focuses on powerboats, people, products, destinations, trends and technological developments in the boating market, as well as cruising, water sports and safety.
Monthly Founded: 1907
Printed in on glossy stock

2898 NASBLA Annual Report
National Association of State Boating Law
1500 Leestown Road
Suite 300
Lexington, KY 40511
859-225-9487
FAX: 859-231-6403
info@nasbla.org www.nasbla.org
John Johnson, Chief Executive Officer
Published by the National Association of State Boating Law Administration.

Mailing list available for rent 56 names

2899 National Numbering & Titling
National Association of State Boating Law
1500 Leestown Road
Suite 330
Lexington, KY 40511
859-225-9487
FAX: 859-231-6403
info@nasbla.org www.nasbla.org
Kim Hermes, Editor
Charles A Sledd, President
Jeff Johnson, VP
John Johnson, Chief Executive Officer
Dr Deb Gona, Research Director
Facilitate ongoing efforts to evaluate and improve the programs' internal procedures and external interactions in the face of resource constraints and in preparation for implementing the Coast Guard's Vessel Identification System. *$14.95*
Founded: 2002
Mailing list available for rent 56 names

2900 Paddle Magazine
Paddle Sport Publishing
PO Box 775450
Steamboat Springs, CO 80477-5450
970-879-1450
FAX: 970-870-1404
Eugene@paddlermagazine.com
www.paddlermagazine.com
Eugene Buchanan, Publisher/Editor
Jeff Moag, Managing Editor
Kevin Thompson, Account Manager
Information to keep the paddle sport equipment dealer up-to-date on issues that will effect their business, industry trends in boats, apparel and accessories, how to articles to assist the reader in selling boats. *$18.00*

Circulation: 5527
Printed in 4 colors on glossy stock

2901 Paddlesports Business
Canoe & Kayak
10526 NE 68th Street
Suite 3
Kirkland, WA 98083-3146
425-827-6363
FAX: 425-827-1893 800-692-2663
Ross Prather, Editor
Chris Callaman, Sales/Marketing Director
Trade publication for the paddlesports industry.

Mailing list available for rent

2902 Practices & Products for Clean Marinas
Association of Marina Industries
444 North Capitol Street NW
Suite 645
Washington, DC 20001
202-379-9768
FAX: 202-628-8679
info@imimarina.org
www.imimarina.org
Gregg Kenney, Chairman
Alex Laidlaw, Vice Chairman
Maureen Healey, Executive Director
Cris McSparen, Treasurer
Brooke Fishel, Manager Communications

This Best Management Practice(BMP) Handbook gives background informtion explaining environmental regulations, as well as the sources and effects of pollution, and successful techniques for controlling pollution. *$39.00*

2903 Professional BoatBuilder
WoodenBoat Publications
86 Great Cove Drive
PO Box 78
Brooklin, ME 04616
207-359-4651
FAX: 207-359-8920
carl@proboat.com www.proboat.com
Paul Lazarus, Editor
Aaron Porter, Associate Editor
Carl Cramer, Publisher
Focuses on materials, design, and construction techniques and repair solutions chosen by marine professionals. Regular technical articles provide detailed, real-world examples to improve the efficiency and quality of their work. *$35.95*
76 pages Founded: 1989
Circulation: 27500
Printed in 4 colors on glossy stock

2904 Propeller
American Power Boat Association
17640 Nine Mile Road
Eastpointe, MI 48021
586-773-9700
FAX: 586-773-6490
propeller@apba-racing.com
www.apba-racing.com
Tana Moore, Editor
Fred Hauenstein, President
Propeller magazine is the mouthpiece of the American Power Boat Association, the nation's leading authority on power boat racing which sanctions over 200 races each year. *$25.00*
32 pages Monthly Founded: 1903
Printed in 4 colors on glossy stock

2905 Reference Guide to State Boating Laws
National Association of State Boating Law
1500 Leestown Road
Suite 300
Lexington, KY 40511
859-225-9487
FAX: 859-231-6403
info@nasbla.org www.nasbla.org
Charles A Sledd, President
Jeff Johnson, VP
John Johnson, Chief Executive Officer
Ron Sarver, Deputy Director
Dr Deb Gona, Research Director
This guide provides a wealth of information that can assist boating law enforcement officers, boating safety education officials and boating safety advocates in their daily work. *$30.00*

Mailing list available for rent 56 names

2906 Small Craft Advisory
National Association of State Boating Law Admnstrs
1500 Leestown Road
Suite 330
Lexington, KY 40511
859-225-9487
FAX: 859-231-6403
editor@nasbla.org www.nasbla.org
John Johnson, Executive Editor
Ron Sarver, Managing Editor
Kimberly Hermes, Editor
Small Craft Advisory, published bimonthly, is for and about the nation's boating law administration professionals. Authoritative articles featuring practices,

procedures, and research in recreational boating safety, marine law enforcement, and boating safety education are presented to enhance the efficiency and effectiveness of recreational boating safety. Each issue highlights successful recreational boating safety programs, NASBLA activities, professional news, and legislative updates *$14.00*

Bi-Monthly Founded: 1998
Circulation: 11000
Mailing list available for rent 56 names

2907 Southern Boating Magazine
330 N Andrews Avenue
Ft Lauderdale, FL 33301
954-522-5515
FAX: 954-522-2260
sboating@southernboating.com
www.southernboating.com

Skip Allen, Jr, Publisher/Editor
Bill Lindsey, Executive Editor
Kenneth Masi, Associate Editor
Risa Merl, Associate Editor
Betsy Dietze, Circulation Manager

Focus is on boating in the southern US, Bahamas, and Caribbean. *$22.95*

Monthly Founded: 1972
Circulation: 42000
Printed in 4 colors on matte stock

2908 US Yacht Racing Union
US Sailing
15 Maritime Drive
PO Box 1260
Portsmouth, RI 02871-0907

FAX: 401-683-0840 800-877-2451
info@ussailing.org www.ussailing.org

Janet Baxter, President
Charlie Leighton, Executive Director
Bobbi Warren, Director Finance
Dan Cooney, Director Marketing

National news of the Union, the latest in yacht racing, and dealers of yachts are covered.

2909 UnderWater Magazine
Doyle Publishing Company
607 Mason
Tomball, TX 77375
281-516-0350
FAX: 281-516-0391
editor@doylepublishing.com
www.underwater.com

William H Doyle III, Publisher
Daron Jones, Managing Editor
Ross Saxon, Executive Editor

It covers the entire spectrum of underwater contracting, vehicles and technology. *$50.00*

Founded: 1993

2910 WoodenBoat
WoodenBoat Publications
Naskeag Road
PO Box 78
Brooklin, ME 04616
207-359-4651
FAX: 207-359-8920 800-877-5284
woodenboat@woodenboat.com
www.woodenboat.com

Mathew P. Murphy, Editor
Carl Cramer, Publisher

Provides readers with a dynamic editorial environment that combines technologies with traditional methods of boat design, construction and repair. The magazine is about craftmanship in wood, and its active boating audience works at all levels of expertise to build, restore, and maintain their boats. *$29.95*

160 pages Bi-Monthly Founded: 1974
Circulation: 98000

2911 WorkBoat
Diversified Business Communications
121 Free Street
PO Box 7437
Portland, ME 04112-7437
207-425-5500
FAX: 207-842-5609
info@divcom.com www.workboat.com

Mike Lodato, Publisher
Ken Hocke, Senior Editor
David Krapf, Editor
Nancy Hasselback, President/CEO
Stephanie Wendel, Circulation Manager

Commercial marine publication serving the North American inland and coastal waterways — the most active sector in the commercial marine market today. Consisting of captains, owners, managers, operators, chief engineers and other industry professionals, the Workboat audience represents important and influential purchasing power in the commercial marine industry. *$39.00*

Monthly Founded: 1949
Circulation: 25000

2912 Yachting Magazine
Time4 Media Marine Group
18 Marshall Street
Suite 114
South Norwalk, CT 06854
203-299-5900
FAX: 203-299-5901 800-999-0869
service@yachting.customersvc.com
www.yachtingmagazine.com

Ed Baker, Associate Publisher
Rich Rasor, East Coast Sales Director

Covers the finest boats, electronics and equipment, including large yachts and yacht charters. It also covers the passions, adventures and lifestyles of active, affluent boat owners.

Monthly Founded: 1907

2913 Yioung Mariners Guide
Yachting Club of America
PO Box 1040
Marco Island, FL 34146
239-642-4448
FAX: 239-642-5284
ycaol@hotmail.com www.ycaol.com
Designed to inform and teach young people about boating in simple and handy pocket book to help them on their way to becoming the future of the yachting fraternity in America. *$5.00*

32 pages Softbound

Trade Shows

2914 Annual American and Canadian Sport, Travel and Outdoor Show
Expositions
Edgewater Branch
PO Box 550
Cleveland, OH 44107-0550
216-529-1300
FAX: 216-529-0311
expoinc@expoinc.com
www.expoinc.com
975 exhibits of hunting and fishing equipment, travel services, boats, recreational vehicles and related equipment, supplies and services.

300k Attendees March Founded: 1935

2915 Annual Boat & Fishing Show at the Lansing Center
Show Span
2121 Celebration Drive NE
Grand Rapids, MI 49525
616-447-2860
FAX: 616-447-2861 800-328-6550
events@showspan.com
www.showspan.com

Adam Starr, Show Manager
Henri Boucher, President
Carolyn Alt, Show Manager

Held in Lansing, Michigan.

March

2916 Annual Boat Show
General Sports Shows
3539 Hennepin Avenue
PO Box 8358
Minneapolis, MN 55408-0358
612-827-5833
FAX: 612-827-1424 800-777-4766

Jennifer Thompson, Show Manager
Bonnie Schuenemann, Special Events Coordinator
Patty Gibbs, Media Contact

Enjoy 5 days of boating fun, education and one-stop shopping with hundreds of boats and exhibits and special attractions all under one roof.

January

2917 Annual Boat Show & Fishing Exposition
Greenband Enterprises
3450 South Highland Drive
Suite 105
Salt Lake City, UT 84106
801-485-7399
FAX: 801-485-0687 800-657-3050
showinfo@greenband.com
www.greenband.com

Jonathan D Greenband, Show Manager
Debra Greenband, Sales Manager

See the latest in Ski Boats, Cruisers, Fishing Boats, everything for boating fun.

45000 Attendees Annual, February
Founded: 1965

2918 Annual Boat, Vacation and Outdoor Show
Showtime Productions
PO Box 4372
Rockford, IL 61110
815-877-8043
FAX: 815-877-9037
brenda@showtimeproduction.net
showtimeproduction.net

Tom Pellant, President
Brenda Rotoco, Event Coordinator

Boat, travel, outdoor equipment, supplies, and services plus demonstrations.

28000 Attendees February Founded: 1970

2919 Annual Conference & Educational Training S ymposia
Society of Accredited Marine Surveyors
4605 Cardinal Boulevard
Jacksonville, FL 32210
904-384-1494
FAX: 904-388-3958 800-344-9077
samshq@aol.com
www.marinesurvey.org

Bob Callahan, Show Director
Heather Palmeter, Show Coordinator
Charles V Corder, Jr, VP Meetings/Conventions

September

2920 **Annual Conference on Sail Training and Tal l Ships**
American Sail Training Association
240 Thames Street
PO Box 1459
Newport, RI 02840
401-846-1775
FAX: 401-849-5400
asta@sailtraining.org
www.tallships.sailtraining.org
Peter A Mello, Executive Director
Adria Lande, Education Coordinator
Robert Hofmann, Development Director
Jonathan Harley, Race Director
Lori A Aguiar, Program Manager
November

2921 **Annual Iowa Boat and Vacation Show**
Iowa Show Productions
PO Box 2460
Waterloo, IA 50704-2460
319-232-0218
FAX: 319-235-8932
info@iowashows.com
www.iowashows.com
John Bunge, Show Manager
Over 25 dealers, 40 brands, 100's of models. Family runabouts, fishing boats, cabin cruisers, cuddies, power boats, waterski boats, personal watercraft, jet boats, bass boats, walleye boats, deck boats, pontoons, fish/ski boats, and marine accessories.
January Founded: 1975

2922 **Annual Lido Yacht Expo**
Duncan McIntosh Company
17782 Cowan, Ste A
Irvine, CA 92614
949-757-5959
FAX: 949-660-6172
boatshow@goboating.com
www.lidoyachtexpo.com
An upscale in-the-water show of yachts and big boats. More than 2,000 feet of floating dock.
May

2923 **Annual National Capital Boat Show**
Royal Productions
PO Box 4197
Chester, VA 23831
804-256-6556
FAX: 804-288-7132
info@royalshows.com
www.royalshows.com
David Posner, President
Nearly 40 dealers form throughout Maryland and Virginia bring a wide range of boats to the National Capital Boat Show including saltware fishing boats, ski boats, runabouts, motor yachts, jet boats, jon boats, PWC, bass boats, inflatables, deck boats and pontoons.
20000 Attendees March

2924 **Annual Spring Boat Show**
Southern California Marine Association
1006 East Chapman
Orange, CA 92866
714-633-7581
FAX: 714-633-9498
scma@scma.com www.scma.com
Terry Tjaden, Show Manager
Ryan Rawlings, Show Coordinator
David Geoffroy, Executive Director
You'll find a assortment of marine accessory booths featuring the latest and newest products filled with everything that floats, affordable family runabounts, ski boats, fishing boats, cruisers, pontoons, performance sportboats and personal watercraft.
June

2925 **Annual Spring New Products Show**
Pacific Expositions
1580 Makaloa Street
Suite 1200
Honolulu, HI 96814-3801
808-945-3594
FAX: 808-946-6399
www.pacificexpos.com
Tara Chanel-Thompson, Director/General Manager
The newest and most exciting products on land and sea with 320 exhibits for trade professionals, buyers, and the general public.
17000 Attendees Annual, April Founded: 1974

2926 **Association of Marina Industries Annual Co nference**
Association of Marina Industries
444 North Capitol Street NW
Suite 645
Washington, DC 20001
202-379-9768
FAX: 202-628-8679
info@imimarina.org
www.imimarina.org
James L Frye, President/CEO
Cris McSparen, Treasurer
Maureen Healey, Executive Director
Brooke Fishel, Manager Communications
May

2927 **Atlanta Boat Show**
National Marine Manufacturers Association
200 E Randolph Drive
Suite 1500
Chicago, IL 60601
954-441-3228
www.atlantaboatshow.com
Melissa Malone, Show Manager
Debbie Harewood, Operations Manager
Showcases the latest in boating products and marine technology. 225 exhibitors.
January

2928 **Atlantic City In-Water Power Boat Show**
In-Water Power Boat Show
1500 Walnut Street
Suite 1202
Philadelphia, PA 19102
215-732-8001
FAX: 215-732-8266
jerryflax@aol.com
www.acinwaterboatshow.com
Jerry Flaxman, Executive Vice President
This show provides space for over 700 boats on land and in-water and over 200 booths in the marine marketplace, including 2 tents and walkways along the piers. Showcases the new models for each coming year.
September

2929 **Atlantic City International Power Boat Show**
National Marine Manufacturers Association
200 Randolph Drive
Suite 1500
Chicago, IL 60601
212-984-7016
www.acboatshow.com
Michael Duffy, Show Manager
Jon Pritko, Operations Manager
Showcases more than 700 all-new models of motor and express yachts, sports fisherman, cruisers and sport boats. Attracts boaters from all of the East Coast.
50000 Attendees February

2930 **Boat Show of Grand Rapids**
Show Span
2121 Celebration Drive NE
Grand Rapids, MI 49525
616-472-2860
FAX: 616-447-2861 800-328-6550
events@showspan.com
www.showspan.com
Adam Star, Show Manager
Mike Wilbraham, VP
Over 400 exhibits of power and sail boats, accessories, clocks, dockominiums and vacation destinations. Held at the Grand Center in Grand Rapids, Michigan.
February Founded: 1945

2931 **Boat Show of New England**
North America Expositions Company
33 Rutherford Avenue
Boston, MA 02129-3795
617-242-6092
FAX: 617-242-1817 800-225-1577
Joseph B O'Neal, Managing Partner
Over 600 boats on display, both power and sailboats ranging from dinghies to 45 foot yachts, along with every conceivable accessory for your new or present boat.
215M Attendees February

2932 **Brokerage Yacht Show**
Yachting Promotions
1115 NE 9th Avenue
Fort Lauderdale, FL 33304-2110
954-764-7642
FAX: 954-462-4140 800-940-7642
info@showmanagement.com
wwww.showmanagement.com
Steve Sheer, Director Advertising
Kaye Pearson, President
The totally in-water presentation features over 500 new and pre-owned vessels.
February

2933 **Education Under Sail Forum**
American Sail Training Association
240 Thames Street
PO Box 1459
Newport, RI 02840
401-846-1775
FAX: 401-849-5400
asta@sailtraining.org
www.tallships.sailtraining.org
Peter A Mello, Executive Director
Adria Lande, Education Coordinator
Robert Hofmann, Development Director
Jonathan Harley, Race Director
Lori A Aguiar, Program Manager
Biennial

2934 **IBEX Annual Conference**
National Marine Manufacturers Association
200 East Randolph Street
Suite 5100
Chicago, IL 60601-4255
312-946-6200
FAX: 312-946-0401 www.nmma.org
William Barrington, Chairman
Robert Selig, Vice Chairman
Thomas Dammrich, President
Ben Wold, Executive Vice President
Craig Boskey, VP Finance/CFO

Exhibition features the products and processes now available that will streamline your boatbuilding business. See the advanced technologies ready for the upcoming model-year. Featuring 800 OEMs and suppliers, the exhibit halls offer you an opportunity to source and compare every tool available to boatbuilders.
November

2935 Industrial Fabircs Association Internation al Expo
1801 Country Road B W
Roseville, MN 55413
651-222-2508
FAX: 651-631-9334 800-225-4324
generalinfo@ifai.com www. ifai.com
Bob Smith, Exhibit Sales Manager
Chris Kohn, Exhibit Sales
George K Ochs, Chairman
Jeffrey W Kirk, President
October

2936 International Boating and Water Safety Sum mit
National Safe Boating Council
PO Box 509
Bristow, VA 20136
703-361-4294
FAX: 703-361-5294
www.safeboatingcouncil.org
Ed Carter, Chairman
Ruth Wood, Vice Chairman
Virgil Chambers, Executive Director
Sandy Smith, Chief Financial Officer
Veronica Floyd, Treasurer
April

2937 International Marina & Boatyard Conference
American Boat Builders and Repairers Association
50 Warren Street
Warren, RI 02885
401-247-0318
FAX: 401-247-0074 www.abbra.org
Jonathan Jones Haven, President
Peter Sabo, VP
Mark Amaral, Managing Director
Charles Teran, Treasurer/Secretary
The conference is designed to meet the growing demand among those delivering the boating experience for an international forum for education and exposition.
Annual

2938 International WorkBoat Show
121 Fine Street
PO Box 7437
Portland, ME 04101-7437
207-842-5500
FAX: 207-842-5503
Liz Plizga, Show Director
Mike Lodato, VP Commerical Marine Products
Vicki Hennin, VP Marketing/Communications
Chris Dimmerling, Manager Sales
A marine trade show and conference serving the offshore, coastal, inland and shore side markets. It features 1000 exhibiting companies and is produced in partnership with WorkBoat magazine.
November Founded: 1978

2939 La Crosse Boat, Sports and Travel Show
Shamrock Productions
14550 Granada Drive
Apple Valley, MN 55124
952-431-9630
FAX: 952-431-9633
info@shamrockprod.com
www.shamrockprod.com
Randy Schauer, President/CEO
Boats, sports and travel equipment, supplies and services.
February

2940 MEGATEX
Industrial Fabrics Association International

1801 County Road B W
Roseville, MN 55413
651-222-2508
FAX: 651-631-9334 800-225-4324
generalinfo@ifai.com www.ifai.com
Bob Smith, Exhibit Sales Manager
Chris Kohn, Exhibit Sales
George K Ochs, Chairman
Jeffrey W Kirk, President
Will be held at the Georgia World Congress Center in Atlanta, Georgia, and is anchored by the IFAI Expo and the ATMW-I shows. Together, the shows are expected to have more than 1,000 exhibitors.
20000 Attendees

2941 Marine Retailers Association of America An nual Convention
Marine Regtailers Association of America
PO Box 1127
Oak Park, IL 60304
708-763-9210
FAX: 708-763-9236
mraa@mraa.com www.mraa.com
Glenn Mazzella, Chairman
Phil Keeter, President/CEO
Larry Innis, Director Government Affairs
Marge Eckenroad, Director Convention/Meetings
November

2942 Mid-America Sail & Power Boat Show
Lake Erie Marine Trade Association
1269 Bassett Road
Cleveland, OH 44145-1116
440-899-5009
FAX: 440-899-5013
lemta@aol.com
www.clevelandboatshow.com
Norm Schultz, President Emeritus
Annual show of 325 manufacturers and suppliers of pleasure boats and related marine equipment, supplies and services.
140M Attendees January

2943 Midwest Boat Show
Lake Erie Marine Trade Association
1269 Bassett Road
Cleveland, OH 44145-1116
440-899-5009
FAX: 440-899-5013
Norm Schultz, President
Annual show and exhibits of boats, equipment, supplies and services.
23M Attendees August Founded: 1980

2944 NMBA Annual Conference
National Marine Bankers Association
200 East Randolph Street
Suite 5100
Chicago, IL 60601
312-812-2777
FAX: 312-946-0388
bmcardle@nmma.org
www.marinebankers.org
Michael Bryant, Director
Donald Parkhurst, President
Jim Meere, VP
Jim Coburn, Treasurer
Bernice McArdle, Association Manager
NMBA hosts a three day member conference where the latest trends relating to marine industry are discussed in detail.
180 Attendees September

2945 National Association of State Boating Law Administrators Annual Conference
National Association of State Boating Law

1500 Leestown Road
Suite 330
Lexington, KY 40511
859-225-9487
FAX: 859-231-6403
george@nasbla.org www.nasbla.org/
Charles A Sledd, President
Jeff Johnson, VP
John Johnson, Chief Executive Officer
Ron Sarver, Deputy Director
Libby Osborne, Chief Financial Officer
Conference provides information that focuses on boating education, industry trends, workshops, and programs that discuss the history of recreational boating safety programs including an overview of state-by-state regulatory laws.
September

2946 National Capital Boat Show
Royal Productions
PO Box 4197
Chester, VA 23831-8475
804-425-6556
FAX: 804-425-6563
www.royalshows.com
Serving the Washington DC and suburban Virginia/Maryland markets. 40 dealers.
March

2947 National Dry Stack Conference
Association of Marina Industries
444 North Capitol Street NW
Suite 645
Washington, DC 20001
202-379-9768
FAX: 202-628-8679
info@imimarina.org
www.imimarina.org
Gregg Kenney, Chairman
Alex Laidlaw, Vice Chairman
Maureen Healey, Executive Director
Cris McSparen, Treasurer
Brooke Fishel, Manager Communications
The Dry Stack is a three-day hybrid school which combines an educational program along with networking among leading operations, developers and vendors.
October

2948 North American Sail & Power Show
Lake Erie Marine Trade Association
1269 Bassett Road
Cleveland, OH 44145-1116
440-899-5009
FAX: 440-899-5013 lemta@aol.com
Norm Schultz, President

Annual show and exhibits of marine equipment, supplies and services.
31M Attendees September

2949 Pacific Marine Expo
Society of Accredited Marine Surveyors
4605 Cardinal Boulevard
Jacksonville, FL 32210
904-384-1494
FAX: 904-388-3958 800-344-9077
samshq@aol.com
www.marinesurvey.org
Bob Callahan, Show Director
Heather Palmeter, Show Coordinator
Charles V Corder, Jr, VP Meetings/Conventions
Presenters spoke on a wide range of topics for the commercial marine professional.

2950 Portland Boat Show
O'Loughlin Trade Shows
3600 SW Multnomah Boulevard
PO Box 80750
Portland, OR 97219-1750
503-246-8291
FAX: 503-246-1066
otssport@earthlink.net
www.oloughlintradeshows.com
Peter O'Loughlin, Show Manager
Robert O'Loughlin Sr, President
Offers hundreds of makes and models, accessories and plenty of expert advice through seminars and hands on demonstrations.
January

2951 Professional Boatbuilder: International Boatbuilders Expo and Conference
WoodenBoat Publications
86 Great Cove Drive
PO Box 78
Brooklin, ME 04616
207-359-4651
FAX: 207-359-8920
info@bibexshow.com
www.ibexshow.com
Carl Cramer, Show Co-Director
Kathleen Clickett, Show Co-Director
Jim Miller, President
Anne Dunbar, Director Marketing/Sales
Stephen Evans, Director Operations
Over 450 booths offering products for boat builders, designers, repairers, surveyors, and boatyard/marina operators.
2.5M Attendees November

2952 SCA Spring Safety Seminar
Shipbuilders Council of America
1455 F Street NW
Suite 225
Washington, DC 20005
202-383-3307
FAX: 202-347-5464
awalker@vesselalliance.com
www.shipbuilders.org
Donald T Bollinger, Chairman
Steve Welch, Vice Chairman
Allen Walker, President
Irene Ringwood, Manager
March

2953 Seattle Boat Show
Northwest Marine Trade Association
1900 North Northlake Way
Suite 233
Seattle, WA 98103-9087
206-634-0911
FAX: 206-632-0078
info@seattleboatshow.com
www.seattleboatshow.com
George Harris, Boat/Show Coordinator/VP
John Thorburn, Media Contact
Boat show and exposition. Containing 450 exhibits.
70M Attendees January

2954 Society of Accredited Marine Surveyors Int ernational WorkBoat Show
Society of Accredited Marine Surveyors
4605 Cardinal Boulevard
Jacksonville, FL 32210
904-384-1494
FAX: 904-388-3958 800-344-9077
samshq@aol.com
www.marinesurvey.org
Bob Callahan, Show Director
Heather Palmeter, Show Coordinator
Charles V Corder, Jr, VP Meetings/Conventions
Mary Stahler, Executive Director
Reconnect with suppliers and distributors, and renew these important relationships; check in with friend, clients and competitors and share in their experiences; and get a pulse on the market on the show floor and at the industry session.
November

2955 St. Petersburg Boat Show
Show Management
1115 NE 9th Avenue
Fort Lauderdale, FL 33304
954-764-7642
FAX: 954-462-4140 800-940-7642
info@showmanagement.com
www.showmanagement.com
Kaye Pearson, Owner/Promoter
Elise Lipoff, Director Public Relations
Steve Sheer, Director Advertising
More than 600 boats of all types and sizes, electronics, engines and a vast selection of marine accessories will be displayed on land and in water.
10000 Attendees December Founded: 1977

2956 Suncoast Boat Show
Show Management
1115 NE 9th Avenue
Fort Lauderdale, FL 33304
954-764-7642
FAX: 954-462-4140 800-940-7642
info@showmanagement.com
www.showmanagement.com
Kaye Pearson, Owner/Promoter
Elise Lipoff, Director Public Relations
Steve Sheer, Director Advertising
Chuck Bolt, Director Sales
Annual show and exhibits of boats and marine equipment, supplies and services.
30000 Attendees April Founded: 1982

2957 US Sailboat Show
Annapolis Boatshows
100 Severn Drive
PO Box 4997
Annapolis, MD 21401-4997
410-268-8828
FAX: 410-280-3903
Dee Newman, Show Manager
Jim Barthold, General Manager
In-water sailboat show offering over 350 booths.
150M Attendees October

2958 Yacht Brokers Association of America Annua l Conference
Yacht Brokers Association of America
105 Eastern Avenue
Suite 104
Annapolis, MD 21403-3300
410-263-1014
FAX: 410-263-1659
info@ybaa.com www.ybaa.com
Joe Thompson, Executive Director
Kristin Thompson, Dir Communications/Conference
Robb Fish, Program Development Manager
Provides members with a unique opportunity to network with industry peers and participate in important educational sessions, roundtable discussions and presentations covering a variety of business and industry topics.

Directories & Databases

2959 American Boat and Yacht Council
3069 Solomons Island Road
Edgewater, MD 21037
410-956-1050
FAX: 410-956-2737
info@abycinc.org www.abycinc.org
Skip Burdon, President/CEO
Marine suppliers, engineers and underwriters, as well as architects and designers for the marine industry are listed.
105 pages Biennial Founded: 1954

2960 Boater's Source Directory
Boat US Foundation
880 South Pickett Street
Alexandria, VA 22304-4606
703-612-2850
FAX: 703-461-2855 800-336-2628
Richard Schwartz, President
Pocket guide for boaters containing safety and regulatory information and resources.
$5.00
Paperback, SemiAnnual

2961 Boating Industry: Marine Buyers' Guide Issue
Ehlert Publishing Group
6420 Sycamore Lane
Suite 100
Maple Grove, MN 55369
763-383-4400
FAX: 763-383-4499 800-848-6247
dvoll@ehlertpublishing.com
www.boating-industry.com
Matt Gruhn, Editor-in-Chief
Liz Walz, Senior Editor
Jon Mohrm, Associate Editor
Tammy Galvin, Group Publisher
Steven Hedlund, President
A who's who directory of services and supplies to the industry. *$29.95*
Annual
Circulation: 30,000

2962 Confined Space Entry Video and Manual
Shipbuilders Council of America
1455 F Street NW
Suite 225
Washington, DC 20005
202-383-3307
FAX: 202-347-5464
awalker@vesselalliance.com
www.shipbuilders.org

Donald T Bollinger, Chairman
Steve Welch, Vice Chairman
Allen Walker, President
Irene Ringwood, Manager

This manual, in combination with the video program, covers some of the more common hazards associated with confined space entry. It also provides you with the information you will need to prevent accidents and injuries. *$50.00*

2963 Consumer Protection Database
Boat Owners Association of the US
800 South Pickett Street
Alexandria, VA 22304
703-412-2770
FAX: 703-461-2847 www.boatus.com

Richard Schwartz, Chairman/Founder
Jim Ellis, President/CEO

Contains consumer complaints and safety information reported by boat owners, the US Coast Guard, manufacturers, marine surveyors and marine technicians.

2964 Crane Safety Video and Workbook
Shipbuilders Council of America
1455 F Street NW
Suite 225
Washington, DC 20005
202-383-3307
FAX: 202-347-5464
awalker@vesselalliance.com
www.shipbuilders.org

Donald T Bollinger, Chairman
Steve Welch, Vice Chairman
Allen Walker, President
Irene Ringwood, Manager

Designed to educate supervisors and trainers on how to identify and correct crane safety-training deficiencies and provides instruction on effective monitoring of day-to-day operations *$75.00*
38 Minute

2965 ISSPA Sports and Vacation Show Directory and Calendar
International Sport Show Producers Association
PO Box 480084
Denver, CO 80248-0084
303-892-6800
FAX: 303-892-6322 800-457-2434
dseymour@iei-expos.com
www.sportshow.org

Dianne Seymour, Executive Secretary

Products of outdoor recreation shows which include boating, travel, RV, hunting, and fishing.
Annual

2966 Marina Operations Manual
Association of Marina Industries
444 North Capitol Street NW
Suite 645
Washington, DC 20001
202-379-9768
FAX: 202-628-8679
info@imimarina.org
www.imimarina.org

Gregg Kenney, Chairman
Alex Laidlaw, Vice Chairman
Maureen Healey, Executive Director
Cris McSparen, Treasurer
Brooke Fishel, Manager Communications

A standard operational guideline useful for all marina operations, private, public, large & small. An important risk management tool to help marina owners and operators more effectively operate and profit in the marina business. Available to Marinas only. *$500.00*

2967 Marine Industry Supplier Information Manua l
National Marine Representative Association
PO Box 360
Gurnee, IL 60031
847-662-3167
FAX: 847-336-7126
info@nmraonline.org
www.nmraonline.org

Jim Hannan, President
Jay Sanders, VP
Norm MacLeod, Treasurer
Tim Luehmann, Secretary

Informational book authored by NMRA reps outlines effective methods for setting up a sales force in the marine industry. Includes guidance on territories, contracts, commissions, and trade shows as it relates to a rep force. *$55.00*
Annual

2968 Marine Products Directory
Underwriters Laboratories
12 Laboratory Drive
PO Box 13995
Research Triangle Park, NC 27709-3995
919-549-1400
FAX: 919-547-6363
paul.r.ouellette@us.ul.com
www.ul.com/marine

UL has been testing and certifying products for marine use since 1969. With a UL Marine Mark on your product, you can show consumers, retailers, surveyors, insurers, government agencies, regulatory and ABTC, NFPA and UL Safety Standards. *$10.00*
176 pages Annual

2969 Membership Directory: Boating Industry Administration
National Association of State Boating Law

1500 Leestown Road
Suite 300
Lexington, KY 40511
859-225-9487
FAX: 859-231-6403
info@nasbla.org www.nasbla.org

John Johnson, Chief Executive Officer

Published by the National Association of State Boating Law Administration.

Mailing list available for rent 56 names

2970 NMRA Membership Directory
National Marine Representative Association
PO Box 360
Gurnee, IL 60031
847-662-3167
FAX: 847-336-7126
info@nmraonline.org
www.nmraonline.org

Jim Hannan, President
Jay Sanders, VP
Norm MacLeod, Treasurer
Tim Luehmann, Secretary

Provides a complete listing of all NMRA sales representatives. Includes contact information for their main and associate offices, the territories they cover, the markets they represent, and the list of companies they represent. *$10.00*

2971 National Marine Manufacturers Association Membership List
200 East Randolf
Suite 5100
Chicago, IL 60601-4255
312-946-6200
FAX: 312-946-0401 www.nmma.org

Thomas Dammrich, President

Directory of services and supplies to the industry.
160 pages Quadrennial

2972 Pacific Boating Almanac
ProStar Publications
8643 Hayden Place
Culver City, CA 90232
310-280-1010
FAX: 310-280-1025 800-481-6277

Peter Griffes, Editor

Consists of three regional volumes. This information includes the latest Coast Pilot, Tide & Current Tables, First Aid, Electronics, Navigation and Safety, Weather, and Yacht Club Burgees. *$26.95*
Annual ISBN 1-577857-05-4
Circulation: 20,000
Mailing list available for rent 19,000 names
Printed in on matte stock

2973 Portbook of Marine Services
Portbook Publications
PO Box 462
Belfast, ME 04915
207-338-1619
FAX: 207-338-6025
info@portbook.net www.portbook.net

Sandra Squire, Publisher

Marinas, yacht clubs, boatyards, dealers, marine supply stores, repair facilities, and other services for yachtsmen. For Annapolis, Maryland and Newport/Narragansett Bay, Rhode Island. Distributed free through advertisers, or four dollars by mail. *$40.00*
100 pages Annual Founded: 1982
Circulation: 35M
Printed in on matte stock

2974 Register of American Yacht Clubs
Yachting Club of America
1400 North Collier Boulevard
PO Box 1040
Marco Island, FL 34146-1040
239-642-4448
FAX: 239-642-5284 www.ycaol.com

A reciprocity guide for yacht and sailing clubs in the United States, Hawaii, Alaska, and the Virgin Islands registered with the Yachting Club of America. 800 yacht clubs registered with the Yachting Club of America. *$35.00*
200 pages Softbound Founded: 1963
Printed in on glossy stock

2975 Sail Tall Ships: Directory of Sail Training and Adventure at Sea
American Sail Training Association
240 Thames Street
PO Box 1459
Newport, RI 02840
401-846-1775
FAX: 401-849-5400
asta@sailtraining.org
www.tallships.sailtraining.org

Lori Aguiar, Editor
Peter A Mello, Executive Director

Offers information on sail training ships, shoreside sail training programs and ships under construction or restoration. *$50.00*

400 pages Annual Founded: 1980 ISBN 0-963648-36-5
Circulation: 15,000

2976 Seafarers
Admiralty Insurance
6353 Argyle Forest Boulevard
Jacksonville, FL 32244
904-777-0042
FAX: 904-777-0279 800-456-8936
Searchable database of boating associations, yacht clubs, boating clubs and source of nautical information and links.

2977 Ship Agents, Owners, Operators
Maritime Association of the Port of New York
17 Battery Place
Suite 913
New York, NY 10004
212-425-5704
FAX: 212-635-9498
themaritimeassoc@erols.com
www.nymaritime.org
Edward Morgan, President
Brian McAllister, VP
Edward J Kelly, Executive Director
Directory of Atlantic, Gulf and West Coasts listing every steamship, owner, and operator in the major ports with lines that they represent and the countries that they serve. *$50.00*
Annual
Circulation: 2,000

2978 Shipyard Ergonomics Video and Workbook CD
Shipbuilders Council of America
1455 F Street NW
Suite 225
Washington, DC 20005
202-383-3307
FAX: 202-347-5464
awalker@vesselalliance.com
www.shipbuilders.org
Donald T Bollinger, Chairman
Steve Welch, Vice Chairman
Allen Walker, President
Irene Ringwood, Manager
Designed to instruct shipyard employees, supervisors and trainers in identifying ergonomic risks and providing tools to allow the development of creative solutions to reduce the hazards. *$75.00*

Industry Web Sites

2979 www.acbs.org
Antique & Classic Boat Society

Since its founding on the shores of Lake George, New York, The Antique and Classic Boat Society - ACBS - has grown into the largest society in the world dedicated to the preservation and enjoyment of historic, antique and classic boats. ACBS brings people with this common interest together to share fellowship, information, experiences and ideas.

2980 www.apba-racing.com
American Power Boat Association

The appetite for speed on water has been a part of mankind since the early ages. The adrenaline pumping sport of powerboat racing can be traced back at least 100 years. The American Power Boat Association -APBA- founded in 1903, is the sole authority for UIM approved powerboat racing in the United States.

2981 www.by-the-sea.com
By the Sea

Everything for the boat professional and enthusiast alike. News of sales and events, message boards and contact information.

2982 www.greyhouse.com
Grey House Publishing

Selected Grey House directories in the fields of business, health and education are available online. Users can search our online databases by several different search criteria, such as product categories, geographic area, sales volume and much, much more. Full Grey House catalog and online ordering also available.

2983 www.imimarina.org
International Marina Institute

International Marina Institute's educational resources include specialized training courses and seminars on fundamental and advanced levels, workshops, conferences the advanced marina management school and the Certified Marina Manager program along with a wide selection of publications.

2984 www.lemta.com
Lake Erie Marine Trade Association

Trade association of more than 100 recreational boat daelers, marina operators and pleasure boat service companies located across northern Ohio. It isn't often that a trade organization, most often formed to protect the interests of its members, also plays the key role in looking out for the consumer, but that's what makes LEMTA a unique association. LEMTA's varied programs provide benifits to everyone concerned with or enjoying recreational boating in Ohio.

2985 www.marinebankers.org
National Marine Bankers Association

Formed in 1980 in response to a request by the National Marine Manufacturers Association - NMMA for additional sources of financing for its members products. The purpose of the NMBA is to educate prospective lenders in marine financing procedures, create new lenders to help finance the sales of the manufacturers products, and to create an information exchange for its members.

2986 www.mraa.com
Marine Retailers Association of America

Manufacturers and dealers of boats, equipment, supplies and services.

2987 www.nauticalworld.com

Dedicated to bringing all related web sites within easy access to watersports enthusiasts. This search engine has been designed to locate advertiser's information within Nautical World but will also offer access to other watersport related web sites as well. Offers sections on marine electronics and hardware, sailing, boats, dock supplies, fishing accessories, diving accessories, industry news, watersports, weather forecasting and more.

2988 www.nauticexpo.com
NauticExpo

This Virtual Boat Show is accessible in five languages and presents all the boats and nautical equipment available on the international market. It offers an accurate and up-to-date source of information to yachtsmen and professionals.

2989 www.nmdaonline.com
National Marine Distributors Association

Engages in exclusively nonprofit activities designed to promote the common business interests and improve the business conditions of wholesale distributors of marine accessories and of the marine industry in general. We believe that the needs of the wholeasle distributor can best serve the needs of the marine industry by selling a minimum of 85% of its volume through independent marine outlets, that it is the misson of the distributor to supply, assist and promote the welfare of independents.

2990 www.nmraonline.org
National Marine Representatives Association

Members are independent boat and marine accessory sales representatives national association.

2991 www.nmta.net
Northwest Marine Trade Association

Oldest and largest regional boating trade organization in the nation representing the interests of approximately 800 member companies. Each year it produces the Seattle Boat Show at the Stadium Exhibition Center and the Seattle Boat Show at Shilshole Bay Marina on behalf of its members.

2992 www.propellerclubhq.com
Propeller Club of the United States

Grassroots, nonprofit organization, whose membership resides throughout the United States and the world. It is dedicated to the enhancement and well-being of all interests of the maritime community on a national and international basis.

2993 **www.pwia.org**
Personal Watercraft Industry Association

Ensuring that personal watercraft and personal watercraft users are treated fairly when local, state, and federal government officials consider boating regulations. PWIA supports and actively advocates for reasonable regulations, strong enforcement of boating and navigation laws, and mandatory boating safety education for all personal watercraft operators.

2994 **www.rbbi.com**
Polson Enterprises

Recreational boat building industry home page. Offering research tools and papers on new product development and new product development services. We have extensive experience in the fields of marine drives, boat building, engine, marine vessels, propeller guards, boating safety. Industry and regulation updates are also available on this site.

2995 **www.tsca.com**
Traditional Small Craft Association

Nonprofit, tax-exempt educational organization which works to preserve and continue the living traditions, skills, lore and legends surrounding working and pleasure watercraft. It encourages the design, construction and use of boats and it embraces contemporary variants and adaptions of traditional design.

2996 **www.ussailing.org**
United States Sailing Association

Encourages participation and promotes excellence in sailing and racing in the US.

Associations

2997 Academy of Television Arts and Science
5220 Lankershim Boulevard
North Hollywood, CA 91601
818-754-2800
FAX: 818-761-2827 www.emmys.com

Dick Askin, Chairman/CEO
John Shaffner, First Vice Chair
Karen Miller, Second Vice Chair
Dan Birman, Secretary
Todd Leavitt, President

Nonprofit corporation devoted to the advancement of telecommunications arts and sciences and to fostering creative leadership in the telecommunications industry. In addition to recognizing outstanding programming and individual achivements for Primetime and Los Angeles area programming, ATAS sponsors meetings, conferences and activities for collaboration on a variety of topics involving traditional broadcast interests, new media and emerging digital technology.
12000 Members Founded: 1957

2998 Alaska Broadcasters Association
700 W 41st Street
Anchorage, AK 99503
907-258-2424
www.akbroadcasters.org

Scott Smith, President
Ric Schmidt, VP
Dianna Rowedder, Secretary/Treasurer
Darlene Simono, Executive Director

To provide assistance, which enables members to serve their communities of license through education, representation and advocacy.

2999 Alliance for Community Media
666 11th Street NW
Suite 740
Washington, DC 20001-4542
202-393-2650
FAX: 202-393-2653
acm@alliancecm.org
www.alliancecm.org

Anthony Riddle, Executive Director

Participants include cable access television and community programmers. Individual membership dues are $70.00, organization $350.00.
1000 Members Founded: 1976 1000 names $200 per M.

3000 Alliance of Motion Picture and Television Producers
15503 Ventura Boulevard
Encino, CA 91436
818-995-3600
FAX: 818-382-1793 www.amptp.org

Nick Counter, President

Trade association with respect to labor issues in the motion picture and television industry. We negotiate 80 industry wide collective bargaining agreements that cover actors, craftspersons, directors, musicians, technicians and writers — virtually all of the people who work on theatrical motion pictures and television programs. In these negotiations, the AMPTP represents over 350 production companies and studios.
350 Members Founded: 1982

3001 American Auto Racing Writers and Broadcasters Association
922 N Pass Avenue
Burbank, CA 91505-2703
818-842-7005
FAX: 818-842-7020
aarwba@compuserve.com
www.aarwba.org

Norma Dusty Brandel, President
Bob Jenkins, VP
George Peters, Secretary Treasurer
Ron Lemasters, VP
Mike Harris, Southern VP

Members are professional journalists who regularly cover auto racing and related sports events.
400 Members Founded: 1955

3002 American Disc Jockey Association
20118 N 67th Avenue
Suite 300-605
Glendale, CA 85308

888-723-5776
office@adja.org www.adja.org

Peter Merry, President

A national, non-profit association for professional mobile and night club entertainers.

3003 American Federation of Television and Radio Artists
260 Madison Avenue
New York, NY 10016-2402
212-532-0800
FAX: 212-532-2242
info@aftra.com www.aftra.com

John Connolly, President
Bob Edwards, First VP
Roberta Reardon, Second VP

Represents its members in four major areas: news and broadcasting; entertainment programing; the recording business; and commercials and non-broadcast, industrial, educational media.
80000 Members Founded: 1952

3004 American Geophysical Union
2000 Florida Avenue NW
Washington, DC 20009-1231
202-462-6900
FAX: 202-328-0566 www.agu.org

John Orcutt, President
Fred Spilhaus Jr, Executive Director
Terry E Tullis, General Secretary
41000 Members Founded: 1919

3005 American Private Radio Association (APRA)
PO Box 4221
Scottsdale, AZ 85261-4221
480-661-5000

Association members are from private radio stations.

3006 American Speaker Association
33365 N Arlington Heights Road
Arlington Heights, IL 60004
847-679-3799

Assists in proceedings involving legislation and arbitration.
37 Members Founded: 1966

3007 American Sportscasters Association
225 Broadway
Suite 2030
New York, NY 10007
212-227-8080
FAX: 212-571-0556
lschwa8918@aol.com
www.americansportscasters.com

Louis O Schwartz, President/Founder
Curt Gowdy, VP

National Association of Sportscasters, radio, television and cable covering the US, Puerto Rico and Canada. Very active web site. Offers seminars, compiles statistics and operates a placement service, maintains a Hall of Fame and biographical archives and library.
500 Members Founded: 1980 3000 names

3008 American Women in Radio and Television
8405 Greensboro Drive
Suite 800
McLean, VA 22102
703-506-3290
FAX: 703-506-3266
info@awrt.org www.awrt.org

Melodie A Virtue, President
Chickie Bucco, VP
Andrea B Cummis, Treasurer
Maria Brennan, Executive Director
Mary Bennett, Director
Founded: 1951

3009 Associated Press Broadcasters
1825 K Street NW
Suite 800
Washington, DC 20006-1202
202-968-8150
FAX: 202-736-1107
www.apbroadcast.com

James R Williams III, VP Broadcast Services
Greg Groce, Director Business Operations and De
Brad Kalbfeld, Deputy Director\Managing Editor
Roger Lockhart, Director Marketing/Communications
George Galt, Director Business Affairs

Seeks to advance journalism through radio and television, and cooperates with the AP to promote accurate and impartial news.
5.9m Members Founded: 1941

3010 Association for Maximum Service Television
4100 Wisconsin Avenue NW
PO Box 9897
Washington, DC 20036-2224
202-966-1956
FAX: 202-966-9617
mstv@mstv.org www.mstv.org

David Donovan, President

Assures the maintenance of an effective nationwide system of free television and seeks to meet present and future needs of the VHF and UHF system.
400+ Members Founded: 1956

3011 Association of Independent Commercial Producers
3 West 18th Street, 5th Floor
New York, NY 10010-5337
212-929-3000
FAX: 212-929-3359
info@aicp.com www.aicp.com

Matt Miller, President/CEO
Renee Paley, VP Communications

The national trade association of television commercial producers who account for in excess of 80% of the commercial production done in the United States annually.
500 Members Founded: 1972

3012 Association of Local Television Stations
1320 19th Street NW
Washington, DC 20036
202-887-1970
www.altv.com

3013 Association of Public Television Stations
666 Eleventh Street NW
Washington, DC 20001
202-654-4200
FAX: 202-654-4236 www.apts.org

John Lawson, President/CEO
Mark Erstling, Senior VP/COO
Marilyn Mohrman-Gillis, VP Policy/Legal Affairs
Lonna Thompson, VP/General Counsel
Jeffrey Davis, VP Communications

Nonprofit membership organization that supports the continued growth and development of a strong and financially sound noncommercial television service for the American public. Provides advocacy for public television interests at the national level, as well as consistent leadership and information in marshaling grassroots and congressional support for its members: the nation's public television stations.
165 Members Founded: 1980

3014 Broadcast Cable Financial Management Association
550 W Frontage Rd
Ste 3600
Northfield, IL 60093-1243
847-716-7000
FAX: 847-716-7004
info@bcfm.com www.bcfm.com

Mary M Collins, President/CEO
Jamie Smith, Director Operations
Mary Teister, Meetings Manager
Joe Barlek, Chairman
Tim Pecaro, Vice Chariman

Professional society of over 1,200 of television, radio and cable TV's top financial, MIS and HR executives, plus associates in auditing, data processing, software development, credit and collections.
1200 Members Founded: 1961
Mailing list available for rent 1100 names $495 per M.

3015 Broadcast Designers Association
2029 Century Park E
Suite 55
Los Angeles, CA 90067
310-712-0040
FAX: 212-376-6202

Jim Chabin, President

3016 Broadcast Designers' Association International
145 W 45th Street
Room 1100
New York, NY 10036-4008
212-376-6222
FAX: 212-376-6202
Association for manufacturers or suppliers of broadcast design equipment, supplies and services.

3017 Broadcast Education Association
1771 N Street NW
Washington, DC 20036-2812
202-429-5355
FAX: 202-429-4199 888-380-7222
beainfo@beaweb.org www.beaweb.org

Alan B Albarran, President
Louisa Nielsen, Executive Director
Gary Corbitt, VP Professional Relations
Steven D Anderson, VP Academic Relations

Serves as a higher education association of professors and industry professionals who teach college students worldwide and prepares them to go into the broadcasting and related emerging technologies professions upon graduation from college.
1400 Members Founded: 1955 1300 names $100 per M.

3018 Broadcast Pioneers
320 W 57th Street
New York, NY 10019-3705
212-862-2000

Del Bryant, President

Honors radio or television stations for excellence in art and community service. Maintains library documents on television broadcasting history.
1.4M Members Founded: 1942

3019 Cable & Telecommunications Association for Marketing
201 N Union Street
Suite 440
Alexandria, VA 22314-2642
703-549-4200
FAX: 703-684-1167
info@ctam.com www.ctam.com

Char Beales, President/CEO
Daniel Cassidy, SVP/Finance/Administration

Dedicated to the discipline and development of consumer marketing excellence in cable television, new media and telecommunications services. As a member, you have the advantage of progressive research, insightful publications and forward thinking conferences all designed to help you and your company gain a competitive edge.
5500 Members Founded: 1976

3020 Cable Television Association: New England
Ten Forbes Road
Suite 440W
Braintree, MA 02184
781-843-3418
FAX: 781-849-6267
info@necta.info www.necta.info

Mark Reilly, Chairman
Paul Cronin, Vice Chairman

NECTA is a six state regional trade association representing sbtstantially all private cable telecommunications companies in Connecticut, Maine, Massachusetts, New Hampshire, Rhode Island and Vermont.

3021 Coalition Opposing Signal Theft
1724 Massachusetts Avenue NW
Washington, DC 20036-1905
202-775-3550
FAX: 202-775-3696 www.ncta.com
Acts as a clearinghouse of information regarding cable signal theft.

3022 Community Antenna Television Association
PO Box 1005
Fairfax, VA 22030-1005
202-775-3550

An association of over 3,000 cable television systems serving over 30 million subscribers.
3M Members

3023 Corporation for Public Broadcasting
401 9th Street
Washington, DC 20004
202-879-9600
FAX: 202-879-9700 www.cpb.org

Kenneth Y Tomlinson, Chair
Frank H Cruz, Vice Chair
Robert Coonrod, Chief Executive Officer

Federally funded and supports the public television and the public radio industry.
Founded: 1967

3024 Country Radio Broadcasters
819 18th Avenue S
Nashville, TN 37203-3227
615-327-4487
FAX: 615-329-4492
info@crb.org www.crb.org

Ed Salamon, Executive Director
RJ Curtis, President
Bill Mayne, VP
Gary Krantz, Secretary
Jeff Walker, Treasurer

Broadcasting forum.

3025 Educational Broadcasting Association
450 W 33rd Street
New York, NY 10001
212-603-3063
FAX: 212-560-1315 www.thirteen.org

William F Bakerns, President/CEO
Stella Giammasi, VP Communication
Daisy Pommer, Manager

Association members are producers and directors of public educational programming, channel 13, PBS.
500 Members

3026 Geospatial Information and Technology Association
14456 E Evans Avenue
Aurora, CO 80014
303-337-0513
FAX: 303-337-1001
information@gita.org www.gita.org

Robert M Samborski, Executive Director
Wilma Kumar-Rubock, Secretary
Susan Ancel, Treasurer

Provides unbiased educational programs, forums and publications for professionals involved with geospatial information and technology.
2200 Members Founded: 1960

3027 Hollywood Radio and Television Society
13701 Riverside
Sherman Oaks, CA 91423
818-789-1182
FAX: 818-789-1210
genehrts@aol.com www.genehrts.com

Andy Friendly, President
Sue Neagle, VP
Dave Ferrara, Executive Director

Sponsors monthly luncheons featuring top industry and government speakers and sem-

inars about broadcasting, maintains film and audio library.
100 Members Founded: 1947

3028 **Intercollegiate Broadcasting Systems**
367 Windsor Highway
New Windsor, NY 12553-7900
845-565-0003
FAX: 845-565-7446
ibshq@aol.com www.ibsradio.org
Jeffrey N Tellis, VP Information Services

Nonprofit association of student staffed radio stations based at schools and colleges across the country. Some 800 member stations operate all sizes and types of facilities including Internet-Webcasting, closed circuit, AM carrier-current, cable radio and FCC-licensed FM and AM stations.
800 Members Founded: 1940

3029 **International Association of Broadcast Monitors**
PO Box 986
Irmo, SC 29063
803-749-9833
FAX: 888-732-9004 800-236-1741
iabm@iabm.com www.iabm.com
Lisa Smith, Executive Director
Kevin Repka, President
Ron Coucil, VP International
John Croll, Secretary
Holly Wine, Treasurer
Worldwide trade association made up of news retrieval services which monitor television, radio, internet and print news mediums. It acts as a clearinghouse or forum for discussion on topics of collective concerns and acts as a united voice for the news monitoring industry.
Founded: 1981

3030 **International Council-National Academy**
142 West 57th Street
New York, NY 10019-3300
212-489-6969
FAX: 212-489-6557
gl@iemmys.tv www.iemmys.tv
Georges Leclere, Executive Director
Camille Bidermann-Roizen, General Manager
Kim Czaplinski, Accounting/Membership
MJ Sorenson, Director Marketing
Furthers the arts and sciences by bestowing International Emmy Awards, George Movshon Fellowship and the Joan Wilson memorial scholarship.
250+ Members Founded: 1969

3031 **International Radio and Television Society Foundation**
420 Lexington Avenue
Suite 1601
New York, NY 10170
212-864-4877
FAX: 212-867-6653 www.irts.org
Timothy M McAuliff, Chairman
Louis Carr, First Vice Chairman
Cristina Schwarz, Vice Chairman
Henry Schleiff, Vice Chairman
Joyce M Tudryn, President
The lines between broadcast televison and radio, cable, telephony and the computer industry may be blurring, but one thing remains clear, we all have an affinity for a business that entertains, informs, educates and serves the American public in a meaningful way. The foundation provides a unique common forum for all segments of the communication industry. Members can enjoy sharing insight and ideas with colleagues during the season's numerous events.
750 Members Founded: 1939

3032 **International Television Academy**
888 Seventh Avenue
5th Floor
New York, NY 10019
212-489-6969
FAX: 212-489-6557
info@iemmys.tv www.iemmys.tv
Bruce Paisner, President
Fred Cohen, Chairman
Organization of global broadcasters, with representatives from over 50 countries based outside of the US, and represents the world's largest production, distribution and broadcast companies.
Founded: 1969

3033 **Jones/NCTI-National Cable Television Institute**
9697 E Mineral Ave
Centennial, CO 80112-3408
303-797-9393
FAX: 303-797-0829
info@ncti.com* www.ncti.com
Thomas W Brooksher, President/CEO
Michael Guilfoyle, Director Market Strategy
Jerry Neese, Director Sales
Ken Ziel, VP/CFO
Mark Johnson, VP Business Development
Workforce performance products, services and education.
30 Members Founded: 1968

3034 **Library of American Broadcasting**
University of Maryland
College Park, MD 20742-7011
301-405-9160
FAX: 301-314-2634
bp50@umail.umed.edu
www.lib.umd.edu
Holds a wide ranging collection of audio and video recordings, books, pamphlets, periodicals, personal collections, oral histories, photographs, scripts and vertical files devoted exclusively to the history of broadcasting.
Founded: 1972

3035 **Manufacturers Radio Frequency Advisory Committee**
899-A Harrison Drive SE
Leesburg, VA 20175
703-690-0320
FAX: 703-619-0322 800-262-9206
jpakla@mrfac.com www.mrfac.com
Mary McKinley, President
Stan Jenkins, First VP
Clark Hart, Second VP
Dan Fiest, Secretary
Jim Pakla, Manager
Representing the voice of the manufacturing industry and private land mobile radio users before the Federal Communications Commision, the responsibe federal regulatory agency for the nation's industrial communications. The leaders of the manufacturing industry, individually and collectively, have an obligation to influence the policies, plans, and procedures which govern the growth, structure and use of our national radio spectrum and telecommunications systems.
14000 Members

3036 **Media Communications Association International**
2810 Crossroads Drive
Suite 3800
Madison, WI 53718
608-443-2464
FAX: 608-443-2474
info@mca-i.org www.mca-i.org
Susan Rees, Executive Director
The community of professional media communications experts recognized as the definitive source of current comprehensive onformation, skills and connections needed to succeed in a highly competitive environment.
Founded: 1968

3037 **National Academy of Television Arts and Sciences**
111 W 57th Street
New York, NY 10019
212-586-8424
FAX: 212-246-8129
www.emmyonline.org
Dennis Swanson, Chairman
Peter O Price, President
Linda Giannecchini, Vice Chairperson
Darryl Cohen, VP
Janice Selinger, Secretary
Dedicated to the advancement of the arts and sciences of television and the promotion of creative leadership for artistic, educational and technical achievements within the television industry. It recognizes excellence in television with the coveted Emmy Award.
12M Members Founded: 1957
Printed in on glossy stock

3038 **National Association of Broadcasters**
1771 N Street NW
Washington, DC 20036
202-429-5300
FAX: 202-429-4199 www.nab.org
Edward O Fritts, President/CEO
Philip J Lombardo, Chairman
Dean Goodman, COO
Full service trade association that represents the interests of free, over-the-air radio and television broadcasters.
7000 Members Founded: 1923

3039 **National Association of Business and Radio Communication**
500 Montgomery Street
Alexandria, VA 22314
703-739-0300

Encourages technological improvements leading to the reduction of radio interference and improved radio communications.
5.5M Members Founded: 1965

3040 **National Association of College Radio/TV Stations**
71 George Street
Providence, RI 2912-1824
401-863-2225
FAX: 401-863-2221
mark.macleod@brown.edu
Kelley Cunningham, Executive Director
Members are student radio/TV stations and interested individuals. Has an annual budget of approximately $300,000.
1600 Members Founded: 1988

3041 National Association of Farm Broadcasters
PO Box 500
Platte City, MO 64079-2294
816-431-4032
FAX: 816-431-4087
info@nafb.com www.nafb.com
Ken Root, Executive Director
Rose Marie Lawrence, Secretary
Gene Millard, Director Marketing & Promotion
Works to improve quantity and quality of farm programming and serves as a clearing-house for new ideas in farm broadcasting.
600 Members Founded: 1944

3042 National Association of Television Program Executives
5757 Wilshire Boulevard
Penthouse 10
Los angeles, CA 90036
323-374-4465
FAX: 310-453-5258
info@natpe.org www.natpe.org
Rick Feldman, President/CEO
Stephen Davis, Co-Chairperson
Tony Vinciquerra, Director
Our mission is a commitment to furthering the quality and quantity of content, which means offering the wealth of our resources and experience to every content creator, no matter the medium. Because the industry encompasses so much more today than ever before, NATPE too is expanding to accommodate this change and encourage progress while continuing to keep our members constantly apprised of the changes occurring daily in the global media environment regardless of the platform used.
2800 Members Founded: 1963
Mailing list available for rent

3043 National Broadcasters Association
1771 N Street NW
Washington, DC 20036
202-429-5300
FAX: 202-429-4199
nab@nab.org www.nab.org

3044 National Cable Television Association
1724 Massachusetts Avenue NW
Washington, DC 20036
202-753-3595
FAX: 202-775-3676
webmaster@ncta.com www.ncta.com
Robert Sachs, President
David Krone, VP
Eleanor Winter, VP Special Projects
Association for those interested in programs about cable television.
200+ Members Founded: 1952

3045 National Council for Families & TV
3801 Barham Boulevard
Los Angeles, CA 90068-1000
323-953-7300
FAX: 310-208-5984
www.salonprofessionals.org
Advances and promotes television awareness for family television shows.

3046 National Federation of Community Broadcasting
1970 Broadway
Suite 1000
Oakland, CA 94612
510-451-8200
FAX: 510- 45- 820
nfcb@aol.com www.nfcb.org
Carol Pierson, President
Brian Terhorst, Board Chair
Kim Bosler, Secretary
Peggy Berryhill, Treasurer

3047 National Federation of Local Cable Programmers
666 11th Street NW
Suite 806
Washington, DC 20001-4542
202-393-2650
FAX: 202-393-2653

3048 National Public Radio Association
635 Massachusetts Avenue NW
Washington, DC 20001-3753
202-132-2000
FAX: 202-513-3329 www.npr.org
Delano E Lewis, President
Emily Rubin, Director Business Development
Ken Stern, Executive VP
Kevin Klose, Chief Executive Officer
Jim Elder, VP Finance/CFO
750 Members Founded: 1970

3049 National Religious Broadcasters
9510 Technology Drive
Manassas, VA 20110
703-330-7000
FAX: 703-330-7100
info@nrb.org www.nrb.org
Dr. Frank Wright, President
David Keith, VP Operations
Tammy Singleton, Director Finance
Steve Cross, Director Marketing
Represents more than 1500 evangelical Christian radio and television stations, program producers, multimedia developers and related organizations around the world. Members are responsible for much of the world's Christian radio and television.
1700 Members

3050 National Sportscasters and Sportswriters Association
PO Box 1545
Salisbury, NC 28145-1545
704-633-4275
FAX: 704-633-2027
www.halloffame.com
Barbara Lockert, President
Meet annually.
1000 Members Founded: 1959

3051 North American Network
3700 Crestwood Parkway
Suite 350
Duluth, GA 30096
770-279-4560
FAX: 770-279-4566
rbeilfuss@pkfnan.org
Rudolf Beilfuss, President
Radio broadcasting agency that provides news and programming services to radio stations and organizations. Programming is sponsored by the corporations, government angencies, associations and nonprofit organizations who are indentified in the program notes and scripts.

3052 Radio Advertising Bureau
1320 Greenway Drive
Suite 500
Irving, TX 75038
972-536-6700
FAX: 972-753-6727 800-232-3131
Gary R Fries, President/CEO
Renee Cassis, VP/Corporate Marketing
Mary Malone, VP Services
Mike Mahone, Executive VP Services
David Casper, Senior VP/Services
Seeks to increase national and local radio advertising. Supports marketing personnel and raises awareness of radio among advertising and business communities.
5600+ Members

3053 Radio Information Service
2100 Wharton Street
Suite 140
Pittsburgh, PA 15203-1942
412-488-3944
FAX: 412-488-3953
info@readingservice.org
www.readingservice.org
Laurie Anderson, Executive Director
Membership is offered to radio reading and information services for the blind or print handicapped.
10000 Members

3054 Radio Television News Directors Association
1600 K Street NW
Suite 700
Washington, DC 20006-2838
202-659-6510
FAX: 202-223-4007 800-807-8632
rtnda@rtnda.org www.rtnda.org
Dan Shelly, Chairman
Barbara Cochran, President
Angie Kucharski, Chairman Elect
Loren Tobia, Treasurer
The world's largest professional organization devoted exclusively to electronic journalism. RTNDA represents local and network news executives in broadcasting, cable and other electronic media in more than 30 countries.
3200 Members Founded: 1946
Mailing list available for rent $500 per M.

3055 Radio and Television Research Council
245 5th Avenue
New York, NY 10016-8728
212-028-8933
FAX: 212-481-3071
Robert M Purcell, Executive Director
Members are professionals actively engaged in radio/television research.
200 Members Founded: 1941

3056 Radio-Television Correspondents Association
1600 K Street NW
Suite 700
Washington, DC 20006-2838
202-659-6510
FAX: 202-223-4007
rtnda@rtnda.org www.rtnda.org
Brian Lockman, Chairman
Barbara Cochran, President
Rick Osmanski, VP
Jane Nassiri, Director Finance
Noreen Welle, Director Marketing/Communications

Supports professional correspondents, reporters, and news analysts assigned to cover Congress for radio and television.
2.5M Members Founded: 1946

3057 Satellite Broadcasting and Communication Association (SBCA)
225 Reinekers Lane
Suite 600
Alexandria, VA 22314-2875
703-549-6990
FAX: 703-549-7640 800-541-5981
info@sbca.org www.sbca.com
David Moskowitz, Chairman
Joy O'Brien, Director Government Affairs
Pat Andrews, Senior VP
Brian Lynch, Director Program Development
National trade organization representing all segments of the satellite consumer services industry. The association is committed to expanding the utilization of satellite technology for the delivery of video, data, voice, interactive and broadband services.
1000 Members Founded: 1986

3058 Society of Broadcast Engineers
9102 N Meridian St
Ste 150
Indianapolis, IN 46260-1896
317-846-9000
FAX: 317-846-9120
lbaun@sbe.org www.sbe.org
Raymond Benedict, President
Samuel Garfield, VP
Ralph R Hogan, Secretary
John Poray, Executive Director
Ted D Hand, Director
Offers a range of services to members including technology updates, idea exchanges, training, examinations and certification. Includes membership and contact details, technical papers and events.
5800 Members Founded: 1963
Mailing list available for rent 5700 names $170 per M.

3059 Society of Motion Picture & Television Engineers
3 Barker Ave
White Plains, NY 10601-1509
914-761-1100
FAX: 914-761-3115
smpte@smpte.org www.smpte.org
Fred Motts, Executive Director
Hans Hoffmann
Thomas A Scott, Engineering Director
Howell W Mette, VP Engineering
Angelo D'Alessio, Managing Director
More than 10,000 members are spread throughout 85 countries. Also, over 250 corporate members belong to SMPTE, allowing networking and contacts to occur on a larger scale. Touching on every discipline, our members include engineers, technical directors, cameramen, editors, technicians, manufacturers educators, and consultants.
6000 Members Founded: 1916 8600 names

3060 Special Industrial Radio Service
1110 N Glebe
Suite 100
Arlington, VA 22201

Provides a license renewal reminder service. Maintains liaison with major radio manufacturers and mediates problems between licensees.
13M Members Founded: 1953

3061 Television Bureau of Advertising
3 E 54th Street
New York, NY 10022
212-486-1111
FAX: 212-935-5631
info@tvb.org www.tvb.org
chris Rohrs, President
Abby Auerbach, Executive VP
Gary Belis, VP Communications
Not-for-profit trade association of America's broadcast television industry. TVB provides a diverse variety of tools and resources to support its members and to help advertisers make the best use of local television.
500 Members Founded: 1954

3062 WGBH Educational Foundation
WGBH
PO Box 200
Boston, MA 02134-1008
617-300-2000
FAX: 617-300-1039 www.wgbh.org
Founded: 1951

Newsletters

3063 American Sportscasters Association Insiders Newsletter
225 Broadway
Suite 2030
New York, NY 10007
212-227-8080
FAX: 212-571-0556
lschwa8918@aol.com
www.americansportscasters.com
Louis O Schwartz, Executive Director
Curt Gowdy, VP
Louis O Schwartz, CEO
Newsletter keeps sportscasters up to date on important issues for the profession.
24 pages Quarterly Founded: 1980
Circulation: 2500

3064 Bandwidth Investor
Kagan World Media
126 Clock Tower Place
Carmel, CA 93923-8746
831-624-1536
FAX: 831-625-3225
info@kagan.com www.kagan.com
George Niesen, Editor
Harvy Carft, Marketing Manager
Tim Baskerville, CEO/President
Harvy Carft, Circulation Manager
$945.00
Monthly Founded: 1969

3065 Broadband Fixed Wireless
Kagan World Media
126 Clock Tower Place
Carmel, CA 93923-8746
831-624-1536
FAX: 831-625-3225
info@kagan.com www.kagan.com
George Niesen, Editor
Tom Johnson, Marketing Manager
$845.00
Monthly

3066 Broadband Systems & Design
Gordon Publications
301 Gibraltar Drive
#650
Morris Plains, NJ 07950-3400
973-292-5100
FAX: 973-539-3476
Terry McCoy Jr, Publisher
Andrea Frucci, Editor
The only product tabloid serving buying influencers, engineers, corporate managers and purchasing professionals in the cable television marketplace.

Circulation: 26,400

3067 Broadband Technology
Kagan World Media
126 Clock Tower Place
Carmel, CA 93923-8746
831-624-1536
FAX: 831-625-3225
info@kagan.com www.kagan.com
George Niesen, Editor
Tom Johnson, Marketing Manager
$1450.00
Monthly Founded: 1969

3068 Broadcast Banker/Broker
Kagan World Media
126 Clock Tower Place
Carmel, CA 93923-8746
831-624-1536
FAX: 831-625-3225 800-307-2529
info@kagan.com www.kagan.com
George Niesen, Editor
Tom Johnson, Marketing Manager
A readers guide to equity deals and debt financing for radio and TV Station buying and selling analyzed. Key details on station trades with critical yardsticks of value. Three month trial is available. *$925.00*
Monthly Founded: 1969

3069 Broadcast Investor
Kagan World Media
One Lower Ragsdale Drive
Building One, Suite 130
Monterey, CA 93940
831-624-1536
FAX: 831-625-3225 800-307-2529
info@kagan.com www.kagan.com/
George Niesen, Editor
Tom Johnson, Marketing Manager
The newsletter on investments in radio and TV stations and publicly held companies. Comprehensive analysis of cash flow multiples and trends that impact value. Three month trial available. *$1295.00*
Monthly Founded: 1969

3070 Broadcast Stats
Kagan World Media
126 Clock Tower Place
Carmel, CA 93923-8746
831-624-1536
FAX: 831-624-5882 800-307-2529
info@kagan.com www.kagan.com
George Niesen, Editor
Tom Johnson, Marketing Manager
The numbers behind the broadcast companies. Exclusive data, analysis and projections of radio and TV market billings, revenues, and cash flows, plus complete data on the buy-sell market. The industry's key reference source. Three month trial available. *$795.00*
Monthly Founded: 1969

3071 **Business Radio**
Nt'l Association of Business & Educational Radio
500 Montgomery Street
Alexandria, VA 22314
703-548-1500
FAX: 703-836-1608

AE Goetz, Publisher

Association news for professionals, owners and consumers regarding radio stations. *$65.00*

Circulation: 3,000

3072 **Cable Program Investor**
Kagan World Media
One Lower Ragsdale
Building One, Suite 130
Monterey, CA 93940
831-624-1536
FAX: 831-624-5882 800-307-2529
info@kagan.com www.kagan.com/

George Niesen, Editor
Tom Johnson, Marketing Manager
Robin Flynn, Senior VP
Sharon Armbrust, Senior Consultant
Derek Baine, Senior Vice President

Covers the economics of basic cable programming networks. Numbers, perspective unavailable from any other source. Programmers applaud its accuracy. Three month trial available. *$1045.00*

Monthly Founded: 1969

3073 **Cable TV Advertising**
Kagan World Media
126 Clock Tower Place
Carmel, CA 93923-8746
831-624-1536
FAX: 831-624-5882
info@kagan.com www.kagan.com

George Niesen, Editor
Tom Johnson, Marketing Manager

Analysis of sales of commercial time by cable TV networks, interconnects and local systems. Detailed reports on national and local spot sales. Case studies and projections, all about the industry's upside. Three month trial available. *$795.00*

Monthly

3074 **Cable TV Finance**
Kagan World Media
126 Clock Tower Place
Carmel, CA 93923-8746
831-624-1536
FAX: 831-624-5882 800-307-2529
info@kagan.com www.kagan.com

George Niesen, Editor
Tom Johnson, Marketing Manager
Larry Gerbrandt, CEO/President
Judy Pinney, Circulation Manager
Tim Baskerville, Publisher

Cable's financial bible. Analyzes sources of funding for cable TV. Selling and buying of cable systems. Financing strategies and trends. Exclusive surveys of capital sources. Three month trial available. *$795.00*

Monthly Founded: 1969

3075 **Cable TV Investor**
Kagan World Media
One Lower Ragsdale Drive
Building One, Suite 130
Monterey, CA 93940-8746
831-624-1536
FAX: 831-625-3225 800-307-2529
info@kagan.com www.kagan.com

George Niesen, Editor
Tom Johnson, Marketing Manager
Tim Baskerville, President

Readers road map to cable stock trends. Chart service tracking stock price movements of 37 publicly held cable TV companies. Each graph shows two years of stock price activity. Three month trial available. *$1295.00*

Monthly Founded: 1969

3076 **Cable TV Law Reporter**
Kagan World Media
One Lower Ragsdale Drive
Building One, Suite 130
Monterey, CA 93940-8746
831-624-1536
FAX: 831-625-3225 800-307-2529
info@kagan.com www.kagan.com

George Niesen, Editor
Tom Johnson, Marketing Manager

The quintessential library of cable court cases, arbitrations, legal precedents. Labeled and catalogued for easy reference. Required reading for attorneys, government regulators and top executives. Three month trial available. *$995.00*

Monthly Founded: 1969

3077 **Cable TV Technology**
Kagan World Media
One Lower Ragsdale Drive
Suite 130
Monterey, CA 93940-8746
831-624-1536
FAX: 831-625-3225 800-307-2529
info@kagan.com www.kagan.com

George Niesen, Editor
Tom Johnson, Marketing Manager

Incisive, thorough reports on technical advances in cable TV, in terms operating executives can grasp and use to implement strategies. Analyzes growth in addressable converters, high definition TV, fiber optics and other advancements. Three month trial available. *$925.00*

Monthly Founded: 1969

3078 **Community Radio News**
National Federation of Community Broadcasting
Fort Mason Center
Building D
San Francisco, CA 94123
510-451-8200
FAX: 510-451-8208
nfcb@aol.com www.nfcb.org

Ryan Bruce, Publications Manager

Contains calendar of events and information on public broadcasting, job listings, and legislative and regulatory updates. Annual Community Radio Conference and Community Radio Program Awards Competition. *$75.00*

12-16 pages Monthly Founded: 1975
Circulation: 400 300 names $25 per M.
Printed in 1 color on matte stock

3079 **Community Television Review**
National Federation of Local Cable Programmers
666 11th Street NW
Suite 806
Washington, DC 20001
202-393-2650
FAX: 202-393-2653

Andrew Lewis, Publisher

Issues of importance to community programming on cable and other areas of telecommunications. *$15.00*

36 pages

3080 **DBS Report**
Kagan World Media
One Lower Ragsdale Drive
Building One, Suite 130
Monterey, CA 93940
831-624-1536
FAX: 831-625-3225 800-307-2529
info@kagan.com www.kagan.com

George Niesen, Editor
Tom Johnson, Marketing Manager
$1045.00

Monthly Founded: 1969

3081 **Dance on Camera Journal**
Dance Films Association
48 W 21st Street
Suite 907
New York, NY 10010-6806
212-727-0764
FAX: 212-727-0764
dfa5@earthlink.net
www.dancefilmsassn.org

Deirdre Towers, Editor
Louise Spain, President

The only service organization in the world dedicated to both the dance and the film community.

Founded: 1956
Printed in on matte stock

3082 **Digital Television**
Kagan World Media
126 Clock Tower Place
Carmel, CA 93923-8746
831-624-1536
FAX: 831-624-5882 800-307-2529
info@kagan.com www.kagan.com

George Niesen, Editor
Tom Johnson, Marketing Manager

News of the Digital Television. Three month trial available. *$945.00*

Monthly Founded: 1969

3083 **Hearsay**
Association of Radio Reading Services
2100 Wharton Street
Suite 140
Pittsburgh, PA 15203-1942
412-488-3944
FAX: 412-488-3953
Newsletter for the Radio Reading industry.

3084 **Inside NRB Newsfax**
National Religious Broadcasters
9510 Technology Drive
Manassas, VA 20110
703-330-7000
FAX: 703-330-7100
info@nrb.org www.nrb.org

Robert K Powers, Director Media/Publisher
Dr. Frank Wright, President

For members only.

Founded: 1944

3085 **Inside Sports Letter**
American Sportscasters Association
225 Broadway
Suite 2030
New York, NY 10007
212-227-8080
FAX: 212-571-0556
lschwa8918@aol.com
www.americansportscasters.com/

Louis O Schwartz, President/Editor
Curt Gowdy, VP
Dick Enberg, Chairman

Elaine Graifer, Associate Editor
Patrick Turturro, Assistant Editor

A quarterly newsletter published by the American Sportscasters Association.

38513 pages Quarterly Founded: 1980
Circulation: 2000 3000 names

3086 Interactive Mobile Investor
Kagan World Media
One Lower Ragsdale Drive
Suite 130
Monterey, CA 93940-8746
831-624-1536
FAX: 831-625-3225 800-307-2529
info@kagan.com www.kagan.com

George Niesen, Editor
Tom Johnson, Marketing Manager
$945.00
Monthly Founded: 1969

3087 Interactive TV Investor
Kagan World Media
One Lower Ragsdale Drive
Suite 130
Monterey, CA 93940-8746
831-624-1536

info@kagan.com www.kagan.com

George Niesen, Editor
Tom Johnson, Marketing Manager
$895.00
Monthly Founded: 1970

3088 Interactive Television
Kagan World Media
One Lower Ragsdale Drive
Building One Suite 130
Monterey, CA 93940-8746
831-624-1536
FAX: 831-624-5882 800-307-2529
info@kagan.com www.kagan.com

George Niesen, Editor
Tom Johnson, Marketing Manager

News of the Interactive Television. Three month trial available. *$795.00*
Monthly Founded: 1969

3089 Internet Media Investor
Kagan World Media
126 Clock Tower Place
Carmel, CA 93923-8746
831-624-1536
FAX: 831-625-3225
info@kagan.com www.kagan.com

George Niesen, Editor
Tom Johnson, Marketing Manager
$945.00
Monthly Founded: 1969

3090 Interval
Society of Cable Telecommunications Engineers
140 Philips Road
Exton, PA 19341-1318
610-363-6888
FAX: 610-363-5898 800-542-5040
scte@scte.org www.scte.org

Howard Whitman, Senior Editor
Marci Dodd, Managing Editor

A monthly member newsletter. Subscription price of $25.00 is for non-members.
$25.00
Monthly Founded: 1969
Circulation: 16000

3091 Kagan Broadband
Kagan World Media
One Lower Ragsdale Drive
Building One, Suite 130
Monterey, CA 93940
831-624-1536
FAX: 831-625-3225 800-307-2529
info@kagan.com www.kagan.com

George Niesen, Editor
Harvy Craft, Marketing Manager
Tim Baskerville, CEO/President
Robert Nayoor, Circulation Manager
Sandie Borthwick, Executive Director

Daily e-mail or fax. *$1295.00*
Monthly Founded: 1970

3092 Kagan Media Money
Kagan World Media
One Lower Ragsdale Drive
Suite 130
Monterey, CA 93940-8746
831-624-1536
FAX: 831- 62- 322 800- 30- 252
info@kagan.com www.kagan.com

George Niesen, Editor
Tom Johnson, Marketing Manager
Sandie Borthwick, Executive Director

Analysts dissect deals, anticipate trends, project revenues, track financings, and value the debt and equity of hundreds of priovately held and publicly traded advertising, broadcasting, cable TV digital TV, home video, Internet media, motion picture, newspaper, pay TV, professional sports and wireless telecommunications companies in the US and abroad. *$1245.00*

Founded: 1970

3093 Kagan Music Investor
Kagan World Media
One Lower Ragsdale
Building One,Suite 130
Monterey, CA 93940-8746
831-624-1536
FAX: 831-625-3225 800-307-2529
info@kagan.com www.kagan.com

George Niesen, Editor
Tom Johnson, Marketing Manager
Sandie Borthwick, Executive Director

News and analysis of the music industry for investors. *$945.00*
Monthly Founded: 1969

3094 Marketing New Media
Kagan World Media
One Lower Ragsdale Drive
Building One, Suite 130
Monterey, CA 93940-8746
831-624-1536
FAX: 831-625-3225 800-307-2529
info@kagan.com www.kagan.com

George Niesen, Editor
Tom Johnson, Marketing Manager

News of the Marketing New Media. Three month trial available. *$795.00*
Monthly Founded: 1969

3095 Media Communications Association News
Media Communications Association International
2810 Crossroads Dr
Ste 3800
Madison, WI 53718-7961
608-275-5034
FAX: 608-831-5122
info@mca-i.org www.mca-i.org

Rene Chapin, Publisher

Coverage of the multimedia industry and association avtivities.
Quarterly
Circulation: 3,000
Printed in on glossy stock

3096 Media Mergers & Acquisitions
Kagan World Media
126 Clock Tower Place
Carmel, CA 93923-8746
831-624-1536
FAX: 831-624-5882
info@kagan.com www.kagan.com

George Niesen, Editor
Tom Johnson, Marketing Manager

Where it all comes together. Exclusive scorecard of deals done by media companies. Dollar amounts, multiples paid, trends captured in succinct summaries of complex transactions. Three month trial available. *$795.00*
Monthly

3097 Media Sports Business
Kagan World Media
One Lower Ragsdale Drive
Building One, Suite 130
Monterey, CA 93940-8746
831-624-1536
FAX: 831-625-3225 800-307-2529
info@kagan.com www.kagan.com

George Niesen, Editor
Tom Johnson, Marketing Manager
$945.00
Monthly Founded: 1969

3098 Monitoring Times
Grove Enterprises
7540 Highway 64 W
Brasstown, NC 28902
828-837-9200
FAX: 828-837-2216 800-438-8155
order@grove-ent.com
www.grove-ent.com

Rachel Baughn, Managing Director
Judy Grove, Publisher/Editor

News on radio communication, scanner monitoring, international radio broadcasts and technical advice. *$28.95*
92 pages Monthly Founded: 1970
Circulation: 50000
Printed in 4 colors on glossy stock

3099 Motion Picture Investor
Kagan World Media
One Lower Ragsdale Drive
Building One Suite 130
Monterey, CA 93940-8746
831-624-1536
FAX: 831-625-3225
info@kagan.com www.kagan.com

George Niesen, Editor
Tom Johnson, Marketing Manager
Tim Baskerville, President *$845.00*
Monthly Founded: 1969

3100 Multichannel News
360 Park Avenue S
New York, NY 10010
212-878-8387
FAX: 646-746-6406
mpaskowski@reedbusiness.com
www.multichannel.com

Larry Dunn, Publishing Director
Marianne Paskowski, Editorial Director
Kent Gibbons, Editor

News of the electronic media industries.
Weekly Founded: 1980
Circulation: 18,875

3101 National Cable Television Association
National Cable Television Association
1724 Massachusetts Avenue NW
Washington, DC 20036-1969
202-753-3595
FAX: 202-775-3676 www.ncta.com
Robert Sachs, Chief Executive Officer
Convention newsletter with programs about cable television.
8-200 pages 7 per year

3102 Networks
Geospatial Information & Technology Association
14456 E Evans Avenue
Aurora, CO 80014
303-337-0513
FAX: 303-337-1001
info@gita.org www.gita.org
Robert Samborski, Executive Director
Ken Goering, Editor
Elizabeth Roberts, Marketing
A bi-monthly newsletter published by the Geospatial Information & Technology Association. *$125.00*
28 pages Monthly Founded: 1978
Circulation: 2200 2000 names

3103 Pay TV Newsletter
Kagan World Media
126 Clock Tower Place
Carmel, CA 93923-8746
831-624-1536
FAX: 831-624-5882
info@kagan.com www.kagan.com
George Niesen, Editor
Tom Johnson, Marketing Manager
The pay TV industry's publication of record since 1973. Exclusive estimates of network subscribers and economics. The pay-per-view business, event-by-event, film-by-film. Three month trial available. *$795.00*
Monthly

3104 Public Broadcasting Report
Warren Communications News
2115 Ward Court NW
Washington, DC 20037-1209
202-872-9200
FAX: 202-293-3435 800-771-9202
info@warren-news.com
www.warren-news.com
Paul Warren, President
R. Michael Feazel, Managing Editor
Albert Warren, Chairman/Editor/Publisher
Gina Storr, Director, Sales/Mkting Support
Industry news, personnel announcements and calendar listings for public broadcasting, digital TV, congress, FCC, and allied friends. *$575.00*
Founded: 1945

3105 Radio & Records
Radio & Records
10100 Santa Monica Boulevard
3rd Floor
Los Angeles, CA 90067-4003
310-553-4330
FAX: 310-203-8450
moreinfo@radioandrecords.com
www.radioandrecords.com
Erica Farber, Publisher/CEO
Henry Mowry, Director Sales
A music newspaper that covers all aspects of the radio and recording industry. *$325.00*
100 pages Weekly
Circulation: 8006
Printed in 4 colors on n stock

3106 Radio Business Report
2050 Old Bridge Road
Suite B-01
Lake Ridge, VA 22192
703-492-8191
FAX: 703-997-8601
radionews@rbr.com www.rbr.com/
Jim Carnegie, Publisher
Jack Messmer, Executive Editor
Cathy Carnegie, VP Administration
Carl Marcucci, MD/Senior Editor
June Barnes, Sales
Focuses on radio business issues, inside news on people and controversial topics. *$220.00*
Daily Founded: 1983
Circulation: 5100
Printed in 4 colors on matte stock

3107 Radio Ink
Streamline Publishing
224 Datura Street
Suite 1015
West Palm Beach, FL 33401-5635
561-655-8778
FAX: 561-655-6164 800-610-5771
Eric Rhoads, Publisher
Reed Bunzel, Editor
Marty Sacks, Marketing
Tom Elmo, Circulation
Geared toward radio broadcast management professionals contains information on marketing trends, special reports, sales and programming issues. *$199.00*
Founded: 1992
Circulation: 5000

3108 Radio World
Industrial Marketing Advisory Services
5827 Columbia Pike
Suite 310
Falls Church, VA 22041-2027
703-998-7600
FAX: 703-998-2966 800-336-3045
Steve Dana, President/Publisher
Lucia Cobo, Editor
A technical trade newspaper for the broadcast radio industry. Accepts advertising.
48 pages Founded: 1978
Circulation: 18000
Printed in 4 colors on newsprint stock

3109 Signal
Society of Broadcast Engineers
9247 N Meridian Street
Suite 305
Indianapolis, IN 46260-2454
317-846-9000
FAX: 317-846-9120
jporay@sbe.org www.sbe.org
John Poray, Executive Director
Angel Bates, Membership Service
David Otey, Frequency Coordination Di
A bi-monthly newsletter published by the Society of Broadcast Engineers.
24 pages Quarterly Founded: 1963
Mailing list available for rent 5000 names $100 per M.
Printed in 4 colors on glossy stock

3110 Streaming Media Investor
Kagan World Media
126 Clock Tower Place
Carmel, CA 93923-8746
831-624-1536
FAX: 831-624-5882
info@kagan.com www.kagan.com
George Niesen, Editor
Harvy Craft, Marketing Manager
Tim Baskerville, CEO/President
News of the Streaming Media Investor. Three month trial available. *$895.00*
Monthly Founded: 1969

3111 TV Program Investor
Kagan World Media
One Lower Ragsdale Drive
Building One, Suite 130
Monterey, CA 93940-8746
831-624-1536
FAX: 831-625-3225 800-307-2529
info@kagan.com www.kagan.com
George Niesen, Editor
Tom Johnson, Marketing Manager
More than just a newsletter, practically a seminar on how much programs cost and what they are worth. Exclusive spreadsheets with estimates of what goes between the commercials. Three month trial available. *$895.00*
Monthly Founded: 1969

3112 Television Digest with Consumer Electronics
Warren Communications News
2115 Ward Court NW
Washington, DC 20037-1209
202-872-9200
FAX: 202-293-3435
info@warren-news.com
www.warren-news.com
Albert Warren, Chairman/Publisher/Editor
Paul Warren, President/Executive Publisher
Paul Gluckman, NY Bureau Chief
R Michael Feazel, Managing Editor
A weekly newsletter providing continuous coverage of broadcasting, cable, consumer electronics and related industries. *$943.00*
12 pages Weekly
Computerized version available: E-Mail

3113 Video Investor
Kagan World Media
126 Clock Tower Place
Carmel, CA 93923-8746
831-624-1536
FAX: 831-624-5882
info@kagan.com www.kagan.com
George Niesen, Editor
Harvy Craft, Marketing Manager
Tim Baskerville, CEO/President
Authoritative look inside the business of renting and selling video cassettes. Exclusive estimates of retail and wholesale transactions and inventories. Tracking movies into the home. Three month trial is available. *$795.00*
Monthly Founded: 1969

3114 Warren Communications News
Warren
2115 Ward Court NW
Washington, DC 20037-1209
202-872-9200
FAX: 202-296-4397 800-771-9202
info@warren-news.com
www.warren-news.com
Michael Taliaferro, Editor
Gaye Nail, Assistant Managing Editor
Brig Easley, Manager
Commercial and noncommercial television stations and networks, including educational, low-power and instructional TV stations, and translators. Lists over 11,000 operating cable systems including subscribers, channel capacities, programming, fees and personnel. *$6.45*

3115 Wireless Market Stats
Kagan World Media
One Lower Ragsdale Drive
Suite 130
Monterey, CA 93940-8746
831-624-1536
FAX: 831-625-3225 800-307-2529
info@kagan.com www.kagan.com

George Niesen, Editor
Tom Johnson, Marketing Manager

News of the Wireless Market Stats. Three month trial available. *$995.00*
Monthly Founded: 1969

3116 Wireless Telecom Investor
Kagan World Media
One Lower Ragsdale Drive
Building One, Suite 130
Monterey, CA 93940-8746
831-624-1536
FAX: 831-625-3225 800-307-2529
info@kagan.com www.kagan.com

George Niesen, Editor
Tom Johnson, Marketing Manager

Exclusive analysis of private and public values of wireless telecommunications companies, including cellular telephone, ESMR and PCS. Exclusive databases of subscribers, market penetrations, market potential, industry growth. Catching super-fast growth in a capsule. Three month trial available. *$895.00*
Monthly Founded: 1969

3117 Wireless/Private Cable Investor
Kagan World Media
One Lower Ragsdale
Building One, Suite 130
Monterey, CA 93940
831-624-1536
FAX: 831-625-3225 800-307-2529
info@kagan.com www.kagan.com/

George Niesen, Editor
Tom Johnson, Marketing Manager

The original bible of the wireless cable, multipoint distribution pay TV industry. Published continuously since 1972, this newsletter is the window on cable competition. Three month trial available. *$1095.00*

Monthly Founded: 1969

Magazines & Journals

3118 Albumn Network
110 Spazier
Burbank, CA 91502-1852
818-842-2600
FAX: 818-972-2899
imc1704@albumn-network-uf
www.musicbiz.com

Steve Smith, Publisher

Editorial emphasis on chart ratings, sales performances, music reviews, and industry news. *$400.00*
Weekly
Circulation: 2,500

3119 Alliance for Community Media
666 11th Street NW
Suite 740
Washington, DC 20001-4542
202-393-2650
FAX: 202-393-2653
briedel@alliancecm.org
www.alliancecm.org

Bunnie Riedel, Executive Director
Denise M Woodson, Membership/Operation Manager

Participants include cable access television and community programmers. Individual membership dues are $60.00, organization $305.00. *$35.00*
36 pages Quarterly Founded: 1985
Circulation: 1500 1000 names $200 per M.

3120 Almanac
International Council of NATAS
888 7th Avenue
5th floor
New York, NY 10019-3300
212-489-6969
FAX: 212-489-6557
info@iemmys.tv www.iemmys.tv/

Camille Bide Roizen, Executive Director
Eva Obadia, Marketing Manager
Georges Leclere, Senior VP

An annual publication with highlights of the International Emmy Program, global preference guides, articles on various facets in and around television today.
Founded: 1969

3121 BE Radio
Primedia
Subscriptions
9800 Metcalf Ave.
Overland Park, KS 66212-2914
913-411-1300
FAX: 402-293-0741 800-441-0294
beradio@intertec.com
www.beradio.com

Dennis Triola, Publisher
Chriss Scherer, Editor
Kirby Asplund, Marketing Director

Provides radio station managers and engineers the information they need to make critical equipment purchase decisions. Presents need-to-know technical information to help readers solve the challenges of technology and the equipment problems they face. BE Radio serves the needs of radio engineers, managers and owners who need to make informed equipment and services buying decisions. *$30.00*
Monthly Founded: 1959
Circulation: 12000

3122 Broadband Advertising
Kagan World Media
One Lower Ragsdale Drive
Building One Suite 130
Monterey, CA 93940-8746
831-624-1536
FAX: 831-625-3225 800-307-2529
hkraft@kagan.com www.kagan.com

Tim Baskerville, President

Reports and analysis of the sale of commercial time by cable TV networks, interconnects and local spot sales. *$1095.00*
Monthly Founded: 1969
Printed in 2 colors on n stock

3123 Broadcast Engineering
Primedia
PO Box 12914
Overland Park, KS 66282-2914
913-341-1300
FAX: 913-967-1903 800-441-0294
editor@intertec.com
www.broadcastengineering.com

Brad Dick, Editor

Aimed at the market that includes corporate management, engineers/technicians and other management personnel at commercial and public TV stations, post-production and recording studios, broadcast networks, cable, telephone and satellite production centers and networks.
Founded: 1960
Circulation: 35000

3124 Broadcasting
Reed Business Information
2000 Clearwater Drive
Oak Brook, IL 60523
630-740-0825
FAX: 630-288-8686 800-446-6551
webmaster@reedbusiness.com
www.reedbusiness.com

J Max Robins, Editor in Chief
Larry Dunn, Publishing Director
Jim Casella, CEO
Michael Farina, Marketing Services Manager
John LaMarca, Group Circulation Director

Offers comprehensive coverage of television, radio, cable, satellite and the attendant equipment and emerging technologies. Accepts advertising. *$189.00*
Founded: 1894

3125 Broadcasting & Cable
Reed Business Information
360 Park Avenue S
New York, NY 10010
212-450-0067
FAX: 630-288-8686
max.robins@reedbusiness.com
www.broadcastingcable.com

Gary Rubin, Associate Publisher
J Max Robins, Editor in Chief
John LaMarca, Circulation
James Reed, Owner

Coverage on developments in programming, advertising, broadcast and cable journalism, finamce, systems operation and management, and trade show and meetings information. *$189.00*

Circulation: 35400

3126 CQ Amateur Radio
CQ Communications
25 Newbridge Road
Suite 405
Hicksville, NY 11801
516-681-2922
FAX: 516-681-2926
cq@cq-amateur-radio.com
www.cq-amateur-radio.com

Richard Ross, Publisher
Rich Moseson, Editor
Richard Ross, CEO
Mellisa Gillgan, Circulation

Information for people interested in the developments of in the field radio communications and electronics. Coverage includes reviews of new operating programs, new products and seasonal promotional ideas. *$32.00*
Monthly Founded: 1950
Circulation: 87000

3127 CTAM Quarterly Marketing Journal
Cable Television Administration & Marketing
201 N Union Street
Suite 440
Alexandria, VA 22314-2642
703-549-4200
FAX: 703-684-1167
info@ctam.com www.ctam.com/

Char Beales, President
Patrick Dougherty, Marketing Manager

A journal offering financial information to persons in the cable television management and executives. *$295.00*
Quarterly

3128 Cable Plus/Cable TV Publications
Cable TV Publications/TV Host
PO Box 1665
Harrisburg, PA 17105-1665

FAX: 610-687-2965 800-922-4678
Frank Dillahey, Sales Manager
Bob Newell, Marketing Director
Custom cable TV listing guides incorporating exclusive cable programming, editorial, movie reviews and TV listings that are sold to cable subscribers nationally. Circulation of this guide is over 1.75 million. *$24.00*
Monthly

3129 Communicator
Radio Television News Directors Association
1600 K Street NW
Suite 700
Washington, DC 20006
202-968-8897
FAX: 202-223-4007 800-807-8632
rtnda@rtnda.org www.rtnda.org
Barbara S Cochran, Publisher
Sarah Stump, Managing Editor
The latest information on technological breakthroughs, cutting edge newsroom practices, and contemporary management techniques. *$ 75.00*
11x/yr
Circulation: 4,000

3130 DV Digital Video Magazine
Miller Freeman Publications
PO Box 1212
Skokie, IL 60076
888-776-7002
FAX: 847-763-9614 888-776-7002
dv@halldata.com www.dv.com
Dominic Milano, Editorial Director
Armand DerHacobian, Associate Publisher
Jarett Cory, Sales Manager
Video production, animation and audio film, broadcast and new media. Includes discussions on training and communications.
Monthly Founded: 1993
Circulation: 64382

3131 Digital TV/Television Broadcast
United Entertainment Media
460 Park Avenue S
9th Floor
New York, NY 10016
212-378-0400
FAX: 212-378-2158
circulation@cmpinformation.com
www.cmpi-us.com
Marty Porter, VP
Michael Silbergleid, Editor
Jim Maywalt, National Sales Manager
Digital TV/Television Broadcast is an in depth analysis and insider views of the business of television. It discusses the individuals, market trends, technology, products and policies that drive the television industry in the digital age.
Monthly Founded: 1978
Circulation: 22000
Mailing list available for rent

3132 EQ Magazine
Miller Freeman Publications
460 Park Avenue S
9th Floor
New York, NY 10016
212-378-0400
FAX: 212-378-2149
eqmagazine@aol.com
www.eqmag.com/
Valerie Pippin, Publisher
Mitch Gallagher, Editor
Joanne McGowan, Speciality Sales Manager
Articles on recording techniques and tips for musicians, producers, and engineers in the broadcast industry.
Monthly
Circulation: 40000

3133 Electronic Media
Crain Communications
6500 Wilshire Boulevard
Suite 2300
Los Angeles, CA 90048-4947
323-370-2400
FAX: 323-651-3710
info@crain.com www.crain.com
David Klein, Editor
Marc White, Advertising/Sales Manager
Gloria Scoby, Group Publisher
This number one television programming publication is written for the management of broadcast stations and networks. Accepts advertising. *$119.00*
38 pages Weekly Founded: 1916
Circulation: 34801

3134 Emmy Magazine
Academy of Television Arts & Sciences
5220 Lakershim Boulevard
North Hollywood, CA 91601
818-754-2800
FAX: 818-761-2827 818-754-2860
emmymag@emmys.org
www.emmys.com/
Todd Leavitt, President/CEO
Laurel Whitcomb, VP Marketing
Barbara Chase, Director Membership
Juan Morales, Editor
Gail Polevoi, Manager
This magazine tells of association news, EMMY information and awards for the broadcasting and media industries. *$28.00*
Founded: 1995

3135 FTTX
Information Gatekeepers
320 Washington Street
Suite 302
Brighton, MA 02135
617-782-5033
FAX: 617-782-5735 800-323-1088
info@igigroup.com
www.igigroup.com
Paul Polishuk, CEO
Beverly Wilson, Production Manager
Bev Wilson, Marketing
Brian Mark, Editor
Covers developments, products, competition, technology, and standards for the use of fiber optics and related techniques in the cable TV industry. *$695.00*
Monthly Founded: 1977
Circulation: 2000

3136 Financial Manager
Broadcast Cable Financial Management Association
550 Frontage Road
Suite 3600
Northfield, IL 60093
847-960-0200
FAX: 847-716-7004
info@bcfm.com www.bcfm.com
Mary M Collins, CEO
Jamie Smith, Director of Operations
A bi-monthly magazine published by the Broadcast Cable Financial Management Association. *$69.00*
36 pages 6 issues per ye
Circulation: 2000
Mailing list available for rent 1100 names
$495 per M.

3137 Folio
Pacifica Foundation
1925 Martin Luther King Jr Way
Berkeley, CA 94704
510-486-6767

contact@pacifica.org
www.pacifica.org
Richard Wolinsky, Editor
Dan Coughlin, Executive Director
Listing of programs heard on Pacific Radio Stations. *$40.00*
28 pages Monthly Founded: 1949

3138 GBH: Member's Magazine
WGBH Educational Foundation
PO Box 55875
Boston, MA 02205-5875
617-300-5400
FAX: 617-300-1026
feedback@wgbh.org www.wgbh.org
Diane Dion, Editor
Jon Abbott, President
Offers information on station programming, personalities and more for members of WGBH, Boston's PBS and NPR station. *$50.00*
Monthly Founded: 1951
Circulation: 175000

3139 Hits Magazine
Color West
3405 Pacific Avenue
Burbank, CA 91505
818-840-8881
FAX: 818-840-2753
chris.oshaunnessy@colorwestprinting.com www.colorwestprinting.com
Dennis Lavinthal, Publisher
Lynn Jensen, President
Karen Jensen, Controller
Chartmakers and hits in contemporary pop music, industry news and happenings, also includes radio news and playlists. *$300.00*
Weekly Founded: 1971
Circulation: 10000

3140 Inside Radio
Inside Radio
365 Union Street
Littleton, NH 03561
603-444-5720
FAX: 603-444-2872 800-248-4242
streaming@insideradio.com
www.insideradio.com
Jerry Del Colliano, Publisher
Tom Taylor, Editor/Circulation Manager
Gene Mckay, General Manager
Features issues that effect the radio industry and individuals involved in it. *$455.00*

Daily
Circulation: 7000

3141 International Cable
Phillips Business Information
1201 Seven Locks Road
Potomac, MD 20854-2931
301-354-1400
FAX: 301-340-0542
intcatv@aol.com www.phillips.com
Nancy Umberger-Maynard, Publisher
Articles on technological advances internationally and the businesses that are making it possible. *$73.75*
Monthly
Circulation: 11,000

3142 Journal of Broadcasting and Electronic Media
Broadcast Education Association
1771 N Street NW
Washington, DC 20036-2812
202-295-5355
FAX: 301-869-8608 888-380-7222
Don.Godfrey@asu.edu
www.beaweb.org
Louisa A Nielsen, Executive Director
Steven D Anderson, President
Donald G Godfrey, Editor *$50.00*
Quarterly Founded: 1955
Printed in 1 color on matte stock

3143 Journal of College Radio
Intercollegiate Broadcasting System
367 Windsor Highway
New Windsor, NY 12553-7900
845-534-0003
FAX: 845-565-7446
IBSHQ@aol.com
www.collegeradio.tv/
Norman Prusslin, President
Jeff Tellis, VP
Magazine of the nonprofit association of student staffed radio stations based at schools and colleges across the country. Accepts advertising. *$20.00*
24 pages Quarterly Founded: 1940

3144 Journal of Radio Studies
Broadcast Education Association
1771 N Street NW
Washington, DC 20036-2891
202-295-5355
FAX: 202-775-2981 888-380-7222
beainfo@beaweb.org
www.beaweb.org
Louisa A Nielsen, Executive Director
Suzanne Charlick, Administrative Assistant
Douglas A Ferguson, Editor
Steven D. Anderson, President *$30.00*
Bi-annually Founded: 1955 1300 names $100 per M.

3145 Journal of the Audio Engineering Society
Audio Engineering Society
60 E 42nd Street
#2520
New York, NY 10165-2520
212-661-8528
FAX: 212-682-0477
hq@aes.org www.aes.org
Daniel R. vo Recklinghausen, Editor
William T McQuaide, Managing Editor
Gerri M Calamusa, Senior Editor
Mary Ellen Ilich, Associate Editor
Theresa Leonard, President
Journal for professionals in the audio engineering field and its allied arts, scientific advancements, theoretical and practical applications. *$190.00*
Monthly Founded: 1955
Circulation: 12000
Printed in 4 colors on glossy stock

3146 Ku-Band World Magazine
Opportunities Publishing
305 Jackson Avenue W
Oxford, MS 38655-2154

FAX: 662-236-5541
Ed Meek, Editor
Business application of developing Ku-band satellite communications systems. *$25.00*
52 pages Monthly Founded: 1985

3147 Millimeter Magazine
2104 Harvell Circle
Bellevue, NE 68005
402-505-7100
FAX: 402-293-0741 866-505-7173
llcs@pbsub.com www.millimeter.com

Cynthia Wisehart, Editorial Director
Gayle Grooms, Audience Marketing
Christina Heil, Marketing
Jeff Victor, Associate Editor
Authoritative resource for more than 33,000 qualified professionals in production, postproduction, animation, streaming and visual effects for motion pictures, television and commercials. *$25.00*
150 pages Monthly

3148 NRB Magazine
National Religious Broadcasters
9510 Technology Drive
Manassas, VA 20110
703-330-7000
FAX: 703-330-7100
cpryor@nrb.org www.nrb.org
Dr Frank Wright, President
Christine L Pryor, Managing Editor
Steve Cross, Director of Marketing
Trade publication for Christian communicators, including radio, TV, Internet and international media. *$24.00*
56 pages Monthly Founded: 1969
Circulation: 9000
Printed in 4 colors on glossy stock : Online

3149 QST
American Radio Relay League
225 Main Street
Newington, CT 06111-1494
860-594-0200
FAX: 860-594-0259 800-326-3942
hq@arrl.org www.arrl.org
Steve Ford, Editor
Jim Haynie, President
Devoted to amateur radio information.
Monthly Founded: 1914

3150 R&B Airplay Monitor
VNU Business Media
770 Broadway
New York, NY 10003
646-545-5100

bmcomm@vnuinc.com
www.vnubusinessmedia.com
Jon Guynn, Publisher
Howard Lander, President
Michael Marchesano, CEO
Articles on music artist, producers, and R&B radio executives and programmers. Includes how they are being played on radio stations.
Weekly Founded: 1964
Circulation: 5300

3151 RPM Weekly
Novasound Productions
PO Box 630071
Irving, TX 75063-71
972-432-8100
FAX: 972-432-8102
jv@rapmag.com www.rapmag.com
Jerry Vigil, Publisher
Shardan Azat, Manager
Information on radio stations and independent production houses, engineering and production directors that manage these studios, industry news and latest technology information. *$115.00*
Monthly Founded: 1988
Circulation: 7500

3152 Radio
1930 Century Park W
Los Angeles, CA 90067-6803
323-263-6991
FAX: 310-203-8450
Dwight Case, Editor
A magazine covering all aspects of the radio communications industry. *$215.00*
Monthly Founded: 1973

3153 Radio Science
American Geophysical Union
2000 Florida Avenue NW
Washington, DC 20009-1277
202-462-6900
FAX: 202-328-0566 800-966-2481
service@agu.org www.agu.org
Tarek M Habashy, Editor
John Orcutt, President
Coverage of radio propagation, communication, and upper atmospheric physics. *$10.00*
Founded: 1919
Circulation: 1200

3154 Radio-TV Interview Report
Bradley Communications
135 East Plumstead Ave
PO Box 1206
Lansdowne, PA 19050-8206
610-591-1070
FAX: 610-284-3704
Circ@rtir.com www.rtir.com
Bill Harrison, President
A source for finding authors and experts to interview about a wide variety of subjects.
88 pages Monthly Founded: 1986
Circulation: 4000

3155 Rock Airplay Monitor
VNU Business Media
770 Broadway
New York, NY 10003-9595
646-545-5100
800-562-2706
monitor@espcomp.com
www.vnuemedia.com
Scott McKenzie, Editor-in-Chief
Katie Hasty, Online Editor
Sam Bell, Dir, Business Development
Paul Leakas, Group Brand Manager
Howard Lander, President
Information on the latest changes facing rock music business, also airplay reports, radio development, trend and personality features. *$299.00*
Weekly Founded: 1964
Circulation: 5,000

3156 Satellite Retailer
Triple D Publishing
1300 S Dekalb Street
Shelby, NC 28152-7210
704-482-9673
FAX: 704-484-9676

Christopher Schulthesis, Editor

Edited for the satellite industry. *$12.00*
72 pages Monthly Founded: 1985

3157 Satvision Magazine
Satellite Broadcasting/Communications Association
1730 M Street
Suite 600
Washington, DC 20036
202-349-3620
FAX: 202-349-3621
info@sbca.org www.sbca.com

Chuck Hewitt, President

Offers information for television satellite dealers. *$35.00*
Monthly
Circulation: 10000

3158 Secure Signals
National Cable Television Association
1724 Massachusetts Avenue NW
Washington, DC 20036-1969
202-753-3595
FAX: 202-775-3692

James S Allen, Editor

Covers legal aspects of theft of cable television services and how to prevent it from happening.
Quarterly
Circulation: 4,000

3159 Society of Motion Picture & Television Engineers Magazine
3 Barker Ave
White Plains, NY 10601-1509
914-761-1100
FAX: 914-761-3115
smpte@smpte.org www.smpte.org

Frederick C Motts, Executive Director
David Juhren, Director of Publications
Dianne Ross Purrier, Managing Editor

Magazine published by Society of Motion Pictures and Television Engineers. Subscription price: $140 US; $155 foreign. *$140.00*
Monthly Founded: 1916
Circulation: 10000 8600 names
Printed in on glossy stock

3160 Teleguia USA: Novedades USA - Buscando Amor
Lancer Productions
1241 S Soto Street
Suite 213
Los Angeles, CA 90023
323-881-6515
FAX: 323-881-6524 teleguia@aol.com

John DiCarlo, Publisher
Elizabeth DiCarlo, Editor
Lorena Mata, Office Manager

Weekly Founded: 1986
Circulation: 100,000
Printed in 4 colors on newsprint stock

3161 Via Satellite
Phillips Business Information
1201 Seven Locks Rd
Ste 300
Potomac, MD 20854
301-541-1400
FAX: 301-309-3847
www.kftv.com/company-30086.html

Scott Chase, Publisher

Covers voice, video and data in global commercial communications, including company profiles, market analysis and new products. *$ 49.00*
Monthly
Circulation: 17446

3162 WNYC Wavelength
1 Centre Street
New York, NY 10007-1602
212-669-7800
FAX: 212-669-3312

Deborah Thomas, Executive Editor
Laura Walker, President

Relays broadcasting news. Accepts advertising.
16 pages Monthly

3163 Wireless Pay TV International
Bobit Publishing Company
3520 Challenger Street
Torrance, CA 90503-1711
310-533-2400
FAX: 310-533-2504
wireless@bobit.com

Catherine Upton, Publisher
Ed Bobit, Chairman/CEO
Ty Bobit, President and COO
Rick Johnson, CFO

Operational, technological and regional issues are covered along with topics that keep readers aware of pressing concerns.
Founded: 1961
Circulation: 8000

3164 Women on the Job: Careers in the Electronic Media
American Women in Radio and Television

8405 Greensboro Drive
Suite 800
McLean, VA 22102
703-506-3290
FAX: 703-506-3266
info@awrt.org www.awrt.org
Association news focusing on women in the workplace, particularly media and communications industries.

3165 World Screen News
1123 Broadway
Suite 401
New York, NY 10010-2007
212-924-7620
FAX: 212-924-6940
wsninc@aol.com
www.worldscreen.com

Richard Guise, President
Anna Carugati, Editor
Ricardo Duise, Manager

Serves the international television cable and satellite industries including advertising agencies within the industry and others allied to the field. Also publishes the following supplements; TV Kids, TV Europe, TV Docs, TV Latina. *$50.00*
Monthly Founded: 1985
Circulation: 4038

3166 WorldRadio
2628 El Camino Ave
Ste A6
Sacramento, CA 95821-5925
916-457-3655
FAX: 916-457-7339 877-472-8643
generalinfo@wr6wr.com
www.wr6wr.com

Armond Noble, Publisher

Features new ideas, news and stories for amateur radio enthusiasts, as well as the latest on public service and emergency preparations. *$16.00*
64 pages Monthly Founded: 1971
Circulation: 31000
Printed in 1 color on newsprint stock

Trade Shows

3167 Annual Community Radio Conference
Fort Mason Center
Building D
San Francisco, CA 94123
415-771-0400
FAX: 415-771-4343
nfcb@aol.com www.nfcb.org

Carol Pierson, President/CEO
Virginia Z Berson, VP Federation Services

National conference for public community radio stations with many workshops, training sessions, plenaries, etc. Exhibit area programming awards. Business meetings for National Federation of Community Broadcasters. There will be 25-35 Booths
300 Attendees April

3168 Association of Local Television Stations Annual Conference
1320 19th Street NW
Suite 300
Washington, DC 20036
202-296-3560
FAX: 202-887-0950
altv@aol.com www.altv.com

Norbert Kraich, Executive Director

Exhibits of commercial, local television broadcasting stations not affiliated with NBC, ABC television networks, national sales representatives, program distributors and other professional groups in the industry.

3169 Atlantic Cable Show
6900 Grove Road
Thorofare, NJ 08086-9447
856-848-8497
FAX: 856-848-5274

Jan Sharley, Marketing Manager

Three hundred thirty five booths of cable-related companies and products.
4M Attendees October

3170 Broadcast Cable Financial Management Association
550 W Frontage Rd
Ste 3600
Northfield, IL 60093-1243
847-716-7000
FAX: 847-716-7004
info@bcfm.com www.bcfm.com

Mary Collins, President/CEO
Mary Teister, Meetings Manager
Charlie Warner, Conference Coordinator

Annual conference with 50 plus booths for financial and business executives from television, radio and cable networks. Products/services of 10-50 vendors include software, investment/tax services, insurance, banking and collection agencies.
800 Attendees May 1,200 names $495 per M.

3171 **Broadcast Designers' Association International Conference & Expo**
Broadcast Designers' Association International
145 W 45th Street
Room 1100
New York, NY 10036-4008
212-376-6222
FAX: 212-376-6202
Annual show and exhibits of broadcast design equipment, supplies and services.

3172 **Cable Television Association: New England**
100 Grandview Road
Braintree, MA 02184-2686
781-843-3418
FAX: 781-849-6267
Rosemary Vozzella
One hundred booths.
1.1M Attendees July

3173 **Cable Television Trade Show and Convention: East**
Convention Show Management Company
6175 Barfield Road NE
Suite 220
Atlanta, GA 30328-4327
404-252-2454
FAX: 404-252-0215
Nancy Horne, Show Manager
Nine hundred booths.
6M Attendees August

3174 **Cable and Satellite: European Broadcasting/Communications Show**
Reed Exhibition Companies
255 Washington Street
Newton, MA 02458-1637
617-584-4900
FAX: 617-630-2222
Elizabeth Hitchcock, International Sales
Communications forum for professionals in the broadcasting industry.
7.9M Attendees April

3175 **Country Radio Broadcasters**
819 18th Avenue S
Nashville, TN 37203-3227
615-327-4487
FAX: 615-329-4492 www.crb.org
Ed Salamon, Executive Director
Broadcasting forum.
2,000 Attendees March

3176 **GA Radio/TV Institute**
8010 Roswell Road
Suite 260
Atlanta, GA 30350-7019
770-395-7200
FAX: 770-395-7235
Bill Sandra, President
Containing 20 booths and 20 exhibits.
250 Attendees February Founded: 1936

3177 **Great Lakes Broadcasting Conference & Expo**
Society of Broadcast Engineers
9247 N Meridian Street
Suite 305
Indianapolis, IN 46260-2454
317-846-9000
FAX: 317-846-9120 800-968-7622
lbaun@sbe.org
www.michmab.com/conferences/glbcmain.html
Raymond Benedict, President
John Poray, Executive Director
Offers broadcast engineers the opportunity to attend educational sessions, see the latest equipment and supplies, and meet with peers. *$249.00*
Annual
Mailing list available for rent 5700 names $170 per M.

3178 **Intercollegiate Broadcasting Systems Convention**
367 Windsor Highway
New Windsor, NY 12553-7900
845-565-0003
FAX: 845-565-7446
IBSHQ@aol.com www.ibsradio.org
Jeffrey Tellis, President
Twenty booths for those involved in programming and operation of college radio stations.
1.2M Attendees March

3179 **MIP-TV: International Television Program Market**
Reed Exhibition Companies
255 Washington Street
Newton, MA 02458-1637
617-584-4900
FAX: 617-630-2222
Elizabeth Hitchcock, International Sales
Spring market for the television industry to buy, sell and distribute television programming.
9M Attendees April

3180 **NATPE**
5757 Wilshire Boulevard
Suite PH10
Los Angeles, CA 90036
310-453-4440
FAX: 310-453-5258
info@natpe.org www.natpe.org
Nick Orfanopoulos, Senior VP Exhibitions
Beth Braen, Senior VP Marketing
The National Association of Television Program Executives (NATPE) is a global alliance of business professionals engaged in the creation, development and distribution of content as well as advertising and financial activities. NATPE is the world's largest non-profit association dedicated to facilitating the continued growth and convergence of all content across all distribution platforms.
8000 Attendees January Founded: 1963

3181 **NATPE: The Alliance of Media Content**
2425 Olympic Boulevard
Suite 600-E
Santa Monica, CA 90404-4034
310-453-4440
FAX: 310-453-5258 800-NAT-PEGO
info@natpe.org www.natpe.org
Nick Orfanapeulos, Senior VP Exhibitions
Beth Braen, Senior VP Marketing
The National Association of Television Program Executives (NATPE) is a global alliance of business professionals engaged in the creation, development and distribution of content as well as advertising and financial activities. NATPE is the world's largest non-profit association dedicated to facilitating the continued growth and convergence of all content across all distribution platforms.
1000 Attendees January Founded: 1963

3182 **National Broadcasters Association Annual Conference and Expo**
1771 N Street NW
Washington, DC 20036
202-429-5300
FAX: 202-429-4199
nab@nab.org www.nab.org
Jank Roeder, VP Convention
Electronic media show held in Las Vegas.
48M Attendees April

3183 **National Cable Television Association**
National Cable Television Association
1724 Massachusetts Avenue NW
Washington, DC 20036-1969
202-753-3595
FAX: 202-775-3676 www.ncta.com
Robert Sachs, Chief Executive Officer
Convention newsletter and programs concerning cable television. 2,000 booths.
14M Attendees Spring

3184 **National Public Radio Association**
635 Massachusetts Avenue NW
Washington, DC 20001-3753
202-513-2000
FAX: 202-513-3329 www.npr.org
Alma Long, Show/Conference Manager
Delano E Lewis, President
Kevin Klose, Chief Executive Officer
Seventy five booths for public radio professionals and providers of resource materials for public radio.
1.2M Attendees April/May

3185 **National Religious Broadcasters Annual Convention and Exposition**
National Religious Broadcasters
9510 Technology Drive
Manassas, VA 20110
703-330-7000
FAX: 703-330-7100
info@nrb.org www.nrb.org
David Keith, VP Conventions
Dr Frank Wright, President
Containing 280 exhibits. Broadcast and communications emphasis.
5,700 Attendees February

3186 **OAB Annual Convention & Engineering Conference**
Society of Broadcast Engineers
9247 N Meridian Street
Suite 305
Indianapolis, IN 46260-2454
317-846-9000
FAX: 317-846-9120 800-968-7622
smith@oabok.org www.sbe.org
Raymond Benedict, President
John Poray, Executive Director
Carl Smith, Trade Show Contact
Nancy Struby, Trade Show Contact
Offers broadcast engineers the opportunity to attend educational sessions, see the latest equipment and supplies, and meet with peers. *$200.00*
Annual/April
Mailing list available for rent 5700 names $170 per M.

3187 Radio Advertising Bureau Annual Managing Sales Conference
Radio Advertising Bureau
1320 Greenway Drive
#500
Irving, TX 75038
972-536-6700
FAX: 972-753-6727 800-232-3131
MLevy@RAB.com www.rab.com
Mark Levy, VP/GSM
Mike Mahone, Manager
International gathering of radio professionals wtih classes, speakers and workshops dedicated to helping those professionals write more radio advertising orders and run their properties better.
1600 Attendees

3188 Recruiting Conference and Expo
Kennedy Information
1 Phoenix Mill Lane
Floor 3
Peterborough, NH 03458
603-924-1006
800-531-0007
conferences@kennedyinfo.com
www.recruiting2006.com
Matt Lyons, Director, Recruiting Group
Learn about the winning strategies, best practices, and tools ou will need to succeed in a challenging talent market.
Nov 8-9 2006 New York

3189 Satellite Broadcasting and Communication Association (SBCA)
Show Management & Services
900 Jorie Boulevard
Suite 200
Oak Brook, IL 60523-3835

FAX: 630-990-2077 800-654-9276
Diana Bubalo, Show Manager
Four hundred fifty booths.
2.5M Attendees

3190 Society Cable Telecommunications Engineers
140 Philips Road
Exton, PA 19341-1318
610-363-6888
FAX: 610-363-5898 800-542-5040
info@scte.org www.scte.org
Lori Bower, Director
John Clark, Chief Executive Officer
Five hundred booths and, exhibits featuring telecommunications and programming equipment.
12M Attendees June/May

3191 Society of Motion Picture & Television Engineers Conference
3 Barker Ave
White Plains, NY 10601-1509
914-761-1100
FAX: 914-761-3115
smpte@smpte.org www.smpte.org
Thomas M Jordan, Conference VP
Each year, SMPTE hosts two national conferences. The first, the Advanced Motion Imaging Conference in February, whose site varies each year, allows individuals from different locations and regions to attend and contribute. The second is the Technical Conference and Exhibition which is held in the fall. This alternates between the east and west coasts, usually in Pasadena and New York.
17M Attendees

3192 Television Bureau of Advertising Annual Meeting
Television Bureau of Advertising
3 E 54th Street
New York, NY 10022
212-486-1111
FAX: 212-935-5631
info@tvb.org www.tvb.org
Abby Auerbach, Executive VP
Gary Belis, VP Communications
Annual show of 20-25 exhibitors of services for television stations, including research, sales and management training programs, incentives, collection agencies, advertiser contests and computer software.

3193 Western Cable Television Conference and Expo
Trade Associates
11820 Parklawn Drive
Suite 250
Rockville, MD 20852-2505
301-519-1610

Susan Rosenstock, Expo Director
One thousand three hundred booths featuring exhibits of programming, mobile aerial devices, video equipment and products and services for the communications and related industry fields.
10M Attendees November/December

3194 Western Show
Trade Associates
11820 Parklawn Drive
Suite 250
Rockville, MD 20852-2505
301-519-1610
FAX: 301-468-3662
Susan Rosenstock, Director
One thousand booths featuring exhibits from cable operators and suppliers to the cable industry. The California Cable Television Association and the Arizona Cable Television Association sponsor this annual event.
10M Attendees December

Directories & Databases

3195 AV Market Place
Information Today
143 Old Marlton Pike
Medford, NJ 08055-8750
609-654-6266
FAX: 609-654-4309
custserv@inftoday.com
www.infotoday.com
Thomas H Hogan, Publisher/President
John Bryans, Publisher/Editor-in-Chief
Books
The complete business directory of audio, audio visual, computersystems, film, video, and programming with industry yellow pages. The only guide needed to mind more than 7,500 companies that create, apply, or distribute AV equipment and services for business, education, science, and government. *$199.95*
1700 pages February ISBN 1-573871-87-7

3196 Arbitron Radio County Coverage
Arbitron Company
142 W 57th Street
New York, NY 10019-3300
212-887-1300
FAX: 212-887-1558 www.arbitron.com
Stephen Morris, Chief Executive Officer
This database offers access to audience listening estimates by county.
Statistical

3197 Bacon's Newspaper & Magazine Directories
Bacon's Publishing Company
332 S Michigan Avenue
Chicago, IL 60604-4434
312-228-8239
800-621-0561
info@bacons.com www.bacons.com
Ruth McFarland, VP/Publisher
Stephen Newman, Chief Executive Officer
Two volume set listing all daily and community newspapers, magazines and newsletters, news service and syndicates, syndicated columists, complete editorial staff listings of each publication provided, covers US, Canada, Mexico,and Carribean
$350.00
4,700 pages Annual Founded: 1951
Printed in 1 color on matte stock : internet

3198 Broadcast Engineering Equipment Reference Manual
Primedia
9800 Metcalf Avenue
Overland Park, KS 66212
913-341-1300
FAX: 913-967-1898
www.primediabusiness.com
Carl Bentz, Editor
Offers a list of more than 1,400 manufacturers and distributors of communications equipment for radio, television and recording applications. *$20.00*
Annual
Circulation: 35,500

3199 Broadcasting & Cable Yearbook
R.R. Bowker LLC
630 Central Avenue
New Providence, NJ 07974-1541
908-861-1090
FAX: 908-464-3553 800-269-5372
info@bowker.com www.bowker.com
Focused exclusively on the broadcasting industry, particularly cable television.
$159.95

Circulation: 15,000

3200 Burrelle's Broadcast Media Directory
Burrelle's Information Services
75 E Northfield Road
Livingston, NJ 07039
973-992-6600
FAX: 973-992-7675 800-631-1160
Robert Waggoner, Chief Executive Officer
This database contains the complete text of more than 150,000 transcripts representing all of the regularly scheduled news and public affairs programs. *$425.00*
Annual

3201 CPB Public Broadcasting Directory

Corporation for Public Broadcasting
901 E Street NW
Washington, DC 20004-2037
202-879-9600
FAX: 202-879-9700
Offers information on public television stations, national and regional public broadcasting association and networks. *$15.00*

152 pages Annual
Circulation: 14,000

3202 **Cable Online Data Exchange**
Nielsen Media Research
770 Broadway
New York, NY 10003
646-548-8300
FAX: 646-654-8363
www.nielsenmedia.com
This database contains information on more than 10,000 US cable television system franchises.
Numeric

3203 **Cable TV Facts**
Cable TV Advertising Bureau
757 3rd Avenue
5th Floor
New York, NY 10017-2013
212-508-1200
FAX: 212-832-3268
www.cabletvadbureau.com
Offers a list of ad-supported cable networks. *$8.00*
Annual

3204 **Directory of Field Contacts for the Coordination of the Use of Radio**
Federal Communications Commission
445 12th Street SW
Washington, DC 20554
202-180-0450
FAX: 866-418-0232
fccinfo@fcc.gov www.fcc.com
Radio frequency coordinating agencies are listed.
170 pages Annual

3205 **Directory of Religious Media**
National Religious Broadcasters
9510 Technology Drive
Manassas, VA 20110
703-330-7000
FAX: 703-330-7100
info@nrb.org www.nrb.org
Karl Stoll, Director Communications
10 per year

3206 **Editors Guild Directory**
Motion Picture Editors Guild
7715 Sunset Boulevard
Suite 200
Hollywood, CA 90046
323-876-4770
FAX: 323-876-0861
www.editorsguild.com
Lisa Churgin, Guild President
Dede Allen, VP
Diane Adler, Secretary
Rachel Igel, Treasurer
Tris Carpenter, Manager
An invaluable resource for producers, directors and post production professionals alike. It lists contact, credit, award and classification information for all of the Guild's active members at the time of publication, as well as a list of Oscar and Emmy winners for every year since the awards began. It also include a retirees section. *$25.00*

3207 **GMRS National Repeater Guide**
Personal Radio Steering Group
PO Box 2851
Ann Arbor, MI 48106-2851
734-662-4533

Corwin Moore, Administrative Director
Lists the 3,500 GMRS repeaters nationally, along with names and addresses of station licensees.
Monthly

3208 **Gale Directory of Publications and Broadcast Media**
Gale Research
27500 Drake Road
Farmington Hills, MI 48331
248-699-4253
FAX: 248-699-8214 800-877-4253
galeord@gale.com www.gale.com
Allen Paschal, Chief Executive Officer
Carolyn Fischer, Editor
Approximately 35,000 publications and broadcasting stations, including newspapers, magazines, journals, radio stations, television stations and cable systems in the US and Canada. *$440.00*
Annual

3209 **International Motion Picture Almanac Intern Televesion & Video Almanac**
Quigley Publishing Company, Incorporated
64 Wintergreen Lane
Groton, MA 01450
978-448-0272
FAX: 978-448-9325
quigleypub@aol.com
www.quigleypublishing.com
William J Quigley, President/Publisher
Eileen Quigley, Editor
Aaron D Pinkham, Associate Editor/Ops Manager
Dee Quigley, Contributingt Editor
Invaluable completely updated information to the most sucscessful people in the business. Are you one of them? With thousands of corporations, 5,000 plus career profiles and the most comprehensive information available on the second largest industry in the US. *$150.00*
780 pages Annual 49th Editor Founded: 1915 ISBN 0-900610-74-3 780 names

3210 **Kagan Media Index**
Kagan World Media
126 Clock Tower Place
Carmel, CA 93923-8746
831-624-1536
FAX: 831-625-3225
info@kagan.com www.kagan.com
George Niesen, Editor
Tom Johnson, Marketing Manager
The most comprehensive collection of media industry databases found anywhere. Current estimates of industry growth for a dozen different media businesses, shown on a 145-line spreadsheet, projected forward and updated monthly. Three month trial available. *$795.00*
Monthly

3211 **National Radio Publicity Outlets**
Volt Directory Marketing
1800 Byberry Road
Suite 800
Huntingdon Valley, PA 19006-3520

FAX: 610-832-0878 800-677-3839
Offers valuable information on over 7,000 radio stations in all major United States and Canadian markets. *$188.00*
640 pages SemiAnnual

3212 **Radio & Records**
Radio & Records
10100 Santa Monica Boulevard
5th Floor
Los Angeles, CA 90067-4003
310-553-4330
FAX: 310-203-8450
moreinfo@rronline.com
www.rronline.com
Erica Farber, Publisher/CEO
Sky Daniels, General Manager
Ron Rodriguez, Editor-in-Chief
Page Beaver, Operations Manager
Henry Mowry, Sales Executive
A music newspaper that covers all aspects of the radio and recording industry. *$299.00*
BiAnnual
Circulation: 10,000

3213 **Radio Advertising Source**
Standard Rate & Data Services
1700 Higgins Road
Des Plaines, IL 60018-5605
847-375-5000
FAX: 847-375-5001 800-851-7737
Tom Drouillar, CEO
Ruth Harman, Marketing Coordinator
Print and online service provides complete planning information on AM/FM commercial radio stations. This proprietary database contains format detail, demographics and contact information. Access to the most current, accurate data from SRDS makes broadcast planning and buying efficient. *$579.00*
1,489 pages Online/Print Quarterly
Founded: 1919
Mailing list available for rent

3214 **Radio Talk Shows Need Guests**
Pacesetter Publications
PO Box 101330
Denver, CO 80250-1330
303-722-7200
FAX: 303-733-2626
jsabah@aol.com www.joesabah.com
Over 950 radio talk shows that interview guests over the telephone are profiled. *$198.00*
SemiAnnual Founded: 1992 $198 per M.

3215 **Radio and Television Career Directory**
Gale Research
27500 Drake Road
Farmington Hills, MI 48331
248-699-4253
FAX: 248-699-8214 800-877-4253
galeord@gale.com www.gale.com
Stations, networks and trade organizations offering entry-level positions. *$17.95*
335 pages Cloth

3216 **TV Cable Publicity Guide**
Volt Directory Marketing
1 Sentry Parkway
Blue Bell, PA 19422
610-825-7720
FAX: 610-835-0878
Over 5,000 cable and broadcast television stations and systems are profiled. *$188.00*
545 pages SemiAnnual

3217 **Talk Show Selects**
Broadcast Interview Source
2233 Wisconsin Avenue NW
Suite 301
Washington, DC 20007-4132
202-333-4904
FAX: 202-342-5411 800-932-7266
davis@yearbook.com
www.yearbook.com

Mitchell Davis, Production Manager

More than 700 contacts at radio and television talk shows. *$185.00*

240 pages Annual Founded: 1984 ISBN 0-934333-35-1 $280 per M.
Printed in on matte stock

3218 Television Yearbook
BIA Research
15120 Enterprise Court
Suite 100
Chantilly, VA 20151-1217
703-188-8115
FAX: 703-803-3299 800-331-5086
pob@bia.com www.bia.com

Thomas Buono, Editor

US television markets and their inclusive stations, television equipment manufacturers and related service providers and trade associations. *$64.00*

Annual

3219 Television and Cable Factbook
Warren Communications News
2115 Ward Court NW
Washington, DC 20037-1209
202-872-9200
FAX: 202-293-3435
info@warren-news.com
www.warren-news.com

Michael Taliaferro, Senior Editor
Marla Shepard, Senior Editor
Gina Storr, Director Sales/Marketing

Commercial and noncommercial television stations and networks are profiled in this comprehensive directory. Educational and instructional stations are also included as one of the many categories of information. *$595.00*

10M pages 5 Volumes Founded: 1932
Computerized version available: CD ROM

3220 Top 200 National TV, News, Talk and Magazine Shows
Todd Publications
PO Box 635
Nyack, NY 10960-0635
845-358-6213
FAX: 845-358-6213 800-747-1056

B Klein, Publisher

The 200 most popular information shows on US television. *$40.00*

Annual

3221 World Broadcast News: International 500 Issue
Primedia
9800 Metcalf Avenue
Overland Park, KS 66212
913-341-1300
FAX: 913-967-1898
www.primediabusiness.com
Directory of services and supplies to the industry. *$10.00*

Annual

3222 World Radio TV Handbook
VNU Business Media
770 Broadway
New York, NY 10003
646-654-5100

bmcomm@vnuinc.com www.vnu.com
Directory of services and supplies to the industry. *$19.95*

610 pages Annual
Circulation: 75,000

Industry Web Sites

3223 www.aicp.com
Association of Independent Commercial Producers

Founded in 1972 by a small group of television commercial production companies concerned with a single issue, today's AICP has grown to represent exclusively, the interests of US companies that specialize in producing commercials on various media - film, video, computer- for advertisers and their agencies. AICP members account for 85 percent of all domestic commercials aired nationally, whether produced for traditional braodcast channels or nontraditional use.

3224 www.alliancecm.org
Alliance for Community Media

Committed to assuring everyone's access to electronic media. The Alliance advances this goal through public education, a progressive legislative and regulatory agenda, coalition building and grassroots organizing. A nonprofit, national membership organization founded in 1976, the Alliance represents over 1,000 Public, Educational and Govermental (PEG) access organizations and community media centers throughout the country.

3225 www.americansportscasters.com
American Sportscasters Association

National Association of Sportscasters, radio, television and cablecovering the United States, Puerto Rico, and Canada. Very active Web site. Offers seminars, compiles statistics and operates a placement service, maintains a Hall of Fame and biographical archives and library.

3226 www.amptp.org
Alliance of Motion Picture & Television Producers

Trade association with respect to labor issues in the motion picture and television industry. We negotiate 80 industry wide collective bargaining agreements that cover actors, craftspersons, directors, musicians, technicians and writers — virtually all of the people who work on theatrical motion pictures and television programs. In these negotiations, the AMPTP represents over 350 production companies and studios.

3227 www.apts.org
Association of Public Televsion Stations

Nonprofit membership organization established in 1980 to support the continued growth and development of a strong and financially sound noncommercial television service for the American public. We provide advocacy for public television interests at the national level, as well as consistent leadership and information in marshalling grassroots and congressional support for its members: the nation's public television stations.

3228 www.bcfm.com
Broadcast Cable Financial Management Association

A professional society of over 1,200 of television, radio and cable TV's top financial, MIS and HR executives, plus associates in auditing, data processing, software development, credit and collections.

3229 www.bdaonline.org
Broad Designers Association

For broadcast designers. Conferences annually in Asia, Australia, Europe, South and North America.

3230 www.ctam.com
Cable Telecommunications Association for Marketing

Dedicated to the discipline and development of consumer marketing excellence in cable television, new media and telecommunication services. Members have the advantage of progressive research, insightful publications and forward thinking conferences all designed to help you and your company gain a competitive edge.

3231 www.emmyonline.org
National Academy of Television Arts & Sciences

Dedicated to the advancement of the arts and sciences of television to the advancement of the arts and sciences of television and the promotion of creative leadership for artistic, educational and technical achievements within the television industry. It recognizes excellence in television with the coveted Emmy Award.

3232 www.genehrts.com
Hollywood Radio and Television Society

Featuring top industry and government speakers and seminars about broadcasting, maintains film and audio library.

3233 www.gita.org
Geospatial Information & Technology Association

Our site has been created with the intent of providing you a variety of information and useful references for your professional and technical needs. We'll do our best to keep this site fresh with descriptions of new programs and services, while also providing you with a stable source of important member contacts, industry news and association related ongoing programs.

3234 www.greyhouse.com
Grey House Publishing

Selected Grey House directories in the fields of business, health and education are available online. Users can search our online databases by several different search criteria, such as product categories, geographic area, sales volume and much, much more. Full Grey House catalog and online ordering also available.

3235 www.halloffame.com
National Sportscasters & Sportswriters Association

3236 www.i-newsrelease.com
Tellmedia Communications

Media research, Internet news, satelite media tours and video news releases.

3237 www.iabm.com
International Association of Broadcast Monitors

Website of world wide trade association made up of news retrieval services which monitor television, radio, Internet and print news mediums.

3238 www.ibsradio.org
Intercollegiate Broadcasting System

For college and university broadcasting stations.

3239 www.iemmys.tv
International Television Academy

Organization of global broadcasters, with representatives from over 50 countries. Sixty percent of the 100-member board of directors come from countries outside the US, and represent the world's largest production, distribution and broadcast companies.

3240 www.irts.org
Int'l Radio & Television Society Foundation

For professionals in radio, broadcast and cable televison, corporate video production, collaborative communication, DVD and new media production, marketing and advertising plus related areas, as well as interested laypeople. The organization provides a unique forum for all segments of the communication industry.

3241 www.itva.org
Media Communications Association International

Website of the global community of professional devoted to the business and art of visual communication.

3242 www.kagan.com
Kagan World Media

For those interested in investments in radio and TV stations and publicly held companies.

3243 www.lib.umd.edu/LAB
Library of American Broadcasting

Devoted to television and radio broadcasting materials and archives.

3244 www.lostremote.com
Lost Remote

Television industry news, job listings and resources.

3245 www.mediabistro.com
Media Bistro

News and articles especially for those in broadcasting and publishing.

3246 www.millimeter.com
Millimeter Magazine

Authoritative resource for more than 33,000 qualified professionals in production, postproduction, animation, streaming and visual effects for motion pictures, television and commercials.

3247 www.mrfac.com
Manufacturer's Radio Frequency Advisory Committee

Representing the voice of the manufacturing industry and private land mobile radio users before the Federal Communications Commision, the responsible federal regulatory agency for the nation's industrial communications. The leaders of the manufacturing industry, individually and collectively, have an obligation to influence the policies, plans and procedures which govern the growth, structure and use of our national radio spectrum and telecommunications systems.

3248 www.nab.org
National Association of Broadcasters

Full service trade association that represents the interests of free, over-the-air radio and television broadcasters.

3249 www.naed.org
National Association of Electrical Distributors

Nonprofit organization dedicated to serving and protecting the electrical distribution channel. As part of that mission, NAED provides networking opportunities through approximately 50 meetings and conferences a year, training through the NAED Education Foundation, industry information and research through TED Magazine, and a marketing campaign for the industry through the NAED Advocacy Initiative.

3250 www.nafb.org
National Association of Farm Broadcasters

Works to improve quantity and quality of farm programming and serves as a clearinghouse for new ideas in farm broadcasting.

3251 www.natpe.org
Nat'l Association of Television Program Executives

Our mission is a commitment to furthering the quality and quantity of content, which means offering the wealth of our resources and experience to every content creator, no matter what the medium. Because the industry encompasses so much more today than ever before, NATPE too is expanding to accommodate this change and encourage progress while continuing to keep our members constantly appraised of the changes occuring daily in the global environment regardless of the platform used.

3252 www.ncta.com
National Cable & Telecommunications Asssociation

National Cable and Telecommunications Association, formerly the National Cable Television Association, is the principal trade association of the cable television industry in the United States. Founded in 1952, NCTA'S primary mission is to provide its members with a strong national presence by providing a single, unified voice on issues affecting the cable and telecommunications industry.

3253 www.ncti.com
National Cable Television Institute

Independent provider of broadband communications training. Broadband cable system operators, contractors and industry vendors have turned to NCTI to train their employees who construct, operate and maintain broadband systems.

3254 www.nrb.org
National Religious Broadcasters

For religious broadcasters and religious media. Hosts national convention featuring trade show and educational workshops.

3255 www.pcia.com
Personal Communications Industry Association

Represents companies that develop, own, manage and operate towers, commercial rooftops and other facilities for the provision of all types of wireless, broadcasting and telecommunications services. PCIA is dedicated to advancing an understanding of the benefits of wireless services and required infrastructure to local and federal government officials and communities at large.

3256 www.productionhub.com
Production Hub

Television producers' news, listings, classifieds, casting notices and events.

3257 www.rab.cpm
Radio Advertising Bureau

For marketing personnel and raises awareness of radio among advertising and business communities.

3258 www.radiospace.com
North American Network

All information contained is provided to radio stations and networks for their free and unrestricted use.

3259 www.rtndf.org
Radio Television News Directors Association

Provides training programs, seminars, scholarship support and research in areas of critical concern to electronic news professionals and their audience. Offers professional development opportunities for working and aspiring journalists and journalism educators.

3260 www.sacredheartprofram.org
Sacred Heart Hour

Producers and syndicators of Public Service Radio Programs, Contact Radio available in, thirty minute, fifteen minute, five minute versions, Pathways, one minute radio spots.

3261 www.sbca.com
Satellite Broadcasting/Communications Association

National trade association representing all segments of the satellite consumer services industry. The association is committed to expanding the utilization of satellite technology for the delivery of video, data, voice, interactive and broadband services.

3262 www.sbe.org
Society of Broadcast Engineers

Our group and the Advanced Television Systems Committee have established a cooperative educational program intended to assist in the ongoing rollout of digital television.

3263 www.smpte.org
Society of Motion Picture & Television Engineers

3264 www.thirteen.org
Educational Broadcasting Association

For producers and directors of public educational programming, channel 13, PBS.

3265 www.tvspy.com
TVSpy

Television industry news, articles and links to other sites of interest.

Associations

3266 ADSC: International Association of Foundation Drilling
Pacific Center I
14180 Dallas Parkway, Suite 510
Dallas, TX 75254
214-343-2091
FAX: 214-343-2384
adsc@adsc-iafd.com
www.adsc-iafd.com

Scott Litke, Executive Director
Ted Ledgard, Administrative Director

ADSC seeks to advance technology in the foundation of drilling and anchored earth retention industries. Represents drilled shaft and anchored earth retention contractors civil engineers and manufacturing firms world wide.
Founded: 1972

3267 America Seniors Housing Association
5100 Wisconsin Avenue NW
Suite 307
Washington, DC 20036-5816
202-237-0900
FAX: 202-237-1616
www.seniorshousing.org

David S Schless, President
Judy Rainey, VP
Doris K Maultsby, VP Member Services

ASHA members are companies participating in the multi-family seniors housing industry including builders, financers and managers.
Founded: 1991

3268 American Concrete Pipe Association
222 W Las Colinas Boulevard
Suite 641
Irving, TX 75039-5423
972-506-7216
FAX: 972-506-7682
info@concrete-pipe.org
www.concrete-pipe.org

Doug Mohrman, Chairman
Ron Metzger, Vice Chairman
Matt Childs, President
Lynn Schuler, Treasurer
Tom Wheelan, Secretary

Composed primarily of manufacturers of concrete pipe and related conveyance products located throughout the United States, Canada and in over 40 foreign countries.
400 Members Founded: 1907

3269 American Concrete Pressure Pipe Association
11800 Sunrise Valley Drive
Suite 309
Reston, VA 20191
703-391-9135
FAX: 703-391-9136 www.acppa.org

David Prosser, President

Serves as the authoritative voice of the industry.
10 Members Founded: 1949

3270 American Concrete Pumping Association
606 Enterprise Drive
Lewis Center, OH 43035
614-431-5618
FAX: 614-431-6944
christi@concretepumpers.com
www.concretepumpers.com

Christi Collins, Executive Director
Pat Inglese, President
Dennis Andrews, VP
Les Ainsworth, Secretary
Bob Weatherton, Treasurer

Provide education, insurance, marketing and much more to companies involved with the concrete pumping industry. Our dedication to the concrete pumping industry has led us to become a key part in the education of safety and business management to everyone involved, from the operators to the management.
270 Members Founded: 1974

3271 American Congress on Surveying and Mapping
6 Montgomery Village Avenue
Suite 403
Gaithersburg, MD 20879
240-632-9716
FAX: 240-632-1321
curtis.summer@acsm.net
www.acsm.net

Curtis W. Summer, Executive Director
Karen Kerrick, Director of Finance

A professional organization representing those who communicate the earth's spatial information using precisely prepared plats, charts, maps, and digital cartographic and related data systems.
7000 Members Founded: 1941

3272 American Council for Construction Education
1717 N Loop 1604 East
Suite 320
San Antonio, TX 78232-1570
210-495-6161
FAX: 210-495-6168
acce@acce-hq.org www.acce-hq.org

Wilson C Barnes, President
Mark Benjamin, VP
Prof. Murray Jones, Secretary
Dr. Walter Dukes, Treasurer/Chair Finance Committee

The accrediting agency for postsecondary construction education programs. *$150.00*

115 Members Individual Annual Fee
Founded: 1974

3273 American Fence Association
800 Roosevelt Road
Building C-20
Glen Ellyn, IL 60137
630-942-6598
FAX: 630-790-3095
afa@mindspring.com
www.americanfenceassociation.com

Phillip Doyle, President
Kent Bailey, Secretary
Lynn Hayworth, Treasurer
Lee Crumbaugh, Executive Director

Promotes the fence industry, sponsors field training schools and certification programs. Holds management and sales workshops and presents awards. Sponsors FENCETECH convention and trade show.
$365.00
2400 Members Membership Fee Founded: 1962

3274 American Institute of Building Design
2505 Main Street
Suite 209B
Stratford, CT 06615
203-783-3480
FAX: 203-378-3568 800-366-2423
smickley@msn.com www.aibd.org

Lyle Breeze, President
Sam Liberti, Internal VP
Dan Sater, Secretary/Treasurer
Bobbi Morgan, Director of Operations
Steven Mickley, Interim Executive Director

Our members consist of professional building designers and architects, who have for the most part chosen residential design as the focus of their practice.
Founded: 1950

3275 American Institute of Constructors
PO Box 26334
Alexandria, VA 22314
703-683-4999
FAX: 703-683-5480
admin@aicnet.org www.aicnet.org

Steven DeSalvo, President
David R Mattson, VP
Bruce Demeter, Secretary
Steven P. Byrne, Treasurer

An organization established to help individual construction practitioners achieve the professional status they deserve. The Institute is the constructor's counterpart of professional organizations found in architecture, engineering, law and other fields.
Founded: 1971

3276 American Institute of Steel Construction
1 E Wacker Dr
Ste 700
Chicago, IL 60601-2000
312-670-2400
FAX: 312-670-5403 www.aisc.org

James A Stori, Chairman
H Louis Gurthet, President
Lawrence A Cox, Treasurer
David B Ratterman, Secretary/General Counsel
John Devantier, Executive Director

Serving the structural steel industry in the US. Our purpose is to promote the use of structural steel through research activities, market development, education, codes and specifications, technical assistance, quality certifacation and standardization.
2.7M Members Founded: 1921

3277 American Public Works Association
2345 Grand Blvd
Ste 700
Kansas City, MO 64108-2625
816-472-6100
FAX: 816-472-1610 800-848-2792
apwa@apwa.net www.apwa.net

Bob Freudenthal, President
Kaye Sullivan, Deputy Executive Director/COO
David Dancy, Director of Marketing
Daniel Armstrong, Director of Information Technology

An international educational and professional association of public agencies, private sector companies, and individuals dedicated to providing high quality public works goods and services.
26000 Members Founded: 1937

3278 American Society of Heating, Refrigerating and Air-Conditioning Engineers
1791 Tullie Circle, NE
Atlanta, GA 30329
404-636-8400
FAX: 404-321-5478 800-527-4723
ashrae@ashrae.org www.ashrae.org

Kent Peterson, President

3279 **American Society of Heating, Refrigeration and Air Conditioning Engineers**
1791 Tullie Circle NE
Atlanta, GA 30329
404-636-8400
FAX: 404-321-5478 800-527-4723
Lee Burgett, President
Terry Townsend, Treasurer
Jeff Littleton, Secretary
ASHRAE will advance the arts and sciences of heating, ventilation, air conditioning and refrigeration and related human factors to serve the evolving needs of the public and ASHRAE. *$40.00*
Member Dues Founded: 1959

3280 **American Society of Professional Estimators National Roster**
2525 Perimeter Place Drive
Suite 103
Nashville, TN 37214
615-316-9200
FAX: 615-316-9800 888-378-6283
info@aspenational.org
www.aspenational.com
Robert R George, President
Edward Walsh, Executive Director
John Stewart, First VP
Frank A Kutilek, Second Vice President
Patsy Smith, Executive Director, Administration
Serving the construction estimators by providing education, fellowship, and opportunity for professional development.
2500 Members Founded: 1956

3281 **Architectural Woodwork Institute**
46179 Westlake Dr
Ste 120
Sterling, VA 20165-5874
703-733-0600
FAX: 703-733-0584 www.awinet.org
Rick Kogler, President
Ed Brewer, VP
Judith Durham, Executive Vice President
Richard Ungerbuehler Sr., Treasurer
Supports all those involved in wood workshops and woodwork products such as casework, fixtures and panelings, equipment and supplies. Hosts annual trade show.
2800 Members Founded: 1953

3282 **Asbestos Information and Training Centers**
Georgia Institute of Real Estate
5784 Lake Forrest Drive
Atlanta, GA 30328
404-252-6768
FAX: 404-257-0354 800-633-3583
Rebecca Fletcher, Executive Director/VP Education
Brenda Heard, Director of Operations
Sponsors the Regional Asbestos Information and Training Centers. The Centers provide information and training in identification and abatement of asbestos hazards with the ultimate goal of training contractors for eventual certification. Each center offers a variety of specialized courses including identification of asbestos hazards and possible remedies of problems and solutions for those involved in the asbestos hazard abatement process.

3283 **Asphalt Emulsion Manufacturers Association**
3 Church Circle
PO Box 250
Annapolis, MD 21401-1933
410-267-0023
FAX: 410-267-7546
memberservices@aema.org
www.aema.org
John Carrick Jr., President
Robert Koleas, VP
Barry Baughman, Treasurer/Secretary
David H Baker, General Counsel
Michael Krissoff, Executive Director
Representing the asphalt emulsion industry. The mission is to expand the use and applications of asphalt emulsions which are the most environmentally sound, energy efficent and cost effective.
150 Members Founded: 1973

3284 **Asphalt Institute**
2696 Research Park Drive
Lexington, KY 40511
859-288-4960
FAX: 859-288-4999
info@asphaltinstitute.org
www.asphaltinstitute.org
Peter T Grass, President
Bernie McCarthy, VP
Conducts education, research and engineering services related to asphaltic products; conducts seminars and sells publications and videos on asphalt technology.
80+ Members Founded: 1919

3285 **Associated Builders and Contractors**
4250 N Fairfax Drive
9th Floor
Arlington, VA 22203
703-812-2000
FAX: 703-812-8203
gotquestion@abc.org www.abc.org
Kirk Pickerel, President/CEO
Rosita Howell, Executive Assistant
Mike Dunbar, VP
Dennis Weller, Treasurer/Secretary
National trade association representing about 23,000 contractors, subcontractors, material suppliers and related firms from across the country and from all specialties in the construction industry.
23000 Members Founded: 1950

3286 **Associated Building Material Distributors of America**
4500 SW Kruse Way
Suite 340
Lake Oswego, OR 97035
503-635-1252
FAX: 503-635-1254
abmda@earthlink.net
www.abmda.com
Larry Baugh, Executive Vice President
Independent wholesale building material distributors who buy and sell their materials on a cooperative basis.
50 Members Founded: 1975

3287 **Associated Construction Distributors**
1605 SE Deleware Avenue, Suite B
PO Box 14552
Ankeny, IA 50306-3552
515-964-1335
FAX: 515-964-7668
info@acdi.net www.acdi.net
Tom Goetz, Executive VP
Tom Person, Director of Sales/Marketing
Jane Zieser, Controller
Associated Construction Distributors International(ACD) is a co-operative association of independently owned and locally operated distributors of specialty construction products and equipment.
34 Members Founded: 1974

3288 **Associated Equipment Distributors**
615 W 22nd Street
Oak Brook, IL 60523
630-574-0650
FAX: 630-574-0132 800-388-0650
info@aesnet.org www.aednet.org
Toby Mack, President
Sandy Brassel, Executive Assistant
Matt Di Iorio, Staff Vice President P
Pam Gruebnau, Director of Communications
Membership organization of 1,200 independent factory authorized dealers, manufacturers and other organizations involved in the distribution of construction equipment and related products and services in North America and throughout the world.
1200 Members Founded: 1919

3289 **Associated General Contractors of America**
2300 Wilson Blvd
Suite 400
Arlington, VA 22201-5426
703-548-3118
FAX: 703-548-3119
info@agc.org www.agc.org
Kelley Keeler, Senior Director
Carla Julian, Director/Commununications
Jordan Ahmad, Director Publications\Business Deve
Lakisha Campbell, Executive Director Marketing/E-Busi
Carolyn Coker, Executive Director Human Resources
The voice of the construction industry, an organization of qualified construction contractors and industry related companies dedicated to skill, integrity, and responsibility.
33000 Members Founded: 1918

3290 **Association of Equipment Manufacturers**
6737 W Washington St
Milwaukee, WI 53214-5647
414-272-0943
FAX: 414-272-1170 www.aem.org
Dennis Slater, President
John Nowak, Chief Financial Officer
Al Cervero, Senior VP
Luca Lee, Managing Director
Bobbi Klim, Membership Manager
Formed from the consolidation of the Construction Industry Manufacturers Association and Equipment Manufacturers Institute. The international trade and business development resource for companies that manufacture equipment, products and services used worldwide in the construction, agricultural, mining, forestry, and utility fields.
Founded: 2002

3291 **Association of the Wall and Ceiling Industry**
513 W Broad Street
Suite 210
Falls Church, VA 22046
703-534-8300
FAX: 703-534-8307
info@awci.org www.awci.org
Michael Heering, President
Kevin Biddle, VP
Steven A Etkin, Executive VP

Marie Batiste, Executive Assistant/Membership Coor

Represents acoustics systems, ceiling systems, drywall systems, exterior insulation and finishing systems, fireproofing, flooring systems, insulation, and stucco contractors, suppliers and manufacturers and those in allied trades.

2000 Members Founded: 1918

3292 Barre Granite Association
PO Box 481
Barre, VT 05641-4229
802-476-4131
FAX: 802-476-4765
BGA@barregranite.org
www.barregranite.org

Robert Couture, President
John Castaldo, VP/Executive Directors

Manufacturers of cemetery monuments, mausoleums, statuary, landscape and architectural granite products.

35 Members Founded: 1889

3293 Brick Industry Association
11490 Commerce Park Drive
Reston, VA 20191-1525
703-620-0010
FAX: 703-620-3928
brickinfo.com www.gobrick.com

Richard Jennison, President/CEO
Sandy Speer, Executive Assistant
Kathy Curtis, VP
Joseph Casper, VP of Environmental Health

National trade association representing distributors and manufacturers of clay brick and suppliers of related products and services. The Association is involved in a broad range of technical, research, marketing, government relations and communications activities. It is the recognized national authority on brick construction.

50 Members Founded: 1935

3294 Bridge Grid Flooring Manufacturers Association
201 Castle Drive
West Mifflin, PA 15122
412-469-3985
FAX: 412-469-3985
bgfma@aol.com
www.abcdpittsburgh.org

Gary B O'Melia, President
Jane Ann Patton, Secretary
William G Ferko, Treasurer

Comprised of companies who manufacture steel grid flooring systems for bridges, and other companies with an interest in the steel grid market. The role of the Association is to promote the use of Grid Reinforced Concrete Bridge Decks through data collection, research/ development, and education.

3 Members

3295 Building Industry Association of Southern California
1330 Valley Vista Drive
Diamond Bar, CA 91765
909-396-9993
FAX: 909-396-1571
lconti@biasc.org www.biasc.org

John Young, President
Dan Leigh, First VP
Richard Lambros, Chief Executive Officer
Dan Leigh, Secretary/Treasurer
Linda Conti, Membership Director

To promote and protect the industry to ensure our member's success in providing homes for all Southern Californians.

1850 Members Founded: 1923

3296 Building Material Dealers Association
12550 SW Main Street
Suite 200
Tigard, OR 97223
503-624-0561
FAX: 503-620-1016 800-666-2632
bmda@bmda.com www.bmda.com

O' Grant Little, President/CEO
Gwyn Matras, Executive Director

We are a Notice of Right to Lien provider, which assists material suppliers and contractors in protecting their lien rights.

3500 Members Founded: 1915

3297 Building Stone Institute
300 Park Boulevard
Suite 335
Itasca, IL 60143
630-775-9130
FAX: 630-775-9134 866-786-6313
jeff@buildingstoneinstitute.org
www.buildingstone.org

Jeff Buczkiewicz, Executive Vice President
Cristia Caramay, Administrative Assistant
Connie Kitzinger, Special Projects Coordinator

Quarries, fabricators, dealers, installers and restorers of all types of natural stone. Membership dues based on sales volume.

350 Members Founded: 1919

3298 Building Systems Councils
National Association of Home Builders
1201 15th Street NW
Washington, DC 20005
202-220-0200
FAX: 202-266-8559 800-368-5242

David F Wilson, President
Jerry Howard, Executive VP/CEO
David L Pressly Jr., First VP
Brian Catalde, VP/Treasurer
Sandy Dunn, Vice President/Secretary

Represents the interests of concrete, log, modular, and panel manufacturers, builders, and suppliers.

22000 Members Founded: 1942

3299 California Redwood Associates
405 Enfrente Drive
Suite 200
Novato, CA 94949
415-382-0662
FAX: 415-382-8531
info@calredwood.org
www.calredwood.org

Christopher Grover, President
Charles J Jourdain, VP

A trade association for redwood lumber producers.

3300 Composite Panel Association
18922 Premiere Court
Gaithersburg, MD 20879-1574
301-670-0604
FAX: 301-840-1252 www.pbmdf.com

Thomas Julia, President
Allyson S O'Sullivan, Director of Member Services

The association of North American wood and agrifiber-based particleboard and medium density fiberboard producers, to broaden the base of participation in industry outreach programs.

190+ Members Annual Membership Dues
Founded: 1989

3301 Construction Financial Management Association
29 Emmons Drive
Suite F-50
Princeton, NJ 08540
609-452-8000
FAX: 609-452-0474
info@cfma.org www.cfma.org

William Schwab, President
Jeff Zogg, Executive Director
Herbert Brownett, SVP Finance
Henry R Waggoner, Treasurer

Non-profit organization dedicated to serving the financial professional in the construction industry.

7000 Members Founded: 1981

3302 Construction Industry Service Corporation
616 Enterprise Drive
Suite 100
Oak Brook, IL 60523
630-472-9411
FAX: 630-472-9413 877-562-9411

Dave Henderson, President
David Barger, VP
Mike Wiedmaier, Secretary
Charles Dunne, Treasurer
John Brining, Executive Director

Labor management association that promotes union construction, union contractors and union apprenticeship programs throughout Northeastern Illinois.

3303 Construction Owners Association of America
2727 Paces Ferry Road
Suite 1710
Atlanta, GA 30339
770-433-0820
FAX: 404-577-3551 800-994-2622
coaa@coaa.org www.coaa.org

Kim Fisher, Finance/Operations Managing Exec.

To act as a focal point and voice for the interests of owners in construction. Comprised of a diverse group of men and women representing construction owners of America.

Founded: 1994

3304 Construction Specifications Institute
99 Canal Center Plaza
Suite 300
Alexandria, VA 22314
703-684-0300
FAX: 703-684-8436 800-689-2900
csi@csinet.org www.csinet.org

Edward L Soenke, President
Walter Marlowe, Executive Director
Christine Day, Marketing Manager
Carole E Schafmeister, Secretary

Our mission is to continuously improve the process of creating and sustainingt the built environment. We do that by facilitating communication among all those involved in that process.

17000 Members

3305 **Deep Foundations Institute**
326 Lafayette Avenue
Hawthorne, NJ 07506
973-423-4030
FAX: 973-423-4031
dfihq@dfi.org www.dfi.org

Richard D Short, President
Tracy Brettmann, VP
Herbert J Engler, Secretary
Maurice Bottiau, Treasurer
Geordie Compton, Executive Director

We can best be described as being a technical association of firms and individuals in the deep foundations and related industry. DFI covers the gamut of deep foundation construction and earth retention systems.
1325 Members Founded: 1976

3306 **Elberton Granite Association**
1 Granite Plaza
PO Box 640
Elberton, GA 30635
706-283-2551
FAX: 706-283-6380
granite@egaonline.com
www.egaonline.com

Manuel Fernadez, President
Thomas A Robinson, Executive VP

Largest trade association of granite quarriers and manufacturers in the United States. We maintain a voice in the national and international granite industry with regard to market development and technology.
150 Members Founded: 1951

3307 **Hollow Metal Door and Buck Association**
National Assn of Architectural Metal Manufacturer
8 S Michigan Avenue
Suite 1000
Chicago, IL 60603
312-332-0405
FAX: 312-332-0706
www.naamm.org/hmma/

C. John Wiley, Division Chairman
Chris Steward, Division Vice Chairman

The largest of four operating divisions of the National Association of Architectural Metal Manufacturers. HMMA is a group composed of companies that manufacture, distribute and promote the use of hollow metal door and frame products.
60 Members Founded: 1969

3308 **ICC: International Code Council**
5203 Leesburg Pike
Suite 600
Falls Church, VA 22041
703-314-4533
FAX: 703-379-1546 888-422-7233
webmaster@iccsafe.org
www.iccsafe.org

Frank P Hodge Jr., President
Henry L Green, VP
Wally Bailey, Secretary/Treasurer
James Witt, Chief Executive Officer

Formerly known as the Building Officials and Code Administrators International, we publish codes that establish minimum performance requirements for all aspects of the construction industry.
16M Members Founded: 1994 16 K names

3309 **Interlocking Concrete Pavement Institute**
1444 I Street NW
Suite 700
Washington, DC 20005-6542
202-080-0285
FAX: 202-408-0285 800-241-3652
icpi@icpi.org www.icpi.org

Charles McGrath, Executive Director
Rali Mileva, Director of Marketing

Self governed, self funded autonomous association representing the interlocking concrete pavement industry in North America. Membership is open to producers, contractors, suppliers, consultants and others who have an interest in the industry. As the industry voice, the membership represents a majority of the concrete paver production in North America.
600+ Members Founded: 1993

3310 **International Door Association**
PO Box 246
West Milton, OH 45383-0246
937-988-8042
FAX: 937-698-6153 800-355-4432

Christopher Long, Executive Director

Formed with the consolidation of the Door & Operator Dealers Association, we are the industry network for professional door and operator dealers and installers, along with their suppliers.
750 Members Founded: 1996

3311 **International Institute for Lath and Plaster**
PO Box 1663
Lafayette, CA 94549
925-283-5160
FAX: 925-283-5161
wf.pruter@gte.net www.iilp.org

Walter F Pruter, President
Frank E Nunes, Secretary
Michael M. Logue, Director Technical Services

Federation of organizations representing contractors, unions and makers of lathing and manufacturing.
20 Members Founded: 1976

3312 **International Slurry Surfacing Association**
3 Church Circle
PO Box 250
Annapolis, MD 21401-2412
410-267-0023
FAX: 410-267-7546
krissoff@slurry.org www.slurry.org

Eric Reimschiissel, President
Nigel Kerrison, First VP
Randy Terry, Second VP
Howie Snyder, Secretary
Michael Krissoff, Manager

Members are contractors and suppliers of asphalt slurry seal. Provides information, and technical assistance. *$500.00*
220+ Members Membership Fee/Associate Founded: 1963

3313 **Interstates Construction Services**
1520 North Main
Po Box 260
Sioux Center, IA 51250
712-722-1662
FAX: 712-722-1667
bdev@interstates.com
www.interstates.com

Larry Den Herder, Chairman & CEO

Believe strongly in and have used the concept of servant leadership, thereby creating a dynamic leadership pipeline throughout the companies.
Founded: 1953

3314 **Manufactured Housing Institute**
2101 Wilson Boulevard
Suite 610
Arlington, VA 22201-3062
703-558-0400
FAX: 703-558-0401
info@mfghome.org
www.manufacturedhousing.org

Chris Stinebert, President
Michael O'Brien, Executive VP
Erik Jennifer, Coordinator of Publications/Office
Bruce Savage, VP of Public Affairs

National trade organization representing all segments of the factory built housing industry. MHI serves its membership by providing industry research, promotion, education, and government relations programs, and by building and facilitating consensus within the industry.
350+ Members Founded: 1936

3315 **Mason Contractors Association of America: Advancing the Masonry Industry**
33 S Roselle Road
Schaumburg, IL 60193
847-301-0001
FAX: 847-301-1110 800-536-2225
madelizzi@masoncontractors.org
www.masoncontractors.org

G. Alan Griffin, President
Frank Campitelli, VP
Tom Daniel, Secretary
Mackie Bounds, Treasurer
Michael Adelizzi, Executive Director

A trade association representing masonry contractors and suppliers in national legislative and political affairs, codes and standards composition, workforce development, education, market promotion and general industry advocacy.
1000 Members Founded: 1950

3316 **Masonry Society**
3970 Broadway
Suite 201-D
Boulder, CO 80304-1135
303-939-9700
FAX: 303-541-9215
info@masonrysociety.org
www.masonrysociety.org

Susan Scheurer, Company Contact
Raymond T. Miller, Secretary/Treasurer
Max Porter, President
Phillip J. Samblanet, Executive Director

Dedicated to the advancement of scientific engineering, architechtural and construction knowledge of masonry. Promotes research and education and disseminates information on masonry materials, design, construction. Publishes a newsletter
$120.00
750 Members Membership Fee Founded: 1977

3317 **Metal Framing Manufacturers Association**
401 N Michigan Avenue
Chicago, IL 60611-4267
312-644-6610
FAX: 312-321-4098
mfma@sba.com
www.metalframingmfg.org

Jack Springer, Executive Director

Promotes the use of metal framing systems and develops industry standards.

8 Members Founded: 1981

3318 **Mississippi Valley Equipment Association**
10805 Sunset Office Drive
Suite 405
Saint Louis, MO 63127
314-966-5757
FAX: 314-966-8438 800-430-6334
mveainfo@mvea.com www.mvea.com

Joe Dykes, Executive Vice President

A regional affiliate of the North American Equipment Dealers Association provides members with a multitude of services designed to assist them in maintaining a profitable business operation.

165 Members Founded: 1907

3319 **Modular Building Institute**
944 Glenwood Station Ln
Ste 204
Charlottesville, VA 22901-1480
434-296-3288
FAX: 434-296-3361 888-811-3288
info@mbinet.org www.mbinet.org

Tom Hardiman, Executive Director
Steven Williams, Director Marketing/Public Relations

Serving the commercial factory-built buildings industry on an international scale. Our regular members are manufacturers and dealers of commercial modular structures, while our associate members are companies supplying building components, services, and financing.

211 Members Founded: 1983

3320 **NEA Association of Union Constructors**
1501 Lee Highway
Suite 202
Arlington, VA 22209-1109
703-524-3336
FAX: 703-524-3364
www.nea-online.org

Noel C Borck, Executive Vice President
Stephen R Lindauer, Senior VP
Todd R. Mustard, Communications Manager
Kevin J. Hilton, VP of Industrial Relations
Nanette Lester, Director of Finance & Personnel

Steel erectors, general contractors, and industrial maintenance firms. Provides labor relations and safety/information.

5000+ Members Founded: 1969

3321 **National Asphalt Pavement Association**
5100 Forbes Boulevard
Lanham, MD 20706
301-731-4748
FAX: 301-731-4621 888-468-6499
mcervarich@hotmix.org
www.hotmix.org

Mike Acott, President
Margaret Cervarich, VP of Marketing & Public Affairs
Carolyn Wilson, VP of Finance & Operataions
Chuck MacDonald, Director of Communications
Tracie Christie, Associate Director of Awards/Media

The only trade association that exclusively represents the interests of the Hot Mix Asphalt producer and paving contractor on the national level with Congress, government agencies, and other national trade and business organizations.

1100+ Members Founded: 1955

3322 **National Association of Architectural Metal Manufacturers**
8 S Michigan Avenue
Suite 1000
Chicago, IL 60603
312-332-0405
FAX: 312-332-0706
naamm@gss.net www.naamm.org

Ron Robertson, President
C John Wiley, VP
Jim Quinn, Treasurer
August Sisco, Manager

Representing manufacturers of a wide range of metal products chiefly used in commercial and industrial building construction. These products include metal stairs and railings, flagpoles, expanded metal, hollow metal doors and frames, steel and aluminum bar grating and metal lathing and furring.

124 Members Founded: 1938

3323 **National Association of Elevator Contractors**
1298 Wellbrook Circle NE
Suite A
Conyers, GA 30012
770-760-9660
FAX: 770-760-9714 800-900-6232
teresa@naec.org www.naec.org

Douglas W Boydston, President
Ed Chmielewski, VP
Michael Hoover, Secretary
Steven P. Wurth, Treasurer
Teresa Shirley, Executive Director

An association of elevator contractors and suppliers serving primarily the interests of independent elevator contractors and independent suppliers of products and services; promoting safe and reliable elevator, escalator and short-range transportation and promoting excellence in the management of member companies.

631 Members Founded: 1950

3324 **National Association of Home Builders**
1201 15th Street NW
Washington, DC 20005
202-220-0200
FAX: 202-266-8559 800-368-5242
info@nahb.com www.nahb.org

David F Wilson, President
David L Pressly Jr., First VP
Brian Catalde, VP/Treasurer
Sandy Dunn, VP/Secretary
Jerry Howard, Executive Vice President/CEO

Represents the building industry by serving its members and affiliated state and local builders associations.

22000 Members Founded: 1942

3325 **National Association of Manufacturers**
1331 Pennsylvania Avenue NW
Washington, DC 20004-1790
202-637-3000
FAX: 202-637-3182
manufacturing@nam.org
www.nam.org

John A Luke Jr, Chairman/CEO
John Engler, President

The nation's largest industrial trade association, representing small and large manufacturers in every industrial sector and in all 50 states. Our mission is to enhance the competitiveness of manufacturers by shaping a legislative and regulatory environment conducive to U.S. economic growth and to increase understanding among policymakers, the media and the general public about the vital role of manufacturing to America's economic future and living standards.

3326 **National Association of Women in Construction**
327 S Adams Street
Fort Worth, TX 76104
817-877-5551
FAX: 817-877-0324 800-552-3506
nawic@nawic.org www.nawic.org

Carol L Chapman, President
Julie K Foret, VP
Donna B. McDurmont, Secretary
Dede Hughes, Executive Vice President

Founded by 16 women working in the construction industry. The founders organized NAWIC to create a support network for women in construction.

5800 Members Founded: 1953

3327 **National Association of the Remodeling Industry**
780 Lee Street
Suite 200
Des Plaines, IL 60016
847-298-9200
FAX: 847-298-9225 800-611-6274
info@nari.org www.nari.org

Joan Stephens, President
Gwen Biasi, Marketing/Communications Director

A voice in the remodeling industry, NARI has an inclusive, encompassing purpose to; establish and maintain a firm commitment to developing and sustaining programs that expand and unite the remodeling industry; to ensure the industry's growth and security; to encourage ethical conduct, sound business practices and professionalism in the remodeling industry; and to present NARI as the recognized authority in the remodeling industry.

Founded: 1935

3328 **National Concrete Masonry Association**
13750 Sunrise Valley Drive
Herndon, VA 20171-4662
703-713-1900
FAX: 703-713-1910
ncma@ncma.org www.ncma.org

Mark B Hogan, President
Amanda M Chowning, Executive Administrator
Jerry R. Harke, VP Marketing
Rick Ardalan, Communications Manager
Jeffrey H. Greewald, VP of Research & Development

Consists of manufacturers of concrete masonry products and suppliers of products to the industry. Offers a variety of technical of technical services and design aids through publications, computer programs, slide presentations and technical training.

Founded: 1918

3329 **National Conference of States on Building Codes & Standards**
505 Huntmar Park Drive
Suite 210
Herndon, VA 20170
703-437-0100
FAX: 703-481-3596
rwible@ncsbcs.org www.ncsbcs.org

Cynthia Wilk, President
Jerry Jones, VP

Tim Nogler, Treasurer
Ila Jones, Secretary
Robert Wible, Executive Director

Serving as a forum for the interchange of information and provides technical services, education and training to our members to enhance the public's social, economic well-being through safe, durable, accessible and efficient buildings.

Founded: 1967

3330 National Council of Acoustical Consultants

66 Morris Avenue
Suite 1A
Springfield, NJ 07081-1409
973-564-5859
FAX: 973-564-7480
info@ncac.com www.ncac.com

David E Marsh, President
Kerrie G Standlee, VP Membershipct
Russ Berger, VP of Marketing & Communications

Strives to safeguard the interests of professional acoustical consulting firms. Managing physics and psychoacoustics to provide optimum lisning environments.

130 Members Founded: 1962

3331 National Demolition Association

16 N Franklin Street
Suite 203
Doylestown, PA 18901-3536
215-348-4949
FAX: 215-348-8422 800-541-2412
info@demolitionassociation.com
www.demolitionassociation.com

Michael Taylor, Executive Director

Representing the demolition industry including demolition contractors, formed to foster goodwill and the exchange of ideas with the public, governmental agencies and contractors engaged in the demolition industry. Also for manufacturers or suppliers of demolition equipment, supplies and services.

900 Members

3332 National Electrical Contractors Association

3 Bethesda Metro Center
Suite 1100
Bethesda, MD 20814
301-657-3110
FAX: 301-215-4500
eie@neca.net.org www.necanet.org

Russell J Alessi, President
Dan Walter, VP/Chief Operating Officer
J. Michael Thompson, Secretary/Treasurer
John Grau, Chief Executive Officer
Robert Colgan, Executive Director of Marketing

Represents a segment of the construction market comprised of over 70,000 electrical contracting firms.

70000 Members Founded: 1901

3333 National Housing Endowment

1201 15th Street NW
Washington, DC 20005
202-220-0483

nhe@nahb.com
www.nationalhousingendowment.com

F Gary Garczynski, Chairman
Mark Ellis Tipton, First Vice Chairman
Thomas Thompson, Second Vice Chairman
Bruce S. Silver, President/CEO
Charles J. Ruma, Secretary

Provides a permanaent source of funds to address long-term industry concerns at the national level including: supporting scholarship progams that encourage students to select home building and related fields as their life's work, assisting colleges and universities in the development of housing related curricula and activities, revitalizing the industry's labor pool and enhancing its professionalism through apprenticeship programs, seminars and continuing education.

Founded: 1987

3334 National Lumber and Building Material Dealers Association

900 2nd Street NE
Suite 305
Washington, DC 20002
202-547-2230
FAX: 202-547-7640 800-634-8645

NLBMDA represents 8000 of America's building material dealers and the largest regional chains across the United States. Their members and the members 400,000 employees supply the majority of the building products sold in the US professional contractors, home builders and remodelers.

38000 Members Founded: 1916

3335 National Railroad Construction and Maintenance Association

122 C Street NW
Suite 850
Washington, DC 20001
202-387-7790
FAX: 202-318-0867 800-883-1557
info@nrcma.org www.nrcma.org

Ray Chambers, President
Chuck Baker, VP/Executive Director
Manny Ramirez, Treasurer

Members are railroad construction and maintenance contractors, engineering firms, manufacturing suppliers and professional associate firms.

100+ Members Founded: 1978

3336 National Ready Mixed Concrete Association

900 Spring Street
Silver Spring, MD 20910
301-587-1400
FAX: 301-585-4219 888-846-7622
info@nrmca.org www.nrmca.org

Robert Garbini, President
Deana Angelastro, Executive Administrator
Michael Forster, VP of Finance & Administration
Glenn Ochsenreiter, VP of Marketing
Thomas Harman, Director of Safety Compliance

Our mission is to provide exceptional value for our members by responsibly representing and serving the entire ready mixed concrete industry through leadership, promotion, education and partnering; to ensure ready mixed concrete is the building material of choice.

1200 Members Founded: 1930

3337 National Slag Association

25 Stevens Avenue
Building A
West Lawn, PA 19609
610-670-0701
FAX: 610-670-0702
info@nationalsagassoc.org
www.nationalslagassoc.org

Terry Wagaman, President

Members are processors of iron and steel slags for use as a aggregate in construction and manufacturing applications.

77 Members Founded: 1918

3338 National Stone, Sand & Gravel Association

1605 King Street
Alexandria, VA 22314
703-525-8788
FAX: 703-525-7782 800-342-1415
info@nssga.org www.nssga.org

Jennifer J Wilson, President/CEO
Charles E Hawkins III, Executive VP/COO

Represents the crushed stone, sand and gravel — or aggregate — industries. Our members account for 90 percent of the crushed stone and 70 percent of the sand and gravel produced annually in the US.

570 Members Founded: 1985

3339 National Terrazzo and Mosaic Association

201 N Maple Avenue
Suite 208
Purcellville, VA 20132
540-510-0930
FAX: 540-751-0935 800-323-9736
info@ntma.com www.ntma.com

George Hardy, Executive Director

Full service nonprofit trade association headquartered in Northern Virginia. The association establishes national standards for all terrazzo floor and wall systems and provides complete specifications, color plates and general information to architects and designers at no cost.

3340 National Tile Contractors Association

626 Lakeland E Drive
PO Box 13629
Jackson, MS 39236
601-939-2071
FAX: 601-932-6117
bart@tile-assn.com www.tile-assn.com

Scott M Carothers, Chairman
Don Scott, President
Frank Canto, First VP
Bart Bettiga, Executive Director
Bob Brown, Membership Director

Serving every segment of the industry, and is recognized as the largest and most respected tile contractors association in the world.

650 Members Founded: 1947
Mailing list available for rent

3341 National Utility Contractors Association

4301 Fairfax Drive
Suite 360
Arlington, VA 22203-1627
703-358-9300
FAX: 703-358-9307
joyce@nuca.com www.nuca.com

Jim Stutler, President
Bill Hillman, CEO
Linda Straub, COO
Vanessa Straub, Executive Assistant

A national association that provides a forum for continuing education and promotes effective public policy, through its grassroots network, to protect and enhance your industry.

1400 Members Founded: 1964

3342 **North American Insulation Manufacturers Association**
44 Canal Center Plaza
Suite 310
Alexandria, VA 22314-1592
703-684-0084
FAX: 703-684-0427
insulation@naima.org
www.naima.org

Howard Deck, Chairman
Jeff Brisley, Vice Chairman
Kenneth Mentzer, President/CEO
Angus Crane, VP of General Counsel & Secretary
George Phelps, VP of Government & Industry Affairs

Manufacturers of fiber glass, rock wool, and slag wool insulation products. NAIMA members manufacture the vast majority of fiber glass, rock and slag wool insulations produced and used in North America.
2 Members Founded: 1933

3343 **Northeastern Retail Lumber Association**
585 N Greenbush Road
Rensselaer, NY 12144
518-861-1932
FAX: 518-286-1755 800-292-6752
heidi@nrla.com www.nrla.org

James Ayotte, President
Rita Ferris, VP

A resource for industry members, consumers, and public officials independent lumber and building material suppliers and associated businesses in New York and the six New England states.
1150 Members Founded: 1894

3344 **Operative Plasterers and Cement Masons International Association**
14405 Laurel Place
Suite 300
Laurel, MD 20707-6102
301-470-4200
FAX: 301-470-2502
opcmiaintl@opcmia.org
www.opcmia.org

John J Dougherty, President
Patrick D Finley, General Secretary/Treasurer
Ronald K. Bowser, Executive VP
David L. Robinson, VP
Thomas Mora, Vice President

AFL-CIO labor organizations representing plasters and cement masons in the US and Canada.
Founded: 1864

3345 **Outdoor Power Equipment Institute**
341 S Patrick Street
Old Town Alexandria, VA 22314
703-549-7600
FAX: 703-549-7604
mroach@opei.org www.opei.org

Jim Wier, Chairman
Dave Zerfoss, Vice Chairman
William G Harley, President/CEO
Ken Melrose, Treasurer/Secretary

International trade association whose members are manufacturers of powered lawn and garden maintenance products, components and attachment supplies, as well as industry related services.
85 Members Founded: 1952

3346 **Painting and Decorating Contractors of America**
11960 Westline Industrial Drive
Suite 201
St. Louis, MO 63146-3209
314-514-7322
FAX: 314-514-9417 800-332-7322
mconnor@conncogroup.com
www.pdca.com

Carol Adkins, President
Mike Connor, VP
Mark Casale, Senior VP/Assistant Treasurer

PDCA exists to lead the industry by providing quality products, programs, services, and opportunities essential to the success of our members. Membership is $215-400 per year.
10M Members Founded: 1884

3347 **Perlite Institute**
4305 North 6th Street
Harrisburg, PA 17110
717-238-9723
FAX: 717-238-9985
info@perlite.org www.perlite.org

Denise Calabrese, Executive Director
Amy Hauf, Financial Advisor
Bethany Dennis, Communications Manager

An international trade association which establishes product standards and specifications, and which encourages the development of new product uses through research.
45 Members Founded: 1949

3348 **Pile Driving Contractors Association**
PO Box 66208
Orange Park, FL 32065-021
904-215-4771
FAX: 904-264-9531 888-311-7322
execdir@piledrivers.org
www.piledrivers.org

Mark Weisz, President
Van Hogan, VP
Stevan A Hall, Executive Director
Van Hogan, Secretary
Trey Ford, Treasurer

An organization of pile driving contractors that advocates the incresed use of driven piles for deep foundations and earth retention systems. To do this we promote the use of driven pile solutions in all cases where they are effective, support educational programs for engineers on the design and efficiency of driven piles and for contractors on improving installation procedures. We also give contractors a larger voice in establishing procedures and standards for pile installation and design.
450 Members Founded: 1996 1500 names $100 per M.

3349 **Pipe Fabrication Institute**
666 5th Avenue
Suite 325
New York, NY 10103
514-634-3434
FAX: 514-634-9736 866-913-3434
pfi@pfi-institute.org
www.pfi-institute.org

George Stuller, Chairman
Gordon Tunberg, Vice Chairman
Steve Brunett, Treasurer
Guy Fortin, Executive Director

Members are companies producing sophisticated high temperature, high pressure piping systems that employ specialists from the United Association of Journeymen and Apprentices of the Plumbing and Pipe Fitting Industry. We exist solely for the purpose of ensuring a level of quality in the pipe fabrication industry that is without compromise.
65-70 Members Founded: 1913

3350 **Portable Sanitation Association International**
7800 Metro Parkway
Suite 104
Bloomington, MN 55425
952-854-8300
FAX: 952-854-7560 800-822-3020
portsan@aol.com www.psai.org

Ray Anthony Jr., President
Rich Vegter, VP
Karen Holm, Treasurer
Tammy Thompson-Oreskovich, Secretary
William Carroll, Executive Director

International trade association that represents firms engaged in the leasing, renting, selling and manufacturing of portable sanitation equipment, services and supplies for construction, recreation, emergency and other uses. Devoted to the proper handling of human waste by the most modern, sanitary means, giving the greatest concern to the preservation of an unspoiled environment.
550+ Members Founded: 1971

3351 **Precast Prestressed Concrete Institute**
209 W Jackson Boulevard
Chicago, IL 60606-6938
312-786-0300
FAX: 312-786-0353
info@pci.org www.pci.org

James G Toscas, President
John S Dick, Structures Director
John A. Lishamer, Information Services Manager
Brian D. Goodmiller, National Marketing Director
Gary H. Munstermann, Administration & Finance Director

Dedicated to fostering understanding and use of precast and prestressed concrete, maintains a full staff of techniocal and marketing specialists.
1400 Members Founded: 1954

3352 **Professional Construction Estimators Association of America**
PO Box 680336
Charlotte, NC 28216-1626
704-987-9978
FAX: 704-987-9979 877-521-7232
pcea@pcea.org www.pcea.org

Denton Wall, President
Trey Shaw, VP
Gail Chapman, Secretary
Gene Moore, Treasurer

Promotes construction estimating as a profession by upholding the code of ethics, and expanding public awareness.
1000 Members Founded: 1956

3353 **Resilient Floor Covering Institute**
401 East Jefferson Street
Suite 102
Rockville, MD 20850
202-408-8580
FAX: 301-340-7283 www.rfci.com

Douglas Wiegand, Executive Director

Industry trade association of North American manufacturers who produce resilient flooring products. Associate members of RFCI supply raw materials to the industry and manufacture installation and maintenance products.

7 Members Founded: 1976

3354 Roof Coatings Manufacturers Association
1156-15th Street NW
Suite 900
Washington, DC 20005
202-207-0919
FAX: 202-223-9741
info@roofcoatings.org
www.roofcoatings.org

Chris Salazar, President
Joseph Mellott, VP
W J Leonard, Treasurer/Secretary

Represents the interests of manufacturers of cold applied roof coatings, cements and waterproofing agents, as well as the suppliers of products, equipment and services to and for the industry. Currently RCMA boasts more than 70 member companies.
70+ Members Founded: 1983

3355 Rubber Pavements Association
1801 South Jentilly Lane
Suite A-2
Tempe, AZ 85281-5738
480-517-9944
FAX: 480-517-9959
dougc@rubberpavements.org
www.rubberpavements.org

Doug Carlson, Executive Director
Donna Carlson, Director of Marketing

Dedicated to encouraging greater usage of high quality, cost effective asphalt pavements containing recycled tire rubber. Conducts national and international seminars.
20 Members Founded: 1985

3356 SPRI: Single Ply Roofing Industry
77 Rumford Avenue
Suite 3B
Waltham, MA 02453
781-647-7026
FAX: 781-647-7222
info@spri.org www.spri.org

Steve Moskowitz, President
Mark DeFreitas, Treasurer/Secretary
Linda King, Managing Director

Comprised of manufacturers and marketers of sheet applied membrane roofing systems and components to the commercial roofing industry.
58 Members Founded: 1982

3357 Safety Glazing Certification Council
PO Box 9
Henderson Harbor, NY 13651
315-646-2234
FAX: 315-646-2297
ams@nnymail.com www.sgcc.org

John G Kent, Administrative Director
Robin Vincent, Administrative Director

Nonprofit corporation that provides for the certifacation of safety glazing materials, comprised of safety glazing manufacturers and other parties concerned with public safety. SGCC is managed by a board of directors comprised of representatives from the safety glazing industry and the public interest sector.
105 Members Founded: 1971

3358 Scaffold Industry Association
PO Box 20574
Phoenix, AZ 85036-0574
602-257-1144
FAX: 602-257-1166
aimee@scaffold.org www.scaffold.org

Bill Breault, Preident Elect
Aimee Siems, Operations Manager
Nicki Santo, Development Director

Promotes safety by developing educational and informational material, conducting educational seminars and training courses, providing audio-visual programs and codes for safe practices, and other training and safety aids; to work with state, federal and other agencies in developing more effective safety standards; to reduce accidents, thereby reducing insurance costs; and to assist members in becoming more efficient and profitable in their businesses.
1000 Members Founded: 1972

3359 Screen Manufacturers Association
2850 S Ocean Boulevard
Suite 114
Palm Beach, FL 33480-6205
561-533-0991
FAX: 561-533-7466
fitzgeraldfscott@aol.com
www.smacentral.org

James W Gulliford, President
Frank S Fitzgerald, Executive VP
Mark A. DeZwarte, VP
Alan Gray, Treasurer

Manufacturers of insect screens, screen frames, window screens, detention screens, sliding screen doors, swinging screen doors, fiberglass insect screening and aluminum insect screening. *$1000.00*
20 Members Membership Fee Founded: 1955

3360 Specialty Tools and Fasteners Distributors Association
PO Box 44
Elm Grove, WI 53122
262-784-4774
FAX: 262-784-5059 800-352-2981
info@stafda.com www.stafda.org

Marshall Jones, President
Doug Hahn, VP
Georgia Foley, Executive Director

International trade association composed of distributors and manufacturers and rep agents of light construction, industrial and related products. Members also include publishers of industry press serving the construction and industrial trades. *$350.00*
2603 Members Membership Fee Founded: 1976

3361 Stark Ceramics
PO Box 8880
Canton, OH 44711
330-488-1211
FAX: 330-488-0333 800-321-0662
info@starkceramics.com
www.starkceramics.com

Mark Rojek, VP
Lorraine Stewart, Manager

Promotes the use of glazed and unglazed facing tile in all phases of construction.
3 Members Founded: 1934

3362 Steel Joist Institute
3127 10th Avenue N
Myrtle Beach, SC 29577-6760
843-626-1995
FAX: 843-626-5565
sji@steeljoist.org www.steeljoist.org

Carol Perry, Director/Office Manager

Composed of active manufacturers, the SJI cooperates with government and business agencies to establish steel joint standards.
40 Members Founded: 1928

3363 Steel Window Institute
1300 Sumner Avenue
Cleveland, OH 44115-2851
216-241-7333
FAX: 216-241-0105
swi@steelwindows.com
www.steelwindows.com

John H Addington, Executive Director
Charles Stockinger, Manager

For United States manufacturers of windows made from hot-rolled, solid steel sections and such related products as castings, trim, mechanical operators, screens and moldings.
7 Members

3364 Structural Insulated Panel Association
PO Box 1699
Gig Harbor, WA 98335
253-858-7472
FAX: 253-858-0272
staff@sips.org www.sips.org

Damian Pataluna, President
Frank Baker, First VP
Terry Dieken, Second VP
Frank Wopperer, Secretary/Treasurer
Bill Wachtler, Executive Director

A trade association representing manufacturers, suppliers, fabriators, distributors, design professionals and builders committed to providing quality structural insulated panels for all segments of the construction industry.
250 Members Founded: 1990

3365 Stucco Manufacturers Association
2402 Vista Nobleza
Newport Beach, CA 92660-3545
949-640-9902
FAX: 949-640-9911
info@stuccomfgassoc.com
www.stuccomfgassoc.com

Norma Fox, Executive Director

Our main purpose is to promote the advantage of 3 coat colored cementitious stucco by educating the building industry and consumers. *$1200.00*
50 Members Membership Fee Founded: 1957

3366 Subcontractors Trade Association
570 Seventh Avenue
New York, NY 10018
212-398-6220
FAX: 212-398-6224
subcontractorstrade@verizon.net
www.stanyc.com

Fred Levinson, President
Alan Nathanson, VP
Robert Samela, VP
W Scott Rives, Secretary
Ronald Berger, Executive Director

Members are specialty and supply companies in the construction industry. Our goal is to improve the economic well being of our members through representation, support and assistance through the process of legislation, legal action, public relations, education and other public information programs.

350+ Members Founded: 1966

3367 Textile Care Allied Trades Association
271 Route 46W
Suite D203
Fairfield, NJ 07004
973-244-1790
FAX: 973-244-4455
info@tcata.org www.tcata.org

David Cotter, CEO

Represents the interests of distributors and manufacturers of equipment and supplies for the cleaning industry.

3368 Thomas Global Register
Thomas Publishing Company
5 Penn Plaza
New York, NY 10001
212-950-0500
www.tgrnet.com

A directory of over 700,000 manufacturers and distributors from 28 countries, classified by 11,000 products and categories. Mission is to bring industrial buyers and sellers together on the web to facilitate the purchasing process.

Founded: 1898

3369 Tile Contractors Association of America
4 East 113th Terrace
Kansas City, MO 64114
816-317-7429
FAX: 816-767-0194 800-655-8453
info@tcaainc.org www.tcaainc.org

Jerry Leva, President/Chairman
John Trendall, Treasurer
Patty Nolte, Executive Director
Carole Damon, Associate Director

An organization representing the finest tile contractors in the United States.

150 Members Founded: 1903

3370 Tile Roofing Institute
230 E Ohio Street
Suite 400
Chicago, IL
773-424-4242
FAX: 312-644-8557 888-321-9236
info@rooftile.org www.rooftile.org

Mike Perry, Chairman
Jeanne Sheehy, Managing Director
Rick Olson, Technical Director
Charles McGrath, Senior Advisor

Manufacturers of clay and concrete roof tiles. Emphasis is on technical issues and codes that involve tile.

Founded: 1971

3371 Tilt-Up Concrete Association
113 First Street W
PO Box 204
Mount Vernon, IA 52314
319-895-6911
FAX: 319-895-8830
info@tilt-up.org www.tilt-up.org

Laurence Smith, President
David P Tomasula, VP
Bob Truitt, Secretary
Glenn Doncaster, Treasurer
Ed Sauter, Executive Director

Represents builders, engineers, architects and suppliers involved with tilt-up concrete construction. Makes a continuing and increasingly important contribution to the success of each member through the most imaginative and efficient application of every appropriate skill, tool and service of the association.

Founded: 1986
Printed in 4 colors on glossy stock

3372 Timber Frame Business Council
217 Main Street
Hamilton, MT 59840
406-375-0713
FAX: 406-375-6401 888-560-9251
nancy@timberframe.org
www.timberframe.org

John Miller, President
Sandy Bennett, VP
Carmen Caprio, Secretary
Christine Benson, Treasurer
Nancy Wilkins, Manager

Advances the business, communications and research interests of companies engaged in the timber framing industry.

Founded: 1995 free names

3373 Timber Framers Guild
PO Box 60
Becket, MA 01223
413-239-9926
FAX: 888-453-0879 888-453-0879
info@tfguild.org www.tfguild.org

Will Beemer, Co-Executive Director
Joel McCarty, Co-Executive Director

The Guild is dedicated to establishing training programs for dedicated timber framers, disseminating information about timber framing and timber frame building design, displaying the art of timber framing to the public, and generally serving as a center of timber framing information for the professional and general public alike. *$85.00*

1700 Members Annual Membership Dues
Founded: 1984

3374 Truck Mixer Manufacturers Bureau
900 Spring Street
Silver Spring, MD 20910-4015
301-587-1400
FAX: 301-587-1605
bgarbini@tmmb.org www.tmmb.org

Robert Garbini, Executive Secretary
Frank Cavaliere, Bureau Coordinator
Nicole Maher, Bureau Administrator

An association of ready mixed concrete truck manufacturers who have joined together in support of the ready mixed industry. TMMB members are required to manufacture equipment in accordance to the TMMB Standards.

7 Members Founded: 1944

3375 Western Building Material Association
909 Lakeridge Drive SW
PO Box 1699
Olympia, WA 98507
360-943-3054
FAX: 360-943-1219
wbna@wbna.org www.wbma.org

Mike Hennick, President
Rick McCartney, VP
Tom Simkins, VP
Casey Voorhees, Executive Director

Regional trade association serving material dealers throughout the states of Alaska, Idaho, Montana, Oregon and Washington and a federated association of the National Lumber and Building Material Dealers Association.

600 Members Founded: 1903

3376 World Floor Covering Association
2211 E Howell Avenue
Anaheim, CA 92806
714-978-6440
FAX: 714-978-6066 800-624-6880
wfca@wfca.org www.wfca.org

Christopher Davis, CEO
Terry Hearne, Director of Operations
Cammie Weitzel, Director of Finance/Administration
Donna Archambault, Membership Operations Manager

Shapes and defines public policy through agressive, national legislative advocacy on behalf of our members. Provides continuing professional educational programming through educational forums and the Regional Installation and Training Education (RITE) program.

45 Members Founded: 1973

Newsletters

3377 ACSM Bulletin
American Congress on Surveying and Mapping
6 Montgomery Village Avenue
Suite 403
Gaithersburg, MD 20879
240-680-0765
FAX: 240-632-1321
info@acsm.net www.acsm.net

Curtis W Sumner, Executive Director
John Hohol, Advertising Director

Covers topics ranging from land surveying to height modernization, from cartography to GIS and LIS, from the national cadastre to flood mapping and the standardization of geographic data, and from LIDAR, CORS and satellites to exploring the universe. *$92.00*

Bi-Monthly

3378 AEC Automation Newsletter
Technology Automation Services
PO Box 904
Salida, CO 81201
719-539-8549
FAX: 719-539-6971
www.aecnews.com/aecnews

David Weisberg, Publisher

Geared at persons in the design, building, operation and maintenance of industrial building industry, includes information on available technologies, CAD, CAM, and CAE support. *$235.00*

Monthly

3379 AHW Reporter
Duane Publishing
51 Park Street
Dorchester, MA 02122
617-282-4885
FAX: 617-282-0320
info@decmagazine.com
www.decmagazine.com

Herbert Duane Jr, Publisher

Asbestos and hazardous waste information.

3380 Asbestos & Lead Abatement Report
Business Publishers
8737 Colesville Road
Suite 1100
Silver Spring, MD 20910-3928
301-587-6300
FAX: 301-587-4530 800-274-6737
bpinews@bpinews.com
www.bpinews.com

Leonard A Eiserer, Publisher
Beth Early, Operations Director

Tracks the major legislative, regulatory and technological developments in asbestos and lead abatement industries. Includes highlights of major research studies on the effect of lead and asbestos on human health. *$371.54*

BiWeekly

3381 Brick News
National Association of Brick Distributors
11490 Commerce Park Drive
Reston, VA 20191-1525
703-620-0010
FAX: 703-620-3928 www.bia.org/
Walter Galanty Jr, Publisher
Diane Griffin, Editor
Gregg Borchelt, Interim Director
News, information and programs of interest to brick distributors.

3382 Building Products News
Palgrave Macmillan
175 5th Avenue
New York, NY 10010
212-982-3900
FAX: 212-777-6359
David Bull, Director of Journals
A unique publication researching the commercial renovation and retrofit market.

3383 Building Stone
Building Stone Institute
300 Park Boulevard
Suite 335
Itasca, IL 60143
630-775-9130
FAX: 630-775-9134 866-786-6313
jeff@buildingstoneinstitute.com
www.buildingstoneinstitute.org
Dorothy Kender, Production Manager
Jeff Buczkiewicz, Editor/Executive VP
Brenda Edwards, President
Rick Jones, VP
State of the industry publication for architects, designers and people in the natural stone industries: granite, marble, limestone, etc. *$65.00*
Quarterly Founded: 1919
Circulation: 17,000

3384 Building and Construction Market Forecast
Reed Business Information
360 Park Avenue South
New York, NY 10014
212-450-0067
corporatecommunications@reedbusiness.com www.reedbusiness.com
Jim Haughey, Publisher
Dan Buchan, Editor
James Reed, Owner
Carel Bos, Chief Information Officer
Rob Wild, Managing Director-Australia
Forecasts and analysis on the construction industry. *$187.00*
6 pages Monthly Founded: 1946

3385 Commercial Low-Slope Roofing Materials Guide
National Roofing Contractors Association
10255 W Higgins Road Suite 600
Ohare International Center
Rosemont, IL 60018-5607
847-299-9070
FAX: 847-299-1183 800-323-9545
nrca@nrca.net www.nrca.net
Carl Good, Executive Director
Frank Kocich, Marketing Director
Comprehencive report on commercial and industrial low-slope roof membrane, insulation board, and roof fastener products on the market offers complete test data on products on a size by size comparison. *$140.00*
Founded: 1886 : CD-ROM

3386 Concrete Pipe News
American Concrete Pipe Association
222 W Las Colinas Boulevard
Suite 641
Irving, TX 75039-5423
972-506-7216
FAX: 972-506-7682
info@concrete-pipe.org
www.concrete-pipe.org
Karen Hunter, Marketing Manager
Matt Childs, President
Doug Mohrman, Chairman
The latest news and information of the Association. *$3.50*
16 pages Quarterly Founded: 1907

3387 Construction Company Strategist
Brownstone Publishers
3 Park Avenue
30th Floor
New York, NY 10016
212-244-0360
FAX: 212-564-0465 800-401-5937
subserve@ioma.com www.ioma.com
Donis Ford, Editor
David Foster, CEO/President
Omer Karabey, Owner
Judy Pagani, Circulation Manager
Strategies, legal tips, and how-to advice for successfully managing a construction company in the 1990's. Features model contract language, forms, guidelines and more. *$269.00*
Monthly Founded: 1971
Circulation: 180000
Printed in 2 colors on matte stock

3388 Construction Computer Application News
CIP Communications
6585 Commerce Boulevard
#E-292
Rohnert Park, CA 94928-7824
707-938-4177
Royal Maul, Publisher
Contains software reviews and construction uses for computers. *$89.00*
6 pages Monthly

3389 Construction Contractor
Federal Publications
1120 20th Street NW
Washington, DC 20036-3406
202-659-6888
FAX: 202-659-2233 800-926-7926
Richard L Shea, Publisher
Bi-weekly newsletter providing in-depth legal insight and analysis for all construction professionals. *$592.00*
BiWeekly

3390 Construction Equipment Monthly
Heartland Communications
1003 Central Avenue
PO Box 1052
Fort Dodge, IA 50501-1052
515-955-1600
FAX: 515-574-2107 800-247-2000
personnel@hlipublishing.com
www.hlipublishing.com
Tony Smith, Publisher
Shannon Bushman, Sales/Operations Manager
Listings by category, equipment and parts for sale. *$125.00*
Annual+ Founded: 1988

3391 Construction Labor Report
Bureau of National Affairs
1231 25th Street NW
Washington, DC 20037-1197
202-452-4200
800-372-1033
customercare@bna.com www.bna.com
Gregory C McCaffery, Publisher
Jerome Ashton, Managing Editor
Robert Gasperbow, Executive Director
A weekly information service that covers union-management relations in the construction industry, reporting on significant legislative, judicial, economic, management and union developments. *$1543.00*
Weekly
Circulation: 1600

3392 Constructor Newsletter
Associated General Contractors of America
333 John Carlyle Street
Suite 200
Alexandria, VA 22314
703-548-3118
FAX: 703-548-3119
info@agc.org www.agc.org
Stephen E Sandherr, CEO
David R Lukens, COO
Mark Shaw, Editor-in-Chief
Mark Kelly, Publisher
Reports on contractors and items of interest to the construction community.
Monthly Founded: 1918
Circulation: 33000

3393 Crow's Weekly Letter
CC Crow Publications
PO Box 25749
Portland, OR 97298-749
503-417-7382
FAX: 503-646-9971
info@crows.com www.crows.com
Frank J Vetorino, Publisher
Sam Sherrill, Editor
Chad Crowe, President
Weekly report on trends and prices in the wood products industry. *$285.00*
12 pages Weekly Founded: 1921
Printed in 4 colors on matte stock
Computerized version available

3394 Demo-Memo
Duane Publishing
51 Park Street
PO Box 130
Dorchester, MA 02122
617-282-4885
FAX: 617-282-0320
info@decmagazine.com
www.decmagazine.com
Faith Wagner, Publisher
Demolition news and information.

3395 Dodge Report & Bulletins
McGraw Hill
PO Box 182604
Columbus, OH 43272-1095
614-304-4000
FAX: 614-759-3749
customer.service@mcgraw-hill.com
www.mcgraw-hill.com
DJ McGrath, Editor
Dodge Reports gives you the information you need to prepare a bid or enter negotiations. The detailed project information will also enable you to sell products or services.
Daily Founded: 1884

3396 Dome Home Mortgage White Paper
National Dome Council
15th and Main Streets NW
Washington, DC 20005
202-588-1697
FAX: 202-588-1244
www.IOAonline.org

Robert Johns, Executive Director

Information for builders and designers.
10 pages Monthly
Circulation: 3000 3000 names
Printed in 3 colors

3397 Environmental Building News
BuildingGreen
122 Birge Street
Suite 30
Brattleboro, VT 05301
802-257-7300
FAX: 802-257-7304
info@buildinggreen.com
www.buildinggreen.com

Alex Wilson, Executive Editor
Nadav Malin, Editor
Daniel Woodbury, Publisher
Charlotte Snyder, Circulation Manager

Featuring comprehensive, practical information on a wide range of topics related to sustainable building—from energy efficiency and recycled-content materials to land-use planning and indoor air quality.
$99.00
Monthly/Individual Rate Founded: 1992

3398 Hard Hat News
Lee Publications
6113 State Highway 5
PO Box 121
Palatine Bridge, NY 13428
518-673-2269
FAX: 518-673-2699 800-218-5586

Sally Taylor, Publisher
Kent Hogeboom, Editor
Larry Price, Sales/Marketing Manager
Fred Lee, Owner
Bruce Button, Vice President

Construction and heavy equipment.
72 pages Monthly

3399 Housing Marketing Report
CD Publications
8204 Fenton Street
Silver Spring, MD 20910
301-588-6380
FAX: 301-588-6385 800-666-6380
info@cdpublications.com
www.cdpublications.com

Mike Gerecht, Publisher
Charles Wisniowski, Editor

Concise analysis of national and regional housing markets, materials and supplies.
$469.00
Founded: 1961
Mailing list available for rent 2,000 names
$160 per M.
Printed in on matte stock

3400 Indoor Air Quality Update
Aspen Publishers
37 Broadway
Suite 1
Arlington, MA 02474-5552
301-644-3599
FAX: 301-698-7100 800-234-1660
info@cutter.com
www.aspenpublishers.com

Carlton Vogt, Editor

A guide to the practical control of building materials. *$440.00*
Circulation: 20000

3401 Industry News
Modular Building Institute
413 Park Street
Charlottesville, VA 22902-4737
434-296-3288
FAX: 434-296-3361
info@mbinet.org www.mbinet.org

Steven Williams, Editor

For members only.

Circulation: 650

3402 Machinery Outlook
Manfredi & Associates
20934 W Lakeview Parkway
Mundelein, IL 60060-9502
847-949-9080
FAX: 847-949-9910
frank@manfredi.com
www.manfredi.com

Frank Manfredi, Publisher

A newsletter about and for the construction and mining machinery industry. *$550.00*
14 pages Monthly Founded: 1984
Printed in 1 color on matte stock

3403 Manufactured Structures Newsletter
Bobbitt Group
1640 Macintosh Way
Hummelstown, PA 17036
717-566-1457
FAX: 717-566-2114
WBobbitt@aol.com
www.bobbittgroup.com

William S Bobbitt, Editor/Publisher
Marci S Bobbitt, Associate Editor/Business Manager

Covers all aspects of the automated building industry with a monthly collection of original feature stories profiling leading and emerging companies in the industry as well as other informative information on the industry, business tips, proven sales and marketing and featured editorials.
Monthly Founded: 1969

3404 NAWIC Image
National Association of Women in Construction
327 S Adams Street
Fort Worth, TX 76104-1002
817-877-5551
FAX: 817-877-0324 800-552-3506
nawic@nawic.org www.nawic.org

Nancy Eaton, Presdient
Dede Hughes, Publisher

Management, trends and techniques in the construction business. *$50.00*
Fortnightly Founded: 1953
Circulation: 6500

3405 News Brief
Granite State Designers & Installers Association
76 South State Street
Concord, NH 03301-3520
603-228-1231
FAX: 603-228-2118
clough@choiceonemail.com
www.gsdia.org

James Hanna, Vice Chairman
Walter Perry, Executive Director

Newsletter for members of GSD1 relative to septic system design, installation and maintenance. *$150.00*
Monthly

3406 Productivity and Management in Construction
CIP Communications
6585 Commerce Boulevard
Rohnert Park, CA 94928-7824
707-584-9874

Roderick Crandell, Publisher

Construction productivity improvement.

3407 Redwood Reporter
California Redwood Association
405 Enfrente Road
Suite 200
Novato, CA 94949-7201
415-382-0662
FAX: 415-382-8531 888-225-7339
info@calredwood.org
www.calredwood.org

Pamela Allsebrook, Publisher
Christopher Grover, President

Information about the redwood business of interest to redwood dealers.
8 pages
Circulation: 8000

3408 Reed Construction Data
60 Technology Parkway S
Suite 100
Norcross, GA 30092
770-093-3730
FAX: 800-465-6475 800-448-8182

Tad Smith, Chief Executive Officer

Offers statistical information for building contractors.

3409 SPEC-DATA Program
Construction Specifications Institute
99 Canal Center Plaza
Suite 300
Alexandria, VA 22314
703-684-0300
FAX: 703-684-8436 800-689-2900
csimail@csinet.org www.csinet.org

Don Ethier, Marketing Director
Edith S Washington, President
Karl F Borgstrom, Executive Director
Dan Merriman Merriman, Communications Manager

Accepts advertising. *$75.00*
Monthly

3410 Scaffold Industry Association Newsletter
Scaffold Industry Association
PO Box 20574
Phoenix, AZ 85036-574
602-257-1144
FAX: 602-257-1166
info@scaffold.org www.scaffold.org

Bruce Powell, Executive Director
Linda Tweten, Marketing
Howard Schapira, Persident

Information on scaffold safety in the construction industry. Offers safe training programs for competent person and hazard awareness. *$65.00*
Monthly Founded: 1972
Circulation: 1600

3411 Scantlings
Timbers Framers Guild
PO Box 60
Becket, MA 98225
413-239-9926
FAX: 888-453-0879 888-453-0879
witter@nas.com www.tfguild.org

Susan Witter, Editor
Will Beemer, Executive Director
Joel McCarty, Executive Director

It is a member benefit that is not available by subscription. Reports on timber framing events, news, business, and people.

Founded: 1984
Circulation: 1700

3412 Specialty Tools and Fasteners Distributors Association Newsletter
PO Box 44
Elm Grove, WI 53122
262-784-4774
FAX: 262-784-5059 800-352-2981
info@stafda.org www.stafda.org

Georgia H Foley, Executive Director
Catherine P Usher, Director Member Services
Marshall Jones, President
Patty Sherd, Controller

Members distribute or manufacture power equipment, anchors, fastening systems, drilling equipment and other related industrial supplies.

Founded: 1976
Circulation: 4,500

3413 TCA Newsletter
113 1st Street W
PO Box 204
Mount Vernon, IA 52314-204
319-895-6911
FAX: 319-895-8830
info@tilt-up.org www.tilt-up.org

J Edward Sauter, Executive Director
James Baty, Technical Director

A quarterly newsletter published by the Tilt-Up concrete Association. *$25.00*

Quarterly Founded: 1986
Circulation: 5500
Printed in 4 colors on glossy stock

3414 Western Building Material Association Newsletter
Western Building Material Association
PO Box 1699
Olympia, WA 98507-1699
360-943-3054
FAX: 360-943-1219
wbna@wbna.org www.wbma.org

Casey Voorhees, Executive Director
Stephanie Masters, Editor

38511 pages Monthly
Circulation: 700
Printed in on matte stock

3415 World Fence News
World Fencing Data Center
6101 W Courtyard Drive
Building 3 Suite 115
Austin, TX 78730-5096
512-349-2536
FAX: 512-349-2567 800-231-0275
editor@worldfencenews.com
www.worldfencenews.com

Rodger Duke, Publisher
Rick Henderson, Editor

Includes the most up to date information on events, products, trends, and services that effect the industry. *$29.95*

Monthly Founded: 1983
Circulation: 12500

Magazines & Journals

3416 ABC Today
Associated Builders and Contractors
4250 N Fairfax Drive
9th Floor
Arlington, VA 22203-1607
703-812-2000
FAX: 703-812-8203
info@abc.org www.abc.org

Lisa A Nardone, Editor
M. Kirk Pickerel, President/CEO
Amanuel Mehri, Manager

The purpose of this magazine is to offer industry updates on the latest trends and developments that affect general construction, labor, management, legislation, education, products and techniques for the building industry. *$36.00*

Monthly Founded: 1950
Circulation: 25000

3417 American Painting Contractor
Douglas Publications
2807 N Parham Road
Suite 200
Richmond, VA 23294
804-762-9600
FAX: 804-217-8999
editapc@douglaspublications.com
www.douglaspublications.com

Andrew Dwyer, Publisher
Susan Helmer, Editor
Mark Spector, Group Publisher

Features include business management, market research, decorating trends, techniques and developments in preparation and specialty coatings. News includes association activities, personnel changes and government actions.

Monthly Founded: 1985
Circulation: 25000

3418 American Public Works Magazine
2345 Grand Blvd
Ste 700
Kansas City, MO 64108-2625
816-472-6100
FAX: 816-472-1610 800-848-2792
apwa@apwa.net www.apwa.net

Martin Manning, President
Kaye Sullivan, Chief Executive Officer
Kevin Clark, Editor
Christine Robinson, Marketing/Publications Coordinator
Connie Hartline, Publications Manager

International educational and professional association of public agencies, private sector companies, and individuals dedicated to providing high quality public works goods and services. The magazine is a forum for public works professionals, agencies and companies. It includes public works-related topics to public attention in local, state and federal areas. *$100.00*

40 pages Monthly Founded: 1937

3419 Architectural Record
McGraw-Hill Construction
2 Penn Plaza
New York, NY 10121-2298
212-042-2000
FAX: 212-904-4256
brian_mcgann@mcgraw-hill.com
www.construction.com

Robert Ivy, Editor-in-Chief
Brian McGann, Circulation Manager
Norbert Young, Owner

Provides original, reliable and useful information to the architectural marketplace worldwide, setting the standards for excellence in architectural design and presenting insights and practical solutions for current challenges in the design, building construction and business practices. *$64.00*

Monthly/Annual Fee
Circulation: 102,000

3420 Asphalt
Asphalt Institute
2696 Research Park Drive
Lexington, KY 40511-8480
859-288-4960
FAX: 859-288-4999
info@asphaltinstitute.org
www.asphaltinstitute.org

Dwight Walker, Editor
Brian Clark, Publisher

A semi-annual magazine published by the Asphalt Institute.

3 issues per ye Founded: 1919
Circulation: 40000

3421 Automated Builder
CMN Associates
1445 Donlon Street
Suite 16
Ventura, CA 93003
805-642-9735
FAX: 805-642-8820 800-344-2537
info@automatedbuilder.com
www.automatedbuilder.com/

Donald O Carlson, Editor
Bob Mendel, Managing Editor
Agnes Carlson, Circulation

Distributed free of charge in the US to executive and management personnel upon written request in companies that are production (big volume) site builders, panelized home manufacturers, modular home manufacturers, special unit manufacturers, component manufacturers and HUD-Code, modular, panelized and commercial building dealers. *$50.00*

Monthly Founded: 1964
Circulation: 25000
Printed in 4 colors on glossy stock

3422 Bonded Builders News
Richard K Nicholson Enterprises
2201 Corporate Boulevard
#100
Boca Raton, FL 33431-7337
561-278-6968
FAX: 561-994-1474 800-749-0381

Richard K Nicholson, Publisher
Howard Head, Editor-in-Chief

Provides builders and developers with information involving new technologies and changing trends in the home building industry. *$ 18.00*

Quarterly
Circulation: 7000

3423 Builder
Hanley-Wood
1 Thomas Circle NW
Suite 600
Washington, DC 20005-5811
202-452-0800
FAX: 202-785-1974 188- 26- 841
wnesbitt@hanleywood.com
www.builderonline.com

Peter Goldstone, President
Warren Nesbitt, Publisher
Boyce Thompson, Editor-in-Chief

News and features of interest to the home building industry. Accepts advertising. Custom publishing, magazine publishing, CD/ROM, on-line and trade show opera-

tions. Effective print advertising combined with the power of a prestigious seminar series and high-volume Internet site. *$29.95*
Monthly Founded: 1947
Circulation: 150000
Mailing list available for rent 100M names
Printed in 4 colors on glossy stock

3424 Builder Insider
PO Box 191125
Dallas, TX 75219-8105
214-871-2930
FAX: 214-871-2931
Michael Anderson, Editor
What is current in the single-family building industry in Texas. *$12.00*
28 pages Monthly Founded: 1976
Circulation: 5200

3425 Builders Trade Journal
Lee Publications
6113 State Highway 5
PO Box 121
Palatine Bridge, NY 13428
518-673-2269
FAX: 518-673-2699 800-218-3237
bbutton@leepub.com
www.leepub.com
Fred Lee, Editor
Bruce Button, VP
Janet Button, VP Sales & Marketing
Edited for the building industry.
Monthly Founded: 1982

3426 Building Design & Construction
Reed Business Information
360 Park Avenue South
New York, NY 10014
212-450-0067
FAX: 630-288-8145
corporatecommunications@reedbusiness.com www.reedbusiness.com
Robert Cassidy, Editor in Chief
Dean Horowitz, Publisher
James Reed, Owner
Gerard Van d Aast, CEO
Serves the needs of the design and construction professionals of commercial, industrial and institutional buildings that include new and retrofit projects. Geared towards the building team that includes professionals from building firms, owning firms and design firms.
Monthly Founded: 1993
Circulation: 76,005

3427 Building Environment Report
IAQ Publications
7920 Norfolk Avenue
#900
Bethesda, MD 20814-2507
301-913-0115
FAX: 301-913-0119 www.iaqpubs.com
Robert Morrow, Publisher
Covers information to help manage building environmental hazards, meet environmental compliance requirements, protect building occupants, conference coverage and meetings of note. *$325.00*
Monthly
Circulation: 1,500

3428 Building Material Dealer
1405 Lilac Drive N
Minneapolis, MN 55422
763-544-1597
800-634-8645
carla@dealer.org www.dealer.org
Carla Waldemar, Executive Editor
Content focuses on a mixture of regional and national news relating to governmental regulations, dealer and supplier news, meetings and seminars affecting the independent building retailer.
Monthly
Circulation: 24,647

3429 Building Operating Management
Trade Press Publishing Corporation
2100 W Florist Avenue
Milwaukee, WI 53209-3799
414-228-7701
FAX: 414-228-1134
bom@tradeoress.com
www.tradepress.com
Edward Sullivan, Editor
Bobbie Reid, Production Director
Dick Yake, VP/Editorial Director
Eric Muench, Director of Circulation
Serves the field of facilities management, encompassing commercial building: office buildings, real estate/property management firms, developers, financial institutions, insurance companies, apartment complexes, civic/convention centers, including members of the Building Owners and Managers Association *$120.00*
Monthly Founded: 1954
Circulation: 70000
Printed in 4 colors on glossy stock

3430 Building Stone Magazine
300 Park Boulevard
Suite 335
Itasca, IL 60143
630-775-9130
FAX: 630-775-9134 866-786-6713
Jeff Buczkiewicz, Executive VP
Brenda Edwards, CEO
State of the industry publication for architects, designers and people in the natural stone industries: granite, marble, limestone, etc. *$65.00*
Founded: 1919
Circulation: 18000
Printed in 4 colors on glossy stock

3431 Building Supply Home Centers
Reed Business Information
360 Park Avenue S
New York, NY 10014
212-450-0067
www.reedbusiness.com
Daniel Cominskey, Editor
James Reed, Owner
For owners, manufacturers and other executives of the retail building market. *$60.00*
Monthly Founded: 1917

3432 Buildings: Facilities Construction & Management Magazine
Stamats Communications
615 5th Street SE
Cedar Rapids, IA 52401
319-364-6167
FAX: 319-364-4278
leah.garris@buildings.com
www.buildings.com
Tony Dellamaria, Publisher
Leah B. Garris, Associate Editor
Jana J. Madsen, Managing Editor
Tim Fixmer, President
Information on construction costs, building design, space planning, fire safety, environment solutions, energy effiency, accessibilty, security, and strategic facilities planning. *$70.00*
Monthly Founded: 1906
Circulation: 56500

3433 CIM Construction Journal
Construction Industries of Massachusetts
1500 Providence Highway Suite 14
PO Box 667
Norwood, MA 02062
781-551-0182
FAX: 781-551-0916
info@cimass.org
www.cimass.org/contact/
Mark Drummey, Editor/Publisher
Digest of horizontal public works projects.
Weekly Founded: 1921
Circulation: 2000

3434 Carpenter
United Brotherhood of Carpenters & Joiners
6801 Placid Street
Las Vegas, NV 89119
702-938-1111
FAX: 702-938-1122
dshoemaker@carpenters.org
www.carpenters.org
Doug Puppel, Managing Editor
Contains news and information on the union and its members, the craft, and the construction industry in whole
Founded: 1881
Circulation: 4,69,822

3435 Catholic Cemetery
National Catholic Cemetery Conference
710 N River Road
Des Plaines, IL 60016-1296
847-824-8131
FAX: 847-824-9608
nccc@ntriplec.com www.ntriplec.com
Irene K Pesce, Editor
Marc Christian, President
News on products and manufacturers and also gives information on maintenance and repairs.
Monthly Founded: 1949
Circulation: 2100

3436 Commerical Modular Construction
Emlen Publications/Modular Building Institute
1241 Andersen Drive
Suite N
San Rafael, CA 94901
415-460-6185
FAX: 415-460-6288 800-965-8876
jay@emlenpub.com
www.modularconstruction.net
Theodore Gordon, Editorial Director
Eli Gage, Group Publisher
Jay W. Schneider, Editor
Contains articles on modular for architects, engineering and spec writers who need building product, specification and address information.

3437 Computer-Aided Engineering
Penton Media
1300 E 9th Street
Cleveland, OH 44114
216-696-7000
FAX: 216-696-1309
information@penton.com
www.penton.com
William Tucker, Editor
Database applications in design and manufacturing. *$50.00*
96 pages Founded: 1982

3438 Concrete Pumping Magazine
American Concrete Pumping Association
606 Enterprise Drive
Lewis Center, OH 43035
614-431-5618
FAX: 614-431-6944
christi@concretepumpers.com
www.concretepumpers.com
Donald Wagner, President
Christi Collins, Executive Director
Packed with articles on industry leaders, new products, and on-site examples.
Quarterly
Circulation: 2,100

3439 Construction Bulletin
9443 Science Center Drive
New Hope, MN 55428-3636
763-537-1122
FAX: 763-537-1363 888-296-9945
George Rekela, Editor
Jone Sanem, Advertising Sales Manager
Serves heavy highway and building construction. *$199.00*
Weekly Founded: 1893
Circulation: 4000

3440 Construction Dimensions
Association of the Wall and Ceiling Industries
513 W Broad Street
Suite 210
Falls Church, VA 22046-3108
703-534-8300
FAX: 703-534-8307
info@awci.org http://www.awci.org
Steven A Etkin, President/Publisher
Laura M Porinchak, Editor
A monthly magazine for manufacturers and suppliers in the wall and ceiling, and related industries. Construction Dimensions is the official publication of the Association of the Wall and Ceiling Industries International. *$40.00*
115 pages Monthly Founded: 1918
Circulation: 23000

3441 Construction Distributors
Cygnus Publishing
1233 Janesville Avenue
Fort Atkinson, WI 53538
920-563-6388
FAX: 920-563-1699 800-308-6397
tom.hammel@cygnuspub.com
www.cygnusb2b.com/
Joe Drochak, Publisher
Tom Hammel, Editor
Elizabeth Gillette, Assistant Editor
Chris McClimon, Sales Manager
Monthly Founded: 1966
Circulation: 16000

3442 Construction Equipment Distribution
Associated Equipment Distributors
615 W 22nd Street
Oak Brook, IL 60523-8807
630-574-0650
FAX: 630-574-0132 800-388-0650
info@aednet.org www.aednet.org
Toby Mack, President
Pam Gruebnau, Publisher/Editorial Director
Al Ramirez, Sales and Advertising Man
Barb Konopasek, Circulation Coordinator
Offers valuable information for executives who sell and rent construction equipment. *$71.40*
72 pages Monthly Founded: 1918
Circulation: 5500

3443 Construction Equipment Guide-Northeast Edition
McKeon Publishing Company
2627 Mount Carmel Avenue
Glenside, PA 19038-2911
215-591-9125
FAX: 215-885-2910 800-523-2200
Beth Baker, Editor
Ted McKeon, Marketing Manager
Construction Equipment Guide is written for executives and top-level managers who are involved in the acquisition or distribution of construction equipment. Editorial topics include new equipment news, economy, finance, politics and job application stories. Accepts advertising. *$60.00*
120 pages BiWeekly Founded: 1957

3444 Construction Equipment Operation and Maintenance
Construction Publications
PO Box 1689
Cedar Rapids, IA 52406-1689
319-366-1597
FAX: 319-362-8808
Clark Parks, Editor
Use and maintenance of construction equipment. *$10.00*
24 pages Monthly Founded: 1948

3445 Construction Industry International
Quarto International
10 Whirling Dun
Collinsville, CT 06022-1239
Andrew Webster, Editor
Serves the administrative construction industry.
80 pages Monthly Founded: 1975

3446 Construction News
Construction Management
10825 Financial Centre Parkway
Suite 133
Little Rock, AR 72211-3587
501-742-2989
FAX: 501-686-6173
William Orth, Editor
Features and general news about construction. *$65.00*
95 pages Monthly Founded: 1934

3447 Construction News West
McGraw Hill
PO Box 182604
Columbus, OH 43272-1095
614-304-4000
FAX: 614-759-3749
customer.service@mcgraw-hill.com
www.mcgrawhill.com/
Elaine Beall, Managing Editor
Bill Davis, Publisher
Harold McGraw, CEO/President
Robert J. Bahash, Executive Vice President/CFO
Provides F.W. Dodge information for general contractors, suppliers, architects and owners in Arizona, Nevada and New Mexico. *$ 368.00*
Weekly Founded: 1902
Circulation: 3000

3448 Construction Specifier
Construction Specifications Institute
99 Canal Center Plaza
Suite 300
Alexandria, VA 22314-1588
703-684-0300
FAX: 703-684-0465 800-689-2900
csi@csinet.org www.csinet.org
Don Ethiel, Director
Offers a variety of information for construction professionals including construction products, systems, specifications, design solutions, legal concerns and economic forecasts. *$36.00*
Monthly Founded: 1956
Circulation: 18000
Printed in on glossy stock

3449 Constructioneer
Associated Construction Publication
30 Technology Parkway S
Suite 100
Norcross, GA 30092
770-093-3730
rcdwebmaster@reedbusiness.com
www.cmdg.com
Brian Faley, Editor
Tad Smith, Chief Executive Officer
Information directed to construction industry of New York, Pennsylvania, New Jersey, and Delaware.
100 pages Fortnightly Founded: 1975
Circulation: 18889
Printed in 4 colors on matte stock

3450 Constructor Magazine
Associated General Contractors of America
333 John Carlyle Street
Suite 200
Alexandria, VA 22314
703-548-3118
FAX: 703-548-3119
info@agc.org www.agc.org
Mark Shaw, Editor-In-Chief
Mark Kelly, Publisher
Paul L. Bonington, VP/Associate Publisher
Voice of the construction industry.
Monthly Founded: 1918
Circulation: 40,000

3451 Contractors Guide
Painting & Decorating Contractors of America
11960 Westline Industrial Drive
Suite 201
St. Louis, MO 63146-3209
314-514-7322
FAX: 314-514-9417 800-332-7322
hbowman@pdca.org www.pdca.com
Heather Bowman, Membership Coordinator
Diana Killian, Member Services Coordinator
What every painting and decorating contractor needs to know, organized for easy use by painting and decorating contractors of all sizes. *$68.00*

3452 Custom Home
Hanley-Wood
One Thomas Circle NW
Suite 600
Washington, DC 20005-5802
202-452-0800
FAX: 202-785-1974
www.hanleywood.com

J Michael Boyle, Publisher
Denise Dersin, Editor

Features materials, products, trends and the latest in designs for custom home construction. *$24.00*

7 issues per ye Founded: 1976
Circulation: 40000

3453 DBA Automated Builder Magazine

CMN Associates
1445 Donlon Street
Suite 16
Ventura, CA 93003-5640
805-642-9735
FAX: 805-642-8820 800-344-2537
info@automatedbuilder.com
www.automatedbuilder.com/

Don O Carlson, Editor/Publisher
Agnes Carlson, Circulation Manager

Magazine for manufacturers and suppliers who have a product line that is of interest to the factory-built housing industry. Covering all seven segments of US, Canadian and foreign housing industry, including: production builders; panelizers; component producers; modular; commercial modular; hud code; and all builder/dealers.

Monthly Founded: 1964
Circulation: 25000 24,800 names $150 per M.

3454 Daily Construction Service

Construction Market Data
142 Arena Street
El Segundo, CA 90245
310-322-9990
FAX: 858-573-0485

Jeanne Peterson, Editor

Offers valuable information for construction workers. *$365.00*

Monthly Founded: 1933

3455 Daily Journal of Commerce

Dolan Media Company/New Orleans Publishing Grp
111 Veterans Memorial Blvd
Ste 1440
Metairie, LA 70005-3050
504-368-8900
FAX: 504-368-8999
kathy.jeansonne@nopg.com
www.djc-gp.com

Mark Singletary, Publisher
Milton Lacoste, Editor
Anne N Lovas, General Manager
Kathy Jeansonne, Assistance Editor

Reports on building and engineering industries. *$456.00*

Monthly Founded: 1922

3456 Deep Foundations

Deep Foundations Institute
326 Lafayette Avenue
Hawthorne, NJ 07506
973-423-4030
FAX: 973-423-4031
dfihq@dfi.org www.dfi.org/

George R Compton, Executive Director
Manuel Fine, Editor
Theresa Rappaport, Circulaition Manager
$95.00

72 pages Quarterly Founded: 1976
Circulation: 1300

3457 Demolition

National Demolition Association
16 N Franklin Street
Suite 203
Doylestown, PA 18901-3536
215-348-4949
FAX: 215-348-8422 800-541-2412
info@demolitionmagazine.com
www.demolitionassociation.com

Michael Taylor, Executive Director

Trade publication for the Demolition Industry. *$40.00*

Founded: 1972
Circulation: 5000 5000 names
Printed in 4 colors on matte stock

3458 Desarrollo National

PO Box 3410
Milford, CT 06460-0942
203-874-1401

James Coffey, Editor

Covers construction and infrastructure projects. *$60.00*

40 pages Monthly Founded: 1953

3459 Design Build

144 Lexington Street
Woburn, MA 01801
781-937-9265
FAX: 781-937-9241
william_angelo@mcgraw-hill.com
www.designbuild.construction.com

Laura Viscusi, Associate Publisher
William J Angelo, Editor-in-Chief
Gary Merrill, Sales Director

Received by all subscribers of Engineering News Record plus 7,500 owners identified by FW Dodge as having an interest in the design-build project delivery system, and 1,000 members of the Design-Build Institute of America.

84 pages Quarterly Founded: 1953
Circulation: 20000

3460 Design Cost & Data

Rector Communications
2300 Chestnut Street
Suite 340
Philadelphia, PA 19103
215-963-9661
FAX: 215-963-9672
info@rector.com www.rector.com

Lee Rector, President
Greg Campbell, Managing Editor

Cost estimating magazine for architects, builders, developers, appraisers, specifiers, insurers and construction financiers.

3461 Design Solutions Magazine

Architectural Woodwork Institute
1952 Issac Newton Square West
Reston, VA 20190
703-733-0600
FAX: 703-733-0584
pduvic@awinet.org www.awinet.org

Philip Duvic, Director of Marketing/Communication
Cheryl Stratos, Advertising Manager

Each issue showcases beautiful examples of fine architectural woodwork manufactured by AWI Manufacturing Member companies. With beautiful four-color images, crisp detailed drawings and thought provoking articles, Design Solutions offers our readers a bountiful resource that's sure to inspire and delight all. *$25.00*

Quarterly/Annual Fee
Circulation: 27,000

3462 Dodge Construction News

McGraw Hill
2 Pennsylvania Plaza
Manhattan, NY 10121-1095
212-904-2000
FAX: 614-759-3749
customerservice@mcgraw-hill.com
www.mcgraw-hill.com

Eugene Ice, Editor
H Thompson, Art Director
Harold McGraw, III, CEO/President

Consists of program edition and proceedings and recap edition for the National Conventions of the American Institute of Architects and Construction Specifications Institute.

Founded: 1884
Circulation: 86400

3463 Dodge Construction News Green Sheet

McGraw Hill
PO Box 182604
Columbus, OH 43272
614-866-5769
FAX: 614-759-3759 877-833-5524
customerservice@mcgraw-hill.com
www.mcgraw-hill.com

Harold McGraw III, CEO/President
John Simpson, Editor

News and information for the world of construction including books, periodicals, sources of information, equipment and supply reviews and more for the professional and consumer. *$8.00*

Monthly Founded: 1884

3464 Door & Window Maker

Key Communications
385 Garrisonville Road
Suite 116
Stafford, Vi 22554
540-577-7174
FAX: 540-720-5687
key-com@glass.com
www.key-com.com

Tara Taffera, Editor/Publisher
Brigid O'Leary, Assistant Editor

9 issues per ye Founded: 1993
Circulation: 23,947

3465 Electrical Contractor

National Electrical Contractors Association
3 Bethesda Metro Center
Suite 1100
Bethesda, MD 20814-5372
301-657-3110
FAX: 301-215-4500
jwm@necanet.org www.ecmag.com

John W.Maisel, Publisher
John Fulmer, Editor
Astra J Benjamin, Circulation Manager
Daniel G. Walter, VP
John Grau, CEO

Offers important information for the electrical contracting industry: power, voice, data, and video. Free to qualified electrical contractors.

180 pages Monthly Founded: 1939
Circulation: 85000
Mailing list available for rent 90,000 names $120 per M.
Printed in 4 colors on glossy stock

3466 Engineering News Record

McGraw Hill
1221 Avenue of the Americas
New York, NY 10020
212-512-2000
FAX: 212-904-2820 www.enr.com

Janice L Tuchman, Editor-in-Chief
John J Kosowatz, Managing Editor

ENR is the definitive weekly source of technical and business intelligence for top construction professionals. ENR provides fast-breaking news, trends and developments strategically focused to help readers seize the latest new business opportunities. *$74.00*

150 pages Weekly Founded: 1874
Circulation: 78,000
Printed in 4 colors on glossy stock

3467 Environmental Design & Construction
Business News Publishing Company
2401 W Big Beaver Road
Suite 700
Troy, MI 48084
248-893-3500
FAX: 248-362-5103
hucalm@bnpmedia.com
www.edcmag.com

Michelle C Hucal, Editor
Diana Brown, Publisher
Monica Hackney, Production Manager
Janel Webster, Circulation Coordinator
Heather Jenkins, National Sales Manager

Founded: 1926

3468 Equipment Today
Cygnus Publishing
1233 Janesville Avenue
Fort Atkinson, WI 53538
920-563-6388
FAX: 920-563-1700 800-547-7377
becky.schultz@cygnuspub.com
www.cygnusb2b.com

Kris Flitcroft, Publisher
Becky Schultz, Editor

Contractors and other users of construction machinery. Editorial is focused on the selection, application and maintenance of equipment as well as new and improved product introductions. Accepts advertising. *$60.00*

54 pages Monthly Founded: 1966
Circulation: 80000

3469 FW Dodge Northwest Construction
McGraw Hill
800 S Michigan Avenue
Seattle, WA 98108
206-378-4700
FAX: 206-378-4721
sheila_bacon@mcgraw-hill.com
www.construction.com

Judy Schriener, Editor-in-Chief
Norbert W. Young, President
Richard Rodriguez, Marketing Director
Lucy Bodilly, Editor
Karen Heck, Publisher

Project news, plans, specifications and analysis data for the construction professional. *$40.00*

Monthly Founded: 1884

3470 Fabric Architecture
Industrial Fabrics Association International

1801 County Road BW
Roseville, MN 55113-4067
651-222-2508
FAX: 651-631-9334 800-225-4324
fabarch@ifai.com www.ifai.com

Bruce N Wright, Editor
Sarah Hyland, Advertising Information Manager
Steve Warner, President
Beth L. Hungiville, Managing Director:

Educates and inspires over 13,000 architects, designers and buildling professionals about the many uses of technical fabric in architectural applications. *$43.00*

Bi-monthly

3471 Facility Management Journal
International Facility Management Association
1 E Greenway Plaza
#1100
Houston, TX 77046
713-623-4362
FAX: 713-623-6124
ifmahq@ifma.org www.ifma.org

Heather Wiederhoeft, Editor
Alana F. Dunoff, President
Stephny Jones, Publisher

Covers industry economic, financial trends and the industries legislative, special emphasis on developments in technology. *$75.00*

Founded: 1990
Circulation: 14000

3472 Facility News Magazines
National Lead Abatement Council
PO Box 535
Olney, MD 20830
301-924-5490
FAX: 301-924-0265

Stephen A Weil, Publisher
Wendy Faxon, Editor

Information on facility maintenance management. *$36.00*

20 pages Monthly Founded: 1981
Circulation: 7500

3473 Factory Built Structures
Modular Building Institute
413 Park Street
Charlottesville, VA 22902-4737
434-296-3288
FAX: 434-296-3361
info@mbinet.org www.mbinet.org

Judy M Smith CMP, Executive Director
Steven Williams, Director Member Services
Matthew Gunning, Dir. Information/Computer Services

Written for users of commerical factory built structures including school, office, assisted living, construction, retail, and correction facility professionals. Offers reports, analysis, and competitive issues about the commercial modular industry. Also distributed at trade shows around the US.

40 pages Bi-Monthly Founded: 1983
Circulation: 25,000
Printed in 4 colors on glossy stock

3474 Fenestration Magazine
Ashlee Publishing
18 E 41st Street
20th Floor
New York, NY 10017-6009
212-376-7722
FAX: 212-376-7723
joel@ashlee.com
www.fenestrationmagazine.com

Joel Bruinooge, Editor

Windows and door industry. *$40.00*

80+ pages 10 per year
Circulation: 17,000

3475 Fine Homebuilding
Taunton Press
63 South Main Street
Box 5506
Newtown, CT 06470
203-270-6206
FAX: 203-270-6753
fh@tauton.com www.taunton.com

Jeanne Todaro, Circulation Manager
Kevin Ireton, Editor
Marissa Latschaw, Marketing Manager

Reviews of new equipment and related building materials and guidelines to successful work techniques and general industry news. *$ 37.95*

Founded: 1980
Circulation: 308,000

3476 Floor Covering Installer
Business News Publishing Company
755 W Big Beaver Road
Suite 1000
Troy, MI 48084-4900
248-362-3700
FAX: 248-362-0317 fci@bnp.com

Dan Lipman, Publisher

Provides the varied information needed by those who engage in floor covering installation with how-to and skill-building articles, how-to-do-it photographic presentations, new installation product information, news of the industry, as well as how and where to get further training in various aspects of floor covering installation.

Bi-Monthly
Circulation: 40,000

3477 Foundation Drilling
ADSC
Pacific Center I
14180 Dallas Parkway,Suite 510
Dallas, Te 75254
214-343-2091
FAX: 214-343-2384
slitke@adsc-iafd.com
www.adsc-iafd.com

S Scott Litke, Executive Director
Teri Dres, Managing Editor

Offers news and technical articles of interest to the foundation drilling and anchored earth retention industry worldwide. *$85.00*

8 issues per ye Founded: 1972
Circulation: 2800
Printed in 4 colors on glossy stock

3478 Frame Building News
Krause Publications
700 E State Street
Iola, WI 54990
715-445-2214
FAX: 715-445-4087 800-942-0673

Bill Bright, CEO
Scott Tappa, Editor
D'ann Jackson, Circulation Manager

Edited for the diversified town & country builders of light-industrial, commercial, agricultural, and residential structures. The majority of the coverage is about post-frame structures. Readers look for the latest in post-frame research and techniques, building code information, equipment, and materials. Regular features include 'Builder Spotlight,' 'New Products,' 'Supplier News,' 'OSHA Updates,' 'Legal Issues,' 'Business Strategies,' and 'Calendar of Events.' Official magazine of NFBA.

56 pages Founded: 1952
Circulation: 19211

3479 Glass Digest
Ashlee Publishing
18 E 41st Street
New York, NY 10017-6009
212-376-7722
FAX: 212-376-7723
publisher@ashlee.com
www.glassdigestmagazine.com/ashlee/glassdigest/index.html

Jordan Wright, Publisher

Merchandising/technical publication for the flat glass industry. *$25.00*
140 pages Monthly Founded: 1922

3480 **HMAT: Hot Mix Asphalt Technology**
National Asphalt Pavement Association
5100 Forbes Boulevard
Lanham, MD 20706
301-731-4748
FAX: 301-731-4621 888-468-6499
napa@hotmix.org www.hotmix.org

Mike Acott, President
Margaret Cervarich, VP/Marketing
Chuck Mac Donald, Editor
Chris Caldwell, Publisher

Bi-monthly magazine published by the National Asphalt Pavement Association.
50 pages Fortnightly Founded: 1955
Circulation: 30000

3481 **Hanley-Wood's Tools of the Trade**
Builderburg Group
One Thomas Circle NW
Suite 600
Washington, DC 20005-5802
202-520-0800
FAX: 202-785-1974
www.hanleywood.com

Rick Rick Schwolsky, Editor In Chief
Nellie Callahan, Publisher
Mary Leiphart, Circulation Manager
Sara Tobin, Senior Marketing Manager
Frank Anton, President/CEO

The wide array of tools and equipment in the construction and renovation industries. *$36.00*
Founded: 1976
Circulation: 65,000

3482 **Home Builders Magazine**
Work-4 Projects
4819 Saint Charles Boulevard
Pierrefonds, Qu 0
514-620-2200
FAX: 514-620-6300
editor@work4.ca
www.homebuildercanada.com/

Nachmi Artzy, Publisher
Cheryl Carvery, Sales

Specializes in educating readers on the latest installation tips, building techniques and materials that can be put into on-site practice everyday. *$30.00*
6 issues per ye Founded: 1988
Circulation: 23265

3483 **House Magazine**
PO Box 235
Jericho, VT 05465-0235

Leslie Hinchiffe, Publisher

Offers information on the residential construction industry in the northeastern United States. *$18.00*
Bi-Monthly

3484 **IEEE Power and Energy Magazine**

IEEE
445 Hoes Lane
Piscataway, NJ 08854-1331
732-981-0060
FAX: 732-981-1721
customer-service@ieee.org
www.ieee.org

Mel Olken, Editor
Bob Smrek, Production Director
Geri Kroline-Taylor, Senior Managing Editor

Network analysis, system stability studies, fault protection and construction management. *$285.00*
82 pages Monthly Founded: 1885
Circulation: 23000
Mailing list available for rent
Printed in on glossy stock

3485 **InTents**
Industrial Fabrics Association International
1801 County Road B W
Roseville, MN 55113
651-222-2508
FAX: 651-631-9334 800-225-4324

Mary Hennessey, Publisher
Katie Harholdt, Editor

For users and buyers of large tent structures for the special event industry and other temporary shelter needs. *$39.00*
Fortnightly Founded: 1994
Circulation: 12000 $250 per M.
Printed in 4 colors on glossy stock

3486 **Insulation Outlook**
National Insulation Association
99 Canal Center Plaza
Suite 222
Alexandria, VA 22314-1588
703-683-6422
FAX: 703-549-4838
niainfo@insulation.org
www.insulation.org

Melissa Jackson, Director of Publications
Beth Michaels, Assistant Editor
Kristin Follin, Circulation Manager

Contains information on new products, industry trends, asbestos abatement and installation practices. *$45.00*
Monthly Founded: 1973
Circulation: 7000
Printed in 4 colors on glossy stock

3487 **Interior Construction**
Ceilings & Interior Systems Construction Assn
1500 Lincoln Highway
Suite 202
Saint Charles, IL 60174-3579
630-584-1919
FAX: 630-584-7228 800-524-7228
info@cisca.org www.cisca.org

Jan R Foxen, Publisher

Offers information designed to keep contractors abreast of the changes in interior construction. *$35.00*
Monthly Founded: 1950
Circulation: 10000

3488 **Interlocking Concrete Pavement Magazine**
Interlocking Concrete Pavement Institute
1444 I Street NW
Suite 700
Washington, DC 20005
202-080-0285
FAX: 202-408-0285 800-241-3652
icpi@icpi.org www.icpi.org

David Smith, Circulation Director
Charles A McGrath, CAE, Executive Director
Robert J Burak, Director of Engineering
Karen Bigham, Director of Administration & Member
Matthew J. Tosiello, Director of Marketing *$5.00*

32 pages Quarterly Founded: 1993
Circulation: 20,000
Printed in 4 colors

3489 **Intermountain Contractor**
McGraw Hill
1743 West Alexander Street
Salt Lake City, UT 84119
801-742-2843
FAX: 801-972-8975 800-393-6343
al_slattery@mcgraw-hill.com
www.intermountain.construction.com

Al Slattery, Publisher
Brian Fryer, Editorial
Jim Arveseth, Owner

For general contractors. *$40.00*
88 pages Weekly
Circulation: 5,247

3490 **International Construction**
Primedia
PO Box 12914
Overland Park, KS 66282-2914
913-341-1300
FAX: 913-967-1903
www.intlconstruction.com
Provides valuable information to help readers succeed in every aspect of their jobs, from planning strategies to targeting growth, from solving engineering problems to selecting the right equipment and materials.

3491 **Job-Site Supervisor**
FMI Corporation
5171 Glenwood Avenue
Suite 200
Raleigh, NC 27612-3267
919-787-8400
FAX: 919-785-9320
webmasters@fminet.com
www.fminet.com

Joyce Watkins King, Editorial Director

Delivers articles on safety, regulations and management; with a special section that examines a challenging construction project. Editorial is presented from a field manager's point-of-view, including charts, graphs, illustrations and industry advice. *$179.00*
Founded: 1953
Circulation: 4000

3492 **Journal of Light Construction**
Hanley-Wood
186 Allen Brook Lane
Williston, VT 05495
802-879-3335
FAX: 802-879-9384 800-552-1951
jlc-cs@hanley-wood.com
www.jlconline.com

Don Jackson, Editor
Rick Strachan, Publisher

Written for builders, remodelers, contractors and architects involved in the design and construction of residential and light commercial buildings. Accepts advertising. *$39.95*
150 pages Monthly Founded: 1982
Circulation: 73000
Mailing list available for rent 70,000 names $120 per M.
Printed in 4 colors on glossy stock

3493 **Journal of Protective Coatings & Linings**
Technology Publishing Company
2100 Wharton Street
Suite 310
Pittsburgh, PA 15203-1951
412-431-8300
FAX: 412-431-5428 800-837-8303
webmaster@paintsquare.com
www.paintsquare.com

Gina Fleitman, VP Sales
Karen Kapsanis, Editor
Dr. Harold Hower, President

The right tools to help you reach the protective and marine coatings industry. *$80.00*
Monthly
Circulation: 15,000

3494 Kitchen & Bath Design News
Cygnus Publishing
1233 Janesville Avenue
Fort Atkinson, WI 53538
920-563-6388
FAX: 920-563-1699
esefrin@kbdn.net
www.cygnusb2b.com/

Janice Costa, Editor
Richard Reiff, President
Lynnell Lischka, Circulation Manager
Eliot Sefrin, Editorial Director & Publisher

Leading business magazine serving the kitchen and bath design, remodeling and new construction market.
Monthly Founded: 1966
Circulation: 50608

3495 Manufactured Home Merchandiser
RLD Group
203 N Wabash Avenue
Suite 800
Chicago, IL 60601-2411
312-236-3528
FAX: 312-236-4024

Herb Teider, Publisher/President
Wayne Beamer, Editor

Offers information for home builders and professionals in the manufactured home industry. *$36.00*
Monthly Founded: 1952
Circulation: 18600

3496 Masonry Magazine
Mason Contractors Association of America
33 S Roselle Road
Schaumburg, IL 60193
847-301-0001
FAX: 847-301-1110 800-536-2225
llewellyn@lionhrtpub.com
www.lionhrtpub.com

John Llewellyn, Publisher
Jennie Farnsworth, Editor
Meredith Schecter, Assistant Editor

This periodical covers every aspect of the mason contractor profession, not only equipment and techniques but topics such as building codes and stanards. *$24.00*
Monthly/Annual
Circulation: 17,000

3497 Metal Roofing
Krause Publications
700 E State Street
Iola, WI 54990
715-445-2214
FAX: 715-445-4087 800-726-9966

William Bright, Publisher
Stephen J Kent, President/CEO

Founded: 1900
Circulation: 25000 27,000 names $95 per M.
Printed in 4 colors on glossy stock

3498 Midwest Contractor
Associated Construction Publication
30 Technology Parkway
Suite 100
Norcross, GA 30092
770-209-3730
FAX: 770-417-4138 800-486-0014
cgrandia@reedbusiness.com
www.acppubs.com

Wayne Curtis, Publisher
Curt G Randia, Editor
Royce Morse, Production Director
Greg Sitek, National Editorial Director
Tad Smith, Chief Executive Officer

Annual equipment buyers' guide, a complete cross reference listing of manufacturers, area distributors and their construction equipment lines. *$96.00*
Founded: 1905

3499 Muir's Original Log Home Guide for Builders and Buyers
Gary J Schroder
1107 NW 4th Street
PO Box 671
Grand Rapids, MN 55744-0671
218-264-4434
FAX: 218-327-7229 888-345-5647

Doris Muir, Author
Allan Muir, Author
Gary Schroeder, Owner

Log home industry. *$12.95*
Monthly Founded: 1978 ISBN 0-967786-90-8

3500 National Association of Demolition Contactors
16 N Franklin Street
Suite 203
Doylestown, PA 18901-3536
215-348-4949
FAX: 215-348-8422 800-541-2412
info@demolitionassociation.com
www.demolitionassociation.com

Michael Taylor, Executive Director

Bimonthly magazine. $40 domestic, $60 foreign. *$40.00*
Founded: 1969
Circulation: 5000
Printed in 4 colors on matte stock

3501 New England Construction
Associated Construction Publication
30 Technology Parkway S
Suite 100
Norcross, GA 30092
770-209-3730
FAX: 770-417-4138 800-486-0014
jweatherhead@reedbusiness.com
www.acppubs.com

Jim Bellin, Publisher
Paul Fournier, Editor
John Weatherhead, Publishing Director
Tad Smith, Chief Executive Officer

Complete reports on contracts awarded, low bids and proposed work; features on highway construction and earthmoving, land development projects, utility construction, industrial building construction in the six-state New England region. *$96.00*
Monthly Founded: 1975
Circulation: 10490

3502 Northwest Construction
McGraw Hill
800 S Michigan Avenue
Seattle, WA 98108
206-378-4700
FAX: 206-378-4721

Al Slattery, Publisher
Sheila Bacon, Editor
Rick Becker, Owner

A regional, monthly magazine with features on Washington and design construction projects. Accepts advertising. *$60.00*
64 pages Monthly Founded: 1997
Circulation: 6,200

3503 Occupational Hazards
Penton Media
1300 E 9th Street
Cleveland, OH 44114
216-696-7000
FAX: 216-696-1752
information@penton.com
www.penton.com

Stephen G Minter, Editor/Associate Publisher
Sandy Smith, Managing Editor
Mary Abood, VP
Jennifer Daugherty, Communications Manager
James L. Nash, Senior Editor

Analysis of qualified recipients who have indicated that they recommend, select and/or buy the safety equipment, fire protection and other occupational health products.
65 pages Monthly Founded: 1892
Circulation: 65,777
Printed in 4 colors on glossy stock

3504 Old House Journal
Old House Journal Group
PO Box 420235
Palm Coast, FL 32142-235
800-234-3797
FAX: 978-283-4629
pkitzke@restoremedia.com
www.oldhousejournal.com

Patricia Poore, Publisher
Gordon Bock, Editor

Covers restoration techniques for the pre-1939 home. *$27.00*
Founded: 1999
Circulation: 140119

3505 Pacific Builder & Engineer
Vernon Publications
30 Technology Parkway S
Suite 100
Norcross, GA 30092
770-093-3730
FAX: 770-417-4138 800-486-0014
cmolesworth@reedbusiness.com
www.acppubs.com/community/846.html

Carl Molesworth, Editor
Cindi V Richardson, Advertising
Tad Smith, Chief Executive Officer

For management level personnel in the highway and heavy construction and non-residential building industries in Washington, Oregon, Idaho, Montana and Alaska. Includes notice of bid calls, low bidders, contract awards on area projects; cost cutting construction methods, unusual techniques and equipment applications, analysis of market conditions and industry trends, new products and literature, general industry news and views, personal news and legal advice. Accepts advertising. *$50.00*
Founded: 1902
Circulation: 100000

3506 **Pavement Maintenance**
Cygnus Publishing
1233 Janesville Avenue
Fort Atkinson, WI 53538
920-563-6388
FAX: 920-568-2305 800-547-7377
allan.heydorn@cygnuspub.com
www.pavementonline.com

Allan Heydorn, Editor
Dave Davel, Publisher

Founded: 1985
Circulation: 20000

3507 **Period Homes**
Historical Trends Corporation
1000 Potomac Street
Suite 102
Washington, DC 20007-3618
202-339-0744
FAX: 202-339-0749
info@restoremedia.com
www.restoremedia.com

Michael J Tucker, Chairman/CEO
Magnolia C Shepherd, Circulation Director
Peter H Miller, President

Lists sources of products for restoration and new construction of residential architecture. *$18.00*
120 pages
Circulation: 24,600 31M names $110 per M.

3508 **Products Finishing**
Scott Walker/Gardner Publications
6915 Valley Avenue
Cincinnati, OH 45244-3029
513-527-8977
FAX: 513-527-8801 800-950-8020
swalker@pfonline.com
www.pfonline.com

Daniel C Luciano, Publisher
Matthew J Little, Editor

Serves the finishing field, including educational services, public administration and other manufacturing industries. *$89.00*
Monthly Founded: 1928
Circulation: 42000
Printed in 4 colors on glossy stock

3509 **Professional Builder**
Reed Business Information
2000 Clearwater Drive
Oak Brook, IL 60523
630-740-0825
FAX: 630-288-8179
slebris@reedbusiness.com
www.reedbusiness.com

Dean Horowitz, Group Publisher
Heather McCune, Editor-in-Chief

New residential construction magazine with a more than 63 year tradition of providing builders the solutions they need to maximize profits.
Monthly Founded: 1931
Circulation: 127002

3510 **Professional Remodeler**
Reed Business Information
360 Park Avenue South
New York, NY 10010
212-450-0067
FAX: 212-384-2745
ksweet@reedbusiness.com
www.reedbusiness.com

David Wood, Publisher
Mike Morris, Editor-in-Chief
Kimberly Sweet, Editor
James Reed, Owner
James A Casella, CEO

Designed to accomodate the needs of residential remodelers and light commercial renovators and focuses on news, features, new products, tech-takes, and management and marketing approaches.
Monthly Founded: 2002
Circulation: 18131

3511 **Professional Roofing**
National Roofing Contractors Association

10255 W Higgins Road
Suite 600
Rosemont, IL 60018-5607
847-299-9070
FAX: 847-299-1183 800-323-9545
nrca@nrca.net
www.professionalroofing.net

Carl Good, Publisher
Ambika-Punia Bailey, Editor
Krista Reisdorf, Associate Editor

Articles on both technical and business aspects of professional roofing.
Monthly Founded: 1886
Circulation: 18131

3512 **Professional Spraying**
88-11TH AVENUE NE
Minneapolis, MN 55413
612-623-6000
FAX: 612-623-6580
CustomerService@graco.com
www.graco.com

Mick Lee, Publisher

Targets new products, industry news, and trade literature.
Monthly Founded: 1926
Circulation: 40000

3513 **Qualified Remodeler**
Cygnus Publishing
1233 Janesville Avenue
Fort Atkinson, WI 53538
920-563-6388
FAX: 920-563-1707 800-547-7377
heidi.riedl@cygnusb2b.com
www.qualifiedremodeler.com/

Pat O'Toole, Editor
Chaya Chang, Managing Editor
Paul Mackler, CEO

Provides residential remodelers, contractors and architects with information to help them succeed in business.
72 pages Monthly Founded: 1975
Circulation: 53000
Mailing list available for rent 84,000 names
Printed in 4 colors on glossy stock

3514 **Reeves Journal**
Business News Publishing Company
2401 W. Big Beaver Rd.
Suite 700
Troy, MI 48084
248-362-3700
FAX: 248-362-0317
katilarson@aol.com
www.bnpmedia.com

Ellyn Fishman, Publisher
Scott Marshutz, Editor *$55.00*

Monthly Founded: 1922
Circulation: 15,535

3515 **Remodeling**
Hanley-Wood
One Thomas Circle NW
Suite 600
Washington, DC 20005-5802
202-452-0800
FAX: 202-785-1974
rm@omeda.com
www.remodeling.hw.net

Rick Strachan, Group Publisher
Sal Alfano, Editorial Director
Ingrid Bush, Managing Editor
Peter Goldtsone, President

News on state-of-the-art in remodeling management, products, construction and techniques. Appeals to the residential and light commercial remodeling contractor.
$44.95
Monthly Founded: 1955
Circulation: 93612

3516 **Rental Equipment Register**
Miramar Publishing Company
745 Fifth Avenue
Malibu, CA 90265-8987
212-745-0100
FAX: 212-745-0121
information@primedia.com
www.primedia.com

Mixchael Roth, Editor
Mark Welterlen, Publisher
Kelly Conlin, CEO

Edited for owners and managers of equipment rental and sales centers. *$45.00*
125 pages Monthly Founded: 1886
Circulation: 21000

3517 **Residential Architect**
Hanley-Wood
One Thomas Circle NW
Washington, DC 20005
202-452-0800
FAX: 202-785-1974 888-269-8410
res@omeda.com
www.hanley-wood.com

S. Claire Conroy, Editor
Stephen Sheikhli, Managing Editor
Michael Boyle, Group Publisher
Frank Anton, CEO *$39.95*

9 issues (1year Founded: 1976
Circulation: 22000

3518 **Rock and Dirt**
174 Fourth Street
Crossville, TN 38555
931-849-9502
FAX: 931-484-2532 800-251-6776
subs@rockanddirt.com
www.rockanddirt.com

Michael Stone, Publisher
Margaret Ironside, Associate Manager

Comprehensive buy/sell publications for heavy construction. Primary target audiences worldwide are contractors and other heavy equipment buyers. A non-editorial tabloid, each issue contains display and classified ads that feature thousand of pieces of heavy machinery and related products and services. The magazine also has a large auction section. *$14.33*
Founded: 1950
Circulation: 170,000
Printed in 4 colors on newsprint stock

3519 **Roofing Contractor**
BNP Media
2401 W Big Beaver Road
Suite 700
Troy, MI 48084-4900
248-362-3700
FAX: 248-362-5103
DelorenzoJ@bnpmedia.com
www.roofingcontractor.com

Jill Nash, Publisher
Kari Rowe, Group Circulation Manager
Jo Delorenzo, Editor
Candace Roulo, Marketing Manager

Focuses on coverage of new technology and its implementation in the field. Regular issues include equipment comparisons,

new product information, safety tips and legal advice.
Monthly Founded: 1926
Circulation: 27205

3520 Roofing/Siding/Insulation
Advanstar Communications
One Park Avenue
NY, NY 10016
212-797-7631
FAX: 212-951-6793
info@advanstar.com
www.advanstar.com

Mike Russo, Editor/Associate Publisher
Sean Carr, Group Publisher

Reaches contractors and wholesalers engaged in the application of roofing, siding, insulation and related products and materials. Focus on roofing technology, application procedures, government regulatory trends, new products and new industry problems and developments. *$36.00*
64 pages Monthly Founded: 1945
Circulation: 23658

3521 Rural Builder
Krause Publications
700 E State Street
Iola, WI 54990
715-445-2214
FAX: 715-445-4087 800-942-0673
rural_builder@krause.com
www.krause.com/static/construction.htm

Scott Tappa, Editor

Focuses on the post frame and metal frame industry. *$18.94*
64 pages Founded: 1952
Circulation: 32000 32000 names $95 per M.

Printed in 4 colors on glossy stock

3522 Services Magazine
Building Service Contractors Association Int'l
10201 Lee Highway
Suite 225
Fairfax, VA 22030
703-359-7090
FAX: 703-352-0493 800-368-3414
danderson@bscai.org www.bscai.org

Carol Dean, Publishing Director
Barbara Woodward, Advertising Director
Denise Anderson, Editor

The Building Service Contractors Association International is the trade association serving the facility services industry through education, leadership, and representatiion. *$30.00*
56 pages Monthly Founded: 1981
Circulation: 20,504
Printed in 4 colors on glossy stock

3523 Shelter
Association Publications
1168 Vickery Lane
Suite 3
Cordoba, TN 38013
901-519-9856

James Powell, Editor

For the national distribution and retail segments of the building products industry. *$6.00*
Monthly Founded: 1962

3524 Southern Building
Southern Building Code Congress International
900 Montclair Road
Birmingham, AL 35213-1206
205-591-3167

webmaster@iccsafe.org
www.sbcci.org

Kalla P Higgs, Editor

Publishes and maintains a set of model building codes called the Standard Codes. Also provides educational and technical support to the codes enforcement industry. *$25.00*
40 pages Founded: 1943
Circulation: 12000

3525 Southwest Contractor
McGraw Hill
3110 N Central Avenue
Suite 155
Phoenix, AZ 85012
602-274-2155
FAX: 602-631-3073 800-393-6343
kelly_wendel@mcgraw-hill.com
www.southwest.construction.com

Karen Heck, Publisher
Kelly Wendel, Editor
Jim Biallas, President

We cover all aspects of the commercial construction industry in Arizona, Nevada and New Mexico. Our mission is to provide news about the projects, the people and the events that affect the building and highway/heavy segments market. *$40.00*
48 pages Monthly Founded: 1938
Circulation: 7000

3526 Structural Insulated Panel
Structural Insulated Panel Association
PO Box 1699
Gig Harbor, WA 98335
253-858-7472
FAX: 253-858-0272 800-792-7477
staff@sips.org www.sips.org

Damian Pataluna, President
William Wachtler, Executive Director

A comprehensive, full color book on building with energy efficient SIPs.
Quarterly Founded: 1990
Circulation: 5000

3527 Structures
Business Journal of Portland
851 SW 6th Avenue
Suite 500
Portland, OR 97204
503-274-8733
FAX: 503-227-2650 866-246-0424
portland@bizjournals.com
www.bizjournals.com/portland

Ray Shaw, CEO
Rob Smith, Editor
Dan McMillan, Managing Editor
Susan McAvoy, Circulation Director

Special edition of The Business Journal that spotlights top construction projects and highlights the design, architecture and construction *$89.00*
52 pages Daily
Circulation: 400000
Printed in 4 colors on newsprint stock

3528 Subcontractor
Subcontractors Education Trust
1004 Duke Street
Alexandria, VA 22314-3588
703-684-3450
FAX: 703-836-3482 800-221-0415
asaoffice@ASA-HQ.com
www.asaonline.com

David Mendes, Publisher
Luke McFadden, Director Government Relations
E Colette Nelson, Executive VP

News from the construction industry, including up-to-date information on legislative and regulatory affairs, and business news concerning the subcontracting industry.
24 pages Quarterly Founded: 1966
Circulation: 9000
Printed in 2 colors

3529 Tileletter
626 Lakeland E Drive
PO Box 13629
Jackson, MS 39232
601-939-2071
FAX: 601-932-6117
tileletter@tile-assn.com
www.tile-assn.com/

Bob Brown, Membership Director
Bart Bettiga, Executive Director/Editor
Michelle Harrell, Assistant Editor

A professionally produced publication which is directed solely to our industry. Circulated to more that 20,000 firms each month and faithfully read by approximately 50,000 individuals within our industry.
100 pages Monthly Founded: 1947
Circulation: 50000
Mailing list available for rent 21,000 names $150 per M.
Printed in on matte stock

3530 Tiling & Decorative Surfaces
Ashlee Publishing
18 E 41st Street
New York, NY 10017
212-376-7722
FAX: 212-376-7723
publisher@ashlee.com
www.ashlee.com

Jordan M Wright, President

Provides information about industry trends and events throughout the world including interviews with manufacturers, distributors and contractors, offering tips on successful merchandising and sales techniques. Issues include product listings and project articles. *$50.00*
Monthly Founded: 1950
Circulation: 27181

3531 Timber Framing
Timbers Framers Guild
PO Box 60
Becket, MA 01223
413-239-9926
FAX: 888-453-0879 888-453-0879
journal@tfguild.org www.tfguild.org

Ken Rower, Editor
Will Beemer, Executive Director
Joel McCarty, Executive Director

Contains in-depth articles on timber framing history, technology, theory, practice, design, and engineering, as well as the work of the guild and its members *$25.00*
Quarterly Founded: 1984

3532 Traditional Building
Historical Trends Corporation
69A 7th Avenue
Brooklyn, NY 11217-3618
718-638-2699
FAX: 718-636-0750
htcstaff@traditional-building.com
www.traditional-building.com

Ray Shepherd, Production Manager
Clem Labine, Editor

Lists sources of products for restoration and new construction of traditional buildings. *$19.95*

Bi-Monthly Founded: 1988
Circulation: 29,000 39M names $110 per M.
Printed in on glossy stock

3533 Underground Construction
Oildom Publishing Company of Texas
PO Box 941669
Houston, TX 77094-8669
281-558-6930
FAX: 281-558-7029
oklinger@oildompublishing.com
www.oildompublishing.com

Oliver C Klinger, President & Publisher
Robert Carpenter, Editor
Rita Tubb, Managing Editor *$25.00*

Monthly
Printed in 4 colors on glossy stock

3534 Underground Focus
Canterbury Communications
PO Box 374
Lowell, IN 46356
815-468-7814
FAX: 715-635-7977
ufmagazine@underspace.com
www.underspace.com

Ron Rosencrans, Editor-in-Chief
Paula Miller, Advertising Manager
Judy Engelbrecht, Circulation

People read Underground Focus magazine because it documents the importance of their work and helps them get the budgets to do the job. It powerfully dramatizes the need for underground damage prevention and excavation safety. *$25.00*

46 pages Founded: 1986
Circulation: 18,000
Printed in 2 colors

3535 Utility Contractor
4301 N Fairfax Drive
Suite 360
Arlington, VA 22203
703-358-9300
FAX: 703-358-9307
susan@nuca.com www.nuca.com

Susan Williams, Senior Editor
Bill Hillman, CEO/President
Joyce Donkor, Marketing Assistant

Serves the underground utility construction industry, including contractors, manufacturers, suppliers, engineering firms, municipal/public/private utilities, and others allied to the field.

Monthly Founded: 1967
Circulation: 20983

3536 Walls & Ceilings
Business News Publishing Company
2401 W Big Beaver Road
Suite 700
Troy, MI 48084-4900
248-362-3700
FAX: 248-362-5103
mazures@bnp.com
www.bnpmedia.com

Sarah Mazure, Publisher
Nick Moretti, Editor

Information regarding management, building methods, technology, government regulations, consumer trends, and product information for the contractor involved in exterior finishes, waterproofing, insulation, metal framing, drywall, fireproofing, partitions, stucco and plaster. *$ 49.00*

140 pages Monthly Founded: 1938
Circulation: 30000
Printed in 4 colors

3537 Welding Journal
American Welding Society
550 NW 42nd Avenue
Miami, FL 33126-5699
305-443-9353
FAX: 305-443-7559 800-443-9353
info@aws.org www.aws.org

Ray Shook, Executive Director
Andy Cullison, Publisher

Serves the metal working field, individuals and organizations engaged in welding, cutting or related processes and equipment for the fabrication, maintenance, design or repair of metal products. *$80.00*

Monthly Founded: 1919
Circulation: 50,000

3538 Western Builder
Western Builder Publishing Company
30 Technology Parkway
Suite 100
Norcross, GA 30092
770-209-3730
FAX: 770-417-4138
michelle.collins@mdg.com
www.acppubs.com

Wayne Curtis, Publisher
Greg Sitek, National Editorial Director
Tad Smith, Chief Executive Officer

Regional construction publication serving the heavy, highway and non-residential construction industry in Wisconsin and the Upper Peninsula of Michigan. *$53.00*

Monthly Founded: 1905
Circulation: 100,000

3539 Window & Door
National Glass Association
8200 Greensboro Drive
Suite 302
McLean, VA 22102-3803
703-442-4890
FAX: 703-442-0630 866-342- 642

Nicole Harris, Publisher
Philip J. James, President
Nancy Davis, Editor-in-Chief

The focus is on technical, new product information, business management and industry issues which focus on manufacturing both new and replacement windows and doors. *$29.95*

Founded: 1948
Circulation: 20000

3540 Window Film Magazine
Key Communications
PO Box 569
Garrisonville, VA 22463
540-577-7174
FAX: 540-720-5687
boleary@glass.com
www.windowfilmmag.com/

Debra Levy, President
Penny Beverage, Assistant Editor
Brigid O'Leary, Editor
Holly Biller, Marketing Director

Provides industry news, supplier and film manufacturer profiles, technical and installation tips, as well as state-by-state legislative breakdowns and consumer marketing issues relevant to the film industry. *$35.00*

Monthly
Circulation: 7000

3541 Window World Magazine
Work-4 Projects
4819 St. Charles Boulevard
Pierrefonds, Quebec H9H-3C7
514-620-2200
FAX: 514-620-6300
windowworld@work4.com

Nachmi Artzy, Publisher
Cheryl Carvery, Sales

Provides new products, announcements, calendar events, and coverage of industry news, technical and maketing information to small and medium window and door manufacturers of North America. *$30.00*

Bi-Monthly
Circulation: 9,877

3542 Wrecking and Salvage Journal
Duane Publishing
51 Park Street
Dorchester, MA 02122
617-282-4885
FAX: 617-282-0320
info@decmagazine.com
www.decmagazine.com

Herbert Duane III, Editor

Business related information for those engaged in demolition and urban renewal. *$35.00*

Monthly Founded: 1967

Trade Shows

3543 ACSM Annual Spring Conference
American Congress on Surveying and Mapping
6 Montgomery Village Avenue
Suite 403
Gaithersburg, MD 20879
240-680-0765
FAX: 240-632-1321
info@acsm.net www.acsm.net

Hachero Hill, Conference Director
Colleen Campbell, Conference Director

Four hundred booths of products and services offered by companies involved in the aerial mapping industry.

2000 Attendees April

3544 AEMA Annual Meeting
Asphalt Emulsion Manufacturers Association
3 Church Circle
PO Box 250
Annapolis, MD 21401-1933
410-267-0023
FAX: 410-267-7546
krissoff@aema.org www.aema.org

Michael Krissoff, Executive Director

Representing close to 150 of the world's leading companies in the pavement preservation and rehabilitation industry. A combined annual meeting with the International Slurry Surfacing Association and the Asphalt Recycling & Reclaiming Association.

400 Attendees Annual/March

3545 AGC CONSTRUCTOR Exhibition

Associated General Contractors of America
333 John Carlyle Street
Suite 200
Alexandria, VA 22314
703-548-3118
FAX: 703-548-3119
meetings@agc.org www.agc.org

Stephen E Sandherr, CEO
David R Lukens, COO

One hundred and seventy-five exhibiors of heavy and light construction equipment, trucks, building materials, management services, computer hardware and software. Contractors, subcontractors and trade professionals attend.

4500+ Attendees March

3546 AIBD Annual Convention

American Institute of Building Design
2505 Main Street
Suite 209B
Stratford, CT 06615
203-783-3480
FAX: 203-378-3568 800-366-2423
bobbi@aibd.org www.aibd.org

Bobbi Currie, Show Manager
Steven Mickley, Executive Director

Exhibition of 25 manufacturers, suppliers, distributors and plan publishers of building products including: roofing, windows, doors, floor covering, fire places, spas/jacuzzis, lumber, intercom systems, alarm systems and appliances; computer-aid design technology, computer hardware/software and plan publishers. Containing 30 booths and 30 exhibits.

1500 Attendees July Founded: 1950

3547 AIC Annual Forum

American Institute of Constructors
PO Box 26334
Alexandria, VA 22314
703-683-4999
FAX: 703-683-5480
admin@aicnet.org www.aicnet.org

Steven DeSalvo, President
David R Mattson, VP

Educational presentations from leading practitioners and educators in the world of construction, panel discussions with major voices in the industry, opportunities to network with other emerging leaders in the construction profession as they fine-tune their leadership skills.

Annual/April

3548 AISC Annual Meeting

American Institute of Steel Construction
1 E Wacker Drive
Suite 3100
Chicago, IL 60601-2001
312-670-2400
FAX: 312-670-5403
lenihan@aisc.org www.aisc.org

John Devantier, Executive Director
Katey Lenihan, Meeting Planner

One hundred booths attended by structural engineers, steel fabricators, educators and construction managers. Those interested in the design fabrication and erection of structural steel for non-residential buildings and bridges.

100 Attendees Annual/September

3549 APWA International Public Works Congress & Expo

American Public Works Association
2345 Grand Boulevard
Suite 700
Kansas City, MO 64108-2641
816-472-6100
FAX: 816-472-1610
dpriddy@apwa.net www.apwa.net

Diana Forbes, Meeting Planner/Exhibit Sales Mgr
Dana Priddy, Director Meetings
Kaye Sullivan, Chief Executive Officer

Offers the benefit of a variety of educational sessions, depth of the exhibit program and endless opportunities for networking. The latest cutting-edge technologies, managerial techniques and regulatory trends designed to keep you focused on the right solutions at the right time.

6500 Attendees Annual/September

3550 APWA North American Snow Conference

American Public Works Association
2345 Grand Boulevard
Suite 700
Kansas City, MO 64108-2641
816-472-6100
FAX: 816-472-1610
snow@apwa.net www.apwa.net

Diana Forbes, Meeting Planner/Exhibit Sales Mgr
Dana Priddy, Director Meetings
Kaye Sullivan, Chief Executive Officer

Education, technical and hands-on for snow and ice management.

1000 Attendees April

3551 ASPE Estimating Academy & Annual Convention

American Society of Professional Estimators
2525 Perimeter Place Drive
Suite 103
Nashville, TN 37214
615-316-9200
FAX: 615-316-9800 888-378-6283
edwalsh@aspenational.org
www.aspenational.com

Edward Walsh, Executive Director
Robert Kruhm, Advertising & Sponsorship

Provides two days of presentations by nationally known speakers in the construction industry. ASPE's Technical Documents Committee prepares a book for each convention attendee that contains papers submitted by the speakers at these educational sessions.

Annual/July

3552 AWI Annual Meeting/Convention

Architectural Woodwork Institute
1952 Issac Newton Square West
Reston, VA 20190
703-733-0600
FAX: 703-733-0584
kkenn@awinet.org www.awinet.org

Kimberly Kennedy, Meeting/Conventions Director
Rachel Schmidt, Meeting Planner

Seminar, workshop and woodwork products such as casework, fixtures and panelings, equipment and supplies.

Annual/October

3553 American Congress on Surveying and Mapping Conference

6 Montgomery Village Avenue
Suite 403
Gaithersburg, MD 20879
240-680-0765
FAX: 240-632-1321
info@acsm.net www.acsm.net

Hachero Hill, Conference Director
Colleen Campbell, Conference Director
Curt Sumner, Executive Director

Four hundred booths of products and services offered by companies involved in the aerial mapping industry.

2000 Attendees April

3554 American Institute of Building Design Convention

2505 Main Street
Suite 209B
Stratford, CT 06615
203-783-3480
FAX: 203-378-3568 800-366-2423
bobbi@aibd.org www.aibd.org

Steven Mickley, Executive Director
Bobbi Currie, Show Manager

Exhibition of 25 manufacturers, suppliers, distributors and plan publishers of building products including: roofing, windows, doors, floor covering, fire places, spas/jacuzzis, lumber, intercom systems, alarm systems and appliances; computer-aid design technology, computer hardware/software and plan publishers. Containing 30 booths and 30 exhibits.

1500 Attendees July Founded: 1950

3555 American Institute of Constructors Forum

PO Box 26334
Alexandria, VA 22314
703-683-4999
FAX: 703-683-5480
admin@aicnet.org www.aicnet.org

Steven DeSalvo, President
David R Mattson, VP

Educational presentations from leading practitioners and educators in the world of construction, panel discussions with major voices in the industry, opportunities to network with other emerging leaders in the construction profession as they fine-tune their leadership skills.

Annual/April

3556 American Institute of Steel Construction Meeting

1 E Wacker Dr
Ste 700
Chicago, IL 60601-2000
312-670-2400
FAX: 312-670-5403
lenihan@aisc.org www.aisc.org

John Devantier, Executive Director
Katey Lenihan, Meeting Planner

One hundred booths attended by structural engineers, steel fabricators, educators and construction managers. Those interested in the design fabrication and erection of structural steel for non-residential buildings and bridges.

100 Attendees Annual/September

3557 Arrowhead Home and Builders Show

Shamrock Productions
14550 Granada Drive
Apple Valley, MN 55124
952-431-9630
FAX: 952-431-9633
info@shamrockprod.com
www.shamrockprod.com/dh.htm

Randy Schauer, President/CEO

Home building, remodeling, landscaping and more.

41960 Attendees April 11-15, 2007

3558 Asphalt Emulsion Manufacturers Association Meeting

3 Church Circle
PO Box 250
Annapolis, MD 21401-1933
410-267-0023
FAX: 410-267-7546
krissoff@aema.org www.aema.org

Michael Krissoff, Executive Director

Representing close to 150 of the world's leading companies in the pavement preservation and rehabilitation industry. A combined annual meeting with the International Slurry Surfacing Association and the Asphalt Recycling & Reclaiming Association.

400 Attendees Annual/March

3559 Associated Builders and Contractors National Convention

Associated Builders and Contractors
1300 N 17th Street
Suite 800
Rosslyn, VA 22209
703-812-2000
FAX: 703-812-8200
meetings@abc.org www.abc.org

Jessica Burney, Meetings Coordinator
Tina Schneider, Meetings/Conventions Director

Exhibits for construction contractors, subcontractors, and associated trades.

3560 Associated General Contractors of America Exhibition

333 John Carlyle Street
Suite 200
Alexandria, VA 22314
703-548-3118
FAX: 703-548-3119
meetings@agc.org www.agc.org

Stephen E Sandherr, CEO
David R Lukens, COO

One hundred and seventy-five exhibiors of heavy and light construction equipment, trucks, building materials, management services, computer hardware and software. Contractors, subcontractors and trade professionals attend.

4500+ Attendees March

3561 Brick Show

Brick Industry Association
11490 Commerce Park Drive
Reston, VA 20191-1525
703-620-0100
FAX: 703-620-3928
sludwig@bia.org www.bia.org

Susan Ludwig, Show Manager

The only national tradeshow and conference for the clay brick industry.

950 Attendees March

3562 Builders Trade Show

Maryland National Capital Building Industry Assn.
1738 Elton Road
Suite 200
Silver Spring, MD 20903-5730
301-493-3000
FAX: 301-445-5499
building@mncbia.org
www.mncbia.org

Kathy Rockinberg, Program Manager
Susan J Matlick, Executive VP

Annual show and exhibits of construction equipment, supplies and services.

3563 Building Industry Show

Building Industry Assn. of Southern California
1330 Valley Vista Drive
Diamond Bar, CA 91765
909-396-9993
FAX: 909-396-1571
sfrias@biasc.org
www.buildingindustryshow.com

Sue Frias, Show Director
Jessica Harders, Exhibitor Coordinator

Annual show of about 400 exhibitors of products and services for the building industry.

8000+ Attendees November 16-17

3564 Business Administration Conference

National Ready Mixed Concrete Association
900 Spring Street
Silver Spring, MD 20910
301-587-1400
FAX: 301-585-4219 888-846-7622
info@nrmca.org www.nrmca.org

Michael Forster, VP of Finance & Administration
Jennifer Leonard, Meetings Manager

A 3-day educational program for financial, information technology, and human resources professionals in the construction and construction materials business.

Annual/October

3565 CFMA Annual Conference & Exhibition

Construction Financial Management Association
29 Emmons Drive
Suite F-50
Princeton, NJ 08540
609-452-8000
FAX: 609-452-0474
info@cfma.org www.cfma.org

Ron Kress, Sales/Advertising Director
William Schwab, President

The source and resource for construction financial professionals.

6000 Attendees May

3566 CONEXPO-CON/AGG

Association of Equipment Manufacturers
6737 W Washington St
Milwaukee, WI 53214-5647
414-272-0943
FAX: 414-272-1170 800-867-6060

Ken Snover, Expo Managing Director
Jim Eldredge, Exhibits Coordinator
Jackie Vnuk, Exhibits Manager
Melissa Magestro, Exhibits Manager

The international gathering place for the worldwide construction, aggregates and ready mixed concrete industries.

124M Attendees March 2008/Every 3 yrs
Founded: 2002

3567 CSI Show

Construction Specifications Institute
99 Canal Center Plaza
Suite 300
Alexandria, VA 22314
703-684-0300
FAX: 703-684-8436 800-689-2900
lderby@csinet.org www.csinet.org

Lisa Derby, Director, Events Manager
Laurie Lowe, Event Manager
Barbara Aston, Exhibit Sales

Annual convention and exhibit of 650 manufacturers, suppliers and distributors of products and services used in non-residential and commercial construction industry. Containing 1,000+ booths.

8500 Attendees April

3568 Composites & Polycon

American Composites Manufacturers Association
1010 North Glebe Road
Suite 450
Arlington, VA 22201
703-525-0511
FAX: 703-525-0743
jmccormack@acmanet.org
www.acmashow.org

Jeanne McCormack, Director Confernces/Meetings

World's largest trade association serving the composites industry. Provides education and support for composites fabricators in the successful operation of businesses, and offers leading-edge services in regulatory compliance and formulation, education and training, management, and market expansion.

1.5M Attendees September/October

3569 Coverings Trade Show

626 Lakeland E Drive
PO Box 13629
Jackson, MS 39236
601-939-2071
FAX: 601-932-6117
www.coverings.com

Bart A Bettiga, Executive Director
Gigi Wall, Administrative/Accounting Manager

The Largest Ceramic Tile and Natural Stone Exposition In The Country. A comprehensive and quality educational program covering all aspects of our industry, from design and specification, to installation and distribution, including both technical and business sessions.

33000 Attendees April
Mailing list available for rent

3570 Delmarva Ag & Construction Show

Lee Publications
6113 State Highway 5
Palatine Bridge, NY 13428
518-732-2269
FAX: 518-673-3245 800-218-5586
kmaring@leepub.com
www.leepub.com

Ken Maring, Trade Show Manager
Tom Mahoney, Corporate Sales Manager
Janet Button, Trade Show Support
Donna LaComb, Trade Show Support
Missy White, Trade Show Support

Hundreds of agriculture and construction exhibitors with products and equipment. Skid steer rodeo for fun. Held at the Wicomico Youth and Civic Center in Maryland.

December

3571 Design & Construction Exposition

Construction Association of Michigan
43636 Woodward
PO Box 3204
Bloomfield Hills, MI 48302
248-972-1000
FAX: 248-972-1001
marketing@cam-online.com
www.cam-online.com

Ron Riegel, Exposition Manager
Jeanny Snowden, Marketing Coordinator

Annual show of 250 manufacturers, suppliers and distributors of construction industry equipment, supplies and services.

11M Attendees February Founded: 1985

3572 **Door & Hardware Institute Annual Conference and Exposition**
Door and Hardware Institute
14150 Newbrook Drive
Suite 200
Chantilly, VA 20151-2223
703-222-2010
FAX: 703-222-2410
conference@dhi.org www.dhi.org

Marcia Wielga Slakie, Meetings/Conferences Director
Julie Walter, Meeting Planner
Stephen R Hildebrand, Exhibit Sales
Gerald Heppes Sr, Executive Director

Annual show of 200 suppliers of doors, hardware and specialty building products. 450 booths.

4000 Attendees September

3573 **Elevator Escalator Safety Awareness Annual Meeting**
Elevator World
356 Morgan Avenue
PO Box 6507
Mobile, AL 36660
251-479-4514
FAX: 251-479-7043 800-730-5093
admin@elevator-world.com
www.elevator-world.com

Linda A Williams, Director of Administration
Dawn Nichols, Executive Administrative Assistant
Barbara Allen, Executive Director

Meetings, discussions and exhibits on the safety of elevators.

February

3574 **Environmental Management Conference and Exposition**
Environmental Information Association
6935 Wisconsin Avenue
Suite 306
Chevy Chase, MD 20815-6112
301-961-4999
FAX: 301-961-3094 888-343-4342
info@eia-usa.org www.eia-usa.org

Lisa Mihalik, Meetings/Membership Coordinator
Brent Kynoch, Managing Director

Annual conference of 85-100 exhibitors of equipment, supplies and services for quantifying, managing or remediating environmental hazards in buildings and facilities.

1200 Attendees

3575 **Equipment Distributors Association Annual Meeting**
Associated Equipment Distributors
615 W 22nd Street
Oak Brook, IL 60523-8807
630-574-0650
FAX: 630-574-0132
info@aednet.org www.aednet.org

Marcia Arger, Convention & Meetings Manager
Janet Dixon, Convention & Meetings Manager

A place where distributor, manufacturer and supplier executives meet, build relationships, do business, and learn new skills.

3.5M Attendees Annual/January

3576 **FENCETECH Convention & Expo**
American Fence Association
2336 Wisteria Drive
Suite 230
Snellville, GA 30078-6163
770-419-2555
FAX: 770-449-8927

Chuck Simanek, Exhibit Contact
Maria Prior, Exhibit Contact
Terry Dempsey, Owner

Four hundred and eighty booths for the fence industry. Educational opportunities that will inform you of the most up-to-date technology.

5883 Attendees January/Febuary

3577 **Glass, Window & Door Expo**
National Glass Association
8200 Greensboro Drive
Suite 302
McLean, VA 22102-3881
703-424-4890
FAX: 703-442-0082 866-342-5642
attend@glass.org www.glass.org

Denise Sheehan, VP
Jeffrey Smith, Exhibit Sales Manager

A trade show encompassing the entire spectrum of the glass industry. From machinery, windows, mirrors, bath enclosures, sealants, metal framing, etc. Containing over 350 exhibitors in about 1,000 booths.

7000+ Attendees September

3578 **Great Lakes Building Products Exposition**
Michigan Lumber & Building Materials Association
5815 Executive Drive
Suite A
Lansing, MI 48911
517-394-5225
FAX: 517-394-5228
assn@mlbma.org www.mlbma.org

Sherry McVicker, Administrative Assistant
Tammy Smith, Executive Assistant

Offering new products and presentations on industry topics for the building material dealer and builders/contractors.

January

3579 **Hard Hat Show**
Lee Publications
6113 State Highway 5
Palatine Bridge, NY 13428-0121
518-732-2269
FAX: 518-673-3245 800-218-5586
kmaring@leepub.com
www.leepub.com

Ken Maring, Trade Show Manager
Larry Price, Sales Manager
Fred Lee, Owner

The premier showcase for heavy construction in the Northeast sharing information about the latest innovations in the construction industry!

3.5M Attendees March Founded: 1989

3580 **Home Improvement & Remodeling Exposition**
Dmg World Media
325 Essjay Road
Suite 100
Williamsville, NY 14221
716-631-2266
FAX: 716-631-2425 800-274-6948
karenmarconi@us.dmgworldmedia.com
www.

Karen Marconi, Show Manager
Sheila Kowalow, Show Assistant
Linda Beck, Exhibit Sales
Kelly Limina, Exhibit Sales
Gary King, Owner

Featuring a spectacular garden, the latest in home technology, thousands of products, celebrity appearances and over 350 exhibits where consumers can find what they need to create their own unique spaces and put their special style to work.

60000 Attendees March

3581 **IDA International Garage Door Expo**
International Door Association
PO Box 246
West Milton, OH 45383-0246
937-988-8042
FAX: 937-698-6153 800-355-4432
roelong@longmgt.com www.doors.org

Roe Long-Wagner, Exhibit Manager
Stephanie Long, Registration Contact

Workshops and Exhibits featuring the latest product innovations as well as the traditional products and services for which the industry is known for.

April

3582 **INTEX Expo System Construction Association**
Association of the Wall and Ceiling Industry
513 West Broad Street
Suite 210
Falls Church, VA 22046
703-534-8300
FAX: 703-534-8307
www.intexconstructionexpo.com

Lee C Morris, III, Trade Show Manager
Karen Bilak, CMP, Convention & Conference Director

The premier interior/exterior wall and ceiling commercial construction trade show. This annual show host exhibitors such as, wall and ceiling contractors, general contractors, architects, specifiers, suppliers, and distributors.

3000 Attendees April

3583 **Independent Electrical Contractors National Convention**
Independent Electrical Contractors
4401 Ford Avenue
Suite 1100
Alexandria, VA 22302
703-549-7351
FAX: 703-549-7448
info@ieci.org www.ieci.org

Larry Mullins, Executive Vice President
Dudley Harris, Executive Director

One hundred booths of electrical equipment, products and services.

1000 Attendees October 3,500 names $225 per M.

3584 **International Builders Show**
National Association of Home Builders
1201 15th Street NW
Washington, DC 20005-2800
202-220-0200
FAX: 202-266-8104 800-368-5242
bfoust@nahb.com
www.buildersshow.com

Geoff Cassidy, Staff Vice President
Bernadette Foust, Senior Secretary for Convention

More than 1,600 suppliers, representing the most comprehensive showcase of home building products and services, are ready to demonstrate how their offerings can help you to corner the market.

90000 Attendees January

3585 International Conference Building Official
International Code Council
5360 Workman Mill Road
Whittier, CA 90601-2298

FAX: 562-692-3853 888-422-7233

Jan Bear, President
Felipe Segovia, VP

1,2M Attendees September

3586 International Construction and Utility Equipment Exposition
Association of Equipment Manufacturers
111 E Wisconsin Avenue
Suite 1000
Milwaukee, WI 53202-4806
414-272-0943
FAX: 414-272-1170 www.aem.org

Sara Mooney Truesdale, Show Manger
Caroline Roberts, Exhibits Coordinator

The only exposition for outdoor demonstrations of utility and construction equipment. Experience the newest technologies for their electric, phone, cable, water, sewer, gas, general construction, landscape, and government jobs.

15000 Attendees September

3587 Lumber and Building Material Expo
Northeastern Retail Lumber Association
585 N Greenbush Road
Rensselaer, NY 12144
518-861-1932
FAX: 518-286-1755 800-292-6752
heidi@nrla.org
www.nrla.org/annualConvention.htm

Heidi Longton, Convention & Meetings Director
Bonnie J Heslin, Convention Coordinator

Largest regional trade show in the lumber and building material industry. Retail lumber dealers in the Northeast are afforded the opportunity to interact with manufacturers, wholesalers, and distributors of lumber, building materials, and related technologies.

7000 Attendees February

3588 MCAA Annual Convention & Masonry Showcase
Mason Contractors Association of America
33 S Roselle Road
Schaumburg, IL 60193
847-301-0001
FAX: 847-301-1110 800-536-2225
jmount@masoncontractors.org
www.masonryshowcase.com

Michael Adelizzi, Executive Director
Joni Mount, Showcase Contact

Featuring in-depth education seminars, high-profile international skills competitions and exhibit display. Attendees includes masonry contracting firms representing all facets of masonry installation, including the largest commercial, residential, institutional, landscape, paving, retaining, glass block, and stone contractors.

March

3589 MIACON Construction, Mining & Waste Management Show
Finocchiaro Enterprises
2921 Coral Way
Miami, FL 33145
305-441-2865
FAX: 305-529-9217
mail@miacon.com www.miacon.com

Michael Finocchiaro, President
Jose Garcia, VP
Justine Finocchiaro, Chief Operations

Annual show of 650 manufacturers, suppliers, distributors and exporters of equipment, machinery, supplies and services for the construction, mining and waste managment industries. There will be 600 booths.

10M Attendees October Founded: 1994

3590 Metalcon International
PSMJ Resources
10 Midland Avenue
Newton, MA 02458-1021
617-965-0055
FAX: 617-928-1670
metalcon@psmj.com
www.metalcon.com

Claire Kilcoyne, Show Manager
Suzanne Maher, Conference Director
Paula Parker, Exhibit Sales

Architects, builders, craftspeople, designers, framers, contractors, and other industry leaders will share their expertise, hone their skills, and make connections that will help their businesses reach new heights.

8000 Attendees October

3591 Modular Building Institute Annual Convention & Trade Show
944 Glenwood Station Ln
Ste 204
Charlottesville, VA 22901-1480
434-296-3288
FAX: 434-296-3361 888-811-3288
info@mbinet.org www.mbinet.org

Tom Hardiman, Executive Director
Steven Williams, Meetings & Marketing Director

The only convention and trade show exclusively for manufacturers and dealers of commerical modular buildings and their suppliers. Includes educational sessions, keynote SP bakers, and networking events. MBI also holds three regional meetings throughout this year at locations in the US and Canada. Containing 50 exhibits.

300 Attendees March

3592 NCSBCS/AMCBO Annual Conference
Int'l Conference of State Bldg Codes & Standards
505 Huntmar Park Drive
Suite 210
Herndon, VA 20170
703-437-0100
FAX: 703-481-3596
rwible@ncsbcs.org www.ncsbcs.org

Robert Wible, Executive Director
Debbie Becker, Administrative Assistant

Providing a wide variety of technical and administrative information of immediate value to the nation's construction and code enforcement community, trade associations, information technology firms and professional societies, academicians, students, and elected officials regarding building codes administration and public safety.

Annual/Sept-Oct

3593 NEA Annual Meeting
1501 Lee Highway
Suite 202
Arlington, VA 22209-1109
703-524-3336
FAX: 703-524-3364
www.nea-online.org

Gwen Jackson, Office Manager

The prime meeting of the year, bringing together our membership from around the country in a relaxed and informal setting. The meeting will provide an opportunity to network and meet our union contractors.

Annual/May Founded: 1970

3594 NEA-The Association of Union Constructors Annual Meeting
1501 Lee Highway
Suite 202
Arlington, VA 22209-1109
703-524-3336
FAX: 703-524-3364
www.nea-online.org

Noel Borck, President
Gwen Jackson, Office Manager

The prime meeting of the year, bringing together our membership from around the country in a relaxed and informal setting. The meeting will provide an opportunity to network and meet our union contractors.

Annual/May Founded: 1970

3595 NECA Convention
National Electrical Contractors Association
3 Bethesda Metro Center
Suite 1100
Bethesda, MD 20814
301-657-3110
FAX: 301-215-4500
eie@neca.net.org www.necashow.org

Bettie Luckman, Manager, Conventions/Expos
Steve Schultz, Executive Director, Convention/Expo
John Grau, Executive VP

The event brings the largest manufacturers, utilities, contractors, engineers, consultants, plant engineers, and distributors from all over North America and 31 foreign countries.

8000 Attendees September

3596 NRC Conference
National Railroad Construction and Maintenance
122 C Street NW
Suite 850
Washington, DC 20001
202-387-7790
FAX: 202-318-0867 800-883-1557
info@nrcma.org www.nrcma.org

Chuck Baker, Executive Director
Judi Meyerhoeffer, Exhibitor Sales
Keith Hartwell, President

For railroad personnel, managers and purchasers in design, construction and maintenance. Information on breakthrough innovations in rail construction, railroad safety, new rail projects of national significance and more.

300+ Attendees January

3597 NRCA Annual Convention
National Roofing Contractors Association

10255 W Higgins Road
Suite 600
Rosemont, IL 60018-5607
847-299-9070
FAX: 847-299-1183 www.nrca.net

William Good, Executive Vice President
Bennett Judson, Associate Executive Director
Michelle Iniguez, Administrative Assistant

Held in conjunction with Hanley Wood's International Roofing Expo. The convention gives you the opportunity to network with fellow roofing professionals from around the world; see the newest industry products, equipment and services; and learn from the industry's leading experts.

7,000 Attendees February

3598 NSSGA Dredging Seminar & Expo
National Stone, Sand & Gravel Association
1605 King Street
Alexandria, VA 22314
703-525-8788
FAX: 703-525-7782 800-342-1415
slenker@nssga.org www.nssga.org

Diana Carmenates, Meetings/Conventions Director
Steven Lenker, VP Operations

Created to specifically meet the needs of aggregate producers who use dredges or have an interest in using dredges in the future. This seminar uses educational seminars, plant tours and manufacturer's exhibits to provide information useful to both novice and experienced dredgers.

June

3599 National Congress & Expo for Manufactured and Modular Housing
Manufactured Housing Institute
2101 Wilson Boulevard
Suite 610
Arlington, VA 22201-3062
703-558-0400
FAX: 703-558-0401
sclegg@mfghome.org
www.manufacturedhousing.org or
www.congressandexpo.com

Suzanne Clegg, Meetings Director
Lauren Lewis, Trade Show Sponsorships

National gathering for the manufactured & modular housing industries. The Expo features over 100 exhibitors where attendees can get a first look at new products and services in the manufactured & modular housing industries. *$75.00*

1500 Attendees April 10-12, 2007

3600 National Demolition Association Annual Convention
National Demolition Association
16 North Franklin Street
Suite 203
Doylestown, PA 18901-3536
215-348-4949
FAX: 215-348-8422 800-541-2412
info@demolitionassociation.com
www.demolitionassociation.com

Michael Taylor, Executive Director

Annual convention and exhibits of demolition equipment, supplies and services. 165 booths.

1500 Attendees Annual/April

3601 National Hardware Show
Reed Exhibitions
383 Main Avenue
Norwalk, CT 06851
203-404-4800
FAX: 203-840-9622 888-425-9377
inquiry@hardware.reedexpo.com
www.nationalhardwareshow.com

Dennis MacDonald, Event Manager
Rob Cappiello, Event Manager

The only housing after-market show, bringing together manufacturers and resellers of all products used to remodel, repair, maintain and decorate the home and its surroundings.

3M Attendees May

3602 New England Home Show
Dmg World Media
45 Braintree Hill Office Park
Suite 302
Braintree, MA 02184
781-849-0990
FAX: 781-849-7544 800-469-0990
lauriemyette@us.dmgworldmedia.com
www.newenglandhomeshow.com

Laurie Myette, Show Manager
Amy Kimball, Administrative Assistant

Annual show of 379 exhibitors of homebuilding and improvement equipment, supplies and services, including bathroom and kitchen supplies, building materials, appliances, doors and windows, swimming pools, hot tubs and spas.

100M Attendees February

3603 North American Quarry Recycling Show
Lee Publications
6113 State Highway 5
PO Box 121
Palatine Bridge, NY 13428-0121
518-732-2269
FAX: 518-673-3245 800-218-5586

Ken Maring, Trade Show Manager
Janet Button, VP Marketing

The North American Quarry Show is the largest trade show in North America for the aggregates industry.

October

3604 North American Steel Construction Conference
One E Wacker Drive
Suite 3100
Chicago, IL 60601-2001
312-670-2400
FAX: 312-670-5403 www.aisc.org

Thorn Hoffman, Exhibit Contact
H Louis Gurthet, President

A premier education event aimed at providing structural engineers, steel fabricators, erectors, and detailers with practical information and the latest design and construction techniques.

2300 Attendees April

3605 Northwestern Building Products Exposition
Northwestern Lumber Association
1405 Lilac Drive N
Suite 130
Minneapolis, MN 55422-4528
763-544-6822
FAX: 612-544-0820

P Siewert, Show Manager
Gary Smith, President

310 booths for retail lumber and building material dealers in Iowa, Minnesota, North Dakota, South Dakota and Wisconsin. Commodities products and services sold or used by retailers are displayed at this regional show.

3.8M Attendees February

3606 PACE: Paint and Coatings Expo
Painting and Decorating Contractors of America
11960 Westline Industrial Drive
Suite 201
St. Louis, MO 63146-3209
314-514-7322
FAX: 314-514-9417 800-332-7322
miller@pace2006.com www.pdca.com

Jennifer Miller, Expo Director
Annette S DeLorenzo, Exhibitor Sales

This mega show is the culmination of months of research and planning by members of the two professional associations (PDCA & SSPC), who joined forces in search of a 'one-stop shop' solution for convening the maximum number of industry professionals in the most cost-effective and productive way.

January-February

3607 SIA Annual Convention & Trade Show
Scaffold Industry Association
PO Box 20574
Phoenix, AZ 85036-0574
602-257-1144
FAX: 602-257-1166
info@scaffold.org www.scaffold.org
Exhibits and classes on scaffold safety and education.

Annual/July

3608 SIPA Annual Meeting & Conference
Structural Insulated Panel Association
PO Box 1699
Gig Harbor, WA 98335
253-858-7472
FAX: 253-858-0272
billw@sips.org www.sips.org

Bill Wachtler, Executive Director

A valuable networking event for both long-time veterans and newcomers to the SIP industry. If you're a builder, architect, developer or entrepreneur interested in employing SIPs in your next commercial or residential project, you'll be interested in this conference

Annual/April

3609 STAFDA Annual Convention & Trade Show
Specialty Tools and Fasteners Distributors Assn.
PO Box 44
Elm Grove, WI 53122-0044
262-784-4774
FAX: 262-784-5059 800-352-2981
ghfoley@stafda.org www.stafda.org

Georgia H Foley, Executive Director
Catherine P Usher, Director Member Services

Members distribute or manufacture power equipment, anchors, fastening systems, drilling equipment and other related industrial supplies.

4000 Attendees November

3610 Surfaces Conference
World Floor Covering Association
2211 E Howell Avenue
Anaheim, CA 92806
714-978-6440
FAX: 714-978-6066 800-624-6880
casey@wbma.org www.wfca.org

Casey Voorhees, Executive Director
Tina Krulich, Administrative Assistant

The event for the floor covering industry with the latest trends to keep your business competitive, proven strategies to increase sales and profitability and all the critical industry information you need to make the right decisions.

40000 Attendees January-February

3611 Technology for Construction

Hanley-Wood
8600 Freeport Parkway
Suite 200
Irving, TX 75063
972-366-6300
FAX: 972-536-6402 866-962-7469
TCindric@hanleywood.com
www.technologyforconstruction.com

Tom Cindric, Show Director
Jackie James, Show Manager

International conference and tradeshow focused on the technology needs and interests of architects and interior designers; civil engineers, contractors, builders, and construction managers, facility managers, building engineers, owners, GIS, surveyors and mapping professionals for private, commercial, institutional and government sectors.

33M Attendees Annual/January

3612 Tilt-Up Convention

Tilt-Up Concrete Association
113 First Street W
PO Box 204
Mount Vernon, IA 52314
319-895-6911
FAX: 319-895-8830
esauter@tilt-up.org www.tilt-up.org

J Edward Sauter, Executive Director
Jim Baty, Technical Director

First annual convention being held which will feature intensive training and education seminars for contractors and engineers, as well as a trade show, building tour and focused sessions on marketing and architecturald design.

Annual/October Founded: 2005
Printed in 4 colors on glossy stock

3613 Utility Construction Expo

National Utility Contractors Association
4301 Fairfax Drive
Suite 360
Arlington, VA 22203-1627
703-358-9300
FAX: 703-358-9307
linda@nuca.com www.nuca.com

Linda Holtz Kinnecome, COOÆ
Paula Ketter, VP of Communications

The latest technologies, products, and services being offered by the leading manufacturers and suppliers in the underground utility construction industry. Next trade show is scheduled to take place in Las Vegas, Nevada.

February

3614 WBMA Annual Convention

Western Building Material Association
909 Lakeridge Drive SW
PO Box 1699
Olympia, WA 98507-1699
360-943-3054

stephanie@wbma.org /
wbma@wbma.com www.wbma.org

Charles Link, Show Manager
Stephanie Masters, Exhibitor Director
Casey Voorhees, Executive Director

One hundred and fourty booths of products stocked and sold by building material dealers.

1.6M Attendees November

3615 World of Asphalt Show & Conference

National Asphalt Pavement Association
5100 Forbes Boulevard
Lanham, MD 20706
301-731-4748
FAX: 301-731-4621 888-468-6499
NLawler@hotmix.org
www.hotmix.org

Nancy Lawler, VP of Conventions & Meetings
Lauren Ward, Administrative Assistant

World of Asphalt focuses exclusively on the asphalt industry, and is the industry's leading exposition and education resource. World of Asphalt features educational sessions, equipment demonstrations and exhibits showcasing the latest innovations in asphalt-related equipment, products and services.

3200+ Attendees March

Directories & Databases

3616 ANSI/SPRI Standard Field Test Procedure

Single Ply Roofing Institute
77 Rumford Avenue
Suite 3B
Waltham, MA 02543
781-647-7026
FAX: 781-647-7222
info@spri.org www.spri.org

Linda King, Managing Director

Standard Field Test Procedure for determining the withdrawal resistance of roofing fasteners. *$5.00*

Free to members

3617 ANSI/SPRI Wind Design Standard

Single Ply Roofing Institute
77 Rumford Avenue
Suite 3B
Waltham, MA 02453
781-647-7026
FAX: 781-647-7222
info@spri.org www.spri.org

Linda King, Managing Director

Written for those who design, specify and install smooth-surfaced, low-slope flexible membrane roof systems. *$5.00*

23 pages

3618 Affirmative Action Compliance Manual for Federal Contractors

Bureau of National Affairs
1231 25th Street NW
Washington, DC 20037-1197
202-452-4200
800-372-1033
edcontactslaborlaw@bna.com
www.bna.com

Gregory C McCaffery, Publisher
Heather Bodell, Managing Editor

A two-binder service containing the official text of the Office of Federal Contract Compliance Programs Manual and reports on related developments. *$611.00*

Monthly

3619 Automated Builder: Top Component Producers Survey Issue

Automated Builder
1445 Donlon Street
Suite 16
Ventura, CA 93003-5640
805-642-9735
FAX: 805-642-8820 800-344-BLDR
info@automatedbuilder.com
automatedbuilder.com

Don Carlson, Editor/Publisher

Over 100 leading industrialized building producers are profiled on the basis of sales. Top HUD-Code home producers, TOP pakelizers, TOP commercial modular builders. Features articles on technology, methods and machinery, sales and marketing for in-plant building. *$6.00*

48 pages Monthly Founded: 1964

3620 Blue Book of Building and Construction

Contractors Register
PO Box 500
Jefferson Valley, NY 10535
914-450-0200
FAX: 914-243-0287 800-431-2584
info@thebluebook.com
www.thebluebook.com

Jeff Fandl, Editor

Regional construction directories in most major markets throughout the US. Online, thebluebook.com provides easy access to continually updated information for each of our regional editions.

4500 pages Annual Founded: 1913
Circulation: 615,000

3621 Building & Construction Trades Department

815 16th Street NW
Suite 209
Washington, DC 20006-4145
202-347-1461
FAX: 202-628-0724 www.bctd.org

Ed Sullivan, President
Joseph Maloney, Secretary/Treasurer

Coordinates activity and provides resources to 15 affiliated trades unions in the construction industry.

386 pages Founded: 1908

3622 Building Materials Directory

Underwriters Laboratories
333 Pfingsten Road
Northbrook, IL 60062-2096
847-120-0136
FAX: 847-509-6243 800-704-4050
directories@us.ul.com www.ul.com

Keith E. Williams, President/CEO

Offers information on companies that have qualified to use the UL listing mark or classification marking on products that have been found to be in compliance with UL requirements. *$30.00*

512 pages Annual/February

3623 Buildings: Who's Who in Commercial Buildings Issue

Stamats Communications
427 6th Avenue SE
Cedar Rapids, IA 52401-1931
319-364-6167
FAX: 319-364-4278
barbara-schrafel@stamats.com
www.bldgsmag.com

Linda K Monroe, Editor

Listing of major building ownership.development/facilities management firms in

North America, as well as leading manufacturers of building supplies. *$7.00*
Annual, August

3624 Cement Americas
Primedia
745 Fifth Avenue
New York, NY 10151
212-745-0100
FAX: 212-745-0121
information@primedia.com
www.primedia.com
Steven Prokopy, Editor
Scott Bieda, Publisher
Offers 100 cement manufacturing companies in the United States, Canada, Mexico, Central and South America. *$78.00*
225 pages Annual
Circulation: 300
Mailing list available for rent
Printed in on glossy stock

3625 Commercial Low-Slope Roofing Materials Guide
National Roofing Contractors Association
10255 W Higgins Road
Suite 600
Rosemont, IL 60018-5613
847-299-9070
FAX: 847-299-1183 www.nrca.net
Carl Good, Publisher
Ambika Puniani Bailey, Director of Communications
Jeff Jarvis, Director of Membership
Two volume guide that features descriptions of roofing materials, including product names, specifications and characteristics. It offers information about industrial, commercial and institutional low-slope roof coverings, fasteners, cements, rigid insulation board and coating products. The guide also includes information about warranties for most membrane roof systems. *$140.00*
900 pages

3626 Construction Equipment: Construction Giants Issue
Reed Business Information
2000 Clearwater Drive
Oak Brook, IL 60523
630-740-0825
FAX: 630-288-8145
rblesi@reedbusiness.com
www.reedbusiness.com
Rick Blesi, Publisher
Rod Sutton, Editor-in-Chief
Listing of approximately 250 of the largest equipment-owning heavy construction contractors, engaged in earthmoving, paving, building and materials production owning over $10 million in equipment.
Monthly Founded: 1949
Circulation: 77010

3627 Construction Planning & Scheduling Manual
National Insulation Association
99 Canal Center Plaza
Suite 222
Alexandria, VA 22314-1588
703-683-6422
FAX: 703-549-4838
editor@insulation.org
www.insulation.org
Melissa Jackson, Director of Publications
Beth Michaels, Assistant Editor
This manual from the Associated General Contractors (AGC) was written to provide guidance to the contractor in the effective use of modern project management techniques. Its primary objective is to provide an educational tool that can be used within the construction industry to teach the concepts of construction planning and scheduling. The content of the book is written for all project personnel, from the working foreman to the project executive. *$155.00*

3628 Construction Specifier: Member Directory Issue
Construction Specifications Institute
990 Canal Center Plaza
Suite 300
Alexandria, VA 22314
703-684-0300
FAX: 703-684-8436 800-689-2900
csi@csinet.org www.csinet.org
Jack Reeder, Editor
Roster of construction specifiers certified by the institute and approximately 17,200 members. *$203.00*
Annual, January

3629 Constructor: AGC Directory of Membership and Services Issue
Associated General Contractors of America
333 John Carlyle Street
Sutie 200
Alexandria, VA 22314
703-548-3118
FAX: 703-548-3119
info@agc.org www.agc.org
Donald Scott, Production Manager
List of more than 8,500 member firms and 24,000 national associate member firms engaged in building, highway, heavy, industrial, municipal utilities and railroad construction.
Annual/July
Circulation: 34,000

3630 Directory of Building Codes & Regulations
National Conference of States on Building Codes
505 Huntmar Park Drive
Herndon, VA 20170-5139
703-370-0100
FAX: 703-481-3596 800-362-2633
Robert Wible, Executive Director
Carolyn Fitch, Membership Services
This directory is a comprehensive guide to the building codes and regulations adopted and enforced in each of the 50 states, Puerto Rico, the District of Columbia, and 53 major U. S. cities in 14 different code areas - building, mechanical, plumbing, electrical, energy conservation, gas, fire prevention, life safety, accessibility, one & two family, modular, ventilation/indoor air quality, manufactured home installation, and elevator. *$78.00*
Annual

3631 Dodge Construction Analysis System
McGraw-Hill
1221 Avenue of the Americas
New York, NY 10020-1095
212-122-2000
800-393-6343
dodge_cust_svc@mcgraw-hill.com
www.dodge.construction.com
Norbert W Young, President
Joseph A Scott, National Marketing Director
This database lists over 4 million time series for construction projects involving more than 200 structural types.

3632 Dodge DataLine
McGraw-Hill
1221 Avenue of the Americas
New York, NY 10020-1095
212-122-2000
800-393-6343
dodge_cust_svc@mcgraw-hill.com
www.dodge.construction.com
Norbert W Young, President, Dodge Construction
Joseph A Scott, National Marketing Director
Dodge DataLine offers the most advanced searching of project leads in the industry. You can search the largest U.S. database of 500,000+ active construction projects.
Daily

3633 ENR Top 400 Contractors Sourcebook
Engineering News Record/McGraw Publishing
2 Penn Plaza
9th Floor
New York, NY 10121
212-046-6217
FAX: 212-904-2820 888-877-8208
constructioninfo@ecnext.com
www.enr.construction.com
Janice L Tuchman, Editor-in-Chief
Joann Gonchar, Associate Editor
William G. Krizan, Assistant Managing Editor
Debra K. Rubin, Managing Senior Editor
Market analysis rankings of the largest U.S.-based general contractors in eight major industry sectors: general building, transportation, manufacturing, industrial process, petroleum, power, environmental and telecommunications. *$25.00*
112 pages

3634 ENR: Top 100 Construction Managers
Engineering News Record/McGraw Publishing
2 Penn Plaza
9th Floor
New York, NY 10121
212-046-6217
FAX: 212-904-2820 888-877-8208
constructioninfo@ecnext.com
www.enr.construction.com
Janice L Tuchman, Editor
John J Kosowatz, Managing Editor
William G. Krizan, Assistant Managing Editor
List of the top 100 leading construction and program management firms with the largest dollar volume in new construction management contracts on a for-fee only basis and an at-risk basis in the previous year. *$250.00*
Annual, June

3635 ENR: Top 400 Contractors
Engineering News Record/McGraw Publishing
2 Penn Plaza
9th Floor
New York, NY 10121
212-046-6217
FAX: 212-904-4178 800-848-9002
constructioninfo@ecnext.com
www.enr.construction.com
Janice L Tuchman, Editor
John J Kosowatz, Managing Editor
Lists over 400 contractors in the United States that received the largest dollar volume of contracts in the preceding calendar year. *$320.00*

128 pages Annual/May Founded: 1965

3636 ENR: Top 600 Specialty Contractors Issue
Engineering News Record/McGraw Hill
2 Penn Plaza
9th Floor
New York, NY
212-046-6217
FAX: 212-904-4178
constructioninfo@ecnext.com
www.enr.construction.com

Janice L Tuchman, Editor
John J Kosowatz, Managing Editor

Lists of the 600 largest US specialty subcontractors with sub-lists of top firms in mechanical contracting, electrical, excavation-foundation, steel erection, rofing, sheet metal, demolition-wrecking, glazing curtain wall, masonry, concrete, utilities, painting, wall/ceiling and asbestos abatement. *$350.00*
Annual, September

3637 ENR: Top Owners Issue
Engineering News Record/McGraw Hill
2 Penn Plaza
9th Floor
New York, NY 10121
212-046-6217
FAX: 212-904-4178
constructioninfo@ecnext.com
www.enr.construction.com

Janice L Tuchman, Editor
John J Kosowatz, Managing Editor

List of 700 companies that had the largest expenditures for building construction and building acquisition in the previous year. *$300.00*
Annual, December

3638 Electrical Construction Materials Directory
Underwriters Laboratories
333 Pfingsten Road
Northbrook, IL 60062-2096
847-120-0136
FAX: 847-272-8129 800-704-4050
directories@us.UL.com www.UL.com

Shaquanda Debbe, Editor

Companies that have qualified to use the UL listing mark or classification marking on or in connection with products which have been found to be in compliance with UL's requirements. *$30.00*
Annual
Printed in on glossy stock

3639 Fastener Selection Guide
Single Ply Roofing Institute
77 Rumford Avenue
Suite 3B
Waltham, MA 02453
781-647-7026
FAX: 781-647-7222
info@spri.org www.spri.org

Linda King, Managing Director

Identifies the various fastener options for each desk type and typical pullout values. *$15.00*

3640 Flexible Membrane Roofing: Guide to Specifications
Single Ply Roofing Institute
77 Rumford Avenue
Suite 3B
Waltham, MA 02453
781-647-7026
FAX: 781-647-7222
info@spri.org www.spri.org

Linda King, Managing Director

Now in it's 7th edition, this is the most complete reference guide on materials, systems and designs for commerical roofing. *$ 50.00*

3641 GreenSpec Directory
BuildingGreen
122 Birge Street
Suite 30
Brattleboro, VT 05301
802-257-7300
FAX: 802-257-7304
info@buildinggreen.com
www.buildinggreen.com

Alex Wilson, Executive Editor
Nadav Malin, Editor
Daniel Woodbury, Publisher
Charlotte Snyder, Circulation Manager

Information on more than 1,850 green building products carefully screened by the editors of Environmental Building News. Directory listings cover more than 250 categories_from access flooring to zero-VOC paints. Included are product descriptions, environmental characteristics and considerations, and manufacturer contact information with internet addresses. *$89.00*
464 pages ISBN 1-929884-15-X

3642 High-Performance Composites Directory
Ray Publishing
4891 Independence
Suite 270
Wheat Ridge, CO 80033
303-467-1776
FAX: 303-467-1777
www.compositesworld.com

Judith Hazen, Publisher
Mike Mussleman, Managing Editor

60 pages Founded: 1993
Printed in 4 colors on glossy stock

3643 MasterFormat
Construction Specifications Institute
99 Canal Center Plaza
Suite 300
Alexandria, VA 22314
703-684-0300
FAX: 703-684-8436 800-689-2900
csi@csinet.org www.csinet.org

Karl Borgstrom, Executive Director
Teresa Sullivan,
Marketing/Communications Director
Christine Day, Marketing Manager

The reengineering of this industry standard sets the present and future pace for organizing construction communication. MasterFormat 2004 Edition simplifies the process of determining where specific subject matter is located. *$159.00*
516 pages Founded: 2004 ISBN 0-976239-90-6

3644 NRC Membership Directory
National Railroad Construction and Maintenance
122 C Street NW
Suite 850
Washington, DC 20001
202-387-7790
FAX: 202-318-0867 800-883-1557
info@nrcma.org www.nrcma.org

Ray Chambers, President
Chuck Baker, VP/Executive Director

A book of the railroad contracting industry, lists all members of the NRC, including their technical specialities ang geographic regions of operation. *$35.00*
Free to Members

3645 Public Works Manual
Hanley-Wood
426 S Westgate Street
Addison, IL 60101
630-543-0870
FAX: 630-543-3112 800-524-2364
arozgus@hanleywood.com
www.pwmag.com

William D Palmer Jr., Editor-in-Chief
Amara Rozgus, Managing Editor
Sharon Glorioso, Associate Editor
Colette Palait, Editorial Assistant

Over 4,000 manufacturers and distributors of equipment, materials, services, computers and software used in the design, construction and maintenance of streets and highways, water systems, wastewater and solid wastes processing and recreation areas. *$30.00*
Annual

3646 Roofing/Siding/Insulation: Trade Directory Issue
Advanstar Communications
1 Park Avenue
New York, NY 10016
212-797-7631
FAX: 212-951-6793
info@advanstar.com
www.advanstar.com

Francis Heid, VP of Publishing Operations
Steve Morris, VP of Market Development

Lists 1,700 contractors, manufacturers and distributors of equipment and products. *$20.00*
Annual
Circulation: 22,000

3647 STAFDA Directory
Specialty Tools & Fasteners Distributors Assn
PO Box 44
Elm Grove, WI 53122-0044
262-784-4774
FAX: 262-784-5059 800-352-2981
info@stafda.org www.stafda.org

Georgia H Foley, Executive Director
Catherine P Usher, Director Member Services

This is a Who's Who of the industry. Listings include who makes over 900 different products: nearly 2,570 member addresses and contacts; brand names; fax numbers: 800 numbers; e-mail; www; and a recap of association services and activities.
500 pages Annual

3648 **Scaffold Industry Association Directory & Handbook**
Scaffold Industry Association
PO Box 20574
Phoenix, AZ 85036-0574
602-257-1144
FAX: 602-257-1166
info@scaffold.org www.scaffold.org
Aimee Siems, Operations Manager
Elouise Schultz, Director of Membership
The SIA Directory and Handbook contains complete membership information, company and individual listings. It also includes federal OSHA scaffold standards for general industry, construction and maritime, scaffold plank grading rules, map and listing of OSHA regional and area offices, scaffold standards for the state of California, glossary of scaffold terms, illustrations of various types of scaffolds, and codes of safe practices. *$125.00*
355 pages

3649 **Source: Buyers' Guide & Dealer Directory**
Northeastern Retail Lumber Association
585 N Greenbush Road
Rensselaer, NY 12144
518-861-1932
FAX: 518-286-1755 800-292-6752
jsacks@nrla.org www.nrla.org
Jeff Sacks, Editor/Publisher/Advertising Mgr.
Melissa Stankovich, Art Director
The industry's guide to names, addresses, phone numbers, fax numbers, and product lines of companies that comprise the independent retail lumber dealers of the Northeast. *$89.95*
Annual

3650 **Store Fixture Buyers' Guide and Membership Directory**
Nat'l Association of Store Fixture Manufacturers
3595 Sheridan
Suite 200
Hollywood, FL 33322
954-893-7300
FAX: 954-893-7500
nasfm@nasfm.org www.nasfm.org
Jo Rossman, Senior Editor
Klein Merriman, Executive Director
This buyers' guide features the products and services of some 400 store fixture manufacturers. Contact information, plant size, number of employees, and company descriptions of all member manufacturers, plant listings by location, and contact and company information on products and services of 200 supplier members is included.
$175.00
80 pages Free to Members

3651 **Sweets Directory**
McGraw-Hill Companies
1221 Avenue of the America
New York, NY 10020-1095
212-122-2000
FAX: 212-512-2000 800-442-2258
sweets_customerservice@mcgraw-hill.com www.sweets.construction.com
Judy Schriener, Editorial
The leading desktop reference and preliminary research guide, featuring more than 10,000 building product manufacturers and their products.
Annual Founded: 1906

3652 **Timber Frame Homes**
Home Buyer Publications
4125 Lafayette Center Drive
Suite 100
Chantilly, VA 20151
703-226-6155
FAX: 703-222-3209 800-850-7279
store@homebuyerpubs.com
www.loghomeliving.com
Peter Lobred, Editor
For individuals wishing to plan, build, decorate, or design a log or timber frame home.
$3.99
Bi-Monthly

3653 **Wind Design Guide**
Single Ply Roofing Institute
77 Rumford Avenue
Suite 3B
Waltham, MA 02453
781-647-7026
FAX: 781-647-7222
info@spri.org www.spri.org
Linda King, Managing Director
Wind Design Guide for Edge Systems Used with Low Slope Roofing Systems outlines design and construction of edge details for wind resistance, including test methods, calculations of design pressures and commentary. *$20.00*

Industry Web Sites

3654 **www.abc.org**
Associated Builders and Contractors

National trade association representing about 23,000 contractors, subcontractors, material suppliers and related firms from across the country and from all specialties in the construction industry.

3655 **www.acdi.net**
Associated Construction Distributors International

Cooperative association of independently owned and locally opearated distributors of specialty construction products and equipment.

3656 **www.acesystems.com**
AEC Systems International/Penton Media

Focuses on Internet/Intranet for the design, engineering and construction industries.

3657 **www.aednet.org**
Associated Equipment Distributors

Membership association of 1,200 independent distributors, manufacturers, and other organizations involved in the distribution of construction equipment and related products and services in North America and throughout the world.

3658 **www.agc.org**
Associated General Contractors of America

The voice of the construction industry, an organization of qualified construction contractors and industry related companies dedicated to skill, integrity and responsibility.

3659 **www.aibd.org**
American Institute of Building Design

Our members consist of professional building designers and architects, who have for the most part chosen residential design as the focus of their practice.

3660 **www.aisc.org**
American Institute of Steel Construction

Serving the structural steel industry in the US. Our purpose is to promote the use of structural steel through research activities, market development, education, codes and specifications, technical assistance, quality certifacation and standardization.

3661 **www.akropolis.net**
Akropolis

To enable firms at all levels of the design and building industry to operate more efficiently with the help of cutting edge technology solutions.

3662 **www.anodizing.org**
Aluminum Anodizers Council

Represents the interests of aluminum anodizers worldwide and is the principal trade organization for the anodizing industry in North America. It promotes the interests of its members through technical exchange, ongoing education, statistical data, market promotion, and industry representation.

3663 **www.apfa.com**
American Pipe Fittings Association

Trade association for any domestic corporation, firm or individual engaged in manufacture in the US or Canada of piping components and accessories, including pipe hangers and supports.

3664 **www.apwa.net**
American Public Works Association

An international educational and professionals association of public agencies, private sector companies, and individuals dedicated to providing high quality public works goods and services.

3665 www.aspenational.com
American Society of Professional Estimators

Serving the construction estimators by providing education, fellowship and opportunity for professional development. ASPE represents individual members involved in the construction industry.

3666 www.automatebuilder.com
CMN Associates

Association of manufacturers and suppliers who have a product line that is of interest to the manufactured and pre-fabricated housing industry.

3667 www.awci.org
Association of the Wall and Ceiling Industries

Represents acoustics systems, ceiling systems, drywall systems, exterior insulation and finishing systems, fireproofing, flooring systems, insulation, and stucco contractors, suppliers and manufacturers and those in allied trades.

3668 www.bia.org
Brick Industry Association

A national trade association representing distributors and manufacturers of clay brick and suppliers of related products and services.

3669 www.build.com
Build.com

Providing consumers, contractors and industry professionals with a valuable resource of products, service and information related to the building and home improvement industry.

3670 www.buildingstone.org
Building Stone Institute

Quarries, fabricators, dealers, installers and restorers of all types of natural stone. Membership dues based on sales volume.

3671 www.buildingsystems.org
Panelized Building Systems Council

Learn more about modular, panelized, and log construction. Search for modular manufacturers that distribute to your state or search for panelized manufacturers by building type, or find designs for your systems built home.

3672 www.calredwood.org
California Redwood Association

A trade association for redwood lumber producers.

3673 www.cfma.org
Construction Financial Management Association

Non-profit organization dedicated to serving the financial professional in the construction industry.

3674 www.cisco.org
Construction Industry Service Corporation

Labor management association that promotes union construction, union contractors and union apprenticeship programs throughout Northeastern Illinois.

3675 www.coaa.org
Construction Owners Association of America

To act as a focal point and voice for the interests of owners in construction. Comprised of a diverse group of men and women representing construction owners.

3676 www.concretepumpers.com
American Concrete Pumping Association

Provides education, insurance, marketing and much more to companies involved with the concrete pumping industry. Our dedication to the concrete pumping industry has led us to become a key part in the education of safety and business management to everyone involved, from the operators to the management.

3677 www.csinet.org
Construction Specifications Institute

Our mission is to continuously improve the process of creating and sustaining the built environment. We do this by facilitating communication among all those involved in that process.

3678 www.demolitionassociation.com
National Association of Demolition Contractors

Representing the demolition industry including demolition contractors, formed to foster goodwill and the exchange of ideas with the public, governmental agencies and constractors engaged in the demolition industry. Also for manufacturers or suppliers of demolition equipment, supplies and services.

3679 www.ebmda.org
Eastern Building Material Dealers Association

Established to foster, protect and promote the welfare and best interest of its members engaged in the retail lumber and building materials business.

3680 www.firstsourceonl.com
First Source Online

Provides A/E/C professionals free access to the industry's most comprehensive, up-to-date library of formatted commercial building product information, plus manufacturers' addresses, telephone numbers, trade names, and regional distributors.

3681 www.floorbiz.com
Floor Biz

Internet's leading creator and operator of a vertical business community for the flooring industry. FloorBiz leverages the interactive features and global reach of the Internet to create a multi-national, targeted business community vertically integrated from consumer to manufacturer.

3682 www.greyhouse.com
Grey House Publishing

Selected Grey House directories in the fields of business, health and education are available online. Users can search our online databases by several different search criteria, such as product categories, geographic area, sales volume and much, much more. Full Grey House catalog and online ordering also available.

3683 www.homebuilder.com
HomeBuilder.com

The web's leading provider of information on newly built homes, with listings for over 125,000 new home and planned developments throughout the US. Supplier of media and technology solutions that promote and connect real estate professionals to consumers before, during and after a move.

3684 www.homeimprovement.com
Hometime

Hometime is a home-improvement television show broadcast on public television, The Learning Channel and in syndication. A comprehensive online resource for your remodeling and home-improvement needs.

3685 www.hotmix.org
National Asphalt Pavement Association

The only trade association that exclusively represents the interest s of the Hot Mix Asphalt producer and paving contractor on the national level with Congress, government agencies, and other national trade and business organizations.

3686 www.iccsafe.org
International Code Council

Formerly known as the Building Officials and Code Administrators International, we publish codes that establish minimum performance requirements for all aspects of the construction industry.

3687 **www.icpi.org**
Interlocking Concrete Pavement Institute

Self governed, self funded, autonomous association representing the interlocking concrete pavement industry in North America. Membership is open to producers, contractors, suppliers, consultants and others who have an interest in the industry. As an industry voice, the membership represents a majority of concrete paver production in North America.

3688 **www.iilp.org**
International Institute for Lathe and Plaster

Federation of organizations representing contractors, unions and makers of lathing and manufacturing.

3689 **www.manufacturedhousing.org**
Manufactured Housing Institute

National trade organization representing all segments of the factory built housing industry. MHI serves its membership by providing industry research, promotion, education, and government relations programs, and by building and facilitating consensus within the industry.

3690 **www.masonryshowcase.com**
Mason Contractors Association of America

Through strong programs, publications and services, the MCAA avtively promotes the interests of its members. By promoting the use of masonry, influencing resonable codes and standards, work force development and public affairs, the association advances the use of masonry.

3691 **www.masonrysociety.org**
Masonry Society

Dedicated to the advancement of scientific engineering, architechtural and construction knowledge of masonry. Promotes research and education and disseminates information on masonry materials, design, construction. Publishes a newsletter.

3692 **www.mbinet.org**
Modular Building Institute

Serving the commercial factory-built buildings industry on an international scale. Our regular members are manufacturers and dealers of commercial modular structures, while our associate members are companies supplying building components, services, and financing.

3693 **www.naamm.org**
Nat'l Assn of Architectural Metal Manufacturers

The largest of four operating divisions of the National Association of Architectural Metal Manufacturers. HMMA is a group composed of companies that manufacture, distribute and promote the use of hollow metal door and frame products.

3694 **www.nahb.org**
National Association of Home Builders

Represents the interests of concrete, log, modular, and panel manufacturers, builders, and suppliers.

3695 **www.nam.org**
National Association of Manufacturers

The nation's largest industrial trade association, representing small and large manufacturers in every industrial sector and in all 50 states.

3696 **www.nari.org**
National Association of the Remodeling Industry

A voice in the remodeling industry, NARI has an exclusive, encompasing purpose to; establish and maintain a firm commitment to developing and sustaining programs that expand and unite the remodeling industry; to ensure the industry's growth and security; to encourage ethical conduct, sound business practices and professionalism in the remodeling industry; and to present NARI as the recognized authority in the remodeling industry.

3697 **www.nationalslagassoc.org**
National Slag Association

Members are processors of iron and steel slags for use as a aggregate in construction and manufacturing applications.

3698 **www.nawic.org**
National Association of Women in Construction

Founded by 16 women working in the construction industry. The founders organized NAWIC to create a support network for women in construction.

3699 **www.ncac.com**
National Council of Acoustical Consultants

Strives to safeguard the interests of professional acoustical consulting firms. Managing physics and psychoacoustics to provide optimum listning environments.

3700 **www.ncma.org**
National Concrete Masonry Association

Manufacturers of concrete masonry products and suppliers of products to the industry. Offers a variety of technical services and design aids through publications, computer programs, slide presentations and technical training.

3701 **www.ncsbcs.org**
National Conference of States on Building Codes

Serving as a forum for the interchange of information and provides technical services, education and training to our members to enhance the public's social, economic well-being through safe, durable, accessible and efficient buildings.

3702 **www.necanet.org**
National Electrical Contractors Association

Represents a segment of the construction market comprised of over 70,000 electrical firms.

3703 **www.nrcma.org**
National Railroad Construction & Maintenance Assn

Railroad construction and maintenance contractors, engineering firms, manufacturing suppliers and professional associate firms.

3704 **www.nrla.org**
Northeastern Retail Lumber Association

A resource for industry members, consumers, and public officials in dependent lumber and building material suppliers and associated businesses in New York and the six New England states.

3705 **www.nrmca.org**
National Ready Mixed Concrete Association

Our mission is to provide exceptional value for our members by responsibly representing and serving the entire ready mixed concrete industry through leadership, promotion, education and partnering; to ensure ready mixed concrete is the building material of choice.

3706 **www.nssga.org**
National Stone, Sand & Gravel Association

Represents the crushed stone, sand and gravel — or aggregate — industries. Our members account for 90 percent of the crushed stone and 70 percent of the sand and gravel produced annually in the US.

3707 **www.ntma.com**
National Terrazzo and Mosaic Association

Full service nonprofit trade association headquartered in Northern Virginia. The association establishes national standards for all terrazzo floor and wall systems and provides complete specifications, color plates and general information to architects and designers at no cost.

3708 **www.nuca.com**
National Utility Contractors Association

A national association that provides a forum for continuing education and promotes effective public policy, through its grassroots network, to protect and enhance your industry.

3709 **www.oikos.com**
Oikos

Devoted to serving professionals whose work promotes sustainable design and construction. Oikos is a Greek word meaning house. Oikos serves as the root for two English words: ecology and economy.

3710 **www.opcmia.org**
Operative Plasterers' & Cement Masons' Int'l Assn

AFL-CIO labor organizations representing plasters and cement masons in the US and Canada.

3711 **www.opei.org**
Outdoor Power Equipment Institute

International trade association whose members are manufacturers of powered lawn and garden maintenance products, components and attachment supplies, as well as industry related services.

3712 **www.pbmdf.com**
Composite Panel Association

The association of North American wood and agrifiber based particle board and medium density fiberboard producers, to broaden the base of participation in industry outreach programs.

3713 **www.pci.org**
Precast Prestressed Concrete Institute

Dedicated to fostering greater understanding and use of precast and prestressed concrete, maintains a full staff of technical and marketing specialists.

3714 **www.perlite.org**
Perlite Institute

International trade association which establishes product standards and specifications, and which encourages the development of new product uses through research.

3715 **www.pfi-institute.org**
Pipe Fabrication Institute

Members are companies producing sophisticated high temperature, high pressure piping systems that employ specialists from the United Association of Journeymen & Apprentices of the Plumbing & Pipe Fitting Industry. We exist solely for the purpose of ensuring a level of quality in the pipe fabrication indusrty that is without compromise.

3716 **www.piledrivers.org**
Pile Driving Contractors Association

Organization of pile driving contractors that advocates the increased use of driven piles for deep foundations and earth retention systems. To do this we promote the use of driven pile solutions in all cases where they are effective, support educational programs for engineers on the design and efficiency of driven piles and for contractors on improving installation procedures. We also give contractors a larger voice in establishing procedures and standards for pile installation and design.

3717 **www.psai.org**
Portable Sanitation Association International

International trade association that represents firms engaged in the leasing, renting selling and manufacturing of portable sanitation equipment, services and supplies for construction, recreation, emergency and other uses. devoted to the proper handling of human waste by the most modern, sanitary means, giving the greatest concern to the preservation of an unspoiled environment.

3718 **www.rfci.com**
Resilient Floor Covering Institute

Industry trade association of North American manufacturers who produce resilient flooring products. Associate members of RFCI supply raw materials to the industry and manufacture installation and maintenance products.

3719 **www.roofcoatings.org**
Roof Coatings Manufacturers Association

Represents the interests for manufacturers of cold applied roof coatings, cements and waterproofing agents, as well as the suppliers of products, equipment, and services to and for the industry. Currently RCMA boasts more than 70 member companies.

3720 **www.rubberpavements.org**
Rubber Pavements Association

Dedicated to encouraging greater usage of high quality, cost effective asphalt pavements containing recycled tire rubber. Conducts national and international seminars.

3721 **www.scaffold.org**
Scaffold Industry Association

Promotes scaffold safety and education through its publications, conventions, tradeshows and training programs. Marketing of your product is available through the monthly magazine, convention and trade show.

3722 **www.sgcc.org**
Safety Glazing Certification Council

Provides for the certification of safety glazing materials, comprised of safety glazing manufacturers and other parties concerned with public safety. SGCC is managed by a board of directors comprised of representatives from the safety glazing industry and the public interest sector.

3723 **www.sips.org**
Structural Insulated Panel Association

A trade association representing manufacturers, suppliers, fabricators, distributors, design professionals and builders committed to providing quality structural insulated panels for all segments of the construction industry.

3724 **www.spri.org**
Single Ply Roofing Institute

Comprised of manufacturers and marketers of sheet applied membrane roofing systems and components to the commerical roofing industry.

3725 **www.stafda.org**
Specialty Tools & Fasteners Distributors Assn

International trade association composed of distributors and manufacturers and rep agents of light construction, industrial and related products. Members also include publishers of industry press serving the construction and industrial trades.

3726 **www.stanyc.com**
Subcontractors Trade Association

Members are specialty and supply companies in the construction industry. Our goal is to improve the economic well being of our members through representation, support and assistance through the process of legislation, legal action, public relations, education and other public information programs.

3727 **www.steelwindows.com**
Steel Window Institute

For United States manufacturers of windows made from hot-rolled, solid steel sections and such related products as castings, trim, mechanical operators, screens and moldings.

3728 **www.swensongranite.com**
Swenson Granite Works

Family owned business that has been quarrying and cutting granite in New England since 1883.

3729 **www.tfguild.org**
Timber Framers Guild of North America

Dedicated to establishing training programs for dedicated timber framers, disseminating information about timber framing and timber frame building design, displaying the art of timber framing to the public, and generally serving as a center of timber framing information for the professional and general public alike.

3730 **www.thebluebook.com**
Contactors Register

Regional construction directories in most major markets throughout the US. Provides easy online access to continually updated information for each of our regional editions.

3731 **www.tile-assn.com**
National Tile Contractors Association

Serving every segment of the industry, and is recognized as the largest and most respected tile contractors association in the world.

3732 **www.tilt-up.org**
Tilt-up Concrete Association

Represents builders, engineers and suppliers involved with tilt-up concrete construction. Makes a continuing and increasingly important contribution to the success of each member through the most imaginative and efficient application of every appropriate skill, tool and service of the association.

3733 **www.wbma.org**
Western Building Material Association

Regional trade association serving building material dealers throughout the states of Alaska, Idaho, Montana, Oregon and Washington and a federated association of the National Lumber and Building Material Dealers Association.

3734 **www.wfca.org**
World Floor Covering Association

Shapes and defines public policy through agressive, national legislative advocacy on behalf of our members. Provides continuing professional educational programming through educational forums and the Regional Installation and Training Education (RITE) program.

3735 **www.windowanddoor.com**
WindowDoor.net

Anyone who is interested in window and door products can find the latest information on products, components and how-to information here.

Associations

3736 **AOAC International**
481 North Frederick Avenue
Suite 500
Gaithersburg, MD 20877
301-924-7077
FAX: 301-924-7089 800-379-2622
aoac@aoac.org www.aoac.org

Maire C Walsh, President
Robert E Koeritzer, Secretary/Treasurer
E James Bradford, Executive Director

Serves the communities of analytical sciences by providing the tools and porcesses necessary for community stakeholders to collaborate and through, consensus building, develop fit for purpose methods and services for assuring quality measurments.

3700 Members Founded: 1884

3737 **Acrylonitrile Group**
1250 Connecticut Avenue NW
Suite 700
Washington, DC 20036
202-314-4383
FAX: 202-659-8037
angroup@regnet.com
www.angroup.org

Robert J Fensterheim, Group Executive Director

Affiliated with the Synthetic Organic Chemical Manufacturers, (TAG) was formed under the Chemical manufacturers Association in the late 1960's to do research. TAG represents producers and users of the industrial chemical used to make plastics, fibers and synthetic rubber products.

3738 **Adhesion Society**
2 Davidson Hall - 0201
Blacksburg, VA 24061
540-231-7257
FAX: 540-231-3971
adhesoc@vt.edu
www.adhesionsociety.org

Lynn Penn, President
Paul J Clark, Treasurer
Esther Brann, Manager

Supports all those who are involved in adhesion's role in coatings, compostie materials, biological tissues and bonded structures.

400 Members Founded: 1978

3739 **Agricultural Retailers Association**
11701 Borman Drive
Saint Louis, MO 63146-4193
314-567-6655
800-844-4900
ara@agretailerassn.org
www.agretailerassn.org
Dedicated to suppliers, manufactureres and distributors of agricultural chemicals and fertilizers.

3740 **Alkyl Amines Council**
1850 M Street NW
Washington, DC 20036-5803
202-721-4100
FAX: 202-296-8120
www.easternfinance.org

Alan Rautio, Executive Director

Data relating to production, processing and application.

6 Members Founded: 1985

3741 **Alkylphenols and Ethoxylates Research Council**
1250 Connecticut Avenue NW
Suite 700
Washington, DC 20036
202-314-4383
FAX: 202-659-8037 866-273-7262
info@aperc.org www.aperc.org

Robert J Fensterheim, Executive Director

Monitors regulatory developments affecting manufacturers in the chemical industry

5 Members Founded: 1998

3742 **Alliance for Responsible Atmospheric Policy**
2111 Wilson Boulevard
Suite 850
Arlington, VA 22201
703-243-0344
FAX: 703-243-2874
info@arap.org www.arap.org

Dave Lewis, Chairman
John Mandyck, Vice Chairman
David Stirpe, Executive Director
Pat Rynd, Secretary
Warren Beeton, Treasurer

Made up of companies who rely on alternatives to ozone depleting chlorofluorocarbons(CFCs). Theses alternatives are HCPCs and HFCs, used primarily as refrigerants, speciality solvents, agents for foamed plastics.

300 Members Founded: 1980

3743 **American Association Textile Chemists & Colorists**
PO Box 12215
Researce Triangle Park, NC 27709-2215
919-549-8141
FAX: 919-549-8933 800-360-5380
chrietb@aatc.org www.aatcc.org

Roland L Connelly, Chairman
John A Darsey, Vice Chairman
Charles E Gavin, Treasurer
Richard A Malachowski, VP
John Daniels, Manager

Supports all those working with colorants and chemical finishes for textile and related industries.

5,000 Members

3744 **American Association for Clinical Chemistry**
1850 K St NW
Ste 625
Washington, DC 20006-2215
202-857-0717
FAX: 202-833-4576 800-892-1400

Richard Flaherty, Executive VP
Penelope Jones, Director

AACC is an international scientific/medical society of clinical laboratory professionals, physicians, research scientists and other individuals involved with clinical chemistry and other clinical laboratory science related disciplines.

3745 **American Association for Crystal Growth**
25 4th St
Somerville, NJ 08876-3205
908-575-0649
FAX: 908-575-0794
aacg@att.net
www.crystalgrowth.org/index.php

David F Bliss, President
Christine A Wang, VP
Laura Bonner, Executive Administrator

Provides support for all professionals in the field of crystal and crystal growth.

3746 **American Association of Bioanalysts**
917 Locust Street
Saint Louis, MO 63101
314-241-1445
FAX: 314-241-1449
aab@aab.org www.aab.org

3747 **American Association of Cereal Chemists**
3340 Pilot Knob Road
St Paul, MN 55121-2097
651-454-7250
FAX: 651-454-0766
aacc@scisoc.org www.aaccnet.org

Steven C Nelson, Executive Director
Betty Ford, Director Meetings and Conventions
Amy Hope, VP Operations

An organization of cereal and food science professionals working in the grain-based foods field and/or studying cereal grains and their products. Encourages research in cereal grains related materials, processing and utilization.

3000 Members Founded: 1915

3748 **American Association of Textile Chemists**
One Davis Drive
PO Box 12215
Research Triangle Park, NC 27709-2215

919-549-8141
FAX: 919-549-8933 800-360-5380
info@textileweb.com
www.textileweb.com

John Daniels, Manager

3749 **American Chemical Society**
1155 Sixteenth Street NW
Washington, DC 20036
202-872-4600
FAX: 202-872-4615 800-227-5558
help@acs.org www.acs.org

James D Burke, Chairman
William F Carroll, President
Madelaine Jacobs, Executive Director
John Crum, CEO

Self-governed individual membership organization that provides a range of opportunities for peer interaction and career development, regardless of professional or scientific interests.

15900 Members Founded: 1876

3750 **American Chemistry Council**
1300 Wilson Boulevard
Arlington, VA 22209-2307
703-741-5000
FAX: 703-741-6000
www.americanchemistry.com

Greg Lebedev, Presiden/CEO
Charlie Van Vlack, Sr. VP
Beth T Hampton, Sr. Director
Fred Webber, President

Committed to improved environmental, health and safety performance through responsible care, common sense advocacy designed to address major public policy issues, health and environmental research and product testing.

190 Members

3751 **American Coke & Coal Chemicals Institute**
1255 23rd Street NW
Washington, DC 20037
202-452-1140
FAX: 202-833-3636
information@accci.org www.accci.org

David A Saunders, President
James L Hansen, Chairman
Kevin Fitzgerald, Vice Chairman
Charles Stewarty, Treasurer/Secretary
Rebecca L Page, Director Meetings

Formed by companies interested in establishing a forum to discuss and act upon issues of common concern to their industry. Today, ACCI represents 8 of the 9 independently owned and operated US merchant coke producers; several integrated steel companies which produce coke; and all 5 of the US and 1 Canadian coal chemical companies which refine coal tar. Nearly 170 representatives from about 60 companies contribute their knowledge and expertise to enhance the effectiveness of the Institute.
160 Members Founded: 1944

3752 **American College of Toxicology Annual Meeting**
9650 Rockville Pike
Bethesda, MD 20814
301-634-7840
FAX: 301-634-7852
ekagan@actox.org www.actox.org

Robert Snyder PhD, President
Patricia Frank PhD, VP
Robert W Kapp Jr. PhD, Treasurer
Suzanne W McMaster PhD, Secretary
Carol C Lemire, Executive Director

Multidisciplinary society composed of professionals having a common interest in toxicology. Our mission is to educate and lead professionals in industry, government and related areas of toxicology and actively promote the exchange of information and perspectives on the current status of safety assessment and the application of new developments in toxicology. Annual meeting,education courses, symposia and exhibits.
500 Members Founded: 1979

3753 **American Fiber Manufacturers Association**
1530 Wilson Boulevard
Suite 690
Arlington, VA 22209
703-875-0432
FAX: 703-875-0907
afma@afma.org www.fibersource.com

Paul O'Day, President
Robert Baker, VP
Kris Bayer, Manager Information Technology
Walter Hubbard, Chairman

Trade association for US companies that manufacture synthetic and cellulostic fibers. The industry employs 30,000 people and produces over 9 billion pounds of fiber in the US. The association maintains close ties to other manufactured fiber trade associations worldwide.
30000 Members Founded: 1933

3754 **American Hydrogen Association**
3349 E Blackhawk Dr
Phoenix, AZ 85050-4826
602-710-0955

aha@clean-air.org www.clean-air.org

Stimulates interest and helping to establish the renewable hydrogen energy economy by the year 2010.

3755 **American Institute of Chemical Engineers**
3 Park Avenue
New York, NY 10016-5991
212-197-7676
FAX: 212-591-8897 800-242-4363
xpress@aiche.org www.aiche.org

John Sofranko, Executive Director
William D Byers, President
Cathy Diana, Director Human Resources
Ken Gruber, Finance/IT Manager

A professional association of members that provide leadership in advancing the chemical engineering profession.
50000 Members Founded: 1908

3756 **American Institute of Chemists**
315 Chestnut Street
Philadelphia, PA 19106-2702
215-873-8224
FAX: 215-925-1954
info@theaic.org www.theaic.org

Sharon Dobson, Executive Director

Supports all individual chemists and chemical engineers involved in the chemical industry.
Founded: 1923

3757 **American Institute of Physics**
One Physics Ellipse
College Park, MD 20740-3843
301-209-3100
FAX: 301-209-0843
aipinfo@aip.org www.aip.org

Marc Brodsky, Executive Director/CEO
Wendy Marriot, Systems/Operations Director
Richard Baccante, Treasurer/CFO
Darlene Walters, VP Pubishing
Douglas LaFrenier, Marketing/Sales Director

Supports all chemists and physicists involved in research and applications of chemical physics technolgy.
40 Members Founded: 1931

3758 **American Leather Chemists Association**
1314 50th Street
Suite 103
Lubbock, TX 79412-2940
806-744-1798
FAX: 806-744-1785
alca@leatherchemists.org
www.leatherchemists.org

Carol Adcock, Executive Secretary

To promote the advancement of the knowledge of science and engineering especially in regard to their application to problems facing the leather and leather products industries.
500 Members Founded: 1903

3759 **American Methanol Institute**
800 Connecticut Avenue NW
Suite 620
Washington, DC 20006
202-467-5050
FAX: 202-331-9055 888-275-0768
MI@methanol.org www.methanol.org

John E Lynn, President/CEO
Gregory A Dolan, VP Communications

Our mission is to expand markets for the use of methanol as a chemical commodity building block, a hydrogen carrier for fuel cell applications, and an alternative fuel.

3760 **American Oil Chemists Society**
2211 W Bradley Avenue
Champaign, IL 61821-1827
217-359-2344
FAX: 217-351-8091 800-336-2627
general@aocs.org www.aocs.org

Jean Wills, Executive VP
Gloria Cook, Director Finance/Operations
Greg Reed, Manager
Lisa Spencer, Director Marketing & Sales
Jeffrey Newman, Director Meetings & Education

An international society focused on the science and technology of fats, oils, lipids and related substances.
4500 Members Founded: 1909 6000 names

3761 **American Society Biochemistry and Molecular Biology**
9651 Rockville Pike
Bethesda, MD 20814
301-634-7145
FAX: 301-634-7126 www.asbmb.org

Supports all those involved in the biomedical and molecular biology industries.
13000 Members Founded: 1905

3762 **American Society for Mass Spectrometry**
2019 Galisteo Street, Building I-1
Santa Fe, NM 87505
505-989-4517
FAX: 505-989-1073
office@asms.org www.asms.org

Judith Sjoberg, Executive Director
Catherine E Costello, President
Alan G Marshall, VP Programs
Susan D Richardson, Treasurer
Carol A Haney, VP

Formed to promote and disseminate knowledge of mass spectrometry and allied topics. Members come from academic, industrial and govermental laboratories. Their interests include advancement of techniques and instrumentation in mass spectrometry, as well as fundamental research in chemistry, geology, biological sciences and physics.
3500 Members Founded: 1969

3763 **American Society for Neurochemistry**
9037 Ron Den Lane
Windmere, FL 34786
407-876-0750
FAX: 407-876-0750
amazing@iag.net
www.asneurochem.org

Sheilah Jewart, Executive Director

Organized in 1968-1969 by US, Canadian and Mexican members of the International Society for Neurochemistry and incorporated in the District of Columbia on August 6, 1969. Membership dues are $75/year.
1000 Members Founded: 1969

3764 **American Society of Brewing Chemists**
3340 Pilot Knob Road
Saint Paul, MN 55121
651-547-7250
FAX: 952-454-0766 800-328-7560
asbcwebmaster@scisoc.org
www.asbcnet.org

Steven C Nelson, Executive Officer
Amy Hope, VP Operations
Susan Kohn, Director Membership/Communication
Karen Cummings, Director of Publications/Production
Kathryn Aro, Director Meetings

Supports all those involved with brewing chemicals, and anything of interests to brewing chemists.
700 Members Founded: 1934

3765 Analytical and Life Science Systems Association
225 Reinekers Lane
Suite 625
Alexandria, VA 22314-2875
703-836-1360
FAX: 703-836-6644 www.alssa.org
ALSSA is the primary trade association for companies that supply instruments, chemical reagents, consumables and software used for analysis and measurement in chemistry and the life sciences.

3766 Aspirin Foundation of America
529 14th Street NW
Suite 807
Washington, DC 20045
202-378-8400
FAX: 202-737-8406 800-432-3247
info@aspirin.org www.aspirin.org
Thomas E Bryant, President
Non profit educational foundation with a membership of companies engaged in the manufacture, preparation, compounding or processing of aspirin and aspirin products.
8 Members Founded: 1981

3767 Association Official Analytical Chemists
481 N Frederick Avenue
Suite 500
Gaithersburg, MD 20877
301-924-7077
FAX: 301-924-7089
aoac@aoac.org www.aoac.org
Marilyn Blakely, Marketing Director
Jonathan W DeVries, President
Maire C Walsh, Secretary/Treasurer
Gayle Lancette, Director
James F Lawrence, Director
Offers scientific information on analytical methodology and high quality analytical measurements in the food industry.
4M Members Founded: 2000

3768 Association of Consulting Chemists and Chemical Engineers
PO Box 297
Sparta, NJ 07871
973-729-6671
FAX: 973-729-7088
info@chemconsult.org
www.chemconsult.org
Linda Townsend, Executive Secretary
A non profit membership corporation chartered in 1928 under the laws of the State of New York. The only organization of its kind and constantlyattracts to its membership qualified technical consultants of all kinds who assist their clients in creating and using chemical knowledge and technology.
150 Members Founded: 1928

3769 Association of Defensive Spray Manufacturers
906 Locust Street
St Louis, MO 1419
314-241-1445
FAX: 314-241-1449
ADSM@pepperspray.org
www.pepperspray.org
Mark S Birenbaum, Executive Director
To permit manufacturers of non lethal chemical weapons to join together to promote the industry as well as to address safety, quality control, marketing and other issues relevant to the industry
6 Members Founded: 1992

3770 Association of Official Analytical Communities: AOAC International
481 N Frederick Avenue
Gaithersburg, MD 20877-2417
301-924-7077
FAX: 301-924-7089 800-379-2622
aoac@aoac.org www.aoac.org
Jonathan W DeVries, President
Maria I Sontoro, Director
Gayle A Lancette, Director
James F Lawrence, Director
Committed to be a proactive, worldwide provider and facilitator in the development, use and harmonization of validated analytical methods and laboratory quality assurance programs and services. AOAC also serves as the primary resource for timely knowledge exchange, networking, and high quality laboratory information for its members.

3771 Association of Official Racing Chemists
PO Box 8400 Station T
Ottawa, ON KIG-3H
613-731-7137
FAX: 613-731-7984
aorc.mclellan@sympatico.ca
Sharon K McLellan, Executive Director
The international membership consits of individuals concerned with detection of drugs in racing samples.
200 Members Founded: 1947

3772 Basic Acrylic Monomer Manufacturers
17260 Vannes Court
Hamilton, VA 20158
540-751-2093
FAX: 540-751-2094
ehunt@adelphia.net www.bamm.net
Elizabeth K Hunt, Executive Director
Addresses the issues facing the basic acrylates. Also represents manufacturers and importers of acrylic acid and its esters.
5 Members Founded: 1986

3773 CIIT Centers for Health Research
Six Davis Drive
PO Box 12137
Research Triangle Park, NC 27709-2137

919-581-1200
FAX: 919-588-1400
wgreenlee@ciit.org www.ciit.org
William F Greenlee PhD, President/CEO
Carol J M Henry, VP Science & Research
Helen N Schinkel, VP Finance & Operations
Studies toxicological and human health risk issues associated with the manufacture, distribution and disposal of industrial chemicals.
130 Members Founded: 1974

3774 Chemical Coaters Association International
PO Box 54316
Cincinnati, OH 45254
513-624-6767
FAX: 513-624-0601 800-926-2848
aygoyer@one.net www.ccaiweb.com
Anne Goyer, Executive Director
A technical and professional organization that provides information and training on surface coating technologies. Users and suppliers of industrial cleaners, paints, coatings, and equipment.
1000 Members Founded: 1970

3775 Chemical Fabrics and Film Association
1300 Sumner Avenue
Cleveland, OH 44115-2851
216-241-7333
FAX: 216-241-0105
cffa@chemicalfabricsandfilm.com
www.chemicalfabricsandfilm.com
Charles M Stockinger, Executive Secretary
International trade association representing manufacturers of polymer-based fabric and film products, used in the building and construction, automotive, fashion and many other industries.
40 Members Founded: 1927

3776 Chemical Heritage Foundation
315 Chestnut Street
Philadelphia, PA 19106
215-925-2222
FAX: 215-925-1954 888-224-6006
kerryo@chemheritage.org
www.chemheritage.org
Miriam Fisher-Shaefer, Chief Financial Officer
Rosiland Remer, Director
Alan Thackray, President
John Van Ness, VP Administration
Supports and maintains the history of the chemical and molecular sciences and industries.
29 Members

3777 Chemical Industry Data Exchange
401 North Michigan Avenue
Chicago, IL 60611-4267
312-321-5145
FAX: 312-212-5971
memberservices@cidx.org
www.cidx.org
JoAnne Norton, Executive Director
Laura Field, Communications
Promotes standards to improve the efficiency of transactions across the chemical industry supply chain. Members include chemical producers and companies active in the chemicals industry.

3778 Chemical Manufacturers Association
1300 Wilson Boulevard
Arlington, VA 22209
703-276-6160
FAX: 603-741-6807
www.coatingstech.org
Supports all those involved in the manufacturer of chemicals.

3779 Chemical Marketing Research Association
60 Bay Street
Suite 702
Staten Island, NY 10301-2514
718-876-8800
FAX: 718-720-4666
cmra@cmra.org
www.netbox.com/cmra/cmra_about.htm
Mary Carrick, President
Keeps members informed on industrial market research, conducts seminars, and

supports business schools in market research.
1000 Members Founded: 1945

3780 Chemical Producers and Distributors Association
1430 Duke Street
Alexandria, VA 22314
703-548-7700
FAX: 703-548-3149 www.cdpa.com
Warren Stickle PhD, President
Diane Schute, Director Legislative Affairs
Bethany Oxer, Exec Asst & Dir Meetings/Membership
Members are samll to medium sized pesticide formulators, manufacturers and distributors
86 Members Founded: 1975

3781 Chemical Specialties Manufacturers Association
1913 I Street NW
Washington, DC 20006
202-872-8110

ipp@halldata.com www.csma.org
Supports all professionals involved in the manufacturer of chemical specialties.

3782 Chemical Strategies Partnership
423 Washington Street
4th Floor
San Francisco, CA 94111
415-421-3405
FAX: 415-421-3304
www.chemicalstrategies.com
Jill Kauffman Johnson, Executive Director
Tom Votta, Deputy Director
CSP seeks to reduce chemical use, waste, risks and cost through the transformation of the chemical supply chain by redefining the way chemicals are used and sold.

3783 Chemtrec/American Chemistry Council (ACC)
1300 Wilson Boulevard
Arlington, VA 22209-2307

FAX: 703-741-6037 800-262-8200
chemtrec@americanchemistry.com
www.chemtrec.com
Carl Reynolds, Director Emergency Response Center
Randy Speight, Managing Director
Nancy White, Manager Communications\Strategic Pr
Randy Speight, Managing Director
A 24 hour emergency communication service center that helps fire fighters and emergency responders protect the public and helps shippers of hazardous materials comply with the US Department of Transportation regulations.
Founded: 1971

3784 Chlorinated Paraffins Industry
1250 Connecticut Avenue NW
Suite 700
Washington, DC 20036
202-419-1500
FAX: 202-659-8037
info@regnet.com
www.regnet.com/cpia
Robert J Fensterheim, Executive Director
Composed of manufacturers, distributors, and users of chlorinated paraffins, used in lubricants, plastics and flame retardants.
2 Members Founded: 1970

3785 Chlorine Chemistry Council
1300 Wilson Boulevard
Arlington, VA 22209
703-741-5000
www.c3.org
A national trade association based in Arlington representing the manufacturers and users of chlorine and chlorine-related products.

3786 Chlorine Free Products Association
19 N Main Street
Algonquin, IL 60102
847-658-6104
FAX: 847-658-3152
info@chlorinefreeproducts.org
www.chlorinefreeproducts.org
Archie Beaton, Owner
A nonprofit association that's primary purpose is to promote total chlorine free policies, programs and technologies throughtout the world.

3787 Chlorine Institute
1300 Wilson Boulevard
Rosslyn, VA 22209-4919
703-741-5760
FAX: 703-741-6068
info@cl2.com
www.chlorineinstitute.org
Supports the chlo-alkali industry and serves the public by promoting the safe handling of chlorine and caustic materials.
220 Members Founded: 1924

3788 Chlorobenzene Producers Association
1850 M Street NW
Suite 700
Washington, DC 20036-1704
202-721-4100
FAX: 202-296-8120
murrayj@socma.com
www.socma.com/amc/listofaffiliates.htm
John F Murray, VP Project Management
Addresses health and environmental issues in response to Environmental Protection Agency.
40 Members Founded: 1981

3789 Color Pigments Manufacturers Association
300 North Washington Street
Suite 102
Alexandria, VA 22314
703-684-4044
FAX: 703-684-1795
cpma@cpma.com www.pigments.org
J Lawrence Robinson, President
An industry trade association representing color pigment companies in Canada, Mexico and the US. Also represents small, medium, and large color pigments manufacturers accounting for 95% of the production of color pigments in North America
50 Members Founded: 1925

3790 Combustion Institute
5001 Baum Boulevard
Suite 635
Pittsburgh, PA 15213-1851
412-687-1366
FAX: 421-687-0340
office@combustioninstitute.org
www.combustioninstitute.org
Sue S Terpack, Executive Administrator
International organizaton with sections in several foreign countries including Canada. A non profit, educational organization with the purpose of promoting and disseminating knowledge in the field of combustion science.
4000 Members Founded: 1954

3791 Consumer Specialty Products Association
900 17th Street NW
Suite 300
Washington, DC 20006
202-872-8110
FAX: 202-872-8114
info@cspa.org www.cspa.org
Christopher Cathcart, President/CEO
Joanne Weaver, Director, VPController
Carlos Underwood, Manager Information\Technology
Nonprofit organization composed of many companies involved in the formulation, manufacture, testing and marketing of chemical specialty products. Our line includes disinfectants that kill germs in homes, hospitals and restaurants, candles and fragrances that eliminate odors, pest management products for home and garden, cleaning products and much more.
200 Members Founded: 1914

3792 Council for Chemical Research
1730 Rhode Island Avenue NW
Suite 302
Washington, DC 20036
202-429-3971
FAX: 202-429-3976
danthony@ccrhq.org www.ccrhq.org
Donald B Anthony, Executive Director
Mary Beth McCutcheon, Director Membership Services
Wayne Madison, Operations Manager
Promotes cooperation in basic research and encourage high quality education in the chemical sciences ans engineering. Membership represents industry, academia, and government.
200 Members Founded: 1979

3793 CropLife America
1156 15th Street NW
Suite 400
Washington, DC 20005
202-296-1585
FAX: 202-463-0474
webmaster@croplifeamerica.org
www.croplifeamerica.org
Jay J Vroom, President/CEO
Patrick Donnelly, Executive VP/COO
Douglas T Nelson, Exec VP/General Counsel/Secretary
A Allen Noe, Direcotr Communications
George Rolofson, Sr VP Government Affairs
A trade association of the manufacturers, formulators, and distributors of agricultural crop protection, pest control, and bitechnology products. Membership is composed of companies that produce, sell and distribute virtually all the active ingredients use in crop protection chemicals.
86 Members Founded: 1933

3794 Drug, Chemical & Associated Technologies Association
1 Washington Boulevard
Suite 7
Robbinsville, NJ 08691
609-448-1000
FAX: 609-448-1944 800-640-3228
info@dcat.org www.dcat.org

Patrick Vazquez, President
Lynda M Doyle, Senior VP
Margaret Timony, Executive Director

The premier business development association whose membership is comprimsed of companies that manufacture, distribute or provide services to the pharmaceutical, chemical, nutritional and related industries.
350 Members Founded: 1890

3795 ETAD North America
1850 M Street NW
Suite 700
Washington, DC 20036
202-721-4154
FAX: 202-296-8120
helmest@socma.com www.etad.com

Dr.C.T. Helmes, Executive Director

Furthers the efforts of the North American dye manufacturing industry in addressing health, safety and environmental issues. It is recognized by regulatory authorities, customers, and the public as an authoritative source of informationon the technical aspects of organic dyes.
14 Members Founded: 1982

3796 Electrochemical Society
65 S Main Street
Building D
Pennington, NJ 08534
609-737-1902
FAX: 609-737-2743
interface@electrochem.org
www.electrochem.org

Carolyn R Wroblewski, Director Finance
Brian Bosak, Director Information Technology
Calvo Roque J., Executive Director
Valerie Yacko, Executive Assistant
Roque Calvo, Manager

Supports all those involved in the fields of electrochemical and solid state science and technology.
8000 Members Founded: 1902

3797 Embalming Chemical Manufacturers
1370 Honeyspot Road Ext
Stratford, CT 06615-7115

Works to develop scientific, technological, and economic data about safety issues of the product.
Founded: 1951

3798 Emulsion Poylmers Council
1250 Connecticut Avenue NW
Suite 700
Washington, DC 20036
202-314-4383
FAX: 202-659-8037
epc@regnet.com www.regnet.com/epc

Robert J Fensterheim, Executive Director

Represents regulatory professionals at companies which produce emulsion polymers, chemical compounds used in a variety of coating and other industril applications.
10 Members Founded: 1995

3799 Environmental Arsenic Council
1250 Connecticut Avenue NW
Suite 700
Washington, DC 20036
202-314-4383
FAX: 202-637-9718 bobf@regnet.com

Robert J Fensterheim, Executive Director

Monitors regulatory developments on behalf of manufacturers in the chemical industry
5 Members Founded: 1996

3800 Ethylene Oxide Sterlization Association
11527 Bertram Street
Lake Ridge, VA 22192-6604
703-897-4444
FAX: 703-897-4646
info@eosa.org www.eosa.org

Joseph E Hadley Jr, General Counsel

EOSA works to educate industry, regulators, and the public on the uses and benefits of ethylene oxide. EOSA also works to improve safety standards, foster industry communication, and provide a forum for issues related to ethylene oxjde sterilization.

50 Members Founded: 1995

3801 Federation of Analytical Chemistry and Spectroscopy Societies
2019 Galisteo Building I-1
Santa Fe, NM 87505
505-888-8800
FAX: 505-989-1073
facssc@@facssc.org www.facss.org

Cindi Lily, Executive Assistant
Michael Boyle, Manager

Exists to combine many small meetings previously organized bythe individual societies into one joint meeting that covers the whole field of Analytical Chemistry.
7 Members Founded: 1972

3802 Federation of Societies for Coatings Technology
492 Norristown Road
Blue Bell, PA 19422-2350
610-940-0777
FAX: 610-940-0292
fsct@coatingstech.org
www.coatingstech.org

Frederick H Walker, President
Rose A Ryntz, Secretary/Treasurer
John F Bartlett, VP

Provides technical education and professional development to its members and to the global industry through its multi-national constituent societies and collectively as a federation.
6000 Members Founded: 1922

3803 Federation of Spectroscopy Societies
13 N Cliffe Drive
Wilmington, DE 19809
302-656-0771

Supports all those involved with analytical chemistry.

3804 Independent Liquid Terminals Association
1444 I Street NW
Suite 400
Washington, DC 20005
202-842-9200
FAX: 202-326-8600
info@ilta.org www.ilta.org

E David Doane, President
Melinda Whitney, Director/Government Affairs

Supports all those involved in the storage and transfer of bulk commercial liquids.
400 Members Founded: 1974

3805 Independent Lubricant Manufacturers Association
400 N Columbus St
Ste 201
Alexandria, VA 22314-2264
703-684-5574
FAX: 703-836-8503
ilma@ilma.org www.ilma.org

Celeste Powers, Executive Director
Christine Hutcherson, Director Member Relations
Martha Jolkovski, Director Publications
Carla Mangone, Managing Editor

Supports all those involved in the US and international independent lubricant industry.

3806 International Cadmium Association
9222 Jeffrey Road
PO Box 924
Great Falls, VA 22066-3223
703-759-7400
FAX: 703-759-7003
icdamorrow@aol.com
www.cadmium.org

Hugh Morrow, Consultant

Provides marketing research and promotion to the industry. Hosts seperate annual meetings in the United States and Europe.
30 Members

3807 International Ozone Association: Pan American Group Branch
98 Warren Ave
Quincy, MA 02170-2608
617-773-4469
www.ioza.org

Robert Jarnis, Executive Director

Represents the interests of environmental and other scientific communities, application engineers, users, and manufacturers of ozone generation and contacting equipment.
810 Members Founded: 1976

3808 Materials Technology Institute
1215 Fern Ridge Parkway
Suite 206
Saint Louis, MO 63141-4405
314-576-7712
FAX: 314-576-6078
mtiadmin@mti-global.org
www.mti-global.org

JM Macki PhD, Executive Director
Deborah Ehret, Operations Director

Provides leadership in materials technology for chemical processing to improve reliability, profitability and safety.
52 Members Founded: 1977

3809 Materials Technology Institute of the Chemical Process Industries
1215 Fern Ridge Parkway
Saint Louis, MO 63141-4405
314-576-7712
FAX: 314-576-6078
mtiadmin@mti-global.org
www.mti-global.org

JM Macki PhD, Executive Director
Deborah Ehret, Operations Director

Provides leadership in materials technology for chemical processing to improve reliability, profitability and safety.
52 Members Founded: 1977

3810 Methanol Institute
4100 N Fairfax Drive
Suite 740
Arlington, VA 22203
703-248-3636
FAX: 703-248-3997 888-275-0768
MI@methanol.org www.methanol.org

Gregory Dolan, VP

Serves as the voice of the methanol. As a trade association, MI's member companies include the principal global producers of methanol, as well as methanol distributors, industry suppliers and consumers. In addition to encouraging the expansion of marketing for reformed gasoline, MI also promotes the use of methanol as a hydrogen carrier for fuel cell technology applications.
20 Members Founded: 1989

3811 National Aerosol Association
PO Box 5510
Fullerton, CA 92828
714-525-1518
FAX: 714-526-1295
naa@industrialhydrocarbons.com
www.nationalaerosol.com

David Shaw, President
Sean Fitzgerald, VP

Individuals, firms and agencies engaged in the development, manufacture, packaging, sale or distribution of aerosol products.
30 Members Founded: 1986

3812 National Association of Chemical Recyclers
1900 M Street NW
Washington, DC 20036
202-296-1725
FAX: 202-296-2530
103612.514@compuserve.com

Christopher Goebel, Executive Director

Members are companies whose primary business is the reclamation of solvents and other chemicals from industrial waste streams and recycling.
Founded: 1979

3813 National Chemical Credit Association
1100 Main Street
Buffalo, NY 14209-2356
716-887-9527
FAX: 716-878-2866 www.ncca#1.org

Don Peters, Contact

Members are major producers of basic chemicals and allied products.
100 Members Founded: 1938

3814 National Pest Management Association
9300 Lee Hwy
Ste 301
Fairfax, VA 22031-6051
703-352-6762
FAX: 703-352-3031 800-678-6722
cmannes@pestworld.org
www.pestworld.org

Cindy Mannes, Executive Director
Robert Lederer, Executive VP
Gary McKenzie, Finance
Jean Neun, Membership
Elizabeth Preston, Director, Communications/Marketing

Represents the interests of its members and the structural pest control industry.
4600 Members October Founded: 1933

3815 North American Catalysis Society
PO Box 80262
Wilmington, DE 19880
302-695-2488
FAX: 302-695-8347
michael.b.damore@usa.dupont.com
www.nacatsoc.org

John N Armor, President
Gary B McVicker, VP
Umit S Ozkan, Secretary
John W Byrne, Treasurer

Fosters an interest in heterogeneous and homogeneous catalysis. Organizes national meetings. Members are chemists and chemical engineers engaged in the study and use of reactions involving catalysts. Publishes a newsletter.
1400 Members Founded: 1956 3400 names

3816 Official Analytical Chemists Association
481 N Frederick Avenue
Gaithersburg, MD 20877
301-924-7077
FAX: 301-924-7089 800-379-2622
International association of scientists including analytical chemists, microbiologists, laboratory managers and other laboratory personnel.

3817 Oxygenated Fuels Association
1401 New York Avenue NW
Suite 520
Washington, DC 20005
202-393-6190
FAX: 202-393-6199
info@ofa.net www.cleanfuels.net

Fred Craft Jr, Executive Director
12 Members Founded: 1983

3818 Phosphate Chemicals Export Association
IMC Global Operations
Suite 300
Lake Forest, IL 60045-2561
847-739-1200
FAX: 847-739-1617
daprichard@imcglobal.com
www.pfa.org

Douglas A Pertz, Chairman/CEO
C Steven Hoffman, Senior VP
David A Prichard, VP Investor/Corporate Relations
Mary Ann Hynes, Senior VP/General Counsel

From lowest cost mines and plants in North America through a highly efficient distribution network, IMC Global serves world agriculture as the largest global producer and supplier of concentrated phosphates and potash fertilizers. The company also is one of the leading providers of phosphorus and potassium feed supplements for the global animal nutrition industry.
3 Members Founded: 1975

3819 Pine Chemicals Association
3350 Riverwood Pkwy SE
Suite 1900
Atlanta, GA 30339
678-278-8157
FAX: 770-984-5341
cmorgan@pinechemicals.org
www.pinechemicals.org

Walter L Jones, President/COO
Gerald Marterer, Chairman/CEO

Association of producers, processors and consumers of pine chemicals. Promotes innovative, safe and environmentally responsible practices to assure a reliable supply of high quality products.
50 Members Founded: 1947

3820 Polyisocyanurate Insulation Manufacturers Association
515 King Street
Suite 420
Alexandria, VA 22314-1137
703-684-1136
FAX: 703-684-6048
pima@pima.org www.pima.org

Alma Garnett, Chairman
Jared O Blum, President

Represents the interests of polyisocyanurate manufacturers and suppliers to the industry. Efforts include education, environmental responsibility, government partnerships and energy conservation.
32 Members Founded: 1970

3821 Polyurethane Foam Association
PO Box 52246
Knoxville, TN 37950-2246
865-546-7661
FAX: 865-523-7300
rluedeka@pfa.org www.pfa.org

Pat Martin, Chairman
Robert Luedeka, Executive Director

Suppliers of raw material and equipment. Associate members are manufacturers of flexible polyurethane foam. Our mission is to educate customers and other groups about flexible polyurethane foam and to promote its use in manufactured and industrial products. This includes providing facts on environmental, health and safety issues related to polyurethane foam to the membership of PFA, polyurethane foam users, regulatory officials, business leaders and the media.
63 Members Founded: 1980

3822 Powder Coating Institute
2121 Eisenhower Avenue
Suite 401
Alexandria, VA 22314-4688
703-684-1770
FAX: 703-684-1771
pci-info@powdercoating.org
www.powdercoating.org

Gregory J Bocchi, Executive Director
Jeff Palmer, Communications Director

Is a trade association representing suppliers of powder coating materials, equipment, and related products and services in North America.
325 Members Annual/Fall Founded: 1981

3823 Process Equipment Manufacturers Association
201 Park Washington Court
Falls Church, VA 22046-4513
703-538-1796
FAX: 703-241-5603 www.pemanet.org

Richard C Neuffer, President
Alan Cohen, VP
Doug Schlepp, Treasurer
Sue Denston, Executive Director
Clay D Tyeryar, CAE, International Exhibit Manager

Manufacturers and suppliers of equipment for food, chemical, pulp and paper, water, wastewater processing.
50 Members Founded: 1960

3824 Society of Cosmetic Chemists
120 Wall Street
Suite 2400
New York, NY 10005
212-668-1500
FAX: 211-268-1504
societycoshem@worldnet.att.net
www.scconline.org

Amy Wyatt, President
Guy Padulo, VP
Theresa Cesario, Executive Director

Supports all those involved in working with and developing cosmetic chemicals.
4000 Members Founded: 1945

3825 Society of Toxicology
1821 Michael Faraday Drive
Suite 300
Reston, VA 20190
703-438-3115
FAX: 703-438-3113
sothq@toxicology.org
www.toxicology.org

Dr. Marion F Ehrich, President
Shawn Lamb, Executive Director

Members are scientists concerned with the effects of chemicals on man and the environment. Promotes the acquisition and utilization of knowledge in toxicology, aids in the protection of public health and facilitates disciplines. The society has a strong commitment to education in toxicology and to the recruitment of students and new members into the profession.
5000 Members Founded: 1961

3826 Synthetic Organic Chemical Manufacturers Association
1850 M Street NW
Suite 700
Washington, DC 20036-5810
202-721-4100
FAX: 202-296-8120
info@socma.com www.socma.com

Michael DeRuosi, Chair
Margaret R Walker, Vice Chairperson
Charles Hinnant, Vice Chairmam
John J Nicols, Secretary
Larry Brotherton, Treasurer

Conducts workshops and seminars. Maintains a library on cancer policies and related subjects. Its more than 320 member companies have more than 2,000 manufacturing sistes and 100,000 employees.
300 Members Founded: 1921

Newsletters

3827 AACG Newsletter
American Association for Crystal Growth
25 4th Street
Somerville, NJ 08876-3205
908-575-0649
FAX: 908-575-0794
aacg@att.net www.crystalgrowth.org

David Matthiesen, Chief Editor
Lara Keefer, Editor

Technical articles and includes calendar of upcoming meetings.
Founded: 1966
Circulation: 600
Printed in 4 colors on glossy stock

3828 Advanced Coatings and Surface Technology
John Wiley & Sons
111 River Street
Hoboken, NJ 07030-5774
201-748-6000
FAX: 201-748-6088
custserv@wiley.com www.wiley.com

Alan Brown, Publisher
William J Pesce, President/CEO

Provides intelligence service reports and puts into perspective significant developments in coatings and surface modification across a broad range of industry lines. ACT interprets developments ranging from traditional coating processes to chemical vapor deposition and iron beam methods, which offers interdisciplinary analyses of those that have true commercial potential.
$530.00
10 pages Monthly Founded: 1807

3829 Amber-Hi-Lites
Rohm And Haas Company
Independence Mail W
Philadelphia, PA 19105
215-592-3000
FAX: 215-592-6808

JC Fanelli, Publisher

Offers discussions of ion exchange resin use in fields of water conditioning.

3830 Analytical Chemistry
American Chemical Society
1155 16th Street NW
Suite 600
Washington, DC 20036-4892
202-872-4600
FAX: 202-872-6067 800-227-5558
help@acs.org www.chemistry.org

Royce W Murray, Editor
Madeleine Jacobs, Executive Director
Elizabeth Zubritsky, Manager

Information and news on the chemical industry.
Founded: 1876

3831 Biochemistry
American Chemical Society
1155 16th Street NW
Suite 600
Washington, DC 20036-4892
202-872-4600
FAX: 202-872-4615 800-333-9511
help@acs.org www.chemistry.org

Gordon G Hammes, Editor
Madeleine Jacobs, Executive Director

News and information for the scientific community. *$137.00*
Weekly Founded: 1876

3832 CSMA Executive Newswatch
Chemical Specialties Manufacturers Association
900 17TH Street NW
Suite 300
Washington, DC 20006-2111
202-872-8110
FAX: 202-872-8114
CSMA@Juno.com www.csma.org/

Ralph Engel, Publisher
Lisa Johns, Editor
Christopher Cathcart, President

Articles cover regulatory and market information.
Monthly Founded: 1914

3833 ChemEcology
Chemical Manufacturers Association
1300 Wilson Boulevard
Arlington, VA 22209-2307
703-741-5502
FAX: 703-741-6807

Rebecca Swinehart, Editor

Issues on health, safety and the environment.

3834 ChemWeek Association
110 Williams Street
11th Floor C3A
New York, NY 10038
212-621-4900
FAX: 212-621-4800
reg@chemweek.com
www.chemweek.com

Lyn Tattum, Publisher/Group Vice-President
Joseph Mennella, National Sales Manager
Alexandra Sheppard, Regional Sales Manager
Brian Languile, President

Comprehensive coverage of the latest developments, uses, production, distribution, and manufacturing of chemicals for all industries. *$159.00*
Monthly Founded: 1977
Circulation: 20779

3835 Chemical Bond
American Chemical Society
1155 16th Street NW
Suite 600
Washington, DC 20036-4892
202-872-4600
FAX: 202-872-6381 800-333-9511
help@acs.org www.chemistry.org

Martha Rhine, Publisher
John Bornmann, Editor

Covers organization activities.

3836 Chemical Bulletin
American Chemical Society
7173 N Austin
Niles, IL 60714-4617
847-647-8405
FAX: 847-647-8364
chicagoacs@ameritech.net
www.chicagoacs.org

Fran Karen Kravitz, Editor

Highlights events and meetings of local chapters, profiles prominent society members, and reports on research and technological advancements in the field. *$20.00*
Monthly
Circulation: 5700

3837 Chemical Economics Handbook Program
SRI Consulting
4300 Bohannon Drive
Suite 200
Menlo Park, CA 94025-3493
650-592-2000
FAX: 650-330-1149
inquiry@sri.com
www.sriconsulting.com/

Eric Linak, Director
John Pearson, President/CEO

Ongoing multiclient program focusing on the chemical and allied products industries. History, status and projected trends for hundreds of chemicals, chemical raw materials, and end-use products. Service includes access to on-line data base and client inquiry privileges. *$12000.00*

Monthly Founded: 1946

3838 Chemical Industries Newsletter
SRI International
333 Ravenswood Avenue
Menlo Park, CA 94025-3453
650-859-2000
FAX: 650-326-5512 www.sri.com
Elizabeth Johnson, Publisher
Articles discuss the activities of SRI International Chemical Industries Centers.

3839 Chemical Industry Monitoring
Cyrus J Lawrence
1290 Avenue of the Americas
New York, NY 10006

Don Pattison, Editor
Prices and technological developments in the industry.

3840 Chemical Product News
US Dept. of Commerce, Business & Defense Service
14th & Constitution NW NW
Washington, DC 20230-0001
202-935-5000

Roger Davis, Publisher
Offers information about chemical products and related issues.

3841 Chemical Regulation Reporter
Bureau of National Affairs
1231 25th Street NW
Washington, DC 20037
202-452-4466
FAX: 202-452-4084 800-372-1033
customercare@bna.com www.bna.com

Gregory C McCaffery, Publisher
Larry E Evans, Managing Editor
A notification and reference service consisting of six binders that comprehensively covers federal chemical regulations. *$1103.00*
Weekly Founded: 1929

3842 Chemical and Engineering News
American Chemical Society
1155 16th Street NW
Suite 600
Washington, DC 20036-4892
202-872-4600
FAX: 202-872-6067 800-227-5558
help@acs.org www.acs.org
Rudy M Baum, Editor-in-Chief
Pamela S Zurer, Managing Editor
Covers news relating to chemical engineering and technology.
Weekly Founded: 1876
Circulation: 137,664

3843 Chemweek's Business Daily
Chemical Week/Access Intelligence
110 William Street
11th Floor
New York, NY 10038
212-621-4900
FAX: 212-621-4800
www.chemweek.com
Lyn Tattum, Publisher
Rob Westervelt, Editor
Daily electronic newsletter covering the latest chemical industry business and financial news, including markets, pricing, regulatory and security issues, research, technologies and new services. *$1049.00*
Daily Founded: 2002
Printed in 4 colors : pdf

3844 Chlor-Alkali Marketwire
Chemical Week/Access Intelligence
110 William Street
11th Floor
New York, NY 10038
212-621-4900
FAX: 212-621-4800
www.chemweek.com
Lyn Tattum, Publisher
Peckwee Sim, Editor
Weekly electronic newsletter covering chlor-alkali market sector, including market trends in supply and demand, pricing fluctuations, production rates in caristic soda and chlorine. Also covers vinyls, soda ash and related derivatives *$1699.00*
Weekly Founded: 2002
Printed in 4 colors : pdf

3845 Chlorine Institute Newsletter
Chlorine Institute
1300 Wilson Boulevard
Arlington, VA 22209
703-741-5760
FAX: 703-741-6068
tkerns@cl2.com
www.chlorintinstitute.org
Dr. Robert Smerko, President
Articles featuring safe handling of chlorine and caustic materials.
5 pages Founded: 1924
Printed in 2 colors on matte stock

3846 Composites and Adhesives Newsletter
T/C Press
223 S Detroit Street
PO Box 36006
Los Angeles, CA 90036
323-971-4665
FAX: 323-938-6923 tcpress@msn.com
Sue Stone, Office Manager
George Epstein, Editor
News about composites and adhesives industry. Accepts very limited and selective advertising. *$190.00*
20 pages Quarterly Founded: 1984
Circulation: 300 Audited Est. Pass-Along Circ: 3000
Computerized version available

3847 Electronic Chemicals News
Chemical Week Associates
1201 seven locks road suite 100
Votomac, MD 20854
301-354-2000
FAX: 301-738-7581
wkch@kable.com
www.chemweek.com
Micheal Kraus, Publisher
Written for and about the chemicals industry and contains industry developments, environmental news, new products, and financial and corporate briefs. *$699.00*

3848 ILTA Newsletter
Independent Liquid Terminals Association

1444 I Street NW
Suite 400
Washington, DC 20005
202-842-9200
FAX: 202-326-8660
info@ilta.org www.ilta.org
E David Doane, President/Editor
Melinda Whitney, Assistant Editor
International trade association representing bulk liquid terminal companies that store commercial liquids in aboveground storage tanks and transfer products to and from oceangoing tank ships, tank barges, pipelines, tank trucks, and tank rail cars.
Monthly Founded: 1974
Circulation: 1200
Printed in 2 colors on matte stock

3849 Inside R&D
John Wiley & Sons
111 River Street
Hoboken, NJ 07030-5774
201-748-6000
FAX: 201-748-6088
subinfo@wiley.com www.wiley.com
Kenneth A Kovaly, Publisher
Charles Joslin, Editor
William J. Pesce, President/CEO
Weekly service offering information about current research and development, concentrating on new and significant developments that create new products/markets in the near-term and this are valuable to a company's bottom line. *$790.00*
6 pages Weekly Founded: 1807
Mailing list available for rent

3850 Langmuir: QTL Biosystems
American Chemical Society
1322 Pouseo de Peralta
Santa Fe, NM 87501
505-989-1907
FAX: 505-989-1979
service@acs.org www.pubs.acs.org
David Whitten PhD, Editor
Edited for an audience involved with high-vacuum surface chemistry and spectroscopy, heterogeneous catalysis, all aspects of interface chemistry involving fluid interfaces and disperse systems.
BiWeekly
Circulation: 1,200

3851 Molecular Crystals & Liquid Crystals Optic Bulletin
Gordon Publications
PO Box 786
New York, NY 10276-0786

Scientific news and information for chemists.

3852 North American Catalysis Society Newsletter
PO Box 80262
Wilmington, DE 19880-262
302-695-2488
FAX: 302-695-8347
michael.b.damore@usa.dupont.com
www.nacatsoc.org
Michael B D Amore, Editor
John N Armor, President
Gary McVicker, VP
Fosters an interest in heterogeneous and homogeneous catalysis. Organizes national meetings. Members are chemists and chemical engineers engaged in the study and use of reactions involving catalysts. *$45.00*
38448 pages Monthly Founded: 1956
Mailing list available for rent 3,500 names $160 per M.

3853 SOCMA Newsletter
Synthetic Organic Chemical Manufacturers Assn
1850 M Street NW
Suite 700
Washington, DC 20036-5810
202-721-4100
FAX: 202-296-8120
info@socma.com www.socma.com
Joseph Acker, President
Kim Fuller, Editor
Liesa Brown, Sr Manager Marketing/Communications
Offers information on the organic chemical industry.
10 pages Bi-monthly Founded: 1921

Magazines & Journals

3854 AICHE Journal
American Institute of Chemical Engineers

3 Park Avenue
New York, NY 10016-5991
212-197-7676
FAX: 212-591-8883 800-242-4363
xpress@aiche.org www.aiche.org/
Stephen Smith, Group Publisher
Jeffrey J Siirola, President
Tim McCreight, Marketing Manager
John Sofranko, Executive Director
Serves as a journal emcompassing data and results of the latest information in significant research and trends in the field. $ 1250.00
Monthly Founded: 1908

3855 Accounts of Chemical Research
American Chemical Society
1155 16th Street NW
Suite 600
Washington, DC 20036-4892
202-872-4600
FAX: 202-776-8258 800-227-5558
webmaster@acs.org
www.chemistry.org
Joan S Valentine, Editor
Madeleine Jacobs, Executive Director
William Carroll, President
Chemical research and statistical information. *$526.00*
Monthly Founded: 1968
Circulation: 159,000

3856 Advanced Coatings and Surface Technology
605 3rd Avenue
New York, NY 10158
212-850-6890
FAX: 212-850-8800

3857 American Laboratory
International Scientific Communications
30 Controls Drive
PO Box 870
Shelton, CT 06484-870
203-926-9300
FAX: 203-926-9310
sandyg@iscpubs.com
www.iscpubs.com
S McCorvie Wham, Associate Publisher
Susan Messinger, Managing Editor
Maureen Magner, Production Manager
Steven J. Morris, CEO/President
American Laboratory serves industry, university, government, independent and foundation research laboratories.
50 pages Monthly Founded: 1969
Circulation: 91611
Printed in 4 colors on glossy stock

3858 Asia Pacific Chemicals
Reed Chemical Publications
2 Rector Street
26th Floor
New York, NY 10006-1819
212-323-3200
FAX: 212-791-4311
jlucas@chemexpo.com
www.reedchemicals.com

3859 Asian Chemical News
Reed Chemical Publications
2 Rector Street
26th Floor
New York, NY 10006-1819
212-323-3200
FAX: 212-791-4311
www.reedchemicals.com

3860 CPI Purchasing
Reed Business Information
2000 Clearwater Drive
Oak Brook, IL 60523
630-740-0825
FAX: 630-288-8686
k.doyle@reedbusiness.com
www.reedbusiness.com/
Kevin Fitzgerald, Editor
Kathy Doyle, Publisher
Trade magazine for purchasing professionals in the chemical/process industry. Accepts advertising. *$74.95*
100 pages Founded: 1983
Circulation: 95078

3861 Cereal Chemistry
American Association of Cereal Chemists

3340 Pilot Knob Road
St Paul, MN 55121-2097
651-454-7250
FAX: 651-454-0766
aacc@scisoc.org www.aaccnet.org
Steven C Nelson, Publisher
Karen Cummings, Director Publications/Production
Phyllis Albertz, Technical Editor
Ina Pfefer, Journals Records Coordinator
Dawn Wuest, Circulation Coordinator
The premier international archival journal in cereal science. Research explores raw materials, processes, products utilizing cereal, oilseeds, and pulses, as wellas analytical procedures, technological tests, and fundamental research in the cereals area. *$79.00*
Bi-Monthly

3862 Chemical & Engineering News
American Chemical Society
1155 16th Street NW
Washington, DC 20036
202-872-4600
FAX: 202-872-8258 800-227-5558
help@acs.org www.chemistry.org
Robert D Bovenschulte, Publishing Director
Madeleine Jacobs, Executive Director
Regular issue features include management, industry and business, sales and marketing, research, production and technology, chemicals, equipment, instrumentation, government and people. *$140.00*
Weekly Founded: 1876
Circulation: 152000

3863 Chemical Engineering
Chemical Week Associates
110 William Street
New York, NY 10038
212-621-4900
FAX: 212-621-4949
rzanetti@che.com www.che.com
Ken Fouhy, Editor
Richard J Zanetti, VP/Publisher
John Pearson, President
Highlights include a calendar of related trade shows, new products listings, operations and maintenance techniques and marketing services ideas. *$59.00*
Monthly Founded: 1902
Circulation: 69000
Printed in 4 colors on glossy stock

3864 Chemical Engineering Progress
American Institute of Chemical Engineers

3 Park Avenue
New York, NY 10016-5991
212-197-7676
FAX: 212-591-8888 800-242-4363
xpress@aiche.org www.aiche.org
Jeffrey J Siirola, President
Kristine Chin, Editor
Offers updated information for chemical engineers. *$245.00*
Quarterly Founded: 1908

3865 Chemical Equipment
Reed Business Information
301 Gibraltar Drive
PO Box 650
Morris Plains, NJ 07950-650
973-920-7000
FAX: 973-539-3476
privacymanager@reedbusiness.com
www.reedbusiness.com
Bud Ramsey, Publisher
Geoffery Bridgman, Editor
Gerard Van de Aast, CEO/President
Chemical Equipment is for engineers, plant management personnel, maintenance engineering and others concerned with design, building, engineering, operating and maintaining chemical process plants.
Monthly Founded: 1959
Circulation: 106032

3866 Chemical Equipment Literature Review
Reed Business Information
St 600
Rockaway
New Jersey, NJ 07866
973-920-7000
FAX: 973-920-7531 800-222-0289
plundy@reedbusiness.com
www.chemicalequipment.com
Geoff Bridgman, Editor
Gail Kirberger, Circulation Manager
Patrick Lundy, Publisher
Colin Ungaro, President
Don Grennan, Marketing Manager
Covers reviews of new catalogs and brochures on products for the chemical industry.
8 pages Monthly Founded: 1985
Circulation: 106038

3867 Chemical Heritage
Chemical Heritage Foundation
315 Chestnut Street
Philadelphia, PA 19106-2702
215-925-2222
FAX: 215-925-1954 888-224-6006
info@chemheritage.org
www.chemheritage.org

Frances Kohler, Editor-in-Chief
Kerry O'Connor, Associate Marketing

An unrivaled resource for the history of the chemical, and molecular sciences, and industries. Reports on programs for chemical researchers, engineers, teachers, and the general public, and collects the papers of outstanding chemical scientists, corporations, and professional organizations.

48 pages Founded: 1982
Circulation: 30000 35M names $90 per M.

3868 Chemical Intelligencer
Springer Verlag
175 5th Avenue
New York, NY 10010-7703
212-460-1500
FAX: 212-533-5587
hargittai@ch.bme.hu
www.springer-ny.com

Isstivan Hargittai, Editor-in-Chief

Written for the scientist interested in the history and culture of chemistry. Includes articles and essays that develop and comment on the current directions and concerns in chemistry, new discoveries and experiments as well as present trends and opportunities in chemistry, philosophy and education. *$79.00*

Quarterly
Circulation: 1,000

3869 Chemical Management Review
Reed Chemical Publications
2 Rector Street
26th Floor
New York, NY 10006-1819
212-323-3200
FAX: 212-791-4311
helga.tilton@chemicalmarketreporter.com
www.reedchemicals.com

Jerry Gosney, Publisher
Helga Tilton, Editor
Keith Jones, CEO/President
Jane Burgess, Marketing

Provides information for senior managers in the chemical industry and other industrial markets. *$195.00*

Monthly Founded: 1871
Printed in 4 colors on glossy stock

3870 Chemical Market Reporter
Schnell Publishing Company
2 Rector Street
26th Floor
New York, NY 10006-1819
212-878-8714
FAX: 212-791-4310
editor@chemexpo.com
www.chemexpo.com

James Hannan, Publisher
Helga Tilton, Editor in Chief

Regular issue highlights include news of the week, coverage of pertinent industry trade shows/meetings, a review of new materials, and periodic insight reports on segments of the industry. *$109.00*

Weekly
Circulation: 14714

3871 Chemical Processing
Putman Media
555 W Pierce Road
Suite 301
Itasca, IL 60143-2649
630-467-1300
FAX: 630-467-1109
chemicalprocessing@putman.net
www.chemicalprocessing.com

Mark Rosenzweig, Editor-in-Chief
Tim Gillerlain, Publisher
John Cappellepti, CEO

Carries technical overview and case history articles presented in a problem-solving environment geared to operations, engineering and R&D management. Topics include instrumentation, pumping, corrosion, heat transfer, mixing and energy conservation. Accepts advertising.

60 pages Monthly Founded: 1938
Circulation: 55000 $125 per M.
Printed in 4 colors

3872 Chemical Times & Trends
Allen Press
900 17th St NW
Washington, DC 20006-2106
202-872-8110
FAX: 202-872-8114
info@csma.org www.allenpress.com

Tom Smith, Executive Editor
Frank Cherry, Marketing Division Director
Guy Dresser, VP Marketing
Theresa Pickel, Director of Publishing

Editorial focus emphasizes trends in legislation, industry events, packaging topics, and marketing concepts. *$27.00*

Quarterly Founded: 1935
Circulation: 7000

3873 Chemist
American Institute of Chemists
315 Chestnut Street
Suite 420
Philadelphia, PA 19106-2702
215-873-8224
FAX: 215-925-1954
info@theaic.org www.theaic.org

Vincent Savage, Administrative Assistant
W Jeffery Hurst, Editor
Richard Bradley, President

Topics of professional, economic, social and legislative interest to individual chemists or chemical engineers. *$35.00*

32 pages Quarterly Founded: 1923
Circulation: 5000

3874 Chemistry Research in Technology
American Chemical Society
1155 16th Street NW
Suite 600
Washington, DC 20036-4892
202-872-4600
FAX: 202-872-4615 800-227-5558
help@acs.org www.chemistry.org

Michael Woods, Editor
William F Carroll, President
Madeleine Jacobs, CEO
Elizabeth Zubritsky, Manager

Information and research summaries of the latest in the chemical industry. *$49.00*

1 Year 3 Issues Founded: 1876

3875 Coatings World
Rodman Publishing
70 Hilltop Road
3 Floor
Ramsey, NJ 07446
201-825-2552
FAX: 201-825-0553
info@rodpub.com
www.rodmanpublishing.com

Dale Pritchett, Publisher
Christine Canning-Esposito, Editor

Cutting edge technical information and the most advanced and pertinent management and distribution techniques.

10 issues per y Founded: 1964
Circulation: 17000

3876 Compoundings
Independent Lubricant Manufacturers Association
651 S Washington Street
Alexandria, VA 22314
703-684-5574
FAX: 703-836-8503
editor@ilma.org
www.compoundings.org

Carla Mangone, Director of Meetings/Communications
Marth Jolkovski, Director of Publications/Advertisin
Celeste Powers, Executive Director

Association and marketing news, meetings and programs, as well as employment and business opportunities to the US and international independent lubricant industry. *$150.00*

Monthly Founded: 1948
Circulation: 2050
Printed in 4 colors on glossy stock

3877 Energy Process
American Institute of Chemical Engineers
345 E 17th Street
New York, NY 10003-3804
212-770-7000

Offers updated information for chemical engineers. *$20.00*

Quarterly

3878 European Chemical News
Reed Chemical Publications
2 Rector Street
26th Floor
New York, NY 10006-1819
212-323-3200
FAX: 212-791-4311
jonathan.sismey@icis.com
www.europeanchemicalnews.com

Sherri Sims, Sales Manager *$711.00*

Weekly
Circulation: 14112

3879 European Journal of Clinical Chemistry and Clinical Biochemistry
Walter De Gruyter
200 Saw Mill Road
Hawthorne, NY 1052

Water De Gruyler, Editor

Up-to-date information on the chemistry industry.

Monthly

3880 Forest Chemicals Review
Kriedt Enterprises
129 S Cortez Street
New Orleans, LA 70119
504-482-3914
FAX: 504-482-4205
info@forestchemicalsreview.com
www.forestchemicalsreview.com

Romney Richard, Publisher
Alan Hodges, Editor

Forest Chemicals Review is the only trade journal covering pine and pulp chemicals within the naval stores industry. It is directed to producers and processors of pine gum and wood naval stores; pulp chemicals and pine derivative chemicals for the adhesives, coatings, printing ink, paper chemicals, flavor and fragrance. *$110.00*

24 pages Monthly Founded: 1990
Circulation: 300
Printed in 4 colors on glossy stock

3881 HAPPI Household and Personal Products Industry
Rodman Publishing
70 Hilltop Road
3rd Floor
Ramsey, NJ 07446
201-825-2552
FAX: 201-825-0553
info@rodpub.com
www.rodmanpublishing.com/
Matthew Montgomery, Executive Vice President
Tom Branna, Editor
Ellen Pfister, Circulation
Melanie Henson, Associate Editor
Art Largar, Publisher
Highlights current developments, marketing, production, formulations, technical innovations, packaging, and management problems. Includes in-depth news on developments abroad as well as in the United States. *$52.00*
Monthly Founded: 1964
Circulation: 140000

3882 Hydrocarbon Processing
Gulf Publishing Company
PO Box 2608
Houston, TX 77252-2608
713-529-4301
FAX: 713-520-4433
mark.peter@gulfpub.com
www.hydrocarbonprocessing.com
Gene Swantek, Publisher
Les A Kane, Editor
John D. Meador, President and CEO
Alexandra Pruner, Senior Vice President
Mark Peters, Vice President and Publisher
Covers the changing technology in the petroleum refining, petrochemical processing, gas processing and synfuel markets. *$120.00*
172 pages Monthly Founded: 1916
Circulation: 35613 35895 names $175 per M.
Printed in 4 colors on glossy stock

3883 I&EC Research
American Chemical Society
1155 16th Street NW
Suite 600
Washington, DC 20036
202-872-4600
FAX: 202-872-4615 800-227-5558
help@acs.org www.chemistry.org
William F Carroll, President
Donald R. Paul, Editor
Offers information and statistical updates for chemists.
Founded: 1876
Circulation: 4600

3884 Industrial & Engineering Chemistry Research
American Chemical Society
1155 16th Street NW
Suite 600
Washington, DC 20036
202-872-4600
FAX: 202-872-4615 800-227-5558
help@acs.org www.chemistry.org
Donald Paul, Editor
William F. Carroll, President
Elizabeth Zubritsky, Manager
Features fundamental research, design methods, process design and development, product research and development for chemists and chemical engineers.
Founded: 1876
Circulation: 4600

3885 Inform
American Oil Chemists Society
2211 W Bradley Avenue
PO Box 3489
Champaign, IL 61821-1827
217-359-2344
FAX: 217-351-8091
bjewett@aocs.org www.aocs.org
Amie Ziegler, Advertising Representative
Allison Ogdon, Advertising Production Coordinator
Barbara Jewett, Editor
A scientific publication that is addressed to professionals interested in science and technology of fats, oils, proteins and related substances. Accepts advertising. *$120.00*
100 pages Monthly Founded: 1990
Circulation: 4500 45000 names $.35 per M.
Printed in 4 colors on glossy stock

3886 Inside Laboratory Management
AOAC International
481 North Frederick Avenue
Suite 500
Gaithersburg, MD 20877
301-924-7077
FAX: 301-924-7089 800-379-2622
tmilor@aoac.org www.aoac.org
Tien Milor, Editor
Brings you the key information you need to successfully manage a quality analytical laboratory. Each issue provides you with the information needed to stay current and knowledgeable about laboratory practices for chemical and ,microbiological analysisof food, drug, agricultural and environmental matrices.
Bi-monthly

3887 International Laboratory
International Scientific Communications
30 Controls Drive
PO Box 870
Shelton, CT 06484-870
203-926-9300
FAX: 203-926-9310
webmaster@iscpubs.com
www.internationallaboratory.com/
Steven J Morris, President
Brian Howard, Editor-in-Chief/Publisher
S. McCorvie Wham, VP Sales
Patricia Ekbatani, Directing Editor
Susan Messinger, Managing Editor
International Laboratory serves the industry, universities, government, independent and foundation research laboratories.
50 pages Founded: 1971
Circulation: 50036
Printed in 4 colors on glossy stock

3888 International Laboratory Pacific Rim Edition
International Scientific Communications
30 Controls Drive
PO Box 870
Shelton, CT 06484
203-926-9300
FAX: 203-926-9310
iscpubs@iscpubs.com
www.iscpubs.com
Steven J Morris, President
Robert Sweeney, Publisher
S McCorvie Wham, Senior VP
Brian Howard, Editor
Edited for chemists and biologists throughout Far East Asia and Australia who have a professional interest in various aspects of modern laboratory practice and basic research.
40 pages Founded: 1986

3889 Journal of AOAC International
AOAC International
481 North Frederick Avenue
Suite 500
Gaithersburg, MD 20877-2417
301-924-7077
FAX: 301-924-7089 800-379-2622
aoac@aoac.org www.aoac.org
Krystyna McIver, Sr Director Publications Sales
Robert Rathbone, Director Publications
Ellen Sellers, Production Editor
Jennifer Diatz, Production Manager
Publishes fully refereed contributed papers in the fields of chemical and biological analysis. *$98.00*

3890 Journal of Analytical Toxicology
Preston Publications
6600 W Touhy Avenue
PO Box 48312
Niles, IL 60714
847-647-2900
FAX: 847-647-1155
webadmin@prestonpub.com
www.jatox.com
S Tinsley Preston III, Publisher/CEO
Dr. Bruce A. Goldberger, Editor
Maria Tamacho, Circulation Manager
An international publication for toxicologists, pathologists, analytical chemists, researchers, educators and others. Dedicated to the isolation, indentification, and quantification of potentially toxic substances. Emphasis is on the practical applications for use in clinical, forensic, industrial, and other toxicology laboratories, drug abuse testing, therapeutic drug monitoring, and environmental pollution. Includes new products and litrature, meetings and short courses. *$475.00*
8 issues per ye Founded: 1977
Circulation: 1148
Mailing list available for rent 9939 names $125 per M.

3891 Journal of Biological Chemistry
9650 Rockville Pike
Bethesda, MD 20814-3998
301-530-7150
FAX: 301-634-7126
Herbert Taber, Editor
Barbara Gordon, Executive Director
Features research papers on biochemistry and molecular biology and other articles of interest to the professional.
TriAnnual

3892 Journal of Chemical Education
Division of Chemical Education
204 N Brooks Street
Madison, WI 53715-1116
608-262-7146
FAX: 608-262-7145 800-991-5534
jce@chem.wisc.edu
www.jce.divched.org
John W Moore, Editor
Mary Virginia ORNA, Publications Coordinator
Diana S. Mason, Editor
Jeffery Kovac, Editor
John Yi, Manager
Provides information about and examples of teaching techniques for classroom and laboratory, curricular innovations, chemistry content, and chemical education research. *$45.00*

136 pages Monthly Founded: 1924
Printed in on glossy stock
Computerized version available: CD ROM

3893 Journal of Chemical Information & Computer Sciences
American Chemical Society
1155 16th Street NW
Suite 600
Washington, DC 20036-4892
202-872-4600
FAX: 202-872-6067 800-227-5558
help@acs.org www.chemistry.org

George WA Milne, Editor

Offers the latest technological information and news directed at the chemical industry. *$27.00*
Bi-Monthly

3894 Journal of Chemical Physics
American Institute of Physics
2 Huntington Quadrangle
Melville, NY 11747-2924
516-576-2200
FAX: 516-349-9704
jcp@aip.org www.aip.org

Donald Levy, Editor

Targets both chemists and physicists involved in research and applications of chemical physics technology.
Weekly
Circulation: 5,000

3895 Journal of Chemical and Engineering Data
American Chemical Society
2 Huntington Quadrangle
Melville, NY 11747-2924
516-576-2200
FAX: 516-349-9704
squarles@acp.org www.aip.org

Donald Levy, Editor
Marc Brodsky, CEO

Offers the latest updates and new information in the chemical industry. *$458.00*
Weekly Founded: 1931
Circulation: 5000

3896 Journal of Chromatographic Science
Preston Publications
6600 W Touhy Avenue
Niles, IL 60714
847-647-2900
FAX: 847-647-1155
tpreston@prestonpub.com
www.j-chrom-sci.com

S Tinsley Preston III, Publisher
Kevin Bailey, Managing Editor
Janice Gordon, Director Marketing

An international publication for scientists, analytical chemists, researchers, educators, and other allied to the field. Provides in depth information about analytical techniques, applications, sample preparation methods, systems problem solving, etc. Articles cover more practical information on all types of separations—gas, liquid, thin layer, supercritical fluid, electrophoresis, spectrometry, hyphenated methods, etc. any other single source. Also problem solving/troubleshooting answers. *$405.00*
Monthly Founded: 1961
Circulation: 1000

3897 Journal of Colloid & Interface Science
Academic Press
525 B Street
#1900
San Diego, CA 92101-4401
619-231-6616
FAX: 619-699-6280 800-321-5068
apads@acad.com www.apnet.com

Jennifer Haddlesten, Editor
Claudia Romas, Publisher

Presents chemical and physiochemical aspects of theory and practice of colloids. *$883.00*
Monthly Founded: 1885
Circulation: 2000

3898 Journal of Medicinal Chemistry
American Chemical Society
1155 16th Street NW
Suite 600
Washington, DC 20036-4892
202-872-4600
FAX: 202-872-4615 800-333-9511

Philip S Portoghese, Editor
Madeleine Jacobs, CEO
Elizabeth Zubritsky, Manager

Information on the chemistry industry, dealing with aspects directly pertaining to the medical profession.
Founded: 1876

3899 Journal of Organic Chemistry
American Chemical Society
1155 16th Street NW
Washington, DC 20036-4800
202-872-4600
FAX: 202-872-6325 800-333-9511
help@acs.org www.chemistry.org

Clayton H Heathcock, Editor
Elizabeth Zubritsky, Manager

Areas emphasized are the multiple facets of organic reactions, natural products, studies of mechanism, theoretical organic chemistry and the various aspects of spectroscopy related to organic chemistry. *$1260.00*
BiWeekly
Circulation: 8,500

3900 Journal of Physical Chemistry
American Chemical Society
GA Institute of Technology
Boggs Building
Atlanta, GA 30332
404-894-0293
FAX: 404-894-0294 800-227-5558
jphyschm@chemistry.gatech
pubs.acs.org

Mostafa A El-Sayed, Editor

Reports on both experimental and theoretical research dealing with the fundamental aspects of physical chemistry and chemical physics.
Weekly
Circulation: 3774

3901 Journal of Society of Cosmetic Chemists
Society of Cosmetic Chemists
120 Wall Street
#2400
New York, NY 10005-4088
212-668-1500
FAX: 212-668-1504
societycoschem@worldnet.att.net
www.scconline.org

Greg Hillebrand, President
Mindy Goldstein, Journal Editor
Doreen Scelso, Publication Coordinator

Features highlight new products, processing techniques, safety issues, and pharmacological features. *$200.00*
Founded: 1945
Circulation: 4200

3902 Journal of Surfactants and Detergents
AOCS Press
12024 Vista Parke Drive
PO Box 200135
Austin, TX 78720-0135
512-331-2441
FAX: 512-331-2387
mfcox@cvcnet.com

Michael F Cox, Editor-in-Chief

Reports on the development and performance of surfactants in all areas, from household detergents to industrial uses, as well as on the development and manufacture of other detergent ingredients and their formulation into finished products. *$85.00*
Quarterly
Circulation: 1,500

3903 Journal of the American Chemical Society
American Chemical Society
1155 16th Street NW
Suite 600
Washington, DC 20036-4892
202-872-4600
FAX: 202-872-4615 800-333-9511
help@acs.org
http://www.chemistry.org

Peter Stang, Editor

Association news, member information and chemical industry information. *$125.00*
Weekly

3904 Journal of the American Leather Chemists Association
American Leather Chemists Association
1314 50th Street
Suite 103
Lubbock, TX 79412
806-744-1798
FAX: 806-744-1785
alca@leatherchemists.org
http://www.leatherchemists.org

Kenneth Boni, Editor
Kadir Donmez, Secretary/Treasurer
Greg Morrison, President *$150.00*
Monthly Founded: 1903
Circulation: 600 1000 names $60 per M.

3905 Journal of the Electrochemical Society
Electrochemical Society
65 S Main Street
Building D
Pennington, NJ 08534-2839
609-737-1902
FAX: 609-737-2743
ecs@electrochem.org
http://www.electrochem.org

Paul Kohl, Editor
Roque J Calvo, Executive Director
Cor Claeys, Associate Editor

Contains technical papers covering basic research and technology. *$110.00*
Monthly Founded: 1902
Circulation: 8300

3906 **LCGC North America**
Advanstar Communications
Woodbridge Corporate Plaza 485 Route 1 South
Building F, First Floor
Iselin, NJ 08830
732-225-9500
FAX: 732-225-0211
lcgcedit@lcgcmag.com
http://www.lcgcmag.com/lcgc/

David Esola, VP/General Manager
Michael Tessalone, Group Publisher
Tria Deibert, Marketing Director

Includes product and literature reports along with meeting and seminar listings. *$67.00*
100 pages Monthly Founded: 1987
Circulation: 56000
Mailing list available for rent 47,543 names $155 per M.
Printed in 4 colors on glossy stock

3907 **Laboratorio y Analisis**
Keller International Publishing Corporation
150 Great Neck
Great Neck, NY 11021
516-829-9722
FAX: 516-829-5414
info@kellerpubs.com
www.kellerpus.com

Terry Beirne, Publisher
Bryan DeLuca, Editor
Jerry Keller, President

3908 **Lipids**
American Oil Chemists Society
2211 W Bradley Avenue
Champaign, IL 61821
217-359-2344
FAX: 217-351-8091
general@aocs.org
http://www.aocs.org

Howard Knapp, Editor
Jean Wills, VP

Designed as a forum for chemists to peruse the latest in scientific research in this peer reviewed publication.
Monthly Founded: 1909
Circulation: 2400

3909 **Nucleus**
American Chemical Society — Northeast
23 Cottage Street
Natick, MA 01760
800-872-2054
FAX: 508-653-6329 800-872-2054
webmaster@nesacs.org
http://www.nesacs.org

Vincent J Gale, Editor
Amy Tapper, Chairman

Content includes local meeting announcements; news of members of the Northeastern Section, American Chemical Society; historical articles; book reviews; calender of events covering all chemistry disciplines in the area. No Company or product information is published. Advertising is accepted.
Monthly Founded: 1888
Circulation: 7500
Printed in 2 colors on matte stock

3910 **PaintSquare**
PaintSquare
2100 Wharton Street
Suite 310
Pittsburgh, PA 15203
412-431-8300
FAX: 412-431-5428 800-837-8303
webmaster@paintsquare.com
http://www.paintsquare.com

Harold Hower, Publisher

Founded: 2002

3911 **Performance Chemicals Europe**
Reed Chemical Publications
2 Rector Street
26th Floor
New York, NY 10006-1819
212-323-3200
FAX: 212-791-4311
cnihelp@cnionline.com
http://www.performancechemicals.com

Christopher Flook, Publisher
Neil Sinclair, Managing Editor *$711.00*

Weekly

3912 **Perfumer & Flavorist**
Allured Publishing Corporation
362 S Schmale Road
Carol Stream, IL 60188-2755
630-653-2155
FAX: 630-653-2192
perfumer@allured.com
http://www.perfumflavor.com

Matt Gronlund, Publisher
Jeb Gleason, Editor
Janet Ludwig, President

Regular features include trade literature, worldwide sources, news, book reviews, creative services and an events calendar. *$ 135.00*
Founded: 1976
Circulation: 1800

3913 **PetroChemical News**
William F Bland
709 Turmeric Lane
Durham, NC 27713
919-544-1717
FAX: 919-544-1999
pcn@petrochemical-news.com
http://www.petrochemical-news.com

Susan Kensil, Publisher
Mollie Bland Sandor, Circulation/Promotion Coordinator

Covers new plants and projects, awards of contracts, mergers and acquisitions, current technology, and related government actions. *$807.00*
Weekly Founded: 1963

3914 **Powder and Bulk Engineering**
CSC Publishing
1155 Northland Drive
St Paul, MN 55120
651-287-5600
FAX: 651-287-5650
powbulk@cscpub.com
http://www.powderbulk.com

Richard Cress, Publisher
Terry O'Neill, Editor
Katherine Davich, Senior Editor

Featured editorial includes technical articles, case histories, test centers, product news and literature, and industry news items.
Monthly Founded: 1986
Circulation: 35379

3915 **Powder/Bulk Solids**
Reed Business Information
301 Gibralter Drive
Box 650
Morris Plains, NJ 07950
973-920-7000
FAX: 973-539-3476
scrow@reedbusiness.com
http://www.reedbusiness.com

Kevin Cronin, Editor-in-Chief
Sabrina Crow, VP/Publishing Director
Patrick Lundy, Publisher
Mike Botta, Editorial Director
Carol Cmielewski, Sales Support Coordinator

Equipment and technological news for dry particulates processors. *$74.95*
Monthly Founded: 1993
Circulation: 45,070

3916 **Processing**
Putman Media Company
555 W Pierce Road
Suite 301
Itasca, IL 60143-2649
630-467-1300
FAX: 630-467-1124
webmaster@putman.net
http://www.processingmagazine.com

Mike Wasson, Publisher
Dennis Van Milligen, Editor-in-Chief
K Heitman, President
John M Cappelletti, CEO

Product areas covered include mechanical and pneumatic conveying, material handling, packaging, and storage. Each issue includes a specific editorial spotlight, product showcase and new literature section.
Monthly Founded: 1972
Circulation: 95035 $125 per M.
Printed in 4 colors

3917 **Quimica Latinoamericana**
Reed Chemical Publications
2 Rector
26th Floor
New York, NY 10006-1819
212-323-3200
FAX: 212-791-4311 888-525-3255
cnihelp@cnionline.com
http://www.quimicalatinoamericana.com/

Jonathan Sismey, Advertising
Christopher Flook, Publisher
Neil Sinclair, Managing Editor
Jeff Evans, CEO/President

3918 **Soap/Cosmetics/Chemical Specialties**
Cygnus Publishing
445 Broad Hollow Road
#21
Melville, NY 11747-3601
631-845-2700
FAX: 631-845-2798 800-308-6397
soap@erols.com
www.cygnuspub.com

Anita Hipius Shaw, Editor-in-Chief

Includes tips on general management, purchasing, as well as new products and market trends, personal care, industrial and institutional markets, especially as they affect chemical, packing and equipment suppliers and their R and D professionals. *$30.00*
Monthly
Circulation: 6,491

3919 Spray Technology & Marketing
Industry Publications
3621 Hill Road
Parsippany, NJ 07054-1001
973-331-9545
FAX: 973-331-9547
info@spraytechnology.com
http://www.spraytechnology.com

Cynthia Hundley, Publisher
Michael L. SanGiovanni, Executive Editor
Shirleen Dorman, Editor
Jas Persaud, Circulation Manager

Features include articles on marketers, chemical and fragrance manufacturers and components manufacturers.
Monthly Founded: 1954
Circulation: 6,491
Printed in 4 colors on glossy stock

3920 Sulfuric Acid Today
BIC Alliance
6378 Quinn
PO Box 40166
Baton Rouge, LA 70835-0166
225-751-9996
FAX: 225-751-9993
bic@bicalliance.com
www.bicalliance.com

Earl B Heard, Publisher

Editorial covers industry news, engineering, technology and upcoming events.
$39.00
SemiAnnual
Circulation: 5,000

3921 Today's Chemist at Work
American Chemical Society
1155 16th Street NW
Washington, DC 20036-4800
202-872-4600
FAX: 202-872-4615 800-227-5558
tcaw@acs.org
http://www.chemistry.org

Mary Warner, Publisher
James Ryan, Editor
William F. Carroll, Jr. President
Madeleine Jacobs, Executive Director

Covers reports on materials, new products, chemical education, analytical chemistry and instrumentation. *$18.00*
Monthly Founded: 1876
Circulation: 120000

Trade Shows

3922 AOAC International Annual Meeting & Exposition
481 North Frederick Avenue
Suite 500
Gaithersburg, MD 20877-2417
301-924-7077
FAX: 301-924-7089 800-379-2622
aoac@aoac.org www.aoac.org

Kenneth Morton, Director Meetings/Education

A great place to meet and network with your colleagues from around the world, enhance your technical knowledge base, and to learn about the latest laboratory products and equipment from more than 100 exhibitors.
1000 Attendees Annual September

3923 ASBC Annual Meeting
American Society of Brewing Chemists
3340 Pilot Knob Road
Saint Paul, MN 55121
651-454-7250
FAX: 651-454-0766 800-328-7560
bford.@asbcnet.org
www.meeting.asbcnet.org

Betty Ford, Meetings Director
Sue Casey, Meetings Coordinator
Steven Nelson, VP

An opportunity to network, learn, build business relationships and hear first-handed the latest brewing science and related research. Contains exhits, technical and keynote presentations and workshops.
$625.00
300 Attendees June/Non-Members Fee
Founded: 1934

3924 Agricultural Retailers Association Convention and Expo
Agricultural Retailers Association
11701 Borman Drive
Suite 110
Saint Louis, MO 63146-4193
314-676-6655
FAX: 314-567-6808 800-844-4900
ara@agretailerassn.org
www.agretailerassn.org
Annual show of 120 manufacturers, suppliers and distributors of agricultural chemicals and fertilizers. Seminar, conference and banquet.
1200 Attendees Annual Founded: 1993

3925 American Association of Cereal Chemists Annual Meeting
3340 Pilot Knob Road
St Paul, MN 55121-2097
651-454-7250
FAX: 651-454-0766
aacc@scisoc.org www.aaccnet.org

Betty Ford, Director Meetings
Sue Casey, Meetings Coordinator
Steven Nelson, VP

The only conference specializing in cereal related items.
1900 Attendees Annual Fall

3926 American Association of Textile Chemists & Colorists International Conference
PO Box 12215
Research Triangle Park, NC 27709-2215
919-549-8141
FAX: 919-549-8933 800-360-5380

B Chrietzberg, Advertising Manager
John Daniels, Manager

Colorants and chemical finishes for the textile trade are on display.
Annual

3927 American Chemical Society, Chemistry Spectroscopy Western Regional
1155 16th Street NW
Washington, DC 20036
202-872-4600
FAX: 202-872-4615 800-227-5558
help@acs.org www.acs.org

John Crum, Chief Executive Officer
Christine Pruitt, Marketing Department Head

50 booths.
1.2M Attendees October

3928 American Chemical Society: Central Region
PO Box 1785
Midland, MI 48641-1785
989-426-1776
FAX: 989-835-8356

Dr. DR Petersen, Executive Secretary

Scientific and educational organization; publisher of technical books and periodicals. Members include chemists and chemical engineers in Indiana, Michigan, Ohio and parts of Pennsylvania and West Virginia.
1M Attendees May/June

3929 American Chemical Society: Middle Atlantic Expo
Fordham University
Bronx, NY 10458
718-817-4430
FAX: 718-817-4432
www.fordham.edu/chemistry

Dr. Donald Clarke, Steering Communications

35 booths.
May

3930 American Chemical Society: National Marketing and Exposition
1155 16th Street NW
Washington, DC 20036
202-872-4600
FAX: 202-872-4615
help@acs.org www.chemistry.org

Evelyn Fuller, Exposition Manager
John Crum, Chief Executive Officer

500 booths featuring exhibits of the chemicals industry.
10M Attendees March/April

3931 American Chemical Society: Southeastern Regional Conference & Exhibition
1155 16th Street NW
Room 214
Washington, DC 20036
202-872-4600
FAX: 202-872-6067 800-227-5558

Evelyn Fuller, Exposition Manager
John Crum, Chief Executive Officer

Booths featuring exhibits of the chemicals industry.
Annual

3932 American Chemical Society: Spring National Exhibition
1155 16th Street NW
Room 214
Washington, DC 20036-4800
202-872-4600
FAX: 202-872-6067 800-227-5558

Evelyn Fuller, Exposition Manager
John Crum, Chief Executive Officer

50 booths featuring exhibits of the chemicals industry, equipment, materials and supplies.
Annual

3933 American College of Toxicology Annual Meeting
9650 Rockville Pike
Bethesda, MD 20814
301-571-1840
FAX: 301-634-7852
clemire@actox.org www.actox.org

Carol Lemire, Executive Director

Education courses and scientific symposia, exhibits of contract laboratories, toxicol-

ogy supplies and equipment and science journal publishing companies.
500 Attendees November

3934 **American Institute Chemical Engineers Petrochemical Refining Expo**
345 E 47th Street
New York, NY 10017-2304
212-660-0761

Marie Stewart, Director
A marketplace for materials used in processing chemicals.
20M Attendees April

3935 **American Oil Chemists Society Annual Meeting & Expo**
American Oil Chemists Society
2211 W Bradley Avenue
Champaign, IL 61821-1827
217-359-2344
FAX: 217-351-8091
meetings@aocs.org www.aocs.org
Jeffry Newman, Meetings Manager
Greg Reed, Manager
184 booths displaying fat and oil processing equipment, instrumentation and related services. Seminar, banquet, luncheon and dinner.
2000 Attendees Annual 2000 names

3936 **American Society Biochemistry and Molecular Biology Expo**
9650 Rockville Pike
Bethesda, MD 20814-3998
301-530-7145
FAX: 301-571-1824
Geri Goodenough, Marketings
600 booths of products used in biomedical research.
8M Attendees

3937 **Analytical Symposium East**
73 Ethel Street
Metuchen, NJ 08840-2941
908-725-0101

Norman Gardner, Show Manager
240 booths.
6M Attendees October

3938 **Association of Official Analytical Communi ties International Trade Show**
481 N Frederick Avenue
Suite 500
Gaithersburg, MD 20877-2417
301-924-7077
FAX: 301-924-7089 800-379-2622
aoac@aoac.org www.aoac.org
Marilyn Blakely, Marketing Director
110 booths. Conference serves as a resource for timely knowledge exchange, networking and high quality laboratory information.
1.4M Attendees September

3939 **Chem Show: Chemical Process Industries Exposition**
International Exposition Company
15 Franklin Street
Westport, CT 06880-5903
203-221-9232
FAX: 203-221-9260
info@chemshow.com
www.chemshow.com
Mark Stevens, VP
Jeff Stevens, Sales VP
Kelley Stevens, Sales Manager
Bringing together in one place major manufacturers of equipment, systems and services for the CPI. Product categories include; process equipment, fluid handling equipment and systems, solids handling equipment and sytems, engineered materials, instruments and controls, environmental and safety equipment and systems and services. *$20.00*
7481 Attendees Biennial/Oct 30-Nov 1
Founded: 1915

3940 **Chem-Distribution**
PennWell Conferences and Exhibitions
1421 S Sheridan Road
Tulsa, OK 74112-6619
918-353-3161
FAX: 918-831-9834
Exhibits of technology for the distribution, transfer and storage of chemicals and petrochemicals.

3941 **Chem-Safe**
PennWell Conferences and Exhibitions
1421 S Sheridan Road
Tulsa, OK 74112-6619
918-353-3161
FAX: 918-831-9834
Exhibits of environmental, safety and health technology for the chemical and process industries.

3942 **Conchem Exhibition and Conference**
Reed Exhibition Companies
255 Washington Street
Newton, MA 02458-1637
617-584-4900
FAX: 617-630-2222
Elizabeth Hitchcock, International Sales
The international event featuring specialty additives and chemicals for the building industry.
November

3943 **Consumer Specialty Products Association**
Chemical Specialties Products Association
900 17th Street NW
Suite 300
Washington, DC 20006
202-872-8110
FAX: 202-872-8114 www.cspa.org
Christopher Cathcart, President
Ann Wheeler, Director Meetings/Conventions
Nonprofit organization trade show for the many companies involved in the formulation, manufacture, testing and marketing of chemical specialty products. 100 booths.
2M Attendees

3944 **Eastern Analytical Symposium and Expo**
RWB Convention Management
4704 Bert Drive
Monroeville, PA 15146-3608
412-372-8965
FAX: 412-372-6748
240 booths providing a forum for analytical chemists.
6M Attendees November

3945 **Federation of Spectroscopy Societies**
13 N Cliffe Drive
Wilmington, DE 19809-1623
302-656-0771

Dr. Edward Brame Jr, Show Manager
120 booths of analytical chemistry.
2M Attendees October

3946 **ILTA Storage Tank & Bulk Liquid Terminal I nt'l Operating Conf. & Trade Show**
Independent Liquid Terminals Association
1444 I Street NW
Suite 400
Washington, DC 20005
202-842-9200
FAX: 202-326-8660
info@ilta.org www.ilta.org
E David Doane, President
Melinda Whitney, Director/Government Affairs
Containing 202 booths and 161 exhibits.
2,700 Attendees June

3947 **Official Analytical Chemists Association**
481 N Frederick Avenue
Suite 500
Gaithersburg, MD 20877
301-924-7077
FAX: 301-924-7089 800-379-2622
Margaret Ridgell, Show Manager
Five day conference that offers a diverse program of symposia, workships, and poster sessions. Specific educational tracks are offered for analytical chemists, microbioligists, laboratory managers and other laboratory personnel. More than 100 exhibits.
1.3M Attendees August

3948 **Powder Bulk Solids Conference and Expo**
Reed Business Information
2000 Clearwater Drive
Oak Brook, IL 60523
630-740-0825
www.reedbusiness.com
Angela Piermartini, Show Manager
1,300 booths.
11M Attendees May

3949 **TRADEWORX**
Chemical Specialties Products Association
900 17th Street NW
Suite 300
Washington, DC 20006
202-872-8110
FAX: 202-872-8114 www.cspa.org
Christopher Cathcart, President
Ann Wheeler, Director Meetings/Conventions
Not-for-profit organization composed of many companies involved in the formulation, manufacture, testing and marketing of chemical specialty products.
2M Attendees May

Directories & Databases

3950 **Adhesives Digest**
International Plastics Selector/DATA Business Pub.
15 Inverness Way E
#6510
Englewood, CO 80112-5710
303-904-0407

A who's who directory of services and supplies to the industry. *$180.00*

Biennial

3951 Advanced Coatings and Surface Technology
John Wiley & Sons
111 River Street
Hoboken, NY 07030
201-748-6000
FAX: 201-748-6088
subinfo@wiley.com www.wiley.com
Offers information on coatings and surface technology, covering breakthroughs in traditional coating processes, chemical vapor deposition and ion beam methods.
Full-text

3952 American Coke & Coal Chemicals Institute Directory and By-Laws
1255 23rd Street NW
Washington, DC 20037
202-452-1140
FAX: 202-833-3636
information@accci.org www.accci.org

David A Saunders, President
Represents merchant oven coke producers, integrated coke producers, tar distillers, sales agents, and industry suppliers.
75 pages Founded: 1944

3953 American Laboratory Buyers Guide
International Scientific Communications
30 Control Drive
Suite 870
Shelton, CT 06484-6139
203-926-9300
FAX: 203-926-9310
Erin MacDonnell, Editor
Manufacturers of and dealers in scientifi instruments, equipment, apparatus, and chemicals worldwide. *$25.00*
Annual January

3954 Available Chemicals Directory
MDL Information Systems
14600 Catalina Street
San Leandro, CA 94577-6608
510-895-1313
FAX: 510-352-2870 800-635-0064
Magnetic tape, covers approximately 240,000 commercially available chemicals, including organic, and inorganic chemicals.

Semiannual

3955 CEH On-Line
SRI International
333 Ravenswood Avenue
#AE208
Menlo Park, CA 94025-3453
650-859-2000
FAX: 650-859-2182
Database containing economic data for more than 1300 major commodity and specialty chemical products.
Full-text

3956 CERCLIS Database of Hazardous Waste Sites
Environmental Protection Agency
Ariel Rios Building
1200 Pennsylvania Avenue NW
Washington, DC 20460
202-272-0167
www.epa.gov
Stands for Comprehensive Environmental Response, Compensation, and Liability Information System. This database contains information on more than 36,000 releases of hazardous substances reported to the US Environmental Protection Agency.

Directory

3957 CHEMEST
Technical Database Services
63 W 38th Street
New York, NY 10018
212-556-0001
FAX: 212-556-0036
This database contains information for estimating the properties of pharmaceuticals and chemicals of environmental concern.
Properties

3958 CLAIMS/Comprehensive Data Base
IFI/Plenum Data Company
302 Swann Avenue
Alexandria, VA 22301-1042

FAX: 910-392-0240 800-368-3093
Harry M Allcock, VP
This database contains enhanced indexing of the US chemical and chemically related patents included in the CLAIMS/UNITERM database.
Bibliographic

3959 Chem Source USA
Chemical Sources International
PO Box 1824
Clemson, SC 29633
864-646-7840
FAX: 864-646-9938 800-222-4531
information@chemsources.com
www.chemsources.com
Mike Desing, Editor
Book containing information on where to obtain chemicals in the US and Canada.
$495.00
1700 pages Annual January Founded: 1958

Circulation: 10000

3960 Chem Sources International
PO Box 1824
Clemson, SC 29633-1824
864-646-7840
FAX: 864-646-9938 800-222-4531
csinfo@chemsources.com
www.chemsources.com
Mike Desing, Editor
Dale Krohn, Owner
The most comprehensive directory ever compiled on the world's chemical industry. Includes the products of more than 8,000 chemical firms spanning 128 countries.
$750.00
Biennial Founded: 1958 : CD-ROM

3961 Chemcyclopedia
American Chemical Society
1155 16th Street NW
Suite 600
Washington, DC 20036-4892
202-872-4600
FAX: 202-872-6067 800-227-5558
chemcy@acs.org pubs.acs.org/chemcy
List of over 900 chemical manufacturers in the US. *$60.00*
Annual

3962 Chemical Abstracts
American Chemical Society
1155 16th Street NW
Suite 600
Washington, DC 20036-4892
202-872-4600
FAX: 202-872-4615 800-333-9511
help@acs.org www.chemistry.org
Newsletter covering this branch of the American Chemical Society.

Monthly

3963 Chemical Exposure and Human Health
McFarland & Company Publishers
PO Box 611
Jefferson, NC 28640-0611
336-246-4460
FAX: 336-246-5018 800-253-2187
Cynthia Wilson, Editor
A list of organizations concerned with the effects of chemical exposure. Government exposure standards on over 300 chemicals.
$ 55.00
ISBN 0-899508-10-3

3964 Chemical Regulations and Guidelines System
Network Management CRC Systems
11242 Waples Mill Road
Fairfax, VA 22030-6079
703-219-3865

This database contains citations, with abstracts, to US government statutes and federal guidelines.
Bibliographic

3965 Chemical Week: Financial Survey of the 300 Largest Companies in the US
Chemical Week Associates
650 Madison Avenue
21st Floor
New York, NY 10022-1029
212-223-6500

Emily Plishner, Editor
Offers information on over 300 chemical process companies in the United States.
$8.00
7 pages Annual
Circulation: 50,615

3966 DRI Chemical
DRI/McGraw-Hill
24 Hartwell Avenue
Lexington, MA 02421-3158
781-863-5100

Linda Ansill, Marketing Coordinator
The coverage of this database encompasses the chemical industry in the United States, including imports and exports, inventories, production, sales, shipments and uses.

3967 DRI Chemical Forecast
DRI/McGraw-Hill
24 Hartwell Avenue
Lexington, MA 02421-3158
781-863-5100

This time series contains over 700 quarterly forecasts on US supply and demand for more than 120 chemical products.

3968 Directory of Bulk Liquid Terminal and Storage Facilities
Independent Liquid Terminals Association

1444 I Street Nw
Suite 400
Washington, DC 20005
202-842-9200
FAX: 202-326-8660
info@ilta.org www.ilta.org
E David Doane, President
Melinda Whitney, Director/Government Affairs

Published annually in April. *$95.00*

3969 **Directory of Chemical Producers US**
SRI Consulting
333 Ravenswood Avenue
Menlo Park, CA 94025-3477
650-859-2000
FAX: 650-859-2182 www.sri-chem.com

Janet R Hardy, Director

Over 1,500 United States basic chemical producers manufacturing almost 10,000 chemicals in commercial quantities at 4,500 plant locations. Providing comprehensive, accurate and timely coverage of the international chemical industry since 1961. *$1460.00*
1100 pages Annual

3970 **Directory of Chemical Producers: East Asia**
SRI Consulting
333 Ravenswood Avenue
Menlo Park, CA 94025-3453
650-859-2000
FAX: 650-859-2182 www.sri-chem.com

Janet R Hardy, Editor

Over 2,000 companies producing over 14,000 chemicals in 2,600 plant locations in Indonesia, Japan, Korea, Taiwan and the Philippines. *$1800.00*
800 pages Annual

3971 **Directory of Chemical Producers: Western Europe**
SRI Consulting
333 Ravenswood Avenue
Menlo Park, CA 94025
650-859-2000
FAX: 650-859-2182 www.sri-chem.com

Janet R Hardy, Editor

Covered are over 2,500 western European chemical producers, chemicals and plant locations. *$1930.00*
Annual
Circulation: 2,100

3972 **Directory of Custom Chemical Manufacturers**
Delphi Marketing Services
400 E 89th Street
Apartment 2J
New York, NY 10128-6728

A list of over 280 custom chemical manufacturers. *$295.00*
220 pages

3973 **Directory of Suppliers of Services**
Independent Liquid Terminals Association
1444 I Street NW
Suite 400
Washington, DC 2005
202-842-9200
FAX: 202-326-8660
info@ilta.org www.ilta.org

E David Doane, President
Melinda Whitney, Director/Government Affairs *$25.00*

3974 **Environmental Fate Data Bases**
Syracuse Research Corporation
6225 Running Ridge Road
North Syracuse, NY 13212
315-452-8000
FAX: 315-452-8100 800-724-0451

Phil Howard, Publisher

This database, consisting of 4 interrelated files of information on the fate of organic chemicals. The files include information in physical/chemical properties, degradation and transport, and monitoring for 16,000 chemicals.
Bibliographic

3975 **Environmental Industry Yearbook and The Gallery**
Environmental Economics
1026 Irving Street
Philadelphia, PA 19107-6707
215-877-2063
FAX: 215-440-0116
More than 80 publicly traded companies, plus Fortune 500 firms that have an impact on environmental concerns. *$75.00*
250 pages SemiAnnual

3976 **Fine Chemicals Database**
Chemron
PO Box 2299
Paso Robles, CA 93447
210-340-8121
FAX: 210-340-8123 800-423-1148
This large database provides supplier information for more than 27,000 chemical products available from over 50 manufacturers and distributors in North America.
Directory

3977 **Index to Chemical Regulations**
Bureau of National Affairs
1231 25th Street NW
Washington, DC 20037-1197
202-452-4200
800-372-1033
customercare@bna.com
www.bna.com

Gregory C McCaffery, Publisher
Inara Z Apinis, Managing Editor

A one-binder index containing more than 80,000 citations by chemical name to the Code of Federal Regulations and the Federal Register. *$988.00*
Monthly

3978 **Information Officers of Member Companies**
Chemical Manufacturers Association
1300 Wilson Boulevard
Arlington, VA 22209-2307
703-741-5502

Thomas J Gilroy, Associate Media Director

About 180 companies.
Biennial

3979 **International Chemical Regulatory Monitoring System**
Ariel Research Corporation
8280 Greensboro Drive
Suite 400
McLean, VA 22102-3015
703-663-1400
FAX: 703-288-3660
This database contains references to regulations and precautionary data on more than 100,000 chemical substances.
Full-text

3980 **Kirk-Othmer Encyclopedia of Chemical Technology Online**
John Wiley & Sons
111 River Street
Hoboken, NJ 07030
201-748-6000
FAX: 201-748-5915 800-825-7550
uscs-wis@wiley.com
www.mrw.interscience.wiley.com
This comprehensive database offers complete text, citations, tables and abstracts of all 1,200 chapters in the 25-volume Encyclopedia of the same name. With no concurrent usage restriction, you can call up information covering the entire chemical industry and allied fields any time with a click of your mouse from the library, office or laboratory.

3981 **McCutcheons Functional Materials**

McCutcheons Division
175 Rock Road
Glen Rock, NJ 07452-1724
201-652-2655
FAX: 201-652-3419
themc@gomc.com www.gomc.com

Michael Allured, Publisher

List of materials commonly used in conjunction with surfactants such as enzymes, lubricants, waxes, corrosion inhibitors, and other chemicals produced worldwide. *$40.00*
Monthly Founded: 1921

3982 **Multilingual Thesaurus of Geosciences**
Information Today
143 Old Marlton Pike
Medford, NJ 08055-8750
609-654-6266
FAX: 609-654-4309
custserv@infotoday.com
www.infotoday.com

J Gravesteijn, Editor
C Kortman, Editor
G N Rassam

Represents the state of the art use of geoscience terminology by informations centers around the world. *$99.00*
654 pages ISBN 1-573870-09-9

3983 **OPIS/STALSBY Electric Power Industry Directory**
OPIS/STALSBY
1255 Highway 70
Suite 32-N
Lakewood, NJ 08701
732-901-8800
FAX: 732-901-9632 877-210-4287
kreng@opisnet.com www.opisnet.com

Karen England, Senior Editor
Karen Reng, Marketing Manager
Christine Kaniuk, Production/Advertising Coordinator

Provides detailed listings of over 1,200 companies and more than 2,700 personnel of the electric power industry. Company categories include producer, marketer, trader, broker, transmission, investor-owned, municipal, rural/co-op/fed/local government and independent. Personnel listings include sales/marketing, supply/purchasing, operations/transmissions, finance/treasury. Company listings include address, direct telephone, fax numbers and e-mails. CD-ROM $495. *$141.00*

2 per year
Circulation: 625 2,700 names
Printed in 4 colors

3984 OPIS/STALSBY Petrochemicals Directory
OPIS/STALSBY
3349d State Route 138
Unit D
Wall Township, NJ 07719-9695
732-302-2500
FAX: 732-901-9632 877-210-4287
kreng@opisnet.com www.opisnet.com

Karen England, Senior Editor
Karen Reng, Marketing Manager
Christine Kaniuk, Production/Advertising Coordinator

Provides detailed listings of over 2,100 companies and more than 7,000 personnel covering all segments of the petrochemical gas industry, including manufacturing, trading and distributing of petrochemicals. Company listings include addresses, telephone, fax, TLX, personal phone/fax numbers, car phones and home addresses, area of responsibility andjob titles. Five separate indices are provided for complete cross-referencing. CD-ROM $995. *$175.00*
2 per year
Circulation: 425 7,100 names
Printed in 4 colors

3985 OPIS/STALSBY Petroleum Supply Americas Directory
OPIS/STALSBY
1255 Highway 70
Suite 32-N
Lakewood, NJ 08701
732-901-8800
FAX: 732-901-9632 877-210-4287
kreng@opisnet.com www.opisnet.com

Karen England, Senior Editor
Karen Reng, Marketing Manager
Christine Kaniuk, Production/Advertising Coordinator

Helps traders, marketers and suppliers of crude oil, refined products and gas liquids to access detailed information on over 2,500 companies and 10,000 personnel in North, Central and South America. Company listings include company address, telephone, fax, TLX, personal phone/fax numbers, car phones, home addresses, area of responsibility and job title. Four separate indices are provided for complete cross-referencing. CD-ROM $995. *$235.00*
2 per year
Circulation: 2,045 10M names
Printed in 4 colors

3986 OPIS/STALSBY Petroleum Supply Europe Directory
OPIS/STALSBY
1255 Highway 70
Suite 32-N
Lakewood, NJ 08701
732-901-8800
FAX: 732-901-9632 877-210-4287
kreng@opisnet.com www.opisnet.com

Karen England, Senior Editor
Karen Reng, Marketing Manager
Christine Kaniuk, Production/Advertising Coordinator

Helps traders, marketers and suppliers of crude oil, refined products and gas liquids to access detailed information on over 1,500 companies and 6,600 personnel in Europe, Eastern Europe, Africa and the Middle East. Listings include company address, telephone, fax, TLX, personal phone/fax numbers, car phones, home addresses, area of responsibility and job titles. Four separate indices are provided for complete cross-referencing. CD-OM $995. *$190.00*
2 per year
Circulation: 425 6,500 names
Printed in 4 colors

3987 OPIS/STALSBY Petroleum Terminal Encyclopedia
OPIS/STALSBY
1255 Highway 70
Suite 32-N
Lakewood, NJ 08701
732-901-8800
FAX: 732-901-9632 877-210-4287
kreng@opisnet.com www.opisnet.com

Karen England, Senior Editor
Karen Reng, Marketing Manager
Christine Kaniuk, Production/Advertising Coordinator

Provides detailed listings of over 2,800 petroleum terminals. Information includes pipeline and rail interconnections and truck facilities for each terminal; berth, waterway and docking information for marine terminals; details on both public and private terminals for market analysis and exchange planning. Three separate indices are provided for complete cross-referencing. CD-ROM $995. *$245.00*
2 per year
Circulation: 825 2,800 names
Printed in 4 colors

3988 OPIS/STALSBY Who's Who in Natural Gas
OPIS/STALSBY
1255 Highway 70
Suite 32-N
Lakewood, NJ 08701
732-901-8800
FAX: 732-901-9632 877-210-4287
kreng@opisnet.com www.opisnet.com

Karen England, Senior Editor
Karen Reng, Marketing Manager
Christine Kaniuk, Production/Advertising Coordinator

Provides detailed listings of over 2,600 companies and more than 11,000 personnel covering all segments of the natural gas industry, including producers, processors, marketers, traders, transporters, major buyers, LDCs, brokers, gas storage, regulatory, etc. Company listings include addresses, telephone, fax, TLX, personal phone/fax numbers, car phones and home addresses, area of responsibility and job titles. Four separate indices are provided for complete cross-referencing. CD-ROM $995. *$200.00*
2 per year
Circulation: 950 11M names
Printed in 4 colors

3989 Purchasing/CPI Edition: Chemicals Yellow Pages
Reed Business Information
2000 Clearwater Drive
Oak Brook, IL 60523
630-740-0825
www.cahners.com

Kevin Fitzgerald, Editor

Manufacturers and distributors of 10,000 chemicals and raw materials; manufacturers and distributors of containers and packaging. *$85.00*
Annual

3990 Refining & Gas Processing
Midwest Publishing Company
PO Box 4468
Tulsa, OK 47159
918-839-9999
FAX: 918-587-9349 800-829-2002
info@midwestdirectories.com
www.midwestdirectories.com

Will Hammack, Editor

Over 5,200 refineries, gas processing plants, engineering contractors, equipment manufacturers and supply companies. *$145.00*
Annual, May Founded: 1943 : Paperback

3991 Regulated Chemical Directory
Chapman & Hall
29 W 35th Street
New York, NY 10001-2299
212-755-5207
FAX: 212-563-2269
List of major federal and selected state and international regulatory and advisory sources of information regarding chemicals in the US, Canada, Australia, Germany and Israel. *$375.00*
Annual, January

3992 Research Services Directory
Grey House Publishing
185 Millerton Road
PO Box 860
Millerton, NY 12546
518-890-0526
FAX: 518-789-0545 800-562-2139
books@greyhouse.com
www.greyhouse.com

Leslie Mackenzie, Publisher
Richard Gottlieb, Editor

This Ninth Edition provides access to well over 7,700 corporate and independent Commercial Research Firms and Laboratories offering contract services for hands-on, basic or applied research. *$550.00*
992 pages Annual ISBN 1-592370-03-9

3993 STN Easy
Chemical Abstracts Service
PO Box 3012
Columbus, OH 43210-0012
614-473-3600
FAX: 614-447-3713 800-848-6533
help@cas.org www.cas.org
Easy web acccess to scientific research and patents. STN Easy provides access to more than 60 databases covering all types of sci/tech information including chemistry, life sciences, buisiness, MSDS, math/computer science, engineering, medicine, pharmaceuticals, general science, food and agriculture, and regulatory information.

3994 Soap/Cosmetics/Chemical Specialties: Blue Book Issue
Cygnus Publishing
445 Broad Hollow Road
Suite 21
Melville, NY 11747-3601
631-845-2700
FAX: 631-845-2723
www.cygnuspub.com

Anita Shaw, Editor-in-Chief
Shelley Colwell, Managing Editor

Sources of raw materials, equipment and services for the chemical, soap and cosmetics industries. Includes a list of trade associations. *$15.00*
Annual, April
Circulation: 19,000

Industry Web Sites

3995 **www.aaccnet.org**
American Association of Cereal Chemists

Nonprofit international organization of nearly 4,000 members who are specialists in the use of cereal grains in foods. AACC has been an innovative leader in gathering and disseminating scientific and technical information to professionals in the grain based foods industry worldwide for over 85 years. We know its not easy to keep up with the latest technology, that's why AACC is here to help you. We're a tool unlike any other in your lab or office. Industry leaders turn to AACC for information.

3996 **www.accci.org**
American Coke & Coal Chemicals Institute Directory

For merchant oven coke producers, integrated coke producers, tar distillers, sales agents, and industry suppliers.

3997 **www.actox.org**
American College of Toxicology

Multidisciplinary society composed of professionals having a common interest in toxicology. Our mission is to educate and lead professionals in industry, government and related areas of toxicology by actively promoting the exchange of information and perspectives on the current status of safety assesment and the application of new developments in toxicology.

3998 **www.aiche.org**
American Institute of Chemical Engineers

Professional association of more than 50,000 members, providing leadership in advancing the chemical engineering profession. Members are those who develop processes and design and operate manufacturing plants, as well as researchers who assure the safe and environmentally sound manufacture, use and disposal of chemical products.

3999 **www.americanchemistry.com**
American Chemistry Council

Committed to improved environmental, health and safety performance through responsible care, common sense advocacy designed to address major public policy issues, health and environmental research and product testing.

4000 **www.aoac.org**
Association of Official Analytical Communities

Calender, publications and training courses. AOAC serves as the primary resource for timely knowledge exchange, networking and high quality laboratory information for its members.

4001 **www.aocs.org**
American Oil Chemists Society

Encourages advancement of technology and research in fats, oils and other associated substances.

4002 **www.aperc.org**
Alkyphenols and Ethoxylates Research Council

4003 **www.arap.org**
Alliance for Responsible Atmospheric Policy

4004 **www.asms.org**
American Society for Mass Spectrometry

Formed to disseminate knowledge of mass spectrometry and allied topics. Members come from academic, industrial and governmental laboratories. Their interests include advancement of techniques and instrumentation in mass specrometry, as well as fundamental research in chemistry, geology, biological sciences and physics.

4005 **www.asneurochem.org**
American Society for Neurochemistry

4006 **www.aspirin.org**
Aspirin Foundation of America

4007 **www.bamm.net**
Basic Acrylic Monomer Manufacturers

4008 **www.ccaiweb.com**
Chemical Coaters Association International

4009 **www.ccrhq.org**
Council for Chemical Research

4010 **www.chemconsult.org**
Assn of Consulting Chemists and Chemical Engineers

4011 **www.chemicalfabricsandfilm.com**
Chemical Fabrics and Film Association

4012 **www.chemistry.org**
American Chemical Society

Encourages advancement in all branches of chemistry. There are 34 ACS divisions and 188 local sections.

4013 **www.chemsources.org**
Chemical Sources Association

4014 **www.chemtrec.org**
American Chemistry Council

Serves as a referral service for non-emergency health and safety information, maintains library and speakers bureaus. Serves as a 24 hour emergency communication service center for hazardous materials, material data sheets, lending library, audio-visual training programs. Health and safety information for registered members.

4015 **www.cidx.org**
Chemical Industry Data Exchange

4016 **www.ciit.org**
CIIT Centers for Health Research

4017 **www.coatingstech.org**
Federation of Societies for Coatings Technology

Provides technical education and professional development to its members and to the global industry through its multi-national constituent societies and collectively as a federation.

4018 **www.combustioninstitute.org**
Combustion Institute

4019 **www.cpda.com**
Chemical Producers and Distributors

4020 **www.croplifeamerica.org**
CropLife America

4021 **www.csma.org**
Chemical Specialties Manufacturers Association

For companies involved in the formulation, manufacture, testing and marketing of chemical specialty products.

4022 **www.cspa.org**
Consumer Specialty Products Association

Nonprofit organization composed of many companies involved in the formulation, manufacture, testing and marketing of chemical specialty products. Our line includes disinfectants that kill germs in homes, hospitals and restaurants, candles that eliminate odors, pest management products for home and garden, cleaning products and much more.

4023 **www.dupont.com/nacs**
DuPont Experimental Station

For chemists and chemical engineers engaged in the study and use of reactions involving catalysts. Publishes a newsletter

4024 **www.electrochem.org**
Electrochemical Society

The society is an international nonprofit, educational organization concerned with phenomena relating to electrochemical and solid state science and technology. Members are individual scientists and engineers, as well as corporations and laboratories.

4025 **www.etad.com**
ETAD North America

4026 **www.fibersource.com**
American Fiber Manufacturers Association

Trade association for US companies that manufacture synthetic and cellulostic fibers. The industry employs 30,000 people and produces over 9 billion pounds of fiber in the US. The association maintains close ties to other manufactured fiber trade associations worldwide.

4027 **www.greyhouse.com**
Grey House Publishing

Selected Grey House directories in the fields of business, health and education are available online. Users can search our online databases by several different search criteria, such as product categories, geographic area, sales volume and much, much more. Full Grey House catalog and online ordering also available.

4028 **www.ilta.org**
Independent Liquid Terminals Association

Representing bulk liquid terminal companies that store commercial liquids in aboveground storage tanks and transfer products to and from oceangoing tanks ships, tank barges, pipelines, tank trucks, and tank rail cars.

4029 **www.imcglobal.com**
IMC Global Operations

From lowest cost mines and plants in North America through a highly efficent distribution network, IMC Global serves world agriculture as the largest global producer and supplier of concentrated phospahtes and potash fertilizers. The company also is one of the leading providers of phosphorus and potassium feed supplements for the global animal nutrition industry.

4030 **www.ioza.org**
International Ozone Assn-Pan American Group Branch

Not for profit educational association which performs its information sharing functions through sponsorship of international symposia, seminars, publications, and the development of personal relationships among ozone specialists throughout the world.

4031 **www.leatherchemists.org**
American Leather Chemists Association

Publishes the Journal of the American Leather Chemists Association where original research reports are published along with abstracts of foreign articles. A four-day technical meeting is held annually. Promotes the advancement of the knowledge of science and engineering in their application to the problems facing the leather and leather products industries.

4032 **www.methanol.org**
American Methanol Institute

Our mission is to expand markets for the use of methanol as a chemical commodity building block, a hydrogen carrier for fuel cell applications, and an alternative fuel. AMI was formed in 1989, during the height of the Clean Air Act debate, and worked to help create the highly successful reformulated gasoline program.

4033 **www.mti-link.org**
Materials Tech. Institute of the Chemical Process

MTI provides leadership in materials technology for chemical processing to improve reliability, profitability and safety.

4034 **www.nacatsoc.org**
North American Catalysis Society

Fosters an interest in heterogeneous and homogeneous catalysis. Organizes national meetings. Members are chemists and chemical engineers engaged in the study and use of reactions involving catalysts. Publishes a newsletter.

4035 **www.pemanet.org**
Process Equipment Manufacturers' Association

Organized in 1960, we represent more than 40 companies in the process equipment field. Member companies serve the liquid-solids separation, food processing, pulp and paper, waste water treatment industry and others.

4036 **www.pepperspray.org**
Association of Defensive Spray Manufacturers

4037 **www.pestworld.org**
National Pest Control Association

For over 65 years, the NPMA has represented the interests of its members and the structural pest control industry. Through the efforts of NPMA, the pest control industry is stronger, more professional, and more unified. Guiding its members and industry through legislative and regulatory initiatives on the federal and state levels, the creation of verifiable training, the changing technologies used by the industry, and public and media relations, NPMA has been a clear, positive voice.

4038 **www.pfa.org**
Polyurethane Foam Association

Educating customers and other groups about flexible polyurethane foam and to promote its use in manufactured and indutrial products. This includes providing facts on environmental, health and safety issues related to polyurethane foam to the memebership of PFA, polyurethane foam users, regulatory officials, business leaders and the media.

4039 **www.pigments.com**
Color Pigments Manufacturers Association

4040 **www.pima.org**
Polyisocyanurate Insulation Manufacturers Assn

National association that advances the use of polyisocyanurate (polyiso) insulation. Polyiso is one of the nation's most widely used and cost-effective insulation products. PIMA's membership consiosts of manufacturers as well as suppliers to the industry.

4041 **www.pinechemicals.org**
Pine Chemicals Association

Association of producers, processors and consumers of pine chemicals. The PCA promotes innovative, safe and environmentally responsible practices to assure a reliable supply of high quality products.

4042 **www.powdercoating.org**
Powder Coating Institute

Founded in 1981 as a nonprofit organization, PCI works to advance the utilization of powder coating as an economical, non-polluting and high quality finish for industrial and consumer products.

4043 **www.regnet.com/cpia**
Chlorinated Paraffins Industry Association

4044 **www.regnet.com/epc**
Emulsion Polymers Council

4045 **www.scisoc.org/asbc**
American Society of Brewing Chemists

News, information, member directory and publications.

4046 **www.simaflavor.org**
Flavor & Extract Manufacturers Assn of the US

Locates suppliers and manufacturers of rare chemicals and oils used in the flavor and fragrance industry.

4047 **www.socma.com**
Synthetic Organic Chemical Manufacturers Assn

Trade association serving the specialty batch and custom chemical industry since 1921. Its more than 320 member companies have more than 2,000 manufacturing sites and 100,000 employees. SOCMA members encompass every segment of the industry - from small specialty producers to large multinational corporations - and manufacture 50,000 products annually that are valued at $60 billion dollars.

4048 **www.toxicology.org**
Society of Toxicology

Members are scientists concerned with the effects of chemicals on man and the environment. Promotes the aquisition and utilization of knowledge in toxicology, aids in the protection of public health and facilitates disiplines. The society has a strong commitment to education in toxicology and to the recruitment of students and new members into the profession.

Associations

4049 Association of Specialists in Cleaning and Restoration International
8229 Cloverleaf Drive
Suite 460
Millersville, MD 21108-1592
410-299-9900
FAX: 410-729-3603 800-272-7012
info@ascr.org www.ascr.org

Lawrence Jacobson, Executive Director
Timothy Horrigan, President/CEO
Charlotte Tull, Manager

International trade association for professionals involved in the cleaning and restoration of interior textiles and structures, including air handling systems. Publishes Cleaning and Restoration magazine monthly, and holds annual convention and exhibition in March. This organization also provides training courses throughout the year, as well as giving full-time technical support to members.
1300 Members Founded: 1946

4050 Building Service Contractors Association International
10201 Lee Highway
Suite 225
Fairfax, VA 22030
703-359-7090
FAX: 703-352-0493 800-368-3414
asaoffice@asa-hq.com www.bscai.org

Carol Dean, Executive VP

Trade association for companies offering security, maintenance and cleaning services. The international membership now represents over 10% of the association's professional membership. *$30.00*
2500 Members Founded: 1965 $75 per M.

4051 Cleaning Equipment Trade Association
968 Lake St S
Ste 202
Forest Lake, MN 55025-2615
651-982-0010
FAX: 651-982-0030 800-441-0111
carol@ceta.org.com www.ceta.org

Carol Wasieleski, Managing Director
Joe Jones, VP
Karl Loeffelholz, Secretary/Treasurer
Curtis Braber, Executive Director

International nonprofit reade association made up of manufacturers, distributors, and suppliers who coordinate their efforts to promote public awareness, professionalism, industry wide safety standards, and education for the advancement of the powered cleaning equipment industry.
300 Members Founded: 1996

4052 Cleaning Management Institute
National Trade Publications
13 Century Hill Drive
Latham, NY 12110-2197
518-783-1281
FAX: 518-783-1386
cmi@ntpmedia.com
www.cminstitute.net

Humphrey Tyler, Owner
Nicole Older, Administrator

Members are individuals involved in building cleaning maintenance operations.
1000 Members Founded: 1964

4053 Coin Laundry Association
1315 Butterfield Road
Suite 212
Downers Grove, IL 60515-5602
630-963-5547
FAX: 630-963-5864 800-570-5629
info@coinlaundry.org
www.coinlaundry.org

Bob Eisenberg, Chairman
Dan Naumann, Vice Chairman
Clay Pederson, Treasurer

Association for self-service laundry and dry cleaning industry.
2700+ Members Founded: 1960

4054 Environmental Management Association
209 Winding Way
Morrisville, PA 19067
215-295-7244
FAX: 215-295-7248

Michael Kneucker, President

Association for manufacturers, suppliers and distributors of sanitation maintenance supplies, products, services.
11 Members Founded: 1994

4055 Halogenated Solvents Industry Alliance
1300 Wilson Boulevard
Arlington, VA 22209
703-741-5780
FAX: 703-741-6077
info@hsia.org www.hsia.org

Steve Risotto, Executive Director

Represents manufacturers of perchloroetheylene and related solvents.

4056 International Drycleaners Congress

4 W Central Avenue
Oxford, OH 45056
513-523-4121
FAX: 513-523-1370 www.idcnews.org

Manfred Wentz, Executive Director

International organization for cleaners.

4057 International Fabricare Institute
14700 Sweitzer Lane
Laurel, MD 20904
301-622-1900
FAX: 240-295-4200 800-638-2627
techline@ifi.org www.ifi.org

Dan Martino, President
Jim Cripe, Chairman
Gary Dawson, Treasurer

With its education, research, testing and professional training, IFI offers solutions that help member businesses provide expert garment care. *$85.00*
8000 Members Founded: 1883
Printed in 4 colors on glossy stock

4058 International Kitchen Exhaust Cleaning Association
1518 K Street NW
Suite 503
Washington, DC 20005
202-593-5955
FAX: 202-638-4833
ikecahq@aol.com www.ikeca.org

Harris Rothenberg, CECS, President
Jeffrey Morris, CECS, VP
Janice Paulat, Treasurer
Joel Berkowitz, Director
Joseph Kenney, CECS, Director

Promotes fire safety in restaurants and professionalism in the kitchen exhaust cleaning industry. This not for profit trade association, has established stringent standards and practices for contractors engaged in kitchen exhaust cleaning, conducted a variety of educational programs, and worked with influential code setting bodies such as the National Fire Protection Association to improve existing codes and regulations.
Founded: 1989

4059 International Maintenance Institute

PO Box 751896
Houston, TX 77275-1896
281-481-0869
FAX: 281-481-8337
george.masterson@irco.com
www.imionline.org

George W Masterson, Chairman
Gerry Goudreau, President
Joyce Rhoden, Executive Secretary
Edward Stedman, Secretary
Gregory Nye, Regional VP

Focuses on plant workers and vendors who have products tailored to the maintenance industry. The philosophy of the organization is to professionalize the maintenance function by helping maintenance managers to work smarter through the exchange of ideas and education.
2.5M Members Founded: 1960

4060 Laundry and Dry Cleaning International
307 4th Avenue
Pittsburgh, PA 15222-2102
412-818-8105

Patrick Jones, Manager

Sponsers and supports The League of Voter Education Political Action Committee.

4061 Multi-Housing Laundry Association
1500 Sunday Drive
Suite 102
Raleigh, NC 27607-7506
919-861-5579
FAX: 919-787-4916
nshore@olsonmgmt.com
www.laundrywise.com

Michael Olson, Executive Director
David Feild, Executive Director
Penney DePas, Director of Meeting Planning

Furnishes information on tax and business development and promotes high business standards. Annual meetings held in June.
40M Members Founded: 1939

4062 National Association of Diaper Services
994 Old Eagle School Road
Suite 1019
Wayne, PA 19087-1866
610-971-4850
FAX: 610-971-4859 800-722-7712

John A Shiffert, Executive Director

Dedicated to promoting the health and environmental benifits of using cotton diapers rather than disposables. We monitor the laundering and sanitation practices of our members and specify the highest standards for what we consider a public health industry.
Founded: 1938

4063 **National Association of Institutional Linen Management**
2130 Lexington Road
Richmond, KY 40475-7923

FAX: 859-624-3580 800-669-0863

Jim Thacker, Executive Director

Seeks improvement of laundry technology. Conducts formal schools.

1.4M Members Founded: 1959

4064 **National Cleaners Association**
252 W 29th Street
New York, NY 10001-5271
212-967-3002
FAX: 212-967-2240
ncaiclean@aol.com www.nca-i.com

Nora Nealis, Executive Director
Stephen Yudelson, President
Sultan Saeed, Treasurer

Professional trade association dedicated to the welfare of well groomed consumers and the professional cleaners who serve them. For over 50 years, NCA has been at the vanguard of education, research, and information distribution concerning garment and household fabric care. Elected officials, government angencies, consumer groups, fashion designers and major media outlets have recognized and responded to NCA's activities, reports and tradition of excellence.

4000 Members Founded: 1946

4065 **North East Fabricare Association**
580 Main Street
Reading, MA 01867
781-942-7630
FAX: 781-942-7393
peteblke@aol.com
www.nefabricare.com

Peter Blake, Executive Director
Mary White, Office Coordinator
Nelson Kravetz, Consumer Affairs Mediator

Serves cleaners in the New England, New Jersey and New York with information and news about the fabricare industry.

Founded: 1992

4066 **Power Washers of North America**
PO Box 2996
Vincetown, NJ 08088
609-268-9776
FAX: 609-268-9778 800-393-7962
pwnahq@pwna.org www.pwna.org

Paul Horsley, President
Tom Bickett, VP
John Hartley, Secretary

Developing and communicating high standards in ethical business practices, environmental awareness and safety through continuing education and active representation of the membership. PWNA educated and trained contractors raise the level of professionalism and value to their customers.

550 Members Founded: 1992 500 names

4067 **Rocky Mountain Fabricare Association**
1166 Huron Street
Suite 27
Denver, CO 80234
303-433-4446
FAX: 303-458-0002
gary@rmfa.org www.rmfa.org

Richard Reese, President
Gary Leeper, Executive Director

Enhancing the image and viability of the fabricare industry through education and development of the skills, talents and professionalism of its membership. Serves cleaners in Colorado, Utah and Wyoming.

900 Members

4068 **Soap and Detergent Association**
1500 K Street NW
Washington, DC 20005
202-347-2900
FAX: 202-347-4110
info@cleaning101.com
www.cleaning101.com

Stanley W Silverman, Chair
Javed Ahmed, Executive VP
Neal Briggi, VP
Thomas J Pekich, Group VP
Ernie Rosenberg, President

Nonprofit trade association representing manufacturers of household, industrial and institutional cleaning products; their ingredients and finished packaging. Dedicated to advancing public understanding of the safety and benefits of cleaning products and protecting the ability of its members to formulate products that best meet consumer needs.

100+ Members Founded: 1926

4069 **South Eastern Fabricare Association**
7373 Hodson Memorial Drive
Building 3
Savannah, GA 31406
912-355-3364
FAX: 912-355-3155 877-707-7332
sefa.clnrs@worldnet.att.net
www.sefa.org

Bubba Dean, Chairman
Perry Bullard, President
Jim Hardy, Executive VP
Barry McElveen, Executive Director

Trade association that represents its members who have an interest in the dry cleaning and laundry industry.

900+ Members Founded: 1972

4070 **Southwest Drycleaners Association**

1800 NE Loop 410
Suite 308
San Antonio, TX 78210
210-826-4684

desda@ix.netcomcom
www.sda-dryclean.com

Andrew Stanley Jr, Executive Director

Serves cleaners in Louisiana, Mississippi, Missouri, Kansas, Arkansa, New Mexico, Oklahoma and Texas.

4071 **Sponge and Chamois Institute**
117 Wilmot Circle
Suite 2
Scarsdale, NY 10583
914-725-4646
FAX: 914-725-1183

Jules Schwimmer, Executive Secretary

Members are dealers and suppliers of natural sponges and chamois leather.

Founded: 1933

4072 **Uniform and Textile Service Association**
1300 17th Street N
Suite 750
Arlington, VA 22209-3801
703-247-2600
FAX: 703-841-4750 800-486-6745
dunlap@utsa.com www.utsa.com

David Hobson, President
David Dunlap, Director Environmental Affairs
Larry Patton, Director Plant Operations
Deborah Hodges, Director Finance/Administration

International trade association representing textile supply and service companies. This association has been in existence for more than 70 years and represents 95% of the annual sales generated by the uniform service industry and 65% of the annual sales generated by the linen supply industry. UTSA members provide, clean, and maintain reusable textile products, such as uniforms, sheets, table linen, shop and print towels, floor mats, mops and other items to thousands of businesses.

100 Members Founded: 1933

Newsletters

4073 **Bulletin**
Neighborhood Cleaners Association
252 W 29th Street
New York, NY 10001
212-967-3002
FAX: 212-967-2240 www.nca-i.com
Technical info for the dry cleaning industry. Government regulation compliance.
$25.00

Circulation: 4,400

4074 **Coin Laundry Association: Journal**

Coin Laundry Association
1315 Butterfield Road
Suite 212
Downers Grove, IL 60515-5602
630-963-5547
FAX: 630-963-5864
info@coinlaundry.org
http://www.coinlaundry.org

Steven Bova, Publisher
Brian Wallace, President
Bob Nieman, Editor
Laurie Moore, Circulation Manager
Bill Gilbert, Marketing Manager

Committed to offering coin-op owners the information necessary to become and remain competitive in today's changing market.

4 pages Monthly Founded: 1960

4075 **Fabricare News**
International Fabricare Institute
14700 Sweitzer lane
Laurel, MD 20707
301-622-1900
FAX: 240-295-4200 800-638-2627
techline@ifi.org http://www.ifi.org

William E Fisher, Publisher
J Calleja, Editor
Barbara Wagner, Marketing Manager

Information of interest to dry cleaners and launderers.

8 pages Monthly Founded: 1883
Circulation: 5000

4076 **Maytag Commercial Newsletter**
Maytag Company
240 Edwards Street
Cleveland, TN 37311
423-723-3333
800-688-9900

Mike Klosterman, Publisher
Debbie White, Executive Director

Self-service laundry industry news.

8 pages BiWeekly

4077 **Reclaimer**
South Eastern Fabricare Association
7373 Hodson Memorial Drive
Building 3, Suite C
Savannah, GA 31406
912-355-3364
FAX: 912-355-3155 877-707-7332
barry@sefa.org http://www.sefa.org

Barry McElveen, Executive Director
Grey Griffin, President

A monthly newsletter dedicated to the service of the drycleaning industry. *$5.00*
Monthly
Circulation: 2200

Magazines & Journals

4078 **American Coin-Op**
Crain Communications
500 N Dearborn St
Suite 1000
Chicago, IL 60610-4464
773-358-8688
FAX: 312-337-8654 800-678-9595
info@crain.com http://www.crain.com

Charles R. Thompson, Publisher
Ian P Murphy, Editor
Scott Segal, Sales Manager
Rance E. Crain, President

For owners of coin-op laundries. Accepts advertising. *$33.00*
40 pages Monthly Founded: 1925
Circulation: 18000
Printed in 4 colors on glossy stock

4079 **American Drycleaner**
American Trade Magazines
500 N Dearborn Street
Chicago, IL 60610-9988
312-337-7700
FAX: 312-337-8654 800-678-9595
info@crain.com http://www.crain.com

Ian P Murphy, Editor
Charles R. Thompson, VP/Publisher
Scott Segal, Eastern Sales Manager
Brett Carr, Western Sales Manager

American Drycleaner is the number one publication serving the drycleaning industry. It carries more pages of editorial and advertising than any other industry publication.
150 pages Monthly Founded: 1935
Circulation: 24,000
Printed in 4 colors on glossy stock

4080 **American Laundry News**
American Trade Magazines
500 N Dearborn Street
Suite 1000
Chicago, IL 60610-9988
312-337-7700
FAX: 312-337-8654 800-678-9595
laundrynews@crain.com
http://www.crain.com/

Charlie Thompson, Publisher
Elise Coyle, Circulation Manager
Bruce Beggs, Editor

American Laundry News specializes in news and investigative reporting by professional journalists who break virtually every major story in the institutional laundry field.
28 pages Monthly Founded: 1974
Circulation: 15600
Printed in 4 colors on glossy stock

4081 **American Window Cleaner Magazine**
12 Twelve Publishing Corp.
PO Box 98
Bedford, NY 10506
914-234-2630
FAX: 914-234-2632
karen@awcmag.com
http://www.awcmag.com

Richard Fabry, Publisher
Norman J Finegold, President
Mark Battersby, Editor

Information on new products, add-on businesses, association and convention news and safety. *$35.00*
Monthly Founded: 1986
Circulation: 9000

4082 **Broom Brush & Mop**
Rankin Publishing Company
204 E. Main Street
PO Box 130
Arcola, IL 61910-130
217-268-4959
FAX: 217-268-4815
DRankin125@aol.com
http://www.rankinpublishing.com

Don Rankin, Co-Publisher
Harrell Kerkhoff, Editor
Ron White, Associate Editor

Reports on import and export totals as well as updates on new products and trade show coverage, also industry trends and market conditions. *$25.00*
Monthly Founded: 1912
Circulation: 1,700

4083 **Brushware**
Brushware
PO Box 98
Bedford, NY 10506
914-234-2630
FAX: 914-234-2632
editors@brushwaremag.com
http://www.brushwaremag.com/

Karen Grinter, Publisher
Norman J Finegold, President

Information on products that apply materials, clean and polish surfaces, covers also industry news, products, methods and trends, market reports, profiles and interviews. *$45.00*
Founded: 1898
Circulation: 2000

4084 **Cleaner**
COLE Publishing
1720 Maple Lake Dam Road
PO Box 220
Three Lakes, WI 54562
715-546-3346
FAX: 715-546-3786 800-994-7990
cole@pumper.com
http://www.cleaner.com

Ted Roulphe, Editor
Geoff Bruss, CEO

The latest tools and equipment promoting safety and efficiency, employment and environmental concerns, as well as industry profiles. *$15.00*
Monthly Founded: 1979
Circulation: 24000

4085 **Cleaner Times**
Advantage Publishing Company
1000 Nix Road
Little Rock, AR 72211
501-280-0007
FAX: 501-280-9233 800-525-7038
advpub@adpub.com
http://www.adpub.com

Charlene Yarbrough, Publisher
Gerry Plus, Circualtion Manager

Application, information, and productivity for persons engaged in the manufacturing, distribution, or the use of high pressure water systems and accessories. The emphasis is on safety, regulatory, which affect the industry as well as cleaning applications. *$36.00*
72 pages Monthly Founded: 1989
Circulation: 25,000
Printed in 4 colors on glossy stock

4086 **Cleanfax Magazine**
National Trade Publications
13 Century Hill Drive
Latham, NY 12110-2197
518-783-1281
FAX: 518-783-1386
asavino@ntpinc.com
http://www.cleanfax.com

Humphrey S Tyler, President
Paul Amos, Editor
Alice Savino, Publisher

Information on carpet cleaning, water and fire damage restoration, industry news and updates.
80 pages Monthly Founded: 1981
Circulation: 20,000 21,000 names $125 per M.
Printed in 4 colors on glossy stock

4087 **Cleaning & Restoration Magazine**
Association of Specialists in Cleaning/Restoration
8229 Cloverleaf Drive
Suite 460
Millersville, MD 21108
410-299-9900
FAX: 410-729-3603 800-272-7012
alhwrite@erols.com
http://www.ascr.org

Patricia Harman, Editor-in-Chief
Tony Greenfield, General Sales Mganager
William Lakin, President/CEO

Offers specialized information and updates for the cleaning and restoration industry. *$69.00*
Monthly Founded: 1947
Circulation: 2000

4088 **Commercial Floor Care**
Business News Publishing Company
22801 Ventura Blvd.
#115
Woodland Hills, CA 91364
818-224-8035
FAX: 818-224-8042 800-835-4398
stoufferj@bnpmedia.com
http://www.icsmag.com

Evan Kessler, Publisher
Jeffrey Stouffer, Editor
Phil Johnson, Group Publisher
Amy Levin, Production Manager
Jim Michaelson, Associate Publisher

Dedicated to floor care in the commercial environment.
40 pages Monthly Founded: 1926
Circulation: 26700
Printed in 4 colors on glossy stock

4089 **Fabricare**
International Fabricare Institute
14700 Sweitzer Lane
Laurel, MD 20707
301-622-1900
FAX: 240-295-0685 800-638-2627
techline@ifi.org http://www.ifi.org

Willam E. Fisher, Executive VP
Jay Calleja, Editor

The central publication of the International Fabricare Institute. This publication provides information, knowledge and education about drycleaning and laundry issues, the industry, as a whole, and the association.

8 pages Monthly Founded: 1883
Circulation: 8,000

4090 **ICS Cleaning Specialist**
Business News Publishing Company
22801 Ventura Boulevard
Suite 115
Woodland Hills, CA 91364-1230
818-224-8035
FAX: 818-224-8042 800-835-4398
johnsonp@bnpmedia.com
http://www.icsmag.com

Phil Johnson, Group Publisher
Evan Kessler, Publisher
Jeffrey Stouffer, Editor
Amy Levin, Production Manager
Jim Michaelson, Associate Publisher

For carpet cleaning, restoration and floor care service providers.

68 pages Founded: 1928 varies names
$120 per M.
Printed in on glossy stock

4091 **Industrial Launderer Magazine**
Uniform & Textile Service Association
1300 N 17th Street
Suite 750
Arlington, VA 22209
703-247-2600
FAX: 703-841-4750 800-486-6745
info@utsa.com http://www.utsa.com

Ken Koepper, Publisher
David Hobson, President/CEO

The authoritative source for information for the uniform and textile service industry. It provides practical guidance and assistance for businesses that rent, lease or sell uniforms and other textiles including linen supply. *$100.00*

Monthly
Circulation: 6000

4092 **International Fabricare Institute**
12251 Tech Road
Silver Spring, MD 20904-1976
301-622-1900
FAX: 301-236-9320 800-638-2627
techline@ifi.org http://www.ifi.org

William Fisher, Executive Director
Bill Fisher, Chief Executive Officer

The association of Professional Dry Cleaners, wetcleaners, and launderers. With its education, research, testing and professional training, IFI offers solutions that help member businesses provide expert garment care.

32 pages Monthly Founded: 1883
Circulation: 8,000
Printed in 4 colors on glossy stock

4093 **Journal of the Coin Laundering and Drycleaning Industry**
Coin Laundry Association
1315 Butterfield Road
Suite 212
Downers Grove, IL 60515-5602
630-963-5547
FAX: 630-963-5864

Kathy Gilbert, Editor

The official voice of the coin laundry and drycleaning industry. It's the most cost effective way to reach over 28,000 small business entrepreneurs. Besides industry specific items these owners operate over 38,000 company vehicles, utilize business management materials and more. Accepts advertising.

52 pages Monthly

4094 **Laundry News**
American Trade Magazines
500 N Dearborn Street
Ste. 1100
Chicago, IL 60610-4900
312-337-7700
FAX: 312-337-8654
info@crain.com
http://www.crain.com

Charles R Thompson, VP
Bruce Beggs, Editor
Donald Feinstein, Production Manager

Information for buyers of institutional laundry and housekeeping products. *$24.00*

Monthly Founded: 1916
Circulation: 15500

4095 **Maintenance Sales News**
Rankin Publishing Company
204 E Main Street
PO Box 130
Arcola, IL 61910-130
217-268-4959
FAX: 217-268-4815 800-598-8083
drankin125@aol.com
http://www.rankinpublishing.com

Harrell Kerkhoff, Editor
Don Rankin, Co-Publisher
Kris Bott, Production

Information on selling techniques, business management, training, merchandise, and seminars.

Circulation: 18,000

4096 **Maintenance Solutions**
Trade Press Publishing Corporation
2100 W Florist Avenue
Milwaukee, WI 53209
414-228-7701
FAX: 414-228-1134
facilitiesnet@tradepress.com
http://www.facilitiesnet.com

Dick Yake, Editoridal Director
Dan Hounsell, Editor

How to articles and features designed to alleviate reader problems as well as new product information and applications. *$45.00*

42 pages Monthly Founded: 1993
Circulation: 35000

4097 **Maintenance Supplies**
Cygnus Publishing
3 Huntington Quadrangle
Suite 301N
Melville, NY 11747-3601
631-845-2700
FAX: 631-845-2798 800-308-6397
Rich.DiPaolo@cygnuspub.com
http://www.cygnusb2b.com

Tracy Rossi, Publisher
Paul Mackler, President
Rich Di Paolo, Editor

Case histories and general industry news, also supply distributors, new methods and equipment in the field. *$66.00*

Monthly Founded: 1966
Circulation: 16,500

4098 **National Association of Institutional Linen Management News Magazine**
2161 Lexington Rd
Ste 2
Richmond, KY 40475-7952
859-624-0177
FAX: 859-624-3580 800-669-0863

Jim Thacker, Executive Director

Offers information for cleaners of fine fabrics.

Monthly

4099 **Sanitary Maintenance**
Trade Press Publishing Corporation
2100 W Florist Avenue
Milwaukee, WI 53201-3799
414-228-7701
FAX: 414-228-1134
msm@tradepress.com
http://www.tradepress.com

Dick Yake, Editorial Director
Rob Geissler, Publisher
Pat Foran, Editor
Eric Muench, Circulation Director

Business management, inventory control and product trends, also includes industrial paper products, cleaning chemicals, safety supplies, janitorial supplies and packaging products.

58 pages Monthly Founded: 1943
Circulation: 16052

4100 **Services Magazine**
Building Service Contractors Association Int'l
10201 Lee Highway
Suite 225
Fairfax, VA 22030
703-359-7090
FAX: 703-352-0493 800-368-3414
ganderson@bscai.org
http://www.bscai.org

Carol Dean, CEO
Barbara Woodward, Advertising Director

The Building Service Contractors Association International is the trade association serving the facility services industry through education, leadership, and representatiion. *$30.00*

56 pages Monthly Founded: 1981
Circulation: 20064 20000 names

4101 **Textile Rental Magazine**
Textile Rental
1800 Diagonal Road
suite 200
Alexandria, VA 22314
703-519-0029
FAX: 703-519-0026
trsa@trsa.org http://www.trsa.org

Roger Cocivera, CEO/President
Jack Morgan, Editor
Debbie Smith, Marketing

The leading voice in the industrial uniform rental, linen, supply, dust control and commercial laundering industries. It provides a marketplace for vendors to share information and documents and reports on industry trends. *$240.00*

100 pages Monthly Founded: 1915
Circulation: 8225
Mailing list available for rent 6M names
Printed in 4 colors on glossy stock

Trade Shows

4102 **Association of Specialists in Cleaning & Restoration Convention**
9810 Patuxent Woods Dr
Ste K
Columbia, MD 21046-1595
443-878-1000
FAX: 443-878-1010 800-272-7012
info@ascr.org www.ascr.org

Tiffany Palcn, Education Director
Charlotte Tull, Manager

Annual convention and exhibits of carpet, upholstery and draperies cleaning and restoration equipment, duct cleaning supplies and services, 130 booths.

600 Attendees Annual Founded: 1945

4103 Building Service Contractors Association International Trade Show
10201 Lee Highway
Suite 225
Fairfax, VA 22030-2222
703-359-7090
FAX: 703-352-0493 www.bscai.org

Carol Dean, Executive Vice President
Elizabeth Price, Exhibitor Director

Containing 400 booths and 185 exhibits.

2000 Attendees March/April Founded: 1965

4104 Clean Show
Riddle & Associates
1874 Piedmont Road NE
Suite 360-C
Atlanta, GA 30324
404-876-1988
FAX: 404-876-5121
info@cleanshow.com
www.cleanshow.com

John Riddle, Manager
Ann Howell, Communications

17000 Attendees Biennial, Odd Years
Founded: 1977

4105 Educational Congress for Laundering & Drycleaning
Coin Laundry Association
1315 Butterfield Road
Suite 212
Downers Grove, IL 60515-5602
630-963-5547
FAX: 630-963-5864

Frank Vitek, Executive Director

Two thousand one hundred booths of equipment and products for the cleaning industry. Service schools and other events planned.

22M Attendees July

4106 National Educational Exposition and Conference
Environmental Management Association
1721 Pheasant Road
Norristown, PA 19403-3333
610-935-5577
FAX: 610-539-8588

Annual show of 15 manufacturers, suppliers and distributors of sanitation maintenance supplies, products, services.

150 Attendees

4107 Power Clean
Cleaning Equipment Trade Association
2440 N Charles Street
Suite 220
North St. Paul, MN 55109

FAX: 651-777-4114 800-441-0111

Annual show of 100 manufacturers and suppliers of cleaning equipment, high pressure washers and related component accessories and products.

1200 Attendees October, Dallas

4108 Southern Drycleaners Show
South Eastern Fabricare Association
500 Sugar Mill Road
Suite 200A
Atlanta, GA 30350-2886
770-433-0340
FAX: 770-998-1441 www.sefa.org

Joel Deutsch, Manager

Trade show for the drycleaning industry with 120 exhibitors and 250 booths.

2500 Attendees August

4109 Tex Care
National Cleaners Association
252 W 29th Street
New York, NY 10001
212-967-3002
FAX: 212-967-2240
ncaiclean@aol.com www.nca-i.com

Nora Nealis, Executive Director

Containing 350 exhibits of interest to member cleaners.

5000+ Attendees April

Directories & Databases

4110 Carpet Cleaners Institute of the Northwest Membership Roster
147 SE 102nd Avenue
Portland, OR 97216-2703
503-253-9091
FAX: 503-253-9172 805-261-8222

Over 330 member companies involved in the carpet cleaning industry in Washington, Oregon, and Montana, USA and Alberta and British Columbia, Canada.

Annual

4111 Cleaning and Maintenance Management: Buyer's Guide Directory Issue
National Trade Publications
13 Century Hill Drive
Latham, NY 12110-2197
518-783-1281
FAX: 518-783-1386
asavino@ntpine.com cmmonline.com

Alice J Savino, Group Publisher
Chris Sanford, Executive Editor

Over 500 manufacturers are profiled that supply equipment used in building maintenance and housekeeping. *$42.00*

84 pages Annual Founded: 1966
Circulation: 42000
Mailing list available for rent 42M names $125 per M.
Printed in 4 colors on glossy stock

4112 Coin Laundry Association of Suppliers
Coin Laundry Association
1315 Butterfield Road
Downers Grove, IL 60515
630-963-5547
FAX: 630-963-5864
info@coinlaundry.org
www.coinlaundry.org

Brian Wallace, Executive Director
Michael Sokolowski, Deputy Executive Director
Bob Nieman, Editor
Kathy Sherman, Director Administration
Sue Lally, Director Membership

Lists over 500 manufacturers and suppliers of products and services to the coin and dry cleaning laundry industries.

2700+ pages Founded: 1960

4113 Inside Textile Service - Directories
Uniform & Textile Service Association
1300 N 17th Street
Suite 750
Arlington, VA 22209
703-247-2600
FAX: 703-841-4750
info@utsa.com www.utsa.com

David Hobson, President

The uniform and textile service industry's most comprehensive guide to US textile service companies. Includes contact data for UTSA's membership, and for hundreds of other textile service companies as well. Contains listings of all UTSA affiliated suppliers with catalog-like data on their products and services. Free to members.

Circulation: 3,000

4114 Textile Rental Services Association Roster
Textile Rental Services Association
1800 Diagonal Road
Suite 200
Alexandria, VA 22314
703-519-0029
FAX: 703-519-0026
trsa@trsa.org www.trsa.org

Roger F Cocivera, President/CEO
Scott Mallan, Finance Manager
Michael Wilson, Director Government Affairs
Jack Morgan, Editor

Offers a list of over 1,800 companies that supply linen, uniforms and other textile products to other industries.

1300 pages Founded: 1913

Industry Web Sites

4115 www.ascr.org
Assn of Specialists in Cleaning and Restoration

For professionals involved in the cleaning and restoration of interior textiles and structures, including air handling systems.

4116 www.bscai.org
Building Service Contractors Association Int'l

For companies offering security, maintenance and cleaning services.

4117 www.ceta.org
Cleaning Equipment Trade Association

For manufacturers and suppliers of cleaning equipment, high pressure washers and related component accessories and products.

4118 www.coinlaundry.org
Coin Laundry Association

For self-service laundry and dry cleaning industry. CLA is a not for profit trade association representing the 30,000 coin laundry owners in the US and the world.

4119 **www.greyhouse.com**
Grey House Publishing

Selected Grey House directories in the fields of business, health and education are available online. Users can search our online databases by several different search criteria, such as product categories, geographic area, sales volume and much, much more. Full Grey House catalog and online ordering also available.

4120 **www.ifi.org**
International Fabricare Institute

With its education, research, testing and professional training, IFI offers solutions that help member businesses provide expert garment care.

4121 **www.ikeca.org**
International Kitchen Exhaust Cleaning Association

Education for members about safety, cleaning techniques and many other areas. Since its inception, IKECA, a not for profit trade association, has established stringent standards and practices for contractors engaged in kitchen exhaust clening, conducted a variety of educational programs, and worked with influential code setting bodies such as the National Fire Protection Association to improve existing codes and regulations.

4122 **www.imionline.org**
International Maintenance Institute

Focuses on plant workers and vendors who have products tailored to the maintenance industry. The philosophy of the organization is to professionalize the maintenace functiuon by helping maintenace managers to work smarter through the exchange of ideas and function.

4123 **www.jriddle.com**
Riddle & Associates

For the laundering, drycleaning and textile care industry - from single-owner coin-operated laundry and drycleaning establishments to giant industrial and institutional laundries. Our management capabilities work for any type of trade show - large or small. Our experience with heavy utility shows, and shows with highly technical requirements, gives us an expertise in these areas that is difficult to find.

4124 **www.nailm.org**
National Assn of Insurance Litigation Management

National educational and research group concerned primarily with the advancement of the art of manageing litigated claims.

4125 **www.natclo.com**
National Clothesline

News of interest to drycleaners. Links to regional and state associations, calendar of events.

4126 **www.nca-i.com**
Neighborhood Cleaners Association

Professional trade association dedicated to the welfare of well-groomed consumers and the professional cleaners and suppliers who serve them. for over 50 years, NCA has been at the vanguard of education, research and information distribution concerning garment and household fabric care. Elected officials, goverment agencies, consumer groups, fashion designers and major media outlets have recognized and responded to NCA's activities, reports and tradition of excellence.

4127 **www.pwna.org**
Power Washers of North America

Developing and communicating the highest standards in ethical business practices, environmental awareness and safety through continuing education and active representation of the membership. PWNA educated and trained contractors raise the level of professionalism and value to their customers.

4128 **www.rmfa.org**
Rocky Mountain Fabricare Association

Enhancing the image and viability of the fabricare industry through education and development of the skills, talents, and professionalism of its membership.

4129 **www.sdahq.org**
Soap and Detergent Association

Nonprofit tade association representing over 100 North American manufacturers of household, industrial and institutional cleaning products; their ingredients and finished packaging. Established in 1926, SDA is dedicated to advancing public understanding of the safety and benefits of cleaning products and protecting the ability of its members to formulate products that best meet consumer needs.

4130 **www.sefa.org**
South Eastern Fabricare Association

Trade association that represents its members who have an interest in the dry cleaning and laundry industry. The not for profit asscoiation provides value through education, research, legislative representation, industry specific information programs, products and services.

4131 **www.uniforminfo.com**
Uniform & Textile Service Association

Uniform companies provide more than just corporate apparel programs. Companies on this site offer a wide variety of products and services that will not only ensure that your unique corporate identity is conveyed consistently, but will help your workplace run more smoothly.

4132 **www.utsa.com**
Uniform & Textile Service Association

One stop place for important industry and UTSA news. It has complete information on upcoming events and activities, including online meeting brochures and secure online registration. Each department at UTSA has its own page where you will find information about committees, projects, regulations, and links to dozens of other pertinent sites such as the Clean Show or government sites.

Associations

4133 Accuracy in Media
4455 Connecticut Avenue NW
Suite 330
Washington, DC 20008
202-364-4401
FAX: 202-364-4098
info@aim.org www.aim.org

Don Irvine, Chairman
Deborah Lambert, Director of Special Projects
Roger Aronoff, Executive Secretary

Nonprofit, grassroots citizens watchdog of the news media that critiques botched and bungled news stories and sets the record straight on important issues that have recieved slanted coverage.

3500 Members Founded: 1969

4134 Agricultural Communications in Education
University of Florida
Mowry Road
Building 16
Gainesville, FL 32611
352-460-0372
FAX: 358-392-7902
ace@mail.ifas.edu www.aceweb.org

Judy Winn, President
Virginia Morgan, VP
Hugh Maynard, Associate Director

Members are writers, editors, broadcasters and communicators who are involved in the dissemination of agricultural, food sciences and natural resource information in land-grant colleges, federal and state agencies, international agencies and other private communications work.

700+ Members Founded: 1970

4135 Alliance for Telecommunication Industry Solutions
1200 G Street NW
Suite 500
Washington, DC 20005-3814
202-628-6380
FAX: 202-393-5453
atispr@artis.org www.atis.org

Susan Miller, President/CEO
Kelly Weiss, Director Information Services
Bill Klein, VP Finance/Operations

Membership organization that provides the tools necessary for the industry to identify standards, guidelines and operating procedures that make the inoperability of existing and emerging telecommunications products and services possible.

1400 Members Founded: 1983

4136 American Chambers of Congress Executives Communications Council
4875 Eisenhower Avenue
Suite 250
Alexandria, VA 22304-1507
703-998-0072
FAX: 703-212-9512 800-394-2223
mfleming@acce.org www.acce.org

Mick Fleming, President
Brenda Luper, VP/CFO
Maryann Niner, Director Administration

National association uniquely serving individuals involved in the management of chambers of all sizes. Chamber executives and professionals hold positions requiring leadership, vision and strong management skills. Devoted to helping chamber executives and their staffs' play a significant leadership role ing their communities.

1300 Members Founded: 1914 5300 names

4137 American Communication Association
College of Business Administration
The University of Northern Iowa
1227 W 27th Street
Cedar Falls, IA 50614-0125
209-667-3374

pdecaro@csustan.edu
www.americancomm.org

Peter A DeCaro PhD, Executive Director
Tyrone L Adams PhD, President

Founded for the purposes of fostering research and scholarship in all areas of human communication behavior, promoting and improving excellence in the pedagogy of communication, providing a voice in communication law and policy, providing evaluation and certification services for academic programs in communication study.

Founded: 1993

4138 American Public Communications Council
625 Slater Lane
Suite 104
Alexandria, VA 22314
703-739-1322
FAX: 703-385-5301 703-739-1324
APPC@apcc.net www.apcc.net

Willard R Nichols, President
Brad Benge, Executive Director
Michael Bright, Director

The American Public Communications Council is the national trade association repesenting the owners, suppliers, and manufacturers of public communications products and services. APCC is dedicated to supporting a public communications environment that promotes the widest deployment of payphones for the use of the American public.

Founded: 1988

4139 Armed Forces Broadcasters Association
Po Box 447
Sun City, CA 92586-0447
951-672-7299
FAX: 951-679-5484

Mary Carnes, President

Enhances comaraderie among former, present, and future members of the military broadcasting community; provides employment search assistance.

600 Members Founded: 1982

4140 Armed Forces Communications and Electronic Association
4400 Fair Lakes Court
Fairfax, VA 22033
703-631-6100
FAX: 703-631-6405 800-336-4583
promo@afcea.org www.afcea.org

Tobey Jackson, Marketing/Public Relations Manger

A non-profit international association, dedicated to supporting global security by providing an ethical environment that encourages a close cooperative relationship among civil government agencies, the military and industry.

31000 Members Founded: 1946

4141 Association for Business Communication
Box B8-240, Baruch College
One Benard Baruch Way
New York, NY 10010
646-312-3727
FAX: 646-349-5297
abcrjm@cs.com www.theabc.org

Linda Beamer, First VP
Marsha Bayless, Second VP
Ken Davis, Director
Dan Dieterich, Director

International organization commited to fostering excellence in business communication scholarship, research, education, and practice.

72 Members Founded: 1935

4142 Association for Communication Administration
1765 N Street, N.W.
Washington, DC 20006
202-464-4622
FAX: 202-464-4600
www.aca.iupui.edu/cq-i/aca-info.html

Roger Smitter, Executive Director

Originally called the Association for Departments and Administrators in Speech Communication, the name and scope of the Association were changed in 1975. During its years of existance, the ACA has grown to become the most dynamic and responsive of the communication-related organizations. It has achieved this prominance by serving the needs of departmental administrators in the communication arts and sciences.

7700 Members Founded: 1972

4143 Association for Conservation Information
Division of Fish Game and Wildlife
Po Box 400
Trenton, NJ 08625-0400
609-984-0837
FAX: 609-984-1414

David Chanda, President

Works to upgrade the quality of all forms of communication in and among agencies devoted to the protection and management of natural resources and wildlife.

110 Members Founded: 1938

4144 Association for Educational Communication
1800 N Stonelake Drive
Suite 2
Bloomington, IN 47408
812-335-7675
FAX: 812-335-7678
aect@aect.org www.aect.org

Wes Miller, President
Lois Wilkins, Secretary/Treasurer
Scott Schaffer, Training Representative
Phillip Harris, Executive Director

For audiovisual and instructional materials specialists, educational technologists, audiovisual and television production personnel, school media specialists.

2200 Members Founded: 1923
Mailing list available for rent $159 per M.

4145 Association for Information Systems
Po Box 2712
Atlanta, GA 30301-2712
404-651-0348
FAX: 404-651-4938
WebMaster@ALSNe.org
www.aisnet.org

James P Tinsley, Deputy Director
Michael Myers, President

AIS members are academics with interest in information systems and related fields.
4300 Members Founded: 1994

4146 Association for Information and Image Management International
1100 Wayne Avenue
Suite 1100
Silver Spring, MD 20910
301-587-8202
FAX: 301-587-2711
aiim@aiim.org www.aiim.org

Martyn Christian, Chair
AJ Hyland, Vice Chair
MS Lee, Treasurer
Chris Ryan, Chair North American Advisory

Global authority on enterprise content management (ECM). ECM Technologies are used to create, capture, customize, deliver, and manage information to support business process.
Founded: 1943

4147 Association for Multi-Media International
PO Box 1897
Lawrence, KS 66044
866-393-4264
FAX: 785-843-1274 hq@ami.org

Vanessa Reilly, Executive Director

The professional objectives of the AMI are to promote the safety and advancement of medical illustration and allied fields of visual communication, and to promote understanding and cooperation with the medical profession and related health science professions.
1M Members Founded: 1974

4148 Association for Postal Commerce
1901 N Fort Myer Drive
Suite 401
Arlington, VA 22209-1609
703-524-0096
FAX: 703-524-1871
cmiller@postcom.org
www.postcom.org

Gene Del Polito, President

National organization representing those who use, or who support, the use of mail as a medium for communication and commerce. Publishes a weekly newsletter covering postal policy and operational issues.
231 Members Founded: 1947

4149 Association for Service Managers Internati onal
1342 Colonial Boulevard
Suite 25D
Fort Myers, FL 33907
239-275-7887
FAX: 239-275-0794 800-333-9786
afsmi@afsmi.org www.afsmi.org

John Schoenewald, CEO
James Gaidry, VP Marketing

A global organization dedicated to furthering the knowledge, understanding, and career development of executives, managers and professionals in the high technology service industry.
3000+ Members Founded: 1975

4150 Association of Federal Communications Consulting Engineers
PO Box 19333
20th Street Station
Washington, DC 20036-0333
941-329-6000
FAX: 703-591-0115 www.afcce.org

Thomas Silliman, President
Alan R Rosner, VP

An organization of professional engineering consultants serving the telecommunications industry.
250 Members Founded: 1948

4151 Association of Medical Illustrators
810 East 10th Street
Lawrence, KS 66044
866-393-4264
FAX: 785-843-1274
hq@ami.org www.ami.org

Vanessa Reilly, Executive Director
Kay Rose, Association Manager
Ethel Ford, Financial Manager

An international organization of media professionals who promote, produce and utilize a wide range of presentation media.
1M Members Founded: 1974

4152 Association of Professional Communication Consultants
211 E 28th st
Tulsa, OK 74114-3329
918-743-4793
FAX: 918-745-0932
www.consultingsuccess.org

Lee Clark Johns, President
Sana Reynolds, Secretary
Sherry Scott, Treasurer
Janet Cherry, Past President
Elizabeth Frick, Managing Editor

Professional community of communication consultants where members can increase their knowledge, grow their business and achieve high standards of professional practice. Services include professional development workshops, online newsletter and referral database and active listserve discussions.
200 Members Founded: 1982

4153 Association of Schools of Journalism and Mass Communications
234 Outlet Pointe Blvd
Columbia, SC 29210-5667
803-798-0271
FAX: 803-772-3509
aejmchq@aol.com www.asjmc.org

Jennifer McGill, Executive Director

Promotes excellence in journalism and mass communication education. Non-profit, educational association composed of some 190 JMC programs at the college level. Eight international journalism and communication schools have joined the association in recent years.
202 Members Founded: 1917

4154 Association of Teachers of Technical Writing
Graduate Studies In English
Po Box 311307
Denton, TX 76203-1307
940-565-2114

sims@unt.edu www.attw.org

Barbara Sims, Executive Secretary

Provides communication among teachers of technical writing and develops technical communications as an academic discipline.
1200 Members Founded: 1973

4155 Association of Women in Communications
780 Ritchie Highway
Suite 28S
Severna Park, MD 21146
410-544-7442
FAX: 410-544-4640
pat@womcom.org www.womcom.org

Patricia Troy, Executive Director
Mary Garner, Accounting Manager

Professional organization that champions the advancement of women across all communications disciplines by recognizing excellence, promoting leadership and positioning its members at the forefront of the evolving communications era.
120+ Members Founded: 1909

4156 Catholic Academy for Communication Arts Professionals
1645 Brook Lynn Dr
Ste # 2
Dayton, OH 45432-1933
937-458-0265
FAX: 937-458-0263
admin@catholicacademy.org
www.catholicacademy.org

Sue West, National Office Adiministrator

Affiliate of SIGNIS.
250 Members Founded: 1972

4157 Cellular Telecommunications and Internet Association
1400 16th Street, N.W.
Suite 600
Washington, DC 20036
202-785-0081
FAX: 202-785-0721 www.ctia.org

Steve Largent, President/C.E.O

The voice of the wireless industry-representing its members in a constant dialogue with policy makers in the Executive Branch, in the Federal Communications Commission, and in Congress. CTIA's industry committees provide leadership in the area of taxation, roaming, safety, regulations, fraud and technology.
396 Members Founded: 1984

4158 College Media Advisors
The University of Memphis
Memphis, TN 38152
901-678-2403
FAX: 901-678-4798
kathyl@mail.utexas.edu
www.collegemedia.org

Ron Spielberger, Executive Director
Kathy Lawrence, President
Lance Speere, VP
Kelly Wolff, VP Member Services
John Ryan, Treasurer

For supervisors and advisers of college media run by students.
800 Members Founded: 1954

4159 Columbia University: Freedom Forum Media
2950 Broadway
New York, NY 10027-7004
212-854-5047
FAX: 212-280-5726 www.iics.org

4160 Communications Fraud Control Association
3030 N. Central Avenue
Suite 707
Phoenix, AZ 85012-2715
602-265-2322
FAX: 602-265-1015
fraud@cfca.org www.cfca.org

Frances Feld, Executive Director

Representing companies and individuals in the communications industry, and agencies and professionals involved in the investigation of communication fraud, CCFA is a leading international association for communications fraud control education and information. Created to foster and promote cooperation inside and outside the communications industry regarding communications fraud control.
300 Members Founded: 1985

4161 Communications Marketing Association
PO Box 36275
Denver, CO 80227
303-988-3515
FAX: 303-988-3517
mercycontreras@comcast.net
www.commktga.com

Mercy Conteras, Executive Director

Members are independent manufacturers, independent sales representative firms and distributors of cellular and two-way radio equipment.
400 Members Founded: 1974

4162 Communications Media Management Association
20423 State Road 7
Suite F6-491
Boca Raton, FL 33498
561-988-2681

cmma@cmma.net www.cmma.net

Warren T. Harmon, President
Kelly L. Bell, VPresident

CMMA is a professional association dedicated to the professional growth of corporate, education and government communications media managers.

4163 Communications Roundtable Association
1250 24th Street NW
Suite 260
Washington, DC 20037
866-279-5172
FAX: 202-466-0544
www.roundtable.org

Michael Reichgut, Chairman

Association of more than 20 public relations, marketing, graphics, advertising, training and other communications organizations with more than 12,000 professional members. The goals include furthering professionalism, cooperation between member organizations, career and employment support, and employer assistance.
12000 Members Founded: 1991

4164 Communications Workers of America
501 Third St. N.W.
Washington, DC 20001-2797
202-434-1100
FAX: 202-434-1279 www.cwa-union.org

Morton Bahr, President

Sponsors and supports the CWA-COPE Political Action Committee.
63000 Members Founded: 1938

4165 Comp TIA Worldwide
1815 S Meyers Road
Suite 300
Oakbrook Terrace, IL 60181-5228
630-788-8320
FAX: 630-268-1384 www.comptia.org

David Smith, Chairman
Gary Gillam, Vice Chairman
Martin Bean, Secretary
Robert J Sartor, Treasurer
Robert Battistich, Director

Global information technology trade association with influence in all areas of the information technology industry.
19000 Members

4166 Computer and Communication Industry Association
666 11th Street N.W.
Washington, DC 20001-4542
202-783-0070
FAX: 202-783-0534
ccia@ccianet.org www.ccianet.org

Edward J Black, President/C.E.O
Dan Johnson, General Counsel

non-profit membership organization. Members are manufacturers and providers of computer information processing and telecommunications-related products and services. Represents the interests of its members in domestic and foreign trade.
35 Members Founded: 1972

4167 Consolidated Tape Association
C/O New York Stock Exchange
11 Wall Street, 21st Floor
New York, NY 10005
212-656-2052
FAX: 212-656-5848 phussey@nyse.com

Patricia Hussey, Administrator

Members are stock exchanges and the National Association of Securities Dealers. CTA melds the reporting of transactions from the various stock exchanges.
9 Members Founded: 1974

4168 Consortium for School Networking
1710 Rhode Island Avenue, N.W.
Suite 900
Washington, DC 20036-3007
202-861-2676
FAX: 202-861-0888 866-267-8747
membership@cosn.org www.cosn.org

Keith Krueger, CEO

Promotes the development and use of internet and information technologies for K-12 learning. Members are school districts, states, nonprofits and commercial organizations, all of whom share the goal of promoting the state of the art in computer networking technologies in schools.
450 Members Founded: 1992

4169 Cooperative Communicators Association
5307 43rd Street
Lubbock, TX 79414-1315
806-795-2783
FAX: 806-795-5289
CCA@communicators.coop
www.communicators.coop

Susie Bullock, Executive Director
Greg Brooks, Director Media/Public Relations
Chuck Lay, Board Member
Leta Mach, Board Member
Sheryl Meshke, Board Member

A teaching and news tool for the Cooperative Communicators Association, CCA consists of 310 communicators, editors, photographers, graphics, designers, public relations specialists who work for cooperatives in 35 states, Canada and Poland.
350 Members Founded: 1953

4170 Council of Communication Management
65 Enterprise
Aliso Viejo, CA 92656
949-715-6932
FAX: 949-715-6931 866-463-6226
membership@ccmconnection.com
www.ccmconnection.com

Fred Droz, Contact

Provides a network through which managers, consultants and educators, who work at the policy level in organizational communication can help one another advance the practice of communication in business.
270 Members Founded: 1955

4171 Council of Science Editors
12100 Sunset Hills Road
Suite 130
Reston, VA 20190-5202
703-437-4377
FAX: 703-435-4390
cse@councilscienceeditors.org
www.councilscience editors.org

Kathy Hoskins, Executive Director

Membership consists of individuals concerned with writing, editing and publishing in the life sciences and related fields.
1200 Members Founded: 1957

4172 Digital Media Association (DiMA)
1029 Vermont Avenue NW
Suite 850
Washington, DC 20005
202-639-9509

info@digmedia.org www.digmedia.org

Jonathan Potter, Director
Lee Knife, General Counsel

National trade organization devoted primarily to the online audio and video industries, and more generally to commercially innovative digital media opportunities.

4173 Drug Information Association
800 Enterprise Road
Suite 200
Horsham, PA 19044-3595
215-442-6100
FAX: 215-442-6199
dia@diahome.org www.diahome.org

David Maola, Executive Director
Carol E Layer, Asst Ex Director Training/Education
William Brassington, CFO
Marlynn Orlando, Worldwide Director Member Services
Lisa Zoks, Worldwide Director Mkting/Commun

Provides a neutral global forum for the exchange and dissemination of information on the discovery, development, evaluation and utilization of medicines and related health care technologies. Through these activities the DIA provides development opportunities for its members.
27000 Members Founded: 1964

4174 EDUCAUSE
1150 18th Street, N.W.
Washngton, DC 20036
202-872-4200
FAX: 202-872-4318
info@educause.edu
www.educause.edu

Brian L Hawkins, President
Mark Luker, VP

Non-profit consortium of colleges, universities and other nonprofit institutions to facilitate the introduction, use and management of information technology.
1990 Members Founded: 1962

4175 Electronic Retailing Association
2000 N. 14th Street
Suite 300
Arlington, VA 22201
703-841-1751
FAX: 703-841-1860 800-987-6462
contact@retailing.org
www.retailing.org

Barbara Tulipane, President/CEO

For companies who use the power of electronics to sell goods and services to the public. The purpose of ERA is to foster growth, development and acceptance of the rapidly growing electronic retailing industry worldwide.
400 Members Founded: 1990

4176 Energy Telecommunications and Electrical Association
5005 Royal Lane
Suite 190
Irving, TX 75063

888-503-8700
blaine@entelec.org www.entelec.org

Blain Siske, Executive Manager

Members are companies and corporations in the energy industries employing personnel having managerial, engineering or technical respnosibility in the electrical, electronics, communications and allied fields.
140 Members Founded: 1928

4177 Forest Industries Telecommunications
1565 Oak Street
Eugene, OR 97401-2200
541-485-8441
FAX: 541-485-7556

Kenton Sturdevant, Executive VP

Organized to assist the forest industry in radio matters before the FCC.
600 Members Founded: 1947

4178 Forestry Conservation Commuications Association
Po Box 3217
Gettysburg, PA 17325
717-338-1505
FAX: 717-334-5656
nfc@fcca-usa.org www.fcca-usa.org

Ralph Haller, Executive Manager

Certified by the FCC as the radio frequency coordinator for the Forestry Conservation Radio Service.
200 Members Founded: 1944

4179 Freedom Information Center
133 Neff Annex University of Missouri
Columbia, MO 65211
573-882-4856
FAX: 573-884-6204
edwardsm@missouri.edu
web.missouri.edu/~foiwww/

Kathleen Edwards, Director
Charles N Davis, Executive Director

Maintains files documenting actions by government, media and society affecting the flow and content of information. Call or write for assistance with researching media topics or instruction in using access laws.
Founded: 1958

4180 Fulfillment Services Association of America
3030 Malmo Drive
Arlington Heights, IL 60005-4728
847-364-1222
FAX: 847-364-1268

Frederick J Herzog, Executive Vice President

Formerly Association of Publishing and fulfillment services.
1450 Members Founded: 1986

4181 Graphic Communications Association
1421 Prince St.
Suite 230
Alexandria, VA 22314-2806
703-371-1060
FAX: 703-548-2867
info@gca.org www.idealliance.org

Chuck Myers, Chair
Ann Marie Bushell, Vice Chair
Dan Minnick, Secretary/Treasurer
David J Steinhardt, President
Sharon Adler, Director

Promotes the interests of graphic communication professionals.
300 Members Founded: 1966

4182 Graphic Communications International Union
1900 L Street NW
Washington, DC 20036-3004
202-462-1400
FAX: 202-721-0600 800-331-5706

George Tedeschi, President
Gerald H Deneau, Secretary/Treasurer
Lawrence Martinez, VP
Duncan K Brown, VP
David A Grabhorn, VP

Combines three independent shows: Printing XPO, Type-X, and Art-X and gives you a complete overview of the most recently introduced technologies and the newest information in the field of graphic arts.
15000 Members Founded: 1983

4183 Health Industry Business Communications Council
2525 East Arizona Biltmore Circle
Suite 127
Phoenix, AZ 85016
602-381-1091
FAX: 602-381-1093
info@hibcc.org www.hibcc.org

Robert A Hankin PhD, President
Sara Polansky, Director Communications

An industry-sponsored nonprofit council which was organized by major health care associations initially to develop a standard for data transfer using uniform bar code labeling, and later as the focal point for many other electronic data interchange standards.
12000 Members Founded: 1984

4184 Industrial Telecommunications Association
8484 Westport Drive
Suite 630
McLean, VA 22102
703-528-5115
FAX: 703-524-1074 800-482-8282
sharpe@enterprisewireless.org
www.ita-relay.com

Mark Crosby, President/CEO
Andre Cote, Senior VP
Howard Levitas, CIO
Karin L Norton, VP Administrations
Donald J Vasek, Executive Director

An FCC-certified frequency advisory committee and national trade association that represents the interests of private wireless industry.
3100 Members Founded: 1953

4185 Information Systems Consultants
4131 Idlevale Drive
Tucker, GA 30084
770-491-1500
800-832-7767

Nonprofit organization of small businesses and individuals providing consulting services to all industries and government.
350 Members Founded: 1986

4186 Instructional Telecommunications Council
One Dupont Circle
Suite 360
Washington, DC 20036-1143
202-720-0060
FAX: 202-822-5014
www.itcnetwork.org

Jon Clements, Owner
Christine Mullins, Executive Director

Members are educators and organizations involved in higher education instructional telecommunications and distance learning
500 Members Founded: 1977

4187 Interactive Multimedia and Collaborative Communications Association
PO Box 756
Syosset, NY 11797-0756
516-818-8184
FAX: 516-922-2170 www.imcca.org

Carol Zelkin, Executive Director

Provides a clearinghouse for the exchange of information between users, researchers, and providers in the field of teleconferencing.
1000 Members Founded: 1982

4188 International Association of Audio Visual Communicators
57 West Palo Verde Avenue
PO Box 250
Ocotillo, CA 92259-0250
760-358-7000
FAX: 760-358-7569
sheemonw@cindys.com
www.iaavc.org

Sheemon Wolfe, Contact

Members are audio-visual professionals using the media of film, video, slides, filmstrips, multi-image and interactive media to communicate information
5200 Members Founded: 1957

4189 International Association of Business Communicators
One Hallidie Plaza
Suite 600
San Francisco, CA 94102
415-544-4700
FAX: 415-544-4747 800-776-4222
service_centre@iabc.com
www.iabc.com

Stephanie M Griffiths, Chair
David C Kistle, Vice Chair
Janice J Thibodeau, Finance Director
Marissa Winstanley, Director Business Development
Lee Anne Snedeker, VP Membership

International knowledge network for professionals engaged in stategic business communication mangement.
13,00 Members Founded: 1982

4190 International Communications Association
1730 Rhode Island Avenue NW
Suite 300
Washington, DC 20036
202-530-9855
FAX: 202-530-9851
icahdq@icahdq.org www.icahdq.org

Wolfgang Donsbach, President/Chair
Jon F Nussbaum, President-Elect
Joseph Cappella, Finance Chairman

International association for scholars interested in the study, teaching and application of all aspects of human mediated communication. ICA began more than 50 years ago as a small association of US reseachers and has matured into a truly international association with more than 3,500 members in 65 countries.
3400+ Members Founded: 1950

4191 International Communications Industry Association
11242 Waples Mill Road
Suite 200
Fairfax, VA 22030
703-273-7200
FAX: 703-278-8082 www.infocomm.org

Harald Thiel, Chairman
Scott Walker, President
Randy Lemke, Executive Director

Centers on the technologies, products and systems for visual display, audio reproduction, video and audio production, interfacing and signal distribution, lighting, control systems, interactive display and audio presentation systems, remote video and web conferencing.

4192 International Digital Enterprise Alliance
1421 Prince St.
Suite 230
Alexandria, VA 22314-2805
703-837-1070
FAX: 703-837-1072
webmaster@idealliance.org
www.idealliance.org

David Steinhardt, President/CEO
Frank Balser, Managing Director

IDEAlliance programs and activities enable its members to strengthen their staff skills, participate in the development of standards, influence the development of tools and technologies, develop strategies and partnerships to deploy technology solutions, and position themselves as industry leaders.
200 Members Founded: 1966

4193 International Documentary Association
1201 West 5th Street
Suite M320
Los Angeles, CA 90017-1461
213-534-3600
FAX: 213-534-3610
info@documentary.org
www.documentary.org

Sandra J Ruch, Executive Director/Publisher
Maria Arzola, Membership Coordinator

A non-profit association to promote non-fiction film and video, to support the efforts of documentary film and video makers around the world and to increase public appreciation and demand for documentary film and television programs.
2700 Members Founded: 1982
Mailing list available for rent 2800 names $250 per M.

4194 International Interactive Communications Society
10160 SW Nimbus Avenue
Portland, OR 97223-4338
503-968-9210
FAX: 503-620-7857
worldhq@iics.org www.iste.org

Debra Palm, Managing Director

Association of communications industry professionals dedicated to the advancement of interactive technologies. Provides a forum to share ideas, applications and techniques for effective use of interactive media.
3000 Members Founded: 1983
Mailing list available for rent 8000 names

4195 International Regional Magazine Association
1320 E University Avenue
Georgetown, TX 78626
512-819-9500
FAX: 512-863-7148
us002848@mindspring.com
www.regionalmagazines.org

Kit Parker, President
Cathy Murphy CMP, VP
Letitia Pollard, Director
Joan Henderson, Director
Kelly Roberson, Treasurer

Formed in 1960, IRMA provides a forum for regional magazine publishers to exchange ideas with the view to improving their respective publications.
250-3 Members Founded: 1960

4196 International Society for Technology in Education
175 W Broadway
Ste 300
Eugene, OR 97401-3042
541-023-3770
FAX: 541-302-3778 800-336-5191
iste@iste.org www.iste.org

Jan Van Dam, President
Leslie Conery, Manager
Chuck Chulvick, Secretary

A large nonprofit organization serving the technology-using educator.
10000 Members Founded: 1979

4197 International Society of Business
7159 Navajo Road
San Diego, CA 92119-1606
619-687-3450

Audio and videotape professionals.
Founded: 1983

4198 Internet Society
1775 Wiehle Avenue
Suite 102
Reston, VA 20190-5108
703-326-9880
FAX: 703-326-9881
info@isoc.org www.isoc.org

Lyn St Amour, President/CEO

Members are technologists, developers, educators, researchers, government representatives, business people and other with an interest in internet technologies and applications.
20000 Members Founded: 1992

4199 Land Mobile Communications Council
8484 Westpark Drive
Suite 630
McLean, VA 22102-5117
703-528-5115
FAX: 703-524-1074
donald.vasek@enterprisewireless.org
www.lmcc.org

Ralph Haller, President
Al Ittner, VP

The Land Mobile Communications Council is a nonprofit association of organizations representing land mobile radio carriers and manufactureres equipment. LMCC membership is comprised of organizations representing diverse telecommunications sectors such as public safety, industrial/ land transportation, private radio, specialized mobile radio and critical infrastructure.
21 Members Founded: 1967

4200 Media Alliance
1904 Franklin St
Ste 500
Oakland, CA 94612-2926
510-329-9000
FAX: 415-546-6218
www.media-alliance.org

Jeff Perlstein, Executive Director

A nonprofit training and resource center for media workers, community organizations and political activists.

4201 Media Communications Association International
7600 Terrace Avenue
Suite 203
Middleton, WI 53562
698-827-5034
FAX: 608-831-5122
info@mca-i.org www.mca-i.org

Emma Justice, President
Susan Rees, Executive Director

Global community that provides its members opportunities for networking, learning and career advancement. Members work in video, film, collaborative communication, distance learning, web design and creation, and all forms of interactive visual communication, along with associated crafts; serving businesses, nonprofit organizations, the government, educational institutions, the medical field, and electronic media. Chapters are throughout the US, with affiliates in Asia and Europe.
Founded: 1968

4202 **Media Research Directors Association**
Ogilvy and Mather
309 W 49th Street
New York, NY 10019-7316
212-375-5502
www.mrda.org
Provides support for research and maintains library.

4203 **NASTD-Telecommunications and Technology Professionals Serving State Gov't**
PO Box 11910
2760 Research Park Drive
Lexington, KY 40578-1910
859-244-8186
FAX: 859-244-8001 www.nastd.org
Jack Ries, President
Concerned with providing a forum for the exchange of ideas and practices and the development of a unified position on matters of national telecommunications policy and regulatory issues.
1000 Members Founded: 1978

4204 **National Association for Community Mediation**
1527 New Hampshire Avenue NW
Washington, DC 20036-1206
202-832-2512
FAX: 202-667-8629
nafcm@nafcm.org www.nafcm.org
Joanne Galindo, Senior Director
Irvin Foster, Executive Director
Erika Acera, Manager Membership/Programs
Supports the maintenance and growth of community-based mediation program and processes: presents a compelling voice in appropriate policy-making, legislative, professional, and other arenas; and encourages the development and sharing of resources for these efforts.
779 Members Founded: 1994

4205 **National Association for Multi-Ethnicity in Communications**
336 West 37th Street
Suite 302
New York, NY 10018
212-594-5985
FAX: 212-594-8391
info@namic.com www.namic.com
Kathy A Johnson, Executive Vice President
Works for the cause of diversity in the telecommunications industry.
200 Members Founded: 1980

4206 **National Association of Air Medical Communication Specialists**
PO Box 28
Otis Orchards, WA 99027-0028
877-396-2227
FAX: 877-396-2227 www.naacs.org
Allan Adler, President
Not for profit professional organization whose mission is to represent the air medical communications specialist on a national level through education, standardization and recognition.
200 Members

4207 **National Association of Aircraft and Communicstion Suppliers**
4301 Connecticut Avenue NW
Suite 453
Washington, DC 20008
202-237-0505
FAX: 202-237-7566
info@naacs.org www.naacs.org
John J Fausti, Executive Director
A national organization of small business who regularly purchase military surplus aircraft and electronics parts from the US Department of Defense.
120 Members

4208 **National Association of Hispnic Publications**
529 14th Street NW
Suite 1085
Washington, DC 20045
202-240-0566
FAX: 202-662-7251
info@nahp.org www.nahp.org
Thomas Oliver, Executive Director/CEO
Rex Nutting, Manager
Founded in the belie that the most effective way to reach the more than 29 million Hispanic Americans in the country is their own language.
234 Members Founded: 1982

4209 **National Association of Media Women**
1185 Niskey Lake Road SW
Atlanta, GA 30331-7229
404-344-5862
www.nawbo-sf.org
Xerona Brady, Executive Director
Sponsors studies, research and seminars to find solutions to problems and create opportunities for women. Presents annual awards.
300 Members Founded: 1965

4210 **National Association of Telecommunications Officers and Advisers**
1800 Diagonal Road
Suite 495
Alexandria, VA 22314
703-519-8035
FAX: 703-519-8036
info@natoa.org www.natoa.org
Libby Beaty, Executive Director
A national association that represents the telecommunication needs and interests of local governments, and those who advise local governments.
800 Members Founded: 1980

4211 **National Cable and Telecommunications Association**
1724 Massachusetts Avenue NW
Washington, DC 20036-1969
202-753-3595
FAX: 202-775-3692 www.ncta.com
Robert Sachs, President/CEO
David Krone, Executive VP
Rob Stoddard, Sr VP Communications/Public Affairs
Eleanor Winter, VP Special Projects
Barbara Yok, Chief Administrative Officer
Members are cable TV systems; associate members are manufacturers, distributors, suppliers of hardware, programmers and other services
3189 Members Founded: 1952

4212 **National Communication Association**
1765 N Street NW
Washington, DC 20036
202-464-4622
FAX: 202-464-460 www.natcom.org
Roger Smitter, Executive Director
Sherry Morreale, Associate Director
Donna Porter, Coordinator Meetings
Members are teachers at all levels and in all aspects of communication arts aons consultants,students,libraries and persons in theatre production
7000 Members Founded: 1914

4213 **National Council of Writing Program Administrators**
Department of English
Miami University
Oxford, OH 45056
513-529-5221
FAX: 513-529-1392
www.wpacouncil.org
John Tassoni
National organization that fosters professional development, communication and community among college and university writing progrma administrators and other interested faculty.
700 Members Founded: 1975

4214 **National Federation Abstracting & Information Services**
1518 Walnut Street
Suite 1004
Philadelphia, PA 19102-3402
215-893-1561
FAX: 215-893-1564
nfais@nfais.org www.nfais.org
Bonnie Lawlor, Executive Director
Jill O'Neill, Director Planning/Communications
Linda Beebe, President
Terence Ford, Secretary
Serves those groups that aggregate, organize, and facilitate access to information. To improve member capabilities and contribute to their ongoing success. Provides opportunities for education, advocacy, and a forum to address common interests.
52 Members Founded: 1958
Printed in on matte stock

4215 **National Speakers Association**
1500 S Priest Drive
Tempe, AZ 85281
480-968-2552
FAX: 480-968-0911
information@nsaspeaker.org
www.nsaspeaker.org
Scott Friedman, President
Rick Jakle, VP
Stacy Tetschner, Manager
Dulce de Leon, Manager Public Relations
The leading organization for experts who speak professionally. NSA's 4000 members include experts in a variety of industries and disciplines, who reach audiences as trainers, educators, humorists, motivators, consultants, authors and more. NSA provides resources and education designed to advance the skills, integrity, and value of its members and speaking profession. NSA the voice of the speaking profession.
3500 Members Founded: 1973 3400 names $500 per M.

4216 National Systems Contractors Association
625 First Street SE
Suite 420
Cedar Rapids, IA 54201
319-366-6722
FAX: 319-366-4164 800-446-6722
jquint@nsca.org www.nsca.org

Chuck Wilson, Executive Director
Kim Doyle, VP Communications
Jeff Quint, Executive VP

The leading not for profit association representing the commercial electronic systems industry. Also a powerful advocate of all who work within the low voltage industry, including systems contractors/integrators, product manufacturers, consultants, sales representatives, a growing number of architects, specifying engineers and others.
2800 Members Founded: 1980

4217 National Translator Association
5611 Kendall Court
Suite 2
Arvada, CO 80002
303-465-5742
FAX: 303-465-4067
stcl@attbi.com
www.tvfmtranslators.com

Byron St. Clair, President
Kent Parsons, VP
Paul Burkholder, Secretary/Treasurer
Arnold Cruze, Director
Dave Sunderman, Director

Dedicated to the preservation of free over-the-air TV in all geographical areas. It works to improve the technology of rebroadcast translators and regulatory climate which governs them. It continously promotes the concept of universal free over-the-air TV and reprsents the ineterests of translator operators before the FCC and other government agencies such as the Forest Service and the Bureau of Land Management. Membership is open to all individuals and organizations that are interested.
Founded: 1967

4218 Networking Institute
505 Waltham Street
West Newton, MA 02465-1928
617-653-3340
FAX: 617-965-2341
info@netage.com www.netage.com

Jessica Lipnack, CEO/Co-Founder
Bruce Bedford, Director
Carrie Kuempel, Director Training
Rich Carpenter, Strategy Advisor

Promotes networks to help people work together. Offers consulting services, educational workshops and seminars. To order: The Age of the Network and The TeamNet Factor call Oliver Wright productions at 800-343-0625.
Founded: 1998

4219 Newspaper Association of America
1921 Gallows Road
Suite 600
Vienna, VA 22182
703-021-1600
FAX: 703-902-1600 www.naa.org

P Anthony Ridder, Chairman
Gregg K Jones, Vice Chairman
Jay R Smith, Secretary
Boisfeuillet Jones, Treasurer
James Abbott, Vice President

Promotes the interests of the newspaper business.
2000 Members Founded: 1992

4220 North American Serials Interest Group
2103 North Decatur Road
PMB 214
Decatur, GA 30033-5305

info@nasig.org www.nasig.org

Joyce Tenney, Secretary

An independent organiation taht promotes communication and sharing of ideas among all members of the serials information chain- anyone working with or concerned about serial publications.
1200 Members Founded: 1985

4221 Organization for the Promotion and Advance Ment of Small Telecommunications Co
21 Dupont Circle NW
Suite 700
Washington, DC 20036-1109
202-332-2775
FAX: 202-659-4619
kkr@opastco.org www.opastco.org

John N Rose, President
Lora Magruder, Director Membership
Kathleen Kelley Riesett, Director Education/Events
Martha Silver, Director Public Relations
Michael Viands, Director Finance

Protects the interests of small, rural, independent commercial telephone companies and cooperatives that have less than 50,000 access lines.
675 Members Founded: 1963

4222 PCIA- The Wireless Industry Association
500 Montgomery Street
Suite 700
Alexandria, VA 22314-1561
703-739-0300
FAX: 703-836-1608 800-759-0300
andrewd@pcia.com www.pcia.com

Don Andrew, Manager Of Operations
Andrea Burns, Director Gov't Relations
Connie Durcksak, Sr Director Industry/Gov't Relation
Rick Harris, Sr Director Press/Public Relations

Represents companies that develop, own, manage and operate towers, commercial rooftops and other facilities for the provision of all types of wireless, broadcasting and telecommunications services.
3000 Members Founded: 1949

4223 Personal Achievement Institute
1 Speaking Success Road
Kingman, AZ 86402-6543
928-753-7546
FAX: 928-753-7554 800-321-1225
burt@burtdubin.com
www.speakingsuccess.com

Burt Dubin

Education that provides advice and business strategies for both novices and experts in mastering the field of professional speaking. Free monthly newsletter is accessible through Website.
Founded: 1978
Printed in 1 color on matte stock

4224 Portable Computer and Communications Association
PO Box 680
Hood River, OR 97031
541-490-5140
FAX: 419-831-4779
gk@gorge.net www.pcca.org

Gloria Kowalski, Director

Represents firms, organizations, and individuals interested in moblie communications.
65 Members

4225 Railway Systems Suppliers
9304 New LaGrange Road
Suite 200
Louisville, KY 40240
502-327-7774
FAX: 502-327-0541
rssi@rssi.org www.rssi.org

Donald F Remaley, Executive Director

A trade association serving the communication and signal segment of the rail transportation industry. Primary activity is to organize and manage a trade show for its members to exhibit their products and services.
250 Members Founded: 1906

4226 Real Estate Information Professionals Association
PO Box 3159
Durham, NC 27715-3159
919-383-0044
FAX: 919-383-0035
reipa@reipa.org www.reipa.org

Mike Borden, Executive Director

Supports professional information providers in the real estate industry.
110 Members Founded: 1995

4227 Religious Communication Association
Department of Communication
Weber St University
Ogden, UT 84409
801-626-7455
FAX: 801-626-7956 bjohns@weber.edu

Dennis Lee Bailey, Executive Secretary

An academic society of individuals interested in the study of all aspects of public religious communication, members include teachers, students, clergy, broadcasters and other scholars and professionals.
210 Members Founded: 1973

4228 Republican Communications Association
PO Box 550
Washington, DC 20515-1

Sponsors professional development and networking programs. Conducts seminars, briefings, and tours.
165 Members Founded: 1970

4229 Satellite Broadcasting and Communications Association
225 Reinekers Lane
Suite 600
Alexandria, VA 22314
703-549-6990
FAX: 703-549-7640 800-541-5981
info@sbca.org www.sbca.com

Richard DalBello, President
Camille Osborne, Director Communications

The national trade organization representing all segments of the satellite industry. It is committed to expanding the utilization of satellite technology for the broadcast delivery of video, audio, data, music, voice, interactive and broadband services.
100 Members Founded: 1986

4230 Society for Technical Communication
901 N Stuart Street
Suite 904
Arlington, VA 22203-1854
703-522-4114
FAX: 703-522-2075
stc@stc.org www.stc.org

Suzanna Laurent, President
Paula R Berger, First VP
Linda Oestreich, Second VP
Rob Moran, Executive Director

Seeks to advance the theory and practice of technical communication in all media. Presents awards and sponsors high school writing contests.

19000 Members Founded: 1953
Mailing list available for rent 9000 names $120 per M.

4231 Society for Visual Anthropology
University of Waterloo Dept of Anthropology
519-885-1221
www.societyforvisualanthropology.org

Anne Zeller, President

Promotes the study of visual representation and media. Members are involved in all aspects of production, dissemination, and analysis of visual forms.

570 Members Founded: 1984

4232 Society of Satellite Professionals International
NY Information and Technology Center
55 Broad Street 14th Floor
New York, NY 10004
212-809-5199
FAX: 212-825-0075
tbond@sspi.org www.sspi.org

Robert Bell, Executive Director
Louis Zacharilla, Director Development

Members are individuals in the fields of businesss, education, entertainment, media, science and industry who share common interests in satellite technology.

1700 Members Founded: 1983

4233 Society of Telecommunications Consultants
13275 State Hwy 89
Po Box 70
Old Station, CA 96071
530-335-7313
FAX: 530-335-7360 800-782-7670
stchdq@stcconsultants.org
www.stcconsultants.org

Cathy Cimaglia, Administrative Manager

International organization of independent telecommunications and informations technology consultants who serve clients in business and government

200 Members Founded: 1976

4234 Telecommunications Benchmarking International Group
4606 FM 1960 West
Suite 250
Houston, TX 77069
281-440-5044
FAX: 281-440-6677 888-739-8244
tbig@benchmarkingnetwork.com
www.tbig.org

Mark T Czarnecki, President

An association of contact center professionals within telecommunications companies dedicated to providing members with an opportunity to identify, document and establish best practices through benchmakring to increase value, effiencies, and profits.

3500+ Members Founded: 1996

4235 Telecommunications Industry Association
2500 Wilson Boulevard
Suite 300
Arlington, VA 22201
703-907-7700
FAX: 703-907-7727 www.tiaonline.org

Matt Flanigan, President

TIA represents providers of communications and information technology products and services for the global marketplace through its core competencies in standards development, domestic and international advocacy, as well as market development and trade promotion programs.

4236 Toastmasters International
PO Box 9052
Mission Viejo, CA 92690-9052
949-858-8255
FAX: 949-858-1207
www.toastmasters.org

Ted Cocoran, President
Jon Greiner, Senior VP
Dilip Abayasekara, Second VP
Johnny Uy, Third VP
Donna Groh, Executive Director

Publishes educational articles on the subjects of communication and leadership. Topics include language, listening, humor, self-improvement, goal setting, success and logical thinking.

19500 Members Founded: 1924

4237 United States Internet Service Providers
1330 Connecticut Avenue NW
Washington, DC 20036
202-862-3816
FAX: 202-261-0604
kdean@steptoe.com www.usispa.org

Kate Dean, Contact

Will serve both as the ISP community's representative during policy debates and as a forum in which members can share information and develop best practices for handling specific legal matters.

7 Members Founded: 1991

4238 United Telecom Council
1901 Pennsylvania Avenue NW
5th Floor
Washington, DC 20006
202-872-0030
FAX: 202-872-1331 800-900-4882
bill.moroney@utc.org www.utc.org

William R Moroney, President/CEO
Jill Lyon, VP and General Counsel

Represents organizations using telecommunications in their operations before various federal and state legislative and regulatory agencies, particularly the FCC

1500 Members Founded: 1948

4239 Utility Communicaotrs International
229 E. Ridgewood Road
Georgetown, TX 78628
512-869-1313
FAX: 512-864-7203
eboardman@att.net
www.uci-online.com

Elliot Boardman, Executive Director

International organization comprimsed of advertising, public relations and marketing professionals from electric, gas and water utilities, energy companies, telephone companies, advertising and public relations agencies, and suppliers who communicate for and about the utility and energy industries.

400 Members Founded: 1922

4240 Wireless Communications Association International
1333 H Street NW
Suite 700W
Washington, DC 20005
202-452-7823
FAX: 202-452-0041
angela@wcai.com www.wcai.com

Andrew T Kreig, President/CEO
Rose DiMartino, Controller
Soraya Fuentes, Office Manager
Horacio A Oyhanarte, Director International Affairs
Angela Wagner, Director Web/IT Services

Non-profit trade and professional association for the Wireless Broadband industry with member compaines on six continents representing the bulk of the sector's leading carriers, vendors and consultants.

250 Members Founded: 1987

4241 Wireless Dealers Association
9746 Tappenbeck Drive
Houston, TX 77055
713-467-0077
800-624-6918
topbox@wirelessindustry.com
www.wirelessindustry.com

Bob Hutchinson, President

Business association made up of cellular and wireless communications agents, dealers, resellers, carriers, manufacturers, distributors and importers.

2500 Members Founded: 1986

4242 Women in Cable and Telecommunications
14555 Avlon Parkway
Suite 250
Chantilly, VA 20151
703-234-9807
FAX: 703-817-1595
rpearson@wict.org www.wict.org

Parthavi Das, Director Research/Advocacy
Robin Pearson, VP Director Development
Robin Burke Zahory, Director Membership/ChapterRelation

Provides opportunitites for leadership, networking, and advocacy in the industry.

4600 Members Founded: 1979

4243 World Teleport Association
NY Information and Technology Center
55 Broad Street 14th Fllor
New York, NY 10004
212-825-0218
FAX: 212-825-0075
lzacharilla@worldteleport.org
www.worldteleport.org

Robert Bell, Executive Director
China Blue, Manager Member Services
Louis Zacharilla, Director Development

Promotes the understanding, development, and use of eleports as a means to achieve economic, political and social progress locally, regionally and worldwide.

606 Members Founded: 1985

4244 **Writers Research Group LLC**
8801 S Kentucky Avenue
PO Box 891568
Oklahoma City, OK 73159
405-681-5074
FAX: 405-685-3390
info@writersresearchgroup.com
www.writersresearchgroup.com
Karen Tingle, Executive Director
Lori Packwood, Executive Director
Writers Research Group is a professional writing and research firm. Our knowledgeable employees gather, examine, edit, and compile data to your company's specifications. Our services include research, writing, directory listing updates and new entries, indexing, copyediting, proofreading, data entry, document markup and permissions negotiations.
Founded: 1999

Newsletters

4245 **411 Newsletter**
United Communications Group
11300 Rockville Pike
Suite 1100
Rockville, MD 20852-3030
301-287-2700
FAX: 301-816-8945
Doug O'Boyle, Publisher
Jim Sweeney, Editor
Business newsletter for professionals in the communications industry. *$339.00*
Founded: 1977

4246 **AV Guide**
Scranton Gillette Communications
380 E Northwest Highway
Suite 200
Des Plaines, IL 60016-2282
847-298-6622
FAX: 847-390-0408 www.spcpubs.com
Natalie Fergusan, Editor
Provides practical information on audio-visual products and new methods of using learning media. *$15.00*
4 pages Monthly Founded: 1921
Circulation: 500

4247 **Business Publisher**
JK Publishing
3105 N Newhall Street
Milwaukee, WI 53211
414-332-1625
FAX: 414-332-0916
John Kenney, Editor
Jean O'Brien, Circulation Manager
Offers information and full coverage of the magazine and business/trade publishing industry. *$335.00*
8 pages BiWeekly

4248 **CMA Newsletter**
College Media Advisers
University
#300
Memphis, TN 38152
512-471-5084
FAX: 901-678-4798
http://www.collegemedia.org
Ken Rosenauer, Publisher
Provides news and information to those who advise/supervise college media run by students (i.e. newspapers, magazines, yearbooks, radios, and TV stations). *$60.00*
6 pages Founded: 1954
Circulation: 750

4249 **Cantu's Newsletter**
Cantu's Comedy Newsletter
PO Box 210495
San Francisco, CA 94121
415-668-2402

info1@HumorMall.com
http://www.humormall.com
John Cantu, Publisher
Articles of interest to public speakers, writers, comedians, comedy writers. *$29.95*
Founded: 1999
Circulation: 3000

4250 **Chamber Executive**
Communications
4875 Eisenhower Avenue
Suite 250
Alexandria, VA 22304
703-998-0072
FAX: 703-212-9512
clada@acce.org http://www.acce.org
Greg Roth, Editor
Mick Fleming, CEO
Catherine Lada, Editor -in-Chief
Newsletter aimed at management level communications professionals. *$99.00*
12 pages Founded: 1914
Printed in 4 colors on matte stock

4251 **Classified Communications Newsletter**
833 alpha lane
Prescott, AZ 86303-4177
928-778-6788
classa@northlink.com
Agnes Franz, Publisher
Information and ad-writing tips for small budget advertisers. Both display and word classifieds addressed. Will also review books on advertising and marketing. *$35.00*
8 pages Monthly Founded: 1989
Circulation: 2000 1,000 names
Printed in 2 colors on glossy stock

4252 **Communication Briefings**
1101 King Street
Suite 110
Alexandria, VA 22314-2944
703-780-7194
FAX: 703-684-2136
customerservice@briefings.com
http://www.combriefings.com
William G Dugan, Group Publisher
Susan Marshall, Executive Editor
Lois Willingham, Marketing Manager
Charles Blakeney, Owner
This newsletter provides subscribers with communications ideas and techniques to use to persuade clients, and motivate employees. *$79.00*
8 pages Monthly Founded: 1981
Circulation: 55000

4253 **Communications Business Daily**
Warren Communications News
2115 Ward Ct NW
Washington, DC 20037

FAX: 202-318-8350 800-771-9202
Albert Warren, Chairman, Editor & Publisher
R Michael Feazel, Managing Editor
Founded: 1945

4254 **Communications Concepts**
Communication Concepts
508 Millstone Drive
Beavercreek, OH 45434-5840
937-426-8600
FAX: 937-429-3811
cci.dayton@pobox.com
http://www.communication-concepts.com/

Rodger Southworth, CEO
Ideas and methods for professional communications.

4255 **DBS Report**
Kagan World Media
One Lower Ragsdale Drive
Building One, Suite 130
Monterey, CA 93940-8746
831-624-1536
FAX: 831-625-3225 800-307-2529
info@kagan.com
http://www.kagan.com
Robin Flynn, VP *$1045.00*
Monthly Founded: 1969

4256 **Daily Deal**
Vicki King
105 Madison Avenue
New York, NY 10016
212-313-9200
FAX: 212-545-8442 888-667-3325
customerservice@thedeal.com
http://www.thedeal.com
Ed Paisley, Managing Editor
Kevin Worth, President/CEO
Vicki King, Publisher
Robert Teitelman, Editor-in-Chief
Emily Griste, Marketing Director
Reports and analyzes all the aspects of the booming, high stakes world of the deal economy. Areas of coverage include mergers and aquisitions, private equity, venture capital and bankruptcies. *$498.00*
26 pages Daily Founded: 1999
Circulation: 40893

4257 **Emerging Media Report**
Knight MediaCom International
97 Sparkill Avenue
Tappan, NY 10983-2210
845-365-1270
FAX: 845-365-1271 800-707-0470
rknight@knightmedia.com
http://www.knightmedia.com
Ron Knight, Editor
Covers VR, TV, CD, PC, and entertainment marketing.
Founded: 1978

4258 **INTRANETS Newsletter**
Information Today
143 Old Marlton Pike
Medford, NJ 08055-8750
609-654-6266
FAX: 609-654-4309
custserv@infotoday
www.infotoday.com
Thomas Hogan, Publisher/President
Lauree Padgett, Editorial Services Manager
Inge Coffey, Circulation Manager
Covers strategies, tips, and tools required to help organizations develop, deploy, and manage intranest, extranets, portals, and other knowledge adnd information management initiatives. *$149.95*
Bi Monthly

4259 Information Advisor
Information Today
143 Old Marlton Pike
Medford, NJ 08055-8750
609-654-6266
FAX: 609-654-4309
custserv@infotoday
www.infotoday.com

Robert Berkman, Editor

Provides comprehensive evlauation of research tools, timely and specific information you will use, new sources valuable to researchers and head to head analysis of the most popular information services. *$165.00*

Monthly

4260 Information Broker
Burwell Enterprises
5619 Plumtree Drive
Dallas, TX 75252
972-331-1951
FAX: 972-733-1951
helen@burwellinc.com
www.burwellinc.com

Helen Burwell, Publisher
Jeanne Paulino, Marketing Director

Covers fee-based information services for practitioners and users of information services. Accepts advertising. *$40.00*

12 pages Bi-Monthly
Circulation: 500
Printed in 1 color on matte stock

4261 Intercom
Society for Technical Communication
901 N Stuart Street
Suite 904
Arlington, VA 22203-1822
703-522-4114
FAX: 703-522-2075
stc@stc.org http://www.stc.org

Peter R Herbst, Publisher
Anita Dosik, Publications Director
Maurice P. Martin, Editor
Antoinette DeSalvo, Marketing Coordinator
Suzanna Laurent, President

A monthly magazine offering Society members with information and articles on communication industry trends and activities. *$95.00*

Founded: 1957
Circulation: 20000 1000 names $120 per M.

4262 Lifestyle Media-Relations Reporter

InfoCom Group
5900 Hollis Street
Suite L
Emeryville, CA 94608-2098
510-533-3035
FAX: 510-596-9331 800-959-1059
bulldogrep@aol.com
http://www.infocomgroup.com

James Sinkinson, Publisher
Jim Sinkinson, Presiden

This newsletter offers information on media placement in lifestyle and consumer media. *$369.00*

Monthly Founded: 1980

4263 MAPNetter
Architecture Technology Corporation
9971 Valley View Road
Eden Prairie, MN 55344
952-829-5864
FAX: 952-829-5871

Kenneth Thurber, Publisher

Monthly newsletter covering important developments in the field of factory communication systems. *$432.00*

12 pages Monthly Founded: 1981

4264 MIN: Media Industry Newsletter
Phillips Business Information
305 Madison Avenue
Suite 4417
New York, NY 10165-0006

FAX: 212-983-5144

Ellen Stuhlman, Publisher

This newsletter reports developments in the media and advertising industries. *$345.00*

8 pages Weekly

4265 MRC Cyberalert
Media Research Center
325 S Patrick Street
Alexandria, VA 22314-3580
703-683-9733
FAX: 703-683-9736 800-672-1423
mrc@mediaresearch.org
http://www.mediaresearch.org

LB Bozell III, President
Brent Baker, Editor

A news-daily report which documents and exposes liberal media bias. MRC is the nation's leading media watchdog. *$29.00*

Monthly Founded: 1987
Circulation: 13000 : HTML

4266 Marketing Library Services
Information Today
143 Old Marlton Pike
Medford, NJ 08055-8750
609-654-6266
FAX: 609-654-4309
custserv@infotoday
www.infotoday.com

Thomas Hogan, Publisher/President
Lauree Padgett, Editorial Services Manager
Inge Coffey, Circulation Manager

Provides information professional in all types of libraries with specfic ideas for marketing their services. *$79.95*

Bi Monthly

4267 Marketing New Media
Kagan World Media
One Lower Ragsdale Drive
Building One, Suite 130
Monterey, CA 93940-8746
831-624-1536
FAX: 831-625-3225 800-307-2529
info@kagan.com
http://www.kagan.com

George Niesen, Editor
Tom Johnson, Marketing Manager

News of the Marketing New Media. Three month trial available. *$795.00*

Monthly Founded: 1878

4268 Media Access
WGBH Educational Foundation
PO Box 200
Boston, MA 02134-1008
617-300-2000
FAX: 617-300-1032
ncam@wgbh.org
http://www.wgbh.org

Henry Becteon, President
Jaenne Hopkins, VP

Includes information on NCAM's research and development projects, which strive to make media and technology accessible to disabled populations.

2 pages Founded: 1951
Circulation: 15000
Printed in 2 colors on matte stock

4269 Media Business News
Summitt Media International
50 S Steele Street
Suite 700
Denver, CO 80209-2812
720-941-1000

Paul Maxwell, Publisher

Up-to-date business and financial news in the communications and media industry.

20 pages Monthly

4270 Media File
Media Alliance
1904 Franklin Street
Suite 500
Oakland, CA 94612
510-832-9000
FAX: 510-238-8557
information@media-allinace.org
http://www.media-alliance.org

Jeff Perlstein, Executive Director
Anna Realini, Membership Director
Sydney Levy, Program Director

Information about media and media workers.

8 pages Quarterly Founded: 1977

4271 Media Law Reporter
Bureau of National Affairs
1231 25th Street NW
Washington, DC 20037-1197
202-452-4200
800-372-1033
customercare@bna.com
http://www.bna.com

Gregory C McCaffery, Publisher
William R McKey, Managing Editor

A weekly reference service containing the full-text of federal and state court decisions and selected agency rulings affecting newspapers, magazines, radio, television, film and other media. *$1856.00*

Weekly Founded: 1929

4272 Media Mergers & Acquisitions
Kagan World Media
One Lower Ragsdale Drive
Building One, Suite 130
Monterey, CA 93940
831-624-1536
FAX: 831-624-5882 800-307-2529
info@kagan.com
http://www.kagan.com

George Niesen, Editor
Tom Johnson, Marketing Manager

Where it all comes together. Exclusive scorecard of deals done by media companies. Dollar amounts, multiples paid, trends captured in succinct summaries of complex transactions. Three month trial available. *$795.00*

Monthly Founded: 1969

4273 Media Sports Business
Kagan World Media
One Lower Ragsdale Drive
Building One, Suite 130
Monterey, CA 93940-8746
831-624-1536
FAX: 831-625-3225
info@kagan.com
http://www.kagan.com

George Niesen, Editor
Tom Johnson, Marketing Manager
$945.00

Monthly Founded: 1969

4274 **Motion Picture Investor**
Kagan World Media
One Lower Ragsdale Drive
Building One, Suite 130
Monterey, CA 93940-8746
831-624-1536
FAX: 831-625-3225 800-307-2529
info@kagan.com
http://www.kagan.com
George Niesen, Editor
Tom Johnson, Marketing Manager
$845.00
Monthly Founded: 1969

4275 **NFAIS Newsletter**
National Federation Abstracting & Info. Services
1518 Walnut Street
Suite 1004
Philadelphia, PA 19102-3403
215-893-1561
FAX: 215-893-1564
nfais@nfais.org http://www.nfais.org
Bonnie Lawlor, Executive Director
Jill O'Neil, Director Communications
Linda Beebe, President
A monthly publication covering feature articles and news items of interest to the information industry. *$135.00*
Monthly Founded: 1958
Circulation: 500 Audited

4276 **Newspaper Investor**
Kagan World Media
One Lower Ragsdale Drive
Building One, Suite 130
Monterey, CA 93940-8746
831-624-1536
FAX: 831-625-3225 800-307-2529
info@kagan.com
http://www.kagan.com
George Niesen, Editor
Tom Johnson, Marketing Manager
$845.00
Monthly Founded: 1969

4277 **Pacific Dialogue**
Robert Miko
33 Ferry Ct
Stratford, CT 06615-6064
FAX: 212-877-2213
Robert Miko, Publisher
Corporate communications of the Pacific Region. *$196.00*
4 pages Weekly
Circulation: 1,000

4278 **Party Line**
Party Line Publishing Company
35 Sutton Place
New York, NY 10022-2464
212-755-3487
FAX: 212-755-4859
info@partylinepublishing.com
http://www.partylinepublishing.com
Morton Yarmon, Publisher
Betty Yarmon, Editor
Betty Yarmon, Marketing
Weekly media placement newsletter with up-to-date news of the media for public relations executives in all aspects of business, hospitals, publishers and associations. *$200.00*
Weekly Founded: 1960
Circulation: 2000
Mailing list available for rent $100 per M.
Printed in 2 colors on matte stock

4279 **Pay TV Newsletter**
Kagan World Media
126 Clock Tower Place
Carmel, CA 93923-8746
831-624-1536
FAX: 831-625-3225
info@kagan.com www.kagan.com
George Niesen, Editor
Tom Johnson, Marketing Manager
$845.00
Monthly

4280 **Pro Motion**
Beyond the Byte
PO Box 388
Fallston, MD 21047-0388
410-877-3524
FAX: 410-877-7064 800-861-1235
elaisy@aol.com
www.pro-motionsnetwork.com
Emily Laisy, President
News of interest to Media Escort and publicists. *$12.00*
4 pages Quarterly Founded: 1986
Circulation: 325 Audited
Printed in 1 color on matte stock

4281 **SIGNAL Connections**
4400 Fairfax Lakes Court
Fairfax, VA 22033
703-631-6100
FAX: 703-631-6169 800-336-4583
promo@afcea.org www.afcea.org
Richard K Ackerman, Editor in Chief
Bridges the gap between issues of SIGNAL by providing additional news and feature articles about the industry and the Association.
Monthly

4282 **Satellite Week**
Warren Communications News
2115 Ward Ct NW
Washington, DC 20037
FAX: 202-318-8350 800-771-9202
Albert Warren, Chairman, Editor & Publisher
R Michael Feazel, Managing Editor
Founded: 1945

4283 **Speech Technology Magazine**
2628 Wilhite Court
Suite 100
Lexington, KY 40503
859-278-2223
FAX: 859-278-7364 877-993-9767
devon@amcommexpos.com
http://www.speechtechmag.com/
John Kelly, Publisher & Editor
Sheila Willison, Circulation Director
Stephanie Owens, Associate Editor
Devon Taylor, Magazine Sales
Kerrie Porath, Sales Coordinator
Divided into four sections: applications, technology, new products, and a special focus section. Authors from the field contribute their expertise to this trade magazine.
73 pages Fortnightly Founded: 1996
Circulation: 25000

4284 **Telecom A.M.**
Warren Communications News
2115 Ward Ct NW
Washington, DC 20037
FAX: 202-318-8350 800-771-9202
Albert Warren, Chairman, Editor & Publisher
R Michael Feazel, Managing Editor
Founded: 1945

4285 **Television A.M.**
Warren Communications News
2115 Ward Ct NW
Washington, DC 20037
FAX: 202-318-8350 800-771-9202
Albert Warren, Chairman, Editor & Publisher
R Michael Feazel, Managing Editor
Founded: 1945

4286 **Washington Internet Daily**
Warren Communications News
2115 Ward Ct NW
Washington, DC 20037
FAX: 202-318-8350 800-771-9202
Albert Warren, Chairman, Editor & Publisher
R Michael Feazel, Managing Editor
Founded: 1945

Magazines & Journals

4287 **15 Minutes Magazine.Com**
7334 173rd Street
Fresh Meadows, NY 11366-1428
718-969-0404
FAX: 718-591-3660
editor@15minutesmagazine.com
http://www.15minutesmagazine.com
Tim Boxer, Editor/Publisher
Nina Boxer, Managing Editor
Bernie Ilson, Public Relations Consulta
Monthly magazine online covering society benefits, with reviews of arts and entertainment, travel and new products. Targets 715,000 readers in affluent market *$50.00*
Monthly Founded: 1999
Circulation: 4,45,000
Printed in 4 colors

4288 **AV Video and Multimedia Producer**
Knowledge Industry Publications
701 Westchester Avenue
#101W
White Plains, NY 10604-3002
914-328-9157
FAX: 914-328-2024
avvmmp@kipi.com
www.kipinet.com/av_mmp/
Ollie Bieniemy, Publisher
Covers product development, graphics and animation, software and equipment, and industry news for readers involved in professional production, multimedia production, and presentation technology. *$53.00*
Monthly
Circulation: 100,000

4289 **American Communication Journal**
American Communication Association
College of Bus Admin, University of Iowa
1227 W 27th Street
Cedar Falls, IA 50614-0125
www.acjournal.org
Robert Schrag PhD, Editor
Deborah H Westmoreland, Associate Editor
Online scholarly journal dedicated to the study of communication.

4290 Applied Microwave & Wireless
Noble Publishing Corporation
630 Pinnacle Court
Norcross, GA 30071
770-449-6774
FAX: 770-448-2839
amw@amwireless.com
www.amwireless.com

Joseph White, Publisher

Edited for the RF and microwave professional.

Circulation: 26,287

4291 Archive Magazine
Showcase Archive
200 Park Avenue South
Suite 1703
New York, NY 10003
212-941-2496
FAX: 212-941-5490 800-894-7469

Walter Lurzer, President

Read by advertising agency executives in 35 countries, archive presents tv commercials and print ads that are currently running around the world. *$13.95*

260 pages 6x a year Founded: 1984
Circulation: 40,000
Printed in 4 colors on glossy stock

4292 Business Communications Review
BCR Enterprises
950 N York Road
Hinsdale, IL 60521-2950
630-986-0950
FAX: 630-986-0926

Fred Knight, Editor
Steven Maxey, Managing Editor
Lynn Svandra, President

Offers a complete package of the latest information for persons associated with the communications industry. *$46.00*

80 pages Monthly

4293 Communication World
Int'l Association of Business Communicators
1 Hallidie Plaza
Suite 600
San Francisco, CA 94102-2842
415-544-4700
FAX: 415-544-4747 800-776-4222
service_centre@iabc.com
http://www.iabc.com

Julie Freeman, President
Natasha Spring, VP Publishing/Research
Joseph Ugalde, VP Marketing/Communications

Association publication for members who are professionals in organizational communications and public relations. *$150.00*

Founded: 1982
Circulation: 13,000
Printed in on matte stock

4294 Communications ASP
Technology Marketing Corporation
One Technology Plaza
Norwalk, CT 06854
203-852-6800
FAX: 203-853-2845 800-243-6002
tmc@tmcnet.com
http://www.tmcnet.com

Rich Tehrani, President

Communication solution magazine. *$2000.00*

Monthly Founded: 1972

4295 Communications Arts
Coyne & Blanchard
110 Constitution Drive
Menlo Park, CA 94025
650-326-6040
FAX: 650-326-1648 800-688-1971
ca@commarts.com
http://www.commarts.com

Mike Krigel, General Manager
Patrick Coyne, Editor

The leading professional journal in the US on graphic arts, commercial photography, illustration and interactive design. Features profile individuals, studios, and agencies with examples of their work. Accepts advertising. *$53.00*

140 pages 1 Year 8 Issues Founded: 1959
Circulation: 74,834
Printed in on glossy stock

4296 Communications Daily
Warren Publishing
2115 Ward Court NW
Washington, DC 20037-1209
202-872-9200
FAX: 202-293-3435
info@warren-news.com
http://www.warren-news.com

Albert Warren, Chairman
Daniel Warren, Executive Editor
Paul Warren, President
Ian Martinez, Production Manager
R Michael Feazel, Director of Advertising

Covers the entire spectrum of the telephone, data communications, broadcasting, cable TV, electronic information distribution, cellulars, PCS and satellite. *$4295.00*

Daily Founded: 1945

4297 Computers in Libraries
Information Today
143 Old Marlton Pike
Medford, CT 08055-8750
609-654-6266
FAX: 609-654-4309 800-248-8466
custserv@infotoday.com
http://www.infotoday.com/

Kathleen Dempsey, Editor in Chief
Lauree Padgett, Editorial Services Manager
Inge Coffey, Circulation Manager

Coverage of news and issues in the field of library information technology. Focuses on practical applications of technology in community, school, academic and special libraries. Includes discussions of the impact of emerging computer technologies on library systems and services and on the library community itself. *$99.95*

10 issues/yr
Mailing list available for rent 4M names
Printed in 4 colors on glossy stock

4298 Darwin
CXO Media
492 Old Connecticut Path
Framingham, MA 01701-4584
508-354-4745
FAX: 508-879-1957 800-343-4935

Joseph Levy, President/CEO
Lew McCreary, Editor in Chief
Cathy O'Leary, VP Marketing
Martha Crowley, Marketing Executive

CXO Media is an executive reach company serving coorporate officers who use technology to thrive and prosper in this new era of business. The company strives to enhance partnerships between CIOs and CXOs as well as create opportunities ofor IIT and consumer marketers to reach them.

180 pages 23 per year
Circulation: 150,000
Printed in 4 colors on glossy stock

4299 Digital Magic
PennWell Publishing Company
10 Tara Boulevard
5th Floor
Nashua, NH 03062-2800
603-891-0123
FAX: 603-891-0539
www.digitalmagicmag.com

Dennis Allen, Publisher

Insights on new technology trends and techniques, covers the latest in hardware and software products to keep digital effects professional competitive and up to date. *$19.95*

Bi-Monthly
Circulation: 30,000

4300 E-Content
Information Today
143 Old Marlton Pike
Medford, CT 08055-8750
609-654-6266
FAX: 609-654-4309 800-248-8466
custserv@infotoday.com
http://www.infotoday.com/

Michelle Manafy, Editor
Jared Bernstein, Editorial Assistant

Delivers essential research, reporting, news and analysis of content related issues. It is essential reading for executive and professionals involved in content creation, management, acquisition, organization and distribution in both commercial and enterprise environments. *$115.00*

10 issues/yr
Mailing list available for rent 4M names
Printed in 4 colors on glossy stock

4301 Electronic Media
Crain Communications
6500 Wilshire Boulevard
Suite 32300
Los Angeles, CA 90048
323-370-2400
FAX: 323-653-4425
emediachi@aol.com
http://www.crain.com

Chuck Ross, Publisher
Alex Block, Editor
Rance Crain, CEO

Covers a full spectrum of electronic media, cable, radio, and television. Includes information on equipment and technology as well as interviews with industry leaders. *$119.00*

Weekly Founded: 1916
Circulation: 35252

4302 Extra!
Fairness & Accuracy in Publishing
112 W 27th Street
New York, NY 10001
212-633-6700
FAX: 212-727-7668
fair@fair.org http://www.fair.org

Deborah Thomas, Publisher
Jim Naureckas, Editor
Marie Hickey, Manager

Progressive media criticism. *$21.00*

Bi-monthly Founded: 1987
Circulation: 21800

4303 Government Video
Miller Freeman Publications
460 Park Avenue S
9th Floor
New York, NY 10016-7315
212-378-0400
FAX: 212-378-2160
gv@psn.com
www.governmentvideo.com
Paul G Gallo, Publisher
Chris Gallo, Associate Publisher
Martin Porter, Senior VP
Articles on audio, video production and technologies, training and presentation, multimedia, video conferencing, and medical and scientific applications.
Monthly
Circulation: 18,000

4304 Hope Reports Media Market Trends
Hope Reports
58 Carverdale Drive
Rochester, NY 14618-4004
585-442-1310
FAX: 585-442-1725
Thomas W Hope, Chairman/CEO
Mabeth S Hope, VP/Corporate Secretary
Covers high technology media for business planning, marketing, consultation and focus reports on media markets equipment, visual communications statistics, contract production, video post-production. Compensation reports. *$165.00*
Printed in 1 color on matte stock

4305 IEEE Wireless Communications
IEEE Communications Society
3 Park Avenue
17th Floor
New York, NY 10016
212-705-8900
FAX: 212-705-8999
publications@comsoc.org
www.comsoc.org
An interdisciplinary bimonthly magazine, covers technical and policy issues relating to personal, location-independent communications in all media and at all protocol layers.
Bi-Monthly

4306 IQ News
ADWEEK
770 Broadway
7th Floor
New York, NY 10003
646-545-5220
FAX: 646-654-5351
publisher@adweek.com
www.adweek.com
Wright Ferguson Jr, VP/Magazine Publisher
Weekly magazine about new media and Internet marketing.

4307 Information Week
CMP Media LLC
600 Community Drive
Manhasset, NY 11030
516-562-5000
www.informationweek.com
Gary Marshall, President & CEO
Scott Vaughan, Publisher

4308 International Communications Association
1730 Rhode Island Avenue NW
Suite 300
Washington, DC 20036
202-530-9855
FAX: 202-530-9851
icahdq@icahdq.org
http://www.icahdq.org
Michael Haley, Executive Director
Wolfgang Donfback, President
Bi-monthly newsletter that supports all students and professionals in the international communications industry. *$30.00*
Founded: 1950
Circulation: 3500
Printed in on matte stock

4309 Journal of Applied Communications
Agricultural Communicators in Education
University of Florida
PO Box 110810
Gainesville, FL 32611-810
352-392-0502
FAX: 352-392-8583
ace@mail.ifas.ufl.edu
http://www.aceweb.org/jac/jac.html
Amanda Chambliss, Editor
Linda Foster Benedict, Editor
A peer-reviewed professional journal which accepts original contributions about communications, research, innovations and other pertinent information. The Journal is provided to all members, libraries and other interested people. *$75.00*
Quarterly Founded: 1990
Circulation: 700

4310 Journal of the Association of Information systems
Case Western Reserve University
Cleveland, OH 44106
216-368-5353
FAX: 216-368-4776
kalle@cwru.edu www.aisnet.org
Kalle Lyytinen, Editor
Publishes the highest quality scholarship in the field of information systems. Covers all aspects of Information Systems and Information Technology. Publishes rigorously developed and forward looking conceptual and empirical contributions.Encourages multidisciplinary and nontraditional approaches.
Quarterly

4311 KM World
Information Today
143 Old Marlton Pike
Medford, CT 08055-8750
609-654-6266
FAX: 609-654-4309 800-248-8466
custserv@infotoday.com
http://www.infotoday.com/
Hugh Mckellar, Editor in Chief
Sandra Haimila, Managing Editor
Andy Moore, Publisher
Serves the knowledge management industry by offering components and processes, including success stories, designed to improve business. *$23.95*
Mailing list available for rent 4M names
Printed in 4 colors on glossy stock

4312 Link-Up Digital
Information Today
143 Old Marlton Pike
Medford, CT 08055-8750
609-654-6266
FAX: 609-654-4309 800-248-8466
custserv@infotoday.com
http://www.infotoday.com/
A web-only product featuring articles, reviews and more for users and producers of electronic information products and services.
Mailing list available for rent 4M names
Printed in 4 colors on glossy stock

4313 MAIL: Journal of Communication Distribution
Gold Key Box 2425
Milford, PA 18337
Offers updated information on electronic mail and mail messaging systems. *$6.00*
105 pages Monthly

4314 Managing Media Relations in a Crisis
NACHA: Electronic Payments Association
13665 Dulles Technology Drive
#300
Herndon, VA 20171
703-561-1100
FAX: 703-787-0996
info@nacha.org www.nacha.org
Elliott McEntee, President/CEO
William B Nelson, Executive VP
Designed to assist your organization to develop, test and execute a crisis communication plan. With this guide, you will understand how to address issues, whom to call and in what order to alert them, which vendors you can count on to help and how to develop a means to track the crisis as it grows or abates.

4315 Media Studies Journal
Columbia University, Freedom Forum Media Center
2960 Broadway
New York, NY 10027-6902
212-854-5573
FAX: 212-678-4817
http://www.columbia.edu
Craig L LaMay, Editor
James D Jordan, Director
Aimed at scholars, practitioners and commentators. Offers information on mass communications issues involving the media and the public at large. *$20.00*
Quarterly Founded: 1754
Circulation: 9000

4316 Novedades USA
Lancer Productions
1241 S Soto Street
Suite 213
Los Angeles, CA 90023
323-881-6515
FAX: 323-881-6524 teleguia@aol.com
John DiCarlo, Publisher
Elizabeth DiCarlo, Editor
Lorena Mata, Office Manager
Weekly Founded: 1986
Circulation: 100,000
Printed in 4 colors on newsprint stock

4317 **ONLINE Magazine**
Information Today
143 Old Marlton Pike
Medford, CT 08055-8750
609-654-6266
FAX: 609-654-4309 800-248-8466
custserv@infotoday.com
http://www.infotoday.com/
Thomas Hogan, Publisher
Marydee Ojala, Editor
Lauree Padgett, Editorial Services Manager
Written for information professionals and provides articles, product reviews, case studies, evaluation and informed opinion aobut selecting, using and managing electronic information products, plus industry and professional information about online database systems, CD-ROMs and the Internet. *$115.00*
6 issues/yr
Mailing list available for rent 4M names
Printed in 4 colors on glossy stock

4318 **Presentations Magazine**
VNU Expositions
50 S 9th Street
Minneapolis, MN 55402-3118
612-333-0471
FAX: 612-333-6526 800-328-4329
tsimons@presentations.com
http://www.presentations.com
Tad Simons, Editor-in-Chief
Richard Ausman, Publisher
Mike Keegan, Marketing Executive
The only magazine dedicated to individuals and organizations that create and deliver presentations. Articles track the latest presentation technology and trends, offer application tips and techniques to help readers build their creative and delivery skills, and identifies best presentation practices of leading presenters and organizations worldwide. *$120.00*
62 pages Monthly Founded: 1988
Circulation: 75000 75000 names $130 per M.
Printed in 4 colors on glossy stock

4319 **Professional Journal: Sbusiness Publication**
AFSM International
1342 Colonial Boulevard
Suite 25D
Fort Meyers, FL 33907
239-275-7887
FAX: 239-275-0794 800-333-9786
jgaidry@afsmi.org
http://www.afsmi.org
John Schoenwald, CEO
Suzanne Kaminski, Senior Editor
A global organization dedicated to furthering the knowledge, understanding, and career development of executives, managers, and professionals in the high-technology services and support industry as well as to provide leadership and direction that helps our individual and corporate members expand their capabilities to meet the growing complexities and challenges of the industry. Sbusiness publication is distributed bi-monthly serving international decision makers. *$95.00*
114 pages Founded: 1975
Circulation: 10000
Printed in 4 colors on matte stock

4320 **Professional Speaker Magazine**
National Speakers Association
1500 S Priest Drive
Tempe, AZ 85281-6266
480-968-2552
FAX: 480-968-0911
information@nsaspeaker.org
http://www.nsaspeaker.org
Cecile Blaine-Dunnke, Manager Publicatiion
Theresa Sullivan, Marketing Assistant
Stacy Tetschner, Manager
Trends, issues and perspectives about and for the professional speaking industry. *$49.00*
Founded: 1973
Circulation: 4000 3400 names $500 per M.
Printed in 4 colors on glossy stock

4321 **Red Herring: The Business of Technology**
Red Herring
19 Davis Drive
Belmont, CA 94002
650-428-2900
FAX: 650-321-5597
info@redherring.com
http://www.redherring.com
Jason Simpson, Editor
Christopher Alden, Editorial Director
Alex Vieux, Publisher
Joel Dreyfuss, Editor-in-Chief
Offers information on new and rising companies, as well as current industrial technology issues and topics.
Weekly Founded: 1993
Circulation: 45000

4322 **Replication News**
Miller Freeman Publications
460 Park Avenue S
9th Floor
New York, NY 10016-7315
212-378-0400
FAX: 212-378-2160 repnews@psn.com
Paul G Gallo, Publisher
Information on electronic and recording media through news coverage and analysis to provide executives with the market for strategic business planning.
Monthly
Circulation: 16,490

4323 **SIGNAL Magazine**
4400 Fair Lakes Court
Fairfax, VA 22033-3899
703-631-6100
FAX: 703-631-6133 800-336-4583
promo@afcea.org www.afcea.org
Robert K Ackerman, Editor in Chief
International news magazine serving the critical information needs of government, military and industry professionals active in the fields of command, control, communications, computers, intelligence, surveillance and reconnaissance (C4ISR); information security, research and development; electronics; and homeland security.
Monthly
Circulation: 90000

4324 **TV Guide**
United Video Satellite Group
1211 Avenue of the Americas
4th Floor
New York, NY 10036-8701
212-852-7500
FAX: 212-852-4914
Richard Porter, Publisher
Focuses on all aspects of network, cable and pay television programming and how it affects and reflects their audience. *$39.88*
Weekly
Circulation: 13mm

4325 **TV Technology**
IMAS Publishing
PO Box 1214
Falls Church, VA 22041
703-998-7600
FAX: 703-998-2966
webmaster@imaspub.com
http://www.tvtechnology.com
Steven Dana, President
Tom Butts, Editor
Eric Trabb, Publisher
Kwentin Keenan, Circulation Manager
News of a technical nature covering topics ranging from regulatory developments through maintenance and new products. *$39.95*
Fortnightly Founded: 1978
Circulation: 37,000

4326 **Tech Trenda**
Association for Educational Communication
1800 N Stonelake Drive
Suite 2
Bloomington, IN 47404
812-335-7675
FAX: 812-335-7678
aect@aect.org www.aect.org
Elizabeth Boiling, Editor-in-Chief
$125.00
Bi-Monthly
Circulation: 3500

4327 **TechNews**
Newspaper Association of America
1921 Gallows Road
Suite 600
Vienna, VA 22182-3900
703-902-1600
FAX: 703-902-0636 http://www.naa.org
Tom Croteau, Publisher
Mark Toner, Editor
John Sturm, CEO
John Kimball, Marketing Senior Vice Presidents
Su-Lin Nichols, Communications/SVP
Serves Newspaper Association of America member and non-member newspaper executives and staff, and others allied to the field. Subscriptions: $55 member, $110 non-member.
Founded: 1992
Printed in 4 colors on glossy stock

4328 **Television International Magazine**
Television International Magazine
PO BOX #2473
Universal City, CA 91610-8471
323-462-1099
FAX: 702-939-4725
tvi@smart90.com
http://www.tvimagazine.com
Josie Cory, Publisher
Mark Soval, Advertising Director
News and information regarding the television industry, includes the who's who of the business; geared toward the executives and professionals of the industry. *$129.00*
Monthly Founded: 1956
Circulation: 16000
Printed in 4 colors on glossy stock

4329 Truman Communications
503 9th Street
Santa Monica, CA 90402-2801
212-593-2825

A comprehensive magazine offering the latest news and information pertaining to the communications industry.

4330 Tyndall Report
ADT Research
135 Rivington Street
#4
New York, NY 10002-2415
212-674-8913
FAX: 212-979-7304
andrew@tyndallreport.com
http://www.tyndallreport.com

Andrew Tyndall, Publisher

This publication measures time spent in covering the current hot topics including the economy.
Weekly Founded: 1987
Circulation: 350

4331 XCHANGE
Virgo Publishing
3300 N. Central Avenue Suite 2500
PO Box 40079
Phoenix, AZ 85012
480-990-1101
FAX: 480-675-8146
pbernier@vpico.com
http://www.xchangemag.com

Megan McCoy, Managing Editor
Marla Ellerman, Group Publisher
Khali Henderson, Group Editor
Paula Bernier, Editor in Chief

Strategic window on developments of vital concern to facilities-based providers in the competitive local exchange marketplace. *$ 75.00*
Monthly Founded: 1986
Circulation: 35,003

Trade Shows

4332 AFCEA TechNet International
Armed Forces Communications and Electronics Assn
4400 Fair Lakes Court
Fairfax, VA 22033-3899
703-631-6200
FAX: 703-654-6931 800-564-4220
technetinternational@jspargo.com
www.afcea.org

Paul doCarmo, Sales Manager
Connie Shaw, Sales Manager

This event draws commanders and staff from every branch of the military, including warfighting integration organizations charged with the most critical responsibilities of synthesizing military power on land, at sea, and in the air.
7500 Attendees June

4333 AM&AA Summer Conference
Alliance of Merger and Acquisition Advisors
150 North Michigan Ave
Suite 2700
Chicago, IL 60601
877-844-2535
FAX: 312-729-9800
aemerson@amaaonline.org
www.amaaonline.org

Ainsley Emerson, Director

Annual

4334 Alpha Graphics Show
Hynes Convention Center
900 Boylston
Boston, MA 02115
617-248-8585
FAX: 617-954-2125 800-845-8800
info@mccahome.com
www.mccahome.com
800 Attendees July

4335 American Public Communications Council Conference & Expo
10302 Eaton Place
Suite 340
Fairfax, VA 22030

FAX: 703-385-5301 800-868-2722

Bruce Renard, President

Conference, luncheon and 100 exhibits of public communications equipment and information including, pay phones, internet, atm, multimedia and more.
Founded: 1988

4336 Association for Business Communication Annual Symposium
17 Lexington Avenue
New York, NY 10010
212-387-1620
FAX: 212-387-1655
abcrjm@cs.com www.theabc.org

Robert J Meyers, Executive Director

Workshop and displays from textbook publishers, speech and business writing, technical publications and corporate communication.
400 Attendees Founded: 1935

4337 Communications
Reed Exhibition Companies
255 Washington Street
Newton, MA 02458-1637
617-584-4900
FAX: 617-630-2222

Elizabeth Hitchcock, International Sales

Offers communications professionals.
21M Attendees April

4338 DISA Customer Partnership AFCEA Technology Showcase
Armed Forces Communications and Electronics Assn
4400 Fair Lakes Court
Fairfax, VA 22033
703-631-6200
FAX: 703-654-6931 800-564-4220
disaexhibits@jspargo.com
www.afcea.org

Paul doCarmo, Assistant Director/Exhibit Sales
Connie Shaw, Exhibit Sales Account Manager

This conference facilitates a continuing interface with customers and strategic partners by allowing attendees to benefit from the perspective of DoD (Department of Defense) and industry speakers. It offers information sessions that provide a forum for questions, concerns and problem resolution.
1200 Attendees April-May

4339 LandWarNet Conference
Armed Forces Communications and Electronics Assn
4400 Fair Lakes Court
Fairfax, VA 22033
703-631-6200
FAX: 703-654-6931 800-564-4220
landwarnet@jspargo.com
www.afcea.org

Nathan Wills, Account Manager

Thousands of key communications/information technology buyers and influencers attend the conference every year. This is an opportunity to network with the best and develop crucial relationships with some of the Army's most influential decision-makers.
3700 Attendees August

4340 MILCOM
Armed Forces Communications and Electronics Assn
4400 Fair Lakes Court
Fairfax, VA 22033
703-631-6200
FAX: 703-654-6931 800-564-4220
milcom@jspargo.com www.afcea.org

Paul doCarmo, Assistant Director/Exhibit Sales
Connie Shaw, Exhibit Sales Account Manager

For over 20 years, MILCOM has been the premier international conference for military communications, with over 3,000 attendees every year. It attracts decision-makers from government, military, academia and industry, including heads of multi-national forces from around the globe, all who contribute key technologies decisions and investments for their agency.
3000 Attendees October

4341 Mailcom
The Art & Science of Mail Communications
Po Box 7045
Philadelphia, PA 19149-0045
732-280-8865
FAX: 732-280-7854
ljhumphries@msn.com
www.mailcom.org

Lance Humphries, Managing Director

Learn how business communications can become strategic corporate tools
9000 Attendees Oct Las Vegas

4342 Multi-Media Association Convention
Association for Multi-Media International
PO Box 270298
Suite 204
Tampa, FL 33688-0298
850-644-4470
FAX: 813-962-7911

Marilyn Kulp, Executive Director

International convention.
1M Attendees August Founded: 1974

4343 National Hispanic Market Trade Show and Media Expo (Se Habla Espanol)
Hispanic Business
360 S Hope Avenue
Suite 300C
Santa Barbara, CA 93105-4031
805-563-1049
FAX: 805-687-4546
info@hispanstar.com
www.hispanstar.com

Luisa Donis, Corporate Communications

Annual show of 100 exhibitors of market/research, media, advertising, public relations, information services and recruitment.
1500 Attendees

4344 Toastmasters Trade Show
Toastmasters International
PO Box 9052
Mission Viejo, CA 92690-9052
949-858-8255
FAX: 949-858-1207
www.toastmasters.org
Suzanne Frey
Focuses on communication in general and public speaking in particular. Topics include language, listening, humor, self improvement, goal setting, success and logical thinking.
2M Attendees August

Directories & Databases

4345 ACCE Communications Council Directory
4875 Eisen Hower Avenue
Stree 250
Alexandria, VA 22304-1507
703-998-0072
FAX: 703-931-5624
webmaster@acce.org
http://www.acce.org
Mick Fleming, President/CEO
Greg Roth, Editor
Offers member information on the council activities.
Annual+ Founded: 1914

4346 ADWEEK Directory
ADWEEK
770 Broadway
7th Floor
New York, NY 10003
646-545-5220
FAX: 646-654-5351
publisher@adweek.com
www.adweek.com
Mitch Tebo, Directory Publisher
For anyone seeking agency-specific information. Over 29,000 personnel listings, more the 6,000 full service advertising agencies and networks, public relations firms, media buying services, recruitment entertainment marketing, yellow pages, health care, interactive, sports marketing, infomercials, direct marketing, creative design, marketing communications and research, consultancies and many more media related listings.

4347 AV Market Place 2005 The Complete Business Directory
Information Today
143 Old Marlton Pike
Medford, NJ 08055-8750
609-654-6266
FAX: 609-654-4309
custserv@infotoday.com
www.infotoday.com
Thomas H Hogan, Publisher/President
John Bryans, Publisher/Editor-in-Chief Books
Lauree Padgett, Editorial Services Manager
Inge Coffey, Circulation Manager
Pat Palatucci, Assistant to the President
The only guide needed to find more than 7,500 companies that create, apply, or distribute AV equipment and services for businesss, education, science and government. *$199.95*
1700 pages February ISBN 1-573871-87-7

4348 American Showcase Illustration
Showcase Archive
200 Park Avenue South
Suite 1703
New York, NY 10003
212-941-2496
FAX: 212-941-5490 800-894-7469
Walter Lurzer, President
Illustrators and graphic designers.

4349 Association For Educational Communications And Technology Membership Directory
Assn. for Educational Communications & Technology
1800 N Stonelake Drive
Suite 2
Bloomington, IN 47404
812-335-7675
FAX: 812-335-7678
aect@aect.org www.aect.org
Phillip Harris, Editor
5,000 audiovisual and instructional materials specialists, educational technologists, audiovisual and television production personnel, school media specialists
Annual

4350 Bacon's Calendar Directory
Bacon's Publishing Company
332 S Michigan Avenue
Chicago, IL 60604-4434
312-228-8239
FAX: 312-922-3126 800-621-0561
info@bacons.com www.bacons.com
Ruth McFarland, VP/Publisher
Stephen Newmna, Chief Executive Officer
Helps you match your story and products ideas with specific issues of publications containing upcoming related editorial features. *$350.00*
Annual
Printed in 1 color on matte stock : internet

4351 Bacon's Computer/Hi-Tech Media Directory
Bacon's Publishing Company
332 S Michigan Avenue
Chicago, IL 60604-4434
312-228-8239
FAX: 312-922-3127 800-621-0561
info@bacons.com www.bacons.com
Ruth McFarland, VP/Publisher
Stephen Newman, Chief Executive Officer
Contains detailed coverage on technology beat — now with expanded freelance listings. *$300.00*
Annual
Printed in 1 color on matte stock : internet

4352 Bacon's International Media Directory
Bacon's Publishing Company
332 S Michigan Avenue
Chicago, IL 60604-4434
312-228-8239
FAX: 312-922-3127 800-621-0561
info@bacons.com www.bacons.com
Ruth McFarland, VP/Publisher
Stephen Newman, Chief Executive Officer
Complete information source to Western European media, from Austria to the UK. *$350.00*
Annual
Printed in 1 color on matte stock : internet

4353 Bacon's New York Publicity Outlelts
Bacon's Publishing Company
332 S Michigan Avenue
Chicago, IL 60604-4434
312-228-8239
FAX: 312-922-3127 800-621-0561
info@bacons.com www.bacons.com
Ruth McFarland, VP/Publisher
Stephen Newman, Chief Executive Officer
Provides in-depth coverage of regional media for professionals who target the New York area, including portions of Connecticut and New Jersey. *$250.00*
Annual
Printed in 1 color on matte stock : internet

4354 Bacon's Newspaper & Magazine Directories
Bacon's Publishing Company
332 S Michigan Avenue
Chicago, IL 60604-4434
312-228-8239
FAX: 312-922-3127 800-621-0561
info@bacons.com www.bacons.com
Ruth McFarland, VP/Publisher
Stephen Newman, Chief Executive Officer
Two volume set listing all daily and community newspapers, magazines and newsletters, news service and syndicates, syndicated columists, complete editorial staff listings of each publication provided, covers US, Canada, Mexico,and Carribean *$350.00*
4,700 pages Annual Founded: 1951
Printed in 1 color on matte stock : internet

4355 Bacon's Radio/TV/Cable Directory
Bacon's Publishing Company
332 S Michigan Avenue
Chicago, IL 60604-4434
312-228-8239
FAX: 312-922-3127 800-621-0561
info@bacons.com www.bacons.com
Ruth McFarland, VP/Publisher
Stephen Newman, Chief Executive Officer
Includes expandedn listings for television and radio stations in major markets. *$350.00*
Annual
Printed in 1 color on matte stock : internet

4356 Brandweek Directory
ADWEEK
770 Broadway
7th Floor
New York, NY 10003
646-545-5220
FAX: 646-654-5351
publisher@adweek.com
www.adweek.com
Mitch Tebo, Directory Publisher
Matt Lennon, Online Product Manager
Featuring in depth information in a clear and easy-to-use format, organized by brand name with marketer, personnel, lead agency and media expenditure data. Contains stand alone listings for over 6,200

brands, including 22,000 personnel at both corporate and brand level.

4357 Burrelle's Media Directory
Burrelle's Information Services
75 E Northfield Road
Livingston, NJ 07039-4501
973-992-6600
FAX: 973-992-7675 800-631-1160
Robert Waggoner, Chief Executive Officer

Approximately 60,000 media listings in North America. Listings cover newspapers, magazines (trades and consumer), broadcast, and internet outlets. *$795.00*
Annual

4358 Corporate Yellow Book
Leadership Directories
104 5th Avenue
New York, NY 10011-6901
212-627-4140
FAX: 212-645-0931
corporate@leadershipdirectories.com
www.leadershipdirectories.com
Vonessa Ruffin, Editor

Contact information for over 48,000 executives at over 1,000 companies and 6,000 subsidiaries and divisions, and more than 9,000 board members and their outside affiliations. *$360.00*
1,400 pages Quarterly Founded: 1986
50,000 names $105 per M. : CD-Rom

4359 Directory of Library Automation Software, Systems and Services
Information Today
143 Old Marlton Pike
Medford, NJ 08055-8750
609-654-6266
FAX: 609-654-4309
custserv@infotoday.com
www.infotoday.com
Thomas H Hogan, Publisher/President
John Bryans, Publisher/Editor-in-Chief Books
Lauree Padgett, Editorial Services Manager
Inge Coffey, Circulation Manager
Pamela Cibbarelli, Editor

Recognized as the primary reference source for software packages used in automating libraries. This entirely new expanded edition provides detailed descriptions of hundreds of currently available microcomputer, minicomputer, and mainframe software packages and services. *$ 89.00*
351 pages Biannually Founded: 1983
ISBN 1-573872-00-8

4360 Film & Video Finder
Information Today
143 Old Marlton Pike
Medford, NJ 08055-8750
609-654-6266
FAX: 609-654-4309
custserv@infotoday.com
www.infotoday.com
Thomas H Hogan, Publisher/President
John Bryans, Publisher/Editor-in-Chief Books
Lauree Padgett, Editorial Services Manager
Inge Coffey, Circulation Manager
Pat Palatucci, Assistant to the President

Contains information on 130,000 films and videos. The most comprehensive reference available to educational films and videos. A three volume hardbound set. *$295.00*
6434 pages Annual ISBN 0-937548-29-4

4361 Gale Database of Publications and Broadcast Media
Gale Research
27500 Drake Road
Farmington Hills, MI 48331
248-699-4253
FAX: 248-699-8214 800-877-4253
galeord@gale.com www.gale.com
Allen Paschal, Chief Executive Officer

Comprehensive directory offers over 65,000 journals, newsletters, radio and television stations, directories and cable companies across the globe.

4362 Gale Ready Reference Database (CD-ROM)
Gale Research
27500 Drake Road
Farmington Hills, MI 48331
248-699-4253
FAX: 248-699-8214 800-877-4253
galeord@gale.com www.gale.com
Allen Paschal, Chief Executive Officer

Contains association and organization data, descriptions and contact information for research centers, directories, publishing and broadcast firms, newsletters, databases, libraries and information centers. *$3500.00*

4363 Gebbie Press All-in-One Directory
Gebbie Press
PO Box 1000
New Paltz, NY 12561-0017
845-255-7560
FAX: 845-256-1239
www.gebbieinc.com
Mark Gebbie, Editor/Publisher

TV and radio stations, daily and weekly newspapers, consumer and trade magazines, black and Hispanic media, news syndicates, networks, AP/UPI bureaus. Compact spiral bound 6x9 inches. *$140.00*
500 pages Also on Disk Founded: 1970

4364 Graphic Communications International Union
1 E 1st Street
Duluth, MN 55802-3004

FAX: 218-723-9583 800-331-5706
Combines three independent shows: Printing XPO, Type-X and Art-X and gives you a complete overview of the most recently introduced technologies and the newest information in the field of graphic arts.

4365 Hoover's Guide to Media Companies
Hoover's
1003 La Posada Drive
Suite 250
Austin, TX 78752-3815
512-579-9925
FAX: 512-374-4501 800-486-8666
More than 250 media industry leaders with in-depth profiles and more than 750 other public and private media industry companies with capsule profiles; international coverage. *$29.95*

4366 Index to AV Producers & Distributors
Information Today
143 Old Marlton Pike
Medford, NJ 08055-8750
609-654-6266
FAX: 609-654-4309
custserv@infotoday.com
www.infotoday.com
Thomas H Hogan, Publisher/President
John Bryans, Publisher/Editor-in-Chief Books
Lauree Padgett, Editorial Services Manager
Inge Coffey, Circulation Manager

Contains over 23,500 producers and distributors of AV materials of all kinds. This handy softbound volume is an indispensible tool for buyers of audiovisual materials of all kinds. *$89.00*
626 pages ISBN 0-937845-30-8

4367 Journalism and Mass Communication Directory
AEJMC
234 Outlet Pointe Boulevard
Suite A
Columbia, SC 29210-5667
803-798-0271
FAX: 803-772-3509
aejmchq@aol.com www.aejmc.org
Felicia Greenlee Brown, Production Manager

Over 3,000 professionals, academics and graduate students; more than 400 journalism and mass communications schools and departments in four-year colleges and universities, including 200 members of the Association of Schools of Journalism and Mass Communication. *$25.00*
Annual Founded: 1983
Circulation: 5000

4368 Kagan Media Index
Kagan World Media
126 Clock Tower Place
Carmel, CA 93923-8746
831-624-1536
FAX: 831-625-3225
info@kagan.com www.kagan.com
George Niesen, Editor
Tom Johnson, Marketing Manager

The most comprehensive collection of media industry databases found anywhere. Current estimates of industry growth for a dozen different media businesses, shown on a 145-line spreadsheet, projected forward and updated monthly. Three month trial available. *$795.00*
Monthly

4369 M Street Radio Directory
M Street Corporation
81 Main Street, Suite 2
PO Box 442
Littleten, NH 03561
603-444-5720
FAX: 603-444-2872 888-256-1156
billing@mstreet.net ww.mstreet.net
Cathy Devine, Editor
Ireve Yeargle, Circulation

Approximately 14,000 AM and FM radio stations in the US and Canada. *$79.00*
Annual
Printed in on matte stock

4370 Mediaweek Directory
ADWEEK
770 Broadway
7th Floor
New York, NY 10003
646-545-5220
FAX: 646-654-5351
publisher@adweek.com
www.adweek.com

Mitch Tebo, Directory Publisher

Focuses on the most powerful segments covering 9,000 media companies from the top 100 media markets for radio, broadcast TV, cable TV and daily newspapers. Also includes the top 300 consumer magazines, the top 150 trade magazines, networks, syndicators, sales representatives, multi-media holding companies, trade associations and rating organizations.

4371 Multilingual Thesaurus of Geosciences
Information Today
143 Old Marlton Pike
Medford, NJ 08055-8750
609-654-6266
FAX: 609-654-4309
custserv@infotoday.com
www.infotoday.com

J Gravesteijn, Editor
C Kortman, Editor
G N Rassam

Represents the state of the art use of geoscience terminology by informations centers around the world. *$99.00*
654 pages ISBN 1-573870-09-9

4372 News Media Directories
PO Box 316
Mount Dora, FL 32757
352-589-9020
FAX: 866-586-7020 800-749-6399
nm0777@aol.com
www.newsmediadirectories.com

Dean Highberger, Editor

Directory for lists, daily papers, new services, magazines, weekly papers, special publications and radio stations. We have directories covering eight states , Alabama, Florida, Georgia, Mississippi, North Carolina, Ohio, South Carolina and Tennessee. Also, we have a condensed southeast edition. Listings include address, phone, fax, e-mail, and key associates.
Annual

4373 News Media Yellow Book
Leadership Directories
104 5th Avenue
New York, NY 10011-6901
212-627-4140
FAX: 212-645-0931
newsmedia@leadershipdirectories.com
www.leadershipdirectories.com

Laura Gibbons, Editor
James M Petrie, Associate Publisher

Contact information for over 39,000 journalists at over 2,500 new services, networks, newspapers, television, radio stations, as well as independent journalists and syndicated columnists. *$325.00*
1,200 pages Quarterly Founded: 1989
Mailing list available for rent 32,000 names $125 per M.
Computerized version available: CD-ROM

4374 O'Dwyer's Directory of Public Relations Firms
JR O'Dwyer Company
271 Madison Avenue
New York, NY 10016
212-791-1032
FAX: 212-683-2750
jack@odwyerpr.com
www.odwyerpr.com

Jack O'Dwyer, Publisher

Exclusive ranking of public relations firms and lists more than 2,900 firms in the US and 55 countries. *$125.00*
400 pages Annual

4375 Pocket Media Guide
Media Distribution Services
307 W 36th Street
Department P
New York, NY 10018-6490
212-279-4800
FAX: 212-643-0576 800-637-3282
services@mdsconnect.com
www.mdsconnect.com

Designed to fit easily into a wallet, the palm size guide includes names and addresses, with phone numbers, of more than 700 major print and media in North America, plus a calendar, annual media statistics, and a publicity primer.
40 pages Annual

4376 Power Media Selects
Broadcast Interview Source
2233 Wisconsin Avenue NW
Suite 301
Washington, DC 20007-4132
202-333-4904
FAX: 202-342-5411 800-932-7266

Mitchell Davis, Owner
Alan Caruba, Production Manager

Approximately 3,000 media contacts throughout the US, including newswire services, syndicates, syndicated columnists, national newspapers, magazines, radio and television talk shows, etc. *$166.50*
Annual

4377 Print Media Production Data
Standard Rate & Data Services
1700 Higgins Road
Des Plaines, IL 60018-5605
847-375-5000
FAX: 847-375-5001 800-851-7737

Tom Drouillard, CEO
Ruth Harman, Marketing Coordinator

Directory of services and supplies to the industry. *$481.00*
1,455 pages Online/Print Quarterly
Founded: 1919
Mailing list available for rent

4378 Sound & Communications
Testa Communications
25 Willowdale Avenue
Port Washington, NY 11050-3779
516-767-2500
FAX: 516-767-9335

David Silverman, Editor
Bob Beoder, Advertising Manager

The systems magazine for contractors and consultants who design, specify, sell, and install audio and display systems. Installation profiles, news, business and product updates, incisive theory and applications reporting. *$15.00*
Monthly Founded: 1955
Circulation: 23,000

4379 Working Press of the Nation
Reed Reference Publishing RR Bowker
121 Chanlon Road
New Providence, NJ 07974-1541
908-665-2834
FAX: 908-464-3553 800-269-5372
info@bowker.com www.bowker.com

Elizabeth Onaron, Editor

Offers, in four separate volumes, syndicates, newspapers, radio and television stations, feature writers, photographers, illustrators and internal house organs. *$399.00*
Set

Industry Web Sites

4380 www.acce.org
American Chamber of Commerce Executives

National organization uniquely serving individuals involved in the management of chambers of all sizes. Chamber executives and their staffs can capitalize on a wealth of information, leadership, skill development, management techniques and innovative program offerings. Also works diligently to upgrade the economic status and professional standing of those active in the chamber field.

4381 www.adweek.com
Adweek

Leading decision makers in the advertising and marketing field go to Adweek.com every day for breaking news, insight, buzz, opinion, analysis, research and classifieds. The resources of all six regional editions of Adweek, as well as the national edition of Brandweek are combined with the knowledge of our editors and the multimedia-interactive capabilities of the Web to deliver vital information quickly and effectively to our target audience.

4382 www.aim.org
Accuracy in Media

Nonprofit, grassroots citizens watchdog of the news media that critiques botched and bungled news stories and sets the record straight on important issues that have recieved slanted coverage.

4383 www.americomm.org
American Communication Association

Founded for the purposes of fostering research and scholorship in all areas of human communication behavior, promoting and improving excellence in the pedagogy of communication, providing a voice in communication law and policy, and providing evaluation and certification services for academic programs in communication study.

4384 **www.amta.org**
Antenna Measurement Techniques Association

Nonprofit professional organization, open to individuals with an interest in antenna measurements. Areas of interest include: measurement facilities, unique or innovative measurement techniques, test instrumentation and systems, RCS measurements, compact range design and evaluation, near-field techniques and their applications, and the practical aspects of measurement problems problems and their solutions.

4385 **www.apcc.net**
American Public Communications Council

APCC proudly offers offers a wide array of services to the public communications industry, from Perspectives magazine to our annual trade show to our involvement in legal and regulatory issues. This site is a place for the public to find out about our industry and for our members to learn of legal and regulatory developments, to become aware of APCC programs events, and to have a forum for discussion.

4386 **www.apco911.org**
Association of Public-Safety Communications

The world's oldest and largest professional organization dedicated to the enhancement of public safety communications and to serving its more than 15,000 members, the people who use public safety communications systems and services.

4387 **www.bowker.com**
Reed Reference Publishing RR Bowker

Offers, in four separate volumes, syndicates, newspapers, radio and television stations, feature writers, photographers, illustrators and internal house organs.

4388 **www.consultingsuccess.org**
Assn of Professional Communication Consultants

Professional community where communication consultants increase their knowledge, grow their business, achieve high standards of professional practice. APCC's mission is to support members as they help clients reach their goals through better communication.

4389 **www.digmedia.org**
Digital Media Association

National trade organization devoted primarily to the online audio and video industries, and more generally to commercially innovative digital media opportunities.

4390 **www.drudgereport.com**

Links to international news sources and columnists.

4391 **www.greyhouse.com**
Grey House Publishing

Selected Grey House directories in the fields of business, health and education are available online. Users can search our online databases by several different search criteria, such as product categories, geographic area, sales volume and much, much more. Full Grey House catalog and online ordering also available.

4392 **www.iaais.org**
Int'l Association of Audio Information Services

Formerly the National Association of Radio Reading Services, we are an organization of services that provide audio access to information for people who are print disabled. People served are blind, visually impared, learning disabled or physically disabled.

4393 **www.iabc.com**
Int'l Association of Business Communications

International knowledge network for professionals engaged in strategic business communication management. IABC links communicators in a global network that inspires, establishes and supports the highest professional standards.

4394 **www.icahdq.org**
International Communications Association

International association for scholars interested in the study, teaching and application of all aspects of human mediated communication.

4395 **www.iics.org**
International Interactive Communication Society

For communications industry professionals dedicated to the advancement of interactive technologies. Provides a forum to share ideas, applications amd techniques for effective use of interactive media.

4396 **www.iste.org**
International Society for Technology in Education

Nonprofit professional organization with a worldwide membership of leaders and potential leaders in educational technology.

4397 **www.kagan.com**
Kagan World Media

For those interested in investments in radio and TV stations and publicly held companies.

4398 **www.kausfiles.com**

Site for journalists and media specialists.

4399 **www.liberty.uc.wlu.edu**
Journalism Resources

Lists of newspapers, film resources, jobs and internships and political advocacy groups.

4400 **www.missouri.edu/~foiwww**
Affiliation of University of Missouri

Maintains files documenting actions by government, media and society affecting the flow and content of information. Call or write for assistance with researching media topics or instruction in using access laws.

4401 **www.netage.com**
Networking Institute

Promotes networks to help people work together. Offers consulting services, educational workshops and seminars.

4402 **www.nfais.com**

Serves those groups that aggregate, organize, and facilitate access to information. To improve member capabilities and contribute to their ongoing success. Provides opportunities for education, advocacy, and a forum to address common interests.

4403 **www.nsaspeaker.org**
National Speakers Association

The leading organization for experts who speak professionally. NSA's 4000 members include experts in a variety of industries and disciplines, who reach audiences as trainers, educators, humorists, motivators, consultants, authors and more. NSA provides resources and education designed to advance the skills, integrity, and value of its members and speaking profession. NSA the voice of the speaking profession.

4404 **www.postcom.org**
Association for Postal Commerce

National Organization representing those who use, or support the use, of mail as a medium for communication and commerce. Postcom publishes a weekly newsletter covering postal policy and operational issues.

4405 **www.poynter.org**

Poynter Institute is dedicated to teaching and inspiring journalists and media leaders.

Promotes excellence and integrity in the practice of craft and in the practical leadership of successful businesses.

4406 **www.regionalmagazines.org**
International Regional Magazine Association

Promotes the interests of international and regional magazine professionals.

4407 **www.retailing.org**
Electronics Retailing Association

For infomercial producers, marketers, product developers, broadcasters and other industries serving the infomercial market.

4408 **www.speakingsuccess.com**
Personal Achievement Institute

4409 **www.theabc.org**
Association for Business Communication

International organization commited to fostering excellence in business communication scholarship, research, education, and practice.

4410 **www.toastmasters.org**
Toastmasters International

Publishes educational articles on the subjects of communication and leadership. Topics include language, listening, humor, self-improvement, goal setting, success and logical thinking.

4411 **www.wgbh.org**
WGBH Educational Foundation

WGBH productions are seen and heard on stations around the country.

Associations

4412 **AIM Global**
125 Warrendale-Bayne Road
Warrendale, PA 15086
724-934-4470
FAX: 724-934-4495
info@aimglobal.org
www.aimglobal.org
Dan Mullen, President
Mary Ann Thompson, Member Service Coordinator
A global trade association comprising providers of components, networks, systems, and services that manage the collection and integration of data with information management systems.
900+ Members Founded: 1972

4413 **ARMA**
ARMA International
13725 W 109th Street
Suite 101
Lenexa, KS 66215
913-341-3808
FAX: 913-341-3742 800-422-2762
hq@arma.org www.arma.org
Peter Hermann, Executive Director
A not-for-profit association and the leading authority on managing records and information - paper and electronic.
Founded: 1956

4414 **Alpha Micro Users Society**
210 N Iris Avenue
Rialto, CA 92376-5727
909-874-6214
FAX: 909-874-2143
info@amus.org www.amus.org
Jeff Kreider, President
An organization supported by members to promote the uses of computers manufactured by Alpha Micro Products of Irvine, California. This basic purpose has expanded, over the years, from merely a focal point for the exchange of technical information on its use and versatility, to promotion of products (Software and Hardware) from Alpha Micro and various third party organizations having an interest in users of Alpha Micro computers.
125 Members Founded: 1978

4415 **American Association for Artificial Intelligence**
445 Burgess Drive
Menlo Park, CA 94025-3442
650-328-3123
FAX: 650-321-4457
info@aaai.org www.aaai.org
Alan Mackworth, President
Ted Senator, Treasurer/Secretary
Nonprofit society devoted to advancing the scientific understanding of the mechanisims underlying thought and intellegent behavior and their embodiment in machines.
6000 Members Founded: 1979

4416 **American Council For Technology**
11350 Random Hills Road
Suite 120
Fairfax, VA 22030
703-218-1955
FAX: 703-218-1960
act@iac@actgov.org www.actgov.org
Barry C West, President
Wilbert Berrios, Executive VP
Ken Allen, Executive Director
Kristin Cleveland, Communications Manger
A membership driven nonprofit organization that leads the IT community to improve government. ACT facilitates and encourages education, communication and collaboration across all levels of government.
50000 Members Founded: 1979

4417 **American Medical Informatics Association**
4915 St. Elmo Avenue
Suite 401
Bethesda, MD 20814
301-657-1291
FAX: 301-657-1296
mail@mail.amia.org www.amia.org
Charles Safran, President
Joan S Ash, Director
Eta S Berner, Secretary
Karen Greenwood, Manager
Patricia Ann Abbott, Director
Support all those involved with commercial and scientific medical informatics software and hardware, supplies and services. Hosts annual trade show.
3200 Members Founded: 1990 2000 names

4418 **American Public Human Services Association Information Systems Management**
810 First Street NE
Suite 500
Washington, DC 20002
202-682-0100
FAX: 202-289-6555 www.aphsa.org
Karl B Kurtz, President
Charisse Mitchel, Chief Operating Officer
Dan Engstrom, VP
John Cuddy, Treasurer
Jerry W. Friedman, Executive Director
The first national group for those concerned with the delivery of government aid to the poor. It was founded as the American Public Welfare Association and later renamed. The mission is to develop, promote and implement public human service policies and practices that improve the health and well-being of families, children and adults.
1,200 Members Founded: 1930

4419 **American Society for Information Science and Technology**
1320 Fenwick Lane
Suite 510
Silver Spring, MD 20910
301-495-0900
FAX: 301-495-0810
asis@asis.org www.asis.org
Michael Leach, President
June Lester, Treasurer
Richard Hill, Executive Director
ASIS&T has been the society for information professionals leading the search for new and better theories, techniques, and technologies to improve access to information.
4000 Members Founded: 1937

4420 **American Society for Precision Engineering**
PO Box 10826
Raleigh, NC 27605-0826
919-839-8444
FAX: 919-839-8039
webmaster@aspe.net www.aspe.net
David L Trumper, President
Steven R Patterson, VP
Vivek G. Badami, Treasurer
Thomas A. Dow, Executive Director
Members are from academia, industry and government, and include professionals in engineering, materials science, physics, chemistry, mathematics and computer science. Multidisciplinary professional and technical society concerned with precision engineering research and development, design and manufacturing of high accuracy components and systems.
Founded: 1986

4421 **Armed Forces Communications & Electronics Association**
4400 Fair Lakes Center
Fairfax, VA 22033-3899
703-311-1397
FAX: 703-631-6169 800-336-4583
service@afcea.org www.afcea.org
Herb Browne, President/CEO
Becky Nolan, Executive VP
John A. Dubia, Executive VP
AFCEA serves as a bridge between government requirements and industry capabilities, representing the top government, industry, and military professionals in the fields of information technology, communications, and intelligence.
31000 Members Founded: 1946

4422 **Association for Computing Machinery**
1515 Broadway
New York, NY 10036
212-697-7440
FAX: 212-302-5826 800-342-6626
mandelbaum@acm.org www.acm.org
John R White, Executive Director/CEO
Patricia Ryan, Deputy Exec Director Operations/COO
Wayne Graves, Director of Information Systems
Russell Harris, Director of Financial Services
Association for advancing the skills of information technology professionals and for interpreting the impact of information technology on society.
80000 Members Founded: 1947

4423 **Association for Educational Communication & Technology**
1800 N Stonelake Drive
Suite 2
Bloomington, IN 47407
812-335-7675
FAX: 812-335-7678 877-677-2328
aect@aect.org www.aect.org
Wes Miller, President
Ken Harmaning, Secretary/Treasurer
Dr. Phillip Harris, Executive Director
Ned Shaw, Director of Marketing/Communication
A professional association of thousands of educators and others whose activities are directed towards improving instruction through technology.
Founded: 1923

4424 **Association for Information and Image Management International**
1100 Wayne Avenue
Suite 1100
Silver Spring, MD 20910
301-587-8202
FAX: 301-587-2711 800-477-2446
aiim@aiim.org www.aiim.org
AJ Hyland, Chair
Larry Wischerth, Vice Chair
Don McMahan, Treasurer
Global authority on enterprise content management (ECM). ECM Technologies are

used to create, capture, customize, deliver, and manage information to support business process.
Founded: 1943

4425 **Association for Services Management International**
1342 Colonial Boulevard
Suite 25-D
Fort Myers, FL 33907-1084
239-275-7887
FAX: 239-275-0794 800-333-9786
afsmi@afsmi.org www.afsmi.org

Herb Kamensky, Chairman/President
Nancy Alm, VP
Tom Schlick, Treasurer
Martin R. Gilday, Secretary

Provides the knowledge, fellowship and career connections that customer services and support managers for technology based products and solutions needed for professional and career development.
$375.00
Membership Fee Founded: 1975

4426 **Association for the Advancement of Computing in Education**
PO Box 1545
Chesapeake, VA 23327-1545
757-366-5606
FAX: 703-997-8760
info@aace.org www.aace.org

Dr Gary H Marks, Executive Director

An international, educational and professional nonprofit organization dedicated to the advancement of the knowledge, theory and quality of learning and teaching at all levels with information technology.
Founded: 1981

4427 **Association of Information Technology Professionals**
401 N Michigana Avenue
Suite 2400
Chicago, IL 60611-4267
312-245-1070
FAX: 312-527-6636 800-224-9371

Brian J Reithel, President
Mark Gilfand, Executive VP/President Elect
Teresa Hickerson, Secretary/Treasurer

Comprised of career minded individuals who seek to expand their potential employers, employees, managers, programmers, and many others. The organization seeks to provide avenues for all their members to be teachers as well as students and to make contacts with other members in the IS field, all in an effort to become more marketable in rapidly changing, technological careers.

Founded: 1951

4428 **Association of Personal Computer User Group**
3155 E Patrick Lane
Suite 1
Las Vegas, NV 89120-3481

800-558-6867

Susy Ball, President
Ash Nallawalla, VP
Jim Evans, Secretary
Steve Peyrot, Treasurer

Dedicated to helping member computer user groups succeed. The APCUG helps to foster communications by operating as informal network between user group organizations and also with companies that provide computer related and internet related goods and services.

4429 **Business Software Alliance**
1150 18th Street NW
Suite 700
Washington, DC 20036
202-725-5501
FAX: 202-872-5501
info@bsa.org www.bsa.org

Robert W Holleyman II, President/CEO
Robert Cresanti, VP Public Policy
Jeffrey Hardee, VP
Diane Smiroldo, VP of Public Affairs
Scott Van Hove, Vice President of Global Operations

An organization dedicated to promoting a safe and legal digital world. BSA educates consumers on software management and copyright protection, cyber security, trade, e-commerce and other internet related issues.
Founded: 1988

4430 **Business Technology Association**
12411 Wornall Road
Kansas City, MO 64145
816-941-3100
FAX: 816-941-2829
info@bta.org www.bta.org

Mark Naylor, President
John Heiser, VP
Bert Darling, Executive Director

Serving independent dealers, value-added resellers, systems integrators, manufacturers and distributors in the business equipment and systems industry. BTA helps its members profit through a wide variety of services, including free legal advice and guidance; business benchmarking studies and reports; information on the latest news, trends, and products in the industry.

4431 **CEMA: Computer Event Marketing Association**
1512 Weiskopf Loop
Round Rock, TX 78664
512-310-8330
FAX: 512-682-0555
info@cemaonline.com
www.cemaonline.com

Mitch Ahiers, President
Joseph Spaccarelli, VP
Billie Little, Treasurer
Alexia Henrie, Secretary
Erika Brunke, Executive Director

Serving marketing professionals in the high technology industry. CEMA has grown to represent the interest of marketing communications professionals in the information technology industry.
500 Members $275-$775 Membership Fee
Founded: 1990

4432 **Carnegie Mellon University: Information Networking Institute**
4616 Henry Street
Pittsburgh, PA 15213
412-682-2905
FAX: 412-268-7196
ini-infobboard@andrew.cmu.edu
www.ini.cmu.edu

Dena Haritos-Tsamitis, Director
Terri Weinberg, Administrative Assistant
Tracey Bragg, Business & Enrollment Manager
Sean O'Leary, Manager

Established as the nation's first research and education center devoted to Information Networking. INI focuses on professional degree programs that combine technologies, economics, and policies of global communication networks and information security.
300 Members Founded: 1989

4433 **CompTIA**
1815 S Meyers Road
Suite 300
Oakbrook Terrace, IL 60181-5228
630-678-8300
FAX: 630-268-1384
info@comptia.org www.comptia.org

Robert J Sartor, Chairman
Martin Bean, Vice Chairman
John Venator, President/CEO
Kevin Gilroy, Secretary
Jon Reardon, Treasurer

CompTIA is the leading association representing the international technology community. Its goal is to provide a unified voice, global advocacy and leadership, and to advance industry growth through standards, professional competence, education and business solutions.
20000 Members Founded: 1984

4434 **Computer Assisted Language Instruction Consortium**
Texas State University
214 Centennial Hall
San Marcos, TX 78666
512-452-2111
FAX: 512-245-9089
info@calico.org www.calico.org

Robert Fischer, Executive Director
Esther Horn, Manager

A professional association for language teachers, linguists, courseware developers and governments who are interested in teaching languages with the use of computer assisted instruction.
780 Members Founded: 1983

4435 **Computer Security Institute**
600 Harrison Street
San Francisco, CA 94107
415-947-6320
FAX: 415-905-2218
csi@cmp.com www.gocsi.com

Chris Keating, Director
Nancy Baer, Marketing Manager
Mary Griffin, Membership Director
Fran Timmerman, Operations Manager

The world's leading membership organization specifically dedicated to serving and training the information, computer and network security professional. *$224.00*
Membership Fee Founded: 1974

4436 **Computerized Medical Imaging**
National Biomedical Research Foundation

3900 Reservoir Road NW
Washington, DC 20007
202-687-2121
FAX: 202-687-1662
ledley@nbrf.georgetown.edu
www.pir.georgetown.edu/nbrf/contact.html

Blaire V Mossman, Chief Administrator

Formerly the Computerized Radiology Society. A source for the exchange of information concerning the medical use of computerized tomography in radiological diagnosis.
Founded: 1977

4437 Computing Research Association
1100 17th Street NW
Suite 507
Washington, DC 20036-4632
202-234-2111
FAX: 202-667-1066
info@cra.org www.cra.org

James D Foley, Chairman
Lori Clark, Vice Chair
Philip Bernstein, Treasurer
Kathleen McKeown, Secretary
Dana Neill, Manager

Our mission is to seek to strengthen research and advanced education in computing and allied fields.
200 Members Founded: 1972

4438 Data Interchange Standards Association (DISA)
7600 Leesburg Pike
Suite 430
Falls Church, VA 22043
703-487-7005
FAX: 703-970-4488 888-363-2334
info@disa.org www.disa.org

David Hutchings, Chairman
Mark Tiggas, Vice Chairman
Jerry C. Connors, President
Steve Bass, Secretary
David Barkley, Treasurer

Nonprofit home for the development of cross-country electronic business interchange standards.
800+ Members Founded: 1986

4439 Data Management Association
126 E Wing Street
Suite 201
Arlington Heights, IL 60004
847-673-2478

vpmembership@damachicago.org
www.damachicago.org

Gordon Benkler, President
Virginia Farell, VP Membership
Olena Dikina, Secretary
Warren Cotton, Treasurer

A vendor independent professional organization dedicated to the advancement of data asset management concepts.
Founded: 1986

4440 Electronics Industries Alliance
2500 Wilson Boulevard
Arlington, VA 22201
703-907-7500
FAX: 703-907-7602 www.eia.org

Dave McCurdy, President/CEO
Charles L Robinson, COO
James Shiring, Secretary/Treasurer

A national trade organization that includes a full spectrum of U.S. manufacturers. The alliance is a partnership of electronic and high-tech associations and companies whose mission is promoting the market development and competitiveness of the U.S. high-tech industry through domestic and international policy efforts.
1300 Members Founded: 1952

4441 Enterprise Computing Solutions
26024 Acero
Mission Viejo, CA 92691-2768
949-609-1980
FAX: 949-609-1981
cbulter@thinkecs.com
www.thinkecs.com

David Butler, President/CEO
Cheryl Butler, CFO
Bruce Underwood, VP of Professional Services

A leading provider of IT infrastructure solutions for Fortune 500 and mid-tier companies throughout California. ECS builds sophisticated IT infrastructure solutions for mission-critical applications, provides enterprise storage solutions that ensure data protection and business continuity, and delivers state-of-the-art server solutions for optimal computing capacity.
500 Members Founded: 1995

4442 Federation of Government Information Processing Councils
11350 Random Hills Road
Suite 120
Fairfax, VA 22030
703-218-1955
FAX: 703-218-1960
fgipc@fgipc.org www.fgipc.org

James D Buckner, President
Mary Ann Emely, Executive Director

Members are information resources management councils, as well as various government professionals.
38M Members Founded: 1979

4443 Independent Computer Consultants Association (ICCA)
11131 S Towne Square
Suite F
St. Louis, MO 63123-7817
314-892-1675
FAX: 314-487-1345 800-774-4222
info@icca.org www.icca.org

Joyce Burkard, Executive Director

Provides professional development opportunities and business support programs for independent computer consultants. Chapters are in many major metropolitan areas representing nearly 1,000 consulting firms nationwide.
1000 Members Founded: 1976

4444 Information Systems Audit & Control Association
3701 Algonquin Road
Suite 1010
Rolling Meadows, IL 60008
847-253-1545
FAX: 847-253-1443
publication@isaca.org www.isaca.org

Marios Damiandes, International President
Susan M Caldwell, CEO

Supports all those involved with IS controls, security and quality assurance, financial and banking institutions, consulting and public accounting groups, and manufacturing organizations and utilities. Publishes bi-monthly magazine.
35000 Members Founded: 1967

4445 Information Technology Management Institute
PO Box 890
Merrifield, VA 22116
703-208-9610
FAX: 703-208-9604
info@itm-inst.com www.itm-inst.com

Dr. Diane Murphy, CEO/Founder

Association for information technology organizations primarily in the US.
90 Members Founded: 1996

4446 Institute of Electrical & Electronics Engineers Computer Society
1730 Massachusetts Avenue NW
Washington, DC 20036-1992
202-371-0101
FAX: 202-728-9614
webmaster@computer.org
www.computer.org

Jeffry W Raynes, Executive Director
Anita Wills, Executive Assistant
Ann Marie Kelly, Associate Executive Director
Henry Buchheit, Operations Associate
David Jundt, Operations Associate

Supports all those involved in use and design of multimedia hardware, software and systems in industry, business, academia and the arts.
10000 Members Founded: 1946

4447 International Association for Computer Systems Security
6 Swarthmore Lane
Dix Hills, NY 11746-4829
631-499-1616
FAX: 631-462-9178
iacssjalex@aol.com www.iacss.com

Robert J Wilk, President/Founder

Offers a testing program and upholds professional ethics. Supports education through workshops and sponsors lectures.
Founded: 1981

4448 International Association of Knowledge Engineers
973 Russell Avenue
Gaithersburg, MD 20879-3292
301-948-5390
FAX: 301-926-4243 www.iake.org

Milton White, Owner
Julie Walker-Lowe, Executive Director

An international association of computer professionals concerned with designing reasoning machines and computer systems to receive, organize and maintain human knowledge.
Founded: 1987

4449 International Society for Technology in Education
175 W Broadway
Ste 300
Eugene, OR 97401-3042
541-023-3770
FAX: 541-302-3778 800-336-5191
iste@iste.org www.iste.org

Kurt Steinhaus, President
Don Knezek, CEO
Leslie Conery, Deputy CEO
Brenda Aspaas, Senior Executive Assistant

A professional organization with a worldwide membership of leaders and potential leaders in educational technology. We are dedicated to providing leadership and service to improve teaching and learning by advancing the effective use of technology in K-12 education and teacher education. We provide our members with information, networking opportunities, and guidance as they face the challenge of incorporating computers, the Internet, and other new technologies into their schools.

4450 **International Technology Law Association/ ITechLaw**
401 Edgewater Pl
Ste 600
Wakefield, MA 01880-6200
781-876-8877
FAX: 781-224-1239
memberservices@itechlaw.org
www.itechlaw.org
Esther B Nunes, President
Amy-Lynne Williams, VP
Richard Allan Horning, Treasurer
Enrique J. Batalla, Secretary
Barbara Fieser, Executive Director
Computer Law Association changed its identity to ITechLaw to better reflect its global activities and expanded focus. Providing benefit to the worldwide community of information technology law professionals.
2000 Members Founded: 1971

4451 **Internet Alliance**
1111 19th Street NW
Suite 1180
Washington, DC 20035-5782
202-284-4380

emilyh@internetalliance.org
www.internetalliance.org
Emily T Hackett, Executive Director
Kaye Caldwell, California Policy Director
Formerly the Interactive Services Association, the Alliance has been the only consisted voice representint internet companies in the 50 states. We have a proven track record of blocking or mitigating privacy and anti-spam legislation, and a high level of expertise in the Internet state tax area.
Founded: 1999

4452 **NaSPA: Association for Corporate Computing Technical Professionals**

NaSPA
7044 S 13th Street
Oak Creek
Milwaukee, WI 53154
414-688-8000
FAX: 414-768-8001 www.naspa.com
Scott Sherer, President/Director
Emit Hurdelbrink, Chairman/Director
Bennie Shearer, Director
Radi Shourbaji, VP of Marketing
Edward J. Krueger, Director of Membership Services
NaSPA once stood for National Systems Programmers Association but as the association evolved over the years the name was eventually changed to Network and Systems Professionals Association. Our mission is to serve the means to enhance the status and promote the advancement of all network and systems professionals; nurture member's technical and managerial knowledge and skills and many more.
50000 Members Founded: 1986

4453 **National Association of Computer Consultant Businesses**
1420 King Street
Suite 610
Alexandria, VA 22314
703-838-2050
FAX: 703-838-3610
staff@naccb.org www.naccb.org
Dave Vadis, Chairman
Mark Roberts, CEO
Mark Granger, President
Jeffrey Neal, Secretary/Treasurer
Members are companies providing technical support services to clients such as programming, systems analysis and software/hardware engineering.
300 Members Founded: 1987

4454 **Online Audiovisual Catalogers**
Minnesota State University
Memorial Library 3097
PO Box 8419
Mankota, MN 56002-2645
507-892-2147
FAX: 904-620-2719
gerhart@u.washington.edu
www.olacinc.org
Rebecca Lubas, President
Amy K Weiss, Secretary
Bobby Bothmann, Treasurer
To establish and maintain a group that could speak for catalogers of audiovisual materials. Provides a means for exchange of information, continuing education, and communication among catalogers of audiovisual materials and with the Library of Congress. Maintaining a voice with the bibliographic utilities that speak for catalogers of audiovisual materials, works toward common understanding of AV cataloging practices and standards.
Founded: 1980

4455 **Open Applications Group**
PO Box 4897
Marietta, GA 30061
678-715-7588
FAX: 770-234-6036
info@openapplications.org
www.openapplications.org
David M Connelly, President/CEO
Michelle Rascoe, Business Manager
George Siegle, Executive Manager
Michelle Rascoe, Business Manager
A not-for-profit open standards group building process-based XML standards for both B2B and A2A integration.
Founded: 1994

4456 **Optical Society of America**
2010 Massachusetts Avenue NW
Washington, DC 20036-1023
202-223-8130
FAX: 202-223-1096
info@osa.org www.osa.org
Tony Keane, Chief Operating Officer
Beth T Hampton, Chief Marketing Officer
Elizabeth A. Rogan, Executive Director
Deborah C. Herrin, Sr. Director of Information
Organized to increase and diffuse the knowledge of optics, pure and applied; to promote the common interests of investigators of optical problems, of designers and of users of optical apparatus of all kinds; and to encourage cooperation among them. *$95.00*
15000 Members Membership Fee Founded: 1916

4457 **Personal Computer Memory Card International Association**
2635 N First Street
Suite 218
San Jose, CA 95134
408-433-2273
FAX: 408-433-9558
office@pcmcia@org www.pcmcia.org

Bradley Saunders, Chairman
Ken Stufflebeam, President
Brian Ikeya, Secretary
Jim Koser, Treasurer
Patrick Maher, Executive Director
Created to establish standards for Integrated Circuit cards and to promote interchangeability among mobile computers where ruggedness, low power, and small size were critical.
200+ Members Founded: 1989

4458 **Polar Microsystems**
1000 Rambler Road
Glenside, PA 19038-7152
215-402-0700

polar@netaxs.com
www.polarmicro.com
Doug C Baer, Senior Systems Engineer
Provides consulting services that enable our clients to advance their businesses through full utilization of the Apple Macintosh hardware and software platform.

4459 **Portable Computer and Communications Association**
PO Box 680
Hood River, OR 97031
541-490-5140
FAX: 419-831-4779
pcca@pcca.org www.pcca.org
Gloria Kowalski, Executive Director
Peter Rysavy, Director
Chris Burke, Director
Boris Fridman, Director
Jim Hobbs, Director
Represents firms, organizations and individuals interested in mobile communications. PCCA publishes information, standards, software and other materials.
$100.00
75 Members Individual Membership Fee Founded: 1992

4460 **Society For Modeling Simulation International**
PO Box 17900
San Diego, CA 92177-7900
858-277-3888
FAX: 858-277-3930
info@scs.org www.scs.org
Francois Cellier, President
John Hamilton Jr., Senior VP
Levent Yilmaz, Secretary
S. Narayanan, Treasurer
Stephen Branch, Executive Director
The only technical Society dedicated to advancing the use of modeling & simulation to solve real-world problems. SCS is the principal technical society devoted to the advancement of simulation and allied computer arts in all fields. *$55.00*
Regular Membership Dues Founded: 1952

4461 **Society for Imaging Science and Technology**
7003 Kilworh Lane
Springfield, VA 22151-4088
703-642-9090
FAX: 703-642-9094
info@imaging.org www.imaging.org
James C King, President
James R Milch, Executive VP
Linda T. Creagh, Treasurer
Gabriel Marcu, Secretary
Peter D. Burns, Treasurer
Our goal is to keep members aware of the latest scientific and technological developments in the field of imaging through conferences, journals and other publications. We focus on imaging in all its aspects, with

particular emphasis on silver halide, digital printing, electronic imaging, photofinishing, image preservation, image assessment, pre-press technologies and hybrid imaging systems.
2000+ Members

4462 Society for Information Display
610 S 2nd Street
San Jose, CA 95112-4006
408-977-1013
FAX: 408-977-1531
office@sid.org www.sid.org
Larry Weber, President
Paul Drzaic, Treasurer
Munisamy Anandan, Secretary
Representing the international and local display communities. Offers opportunites to network, recieve information and publications and news about trade shows.
6000 Members Founded: 1962

4463 Society for Materials Engineers and Scientists
3440 E University Drive
Phoenix, AZ 85034
602-470-5700
FAX: 602-437-8497
general.inquiries@asm.com
www.asm.com
Arthur H del Prado, President/CEO
Robert L de Bakker, CFO
Haijo D J Pietersma, Deputy CEO
Han F M Westendorp, COO of Front End Operations
Chuck D del Prado, General Manager
A leading supplier of semiconductor process equipment in both front and back end markets. The Company possesses a strong technological base, state-of-the-art manufacturing facilities, a competent and qualified workforce and a highly trained, strategically distributed support network.
Founded: 1968

4464 Society of Manufacturing Engineers International
1 SME Drive
Dearborn, MI 48121
313-271-1500
FAX: 313-425-3401 800-733-4763
service@sme.org www.sme.org
William J Geary, President
Edward H Abbott, VP
F. Brian Holmes, Secretary/Treasurer
Nancy S. Berg, Executive Director/General Manager
An association that provides information on various automated and computerized systems.
33 Members Founded: 1932

4465 Software Engineering Institute
Carnegie Mellon University
Pittsburgh, PA 15213-3890
412-687-7700
FAX: 412-268-6257
customer-relations@sei.cmu.edu
www.sei.cmu.edu
Paul D Nielsen, Chief Executive Officer
Clyde Chittister, Chief Operating Officer
A federally funded research and development center sponsored by the U.S. Department of Defense through the Office of the Under Secretary of Defense for Acquisition, Technology, and Logistics. Supports all those engineers involved in the software industry.

4466 Software Management Network
4546 El Camino Real
B10 - Suite 237
Los Altos, CA 94022
650-941-4027
FAX: 650-941-4028
jmgolub@softwaremanagement.com
www.softwaremanagement.com
Nicholas Zvegintzov, President/Chief Technical Officer
Judith Marx Golub, VP/CFO
A publishing, consulting, and training group that serves professional software teams responsible for working, installed software systems. Its unique mission is to make available the most effective resources for managing active software.
Founded: 1981

4467 Uni Forum Association
PO Box 3177
Annapolis, MD 21403
410- 71-5950
FAX: 240-465-0207 800-333-8649
afedder@uniforum.org
www.uniforum.org
Alan Fedder, President
Deborah Murray, VP
John Lehmann, Board Member
Phil Hughes, Board Member
Jon Hall, Board Member
Professional association for end users, developers and vendors. Promotes and exchanges information about the practices and benefits of open technologies and related hardware, software, applications and standards.
Founded: 1981

4468 Vmebus International Trade Association
PO Box 19658
Fountain Hills, AZ 85269
480-837-7486

info@vita.com www.vita.com
Ray Alderman, Executive Director
Jerry Gipper, Marketing Director
Association for manufacturers of microcomputer boards, hardware, software, military products, controllers, bus interfaces and other accessories compatible with VMEbus architecture. *$2500.00*
150 Members Regular Membership Fee
Founded: 1984

Newsletters

4469 AAR Newsletter
School of Information Technology & Engineering
University of Ottawa
800 King Edward Avenue
Ottawa, Canada
613-562-5738
FAX: 613-562-5664
pieper@mcs.anl.gov
www-unix.mcs.anl.gov
Gail W Pieper, Editor
Represents research notes and problem sets, discusses software advances and announces conferences and workshops.
Quarterly

4470 ADAIC News
Ada Information Clearinghouse
201 ILR Extension Building
Cornell University
Ithaca, NY 14853-3901
607-255-2763
800-949-4232
northeastada@cornell.edu
http://www.northeastada.org
Susan Carlson, Publisher
Information on Ada-an internationally standardized, general purpose computer language used in a variety of applications includes news of the Ada community.
Founded: 2001
Circulation: 20,000

4471 AEC Automation Newsletter
Technology Automation Services
PO Box 3593
Englewood, CO 80155-3593
303-770-1728
FAX: 303-770-3660
david@aecnews.com
http://www.aecnews.com
Jeff Rowe, Editor
David Weisberg, Circulation Director
Randall S Newton, Editor-In-Chief
W Bradley Holtz, Group Publisher
Joel N Orr, Senior Editor
Reports on computer hardware and software issues relevant to architectural design, civil engineering, structural design, process plant design and geographic information management. Includes articles on software developments, new computer hardware, business issues, operating systems, application software, networking and technology developments. *$235.00*
16 pages Monthly Founded: 1977
Printed in 1 color on matte stock

4472 AI Interactions
Academy of International Business
Michigan State University
7 Eppley Center
East Lansing, MI 48824-1121
517-432-4336
FAX: 517-432-1009
ciber@msu.edu
http://ciber.msu.edu/events/cibernews
G Tomas M Hult, Executive Secretary
Irem Kiyak, Associate Director
Calls for papers, meeting notices and membership news of interest to professors of international business around the world.
$57.00
Founded: 1959
Circulation: 2700

4473 Acronyms
Computer Laboratory Michigan State University
40F Computer Ctr
East Lansing, MI 48824-1042
517-355-3600
FAX: 517-355-5176
Linda Dunn, Publisher
A listing of procedures, policies, hardware and software for computer users.
Quarterly

4474 Advanced Office Technologies Report
DataTrends Publications
PO Box 4460
Leesburg, VA 20177-8541
703-779-0574
FAX: 703-779-2267 800-766-8130
Offers information on products, technological breakthroughs and industry developments in office automation technology.

Full-text

4475 **Alpha Forum**
Pinnacle Publishing
316 N Michigan Avenue
Suite 300
Chicago, IL 60601
312-272-2401
FAX: 312-960-4106 800-493-4867
pinpub@ragan.com
http://www.pinpub.com
Brent Smith, Publisher
David Stevenson, Editor
Technical newsletter for application developers and users. Hands-on articles with specific usage and programming techniques, tips and product updates.
16 pages Monthly Founded: 1990
Circulation: 8000 Audited
Mailing list available for rent
Printed in 2 colors on matte stock

4476 **Applications Software**
Thomson Media
1 State Street Plaza
27th Floor
New York, NY 10004
212-258-8445
FAX: 212-843-9600
James Malkin, President/CEO
William Johnson, CFO
General business management and word processing, reference services, custom services and CD-ROM services.
Monthly

4477 **Artificial Intelligence Letter**
Kluwer Academic Publishers
101 Philip Drive
Norwell, MA 02061-1677
781-871-6600
FAX: 781-871-6528
Masoud Yazdani, Publisher
Provides a forum for the work of researchers and application developers from artificial intelligence, cognitive science and related disciplines.

Circulation: 625

4478 **Bits and Bytes Review**
Bits and Bytes Computer Resources
623 Iowa Avenue
Whitefish, MT 59937-2336
406-862-7280
FAX: 406-862-1124 800-361-7280
Info@bitsbytescomputer.com
http://www.bitsbytescomputer.com
John Hughes, Publisher
Resources and products for the academic field. *$56.90*
Monthly

4479 **Branch Automation News**
Phillips Publishing
7811 Montrose Road
Potomac, MD 20854-2958
301-340-2100
FAX: 301-309-3847
feedback@healthydirections.com
http://www.healthydirections.com
David Smith, Publisher
Kathleen Hawk, Editor
Edward Hauck, President
Kevin Donoghue, CEO
Strategies for planning, implementing and managing bank technology. *$495.00*
Founded: 1974
Circulation: 1000 Est. Pass-Along Circ: 7000
Mailing list available for rent 30342 names
$125 per M.
Printed in 2 colors on matte stock
Computerized version available

4480 **Builders Computer Newsletter**
CMA Microcomputers
113 Wattenbarger
County Road 28
Sweetwater, TN 37874-6135

FAX: 423-337-0222 800-484-4074
Charles W Mann, Editor
Case studies and new technologies related to the use of computers within the construction trades.
Monthly

4481 **Business Computer Report**
Guidera Publishing Corporation
3 Myrtle Bank Road
Hilton Head Island, SC 29926-1809

Lawrence C Oakley, Editor
Hands-on review of business related software, as well as hardware, primarily for the PC world (as opposed to the MAC World). Readers are primarily owners of small to medium-sized businesses. *$95.00*
8 pages Monthly
Circulation: 125,000 Audited
Printed in 1 color on matte stock

4482 **Business Software News**
110 N Bell Avenue
Suite 300
Shawnee, OK 74801-6967
405-275-3100
FAX: 405-275-3101
http://www.cpatechadvisers.com
Shari Bodger, Publisher
Melody Wrinkle, Editor
Shari Bodger, Marketing Manager
Offers updated information on computer software, marketing and technology news. Columnists address networks, sales and management with every issue including independent, comparative software reviews. *$40.00*
8 pages Founded: 1991
Circulation: 1000
Printed in 4 colors on matte stock

4483 **C/C & Users Journal**
Miller Freeman Publications
2800 Campus Drive
San Mateo, CA 94403
650-513-4300
FAX: 650-513-4601 800-365-1364
cuj@neodata.com http://www.cuj.com

Peter Westerman, Publisher
Jon Erickson, Editorial Director
Jessica Marty, Director of Marketing
Amy Stephens, Managing Editor
Information for intermediate and advanced C and C++ programmers. Includes programming techniques, tutorials and software reviews. *$29.95*
Monthly Founded: 1988
Circulation: 39,048

4484 **C/Net News.Com**
CNET
150 Chestnut Street
San Francisco, CA 94111-1004
415-098-8900
FAX: 415-395-9254
Janice.Chen@cnet.com
http://www.cnet.com
Janice Chen, Editor in Chief
John Morris, Editor
Christina Koukkos, Managing Editor
Provides information for high end audiences in the market for tech news, including the IS community, the technology business itself and the financial community.
Daily Founded: 1992

4485 **COM-AND: Computer Audit News & Developments**
Management Advisory Services & Publications
PO Box 81151
Wellesley Hills, MA 02481
781-235-2895
FAX: 781-235-5446
jaykmasp@aol.com
http://www.masp.com
J Kuong, Publisher
JF Kuong, Editor
New standards and practices. Tutorials on impact of EDP on audit and control matters. Practical coverage of technical EDP developments for auditors and internal controls specialists. *$70.00*

The above price is for North America, $82.00 Overseas

8 pages Founded: 1972
Printed in 2 colors on matte stock

4486 **COMDEX Show Daily**
Key 3 Media Group
795 Folsom Street
6th Floor
San Francisco, CA 94107-1243
415-905-2300
FAX: 415-905-2329
sean.cassidy@key3media.com
http://www.medialiveinternational.com
Sean Cassidy, Marketing Manager
Robert Priest-Heck, President/CEO
Tabloid newspaper of computer related exhibits.
Daily
Circulation: 3445

4487 **CPA Technology Advisor**
Harcourt Brace Professional Publishing
525 B Street
Suite 1900
San Diego, CA 92101
619-231-6616
800-831-7799
propub@harcourtbrace.com
http://www.hbpp.com
Jerry Huss, Publisher
Frank Peterson, Editor
Concise unbiased recommendations on hardware and software for CPA's. *$19.00*

4488 **Client/Server Economics Letter**
Computer Economics
2082 Business Center Drive
Suite 240
Irvine, CA 92612
949-831-8700
FAX: 949-442-7688 800-326-8100
Bruno Bassi, Publisher
Don Trevillian, Editor
Economic look at the client/server revolution. Provides critical economic data on costs and risks of client/server computing, backed up with research and presentation-quality graphs and tables. Provides the information you need to make sound business decisions. *$395.00*

Daily Founded: 1978

4489 Comp-U-Fax Computer Trends Newsletter
Microcomputers Software and Consulting
28 S 12th Avenue
Mount Vernon, NY 10550-2913

Bob James, Publisher

Corporate information resource newsletter.

4490 Computer Aided Design Report
CAD/CAM Publishing
1010 Turquoise Street
Suite 320
San Diego, CA 92109-1268
619-379-9420
FAX: 858-488-6052
circulation@cadcamnet.com
www.cadcamnet.com

Jeannette DeWyze, Editor
Shari Glave, Circulation Director

Uses of computers by engineers in the manufacturing trades. *$195.00*

4491 Computer Architecture
IEEE Computer Society
1730 Massachusetts Avenue NW
Washington, DC 20036-1992
202-371-1013
FAX: 202-728-9614

Henry Ayling, Publisher
Lee Blue, Production Manager

Current trends in computer networks, hardware description languages, performance.

Circulation: 2303

4492 Computer Business
Round Table Association SAB
5340 W 57th Street
Los Angeles, CA 90056-1339
310-649-2846

A Hassan, Publisher/Editor
J Hassan, Circulation Manager

Best computer/communications articles of previous month, briefly abstracted. *$20.00*

4493 Computer Economics Report
Computer Economics
2082 Business Center Drive
Ste 240
Irvine, CA 92712
949-831-8700
FAX: 949-442-7688 800-326-8100
custserv@compecon.com
http://www.computereconomics.com

Bruno Bassi, Publisher
Don Trevillian, Editor

Written from an end-user perspective, this monthly newsletter provides analyses of new IBM technologies, plus acquisition and financial management strategies. Regular features include cost comparisons, price/performance analysis, new product forecasts, and evaluations of acquisition techniques for medium and large computer systems. *$595.00*
Monthly Founded: 1978

4494 Computer Industry Report
International Data Corporation
5 Speen Street
#955
Framingham, MA 01701-4674
508-728-8200
FAX: 508-935-4015
http://www.idc.com/

PJ McGovern, Chief Marketing Manager
Doug McLeod, Editor

Research and analysis of the computer processing industry.
Founded: 1964

4495 Computer Integrated Manufacture and Engineering
Lionheart Publishing
2555 Cumberland Parkway SE
Suite 299
Atlanta, GA 30339-3908
770-234-9360
FAX: 770-432-6969

Explores cutting edge developments in manufacturing systems operation management.

Circulation: 24,000

4496 Computer Modeling and Simulation in Engineering
Sage Science Press
2455 Teller Road
Thousand Oaks, CA 91320-2218
805-499-0721
FAX: 805-375-1700
http://www.sagepub.com

S N Alturi, Editor
Blaise Simqu, CEO/President
Ben Bagger, Marketing
Mary Nugent, Circulation Manager

Publishes application-oriented papers that utilize computer modeling and simulation techniques to understand and resolve industrial problems or processes that are of immediate and contemporary interest.
Monthly

4497 Computer Protocols
Worldwide Videotex
PO Box 3273
Boynton Beach, FL 33424-3273
561-738-2276

markedit@juno.com
http://www.wvpubs.com

Mark Wright, Editor/President
Linda Dera, Marketing Manager
Linda Dera, Circulation Manager

Covers news and developments of bridges, gateway and LAN. Coverage also provided on the development of internal protocols. *$165.00*
Monthly Founded: 1981
Circulation: 30000

4498 Computer Reseller News
CMP Publications
One Jericho Plaza
Jericho, NY 11753-1680
516-562-5000
FAX: 516-562-7243
shadowram@mcimail.com
www.crn.com

John Russell, Publisher

Computer news for resellers and distributors.

4499 Computer and Communications Buyer
Technology News of America Company
PO Box 20008
New York, NY 10025-1510
212-966-4466
800-638-7257
subs@eintelligence.com
http://www.eintelligence.com

Yao Yung Chang, Owner
Edward Rosenfeld, Publisher/Editor

Annotated statistical reports on capital equipment. $450.00 outside of United States. *$395.00*
8 pages Monthly Founded: 1984

4500 Computer and Computer Management News and Developments
Management Advisory Services & Publications
PO Box 81151
Wellesley Hills, MA 02481-1301
781-235-2895
FAX: 781-235-5446
jaymasp@aol.com www.masp.com

J Kuong, Publisher

Newsletter aimed at the management level of the computer industry.

4501 Computers & Security
Elsevier Science
6277 Sea Harbor Drive
Orlando, FL 32887
407-345-4020
FAX: 407-363-1354 877-839-7126
usjcs@elsevier.com
http://www.elsevier.com

Andrew Fletcher, Publisher
E Schultz, CEO/President
Ann Dudley, Circulation Manager
Carl Lampert, Editor

International newsletter for the management of computer and information security.

Circulation: 1500

4502 Computers & Structures
Elsevier Science
PO Box 945
New York, NY 10010-945
212-989-5800
FAX: 212-633-3680 888-437-4636
usinfo@sciencedirect.com
http://www.sciencedirect.com

Keith Lambert, Publisher/Editor

Analyzes the many relationships between computer technology and the different fields of engineering.
Founded: 1962
Circulation: 1500

4503 Computers, Foodservice and You
Mike Pappas
1201 S 2nd Street
#338
Raton, NM 87740-2201
505-459-9811
FAX: 505-445-8252

Mike Pappas, Publisher

A newsletter focusing on computers for the hospitality industry. *$119.00*
16 pages Bi-Monthly
Circulation: 450 Audited
Printed in 1 color on matte stock

4504 DM Direct
126 E Wing Street
Suite 201
Arlington Heights, IL 60004
847-673-2478

dmdirect@dmreview.com
www.dmreview.com
In this e-mail newsletter you will find articles, online columnists, news and industry events exclusive to you, the online reader. Our goal is to ensure that DM Direct provides the information you need to compete in the business intelligence, data warehousing and analytics marketplace.

4505 DP Budget
Computer Economics
2082 Business Center Dr.
Ste 240
Irvine, CA 92612
949-831-8700
FAX: 949-442-7688 800-326-8100
Bruno Bassi, Publisher
Michael Erbschloe, Editor-in-Chief
Frank Scavo, President
Report analyzing DP expenses, salary issues and acquisition costs. Focuses on increasing productivity and improving the return on your DP investment. *$495.00*
Monthly

4506 DPFN
Directory & Database Publishers Forum & Network
352 Seventh Avenue
New York, NY 10001-546
212-643-5458
845-358-8034
gstone@ptmcomm.com
http://www.dpfn.com
Barry Lee, Membership Chair
Jeff Fandl, President
Contains events, seminar information, publishers story, industry snapshots, and news pertaining to the industry. Members are large and small directory publishers, vendors to the trade and consultants. Provides networking opportunities and exposure to industry experts through their meetings and workshops.
Founded: 1990
Printed in on matte stock

4507 Data Channels
Phillips Publishing
7811 Montrose Road
Suite 2
Potomac, MD 20854-3394
301-340-2100
FAX: 301-424-4297 800-777-5006
Christopher Scrotton, Publisher
Lane Cooper, Editor
Source of intelligence for executives making data communications decisions. Accepts advertising. *$397.00*
9 pages

4508 Data Security Management
Auerbach Publications
535 5th Avenue
Room 806
New York, NY 10017-3610

800-737-8034
ro'hamley@crepress.com
www.auerbach-publications.com
Rich O'Hanley, Editor
Technical and management information for security managers, networks and systems administrators and data center managers. *$495.00*
Bi-Monthly
Circulation: 1,500
Printed in on matte stock : CD- Room

4509 Dental Computer Newsletter
Andent
1000 N Avenue
Waukegan, IL 60085-2938
847-223-5077

info@andent.net
http://www.andent.net
S Neiburger, Editor
For and by an international group of Dentists, Physicians and allied health professionals interested in computers. Emphasis is on the practical use of all brands of computers for the professional office. *$25.00*
Quarterly
Circulation: 3100

4510 Digital Directions Report
Computer Economics
2082 Business Center Drive
Ste 240
Irvine, CA 92612-6500
949-831-8700
FAX: 949-442-7688 800-326-8100
Bruno Bassi, Publisher
Barbara McDonald, Editor
Frank Scavo, CEO/President
Ed Pasahow, Senior Editor
Provides details on the financial ramifications of future DEC products. The information is critical for decision makers involved with cost-control, strategy planning and new product analysis. *$525.00*
Monthly

4511 Directory of Top Computer Executives
Applied Computer Research
11242 N 19th Avenue
PO Box 82266
Phoenix, AZ 85029-2266
602-216-9100
FAX: 602-216-9200 800-234-2227
taras@acrhq.com
http://www.itmarketintelligence.com
Alan Howard, Managing Editor
Alice Howard, Associate Editor
Computer performance and management. *$370.00*
Founded: 1972
Circulation: 1000 $140 per M.
Printed in 1 color on matte stock

4512 Document Imaging Report
Corry Publishing
5539 Peach Street
Erie, PA 16509
814-380-0025
FAX: 814-864-2037
corrypub@corrypub.com
http://www.corrypub.com
john Coiston, Publisher
Terry Peterson, CEO
Micole Hykes, Editor
Karrie Boocious, Marketing
Melinda Fadden, Circulation Manager
Timely and actionable information on electronic imaging applications, products and user implementation.
Monthly
Circulation: 43000

4513 Dvorak Developments
Freelance Communications
PO Box 666
Ridgway, CO 81432
970-626-2255

Randy Cassingham, Publisher
Promotes the use of the Dvorak keyboard for typewriters and computers. Dvorak is more ergonomic than the common Qwerty keyboard. Accepts advertising.
8 pages

4514 E-News
Patricia Seybold Group
210 Commercial Street
Boston, MA 02109-3504
617-742-5200
FAX: 617-742-1028 800-826-2424
Patricia Seybold, Publisher
E-mail newsletter includes perspectives on the e-commerce industry, research and upcoming events.

4515 EDI News
Phillips Publishing
7811 Montrose Road
Suite 2
Potomac, MD 20854-3394
301-340-2100
FAX: 301-309-3847
Chrisopher Scotton, Publisher
Lane Cooper, Editor
Electronic data interchange marketplace information. *$397.00*
9 pages

4516 EDP Weekly
Millen Publishing Group
1150 Connecticut Avenue NW
Suite 900
Washington, DC 20036
202-624-4330
FAX: 202-659-3493 888-739-8500
SL Millin, Publisher
Tom Shack, Editor
Computer industry publication delivers comprehensive and up-to-date news coverage on the entire industry. *$495.00*
Weekly
Circulation: 1,250

4517 Education Technology News
Business Publishers
8737 Colesville Road
10thFloor
Silver Spring, MD 20910-3928
301-587-6300
FAX: 301-587-4530 800-274-6737
bpinews@bpinews.com
http://www.bpinews.com
Leonard Eiserer, Publisher
Information on educational hardware and software, trends in computer-aided teaching and computer uses in the classroom. *$217.00*
Founded: 1963
Circulation: 500

4518 Electronic Education Report
Simba Information
60 Long Ridge Road
Suite 300
Stamford, CT 06902
203-325-8193
FAX: 203-325-8915 800-307-2529
info@simbanet.com
www.simbanet.com
Linda Kopp, Editorial Director
Donna Devall, Marketing Director

Charlie Friscia, Director of Advertising S
R.R. Bowker, President

News and analysis from a business perspective on software, multimedia/CD-ROM, videodisc, distance learning, Internet/online services and educational videocassettes. *$625.00*

Founded: 1989

4519 Electronic Marketing News
Software Assistance International
PO Box 750
Morris Plains, NJ 07950-0750
973-644-0022
FAX: 973-539-3253

George Papov, Editor

Supplier of electronic catalogs to business and industries.

Circulation: 6,000

4520 End-User Computing Management
Auerbach Publications
535 5th Avenue
Room 806
New York, NY 10017-3610

FAX: 212-297-9176 800-737-8034

Kim Hovan Kelly, Publisher

Technical and mangement information. *$495.00*

BiWeekly
Circulation: 1,000

4521 Engineering Automation Report
Technology Automation Services
711 Chuckanut Drive North
Bellingham, CO 80155-3593
303-689-9099
FAX: 303-770-3660
david@eareport.com
http://www.eareport.com

Dave White, President
David Weisberg,
Publisher/Editor-in-Chief
Rachael Taggart, Assistant Editor
W. Bradley Holtz, Group Publisher
L. Stephen Wolfe, Senior Editor

Reports on computer hardware and software issues relevant to the design, manufacturing and support of mechanical products. Includes articles on software developments, new computer hardware, business issues including financial results, operating systems, application software, networking and technology developments. *$235.00*

Monthly
Circulation: 800 Audited Est. Pass-Along Circ: 2000
Mailing list available for rent 2000 names $100 per M.
Printed in 2 colors on glossy stock

4522 Federal Computer Week
101Communications
3141 Fairview Park Drive
#777
Falls Church, VA 22042-4507
703-876-5100
FAX: 703-876-5126
http://www.fcw.com

Anne Armstrong, Publisher
Jeff Calore, General Manager

The Federal Computer Week provides practical news, analysis and insight on how to buy, build and manage technology in government.

Circulation: 93000

4523 Forestry Computer Applications
Michaelsen's Micro Magic Publishers
PO Box 7332
Fredericksburg, VA 22404-7332

Nancy Michaelsen, Publisher

Offers news and information on computers and electronics used in the forestry services industry, including manufacturing, building, construction and architecture. *$29.95*

4524 Frontline
Computer Security Institute
600 Harrison Street
San Francisco, CA 94107
415-947-6320
FAX: 818-487-4550
rrichardson@cmp.com
www.gocsi.com

Robert Richardson, Editorial Director
Chris Keating, Director

This quarterly newsletter is to improve the security practices of your entire organization to increase end-user awareness of critical security topics pertaining to them. *$1860.00*

4 pages Annual Subscription

4525 GCN Tech Edition
Post Newsweek Tech Media
10 G Street NE
Suite 500
Washington, DC 20002
202-772-2500
FAX: 202-772-2511 866-447-6864
editorial@gcn.com
http://www.gcn.com

Tom Trezza, Publisher
Tom Temin, Editor-in-Chief
Dave Greene, CEO/President
Kirstin Crane, Marketing Manager
Bar Blaskowsky, Circulation Manager

Evaluates performance, cost and applications of hardware, software, peripheral and communication products available to government agencies and businesses. *$95.00*

Founded: 1998
Circulation: 87500
Printed in on glossy stock

4526 Government Computer News
Reed Business Information
2000 Clearwater Drive
Oak Brook, IL 60523
630-740-0825
www.reedbusiness.com

Thomas Temin, Editor

The national newspaper of government computing. *$53.00*

55 pages Monthly Founded: 1982

4527 Graphic Communications Today
IDEA Alliance
100 Daingerfield Road
4th Floor
Alexandria, VA 22314-2886
703-837-1070
FAX: 703-837-1072
info@idealliance.org
http://www.idealliance.org

Alan Kotok, Editor
David Steinhardt, CEO

Electronic commerce, direct marketing, printing and paper aspects, and graphics updates.

Daily Founded: 1966
Circulation: 200

4528 HIS Insider
United Communications Group
11300 Rockville Pike
Street 1100
Rockville, MD 20852-3030
301-287-2700
FAX: 301-816-8945
webmaster@ucg.com
http://www.ucg.com

Sara Jackson, Editor
Glynn Willet, CEO/President

News and reports on new hospital and clinical information system technologies, upcoming vendor merger acquisitions, analyses of telecommunicaiton systems used in health care. *$427.00*

Weekly Founded: 1977

4529 IN SYNC Magazine
Agate Publishing
21 West 26th Street
New York, NY 10010
847-475-4457
FAX: 651-221-0124 800-283-3572

News and how-to for distributed and cooperative applications. Particularly how to link multiple computer systems to gain best advantage from each. *$8.00*

Circulation: 1000

4530 IS Budget
Computer Economics
2082 Business Center
Dr. Ste 240
Irvine, CA 92612-6500
949-831-8700
FAX: 949-442-7688 800-326-8100

Ed Pasahow, Senior Editor
Jim Miller, Director Sales
Frank Scavo, CEO/President

Tackles today's toughest IS budgeting issues head-on with exhaustively researched line-item cost comparisons by type of industry, installation size, company revenue and type of expenditure. Regular features include MIS spending comparisons, analyses of budgeting issues and inside information on vendor discounts. *$495.00*

Monthly Founded: 1978

4531 Imaging Service Bureau Newsletter
Image Publishing
PO Box 686
Wilton, CT 06897-0686
203-761-9003
FAX: 203-222-7871

Charles Miles, Publisher
John Bryans, Editor
David Miles, Production

Data entry and data conversion service bureaus, CD-ROM and optical disc service bureau profiles. Accepts advertising. *$190.00*

28 pages Bi-Monthly
Circulation: 1,000 Audited
Mailing list available for rent 30000 names $125 per M.

4532 Independent Computer Consultants Newsletter
Independent Computer Consultants Association
11131 S Towne Square
Suite F
St Louis, MO 63123
314-892-1675
FAX: 314-487-1345 800-774-4222
info@icca.org http://www.icca.org

Joyce Burkard, Executive Director

Promotes professional standards in the industry. Conducts educational programs and

maintains local chapters in many major cities. Available to members only.
Founded: 1976
Circulation: 1000
Mailing list available for rent 1200 names $500 per M.
Printed in 2 colors

4533 Inside Microsoft Windows
Cobb Group
115 6th Avenue
Dayton, KY 41074
859-291-1146
FAX: 859-655-2482 800-733-2040
prepress@cobbinc.com
http://www.cobbinc.com
Mark Crane, Publisher
Charity Edelen, Editor
Tom Bell, CEO/President
Tips and techniques for Microsoft Windows. *$49.00*
12 pages Monthly
Circulation: 48630 Audited Est.
Pass-Along Circ: 2610
Printed in 2 colors on matte stock

4534 Inside the Internet
Cobb Group
115 6th Avenue
Dayton, KY 41074
859-291-1146
FAX: 859-655-2482 800-733-2040
Practical advice and instructions for Internet users.

4535 Intelligence: The Future of Computing
Intelligence
PO Box 20008
New York, NY 10025-1510
212-222-1123
800-638-7257
i@eintelligence.com
http://www.eintelligence.com
Edward Rosenfeld, Editor
Edward Rosenfeld, Publisher
Provides coverage of advanced computing: neutral networks, AI, genetic algorithms, fuzzy systems, wavelets, et. al., and the Net, the Web, Nanotechnologies quanteum, molecular and DNA computing. *$395.00*
8 pages Monthly Founded: 1984
Printed in 1 color on matte stock
Computerized version available

4536 Intelligent Software Strategies
Cutter Information Corporation
37 Broadway
Arlington, MA 02474-5552
781-641-2886
Karen Fine Coburn, Publisher
Paul Harmon, Editor
Trends and forecasts for software/hardware industries. *$395.00*
Monthly

4537 International Spectrum
International Spectrum Magazine & Conferences
8956 Fox Drive
Ste 102
Thornton, CO 80260
720-259-1356
FAX: 603-250-0664
nathan@intl-spectrum.com
http://www.intl-spectrum.com
Nathan Rector, President
Monica Giobbi, Manager
Clif Oliver, Editor
Trade magazine for PICK/UNIX/DOS computer industry which covers hardware, software and peripherals. Company produces major trade show held annually in Southern California and regional exhibitions and conferences across the country.
88 pages 6 issues/Yr Founded: 1982
Circulation: 50,000
Mailing list available for rent 80M names
Printed in 4 colors on glossy stock

4538 Managing Human Resource Information Systems
Institute of Management & Administration
29 W 35th Street
5th Floor
New York, NY 10001-2299
212-244-0360
FAX: 212-564-0465 800-401-5937
subserve@ioma.com
http://www.ioma.com/
David Foster, CEO/President
Sue Sangler, Editor
Harry Pateron, Publisher
Covers management issues critical to building and maintaining state-of-the-art HRIS software, hardware, and Internet/intranet activities. It is intended to help control costs of HRIS, make better use of new technologies, migrate HRIS from mainframe, mini, and client/server systems. *$259.00*
Monthly Founded: 1982
Circulation: 180000

4539 Micro Publishing
Cygnus Publishing
445 Broad Hollow Road
Melville, NY 11747
631-845-2700
FAX: 631-845-2798 800-308-6397
James Cavuoto, Publisher
Nancy Whelan, Advertising/Sales
Kenneth Spears, Production
Mark Erikson, Circulation Manager
A newsletter for hardware and software vendors that examines the micro-based publishing systems market, including workstation publishing, printers, scanners, networks, technology and data-based publishing, production methods and page layout software. The editorials consists of microcomputer publishing product reviews, notes, and trend analysis, and new product announcements. *$295.00*
10 pages Monthly
Printed in on matte stock

4540 Network Economics Letter
Computer Economics
5841 Edison Place
Carlsbad, CA 92008-6500
760-438-8100
FAX: 760-431-1126 800-326-8100
Bruno Bassi, Publisher
Don Trevillian, Editor
Provides an executive overview for MIS and network professionals who are involved in network strategic planning and implementation. It covers such topics as comparative analysis of hardware and software systems, cost of ownership studies, analysis of emerging protocols and standards and cost-saving opportunities. *$395.00*
Monthly

4541 OSINetter Newsletter
Architecture Technology Corporation
9971 Valley View Road
Eden Prairie
Minneapolis, MN 20036-9998
952-829-5864
FAX: 952-829-5871
info@atcorp.com
http://www.atcorp.com
Gordon A Palzer, Editor
Rick Edin, CEO
D Thurber, Author
Covers products and company activity in the area of open systems interconnection. *$50.00*
Founded: 1955

4542 Official Memory News
Phillips Publishing
7811 Montrose Road
Suite 2
Potomac, MD 20854-3394
301-340-2100
FAX: 301-309-3847 800-777-5006
Provides the latest news and analysis on OSI standards developments. Accepts advertising. *$497.00*
9 pages Founded: 1974

4543 Open Systems Economics Letter
Computer Economics
2082 Business Center Dr.
Ste. 240
Irvine, CA 92612-6500
949-831-8700
FAX: 949-442-7688 800-326-8100
Bruno Bassi, Publisher
Barbara McDonald, Editor
Frank Scavo, CEO/President
Mark McManus, VP
Addresses the critical economic issues associated with the worldwide transformation to open systems. In a concise, monthly format, this report provides the information that you must have to successfully adopt an open systems strategy, manage your transition to open standards, and protect your corporate investment in new technology. *$395.00*
Monthly

4544 Optical Memory News
Phillips Publishing
7811 Montrose Road
Suite 2
Potomac, MD 20854-3394
301-340-2100
FAX: 301-309-3847
Ellen Stuhlman, Publisher
Marc Osgoode Smith, Editor
Ruth Zellers, Advertising/Sales
Provides the latest news and analysis on the optical storage marketplace from vendor perspective. Accepts advertising. *$397.00*
9 pages BiWeekly
Printed in 1 color on matte stock

4545 Packaged Software Reports
Phillips Decision Point Resources
1111 Marlkress Road
#5062
Cherry Hill, NJ 08003-2334
856-424-1100
FAX: 856-424-1999
Lawrence Feidelman, Publisher
Mark Kistre, Editor
Jerry Phillips, Manager
Evaluations of business application packages that run on micro and mini computers.

4546 **Product Data Management Report**
CAD/CAM Publishing
1010 Turquoise Street
Suite 320
San Diego, CA 92109-1268
619-379-9420
FAX: 858-488-6052
circulation@cadcamnet.com
www.cadcamnet.com

L Wolf, Production
Shari Galve, Circulation

Devoted to product data management software and systems that are used by major manufacturing firms to store, control, and distribute CAD and other engineering data. *$345.00*

4547 **Rapid Prototyping Report**
CAD/CAM Publishing
2880 Stone Trail Dr
Bethesda, MD 20817-4556
240-425-4004
FAX: 301-365-4586
info@cadcamnet.com
http://www.cadcamnet.com

Geoff Smith-Moritz, Editor
L Wolf, Production Manager

Gives in-depth objective appraisals of strengths and weaknesses of rapid prototyping technology. Includes applications on how RP technology is used in the industry. *$295.00*
Monthly

4548 **Release 1.0**
EDventure Holdings
104 5th Avenue
20th Floor
New York, NY 10011-6987
212-924-8800
FAX: 212-924-0240

Daphne Kis, Publisher
Esther Dyson, Editor

Latest developments in the personal computer software industry.

Printed in 2 colors on matte stock

4549 **Report on IBM**
DataTrends Publications
PO Box 4460
Leesburg, VA 20177-8541
703-779-0574
FAX: 703-779-2267
info@datatrendspublications.com
http://www.datatrendspublications.com

Paul Ochs, Publisher

For information technology professionals. *$495.00*
Founded: 1983

4550 **Retail Price Week**
Personal Technology Research
63 Fountain Street
#400
Framingham, MA 01702-6262
508-875-5858
retailweek@aol.com

Casey Dworkin, Publisher

Product-specific advertising and pricing data on microcomputer software, perhipherals and desktop retail commodities.
Weekly
Circulation: 300

4551 **Semiconductor Economics Report**
Relayer Group
8232 E Buckskin Trail
Scottsdale, AZ 85255-2132

Howard Dicken, Publisher

Economics in the microelectronics industry.

4552 **Small Business Systems**
Charles Moore Associates
PO Box 6
Southampton, PA 18966-0006
215-556-6084
FAX: 215-364-2212

Charles Moore, Editor
Nancy Hannigan, Circulation Manager

Case histories which apply computers to solve small business problems.

4553 **Softletter**
Mercury Group
990 Washington Street
Suite 308 S
Dedham, MA 02026
781-518-8600
FAX: 301-816-8945 860-663-0552
jtarter@softletter.com
http://www.softletter.com

Merrill R. Chapman, Publisher
Gail Wertheimer, Editor
Rick Chapman, Marketing Manager

Trends in the microcomputer software industry. *$596.00*
Fortnightly Founded: 1983
Printed in 2 colors : offset

4554 **Softrader**
Amerasia Group
PO Box 53114
Indianapolis, IN 46253-0114

Ben Yanto, Publisher

Shareware public domain programs guide. Accepts advertising.
16 pages BiWeekly

4555 **Software Economics Letter**
Computer Economics
5841 Edison Place
Carlsbad, CA 92008-6500
760-438-8100
FAX: 760-431-1126 800-326-8100

Bruno Bassi, Publisher
Don Trevillian, Editor

Devoted to management and cost control of software investments. Provides the corporate user and information systems communities with a concise analysis of software issues. Profiles the latest trends in software and software licensing and includes analysis of vendor policies and practices. *$395.00*
Daily

4556 **Software Law Bulletin**
Andrews Publications
175 Strafford Avenue
Building 4, Suite 140
Wayne, PA 19087
610-225-0510
FAX: 610-225-0501 800-345-1101

Donna Higgins, Editor
Marry Fox, Publisher

As patenting becomes the predominant method of protecting software, and as cases involving technological copy protection measures wind through the court system, Andrews' Software Law Bulletin provides coverage of decisions and opinions in the key cases. Detailed articles put individual developments into the big picture of the changing software law landscape.

4557 **Software Success**
400 Group
990 Washington
Suite 308 S
Deham, MA 02026
781-518-8600
FAX: 781-320-9466
info@softwaresuccess.com
http://www.softwaresuccess.com

Rob Shapiro, Publisher
Merrill R Chapman, Managing Editor

Reports on the software industry, including compensation, software operating ratio guidelines, company valuation, business management, and coverage of related events and trade shows. *$395.00*
Monthly
Circulation: 1500

4558 **Step-By-Step Electronic Design**
Dynamic Graphics
6000 N Forest Park Drive
Peoria, IL 61614-3592
309-688-8851
FAX: 309-688-6579
servicedgm@dgusa.com
http://www.dgusa.com

Tom Biederbeck, Editor
Kris Elwell, Publisher
Alan Meckler, CEO/President
Mike Demilt, Marketing
Marcy Slane, Manager

For electronic designers, illustrators and prepress professionals, how-to articles with step-by-step techniques. *$36.00*
Founded: 1995
Circulation: 24000

4559 **System Development**
Applied Computer Research
PO Box 82266
Phoenix, AZ 85071-2266
602-216-9100
FAX: 602-216-9200 800-234-2227

Philip Howard, Publisher
Allen Howard, CEO
Tara Saenz, Circulation Manager

Improvement ideas and techniques for software development. *$630.00*
12 pages Bi-annually Founded: 1971
Mailing list available for rent 20M names
$105 per M.
Printed in 1 color on matte stock

4560 **Systems Reengineering Economics Letter**
Computer Economics
2082 Business Center Drive
Suite 240
Irvine, CA 92612-6500
949-831-8700
FAX: 949-442-7688
http://www.computereconomics.com

Bruno Bassi, Publisher
Don Trevillian, Editor

Economic look at the re-engineering explosion, delivering critical information on the methods, costs and risks of systems and business process re-engineering. Updates on the analyses, data, opinions, and case studies you need to make sound business decisions and capitalize on your re-engineering process. *$395.00*

Daily Founded: 1978

4561 **TechTarget**
117 Kendrick Street
Suite 800
Needham, MA 02494
781-657-1000
FAX: 781-657-1100 888-274-4111
info@techtarget.com
http://www.techtarget.com

Carol Crowell, Publisher
Don Hawk, President
Greg Strakosch, CEO
Lisa Johnson, VP Marketing
Catherine Engelke, Director Public Relations

IBM iSeries focused media. The IBM e-Server iSeries (formerly the AS/400) is considered to be the world's most often used multi-user business computer. The installed base worldwide is huge and will get bigger, fueled by incresed Web development. The iSeries come with an integrated Web application server and all the tools needed to build internet, intranet, extranet, and e-commerce sites quickly and will figure promenently into IT strategy and implementation for years to come.
Monthly Founded: 1999

4562 **Technical Computing**
STICS
9714 S Rice Avenue
Houston, TX 77096-4138

AW Crull, Publisher

Computer news and views.

4563 **Technology Advertising & Branding Report**
Simba Information
60 Long Ridge Road
Suite 300
Stamford, CT 06902-234
203-325-8193
FAX: 203-325-8915
info@simbanet.com
http://www.simbanet.com

John McManus, COO/Editorial Direct
John Fuller Fuller, Executive Editor
Charlie Friscia, Director of Advertising S

Offers news, statistics and analysis of advertising strategies in the technology industry. Provides competitive information on the advertising and marketing activities of computer hardware and software companies. Helps computer publishers target advertising sales by reporting the plans of computer advertisers. Shows computer advertisers how to get best buys. *$549.00*
8 pages

4564 **Techweek**
Metro States Media
1156 Aster Avenue
#B
Sunnyvale, CA 94086-6810
408-249-8300
FAX: 408-249-0727
editor@techweek.com
www.techweek.com

John Leggett, Publisher

Provides articles for the local high technology industry programmers. Includes information about the internet, finances, job market, and new products for technology professionals.
BiWeekly
Circulation: 100,000

4565 **TidBITS**
TidBITS
27541 SE 154th Place
Issaquah, WA 98027-7340
425-392-0553

info@tidbits.com
http://www.tidbits.com

Adam Engst, Publisher
Tonya Engst, Editor

Online newsletter and web site, devoted to the person behind the most personal of personal computers, the Macintosh. TidBITS relates events and products to real life uses and concerns. New TidBITS issues go out every Monday night; breaking news and important updates appear on the web site more frequently.
Weekly Founded: 1990
Circulation: 150000 65,000 names : web, email

4566 **Virtual**
Virtual Fusion
5160 Calle Bonita
Sierra Vista, AZ 85635-4692

A newsletter for the online business community.

4567 **Virtual Reality: An International Directory of Research Projects**
Mecklermedia Corporation
11 Ferry Lane W
Westport, CT 06880-5808

Over 200 research projects related to virtual reality are listed, worldwide. *$60.00*
235 pages

4568 **Wildlife Computer Applications**
Michaelsen's Micro Magic Publishers
PO Box 7332
Fredericksburg, VA 22404-7332

Nancy Michaelsen, Publisher

Offers information on the use of computers and electronics in the environment and conservation fields. *$29.95*

4569 **Wireless LAN**
Information Gatekeepers
320 Washington Street
Suite 302
Brighton, MA 02135
617-782-5033
FAX: 617-782-5735 800-323-1088
editor@igigroup.com
http://www.igigroup.com

Paul Polishuk, Publisher/CEO
Cathey Mallen, Production Manager
Brian Mark, Newsletter Managing Edito
Bev Wilson, Marketing Manager

LAN technological trends and market opportunities. *$695.00*
Monthly Founded: 1977 20,000 names $150 per M.

4570 **Word for Word**
Cobb Group
9420 Bunsen Parkway
Suite 300
Louisville, KY 40220-4206

FAX: 502-491-3433 800-223-8720

Mark Crane, Publisher
Charity Edelen, Editor
Tracee Bell Trout, Advertising/Sales
Tara Dickerson, Production
Brent Shean, Circulation Manager

Tips and techniques for using Microsoft Windows on a network. *$49.00*
16 pages Monthly
Printed in 2 colors on matte stock

4571 **Work Process Improvement Today**
Recognition Technologies Users Association
185 Devonshire Street
Suite 710
Boston, MA 02110-1413
617-426-1167
FAX: 617-521-8675 800-99 -2974
kguarino@tawpi.org
http://www.aiimondemand.com

Dan Bllida, Editor
Debra Sanderson, Publisher
Frank Moran, Owner

Accepts advertising. *$60.00*

Circulation: 10000

Magazines & Journals

4572 **2600 Magazine**
PO Box 752
Middle Island, NY 11953
631-751-2600
FAX: 631-474-2677
subs@2600.com
http://www.2600.com/

Emanuel Golstein, Editor

Written for computer hackers. *$20.00*
Quarterly Founded: 1984

4573 **A-com Magazine**
Virgo Publishing
3300 N Central Avenue, Suite 2500
PO Box 40079
Phoenix, AZ 85067-0079
480-990-1101
FAX: 480-675-8146
www.a-cominteractive.com

Marla Ellerman, Publisher

Serves the applications commerce marketplace.
Monthly

4574 **ACM QUEUE**
1515 Broadway
17th Floor
New York, NY 10036-5701
212-869-7440
FAX: 212-302-5826 800-342-6626
SIGS@acm.org http://www.acm.org

Mark Mandelbaum, Director Publication
John R. White, CEO/President

Published by the Association for Computing Machinery.
Founded: 1947
Circulation: 25000

4575 **AFSM International Professional Journal and High-Technology Service Mgmt.**
AFSM International
1342 Colonial Boulevard
Suite 25
Fort Myers, FL 33907-1084
239-275-7887
FAX: 239-275-0794 800-333-9786
afsmi@afsmi.org www.afsmi.org
David Henault, Publisher
Suzanne Tissier, Senior Editor
Sue Kaminski, Managing Editor
For trade association members. *$150.00*
86 pages Monthly Founded: 1975
Circulation: 20000
Printed in 4 colors on glossy stock

4576 **AI Expert**
Miller Freeman Publications
2655 Seely Avenue
San Jose, CA 95134
408-943-1234
FAX: 408-943-0513
Regina Star Ridley, Editor
Practical applications of artificial intelligence in any field. *$37.00*
42 pages Monthly Founded: 1986

4577 **AI Magazine**
American Association for Artificial Intelligence
445 Burgess Drive
Menlo Park, CA 94025-3442
650-328-3123
FAX: 650-321-4457
aiide05@aaai.org
http://www.aimagazine.org
David Leake, Editor
David M Hamilton, Managing Editor
Michael Wellman, Book Review Editor
Carol McKenna Hamilton, Executive Director, AAAI
Quarterly issued magazine, available through AAAI membership. AI Magazine features articles regarding research in the field of artificial intelligence.
128 pages Quarterly Founded: 1980
Circulation: 7000 5000 names $210 per M.
Printed in on matte stock

4578 **ASR News**
Voice Information Associates
PO Box 253
Concord, MA 01742-6
978-266-1966
FAX: 978-263-3461
webmaster@asrnews.com
http://www.asrnews.com
Walt Tetschner, Publisher and Editor
Developments in products, marketing, technology, and investments in the automatic speech recognition industry. *$345.00*
Monthly Founded: 1990

4579 **Advanced Imaging**
Cygnus Publishing
3 Huntington Quadrangle
Suite 301N
Melville, NY 11747-3601
631-845-2700
FAX: 631-845-2736 800-308-6397
info@advancedimaging.com
http://www.advancedimagingmag.com
Dave Brambert, Publisher
Larry Adams, Editor-in-Chief
Paul Mackler, CEO
The only international magazine specifically designed to meet the needs of professionals using all forms of electronic imaging technologies. Offering monthly coverage of imaging application solutions for medical/diagnostic, industrial machine vision, government/security, and scientific imaging markets.
Monthly Founded: 1966
Circulation: 44009

4580 **Aixpert**
IBM Corporation
1133 Westchester Avenue
White Plains
New York, NY 10604-3406
914-423-3000
FAX: 866-722-9226
http://www.ibm.com
George Noren, Editor-in-Chief
Provides timely up-to-date technical material to help developers plot, develop, and enhance applications for IBM AIX products.
Quarterly
Circulation: 10,000

4581 **Aldus Magazine**
Aldus Corporation
801 N 34th Street
Seattle, WA 98103-8882
Carla Noble, Publisher
Harry Edwards, Editor
Supports and educates graphics professionals using ALDUS software. Covers tips, tricks and how-to pointers for maximizing Pagemaker, Freehand, PhotoStyler and Persuasion. Also covers trends in electronic publishing. *$24.00*
68 pages 8 per year Founded: 1989
Circulation: 220,000

4582 **Algorithmica**
Springer Verlag
233 spring st.
New York, NY 10013
212-208-8000
FAX: 212-473-1575
service@springer-ny.com
http://www.springer-ny.com
C K Wong, Editor-in-Chief
D T Lee, Application Editor
Provides an in-depth look into distributed computing, parellel processing, automated design, and software tools. *$1008.00*
Quarterly Founded: 1855
Circulation: 1000

4583 **Analysis Solutions**
ConnectPress
2530 Camino Entrada
Santa Fe, NM 87505-4807
505-474-5000
FAX: 505-474-5001
cmascarenas@hmp.com
www.analysismag.com
Carolyn Mascarenas, Publisher
Design analysis and optimization for ANSYS technology users. Covers engineering simulation, acousitc analysis, model meshing, new products and case studies. *$90.00*
Quarterly
Circulation: 27,575

4584 **Application Development Trends**
600 Worcester Road
Suite 301
Framingham, MA 01702
508-875-6644
FAX: 508-875-6622
info@101com.com
http://www.adtmag.com
Sheryl Katz, Publisher
Michael Alexander, Editorial-in-Chief
Tracy S. Cook, Marketing Director
Christina Schaller, Managing Editor
The number one information source on today's key application development options delivering a high powered, management-oriented editorial that covers the application development industry in greater depth and breadth than any other publication.
Monthly Founded: 1998
Circulation: 45000

4585 **Applied Computing Technologies**
9047 Executive Park Drive
Suite 222
Knoxville, TN 37923
865-694-9099
FAX: 865-694-9096
Peyman Dehkordi, Owner

4586 **Automatic ID News**
Advanstar Communications
545 Boylston Street
Boston, MA 02116
617-514-4600
FAX: 617-267-6900
info@advanstar.com
www.advanstar.com
Information for decision-makers in all industries seeking definitive information about automatic data collection technology. The technology includes optical, magnetic, radio frequency and voice recognition systems and peripherals.
Monthly

4587 **BAM Publications**
BAM Publications
3470 Buskirk Avenue
Pleasant Hill, CA 94523-4340
925-932-5900
Dennis Erokan, Editor
Provides regionally focused product and channel news to computer products and services. *$120.00*
60 pages Monthly Founded: 1988

4588 **Better Channel**
ABCD: The Microcomputer Industry Association
450 E 22nd Street
Suite 230
Lombard, IL 60148-6158
630-268-1818
FAX: 630-268-1384
John Venator, Executive VP
A professional magazine that is exclusively dedicated to representing and serving all segments of the microcomputer industry. Accepts advertising. *$150.00*
32 pages Monthly

4589 **CADALYST**
Advanstar Communications
545 Boylston Street
Boston, MA 02116
617-514-4600
FAX: 617-267-6900
info@advanstar.com
http://www.advanstar.com
John Kiesewetter, Publisher
David Cohn, Editor
Expert coverage of the latest developments in auto CAD systems, their products and the various CAD applications. *$4.00*

Monthly
Circulation: 70000

4590 CASE Strategies
Cutter Information Corporation
37 Broadway
Arlington, MA 02474-5552
781-641-2886
FAX: 781-648-8707 800-888-8939
Kim Leonard, Editor
Implementation strategies, reviews and case studies in areas of computer-aided systems engineering. *$295.00*

4591 CBT Solutions
SB Communications
183 Whiting Street
#15
Hingham, MA 02043-3845
781-749-2151

cbstol@ziplink.net
www.cbtsolutions.com
Steve Blumberg, Publisher
Featured editorials include advanced technology in the past and future, interactive web programs, new methods to access and control information, and personal profiles.

Bi-Monthly
Circulation: 15,000

4592 CD-ROM Enduser
Disc Company
6609 Rosecroft Pl
Falls Church, VA 22043-1828

Linda Helgerson, Editor
For people who use CD-ROM applications. *$3.00*
Monthly Founded: 1989

4593 CD-ROM Librarian
Mecklermedia Corporation
20 Ketchum Street
Westport, CT 06880-5808
203-226-6967
FAX: 203-454-5840
Alan Meckler, Editor
A periodical intended for the library professional. *$80.00*
Monthly Founded: 1986

4594 CHANCE: New Directions for Statistics and Computing
Springer Verlag
233 Spring Street
New York, NY 10013
212-208-8000
FAX: 212-460-1575
service@springer-ny.com
http://www.springer-ny.com
Jolanda Von Hagen, Publisher
John E Rolph, Editor
Derk Haank, CEO
Peter Hendriks, Head of Marketing and Sales
Covers both statistics and computing. Designed for everyone who has an interest in the analysis of data. The informal style highlights and encourages sound statistical practice. *$7.00*
Monthly Founded: 1842
Circulation: 4500

4595 Cadence
Miller Freeman Publications
2655 Seely Avenue
San Jose, CA 95134
408-468-8603
FAX: 408-468-1902
lily.yu@gartner.com
www.gartner.com
Johanna Kleppe, Publisher
Kathleen Maher, Managing Editor
Michael Fister, Chief Executive Officer
For users of Autocad - a construction/architecture program. *$6.00*

Circulation: 72664

4596 Catalyst
Western Center for Microcomputers
1259 El Camino Real
#275
Menlo Park, CA 94025
650-855-8064

thecatalyst@mail.earthlink.net
www.home.earthlink.net/~thecatalyst/index.html
Sue Swezey, Editor
Reporting on both the increasing sophistication of technology and the increasing complexity special education. We've covered the profound changes in the lives of children and adults with special needs as they have benefited from computer use, as well as on the obstacles confronting them and those who serve them. *$18.00*
Quarterly

4597 Christian Computing
PO Box 319
Belton, MO 64012-0319

FAX: 800-456-1868 800-456-1868
steve@ccmag.com
http://www.ccmag.com
Steve Hewitt, Editor-in-Chief
Monthly Founded: 1989

4598 CircuiTree
Business News Publishing Company
2401 w big
Suite700
Troy, MI 48084
248-362-3700
FAX: 248-362-0317
http://www.bnpmedia.com
Steve Gold, Publisher
Roy Sakelson, Editor *$64.00*
Monthly Founded: 1926
Circulation: 12000

4599 Civic.com
FCW Government Technology Group
3141 Fairview Park Drive
Suite 777
Falls Church, VA 22042-4507

FAX: 703-876-5126 www.fcw.com
Edith Holmes, President
Steve Vito, Publisher
Agnes Vanek, Circulation Director
Margo Dunn, Production Manager
Anne Armstrong, Editor
A print magazine and electronic companion designed for volume IT buyers, chief information officers and IT planners in state and local government.

4600 CleanRooms Magazine
PennWell Publishing Company
98 Spit Brook Road
Suite 100
Nashua, NH 03062-5723
603-891-0123
FAX: 603-891-9200
johnh@pennwell.com
http://www.cleanrooms.com
John Haystead, Editor-in-Chief
James Enos, Publisher
Angela Godwin, Managing Editor
Steve Smith, News Editor
Bob Johnson, National Sales Manager
Serves the contamination control and ultrapure materials and process industries. Written for readers in the microelectronics, pharmaceutical, biotech, health care, food processing and other user industries. Provides technology and business news and new product listings. *$97.00*
Monthly Founded: 1987
Circulation: 35031

4601 Com-SAC, Computer Security, Auditing & Controls
Management Advisory Services & Publications
PO Box 81151
Wellesley Hills, MA 02481-1
781-235-2895
FAX: 781-235-5446
jaykmasp@aol.com
http://www.masp.com
J. Kuong, Editor
A quarterly journal of in-depth tutorials in computer security, auditing and the most comprehensive digest service of all publications in computer security and controls. *$98.00*
Quarterly Founded: 1973

4602 Common Knowledge
230 W Monroe
Suite 220
Chicago, IL 60606
312-600-0925
FAX: 312-279-0227 800-777-6734
common@common.org
www.common.org
Kris Neeley, Publisher
Features interviews with industry experts, case studies, tutorials, the latest industry news and overviews of management concerns.
Quarterly
Circulation: 15,000

4603 Communications of the ACM
Association for Computing Machinery
1515 Broadway
17th Floor
New York, NY 10036-8901
212-697-7440
FAX: 212-302-5826 800-342-6626
acmhelp@acm.org
http://www.acm.org
Jerry Ashton, President
John R White, CEO
Edward Grossman, Publisher
Diane Crawford, Executive Editor
Brian Hebert, Marketing/Communications Manager
Technical magazine covering developments in computer science for professional scientific and business dp, systems programming, database techniques and more. *$17.00*
Monthly Founded: 1947
Circulation: 82,867

4604 **CompactPCI Systems**
CompactPCI Systems
13253 La Montana
Dr 207
Fountain Hills, AZ 85268-5328
480-967-5581
FAX: 480-837-6466
editor@compactpci-systems.com
http://www.compactpci-systems.com

Mike Hopper, Publisher
Joe Pavlat, Editor

Features application success stories that demonstrate how and where CompactPCI technology has provided solutions.

Circulation: 20000

4605 **Component Development Strategies**

Cutter Information Corporation
37 Broadway
Suite 1
Arlington, MA 02474
781-648-8700
FAX: 781-648-1950 800-964-5118
press@cutter.com
http://www.cutter.com

Karen Coburn, President and CEO
Tom Welsh, Editor

Editorial content covers the latest information and technology on object-oriented programming, databases, and analysis and design. *$2400.00*
Monthly Founded: 1991

4606 **CompuServe Magazine**
5000 Arlington Centre Boulevard
Columbus, OH 43220-5439
614-457-8600
FAX: 614-457-0348

John Miller, Chief Executive Officer
Richard A Baker, Executive Director

Offers updated and statistical information for computer professionals.

4607 **Computer**
IEEE Computer Society
10662 Los Vaqueros Circle
P. O. Box 3014
Los Alamitos, CA 90720-1314
714-821-8380
FAX: 714-821-4010 800-272-6657
computer@computer.org
http://www.computer.org/

Matt Loeb, Publisher
Doris L. Carver, Editor in Chief
Bill Schilit, Associate Editors in Chie
Judi Prow, Managing Editor
Jim Sanders, Senior Editor

Information on late breaking news, business trends, and a variety of technology specific departments. *$63.00*
Monthly Founded: 1988
Circulation: 84340

4608 **Computer Business Review**
ComputerWire
245 5th Avenue
4th Floor
New York, NY 10016
212-770-0409
FAX: 212-686-2626
info@computerwire.com
http://www.computerwire.com/cbr

Jake Sharp, Publisher
Micheal Danzon, CEO
Jason Stamper, Editor

Company profiles, computer market coverage and technology trends and news for investors and professionals in the computer, communications and microelectronics industries. *$195.00*
Monthly Founded: 1984
Circulation: 20450

4609 **Computer Buyer's Guide & Handbook**
Bedford Communications
1410 Broadway
21st Floor
New York, NY 10018
212-807-8220
FAX: 212-807-1098
http://www.bedfordmags.com

Leigh Sprimont, Editor-In-Chief

A guide to buying peripherals and software, as well as general advice and news on the world of computing. *$36.00*
128 pages Monthly Founded: 1981
Circulation: 50000

4610 **Computer Design**
PennWell Publishing Company
10 Tara Boulevard
5th Floor
Nashua, NH 03062-2800
603-891-0123
FAX: 603-891-0514
www.computer-design.com

John Carroll, Group Publisher

Each issue contains in-depth articles and timely features written by experienced senior editors who concentrate on the critical technologies, components and tools needed to design microprocessor and computer based OEM products and systems.
Monthly
Circulation: 105,028

4611 **Computer Graphics Review**
Primedia
9800 Metcalf Avenue
Overland Park, KS 66212
913-341-1300
FAX: 913-967-1898
inquiries@primediabusiness.com *uirie*
http://www.primediabusiness.com/

Duance Hefner, Editor

To identify and interpret significant technological and business developments. *$48.00*
120 pages Monthly Founded: 1986

4612 **Computer Graphics World**
PennWell Publishing Company
98 Spit Brook Road
Nashua, NH 03062
603-891-0123
FAX: 603-891-9492 800-225-0556
phil@pennwell.com
http://cgw.pennnet.com

Phile LoPicccolo, Editor-in-Chief
Jenny Donelan, Managing Editor

Covers specific applications of computer graphics, written by users and vendors of equipment and services to the industry. The magazine of 3D computer graphics for engineering and animation professionals.
Monthly Founded: 1978
Printed in 4 colors on glossy stock

4613 **Computer Industry Almanac**
304 W White Oak
Arlington Heights, IL 60005
847-758-3687
FAX: 847-758-3686
ej@c-i-a.com www.c-i-a.com

Egil Juliussen, President

Annual reference book for and about the computer industry. The Almanac has ranking and awards of products, people and companies. Includes salary information, market forecasts, technology trends and directories of companies, publications, market research firms, associations and trade shows. *$45.00*
Annual

4614 **Computer Journal**
Oxford University Press
2001 Evans Road
Cary, NC 27513
919-677-0977
FAX: 919-677-1714 800-852-7323
patricia.thomas@oupjournals.org
http://www3.oup.co.uk/computer_journal/

F Leroy, Editorial Assistant:
F Murtagh, Editor-in-Chief
Julie Gribben, Special Sales Manager

Provides information on web sites, personal computers, hardware, software and online uses. *$920.00*

Circulation: 18000

4615 **Computer Language**
600 Harrison Street
San Francisco, CA 94107-1387
415-905-2200
FAX: 415-905-2234

Larry O'Brien, Editor

Computer news and information.

4616 **Computer Link Magazine**
Millennium Publishing
100 Mobile Dr
Ste 1
Rochester, NY 14616-2145
585-797-4399

info@computerlinkmag.com
www.techny.com

Justin Ziemniak, Editor-in-Chief

Website reviews, employment opportunities, and women's involvement in the technology age. Includes reports on the Western New York computer market. *$20.00*
Monthly
Circulation: 20000

4617 **Computer Manager**
Story Communications
116 N Camp Street
Seguin, TX 78155-5600
830-303-3328
FAX: 830-372-3011
story@storycomm.com
http://www.compumgr.com

James M Story, Publisher
K Wiemann, Circulation Manager

Information to help corporate end users purchase computers and communications equipment easily.
Quarterly
Circulation: 50000

4618 **Computer Price Guide**
Computer Merchants
22 Saw Mill River Road
Hawthorne, NY 10532-1533
914-347-0290
FAX: 914-347-0292

Svend Hartmann, Publisher

Market trends and developments, prices on used IBM computer equipment. *$70.00*
Quarterly
Circulation: 3500

4619 Computer Security Journal
Computer Security Institute
600 Harrison Street
San Francisco, CA 94107
415-947-6320
FAX: 415-947-6023 866-271-8529
csi@cmp.com http://www.gocsi.com
Russell Kay, Publisher
Chris Keating, Director
Robert Richardson, Editorial Director
Nancy Baer, Marketing Manager
Keeps you informed with comprehensive, practical articles, case studies, reviews and commentaries written by knowledgeable computer security professionals. *$25.00*
Quarterly Founded: 1974
Circulation: 3000

4620 Computer Security, Auditing and Controls (COM-SAC)
Management Advisory Services & Publications
PO Box 81151
Wellesley Hills, MA 02481-1
781-235-2895
FAX: 781-235-5446
jaykmasp@aol.com
http://www.masp.com
J Kuong, Publisher
N Lagos, Manager
Indepth tutorials in computer security and auditing and the most comprehensive digest service of all publications in computer security, auditing and internal controls. Security hardware-software news. *$98.00*
Quarterly Founded: 1973
Printed in on glossy stock

4621 Computer Shopper
Segal Company
1 Park Avenue
New York, NY 10016-5895
212-251-5000
FAX: 212-251-5490 info@segalco.com
Charlie Cooper, Senior Editor
A buyer's guide of sorts, listing the latest information and equipment for the world of computers.

4622 Computer Survival Journal
Enterprise Publishing
138 N 16 Street
Blair, NE 68008
402-426-2121
FAX: 402-426-2227
http://www.enterprisepub.com
Tom Weston, Director, Editor, Publisher, Marketing
Reviews and features on all areas of computer, office and home products (hardware and software). Also includes information on cellular phones, TV's and appliances, home electronics and television. *$250.00*
50 pages

4623 Computer Technology Review
West World Productions
420 N Camden Drive
Beverly Hills, CA 90210-4507
310-327-7100
FAX: 310-246-1405 888-889-3130
sinan@kanatsiz.com
http://www.wwpi.com
Kathenne Diaz, Assistant Editor
Computer Technology Review is an all-inclusive tabloid that covers the full spectrum of new and emerging technologies vital to systems integrators, high-end VARS, and OEM. *$10.00*
60 pages Monthly Founded: 1981
Circulation: 64044 72,000 names $185 per M.
Printed in 4 colors on matte stock

4624 Computer User Magazine
Key Professional Media
220 S 6th Street
Suite 500
Minneapolis, MN 55402-4501
612-339-7571
FAX: 612-339-5806 800-788-0204
matt@computeruser.com
http://www.computeruser.com
Sarah Rudish, Group Publisher
Elizabeth Milllard, Associate Publisher
For small to medium-size business professionals and computer owners, ComputerUser is published in 13 markets nationally. *$14.00*
60 pages Monthly Founded: 1981
Circulation: 64000
Printed in 4 colors on newsprint stock

4625 Computer World/Focus
PO Box 9171
Framingham, MA 01701-9171
Joe Maglitta, Feature Editor
A comprehensive magazine offering information on the computer industry.

4626 Computer-Aided Engineering
Penton Media
1300 E 9th Street
Cleveland, OH 44114
216-696-7000
FAX: 216-696-1752
caenetmaster@penton.com
www.penton.com/cae/
Larry Boulden, Publisher
Applications, news, trends and products for CAD/CAM technology as applied in manufacturing, electronics, architectural and construction industries. *$50.00*
Monthly
Circulation: 56,062

4627 Computers & Industrial Engineering
Elsevier Science
NIU, Industrial Engineering Department
Dekalb, IL 60174
815-753-9980
FAX: 815-753-0823
eldin@icaen.iowa.edu
www.umoncton.ca/cie/
Mohamed Dessouky, Editor
Computerized industrial engineering applications, develoment of computer problem solving, and implementation of different computer techniques.
Quarterly
Circulation: 2M

4628 Computers User
220 S 6th Street
Suite 500
Minneapolis, MN 55042
612-339-7571
matt@computeruser.com
http://www.computeruser.com
David Needle, Editor
Matt Kusilek, Publisher
End user computer magazine for business and professional users of PC and Macintosh computers, software and peripherals. *$24.99*
Monthly

4629 Computers and Biomedical Research
Academic Press
1901 E South Campus Drive
Suite 1195
Salt Lake City, UT 84112-9359
801-581-6461
FAX: 801-585-5414 www.aoce.utah.edu
T Allan Pryor, Editor
Information on application of computer technology in biomedical research for medical professionals. Evaluates and discusses various techniques. Accompanied by photographs, charts, graphs and figures. *$325.00*
6 per year
Circulation: 1,425

4630 Computers in Graphics
Virgo Publishing
3300 N Central Avenue, Suite 2500
PO Box 40079
Phoenix, AZ 85067-0079
480-990-1101
FAX: 480-675-8146
Jennifer Lutener, Editor
Explores the use of computer technology in the graphics industries. *$35.00*
Monthly Founded: 1990

4631 Computers in Libraries
Information Today
143 Old Marlton Pike
Medford, NJ 08055-8750
609-654-6266
FAX: 609-654-4309 800-300-9868
custserv@infotoday.com
http://www.infotoday.com
Thomas Hogan, Publisher
John Brokenshire, Chief Financial Officer
Complete coverage of news and issues in the evolving field of library information technology. Emphasis on practical application of technology in public, school, academic, and special libraries. *$99.95*
Founded: 1997
Circulation: 6000+

4632 Computers in the Schools
Haworth Press
10 Alice Street
Binghamton, NY 13904
607-722-5857
FAX: 607-722-1424 800-429-6784
getinfo@haworthpress.com
http://www.haworthpress.com/web/cits
D. LaMont Johnson, Editor
Bill Cohen, Publisher
Mary L. Johnson, Managing Editor
Assists educators in using the small computer in the classroom. *$75.00*
Quarterly Founded: 1978

4633 Computertalk
Computertalk Associates
492 Norristown Road
Suite 160
Blue Bell, PA 19422
610-825-7686
FAX: 610-825-7641
wal@computertalk.com
http://www.computertalk.com
William A Lockwood Jr, President
Will Lockwood, Director of Editorial Content/Senio
Maggie L. Lockwood, Director of Publications/

Profiles on various sytems available for pharmacists purchasing and using computers. *$50.00*
Monthly Founded: 1980
Circulation: 32,000
Printed in 4 colors on glossy stock

4634 Computerworld
CW Publishing
One Speen Street
PO Box 9171
Framingham, MA 01701-4653
508-879-0700
FAX: 508-626-2705 800-343-6474
don_tennant@computerworld.com
http://www.computerworld.com
Mitch Betts, Executive Editor
Don Tennant, VP/Editor in Chief
Matt Sweeney, Chief Executive Officer
For computer professionals who evaluate and implement information systems. *$99.99*
170 pages Founded: 1967
Circulation: 170000

4635 Computing Surveys
Association for Computing Machinery
One Astor Place
1515 Broadway
New York, NY 10036-5701
212-869-7440
FAX: 212-302-5826 800-342-6626
acmhelp@acm.org http://www.acm.org
Mark Mandelbaum, Director Publication
John R. White, CEO
Gul Agha, Editor in Chief
Carefully planned and presented introductions to complex issues, supported by exhaustive and comprehensive notations on the relevant literature. *$170.00*
Quarterly Founded: 1947

4636 Computing in Science & Engineering
American Institute of Physics
2 Huntington Quadrangle
Melville, NY 11747
516-576-2200
FAX: 516-349-9704
cip@aip.org http://www.aip.org/cip
Jenny Ferrero, Senior Editor
Angela Burgess, Publisher
Georgann Carter, Marketing/Circulation Man
Computer science's interdisciplinary juncture with physics, astronomy and engineering. *$55.00*

4637 Control Solutions
PennWell Publishing Company
1421 S Sheridan Road
Tulsa, OK 74112
918-835-3161
FAX: 918-831-9497 800-331-4463
Matt O'Shea, Publisher
Ron Kuhfeld, Editor-in-Chief
Represents control technology for engineers and engineering manage4ment.

4638 Cryptosystems Journal
Cryptosystems Journal
485 Middle Holland Road
Holland, PA 18966-2870
Tony Patti, Publisher/Editor
Unique international journal devoted to implementation of cryptographic systems on IBM-PC's and compatibles.

4639 Cyber Defense Magazine
PO Box 71748
Phoenix, AZ 85050
480-990-0407
FAX: 480-990-7306 866-487-6652
editor@cyberdefensemag.com
www.cyberdefensemag.com
John Riccio, Publisher
Curt Blakeney, Editor
Computer/Network security magazine. *$31.00*
64 pages 12 issues Founded: 2003
Circulation: 64,000 64000 names $200 per M.
Printed in 4 colors on glossy stock

4640 DBMS-Database Management Systems
Miller Freeman Publications
2655 Seely Avenue
San Jose, CA 95134
408-943-1234
FAX: 408-943-0513
Phillip Chapnick, Publisher
David Kohman, Editor
Covers the database and database applications marketplace.
Circulation: 69,029

4641 DG Review
Data Base Publications
9390 Research Boulevard
Suite 300
Austin, TX 78759-6585
512-388-8181
FAX: 512-794-0860
John Moore, Publisher
Gloria Trent, Editor
For Data General and compatible computer users. *$48.00*
64 pages Monthly Founded: 1981

4642 DM Review
Powell Publishing Company
240 Regency Court
Suite 201
Brookfield, WI 53045
262-800-0202
FAX: 414-771-8058
http://www.dmreview.com
Brian Cronin, Publisher
Val Latzke, Editor
Jean Schauer, Editor in Chief
Mary Jo Nott, Manager
Provides a wealth of knowledge through columns by top industry experts, data warehouse success stories, timely and informative articles, third-party product reviews, and executive interviews.
Monthly Founded: 1994
Circulation: 75012

4643 DSP Engineering
13253 La Montana Dr
Suite 207
Fountains Hills, AZ 85268
480-967-5581
FAX: 480-837-6466
subscriptions@opensystems-publishing.com http://wwwdspengineering.com
Rosemary Kristoff, VP
Phyllis Thompson, Circulation Manager
Patrick Hopper, VP Marketing
Mike Hopper, Publisher

4644 Data Bus
AM Publications
PO Box 20044
Saint Petersburg, FL 33742
727-577-5500
FAX: 727-576-0622 ampubs@aol.com
Al Martino, Publisher/Editor
Contains new product reviews, trade literature and personnel announcements.
Monthly
Circulation: 24000

4645 Data Communications
McGraw Hill
PO Box 182604
Columbus, OH 43272
614-866-5769
FAX: 614-759-3759
customer.service@mcgraw-hill.com
www.mcgraw-hill.com
Kevin Harold, Publisher
Steve Weiss, Production Manager
Networking magazine edited for the technical managers responsible for the implementation and integration of computer information networks. *$5.00*
Circulation: 112,941

4646 Data Sources
Ziff Davis Publishing Company
28 E 28th Street
New York, NY 10016
212-503-3500
randyzane@ziffdavis.com
http://www.ziffdavis.com
Randy Zane, Director Communication
Leo Greisman, Owner *$240.00*
Monthly Founded: 1981
Circulation: 700000

4647 Data Storage
PennWell Publishing Company
10 Tara Boulevard
5th Floor
Nashua, NH 03062-2800
603-891-0123
www.datastorage.com
Becky Adams, Publisher
Features news and information on all types of systems such as magnetic disk drives, media and magnetic tape drives, CD-ROM, optical, magneto-optical, holographic and nonvolative semiconductor storage devices.
Monthly
Circulation: 15,140

4648 Data to Knowledge
Business Rule Solutions
2476 Bolsover Street
#488
Houston, TX 77005-2518
713-681-1651
FAX: 604-681-7223
datatoknow@brsolutions.com
http://www.brcommunity.com
Gladys S W Lam, Publisher
Ronald G Ross, Executive Editor
Keri Anderson Healy, Editor
Marie Yang, Director, Marketing & Business Deve
John Hall, Technology Review Editor
Provides analysis, news and tutorials for data management professionals, data administrators, DBA's and other involved in the planning, design and construction of large-scale information systems.

Founded: 1973
Circulation: 4603

4649 **Database Searcher**
Mecklermedia Corporation
11 Ferry Lane W
Westport, CT 06880-5808

Alan Meckler, Editor

Covers online and micro-computer techniques. *$95.00*
Monthly Founded: 1985

4650 **Datamation**
Reed Business Information
2000 Clearwater Drive
Oak Brook, IL 60523
630-740-0825
FAX: 630-320-7457
www.reedbusiness.com

Carole Sacino, Publisher
William Semich, Editor-in-Chief

The magazine that interprets products, events and technologies for computer professionals in large companies worldwide. *$4.00*

Circulation: 189,101

4651 **Design Automation**
Miller Freeman Publications
2655 Seely Avenue
San Jose, CA 95134
408-943-1234
FAX: 408-943-0513

Lindsey Vereen, Editor

Targeted to computer design engineers.
Monthly

4652 **Designfax**
Adams Business Media
6001 Cochran Road
Suite 104
Solon, OH 44139
440-248-1125
FAX: 440-248-0187
designfax@designfaxmag.com
http://www.designfax.net

Tom W Corcoran, Group Publisher
Richard Mandel, Editor
Michael E Hilts, Publisher
Betty Johnson, Subscriptions
Laura Moulton, Advertisments

Technological advancements, computer software and equipment, engineering materials and book reviews are featured. *$54.00*
Monthly Founded: 1979
Circulation: 128,000
Printed in 4 colors on glossy stock

4653 **Desktop Engineering**
Helmers Publishing
174 Concord Street
PO Box 874
Peterborough, NH 03458
603-924-9631
FAX: 603-924-4004
de-editors@helmers.com
http://www.deskeng.com

Brian Vaillancourt, Publisher
Anthony J. Lockwood, Editorial Director
Bill Fahy, Circulation Director
Carol Laughner, Marketing Director

Magazine providing design solutions from concept throughout manufacture, focuses on hardware, software, and technologies for hands-on design engineers and engineering management in the manufacturing solutions throughout extensive product reviews, comparisions, technology updates, real-world application stories, news, product resource guides, and new product reports.
60 pages Monthly Founded: 1995
Circulation: 63000 63000 names $89 per M.
Printed in 4 colors on glossy stock

4654 **Distributed Computing Monitor**
Patricia Seybold Group
85 Devonshire Street
5th Floor
Boston, MA 02109-3504
617-742-5200
FAX: 617-742-1028
info@psgroup.com
http://www.psgroup.com

Patricia Seybold, Publisher
Anne Thomas, Editor
Patricia Seybold, CEO and Founder
Mitchell Kramer, Senior Vice President

The editors give advanced technologists and strategic technology architects the technical details and business perspective necessary to sell upper management on how, why and when to implement the leading edge.
Monthly Founded: 1978

4655 **Distributing Computing**
DC Corporation
236 W 26th Street
#7SW
New York, NY 10001-6736
212-446-9330
www.distributedcomputing.com

Hal Avery, Publisher

Editorial includes case studies of applications, technical, management, organizational, and cultural techniques.
Monthly
Circulation: 40000

4656 **E-Content**
Information Today
143 Old Marlton Pike
Medford, CT 08055-8750
609-654-6266
FAX: 609-654-4309 800-248-8466
custserv@infotoday.com
http://www.infotoday.com/

Michelle Manafy, Editor
Jared Bernstein, Editorial Assistant

Delivers essential research, reporting, news and analysis of content related issues. It is essential reading for executive and professionals involved in content creation, management, acquisition, organization and distribution in both commercial and enterprise environments. *$115.00*
10 issues/yr
Mailing list available for rent 4M names
Printed in 4 colors on glossy stock

4657 **E-doc**
Association for Information and Image Management
1100 Wayne Avenue
Suite 1100
Silver Spring, MD 20910-5603
301-587-8202
FAX: 301-587-2711 800-477-2446
aiim@aiim.org http://www.aiim.org

John Harney, Editor
John F. Mancini, President
Peggy Winton, Sales and Marketing Direc

Association magazine on electronic document management.

Founded: 1943
Circulation: 40000

4658 **EServer Magazine**
IBM Corporation
220 S 6th Street
Suite 500
Minneapolis, MN 55402
612-339-7571
FAX: 612-336-9220
eservermagazine@msptechmedia.com
http://www.eservercomputing.com

Doug Rock, Editor/Publisher
Mari Adamson-Bray, Marketing Manager
Kelly McManus, Production Manager

New products and services, technological information, and related topics that benefit the decision makers in the optimization and management of these systems are included.

80 pages Monthly Founded: 1993
Circulation: 45000 40,000 names $185 per M.
Printed in 4 colors on glossy stock

4659 **Educational Technology**
Educational Technology Publications
700 Palisade Avenue
PO Box 1564
Englewood Cliffs, NJ 07632-564
201-871-4007
FAX: 201-871-4009 800-952-2665
edtecpubs@aol.com
http://www.bookstoread.com/etp

Lawrence Lipsitz, Publisher/Editor

Systematic design of software and applications, and their impact on the educational community worldwide. Emphasis on computer-based instruction, the Internet, multimedia, electronic performance support, television and videoconferencing. *$139.00*
Bi-annually Founded: 1960
Printed in on glossy stock

4660 **Educational Technology Research and Development**
Assn. for Educational Communications & Technology
1800 N Stonelake Drive
Suite 2
Bloomington, IN 47404
812-335-7675
FAX: 812-335-7678
aect@aect.org http://www.aect.org

Michael Spector, Editor
Charlie White, President

Communcations, technology and instructional development news. *$75.00*
Quarterly Founded: 1923 6000 names $150 per M.

4661 **Educational Technology Review**
AACE International
PO Box 3728
Norfolk, VA 23514
757-623-7588
FAX: 703-977-8760
info@aace.org http://www.aace.org

Gary H Marks, Editor, Publisher, CEO/President, Marketing,

Promotes the use of information technology in education. New products including software, hardware and related materials. *$38.00*
Founded: 1981

4662 **Electronic Design**
Penton Media
1300 E 9th Street
Cleveland, OH 44114
216-696-7000
FAX: 216-696-0836
information@penton.com
http://www.penton.com
Mark David, Editor
David B. Nussbaum, CEO
Celebrating 50 years of innovation, this authoritative magazine provides leading-edge technical information to electronic and engineering managers around the world. *$105.00*
Founded: 1890
Circulation: 145000

4663 **Embedded Systems Programming**
Miller Freeman Publications
600 Harrison Street
Suite 400
San Francisco, CA 94107-1391
415-905-2200
FAX: 415-905-2232 800-956-1215
jturley@cmp.com http://www.mfi.com
Eric Berg, Publisher
Jim Turley, Editor
Kerry Gates, Senior Marketing Events M
Charles J. Murray, Ceo
Monthly Founded: 1986
Circulation: 45,000

4664 **Enterprise Management Issues**
AFCOM
742 E Chapman Avenue
Orange, CA 92866-1621
714-997-7966
FAX: 714-997-9743
afcom@afcom.com www.afcom.com
Leonard Eckhaus, Editor-in-Chief
Content includes an in-depth cover story and features on current developments and the impact of advancing technology. Regular departments are devoted to automation issues and data processing news.
Bi-Monthly
Circulation: 4,000

4665 **European Sources and News**
SSC Group
3126 Woodley Road NW
Washington, DC 20008-3448
202-232-0822
FAX: 202-337-5354
info@euroreseller.com
http://www.euroreseller.com
Robert Snyder, Publisher
Steve Solomon, Editor
Provides European resellers, VAR, systems integrators and OEM with information on product sources and reseller management strategies.
Circulation: 49000

4666 **Federal Computer Week**
FCW Government Technology Group
3141 Fairview Park Drive
Suite 777
Falls Church, VA 22042-4507
703-876-5100
FAX: 703-876-5126 866-293-3194
info@fcw.com http://www.fcw.com
Jeffrey Calore, General Manager, Sales & Marketing
Anne Armstrong, Publisher
John Zyskowski, Senior Editor
The markets leading newspaper for influential users and volume buyers of federal information technology. *$100.00*
48 pages Weekly Founded: 1987
Circulation: 100000

4667 **Foghorn**
FOG Publications
PO Box 1030
Dixon, CA 95620-1030
Gale Rhoades, Editor
For users of 16 and 32 bit systems. *$30.00*
64 pages Monthly Founded: 1985

4668 **GEOWorld**
Adams Business Media
833 W Jackson
7th Floor
Chicago, IL 60607
312-846-4600
FAX: 312-846-4638
admin@gisworld.com
http://www.geoplace.com
Jo Treadwell, VP/Publisher
Todd Danielson, Executive Editor
Joanne Juda, Circulation Manager
Melisa Harder, Business Development Manager
Matt Ball, Associate Publisher
Reports news, events, business, projects, meetings and conventions, and features analysis, technical tutorials and GIS applications for engineering, natural resources, federal and local government, utilities and business. *$72.00*
Monthly
Circulation: 25,000

4669 **Game Developer Magazine**
CMP Media
2800 Campus Drive
San Mateo, CA 94403
650-513-4300
FAX: 650-513-4446
jduffy@cmp.com http://www.cmp.com
Michele Maguire, Publisher
Jamil Moledina, Editor
Jana Scandurra, Marketing
Afton Thatcher, Marketing *$49.95*
Founded: 1971
Circulation: 35,000

4670 **Genealogical Computing**
Ancestry
360 West 4800 North
Provo, UT 84604
801-426-3500
FAX: 801-426-3501 800-262-3787
gceditor@ancestry-inc.com
http://www.ancestry.com
Loretto Dennis Szucs, Vice-President of Publishing
Elizabeth Kelley Kerstens, Managing Editor
Jennifer Browning, Senior Editor
For readers who use computers and technology to organize and enhance their research into accounts of ancestries and descent. *$ 25.00*
Quarterly

4671 **Gilder Technology Report**
Gilder Publishing
291A Main Street
Great Barrington, MA 01230
413-644-2100
FAX: 413-644-2123
info@gilder.com
http://www.gildertech.com
George Gilder, Editor in Chief
Focuses on the ascendence of the telecoms and the centrality of the Internet. *$195.00*
Monthly Founded: 1995

4672 **Global Technology Business**
Global Technology Business Publishing
1157 San Antonio Road
Mountain View, CA 94043
650-934-2300
FAX: 650-934-2306
http://www.gtbusiness.com
Alex Vieux, Publisher
Laurence Scott, Editor
Bob Beauchamp, CEO
Emphasizes the business aspects of the global computer and communications industries through corporate strategies, financial performance, technological directions.
Monthly
Circulation: 45000

4673 **Global Techventures Report**
Miller Freeman Publications
2655 Seely Avenue
San Jose, CA 95134
408-943-1234
FAX: 408-943-0513 gtvr@mfi.com
Annie Feldman, Publisher
Editorial content profiles vital capital investments and start-up companies, and addresses a variety of legislation, security and communication issues as they relate to today's technology.
SemiMonthly

4674 **Government Best Buys**
FCW Government Technology Group
3141 Fairview Park Drive
Suite 777
Falls Church, VA 22042-4507
703-876-5100
FAX: 703-876-5126 866-293-3194
info@fcw.com http://www.fcw.com
Edith Holmes, President
John Stein Monroe, Editor-in-Chief
Christopher J. Dorobek, Executive Editor
Covers the hardware and software products available to government buyers on agency contracts and the General Services Administration schedule.
Founded: 1987

4675 **Hard Copy Observer**
Lyra Research
320 Nevada Street 1st Floor
PO Box 9143
Newtonville, MA 02640-9143
617-454-2600
FAX: 617-454-2601
mail@lyra.com http://www.lyra.com
Charles LeCompte, President
Ann Priede, Managing Editor and Publisher
News on the latest products, market news, supplies, end-user reponse and product testing for the computer printer industry. *$ 617.00*
80 pages Monthly Founded: 1991

4676 **Heller Report on Educational Technology Markets**
Nelson B Heller & Associates
810 S Alfred Street
#1
Alexandria, VA 22314
303-209-9410
FAX: 303-209-9444
info@hellerreports.com
www.hellerreports.com
Anne Wujcik, Publisher/Managing Editor

Information on the marketing of technology and telecommunications equipment to educators at all levels. *$395.00*
Monthly
Circulation: 1,100

4677 Home Networking News
111 Spleen
Suite 200
Framingham, MA 01701-2000
508-663-1500
FAX: 508-663-1599
kmoyes@ehpub.com
http://www.ehpub.com

Kenneth Moyes, CEO/President
Kenneth Moyes, Publisher
Cindy Tazis, Editor
Elizabeth Cruze, Marketing Manager
Christine Ayers, Circulation Manager
$14.95
Monthly Founded: 1994
Circulation: 100000

4678 IEEE Computational Science & Engineering
IEEE Computer Society
PO Box 3014
Los Alamitos, CA 90720-1314
714-821-8380
FAX: 714-821-4010
mloeb@computer.org
http://computer.org

Matt Loeb, Publisher
Scott Andresen, Editor
Monette Velasco, Production Manager

Developments in computation and algorithms, high-performance evaulation, and visualization techniques in the computational science field. *$98.00*
Quarterly Founded: 1946
Circulation: 5713

4679 IEEE Computer
IEEE Computer Society
10662 Los Vaqueros Circle
PO Box 3014
Los Alamitos, CA 90720-1314
714-218-8380
FAX: 714-821-4010 800-272-6657

Angela Burgess, Publisher
Marilyn Potes, Managing Editor
Rakesh Gupta, Editor in Chief

Examines a wide range of computer-related technologies. Written and refereed by experts, it features articles on the latest developments in computer technology, applications and research in the computer field. *$37.00*
Founded: 1946
Circulation: 85930

4680 IEEE Computer Graphics and Applications
IEEE Computer Society
10662 Los Vaqueros Circle
PO Box 3014
Los Alamitos, CA 90720-1314
714-821-8380
FAX: 714-821-4010 800-272-6657
help@computer.org
http://www.computer.org/

Angela Burgess, Publisher
Sandy Brown, Marketing Director
Robin Baldwin, Managing Editor
Christine Kelly, Staff Editor
Tammi Titsworth, Staff Editor

Focuses on the design and use of computer graphics and systems. Addresses topics such as solid modeling, animation, CAD/CAM, tools for rendering graphics and graphics in medicine, science and business. *$70.00*
Founded: 1946
Circulation: 10028

4681 IEEE Computer Society of Computing Software Magazine
10662 Los Vaqueros Circle
Los Alamitos, CA 90720-2578
714-821-8380
FAX: 714-821-4010
membership@computer.org
http://www.computer.org

Angela Burgess, Publisher
Warren Harrison, Editor

Offers information on the latest software programs for computer professionals.
Founded: 1945
Circulation: 10000

4682 IEEE Expert
IEEE Computer Society
10662 Los Vaqueros Circle
P. O. Box 3014
Los Alamitos, CA 90720
714-821-8380
FAX: 714-821-4010 800-272-6657
membership@computer.org
http://www.computer.org

Crystal Shif, Managing Editor
Angela Burgess, Publisher
Matthew Bertholf, Advertising Manager
Sandy Brown, Business Development Manager
David Hennage, Executive Director

Accepts advertising. *$58.00*
Founded: 1986
Circulation: 3,463

4683 IEEE Intelligent Systems
IEEE Computer Society
10662 Los Vaqueros Circle
PO Box 3014
Los Alamitos, CA 90720-1314
714-821-8380
FAX: 714-821-4010 800-272-6657
mloeb@computer.org
http://www.computer.org

Angela Burgess, Publisher
Deborah M Cooper, President
Doris L Carver, Editor-in-Chief

Features emphasize advanced research that is ready to be used in the real world. Departments include interviews, books and product reviews, opinion pieces, and conference calendars. *$47.00*
Founded: 1946
Circulation: 15355

4684 IEEE Network
Institute of Electrical & Electronics Engineers
3 Park Avenue
17th Floor
New York, NY 10016-5902
212-419-7900
FAX: 212-705-8999
postmaster@iee.org http://www.iee.org

Carol Lof, Publisher
Dr. Warren Gifford, Editor

Technical magazine serving both users and designers of multimedia hardware, software and systems in industry, business, academia and the arts.
Founded: 1871
Circulation: 14388

4685 IEEE Transactions on Computers
IEEE Computer Society
10662 Los Vaqueros Circle
P. O. Box 3014
Los Alamitos, CA 90720
714-821-8380
FAX: 714-821-4010
help@computer.org
http://www.computer.org

Jean-Luc Gaudidt, Editor-in-Chief
Angela Burgess, Publisher

Includes technical research reports and papers on the theory, design and applications of computer systems. *$72.00*
Monthly Founded: 1979
Circulation: 8000

4686 IS Audit & Control Journal
Information Systems Audit & Control Association
3701 Algonquin Road
#1010
Rolling Meadows, IL 60008-3127
847-253-1545
FAX: 847-253-1443
publication@isaca.org
http://www.isaca.org/

Jennifer Blader, Publications Manager
Jane Seago, Editor
Micheal Cangemi, Editor-in-Chief
Susan Caldwell, CEO

Few publications enable you to precisely target your market like the Information Systems Control Journal. The primary audience of this award-winning publication is IT and IS professionals - the very individuals you want to reach. In 2004, we renew our dedication to helping you promote your products and services to this key audience segment. *$75.00*
Founded: 1969
Circulation: 35000
Printed in 4 colors on glossy stock

4687 ISR: Intelligent Systems Report
Lionheart Publishing
2555 Cumberland Parkway
#299
Atlanta, GA 30339-3908
770-431-0867
FAX: 770-432-6969
www.lionhrtpub.com

John Llewellyn, Publisher

Provides an in-depth look into the integration and application of advanced decision support technologies including artificial intelligence, speech recognition, neural networks, fuzzy logic, expert systems, multimedia and virtual reality, and artificial life.
Monthly

4688 Imaging World
American Business Media
1300 Virginia Drive
Suite 400
Fort Washington, PA 19034-3297
215-643-8000
FAX: 215-643-8159
webmaster@boucher1.com
http://www.boucher1.com

Robert Boucher Jr, President/CEO
Dan Marsh, Publisher, Eyecare Business
Stephanie De Long, Editor-in-Chief, Eyecare

Serves the needs of vendors wishing to reach the North American market for electronic imaging and document-based information management and workflow.
Monthly Founded: 1997
Circulation: 75000

4689 InTech Computing Magazine
ISA Services
67 Alexander Drive
PO Box 12277
Research Triangle Park, NC 27709
919-549-8411
FAX: 919-549-8288
info@isa.org http://www.isa.org
Gregory Hale, Editor
Richard T Simpson, Publisher
Key source of information on automating manufacturing processes. *$45.00*
Monthly Founded: 1945
Printed in 4 colors on glossy stock : web offset

4690 Info Log Magazine
BBS Press Service
785-286-4272
FAX: 239-992-4862
Alan Bechtold, Editor
A comprehensive magazine offering the latest information on aspects of the computer industry.
Monthly Founded: 1982

4691 Information Display
610 S 2nd Street
San Jose, CA 95112-4006
408-977-1013
FAX: 408-977-1531
office@sid.org http://www.sid.org
Ken Werner, Editor
Jenny Needham, Circulation Manager
Shigeo Nikoshiba, CEO/President
A magazine published by the Society for Information Display. *$55.00*
Monthly Founded: 1964
Circulation: 12000

4692 Information Management Journal
ARMA International
2400 Somerset Drive
#215
Prairie Village, KS 66208
913-341-3808
FAX: 913-341-3742 800-422-2762
hq@irma.org http://www.arma.org
Cynthia Launchbaugh, Editor
Peter Hermann, CEO
Articles about information management. *$95.00*
Bi-monthly Founded: 1972
Circulation: 10000
Printed in 4 colors on glossy stock

4693 Information Systems Control Journal
Information Systems Audit & Control Association
3701 Algonquin Road
Suite 1010
Rolling Meadows, IL 60008
847-253-1545
FAX: 847-253-1443
publication@isaca.org www.isaca.org
Debra Cutts, Marketing
Jen Blader, Editorial
Richard Lockman, Advertising
Susan Caldwell, Chief Executive Officer
Bi-Monthly
Circulation: 25000 21000 names $250 per M.
Printed in 4 colors

4694 Information Systems Management
Auerbach Publications
3701 Algonquin Road
Suite 1010
Rolling Meadows, IL 60008
847-253-1545
FAX: 847-253-1443
publication@isaca.org
http://www.isaca.org
Debra Cutts, Marketing
Jen Blader, Editorial
Susan Caldwell, Chief Executive Officer
Coverage includes information technology developments and business applications, financial issues, IS staff development, and relationships with business management.
$75.00
Bi-monthly Founded: 1969
Circulation: 40,000 : web

4695 Information World Review
143 Old Marlton Pike
Medford, NJ 08055-8750
609-654-7777
FAX: 609-654-4309
Offers a full overview of the computer industry overseas.

4696 InformationWEEK
CMP Publications
600 Community Drive
Manhasset, NY 11030
516-562-5000
FAX: 516-562-5036
llally@cmp.com http://www.cmp.com
Stephanie Stahl, Editor-in-Chief
Mike Friedenberg, Publisher
For information systems management.
Weekly Founded: 1985
Circulation: 440,000

4697 Infostor
PennWell Publishing Company
98 Spit Brook Road
Nashua, NH 03062-5737
603-891-0123
FAX: 603-891-9297
mark@pennwell.com
http://www.infostor.com
Mark Finkelstein, Publisher
Jill Davis, Marketing Communications
News and information for enterprise storage professionals. *$120.00*
Monthly Founded: 1997
Circulation: 38000

4698 Infoworld Magazine
Infoworld
501 Second Street
San Francisco, CA 94107
847-291-5217

customerservice@infoworld.com
http://www.infoworld.com/
Bob Ostrow, President/Publisher
Paul Calento, VP Marketing
Kevin McKean, Chairman and Editorial Di
Steve Fox, Editor-in-Chief
Kathy Badertscher, Executive Managing Editor
Offers information for computer professionals.
Weekly

4699 Inside DPMA
Data Processing Management Association
505 Busse Highway
Park Ridge, IL 60068-3143
847-825-0880
FAX: 847-825-1693
Paul Zuziak, Editor
A monthly newspaper for the DPMA and the information management profession. Accepts advertising. *$16.00*
Monthly Founded: 1988

4700 Inside Technology Training
Ziff Davis Publishing Company
500 Unicorn Park Drive
Woburn, MA 01801
781-938-2600

editor@itrain.com www.itrain.com/
Nancy J Weingarten, Publisher
Targets management level executives, technology trainers, information technology training managers, CIO's and independent training consultants. Includes reports on new software, new media and new career paths. Also features designed to help training managers create and successfully implement strategy training and reskilling programs that anyone on any level can use.
10 per year
Circulation: 40,000

4701 Inside Visual Basic
ZD Journals
500 Canal View Boulevard
Rochester, NY 14623-2800
585-407-7301
FAX: 585-240-7760
visual_basic@elementkjournal.com
www.zdjournals.com
Jon Pyles, Publisher
Authors discuss subjects covering the building and creating of external objects, as well as topics surrounding class development. The publication informs readers of Visual Basic online resources, and addresses real world questions reagrding controls written in the program, uses of the status bar and extending functions capabilities.
Monthly

4702 Integrated System Design
Verecom Group
954 San Rafael Avenue
Mountain View, CA 94043-1926
650-988-9677

rwallace@cmp.com
http://www.isdmag.com
James Uhl, Publisher
Richard Wallace, VP
Articles are written by designers who explain unique methods for solving design challenges. Publication supplies information on design methodologies and the use of tools and semiconductor capabilities.
Monthly
Circulation: 58082

4703 Intelligent Enterprise
Miller Freeman Publications
411 Boral Avenue
#100
San Mateo, CA 94402-3522
650-573-3210
FAX: 650-655-4350
dbpd@mfi.com
www.intelligententerprise.com
David Kalman, Publisher
Each issue provides detailed analyses of the products, trends and strategies that help accelerate the creation of the enterprise's information infrastructure. Topics include: business intelligence; enterprise resource planning; knowledge management; transaction processing and performance monitor-

ing; applications and systems management.
18 per year
Circulation: 103,000

4704 Interactions
Association for Computing Machinery
One Astor Place
1515 Broadway
New York, NY 10036-5701
212-697-7440
FAX: 212-302-5826 800-342-6626
usacm@acm.org http://www.acm.org
Mark Mandelbaum, Director Publication
Jonathan Arnowitz, Editors in Chief
Editorial content covers business, design, methods and tools, book previews, conference previews and current events pertaining to designers, developers and researchers.
Founded: 1947

4705 International Journal of IT Standards and Standardization Research
Information Resources Management Association
701 E Chocolate Avenue
Suite 200
Hershey, PA 17033
717-533-8879
717-533-8661
members@irma-international.org
www.irma-international.org
Kai Jakobs, Editor
An authoritative source and information outlet for the diverse community of IT standards researchers. *$85.00*
Semi-Annual

4706 International Journal of Information and Communication Technology Education
Information Resources Management Association
701 E Chocolate Avenue
Suite 200
Hershey, PA 17033
717-533-8879
FAX: 717-533-8861
member@irma-international.org
www.irm-international.org
Lawrence A Tomei, Editor
Includes new applications of technology for teaching and learning, and document those practices that contribute irrefutable verification of information technology education as a discipline. *$85.00*
Quarterly

4707 Interpersonal Computing and Technology Journal
Assn. for Educational Communications & Technology
1800 N Stonelake Drive
Suite 2
Bloomington, IN 47404
812-335-7675
FAX: 812-335-7678 877-677-AECT
aect@aect.org www.aect.org
Sue Barnes, Editor
Mauri Collins, Managing Editor
The focus is on computer-mediated communication, and the pedagogical issues surrounding the use of computers and technology in educational settings.
2-4 times a year

4708 Iris Universe: Magazine of Visual Computing
Silicon Graphics
1500 Crittenden Lane
Mountain View, CA 94043
650-960-1980
FAX: 650-932-6102 800-800-7441
Warren C. Pratt, CEO/President
Gaye Graves, Features Editor
Anne Marie Gambelin, Publisher
Written to appeal to all users of computer visualization, from the most technically oriented to the novice. Devoted to cutting edge techniques and technology used and presents the best in new products available.

Quarterly Founded: 1981

4709 Journal of American Society for Information Science
John Wiley & Sons
111 River Street
Hoboken, NJ 07030
201-748-6000
FAX: 201-748-6088
customer@wiley.com
www.wiley.com
Therese Zak, Publisher
Chris Shepherd, Production Manager
Communications, management, applications, economics, and other news of interest in the science field. *$95.00*
72 pages Bi-Monthly

4710 Journal of Imaging Science and Technology
Society for Imaging Science & Technology
7003 Kilworh Lane
Springfield, VA 22151-4088
703-642-9090
FAX: 703-642-9094
info@imaging.org
http://www.imaging.org
Mae Sahyun, Editor
Donna Smith, Managing Editor
Provides the imaging community documentation of a broad range of research, development, and applications in imaging. The selection of papers reflects the role of IS&T as the window on imaging, promoting communication and understanding across the boundaries of the many disciplines involved in modern imaging. *$95.00*

Founded: 1947
Circulation: 2000

4711 Journal of Interactive Learning Research
AACE International
1 Morton Drive
Suite 500
Charlottesville, VA 22903
434-977-5029
FAX: 434-977-5431
aace@virginia.edu www.aace.org
John Self, Editor
Reports on the research, developments, applications, and integration of intelligent computer technologies in education.
Quarterly
Circulation: 3M

4712 Journal of Object-Oriented Programming
SIGS Publications
9121 Oakdale Avenue
Chatsworth, CA 91311
818-734-1520
FAX: 818-734-1522
info@101com.com
http://www.101com.com
Richard S Weiner, Editor
Provides an international forum for research, developments, applications, and new products in the field.
Founded: 1998
Circulation: 3,50,000

4713 KM World
Information Today
143 Old Marlton Pike
Medford, CT 08055-8750
609-654-6266
FAX: 609-654-4309 800-248-8466
custserv@infotoday.com
http://www.infotoday.com/
Hugh Mckellar, Editor in Chief
Sandra Haimila, Managing Editor
Andy Moore, Publisher
Serves the knowledge management industry by offering components and processes, including success stories, designed to improve business. *$23.95*

Mailing list available for rent 4M names
Printed in 4 colors on glossy stock

4714 LAN Magazine
Miller Freeman Publications
600 Harrison Street
Suite 400
San Francisco, CA 94107-1391
415-905-2200
FAX: 415-905-2232 800-956-1215
Steve Schneiderman, Publisher
Kerry Gates, Senior Marketing Events Manager
Charles J. Murray, CEO
Covers Local Area Networks. *$20.00*
180 pages Monthly Founded: 1986

4715 Law Office Computing
James Publishing
PO Box 25202
Santa Ana, CA 92799-5202
714-755-5450
FAX: 714-751-5508
jamessale@jamespublishig.com
http://www.jamespublishing.com
Jamie Tyo, Managing Editor
Amanda Flatten, Editor & Publisher
Jim Pawell, Marketing and Circulation
Legal software reviews, productivity enhancing tips and resources to improve law office automation. *$39.00*
Founded: 1981

4716 Learning and Leading with Technology
International Society for Technology in Education
175 W Broadway
Ste 300
Eugene, OR 97401-3042
541-302-3777
FAX: 541-302-3778 800-336-5191
iste@iste.org http://www.iste.org
Anita McAnear, Production Manager
Don Knezek, CEO
Dr. Jan Van Dam, President
Authors and teachers include school and state administrators, classroom and lab teachers, tech coordinators, and teachers

educators. Most are involved in tech-purcahsing decisions for their school and district. Every issue of L&L includes: a feature subject of broad appeal, articles about using tech in specific subject areas, lesson plans, reproducible worksheets, professional development advice, and referral to supplementary information on the L&L web site at www.iste.org. *$89.00*
Founded: 1989
Circulation: 17000

4717 Library Software Review
Sage Publications
Vanderbilt University
419 21st Avenue S
Nashville, TN 37240-0001
615-343-6094
FAX: 615-343-8834
info@sagepub.com www.sagepub.com

Marshall Breeding, Editor

Provides the library professional with information necessary to make intelligent software evaluation, procurement, integration and installation decisions. Issues review software and software books and periodicals. *$52.00*
Quarterly
Circulation: 1M

4718 Link-Up Digital
Information Today
143 Old Marlton Pike
Medford, CT 08055-8750
609-654-6266
FAX: 609-654-4309 800-248-8466
custserv@infotoday.com
http://www.infotoday.com/
A web-only product featuring articles, reviews and more for users and producers of electronic information products and services.

Mailing list available for rent 4M names
Printed in 4 colors on glossy stock

4719 MC Technology Marketing Intelligence
VNU Business Media
770 Broadway
New York, NY 10003
646-654-5100

bmcomm@vnuinc.com www.vnu.com
News of trends and developments affecting marketing strategies of sales and marketing professionals in the high-tech industry. *$ 45.00*
Monthly
Circulation: 15,158

4720 MD Computing
Springer Verlag
175 5th Avenue
New York, NY 10010
212-460-1521
FAX: 212-533-5617
mdcomputing@springer-ny.com
www.mdcomputing.com

Nhora Cortes-Comerer, Executive Editor
Kelley Suttenfield, Assistant Editor

Provides comprehensive and up-to-date information about the various segments of medical and healthcare informatics, such as clinical computing, health care information and delivery systems, telemedicine, radiology, and many others. *$69.00*
74 pages Bi-Monthly
Circulation: 19,771
Printed in 4 colors on glossy stock

4721 MacWeek
MacWorld Communications
501 2nd Street
San Francisco, CA 94107
415-243-0505
FAX: 415-442-0766

Daniel Farber, Editor
David Ezequelle, Publisher
Rick Lepage, President

Covers Apple's Macintosh computers. Accepts advertising. *$99.00*
72 pages 44 per year Founded: 1987

4722 MacWorld Magazine
Mac Publishing
501 2nd Street
San Francisco, CA 94107-2252
415-243-0505
FAX: 415-243-3543
letters@macworld.com
www.macworld.com

Jason Snell, Editorial Director
Dan Miller, Executive Editor
Scholle Sawyer McFarland, Senior Editor
Dan Frakes, Senior Writer

The ultimate resource for Mac professionals and savvy Mac users. Each issue is packed with practical how-tos, in-depth features, the latest troubleshooting tips and tricks, industry news, future trends and more. *$19.97*
Year Subscription

4723 Marketing Computers
V&U
770 Broadway
F18
New York, NY 10003-9595
646-654-5000
FAX: 646-654-5374
http://www.marketingcomputers.com

Donna Tapellini, Editor
Tony DiCamillo, Publisher

Edited for advertising and marketing executives in the high-tech industries. The publication covers interpretive news, timely big picture features, departments and analysis by staff editors and industry experts. *$149.00*
100 pages Weekly
Circulation: 15484

4724 Mobile Office
21800 Oxnard Street
Suite 250
Woodland Hills, CA 91367-3651
818-598-2405

Jeff Hecox, Editor

Office equipment, computer technology and information.

4725 Motion System Distributor
Penton Media
1300 E 9th Street
Cleveland, OH 44114-1503
216-696-7000
FAX: 216-696-1752
information@penton.com
http://www.penton.com

Jack C Lyttle, Publisher
David B. Nussbaum, Ceo
Larry Berardinis, Editor

Provides selling and technical information to individuals and distributors, specializing in power transmission, motion control and fluid products.
Monthly Founded: 1892
Circulation: 54000

4726 NCR Connection
Publications & Communications
505 Cypress Creek Road
Suite B
Cedar Park, TX 78613
512-250-9023
FAX: 512-331-3900

Mary Wilson, Editor

For users of NCR computer systems. *$92.00*
32 pages Monthly Founded: 1983

4727 NEWS 3X/400
Duke Communications International
221 E 29th Street
Loveland, CO 80538-2769
970-634-4700
FAX: 970-667-2321

Tim Fixmer, Publisher
Trish Faubion, Editor

Leading technical journal for IBM Systems. *$119.00*
220 pages 16 per year Founded: 1982
Circulation: 31,000

4728 Network Support Magazine
Technical Enterprises
7044 S 13th Street
Oak Creek, WI 53154-1429
414-768-8000
FAX: 414-768-8001
mbrships@naspa.com www.naspa.com

Denise Rockhill, Publisher/Advertising Sales
Rachael Zimmerman, Editor
Matthew Jossart, Art Director

The most comprehensive how to publication in the industry. Orientedtoward professionals involved with a myriad of computing technologies and discusses the topic of importance in mainframe, host based and network oriented environments. *$5.00*
68 pages Monthly Founded: 1987
Circulation: 50,000

4729 Network World
Network World
118 Turnpike Road
Southborough, MA 01772-9108
508-756-6400
FAX: 508-460-1192 800-622-1108
bcruse@nww.com
http://www.networkworld.com

Evilee T Ebb, CEO/Publisher
John Gallant, President/Editorial Director

For network IS professionals with direct responsibility for planning and managing their companies network computing environment. *$129.00*
100 pages Weekly Founded: 1986
Circulation: 170,000

4730 Newmedia Age
HyperMedia Communications
PO Box 299
Brooklin, ME 04616
207-359-6573
FAX: 207-359-9809 800-935-0040

Ben Calica, Editor

Covers new products and technology trends in audio and video computing. *$24.00*
Quarterly
Circulation: 40,000

4731 **ONLINE Magazine**
Information Today
143 Old Marlton Pike
Medford, NJ 08055-8750
609-654-6266
FAX: 609-654-4309
marydee@xmission.com
www.onlinemag.net

Marydee Ojala, Editor

Written for information professionals and provides articles, product reviews, case studies, evaluation, and informed opinion about selecting, using, and managing electronic information products, plus industry and professional information about online database systems, CD-ROM, and the Internet. *$115.00*
Bi-Monthly
Printed in 4 colors on glossy stock

4732 **OfficeWorld News**
366 Ramtown Greenville Road
Howell, NJ 07731-2789
732-785-5976
FAX: 732-785-1347

William Urban, Publisher
Kim Chandlee McCabe, Editor-in-Chief

Provides a diverse population of business products resellers the news and information to best serve the needs of small, mid and large business customers. Provides insight into partnering with their peers in this diverse marketplace.
Monthly
Circulation: 31,500
Printed in 4 colors on glossy stock

4733 **PC Arcade**
Softdisk Publishing
606 Common Street
Shreveport, LA 71101-3437
318-218-8718
FAX: 318-221-8870

Al Vekovius, President
Ronda Farries, Circulation Director

Publisher of software subscriptions for DOS, Windows and Macintosh computers. *$19.95*
Monthly Founded: 1990

4734 **PC Sources**
Ziff Davis Publishing Company
500 Unicorn Park Drive
Woburn, MA 01801
781-938-2600
FAX: 781-938-2626
opportunities@ziffdavis.com
http://www.ziffdavis.com

Peter McKie, Editor
Robert F Callahan, CEO
Michael J Miller, Editor-in-chief

Serves experienced PC users. *$149.75*
Monthly Founded: 1985

4735 **PC Systems and Support**
Technical Enterprises
7044 S 13th Street
Oak Creek, WI 53154
414-325-3366
FAX: 414-768-8001

Scott Sherer, President
Amy Birschbach, Editor

Offers solutions with tutorials on hardware and software implementation/upgrade techniques, workstation customization, integration and optimization. The how-to material presented each month guides those professionals in evaluating, selecting, acquiring, implementing, and supporting PC distributed resources. Presents in-depth technical information that can be applied at work.

4736 **PC Techniques**
Coriolis Group
14455 N Hyden Road
Suite 220
Scottsdale, AZ 85260
480-483-0192

Keith Weiskamp, Publisher
Jeff Duntemann, Editor

Covers information on a wide variety of computer systems and language technology. *$22.00*
104 pages Bi-Monthly Founded: 1990

4737 **Pen Computing Magazine**
Aeon Publishing Group
PO Box 408
Plainview, NY 11803-0408

biz@pencomputing.com
http://www.pencomputing.com

Conrad H Blickenstorfer, Editor-in-Chief
Howard Borgen, Publisher
Wayne Laslo, Advertising Manager

In-depth coverage of pen technology, wireless communications and mobile computing. *$18.00*
Monthly Founded: 1993
Circulation: 79515

4738 **Physicians & Computers**
Moorhead Publications
600 S Waukegan Road
#200
Lake Forest, IL 60045-2672
847-615-8333

physcomp@aol.com
http://www.physicians-computers.com

Tom Moorhead, Publisher

Provides physicians with information on computer advances helpful in the private practice of medicine. Practice management, current medical and nonmedical software, computer diagnostics, etc. *$50.00*
Monthly

4739 **Powerbuilding Developer's Journal**

SYS-CON Publications
135 Chesnut Ridge Road
Montvaleer, NJ 07645-2306
201-802-3000
FAX: 201-782-9601 800-513-7111

Fuat Kircaali, Publisher

Covers provide an advanced look at Powerbuilder techniques, new products, reader feedback and interaction, and training in the Powerbuilder language.
Monthly
Circulation: 20000

4740 **Precision Engineering Journal**
Elsevier Science Publishing
6277 Sea Harbor Drive
Orlando, FL 32887-4800
407-345-4020
FAX: 407-363-1354 877-839-7126
usjcs@elsevier.com
www.elsevier.com /www.aspe.net

W T Estler, Editor-in-Chief
D G Chetwynd, Editor
T. Moriwaki, Co-Editor

Provides an integrated approach to all subjects related to the development, design, manufacture, and application of high-precision machines, systems, and components. International news, reviews, conference reports, informed comment, and a calendar of forthcoming events complete the spectrum of coverage designed to keep readers abreast with a fast-moving technology. *$1014.00*
Founded: 1979

4741 **Processor**
Peed Corporation
PO Box 85518
Lincoln, NE 68501-5518
402-479-2141
FAX: 402-479-2120 800-819-9014
feedback@processor.com
http://www.processor.com

Susy Miller, Publisher
Rhonda Peed, CEO

Information on computer products and services. *$26.00*
84 pages Weekly Founded: 1978

4742 **Products for Document Management**
Acron Publishing
1306 Gaskins Road
Richmond, VA 23233-4919
804-754-2101
FAX: 804-754-1534

Irwin Posner, Publisher

News and reviews of latest technology and applications for document management world, including hardware, software, supplies and services.
Quarterly
Circulation: 10,963

4743 **Public Human Services Directory**
American Public Human Services Association
810 First Street NE
Suite 500
Washington, DC 20002
202-682-0100
FAX: 202-289-6555
pubs@aphsa.org www.aphsa.org

Amy Plotnick, Publications Manager
Jerry W Friedman, Executive Director

A must-have for all human service professionals. Backed by APHSA, the Directory has consistently help steer people to the right contacts. Program contacts for such programs as Temporary Assistance for Needy Families, Child Welfare, Medicaid, Nutrition Assistance, Long-Term Care, Mental Health, Workforce Investment Act, and the Social Services Block Grant are available at a glance. *$115.00*

4744 **Pure Java Developer's Journal**
ZD Journals
500 Canal View Boulevard
Rochester, NY 14623-2800
585-407-7301
FAX: 585-240-7760
purejavadj@zdjournals.com
www.elementkjournal.com

Jon Pyles, Publisher

Offers tips for Java developers and answers questions regarding serving side and the aspects of BeanInfo, writing, and mathematical equations
Monthly

4745 RIS/Retail Info Systems News
Edgell Communications
4 Middlebury Boulevard
Randolph, NJ 07869-4221
973-252-0100
FAX: 973-252-9020
agaffney@edgellmail.com
http://www.risnews.com

Andrew Gaffney, Publisher
Jeff zabe, Circualtion Manager
Gabriele A. Edgell, CEO
Gerald C Ryerson, President

Updates on the latest development in retail management technologies with articles that focus on the application of managerial and hi-tech advancements.
Monthly Founded: 1984
Printed in 4 colors on glossy stock

4746 RTC
RTC Group
27312 Calle Arroyo
San Juan Capistrano, CA 92675-2768
949-443-4400
FAX: 949-489-8502 www.rtcgroup.com

John Reardo, Publisher

Provides information to answer real life questions about the open systems computer market. Also news, product updates, tech updates and standard tracking.
Monthly
Circulation: 29,500

4747 Real Time Graphics
Computer Graphic Systems Development Corporation
2483 Old Middlefield Way
#140
Mountain View, CA 94043-2330
650-903-4920
FAX: 650-967-5252
rtg@cgsd.com www.cgsd.com

Roy Latham, Publisher/Editor-in-Chief

In-depth information on the technology of real time graphics, VR, simulations and coverage of industry news. *$205.00*
Monthly
Circulation: 1M

4748 Real-Time Engineering
Micrology PBT
2618 S Shannon
Tempe, AZ 85282-2936
480-967-5581
FAX: 480-968-3446
micrology@aol.com
www.realtime-engineering.com

John Black, Editor-in-Chief

Focuses on software and operating systems.

Quarterly
Circulation: 10,000

4749 Red Herring: The Business of Technology
Red Herring Communications
1550 Bryant Street
Suite 450
San Francisco, CA 94103
415-862-2819
FAX: 415-865-2280
www.redherring.com

4750 Report on Healthcare Information Management
Aspen Publishers
1101 King Street
#444
Alexandria, VA 22314
703-683-4100
FAX: 703-739-6517
mbrown@aspenpubl.com
http://www.healthcarenet.com

Mike Brown, Publisher
H. Stephen Lieber, CEO/President
Timothy B Clark, Marketing & Business Deve

System development, clinical information systems, cost-effective clinical integration, data collection, network security and confidentiality for the health care industry.
$358.00
Monthly

4751 Reseller Management
Elsevier Communications
301 Gibraltar Drive
Morris Plains, NJ 07950-3409
973-292-5100
FAX: 973-898-9281

Michael Doyle, Editor

Targeted to managers at VARs and VADs.
$60.00
Monthly Founded: 1978

4752 Retail Systems Alert
Retail Systems Alert Group
377 Elliot Street
PO Box 332
Newton Upper Falls, MA 02464
617-527-4626
FAX: 617-527-8102
info@retailsystems.com
http://www.retailsystems.com

Tom Friedman, President
Hideo Funamoto, Contributing Editor

Provides updated information on automation news and trends, including decision systems, information systems implementation, in-store merchandise management, and case studies of retailers. *$295.00*
8 pages Monthly Founded: 1988

4753 Retail Systems Reseller
Edgell Communications
4 Middlebury Boulevard
Suite 1
Randolph, NJ 07869-1111
973-252-0100
FAX: 973-252-9020
cboughton@edgellmail.com
http://www.edgellcommunications.com

michael Kachmar, Publisher
Joe Skorupa, Editor-in-Chief
Gabriele Edgell, CEO
Gerald C. Ryerson, President
John Chiego, Vice President

Offers information to retailers, dealers, systems integraters, VARs, VADs, etc., on retail technology for small to mid-size retailers. *$190.00*
Monthly Founded: 1984

4754 RetailTech
Progressive Grocer Associates
23 Old King's Highway South
Darien, CT 06820-4538
646-654-7561
FAX: 203-656-3800
info@progressivegrocer.com
http://www.progressivegrocer.com

John Failla, Publisher
Jenny McTaggart, Senior Editor
Stephen Dowdell, Editor-in-Chief
Joseph Tarnowski, Tech Editor, Equipment & Design

Editoral content covers software, computer peripherals, communications, electronic retailing, point-of-sale systems, networking, data warehousing, logistics/distribution systems, and the Internet. *$99.00*
Monthly

4755 Robot Explorer
Appropriate Solutions
85 Grove Street
PO Box 458
Peterborough, NH 03458
603-924-6079
FAX: 603-924-8668
asi@appropriatesolutions.com
www.appropriatesolutions.com

Raymond Cote, Editor

Targets the world of non-industrial robots. From eight-legged walking machines exploring Antarctic volcanoes, to microscopic nano-machines, Robot Explorer provides practical construction details and fascinating reviews of current technology.
$14.95

Circulation: 500

4756 SCO Magazine
600 Community Drive
Manhasset, NY 11030-3847
516-562-5836
FAX: 516-562-5466

H Newton Barrett, Publisher

4757 SIGNAL Magazine
4400 Fair Lakes Center
Fairfax, VA 22033-3899
703-631-6100
FAX: 703-631-6169 800-336-4583
bmowery@afcea.org www.afcea.org

Beverly Mowery, Associate Publisher
Robert K Ackerman, Editor-in-Chief

A news magazine targeted to serve the critical information needs of government, military and industry professionals active in the fields of command, control, communications, computers, intelligence, surveillance and reconnaissance, or C4ISR; information security; research and development; electronics; and homeland security. *$56.00*
Monthly/Year Subscription

4758 SQL Forum Online
Informant Communications Group
10519 E Stockton Boulevard
Suite 100
Elk Grove, CA 95624-9703
916-863-3700
FAX: 916-379-0610
www.informant.com

Forrest Freeman, Owner
Tom Bondur, Publisher

Written for data-base professionals to share and exchange ideas. Has papers and articles that are filled with answers to common data-base questions.
Monthly

4759 Sawtooth News
Sawtooth Technologies
1500 Skokie Boulevard
Suite 510
Northbrook, IL 60062
847-239-7300
FAX: 847-239-7301
info@sawtooth.com
http://www.sawtooth.com

Nicole Garneau, Editor

Articles on computer aided telephone interviewing, computer interviewing, conjoint analysis, and other advanced research techniques.
Founded: 1995

4760 Scan Tech News
Reed Business Information
2000 Clearwater Drive
Oak Brook, IL 60523
630-740-0825
FAX: 630-288-8686 www.scantech.com

Peter M Boniface, Publisher

Updates in trends in ADC technology and standards, the latest news from leading industry events, and product developments that streamline the flow of essential information in industrial settings.
Monthly
Circulation: 82M

4761 Scan: Data Capture Report
Corry Publishing
5905 Beacon Hill Lane
Erie, PA 16509
814-380-0025
FAX: 814-864-2037
rickm@scandcr.com
http://www.rmgenterprises.com/

Larry Roberts, CEO and Publisher
(Jon) Rick Morgan, President and Editor

Developments in bar code scanning, biometric identification, electronic commerce and areas of automatic data capture. *$597.00*
Fortnightly Founded: 1996

4762 Scientific Computing & Automation
Reed Business Information
2000 Clearwater Drive
Oak Brook, IL 60523
630-740-0825
FAX: 630-288-8686
mlally@cahners.com
www.scamag.com

Matt Lally, Publisher

Provides the scientists working in industrial/analytical labs, clinical labs, life science labs and electronics R&D labs with information on developments in computing and automation technology for the laboratory. *$60.00*
Monthly
Circulation: 50,059

4763 Scientific Computing & Instrumentation
Reed Business Information
350 Hudson Street
4th Floor
New York, NY 10014
212-959-9550
FAX: 630-288-8686
subsmail@reedbusiness.com
http://www.scimag.com

Matt Lally, Publisher
Suzanne Tracy, Editor in Chief

4764 Searcher: The Magazine for Database Professionals
Information Today
143 Old Marlton Pike
Medford, NJ 08055-8750
609-654-6266
FAX: 609-654-4309
custserv@infotoday.com
http://www.infotoday.com/

Thomas Hogan, Publisher

Information on applications and software in computer database technology. Includes news from the industry, buying guides, and pricing information. *$62.95*

Circulation: 3200

4765 Semiconductor Magazine
Semiconductor Equipment & Materials International
3081 Zanker Road
San Jose, CA 95134
408-943-6900
FAX: 408-428-9600
semihq@semi.org
http://www.semi.org

T Buehler, Editor-in-Chief
Chris Bucholtz, Editor
Marie Claussell, Circulation Manager
Barbara Wietzel, Marketing Manager

Covers the technical and business information needs of inportant worldwide semiconductor manufacturers, including captive manufacturers, merchant manufacturers, research and development laboratories, equipment suppliers, government/military installations and consortiums. *$125.00*
Monthly Founded: 1980

4766 Sensors Magazine
Advanstar Communications
275 Grove Street
Suite 2-130
Newton, MA 02466
603-924-5400
FAX: 603-924-5401
bgoode@advanstar.com
http://www.sensormag.com

Barbara Goode, Group Editorial Director
Stephanie Henkel, Executive Editor
Jill Thiry, Group Publishing Director

Source among design and production engineers of information on sensor technologies and products, and topic integral to sensor-based systems and applications. Provides practical and in-depth yet accessible information on sensor operation, design, application, and implementation within systems. Covers the effective use of state-of-the-art resources and tools that enable readers to get the maximum benefit from their use of sensors.
Monthly Founded: 1999
Circulation: 66676

4767 Serverworld Magazine
Publications & Communications
11675 Jollyville Rd
Ste 150
Austin, TX 78759
512-250-9023
FAX: 512-331-3900 800-678-9724
subscriptions@pcinews.com
http://www.pcinews.com

David Wohlbrueck, Editor
Gary Pittman, CEO/President
Bill Lifland, VP Operations

Dedicated to Hewlett-Packard computing. *$45.00*
60 pages Monthly Founded: 1979

4768 Simulation
Simulation Councils
PO Box 17900
San Diego, CA 92177-7900
858-277-3888
FAX: 858-277-3930
info@scs.org http://www.scs.org

William Gallagher, Publisher
Richard Fujimoto, Editor-in-Chief
Steve Branch, Executive Director

Information on computer simulation including, applications, methodologies and techniques of computer simulation. *$195.00*
Monthly Founded: 1952
Circulation: 3800

4769 Small Business Advisor: Software News
Software News Publishing Company
110 N Bell Avenue
Suite 300
Shawnee, OK 74801-6967
405-275-3100
FAX: 405-275-3101 800-456-0864
circulation@cpasn.com
http://www.cpatechadvisor.com

Sharie Dodgen, Publisher
Melody Wrinkle, Editor

Published for advisers to small businesses and for software installers for small businesses. *$48.00*
Founded: 1991
Circulation: 50000

4770 Smart Reseller
Ziff Davis Publishing Company
500 Unicorn Park Drive
Woburn, MA 01801-4874
781-938-2600
FAX: 781-938-2626
sloan_seymour@zd.com
www.smartreseller.com

Sloan Seymour, Publisher

Identifies the most lucrative new business opportunities and details how to profitably take advantage of them. In-depth business management strategies and trusted new technology solutions-based reviews.
SemiMonthly
Circulation: 60M

4771 Software Development
Miller Freeman Publications
2655 Seely Avenue
San Jose, CA 95134
408-943-1234
FAX: 408-943-0513 800-227-4675

Veronica Costanza, Publisher
Nicole Freeman, Editor
Laura Merling, Executive Director

For corporate developers and technical managers involved in the development of software applications within the industries.

Circulation: 73297

4772 Software Digest
National Software Testing Laboratories
670 Sentry Parkway
2nd Floor
Blue Bell, PA 19422
610-832-8400
FAX: 610-941-9952
info@nstl.com http://www.nstl.com/

Lowrenie Goldstein, Publisher
Andrew Froning, Editor

Independent and comparative ratings on IBM PC software. All categories tested free of bias. No advertising is accepted.
Monthly Founded: 1983

4773 Solid Solutions
ConnectPress
551 W. Cordova Road
Suite 701
Santa Fe, NM 87505-4100
505-474-5000
FAX: 505-474-5001
info@solidprofessor.com
http://www.solidmag.com

Dale Bennie, Publisher

Covers the latest market developments and tracks the growth of SolidWorks software in the CAD/CAM/CAE market. Reviews of workstations, 3D printers, and Windows NT graphic accelerators. *$99.00*

Monthly

4774 Solutions Integrator
International Data Group
3 Post Office Square
4th Floor
Boston, MA 02109
617-239-9030
FAX: 617-423-0240
howard_sholkan@idg.com
http://www.solutionsintegrator.com

Keith Newman, CEO
Joel Shore, Editor-In-Chief

Provides accessment of technology, IT buying practices and plans, business strategies and vendor technology roadmaps.

Circulation: 90000

4775 Speech Recognition Update
CI Publishing
PO Box 570730
PO Box 4109
Tarzana, CA 91357-730
818-708-0962
FAX: 818-345-2980 888-632-7419
info@tmaa.com http://www.tmaa.com

William S Meisel, President
Bill Meisel, Editor

News and analysis of speech recognition markets, companies and technologies. *$195.00*

Monthly Founded: 1993

4776 Storage Management Solutions
West World Productions
420 N Camden Drive
Beverly Hills, CA 90210-4507
310-327-7100
FAX: 310-246-1405
http://www.wwpi.com/

Mark Ferelli, Editor
Yuri Spiro, CEO/President
Yuri Spiro, Publisher
Steve Schone, Circulation Manager

Articles on tutorials, case studies, lab tests and new products that offer solutions to issues of data accessibility, availablity and protection and network storage. *$10.00*

72 pages Monthly Founded: 1995
Circulation: 64044 26,000 names $195 per M.
Printed in 4 colors on glossy stock : html

4777 Studio City
Resource Central
4126 Pennsylvania Avenue
Suite 3
Kansas City, MO 64111-3018

Tom Weishaar, President

Information on using the multimedia package Hyper Studio, mailed on 3.5 inch disk, 6 times a year. Available in Macintosh and Apple II versions.

Bi-Monthly

4778 Sun Observer
Publications & Communications
11675 Jollyville Rd
Ste 150
Austin, TX 78759
512-250-9023
FAX: 512-331-3900 800-678-9724
robertm@pcinews.com
http://www.pcinews.com

Gary Pittman, CEO/President
Robert Martin, Editor

Journal of news and information devoted to the users of Sun Microsystems. *$14.95*

80 pages Founded: 1980

4779 Supply Chain Systems Magazine
Helmers Publishing
174 Concord Street
P O Box 874
Peterborough, NH 03458-1291
603-924-9631
FAX: 603-924-7408
dandrews@helmers.com
http://www.scs-mag.com

David Andrewso, Publisher/Editorial
Bill Fahy, Circulation Director
Paul Quinn, Editor/Senior Writer

Educates its readers about the benefits and bast practices of supply chain management in manufacturing and service industries. We educate our readers about how e-business, Enterprises Resource Planning, asset management, data capture, warehouse management and management can be integrated to create effective and efficient supply chain systems.

60 pages Weekly Founded: 1979
Circulation: 53000 53000 names
Printed in 4 colors on glossy stock

4780 Synapps
Synergis Technologies
472 California Road
Quakertown, PA 18951-2408
215-529-9900
FAX: 215-536-9249 www.synergis.com

David B Sharp III, Publisher

Information for professional management of AutoCAD systems and includes application articles.

Quarterly
Circulation: 25000

4781 Sys Admin
CMP Media
4601 West 6th Street
Suite B
Lawrence, KS 66046
785-841-1631
FAX: 785-841-2047
samag@neodata.com
http://www.sysadminmag.com

Edwin Rothrock, Publisher
Amber Ankerholz, Editor
Gary Marshall, President
Bob Cucciniello, Marketing

SYS ADMIN serves the Unix and Linux system administration market. *$43.00*

100 pages Monthly Founded: 1992
Circulation: 29121 27000 names $195 per M.
Printed in on glossy stock

4782 Systematic Magazine
American Payroll Association
711 Navarro Street
Suite 100
San Antonio, TX 78205-1710
210-226-4600
FAX: 210-226-4027
apa@apa-ed.com
www.americanpayroll.org

Daniel J Maddux, Publisher

Covers new systems and implementation, the latest technology and its relation to human resources, payroll and accounting for CFOs, MIS department heads and top management in companies that use information technology for communication.

Quarterly
Circulation: 14M

4783 Systems Development Management
Auerbach Publications
535 5th Avenue
Room 806
New York, NY 10017-3610

FAX: 212-297-9176 800-737-8034

Rich O'Hamley, Publisher
Janet Butler, Editor

Technical and managerial information on systems development. *$495.00*

Bi-Monthly
Circulation: 1,000
Printed in on matte stock : CD-Room

4784 Systems Integration
Reed Business Information
360 Park Avenue South
New York, NY 10014
212-450-0067
FAX: 646-746-7583
slebris@reedbusiness.com
http://www.reedbusiness.com

Susan Chouland, Publisher
Thomas Temin, Editor
James Reed, Owner
Jim Casella, CEO

Covers trade and developments for mini-micro based computer systems. *$75.00*

Monthly Founded: 1968

4785 TAAR: The Automated Agency Report
Automation Management Group
4964 Sundance Square
Boulder, CO 80301-3739
303-581-0525

joannem@taarreport.com
www.taan.com

Rick Morgan, Editor

Covers trends, developments and news, reviews new and current technology, and offers ideas and profiles on the productivity benefits. *$175.00*

Monthly

4786 Tech Week
1156 Aster Avenue
Suite B
Sunnyvale, CA 94086
408-249-8300
FAX: 408-249-0727
advert@techweek.com

4787 Techlinks
3350 Riverwood Parkway
Suite 1900
Atlanta, GA 30339
678-627-8157
FAX: 678-627-8159

4788 **Technical Services Quarterly**
Haworth Press
10 Alice Street
Binghamton, NY 13904-1580
607-722-5857
FAX: 607-771-0012 800-429-6784
getinfo@haworthpress.com
http://www.haworthpress.com/web/tsq

Gary M Pitkin, Editor
Laverna Saunders, Acting VP

Provides updated information concerning the technology that technical service professionals in library surroundings utilize, including new trends in computer automation and related systems. *$75.00*
Quarterly Founded: 1978

4789 **Technical Support Magazine**
Technical Enterprises
7044 S 13th Street
Oak Creek, WI 53154
414-908-4945
FAX: 414-768-8001
editor@naspa.com
http://www.naspa.com

Rachael Zimmerman, Editor
Denise Rockhill, Publisher

Provides tips and techniques for MVS, VM and VSE mainframe operating systems and NT environments. It also examines security and system performance, product installation experiences and a host of other related enterprise concerns.
68 pages Monthly Founded: 1986
Circulation: 50,000 80,000 names $170 per M.
Printed in 4 colors on glossy stock

4790 **Technical Training**
American Society for Training & Development
1640 King Street
Box 1443
Alexandria, VA 22313-2043
703-836-4606
FAX: 703-683-8103
csc4@astd.org www.astd.org

Curtis E Plott, Publisher

Industry trends, technologies and techniques within computer, manufacturing, telecommunications and government industries. *$59.00*
Bi-Monthly
Circulation: 11M

4791 **Technology & Learning**
CMP Media
600 Harrison Street
San Francisco, CA 94107-1387
415-728-8947
FAX: 415-947-6041
techlearning_editors@cmp.com
http://www.techlearning.com

Jo-Ann McDevitt, Publisher
Susan McLester, Editor in Chief
Michelle Thatcher, Managing Editor

Listings of new software education programs, new computer systems, and industry news for administrators and educators at the K-12 level. *$44.00*
Monthly Founded: 1971
Circulation: 81000
Printed in on glossy stock

4792 **Technology and Practice Guide**
ABA Publishing
750 N Lake Shore Drive
Chicago, IL 60611-4403
312-988-5000
FAX: 312-988-6081 www.abanet.org

Mary Kay Rockwell, Publisher

Helps law professionals of general practice in making decisions about legal information management and technology. *$18.00*
SemiAnnual
Circulation: 13,477

4793 **Techscan: The Managers Guide to Technology**
Richmond Research
Village Station
PO Box 537
New York, NY 10014-0537
212-915-5318
techscan@pipeline.com

Lou Giacalone, Publisher

Information and insights on how various new technologies, products and design techniques are used to solve business problems. *$ 87.50*
Monthly
Circulation: 2,500

4794 **Text Technology: The Journal of Computer Text Processing**
McMaster University
1280 Main Street W
Hamilton, On 0
905-525-9140
FAX: 905-577-6930
buckleyj@mcmaster.ca
http://texttechnology.mcmaster.ca

Joanne Buckley, Editor
Edie Rasmussen, Editor

Tips, techniques and programs for TEXT, Icon, Macintosh and other software and word-processing programs, desktop publishing and Internet as they apply to educational applications. *$45.00*
Quarterly
Circulation: 800

4795 **Trends in Computing**
Scientific American
415 Madison Avenue
New York, NY 10017-1179
212-540-0525
FAX: 212-832-2998 800-333-1199
gbronson@sciam.com
http://www.sciam.com

Harry Myers, Editor
Elias Arnett, Owner

Targets computer managers and professionals. *$24.97*
Annual+ Founded: 1845

4796 **Unicenter TNG Advisor**
Advisor Media
PO Box 429002
San Diego, CA 92142-9002
858-278-5600
FAX: 858-278-0300
http://www.advisor.com

John Hawkins, CEO

Advice on TNG programs and equipment, covers end to end management in support of multi-platform infrastructure, integration of management functions and open extensibility. *$39.00*
Monthly
Circulation: 35000

4797 **Unisys World/Network Computing News**
Publications & Communications
505 Cypress Creek Road
Suite B
Cedar Park, TX 78613-1868
512-250-9023
FAX: 512-331-3900

Larry Storer, Editor

Dedicated to the users and OEMs of convergent technologies products.' *$48.00*
24 pages Monthly Founded: 1983

4798 **VAR Business**
CMP Media
One Jericho Plaza
Wing A
Jericho, NY 11753-1680
516-733-6700

ljeffrey@cmp.com
www.varbusiness.com

Leslie Jeffrey, Publisher

Focuses on management issues and trends, and includes business news and the latest products and technology. *$89.00*
BiWeekly
Circulation: 95,072

4799 **Varindustry Products**
VIPublishing
30506 Palos Verdes Drive W
Rancho Palos Verdes, CA 90275-4471

Kenneth Allen, Editor

Focuses on new products and services.
Monthly Founded: 1990

4800 **Vision Systems Design**
PennWell Publishing Company
98 Spit Brook Road
5th Floor
Nashua, NH 03062
603-891-0123
FAX: 603-891-9279
cholton@pennwell.com
http://www.vision-systems.com

W.Conard Holton, Editor-in-Chief
Andrew Wilson, Editor
Bonnie Heines, Managing Editor

Each issue discusses the development of leading edge industrial, scientific, medical, military, and aerospace machine vision applications. *$85.00*
Monthly Founded: 1910
Circulation: 32000
Printed in 4 colors

4801 **Visual Basic Programmer's Journal**
Fawcette Technical Publications
2600 S El Camino Real
Suite 300
San Mateo, CA 94403-2332
650-378-7100
FAX: 650-570-6307 800-848-5523
hr@fawcette.com
http://www.fawcette.com/vsm/

James E Fawcette, Publisher/
Tina Fontenot, Marketing
Karin Becker, Associate Publisher
Karen Koenen, Sr. Circulation Director
James E Fawcette, CEO

Provides technical news on how to increase productivity and process applications more efficiently. *$71.40*
Monthly Founded: 1990
Circulation: 109874

4802 **WINDOWS Magazine**
CMP Publications
600 Community Drive
Manhasset, NY 11030-3847
516-562-5000
FAX: 516-562-5995

Scott Wolfe, Publisher

Offers the latest information and updates for the WINDOWS user.

4803 **Wall Street Computer Review**
Miller Freeman Publications
1199 S Belt Line Road
Suite 100
Coppell, TX 75019-4667
972-906-6500
FAX: 972-419-7825

Elizabeth Katz, Publisher
Pavan Sahgal, Editor

For financial and investment professionals and individual investors. *$5.00*

Circulation: 34,000

4804 **Waters**
Waters Information Services
270 Lafayette Street
Suite 700
New York, NY 10012
212-130-0711
FAX: 212-925-7585
jkotz@riskwaters.com
http://www.watersinfo.com

Andrew Delaeny, Editor-in-Chief
Phil Albinus, Editor
John Waters, Chief Executive Officer
Farrell McManus, Advertising Manager

Articles on technology applications leading strategic business success, career enhancements and workplace changes. *$240.00*
Monthly Founded: 1993
Circulation: 20000

4805 **Windows & Dot Net**
Duke Communications International
221 E 29th Street
Loveland, CO 80538
970-663-4700
FAX: 970-667-2321 800-621-1544
information@penton.com
http://www.penton.com

Bart Taylor, Group Publisher
Kim Paulsen, Publisher
David B. Nussbaum, CEO *$49.95*

Monthly Founded: 1982
Circulation: 100000

4806 **Windows Developer's Journal**
600 Harrison Street
San Francisco, CA 94107
415-947-6000
FAX: 415-947-6027
wdeditor@cmp.com
http://www.wdj.com

John Dorsey, Editor in Chief
Kerry Gates, Publisher
Holly Vessichelli, Director of Marketing

Publication for professional Windows developers.
Founded: 1990

4807 **Windows NT Magazine**
Duke Communications International
221 E 29th Street
PO Box 447
Loveland, CO 80539-447
970-663-4700
FAX: 970-203-2996 800-621-1544
mark@winntmag.com
http://www.winntmag.com

Mark Smith, Publisher
Karen Forster, Editor

Serves technical decision makers using the Windows NT application, and related systems. *$49.95*
Monthly
Circulation: 75000

4808 **Windows/DOS Developer's Journal**
R&D Associates
6701 W 121st Street
Suite 310
Overland Park, KS 66209
913-491-0345
FAX: 785-841-2624
http://www.rndassociates.com

Ron Burk, Editor

Information for professional Windows and DOS programmers. *$29.00*
Monthly Founded: 1996
Circulation: 22000

4809 **Windowspro Magazine**
Ziff Davis Publishing Company
500 Unicorn Park Drive
Woburn, MA 01801
781-938-2600
FAX: 781-938-2626
jason_young@zd.com
www.windowspro.com

Jason Young, Publisher
Jacquelyn Gavron, Editor-in-Chief

Serves technology-experts responsible for Windows NT based support. Includes technologies, products, solutions, and how-to instructions.
Monthly
Circulation: 150,000

4810 **Wired**
Wired News
660 3rd Street
1st Floor
San Francisco, CA 94107
415-276-5000
FAX: 415-276-8500 800-769-4733
subscriptions@wiredmag.com
http://www.wired.com

Evan Hansen, Editor-in-Chief
Jeremy Barna, Production Manager
Alison Macondray, General Manager
Drew Schutte, Publisher

Focuses on people and ideas behind digital technology.
Monthly
Circulation: 305097

4811 **Workstation News**
Data Base Publications
9390 Research Boulevard
Suite 300
Austin, TX 78759-7367
512-372-8216
FAX: 512-794-0860

Aimed at workstation users and volume buyers.
Monthly Founded: 1990

Trade Shows

4812 **AAAI National Conference**
American Association for Artificial Intelligence
445 Burgess Drive
Menlo Park, CA 94025-3442
650-328-3123
FAX: 650-321-4457 800-968-1738
ncai@aaai.org www.aaai.org

Keri Vasser Harvey, Senior Conference Coordinator
Corina Anzaldo, Conference Coordinator

The conference provides a forum for a broad range of topics, including knowledge representation and automated reasoning, planning, machine learning and data mining, autonomous agents, robotics and machine perception, probabilistic inference, constraint satisfaction, search and game playing, natural language processing, neural networks, multi-agent systems, computational game theory and cognitive modeling.

1.2M Attendees July Founded: 1980

4813 **ACUI Annual Conference**
Association of College Unions International
1 City Centre, Suite 200
120 W. 7th Street
Bloomington, IN 47404-3925
812-855-8550
FAX: 812-855-0162
melletso@pcc.edu www.acui.org

Mandy Ellertson, Conference Team Chairperson
David Mucci, Conference Host

One hundred exhibits of graphic supplies, recreation equipment, computer hardware & software, furnishings, entertainment and speaker bureau information, food service equipment, and more related information and supplies.
1000 Attendees March 2006 Founded: 1951

4814 **AIA Business Conference**
Automated Imaging Association
900 Victors Way
Suite 140
Ann Arbor, MI 48108
734-994-6088
FAX: 734-994-3338 800-994-6099
jburnstein@robotics.org
www.machinevisiononline.org

Jeff Burnstein, Executive Director

The annual AIA Business Conference has become the machine vision industry's most important networking event. The Conference gathers top industry executives to do business with their peers and hear presentations on issues affecting the global economy in general and the machine vision industry specifically.
300+ Attendees February

4815 **AIIM Annual Expo Conference & Exposition**
Association for Information and Image Management
1100 Wayne Avenue
Suite 1100
Silver Spring, MD 20910
301-587-8202
FAX: 301-587-2711 888-824-3004
aiim@aiim.org www.aiim.org

Don Post, Conference/Expo Chairman
John Mancicni, President

The largest enterprise content & document management conference and exposition showcasing the technologies and solutions that provide intelligence behind information. For more than 50 years, this annual event attracts business professionals and executive management seeking the latest technologies.
May

4816 **AMIA Annual Symposium**
American Medical Informatics Association

4915 St Elmo Avenue
Suite 401
Bethesda, MD 20814
301-657-1291
FAX: 301-657-1296
mail@amia.org www.amia.org

Charles P Friedman, Meeting Chairman
Karen Greenwood, Manager

Features an outstanding program of scientific papers, posters, tutorials and other educational events that provide information about cutting-edge work in medical informatics.

2000 Attendees Annual/October Founded: 1977 2000 names

4817 **ARMA Annual Conference & Exposition**
ARMA International
13725 W 109th Street
Suite 101
Lenexa, KS 66215
913-341-3808
FAX: 913-341-3742 800-422-2762
hq@arma.org www.arma.org

Wanda Wilson, Conference Manager
Sarah G Pratt-Pronek, Trade Show Director
Peter Hermann, Chief Executive Officer

Conference, seminar, workshop, banquet, award ceremony and 200 exhibits of micrographics, optical disk, automated document storage and retrieval systems and more technology of interest to information professionals.

3000 Attendees September Founded: 1956

4818 **ASIS&T Annual Meeting**
American Society for Information Science & Techn.
1320 Fenwicka Lane
Suite 510
Silver Spring, MD 20910
301-495-0900
FAX: 301-495-0810
meetings@asis.org www.asis.org

Richard B Hill, Executive Director
Vanessa Foss, Director of Meetings & Membership

Focus on the diversity of perspectives and insights from all those participating in the information science and technology community, as they generate innovative ideas, define theoretical concepts or work out the nuts and bolts of implementing well-tested ideas in new ways and in new settings.

Annual/Oct-Nov

4819 **ASPE Annual Meeting**
American Society for Precision Engineering
PO Box 10826
Raleigh, NC 27605-0826
919-839-8444
FAX: 919-839-8039
erika_layne@aspe.net www.aspe.net

Erika Deutsch Layne, Meetings Manager
Thomas A Dow, Executive Director

Offering the latest in precision engineering research through presentations from national and international speakers. Participants in the Annual Meeting have the opportunity to exchange ideas with internationally renowned experts in the field.

Annual/Oct-Nov

4820 **AWWA Annual Conference and Exposition**
American Water Works Association
6666 W Quincy Avenue
Denver, CO 80235
303-794-7711
FAX: 303-347-0804 800-926-7337

Melanie Fahrenbruch, Convention Services
Jack W Hoffbuhr, Executive Director
Paula I. Macllwaine, Deputy Executive Director

The source of knowledge and information for water professionals who work to improve the quality and supply of drinking water in North America and beyond. You'll learn from industry experts in the field, hear about cutting edge research and exceptional best practices, and have the opportunity to ask questions, seek advice, and interact with other water professionals regarding both universal topics and items specifically focused to meet your needs.

Annual/June

4821 **AWWA Information Management & Technology Conference**
American Water Works Association
6666 W Quincy Avenue
Denver, CO 80235
303-794-7711
FAX: 303-347-0804 800-926-7337

Melanie Fahrenbruch, Convention Services
Jack W Hoffbuhr, Executive Director
Paul Macllwaine, Deputy Executive Director

This event is North America's premier conference in the area of water supply information management technology and applications for the water and wastewater industry.

March

4822 **Association For Services Management World Conference Expo**
AFSM International
1342 Colonial Boulevard
Suite 25
Fort Myers, FL 33907-1084
239-275-7887
FAX: 239-275-0794 800-333-9786
sstidinger@afsmi.org www.afsmi.org

Stephen Stidinger, Director of Events Planning

World's largest gathering of executives in the services and support industry.

October

4823 **Autodesk Expo**
AEC Systems International/Penton Media
1300 E 9th Street
Cleveland, OH 44114

FAX: 610-280-7106 800-451-1196
info@aecsystems.com
www.acesystems.com

Philip McKay, Manager

Highlights AutoCAD and related products from Autodesk and third party developers. 500 exhibits.

20M Attendees May

4824 **Bentley MicroStation Mail**
AEC Systems International/Penton Media
1300 E 9th Street
Cleveland, OH 44114

FAX: 610-280-7106 800-451-1196
info@aecsystems.com
www.acesystems.com

Philip McKay, Manager

Showcases a comprehensive line-up of intergrated design, facility management and GIS solutions built around MicroStation software. 500 exhibits.

20M Attendees May

4825 **CALICO Annual Meeting**
Computer Assisted Language Instruction Consortium
Southwest Texas State University
116 Centennial Hall
San Marcos, TX 78666
512-245-1417
FAX: 512-245-8298
info@calico.org www.calico.org

Robert Fischer, Executive Director
Esther Horn, Manager

Providing a forum for discussions of state-of-the-art educational technology and its applications to the more effective teaching and learning of languages. The symposia accommodate workshops, papers, demonstrations, panels, and special interest groups for participants at all levels of expertise.

Annual/May

4826 **CLA World Computer and Internet Law Congress Conference**

Computer Law Association
3028 Javier Road
Suite 402
Fairfax, VA 22031
703-560-7747
FAX: 703-207-7028
askcla@cla.org www.cla.org

Barbara Fieser, Executive Director

This conference will provide you with proven strategies and best practices that will enable you to effectively address your existing clients' IT-related challenges and problems and seek out clients whom you can assist with knowledge you will gain from the conference.

2000+ Attendees May

4827 **CSI Annual Computer Securtiy Conference & Exhibition**
CMP Media/Computer Security Institute Services
600 Community Drive
Manhasset, NY 11030
516-562-5000
FAX: 818-487-4550 866-271-8529
jstevens@cmp.com www.cmp.com

Jennifer Stevens, Conference Manager
Kimber Heald, Registration Manager
Annette Campo, Manager

The exhibition features 150 security vendors, from the industry leaders to the up-and coming, displaying the latest security technologies.

950 Attendees November

4828 **CUMREC**
Educause
4772 Walnut Street
Suite 206
Boulder, CO 80301-2538
303-449-4430
FAX: 303-440-0461
info@curec.org www.educause.edu

Beverly Williams, Director of Conference Activities
Lisa Gesner, Assistant Director of Marketing

Higher education administrative technology conference. The purpose of CUMREC is to provide a forum for higher education professionals to share their expertise and experiences with computer systems in our ever changing world of technology. The CUMREC annual conference, founded in 1956, is devoted to promoting the understanding and use of information technology in higher education.

3M Attendees May Founded: 1956

4829 Comdex Spring and Fall Shows
MediaLive International
795 Folsom Street
6th Floor
San Francisco, CA 94107-1243
415-905-2300
FAX: 415-905-2FAX
eric.faurot@mlii.com
www.medialiveinternational.com

Eric Faurot, VP
Marco Pardi, Exhibit Sales

COMDEX is the global marketplace for the IT industry. Buyers and sellers from around the world converge to learn how best to use technology to solve their business challenges and remain competitive. COMDEX is where hardware manufacturers, software vendors and service providers launch new products, where thought-leaders discuss industry trends, and where the media reports on the latest in the IT industry and considers its future.
100M+ Attendees November

4830 CompTIA Annual Breakaway Conference
CompTIA
1815 S Meyers Road
Suite 300
Oakbrook Terrace, IL 60181-5228
630-678-8300
FAX: 630-268-1384
breakaway@comptia.org
www.comptia.org

Robert J Sartor, Chairman
Martin Bean, Vice Chairman

The annual CompTIA Breakaway conference is the computing industry's premier partnering event. The conference focuses on business-building solutions, networking forums, and the latest industry trends and technologies.
Annual/August

4831 Design Automation Conference
Design Automation
5405 Spine Road
Suite 102
Boulder, CO 80301
303-530-4333
FAX: 303-530-4334
kevin@mpassociates.com
www.dac.com

Kevin Lepine, Conference Manager
Lee Wood, Exhibits Manager
Nannette Jordan, Registration Coordinator

The premier Electronic Design Automation (EDA) and silicon solution event. DAC features over 50 technical sessions covering the latest in design methodologies and EDA tool developments, and an Exhibition and Demo Suite area with over 250 of the leading EDA, silicon, and IP Providers.
11M+ Attendees June

4832 Embedded Systems Conference
CMP Media Headquarters
600 Community Drive
Manhasset, NY 11030
516-562-5000

cfahlen@cmp.com
www.esconline.com

Christian Fahlen, Senior Conference Manager
Ardis Gough, Conference Manager
Kara Pistochini, Conference Assistant
Annette Campo, Manager

The only conference to focus on the art and science of microcomptroller and microprocessor based development, covering the needs of real-time software engineers.
2.7M Attendees September

4833 FOSE
Post Newsweek Tech Media
10 G Street NE
Suite 500
Washington, DC 20002-4228
202-772-2500
FAX: 202-772-2511 800-791-FOSE
lnichols@postnewsweektech.com
www.ntpshow.com

Lauri Nichols, Trade Show Operations Manager
Melanie Woodfolk, Show Marketing Manager
David Greene, President

Largest information technology exposition serving the government marketplace.
4000 Attendees April

4834 Frontline Solutions Conference & Expo
AIM/Advanstar Technology Group
275 Grove Street
Suite 2-130
Newton, MA 02466
617-219-8300
FAX: 617-219-8311
info@aimglobal.org
www.aimglobal.org /
www.frontlineexpo.com

Priya Chan, Event Services
Kara Boudreau, Exhibit Sales

The world's largest industry forum focused on the application of RFID, Auto-ID and data management technologies and solutions to the supply chain.
1100 Attendees September

4835 GeoExpo
AEC Systems International/Penton Media
1300 E 9th Street
Cleveland, OH 44114

FAX: 610-280-7106 800-451-1196
info@aecsystems.com
www.aecsystems.com

Philip McKay, Manager

Latest GIS/mapping/survey technology. 500 exhibits.
20M Attendees May

4836 Graph Expo & Convention
Graphic Arts Show Company
1899 Preston White Drive
Reston, VA 20191
703-264-7200
FAX: 703-620-9187
info@gasc.org www.gasc.org

Kelly Kilga, Conference/Show Operations Director
Lilly Kinney, Conference Manager

The largest, most comprehensive prepress, printing, converting and digital equipment trade show and conference in the Americas.
40000 Attendees October

4837 Graphics of the Americas
Printing Association of Florida
6275 Hazeltine National Drive
Orlando, FL 32822
407-240-8009
FAX: 407-240-8333 800-331-0461

Anne Gaither, Convention Director
Michael H Streibig, Staff Executive

We are the second largest Graphic Arts and Converting show in America. We give you two vital markets — southeast US and Latin America: Mexico, South America, Central America and the Caribbean. Our 28 year track record reflects our success with both exhibitors and show visitors.
20000 Attendees Feb

4838 Healthcare Information and Management Systems Society Conference
Healthcare Information and Management Systems
230 E Ohio
Suite 500
Chicago, IL 60611-3269
312-664-4467
FAX: 312-664-6143
kmalone@himss.org www.himss.org

Karen Malone, Director of Meetings

An opportunity to learn the latest industry intelligence, find solutions to your most pressing professional challenges, and network with your peers. Pre-conference workshops and education session, see industry newsmakers, explore the latest technologies in more than 600 exhibits and earn continuing education credit and certification.
20000 Attendees February

4839 IAAP International Convention and Education Forum
Int'l Association of Administrative Professionals
10502 NW Ambassador Drive
Kansas City, MO 16415
816-891-6600
FAX: 816-891-9118
meetings@iaap-hq.org
www.iaap-hq.org

Inge Hafkemeyer, Convention/Meetings/Exhibit Manager
Don Bretthauer, Executive Director

An opportunity to showcase your product or service to this important audience. Office Expo exhibitors include major office product manufacturers, publishers, software vendors, staffing firms, gift suppliers, paper companies, and many more.
2000 Attendees July

4840 IAPP Privacy and Data Security Academy Expo
Internet Alliance
1111 19th Street NW
Suite 1180
Washington, DC 20035-5782
202-284-4380
FAX: 202-955-8081
emilyh@internetalliance.org
www.internetalliance.org

Emily T Hackett, Executive Director
Katy Caldwell, California Policy Director

The conference will showcase the latest thinking on important privacy issues in healthcare, financial services, technology and marketing. Attendees will gain a deeper understanding of strategies and tools required to meet today's privacy challenges.
1000 Attendees October Founded: 1981

4841 IRGA Annual Convention and Trade Show
International Reprographic Association
401 N Michigan Avenue
Chicago, IL 60611-1929
312-245-1026
FAX: 312-527-6705
ejohnson@irga.com www.irga.com

Steve Bova, Executive Director
Eric Johnson, Director of Convention/Exhibits

Jen Marcus, Trade Show Coordinator
Nicole Boland, Sponsorship Sales

A host to the reprographic and digital imaging industry's premiere suppliers of small-format copiers, wide-format printers, print management solutions, finishing equipment, scanners, media and other related products and services.

Annual/May

4842 IS&T/SPIE Annual Symposium Electronic Imaging
International Society for Optical Engineering
1000 20th Street
PO Box 10
Bellingham, WA 98227-6705
360-763-3290
FAX: 360-647-1445
meetinginfo@spie.org www.spie.org

Giordano B Beretta, Director
Robert L Stevenson, Co-Director
Eugene Arthurs, Executive Director

Electronic Imaging's top-notch technical program gathers the world's prominent experts to discuss and push the forefront of imaging technology and it's applications.

1200 Attendees Annual/January

4843 ISACA International Conference
Information Systems Audit & Control Association
3701 Algonquin Road
Suite 1010
Rolling Meadows, IL 60008
847-253-1545
FAX: 847-253-1443
conference@isaca.org www.isaca.org

Sandy Arens, Registration

The International Conference has long been recognised throughout the world for providing in-depth coverage of the leading-edge technical and managerial issues facing IT governance, control, security and assurance professionals.

June

4844 Industrial Virtual Reality
Reed Exhibitions
US Consumer Show Division
225 Wyman Street
Waltham, MA 02451
781-622-8616
FAX: 781-622-8042
inquiry@sport.reedexpo.com
www.reedexpo.com

Elizabeth Hitchcock, International Sales

The first trade show focusing on industrial applications of virtual reality and tele-existence.

June

4845 Information Technology Week
Information Week/CMP Media
600 Community Drive
Manhasset, NY 11030
516-562-5000
FAX: 516-562-5036
lmonvign@cmp.com
www.informationweek.com

Lisa Monvigner, Events Associate Director
Stephanie Iannuzzi, Sr. Marketing Manager
Michael Friedenberg, Publisher

A forum for computer technicians and professionals.

May

4846 International Conference on Software Engineering
Software Engineering Institute
Carnegie Mellon University
Pittsburgh, PA 15213-3890
412-687-7700
FAX: 412-268-6257
register@computer.org
www.sei.cmu.edu

John Foreman, Program Director
Kelly Kimberland, Public Relations Director

ICSE is the premier software engineering conference, providing a forum for researchers, practitioners and educators to present and discuss the most recent innovations, trends, experiences, and concerns in the field of software engineering.

800 Attendees May

4847 International Consumer Electronics Technology Show
Consumer Electronics Association
2500 Wilson Boulevard
Arlington, VA 22201-3834
703-077-7600
FAX: 703-907-7601 866-233-7968
tdunion@ce.org www.cesweb.org

Tara Dunion, Event Director
Kristen Peifer, Event Manager
Leah Arnold, Exhibitor Coordinator

The largest annual consumer technology tradeshow offering a wealth of opportunity for your business.

140M Attendees Annual/January

4848 International Spectrum MultiValue Conference & Exhibition
International Spectrum
715 J Street
Suite 301
San Diego, CA 92101-2478
619-515-9930
FAX: 619-515-9933
requests@intl-spectrum.com
www.intl-spectrum.com

Monica Giobbi, President
Gus Giobbi, Chairman

A conference and exhibition showcasing MultiValue products and services. *$795.00*

6M Attendees March

4849 Interop Conference
Interop
C/O MediaLive International
795 Folsom Street, 6th Floor
San Francisco, CA 94107-1243
415-905-2300
FAX: 415-905-2FAX
jennifer.sioteco@mlii.com
www.interop.com

Jennifer Sioteco, Conference Program Manager
Lenny Heymann, General Manager

Provides you an overview of the robust conference offerings, workshops and tutorials, and special programs.

60000 Attendees

4850 Java One Conference
Sun Microsystems
4150 Network Circle
Santa Clara, CA 95054
650-960-1300
866-382-7151
javaoneinfo@eventreg.com
www.java.sun.com

Jonathan Schwartz, President/CEO
Anil Gadre, EVP/Chief Marketing Officer

Gain knowledge and Java technology education directly from Sun Microsystems, Inc. and other industry leaders. Get expert advice on solving the most common Java challenges. Benefit from four full days of content. Choose from hundreds of technical sessions and test drive real-world Java technology solutions.

5000 Attendees June

4851 MacWorld Conference & Expo
1400 Providence Highway
Norwood, MA 02062-5015
781-539-9800
FAX: 781-440-0351
nora_risti@idg.com
www.macworldexpo.com

Jessica Taylor, Conference Coordinator
Nora Risti, Event Operations Manager

Annual show of 400 exhibitors of MacIntosh equipment, supplies and services. We provide the education, networking and thought leadership that professionals and consumers alike need to get the most from their technology investment.

65000 Attendees Jan & July

4852 Marketechnics
Food Marketing Institute
655 15th Street NW
Washington, DC 20005
202-200-0600
FAX: 202-429-4519 www.fmi.org

Aileen Dullaghan Munster, Contact Person

Provides a once-a-year opportunity to hear, see and discuss new technologies and their impact on the supply chain, store operations and marketing/merchandising strategies.

7000 Attendees Jan-Feb

4853 NACCB Annual Conference
National Association of Computer Consultants
1420 King Street
Suite 610
Alexandria, VA 22314
703-838-2050
FAX: 703-838-3610
susan@naccb.org www.naccb.org

Susan Donohoe, Director of Programs/Public Policy
Beth Berman, Program & Administrative Coord.

The only educational, networking, and leadership event exclusively for the IT Services Industry. The NACCB conference provides a platform where IT services firms connect to address issues and solutions most affecting business today.

Annual/November Founded: 1988

4854 National Ergonomics Conference and Exposition
Continental Exhibitions
370 Lexington Avenue
Suite 1407
New York, NY 10017-6503
212-370-5005
FAX: 212-370-5699
information@ergoexpo.com
www.ergoexpo.com

Larry L Elyea, Executive Program Director
Pedro Caceres, Senior VP of Operations

The NECE maximizes your time and effort by providing direct contact with industry leaders that comprise our speaker faculty, direct contact with leading providers of ergonomics products and services, and direct

contact with your peers at networking receptions during the exposition.
Nov-Dec

4855 Object World Conference
Object Management Group/IDG Management
111 Speen Street
PO Box 9107
Framingham, MA 01701-9514

FAX: 508-872-8237 800-225-4698
omg@omg.com www.omg.com

Mary DeCristoforo, Conference Director
David Elliott, Exhibit Sales Manager

An annual conference sponsored by the Object Management Group and IDG Management Group to advance object-oriented technology in commercial software development. The event features tutorials and conference sessions.
6.5M Attendees October

4856 Optical Fiber Communications Conference
Optical Society of America
2010 Massachusetts Avenue NW
Washington, DC 20036
202-238-8130
FAX: 202-416-6140
info@ofcconference.org
www.ofcnfoec.org

Colleen Morrison, Media Relations Director
Melissa Russell, Exhibit Sales Director
Colleen Morrison, Media Relations Manager

Provides leading edge, peer reviewed educational programming along with a high powered, commerce driven exhibition. This unique combination attracts the field's most progressive professionals and exhibiting companies.
13111 Attendees March Founded: 1916

4857 PCB Design Conference West
UP Media Group
2400 Lake Park Dr Se
Ste 440
Smyrna, GA 30080-7695
678-589-8800
FAX: 678-589-8850
askarbek@upmediagroup.com
www.pcbwest.com

Alyson Skarbek, Show Operations Manager
Andy Shaughnessy, Conference Chairperson
Brooke Anglin, Exhibit Sales Manager

The first and only conference 100% dedicated to the needs of the PCB designer.
750 Attendees March

4858 PIMA Leadership Conference
Paper Industry Management Association
4700 W Lake Avenue
Glenview, IL 60025-1485
847-375-6860
FAX: 732-460-7333 877-527-5973
info@pimaweb.org
www.pima-online.org

Carol Waugh, Meetings Manager
Julie Weir, Senior Manger

Three-day conference to bring together IT and process control professionals from around the world to share their knowledge of information technology in the pulp and paper industry and to promote systems applications. The only IT conference planned for and by IT professionals.
500 Attendees Annual/June

4859 Pacific Telecommunications Council Conference: PTC Conference
Pacific Telecommunications Council
2454 S Beretania Street
3rd Floor
Honolulu, HI 96826-1596
808-941-3789
FAX: 808-944-4874
snakama@ptc.org www.ptc.org

Sharon Nakama, Conference Director
Dolores Fung, Conference/Seminar Coordinator
Claudine Naruse, Conference/Seminar Coordinator
Justin Riel, Conference/Seminar Assistant

Provides an opportunity to learn and to analyze current issues. Registrants from the ranks of senior corporate officers and management, experts from law and consulting firms, noted analysts and scholars, and technical experts provide a wide diversity of ideas.
1500 Attendees January

4860 SC: High Performance Networking & Computing
Hall-Erickson
98 E. Naperville Road
Westmont, IL 60559
630-639-9185
FAX: 630-434-1216
www.sc-conference.org

William Kramer, Conference General Chair
Barbara Horner-Miller, Conference Deputy Chair

The world's leading conference on high performance computing, networking and storage. Representatives from many technical communities together to exchange ideas, celebrate past successes and plan for the future.
6000 Attendees Annual/November Founded: 1988

4861 SCSC: Summer Simulation Multiconference
Society for Modeling and Simulation International
PO Box 17900
San Diego, CA 92177-7900
858-277-3888
FAX: 858-277-3930
scs@scs.org www.scs.org

Steve Branch, Executive Director
Mark Yen, Event Coordinator

Focusing on Innovative Technologies for Simulation this year. Modeling and Simulation is a very critical area for supporting Research and Development as well as competitiveness worldwide; new technologies are enabling new use of M&S and increasing its impact in new areas; SCSC provides an international forum for presenting the state of the art in the international simulation community.
600 Attendees July

4862 SEMICON/West
Semiconductor Equipment & Materials International
3081 Zanker Road
San Jose, CA 95134
408-943-6900
FAX: 408-428-9600
semiexpositions@semi.org
www.semi.org

Ana Christiansen, Exposition Marketing
Leslie Schade, Exhibitor Services

Showcasing the latest products and technologies used in manufacturing today and the technology of tomorrow.
1500 Attendees June

4863 SID International Symposium, Seminar and Exhibition
Society for Information Display
610 S 2nd Street
San Jose, CA 95112
408-977-1013
FAX: 408-977-1531
office@sid.org www.sid.org

Mark Goldfab, Conference Coordinator
Bill Klein, Symposium Coordinator
Kate Dickie, Exhibition/Sponsorship Sales Mgr.
Danielle Rocco, Exhibition/Sponsorship Coordinator
Jenny Needham, Manager

The premier international gathering of scientists, engineers, manufacturers and users in the electronic display industry. The event provides access to a wide range of technology and applications from high-definition flat-panel displays using both emissive and liquid-crystal technology to the latest in OLED displays and large-area projection-display systems.
6000 Attendees May Founded: 1962

4864 SIGGRAPH Conference
Association for Computing Machinery
1515 Broadway
17th Floor
New York, NY 10036
212-697-7440
FAX: 212-944-1318
acmhelp@acm.org www.siggraph.org

Dino Schweitzer, Conference Chief Staff Executive
James Mohler, Conference Chairperson

The annual conference and its year round initiatives provide unique crossroads for a diverse community of researchers, developers, creators, educators and practitioners. Our continuing mission is to be the premier annual conference on leading edge theory and practice of computer graphics and interactive techniques, inspiring progress through education, excellence, and interaction.
50000 Attendees July-August

4865 SMC: Spring Simulation Multiconference
Society for Modeling and Simulation International
PO Box 17900
San Diego, CA 92177-7900
858-277-3888
FAX: 858-277-3930
sbranch@scs.org www.scs.org

Drew Hamilton, Conference General Chair
Steve Branch, Executive Director

Bringing together eight symposia and providing a forum for academia, industry, business and government covering a wide variety of disciplines and domains that utilize modeling and simulation to present their work in a unique setting.
400 Attendees April

4866 **Seybold Seminars**
MediaLive International
795 Folsom Street
6th Floor
San Francisco, CA 94107-1243
415-905-2300
FAX: 415-905-2FAX
jackie.rees@mlii.com
www.medialiveinternational.com

Jackie Rees, Program Director
Cynthia Wood, Conference Content Director

Four focused conferences; Chicago, New York, San Francisco, that will deliver new solutions, emerging technologies and real world examples of businesses that have successfully implemented new digital publishing workflow and content management strategies.

21000 Attendees Sept, Oct, Nov

4867 **Southwest Users Group Conference**
18727 Nadal Street
Canyon Country, CA 91351

swugconf@usa.net
www.swugconf.org

Judy Taylour, Conference Director
Patricia Hill, Sponsorship Sales

Interface with user group leaders having similar interests to share ideas and experiences, as well as solutions to problems.

260+ Attendees August

4868 **TAWPI Annual Forum & Exposition**
Association for Work Process Improvement
185 Devonshire Street
Suite M102
Boston, MA 02110-1407
617-426-1167
FAX: 617-521-8675 800-998-2974
info@tawpi.org www.tawpi.org

Sandra Savage, Conference Planner
Jenny Star, Forum/Expo Communications

Leading event for technology and management professionals in data capture, mail, imaging, payment/remittance, document and forms processing.

1500 Attendees July

4869 **TechNet International**
Armed Forces Communications and Electronics Assn
4400 Fair Lakes Court
Fairfax, VA 22033
703-311-1397
FAX: 703-631-6133 800-336-4583
events@afcea.org
www.technet2006.org

Becky Nolan, Executive Vice President
LTG John A Dubia, Executive VP

An annual event representing top government, industry and military professionals in the fields of communications, electronics, intelligence, information systems, imaging and multi-media.

Annual/June

4870 **UNITE Golden Opportunities Annual Technology Conference**
UNITE
21523 Harper Avenue
St Clair Shores, MI 48080-2209
586-443-6901
FAX: 586-443-6902
cathmurphy39@hotmail.com
www.unite.org

Catherine Murphy, Conference Chair
George Gray, Conference Vice Chair

Held in mid October. Development and use of information technology. Pre-registration for full conference attendees: $1,095; daily attendees: $740.

October

4871 **Usenix Annual Technical Conference**
Usenix
2560 9th Street
Suite 215
Berkeley, CA 94710-2573
510-528-8649
FAX: 510-548-5738
conference@usenix.org
www.usenix.org

Jennifer Joost, Conference Manager
Devon Shaw, Conference Coordinator

A 5 day training running alongside a 3 day conference program filled with the latest research, security breakthroughs, sessions devoted to Linux and open source software and practical approaches to the puzzles and problems you wrestle with.

3M Attendees June

4872 **Vue/Point Conference**
Graphic Arts Show Company
1899 Preston White Drive
Reston, VA 20191
703-264-7200
FAX: 703-620-9187
info@gasc.org www.gasc.org

Kelly Kilga, Conference/Show Operations Director
Lilly Kinney, Conference Manager

The only interactive, peer-to-peer conference event in the graphic communications industry.

April

4873 **WMC: Western Simulation Multiconference**
Society for Modeling and Simulation International
PO Box 17900
San Diego, CA 92177-7900
858-277-3888
FAX: 858-277-3930
sbranch@scs.org www.scs.org

Steve Branch, Executive Director
Mark Yen, Events & Publications Coordinator

15 booths of technical and scientific papers.

300+ Attendees January

4874 **Wall Street on Java Show**
Flagg Management
353 Lexington Avenue
New York, NY 10016
212-286-0333
FAX: 212-286-0086
flaggmgmnt@msn.com
www.flaggmgmt.com

Russell Flagg, President

1000 Attendees February Founded: 2001

4875 **Wescon North America Exposition**
234 Main Street
Pleasanton, CA 95466
925-249-0866
FAX: 925-931-1334 800-877-2668
info@ieee-wescon.org
www.wescon.org

Leonard Cross, Press Relations

An event that offers attendees the opportunities to experience electronics from theoretical, innovative idea all the way to end products used in everyday life.

20000 Attendees August

4876 **Western Conference & Exposition**
Armed Forces Communications and Electronics Assn
4400 Fair Lakes Court
Fairfax, VA 22033
703-631-1397
FAX: 703-818-9177
gmcgovern@afcea.org www.afcea.org

Gina McGovern, Patron/Sponsor Director
Kim Couranz, Program Director

Largest event on the West Coast for communications, electronics, intelligence, information systems, imaging, military weapon systems, aviation, shipbuilding, and more. Featuring the people you need to hear from, the products and services you need to do your job, and the critical issues of today and tomorrow.

7000 Attendees January

Directories & Databases

4877 **ACM-SIGGRAPH Computer Graphics Education Directory**
Association for Computing Machinery
1515 Broadway
17th Floor
New York, NY 10036-8901
212-869-7440
FAX: 212-944-1318 800-342-6626
acmhelp@acm.org www.acm.org

Lynn D'Addesio-Kraus, Production Manager
Roma Simon, Managing Editor

Compiled to create a unified site where educators, students, and others can find information about computer graphics educational programs, computer graphics curriculum, computer graphics text.

$20.00

0 pages Biennial

4878 **AV Market Place**
Information Today
143 Old Marlton Pike
Medford, NJ 08055-8750
609-654-6266
FAX: 609-654-4309
custserv@infotoday.com
www.infotoday.com

Thomas H Hogan, Publisher/President
John Bryans, Publisher/Editor-in-Chief Books
Lauree Padgett, Editorial Services Manager
Inge Coffey, Circulation Manager
Pat Palatucci, Assistant to the President

The complete business directory of audio, audio visual, computer systems, film, video, and programming with industry yellow pages. The only guide needed to find more than 7,500 companies that create, apply or distribute AV equipment and ser-

vices for business, education, science, and government. *$199.95*
1700 pages February ISBN 1-573871-87-7

4879 Bacon's Computer/Hi-Tech Media Directory
Bacon's Publishing Company
332 S Michigan Avenue
Chicago, IL 60604-4434
312-228-8239
FAX: 312-922-3127 877-922-2400
info@bacons.com www.bacons.com
Ruth McFarland, Sr. VP & Publisher
Tim McManus, Sr. VP of Product Management
Stephen Newman, Chief Executive Officer
Contains detailed coverage on technology beat — now with expanded freelance listings. *$395.00*
Annual
Printed in 1 color on matte stock : internet

4880 CD-ROM Databases
Worldwide Videotex
PO Box 3273
Boyton Beach, FL 33424
561-738-2276

markedit@juno.com
www.wvpubs.com
Contains information on currently marketed databases available on CD-ROM.
Directory

4881 CD-ROMs in Print
Thomson Gale
27500 Drake Road
Farmington Hills, MI 48331
248-994-4253
FAX: 800-414-5043 800-877-4253
gale.salesassistance@thomson.com
www.galegroup.com
Dennis Poupard, Executive VP of Editorial
Rich Foley, Executive VP of Sales & Marketing
International guide to CD-ROM, Cdi, 3Do, Mmcd, Cd32, Multimedia, Laserdisc and Electronic Products. *$205.00*
ISBN 0-787671-33-9
Circulation: 13,000

4882 Computer & Consumer Electronics Retailers
Chain Store Guide
3922 Coconut Palm Drive
Tampa, FL 33619
813-276-6700
FAX: 813-627-6882 800-778-9794
info@csgis.com www.csgis.com
Chris Leedy, Marketing/Advertising Director
Shami Choon, Manager
An in-depth look at the mass-merchandising segment, bringing you access to more than 7,000 listings of US and Canadian computer and consumer electronics retailers. *$335.00*

4883 Computer Database
Information Access Company
362 Lakeside Drive
Foster City, CA 94404-1171
650-378-5200
FAX: 650-378-5368 800-227-8431
info@informationaccess.com
www.iacnet.com
Robert Howells, President
Comprehensive database offering over 500,000 citations, with abstracts, to literature from over 150 trade journals, industry newsletters and platform-specific publications covering the computer, telecommunications and electronics industries.
Bibliographic

4884 Computer Industry Almanac
Computer Industry Almanac
304 W White Oak
Arlington Heights, IL 60005-3201
847-758-3687
FAX: 847-758-3686
ej@c-i-a.com www.c-i-a.com
Egil Juliussen, Editor
Karen Petska-Juliussen, Editor
A reference book about the computer industry. *$63.00*
800 pages Annual ISBN 0-942107-08-X

4885 Computer Industry Market Intelligence System
Hart-Hanks Market Intelligence
9980 Huennekens Street
San Diego, CA 92121
858-450-1667
FAX: 858-452-6857
www.hartehanksmi.com
Randy Wussler, Managing Director
Randy Ilas, Product Management Director

Database of more than 250,000 business locations with mainframe, mini or micro computer systems.

4886 Computer Review
Computer Review
19 Pleasant Street
Gloucester, MA 01930-5937
978-283-2100

info@computerreview.com
www.computerreview.com
Robert D. MacCormack, Editorial Director
George Luhowy, Owner
Your personal business tool for mining the Knowledge economy. This is a well organized hardcopy directory with a daily online monitor. It shows you what's happening in 12,000 companies from 77 technology sectors. *$495.00*
750 pages Annual ISBN 0-914730-02-9 : web

4887 Computers and Computing Information Resources Directory
Gale Research
27500 Drake Road
Farmington Hills, MI 48331
248-699-4253
FAX: 800-414-5043 800-877-4253
gale.customerservice@thomson.com
www.gale.com
Dennis Poupard, Executive VP, Editorial/Production
Rich Foley, Executive VP, Sales/Marketing
Computer related information sources, including consultant and training organizations, trade and professional associations or user groups, special libraries and information centers, university computer facilities and research centers, for-profit research services, online services, etc. *$195.00*

4888 Computing and Software Design Career Directory
Gale Research
27500 Drake Road
Farmington Hills, MI 48331
248-699-4253
FAX: 248-699-8214 800-877-4253
galeord@gale.com www.gale.com
Bradley J Morgan, Editor
Joseph M Palmisano, Editor
Directory of services and supplies to the industry. *$34.00*
300 pages ISBN 0-810395-12-X

4889 DACS Annotated Bibliography
Data & Analysis Center for Software
775 Daedalian Drive
Rome, NY 13441-4909
315-334-4905
FAX: 315-334-4964 800-214-7921
cust-liasn@dacs.dtic.mil
www.iac.dtic.mil/dacs
Thomas McGibbon, Director
Offers citations on over 9,000 technical reports, articles, papers and books concerned with software development and engineering. *$60.00*
400 pages

4890 DIALOG Publications
Dialog, Thomas Business
11000 Regency Parkway
Suite 10
Cary, NC 27511
919-462-8600
FAX: 919-468-9890 800-3DI-ALOG
Mike Eastwood, VP Finance & Administration
Al Zink, VP Human Resources
Roy Martin, Chief Executive Officer
Offers descriptions of DIALOG system and database publications that are available for purchase.
Bibliographic

4891 DP Directory
525 Goodale Hill Road
Glastonbury, CT 06033-4022
860-659-1065

al@dpdirectory.com
www.dpdirectory.com
Al Harberg, President
Offers mailing lists for the computer trade as well as information on the value and uses of press releases for marketers.

4892 Datapro Directory of Microcomputer Hardware
S. Karger Publishers
26 W. Avon Road
PO Box 529
Farmington, CT 06085
860-675-7834
FAX: 860-675-7302 800-828-5479
karger@snet.net www.libri.ch
Martin Buess, Managing Director
Andrea Murdoch, Manager of Journals Administration
Offers valuable information on over 1,500 manufacturers of microcomputers and peripheral equipment. *$675.00*
1000 pages Monthly

4893 Directory of Computer and High Technology Grants
Research Grant Guides
PO Box 1214
Loxahatchee, FL 33470-1214
561-795-6129

Richard M Eckstein, Author

Offers information on over 750 foundations and corporations that award grants to nonprofit organizations for computers, computer training and software. *$52.50*
200 pages Biennial ISBN 0-945078-07-2

4894 Directory of Library Automation Software, Systems and Services
Information Today
143 Old Marlton Pike
Medford, NJ 08055-8750
609-654-6266
FAX: 609-654-4309
custserv@infotoday.com
www.infotoday.com

Pamela Cibbarelli, Editor

Recognized as the primary reference source for software packages used in automating libraries. This entirely new expanded 2004-2005 edition provides detailed descriptions of hundreds of currently available microcomputer, minicomputer, and mainframe software packages and services. *$89.00*
351 pages Bi-Annually Founded: 1983

4895 Directory of Simulation Software
Society for Modeling and Simulation International
4838 Ronson Ct
PO Box 17900
San Diego, CA 92177-7900
858-277-3888
FAX: 858-277-3930
info@scs.org www.scs.org

Amy Shapiro, Publications Manager & Editor
Steve Branch, Executive Director

About 200 simulation software packages and their suppliers. *$40.00*
Annual
Circulation: 2,000

4896 Directory of Top Computer Executives
Applied Computer Research
PO Box 82266
Phoenix, AZ 85071-2266
602-216-9100
FAX: 602-216-9200 800-234-2ACR
alan@acrhq.com
www.itmarketingintelligence.com
Contains the names of more than 52,000 of the most influential information technology managers in the US and Canada. Entepreneurs and corporate executives have used this data base to build successful businesses for over 30 years. *$245.00*
Semi-Annual Founded: 1972

4897 Directory of US Government Software for Mainframes and Microcomputers
US National Technical Information Service
5285 Port Royal Road
Springfield, VA 22161
703-605-6000
FAX: 703-605-6900 800-553-6847
info@ntis.gov www.ntis.gov
Contains descriptions of some 550 mainframe and microcomputer programs made available from more than 100 federal agencies, or their contractors since 1984. The directory is an essential reference tool for users who wish to tap the wealth of U.S. Government software. *$65.00*
174 pages Annual ISBN 0-934213-37-2

4898 Electronic Imaging an Image Processing: An Assessment of Technology & Products
Richard K Mill & Associates
5880 Live Oak Parkway
Suite 270
Norcross, GA 30093-1707
770-416-0006
FAX: 770-416-0052

Richard K Miller, Editor/President
Kelli D Washington, Editor-in-Chief

List of producers and suppliers of electronic imaging computer software and hardware. *$485.00*
ISBN 0-896711-12-9

4899 Guide to Free Films, Flimstrips and Slides
Educators Progress Service
214 Center Street
Randolph, WI 53956
920-326-3126
FAX: 920-326-3127 888-951-4469
questions@freeteachingaids.com
www.freeteachingaids.com

Kathleen Suttles Nehmer, Editor

Offers sources for films, filmstrips, slide sets, audiotapes and videotapes. *$37.95*
135 pages Annual ISBN 0-877083-51-7

4900 Hoover's Guide to Computer Companies
Hoover's
5800 Airport Boulevard
Austin, TX 78752-3826
512-374-4500
FAX: 512-374-4501 800-486-8666
orders@hoovers.com
www.hoovers.com

Dwayne Spradlin, President
Paul Pellman, Executive VP Marketing/Products

250 of the largest public and private computer industry companies in in-depth profiles. *$34.95*
737 pages Annual ISBN 1-878753-80-0

4901 IT Computer Economics Report Journal
Computer Economics
2082 Business Center Drive
Suite 240
Irvine, CA 92612
949-831-8700
FAX: 949-442-7688
www.computereconomics.com

Barbara McDonald, Editor
Deb Dismuke, Director of Client Services

Provides decision makers throughout the world with timely insights into the management of information systems.
Monthly Founded: 1978

4902 Index to AV Producers & Distributors 10th Edition
Information Today
143 Old Marlton Pike
Medford, NJ 08055-8750
609-654-6266
FAX: 609-654-4309
custserv@infotoday.com
www.infotoday.com

Thomas H Hogan, Publisher/President
John Bryans, Publisher/Editor-in-Chief
Lauree Padgett, Editorial Serives Manager
Inge Coffey, Circulation Manager

Contains over 23,500 producers and distributors of AV materials of all kinds. This handy softbound volume is an indispensible tool for buyers of audiovisual materials of all kinds. *$89.00*
626 pages ISBN 0-937548-30-8

4903 Internet & Personal Computing Abstracts Journal
Information Today
143 Old Marlton Pike
Medford, NJ 08055-8750
609-654-6266
FAX: 609-654-4309
custserv@infotoday.com
www.infotoday.com

Daniel R Franzen, Editor
Marie A Pitman, Editor

This comprehensive database contains over 150,000 citations, with abstracts to reviews of commentaries on the use and applications of microcomputers and software packages: *$235.00*
Quarterly Founded: 1980
Circulation: 10,000

4904 Inventor's Desktop Companion: A Guide to Successfully Marketing Ideas
Visible Ink Press/Gale Research
27500 Drake Road
Farmington Hills, MI 48331
248-994-4253
FAX: 313-961-6741 800-877-GALE

Richard C Levy, Editor

Offers information on agencies and organizations of interest to inventors, including regional and national associations, university innovation research centers and business incubators for the computer and desktop industries. *$24.95*
470 pages

4905 Micro Publishing Report's Directory of Desktop Publishing Suppliers
Cygnus Publishing
1233 Janesville Avenue
Fort Atkinson, WI 53538
920-636-6388
800-547-7377
rich.reiff@cygnuspub.com
www.cygnuspub.com

Rich Reiff, President
Tom Martin, Production VP

Offers valuable information on over 200 suppliers of microcomputer systems for desktop publishing. *$35.00*
30 pages Annual

4906 Microcomputer Market Place
Random House
201 E 50th Street
New York, NY 10022-7703
212-782-9000

Offers information on manufacturers and suppliers of computer equipment and accessories. *$29.95*
795 pages

4907 Microprocessor Integrated Circuits

DATA Digest
15 Inverness Way E
Englewood, CO 80112-5710
303-790-0600

Offers a list of over 185 manufacturers and distributors of microprocessor integrated circuits. *$205.00*
SemiAnnual

4908 **Microsoft Applications and Systems Forums**
Microsoft Corporation
1 Microsoft Way
Redmond, WA 98052-8300
425-882-8080
FAX: 425-883-8101 800-426-9400
Steven Ballmer, Chief Executive Officer
This database provides an exchange of information and tips on Microsoft computer systems for participants.

4909 **Modern Machine Shop's Handbook for Metalworkingi Industries on CD-ROM**
Gardner Publications
6915 Valley Avenue
Cincinnati, OH 45244-3029
513-278-8977
FAX: 513-527-8801 800-950-8020
Woodrow Chapman, Editor
Richard Kline, President
Provides a balanced blend of traditional and modern topics. In addition to containing a wide range of reference tables covering all aspects of machining, composition of materials, and dimensions of tooling and machine components. *$55.00*
2368 pages Founded: 2002 ISBN 1-569903-55-7

4910 **National Directory of Bulletin Board Systems**
Penton Media
1300 E 9th Streetnue E
Cleveland, OH 44114
216-696-7000
FAX: 216-696-1309
information@penton.com
www.penton.com
Computer bulletin board systems that display notices of special events or new products are profiled. *$45.00*
400 pages Annual

4911 **NetWire**
Novell
122 E 1700 S
Provo, UT 84606-6194
801-297-7000
800-453-2167
This database concentrates on Novell computer software and hardware information.

4912 **Network Magazine Buyers Guide**
Miller Freeman Publications
600 Harrison Street
Suite 400
San Francisco, CA 94107-1391

FAX: 415-905-2239
Michelle Henry, Editor
List of companies that produce software and hardware to support local area networks. *$4.95*
Annual

4913 **Online Networks, Databases & Bulletin Boards on Assistive Technology**
ERIC Document Reproduction Service
7420 Fullerton Road
Suite 110
Springfield, VA 22153-2852
703-440-1400
FAX: 703-440-1408 800-443-ERIC
Directory of electronic networks that focus on technology-related services.

4914 **Orion Blue Book: Computer**
Orion Research Corporation
14555 N Scottsdale Road
Suite 330
Scottsdale, AZ 85254-3487
480-951-1114
FAX: 480-951-1117 800-844-0759
orion@orionbluebook.com
www.orionbluebook.com
Roger Rohrs, Publisher
63,053 products listed from 1970's to present. Over 1,000 manufacturers listed.
695 pages Annual Founded: 1985

4915 **PC-Link**
America Online
8619 Westwood Center Drive
Suite 200
Vienna, VA 22182-2238

Provides access to a variety of databases and computer services of interest to users of IBM and compatible computers running MS-DOS.
Directory

4916 **ParaTechnology Directory of Systems and Network Integrators**
ParaTechnology
1215 120th Avenue NE
Suite 101
Bellevue, WA 98005-2135
425-451-9500
FAX: 425-451-9500 800-377-2021
One thousand computer system and network integrators in North America. *$495.00*
Annual

4917 **Personal Computing Directory**
Resources
PO Box 1067
Cambridge, MA 02238-1067

Directory of services and supplies to the industry. *$29.95*
Annual

4918 **Pocket Guides to the Internet: Telnetting**
Information Today
143 Old Marlton Pike
Medford, NJ 08055-8750
609-654-6266
FAX: 609-654-4309
George Hartnell, Editor
Mark Veijkov, Editor
Logon information and resources available via telnetting. *$9.95*

4919 **Q-Link**
America Online
8619 Westwood Center Drive
Suite 200
Vienna, VA 22182-2238

FAX: 540-265-2135 800-227-6364
Anne Botsford
This database consists of several files of general interest news and information for users of Commodore computers.
Full-text

4920 **Shareware Magazine: PC SIG's Encyclopedia of Shareware Section**
Shareware Magazine
1030 E Duane Avenue
Suite D
Sunnyvale, CA 94086-2624
408-733-8900

Offers a variety of software programs for the IBM PC and its compatibles. *$19.95*
Bi-Monthly

4921 **SoftBase**
Information Resources
PO Box 8120
Berkeley, CA 94707-8120
510-525-6220
FAX: 510-525-1568
softbase@searchsoftbase.com
www.searchsoftbase.com
Ruth K Koolish, Editor
It produces software products, services and companies abstracted from more than 200 business, computer, technical, trade and consumer publications.
Monthly

4922 **Software Encyclopedia**
RR Bowker
630 Central Avenue
New Providence, NJ 07974
908-286-1090
800-526-9537
info@bowker.com www.bowker.com
Lisa Heft, Managing Editor
A comprehensive, easy-to-navigate guide filled with detailed information on micro-computer software. Listings of over 47,225 software programs from 4,840 publishers and distributors are fully annotated to facilitate research and acquisition. *$300.00*
2000 pages 2 Volume set ISBN 0-835246-35-3

4923 **Software Engineering Bibliography**
Kaman Sciences Corporation
258 Genesse Street
Utica, NY 13502
315-732-1955

dacs@rome.kaman.com
www.dacs.com
Citation for over 15,000 technical reports, articles, theses, papers and books concerned with software technology. *$30.00*
Annual

4924 **Software Life Cycle Tools Directory**

Data & Analysis Center for Software
PO Box 1400
Rome, NY 13442-1400
315-334-4905
FAX: 315-334-4964 800-214-7921
cust-liasn@dacs.dtic.mil
www.iac.dtic.mil/dacs

Offers sources of more than 400 software packages for software engineering and maintenance. *$40.00*
500 pages

4925 **Telecom Internet Directory**
Information Gatekeepers Group
320 Washington Street
Suite 302
Boston, MA 02135
617-782-5033
FAX: 617-782-5735 800-323-1088
info@igigroup.com
www.igigroup.com
Will Ashley, Information Systems Manager
Bev Wilson, Marketing Manager
Developed to help find information in telecommunications efficiently and timely manner. A wide range of researchers, market analysts, information specialists, librarians and others will find the directory useful in finding information about telecommunications on the Internet. *$195.00*

4926 **Top 100 Service Companies**
Coordinated Service
20A Court Street
Groton, MA 01450-4217
978-448-2472

100 of the largest US based independent computer service companies.

4927 **UNISYS World Software Directory**

Publications & Communications
Cypress Creek Road
Suite B
Cedar Park, TX 78613
512-250-9023

Offers valuable information on suppliers of computer software packages compatible with UNISYS Corporation computer systems.
140 pages SemiAnnual
Circulation: 650

4928 **Uplink Directory**
Virginia A Ostendorf
PO Box 2896
Littleton, CO 80161-2896
303-797-3131

Directory of services and supplies to the industry. *$150.00*
200 pages Annual
Circulation: 1,000

4929 **User's Directory of Computer Networks**
Digital Press
129 Parker Street
Maynard, MA 01754-2199
978-493-1770

Offers a list of hosts, site contacts and administrative domains. *$35.95*
630 pages

Industry Web Sites

4930 **www.4w.com**
Information Analytics

Dedicated to the non-profit professional development of information systems managers, directors and analysts.

4931 **www.aaai.org**
American Association for Artificial Intelligence

A scientific society devoted to advancing the scientific understanding of the mechanisms underlying thought and intelligent behavior and their embodiment in machines.

4932 **www.aace.org**
Assn for the Advancement of Computing in Education

Promotes the use of computers and the internet in educational settings.

4933 **www.adweek.com**
Adweek

Leading decision makers in the advertising and marketing field go to Adweek.com every day for breaking news, insight, buzz, opinion, analysis, research and classifieds. The resources of all six regional editions of Adweek, as well as the national edition of Brandweek are combined with the knowledge of our online editors and the multimedia-interactive capabilities of the web to deliver vital information quickly and effectively to our target audience.

4934 **www.afsmi.org**
Association for Services Management International

Provides the knowledge, fellowship and career connections that customer services and support managers for technology based products and solutions needed for professional and career development.

4935 **www.aiim.org**
Association for Information and Image Management

The leading international organization focused on helping users to understand the challenges associated with managing documents, content, and business processes.

4936 **www.aitp.org**
Association of Information Technology Professional

Comprised of career minded individuals who seek to expand their potential employers, employees, managers, programmers and many others. This organization seeks to provide avenues for all their members to be teachers as well as students and to make contacts with other members in the IS field, all in an effort to become more marketable in rapidly changing technological careers.

4937 **www.apple.com**
Apple

Official web site for Apple; Macintosh computers and software.

4938 **www.asm.com**
Society for Materials Engineers and Scientists

A leading supplier of semiconductor process equipment in both front and back end markets. The Company possesses a strong technological base, state-of-the-art manufacturing facilities, a competent and qualified workforce and a highly trained, strategically distributed support network.

4939 **www.bta.org**
Business Technology Association

Serving independent dealers, value added resellers, system integrators, manufacturers and distributors in the business equipment and system industry. BTA helps its members profit through a wide variety of services, including free legal advice and guidance; business benchmarking studies and reports; information on the latest news, trends, and products in the industry.

4940 **www.calico.org**
Computer Assisted Language Instruction Consortium

For language teachers, linguists, courseware developers and governments who are interested in teaching languages with the use of computer assisted instruction.

4941 **www.comptia.org**
CompTIA

Representing the international technology community. The goal is to provide a unified voice, global advocacy and leadership and to advance industry growth through standards, professional competence, education and business solutions.

4942 **www.devx.net**
DevX

The leading provider of technical and services that enable corporate application development teams to efficiently conquer development challenges and keep projects moving.

4943 **www.disa.org**
Data Interchange Standards Association

Many industries are looking to develop and implement eXtensible Markup Language (XML) specifications to eliminate paperwork, improve data accuracy, increase productivity, and reduce operating costs. This effort requires technical and administrative support. DISA can help.

4944 **www.greyhouse.com**
Grey House Publishing

Selected Grey House directories in the fields of business, health and education are available online. Users can search our online databases by several different search criteria, such as product categories, geographic area, sales volume and much, much more. Full Grey House catalog and online ordering also available.

4945 **www.guide.sbanetweb.com**
Guide to Computer Vendors

Planning and project management involved in the installation and implementation of client server accounting systems. We provide consulting assitance to a wide range of services such modeling agencies, publishing firms as well as manufacturing and distributors.

4946 **www.icca.org**
Independent Computer Consultants Association

Represents a wide variety of information technology consultants who provide consulting, implementation, support, training, strategic planning, and business analysis services.

4947 **www.internet.com**
Internet.Com/Mecklermedia

A leading source of global Internet news, and analyses. To learn about Internet.com's latest activities

4948 **www.intl-spectrum.com**
International Spectrum

The independent source of information for users and vendors of IBM's UniVerse and UniData; jBASE International's jBASE; Northgate information Solutions Reality; ONgroup's ONware; Raining Data's D3, mvBASE and mvEnterprise; Revelation Software's Opensight and VIA Systems UniVision Databases.

4949 **www.ioma.com**
IOMA

Supports managers involved in building and maintaining state-of-the-art HRIS software, hardware, and Internet/intranet activities. Publishes newsletter.

4950 **www.irga.com**
International Reprographic Association

Provides a framework for the exchange of information and support for the reprographic industry. The IRgA continues to be the only independent association serving the reprographics industry and the AEC community.

4951 **www.iste.org**
International Society for Technology in Education

A worldwide membership of leaders and potential leaders in educational technology. We are dedicated to providing leadership and service to improve teaching and learning by advancing the effective use of technology in K-12 education and teacher education. We provide our members with information, networking opportunities, and guidance as they face the challenge of incorporating computers, the Internet, and other new technologies into their schools.

4952 **www.openapplications.org**
Open Applications Group

A open standards group building process-based XML standards for both B2B and A2A integration.

4953 **www.pcca.org**
Portable Computer and Communications Association

A forum for disparate industries to meet, learn about each other, and collaborate on the interaction of the multiple technologies involved in wireless solutions.

4954 **www.polarmicro.com**
Polar Microsystems

Provides consulting services that enable our clients to advance their businesses through full utilization of the Apple Macintosh hardware and software platform.

4955 **www.sme.org**
Automated Systems Technical Group/SME

This group harnesses the power of information technology for advancing product development and design, manufacturing automation, enterprise integration, and communication throughout the product life cycle and supply chain.

4956 **www.spie.org**
International Society for Optical Engineering

Serves the international technical community as the premier provider of education, information, and resources covering optics, photonics, and their applications.

4957 **www.thinkecs.com**
Enterprise Computing Solutions

A leading provider of IT infrastructure solutions for Fortune 500 and mid-tier companies throughout California. ECS builds sophisticated IT infrastructure solutions for mission critical applications, provides enterprise storage solutions that ensure data protection and business continuity and delivers state of the art server solutions for optimal computing capacity.

4958 **www.unf.edu/library**
University of North Florida, Carpenter Library

For catalogers of audiovisual materials and electronic resources. Provides information exchange, continuing education, and works toward a common understanding of practices and standards.

4959 **www.vita.com**
VMEbus International Trade Association

For manufacturers of microcomputer boards, hardware, software, military products, controllers, bus interfaces and other accessories compatible with VMEbus architecture. VITA is an incorporated, nonprofit organization of vendors and users having a common market interest.

4960 **www.webdeveloper.com**
Mecklermedia/Internet.Com

Information on maintaining and growing business web sites and intranets.

4961 **www1.hp.com**
Hewlett Packard /Compaq

The official Web site for the Compaq PCs.

Associations

4962 Aesthetics' International Association
2611 N BeltLine Road
Suite 140
Sunnyvale, TX 75182-9357
972-038-8530
FAX: 972-962-1480 877-968-7539
AIAtheKey@aol.com
www.beautyworks.com/aia
The association for the advancement of education and public awareness on aesthetics. Paramedical aesthetics and body spa therapy. Professionals from the medical, paramedical and beauty industries working together for the most advanced techniques for the patients and clients.
Founded: 1972

4963 Alpine Aromatics
51 Ethel Road W
Piscataway, NJ 08854
732-572-5600
FAX: 732-572-0944
www.alpinearomatics.com
John Yorey Jr, President
At Alpine, each fragrance is created after careful planning, testing, revising and re-formulating until the perfumer is completely satisfied that the fragrance is right.

4964 American Association for Esthetics Education
401 N Michigan Avenue
Chicago, IL 60611
312-245-1570
FAX: 312-245-1080 800-648-2505
Paul Dykstra, CEO
Provides access to educational experts, methods for increasing profits, and infomation on the latest products and techniques. *$ 105.00*

4965 American Beauty Association
401 N Michigan Avenue
Chicago, IL 60611
312-245-1595
FAX: 312-245-1080 800-868-4265
steve@bbsi.org www.abbies.org
Tom Clifford, President
Myriam Clifford, VP
Bruce Selan, First VP
Lydia Sarfati, Second VP
George Schaeffer, Secretary
ABA members are manufacturers, manufacturer reps and consultants in the professional beauty industry. Associate members are made up of trade publications, distributors and salons. The ABA's mission is to expand, serve and protect the interests of the professional beauty industry.
200 Members Founded: 1985

4966 American Hair Loss Association
23679 Calabasas Road # 254
Calabasas, CA 91301-1502
The American Hair Loss Association is the only national, non-profit membership organization dedicated to educating the public, healthcare professionals, main stream media and legislators about the emotionaally devastating disease of hair loss (alopecia). Committed to the prevention and treatment of hair loss, the ALHA is dedicated to supporting research that will ultimately treat and cure thoses who suffer from this silent epidemic.

4967 American Hair Loss Council
30 South Main
Shenandoah, PA 17976
412-765-3666
FAX: 412-765-3669
info@ahlc.org www.ahlc.org
Susan Kettering, Executive Director
The nation's only, unbiased, not for profit agency, dedicated to sorting through this information, discovering what works and what doesn't,a nd presenting our findings to the consumer.

4968 American Health & Beauty Aids Institute
PO Box 19510
Chicago, IL 60619-0510
708-333-8740
FAX: 708-333-8741
ahbail@bcglopal.net www.ahbai.org
Joe Dudley, Senior President
Jory Luste, President
Nathaniel Bronner, Jr. Executive VP
AHBAI reresents leading, African American-owned companies manufacturing ethnic hair care and beauty products. Members serve African Americans through employment, scholarships and education.

4969 American Society of Hair Restoration Surgery
737 North Michigan Avenue
Suite 2100
Chicago, IL 60611
312-981-6760
FAX: 312-981-6787
info@cosmeticsurgery.org
www.cosmeticsurgery.org
Jeffrey P Knezovich, Executive Vice President
1600 Members

4970 American Society of Perfumers
PO Box 1551
West Caldwell, NJ 07004
201-991-0040
FAX: 201-991-0073
www.perfumers.org
Steven Claisse, Chairman
Alice Rebeck, President
Jim Krivda, VP
Angela Kohut, Secretary
John Gamba, Treasurer
Nonprofit organization fosters and encourages the art and science of perfumery in the US while promoting professional exchange and a high standard of professional conduct within the fragrance industry. The ASP holds yearly symposiums in the New York City area where leading members of the fragrance industry are invited to speak and present information on all aspects of the industry.
Founded: 1947

4971 Association Accredited Cosmetology Schools
5201 Leesburg Pike
Falls Church, VA 22041-3244
Ronald Smith, Publisher
Association for those concerned with cosmetology.
6 Members

4972 B-cause
PO Box 4814
Poughkeepsie, NY 12601
845-431-6670
rudy@bcause.org www.bcause.org
Rudy Sprogis, Founder
Non-profit organization that advances charitable causes for salon owners and beauty industry professionals.
Founded: 2000

4973 Chain Drug Marketing Association
43157 W. Nine Mile Road
Po Box 995
Novi, MI 48376-0995
248-449-9300
FAX: 248-449-4634
www.chaindrug.com
James R Devine, President
Judy Aspinall, VP
Brandon Curtis, Director/Information Technology
Members are regional drug chains from across North ASmerica Association markets over 800 products under the name Quality Choice to its members.
101 Members

4974 Consumer Healthcare Manufacturers Association
900 19th Street, NW,
Suite 700
Washington, DC 20006
202-429-9260
FAX: 202-223-6835
eassey@chpa-info.org
www.chpa-info.org
Linda A Suydam, President
Priya Samuel, Executive Assistant
Promotes industry growth through consumer understanding, appreciation, and acceptance of responsible self-care in America's health care system by developing and sustaining a climate that provides consumers with convenient access to safe and effective nonprescription medicines and other self-care products marketed without undue restrictions.

4975 Cosmetic Executive Women
21 E 40th Street
Suite 1700
New York, NY 10016
212-685-5955
FAX: 212-685-3334
cew@cew.org www.cew.org
Carlotta Jacobson, President
Margie French, Chief Businees Officer
Siobhan McManus, Director Finance
Nonprofit, trade organization of approximately 1,500 executives in the beauty, cosmetics, fragrance and related industries. Based in New York City, CEW has associated organizations in France and the United Kingdom. As a leading trade organization in the beauty industry, CEW helps develop contacts, knowledge and skills of its members so that they may advance on both professional and personal levels.
2500+ Members Founded: 1954

4976 Cosmetic Industry Buyers and Suppliers
36 Lakeville Road
New Hyde Park, NY 11040
516-775-0220
FAX: 516-328-9789
webmaster@cibsonline.com
www.cibsonline.com

Joseph A Palazzolo, Executive Director

Members are individuals providing and obtaining essential oils, chemicals, packaging and other goods for the cosmetic industry.
800 Members Founded: 1948

4977 Cosmetic, Toiletry & Fragrance Association
1101 17th Street NW
Suite 300
Washington, DC 20036-4702
202-331-1770
FAX: 202-331-1969
membership@ctfa.org www.ctfa.org

Pamela Bailey, President
Mark Pollak, VP
Cheryl Mason, Secretary

Provides a complete range of services that support the personal care products industry's needs and interests in the scientific, legal, regulatory, legislative and international fields. CTFA strives to ensure the personal care products industry has the freedom to pursue creative product development and compete in a fair and responsible marketplace.
525 Members Founded: 1894

4978 Cosmetologists Chicago
401 N Michigan Avenue
Suite 2200
Chicago, IL 60611
312-321-6809
FAX: 312-245-1080 800-648-2505

Jerry Gordon, President
Luz Segovia, First VP
Paul Dykstra, Chief Executive Officer
Lynn Weber, Assistant Event/Show Manager
Lisa Newman, Director Marketing

A beauty voice and presenter of cosmetology shows.

4979 Drug, Chemical & Associated Technologies Association
1 Washington Boulevard
Suite 7
Robbinsville, NJ 08691
609-448-1000
FAX: 609-448-1944
info@dcat.org www.dcat.org

Patrick Vazquez, President
Lynda M Doyle, Senior VP
Margaret Timony, Executive Director

Members include more than 350 companies, in the US and abroad, who manufacture, distribute or provide services to the chemical, pharmaceutical, nutritional and related industries. Services, programs and activities are designed to support business development objectives. These programs and events provide opportunities for member representatives to make important contacts, learn new industry information, dialogue with counterparts in other companies and build relationships with customers.

Founded: 1890

4980 Esthetics Manufacturers and Distributors
401 N Michigan Avenue
Chicago, IL 60611
312-215-5120
FAX: 312-245-1080 800-868-4265
steve@bbsi.org www.manebs.com

Paul Dykstra, Executive Director
Paul Scott Premo, President
Charles Mizelle, VP
Mark Lees, Chairman
Julianne Bendel, Manager

A member of the American Beauty Association, whose members are manufacturers of specific products related to the professional beauty industry. EMDA is dedicated to meeting the needs of skin care and body care manufacturers and distributors and the salons they service. The mission of the American Beauty Association and all of its sub-groups is to expand, serve and protect the interests of the professional beauty industry.
40 Members Founded: 1993

4981 Fragrance Foundation
145 E 32nd Street
New York, NY 10016-6002
212-725-2755
FAX: 212-779-9058
info@fragrance.org
www.fragrance.org

Rochelle R Bloom, President
Mary Lapsansky, Executive Director
Elizabeth Bonafiglio, Special Projects Assistant

Nonprofit, educational arm of the international fragrance industry. Devotes its energies to creating an atmosphere of understanding and appreciation of the benefits and pleasures of fragrance in all its many forms.
160 Members Founded: 1949

4982 Fragrance Materials Association of the US
1620 I Street NW
Suite 925
Washington, DC 20006
202-293-5800
FAX: 202-463-8998
info@fmafragrance.org
www.fmafragrance.org

Sean Traynor, President
Daniel J Carey, VP
Robert Bedoukian, Secretary
Stephen A Block, Treasurer
Glenn Roberts, Executive Director

Manufacturers of fragrance ingredients.
90 Members Founded: 1927

4983 Fragrance Research Fund
142 E 30th Street
New York, NY 10016-7319
212-684-4646

Annette Green, Administrator

Offers financial support for doctors and clinical researchers. Bestows awards.

4984 Independent Cosmetic Manufacturers and Distributors
1220 W Northwest Highway
Palatine, IL 60067
847-991-4499
FAX: 847-991-8161 800-334-2623
info@icmad.org www.icmad.org

Penni Jones, Executive Director
Sheila Sebor, Associate Executive Director

Represents 600 cosmetic manufacturers, distributors and suppliers to industry. Mission: to represent, educate and foster the growth and profitability of entrepreneurial companies in the cosmetic and personal care industries worldwide.
540 Members Founded: 1974

4985 International Aloe Science Council
415 East Airport Freeway
Suite 150
Irving, TX 75062
972-258-8772
FAX: 972-258-8777
iasc1@msn.com www.iasc.org

Gene Hale, Executive Director

Explores the use of aloe in cosmetic industries, hair products, herb preparations, pharmaceuticals and drinks.
300 Members Founded: 1981

4986 International Association of Color
1620 I Street NW
Suite 925
Washington, DC 20006
202-293-5800
FAX: 202-463-8998
info@iacmcolor.org
www.iacmcolor.org

Glenn Roberts, Owner

Actively represents the interests of the regulated color industry by demonstrating the safety of color additives and promotes the industry's economic growth by participating in new color approvals, regulatory and legislative issues that affect the industry worldwide.
15 Members Founded: 1972

4987 International Perfume Bottle Association
PO Box 1299
Paradise, CA 95967

paradise@sunset.net
www.perfumebottles.org

Connie Linne, President
Shari Hooper, Membership Secretary

Worldwide non-profit organization of people who collect and deal in the variety of perfume containers. *$45.00*
2000+ Members

4988 International SPA Association
2365 Harrodsburg Road
Lexington, KY 40504
859-226-4326
FAX: 859-226-4445 888-651-4772
ispa@ispastaff.com
www.experienceispa.com

Kate Mearns, Chairman
Jim Root, Secretary/Treasurer

International community of spa professionals, product manufacturers and service providers. *$530.00*

4989 International Tanning Manufacturers Association
3820 Premier Avenue
Memphis, TN 38118
901-368-3333
FAX: 901-368-1144

William C Richey, President

Members are manufacturers of suntannning equipment. Promotes quality and safety of tanning.

4990 Nail Manufacturers Council
401 N Michigan Avenue
Chicago, IL 60611

FAX: 312-245-1080 800-868-4265

Paul Dykstra, Executive Director

A member of the American Beauty Association, whose members are manufacturers of specific products related to the professional beauty industry. The NMC's mission is to inform, serve and protect the interests of the professional nail industry. Membership is complimentary to members of the American Beauty Association.
50 Members Founded: 1989

4991 National Coalition of Estheticians Manufactures/Distributors Assoc
484 Spring Avenue
Ridgewood, NJ 07450-4624
201-670-4100
FAX: 201-670-4265
nceaorg@aol.com www.ncea.tv

Susan S Warfield, Executive Director

Represents and promotes the esthetic and related professions industry by sharing information, building consensus and providing a unified voice on behalf of the industry.
100+ Members

4992 National Cosmetology Association
401 N Michigan Avenue
22nd Floor
Chicago, IL 60611
312-527-6765
FAX: 312-245-1080
www.salonprofessionals.org

Gordon Miller, Executive Director

Nationwide community of 30,000 salon professionals, connected by a common passion for learning, growing and raising the professionalism of the entire salon industry. As a group we have a storng voice in our communities, our industry and with our government because ithe NCA is for everyone in the professional salon industry. Members have access to education, fashion events, community service and inurance — all the tools needed to build your career.
30000 Members

4993 National Interstate Council of State Boards of Cosmetology
7622 Briarwood Circle
Little Rock, AR 72205
501-227-8262
FAX: 501-227-8212
dnorton@nictesting.org
www.nictesting.org

Debra Norton, Executive Director

Merger of National Council of State Boards of Cosmetology and Interstate Council of State Boards of Cosmetology. Persons commissioned by the state governments to administer cosmetology laws and examine applicants for cosmetology licenses.
3200 Members Founded: 1950

4994 Professional Beauty Association
15825 N 71st Street
Suite 100
Scottsdale, AZ 85254
480-281-0424
FAX: 480-905-0708 800-468-2274

Steven Sleeper, Executive Director
Mark Kochman, Senior Director
Jill Jensen, Marketing Coordinator

Roof is a professional salon industry community of nonprofit associations, show divisions, charitable foundations and industry wide educational programs.
Founded: 2004

4995 Professional Beauty Foundation
4401 Ford Avenue
Suite 1300
Alexandria, VA 22302
703-600-7600
FAX: 703-379-2200
mkgross@naccas.org
www.probeautyfederation.org
A nonprofit organization made up of professional beauty organizations dedicated to promote and protect the professional beauty industry as it relates to government laws and regulation.

4996 RIFM: Research Institute for Fragrance Materials
50 Tice Boulevard
Woodcliff Lake, NJ 07677-7654
201-689-8089
FAX: 201-689-8090
rifm@rifm.org www.rifm.org

Ladd W Smith, President
Marie Gartshore, Communications Specialist

Evaluates and distributes scientific data on the safety of fragrance raw materials found in cosmetics, perfumes, shampoos, acndles, air fresheners and other personal products, to encourage uniform safety standards. Membership is open to all companies that manufacture , sell, distribute or engage in business related to the fragrance industry for at least one year.
Founded: 1966

4997 Regulatory Affairs Professionals Society
11300 Rockville Pike
Suite 1000
Rockville, MD 20852-3048
301-770-2920
FAX: 301-770-2924
raps@raps.org www.raps.org

Sherry Keramidas PhD, Executive Director
Susan Alpert, Chair
A Cedric Calhoun, Director Member/Component Relations
Jennifer Gibson, Director Communications
Iris Rush, Vice President Administration

The foremost worldwide member organization creating and upholding standards of ethica, credentialing and education for the regulatory affairs professicn within the health product sector.
10000 Members Founded: 1976

4998 Scent Marketing Institute
7 Fox Meadow Road
Scarsdale, NY 10583
646-236-4606
FAX: 914-470-2416
info@scentmarketing.org
www.scentmarketing.org

Harald H Vogt, Founder/Chief Marketer
Avery Gilbert PhD, Chief Scientist

Supports and facilitates the development of scent branding efforts and scent-centered marketing.

4999 Sense of Smell Institute
145 E 32nd Street
New York, NY 10016
212-725-2755
FAX: 212-779-9072
info@senseofsmell.org
www.senseofsmell.org

Theresa Molnar, Executive Director
Rachel Vandiver, Project Coordinator

Research and education division of the Fragrance Foundation.

5000 Society of Clinical and Medical Hair Removal
2810 Crossroads Drive,
Suite 3800
Madison, WI 53718
608-443-2470
FAX: 608-443-2474
homeoffice@scmhr.org
www.scmhr.org

Lisa Nelson, Executive Secretary

An international non profit organization with members in the United States, Canada, Australia, Japan and beyond. Supports all methods of hair removal and is dedicated to the research of new technology that will keep its members at the pinnacle of thier professsion, offering safe, effective hair removal to their clients.
350 Members Founded: 1985

5001 Society of Cosmetic Chemists
120 Wall Street
Suite 2400
New York, NY 10005-4088
212-668-1500
FAX: 212-668-1504
scc@scconline.org
www.scconline.org

Guy Padulo, President
Greg Hillebrand PhD, VP
Nick Morante, Secretary
John Wagner, Treasurer
Theresa Cesario, Executive Director

Dedicated to the advancement of cosmetic science, the Society strives to increase and disseminate scientific information through meetings and publications. By promoting research in cosmetic science and industry, and by setting high ethical, professional and educational standards, we reach our goal of improving the qualifacations of cosmetic scientists.
3600 Members Founded: 1945

5002 Women in Flavor & Fragrance Commerce
Association of Food Industries
3301 Route 66, Building C
Suite 205
Neptune, NJ 07753
732-223-3008
FAX: 732-922-0560
info@wffc.org www.wffc.org

Pia Henzi, President
Nancy Poulos, VP
Pia Henzi, Secretary
Nancy Poulos, Treasurer
Bob Bauer, Executive Director

Provides a center of education, camaraderie, support and networking opportunities for women in our industry. Our membership encompasses women involved in sales, purchasing, customer service as well as technical and laboratory careers. WFFC has timely seminars as well as social and networking opportunities for our members and the industry as a whole.
300 Members Founded: 1982

5003 **World International Nail and Beauty**
606 W Katella
Orange, CA 92667
714-532-2553
800-541-9838
Represents industry, promotes effective use of products, sponsors competition and bestows awards. Also offers world championship competitions for nails, hair and makeup.
8M Members Founded: 1981

Newsletters

5004 **FDC Reports: Rose Sheet**
FDC Reports
5550 Friendship Boulevard
Suite 1
Chevy Chase, MD 20815-7256
301-657-9830
FAX: 301-664-7238 800-332-2181
Brooke Mcmanus, Editor
Susan Easton, Publisher
Mike Squires, President
Shaun Smith, Marketing
Nicole Tesschamts, Circulation Manager
For executives in the cosmetics, toiletries, fragrances and skin care industries. Provides, coverage of the regulatory and legal environment for cosmetics, major scientific developments and testing methods product marketing news, new product launches; promotions and advertising, retail weekly trademark listings, mergers and acquisitions and developments in the European community. *$1050.00*
Weekly Founded: 1939
Computerized version available

5005 **Olfactory Research Fund/Aromachology Review**
The Fragrance Foundation
145 E 32nd Street
New York, NY 10016-6002
212-725-2755
FAX: 212-779-9058
info@fragrance.org
http://www.fragrance.org
Mary Ellen Lapsansky, Executive Director
Rochelle Bloom, President
Mary Ellen Lapsansky, Executive Director
Aislinn Madden, Special Event & Project Manager
Focuses on fragrance and olfactory developments around the world. Tracks international news in medical, technical, physical and social sciences which may be applied to the study of the sense of smell and the psychological benefits of aromas. *$40.00*
Quarterly Founded: 1982
Circulation: 500

5006 **Perfume Bottle Quarterly**
PO Box 1299
Paradise, CA 95967

paradise@sunset.net
www.perfumebottles.org
Ed Lefkowith, President
Anne Conrad, Publications Chair
Features association news bottle photos, people, literature reviews, trade events, and classified ads.
24 pages Quarterly Founded: 1997
Printed in 4 colors

5007 **Sierra Soap**
Parodon
PO Box 3005
Diamond Springs, CA 95619
530-647-8900
800-223-0650
sierra@inercite.com
www.sierrasoap.com
Toni Hughes, Owner
Jeff Hughes, Publisher
Offers information on natural products and beauty aids.
Bi-Monthly Founded: 2000

Magazines & Journals

5008 **American Looks**
National Cosmetology Association
401 N Michigan Avenue
Chicago, IL 60611-4255
312-527-6765
FAX: 312-245-1080
nca1@ncacares.org
http://www.salonprofessionals.org
Josephine Zeppieri, President
Gordon Miller, Executive Director
Information and news for the cosmetology industry.
Monthly Founded: 1921

5009 **Beauty Education Magazine**
Milady Publishing Company
5 Maxwell Drive
Clifton Park, NY 12605

FAX: 518-373-6200 800-998-7498
Dawn Gerrain, President
Donna Lewis, Executive Marketing Manager
Joyce Wynne, Production Manager
Offers information of interest to cosmetology educators and cosmetology school owners. *$34.50*
Bi-Monthly
Circulation: 4,500

5010 **Beauty Fashion**
Ledes Group
8 W 38th Street
Suite 200
New York, NY 10018
212-408-8800
FAX: 212-840-7246
cwhitman@boxingdigest.com
http://www.beautyfashion.com
Adelaide Farah, Group Editorial Director
Michelle Krell Kydd, Marketing
John Ledes, Owner
The authoritative magazine in the field of cosmetics, toiletries, fragrances and personal care. *$25.00*
131 pages Monthly
Circulation: 18672
Printed in 4 colors on glossy stock

5011 **Beauty Fashion: Body/Bath/Sun Issue**
Beauty Fashion
16 E 40th Street
New York, NY 10016
212-328-6789
FAX: 212-840-7246
www.beautyfashion.com
Offers listings of body/bath and sun products as well as manufacturers and US distributors. *$25.00*
Annual
Circulation: 17,000

5012 **Beauty Fashion: CTFA Convention Issue**
Beauty Fashion
16 E 40th Street
New York, NY 10016
212-328-6789
FAX: 212-840-7246
www.beautyfashion.com
Offers various suppliers of goods and services to the cosmetics industry manufacturers represented at Cosmetic, Toiletry and Fragrance Association convention. *$25.00*
Annual
Circulation: 17,000

5013 **Beauty Fashion: Cosmetics Issue**
Beauty Fashion
16 E 40th Street
New York, NY 10016
212-328-6789
FAX: 212-840-7246
www.beautyfashion.com
Offers listings of color cosmetics products for women as well as manufacturers and US distributors. *$25.00*
Annual
Circulation: 17,000

5014 **Beauty Fashion: Women's Fragrance Issue**
Beauty Fashion
16 E 40th Street
New York, NY 10016-5101
212-328-6789
FAX: 212-840-7246
mkrellkydd@cosmeticworld.com
http://www.beautyfashion.com/
Michelle Kre Kydd, Marketing
Veronica Kelly, Circulation Manager
Adelaide Farah, Editor
Offers listings of women's fragrance products including perfumes, eau de toilettes, and colognes as well as manufacturers and US distributors. *$25.00*
Monthly
Circulation: 17000

5015 **Beauty Fashion: Women's Treatment Issue**
Beauty Fashion
8 West 38th Street
Suite 200
New York, NY 10018
212-840-8800
FAX: 212-840-7246
http://www.beautyfashion.com/
Adelaide Farah, Group Editorial Director
Veronica Kelly, Subscription
Michelle Krell Kydd, Marketing
Offers listings of products and manufacturers and US distributors of cosmetics called treatment products. *$25.00*
Monthly

5016 **Cosmetic Ingredient Review**
1101 17th Street NW
Suite 310
Washington, DC 20036-4702
202-331-0651
FAX: 202-331-0088
cirinfo@cir-safety.org
http://www.cir-safety.org
F Alalan Andersen, Director and Scientific Coordinator
Wilma F. Bergfeld, Chairman
Assesses the safety of ingredients used in cosmetics in an unbiased manner and publishes the result in open, peer written literature. *$100.00*

Annual+ Founded: 1976

5017 **Cosmetic Packaging & Design**
Rodman Publications
70 Hilltop Road
Ramsey, NJ 07446
201-825-2552
FAX: 201-825-0553
donnaf@rodpub.com
http://www.cosmeticpackaginganddesign.com
Rodman J Zilenziger, President
Art Larger, Publisher
Leah Genuario, Editor
Allen Pfister, Circulation Director
Richard Devoto, Circulation Manager
$40.00
Founded: 1965
Circulation: 17387

5018 **Cosmetic World**
Ledes Group
8 W 38th Street
Suite 200
New York, NY 10018
212-840-8800
FAX: 212-840-7246
dkaplan@cosmeticworld.com
http://www.cosmeticworld.com
John G Ledes, Publisher
Dorene Kaplan, Managing Editor
Current industry events, legislation, management changes and corporate activities, as well as marketing developments and financial analysis. *$175.00*
Weekly
Circulation: 5397

5019 **Cosmetics & Toiletries**
Allured Publishing Corporation
362 S Schmale Road
Carol Stream, IL 60188-2787
630-653-2155
FAX: 630-653-2192
customerservice@allured.com
http://www.allured.com
Laurie Di Berardino, Editor
Matt Gronlund, Publisher
This magazine presents a full range of products covering the international cosmetic technology field - including the magazine, a tradeshow, conferences, books and extensive Web sites. The magazine brings the most current technologies in formulating, research, regulations and new ingredients. It also delivers for you a devoted readership base of cosmetic chemists and scientists around the world. *$98.00*
110 pages Monthly
Circulation: 15,000
Printed in 4 colors on glossy stock

5020 **DaySpa Magazine**
Creative Age Publications
7628 Densmore Avenue
Van Nuys, CA 91406-2042
818-782-7328
FAX: 818-782-7450 800-442-5667
dayspa@creativeage.com
http://www.dayspamagazine.com
Linda Lewis, Editor
Linda Kossoff, Marketing Manager
$22.00
Monthly Founded: 1971

5021 **Delicious Living**
New Hope Natural Media
1401 Pearl Street
Suite 200
Boulder, CO 80302-5346
303-939-8440
FAX: 303-939-9886
info@newhope.com
http://www.newhope.com
Jean Weiff, Managing Editor
Pamela Emanoil, Advertising Manager
$12.99
Monthly

5022 **Dermascope Magazine**
Aesthetics International Association
2611 N Belt Line Road
Suite 101
Sunnyvale, TX 75182-9357
972-038-8530
FAX: 972-226-2339 800-961-3777
dermascope@aol.com
http://www.dermascope.com
William Strunk, Publisher
Rachel Valma, Circulation Director
Casey Fore, Editor
The official publication for the advancement of education and public awareness. Variety of articles on skin care, makeup, body spa therapy and paramedical articles where medical and beauty specialists interact. *$45.00*
Monthly Founded: 1972
Circulation: 80000

5023 **Global Cosmetic Industry**
Allured Publishing Corporation
362 S Schmale Road
Carol Stream, IL 60188
630-344-6054
FAX: 630-597-0118
kjednachowski@allured.com
www.gcimagazine.com
Karen A Newman, Editor
Kim Jadnackowski, Sales/Account Manager
The business magazine for the cosmetics and personal care industry, covering the latest trends, products, packaging and technologies.

Circulation: 36,500

5024 **HSR: Health Supplement Retailer**
Virgo Publishing
3300 N Central Avenue, Suite 300
Phoenix, AZ 85012
480-990-1101
FAX: 480-675-8154
asharman@vpico.com
www.hsrmagazine.com
Peggy Jackson, Publisher
Heather Granato, Editor
Publication for the dietary supplement industry, focusing on the latest news, products and trend analysis to keep retailers informed and ahead of the competition.
50 pages Monthly + Buyer's Guide
Founded: 1995
Circulation: 17000+
Mailing list available for rent 17000+ names $var per M.
Printed in 4 colors on glossy stock

5025 **Happi**
Rodman Publications
70 Hilltop Raod
Ramsey, NJ 07446
201-825-2552
FAX: 201-825-0553
mmontgomery@rodpub.com
http://www.happi.com
Matthew Montgomery, Executive Vice President
Ellen Pfister, Circulation Manager
Tom Branna, Editor
Art Largar, Publisher
Serves the manufacturers and fillers of cosmetics, toiletries, fragrances, pharmaceuticals, detergents and chemical specialties inclusing household cleaning products and others product lines allied to the field.
Monthly Founded: 1964
Circulation: 15783
Printed in 4 colors on glossy stock

5026 **Health Products Business**
Cygnus Publishing
2 Huntington Quad
Suite 301n
Melville, NY 11747-4618
631-845-2700
FAX: 631-845-2723
feedback@magazines.com
www.healthproducts.com
Susanne Alberto, Editor/Features
Bruce Leftakels, Publisher
This is a trade magazine that covers news and trends in the natural health products industry vitamins, herbs, dietary supplements and other products. Publishes annual raw materials directory and purchasing guide. Target audience, natural products retail store owners, buyers and managers. Qualified subscription only.
Monthly Founded: 1996

5027 **Journal of Essential Oil Research/JEOR**
Allured Publishing Corporation
362 S Schmale Road
Carol Stream, IL 60188
630-653-2155
FAX: 630-597-0118
jeor@allured.com
www.perfumerflavorist.com/jeor
Brian M Lawrence, Editor-in-Chief
Forum for the publication of essential oil research and analysis. *$660.00*

5028 **Perfume 2000 Magazine**
Nathalie Publishing Corp
444 Brickell Avenue
Ste 510
Miami, FL 33131
305-669-4602
FAX: 305-669-6116
magazine@perfume2000.com
www.perfume2000.com
Bernard Pommier, Circulation Manager
Joseph P Quick, Publisher
Provides an inside look at the American and international prefume industry. *$18.00*

Bi-Monthly

5029 **Perfumer & Flavorist**
Allured Publishing Corporation
362 S Schmale Road
Carol Stream, IL 60188
630-653-2155
www.perfumeflavorist.com
Jeb Gleason, Editor
Matt Gronlund, Publisher
Helps readers to analyze global trends, discover new ingredients and innovations, and keep up-to-date with industry news and analysis. *$135.00*
8 Issues + 3 Bonus Issues

5030 **Rite Aid Be Healthy & Beautiful**
Drug Store News Consumer Health Publications
425 Park Avenue
New York, NY 10022
212-565-5220
FAX: 212-756-5290 800-766-6999
jtanzola@lf.com
http://www.consumerhealthpubs.com
John Tanzola, Marketing Manager
Provides health and beauty tips to millions of women who visit Rite Aid stores.
Quarterly Founded: 2002
Circulation: 450,000

5031 **SalonOvation Magazine**
Milady Publishing Company
5 Maxwell Drive
Clifton Park, NY 12065-2919
518-348-2300
FAX: 518-373-6200 800-998-1498
esales@thomsonlearning.com
http://www.delmarlearning.com
Dawn Gerrain, President
Donna Lewis, Executive Marketing Director
Ron Schlosser, President/CEO
Dedicated to furthering the education of new and established beauty professionals, available by paid subscription to cosmetology students, and practicing massage therapists, cosmetologists, nail technicians, barber-stylists and estheticians. *$20.00*
Monthly Founded: 1945
Circulation: 80000

5032 **Sun-Wellness**
Virgo Publishing
3300 N Central Avenue, Suite 2500
PO Box 40079
Phoenix, AZ 85067-79
480-990-1101
FAX: 480-990-0819
jlbolton@vpico.com
http://www.sun-wellness.com/
Jenny Bolton, Publisher
Judie Bizzozero, Editor
Russ Titsch, Marketing
Jenny Bolton, CEO/President
Simone Kjolsrud, Circulation Manager
Of interest to those watching fitness and health.
Founded: 1986

5033 **Supermarket News: Home & Health**
Fairchild Publications
7 W 34th Street
New York, NY 10001
212-630-4000
FAX: 212-630-4201 800-424-8698
custserv@espcomp.com
http://www.supermarketnews.com
Dan Bagan, Publisher Director
David Merrefield, Editorial Director
Dan Alaimo, Editor
Mary Berner, President/CEO *$195.00*
Weekly Founded: 1892
Circulation: 36346

5034 **Today's Image**
Today's Image
7628 Densmore Ave
Van Nuys, CA 91406-2042
818-782-7328
FAX: 818-782-7450
timcs@magserv.com
http://www.todaysimage.com/
John Dancer, Editor
Monica Smiley, Editor
Trade magazine for the tanning industry. Accepts advertising.
80 pages Monthly Founded: 1971

5035 **WWD Beauty Biz**
Fairchild Publications
7 West 34th Street
New York, NY 10001
212-630-4000
FAX: 212-630-3610 800-289-0273
customerservice@fairchildpub.com
http://www.fairchildpub.com
Mary Berner, President
Jenny B. Fine, Editor-in-Chief
Sarah Murphy, Publisher
The premier guide to the beauty industry. Provides in-depth coverage and analysis on all aspects of the industry, including trends, brands, retailers, and personalities driving both the general comsumer and insider sides of the business. *$60.00*
Monthly
Circulation: 40056

Trade Shows

5036 **Aesthetics' and Spa World Conference**
Aesthetics' International Association
2611 N Belt Line Road
Suite 140
Sunnyvale, TX 75182
972-038-8530
800-961-3777
2000 Attendees

5037 **America's Expo for Skin Care & Spa**
Allured Publishing Corporation
362 S Schmale Road
Carol Stream, IL 60188
630-653-2155
FAX: 630-653-2192
lludwig@allured.com
www.americasexpo.com
Laura Ludwig, Account Executive
Interactive exhibition focuses on professional skin care and spa services. Showcases the newest products, services and technologies from industry manufacturers and suppliers.
May

5038 **American Association of Cosmetology Schools**
American Association of Cosmetology Schools
15825 N 71st Street
Suite 100
Scottsdale, AZ 85254-2187
480-810-0431
800-831-1086
jim@beautyschools.org
www.beautyschools.org
Ronald E Smith, President
Jim Cox, Executive Director
Attended by over 300 schools owners, with over 75 exhibits of beauty supplies, products and services.
Annual

5039 **Association of Image Consultants Annual Convention & Exhibitor Showcase**
Association of Image Consultants International
910 Charles Street
Fredericksburg, VA 22401
540-370-0311
FAX: 540-370-0015 800-383-8831
aici@worldnet.att..net www.aici.org
Conference and industry related exhibits.
250 Attendees Founded: 1991

5040 **Beauty Exposition USA**
5839 Delmar Blvd
Saint Louis, MO 63112-2307
314-454-1112
FAX: 314-454-6668
btexpo@aol.com
www.beautyexpousa.com
Leon Beatty, Owner
Ann Park, Marketing Director
Hair and beauty supply trade show.
2,000 Attendees February

5041 **Beauty Supply Show: West Coast**
West Coast Beauty Supply
5001 Industrial Way
Benicia, CA 94510
707-484-4800
FAX: 707-748-4623 800-233-3141
info@westcoastbeauty.com
www.westcoastbeauty.com
Jennifer Coleman, Director
Wayne Clark, President
Jane West, Principal
200 booths.
15M Attendees March

5042 **Chain Drug Marketing Association Trade Show**
43157 W 9 Mile Road
Novi, MI 48375
248-499-9300

pritchard@chaindrug.com
www.chaindrug.com
James R Devine, President
Dennis Wasko, VP
Susan Pritchard, Marketing Coordinator
Two hundred booths of health and beauty aids, cosmetics and electronics.
350 Attendees March/September

5043 **Chicago Midwest Beauty Show**
401 N Michigan Avenue
Ste 2200
Chicago, IL 60611
312-321-6809
800-883-7808
info@chicagomidwestbeautyshow.com
www.chicagomidwestbeautyshow.com
Lynn Weber, Assistant Show Manager
Lisa Newman, Director/Marketing
Evaluate new products, meet with distributors, continuing education classes on the show floor, and purchase product.
50000 Attendees March

5044 **Cosmetic Toiletry & Fragrance Association Scientific Conference and Exchange**
1101 17th Street NW
Suite 300
Washington, DC 20036-4702
202-331-1770

Constance Cantin, Director Meetings
Pamela Bailey, President

Fifty five booths of senior management firms from cosmetics companies with exhibits of supplies and raw materials for the cosmetic industry.
550 Attendees October

5045 Cosmetologists Association: Cosmo Expo
526 Mission Street
South Pasadena, CA 91030-3036
626-441-4228
FAX: 626-441-1672
Karen Johnson, Show Manager
380 booths.
30M Attendees August

5046 Cosmetologists Association: Spring Annual Beauty Trade Show
526 Mission Street
South Pasadena, CA 91030-3036
626-441-4228
FAX: 626-441-1672
Karen Johnson, Show Manager
180 booths.
12M Attendees

5047 Cosmoprof North America
Professional Beauty Association
15825 N. 71st Street
Suite 100
Scottsdale, AZ 85254

FAX: 480-905-0708 800-468-2274
Jen Ingalls, Trade Show Manager
Nathan Miner, Sales Manager
Melissa Coe, Registration Manager
Bonnie Bonadeo, Director Education
Best in hair,cosmetics,packagin and style. Attracted 25,000 professionals from 32 countries with 760 exhibitors.
10M Attendees July Founded: 2002

5048 DCAT Western Education Conference
Drug, Chemical & Associated Technologies
1 Washington Boulevard
Suite 7
Robbinsville, NJ 08691
609-448-1000
FAX: 609-448-1944 800-640-3228
brooke@dcat.org www.dcat.org
Brooke DiGiuseppe, Meeting Services
Margaret Timony, Executive Director
Gain important insights into issues and trends that will affect the future of the nutrition and health industry. Participate in discussion on key business issues with industry experts.
April

5049 Extracts: Essentials for Spa, Home, & Travel
George Little Management
10 Bank Street
Suite 1200
White Plains, NY 10606
914-486-6070
FAX: 914-948-6289 800-292-4560
laura_woodward@glmshows.com
www.extractsny.com/www.glmshows.com
Rita Malek, Show Manager
Laura Anne Woodward, Show Coordinator
George Little II, President
EX-TRACTS: Essentials for Spa, Home and Travel is co-located with the International Hotel/Motel Restaurant Show® (IH/MRS). Presenting the finest Apparel & Accessories, Aromatherapy Products & Candles, Baby and Cildren's Spa Products, Bathrobes and Loungewear, Business Services, Cosmetics, Cosmeceuticals, Home Environment Products, Essential Oils, Frangrances, Home Spa Electrics, Massage/Reflexology, Men's Spa Products, Music & Recordings.
10000 Attendees Nov 12-14 Founded: 1997

5050 Extracts: New Discoveries in Beauty and Wellness
George Little Management
10 Bank Street
Suite 1200
White Plains, NY 10606
914-486-6070
FAX: 914-948-6289 800-292-4560
laura_woodward@glmshows.com
www.extractsny.com
Rita Malek, Show Manager
Laura Anne Woodward, Show Coordinator
George Little II, President
EXTRACTS® at the NYIGF is a unique, high-quality environment, showcasing the most innovative personal care and wellness products for the gift industry: aromatherapy, bath & bodycare, cosmetics, beauty accessories, candles, home fragrances, massage oils, music & recordings, natural/organic products, perfumes, potpourri and skincare.
43M Attendees Jan 28-31/Aug 13-16 Founded: 1997

5051 General Merchandise/Health and Beauty Care Conference
Food Marketing Institute
800 Connecticut Avenue NW
Washington, DC 20006-2709
202-220-0600
FAX: 202-429-4519
Don McWhirter, Owner
Annual show of 150 exhibitors of health and beauty care products.
3000 Attendees

5052 HAIRCOLOR USA
International Beauty Show Group
440 Wheelers Farm Road
Suite 101
Milford, CT 06460
203-882-1300
FAX: 203-882-1800 800-301-3976
Mike Boyce, Show Manager
Haircolor USA offers superior education from world class color manufacturers for hair colorists and salon owners.
1500 Attendees June

5053 Health & Beauty America
HBA
11 West 19th Street
3rd Fl
New York, NY 10011
212-600-3000
FAX: 212-600-3045
jgonzalez@cmprinceton.com
www.hbaexpo.com
Jack Gonzalez, Director Health/Beauty Events
Sal Pecoraro, Sales Manager
America's largest industry-specific educational conference and exposition for cosmetics, toiletries, fragances and personal care.
16500 Attendees

5054 International Beauty Show
International Beauty Show Group
440 Wheelers Farm Road
Suite 101
Milford, CT 06460

800-736-7170
Peter Lucibelli, Exhibit Director
Annual exposition of hair and skin care products manufacturers and beauty technicians. Held in New York city.
75000 Attendees March

5055 Kayser Show
337 Elm Street
Buffalo, NY 14203-1634
716-548-8443
FAX: 716-894-1491 800-937-8445
Melissa Rondenell, Trade Show Coordinator
Ninety booths. A two day educational event for the salon professionals, students and nail technicians. The conference features exhibit booths, round table discussions, private classes and hands on workshops.
6M+ Attendees October

5056 National Beauty Culturists League Conference
25 Logan Circle NW
Washington, DC 20005-3725
202-332-2695
FAX: 202-332-0940
DrLindsay@nbcl.org www.nbcl.org
Dr. Katie B Catalon, President
Dr. William Lindsay, Executive Manager
One hundred booths of beauty industry associates, manufacturing companies and other businesses.
3M Attendees July Founded: 1919

5057 National Cosmetology Association Annual Convention
401 N Michigan Avenue
22nd Floor
Chicago, IL 60611
312-527-6765
FAX: 312-245-1080
www.salonprofessionals.org
Gordon Miller, Executive Director
One hundred booths or more of interest to hairdressers, estheticians, nail technicians, educators, distributors and manufacturers in the beauty industry.
3M Attendees July

5058 Natural Products Exposition East
New Hope Natural Media
1301 Spruce Street
Boulder, CO 80302
303-939-8440
FAX: 303-939-9559
20000 Attendees

5059 Natural Products Exposition West
New Hope Communications
1301 Spruce Street
Boulder, CO 80302
303-939-8440
FAX: 303-939-9559
31000 Attendees

5060 Personal Care Ingredients & Technology Expo (PCITX)
HBA/CMP Princeton Inc
125 Village Boulevard, #220
Princeton, NJ 08540-5703
609-452-2800
FAX: 609-452-2880
eevers@cmpprinceton.com
www.personalcareexpo.com
Jack Gonzalez, Group Beauty Show Director
Ellen Evers, Exhibit Sales Representative
Focuses on the latest developments and recent advances in ingredient technologies, bioengineering and delivery systems for a new generation of cosmetics and personal care products.
September

5061 Professional Beauty Association Annual Convention
Professional Beauty Association
15825 North 71st Street
Suite 100
Scottsdale, AZ 85254
480-281-0424
FAX: 480-905-0708 800-468-2274
info@probeauty.org
www.probeauty.org
Susan Howard, Director Event Operations
Jen Burns, Manager Trade Shows
John Heffner, Chair
Sasha Rash, Secretary/Treasurer
Steven Sleeper, Executive Director
Annual show of 700 exhibitors of industry related equipment, supplies and services.
10M Attendees

5062 Salon Focus
Advanstar Communications
545 Boylston Street
Boston, MA 02116
617-514-4600
FAX: 617-267-6900
info@advanstar.com
www.advanstar.com
Thomas Beger, Executive Director
Joyce DeRemer, Sales
Educational and exhibiting forum for the Southwest professional salon industry. 140 booths.
6.5M Attendees November

5063 Science Executive Leadership Conference
Cosmetic, Toiletry & Fragrance Association
1101 17th Street NW
Suite 300
Washington, DC 20036-4702
202-331-1770
FAX: 202-331-1969 www.ctfa.org
Pamela Bailey, President/CEO
Emphasizing leadership training for science management staff. Speakers will cover topics designed specifically for science executives in the cosmetic and personal care products industry. Receptions and luncheons are available.
700 Attendees October

5064 Techniques
New Dimensions Advertising
47 W Main Street
Mechanicsburg, PA 17055-6262
717-697-4181
FAX: 717-790-9441 800-845-4694
Triennial show of 25 exhibitors of cosmetics and accessories.
1500 Attendees

5065 West Coast Spring Style and Beauty Show
West Coast Beauty Supply
5001 Industrial Way
Benicia, CA 94510
707-484-4800
FAX: 707-748-4623 800-233-3141
info@westcoastbeauty.com
www.westcoastbeauty.com
Paul Eggert, Show Director
Wayne Clark, President
John Golliher, Manager
200 booths.
15M Attendees March

5066 World International Nail and Beauty Trade Show
1221 N Lakeview Avenue
Anaheim, CA 92807-1830
714-779-9883
FAX: 714-779-9971 800-624-5777
James George, President
Mitch Cohen, Show Manager
World's largest fingernail and beauty trade shows in California and Arizona. 200 to 500 booths.
17M+ Attendees May/September

Directories & Databases

5067 Beauty Fashion: Men's Issue
Beauty Fashion
16 E 40th Street
New York, NY 10016
212-328-6789
FAX: 212-840-7246
www.beautyfashion.com
Offers listings of men's fragrances, toiletries and related products as well as manufacturers and US distributors. *$25.00*
Annual
Circulation: 17,000

5068 Complete Directory of Cosmetic Specialties
Sutton Family Communications & Publishing Company
155 Sutton Lane
Fordsville, KY 42343
270-740-0870

jlsutton@apex.net
www.fleamarketeer.net
Theresa Sutton, Editor
Lee Sutton, General Manager
Print-out from database of wholesalers, manufacturers, distributors, importers and close-out houses. Database is updated daily to guarantee the most current and up-to-date sources available. *$39.50*
100+ pages

5069 Complete Directory of Personal Care Items
Sutton Family Communications & Publishing Company
155 Sutton Lane
Fordsville, KY 42343
270-740-0870

jlsutton@apex.net
www.fleamarketeer.net
Theresa Sutton, Editor
Lee Sutton, General Manager
Print-out from database of wholesalers, manufacturers, distributors, importers and close-out houses. Database is updated daily to guarantee the most current and up-to-date sources available. *$39.50*
100+ pages

5070 Cosmetics & Toiletries: Cosmetic Bench Reference
Allured Publishing Corporation
362 S Schmale Road
Carol Stream, IL 60188-2787
630-653-2155
FAX: 630-653-2192
Offers a full list of cosmetics ingredient suppliers. *$95.00*
Biennial

5071 Cosmetics & Toiletries: Who's Who in R&D Directory Issue
Allured Publishing Corporation
362 S Schmale Road
Carol Stream, IL 60188-2787
630-653-2155
FAX: 630-653-2192
Offers a list of cosmetic manufacturers and consultants for product development, legal, safety and regulatory assistance. *$25.00*
Annual
Circulation: 3,200

5072 Fragrance Foundation Reference Guide
Fragrance Foundation
145 E 32nd Street
New York, NY 10016-6002
212-725-2755
FAX: 212-779-9058
info@fragrence.org
www.fragrance.org
Rochelle R Bloom, President
Over 1100 fragrances are listed that are available in the US, with dates of introduction and description, alphabetically indexed with company name, address and phone number. *$60.00*
112 pages Annual

5073 Fragrance and Olfactory Dictionary
Fragrance Foundation
145 E 32nd Street
New York, NY 10016-6002
212-725-2755
FAX: 212-779-9058
Rbloom@fragrence.org
www.fragrence.org
Rochell R Bloom, President
Definitions of ingredients, techniques, language of fragrance and olfactory references. *$7.00*
32 pages

5074 Perfume 2000
Perfume 2000
444 Brickell Avenue
Ste 510
Miami, FL 33131
305-374-6849
FAX: 305-374-6850
ana@perfume2000.com
www.perfume2000.com
Ana Murias, Public Relations
Comprehensive database; services encourage industry networking and integration.

5075 RIFM Database of Fragrance & Flavor Materials
50 Tice Boulevard
Woodcliff Lake, NJ 07677-7654
201-689-8089
FAX: 201-689-8090 www.rifm.org/nd
Ladd W Smith, President

A comprehensive source offering safety evaluations and toxicology data on more than 4,500 fragrance and flavor materials. Operated in full cooperation with Flavor & Extracts Manufacturing Association (FEMA).
Founded: 1966

5076 Rauch Guide to the US Cosmetics & Toiletri es Industry
Grey House Publishing
PO Box 860
Millerton, NY 12546
518-789-8700
FAX: 518-789-0545 800-562-2139
books@greyhouse.com
www.greyhouse.com
Leslie Mackenzie, Publisher
Richard Gottlieb, President
Guide is organized into several information-packed chapters. Chapters consists of economics, technology & raw materials, products & markets, industry activities, organizations & sources of information, company directory and appendices.
$895.00
Annual

5077 Who's Who: Membership Directory of the Cosmetic, Toiletry & Fragrance Assn
Cosmetic, Toiletry & Fragrance Association
1101 17th Street NW
Suite 300
Washington, DC 20036-4702
202-331-1770
FAX: 202-331-1969 www.ctfa.org
Gwen Hallill, Director Publications/Comm
Pamela Bailey, President
About 500 member companies of the cosmetics industry. *$75.00*
Annual, June

Industry Web Sites

5078 www.abbies.org
American Beauty Association

Mission is to expand, serve and protect the interests of the professional beauty industry.

5079 www.ahbai.org
American Health and Beauty Aids Institute

Trade association representing leading Black-owned companies manufacturing ethnic hair care and beauty products that feature the Proud Lady symbol. Members serve Black America through employment, scholarships and education of consumers on recycling their dollars into the Black community.

5080 www.bbsi.org
Beauty and Barber Supply Institute

Our members are wholesaler-distributors, manufacturers and manufacturers' representatives from around the world. Our mission is to maximize the potential of the salon industry.

5081 www.beautyworks.com/aia
Aestheticis International Association

For the advancement of education and public awareness on aesthetics. Paramedical aesthetics and body spa therapy. Professionals from the medical, paramedical and beauty industries working together for the most advanced techniques for the patients and clients.

5082 www.cew.org
Cosmetic Executive Women

Nonprofit trade organization of approximately 1,500 executives in the beauty, cosmetics, fragrance and related industries. Based in New York City, CEW has associated organizations in France and the United Kingdom. As a leading trade organization in the beauty industry, CEW helps develop the career contacts, knowledge and skills of its members so that they may advance on both professional and personal levels.

5083 www.cibsonline.com
Cosmetic, Toiletry & Fragrance Association

Provides a complete range of services that support the personal care products industry's needs and interests in the scientific, legal, regulatory, legislative and international fields. CTFA strives to ensure that the personal care products industry has the freedom to pursue creative product development and compete in a fair and responsible marketplace.

5084 www.cosmeticindex.com
CosmeticIndex.Com

www.cosmeticindex.com
Online source for cosmetics, resources and services.

5085 www.fragrance.org
Fragrance Foundation

5086 www.greyhouse.com
Grey House Publishing

Selected Grey House directories in the fields of business, health and education are available online. Users can search our online databases by several different search criteria, such as product categories, geographic area, sales volume and much, much more. Full Grey House catalog and online ordering also available.

5087 www.iacmcolor.org
International Association of Color Manufacturers

Actively represents the interests of the regulated color industry by demonstrating the safety of color additives and to promote the industry's economic growth by participating in new color approvals, regulatory and legislative issues that affect the industry worldwide.

5088 www.iasc.org
International Aloe Science Council

Nonprofit trade organization for the Aloe Vera Industry world-wide. Its membership includes Aloe growers, processors, finished goods manufacturers, marketing companies, insurance companies, equipment suppliers, printers, sales organizations, physicians, scientists and researchers.

5089 www.icmad.org
Independent Cosmetic Manufacturers & Distributors

Information on government consumers and the media. Provides group programs for product liability.

5090 www.inmnails.com
World International Nail and Beauty Association

Promotes effective use of products, sponsors competition and bestows awards. Also offers world championship competitions for nails, hair and makeup.

5091 www.isnow.com
Cosmetologists Chicago

Voice of the salon industry. For over eight decades, we have been a beauty authority and presenter of the Chicago Midwest Beauty Show. We are stylists, estheticians, color technicians, salon owners, educators and nail technicians.

5092 www.perfume2000.com

www.perfume2000.com

5093 www.perfumers.org
American Society of Perfumers

Nonprofit organization fostering and encouraging the art and science of perfumery in the US while promoting professional exchange and a high standard of professional conduct within the fragrance industry. The ASP holds symposiums in the New York City area where leading members of the fragrence community are invited to speak and present information on all aspects of the industry.

5094 www.salonprofessionals.org
National Cosmetology Association

Nationwide community of 30,000 salon professionals, connected by a common passion for learning, growing and raising the professionalim of the entire salon industry. As a group, we have a strong voice in our communities, our industry and with our government because the NCA is for everyone in the professional community. Members have access to education, fashion events, community service and insurance—all the tools needed to build your career.

5095 www.shopvmall.com/beabarb.html

Links to beauty salons, nail salons, hair, skin makeup studios and much more. In association with Martin County, Florida's Beauty Salon and Barber Shop Emporium.

Associations

5096 **ACA International**
PO Box 390106
Minneapolis, MN 55439
952-926-6547

membership@acainternational.org
www.acainternational.com
International trade organization of over 5,300 credit and collection professionals providing a variety of accounts receivable management services to over 1,000,000 credit grantors.
5300 Members Founded: 1995

5097 **Advertising Media Credit Executives**
8840 Columbia 100 Parkway
Columbia, MD 21045-2158
410-992-7609
FAX: 410-740-5574
amcea@amcea.org www.amcea.org
Kay Rice, President
Mark Stepuszek, First VP
Mark Lee, Second VP
Michael Murphy, Secretary/Treasurer
Judith K Bennett, Director
Improving the professionalism, principles, understanding and techniques of media credit management by encouraging the exchange of ideas, methods and procedures within the membership. Providing additional education and training in the business fundamentals of media credit and credit policies and in the related areas of finance, accounting, law and economics for the purpose of enhancing the career development of the members.
60 Members Founded: 1953

5098 **Affordable Housing Tax Credit Coalition**
1900 K St Nw
Ste 1200
Washington, DC 20006-1109
202-551-1500
FAX: 202-585-8080
info@taxcreditcoalition.org
www.taxcreditcoalition.org
Linda D Kirk, Executive Director
Plays a major role in assuring the continuance of the low income housing tax credit, with the primary goal of achieving permanent extension of the low income housing tax credit program.
105 Members Founded: 1988

5099 **American Association of Credit Union**
5710 Mineral Point Road
Madison, WI 53701
608-314-4000
FAX: 608-231-4263 800-356-9655
dorothy@cuna.org www.cuna.org
Paul Mercer, Chairman
Rick Pillow, First Vice Chairman
Rosie Holub, Second Vice Chairman
Brett Thompson, Treasurer
Bill Mellin, Secretary
Association of state credit union leagues.
51 Members Founded: 1942

5100 **American Bankruptcy Institute**
44 Canal Center Plaza
Suite 404
Alexandria, VA 22314
703-739-0800
FAX: 703-739-1060
info@abiworld.org www.abiworld.org
Andrew W Caine, Chairman
Samuel J Gerdano, Executive Director
Michael P Richman, President
Neil P Olack, VP Education
Professional association providing a multidisciplinary forum for the exchange of ideas and information on bankruptcy issues. Sponsors educational programs on current developments. Publishes ABI Law Review and the ABI Journal and periodic bulletins on court cases or legislative developments.
10000 Members Founded: 1982

5101 **American Financial Services Association**
919 18th Street NW
Suite 300
Washington, DC 20006
202-296-5544
FAX: 202-223-0321
afsa@afsaonline.org
www.afsaonline.org
Tom Hallman, Chairperson
Randy Lively, President/CEO
Isaac Templeton, Consumer Affairs/Program Manager
Lynne B Strang, VP Communications
A national trade association for market funded providers of financial services to consumers and small businesses.
400 Members Founded: 1916

5102 **American Recovery Association**
PO Box 231565
New Orleans, LA 70183-1565
504-738-6404
FAX: 504-738-7910
homeoffice@americanrecoveryassn.org
www.repo.org
Paul Hallock, President
Lloyd Swor, VP
Les McCook, Secretary/Treasurer
Approximately 500 offices around the US, Canada and Germany, providing repossesion services around the world.
280 Members Founded: 1965

5103 **Association of Professionals in Finance**
8840 Columbia 100 Parkway
Columbia, MD 21045-2158
410-423-1840
FAX: 410-423-1845 888-256-3242
fcib_info@fcibglobal.com
www.fcibglobal.com
Kenneth F Garrison Jr, President/CEO
William Bastiaan, Chairman
Betsy Gardner, Executive Assistant
Provider of products and services to many small, medium and large size exporters as well as major multinational corporations in 30 countries around the world. Its international dimension and superior products and services enable international professionals achieve business objectives, professional growth, recognition and prosperity.
800 Members Founded: 1919

5104 **Broadcast Cable Credit Association**
550 W Frontage Rd
Ste 3600
Northfield, IL 60093-1243
847-960-0200
FAX: 847-827-1653
info@bccacredit.com
www.bccacredit.com
Mary Collins, President/CEO
Jamie Smith, Operations Manager
Doreen Colleti-Muhs, Sales/Membership Manager
Subsidiary of the Broadcast Cable Financial Management Association. BCCA provides industry specific credit reports on individual agencies, advertisers or buying services both national and local. These reports may be obtained upon request online and by phone or fax. Its mission is to provide tools and services that will allow members to perform their functions to the best of their abilities, and help them achieve a profitable bottom line.
425 Members Founded: 1972

5105 **Business Products Credit Association**
607 Westridge Drive
O'Fallon, MO 63366
636-272-3005
FAX: 636-272-2973
service@bcpa.org www.bcpa.org
C David Schmucker, President/CEO
Debbie Schmucker, Manager
Credit Trade Association for manufacturers and wholesalers.
Founded: 1875

5106 **CDC Consumer Debt Counseling**
1300 Hampton Avenue
Saint Louis, MO 63139-3163
314-647-9006
FAX: 314-647-1359 800-966-3328
Philip Johnston, President
Nonprofit provider of quality, face-to-face and telephone budget and debt counseling education.

5107 **Callahan & Associates**
1001 Connecticut Avenue NW
10th Floor
Washington, DC 20036
202-223-3920
FAX: 202-223-6098 800-446-7453
Charles Filson, President/CEO
Jay Johnson, VP
National credit union research and consulting firm specializing in finacial publications and analysis software, strategic planning and investment management. Callahan's goal is to help credit unions position themselves at the leading edge of the ever changing financial service industry.
Founded: 1985

5108 **Capital Markets Credit Analysts Society**
151 Hendricks Road
Suite 1
Garden City Park, NY 11040
516-739-2510
FAX: 516-739-3803 800-284-6228
cmcas@cmcas.org www.cmcas.org
Matthew V Hansen, Executive Director
A professional society whose membership consists primarily of managers and analysts in credit risk departments that directly support their employers' capital market activities.
500 Members Founded: 1989

5109 **Coalition of Higher Education Assistance Organizations**
1101 Vermont Avenue NW
Suite 400
Washington, DC 20005
202-289-3903
FAX: 202-371-0197
hwadsworth@wpllc.net
www.coheao.com
Harrison Wadsworth, Executive Director

Focus is on legislative and regulatory advocacy for Federal Perkins and other campus based student loan programs.
365 Members Founded: 1980

5110 Commercial Finance Association
225 W 34th Street
New York, NY 10122
212-594-3490
FAX: 212-564-6053
info@cfa.com www.cfa.com
Richard P Palmieri, Chairman
Bruce H Jones, Executive Director/Secretary
Michael D Sharkey, President
Joseph F Nemia, VP Finance
Deborah J Monosson, VP
Trade group of the asset-based, financial services industry, with members throughout the US, Canada and around the world. Members include the asset-based lending arms of domestic and foreign commercial banks, small and large independent finance companies, floor plan financing organizations, factoring organizations and financing subsidiaries of major industrial corporations. CFA membership is by organization, not by individual.

5111 Commercial Mortgage Securities Association
30 Broad Street
28th Floor
New York, NY 10004-2304
212-509-1844
FAX: 212-509-1895
info@cmbs.org www.cmbs.org
Dottie Cunningham, CEO
Jane Gelfand, Managing Director Finance/Admin
Marcus Henderson, Coordinator Membership/Facilities
Trish Madonia, Director Meetings
International trade organization for the commercial real estate capital markets. Also represents and promotes an orderly and ethical global institutional secondary market for the sale of commercial mortgage loans and equity investments.
309 Members Founded: 1994

5112 Consumer Credit Insurance Association
542 South Dearborn
Suite 400
Chicago, IL 60605
312-394-4371
FAX: 312-939-8287
bburfeind@cciaonline.com
www.cciaonline.com
William F Burfeind III, Executive Vice President
To preserve, promote and enhance the availability, utility and integrity of insurance and related products and services delivered in connection with financial transactions.
140 Members Founded: 1951

5113 Consumer Data Industry Association
1090 Vermont Avenue NW
Suite 200
Washington, DC 20005
202-821-1699
FAX: 202-371-0134
tmhorn@cdiaonline.org
www.cdiaonline.org
Kim Alfano, Chief Executive Officer
Tina Horn, Membership Services
Trade association representing consumer information companies that provide fraud prevention and risk management products, credit and mortgage reports, tenant and employment screening services, check fraud and verification services and collection services. Sets industry standards and provides education for its members. Provides educational materials for consumers regarding their credit rights and how consumer credit reporting agencies can better serve their needs.
360 Members Founded: 1906

5114 Credit Professionals International
525-B N Laclede Station Road
St. Louis, MO 63119
314-961-0031
FAX: 314-961-0040
creditpro@creditprofessionals.org
www.creditprofessionals.org
Linda Bridgeford, President
Joyce Jones, First VP
Barbara Chapin, Secretary/Treasurer
Conducts educational seminars and conferences for the credit industry.
475 Members Founded: 1927

5115 Credit Research Foundation
8840 Columbia 100 Parkway
Columbia, MD 21045
410-740-5499
FAX: 410-740-4620
crf_info@crfonline.org
www.crfonline.org
Rob Olsen, Chairman
Sheryl Mott, Vice Chairman Finance
Michael W Durant, Vice Chairman Research
Alex Behm, Vice Chairman Membership
Terry Callahan, President
Independent, member-run organization, consisting of a dynamic community of like minded business professionals with a vested interest in improving and fostering the field of business credit — more specifically — the practices and technologies of business credit. CRF is your industry advocate; the bridge in the customer financial relationship. With our variety of member benefits, we're here to provide help to the real problems and challenges your business faces every day.
550 Members Founded: 1949

5116 Credit Union Executives Society
5510 Research Park Drive
Madison, WI 53711
608-271-2664
FAX: 608-271-2303 800-252-2664
cues@cues.org www.cues.org
Fred Johnson, President/CEO
Mary Arnold, VP Publications
Gary W Irvin, Vice Chairman
Catherine S Robertson, Treasurer
Rose Bartolomucci, Secretary
An independent membership organization for credit union executives. CUE'S mission is to advance the professional development of credit union CEO's senior management, and directors.
3500 Members Founded: 1962

5117 Credit Union National Association
5710 Mineral Point Road
Madison, WI 53705
608-314-4000
FAX: 608-231-4263
rensweiler@tcul.coop www.cuna.org
Dick Ensweiler, Chairman
Juri Valdov, Vice Chairman
Donald L Larsen, Secretary
Daniel Mica, Chief Executive Officer, Director
With its network of affiliated state credit union leagues, CUNA serves more than 90 percent of America's 10,000 credit unions, which are based in Washington, DC and Madison, Wisconsin. This nonprofit trade group is governed by volunteer directors who are elected by their credit union peers.
Founded: 1970

5118 Education Credit Union Council
PO Box 7558
Spanish Fort, AL 36577
251-626-3399
FAX: 251-626-3565
webster@ecuc.org www.ecuc.org
Lorraine B Zerfas, Executive Director
Organization dedicated to providing educational and networking opportunities to credit unions who serve educational communities. Whether educators compose the majority or small segment of your membership, you will benefit from the exchange of ides offered by our ECUC members. Any goup involved in the field of education — teachers, administrators, students, support staff and others constitutes the educational community.
330 Members Founded: 1972

5119 Electronic Transactions Association
1101 16th Street NW
Washington, DC 20036

800-695-5509
info@electran.org www.electran.org
Carla Balakgie CAE, Executive Director
International trade association serving the needs of organizations offering transaction processing products and services.

5120 FCIB-NACM Corporation
8840 Columbia 100 Parkway
Columbia, MD 21045-2158
410-303-3424
FAX: 410-423-1845 888-256-3242
fcib_info@fcibglobal.com
www.fcibglobal.com
Robin Schauseil, President
A subsidiary of the National Association of Credit Management and formely the Foreign Credit Interchange Bureau.
850 Members Founded: 1919

5121 Farm Credit Council
50 F Street NW
Suite 900
Washington, DC 20001
202-471-1184
FAX: 202-626-8718 800-525-2345
morrill@fccouncil.com
www.fccouncil.com
Ken Auer, President/CEO
Jennifer Morrill, Director Communications
The national trade association of the Farm Credit System and represents the system's legislative and regulatory interests, and provides a wide range of businesss services to Farm Credit institutions.
5 Members Founded: 1982

5122 First Entertainment Credit Union
6735 Forest Lawn Drive
Hollywood, CA 90068
323-512-2412
FAX: 323-851-0383 888-800-3328
Nonprofit, financial institution for the entertainment community. Profits after operating expenses are returned directly to members in the form of high dividend rates,

low loan rates and reduced fees for services. FECU serves more than 700 entertainment-based companies, with more than $340,000,000 in assets.
52000 Members Founded: 1967

5123 **Fraud & Theft Information Bureau**
9770 S Military Trail
Suite 380
Boynton Beach, FL 33436
561-737-8700
FAX: 561-737-5800
sales@fraudandtheft.com
www.fraudandtheft.com
Larry Schwartz, President
Pearl Sax, VP
Publishers of manuals and fraud-blocker databases relating to credit card and check fraud control and loss prevention. Consultants to merchants, credit card companies, banks and other credit grantors.
Founded: 1982

5124 **Information Technologies Credit Union Association**
PO Box 160
Del Mar, CA 92014-0160
858-792-3883
FAX: 858-792-3884
itcua@itcua.org www.itcua.org
Katherine E Clark, Executive Director
To provide information, education, networking, products, services and constituent representation to credit unions serving the information technology industry.
300 Members Founded: 1959

5125 **International Association of Commercial Collectors**
4040 W 70th Street
Minneapolis, MN 55435
952-925-0760
FAX: 952-926-1624
iacc@commercialcollector.com
www.commercialcollector.com
David Ware, President
Ted M Smith, Executive Director
International trade association comprised of more than 200 collection specialists and 140 commercial attorneys, with members throughout the US and 38 international countries. IACC's mission is to promote the commercial collection profession by providing IACC members with the resources to excel in the industry.
350 Members Founded: 1970

5126 **International Energy Credit Association**
8325 Lantern View Lane
St John, IN 46373
219-365-7313
FAX: 219-365-0327
rprco@aol.com www.ieca.net
Robert Raichle, Executive Vice President
The oldest international industry credit association in the United States. Membership includes companies located in the Uited States, Canada, most Western European countries, Mexico, South America and Asia.
700 Members Founded: 1923

5127 **Jewelers Board of Trade**
95 Jefferson Boulevard
Warrick, RI 02888-1046
401-467-0055
FAX: 401-467-1199
jbtinfo@jewelersboard.com
www.jewelersboard.com
Dione D Kenyon, President
A nont for profit jewelry trade association whose primary function is to compile and disseminate accurate and reliable credit information among its members as to the financial standing, credit history and background of dealers of jewelry and related products.
3200 Members Founded: 1884

5128 **Mortgage Bankers Association**
1919 Pennsylvania Avenue NW
Washington, DC 20006-3438
202-557-2700
FAX: 202-721-0246
membership@mortgagebankers.org
www.mortgagebankers.org
Jonathan L Kemper, President/CEO
Dan Thoms, VP
Representing the real estate finance industry, MBA serves its membership by representing their legislative and regulatory interests before the US Congress and federal agencies; by meeting their educational needs through programs and a range of periodicals and publications; and by supporting their business interests with a variety of research initiatives and other products and services.
2900 Members Founded: 1918

5129 **NACUSO**
PMB 3419 Via Lido
#135
Newport Beach, CA 92663
949-645-5296
FAX: 949-645-5297 888-462-2870
info@nacuso.org www.nacuso.org
Victor Pantea, Interim CEO
Pete Snyder, Treasurer
Dennis Pierce, Secretary
400 Members Founded: 1985

5130 **National Association of Consumer Credit**
PO Box 20871
Columbus, OH 43220-871
614-326-1165
FAX: 614-326-1162
nacca2001@aol.com
www.naccaonline.org
Laura Udis, President
C Dean Bratton, First VP
Kevin Glendening, Second VP
Bob Tedcastle, Third VP
Theresa Brady, Secretary-Treasurer
Improving the supervision of consumer credit agencies; facilitating the administration of laws governing these agencies by providing a forum for the exchange of information, ideas and experiences among public officials having supervision of such agencies and changes with the administration of such laws; facilitating intercommunication among its members and developing standard information collection concerning consumer credit agencies in each state.
55 Members Founded: 1935

5131 **National Association of Credit Management**
8840 Columbia 100 Parkway
Columbia, MD 21045
410-740-5560
FAX: 410-740-5574
nacm_info@nacm.org www.nacm.org
Ralph Rimualdo, Chairman
Faith Anderson, Senior Vice Chairman
David Beckel, Junior Vice Chairman
Mark Tuniewicz, Senior Vice Chairman
Robin Schauseil, President
NACM and its network of affiliated associations are the leading resource for credit and financial management information and education, delivering products and services which improve the management of business credit and accounts receivable. Our collective voice has influenced legislative results concerning commercial business and trade credit to our nation's policy makers for more than 100 years, and continues to play an active part in legislative issues pertaining to business credit.
25000 Members Founded: 1896

5132 **National Association of Credit Union Service Organizations**
PMB 3419 Via Lido
Suite 135
Newport Beach, CA 92663
949-645-5296
FAX: 949-645-5297 888-462-2870
info@nacuso.org www.nacuso.org
Shawna Luna, Executive Assistant
Thomas Davis, Chairman
Leading professional trade association for credit unions and CUSO's seeking to provide a full aray of services, such as mortgages, business lending and business lending depository services, trust services, investments and insurance to their members and non members alike.
412 Members Founded: 1985

5133 **National Association of Federal Credit Unions**
3138 10th Street North
Arlington, VA 22201-2149
703-522-4770
FAX: 703-524-1082 800-336-4644
lcorbin@nafcu.org www.nafcu.org
Fred Becker, President
Diane Swenson, Executive VP
Jay Morris, VP Communications
William J Donovan, General Counsel/Senior VP
Sara J Romanick, Director Education
Influential trade association that exclusively represents the nterests of federal credit unions before the federal government and the public.
804 Members Founded: 1967

5134 **National Association of State Credit Union Supervisors**
1655 North Fort Myer Drive
Suite 300
Arlington, VA 22209
703-528-8351
FAX: 703-528-3248 800-728-7927
offices@nascus.org www.nascus.org
Mary Martha Fortney, President/CEO
Sandra Troutman, Executive VP
Jennifer Champagne, Director Education
State chartered credit unions and state credit union supervisors.
900 Members Founded: 1965

5135 National Chemical Credit Association
1100 Main Street
Buffalo, NY 14209-2356
716-887-9527
FAX: 716-878-2866 www.ncca#1.org

Don Peters, Contact

Members are major producers of basic chemicals and allied products.
100 Members Founded: 1938

5136 National Council of Postal Credit Unions
PO Box 160
Del Mar, CA 92014-0160
858-792-3883
FAX: 858-792-3884
ncpcu@ncpcu.org www.ncpcu.org

Robert P Spindler, Executive Director

Organized to represent the special interests of postal credit unions.
160 Members Founded: 1984

5137 National Credit Reporting Association
125 East Lake Street
Suite 200
Bloomingdale, IL 60108
630-539-1525
FAX: 630-539-1526
tclemans@ncrainc.org
www.ncrainc.org

Terry W Clemans, Executive Director

Purpose is to promote the general welfare of its members. Also provides leadership in education, legislation, ethics and enhanced vendor's relation
150 Members Founded: 1992

5138 National Credit Union Administration
1775 Duke Street
Alexandria, VA 22314-3428
703-518-6300
FAX: 703-518-6319
csdesk@ncua.gov www.ncua.gov

Joann Johnson, Chairman
Deborah Matz, Board Member

Governed by a three member board appointed by the President and confirmed by the US Senate, this independent federal agency charters and supervises federal credit unions. NCUA, with the backing of the full faith and credit of the US government, operates the National Credit Union Share Insurance Fund, insuring the savings of 80 million account holders in all federal credit unions and many state chartered credit unions.
82M Members Founded: 1970

5139 National Federation of Community Development Credit Unions
120 Wall Street
10th Floor
New York, NY 10005
212-809-1850
FAX: 212-809-3274
mstrange@natfed.org www.natfed.org

Clifford N Rosenthal, Executive Director

Serve and represent financial cooperatives in low income communities. Members are community based credit unions. Provides training and management support to CDCU's and asists groups in organizing new credit unions.
200 Members Founded: 1974

5140 National Foundation for Credit Counseling
801 Roeder Road
Suite 900
Silver Spring, MD 20910
301-589-5600
FAX: 301-495-5623 800-388-2227

Susan C Keating, President/CEO
Paul Weiss, Senior VP/CFO
Lydia Sermons-Ward, Senior VP Marketing

Sets the standard for quality credit counseling, debt reduction services and education for financial wellness.
1200 Members

5141 New York Media Credit Group
3 East 54th Street
New York, NY 10022
212-230-5737
FAX: 212-230-5996 800-746-9428

Michael Denson, Chairman

The New York Media Credit Group is one of the most active credit association for the media credit professionals today
850 Members Founded: 1903

5142 Risk Management Association
One Liberty Place
1801 Market St
Ste 300
Philadelphia, PA 19103-1613
215-519-9000
FAX: 415-446-4101 800-677-7621
customers@rmahq.org
www.rmahq.org

W Kendall Chalk, Chair
Glenn L Wilson, Vice Chair
Maurice H Hartigan II, President/CEO
Reid Adamson, Senior VP
William S Aichele, President/CEO

Champions risk management while also monitoring emerging trends. Our strong relationship with members and regulators helps us develop new risk management techniques, innovative products and education and training programs geared to risk management professionals at different stages of their careers.
3000 Members Founded: 1914

Newsletters

5143 ARA News & Views
American Recovery Association
PO Box 231565
New Orleans
Louisiana, LA 70183-1565
504-738-6404
FAX: 504-738-7910
homeoffice@americanrecoveryassn.org
http://www.repo.org/

Don Thornton, President
Paul Hallock, VP
Judy Roth, Administrative Director
Charlene Miller, Office Assistant

Provides news, information and coverage of the recovery industry. Free to members only in print. Available to all others online
28 pages Quarterly Founded: 1965

5144 Bankcard Barometer
RAM Research Group
1230 Avenue
7th Floor
New York, NY 10020
212-745-1362
FAX: 917-639-4005
cardstaff@ramresearch.com
http://www.ramresearch.com

Robert B McKinley, Chairman
Robert B McKinley, Publisher

Reports on the pricing and performance of US bank credit card portfolios. Trendline charts follow deliquency, charge-offs, attrition, payment rates, bankruptcy rates, fraud losses, interest yield, operating expenses, net interest margin and return on assets. *$1295.00*
40 pages Monthly Founded: 1986
Printed in 4 colors

5145 Bankcard Dispatch
RAM Research Group
PO Box 1916
Frederick, MD 21702
301-695-4660
FAX: 301-695-0160
staff@ramresearch.com
www.cardweb.com

Robert B McKinley, Editor

Covers the entire payment card industry as it affects the US market. Comprehensive periodical is prepared for payment card executives. *$1295.00*
40 pages Monthly
Printed in 4 colors

5146 Bankcard Update
RAM Research Group
PO Box 1916
Frederick, MD 21702
301-695-4660
FAX: 301-695-0160
staff@ramresearch.com
http://www.ramresearch.com/

Robert B McKinley, Editor/chairman

Updated printed report and CD-ROM on quarterly statistics of the top US issuers. Covers hundreds of portfolios comprising more than 95 percent of the US market. Subscription includes both the printed version and CD-ROM. *$1295.00*
40 pages Monthly Founded: 1986
Printed in 4 colors

5147 Capitol Watch
National Association of Credit Unions
3138 10th Street N
Suite 300
Arlington, VA 22201-2149
703-522-4770
FAX: 703-524-1082 800-336-4644
jbruce@nafcu.org www.nafcu.org

Fred Becker, President
Jerome Bruce, Exhibits/Advertising Manager

This members only electronic format newsletter is NAFCU's monthly communication for credit unions with assets of $50 million or less.

5148 Collection Agency Report
First Detroit Corporation
PO Box 5025
Warren, MI 48090-5025
586-573-0045
FAX: 586-573-9219 800-366-5995
info@firstdetroit.com
http://www.firstdetroit.com

Albert Scace, President
Patricia Herrick, Marketing Manager
Patricia Herrick, Circulation Manager

Provides financially oriented news on the collection agency and bad debt buying industries worldwide. *$420.00*

8 pages Monthly Founded: 1988
Mailing list available for rent $110 per M.

5149 Communicator
Consumer Data Industry Association
1090 Vermont Avenue NW
Suite 200
Washington, DC 20005-4905
202-821-1699
FAX: 202-371-0134
http://www.cdiaonline.org

Kim Alfano, Chief Executive Officer
Alicia Payne, Contact

Comprehensive online news about the consumer reporting industry, legislation, member news and schedule of industry events. Members only benefit.

16 pages Monthly Founded: 1906
Circulation: 3000

5150 Consumer Bankruptcy News
LRP Publications
360 Hiatt Drive
Palm Beach Gardens, FL 33418
561-622-6520
FAX: 215-784-9639 800-341-7874
custserv@lrp.com www.lrp.com

Keeps readers up-to-date on the latest news and cases involving consumer bankruptcy. A must-have for every bankruptcy professional. *$290.00*

Mailing list available for rent
Printed in 2 colors on matte stock

5151 Covering Credit Newsletter
Covering Credit
13 Calle Larspur
Rancho Santa Margarita, CA 92688
949-460-7609
FAX: 949-460-7609
newsletter@coveringcredit.com
http://www.coveringcredit.com

Michael C Dennis, Communications Advisor
Steve Kozack, Financial Consultant

Intended for business professionals dealing with credit risk management and/or commercial debt collection and their advsiors. Free and online.

Monthly Founded: 1989

5152 Credit Union News Watch
Credit Union National Association
PO Box 431
Madison, WI 53701-431
608-314-4000
FAX: 608-231-4263 800-348-3646
bmerrick@cuna.com
http://www.creditunionmagazine.com

Bill Merrick, Managing Editor
Daniel A. Mica, CEO/President
Leah Knope, Director of Circulation

Offers news and reports on credit and lending services. *$50.00*

Weekly Founded: 1970

5153 Credit Union Report
Callahan & Associates
1001 Connecticut Avenue NW
10th Floor
Washington, DC 20036
202-223-3920
FAX: 202-223-6098 800-446-7453
pubs@creditunions.com
www.creditunions.com

Catherine Hassinger, Publications
Charles Filson, President/CEO

Keeps an eye on the future, providing stategic vision for every level of credit union management. Each issue includes leading-edge ideas from the industry's top consultants and CEO's, as well as financial trend analysis to help credit unions operate more effectively. Available in print and electronic formats. *$149.00*

Monthly : PDF

5154 Credit Union Times
560 Village Boulevard
Suite 325
West Palm Beach, FL 33409-1962
561-683-8515
FAX: 561-683-8514 800-345-9936
subscriptions@cutimes.com
http://www.cutimes.com

Mike Welch, Publisher
Paul Gentile, Editor
Elaine Barr, Managing Editor

Reports on marketing, regulation, technology and developing trends. *$120.00*

Weekly
Circulation: 9337
Printed in 4 colors on matte stock

5155 Inside MBS & ABS
Inside Mortgage Finance Publishers
7910 Woodmont Avenue
Suite 1010
Bethesda, MD 20814
301-951-1240
FAX: 301-656-1709
service@imfpubs.com
http://www.imfpubs.com

Guy Cecala, Publisher
John Bancroft, Managing Editor

If you're involved in issuing, underwriting, investing, research, rating or trading mortgage-backed securities and asset-backed securities, this publication is for you. *$1699.00*

Founded: 1984

5156 Jumbo Rate News
Bauer Financial
2655 LeJeune Road - PH 1-A
Coral Gables, FL 33114
305-445-9500
FAX: 305-445-6775 800-388-6686
customerservice@bauerfinancial.com
http://www.bauerfinancial.com

Paul Bauer, Circulation Manager
Karen Dorway, President

Each issue contains over 1,000 separate Jumbo CD rates in seven categories from over 200 creditworthy banks and thrifts nationwide. Includes star ratings, wire transfer fees, deposit requirements and financial highlights for each institution. *$4150.00*

Weekly Founded: 1986
Printed in 2 colors on matte stock

5157 MBA Newslink
Mortgage Bankers Association of America
1919 Pennsylvania Avenue NW
Washington, DC 20006-3438
202-557-2700
FAX: 202-721-0167 800-793-6222
mbanewslink@mortagagebankers.org
http://www.mortgagebankers.org

Jonathan Kempner, CEO/President
Mike Sorohan, Editor
Cheryl Crispen, Publisher
Prudence Roberts-Milligan, Marketing Manager
Christine Rene, Circulation Manager

Learn the latest residential, commercial, and multifamily real estate finance news. Hear what's happening at our association, free to members. Electronic format.

20 pages Daily Founded: 2003
Circulation: 42,500 2,800 names $100 per M.
Printed in 2 colors on newsprint stock

5158 NACM E-News
National Association of Credit Management
8840 Columbia 100 Parkway
Columbia, MD 21045-2158
410-740-5560
FAX: 410-740-5574
nacm_info@nacm.org
www.nacm.org/enews

Robin Schauseil, President

News items of interest to credit and business professionals. Free online.

5159 National Mortgage News
Thomson Financial Publishing
1 State Street Plaza
27th Floor
New York, NY 10004
212-258-8445
FAX: 800-235-5552 800-221-1809
custserv@thomsonmedia.com
http://www.nationalmortgagenews.com

James Malkin, CEO
Jose Thomas, Manager

Mortgage information, legislation and news. *$228.00*

Weekly
Printed in 2 colors on newsprint stock

5160 News and Views
Advertising Media Credit Executives Association
8840 Columbia 100 Parkway
Columbia, MD 21045-2158
410-992-7609
FAX: 410-740-5574
amcea@amcea.org
http://www.amcea.org

Delores Richman, Editor
Charles Wilson, VP

Improving the professionalism, principles, understanding and techniques of media credit management by encouraging the exchange of ideas, methods and procedures within the membership. Providing additional education and training in the business fundamentals of media credit and credit policies and in the related areas of finance, accounting, law and economics for the purpose of enhancing the career development of its members. *$185.00*

Quarterly Founded: 1953

5161 Newsbreak
First Entertainment Credit Union
PO Box 100
Hollywood, CA 90078
323-513-3673
FAX: 323-876-9810 888-800-3328
mail@firstent.org www.firstent.org

Provides industry, resources and investment news and information for the First Entertainment Credit Union member. Free online.

Quarterly

5162 SNL Daily ThriftWatch
SNL Financial
321 E Main Street
Charlottesville, VA 22902
434-977-1600
FAX: 434-977-4466
CustMerDept@snl.com
http://www.snl.com

Virginia Needham, Editor
Reid Nagle, Publisher

Provides the information that thrift executives and investors require to stay on top of the industry. Available in print and electronic formats.
5 pages Daily Founded: 1987

5163 Scope
International Association of Commercial Collectors
4040 West
70th Street
Minneapolis, MN 55435
952-925-0760
FAX: 952-926-1624
iacc@commercialcollector.com
http://www.commercialcollector.com

Ted Smith, Executive Director
David Ward, President

Provides updates on developments in the industry, important legislative and legal issues, and IACC events and resources. Free to members only.
Monthly
Circulation: 350
Printed in on glossy stock

5164 Trade Vendor Quarterly
Blakeley & Blakeley
2030 Main Street Suite 210
Wells Fargo Tower
Irvine, CA 92614
949-260-0611
FAX: 949-260-0613
administrator@vendorland.com
http://www.vendorlaw.com

Scott Blakeley, Editor

Highlights developments in commercial, creditors' rights, e-commerce and bankruptcy law of interest to the credit and financial professional. Free online.
Quarterly

Magazines & Journals

5165 Affordable Housing Finance
Alexander & Edwards Publishing
111 Sutter Street
Suite 975
San Francisco, CA 94104-4547
415-315-1241
FAX: 415-315-1248 800-989-7255
ahf@housingfinance.com
http://www.housingfinance.com/

Andre Shashaty, Editor/Publisher
Susan Piel, Business Manager
Christine Serlin, Managing Editor
Michael Premsrirat, Circulation Manager

Offers practical information on obtaining debt and equality financing from federal, state, and local governments as well as private resources. In-depth coverage on the federal low-income housing tax credit program, tax-exempt bond financing, corporate tax credit investigation. *$83.00*
88 pages Monthly Founded: 1993
Circulation: 9000 9000 names $100 per M.
Printed in 4 colors on glossy stock

5166 American Bankruptcy Institute Journal
American Bankruptcy Institute
44 Canal Center Plaza
Suite 404
Alexandria, VA 22314
703-739-0800
FAX: 703-739-1060
marketing@abiworld.org
http://www.abiworld.org

Samuel J Gerdano, Publisher/Executive Director
Pat Noboa, Publications Fulfillment / Staff As
Melissa Lanning Trumpower, Director of Communication

Benefit to ABI members. Written by experts in the insolvency community, the Journal addresses timely issues involving consumer bankruptcy, the intersection of state laws and the Bankrupcy Code, valuation, turnaround management concerns, recent legislative developments, the US trustee system and more. Available in print or online. *$225.00*
1 Year 10 Issue Founded: 1982
Circulation: 10500 $200 per M.
Printed in 5 colors on matte stock

5167 Apartment Finance Today Magazine
Alexander & Edwards Publishing
111 Sutter Street
Suite 975
San Francisco, CA 94104-4547
415-151-1241
FAX: 415-315-1248 800-989-7255
aft@housingfinance.com
http://www.housingfinance.com

Andre Shashaty, Editor-in-chief
Christine Serlin, Managing Editor
Michael Premsrirat, Circulation Manager
Tom Borsellino, Ad Sales Director

AFT serves the apartment finance industry including apartment building owners, building/constructing property managers, developers, financial services, government agencies, consulting services, asset managers, legal/accounting, institutional investment, suppliers, manufacturers and other allied to the field. *$29.00*
80 pages Founded: 1995
Printed in 4 colors on glossy stock

5168 Business Credit
National Association of Credit Management
8840 Columbia 100 Parkway
Columbia, MD 21045-2107
410-740-5560
FAX: 410-740-5574
bcm@nacm.org http://www.nacm.org

Norma J Heim, Editor-in-Chief

For professionals responsible for extending credit and collecting receivables. Topics include business law, lein law, technology, credit management, collections, deductions, fraud, credit risk, credit scoring, outsourcing, information services, trade finance and more. *$54.00*
72 pages
Circulation: 32000
Printed in 4 colors on matte stock

5169 Card Technology
Thomson Financial Publishing
1 State Street Plaza
27th Floor
New York, NY 10004
212-825-8445
FAX: 212-843-9622 800-221-1809
custserv@thomsonmedia.com
http://www.tfn.com

Richard Harrington, President
Jose Thomas, Manager

Store-value cards, optical-memory cards, biometrics, cards on the Internet, cards for electronic data storage, and devices used with these cards in banking, government, telecommunications, transportation and education. *$98.00*
Monthly Founded: 1961
Circulation: 25000
Printed in 4 colors on glossy stock

5170 Collections & Credit Risk
Thomson Financial Publishing
1 State Street Plaza
27th Floor
New York, NY 10004
212-258-8445
FAX: 800- 23- 555 800-221-1809
custserv@sourcemedia.com
http://www.creditcollectionsworld.com

Catherine Ladwig, Editor
Jose Thomas, Manager

Focuses on news and trends of strategic and competitive importance to collections and credit policy executives. Covers the credit risk industry's growth, diversification and technology in both commercial and consumer credit. *$98.00*
66 pages Monthly Founded: 1996
Circulation: 25000

5171 Collector Magazine
ACA International
4040 W 70th Street
PO Box 390106
Minneapolis, MN 55439-106
952-926-6547
FAX: 952-926-1624
comm@acainternational.org
http://www.acainternational.org

Timothy Dressen, Editor
Gary D Rippentrop, CEO
Anne Rosso, Associate Editor

Read and circulated by more than 6,000 credit and collection professionals across the country and around the world, Collector brings you vital, up to the minute information on credit and collection industry trends, regulations and legislation each month. *$70.00*
Monthly

5172 Commercial Mortgage Insight
Zackin Publications
PO Box 2180
Waterbury, CT 06722-2180
203-755-0158
FAX: 203-755-3480 800-325-6745
info@cmi-online.com
http://www.cmi-online.com

Paul Zackin, Publisher
Joe Caton, Editor
June Han, Marketing

For desicion making executives in commercial mortgage banking and brokerage firms, commercial banks and community/savings institutions. Provides professionals with timely and comprehensive market news, trends and know-how needed to make informed decisions and choices. *$48.00*
32 pages Monthly Founded: 1997
Circulation: 18000 17505 names $100 per

M.
Printed in 4 colors

5173 **Credit & Financial Management Review**
Credit Research Foundation
8840 Columbia 100 Parkway
Columbia, MD 21045
410-740-5499
FAX: 410-740-4620
info@crfonline.org
http://www.crfonline.org

Rogelio Lara, Chief Financial Officer

Referred journal that publishes original material concerned with all aspects of credit, accounts receivable and customer financial relationships. It is devoted to the improvement and further development of the theory and practice of credit management. *$80.00*

56 pages Quarterly
Circulation: 3000
Printed in 2 colors

5174 **Credit Card Management**
Thomson Financial Publishing
1 State Street Plaza
27th Floor
New York, NY 10004
212-825-8445
FAX: 212-292-5216 800-221-1809
custserv@thomsonmedia.com
www.tfn.com

James Daly, Editor
Jose Thomas, Manager

Information on the major developments in the credit card industry. *$98.00*

74 pages Monthly
Circulation: 19000
Printed in 4 colors on glossy stock

5175 **Credit Professional**
Credit Professionals International
525 N Laclede Station Road
Suite B
Webster Groves, MO 63119
314-961-0031
FAX: 314-961-0040
creditpro@creditprofessionals.org
http://www.creditprofessionals.org
A bi-annual magazine published by Credit Professionals International. *$15.00*

Bi-annually Founded: 1989
Circulation: 550

5176 **Credit Union Magazine**
Credit Union National Association
PO Box 431
Madison, WI 53701
608-314-4000
FAX: 608-231-4370 800-348-3646
bmerrick@cuna.com
http://www.cuna.org

Dick Ensweiler, Chairman
Bill Merrick, Managing editor
Kathy Kuehn, Manager Periodicals

The role and operations of modern credit unions. *$50.00*

100 pages Monthly
Circulation: 34401
Printed in 4 colors on glossy stock

5177 **Federal Credit Union Magazine**
National Association of Federal Credit Unions
3138 N 10th Street
Suite 300
Arlington, VA 22201-2149
703-522-4770
FAX: 703-524-1082 800-336-4644
jbruce@nafcu.org
http://www.nafcu.org

Jerome Bruce, Exhibits/Advertising
Fred Becker, President /CEO

Written for CEO's, senior staff and volunteers of Federal Credit Unions. Offers legislative and regulatory news, as well as technology and operational issues. Call for rates.

50 pages Founded: 1967
Circulation: 1500
Printed in 4 colors on glossy stock

5178 **Financial Manager for the Media Professional**
Broadcast Cable Financial Management Association
550 Frontage Road
Suite 3600
Northfield, IL 60093
847-960-0200
FAX: 847-716-7004
sschley@bcfm.com
http://www.bcfm.com

Stewart Schley, Editor
Mary Collins, CEO/President

Feaures issues, trends, ideas and information about broadcast and cable finance, taxation, personnel, credit/collections, management and automation. Paid subscriptions available, or free with membership. *$69.00*

40 pages
Circulation: 2500

5179 **Inside B&C Lending**
Inside Mortgage Finance Publishers
7910 Woodmont Avenue
Suite 1010
Bethesda, MD 20814
301-951-1240
FAX: 301-915-0143
ibcl@imfpubs.com
http://www.imfpubs.com/

Andrew Analore, Editor
Guy Cecala, Publisher

Covers this dynamic market of lending thoroughly and exclusively with less than perfect credit with news, analysis and truly useful market intelligence. *$763.00*

14 pages Founded: 1984
Circulation: 1000 1,150 names
Printed in 2 colors on matte stock

5180 **MBA Uplink**
Mortgage Bankers Association of America
1919 Pennsylvania Avenue NW
Washington, DC 20006-3438
202-557-2700
FAX: 202-721-0167 800-793-6222
mbanewslink@mbaa.org
http://www.mbaa.org

Jonathan L. Kempner, President
Cheryl Crispen, VP.Marketing

Learn the latest residential, commercial, and multifamily real estate finance news. Hear what's happening at our association, free to members only. Electronic format.

Daily Founded: 1914
Circulation: 20000 2,800 names $100 per M.
Printed in 4 colors on glossy stock

5181 **Mortgage Banking**
Mortgage Bankers Association of America (MBA)
1919 Pennsylvania Avenue NW
Washington, DC 20006-3404
202-557-2700
FAX: 202-721-0198 800-348-8653
janet_hewitt@mbaa.org
http://www.mortgagebankingmagazine.com

Janet Hewitt, Editor

Provides in-depth coverage of the real estate finance industry. Itelligent analysis of news and the most important issues and trends affecting the industry. Association discount available. *$69.95*

120 pages Monthly Founded: 1939
Circulation: 6000 2800 names $100 per M.
Printed in 4 colors on glossy stock

5182 **News & Views**
Advertising Media Credit Executives Association
8840 Columbia 100 Parkway
Columbia, MD 21045-2158
410-992-7609
FAX: 410-740-5574
amcea@amcea.org
http://www.amcea.org

Charles Wilson, President
Kay Rice, VP

A quarterly magazine published by Advertising Media Credit Executives Association International.

Quarterly Founded: 1953
Circulation: 400

5183 **RMA Journal**
Risk Management Association
One Liberty Place
1650 Market Street, Suite 2300
Philadelphia, PA 19103
215-446-4000
FAX: 215-446-4101 800-677-7621
customers@rmahq.org
http://www.rmahq.org

Beverly Foster, Publisher
Marla Katz, Marketing Media Coor
Maurice H. Hartigan II, President/CEO
Valerie Morris, Marketing Director

Journal coverage spans the gamut of risk management issues from credit operations, problem loans and workouts, small business lending, loan training and loan management to analyzing customer profitability, risk management, loan pricing, lender compensation, and the effect of reengineering. Discount on subscription with membership. *$95.00*

Founded: 1918
Circulation: 23000
Printed in 4 colors on glossy stock

5184 **Secured Lender**
Commercial Finance Association
225 W 34th Street
Suite 1815
New York, NY 10122
212-594-3490
FAX: 212-564-6053
postmaster@cfa.com
http://www.cfa.com/

Bruce H Jones, Editor-in-Chief
Michele A Ocejo, Executive Editor
Michael D. Sharkey, Chairman
Jack R. Hoekstra, President
Joseph F. Nemia, Vice President

Provides in-depth reporting on federal and state legislation affecting the industry, legal notes on a wide range of issues, a full calandar year of industry workshops, meetings and seminars, personnel shifts, industry news and reviews of publications covering the industry. Discouned subscription rates for members. *$56.00*

Founded: 1944
Circulation: 27000
Printed in 4 colors on glossy stock

5185 **Transaction Trends**
Electronic Transaction Association
1101 16th Street N.W.
Suite 402
Washington, DC 20036
202-828-2635
FAX: 202-828-2639 800-695-5509
michelek@robstan.com
http://www.electran.org
Jeff Colchamiro, Editor
Drew MacFadyen, Advertising
Magazine for bankcard service providers who are actively engaged in providing a full range of services to qualified merchants. *$ 150.00*
50 pages Monthly Founded: 1990
Circulation: 1500
Printed in 4 colors on glossy stock

Trade Shows

5186 **American Bankruptcy Institute's Annual Spring Meeting**
American Bankruptcy Institute
44 Canal Center Plaza
Suite 404
Alexandria, VA 22314-5810
703-739-0800
FAX: 703-789-1060
jdannemiller@abiworld.org
www.abiworld.org
Samuel Gerdano, Executive Director
Meeting for the exchange of ideas and information on bankruptcy issues.
April

5187 **American Recovery Association Annual Convention**
PO Box 231565
New Orleans, LA 70183
504-738-6404
FAX: 504-738-7910
homeoffice@americanrecoveryassn.org
www.repo.org
Andrew T Hale, Executive Director
Over 10 exhibits of repossession and recovery industry equipment, telephones, computers, tow truck equipment, key machines and more.
250 Attendees August

5188 **Commercial Real Estate Finance & Multi-Fam ily Housing Conference**
Mortgage Bankers Association of America

1919 Pennsylvania Avenue NW
Washington, DC 20006-3438
202-557-2700
FAX: 202-721-0198 800-793-6222
Edward Callahan, Show Manager
Annual conference and exhibits for commercial real estate and multi-family housing professionals.
February

5189 **Credit Union Executive Society Annual Conv ention: CUES**
5510 Research Park Drive
Madison, WI 53711-5377
608-712-2664
FAX: 608-271-2303 800-252-2664
cues@cues.org www.cues.org
Fred Johnson, Chief Executive Officer
Offers a rainbow of marketing and technology topics, as well as a supplier showcase, geared toward board members.
June

5190 **Credit Union National Association Governmental Affairs Conference**
Credit Union National Association
5710 Mineral Point Road
Madison, WI 53705
608-231-4000
FAX: 608-231-4998 800-356-9655
dorothy@cuna.coop www.cuna.org
Daniel Mica, President
Annual conference held in Washington, DC, with a focus on legislative issues impacting credit unions.
February

5191 **Credit Union National Association Future Forum**
5710 Mineral Point Road
Madison, WI 53705-0
608-231-4000
FAX: 608-231-4263 800-356-9655
dorothy@cuna.coop www.cuna.org
Daniel Mica, President
Convention and annual general meeting with exhibit hall, educational sessions, and other events.
September

5192 **Defense Credit Union's Annual Conference**
Defense Credit Union Council
601 Pennsylvania Avenue NW
Suite 600
Washington, DC 20004
202-829-9110
FAX: 202-638-3410
dcuc1@cuna.com www.dcuc.org
Janet Sked, Conference Coordinator
Roland Arty Arteaga, President/CEO
Conference and exhibits of equipment, supplies and services for credit unions that serve Department of Defense personnel with problems peculiar to military installations and personnel.
200 Attendees August

5193 **Education Credit Union Council Annual Conference**
Education Credit Union Council
PO Box 7558
Spanish Fort, AL 36577-7558
251-626-3399
FAX: 251-626-3565 www.ecuc.org
Lorraine B Zerfas, Executive Director
Any CEOs, directors, committee members and top management active in the operations of any credit union that serves the educational community who want to achieve professional excellence should attend. Interact with peers from across the US serving the fields of education, introduce executive staff and managers to credit union ideas and philosophy on a national level and discuss issues important to your credit union in the coming year.
February

5194 **Finance, Credit & International Business Global Conference**
Finance, Credit & International Business
8840 Columbia 100 Parkway
Columbia, MD 21045-2158
410-423-1840
FAX: 410-423-1845 888-256-3242
fcib_info@fciglobal.com
www.fciglobal.com
Annual gathering of international credit and finance professionals draws upon the combined expertise of financial executives from all regions of the world to provide attendees with practical insight for managing in a rapidly evolving international environment.
November

5195 **Fleet/Lease Remarketing**
S&A Conferences Group
Fleet/Lease Remarketing 2002 Conference
1150 SE Maynard Road, Suite 210
Cary, NC 27511

FAX: 919-481-2658 800-608-7500
Shannon Smith, Contact
Executive conference focused on remarketing strategies for manufacturer, bank, finance, commercial and rental fleet/lease vehicles.
February

5196 **International Association of Commercial Collectors Annual Convention**
4040 W 70th Street
Minneapolis, MN 55435
952-925-0760
FAX: 952-926-1624
iacc@collector.com
www.commercialcollector.com
Jim Bessenbacher Jr, President
Ted M Smith, Executive Director
125 Attendees January Founded: 1970

5197 **Mortgage Bankers Association Annual Convention & Expo**
1919 Pennsylvania Avenue NW
Washington, DC 20006-3438
202-557-2700
FAX: 202-721-0246
membership@mortgagebankers.org
www.mortgagebankers.org
Jonathan L Kemper, President/CEO
Elaine Howard, VP Meetings/Conferences
Dan Thoms, VP
Brings members up to speed on industry trends and resources and encourages cooperative interaction among members.
2900 Attendees October Founded: 1918

5198 **National Association of Credit Management: Annual Credit Congress**
National Association of Credit Management
8840 Columbia 100 Parkway
Columbia, MD 21045
410-740-5560
FAX: 410-740-5574
conventions_info@nacm.org
www.nacm.org
Robin Schauseil, President
Jill Leimbach, Director Meetings
The event for the business credit and financial professional offering relevant, timely educational offerings, including industry specific programs, over 100 specialized service providers on the expo floor, showcasing the latest products and services, countless networking and relationship-building events to facilitate the sharing of knowlege and expertise.
2000 Attendees May/June

5199 **National Foundation for Credit Counseling Annual Leaders Conference**
801 Roeder Road
Suite 900
Silver Spring, MD 20910
301-589-5600
FAX: 301-576-2518 www.nfcc.org

Susan C Keating, President/CEO
Paul Weiss, Senior VP/CFO
William Binzel, Chief Counsel

Three-day conference to discuss credit counceling industry practices, trends and issues.

September Founded: 1951

5200 National Mortgage Servicing Conference
Mortgage Bankers Association of America
1919 Pennsylvania Avenue NW
Washington, DC 20006-3438
202-557-2700
FAX: 202-721-0198 800-793-6222

Edward Callahan, Show Manager

Annual conference and exhibits of equipment supplies and services for lending, pensions and mortgaging.

February

5201 National Technology in Mortgage Banking Conference
Mortgage Bankers Association of America
1919 Pennsylvania Avenue NW
Washington, DC 20006-3438
202-557-2700
FAX: 202-721-0198 800-793-6222

Edward Callahan, Show Manager

Annual conference and exhibits for those responsible for evaluating and implementing information systems for the mortgage banking industry.

March

5202 Risk Management Conference
Risk Management Association
1801 Market Street
Suite 300
Philadelphia, PA 19103
215-635-5398
FAX: 215-446-4101
jgermanotta@rmahg.org
www.rmahq.org

Jennifer Germanotta, Coordinator Events/Sponsors
Valerie Morris, Director Marketing
William F Githens, Director Member Relations

Educates and helps risk management professionals develop new techniques and learn about new innovative products at different stages of their careers. Mailing list available for exhibitors and sponsors only.

800 Attendees October

Directories & Databases

5203 American Recovery Association Directory
American Recovery Association
PO Box 231565
New Orleans, LA 70183-1565
504-738-6404
FAX: 504-738-7910
homeoffice@americanrecoveryassn.org
www.repo.org

Don Thornton, President
Paul Hallock, VP
Lloyd M Swor, Secretary/Treasurer

Contain's listings of ARA's members, offices and services. Available in hardcopy and electronic formats.

308 pages Annual Founded: 1965

5204 Banksearch Book
Sheshunoff Information Services
505 Barton Springs Road
Suite 1200
Austin, TX 78704
512-472-2244
FAX: 512-305-6575 800-456-2340
editorialqueries.sis@thomsonmedia.com
www.tfn.com

Offers information on savings and loans, savings banks and credit unions with assets over 10 million. Customized for your institutution type: bank thrift, bank holding company or credit union. You buy only the data you want — by state, region or nation. *$295.00*

Annual

5205 Business Products Credit Association
BCPA
607 Westridge Drive
O'Fallon, MO 63366
636-272-3005
FAX: 636-394-7099
service@bcpa.org www.bcpa.org

C David Schmucker, President/CEO

BPCA has a database of over 400,000 companies and their payment histories. This is available to members over the Internet.

5206 Callahan's Credit Union Directory
Callahan & Associates
1001 Connecticut Avenue NW
10th Floor
Washington, DC 20036
202-223-3920
FAX: 202-223-6098 800-446-7453

Catherine Hassinger, Publications
Charles Filson, President

This directory turns raw data into research, giving you the tools you need to keep up with the credit union industry. Access all the credit union information found in the print edition through the Online Edition on this website. In a special Users Area only for purchasers of the print edition, you can access updated finacials four times a year, conduct searches on key information and save those search results to return to over and over again. Real time updates directly from our database. *$135.00*

Annual

5207 Collection Agency Directory
First Detroit Corporation
PO Box 5025
Warren, MI 48090-5025
586-573-0045
FAX: 586-573-9219 800-366-5995
info@firstdetroit.com
www.firstdetroit.com

Albert W Scace, Publisher

Offers information and statistics on nearly 900 collection agencies throught the world. *$347.00*

301 pages Annual, Paperback Founded: 1991

Mailing list available for rent 11,000 names $150 per M.

Printed in 1 color on matte stock

5208 Credit
American Financial Services Association
919 18th Street NW
Washington, DC 20006-5503
202-296-5544
FAX: 202-223-0321
afsa@afsamail.org
www.afsaonline.org

Lee Westell, Director Publications

Focuses on breaking developments on legislative and regulatory issues on the federal and state levels, as well as consumer education initiatives, industry news, news inside AFSA and information on meetings and conferences. Free online access.

1500 pages Bi-Monthly 1500 names

5209 Credit Card and Check Fraud: A Stop-Loss Manual
Fraud & Theft Information Bureau
PO Box 400
Boynton Beach, FL 33425-4011
561-323-3653
FAX: 561-737-5800
sales@fraudandtheftinfo.com
fraudandtheftinfo.com

Larry Schwartz, President/Publisher

Inside information on how the FBI, Secret Service, police, attorneys general, distric attorneys, US Postal Inspection Service work with businesses to identify credit card and check thieves and counterfeiters. Instructions for every business to prevent fraud and changeback losses. *$199.95*

300 pages Founded: 1982

5210 Credit Union Attorneys Legal Directory
Legal Directory
PO Box 1967
Montgomery, AL 36102-1967
334-265-8551
FAX: 334-261-3489 800-448-0461

George B Azar, President

Information is offered on attorneys and lawyers who represent credit unions or are willing to do so. *$70.00*

265 pages Annual
Circulation: 8,500

5211 Credit Union Cooperatives
Callahan & Associates
1001 Connecticut Avenue NW
10th Floor
Washington, DC 20036
202-223-3920
FAX: 202-223-6098 800-446-7453

Catherine Hassinger, Publications
Charles Filson, President

Your source for information on credit union service organizations (CUSOs) and other cooperative providers to the credit industry. The directory has up-to-date contact names, addresses and phone numbers for more than 700 CUSOs and their associated credit unions. Use this publication to compare services offered by CUSOs or if you're looking to start or expand an existing CUSO. *$165.00*

5212 Credit Union Directory
National Credit Union Administration
1775 Duke Street
Alexandria, VA 22314
703-518-6300
FAX: 703-518-6319 www.ncua.gov

Federal credit and state-chartered credit unions are the focal point of this directory. Free online.

Annual

5213 Credit Union Financial Yearbook
Callahan & Associates
1001 Connecticut Avenue NW
10th Floor
Washington, DC 20036
202-223-3920
FAX: 202-223-6098 800-446-7453

Catherine Hassinger, Publications

Each quarter Callahan publishes a comprehensive study on the state of the industry that includes detailed financials for all credit unions over $50 million. The third quarter edition is published in 3 volumes based on asset size. Fourth quarter edition is based on total assets for the year. Asset sizes considered are $50 to $100 million, $100 - $250 million and over $250 million. *$565.00*
Complete Year Price

5214 **DRI Financial and Credit Statistics**
DRI/McGraw-Hill
24 Hartwell Avenue
Lexington, MA 02421-3158
781-863-5100

This database contains over 25,000 financial time series, including releases of the Federal Reserve and the US Department of the Treasury.

5215 **Defense Credit Union Directory**
Defense Credit Union Council
601 Pennsylvania Avenue NW
Suite 600
Washington, DC 20004-2601
202-829-9110
FAX: 202-638-3410
dcuc1@cuna.com www.dcuc.org
Roland Arteaga, President/CEO
Listing of about 360 credit unions with membership consisting wholly or partly of the military and civilian personnel of the United States and worldwide. *$150.00*
60 pages Biennial

5216 **Dun's Credit Guide**
Dun & Bradstreet Information Service
1 Diamond Hill Road
New Providence, NJ 07974-1218
908-665-5000
FAX: 908-665-5803 800-362-3425
Providing a dollar-specific credit guideline on manufacturers, wholesalers and retailers, this database is updated continuously for the interested business person.

5217 **National Credit Union Administration Directory**
National Credit Union Administration
1775 Duke Street
Alexandria, VA 22314
703-518-6300
FAX: 703-518-6319 www.ncua.gov
JoAnn Johnson, Chairperson
J Leonard Skiles, Executive Director
Chrisanthy J Loizos, Director Equal Opportunity Programs
Directory of credit unions governed by a three member board appointed by the President and confirmed by the US Senate, by the independent federal agency that charters and supervises federal credit unions. NCUA, with the backing of the full faith and credit of the US government, operates the National Credit Union Share Insurance Fund, insuring the savings of 80 million account holders in all federal credit unions and many state chartered credit unions.

5218 **Thomson Credit Union Directory**
Thomson Financial Publishing
4709 Golf Road
6th Floor
Skokie, IL 60076-1231
847-778-8037
FAX: 847-933-8101 800-321-3373
Glenn Gottfried, Chief Operating Officer
Sarah Frazer, Product Manager
Semi-annual directory that includes valuable industry statistics, a quick telephone lookup index of all credit unions and a resource guide featuring vendors within the credit union marketplace. Includes over 12,500 major credit unions and 5,500 branches, with asset rankings, membership totals and more. Published in partnership with the Credit Union National Association. *$199.00*
January/July ISBN 1-563103-24-9 : Paperback

5219 **Who's Who in Credit and Financial Management**
New York Credit and Financial Management Assn
520 8th Avenue
New York, NY 10018-6507
212-695-4807

Directory of services and supplies to the industry.
100 pages Annual

5220 **World Council of Credit Unions Directory**
World Council of Credit Unions
PO Box 2982
Madison, WI 53701-2982
608-231-7130
FAX: 608-238-8020
Lists over 100 World Council of Credit Union leaders and member organizations in each of seven confederations. African, Asian, Australian, Canadian, Caribbean, Latin-American and the United States.

Industry Web Sites

5221 **www.aacul.org**
American Association of Credit Union Leagues

Voluntary membership association for credit union leagues that are members of the Credit Union National Association. AACUL provides representation, products, services and programs to its members.

5222 **www.abiworld.org**
American Bankruptcy Institute

ABI is the largest multi-diciplinary, non-partisan organization dedicated to research and education on matters related to insolvency. The ABI membership provides a forum for the exchange of ideas and information. ABI is engaged in numerous educational and research activities, as well as the production of a number of publications both for the insolvency practitioner and the public.

5223 **www.afsaonline.com**
American Financial Services Association

National trade association for market funded providers of financial services to consumers and small businesses. These providers offer an array of finacial services, including unsecured personal loans, automobile loans, home equity loans and credit cards through specialized bank institutions.

5224 **www.amcea.org**
Advertising Media Credit Executives Association

Improving the professionalism, principles, understanding and techniques of media credit management by encouraging the exchange of ideas, methods and procedures within the membership. Providing additional education and training in the business fundamentals of media credit and credit policies and in the related areas of finance, accounting, law and economics for the purpose of enhancing the career development of members.

5225 **www.bccacredit.com**
Broadcast Cable Credit Association

Subsidiary of the Broadcast Cable Financial Management Association. BCCA provides industry specific credit reports on individual agencies, advertisers, or buying services (national and local). These reports may be obtained upon request online, phone or fax. It's mission is to provide tools and services that will allow our members to perform their functions to the best of their abilities, and help them achieve a profitable bottom-line.

5226 **www.bcpa.org**
Business Products Credit Association

Nonprofit trade association for credit personnel of manufacturers, wholesalers and factors. BPCA has credit groups based on the channel you sell. The national credit group consists of discount stores, superstores, commercial stationers, printing and publications, business machines, computer peripherals and software, plus mass merchandisers. In addition, BPCA has the following industry specific groups: school supply, janitorial and sanitary supplies, fine pen and promotional products.

5227 **www.cdiaonline.org**
Consumer Data Industry Association

Trade association representing consumer information companies that provide fraud prevention and risk management products, credit and mortgage reports, tenant and employment screening services, check fraud and verifacation services and collection services. Sets industry standards and provides education for it's members. Provides educational materials for consumers regarding their credit rights and how consumer credit reporting agencies can better serve their needs.

5228 **www.cfa.com**
Commercial Finance Association

Trade group of the asset-based financial services industry, with members throughout the US, Canada and around the world. Members include the asset-based lending arms of domestic and foreign commercial banks, small and large independent finance companies, floor plan financing organizations, factoring organizations and financing subsidiaries of major industrial corporations.

5229 **www.collector.com**
American Collectors Association

International trade organization of credit and collection professionals that provides a variety of accounts recievable management services to over 1,000,000 credit grantors.

5230 **www.commercialcollector.com**
International Association of Commercial Collectors

International trade association comprised of more than 200 collection specialists and 140 commercial attorneys, with members throughout the US and in 38 international countries. IACC's mission is to promote the commercial collection profession by providing IACC members with the resources to excel in the industry.

5231 **www.consumerdebtcounseling.org**
CDC Consumer Debt Counseling

Nonprofit provider of quality, face-to-face and telephone debt counseling education.

5232 **www.creditunions.com**
Callahan & Associates

National credit union research and consulting firm specializing in financial publications and analysis software, strategic planning and investment management. Callahan's goal is to help credit unions position themselves at the leading edge of the ever changing financial service industry.

5233 **www.crfonline.org**
Credit Research Foundation

Independent, member run organization, consisting of a dynamic community of like minded business professionals with a vested interest in improving and fostering the field of business credit — more specifically, the practices and technologies of business credit. CRF is your industry advocate, the bridge in the consumer financial relationship. With our variety of member benefits, we're here to provide help to the real problems and challenges your business faces every day.

5234 **www.cues.org**
Credit Union Executives Society

For credit union executives. Our mission is to advance the professional development of credit union CEOs, senior management and directors.

5235 **www.cuna.org**
Credit Union National Association

With its network of affiliated state credit union leagues, CUNA serves more than 90 percent of America's 10,000 credit unions, wich are owned by more than 83 million consumer members. Based in Washington, DC and Madison, Wisconsin, this nonprofit trade group is governed by volunteer directors who are elected by their credit union peers.

5236 **www.ecuc.org**
Education Credit Union Council

Dedicated to providing educational and networking opportunities to credit unions who serve educational communities. Whether educators compose the majority or a small segment of your membership, you will benefit from the exchange of ideas offered by our ECUC members. Any group involved in the field of education — teachers, administrators, students, support staff and others constitute the educational community.

5237 **www.electran.org**
Electronic Transaction Association

International trade association serving the needs of organizations offering transaction processing products and services.

5238 **www.fcibglobal.com**
Executives Finace, Credit & International Business

Provider of products and services to many small, medium and large size exporters as well as major multinational corporations in 30 countries around the world. Its international dimension, superior products and services enable international professionals to achieve business objectives, professional growth, recognition and prosperity.

5239 **www.firstent.org**
First Entertainment Credit Union

Nonprofit institution is the financial resource for the entertainment community. Profits after operating expenses, are returned directly to members in the form of high dividend rates, low loan rates, and reduced fees for services. FECU serves more than 700 entertainment based companies with more than $34O million in assets.

5240 **www.fraudandtheftinfo.com**
Fraud & Theft Information Bureau

Provides problem solving, crime prevention, money saving manuals and fraud blocker databases.

5241 **www.greyhouse.com**
Grey House Publishing

Selected Grey House directories in the fields of business, health and education are available online. Users can search our online databases by several different search criteria, such as product categories, geographic area, sales volume and much, much more. Full Grey House catalog and online ordering also available.

5242 **www.mbaa.org**
Mortgage Bankers Association of America

Representing the real estate finance industry, MBA serves its membership by representing their legislative and regulatory interests before the US Congress and federal agencies; by meeting their educational needs through programs and a range of periodicals and publications; and by supporting their business interests with a variety of research initiatives and other products and services.

5243 **www.nacm.org**
National Association of Credit Management

Assures good laws for sound credit. Promotes honest and fair dealings in credit transactions, fosters and encourages research in the field of credit.

5244 **www.nfcc.org**
National Foundation for Credit Counceling

National nonprofit credit counseling oranization with 1,200 offices helping 1.5 million households annually. Identify NFCC members (Consumer Credit Counseling Service CCCS) by the NFCC member seal representing high standards, free and low-cost confidential services.

5245 **www.nuca.gov**
National Credit Union Administration

Governed by a three-member board appointed by the President and confirmed by the US Senate, this is the independent federal agency that charters and supervises the nation's federal credit unions. Operates the National Credit Union Share Insurance Fund, insuring the savings of 80 million account holders and many state chartered credit unions.

5246 **www.repo.org**
American Recovery Association

Approximately 500 offices throughout the US, Canada and Germany, providing repossesion services around the world.

5247 **www.rmahg.org**
Risk Management Association

Finacial services association champions best practices in risk management while also monitoring emerging trends. Our strong relationship with members and regulators helps us develop new risk management techniques, innovative products, and education and training programs geared to risk management professionals at different stages of their careers.

Associations

5248 Advertising Mail Marketing Association
Advertising Mail Marketing Association
1333 F Street NW
Suite 710
Washington, DC 20004-1108
202-347-0055
FAX: 202-347-0789
chadr@amma.org www.amma.org
Gene A DelPolito, Publisher
Chad W Robbins, Editor
For those who use mail for fundraising or business purposes.
Founded: 1947

5249 American Marketing Association
311 S Wacker Drive
Suite 5800
Chicago, IL 60606
312-542-9000
FAX: 312-542-9001 800-262-1150
info@ama.org
www.marketingpower.com
Dennis Dunlap, Chief Executive Officer
An association for marketers with members worldwide in every area of marketing.
38000 Members

5250 American Mobile Telecommunications
1150 18th Street NW
Suite 250
Washington, DC 20036
202-835-7819
FAX: 202-331-9062
online@amtausa.org
www.amtausa.org
Alan R Shark, President/CEO
Elizabeth R Sachs, General Counsel
Joe Vestal, Chairman
Mark Abrams, Vice Chairman
Ralph Haller, Secretary
Membership is made up of operators on the 220 MHz, 450 MHz, 800 MHz and 900 MHz bands, as well as product and service providers for the industry. Many members are exploring other areas of the mobile telecommunications industry — digital SMR, Personal Communications Services, data communications, mobile satellite, cable telephony and international wireless interests. AMTA is working with its members and with government to insure that these areas can be pursued successfully.
400 Members Founded: 1985

5251 American Teleservices Association
3815 River Crossing Parkway
Suite 20
Indianapolis, IN 46240
317-816-9336
FAX: 317-218-0323 877-779-3974
contact@ataconnect.org
www.ataconnect.org
Tim Searcy, Chief Executive Officer
Represents the call centers, trainers, consultants and equipment suppliers that initiate, facilitate and generate telephone, Internet and e-mail sales, service and support.
240 Members

5252 Art Directors Annual
Art Directors Club
106 W 29th Street
New York, NY 10001
212-643-1440
FAX: 212-643-4293
info@adcglobal.org
www.adcglobal.org
Emily Warren, Editor
Myrna Davis, Executive Director
The work featured in these pages is nothing less than the year's most innovative in the fields of advertising, design, publishing, photography, illustration, film, video, and interactive media. The 83rd Annual marks the introduction of the Multi-Channel hybrid media campaign category, as well as continuing to represent student work submitted at a professional caliber.
$65.00
520 Members
Circulation: 7,000
Mailing list available for rent

5253 Art Directors Club
106 W 29th Street
New York, NY 10001
212-643-1440
FAX: 212-643-4293
info@adcglobal.org
www.adcglobal.org
Robert Greenberg, President
Jon Kamen, VP
Vickie Peslak, Second VP
Thomas Mueller, Secretary
Myrna Davis, Executive Director
An international nonprofit organization of leading creatives in advertising, graphic design, interactive media, broadcast design, typography, packaging, environmental design, photography, illustration and related disciplines.
1200 Members Founded: 1920
Mailing list available for rent

5254 Association of Direct Marketing Agencies
Cohn & Wells
350 Hudson Street
New York, NY 10014-4504
212-192-2278
FAX: 212-973-1789
jwpgroup@aol.com
www.cyberdirect.com/ADMA
John A Greco Jr, President/CEO
Members are direct response advertising agencies.
100 Members

5255 Color Marketing Group
5845 Richmond Highway #410
Alexandria, VA 22303
703-329-8500
FAX: 703-329-0155
cmg@colormarketing.org
www.colormarketing.org
Kathleen Conroy, Executive Director
Amy Larrabee, Manager/Communications
Jaime Stephens, Director/Conferences
A nonprofit international association of color designers involved in the use of color as it applies to the profitable marketing of goods and services.
1300 Members Founded: 1962

5256 Digital Concepts for Business
1301 Pyott Road
Suite 102
Lake in the Hills, IL 60156
847-458-5129
FAX: 847-458-5134
info@dcfb.com www.dcfb.com
Mary Owens, Owner
Provides services to companies throughout the US and is dedicated to providing high-quality business communcations solutions using the latest hardware and software for both PC and Macintosh.

5257 Direct International
1501 3rd Avenue
New York, NY 10028-2101
212-861-4188
FAX: 212-986-3757
Alfred Goodloe, President
Offers publications and services for the international direct marketing executive.

5258 Direct Marketing Association
1120 Avenue of the Americas
New York, NY 10036-6700
212-768-7277
FAX: 212-398-6725
lrc@the-dma.org www.the-dma.org
Markus Wilhelm, Chairman
Donn Rappaport, Vice Chairman
Kelly B Browning, Treasurer
Arun Sinha, Secretary
John A Greco, Jr, President/CEO
For businesses interested in direct, database and interactive global marketing, with about 4,700 member companies from the US and 53 foreign nations on six continents. Members include catalog companies, direct mailers, teleservices firms, Internet marketers and other at-distance marketers from every consumer and business-to-business segment, both commercial and nonprofit as well as companies that provide supplies and services to marketers.
3.5M Members Founded: 1917

5259 Direct Selling Association
1667 K St NW
Ste 1100
Washington, DC 20006-1660
202-452-8866
FAX: 202-452-9010
info@dsa.org www.dsa.org
Brian C Connolly, Chairman
Douglas L DeVos, Vice Chairman
Neil H Offen, President
John A Addison Jr, Director
Mark Bosworth, Director
National trade of the leading firms that manufacture and distribute goods and services sold directly to consumers. More than 150 companies are members of the association, including many well-known brand names. The association's mission is to protect, serve and promote the effectiveness of member companies and the independent business people they represent.
Founded: 1973

5260 Directo-Direct Marketing Association Council for Hispanic Marketing
Direct Marketing Association
1120 Avenue of the Americas
New York, NY 10036-6700
212-768-7277
FAX: 212-768-6714

Allison Longley, Manager

Provides education, information and networking opportunities for direct marketing professionals targeting the Hispanic market.

120 Members Founded: 1992

5261 EMarketing Association
5600 Post Road #114-312
East Greenwich, RI 02818
401-884-0614
FAX: 408-884-2461
admin@emarketingassociation.com
www.emarketingassociation.com

Robert Fleming, President
Alan Brown, VP
John Hastings, VP
Linda Jaffe, VP

An international association of emarketing professionals. Members include government, companies, professionals and students involved with the emarketing arena.

5262 Mail Advertising Service Association
1421 Prince Street
Suite 410
Alexandria, VA 22314
703-519-0801
FAX: 703-548-8204
mfsa-mail@mfsanet.org
www.masa.org

James E Pinkin, Chairman
Charles G Klasek, Vice Chairman
John Rafner, Second Vice Chairman
C Scott Schuh, Treasurer

Supports all those involved in the mailing, addressing, and inserting industries.

5263 Mailing & Fulfillment Service Association
1421 Prince Street
Alexandria, VA 22314
703-836-9200
FAX: 703-548-8204 800-333-6272
daweaver@mfsanet.org
www.mfsanet.org

David Weaver, President
Eric Casey, VP
Leo Raymond, Director Postal Affairs
Anita Shelton, Administrative Secretary
Ruth M Clark, Manager Accounting

80-year-old trade association which provides education/training, information, surveys and industry representation for companies which offer 3rd party mailing and fulfillment services.

750 Members Founded: 1920

5264 Midwest Direct Marketing Association
4248 Park Glen Road
Minneapolis, MN 55416-4775
952-928-4643
FAX: 952-929-1318
mdma@mdma.org www.mdma.org

Lisa Ferrier, Executive Director
Dennis Bell, President
Ed Harrington, Manager

Advancing the professional and ethical practice of direct response marketing by members throughout the Upper Midwest. The MDMA seeks to accomplish this by sponsoring educational and professional networking events to share and encourage the best practices in telemarketing, direct mail and online marketing techniques and strategies.

725 Members Founded: 1960

5265 National Mail Order Association
2807 Polk St NE
Minneapolis, MN 55418
612-788-1673
FAX: 612-788-1147
info@nmoa.org www.nmoa.org

John D Schulte, Chairman, Editor
Dan Argenas, Director Marketing Services
Ken Boone, President
Peter Candito, President Database Marketing

Offers the strongest and lowest cost means for people to come together for the purpose of conducting business and creating sales. Small to medium-sized organizations come for education, information, ideas, resources and new contacts.

4M Members Founded: 1972

5266 New England Direct Marketing Association
354 Washington Street
Suite 223
Wellesley Hills, MA 02481
781-237-1366
FAX: 781-431-8118
info@nedma.com www.nedma.com

Alexander Macaaron, President
Tom Tringale, VP
Dennis Driscoll, Treasurer
Craig Blake, Secretary
Beth Drysdale, Executive Director

Regional, professional association for all those interested in direct marketing. Membership is composed of leading area companies that use direct marketing, direct marketing agencies, independent professionals, educators and students.

5267 Rocky Mountain Direct Marketing Association
PO Box 620822
Littleton, CO 80162
303-914-8407
FAX: 720-922-9414 www.rmdma.org

Sandi Rhynard, Executive Director
Carol DeVita, Coordinator

To provide direct marketing users and suppliers in the rocky mountain region with the resources needed to achieve bottom line results.

5268 Society of Publication Designers
17 East 47th Street
Floor 6
New York, NY 10017
212-223-3332
FAX: 212-223-5880
mail@spd.org www.spd.org

Jennifer Crandall, Chair

The society encourages artistic excellence by judging annually the work of thousands of design professionals in the United States and abroad.

5269 Women In Direct Marketing International
224 7th Street
Garden City, NY 11530-5781
516-746-6700

Seeks to advance the interests and influence of women in the direct response industry.

600 Members Founded: 1970

5270 World Federation of Direct Selling
1666 K Street NW
Suite 110
Washington, DC 20006
202-452-9010
FAX: 202-347-0055
info@wfdsa.org www.wfdsa.org

Offers worldwide supports to all those involved in the direct selling industry. WFDS is a non-governmental, voluntary organization representing direct selling associations.

5271 Writers Research Group LLC
8801 S Kentucky Avenue
Oklahoma City, OK 73159
405-681-5074
FAX: 405-685-3390
info@writersresearchgroup.com
www.writersresearchgroup.com

Karen Tingle, Executive Director
Lori Packwood, Executive Director

Writers Research Group is a professional writing and research firm. Our knowledgeable employees gather, examine, edit, and compile data to your company's specifications. Our services include research, writing, directory listing updates and new entries, indexing, copyediting, proofreading, data entry, document markup and permissions negotiations.

Newsletters

5272 Business Marketing Notepad
Direct Marketing Publishers
1304 University Drive
Yardley, PA 19067-2829
215-321-3068
FAX: 215-321-9647 800-663-8387
info@dmpublishers.com
http://www.dmpublishers.com

Bernie Goldberg, Editor
Bernie Goldberg, Publisher

Techniques and relevent pointers about how to improve business-to-business selling, lead generation and telephone sales. *$69.00*

Founded: 1987

5273 CC Ideas
Communication Concepts
508 Millstone Drive
Beavercreek, OH 45434
937-426-8600

http://www.communication-concepts.com/

Rodger Southworth, President/CEO

Covers direct marketing and direct mail trends.

4 Issues

5274 DMA List Readers Basic Training
Direct Marketing Association
1120 Avenue of the Americas
14th Floor
New York, NY 10036-6700
212-768-7277
FAX: 212-302-6714
customerservice@the-dma.org
http://www.the-dma.org

John A Greco Jr, Chief Executive Officer
Allison Longley, Manager

Information and practical introductory training for new professionals in the direct marketing list industry.

Founded: 1917

5275 DMAW Marketing Events
Direct Marketing Association
1120 Avenue of the Americas
New York, NY 10036-6700
212-768-7277
FAX: 212-302-6714
customerservice@the-dma.org
http://www.the-dma.org
John Jay Daly, Publisher
John A Greco Jr, Chief Executive Officer

Newsletter for members of the Direct Marketing Association of Washington.
Founded: 1917

5276 Direct Line
Direct Marketing Association
11 W 42nd Street
New York, NY 10036-8002
212-391-9683
FAX: 212-768-4546
A membership newsletter of the Direct Marketing Association offering information to industry professionals.
Monthly

5277 Direct Mail
North American Publishing Company
401 N Broad Street
Philadelphia, PA 19108-1001
215-238-5300
FAX: 215-238-5270
www.insidedirectmail.com
Peggy Hatch, Publisher
Hailie Mummet, Editor
Analyzes direct mail pieces mailed in the United States. Has archives that can be accessed for samples of over 100,000 mailing pieces. *$195.00*
32 pages Monthly
Printed in 4 colors on matte stock

5278 Direct Marketing Hints and Secrets
Bookfinders General
145 E 27th Street
New York, NY 10016
212-689-0772
FAX: 212-481-0552
Martin Gross, Editor
John A Greco Jr, Chief Executive Officer

Direct marketing strategy, tactics, and techniques. *$150.00*
Monthly Founded: 1994

5279 Direct Marketing Success Letter
Nicholas Direct
2454 McMullen Booth Road
Building C
Clearwater, FL 33759
727-260-0763
FAX: 727-726-2140 800-237-2721
Bethany Waller, Editor/Publisher
marketing strategies: writing powerful copy, preparing sales letters, space ads and media buying. *$177.00*
Monthly

5280 Direct Response
Creative Direct Marketing Group3
2360 Plaza Del Amo
Suite 105
Torrance, CA 90501
310-125-5727
FAX: 310-212-5773
cdmg@cdmginc.com
http://www.directmarketingcenter.net
Craig Huey, President/Publisher
Kent Komae, Editor
Direct marketing information. *$79.00*
Monthly

5281 Direct Selling Association International Bulletin
World Federation of Direct Selling Association
1667 K St Nw
Ste 1100
Washington, DC 20006-1660
202-452-8866
FAX: 202-452-9010 info@wfdsa.org
Neil Offen, Editor
Association activities, legislation affecting direct selling and trends.

Circulation: 1200

5282 Direction
Direct Marketing Consultants
705 Franklin Tpke
Allendale, NJ 07401-1637
201-327-9213

Hugh P Curley, Publisher
'How to' information on motivating buying decisions via more creative use of direct mail, sales promotion, newsletters, and other marketing tools. *$40.00*

Circulation: 3800

5283 Fred Goss' What's Working in Direct Marketing
United Communications Group
11300 Rockville Pike
Ste. 1100
Rockville, MD 20852-3030
301-287-2700
FAX: 301-816-8945
http://www.ucg.com/
Fred Goss, Editor/Publisher
Brian Crotty, President
Direct response marketing-all forms. *$242.00*
Founded: 1977

5284 Friday Report
Hoke Communications
224 7th Street
Garden City, NY 11530-5771
516-746-6700
FAX: 516-294-8141 800-229-6700
dmmagazine@aol.com
http://www.directmarketingmag.com
Henry R Hoke, Publisher
Joseph D Gatti, Editor
Stuart W Boysen, President/Circulation Man
Edson Georges, Mailing Systems Manager
Weekly newsletter of direct marketing. *$165.00*
8 pages Weekly Founded: 1951

5285 General Encouragement, Motivation and Inspirational Handbook
Economics Press
12 Daniel Road
Fairfield, NJ 07004-2565
973-227-1224
FAX: 973-227-3558
info@epinc.com
http://www.epinc.com
Allan Yahalen, President
Rob Gilbert, Editor *$20.00*
24 pages Monthly
Circulation: 200000 200,000 names
Printed in 4 colors on matte stock

5286 Inside Mail Order
Mellinger Company
PO Box 956
Santa Clarita, CA 91380-9056
661-259-2303
FAX: 805-257-4840
mell@tradezone.com
www.tradezone.com
BL Mellinger III, Publisher
A newsletter offering the latest information to businesses on marketing and advertising through direct mail.

5287 Mail Order Digest & Washington Newsletter
National Mail Order Association
2807 Polk Street NE
Minneapolis, MN 55418-2954
612-788-1673
FAX: 612-788-1147
editor@nmoa.org
http://www.nmoa.org
John D Schulte, President
J Bradley, Editor
Paul Muchnick, Founder Director
Contains information of interest to small to midsize mail marketers including new products available, money saving techniques, industry contacts, help for beginners, new concepts for mail order selling, and postal changes and regulations. *$99.00*

Monthly Founded: 1972
Circulation: 7000

5288 Memo to Mailers
US Postal Service
475 Lenfant Plaza SW
Room 10523
Washington, DC 20260
202-268-2900
FAX: 202-268-5211 800-275-8777
mmailers@usps.com
http://www.usps.com
Jon Leonard, Editor
Carries information and news about the Postal Service as well as value added information about using the mail effectively and efficiently. Also offers information to mail center managers on ways to cut costs.
8 pages Daily
Circulation: 100000

5289 Nonprofit Mailers Foundation
125 Michigan Avenue NE
#239
Washington, DC 20017-1004
202-628-4380

Esther Huggins, Manager
Promotes welfare of groups using nonprofit mail rates for communications and fundraising.
600 pages Founded: 1982

5290 PD&D Direct Mail List
Chilton Way
Radnor, PA 19089-0001

This list is a proven response vehicle for product promotion, seminar announcements and trade show promotions.

5291 TeleResponse
InfoCision Management
325 Springside Drive
Akron, OH 44333-4504
330-668-1400
FAX: 330-668-1407

Jerry Harris, Editor

Specializes in making outbound sales calls for the infomercial, catalog and direct marketing industries.

5292 Telemarketing Update
Prosperity & Profits Unlimited
PO Box 416
Denver, CO 80201-0416
303-573-5564

AC Doyle, Publisher

Telemarketing script presentation suggestions and ideas. *$200.00*

8 pages Annual
Circulation: 2,000
Printed in on matte stock

5293 Telemarketing Update-Catering Service Business Script Presentations
Prosperity & Profits Unlimited
PO Box 416
Denver, CO 80201-0416
303-573-5564

A Doyle, Editor

Catering service telemarketing script presentations. *$21.95*

10 pages Annual Founded: 1992
Circulation: 2,100 Audited
Printed in 1 color on matte stock

5294 Telephone Selling Report
Business By Phone
13254 Stevens Street
Omaha, NE 68137-1728
402-455-1111
FAX: 402-896-3353 800-326-7721
arts@businessbyphone.com
www.businessbyphone.com

Art Sobczak, Production Manager

For businesses that use the phone to prospect, service and sell. How-to information on getting through screens; creating interest-grabbing openings; closes that work; overcoming tough objections; and beating call reluctance. Accepts advertising inserts. *$109.00*

8 pages Monthly
Mailing list available for rent 2M names
Printed in 2 colors

5295 Venture Views & News
Venture Communications
60 Madison Avenue
New York, NY 10010-1600
212-684-4800
FAX: 212-576-1129
sales@ven.com
http://www.venturedirect.com

Rachel Krasny, Editor
Richard Baumer, CEO/President
Neal Mandel, Group Division Sales Mana

News and practical advice in the field of direct response marketing.

Weekly Founded: 1983

5296 What's Working in DM and Fulfillment
United Communications Group
11300 Rockville Pike
Suite 1100
Rockville, MD 20852-3030
301-816-8950
FAX: 301-816-8945 800-929-4824
webmaster@ucg.com
http://www.ucg.com/

Barbara W Kaplowitz, Publisher
Monica Brown, Circulation Manager
Brian Crotty, CEO/President, Editor

Tested tips, tactics and techniques for direct marketers in all industries, news, legislative updates and winning (and losing) DM ideas including hard costs and how to's. *$242.00*

8 pages Founded: 1977
Mailing list available for rent $125 per M.
Printed in 2 colors on matte stock

Magazines & Journals

5297 B-to-B
Crain Communications
1155 Gratiot Avenue
Detroit, MI 48207-2997
313-446-6000
FAX: 313-446-1687 800-678-9595
info@crain.com
http://www.btobonline.com

Keith Crain, CEO/President
Ellis Booker, Editor
Bob Fenthan, Publisher
Tera Curran, Marketing
Hamilton Maher, Circulation Manager
$59.00

Monthly Founded: 1916
Circulation: 45402

5298 Customer Interface
Advanstar Communications
One Park Avenue
New York, NY 10016
212-797-7631
FAX: 212-951-6793 888-835-3773
info@advanstar.com
http://www.advanstar.com/

Ross M Scovotti, Publisher
Robert E Van Voorhis Jr, Editor-in-Chief
Kerry Gumas, VP

Magazine for decision-makers actively involved in planning, managing or operating a business call center. *$39.00*

104 pages Founded: 1992
Circulation: 50000

5299 DM News
Mill Hollow Corporation
100 Ave of the Americas
New York, NY 10013-6805
212-259-9251
FAX: 212-925-8752
dmnews@halldata.com
http://www.dmnews.com

Adrian Courtenay III, President/CEO
Tad Clarke, Editor-in-Chief
Ronald L. Sichler, Publisher

Valuable information on the newest trends in direct marketing, catalog statistics and advertising information for persons working in the direct mail industry. *$49.00*

Weekly Founded: 1979

5300 Dateline: DMA
Direct Marketing Association
11 W 42nd Street
New York, NY 10036-8002
212-391-9683
FAX: 212-768-4546

Offers comprehensive information on the Direct Marketing Association, trends in the industry, technological advances and more for the marketing and advertising professional.

Quarterly

5301 Direct
Primedia
249 W 17th Street
New York, NY 10011
646-860-0340
FAX: 212-206-3622
cvietri@primediabusiness.com
http://www.primediabusiness.com

Jack Condon, Chief Operating Officer
Ray Schultz, Editorial Director
Charles Vietri, Managing Editor
Elizabeth O'Connor, Publisher

Magazine of direct marketing management. *$85.00*

Founded: 1989
Circulation: 46,527

5302 Direct Marketing Magazine
Hoke Communications
224 7th Street
Garden City, NY 11530-5771
516-746-6700
FAX: 516-294-8141 800-229-6700
dmmagazine@aol.com
http://www.directmarketingmag.com

Stuart W. Boysen, Presdident
Joseph D. Gatti, Editor
Henry R Hoke, Publisher

Covers all aspects of direct marketing including production, creative campaigns, telemarketing, interactive marketing, direct response, TV/radio, legal issues and more. Profiles professionals in the field and offers statistical information to the industry. *$52.00*

80 pages Monthly Founded: 1948

5303 Education Job Finder
Planning/Communications
7215 Oak Avenue
River Forest, IL 60305-1935
708-366-5200
FAX: 708-366-5280 888-366-5200
dl@planningcommunications.com
www.jobfindersonline.com

Daniel Lauber, President

Details over 1,300 sources of jobs in all levels of education, from preschool through graduate and professional schools: online job databases, resume banks, job-matching services, email job alerts, directories, salary surveys, newsletters, and magazines. *$16.95*

300 pages Founded: 2005
Printed in 1 color on matte stock

5304 Journal of Direct Marketing
John Wiley & Sons
111 River Street
Hoboken, NJ 07030
201-748-6000
FAX: 201-748-6088 800-825-7550
customer@wiley.com
http://www.wiley.com

William J. Pesce, CEO/President
Russell S. Winer, Editor
Jill Gottlieb, Journal Supplement Manage
Kenneth Gesser, Publisher

Publication featuring research articles from some of the best minds in the field of direct marketing. Offers creative ideas for marketing products, analysis of what works, pioneering research from the nation's top universities, articles from other direct marketing publications and special reports on overseas direct marketing. *$1000.00*
Quarterly Founded: 1807

5305 **Operations & Fulfillment**
Primedia
9800 Metcalf Avenue
Overland Park, KS 66212
913-341-1300
FAX: 913-967-1898 800-775-3777
rramaswami@primediabusiness.com
http://www.opsandfulfillment.com
Rama Ramaswami, Editorial Director
Glenn Laudenslager, Marketing Manager
Leslie Bacon, Publisher
Leonard Roberto, Circulation Manager
John French, President
Provides executives information they can't get anywhere else and reach executives and managers with purchasing authority in all areas of operations management. Information on direct to customer fulfillment.. *$36.00*
Monthly Founded: 1905

5306 **Target**
North American Publishing Company
401 N Broad Street
Philadelphia, PA 19108-1001
215-238-5300
FAX: 215-238-5270
editor.tm@napco.com
http://www.targetmarketingmag.com
Hallie Mummert, Editor
Peggy Hatch, Publisher
Lois Boyle, President
This monthly magazine is the authoritative information source for direct marketers with hands-on, how-to-do-it, ideas you can take to the bank. *$24.95*
Monthly Founded: 1977
Circulation: 35000
Printed in 4 colors on glossy stock

5307 **Telemarketing Magazine**
Technology Marketing Corporation
1 Technology Plaza
Norwalk, CT 06854
203-852-6800
FAX: 203-853-2845 800-243-6002
tmc@tmcnet.com
http://www.tmcnet.com
Nadji Tehrani, Publisher/President
Linda Driscoll, Editor/VP
Rich Tehrani, President/Editor-in-Chief
Serves telemarketing, marketing, customer service, sales and telecommunications professionals. Features legislative updates, new product and service releases, techniques and beginner information. *$49.00*
Monthly Founded: 1972

5308 **Washington Report and Washington Update**
Direct Marketing Association
1111 19th Street NW
Washington, DC 20036-3603
202-955-5030
FAX: 202-955-0085
customerservice@the-dma.org
http://www.the-dma.org
Elizabeth Kitsinger, Editor
For DMA members only; covers state and federal legislative and regulatory issues.
Monthly Founded: 1917

Trade Shows

5309 **Annual Conference for Catalog and Multichannel Merchants**
PRISM Business Exhibitions
11 River Bend Drive South
Stamford, CT 06907
203-358-9900
FAX: 203-358-5816 800-927-5007
registration@prismb2b.com
www.accmshow.com
Ed Berkowitz, Sales Director
Angela Eastin, Group Show Director
Co-presented by the Direct Marketing Association and Multichannel Merchant Magazine, ACCM offers the latest advances, technology and information and solutions for cataloger, retailers and multichannel merchants.
May

5310 **Business-to-Business Database Marketing Conference**
Interlect Events
11 Riverbend Drive S
Stamford, CT 06907
203-852-4200
Robin Altman, Contact
The only database marketing conference that is focused exclusively on business-to-business marketing database strategies and tactics. 40 tabletop exhibits.
500 Attendees Fall

5311 **DMD New York Conference & Expo**
Direct Marketing Conferences
20 Academy Street
Norwalk, CT 06850-4032
203-854-9166
800-969-6566
connecticut@dmdays.com
www.dmdays.com
Direct Marketing Days New York offers new ideas in media, creative, database, eCommerce and technology. Hundreds of exhibits showcase the newest technologies, products and services. Over 85 sessions and 25 consultation centers led by A level speakers. Network with top-level executives.
June

5312 **MFSA Mailing and Fulfillment Expo**
Mailing & Fulfillment Service Association
1421 Prince Street
Suite 100
Alexandria, VA 22314-2805
703-369-9200
FAX: 703-548-8204 800-333-6272
wecasey@mfsanet.org
www.mfsanet.org
Eric Casey, Manager
David Weaver, President
Annual exposition of suppliers to mailing and fulfillment companies. Containing 60 booths and 50 exhibits.
250 Attendees June

5313 **Marketing in the Millennium**
Florida Direct Marketing Association
8851 NW 10th Pl
Plantation, FL 33322-5007
954-472-6374
FAX: 954-472-8165 800-520-FDMA
fdma@juno.org www.fdma.org
Beth Kaufman, Manager
Yearly exhibit of legislative updates and more for members of the direct marketing industry.
February Founded: 1999

5314 **National Catalog Operations Forum**
Primedia
9800 Metcalf Avenue
Overland Park, KS 66212
913-341-1300
FAX: 913-967-1898
www.primediabusiness.com
Robin Altman, Contact
The only major national conference devoted exclusively to the sharing of vital catalog operations information. This conference is dedicated to the crucial background of the catalog business, and brings operations management together to meet and learn; 140 booths.
1.2M+ Attendees April/May

5315 **Telemarketing and Business Telecommunications Conference**
1 Technology Plaza
Norwalk, CT 06854-1924
FAX: 203-853-2845
Laura Driscoll, Meeting Coordinator
The world's foremost forum on telemarketing, sales automation and customer service.
4.5M Attendees June

Directories & Databases

5316 **ADWEEK Directory**
ADWEEK
770 Broadway
7th Floor
New York, NY 10003
646-545-5220
FAX: 646-654-5351
publisher@adweek.com
www.adweek.com
Mitch Tebo, Directory Publisher
For anyone seeking agency-specific information. Over 29,000 personnel listings, more the 6,000 full service advertising agencies and networks, public relations firms, media buying services, recruitment entertainment marketing, yellow pages, health care, interactive, sports marketing, infomercials, direct marketing, creative design, marketing communications and research, consultancies and many more media related listings.

5317 **Annual Guide to Telemarketing**
Marketing Logistics
1460 Cloverdale Avenue
Highland Park, IL 60035-2817
847-831-1575
Arnold Fishman, Editor
About 400 telemarketing services bureaus in the United States. *$475.00*

Irregular

5318 Associations Yellow Book
Leadership Directories
104 5th Avenue
New York, NY 10011-6901
212-627-4140
FAX: 212-645-0931
associations@leadershipdirectories.com
www.leadershipdirectories.com
Christiane Muntone, Editor
James M Petrie, Associate Publisher
Contact information for over 41,000 officers and board members at 1,000 trade and professional associations, coalitions, PACs, and foundations. *$245.00*
1,300 pages SemiAnnual Founded: 1991
Mailing list available for rent 37,000 names
$125 per M.
Computerized version available: CD-ROM

5319 Catalog Success
North American Publishing Company
4001 S Business Park Avenue
Marshfield, WI 54449-9027
715-387-3400
FAX: 715-486-4185
daniel.gust@donnelleymarketing.com
www.catalogsuccess.com
Putting marketing management to the test.
Monthly
Printed in 4 colors

5320 Corporate Yellow Book
Leadership Directories
104 5th Avenue
New York, NY 10011-6901
212-627-4140
FAX: 212-645-0931
corporate@leadershipdirectories.com
www.leadershipdirectories.com
Vonessa Ruffin, Editor
Contact information for over 48,000 executives at over 1,000 companies and more than 9,000 board members and their outside affiliations. *$360.00*
1,400 pages Quarterly Founded: 1986
50,000 names $105 per M. : CD-Rom

5321 Customer Interaction Solutions
Technology Marketing Corporation
1 Technology Plaza
Norwalk, CT 06854
203-852-6800
FAX: 203-853-2845 800-243-6002
Rich Tehrani, President/Editor-in-Chief
Tracy Schelmetic, Editor
Over 1100 domestic and foreign suppliers of equipment products and services to the telecommunications/telemarketing industry. *$ 25.00*
Annual/December/89 Pages Founded: 1982
Mailing list available for rent 63,000 names
$25 per M.

5322 D&B Million Dollar Directory
Dun & Bradstreet Information Service
3 Sylvan Way
Parsippany, NJ 07054-3805
973-455-0900
FAX: 973-605-6911 800-526-0651
160,000 public and private businesses with either a net worth of 500,000 or more, 250 emplyees at that location or 25,000,000 or more in sales volume. *$1395.00*

5323 D&B Million Dollar Directory: Top 50,000
Dun & Bradstreet Information Service
3 Sylvan Way
Parsippany, NJ 07054-3805
973-455-0900
FAX: 973-605-6911 800-526-0651
50,000 top corporations, utilities, transportation companies, bank and trust companies, stock brolers, mutual and stock insurance companies, wholesalers, retailers, and domestic susidiaries of foreign corporations. *$500.00*

5324 Direct Mail Service
Information Resource Group
50495 Corporate Drive
Suite 112
Shelby Township, MI 48315-3132
586-726-6237

This database offers over 1,000,000 MIS and corporate professionals at over 150,000 companies throughout the United States. *$ 150.00*

5325 Direct Marketing Association Fact Book
Direct Marketing Association
1120 Avenue of Americas
New York, NY 10036-8002
212-768-7277
FAX: 212-398-6725
Anna Cheknis, Market Research Associate
John A Greco Jr, Chief Executive Officer
Annual directory of statistical information and trends in the direct marketing industry. The most sought-after direct marketing statistics, benchmarks, projections and information from more than 65 leading research sources.
Annual Founded: 1978

5326 Direct Marketing Association's Great Catalog Guide
Direct Marketing Association
1120 Avenue of the Americas
New York, NY 10036-8002
212-768-7277
FAX: 212-302-6714
Anna Cheknis, Market Research Associate
John A Greco Jr, Chief Executive Officer
Offers valuable information on more than 260 mail order catalog companies. *$3.00*
35 pages Biennial

5327 Direct Marketing Market Place
Reed Reference Publishing RR Bowker
121 Chanlon Road
New Providence, NJ 07974-1541
908-665-2834
FAX: 908-464-3553
info@bowker.com www.bowker.com
Offers over 9,000 direct marketing companies, service firms and consulting services concerned with direct marketing. *$179.99*
1200 pages Annual

5328 Direct Selling World Directory
World Federation of Direct Selling Association
1776 K Street NW
Suite 600
Washington, DC 20006-2304
202-194-4901
FAX: 202-463-4569 www.dsa.org
Over 50 direct selling associations and over 1,000 associated member companies are offered in this comprehensive directory.
90 pages Annual

5329 Directory of Mail Order Catalogs
Grey House Publishing
185 Millerton Road
PO Box 860
Millerton, NY 12546
518-890-0526
FAX: 518-789-0545 800-562-2139
books@greyhouse.com
www.greyhouse.com
Leslie Mackenzie, Publisher
Richard Gottlieb, Editor
The premier source of information on the mail order catalog industry. Covers over 12,000 consumer and business catalog companies with 44 different product chapters from Animals to Toys and Games. *$350.00*
1600 pages Annual Founded: 1980 ISBN 1-592370-66-7

5330 Directory of Mailing List Companies
Todd Publications
PO Box 635
Nyack, NY 10960-0635
845-358-6213
FAX: 845-358-1059 800-747-1056
Over 1,000 mailing list compilers, brokers and managers are previewed in this directory. *$40.00*
150 pages Biennial
Circulation: 5,000

5331 Directory of Major Mailers
North American Publishing Company
401 N Broad Street
Philadelphia, PA 19108-1001
215-238-5300
FAX: 215-238-5412
Nancy Danon-Smith, Editor
Offers over 7,500 major direct mailers and the key players with their names, addresses, phones and fax numbers, executive contacts, types of business, and the size of the house file. The Directory also contains actual reproductions of these mailings - letters, envelopes, order cards, brochures, etc. You'll see what was mailed, what worked and what didn't. *$395.00*
Annual Founded: 1994
Printed in 1 color on matte stock

5332 International Job Finder: Where the Jobs are Worldwide
Planning/Communications
7215 Oak Avenue
River Forest, IL 60305-1935
708-366-5200
FAX: 708-366-5280 888-366-5200
dl@planningcommunications.com
www.jobfindersonline.com
Daniel Lauber, President
Describes in detail over 1,200 print and online sources of jobs outside the USA; newsletters, magazines, directories, web sites, online job databases, resume banks, email job alerts, and salary surveys. *$19.95*
384 pages Every 4 Years Founded: 2002
ISBN 1-884587-10-0
Circulation: 8,000
Printed in 1 color on matte stock

5333 **Nonprofit Sector Yellow Book**
Leadership Directories
104 5th Avenue
New York, NY 10011-6901
212-627-4140
FAX: 212-645-0931
info@leadershipdirectories.com
www.leadershipdirectories.com
Michelle Barile, Editor
James M Petrie, Associate Publisher
Contact information for over 51,000 nonprofit executives and trustees at over 1,300 nonprofit organizations, including foundations, colleges and universities, museums, performing arts group and centers, medical institutions, library systems, preparatory schools, and charitable service organizations. *$245.00*
1,200 pages SemiAnnual Founded: 1999
Mailing list available for rent 45,000 names $125 per M.
Computerized version available: CD-ROM

5334 **Nonprofits Job Finder: Where the Jobs are in Charities and Nonprofits**
Planning/Communications
7215 Oak Avenue
River Forest, IL 60305-1935
708-366-5200
FAX: 708-366-5280 888-366-5200
dl@planningcommunications.com
www.jobfindersonline.com
Daniel Lauber, President
Describes in detail over 1,500 sources of jobs in the nonprofit sectors job database online, resume banks, email job alerts, directories, salary surveys, newsletters, and magazines. *$17.95*
300 pages Founded: 2005 ISBN 1-884587-06-2
Circulation: 6,000
Printed in 1 color on matte stock

5335 **SRDS Direct Marketing List Source**
Standard Rate & Data Services
1700 Higgins Road
Des Plaines, IL 60018-5605
847-375-5000
FAX: 847-375-5001 800-851-7737
Pat Kagan, Publisher
Marty Hooks, Advertising Manager
Kevin McNally, Controller
Leading provider of media rates and data to the advertising industry. Offers comprehensive coverage of traditional media, such as magazines, newspapers, television and radio as well as today's alternative marketing opportunities, such as online, out-of-home and direct marketing. *$586.00*
3238 pages Bi-Monthly
Circulation: 2077 87,648 names $140 per M.

5336 **Yellow Pages & Directory Report**
SIMBA Information
11 Riverbend Drive S
PO Box 4234
Stamford, CT 06907-2524
203-258-8193
FAX: 203-358-5825 800-307-2529
simba99@aol.com www.simba.com
Natalie Schwartz, Editor
Alan Brigish, Publisher
Covers directory publishing, advertising, printing and releases from national yellow pages accounts. *$549.00*
Bi-Monthly Founded: 1985

Industry Web Sites

5337 **www.adweek.com**
Adweek

Leading decision makers in the advertising and marketing field go to Adweek.com everyday for breaking news, insight, buzz, opinion, analysis, research and classifieds. The resources of all six regional editions of Adweek, as well as the national edition of Brandweek are combined with the knowledge of our online editors and the multimedia-interactive capabilities of the web to deliver vital information quickly and effectively to our target audience.

5338 **www.amma.org**
Advertising Mail Marketing Association

Represents the interests of those who use mail for fundraising or business purposes.

5339 **www.ataconnect.org**
American Teleservices Association

Represents the call centers, trainers, consultants and equipment suppliers that initiate, facilitate and generate telephone, Internet and e-mail sales, service and support.

5340 **www.cadm.org**
Chicago Association of Direct Marketing

Promotes the interests of Chicago's direct marketing professionals. Fosters member development through business, educational and social opportunities and provides a high-quality forum for the exchange of ideas by direct marketing professionals.

5341 **www.cyberdirect.com/ADMA**
Cohn & Wells

Members are direct response advertising agencies.

5342 **www.dmad.org**
Direct Marketing Association of Detroit

Not for profit organization dedicated to providing networking and educational opportunities to a dymamic group of direct marketing professionals. It is the premier resource for direct response marketing information, and is committed to recognizing outstanding direct marketing achievements in the Detroit area.

5343 **www.dsa.org**
Direct Selling Association

National trade association of the leading firms that manufacture and distribute goods and services sold directly to consumers. More than 150 companies are members of the association, including many well-known brand names. The association's mission is to protect, serve and promote the effectiveness of member companies and the independent business people they represent.

5344 **www.fraudandtheftinfo.com**
Fraud & Theft Information Bureau

Provides problem solving, crime prevention, money saving manuals and fraud blocker databases.

5345 **www.greyhouse.com**
Grey House Publishing

Selected Grey House directories in the fields of business, health and education are available online. Users can search our online databases by several different search criteria, such as product categories, geographic area, sales volume and much, much more. Full Grey House catalog and online ordering also available.

5346 **www.ims-lists.com/links**
IMS Direct Marketing Links

Professional associations links.

5347 **www.mdma.org**
Midwest Direct Marketing Association

Advancing the professional and ethical practice of direct response marketing by members throughout the Upper Midwest. The MDMA seeks to accomplish this by sponsoring educational and professional networking events to share and encourage the best practices in telemarketing, direct mail and online marketing techniques and strategies.

5348 **www.mfsanet.org**
Mailing & Fulfillment Service Association

80 year old trade association which provides education/training, information, surveys and industry representation for companies which offer 3rd party mailing and fulfillment services.

5349 **www.nedma.com**
New England Direct Marketing Association

5350 **www.nmoa.org**
National Mail Order Association

Offers the stongest and lowest cost means for people to come together for the purpose of conducting business and creating sales. Small to medium sized organizations come for education, information, ideas, resources and new contacts.

5351 **www.the-dma.org**
Direct Marketing Association

Trade association in the direct marketing field with more than 3,500 member companies from the United States and 54 foreign nations. Included are catalogers, direct marketers from consumer to business-to-business, publishers, retail stores as well as service industries that support them.

Associations

5352 **Academy of Managed Care Pharmacy**
100 N Pitt Street
Suite 400
Alexandria, VA 22314-3134
703-683-8416
FAX: 703-683-8417 800-827-2627
sandres@amcp.org www.amcp.org

Steven W Gray PharmD, President
Elaine Manieri, Director
Judith A Cahill, Executive Director/Secretary
Cathryn A Carroll, PhD, Treasurer

Promotes the development and application of appropriate and accessible medication therapy. Represents professional pharmacists and associates practicing in managed care settings.

4800 Members Founded: 1989
Mailing list available for rent

5353 **American Association of Colleges of Pharmacy**
1426 Prince Street
Alexandria, VA 22314
703-739-2330
FAX: 703-836-8982
mail@aacp.org www.aacp.org

Susan M Meyer, Senior Vice President
Lucinda L Maine, Executive VP
Barbara A Gustis, Manager Meetings

National organization representing the interests of pharmaceutical education and educators. Comprising all 83 US pharmacy colleges and schools including more than 4,000 faculty, 36,000 students enrolled in professional programs and 3,600 individuals pursuing graduate study. AACP is committed to excellence in pharmaceutical education.

40M+ Members Founded: 1900

5354 **American Association of Pharmaceutical Scientists**
2107 Wilson Boulevard
Suite 700
Arlington, VA 22201-3042
703-243-2800
FAX: 703-243-9650
aaps@aaps.org www.aaps.org

John Lisack, Jr, Executive Director
Maureen Downs, Director Finance
Peter Inchauteguiz, Director Marketing/Members Svcs
James Greif, Communcations Specialist
Jerry Skelly, President

Aims to advance science through the open exchange of scientific knowledge, serve as an information resource and contribute to human health through pharmaceutical research and development.

11000 Members Founded: 1986
Mailing list available for rent

5355 **American Association of Pharmacy**

PO Box 1447
Greensboro, NC 27402
877-368-4771
FAX: 336-333-9068
aapt@pharmacytechnician.com
www.pharmacytechnician.com

Ryan C Lee CPhT, President
Philip H Martin, Director
Marion K Keener, AS, Treasurer
Michele Poarch, CPhT, Secretary

Provides leadership and represents the interests of its members to the public as well as health care organizations. Promotes safe efficacious and cost effective dispensing, distribution and use of medications. Provides continuing education programs and services to help technicians update their skills and keep pace with changes in pharmacy services. Promotes pharmacy technicians as an integral part of the patient care team.

5356 **American Chemical Society**
1155 16th Street NW
Washington, DC 20036
202-872-4600
FAX: 202-872-4615 800-227-5558
help@acs.org www.chemistry.org

James D Burke, Chair
E Ann Nalley, President
John Crum, Executive Director
C Gordon McCarty, Director
Madeleine Jacobs, Executive Director

Supports scientists and other professionals working in the field of drug discovery. Publishes monthly magazine.

159K Members Founded: 1876

5357 **American Clinical Laboratory Association**
1250 H Street NW
Suite 880
Washington, DC 20005
202-637-9466
FAX: 202-637-2050
info@clinical-labs.org
www.clinical-labs.org

Thomas P MacMahon, Chair
Alan Mertz, President
Joanne Glisson, Senior VP
Gary Hilburn, Chief Executive Officer
Peter M Kazon, Legal Counsel

Members are clinical laboratories licensed and regulated under medicare and the interstate laboratory program.

Founded: 1971

5358 **American College of Apothecaries**
2830 Summer Oaks Drive
Bartlett, TN 38134-3811
901-383-8119
FAX: 901-383-8882
aca@acainfo.org www.acainfo.org

John S Oftebro, Chairman
Jeffrey Denton, President
Randall S Myers, VP
D Huffman, Executive Vice President

Disseminates and translates knowledge, research data and recent developments in professional pharmacy practice for the benefit of pharmacists, pharmacy students and the public. This is achieved through regular distribution of periodicals, development of major publications and continuing education courses on clinical and administrative topics and conducting educational conferences.

1M Members Founded: 1940

5359 **American College of Clinical Pharmacy**
3101 Broadway Street
Suite 650
Kansas City, MO 64111-2416
816-531-2177
FAX: 816-531-4990 www.accp.com

Michael Maddux, Executive Director

Professional and scientific society that provides leadership, education, advocacy and resources enabling clinical pharmacists to achieve excellence in practice and research. Membership is composed of practitioners, scientists, educators, administrators, students, residents, fellows and others committed to excellence in clinical pharmacy and patient pharmacotherapy.

Founded: 1979

5360 **American College of Medical Quality**
4334 Montgomery Avenue
Suite B
Bethesda, MD 20814
301-913-9149
FAX: 301-913-9142 800-924-2149
acmq@acmq.org www.acmq.org

Bridget Brodie, Executive Vice President
Eric Silfen, VP

5361 **American Council on Pharmaceutical Education**
20 N Clark Street
Suite 2500
Chicago, IL 60602
312-664-3575
FAX: 312-664-4652

Robert Buchman, Executive Director

Promotes the education of pharmaceutical medicine.

5362 **American Institute of the History of Pharmacy**
777 Highland Avenue
Madison, WI 53705-2222
608-262-5378
FAX: 608-262-3397
aihp@mace.wisc.edu
www.pharmacy.wisc.edu/aihp

Dr. Gregory Higby, Executive Director
Dr. Elaine C Stroud, Assistant Director
Beth D Fisher, Program Manager
Greg Bond, Project Assistant

Non-profit national organization devoted to advancing knowledge and understanding of the place of pharmacy in history. Contributes to the understanding of the development of civilization by fostering the creation, preservation, and dissemination of knowledge concerning the history and related humanistic aspects of the pharmaceutical field.

900 Members Founded: 1941

5363 **American Oil Chemists Society**
2211 W Bradley Avenue
Champaign, IL 61821-1827
217-359-2344
FAX: 217-351-8091
general@aocs.org www.aocs.org

Jean Wills, Executive VP
Gloria Cook, Finance/Operations Director
Greg Reed, Manager
Lisa Spencer, Marketing/Sales
Kathleen Atchley, Membership Programs

A global forum to promote the exchange of ideas, information, and experience, to enhance personal excellence, and to provide high standards of quality among those with a professional interest in the science and technology of fats, oils, surfactants, and related materials.

5364 **American Pharmaceutical Association Foundation**
2215 Constitution Avenue NW
Washington, DC 20037
202-297-7524
FAX: 202-429-6300 800-237-APHA
info@aphafoundation.org
www.aphanet.org

John A Gans, Executive VP/CEO
Linda K Gainey, Director Executive Operations
Roger K Browning, VP Finance & Admin/CFO
Susan Winckler, VP Policy & Communications
Gwen Norheim, Library Services

National, professional society of pharmacists practicing in every practice setting and influencing the industry, distribution and utilization of medications.
50000 Members Founded: 1852

5365 **American Public Health Association**
800 I Street NW
Washington, DC 20001-3710
202-777-2742
FAX: 202-777-2534
coments@apha.org www.apha.org

Jay M Bernhardt, Vice Chair
Gene Lutz, President
Georges Benjamin, Executive Director
Jose F Cordero, Member
Louise A Anderson, Director Operations

Brings together researchers, health service providers, administrators, teachers and other health workers in a unique, multidisciplinary environment of professional exchange, study and action in the effort to prevent disease and promote health.
50000 Members Founded: 1872

5366 **American Society for Automation in Pharmacy**
492 Norristown Road
Suite 160
Blue Bell, PA 19422
610-825-7783
FAX: 610-825-7641
wal@computertalk.com
www.asapnet.org

Jim Wilson, President
Ken Whittemore, RPh, VP
Kevin Kite-Powell, Director
Bill Lockwood, Executive Director
Tom Weiss, RPh, Secretary/Treasurer

Assists its members in advancing the application of computer technology in the pharmacist's role as care giver, in the efficient operation of a pharmacy and promoting standards, legislation and guidelines.
350 Members Founded: 1988

5367 **American Society for Parenteral & Enteral Nutrition**
8630 Fenton Street
Suite 412
Silver Spring, MD 20910
301-587-6315
FAX: 301-587-2365 800-727-4567
aspen@nutr.org www.nutritioncare.org

Marion F Winkler, President
Vincent W Vanek, VP
Robin Kriegel, CAE, Executive Director
Joanne Kieffer, Director Finance

Promotes professional communication among and within professional disciplines in the broad field of clinical nutrition including parenteral and enteral nutrition (tube feeding) through national and regional meetings, local seminars, scientific, clinical and educational exhibits and publications.
6000 Members Founded: 1979

5368 **American Society for Pharmacy Law**
1224 Centre W
Suite 400B
Springfield, IL 62704
217-391-0219
FAX: 217-793-0041 www.aspl.org

Melissa Madigan, President
Francis B Paulumbo, Director
Pamela Tolson, CAE, Executive Director
William Fassett, Treasurer

An organization of pharmacists and lawyers who are interested in the law as it applies to the pharmacy industry.

5369 **American Society of Consultant Pharmacists**
1321 Duke Street
Alexandria, VA 22314
703-739-1300
FAX: 800-220-1321 800-355-2727
info@ascp.com www.ascp.com

John Feather, Executive Director/CEO
Phylliss M Moret, Associate Executive Director/COO
Robert Appel, Director Communications
Doug McAdoo, Chief Financial Officer

The international professional association that provides leadership, education, advocacy and resources to advance the practice of senior care pharmacy.
6500+ Members

5370 **American Society of Health-System Pharmacists**
7272 Wisconsin Avenue
Bethesda, MD 20814-4836
301-657-3000
FAX: 301-664-8857 www.ashp.org

Jill E Martin, President
Henri R Manasse Jr, EVP/CEO

An association that brings together health-system pharmacists who practice in hospitals, health maintenance organizations, long-term care facilities, home care, and other components of health care systems. ASHSP has a long history of medication error prevention efforts and believe the mission of pharmacists is to help people make the best use of medicines.
31M Members Founded: 1942
Mailing list available for rent

5371 **Association of Clinical Research Professionals**
500 Montgomery Street
Suite 800
Alexandria, VA 22314
703-254-8100
FAX: 703-254-8101
acrp@associationhq.com
www.acrpnet.org

Robin Newman, Vice Chair
Thomas L Adams, CAE, President/CEO
Larry J Medley, CAE, Director Finance
Alan Armstrong, Director Marketing/COO

The Academy of Clinical Research Professionals and the Academy of Pharmaceutical Physician and Investigators are affiliates of ACRP. The Academy asministers non-physician certification programs and govermmental affairs activities. APPI represents all physician members of ACRP.
17000 Members Founded: 1976

5372 **Drug Information Association**
800 Enterprise Road
Suite 200
Horsham, PA 19044-3595
215-442-6100
FAX: 215-442-6199
dia@diahome.org www.diahome.org

Eleanor M Perfetto, President
Gaby L Danan, Director
Richard O Day, Director
Francoise de Cremiers, Director
David Maola, Executive Director

Provides a neutral global forum for the exchange and dissemination of information on the discovery, development, evaluation and utilization of medicines and related health care technologies. Through these activities the DIA provides development opportunities for its members.
27000 Members Founded: 1964

5373 **Drug, Chemical & Associated Technologies**
1 Washington Boulevard
Suite 7
Robbinsville, NJ 08691
609-448-1000
FAX: 609-448-1944
mtimony@dcat.org www.dcat.org

Patrick Vasquez, President
Lynda M Doyle, Senior VP
Joseph Colleluori, Treasurer
Margaret M Timony, Executive Director

Members include more than 350 companies, in the US and abroad, who manufacture, distribute or provide services to the chemical, pharmaceutical, nutritional and related industries. Services, programs and activities are designed to support business development objectives. These programs and events provide opportunities for member representatives to make important contacts, learn new industry information, dialogue with counterparts in other companies and build relationships with customers.

Founded: 1890

5374 **Food & Drug Law Institute**
1000 Vermont Avenue NW
Suite 200
Washington, DC 20005
202-371-1420
FAX: 202-371-0649 800-956-6293
comments@fdli.org www.fdli.org

Patrick M McLain, Chairman
Sheritta Lancaster, Membership Manager
Matthew Weinberg, Treasurer
Rafaek N Manalac, Director Finance
Frederick Degnan, Secretary

A nonprofit, educational organization dedicated to improving the understanding of the laws, regulations, and policies affecting health care technologies, food and cosmetics. FDLI is neutral, nonpartisan and does not lobby or advocate positions on any issue.
550+ Members Founded: 1949

5375 **Generic Pharmaceutical Association**
2300 Clarendon Boulevard
Suite 400
Arlington, VA 22201
703-647-2480
FAX: 703-647-2481
info@gphaonline.org
www.gphaonline.org

Kathleen Jaeger, President/CEO
Christine Simmon, VP of Public Affairs/Development

Represents the manufacturers and distributors of finished generic pharmaceutical products, manufacturers and distributors of bulk active pharmaceutical chemicals, and suppliers of other goods and services to the generic pharmaceutical industry.

5376 Healthcare Distribution Management Association
900 N Glebe Road
Suite 1000
Arlington, VA 22203
703-787-0000
FAX: 703-935-3200
www.healthcaredistribution.org

John M Gray, President/CEO
Nancy E Hanagan, Executive VP/COO
Susan Mirvis, Senior VP Marketing/Communications

An organization representing all major constituents of healthcare product distribution management.

5377 Independent Pharmacy Cooperative
1550 Columbus Street
Sun Prairie, WI 53590
608-259-9556
FAX: 800-274-5525 800-755-1531
staff@iperx.com www.ipcrx.com

Steve Niebauer, President/CEO
Mike Flint, VP
Chuck Benjamin, Chief Financial Officer
Mindy Hermann, Director Marketing/Sales

Provides member pharmacies with the lowest possible contract pricing on quality products and services.
4000 Members Founded: 1984

5378 International Pharmaceutical Excipients Council of the Americas

1655 North Fort Myer Drive
Suite 700
Arlington, VA 22209
703-875-2127
FAX: 703-525-5157
info@ipecamericas.org
www.ipecamericas.org

Alan W Mercill, Secretary/Treasurer

Members are companies with an interest in the otherwise inert chemicals used as vehicles for medicines. IPEC is a federation of three independent regional associations headquartered in the US. and Japan. Each association focuses its attention on the applicable laws, regulations, science and business practices of its region to accomplish its members goals.
300 Members Founded: 1991

5379 International Society for Pharmaceutical Engineering (ISPE)
3109 West Drive Martin Luther King Jr Blvd
Suite 250
Tampa, FL 33607
813-960-2105
FAX: 813-264-2816
customerservice@ispe.org
www.ispe.org

Gert Moelgaard, Chairman
Jane R Brown, Vice Chairman
Bruce Davis, Treasurer

Supports pharmaceutical manufacturing professionals with a particular focus on the design, construction, supervision and maintenance of process equipment, plant systems, instrumentation and facilities. Publishes bi-monthly magazine.
23000 Members Founded: 1980

5380 National Association of Boards of Pharmacy
700 Busse Highway
Park Ridge, IL 60068
847-698-6227
FAX: 847-698-0124 800-774-6227
custserv@nabp.net www.nabp.net

Donna S Wall, Chairperson
Donna M Horn, President
Lawrence H Mokhiber, Treasurer

Serves all American boards of pharmacy in matters of interstate reciprocity of licensure and licensing as well as other matters of mutual concern.

5381 National Association of Chain Drug Stores
413 N Lee Street
PO Box 1417-D49
Alexandria, VA 22313-1480
703-549-3001
FAX: 703-836-4869 www.nacds.org

Mary F Sammons, Chairman
Anthony Civello, Vice Chairman
Craig L Fuller, President/CEO
Mark Griffin, Director
David Bernauer, Treasurer

Association for manufacturers or suppliers of chain drug store equipment, supplies and services.
210 Members Founded: 1933

5382 National Community Pharmacists Association
100 Daingerfield Road
Alexandria, VA 22314
703-683-8200
FAX: 703-683-3619 800-544-7447
info@ncpanet.com www.ncpanet.org

James R Rankin PD, President
Donnie Calhoun, First VP
Bruce Roberts, RPh, EVP/Chief Executive Officer
Lonny Wilson, Secretary/Treasurer

Represents pharmacy owners, managers and employees of nearly 25,000 independent community pharmacies across the US.
60000 Members Founded: 1898

5383 National Council for Prescription Drug Programs
9240 E Raintree Drive
Scottsdale, AZ 85260-7518
480-477-1000
FAX: 480-767-1042
ncpdp@ncpdp.org www.ncpdp.org

Lee Ann Stember, President
Dennis Kitterman, Director Marketing Communications
Phillip D Scott, SVP Sales/Marketing
Joanne Longie, VP Operations

Members are computer companies, drug manufacturers, drug store chains, drug wholesalers, insurers, mail order prescription drug companies, pharmaceutical claim processors, prescription drug providers, software vendors, service organizations, government agencies and others with a interest in drug program administration standardization.
1350 Members Founded: 1977

5384 National Council of State Pharmacy Association Executives
5501 Patterson Avenue
Suite 200
Richmond, VA 23226
804-285-4145
FAX: 804-285-4227
becky@ncspae.org www.ncspae.org

Jim Bracewell, President
Craig Burridgel, First VP
Lawrence Sage, Second Vice President
Bateena Black, Secretary/Treasurer

Represents high level executives in pharmacy and pharmaceutical education.

5385 National Institute for Pharmacist Care Outcomes
100 Daingerfield Road
Alexandria, VA 22314
703-481-1518
FAX: 703-683-3619
kathryn.kuhn@ncpanet.org
www.ncpanet.org

Kathryn Kuhn, Executive Director, NIPCO Programs
Eleanor Nespica, Coordinator, NIPCO Programs
Mike Clark, Manager

The national accrediting organization for pharmacist care education and training programs leading to the pharmacist care diplomate credential. A leading authority in helping community pharmacists develop new market niches in disease management and wellness.

5386 National Pharmaceutical Alliance
427 King Street
Suite 222
Alexandria, VA 22314
703-836-8816
FAX: 703-549-4749 www.npa.org

Cristina Sizemore, Executive Director
Deborah Kline, Manager Communications

Represents the interests of small pharmaceutical companies and allied industries.

5387 National Pharmaceutical Council
1894 Preston White Drive
Reston, VA 20191-5433
703-620-6390
FAX: 703-476-0904
info@npcnow.com www.npcnow.org

Karen Williams, President
Pat Adams, VP Business Operations
Gary Persinger, VP Health Care Systems
Richard Levy, VP Scientific
Jeffery Warren, Senior Advisor

Represents major, research-intensive, pharmaceutical companies. Conducts national and state studies, holds educational forums and generates publications for consumer and for health care cost containment programs.
31 Members Founded: 1953

5388 Parenteral Drug Association
3 Bethesda Metro Center
Suite 1500
Bethesda, MD 20814
301-860-0293
FAX: 301-986-1093
info@pda.org www.pda.org

Vince R Anicetti, Chairman
Robert Myers, President
Wanda Neal-Ballard, Director Programs/Meetings

Lance K Hoboy, MBA, VP Finance
Matthew Clark, Director Marketing

A non-profit international association of more than 10,500 scientists involved in the development, manufacture, quality control and regulation of pharmaceuticals/biopharmaceuticals and related products. The association also provides educational opportunities for government and university sectors that have a vocational interest in pharmaceutical/biopharmaceutical sciences and technology.

10500 Members Founded: 1946

5389 Pharmaceutical Outsourcing Management Association
8865 W Okeechobee Boulevard
Suite 202
West Palm Beach, FL 33411
561-795-5503
FAX: 561-795-5503 www.pomasite.com

Shannon Brome-Ward, President
Linda Wauk, VP
Charles Calvert, Treasurer
Fran Grote, Secretary

Established as a forum to exchange ideas and experiences about outsourcing in the pharmaceutical industry.

Founded: 1995

5390 Pharmaceutical Research and Manufacturers
1100 15th Street NW
Washington, DC 20005
202-835-3400
FAX: 202-835-3414
webmaster@phrma.org
www.phrma.org

Billy Tauzin, President/CEO

Members are pharmaceutical companies that manufacture market finished, dosage-form pharmaceuticals under their own brand name and conduct a significant amount of R&D within the US.

100 Members Founded: 1958

Newsletters

5391 AACP News
American Association of Colleges of Pharmacy
1426 Prince Street
Alexandria, VA 22314-2815
703-739-2330
FAX: 703-836-8982
mail@aacp.org http://www.aacp.org

Norida Torrente, Director
Janice Zooler, Publisher
Lucinda Maine, CEO

Activities and issues in pharmacy education. 12 pages, free to members. Published since 1874. *$35.00*

Monthly Founded: 1800
Circulation: 300 300 names
Printed in on newsprint stock

5392 ACCP Report
American College of Clinical Pharmacy
3101 Broadway Street
Suite 650
Kansas City, MO 64111-2416
816-531-2177
FAX: 816-531-4990
accp@accp.com http://www.accp.com

George Puiges, Publisher
Bruce Mueller, Editor
Micheal Maddux, Executive Director
Nancy Terrin, Marketing Manager
Timothy Ives, President

Offers the latest research on drugs and pharmaceuticals. *$45.00*

Monthly
Circulation: 12000

5393 Alternative Medicine Alert
American Health Consultants
3525 Piedmont Road NE
Building Six, Suite 400
Atlanta, GA 30374-56
404-262-7436
FAX: 404-262-7837 800-688-2421

Leslie Copeland, Publisher

Reports on studies of herbs in medicine, reactions in relation to different herbs. Studies that are out and those being done. *$ 299.00*

Monthly
Printed in 4 colors on matte stock

5394 American Pharmaceutical Association
2215 Constitution Avenue NW
Washington, DC 20037-2907
202-429-7524
FAX: 202-783-2351 800-237-2742

Lucinda L Maine, Staff Liason
Gwen Norheim, Library Services

Part of the American Pharmaceutical Association which promotes the professional growth of scientists and serves as a resource of scientific knowledge for the practitioner.

5395 Annals of Pharmacotherapy
Harvey Whitney Books Company
PO Box 42696
8044 montgomery road
Cincinnati, OH 45236-696
513-793-3555
FAX: 513-793-3600 877-742-7631
customer-services@theannals.com
http://www.theannals.com

Harvey Whitney, Publisher/Editor
Eugene Sorkin, Associate Editor
Harvey Whitney, CEO
Greg Johnson, Marketing
Ann Brandwieve, Circulation Manager

For 38 years this independent peer reviewed journal has been dedicated to the advancement of pharmacotherapy. Article categories include; original research, comprehensive reviews, case reports, editorials, and letters. special article features include new drug evaluations, therapeutic controversies, recent theraputic advances, international reports, continuing education articles, and more. *$158.00*

Monthly Founded: 1967
Circulation: 50000
Printed in 4 colors on glossy stock

5396 Chapter News
American College of Cardiology
76 S State Street
Concord, NH 03301-3520
603-228-1231
FAX: 603-228-2118 assnrhc@aol.com

Walter Perry, Executive Director

Newsletter for cardiovascular specialists in Maine, New Hampshire and Vermont.

Quarterly

5397 Clin-Alert-Newsletter
Technomic Publishing Company
300 S Riverside Plaza
Suite 1940 S
Chicago, IL 60606
312-760-0004
FAX: 312-876-1158
www.technomic.com

Amy Flannery, Marketing

This unique adverse drug reaction/interaction reporting service presents-in newsletter format-a summary of adverse clinical events, collected from 103 key medical and research journals from around the world. Approximately 360 abstracts per year. *$155.00*

8 pages Semimonthly
Printed in 2 colors : On-Line

5398 Clinical Investigator News
CTB International Publishing
PO Box 218
Maplewood, NJ 07040-218
973-966-0997
FAX: 973-966-0242
info@ctbintl.com
http://www.ctbintl.com

FG Racioppi, Marketing Director
William Robison, Circulation Manager

Alerts independent investigators to existing or emerging opportunities to participate in clinical trials of drugs and maintain a steady flow of studies. Covers preclinical development through Phase II/III, approvals and post-marketing surveillance (PMS) studies. *$647.00*

48 pages Monthly Founded: 1980
Printed in 1 color on newsprint stock

5399 Clinical Trials Monitor
CTB International Publishing
PO Box 218
Maplewood, NJ 07040-218
973-966-0997
FAX: 973-379-0242
info@ctbintl.com
http://www.ctbintl.com

Oykue Brogna, Publisher
Christopher Brogna, Editor

Tracks clinical trials planned, underway, completed or abandoned. Lists the drug, the company, the indication, phase or stage, principal investigator, where and when trials will be held, enrollment plans and proposed end points. Reports results at meetings, and in journals. *$1197.00*

64 pages Monthly Founded: 1985
Printed in 1 color on newsprint stock

5400 Consumer Pharmacist
Elba Medical Foundation
PO Box 494
Metairie, LA 70004
504-889-7070
FAX: 504-889-7060

John DiMaggio, Publisher

Drug information newsletter. *$30.00*

Monthly

5401 DIA Newsletter
Drug Information Association
800 Enterprise Road
Suite 200
Horsham, PA 19044-3595
215-442-6100
FAX: 215-442-6199
dia@diahome.org
http://www.diahome.org

Thomas Teal, Publisher
David Maola, Executive Director

Association activities, technical developments, supplying, and production of drugs. *$40.00*
20 pages Monthly Founded: 1964

5402 Diagnostics Intelligence
CTB International Publishing
PO Box 218
Maplewood, NJ 07040-218
973-966-0997
FAX: 973-966-0242
info@ctbintl.com
http://www.ctbintl.com
Oyque Brogna, CEO/President
F Racioppi, Marketing Director
Covers the latest in research, development, new product language, regulatory affairs, patents, litigations, opportunities and finance in the invitro diagnostics business. *$578.00*
20 pages Monthly
Printed in 1 color on newsprint stock

5403 Drug Development Pipeline
CTB International Publishing
PO Box 218
Maplewood, NJ 07040
973-966-0997
FAX: 973-966-0242
info@ctbintl.com
http://www.ctbintl.com/
FG Racioppi, Marketing Director
Chris Brogna, President
Laszlo Novak, Editor
Newsletter that summarizes the changes in the drug development plans of US and Canadian pharmaceutical companies. Each issue will alert the reader to more than 120 products that are moving through the pipeline. *$198.00*
Monthly Founded: 1982
Printed in 1 color on newsprint stock

5404 Emerging Pharmaceuticals
CTB International Publishing
PO Box 218
Maplewood, NJ 07040-218
973-966-0997
FAX: 973-966-0242
info@ctbintl.com
http://www.ctbintl.com
FG Racioppi, Marketing Director
Covers the earliest stage of drug development, from discovery through preclinical trials. Alerts readers to news and insights about novel compounds, innovative screening methods and candidates for the R&D pipeline. *$542.00*
14 pages Monthly
Printed in 1 color on newsprint stock

5405 FDC Reports: Gold Sheet
FDC Reports
5550 Friendship Boulevard
Suite 1
Chevy Chase, MD 20815-7278
301-657-9830
FAX: 301-656-3094 800-332-2181
fdc.customer.service@elsevier.com
http://www.fdcreports.com
Bill Paulson, Editor
Michael Magoulias, VP Sales/Marketing
Mike Squires, CEO/President
William Paulson, Executive Editor
A specialized publication which focuses each month on important changes in FDA's policies for regulating good manufacturing practices for pharmaceutical companies and their suppliers. Since 1967, this publication has provided quality control officials with the latest useful information on state-of-the-art production and quality control techniques. *$595.00*
Monthly Founded: 1939
Printed in 2 colors on matte stock

5406 FDC Reports: Green Sheet
FDC Reports
5550 Friendship Boulevard
Suite 1
Chevy Chase, MD 20815-7256
301-657-9830
FAX: 301-656-3094
http://www.fdcreports.com
Mike Squires, President
Michael Koppenhoffer, Editor
For nearly 40 years The Green Sheet has been an independent source of news and information on the pharmacy profession and the pharmaceutical distribution system. This four-page publication provides pharmacists, wholesalers, drugstore managers and trade relations executives with concise coverage of: professional policy; national and state pharmacy association activities; reimbursement issues; new drug introductions and pharmaceutical pricing and deals. *$65.00*
4 pages Weekly Founded: 1939
Computerized version available

5407 FDC Reports: Pink Sheet
FDC Reports
5550 Friendship Boulevard
Suite 1
Chevy Chase, MD 20815-7256
301-657-9830
FAX: 301-656-3094 800-332-2181
PinkEditor@elsevier.com
http://www.fdcreports.com
Wallace Werble Jr, Publisher
Janet Coleman, Editor
Mike Squires, CEO/President
Shawn Smith, Marketing
Emily Brainard, Circulation Manager
Provides in-depth weekly news and analysis about developments affecting the prescription medicines. The publication closely tracks regulatory policies and actions by FDA, FTC, HCFA, Congress, the courts and other key federal and state agencies with jurisdiction over the drug industry. Regular coverage areas include: NDA and Generic Drug approvals, FDA recalls and seizures, mergers, the R&D pipeline, biotechnology start-ups and new product activity. *$1580.00*
35 pages Weekly Founded: 1939
Computerized version available

5408 FDC Reports: Tan Sheet
FDC Reports
5550 Friendship Boulevard
Suite 1
Chevy Chase, MD 20815-7256
301-657-9830
FAX: 301-656-3094
FDC.Customer.Service@Elsevier.com
http://www.fdcreports.com
Mike Squires, CEO/President
Ramsey Baghdadi, Editor
Michael Magoulias, Marketing Manager
Emily Brainard, Circulation Manager
Provides in-depth coverage of nonprescription pharmaceuticals and dietary supplement/nutritionals. Spectrum of coverage includes: regulatory activities of FTC, CPSC and FDA, including monograph and non-monograph decisions, enforcement actions, advisory committee reviews and approvals; Congressional hearings and legislation; business and marketing news such as Rx-to-OTC switches, product development and new product introductions; FDA recalls and seizures and regular listing of product trademarks *$1285.00*
Weekly Founded: 1939
Computerized version available

5409 Food and Drug Letter
FDAnews
300 N Washington Street
Suite 200
Falls Church, VA 22046-3431
703-538-7600
FAX: 703-538-7676 888-838-5578
customerservice@fdanews.com
http://www.fdanews.com
Matt Salt, Publisher
Cindy Carter, President
Michael Miven, Editor
Maritva Lizama, Marketing
J T Hrontith, Sales Director
Provides reliable, in-depth analysis of how FDA's regulations and procedures will affect your current decisions and long-term plans and gives you in-depth interpretation to tell you why FDA is making or proposing revisions. *$1095.00*
8 pages Annual+

5410 Health News Daily
FDC Reports
5550 Friendship Boulevard
Suite 1
Chevy Chase, MD 20815-7256
301-657-9830
FAX: 301-656-3094 800-332-2181
Jim Chicca, Editor
Mike Squires, Executive Director
Provides up-to-the-minute coverage on a broad spectrum of health care issues including pharmaceuticals, medical devices and diagnostics, biomedical research, federal health policy and legislation, Medicare-Medicaid, technology reimbursement and cost-containment. Special emphasis is placed on federal regulatory and legislative developments. Published each business day, the publication draws on the expertise of more than 40 F-D-C reports editors and reporters. *$1480.00*
Daily Founded: 1939

5411 International Pharmaceutical Regulatory Monitor
Omniprint
9700 Philadelphia Court
Lanham, MD 20706-4405
301-731-7000
FAX: 301-731-5203 800-345-2611
editor@omniprint.net
http://www.pharmaceuticalmonitor.com
Michael Nagan, Publisher
Joanie Eglovitch, Editor
Comprehensive reports on the world's drug and biotechnology regulations for testing and marketing; provides actual regulatory documents (English texts). *$595.00*
60 pages Monthly Founded: 1973
Printed in 2 colors on matte stock

5412 Mealey's Emerging Drugs & Devices
LexisNexis Mealey's
1018 W Ninth Avenue
Third Avenue
King of Prussia, PA 19406-1225
610-768-7800
FAX: 610-768-0880
mealeyinfo@lexisnexis.com
www.lexisnexis.com/mealeys
Tom Hagy, VP/General Manager
Maureen McGuire, Editorial Director
Tom Moylan, Editor

The report covers cases involving a variety of prescription drug vaccines, implants and devices. Duract, Parlodel, Accutane, fen-phen, Rezulin, Propulsid, dietary supplements and blood products are among the topics tracked. Medical devices covered include heart catheters, breast implants, heart valves, intraocular lenses, jaw implants, joint replacements, latex gloves, pacemakers, pedicle screws, penile implants, and surgical lasers. *$1249.00*

100 pages Semi-Monthly Founded: 1996

5413 Mealey's Litigation Report: Baycol
LexisNexis Mealey's
1018 W Ninth Avenue
Third Avenue
King of Prussia, PA 19406-1225
610-768-7800
FAX: 610-768-0880
mealeyinfo@lexisnexis.com
www.lexisnexis.com/mealeys

Tom Hagy, VP/General Manager
Maureen McGuire, Editorial Director
Dylan McGuire, Editor

This report tracks the litigation surrounding Baycol and other statin-based anti-cholesterol drug cases. Since the voluntary withdrawl of Bayer's Baycol and Lipobay brand cerivastatin anti-cholesterol drugs, numerous complaints have been filed. The report will cover hard-to-find filings, new complaints, class actions, MDL developments, trial updates and more. *$950.00*

100 pages Monthly Founded: 2002

5414 Mealey's Litigation Report: Fen-Phen/Redux
LexisNexis Mealey's
1018 W Ninth Avenue
Third Avenue
King of Prussia, PA 19406-1225
610-768-7800
FAX: 610-768-0880
mealeyinfo@lexisnexis.com
www.lexisnexis.com/mealeys

Tom Hagy, VP/General Manager
Maureen McGuire, Editorial Director
Michael Lefkowitz, Editor

The report provides detailed coverage of the litigation surrounding fen-phen, Redux and other diet drugs. The report covers new filings, class actions, MDL proceedings, trials, settlements, rulings, medical studies, FDA activity and more. *$995.00*

100 pages Monthly Founded: 1997

5415 NABP Newsletter
National Association of Boards of Pharmacy
700 Busse Highway
Park Ridge, IL 60068
847-698-6227
FAX: 847-698-0124 800-774-6227
custserv@nabp.net www.nabp.net

Donna S Wall, Chairperson
Donnal M Horn, President
Lawrence H Mokhiber, Treasurer

Provides coverage of issues important to those who practice pharmacy and those who regulate that practice. Information about NABP's competency assessment and licensure transfer programs, news about the boards of pharmacy, and articles that impact the practice and regulation of pharmacy appear in each issue. *$35.00*

10 Per Year

5416 NCPA Newsletter
National Community Pharmacists Association
100 Daingerfield Road
Alexandria, VA 22314
703-683-8200
FAX: 703-683-3619 800-544-7447
info@ncpanet.com www.ncpanet.org

Mike Conlan, VP Publications
Chris Linville, Managing Editor

Stay up-to-date on the latest developments in legislation, federal regulation, pharmacy news, and other important events with the NCPA Newsletter. Independent pharmacists get the information they need to understand the policies, politics, and government actions that affect independent pharmacy practice. Annual subscription is included in NCPA memership dues. *$50.00*

5417 Nation's Health
American Public Health Association
800 I Street NW
Washington, DC 20001-3710
202-777-2742
FAX: 202-777-2534
coments@apha.org www.apha.org

Georges C Benjamin, Publisher
Kim Krisberg, Senior Editor
Michele Late, Executive Editor

For the latest news on public health, public health professionals, legislators and decision-makers. This newsletter is part of APHA membership. *$50.00*

10 Per Year

5418 PDA Letter
Parenteral Drug Association
1894 Preston White Drive
Reston, VA 20191-5433
703-620-6390
FAX: 703-476-0904
info@npcnow.org www.npcnow.org

Walter L Morris, III, Senior Editor

Designed to keep members informed of the latest information in the regulatory arena along with scientific happenings within the Association and the industry. It also contains details on upcoming PDA events, as well as worldwide Chapter activities.

Monthly Founded: 1949

5419 PMA Newsletter
Pharmaceutical Manufacturers Association

1100 15th Street NW
Washington, DC 20005-1707
202-835-3400
FAX: 202-835-3414
http://www.phrma.org/

Duffy Miller, Publisher
Billy Tauzin, President

Association news, technological developments, design, implementation and production of drugs and pharmaceuticals, here and abroad.

Founded: 1965

5420 Pharmaceutical & Med Packaging News
Canon Communications
11444 W Boulevard
Los Angeles, CA 90064-1549
310-445-4200
FAX: 310-445-4299
feedback@cancom.com
http://www.cancom.com

Daphne Allen, Editor
Dan Cutrone, Marketing Manager
Sandra Martin, Circulation Manager

Monthly

5421 Pharmaceutical News Daily
CTB International Publishing
PO Box 218
Maplewood, NJ 07040
973-966-0997
FAX: 973-966-0242
info@ctbintl.com
http://www.ctbintl.com

Kris Brogina, CEO/President
Kistine Yanicek, Editor
Oykue Brogina, Publisher
T Tseng, Circulation Manager

This daily electronic newsletter updates the highly competitive pharmaceutical and biotechnology industries. Delivered by e-mail. *$279.00*

Daily Founded: 1984
Printed in 1 color on newsprint stock

5422 Pharmaceutical Production
Pharmaceutical Production Tech Source
106 N 4th Avenue
Ann Arbor, MI 48104
734-998-0098
FAX: 734-998-0816 www.ic.net/~ppt/

Offers full coverage of pharmaceutical services and drug development in the US. If you don't have a great deal of time we supply you with the latest technical information and knowledge through educational conferences, courses, books, professional contacts, and mini table top exibits.

Monthly

5423 Pharmacist's Letter
Therapeutic Research
3120 W. March Lane PO Box 8190
Stockton, CA 95208-190
209-472-2240
FAX: 209-472-2249
http://www.pletter.com

Jeff Jellin, Publisher

A newsletter to pharmacists offering coverage of drug development, production, distribution, legislation, safety and other issues concerning the industry. *$85.00*

5424 Pharmacy Practice News
McMahon Group
545 W 45th Street
8th Floor
New York, NY 10036-3409
212-957-5300
FAX: 212-957-7230
davidb@mcmahonmed.com
http://www.mcmahonmed.com

Raymond E McMohan, Publisher
Van Velle, President
David Bronstein, Editor-in-Chief
Marsha Radebaugh, Circulation Manager
Michelle McMohan, Creative Director

Created to inform hospital pharmacists of the latest news on drugs, nutrition, research and trends in the pharmaceutical industry. *$60.00*

Monthly Founded: 1972
Circulation: 45460

5425 Pharmacy Student
APLA
2215 Constitution Avenue NW
Washington, DC 20037-2977
202-429-7576

Rick Harding, Publisher

Practical information to help pharmacy students grow. *$35.00*

Monthly
Circulation: 100000

5426 Pharmacy Today
APLA
2215 Constitution Avenue NW
Washington, DC 20037-2977
202-429-7576
FAX: 202-429-7596 800-363-8012
Rick Harding, Publisher
Rick Harding, President
Industry and practice news and reports on practice, medication usage, drug delivery, selection, and all areas of pharmacy practice.
Founded: 1962
Circulation: 100000

5427 Prescriber's Letter
Therapeutic Research
PO Box 8190
Stockton, CA 95208
209-472-2240
FAX: 209-472-2249 www.pletter.com
Jeff Jellin PharmD, Publisher
A newsletter to pharmacists offering coverage of drug development, production, distribution, legislation, safety and other issues concerning the industry. *$85.00*

5428 Preventive Medicine Update
HealthComm International
5800 Soundview Drive
PO Box 1729
Gig Harbor, WA 98335-2000
253-858-3315
FAX: 253-851-9749 800-843-9660
Jeffrey Bland, CEO/Contact

5429 Psoriasis Resource
National Psoriasis Foundation
6600 SW 92nd Avenue
Suite 300
Portland, OR 97223-7195
503-244-7404
FAX: 503-245-0626 800-723-9166
getinfo@npfusa.org
http://www.psoriasis.org
Sheri Decker, Editor
Bill Taggart, Managing Editor
Gail Zimmerman, Chief Executive Officer
A newsletter published for members of the National Psoriasis Foundation. Highlights interesting articles on psoriasis products and medications andother health related topics. Contains advertisements for psoriasis-related products and services.
16 pages
Circulation: 40000
Mailing list available for rent 28000 names
Printed in 2 colors on matte stock : website

5430 Rx Ipsa Loquitur
American Society for Pharmacy Law
1224 Centre W
Suite 400B
Springfield, IL 62704
217-391-0219
FAX: 217-793-0041 www.aspl.org
Melissa Madigan, President
Francis B Palumbo, Director
Pamela Tolson, CAE, Executive Director
William Fassett, Treasurer
Featuring recent court decisions, legislative and regulatory news, and other current pharmacy law news and articles.
Bi-Monthly

5431 Washington Drug Letter
FDAnews
300 N Washington Street
Suite 200
Falls Church, VA 22046-3431
703-538-7600
FAX: 703-538-7676 888-838-5578
customerservice@fdanews.com
http://www.fdanews.com
David Swit, Publisher
Cynthia Carter, President
Maritza Lizama, Marketing Director
Summaries of FDA regulatory changes and key legislation that affects prescription and over the counter drugs. Each weekly issue brings you up-to-date on pre approval and post approval issues that directly impact your operation. *$897.00*
Weekly

Magazines & Journals

5432 A Practical Guide to Food and Drug Law and Regulation
Food & Drug Law Institute
1000 Vermont Avenue NW
Suite 200
Washington, DC 20005
202-371-1420
FAX: 202-371-0649 800-956-6293
comments@fdli.org www.fdli.org
Kenneth R Pina, Author
Wayne L Pines, Author
Includes a new user friendly format with comprehensive indexing to make locating the help you need faster and easier, updated text by the original authors, and a new chapter on dietary supplements. 2nd Edition. *$99.00*
354 pages Soft Cover ISBN 1-885259-73-5

5433 AAPS Newsmagazine
American Association of Pharmaceutical Scientists
2107 Wilson Boulevard
Suite 700
Arlington, VA 22201-3046
703-243-2800
FAX: 703-243-9054
aaps@aaps.org www.aaps.org
Jake Harris, Publications Associate Director
Rebecca Jensen, Managing Director
Janelle Kihlstrom, Editorial Assistant
Exclusive to AAPS members. Features expanded coverage of the industry, complete with expert information on marketplace trends, regulatory matters, and career opportunities.
Mailing list available for rent

5434 AAPS Online Buyers Guide
American Association of Pharmaceutical Scientists
2107 Wilson Boulevard
Suite 700
Arlington, VA 22201-3046
703-243-2800
FAX: 703-243-9054
aaps@aaps.org www.aaps.org
Jake Harris, Publications Associate Director
Rebecca Jensen, Managing Director
Janelle Kihlstrom, Editorial Assistant
comprehensive sourcebook you need as a pharmaceutical scientist. Research the more than 500 companies providing the products and service you need. You can browse the entire Online Buyers Guide or you can refine your search by Company Name, Region, Business Category, or Keyword.
Mailing list available for rent

5435 AAPS PharmSciTech Journal
American Association of Pharmaceutical Scientists
2107 Wilson Boulevard
Suite 700
Arlington, VA 22201-3046
703-243-2800
FAX: 703-243-9054
pharmscitech-edoffice@aaps.org
www.aapspharmaceutica.com
Patrick P DeLuca, Editor-in-Chief
James Greif, Communications Specialist
An online-only journal published and owned by the American Association of Pharmaceutical Scientists. The journal's mission is to disseminate scientific and technical information on drug product design, development, evaluation and processing to the global pharmaceutical research community, taking full advantage of web-based publishing by presenting innovative text with 3-D graphics, interactive figures and databases, video and audio files.
Mailing list available for rent

5436 America's Pharmacist
National Community Pharmacists Association
100 Daingerfield Road
Alexandria, VA 22314
703-683-8200
FAX: 703-683-3619 800-544-7447
info@ncpanet.com www.ncpanet.org
Mike Conlan, VP Publications/Editor
Chris Linville, Managing Editor
This informative magazine gives 25,000 independent pharmacists insight into current issues that affect independent pharmacy and NCPA's activities to address those issues. Also; it serves the readers by including monthly articles on clinical topics, a continuing education series for pharmacists who want to earn CE credit, information on how to manage finances, and proven tips on better marketing, as well as profiles of NCPA members from across the country. Annual subscription included in dues. *$50.00*
Monthly

5437 American Institute of the History of Pharmacy
777 Highland Avenue
Madison, WI 53705-2222
608-262-5378
FAX: 608-262-3397
aihp@aihp.org http://www.aihp.org/
Dr. Gregory Higby, Executive Director
Margaret Sherwood, Circulation Manager
Articles on pharmaceutical history and usage. *$50.00*
200 pages Quarterly Founded: 1960
Circulation: 1200
Printed in on glossy stock

5438 **American Journal of Health-System Pharmacy**
American Society of Health-System Pharmacists
7272 Wisconsin Avenue
Bethesda, MD 20814-4836
301-657-3000

ajhp@ashp.org www.ashp.org
C Richard Talley, Editor
Maryann R Mohassel, Managing Editor
The journal for pharmacists practicing in all area's of acute care, ambulatory care, home care, long term care, HMO's, PPO's, and PBM's. *$165.00*
54 pages Bi-Weekly
Circulation: 42,000
Printed in 2 colors on glossy stock

5439 **American Journal of Pharmaceutical Education**
American Association of Colleges of Pharmacy
1426 Prince Street
Alexandria, VA 22314
703-739-2330
FAX: 703-836-8982
jdipiro@mail.mcg.edu www.aacp.org
Joseph Dipiro, Editor
Karen Shipp, Assistant Editor
Gayle A Brazeau, PhD, Associate Editor
Jack E Finchman, PhD, Associate Editor
Official publication of the American Association of Colleges of Pharmacy. Dedicated to all those with interest in professional, graduate, and postgraduate pharmaceutical education. Its purpose is to documnet and advance pharmaceutical education in the United States and Internationally. Features original research articles, editorials, reports on the state of pharmaceutical education, descriptions of teaching innovations, and book reviews. *$65.00*
120 pages Quarterly Founded: 1937
Circulation: 3200
Printed in 1 color on matte stock

5440 **American Journal of Public Health**
American Public Health Association
CJ-1020
Medical College of Georgia
Augusta, GA 30912-2450
706-721-4915
FAX: 706-721-3994
AJPE@mail.mcg.edu
http://www.ajpe.org
Joseph T Dipiro, Editor
Gayle Brazeau, Associate Editor
Dedicated to original work in research, research methods, and program evaluation in the field of public health. This prestigious journal also regularly publishes authoritative editorials and commentaries and serves as a forum for the analysis of health policy. *$100.00*
120 pages Quarterly Founded: 1990
Circulation: 3200

5441 **American Society of Health-System Pharmacists**
7272 Wisconsin Avenue
Bethesda, MD 20814-4836
301-657-3000
FAX: 301-657-1615
webcustsvc@ashp.org
http://www.ashp.org
Cynthia Brennan, President
Henri R Manasse Jr, Executive VP
Supports all pharmacists in a hospital environment.
Monthly Founded: 1942

5442 **BioPharm**
Advanstar Communications
One Park Avenue
New York, NY 10016
212-797-7631
FAX: 212-951-6793
info@advanstar.com
http://www.advanstar.com
Joseph Loggia, Chief Executive Officer
Tom Larranaga, Group Publisher
Francis Heid, VP Publishing
David Esola, VP Pharmaceutical and Science Group
Tom Cermak, Marketing Development
Publication taking a practical approach to the technology and business of developing and manufacturing biotechnology-derived pharmaceutical products. Regular topics include process development, downstream processing, facilities design, emerging technologies and regulatory compliance. *$64.00*
Monthly Founded: 1987
Circulation: 29,200

5443 **Certificate of Analysis Guide for Bulk Pharmaceutical Excipients**
Int'l Pharm. Excipients Council of the Americas
1655 N Fort Myer Drive
Suite 700
Arlington, VA 22209
703-515-5266
FAX: 703-525-5157
info@ipecamericas.org
http://www.ipecamericas.org
R Christian Moreton PhD, Chairman
Alan W Mercill, Secretary/Treasurer
Joel Bleustein, Owner
Published by the International Pharmaceutical Excipients Council of the Americas. *$10.00*
Founded: 2000

5444 **Chain Drug Review**
Racher Press
220 5th Avenue
New York, NY 10001
212-213-6000
FAX: 212-725-3961
info@racherpress.com
http://www.racherpress.com
Kevin Burke, VP/Group Advertising
Jeff Woldt, VP/Editorial Director
David Pinto, Editor
Chain Drug Review serves the chain drug industry. *$185.00*
Bi-weekly Founded: 1978
Circulation: 54000 54M names $100 per M.
Printed in 4 colors on glossy stock

5445 **Chemistry**
American Chemical Society
1155 16th Street NW
Washington, DC 20036
202-724-4600
FAX: 202-872-4615 800-227-5558
help@acs.org www.chemistry.org
James D Burke, Chair
E Ann Nalley, President
Elizabeth Zubritsky, Manager
C Gordon McCarty, Director
Madeleine Jacobs, Executive Director
Published for members, student affiliates, and those interested in learning more about the chemical sciences and the American Chemical Society.

5446 **CleanRooms Magazine**
PennWell Publishing Company
98 Spit Brook Road
Suite 100
Nashua, NH 03062-5723
603-891-0123
FAX: 603-891-9200
georgem@pennwell.com
http://www.cleanrooms.com
John Haystead, Editorial Director
James Enos, Publisher
Bob Johnson, Sales & Marketing Manager

Serves the contamination control and ultrapure materials and process industries. Written for readers in the microelectronics, pharmaceutical, biotech, health care, food processing and other user industries. Provides technology and business news and new product listings. *$97.00*
Monthly Founded: 1987
Circulation: 35031

5447 **Community Pharmacist**
ELF Publications
5285 W Louisiana Avenue
Lakewood, CO 80232
303-975-0075
FAX: 303-975-0132 800-922-8513
mcasey@elfpublications.com
http://www.elfpublications.com
Judith D Lane, Editor/Publisher
Ronald R Quam, Editor/Publisher
Pharmacy trade journal that meets the professional educational needs of today's practitioner *$12.00*
40 pages Founded: 1972 50,000 names $50 per M.
Printed in 4 colors on glossy stock

5448 **Consultant Pharmacist**
American Society of Consultant Pharmacists
1321 Duke Street
Suite 120
Alexandria, VA 22314
703-739-1300
FAX: 703-739-1321 800-355-2727
info@ascp.com http://www.ascp.com
H. Edward Davidson, Editor-in-Chief
Marlene Bloom, Managing Editor
Official peer reviewed journal of the American Society of Consultant Pharmacists. Editorial deals with geriatric pharmacotherapy. *$50.00*
76 pages Founded: 1982
Circulation: 13000
Printed in 4 colors on glossy stock

5449 **Contract Pharma**
Rodman Publications
70 Hilltop Road
Ste. 3000
Ramsey, NJ 07446
201-825-2552
FAX: 201-825-0553
info@contractpharma.com
http://www.contractpharma.com
Matthew Montgomery, Executive Vice President
Gil Y Roth, Editor
Gary Durr, Publisher
Ellen Pfister, Circulation Manager
A global publication providing most up-to-date news, outsourcing information, business trends, commentary, and viewpoints to the Pharmaceutical and Biopharmaceutical outsourcing industry.
Monthly Founded: 1999
Circulation: 20026

5450 **DIA Today**
Drug Information Association
800 Enterprise Road
Suite 200
Horsham, PA 19044-3595
215-442-6100
FAX: 215-442-6199
dia@diahome.org www.diahome.org
Fran Klass, Managing Editor
David Maola, Executive Director
Features important news coming out of major DIA conferences and workshops, as well as reports on the actions of the Board of Directors and the Regional Steering Committees that directly impact DIA members.

5451 **DVM News**
Advanstar Communications
One Park Avenue
New York, NY 10016
212-797-7631
FAX: 617-267-6900 800-598-6008
info@advanstar.com
http://www.advanstar.com
Maureen Hrehocik, Editor
Information from veterinary medicine covering news, features, practice management and new products and services. *$4.00*
Monthly Founded: 1987

5452 **Drug Information Journal**
Drug Information Association
800 Enterprise Road
Suite 200
Horsham, PA 19044-3595
215-442-6100
FAX: 215-442-6199
dia@diahome.org
http://www.diahome.org
David M Maola Esq, Executive Director
Carol Layer, Administrative Director
Fran Klass, Managing Editor
Cheryl Buckage, Administrative Assistant
Mark Eberhardt, Member Services Manager
Provides a neutral global forum for the exchange and dissemination of information on the discovery, development, evaluation and utilization of medicines and related health care technologies. Through these activities the DIA provides development opportunities for its members.
Quarterly Founded: 1964
Circulation: 27500

5453 **Drug Store News**
Lebhar-Friedman
425 Park Avenue
New York, NY 10022
212-756-5088
FAX: 212-756-5250
editor@drugstorenews.com
http://www.drugstorenews.com
Tony Lasanti, Editor
J Rodger Friedman, CEO
Publication consists of merchandising trends and pharmacy developments. Provides extensive coverage of every major segment of chain drug retailing and combination stores. *$119.00*
Founded: 1925
Circulation: 45000

5454 **Drug Topics**
Medical Economics Publishing
5 Paragon Drive
Montvale, NJ 07645-1742
973-447-7777
FAX: 973-847-5303
drug.topics@Medec.com
http://www.drugtopics.com
Judy Chi, Managing Editor
Information on the distributing and dispensing drug trade. *$61.00*
Printed in 4 colors on glossy stock

5455 **Food & Drug Packaging**
Stagnito Publishing Group
155 Pfingston Road
Suite 205
Deerfield, IL 60015
847-205-5660
FAX: 847-205-5680
gvansomeren@stagnito.com
http://www.fdp.com
Lisa McTigue Pierce, Editor-in-Chief
Blayne Long, Senior Marketing Manager
Geneine Van Someren, Circulation Manager
Food and Drug Packaging serves industries engaged in packaging food, beverages, pharmaceuticals, cosmetics and consulting/engineering firms.
Monthly Founded: 1959
Circulation: 75140

5456 **Formulary**
Advanstar Communications
One Park Avenue
New York, NY 10016
212-797-7631
FAX: 212-951-6793 800-225-4569
info@advanstar.com
http://www.advanstar.com
Tara Stultz, Editor-in-Chief
Steven Reichenstein, Publisher
Peer-reviewed publication providing drug information for physicians, pharmacists, and other health care professionals who influence the selection and use of drugs in hospitals, HMO's, and other managed care settings. *$61.00*
Monthly Founded: 1992
Circulation: 51402

5457 **Framework for Pharmaceutical Risk Management**
Food & Drug Law Institute
1000 Vermont Avenue NW
Suite 200
Washington, DC 20005
202-711-1420
FAX: 202-371-0649 800-956-6293
comments@fdli.org www.fdli.org
Jeffrey E Fetterman, Author
Wendy K Nickel, Author
Wayne L Pines, Author
Gary H Slatko, MD, Author
Provides decision makers within drug development, regulatory affairs and marketing disciplines with timely, insightful and practical recommendations to help answer key questions and provide direction for program development. *$99.00*
191 pages Soft Cover ISBN 1-885259-79-4

5458 **GMP Audit Guideline for Bulk Pharmaceutical Excipients**
Int'l Pharm. Excipients Council of the Americas
1655 N Fort Myer Drive
Suite 700
Arlington, VA 22209
703-351-5266
FAX: 703-525-5157
www.ipecamericas.org
R Christian Moreton PhD, Chairman
Alan W Mercill, Secretary/Treasurer
Kimberly Beals, Director Member Services
Published by the International Pharmaceutical Excipients Council of the Americas. *$10.00*
Founded: 1998

5459 **GMP Audit Guideline for Distributors of Bulk Pharmaceutical Excipients**
Int'l Pharm. Excipients Council of the Americas
1655 N Fort Myer Drive
Suite 700
Arlington, VA 22209
703-351-5266
FAX: 703-525-5157
info@ipecamericas.org
http://www.ipecamericas.org
Dr Arthru J Falk, Chairman
Alan W Mercill, Secretary/Treasurer
Published by the International Pharmaceutical Excipients Council of the Americas. *$10.00*
Founded: 1991

5460 **GMP Guide for Bulk Pharmaceutical Excipients**
Int'l Pharm. Excipients Council of the Americas
1655 N Fort Myer Drive
Suite 700
Arlington, VA 22209
703-351-5266
FAX: 703-525-5157
info@ipecamericas.org
http://www.ipecamericas.org
Arthur Folk, Chairman
Alan W Mercill, Secretary/Treasurer
Published by the International Pharmaceutical Excipients Council of the Americas. *$10.00*
Founded: 1991

5461 **Happi**
Rodman Publications
70 Hilltop Raod
Ramsey, NJ 07446
201-825-2552
FAX: 201-825-0553
resource@intac.com
http://www.happi.com
Art Largar, Publisher
Sharon Messner, Manager
Rodman J. Zilenziger, Jr., President
Tom Branna, Editor
Serves the manufacturers and fillers of cosmetics, toiletries, fragrances, pharmaceuticals, detergents and chemical specialties inclusing household cleaning products and other product lines allied to the field.
Monthly Founded: 1964
Circulation: 15783
Printed in 4 colors on glossy stock

5462 HealthCare Distributor
ELF Publications
5285 W Louisiana Avenue
Lakewood, CO 80232
303-975-0075
FAX: 303-975-0132 800-922-8513
elfpub@qwest.net
http://www.elfpublications.com

Judith D Lane, Editor/Publisher/CEO
Ronald R Quam, Editor/Publisher
Chuck Austin, Senior Editor
Jerry Lester, Director of Sales

Multi-market publication devoted to the issues and opportunities facing the wholesale drug, chain drug, medical/surgical and home care products distribution industries *$12.00*

80 pages Bi-annually Founded: 1972
Circulation: 12000
Printed in 4 colors on glossy stock

5463 Hospital Pharmacy
Facts and Comparisons
111 W Port Plaza
Suite 300
Saint Louis, MO 63146-3098
314-878-2515
FAX: 314-878-5563 800-223-0554
service@drugfacts.com
www.drugfacts.com

Neil M Davis, Editor-in-Chief

Provides pharmacists with peer-reviewed articles and monthly features covering clinical and administrative areas such as drug use, drug distribution systems in hospitals and health-systems, automation, medication errors and adverse events, Joint Commission drug-related material and current FDA drug information. *$124.95*

Monthly Founded: 1965

5464 Inform
American Oil Chemists Society
2211 W Bradley Avenue
Champaign, IL 61821-1827
217-359-2344
FAX: 217-351-8091
general@aocs.org http://www.aocs.org

James B Rattray, Editor-in-Chief
Barbara Jewett, Managing Editor

Provides business and scientific news to readers interested in research, development and processing of fats and oils and their derivative products. *$120.00*

462 pages Monthly Founded: 1909
Circulation: 3700 $210 per M.
Printed in on glossy stock

5465 International Pharmaceutical Abstracts
American Society of Health-System Pharmacists
7272 Wisconsin Avenue
Bethesda, MD 20814-4836
301-657-3000

ipa@ashp.org http://www.ashp.org

Dwight Tousignaut, Production Manager
Henri Manasse Jr., President/CEO

These reports offering the latest in the development of drugs overseas, clinical use, cosmetics and, alternative and herbal medicine. Reports on pharmacy practice are also included. *$240.00*

Monthly Founded: 1936
Circulation: 31,000

5466 Journal of Managed Care Pharmacy
Academy of Managed Care Pharmacy
100 N Pitt Street
Suite 400
Alexandria, VA 22314-3134
703-683-8416
FAX: 703-683-8417 800-827-2627
sandres@amcp.org www.amcp.org

Frederic R Curtiss, PhD, Editor-in-Chief
Judy Cahill, Executive Director

Features articles on trends and recent developments in managed care pharmacy, updates from pharmacy educators about the inclusion of managed care topics in cirricula and news and information about the academy and it's activities. *$60.00*

Bi-Monthly

5467 Journal of Parenteral and Enteral Nutrition
Amer. Society for Parenteral & Enteral Nutrition
8630 Fenton Street
Suite 412
Silver Spring, MD 20910-3803
301-587-6315
FAX: 301-587-2365 800-727-4567
jpen@nutr.org
http://www.nutritioncare.org

Robin Kriegel, Executive Director
Karyn Butts, Research Administrator
Bridget Hollick, Managing Editor
Natalie Ortiz-Ramos, Executive Assistant
Charles W. Van Way III, Editor-in-Chief

Is the premier scientific journal of nutrition and metabolic support. It publishes original, peer-reviewd studies that define the cutting edge of basic and clinical research in the field. It explores the science of optimizing the care of patients receiving enteral or IV therapies. This is included as benefits of membership in ASPEN. *$90.00*

Fortnightly Founded: 1977
Circulation: 7800

5468 Journal of Pharmaceutical Marketing and Management
Haworth Press
10 Alice Street
Binghamton, NY 13904-1580
607-722-5857
FAX: 607-771-0012 800-429-6784
getinfo@haworthpress.com
www.haworthpress.com/web/jpmm/

Mick Kolassa PhD, Editor

Multidisciplinary journal devoted to solving the problems inherent in the mangement and marketing of pharmaceutical products and services. This journal maintains a rigorous policy of publishing quality research reports of interest to individuals involved in the manufacturing, wholesale, institutional, retail, regulatory, organizational and academic components of the pharmaceutical industry. *$75.00*

Quarterly

5469 Journal of Pharmaceutical Sciences

10 Alice Street
Binghamton, NY 13904-1580
607-722-5857
FAX: 607-771-0012 800-429-6784
getinfo@haworthpress.com
http://www.haworthpress.com

Mick Kolassa, Editor
Julie Fisher, Assistant Editor
Roger Hall, VP
Laurie Beagell, Circulation Manager

A comprehensive look at the world of drugs and pharmaceuticals. *$75.00*

Quarterly Founded: 1979
Circulation: 225

5470 Journal of Pharmacy Practice
Technomic Publishing Company
PO Box 3535
Lancaster, PA 17601
717-291-5609
FAX: 717-295-4538 800-233-9936
aflannery@techpub.com
http://www.techpub.com

Amy Flannery, Marketing

The journal provides useful, timely reports on the most challenging issues of pharmacy today and anticipates the unique demands of this rapidly changing field. Each issue's single-topic format and thoughtful, readable analysis gives a better grasp of difficult problems and provides immediately useful information. *$210.00*

80 pages
Printed in 2 colors on matte stock : On-Line

5471 Journal of Pharmacy Technology
Harvey Whitney Books Company
PO Box 42696
Cincinnati, OH 45242-696
513-793-3555
FAX: 513-793-3600 877-742-7631
customerserv@jpharmtechnol.com
http://www.jpharmtechnol.com

Harvey Whitney, Publisher/Editor
Eugene Sorkin, Associate Editorial
Ann Brandewiede, Circulation Manager

Latest information on drugs, for health professionals. Topics covered include new drug profiles, education and training, legal dilemmas, drug distribution, products and equipment and continuing education. *$122.00*

Circulation: 1000

5472 Journal of Surfactants and Detergents
American Oil Chemists Society
2211 W Bradley Avenue
Champaign, IL 61821-1827
217-359-2344
FAX: 217-351-8091
general@aocs.org www.aocs.org

V Mark Nace, Editor-in-Chief
Brian Moore, Managing Editor

A science and news journal dedicated to the practical and theoretical aspects of oleochemical and petrochemical surfactants, soaps, and detergents. This journal publishes peer-reviewed research papers, reviews, and news related to surfactants and detergents technologies.

Quarterly Founded: 1998

5473 Journal of the American Oil Chemists' Society
American Oil Chemists Society
2211 W Bradley Avenue
Champaign, IL 61821-1827
217-359-2344
FAX: 217-351-8091
general@aocs.org www.aocs.org

John P Cherry, Editor-in-Chief

This is a peer reviewed journal devoted to fundamental and practical research, production, processing, packaging, and distribution in the field of fats, oils, proteins, and other related substances.

Monthly Founded: 1947

5474 Lipids
American Oil Chemists Society
2211 W Bradley Avenue
Champaign, IL 61821-1827
217-359-2344
FAX: 217-351-8091
general@aocs.org www.aocs.org

Howard R Knapp, Editor-in-Chief
Pam Landman, Production Editor

This journal features full length original research articles, short communications, methods papers, and review articles on timely topics. All papers are meticulously peer-reviewed and edited by some of the foremost experts in their respective fields.
Monthly Founded: 1966

5475 MPMN: Medical Product Manufacturing News
Canon Communications
11444 W Olympic Boulevard
Los Angeles, CA 90064-1549
310-445-4200
FAX: 310-445-4299
john.bethune@cancom.com
www.devicelink.com

Susan Wallace, Editor
John Bethune, Editorial Director

A product tabloid magazine that provides information on the new products and services available to medical device manufacturers.
10x/yr

5476 Medical Advertising News
Engel Publishing Partners
828A Newtown-Yardley
Newtown, PA 18940
215-867-0044
FAX: 215-867-0053
interactivemedia@engelpub.com
http://www.engelpub.com

Jim Hannan, CEO
Chris Truelove, Editor
Glenn Glasberg, Marketing Manager

News and events affecting the medical and pharmaceutical marketing industry. *$50.00*
40 pages Monthly

5477 Modern Drug Discovery
American Chemical Society
1155
16th Street NW
Washington, DC 20036-4800
202-872-4600
FAX: 202-872-4615 800-227-5558
help@acs.org
http://www.pubs.acs.org
Reports matters of interest to scientists and other professionals working in the field of drug discovery.
Monthly

5478 Monitor
Association of Clinical Research Professionals
1012 14th Street NW
Suite 108
Washington, DC 20006
202-737-8100
FAX: 202-737-8101
acrp@associationhq.com
www.acrpnet.org

Sharada Gilkey, Editor-in-Chief

Features peer-reviewed articles, columns, and home study.
Quarterly

5479 Nutrition in Clinical Practice
Amer. Society for Parenteral & Enteral Nutrition
8630 Fenton Street
Suite 412
Silver Spring, MD 20910
301-587-6315
FAX: 301-587-2365 800-727-4567
aspen@nutr.org
www.nutritioncare.org

Bridget Hollick, Managing Editor

This compliments the Journal of Parenteral and Enteral Nutrition with practical information and advice. It provides peer-reviewed clinical studies, reviews, techniques and procedures, teaching cases, clinical observations, and nutrition news. Included as benefits of membership is ASPEN. *$45.00*
Bi-Monthly

5480 PDA Journal of Pharmaceutical Science and Technology
Parenteral Drug Association
1894 Preston White Drive
Reston, VA 20191-5433
703-620-6390
FAX: 703-476-0904
infoQnpcnow.com www.npcnow.org

Lee Kirsch, Editor

One of the most relevant and outstanding peer-reviewed scientific and technical papers in the pharmaceutical/biopharmaceutical industry. The Journal is distributed to members as a membership benefit.
Bi-Monthly

5481 Pharmaceutical & Medical Packaging News
Canon Communications
11444 W Olympic Boulevard
Suite 900
Los Angeles, CA 90064
310-445-4200
FAX: 310-445-4269
feedback@cancom.com
http://www.pmpnews.com

Bill Cobert, Publisher
Daphne Allen, Editor
Justine Hamilton, Marketing Director

Information and news on events, new technology, industry trends, regulatory matters, and health care trade associations for professionals involved in the pharmaceutical and medical product packaging industry. *$150.00*
Monthly Founded: 1978
Circulation: 20,000

5482 Pharmaceutical Engineering
Int'l Society for Pharmaceutical Engineering
3109 W Dr. Martin Luther King Jr Blvd
Suite 250
Tampa, FL 33607
813-960-2105
FAX: 813-264-2816
customerservice@ispe.org
http://www.ispe.org

Gloria N Hall, Editor
Linda Brady, Director Marketing
Bob Best, CEO

Journal is published bi-monthly for members only and is considered by ISPE members to be the number one member benefit. Feature articles provide practical application and specification information on the design, construction, supervision and maintenance of process equipment, plant systems, instrumentation and facilities.
Bi-monthly Founded: 1980
Circulation: 23000

5483 Pharmaceutical Executive
Advanstar Communications
131 W First Street
Duluth, MA 55802
218-723-9200
FAX: 218-723-9537 800-598-6008
info@advanstar.com
http://www.advanstar.com

Wayne Koberstein, Editor
Kim Brown, Producation Manager

Publication designed to meet the diverse management and marketing needs of professionals in the pharmaceutical industry worldwide. Editorial provides useful information on marketing, sales and promotion, as well as legal and regulatory issues. *$70.00*
Monthly Founded: 1987
Circulation: 16237

5484 Pharmaceutical Formulation & Quality
Carpe Diem Communications
208 Floral Vale Boulevard
Yardley, PA 19067
215-860-7800
FAX: 215-860-7900
pharmaeditor@carpediemcomm.com
http://www.pharmaquality.com

Sangita Viswanathan, Editor-in-Chief
Rick Biros, Publisher/President
Karen Devlin, Production Manager

A dynamic magazine written to keep the pharmaceutical and related industries informed about the very latest technologies, techniques and regulations affecting product development and formulation. PFQ's coverage extends throughout the full product lifecycle, from initial development through clinical trials and scale up top manufacturing, focusing on current issues in the competitive business of producing pharmaceuticals and biopharmaceuticals. *$90.00*
100 pages Founded: 1998
Circulation: 20000
Mailing list available for rent 20000 names $185 per M.
Printed in 4 colors on glossy stock

5485 Pharmaceutical Industry Profile
Pharmaceutical Research and Manufacturers
1100 15th Street NW
Washington, DC 20005
202-835-3400
FAX: 202-833-3414
webmaster@phrma.org
www.phrma.org

Billy Tauzin, President/CEO

Focuses on pharmaceutical research and development, a responsibility that our industry shoulders for much of the world. America's biopharmaceutical companies are expected to take the lead in defeating crippling and deadly diseases.

5486 Pharmaceutical Processing
Reed Business Information
100 Enterprise drive
Suite 600
Rockaway, NJ 07866-912
973-920-7000
FAX: 973-920-7531 800-222-0289

Tim Canny, Publisher
Mike Auerbach, Editor
R Reed, Owner

Contents include news on new products/equipment/services, case history and application articles focusing on equipment, instrumentation, process systems, packaging, validation and outsourcing services offered to the pharmaceutical marketplace.
Monthly Founded: 1984
Circulation: 31075

5487 Pharmaceutical Research
Plenum Publishing Corporation
233 Spring Street
New York, NY 10013-1522
212-421-1490
FAX: 212-807-1047
info@plenum.com
http://www.plenum.com
Wolfgang Sadee, Editor
Research reports and summaries of the latest in development of certain drugs and pharmaceuticals. *$49.95*
Monthly Founded: 1998

5488 Pharmaceutical Technology Magazine
Advanstar Communications
485 Route One South
Building F, First Floor
Iselin, NJ 08830
732-596-0276
FAX: 732-596-0005
mtracey@advanstar.com
http://www.pharmtech.com
Mike Tracey, Publisher
Douglas McCormick, Editor in Chief
Paul Milazzo, Director of Sales
Tria Deibert, Marketing Director
Provides authoritative and timely information covering all aspects of conventional and biotech pharmaceutical manufacturing including: applied research and development, drug delivery, solid dosage, manufacturing machinery and equipment, information technologies, contract services, biotechnology trends, and regulatory issues.
Monthly Founded: 1987
Circulation: 33691

5489 Pharmacy Times
Romaine Pierson Publishers
241 Forsgate Drive
Jamesburg, NJ 08831
732-560-0200
FAX: 732-656-1148
cms@skainfo.com
http://www.pharmacytimes.com
Emilie McCardell, Editor-In-Chief
Cam Bishop, CEO
James Granato, Publisher
James Marshal, Production Director
Margaret P. Roeske, Associate Editor
News, analysis and trends in the pharmaceutical business. *$65.00*
Monthly Founded: 1897
Circulation: 174,104

5490 Pharmacy West
Western Communications
1777 SW Chandler Avenue
Bend, OR 97702
303-806-8952
FAX: 541-383-0372
Elroy FitzHenry, Editor
Distributed to pharmacies in the thirteen western states. *$18.00*
Monthly

5491 Profile of Pharmacy Faculty
American Association of Colleges of Pharmacy
1426 Prince Street
Alexandria, VA 22314
703-739-2330
FAX: 703-836-8982
mail@aacp.org www.aacp.org
Susan M Meyer, Senior Vice President
Lucinda L Maine, Executive VP
Provides statistics describing faculty at U.S. colleges and schools of pharmacy including a summary of the demographics, teaching discipline, rank, highest degree earned, tenure status, type of appointment, and salary of over 3,000 full time faculty members. Updated annually. *$25.00*

5492 Scrip Magazine
1775 Broadway
Suite 511
New York, NY 10019
212-262-8230
FAX: 212-262-8234
chonour@ThetaReports.com
An in-depth view of the issues and challenges facing all sectors of the pharmaceutical industry worldwide. Analytical features are written by pharmaceutical experts and opinion leaders as well as specialist journalists.
Monthly

5493 Significant Change Guide for Bulk Pharmaceutical Excipients
Int'l Pharm. Excipients Council of the Americas
1655 N Fort Myer Drive
Suite 700
Arlington, VA 22209
703-515-5266
FAX: 703-525-5157
info@ipecamericas.org
http://www.ipecamericas.org
R Moreton, Chairman
Alan Mercill, Secretary/Treasurer
Published by the International Pharmaceutical Excipients Council of the Americas. *$10.00*
Founded: 2000

Trade Shows

5494 AACP Annual Meeting and Seminars
American Association of Colleges of Pharmacy
1426 Prince Street
Alexandria, VA 22314
703-739-2330
FAX: 703-836-8982
mail@aacp.org www.aacp.org
Barbara A Gustis, Manager Meetings
A chance to learn and exchange ideas on pharmacy education and recent innovations in health care.
July

5495 AACP Institute
American Association of Colleges of Pharmacy
1426 Prince Street
Alexandria, VA 22314
703-739-2330
FAX: 703-836-8982
mail@aacp.org www.aacp.org
Barbara A Gustis, Manager Meetings
May

5496 AAPS Annual Meeting & Expo
2107 Wilson Boulevard
Suite 700
Arlington, VA 22201-3046
703-243-2800
FAX: 703-243-9054
aaps@aaps.org www.aaps.org
Sharon Pichon, Director Meetings/Expositions
925 booths of raw materials, supplies and equipment, research and contract service labs, computer software, packaging and more.
Annual November
Mailing list available for rent

5497 AAPT Annual Convention
American Association of Pharmacy Technicians
PO Box 1447
Greensboro, NC 27402
877-368-4771
336-333-9068
aapt@pharmacytechnician.com
www.pharmacytechnician.com
Ryan C Lee CPhT, President
Philip H Martin, Director
Marion K Keener, AS, Treasurer
Michele Poarch, CPhT, Secretary
Education programs and services to help technicians update their skills to keep pace with changes in the pharmacy services.
August

5498 ACLA Annual Meeting
American Clinical Laboratory Association
1250 H Street NW
Suite 880
Washington, DC 20005
202-637-9466
FAX: 202-637-2050
chawk@clinical-labs.org
www.clinical-labs.org
Cheryl Hawkins, Meeting Director
Alan Hertz, President
Dedicated to providing the latest information for clinical laboratories.
January Founded: 1971

5499 ACMP Conference
Academy of Managed Care Pharmacy
100 N Pitt Street
Suite 400
Alexandria, VA 22314-3134
703-683-8416
FAX: 703-683-8417 800-827-2627
sadres@amcp.org www.amcp.org
Aimee Hickox, Director Education/Meetings
Offers an exciting lineup of speakers, workshops, and topical sessions designed to meet the challenges of today's pharmacist practicing in a dynamic and constantly evolving managed care environment.
October

5500 APHA Annual Meeting & Exposition
American Public Health Association
800 I Street NW
Washington, DC 20001-3710
202-777-2742
FAX: 202-777-2534
diane.lentini@apha.org www.apha.org
Diane Lentini, Meetings Manager
Gene Lutz, President
Georges C Benjamin, Executive Director
Jose F Cordero, Member
Louise A Anderson, Director Operations

The premier platform to share successes and failures, discover exceptional best practices and learn from expert colleagues and the latest reasearch in the field.
13000 Attendees November

5501 APhA Annual Meeting
American Pharmaceutical Association Foundation
2215 Constitution Avenue NW
Washington, DC 20037
202-297-7524
FAX: 202-429-6300 800-237-APHA
tmcdonald@aphanet.org
www.aphameeting.org

Laura Larson, Exposition Director
Todd McDonald, Meeting Schedule Director
Hazel Pipkin, VP
Marie Michnich, Director Health Policy Program
Michael Stewart, Director Public Relations

A place to learn the latest about prescription drugs, natural products, and over-the-counter remedies. Gain knowledge and insights to better aid patients and advance your career. Discover new products and services from the industry's leading manufacturers.
Annual/March

5502 ASHP Summer Meeting
American Society of Health-System Pharmacists
7272 Wisconsin Avenue
Bethesda, MD 20814-4836
301-657-3000
FAX: 301-664-8857
info@ascp.com www.ascp.com

Frances Byrnes, Manager Meetings/Conferences
Jill E Martin, President

Offers a variety of programming, and delivers expertise on subject areas that are crucial to advancing a professional practice. Series programming, learning communities, and updates on hot topics, combined with exhibits and a variety of networking opportunities.
June

5503 ASPL Developments in Pharmacy Law Seminar
American Society for Pharmacy Law
1224 Centre W
Suite 400B
Springfield, IL 62704
217-391-0219
FAX: 217-793-0041 www.aspi.org

Melissa Madigan, President
Francis B Paulumbo, Director
Pamela Tolson, CAE, Executive Director
William Fassett, Treasurer

An annual highlight with nationally renowned speakers and panelists discussing issues pertaining to pharmacy law. This seminar has evolved into an excellent educational opportunity for practicing pharmacists, attorneys, and academicians with the opportunity to gain both pharmacy and legal continuing education credits.
Annual

5504 Academy of Pharmaceutical Research and Science Convention
American Pharmaceutical Association
2215 Constitution Avenue NW
Washington, DC 20037
202-429-7524
FAX: 202-628-0443 800-237-2742

Windy K Christner, Meetings/Expositions

Main exhibits, pharmaceutical equipment supplies and services.
Annual

5505 American Association of College Pharmacies
1426 Prince Street
Alexandria, VA 22314-2815
703-739-2330
FAX: 703-836-8982

Mary Bassler, Administrative Director

Educational association representing pharmacy scientists, educators and administrators.
2.3M Attendees July

5506 American College of Medical Quality Annual Meeting
American College of Medical Quality
4334 Montgomery Avenue
Suite B
Bethesda, MD 20814
301-913-9149
FAX: 301-913-9142 800-924-2149
acmq@aol.com www.acmq.org

Bridget Brodie, Executive Vice President

Annual show and 10-20 exhibits of computer hardware and software, pharmaceuticals, medical publications and related equipment, supplies and services.
150 Attendees

5507 American Pharmaceutical Association Trade Show
2215 Constitution Avenue NW
Washington, DC 20037-2975
202-628-4410
FAX: 202-783-2351 www.aphanet.org

Windy K Christner, Meetings/Exposition
Gwen Norheim, Library Services

Trade show featuring pharmaceutical products, pharmacy-management software, pharmacy equipment, publications and services for the pharmacy profession. 300 booths; 160 exhibitors.
6500 Attendees April

5508 Annual NCPA Convention & Trade Exposition
National Community Pharmacists Associations
100 Daingerfield Road
Alexandria, VA 22314
703-683-8200
FAX: 703-683-3619 800-544-7447
info@ncpanet.com www.ncpanet.org

Litsa Deck, Director Convention/Trade Expos

Workshops and education programs pretaining to Pharmacy industry.
October

5509 Annual North American Conference and European Annual Conference
Association of Clinical Research Professionals
1012 14th Street NW
Suite 108
Washington, DC 20006
202-737-8100
FAX: 202-737-8101
acrp@associationhq.com
www.acrpnet.org

Robin Newman, Vice Chair
Thomas L Adams, CAE, President/CEO
Larry J Medley, CAE, Director Finance
Alan Armstrong, Director Marketing/COO

The world's leading conferences for clinical research professionals, presenting diverse educational opportunities and face-to-face interactions with industry experts.
April, September

5510 Annual Physician Assistant Conference
American Academy of Physician Assistants
950 N Washington Street
Alexandria, VA 22314-1552
703-836-2272
FAX: 703-684-1924
aapa@aapa.org www.aapa.org

Amy Phillips, Dir Meetings/Industry Relations
Lauren Miller, Mgr Meetings/Industry Relations
Stephen Crane, Executive VP

250 educational sessions, plus 225 exhibits of medical software, books, pharmaceuticals, equipment and supplies, as well as sponsored symposia and adjuncts.
8000 Attendees May Founded: 1973
2M-5M names $500 per M.

5511 DCAT Western Education Conference
Drug, Chemical & Associated Technologies
1 Washington Boulevard
Suite 7
Robbinsville, NJ 08691
609-448-1000
FAX: 609-448-1944 800-640-3228
brooke@dcat.org www.dcat.org

Brooke DiGiuseppe, Meeting Services
Margaret Timony, Executive Director

Gain important insights into issues and trends that will affect the future of the nutrition and health industry. Participate in discussion on key business issues with industry experts.
April

5512 DIA Forum
Drug Information Association
800 Enterprise Road
Suite 200
Horsham, PA 19044-3595
215-442-6100
FAX: 215-442-6199
dia@diahome.org www.diahome.org

Eleanor M Perfetto, President
Gaby L Danan, Director
Richard O Day, Director
Francoise de Cremiers, Director
David Maola, Executive Director

Delivers practical, experience-based articles as well as comprehensive meeting proceedings, for selected conference sessions and workshops. Articles will be presented in a style that makes for easy reading while sharing useable information on working in an environment that is changing daily.

5513 Distribution & Logistics Conference
National Association of Chain Drug Stores
413 N Lee Street
PO Box 1417 D-49
Alexandria, VA 22313-1480
703-549-3001
FAX: 703-836-4869 www.nacds.org

Mary F Sammons, Chairman
Anthony Civello, Vice Chairman
Craig L Fuller, President/CEO
Mark Griffin, Director
David Bernauer, Treasurer

This unique conference explores and evaluates current systems and emerging technologies, and helps retailers and suppliers forge stronger links through supply chain management. The exhibit hall allows leading industry consultants and vendors to demonstrate their products and services.

March

5514 **Distribution Management Conference & Expo**
Healthcare Distribution Management Association
900 N Glebe Road
Suite 1000
Arlington, VA 22203
703-787-0000
FAX: 703-935-3200
lburke@hdmanet.org
www.healthcaredistribution.org

Lori Burke, Director Meetings/Conferences
Denise Woodson, Meerings Coordinator

Provides the latest information on the most important topics affecting healthcare distribution.

June

5515 **HDMA Annual Meeting**
Healthcare Distribution Management Association
900 N Glebe Road
Suite 1000
Arlington, VA 22203
703-787-0000
FAX: 703-935-3200
lburke@hdmanet.org
www.healthcaredistribution.org

Lori Burke, Director Meetings/Conferences
Denise Woodson, Meetings Coordinator

Provides a unique opportunity for senior-level retailer and supplier member executives to interact and discuss strategic issues.

October

5516 **IPC Annual Meeting**
Independent Pharmacy Cooperative
1550 Columbus Street
Sun Prairie, WI 53590
608-259-9556
FAX: 800-274-5525 800-755-1531
staff@ipcrx.com www.ipcx.com

Steve Niebauer, President/CEO
Mike Flint, VP
Chuck Benjamin, Chief Financial Officer
Mindy Hermann, Director Marketing/Sales

A venue to provide independent pharmacies vital information to maximize their store's profitability

July

5517 **ISPE Washington Conference**
Int'l Society for Pharmaceutical Engineering
3109 W Dr. Martin Luther King Jr Blvd
Suite 250
Tampa, FL 33607
813-960-2105
FAX: 813-264-2816
customerservice@ispc.org
www.ispe.org

Gert Moelgaard, Chairman
Elizabeth Barreto, Traffic Coordinator
Robert E Chew, PE, Director
Robert Best, Chief Executive Officer
Bruce Davis, Secretary

Education and training on topics pretaining to the pharmaceutical manufacturing industry.

June

5518 **Midyear Industry & Technology Issues Conference**
American Society for Automation in Pharmacy
492 Norristown Road
Suite 160
Blue Bell, PA 19422
610-825-7783
FAX: 310-825-7641
wal@computertalk.com
www.asapnet.org

Bill Lockwood, Executive Director
Tom Weiss, Secretary/Treasurer

Learn about the industry and technology issues facing the pharmacy market today.

June

5519 **NABP's Annual Meeting**
National Association of Boards of Pharmacy
700 Busse Highway
Park Ridge, IL 60068
847-698-6227
FAX: 847-698-0124 800-774-6227
custserv@nabp.net www.nabp.net

Carmen A Catizone, Executive Director/Secretary

Building regulatory foundation for patients safety.

May

5520 **NABP's Fall Educational Conference**
National Association of Boards of Pharmacy
700 Busse Highway
Park Ridge, IL 60068
847-698-6227
FAX: 847-698-0124 800-774-6227
custserv@nabp.net www.nabp.net

Donna S Wall, Chairperson
Donna M Horn, President
Lawrence H Mokhiber, Treasurer

December

5521 **NCPA Annual Conference on National Legislation and Government Affairs**
National Community Pharmacists Associations
100 Daingerfield Road
Alexandria, VA 22314
703-683-8200
FAX: 703-683-3619 800-544-7447
info@ncpanet.com www.ncpanet.org

Litsa Deck, Director Convention/Trade Expos

An opportunity to be an insider to discuss community pharmacy issues on Capitol Hill with the people that can make things happen. It will enhance your understanding of the political process and the many legislative issues that will have a dramatic impact on the way you deliver health care in the coming years.

April

5522 **NCPA Annual Meeting**
National Council of State Pharmacy Association
5501 Patterson Avenue
Suite 200
Richmond, VA 23226
804-285-4145
FAX: 804-285-4227
becky@ncspae.org www.ncspae.org

Rebecca P Snead, Administrative Manager

Offers cutting-edge training for professionals from every facet of the pharmacy industry. Learn the latest about prescription drugs, natural products, and over-the-counter remedies. Discover new products and services from the industry's leading manufacturers, and gain knowledge and insights to better aid patients and advance your career.

October

5523 **NCPDP's Annual Conference**
National Council for Prescription Drug Programs
9240 E Raintree Drive
Scottsdale, AZ 85260-7518
480-477-1000
FAX: 480-767-1042
ncpdp@ncpdp.org www.ncpdp.org

Beth Fagan, Meeting Planning
Lee Ann Stember, President

Topic will be Building New Technologies. Offers educational sessions, a trade show, kenote speakers and more.

March 2006

5524 **National Association of Chain Drug Stores Annual Meeting**
413 N Lee Street
PO Box 1417-D49
Alexandria, VA 22313-1480
703-549-3001
FAX: 703-836-4869 www.nacds.org

Jodi Witmer, Executive Director
Terry Arth, VP Meetings/International Programs
Larry Lotridge, VP Conference Exhibits

This meeting provides a unique and educational retreat for executive with general sessions and specific breakout sessions focusing on legal issues, finance, human resources and loss prevention issues.

1M Attendees April

5525 **National Clinical Issues Forum: Metabolic Syndrome**
American Pharmaceutical Association Foundation
2215 Constitution Avenue NW
Washington, DC 20037
202-297-7524
FAX: 202-429-6300 800-237-APHA
info@aphafoundation.org
www.aphafoundation.org

Carol Bugdalski-Stutrud, Director
Carl Emswiller, Director
Hazel Pipkin, VP
Marie Michnich, Director Health Policy Program
Michael Stewart, Director Public Relations

To provide an opportunity for the exchange of information between leading clinical pharmacists from across the U.S. who are providing innovative patient care services for people afflicted with the co-morbidities of diabetes, hypertension and hyperlipidemia.

May

5526 **National Community Pharmacists Association Convention and Exhibition**
National Community Pharmacists Association
100 Daingerfield Road
Alexandria, VA 22314-2833
703-683-8200
FAX: 703-683-3619 800-544-7447
Litsa Deck, Director Convention/Meetings
Faith James, Coordinator Convention/Meetings
Deleisa Johnson, VP Public Relations
Annual show of 450 exhibitors of pharmaceutical and related equipment, supplies and services.
October, Florida

5527 **National Conference on Advances in Perinatal and Pediatric Nutrition**
Amer. Society for Parenteral & Enteral Nutrition
8630 Fenton Street
Suite 412
Silver Spring, MD 20910
301-587-6315
FAX: 301-587-2365 800-727-4567
aspen@nutr.org
www.nutritioncare.org
Marion F Winkler, President
Vincent W Vanek, VP
Robin Kriegel, CAE, Executive Director
Joanne Kieffer, Director Finance
The purpose of the conference is to increase knowledge and awareness of the nutritional requirements of these special need patients. Has been planned for dieticians, nurses, obstetricians, neonatologiests, pediatricians, pediatric gastroenterologists, pharmacists, and other health care professionals involved in the care of high risk pregnant mothers, premature infants, and pediatric patients.
July

5528 **RX Expo: An Educational Forum and Buying Show**
National Community Pharmacists Association
205 Daingerfield Road
Alexandria, VA 22314-2833
703-683-8200
FAX: 703-683-3619 www.ncpanet.org
Annual show and exhibits of general gifts, sundries and seasonal items, over the counter products, health and beauty aids, electronic products, prescription drug products, personal care products, home health care products, IV products and related products.
1700 Attendees

5529 **Senior Care Pharmacy: ASCP's Annual Meeting**
American Society of Consultant Pharmacists
1321 Duke Street
Alexandria, VA 22314-3563
703-739-1300
FAX: 703-739-1321 800-355-2727
info@ascp.com www.ascp.com
Jackie Hajji, Director Meetings/Conventions
Annual meeting of 300 exhibitors of pharmaceuticals, drug distribution systems, packaging equipment, computers, durable medical equipment and medical supplies.
2000 Attendees November Founded: 1969
6500 names

5530 **USP Annual Scientific Meeting**
United States Pharmacopeial Convention
12601 Twinbrook Parkway
Rockville, MD 20852-1790
301-810-0667
FAX: 301-816-8148 800-227-8772
custsvc@usp.org www.usp.org
Anju K Malhotra, Manager Conferences/Meetings
Roger Williams, Executive Director
Open to the public and serves as an interactive forum where USP and its stakeholders can discuss new direction and standards that affect the pharmaceutical industry. The meeting provides attendees an opportunity to better understand the scope of USP's scientific work and provide input on key standards-setting issues.
September

5531 **United States Pharmacopeial Convention**
12601 Twinbrook Parkway
Rockville, MD 20852-1790
301-810-0667
FAX: 301-816-8299 800-227-8772
custsvc@usp.org www.usp.org
Anju K Malhotra, Manager Conferences/Meetings
Roger Williams, Executive Director
Composed of representatives of medical and pharmaceutical organizations.

5532 **Western Section Meeting of the Triological Society**
Triological Society
555 N 30th Street
Omaha, NE 68131-2136
402-346-5500
FAX: 402-346-5300
www.triological.org
I Kaufman Arenberg, MD, Executive Director
Annual show of 30 exhibitors of medical services and supplies related to Otolaryngology.
152 Attendees May

Directories & Databases

5533 **American Drug Index**
Lippincott Williams & Wilkins
16522 Hunters Green Pkwy
PO Box 1600
Hagerstown, MD 21740
301-223-2300
FAX: 301-223-2400 800-638-3030
Norman Billups, Editor
Shirley Billups, Editor
Contains more than 22,000 entries. Practical features include: alphabetically listed drug names, extensive cross-indexing, complete information on the distributor's brand name, manufacturer, generic and/or chemical names, chemical strength and much more useful information. Electronic version available. *$69.95*
1088 pages Annual, Hardcover ISBN 1-574391-33-X

5534 **Annual Meeting & Showcase**
Academy of Managed Care Pharmacy
100 N Pitt Street
Suite 400
Alexandria, VA 22314-3134
703-683-8416
FAX: 703-683-8417 800-827-2627
sandres@amcp.org www.amcp.org
Aimee Hickox, Director Education/Meetings
Nationally reowned keynote speakers, new research presentations, achievement awards, competitions and Board inaugurations fill the agenda for managed care pharmacy's premier event.
April

5535 **CSO Directory**
Drug Information Association
800 Enterprise Road
Suite 200
Horsham, PA 19044-3595
215-442-6100
FAX: 215-442-6199
dia@diahome.org www.diahome.org
Eleanor M Perfetto, President
Gaby L Danan, Director
Richard O Day, Director
Francoise de Cremiers, Director
Stuart W Cummings, Secretary/Treasurer
One of the industry's most respected and comprehensive reference guides, compiles company descriptions and contact information from hundreds of companies that provide services for every phase of the clinical trial and drug development process.

5536 **DCAT Digest and Directory of Membership**
Drug, Chemical & Associated Technologies
1 Washington Boulevard
Suite 7
Robbinsville, NJ 08691
609-448-1000
FAX: 609-448-1944 800-640-3228
info@dcat.org www.dcat.org
Patrick Vasquez, President
Lynda M Doyle, Senior VP
Margaret Timony, Executive Director
Keeping members in touch with their colleagues throughout the industry.

5537 **DIOGENES**
FOI Services
11 Firstfield Road
Gaithersburg, MD 20878-1704
301-975-9400
FAX: 301-975-0702
infofoi@foiservices.com
www.foiservices.com
John Carey, President
Marlene Bobka, VP
This comprehensive database contains citations to more than 1 million unpublished US Food and Drug Administration regulatory documents covering prescription and over-the-counter drugs.
Bibliographic Founded: 1975

5538 **DRUGDEX System**
Thompson Micromedex
6200 South Syracuse Way
Suite 300
Greenwood Village, CO 80111-4740
303-679-9500
FAX: 303-486-6464 800-525-9083

This comprehensive database covers all aspects of drugs and their use, including investigational, FDA-approved, and OTC preparations.
Full-text

5539 DataStat
NDCHealth
NDC Plaza
Atlanta, GA 30329-2010
404-728-2000
800-225-5632

Walter M Hoff, Chairman/CEO
Lee Adrean, EVP Finance
Randolph Hutto, EVP Business Development
Charles W Miller, EVP Corporate Initiatives

This comprehensive database offers descriptions of drug interactions at the ingredient level for individual drugs and therapeutic classes of drugs.
Full-text Founded: 1967

5540 Drug Store and HBC Chains
Chain Store Guide
3922 Coconut Palm Drive
Tampa, FL 33619
813-276-6700
FAX: 813-627-6882 800-778-9794
info@csgis.com www.csgis.com

Arthut Sciarrotta, Senior Vice President
Chris Leedy, Advertising Sales

Tap into the lucrative drug industry with profiles on more than 1,700 US and Canadian companies operating two or more retail drug stores, deep discount stores, health and beauty care (HBC) stores, cosmetic stores or vitamin stores that have industry sales of at least $250,000. This powerful database empowers you to sell and market your products successfully by reaching more than 8,300 key decision makers. *$335.00*

5541 Drug and Cosmetic Industry Catalog
Advanstar Communications
One Park Avenue
New York, NY 10016
212-797-7631
FAX: 212-951-6793
info@advanstar.com
www.advanstar.com

Eric Lisman, Executive Vice President

Over 1,000 manufacturers and suppliers of packaging equipment, private formulas and raw materials used in the drug and cosmetics industries are profiled. *$25.00*
270 pages Annual
Circulation: 4,000

5542 FDC Reports: The NDA Pipeline
FDC Reports
5550 Friendship Boulevard
Suite 1
Chevy Chase, MD 20815-7278
301-657-9830
FAX: 301-664-7238
fdc.customer.service@elsevier.com
www.fdcreports.com

Karl Uhlendo, Executive Editor
Mike Squires, President

The NDA Pipeline is a searchable database available through the Web that contains up-to-date coverage of over 900 companies and more than 7,00 approval records. The NDA Pipeline tracks drug and biological product research, clinical trials and approvals. It also includes a comprehensive listing of products in research, descriptions of phases of development and licensing information and linked articles from The Pink Sheet and other FDC Reports publications.
900 pages Annual Founded: 1939
Computerized version available

5543 GAMP Good Practice Guide
Int'l Society for Pharmaceutical Engineering
3109 W Dr. Martin Luther King Jr Blvd
Suite 250
Tampa, FL 33607
813-960-2105
FAX: 813-264-2816
customerservice@ispe.org
www.ispe.org

Paul N D'Eramo, Chairman
Gert Moelgaard, Vice Chairman
Robert E Chew, PE, Director
Jane R Brown, Treasurer
Bruce Davis, Secretary

Provides new comprehensive guidance on meeting current regulatory expectations for compliant electronic records and signatures, which includes the need for record integrity, security, and availability throughout the required retention period. This is achieved by well documented, validated systems, and the application of appropriate operational controls. *$145.00*

5544 HDMA Industry Profile and Healthcare Factbook
Food & Drug Law Institute
1000 Vermont Avenue NW
Suite 200
Washington, DC 20005
202-371-1420
FAX: 202-371-0649 800-956-6293
comments@fdli.org www.fdli.org

M Cathryn Butler, Editor-in-Chief
Margaret C Deegan, Managing Editor

Offers the most comprehensive statistics available on the pharmaceutical and healthcare industry. Gathered from more than 50 industry leaders, you can put the Factbook's critical information to work for your company. FDLI or HDMA member, book only. *$149.00*

5545 ISPE Good Practice Guide
Int'l Society for Pharmaceutical Engineering
3109 W Dr. Martin Luther King Jr Blvd
Suite 250
Tampa, FL 33607
813-960-2105
FAX: 813-264-2816
customerservice@ispe.org
www.ispe.org

Paul N D'Eramo, Chairman
Gert Moelgaard, Vice Chairman
Robert E Chew, PE, Director
Robert Best, Chief Executive Officer
Bruce Davis, Secretary

Provides a standard methodology for use in testing the containment efficiency of solids handling systems used in the pharmaceutical industry under closely defined conditions. It covers the main factors that affect the test results for specific contained solids handling systems, including material handled, room environment, air quality, ventilation and operator technique. *$145.00*

5546 Ident-A-Drug Reference
Therapeutic Research
3120 W March Lane
PO Box 8190
Stockton, CA 95219-0190
209-472-2240
FAX: 209-472-2249 www.pletter.com

Jeff Jellin, PharmD, Editor

It gives you all the drug identification information found on this web site for more than 30,000 entries. *$85.00*
704 pages ISBN 0-967613-65-5

5547 InVitro Diagnostics Industry Directory
CTB International Publishing
PO Box 218
Maplewood, NJ 07040-0218
973-966-0997
FAX: 973-966-0242
info@ctbintl.com www.ctbintl.com

Lists address, phone and fax number of invitro diagnostics companies, suppliers, distributors, regulatory agencies, professional societies and trade associations worldwide and contains over 2,300 entries worldwide-more than 1,200 contact names. *$277.00*
ISBN 1-887566-17-1
Printed in 1 color on matte stock

5548 International Pharmaceutical Abstracts Database
Thomson Scientific
3501 Market Street
Philadelphia, PA 19104-4836
215-386-0100
FAX: 215-386-2911 800-336-4474
ts.info.na@thomson.com
www.thomson.com

Robert C Cullen, President/CEO
Craig Soderstrom, VP Office of CEO
Kristen McCarthy, VP Marketing/Communications

These reports offering the latest in the development of drugs overseas, clinical and inventigotional use, cosmetics and, alternative and herbal medicine. Reports on pharmacy practice are also included.

5549 NABP Manual
National Association of Boards of Pharmacy
700 Busse Highway
Park Ridge, IL 60068
847-698-6227
FAX: 847-698-0124 800-774-6227
custserv@nabp.net www.nabp.net

Donna S Wall, Chairperson
Donna M Horn, President
Lawrence H Mokhiber, Treasurer

Developed to be read in conjunction with state laws. It presents general information essential to all board of pharmacy members, and serves as a valuable reference for new board members. The manual is ideal for compiling and cross-referencing amendments and other records. *$25.00*

5550 Natural Medicines Comprehensive Database
Therapeutic Research
PO Box 8190
Stockton, CA 95208-0190
209-472-2240
FAX: 209-472-2249 www.pletter.com

Jeff Jellin, PharmD, Editor

Provides you with monographs on each natural ingredient plus updated helpful charts and tables. *$85.00*
2000 pages ISBN 0-967613-68-X

5551 **Pharma Industry Directory**
CTB International Publishing
PO Box 218
Maplewood, NJ 07040
973-966-0997
FAX: 973-966-0242
info@ctbintl.com www.ctbintl.com
This is divided into 4 sections. The first section contains a complete alphabetical listing of the names, addresses, and phone and fax numbers of over 1,300 companies. The other sections are alphabetical listings of the companies with tables identifying them as to the fields they are involved in. The last section is a business index. *$250.00*
ISBN 1-887566-21-X
Printed in 1 color on matte stock

5552 **Pharmaceutical News Index**
UMI/Data Courier
620 S 3rd Street
Suite 400
Louisville, KY 40202-2475
502-583-4111
FAX: 502-589-5572 800-626-2823
Contains the latest US and international information about pharmaceutial, cosmetics, medical devices, and related health industries.
Bibliographic

5553 **Pharmacy School Admission Requirements**
American Association of Colleges of Pharmacy
1426 Prince Street
Alexandria, VA 22314
703-739-2330
FAX: 703-836-8982
mail@aacp.org www.aacp.org
Susan M Meyer, Senior Vice President
Lucinda L Maine, Executive VP
This reference guide provides prospective pharmacy students and school counselors with specifics about admission requirements for all the professional pharmacy degree programs in the U.S. recognized by the American council on Pharmaceutical Education. The guide contains informative narratives about each school outlining environmental factors, program descriptions, and selection factors. Updated annually. Will not be available until the end of July. *$25.00*
116 pages

5554 **Physicians' Desk Reference**
Thomson Medical Economics
5 Paragon Drive
Montvale, NJ 07645-1742
201-358-7500
FAX: 201-573-8999 800-442-6657
PDRbookstore@medec.com
www.pdr.net
Physicians have turned to PDR for the latest word in prescription drugs for 57 years. Today, it is considered the standard prescription drug reference and can be found in virtually every phyician's office, hospital and pharmacy in the US. *$92.95*
3,000 pages Hardcover

5555 **Roster of Faculty and Professional Staff**
American Association of Colleges of Pharmacy
1426 Prince Street
Alexandria, VA 22314
703-739-2330
FAX: 703-836-8982
mail@aacp.org www.aacp.org
Susan M Meyer, Senior Vice President
Lucinda L Maine, Executive VP
A directory of more than 5,000 full and part-time pharmacy faculty members including mailing and e-mail addresses, phone and fax numbers, degrees, and disciplines. Also included is valuable information about AACP such as officers, committee members, staff, and addresses and phone numbers for affiliated associations and corporations. $10 AACP Member. *$100.00*
November

Industry Web Sites

5556 **www.aacp.org**
American Association of Colleges of Pharmacy

National organization representing the interests of pharmaceutical education and educators. Comprising all 83 US pharmacy colleges and schools including more than 4,000 faculty, 36,000 student enrolled in professional programs and 3,600 individuals pursuing graduate study, AACP is committed to excellence in pharmaceutical education.

5557 **www.aaps.org**
American Association of Pharmaceutical Scientists

Aims to advance science through the open exchange of scientific knowledge, serve as an information resource and contribute to human health through pharmaceutical reseach and development.

5558 **www.accp.com**
American College of Clinical Pharmacy

Professional and scientific society that provides leadership, education, advocacy and resources enabling clinical pharmacists to achieve excellence in practice and research.

5559 **www.acrpnet.org**
Association of Clinical Research Professionals

Provides global leadership for the clinical research profession by promoting and advancing the highest ethical standards and practices.

5560 **www.aihp.org**
American Instiute of the History of Pharmacy

Supplies information regarding pharmaceutical history and usage.

5561 **www.apha.org**
American Public Health Association

Brings together researchers, health service providers, administrators, teachers and other health workers in a unique, multidisciplinary environment of professional exchange, study and action on the effort to prevent disease and promote health.

5562 **www.aphanet.org**
American Pharmaceutical Association

National, professional society of pharmacists practicing in every practice setting and influcencing the industry, distribution and utilization of medications.

5563 **www.asapnet.org**
American Society for Automation in Pharmacy

Is to assist its members in advancing the application of computer technology in the pharmacists role as caregiver and in the efficient operation and management of a pharmacy.

5564 **www.ashp.org**
American Society of Health-System Pharmacy

An association that brings together health-system pharmacists and addresses their concerns.

5565 **www.aspl.org**
American Society for Pharmacy Law

An organization of pharmacists and lawyers who are interested in the law as it applies to the pharmacy industry.

5566 **www.diahome.org**
Drug Information Association

Association for those interested in technical developments, supply, and production of drugs. Exchanges and disseminates information by continuing to provide a neutral forum, respecting and welcoming all participants and offering quality driven programming.

5567 **www.fdli.org**
Food and Drug Law Institute

Nonprofit educational organization dedicated to improving the understanding of the laws, regulations and policies affecting the food, drug, medical device and biologics industries. A neutral, non-partisan organization that does not lobby.

5568 **www.greyhouse.com**
Grey House Publishing

Selected Grey House directories in the fields of business, health and education are available online. Users can search our online databases by several different search criteria, such as product categories, geographic area, sales volume and much, much more. Full Grey House catalog and online ordering also available.

5569 **www.ipecamericas.org**
International Pharmaceutical Excipients Council

Members are companies with an interest in the otherwise inert chemicals used as vehicles for medicines. Federation of three independent regional industry associations headquartered in the US. Each association focuses its attention on the applicable law, regulations, science and business practices of its region. The three associations work together on excipient safety and public health issues, in connection with international trade matters, and to achieve harmonization of regulatory standards.

5570 **www.ncpanet.org**
National Community Pharmacists Association

Represents independent pharmacists, provides support for undergraduate pharmacy education.

5571 **www.npa.org**
National Pharmaceutical Alliance

Represents the interests of small pharmaceutical companies and allied industries.

5572 **www.nutritioncare.org**
American Soc. for Parenteral & Enteral Nutrition

Strives to be a conduit amoung those interested in Nutrition Support.

5573 **www.pda.org**
Parenteral Drug Association

Members are makers of parenteral (injectable) drugs and other pharmaceuticals, as well as suppliers, academia and regulatory bodies. Our mission is to advance the pharmaceutical and biopharmaceutical technology internationally by promoting scientifically sound and practical technical information and education for industry and regulatory issues.

5574 **www.pdr.net**
Thomson Medical Economics

Physicians have turned to PDR for the latest word on prescription drugs for 57 years. Today it is considered the standard prescription drug reference and can be found in virtually every phyician's office, hospital and pharmacy in the US.

5575 **www.pharmacytechnician.com**
American Association of Pharmacy Technicians

Provides leadership and represents the interests of its members to the public as well as healthcare organizations. Promotes the safe, effectacious, and cost effective dispensing distribution and use of medications. Provides continuing education programs and services to help technicians update their skills to keep pace with changes in pharmacy services.

5576 **www.thompson.com**
Thompson Scientific and Healthcare

Professionals in business, government, law and academia have reliedon us for the most authorative, timely and practical guidance available.

5577 **www.usp.org**
United States Pharmacopeia

Helps to ensure that consumers recieve quality medicines by establishing state-of-the-art standards that pharmaceutical manufacturers must meet. We provide standards for more than 3,800 medicines, dietary supplements and other health care products.

Associations

5578 American Automatic Control Council
3640 Col Glenn Hwy
Dayton, OH 45435
937-775-5062
FAX: 937-775-3936
pmisra@cs.wright.edu www.a2c2.org
A Galip Vlsoy, President
Pradeep Misra, Secretary
Supports all those involved in the manufacturer and distribution of automatic controls. Hosts annual trade show.

5579 Association for High Technology Distributors
1900 Arch Street
Philadelphia, PA 19103-1498
215-564-3484
FAX: 215-564-2175
ahtd@ahtd.org www.ahtd.org
Dan O'Brien, President
Patricia A Lilly, Executive Director
Paul Lewis, VP
Steve Earley, Secretary/Program Chair
James H Norton, Treasurer
Works to increase productivity and profitability of high technology automation solutions, providers and manufacturers.
250 Members Founded: 1985

5580 Association of Edison Illuminating
600 18th Street N
PO Box 2641
Birmingham, AL 35291
205-257-2530
FAX: 205-257-2540
diraeic@bellsouth.ne www.aeic.org
Robert E Huffman, Executive Director
Len Holland, Manager AEIC Services
Sally Veazey, Secretary
Association of public-owned utilities concerned with lighting and electricity. This organization supplies information and support to the industry.
78 Members Founded: 1885

5581 Bioelectromagnetics Society
2412 Cobblestone Way
Frederick, MD 21702-3519
301-663-4252
FAX: 301-694-4948
bemsoffice@aol.com
www.bioelectromagnetics.org
Bruce R McLeod, President
Stephan Engstrom, VP
Gloria Parsley, Executive Director
Robert F Cleveland, Treasurer
Robert B Goldberg, Secretary
Nonprofit organization and international resource for excellence in scientific research, knowledge and understanding of the interaction of electromagnetic fields with biological systems. Members are biological and physical scientists, physicians and engineers interested in the interactions of nonionizing radiation with biological systems.
700 Members Founded: 1979

5582 Contract Services Association of America
1000 Wilson Boulevard
Suite 1800
Arlington, VA 22209
703-243-2020
FAX: 703-243-3601
info@csa-dc.org www.csa-dc.org
Jenny Adlakha, Marketing Specialist
Cathy Gannann, Sr VP Public Policy
Chris Jahn, President
Kate Hannon, Executive Assistant to President
Isiah Harris, Secretary
Represents the government services contracting industry. Membership ranges from small businesses and corporations servicing federal and state government in numerous capacities. CSA acts to foster the effective implementation of the government's policy of reliance on the private sector for support services. Largest DOD association of service contractors.
650 Members Founded: 1965

5583 Edison Electric Institute
701 Pennsylvania Avenue NW
Washington, DC 20004-2696
202-085-5995
FAX: 202-508-5335
eblume@eei.org www.eei.org
Tom Kuhn, President
David Owens, Executive VP
Advocates public policy, expands market opportunities and provides strategic business information for the shareholder-owned, electric utility industry.
180 Members Founded: 1930

5584 Electric Association
4100 Madison Street
Suite 4
Hillside, IL 60162
708-547-9910
FAX: 708-547-9920
cspaeth@eachicago.org
www.eachicago.org
Carrie Spaeth, Executive Director
Amy Kasser, Coordinator of Administration
Carrie Spaeth, Managing Director
Jim Paplaczyk, Treasurer
Bob Porter, Secretary
Provides members of the electrical industry of Chicagoland and their employees with formal educational opportunities, professional development, information exchange, and member services.
Founded: 1926

5585 Electric Power Research Institute
3412 Hillview Avenue
Palo Alto, CA 94304-1395
650-552-2354

askepri@epri.com www.epri.com
Eugene W Zeltmann, Chairman
Steven R Specker, President/CEO
William J Clark, VP/CFO/Treasurer
Richard Rudman, Executive VP/COO
Judith Mills, Technical Information Specialist
Nonprofit, energy research consortium for the benefit of utility members, their customers and society. Mission is to provide science and technology-based solutions of indispensable value to our global energy customers by managing a far-reaching program of scientific research, technology development and product implementation.
660 Members Founded: 1973

5586 Electrical Apparatus Service Association
1331 Baur Boulevard
Saint Louis, MO 63132-1903
314-993-2220
FAX: 314-993-1269
easainfo@easa.com www.easa.com
Bill Nielsen, Chair
Linda J Raynes, President/CEO
Randy D Joslin, Communications Manager
Dale Shuter, CMP, Meetings/Expositions Manager
Maintains data files on rewinding and repair of electrical equipment. Sponsors seminars.
2200 Members Founded: 1937
Mailing list available for rent 2200 names

5587 Electrical Equipment Representatives
PO Box 419264
Kansas City, MO 64141-6264
816-561-5323
FAX: 816-561-1249
jmale@eera.org www.eera.org
Randy Sutton, Chairman
Robert D Chapman, President
Scott Dashiell, VP
John Commons, Treasurer
Sales agents for manufacturers of electrical equipment used by utilities. Advances the quality and increases the effectiveness of manufacturers' representatives in the electrical equipment industry.
98 Members Founded: 1948

5588 Electrical Generating Systems Association
1650 S Dixie Highway
Suite 500
Boca Raton, FL 33432
561-750-5575
FAX: 561-395-8557 www.egsa.org
Dale Slemp, President
Jalane Kellough, Executive Director
Warner Bauer, Secretary/Treasurer
A trade association made up of nearly 600 companies in the USA and around the world that design, manufacture, sell, distribute, rent, specify, service and use on site power equipment.
Founded: 1965

5589 Electrical Safety Foundation International
1300 N 17th Street
Suite 1847
Rosslyn, VA 22209
703-413-3209
FAX: 703-841-3329
info@esfi.org
www.electrical-safety.org
Grant J Carter, Chair
David Tallman, Vice Chair
Brett Brenner, President
Michael Clendenin, Executive Director
The ESFI's mission is to reduce electrically related deaths and injuries through vigilant public education keeping electrical safety top of mind and to give the general public, school children and the workfoce tips and tools to use to prevent deadly and destructive electrical accidents.

Founded: 1994

5590 Electrochemical Society
65 S Main Street
Building D
Pennington, NJ 08534-2839
609-737-1902
FAX: 609-737-2743
webmaster@electrochem.org
www.electrochem.org
Carolyn Wroblewski, Director Finance
Brian Bosak, Director Information Technology

Valerie Yacko, Executive Assistant
Roque Calvo, Manager

Members are electrochemists and professionals in related industries.
8000 Members Founded: 1902

5591 **Electronic Industries Association**
2500 Wilson Boulevard
Arlington, VA 22201-3834
703-907-7500
FAX: 703-907-7767 www.eia.org

Ronald L Turner, Chairman
Mike Kennedy, Vice Chairman
Dave McCurdy, President
Charles Robinson, Chief Operating Officer
James Shiring, Secretary/Treasurer

Is a national trade organization that includes the full spectrum of U.S. manufacturers.
1300 Members

5592 **Electronic Technicians Association**
5 Depot Street
Greencastle, IN 46135
800-288-3824
FAX: 765-653-4287 765-653-4301
eta@eta-i.org www.eta-i.org

Richard Glass, President
Teresa Maher, VP
Richard Glass, President
Ben Longwood, Treasurer
Tom Janca, Secretary

Association for electronic technicians worldwide offering 23 technical certifications.
3100 Members Founded: 1978

5593 **Electrostatic Discharge Association**
7900 Turin Road
Building 3
Rome, NY 13440-2069
315-339-6937
FAX: 315-339-6793
info@esda.org www.esda.org

Kay Adams, President
Dave Swenson, Senior VP
Donn Bellmore, Treasurer
Michele McSwain, Secretary
Lisa Pimpinella, Operations Manager

Professional voluntary association dedicated to advancing the theory and practice of electrostatic discharge avoidance. Initial emphasis on the effects of ESD on electronic components has broadened to include textiles, plastics, web processing, explosives, clean rooms and graphic arts. Expands ESD awareness through educational programs, development of standards, tutorials, publications, local chapters, symposia and certification.
1300 Members Founded: 1982
Mailing list available for rent

5594 **IPC: Association Connecting Electronics**
3000 Lakeside Drive
Suite 309 S
Bannockburn, IL 60015
847-615-7100
FAX: 847-615-7105
webmaster@ipc.org www.ipc.org

Denny McGuirk, President
Dick Crowe, Executive Director
Tom McCabe, CPA, CFO/VP Administration
Jennifer Sandahl, Controller

A trade association for the printed circuit boards and electronics assembly industries, offering programs and resources to board manufacturers and electronic assemblers, designers, industry suppliers and original equipment manufacturers.
2200 Members Founded: 1957

5595 **Independent Electrical Contractors Association**
4401 Ford Avenue
Suite 1100
Alexandria, VA 22302
703-549-7351
FAX: 703-549-7448
info@ieci.org www.ieci.org

J B Wise, National President
Larry Mullins, Executive VP

The mission of IEC is to create success among independent electrical conteractors by developing a professional workforce, communicating clearly with government, promoting ethical business practices, and providing leadership for the electrical industry.
73000 Members Founded: 1957

5596 **Institute of Electrical/Electronic Engineers**
3 Park Avenue
17th Floor
New York, NY 10016
212-419-7900
FAX: 212-752-4929 www.ieee.org

Michael R Lightner, President
Joseph V Lillie, Director/Treasurer
Dr Mohamed El-Hawary, Director/Secretary
Daniel Senese, Chief Executive Officer

Supports all those involved in the field of electrical engineering.Publishes newsletter and hosts trade show.
365K Members Founded: 1963

5597 **Instrumentation and Measurement Society**
3 Park Avenue
17th Floor
New York, NY 10016
212-419-7900
FAX: 212-752-4929
webmaster@ieee.org
www.ewh.ieee.org

Michael R Lightner, President/CEO
Joseph V Lillie, Director/Treasurer
Dr Mohamed El-Hawary, Director/Secretary

A subsidary of the Institute of Electrical and Electronics Engineers. Provides support to scientists and technicians who design and develop electrical and electronic measuring instruments and equipment.
36000 Members Founded: 1980

5598 **Instrumentation, Systems, and Automation Society**
67 Alexander Drive
Box 12277
Research Triangle Park, NC 27709
919-549-8411
FAX: 919-549-8288
info@isa.org www.isa.org

Ken Baker, President
Rob Renner, Executive Director
Debbie Eby, Executive Assistant
Leo Staples, Treasurer

Nonprofit, educational organization connecting people and ideas in automation. The Society fosters advancement in the theory, design, manufacture, and use of sensors, instruments, computers, and systems for automation in a wide variety of applications.
33000 Members Founded: 1945

5599 **Insulated Cable Engineers Association**
PO Box 1568
Carrollton, GA 30112
770-830-0369
FAX: 770-830-8501
ieeeusa@ieee.org www.icea.net

Lauri J Hiivala, President

Professional organization dedicated to developing cable standards for the electric power, control and telecommunications industries. Ensures safe, economical and efficient cable systems utilizing proven, state-of-the-art materials and concepts. ICEA documents are of interest to cable manufacturers, architects and engineers, utility and manufacturing plant personnel, telecommunication engineers, consultants and OEMs.
Founded: 1925

5600 **International Electrical Testing Association**
106 Stone Street
Morrison, CO 80465
303-697-8441
FAX: 303-697-8431 888-300-6382
neta@netaworld.org
www.netaworld.org

Stuart Jackson, President
John White, First VP
Kerry Heid, Second VP
Charles K Blizard, Secretary
Mary Jordan, Executive Director

Defines the standards by which electrical equipment is deemed safe and reliable. Creates specifications, procedures, testing and requirements for commissioning new equipment and testing the reliability and performance of existing equipment.
2000 Members Founded: 1972

5601 **International Institute of Connector and Interconnection**
PO Box 20002
Sarasota, FL 34276
941-929-1806
FAX: 941-929-1807 800-854-4248
sromeo@iicit.com www,iicit.org

Darrell Fernald, International President

Dedicated to the spread of technological information throughout teh industry. In a time of global competition, success depends on communicating technological breakthroughs, innovations and changes in specifications to engineers, designers, specifiers, consultants and other professionals using your product or services.
2640 Members Founded: 1958

5602 **International League of Electrical Associations**
12165 West Center Road
Suite 59
Omaha, NE 68144
402-330-7227
FAX: 402-330-7283
niec2006@aol.com www.ileaweb.org

Bill Regan, President
Jane Male, VP
R E Morris, Executive Manager

An organization of professional electric association and electric league managers from more than thirty US and seven Canadian cities.
Founded: 1936

5603 International Magnetics Association
Eight South Michigan Avenue
Suite 1000
Chicago, IL 60603-3310
312-456-5590
FAX: 312-580-0165
ima@gss.net www.inti-magnetics.org

August Sisco, Chair
Lowell Bosley, President
George Orenchak, Secretary/Treasurer

Is the worldwide trade association representing manufacturers of magnetic materials, distributors and fabricators, suppliers to the magnetics industry and others with an interest in magnetics.
35 Members Founded: 1959

5604 International Microelectronics and Packaging Society
611 2nd Street NE
Washington, DC 20002
202-548-4001
FAX: 202-548-6115 888-464-6277
imaps@imaps.org www.imaps.org

Dr Bruce M Romenesko, President
Michael O'Donoghue, Executive Director
Steve Capp, Treasurer
Lawrence J Rexing, Secretary

Promotes interaction among technologies of ceramics, thin and thick films, semiconductor packaging, surface mount technology, multichip modules, semiconductor devices and monolithic circuits. Dedicated to the advancement and growth of the use of microelectronics and electronic packaging through education. Disseminates information through symposia, workshops and conferences.
11000 Members Founded: 1967

5605 International Microwave Power Institute
7076 Drinkard Way
Mechanicsville, VA 23111-5007
804-596-6667
FAX: 540-961-1463
info@impi.org www.impi.org

Kimberly D Thies, Executive Director
Neal Cooper, President
Matthew Lorence, Secretary
David Baron, Treasurer

IMPI's members include scientists, researchers, lab technicians, product developers, marketing managers and a variety of other professionals in the microwave industry. The Institute serves the information needs of all specialists working with dielectric (microwave and RF) heating systems, and was expanded in 1977 to meet the information needs relating to consumer microwave ovens and related products.
700 Members Founded: 1966

5606 Laser Institute of America
13501 Ingenuity Drive
Suite 128
Orlando, FL 32826
407-380-1553
FAX: 407-380-5588
lia@laserinstitute.org
www.laserinstitute.org

Peter Baker, Executive Director

The Laser Institute of America is the professional membership society dedicated to fostering lasers, laser applications and safety worldwide.
1200 Members Founded: 1968

5607 Laser and Electro-Optic Manufacturers
123 Kent Road
Pacifica, CA 94044-3923
650-738-1492
FAX: 650-738-1769
info@leoma.com www.leoma.com

John Ambroseo, President
Breck Hitz, Executive Director
Lynn Strickland, Treasurer
Brian Lula, Secretary

Is the trade association for North American manufacturers of lasers and associated electro-optics equipment.
Founded: 1986

5608 National Association of Electrical Distributors
1100 Corporate Square Drive
Suite 100
St. Louis, MO 63132
314-991-9000
FAX: 314-991-3060 888-791-2512
info@naed.org www.naed.org

Tom Naber, President
Michelle Jaworowski, VP/Executive Director
Tim Dencker, Controller
Laurie Mueller-Bevirt, Director Marketing

Supports manufacturers and distributors of electrical components, supplies and equipment. Publishes directory.

5609 National Electrical Contractors
3 Bethesda Metro Center
Suite 1100
Bethesda, MD 20814
301-657-3110
FAX: 301-215-4500
webmaster@necanet.org
www.necanet.org

William B Cook, Jr, President
Stuart Binstock, Executive Director
John Grau, Chief Executive Officer
Robert Colgan, Director Marketing
J Michael Thompson, Secretary-Treasurer

Represents a segment of the construction market comprised of over 70,000 electrical contracting firms.
65000 Members Founded: 1901

5610 National Electrical Manufacturers Representatives Association
660 White Plains Road
Suite 600
Tarrytown, NY 10591-1504
914-524-8650
FAX: 914-524-8655
nemra@nemra.org www.nemra.org

Stephen Gallagher, Chairman
Henry P Bergson, President
Michael Rowe, Secretary/Treasurer

Promotes the function of the independent manufacturer's representative as the most effective way to market electrical products. Increases the income of the rep's firm employees and sales staff by increasing the value of the rep firm to owners and customers. Offers educational opportunities that help representatives strengthen the management, technical and professional capabilities of their firms. Promotes communication between independent electrical representatives and manufacturing partners.

5611 National Electronics Service Dealers
3608 Pershing Avenue
Fort Worth, TX 76107-4527
817-921-9061
FAX: 817-921-3741 800-797-9197
webmaster@nesda.com
www.nesda.com

Brian Gibson Cet, President
Don Cressin, VP
Mack Blakely, Executive Director
Fred Paradis CSM, Treasurer
Wayne Markman, Secretary

Supports manufacturers, suppliers and distributors of electronics, receivers, recorders, and supplies, software, telecommunications equipment, computers, videocassette recorders, parts and accessories. Publishes monthly magazine and hosts annual trade show.
Founded: 1964

5612 National Rural Electric Cooperative Association
4301 Wilson Boulevard
Suite 1
Arlington, VA 22203-1860
703-907-5500
FAX: 703-907-5514 www.nreca.org

Glenn L English, CEO

Organized specifically to overcome World War II shortages of electric construction materials, to obtain insurance coverage for newly constructed rural electric cooperatives, and to mitigate wholesale power problems. Since those early days, NRECA has been an advocate for consumer owned cooperatives on energy and operational issues as well as rural community and economic development.
1000 Members Founded: 1942

5613 National Systems Contractors Association
625 1st Street SE
Suite 420
Cedar Rapids, IA 52401
319-366-6722
FAX: 319-366-4164 800-446-6722
randy.vaughan@ae-systems.com
www.nsca.org

Randy Vaughan, President
Nancy Emerson, VP
Chuck Wilson, Executive Director
Kirsten Poggenklass, Marketing Manager
Andy Musci, Secretary/Treasurer

Represents the commercial electronic systems industry. Serves as an advocate for all those who work within the low-voltage industry, including systems contractors/integrators, product manufacturers, consultants, sales representatives and a growing number of architects, specifying engineers and others.
2500 Members Founded: 1980

5614 North American Electric Reliability Council
116 Village Boulevard
Suite 390
Princeton, NJ 08540-5731
609-452-8060
FAX: 609-452-9550
info@nerc.com www.nerc.com

Richard Drouin, Chairman
Thomas W Berry, Vice Chairman
Michehl R Gent, President/CEO
David R Nevius, Senior Vice President
Joseph K Conner, Jr, Chief Financial Officer

Principal organization for coordinating and promoting North America's electrical supplies, demands and reliability issues.
11 Members Founded: 1968

5615 North Central Electrical League
2901 Metro Drive
Suite 203
Bloomington, MN 55425
952-854-4405
FAX: 952-854-7076 800-925-4985
dale@ncel.org www.ncel.org

Lane Hersey, Chair
Greg Hames, Vice Chair
Dale Yohnke, Executive Director
Jeff Keljik, Treasurer

Trade association representing all segments of the electrical industry in the Upper Midwest.
1500 Members Founded: 1936

5616 Power Sources Manufacturers Association
PO Box 418
Mendham, NJ 07945-0418
973-543-9660
FAX: 973-543-6207
power@psma.com www.psma.com

Bruce Miller, Chairman
Chavonne Yee, President
Kevin Parmenter, VP
Joe Horzepa, Executive Director

Worldwide membership consists of manufacturers of power sources and conversion equipment. Nonprofit association strives to integrate the resources of the power sources industry to more effectively and profitably serve the needs of the power sources users.
156 Members Founded: 1985

5617 Relay and Switch Industry Association
2500 Wilson Boulevard
Arlington, VA 22201
703-907-8025
FAX: 703-858-908
narm@ecaus.org
www.ec-central.org/RSIA

Dave Bauchaine, Chairman
Jeffrey Boyce, President

Offers its members an opportunity to keep current with all aspects of this fascinating industry through available information and participated int the various programs. The organization serves as a clearing house for information about the many government directives concerning the relay industry as well as promoting the establishment of relay standards and specifications.
Founded: 1947

5618 SMMA: The Motor & Motion Association
PO Box P182
South Dartmouth, MA 02748
508-979-5935
FAX: 508-979-5845
info@smma.org www.smma.org
Manufacturing trade association of electric motor and motion control companies, suppliers, users and associated businesses such as consultants, universities and distributors.
110 Members Founded: 1975

5619 Semiconductor Environmental, Safety & Health Association
1313 Dolly Madison Boulevard
McLean, VA 22101
703-790-1745
FAX: 703-790-2672
sesha@burkinc.com
www.seshaonline.org

John D Cox, President
Brett Burk, Executive Director
Brian Sherin, Treasurer
Karl Albrecht, Secretary

Members are individuals employed within the electronics and related high technology industries with an interest in environmental, health and safety issues.
1500 Members Founded: 1978

5620 Semiconductor Equipment and Materials International
1401 K Street NW
Suite 601
Washington, DC 20005
202-289-0440
FAX: 202-289-0441
semidc@semi.org www.semi.org

Stanley T Myers, President/CEO
Victoria Hadfield, Executive VP/President, N America

An international trade association representing firms supplying equipment, materials and services to the semiconductor industry. Strengthens the performance of members through promotion, lobbying, education and statistical research.
2300 Members Founded: 1970

5621 Semiconductor Industry Association
181 Metro Drive
San Jose, CA 95110
408-436-6600
FAX: 408-436-6646
mailbox@sia-online.org
www.sia-online.org

Steven R Appleton, Chairman
Brian L Halla, Vice Chairman
George Scalise, President
Chuck Fraust, Director Environment Health/Safety
Daryl Hatano, VP Public Policy

Trade association representing the US microchip industry. Provides a forum for working collectively to enhance the competitiveness of the US chip industry.
70 Members Founded: 1977

5622 Society of Manufacturing Engineers

1 SME Drive
PO Box 930
Dearborn, MI 48121
313-271-1500
FAX: 313-425-3401 800-733-4763
service@sme.org www.sme.org

Nancy Berg, Executive Director
Karen Manardo, Director Communications
Rob Fekaris, Director Finance

Supports all those engineers involved in electrical manufacturing. Hosts trade show.

40K Members Founded: 1932

5623 Surface Mount Technology Association
5200 Willson Road
Suite 100
Mineapolis, MN 55424
952-920-7682
FAX: 952-926-1819
joann@smta.org www.smta.org

David Raby, President
JoAnn Stromberg, Executive Administrator
Paul Vianco, Treasurer
Evelyn Baldwin, VP Communications
Irene Sterian, Secretary

Network of professionals building skills, sharing practical experience and developing solutions in electronic assembly technologies and related business operations.
3200 Members Founded: 1984

5624 Variable Electronic Components Institute
PO Box 1070
Vista, CA 92085-1070
760-631-0178
FAX: 760-631-7827
vrci@aol.com www.veci-vrci.com

Stanley Kukawka, Executive Director

Trade association of manufacturers of variable resistive products, panel pots, trimmers, precision potentiometers and encoders.
30 Members Founded: 1960

Newsletters

5625 Advanced Battery Technology
Seven Mountains Scientific
913 Tressler Street
PO Box 650
Boalsburg, PA 16827
814-466-6559
FAX: 814-466-2777
jo@7ms.com www.7ms.com

E Thomas Chesworth, Technical Editor
Josephine Chesworth, Managing Editor

The oldest, most widely read international newsletter reporting on battery technology, marketing and industry events including new products and financial news. Accepts advertising. Print and online versions available. *$180.00*

Circulation: 1000 Audited
Printed in 4 colors on matte stock
Computerized version available

5626 Cleanroom Markets Newsletter
McIlvaine Company
191 Waukegan Road
Suite 208
Northfield, IL 60093
847-784-0012
FAX: 847-784-0061
editor@mcilvainecompany.com
www.mcilvainecompany.com

Robert McIlvaine, President
Marilyn McIlvaine, Managing Editor

Information on cleanrooms markets worldwide. *$460.00*
8 pages Monthly
Printed in on newsprint stock

5627 **Cleanroom Technology Newsletter**
McIlvaine Company
191 Waukegan Road
Suite 208
Northfield, IL 60093
847-784-0012
FAX: 847-784-0061
Robert McIlvaine, Publisher
Marilyn McIlvaine, Editor
Information on cleanroom technology.

5628 **Continuous Improvement**
James Publishing
3505 Cadillac Avenue
Suite H
Costa Mesa, CA 92626-1430
714-755-5450
FAX: 714-751-2709
Robert Sperker, Publisher
Stephen Sicillan, Editor
Tutorial and news on new quality assurance technologies and ISO 9000, QS 9000 and ISO 14000. *$20.00*
Circulation: 2000

5629 **Currents**
Electrical Apparatus Service Association
1331 Baur Boulevard
Saint Louis, MO 63132-1903
314-993-2220
FAX: 314-993-1269
easinfo@easa.com www.easa.com
Bill Nielsen, Chair
Linda J Raynes, President/CEO
Randy D Joslin, Communications Manager
Dale Shuter, CMP, Meetings/Expositions Manager
Provides information on EASA's programs, seminars, technical articles and industry trends and events. Members receive a copy each month.
Monthly

5630 **Display Technology News**
Business Communications Company
25 Van Zant Street
Suite 13
Norwalk, CT 06855-1713
203-853-4266
FAX: 203-853-0348
sales@bccresearch.com
http://www.bccresearch.com
Louis Naturman, Publisher
Robert Moran, Editor
Alan Hall, Editorial Director
Market reports and technology updates of topics such as news materials, news applications, patents, technology transfer, processing and equipment. *$500.00*
Monthly Founded: 1971

5631 **Document Imaging Report**
Corry Publications
5539 Peech St
Erie, PA 16509
814-838-0025
FAX: 301-340-0542
corrypub@corrypub.com
http://www.corrypub.com
Nicole Hykes, Editor
John Toiston, Publisher
Carry Procious, Marketing
Mindy Sadden, Circulation Manager
Presents the most timely and actionable information on electronic imaging applications, products and user implementation.
Monthly
Circulation: 50

5632 **EEI Washington Letter**
Edison Electric Institute
701 Pennsylvania Avenue NW
Washington, DC 20004-2696
202-085-5995
www.eei.org
Weekly electronic newsletter covers significant Washington energy development news, including legislative, regulatory and judicial actions; member company announcements; and activities of outside groups of interest to electric utilities. Includes calendar of upcoming events. Free to EEI electric company members and associate members.

5633 **Electrical Product News**
Business Marketing & Publishing
PO Box 7457
Wilton, CT 06897
203-834-9959
info@epnweb.com
http://www.epnweb.com
George Young, Editor/Publisher
Accepts advertising. *$39.50*
20 pages Monthly
Circulation: 3500 3500 names
Printed in 2 colors on newsprint stock

5634 **Electro Manufacturing**
Worldwide Videotex
PO Box 3273
Boynton Beach, FL 33424-3273
772-738-2276
markedit@juno.com
www.wvpubs.com
Computer and electronic technologies used to help improve manufacturing efficiency. *$165.00*

5635 **Executive Newsline**
Electric Power Research Institute
3412 Hillview Avenue
Palo Alto, CA 94304-1395
650-552-2354
800-313-3774
askepri@epri.com www.epri.com
Christine Hopf-Lovette, Editor
Jackie Turner, Editor
Contains brief highlights of EPRI science and technology developments and announcements of interest to utility executives.

5636 **Global Electronics**
Pacific Studies Center
222B View Street
Mountain View, CA 94041-1344
650-969-1545
FAX: 650-961-9818
Leonard Siegel, Editor
News items detailing the industry throughout the world and the social, environmental and military implications of production and application. *$1.00*
Circulation: 400

5637 **High Tech News**
Electronics Technicians Association International
5 Depot Street
Greencastle, IN 46135
765-653-8262
FAX: 765-653-4287 800-288-3824
eta@eta-i.org http://www.eta-i.org
Dick Glass, President
Bryan Allen, Co-Editor
Contains job opportunities, technical articles, industry news and newly ETA-I certified technicians. *$59.00*
Monthly Founded: 1978
Circulation: 5000 16-24 names
Printed in 2 colors on glossy stock

5638 **IEEE Transactions on Applied Superconductivity**
IEEE Instrumentation and Measurement Society
67 Alexander Drive
PO Box 12277
Research Triangle Park, NC 27709
919-549-8411
FAX: 919-549-8288
info@isa.org www.isa.org
Ken Baker, President
Rob Renner, Executive Director
Jerry Clemons, Department VP
Leo Staples, Treasurer
Concentrates on materials and their applications to electronics and power systems where superconductivity is central to the work.

5639 **IEEE Transactions on Mobile Computing**
IEEE Instrumentation and Measurement Society
67 Alexander Drive
PO Box 12277
Research Triangle Park, NC 27709
919-549-8411
FAX: 919-549-8288
info@isa.org www.isa.org
Ken Baker, President
Rob Renner, Executive Director
Jerry Clemons, Department VP
Leo Staples, Treasurer
Research papers are presented in this publication dealing with mobile computing, wireless networks, reliability, quality assurance, distributed systems architecture and high-level protocols.
Quarterly

5640 **IFAC Newsletter**
American Automatic Control Council
3640 Col Glenn Hwy
Dayton, OH 45435
937-775-5062
FAX: 937-775-3936
pmisra@cs.wright.edu www.a2c2.org
Gustav Hencsey, Editor
It contains up-to-date information about forthcoming IFAC events as well as brief announcements of other IFAC related activities. It is sent free of charge to NMO's, IFAC Affiliates and libraries.
Bi-Monthly

5641 **Inside FERC**
McGraw Hill
3333 Walnut Street
Boulder, CO 80301
720-485-5000
FAX: 720-548-5701 800-424-2908
Larry Foster, Publisher

Provides coverage of the Federal Energy Regulatory Commission's activities and federal regulations. *$975.00*
14 pages Monthly Founded: 1884

5642 Inside NRC
McGraw Hill
PO Box 182604
Columbus, OH 43272
614-304-4000
FAX: 614-759-3749 800-424-2908
customer.service@mcgraw-hill.com
http://www.mcgraw-hill.com
Michael Knapik, Publisher
Focuses exclusively on the US Nuclear Regulatory Commission. *$1310.00*
13 pages Founded: 1800

5643 SMMA: Newsletter
SMMA: Small Motors & Motion Association
PO Box P182
S Dartmouth, MA 02748
508-979-5935
FAX: 508-979-5845
info@smma.org www.smma.org
Elizabeth B Chambers, Executive Director
William H Chambers, Operations Director
The SMMA is a manufacturing trade association of electric motor and motion control companies, suppliers, users and associated businesses such as consultants, universities and distributors.
Founded: 1975

5644 SMT Trends
New Insights
303 Vallejo Street
Crockett, CA 94525-1237
510-787-2273
FAX: 415-389-8671
Michael New, Publisher/Editor
Marketing and business news for the surface mount industry. Covers component and packaging trends, CAD, CAE, pick and place, robotics and test inspection.
Printed in 1 color on matte stock

5645 Seven Mountain Scientific
PO Box 650
Boalsburg, PA 16827-651
814-466-6559
FAX: 814-466-2777
abt@7ms.com http://www.7ms.com
E Thomas Chesworth, President
Industry news in battery and fuel cell technology, marketing and industry events including new products, electric vehicle, R&D and environmental news. *$180.00*
Founded: 1965

5646 Tech Notes
National Technical Information Service
S U 5285 Port Royal Road
Springfield, VA 22161-0001
703-874-4650
Edward Lehmann, Editor
Describes new processes, equipment, materials and techniques developed by Federal laboratories. *$8.00*

5647 Threshold Newsletter
Electrostatic Discharge Association
7900 Turin Road
Building 3
Rome, NY 13440-2069
315-339-6937
FAX: 315-339-6793
info@esda.org www.esda.org
Lynn Babiarz, Marketing & Communications Admnstr
Kay Adams, President
Dave Swenson, Senior VP
Donn Bellmore, Treasurer
Michele McSwain, Secretary
Benefits of ESD membership include a subscription to the Threshold Newsletter in addition to other Association activites and programs such as educational tutorials and seminars; the EOS/ESD Symposium; participation in local chapters; discounts on Association standards and other publications; extensive networking; membership roster, and participation in standards development. *$60.00*
Bi-Monthly

5648 Transformers for Electronic Circuits
Power Sources Manufacturers Association
PO Box 418
Mendham, NJ 07945-0418
973-543-9660
FAX: 973-543-6207
power@psma.com www.psma.com
Judy Horzepa, Associate Director/Managing Editor
It is a complete, one-stop guide to transformer and inductor design and applications for everyone who designs, builds, or uses power magnetics components. Throughout this book, the author combines analysis and synthesis, and all theory is related to the solution of real world problems. *$75.00*
Second Edition

5649 Vision
Society of Manufacturing Engineers
1 Sme Drive
PO Box 930
Dearborn, MI 48128
313-271-1500
FAX: 313-425-3417 800-733-4763
service@sme.org http://www.sme.org
Dianna Helka, Associate Editor
The newsletter highlights the latest developments in the machine vision industry including applications, techniques and methods. *$85.00*
Quarterly
Circulation: 1100

5650 Wafer News Confidential
PennWell Publishing Company
98 Spit Brook Road
Nashua, NH 03062-2800
603-891-0123
FAX: 603-891-0574
ATD@PennWell.com
http://www.pennwell.com
Philip Lopiccolo, Editor
Barbara Pennwell, CEO/President
Provides semiconductor equipment industry executives with information on developments, trends, news and market insights. *$15.00*
Monthly Founded: 1910

Magazines & Journals

5651 Bioelectromagnetics Journal
John Wiley & Sons
2412 Cobblestone Way
Frederick, MD 21702-3519
301-663-4252
FAX: 301-694-4948
bemsoffice@aol.com
www.bioelectromagnetics.org
Ben Greenebaum, Editor-in-Chief
James C Lin, Associate Editor
Gloria Parsley, Executive Director
It is a peer-reviewed, internationally circulated scientific journal that specializes in reporting original data on biological effect and applications of electromagnetic fields that range in frequency from zero hertz(static fields) to the terahertz undulations of visible light.

5652 Contact
1000 McKee Street
Batavia, IL 60510-1682
630-879-6000
FAX: 630-879-0867
Steve Wilcox, Editor
Application of electric motor controls to electrically operated machinery and equipment.
Circulation: 4,000

5653 Control Solutions
PennWell Publishing Company
1421 S Sheridan Road
Tulsa, OK 74112
918-835-3161
FAX: 918-831-9497 800-331-4463
Headquarters@PennWell.com
http://www.pennwell.com
Matt O'Shea, Publisher
Ron Kuhfeld, Editor-in-Chief
Monthly

5654 Diesel & Gas Turbine Worldwide
Diesel & Gas Turbine Publications
20855 Watertown Road
Waukesha, WI 53186-1873
262-325-5000
FAX: 262-832-5075 www.dieselpub.com
Robert A Wilson, Publisher
Lynne Diefenbach, Advertising Manager
Concentrates its editorial on the design, packaging, operation and maintenance of medium and slow-speed, high output diesel, natural gas and gas turbine engine systems used in the electrical power generation, cogeneration, oil and gas, marine propulsion and railroad markets throughout the world. *$65.00*
10 per year Founded: 1969
Circulation: 22,000

5655 ECN Magazine
Reed Business Information
360 Park Avenue South
4th Floor
New York, NY 10014
212-450-0067
FAX: 630-288-8686
subsmail@reedbusiness.com
www.ecnmag.com
Jeff Rovner, Circulation Manager
Aimee Kalnoskas, Editor

Steve Wirth, Publisher Director
James Reed, Owner

Provides product solutions for designed engineers in the electronics industry.
$96.19
Monthly

5656 **EE Product News**
Penton Media
1300 E 9th Street
Cleveland, OH 44114
216-696-7000
FAX: 216-696-1752 800-249-9365
information@penton.com
http://www.eepn.com

Joseph Desposito, Editor-in-Chief
David B. Nussbaum, Ceo

Source of information on new products necessary to successfully design, assemble and test prototypes of commercial, industrial, military and aerospace electronic products.
Monthly Founded: 1892
Circulation: 111968

5657 **EE: Evaluation Engineering**
Nelson Publishing
2500 Tamiami Trail North
Nokomis, FL 34275
941-966-9521
FAX: 941-966-2590 800-226-6113
pmilo@evaluationengineering.com
http://www.nelsonpub.com

Paul Milo, Editor
Mike Hughes, Sales

Magazine devoted exclusively to companies that test, evaluate, design and manufacture electronic products and equipment.
$43.00
84 pages Monthly Founded: 1962
Mailing list available for rent 65,000 names
Printed in 4 colors on glossy stock

5658 **ElectriCITY Magazine**
Electric Association
4100 Madison Street
Suite 4
Hillside, IL 60162
708-547-9910
FAX: 708-547-9920
admin@eachicago.org
www.eachicago.org

Chuck Currie, Jr, President
Michael McInerney, VP
Carrie Spaeth, Managing Director
Jim Paplaczyk, Treasurer
Bob Porter, Secretary

Corporate news, timely articles, career announcements, product line changes, industry-dates calendars, career placement services, and government legislation updates; circulation across the Midwest.
Quarterly

5659 **Electric Co-op Today**
National Rural Electric Cooperative Association
4301 Wilson Boulevard
Suite 1
Arlington, VA 22203-1860
703-907-5500
FAX: 703-907-5514

Ruth Coates, Senior Editorial Advisor

Devoted to accurate, critical coverage of electric cooperative developments and electric cooperative industry news, unavailable in any other publication. The only weekly publication covering electric cooperative industry news, legislation and regulation, and community and economic development. Each issue highlights what you need to know to understand key industry issues clearly, quickly, and easily.
$40.00
45 Issues Founded: 1994

5660 **Electric Light & Power**
PennWell Publishing Company
1421 S Sheridan Road
Tulsa, OK 74112
918-835-3161
FAX: 918-831-9497 800-331-4463
Headquarters@PennWell.com
http://www.elp.com

Michael Gros Boschee, Publisher
Steven M Brown, Editor
Kathleen Davis, Associate Editor
Timothy P Adams, Assistant Associate Editor

Serves the North American Electric Utility Industry including electric power generation, delivery, and information technology operations in investor-owned electric utilities.
Monthly Founded: 1902

5661 **Electric Perspectives**
Edison Electric Institute
701 Pennsylvania Avenue NW
3rd Floor
Washington, DC 20004-2696
202-085-5995
FAX: 202-508-5759 800-334-5453
feedback@eei.org http://www.eei.org/

Eric Blume, Editor & Publisher
William Mambert, Advertising Director
Mark Hand, Associate Editor
LaVonne M. Rose, Editorial Assistant
Thomas Kuhn, President

The magazine for executives and managers in shareholoder-owned electric companies—an intelligent business audience t hat wants to understand the issues shaping the industry. Free to management level employees at EEI member companies. *$50.00*

Founded: 1933
Circulation: 15000
Printed in 4 colors on glossy stock

5662 **Electrical Apparatus**
Barks Publications
400 N Michigan Avenue
Suite 900
Chicago, IL 60611-4289
312-321-9440
FAX: 323-321-1288
info@barks.com
http://www.barks.com

Horace B. Barks, Editor
Elsie Dickson, Associate Publisher
Horace Barks, CEO
Joseph Hoff, Manager

Serves the electromechanical and electronic maintenance and application industries, including manufacturing plants, institutional facilities and service companies. *$45.00*
Monthly Founded: 1969
Circulation: 15500

5663 **Electrical Construction & Maintenance**
Primedia
9800 Metcalf Avenue
Overland Park, KS 66212
913-341-1300
FAX: 913-967-1898
mhalverson@primediabusiness.com
www.primediabusiness.com

John Dedad, Editorial Director
Michael Eby, Editor-in-Chief
David Miller, Publisher

Owners and company officials, engineers, electrical personnel, electrical inspectors, architects and designers, purchasing and other related personnel.

Circulation: 104344

5664 **Electrical Contractor**
National Electrical Contractors Association
3 Bethesda Metro Center
Suite 1100
Bethesda, MD 20814-5372
301-657-3110
FAX: 301-215-4501
jfulmer@necanet.org
http://www.ecmag.com

John W. Maisel, Publisher
John Fulmer, Editor
Astra Benjamin, Circulation Manager
John Grau, CEO/President

Offers important information for the electrical contracting industry: power, voice, data, and video. Free to qualified electrical contractors.
180 pages Founded: 1939
Circulation: 35000
Mailing list available for rent 90,000 names
$120 per M.
Printed in 4 colors on glossy stock

5665 **Electrical Contractor Magazine**
National Electrical Contractors Association
3 Bethesda Metro Center
Suite 1100
Bethesda, MD 20814
301-657-3110
FAX: 301-215-4500
webmaster@necanet.org
www.necanet.org

John W Maisel, Publisher
Donna Bailey, Associate Publisher

The magazine has been the complete information source for electrical construction professionals. Its goal is to serve all participants in the power and integrated building systems industries. It delivers the latest information in the areas of power, communications and controls in both high voltage and low voltage applications to electrical contractors who compete in residential, commercial, industrial and institutional market segments of the construction arena.

Founded: 1939
Circulation: 85,000

5666 **Electrical Distributor Magazine**
National Association of Electrical Distributors
1100 Croporate Square Drive
Suite 100
St Louis, MO 63132
314-991-9000
FAX: 314-991-3060 888-791-2512
info@naed.org www.naed.org

Tom Naber, President
Tim Dencker, Controller
Laurie Mueller-Bevirt, Director Marketing

An informative, insightful publication that offers electrical distributors the latest information affecting their business. Subscriptions are free to NAED members.

5667 **Electrical Wholesaling**
Primedia
9800 Metcalf Avenue
Overland Park, KS 66212
913-341-1300
FAX: 913-967-1898
kevinadamson@intertec.com
http://www.primediabusiness.com

Andrea Herbert, Editor
David Miller, Publisher

Offers information on manufacturers, suppliers, prices and marketing of electrical products. *$25.00*
Monthly Founded: 1905
Circulation: 22,500

5668 **Electricity Today**
215-1885 Clements Road
Pickering, Ontario Canada L1W-3V4
905-686-1040
FAX: 905-686-1078
info@electricty-today.com
www.electricty-today.com

Randy Hurst, Publisher

5669 **Electronic Design**
Penton Media
1300 E 9th Street
Cleveland, OH 44114
216-696-7000
FAX: 216-696-1752
information@penton.com
http://www.edmediafile.com

Mark David, Editor-in-Chief
Bill Baumann, Publisher
Roger Engelke, Issue Editor

Celebrating 50 years of innovation, this authoritative source provides leading-edge information to electronic and engineering managers around the world.

5670 **Fringe Ware Review**
Fringe Ware
PO Box 49921
Austin, TX 78765-4858
512-444-2393

Jon Lebkowsky, Publisher
Don Lebkowsky, Editor

Stories and review on electronic products made by smaller producers. *$4.00*

5671 **Handbook of Standardized Terminology for the Power Sources Industry**
Power Sources Manufacturers Association
PO Box 418
Mendham, NJ 07945-418
973-543-9660
FAX: 973-543-6207
power@psma.com
http://www.psma.com

Arnold Alderman, President
Chuck Mullett, Chairman
Judy Horzepa, Managing Editor

This handbook provides a current common language for the industry, covering every facet of power sources and conversion. All member companies receive a copy of this report as a benefit of membership. *$25.00*
Annual+ Founded: 1987

5672 **IEEE Instrumentation and Measurement Magazine**
IEEE Instrumentation and Measurement Society
67 Alexander Drive
PO Box 12277
Research Triangle Park, NC 27709
919-549-8411
FAX: 919-549-8288
info@isa.org www.isa.org

Kim Fowler, Editor-in-Chief

This publication is included in member dues, it contains applications-oriented articles and news nominations, awards, highlights of conferences, Technical Committee news, book reviews, tutorials and contributions from the membership.
Quarterly

5673 **IEEE Sensors Journal**
IEEE Instrumentation and Measurement Society
67 Alexander Drive
PO Box 12277
Research Triangle Park, NC 27709
919-549-8411
FAX: 919-549-8288
info@isa.org www.isa.org

Ken Baker, President
Rob Renner, Executive Director
Jerry Clemons, Department VP
Leo Staples, Treasurer

Specializes in the theory, design, fabrication, manufacturing and applications of devices for sensing and transducing physical, chemical and biological phenomena.
Bi-Monthly

5674 **IEEE Transactions on Intelligent Transportation Systems**
IEEE Instrumentation and Measurement Society
67 Alexander Drive
PO Box 12277
Research Triangle Park, NC 27709
919-549-8411
FAX: 919-549-8288
info@isa.org www.isa.org

Ken Baker, President
Rob Renner, Executive Director
Jerry Clemons, Department VP
Leo Staples, Treasurer

This journal contains basic and applied research to expand the knowledge base on transportation for improved design, management and control of future transportation systems.
Quarterly

5675 **IEEE Transactions on Nanotechnology**
IEEE Instrumentation and Measurement Society
67 Alexander Drive
PO Box 12277
Research Triangle Park, NC 27709
919-549-8411
FAX: 919-549-8288
info@isa.org www.isa.org

Ken Baker, President
Rob Renner, Executive Director
Jerry Clemons, Department VP
Leo Staples, Treasurer

The journal is devoted to the dissemination of new results and discussions related to understanding the physical basis and engineering applications of phenomena at the nanoscale level.
Quarterly

5676 **Industrial Laser Solutions**
PennWell Publishing Company
98 Spit Brook Road
5th Floor
Nashua, NH 03062-5737
603-891-0123
FAX: 603-891-0574 www.ilr.com

Florence Oreiro, Publisher
David Belforte, Editor

For all industries that use industrial lasers. *$260.00*
45 pages Monthly Founded: 1986
Circulation: 10,000

5677 **Industrial Market Place**
Wineberg Publications
7842 Lincoln Avenue
Skokie, IL 60077
847-676-1900
FAX: 847-676-0063 800-323-1818
info@industrialmktpl.com
http://www.industrialmktpl.com

Eliot Wineberg, President
Joel Wineberg, Publisher

Advertising sales on new and used machinery and equipment and industrial auctions. *$175.00*
60 pages Bi-weekly Founded: 1951
Circulation: 10,000 100000 names $70 per M.
Printed in 4 colors on glossy stock

5678 **Interface Magazine**
Electrochemical Society
65 S Main Street
Building D
Pennington, NJ 08534-2839
609-737-1902
FAX: 609-737-2743
interface@electrochem.org
http://www.electrochem.org

Krishnan Rajeshwar, Editor
Elisha Nicholson, Circulation Manager

Is an authoritative accessible publication for those in the field of solid-state and electrochemical science and technology which contains technical articles about the latest developments in the field, and presents news and information about and for members of ECS. *$40.00*
Quarterly Founded: 1902
Circulation: 9000
Printed in 4 colors

5679 **Journal of Laser Applications**
Laser Institute of America
13501 Ingenuity Drive
Suite 128
Orlando, FL 32826
407-380-1553
FAX: 407-380-5588
lia@laserinstitute.org
www.laserinstitute.org

Jyoti Mazumder, Editor-in-Chief
Anja Selnau, Managing Editor
Peter Baker, Executive Director

The official journal of the Laser Institute of America and serves as the major international forum for exchanging ideas and information in disciplines that apply laser technology. *$360.00*

5680 **Journal of Lightwave Technology**
IEEE Instrumentation and Measurement Society
67 Alexander Drive
PO Box 12277
Research Triangle Park, NC 27709
919-549-8411
FAX: 919-549-8288
info@isa.org www.isa.org

Ken Baker, President
Rob Renner, Executive Director
Jerry Clemons, Department VP
Leo Staples, Treasurer

The Journal is concerned with research, applications and methods used in all aspects of lightwave technology and fiber optics.

Monthly

5681 Journal of Microwave Power and Electro- magnetic Energy
International Microwave Power Institute
1916 Sussex Road
Blacksburg, VA 24060
540-552-3070
FAX: 540-961-1463
info@impi.org www.impi.org

John A Pearce, Editor-in-Chief

A peer reviewed, technical journal of the Institute focusing on the industrial, scientific, medical and instrumentation interest areas of the profession. The publication is free to members and also available for yearly subscription to nonmembers for an annual fee of $250.00.

Quarterly

5682 Journal of the Electrochemical Society
Electrochemical Society
65 S Main Street
Building D
Pennington, NJ 08534-2839
609-737-1902
FAX: 609-737-2743
webmaster@electrochem.org
http://www.electrochem.org

Paul Kohl, Editor
Roque Calvo, Manager

This peer reviewed journal publishes 60 articles each month. Articles are posted on-line, with a monthly paper edition following electronic publication. The ECS membership benefits package includes access to the electronic edition of this journal. Free with membership. *$ 110.00*

Monthly Founded: 1902
Circulation: 8300

5683 LIA Today
Laser Institute of America
13501 Ingenuity Drive
Suite 128
Orlando, FL 32826
407-380-1553
FAX: 407-380-5588
lia@laserinstitute.org
www.laserinstitute.org

Peter M Baker, Managing Director

This journal strives to educate and inform laser professionals on laser safety and new trends related to laser technology. LIA members receive a free subscription.

Bi-Monthly

5684 Laser Tech Briefs
Associated Business Publications International
317 Madison Avenue
New York, NY 10017
212-490-3999
FAX: 212-986-7864 www.abpi.net
For purchasers of laser/optical products.

Circulation: 40,000

5685 Lighting Dimensions
Primedia Business
249 W 17th Street
New York, NY 10011
212-716-8449
FAX: 212-514-3719 800-827-3322

Doug MacDonald, Group Publisher
David Johnson, Associate Publisher/Editorial
Marian Sandberg-Dierson, Editor
Mark Newman, Managing Editor

Trade publication for lighting professionals in film, theatre, television, concerts, clubs, themed environments, architecctural, commercial, and industrial lighting. Sponsors of the LDI Trade Show and the Broadway Lighting Master Classes. *$34.97*

12/year Founded: 1989
Circulation: 14,177

5686 Market Trends
Electronic Industries Association
2500 Wilson Boulevard
Arlington, VA 22201-3834
703-907-7500
FAX: 703-907-7767
Statistical information and marketing trends in the electronics industry. *$195.00*

Monthly

5687 Motion Control
ISA Services
2807 N Parham Road
Suite 200
Richmond, VA 23294
804-762-9600
FAX: 804-217-8999
editroboQ@douglaspublications.com
http://www.douglaspublications.com

Janine Nunes, Editor
Edward Mueller, Publisher

Information for those who design and maintain motion control systems.

56 pages Monthly Founded: 1985
Circulation: 16,490
Printed in 4 colors on glossy stock

5688 NETA World
International Electrical Testing Association
106 Stone Street
Morrison, CO 80465
303-697-8441
FAX: 303-697-8431 888-300-6382
neta@netaworld.org
www.netaworld.org

Stuart Jackson, President
John White, First VP
Kerry Heid, Second VP
Ken Bassett, Treasurer
Charles K Blizard, Secretary

Features articles of interest to electrical testing and maintenance companies, consultants, engineers, architects, and plant personnel directly involved in electrical testing and maintenance. Free with membership.

Quarterly

5689 Power Conversion & Intelligent Motion
Primedia
9800 Metcalf Avenue
Overland Park, KS 66212
913-341-1300
FAX: 913-967-1898
www.primediabusiness

Myron A Miller, Publisher
Sam Davis, Editor

Directed to engineers, designers and manufacturers of power electronic and electronic motion control components, subsystems and systems. Feature articles interpret trends and innovation in these subjects.

Circulation: 31,113

5690 Power Engineering International
PennWell Publishing Company
1421 S Sheridan Road
Tulsa, OK 74112
918-353-3161
FAX: 918-831-9776
brians@pennwell.com
http://pepei.pennnet.com/

Junior Isles, Publisher/Editor

Serves the global electric power generation and transmission industry.

Monthly Founded: 1896
Circulation: 34000

5691 Powerline Magazine
Electrical Generating Systems Association
1650 S Dixie Highway
Suite 500
Boca Raton, FL 33432
561-750-5575
FAX: 561-395-8557 www.egsa.org

Donald M Ferreira, Director Publications

Focuses on the entire on-site power generation industry. *$5.00*

Bi-Monthly

5692 ProService Magazine
National Electronics Service Dealers Association
3608 Pershing Avenue
Fort Worth, TX 76107-4527
817-921-9061
FAX: 817-921-3741 800-797-9197
webmaster@nesda.com
www.nesda.com

Mary M Bauer, Associate Editor

Published for members of NESDA/ISCET.

24 pages Bi-Monthly

5693 Process Heating
Business News Publishing Company
755 W Big Beaver Road
Suite 100
Troy, MI 48084-4900
248-362-3700
FAX: 248-362-0317
beckerL@bnpmedia.com
http://www.process-heating.com

Linda Becker, Editor
Anne Armel, Publisher

Covers heat processing at temperatures up to 1000 degrees F at end user and OEM plants in 9 industries.

Founded: 1994
Circulation: 25000

5694 RE Magazine
National Rural Electric Cooperative Association
4301 Wilson Boulevard
Suite 1
Arlington, VA 22203-1860
703-907-5500
FAX: 703-907-5514

Frank Gallant, Editor

Editorial content covers utility operations, deployment of the latest industry products and services; a showcase of new products, services, and catalogs; online resources; safety; member(customer) services; business and management trends; marketing tools; community and economic development; local leaders and rural issues; co-op personnel news; and politics and regula-

tory policies impacting electric co-ops. *$43.00*
Monthly Founded: 1942

5695 **Rural Electrification**
National Rural Electric Cooperative Association
4301 Wilson Boulevard
Arlington, VA 22203-1860
703-907-5500
FAX: 703-907-5531
http://www.nreca.org
Frank Gallant, Editor
Glenn English, CEO/President
Serves people involved in the rural electric cooperative industry including generation and transmission cooperatives, distribution systems and public utility district members of NRECA; electric equipment manufacturers; US Congress, state and federal regulatory agencies and commissions; and others allied to the field. *$85.00*
Monthly Founded: 1942

5696 **Service Contractor Magazine**
Contract Services Association of America
1000 Wilson Boulevard
Suite 1800
Arlington, VA 22209
703-243-2020
FAX: 703-243-3601
info@csa-dc.org www.csa-dc.org
Larry Trammell, Chairman
Michael W Shelton, Vice Chairman
Chris Jahn, President
Kate Hannon, Executive Assistant to President
Isiah Harris, Secretary
Focuses on industry developments, regulatory and legislative issues, and any issues encountered in the process of competing for and securing contracts, such as changes in the acquisitions or procurement process. It tailors its content exclusively to government contractors.
Bi-Annual

5697 **Standard for Certification of Electrical Testing Technicians**
International Electrical Testing Association
106 Stone Street
Morrison, CO 80465
303-697-8441
FAX: 303-697-8431 888-300-6382
neta@netaworld.org
www.netaworld.org
Stuart Jackson, President
John White, First VP
Kerry Heid, Second VP
Ken Bassett, Treasurer
Charles K Blizard, Secretary
Specifying requisite levels of training, experience, and education for the evaluator of electrical power equipment is an important test procedure itself. The requirements parallel those of the National Skill Standards Board in Washington, DC, which promulgates for various occupations. *$55.00*
36 pages Hard Cover : Bound

5698 **Standard for Electrical Maintenance Testing of Dry-Type Transformers**
International Electrical Testing Assocaition
106 Stone Street
Morrison, CO 80465
303-697-8441
FAX: 303-697-8431 888-300-6382
neta@netaworld.org
www.netaworld.org
Stuart Jackson, President
John White, First VP
Kerry Heid, Second VP
Ken Bassett, Treasurer
Charles K Blizard, Secretary
This Standard has been an individual section within the NETA document entitled Maintenance Testing Specifications for Electrical Power Distribution Equipment and Systems since 1975. The Maintenance Testing Specifications along with NETA's Acceptance Testing Specifications have long been in general use by organizations and individuals involved with testing of electrical apparatus. *$55.00*
18 pages Hard Cover : Bound

5699 **Standard for Electrical Maintenance Testin g of Liquid-Filled Transformers**
International Electrical Testing Association
106 Stone Street
Morrison, CO 80465
303-697-8441
FAX: 303-697-8431 888-300-6382
neta@netaworld.org
www.netaworld.org
Stuart Jackson, President
John White, First VP
Kerry Heid, Second VP
Ken Bassett, Treasurer
Charles K Blizard, Secretary
The Standard has been an individual section within the NETA document entitled Maintenance Testing Specifications for Electrical Power Distribution Equipment and Systems since 1975. The Maintenance Testing Specifications along with NETA's Acceptance Testing Specifications have long been in general use by organizations and individuals involved with testing of electrical apparatus. *$55.00*
21 pages : Bound

Trade Shows

5700 **AHTD Trade Show**
Association for High Technology Distributors
1900 Arch Street
Philadelphia, PA 19103-1498
215-564-3484
FAX: 215-564-2175
ahtd@ahtd.org www.ahtd.org
Dan O'Brien, President
Patricia A Lilly, Executive Director
Paul Lewis, VP
Steve Earley, Secretary/Program Chair
James H Norton, Treasurer
Worked to increase the productivity and profitability of the high technology automation solutions provider and manufacturer who satisfy the automation needs of general industry and OEM manufacturers. Through a wide spectrum of association programs and services for members, AHTD is the primary resource for all member companies to achieve their ultimate and common goals.
September

5701 **American Control Conference**
American Automatic Control Council
2145 Sheridan Road
Evanston, IL 60208-3118
847-491-8175
FAX: 847-491-4455
aacc@ece.northwestern.edu
www.a2c2.org
A Galip Ulsoy, President
R Russell Rhinehart, Treasurer
Pradeep Misra, Secretary
Covers a broad range of topics relevant to the theory and practice of control and automation, including robotics, manufacturing, guidance and control, power systems, process control, identification and estimation, signal processing, modeling and advanced simulation.
800 Attendees June

5702 **Annual Connector & Interconnection Technology Symposium and Trade Show**
International Institute of Connector and Intercon
PO Box 20002
Sarasota, FL 34276
941-929-1806
FAX: 941-929-1807 800-854-4248
Darrell Fernald, International President
Offers the opportunity to meet with other connector/interconnection industry users and vendors to learn about the latest advances in interconnection technology in the areas of radio frequency interconnection, quality, high speed connectors, personal computer interconnections, automotive Interconnections, materials, finishes, and platings, test methods, automation, surface mount technology, fiber optics, spaceflight connector technology, and medical applications.

5703 **Annual Legislative & Regulatory Roundtable**
Electronic Industries Association
2500 Wilson Boulevard
Arlington, VA 22201-3834
703-907-7500
FAX: 703-907-7767 www.eia.org
Gail Tannenbaum, CMP, Manager Meetings
Panel topics in the past have included Broadband, Tax, Trade, Environment, Defense, Space, and the Congressional Leadership Agenda.
August

5704 **Bioelectromagnetics - Stun Gun Mini Symposium**
Bioelectromagnetics Society
2412 Cobblestone Way
Frederick, MD 21702-3519
301-663-4252
FAX: 301-694-4948
bemsoffice@aol.com
www.bioelectromagnetics.org
Bruce R McLeod, President
Gloria Parsley, Executive Director
Stefan Engstrom, VP
Robert F Cleveland, Treasurer
Robert B Goldberg, Secretary
The focus of this symposium will be the technology, physiology and potential adverse side effects of the use of electronic weapons or stun guns, which are rapidly being deployed in military and police use.
June

5705 **Bioelectromagnetics - U.S. Air Force Workshop**
Bioelectromagnetics Society
2412 Cobblestone Way
Frederick, MD 21702-3519
301-663-4252
FAX: 301-694-4948
bemsoffice@aol.com
www.bioelectromagnetics.org

Bruce R McLeod, President
Gloria Parsley, Executive Director
Stefan Engstrom, VP
Robert F Cleveland, Treasurer
Robert B Goldberg, Secretary

Will focus on the use of molecular biology to identify changes in genes and proteins that may lead to physiological, pathological, or behavioral events.
June

5706 **Bioelectromagnetics Society Meeting**
Bioelectromagnetics Society
2412 Cobblestone Way
Frederick, MD 21702-3519
301-663-4252
FAX: 301-694-4948
bemsoffice@aol.com
www.bioelectromagnetics.org

Bruce R McLeod, President
Gloria Parsley, Executive Director
Stefan Engstrom, VP
Robert F Cleveland, Treasurer
Robert B Goldberg, Secretary

This is a joint meeting of The Bioelectromagnetics Society and The European BioElectromagnetics Association. Topics will be: Electric Fields, Human Studies, Exposure Assessment, Dosimetry, In Vitro ELF, Epidemiology, Unique EMF Signals, Medical applications, Mechanisms, Electromagnetic Therapy.
June, Dublin Ireland

5707 **CSA Winter Meeting**
Contract Services Association of America

1000 Wilson Boulevard
Suite 1800
Arlington, VA 22209
703-243-2020
FAX: 703-243-3601
info@csa-dc.org www.csa-dc.org

Larry Trammell, Chairman
Michael W Shelton, Vice Chairman
Chris Jahn, President
Kate Hannon, Executive Assistant to President
Isiah Harris, Secretary

This one day workshop is a free flowing exchange of information with real time interaction and information exchange.
January, Hawaii

5708 **Coherence and Electromagnetic Fields in Biological Systems**
Bioelectromagnetics Society
2412 Cobblestone Way
Frederick, MD 21702-3519
301-663-4252
FAX: 301-694-4948
bemsoffice@aol.com
www.bioelectromagnetics.org

Bruce R McLeod, President
Gloria Parsley, Executive Director
Stefan Engstrom, VP
Robert F Cleveland, Treasurer
Robert B Goldberg, Secretary

Highlights of the symposium organized by the Institute of Radio Engineering and Electronics, the Academy of Sciences of the Czech Republic and others are expected to include biophysical principles of coherence, role of endogenous EMF in the organization of biological systems, biophysical mechanisms of interaction of biological systems with EMF and more.
July

5709 **Consulting Electrical Engineers(CEE) Technical Forum & Table-Top**
Electric Association
4100 Madison Street
Suite 4
Hillside, IL 60162
708-547-9910
FAX: 708-547-9920
admin@eachicago.org
www.eachicago.org

Chuck Currie, Jr, President
Michael McInerney, VP
Carrie Spaeth, Managing Director
Jim Paplaczyk, Treasurer
Bob Porter, Secretary

This event will feature a free technical forum for engineers, specifiers, and designers on Short Circuit analysis, Coordination, and Arc Flash Hazard analysis using conventional and computerized methods. The Table Top tradeshow will feature 45 vendors and their latest technology.
May

5710 **EEI Annual Convention**
Edison Electric Institute
701 Pennsylvania Avenue NW
Washington, DC 20004-2696
202-085-5995
FAX: 202-508-5335
eblume@eei.org www.eei.org

Tom Kuhn, President
David Owens, Executive VP

Provides the top showcase for the tools to improve your business. Equipment, software, top-of-the-line consulting will be offered in the exhibit hall.

5711 **EEI Financial Conference**
Edison Electric Institute
701 Pennsylvania Avenue NW
Washington, DC 20004-2696
202-085-5995
FAX: 202-508-5335
eblume@eei.org www.eei.org

Tom Kuhn, President
David Owens, Executive VP

Provides a unique forum for exchange of ideas and experience; and to give you insight into emerging critical issues.
November

5712 **EERA Annual Meeting**
Electrical Equipmnet Representation
PO Box 419264
Kansas City, MO 64141-6264
816-561-5323
FAX: 816-561-1249
jmale@erra.org www.eera.org

Randy Sutton, Chairman
Robert D Chapman, President
Scott Dashiell, VP
John Commons, Treasurer

Provide a forum where indsutry representatives may discuss matters pertinent to the success of their business and to the interest of the industy.
May

5713 **EGSA Annual Spring Convention**
Electrical Generating Systems Association
1650 S Dixie Highway
Suite 500
Boca Raton, FL 33432
561-750-5575
FAX: 561-398-8557 www.egsa.org

Lynn Grant, Director Conventions/Meetings

Offers educational sessions covering a broad range of issues effecting the on-site power industry.
March, Florida

5714 **EIA's Congressional Technology Forum**
Electronic Industries Association
2500 Wilson Boulevard
Arlington, VA 22201-3834
703-907-7500
FAX: 703-907-7767 www.eia.org

Gail Tannenbaum, CMP, Manager Meetings

Discusses the issues most relevant for the electronics and high-tech industries.
October

5715 **EOS/ESD Symposium & Exhibits**
Electrostatic Discharge Association
7900 Turin Road
Building 3
Rome, NY 13440-2069
315-339-6937
FAX: 315-339-6793
info@esda.org
www.esda.org/symposia.html

Lisa Pimpinella, Operations Mgr/Symposium Exhibits
Lynn Barbiarz, Marketing & Communications Admnstr

International technical forum on electrical overstress and electrostatic discharge that features research, technology, and solutions to increase understanding, enhance quality and reliability, reduce and control costs, and improve yields and productivity.

1M Attendees September

5716 **Electric West Conference**
PRIMEDIA Business Exhibitions
11 River Bend Drive S
PO Box 4232
Stamford, CT 06907-0232
203-358-9900
FAX: 203-358-5816
www.primediaevents.com

David Small, Show Director
Tara Keating-Magee, Show Coordinator

Educational sessions attract electrical professionals from contracting companies, industrial plants, consulting engineering firms, datacom installers and electricians. Presentations focus on such topics as power quality, lighting, the NEC, project management, claims management and fiber optics. Also provides in-depth coverage of National Electrical Code changes that directly impact the work of electrical professionals. 250 Exhibitors.
6000 Attendees March

5717 **Electrical Apparatus Services**
1331 Baur Boulevard
Saint Louis, MO 63132-1903
314-993-2220
FAX: 314-993-1269
easainfo@easa.com www.easa.com

Linda J Raynes, President/CEO
Dale Shuter, CMP, Meetings/Exposition Manager

Provides members with a means of keeping up to date on materials, equipment, and state-of-the-art technology. 150 booths.

Mailing list available for rent 2200 names $193 per M.

5718 Electromagnetic Compatibility International Expo
SEI
111 1/2 East Main Street
Richardson, TX 75081
972-690-9881
FAX: 972-669-8847
joe@swelectronic.com
www.swelectronic.com

Joe Stanfield, Administrator

Representing electronic factories and companies in the following areas: components, magnetic and shielding materials, RF and regulatory qualitication and consulting, factory authorized distributors. View our on-line capabilities presentation and technical standard links and other information. 80 booths available.

1.5M Attendees August

5719 Electronic Distribution Show Corporation
222 S Riverside Plaza
Suite 2160
Chicago, IL 60606-6160
312-648-1140
FAX: 312-648-4282
eds@edsc.org www.edsc.org

Gretchen Oie-Weghorst, Director
Gerald M Newman, Executive VP

Attendees are manufacturers of electronic components who sell their products through electronics distributors.

6M Attendees May Founded: 1937

5720 Energy - Exhibit Promotions Plus
US Department of Energy/US Dept. of Defense/GSA
11620 Vixens Path
Ellicott City, MD 21042
301-596-3028
FAX: 410-997-0764
energy@epponline.com
www.energy2003.ee.doe.gov

Harve Horowitz, President
Kevin Horowitz, Senior Association Manager

Energy is an exclusive Federal Grant sponsored annual educational forum and exhibition.

1000+ Attendees August 1,000+ names

5721 Fall Technical and Marketing Conference
Electrical Generating Systems Association
1650 S Dixie Highway
Suite 500
Boca Raton, FL 33432
561-750-5575
FAX: 561-395-8557 www.egsa.org

Lynn Grant, Director
Conventions/Meetings

Will focus on technical presentations and marketing efforts.

September

5722 ICALEO
Laser Institute of America
13501 Ingenuity Drive
Suite 128
Orlando, FL 32826
407-380-1553
FAX: 407-380-5588
lia@laserinstitute.org
www.laserinstitute.org

Beth Cohen, Show Manager

Devoted to the field of laser materials processing and is viewed as the premier source of technical information in the field.

5723 IETA Annual Technical Conference

International Electrical Testing Association
106 Stone Street
Morrison, CO 80465
303-697-8441
FAX: 303-697-8431 888-300-6382
neta@netaworld.org
www.netaworld.org

Stuart Jackson, President
John White, First VP
Kerry Heid, Second VP
Ken Bassett, Treasurer
Charles K Blizard, Secretary

Targets the electrical testing industry.

March, Tennessee

5724 IFAC World Congress
American Automatic Control Council
3640 Col Glenn Hwy
Dayton, OH 45435
937-775-5062
FAX: 937-775-3936
pmisra@cs.wright.edu www.a2c2.org

A Galip Ulsoy, President
R Russell Rhinehart, Treasurer
Pradeep Misra, Secretary

You will have the opportunity to take part in the wide spectrum of categories for technical presentations, including plenary lectures, survey papers, regular papers of both lecture and poster session types, panel discussions and case studies.

July

5725 ILEA Annual Conference
International League of Electrical Association
12165 West Center Road
Suite 59
Omaha, NE 68144
402-330-7227
FAX: 402-330-7283
niec2005@aol.com www.ileaweb.org

Chuck Eckert, President
Jane Male, VP
Bill Regan, Treasurer
Susan Crow-Jones, Secretary

Provides a venue through which information and ideas exchanged and by encouraging all members to attend and share ideas.

July, Vancover BC

5726 IMA Spring Meeting
International Magnetics Association
8 S Michigan Avenue
Suite 1000
Chicago, IL 60603-3310
312-456-5590
FAX: 312-580-0165
www.intl-magnetics.org

August Sisco, Chair
Lowell Bosleyeo, President
George Orenchak, Secretary/Treasurer

Promote the worldwide growth, development, and use of magnetic materials through: collection and dissemination of global trade statistics, publication of industry standards and user and industry education.

May

5727 IMAPS International Symposium on Microelectronics
International Microelectronics & Packaging Society
611 2nd Street NE
Washington, DC 20002
202-548-4001
FAX: 202-548-6115 888-464-6277

Michael O'Donoghue, Executive Director
Ann Bell, Manager
Marketing/Communications

Symposium for the microelectronics and electronics packaging industries. Features a powerful technical program, progressive professional development courses and many forums to share the latest developments in microelectronics. Comprehensive exhibition of materials and equipment for the industry.

3000 Attendees September

5728 IMPI's Annual Symposium
International Microwave Power Institute
1916 Sussex Road
Blacksburg, VA 24060
540-552-3070
FAX: 540-961-1463
info@impi.org www.impi.org

Neal Cooper, President
Kimberly D Thies, Executive Director

Is the major global technology exchange forum for microwave and radio frequency specialists in 2005. The IMPI Symposium is designed to benefit all persons interested in advancing their knowledge of microwave/RF heating technology.

July

5729 IPC Printed Circuits Expo
IPC: Association Connecting Electronics
3000 Lakeside Drive
Suite 309 S
Bannockburn, IL 60015
847-615-7100
FAX: 847-615-7105
webmaster@ipc.org www.ipc.org

Sabrina Neamand, Director
Meetings/Special Events
Sarah Martino, Exhibits Operations Coordinator

Meet with everyone who designs, manufactures, and assembles printed circuit boards and electronics assemblies.

February, California

5730 ISA Expo
ISA
67 Alexander Drive
Box 12277
Research Triangle Park, NC 27709
919-549-8411
FAX: 919-549-8288
info@isa.org www.isa.org

Tracey Berrett-Noble, Event Manager
Rodney Jones, Conference Coordinator
Cyrus Taft, Program Chair
Dale Lee, Director Convention Services
Tracey Berrett, Manager Convention Services

Features the latest and most extensive products and services exhibition, a strategically relevant technical conference, and a prominent continuing education and training program. With practitioners from over 70 countries. Offers the most complete automation and control experience in today's marketplace.

15000 Attendees October 17-19, 2006

5731 ISA Fugitive Emissions LDAR Symposium and Training
Instrumentation, Systems, and Automation Society
67 Alexander Drive
Box 12277
Research Triangle Park, NC 27709
919-549-8411
FAX: 919-549-8288
info@isa.org www.isa.org

Dale Lee, Director Convention Services
Tracey Berrett, Manager Convention Services

Covers topics including, but not limited to leak detection repair methods and fugitive emissions management systems. Industry experts in leak detection and repair will discuss implementations and improvements in LDAR programs in plant facilities.

May

5732 Innovation in Power Generation Measurement & Control Conference

Instrumentation, Systems, and Automation Society
67 Alexander Drive
Box 12277
Research Triangle Park, NC 27709
919-549-8411
FAX: 919-549-8288
info@isa.org www.isa.org

Denny Younie, Conference General Chair
Rodney Jones, Conference Coordinator
Cyrus Taft, Program Chair
Dale Lee, Director Convention Services
Tracey Berrett, Manager Convention Services

Dedicated to instrumentation and control in the fossil and nuclear power generation industry. This year's conference includes approximately 50 technical papers presented in 8 sessions over two and a half days, a vendor exhibition area, 5 training courses, several ISA committee meetings, and the EPRI I&C Interest Group meeting and a Sunday evening welcome reception.

June

5733 International Conference and Exhibition on Device Packaging

International Microelectronics & Packaging Society
611 2nd Street NE
Washington, DC 20002
202-548-4001
FAX: 202-548-6115 888-464-6277
imaps@imaps.org www.imaps.org

Jim Drehle, President
Michael O'Donoghue, Executive Director
Steve Capp, Treasurer
Lawrence J Rexing, Secretary

Will provide a comprehensive technical program addressing the challenges of applications, and the latest developments in packaging for emerging devices, circuits, MEMS, sensors as well as materials and processes.

March

5734 International Congress Applications of Lasers and Electro-Optics

Laser Institute of America
13501 Ingenuity Drive
Suite 128
Orlando, FL 32826-3204
407-380-1553
FAX: 407-380-5588
icaleo@laserinstitute.org
www.laserinstitute.org

Beth Cohen, Show Manager
Amanda Criner, Conference Dept. Assistant

Provides an international forum for the exchange of technical information between the people in the industrial, government and academic communities who apply laser/electro-optic technologies and the scientists, engineers and technicians engaged in developing these technologies. Accepts advertising.

5M Attendees October

5735 International Instrumentation Symposium

Instrumentation, Systems, and Automation Society
67 Alexander Drive
Box 12277
Research Triangle Park, NC 27709
919-549-8411
FAX: 919-549-8288
info@isa.org www.isa.org

Denny Younie, Conference General Chair
Rodney Jones, Conference Coordinator
Cyrus Taft, Program Chair
Dale Lee, Director Convention Services
Tracey Berrett, Manager Convention Services

Provides an outstanding opportunity to gain valuable technical information and training in the traditional areas of measurements/sensors, instrumentation systems, data and advanced system/sensor technology as well as innovative papers in many other state of the art areas.

May

5736 International Laser Safety Conference

Laser Institute of America
13501 Ingenuity Drive
Suite 128
Orlando, FL 32826
407-380-1553
FAX: 407-380-5588
lia@laserinstitute.org
www.laserinstitute.org

Beth Cohen, Show Manager
Peter Baker, Executive Director

A comprehensive four-day conference covering all aspects of laser safety practice and hazard control. Technical sessions and workshops will address developments in regulatory, mandatory and voluntary safety standards for laser products and laser use.

March

5737 International Relay & Switch Technology Conference

Relay and Switch Industry Association
2500 Wilson Boulevard
Arlington, VA 22201
703-907-8025
FAX: 703-875-8908
narm@ecaus.org
www.ec-central.org/RISA

Dave Bauchaine, Chairman
Jeffrey Boyce, President

To promote the exchange of ideas and new development.

April

5738 International Symposium on Bioelectrochemi stry and Bioenergetics

Bioelectromagnetics Society
2412 Cobblestone Way
Frederick, MD 21702-3519
301-663-4252
FAX: 301-694-4948
bemsoffice@aol.com
www.bioelectromagnetics.org

Bruce R McLeod, President
Gloria Parsley, Executive Director
Stefan Engstrom, VP
Robert F Cleveland, Treasurer
Robert B Goldberg, Secretary

Covers analytical chemistry.

June

5739 Joint Conference on Decision and Control & European Control Conference

American Automatic Control Council
3640 Col Glenn Hwy
Dayton, OH 45435
937-775-5062
FAX: 937-775-3936
pmisra@cs.wright.edu www.a2c2.org

A Galip Ulsoy, President
R Russell Rhinehart, Treasurer
Pradeep Misra, Secretary

Dedicated to the advancement of the theory and practice of systems and control. It brings together an international community of experts to discuss the state-of-the-art, new research results, perspectives of future developments, and innovative applications relevant to decision making, control, automation, and related areas.

December

5740 Magnetism Conference: Institute of Electrical/Electronics Engineers

Courtesy Associates
2000 L Street NW
Suite 710
Washington, DC 20036
202-331-2000
FAX: 202-331-0111
magnetism@courtesyassoc.com
www.magnetism.org

Wendy Acevdo, Manager Meetings/Events

Conference brings together scientists and engineers interested in recent developments in all branches of fundamental and applied magnetism. Emphasis is placed on experimental and theoretical research in magnetism, the properties and synthesis of new magnetic materials and advances in magnetic technology. Program consists of invited and contributed papers.

1.1M Attendees October

5741 Meeting of the Electrochemical Society

Appliance Manufacturer
5900 Harper Road
Suite 105
Solon, OH 44139-1935
609-737-1902
FAX: 609-737-2743
www.electrochem.org

Mitch Henderson, Group Publisher
Joe Jancsurak, Editor

Has become the leading society for solid-state and electrochemical science and technology. ECS has 8000 scientists and engineers in over 75 countries worldwide who hold individual membership, as well as roughly 100 corporations and laboratories who hold corporate membership.

May Founded: 1902

5742 Mid-Atlantic Electrical Exposition

S&L Productions
1916 Crain Highway S
Suite 16
Glen Burnie, MD 21061-5572
410-863-1180
FAX: 410-863-1187 888-532-3669

Triennial show and 150 exhibits with 200 booths of electrical supplies, hardware and services.

3000 Attendees October Founded: 2000

5743 **NAED Annual Meeting**
National Association of Electrical Distributors
1100 Corporate Square Drive
Suite 100
St Louis, MO 63132
314-991-9000
FAX: 314-991-3060 888-791-2512
info@naed.org www.naed.org

Becky Burgess, Director Meetings/Conferences
Lesley Wall, Senior Conference Manager
Tom Naber, President

The only event to bring the entire industry together in the same place at the same time. In addition to offering strong topical and informational programming, the NAED Annual Meeting provides distributors access to the top management of more than 225 electrical product suppliers.

5744 **NECA**
National Electrical Contractors Association
3 Bethesda Metro Center
Suite 1100
Bethesda, MD 20814
301-657-3110
FAX: 301-215-4500
webmaster@necanet.org
www.necanet.org

Steve Schultz, Executive Director Conventions
Bettie Luckman, Manager Conventions/Meetings
John Grau, Executive VP

Brings the largest manufacturers, utilities, contractors, engineers, consultants, plant engineers, and distributors from all over North America and 31 foreign countries.
8000 Attendees September

5745 **NEMA Annual Meeting**
National Electrical Manufacturers Association
1300 North 17th Street
Suite 1847
Rosslyn, VA 22209
703-841-3200
FAX: 703-841-5900 www.nema.org

Evan Gaddis, President
Al Scolnik, VP Technical Services
Tim Feldman, VP Industry Programs

Provides a forum for the standardization of electrical equipment, enabling consumers to select from a range of safe, effective and compatible electrical products.
November Founded: 1926

5746 **NEMRA Annual Conference**
Nat'l Electrical Mfgs Representatives Association
660 White Plains Road
Suite 600
Tarrytown, NY 10591-1504
914-524-8650
FAX: 914-524-8655
nemra@nemra.org www.nemra.org

Brian Chase, Chairman
Henry P Bergson, President
Michael Rowe, Secretary/Treasurer

Provides a forum for the standardization of electrical equipment, enabling consumers to select from a range of safe, effective, and compatible electrical products.
March

5747 **NORTHCON**
Electronic Conventions
8110 Airport Boulevard
Los Angeles, CA 90045-3119

FAX: 310-641-5117 800-877-2668

Donna Ybarra, Show Manager

400 booths featuring exhibits of components and microelectronics instrumentation.
6057 Attendees October

5748 **NOx Emissions & Source Monitoring Technical Conference and Training**
Instrumentation, Systems, and Automation Society
67 Alexander Drive
Box 12277
Research Triangle Park, NC 27709
919-549-8411
FAX: 919-549-8288
info@isa.org www.isa.org

Denny Younie, Conference General Chair
Rodney Jones, Conference Coordinator
Cyrus Taft, Program Chair
Dale Lee, Director Convention Services
Tracey Berrett, Manager Convention Services

Will present experiences with the measurement and control of low level NOx emissions, new concepts for NOx reduction techniques, and innovative monitoring systems. Presenters will participate in Q&A sessions, panel discussions, and be accessible throughout the two days to answer your questions.
August

5749 **NRECA's Annual Meeting**
National Rural Electric Cooperative Association
4301 Wilson Boulevard
Suite 1
Arlington, VA 22203-1860
703-907-5500
FAX: 703-907-5514 www.nrcea.coop

Glenn L English, CEO

The national service organization dedicated to representing the national interests of cooperative electric utilities and the consumers they serve. An advocate for consumer-owned cooperatives on energy and operational issues as well as rural community and economic development.
February, Florida Founded: 1942

5750 **NSCA Systems Integration Expo**
National Systems Contractors Assocaition
625 1st Street SE
Suite 420
Cedar Rapids, IA 52401
319-366-6722
FAX: 319-366-4164 800-446-6722
randy.vaughan@ae-systems.com
www.nsca.org

Randy Vaughan, President
Nancy Emerson, VP
Chuck Wilson, Executive Director
Kirsten Poggenklass, Marketing Manager
Andy Musci, Secretary/Treasurer

Dedicated to building connections between the people, knowledge and new ideas of the commercial electronic systems industry. A leading not-for-profit association representing the commercial electronic systems industry. A powerful advocate of all who work within the low-voltage industry, including systems contractors/integrators, product manufacturers, consultants, sales representatives, growing number of architects, engineers and others. 600 exhibitors
11000 Attendees March

5751 **National Electrical Equipment Show**
Reed Exhibition Companies
255 Washington Street
Suite 275
Newton, MA 02458-1649
617-584-4900
FAX: 617-630-2222

Mike Rusbridge, Chairman/CEO

Serves the electrical and electronic industries.
7.5M Attendees March

5752 **National Electrical Wire Processing Technology Expo**
Expo Productions
510 Hartbrook Drive
Hartland, WI 53029
262-367-5500
FAX: 262-367-9956 800-367-5520
cherylluck@sbcglobal.net
www.electricalwireshow.com

Cheryl L Luck, Sales Manager

Only trade show tailored expressly to the electrical wire cable processing industry.
2000 Attendees May

5753 **National Lighting Fair**
Dallas Market Center
2100 N Stemmons Freeway
Suite 1000
Dallas, TX 75207-3009
214-556-6100
FAX: 214-655-6100

Charlie Sullivan, Executive Director
Cindy Morris, Chief Operating Officer

250 booths.
5M Attendees February

5754 **National Professional Service Convention**
National Electronics Service Dealers Association
3608 Pershing Avenue
Fort Worth, TX 76107
817-921-9061
FAX: 817-921-3741
npsc@nesda.com www.nesda.com

PAtricia Bohon, Trade Show Manager

Annual show of 55 manufactures, suppliers and distributor of electronics, receivers, recorders, and supplies, software, telecommunications equipment, computers, videocassette recorders, parts and accessories, business forms, warranty companies and magazines/associations. Containing 100 booths and 70 exhibits.
950 Attendees July Founded: 1964

5755 **Pacific International Conference on Applications of Lasers and Optics**
Laser Institute of America
13501 Ingenuity Drive
Suite 128
Orlando, FL 32826
407-380-1553
FAX: 407-380-5588
lia@laserinstitute.org
www.laserinstitute.org

Milan Brandt, Conference General Chair

Will focus on growth and application of lasers and optics in the Pacific region.
April

5756 Power-Gen International Trade Show
Electrical Generating Systems Association
1650 S Dixie Highway
Suite 500
Boca Raton, FL 33432
561-750-5575
FAX: 561-395-8557 www.egsa.org
Lynn Grant, Director Conventions/Meetings
This is a special section of a larger show where we concentrate booths of firms that make, sell, and distribute on-site power products.
December, Las Vegas

5757 Product Safety and Liability Conference
National Electrical Manufacturers Association
1300 North 17th Street
Suite 1847
Rosslyn, VA 22209
703-841-3200
FAX: 703-841-5900 www.nema.org
Evan Gaddis, President
Al Scolnik, VP Technical Services
Tim Feldman, VP Industry Programs
Provides a forum for the standardization of electrical equipment, enabling consumers to select from a range of safe, effective and compatible electrical products.
September

5758 Reliability and Maintenance Symposium
Consulting Services
1768 Lark Lane
Cherry Hill, NJ 08003-3215
856-428-2342
FAX: 856-616-9315
vrmonshaw@ieee.org www.rams.org
V R Monshaw, Administrator
The symposium offers the opportunity to explore and learn more about this and other related R&M subjects. 50 booths.
1M Attendees January

5759 Rocky Mountain Electronics Expo
Conference and Management Specialists
138 Garfield St
Denver, CO 80206-5517
303-568-8028
FAX: 303-799-0678
Karen Hone, Executive Director
Annual show and exhibits of products and services related to the hi-tech electronics industry.

5760 SESHA Annual Symposium
Semiconductor Environmental, Safety & Health Assn
1313 Dolly Madison Boulevard
Suite 402
McLean, VA 22101
703-790-1745
FAX: 703-790-2672
sesha@burkinc.com seshaonline.org
John D Cox, President
Brett Burk, Executive Director
For individuals employed within the electronics and related high technology industries with an interest in environmental, health and safety issues.
1235 Attendees May Founded: 1978

5761 SMMA: Fall Technical Conference
SMMA: The Motor & Motion Association
PO Box P182
South Dartmouth, MA 02748
508-979-5935
FAX: 508-979-5845
info@smma.org www.smma.org
William H Chambers, Operations Director
Elizabeth B Chambers, Executive Director
Presentations of interest to motor industry engineers. Table-top exhibits for suppliers.
October

5762 SMMA: Spring Management Conference
SMMA: The Motor & Motion Association
PO Box P182
S Dartmouth, MA 02748
508-979-5935
FAX: 508-979-5845
info@smma.org www.smma.org
Presentations of interest to motor and motion indusrty executives. Table-top exhibits for suppliers.
May

5763 SMTA International
Surface Mount Technology Association
5200 Wilson Road
Suite 100
Minneapolis, MN 55424
952-920-7682
FAX: 952-926-1819
joann@smta.org www.smta.org
David Raby, President
JoAnn Stromberg, Executive Administrator
Paul Vianco, Treasurer
Evelyn Baldwin, VP Communications
Irene Sterian, Secretary
A network of professionals who build skills, share practical experience and develop solutions in electronics assembly technologies and related business operations.
September

5764 SOUTHCON
Electronic Conventions
12340 Rosecrans Avenue
Suite 100
Manhattan Beach, CA 90266
310-524-4100
FAX: 310-643-7328 800-877-2668
exhibits@ecmshows.com
www.southcon.org
Donna Ybarra, Show Manager
Companies attending represent a major cross-section of the electronics industry including consumer, computer, medical, automotive and others. Offers conference sessions, in-depth technical sessions, product demonstrations and exhibits by vendors.
10M Attendees March

5765 Semicon
Semiconductor Equipment & Materials International
1401 K Street NW
Suite 601
Washington, DC 20005
202-289-0440
FAX: 202-289-0441
semide@semi.org www.semi.org
Stanley T Myers, President/CEO
Victoria Hadfield, Executive VP/President, N America
Offers a series of technical conferences, business programs, standards workshops and industry networking events for the regional semiconductor community.
12000 Attendees May, Singapore

5766 Semicon East
805 E Middlefield Road
Mountain View, CA 94043-4025
650-964-5111
FAX: 650-940-7919 semihq@semi.org
500 booths of new technologies in equipment, materials and products used in the manufacture of semiconductors and flat panel displays.
8M Attendees October

5767 TechAdvantage Conference
National Rural Electric Cooperative Association
4301 Wilson Boulevard
Suite 1
Arlington, VA 2203-1860
703-907-5500
FAX: 703-907-5514
Glenn L English, CEO
The only utility industry trade show exclusively for electric cooperative network management; engineering and operations; information services and technology; and purchasing employees.

5768 Upper Midwest Electrical Expo
North Central Electrical League
2901 Metro Drive
Suite 203
Bloomington, MN 55425
952-854-4405
FAX: 952-854-7076 800-925-4985
dale@ncel.org www.ncel.org
Lane Hersey, Chair
Greg Hames, Vice Chair
Dale Yohnke, Executive Director
Jeff Keljiik, Treasurer
Unites our electrical industry by providing vital industry commerce, educational discussion forums and offering various outlets for peer interaction. NCEL is the bridge between industry sectors and our electrical industry joins together to develop, expand and to protect all stakeholder interests in our Upper MIdwest Electrical Industry.
10213 Attendees Every 2 Years / Next 2008

Directories & Databases

5769 Buyer's Guide and Member Services Directory
Diesel & Gas Turbine Publications
1650 S Dixie Highway
Suite 500
Boca Raton, FL 33432
561-750-5575
FAX: 561-395-8557 www.egsa.org
Donald M Ferreira, Director Publications
It is the ultimate gen-set industry buyer's guide, because the members are listed in one or more of 23 different product categories. Each member's listing also shows whether they sell, rent, and/or service equipment. *$6.00*
Hard Copy

5770 Circuits Assembly: Buyers' Guide Issue
Miller Freeman Publications
600 Harrison Street
Suite 400
San Francisco, CA 94107-1391

FAX: 415-905-2239

Ron Daniels, Editor-in-Chief

List of suppliers of products and services to the surface mount industry; representatives and distributors. *$7.00*
Annual, November
Circulation: 40,500

5771 Compressor Tech Two
Diesel & Gas Turbine Publications
20855 Watertown Road
Suite 220
Waukesha, WI 53186-1873
262-832-5000
FAX: 262-832-5075 www.dieselpub.com

Joseph M Kane, Founder
Phil Burnside, Editor-in-Chief
Brent Haight, Managing Editor
Kara Kane, Advertising Manager
Sheila Lizdas, Circulation Manager

Covers the operation, application and design of gas compression systems, as used in the gas gathering, transportation, storage, processing and related industries worldwide. Featured are new products, new technologies and interesting new applications related to gas compression systems and components. *$45.00*
6 per year Founded: 1996
Circulation: 13,000

5772 Diesel Progress: International Edition
Diesel & Gas Turbine Publications
20855 Watertown Road
Suite 220
Waukesha, WI 53186-1873
262-832-5000
FAX: 262-832-5075 www.dieselpub.com

Michael J Osenga, Senior Vice President
Michael J Brezonick, Editor-in-Chief
Katie Evans, Advertising Sales Manager

Covers the design of engine-powered equipment manufactured outside of North America. This includes various types of mobile on-and-off-highway equipment including construction, mining, forestry, agricultural and turf maintenance vehicles, trucks and buses; specialty vehicles; pleasure boats; and generator, pump and compressor set manufacturers. Editoiral focus is on new products and technology for these markets. *$40.00*
6 per year Founded: 1981
Circulation: 12,000

5773 Diesel Progress: North American Edition
Diesel & Gas Turbine Publications
20855 Watertown Road
Suite 220
Waukesha, WI 53186-1873
262-832-5000
FAX: 262-832-5075 www.dieselpub.com

Michael J Brezonick, Editor-in-Chief
Michael J Osenga, Senior VP
Patricia May, Advertising Sales Manager

Published for those concerned with the design, distribution and service of equipment powered by diesel, gasoline, or alternatively fueled engines. This includes all types of mobile on-and-off-highway equipment and stationary equipment. Markets covered include: construction, mining, forestry, agricultural and turf maintenance equipment; trucks and buses; pleasure boats; and generator, pump and compressor sets. Editorial focus is on new products and technology for these markets. *$75.00*
Monthly Founded: 1935
Circulation: 30,000

5774 Directory of Electrical Wholesale Distributors
Primedia
9800 Metcalf Avenue
Overland Park, KS 66212
913-341-1300
FAX: 913-967-1898
www.primediabusiness.com

Features a full search and download capabilities, you can easily assess your current distributor network and look for new distributors for your products. Search by MSA market, location square footage, employee count and many other critical variables. The handy main house and branch cross-reference brings the ever-changing electrical distribution market into focus. Using the simple search functions, you can build and download highly targeted lists in just seconds.
Cd-Rom

5775 Electrical Construction Materials Directory
Underwriters Laboratories
333 Pfingsten Road
Northbrook, IL 60062-2096
847-120-0136
FAX: 847-509-6243 800-704-4050
directories@us.UL.com www.UL.com

Shaquanda Debbe, Editor

Offers information on companies that have qualified to use the UL listing mark or classification marking with products that have been found to be in compliance with UL regulations. *$40.00*
912 pages Annual
Printed in on glossy stock

5776 Electrical Distributor
National Association of Electrical Distributors
1100 Corporate Square Drive
Suite 100
St. Louis, MO 63132
314-991-9000
FAX: 314-991-3060 888-791-2512
info@naed.org www.naed.org

Jack Foster, Editor

List of manufacturers and distributors of electrical components, supplies and equipment. *$295.00*
Biennial
Circulation: 3,500

5777 Electrical Equipment Representatives Association Membership Directory
Electrical Equipment Representatives Association
PO Box 419264
Kansas City, MO 64141-6264
816-561-5323
FAX: 816-561-1249
jflora@eera.org www.eera.org

Jack W Keegan, President
Jeffrey H Flora, Chief Executive Officer

More than 105 manufacturers representatives of electrical equipment companies.
Annual, October Founded: 1948

5778 Engineers Relay Handbook
Relay and Switch Industry Association
2500 Wilson Boulevard
Arlington, VA 22201
703-907-8025
FAX: 703-875-8908
narm@ecaus.org
www.ec-central.org/RSIA

Dave Baicjaome, Chairman
Jeffrey Boyce, President

In summary, special effort has been made by the editors to cover specification parameters in sufficient detail to provide systems and product design engineers with all the information they need to obtain the correct types of relays for their applications. *$60.00*
Fifth Edition

5779 Global Sourcing Guide
Diesel & Gas Turbine Publications
20855 Watertown Road
Suite 220
Waukesha, WI 53186-1873
262-832-5000
FAX: 262-832-5075 www.dieselpub.com

Mark McNeely, Publisher/Editor
Michael J Mercer, Managing Editor
Kara Kane, Publication Manager
Christa Stern, Production Manager
Sheila Lizdas, Circulation Manager

The Global Sourcing Guide is one of the premier references and purchasing guides for the power systems and components industry. Covering products and systems used across the mobile and stationary engine-powered equipment industries, this guide incorporates information in a wide range of classifications. *$110.00*
Annual Founded: 1935

5780 High-Performance Composites
Ray Publishing
4891 Independence
Suite 270
Wheat Ridge, CO 80033
303-467-1776
FAX: 303-467-1777
www.compositesworld.com

Judith Hazen, Publisher/Editor
Mike Mussleman, Managing Editor

60 pages Founded: 1993
Printed in 4 colors on glossy stock

5781 Indoor Electrical Safety Check Booklet
Electrical Safety Foundation International
1300 N 17th Street
Suite 1847
Rosslyn, VA 22209
703-413-3209
FAX: 703-841-3329
info@esfi.org
www.electrical-safety.org

Grant J Carter, Chair
David Tallman, Vice Chair
Michael Clendenin, Executive Director
Barbara R Guthrie, Secretary

Instructions on running an electrical safety audit of your home and at the same time learn about electrical inspections, circuit maps, power audits, and potential electrical hazards and safety tips from your circuit breaker or fuse panel to your outlets, power cords and extension cords, light bulbs, space heaters, ground fault circuit interrupters (GFCIs), arc fault circuit interrupters (AFCIs), batteries, and much more.
Hard Copy

5782 **NEMA Database**
National Electrical Manufacturers Association
1300 North 17th Street
Suite 1847
Rosslyn, VA 22209
703-841-3200
FAX: 703-841-5900 www.nema.org
Evan Gaddis, President
Al Scolnik, VP Technical Services
Tim Feldman, VP Industry Programs
This database offers time series on orders, shipments and unfilled orders for 6 major segments of the electrical manufacturing industry.

5783 **NETA Electrical Acceptance Testing Specifications for Electrical Power**
International Electrical Testing Association
106 Stone Street
Morrison, CO 80465
303-697-8441
FAX: 303-697-8431 888-300-6382
neta@netaworld.org
www.netaworld.org
Stuart Jackson, President
John White, First VP
Kerry Heid, Second VP
Ken Bassett, Treasurer
Charles K Blizard, Secretary
A document to assist designers, specifiers, architects, and users of electrical equipment and systems in specifying required tests on newly-installed power systems and apparatus, before energizing, to ensure that the installation and equipment comply with specifications and intended use as well as with regulatory and safety requirements.
$95.00
205 pages : Bound

5784 **NETA Electrical Maintenance Testing Specifications for Electrical Power**
International Electrical Testing Association
106 Stone Street
Morrison, CO 80465
303-697-8441
FAX: 303-697-8431 888-300-6382
neta@netaworld.org
www.netaworld.org
Stuart Jackson, President, First VP
Kerry Heid, Second VP
Ken Bassett, Treasurer
Charles K Blizard, Secretary
Developed for use by those responsible for the continued operation of existing electrical systems and equipment to guide them in specifying and performing the necessary tests to ensure that these systems and apparatus perform satisfactorily, minimizing downtime and maximizing life expectancy.
$125.00
265 pages : Bound

5785 **National Electrical Manufacturers Represen tatives Association Locator**
National Electrical Manufacturers Rep Assoc
660 White Plains Road
Suite 600
Tarrytown, NY 10591-1504
914-524-8650
FAX: 914-524-8655
nemra@nemra.org www.nemra.org
Henry P Bergson, Editor/President
Brian Chase, Chairman
Stephen Gallagher, Chairman-Elect
Approximately 1,000 electrical manufacturers representative companies. *$200.00*
Annual

5786 **National Electronic Distributors Association Membership Directory**
National Electronic Distributors Association
1111 Alderman Drive
Suite 400
Alpharetta, GA 30005-4175
678-393-9990
FAX: 678-393-9998 800-347-6332
Robin B Gray, Jr, Executive Vice President
Debbie Conyers, Director Marketing
Michelle Meyer, Director/Meetings
Janet Wood, VP/Administration
Approximately 300 member distributors and 180 member manufacturers of electronics products, plus 1,100 branch offices.

5787 **On-Site Power Generation: A Reference Book**
Electrical Generating Systems Association
1650 S Dixie Highway
Suite 500
Boca Raton, FL 33432
561-750-5575
FAX: 561-395-8557 www.egsa.org
Donald M Ferreira, Director Publications
This book contains the most complete and up-to-date technical information covering on-site electrical power generation.
$95.00
600 pages

5788 **Outdoor Electrical Safety Check Booklet**
Electrical Safety Foundation International
1300 N 17th Street
Suite 1847
Rosslyn, VA 22209
703-413-3209
FAX: 703-841-3329
info@esfi.org
www.electrical-safety.org
Grant J Carter, Chair
David Tallman, Vice Chair
Michael Clendenin, Executive Director
Barbara R Guthrie, Secretary
Use this handy booklet to learn about available electrical safety devices, and the safety rules related to hot tubs, spas and pools, extension cords, electrical lawn and garden products, battery operated products and power tool safety.

5789 **Product and Supplier Information**
Electrical Generating Systems Association
1650 S Dixie Highway
Suite 500
Boca Raton, FL 33432
561-750-5575
FAX: 561-395-8557 www.egsa.org
Donald M Ferreira, Director Publications
EGSA publishes a new Buyer's Guide and Member Services Directory listing every member.

5790 **SMMA: Directory**
SMMA: Small Motors & Motion Association
PO Box P182
S Dartmouth, MA 02748
508-979-5935
FAX: 508-979-5845
info@smma.org www.smma.org
David E Beth, President
Elizabeth Chambers, Executive Director
Eric S Cole, VP Engineering
William H Chambers, Operations Director
Manufacturers, suppliers and users of fractional and subfractional horsepower electric motors.
Founded: 1975

5791 **Transmission and Distribution: Specifiers and Buyers Guide Issue**
Primedia
9800 Metcalf Avenue
Overland Park, KS 66212
913-341-1300
FAX: 913-967-1629
www.primediabusiness.com
Rick Bush, Editor
Pete May, Senior VP
John French, Executive VP
Eric Jacobson, SVP Business Development
Jack Condon, Chief Operating Officer
List of manufacturers and distributors of equipment for electric power transmission and distribution. *$20.00*
Annual, September
Circulation: 49,000

5792 **Wholesale Source Directory of Electrical Products, Supplies & Accessories**
Sutton Family Communications & Publishing Company
155 Sutton Lane
Fordsville, KY 42343
270-740-0870
jlsutton@apex.net
www.fleamarketeer.net
Theresa Sutton, Editor
Lee Sutton, General Manager
Listings include names, addresses, phone/fax numbers and product descriptions for wholesale distributors, importers, manufacturers, close-out houses and liquidators. Every item needed to become an electrical contractor, open an electrical store or sell this type of merchandise in a hardware store, flea market or other market. Daily updated laser printed copy. Price includes shipping and handling. *$57.20*
100+ pages Founded: 1977

Industry Web Sites

5793 **www.7ms.com**
Seven Mountains Scientific
Industry news in battery technology, marketing and industry events including new products, electric vehicles, R&D and environmental news.

5794 **www.ahtd.org**
Association for High Technology Distributors

Promotes an open forum for discussion for high technology distributors. Works to increase productivity and profitability of high technology automation solutions providers and manufacturers.

5795 **www.bioelectromagnetics.org**
Bioelectromagnetics Society

International resource for excellence in scientific research, knowledge and understanding of the interaction of electromagnetic fields with biological systems. Members of the society are biological and physical scientists, physicians and engineers interested in the interactions of nonionizing radiation with biological systems.

5796 **www.csa-dc.org**
Contract Services Association of America

Represents the government services contracting industry in Washington, DC. Members range from small businesses to large corporations servicing federal and state government in numerous capacities. CSA acts to foster effective implementation of the government's policy of reliance on the private sector for support services.

5797 **www.eachicago.org**
Electric Association

Its purpose is to serve as the umbrella organization for the various electrical disciplines in the Chicagoland area.

5798 **www.ec-central.org/RSIA**
Relay and Switch Industry Association

The purpose and aims shall be to encourage the advancement of the art and science of making and using those switching devices generally known as relays; to promote and further interest of relay manufacturers consistent with the best interest of relay users; to create a spirit of mutual esteem, respect and recognition among members, and between the members and their customers and suppliers.

5799 **www.eei.org**
Edison Electric Institute

Advocates public policy, expands market opportunities and provides strategic business information for the shareholder-owned electric utility industry. Find out more about EEI's members, upcoming meetings, career opportunities and products and services.

5800 **www.eera.org**
Electrical Equipment Representatives Association

Sales agents for manufacturers of electrical equipment used by utilities. Mission is to advance the quality and increase effectiveness of manufacturer's representatives in the electrical equipment industry.

5801 **www.electric-find.com**
Electric Find

A directory/search engine for the electrical construction industry. Search results have been screened by electrical professionals.

5802 **www.electrochem.org**
Electrochemical Society

The society is an international nonprofit, educational organization concerned with phenomena relating to electrochemical and solid state science and technology. Members are individual scientists and engineers, as well as corporations and laboratories.

5803 **www.epri.com**
Electric Power Research Institute

Research relating to the production, transmission, distribution and utilization of electric power.

5804 **www.ewh.ieee.org**
Instrumentation and Measurement Society

A subsidiary of the Institute of Electrical and Electronics Engineers. Provides support to scientists and technicians who design and develop electrical and electronic measuring instruments and equipment.

5805 **www.greyhouse.com**
Grey House Publishing

Selected Grey House directories in the fields of business, health and education are available online. Users can search our online databases by several different search criteria, such as product categories, geographic area, sales volume and much, much more. Full Grey House catalog and online ordering also available.

5806 **www.icea.net**
Insulated Cable Engineers Association

Professional organization dedicated to developing cable standards for the electric power, control and telecommunications industries. Ensures safe, economical and efficient cable systems utilizing proven state-of-the-art materials and concepts. ICEA documents are of interest to cable manufacturers, architects and engineers, utility and manufacturing plant personnel, telecommunication engineers, consultants and OEMs.

5807 **www.imaps.org**
International Microelectronics & Packaging Society

Dedicated to the advancement and growth of the use of microelectronics and electronic packaging through public and professional education, dissemination of information by means of symposia, workshops and conferences and promotion of the Society's portfolio of technologies.

5808 **www.impi.org**
International Microwave Power Institute

IMPI's members include scientists, researchers, lab technicians, product developers, marketing managers and a variety of other professionals in the microwave industry. The Institute serves the information needs of all specialists working with dielectric (microwave and RF) heating sytems, and was expanded in 1977 to meet the information needs relating to consumer microwave ovens and related products.

5809 **www.ipc.org**
IPC:Association Connecting Electronics

Works to develop standards in circuit board assembly equipment. Brings together all players in the electronic interconnection industry, including designers, board manufacturers, assembly companies, suppliers and original equipment manufacturers. Offers workshops, conferences, meetings and online communications.

5810 **www.ncel.org**
North Central Electrical League

Trade association representing all segments of the electrical industry in the Upper Midwest.

5811 **www.necanet.org**
National Electrical Contractors Association

Represents a segment of the construction market comprised of over 70,000 electrical firms.

5812 **www.nerc.com**
North American Electric Reliability Council

Voluntary organization promoting bulk electric system reliability and security.

5813 **www.netaworld.org**
International Electrical Testing Association

Defines the standards by which electrical equipment is deemed safe and reliable. Creates specifications, procedures, testing and requirements for commissioning new equipment and testing the reliability and performance of existing equipment.

5814 **www.nsca.org**
National Systems Contractors Association

Not-for-profit association representing the commercial electronic systems industry. Serves as an advocate for all those who work within the low-voltage industry including systems contractors/integrators, product manufacturers, consultants, sales representatives and a growing number of architects, specifying engineers and others.

5815 www.platts.com
Electrical World

The latest trends in utility engineering and IT, equipment and services, best business practices and critical industry thinking. For managers, engineers and technicians who plan, design, build, maintain and upgrade electric T&D systems around the world.

5816 www.psma.com
Power Sources Manufacturers Association

Worldwide membership consists of manufacturers of power sources and conversion equipment. Nonprofit association strives to integrate the resources of the power sources industry to more effectively and profitably serve the needs of the power sources users, providers and PSMA members. Educates the electronics industry and others on the relevant applications for power sources and conversion devices.

5817 www.semi.org
Semiconductor Equipment & Materials International

Strengthens the performance of member companies through lobbying, promotion, education and statistical research.

5818 www.seshaonline.org
Semiconductor Environmental, Safety & Health Assn

Members are individuals employed within the electronics and related high technology industries with an interest in environmental, health and safety issues.

5819 www.sia-online.org
Semiconductor Industry Association

Trade association representing the US microchip industry.

5820 www.smma.org
SMMA: Small Motors & Motion Association

Manufacturing trade association. Members include electric motor and motion control companies, as well as suppliers, users, and associated businesses such as consultants, universities and distributors.

5821 www.smta.org
Surface Mount Technology Association

A network of professionals building skills, sharing practical experience and developing solutions in electronic assembly technologies and related business operations.

Associations

5822 **AG Electronic Association**
10 S Riverside Plaza
Suite 1220
Chicago, IL 60606-3710
312-321-1470
FAX: 312-321-1480
age@agelectronicsassn.org
www.agelectronicsassn.org

Darrin Dollinger, Marketing Manager

Identifies, develops & or facilitates appropriate action aimed at furthering the compatibility & interchangeability of electronics and information systems used in agriculture.

5823 **AVS Science & Technology Society**
120 Wall Street
32nd Floor
New York, NY 10005-3993
212-248-0200
FAX: 212-248-0245
angela@avs.org www.avs.org

Christie R Marrian, President
John Coburn, Treasurer
Joseph E Greene, Clerk/Secretary
Yvonne Towse, Executive Director

Supports all those involved with all aspects of science and technology through research, education, new products, publications and conferences.
5500 Members Founded: 1953

5824 **Aircraft Electronics Association**
4217 S Hocker
Independence, MO 64055
816-373-6565
FAX: 816-478-3100
info@aea.net www.aea.net

Paula Derks, President
Mark Gibson, VP Administration
Mike Adamson, Information Services Director
Linda Adams, Director Communications

AEA represents over 1250 aviation businesses, including repair stations that specialize in maintenance, repair and installation of avionics and electronic systems in general aviation aircraft.

5825 **American Electronics Association**
5201 Great America Parkway
Santa Clara, CA 95054
408-987-4200
FAX: 408-987-4298 800-284-4232
csc@aeanet.org www.aeanet.org

John V Harker, Chairman
William T Archey, President/CEO
Samuel J Block, VP/Controller
Tim Bennett, COO/EVP

Works to foster a healthy business climate by providing services education and research programs.
3500 Members Founded: 1943

5826 **Armed Forces Communications and Electronics Association**
4400 Fair Lakes Court
Fairfax, VA 22033-3899
703-311-1397
FAX: 703-631-6169 800-336-4583
promo@afcea.org www.afcea.org

Eugene C Renzi, Chairman
Herb Browne, President/CEO
Becky Nolan, Executive VP
Paul E Tobin, Jr, Executive Director
Robert Howell, RN, General Manager

Provides an ethical forum for government and industry leaders in the technical disciplines of communications, electronics, intelligence and information systems.
30000 Members Founded: 1946

5827 **Association for Electronics Manufacturing**
1 SME Drive
PO Box 930
Dearborn, MI 48121
313-271-1500
FAX: 313-425-3401 800-733-4763
hr@sme.org www.sme.org

Rick Peters, President
Nancy Berg, Executive Director
Gary Mikola, Director Expositions
Rob Fekaris, Director Finance
Edward McCallum, Director

Represents the electrical manufacturers.
3.6M Members

5828 **Association of Progressive Rental Merchandise**
1504 Robin Hood Trail
Austin, TX 78703
512-794-0095
FAX: 512-794-0097 800-204-APRO
rmay@aprovision.org
www.aprovision.org

Shannon Strunk, President
John C Cleek, First VP
Kevin Quinn, Secretary
Jeannie Hutchison, Program Coordinator
Bill Keese, Manager

Members include television, appliance and furniture dealers who rent merchandise with an option to purchase.
2000 Members Founded: 1980

5829 **Consumer Electronics Association**
2500 Wilson Boulevard
Arlington, VA 22201-3834
703-907-7600
FAX: 703-907-7690
communications@ce.org www.ce.org

Gary Shapiro, President/CEO
Lisa Fasold, Director
Stephen Gates, Senior Manager
Brad Jones, Communications Manager

Supports all those involved in the manufacturing of consumer electronics. Publishes bi-monthly magazine and hosts trade show.
1700 Members

5830 **Consumer Electronics Forum**
CompuServe Information Service
5000 Arlington Center Blvd
PO Box 20212
Columbus, OH 43220-0212
614-457-8600
FAX: 614-457-0348

Dawn Gordon, Forum Administrator

Offers valuable information on electronic consumer products, including audio, video and satellite systems and radar detectors.

5831 **Electronic Industries Alliance**
2500 Wilson Boulevard
Arlington, VA 22201-3834
703-907-7500
FAX: 703-907-7500 www.eia.org

Ronald L Turner, Chairman
Mike Kennedy, Vice Chairman
Dave McCurdy, President/CEO
Neal McDonald, Senior Coordinator
James Shiring, Secretary/Treasurer

Trade organization representing the entire spectrum of manufacturers and consumer manufacturers involved in electronic products.
1.5M Members Founded: 1924

5832 **Electronic Service Dealers Association**
4925 W Irving Park Road
Chicago, IL 60641-2620
773-282-9400

George Weiss, Publisher

Association for those interested in industry news and developments and governmental and legislative issues.
8 Members Founded: 1950
Mailing list available for rent 4000 names $60 per M.

5833 **Electronic Transactions Association**
1101 16th Street NW
Suite 402
Washington, DC 20036
202-828-2635
FAX: 202-828-2639 800-695-5509

Daniel J Neistadt, President
Joe Kaplan, Treasurer
James Baumgartner, Secretary

ETA is the international trade association serving the needs of organizations offering transaction processing products/services.
400M Members Founded: 1990

5834 **Electronics Representatives Association**
444 N Michigan Avenue
Suite 1960
Chicago, IL 60611
312-527-3050
FAX: 312-527-3783 800-776-7377
info@era.org www.era.org

Mark Motsinger, Chairman
Dave Rossi, Vice Chairman
Mike Kunz, President
Thomas Shanahan, Interim Executive VP
William R Warfield, Director Finance/Operations

Provides services and benefits to electronic industry manufacturers' representatives.
$48.00
1600 Members Founded: 1935

5835 **Electronics Technicians Association International**
5 Depot Street
Greencastle, IN 46135
765-653-8262
FAX: 765-653-4287 800-288-3824
eta@eta-i.org www.eta-i.org

Randy Reusser, Chairman
Glen L Wolfe, Vice Chairman
Richard Glass, President
Teresa Maher, VP
Carolyn Carson, Special Projects Manager

Association for electronic technicians nationwide offering 23 technical certifications.
3100 Members Founded: 1978

5836 **IPC: Association Connecting Electronics**
2215 Sanders Road
Northbrook, IL 60062-6135
847-509-9700
FAX: 847-509-9798
webmaster@ipc.org www.ipc.org

Denny McGuirk, President
Betty Johnson, Executive Assistant to President
Dick Crowe, Executive Director

Tom McCabe, VP/CFO
Jennifer Sandahl, Controller

A trade association for the printed circuit boards and electronics assembly industries, offering programs and resources to board manufacturers and electronic assemblers, designers, industry suppliers and original equipment manufacturers.
2000 Members Founded: 1957

5837 Instrumentation and Measurement Society
799 N Beverly Glen
Los Angeles, CA 90077
310-446-8280
FAX: 310-446-8390
bob.myers@ieee.org
www.ewh.ieee.org

Robert Myers, Executive Director
Lee Myers, Assistant Director
Robert Rassa, President
Barry Oakes, VP Finance

A subsidiary of the Institute of Electrical and Electronics Engineers. Provides support to scientists and technicians who design and develop electrical and electronic measuring instruments and equipment.
6500+ Members Founded: 1950

5838 International Microelectronics and Electronic Packaging
611 2nd Street NE
Washington, DC 20002
202-548-4001
FAX: 202-548-6115 888-464-6277
imaps@imaps.org www.imaps.org

Michael O'Donoghue, Executive Director
Rick Mohn, Operations Manager
Brian Schieman, Director Information Technology
Ann Bell, Manager Marketing/Communications

Promotes interaction among technologies of ceramics, thin and thick films, semiconductor packaging, surface mount technology, multichip modules, semiconductor devices and monolithic circuits. Dedicated to the advancement and growth of the use of microelectronics and electronic packaging through education. Disseminates information through symposia, workshops and conferences.
11000 Members Founded: 1967

5839 International SEMATECH
2706 Montopolis Drive
Austin, TX 78741
512-356-3500

information@ismi.sematech.org
www.sematech.org

O B Bilous, Chairman
Mike Polcari, President/CEO
John Schmitz, COO
David Saathoff, CAO

A global consortium of leading semiconductor manufacturers who engage in cooperative precompetitive efforts to improve semiconductor manufacturing technology through the support of their members.
Founded: 1987

5840 International Society of Certified Electronic Technicians
3608 Pershing Avenue
Fort Worth, TX 76107-4527
817-921-9101
FAX: 817-921-3741
info@iscet.org
www.iscetstore.org/about

Mack Blakely, Executive Director
Ed Clingman, Administrator
Sheila Fredrickson, Director Communications

Seeks to provide awareness of and services to certified electronics technicians. Provides educational materials in electronics training to schools, technical institutes and junior colleges. Offers certification programs for electronics technicians in associate and journeyman levels.
46000 Members Founded: 1965

5841 Minerals, Metals & Materials Society
184 Thorn Hill Road
Warrendale, PA 15086-7514
724-776-9000
FAX: 724-776-3770
foundation@tms.org www.tms.org

Tresa Pollock, President
Brajendra Mishra, VP
Alexander Scott, Executive Director
John Parsey, Financial Planning Officer
Marc DeGraef, Director Information Technology

Supports all those in the minerals, metals and materials industries with education, publications, trade shows and conferences.

Founded: 1971

5842 National Association of Relay Manufacturers
2500 Wilson Boulevard
Arlington, VA 22201
703-907-8025
FAX: 703-875-8908
narm@ecaus.org
www.ec-central.org/NARM

Dave Bauchaine, Chairman
Jeffrey Boyce, President

NARM is a trade association for the electro-mechanical relay and associated switching devices industry. An affiliate of Electronic Industries Alliance.
32 Members Founded: 1947

5843 National Electronic Distributors Association
1111 Alderman Drive
Suite 400
Alpharetta, GA 30005-4175
678-393-9990
FAX: 678-393-9998
admin@nedassoc.org
www.nedassoc.org

Francis Flynn Jr, President
Robin B Gray Jr, President-Elect
Debbie Conyers, Director Marketing
Barney Martin, VP Industry Practices

Conducts research and offers educational programs for wholesale distributors of electronic components.
Founded: 1939

5844 National Electronics Service Dealers
3608 Pershing Avenue
Fort Worth, TX 76107-4527
817-921-9061
FAX: 817-921-3741 800-797-9197
webmaster@nesda.com
www.nesda.com

Brian Gibson, President
Don Cressin, VP
Mack Blakely, Executive Director
Fred Paradis, CSM, Treasurer
Wayne Markman, Secretary

A national trade association for professionals in the business of repairing consumer electronics equipment, appliances, and computers. NESDA has an e-mail group of over 600 members and manufacturers that communicate daily for information sharing. NESDA also has an annual convention and trade show.
1000 Members Founded: 1965

5845 National Marine Electronics Association
Seven Riggs Avenue
Severna Park, MD 21146
410-975-9425
FAX: 410-975-9450
info@nmea.org www.nmea.org

Mark Young, Chairman
Jules Rutstein, Vice Chairman
Beth Kahr, Executive Director
Michael Cerchiaro, Treasurer
Christopher Harley, Secretary

Is the unifying force behind the entire marine electronics industry, bringing together all aspects of the industry for the betterment of all in our business.
400 Members Founded: 1957

5846 Optical Society of America
2010 Massachusetts Avenue NW
Washington, DC 20036-1023
202-223-8130
FAX: 202-223-1096
info@osa.org www.osa.org

Elizabeth A Rogan, Executive Director
Tony Keane, COO
John Childs, Senior Director Publications
Cynthia Gady, Senior Director Meetings
Deborah C Herrin, Senior Director IT

A professional society of optical engineers and scientists concerned with the fields of optics and photonics.
15000 Members Founded: 1916

5847 Power Electronics Society
799 N Beverly Glen
Los Angeles, CA 90077
310-446-8280
FAX: 310-446-8390
bob.myers@ieee.org www.pels.org

Jerry Hudgins, President
Robert Myers, Executive Director
Steven Leeb, Treasurer
Ronald Harley, VP Operations

A subsidiary of the Institute of Electrical & Electronics Engineers. Supports professionals working in the field of power electronics technology.
5000 Members Founded: 1987

5848 Power Sources Manufacturers Association
PO Box 418
Mendham, NJ 07945
973-543-9660
FAX: 973-543-6207
power@psma.com www.psma.com

Arnold Alderman, Chairman
Marshall Miles, President
Bruce Miller, VP
Kevin Parmenter, Secretary
Joe Horzepa, Executive Director

Worldwide membership consists of manufacturers of power sources and conversion equipment. Nonprofit association strives to integrate the resources of the power sources industry to more effectively and profitably serve the needs of the power sources users, providers and PSMA members. Educates the electronics industry and others on the relevant applications for power sources and conversion devices.
133 Members Founded: 1985

5849 Semiconductor Environmental, Safety & Health Association
1313 Dolly Madison Boulevard
Suite 420
McLean, VA 22101
703-790-1745
FAX: 703-790-2672
sesha@burkinc.com
www.seshaonline.org

Bernie Firstn, President
Brett Burk, Executive Director
Brian Sherin, Treasurer
Karl Albrecht, Secretary

Members are individuals employed within the electronics and related high technology industries with an interest in environmental, health and safety issues.
1500 Members Founded: 1978

5850 Semiconductor Equipment and Materials International
1401 K Street NW
Suite 601
Washington, DC 20005
202-289-0440
FAX: 202-289-0441
semidc@semi.org www.semi.org

Stanley T Myers, President/CEO
Victoria Hadfield, Executive VP/President, N America

An international trade association representing firms supplying equipment, materials and services to the semiconductor industry. Strengthens the performance of members through promotion, lobbying, education and statistical research.
2300 Members Founded: 1970

5851 Semiconductor Industry Association
181 Metro Drive
Suite 450
San Jose, CA 95110
408-436-6600
FAX: 408-436-6646
mailbox@sia-online.org
www.sia-online.org

WJ Sanders III, Founder
Wilfred J Corrigan, Chairman/CEO
George Scalise, President
John Kelly III, Director

Trade association representing the US microchip industry. Provides a forum for working collectively to enhance the competitiveness of the US chip industry.
70 Members Founded: 1977

5852 Society of Manufacturing Engineers
1 SME Drive
Dearborn, MI 48121
313-271-1500
FAX: 313-271-2861 800-733-4763
service@sme.org www.sme.org

Donna Bibber, VP
Nancy Berg, Executive Director
Robert L Wolff, Professor/Program Coordinator
George E West, VP Manufacturing
Guenter Warnecke, Professor Manufacturing

Supports all engineers in electronics manufacturing. Publishes quarterly newsletter.
70M Members Founded: 1932

5853 Surface Mount Technology Association
5200 Willson Road
Suite 215
Edina, MN 55424
952-920-7682
FAX: 952-926-1819
phyllis@smta.org www.smta.org

Dan Baldwin, Chairperson
David Raby, President
JoAnn Stromberg, Executive Administrator
Jesse Katzman, Director Communications
Irene Sterian, Secretary

Network of professionals building skills, sharing practical experience and developing solutions in electronic assembly technologies and related business operations.
3.5M Members Founded: 1984

Newsletters

5854 AEA Monthly News
American Electronics Association
5201 Great America Parkway
Santa Clara, CA 95054
408-987-4200
FAX: 408-987-4298 800-284-4232
csc@aeanet.org www.aeanet.org

John V Harker, Chairman
William T Archey, President/CEO
Samuel J Block, VP/Controller
Tim Bennett, COO/EVP

AEA Advancing the Business of Technology, Access to Investors, State, Federal & International Lobbying, Insurance Services, Government Procurement, Business Networking, Foreign Market Access, Select Business Services, Executive Education.
Monthly

5855 AEA by the Bay
American Electronics Association
5201 Great America Parkway
Santa Clara, CA 95054
408-987-4200
FAX: 408-987-4298 800-284-4232
info@aeanet.org www.aeanet.org

John V Harker, Chairman
William T Archey, President/CEO
Samuel J Block, VP/Controller
Tim Bennett, COO/EVP

Newsletter for the AEA Bay Area Council.
Monthly

5856 AEA's Californica Monday Morning Report
American Electronics Association
5201 Great America Parkway
Santa Clara, CA 95054
408-987-4200
FAX: 408-987-4298 800-284-4232
csc@aeanet.org www.aeanet.org

John V Harker, Chairman
William T Archey, President/CEO
Samuel J Block, VP/Controller
Tim Bennett, COO/EVP

A weekly report of what is going on in Californica policy relating to the high-tech industry, and how to change it.
Weekly

5857 American Electronics Association Impact
American Electronics Association
5201 Great America Parkway
Santa Clara, CA 95054-1122
408-987-4200
FAX: 408-970-8565
csc@aeanet.org http://www.aeanet.org

William Archey, President

Representing the electronics software and information technology industries. Covers business and management issues for electronics executives.
Monthly Founded: 1945
Circulation: 25000

5858 Consumer Electronic and Appliance News
Kasmar Publications
PO Box 12638
Palm Desert, CA 92255-3611
760-773-2874
800-253-9992

Donald Martin, Editor

Home entertainment, consumer electronics and major appliances.
28 pages Founded: 1970

5859 Electronic Advertising Marketplace Report
Simba Information
PO Box 4234
Stamford, CT 06907-0234
203-258-8193
FAX: 203-358-5825
simbainfo@simbanet.com
www.simbanet.com

Linda Kopp, Editor
Donna Devall, Marketing Director
Joyce Brigish, Circulation Manager

Provides news, analysis and opinion for the emerging business of electronic advertising and shopping and commerce. Discover how publishers, telephone companies, distributors, and retailers are now using information technologies to build the information infrastructure that will reach new customers and match buyers with sellers. Covers electronic marketing, new electronic classified and transactional services, the role of the Internet, electronic yellow pages, etc.
$499.00
BiWeekly

5860 Electronic Education Report
Simba Information
PO Box 4234
Stamford, CT 06907-0234
203-258-8193
FAX: 203-358-5825
simbainfo@simbanet.com
www.simbanet.com

Megan St. John, Manager
Patrick Quinn, Editor

Provides information on the multi-billion dollar market for electronic instructional materials. Includes company rankings, financial profiles, sales and distrbution trends, funding and adoptions, enrollement and demographics, trademark and copyright issues, strategic alliances and mergers. *$445.00*
BiWeekly

5861 Electronic Imaging Report
Phillips Publishing
7811 Montrose Road
Suite 2
Potomac, MD 20854-3394
301-340-2100
FAX: 301-309-3847

Christopher Scotton, Publisher
Lane Cooper, Editor

Written for top-level executives interested in learning how imaging technology can streamline their operations, cut their overhead costs and boost their competitiveness. Accepts advertising. *$397.00*

9 pages BiWeekly

5862 Electronic Information Report
Simba Information
PO Box 4234
Stamford, CT 06907-234
203-258-8193
FAX: 203-358-5825
simbainfo@simbanet.com
http://www.simbanet.com

Linda Kopp, Editor
Charlie Friscia, Marketing Director

The original information industry newsletter. Every week, this report monitors, analyzes, and reports on trends and developments in information services. It covers new storage and distribution media, databases, electronic publishing, value-added fax, online, multimedia and voice services. Readers will receive up-to-the-minute news written from a product, financial and marketing viewpoint. *$685.00*

46 Issues Per Y Founded: 1989

5863 Electronic Materials Technology News
Business Communications Company
25 Van Zant Street
Suite 13
Norwalk, CT 06855-1713
203-853-4266
FAX: 203-853-0348
sales@bccresearch.com
http://www.bccresearch.com

Louis Naturman, President
Marc Favrean, Editor
Alan Hall, Editorial Director
Thomas Abraham, VP Research
Marc Favreau, VP Development

Reports on electronic materials and processes, patents, companies involved, trends and business opportunities. *$35.00*

Founded: 1971

5864 Electronics Manufacturing Engineering
Society of Manufacturing Engineers
1 Sme Drive
po box#930
Dearborn, MI 48128-2408
313-271-1500
FAX: 313-425-3400 800-733-4763
services@sme.org
http://www.sme.org

Thomas Drozda, Publisher
Gene Korte, Editor
Gene Nelson, President
Greg Shermet, Circulation Manager
Richard Becker, Owner

Covers various aspects of electronics manufacturing. *$60.00*

8 pages Quarterly
Circulation: 2147 Audited
Mailing list available for rent 18190 names $95 per M.
Printed in 2 colors on matte stock

5865 Electronics Technicians Association Newsletter
Electronics Technicians Association International
5 Depot Street
Greencastle, IN 46135-1035
765-653-8262
FAX: 765-653-4287 800-288-3824
eta@tds.net http://www.eta-i.org/

Dick Glass, Publisher
Carolyn Carson, Circulation Director
Harry Maher, CEO/President
Jess Osborn, Marketing Manager

Accepts advertising. *$25.00*

Monthly Founded: 1978
Circulation: 4000

5866 IEEE All-Society Periodicals Package(ASPP)
Power Electronics Society
799 N Beverly Glen
Los Angeles, CA 90077
310-446-8280
FAX: 310-446-8390
bob.myers@ieee.org www.pels.org

Jerry Hudgins, President
Robert Myers, Executive Director
Steven Leeb, Treasurer
Ronald Harley, VP Operations

Provides access to our core collection of engineering, electronics, and computer science periodicals.

5867 ISCET Update
Int'l Society of Certified Electronics Technicians
3608 Pershing
Fort Worth, TX 76107-4527
817-921-9101
FAX: 817-921-3741 800-946-0201
info@iscet.org http://www.iscet.org

Mike Tlelikly, Publisher
Sheila Fred, Editor
Brian Gibbson, Circulation Manager

News and information for the electronics community.

Monthly
Circulation: 1300

5868 Integrated Circuit Manufacturing Synopsis
Semiconductor Equipment & Materials International
1401 K Street NW
Suite 601
Washington, DC 20005
202-890-0440

Michael Heynes, PhD, Author
Anne Miller, Author
Victoria Hadfield, Executive VP/President, N America

An illustrated booklet that provides an excellent introduction to the semicconductor industry and makes a great handout for new employee orientation or as a resource for industry suppliers. It is easy to understand and free of technical terminology. *$15.75*

35 pages

5869 Manufacturing Market Insider
JBT Communications
PO Box 782
Needham Heights, MA 02494-0006
781-444-2154
FAX: 781-455-8409 www.mtgmkt.com

John B Tuck, Publisher/Editor
Ann Connors, Circulation Manager

Specializes in contract manufacturing of electronics. Includes acquisitions, expansions, financial results and contract awards announced by contract manufacturers of electronics. *$420.00*

8 pages Monthly Founded: 1991
Printed in 1 color on matte stock

5870 Military & Aerospace Electronics
PennWell Publishing Company
98 Spit Brook Road
Nashua, NH 03062-5737
603-891-0123
FAX: 603-891-0574
ATD@PennWell.com
http://www.pennwell.com

John C Miklosz, Publisher
Tobias Naegele, Editor

Engineering newspaper written exclusively for military-aeronautical electronic systems designers, buyers and project managers. *$ 10.00*

Monthly Founded: 1910
Circulation: 48,100

5871 Optics and Photonics News
Optical Society of America
2010 Massachusetts Avenue NW
Washington, DC 20036-1023
202-223-8130
FAX: 202-223-1096
info@osa.org http://www.osa.org/

Beth T Hampton, Chief Marketing Officer
Tony Keane Rogin, Chief Operating Officer
Elizabeth A Rogan, Executive Director
John Childs, Director of Publications

Promotes the generation application, archiving and worldwide dissemination of knowledge in optics and photonics.

Monthly
Circulation: 17000

5872 Representor
Electronics Representatives Association
444 N Michigan Avenue
Suite 1960
Chicago, IL 60611-3977
312-527-3050
FAX: 312-527-3783
info@era.org http://www.era.org

Bettina Lee, Editor
Tess Hill, Features Editor
Thomas Shanahan, Interim Executive VP

Offers membership information on the Electronics Representatives Association. *$72.00*

40 pages
Circulation: 5000

5873 SITE
American Electronics Association
5201 Great America Parkway
Santa Clara, CA 95054
408-987-4200
FAX: 408-987-4298 800-284-4232
csc@aeanet.org www.aeanet.org

John V Harker, Chairman
William T Archey, President/CEO
Samuel J Block, VP/Controller
Tim Bennett, COO/EVP

Brings High-Tech HR professionals important information about compensation and benefits, employment law, relevant legislation, education and training.

Bi-Monthly

5874 SouthWest Technology Report
Communications
PO Box 23899
Tempe, AZ 85285-3899
480-345-1118
FAX: 480-345-1119

Walter J Schuch, Publisher

Focused on business and technology news related to high tech and electronics companies and organizations based in the Southwestern United States. *$69.00*

8 pages Monthly
Printed in 1 color on matte stock

5875 Technician Association News
Electronic Technicians Association International
5 Depot Street
Greencastle, IN 46135-1035
765-653-8262
FAX: 765-653-4287 800-288-3824
eta@tds.net
http://www.etainternational.org

Dick Glass, President
Carolyn Carson, Circulation Director
Jeff Osborn, Marketing Director
Delores Andrews, Circulation Manager

A professional and trade journal servicing electronic technicians nationwide. Lists new certified electronics technicians, technical repair services, upcoming seminars and satellite training sessions.

Monthly Founded: 1978
Printed in 2 colors

5876 Technology News Today
American Electronics Association
5201 Great America Parkway
Santa Clara, CA 95054
408-987-4200
FAX: 408-987-4298 800-284-4232
csc@aeanet.org www.aeanet.org

John V Harker, Chairman
William T Archey, President/CEO
Samuel J Block, VP/Controller
Tim Bennett, COO/EVP
Melissa La vigna, Contact

Aims to benefit investors with exclusive information on high-tech industry trends available only through AEA's extensive research, legislative monitoring and high-leveled networking capabilities.

Quarterly

5877 Twice: This Week in Consumer Electronics
Reed Business Information
360 Park Avenue South
15th Floor
New York, NY 10010
212-450-0067
FAX: 646-746-7066 800-826-6270
mgrand@reedbusiness.com
http://www.twice.com

Marcia Grand, Publisher
Jeff Greisch, Editor/CEO/President
Stephen F Smith, Editor-in-Chief
James Reed, Owner
Patricia Kennedy, Production Manager

Features include industry news, statistics, financial reports and new product trends and announcements. *$94.90*

Monthly
Circulation: 41000

Magazines & Journals

5878 Advancing Microelectronics
ISHM-Microelectronics Society
611 2nd street
North East Washington Dc, VA 20002
202-548-4001
FAX: 202-548-6115
imaps@imaps.org
http://www.imaps.org

Michael Odonoghue, President
Ann Bell, Circulations Manager

For the Microelectronics Society.

Circulation: 4010

5879 Applied Microwave & Wireless
Noble Publishing Corporation
1334 Meridian Rd
Thomasville, GA 31792
229-377-0587
FAX: 229-377-0589
randy@noblepub.com
http://www.noblepub.com

Joseph White, Publisher
Randy W Rhea, CEO

Edited for the RF and microwave professional. *$30.00*

Monthly Founded: 1994
Circulation: 26287

5880 AudioXpress
Audio Amateur Publications
PO Box 876
Peterborough, NH 03458
603-924-9464
FAX: 603-924-9467 888-924-9465
editorial@audioxpress.com
www.audioxpress.com

Edward Dell, Publisher

Focuses on the developments in sound production and enhancements in audio equipment and contains information on the construction of new and modification of existing audio equipment. Projects include schematics, parts lists and instructions necessary for completion aimed at electronic engineers and hobbyists. *$34.95*

72 pages Monthly Founded: 2001
Circulation: 11000
Printed in 4 colors on glossy stock

5881 Avionics News Magazine
Aircraft Electronics Association
4217 S Hocker
Independence, MO 64055
816-373-6565
FAX: 816-478-3100
info@aea.net www.aea.net

Debra McFarland, Publisher
Tracy Lykins, Editor
Linda Adams, Managing Editor

This publication is the voice of the general aviation electronics industry. It is recognized as one of the leading publications for the latest information in avionics technology. Subscriptions are complimentary within North America, however, subscribers must be employed within the aviation industry to receive the magazine. *$132.00*

Monthly

5882 Channel Magazine
Semiconductor Equipment & Materials International
3081 Zanker Road
San Jose, CA 95134-4080
408-943-6900
FAX: 408-428-9600
semihq@semi.org http://www.semi.org

Karen Savala, Publisher
Steve Buehler, Editor

A forum for equipment and material suppliers committed to the environment, health and safety as a Global Care member.

Founded: 1970

5883 Circuits Assembly
CMP Media
600 Community Drive
Manhasset, NY 11030
516-562-5000
FAX: 516-562-5049
www.circuitassembly.com

Laura Brown Sims, Associate Publisher

Devoted to the global electronics assembly industry.

Monthly

5884 CleanRooms Magazine
PennWell Publishing Company
98 Spit Brook Road
Nashua, NH 03062
603-891-0123
FAX: 603-891-9200 800-225-0556
jhaystead@pennwell.com
http://www.cleanrooms.com

John Haystead, Editor-in-Chief
Angela Godwin, Managing Editor
Heidi Barns, Circulation Manager
Lisa Bergevin, Marketing
James Enos, Publisher

Serves the contamination control and ultrapure materials and process industries. Written for readers in the microelectronics, pharmaceutical, biotech, health care, food processing and other user industries. Provides technology and business news and new product listings.

Monthly Founded: 1987
Circulation: 35031

5885 CommVerge
Reed Business Information
2000 Clearwater Drive
Oak Brook, IL 60523
630-740-0825
FAX: 630-288-8686
www.reedbusiness.com
The world leading publisher and information provider. Provides a range of communication and information channels, magazines, exhibitions, directories, online media, marketing services across five continents. Prestige brands in leading positions in key business sectors we deliver unrivalled access to business professionals across a diverse range of industries.

5886 Computer Business Review
ComputerWire
150 Post Street
#520
San Francisco, CA 94108-4707
415-274-8290
FAX: 415-274-8281
cbred@computerwire.com
www.computerwire.com/cbr

Tim Langford, Publisher

Company profiles, computer market coverage and technology trends and news for investors and professionals in the computer, communications and microelectronics industries. *$195.00*

Monthly
Circulation: 23M

5887 Computer-Aided Engineering
Penton Media
1300 E 9th Street
Cleveland, OH 44114
216-696-7000
FAX: 216-696-1752
caenetmaster@penton.com
www.penton.com/cae/

Larry Boulden, Publisher

Applications, news, trends and products for CAD/CAM technology as applied in manu-

facturing, electronics, architectural and construction industries. *$50.00*
Monthly
Circulation: 56,062

5888 **Consumer Electronics Vision**
Consumer Electronics Association
2500 Wilson Boulevard
Arlington, VA 22201-3834
703-907-7600
FAX: 703-907-7675 866-858-1555
cea@ce.org http://www.ce.org

Cindy Stevens, Manager Publications
Gary Shapiro, Chief Executive Officer

Provides the latest information on industry standards, public policy, market research, CEA events and training opportunities. Is the premier source of information for the top management of more than 1,000 US corporations that design, develop, manufacture and distribute audio, video, mobile electronics, wireless and landline communications, IT, multimedia, accessory products and related services sold through consumer channels.
Monthly Founded: 1844
Circulation: 1000

5889 **Control Solutions**
PennWell Publishing Company
1421 S Sheridan Road
Tulsa, OK 74112
918-835-3161
FAX: 918-831-9497 800-331-4463
headquarters@pennwell.com
http://www.pennwell.com

Matt O'Shea, Publisher
Ron Kuhfeld, Editor-in-Chief

Monthly Founded: 1910

5890 **Dealerscope**
North American Publishing Company
401 N Broad Street
5th Floor
Philadelphia, PA 19108
215-238-5300
FAX: 215-238-5346 800-627-2689
webmaster@napco.com
http://www.napco.com

Grant Clauser, Editorial Director
Rhoda Dixon, Circulation Manager
Eric Schwartz, President/Publishing Dire

Dedicated to delivering peer-based knowledge and experience, Dealerscope is the ultimate vehicle for presenting product and service solutions to the consumer.
Monthly Founded: 1958

5891 **ECN Magazine**
Reed Business Information
360 Park Avenue South
4th Floor
New York, NY 10010
212-450-0067

subsmail@reedbusiness.com
www.ecnmag.com

Jim Casella, CEO
James Reed, Owner

Provides product solutions for designed engineers in the electronics industry.
Founded: 1957
Circulation: 117923

5892 **EDN Asia**
Reed Business Information
350 Hudson Street
4th Floor
New York, NY 10014
212-959-9550
FAX: 630-288-8686
mike.pan@rbi-asia.com
http://www.edn.com/

Kirtimaya Varma, Editor in chief
Mike Pan, Editor
Robin Peter Lange, Managing Editor
Raymond Wong, Publishing Director
Chen Wai Chun, Publisher

A source for all the design features, technology trends, design ideas, hands-on applications and product updates.
Monthly Founded: 1990
Circulation: 30000

5893 **EDN China**
Reed Business Information
350 Hudson Street
4th Floor
New York, NY 10014
212-959-9550
FAX: 630-288-8686
john.dodge@reedbusiness.com
http://www.edninteractive.com

John Dodge, Editor-in-Chief
William Zhang, Publisher Director
John Mu, Executive Editor
Stephen D. Moylan, President

A source for design, development, & applications information foe electronics engineers & managers.
Monthly Founded: 1946
Circulation: 30018

5894 **EDN Europe**
Reed Business Information
350 Hudson Street
4th Floor
New York, NY 10014
212-959-9550
FAX: 630-288-8686
gprophet@reedbusiness.com
http://www.edninteractive.com

John Dodge, Editor-in-Chief
Martin Savery, Publisher
Graham Prophet, Editor

A focused product specific to, and unique in, its own region, that draws on a unique international network of editorial expertise. EDN serves design engineers, providing exactly the information they need to conceive and create tomorrow's electronic products.

Circulation: 35,024

5895 **EE Product News**
Penton Media
1300 E 9th Street
Cleveland, OH 44114
216-696-7000
FAX: 216-696-1752
information@penton.com
http://www.eepn.com

Joseph Desposito, Editor-in-Chief
David B. Nussbaum, CEO

Source of information in new products necessary to successfully design, assemble and test prototypes of commerical, industrial, military and aerospace electronic products.
Monthly Founded: 1892
Circulation: 111968

5896 **EE: Evaluation Engineering**
Nelson Publishing
2500 Tamiami Trail N
Nokomis, FL 34275
941-966-9521
FAX: 941-966-2590 800-226-6113
pmilo@evaluationengineering.com
http://www.nelsonpub.com

Paul Milo, Publisher & Editorial Director
Michael Hughes, Sales

Magazine devoted exclusively to companies that test, evaluate, design and manufacture electronic products and equipment.
$43.00
84 pages Monthly Founded: 1962
Mailing list available for rent 65,000 names
Printed in 4 colors on glossy stock

5897 **Electronic Business**
Reed Business Information
1101 South Winchester Boulevard
Building N
San Jose, CA 95128
408-454-4488
FAX: 408-345-4400
subsmail@reedbusiness.com
http://www.reedbusiness.com

Steven Drace, Publishing Director
Kathleen Doler, Editor-in-Chief
James A Casella, CEO
Shahrokh Rad, Owner
Salina Le Bris, Corporate Communications/PR

Monthly Founded: 1975
Circulation: 65732

5898 **Electronic Components**
Global Sources
7341 Washington Avenue
Suite C
Whittier, CA 90602
562-945-4612
FAX: 562-945-4192
mktgserv@globalsources.com
http://www.globalsources.com

Anna Maria Anguiano, Account Manager
Mark Sanderson, Publisher
Dan Katz, Managing Director *$75.00*

Monthly Founded: 1971

5899 **Electronic Design**
Penton Media
1300 E 9th Street
Cleveland, OH 44114
216-696-7000
FAX: 216-696-1752
information@penton.com
http://www.edmediafile.com

Tom Morgan, Group Publisher
Mark David, Editor in Chief
Janet Connors, Marketing

Celebrating 50 years of innovation, this authoritative source provides leading-edge technical information to electronic and engineering managers around the world.
Monthly Founded: 1892
Circulation: 145000

5900 **Electronic Packaging & Production**

Reed Business Information
1350 E Touhy Avenue
Des Plaines, IL 60018
630-320-7000
FAX: 630-288-8686
epp@cahners.com www.cahners.com

Vicky Steen, Publisher
Michael Sweeney, Editorial Director

Edited for engineers and managers who are involved in packaging designed, printed circuit board fabrication and assembly, and production testing of electronic circuits, systems, products and equipment.

5901 Electronic Products
Hearst Business Communications
645 Stewart Avenue
Garden City, NY 11530-4709
516-227-1300
FAX: 516-227-1342
ralphr@electronicproducts.com
http://www.elecprod2.com
Todd Christenson, Publisher
Gail Meyer, Production Manager
R Pell, Editor-in-Chief
News about developments in electronic components and equipment.
Monthly Founded: 1958
Circulation: 123767 123767 names
Printed in 4 colors on glossy stock

5902 Electronics Manufacturing Engineering
Society of Manufacturing Engineers
1 SME Drive
#930
Dearborn, MI 48128-2408
313-271-1500
FAX: 313-271-2861
Tom Drozda, Publications/Advertising Director
John Coleman, Editor-in-Chief
Richard Becker, Owner
For manufacturing engineers and managers involved with electronics manufacturing.
Circulation: 3,300

5903 Handbook of Standardized Terminology for the Power Sources Industry
Power Sources Manufacturers Association
PO Box 418
Mendham, NJ 07945-0418
973-543-9660
FAX: 973-543-6207
power@PSMA.com www.psma.com
Arnold Alderman, President
Chuck Mullett, Chairman
Joe Horzepa, Executive Director
This handbook provides a current common language for the industry, covering every facet of power sources and conversion. All member companies receive a copy of this report as a benefit of membership.

5904 High Density Interconnect
CMP Media
600 Community Drive
Manhasset, NY 11030
516-562-5000
FAX: 415-947-6090 www.cmp.com

5905 IEEE Control Systems Magazine
IEEE Control Systems Society (CSS)
445 Hoes Lane
PO Box 1331
Piscataway, NJ 08854-1331
732-981-0060
FAX: 732-981-1721
tariq_samad@htc.honeywell.com
http://www.ieee.org
Dennis S. Bernstein, Editor
Susan Schneiderman, Manager
Focuses on applications of technical knowledge and concentrates on industrial implementations, design tools, technology review, control education and applied research. Geared towards readers with many different responsibilities including applied research, device design, product development and design including software and semiconductor components. *$210.00*
Founded: 1973
Mailing list available for rent

5906 Journal of Electronic Materials
Minerals, Metals & Materials Society
184 Thorn Hill Road
Warrendale, PA 15086-7528
724-776-9000
FAX: 724-776-3770 800-759-4867
jem@tms.org http://www.tms.org
Theodore C. Harman, Editor
Shirley A. Litzinger, Production Editor
Reports on the science and technology of electronic materials, while examining new applications for semiconductors, magnetic alloys, insulators, optical and display materials. *$131.00*
Monthly Founded: 1993
Circulation: 1400 1400 names
Printed in 2 colors on glossy stock

5907 Journal of Microelectronics and Electronic Packaging
International Microelectronics & Electronics
611 2nd Street NE
Washington, DC 20002
202-548-4001
FAX: 202-548-6115 888-464-6277
impas@imaps.org www.imaps.org
Michael O'Donoghue, Executive Director
Rick Mohn, Operations Manager
Brian Schieman, Director Information Technology
Ann Bell, Manager Marketing/Communications
Dedicated to publishing peer-reviewed papers in microelectronics, multichip module technologies, electronic packaging, electronic materials, surface mount and other related technologies, interconnections, RF and microwaves, wireless communications, manufacturing, design, test, and reliability. *$35.00*

5908 Laser Focus World
PennWell Publishing Company
Advance Technology Divison
98 Spit Brook Road
Nashua, NH 03062-5737
603-891-0123
FAX: 603-891-0574
allisono@pennwell.com
http://www.optoelectronics-world.com
Stephen G Anderson, Associate Publisher, Editor-in-Chie
Carol Settino, Managing Editor
Christine Shaw, Group Publisher
The world of optoelectronics. *$150.00*
173 pages Monthly Founded: 1965
Circulation: 70004
Printed in 4 colors on glossy stock

5909 Modeling Power Devices and Model Validation
Power Sources Manufacturers Association
PO Box 418
Mendham, NJ 07945
973-543-9660
FAX: 973-543-6207
power@psma.org www.psma.org
Peter O Lauritzen, Author
H Alan Manthooth, Author
Alexander Craig, Author
This report consists of two parts, one devoted to modeling, and the other, model validation. The first article in the report reviews commonly used device models used in circuit simulations, and applies these to simulation designed power converters and rectifers. The second article establishes processes by which the features and accuracy of a model are determined by simulating the results of test circuits containing power devices and comparing these results with the results of actual measurements *$20.00*

5910 Optics Letters
Optical Society of America
2010 Massachusetts Avenue NW
Washington, DC 20036-1023
202-223-8130
FAX: 202-223-1096
info@osa.org www.osa.org
John Childs, Director Publications
Alan Tourtlotte, Associate Publisher
Anthony J Campillo, Editor-in-Chief
Christopher Videll, Managing Editor
Offers rapid dissemination of new results in all areas of optics with short, original, peer-reviewed communications. Optics Letters covers the latest research in optical science, including atmospheric optics, quantum electronics, Fourier optics, integrated optics, and fiber optics.
24 issues per year

5911 PCIM Power Electronics Systems
Adams Business Media
2472 Eastman Avenue
#33
Ventura, CA 93003-5792
805-509-9990
FAX: 805-650-7054
sales@pcim.com
www.powersystems.com
Dann Daggett, Publisher
Sam Davis, Publisher/Editor
Terri Adams, Executive Director
PCIM Power Electronics Systems serves the manufacturers of automotive electronics, batteries/chargers/monitors, communication/Telecom, and others allied to the field.
Monthly Founded: 1975
Circulation: 40,050

5912 Power Conversion & Intelligent Motion
Primedia
9800 Metcalf Avenue
Overland Park, KS 66212
913-341-1300
FAX: 913-967-1898
www.primediabusiness.com
Myron A Miller, Publisher
Sam Davis, Editor
Directed to engineers, designers and manufacturers of power electronic and electronic motion control components, subsystems and systems. Feature articles interpret trends and innovation in these subjects.
Circulation: 31,113

5913 Printed Circuit Fabrication
CMP Media
600 Community Drive
Manhasset, NY 11030
516-562-5000
FAX: 415-947-6090

5914 ProService
Int'l Society of Certified Electronics Technicians
3608 Pershing Avenue
Fort Worth, TX 76107-4527
817-921-9101
FAX: 817-921-3741 800-946-0201
info@iscet.org http://www.iscet.org

Mack Blakely, Executive Director
Ed Clingman, ISCET Administrator
Shiela Fredrickson, Publisher

A bi-monthly magazine published by the International Society of Certified Electronics Technicians.
24 pages Founded: 1965

5915 ProService Magazine
National Electronics Service Dealers Association
3608 Pershing Avenue
Fort Worth, TX 76107-4527
817-921-9061
FAX: 817-921-3741 800-797-9197
webmaster@nesda.com
www.nesda.com

Brian Gibson, President
Don Cressin, VP
Mack Blakely, Executive Director
Fred Paradis, CSM, Treasurer
Wayne Markman, Secretary

For members of NESDA/ISCET, and a printed magazine is mailed to the membership address on file in April and August.
Bi-Monthly

5916 Representor Magazine
Electronics Representatives Association
444 N Michigan Avenue
Suite 1940
Chicago, IL 60611
312-527-3050
FAX: 312-527-3783 800-776-7377
info@era.org www.era.org

Mark Motsinger, Chairman
Dave Rossi, Vice Chairman
Mike Kunz, President
Thomas Shanahan, Interim Executive Vice President
William R Warfield, Director Finance/Operations

Devoted to fulfilling the management, informational, educational and communications needs of representatives and manufacturers in the electronics industry.

5917 Review of the Electronic and Industrial Distribution Industries
National Electronic Distributors Association
1111 Alderman Drive
Suite 400
Alpharetta, GA 30005-4175
678-393-9990
FAX: 678-393-9998
admin@nedassoc.org
www.nedassoc.org

Francis Flynn Jr, President
Robin B Gray Jr, Executive VP
Debbie Conyers, Director Marketing
Barney Martin, VP Industry Practices

Contains academic articles on topics pertinent to our members' business. Leading electronic and industrial distribution academicians provides the content. Offers insightful articles aimed at improving industry practices. $12.00 per volume or $20.00 for an annual subscription. *$ 20.00*
Bi-Annually

5918 SIGNAL Magazine
Armed Forces Communications and Electronics Assn
4400 Fair Lakes Court
Fairfax, VA 22033-3899
703-311-1397
FAX: 703-631-6169 800-336-4583
promo@afcea.org www.afcea.org

Eugene C Renzi, Chairman
Herb Browne, President/CEO
Becky Nolan, Executive VP
Paul E Tobin, Jr, Executive Director
Robert Howell, RN, General Manager

Is a international news magazine serving the critical information needs of government, military and industry professionals active in the fields of command, control, communications, computers, intelligence, surveillance and reconnaissance (C4ISR); information security; research and development; electronics; and homeland security.
Monthly

5919 Semiconductor Manufacturing Magazine
Semiconductor Equipment & Materials International
3081 Zanker Road
San Jose, CA 95134
408-943-6900
FAX: 408-428-9600
semihq@semi.org www.semi.org

Stanley T Myers, President/CEO

Covers the technical and business information needs of important worldwide semiconductor manufacturers, including captive manufacturers, merchant manufacturers, research and development laboratories, equipment suppliers, government/military installations and consortiums. *$90.00*
Monthly

5920 Sensors Magazine
Questex Media
275 Grove St
Ste 2-130
Newton, MA 02466
617-219-8300
FAX: 617-219-8310 888-552-4346
seninfo@sensorsmag.com
http://www.sensorsmag.com

Barbara G Goode, Editor-in-Chief
Stephanie Henkel, Executive Editor

Source among design and production engineers of information on sensor technologies and products, and topic integral to sensor-based systems and applications. Provides practical and in-depth yet accessible information on sensor operation, design, application, and implementation within systems. Covers the effective use of state-of-the-art resources and tools that enable readers to get the maximum benefit from their use of sensors. *$99.00*
Monthly Founded: 1984
Circulation: 75000

5921 Tech Briefs
Associated Business Publications International
1466 Broadway
Ste. 910
New York, NY 10036
212-490-3999
FAX: 212-986-7864
alfredo@abpi.net
http://www.nasatech.com

Domenic Mucchetti, CEO
Hugh Dowling, Circualtion Manager
Linda Bell, Chief Editor

Serves design engineers, managers and scientists in the industries of electronics, industrial equipment, computers, communications, bio-medical, transportation/automotive, power and energy, materials, chemicals and many more related fields. *$75.00*
Monthly Founded: 1958

5922 Test & Measurement World
Reed Business Information
275 Washington Street
Ste 275
Newton, MA 02458
617-964-3030
FAX: 617-558-4470
tmswales@cahners.com
http://www.tmworld.com

Rick Nelson, Chief Editor
Deborah M Sargent, Managing Editor
Russ Pratt, Publisher

The magazine on test, measurement and inspection in the electronics industry
Monthly Founded: 1981
Circulation: 65000

5923 Wideband
Advanstar Communications
545 Boylston Street
Boston, MA 02116
617-514-4600
FAX: 617-267-6900
wbandmag@aol.com
www.widebandmag.com

Les Hamaguchi, Publisher

Covers accessories, equipment, services, products, and an anlysis of major market trends, industry news, statistics, new products, and personnel changes are featured in every issue.
SemiMonthly
Circulation: 26,000

Trade Shows

5924 AEA Annual Convention & Trade Show
Aircraft Electronics Association
4217 S Hocker
Independence, MO 64055
816-373-6565
FAX: 816-478-3100
info@aea.net www.aea.net

Paula Derks, President
Debra McFarland, VP
Tracy Lykins, Director Communications
Mark Gibson, Administration/Meeting Management

Annual show of 131 exhibitors of industry related equipment and supplies.
1500 Attendees Annual Founded: 1957

5925 AFCEA Sponsored Conferences/Symposia
Armed Forces Communications and Electronics Assn
4400 Fair Lakes Court
Fairfax, VA 22033-3899
703-311-1397
FAX: 703-631-6169 800-336-4583
promo@afcea.org www.afcea.org

Tobey Jackson, Marketing/PR Manager
Herb Browne, President/CEO
Becky Nolan, Executive VP
Paul E Tobin, Jr, Executive Director
Robert Howell, RN, General Manager

Offers problem solving and networking opportunities through exhibits, technical panels, and featured speakers. Decision-makers from around the world attend AFCEA conferences for hands-on demonstrations, question-and-answer sessions and system solutions.

5926 **AFCEA TechNet Asia-Pacific**
Armed Forces Communications and Electronics Assn
4400 Fair Lakes Court
Fairfax, VA 22033-3899
703-631-6200
FAX: 703-654-6931 800-654-4220
technet@jspargo.com www.afcea.org
Paul doCarmo, Assistant Director/Exhibit Sales
Connie Shaw, Exhibit Sales Account Manager
Military, government and industry communications and electronics professionals gather to see exhibits of communications and electronics equipment, supplies and services. Seminar, conference, dinner and luncheon. Co-sponsored by AFCEA International and AFCEA Hawaii.
2000 Attendees Nov 7-9 Founded: 1985

5927 **AFCEA TechNet International**
Armed Forces Communications and Electronics Assn
4400 Fair Lakes Court
Fairfax, VA 22033-3899
703-631-6200
FAX: 703-654-6931 800-564-4220
technetinternational@jspargo.com
www.afcea.org
Paul doCarmo, Sales Manager
Connie Shaw, Sales Manager
This event draws commanders and staff from every branch of the military, including warfighting integration organizations charged with the most critical responsibilities of synthesizing military power on land, at sea, and in the air.
7500 Attendees June

5928 **AFCEA/USNI West Conference & Exposition**
Armed Forces Communications and Electronics Assn
4400 Fair Lakes Court
Fairfax, VA 22033
703-631-6200
FAX: 703-654-6931 800-564-4220
west@jspargo.org www.afcea.org
Paul doCarmo, Assistant Direct/Exhibit Sales
Connie Shaw, Exhibit Sales Account Manager
Over 350 of the industry's most recognized defense and technology organizations showcase their technology products and services to top decision-makers from the US Pacific Fleet, Naval Station San Diego, Space & Warfare Command, Naval Base Coronado, Camp Pendleton Marine Corps Base and many other west coast military and government facilities.
6000 Attendees January Founded: 1980

5929 **ASM/TMS Spring Symposium**
Minerals, Metals & Materials Society
184 Thorn Hill Road
Warrendale, PA 15086-7514
724-776-9000
FAX: 724-776-3770
foundation@tms.org www.tms.org
Tresa Pollock, President
Brajendra Mishra, VP
Alexander Scott, Executive Director
John Parsey, Financial Planning Officer
Marc DeGraef, Director Information Technology
This symposium, organized by the local chapters of TMS and ASM, will focus on materials for extreme environments, with sessions on materials characterization in three dimensions, structural materials for high temperature, materials for space applications, and materials by design.
May

5930 **ATE and Instrumentation West**
Miller Freeman Publications
600 Harrison Street
Suite 400
San Francisco, CA 94107-1391
415-905-2354
FAX: 415-905-2232
Steve Schulderfrei, Trade Show Director
Geared to the test and measurement of electronics.
5.8M Attendees January

5931 **AVS International Symposium and Exhibition**
AVS Science & Technology Society
120 Wall Street
32nd Floor
New York, NY 10005-3993
212-248-0200
FAX: 212-248-0245
angela@avs.org www.avs.org
Christie R Marrian, President
John Coburn, Treasurer
Joseph E Greene, Clerk/Secretary
Yvonne Towse, Executive Director
This conference has been developed to address cutting edge issues associated with vacuum science and technology in both the research and manufacturing communities. The equipment exhibition is one of the largest in the world and provides an excellent opportunity to view the latest products and services offered by over 200 participating companies.
3000 Attendees

5932 **AVS: Science & Technology Society**
120 Wall Street
32nd Floor
New York, NY 10005
212-248-0200
FAX: 212-248-0245 www.avs.org
Christie R Marrian, President
John Coburn, Treasurer
Joseph E Greene, Clerk/Secretary
Yvonne Towse, Executive Director
Promotes communication, dissemination of knowledge, recommended practices, research, and education in the use of vacuum and other controlled environments to develop new materials, process technology, devices, and related understanding of material properties for the betterment of humanity.
February

5933 **All-Service Convention**
Electronic Technicians Association International
5 Depot Street
Greencastle, IN 46135-1035
765-653-8262
FAX: 765-653-4287 800-288-3824
eta@tds.net www.eta-i.org
Richard Glass, President
Teresa Maher, VP
Jeff Osborn, Director Marketing
Carolyn Carson, Special Projects Manager
Appliances and electronic service products and services. Third party administrators. Certification exams and study materials. Tools and test equipment. Containing 40 booths and 50 exhibits.

5934 **Annual Interactive Service Association Conference**
Internet Alliance
1111 19th Street NW
Suite 1180
Washington, DC 20036
202-284-4380
FAX: 202-955-8081
ia@internetalliance.org
www.internetallaince.com
Emily Hackett, Executive Director
Conference and 100 exhibits of computer hardware and software & interactive electronics. Services for home and business of interest to corporate executives concerned with delivering interactive electronic services to mass markets.
1000 Attendees Annual Founded: 1981

5935 **Annual Legislative & Regulatory Roundtable**
Electronic Industries Alliance
2500 Wilson Boulevard
Arlington, VA 22201-3834
703-907-7500
703-907-7500
Gail Tannenbaum, CMP, Manager Meetings/Industry Relations
August

5936 **Asia Card Technology Exhibition**
Reed Exhibition Companies
383 Main Avenue, Suite 3
PO Box 6059
Norwalk, CT 06851
203-840-4800
FAX: 203-840-9628
Emily Hackett, Executive Director
Peter DiLeo, Marketing Director
Deborah Luongo, Conference Manager
Trade professionals see exhibits on computers and electronics.
Annual

5937 **Assembly Northeast Exhibition**
Reed Exhibition Companies
383 Main Avenue, Suite 3
PO Box 6059
Norwalk, CT 06851
203-840-4800
FAX: 203-840-9628
Emily Hackett, Executive Director
Peter DiLeo, Marketing Director
Deborah Luongo, Conference Manager
Gregg Vautrin, Chief Executive Officer
Assembly industry equipment, supplies and services for engineers and managers from electronic and automated assembly operations.
1365 Attendees Annual Founded: 1999

5938 **Assembly Technology Exposition**
Reed Exhibition Companies
383 Main Avenue, Suite 3
PO Box 6059
Norwalk, CT 06851
203-840-4800
FAX: 203-840-9686 800-267-3796
Emily Hackett, Executive Director
Peter DiLeo, Marketing Director
Deborah Luongo, Conference Manager
525 exhibitors with robotics, vision systems, electronics and production machinery

of interest to engineers and managers from automated assembly plants.
14000 Attendees Annual Founded: 1979

5939 **Assembly West Exhibition**
Reed Exhibition Companies
383 Main Avenue, Suite 3
PO Box 6059
Norwalk, CT 06851
203-840-4800
FAX: 203-840-9628
Emily Hackett, Executive Director
Peter DiLeo, Marketing Director
Deborah Luongo, Conference Manager
Gregg Vautrin, Chief Executive Officer
Assembly industry equipment, supplies and services for engineers and managers from electronic and automated assembly operations.
3000 Attendees Annual

5940 **Association of Progressive Rental Organizations Convention**
1504 Robin Hood Trail
Austin, TX 78703
512-794-0095
FAX: 512-794-0097 800-204-APRO
cmay@aprovision.org
www.aprovision.org
Shannon Strunkec, President
John C Cleek, First VP
Jeannie Hutchison, Program Coordinator
Bill Keese, Manager
Seminar, reception and tours, plus 280 exhibits of products and services of interest to rent to own dealers: stereos, televisions, furniture, fabric protection and more.
1400 Attendees Annual

5941 **Automated Manufacturing Exposition: New En gland**
TEC
2001 Assembly Street
Suite 204
Columbia, SC 29201
803-779-7123
www.amexpo.com/newengland
Tony Smith, Founder
Rafael Pastor, Chairman/CEO
Richard Carr, President/Vice Chairman
Jerry Schneider, Chief Financial Officer
In addition to the exhibits, the conference will feature seminars that focus on topics such as continuous improvement and lean manufacturing.

5942 **CEA Industry Forum**
Consumer Electronics Association
2500 Wilson Boulevard
Arlington, VA 22201
703-907-7600
FAX: 703-907-7675 866-858-1555
Loyd Ivey, Chair
Pat Lavelle, Vice Chair
Gary Shapiro, President/CEO
This is your chance to help guide the consumer electronics industry and CEA's leadership in findings the right focus for the coming year. Plus, get key knowledge and insight on how to improve your CE business.
October

5943 **CEA Winter Technology & Standards Forum**
Consumer Electronics Association
2500 Wilson Boulevard
Arlington, VA 22201-3834
703-907-7600
FAX: 703-907-7675 866-858-1555
Loyd Ivey, Chair
Pat Lavelle, Vice Chair
Gary Shapiro, President/CEO
March, Florida

5944 **CEO Summit**
Consumer Electronics Association
2500 Wilson Boulevard
Arlington, VA 22201
703-907-7600
FAX: 703-907-7675 866-858-1555
Loyd Ivey, Chair
Pat Lavelle, Vice Chair
Gary Shapiro, President/CEO
Presents a rare opportunity to network in a qualified, executive-only environment, to gather insight helpful to your business and to focus on the issues most critical to the industry.
June

5945 **CLEO/QELS Conference**
Optical Society of America
2010 Massachusetts Avenue NW
Washington, DC 20036-1023
202-223-8130
FAX: 202-223-1096
info@osa.org www.osa.org
Elizabeth A Rogin, Executive Director
Tony Keane, COO
John Childs, Senior Director Publications
Cynthia Gady, Senior Director Meetings
Deborah C Herrin, Senior Director IT
Is a unique conference that gathers distringuished leaders to discuss the latest research in the fields of optics and photonics. The conference includes application-focused forums, educational sessions and an applications-oriented exhibit.
May

5946 **COM Conference of Metallurgists**
Minerals, Metals & Materials Society
184 Thorn Hill Road
Warrendale, PA 15086-7514
724-776-9000
FAX: 724-776-3770
foundation@tms.org www.tms.org
Tresa Polloc, President
Brajendra Mishra, VP
Alexander Scott, Executive Director
John Parsey, Financial Planning Officer
Marc DeGraef, Director Information Technology
Topic: Challenges for the Metals and Materials Industry. This conference will feature symposia on computational analysis in hydrometallurgy; nickel and cobalt; pipelines for the 21st century; materials degradation: innovation, inspection, control, and rehabilitation; light metals; fuel cell and hydrogen technologies; recruitment and early career development programs; and the treatment of gold ores.
August

5947 **Ceramic Interconnect and Ceramic Microsystems**
International Microelectronics & Electronics
611 2nd Street
Washington, DC 20002
202-548-4001
FAX: 202-548-6115 888-464-6277
imaps@imaps.org www.imaps.org
Michael O'Donoghue, Executive Director
Rick Mohn, Operations Manager
Brian Schieman, Director Information Technology
Ann Bell, Manager Marketing/Communications
April

5948 **DistribuTech Conference**
PennWell Conferences and Exhibitions
350 Post Oak Blouevard
Suite 205
Houston, TX 77056
713-621-8833
FAX: 713-963-6284
www.pennwell.com
Bob Biolchini, Chief Executive Officer
Is the leading automation and information technology conference and exhibition in the utility industry; and provides the best resources, tools and networking opportunities relating to electric utility automation and control systems, IT, T&D engineering, power and delivery equipment, and water utility technology.
3000 Attendees January

5949 **EASA Conference**
Electrical Apparatus Service Association
1331 Baur Boulevard
Saint Louis, MO 63132-1903
314-993-2220
FAX: 314-993-1269
www.easainfo@easa.com
www.easa.com
Linda J Raynes, President/CEO
Dale Shuter, CMP, Expositions Manager
2200 Attendees June Founded: 1937
Mailing list available for rent 2200 names

5950 **EIA's Congressional Technology Forum**
Electronic Industries Alliance
2500 Wilson Boulevard
Arlington, VA 22201-3834
703-907-7500
FAX: 703-907-7500 www.eia.org
Gail Tannenbaum, CMP, Manager Meetings/Industry Relations
October

5951 **EOS/ESD Symposium & Exhibits**
Electrostatic Discharge Association
7900 Turin Road
Building 3
Rome, NY 13440-2069
315-339-6937
FAX: 315-339-6793
info@esda.org
www.esda.org/symposia.html
Lisa Pimpinella, Operations Mgr/Symposium Exhibits
Lynn Barbiarz, Marketing & Communications Admnstr
International technical forum on electrical overstress and electrostatic discharge that features research, technology, and solutions to increase understanding, enhance quality and reliability, reduce and control costs, and improve yields and productivity.
1M Attendees September

5952 **ETA Annual Meeting and Expo**
Electronic Transactions Association
1101 16th Street NW
Suite 402
Washington, DC 20036
202-828-2635
FAX: 202-828-2639 800-695-5509
Jennifer Leo, Meetings Manager
Featuring valuable networking opportunities, outstanding speakers and educational seminars.
April, Las Vegas

5953 ETA Expo Network
Electronic Transactions Association
1101 16th Street NW
Suite 402
Washington, DC 20036
202-828-2635
FAX: 202-828-2639 800-695-5509
Jennifer Leo, Meetings Manager
Offers conference events that focus specifically on delivering need to know education to ISOs and sales agents. ETA created these meetings to increase educational and business development opportunities for the industry. These affordable and easily accessible conferences are the ideal opportunity to increase your knowledge and meet new business partners.

5954 East Coast Video Show
Expocon Management Associates
363 Reef Road
PO Box 915
Fairfield, CT 06430-0915
203-882-1300
FAX: 203-256-4730
Diane Stone, Show Director
8000 Attendees

5955 Electronic Distribution Show and Conference
Electronic Distribution Show Corporation
222 S Riverside Plaza
Suite 2160
Chicago, IL 60606-6160
312-648-1140
FAX: 312-648-4282
eds@edsc.org www.edsc.org
Gretchen Oie-Weghorst, Show Manager
Annual conference and exhibits of 500 manufacturers of electronic components who sell through distribution. Containing 700 booiths and 500 exhibits.
10M Attendees May

5956 Electronic Imaging East
Miller Freeman Publications
600 Harrison Street
Suite 400
San Francisco, CA 94107-1391
415-905-2354
FAX: 415-905-2232
Stephen Schuldenfrei, Trade Show Director
300 booths consisting of electrical equipment and services.
5.3M Attendees October

5957 Electronic Imaging West
Miller Freeman Publications
600 Harrison Street
Suite 400
San Francisco, CA 94107-1391
415-905-2534
FAX: 415-905-2232
Stephen Schuldenfrei, Trade Show Director
Exhibits of equipment, supplies and services for the computer and electronics industries.
3M Attendees

5958 Electronic Materials Conference
Minerals, Metals & Materials Society
184 Thorn Hill Road
Warrendale, PA 15086-7514
724-776-9000
FAX: 724-776-3770
foundation@tms.org www.tms.org
Tresa Pollock, President
Brajendra Mishra, VP
Alexander Scott, Executive Director
John Parsey, Financial Planning Officer
Marc DeGraef, Director Information Technology
This conference will provide a forum for topics of current interest and significance related to the preparation and characterization of electronic materials. Individuals actively engaged or interested in electronic materials research and development are encouraged to submit an abstract or attend the meeting. A technological exhibition will also be held.
June

5959 Electronic West: Annual Western Electrical Exposition Conference
Continental Exhibitions
370 Lexington Avenue
Suite 1401
New York, NY 10017
212-370-5005
FAX: 212-370-5699
10000 Attendees

5960 Embedded Systems Conference - West
Miller Freeman Publications
600 Harrison Street
Suite 400
San Francisco, CA 94107
415-905-2354
FAX: 415-905-2220 www.esconline.com
Lisa Ostrom, Electronics Show Director
Christian Fahlen, Senior Conference Manager
This is an ideal forum to learn relevant new skills, and about the latest technologies and products; to network with industry experts, vendors and your peers; and to discover an exhibits floor featuring leading companies showcasing cutting edge products.
13000 Attendees March

5961 Executive Leadership Forum & Board of Governors Meeting
Electronic Industries Alliance
2500 Wilson Boulevard
Arlington, VA 22201-3834
703-907-7500
FAX: 703-907-7500 www.eia.org
Gail Tannenbaum, CMP, Manager Meetings/Industry Relations
February, California

5962 IS&T/SPIE's Electronic Imaging
International Society for Optical Engineering
1000 20th Street
PO Box 10
Bellingham, WA 98227-0010
360-763-3290
FAX: 360-647-1445
meetinginfo@spie.org www.spie.org
Electronic Imaging's top-notch technical program gathers the world's most prominent experts to discuss and push the forefront of imaging technology and it's applications.
1200 Attendees Annual/January

5963 Industry Wide Service and Retail Convention
Electronic Technicians Association International
5 Depot Street
Greencastle, IN 46135
765-653-8262
FAX: 765-653-4287 800-288-3824
eta@tds.net www.eta-i.org
Richard Glass, President
Tresa Maher, VP
Jeff Osborn, CSS, Director Marketing
Carolyn Carson, Special Projects Manager
Three groups united to offer the largest schedule of business management and technical seminars and trade show for educators, servicers and retailers. Thirty booths.
200 Attendees February

5964 International CES
Consumer Electronics Association
2500 Wilson Boulevard
Arlington, VA 22201-3834
703-907-7600
FAX: 703-907-7695
communications@ce.org www.ce.org
Gary Sharpiro, President/CEO
Lisa Fasold, Director
Stephen Gates, Senior Manager
Brad Jones, Communications Manager
Offers a glimpse into the digital future.

5965 International Conference and Exhibition on Device Packaging
International Microelectronics & Electronics
611 2nd Street NE
Washington, DC 20002
202-548-4001
FAX: 202-548-6115 888-464-6277
imaps@imaps.org www.imaps.org
Michael O'Donoghue, Executive Director
Rick Mohn, Operations Manager
Brian Schieman, Director Information Technology
Ann Bell, Manager Marketing/Communications
March

5966 International Conference on Trends in Welding Research
Minerals, Metals & Materials Society
184 Thorn Hill Road
Warrendale, PA 15086-7514
724-776-9000
FAX: 724-776-3770
foundation@tms.org www.tms.org
Tresa Pollock, President
Brajendra Mishra, VP
Alexander Scott, Executive Director
John Parsey, Financial Planning Officer
Marc DeGraef, Director Information Technology
This conference will feature five days of technically intensive programming focusing on both fundamental and applied topics related to welding and joining. Top researchers from industry, government, and academia will present the latest in experimental and modeling developments.
May

5967 International Symposium on Microelectronics
International Microelectronics & Electronics
611 2nd Street NE
Washington, DC 20002
202-548-4001
FAX: 202-548-6115 888-464-6277
imaps@imaps.org www.imaps.org
Michael O'Donoghue, Executive Director
Rick Mohn, Operations Manager
Brian Schieman, Director Information Technology
Ann Bell, Manager Marketing/Communications

Seeks original papers that demonstrate how new technologies and applications are expanding and redefining microelectronics between the chip and the system. All abstracts submitted must represent original, previously unpublished work.
September

5968 Materials, Science & Technology
Minerals, Metals & Materials Society
184 Thorn Hill Road
Warrendale, PA 15086-7514
724-776-9000
FAX: 724-776-3770
foundaton@tms.org www.tms.org
Tresa Pollock, President
Brajendra Mishra, VP
Alexander Scott, Executive Director
John Parsey, Financial Planning Officer
Marc DeGraef, Director Information Technology
Offers a materials science and applied technology event unlike any other. More than 40 symposia make MS&T 2005 the largest gathering.
September

5969 NCSLI Workshop & Symposium
NCSL
1800 30th Street
Suite 305 B
Boulder, CO 80301
303-440-3339
FAX: 303-440-3384 www.ncsli.org
Harry J Moody, President
William T Pound, Executive Director
Will provide a forum to discuss the impact of these advances have had on metrology, as well as other related issues. Please join us as we reflect on how far and fast metrology has progressed over the past quarter of a century and to discuss its future needs and directions.
1200 Attendees August, Washington

5970 NEDA Executive Conference
National Electronic Distributors Association
1111 Alderman Drive
Suite 400
Alpharetta, GA 30005-4175
678-393-9990
FAX: 678-393-9998
admin@nedassoc.org
www.nedassoc.org
Francis Flynn Jr, President
Robin B Gray Jr, Executive VP
Debbie Conyers, Director Marketing
Barney Martin, VP Industry Practices
November

5971 NMEA Convention & Expo
National Marine Electronics Association
Seven Riggs Avenue
Severna Park, MD 21146
410-975-9425
FAX: 410-975-9450
info@nmea.org www.nmea.org
Mark Young, Chairman
Jules Rutstein, Vice Chairman
Beth Kahr, Executive Director
Michael Cerchiaro, Treasurer
Christopher Harley, Secretary
October

5972 NPSC Meeting
National Electronics Service Dealers Association
3608 Pershing Avenue
Fort Worth, TX 76107-4527
817-921-9061
FAX: 817-921-3741 800-797-9197
webmaster@nesda.com
www.nesda.com
Brian Gibson, President
Don Cressin, VP
Mack Blakely, Executive Director
Fred Paradis, CSM, Treasurer
Wayne Markman, Secretary
Featuring Training, Sponsored Meal Events, Meetings, and Opportunities to Network with other service professionals as well as key service industry representatives.
July

5973 Northwest Electronics Technology Conference
Electronic Conventions Management
8110 Airport Boulevard
Los Angeles, CA 90045-3119
310-215-3976
FAX: 310-641-5117 800-877-2668
northcon@ieee.org www.northcon.org

James Lipman, PhD, Conference Director
Sue Kingston, Trade Show Manager
Offers a concentrated technical conference with complimenting exhibits. It provides a venue where those involved with the design, production and marketing of electronics-related products can converge in a real time, interactive atmosphere.
7000 Attendees May

5974 OEMBoston
Canon Communications
11444 W Olympic Boulevard
Suite 900
Los Angeles, CA 90064-1549
310-445-4200
FAX: 310-445-4299
exhibit@concom.com
www.oemboston,com
William F Cobert, President/CEO
Diane O'Conner, Trade Show Director
Dan Cutrone, Show Marketing Director
The creation of two seperate shows, OEM Electronics and OEMed, the OEMBoston is accessible to thousands of electronics and medical OEMs, who can benefit from the combination of the two shows. The different product classification found at this show include Contract Manufacturing, Electronics Components, Component Fabrication, Production/Assembly Equipment, Packaging Equipment & Supplies, Tubing and more. Held at the Bayside Expo Center in Boston, Massachusetts.
1604 Attendees September

5975 OFC/NFOEC
Optical Society of America
2010 Massachusetts Avenue NW
Washington, DC 20036
202-223-8130
FAX: 202-223-1096
info@osa.org www.osa.org
Eric W Van Stryland, President
Elizabeth A Rogin, Executive Director
Colleen Morrison, Media Relations Manager
With more than 750 presentations focused on the industry's hottest topics, FTTx and ROADMs at the top of the list, the conference again established itself as the leading technical conference for optical communications. OFC/NFOEC is the show to present new product and corporate announcements.
15000 Attendees March Founded: 1916

5976 PhAST Conference
Optical Society of America
2010 Massachusetts Avenue NW
Washington, DC 20036-1023
202-223-8130
202-223-1096
info@osa.org www.osa.org
Elizabeth A Rogin, Executive Director
Tony Keane, COO
John Childs, Senior Director Publications
Cynthia Gady, Senior Director Meetings
Deborah C Herrin, Senior Director IT
Will feature previews of new application areas, access to industry innovators and discussions of the engineering ideas behind new products.
May

5977 SEMI Expo CIS
Semiconductor Equipment & Materials International
1401 K Street NW
Suite 601
Washington, DC 20005
202-289-0440
FAX: 202-289-0441
semide@semi.org www.semi.org
Stanley T Myers, President/CEO
Victoria Hadfield, Executive VP/President, N America
Will highlight CIS as a region with huge potential and a new developing market for the world semiconductor equipment and materials manufacturers.
September

5978 SEMICON/West
Semiconductor Equipment & Materials International
805 E Middlefield Road
Mountain View, CA 94043-4080
650-964-5111
FAX: 650-967-5375
semihq@semi.org www.semi.org
Stanley T Myers, President/CEO
Leslie Schade, Exhibitor Services
Anna Christiansen, Marketing
Offers a wide range of programs for 2005 - from exciting keynotes speakers to the latest in Emerging Technologies.
45000 Attendees July

5979 SESHA Annual Symposium
Semiconductor Environmental, Safety & Health Assn
1313 Dolly Madison Boulevard
Suite 402
McLean, VA 22101
703-790-1745
FAX: 703-790-2672
sesha@burkinc.com seshaonline.org
Bernie First, President
Brett Burk, Executive Director
Brian Sherin, Treasurer
Karl Albrecht, Secretary
For individuals employed within the electronics and related high technology industries with an interest in environmental, health and safety issues.
1235 Attendees May Founded: 1978

5980 SOUTHCON
Electronic Conventions
12340 Rosecrans Avenue
Suite 100
Manhattan Beach, CA 90266
310-524-4100
FAX: 310-643-7328 800-877-2668
exhibits@ecmshows.com
www.southcon.org

Susan Kingston, Show Manager

Companies attending represent a major cross-section of the electronics industry including consumer, computer, medical, automotive and others. Offers conference sessions, in-depth technical sessions, product demonstrations and exhibits by vendors.

10M Attendees March

5981 Semiconductor
Semiconductor Equipment & Materials International
1401 K Street NW
Suite 601
Washington, DC 20005
202-289-0440
FAX: 202-289-0441
semide@semi.org www.semi.org

Stanley T Myers, President/CEO
Victoria Hadfield, Executive VP/President, N America

The future of the European Semiconductor Industry.

June

5982 Sensors Expo & Conference
Advanstar Technology Group
7500 Old Oak Boulevard
Cleveland, OH 44130
440-243-8100
800-225-4569
pchan@advanstar.com
www.sensorsexpo.com
/www.advanstartech.com

Jeanne Duval, Exhibit Sales
Cathy Walters, Exhibit Contact

Leading sensors event in North America, featuring a conference program exploring the most up-to-date innovations in sensor technology including physical sensors, sensor networks, biosensors, MEMS/Nanotechnology, instrumentation and controls, intelligent systems, machine-to-machine communication, wireless sensing and IT technology.

June

5983 Service & Retail Convention
Electronics Technicians Association International
5 Depot Street
Greencastle, IN 46135
765-653-8262
FAX: 765-653-4287 800-288-3824
eta@eta-i.org www.eta-i.org

Randy Reusser, Chairman
Glen L Wolfe, Vice Chairman
Richard Glass, President
Teresa Maher, VP
Carolyn Carson, Special Projects Manager

February, Las Vegas

5984 Southeastern Technology Week
TEC
2001 Assembly Street
Suite 204
Columbia, SC 29201
803-779-7123
FAX: 803-772-9964 www.teconline.com

5985 Strategic Leadership and Networking Forum
Electronic Transactions Association
1101 16th Street NW
Suite 402
Washington, DC 20036
202-828-2635
FAX: 202-828-2639 800-695-5509

Jennifer Leo, Meetings Manager

A unique event designed to help executives thrive in the new payments industry. The Forum goes far beyond fundamental education to tackle the strategic, big-picture issues that today's payment executives and CEOs deal with each day. ETA takes a distinct approach to executive education and has adopted interactive formats conducive to peer-to-peer learning and business-to-business networking.

5986 Summer Technology & Standards Forum
Consumer Electronics Association
2500 Wilson Boulevard
Arlington, VA 22201
703-907-7600
FAX: 703-907-7675 866-858-1555

Loyd Ivey, Chair
Pat Lavelle, Vice Chair
Gary Shapiro, President/CEO

Focus on development of emerging industry standard, contribute your company's viewpoint, and gain networking opportunities. Take advantage of valuable opportunities to interface with industry technical leaders as they consider, develop, and finalize, crucial CE standards.

July

5987 TABES Technical Business Exhibition & Symposium
Huntsville Association of Technical Societies
3414 Governors Dr SW
PO Box 1964
Huntsville, AL 35805
256-882-1234
FAX: 205-837-4275
www.hats.org/society

J Tardy, Manager

Brings new business into the community.

10000 Attendees Founded: 1969

5988 TMS Annual Meeting & Exhibition
Minerals, Metals & Materials Society
184 Thorn Hill Road
Warrendale, PA 15086-7514
724-776-9000
FAX: 724-776-3770
foundation@tms.org www.tms.org

Teresa Pollock, President
Brajendra Mishra, VP
Alexander Scott, Executive Director
John Parsey, Financial Planning Officer
Marc DeGraef, Director Information Technology

Offers the latest breakthroughs in materials research, the most important technological advances, and the newest product developments to solutions for current issues in your workplace.

March

5989 Tech Advantage Exposition
National Rural Electric Cooperative Association
4301 Wilson Blouevard
Arlington, VA 22203
703-907-5500
FAX: 703-907-5528 www.nreca.org

Gary Pfann, Conference Contact
Barbara Christiana, Expo Contact

11000 Attendees

5990 Technical Conference
Optical Society of America
2010 Massachusetts Avenue NW
Washington, DC 20036
202-223-8130
FAX: 202-223-1096
info@osa.org www.osa.org

Elizabeth A Rogin, Executive Director
Tony Keane, COO
John Childs, Senior Director Publications
Cynthia Gady, Senior Director Meetings
Deborah C Herrin, Senior Director IT

Connect with the most accomplished international scientists, researchers, engineers and business leaders as they shape the future of optics, photonics, and laser science.

October

5991 WESCON
Electronic Conventions Management
12340 Rosecrans Avenue
Manhattan Beach, CA 90266
310-524-4100
FAX: 310-641-5117

40000 Attendees

5992 Xplor Int'l Global Electronic Document Systems Conference Exhibition
Xplor International
24238 Hawthorne Blouevard
Torrance, CA 90505
310-373-3633
FAX: 310-375-4240
info@xplor.org www.xplor.org/contact

Phyllis Palmer, President

20000 Attendees

Directories & Databases

5993 Antenna Book
Electronic Technicians Association International
5 Depot Street
Greencastle, IN 46135-1035
765-653-8262
FAX: 765-653-4287 800-288-3824
eta@tds.net www.eta-i.com

Richard Glass, President
Teresa Maher, VP
Jeff Osborn, CSS, Director Marketing
Carolyn Carson, Special Projects Manager

Written by professional technicians who have worked closely with antennas, this two book series is the ultimate study guide for technicians seeking certification through ETA-I's Video Distribution, Certified Satellite Installer and TVRO programs. It can also serve as study materials for electronics classes, employee training, or as a quick reference guide your whole shop can use. Includes shipping & handling. *$33.00*

ISBN 1-891749-14-5
Printed in on matte stock

5994 Battery Report
Power Sources Manufacturers Association

PO Box 418
Mendham, NJ 07945
973-543-9660
FAX: 973-543-6207
power@psma.org www.psma.org

Arnold Alderman, Chairman
Marshall Miles, President
Joe Horzepa, Executive Director
Bruce Miller, VP/Treasurer
Kevin Parmenter, Secretary

Is a comprehensive report describing the state-of-the-art, current problems and R&D needs for numerous battery systems. The report also includes battery global market trends, status of electric/hybrid vehicle battery development and UN requirements for shipping lithium. *$ 125.00*

5995 Color TFT Liquid Crystal Displays

Semiconductor Equipment & Materials International
1401 K Street NW
Suite 601
Washington, DC 20005
202-289-0440
FAX: 202-289-0441
semide@semi.org www.semi.org

Stanley T Myers, President/CEO
Victoria Hadfield, Executive VP/President, N America

The book discribes the fundamentals of liquid crystal materials, including an explanation of the optical principles necessary to achieve usable images. *$95.00*
280 pages

5996 Computer & Consumer Electronics Products
Chain Store Guide
3922 Coconut Palm Drive
Tampa, FL 33619
813-276-6700
FAX: 813-627-6882 800-778-9794
info@csgis.com www.csgis.com

Chris Leedy, Advertising Sales
Shami Choon, Manager

Directory of US and Canadian computer and consumer electronics retailers. Bringing you access to more than 7,000 listings along with over 23,000 key personnel. *$335.00*

5997 Connecting Resources: A Primer for the Electronics Distribution
National Electronic Distributors Association
1111 Alderman Drive
Suite 400
Alpharetta, GA 30005-4175
678-393-9990
FAX: 678-393-9998
admin@nedassoc.org
www.nedassoc.org

Laurie Kane-Sellers, Author
Joan Koerber Walker, Author
Dr Ben Zoghi, Author

A complete reference manual for building lasting and profitable distribution relationships! This book deliver a comprehensive overview of the structure and challenges within the electronics distribution industry including: the history, players, business practices, policies and procedures, programs, systems, and trends. *$95.00*

5998 ERA Rep Locator
Electronics Representatives Association
444 N Michigan Avenue
Suite 1960
Chicago, IL 60611
312-527-3050
FAX: 312-527-3783 800-776-7377
info@era.org www.era.org

Mark Motsinger, Chairman
Dave Rossi, Vice Chairman
Mike Kunz, President
Raymond J Hall, EVP/CEO
William R Warfield, Director Finance/Operations

Manufacturers match your products and territories with qualified, professional representatievs firms. The Locator lists ERA member companies with informtion on size of firm, territories covered, type of products represented and customer bases. *$90.00*
Annually

5999 Electronic Buyers News: Specialized and Local/Regional Directory
CMP Publications
600 Community Drive
Manhasset, NY 11030-3847
516-625-5000
FAX: 516-562-5123

Hailey McKeefry, Editor

List of about 325 distributors of electronic products and supplies operating on less than national scale, or offering only one or a few produst nationwide.

6000 Electronic Buyers News: Top 50 Distributors Issue
CMP Publications
600 Community Drive
Manhasset, NY 11030-3847
516-625-5000
FAX: 516-562-5123

David Gabel, Editor

List of electronic distributors ranked by annual gross sales.

6001 Electronic Distribution Directory
Electronic Distribution Show Corporation
222 S Riverside Plaza
Suite 2160
Chicago, IL 60606-6160
312-648-1140
FAX: 312-648-4282
eds@edsc.org www.edsc.org

Gretchen Oie-Weghurst, Trade Show Manager

6002 Electronic Industries Association: Trade Directory and Membership List
Electronic Industries Alliance
2500 Wilson Boulevard
Arlington, VA 22201-3834
703-907-7500
FAX: 703-907-7501 www.eia.org

Dave McCurdy, President/CEO
Charles L Robinson, Chief Operating Officer

More than 1,200 member companies in the electronic manufacturing industry.
Annual

6003 Electronic Materials & Process Handbook
International Microelectronics & Electronics
611 2nd Street NE
Washington, DC 20002
202-548-4001
FAX: 202-548-6115 888-464-6277
imaps@imaps.org www.imaps.org

Charles A Harper, Editor
Ronald M Sampson, Editor

Offers guidance on insulations, conductors, and semiconductor materials, defines critical manufacturing parameters, and shows how these parameters can be combined to create successful electronic devices. *$80.00*
ISBN 0-070542-99-6

6004 Electronic Representatives Directory
Harris Publishing Company
360 B Street
Idaho Falls, ID 83402-1938
208-524-4217
FAX: 208-522-5241
www.harrispublishing.com
Directory of services and supplies to the industry. *$25.00*
320 pages Annual
Circulation: 7,500

6005 Electronics Manufacturers Directory on Diskette
Harris InfoSource International
2057 E Aurora Road
Twinsburg, OH 44087-1938
330-425-9000
FAX: 330-425-7150 800-888-5900

Frances Carlsen, Editor

Diskette. Covers approximately 1,000,000 manufacturers of electronic equipment and products. *$329.00*
Annual

6006 Handbook of Hybrid Microelectronics
International Microelectronics & Electronics
611 2nd Street NE
Washington, DC 20002
202-548-4001
FAX: 202-548-6115 888-464-6277
imaps@imaps.org www.imaps.org

Jerry Sergent, Editor
Charles Harper, Editor

Provides data, information, and guidelines to all who design, manufacture, and use hybrid microcircuits, as well as thos who develop and market parts and materials for hybrids. *$90.00*
800 pages ISBN 0-070266-91-3

6007 Low Voltage Study - The Workshop Report
Power Sources Manufacturers Association

PO Box 418
Mendham, NJ 07945
973-543-9660
FAX: 973-543-6207
power@psma.com www.psma.com

Arnold Alderman, Chairman
Marshall Miles, President
Joe Horzepa, Executive Director
Bruce Miller, VP/Treasurer
Kevin Parmenter, Secretary

This workshop concentrated on the effects that constantly declining microprocessor voltages have on the power products. The companies and individuals that participated in the workshop represented a good cross section of the power supply industry and the end user companies. *$ 125.00*

6008 Microchip Fabrication
Semiconductor Equipment & Materials International
1401 K Street NW
Suite 601
Washington, DC 20005
202-289-0440
FAX: 202-289-0441
semide@semi.org www.semi.org
Peter Van Zant, Author
Victoria Hadfield, President North America
This textbook is written specificaly for industry personnel - such as semiconductor plant operators, new engineers and support staff in training, production control, design, and administration who need this kind of comprehensive information. In addition, salespeople, marketing and communications managers, and product designers who supply the industry with high-tech equipment and materials will find this book a valuable resource. *$58.50*
Fourth Edition

6009 Microchip Manufacturing
Semiconductor Equipment & Materials International
1401 K Street NW
Suite 601
Washington, DC 20005
202-289-0440
FAX: 202-289-0441
semide@semi.org www.semi.org
Stanley Wolfe, PhD, Author
Provides detailed technical content about microchip manufacturing in an easy-to-read format. It explains all aspects of this fascinating and important technology, from introductory material on the semiconductor industry, to test, chemicals and safety. It also describes the latest technologies, including copper interconnects, CMP, dual-damascene, low-k dielectrics, and 300-mm wagers, and provides a discussion of diffusion, oxidation, lithography, ion implantation, etching CVD, and PVD. *$113.00*
564 pages

6010 North American Directory of Contract Electronic Manufacturers
Miller Freeman Publications
600 Harrison Street
Suite 400
San Francisco, CA 94107-1391

FAX: 415-905-2239
www.cassembly.com
Kimberly Cassidy, Editor
Over 1,350 electronics manufacturers facilities in the United States, Canada, and Mexico. *$295.00*
Annual

6011 Power Technology Roadmap from APEC
Power Sources Manufacturers Association
PO Box 418
Mendham, NJ 07945
973-543-9660
FAX: 973-543-6207
power@psma.org www.psma.org
Arnold Alderman, Chairman
Marshall Miles, President
Joe Horzepa, Executive Director
Bruce Miller, VP/Treasurer
Kevin Parmenter, Secretary
Focuses on the needs of the users and identifies technology trends over the next five years. Then, the power supply designers and manufacturers discussed the same topic from their perspective, responding to the challenges set forth by the users. *$495.00*

6012 ProService Directory and Yearbook

National Electronics Service Dealers Association
3608 Pershing Avenue
Fort Worth, TX 76107-4527
817-921-9061
FAX: 817-921-3741 800-797-9197
webmaster@nesda.com
www.nesda.com
Clyde Nabors, Publisher
Wallace Harrison, Editor
Mary Margaret Merill, Production Manager
The yearbook is an annual resource listing for servicers. This directory is sent each January to current members.
Annual

6013 Product Source Guide for Electronic Devices
Reed Business Information
275 Washington Street
Newton, MA 02458
617-964-3030
FAX: 617-558-4470
sales@eb-mag.com
www.reedbusiness.com
Donald Swanson, Editor
List of over 4,000 manufacturers and suppliers of equipment and materials used in the production, testing, and packaging of electronic devices and systems. *$25.00*
Annual

6014 Report from the PSMA Silicon Integration Project
Power Sources Manufacturers Association
PO Box 418
Mendham, NJ 07945
973-543-9660
FAX: 973-543-6207
power@psma.org www.psma.org
Arnold Alderman, Chairman
Marshall Miles, President
Joe Horzepa, Executive Director
Bruce Miller, VP/Treasurer
Kevin Parmenter, Secretary
Experts from the industry reviewed three paths to Integration and provided PSMA members insight as to how best to approach these difficult alternatives. The Silicon Integration Workshop Report includes all of the Workshop presentation material plus a set of decision tree flow charts to walk the reader through their own path to integration. *$249.00*
Two-Volume

6015 Source Book
Armed Forces Communications and Electronics Assn
4400 Fair Lakes Court
Fairfax, VA 22033-3899
703-311-1397
FAX: 703-631-6169 800-336-4583
promo@afcea.org www.afea.org
Eugene C Renzi, Chairman
Herb Browne, President/CEO
Becky Nolan, Executive VP
Paul E Tobin, Jr, Executive Director
Robert Howell, RN, General Manager
The Source Book published in the January issue, contains the company profiles and contacts of AFCEA's corporate members. It is the who's who of C$ISR and homeland security organizations. The annual Security Directory, published in the February issue, focuses on security solutions and the organizations that provide them.

6016 Transformers for Electronic Circuits
Power Sources Manufacturers Association
PO Box 418
Mendham, NJ 07945
973-543-9660
FAX: 973-543-6207
power@psma.com www.psma.com
Arnold Alderman, Chairman
Marshall Miles, President
Joe Horzepa, Executive Director
Bruce Miller, VP/Treasurer
Kevin Parmenter, Secretary
It is a complete, one-stop guide to transformer and inductor design and applications for everyone who designs, builds, or uses power magnetics components. *$75.00*
Second Edition Reprint

6017 Who's Who in Electronics Buyer's Guide
Harris Publishing Company
360 B Street
Idaho Falls, ID 83402-1938
208-524-4217
FAX: 208-522-5241
www.harrispublishing.com
A list of over 15,000 manufacturers and distributors of electronics products in five regional volumes. *$65.00*
Annual
Circulation: 60,000

6018 Wire Bonding in Microelectroncis Materials , Processes, Reliability & Yield
International Microelectronics & Electronics
611 2nd Street NE
Washington, DC 20002
202-548-4001
FAX: 202-548-6115 888-464-6277
imaps@imaps.org www.imaps.org
George Harman, Editor
Offers the hands-on guidance that is needed to test wire bonds, clean bond pads to improve bonability and reliability, solve other mechanical problems, bond wires to multichip modules, and much, more. The book also includes up-to-the-minute details on utilizing fine pitch, and applying new bonding metallurgies, wire sweep, and the wire bonding mechanism. *$65.00*

Industry Web Sites

6019 www.afcea.org
Armed Forces Communications and Electronics Assn

An association that represents the professional communications, electronics, intelligence and information systems community.

6020 **www.aprovision.org**
Association of Progressive Rental Organizations

Members include television, appliance and furniture dealers who rent merchandise with an option to purchase.

6021 **www.era.org**
Electronics Representatives Association

Provides services and benefits to electronic industry manufacturers representatives.

6022 **www.eta-i.org**
Electronic Technicians Association International

A worldwide professional association founded by electronics technicians and servicing dealers.

6023 **www.ewh.ieee.org**
Instrumentation and Measurement Society

A subsidiary of the Institute of Electrical and Electronics Engineers. Provides support to scientists and technicians who design and develop electrical and electronic measuring instruments and equipment.

6024 **www.greyhouse.com**
Grey House Publishing

Selected Grey House directories in the fields of business, health and education are available online. Users can search our online databases by several different search criteria, such as product categories, geographic area, sales volume and much, much more. Full Grey House catalog and online ordering also available.

6025 **www.imaps.org**
International Microelectronics & Packaging Society

Dedicated to the advancement and growth of the use of microelectronics and electronic packaging through public and professional education, dissemination of information by means of symposia, workshops and conferences and promotion of the Society's portfolio of technologies.

6026 **www.ipc.org**
IPC-Association Connecting Electronics Industries

Works to develop standards in circuit board assembly equipment. Brings together all players in the electronic interconnection industry, including designers, board manufacturers, assembly companies, suppliers and original equipment manufacturers. Offers workshops, conferences, meetings and online communications.

6027 **www.iscet.org**
Int'l Society of Certified Electronics Technicians

Designed to measure the degree of theoretical knowledge and technical proficiency of practicing technicians.

6028 **www.nesda.com**
National Electronics Service Dealers Association

A national trade association for professionals in the business repairing consumer electronics equipment, appliances, and computers. NESDA has an e-mail group of over 600 members and manufacturers that communicate daily for information sharing. NESDA also has an annual convention and trade show.

6029 **www.nmea.org**
National Marine Electronics Association

The unifying force behind the entire marine electronics industry, bringing together all aspects of the industry for the betterment of all in the business.

6030 **www.psma.com**
Power Sources Manufacturers Association

Worldwide membership consists of manufacturers of power sources and conversion equipment. Nonprofit association strives to integrate the resources of the power sources industry to more effectively and profitably serve the needs of the power sources users, providers and PSMA members. Educates the electronics industry and others on the relevant applications for power sources and conversion devices.

6031 **www.semi.org**
Semiconductor Equipment & Materials International

Strengthens the performance of member companies through lobbying, promotion, education and statistical research.

6032 **www.seshaonline.org**
Semiconductor Environmental, Safety & Health Assn

Members are individuals employed within the electronics and related high technology industries with an interest in environmental, health and safety issues.

6033 **www.sia-online.org**
Semiconductor Industry Association

Trade association representing the US microchip industry.

6034 **www.sme.org**
Society of Manufacturing Engineers

Represents the electrical manufacturers.

6035 **www.smta.org**
Surface Mount Technology Association

A network of professionals building skills, sharing practical experience and developing solutions in electronic assembly technologies and related business operations.

Associations

6036 **ASFE/The Best People on Earth**
8811 Colesville Road
Suite G106
Silver Spring, MD 20910
301-565-2733
FAX: 301-589-2017
info@asfe.org www.asfe.org

John P Bachner, Executive Vice President

Not-for-profit trade association. Helps geo professional, environmental and civil engineering firms profit through professionalism.

300 Members Founded: 1969 2,500 names $100 per M.

6037 **ASME International Gas Turbine Institute**
5775-C Glenridge Drive
Suite 115
Atlanta, GA 30328-5364
404-847-0072
FAX: 404-847-0151
bob.macdonald@airqualityweb.com
www.asme.org

Richard E Feigel, President
Virgil R Carter, Executive Director
David Soukup, Managing Director Operations

Supports all those involved with engineering and energy technology.

12500 Members Founded: 1958

6038 **ASTM International**
100 Barr Harbor Drive
PO Box C700
West Conshohocken, PA 19428-2959
610-329-9500
FAX: 610-832-9555
service@astm.org www.astm.org

James Thomas, President
Kenneth Pearson, VP
Kathleen Kono, VP Global Cooperation
Teresa Cendrowska, Director External Relations

Not-for-profit organization that provides a global forum for the development and publication of voluntary consensus standards for materials, products, systems and services. Members are over 30,000 individuals who are users, producers, consumers and representatives of academia and government. Formerly known as the American Society for Testing and Materials.

30000 Members Founded: 1898

6039 **AVS Science & Technology Society**
120 Wall Street
32nd Floor
New York, NY 10005-3993
212-248-0200
FAX: 212-248-0245 www.avs.org

Christie R Marian, President
John Coburn, Treasurer
Joseph J Greene, Clerk/Secretary
Yvonne Towse, Executive Director

AVS is a resource for scientists, engineers, industrialists, students and educators.

6000 Members Founded: 1963

6040 **Abrasive Engineering Society**
141 Moore Road
Butler, PA 16001
724-282-6210
FAX: 724-234-2376
aes@abrasiveengineering.com
www.abrasiveengineering.com

Doug Haynes, President
Ted Giese, Executive Director

Technical society promoting knowledge and understanding of abrasives.

500 Members Founded: 1957

6041 **Accreditation Board for Engineering and Technology**
111 Market Place
Suite 1050
Baltimore, MD 21202-4012
410-347-7700
FAX: 410-625-2238
info@abet.org www.abet.org

George D Peterson, Executive Director
Kate Aberle, Associate Executive Director
Mimi Traynor, Senior Administrative Assistant
Daniel B Hodge, Accreditation Director

Accreditation of engineering, technology and applied science educational programs.

31 Members Founded: 1932

6042 **Acoustical Society of America**
2 Huntington Quadrangle
Suite 1N01
Melville, NY 11747-4502
516-576-2360
FAX: 516-576-2377
asa@aip.org asa.aip.org

William A Yost, President
Donna L Neff, VP
Charles E Schmid, Executive Director
Elaine Moran, Manager

Supports all those involved with the acoustics industry.

7000 Members Founded: 1929

6043 **Adhesive & Sealant Council**
7979 Old Georgetown Road
Suite 500
Bethesda, MD 20814
301-986-9700
FAX: 301-986-9795
info@ascouncil.org
www.ascouncil.org

Alan R Longstreet, Chairman
Lawrence Sloan, President
Joseph Stevenson, Director Member Services

Supports all those involved in manufacturing products and equipment, raw materials, and consulting to the adhesive and sealant industry.

124 Members Founded: 1958

6044 **American Academy of Environmental Engineers**
130 Holiday Court
Suite 100
Annapolis, MD 21401
410-266-3311
FAX: 410-266-7653
academy@aaee.net www.aaee.net

Alan H Victory Jr, President
Stephen R Kellogg, VP
David Asselin, Executive Director
Matthew Dominy, Treasurer

Improves the standards of environmental engineering. Certifies those with the special knowledge of environmental engineering and supplies a list of certified engineers to the public. Publishes reference books and other matters of interest for the profession.

2500 Members Founded: 1955

6045 **American Association of Cost Engineers**
209 Prairie Avenue
Suite 100
Morgantown, WV 26501
304-296-8444
FAX: 304-291-5728 800-858-2678
info@aacei.org www.aacei.org

Philip D Larson, President
William E Kraus, VP Administration
Robert B Brown, VP Finance
Andy Dowd, Executive Director

Individuals interested in applying scientific principles to the solution of problems.

5500 Members Founded: 1956

6046 **American Association of Engineering Scientists**
1620 I (Eye) Street, NW
Suite 210
Washington, DC 20006-4028
202-296-2237
FAX: 202-296-1151 888-400-2237
info@aaes.org www.aaes.org

Thomas Price, Executive Director
Dan Bateson, Dir Engineering Workforce Commiss
Connie L Kyle, Office/Accounting Manager

Association for national, international, regional and Canadian organizations concerned with engineering and related fields.

10 Members Founded: 1958

6047 **American Automatic Control Council**
Northwestern University
c/o Dept of Electrical Eng, Wright State Univ
3640 Col Glenn Highway
Dayton, OH 45435
937-775-5062
FAX: 937-775-3936
pmisra@cs.wright.edu www.a2c2.org

A Galip Ulsoy, President
R Russell Rhinehart, Treasurer
Pradeep Misra, Secretary

Supports industry of automatic controls producers.

1M Members Founded: 1960

6048 **American Council of Engineering Companies**
1015 15th Street
8th floor NW
Washington, DC 20005-2605
202-347-7474
FAX: 202-898-0068
acec@acec.org www.acec.org

David A Raymond, President
Mary Ann Emely, VP Operations
TJ Schulz, Director Transportation
Steven Hall, Director Government Affairs
Charles Kim, General Counsel

Membership includes over 5,500 US firms engaged in a range of engineering works. Mission is to contribute to the nation's prosperity through advancing the interests of member firms.

55000 Members Founded: 1905

6049 **American Crystallographic Association**
Ellicott Station
PO Box 96
Buffalo, NY 14205-0096
716-569-9600
FAX: 716-898-8695
aca@hwi.buffalo.edu
www.hwi.buffalo.edu/aca

Louis Delbaere, President
Robert Bau, VP
Douglas Ohlendorf, Treasurer
Lisa J Keefe, Secretary

Supports all those involved with hardware, software, and x-ray equipment for the crystal industry.

2200 Members May Founded: 1949

6050 American Engineering Assocation
4116 S Carrier Parkway
Suite 280-809
Grand Prairie, TX 75052
972-264-6428

info@aea.org www.aea.org

A national nonprofit professional association founded for the protection of high-wage American technology jobs.

Founded: 1979

6051 American Institute of Chemical Engineers
3 Park Avenue
New York, NY 10016-5991
212-197-7676
FAX: 301-843-0159
xpress@aiche.org www.aiche.org

Joe Cramer, Director Programming
Darlene Schuster, Senior Director
Betty Feehan, Senior Manager Career Services
Cathy Diana, Director Human Resources
John Sofranko, Executive Director

Professional association of more than 50,000 members, providing leadership in advancing the chemical engineering profession. Members are those who develop processes and design and operate manufacturing plants, as well as researchers who assure the safe and environmentally sound manufacture, use and disposal of chemical products.

50000 Members Founded: 1908

6052 American Institute of Physics
One Physics Ellipse
College Park, MD 20740-3843
301-209-3100

asa@aip.org www.aip.org

Marc Brodsky, Executive Director/CEO
Richard Baccante, Treasurer/CFO
Wendy Marriott, Director Business Systems & Ops

Supports all those involved with the principles, devices and techniques in scientific instrumentation.

Founded: 1931

6053 American Nuclear Society
555 North Kensington Avenue
La Grange Park, IL 60526
708-352-6611
FAX: 708-352-0499 www.ans.org

E James Reinsch, President
Harry Bradley, Executive Director
William F Naughton, Treasurer

Serves its members in their efforts to develop and safely apply nuclear science and technology for public benefit through knowledge exchange, professional development, and enhanced public understanding.

Founded: 1954

6054 American Oil Chemists Society
2211 W Bradley Avenue
Champaign, IL 61821
217-359-2344
FAX: 217-351-8091
general@aocs.org www.aocs.org

Michael Haas, President
Howard Knapp, VP
Jean Wills, Executive VP
Casimir Akoh, Secretary
Greg Reed, Manager

A global forum to promote the exchange of ideas, information, and experience, to enhance personal excellence, and to provide high standards of quality among those with a professional interest in the science and technology of fats, oil, surfactants, and related materials.

5400+ Members Founded: 1909

6055 American Society for Engineering Education
1818 N Street NW
Suite 600
Washington, DC 20036-2476
202-331-3500
FAX: 202-265-8504
prism@asee.org www.asee.org

Ronald E Barr, President
Frank L Huband, Executive Director
Arthur T Murphy, VP/Finance

Supports all those educators in the engineering technology fields.

12000 Members Founded: 1893

6056 American Society for Precision Engineering
PO Box 10826
Raleigh, NC 27605-0826
919-839-8444
FAX: 919-839-8039
webmaster@aspe.net www.aspe.net

Michele H Miller, Chairperson
David L Trumper, President
Steven R Patterson, VP
Thomas Dow, Executive Director
Vivek G Badami, Director at Large/Secretary

Members are from academia, industry and government, and include professionals in engineering, materials science, physics, chemistry, mathematics and computer science. Multidisciplinary professional and technical society concerned with precision engineering research and development, design and manufacturing of high accuracy components and systems. Member and nonmember rates for annual meetings, spring and summer topical meetings, books and video tapes. Membership is $65 regular, $30 student.

Founded: 1986

6057 American Society for Quality
600 N Plankinton Avenue
Milwaukee, WI 53203
414-272-8575
FAX: 414-272-1734 800-248-1946
help@asq.org www.asq.org

Kenneth E Case, Chairman
Jerry Mairani, President
Gary D Floss, VP
Paul Borawski, Executive Director

ASQ's mission is to facilitate continuous improvement and increase customer satisfaction. Promotes quality principles, concepts and technologies. Provides information, contacts and opportunities to make things better in the workplace, in communities and in people's lives.

104M Members Founded: 1946

6058 American Society of Agricultural and Biological Engineers
2950 Niles Road
Saint Joseph, MI 49085
269-429-0300
FAX: 269-429-3852 800-371-2723
hq@asabe.org www.asabe.org

Melissa Moore, Executive VP
Donna Hull, Publication Director
Michael Chesser, Director Meetings/Conferences
Scott Cedarqurst, Standards Director
Mark Crossley, Membership Director

A professional association of members with an international interest in engineering knowledge and technology for the food industry. *$10.00*

9000 Members Membership Fees Vary
Founded: 1907

6059 American Society of Certified Engineering
PO Box 1348
Flowery Branch, GA 30542
770-967-9173
FAX: 770-967-8049
kurt_schuler@ascet.org
www.ascet.org

Russell E Freier, Chairman
Leo Saenz, CET, President
Kurt Schuler, Secretary/Treasurer

Strives to obtain recognition of engineering technicians as essential to the engineering scientific team. Provides a forum for discussion of employment issues and improvement of the professional status of engineering technicians.

2000 Members Founded: 1964

6060 American Society of Civil Engineers
1801 Alexander Bell Drive
Reston, VA 20191-4400
703-295-6000
FAX: 703-295-6222 800-548-2723
cybrarian@asce.org www.asce.org

Patricia Galloway, President
Lawrence Roth, Deputy Executive Director
Patrick Natale, Secretary/Treasurer

Professional association of engineers and scientists working in civil and structural engineering, applied mechanics and engineering science, aeronautics and astronautics.

Annual

6061 American Society of Gas Engineers

2805 Barranca Parkway
Irvine, CA 92606
949-733-4304
FAX: 949-733-4320
jerry.moore@csa-international.org
www.asge-national.org

Daryl Hosler, President
Dante Cantal, VP
Jerry Moore, Executive Director

Supports all engineers in the gas industry.

300 Members Founded: 1954

6062 American Society of Heating, Refrigeration & Air-Conditioning Engineers
1791 Tullie Circle NE
Atlanta, GA 30329
404-636-8400
FAX: 404-321-5478 800-527-4723
ashrae@ashrae.org www.ashrae.org

Terry E Townsend, President
Jeff H Littleton, Executive VP

W Stephen Comstock, Director Communications & Pubs

ASHRAE will advance the arts and sciences of heating, ventilation, air-conditioning and refrigeration and related human factors to serve humanity and promote a sustainable world. *$590.00*

55000 Members Monthly Founded: 1894 Circulation: 55000

6063 American Society of Mechanical Engineers
Three Park Avenue
New York, NY 10016-5990
212-917-7740
FAX: 973-882-1167 800-843-2763
infocentral@asme.org www.asme.org

Richard E Feigel, President
Virgil Carter, Executive Director
David Soukup, Managing Director Operations
John Panza, List Rental Manager

Supports the training and education of mechanical engineers.

12000 Members Founded: 1880

6064 American Society of Naval Engineers
1452 Duke Street
Alexandria, VA 22314-3458
703-836-6727
FAX: 703-836-7491
asnehq@navalengineers.org
www.navalengineers.org

David Sargent, President
Paul Sullivan, VP
Capt Dennis Krusent, Executive Director

Naval engineering includes all arts construction and sciences as applied in research, development design, construction, operation, maintenance, and logistic support of: surface/sub-surface ships and marine craft.

Founded: 1946

6065 American Society of Petroleum Operations Engineers
301 East Culpeper Street
Culpeper, VA 22701
703-768-4159
800-918-8962
info@aspoe.org www.aspoe.org

John B Stanley, President
Gerald Holton, VP
Harry Lyon, Executive VP
Coles Marsh, Treasurer
Cheryl George, Secretary

Works to stimulate interest from the academic world in the qualifications necessary to become a Petroleum Operations Engineer.

Founded: 1976

6066 American Society of Plumbing Engineers
8614 Catalpa Avenue
Suite 1007
Chicago, IL 60656-1116
773-693-2773
FAX: 773-695-9007
info@aspe.org www.aspe.org

J Joe Scott II, President
Norman Parks, VP Education
Julius A Ballanco, VP Technical
Ray W Moore, VP Membership
Stan Wolson, Executive Director

Supports all those engineers in the plumbing industry.

7500 Members Founded: 1964

6067 American Society of Safety Engineers
1800 E Oakton Street
Des Plaines, IL 60018
847-699-2929
FAX: 847-768-3434
customerservice@asse.org
www.asse.org

Jack H Dobson Jr CSP, President
Donald S Jones, SVP
Fred J Fortman, Executive Director/Secretary
Richard Nugent, VP Finance

Nonprofit, global organization that works to advance the technical, scientific, managerial and ethical knowledge and skills of occupational safety, heath and envionmental professionals, and is committed to protecting people, property and the envionnment. Offers education, technical publications, involvement in safety standards development, annual conferences, and more.

30000 Members Founded: 1911

6068 American Society of Sanitary Engineering
901 Canterbury
Westlake, OH 44145
440-835-3040
FAX: 440-835-3488
info@asse-plumbing.org
www.asse-plumbing.org

Rand Ackroyd, President
Sean Cleary, First VP
Robert Cross, Second VP
Shannon Corcoran, Executive Director
Marla Gasser, Manager

Members are from all segments of the plumbing industry, including contractors, engineers, inspectors, journeymen, apprentices and others who are involved in various segments of the industry. Provides information, an opportunity to exchange ideas, solve problems and offers a forum where all sides can express their views.

300 Members

6069 American Water Works Association

6666 W Quincy Avenue
Denver, CO 80235
303-794-7711
FAX: 303-347-0804 800-926-7337

Jack W Hoffbuhr, Executive Director

Dedicated to the improvement of drinking water quality and supply. AWWA is defined by six core competencies, through which we communicate and interact with all of our audiences.

57K Members Founded: 1881

6070 Applied Technology Council
201 Redwood Shores Parkway
Suite 240
Redwood City, CA 94065
650-595-1542
FAX: 650-593-2320
atc@atcouncil.org www.atcouncil.org

Tom Mclane, Director Business Development
Christopher Rojahn, Executive Director
Bernadette Mosby, Operations Manager

Nonprofit, tax-exempt corporation established through the efforts of the Structural Engineers Association of California. ATC's mission is to develop and promote state-of-the-art, user-friendly, engineering resources and applications for use in mitigating the effects of natural and other hazards on the built environment.

300 Members Founded: 1973 350 names

6071 Associated Soil and Foundation Engineers
8811 Colesville Road
Suite G106
Silver Spring, MD 20910
301-565-2733
FAX: 301-589-2017
info@asfe.org www.asfe.org

Daniel L Harpstead PE, President
John P Bachner, Executive VP
Joseph Cibor, Secretary/Treasurer

Supports all those employees of engineering companies.

Founded: 1969

6072 Association for Facilities Engineering
8160 Corporate Park Drive
Suite 125
Cincinnati, OH 45242
513-489-2473
FAX: 513-247-7422
webmaster@afe.org www.afe.org

Ben Berrett, President
Michael Ireland, Executive Director
Lane T Pierce, CPE, Treasurer
Fred King, VP Marketing/Communications

Provides education, certification, technical information and other relevant information for plant and facility engineering operations and maintenance professionals worldwide.

5000 Members Founded: 1954

6073 Association for the Advancement of Cost
Advancement Cost Engineering Council
209 Prairie Avenue
Suite 100
Morgantown, WV 26501
304-296-8444
FAX: 304-291-5728 800-858-2678
info@aacei.org www.aacei.org

Philip D Larson, President
Andrew S Dowd Jr, Executive Director
Robert Brown, VP Finance
William Kraus, VP Administration

Serves cost management professionals, cost engineers, project managers, planners, estimators and bidders.

6000 Members Founded: 1956

6074 Association of Energy Engineers
4025 Pleasantdale Road
Suite 420
Atlanta, GA 30340
770-447-5083
FAX: 770-446-3969
webmaster@aeecenter.org
www.aeecenter.org

Timothy B Janos, President
Albert Thumann, Executive Director
Paul Goodman, Treasurer
Laurie Wiegand-Jackson, Secretary

Membership organization of over 8,000 professionals and certification programs in the fields of energy efficiency, utility deregulation, facility management, plant engineering and environmental compliance. Offers seminars, conferences, books to critical buyer-seller, networking trade shows, job listings and certification programs.

8.2M Members Founded: 1977

6075 Association of Engineering Firms
8811 Colesville Road
Suite G106
Silver Spring, MD 20910-4343
301-585-0860
FAX: 301-589-2017
info@asfe.org www.asfe.org
Supports all those employees of engineering companies.

6076 Association of Engineering Geologists
300 South Jackson Street, Suite 100
PO Box 460518
Denver, CO 80246-0518
303-757-2926
FAX: 303-757-2969
aeg@aegweb.org www.aegweb.org
David Bieber, President
Darrel Schmitz, VP
Becky Roland, Chief Staff Executive
Meets the professional needs of geologists who are applying their scientific training and experience to the broad field of civil and environmental engineering. Mission is to provide leadership in the development and application of geologic principles and knowledge to serve engineering, environmental and public needs.
3000 Members Founded: 1957
Mailing list available for rent 3000 names $100 per M.

6077 Association of Higher Education Facilities
1643 Prince Street
Alexandria, VA 22314-2818
703-684-1446
FAX: 703-549-2772
maryjane@appa.org www.appa.org
Brooks H Baker III, President
E Lander Medlin, Executive VP
Chong-Hie Choi, Senior Director Finance
James O Roberts, Director Plant Operations
Vickie Younger, VP Educational Program

Supports those administrators involved with equipment and supplies for physical sites of higher education.
4500+ Members Founded: 1914

6078 Audio Engineering Society
60 E 42nd Street
Room 2520
New York, NY 10165-2520
212-661-8528
FAX: 212-682-0477
HQ@aes.org www.aes.org
Neil Gilchrist, President
Roger K Furness, Executive Director
Marshall Bcuk, Treasurer
Louis Fielder, Treasurer-Elect
Professional society devoted to audio technology. Membership includes leading engineers, scientists and other authorities in the field. Serves its members, the industry and the public by stimulating and facilitating advances in the constantly changing field of audio.

6079 BOCA Evaluation Services
4051 W Flossmoor Road
Country Club Hills, IL 60478-5795
708-799-2300
FAX: 800-214-7167 888-422-7233
boca@bocai.org
www.icsafe.org/news/about/#origin
John Nosse, President
James Lee Witt, Chief Executive Director
Karl Meuer, CFO/Finance & Administration
Carolina Khoury, Secretary
An independent nonprofit organization which conducts a voluntary program of evaluation of both traditional and innovative building materials, products and systems for compliance with BOCA National Codes.
14000 Members Founded: 1994

6080 Biomedical Engineering Society
8401 Corporate Dr
Ste 140
Hyattsville, MD 20785-2263
301-459-1999
FAX: 301-459-2444
info@bmes.org www.bmes.org
Frank C P Yin, President
Patricia I Horner, Executive Director
George A Truskey, Treasurer
Arthur T Johnson, Secretary
Supports all those involved in the biomedical engineering industry. *$150.00*
171 Members Monthly Founded: 1977

6081 Carnegie Mellon University: Information Networking Institute
Carnegie Mellon University
Electrical & Computer Engineering Department
4616 Henry Street
Pittsburgh, PA 15213
412-682-2905
FAX: 412-268-7196 www.ini.cmu.edu
Pradeep Khosia, Dean
Mike Niederberger, Business/Finance Administrator
Donald Shields, Director Development
Dean Haritos Tsamitis, Director Information Networking
Sean O'Leary, Manager
Focusing on professional degress programs combining economics, technologies and global communication networks - information security policies.
Founded: 1989

6082 Cold Regions Research and Engineering Laboratory
US Army Corps of Engineers
72 Lyme Road
Hanover, NH 03755-1290
603-646-4100
FAX: 603-646-4278
info@crrel.usace.army.mil
www.crrel.usace.army.mil/welcome
James L Wuebben, PE, Director
Dr Mary Albert, Research Mechanical Engineer
The mission of this Laboratory is to understand the characteristics of the cold regions of the world and to apply this knowledge to make it easier for people to live and work in those regions. For example, CRREL engineers have conducted a long-term program on the correct design of roofs in heavy snowfall areas.

6083 Conveyor Equipment Manufacturers Association (CEMA)
6724 Lone Oak Boulevard
Naples, FL 34109
239-514-3441
FAX: 239-514-3470
cema@cemanet.org www.cemanet.org
Tom Easterhouse, President
Fred Thimmel, VP
Robert Reinfreid, Executive Director
Involved in writing industry standards, the CEMA seeks to promote among its members and the industry standardization of design manufacture and application on a voluntary basis and in such manner as will not impede development of conveying machinery and component parts or lessen competition. CEMA sponsors an annual Engineering Conference that allows Member Company Engineers to meet and develop or improve CEMA Consensus Industry Standards and National Standards that affect the conveyor industry.
99 Members Founded: 1933

6084 Council of Engineer and Scientific Specialty Board
PO Box 1448
Annapolis, MD 21401-1448
410-266-3766
FAX: 410-721-1746
academy@aaee.net www.cesb.org
William C Anderson PE DEE, Executive Director
Accredits engineering, science and technology certification programs from professional to technician certificates.
Founded: 1990
Mailing list available for rent

6085 Engineering Workforce Commission
1828 L Street NW
Suite 906
Washington, DC 20036
202-331-1830
FAX: 202-296-1151 888-400-2237
info@aaes.org
www.ewc-online.org/contact
Dan Bateson, Director
David Gately, Media Contact
Carlos Miro, Manager
Provides representation to government groups dealing with professional manpower policy. Conducts surveys of engineering school enrollment degrees and salaries.
35 Members Founded: 1950

6086 Environmental Information Association
6935 Wisconsin Avenue
Suite 306
Chevy Chase, MD 20815
301-961-4999
FAX: 301-961-3094 888-343-4342
info@eia-usa.org www.eia-usa.org
Brent Kynoch, Managing Director
Kelly Rutt, Development & Communications Mgr
Lisa Mihalik, Membership/Meetings Coordinator
BJ Fungaroli, Board President
Vince Brennan, Board VP
Nonprofit organization dedicated to providing environmental information to individuals, members and industry. Disseminates information on the abatement of asbestos and lead-based paint, indoor air quality, safety and health issues, analytical issues and environmental site assessments.

6087 Ergosyst Associates
4840 W 15th Street
Suite 1012
Lawrence, KS 66049
785-842-7334
FAX: 785-842-7348

John Burch, Publisher

Association for those interested in economics/human factors.

6088 Federation of Materials Societies
910 17th Street NW
Suite 800
Washington, DC 20006
202-296-9282
FAX: 202-833-3014
betsyhou@ix.netcom.com
www.materialsocieties.org

Betsy Houston, FMS Executive Director
Iver Anderson, President

Promotes cooperation among societies concerned with the understanding, development and application of materials and processes.
700K Members Founded: 1972

6089 ICC Evaluation Service
5360 Workman Millroad
Whittier, CA 90601
562-699-0543
FAX: 562-695-4694
es@icc-es.org www.icc-es.org

Billy R Manning, President
Gary Nichols, VP

An independent, nonprofit organization that conducts a voluntary program of evaluation of both traditional and innovative building materials, products and systems for compliance with the three major model codes in the United States.
3 Members Founded: 2003

6090 Illuminating Engineering Society of North America
120 Wall Street
Floor 17
New York, NY 10005
212-248-5000
FAX: 212-248-5018
iesna@iesna.org www.iesna.org

Alan L Lewis OD PhD, President
William Hanley, Executive Director
Boyd Corbett, Treasurer
Sue Foley, Marketing Manager

To advance knowledge and disseminate information for the improvement of the lighted environment to the benefit of society. Publishes a monthly magazine.
10000 Members Founded: 1906

6091 Industrial Designers Society of America
45195 Business Court
Suite 250
Dulles, VA 20166
703-707-6000
FAX: 703-787-8501
idsa@idsa.org www.idsa.org

Bruce Claxton, Board Chair
Ron B Kemnitzer, President
Tim P Fletcher, Chapter VP
Kristina Goodrich, Executive Director/CEO
Larry Allen, Deputy Executive Director

Provides resources on research, industrial design processes, trends and viewpoints, new processes and materials, marketing, managing, and computer-aided designs for all those involved in industrial design.

6092 Industrial Fabrics Association International
1801 County Road BW
Roseville, MN 55113
651-222-2508
FAX: 651-631-9334 800-225-4324
generalinfo@ifai.com
www.ifai.com/index

George K Ochs, Chairman
Jeffrey W Kirk, IFM, First Vice Chairman
Scott C Campbell, Second Vice Chairman
Stephen M Warner, President
Mary J Hennessy, VP Communications
2000 Members

6093 Industrial Research Institute
2200 Clarendon Boulevard
Suite 1102
Arlington, VA 22201
703-647-2580
FAX: 703-647-2581 www.iriinc.org

Susan M Gaud, Chairman
R Kent Crawford, Vice Chairman
F M Ross Armbrecht, Jr, President
Margaret Grucza, Executive Director

The mission is to enhance the effectiveness of technological innovation industry.
Founded: 1938

6094 Institute of Industrial Engineers
3577 Parkway Lane
Suite 200
Norcross, GA 30092-2928
770-490-0461
FAX: 770-441-3295 800-494-0460

Susan M Sinclair, President
Don Greene, Executive Director
Christopher Barnes, Treasurer
Marc Resnick, PhD, Secretary

Supports all indutrial engineers with training, education, publications, conferences, etc.

6095 Institute of Noise Control Engineering
210 Marston Hall
Ames, IA 50011-2353
515-294-6142
FAX: 515-294-3528
ibo@inceusa.org www.inceusa.org

Paul Donavan, President
Joseph M Cuchieri, Interim Executive Director

Supports those involved with hearing protection, modal analysis, and signal processing.
1200 Members

6096 Instrumentation and Measurement Society
799 N Beverly Glen
Los Angeles, CA 90077
310-446-8280
FAX: 310-446-8390
bob.myers@ieee.org
www.ewh.ieee.org

Robert Myers, Executive Director

A subsidiary of the Institute of Electrical and Electronics Engineers. Provides support to scientists and technicians who design and develop electrical and electronic measuring instruments and equipment.
6500 Members Founded: 1950

6097 Insulated Cable Engineers Association
PO Box 1568
Carrollton, GA 30112
770-830-0369

info@icea.net www.icea.net

Lauri J Hiivala, President

Professional organization dedicated to developing cable standards for the electric power, control and telecommunications industries. Ensures safe, economical and efficient cable systems utilizing proven, state-of-the-art materials and concepts. ICEA documents are of interest to cable manufacturers, architects and engineers, utility and manufacturing plant personnel, telecommunication engineers, consultants and OEMs.
Founded: 1925

6098 International Reprographic Association
401 N Michigan Avenue
Chicago, IL 60611
312-245-1026
FAX: 312-527-6705 www.irga.com

Chuck Gremillion, President
Michael Shaw, VP
Steve Bova, CAE, Executive Director
Jeff Mitchell, Director Marketing
Mike Carter, Secretary/Treasurer

Represents entrepreneurial businesses serving the wide-format imaging needs of graphic arts, architectural, engineering, manufacturing, corporate, legal, retail, and POP industries.
Founded: 1927

6099 International Society Weighing/Measurement
15245 Shady Grove Road
Suite 130
Rockville, MD 20850
301-258-1115
FAX: 301-990-9771
staff@iswm.org www.iswm.org

Tom Mikan, Chairman
Steve Kendra, President
Richard Sharpe, VP
Douglas Morse, Treasurer
Bernd K Rau, Secretary

Supports all those involved in the weighing and measurement industry.

6100 International Society for Optical Engineering
1000 20th Street
P O Box 10
Bellingham, WA 98225-6705
360-676-3290
FAX: 360-647-1445 888-504-8171
spie@spie.org www.spie.org/

Dr Paul F McManamona, President
Kevin Harding, VP
Eugene G Arthurs, Executive Director
Robert E Fischer, Secretary/Treasurer

Serves the international, technical community as the premier provider of education, information, and resources covering optics, photonics, and their applications.
16000 Members Founded: 1955

6101 NACE International
1440 S Creek Drive
Houston, TX 77084-4906
281-228-6200
FAX: 281-228-6300 800-797-6223
trevor.eade@mail.nace.org
www.nace.org

Neil Thompson, President
Ralph G Pontillo, Executive Director/CAE
Cassie Davies, Director/Conferences/Exhibitions
Teri Elliott, Director/Marketing/Communications
Cliff Johnson, Director/Public Affairs

Advances the knowledge of corrosion engineering and science in all major industries through education, certification, standards, publications, and public awareness.

16000 Members Founded: 1943

6102 National Academy of Engineering
500 5th Street NW
Washington, DC 20001
202-334-3200
FAX: 202-334-2290 www.nae.edu

William A Wulf, President
Lance Davis, Executive Officer
Mary Lee Berger-Hughes, Membership Director

Promotes public understanding of the role that engineering plays in the technical fields. Sponsors programs aimed at meeting national needs in the field. Encourages research.

2000 Members Founded: 1964

6103 National Association of Minority Engineers
1133 W Morse Boulevard
Suite 201
Winter Park, FL 32789
407-647-8839
FAX: 407-629-2502
namepa@namepa.org
www.namepa.org

Leo Osgood, President
Phil Pyster, CAE, Executive VP
Latisha Moore, Assistant Executive Director
David Aragon, Treasurer
Carolyn Vallas, Secretary

Provides a communication network among college-level administrators of minority engineering programs.

575 Members

6104 National Board of Boiler and Pressure Vessel Inspectors
1055 Crupper Avenue
Columbus, OH 43229
614-888-8320
FAX: 614-888-0750
getinfo@nationalboard.org
www.nationalboard.org

Donald E Tanner, Executive Director
Connie Homer, Senior Executive Secretary

Membership is composed of chief boiler inspectors of states, major US cities and Canadian provinces having boiler laws.

55 Members Founded: 1919

6105 National Council of Examiners for Engineering and Surveying
280 Seneca Creek Road
PO Box 1686
Clemson, SC 29633-1686
864-654-6824
FAX: 864-654-6033 800-250-3196
pfenno@ncees.org www.ncees.org

Martin A Pederson LS, President
Betsy Browne, Executive Director
Jerry Carter, Associate Executive Director
Gregg E Brandow, PhD PE, Treasurer

Promotes uniform standards of registration and coordinates interstate registration of engineers and surveyors.

68 Members Founded: 1920

6106 National Institute for Certification in Technologies
1420 King Street
Alexandria, VA 22314
703-548-1518
800-787-0034
certify@nicet.org www.nicet.org

E Terence Foster, PhD PE, Chair
Lori A Allison, SET, Chair-Elect
Michael A Clark, General Manager

Issues certification to engineering technicians and technologists who voluntarily apply for certification and satisfy competency criteria through examinations and verification of work experience.

113K Members Founded: 1961

6107 National Society of Black Engineers
1454 Duke Street
Alexandria, VA 22314
703-549-2207
FAX: 703-683-5312
info@nsbe.org www.nsbe.org

Chancee Lundy, Chairperson
Candice M Dixon, Vice Chairperson
Justin Brown, National Parliamentarian
Jennifer Jasper, National Secretary
Carl Mack, Executive Director

Supports all black technical professionals involved in the manufacturing engineering industry.

15000 Members Founded: 1971

6108 National Society of Professional Engineers
1420 King Street
Alexandria, VA 22314-2794
703-684-2800
FAX: 703-836-4875
customer.service@nspe.org
www.nspe.org

Kathryn A Gray, President
Bradley F Aldrich, VP
Robert Miller, III, Treasurer

The mission of the Society is to promote the ethical, competent and licensed practice of engineering and to enhance the professional, social and economic well-being of its members.

60000 Members Founded: 1934

6109 North American Die Casting Association
241 Holbrook Drive
Wheeling, IL 60090-5809
847-279-0001
FAX: 847-279-0002
twarog@diecasting.org
www.diecasting.org

Daniel Twarog, President

The organization serves as the voice of the industry, promoting growth and enhancing member's ability to compete domestically in the gobal marketplace.

3700 Members Founded: 1989

6110 North American Manufacturing Research Institute
1 SME Drive
PO Box 930
Dearborn, MI 48121
313-271-1500
FAX: 313-271-2861 800-733-4763

Kristen Dudash, Manager

Members are engaged in manufacturing, research and technology development.

180 Members Founded: 1981

6111 Professional Engineers in Private Practice
1420 King Street
Alexandria, VA 22314-2750
703-684-2800
FAX: 703-836-4875 www.nspe.org

Fred Palmerton, PE, Chair
Larry L Britt, PE, Chair-Elect
Steve M Theno, PE, Secretary

Addresses the concerns of individual engineers in private practice, primarily working in design for construction. Offers resources, standard contracts, newsletters and management guidance in the forms of videos, books, and newsletters.

24M Members

6112 Railway Engineering: Maintenance Suppliers Association
417 West Broad Street
Suite 203
Falls Church, VA 22046
703-241-8514
FAX: 703-241-8589
home@remsa.org www.remsa.org

Thomas E Dickey, President
Jonathan D Reilly, VP
Judi Meyerhoeffer, Executive Director
Ronald C Olds, Secretary/Treasurer

Members are distributors and manufacturers of railway track machinery supplies and services.

199 Members Founded: 1965

6113 Refrigerating Engineers & Technicians Association
PO Box 1819
Salinas, CA 93902
831-455-8783
FAX: 831-455-7856
info@reta.com www.reta.com

Dave Murphy, President
Doug Sweet, Chairman
Stephan Shaub, Executive VP
Jim Barron, Treasurer
Edward Seffens, Vice President

Seeks to upgrade the skills and knowledge of experienced members. Offers home-study courses on refrigeration and air conditioning.

2300 Members Founded: 1910

6114 Refrigeration Service Engineers Society
1666 Rand Road
Des Plaines, IL 60016
847-976-6464
FAX: 847-297-5038
general@rses.org www.rses.org

Robb Isaacs, Executive VP
Mark Lowry, Director Operations
Jean Birch, Director Conferences
Kim Heselbarth, Marketing Director
Tim Gioe, Director Education

A leading education, training and certification association for heating, ventilation, air conditioning and refrigeration professionals. RSES certification includes the CM/CMS exam series (since 1935), National Technician certification (since 1985) and one of the largest EPA section 608 programs in the industry. A nonprofit organization of more than 18,700 members in the U.S. and Canada, as well as affiliate organizations world-wide.

19000 Members Founded: 1933

6115 **Reliability Engineering and Management Institute**
7340 N La Oesta Avenue
Tucson, AZ 85704-3119
520-297-2679
FAX: 520-621-8191
dimitri@u.arizona.edu
www.u.arizona.edu/~dimitri

Dr. Dimitri B Kececioglu, Executive Director

Supports all engineers and managers who deal with the issue of Reliability Engineering. Provides publications, training, education, new techniques and product forums and two annual conference.
Founded: 1963
Mailing list available for rent 44000 names

6116 **Research Council on Structural Connections**
Sargent & Lundy
55 E Monroe Street
Chicago, IL 60603-5780
312-269-2000
FAX: 312-269-3681
rshaw@steelstructures.com
www.boltcouncil.org

Ray Tide, Chairman Executive Committee
Geoff Kulak, Vice Chairman
Charles Carter, Chairman Membership/Funding
Emile Troup, Secretary/Treasurer

Researches the effects of stress on bolted and riveted joints for its member companies and institutions.
45 Members Founded: 1946

6117 **Robotics Industries Association**
900 Victors Way
PO Box 3724
Ann Arbor, MI 48106
734-994-6088
FAX: 734-994-3338
webmaster@robotics.org
www.robotics.org

Don Vincent, Executive VP
Brian Huse, Director Marketing/PR
Jim Adams, Marketing Manager
Sharon Adams, Accounting Manager
Jeff Burnstein, Executive Director

Trade group organized specifically to serve the robotics industry. Member companies inlude leading robot manufacturers, users, system integrators, component suppliers, research groups and consulting firms. Trade show is held every two years.
250+ Members Founded: 1974

6118 **Science and Technology Society**
120 Wall Street
32nd Floor
New York, NY 10005-3993
212-248-0200
FAX: 212-248-0245 www.avs.org

Christie R Marrian, President
John Coburn, Treasurer
Joseph E Greene, Clerk/Secretary

Supports all those in the vacuum industry, especially scientists and engineers.
6000 Members Founded: 1953

6119 **Sigma Phi Delta**
438 Smithfield Street
East Liverpool, OH 43920-1723
330-385-5287

webmaster@sigphi.org
www.sigphi.org

Derek R Troy, Grand President
Alixandre R Minden, Grand VP
Steven A Weiss, Communications Director
Edward A Hurst, Treasurer
Robert Featheringham, Manager

A professional and social fraternity in engineering.
7200 Members Founded: 1924

6120 **Society for Experimental Mechanics**
7 School Street
Bethel, CT 06801-1405
203-790-6373
FAX: 203-790-4472
sem@sem1.com www.sem.org

Eddie O'Brien, President
Mashisa Takashi, VP
Tom Proulx, Executive Director
Jonathan D Rogers, Treasurer

Supports all those involved with general experimental mechanics and the measurement of stresses and strains in metals and other materials.

6121 **Society for the Advancement of Material and Process Engineering**
1161 Parkview Drive
Covina, CA 91724-3751

FAX: 626-332-8929 800-562-7360
sampeibo@sampe.org www.sampe.org

Gregg Balko, Executive Director
Marcelo Beleber, Finance Manager
Dr Scott Beckwith, Technical Director

An international, professional, member society that provides information on new materials and processing technology via technical forums and publications.
Founded: 1944

6122 **Society of Allied Weight Engineers**
204 Hubbard Street
Glastonbury, CT 06033-3063
860-633-0850
FAX: 860-633-8971
exdirector@sawe.org www.sawe.org

Roger L Belt, President
James L Valentine, VP
William M Childers, Treasurer
Andreas R Schuster, VP Transportation
Brandy R Meyer, Secretary

Consists of engineers in the aerospace industry.
860 Members Founded: 1941

6123 **Society of American Military Engineers**
607 Prince Street
Alexandria, VA 22314-3117
703-549-3800
FAX: 703-684-0231 800-336-3097
webmanager@same.org
www.same.org

Dr Robert D Wolff, Executive Director
Jennifer Nichols, Marketing Manager
Jenni Ford, CPA, Director Finance/Accounting
L Eileen Erickson, Director Communications

Brings together professional engineers and those in engineering related fields to improve and increase the engineering capabilities of the nation and to exchange and advance the knowledge of engineering technologies, applications and practices.
22500 Members Founded: 1920

6124 **Society of Manufacturing Engineers**

1 SME Drive
Dearborn, MI 48121
313-271-1500
FAX: 313-425-3401 800-733-4763
service@sme.org www.sme.org

Nancy Berg, Executive Director
William J Geary, VP
F Brian Holmes, Director
George E West, Director
Richard C Peters, President

Professional society dedicated to advancing scientific knowledge in the field of manufacturing and to applying its resources for researching, writing, publishing and disseminating information.
70M Members Founded: 1932

6125 **Society of Petroleum Engineers**
PO Box 833836
Richardson, TX 75083-3836
972-529-9300
FAX: 972-952-9435 800-456-6863
spedal@spe.org www.spe.org

Giovanni Paccaloni, President
Bill Cobb, VP Finance
John E Bethancourt, Director Management/Information
Ian Gorman, Director Production/Operations
Mark Rubin, Executive Director

To provide the means for collection, dissemination and exchange of technical information concerning the development of oil and gas resources, subsurface fluid flow and production of other materials through well bores for the public benefit.
64000 Members Founded: 1957

6126 **Society of Rheology**
University Of California/Department of Chemical
Engineering
Meville, NY
516-576-2403
FAX: 516-576-2223
jbennett@aip.org www.rheology.org

Robert Prus'homme, VP
Andrew M. Kraynik, President

Composed of physicists, chemists, biologists, engineers, and mathematicians interested in advancing and applying rheology, which is defined as the science of deformation and flow of matter.
1700 Members

6127 **Society of Tribologists & Lubrication**
840 Busse Highway
Park Ridge, IL 60068-2376
847-825-5536
FAX: 847-825-1456
information@stle.org www.stle.org

Robert Baker, Presidential Council Chairman
William E Wambach, President
Edward Salek, Executive Director
Robert Bruce, Treasurer
Edward P Becker, Secretary

Strives to advance the science of lubrication tribology and related arts and sciences. Sponsors courses and an annual meeting.
4400 Members Founded: 1960

6128 **Tau Beta Pi Association**
PO Box 2697
Knoxville, TN 37901-2697
865-546-4578
FAX: 865-546-4579
tbp@tbp.org www.tbp.org

The National Engineering honor society recognizes engineering students of superior scholarship and exemplary character and practitioners of engineering. The organization includes 230 collegiate chapters and 16 alumnus chapters.
483K Members Founded: 1885

6129 Theta Tau
815 Brazos
Suite 710
Austin, TX 78701
512-482-1904
FAX: 512-472-4820 800-264-1904
central@thetatau.org
www.thetatau.org
Michael T Abraham, Executive Director
Dana Wortman, Grand Treasurer
Brandon J Satterwhite, Western Regional Director
A professional fraternity in engineering. Founded at the Univerity of Minnesota. Purpose of the fraternity is to develop and maintain a high standard of professional interest among its members, and to unite them in a strong bond of fraternal fellowship.
30000 Members Founded: 1904

6130 United Engineering Foundation
PO Box 70
Mount Vernon, VA 22121-070
973-244-2328
FAX: 973-882-5155
engfnd@aol.com
www.uefoundation.org
Sidney F Sapakie, President
Dr David L Belden, Executive Director
Supports research in engineering science and seeks to advance the profession of engineering.
19 Members Founded: 1904

6131 United Engineering Trustees
Three Park Avenue
27th Floor
New York, NY 10016-5902
212-591-7829
FAX: 212-591-7441
engfnd@aol.com
www.uefoundation.org
Sidney F Spakie, President
Dr David L Belden, Executive Director
Rosa Landinez, Conference Director
Joel B Snyder, Assistant Treasurer
Aims to advance engineering arts and sciences.
Founded: 1904

Newsletters

6132 AEG News
Association of Engineering Geologists
PO Box 460518
Denver, CO 80246
303-757-2926
FAX: 303-757-2969
aeg@aegweb.org www.aegweb.org
Dave Bieber, President
Darrel Schmitz, President-Elect/VP
Becky Roland, Chief Staff Executive
Terry West, Treasurer
Dorian Kuper, Secretary
Includes reports of committee activities, section news, and other news items of interest to the profession.
Quarterly

6133 AIP History Newsletter
American Institute of Physics
One Physics Ellispe
College Park, MD 20740-3843
301-209-3100
www.aip.org
Randolph Nanna, Publisher

6134 ASEF
8811 Colesville Road
Suite G106
Silver Spring, MD 20910-4343
301-565-2733
FAX: 301-589-2017
info@asfe.org http://www.asfe.org
John P Bachner, Executive VP
Daniel L Harpstead, President
John.P Bachner, Editor
Information on geo professional, environmental, and civil engineering firms. *$240.00*
16 pages Founded: 1969
Circulation: 5000

6135 ASTM International Business Link
ASTM International
100 Barr Harbor Drive
PO Box C700
West Conshohocken, PA 19428-2959
610-329-9500
FAX: 610-832-9555
service@astm.org www.astm.org
James Thomas, President
John Pace, VP Publications/Marketing
Provides information on the topics connecting the business and technical communities.
Semi-Annual

6136 Access ASTM International
ASTM International
100 Barr Harbor Drive
PO Box C700
West Conshohocken, PA 19428-2959
610-329-9500
FAX: 610-832-9555
service@astm.org www.astm.org
James Thomas, President
John Pace, VP Publications/Marketing
This is for ASTM's global customers.
Semi-Annual

6137 American Automatic Control Council Newsletter
AACC Secretariat
2145 Sheridan Road
Evanston, IL 60208-3118
847-491-8175
FAX: 847-491-4455
aacc@ece.northwestern.edu
http://www.a2c2.org
Bonnie Heck, Publisher
William Levine, President
A Ulsoy, Vice-President
Automatic control council information.
4 pages Quarterly Founded: 1961

6138 BMES Bulletin
Biomedical Engineering Society
8401 Corporate Drive
Suite 225
Landover, MD 20785-2224
301-459-1999
FAX: 301-459-2444
info@bmes.org http://www.bmes.org
Steven Slack, Editor
Patricia Horner, CEO
The Bulletin presents bioengineering science articles, student chapter news, Society and public policy announcements, employment opportunities, and a calendar of conference and events. It is also a forum for member opinions through editorials and letters. *$30.00*
Monthly Founded: 1969
Circulation: 3500 3700 names
Printed in 2 colors on matte stock

6139 Be Your Own Cotton Doctor
Potash and Phosphate Institute
655 Engineering Drive
Suite 110
Norcross, GA 30092-2837
770-447-0335
FAX: 770-448-0439
ppi@ppi-ppic.org www.ppi-ppic.org
David W Dibb, President
Terry Roberts, SVP Communications
Paul Fixen, Senior VP
Offers cotton growers and their advisers and consultants a new tool. The booklet features 40 color illustrations showing typical symptoms of nutrient deficiencies, toxicities, diseases, and other discorders in cotton production. *$.50*
8 pages

6140 Bulletin of Tau Beta Pi
Tau Beta Pi Association
PO Box 2697
Knoxville, TN 37901-2697
865-546-4578
FAX: 865-546-4579
tbp@tbp.org www.tbp.org
R E Hawks, Editor
Disseminate news and information about Tau Beta Pi of special interest to the collegiate chapters. It is an important vehicle for the annual repetition of instructions from the Executive Council and national headquarters to the chapters on election and initiation procedures and for the exchange of chapter project ideas and experience.
3x Annually

6141 Computer Integrated Manufacture and Engineering
Lionheart Publishing
506 Roswell Street
Suite 220
Marietta, GA 30060
770-431-0867
FAX: 770-432-6969
lpi@lionhrtpub.com
http://www.lionhrtpub.com/
Explores cutting edge developments in manufacturing systems operation management.
Circulation: 24000

6142 Cross Connection Protection Devices
American Society of Sanitary Engineering
901 Canterbury
Westlake, OH 44145
440-835-3040
FAX: 440-835-3488
info@asse-plumbing.org
ww.asse-plumbing.org
James C Church, PE, Editor
Joseph C Zaffuto, PE, Editor
Summary of backflow conditions and method of eliminating or minimizing their possible dangers. *$15.00*

6143 Echoes Newsletter
Acoustical Society of America
2 Huntington Quadrangle
Suite 1N01
Melville, NY 11747-4502
516-576-2360
FAX: 516-576-2377
asa@aip.org www.asa.aip.org
Allan D Pierce, Editor-in-Chief
Covers current and topical happenings of general interest and features articles about current research and personalities. Distributed free to members.
Quarterly

6144 Engineering Department Management and Administration Report
Institute of Management & Administration
29 W 35th Street
5th Floor
New York, NY 10001-2299
212-244-0360
FAX: 212-564-0465
subserve@ioma.com
http://www.ioma.com
Mark Baven, Publisher
Perry Patterson, Editor
Carlene Micheletto, President
Jim Bell, CEO
Focuses on improving efficiency and productivity. *$245.00*
16 pages Monthly

6145 Engineering Times
National Society of Professional Engineers
1420 King Street
Alexandria, VA 22314-2750
703-684-2800
FAX: 703-836-4875
customer.service@nspe.org
http://www.nspe.org
David Siegel, Editor
Robert Grey, CEO/President
Reports on issues affecting the engineering profession; featured monthly series on ethics. Free to members. *$30.00*
24 pages

6146 Engineers
Engineering Workforce Commission
1828 L Street NW
Suite 906
Washington, DC 20036
202-331-1830
FAX: 202-296-1151 888-400-2237
Dan Bateson, Director
David Gately, Media Contact
Carlos Miro, Manager
Provides an in-depth look at the current trends in engineering. *$105.00*
Quarterly

6147 High-Tech Materials Alert
Technical Insights
605 3rd Avenue
New York, NY 10158
212-850-6890
FAX: 212-850-8800 800-245-6217
dstrose@wiley.com
www.wiley.com/technical-insights/
Kenneth Kovaly, Publisher
Opportunities in advanced materials. *$867.00*
12 pages

6148 Hufact Quarterly: A Current Awareness Resource
Ergosyst Associates
123 W 8th Street
Suite 210
Lawrence, KS 66044-2687
FAX: 785-842-7348
John Burch, Publisher
Covers economics/human factors. *$100.00*

6149 IE News: Ergonomics
Institute of Industrial Engineers
3577 Parkway Lane
Suite 200
Norcross, GA 30092-2928
770-490-0461
FAX: 770-441-3295 800-494-0460
Dona Brown, Publisher
Joseph Hartman, Editor-in-Chief
Newsletter for Ergonomics Division.
4 pages Quarterly Founded: 1948

6150 IE News: Facilities Planning and Design
Institute of Industrial Engineers
25 Technology Parkway S
Norcross, GA 30092-2928
770-417-1788
FAX: 770-263-8532
Dona Brown, Publisher
Accepts advertising.
4 pages

6151 IE News: Operations Research
Institute of Industrial Engineers
25 Technology Parkway S
Norcross, GA 30092-2928
770-417-1788
FAX: 770-263-8532
Dona Brown, Publisher
News for industrial engineers. Accepts advertising.
4 pages

6152 IE News: Quality Control and Reliability Engineering
Institute of Industrial Engineers
25 Technology Parkway S
Norcross, GA 30092-2928
770-417-1788
FAX: 770-263-8532
Dona Brown, Publisher
Association news.
4 pages

6153 Innovators Digest
InfoTeam
PO Box 15640
Plantation, FL 33318-5640
954-473-9560
FAX: 954-473-0544
infoteamma@aol.com
Merton Allen, Editor
A multidisciplinary publication covering developments in science, engineering, products, markets, business development, manufacturing and other technological developments having industrial or commercial significance.
2 per year
Computerized version available

6154 Instrumentation Newsletter
National Instruments
6504 Bridge Point Parkway
Austin, TX 78730-5017
512-389-9119
FAX: 512-794-8411 888-280-7645
info@natinst.com
http://www.natinst.com
Gail Folkins, Managing Editor
John Graff, VP Marketing
James Truchard, President
Quarterly Founded: 1976
Circulation: 150000

6155 Last Word
American Council of Engineering
1015 15th Street NW
8th Floor
Washington, DC 20005-2605
202-347-7474
FAX: 202-898-0068
acec@acec.org http://www.acec.org
David Raymond, CEO/President
Ann Randstapter, Editor
Sheila Mahoutchian, Marketing Manager
Mary Jaffe, Director, Publications
Alan Crockett, Director, Public Relations and Comm
Independent private practice engineering companies. *$90.00*
2 pages Monthly Founded: 1905
Circulation: 5800 5800 names
Printed in on glossy stock

6156 Leadership and Management in Engineering
American Society of Civil Engineers
1801 Alexander Bell Drive
Reston, VA 20191
703-295-6000
FAX: 703-295-6222 800-548-2723
cybrarian@asce.org www.asce.org
Patricia Galloway, President
Lawrence Roth, Deputy Executive Director
Patrick Natale, Secretary/Treasurer
A cutting-edge periodical focusing on the art and practice of management and leadership in the civil engineering community.
Quarterly

6157 Licensure Exchange
National Council of Examiners for Engineering
280 Seneca Creek Road
PO Box 1686
Clemson, SC 29633
864-654-6824
FAX: 864-654-6033 800-250-3196
pfenno@ncees.org www.ncees.org
Keri Anderson, Editor
Ashley Cheney, Managing Editor
Provides information, opinion, and ideas regarding the licensure of engineers and land surveyors.
Bi-Monthly

6158 NSBE Magazine
National Society of Black Engineers
1454 Duke Street
Alexandria, VA 22314-3403
703-549-2207
FAX: 703-683-5312
office@nsbe.org http://www.nsbe.org
Pamela D Sharif, Publisher
Carl Mack, Executive Director
Coverage of all aspects of manufacturing engineering, geared towards black technical professionals. *$30.00*

Circulation: 100000
Printed in 4 colors on glossy stock

6159 **NewsLog**
ASFE
8811 Colesville Road
Suite G106
Silver Spring, MD 20910
301-565-2733
FAX: 301-589-2017
info@asfe.org www.asfe.org
John P Bachner, Editor
Alpha Moore, Publications Coordinator
Steve Johnson, President
Provides the latest information on effective practices, client relations, legal rulings, educational events, limitation of liability, contract clauses, professional selling techniques, human resources management, and ASFE itself. It also includes information about member news, committee work, ASFE publications, and new members.
Bi-Monthly Founded: 1969

6160 **Nuclear News**
American Nuclear Society
555 North Kensington Avenue
La Grange Park, IL 60526
708-352-6611
FAX: 708-352-0499 www.ans.org
Sarah Wells, Editor
Covers the latest developments in the nuclear field, a large part of which concerns nuclear energy - in particular, the 104 operating U.S. nuclear power plants, and another 334 operating elsewhere around the globe. *$365.00*
Monthly Founded: 2005

6161 **Plumbing Systems & Design**
American Society Of Plumbing Engineers
8614 W Catalpa Avenue
Suite 1007
Chicago, IL 60656
773-693-2773
FAX: 773-695-9007
info@psdmagazine.com
http://www.psdmagazine.org/
Tom Govedarica, Executive Publisher
Gretchen Pienta, Managing Editor
Maria Barriga, Circulation Manager
Jill Dirksen, Technical Director
David Ropinski, Graphic Designer
Industry leading technical publication with ASPE news and features. Free to ASPE members and subscribers. *$150.00*

Circulation: 25500
Printed in 4 colors on glossy stock

6162 **Power**
McGraw Hill
3333 Walnut Street
Boulder, CO 80301
720-485-5000
FAX: 720-548-5701 800-424-2908
customer.service@mcgrawhill.com
http://www.mcgraw-hill.com
Robert Schwieger, Publisher
Robert Peltier, Editor
Terry McGraw, CEO/President
Published for engineers who design, construct, operate and maintain power operating facilities in cogeneration and independent power plants in electric utilities. Accepts advertising. *$50.00*
Monthly Founded: 1888

6163 **RETA Breeze**
Refrigerating Engineers & Technicians Association
PO Box 1819
Salinas, CA 93902
831-455-8783
FAX: 831-455-7856
info@reta.com www.reta.com
Mark Broomer, Chairman
Doug Sweet, President
Stephan Shaub, VP
Dave Murphy, EVP
Edward Seffens, Treasurer
Provides information on meetings, chapter happenings and industry related topics. Advertising opportunities are available with special discounts for members.

6164 **RETA Technical Reports**
Refrigerating Engineers & Technicians Association
PO Box 1819
Salinas, CA 93902
831-455-8783
FAX: 831-455-7856
info@reta.com www.reta.com
Mark Broomer, Chairman
Doug Sweet, President
Stephan Shaub, VP
Dave Murphy, EVP
Edward Seffens, Treasurer
Combined with the RETA Breeze, the Tech Report is a series of reports written by industry experts on technical topics related to the refrigeration industry.

6165 **Report on Performance Materials**
McGraw Hill
PO Box 182604
Columbus, OH 43272-1095
614-304-4000
FAX: 614-759-3749 800-525-5003
customer.service@mcgrow-hill.com
http://www.mcgraw-hill.com
Thomas Woodall, Publisher
Covers materials for high-tech materials in aerospace. *$417.00*
Founded: 1909

6166 **Robotics Today**
Society of Manufacturing Engineers
1 Sme Drive
#930
Dearborn, MI 48128-2408
313-271-1500
FAX: 313-271-2861 800-733-4763
Thomas Drozda, Publisher
Gene Korte, Editor
Gene M Nelson, CEO/President
Reports on robotics used in manufacturing. *$60.00*
8 pages Quarterly
Mailing list available for rent $95 per M.
Printed in 2 colors on matte stock

6167 **SAWE Newsletter**
Society of Allied Weight Engineers
204 Hubbard Street
Glastonbury, CT 06033-3063
860-633-0850
FAX: 860-633-8971
exdirector@sawe.org www.sawe.org
Roger L Belt, President
James L Valentine, VP
Andreas R Schuster, VP Transportation
William M Childers, Treasurer
Brandy R Meyer, Secretary
The Technical Paper Index.
issued every 3 years

6168 **Systems**
Institute of Industrial Engineers
25 Technology Parkway S
Norcross, GA 30092-2928
770-417-1788
FAX: 770-263-8532
SL Browder, Publisher
Newsletter for IIE's society.
4 pages Quarterly

6169 **Tribology Letters**
Kluwer Academic/Plenum Publishers
840 Busse Highway
Park Ridge, IL 60068-2376
847-825-5536
FAX: 847-825-1456
information@stle.org www.stle.org
Karl Phipps, Associate Managing Editor
Devoted to the development of the science of Tribology and to its applications. It also serves as the depository for new information on the mechanical properties of surfaces.
95 per year

6170 **Velocitus Officers Newsletter**
Theta Tau
815 Brazos
Suite 710
Austin, TX 78701
512-482-1904
FAX: 512-472-4820 800-264-1904
central@thetatau.org
www.thetatau.org
Michael T Abraham, Executive Director
Dana Wortman, Grand Treasurer
Brandon J Satterwhite, Western Regional Director
Available by request via email or calling our 800 number.

Magazines & Journals

6171 **AFE Facilities Engineering Journal**
Association for Facilities Engineering
8160 Corporate Park Drive
#125
Cincinnati, OH 45242-3309
513-489-2473
FAX: 513-247-7422
mail@afe.org http://www.afe.org
Gabriella Jacobs, Communications Manager
Bob Kruhm, Advertising Manager
Patrick Janszen, Art Director
Michael Ireland, Executive Director
Information on maintenance management, energy conservation, safety and security, computerized maintenance management systems, evironmental compliance, telecommunications and related issues.
$225.00
Monthly Founded: 1956
Circulation: 6000
Mailing list available for rent 10000 names $100 per M.
Printed in 4 colors on glossy stock

6172 ASEE Prism
American Society for Engineering Education
1818 N Street NW
#600
Washington, DC 20036-2479
202-331-3500
FAX: 202-265-8504
prism@asee.org http://www.asee.org
Frank L Huband, Publisher
Mary Dalheim, Editor
Sherra E. Kerns, President
Frank L. Huband, Executive Director
Geared towards educators in the engineering technology fields.
Monthly Founded: 1893
Circulation: 12000

6173 ASME News
American Society of Mechanical Engineers
Three Park Avenue
New York, NY 10016-5990
212-917-7740
FAX: 212-591-7674 800-843-2763
infocentral@asme.org
http://www.asme.org
Thomas G Loughlin, Publisher
John G Falcioni, Editor-in-Chief
Virgil Carter, Chief Executive Officer
News, profiles and more from the American Society of mechanical engineers. *$125.00*
Monthly Founded: 1880
Circulation: 125000 350000 names $125 per M.
Printed in 4 colors on matte stock

6174 ASTM Standardization News
ASTM International
100 Barr Harbor Drive
West Conshohocken, PA 19428-2959
610-329-9500
FAX: 610-832-9555 800-262-1373
service@astm.org http://www.astm.org
Barbara Schnider, Editor
James Thomas, President
Maryann Gorman, Editor in Chief
Reports events in materials research and standardization. *$18.00*
88 pages Monthly Founded: 1898
Circulation: 30000

6175 Advanced Materials & Processes
ASM International
9639 Kinsman Road
Materials Park, OH 44073-2
440-338-5151
FAX: 440-338-4634 800-336-5152
cust-srv@asminternational.org
http://www.asminternational.org
Margaret Hunt, Editor
Don Baxter, Managing Editor
Lana Shapowal, Marketing/Publications Ma
Tina Long, Circulation Manager/Leads and Billi
Vincent LeGendre, Publisher
Engineered materials, manufacturing processes.
Monthly Founded: 1913

6176 Aerospace Engineering
400 Commonwealth Drive
Warrendale, PA 15096-1
724-776-4841
FAX: 724-776-9765
magazines@sae.org
http://www.sae.org
J. E. Robertson, PE, President
Robert E. Spitzer, VP Aerospace
Raymond Morris, Executive VP
Richard Schaum, VP Automotive
Serves the international aerospace design and manufacturing field which consists of producers of airliners, helicopters, spacecraft, missles; their powerplants, propulsion systems, avionics, electronic/electrical systems, parts and components. *$75.00*
Founded: 1905
Circulation: 28440

6177 American Consulting Engineer
American Council of Engineering
1015 15th Street NW
8th Floor
Washington, DC 20005-2605
202-347-7474
FAX: 202-898-0068
acec@acec.org http://www.acec.org
Joseph A Salimando, Editor-in-Chief
David A. Raymond, President
American Consulting Engineer serves engineers and surveyors who are employed by Consulting Engineering Firms, Architectural/Engineering Firms, Engineering/Architectural Firms, and Surveying Firms. *$45.00*
42 pages Monthly Founded: 1905
Circulation: 15841
Printed in 4 colors on glossy stock

6178 Annals of Biomedical Engineering
Biomedical Engineering Society
8401 Corporate Dr
Ste 140
Hyattsville, MD 20785-2263
301-459-1999
FAX: 301-459-2444
info@bmes.org www.bmes.org
Larry V McIntire, Editor-in-Chief
Presents original research in the following areas: tissue and cellular engineering and biotechnology; biomaterials and biological interfaces; biological signal processing and instrumentation; biomechanics, rheology, and molecular motion; dynamical, regulatory, and integrative biology; transport phenomena, systems analysis and electrophysiology; imaging.
Monthly

6179 Automotive Engineering International
Society of Automotive Engineers
400 Commonwealth Drive
Warrendale, PA 15096-1
724-776-4841
FAX: 724-776-0790 877-606-7323
magazines@sae.org
http://www.sae.org
Larry Schneider, Publisher
Kevin Jost, Editor
J Robertson, President
For engineers involved in the auto design industry. *$120.00*
125 pages Monthly Founded: 1905
Circulation: 124451

6180 Bent
Tau Beta Pi Association
PO Box 2697
Knoxville, TN 37901-2697
865-546-4578
FAX: 865-546-4579 800-250-3196
tbp@tbp.org http://www.tbp.org
James D Froula, Publisher/CEO
Roger E Hawks, Circulation Manager
The National Engineering honor society recognizes engineering students of superior scholarship and exemplary character and practitioners of engineering. The organization includes 226 collegiate chapters and 16 alumnus chapters. *$10.00*
Quarterly Founded: 1885
Circulation: 90000

6181 Bent of Tau Beta Pi
Tau Beta Pi Association
PO Box 2697
Knoxville, TN 37901-2697
865-546-4578
FAX: 865-546-4579
tbp@tbp.org www.tbp.org
James B Froula, Editor
Carries advertising of numerous major business firms and universities in the engineering field. *$10.00*
Founded: 1905
Circulation: 94,000

6182 Better Crops International Magazine
Potash and Phosphate Institute
655 Engineering Drive
Suite 110
Norcross, GA 30092-2837
770-447-0335
FAX: 770-448-0439
ppi@ppi-ppic.org www.ppi-ppic.org
David W Dibb, President
Terry Roberts, SVP Communications
Paul Fixen, Senior VP
Researchers report on nutrient-related topics for corn, wheat, groundnut, oil palm, sugarcane, rice, crop rotations, and fish ponds. The issue concludes with a backcover commentary explaining why support of agricultural development is the right thing to do.

6183 Biomedical Engineering Society
8401 Corporate Dr
Ste 140
Hyattsville, MD 20785-2263
301-459-1999
FAX: 301-459-2444
info@bmes.com http://www.bmes.org
Patricia I. Horner, Executive Director
Denise Silver, Associate Director
Of interest to those in the biomedical engineering field. To promote the increase of biomedical engineering knowledge and its utilization. *$175.00*
Monthly Founded: 1968
Printed in 8 colors on matte stock

6184 Bridge
National Academy of Engineering
500 Fifth Street NW
Washington, DC 20001
202-334-3200
FAX: 202-334-2290
carenber@nae.edu http://www.nae.edu
George Bugliarello, Editor-in-Chief
Carol Aronberg, Editor
In-depth feature articles on issues in engineering, science, technology and public policy, and news from the National Academy of Engineering.
Quarterly Founded: 1954
Circulation: 5000

6185 Bridge Magazine
National Society of Black Engineers
1454 Duke Street
Alexandria, VA 22314
703-549-2207
FAX: 703-683-5312
info@nsbe.org www.nsbe.org

Chancee Lundy, Chairperson
Candice M Dixon, Vice Chairperson
Justin Brown, National Parliamentarian
Lee V Pham, National Treasurer
Jennifer Jasper, National Secretary

The cornerstone publication of the NSBE pre-college initiative. Presents math, science and engineering topics in a lively, engaging editorial style.
4 issues

6186 CET Magazine
American Society of Certified Engineering
PO Box 1348
Flowery Branch, GA 30542-0023
770-967-9173
FAX: 770-967-8049
kurt_schuler@ascet.org
www.ascet.org

Russell E Freier, Chairman
Leo Saenz, CET, President
Kurt Schuler, Secretary/Treasurer

It contains technical, educational, notices of upcoming events, employment opportunities, legislative and informational articles. Also included are national, regional and local society news, reports and activities.
32 pages Bi-Monthly
Printed in 1 color

6187 Certified Engineering Technician Magazine
American Society of Certified Engineering Techs.
PO Box 1348
Flowery Branch, GA 30542
770-967-9173
FAX: 770-967-8049
kurt-schuler@ascet.org
http://www.ascet.org

Leo Saenz, President
Russel E Freier, Chairman *$12.00*
30 pages Founded: 1964
Circulation: 2500

6188 Chemical & Engineering News
American Chemical Society
1155 16th Street NW
Suite 600
Washington, DC 20036-4892
202-872-4600
FAX: 202-872-4615 800-333-9511
help@acs.org
http://www.chemistry.org

Michael Heylin, Editor
William F. Carroll, President

Professional magazine which covers all areas of interest to the chemical community, including business, science and government.
Weekly Founded: 1934

6189 Civil Engineering
American Society of Civil Engineers
1801 Alexander Bell Drive
Reston, VA 20191-4400
703-956-6000
FAX: 703-295-6211 800-548-2723
member@asce.org
http://www.pubs.asce.org

David Dresia, Publisher
Virginia Fairweather, Editor-in-Chief
Anne Powell, Editor

Comprised of news, information and updates for the civil engineering industry.
$180.00
Monthly Founded: 1855
Circulation: 107,000
Printed in 4 colors

6190 Civil Engineering Magazine
American Society of Civil Engineers
1801 Alexander Bell Drive
Reston, VA 20191
703-295-6000
FAX: 703-295-6222 800-548-2723
cybrarian@asce.org www.asce.org

Anne Powell, Editor

Reports on a wide variety of pivotal civil engineering projects and structures, as well as contemporary problems, trends, controversies, and achievements in civil engineering. Court decisions, engineering applications, new products, manufacturers literature, computer systems marketplace, and legal trends are just a few of the magazine's regular departments. *$180.00*

6191 Composites Technology
Ray Publishing
4891 Independence Street
Suite 270
Wheat Ridge, CO 80033
303-467-1776
FAX: 303-467-1777
info@raypubs.com
http://www.raypubs.com

Judith Ray Hazen, Publisher/Editor
Michael Musselman, Managing Editor
Donna K. Dawson, Senior Editor
Susan Rush, Copy Editor
Dirk Weed, Global Sales Manager

To provide comprehensive coverage of the composites industry by focusing on the design, engineering, manufacture and performance of products made from this type of material. Particular attention is given to the transfer of technology from traditional end-use markets into high-volume commercial and industrial arenas. *$15.00*
44 pages Founded: 1993
Circulation: 24000
Printed in 4 colors on glossy stock

6192 Composites in Manufacturing
Society of Manufacturing Engineers
One SME Drive
Dearborn, MI 48128-2408
313-271-1500
FAX: 313-425-3401 800-733-4763
service@sme.org http://www.sme.org

Thomas Drozda, Publisher
Gene Korte, Editor
James N Brecker, President
Paul D. Bradley, Managing Director

Covers various aspects of composite materials used in manufacturing.
Bi-annually Founded: 1932
Circulation: 20000 Audited
Mailing list available for rent 13727 names $95 per M.

6193 Computer-Aided Engineering
Penton Media
1300 E 9th Street
Cleveland, OH 44114
216-696-7000
FAX: 216-696-1309
information@penton.com
www.penton.com

William Tucker, Editor

Database applications in design and manufacturing. *$50.00*
96 pages Founded: 1982

6194 Computing in Science & Engineering
American Institute of Physics
2 Huntington Quadrangle
Suite 1NO1
Melville, NY 11747
516-576-2200
FAX: 516-349-9704
cip@aip.org http://www.aip.org

Stephen Benka, Editor
Angela Dombroski, CEO
Randolph Nanna, Publisher

Computer science's interdisciplinary juncture with physics, astronomy and engineering. *$42.00*
Monthly Founded: 1931

6195 Consulting-Specifying Engineer
Reed Business Information
2000 Clearwater Drive
Oak Brook, IL 60523
630-740-0825
FAX: 630-288-8681 877-422-4637
e-letters@reedbusiness.com
http://www.csemag.com

Jim Langhenry, Publisher
Jim Crockett, Chief Editor
Scott Siddens, Senior Editor

Serves engineering management and engineering personnel who perform mechanical and/or electrical engineering activities.

100 pages Monthly Founded: 1958
Circulation: 46,157
Printed in 4 colors on glossy stock

6196 Contracting Business
Refrigerating Engineers & Technicians Association
PO Box 1819
Salinas, CA 93902
831-455-8783
FAX: 831-455-7856
info@reta.com www.reta.com

Mark Broomer, Chairman
Doug Sweet, President
Stephan Shaub, VP
Dave Murphy, EVP
Edward Seffens, Treasurer

A trade publication focusing on the issues related to the refrigeration and air-conditioning industry.

6197 Control Engineering
Reed Business Information
350 Park Avenue S
New York, NY 10010
212-659-9351
800-446-6551
dharvey@cahners.com
http://www.controleng.com

David Harvey, Publisher
Jim Casella, President

Stresses the how-to aspect of the field. Highlights the practical application of instrumentation, and new analytical and systems design techniques. *$195.00*
Monthly Founded: 1900
Circulation: 31050

6198 Control Engineering International
Reed Business Information
350 Park Avenue S
New York, NY 10010
212-659-9351

dharvey@cahners.com
www.controleng.com

David Harvey, Publisher

Focuses on the design and use of control instrumentation systems, components and equipment in manufacturing and non-manufacturing industries.

9 per year
Circulation: 31,050

6199 Control Solutions
PennWell Publishing Company
1421 S Sheridan Road
Tulsa, OK 74112
918-835-3161
FAX: 918-831-9497 800-331-4463

Matt O'Shea, Publisher
Ron Kuhfeld, Editor-in-Chief

A highly diversified, business-to-business media company providing authoriative print and online publications, conferences and exhibitions, research, databases, online exchanges and information products to strategic global markets.

Founded: 1910

6200 Corrosion Journal
NACE International
1440 S Creek Drive
Houston, TX 77084-4999
281-228-6200
FAX: 281-228-6359
http://www.nace.org

Angela Jarrell, Managing Editor
Melanie Chmiel, Production Manager
Suzanne Moreno, Editorial Assistant

Corrosion is the monthly permanent record of progress in corrosion control and prevention with more than 50 years of published research from engineers and scientists to draw upon. *$220.00*

Monthly Founded: 1945
Circulation: 7800

6201 Cost Engineering Journal
AACE International
209 Prairie Avenue
Suite 100
Morgantown, WV 26501-5949
304-296-8444
FAX: 304-291-5728 800-858-3678
info@aacei.org http://www.aacei.org

Marvin Gelhausen, Editor
Andrew Dowd, Interim Executive

International journal of cost estimation, cost/schedule control, and project management read by cost professionals around the world to get the most up-to-date information about the profession. *$65.00*

Monthly Founded: 1956
Circulation: 5500
Mailing list available for rent

6202 Cutting Tool Engineering
CTE Publications
400 Skokie Boulevard
Suite 395
Northbrook, IL 60062-7903
847-498-9100
FAX: 847-559-4444
alanr@jwr.com
http://www.ctemag.com

Alan Richter, Editor
Don Nelson, Publisher
John Wm. Roberts, CEO

Serves manufacturing plants in the metal working industries. *$65.00*

72 pages Monthly Founded: 1955
Circulation: 34871
Printed in 4 colors on glossy stock

6203 Design News
Reed Business Information
225 Wyman Street
Waltham, MA 02451
617-643-3030
FAX: 781-290-3178
amorrow@reedbusiness.com
http://www.designnews.com

Daniel Hirsh, Publisher
Karen Auguston Field, Chief Editor
Jim Sacella, CEO
Tracey Farina, Marketing,
Reck Allis, Circulation Manager

A magazine devoted exclusively to engineering design.

Monthly Founded: 1946
Circulation: 170114
Printed in 4 colors on glossy stock

6204 EE: Evaluation Engineering
Nelson Publishing
2500 Tamiami Trail N
Nokomis, FL 34275
941-966-9521
FAX: 941-966-2590 800-226-6113
subscriptions@nelsonpub.com
http://www.nelsonpub.com

Paul Milo, Editor
Michael Hughes, Sales Manager

Magazine devoted exclusively to companies that test, evaluate, design and manufacture electronic products and equipment.
$43.00

84 pages Monthly Founded: 1962
Circulation: 80000
Mailing list available for rent 65,000 names
Printed in 4 colors on glossy stock

6205 Energy Engineering Journal
The Fairmont Press, Association of Energy Engineer
4025 Pleasantdale Road
Suite 420
Atlanta, GA 30340
770-447-5083
FAX: 770-446-3969
webmaster@AEEcenter.org
http://www.aeecenter.org

Wayne Turner, Editor-in-Chief
Larry Good, President

Engineering solutions to cost efficiency problems and mechanical contractors who design, specify, install, maintain, and purchase non-residential heating, ventilating, air conditioning and refrigeration equipment and components. *$160.00*

Circulation: 8000

6206 Energy Services Marketing Institute News
Association of Energy Engineers
4025 Pleasantdale Road
Suite 420
Atlanta, GA 30340
770-447-5083
FAX: 770-446-3969
webmaster@aeecenter.org
www.aeecenter.org

Stephen A Roosa, President
Timothy B Janos, President-Elect
Albert Thumann, Executive Director
Paul Goodman, Treasurer
Laurie Wiegand-Jackson, Secretary

Subjects addressed include IPMVP Management and Verification Standard; Performance Contracting; Energy Project Financing and Energy Procurement.

3x/year

6207 Engineered Systems
Refrigerating Engineers & Technicians Association
PO Box 1819
Salinas, CA 93902
831-455-8783
FAX: 831-455-7856
info@reta.com www.reta.com

Mark Broomer, Chairman
Doug Sweet, President
Stephen Shaub, VP
Dave Murphy, EVP
Edward Seffens, Treasurer

A trade publication focusing on the theory and practical applications of refrigeration practices.

6208 Engineering Automation Report
Technology Automation Services
PO Box 3593
Englewood, CO 80155-3593
303-689-9099
FAX: 303-770-3660
www.eareport.com/eareport

David Weisberg, Publisher
Steve Weisberg, Editor
Dave White, President

Internet/intranet technologies for use in engineering design are covered along with software news. *$235.00*

Monthly

6209 Engineering News Record
McGraw Hill
PO Box 182604
9th Floor
Columbus, OH 43272
614-304-4000
877-876-8208
scott_lewis@mcgraw-hill.com
http://www.enr.com

Judy Schriener, Editor-in-Chief
James H McGraw, Publisher
Richard Rodriguez, Marketing Director
Norbert Young, President
Dora Chomiak, Sales Director

ENR is the definitive weekly source of technical and business intelligence for top construction professionals. ENR provides fast-breaking news, trends and developments strategically focused to help readers seize the latest new business opportunities.
$82.00

150 pages Weekly Founded: 1874
Circulation: 76,000
Printed in 4 colors on glossy stock

6210 Engineering and Mining Journal
Primedia Business
29 N Wacker Drive
10th Floor
Chicago, IL 60606-2802
312-726-2802
FAX: 312-726-2574
pjohnson@mining-media.com
http://www.mining-media.com

Peter Johnson, Publisher
Steve Fiscor, Editor

Serves the field of mining including exploration, development, milling, smelting, refining of metals and nonmetallics. *$79.00*

Founded: 1989
Circulation: 20589
Mailing list available for rent
Printed in 4 colors

6211 Engineering in Medicine and Biology
445 Hoes Lane
Piscataway, NJ 08854-1331
732-981-0060
FAX: 732-981-1721 800-678-4333
customer-service@ieee.org
http://www.spectrum.ieee.org/ieeemedia

Desirée de Myer, Managing Editor
John Enderle, Editor
Susan Schneiderman, Business Development Mana

Focuses on up-to-date biomedical engineering applications for engineers who are at the forefront of electrotechnology innovation. *$300.00*
Founded: 1988
Circulation: 7983

6212 Environmental Engineer
American Academy of Environmental Engineers
130 Holiday Court
Suite 100
Annapolis, MD 21401-7003
410-266-3311
FAX: 410-266-7653
academy@aaee.net
http://www.aaee.net

David A. Asselin, Executive Director
Yolanda Y. Moulden, Production Manager

Articles dealing with environmental engineering practice issues and history. *$20.00*

Quarterly Founded: 1955
Circulation: 12000
Mailing list available for rent

6213 Environmental and Engineering Geosciences
Association of Engineering Geologists
PO Box 460518
Denver, CO 80246
303-757-2926
FAX: 303-757-2969
aeg@aegweb.org www.aegweb.org

Dave Bieber, President
Darrel Schmitz, President-Elect/VP
Becky Roland, Chief Staff Executive
Terry West, Treasurer
Dorian Kuper, Secretary

Presents reviewed technical papers and discussions and book reviews related to the general field of engineering geology.
Quarterly

6214 Experimental Mechanics
Society for Experimental Mechanics
2455 Teller Road
Thousand Oaks, CA 91320-1855
800-818-7243
FAX: 805-499-0871
sem@sem1.com
http://www.sagepub.com

Thomas W Proulx, Publisher
N R Sottos, Editor
Hugh Bruck, Associate Technical Edito

Concentrates on advanced research and development. EM is the archival publication of the Society and is recognized as one of the many journals in engineering mechanics. Members receive free electronic access. *$767.04*
Quarterly Founded: 1965
Circulation: 4500

6215 Experimental Techniques
Society for Experimental Mechanics
Seven School Street
Bethel, CT 06801-1855
203-790-6373
FAX: 203-790-4472
sem@sem1.com http://www.sem.org

Jenniffer Proulx, Editor
Thomas Proulx, Execetive Director

Focused on the techniques utilized in experimental mechanics. ET includes Society news, peer-reviewed technical articles and notes, new product information and much more. All members receive a printed copy of the journal and free electronic access. *$145.00*
48 pages Founded: 1943
Circulation: 4000
Printed in 4 colors on glossy stock

6216 Exponent
Iowa Engineering Society
1000 Walnut
#102
Des Moines, IA 50309
515-284-7055
FAX: 515-284-7301
ies@iaengr.org http://www.iaengr.org

David H Scott, Editor/Publisher/Circulation Manage
Brian E. E. Roth, President

Supplies the Iowa engineering society members with vital information on issues and activities such as state legislation, education, ethics. *$6.00*
26 pages Quarterly
Circulation: 1000

6217 Facilities Engineering Journal
Association for Facilities Engineering
8160 Corporate Park Drive
Suite 125
Cincinnati, OH 45242
513-489-2473
FAX: 513-247-7422
webmaster@afe.org www.afe.org

Gabriella Jacobs, Editor/Communications Manager

Provides you with practical, in-depth information on the key issues you face on the job every day.

6218 Fiberoptic Product News
Reed Business Information
100 Enterprise Drive
Suite 600
Rockaway, NJ 07866-912
973-920-7000
FAX: 973-920-7534
dhimes@cahners.com
http://www.fpnmag.com

Steve Wirth, VP/Group Publisher
Diane Himes, Editor
Kim Potts, Managing Editor
Ernest Worthman, Technical Editorial Director
R Reed, Owner

Edited for designers, engineers, researchers and management personnel who design, install and the buy the products and services that make up the fiberoptic marketplace.
Monthly Founded: 1986
Circulation: 35000
Printed in 4 colors on glossy stock

6219 Fusion Science and Technology
American Nuclear Society
555 North Kensington Avenue
La Grange Park, IL 60526
708-352-6611
FAX: 708-352-0499 www.ans.org

James S Tulenko, President
E James Reinsch, President-Elect/VP
Harry Bradley, Executive Director
William F Naughton, Treasurer

Is the source of information on fusion plasma physics and plasma engineering, fusion plasma enabling science and technology, fusion nuclear technology and material science, fusion applications, fusion design and system studies. *$1425.00*
8x/year Founded: 2005

6220 Geotechnical Fabrics Report
Industrial Fabrics Association International
1801 County Road B W
Roseville, MN 55113
651-222-2508
FAX: 651-631-9334 800-225-4324
generalinfo@ifai.com
http://www.ifai.com

Mary J Hennessey, Publisher
Chris Kelsey, Editor
Susan.B Smeed, Assistant Circulation Man

Peer reviewed technical journal for civil engineers using geosynthetics in road construction, errosion control, hazardous waste, drainage, containment and reinforcement. *$49.00*
Founded: 1982
Circulation: 16000 $250 per M.
Printed in 4 colors on glossy stock

6221 Geotechnical Testing Journal
ASTM International
100 Barr Harbor Drive
PO Box C700
West Conshohocken, PA 19428-2959
610-329-9500
FAX: 610-832-9555
service@astm.org www.astm.org

L David Suits, Co-Editor
Dr Thomas C Sheahan, Co-Editor
John Pace, VP Publications/Marketing

Provides a high quality publication that informs the profession of new developments in soil and rock testing and related fields; provides a forum for the exchange of information, particularly that which leads to the development of new test procedures; and to stimulate active participation of the profession in the work of ASTM International Committee D18 on Soil and Rock and related information. *$229.00*
Bi-Monthly

6222 Global Design News
Reed Business Information
2000 Clearwater Drive
Oak Brook, IL 60523
630-740-0825
FAX: 630-288-8686
dhirsh@reedbusiness.com
http://www.reedbusiness.com

Dan Hirsh, Publisher
Jim Casella, CEO
Karen Auguston Field, Editor-in-Chief

Publication includes articles that cover the key product areas necessary for product development; reports on new technologies in the OEM industries, developments in the field of engineering design; and regular features on European product listings, technique and system updates.

Founded: 1977
Circulation: 30173

6223 Heat Transfer Engineering
Taylor & Francis
325 Chestnut Street
Suite 800
Philadelphia, PA 19106-2614
215-625-8900
FAX: 215-625-8914
info@taylorandfrancis.com
http://www.taylorandfrancis.com

James Edward, Publisher
Afshin Ghajar, Editor-in-Chief
Jack Taylor, Owner

Information on refereed papers of original work, state-of-the-art reviews, articles on new developments in equipment and practices and news items on people and companies in the field. *$355.00*
Founded: 1798
Circulation: 2000

6224 High Tech Materials Alert
605 3rd Avenue
New York, NY 10158
212-850-6890
FAX: 212-850-8800

6225 Hispanic Engineer & Information Technology
Career Communications Group
729 E Pratt Street
Suite 504
Baltimore, MD 21202
410-244-7101
FAX: 410-752-1834
eaddison@ccgmag.com
http://www.hispanicengineer.com

Tyrone D Taborn, Editor/Publisher/CEO
Vishal Thakkar, Marketing Team Leader

Devoted to science and technology and to promoting opportunities in those fields for Hispanic Americans. *$13.00*
56 pages Founded: 1982
Printed in 4 colors on glossy stock

6226 Hydraulics & Pneumatics
Penton Media
1300 E 9th Street
Cleveland, OH 44114
216-696-7000
FAX: 216-696-1309
hp@penton.com
http://www.penton.com

Paul J. Heney, Senior Editor
Mike Ference, Advertising

Issues highlight the application of new hydraulic and pneumatic components, new equipment research and listings, new design and literature innovations in fluid power and motion control systems. *$65.00*
Monthly Founded: 1892
Circulation: 49,878

6227 ID International Design
F&W Publications
38 East 29th Street
Floor 3
New York, NY 10016
212-447-1400
FAX: 212-447-5231
idedit@fwpubs.com
http://www.idonline.com

Caroline G Rhame, Publisher
Julie Lasky, Editor - in - chief
Nicole Martin, Circualtion Manager
Barbara Schmitz, VP

The issues include news and features on computers, new technologies, case studies, design management, materials, aesthetics, new components and design trends. They also cover new sources, a calendar of events, personnel news, book reviews and products. *$30.00*
Founded: 1954
Circulation: 19852

6228 IESNA Technical Memorandum on Light Emitt- ing Diode (LED) Sources and Systems
Illuminating Engineering Society of North America
120 Wall Street
Floor 17
New York, NY 10005
212-248-5000
FAX: 212-248-5018
iesna@iesna.org www.iesna.org

Albert Suen, Publications Fulfillment

In addition to a brief history of LED development, a description of LED technologies, and an overview of LED produt design and related thermal management issues, this Technical Memorandum discusses unique applications in which LEDs are used - traffic and commerical signage; architectural lighting (exterior and interior); automotive applications; display lighting; task lighting and medical lighting. *$24.50*
17 pages Softcover Founded: 2005

6229 IIE Solutions
Institute of Industrial Engineers
3577 Parkway Lane
Suite 200
Norcross, GA 30092-2928
770-490-0461
FAX: 770-441-3295 800-494-0460
editor@iienet.org
http://www.iienet.org

Cliff Cary, Publisher
Jane Gaboury, Editor

Listings, literature and news for executive engineers. *$66.00*
Monthly Founded: 1948
Circulation: 26276

6230 ITE Solutions
Institute of Industrial Engineers
3577 Parkway Lane
Suite 200
Norcross, GA 30092
770-490-0461
FAX: 770-441-3295 800-494-0460
cs@iienet.org http://www.iienet.org

Monica Elliott, Managing Editor
Don Greene, Executive Director
Joan Milczarski, Marketing Director

Monthly Founded: 1948

6231 InTents
Industrial Fabrics Association International

1801 Country Road BW
Roseville, MN 55113
651-222-2508
FAX: 651-631-9334 800-225-4324
generalinfo@ifai.com
www.ifai.com/index

Mary Hennessy, Publisher
Katie Harboldt, Editor
Galynn Nordstrom, Editorial Director

Promotes the use of tents and accessories to the special-event and general-rental industries. The publication features the latest innovations in fabric structures and event products, showcases the world's best tent installations, profiles leading figures and firms, offers tips from experienced professionals, covers new trends, and reports on the activities and services of trade support groups, including IFAI's Tent Rental Division. *$39.00*
Bi-Monthly
Circulation: 12,000

6232 Industrial Equipment News
Thomas Publishing Company
5 Penn Plaza
New York, NY 10001
212-950-0500
800-733-1127
subscriptioninfo@ienonline.com
http://www.ienonline.com/

Ciro Buttacavoli, Publisher
Joseph Rosta, Editor-in-Chief
Debbie Maskin, Managing Editor
Gregory Mottola, Associate Editor
Marie Urbanowicz, Marketing Manager

Serves the industrial field including manufacturing, mining, utilities, construction, transportation,governmental establishments, and educational services.
Monthly Founded: 1933
Circulation: 205000

6233 Innovation
Industrial Designers Society of America
45195 Business Court
Suite 250
Dulles, VA 22066-6717
703-707-6000
FAX: 703-787-8501
idsa@idsa.org http://www.idsa.org

Kristina Goodrich, CEO/Executive Director
Karen Berube, Managing Editor

Feature articles contain research, industrial design processes, trends and viewpoints, new processes and materials, marketing, managing, and computer-aided designs. *$50.00*
Quarterly Founded: 1965
Circulation: 3500

6234 Interface Magazine
Electrochemical Society
65 S Main Street
Building D
Pennington, NJ 08534-2839
609-737-1902
FAX: 609-737-2743
interface@electrochem.org
http://www.electrochem.org

Krishnan Rajeshwar, Editor
Elisha Nicholson, Circulation Manager

Editorial material contains news, reviews, advertisements and articles on technical matters in the fields of electrochemical and solid state science and technology. *$61.97*
Quarterly Founded: 1902
Circulation: 8000

6235 International Dredging Review
PO Box 1487
Fort Collins, CO 80522-1487
970-416-1903
FAX: 970-416-1878
editor@dredgemag.com
http://www.dredgemag.com

Judith Powers, Publisher
Leonard F Cors, Advertising/Business Manager
Judith Powers, Editor
Julia Leach, Production Manager

Targeted to dredging company executives, project managers and dredge crew members, suppliers and service people such as pump manufacturers, hydrographic surveyors, consulting engineers, etc. *$85.00*
Founded: 1981
Circulation: 3300

Mailing list available for rent
Printed in 4 colors on glossy stock

6236 JSME International Journal
American Society of Mechanical Engineers
Three Park Avenue
New York, NY 10016-5990
212-917-7740
FAX: 973-882-1167 800-843-2763
infocentral@asme.org www.asme.org

Harry Armen, President
Richard E Feigel, President-Elect
Virgil Carter, Executive Director
David Soukup, Managing Director Operations

Provides advanced scientific and technological information for the mechanical engineering industry to facilitate the international exchange and transfer of technology. *$200.00*
Monthly

6237 Journal of Applied Mechanics
American Society of Mechanical Engineers
Three Park Avenue
New York, NY 10016-5990
212-917-7740
FAX: 973-882-1167 800-843-2763
infocentral@asme.org www.asme.org

Mike Kiley, President
Robert M McMeeking, Editor

Is to serve as a vehicle for the communication of original research results of permanent interest in all branches of mechanics.
$ 60.00
Bi-Monthly

6238 Journal of Biomechanical Engineering
American Society of Mechanical Engineers
Three Park Avenue
New York, NY 10016-5990
212-917-7740
FAX: 973-882-1167 800-843-2763
infocentral@asme.org www.asme.org

Dr Frank C Yin, Editor

Reports research results involving the application of mechanical engineering knowledge, skills and principles to the conception, design, development, analysis, and operation of biomechanical systems, inlcuding: artifical organs and prostheses; bioinstrumentation and measurements; bioheat transfer; biomaterials; biomechanics; bioprocess engineering; cellular mechanics; design and control of biological systems; and physiological systems. *$60.00*
Bi-Monthly

6239 Journal of Construction Engineering and Management
American Society of Civil Engineers
1801 Alexander Bell Drive
Reston, VA 20191
703-295-6000
FAX: 703-295-6222 800-548-2723
cybrarian@asce.org www.asce.org

Patricia Galloway, President
Lawrence Roth, Deputy Executive Director
Patrick Natale, Secretary/Treasurer

Quality papers that aim to advance the science of construction engineering, to harmonize construction practices with design theories, and to further education and research in construction engineering and management.

6240 Journal of Engineering Education
American Society for Engineering Education
1818 N Street NW
Suite 600
Washington, DC 20036-2476
202-331-3500
FAX: 202-265-8504
prism@asee.org www.asee.org

Dr Jack R Lohmann, Editor
Frank Huband, Executive Director

It serves as an archival record of scholarly research in engineering education.
Quarterly

6241 Journal of Engineering for Industry
American Society of Mechanical Engineers
Three Park Avenue
New York, NY 10016-5990
212-917-7740
FAX: 973-882-1717 800-843-2763
infocentral@asme.org
http://www.asme.org

Joe Sansone, Publisher
Cornelia Monahan, Editor/Production Manager
William T. Cousins, President

Covers interfaces of mechanical engineering.
Quarterly Founded: 1880
Circulation: 2162

6242 Journal of Forensic Sciences
ASTM International
100 Barr Harbor Drive
PO Box C700
West Conshohocken, PA 19428-2959
610-329-9500
FAX: 610-832-9555
service@astm.org www.astm.org

James Thomas, President
John Pace, VP Publications/Marketing

Is the offical publication of the American Academy of Forensic Sciences (AAFS). It is devoted to the publication of original investigations, observations, scholarly inquiries, and reviews in the various branches of the forensic sciences. *$249.00*
Bi-Monthly

6243 Journal of Management in Engineering
American Society of Civil Engineers
1801 Alexander Bell Drive
Reston, VA 20191
703-295-6000
FAX: 703-295-6222 800-548-2723
cybrarian@asce.org www.asce.org

Patricia Galloway, President
Lawrence Roth, Deputy Executive Director
Patrick Natale, Secretary/Treasurer

Examines contemporary issues associated with leadership and management for the twenty-first century civil engineer.

6244 Journal of Petroleum Technology
Society of Petroleum Engineers
PO Box 833836
Richardson, TX 75083-3836
972-529-9300
FAX: 972-952-9435 800-456-6863
spedal@spe.org www.spe.org

Giovanni Paccaloni, President
Bill Cobb, VP Finance
John E Bethancourt, Director Management/Information
Ian Gorman, Director Production/Operations

A suite of peer-reviewed, discipline-centered journals; books wrtitten by the industry's most honored professionals; and an online, 35,000-paper library. *$15.00*
Monthly

6245 Journal of Process Control
Butterworth Heinemann
313 Washington Street
Suite 302
Newton, MA 02458-1626
617-928-5460
FAX: 617-928-5494

JD Perkins, Editor
T McAvoy, Regional Editor

Covers the application of control theory, operations research, computer science and engineering principles to the solution of process control problems.

6246 Journal of Testing and Evaluation
ASTM International
100 Barr Harbor Drive
PO Box C700
West Conshohocken, PA 19428-2959
610-329-9500
FAX: 610-832-9555
service@astm.org www.astm.org

Dr Donald R Petersen, Editor-in-Chief
Dr Richard Link, Associate Editor

Provides a multidisciplinary forum for applied sciences and engineering. *$249.00*
Bi-Monthly

6247 Journal of the Acoustical Society of America
Acoustical Society of America
2 Huntington Quadrangle
Suite 1N01
Melville, NY 11747-4502
516-576-2360
FAX: 516-576-2377
asa@aip.org www.asa.aip.org

Allan D Pierce, Editor-in-Chief

Distributed free to members. *$1545.00*
7000 pages Monthly

6248 Journal of the Electrochemical Society
Electrochemical Society
65 S Main Street
Building D
Pennington, NJ 08534-2839
609-737-1902
FAX: 609-737-2743
ecs@electrochem.org
http://www.electrochem.org

Paul.A Kohl, Editor
Mary Yess, Publication Manager
Roque Calvo, Manager

Contains technical papers covering basic research and technology. *$63.00*
Founded: 1902
Circulation: 8300

6249 LD+A
Illuminating Engineering Society of North America
120 Wall Street
Floor 17
New York, NY 10005
212-248-5000
FAX: 212-248-5018
iesna@iesna.org www.iesna.org

Paul Tarricone, Editor
John Michael Kobes, Associate Editor

Is a magazine for professionals involved in the art, science, study, manufacture, teaching and implementation of lighting. LD+A is designed to enhance and improve the practice of lighting. Every issue of LD+A includes feature articles on design projects, technical articles on the science of illumination, new product developments, industry trends, news of the Illuminating Engineering Society and vital information about the illuminating profession. *$32.00*
Monthly

6250 Low Temperature Physics
200 Huntington Quadrangle
Suite 1N01
Melville, NY 11747-4502
516-516-2270
FAX: 516-349-9704

6251 Machine Design
1300 E 9 Street
Cleveland, OH 44114-2518
216-696-7000
FAX: 216-696-0177 847-763-9670
mdeditor@penton.com
http://www.machinedesign.com

Joe DiFranco, Publisher
Ronald Khol, Editor
Kenneth J. Korane, Managing Editor
Bobbie Macy, Circulation Manager

The only magazine for applied technology for design engineering edited for design engineers and engineering managers. It covers new products and design practices in the fields of mechanical, electromechanical, electronics, motion control and process engineering.
Founded: 1929
Circulation: 180000

6252 Maintenance Solutions
Trade Press Publishing Corporation
2100 W Florist Avenue
Milwaukee, WI 53209
414-228-7701
FAX: 414-228-1134
dan.hounsell@tradepress.com
http://www.facilitiesnet.com/

Dick Yake, Editorial Director
Dan Hounsell, Editor
Brad R. Ehlert, VP
Brian Terry, Publisher
Renee Gryzkewicz, Associate Editor

How to articles and features designed to alleviate reader problems as well as new product information and applications. *$45.00*
42 pages Monthly Founded: 1993
Circulation: 35000

6253 Maintenance Technology
Applied Technology Publications
1300 S Grove Avenue
Suite 105
Barrington, IL 60010
847-382-8100
FAX: 847-304-8603
editors@mt-online.com
http://www.mt-online.com

Tom Madding, Publisher
Robert Baldwin, Editor
Susan Dahlberg, Managing Editor

Techniques, tools, equipment, strategies, procedures, and services for managing and maintaining capital assets are emphasized.
Monthly
Circulation: 50000

6254 Marine Fabricator
Industrial Fabrics Association International

1801 County Road BW
Roseville, MN 55113
651-222-2508
FAX: 651-631-9334 800-225-4324
generalinfo@ifai.com www.ifai.com

Mary Hennessy, Publisher
Melissa Kaudy, Editor
Galynn Nordstrom, Editorial Director

Features include fabrication techniques, fabricator profiles, case studies, business tips and solutions, a buyer's guide showcase. MFA news, and more. Marine Fabricator provides reportage that reflects the innovations and trends of the industry, in support of the Marine Fabricators Association. *$35.00*
Quarterly

6255 Material Handling Business
Penton Media
1300 E 9th Street
Cleveland, OH 44114
216-696-7000
FAX: 216-696-1752
information@penton.com
http://www.penton.com

Newt Barrett, Publishing Director
Tom Andel Reilly, Cheif Editor
Antoinette Sanchez Perkins, Circulation Manager

Journal written for design engineering managers, system integrates, material handling distributors and manufacturing sales executives.
86 pages Founded: 1892
Circulation: 92836
Printed in 4 colors on glossy stock

6256 Materials Performance
NACE International, The Corrosion Society
1440 S Creek Drive
Houston, TX 77084-4999
281-228-6200
FAX: 281-228-6300 1 8-0 7-7 62
pubs@mail.nace.org
http://www.nace.org

Gretchen Jacobson, Editor
Michele Sandusky, Production Manager
Angela Jarrell, Publisher
Helena Alexander, Director

Materials Performance, the monthly membership magazine for NACE International, is the primary source of corrosion-related information for engineers and specialists around the world. MP presents articles offering practical solutions to corrosion problems experienced in marine, underground, atmoshperic, and industrial environments and includes case histories, failure analyses, and general overviews. *$20.00*
Monthly Founded: 1943
Circulation: 17000
Printed in 4 colors

6257 Materials at High Temperatures
Butterworth Heinemann
313 Washington Street
Newton, MA 02458-1626
617-928-5460
FAX: 781-933-6333

T Suzuki, Co-Editor
TB Gibbons, Co-Editor

Serves the needs of those developing and using materials for high temperature applications in the power, chemical, engine, processing and furnace industries.

6258 Measurements and Control News
Measurements and Data Corporation
100 Wallace Avenue
Suite 100
Sarasota, FL 34237
941-954-8405
FAX: 941-366-5743
editor@mac-mag.com

Ken Kemski, Editor-in-Chief
Kristine Burmester, Associate Editor

Serves engineers, technichians, scientists, and other professionals involved in the recommendation and specification, of instuments and devices for measurement, inspection, testing, analysis, computing, and control.
Bi-Monthly

6259 Mechanical Engineering Magazine
American Society of Mechanical Engineers
Three Park Avenue
New York, NY 10016-5990
212-917-7740
FAX: 212-591-7674 800-843-2763
infocentral@asme.org
http://www.asme.org

Joe Sansone, Publisher
Cornelia Monahan, Editor/Production Manager
William T Cousin, President
John G. Falcioni, Editor in Chief *$25.00*

Monthly Founded: 1880

6260 Medical Equipment Designer
Adams Business Media
6001 Cuchran Road
Suite 300
Cleveland, OH 44139
216-249-9444
FAX: 440-248-0187
med@medicaldesigner.com
www.medicaldesigner.com

Terry Person, Publisher
Steve Wafalosky, Publisher

Published for the design function as it relates specifically to medical manufacturing and design of materials, components and complete systems.
1004 pages Bi-Monthly Founded: 1985
Circulation: 15,000
Printed in 4 colors on glossy stock

6261 Medical Physics
2 Huntington Quadrangle
Suite 1N01
Melville, NY 11747
516-576-2200
FAX: 516-576-2481 http://www.aip.org
Founded: 1931

6262 Microwave and RF
Penton Media
45 Eisenhower Drive
5th Floor
Paramus, NJ 07652
201-452-2400
FAX: 201-845-2493 800-829-9028
dprior@Penton.com
http://www.mwrf.com

Jack Browne, Publisher/Editor
Dawn Prior, Editorial Assistant

Dedicated to educating senior level design engineers, engineering managers, both domestic and foreign, who work all types of microwave systems, subsytems and components. *$81.00*
Monthly Founded: 1967
Circulation: 47000

Mailing list available for rent
Printed in on glossy stock

6263 Modern Materials Handling
Reed Business Information
275 Washington Street
Newton, MA 02158
617-558-4240
FAX: 617-630-3925
subsmail@reedbusiness.com
http://www.reedbusiness.com

Peter Boniface, Publisher
Raymond Kulwiec, Editor
James A Casella, CEO
Jason Cassidy, VP
Greg Flores, Senior Vice President

The magazine for managers and engineers responsible for handling materials and managing inventories in manufacturing, warehousing and distribution.
14 per year Founded: 1977
Printed in 4 colors on glossy stock

6264 Motion Control
ISA Services
67 Alexander Drive
Research Triangle Park, NC 27709
919-549-8411
FAX: 919-990-9434
sbatman@isa.org http://www.isa.org

Sam Batman, Editor

Information for those who design and maintain motion control systems. *$54.00*
56 pages Founded: 1945
Circulation: 41000
Printed in 4 colors on glossy stock

6265 Motion System Distributor
Penton Media
1300 E 9th Street
Cleveland, OH 44114
216-696-7000
FAX: 216-696-1752 800-249-9365
information@penton.com
http://www.penton.com

Jack C Lyttle, Publisher
David B Nussbaum, CEO
Larry Berardinis, Editor

Provides selling and technical information to individuals and distributors specializing in power transmission, motion control and fluid products. *$65.00*
Monthly Founded: 1892
Circulation: 54,000

6266 NACE International
NACE
1440 South Creek Drive
Houston, TX 77084-4906
281-228-6200
FAX: 281-228-6300 800-797-6223
msd@nace.org http://www.nace.org/

Helena Alexandera, Interim Director
Gretchen Jacobson, Editor
Neil Thompson, President *$105.00*
Monthly Founded: 1943
Circulation: 25000

6267 Naval Engineers Journal
American Society of Naval Engineers
1452 Duke Street
Alexandria, VA 22314-3458
703-836-6727
FAX: 703-836-7491
asnehq@navalengineers.org
www.navalengineers.org

Susan King, Editor

It contains technical papers authored by professionals engaged in naval and related engineering fields. Its high quality content is sought by those with an interest in topics of importance to the advancement of naval engineering.
Quarterly

6268 New Equipment Digest
Penton Media
1300 E 9th Street
Cleveland, OH 44114
216-696-7000
FAX: 216-696-1752
information@penton.com
http://www.newequipment.com

John Dipaula, VP
Dave Madonia, Publisher
Robert.F King, Editor

New Equipment Digest serves the general industrial field which includes manufacturing, processing, engineering services, construction, transportation, mining, public utilities, wholesale distributors, educational services, libraries and governmental establishments. *$65.00*
Monthly Founded: 1936
Circulation: 206006

6269 Noise Control Engineering Journal
Institute of Noise Control Engineering
62 Timberline Drive, Arlington Branch
PO Box 3206
Poughkeepsie, NY 12603-0206
845-462-4006
FAX: 845-463-0201
hq@ince.org www.ince.org

Alan Marsh, Editor

Includes articles on hearing protection, modal analysis, and signal processing. Information is refereed, authoritative, and technical. *$110.00*
Bi-Monthly
Circulation: 2,000

6270 Noise/News International
Institute of Noise Control Engineering
212 Marston Hall
Ames, IA 50011-2353
515-294-6142
FAX: 515-294-3528
ibo@inceusa.org www.inceusa.org

James K Thompson, VP Publications
Rich Peppin, Advertising/Expo Manager

Contains not only news items but also feature articles on a wide variety of topics of braod interest in noise control engineering. *$60.00*
Quarterly

6271 Nuclear Science and Engineering
American Nuclear Society
555 North Kensignton Avenue
La Grange Park, IL 60526
708-526-6611
FAX: 708-352-0499 www.ans.org

James S Tulenko, President
E James Reinsch, President-Elect/VP
Harry Bradley, Executive Director
William F Naughton, Treasurer

The journal is widely recognized as an outstanding source of information on research in all scientific areas related to the peaceful use of nuclear energy and radiation. Technical papers, notes, critical reviews, and computer code abstracts are presented. *$1200.00*
9x/year Founded: 1956

6272 Nuclear Technology
American Nuclear Society
555 North Kensington Avenue
La Grange Park, IL 60626
708-352-6611
FAX: 708-352-0499 www.ans.org

James S Tulenko, President
E James Reinsch, President-Elect/vP
Harry Bradley, Executive Director
William F Naughton, Treasurer

Leading international publication reporting on new information in all areas of the practical application of nuclear science. Topics include all aspects of reactor technology: operations, safety materials, instrumentation, fuel, and wast management. Also covered are medical uses, radiation detection, production of radiation, health physics, and computer applications, *$1315.00*
Monthly Founded: 2005

6273 Off-Highway Engineering
SAE
400 Commonwealth Drive
Warrendale, PA 15096-1
724-772-8548
FAX: 724-776-1665
magazines@sae.com
http://www.sae.org

Lawrence C Schneider, Publisher
Mark Davies, Editor-In-Chief

Off-Highway Engineering serves the international off highway design and manufacturing field which consists of producers of construction, lawn and garden, agricultural equipment, and industrial vehicles. Also served are makers of engines and parts and components and others allied to the field. *$70.00*
66 pages Founded: 1905
Circulation: 16308
Printed in 4 colors on glossy stock

6274 Optics and Spectroscopy
2010 Massachusetts Avenue NW
Washington, DC 20036-1023
202-223-8130
FAX: 202-223-1096 800-582-0416
nfo@osa.org http://www.osa.org

Elizabeth A Rogin, Executive Director
Colleen Morrison, Media Relations Mana
John Childs, Publication Director
$2850.00
Monthly Founded: 1916

6275 PM Engineer
Business News Publishing Company
2401 W Big Beaver Road
Suite 700
Troy, MI 48084
248-362-3700
FAX: 248-244-6439
wrdwzrd@aol.com
http://www.pmengineer.com

Julius Ballanco, Editorial Director
George Zebrowski, Group Publisher
Kelly Johnson, Editor
Joseph Mayton, Circulation Coordinator
Debora Reda, Marketing

Provides technical sheets, manufacturer product brochures, news features and analysis of useful industry information on the engineering and design of plumbing, piping, hydronics, cooling/heating, and fire protection/sprinkler systems. Free to trade engineers. *$64.00*
80 pages Monthly Founded: 1970
Circulation: 25000
Printed in 4 colors on glossy stock

6276 **PT Design**
Penton Media
1300 E 9th Street
Cleveland, OH 44114
216-696-7000
FAX: 216-696-1752
information@penton.com
http://www.penton.com

Jack Lyttle, Publisher
David B. Nussbaum, Ceo

Blends state-of-the-art motion system designs with traditional electrical and mechanical technology for the system designer. Also features articles on new products and technology, industry trends and application ideas. *$65.00*
Monthly Founded: 1892
Circulation: 54000

6277 **PT Distributor**
Reed Business Information
2000 Clearwater Drive
Oak Brook, IL 60523
630-740-0825
FAX: 630-288-8686 www.pddnet.com

Thomas H King, Publisher

provides information on selling techniques, fiscal and personnel management, purchasing, improving profits, training, and inventory and warehousing control. *$30.00*
Bi-Monthly
Circulation: 10,000

6278 **Pharmaceutical Engineering**
Int'l Society for Pharmaceutical Engineering
3109 W Dr. Martin Luther King Jr Blvd
Suite 250
Tampa, FL 33607
813-960-2105
FAX: 813-264-2816
customerservice@ispe.org
http://www.ispe.org

Gloria N Hall, Editor
Linda Brady, Director Marketing
Robert P. Best, President

Journal is published bi-monthly for members only and is considered by ISPE members to be the number one member benefit. Feature articles provide practical application and specification information on the design, construction, supervision and maintenance of process equipment, plant systems, instrumentation and facilities. *$60.00*

Founded: 1980
Circulation: 13138

6279 **Plant Engineering**
Reed Business Information
8878 Barrons Blvd
Highlands Ranch, CO 80129-2345
303-704-4000
FAX: 303-470-4280 800-446-6551
subsmail@reedbusiness.com
http://www.reedbusiness.com

Jim Langhenry, Publisher
Bobbie Wisniewski, Advertising Production Manager
Rick Ellis, Circulation Manager
Rick Dunn, Editor
Jim Silvestri, Managing Editor

Provides a constant reminder of engineering products and services and helps keep your company at the top of your customers' minds.
Monthly Founded: 1947
Circulation: 100034

6280 **Plant Services**
Putman Media
555 W Pierce Road
Suite 301
Itasca, IL 60143-2649
630-467-1300
FAX: 312-644-1131 800-984-7644
mbrener@putman.net
http://www.putmanmedia.com

Mike Brenner, Publisher
Paul Studebaker, Editor
Keith Larson, VP

For maintenance and engineering managers responsible for keeping manufacturing plants running efficiently. *$3.00*
Monthly Founded: 1938
Circulation: 500,000
Mailing list available for rent 10,000 names
Printed in 4 colors on glossy stock

6281 **Plastics Engineering**
Society of Plastics Engineers
14 Fairfield Drive
PO Box 403
Brookfield, CT 06804
203-775-0471
FAX: 203-775-8490
info@4spe.org http://www.4spe.org

Roger Ferris, Editor
Daniel J Domoff, Managing Editor
Susan Oderwald, Executive Director

Plastics publication dealing with breakthrough plastics technology. *$142.00*
Monthly Founded: 1942
Circulation: 86000

6282 **Plumbing Engineer**
Delta Communications
1167 W Bluemound Road
Wauwatosa, WI 53226
262-542-8820
FAX: 262-542-9111
delta@deltacommunications.com
www.deltacommunications.com

Edwin Scott, Editor

Offers news and updates to plumbing engineers and manufacturers. *$35.00*
Monthly Founded: 1973

6283 **Plumbing Standard Magazine**
American Society of Sanitary Engineering
901 Canterbury
Westlake, OH 44145
440-835-3040
FAX: 440-835-3488
info@asse-plumbing.org
www.asse-plumbing.org

Rand Ackroyd, President
Sean Cleary, First VP
Robert Cross, Second VP
Joseph Fugelo, IPP, Third VP
Shannon Corcoran, Executive Director

This magazine includes technical articles, current information on codes, standards, and other developments in the plumbing industry and related fields. Free with membership. *$12.00*
Quarterly

6284 **Powder Diffraction**
International Center for Diffraction Data
12 Campus Boulevard
Newton Square, PA 19073-3200
610-325-9814
FAX: 610-325-9823
info@icdd.com http://www.icdd.com

Timothy Fawcett, Executive Director
Cathyann Colaiezzi, Managing Editor
Theresa Kahmer, Publication Manager

A quarterly journal devoted to the use of the powder method for material characterization is available on annual subscription. The journal focus is on materials. Characterization employing x-ray powder diffraction and related techniques. *$90.00*
Quarterly Founded: 1941

6285 **Powder and Bulk Engineering**
CSC Publishing
1155 Northland Drive
St Paul, MN 55120
651-287-5600
FAX: 651-287-5650
powbulk@cscpub.com
http://www.powderbulk.com

Rich Cress, Publisher
Terry O' Neill, Editor

Featured editorial includes technical articles, case histories, test centers, product news and literature, and industry news items. *$100.00*
Monthly

6286 **Power Engineering International**
PennWell Publishing Company
1421 S Sheridan Road
Tulsa, OK 74112-6600
918-835-3161
FAX: 918-831-9497 800-331-4463
candiced@pennwell.com
http://www.peimagazine.com

Junior Isles, Publisher
Brian Schimmoller, Managing Editor

Serves the global electric power generation and transmission industry. *$180.00*
Monthly Founded: 1896

6287 **Precision Engineering**
Elsevier Science
PO Box 10826
Raleigh, NC 27605-0826
919-839-8444
FAX: 919-839-8039
webmaster@aspe.net www.aspe.net

W T Estler, Editor-in-Chief

Is the foremost international journal devoted to the study of ultra-high precision engineering and metrology.

6288 **Precision Engineering: An Evolutionary View**
Cranfield
PO Box 10826
Raleigh, NC 27605-0826
919-839-8444
FAX: 919-839-8039
webmaster@aspe.net www.aspe.net

Chris Evans, Editor

Gives an historical reference and development workers in the precision engineering field who want to understand the roots from which further precision engineering technology is to be developed. *$60.00*

6289 **Printed Circuit Design**
CMP Media
600 Community Drive
Manhasset, NY 11030
516-562-5000
FAX: 415-947-6090 www.cmp.com

6290 **Process Cooling & Equipment**
Refrigerating Engineers & Technicians Association
PO Box 1819
Salinas, CA 93902
831-455-8783
FAX: 831-455-7856
info@reta.com www.reta.com

Mark Broomer, Chairman
Doug Sweet, President
Stephan Shaub, VP
Dave Murphy, EVP
Edward Seffens, Treasurer

The only magazine that devotes itself to the industrial cooling side of the manufacturing process, including industrial refrigeration.

6291 Process Heating
Business News Publishing Company
755 W Big Beaver Road
Suite 100
Troy, MI 48084-4900
248-362-3700
FAX: 248-362-0317
ArmelA@bnpmedia.com
http://www.process-heating.com

Anne Armel, Publisher/Editor
Diane Bowles, Circulation Director

Covers heat processing at temperatures up to 1000 degrees F at end user and OEM plants in 9 industries.
Founded: 1994
Circulation: 25000

6292 Processing
Putman Media
PO Box 698
Birmingham, AL 35243
888-431-2877
FAX: 205-408-3797
webmaster@grandviewmedia.com
http://www.grandviewmedia.com

Dennis Van Milligen, Editor in Chief
Mike Wasson, Publisher

Offers information on printing, publishing and processing. Information is given on the latest technology in these and other desktop industries. *$15.00*
53 pages Monthly Founded: 1960

6293 Product Design and Development
Reed Business Information
301 Gibraltar Drive
Box 650
Morris Plains, NJ 07950
973-292-5100
FAX: 630-288-8686
www.reedbusiness.com

6294 Product Development Best Practices Report
Management Roundtable
92 Crescent Street
Waltham, MA 02453-3471
781-891-8080
FAX: 781-398-1889
editor@roundtable.com

Alex Cooper, Publisher

The goal of this publication is to help firms market, manufacture and design better products at a lower rate. *$219.00*
Monthly

6295 Professional Safety
American Society of Safety Engineers
1800 E Oakton Street
Des Plaines, IL 60018
847-699-2929
FAX: 847-768-3434
customerservice@asse.org
www.asse.org

Gene Barfield, CSP, President
Jack H Dobson, Jr CSP, President-Elect
Donald S Jones, SVP
Fred J Fortman, Executive Director/Secretary
Richard Nugent, VP Finance

Sharing the latest technical knowledge in SH&E information that is constantly being developed through research and on-the-job experience. *$60.00*
Monthly

6296 REPRO REPORT Magazine
International Reprographic Association
401 N Michigan Avenue
Chicago, IL 60611
312-245-1026
FAX: 312-527-6705 www.irga.com

Chuck Gremillion, President
Michael Shaw, VP
Steve Bova, CAE, Executive Director
Jeff Mitchell, Director Marketing
Mike Carter, Secretary/Treasurer

A primary technolgy and business resource for reprographic and wide-format color businesses. Subscriptions free to members
Bi-Monthly

6297 RSES Journal
Refrigeration Service Engineers Society
1666 Rand Road
Des Plaines, IL 60016-3552
847-297-6464
FAX: 847-297-5038 800-297-5660
jferenc@rses.org http://www.rses.org

Jeff Ferenc, Publisher
John Dyslin, Managing Editor
Robb Isaacs, Executive VP

Dedicated to HVACR professionals. Provides information on changing technology and marketplace demands, current government regulations, working methods and business strategy. Includes industry news, society and chapter program news, new products and services. *$48.00*
Monthly Founded: 1933
Circulation: 19200
Printed in 4 colors on glossy stock

6298 Radwaste Solutions
American Nuclear Society
555 North Kensington Avenue
La Grange Park, IL 60526
708-352-6611
FAX: 708-352-0499 www.asn.org

James S Tulenko, President
E James Reinsch, President-Elect/VP
Harry Bradley, Executive Director
William F Naughton, Treasurer

Containing articles that discuss practical approaches and solutions to everyday problems and issues in all fields of radioactive waste management and environmental restoration. *$455.00*
Bi-Monhtly Founded: 2005

6299 Reliability Engineering and Management Proceedings
7340 N La Oesta Avenue
Tucson, AZ 85704-3119
520-297-2679
FAX: 520-621-8191
dimitri@u.arizona.edu
http://www.u.arizona.edu/~dimitri

Dimitri Kececioglu, Executive Director

Proceedings where over 15 leading corporations present their latest techniques in this field. *$50.00*
Annual+ Founded: 1963
Circulation: 50
Mailing list available for rent 43000 names $152 per M.

6300 Repro Report
International Reprographic Association
401 N Michigan Avenue
Chicago, IL 60611
312-245-1026
FAX: 312-527-6705
info@irga.com http://www.irga.com

Steve Bova, Executive Director
Amy Carlton, Editor
Jeff Mitchell, Director of Marketing

Articles on blueprint service companies, engineering equipment manufacturers and suppliers. *$150.00*
Founded: 1927
Circulation: 1000

6301 Research-Technology Journal
Industrial Research Institute
2200 Clarendon Boulevard
Suite 1102
Arlington, VA 22201
703-647-2580
FAX: 703-647-2581 www.iriinc.org

Susan M Gaud, Chairman
R Kent Crawford, Vice Chairman
F M Ross Armbrecht, Jr, President
Margaret Grucza, Executive Director

It contains peer-reviewed articles covering the entire spectrum of technological innovation, from research and development through product development to marketing. *$95.00*
Bi-Monthly Founded: 1958

6302 Resource
American Society of Agricultural Engineers
2950 Niles Road
Saint Joseph, MI 49085-8607
269-429-0300
FAX: 269-429-3852 800-371-2723
hq@asae.org http://www.asae.org

Melissa Moore, Executive VP
Pam Bakken, Advertising Sales Manager
Sue Mitrovich, Editor

Accepts advertising. *$75.00*
Founded: 1907
Circulation: 9000 $120 per M.
Printed in on matte stock

6303 Review of Scientific Instruments
American Institute of Physics
Suite 1NO1
2 Huntington Quadrangle
Melville, NY 11747-2924
516-576-2200
FAX: 516-349-9704
rsi@aip.org http://www.aip.org

Thomas Braid, Editor
Douglas LaFrenier, Marketing Director

Presents original articles on new principles, devices and techniques in scientific instrumentation. *$90.00*
Monthly Founded: 1931
Circulation: 3100

6304 Robotics and Computer-Intergrated Manufacturing
Elsevier Science
PO Box 945
New York, NY 10159
212-895-5800
FAX: 212-633-3680
usinfo-f@elsevier.com
http://www.elsevier.com

Nam P Sata, Editor
A. Sharon, Editor-in-Chief:

Cotains original papers on theoretical, applied and experimental robotics and computer-integrated manufacturing, with

emphasis on flexible manufacturing systems. *$1156.00*
Founded: 1880
Circulation: 2500

6305 SAMPE Journal
Society for the Advancement of Material
1161 Parkview Drive
Covina, CA 91724-3751

FAX: 626-332-8929 800-562-7360
sampe@sampe.org www.sampe.org

Dr Scott Beckwith, Editor

An informative and acclaimed publication provides a steady stream of technical articles, industry and international technical news, product and new literature announcements, book reviews, technical events calendars, and local SAMPE information. This publication is mailed complimentary to all SAMPE members. *$70.00*
Bi-Monthly

6306 SPE Drilling & Completion
Society of Petroleum Engineers
PO Box 833836
Richardson, TX 75083-3836
972-529-9300
FAX: 972-952-9435 800-456-6863
spedal@spe.org www.spe.org

Giovanni Paccaloni, President
Bill Cobb, VP Finance
John E Bethancourt, Director
Management/Information
Ian Gorman, Director
Production/Operations

Features papers covering bit technology, completions, drilling fluids and operations, equipment and instrumentation, perforation and sand control, simulations tubulars, well control, and workover well construction related topics. *$30.00*
Quarterly

6307 SPE Journal
Society of Petroleum Engineers
PO Box 833836
Richardson, TX 75083-3836
972-529-9300
FAX: 972-952-9435 800-456-6863
spedal@spe.org www.spe.org

Giovanni Paccaloni, President
Bill Cobb, VP Finance
John E Bethancourt, Director
Management/Inforamtion
Ian Gorman, Director
Production/Operations

Includes full length technical papers covering all aspects of petroleum technology. SPE Journal covers the theories and emerging concepts that will become the new technologies of tomorrow. *$60.00*
Quarterly

6308 SPE Production & Facilities
Society of Petroleum Engineers
PO Box 833836
Richardson, TX 75083-3836
972-529-9300
FAX: 972-952-9435 800-456-6863
spedal@spe.org www.spe.org

Giovanni Paccaloni, President
Bill Cobb, VP Finance
John E Bethancourt, Director
Management/Information
Ian Gorman, Director
Production/Operations

It includes papers on artificial lift, chemical treatments, design and operation of surface facilities and downhole equipment, formation damage control, fracturing, gas production and storage, offshore operations, production logging and optimization systems, sand control, separation and processing, and workover-production improvement. *$30.00*
Quarterly

6309 SPE Reservoir Evaluation & Engineering
Society of Petroleum Engineers
PO Box 833836
Richardson, TX 75083-3836
972-529-9300
FAX: 972-952-9435 800-456-6863
spedal@spe.org www.spe.org

Giovanni Paccaloni, President
Bill Cobb, VP Finance
John E Bethancourt, Director
Management/Information
Ian Gorman, Director
Production/Operations

The journal covers a wide range of topics, including the following: Reservoir Engineering. *$40.00*
Bi-Monthly

6310 Sea Technology
Compass Publications
1501 Wilson Boulevard
Suite 1001
Arlington, VA 22209
703-524-3136
FAX: 703-841-0852 877-263-4496
seatechorder@sea-technology.com
http://www.sea-technology.com

Amos Bussmann, Publisher
Carol Foster, Circulation Manager
Travis Talnt, Editor
Michele Umansky, Managing Editor

Worldwide information leader for marine business, science and engineering. Read in more than 100 countries by management, engineers, scientists and technical personnel working in industry, government and educational research institutions. Readers are involved with oceanographic research, fisheries management, offshore oil and gas exploration and production, and undersea defense including antisubmarine warfare, ocean mining and commercial diving. *$40.00*
Monthly Founded: 1960
Circulation: 16304
Mailing list available for rent $80 per M.
Printed in 4 colors

6311 Standardization News
ASTM International
100 Barr Harbor Drive
PO Box C700
West Conshohocken, PA 19428-2959
610-329-9500
FAX: 610-832-9555
service@astm.org www.astm.org

Maryann Gorman, Editor-in-Chief
John Pace, VP Publications/Marketing

Provides news and feature articles on ASTM's standards development activities and global standardization trends.
Monthly

6312 TEST Engineering & Management
Mattingley Publishing Company
3756 Grand Avenue
#205
Oakland, CA 94610-1545
510-839-0909
FAX: 510-839-2950
testmag@mattingley-publ.com
http://www.mattingley-publ.com

Eve Mattingley-Hannigan, Publisher
Nora Archambeau, Advertising Sales Manager

Includes mechanical testing, environmental simulation, and related technologies in industry, government, testing labs, and universities. *$45.00*
Monthly Founded: 1959
Circulation: 9500 9000 names
Printed in 4 colors on glossy stock

6313 Tribology & Lubrication Technology
Society of Tribologists & Lubrication
840 Busse Highway
Park Ridge, IL 60068-2376
847-825-5536
FAX: 847-825-1456
information@stle.org www.stle.org

Thomas T Astrene, Editor-in-Chief
Karl Phipps, Associate Editor
Dr Neil Canter, Contributing Editor

Technical magazine that serves an audience of interdisciplinary professionals from industry, academic institutions and government. Included in this group are scientists, engineers, corporate leaders, researchers and product developers, plant managers and maintenance professionals, sales and marketing people and more.
Monthly
Circulation: 7,000

6314 Tribology Transaction
Society of Tribologists & Lubrication
840 Busse Highway
Park Ridge, IL 60068-2376
847-825-5536
FAX: 847-825-1456
information@stle.org www.stle.org

Dr Andrew Jackson, Editor

Provides you with new and useful reports and analysis of every aspect of tribology and lubrication presented by renowned authors from around the globe. Available online as well.
Quarterly

6315 US Black Engineer & Information Technology
Career Communications Group
729 E Pratt Street
Suite 504
Baltimore, MD 21202
410-244-7101
FAX: 410-752-1834
customer_service@ccgmag.com
http://www.ccgmag.com

Tyrone D Taborn, Editor-in-Chief, Publisher & CEO
Lango Deen, Technology Editor
Antonio Watson, VP Sales
Guy Madison, Publisher

Devoted to engineering, science, and technology and to promoting opportunities in those fields for Black Americans. *$26.00*
84 pages Quarterly
Circulation: 100,000
Printed in 4 colors on glossy stock

6316 Upholstery Journal
Industrial Fabrics Association International

1801 County Road BW
Roseville, MN 55113
651-222-2508
FAX: 651-631-9334 800-225-4324
generalinfo@ifai.com www.ifai.com

Mary Hennessy, Publisher
Janet Cass, Editor
Galynn Nordstrom, Editorial Director

Recent topics have included shop safety, the art of wood finish touch-ups, leather's continuing popularity and diversity, and trends in the boating industry. Upcoming issues

will feature a review of the latest furniture frame designs, how to deal with down-time, recycling shop leftovers, trends in vinyl, sewing machine showcase, and upholsterers of the year profiles.
$39.00
Bi-Monthly

6317 VXI Journal
30233 Jefferson Avenue
Saint Clair Shores, MI 48282
586-415-6500
FAX: 586-415-4882
Magazine is geared towards test engineers who are using or considering VXI bus systems and equipment.
Quarterly
Circulation: 8000

6318 Water Engineering & Management

Scranton Gillette Communications
380 E Northwest Highway
Suite 200
Des Plaines, IL 60016-2282
847-298-6622
FAX: 847-390-0408
www.waterinfocenter.com
Bill Swichtenberg, Editorial Director
Edited for managers and engineers at municipal and privately held water/wastewater treatment facilities. *$40.00*

100 pages Monthly Founded: 1982
Circulation: 41,000

6319 Way Ahead Magazine
Society of Petroleum Engineers
PO Box 833836
Richardson, TX 75083-3836
972-529-9300
FAX: 972-952-9435 800-456-6863
spedal@spe.org www.spe.org
Giovanni Paccaloni, President
Bill Cobb, VP Finance
John E Bethancourt, Director Management/Information
Ian Gorman, Director Production/Operations
Designed for and written by young professionals in the oil and gas industry. In it, you will find items of particular interest to the younger members of our industry, including articles on the current state of the job market, how to improve communication skills, and what SPE young professionals are doing will be.
3x/year

6320 Weighing & Measurement
Key Markets Publishing Company
4729 Charles Street
PO Box 5867
Rockford, IL 61125-0867
815-636-7739
dwam34@inwave.com
David M Mathieu, Publisher
Articles on new products, industry news, previews and reviews of events, and technical approaches to measurement.
Bi-Monthly
Circulation: 12,000

6321 Weight Engineering Journal
Society of Allied Weight Engineers
204 Hubbard Street
Glastonbury, CT 06033-3063
860-633-0850
FAX: 860-633-8971
exdirector@sawe.org www.sawe.org
Roger L Belt, President
James L Valentine, VP
William M Childers, Treasurer
Adreas R Schuster, VP Transportation
Brandy R Meyer, Secretary
Reports topics of interest from both the international office and the individual chapters.
Periodic

6322 Wireless Design & Development
Reed Business Information
301 Gibraltar Drive
PO Box 650
Morris Plains, NJ 07950-0650
973-292-5100
FAX: 973-292-0783
wcurtis@cdhners.com
www.wirelessdesignmag.com
Wayne Curtis, Group Publisher
Kim Stokes, Editor
Edited for wireless component and system design engineers in the commerical RF and microwave market.
Monthly

Trade Shows

6323 AACE International Annual Meeting & Exposition
AACE International
209 Prairie Avenue
Suite 100
Morgantown, WV 26507
304-296-8444
FAX: 304-291-5728 800-858-2678
info@aacei.org www.aacei.org
Teri Jefferson, Meetings Coordinator
Andy Dowd, Executive Director
Offers a unique opportunity to learn, network, and expand your professional horizons in a cost-effective manner. Our goal is to provide cost professionals with the knowledge necessary for survival in today's incredibly fast-changing marketplace. AACE's technical presentations, skills and knowledge track, exhibitors, transactions, certification program and social events combine to create an experience you can't afford to miss.
800 Attendees June 5000+ names $100 per M.

6324 AES Convention
Audio Engineering Society
60 E 42nd Street
Room 2520
New York, NY 10165-2520
212-661-8528
FAX: 212-682-0477
HQ@aes.org www.aes.org
Theresa Leonard, President
Neil Gilchrist, President-Elect
Roger K Furness, Executive Director
Marshall Buck, Treasurer
Louis Fielder, Treasurer-Elect
October

6325 AHR Expo
Refrigeration Service Engineers Society
1666 Rand Road
Des Plaines, IL 60016
847-976-6464
FAX: 847-297-5038 800-297-5660
general@rses.org www.rses.org
Jean Birch, Director Conferences
Attracts thousands of attendees from all facets of the industry, including contractors, engineers, dealers, distributors, wholesalers, OEM's, architects and builders, industrial plant operators, facility owners and managers, agents and reps.
January, Chicago

6326 ANS Annual Meeting
American Nuclear Society
555 North Kensington Avenue
La Grange Park, IL 60526
708-352-6611
FAX: 708-352-0499 www.ans.org
Dr Lawrence Papay, General Chair
Dr Atambir Rao, Technical Program Chair
Harry Bradley, Executive Director
Topic: The Next 50 Years Creating Opportunities.
June

6327 AOCS Annual Meeting & Expo
American Oil Chemists Society
2211 W Bradley Avenue
Champaign, IL 61821
217-359-2344
FAX: 217-351-8091
general@aocs.org www.aocs.org
Mary Belding, Conference Contact
Connie Hilson, Exhibit Information
April, Missouri

6328 APPA Institute for Facilities Management
1643 Prince Street
Alexandria, VA 22314-2818
703-684-1446
FAX: 703-549-2772
www.appa.org/education
Suzanne Healy, Director Conventions/Education
Next show dates are January, February, March, June, July, and September.

6329 APPA's Educational Facilities Leadership Forum
Association of Higher Education Facilities

1643 Prince Street
Alexandria, VA 22314-2818
703-684-1446
FAX: 703-549-2772 www.appa.org
Suzanne Healy, Director Conventions/Education
August

6330 ASA: Drive Systems-Control Units-Automation
Stygar Associates
1202 Allanson Road
Mundelein, IL 60060
847-566-4566
FAX: 847-566-4580
estygariii@aol.com
www.stygarassociates.com
376 exhibitors of hydraulic and pneumatic elements, compressed air systems, automation components, openloop and measuring controls.
40000 Attendees Biennial

6331 ASCE Annual Meeting
American Society of Certified Engineering
PO Box 1348
Flowery Branch, GA 30542-0023
770-967-9173
FAX: 770-967-8049
kurt_schuler@ascet.org
www.ascet.org
Russell E Freier, Chairman
Leo Saenz, CET, President
Kurt Schuler, Secretary/Treasurer

June

6332 **ASEE Annual Conference & Exposition**
American Society for Engineering Education
1818 N Street NW
Suite 600
Washington, DC 20036-2476
202-331-3500
FAX: 202-265-8504
prism@asee.org www.asee.org
Patti Greenawalt, Director Meetings/Conventions
Frank Huband, Executive Director
June, Chicago

6333 **ASFE Fall Meeting**
ASFE
8811 Colesville Road
Suite G106
Silver Springs, MD 20910
301-565-2733
FAX: 301-589-2017
info@asfe.org www.asfe.org
Gerald J Salontai, PE, President
Daniel L Harpstead, PE, President-Elect
John P Bachner, Executive VP
Phil Pettway, Controller
Joseph Cibor, Secretary/Treasurer
October

6334 **ASFE Winter Leadership Conference**
ASFE
8811 Colesville Road
Suite G106
Silver Springs, MD 20910
301-565-2733
FAX: 301-589-2014
info@asfe.org www.asfe.org
Gerald J Salontai, PE, President
Daniel L Harpstead, PE, President-Elect
John P Bachner, Executive VP
Phil Pettway, Controller
Joseph Cibor, Secretary/Treasurer
January, Colorado

6335 **ASM Heat Treating Society Conference and Heat Treating Show**
ASM International
9639 Kinsman Road
Materials Park, OH 44073-0002
440-385-5151
FAX: 440-338-4634 800-336-5152
asmexpos@asminternational.org
www.asminternational.org
Kim Simpson, Conference Manager
Charles Dec, Exposition Manager
Conference and 300 exhibits of heat treating equipment and supplies plus information of interest to metallurgists, manufacturing, research and design technical professionals.
4500 Attendees September, Bi-Annual
Founded: 1974

6336 **ASM Materials Solutions Conference and Exposition**
ASM International
9639 Kinsman Road
Materials Park, OH 44073-0002
440-338-5151
FAX: 440-338-4634 800-336-5152
asmexpos@asminternational.org
www.asminternational.org
Annual event focusing on testing, analysis, characterization and research of materials such as engineered materials, high performance metals, powdered metals, metal forming, surface modification, welding and joining.
4,000 Attendees October

6337 **ASME International Gas Turbine Institute**
American Society of Mechanical Engineers
5775-B Glenridge Drive
#370
Atlanta, GA 30328-5364
404-847-0072
FAX: 404-847-0151
igti@asme.org www.asme.org
Virgil Carter, Executive Director
A show focused on the role gas turbines will play in meeting the nation's future energy demands.
1.9MM Attendees

6338 **ASME Summer Annual Meeting**
American Society of Mechanical Engineers
Three Park Avenue
New York, NY 10016-5990
212-917-7740
FAX: 973-882-1167 800-843-2763
infocentral@asme.org www.asme.org
Harry Armen, President
Richard E Feigel, President-Elect
Virgil Carter, Executive Director
David Soukup, Managing Director Operations
June

6339 **ASME: American Society of Mechanical Engineers Winter Annual Meeting**
345 E 47th Street
New York, NY 10017

FAX: 973-882-1717 800-843-2763
leadhj@asme.org
www.asme.org/events
June Leach-Barnaby, Meetings Manager
100 exhibits of engineering and consulting information, supplies and services including specialized software.
3200 Attendees

6340 **ASPE Technical Symposium**
American Society of Plumbing Engineers
8614 Catalpa Avenue
Suite 1007
Chicago, IL 60656-1116
773-693-2773
FAX: 773-695-9007
info@aspe.org www.aspe.org
Pat Delaney, Convention/Symposium Information
Stan Wolson, Executive Director
For professional plumbing engineers, designers and contractors to improve their skills, learn original design concepts and make important networking contacts to help them stay abreast of current trends, codes and technologies.
October

6341 **ASPE's Annual Meeting**
American Society for Precision Engineering
PO Box 10826
Raleigh, NC 27605-0826
919-839-8444
FAX: 919-839-8039
webmaster@aspe.net www.aspe.net
Erika Deutsch-Layne, Meetings Manager
Offers the latest in precision engineering research through presentations from national and international.
October

6342 **ASQ World Conference on Quality and Improvement**
American Society for Quality
600 N Plankinton Avenue
Milwaukee, WI 53203
414-272-8575
FAX: 414-272-1734 800-248-1946
help@asq.org www.asq.org
Kenneth E Case, Chairman
Jerry Mairani, President
Gary D Floss, VP
Paul Borawski, Executive Director
May

6343 **ASQ's Annual Six Sigma Forum Roundtable**
American Society for Quality
600 N Plankinton Avenue
Milwaukee, WI 53203
414-272-8575
FAX: 414-272-1734 800-248-1946
help@asq.org www.asq.org
Kenneth E Case, Chairman
Jerry Mairani, President
Gary D Floss, VP
Paul Borawski, Executive Director
An exclusive two-day briefing and networking event designed by and for the top practitioners in the Six Sigma community.
September

6344 **ATCE**
Society of Petroleum Engineers
PO Box 833836
Richardson, TX 75083-3836
972-529-9300
FAX: 972-952-9435 800-456-6863
spedal@spe.org www.spe.org
Giovanni Paccaloni, President
Bill Cobb, VP Finance
John E Bethancourt, Director Management/Information
Ian Gorman, Director Production/Operations
40482 Attendees October

6345 **AVS International Symposium and Exhibition**
AVS Science & Technology Society
120 Wall Street
32nd Floor
New York, NY 10005-3993
212-248-0200
FAX: 212-248-0245 www.avs.org
David E Aspnes, President
Christie R Marrian, President-Elect
John Coburn, Treasurer
Joseph J Greene, Clerk/Secretary
Yvonne Towse, Executive Director
This has been developed to address cutting-edge issues associated with vacuum science and technology in both the research and manufacturing communities. The Symposium is a week long forum for science and technology exchange featuring papers from technical divisions and technology groups, and topical conferences on emerging technologies.
3000 Attendees Founded: 1953

6346 **AVS New Mexico Chapter Annual Symposium Short Courses/Vendor Show**
AVS Science & Technology Society
120 Wall Street
32nd Floor
New York, NY 10005-3993
212-248-0200
FAX: 212-248-0245 www.avs.org

David E Aspnes, President
Christie R Marrian, President-Elect
John Coburn, Treasurer
Joseph J Greene, Clerk/Secretary
Yvonne Towse, Executive Director

May

6347 AWWA Annual Conference and Exposition
American Water Works Association
6666 W Quincy Avenue
Denver, CO 80235
303-794-7711
FAX: 303-347-0804 800-926-7337

Jack W Hoffbuhr, Executive Director

Served as the source of knowledge and information for water professionals who work to improve the quality and supply of drinking water in North America and beyond.

June

6348 Acoustical Society of America Conference
2 Huntington Quadrable
Suite 1NO1
Melville, NY 11747
516-576-2360
FAX: 516-576-2377
asa@aip.org asa.aip.org

Charles E Schmid, Executive Director
Elaine Moran, Manager

15 booths

1M Attendees May

6349 Adhesion Society Annual Meeting
Adhesion Society
2 Davidson Hall-0201
Blacksburg, VA 24061
540-231-7257
FAX: 540-231-3971
adhesoc@vt.edu
www.adhesionsociety.org

Ken Shull, Program Chair
Leonardo Lopez, Exhibition Chair
Esther Brann, Manager

Engineers, chemists, biologists, mathmaticians, physicists, physicians and dentists visit exhibits relating to the study of adhesion's role in coatings, composite materials, the function of biological tissues, and the performance of bonded structures.

400 Attendees February, Annual

6350 Adhesive & Sealant Council Convention
Adhesive & Sealant Council
7979 Old Georgetown Road
Suite 500
Bethesda, MD 20814
301-986-9700
FAX: 301-986-9795 www.ascouncil.org

Rick McConnell, Senior Show Director
Bob Willis, Conventions Manager
Lawrence Sloan, President

SemiAnnual convention for middle to senior level executives featuring concurrent sessions, meal programs, and an exhibition of small product samples, literature and lightweight equipment, as well as raw materials, and consulting services to the adhesive and sealant industry. 40-50 booths of exhibits.

400 Attendees April, Tennessee

6351 Airlines Engineering Committee
Aeronautical Radio
2551 Riva Road
Annapolis, MD 21401-7435
410-266-4000
FAX: 410-266-4040

Daniel Martinec, Director Avionics

Commercial airline and other transport aircraft avionics engineers.

800 Attendees October

6352 American Conference on Crystal Growth and Epitaxy
American Association for Crystal Growth
25 4th Street
Somerville, NJ 08876
908-575-0649
FAX: 908-575-0794
aacg@att.net www.crystalgrowth.org

Darrell Schlom, Conferene Chair
Alexana Roshko, NIST, Program Chair

The meeting will be held jointly with the US Biennial Workshop on Organometallic Vapor Phase Epitaxy. Will provide a forum for the presentation and discussion of recent research and development activities in all aspects of bulk crystal growth and epitaxial thin film growth, with sessions integrating fundamentals, experimental and industrial growth processes, characterization, and applications.

350+ Attendees July

6353 American Crystallographic Association Annual Meeting
Ellicott Station
PO Box 96
Buffalo, NY 14205-0096
716-856-9600
FAX: 716-852-4846
marcia@hwi.buffalo.edu
www.hwi.buffalo.edu/aca

Marcia Evans, Administration

75 manufacturers exhibits of commercial hardware and software, and x-ray equipment. Conference, dinner and reception.

1000 Attendees Annual Founded: 1955

6354 American Institute Industrial Engineers Int'l Maintenance Conference
3577 Parkway Lane
Suite 200
Norcross, GA 30092
770-449-0460
FAX: 770-441-3295 800-494-0460

Don Greene, Executive Director
Bill Gibbs, Continuing Education/Conferences

75 booths.

2M Attendees May

6355 American Oil Chemists Society Annual Meeting & Expo
American Oil Chemists Society
2211 W Bradley Avenue
Champaign, IL 61821-1827
217-359-2344
FAX: 217-351-8091
meetings@aocs.org www.aocs.org

Jeffry Newman, Manager Meetings
Greg Reed, Manager

184 booths displaying fat and oil processing equipment, instrumentation and related services. Seminar, banquet, luncheon and dinner.

2000 Attendees April, Missouri 2000 names

6356 American Society Civil Engineers Annual Convention and Expo
1801 Alexander Bell Drive
Reston, VA 20191-4400
703-295-6000
FAX: 703-295-6144 www.asce/org

Sean Scully, Exhibits Manager
Patrick Natale, Executive Director

focus on the challenges faced by companies and agencies already implementing the next generation of infrastructure in Water(e.g. dams, desalinmation, and recycling) and Transportation(e.g. seaports, rail, and roads). 100 booths.

24M Attendees October

6357 American Society for Engineering Education Conference and Exposition
American Society for Engineering Education
1818 N State Street
Suite 600
Washington, DC 20036
202-331-3500
FAX: 202-265-8504
conferences@asee.org www.asee.org

Patti Greenawalt, Director Conventions/Meetings
Jennifer Atkinson, Meetings Assistant
Kathi J Springer, Manager Exhibits/Sponsorships
Frank Huband, Executive Director

Annual conference of 150 publishers, manufacturers, producers, suppliers, designers of scientific instrumentation and distributors. Exhibits include publications, engineering supplies and equipment, computers, software and research companies all products and services related to engineering education.

1700 Attendees June

6358 American Society for Nondestructive Testing Conference

1711 Arlingate Lane
PO Box 28518
Columbus, OH 43228-0518
614-274-6003
FAX: 614-274-6899 800-222-2768
kthomas@asnt.org www.asnt.org

Thomas Kelly, Exhibit/Event Supervisor

Seminar, conference and 150 exhibits of nondestructive testing equipment, services, supplies and laboratory representatives. Holds a smaller conference in the spring.

3000 Attendees October

6359 American Society of Civil Engineers Annual Conference and Exposition
1801 Alexander Bell Drive
Reston, VA 20191-4400
703-295-6000
FAX: 703-295-6144 800-548-2723
conf@asce.org www.asce.org

Patrick Natale, Executive Director

175 exhibits of industry related products and services, seminars, workshops and banquet plus continuing education classes.

3000 Attendees November

6360 **American Society of Mechanical Engineers Winter Annual Meeting & Exhibition**
American Society of Mechanical Engineers
Three Park Avenue
New York, NY 10016-5990
212-917-7740
FAX: 212-591-7674 800-843-2763
infocentral@asme.org www.asme.org
Thomas Loughlin, Managing Director/Engineer
Virgil R Carter, Executive Director
Annual meeting of 40 exhibitors of software, publications, equipment and services.
3200 Attendees November 100 names $125 per M.

6361 **American Society of Plumbing Engineers Meeting**
American Society of Plumbing Engineers
8614 Catalpa Avenue
Suite 1007
Chicago, IL 60656-1116
773-693-2773
FAX: 773-695-9007
info@aspe.org www.aspe.org
Pat Delaney, Convention/Symposium Contact
Stan Wolson, Executive Director
Biennial meeting and exhibits for the plumbing engineering industry. 600 booths.
7000 Attendees Founded: 1964

6362 **American Society of Safety Engineers Professional Development Conference**
American Society of Safety Engineers
1800 E Oakton Street
Des Plaines, IL 60018-2187
847-699-2929
FAX: 847-296-3769
customerservice@asse.org
www.asse.org
Diane Hurns, Manager Public Relations
Annual conference and expo of 250 manufacturers and suppliers of safety equipment and health products.
3500 Attendees June

6363 **American Vacuum Society National Symposium**
120 Wall Street
32nd Floor
New York, NY 10005
212-248-0200
FAX: 212-248-0245
avsnyc@avs.org www.avs.org
Steve George, Program Chair
Angus Rockett, Program Vice Chair
Heather Korff, Events/Office Coordinator
Yvonne Towse, Executive Director
230 booths of vacuum instruments and component systems of interest to scientists and engineers.
4200 Attendees November Founded: 1963

6364 **Annual Applied Reliability Engineering and Product Assurance**
The University of Arizona
Aerospace and Mechanical Engineering Department
Building 119, PO Box 210119
Tucson, AZ 85721-0119
520-215-5511
FAX: 520-621-8191
dimitri@u.arizona.edu
www.u.arizona.edu/~dimitri
Dimitri B Kececioglu PE, Professor Aerospace/Mechanical Eng.
July 43,000 names $150 per M.

6365 **Annual Canadian Conference on Intelligent Systems**
Robotics Industris Association
900 Victors Way
PO Box 3724
Ann Arbor, MI 48106
734-994-6088
FAX: 734-994-3338
webmaster@robotics.org
www.robotics.org
Don Vincent, Executive VP
Brian Huse, Director Marketing/PR
Jim Adams, Marketing Manager
Sharon Adams, Accounting Manager
Canada's leading showcase of research excellence and breakthroughs in robotics and intelligent systems, featuring technology displays, demonstrations, presentations and workshops.
June

6366 **Annual Lean Management Solutions Conference**
Institute of Industrial Engineers
3577 Parkway Lane
Suite 200
Norcross, GA 30092
770-490-0461
FAX: 770-441-3295 800-494-0460
cs@iienet.org www.iienet.org
Allen L Soyster, PhD, President
Susan M Sinclair, President-Elect
Don Greene, Executive Director
Christopher Barnes, Treasurer
Marc Resnick, PhD, Secretary
Will enable you to significantly improve performance, reduce costs, and increase customer satisfaction. With over 60 presentations and new tracks in MRO, Food Processing, Aviation, Healthcare, and Product Design, you will find what you need.
December

6367 **Annual Physical Electronics Conference**
AVS Science & Technology Society
120 Wall Street
32nd Floor
New York, NY 10005-3993
212-248-0200
FAX: 212-248-0245 www.avs.org
David E Aspnes, President
Christie R Marrian, President-Elect
John Coburn, Treasurer
Joseph J Greene, Clerk/Secretary
Will provide a forum for the dissemination and discussion of new research results in the physics and chemistry of surfaces and interfaces. The conference will continue to emphasize fundamental science in materials systems, including metals, semiconductors, insulators and biomaterials.
June

6368 **Annual Quality Audit Conference**
American Society for Quality
600 N Plankinton Avenue
Milwaukee, WI 53203
414-272-8575
FAX: 414-272-1734 800-248-1946
help@asq.org www.asq.org
Kenneth E Case, Chairman
Jerry Mairani, President
Gary D Floss, VP
Paul Borawski, Executive Director
Topics of interest: New Innovating Audit/Process Approaches, Value Added Involvement, Corporate Expectations, Corporate/Social Responsibility, Auditing in the Overall Corporate Scheme.
October 2006

6369 **Annual RSES Conference & Expo**
Refrigeration Service Engineers Society
1666 Rand Road
Des Plaines, IL 60016
847-976-6464
FAX: 847-297-5038 800-297-5660
general@rses.org www.rses.org
Jean Birch, Director Conferences
September

6370 **Annual Reliability Engineering and Management Institute**
The University of Arizona
Aerospace and Mechanical Engineering Department
Building 119
Tucson, AZ 85721
520-621-5511
FAX: 520-621-8191
dimitri@u.arizona.edu
www.u.arizona.edu/~dimitri
Dimitri B Kececioglu PE, Professor Aerospace/Mechanical Eng.
To provide all engineers, and particularly Reliability Managers and Engineers, and Product assurance Managers and Engineers in government and Industry, with a working knowledge of Reliability Engineering Theory and Practice; Mechanical Reliability Prediction; Reliability Testing and Demonstration; Accelerated Testing; Failure Analysis Techniques; Complete Industry Product Assurance; Maintainability; Quality Management; Concurrent Reliability plus many more!
65 Attendees November 43,000 names $150 per M.

6371 **Annual Service Quality Conference**
American Society for Quality
600 N Plankinton Avenue
Milwaukee, WI 53203
414-272-8575
FAX: 414-272-1734 800-248-1946
help@asq.org www.asq.org
Kenneth E Case, Chairman
Jerry Mairani, President
Mairani
Gary D Floss, VP
Paul Borawski, Executive Director
The sessions we plan will help you to navigate through unpredictable consumer behavior and increasing competition to build a strong foundation for reaching superior levels of quality service.
October

6372 **Annual Simulation Solutions Conference**
Institute of Industrial Engineers
3577 Parkway Lane
Suite 200
Norcross, GA 30092
770-490-0461
FAX: 770-441-3295 800-494-0460
cs@iienet.org www.iienet.org
Ed Williams, Conference Chair
You will have a rich menu of over forty presentations by successful practitioners of simulation in transportation and military applications; management strategies; manufacturing; lean scheduling and operations; healthcare; simulation skills; supply chain, material handling, and distribution; and service and business processes.
May

6373 **Association of Energy Engineers**
4025 Pleasantdale Road
Suite 420
Atlanta, GA 30340
770-447-5083
FAX: 770-446-3969
info@aeecenter.org
www.aeecenter.org

Helen Ardavin, Conference Director
Ted Kurklis, Exhibit Manager
Ruth Marie, Director Information Services
Albert Thumann, Executive Director

Membership organization of over 8,000 professionals and certification programs in the fields of energy efficiency, utility deregulation, facility management, plant engineering and environmental compliance. Offers seminars, conferences, books to critical buyer-seller networking trade shows, job listings and certification programs.
8.2M Attendees
Mailing list available for rent

6374 **Association of Higher Education Facilities Officers Annual Meeting/Exhibition**
1643 Prince Street
Alexandria, VA 22314-2818
703-684-1446
FAX: 703-549-2772
diana@appa.org www.appa.org

Suzanne Healy, Director Conventions/Education
E Lander Medlin, Executive VP

Conference and 210 exhibits relating to consulting services and publications, equipment and supplies for physical site administrators.
1500 Attendees

6375 **Atlantic Design & Manufacturing**
Canon Communications
11444 W Olympic Boulevard
Suite 900
Los Angeles, CA 90064-1549
310-445-4200
FAX: 310-445-4299
diane.o'conner@cacom.com
www.cancom.com

Diane O'Conner, Trade Show Director
Dan Cutrone, Show Marketing Manager

Serves the East Coast's dynamic design, process, and manufacturing marketplace. This exposition, recently acquired by Canon Communications, is now co-located with Medical Design and Manufacturing East. Product classifications include: Coatings and Finishes, Composites, Computer Aided Design/Computer Aided Manufacturing, Electrical/Electronic, Electrc Optical Compnents and Equipment, Engineered Safety Products, Engineering Management and Tools, Fasteners, Fluid Media, Fluid Power and Control.
May

6376 **Atomic Layer Deposition**
AVS Science & Technology Society
120 Wall Street
32nd Street
New York, NY 10005-3993
212-248-0200
FAX: 212-248-0245 www.avs.org

David E Aspnes, President
Chrisitie R Marrian, President-Elect
John Coburn, Treasurer
Joseph J Greene, Clerk/Secretary

Conference will be a three-day meeting, dedicated to the science and technology of atomic layer controlled deposition of thin films, in particular atomic layer deposition.
August

6377 **Audio Engineering Society Meeting**
60 E 42nd Street
Room 2520
New York, NY 10165-2520
212-661-8528
FAX: 212-682-0477 www.aes.org

Roger K Furness, Executive Director

250 booths, held in the fall and spring of each year.
5M Attendees October

6378 **BMES Annual Fall Meeting**
Biomedical Engineering Society
8401 Corporate Drive
Suite 225
Landover, MD 20785-2224
301-459-1999
FAX: 301-459-2444
info@bmes.org www.bmes.org

Diane Solomon, Meetings Coordinator
September

6379 **Corrosion Expo**
NACE International, Corrosion Society
1440 S Creek Drive
Houston, TX 77084-4906
281-228-6200
FAX: 281-228-6300
msd@mail.nace.org www.nace.org

Cassie Davie, Director Conferences/Expositions

Corrosion is a complete professional program offering extensive technical information to managers, end users, and researchers in the field of corrosion prevention materials, control products and services, coatings and linings.
6000 Attendees March, California

6380 **Corrosion Technology Week**
NACE International
1440 S Creek Drive
Houston, TX 77084-4906
281-228-6200
FAX: 281-228-6300 800-797-6223
trevor.eade@mail.nace.org
www.nace.org

Cassie Davie, Director Conferences/Expositions

To provide a series of technical committee meetings focusing on various methods of identifying, preventing, and combating corrosion problems in many industries.
September

6381 **ESTECH, IEST's Annual Technical Meeting and Exposition**
American Institute of Physics
One Physics Ellipse
College Park, MD 20740-3843
301-209-3100
www.aip.org

Cecelia Brescia, Executive Director/CEO
Richard Baccante, Treasurer/CFO

Will feature a cutting-edge technical program, hot-topic tutorials, must attend Working Group meetings, and a state-of-the-art exposition.
May

6382 **Earth and Space**
American Society of Civil Engineers
1801 Alexander Bell Drive
Reston, VA 20191
703-295-6000
FAX: 703-295-6222 800-548-2723
cybrarian@asce.org www.asce.org

Patricia Galloway, President
Lawrence Roth, Deputy Executive Director
Patrick Natale, Secretary/Treasurer

You will be among experts from a variety of disciplines and have ample, enjoyable opportunities to discuss exploration, engineering, construction, and operations in challenging environments on Planet Earth, in Space, and on other planetary bodies such as the Moon and Mars.
March

6383 **Electric West**
PRIMEDIA Business Exhibitions
11 River Bend Drive S
PO Box 4949
Stamford, CT 06907-0949
203-358-9900
FAX: 203-358-5816
ewylie@primediabusiness.com
www.primediaevents.com

Liza Wylie, Show Director
Mandy Ferreira-Nunez, Operations Manager

Educational sessions attract electrical professionals from contracting companies, industrial plants, consulting engineering firms, datacom installers and electricians. Presentations focus on such topics as power quality, lighting, the NEC, project management, claims management and fiber optics. Also provides in-depth coverage of National Electrical Code changes that directly impact the work of electrical professionals.
March, Las Vegas

6384 **European Symposium of the Protein Society**
American Institute of Physics
One Physics Ellipse
College Park, MD 20740-3843
301-209-3100
www.aip.org

Cecelia Brescia, Executive Director/CEO
Richard Baccante, Treasurer/CFO

The meeting features sessions on nanotechnology, biosensors and proteins as materials, proteomics, protein networks and systems biology. membrane proteins and diseases, protein folding and diseases, protein flexibility, and molecular recognition.
May

6385 **Finishing Expo**
Society of Manufacturing Engineers
1 SME Drive
PO Box 930
Dearborn, MI 48121
313-271-1500
FAX: 313-425-3400 www.sme.org

Nancy S Berg, Executive Director

The conference will include workshops, tutorials, and technical sessions. 200 booths.
25M Attendees

6386 General Convention
Sigma Phi Delta
438 Smithfield Street
East Liverpool, OH 43920-1723
330-385-5287

webmaster@sigphi.org
www.sigphi.org

Derek R Troy, Grand President
Alixandre R Minden, Grand VP
Steven A Weiss, Communications Director
Edward A Hurst, Treasurer
Levon Haig Barsoumian, Executive Secretary

Includes a tentative schedule of business sessions, symposiums and events.
July

6387 Geoline Expo
Association of Engineering Geologists
PO Box 460518
Denver, CO 80246
303-757-2926
FAX: 303-757-2969
aeg@aegweb.org www.aegweb.org

Becky Roland, Chief Staff Executive

The symposium will cover three major topics. Session 1 Field investigations: Strategy, Organization, Methods, and Uncertainties, Session 2 Inserting the Structure in its Environment, Session 3 Construction, Monitoring, Evolution and Maintenance.
400 Attendees December 2006

6388 Globalcon
Association of Energy Engineers
4025 Pleasantdale Road
Suite 420
Atlanta, GA 30340
770-447-5083
FAX: 770-446-3969
webmaster@aeecenter.org
www.aeecenter.org

Helen Ardavin, Conference Director
Ted Kurklis, Exhibit Manager

This event is for commerical, industrial, institutional or government energy users who want to explore first-hand the latest technologies and strategies available to reduce costs, upgrade and improve equipment performance, and increase overall operational efficiency.
March, Pennsylvania

6389 Government Affairs Briefing
North American Die Casting Association
241 Holbrook Drive
Wheeling, IL 60090-5809
847-279-0001
FAX: 847-279-0002
twarog@diecasting.org
www.diecasting.org

Daniel Twarog, President

Will provide you with important information in the following informative sessions, state of US manufacturing, trade and global competition, metalcasting research programs, health care & other worker issues, new air standards & other environmental issues, and capitol hill visits.
June

6390 IDSA National Conference
Industrial Designers Society of America
45195 Business Court
Suite 250
Dulles, VA 20166
703-707-6000
FAX: 703-787-8501
isda@isda.org www.idsa.org

Bruce Claxton, Board Chair
Ron B Kemnitzer, President
Tim P Fletcher, Chapter VP
Kristina Goodrich, Executive Director/CEO
Larry Allen, Deputy Executive Director

Inspire and motivate designers worldwide to begin thinking about the opportunity to utilize design as a force for good and a catalyst for change, few among us have done much more than just think about it.
800 Attendees August

6391 IESNA Annual Conference
Illuminating Engineering Society of North America
120 Wall Street
Floor 17
New York, NY 10005
212-248-5000
FAX: 212-248-5018
iesna@iesna.org www.iesna.org

Craig A Bernecker, President
Alan L Lewis, OD PhD, President-Elect/SVP
William Hanley, Executive VP
Boyd Corbett, Treasurer
Sue Foley, Marketing Manager

January, New York

6392 IFAI Expo
Industrial Fabrics Association International

1801 Country Road B W
Roseville, MN 55113
651-222-2508
FAX: 651-631-9334 800-225-4324
generalinfo@ifai.com www.ifai.com

Jennifer E Thompson, Director Conference Management

Will offer exhibits, educational programs, dynamic speakers, recognition opportunities, certification testing, and many networking opportunities - everything specialty fabrics industry professionals could want or need to develop their businesses.
October

6393 IFAI Outlook
Industrial Fabrics Association International

1801 Country Road BW
Roseville, MN 55113
651-222-2508
FAX: 651-631-9334 800-225-4324
generalinfo@ifai.com www.ifai.com

Jennifer E Thompson, Director Conference Management

Will bring industry leaders together to discuss important issues and challenges faced by the United States textile industry.
May

6394 IIE Annual Conference
Institute of Industrial Engineers
3577 Parkway Lane
Suite 200
Norcross, GA 30097
770-490-0461
FAX: 770-441-3295 800-494-0460

Bill Gibbs, Show Manager

With over 600 content filled presentations and expert speakers, it is the productivity event of the year. Discover the latest tools, techniques and solutions from top professionals in the field. Network with peers, decision makers, and leaders during the conference.
1,100 Attendees May

6395 IIE Annual Conference and Exposition
Institute of Industrial Engineers
3577 Parkway Lane
Suite 200
Norcross, GA 30092
770-490-0461
FAX: 770-441-3295 800-494-0460
cs@iienet.org www.iienet.org

Allen L Soyster, PhD, President
Susan M Sinclair, President-Elect
Don Greene, Executive Director
Christopher Barnes, Treasurer
Marc Resnick, PhD, Secretary

With over 600 content filled presentations and expert speakers, it is the productivity event of the year. Topical conferences and in-depth seminars are designed to keep members informed of current industrial engineering processes and to educate them about the latest innovations in their profession.
May

6396 IPTC
Society of Petroleum Engineers
PO Box 833836
Richardson, TX 75083-3836
972-529-9300
FAX: 972-952-9435 800-456-6863
spedal@spe.org www.spe.org

Giovanni Paccaloni, President
Bill Cobbs, VP Finance
John E Berthancourt, Director Management/Information
Ian Gorman, Director Production/Operations

The theme for the conference is Sustaining World Growth - Technology and People. A new meeting brought to you by four leading industry societies (AAPG, EAGE, SEG, and SPE). Natural gas will be a major focus of this meeting.
November

6397 IRI Shaping Innovation Leaders at Kellogg
Industrial Research Institute
2200 Clarendon Bouleavard
Suite 1102
Arlington, VA 22201
703-647-2580
FAX: 703-647-2581 www.iriinc.org

Susan M Gaud, Chairman
R Kent Crawford, Vice Chairman
F M Ross Armbrecht, Jr, President
Margaret Grucza, Executive Director

Create a program specifically designed to meet the needs of those promising, mid-level managers in research, development and engineering whose further success may very well depend on their ability to fully understand and effectively communicate with the non-technical executives of their organizations.
June

6398 IRgA Annual Convention and Trade Show
International Reprographic Association
401 N Michigan Avenue
Chicago, IL 60611
312-245-1026
FAX: 312-527-6705 www.irga.com

Eric Johnson, Director Convention/Exhibits
Jen Marcus, Trade Show Coordinator

You will gain first hand knowledge and experience from technical sessions presented by experts in their field, access to the latest products and services available to enhance your company's performance at the trade

show, re-establish and contacts connections as you interact with peers to find out how they are handling the latest challenges.
May

6399 International Cod Council Annual Conference
BOCA Evaluation Services
4051 W Flossmoor Road
Country Club Hills, IL 60478-5795
708-799-2300
FAX: 800-214-7167 888-422-7233
John Noose, President
James Lee Witt, Chief Executive Officer
Karl Meyer, CFO/Finance & Administration
Carolina Khoury, Secretary
The conference features the Final Action Hearings, the Education Program, the Annual Business Meeting, the International Code Council Expo and networking opportunities with your peers in the building safety and fire prevention fields.
September

6400 International Conference on Construction Engineering/Management
American Society for Civil Engineers
1801 Alexander Bell Drive
Reston, VA 20191
703-295-6000
FAX: 703-295-6222 800-548-2723
cybrarian@asce.org www.asce.org
Patricia Galloway, President
Lawrence Roth, Deputy Executive Director
Patrick Natale, Secretary/Treasurer
October

6401 International Conference on Deburring and Surface Finishing
Abrasive Engineering Society
141 Moore Road
Butler, PA 16001
724-282-6210
FAX: 724-234-2376
aes@abrasiveengineering.com
www.abrasiveengineering.com
Doug Haynes, President
Ted Giese, Executive Director
The program, which is part of series of international conferences, is scheduled for June. This conference will include a Technical Exhibition and Tours. A special course on deburring and surface finishing will be taught following the conference.
June

6402 International Conference on Metallurgical Coatings and Thin Films
AVS Science & Technology Society
120 Wall Street
32nd Floor
New York, NY 10005-3993
212-248-0200
FAX: 212-248-0245 www.avs.com
David E Aspnes, President
Christie R Marrian, President-Elect
John Coburn, Treasurer
Joseph J Greene, Clerk/Secretary
Internationally recognized as a vibrant technical conference that integrates fundamentals and applied research focused on thin film deposition, characterization, and advanced surface modification techniques leading-edge technology.
May

6403 International Society Weighing/Measurement Annual Meeting
15245 Shady Grove Road
Suite 130
Rockville, MD 20850
301-258-1115
FAX: 301-990-9771
staff@iswm.org www.iswm.org
Steve Kendra, President
Richard Sharpe, VP
150 booths.
1.8M Attendees

6404 International Symposium on Advances in Abrasives Technology
Abrasive Engineering Society
141 Moore Road
Butler, PA 16001
724-826-6210
FAX: 742-234-2376
aes@abrasiveengineering.com
www.abrasiveengineering.com
Doug Haynes, President
Ted Giese, Executive Director
Jointly sponsored by the International Committee for Abrasives Technology and the Japan Society for Abrasive Technology, which has conducted eight international conferences on abrasives technologies. Topics including abrasive machining, finishing, assessment of grinding performance, machine tools and systems, coolant and other topics.
November

6405 International Workshop on Deep Inelastic Scattering - DIS05
American Institute of Physics
One Physics Ellipse
College Park, MD 20740-3843
301-209-3100
www.aip.org
Cecelia Brescia, Executive Director/CEO
Richard Baccante, Treasurer/CFO
The aim of these workshops is to review the progress in the field of DIS and QCD and to discuss and lay the groundwork for the future. DIS 2005 will bring together about 250 experimentalists and theorists. The workshop format will involve plenary sessions with review talks and parallel working group sessions with shorter contributions.
April

6406 Material Handling Industry of America Trade Show
ProMat
8720 Red Oak Boulevard, Suite 201
Charlotte, NC 28217-3992
704-676-1190
FAX: 704-676-1199 800-345-1815
Carol Miller, Senior Director Marketing
John Nossinger, Chief Executive Officer
You can compare the latest solutions essential to the productivity of your manufacturing, warehousing, and distribution operations. The material handling & logistics solutions you discover at ProMat will help you differentiate your product, improve customer service and increase overall corporate profitability. 700 exhibits.
January

6407 Mechanical Contractors Association America Conference
1385 Piccard Drive
Rockville, MD 20850-4340
301-869-5800
FAX: 301-990-9690
cynthia@mcaa.org www.mcaa.org
John Gentille, Executive Vice President
Containing 100 booths and 95 exhibits.
February

6408 Meeting of the Acoustical Society of America
Acoustical Society of America
2 Huntington Quandrangle
Suite 1N01
Melville, NY 11747-4502
516-576-2360
FAX: 516-576-2377
asa@aip.org www.asa.aip.org
William A Kuperman, President
William A Yost, President-Elect
Mark F Hamilton, VP
Donna L Neff, VP Elect
Charles E Schmid, Executive Director
May

6409 Metalcasting Congress
North American Die Casting Association
241 Holbrook Drive
Wheeling, IL 60090-5809
847-279-0001
FAX: 847-279-0002
twarog@diecasting.org
www.diecasting.org
Daniel Twarog, President
With the wide range of opportunities for technology transfer, it promises to be the industry's premier show. The American Foundry Society and the North American Die Casting Association are joining together.
April, Ohio

6410 Mid-Atlantic Job Shop Show
Edward Publishing
16 Waterbury Road
Prospect, CT 06712-1215
203-758-6658
FAX: 203-758-4476
www.jobshoptechnology.com
Jennifer Bryda, Production Manager
The show is designed to attract the highest caliber engineers and buyers from your major DEM product manufacturers. There will be 260 exhibitors and booths.
2500 Attendees May Founded: 1999

6411 NADCA Sales Training
North American Die Casting Association
241 Holbrook Drive
Wheeling, IL 60090-5809
847-279-0001
FAX: 847-279-0002
twarog@diecasting.org
www.diecasting.org
Daniel Twarog, President
NADCA will be providing a one day seminar to address the challenges we face in today's marketplace.
June

6412 NSPE Annual Convention and Expo
National Society of Professional Engineers
1420 King Street
Alexandria, VA 22314-2794
703-684-2800
FAX: 703-836-4875 888-285-2853
advertising@nspe.org www.nspe.org

Katrina Robinson, Marketing Manager

The National Society of Professional Engineers is the only engineering society that represents individual engineering professionals and liscensed engineers across all disciplines. Founded in 1934, NSPE serves some 60,000 members and the public through 53 state and territorial societies and more than 500 chapters nationally and internationally. The conference brings together the decision makers of engineering companies and business owners nationwide to network and discuss issues of importance.

700 Attendees July
Mailing list available for rent 50,000+ names $130 per M.

6413 National Industrial Automation, Integration & Control Show
Reed Exhibition Companies
383 Main Avenue, Suite 3
PO Box 6059
Norwalk, CT 06851-1543
203-840-4800
FAX: 203-840-9570

Peter DiLeo, Marketing Director

Annual show of 200 exhibitors of chemical engineering and processing, electronics, machinery equipment, supplies and services.

19M Attendees

6414 National Quality Education Conference
American Society for Quality
600 N Plankinton Avenue
Milwaukee, WI 53203
414-272-8575
FAX: 414-272-1734 800-248-1946
help@asq.org www.asq.org

Kenneth E Case, Chairman
Jerry Mairani, President
Gary D Floss, VP
Paul Borawski, Executive Director

Provides teachers, administrators, and support personnel opportunities to examine continuous improvement principles used in education. It provides resources and best practices to help you address requirements of No Child Left Behind, while helping you increase student achievement and improve overall performance.

November

6415 New England Spring Job Show
Edward Publishing
16 Waterbury Road
Prospect, CT 06712-1215
203-758-6658
FAX: 203-758-4476
www.jobshoptechnology.com

Gerald Schmidt, President
Jennifer Bryda, Production Manager

The show is designed to attract the highest caliber engineers and buyers from your major DEM product manufacturers.

2000 Attendees April Founded: 1999

6416 Ninth International Conference on Quasicrystals
AVS Science & Technology Society
120 Wall Street
32nd Floor
New York, NY 10005-3993
212-248-0200
FAX: 212-248-0245 www.avs.org

David E Aspnes, President
Christie R Marrian, President-Elect
John Coburn, Treasurer
Joseph J Greene, Clerk/Secretary

This is the premier conference for researchers in this field. Held every 2-3 years, the ICQ's typically attract a highly international group of scientists.

May

6417 Northern American Material Handling Show & Forum
Appliance Manufacturer
5900 Harper Road
Suite 105
Solon, OH 44139-1935
440-349-3060
FAX: 440-498-9121 800-345-1815
cmiller@mhia.org www.mhia.com

Carol Miller, Senior Director Marketing

Bi-Annual

6418 Northwest Plant Engineering & Maintenance Show and Conference (NWPE)
Cygnus Expositions
3167 Skyway Court
Fremont, CA 94539
510-543-3131
FAX: 510-354-3159
showinfo@proshows.com
proshows.com

Erin Sparks, Marketing Manager

Annual show of 233 exhibitors of low-tech cleaning systems, high-tech computerized maintenance management systems, diagnostic problem software, indoor air quality controllers and related products and services.

5000 Attendees May

6419 OTC Expo
Society of Petroleum Engineers
PO Box 833836
Richardson, TX 75083-3836
972-529-9300
FAX: 972-952-9435 800-456-6863
spedal@spe.org www.spe.org

Giovanni Paccaloni, President
Bill Cobbs, VP Finance
John E Bethancourt, Director Management/Information
Ian Gorman, Director Production/Operations

51300 Attendees

6420 Pacific Design & Manufacturing
Canon Communications
11444 W Olympic Boulevard
Suite 900
Los Angeles, CA 90064-1549
310-445-4200
FAX: 310-445-4299
register@cancom.com
www.pacdesignshow.com

Diane O'Conner, Trade Show Director
Dan Cutrone, Show Marketing Manager

The Pacific Design Engineering show is the most comprehensive eventserving the West Coast's design, process and manufacturing marketplace. Product classsifications include Coatings & Finishes, Composites, Computer Aided Design/Computer Aided Manufacturing, Electrical/Electronic, ElectroOptical Components & Equipment, Engineered Sarety products, Engineering Management & Tools and more. Held at the Anaheim Convention Center in Anaheim, California.

35970 Attendees January

6421 Pro Audio Expo & Convention
Audio Engineering Society
60 E 42nd Street
Room 2520
New York, NY 10165-2520
212-661-8528
FAX: 212-682-0477
HQ@aes.org www.aes.org

Theresa Leonard, President
Neil Gilchrist, President-Elect
Roger K Furness, Executive Director
Marshall Buck, Treasurer
Louis Fielder, Treasurer-Elect

The AES has been the forum where new products such as CD, SACD, digital consoles, multi-channel and many more products were first introduced to the audio community.

May, Spain

6422 REMSA and AREMA Meeting
Railway Engineering: Maintenance Supplies Assn
417 West Broad Street
Suite 203
Falls Church, VA 22046
703-241-8514
FAX: 703-241-8589
home@remsa.org www.remsa.org

Thomas E Dickey, President
Jonathan D Reilly, VP
Judi Meyerhoeffer, Executive Director
Ronald C Olds, Secretary/Treasurer

Holding the exhibits and technical conference simultaneously in Louisville give added benefit to REMSA members.

September

6423 REMSA and NRC: Synergy in Action
Railway Engineering: Maintenance Supplies Assn
417 West Broad Street
Suite 203
Falls Church, VA 22046
703-241-8514
FAX: 703-241-8589
home@remsa.org www.remsa.org

Thomas E Dickey, President
Jonathan D Reilly, VP
Judi Meyerhoeffer, Executive Director
Ronald C Olds, Secretary/Treasurer

Members and other industry suppliers discuss their products, services and equipment with attendees representing a broad spectrum of railroaders: transits, short lines, commuter and Class I railroads. There were 56 exhibiting companies.

January

6424 RSES HVACR Expo
Refrigeration Service Engineers Society
1666 Rand Road
Des Plaines, IL 60016
847-976-6464
FAX: 847-297-5038 800-297-5660
general@rses.org www.rses.org

Jean Birch, Director Conferences/Seminars
Robb Isaacs, Executive VP

An international annual exposition where suppliers of heating, ventilation, air conditioning and refrigeration equipment and services display their products for HVACR technicians, contractors and businesses.

October

6425 RoboBusiness Conference and Exposition
American Institute of Physics
One Physics Ellipse
College Park, MD 20740-3843
301-209-3100
www.aip.org

Cecelia Bresica, Executive Director/CEO
Richard Baccante, Treasurer/CFO

Focuses on the business development and technical issues involved with the commercial application of mobile robotics and intelligent systems technology to develop entirely new markets and product categories, open additional lines of business and enhance existing product lines.
May

6426 SAFETY Expo
American Society of Safety Engineers
1800 E Oakton Street
Des Plaines, IL 60018
847-699-2929
FAX: 847-768-3434
customerservice@asse.org
www.asse.org

Gene Barfield, CSP, President
Jack H Dobson, Jr CSP, President-Elect
Donald S Jones, SVP
Fred J Fortman, Executive Director/Secretary
Richard Nugent, VP Finance

A full 3-day conference featuring more than 200 sessions, an exposition with 300 exhibitors, special pre- and post-conference seminars, conference proceedings on CD, numerous networking events and more.
July

6427 SME Annual Meeting
Society of Manufacturing Engineers
1 SME Drive
PO Box 930
Dearborn, MI 48121
313-271-1500
FAX: 313-271-2861 800-733-4763
service@sme.org www.sme.org

Nancy S Berg, Executive Director/GM

Bringing together hundreds of SME members to interact and exchange ideas with their fellow practitioners. This yearly forum offers technical training, special sessions for members, and a celebration of the best that manufacturing has to offer through our International Honor Awards Banquet.
June

6428 STL Annual Meeting
Society of Tribologists & Lubrication
840 Busse Highway
Park Ridge, IL 60068-2376
847-825-5536
FAX: 847-825-1456
information@stle.org www.stle.org

Merle Hedland, Meetings Manager

Expect more than 300 technical and practical presentations will be selected for the Calgary program.
May, Canada

6429 Society for the Advancement of Material and Process Engineering (SAMPE)
1161 Park View Drive
Covina, CA 91724-3748
626-331-0616
FAX: 626-332-8929 800-562-7360
sampeibp@aol.com www.sample.org

Gregg Balko, Executive Director
Rosemary Loggia, Exhibits Manager
Priscilla Heredia, Conference/Symposia Assistant Mgr

Theme: New Horizons for Materials and Processing Technology. Over 275 technical papers will be presented, as well as over 200 industry manufacturers, supplier and service companies will showcase the largest variety of latest technologies on our exhibit floor.
8M Attendees May

6430 Street & Area Lighting Conference
Illuminating Engineering Society of North America
120 Wall Street
Floor 17
New York, NY 10005
212-248-5000
FAX: 212-248-5018
iesna@iesna.org www.iesna.org

Craig A Bernecker, President
Alan L Lewis, OD PhD, President-Elect/SVP
William Hanley, Executive Director
Boyd Corbett, Treasurer
Sue Foley, Marketing Manager
October

6431 TBPA Annual Convention
Tau Beta Pi Association
PO Box 2697
Knoxville, TN 37904-2697
865-546-4578
FAX: 865-546-4579
tbp@tbp.org www.tbp.org

Matthew W Ohland, President
Ellen D Styles, VP
James D Froula, Executive Director/Treasurer
Roger Hawks, Assistant Secretary/Treasurer
Patricia McDaniel, Director Communications

Provides an opportunity for delegates from all parts of the country to meet each other and to see another major engineering college. National officers are afforded a special opportunity to meet with chapter representatives and to learn first-hand about their problems, solutions, and opinions on the role ofTau Beta Pi on the nation's campuses.
October

6432 Texoma Regional Education & Training Conference
Society of American Military Engineers
607 Prince Street
Alexandria, VA 22314-3117
703-549-3800
FAX: 703-684-0231 800-336-3097
webmanager@same.org
www.same.org

Dr Robert D Wolff, Executive Director
Jennifer Nichols, Marketing Manager
L Eileen Erickson, Director Communications

Will provide opportunities to attend SAME sponsored sessions as well as TSPE sponsored training sessions. This diversity of training venues is intended to provide the attendee with exposure to a wide variety of topics and will provide a beneficial learning experience.
June

6433 Total Product Development
American Supplier Institute
17333 Federal Drive
Suite 220
Allen Park, MI 48101-3614
313-336-8877
FAX: 313-336-3187 800-462-4500
sandy@amsup.com www.amsup.com

Dr Genichi Taguchi, Executive Director

Annual show and exhibits relating to the encouragement of change in US industry through development and implementation of advanced manufacturing and engineering technologies.
200 Attendees

6434 UNYVAC's Co-Sponsored Symposium
AVS Science & Technology Society
120 Wall Street
32nd Floor
New York, NY 10005-3993
212-248-0200
FAX: 212-248-0245 www.avs.org

David E Aspnes, President
Christie R Marrian, President-Elect
John Coburn, Treasurer
Joseph J Greene, Clerk/Secretary

Topic: Functional Coatings and Surface Engineering (FCSE-2005). Will provide a forum for training and discussion of the physics and chemistry of functional coatings and surfaces.
June, Bi-Annual

6435 West Coast Energy Management Congress EMC
Association of Energy Engineers
4025 Pleasantdale Road
Suite 420
Atlanta, GA 30340
770-447-5083
FAX: 770-446-3969
webmaster@aeecenter.org
www.aeecenter.org

Helen Ardavin, Conference Director
Ted Kurklis, Exhibit Manager

Specifically for business, industrial and institutional energy users. It brings together the top experts in all areas of the field to help you set a clear, optimum path to both energy cost control and energy supply security.
June

6436 Winter Meeting and Nuclear Technology Expo
American Nuclear Society
555 North Kensington Avenue
La Grange Park, IL 60526
708-352-6611
FAX: 708-352-0499 www.ans.org

Thomas A Christopher, General Co-Chair
Michael Wallac, General Co-Chair

Topic: Talk About Nuclear Differently: A Good Story Untold.
November

6437 World Energy Engineering Congress
Association of Energy Engineers
4025 Pleasantdale Road
Suite 420
Atlanta, GA 30340
770-447-5083
FAX: 770-446-3969
webmaster@aeecenter.org
www.aeecenter.org

Helen Ardavin, Conference Director
Ted Kurklis, Exhibit Manager

A comprehensive forum where participants can fully assess the big picture and see exactly how the economic and market forces, new technologies, regulatory developments and industry trends all merge to shape their critical decisions on their organizations' energy and economic future.
September

Directories & Databases

6438 **AEG Annual Directory**
Association of Engineering Geologists
300 S Jackson Street, Suite 100
PO Box 460518
Denver, CO 80246
303-757-2926
FAX: 303-757-2969 www.aegweb.org
Dave Bieber, President
Darrel Schmitz, President-Elect/VP
Becky Roland, Chief Staff Executive
Terry West, Treasurer
Dorian Kuper, Secretary
Contains member and Association information.

6439 **ANS Buyers Guide**
American Nuclear Society
555 North Kensington Avenue
La Grange Park, IL 60526
708-352-6611
FAX: 708-352-0499 www.ans.org
James S Tulenko, President
E James Reinsch, President-Elect/VP
Harry Bradley, Executive Director
William F Naughton, Treasurer
Buyer's Guide Directory lists approximately 1150 suppliers of products and services to the nuclear industry. This comprehensive listing contains approximately 500 categories representing the wide range of nuclear components and services available today. *$110.00*
Annual Founded: 2005

6440 **ASME Database**
American Society of Mechnical Engineers
Three Park Avenue
New York, NY 10016-5990
212-917-7740
FAX: 973-882-1167 800-843-2763
infocentral@asme.org www.asme.org
Harry Armen, President
Richard E Feigel, President-Elect
Virgil Carter, Executive Director
David Soukup, Managing Director Operations
Provides proven direct mail buyers and selection options that enable you to customize lists to achieve your objective.

6441 **AWWA Buyer's Guide**
American Water Works Association
6666 W Quincy Avenue
Denver, CO 80235
303-794-7711
FAX: 303-347-0804 800-926-7337
Jack W Hoffbuhr, Executive Director
The official resource guide to water industry products and services.

6442 **Advanced Energy Design Guide for Small Office Buildings**
Illuminating Engineering Society of North America
120 Wall Street
Floor 17
New York, NY 10005
212-248-5000
FAX: 212-248-5018
iesna@iesna.org www.iesna.org
Albert Suen, Publications Fulfillment
Provides a sensible approach by including practical products and readily-available, off-the-shelf technology. The Guide offers you all the tools you need to create an energy-efficient building where the owners will see a 30 percent energy savings compared to buildings that only meet the minimum requirements of Standard 90.1. *$47.00*
390 pages Softcover Founded: 2004

6443 **Advances in Abrasive Technology**
Trans Tech Publications
141 Moore Road
Butler, PA 16001
724-282-6210
FAX: 724-234-2376
aes@abrasiveengineering.com
www.abrasiveengineering.com
Yongsheng Gao, Editor
With some exceptions, the compilation focuses on technologies for advanced materials and ultra precision machining. Short notes on select papers follow. Hover the cursor over the paper and a brief review will appear in the right column for many papers. *$165.00*
426 pages Founded: 2002 ISBN 0-878499-10-5

6444 **American Association of Cost Engineers Membership Directory**
Association for Total Cost Management
209 Prairie Avenue
#100
Morgantown, WV 26501-5949

FAX: 304-291-5728
Andy Dowd, Executive Director
Member directory. *$35.00*
100 pages Annual

6445 **American Consulting Engineers Council**
1015 156th Street NW
Washington, DC 20005
202-472-2483
FAX: 202-898-0068
acec@acec.org www.acec.org
David Raymond, President
Howard Messner, Executive Director
Conducts programs concerned with public relations, business practices, governmental affairs, insurance and employment. Holds professional seminars.
5.2M pages

6446 **American Society for Engineering Education Membership Directory**
1818 N Street NW
Suite 600
Washington, DC 20036-2476
202-331-3500
FAX: 202-265-8504 www.asee.org
Frank Huband, Executive Director
Offers information on over 10,000 colleges and university engineering professors and personnel, practicing engineers and industry executives who are members of the ASEE.
200 pages Annual
Circulation: 10,000

6447 **American Society of Civil Engineers Official Register**
1801 Alexander Bell Drive
Reston, VA 20191-4400
703-295-6000
FAX: 703-295-6144 800-548-2723
conf@asce.org www.asce.org
Patrick Natale, Executive Director
Provides ready acces to governing documents, statistics, and general information about ASCE for leadership, members, and staff. *$ 24.00*
640 pages Softcover, Annual Founded: 2005 ISBN 0-784407-73-8

6448 **Audio Engineering Society: Directory of Educational Programs**
Audio Engineering Society
60 E 42nd Street
Room 2520
New York, NY 10165-2520
212-661-8528
FAX: 212-682-0477
HQ@aes.org www.aes.org
Roger Furness, Executive Director
Over 100 institutions are listed that offer postsecondary programs and seminars in audio technology and engineering. *$6.00*
40 pages

6449 **BMES Membership Directory**
Biomedical Engineering Society
8401 Corporate Drive
Suite 225
Landover, MD 20785-2224
301-459-1999
FAX: 301-459-2444
info@bmes.org www.bmes.org
Wolf W von Maltzahn, President
Frank C P Yin, President-Elect
Patricia I Horner, Executive Director
George A Truskey, Treasurer
Arthur T Johnson, Secretary
A directory listing members' names, mailing addresses, telephone numbers, e-mail addresses, areas of specialization, as well as indexes of professional interest and geographic location.
Annual

6450 **Basics of Code Division Multiple Access (CDMA)**
International Society for Optical Engineering
PO Box 10
Bellingham, WA 98227-0010
360-676-3290
FAX: 360-647-1445
spie@spie.org www.spie.org
Raghuveer Rao, Editor
Sohail Dianat, Editor
This text, aimed at the reader with a basic background in electrical or optical engineering, covers CDMA fundamentals: from the basics of the communication process and digital data transmission, to the concepts of code division multiplexing, direct sequence spreading, diversity techniques, the near-far effect, and the IS-95 CDMA standard form. *$35.00*
120 pages Softcover ISBN 0-819458-69-4

6451 **CED Directory of Engineering and Engineering Technology Programs**
Mississippi State University
PO Box 6046
Mississippi State, MS 39762-6046
662-258-8122
FAX: 662-325-8733
coop@coop.msstate.edu
Mike Mathews, Editor
Over 150 colleges and universities with cooperative education programs in engineering and engineering technology are listed. *$ 50.00*
250 pages Biennial

6452 **CPD Examination Review Manual**
American Society of Plumbing Engineers
8614 Catalpa Avenue
Suite 1007
Chicago, IL 60656-1116
773-693-2773
FAX: 773-695-9007
info@aspe.org www.aspe.org
Tom Govedarica, Executive Publisher
Richard Albrecht, Publication Coordinator
Gretchen Pienta, Managing Editor
$49.95

6453 **CRC Press**
2000 NW Corporate Boulevard
Boca Raton, FL 33431
561-994-0555
FAX: 772-998-0876 800-272-7737
info@crcpress.com
www.crcpress.com
Eleanor Riemer, Publisher
Emmett Dages, Chief Executive Officer
Publisher in science, medicine, environmental science, forensic, engineering, business, technology, mathematics, and statistics. Our food science and nutrition books and our journal, Critical Reviews in Food and Nutrition, are well established and respected publications in the food science industry.

6454 **CSA Engineering**
Cambridge Scientific Abstracts
7200 Wisconsin Avenue
Suite 601
Bethesda, MD 20814
301-961-6700
FAX: 301-961-6720
market@csa.com www.csa.com
Robert Hilton, Editor
Martin Nowicki, Editor, Engineering
This database offers information on more than 500,000 citations, with abstracts, to international periodical and other research literature covering all fields of engineering and science. *$945.00*
Monthly

6455 **Characterization and Properties of Petroleum Fractions**
ASTM International
100 Barr Harbor Drive
PO Box C700
West Conshohocken, PA 19428-2959
610-329-9500
FAX: 610-832-9555
service@astm.org www.astm.org
M R Riaza, Author
Presents over 600 predictive methods from theoretical to empirical, including the most widely used and most accurate ones for a wide range of conditions. Both petroleum professionals and those without a technical engineering background will find this unique new manual to be a vital and comprehensive reference for the petroleum industry in both processing and production. *$197.00*
435 pages Hardcover Founded: 2005
ISBN 0-803133-61-8

6456 **Coolant Filtration-Additional Technologies**
Society of Tribologists & Lubrication
840 Busse Highway
Park Ridge, IL 60068-2376
847-825-5536
FAX: 847-825-1456
information@stle.org www.stle.org
James Joseph, Editor
The text covers coolant cleaning and handling for metalworking operations where coolants are used as part of the process. The publication also provides the latest thinking on specific metalworking applications with some comprehensive guidelines. 76 illustrations. *$56.00*
223 pages Softcover

6457 **Decommissioning Handbook**
American Nuclear Society
555 North Kensington Avenue
La Grange Park, IL 60526
708-352-6611
FAX: 708-352-0499 www.ans.org
A Taboas, Editor
A Moghissi, Editor
T LaGuardia, Editor
Provides both a full introduction for those new to the field and a current desk reference on regulations, resources, and experience. *$100.00*
500 pages Hardcover Founded: 2004
ISBN 0-894480-41-3

6458 **Die Casting Benchmark Study**
North American Die Casting Association
241 Holbrook Drive
Wheeling, IL 60090-5809
847-279-0001
FAX: 847-279-0002
twarog@diecasting.org
www.diecasting.org
Daniel Twarog, President
This benchmarking study of the die casting industry covers major aspects of die casting production. The aspects include business, materials and energy, quote preparation, design, die manufacturing, melt handling, quality and more. The results of this study are presented and compared to the 1999 benchmarking study, citing the changes that have taken place since 1999. *$100.00*
82 pages Founded: 2005

6459 **Die Casting Safety**
North American Die Casting Association
241 Holbrook Drive
Wheeling, IL 60090-5809
847-279-0001
FAX: 847-279-0002
twarog@diecasting.org
www.diecasting.org
Daniel Twarog, President
This seven module, interactive CD-ROM course, teaches the student to recognize and better understand what causes accidents, how to help prevent them and to work more safely. *$600.00*
100 pages Training CD-ROM w/Book
Founded: 2005

6460 **Directory of Accredited Engineering & Technology Certification Programs**
Council of Engineer and Scientific Specialty Board
PO Box 1448
Annapolis, MD 21404-1488
410-266-3766
FAX: 410-721-1746
academy@aaee.net www.cesb.org
Ronald Council, Owner
William C Anderson PE DEE, Executive Director
Provides a description of existing programs for persons interested in being certified and for those seeking an objective assessment of an expert's capability and competence.

6461 **Directory of Engineering Document Sources**
Global Engineering Documents
15 Inverness Way E
Englewood, CO 80112-5710
303-900-0600
FAX: 303-397-2740 800-854-7179
global@ihs.com www.global.ihs.com
Charles Picasso, Chief Executive Officer
Offers over 10,000 document initialisms and acronyms for governmental, military and industry specifications and related publications. *$145.00*
274 pages Annual

6462 **Directory of Engineering Societies and Related Organizations**
American Association of Engineering Societies
1828 L Street, NW
Suite 906
Washington, DC 20036-3626
202-678-8810
FAX: 202-298-1151
aaes@aaes.org www.aaes.org
Over 1,000 national, international, regional and Canadian organizations concerned with engineering and related fields. *$295.00*
500 pages ISBN 0-876150-09-1

6463 **Directory of Engineers in Private Practice**
National Society of Professional Engineers
1420 King Street
Suite 500
Alexandria, VA 22314-2750
703-684-2800
FAX: 703-836-4875
Consulting engineering firms and individuals who are members of the Society's Professional Engineers in Private Practice division. *$85.00*
260 pages Annual

6464 **EI Page One**
Engineering Information
1 Castle Point Terrace
Hoboken, NJ 07030-5906

FAX: 201-356-6801 800-221-1044
eicustomersupport@elsevier.com
www.ei.org
This database contains a table of contents listing citations to more than 350,000 journal articles and conference papers and proceedings in all fields of engineering.
Bibliographic

6465 ENR: Top International Design Firms Issue
McGraw Hill
1221 Avenue of the Americas
47th Floor
New York, NY 10020-1001
212-512-3916
www.mcgraw-hill.com
Offers a list of over 200 design firms competing outside their own national borders who received largest dollar volumes in foreign contracts. *$270.00*
Annual
Circulation: 900,000

6466 Energy Saving Manual
North American Die Casting Association
241 Holbrook Drive
Wheeling, IL 60090-5809
847-279-0001
FAX: 847-279-0002
twarog@diecasting.org
www.diecasting.org
Daniel Twarog, President
NADCA's newly revised Energy Saving Manual is designed to assist the die caster in establishing a strong, profitable energy management program for his or her organization. *$60.00*
80 pages Founded: 2004

6467 Field Guide to Polarization
International Society for Optical Engineering
PO Box 10
Bellingham, WA 98227-0010
360-676-3290
FAX: 360-647-1445
spie@spie.org www.spie.org
Edward Collett, Editor
To provide an introduction to the developments in polarized light that have taken place over the past half-century, and present the most salient topics of the subject matter such as Mueller matrices, Stokes polarization parameters, and Jones matrices. *$29.00*
130 pages Spiral Bound ISBN 0-819458-68-6

6468 Financial Survey
North American Die Casting Association
241 Holbrook Drive
Wheeling, IL 60090-5809
847-279-0001
FAX: 847-279-0002
twarog@diecasting.org
www.diecasting.org
Daniel Twarog, President
This provides a snapshot view of the financial performance expected from a company in the die casting industry. Productivity, sales performance, profitability and manufacturing efficiency are all measured and reported. *$200.00*
9 pages w/CD-ROM

6469 Guidelines for Professional Filming or Photographing Works of Art
Illuminating Engineering Society of North America
120 Wall Street
Floor 17
New York, NY 10005
212-248-5000
FAX: 212-248-5018
iesna@iesna.org www.iesna.org
Albert Suen, Publications Fulfillment
This guide addresses conccepts and criteria for single-camera videoconference systems for small audiences in any small video-based communication environment. It does not address more complex distance learning facilities, corporate studios or educational broadcast facilities. *$17.50*
25 pages Softcover Founded: 2005

6470 Handbook: Pumps and Pump Systems
American Society of Plumbing Engineers
8614 Catalpa Avenue
Suite 1007
Chicago, IL 60656-1116
773-693-2773
FAX: 773-695-9007
info@aspe.org www.aspe.org
Tom Govedarica, Executive Publisher
Richard Albrecht, Publication Coordinator
Gretchen Pienta, Managing Editor
A valuable resource that provides in-depth coverage, diagrams, illustrations and graphs for pump systems. *$12.00*

6471 Handbook: Solar Energy System Design
American Society of Plumbing Engineers
8614 Catalpa Avenue
Suite 1007
Chicago, IL 60656-1116
773-693-2773
FAX: 773-695-9007
info@aspe.org www.aspe.org
Tom Govedarica, Executive Publisher
Richard Albrecht, Publication Coordinator
Gretchen Pienta, Managing Editor
This manual provides the know-how on solar hot-water systems, collectors, thermal storage and much more. *$20.00*

6472 Human Foundations of Advanced Computing Technology
Ergosyst Associates
4840 W 15th Street
Suite 102
Lawrence, KS 60049
785-842-7334
FAX: 785-842-7348
Bernard O Williams, Editor
John L Burch, Editor
The Guide in the field of Select Literature.
259 pages Founded: 1985 ISBN 0-916313-11-5

6473 IES Manufacturers' Directory
Illuminating Engineering Society of North America
120 Wall Street
Floor 17
New York, NY 10005
212-248-5000
FAX: 212-248-5018
iesna@iesna.org www.iesna.org
Albert Suen, Publications Fulfillment
Manufacturers are listed alphabetically, by state, and by product.
Annual

6474 Introduction to Aircraft Weight Engineering
Society of Allied Weight Engineers
204 Hubbard Street
Glastonbury, CT 06033-3063
860-633-0850
FAX: 860-633-8971
exdirector@sawe.org www.sawe.org
Roger L Belt, President
James L Valentine, VP
Andreas R Schuster, VP Transportation
William M Childers, Treasurer
Brandy R Meyer, Secretary
This textbook is segregated into 31 chapters covering topics important to anyone involved in any aspect of weight egnieering. *$ 25.00*
265 pages

6475 Laser Beam Propagation through Random Media, Second Edition
International Society for Optical Engineering
PO Box 10
Bellingham, WA 98227-0010
360-676-3290
FAX: 360-647-1445
spie@spie.org www.spie.org
Larry C Andrews, Editor
Ronald L Phillips, Editor
New to this edition are models for the scintillation index under moderate-to-strong irradiance fluctuations; models for aperture averaging based on ABCD ray matrices; beam wander and its effects on scintillation; theory of partial coherence of the source; models of rough targets for LADAR applications; phase fluctuations; analysis of other beam shapes; plus expanded analysis of free-space optical communication systems and imaging systems. *$89.00*
820 pages Hardcover Founded: 1998
ISBN 0-819459-48-8

6476 Lubricant Additives - Chemistry and Applications
Society of Tribologists & Lubrication
840 Busse Highway
Park Ridge, IL 60068-2376
847-825-5536
FAX: 847-825-1456
information@stle.org www.stle.org
Dr Leslie R Rudnick, Editor *$235.00*
760 pages Hardcover

6477 Lubrication Fundamentals
Society of Tribologists & Lubrication
840 Busse Highway
Park Ridge, IL 60068-2376
847-825-5536
FAX: 847-825-1456
information@stle.org www.stle.org
D M Pirro, Editor
A A Wessol, Editor *$110.00*
540 pages Hardcover

6478 MOEMS: Micro-Opto-Electro-Mechanical Systems
International Society for Optical Engineering
PO Box 10
Bellingham, WA 98227-0010
360-676-3290
FAX: 360-647-1445
spie@spie.org www.spie.org
Manouchehr E Motamedi, Editor
This book introduces the exciting and fast-moving field of MOEMS to graduate students, scientists, and engineers by providing a foundation of both micro-optics and MEMS that will enable them to conduct future research in the field. Born from the relatively new fields of MEMS andmicro-optics, MOEMS are proving to be an attractive and low-cost solution to a range of device problems requiring high optical functionality and high optical performance. *$89.00*
676 pages Hardcover ISBN 0-819450-21-9

6479 **Manufacturer and Repair Directory**
National Board of Boiler & Pressure Vessel
1055 Crupper Avenue
Columbus, OH 43229
614-888-8320
FAX: 614-888-0750
getinfo@nationalboard.org
www.nationalboard.org

Donald E Tanner, Executive Director
Connie Homer, Senior Executive Secretary

Manufacturers of boilers, pressure vessels, or other pressure-retaining items who are authorized to register these items with the National Board, Repair organizations holding National Board certificates of authorization for use of either the R, VR, or NR stamps.

6480 **Mechanical Contractor Directory Marketing**
Mechanical Contractors Association America
1385 Piccard Drive
Rockville, MD 20850-4340
301-869-5800
FAX: 301-990-9690
cynthia@mcaa.org www.mcaa.org

Cheryl Stratos, Publisher
John Gentille, Executive VP

6481 **Mechanical Seal Handbook**
Society of Tribologists & Lubrication
840 Busse Highway
Park Ridge, IL 60068-2376
847-825-5536
FAX: 847-825-1456
information@stle.org www.stle.org

Karl Phipps, Associate Managing Editor

This book provides valuable information to aid in the selection and use of the most popular mechanical seal designs, configurations, and materials. *$15.00*

48 pages

6482 **Membership Directory**
Society of Tribologists & Lubrication
840 Busse Highway
Park Ridge, IL 60068-2376
847-825-5536
FAX: 847-825-1456
information@stle.org www.stle.org

Karl Phipps, Associate Managing Editor

Directory highlights include: comprehensive listing of all 4,400 STLE members in the U.S., Canada and around the world; E-mail addresses for many members (about 2,500); Contact information for leadership volunteers on the Board of Directors, techncial committees and councils and local sections; STLE program information about publishing, scholarships, future annual meetings, and much more; Guide to STLE headquarters staff contacts. *$35.00*

300 pages

6483 **Metalworking Fluids**
Society of Tribologists & Lubrication
840 Busse Highway
Park Ridge, IL 60068-2376
847-825-5536
FAX: 847-825-1456
information@stle.org www.stle.org

Jerry P Byers, Editor *$150.00*

6484 **Optical Imaging in Projection Microlithogr aphy**
International Society for Optical Engineering
PO Box 10
Bellingham, WA 98227-0010
360-676-3290
FAX: 360-647-1445
spie@spie.org www.spie.org

Alfred K Wong, Editor

Offers rigorous underpinning, clarity in systematic formulation, physical insight into emerging ideas, as well as a system level view of the parameter tolerances required in manufacturing. *$46.00*

276 pages Softcover ISBN 0-819458-29-5

6485 **Organic Electroluminescence**
International Society for Optical Engineering
PO Box 10
Bellingham, WA 98227-0010
360-676-3290
FAX: 360-647-1445
spie@spie.org www.spie.org

Zakya H Kafafi, Editor

This book covers the principles of organic electroluminescence as well as recent trends, current applications, and future potential. *$118.00*

368 pages Hardcover ISBN 0-819458-59-7

6486 **Plumbing Directory**
American Society of Sanitary Engineering

901 Canterbury
Westlake, OH 44145
440-835-3040
FAX: 440-835-3488
info@asse-plumbing.org
www.asse-plumbing.org

I D Jacobson, Editor

Contains more than 4,000 plumbing words and terms, abbreviations, cross references, helpful charts and illustrations, solar energy terms. A great teaching tool for plumbing and related fields. *$21.00*

6487 **Plumbing Technology**
American Society of Plumbing Engineers
8614 Catalpa Avenue
Suite 1007
Chicago, IL 60656-1116
773-693-2773
FAX: 773-695-9007
info@aspe.org www.aspe.org

Tom Govedarica, Executive Publisher
Richard Albrecht, Publication Coordination
Gretchen Pienta, Managing Editor

Is a comprehensive reference tool that approaches plumbing from a practical standpoint. It offers detailed, hands-on methods for the design and maintenance of modern plumbing systems. Everything form the securing of permits, to the installation of piping and fixtures is included in this complete and valuable guide. *$59.95*

6488 **Practical Plumbing Engineering**
American Society of Plumbing Engineers
8614 Catalpa Avenue
Suite 1007
Chicago, IL 60656-1116
773-693-2773
FAX: 773-695-9007
info@aspe.org www.aspe.org

Cyril M Harris, Editor

An authoritative and up-to-date guide that provides everything you need to know to design and install plumbing systems in residential and commercial facilities. This comprehensive source gives you a solid grasp of all aspects of plumbing engineering and design—from the basics of water quality, treatment, supply, distribution, and pressure to the latest advances in earthquake protection, cross-connection control, and specifications for plumbing systems. *$79.95*

6489 **Principles of Lithography**
International Society for Optical Engineering
PO Box 10
Bellingham, WA 98227-0010
360-676-3290
FAX: 360-647-1445
spie@spie.org www.spie.org

Harry J Levinson

Addresses several needs, and the revisions for the second edition were made with those original objectives in mind. Many new topics have been included in this text communsurate with the progress that has taken place during the past few years, and several subjects are discussed in more detail. *$71.00*

438 pages Hardcover ISBN 0-819456-60-8

6490 **Research Services Directory**
Grey House Publishing
185 Millerton Road
PO Box 860
Millerton, NY 12546
518-890-0526
FAX: 518-789-0545 800-562-2139
books@greyhouse.com
www.greyhouse.com

Leslie Mackenzie, Publisher
Richard Gottlieb, Editor

This Ninth Edition provides access to well over 7,700 independent Commercial Research Firms, Corporate Research Centers and Laboratories offering contract services for hands-on, basic or applied research. *$550.00*

1200 pages Annual ISBN 1-592370-03-9

6491 **Research, Training, Test, and Production Reactor Directory**
American Nuclear Society
555 North Kensington Avenue
La Grange Park, IL 60526
708-352-6611
FAX: 708-352-0499 www.asn.org

James S Tulenko, President
E James Reinsch, President-Elect/VP
Harry Bradley, Executive Director
William F Naughton, Treasurer

This comprehensive directory includes administrative, operational, and technical data for all nonpower reactors in the United States. *$400.00*

876 pages Softcover Founded: 1988 ISBN 0-894485-12-1

6492 **Residential Plumbing Inspector's Manual**
American Society of Sanitary Engineering

901 Canterbury
Westlake, OH 44145
440-835-3040
FAX: 440-835-3488
info@asse-plumbing.org
www.asse-plumbing.org

Mario J Fala, Editor

An excellent guide to the basic essentials of plumbing installation in residential one and two family buildings. Includes a section on swimming pools as well as DWV, traps, joints and connections, water piping, fuel gas piping, water heaters and vents and much, much more. Numerous drawings and illustrations. *$18.75*

6493 Scientific and Technical Organizations and Agencies Directory
Gale Research
27500 Drake Road
Farmington Hills, MI 48331
248-699-4253
FAX: 248-699-8214 800-877-4253
jeryan@gale.com www.gale.com
Over 25,600 national and international organizations and agencies concerned with the physical and applied sciences, engineering and technology. *$195.00*

6494 Sculptured Thin Films: Nanoengineered Morphology and Optics
International Society for Optical Engineering
PO Box 10
Bellingham, WA 98227-0010
360-676-3290
FAX: 360-647-1445
spie@spie.org www.spie.org
Akhlesh Lakhtakia, Editor
Russell Messier, Editor
This text, presented as short course at the SPIE Optical Science and Technology Symposium, couples detailed knowledge of thin-film morphology with the optical response characteristics of STF devices. *$63.00*
336 pages Hardcover ISBN 0-819456-06-3

6495 Shot Systems Components User's Guide
North American Die Casting Association
241 Holbrook Drive
Wheeling, IL 60090-5809
847-279-0001
FAX: 847-279-0002
twarog@diecasting.org
www.diecasting.org
David Twarog, President
This book provides information on the impact of the shot sleeve, shot cylinder, and plunger rod on the shot tip. Suggested guideline for alignment, lubrication, and thermal management are discussed as well and various examples of commercial shot tips are provided. *$80.00*
41 pages Founded: 2005

6496 Synthetic Lubricants and High-Performance Functional Fluids
Society of Tribologists & Lubrication
840 Busse Highway
Park Ridge, IL 60068-2376
847-825-5536
FAX: 847-825-1456
information@stle.org www.stle.org
Dr Leslie R Rudnick, Editor
Ronald L Shubkin, Editor *$235.00*
904 pages Hardcover

6497 Tau Beta Pi Information Book
Tau Beta Pi Association
PO Box 2697
Knoxville, TN 37901-2697
865-546-4578
FAX: 865-546-4579
tbp@tbp.org www.tbp.org
Matthew W Ohland, President
Ellen D Styles, VP
James D Froula, Executive Director/Treasurer
Roger Hawks, Assistant Secretary/Treasurer
Patricia McDaniel, Director Communications
The book also serves as a reference to membership and alumni giving statistics as well as names of past and present officers, fellows, scholars, and other award winners.
Yearly

6498 Transaction CD-ROM
North American Die Casting Association
241 Holbrook Drive
Wheeling, IL 60090-5809
847-279-0001
FAX: 847-279-0002
twarog@diecasting.org
www.diecasting.org
Daniel Twargo, President
This CD-ROM contains the die casting papers that were presented at CastExpo 05, April 16-19, 2005. Both the paper and the presentation are included on this CD. This cd-rom requires a Pentium 133 or higher processor, 32 MB RAM, and Microsoft Windows 98. NT Service Pack 6, 2,000, or XP to run properly. *$120.00*

6499 Tribology of Abrasive Machining Processes
Abrasive Engineering Society
141 Moore Road
Butler, PA 16001
724-282-6210
FAX: 724-234-2376
aes@abrasiveengineering.com
www.abrasiveengineering.com
Ioan D Marinescu et al, Editor
This book is a fundamental rethinking element of abrasive machining in terms of tribology; the interdiscplinary study of the interaction of surfaces. *$160.00*
650 pages Hardcover

6500 US Abrasives Industry Directory
Abrasive Engineering Society
141 Moore Road
Butler, PA 16001
724-282-6210
FAX: 724-234-2376
aes@abrasiveengineering.com
www.abrasiveengineering.com
Doug Haynes, President
Ted Giese, Executive Director
Though the scene for industrial abrasive manufacturers has changed significantly over the last decade, the US continues as one of the world's largest manufacturers of abrasive products developing new abrasive grains and products that set international standards for quality and performance.

6501 Wage & Benefit Survey
North American Die Casting Association
241 Holbrook Drive
Wheeling, IL 60090-5809
847-279-0001
FAX: 847-279-0002
twarog@diecasting.org
www.diecasting.org
Daniel Twarog, President
This survey provides a comprehensive look at 13 different job classifications of hourly wage earners, how they are compensated, what benefits they receive and how practices vary by company size and location. *$200.00*
42 pages w/CD-ROM Founded: 2004

6502 Weight Engineers Handbook
Society of Allied Weight Engineers
204 Hubbard Street
Glastonbury, CT 06033-3063
860-633-0850
FAX: 860-633-8971
exdirector@sawe.org www.sawe.org
Roger L Belt, President
James L Valentine, VP
Andreas R Schuster, VP Transportation
William M Childers, Treasurer
Brandy R Meyer, Secretary
Contains technical information for generally used materials, engineering formulas, as well as other general engineering reference material of use to both mass properties engineers and engineers in other related disciplines. *$40.00*
348 pages Hardcopy or CD format

6503 Who's Who in Environmental Engineering
American Academy of Environmental Engineers
130 Holiday Court
Suite 100
Annapolis, MD 21401
410-266-3311
FAX: 410-266-7653
academy@aaee.net www.aaee.net
David A Asselin, Executive Director
A recognized reference for industry, consultants, recruiters, attorneys and health professionals who need to identify and locate experts in the environmental engineering profession.
Annual
Mailing list available for rent

6504 World Directory of Nuclear Utility Management
American Nuclear Society
555 North Kensington Avenue
La Grange Park, IL 60526
708-352-6611
FAX: 708-352-0499 www.ans.org
James S Tulenko, President
E James Reinsch, President-Elect/VP
Harry Bradley, Executive Director
William F Naughton, Treasurer
Is a handy desk reference listing key personnel at nuclear utility headquarters and nuclear plant sites, including plant managers, maintenance superintendents, radwaste managers, contacts for purchasing and public relations, and more. *$850.00*
249 pages Softcover + CD-ROM Founded: 2005

Industry Web Sites

6505 www.aacei.org
Association for Advancement of Cost Engineering

Individuals interested in applying scientific principals to the solution of problems.

6506 www.aaee.net
American Academy of Environmental Engineers

Improves the standards of environmental engineering. Certifies those with the special knowledge of environmental engineering and supplies a list of certified engineers to the public. Publishes reference books and other matters of interest for the profession.

6507 www.aaee.org
American Association for Employment in Education

Provides information and other resources to assist colleges and universities in the employment of education.

6508 www.aaes.org
American Association of Engineering Societies

A multidisciplinary organization dedicated to advancing the knowledge, understanding and practice of engineering in the public interest.

6509 www.abet.org
Accreditation Board for Engineering and Technology

Accreditation of engineering, technology and applied science educational programs.

6510 www.acec.org
American Council of Engineering

Membership includes more than 5,800 US firms engaged in a range of engineering works. Mission is to contribute to the nation's prosperity through advancement of the business interests of member firms.

6511 www.acesystems.com
AEC Systems International/Penton Media

Focuses on Internet/Intranet for the design, engineering and construction industries.

6512 www.aeecenter.org
Association of Energy Engineers

Source of information on the field of energy efficiency, utility deregulation, plant engineering, facility management and environmental compliance. Membership includes more than 8,000 professionals and certification programs. Offers seminars, conferences, job listings and certification programs.

6513 www.aegweb.org
Association of Engineering Geologists

Meets the professional needs of geologists who are applying their scientific training and experience to the broad field of civil and environmental engineering. Mission is to provide leadership in the development and application of geologic principles and knowledge to serve engineering, environmental and public needs.

6514 www.aes.org
Audio Engineering Society

Professional society devoted to audio technology. Membership includes leading engineers, scientists and other authorities in the field. Serves its members, the industry and the public by stimulating and facilitating advances in the constantly changing field of audio.

6515 www.aiche.org
American Institute of Chemical Engineers

Professional association of more than 50,000 members, providing leadership in advancing the chemical engineering profession. Members are those who develop processes and design and operate manufacturing plants, as well as researchers who assure the safe and environmentally sound manufacture, use and disposal of chemical products.

6516 www.akropolis.net
Akropolis

Directory of architects, engineers, designers, construction professionals and others in related fields. Web portal to showcase modules and applications developed by our company.

6517 www.aocs.org
American Oil Chemists Society

Largest international society focused on the science and technology of fats, oils, lipids, and related substances.

6518 www.ascet.org
American Society of Certified Engineering

Strives to obtain recognition of engineering technicians as essential to the engineering scientific team. Provides a forum for discussion of employment issues and improvement of the professional status of engineering technicians.

6519 www.asem.org
American Society for Engineering Management

Strives to promote the profession of engineering management as well as assisting its members in developing and improving their skills as practicing managers of engineering and technology. Members are from academic, field, industrial and governmental organizations.

6520 www.asfe.org
ASFE

Not-for-profit trade association. Helps geoprofessional, environmental and civil engineering firms profit through professionalism.

6521 www.asnt.org
American Society for Nondestructive Testing

Helps create a safer world by serving the nondestructive testing professions and promoting NDT technologies through publishing, certification, research and conferencing.

6522 www.aspe.net
American Society for Precision Engineering

Technical society emphasizing research, design, development, manufacture and measurement of high accuracy components and systems. Members come from the fields of engineering, materials science, physics, chemistry, mathematics and computer science, and work in industry, academia and national labs.

6523 www.asq.org
American Society for Quality

ASQ's mission is to facilitate continuous improvement and increase customer satisfaction. Promotes quality principles concepts and technologies. Provides information, contacts and opportunities to make things better in the workplace, in communities and in people's lives.

6524 www.asse-plumbing.org
American Society of Sanitary Engineering

Members are from all segments of the plumbing industry, including contractors, engineers, inspectors, journeymen, apprentices and others involved in the industry. Provides information, the opportunity to exchange ideas, solve problems and offers forum where all sides can express their views.

6525 www.astm.org
ASTM International

Not-for-profit organization providing a global forum for development and publication of voluntary consensus standards for materials, products, systems and services. Over 30,000 members from 100 nations include producers, users, consumers and representatives of academia and government. Formerly known as the American Society for Testing and Materials.

6526 www.atcouncil.org
Applied Technology Council

Nonprofit corporation. Mission is to develop and promote state-of-the-art, user-friendly engineering resources and applications for use in mitigating the effects of natural and other hazards on the built environment. Seeks to help structural and earthquake engineers keep abreast of technological changes in the field. Conducts seminars.

6527 www.eia-usa.org
Environmental Information Association

Nonprofit organization dedicated to providing environmental information to individuals, members and the industry. Disseminates information on the abatement of asbestos and lead-based paint, indoor air quality, safety and health issues, analytical issues and environmental site assessments.

6528 www.electrochem.org
Electrochemical Society

The society is an international nonprofit, educational organization concerned with phenomena relating to electrochemical and solid state science and technology. Members are individual scientists and engineers, as well as corporations and laboratories.

6529 www.ewh.ieee.org
Instrumentation and Measurement Society

A subsidiary of the Institute of Electrical and Electronics Engineers. Provides support to scientists and technicians who design and develop electrical and electronic measuring instruments and equipment.

6530 www.greyhouse.com
Grey House Publishing

Selected Grey House directories in the fields of business, health and education are available online. Users can search our online databases by several different search criteria, such as product categories, geographic area, sales volume and much, much more. Full Grey House catalog and online ordering also available.

6531 www.icc-es.org
ICC Evaluation Service

An independent, nonprofit organization that conducts a voluntary program of evaluation of both traditional and innovative building materials, products and systems for compliance with the three major model codes in the United States.

6532 www.iccsafe.org
International Code Council

Nonprofit membership association with more than 16,000 members who span the building community, from code enforcement officials to materials manufacturers. Dedicated to preserving the public health, safety and welfare in the built environment through the effective use and enforcement of model codes.

6533 www.icea.net
Insulated Cable Engineers Association

Professional organization dedicated to developing cable standards for the electric power, control and telecommunications industries. Ensures safe, economical and efficient cable systems utilizing proven state-of-the-art materials and concepts. ICEA documents are of interest to cable manufacturers, architects and engineers, utility and manufacturing plant personnel, telecommunication engineers, consultants and OEMs.

6534 www.iienet.org
Institute of Industrial Engineers

Founded in Columbus, Ohio as the American Institute of Industrial Engineers.

6535 www.irga.com
International Reprographic Association

Represents entrepreneurial businesses serving the wide-format imaging needs of graphic arts, architectural, engineering, manufacturing, corporate, legal, retail, and POP industries.

6536 www.manufacturing.net
Manufacturing Marketplace

Manufacturing industry news and resources for the engineering, design, purchasing, logistics and distribution professional.

6537 www.materialsocieties.org
Federation of Materials Societies

Promotes cooperation among societies concerned with the understanding, development and application of materials and processes.

6538 www.nace.org
National Association of Corrosion Engineers

Conducts research on corrosion control. Sponsors short courses annually at universities.

6539 www.nationalboard.org
National Board of Boiler & Pressure Vessel Inspec.

Membership is composed of chief boiler inspectors of states, major US cities and Canadian provinces having boiler laws.

6540 www.naval.org
American Society of Naval Engineers

Includes all arts construction and sciences as applied in research, development design, construction, operation, maintenance, and logistic support of surface/sub-surface ships and marine craft.

6541 www.ncees.org
Natl Council of Examiners for Engineering & Survey

Promotes uniform standards of registration and to coordinate interstate registration of engineers and surveyors.

6542 www.nspe.org
National Society of Professional Engineers

The mission of the Society is to promote the ethical, competent and licensed practice of engineering and to enhance the professional, social and economic well-being of its members.

6543 www.ppi-ppie.org
Potash and Phosphate Institute

6544 www.remsa.org
Railway Engineering-Maintenance Suppliers Assn

Members are distributors and manufacturers of railway track machinery supplies and services.

6545 www.reta.com
Refrigerating Engineers & Technicians Association

Seeks to upgrade the skills and knowledge of experienced members. Offers home-study courses on refrigeration and air conditioning.

6546 www.rses.org
Refrigeration Service Engineers Society

RSES is the leading training and education association for heating, ventilation, air conditioning and refrigeration professionals. It is a non-profit organization of 25,000 members in 421 chapters in the US and Canada, as well as affiliate organizations in other countries.

6547 **www.same.org**
Society of American Military Engineers

Brings together professional engineers and those in engineering-related fields to improve and increase the engineering capabilities of the nation, and to exchange and advance the knowledge of engineering technologies, applications, and practices.

6548 **www.sawe.org**
Society of Allied Weight Engineers

Consists of engineers in the aerospace industry.

6549 **www.sme.org**
Society of Manufacturing Engineers

Members are engaged in manufacturing, research and technology development.

6550 **www.spe.org**
Society of Petroleum Engineers

To provide the means for collection, dissemination and exchange of technical information concerning the development of oil and gas resources, subsurface fluid flow and production of other materials through well bores for the public benefit. To provide opportunities through its programs for interested individuals to maintain and upgrade their individual technical competence in the aforementioned areas for the public benefit.

6551 **www.tbp.org**
Tau Beta Pi Association

The National Engineering honor society recognizes engineering students of superior scholarship and exemplary character and practitioners of engineering. Founded in 1885, the world's largest engineering organization includes 218 collegiate chapters and 220 alumnus chapters.

6552 **www.thetatau.org**
Theta Tau

A professional fraternity in engineering. Founded at the Univerity of Minnesota. Purpose of the fraternity is to develop and maintain a high standard of professional interest among its members, and to unite them in a strong bond of fraternal fellowship.

6553 **www.u.arizona.edu/n aimitril**
Reliability Engineering and Management Institute

This is an annual conference on Reliability Engineering and Management of all types of products. Over 15 leading corporations present their latest techniques in this field, and the proceedings thereof are published.

6554 **www.uefoundation.org**
United Engineering Foundation

Aims to advance engineering arts and sciences.

6555 **www.usace.army.mil**
US Army Corps of Engineers

Information on flood control, environmental protection, disaster response, military construction and support of others through the sharing of engineering expertise with other agencies, state and local governments, academia and foreign nations.

Associations

6556 **ASFE**
8811 Colesville Road
Suite G106
Silver Spring, MD 20910
301-565-2733
FAX: 301-589-2017
info@asfe.org www.asfe.org

Joseph Cifor, President
John Bachner, Executive VP
Zach Fletcher, Chief Information Officer

Not-for-profit trade association. Helps geoprofessional, environmental and civil engineering firms profit through professionalism.

300 Members Founded: 1969 2,500 names $100 per M.

6557 **Abundant Life Seed Foundation**
PO Box 772
Port Townsend, WA 98368-0772
360-385-5660
FAX: 425-385-7455

Katie Wayland, Co-Director
Susan Herman, Co-Director

A nonprofit organization which also sell seeds of vegetables, herbs, flowers, wild flowers, trees and shrubs.

25M Members Founded: 1975

6558 **Acrylonitrile Group**
1250 Connecticut Avenue NW
Suite 700
Washington, DC 20036
202-314-4383
FAX: 202-659-8037
angroup@regnet.com
www.angroup.org

Robert J Fensterheim, Executive Director

Represents producers and users of the industrial chemical used to make plastics, fibers and synthetic rubber products.

Founded: 1981

6559 **Adirondack Council**
103 Hand Avenue, Suite 3
PO Box D2
Elizabethtown, NY 12932-0640
518-873-2240
FAX: 518-873-6675 877-873-2240
info@adirondackcouncil.org
www.adirondackcouncil.org

George Huttig, Owner
Brian L Houseal, Executive Director

Research, education and advocacy to protect the natural character and communities of the Adirondack Park. Also publishes an annual State of Park Report and quarterly newsletters.

Founded: 1975
Mailing list available for rent

6560 **Adirondack Land Trust**
PO Box 65
Keene Valley, NY 12943-65
518-576-2082
dfeeley@tnc.org

Michael T Carr, Director
Timothy I Barnett, VP
Michael G Clarke, Executive Director
Melissa Mack Eisinger, Acting Director
Todd W Dunham, Director Land Protection

Insures the preservation of land and natural resources.

Founded: 1984

6561 **Agricultural Research Institute**
9650 Rockville Pike
Bethesda, MD 20814-3998
301-530-7178
FAX: 301-530-7007
info@aai.org www.aai.org

Michelle Hogan, Executive Director
Laurie Glimcher, President
Susan Swian, VP

One hundred and twenty-five member institutions concerned with environmental issues, pest control, agricultural meteorology, biotechnology, food irradiation, agricultural policy, research and development, food safety, technology transfer and remote sensing. *$50.00*

6562 **Air & Waste Management Association**
420 Fort Duquesne Boulevard
One Gateway Center, 3rd Floor
Pittsburgh, PA 15222-1435
412-652-2458
FAX: 412-232-3450
info@awma.org www.awma.org

Joseph A Martone, President
Peter F Hess, VP
Scott A Freeburn, VP
Richard C Scherr, Secretary
Amy Gilligan, Treasurer

Supports all those involved with the environment, specifically the air and waste management industry. Publishes a magazine.

9000 Members Founded: 1907

6563 **Air Conditioning Contractors of America**
2800 Shirlington Road
Suite 300
Arlington, VA 22206
703-575-4477
FAX: 703-575-4449
michael.honeycutt@acca.org
www.acca.org

Paul T Stalknecht, President/CEO
Hilary Atkins, Esq, General Counsel
Michael Honeycutt, SVP/Chief of Staff
Glenn Hourihan, PE, VP Research/Technology

Formed by a consolidation of Air Conditioning and Refrigeration Contractors of America with the contractors of the National Warm Air Heating and Air Conditioning Association.

4030 Members Founded: 1969

6564 **Air Pollution Control Association**
420 Fort Duquesne Boulevard
One Gateway Center, 3rd Floor
Pittsburgh, PA 15222
412-232-3444
FAX: 412-232-3450
info@awma.org www.awma.org

Joseph Martone, President
Giggs Scherr, Executive Director

Association for the environment and conservation industry.

9000 Members Founded: 1907

6565 **America the Beautiful Fund**
725 15th Street NW
Suite 605
Washington, DC 20005
202-638-1649
FAX: 202-638-2175
katie@america-the-beautiful.org
www.freeseeds.us

Nanine Bilski, President/CEO
Kathleen Rehicaldt, Program Director
Daniel Schneider, Secretary

Groups and private citizens that improve the quality of the environment.

1M Members Founded: 1965

6566 **American Association for Aerosol Research**
15000 Commerce Parkway
Suite C
Mount Laurel, NJ 08054
856-439-9080
FAX: 856-439-0525
info@aaar.org www.aaar.org

Amy Williams, President
Deanna Bright, Executive Assistant
Evan R Whitby, Secretary
Beverly S Cohen, Treasurer

Supports all those involved in aerosol research, especially in areas of industrial process, air pollution, and industrial hygiene.

1000 Members Founded: 1982

6567 **American Association for the Advancement of Science**
1200 New York Avenue NW
Washington, DC 20005-3941
202-266-6721
FAX: 202-371-9227
membership@aaas.org www.aaas.org

Dr John Holdren, President
Dr David E Shaw, Treasurer
Dr. Alan I. Leshner, Chief Executive Officer
Phil Blair, Chief Admin/Financial Officer

An international non-profit organization dedicated to advancing science around the world by serving as an educator, leader, spokesperson and professional association.

262 Members Founded: 1848

6568 **American Council on Science and Health**
1995 Broadway
2nd Floor
New York, NY 10023-5860
212-362-7044
FAX: 212-362-4919
acsh@acsh.org www.acsh.org

Gilbert Ross, Executive/Medical Director
Jeff Stier, Associate Director
Dr Elizabeth Whelan, President

A consumer education organization providing the public with scientifically accurate evaluations of food, chemicals, the environment and health.

2500 Members Founded: 1978

6569 **American Council on the Environment**
1301 20th Street NW
Washington, DC 20036-6003
202-659-1900

David Ward, President

Conducts seminars.

6570 **American Fisheries Society**
5410 Grosvenor Lane
Suite 110
Bethesda, MD 20814-2199
301-897-8616
FAX: 301-897-8096
main@fisheries.org www.fisheries.org

Gus Rassam, Executive Director

Supports all those involved in the fishing industry, specifically environmental issues that the profession addresses.

Founded: 1870

6571 **American Gas Association**
400 N Capitol Street NW
Washington, DC 20001
202-477-7337
FAX: 202-824-7115
ykorolevich@aga.org www.aga.org
David Parker, President/CEO
Kevin Hardardt, CFO
Advocates the interest of its energy utility members and their customers, and provides information and services promoting demand and supply growth and operational excellence in the safe, reliable and cost-competitive delivery of natural gas.

6572 **American Institute of Biological Sciences**
1444 I Street NW
Suite 200
Washington, DC 20005
202-628-1500
FAX: 202-628-1509 800-992-2427
rogrady@aibs.org www.aibs.org
Supports professionals involved with the biological sciences, including research, products, education; sponsors annual conference.

6573 **American Institute of Hydrology**
300 Village Green Circle
Suite 2001
Smyrna, GA 30080
770-384-1634
aihydro@aol.com www.aihydro.org
Cathryn Seaburn, Manager
Registers and certifies hydrologists and hydrogeologists, provides a forum to discuss national and international issues, and provides educational courses.
1000 Members Founded: 1981

6574 **American Methanol Institute**
800 Connecticut Avenue NW
Suite 620
Washington, DC 20006
202-467-5050
FAX: 202-331-9055 888-275-0768
MI@methanol.org www.methanol.org
John E Lynn, President/CEO
Gregory A Dolan, VP Communications/Policy
Represents the global methanol industry. Expands markets for methanol as a chemical commodity component, a hydrogen carrier for fuel cells and alternative fuel.

6575 **American Nuclear Society**
555 N Kensington Avenue
LaGrange Park, IL 60526
708-352-6611
FAX: 708-352-0499 800-682-6397
advertising@ans.org www.ans.org
Larry R Foulke, President
James S Tulenko, VP
William F Naughton, Treasurer
Harry Bradley, Executive Director
Supports all those involved in the fields of radioactive waste management, removal, handling, disposal, treatment, cleanup and environmental restoration.
10500 Members Founded: 1954

6576 **American Phytopathological Society**
3340 Pilot Knob Road
Saint Paul, MN 55121
651-454-7250
FAX: 651-454-0766 800-328-7560
aps@scisoc.org www.apsnet.org
Don E Mathre, Chair
Ann R Chase, Vice Chair
William E Fry, Secretary
Erik L Stromberg, Treasurer
Steven Nelson, Vice President
Supports all those involved in the research of molecular biology and molecular genetics of pathological, symbiotic and associative interactions of microbes with plants, including plant response.
5000 Members Founded: 1908

6577 **American Public Works Association**
2345 Grand Blvd
Ste 700
Kansas City, MO 64108-2625
816-472-6100
FAX: 816-472-1610 800-848-2792
apwa@apwa.net www.apwa.net
Dwayne E Kalynchuk, President
A Thomas De Maio, Director Region I
Howard B LaFever, Director Region II
Bob Freudenthal, Director Region III
Kaye Sullivan, Chief Executive Officer
International educational and professional association of public agencies, private sector companies, and individuals dedicated to providing high quality public works, goods and services. APWA provides a forum brings important public works-related topics to public attention in local, state, and federal areas. Mailing list for members only. *$100.00*
26000 Members Founded: 1937

6578 **American Shore and Beach Preservation Association**
5460 Beaujolais Lane
Fort Myers, FL 33919
239-892-2616
FAX: 238-489-9917
business@asbpa.org www.asbpa.org
Harry Simmons, President
Federal, state and local government agencies and individuals interested in conservation, development and restoration of beaches and shorefronts.
1M Members Founded: 1926

6579 **American Society for Environmental History**
119 Pine Street
Suite 301
Seattle, WA 98101
206-343-0226
FAX: 206-343-0249
mighetto@hrassoc.com www.aseh.net
Lisa Mighetto, Acting Executive Director
ASEH members are techers and researchers with an interest in human ecology and environmental history.
1200 Members Founded: 1976

6580 **American Society for Nondestructive Testing**
1711 Arlingate Lane
Columbus, OH 43228-0518
614-274-6003
FAX: 614-274-6899 800-222-2768
wholliday@asnt.org www.asnt.org
Henry Stephens, President
Sharon Vukelich, VP
Technical society which is involved in nondestructive testing. ASNT publishes journals, including materials evaluation. The fall conference and quality testing show of this association is the society's largest annual show.
10000 Members Founded: 1941

6581 **American Society of Agronomy**
677 S Segoe Road
Madison, WI 53711
608-273-8080
FAX: 608-273-2021
headquarters@agronomy.org
www.agronomy.org
Ellen Bergfeld, Executive VP
L E Moser, President
Supports educators and scientists interested in the impacts of environmental perturbations on the biological and physical sciences.
10000 Members Founded: 1907

6582 **American Society of Mining and Reclamation**
3134 Montavesta Road
Lexington, KY 40502
859-351-9032
FAX: 859-335-6529
asmr@insightbb.com
http://ces.ca.uky.edu/asmr
Richard I Barnhisel, Executive Secretary
ASMR members are mining companies, federal and state agencies, academics and otehrs with an interest in reclamation of mined land.
450 Members Founded: 1973

6583 **American Society of Safety Engineers**
1800 E Oakton Street
Des Plaines, IL 60018
847-699-2929
FAX: 847-768-3434
customerservice@asse.org
www.asse.org
James Kendrick, President
Jack Dobson, Senior VP
Richard Nugent, VP Finance
Fred J Fortman, Executive Director/Secretary
Nonprofit, global organization that works to advance the technical, scientific, managerial and ethical knowledge and skills of occupational safety, heath and envionmental professionals, and is committed to protecting people, property and the envionnment. Offers education, technical publications, involvement in safety standards development, annual conferences, and more.
30000 Members Founded: 1911

6584 **American Solar Energy Society**
2400 Central Avenue
Suite A
Boulder, CO 80301
303-443-3130
FAX: 303-443-3212
ases@ases.org www.ases.org
Thomas Starrs, Chair
Ronal W Larson, Chapter Representative
Renate Boer, Treasurer
Cecile Warner, Secretary
Individuals and professionals working in the field of solar energy and conservation.

6585 **American Zoo & Aquarium Association**
8403 Colesville Road
Suite 710
Silver Spring, MD 20910-3314
301-562-0777
FAX: 301-562-0888
membership@aza.org www.aza.org

Anne M Baker, President
Elizabeth Stevens, VP
Syd Butler, Executive Director

Formerly the American Association of Zoological Parks and Aquariums, this nonprofit organization dedicated to the advancement of zoos and aqariums in the areas of conservation, education, science and recreation. AZA's vision is to work cooperatively to save and protect the wonders of the living natural world.
5500 Members Founded: 1924

6586 **Aquatic Plant Management Society**
PO Box 1477
Lehigh Acres, FL 33970-1477

dpetty@ndrsite.com www.apms.org

Wendy Andrew, Secretary

Individuals and companies interested in the control of water plants that hinder recreation or navigation.

6587 **Aspirin Foundation of America**
529 14th Street NW
Suite 807
Washington, DC 20045
202-378-8400
FAX: 202-737-8406 800-432-3247
info@aspirin.org www.aspirin.org

Thomas E Bryant, MD JD, President

Is a non-profit educational foundation with a membership of companies engaged in the manufacture, preparation, compounding or processing of aspirin and aspirin products.
8 Members Founded: 1981

6588 **Associated Soil and Foundation Engineers**
8811 Colesville Road
Suite G106
Silver Spring, MD 20910
301-565-2733
FAX: 301-589-2017
info@asfe.org www.asfe.org

Phil Pettway, Controller
Gerry Salontai, President
Joseph Cibor, Secretary/Treasurer
John Bachner, Executive VP
Ann Reed, Operations Manager

Not-for-profit, trade association. Helps geoprofessional, environmental and civil engineering firms profit through professionalism.
65000 Members Founded: 1969

6589 **Association for Population/Family Planning Libraries & Information Conference**
Family Health International Library
PO Box 13950
Research Triangle Park, NC 27709
919-447-7040
lnewman@pop.upenn.edu

Lisa A Newman

Offers support for all those involved in issues concerning population and family planning, including publications, training and conferences.
Annual

6590 **Association for the Environmental Health of Soils**
150 Fearing Street
Amherst, MA 01002
413-549-5170
FAX: 413-549-0579 www.aehs.com

Paul T Kostecki, PhD, Executive Director

AEHS is a multi-disciplinary association providing a forum for individual professionals concerned with soil protection and cleanup. Fields represented include chemistry, geology, hydrogeology, law, engineering, modeling, toxicology, regulatory science, public health and public policy.
600 Members Founded: 1989

6591 **Association of Energy Engineers**
4025 Pleasantdale Road
Suite 420
Atlanta, GA 30340
770-447-5083
FAX: 770-446-3969
webmaster@aeecenter.org
www.aeecenter.org

Lawrence L Good, President
James P Waltz, Secretary
Paul Goodman, Treasurer
Albert Thumann, Executive Director

Membership organization of over 8,000 professionals and certification programs in the fields of energy efficiency, utility deregulation, facility management, plant engineering and environmental compliance. Offers seminars, conferences, books to critical buyer-seller networking trade shows, job listings and certification programs.
8.2M Members Founded: 1977

6592 **Association of Engineering Geologists**
300 South Jackson Street, Suite 100
PO Box 460518
Denver, CO 80246-0518
303-757-2926
FAX: 303-757-2969
aeg@aegweb.org www.aegweb.org

David Bieber, President
Darrel Schmitz, VP
Becky Roland, Chief Staft Executive

Meets the professional needs of geologists who are applying their scientific training and experience to the broad field of civil and environmental engineering. Mission is to provide leadership in the development and application of geologic principles and knowledge to serve engineering, environmental and public needs.
3000 Members Founded: 1957
Mailing list available for rent 3000 names $100 per M.

6593 **Association of Environmental Engineering and Science Professors**
2303 Naples Court
Champaign, IL 61822
217-398-6969
FAX: 217-355-9232 www.aeesp.org

Joanne Fetzner, Business Secretary

Individuals working or teaching in the field of environmental engineering, including water quality and treatment, air quality, air pollution control and solid and hazardous waste management.
700 Members Founded: 1963

6594 **Association of Environmental and Resource Economists**
1616 P Street NW
Suite 400
Washington, DC 20036
202-328-5077
FAX: 202-939-3460
voigt@rff.org www.aere.org

Marilyn Voigt, Executive Secretary

AERE serves as an information resource for economists involved in natural resources policy planning and research. It was estabilshed as a way to exchange ideas, stimulate research, and promote graducate research in environmental economics.
900 Members Founded: 1979

6595 **Association of Fish & Wildlife Agencies**
444 N Capitol Street NW
Suite 725
Washington, DC 20001
202-624-7890
FAX: 202-624-7891
info@fishwildlife.org
www.fishwildlife.org

John Cooper, President
Edward Parker, VP
Rachel Brittin, Director Public Affairs

Established as the National Association of Game Commissioners. State and Canadian provincial fish and wildlife resources.
425 Members Founded: 1902

6596 **Association of State Floodplain Managers**
2809 Fish Hatchery Road
Suite 204
Madison, WI 53713
608-274-0123
FAX: 608-274-0696
Larry@floods.org www.floods.org

Chad Berginnis, Chair
Pam Pogue, Vice Chair
Rhonda Montgomery, Secretary
Larry Larson, Executive Director
Bill Nechamen, Treasurer

Promotes common interest in flood damage abatement, supports environmental protection for floodplain areas, provides education on floodplain management practices and policy and urges incorporating multi-objective management approaches to solve local flooding problems.
6500 Members Founded: 1977

6597 **Coastal Conservation Association**
6919 Portwest
Suite 100
Houston, TX 77024-1886
713-626-4234
FAX: 713-951-3801 800-201-3174
ccantl@joincca.org www.joincca.org

Pat Murray, VP

Seeks to advance protection and conservation of all marine life. Conducts seminars and bestows awards.
85000 Members Founded: 1977

6598 **Community Alliance with Family Farmers**
PO Box 363
Davis, CA 95617-363
916-786-5155
FAX: 530-756-7857 800-892-3832
will@mail.caff.org www.caff.org

Judith Redmond, President
Becki Spector, VP
Poppy Davis, Treasurer
Pete Price, Secretary *$47.95*

6599 Conservation Education Association
Department of Conservation
PO Box 180
Jefferson City, MO 65102-0180
573-751-4115
FAX: 573-751-4467
www.conservation.state.mo.us

John Hoskins, Director
Lorna Domke, Outreach/Education
Tom Cwyner, Editor

Focuses on conservation and the importance of protecting the environment.
Founded: 1937

6600 Conservation Fund
1655 Fort Myer Dr
Ste 1300
Arlington, VA 22209-3199
703-525-6300
FAX: 703-525-4610
postmaster@conservationfund.org
www.conservationfund.org

Jessica Catto, President
Charles Jordan, Chairman
J Rutherford Seydel II, Vice Chairman/Treasurer
Riley Bechtel, CEO
Patrick Noonan, Manager

Works with private and public agencies and organizations to protect wildlife habitats, historic sites and parks.
Founded: 1985

6601 Conservation International
1919 M Street NW
#600
Washington, DC 20036
202-912-1000
FAX: 202-912-1030 800-406-2306

Gustavo Fonseca, Executive VP
Russel Mittermeier, Executive Director
Peter Seligmann, Chief Executive Officer

Cooperates with government to sustain biological diversity and sponsors research programs and outreach programs.
60M Members Founded: 1987

6602 Conservation Treaty Support Fund

3705 Cardiff Road
Chevy Chase, MD 20815
301-654-3150
FAX: 301-652-6390 800-654-3150
ctsf@conservationtreaty.org
www.conservationtreaty.org

George A Furness Jr, President
John C Goldsmith, VP International

Promotes awareness, understanding and support of conservation treaties and their goals. Through the International Endangered Species Treaty, the Wetlands Convention, and other conservation agreements, more than 150 nations are committed to work together to preserve the wildlife and habitats that are our shared natural heritage.
Founded: 1986

6603 Conservation and Preservation Charities of America
21 Tamal Vista Boulevard
Suite 209
Corte Maera, CA 94925

800-626-6685

Patrick Mcguire, President

CPCA is a consortium of environmental stewardship organizations. CPCA acts as a central focus for charitable giving dedicated to the protection of the natural habitat and historic treasures. Sponsors workplace giving campaigns in support of its member organizations.

6604 Council on Certification of Heatlh, Environmental & Safety Technologist
208 Burwash Avenue
Savoy, IL 61874-9912
217-359-2686
FAX: 217-359-0055
cchest@cchest.org www.cchest.org

Roger L Brauer, PhD CSP CPE, Executive Director

CCHEST examines and certifies safet practitioners and establishes standards for certification. CCHEST is administered by the Board of Certified Safety Professionals.

6605 ETAD North America
1850 M Street NW
Suite 700
Washington, DC 20036
202-721-4154
FAX: 202-296-8120 www.etad.com

Dr C Tucker Helmes, Executive Director

Represents the interests of manufacturers and formulators of dyes in the region with regard to environmental and health hazards in the manufacture, processing, shipment, use and disposal of thier products.
Founded: 1982

6606 Earth Island Institute
300 Broadway
#28
San Francisco, CA 94133-3312
415-788-3666
FAX: 415-788-7324
arch@earthisland.org
www.earthisland.org

Dave Phillips, Executive Director

Seeks to prevent destruction of environment and sponsors fund drives and activist projects to protect wildlife.
33M Members Founded: 1985

6607 Earth Regeneration Society
1442A Walnut Street
#57
Berkeley, CA 94709-1405
510-849-4155
FAX: 510-849-0183 csiri@igc.apc.org
Organized to develop and study scientific and practical solutions to environmental issues.

6608 Earth Society Foundation
41 Park Avenue
Apartment 17-C
New York, NY 10016
212-758-4802
FAX: 212-686-4900 800-3EA-THDA
info@earthsocietyfoundation.org
www.earthsocietyfoundation.org

Monica Getz, Chairperson
Stan Cohen, President
Tom Dowd, VP

News of interest in environmental and sociological issues. Purpose is to promote Earth Day and the Earth Trustee agenda; Every individual and institution should seek choices in ecology, economics, and ethics that will eliminate pollution, poverty, and violence.

6609 Ecological Farming Association
406 Main Street
#313
Watsonville, CA 95076
831-763-2111
FAX: 831-763-2112
info@eco-farm.org
www.eco-farm.org

Kristian Rosenow, Executive Director

Supports organic farmers, farm suppliers and consultants, produce handlers, researchers, extension, agents, and students involved in the ecological farming industry.
800 Members Founded: 1986

6610 Environmental & Energy Study Institute
122 C Street NW
Suite 630
Washington, DC 20001-2148
202-628-1400
FAX: 202-628-1825
eesi@eesi.org www.eesi.org

Carol Werner, Executive Director
Ruth Lampi, Director Development

Provides information to educate the public and affect policy in order to improve and sustain the environment.

6611 Environmental Alliance for Senior Involvem ent
5615 26th St N
Arlington, VA 22207-1407
703-241-4927
FAX: 703-538-5504
easi@easi.org www.easi.org

Thomas Benjamin, President
Roy Geiger, VP Administration
Peggy Knight, VP Programs

Engaging senior volunteers to use their experience in the restoration and maintenance of environmentally sound environments. International network.
Founded: 1990

6612 Environmental Arsenic Council
1250 Connecticut Avenue NW
Suite 700
Washington, DC 20036
202-637-9040
FAX: 202-637-9178 bobf@regnet.com

Robert J Fensterheim, Executive Director

Monitors regulatory developments on behalf of manufacturers in the chemical industry.
Founded: 1996

6613 Environmental Assessment Association
1224 N Nokomis NE
Alexandria, MN 56308
320-763-4320
FAX: 320-763-9290
eaa@iami.org www.iami.org

Robert Johnson, Executive Director

Supports all those involved in environmental assessment, including training and education, publications, conferences and research resources.

6614 Environmental Bankers Association

510 King Street
Suite 410
Alexandria, VA 22314
703-549-0977
FAX: 703-548-5945 800-966-7475
eba@envirobank.org
www.envirobank.org

D J Telego, Executive Co-Director

EBA voting members are banks, trust companies, credit unions, savings and loan associations, and other financial services organizations with an interest in environmental risk management and related issues. Active participants are bankers from Trust or Credit offices with responsibility for environmental liability, and financial services officers with environmental interests. Affiliate members are from law firms, consulting and insurance organizations.
Founded: 1994

6615 Environmental Business Association
1150 Connecticut Avenue NW
9th Floor
Washington, DC 20036-4129
202-624-4363
FAX: 202-828-4130 wbode@bode.com

William H Bode, President

TEBA members represent all segments of the environmental industry—consultants, labaoratories, remediation companies, disposal firms, recyclers and technology innovators. TEBA facilitates arrangements and information exchange among members to develop business opportunities. Services include sponsoring seminars, monthly meetings, industry trends, changes in technology and legislation.
Founded: 1989

6616 Environmental Coalition on Nuclear Power
433 Orlando Avenue
State College, PA 16803
814-237-3900
johnstrud@link.net

Judith H Johnsrud, Director

Groups and individuals concerned with the nuclear power and energy policies. Maintains speakers' bureau and conducts research and educational programs.
Founded: 1970

6617 Environmental Compliance Institute
2350 Lakeside Boulevard
Richardson, TX 75082-4310
972-669-1068

Attorneys and corporations interested in environmental law and federal regulations governing waste disposal and other matters related to the environment.

6618 Environmental Design Research Association
PO Box 4176
Edmond, OK 73083-7146
405-330-4863
FAX: 405-330-4150
edra@telepath.com www.edra.org

Janet Singer, Executive Director

Is to advance the art and science of environmental design research, to improve understanding of the interrelationships between people and their built and natural surroundings, and to help create environments responsive to human needs. EDRA members are designers and other professionals with an interest in environmental design research.
700 Members Founded: 1968

6619 Environmental Industry Association
4301 Connecticut Avenue NW
#300
Washington, DC 20008-2304
202-664-4701
FAX: 202-966-4868
wa@envasns.org www.envasns.org

Bruce Parker, President

Supports all those involved with technology of recycling, resource recovery and sanitary landfills. Publishes magazine.

6620 Environmental Information Association
6935 Wisconsin Avenue
#306
Chevy Chase, MD 20814
301-961-4999
FAX: 301-961-3094
info@eia-usa.org www.eia-usa.org

Brent Kynoch, Managing Director
Kelly Rutt, Development Manager

Nonprofit organization dedicated to providing environmental information to individuals, members and industry. Disseminates information on the abatement of asbestos and lead-based paint, indoor air quality, safety and health issues, analytical issues and environmental site assessments.

6621 Environmental Law Institute
2000 L St NW
Ste 620
Washington, DC 20036-4919
202-939-3800
FAX: 202-939-3868 800-433-5120
law@eli.org www.eli.org

Leslie Carothers, President
Martin Dickinson, VP Development
Tess Doheny, Director Membership Development
Erik Meyers, Director Associates Programs
Vivian Buckingham, Director Public Interest Program

Supports all those involved in environmental issues from a legal perspective, fostering the exchange of ideas and solutions for pressing environmental issues.

6622 Environmental Mutagen Society
1821 Michael Faraday Drive
Suite 300
Reston, VA 20190
703-438-8220
FAX: 703-438-3113
emshq@ems-us.org www.ems-us.org

Tonia Masson, Executive Director

Members are scientists of diverse backgrounds and varied interests working in the field of molecular genetics and mutagenesis, whether in academia, industry or government. Focus is to encourage the study mutagens in the human environment particularly as they affect public health.
1500 Members Founded: 1969

6623 Environmental Protection Agency
Ariel Rios Building
1200 Pennsylvania Avenue NW
Washington, DC 20460
202-272-0167

internet_support@unixmail.rtpnc.epa.gov
www.epa.gov

Mike Leavitt, Administrator
Stephen L Johnson, Deputy Administrator

Federal agency concerned with maintaining land, air and water quality.
18000 Members Founded: 1970

6624 Federation of Environmental Technologists
9451 N 107th St
Milwaukee, WI 53224-1105
414-540-0070
FAX: 262-244-7106
info@fetic.org www.fetinc.org

Triese Haase, Administrator

FET assists members in interpretation of and compliance with environmental regulations.
700 Members Founded: 1981

6625 Forest History Society
701 Wm Vickers Avenue
Durham, NC 27701-3162
919-682-9319
FAX: 919-682-2349
recluce2@duke.edu
www.foresthistory.org

Steven Anderson, President/Secretary
Larry Tomkaush, Chairman
Yvan Hardy, Co-Vice Chairman
Larry Tombaugh, Co-Vice Chairman
Cheryl Oakes, Manager

Nonprofit, educational institution that explores the history of the environment, forestry and conservation.
2000 Members Founded: 1946
Mailing list available for rent 1,500 names $300 per M.

6626 Forestry, Conservation Communications Association
444 N Capitol Street
Washington, DC 20001-1512
202-245-5416
FAX: 202-624-5407
fcca@sso.org www.fcca.info

John Mcintosh, President
Paul M Leary, First VP
Joseph W Schaefer, Second VP
Thomas Tuttle, Treasurer
Joe Friend, Executive Director

Association for manufacturers or suppliers of forestry and conservation communications equipment, systems and procedures.

6627 Friends of the Trees Society
PO Box 253
Twisp, WA 98856
360-927-1274

friendsofthetrees@yahoo.com
www.friendsofthetrees.net

Michael Pilarski, Director

Nonprofit organization helping tree lovers worldwide.
Founded: 1978

6628 Great Lakes United
State University College at Buffalo
1300 Elmwood Avenue
Buffalo, NY 14222
716-886-0142
FAX: 716-886-0303
glu@glu.org www.glu.org

Patty O'Donnell, President
Jim Mahon, VP
Loretta Michaud, Secretary

An international, environmental coaltion working to preserve and protect the Great Lakes and St. Lawrence River. Memberships are as follows: $100 organizational members, $25 organizational members w/bugdets below $15,000, $25 individuals, and $50 family members.
1.1M Members Founded: 1982

6629 Greenpeace USA
702 H Street NW
Suite 300
Washington, DC 20001
202-462-1177
FAX: 202-462-4507
goa@wdc.greenpeace.org
www.greenpeaceusa.org

John Passacantando, Executive Director
Ellen McPeake, COO

Leading independent campaigning organization that uses non-violent direct action and creative communication to expose global environmental problems and to promote solutions that are essential to a green and peaceful future.
2.5M Members Founded: 1971

6630 Hazardous Materials Information Resource S ystem
One Church Street
Suite 200
Rockville, MD 20850
301-577-1842
FAX: 301-738-2330
The Hazardous Materials Information Resource System is a Department of Defense (DOD) automated system developed and maintained by the Defense Logistics Agency. HMIRS is the central repository for Material Safety Data Sheets (MSDS) for the United States Government military services and civil agencies.

6631 Imaging and Geospacial Information Society
5410 Grosvenor Lane
Suite 210
Bethesda, MD 20814-2160
301-493-0290
FAX: 301-493-0208
asprs@asprs.org www.asprs.org

Temperance Baltee

Supports all those involved in mapping, photogrammetry, environmental management, remote sensing, geographic infromation, and natural resources.

6632 Institute for Environmental Auditing
1775 Duke Street
Alexandria, VA 22314-3457
703-739-6196

A professional organization of environmental auditors.
100 Members

6633 Institute for Polyacrylate Absorbents
1850 M Street NW
Suite 700
Washington, DC 20036-5810
202-721-4145
FAX: 202-296-8120

Dr C Tucker Helmes, Executive Director

Represents manufacturers and users of absorbent polymers made of cross-linked polyacrylates and manufacturers and users of acrylic acid or its salts. It addreses the scientific, regulatory and related issues which are likely to impact the manufacture, use and disposal of fluid-absorhing polyacrylates.
Founded: 1985

6634 Institute for World Resource Research
PO Box 5275
Woodridge, IL 60517
630-910-1551
FAX: 630-910-1561
www.globalwarming.net

BJ Jefferson, Advertising/Sales

Supports those involved in all phases of developments in forestry and reforestation of northern nations including the US, Canada, Russia, Sweden, Finland, Norway, China, Japan and others. Its goal is to increase the worldwide understanding of the ecological and economic roles of the northern forest regions of the world.

6635 Institute of Environmental Sciences and Technology
5005 Newport Drive
Suite 506
Rolling Meadows, IL 60008-3841
847-255-1561
FAX: 847-255-1699
iest@iest.org www.iest.org

Julie Kendrick, Executive Director
Robert Burrows, Director
Communications Services
Corrie Roesslein, Director
Programs/Administration

Is an international professional society that serves members and the industries they represent through education and the development of recommended practices and standards.
1600 Members Founded: 1953

6636 Institute of Gas Technology
1700 South Mount Prospect Road
Des Plaines, IL 60018-1804
847-680-0664
FAX: 609-243-3750

Steven W Gauthier, VP
Michael Dugan, Executive Director
Carol Worster, Supervisor

Supports all those involved in the gas industry worldwide, including energy industry production, consumption, reserves, imports and prices.

6637 Institute of Scrap Recycling Industries
1352 G Street
Suite 1000
Washington, DC 20005-3104
202-731-1770
FAX: 202-626-0900
isri@isri.org www.isri.org

Robin Wiener, President
Charles William Jr, Chairman
Frank J Cozzi, Vice Chair
George Adams, Secretary/Treasurer

Supports all those involved in the scrap processing and recycling industry.

6638 International Academy of Indoor Air
343 Soquel Avenue PMB 312
Santa Cruz, CA 95062
831-426-0148
FAX: 831-426-6522
info@indoorair2002.org
www.indoorair2002.org
Supports all those involved with indoor air quality and climate with training, education, resource materials and an annual conference.

6639 International Association for Energy Economics
28790 Chagrin Boulevard
Suite 350
Cleveland, OH 44122-4630
216-464-5365
FAX: 216-464-2737
iaee@iaee.org www.iaee.org

David Williams, Executive Director
Arnold Baker, President
Majid Abbaspour, VP/Secretary

Association for those involved in energy economics including publications, consultants, energy database software.
3400 Members Founded: 1977

6640 International Association for Food Protection
6200 Aurora Avenue
Suite 200W
Des Moines, IA 50322
515-276-3344
FAX: 515-276-8655 800-369-6337
info@foodprotection.org
www.foodprotection.org

Kathy Glass, President
Jeffrey M Farber, VP
Frank Yiannas, Secretary
David W Tharp, Executive Director

Nonprofit, educational association of food protection professionals. The association is dedicated to the education and service of its members, specifically, as well as industry personnel.
3000 Members Founded: 1911

6641 International Association of Fire Chiefs
4025 Fair Ridge Drive
Suite 300
Fairfax, VA 22033
703-273-0911
FAX: 703-273-9363 www.iafc.org

Gary L Briese, Executive Director
Ernie Mitchell, President
Bob DiPoli, First VP
William D Killen, Second VP
Julian Taliaferro, Treasurer

Supports fire chiefs and their efforts surrounding environmental conservation issues.
12000 Members Founded: 1873

6642 International Association of Wildland Fire
Po Box 261
Hot Springs, SD 57747-0261
605-890-2348
888-440-4293
iawf@iawfonline.org
www.iawfonline.org

Chuck Bushey, President
Paul Woodard, VP

IWAF members are academics and professionals with an interest in wildland fires.

700 Members Founded: 1983

6643 International Ecotourism Society
1333 H St Nw
300 East Tower
Washington, DC 20005-4707
202-347-9203
FAX: 202-789-7279
info"at"ecotourism.org
www.ecotourism.org

Kelly Bricker, Chair
Tony Charters, Voce Chair
Neal Inamdar, Director Finance/Administration

Society members include park managers, tour operators, conservation professionals, and others with an interest in the development of ecology-centered tourism.

900 Members Founded: 1990

6644 International Lead Zinc Research Organiz- ation
2525 Meridian Parkway, Suite 100
PO Box 12036
Research Triangle Park, NC 27709-2036
919-361-4647
FAX: 919-361-1957
rputnam@ilzro.org www.ilzro.org

Stephen Wilkinson, President
Frank Goodwin, VP Materials Sciences
Scott Mooneyham, Treasurer
Rob Putnam, Director Communications

ILZRO members are miners and refiners of lead and zinc. Trade association of the lead and zinc industry worldwide. Focus on research and development to detect new uses for the metals and refine existing uses.

Founded: 1958

6645 International Molded Pulp Environmental Packaging Association
1425 W Mequon Road
Suite C
Mequon, WI 53092
262-410-0522
FAX: 414-241-3766
info@impega.org www.impega.org

HO Ranger, Executive Director

Founded: 1996

6646 International Society for Ecological Economics
1313 Dolley Madison Boulevard
Suite 402
McLean, VA 22101
703-790-1745
FAX: 703-790-2672
jochamber1@aol.com www.ecoeco.org

Joan Martinez-Alier, President

Members are researchers, academics, and other professionals who study the impact of economic models and policies on the environment.

750 Members Founded: 1989

6647 Isaak Walton League
707 Conservation Lane
Gaithersburg, MD 20878
301-268-8713
FAX: 301-548-0146 800-453-5463
general@iwla.org www.iwla.org

Nathaniel P Reed, President
Raymond J Koffler, Secretary
William R West, Treasurer
Timothy W Reid, VP
Paul Hansen, Executive Director

Conducts research and education on river ecosystems and healthy fisheries.

50000 Members Founded: 1922

6648 Marine Technology Society
5565 Sterrett Place
Suite 108
Columbia, MD 21044
410-884-5330
FAX: 410-884-9060
mtsmbrship@erols.com
www.mtsociety.org

Ted Brockett, President
Daniel Schwartz, VP Technical Affairs
John Head, Secretary/Treasurer
Judith Krauthamer, Executive Director

Addresses coastal zone management, marine, mineral and energy resources, marine environmental protection, and ocean engineering issues.

2M Members Founded: 1963

6649 Midwest for Environmental Science and Public Policy
1845 N Farwell Avenue
Suite 100
Milwaukee, WI 53202
414-271-7280
FAX: 414-273-7293
mcespp@mcespp.org www.mcespp.org

Patrice Ann Morrow, Chair
Jeffery A Foran, President/CEO

For citizens concerned with environmental protection.

6650 NORA: an Association of Reponsible Recyclers
5965 Amber Ridge Road
Haymarket, VA 20169
703-753-4277
FAX: 703-753-2445
sparker@noranews.org
www.noranews.org

Scott D Parker, Executive Director

Is a trade association representing the interests of companies in the United States engaged in the safe recycling of used oil, antifreeze, waste water and oil filters.

Founded: 1984

6651 National Association for Environmental Management
1612 K Street NW
Suite 1102
Washington, DC 20006
202-986-6616
FAX: 202-530-4408 800-391-6236
programs@naem.org www.naem.org

Carol Singer Neuvelt, Executive Director
Michael E McGuire, President
Gisella Spreizer, Treasurer

Dedicated to advancing the profession of environmental management and supports the professional corporate and facility environmental manager.

1000+ Members Founded: 1990

6652 National Association for PET Containers
10800 Sikes Place
Suite 240
Charlotte, NC 28277
704-845-5070
FAX: 704-845-5276
information@napcor.com
www.napcor.com

Luke Schmidt, President
Mike Schedler, VP Technology
Don Kneass, Director
Sandi Childs, Director

National association for the PET plastic industry. Promotes the use of PET plastic packaging and facilitates the recycling of PET containers.

Bi-Monthly Founded: 1987

6653 National Association of Conservation Districts (NACD)
509 Capitol Court Northeast
Washington, DC 20002-4937
202-547-6223
FAX: 202-547-6450
Bill-Wilson@nacdnet.org
www.nacdnet.org/

Bill Wilson, President
Krysta Harden, Chief Executive Officer
John Redding, Secretary/Treasurer
Arthur Ganta, Director Finance & Administration
Keira Franz, Director Government Affairs

NACD develops national conservation policies, influences lawmakers and builds partnerships with other agencies and organizations. NACD also provides services to its districts to help them share ideas in order to better serve their local communities.

17000 Members Founded: 1946

6654 National Association of Environmental Professionals
PO Box 2086
Bowie, MD 20718-2086
301-860-1140
FAX: 301-860-1141 888-251-9902
office@naep.org www.naep.org

Sandi Worthman, Administrator

NAEP is a multidisciplinary, non-profit professional association dedicated to the promotion of a code of ethics and standards of practice in the environmental field. NAEP's focus brings together specialists from each of the major segments of the environmental profession.

1200 Members Founded: 1975

6655 National Association of Local Government Environmental Professionals
1333 New Hampshire Avenue NW
Washington, DC 20036
202-638-6254
FAX: 202-393-2866
nalgep@spiegelmcd.com
www.nalgep.org

Kenneth Brown, Executive Director
David Dickson, Project Manager

Is a national organization representing local government professionals responsible for environmental compliance and the development of local environmental policy. NALGEP brings together local environmental officials to share information on practices, conduct policy projects, promote environmental training and education, and communicate the view of local officials on national environmental issues.

150 Members Founded: 1993

6656 National Association of Noise Control
53 Cubberly Avenue
West Windsor, NJ 08550-3400

Members are employees of the state and federal governments.

70 Members

6657 National Audubon Society
700 Broadway
New York, NY 10003
212-979-3000
FAX: 212-979-3188
webmaster@audubon.org
www.audubon.org

John Flicker, President

Conserves and restores natural ecosystems, focusing on birds, other wildlife, and thier habitats for the benefit of humanity and the earth's biological diversity.

50000 Members Founded: 1992

6658 National Center for Appropriate Technology
3040 Continental Drive
Butte, MT 59702
406-494-4572
FAX: 406-494-2905 800-275-6228
info@ncat.org www.ncat.org

Adolfo G Alayon, Chairman
George Ortiz, Vice Chairman
Jeannie Jertson, Secretary
Gene Brady, Treasurer
Kathy Hadley, Executive Director

A resource center for information and expertise on methods of promoting conservation and energy self-sufficiency. The term, appropriate technology, is defined as a small-scale, environmentally sound, low-cost, locally based approach to problems with an emphasis on self help.

Founded: 1976

6659 National Conference of Local Environmental Health Administrators
c/o NEHA, 720 S Colorado Boulevard
South Tower, Suite 970
Denver, CO 80246-1925
303-756-9090
FAX: 303-691-9490 nfabian@neha.org

Nelson E Fabian, Executive Director

An organization of environmental health administrators employed at the local level, at universities, and in industry. Purpose is to promote efficient and effective local environmental health programs.

300 Members Founded: 1938

6660 National Environmental Balancing Bureau
8575 Grovemont Circle
Gaithersburg, MD 20877
301-977-3698
FAX: 301-977-9589 www.nebb.org

Jim Bochat, President
Michael Dolim, VP
John G Cappell, Treasurer

Supports all those involved with testing and balancing equipment, supplies and services.

6661 National Environmental Development Association
One Thomas Circle NW
10th Floor
Washington, DC 20006
202-332-2933
FAX: 202-530-0659

Phil Clapp, President
Steve Hellem, Executive Director

NEDA members are companies and other organizations concerned with balancing environmental and economic interests to obtain both a clean environment and a strong economy.

Founded: 1973

6662 National Environmental Health Association
720 S Colorado Boulevard
Suite 970-S
Denver, CO 80246-1925
303-756-9090
FAX: 303-691-9490
staff@neha.org www.neha.org

Nelson F Fabian, Executive Director
Tabby Bernardo, Executive Coordinator

The National Environmental Heath Association is a unique organization representing all professionals in environmental health. NEHA offers credentials, publications, training, Journal of Environmental Health, and discounts for members; also hosts an annual trade show.

5000 Members Founded: 1937

6663 National Environmental, Safety and Health Training Association
5320 N 16th Street
Suite 114
Phoenix, AZ 85016-3241
602-956-6099
FAX: 602-956-6399
info@neshta.org www.neshta.org

Charles L Richardson, Executive Director
Joan J Jennings, Manager Association Services
Suzanne Lanctot, Manager Certification/Membership

1100 Members Founded: 1977

6664 National Institutes for Water Resources
47 Harkness Road
Pelham, MA 10002
413-253-5686
FAX: 413-253-1309
godfrey@tei.umass.edu

Paul Joseph Godfrey, PhD, Executive Secretary

To coordinate the institute program both internally and externally. Membership consists of the directors of 54 institutes.

54 Members Founded: 1974

6665 National Registry of Environmental Professionals
PO Box 2099
Glenview, IL 60025
847-724-6631
FAX: 847-724-4223
nrep@nrep.org www.nrep.org

Richard A Young, PhD, Executive Director
Edward Beck, PhD, Senior Director
Carol Schellinger, Director

To promote legal and professional recognition of individuals possessing education, training and experience as environmental managers, engineers, technologists, scientists and technicians; and to consolidate that recognition in one centralized source.

17000 Members Founded: 1983
Mailing list available for rent

6666 National Society of Environmental Consultants
303 W Press Street
San Antonio, TX 78212
800-486-3676
800-486-3676

Supports all activities of environmental consultants.

900 Members Founded: 1992

6667 National Solid Wastes Management Association
4301 Connecticut Avenue NW
#300
Washington, DC 20008-2304
202-664-4701
FAX: 202-966-4868
wa@envasns.org www.envasns.org

Bruce Parker, President

Supports all those involved in the environment industry, especially the handling, transportation and disposal of infectious wastes.

6668 National Trust for Historic Preservation
1785 Massachusetts Avenue NW
Washington, DC 20036-2117
202-886-6295
FAX: 202-588-6038
members@nthp.org
www.nationaltrust.org

Richard Moe, President/Executive Director
Sam Kilpatrick, Controller

Association for those involved in preservation law.

25000 Members Founded: 1949

6669 National Wildlife Federation
11100 Wildlife Center Drive
Reston, VA 20190-5362
703-386-6000
www.nwf.org

Mark Van Putten, Chief Executive Officer

Encourages management of natural resources. Gives financial aid to local groups and graduate studies. Conducts guided nature trail tours, produces programs and sponsors competitions.

4.5MM Members Founded: 1936

6670 National Woodland Owners Association
374 Maple Avenue E
Vienna, VA 22180-4718
703-255-2700
800-470-8733
argow@nwoa.net
www.woodlandowners.org

Keith A Argow, President
Bert Udell, Executive Committee Chair
Gerald A Rose, Midwest Regional VP

Provides timely information about forestry and forest practices with news from Washington,DC and state capitals. Written for non-industrial land owners. Includes state landowner association news.

39M Members Founded: 1983

6671 Natural Renewable Energy Laboratory
United States Department of Energy
1617 Cole Boulevard
Golden, CO 80401-3393
303-275-3000
FAX: 303-275-4053
client_services@nrel.gov
www.nrel.gov

Richard H Truly, Director

Created by the Solar Energy Research, Development and Demonstration Act of 1974, which authorized a federal program aimed at developing solar energy as a viable source of the nation's future energy needs. As a primary federal laboratory for solar energy research, SERI conducts and coordinates solar research, technology devel-

opment and testing functions as developed by the US Department of Energy.
Founded: 1977

6672 Natural Resources Defense Council
40 W 20th Street
New York, NY 10011
212-727-2700
FAX: 212-727-1773
nrdcinfo@nrdc.org www.nrdc.org

Frances Beinecke, President

Dedicated to the wise management of natural resources through research, public education and the development of effective public policies.
50000 Members Founded: 1970

6673 North American Association for Environment al Education
2000 P Street NW
Suite 540
Washington, DC 20036
202-419-0412
FAX: 202-419-0415
email@naaee.org www.naaee.org

William H Dent, Jr, Executive Director
Barbara Eager, Conference Coordinator
Paul Werth, Owner

Purpose is to assist and support the work of individuals and groups engaged in environmental education, research and service. NAAEE is organized into four interactive sections: Elementary and Secondary Education Section; Environmental Studies Section; the Non-Formal Section; and the Conservation Education Section.
600 Members Founded: 1971

6674 North American Chapter - International Society for Ecological Modelling
One Shields Avenue
Davis, CA 95616-8521
530-752-5362
FAX: 530-752-0175 www.isemna.org

Wolfgang Pittroff, Secretary-General

Promotes the international exchange of general knowledge, ideas and scientific results in the area of the application of systems analysis and simulation to ecology, environmental science and natural resource management using mathematical and computer modelling of ecological systems.
150 Members Founded: 1983

6675 North American Lake Management Society
4513 Vernon Boulevard, Suite 100
PO Box 5443
Madison, WI 53705-443
608-233-2836
FAX: 608-233-3186
nalms@nalms.org www.nalms.org

Steve Heiskary, President
Sharon Campbell, Secretary
Dick Osgood, Treasurer
Carol Winge, Manager

Members are academics, lake managers and others interested in furthering the understanding of lake ecology. The North American Lake Management Society's mission is to forge partnerships among citizens, scientists and professionals to foster the management and protection of lakes and reservoirs for today and tomorrow. Please call for rate information.
1700 Members Founded: 1980

6676 Northeast Sustainable Energy Association
50 Miles Street
Greenfield, MA 01301
413-774-6051
FAX: 413-774-6053
nesea@nesea.org www.nesea.org

John Walsh, Chair
Sonia Hamel, Vice Chair
Daniel Sagan, Secretary
Michael Skelly, Treasurer
Nancy Hazard, Executive Director

The nation's leading regional membership organization focused on promoting the understanding, development and adoption of energy conservation and non-polluting, renewable energy technologies.
1802 Members Founded: 1974
Mailing list available for rent

6677 Plant Growth Regulator Society of America
Rhone-Poulenc, Ag Company
PO Box 2945
LaGrange, GA 30241
706-845-9085
FAX: 706-883-8215
assocgroup@mindspring.com

Dr Eric A Curry, President
Dr Louise Ferguson, VP
Dr Ed Stover, Secretary

Functions as a nonprofit educational and scientific organization.
325 Members Founded: 1973

6678 Rachael Carson Council
PO Box 10779
Silver Springs, MD 20914
301-593-7507
FAX: 301-593-6251 rccouncil@aol.com

Dr David Pimentel, President
Martha Hayne Talbot, VP
David B McGrath, Treasurer
Dr Diana Post, Secretary

Library and clearinghouse on pesticide toxicity, lower risk alternatives for pest control, and Rachel Carson. Produces publications and sponsors conventions/meetings on these topics, issues newsletter. Nonprofit.
Founded: 1965

6679 Renewable Fuels Association
One Massachusetts Avenue
Suite 820
Washington, DC 20001
202-289-3835
FAX: 202-289-7519
info@ethanolrfa.org
www.ethenolrfa.org

Bob Dinneen, President/CEO
Mary Giglio, Director Public Affairs
Larry Schafer, Legislative Counsel
Monte Shaw, Director Communications

Members are companies and individuals involved in the production and use of ethanol.

55 Members Founded: 1981

6680 Renewable Natural Resources Foundation
5430 Grosvenor Lane
Bethesda, MD 20814-2193
301-493-9101
FAX: 301-493-6148
info@rnrf.org www.rnrf.org

Robert D Day, Executive Director
Ryan M Colker, Director Programs
Chandru Krishna, Director Administration

A consortium of professional and scientific societies whose members are concerned with the advancement of research, education, scientific practice and policy formulation for the conservation, replenishment and use of the earth's renewable natural resources.
14 Members Founded: 1972

6681 Resource Policy Institute
1525 Selby Avenue
Los Angeles, CA 90024-5796

Dr Arthur Purcell, Director/Founder

Education, amd consulting research group concerned with environmental policies, technologies, and management strategies..
Founded: 1975

6682 Safe Buildings Alliance
Metropolitan Square
655 15th Street NW
Suite 1200
Washington, DC 20005-5701
202-879-5120
FAX: 202-638-2103

An association of building products companies that formerly manufactured asbestos-containing materials for building construction. Its main focus is to provide public information on issues relating to asbestos in building. SBA promotes a reasonable, safe response to the problem of asbestos in buildings, including the development of uniform, objective Federal and State standards for asbestos identification and abatement, nonremoval alternatives and the regulation of inspectors.
Founded: 1984

6683 Sagamore Institute
PO Box 40
Raquette Lake, NY 13436-40
315-354-4600
FAX: 315-354-5851
sagamore@telenet.net
www.sagamore.org

Educational programs on history, ecology and culture of Adirondack Park.

6684 Silicones Environmental Health and Safety
11921 Freedom Drive
Suite 550
Reston, VA 20190-5332
703-904-4322
FAX: 703-925-5955
sehsc@sehsc.com www.sehsc.com

Reo Menning, Executive Director
Margaret Newman, Manager

An organization of organosilicones manufacturers. Formed to coordinate programs dealing with health, environmental and safety issues.
6 Members Founded: 1971

6685 Society for Ecological Restoration
285 West 18th Street #1
Tucson, AZ 85701
520-622-5485
FAX: 520-622-5491
info@ser.org www.ser.org

Mary Kay C LeFevour, Executive Director
Jane Cripps, Membership
Julie St John, Communications

SER members are academics, scientists, environmental consultants, government agencies and others with an interest in ecological restoration.

2300 Members Founded: 1988

6686 Society for Environmental Geochemistry and Health
4698 S Forrest Avenue
Springfield, MO 65810
417-851-1166
FAX: 417-881-6920
DRBGWIXSON@aol.com
www.segh.net

Bobby G. Wixson, Secretary

To promote a multi-disciplinary approach to research in fields of geochemistry and health to facilitate and expand communication among scientists within these disciplines and to advance knowledge in the area.
400 Members Founded: 1971

6687 Society for Human Ecology
College of the Atlantic
105 Eden Street
Bar Harbor, ME 04609-0180
207-288-5015
FAX: 207-288-3780
carter@ecology.coa.edu
www.societyforhumanecology.org

Barbara Carter, Assistant to Executive Director

SHE members are academics, scientists, health professionals and others with an interest in studying the interrelationship of man's actions and his environment.
150 Members Founded: 1981

6688 Society for Occupational and Environmental Health
6728 Old Mclean Village Drive
McLean, VA 22101
703-556-9222
FAX: 703-556-8729
soeh@degnon.org www.soeh.org

George K Degnon, CAE, Executive Director
Laura Degnon, Manager

Members include physicians, hygienists, economists, laboratory scientists, academicians, labor and industry representatives, or anyone interested in occupational and/or environmental health. Serves as a forum for the presentation of scientific data and the exchange of information among members; sponsors conferences and meetings which address specific problem areas and policy questions.
300 Members Founded: 1972

6689 Society of Environmental Journalists
PO Box 2492
Jenkintown, PA 19046
215-884-8174
FAX: 215-884-8175
sej@sej.org www.sej.org

Beth Parke, Executive Director
Tim Wheeler, President

SEJ works toward an informed society through excellence in environmental journalism. Members are journalists and educators united to enhance the quality, accuracy and visibility of reporting on environmental issues.
1500 Members Founded: 1990

6690 Society of Environmental Toxicology and Chemistry
1010 N 12th Avenue
Pensacola, FL 32501-3367
850-469-1500
FAX: 850-469-9778
setac@setac.org www.setac.org

Mike Mozur, Executive Director

Is a professional society established to promote the use of multidisciplinary approaches to solving problems of the impact of chemicals and technology on the environment. SETA members are professionals in the fields of chemistry, toxicology, biology, ecology, atmospheric sciences, health sciences, earth sciences, and environmental engineering.
4000 Members Founded: 1979

6691 Society of Exploration Geophysicists
8801 South Yale
Tulsa, OK 74137-2740
918-497-5500
FAX: 918-497-5557
web@seg.org
www.seg.org/index.shtml

Terry K Young, President
Maria Angela Capello, VP
Yonghe Sun, Editor
Frank D Brown, Secretary/Treasurer
Mary Fleming, Executive Director

The Society of Exploration Geophysicists/SEG is a not-for-profit organization that promotes the science of geophysics and the education of applied geophysicists. SEG fosters the expert and ethical practice of geophysics in the exploration and development of natural resources, in characterizing the near surface, and in mitigating earth hazards.
25000 Members Founded: 1930

6692 Soil and Plant Analysis Council
621 Rose Street
Lincoln, NE 68502-2040

FAX: 402-476-7598
spcouncil@aol.com
Supports all those involved in the analysis of soil and plants.

6693 Soil and Water Conservation Society
945 SW Ankeny Road
Ankeny, IA 50021-9764
515-289-2331
FAX: 515-289-1227 800-843-7645
webmaster@swcs.org www.swcs.org

Deborah Cavanaugh-Grant, President
Jeffrey Vonk, VP
Rebecca Fletcher, Treasurer
Ross Braun, Secretary

Supports all professional conservationists with publications, training, education and conferences.

6694 Solar Energy Research Institute
United States Department of Energy
1617 Cole Boulevard
Golden, CO 80401-3305
303-275-4700
FAX: 303-275-4788
Created by the Solar Energy Research, Development and Demonstration Act of 1974, which authorized a federal program aimed at developing solar energy as a viable source of the Nation's future energy needs. As a primary Federal laboratory for solar energy research, SERI conducts and coordinates solar research, technology development and testing functions as developed by the US Department of Energy.
Founded: 1977

6695 Steel Recycling Institute
680 Andersen Drive
Pittsburgh, PA 15220-2700
412-922-2772
FAX: 412-922-3213 800-876-7274

William H Heenan Jr, President

Promotes steel recycling and works to forge a coalition of steelmakers, can manufacturers, legislators, government officials, solid waste managers, business and consumer groups.
Founded: 1988

6696 Student Conservation Association
689 River Road
PO Box 550
Charlestown, NH 03603-550
603-543-1700
FAX: 603-543-1828
jcota@thesca.org www.sca-inc.org

Kurt Merrill, Director Conservation Crew
Bob Bland, Director Membership
Carla Chandler, Director Program Services
Don Hunger, Director National Program
Dale Penny, President
35000 Members Founded: 1957

6697 Surfaces in Biomaterials Foundation
1000 Westgate Dr
Ste 252
Saint Paul, MN 55114-8679
651-290-6295
FAX: 651-290-2266
surfacesinbiomaterials@ewald.com
www.surfaces.org

Bill Monn, Executive Director
Victoria Carr-Bredel, President

An international society of research professionals interested in the manufacture and development of new biomaterials.
250 Members

6698 Synthetic Organic Chemical Manufacturers Association
1850 M Street NW
Suite 700
Washington, DC 20036
202-721-4100
FAX: 202-296-8120
info@socma.com www.socma.com

Joseph Acker, President
Diane McMahon, VP Commercial Development
Charlene Patterson, Director Human Resources

Represents and serves the batch, custom and small chemical industry, which produces products important to the life, health and well-being of people worldwide. SOCMA operations that are internationally competitive and contribute to a healthy, productive economy. We offer two publications online: Online Membership Directory and Chemical Bond Express Newsletter.
Founded: 1921

6699 Test Boring Association
Five Mapleton Road
Suite 200
Princeton, NJ 08540
609-514-2600
FAX: 609-514-2660

Patrizia Zita, Management Executive
Founded: 1941

6700 United Association of Used Oil Services
318 Newman Road
Sebring, FL 33870-6702
941-655-3880
800-877-4356
Established to be an effective presence in dealing with regulations and to provide a network for those with an interest in the collection and proper disposition of used lubricating oils.
Founded: 1987

6701 Water Environment Federation
601 Wythe Street
Alexandria, VA 22314-1994
703-842-2400
FAX: 703-684-2492 800-666-0206
thardwick@wef.org www.wef.org
Phyllis Eastman, Managing Director
Dianne Crilley, Manager Member Association Programs
Teresa Evans-Hunter, Manager Membership Development
Bill Bertera, Executive Director
Tracy Hardwick, Manager Publications
Supports those involved in issues that affect the international water environment.
79 Members Founded: 1928

6702 Water Quality Association
4151 Naperville Road
Lisle, IL 60532-3696
630-505-0160
FAX: 630-505-9637
info@wqa.org www.wqa.org
Gerald Dierolf, VP
Richard F Elliott, Governor at Large
Greg Norgaard, President
Dennis Rupert, Secretary
Peter Censky, Executive Director
An international, nonprofit trade association representing retail/dealers and manufacturer/suppliers in the point of use/entry water quality improvement industry. Membership benefits and services include technical and scientific information, educational seminars and home correspondence course books, professional certification and discount services.
2.5M Members Founded: 1974

6703 Wilderness Society
1615 M Street NW
Washington, DC 20036
202-833-2300
FAX: 202-429-3958
www.wilderness.org
William H Meadows, President
Ben Beach, Senior Editor
Establishes the land ethic as a basic element of the American culture and educates people on the importance of wilderness preservation and land protection.
200M Members Founded: 1935
Mailing list available for rent 178000 names $90 per M.

6704 Wildlife Conservation Society
718-205-5090
FAX: 718-584-2625
John Robinson, Plant Manager
Supports all those involved in the conservation of wildlife, especially the most rare and endangered species.

6705 Wildlife Habitat Council
8737 Colesville Road
Suite 800
Silver Spring, MD 20910
301-588-8994
FAX: 301-588-4629
whc@wildlifehc.org
www.wildlifehc.org
Stephen A Elbert, Chairman
Lawrence A Selzer, Vice Chairman
William W Howard, President
David Carroll, Secretary/Treasurer
Supports corporate, government and conservation leaders from around the globe involved in environmental stewardship.
120+ Members Founded: 1988

6706 Wildlife Management Institute
1146 19th Street NW
Suite 700
Washington, DC 20036
202-371-1808
FAX: 202-408-5059
www.wildlifemanagementinstitute.org
Richard E McCabe, Executive VP
Scot J Williamson, VP
Carol J Peddicord, Finance Manager
Robert L Byrne, Wildlife Program Coordinator
Ronald R Helinski, Conservation Policy Specialist
Supports all those involved with the challenges of modern conservation.

6707 Wildlife Society
5410 Grosvenor Lane
Suite 200
Bethesda, MD 20814-2144
301-897-9770
FAX: 301-530-2471
tws@wildlife.org www.wildlife.org
Harry E Hodgdon, Executive Director
Thomas M Franklin, Wildlife Policy Director
Supports all those involved in wildlife conservation, including wildlife artists, environmental consultants, conservation groups, scientific associations and natural resource companies, industry groups and government agencies.
9000 Members Founded: 1937

6708 Women's Council on Energy and the Environment
PO Box 33211
Washington, DC 20033-0211
Supports women involved in the environmental community with education, research, new trend information and several publications.

6709 World Research Foundation
41 Bell Rock Plaza
Sedona, AZ 86351
928-284-3300
FAX: 928-284-3530
laverne@wrf.org www.wrf.org
LaVerne Boeckman, Co-Founder
Steven Ross, Co-Founder
A unique, international, health information network, so that people could be informed of all available treatments around the world, and so that they could have the freedom to choose, based on complete and in-depth information.
41000 Members Founded: 1977

6710 World Resources Institute
10 G Street NE
Suite 800
Washington, DC 20002
202-729-7600
FAX: 202-729-7610
front@wri.org www.wri.org
Jonathan Lash, President
William D Ruckelshaus, Chairman
Julia Marton Lefèvre, Vice Chair
Frances G Beinecke, Executive Director
Agatha Barclay, Secretary-Treasurer
Compiles information, conducts research, publishes the Environmental Almanac and more.
Founded: 1982

6711 World Society for the Protection of Animals
34 Deloss Street
Framingham, MA 01702
508-879-8350
FAX: 508-620-0786
wspa@wspausa.com
www.wspa.usa.org
Laura Salter, USA Director
Andrew Dickson, Chief Executive
John Walsh, Director International Projects
International animal protection news reports. Lobbies for effective animal welfare laws and provides educational material.
12 Members

6712 World Wildlife Fund
1250 24th Street NW
Washington, DC 20037-1175
202-293-4800
FAX: 202-293-9211
archer@wwfus.org www.panda.org
Kathryn Fuller, President
William K Reilly, Chairman
Edward P Bass, Vice Chairman
William T Lake, Treasurer
Alison Richard, Secretary
Supports all those involved in maintaining wildlife and their environment. Monitors human development, and seeks to influence public opinion and policy makers in favor of ecologically sound practices.
4M Members Founded: 1961

Newsletters

6713 AEESP Newsletter
Association of Environmental Engineering and
2303 Naples Court
Champaign, IL 61822
217-398-6969
FAX: 217-355-9232 www.aeesp.org
Joanne Fetzner, Business Secretary
Quarterly

6714 AERE Newsletter
Association of Environmental and Resource
1616 P Street NW
Suite 400
Washington, DC 20036
202-328-5077
FAX: 202-939-3460
voigt@rff.org www.aere.org
Marilyn Voigt, Executive Secretary
Ralph Metts, President
Semi-Annual

6715 AIH Bulletin
American Institute of Hydrology
300 Village Green Circle
Suite 201
Smyrna, GA 30080
770-269-9388

aihydro@aol.com www.aihydro.org
Cathy Lipsett, Owner
Cathryn Seaburn, Manager
Quarterly

6716 ASMR Newsletter
American Society of Mining and Reclamation
3134 Montavesta Road
Lexington, KY 40502
859-335-6529

asmr@insightbb.com
www.ca.uky.edu/assmr
Richard I Barnhisel, Executive Secretary
10/year

6717 Advisor
Great Lakes Commission
2805 S Industrial Highway
Ann Arbor, MI 48104
734-971-9135
FAX: 734-971-9150
glc@great-lakes.net
http://www.glc.org
Christen Manninen, Production Manager
Cook Havtrkamp, Author
Thomas Crane, Executive Director
Covers economic and environmental issues of the Great Lakes region with a special focus on activities of the Great Lakes Commission.
12 pages Quarterly Founded: 1955
Printed in 1 color on matte stock
Computerized version available

6718 Air Water Pollution Report's Environment Week
Business Publishers
8737 Colesville Road
Suite 1100
Silver Spring, MD 20910-3928
301-876-6300
FAX: 301-589-8493 800-274-6737
custserv@bpinews.com
http://www.bpinews.com
Leonard A Eiserer, Publisher
Beth Early, Operations Director
David Goeller, Editor
Provides a balanced, insightful update on the week's most important environmental news from Washington, D.C. *$595.00*
Weekly Founded: 1963

6719 Annual Research Program Report
National Institutes for Water Resources
47 Harkness Road
Pelham, MA 10002
413-253-5686
FAX: 413-253-1309
godfrey@tei.umass.edu
Paul Joseph Godfrey, PhD, Executive Director
Annual

6720 Archives of Environmental Health
Society for Occupational and Environmental Health
6728 Old McLean Village Drive
McLean, VA 22101
703-556-9222
FAX: 703-556-8729
soeh@degnon.org www.soeh.org
George K Degnon, CAE, Executive Director
Bi-Monthly

6721 BNA's Environmental Compliance Bulletin
Bureau of National Affairs
1231
25th Street NW
Washington, DC 20037-1157
202-452-4200
800-372-1033
customercare@bna.com
http://www.bna.com
Gregory C McCaffery, Publisher
Kevin Fetherston, Managing Editor
Cover the water and air pollution, waste management and regulatory updates, as well as a summary of selected regulatory actions and a list of key environmental compliance dates. *$649.00*
Annual+ Founded: 1929

6722 Bank Notes
Environmental Bankers Association
510 King Street
Suite 410
Alexandria, VA 22314
703-549-0977
FAX: 703-548-5945 800-966-7475
eba@envirobank.org
www.envirobank.org
D J Telego, Executive Co-Director
Bi-Monthly

6723 Bulletins
World Research Foundation
41 Bell Rock Plaza
Sedona, AZ 86351
928-284-3300
FAX: 928-284-3530
laverne@wrf.org www.wrf.org
LaVerne Boeckman, Founder
Quarterly

6724 Business and the Environment
Cutter Information Corporation
37 Broadway
Suite 1
Arlington, MA 02474-5552
781-488-8700
FAX: 617-648-8707 800-888-8939
Karen Fine Coburn, Publisher
Kathleen Victory, Editor
Environmental investment trends, deals and market developments. *$497.00*
Monthly

6725 CCHEST Newsletter
Council on Certification of Health, Environmental
208 Burwash Avenue
Savoy, IL 61874-9912
217-359-2686
FAX: 217-359-0055
cchest@cchest.org www.cchest.org
Roger L Bauer, PhD CSP CPE, Executive Director
Annual

6726 Clean Water Report
CJE Associates
301-589-5103
FAX: 301-589-8493 800-274-6737
custserv@bpinews.com
www.bpinews.com
Follows the latest news from the EPA, Congress, the states, the courts, and private industry. A key information source for environmental professionals, covering the important issues of ground and drinking water, wastewater treatment, wetlands, drought, coastal protection, non-point source pollution, agrichemical contamination and more.
8 pages

6727 Conference Proceedings
North American Association for Environmental
2000 P Street NW
Suite 540
Washington, DC 20036
202-419-0412
FAX: 202-419-0415
email@naaee.org www.naaee.org
William H Dent, Jr, Executive Director
Barbara Eager, Conference Coordinator
Paul Werth, Owner
Annual

6728 Conservation Commission News
New Hampshire Association of Conservation Comm.
54 Portsmouth Street
Concord, NH 03301-5486
603-225-3431
FAX: 603-228-0423
Marjory Swope, Publisher
Encourage conservation and appropriate use of New Hampshire's natural resources by providing assistance to New Hampshire's municipal conservation commissions and by facilitating communication among commissions and between commissions and other public and private agencies involved in conservation. *$5.00*
8 pages Quarterly
Circulation: 1,650
Printed in 1 color on matte stock

6729 Conservogram
Soil and Water Conservation Society
945 SW Ankeny Road
Ankeny, IA 50021-9764
515-289-2331
FAX: 515-289-1227 800-843-7645
swcs@swcs.org http://www.swsc.org
Jean Steiner, CEO/President
Deb Happe, Editor
The professional conservationist's newslwetter, Conservogram is produced for members of the Soil and Water Conservation Society.
Monthly Founded: 1943

6730 Convention Proceedings
Society for Human Ecology
College of the Atlantic
105 Eden Street
Bar Harbor, ME 04609-0180
207-288-5015
FAX: 207-288-3780
carter@ecology.coa.edu
www.societyforhumanecology.org
Barbara Carter, Assistant to Executive Director
1/18 months

6731 Daily Environment Report
Bureau of National Affairs
1231 25th Street NW
Washington, DC 20037-1197
202-452-4200
800-372-1033
customercare@bna.com
www.bna.com
Gregory C McCaffery, Publisher
Larry E Evans, Managing Editor
A 40-page daily report providing comprehensive, in-depth coverage of national and international environmental news. Each

issue contains summaries of the top news stories, articles, and in-brief items, and a journal of meetings, agency activities, hearings and legal proceedings. Coverage includes air and water pollution, hazardous substances, and hazardous waste, solid waste, oil spills, gas drilling, pollution prevention, impact statements and budget matters. *$3537.00*
40 pages Daily

6732 Defense Cleanup
Business Publishers
8737 Colesville Road
Suite 1100
Silver Spring, MD 20910-3928
301-587-6300
FAX: 301-587-4530 800-274-6737
bpinews@bpinews.com
www.bpinews.com
Leonard Eiserer, Publisher
Kathy Thorne, Circulation Manager
Vicki Miller, Owner
Covers the lates news and analysis of defense cleanup activity, including base remediation and closure, contract awards, and site cleanups. *$627.00*
8 pages Weekly
Printed in on matte stock : Newsletter

6733 E&P Environment
Pasha Publications
1616 N Fort Myer Dr
Suite 1000
Arlington, VA 22209-3107
703-528-1244
FAX: 703-528-1253 800-424-2908
epenvr@pasha.com
http://www.newsletteraccess.com
Harry Baisden, Group Publisher
Jerry Grisham, Editor
Reports on environmental regulations, advances in technology and litigation aimed specifically at the exploration and production segments of the oil and gas industry. *$395.00*

6734 E-Scrap News
Resource Recycling
PO Box 42270
Portland, OR 97242-270
503-233-1305
FAX: 503-233-1356
info@resource-recycling.com
http://www.resource-recycling.com
Jerry Powell, Publisher/Editor
Andrew Santosusso, Managing Editor
Betsy Loncar, Circulation Director
Monthly newsletter covering all aspects of recovering, recycling, and managing electronics scrap. Coverage includes market prices and trends, collection events, product stewardship developments and global trends. *$99.00*
6 pages Monthly Founded: 1983
Circulation: 1000
Mailing list available for rent 40,000 names $100 per M.
Printed in 2 colors on matte stock

6735 ECODMOD Newsletter
International Society for Ecological Modelling
University of California, Animal Sciences Dept
One Shields Avenue
Davis, CA 95616-8521
530-752-5362
FAX: 530-752-0175 www.isemna.org
Wolfgang Pittroff, Secretary-General
Quarterly

6736 EH&S Software News Online
Donley Technology
PO Box 152
Colonial Beach, VA 22443-152
804-224-9427
FAX: 804-224-7958 800-201-1595
donleytech@donleytech.com
http://www.donleytech.com
John Donley, Editor
Reports on news and upgraded software products, database, and on-line systems from commercial developers and government resources. *$125.00*
Founded: 1988

6737 EMS Newsletter
Environmental Mutagen Society
1821 Michael Faraday Drive
Suite 300
Reston, VA 20190
703-438-8220
FAX: 703-438-3113
emshq@ems-us.org www.ems-us.org
Tonia Masson, Executive Director
Bi-Annual

6738 Economic Opportunity Report
Business Publishers
8737 Colesville Road
Suite 1100
Silver Spring, MD 20910-3928
301-587-6300
FAX: 301-587-4530 800-274-6737
bpinews@bpinews.com
www.bpinews.com
Leonard A Eiserer, Publisher
Beth Early, Operations Director
Antipoverty news coverage and analysis which gives insight into developments that affect social programs. *$383.00*
Weekly

6739 Environment Reporter
Bureau of National Affairs
1231 25th Street NW
Washington, DC 20037-1197
202-452-4200
800-372-1033
customercare@bna.com
http://www.bna.com
Gregory C McCaffery, Publisher
Patricia Spencer, Managing Editor
Larry Evans, Manager
A weekly notification and reference service covering the full-spectrum of legislative, administrative, judicial, industrial and technological developments affecting pollution control and environmental protection. *$3776.00*
Weekly Founded: 1929

6740 Environmental Health Letter
Business Publishers
8737 Colesville Road
Suite 1100
Silver Spring, MD 20910-3928
301-587-6300
FAX: 301-587-4530 800-274-6737
bpinews@bpinews.com
http://www.bpinews.com
Leonard A Eiserer, Publisher
Beth Early, Operations Director
Ami Dodson, Editor
Comprehensive coverage of the latest policies and ground-breaking research that explores the potential links between environmental factors and human health. *$567.00*
8 pages Monthly Founded: 1963
Mailing list available for rent
Printed in 2 colors on matte stock

6741 Environmental Health Newsletter
International Lead Zinc Research Organization
2525 Meridian Parkway, Suite 100
PO Box 12036
Research Triangle Park, NC 27709-2036
919-361-4647
FAX: 919-361-1957
jhendric@ilzro.org www.ilzro.org
Stephen Wilkinson, President
Frank Goodwin, VP Materials Sciences
Scott Mooneyham, Treasurer
Rob Putnam, Director Communications
Quarterly

6742 Environmental Nutrition
52 Riverside Drive
Suite 15A
New York, NY 10024
212-362-0424
FAX: 212-362-2066 800-424-7887
betty@environmentalnutrition.com
http://www.environmentalnutrition.com
Betty Goldblatt, Publisher
Susan Male Smith, Editor
Monthly nutrition newsletter on nutrition and health. Written and edited by registered dietitians. *$24.00*
Monthly Founded: 1977
Circulation: 50000 Audited
Printed in 2 colors on matte stock

6743 Environmental Policy Alert
Inside Washington Publishers
1225 South Clark Street
Suite 1400
Arlington, VA 22202-4301
703-416-8500
FAX: 703-416-8543 800-424-9068
iwp@sprintmail.com
http://www.iwpnews.com
Rick Weber, CEO/President
Adresses the legislative news and provides reports on the federal environmental policy process. *$560.00*
Founded: 1980

6744 Environmental Problems & Remediation
InfoTeam
PO Box 15640
Plantation, FL 33318-5640
954-473-9560
FAX: 954-473-0544
infoteamma@aol.com
Merton Allen, Editor
Concerned with environmental problems and effects, the methods and approaches for mitigation and remediation. Covers air pollution; surface and ground water pollution; wastewater; soil contamination; waste recycling; medical wastes; landfills and waste sites; stack gases; combustion and incineration; earth warming and more. *$289.00*
Monthly

6745 Environmental Regulation
State Capitals Newsletters
PO Box 7376
Alexandria, VA 22307-7376
703-768-9600
FAX: 703-768-9690
newsletters@statecapitals.com
http://www.statecapitals.com
Keyes Walworth, Publisher
Ellen Klein, Editor *$245.00*

Weekly

6746 Environmental Regulation: From the State Capitals
Wakeman Walworth
300 N Washington Street
Suite 204
Alexandria, VA 22314-2530
703-768-9600
FAX: 703-768-9690
newsletters@statecapitals.com
http://statecapitals.com/environreg.html

Keyes Walworth, Publisher

Wide-ranging source of information on state laws affecting air and water pollution, solid waste, resource recovery and recycling, hazardous waste, acid rain, sewage disposal, pesticide policies, insurance protection, ground water protection. Also includes special industry news section which covers current developments in the pollution control industry - new contracts, products, facilities and acquisitions. *$235.00*

8 pages Weekly
Printed in 1 color on matte stock
Computerized version available

6747 Environmental Regulatory Advisor

JJ Keller
3003 W. Breezewood Lane
Neenah, WI 54956-368
920-722-2848
FAX: 800-727-7516 800-327-6868
sales@jjkeller.com
http://www.jjkeller.com

Webb Shaw, Editor
Robert Keller, Chief Executive Officer

Covers developments at the EPA. *$90.00*

12 pages Monthly Founded: 1953

6748 Environotes Newsletter
Federation of Environmental Technologists
PO Box 624
Slinger, WI 53086-0624
414-540-0070
FAX: 262-644-7106
info@fetinc.org www.fetinc.org

Triese Haase, Administrator

Monthly

6749 Fibre Market News
GIE Media
4012 Bridge Avenue
Cleveland, OH 44113-3320
216-961-4130
FAX: 216-961-0364 800-456-0707

Richard Foster, Publisher
Daniel Sandoval, Editor

Covers the international paper recycling industry. Trends, markets, expansions, economics covered in an in-depth fashion. Also have weekly fax update covering late-breaking news. *$115.00*

16 pages BiWeekly

6750 Forest History Society
701 William Vickers Avenue
Durham, NC 27701
919-682-9319
FAX: 919-682-2349
recluce2@duke.edu
http://www.foresthistory.org

Steven Anderson, President
Cheryl Oakes, Manager

Nonprofit educational institution that explores the history of the environment, forestry and conservation.

Mailing list available for rent 2000 names $150 per M.

6751 From the Ground Up
Ecology Center
117 Division Street
Ann Arbor, MI 48104-1523
734-761-3186
FAX: 734-663-2414
info@ecoocenter.org
http://www.ecocenter.org

Ted Sylvester, Editor
Mike Wallad, President
Michael Garfield, Director

Progressive environmental news from southeast Michigan. *$30.00*

32 pages Monthly Founded: 1970
Circulation: 5000
Printed in 4 colors on newsprint stock

6752 Global Environmental Change Report
Aspen Publishers
37 Broadway
Arlington, MA 02474-5552
781-641-2886
FAX: 301-698-7100 800-234-1660

Brad Hurley, Editor

News and analysis of policy, science and industry developments in the areas of global warming and acid rain. *$447.00*

BiWeekly

6753 HazTECH News
Haztech News
14120 Huckleberry Lane
Silver Spring, MD 20906
301-871-3289
FAX: 301-460-5859
HazTECH@ix.netcom.com

Cathy Dombrowski, Editor/Publisher

Describes technologies for hazardous waste management, site remediation, industrial wastewater treatment and VOC control. *$385.00*

8 pages Bi-Weekly
Printed in 1 color

6754 Hazardous Materials Intelligence Report
World Information Systems
PO Box 535
Cambridge, MA 02238-535
617-492-3312
FAX: 617-492-3312
http://members.aol.com/socejp/hmir.html

Richard S Golob, Publisher
Roger B Wilson Jr, Editor

Provides news analysis on environmental business, hazardous materials, waste management, pollution prevention and control. Covers regulations, legislation and court decisions, new technology, contract opportunities and awards and conference notices. *$375.00*

Weekly
Circulation: 50000

6755 Hazardous Materials Transportation
Bureau of National Affairs
1231 25th Street NW
Washington, DC 20037-1197
202-524-4466
800-372-1033
customercare@bna.com
http://www.bna.com

Gregory C McCaffery, Publisher
Patricia Spencer, Managing Editor
Alan Roberts, President

A two-binder service containing the full-text of rules and regulations governing shipment of hazardous material by rail, air, ship, highway and pipeline, including DOT's Hazardous Materials Tables and EPA's rules for its hazardous waste tracking system. *$933.00*

Monthly

6756 Hazardous Waste Business
McGraw Hill
3333 Walnut Street
Boulder, CO 80301
720-485-5000
FAX: 720-548-5701 800-424-2908
customer.service@mcgrawhill.com
http://www.mcgraw-hill.com/

Kevin Hamilton, Publisher
James Keener, Manager
Karen Cleale, Marketing Manager

Focuses on the control and cleanup of hazardous wastes. *$675.00*

8 pages Founded: 1996

6757 Hazardous Waste Consultant
Aspen Publishers
8400 east cresent parkway
6 floor greenwood village
Lakewood, CO 80111
720-528-4270
FAX: 212-597-0335 800-638-8437

A unique approach to hazardous waste issues. It is written by engineers and regulatory specialists who have an extensive background in the field and understand the problems that industry, consultants, and regulators face. *$475.00*

6758 Hazardous Waste News
Business Publishers
8737 Colesville Road
Suite 1100
Silver Spring, MD 20910-3928
301-587-6300
FAX: 301-587-4530 800-274-6737
bpinews@bpinews.com
www.bpinews.com

Leonard A Eiserer, Publisher
Beth Early, Operations Director

Comprehensive federal, state and local coverage of legislation and regulation affecting all aspects of the hazardous waste industry including Superfund, Resource Conservation and Recovery Act, US EPA, incineration, land disposal and more. *$597.00*

8 pages Weekly
Mailing list available for rent
Printed in 2 colors

6759 Hazardous Waste Report
Aspen Publishers
7201 McKinney Cir
Frederick, MD 21704-8356
301-987-7100
FAX: 212-597-0335 800-638-8437
paul.gibson@aspenpubl.com
http://www.aspenpubl.com

Paul Gibson, Publisher
Sally Almeria, Editor
Bruce Becker, CEO/President
Tom Ceodi, Marketing

Provides information on industry news. *$875.00*

8 pages Founded: 1958

6760 **Health Facts and Fears.com**
American Council on Science and Health
1995 Broadway
2nd Floor
New York, NY 10023-5860
212-362-7044
FAX: 212-362-4919
acsh@acsh.org www.acsh.org
Gilbert Ross, Executive/Medical Director
Jeff Stier, Associate Director
Dr Elizabeth Whelan, President
Weekly

6761 **IALR Newsletter**
American Society of Mining and Reclamation
3134 Montavesta Road
Lexington, KY 40502
859-335-6529
asmr@insightbb.com
www.ca.uky.edu/assmr
Richard I Barnhisel, Executive Secretary
Annual

6762 **IES Quarterly Newsletter**
International Ecotourism Society
733 15th Street NW
Suite 1000
Washington, DC 20005
202-547-9203
FAX: 202-387-7915
ecomail@ecotourism.org
www.ecotourism.org
Martha Honey, Executive Director
Amos Bien, Director International Programs
Neal Inamdar, Director Finance/Administration
Quarterly

6763 **Industrial Health & Hazards Update**
InfoTeam
PO Box 15640
Plantation, FL 33318-5640
954-473-9560
FAX: 954-473-0544
infoteamma@aol.com
Merton Allen, Editor
Covers occupational safety, health, hazards, and disease, mitigatioin and control of hazardous situations; waste recycling and treatment; environmental pollution and control; product safety and liability; fires and explosions; plant and computer security,; air pollution; surface and ground water; wastewater; soil gases; combustion and incineration; earth warming; ozone layer depletion; electromagnetic radiation; toxic materials; and many other related topics.
Monthly
Computerized version available

6764 **Infectious Wastes News**
National Solid Wastes Management Association
4301 Connecticut Avenue NW
#300
Washington, DC 20008-2304
202-664-4701
FAX: 202-966-4868
wa@envasns.org www.envasns.org
John T Aquino, Editor-in-Chief
Bruce Parker, President
A publication by the Environmental industry association geared toward providing readers with timely news and information about the handling, transportation and disposal of infectious wastes.
BiWeekly

6765 **Integrated Environmental Assessment and Management**
Society of Environmental Toxicology and Chemistry
1010 N 12th Avenue
Pensacola, FL 32501-3367
850-469-1500
FAX: 850-469-9778
rparrish@setac.org www.setac.org
Rodney Parrish, Executive Director
Quarterly

6766 **Integrated Waste Management**
McGraw Hill
1221 Avenue of the Americas
Suite C3A
New York, NY 10020-1095
212-512-3916
FAX: 212-512-2723 800-372-1033
Kevin Hamilton, Publisher
Articles geared toward integration of solid waste management. *$745.00*
8 pages BiWeekly

6767 **Interface Newsletter**
Society for Environmental Geochemistry and Health
4698 S Forrest Avenue
Springfield, MO 65810
417-885-1166
FAX: 417-881-6920
drbgwixson@wixson.com
www.segh.net
Bobby Wixson, Director Membership

6768 **International Environment Reporter**
Bureau of National Affairs
1231 25th Street NW
Washington, DC 20037-1197
202-452-4200
800-372-1033
customercare@bna.com www.bna.com
Gregory C McCaffery, Publisher
Susan McInerney, Managing Editor
Larry Evans, Manager
A four-binder information and reference service covering international environmental law and developing policy in the major industrial nations. *$2555.00*

6769 **Marine Conservation News**
Center for Marine Conservation
2029 K Street
Washington, NW 20006
202-750-0574
FAX: 202-872-0619 800-519-1541
cmc@dccmc.org
http://www.cmc-ocean.org
Rose Bierce, Publisher
Roger Rufe, President
Stephanie Drea, VP Commun
Matt Schatzle, VP Membership & Development
Wanda Cantrell, Manager
Updates members of CMC on the organization projects and activities.
24 pages Quarterly
Circulation: 100000
Printed in 2 colors on matte stock

6770 **Matrix Newsletter**
Association for the Environmental Health of Soils
150 Fearing Street
Suite 21
Amherst, MA 01002
413-549-5170
888-540-2347
info@aehs.com www.aehs.com
Paul T Kostecki, PhD, Executive Director
Bi-Annual

6771 **McCoy's Hazardous Waste Regulatory Update Service**
McCoy & Associates
25107 Genesee Trail Road
Suite 200
Golden, CO 80228-4173
303-526-2674
FAX: 303-526-5471
info@mccoyseminars.com
http://www.mccoyseminars.com/contact.cfm
Offers a complete text of the federal hazardous waste regulations, summaries, interpretations and indexes. *$350.00*
Quarterly Founded: 1983

6772 **McCoy's Regulatory Analysis Service**
McCoy & Associates
25107 Genesee Trail Road
Golden, CO 80401-5708
303-526-2674
FAX: 303-526-5471
info@mccoyseminars.com
http://www.mccoyseminars.com
Provides timely, in-depth analyses of hazardous waste regulations within 10 working days after their publication in the Federal Register. *$550.00*
Founded: 1983

6773 **Mealey's Litigation Report: Insurance**
LexisNexis Mealey's
1018 W Ninth Avenue
Third Avenue
King of Prussia, PA 19406-1225
610-768-7800
FAX: 610-768-0880
mealeyinfo@lexisnexis.com
www.lexisnexis.com/mealeys
Tom Hagy, VP/General Manager
Maureen McGuire, Editorial Director
Vivi Gorman, Editor
Shawn Rice, Co-Editor
The report tracks declaratory judgment actions regarding coverage for litigation arising from long-tail claims, including environmental contamination and latent damage and injury allegedly caused by asbestos, tox chemicals and fumes, lead, breast implants, medical devices, construction defects, and more. Key issues: allocation, occurrence, policy exclusion, choice of law, discovery, duty to defend, notice, trigger of coverage and known loss. *$2115.00*
100 pages Weekly Founded: 1984

6774 **Meeting Proceedings**
American Society of Mining and Reclamation
3134 Montavesta Road
Lexington, KY 40502
859-335-6529
asmr@insightbb.com
www.ca.uky.edu/assmr
Richard I Barnhisel, Executive Secretary

Annual

6775 **Monographs**
North American Association for Environmental
2000 P Street NW
Suite 540
Washington, DC 20036
202-419-0412
FAX: 202-419-0415
emai@naaee.org www.naaee.org

William H Dent, Jr, Executive Director
Barbara Eager, Conference Coordinator
Paul Werth, Owner

1-3/year

6776 **NEHA Annual Meeting**
National Conference of Local Environmental Health
c/o NEHA, 720 S Colorado Boulevard
South Tower, Suite 970
Denver, CO 80246-1925
303-756-9090
FAX: 303-691-9490 nfabian@neha.org

Nelson E Fabian, Executive Director

3/year

6777 **NORA News**
NORA: an Association of Responsible Recyclers
5965 Amber Ridge Road
Haymarket, VA 20169
703-753-4277
FAX: 703-753-2445
sparker@noranews.org
www.noranews.org

Scott D Parker, Executive Director

Quarterly

6778 **News Flash**
National Association of Local Government
1333 New Hampshire Avenue NW
Washington, DC 20036
202-638-6254
FAX: 202-393-2866
nalgep@spiegelmcd.com
www.nalgep.org

Kenneth Brown, Executive Director
David Dickson, Projects Manager

Bi-Weekly

6779 **Noise Regulation Report**
Business Publishers
8737 Colesville Road
Suite 1100
Silver Spring, MD 20910-3928
301-587-6300
FAX: 301-587-4530 800-274-6737
custserv@bpinews.com
www.bpinews.com

Leonard A Eiserer, Publisher

Exclusive coverage of airport, highway, occupational and open space noise, noise control and mitigation issues. *$511.00*

10 pages 12 per year
Printed in on matte stock : Newsletter

6780 **Nuclear Monitor**
Nuclear Information & Resource Services

1424 16th Street NW
Suite 404
Washington, DC 20036-2239
202-328-0002
FAX: 202-462-2183
nirsnet@nirs.org http://www.nirs.org

Michael Mariotte, Editor
Linda Gunder, Media Manager

Nuclear power, radioactive waste and sustainable energy news for environmental activities, state and local officials and investment communities. *$250.00*

12 pages 18 issues per y Founded: 1978
Circulation: 1200 Audited Est. Pass-Along Circ: 3600
Printed in 1 color on matte stock

6781 **Nuclear Waste News**
Business Publishers
8737 Colesville Road
Suite 1100
Silver Spring, MD 20910-3928
301-587-6300
FAX: 301-587-1081 800-274-6737
custserv@bpinews.com
http://www.bpinews.com

Adams Goldstien, Publisher
Mautess Patt, Circulation Manager
Nancy Roth, Editor
Adams Goldstien, CEO/President

Worldwide coverage of the nuclear waste management industry including waste generation, packaging, transport, processing and disposal. *$697.00*

10 pages 25 issues per y
Mailing list available for rent
Printed in 2 colors on matte stock : Newsletter

6782 **Plastics Recycling Update**
Resource Recycling
PO Box 42270
Portland, OR 97242-270
503-233-1305
FAX: 503-233-1356
pru@resource-recycling.com
http://www.resource-recycling.com

Jerry Powell, Publisher

Monthly newsletter dealing with all aspects of recycling. Covers markets pricing and trends, collection and processing developments. Annual directory of scrap plastic buyers is also available. *$59.00*

6 pages Monthly Founded: 1981
Circulation: 1000
Mailing list available for rent 40,000 names $100 per M.
Printed in 1 color on matte stock

6783 **Proceedings**
Institute of Environmental Sciences and Technology
5005 Newport Drive
Suite 506
Rolling Meadows, IL 60008-3841
847-255-1561
FAX: 847-255-1699
iest@iest.org www.iest.org

Julie Kendrick, Executive Director
Robert Burrows, Director Communications Services
Corrie Roesslein, Director Programs/Administration

Annual

6784 **Proceedings of Annual Meetings**
Environmental Design Research Association
PO Box 7146
Edmond, OK 73083-7146
405-330-4863
FAX: 405-330-4150
edra@telepath.com www.edra.org

Janet Singer, Executive Director

Annual

6785 **Questions and Answers About the Use and Handling of Dyes**
ETAD North America
1850 M Street NW
Suite 700
Washington, DC 20036
202-721-4154
FAX: 202-296-8120 www.etad.com

Dr C Tucker Helmes, Executive Director

6786 **RCRA Land Disposal Restrictions: A Guide to Compliance**
McCoy & Associates
13701 W Jewell Avenue
Suite 202
Lakewood, CO 80228-4173
303-870-0835
FAX: 303-989-7917

Drew McCoy, Publisher
Deborah McCoy, President

Land disposal restrictions for hazardous waste.

300 pages Annual

6787 **Registry Report**
National Registry of Environmental Professionals
PO Box 2099
Glenview, IL 60025
847-724-6631
FAX: 847-724-4223
nrep@nrep.org www.nrep.org

Richard A Young, PhD, Executive Director
Edward Beck, PhD, Senior Director
Carol Schellinger, Director

Bi-Monthly

6788 **Resource Development Newsletter**
University of Tennessee
PO Box 1071
Knoxville, TN 37996-1071
865-974-1000
FAX: 865-974-7448 rpdavis@utk.edu

Alan Barefield, Publisher

Community development information.

4 pages Quarterly Founded: 1794
Circulation: 2000 Est. Pass-Along Circ: 500
Printed in 1 color on matte stock

6789 **Resource Recovery Report**
PO Box 3356
Warrenton, VA 20188-1956
540-347-4500
FAX: 540-349-4540 800-627-8913
rwill@coordgrp.com
http://www.coordgrp.com

Richard Will, Production Manager

Covers all alternatives to landfills, i.e., recycling, energy recovery, composting in North America, Government, industry, associations, universities, etc. are included. *$227.00*

12 pages Monthly
Mailing list available for rent 12M names
Printed in 1 color on matte stock

6790 **Restoration and Management Notes**
Society for Ecological Restoration
285 W 18th Street #1
Tucson, AZ 85701
520-622-5485
FAX: 520-622-5491
info@ser.org www.ser.org

Mary Kay C LeFevour, Executive Director

Jane Cripps, Membership
Julie St John, Communications
Semi-Annual

6791 **Reuse/Recycle Newsletter**
Technomic Publishing Company
2455 Teller Road
Thousand Oaks, CA 91320
800-818-7243
FAX: 800-583-2665
aflannery@techpub.com
http://rrn.sagepub.com/
Amy Flannery, Marketing Manager
Susan Selke, Editor
Provides news and information on important developments in both industrial and municipal recycling, and focuses on large-scale post-consumer, post-commercial, and post-industrial waste recycling.
8 pages Monthly Founded: 1965
Printed in 2 colors : On-Line

6792 **SER News Newsletter**
Society for Ecological Restoration
285 W 18th Street #1
Phoenix, AZ 85701
520-622-5485
FAX: 520-622-5491
info@ser.org www.ser.org
Mary Kay C LeFevour, Executive Director
Jane Cripps, Membership
Julie St John, Communications
Quarterly

6793 **SOCMA Newsletter**
Synthetic Organic Chemical Manufacturers Assn
1850 M Street NW
Suite 700
Washington, DC 20036
202-721-4100
FAX: 202-296-8120
info@socma.org www.socma.org
Joseph Acker, President
Diane McMahon, VP Commercial Development
Charlene Patterson, Director Human Resources
Offers information on the organic chemical industry.
10 pages Bi-Weekly

6794 **SOEH Letter**
Society for Occupational and Environmental Health
6728 Old McLean Village Drive
McLean, VA 22101
703-556-9222
FAX: 703-556-8729
soeh@degnon.org www.soeh.org
George K Degnon, CAE, Executive Director
Quarterly

6795 **SPAC Newsletter**
Soil and Plant Analysis Council
621 Rose Street
Lincoln, NE 68502-2040
402-437-4944
FAX: 402-476-7598
bvaug12345@aol.com
http://www.spcouncil.com/
Byron Vaughan, Circulation Director
Mark Flock, President
Quarterly newsletter. *$80.00*

Circulation: 250

6796 **Salt & Highway Deicing**
Salt Institute
700 N Fairfax Street
Suite 600
Alexandria, VA 22314-2040
703-549-4648
FAX: 703-548-2194
info@saltinstitute.org
http://www.saltinstitute.org/
Richard Hanneman, CEO/President
A quarterly e-newsletter published by the Salt Institute.
Quarterly Founded: 1914
Circulation: 77000
Printed in on glossy stock

6797 **State Recycling Laws Update**
Raymond Communications
5111 Berwin Road
Suite no#115
College Park, MD 20740
301-345-4237
FAX: 301-345-4768
ciculations@raymond.com
http://www.raymond.com
Lorah utter, Editor
Bruce Popka, VP
Allyn Weet, Circulation Manager
Contains analysis and reports, provides coverage of recycling legislation affecting business, as well as the outlook on future legislation across the states and Canada. Also publishes special reports on related topics, for example, Transportation Packaging and the Environment. *$367.00*
Monthly Founded: 1991
Circulation: 200 17000 names $155 per M. : acrobat

6798 **Superfund Week**
Pasha Publications
8737 Colesville Road
Suite 1100
Silver Spring, MD 20910-3928
301-589-5103
FAX: 301-589-8493 800-274-6737
custserv@bpinews.com
http://www.bpinews.com
Harry Baisden, Group Publisher
Michael Hopps, Editor
A weekly newsletter reporting the most recent developments in Congress, the Environmental Protection Agency and other government offices affecting hazardous waste investigations and cleanups in the federal Superfund and RCRA programs.
$525.00
Weekly Founded: 1963

6799 **Tuesday Letter**
National Association of Conservation Districts
509 Capitol Ct NE
Washington, DC 20002-4937
202-547-6223
FAX: 202-547-6450
http://www.nacdnet.org
Ellen Dougherty, Publisher
Bill Wilson, President
Association news and information on the environment. *$35.00*
12 pages Monthly Founded: 1937
Circulation: 25000

6800 **Underwater Letter**
Callahan Publications
PO Box 1173
Mc Lean, VA 22101-1173
703-356-1925
FAX: 703-356-9614
http://www.newsletteraccess.com
Vincent F Callahan Jr, Editor
A non-technical report for businessmen and others who want to share in the nation's mushrooming underwater-related budget. The Letter provides vital contracting, marketing and development data in military, civilian government, private industry, and academic ocean-related programs. With a reorienting of priorities for federal budgets, including increased emphasis on new energy sources, the oceans offer a vast potential for thousands of companies and institutions in the underwater field.
$190.00
Bi-monthly
Printed in 1 color

6801 **Washington Environmental Compliance Update**
M Lee Smith Publishers
PO Box 5094
Bentwood, TN 37024-5094
615-737-7517
800-274-6774
F Lee Smith, Publisher
Douglas S Little, Editor
Review of environmental laws. *$225.00*
8 pages Daily
Mailing list available for rent
Printed in 2 colors on matte stock

6802 **Washington Environmental Protection Report**
Callahan Publications
PO Box 1173
Mc Lean, VA 22101-1173
703-356-1925
FAX: 703-356-9614
sue@newsletteraccess.com
http://www.newsletteraccess.com
Vincent Callahan, Editor
Twice-monthly letter on contracting opportunities, legislation, research and development, and rules and regulations for the nation's environmental programs. The war on pollution, in all its forms, is coming to the forefront of federal priorities and could be the answer to the many economic problems facing America. *$190.00*
8 pages Bi-monthly Founded: 1990
Printed in 1 color

6803 **Waste Recovery Report**
Icon: Information Concepts
211 S 45th Street
Philadelphia, PA 19104-2918
215-349-6500
FAX: 215-349-6502
info@iconworldwide.com
http://www.iconworldwide.com
Alan Krigman, Publisher/Editor
Contains information on waste-to-enery, recycling, composting and other technologies. *$60.00*
6 pages Monthly
Circulation: 500

6804 **Weather & Climate Report**
Nautilus Press
1054 National Press Building
Washington, DC 20045-2001
202-347-6643

John R Botzum, Editor
Reports on federal actions which impact weather, climate research and global changes in climate.
Monthly

6805 Woodland Report
National Woodland Owners Association
374 Maple Avenue E
Suite 10
Vienna, VA 22180-4718
703-790-4000
800-470-8033

Keith A Argow, Editor

Provides timely information about forestry and forest practices with news from Washington, DC and state capitals. Written for non-industrial, private woodland owners. Includes state landowner association news. *$15.00*

2 pages 8 per year
Circulation: 2,200 Audited
Printed in 1 color on matte stock

6806 World Research News
World Research Foundation
41 Bell Rock Plaza
Sedona, AZ 86351
928-284-3300
FAX: 928-284-3530
laverne@wrf.org www.wrf.org

LaVerne Boeckman, Co-Founder
Steven Ross, Co-Founder

Quarterly

6807 World Wildlife Fund: Focus
1250 24th Street NW
Washington, DC 20037-1124
202-293-4800
FAX: 202-293-9211
archer@wwfus.org
http://www.worldwildlife.org

Pamela Cubberty, Publisher
Jennifer Seeger, Editor
Kathryn Fuller, Chief Executive Officer

WWF projects are highlighted around the world in 450 national parks and nature reserves, with emphasis on coverage of programs and activities in the US.

8 pages Monthly Founded: 1960

Magazines & Journals

6808 ACCA News
Air Conditioning Contractors of America
2800 Shirlington Road
Suite 300
Arlington, VA 22206
703-575-4477
FAX: 703-575-4449
michael.honeycutt@acca.org
www.acca.org

Paul T Stalknecht, President/CEO
Hilary Atkins, Esq, General Counsel
Michael Honeycutt, SVP/Chief of Staff
Glenn Hourihan, PE, VP Research/Technology

6809 ASEH News
American Society for Environmental History
119 Pine Street
Suite 301
Seattle, WA 98101
206-343-0226
FAX: 206-343-0249
mighetto@hrassoc.com www.aseh.net

Lisa Mighetto, Acting Executive Director

Quarterly

6810 Alternative Energy
PWG
205 S Beverly Drive
#208
Beverly Hills, CA 90212-3827
310-273-3486

Irwin Stambler, Publisher
Ahmad Taleban, President

Reports on future economic and technological trends. *$95.00*

12 pages Monthly
Printed in 2 colors on matte stock

6811 Alternative Energy Retailer
Zackin Publications
PO Box 2180
Waterbury, CT 06722-2180
203-755-0158
FAX: 203-755-3480 800-325-6745
info@aer-online.com
http://www.aer-online.com

Michael Griffin, Editor
Jeanette Laliberte, Subscription
Andrew Wold, Associate Publisher
Paul Zackin, Publisher
June Han, Marketing Manager

Covers solid fuel burning, marketing, technology, and sales. *$32.00*

Monthly Founded: 1970
Circulation: 10,000

6812 American Environmental Laboratory
International Scientific Communications
30 Controls Drive
PO Box 870
Shelton, CT 06484-870
203-926-9300
FAX: 203-926-9310
iscpubs@iscpubs.com
http://www.iscpubs.com

Brian Howard, Publisher/Editor
Patricia Ekbatani, Directing Editor
Susan Messinger, Managing Editor
Jane Deyoe, Sales Promotion Manager
Steven J. Morris, President

Laboratory activities, new equipment, and analysis and collection of samples are the main topics. *$282.42*

Monthly
Circulation: 185000

6813 American Forests
734 15th Street NW
Suite 800
Washington, DC 20005
202-371-1944
FAX: 202-955-4588
info@amfor.org
http://www.americanforests.org

Michelle Robbins, Publisher/ Editor
Deborah Gangloff, Executive Director
Jeff Olson, VP Marketing *$25.00*

Quarterly Founded: 1875

6814 American Public Works Association
2345 Grand Blvd
Ste 700
Kansas City, MO 64108-2625
816-472-6100
FAX: 816-472-1610
apwa@apwa.net http://www.apwa.net

Thomas W Trice, President
Kaye Sullivan, Chief Executive Officer
Kevin Clark, Editor

International educational and professional association of public agencies, private sector companies, and individuals dedicated to providing high quality public works goods and services. APWA provides a forum in which public works professionals competency, increase the performance of their agencies and companies, and bring important public works-related topics to public attention in local, state, and federal areas. Mailing list for members only. *$100.00*

40 pages Monthly Founded: 1933
Circulation: 27000

6815 American Waste Digest
Charles G Moody
226 King Street
Pottstown, PA 19464-9150
610-326-9480
FAX: 610-326-9752 800-442-4215
awd@americanwastedigest.com
http://www.americanwastedigest.com

Charles G Moody III, Publisher/Editor
Shannon Costa, Circulation Manager
J. Robert Tagert, Sales Manager
Carasue B. Moody, Marketing Manager

Provides reviews on new products, profiles on sucessful waste removal businesses, and provides discussion on legislation on municipal regulations on recycling. *$24.00*

86 pages Monthly
Circulation: 33000
Printed in 4 colors on glossy stock

6816 Annual Conference Proceedings
National Association of Environmental Professional
PO Box 2086
Bowie, MD 20718-2086
301-860-1140
FAX: 301-860-1141 888-251-9902
office@naep.org www.naep.org

Sandi Worthman, Administrator

Annual

6817 Annual Review
International Lead Zinc Research Organization
2525 Meridian Parkway, Suite 100
PO Box 12036
Research Triangle Park, NC 27709-2036

919-361-4647
FAX: 919-361-1957
jhendirc@ilzro.org www.ilzro.org

Stephen Wilkinson, President
Frank Goodwin, VP Materials Sciences
Scott Mooneyham, Treasurer
Rob Putnam, Director Communications

Annual

6818 Asbestos & Lead Abatement Report
Business Publishers
8737 Colesville Road
Suite 1100
Silver Spring, MD 20910-3928
301-876-6300
FAX: 301-589-8493 800-274-6737
custserv@bpinews.com
http://www.bpinews.com

Leonard Eiserer, Publisher

Contains articles on regulation compliance, environmental trends, and business opportunities. *$382.00*

Monthly Founded: 1963

6819 Bio-Mineral Times
Allen C Forter & Son
3450 W Central Avenue
#328
Toledo, OH 43606-1418
419-535-6374
FAX: 419-535-7008
nviroint@aol.com www.nviro.com
Bonnie Hunter, Publisher
Issues focus on environmental legislation efforts, regulation compliance, and finding answers to the mechanics and practical applications of the distribution and management of biosolids derived products.
Quarterly
Circulation: 25,000

6820 C&D Recycler
Gie Publishing
4012 Bridge Avenue
Cleveland, OH 44113
216-961-4130
FAX: 216-961-0364 800-456-0707
btaylor@gie.net
http://www.recyclingtoday.com
Bryan Tailor, Editor
Jim Keefe, Publisher
Helen Duerr, Production Manager
$17.00
Monthly Founded: 1963
Circulation: 7000

6821 Code of Professional Practice
National Registry of Environmental Professionals
PO Box 2099
Glenview, IL 60025
847-724-6631
FAX: 847-724-4223
nrep@nrep.org www.nrep.org
Richard A Young, PhD, Executive Director
Edward Beck, PhD, Senior Director
Carol Schellinger, Director
Annual

6822 Composting News
McEntee Media Corporation
9815 Hazelwood Avenue
Cleveland, OH 44149-2305
440-238-6603
FAX: 440-238-6712
ken@recycle.cc http://www.recycle.cc
Ken McEntee, Publisher/President
New composting projects, research, regulations and legislation, as well as the latest news in the composting industry. *$83.00*
Monthly Founded: 1990
Circulation: 2000

6823 Conservogram
Soil and Water Conservation Society
945 SW Ankeny Road
Ankeny, IA 50021-9764
515-289-2331
FAX: 515-289-1227
swcs@swcs.org http://www.swcs.org
Deb Happe, Editor
Jean L. Steiner, President
Lindey Krug, Membership Assistant
Published for the professionals in the natural resource fields, and contains highlights on the news and ideas in the preservation of natural resources.
Monthly Founded: 1943
Circulation: 10000

6824 Dairy, Food and Environmental Sanitation
International Association for Food Protection
6200 Aurora Avenue
Suite 200W
Des Moines, IA 50322-2864
515-276-3344
FAX: 515-276-8655 800-369-6337
info@foodprotection.org
http://www.foodprotection.org
Bev Corron, Public Relations Officer
David Tharp, Executive Director
Lessa Halvey, Managing Editor
Published as the general membership publication by the International Association for Food Protection, each issue contains referenced articles on applied research, applications of current technology and general interest subjects for food safety professionals. Regular features include industry and association news, an industry related product section and a calendar of meetings, seminars and workshops. Updates of government regulations and sanitary design is also featured. All members receive DFES. *$227.00*
Monthly Founded: 1911
Circulation: 4000
Mailing list available for rent 3000+ names $150 per M.
Printed in 4 colors on glossy stock

6825 Design Research News
Environmental Design Research Association
PO Box 7146
Edmond, OK 73083-7146
405-330-4863
FAX: 405-330-4150
erda@telepath.com www.edra.org
Janet Singer, Executive Director
Quarterly

6826 Digital Traveler
International Ecotourism Society
733 15th Street NW
Suite 1000
Washington, DC 20005
202-547-9203
FAX: 202-387-7915
ecomail@ecotourism.org
www.ecotourism.org
Martha Honey, Executive Director
Amos Bien, Director International Programs
Neal Inamdar, Director Finance/Administration
Monthly

6827 E/Environmental Magazine
28 Knight Street
Norwalk, CT 06851-4719
203-854-5559
FAX: 203-866-0602 800-967-6572
info@emagazine.com
http://www.emagazine.com
Jim Motavalli, Editor
Karen Soucy, Associate Publisher
Doug Moss, Publisher & Executive Dir
A comprehensive magazine dealing with environmental issues and national conservation concerns. *$19.95*
Founded: 1988
Circulation: 185,000

6828 ECON: Environmental Contractor
Duane Publishing
51 Park Street
Dorchester, MA 02122
617-282-4885
FAX: 617-282-0320
info@decmagazine.com
http://www.decmagazine.com
Herbert Duane, Editor
Information and news of the environment.
$35.00
90 pages Monthly Founded: 1986

6829 EI Digest: Hazardous Waste Marketplace
Environmental Information
PO Box 390266
Minneapolis, MN 55439
952-831-2473
FAX: 952-831-6550
ei@enviro-information.com
http://www.envirobiz.com
Cary Perket, President
Contains market studies of commercial hazardous waste management companies with in-depth analysis of trends in policy, regulations, technology and business.
Founded: 1983
Printed in 2 colors

6830 EM, Air & Waste Management Environmental Managers
Air & Waste Management Association
One Gateway Center 3rd Floor
420 Fort Duquesne Blvd.
Pittsburgh, PA 15222-1435
412-652-2458
FAX: 412-232-3450 800-270-3444
info@awma.org http://www.awma.org
Todd Zahniser, Publisher/Editor
Edith M. Ardiente, President
A magazine that contains sections of Washington and Canadian reports, a calendar of events, government affairs, news focus, campus research, business briefs, district control news, professional development programs, professional services and other issues facing the environmental professionals.
Monthly Founded: 1901
Circulation: 15000

6831 Ecological Economics Journal
International Society for Ecological Economics
1313 Dolley Madison Boulevard
Suite 402
McLean, VA 22101
703-790-1745
FAX: 703-790-2672
iseemembership@burkinc.com
www.ecologicaleconomics.org
Heide Scheiter-Rohland, Director Membership
Monthly

6832 Ecology
Johnson Publishing Company
820 S Michigan Avenue
Chicago, IL 60605-2103
312-322-9200

Linda Johnson Rice, Chief Executive Officer
News on the environment and conservation industries. *$16.00*

6833 Ecosphere
Forum International
91 Gregory Lane
Suite 21
Pleasant Hill, CA 94523
925-671-2900
FAX: 925-671-2993 800-252-4475
fti@foruminternational.com
http://www.foruminternational.com

Dr. Nicolas Hetzer, Production Manager
J McCormack, Circulation Director

Accepts advertising. *$12.00*
16 pages Quarterly Founded: 1956
Circulation: 36000

6834 Energy Engineering
Association of Energy Engineers
4025 Pleasantdale Rd
Suite 420
Atlanta, GA 30340
770-447-5083
FAX: 770-446-3969
webmaster@AEEcenter.org
http://www.aeecenter.org

Wayne Turner, Editor-in-Chief
Larry Good, President
Albert Thumann, Executive Director
Ruth Marie, Managing Editor

Engineering solutions to cost efficiency problems and mechanical contractors who design, specify, install, maintain, and purchase non-residential heating, ventilating, air conditioning and refrigeration equipment and components.
Founded: 1976
Circulation: 8000

6835 Environ: A Magazine for Ecologic Living and Health
Environ
1616 Seventeenth Street
Suite 468
Denver, CO 80202
303-285-5543
FAX: 303-628-5597
http://www.environcorp.com

Suzanne Randegger, Publisher/Editor
Ed Randegger, Co-Publisher/Ad Director
John Haasbeek, Senior Manager

Designed to keep health and ecology conscious readers aware of circumstances hazardous to human health, and provide alternatives - practical, political, and global. Coverage of environmental legislation, ecologic food-growing practices and certification, geographically and climatically safe and hazardous locations, and a view of today's health problems with active solutions. Supported by screened advertisers. *$15.00*
40 pages Quarterly

6836 Environment
Helen Dwight Reid Educational Foundation
1319 18th Street NW
Washington, DC 20036-1802
202-296-6267
FAX: 202-296-5149
brichman@heldref.org
http://www.heldref.org

Douglas Kirkpatrick, Publisher
Barbara Richman, Editor
Fred Huber, Circulation Manager
Emily Tawlowski, Marketing Manager
Steve Hellem, Executive Director

Provides environment professionals and concerned citizens with comprehensive articles, book recommendations, commentaries, news briefs, and reviews on environmental websites, major governmental and institutional reports. *$51.00*
Monthly Founded: 1956
Circulation: 11,408

6837 Environmental Business Journal
Environmental Business International
4452 Park Blvd. Suite 306
PO Box 371769
San Diego, CA 92116-1769
619-295-7685
FAX: 619-295-5743
ebi@ebiusa.com
http://www.ebiusa.com

Grant Ferrier, Publisher
Dan Johnson, Manager

An overview piece, segment analysis by country, profiles of domestic and foreign firms, financial data on listed environmental companies in the region, the latest developments on government initiatives and regulations, company news and projects are included in the features of this publications. *$495.00*
Founded: 1988
Printed in 2 colors

6838 Environmental Communicator
North American Association for Environmental
2000 P Street NW
Suite 540
Washington, DC 20036
202-419-0412
FAX: 202-419-0415
email@naaee.org www.naaee.org

William H Dent, Jr, Executive Director
Barbara Eager, Conference Coordinator
Paul Werth, Owner

Bi-Monthly

6839 Environmental Compliance Update

High Tech Publishing Company
PO Box 1275
Amherst, MA 01004-1275
413-534-4500
FAX: 413-256-6378

Lori Reilly, Editor

Identifies and analyzes the issues and business and economic impact of environmental compliance laws and regulations. Monitors the relevant changes due to legislation, court decisions, private rulings and technology. *$395.00*
Monthly

6840 Environmental Engineering Science
Mary Ann Liebert
140 huguenot st
Larchmont, NY 10801-1961
914-343-3100
FAX: 914-740-109
info@liebertpub.com
http://www.liebertpub.com/

Mary Ann Liebert, Publisher
Dumpnico Grosso, Editor-in-Chief
Stephanie Paul, Production Editor
Lisa Cohen, Associate Editors

The focus is on pollution control of the suface, ground, and drinking water, and highlight research news and product developments that aid in the fight against pollution. *$330.00*
Monthly Founded: 1980
Circulation: 1800

6841 Environmental Geochemistry and Health
Society for Environmental Geochemistry and Health
4698 S Forrest Avenue
Springfield, MO 65810
417-885-1166
FAX: 417-881-6920
drbgwixson@wixson.com
www.segh.net

Bobby Wixson, Director Membership

Quarterly

6842 Environmental History
American Society for Environmental History
119 Pine Street
Suite 301
Seattle, WA 98101
206-343-0226
FAX: 206-343-0249
mighetto@hrassoc.com www.aseh.net

Lisa Mighetto, Acting Executive Director

Quarterly

6843 Environmental Management Report
McGraw Hill
PO Box 182604
Columbus, OH 43272
614-304-4000
FAX: 614-759-3749
customer.service@mcgraw-hill.com
http://www.mcgraw-hill.com

Paul Scicchitano, Executive Editor
Harold McGraw III, President/CEO

Emphasises the interest and needs of the companies and individuals involved in site assessments, regulations, and environmental auditing. *$195.00*
Monthly Founded: 1902

6844 Environmental Manager
Air & Waste Management Association
1 Gateway Center
3rd Floor, 420 Fort Duquesne Blvd.
Pittsburgh, PA 15222-1435
412-652-2458
FAX: 412-232-3450 800-270-3444
info@awma.org http://www.awma.org

Todd E Zahniser, Editor
Lisa Bucher, Managing Editor
Frank Nass, Owner
Edith M Ardiente, VP Environmental Affairs

Features timely articles on business, regulatory, and technical issues of interest to the environmental industry. *$220.00*
Monthly Founded: 1908
Circulation: 9000

6845 Environmental Practice
National Association of Environmental Professional
PO Box 2086
Bowie, MD 20718-2086
301-860-1140
FAX: 301-860-1141 888-251-9902
office@naep.org www.naep.org

Sandi Worthman, Administrator

Quarterly

6846 **Environmental Protection**
Stevens Publishing Corporation
5151 Betline Road
10th Floor
Dallas, TX 75240
972-687-6700
FAX: 972-687-6770
aneville@stevenspublishing.com
http://www.stevenspublishing.com

Craig Stevens, CEO
Dana Cornett, President/COO
Randy Dye, Publisher
Angela Neville, Editor
Margaret Perry, Circulation Director

Founded: 1925
Circulation: 63000

6847 **Environmental Regulation & Permitting**
John Wiley & Sons
111 River Street
Hoboken, NJ 07030-5774
201-748-6000
FAX: 201-748-6088 800-825-7550
subinfo@wiley.com
http://www.wiley.com

Joseph Guida, Editor

Furnishes practical information on workable solutions to winning permits that both society and the industry will approve. *$170.00*
Quarterly Founded: 1807
Circulation: 1800

6848 **Environmental Science and Technology**
American Chemical Society
1155 Sixteenth St., NW
Washington, DC 20036
202-872-4600
FAX: 202-872-4615 800-227-5558
acspubs@acs.org
http://www.chemistry.org/portal/a/c/s/1/home.html

Bruce Poorman, Ad Manager
Jerald Schnoor, Managing Editor

Articles on pollution control, waste treatment, climate changes and various other environmental interests. *$156.00*
110 pages Monthly Founded: 1966
Circulation: 13000

6849 **Environmental Times**
Environmental Assessment Association
1224 N Nokomis NE
Alexandria, MN 56308
320-763-4320
FAX: 320-763-9290
eaa@iami.org
http://www.iami.org/eaa.html

Robert Johnson, Executive Director

This publications contents contain environment conferences and expos, industry trends, federal regulations related to the environment and industry assessments. *$19.95*
24 pages Founded: 1972
Circulation: 7000 5000 names $125 per M.
Printed in 4 colors on newsprint stock

6850 **Environmental Toxicology and Chemistry**
Society of Environmental Toxicology and Chemistry
1010 N 12th Avenue
Pensacola, FL 32501-3367
850-469-1500
FAX: 850-469-9778
rparrish@setac.org www.setac.org

Rodney Parrish, Executive Director

6851 **Environmental and Molecular Mutagensis**
Environmental Mutagen Society
1821 Michael Faraday Drive
Suite 300
Reston, VA 20190
703-438-8220
FAX: 703-438-3113
emshq@ems-us.org www.ems-us.org

Tonia Masson, Executive Director

8/year

6852 **Executive Briefing Magazine**
Synthetic Organic Chemical Manufacturers Assn
1850 M Street NW
Suite 700
Washington, DC 20036
202-721-4100
FAX: 202-296-8120
info@socma.org www.socma.org

Joseph Acker, President
Diane McMahon, VP Commercial Development
Charlene Patterson, Director Human Resources

6853 **Fisheries**
American Fisheries Society
5410 Grosvenor Lane
Suite 110
Bethesda, MD 20814-2199
301-897-8616
FAX: 307-897-8096
main@fisheries.org
http://www.fisheries.org

Beth Beard, Managing Editor
Charles Moseley, Journals Manager

Peer reviewed articles that address contemporary issues and problems, techniques, philosophies and other areas of interest to the general fisheries profession. Monthly features include letters, meeting notices, book listings and reviews, environmental essays and organization profiles. *$76.00*
50 pages Monthly Founded: 1870
Mailing list available for rent 8500 names $250 per M.

6854 **Food Protection Trends**
International Association for Food Protection
6200 Aurora Avenue
Suite 200W
Des Moines, IA 50322-2864
515-276-3344
FAX: 515-276-8655 800-369-6337
info@foodprotection.org
http://www.foodprotection.org

Kathleen Glass, President
Lisa Hovey, Editor

Each issue contains refereed articles on applied research, applications of current technology and general interest subjects for food safety professionals. *$227.00*
Monthly Founded: 1911 ISSN 0362-028X
Circulation: 3000
Mailing list available for rent
Printed in 4 colors on glossy stock

6855 **Global Risk Assessments: Issues, Concepts and Applications**
Global Risk Assessment
3638 University Avenue
Suite 215
Riverside, CA 92501-3331
909-447-5690
FAX: 909-788-0672
jrogers@grai.com
http://www.grai.com

Jerry Rogers, President

Issues concepts and applications in business environment risk assessment and political risk assessment and management. *$42.50*
Annual+ Founded: 1981
Circulation: 2000

6856 **Hauler**
Hauler Magazine
166 S Main Street
PO Box 508
New Hope, PA 18938
800-220-6029
FAX: 215-862-3455 800-220-6029
mag@thehauler.com
http://www.thehauler.com

Thomas N Smith, Publisher/Editor
Barbara Gibney, Circulation Manager
Leslie T. Smith, Marketing Director

This magazine serves as an advertising guide to new products in the waste management, recycling, and environmental industries. *$ 12.00*
Monthly Founded: 1978
Circulation: 18630

6857 **Hazard Technology**
EIS International
1401 Rockville Pike
Suite 500
Rockville, MD 20852-1436

FAX: 301-738-1026 800-999-5009

James W Morentz PhD, Publisher
Leslie Atkin, Managing Editor

Application of technology to the field of emergency and environmental management to save lives and protect property.
Quarterly Founded: 1990
Circulation: 50,000

6858 **Hazardous Management**
Ecolog
1450 Don Mills Road
Don Mills, Ontario M3B-2X7
416-442-2292
FAX: 416-442-2204 888-702-1111

Lynda Reilly, Publisher

The latest environmental regulations and programs as well as the evolving technology and equipment needed to achieve compliance. *$39.50*
Bi-Monthly Founded: 1989
Circulation: 16,000
Mailing list available for rent $250 per M.
Printed in 4 colors on glossy stock

6859 **Hazardous Materials Control**
Hazardous Materials Control Resources Institute
7237 Hanover Highway
Greenbelt, MD 20770
301-577-1842
FAX: 301-220-3870

Patricia Segato, Managing Editor
Victoria Mellin, Advertising Coordinator

Accepts advertising. *$18.00*
64 pages Bi-Monthly Founded: 1988

6860 Hazmat World
Advanstar Communications
545 Boylston
Boston, MA 02116
617-514-4600
FAX: 617-267-6900
info@advanstar.com
www.advanstar.com

Sheldon Schultz, Editor

Business and news publication edited for the environmental world. *$30.00*
100 pages Monthly Founded: 1988

6861 Human Ecology Review
Society for Human Ecology
College of the Atlantic
105 Eden Street
Bar Harbor, ME 04609-0180
207-288-5015
FAX: 207-288-3780
carter@ecology.coa.edu
www.societyforhumanecology.org

Barbara Carter, Assistant to Executive Director

Semi-Annual

6862 Hydrological Science and Technology
American Institute Of Hydrology
300 Village Green Circle
Suite 201
Smyrna, GA 30080
770-269-9388

aihydro@aol.com www.aihydro.org

Cathy Lipsett, Owner
Cathryn Seaburn, Manager

Quarterly

6863 IEEE Power and Energy Magazine

IEEE
PO Box 1331
Piscataway, NJ 08855
732-981-0061
FAX: 732-981-9667
custome-service@ieee.org
http://www.ieee.org

Mel Olken, Editor
Susan Schneiderman, Business Development

Network analysis, system stability studies, fault protection and construction management. *$260.00*
82 pages Monthly Founded: 2003
Circulation: 23000
Mailing list available for rent
Printed in on glossy stock

6864 Indoor Environment Review
IAQ Publications
7920 Norfolk Avenue
#900
Bethesda, MD 20814-2507
301-913-0115
FAX: 301-913-0119
iaqpubs@aol.com www.iaqpubs.com

Robert Morrow, Publisher

New technology, research and legislation concerning all indoor air and water quality issues.
Monthly
Circulation: 10000

6865 Industrial Safety & Hygiene
Business News Publishing Company
755 W Big Beaver
Suite 1000
Troy, MI 48084
248-362-3700
FAX: 248-362-0317

6866 Inside EPA
Inside Washington Publishers
Inside Washington Publishers
1225 South Clark Street, Suite 1400
Arlington, VA 22202
703-416-8500
FAX: 703-416-8543 800-424-9068
iwp@iwpnews.com
http://www.iwpnews.com

Al Sosenko, Publisher

Gives timely information on all facets of waste, water, air, and other environmental regulatory programs.
Weekly Founded: 1980

6867 Inside Waste
John Cupps Associates
2757 13th Street
Sacramento, CA 95818-2907
916-448-5272
FAX: 916-448-7862

John A Cupps, Publisher/Editor

Covers the legislative and regulatory policy issues related to solid waste management issues.
Monthly

6868 International Dredging Review
PO Box 1487
Fort Collins, CO 80522-1487
970-416-1903
FAX: 970-416-1878
editor@dredgemag.com
http://www.dredgemag.com

Judith Powers, Publisher
Julia Leach, Production Manager

Targeted to dredging company executives, project managers and dredge crew members, suppliers and service people such as pump manufacturers, hydrographic surveyors, consulting engineers, etc. *$85.00*
Monthly Founded: 1967
Circulation: 3300

6869 International Environmental Systems Update
CEEM
3975 University Drive
Suite 230
Fairfax, VA 22030-3223
703-437-9000
FAX: 703-437-9001 800-745-5565
jleonard@qsuonline.com
http://www.qsuonline.com

Paul Scicchitano, Publisher
Paul Scicchitano, CEO/President
Suzanne Leonard, Senior Editor

Provides information covering the emerging environmental issues that affect business and industry around the globe including competitive advantages, global updates, strategies, management systems and company profiles. *$390.00*
24 pages Monthly Founded: 1994
Circulation: 50000
Mailing list available for rent
Printed in 2 colors on matte stock
Computerized version available: Paper Sub

6870 International Journal of Phytoremediation
Association for the Environmental Health of Soils
150 Fearing Street
Amherst, MA 01002
413-549-5170
888-540-2347
info@aehs.com www.aehs.com

Paul T Kostecki, PhD, Executive Director

Quarterly

6871 International Journal of Wildland Fire
International Association of Wildland Fire

4025 Fair Ridge Drive
Fairfax, VA 22033
785-423-1818
FAX: 785-542-3511
info@awfonline.org
www.iawfonline.org

Sacha Dick, Programs Manager

Quarterly

6872 Journal of Air & Waste Management Association
Air & Waste Management Association
1 Gateway Center
3rd Floor
Pittsburgh, PA 15222-1435
412-652-2458
FAX: 412-232-3450 800-270-3444
info@awma.org http://www.awma.org

Andy Knopes, Production Manager/Editor
Richard Sherr, Execetive Director

Publishes original, peer-reviewed research on a range of environmental topics. *$330.00*
Monthly Founded: 1907
Circulation: 3500

6873 Journal of Environmental Economics and Management
Association of Environmental and Resource
1616 P Street NW
Suite 400
Washington, DC 20036
202-328-5077
FAX: 202-939-3460
voigt@rff.org www.aere.org

Ralph Metts, President
Marilyn Voight, Executive Secretary

Bi-Monthly

6874 Journal of Environmental Education
Heldref Publications
1319 18th Street NW
Washington, DC 20036-1826
202-296-6267
FAX: 202-296-5149
jee@heldref.org
http://www.heldref.org

Douglas J. Kirkpatrick, Publisher
J. Heldref, Editor

The issues featured are case studies, environmental philosophy and policy discussions, new research evaluations, and information on environmental education. *$58.00*
Quarterly Founded: 1970
Circulation: 1250

6875 Journal of Environmental Engineering
American Society of Civil Engineers
1801 Alexander Bell Drive
Reston, VA 20191-4400
703-295-6000
FAX: 703-295-6222 800-548-2723
member@asce.org
http://www.asce.org

Henry Petrosky, Chairman
M. Kathy Banks, Editor

Emphasizes on the implementaion of effective and safe methods for handling, transporting, and treating waste materials. *$308.00*
Monthly Founded: 1852
Circulation: 2,500

6876 Journal of Environmental Health
National Environmental Health Association
720 S Colorado Boulevard
Suite 970S
Denver, CO 80246-1925
303-756-9090
FAX: 303-691-9490
staff@neha.org www.neha.org
Nelson Fabain, Executive Director
Julie Collins, Research
Kim Brandow, Marketing/Sales Manager
A practical journal containing information on a variety of environmental health issues. *$90.00*
70 pages 10 per year Founded: 1937
Circulation: 20,000 5046+ names $90 per M.
Printed in 4 colors on glossy stock : indexed

6877 Journal of Food Protection
International Association for Food Protection
6200 Aurora Avenue
Suite 200W
Des Moines, IA 50322-2864
515-276-3344
FAX: 515-276-8655 800-369-6337
info@foodprotection.org
http://www.foodprotection.org
Bev Corron, Public Relations
David W Tharp, Executive Director
Bev Brannen, Administrative Editor
Each issue contains scientific research and authoritative review articles reporting on a variety of topics in food science pertaining to food safety and quality. *$335.00*
Monthly Founded: 1919 ISSN 0362-028X
Circulation: 11000
Mailing list available for rent 3000+ names $150 per M.
Printed in 4 colors on glossy stock

6878 Journal of Soil and Water Conservation
Soil and Water Conservation Society
7515 NE Ankeny Road
Ankeny, IA 50021-9764
515-289-2331
FAX: 515-289-1227 800-843-7645
swcs@swcs.org http://www.swcs.org
Deb Happe, Communications Director/Editor
Jody Ogg, Business Manager
Craig Cox, Executive Director
Jean L Steiner, President
Publication includes a variety of conservation subjects, as well as international conservation issues. *$83.00*
Fortnightly Founded: 1945
Circulation: 2000

6879 Journal of the Air & Waste Management Association
Air & Waste Management Association
One Gateway Center 3rd Floor
420 Fort Duquesne Blvd.
Pittsburgh, PA 15222-1416
412-652-2458
FAX: 412-232-3450
info@awma.org http://www.awma.org
Tim Keener, Technical Editor-in-Chief
George Hidy, Co-Editor
Lisa Bucher, Managing Editor
Nancy Bernheisel, Publications Coordinator
Published for the working environmental professional and carries peer-reviewed technical papers on a variety of topics form control technology to science. *$315.00*
Monthly Founded: 1908
Circulation: 14000

6880 Journal of the Air Pollution Control Association
Air Pollution Control Association
1 Gateway Center 3rd Floor
420 Fort Duquesne Blvd.
Pittsburgh, PA 15222-1435
412-232-3444
FAX: 412-232-3450 800-270-3444
info@awma.org http://www.awma.org/
Tim Keener, Technical Editor-in-Chief
George Hidy, Co-Editor
Jeffrey Brook, Associate Editor
A comprehensive journal offering information to the environment and conservation industry. *$95.00*
Monthly Founded: 1907
Circulation: 700

6881 Journal of the Institute of Environmental Sciences and Technology
Institute of Environmental Sciences and Technology
5005 Newport Drive
Suite 506
Rolling Meadows, IL 60008-3841
847-255-1561
FAX: 847-255-1699
iest@iest.org www.iest.org
Julie Kendrick, Executive Director
Robert Burrows, Director Communications Services
Corrie Roesslein, Director Programs/Administration
Annual

6882 Land and Water Magazine
Land and Water
320 A. Street
Fort Dodge, IA 50501-1197
515-576-3191
FAX: 515-576-2606
landandwater@dodgenet.com
http://www.landandwater.com
Amy Dencklau, Publishing Editor
Shanza Dencklau, Assistant Editor
Rasch M. Kenneth, President
Edited for contractors, engineers, architects, government officials and those working in the field of natural resource management and restoration from idea stage through project completion and maintenance. *$20.00*
72 pages Founded: 1959
Circulation: 20000
Mailing list available for rent 20M names
Printed in 4 colors on glossy stock

6883 Leading Edge
Society of Exploration Geophysicists
8801 S Yale
Tulsa, OK 74137
918-975-5500
918-497-5557
web@seg.org http://www.seg.org
Dean Clark, Editor
Merrily Sanzalone, Senior Publications Coordinator
Jim Lawnick, Marketing Director
Addresses a broad spectrum of topics related to applied geophysics. Material immediately accessible to a broad audience. *$70.00*
116 pages Monthly Founded: 1930
Printed in 4 colors on glossy stock

6884 MSW Management
Forester Communications
2946 De La Vina street
Santa Barbara, CA 93105
805-682-1300
FAX: 805-682-0200
customerservice@forester.net
http://www.foresterpress.com
Daniel Waldman, Publisher/President
John Trotti, Group Editor
Provides general news on facility construction, financing, new equipment and revenue issues. *$94.95*
Founded: 1990
Circulation: 25000

6885 Materials Evaluation
American Society for Nondestructive Testing
1711 Arlingate Lane
PO Box 28518
Columbus, OH 43228
614-274-6003
FAX: 614-274-6899 800-222-2768
kwies@asnt.org http://www.asnt.org
Paul McIntire, Senior Manager, Publications
Tim Jones, Periodicals Manager
David Fanning, Materials Evaluation Edit
Shelby Reeves, Owner
Research, reviews and information of nondestructive testing materials for nondestructive testing (NDT) professionals. Provides members and subscribers the latest industry news and technical information. *$105.00*
90 pages Monthly Founded: 1942
Circulation: 10000
Printed in 4 colors on glossy stock

6886 NAESCO Newsletter
NAESCO
1615 M Street NW
Suite 800
Washington, DC 20036-3219
202-822-0950
FAX: 202-822-0955
http://www.naesco.org
Terry E Singer, Executive Editor
Michael Hamilton, Marketing Manager
Mary Lee Berger-Hughes, Publisher
Wallace Duncan, Counsel
Targets energy service companies, electric and gas utilities amd other energy providers. Highlights industry news and features energy conservation. *$12500.00*
Founded: 1985
Circulation: 200

6887 NETAnews
National Environmental, Safety and Health Training
5320 N 16th Street
Suite 114
Phoenix, AZ 85016-3241
602-956-6099
FAX: 602-956-6399
info@neshta.org www.neshta.org
Charles L Richardson, Executive Director
Joan J Jennings, Manager Association Services
Suzanne Lanctot, Manager Certification/Membership
Quarterly

6888 **Natural History Magazine**
American Museum of Natural History
Central Park W at 79th Street
New York, NY 10024
212-695-5150
FAX: 212-769-5427
communications@amnh.org
http://www.naturalhistory.com

Allen Futter, CEO/President
Victor W Fazio, Editor *$55.00*

6889 **Natural Resources and Environment**
American Bar Association
321 North Clark Street
Chicago, IL 60610-4497
312-988-5000
FAX: 312-988-6281 1 8-0 2-5 22
environ@abanet.org
http://www.abanet.org

Robert J Grey, Jr, President/Publisher
Lori T. King, Staff Editor
Stephen Gidiere, Executive Editor

Practical magazine on the latest developments in the field of natural resources law.
$60.00
Quarterly Founded: 1878

6890 **Northeast Sun**
NE Sustainable Energy Association
50 Miles Street
Greenfield, MA 01301-3212
413-774-6051
FAX: 413-774-6053
nesea@nesea.org
http://www.nesea.org

Nancy Hazard, Executive Director
Paul Horowitz, Chairman

Addresses the current issues of solar energy and natural gas power. Also provides an exchange of ideas for those seeking other environmentally sound energy sources.
Quarterly Founded: 1974
Circulation: 5000

6891 **Phytopathology**
American Phytopatholgical Society
3340 Pilot Knob Road
Saint Paul, MN 55121-2097
651-454-7250
FAX: 651-454-0766 800-328-7560
aps@scisoc.org http://www.apsnet.org

Miles Wimer, Publishing Head
Diana Roeder, Editorial/Publishing
Michelle Bjerkness, Marketing Director

Phytopathology is the premier journal for publication of articles on fundamental research that advances understanding of the nature of plant diseases, the agents that cause them, their spread, the losses they cause, and measures that can be used to control them. In addition to research articles, mini reviews provide up to date summaries of recent advances, and letters to the editor provide a forum for evaluation and discussion of ideas and concepts that impact understanding of plant pathology.
$531.00
Monthly Founded: 1908
Circulation: 2238
Printed in 4 colors : online

6892 **Plant Disease**
American Phytopatholgical Society
3340 Pilot Knob Road
Saint Paul, MN 55121-2097
651-454-7250
FAX: 651-454-0766 800-328-7560
aps@scisoc.org http://www.apsnet.org

Steven C Nelson, Publisher
Kira Bowen, Editor
Michelle Bjerkness, Marketing

Plant Disease is the leading international journal for rapid reporting of research on new diseases, epidemics and methods of disease control. It covers basic research which focuses on practical aspects of disease diagnosis and treatment. Monthly feature articles summarize current information on specific diseases. The popular Disease Notes section contains brief and timely reports of new diseases, new disease outbreaks, new hosts and pertinent new observations of plant diseases and pathogens. *$531.00*
Monthly Founded: 1908
Circulation: 2029
Printed in 4 colors : online

6893 **Pollution Engineering**
Business News Publishing Company
2401 W. Big Beaver Road
Suite 700
Troy, MI 48084
248-244-3500
FAX: 248-244-6429
Roy@PollutionEngineering.com
http://www.pollutionengineering.com

Barbara Olsen, Publisher
Roy Bigham, Managing Editor
Seth Fisher, Products Editor

Serves the field of pollution control in manufacturing industries, utilities, consulting engineers and constructors. Also serves government agencies including administration of federal, state and local environmental programs.
Monthly Founded: 1969

6894 **Pollution Equipment News**
Rimbach Publishing
8650 Babcock Boulevard
Pittsburgh, PA 15237-5010
412-364-5366
FAX: 412-369-9720 800-245-3182
info@rimbach.com
http://www.rimbach.com

Raquel Rimbach, Managing Editor
Karen Galante, Circulation Manager
Heinz Schneider, President/CEO
Paul Henderson, VP of Sales and Marketing

Provides information to those responsible for selecting products and services for air, water, wastewater and hazardous waste pollution abatement.
Founded: 1968
Circulation: 91000

6895 **Pollution Prevention News**
US EPA
Ariel Rios Building
1200 Pennsylvania Avenue NW
Washington, DC 20460
202-272-0167
FAX: 202-564-0575
join-p2news2@lists.epa.gov
http://www.epa.gov

Maureen Eichelberger, Editor

Articles include recent information on source reduction and sustainable technologies in industry, transportation, consumer, agriculture, energy, and the international sector.
Monthly Founded: 1970
Circulation: 12000

6896 **Popular Science**
2 Park Avenue
9th Floor
New York, NY 10016-5675
212-779-5000
FAX: 212-779-9468
letters@popsci.com
http://www.popsci.com

Howard Mittman, Marketing/Advertising Sales
Robert Novick, General Manager
$48.00
Monthly Founded: 1964

6897 **Pumper**
COLE Publishing
PO Box 220
Three Lakes, WI 54562-220
715-546-3346
FAX: 715-546-3786
cole@pumper.com
http://www.pumper.com

Ted Rulseh, Editor
Jeff Bruss, President

Emphasis on companies, individuals and industry events while focusing on customer service, environmental issues and employment trends. *$16.00*
Monthly Founded: 1978
Circulation: 20,740

6898 **R&D Focus**
International Lead Zinc Research Organization
2525 Meridian Parkway, Suite 100
PO Box 12036
Research Triangle Park, NC 27709-2036

919-361-4647
FAX: 919-361-1957
jhendric@ilzro.org www.ilzro.org

Stephen Wilkinson, President
Frank Goodwin, VP Materials Sciences
Scott Mooneyham, Treasurer
Rob Putnam, Director Communications
Quarterly

6899 **Radwaste Solutions**
American Nuclear Society
555 N Kensington Avenue
LaGrange Park, IL 60526-5535
708-352-6611
FAX: 708-352-6464 800-323-044
advertising@ans.org
http://www.ans.org/advertising

Nancy J Zacha, Editor-in-Chief
Sarah Wells, Editor
Harry Bradley, Executive Director
Gloria Naurocki, Membership & Marketing
Mary Beth Gardner, Scientific Publications

Addresses issues in all fields of radioactive waste management, removal, handling, disposal, treatment, cleanup and environmental restoration. *$455.00*
Fortnightly Founded: 1954
Circulation: 2000 11,000 names $210 per M.
Printed in on matte stock

6900 **Recharger Magazine**
Recharger Magazine
1050 E Flamingo Rd
Ste 237
Las Vegas, NV 89119-7479
702-505-9530
FAX: 702-873-9671
info@rechargermag.com
http://www.rechargermag.com

Phyllis Gurgeview, Publisher
Amy Turner, Managing Editor
Brenda Potts, Circulation Manager

Information on remanufacturing imaging supplies including articles that cover business and marketing, technical updates, association and industry news, and company profiles. Related features focus on supply sales and equipment service. *$45.00*

250 pages Monthly
Circulation: 8000 15000 names $250 per M.

Printed in 4 colors

6901 **Recycling Laws International**
Raymond Communications
5111 Berwin Road
#115
College Park, MD 20740
301-345-4237
FAX: 301-345-4768
circulation@raymond.com
http://www.raymond.com

Lorah Utter, Editor
Allyn Sweet, Circulation Manager
Michele Raymond, President

Covers recycling, takeback, green labeling policy for business in 35 countries. Also contains a country page document that is updated annually. *$485.00*

200 pages Founded: 1991
Circulation: 150 17000 names $155 per M. : acrobat

6902 **Recycling Markets**
NV Business Publishers Corporation
43 Main Street
Avon by the Sea, NJ 07717-1015
732-502-0500
FAX: 732-502-9606
nvrecycle@aol.com
http://www.nvpublications.com

Jim Curley, VP/Editor-in-Chief
Anna Dutko, Managing Editor
Tom Vilardi, President / Publisher
Ted Vilardi Jr., Co-Chairman

Contains profiles on recycling mills, as well as large users and generators of recycled materials for the broker, dealers and processors of paper stock, scrap metal, plastics and glass. *$180.00*

Weekly
Circulation: 3315
Printed in 4 colors on newsprint stock

6903 **Recycling Product News**
Baum Publications
2323 Boundary Road
#201
Vancouver, BC 0
604-291-9900
FAX: 604-291-1906
webadmin@baumpub.com
http://www.baumpub.com

Engelbert J Baum, Publisher
Keith Barker, Editor

Published for the recycling center operators and other waste mangers, articles discuss technology and new products.

Circulation: 14000

6904 **Recycling Today**
GIE Media
4012 Bridge Avenue
Cleveland, OH 44113-3320
216-961-4130
FAX: 216-961-0364 800-456-0707
info@recyclingtoday.com
http://www.recyclingtoday.com/

James R Keefe, Group Publisher
Brian Taylor, Editor
Richard Foster, Chief Executive
Debbie Kean, Manager

Published for the secondary commodity processing/recycling market. *$30.00*

Monthly
Circulation: 15000

6905 **Renewable Resources Journal**
Renewable Natural Resources Foundation
5430 Grosvenor Lane
Suite 220
Bethesda, MD 20814-2193
301-493-9101
FAX: 301-493-6148
info@rnrf.org http://www.rnrf.org/

Robert D Day, Executive Director/Editor
Ryan M Colker, Programs Director
Chandru Krishna, Circulation

A quarterly journal published by the Renewable Natural Resources Foundation. Examines critical issues in natural resource policy. *$25.00*

32 pages Quarterly Founded: 1975
Circulation: 1800
Printed in 2 colors on matte stock

6906 **Resource Recycling**
Resource Recycling
PO Box 42270
Portland, OR 97242-270
503-233-1305
FAX: 503-233-1356
info@resource-recycling.co
http://www.resource-recycling.com

Jerry Powell, Editor/Publisher
Rick Downing, Advertising Director

The nation's leading recycling and composting magazine. This monthly journal focuses on efforts in the US and Canada to recover materials from homes and businesses for recycling. Accepts advertising. *$52.00*

64 pages Monthly Founded: 1982
Circulation: 14000+ 40,000 names $100 per M.
Printed in 4 colors on glossy stock

6907 **Restoration Ecology**
Blackwell Science
350 Main Street
Malden, MA 02148-5089
781-388-8250
FAX: 781-388-8270
subscrip@bos.blackwellpublishing.com
http://www.blackwellpublishing.com

James Krosschell, Publisher
Richard Hobbs, Editor

Provides the most recent developments in the ecological and biological restoration field for both the fundamental and practical implications of restorations. *$200.00*

Quarterly Founded: 1897
Circulation: 2000

6908 **Restoration Ecology Journal**
Society for Ecological Restoration
285 West 18th Street #1
Tucson, AZ 85701
520-622-5485
FAX: 520-622-5491
info@ser.org www.ser.org

Mary Kay C LeFevour, Executive Director
Jane Cripps, Membership
Julie St John, Communications

Quarterly

6909 **Risk Policy Report**
Inside Washington Publishers
1225 South Clark Street
Suite 1400
Arlington, VA 22202-4301
703-416-8500
FAX: 703-415-8543
iwp@sprintmail.com
http://www.iwpnews.com

David Clarke, Publisher
David Clarke, Editor

Contains analysis, great perspectives, industry news, policymaking profiles and a calendar of events. *$295.00*

Monthly Founded: 1980

6910 **SEJournal**
Society of Environmental Journalists
PO Box 2492
Jenkintown, PA 19046
215-884-8174
FAX: 215-884-8175
sej@sej.org www.sej.org

Beth Parke, Executive Director

Quarterly

6911 **SETAC Globe**
Society of Environmental Toxicology and Chemistry
1010 N 12th Avenue
Pensacola, FL 32501-3367
850-469-1500
FAX: 850-469-9778
rparrish@setac.org www.setac.org

Rodney Parrish, Executive Director
Greg Schifer, Manager

Bi-Monthly

6912 **Science Magazine**
American Assn for the Advancement of Science
1200 New York Avenue NW
Washington, DC 20005-3941
202-266-6721
FAX: 202-371-9227
membership@aaas.org www.aaas.org

Kathy Fishback, Publication Services Director
Allen Lansher, President

A thorough on-the-spot coverage of events in the scientific community, research news, scholarly reports on developments in all fields of science and original research papers, book reviews and editorials.

6913 **Scrap**
Institute of Scrap Recycling Industries
1352 G Street
NW 1000
Washington, DC 20005
202-731-1770
FAX: 202-626-0900
dennywhite@scrap.org www.scrap.org

Denny White, Publisher
Kent Kiser, Editor

Serves the scrap processing and recycling industry. Subscription: $32.95.

6 per year
Printed in 4 colors on glossy stock

6914 Soil & Groundwater Cleanup Magazine
Association for the Environmental Health of Soils
150 Fearing Street
Suite 21
Amherst, MA 01002
413-549-5170
888-540-2347
info@aehs.com www.aehs.com
Paul T Kostecki, PhD, Executive Director
Bi-Monthly

6915 Soil and Sediment Contamination
Association for the Environmental Health of Soils
150 Fearing Street
Suite 21
Amherst, MA 01002
413-549-5170
888-540-2347
info@aehs.com www.aehs.com
Paul T Kostecki, PhD, Executive Director
Bi-Monthly

6916 Solar Energy
Elsevier Science
655 Avenue of the Americas 4th Floor
PO Box 945
New York, NY 10010-945
212-989-5800
FAX: 212-633-3680
usinfo-f@elseview.com
http://www.elsevier.com/wps/fin/d
John A Duffie, Editor
Monthly
Circulation: 6400

6917 Solar Today
American Solar Energy Society
2400 Central Avenue
Suite G1
Boulder, CO 80301-2843
303-443-3130
FAX: 303-443-3212
ases@ases.org http://www.ases.org
Maureen Mcintyre, Editor
Brad Collins, Publisher
Provides information, case histories and reviews of a variety of renewable energy technologies, including solar, wind, biomass and geothermal. *$29.00*
90 pages Founded: 1987
Circulation: 7000

6918 Solid Waste & Recycling
Southam Environment Group
1450 Don Mills Road
Don Mills, ON 0
905-305-6155
FAX: 416-442-2026 888-702-1111
bobrien@solidwastemag.com
http://www.solidwastemag.com
Brad O'Brien, Publisher
Bibi Khan, Circualtion Manager
Guy Crittenden, Editor-in-Chief
Emphasizes municipal and commercial aspects of collection, handling, transportation, hauling, disposal and treatment of solid waste , including incineration, recycling and landfill technology. *$29.95*
Weekly
Circulation: 10000

6919 Solid Waste Report
Business Publishers
8737 Colesville Road
Suite 1100
Silver Spring, MD 20910-3928
301-587-6300
FAX: 301-587-4530 800-274-6737
custserv@bpinews.com
http://www.bpinews.com
Leonard A Eiserer, Publisher
Beth Early, Operations Director
Comprehensive news and analysis of legislation, regulation and litigation in solid waste management including resource recovery, recycling, collection and disposal. Regularly features international news, state updates and business trends. *$567.00*
Founded: 1963

6920 State Environmental Monitor
Inside Washington Publishers
1225 South Clark Street
Suite 1400
Arlington, VA 22202
703-416-8500
FAX: 703-415-8543 800-424-9068
service@iwpnews.com
http://www.iwpnews.com
Paul Singer, Editor
Contains comperhensive coverage of innovations in state environmental programs and the growth of state authority over environmental regulations. *$245.00*
Monthly Founded: 1980

6921 Tide
Coastal Conservation Association
6919 Portwest
Suite 100
Houston, TX 77024-1888
713-264-4234
800-626-4222
ccatx@ccatexas.org
http://www.ccatexas.org
Ted Venker, Editor
Covers recent conservation news.
Fortnightly Founded: 1977
Circulation: 70000

6922 Urban Land
Urban Land Institute
1025 Thomas Jefferson Streer NW
Suite 500 W
Washington, DC 20007-5201
202-624-7000
FAX: 202-624-7140 800-321-5011
reliance@uli.org http://www.uli.org
Kristina Kessler, Editor in Chief
Karen Schaar, Managing Editor
Joan Campbell, Manager *$165.00*
Monthly Founded: 1936
Circulation: 23000

6923 Waste Age
Environmental Industry Association
4301 Connecticut Avenue NW
#300
Washington, DC 20008-2304
202-664-4701
FAX: 202-966-4868
wa@envasns.org
http://www.envasns.org
Gregg Herring, Group Publisher
Patricia-Ann Tom, Editor
Laura Magliola, Marketing Manager
Bruce Parker, President
Contents focus on new system technologies, recycling, resource recovery and sanitary landfills with regular features on updates in the status of government regulations, new products, guides, company profiles, exclusive survey information, legislative implications and news.
Monthly
Circulation: 38000

6924 Waste Age's Recycling Times
Environmental Industry Association
4301 Connecticut Avenue NW
#300
Washington, DC 20008-2304
202-664-4701
FAX: 202-966-4868
rct@envasns.org
http://www.wasteage.com
Katja Adams, Senior Art Director
Wendy Angel, Assistant Editor
Gregg Herring, Group Publisher
Bruce Parker, President
Features municipalities, recycling goals and rates, program innovations, waste habits, and new materials being recycled. *$99.00*
Monthly
Circulation: 5000

6925 Waste Handling Equipment News
Lee Publications
6113 Strate Highway 5
PO Box 121
Palatine Bridge, NY 13428
518-673-3237
FAX: 518-673-2381 800-218-5586
mstanley@leepub.com
http://www.wastehandling.com
Fred Lee, Publisher
Matt Stanley, Sales Manager
Holly Rieser, Editor
Monthly Founded: 1993
Circulation: 14000
Printed in on newsprint stock

6926 Waste News
Crain Communications
1725 Merriman Road
Suite 300
Akron, OH 44313-5282
330-369-9180
FAX: 330-836-1692 800-678-9595
editorial@wastenews.com
http://www.wastenews.com
Rance E Crain, President
Allan Gerlat, Editor
Keith E. Crain, Chairman/Publisher
Robert C. Adams, Circulation Manager
Glen Stout, Publisher
Articles cover emerging technologies, legislative and regulatory environment issues, public opinion and attitudes, political developments, commodity market prices, mergers, aquisitions and expansions, litigation, competition and policy implementations. Solid waste, hazardous waste, and air and water containment disposal issues. *$49.00*
Founded: 1916
Circulation: 51400 45000 names
Printed in 4 colors on matte stock

6927 Water & Wastes Digest
Scranton Gillette Communications
380 E NW Highway
Suite 200
Des Plaines, IL 60016-2282
847-986-6622
FAX: 847-390-0408
hgillette@sgcmail.com
http://www.scrantongillette.com
Denise Covelli, Editor
Dennis Martyka, Publisher
This serves both municipal and industrial water/watewater facilities. *$40.00*

128 pages Monthly Founded: 1961
Circulation: 101000

6928 **Water Quality Products**
Scranton Gillette Communications
380 E NW Highway
Suite 200
Des Plaines, IL 60016-2282
847-298-6622
FAX: 847-390-0408 800-220-7851
wqpeditor@sgcmail.com
http://www.wqpmag.com

Neda Simeonoza, Editor
Dennis Martyka, Publisher

Published for retailers, dealers, distributors and plumbing contractors of residential and commercial point of use and point of entry water enhancement products. *$40.00*

68 pages Monthly Founded: 1995
Circulation: 19000

6929 **Wildfire Magazine**
International Association of Wildland Fire
4025 Fair Ridge Drive
Fairfax, VA 22033
785-423-1818
FAX: 785-542-3511
info@iawfonline.org
www.iawfonline.org

Sacha Dick, Programs Manager

Monthly

6930 **Wildlife Conservation Magazine**
2300 S Boulevard
Bronx, NY 10460
718-220-5121
FAX: 718-584-2625 800-786-8226
magazine@wcs.org
http://www.wildlifeconservation.org/

Debby Bahler, Editor
Diana Warren, Advertising Director
4teve Sanderson, President

A national nature and science magazine. Contains stunning photography, conservation news and special updates on endangered species. Learn how to help protect local wildlife, and the secrets of the world's rarest and most mysterious animals. *$19.95*

96 pages Founded: 1895
Circulation: 150000

6931 **World Resource Review**
SUPCON International
International Headquarters 2W381
75th Street
Naperville, IL 60565-9245
630-910-1551
FAX: 630-910-1561
syshen@megsinet.net
http://www.globalwarming.net

Dr. Sinyan Shen, Production Manager

For business and government readers, provides expert worldwide reviews of global warming and extreme events in relation to the management of natural, mineral and material resources. Subjects include global warming impacts on agriculture, energy, and infrastructure, monitoring of changes in resources using remote sensing, actions of national and international bodies, global carbon budget, greenhouse budget and more. *$ 72.00*

Quarterly
Circulation: 12000

6932 **World Wastes: The Independent Voice**
Communication Channels
6151 Powers Ferry Road NW
Atlanta, GA 30339-2959
770-953-4805
FAX: 770-618-0348

Bill Wolpin, Editor
Jerrold France, President Argus Business

Reaches individuals and firms engaged in the removal and disposal of solid wastes. *$48.00*

Monthly
Circulation: 36,000

6933 **World Watch**
Worldwatch Institute
1776 Massachusetts Avenue NW
Suite 800
Washington, DC 20036-1995
202-452-1999
FAX: 202-296-7365
worldwatch@worldwatch.org
http://www.worldwatch.org

Christopher Flavin, President
Tom Prugh, Editor
Lisa Mastny, Senior Editor

Magazine on global environmental issues. *$27.00*

40 pages Founded: 1974
Circulation: 10000 10000 names
Printed in 4 colors on glossy stock

Trade Shows

6934 **AAAR Annual Meeting**
American Association for Areosol Research
17000 Commerce Parkway
Suite C
Mount Laurel, NJ 08054
856-439-0500
FAX: 856-439-0525
aaar@ahint.com www.aaar.org

Beth Wood, Show Manager

Exibits related to aerosol research in areas including industrial process, air pollution, and industrial hygiene. Over 600 professionals attend.

600 Attendees Annual, October

6935 **ACCA Annual Meetings**
Air Conditioning Contractors of America
280 Shirlington Road
Suite 300
Arlington, VA 22206
703-575-4477
FAX: 703-575-4449
michael.honeycutt@acca.org
www.acca.org

Paul T Stalknecht, President/CEO
Hilary Atkins, Esq, General Counsel
Michael Honeycutt, SVP/Chief of Staff
Glenn Hourihan, PE, VP
Research/Technology

February/March

6936 **AEESP Annual Meeting**
Association of Environmental Engineering and
2303 Naples Court
Champaign, IL 61822
217-398-6969
FAX: 217-355-9232 www.aeesp.org

Joanne Fetzner, Business Secretary

With the Water Environment Federation

Fall

6937 **AEHS Annual Meeting**
Association for the Environmental Health of Soils
150 Fearing Street
Suite 21
Amherst, MA 01002
413-549-5170
888-540-2347
info@aehs.com www.aehs.com

Paul T Kostecki, PhD, Executive Director

March

6938 **AERE Annual Meeting**
Association of Environmental and Resource
1616 P Street NW
Suite 400
Washington, DC 20036
202-328-5077
FAX: 202-939-3460
voigt@rff.org www.aere.org

Ralph Metts, President
Marilyn Voight, Executive Secretary

In conjunction with Allied Social Science Association.

January

6939 **APWA International Public Works Congress & Expo**
American Public Works Association
2345 Grand Boulevard
Suite 700
Kansas City, MO 64108-2641
816-472-6100
FAX: 816-472-1610
dpriddy@apwa.net www.apwa.net

Dana Priddy, Meetings Director
Kaye Sullivan, Chief Executive Officer

Offers the benefit of a variety of educational sessions, depth of the exhibit program and endless opportunities for networking. The latest cutting-edge technologies, managerial techniques and regulatory trends designed to keep you focused on the right solutions at the right time.

6500 Attendees Annual/September Founded: 1894

6940 **ASEH Annual Meeting**
American Society for Environmental History
119 Pine Street
Suite 301
Seattle, WA 98101
206-343-0226
FAX: 206-343-0249
mighetto@hrassoc.com www.aseh.net

Lisa Mighetto, Acting Executive Director

Spring, Texas

6941 **ASFPM Annual Conference**
Association of State Floodplain Managers
2809 Fish Hatchery Road
Suite 204
Madison, WI 53713
608-274-0123
FAX: 608-274-0696
memberhelp@floods.org
www.floods.org

Larry Larson, Executive Director
Alison Stierli, Member Services Coordinator

Focus on floodproofing techniques, materials, floodproofing and elevation contractors, current issues and programs, new federal tax impications and the various means of funding floodproofing projects. implications.

Annual

6942 **ASMR Meeting & Conference**
American Society of Mining and Reclamation
3134 Montavesta Road
Lexington, KY 40502
859-335-6529

asmr@insightbb.com
www.ca.uky.edu/assmr
Richard I Barnhisel, Executive Secretary
June

6943 **ASPRS Annual Conference**
Imaging and Geospacial Information Society
5410 Grosvenor Lane
Suite 210
Bethesda, MD 20814-2160
301-493-0290
FAX: 301-493-0208
asprs@asprs.org www.asprs.org
Temperance Baltee
One hundred exhibits of mapping, photogrammetry, environmental management, remote sensing, geographic infromation, natural resources and much more.
2000 Attendees Founded: 1934

6944 **Air and Waste Management Association Annual Conference and Exhibition**
Air and Waste Management Association
1 Gateway Center
3rd Floor
Pittsburgh, PA 15222-1435
412-652-2458
FAX: 412-232-3450 800-270-3444
info@awma.org www.awma.org
Deborah Hilfman, Show Manager
Robert Greenbaum, Exhibit Manager
Environmental professionals from all sectors of the economy including colleges, universities, natural resource manufacturing and process industries, consultants, local state, provincial, regional and federal governments, construction, utilities industries. Over 300 exhibits of envirnomental control products.
6000 Attendees Founded: 0907

6945 **American Institute of Biological Sciences Annual Meeting**
1444 I Street NW
Suite 200
Washington, DC 20005
202-628-1500
FAX: 202-628-1509 800-992-2427
50 exhibits of scientific equipment, supplies and publications, banquet, breakfast and luncheon.
Annual Founded: 1947

6946 **American Occupational Health Conference & Exhibits**
Slack
6900 Grove Road
Thorofare, NJ 08086
856-848-1000
FAX: 856-848-3522
Peter Slack, President
400 exhibits of pharmaceuticals, equipment, software and supplies for health professionals, offices and labs.
4500 Attendees

6947 **American Society of Safety Engineers Professional Development Conference**
American Society of Safety Engineers
1800 E Oakton Street
Des Plaines, IL 60018-2187
847-699-2929
FAX: 847-296-3769
customerservice@asse.org
www.asse.org
Hall Erickson, Trade Show Director
Annual conference and expo of 250 manufacturers and suppliers of safety equipment and health products.
3500 Attendees June

6948 **Association for Population/Family Planning Libraries & Information Centers**
Assn for Population Family Planning Libraries
Surgical Contraception-79 Madison
New York, NY 10016
212-780-2687
FAX: 212-779-9439
William Record
Annual conference and exhibits for effective documentation, information systems and services in the field of population/family planning.

6949 **Association of Energy Engineers**
4025 Pleasantdale Road
Suite 420
Atlanta, GA 30340
770-447-5083
FAX: 770-446-3969
info@aeecenter.org
www.aeecenter.org
Ruth Marie, Director Information Services
Albert Thumann, Executive Director
Membership organization of over 8,000 professionals and certification programs in the fields of energy efficiency, utility deregulation, facility management, plant engineering and environmental compliance. Offers seminars, conferences, books to critical buyer-seller networking trade shows, job listings and certification programs.
8.2M Attendees

6950 **EBA Annual Meeting**
Environmental Business Association
1150 Connecticut Avenue NW
9th Floor
Washington, DC 20036-4129
202-624-4363
FAX: 202-828-4130 wbode@bode.com

William H Bode, President
June

6951 **EBA Semi-Annual Meeting**
Environmental Bankers Association
510 King Street
Suite 410
Alexandria, VA 22314
703-549-0977
FAX: 703-548-5945 800-966-7475
eba@environbank.org
www.environbank.org
D J Telego, Executive Co-Director
January, June

6952 **EDRA Annual Meetings**
Environmental Design Research Association
PO Box 7146
Edmond, OK 73083-7146
405-304-4863
FAX: 403-330-4150
edra@telepath.com www.edra.org
Janet Singer, Executive Director
Spring-Summer

6953 **EMS Annual Meeting**
Environmental Mutagen Society
1821 Michael Faraday Drive
Suite 300
Reston, VA 20190
703-438-8220
FAX: 703-438-3113
emshq@ems-us.org www.ems-us.org
Tonia Masson, Executive Director
Spring

6954 **ESTECH Annual Technical Meeting and Exposition of IEST**
Institute of Environmental Sciences and Technology
5005 Newport Drive
Suite 506
Rolling Meadows, IL 60008-3841
847-255-1561
FAX: 847-255-1699
iest@iest.org www.iest.org
Heather Dvorak, Marketing Associate
IEST's annual technical meeting and exposition presents the finest educational program with tutorials, technical sessions, and working group meeting, as well as displays in the tabletop exhibition for design, test and evaluation.
300 Attendees May

6955 **ETAD Annual Meeting**
ETAD North America
1850 M Street NW
Suite 700
Washington, DC 20036
202-721-4154
FAX: 202-296-8120 www.etad.com
Dr C Tucker Helmes, Executive Director
Spring

6956 **Earth Technologies Forum**
2111 Wilson Boulevard
8th Floor
Arlington, VA 22201
703-515-5045
FAX: 703-528-1734
earthforum@alcalde-fay.com
www.earthforum.com
Mitch Henderson, Group Publisher
Joe Jancsurak, Editor
Provides information on two of the biggest environmental issues affecting industry today — climate change and stratospheric ozone protection.

6957 **Enviro Expo**
Industrial Shows Northeast
333 Trapelo Road
Belmont, MA 02478-1856
617-489-2302
FAX: 781-489-5534 800-543-5259
rryan@enviro.com
www.enviroexpo.com
Russ Ryan, President
Diane Fisher, Show Manager
Annual show of 400 manufacturers and suppliers of environmental products and services catering to industry and municipalities.

5,000 Attendees May Founded: 1987

6958 **Environmental Business: West**
World Information Systems
PO Box 535
Cambridge, MA 02238-0535

FAX: 617-492-3312

Richard S Golob, Editor-in-Chief
Roger B Wilson Jr, VP

Attracts business leaders in hazardous waste and other key segments of the environmental industry. The events have earned a reputation as summit meetings of environmental business leaders. Speakers have included presidents of major environmental firms, along with well known consultants, financiers and government officials. The two-and-a-half day programs concentrate exclusively on the business issues facing the rapidly growing environmental industry. 25 booths.
800+ Attendees

6959 **Environmental Technology Expo**
Association of Energy Engineers
4025 Pleasantdale Road
Suite 420
Atlanta, GA 30340-4264
770-447-5083
FAX: 770-446-3969
info@aeecenter.org
www.aeecenter.org

Ruth Bennett, Information Services Director

Annual show and exhibits of air and water pollution contrasts, waste-to-energy services information, asbestos abatement and monitoring instruments and equipment.
October

6960 **FET Annual Meeting**
Federation of Environmental Technologists
PO Box 624
Slinger, WI 53086-0624
414-540-0070
FAX: 262-644-7106
info@fetinc.org www.fetinc.org

Triese Haase, Administrator

March

6961 **Forestry, Conservation Communications Association Annual Meeting**
Forestry, Conservation Communications Association
Hall of the States
444 N Capitol
Washington, DC 20001
202-624-5416
FAX: 202-751-9099

Joe Friend, Executive Director

Annual meeting and exhibits of forestry and conservation communications equipment, systems and procedures.

6962 **Global Warming International Conference & Expo**
SUPCON International
PO Box 5275
Woodridge, IL 60517-0275
630-910-1551
FAX: 630-910-1561
syshen@megsinet.net
www.globalwarming.net
Environmental and energy technology, global warming mitigation, journals, publications and software, greenhouse gas measurements, alternative vehicles and alternative energy. Containing 100 booths and exhibits.
2000 Attendees April Boston

6963 **GlobalCon**
Association of Energy Engineers
4025 Pleasantdale Road
Suite 420
Atlanta, GA 30340-4264
770-447-5083
FAX: 770-446-3969
info@aeecenter.org
www.aeecenter.org

Ruth Bennett, Information Services Director

Annual show and exhibits of integrated energy and environmental technological equipment, supplies and services.
April

6964 **HydroVision**
HCI Publications
410 Archibald Street
Kansas City, MO 64111-3001
816-931-1311
FAX: 816-931-2015
hydrovision@hcipub.com
www.hcipub.com

Leslie Eden, Manager

Major conference and trade show serving hydroelectric industry and related water resource management sectors. Containing approximately 150 exhibits.
1,600 Attendees July-August

6965 **IAWF Annual Meetings**
International Association of Wildland Fire
4025 Fair Ridge Drive
Fairfax, VA 22033
785-423-1818
FAX: 785-542-3511
info@iawfonline.org
www.iawfonline.org

Sacha Dick, Programs Manager

Three year rotation: United States, Canada, Australia.

6966 **IEST Annual Meeting**
Institute of Environmental Sciences and Technology
5005 Newport Drive
Suite 506
Rolling Meadows, IL 60008-3841
847-255-1561
FAX: 847-255-1699
iest@iest.org www.iest.org

Julie Kendrick, Executive Director

Spring

6967 **ILZRO Annual Meeting**
International Lead Zinc Research Organization
2525 Meridian Parkway, Suite 100
PO Box 12036
Research Triangle Park, NC 27709-2036
919-361-4647
FAX: 919-361-1957
jhenric@ilzro.org www.ilzro.org

Stephen Wilkinson, President
Frank Goodwin, VP Materials Sciences
Scott Mooneyham, Treasurer
Rob Putnam, Director Communications

November

6968 **ISEE Annual Meetings**
International Society for Ecological Economics
1313 Dolley Madison Boulevard
Suite 402
McLean, VA 22101
703-790-1745
FAX: 703-790-2672
iseemembership@burkinc.com
www.ecologicaleconomics.org

Heide Scheiter-Rohland, Director Membership

Summer or Fall

6969 **ISEMNA Annual Meeting**
International Society for Ecological Modelling
University of California, Animal Sciences Dept
One Shields Avenue
Davis, CA 95616-8521
530-752-5362
FAX: 530-752-0175 www.isemna.org

Wolfgang Pittroff, Secretary-General

August

6970 **International Association for Energy Economics Conference**
International Association for Energy Economics
28790 Chagrin Boulevard
Suite 350
Cleveland, OH 44122-4630
216-464-5365
FAX: 216-464-2737
iaee@iaee.org www.iaee.org

David Williams, Executive Director

Semi-annual conference and exhibits relating to energy economics including publications, consultants, energy database software.
325 Attendees 330 names $150 per M.

6971 **International Conference on Indoor Air Quality and Climate**
International Academy of Indoor Air Sciences
343 Soquel Avenue
PMB 312
Santa Cruz, CA 95062
831-426-0148
FAX: 831-426-6522
info@indoorair2002.org
www.indoorair2002.org
June-July

6972 **International Hazardous Materials Response Teams Conference**
International Association of Fire Chiefs
4025 Fair Ridge Drive
Fairfax, VA 22033
703-273-0911
FAX: 703-273-9363

6973 **MIACON Construction, Mining & Waste Management Show**
MIACON
2921 Coral Way
Miami, FL 33145-3053

FAX: 305-529-9217 www.miacon.com

Michael Finocchiaro, President
Jose Garcia, VP
Justine Finocchiaro, Chief Operations

Annual show of 650 manufacturers, suppliers, distributors and exporters of equipment, machinery, supplies and services for the construction, mining and waste managment industries. There will be 600 booths.

10M Attendees December Founded: 1994

6974 NAAEE Annual Meeting
North American Association for Environmental
2000 P Street NW
Suite 540
Washington, DC 20036
202-419-0412
FAX: 202-419-0415
email@naaee.org www.naaee.org
William H Dent, Jr, Executive Director
Barbara Eager, Conference Coordinator
Paul Werth, Owner
Fall

6975 NAEP Annual Meeting
National Association of Environmental Professional
PO Box 2086
Bowie, MD 20718-2086
301-860-1140
FAX: 301-860-1141 888-251-9902
office@naep.org www.naep.org
Sandi Worthman, Administrator
Spring

6976 NALGEP Annual Meetings
National Association of Local Government
1333 New Hampshire Avenue NW
Washington, DC 20036
202-638-6254
FAX: 202-393-2866
nalgep@spiegelmcd.com
www.nalgep.org
Kenneth Brown, Executive Director
David Dickson, Project Manager
Regional Workshops

6977 NEDA Annual Meeting
National Environmental Development Association
One Thomas Circle NW
10th Floor
Washington, DC 20006
202-878-8800
FAX: 202-530-0659
Steve Hellem, Executive Director
Washington, DC

6978 NEHA Annual Educational Conference and Exhibition
National Environmental Health Association
720 S Colorado Boulevard
Suite 970-S
Denver, CO 80246-1925
303-756-9090
FAX: 303-691-9490
staff@neha.org www.neha.org
Toni Roland, Conference Coordinator
Kim Brandow, Marketing/Sales Manager
The National Environmental Health Association (NEHA) is a unique organization representing all professionals in environmental health. NEHA offers credentials, publications, training, Journal of Environmental Health, and discounts for members. Each year NEHA conducts the Annual Educational Conference and Exhibition, this year it will be at the Minneapolis Hilton in Minneapolis, MN.
2000 Attendees June-July

6979 NEHA Annual Meeting
National Conference of Local Environmental Health
c/o NEHA, 720 S Colorado Boulevard
South Tower, Suite 970
Denver, CO 80246-1925
303-756-9090
FAX: 303-691-9490 nfabian@neha.org
Nelson E Fabian, Executive Director
Held with the National Environmental Health Association.
June

6980 NESHTA Annual Meetings
National Environmental, Safety and Health Training
PO Box 10321
Phoenix, AZ 85064-0321
602-956-6099
FAX: 602-956-6399
info@neshta.org www.neshta.org
Charles L Richardson, Executive Director
Joan J Jennings, Manager Association Services
Suzanne Lanctot, Manager Certification/Membership
June

6981 NIWR Annual Meeting
National Institutes for Water Resources
47 Harkness Road
Pelham, MA 10002
413-253-5686
FAX: 413-253-1309
godfrey@tei.umass.edu
Paul Joseph Godfrey, PhD, Executive Director
Spring

6982 NORA Semi-Annual Meetings
NORA: Association of Responsible Recyclers
5965 Amber Ridge Road
Haymarket, VA 20169
703-753-4277
FAX: 703-753-2445
sparker@noranews.org
www.noranews.org
Scott D Parker, Executive Director
May, November

6983 NREP Annual Meetings
National Registry of Environmental Professionals
PO Box 2099
Glenview, IL 60025
847-724-6631
FAX: 847-724-4223
nrep@nrep.org www.nrep.org
Richard A Young, PhD, Executive Director
October 16-19 Opryland Hotel, Nashville, TN; October 16-17 Certification Workshops-Environmental and Homeland Security; October 18-19; Technical Presentations.
1000 Attendees Semi-Annual
Mailing list available for rent

6984 National Association Civilian Conservation Corps Alumni
52 Woods Road
Little Falls, NJ 07424-2051
201-652-5220
John Moscinski, Executive Director
10 booths.
1.3M Attendees September

6985 National Environmental Balancing Bureau Meeting
National Environmental Balancing Bureau
8575 Grovemont Circle
Gaithersburg, MD 20877-4121
301-977-3698
FAX: 301-977-9589
Michael Dolim, VP
Annual meeting and exhibits of testing and balancing equipment, supplies and services.

6986 National Environmental Training Association Show
2430 E Camelback Road
Suite 185
Phoenix, AZ 85016-4202
602-956-6099
FAX: 602-956-6390
CL Richardson, Show Manager
20 booths.
April

6987 National Real Estate Environmental Conference
National Society of Environmental Consultants
PO Box 12528
San Antonio, TX 78212-0528
210-225-2897
FAX: 956-225-8450 800-486-3676
Annual conference and exhibits related to the environmentally responsible use of real estate.

6988 North American Wildlife and Natural Resources Conference
Wildlife Management Institute
1101 14th Street NW
Suite 801
Washington, DC 20005
202-371-1808
FAX: 202-408-5059
www.wildlifemanagementinstitute.org
Meeting the challenges of modern conservation.

6989 Plant & Facilities Expo (PFE)
Association of Energy Engineers
4025 Pleasantdale Road
Suite 420
Atlanta, GA 30340-4264
770-447-5083
FAX: 770-446-3969
info@aeecenter.org
www.aeecenter.org
Ruth Bennett, Information Services Director
Annual show of 375 manufacturers, suppliers and distributors of environmental, occupational health and safety systems and services.
5000 Attendees October

6990 SBF Annual Meeting
Surfaces in Biomaterials Foundation
13355 10th Avenue North
Suite 108
Minneapolis, MN 55441-5554
763-512-9103
FAX: 763-765-2329
director@surfaces.org
www.surfaces.org
Margaret I Winchell, Executive Director
Fall

6991 **SEGH Annual Meetings**
Society for Environmental Geochemistry and Health
4698 S Forrest Avenue
Springfield, MO 65810
417-885-1166
FAX: 417-881-6920
drbgwixson@wixson.com
www.segh.net
Bobby Wixson, Director Membership
Summer-Fall

6992 **SEJ Annual Meeting**
Society of Environmental Journalists
PO Box 2492
Jenkintown, PA 19046
215-884-8174
FAX: 215-884-8175
sej@sej.org www.sej.org
Beth Parke, Executive Director
Chris Riger, Associate Director
Organized by journalists for journalists who cover environment and related issues. Co-hosted by the University of Vermont and Vermont Law School.
Fall/Oct

6993 **SER Annual Meeting**
Society for Ecological Restoration
285 West 18th Street #1
Tucson, AZ 85701
520-622-5485
FAX: 520-622-5491
info@ser.org www.ser.org
Mary Kay C LeFevour, Executive Director
Jane Cripps, Membership
Julie St John, Communications
Fall

6994 **SETAC Annual Meeting**
Society of Environmental Toxicology and Chemistry
1010 N 12th Street
Pensacola, FL 32501-3367
850-469-1500
FAX: 850-469-9778
rparrish@setac.org www.setac.org
Rodney Parrish, Executive Director
Greg Schifer, Manager
Fall

6995 **SHE Bi-Ennial Meetings**
Society for Human Ecology
College of the Atlantic
105 Eden Street
Bar Harbor, ME 04609-0180
207-288-5015
FAX: 207-288-3780
carter@ecology.coa.edu
www.societyforhumanecology.org
Barbara Carter, Assistant to Executive Director

6996 **SOCMA Annual Meeting**
Synthetic Organic Chemical Manufacturers Assn
1850 M Street NW
Suite 700
Washington, DC 20036
202-721-4100
FAX: 202-296-8120
info@socma.com www.socma.com
Joseph Acker, President
Diane McMahon, VP Commerical Development
Charlene Patterson, Director Human Resources
Early Spring

6997 **SOEH Annual Meeting**
Society for Occupational and Environmental Health
6728 Old McLean Village Drive
McLean, VA 22101
703-556-9222
FAX: 703-556-8729
soeh@degnon.org www.soeh.org
George K Degnon, CAE, Executive Director
Spring

6998 **Take It Back**
Raymond Communications
5111 Berwin Road
#115
College Park, MD 20740
301-345-4237
FAX: 301-345-4768
michele@raymond.com
www.raymond.com
Michele Raymond, Publisher/Editor
The conference brings in the top recycling policy experts from around the world to brief customers. We also have practical sessions with case histories on such issues as packaging design, design for environment in electronics, and lifecycle issues.
150 Attendees March Founded: 1996 $137 per M.

6999 **Waterpower XIII**
HCI Publications
410 Archibald Street
Kansas City, MO 64111-3001
816-931-1311
FAX: 816-931-2015
waterpower@hcipub.com
www.hcipub.com
Leslie Eden, Manager
The conference offers industry professionals a forum in which to share new ideas and approaches to move hydropower forward as the world's leading source of renewable energy. Containing 120 booths.
1,000 Attendees July-August

7000 **Wildlife Habitat Council Annual Symposium**
Wildlife Habitat Council
8737 Colesville Road
Suite 800
Silver Spring, MD 20910
301-588-8994
FAX: 301-588-4629
whc@wildlifehc.org
www.wildlifehc.org
Bill Howard, President
The annual symposium brings together corporate, government and conservation leaders from around the globe for informative sessions, exhibits and field trips on environmental stewardship.
400 Attendees November

7001 **Wildlife Society Annual Conference**
Wildlife Society
5410 Grosvenor Lane
Suite 200
Bethesda, MD 20814-2144
301-897-9770
FAX: 301-530-2471
tws@wildlife.org www.wildlife.org
Lisa Moll, Program Assistant/Membership
1200 Attendees September Founded: 1994

7002 **World Energy Engineering Congress**
Association of Energy Engineers
4025 Pleasantdale Road
Suite 420
Atlanta, GA 30340-4264
770-447-5083
FAX: 770-446-3969
info@aeecenter.org
www.aeecenter.org
Ruth Bennett, Information Services Director
Annual show of 150 exhibitors of air and water pollution controls, waste-to-energy services information, asbestos abatement and monitoring instrumentations.
5000 Attendees October

Directories & Databases

7003 **ACCA Membership Directory**
Air Conditioning Contractors of America
2800 Shirlington Road
Suite 300
Arlington, VA 22206
703-575-4477
FAX: 703-575-4449
michael.honeycutt@acca.org
www.acca.org
Paul T Stalknecht, President/CEO
Hilary Atkins, Esq, General Counsel
Michael Honeycutt, SVP/Chief of Staff
Glenn Hourihan, PE, VP Research/Technology

7004 **ACSH Media Update**
American Council on Science and Health
1995 Broadway
2nd Floor
New York, NY 10023-5860
212-362-7044
FAX: 212-362-4919
acsh@acsh.org www.acsh.org
Gilbert Ross, Executive/Medical Director
Jeff Stier, Associate Director
Dr Elizabeth Whelan, President
Semi-Annual

7005 **ASMR Membership Directory**
American Society of Mining and Reclamation
3134 Montavesta Road
Lexington, KY 40502
859-335-6529
asmr@insightbb.com
www.ca.uky.edu/assmr
Richard I Barnhisel, Executive Secretary
Annual

7006 **Aboveground Storage Tank Management and SP CC Guide**
ABS Group
PO Box 846304
Dallas, TX 75284-6304
FAX: 301-921-0264

7007 **Acid Rain**
Watts, Franklin
90 Sherman Turnpike
Danbury, CT 06816
203-797-3500
FAX: 203-797-3657 800-621-1115
Lists over 4,000 citations, with abstracts, to the worldwide literature on the sources of acid rain and its effects on the environment.

Bibliographic

7008 Alternative Energy Network Online
Environmental Information Networks
119 S Fairfax Street
Alexandria, VA 22314-3301
703-548-1202

Reports on news of all energy sources designed as alternatives to conventional fossil fuels, including wind, solar and alcohol fuels.
Full-text

7009 American Recycling Market: Directory/Reference Manual
Recycling Data Management Corporation
PO Box 577
Ogdensburg, NY 13669-0577
315-785-9072

Offers information, in three volumes, encompassing over 15,000 recycling companies and centers. *$175.00*
1000 pages Annual

7010 American Solar Energy Society Membership Directory
2400 Central Avenue
Suite A
Boulder, CO 80301-2843
303-443-3130
FAX: 303-443-3212
ases@ases.org www.ases.org
Regina Johnson, Editor
Offers information on over 2,000 manufacturers, professors, architects, engineers and others in the solar energy field.

7011 An Electronic Database
National Institutes for Water Resources
47 Harkness Road
Pelham, MA 10002
413-253-5686
FAX: 413-253-1309
godfrey@tei.umass.edu
Paul Joseph Godfrey, PhD, Executive Director
Bi-Annual

7012 Book of Lists for Regulated Hazardous Substances
ABS Group
PO Box 846304
Dallas, TX 75284-6304

FAX: 301-921-0264

7013 Business and the Environment: A Resource Guide
Island Press
1718 Connecticut Avenue NW
Suite 300
Washington, DC 20009-1148
202-232-7933
FAX: 202-234-1328
info@islandpress.org
www.isalndpress.org
Charles Savitt, Owner
Allison Pennell, Editor
List of approximately 185 business and environmental educators working to integrate environmental issues into management, research, education and practices. *$60.00*

7014 Carcinogenicity Information Database of Environmental Substances
Technical Database Services
10 Columbus Circle
New York, NY 10019-1203
212-556-0001
FAX: 212-556-0036
This database contains test results on the carcinogenic and mutagenic effects of approximately 1000 substances of environmental or health concerns.
Numeric

7015 Commercial Guide
Synthetic Organic Chemical Manufacturers Assn
1850 M Street NW
Suite 700
Washington, DC 20036
202-721-4100
FAX: 202-296-8120
info@socma.org www.socma.com
Joseph Acker, President
Diane McMahon, VP Commercial Development
Charlene Patterson, Director Human Resources
Annual

7016 Conservation Directory
National Wildlife Federation
11100 Wildlife Center Drive
Reston, VA 20190-5362
703-386-6000
FAX: 703-438-6061 800-822-9919
Robin Assa, Sales Assistant
Federal agencies, national and international organizations and state government agencies. *$20.00*
500 pages Annual

7017 Department of Energy Annual Procurement and Financial Assistance Report
US Department of Energy
1000 Independence Avenue SW
Washington, DC 20585
202-586-5000
FAX: 202-586-4403 www.energy.gov
Offers a list of universities, research centers and laboratories that represent the Department of Energy.
Annual

7018 Directory of Environmental Information Sources
Government Institutes
4 Research Place
Suite 200
Rockville, MD 20850-6209
301-921-2300
FAX: 301-548-0146
Over 1,400 federal and state government agencies, professional and scientific organizations and trade associations are profiled. *$78.00*
322 pages

7019 Directory of Environmental Websites: Online Micro Edition
US Environmental Directories
PO Box 65156
Saint Paul, MN 55165-0156
612-331-6050

www.geocities.com/usenvironmentaldirectories
Roger N McGrath, Publisher
John C Brainard, Editor
The Directory is a complete guide to the environmental movement on the Internet, provides a concise, practical listing of over 190 of the major Internet addresses of the Environmental Movement. A clear, understandable and comprehensive guide to national and international environmental organizations, directories, networks and services on the Internet. *$25.75*
48 pages Founded: 1998

7020 Directory of Institute Programs
National Institutes for Water Resources
47 Harkness Road
Pelham, MA 10002
413-253-5686
FAX: 413-253-1309
godfrey@tei.umass.edu
Paul Joseph Godfrey, PhD, Executive Director
Bi-Annual

7021 Directory of International Periodicals & Newsletters on Built Environments
Division of Mineral Resources
PO Box 3667
Charlottesville, VA 22903-0667
434-951-6341
FAX: 434-951-6365
www.mme.state.va.us
More than 1,400 international periodicals and newsletters that cover architectural design and the building industry, and the aspects of the environment that deal with the industry are covered. *$6.00*
29 pages

7022 EDOCKET
Environmental Protection Agency
1200 Pennsylvania Avenue NW
Mail Code 3213A
Washington, DC 20460
202-260-2090
FAX: 202-566-0545 www.epa.gov
An electronic public docket and on-line comment system designed to expand access to documents in EPA's major dockets.
Full-text

7023 EH&S Compliance Auditing & Teaching Software Report
Donley Technology
PO Box 152
Colonial Beach, VA 22443-0152
804-224-9427
FAX: 804-224-7958 800-201-1595
donleytech@donleytech.com
www.donleytech.com
Elizabeth Donley, Editor
Profiles 25 software packages for achieving and maintaining compliance, including detailed product descriptions, tables comparing system features, and contact information. *$195.00*
240 pages Every 2 Years Founded: 1997
ISBN 1-891682-08-3
Printed in on matte stock

7024 EMS Membership Roster
Environmental Mutagen Society
1821 Michael Faraday Drive
Suite 300
Reston, VA 20190
703-438-8220
FAX: 703-438-3113
emshq@ems-us.org www.ems-us.org
Tonia Masson, Executive Director
Irregular

7025 ETAD Annual Report
ETAD North America
1850 M Street NW
Suite 700
Washington, DC 20036
202-721-4154
FAX: 202-296-8120 www.etad.com
Dr C Tucker Helmes, Executive Director
Annual

7026 Ecological Farming Conference Participants Directory
Ecological Farming Association
406 Main Street
Suite 313
Watsonville, CA 95076
831-763-2111

info@eco-farm.org www.eco-farm.org
ME Smedsrud, CEO
Kristin Rosenow, Executive Director
About 1,000 organic farmers, farm suppliers and consultants, produce handlers, researchers, extension, agents, students, organization representatives, and others who attended the annual Ecological Farming conference. *$5.00*

7027 Ecology Abstracts
Cambridge Scientific Abstracts
7200 Wisconsin Avenue
Suite 601
Bethesda, MD 20814-4823
301-961-6750
FAX: 301-961-6720 800-843-7751
market@csa.com www.csa.com
James P McGinty, President
Theodore Caris, Publisher
Robert Hilton, Editor
Mark Furneaux, VP Marketing
Angela Hitti, Production Manager
This large database updated continuously, offers over 150,000 citations, with abstracts, to the worldwide literature available on ecology and the environment. *$945.00*
Monthly

7028 Education for the Earth: A Guide to Top Environmental Studies Programs
Peterson's Guides
202 Carnegie Center
#2123
Princeton, NJ 08540-6239

FAX: 609-869-4531 800-338-3282
Colleges and universities that offer programs in environment and conservation are listed. *$10.95*
192 pages

7029 Educational Communications
Educational Communications
PO Box 351419
Los Angeles, CA 90035-9119
310-559-9160
FAX: 310-559-9160
ECNP@aol.com www.ecoprojects.org
Nancy Pearlman, Editor
Directory of over 6,500 environmental organizations worldwide are the focus of this comprehensive directory. Over 400 1/2 hour television shows on the environment. Environmental directions - radio has over 1,500 interviews with ecological experts. Monthly newsletter, TV and radio series about ecological problems and solutions; promotion of ecotourem. Audo/video cassettes available. *$20.00*
244 pages Annual Paperback
Mailing list available for rent

7030 El Environmental Services Directory
Environmental Information Networks
7301 Ohms Lane
Suite 460
Eding, MN 55439
952-831-2473
FAX: 952-831-6550
ei@mr.net www.envirobiz.com
Cary Perket
Waste-handling facilities, transportation and spill response firms, laboratories and the broad scope of environmental services. Online versions are also available. *$1250.00*
Biennial Founded: 1984

7031 Emergency Response Directory for Hazardous Materials Accidents
Odin Press
PO Box 536
New York, NY 10021-0011
212-605-0338

Pamela Lawrence, Editor
Over 1,000 federal, state and local governmental agencies, chemical manufacturers and transporters, hotlines and strike teams, burn care centers, civil defense and disaster centers and other organizations concerned with the containment and cleanup of chemical spills and other hazardous materials accidents. *$36.00*
Biennial

7032 Energy
WEFA Group
800 Baldwin Tower Boulevard
Eddystone, PA 19022-1368
610-490-4000
FAX: 610-490-2770
info@wefa.com www.wefa.com
Peter McNabb
This database covers energy supply and demand, including weekly rig count and gasoline prices by states; reserves, stocks, production, consumption and trade of petroleum products.

7033 Energy Data Base
Newport Associates
7400 E Orchard Road
Suite 320
Englewood, CO 80111-2528

FAX: 303-779-0908
This database covers financial, as well as reserves and production data, for over 450 oil companies in over 20 world regions.
Numeric

7034 Energy Engineering: Directory of Software for Energy Managers and Engineers
Fairmont Press
700 Indian Trail
Liburn, GA 30347
770-259-9388
FAX: 770-381-9865
Wayne C Turner
Directory of services and supplies to the industry. *$15.00*

Circulation: 8,500

7035 Energy Science and Technology
US Department of Energy
PO Box 62
Oak Ridge, TN 37831-0062
865-574-1000
FAX: 865-576-2865
OSTIWebmaster@osti.gov
www.osti.gov
This large database offers over 3 million citations, with abstracts, to literature pertaining to all fields of energy.
Bibliographic

7036 Energy Statistics Spreadsheets
Institute of Gas Technology
1700 S Mount Prospect Road
Des Plaines, IL 60018-1804
847-680-0664
FAX: 847-768-0501
The coverage of this database encompasses worldwide energy industry statistics, including production, consumption, reserves, imports and prices.

7037 Energy User News: Energy Technology Buyers Guide
Chilton Company
360 Park Avenue S
New York, NY 10014-0001
212-513-3596
FAX: 646-746-7433
Kevin Heslin, Editor
Richard Chilton Jr, Owner
A list of about 1,500 manufacturers, dealers and distributors of energy conservation and used equipment. *$10.00*
Annual
Circulation: 40,000

7038 Environmental Bibliography
International Academy at Santa Barbara
5385 Hollister Avenue
#210
Santa Barbara, CA 93111
805-683-8889
FAX: 805-965-6071
info@iasb.org www.iasb.org
Over 615,000 citations are offered in this database, aimed at scientific, technical and popular periodical literature dealing with the environment. *$1750.00*
Bibliographic Founded: 1972 : online

7039 Environmental Career Directory
Gale Research
27500 Drake Road
Farmington Hills, MI 48331
248-699-4253
FAX: 248-699-8214 800-877-4253
galeord@gale.com www.gale.com
Companies and organizations that offer entry-level positions in environment related careers are listed. *$34.00*
350 pages Cloth

7040 Environmental Cost Estimating Software Report
Donley Technology
PO Box 152
Colonial Beach, VA 22443-0152
804-224-9427
FAX: 804-224-7958 800-201-1595
donleytech@donleytech.com
www.donleytech.com
Elizabeth Donley, Editor
John Donley, Editor
Profiles 20 software packages for estimating the cost of environmental projects, including detailed product descriptions, tables comparing system features, and contact information. *$195.00*

162 pages Founded: 1996 ISBN 1-891682-05-9
Printed in on matte stock

7041 **Environmental Health & Safety Dictionary**
ABS Group
PO Box 846304
Dallas, TX 75284-6304

FAX: 301-921-0264

Lydia Simpson, Manager

7042 **Environmental Industries Marketplace**
Gale Research
27500 Drake Road
Farmington Hills, MI 48331
248-699-4253
FAX: 248-699-8214 800-877-4253
galeord@gale.com www.gale.com
List of over 10,000 companies in environment-related activities. *$190.00*
800 pages

7043 **Environmental Law Handbook**
ABS Group
PO Box 846304
Dallas, TX 75284-6304

FAX: 301-921-0264

7044 **Environmental Protection Agency Headquarters Telephone Directory**
Environmental Protection Agency
1200 Pennsylvania Avenue NW
Pittsburgh, PA 15250-7954
412-442-4000
FAX: 202-512-2250
www.epa.gov/customerservice/phonebook/

Ken Bowman, Executive Director

Directory of services and supplies to the industry. *$15.00*
400 pages

7045 **Environmental Resource Handbook**
Grey House Publishing
185 Millerton Road
PO Box 860
Millerton, NY 12546
518-890-0526
FAX: 518-789-0545 800-562-2139
books@greyhouse.com
www.greyhouse.com

Leslie Mackenzie, Publisher
Richard Gottlieb, Editor

The most up-to-date and comprehensive source for Environmental Resources and Statistics. *$155.00*
1200 pages ISBN 1-592370-90-X

7046 **Environmental Statutes**
Government Institutes
4 Research Place
Suite 200
Rockville, MD 20850-3226
301-921-2323
FAX: 301-921-0264 www.govinst.com
Two-volume set. Complete and exact text of the statues and amendments made by Congress concerning environmental law. *$125.00*
1678 pages Paperback ISBN 0-865879-33-8

7047 **Fibre Market News: Paper Recycling Markets Directory**
Recycling Media Group GIE Publishers
4012 Bridge Avenue
Cleveland, OH 44113-3320
216-961-4130
FAX: 216-961-0364 800-456-0707
A list of over 2,000 dealers, brokers, packers and graders of paper stock in the United States and Canada. *$28.00*
Annual
Circulation: 3,000

7048 **Floodplain Management: State & Local Programs**
Association of State Floodplain Managers

2809 Fish Hatchery Road
Suite 204
Madison, WI 53713
608-274-0123
FAX: 608-274-0696
asfpm@floods.org www.floods.org

Larry A Larson, Executive Director
Alison Stierli, Member Services Coordinator
Anita Larson, Member Services
Mark Riebau, Project Manager

The most comprehensive source assembled to date, this report summarizes and analyzes various state and local programs and activities. *$25.00*

7049 **Gale Environmental Almanac**
Gale Research
27500 Drake Road
Farmington Hills, MI 48331
248-699-4253
FAX: 248-699-8214 800-877-4253
galeord@gale.com www.gale.com

Allen Paschal, Chief Executive Officer

List of environmental organizations, national parks and federally protected lands is available through this directory. *$79.95*

7050 **Gale Environmental Sourcebook**
Gale Research
27500 Drake Road
Farmington Hills, MI 48331
248-699-4253
FAX: 248-699-8214 800-877-4253
galeord@gale.com www.gale.com

Allen Paschal, Chief Executive Officer

Thousands of organizations, government agencies and educational programs dealing with environmental issues are listed. *$80.00*
934 pages Biennial

7051 **Geothermal Progress Monitor**
Office of Geothermal Technologies EE-12

1000 Independence Avenue SW
Washington, DC 20585-0001
202-586-1361
FAX: 202-586-8185

Allan J Jelacic, Director

Lists of operating, planned and under construction geothermal electric generating plants; geothermal articles and publications; federal and state government employees active in geothermal energy development.
Annual

7052 **Grey House Safety & Security Directory**
Grey House Publishing
185 Millerton Road
PO Box 860
Millerton, NY 12546
518-890-0526
FAX: 518-789-0545 800-562-2139
books@greyhouse.com
www.greyhouse.com

Leslie Mackenzie, Publisher
Richard Gottlieb, Editor

Two-volume guide to the safety and security industry, including articles, checklists, OSHA regulations and product listings. The 16 chapters focus on creating and maintaing a safe and secure enviroment, and deal specifically with hazardous materials, noise and vibration, workplace preparation and maintenance, electrical and lighting safety, fire and rescue and more. Accepts advertising. *$225.00*
1500 pages Annual ISBN 1-592370-67-5

7053 **Handling Dyes Safely - A Guide for the Protection of Workers Handling Dyes**
ETAD North America
1850 M Street NW
Suite 700
Washington, DC 20036
202-721-4154
FAX: 202-296-8120 www.etad.com

Dr C Tucker Helmes, Executive Director

7054 **Hazardous Materials Guide**
JJ Keller
PO Box 368
Neenah, WI 54957-0368
920-722-2848
FAX: 800-727-7516 800-327-6868
sales@jjkeller.com www.jjkeller.com

Webb Shaw, Editor

A complete reference guide of hazardous materials regulations.

7055 **Hazardous Waste Guide**
JJ Keller
PO Box 368
Neenah, WI 54957-0368
920-722-2848
FAX: 800-727-7516 800-327-6868
sales@jjkeller.com www.jjkeller.com

Webb Shaw, Editor

Contains word-for-word regulations.

7056 **Hydro Review: Industry Sourcebook Issue**
HCI Publications
410 Archibald Street
Kansas City, MO 64111-3001
816-931-1311
FAX: 816-931-2015
hci@aol.com www.hcipub.com

Carl Vansant, Editor-in-Chief

List of over 800 manufacturers and suppliers of products and services to the hydroelectric industry in the US and Canada. *$20.00*
180 pages Annual December Founded: 1984
Circulation: 5000
Printed in 4 colors on glossy stock

7057 **IES Membership Directory**
International Ecotourism Society
733 15th Street NW
Suite 1000
Washington, DC 20005
202-547-9203
FAX: 202-387-7915
ecomail@ecotourism.org
www.ecotourism.org

Martha Honey, Executive Director
Amos Bien, Director International Programs
Neal Inamdar, Director Finance/Administration

Annual

7058 **International Directory of Human Ecologists**
Society for Human Ecology
College of the Atlantic
105 Eden Street
Bar Harbor, ME 04609-0180
207-288-5015
FAX: 207-288-3780
carter@ecology.coa.edu
www.societyforhumanecology.org

Barbara Carter, Assistant to Executive Director

Irregular

7059 **LEXIS Environmental Law Library**
Mead Data Central
9443 Springboro Pike
Dayton, OH 45401

FAX: 518-487-3584 888-223-6337

Andrew Prozes, Chief Executive Officer

This database contains decisions related to environmental law from the Supreme Court and other legislative bodies.

Full-text

7060 **National Directory of Conservation Land Trusts**
Land Trust Alliance
1319 F Street NW
Suite 501
Washington, DC 20004-1106
202-638-4725
FAX: 202-638-4730
lta@lta.org www.lta.org

More than 1,200 nonprofit land conservation organizations at the local and regional levels are profiled. *$12.00*

210 pages Biennial

7061 **National Environmental Data Referral Service**
US National Environmental Data Referral Service
1825 Connecticut Avenue NW
Washington, DC 20235-0003
202-606-4089

More than 22,200 data resources that have available data on climatology and meteorology, ecology and pollution, geography, geophysics and geology, hydrology and limnology, oceanography and transmissions from remote sensing satellites.

Quarterly

7062 **National Organic Directory**
Community Alliance with Family Farmers
PO Box 363
Davis, CA 95617-0363
530-756-8518
FAX: 530-756-7857 800-892-3832
nod@caff.org www.caff.org

Wriiten for all sectors of the booming organic food and fiber industry. Offers international listing with full contact information and extensive, cross-referenced index - Also provides regulatory updates, essays by industry leaders and other ressources. *$47.95*

324 pages Annual Founded: 1983 ISBN 1-891894-04-8
Circulation: 2,500

7063 **Occupational Safety and Health Law Handbook**
ABS Group
PO Box 846304
Dallas, TX 75284-6304

FAX: 301-921-0264

7064 **POWER**
US Department of Energy
Forrestal Building
5H - 021
Washington, DC 20585-0001
202-646-5095
FAX: 202-586-1605
roger.meyer@hd.doe.gov
www.eren.doe.gov

A large database offersing information on all forms of energy, including fossil, nuclear, solar, geothermal and electrical.

Bibliographic

7065 **Pollution Abstracts**
Cambridge Scientific Abstracts
7200 Wisconsin Avenue
Suite 601
Bethesda, MD 20814-4823
301-961-6750
FAX: 301-961-6720
market@csa.com www.csa.com

James P McGinty, President
Ted Caris, Publisher
Evelyn Beck, Editor
Mark Furneaux, VP Marketing
Angela Hitti, Production Manager

This database offers information on environmental pollution research and related engineering studies. *$985.00*

Monthly

7066 **Public Citizen Organizations**
Public Citizen
215 Pennsylvania Avenue SE
Washington, DC 20003-1155
202-546-4996
FAX: 202-547-7392 cmep@citizen.org

Neol Pettie, Organizer
Patricia Lovera, Organizer
Ronald Taylor, Manager

We provide many publications regarding nuclear safety, nuclear waste, water, food, and energy deregulation.

Annual

7067 **RCRA Hazardous Wastes Handbook**
ABS Group
PO Box 846304
Dallas, TX 75284-6304

FAX: 301-921-0264

7068 **Recycling Sourcebook**
Gale Research
27500 Drake Road
Farmington Hills, MI 48331
248-699-4253
FAX: 248-699-8214 800-877-4253
galeord@gale.com www.gale.com

Organizations concerned with policies and programs of recycling in the US are listed. *$80.00*

563 pages

7069 **Recycling Today: Recycling Products & Services Buyers Guide**
Recycling Today GIE Publishers
4012 Bridge Avenue
Cleveland, OH 44113-3320
216-961-4130
FAX: 216-961-0364

Richard Foster, President
James Keefe, Publisher
Mark Phillips, Editor
Rosalie Slusher, Circulation Director
Jami Childs, Production Manager

Directory of services and supplies to the industry. *$19.95*

Annual
Circulation: 22,000

7070 **Research Services Directory**
Grey House Publishing
185 Millerton Road
PO Box 860
Millerton, NY 12546
518-890-0526
FAX: 518-789-0545 800-562-2139
books@greyhouse.com
www.greyhouse.com

Leslie Mackenzie, Publisher
Richard Gottlieb, Editor

This Ninth Edition provides access to well over 7,700 independent Commercial Research Firms, Corporate Research Centers and Laboratories offering contract services for hands-on, basic or applied research. *$550.00*

992 pages Annual ISBN 1-592370-03-9

7071 **US Environmental Law and Regulations**
ABS Group
PO Box 846304
Dallas, TX 75284-6304

FAX: 301-921-0264

7072 **Using Multiobjective Management to Reduce Flood Losses in Your Watershed**
Association of State Floodplain Managers
2809 Fish Hatchery Road
Suite 204
Madison, WI 53713
608-274-0123
FAX: 608-274-0696
asfpm@floods.org www.floods.org

Larry A Larson, Executive Director
Alison Stierli, Member Services Coordinator

Introduction to multiobjective management and planning process that helps a community select suitable flood loss reduction measures. *$15.00*

7073 **Waste Manifest Software Report**
Donley Technology
PO Box 152
Colonial Beach, VA 22443-0152
804-224-9427
FAX: 804-224-7958 800-201-1595
donleytech@donleytech.com
www.donleytech.com

Elizabeth Donley, Editor

Profiles 30 software packages for solid and hazardous waste management, including detailed product descriptions, tables comparing system features, and contact information. *$97.50*

118 pages Founded: 1996 ISBN 1-891682-01-6
Printed in on matte stock

7074 Water Environment and Technology Buyers Guide/Yearbook
Water Environment Federation
601 Wythe Street
Alexandria, VA 22314-1994
703-684-2400
FAX: 703-684-2492 800-666-0206
Glenn Reinhardt, Executive Director
Offers listings of the Water Environment Federation and consultant members.
$28.00
Annual

7075 Water Environmental Federation
601 Wythe Street
Alexandria, VA 22314-1919
703-684-2400
FAX: 703-684-2492 800-666-0206
Mike Nutter, Controller
Matt Rowan, Marketing Manager
Bill Bertera, Executive Director
Book publishing

7076 Weather America
Grey House Publishing
185 Millerton Road
PO Box 860
Millerton, NY 12546
518-890-0526
FAX: 518-789-0545 800-562-2139
books@greyhouse.com
www.greyhouse.com
Leslie Mackenzie, Publisher
David Garoogian, Editor
Provides extensive climatological data for over 4,000 national and cooperative weather stations throughout the US.
$175.00
2,013 pages ISBN 1-891482-29-7

7077 Who's Who in Training
National Environmental, Safety and Health Training
5320 N 16th Street
Suite 114
Phoenix, AZ 85016-3241
602-956-6099
FAX: 602-956-6399
info@neshta.org www.neshta.org
Charles L Richardson, Executive Director
Joan J Jennings, Manager Association Services
Suzanne Lanctot, Manager Certification/Membership
Annual

7078 Wilderness Preservation: A Reference Handbook
ABC-CLIO
PO Box 1911
Santa Barbara, CA 93116-1911
805-705-9339
Offers a list of agencies and organizations concerned with wilderness preservation.

7079 Wind Energy Conversion Systems
South Dakota Renewable Energy Association
PO Box 491
Pierre, SD 57501-0491
605-224-8641
Offers valuable information for electrical-output wind machine manufacturers.
$2.00
45 pages Annual

7080 World Directory of Environmental Organizations
California Institute of Public Affairs
517 19th Street
#189040
Sacramento, CA 95814-1103
916-442-2472
FAX: 916-442-2478
info@cipahq.org
www.cipahq.org/cipa.htm
Over 2,500 governmental, intergovernmental and United Nations organizations are covered. *$47.00*
232 pages

7081 Your Financial Institution & the Environ- ment
Environmental Bankers Association
510 King Street
Suite 410
Alexandria, VA 22314
703-549-0977
FAX: 703-548-5945 800-966-7475
eba@envirobank.org
www.envirobank.org
D J Telego, Executive Co-Director
Annual

7082 Your Resource Guide to Environmental Organizations
Smiling Dolphin Press
4 Segura
Irvine, CA 92612-1726

Information is offered, in three separate sections, on nongovernmental organizations, federal agencies and state agencies that address environmental concerns.
$15.95
514 pages

Industry Web Sites

7083 www.adirondackcouncil.org
Adirondack Council

Research, education and advocacy to protect the natural character and communities of the Adirondack Park. Also publishes an annual State of Park Report and quarterly newsletters.

7084 www.aeecenter.org
Association of Energy Engineers

Source of information on the field of energy efficiency, utility deregulation, plant engineering, facility management and environmental compliance. Membership includes more than 8,000 professionals and certification programs. Offers seminars, conferences, job listings and certification programs.

7085 www.aga.org
American Gas Association

Association for the natural gas industry.

7086 www.america-the-beautiful-fund.or g
America the Beautiful Fund

Groups and private citizens that improve the quality of the environment.

7087 www.apwa.net
American Public Works Association

The American Public Works Association is an international educational and professional association of public agencies, private sector companies, and individuals dedicated to providing high quality public works goods and services. APWA provides a forum in which public works professionals competency, increase the performance of their agencies and companies, and bring important public works-related topics to public attention in local, state, and federal areas. Mailing list for members only.

7088 www.asbpa.org
American Shore and Beach Preservation Association

Federal, state and local government agencies and individuals interested in conservation, development and restoration of beaches and shorefronts.

7089 www.ases.org
American Solar Energy Society

Individuals and professionals working in the field of solar energy and conservation.

7090 www.asfe.org
ASFE

Not-for-profit trade association. Helps geoprofessional, environmental and civil engineering firms profit through professionalism.

7091 www.audbon.org
National Audubon Society

Conserves and restores natural ecosystems, focusing on birds, other wildlife, and thier habitats for the benefit of humanity and the earth's biological diversity.

7092 www.bisoncentral.com
National Bison Association

The National Bison Association was formed to promote the production, marketing, and preservation of bison.

7093 www.blr.com
Business & Legal Reports

Provides essential tools for safety and environmental compliance and training needs

7094 **www.cbemw.org**
Citizens for a Better Environment

For citizens concerned with environmental protection. Maintains library.

7095 **www.cnie.org/nle**
National Library for the Environment

Environment-related information: daily environment and congressional news, upcoming conferences, education resources and congressional research reports.

7096 **www.conservation.state.mo.us**
Department of Conservation

Focuses on conservation and the importance of protecting the environment.

7097 **www.conservationfund.org**
Conservation Fund

Works with private and public agencies and organizations to protect wildlife habitats, historic sites and parks.

7098 **www.conservationtreaty.org**
Conservation Treaty Support Fund

Promotes awareness, understanding and support of conservation treaties and their goals.

7099 **www.earthisland.org/ei**
Earth Island Institute

Seeks to prevent destruction of environment and sponsors fund drives and activist projects to protect wildlife.

7100 **www.earthsite.org**
Earth Society Foundation

News of interest in environmental and sociological issues. Purpose is to promote Earth Day and the Earth Trustee agenda.

7101 **www.eia-usa.org**
Environmental Information Association

Nonprofit organization dedicated to providing environmental information to individuals, members and the industry. Disseminates information on the abatement of asbestos and lead-based paint, indoor air quality, safety and health issues, analytical issues and environmental site assessments.

7102 **www.epa.gov**
US Environmental Protection Agency

7103 **www.ethenolrfa.org**
Renewable Fuels Association

Members are companies and individuals involved in the production and use of ethanol.

7104 **www.floods.org**
Association of State Floodplain Managers

Promotes common interest in flood damage abatement, supports environmental protection for floodplain areas, provides education on floodplain management practices and policy, and urges incorporating multi-objective management, approaches to solve local flooding problems.

7105 **www.greyhouse.com**
Grey House Publishing

Selected Grey House directories in the fields of business, health and education are available online. Users can search our online databases by several different search criteria, such as product categories, geographic area, sales volume and much, much more. Full Grey House catalog and online ordering also available.

7106 **www.ia-usa.org**
National BioEnergy Industries Association

7107 **www.iaee.org**
International Association for Energy Economics

Association for those involved in energy economics including publications, consultants, energy database software.

7108 **www.iaia.org**
International Association for Impact Assessment

IAIA provides a forum for the exchange of the ideas and experiences to stimulate innovation in assessing, managing and mitigating the consequences of development.

7109 **www.iwla.org**
Isaak Walton League

Conducts research and education on river ecosystems and healthy fisheries.

7110 **www.joincca.org**
Coastal Conservation Association

Seeks to advance protection and conservation of all marine life. Conducts seminars and bestows awards.

7111 **www.lib.duke.edu/forest/**
Forest History Society

Non-profit educational institution that explores the history of the environment, forestry, and conservation.

7112 **www.members.aol.com/rccouncil**
Rachael Carson Council

Seeks to promote awareness of the problems of environmental contamination and by serving as an information clearing house on chemical contaminates, especially pesticides.

7113 **www.mtsociety.org**
Marine Technology Society

Addresses coastal zone management, marine mineral and energy resources, marine environmental protection, and ocean engineering issues.

7114 **www.nacdnet.org**
National Association of Conservation Districts

Association for those interested in the environment.

7115 **www.naem.org**
National Association for Environmental Management

Dedicated to advancing the profession of environmental management and supports the professional corporate and facility environmental manager.

7116 **www.nalms.org**
North American Lake Management Society

Members are academics, lake managers and others interested in furthering the understanding of lake ecology.

7117 **www.napcor.com**
National Association for Pet Container Resources

National trade association which promotes the recycling of food containers made from PET plastic (containers with recycle code #1).

7118 **www.nationalwoodlands.org**
National Woodland Owners Association

Provides timely information about forestry and forest practices with news from washington,Dc and state capitals. written for non-industrial land owners. Includes state landowner association news.

7119 **www.ncat.org**
National Center for Appropriate Technology

A resource center for information and expertise on methods of promoting conservation and energy self sufficiency. The term, appropriate technology, is defined as a small-scale, environmentally sound, low-cost, locally based approach to problems with an emphasis on self help.

7120 **www.neha.org**
National Environmental Health Association

Association for suppliers of environmental educational materials.

7121 **www.noaa.gov**
National Oceanic and Atmospheric Administration

National weather forecasts, statistics, searchable databases, agency directory and links to related agencies and sites.

7122 **www.pollutiononline.com**
Pollution Online

For vendors and professionals in pollution equipment and control industries. News, product information, links to related web sites and business information.

7123 **www.purezone.com**
PureZone

Devoted to indoor air quality. Discussion forum moderated by industry experts on topics such as sensors and transducers technology.

7124 **www.recycle-steel.srs**
Steel Recycling Institute

Promotes steel recycling and works to forge a coalition of steelmakers, can manufacturers, legislators, government officials, solid waste managers, business and consumer groups.

7125 **www.rnrf.org**
Renewable Natural Resources Foundation

A consortium of professional and scientific societies whose members are concerned with the advancement of research, education, scientific practice and policy formulation for the conservation, replenishment and use of the earth's renewable natural resources.

7126 **www.sca-inc.org**
Student Conservation Association

7127 **www.socma.com**
Silicone Health Council

Coordinates health, environmental and safety programs. Conveys scientifically sound information about silicones.

7128 **www.techknow.org**
TechKnow

Lists environmentally friendly remediation and ozone-depleting substance management resources.

7129 **www.terrassa.pnl.gov:2080/hydrology**
Hydrology Web

Lists of related internet resource lists.

7130 **www.usace.army.mil**
US Army Corps of Engineers

Information on flood control, environmental protection, disaster response, military construction and support of others through the sharing of engineering expertise with other agencies, state and local governments, academia and foreign nations.

7131 **www.woodlandowners.org**
National Woodland Owners Association

Provides timely information about forestry and forest practices with news from washington,Dc and state capitals. written for non-industrial land owners. Includes state landowner association news.

7132 **www.wqa.org**
Water Quality Association

An international nonprofit trade association representing retail/dealers and manufacturer/suppliers in the point of use/entry water quality improvement industry. Membership benefits and services include technical and scientific information, educational seminars and home correspondence course books, professional certification and discount services.

Associations

7133 American Academy of Equine Art
c/o Kentucky Horse Park
4089 Iron Works Parkway
Lexington, KY 40511
859-281-6031
FAX: 859-281-6043
julieb@aaea.net www.aaea.net
Shelley Hunter, Executive Director
Julie Buchanan, Director
Members are professional artists who are willing and qualified to exhibit works of equine art and to teach the subject.
90 Members Founded: 1980

7134 American Association of Museums
1575 Eye Street NW
Suite 400
Washington, DC 20005
202-289-1818
FAX: 202-289-6578
webmaster@aam-us.org
www.aam-us.org
Louis B Casagrande, Chairman
Jeffrey N Rudolph, Vice Chair
Edward Able, Chief Executive Officer
Patrick Gossett, Executive Assistant
Dedicated to promoting excellence within the museum community. Through advocacy, professional education, information exchange, accreditation and guidance on current professional standards of performance, AAM assists museum staff, boards and volunteers across the country to better serve the public.
16000 Members Founded: 1906

7135 American Business Media
675 3rd Avenue
New York, NY 10017-5704
212-661-6360
FAX: 212-370-0736
info@abmmail.com
www.americanbusinessmedia.com
Gordon Hughes, President/CEO
Jean St George, CFO
John Holden, VP
Melanie Rose, VP
An association for business-to-business information providers, including producers of print publications, websites, trade shows and other media.
Founded: 1906

7136 American Society of Association Executives
1575 I Street NW
Washington, DC 20005
202-626-2723
FAX: 202-371-8315
service@asaenet.org www.asaenet.org
Anetha W Grant, Vice Chair Development
Richard B Green, Chair
Michael E Gallery, Vice Chair Research
John Graham, President
Seeks to provide a medium for the basic principles of association organization.
21M Members Founded: 1920

7137 Association Management Companies Companies
100 North 20th Street
4th Floor
Philadelphia, PA 19103
215-564-3484
FAX: 215-564-2175
Info@AMCinstitute.org
www.iaamc.org
Robert Waller Jr, President
Suzanne Pine, VP
John Ruffin, Sec/Treasurer
The IAAMC includes active member companies through the United States, Canada and Europe. Associate memberships are granted to companies that provide services to association management companies.
175 Members

7138 Association for Advancement of Cost
209 Prairie Avenue
Suite 100
Morgantown, WV 26501
304-296-8444
FAX: 304-291-5728 800-858-2678
info@aacei.org www.aacei.org
William Kraus, President
James R Baxter, Executive Director
Robert B Brown, VP Finance
Barry G McMillan, Executive Director
Provides its members with the resources they need to enhance their performance and ensure continued growth and success. Serves cost management professionals: cost management and engineers, project managers, planners and schedulers, estimators and bidders, and value engineers.
5500 Members Founded: 1956

7139 Association for Convention Marketing
204 E Street NE
Washington, DC 20002
202-547-8030
FAX: 202-547-6348
info@acmenet.org www.acmenet.org
Sheila Crowley, Executive VP
R Frederick Wise, President
Shawn Corwin, First VP
Michelle L Bucks, Active-Member Director
John Oliver, Affiliate-Member Director
Annual meetings for marketing and sales executives.

7140 Association for Convention Operations
191 Clarksville Road
Princeton Junction, NJ 08550
609-799-3712
FAX: 609-799-7032
info@acomonline.org
www.acomonline.org
Larry W Wilson Jr, President
Norman Ford, First VP
Convention service directors and managers from hotels, convention centers and convention visitors bureaus.
400 Members Founded: 1988

7141 Association of Collegiate Conference and Special Events
Colorado State University
8037 Campus Delivery
Fort Collins, CO 80523-8037
970-491-5151
FAX: 970-491-0667 970-877-2233
Deborah Blom, Executive Director
Becky Dakin, Member Services Manager
Lori Everhart, Electronic Communications
Members are college and university conference and special events directors, professionals and others who design, market and coordinate conferences and special events.
1400 Members Founded: 1980

7142 Association of International Meeting Planners
2547 Monroe Street
Dearborn, MI 48124-3013
313-563-0360
FAX: 313-563-1448
Meeting planners.
40 Members Founded: 1986

7143 Association of Science-Technology Centers
1025 Vermont Avenue NW
Suite 500
Washington, DC 20005-3516
202-783-7200
FAX: 202-783-7207
info@astc.org www.astc.org
Per-Edvin Persson, President
Lesley Lewis, VP
Wit Ostrenko, Secretary/Treasurer
William Booth, Member at Large
Bonnie VanDorn, Executive Director
Organization of science centers and museums dedicated to futhering the public understanding of science among increasingly diverse audiences. Encourges excellence and innovation in informal science learning by serving and linking its members worldwide and advancing their common goals.
550 Members Founded: 1973

7144 Center for Exhibition Industry Research
2301 S Lake Shore Drive
Suite 1002
Chicago, IL 60616
312-808-2347
FAX: 312-949-3472
ceir@mpea.com www.ceir.org
Charles D Yuska, Chair
Paul Dykstra, Vice Chair
David A Korse, Secretary/Treasurer
Douglas L Ducate, Staff
Thomas Ackert, Executive Director
The Center for Exhibition Industry Research is an apolitical, nonprofit orgnization with the dual mission of producing research that supports the unique features and value of exhibitors; then, using that research and other tools to promote the image and growth of the exhibition industry

7145 Computer Event Marketing Association
19 Intermediate Unit Drive
Suite 203
Coal Center, PA 15423
724-938-0432
FAX: 724-938-8175
cema@cemaonline.com
www.cemaonline.com
Kimberley Gishler, President
Mitch Ahiers, VP
Alexia Henrie, Secretary
Trinette R Cunningham, Executive Staff
Professionals from the event, trade show and marketing communications industry. Striving to be the definitive resource for event marketing professionals in the information technology industry.
250 Members Founded: 1990

7146 Connected International Meeting
9200 Bayard Place
Fairfax, VA 22032
703-286-2142
FAX: 703-991-2292
info@cimpa.org www.cimpa.org
Andrea Sigler, President/CEO

Members are conference and convention planners with a certificate in convention management. Specializes in planning meetings events, incentives, using the internet.
8000 Members Founded: 1982

7147 Convention Industry Council
1620 Eye St NW
Ste 615
Washington, DC 20006
202-429-8634
FAX: 202-463-8498 877-429-8634

Thomas M Mobley Jr, Chair
John H Graham, Vice Chair
Mary Power, President/CEO
Amy Hawthorne, Project Coordinator

An organization that represents more than 98,000 individuals as well as 15,000 firms and properties involved in the meetings, conventions and exhibitions industries.
Founded: 1949

7148 Convention Liaison Council
10200 W 44th Avenue
Suite 310
Wheat Ridge, CO 80033-2840
303-420-2902
FAX: 303-422-8894
clc@resourcenter.com www.clc.org

Francine Butler, Executive VP

Members are associations which are directly involved in the convention, exposition, trade show and meeting industry.

7149 Display Distributors Association
Modern Display
424 S 700 E
Salt Lake City, UT 84102-2864
801-355-7427
FAX: 801-521-3040
Members are distributors of display equipment.
16 Members Founded: 1950

7150 Exhibit Designers & Producers Association
1100 Johnson Ferry Road
Suite 300
Atlanta, GA 30342
404-303-7310
FAX: 404-252-0774
pdicks@edpa.com www.edpa.com

Peter A. Dicks, Executive Director
Wendy M. McGar, Associate Director
Norm Friedrich, President
Mark Johnson, VP
Dan Cantor, Treasurer

Internationally recognized, national trade association with more than 370 corporate members from 18 countries that are engaged in the design, manufacture, transport, installation and service of displays and exhibits primarily for the trade show industry.
370 Members Founded: 1956

7151 Exhibition Services and Contractors Association
2340 E Trinity Mills Road
#100
Carrollton, TX 75006
469-574-0698
FAX: 469-574-0697
larry@esca.org www.esca.org

Larry Arnaudet, Executive Director

Members are full-service general exposition contractors, and specialty firms related to the exposition service industry such as security, audio-visual, electrical and floral companies.
Founded: 1970

7152 Exposition Service Contractors Association
400 S Houston Street
Suite 210
Dallas, TX 75202-4830
214-742-9217
FAX: 214-741-2519 www.esca.org

ED Simmons, Associate Director

Annual guide to exposition service is distributed annually and lists safety regulations and building rules in major US convention centers.
120 Members Founded: 1970

7153 Goldstein and Associates
1150 Yale Street
Suite 12
Santa Monica, CA 90403-4734
310-828-1309
FAX: 310-829-1169

Steve Goldstein, Publisher

Association for exhibit managers, tradeshow managers and other exhibition professionals.
Founded: 1987

7154 Healthcare Convention & Exhibitors Association
1100 Johnson Ferry Road
Suite 300
Atlanta, GA 30342
404-252-3663
FAX: 404-252-0774
hcea@kellencompany.com
www.hcea.org

Eric Allen, Executive Vice President
Jackie Beaulieu, Associate Director

HCEA's Mission to improve the effectiveness of all convention, meetings and exhibitions for the healthcare industry. The HealthcareConvention @ Exhibitions Association (HCEA) is a trade association of more then 700 oganizations united by their common desire to increase the effectiveness and efficiency of healthcare conventions and exhibitions as as educational marketing medium.
700 Members Founded: 1930

7155 Hospitality Sales & Marketing Association International
8201 Greensboro Drive
Suite 300
McLean, VA 22102
703-610-9024
FAX: 703-610-9005
info@hsmai.org www.hsmai.org

Mary Hanger, Manager/Programs

HSMAI is a global organization of sales and marketing professionals representing all segments of the hospitality industry.
7000 Members Founded: 1927

7156 Industrial Fabrics Association
1801 County Road B W
Roseville, MN 55113-4061
651-222-2508
FAX: 651-631-9334 800-225-4324
generalinfo@ifai.com www.ifai.com

Stephen M Warner, President
Mary J Hennessey, VP Communications

7157 International Association for Exhibition Management
811 LBJ Freeway
Suite 750
Dallas, TX 75251-1313
972-458-8002
FAX: 972-458-8119
iaem@iaem.org www.iaem.org

Steven G Hacker, CAE, President
Cathy Breden, CAE, SVP
Susan Brower, Director
Marketing/Communications

Members are managers of shows, exhibits and expositions; associate members are industry suppliers.
3500 Members Founded: 1928

7158 International Association for Modular Exhibitry
155 W Street
Suite 3
Wilmington, MA 01887-3064
978-988-1200

Irving Sacks, Executive Director

Members are companies that promote the use of modular exhibits for trade shows and museums.
47 Members Founded: 1987

7159 International Association of Assembly Management
635 Fritz Drive
Coppell, TX 75019
972-906-7441
FAX: 972-906-7418 800-935-4226
don.hancock@iaam.org
www.iaam.org

Mike Kelly, CFE

Members are managers of auditoriums, arenas, convention centers, stadiums and performing arts centers.
400 Members Founded: 1924

7160 International Association of Conference Centers
243 N Lindbergh Boulevard
Saint Louis, MO 63141
314-991-4100
FAX: 314-993-8919
info@iacconline.org
www.iaccnorthamerica.org

Tom Bolman, Executive VP
Geoff Lawson, President
James Mahon, Director Marketing/PR

Facilities-based organization which advances the understanding and awareness of conference centers as distinct within the training, education, hospitality and travel fields.
377 Members Founded: 1981

7161 International Association of Fairs and Expositions
Box 985
Springfield, MO 65801
417-862-5771
FAX: 417-862-0156
www.fairsandexpos.com

Jim Tucker, President
Max Wilis, COO/CFO

Membership consists of individual agricultural fairs and regional associatins of agricultural fairs.
Founded: 1920

7162 International Festivals and Events Association
2601 Eastover Terrace
Boise, ID 83706
208-433-0950
FAX: 208-433-9812
kaye@ifea.com www.ifea.com
Steve Schmader, CFE, President/CEO
Kaye Campbell, CFE, SVP
Dolores Gorczyca, Secretary/Treasurer
Candace R Rhett, Communications
2500 Members Founded: 1956

7163 International Laser Display Association
3721 S.E. Henry Street
Portland, OR 97202
503-407-0289
FAX: 503-775-9358 www.laserist.org
David Lytle, Executive Director
ILDA members are individuals involved in the laser entertainment and display industry.
28 Members Founded: 1986

7164 International Special Events Society
401 N Michigan Avenue
Chicago, IL 60611-4267
312-091-1388
FAX: 312-673-6953 800-688-4737
info@ises.com www.ises.com
Kevin Hacke, Executive Director
Julianne Bendel, Operations Director
Cassie Lapekas, Operations Coordinator
Kristin Kindsvater, Membership Coordinator
Three thousand professionals in over a dozen countries representing special event producers, caterers, decorators, florists, destination management companies, rental companies, special effects experts, tent suppliers, audio-visual technicians, party and convention coordinators, ballon artists, educators, journalists, hotel sales managers, specialty entertainers, convention center managers and more.
4000 Members Founded: 1987

7165 Meeting Planners International
4455 LBJ Freeway
#1200
Dallas, TX 75244-5903
972-702-3000
FAX: 972-702-3070
feedback@mpiweb.org
www.mpiweb.org
Theresa Breining, Chairperson
Hugh Lee, Chairman
Christine Duffy, Vice Chairwoman Administration
John Parke, Vice Chairman Finance
Colin Rorrie, President
Meeting industry professionals who plan and/or manage meetings, trade shows and conferences for corporations, educational institutions and associations.
9M Members Founded: 1972

7166 Meeting Professionals International
3030 LBJ Freeway
Suite 1700
Dallas, TX 75234
972-023-3000
FAX: 972-702-3070
feedback@mpiweb.org
www.mpiweb.org
Colin C Rorrie, Jr PhD CAE, President/CEO
MPI members manage meetings and related activities for association, corporations, and educational institutions, or provide goods and services to the meetings industry.
1900 Members Founded: 1972

7167 National Association for Campus Activities
13 Harbison Way
Columbia, SC 29212
803-732-6222
FAX: 803-749-1047 800-845-2338
info@naca.org www.naca.org
Steve Westbrook, Director Student Affairs
Alan Davis, Executive Director
Gordon Schell, Manager/Member Services
Dawn Thomas, Director/Educational/Events
Erin Wilson, Manager Communications
Largest collegiate organization for campus activities. Purpose is to assist in marketing entertainment services to educational institutions and providing student leadership development programs and services.
1100 Members Founded: 1960

7168 National Association of Agricultural Fair Agencies
MI State Department of Agriculture
PO Box 30017
Lansing, MI 48909
517-373-9766
FAX: 517-373-9146
Carol Carlson, Secretary/Treasurer
U.S. and Canadian representatives of state/provincial agencies that are responsible for the support of education and agricultural fairs.
Founded: 1966

7169 National Association of Consumer Shows
147 SE 102nd Avenue
Portland, OR 97216
503-253-0832
FAX: 503-253-9172 800-728-6227
info@publicshows.com
www.publicshows.com
Michael Fisher, Executive Director
Todd Jameson, President
Nelson Ligori, Director
Nonprofit organization dedicated to furthering the interests of consumer show producers and suppliers.
265 Members Founded: 1987

7170 National Association of Professional Organizers
4700 W Lake Avenue
Glenview, IL 60025
847-375-4746
FAX: 877-734-8668
hq@napo.net www.napo.net
Louise Miller, Executive Director
Nicole Travis, Association Administrator
Members are time, productivity and organization management consultants.
1800 Members Founded: 1985

7171 National Catholic Educational Exhibitors
2621 Dryden Road
Suite 300
Dayton, OH 45439
937-293-1415
FAX: 937-293-1310 888-555-8512
Bret Thomas, Executive Director
Members are companies and individuals who exhibit at Catholic shows. Associate members are 150 Catholic school superintendents and administrators.
500 Members Founded: 1950

7172 National Coalition of Black Meeting Planners
8630 Fenton Street
#126
Silver Spring, MD 20910
301-879-9100
FAX: 301-588-0011
ncbmp@compuserve.com
www.ncbmp.com
John Crump, Chairman
Ana Aponte Curtis, President
Founded in 1983, nonprofit organization dedicated to the training needs of African American meeting planners.

7173 North American Farm Show Council
590 Woody Hayes Drive
Columbus, OH 43210-6131
614-292-4278
FAX: 614-292-9448
fendrick.1@osu.edu
www.farmshows.org
Craig Fendrick, Executive Coordinator
NAFSC members are agricultural equipment trade shows. Suppliers of services to shows can obtain an associate membership.
Founded: 1972

7174 Professional Convention Management
2301 S Lake Shore Drive
Chicago, IL 60616-1419
312-423-7262
FAX: 312-423-7222 877-827-7262
communications@pcma.org
www.pcma.org
Michael Payne, Chair
Lee Ann Burr, Vice Chair
Deborah Sexton, Chief Executive Officer
Supports business travel, the hospitality/hotel industry, and related event planning communities.

7175 Professional Show Managers Association
One Regency Drive
PO Box 30
Bloomfield, CT 06002
860-243-3977
FAX: 860-286-0787
msorensen@ssmgt.com
www.psmashows.org
Mitch Sorensen, Executive Director

7176 Religious Conference Management Assocation
One RCA Dome
Suite 120
Indianapolis, IN 46225
317-632-1888
FAX: 317-632-7909
rcma@rcmaweb.org
www.rcmaweb.org
Dewayne S Woodring, Executive Director/CEO
3200 Members Founded: 1972

7177 Society of Government Meeting Planners
908 King Street
Lower Level
Alexandria, VA 22314
703-549-0892
FAX: 703-549-0708
info@sgmp.org www.sgmp.org
Donna E Carey, President
Carl C Thompson, Executive Director
Ruth Harris, First VP
Claudette Ferris, Secretary
Trade association for government meeting planners and exhibitors.
3100 Members Founded: 1981

7178 Society of Independent Show Organizers
7000 W Southwest Highway
Chicago Ridge, IL 60415
708-361-0900
FAX: 708-361-6166
siso@tradeshownet.com
www.siso.org
James A Bracken, Chairman
Margaret Pederson, Vice Chair
Jason Chudnofsky, Director
Galen Poss, Treasurer
James Forlenza, Secretary
200 Members Founded: 1990

7179 Trade Show Exhibitors Association
McCormick Place, 2301 S Lane Shore Drive
Suite 1005
Chicago, IL 60616
312-842-8732
FAX: 312-842-8744
tsea@tsea.org www.tsea.org
Sal Cavallaro, Chairman
Arthur Veale, Vice Chairman
Ron Stevenson, Director
Supports marketing and management professionals.

7180 Visitor Studies Association
8175-A Sheridan Boulevard
Suite 362
Arvada, CO 80003-1928
303-467-2200
FAX: 303-467-0064
info@visitorstudies.org
www.visitorstudies.org
Alan Friedman, President
Ellen Cox, Manager
Members are professionals at various institutions interested in studying audience experiences at museums, zoos, parks, etc. Promotes research in visitor participation and application of such research to programming and policy.
365 Members Founded: 1991

Newsletters

7181 Affiliate Connection
International Festivals and Events Association
2601 Eastover Terrace
Boise, ID 83706
208-433-0950
FAX: 208-433-9812
kaye@ifea.com www.ifea.com
Steve Schmader, President/CEO
Kaye Campbell, SVP
Monthly

7182 Annual Conference Abstracts
Visitor Studies Association
8175-A Sheridan Boulevard
Suite 362
Arvada, CO 80003-1928
303-467-2200
FAX: 303-467-0064
info@visitorstudies.org
www.visitorstudies.org
Alan Friedman, President
Ellen Cox, Manager
Annual

7183 Aviso
American Association of Museums
1575 Eye Street NW
Suite 400
Washington, DC 20005-1113
202-289-1818
FAX: 202-289-6578
aviso@aam-us.org
http://www.aam-us.org
Susan Ciccotti, Senior Editor
Edward Able, CEO
John Strand, Publisher
Barry Pilson, Marketing Manager
Monthly newletter providing information on the museum world federallegislation, AAM activities and services and a job bank. *$40.00*
Monthly Founded: 1906
Circulation: 16500
Mailing list available for rent

7184 CEMA Communicator
Computer Event Marketing Association
1512 Weiskopf Loop
Round Rock, TX 78664
512-108-8330
FAX: 978-443-4715
info@cemaonline.com
http://www.cemaonline.com
Mitch Ahiers, President
Newsletter posted directly on the Internet.
Monthly Founded: 1990

7185 ESCA Voice Newsletter
Exhibition Services and Contractors Association
2260 Corporate Circle
Suite 400
Henderson, NV 80914
702-319-9561
FAX: 702-450-7732 877-792-3722
askus@esca.org www.esca.org
Susan L Schwartz, Director Communications
Quarterly

7186 Exhibition Perspectives
American Academy of Equine Art
c/o Kentucky Horse Park
4089 Iron Works Parkway
Lexington, KY 40511
859-281-6031
FAX: 859-281-6043
julieb@aaea.net www.aaea.net
Julie Buchanan, Director
Annual

7187 Fairs and Expositions
International Association of Fairs & Expositions
Box 985
Springfield, MO 65801
417-862-5771
FAX: 417-862-0156
www.fairsandexpos.com
Jim Tucker, President
Max Willis, COO/CFO
10/year

7188 Healthcare Convention and Exhibitors Association Newsletter
5775 Peachtree Dunwoody Road
Building G, Suite 500
Atlanta, GA 30342
404-252-3663
FAX: 404-252-0774
hcea@kellencompany.com
http://www.hcea.org
Eric Allen, Executive Director
Carol Wilson, Director Meetings
James Hladnik, President
News and events of the trade association of over 700 organizations involved in healthcare exhibiting or providing services to healthcare conventions, exhibitions and/or meetings. *$245.00*
Founded: 1930

7189 IEG Endorsement Insider
IEG
640 N La Salle Drive
Suite 600
Chicago, IL 60610-3777
312-944-1727
FAX: 312-944-1897 800-834-4850
ieg@endoresments.com
www.endoresments.com
Jim Andrews, Editor
John Ukman, Publisher
A newsletter covering the use of sports and entertainment personalities for endorsements, appearances and other marketing purposes. *$295.00*
Monthly

7190 IEG Sponsorship Report
IEG
640 N La Salle Drive
Suite 600
Chicago, IL 60610-3777
312-944-1727
FAX: 312-944-1897 800-834-4850
ieg@sponsorship.com
http://www.sponsorship.com
Lesa Ukman, Editor
John Ukman, Publisher
Bart Zautcke, CEO
Brad Smith, Marketing
Newsletter on sports, arts, event, entertainment and cause marketing. *$415.00*
8 pages Biweekly Founded: 1982
Circulation: 15000

7191 Insight
Healthcare Convention & Exhibitors Association
5775 Peachtree Dunwoody Road NE
Building G, Suite 500
Atlanta, GA 30342-1542
404-252-3663
FAX: 404-252-0774
hcea@kellencompany.com
http://www.assnhq.com
Robert Gelardi, Executive Director
Bill Anderson, Associate Director
These guidelines have been developed to assist association personnel in the planning of exhibits and conventions. The booklet includes information that should be contained in an exhibit prospectus.
Founded: 1964
Printed in 4 colors on glossy stock

7192 **NAAFA Newsletter**
National Association of Agricultural Fair Agencies
MI State Department of Agriculture
PO Box 30017
Lansing, MI 48909
517-373-9766
FAX: 517-373-9146
Carol Carlson, Secretary/Treasurer
Annual

7193 **NAFSC Brochure**
North American Farm Show Council
590 Woody Hayes Drive
Columbus, OH 43210-6131
614-292-4278
FAX: 614-292-9448
www.farmshows.org
Craig Fendrick, Executive Coordinator
Bi-Ennial

7194 **NCEE Bulletin**
National Catholic Educational Exhibitors
2621 Dryden Road
Suite 300
Dayton, OH 45439
937-293-1415
FAX: 937-293-1310 888-555-8512
Bret Thomas, Executive Director
Quarterly

7195 **Newsbytes**
Meeting Professionals International
3030 LBJ Freeway
Suite 1700
Dallas, TX 75234
972-023-3000
FAX: 972-702-3070
feedback@mpiweb.org
www.mpiweb.org
Colin C Rorrie, Jr PhD CAE, President/CEO
Weekly

7196 **Newsletter**
American Academy of Equine Art
c/o Kentucky Horse Park
4089 Iron Works Parkway
Lexington, KY 40511
859-281-6031
FAX: 859-281-6043
julieb@aaea.net www.aaea.net
Julie Buchanan, Director
Semi-Annual

7197 **Workshop Brochure**
American Academy of Equine Art
c/o Kentucky Horse Park
4089 Iron Works Parkway
Lexington, KY 40511
859-281-6031
FAX: 859-281-6043
julieb@aaea.net www.aaea.net
Julie Buchanan, Director
Annual

Magazines & Journals

7198 **Association Meetings**
Primedia
9800 Metcalf Avenue
Overland Park, KS 66212
913-341-1300
FAX: 913-967-1898
bblair@primediabusiness.com
http://www.meetingsnet.com
Betsy Blair, Editorial Director
Larry Keltto, Editor
Directed to association executive directors and meeting planners with the objective of aiding the planning, site selection, and organization of meetings and conventions. *$223.65*

Circulation: 20065
Printed in 4 colors

7199 **Convene**
Professional Convention Management Association
2301 S Lake Shore Drive
Suite 1001
Chicago, IL 60616-1419
312-423-7262
FAX: 312-423-7222 877-827-7262
sales@pcma.org http://www.pcma.org
David Kushner, Publisher
Michelle Russell, Editor
Peggy Swisher, Managing Editor
Deborah Sexton, CEO
Features emphasize solutions of practical and logistical problems concerning business travel, the hospitality/hotel industry, and related event planning topics
Monthly Founded: 1957
Circulation: 31608

7200 **Convention South**
2001 W First Street
2001 West First Street
Gulf Shores, AL 36542
251-968-5300
FAX: 251-968-4532
info@conventionsouth.com
http://www.conventionsouth.com
J Talty O'Connor, Editor/Publisher
Kristen S McIntosh, VP/Executive Editor
Pamela Redden, Marketing Services Manage
Suzanne Kellams, Manager, Circulation Development
For planners of meetings, conferences, seminars and similar events that are held in the South
Monthly Founded: 1983
Circulation: 18000
Printed in 4 colors on glossy stock

7201 **Corporate Meetings & Incentives**
Primedia
9800 Metcalf Avenue
Overland Park, KS 66212-2216
913-341-1300
FAX: 913-967-1898
bbair@primediabusiness.com
http://www.meetingsnet.com
Betsy Bair, Editorial Director
Melissa Fromento, Publisher
Senior executives guide to decision-making.
138 pages Monthly Founded: 1980
Circulation: 34246
Printed in 4 colors on glossy stock

7202 **ESCA Extra Magazine**
Exhibition Services and Contractors Association
2260 Corporate Circle
Suite 400
Henderson, NV 80914
702-319-9561
FAX: 702-450-7732 877-792-3722
askus@esca.org www.esca.org
Susan L Schwartz, CEM, Executive Director
Heather Geldner, Communications Director
Monthly

7203 **EXPO Magazine**
Expo Magazine
11600 College Boulevard
Overland Park, KS 66210
913-469-1185
FAX: 913-344-1486 800-444-4388
expo@halldata.com
http://www.expoweb.com
Susi Cordill, Circulation Manager
Donna Sanford, Publisher
Danica Tormohlen, Editor-in-Chief
Magazine for exposition managment. *$48.00*
134 pages Founded: 1989
Circulation: 7500 5830 names $130 per M.
Printed in 4 colors on glossy stock

7204 **Event Solutions**
Virgo Publishing
3300 N Central Avenue, Suite 2500
PO Box 40079
Phoenix, AZ 85067-0079
480-990-1101
FAX: 480-675-8151
esmag@vpico.com www.vpico.com/es
John Baragona, Group Publisher
Topics featured include decor, themes, high tech support, indoor facility equipment, food and beverage ideas, special effects, new products, and financial issues and regulations. Provides corporate, product and even profiles with suggestions from experts in the field. *$45.00*
Monthly
Circulation: 25,000

7205 **Events World**
International Special Events Society: Indiana
401 North Michigan Avenue
Suite 200
Chicago, IL 60611-4267
312-091-1388
FAX: 312-673-8206 800-688-4737
info@isesindiana.com
http://www.isesindiana.com
Sharon R Gorup, Editor
Gene Huddleson, President
Editorial contents include practical information on each of the seven disciplines, news on promotions, job banks, people in the industry, ISES activities and events, technology trends, and global vision information about environmental, legal and political issues relating to the special events industry.
Monthly Founded: 1987
Circulation: 20000

7206 **Exhibit Builder**
Exhibit Builder
22900 Ventura Boulevard #245
PO Box 4144
Woodland Hills, CA 91365
818-225-0100
FAX: 818-225-0138 800-356-4451
jillb@exhibitbuilder.net
http://www.exhibitbuilder.net
Jill Brookman, CEO/President
Judy Pomerantz, Managing Editor
Jollen Ryan, Circulation Manager
Scott Gray, Editors
Devoted to the business and technical interest of the designers and fabricators of exhibits for trade shows, museums and point of purchase displays, includes application articles, new products, and new technology for creating booths. *$40.00*

72 pages Annual+ Founded: 1983
Circulation: 15000
Printed in 4 colors on glossy stock

7207 **Exhibit Marketing Magazine**
Eaton Hall Publishing
256 Columbia Turnpike
Florham Park, NJ 07932-1231
973-514-5900
FAX: 973-514-5977 800-746-9646
info@eatonhall.com
www.eatonhall.com
Scott Goldman, Publisher
Eaton Hall is a publishing and trade show firm which specializes in bringing buyers and sellers together. *$5.00*
52 pages Quarterly Founded: 1990
Circulation: 31000
Printed in 4 colors on glossy stock

7208 **Exhibitor**
Exhibitor Magazine Group
206 S Broadway
Suite 745
Rochester, MN 55904-6565
507-289-6556
FAX: 507-289-5253 888-235-6155
lee@exhibitormagazine.com
http://www.exhibitornet.com
Lee Knight, CEO
John Pavek, VP Publishing
Cara Schulz, National Sales Manager
Nicole Brudos Ferrara, Managing Editor
Whitney Archibald, Editor
The magazine for trade show and event marketing management. *$78.00*
122 pages Monthly Founded: 1982
Circulation: 30000
Printed in 4 colors on glossy stock

7209 **Exhibitor Times**
Virgo Publishing
3300 N Central Avenue, Suite 2500
PO Box 40079
Phoenix, AZ 85067-0079
480-990-1101
FAX: 480-675-8146
etmag@vpico.com
www.exhibitor-times.com
Troy Bix, Publisher
Articles discuss the latest technology in booth displays, lighting, and location, and gives suggestions on creating memorable displays. *$70.00*
Monthly
Circulation: 15.000

7210 **Facilities & Destinations**
Bedrock Communications
650 1st Avenue
7th Floor
New York, NY 10016
212-532-4150
FAX: 212-213-6382
mikecaffin@aol.com
http://www.facilitiesonline.com
Stella Johnson, Senior Executive Editor
Serves the association meeting industry defined as finance, banking, health, education,religious, trade, labor, fraternal, manufacturing, civic, social, professional, government/military, association management companies, independent meeting planners, destination management companies, trade show/event production companies and other groups who use the facilities industry for meetings, conferences, exhibitions, trade shows and conventions.
45 pages Founded: 1988
Circulation: 34000+

7211 **Facilities & Event Management**
Bedrock Communications
650 1st Avenue
7th Floor
New York, NY 10016-3240
212-387-0155
FAX: 212-213-6382
mikecaffin@aol.com
http://www.facilitiesonline.com/
Michael Caffin, Managing Editor
Glen O'Grady, Sales Manager
Editorial articles solve problems based on industry facts and statistics and coverage encompasses various segments of the facilities industry, including: convention centers, exhibition halls, hotel/conference centers, civic centers, arenas, stadiums, arts centers, etc. Monthly features detail facility business activity and provide coverage of the products and services available. Subscription, $48.00 *$4.95*
52 pages Monthly
Circulation: 30000

7212 **IE - Business of International Events Magazine**
International Festivals and Events Association
2601 Eastover Terrace
Boise, ID 83706
208-433-0950
FAX: 208-433-9812
kaye@ifea.com www.ifea.com
Steve Schmader, President/CEO
Kaye Campbell, SVP
Quarterly

7213 **Inside Events**
Trio Communications
8899 Beverly Boulevard
#408
Los Angeles, CA 90048-2431
310-888-8566
FAX: 310-888-1866 trio8888@aol.com
Elisabeth Familian, Publisher
Articles include area listings of sites and vendors for any type of gathering. Profiles the creative ideas of industry professionals.
Quarterly
Circulation: 20,000

7214 **Insight**
Healthcare Convention & Exhibitors Association
5775-G Peachtree Dunwoody Road
Suite 500
Atlanta, GA 30342-1542
404-252-3663
FAX: 404-252-0774
hcea@kellencompany.com
http://www.hcea.org
Eric Allen, Executive Vice President
Carol Wilson, Meetings Director
Lyn Nabors, Manager
Providing health care convention education and news. *$29.00*
500 pages Founded: 1930
Circulation: 700

7215 **Insurance Conference Planner**
Primedia
9800 Metcalf Avenue
Overland Park, KS 66212
913-341-1300
FAX: 913-967-1898 866-505-7173
Betsy Bair, editorial director
Melissa Fromento, Publisher
Meeting and incentive strategies for the financial services industry.
148 pages Monthly Founded: 1965
Circulation: 8005
Printed in 4 colors on glossy stock

7216 **Laserist**
International Laser Display Association
3721 S.E. Henry Street
Portland, OR 97202
503-407-0289
FAX: 503-775-9358 www.laserist.org
David Lytle, Executive Director
Quarterly

7217 **Medical Meetings**
Primedia
11 Riverbend Dr South
Stamford, CT 06907
203-358-9900
FAX: 203-358-5812
mfromento@primediabusiness.com
http://www.meetingsnet.com
Betsy Bair, Editor Director
Melissa Framento, Publisher
International guide for health care and meeting planners.
106 pages Monthly Founded: 1973
Circulation: 10,823
Printed in 4 colors on glossy stock

7218 **Meeting Professional**
Meeting Professionals International
3030 LBJ Freeway
Suite 1700
Dallas, TX 75234
972-023-3000
FAX: 972-702-3070
feedback@mpiweb.org
www.mpiweb.org
Colin C Rorrie, Jr PhD CAE, President/CEO
Monthly

7219 **Meeting Professionals**
Meeting Professionals International
3030 LBJ Freeway
Suite 1700
Dallas, TX 75234-2759
972-702-3000
FAX: 972-702-3070
publications@mpiweb.org
http://www.mpiweb.org
Colin Rorrie, Jr, President/Chief Executive Officer
John Delavan, Editor-in-Chief
Blair Potter, Managing Editor
Stacy Clark, Marketing Manager
Furthers the professional development and education of all those who participate in the meetings industry. *$99.00*
Monthly Founded: 1972
Circulation: 28,000

7220 **Meetings & Conventions**
Reed Business Information
500 Plaza Drive
Secaucus, NJ 07094
201-021-1960
FAX: 201-902-2053
lcioffi@ntmllc.com
http://www.meetings-conventions.com
Bernard Lynch, Associate Editor
Lori Cioffi, Editor in Chief
Loren G. Edelstein, Executive Editor
Allen Sheinman, Managing Editor
Lisa Grimaldi, Senior Editor
Serves the corporate and independent travel and meeting planner with features on meeting facilities, hotels/airports/car rental, incentive travel options, trade show coverage, entertainment/leisure options and industry news. *$70.00*

Monthly Founded: 1965
Circulation: 70013

7221 **Meetings Industry**
Dunn Enterprises
513 Commerce Drive
Upper Marlboro, MD 20774-7434
301-249-4600
FAX: 301-249-9100
webmaster@jtdunnic.com
www.meetingsquest.com
Rob Davis, VP Marketing
Profiles meetings sites and accomodations for meetings of all sizes. Includes personnel appointments of other meeting planners.

Circulation: 35000

7222 **Museum News**
American Association of Museums
1575 Eye Street NW
Suite 400
Washington, DC 20005-1113
202-289-1818
FAX: 202-289-6578
aviso@aam-us.org
http://www.aam-us.org
Susan Breitkopf, Senior Editor
John Strand, Publisher
Jane Lusaka, Director/Publication
Edward Able, Chief Executive Officer
Includes articles about museum management, curatorship, marketing, culture touring, funding, security, ethics and politics. Readers will find practical information as well as philosophical debate. *$38.00*
Founded: 1906
Mailing list available for rent

7223 **Programming Magazine**
National Association for Campus Activities
13 Harbison Way
Columbia, SC 29212-3401
803-732-6222
FAX: 803-749-1047 800-845-2338
info@naca.org http://www.naca.org
Glenn Farr, Editor
Erin Wilson, Circulation
Features cover facilities and financial management, promotions, and student development to help plan a wide range of events. *$ 70.00*
Founded: 1960
Circulation: 4300

7224 **RCM**
1 RCA Dome
Suite 120
Indianapolis, IN 46225-1023
317-632-1888
FAX: 317-632-7909
rcma@rcmaweb.com
http://www.rcmaweb.org
Dewayne S Woodring, Executive Director

A magazine published six times per year by the Religious Conference Management Association. For members only.
100 pages Monthly Founded: 1972
Circulation: 4,000

7225 **Religious Conference Manager**
Primedia
9800 Metcalf Avenue
Overland Park, KS 66212-2216
913-341-1300
FAX: 913-967-1898
mfromento@primediabusiness.com
http://www.meetingsnet.com
Melissa Fromento, Publisher
Larry Reitto, Editor
Betsy Bair, Editorial Director
Contains ideas and suggestions for successful meetings.
Monthly Founded: 1972
Circulation: 6957
Printed in 4 colors

7226 **Resorts, Hotels, Meetings & Incentives**
Publishing Group
PO Box 318
Trumbull, CT 06611-0318
860-279-0149

John Mortimer, Publisher
Editorial contents include indepth articles on industry trends, budgeting, planning tips, and profiles of the top meeting facilities in the world.
Monthly
Circulation: 58,601

7227 **Special Events Magazine**
Primedia Publication
17383 Sunset Blvd
Suite A220
Pacific Palisades, CA 90272
310-230-7160
FAX: 310-230-7168 800-543-4116
inquiries@primediapublicatio.com
http://www.specialevents.com
Lisa Hurley, Editor
Lisa Perrin, Publisher
Resource for event professionals who design and produce special events (including social, corporate and public events) in hotels, resorts, banquet facilities and other venues. *$48.43*
Monthly Founded: 1982
Circulation: 2000+

7228 **Tradeshow & Exhibit Manager**
Goldstein & Associates
1150 Yale Street
Suite 12
Santa Monica, CA 90403-4734
310-828-1309
FAX: 310-829-1169
sgold@lainet.com
http://www.tradeshowpub.com/
Steve Goldstein, Publisher
Featured articles focus on the issues, trends and products of interest connected to the tradeshow industry. Topics include security, boothmanship, legislation and shipping. *$80.00*

Circulation: 14600

7229 **Tradeshow Week**
Reed Business Information
5700 Wilshire Boulevard
Suite 120
Los Angeles, CA 90036-5804
323-576-6600
FAX: 323-965-2407
amy.lacey@reedbusiness.com
http://www.tradeshowweek.com
Amy Lacey, Marketing Director
Adam Schaffer, Publisher
Michael Hart, Editor-in-Chief
Carlos Lopez, Production Director
Heidi Genoist, Senior Associate Editor
For corporate exhibit managers, independent show managers, special event and meeting planners, association show managers and industry suppliers. Focuses on changing trends, new ideas and issues shaping the exposition industry in the US/Canada and abroad. Each issue contains a national and international show calendar. *$439.00*
Weekly Founded: 1971
Circulation: 2394
Printed in 4 colors on matte stock

7230 **Visitor Studies Today**
Visitor Studies Association
8175-A Sheridan Boulevard
Suite 362
Arvada, CO 80003-1928
303-467-2200
FAX: 303-467-0064
info@visitorstudies.org
www.visitorstudies.org
Alan Friedman, President
Ellen Cox, Manager
3/year

Trade Shows

7231 **AACE International Annual Meeting & Exposition**
AACE International
209 Prairie Avenue
Suite 100
Morgantown, WV 26501
304-296-8444
FAX: 304-291-5728 800-858-2678
info@aacei.org www.aacei.org
Andrew S Dowd, Interim Executive Director
Christian Heller, Staff Director Technical
Charla Miller, Staff Director Education
Carol S Rogers, Manager Finance
Offers a unique opportunity to learn, network, and expand your professional horizons in a cost-effective manner. Our goal is to provide cost professionals with the knowledge necessary for survival in today's incredibly fast-changing marketplace. AACE's technical presentations, skills and knowledge track, exhibitors, transactions, certification program and social events combine to create an experience you can't afford to miss.
1000 Attendees June 5000+ names $100 per M.

7232 **AAEA Annual Meetings**
American Academy of Equine Art
c/o Kentucky Horse Park
4089 Iron Works Parkway
Lexington, KY 40511
859-281-6031
FAX: 859-281-6043
julieb@aaea.net www.aaea.net
Shelley Hunter, Executive Director
Julie Buchanan, Director
April, September

7233 **Affordable Meetings Exposition and Conference**
George Little Management
10 Bank Street
Suite 1200
White Plains, NY 10606-1954
914-486-6070
FAX: 914-948-6180 800-272-7469
Susan Sloan, Show Manager
George Little II, President
Focuses on the needs of meeting planners from all types and sizes of organizations who are responsible for producing successful yet cost effective meetings. 430 booths.
3M Attendees September

7234 Association for the Convention of Operations Management
1819 Peachtree Road NE
Atlanta, GA 30309-1848
404-355-9688
FAX: 404-351-3348
William Just, Executive VP
50 booths.
400 Attendees January

7235 Association of Collegiate Conference & Events Directors Conference
Assn of Collegiate Conference & Events Directors
1301 S College Avenue
Fort Collins, CO 80523-8037
970-491-5151
FAX: 970-491-0667 970-877-2233
acced@lamar.colostate.edu
acced-i.colostate.edu
Deborah Blom, Executive Director
Workshop, conference, banquet and luncheon plus exhibits of conference and special event planning supplies, equipment and service information.
1300 Attendees March Founded: 1980

7236 Association of Science-Technology Centers Annual Conference
1025 Vermont Avenue NW
Suite 500
Washington, DC 20005-3516
202-783-7200
FAX: 202-783-7207
info@astc.org www.astc.org
Bonnie VanDorn, Executive Director
Workshop, conference and 150 exhibits for science and technology museums to improve design, plan displays, fund raise, exhibitions for rent & purchase, film/spacetheater/planetarium equipment, museum shop merchandise, publications and more.
1500 Attendees Founded: 1973

7237 Business to Business Exposition
Trade Shows West
2880 S Main
Suite 110
Salt Lake City, UT 84115
801-485-0176
FAX: 801-485-0241
16000 Attendees

7238 Conventions and Expositions
American Society of Association Executives
1575 I Street NW
Washington, DC 20005-1105
202-262-2723
FAX: 202-626-8825
Judy Comeaux, Advertising
John Young, Production
Exposition planners trade show; 500-700 booths.
2-5M Attendees March

7239 ESC Semi-Annual Meetings
Exhibition Services and Contractors Association
2260 Corporate Circle
Suite 400
Henderson, NV 80914
702-319-9561
FAX: 702-450-7732 877-792-3722
askus@esca.org www.esca.org
Susan L Schwartz, CEM, Executive Director
Heather Geldner, Communications Director
December Meeting with International Association for Exposition Management and Summer Educational Conference.
December, Summer

7240 Exhibit Builder
1600 Golf Road
Suite 550
Rolling Meadows, IL 60008-4273

FAX: 847-506-1030 800-638-6296
Russ Eisenhardt, Show Manager
Two booths for equipment, services and supplies for the production of trade show and museum exhibits.
2.5M Attendees August

7241 Exhibit Ideas Show
Exhibit Builder
1600 Golf Road
Suite 550
Rolling Meadows, IL 60008-4273

FAX: 847-280-0771 800-638-6396
Russ Eisenhardt, Show Manager
Jill Brookman, Publisher
Marketplace for products, services and technologies for exhibit builders and buyers. Elements included in trade show, museum and point of purchase booth construction are displayed, as are portable, modular and custom exhibit systems. 700 booths.
20M Attendees April

7242 Exhibit Industry Conference & Exposition
Trade Show Exhibitors Association
2301 S Lake Shire Drive
Suite 1005
Chicago, IL 60616
312-842-8732
FAX: 312-842-8744
iea@ieabbs.org www.tsea.org
July

7243 Exhibitor Conference
Exhibitor Magazine Group
98 E Naperville Road
Westmont, IL 60559
630-434-7779
FAX: 630-434-1216 800-752-6312
exhibitorshow@heiexpo.com
www.exhibitorshow.com
Carol Fojtik, Managing Director/Sr Vice President
Conference program combined with exhibit hall featuring latest products and resources shaping the future of exhibiting and corporate event programs. Anyone responsible for planning, managing or implementing trade show or corporate event marketing functions should attend. Conference is held annually in Las Vegas, NV.
5M Attendees March 25-29 2007 Founded: 1989

7244 Exposition Service Contractors Association
400 S Houston Street
Suite 210
Dallas, TX 75202-4830
214-742-9217
FAX: 214-741-2519 www.esca.org
Ed Simmons, Associate Director
Carpet manufacturers, drape, banner and flag manufacturers. 25 booths.
200 Attendees June

7245 IAEM Semi-Annual Meetings
International Association for Exhibition Mgmt
8111 LBJ Freeway, Suite 750
PO Box 802425
Dallas, TX 75251-1313
972-458-8002
FAX: 972-458-8119
iaem@iaem.org www.iaem.org
Steven G Hacker, CAE, President
Cathy Breden, CAE CMP, SVP
Susan Brower, Director Marketing/Communications
Annual show of 250 exhibitors of conventions and visitor bureaus, hotels, travel airlines, car rental, shippers, insurance, computer hardware and software, service contractors, printing products, specialty advertisement products, photography equipment and audio-visual equipment.
2200 Attendees June, December

7246 IAFE Annual Meeting
International Association of Fairs & Expositions
Box 985
Springfield, MO 65801
417-862-5771
FAX: 417-862-0156
www.fairsandexpos.com
Jim Tucker, President
Max Willis, COO/CFO
5000 Attendees Fall, Neveda

7247 IFEA Annual Meeting
International Festivals and Events Associations
2601 Eastover Terrace
Boise, ID 83706
208-433-0950
FAX: 208-433-9812
kaye@ifea.com www.ifea.com
Steve Schmader, CFE, President/CEO
Kaye Campbell, CFE, SVP
800 Attendees Fall

7248 ILDA Annual Meeting
International Laser Display Association
3721 S.E. Henry Street
Portland, OR 97202
503-407-0289
FAX: 503-775-9258 www.laserist.rg
David Lytle, Executive Director
November

7249 Interaction
16 W 22nd Street
5th Floor
New York, NY 10010-5803
212-271-1662

Astrida Valigorsky, Owner
Dori White, Coordinator
For the meeting planning industry. 560 booths.
350 Attendees October/November

7250 International Association for Exhibition Management Annual Meeting
8111 LBJ Freeway, Suite 750
PO Box 802425
Dallas, TX 75251
972-458-8002
FAX: 972-458-8119
iaem@iaem.org www.iaem.org
Julie Anderson, Director of Show Development
Annual show of 250 exhibitors of conventions and visitor bureaus, hotels, travel air-

lines, car rental, shippers, insurance, computer hardware and software, service contractors, printing products, specialty advertisement products, photography equipment and audio-visual equipment.

2200 Attendees December Founded: 1928 Circulation: 3,500

7251 International Association of Assembly Managers Annual Conference
4425 W Airport Freeway
Suite 590
Irving, TX 75062-5831
972-252-1957
FAX: 972-255-9582 800-935-4226
jackzimmer@iaam.org www.iaam.org

John R Zimmer, CAE/Executive Director
JoAnn Ramsey, Show Manager

Members are managers of auditoriums, arenas, convention centers, stadiums and performing arts centers.

3000 Attendees July Founded: 1925 2800 names $300 per M.

7252 International Technology Meetings & Incentives Conference
Techno-Savvy Meeting Professional
9200 Bayard Place
Fairfax, VA 22032-2103
703-978-6287
FAX: 703-978-5524
cimpa@cimpa.org www.cimpa.org

Andrea Sigler, Manager

Containing 100 booths and 100 exhibits.

November

7253 MPI Semi-Annual Meetings
Meeting Professionals International
3030 LBJ Freeway
Suite 1700
Dallas, TX 75234
972-023-3000
FAX: 972-702-3070
feedback@mpiweb.org
www.mpiweb.org

Colin C Rorrie, Jr PhD CAE, President/CEO

Summer, Winter

7254 Marketing Planners International
1950 N Stemmons Freeway
Dallas, TX 75207-3107
214-746-3630

Le Wayne Raetz Sr, Meeting Manager

For vendors to the meetings industry such as resorts, hotels, airlines and auto rental firms. 300 booths.

1.5M Attendees June

7255 MuseumExpo
American Association of Museums
1575 Eye Street NW
Suite 400
Washington, DC 20005
202-289-1818
FAX: 202-289-6578
museumexpo@aam-us.org
www.aam-us.org

Edward Able, Chief Executive Officer

Cultural exposition with more than 5,000 decision-makers from every type of museum in attendance. This audience includes museum CEOs, directors, exhibit designers, curators, registrars, educators, marketing and public relations personnel, security directors, store managers and other professionals from art museums, history museums, science and technology centers, natural history museums, youth museums, aquariums, zoos and botanical gardens.

5,000 Attendees May

7256 NAAFA Semi-Annual Meetings
National Association of Agricultural Fair Agencies
MI State Department of Agriculture
PO Box 30017
Lansing, MI 48909
517-373-9766
FAX: 517-373-9146

Carol Carlson, Secretary/Treasurer

Summer, Winter

7257 NAFSC Annual Meeting
North American Farm Show Council
590 Woody Hayes Drive
Columbus, OH 43210-6131
614-292-4278
FAX: 614-292-9448
fendrick.1@osu.edu
www.farmshows.org

Craig Fendrick, Executive Coordinator

May

7258 NCEE Annual Meeting
National Catholic Educational Exhibitors
2621 Dryden Road
Suite 300
Dayton, OH 45439
937-293-1415
FAX: 937-293-1310 888-555-8512

Bret Thomas, Executive Director

In conjunction with the National Catholic Educational Association.

March

7259 Special Event Magazine Exposition
PO Box 8987
Malibu, CA 90265-8987
310-317-4522
FAX: 310-317-0264 800-543-4116
lhurley@primedia.com
www.specialevents.com

Lisa Hurley, Editor/Event Director

Brings together those in the special events industry for new product displays, education, networking and learning. 275 booths.

3M Attendees January

7260 VSA Annual Meeting
Visitor Studies Association
8175-A Sheridan Boulevard
Suite 362
Arvada, CO 80003-1928
303-467-2200
FAX: 303-467-0064
info@visitorstudies.org
www.visitorstudies.org

Alan Friedman, President
Ellen Cox, Manager

Summer

Directories & Databases

7261 Association Management: Convention Bureau and Convention Hall Issue
American Society of Association Executives
1575 I Street NW
Washington, DC 20005-1105
202-262-2723
FAX: 202-371-8825
pr@asaenet.org www.asaenet.org

A list of halls, centers, auditoriums, arenas and visitors bureaus in the United States and Canada. *$4.00*

Circulation: 20,000

7262 Audarena International Guide & Facility Buyers Guide
VNU Business Publications
49 Music Square W
4th Floor
Nashville, TN 37203
615-214-4240
FAX: 615-320-0454 www.billboard.com

Ken Schlager, Executive Editor
Mitch Tebo, Directory Marketing Director
George Van, President *$99.00*

310 pages October

7263 CEMA Member Directory and Meeting Planner
Computer Event Marketing Association
19 Intermediate Unit Drive
Suite 203
Coal Center, PA 15423
724-938-0432
FAX: 724-938-8175 866-702-2362
CEMA@ndegree.com
www.cemaonline.com

All event managers and primary IA members.

500 pages Founded: 1990

7264 Constitution and Membership Roster
National Association of Agricultural Fair Agencies
MI State Department of Agriculture
PO Box 30017
Lansing, MI 48909
517-373-9766
FAX: 517-373-9146

Carol Carlson, Secretary/Treasurer

Annual

7265 Corporate and Incentive Travel: Official Corporate Directory Issue
Coastal Communications Corporation
2600 N Military Trail
Suite 250
Boca Raton, FL 33431-5702
561-989-0600
FAX: 561-989-9509
ccceditor@worldnet.att.net
www.corporate-inc-travel.com

Read by over 40,000 ABC audited meeting and incentive travel planners and key executives responsible for meeting decisions. Articles range monthly from in-depth how-to's, to issue oriented features, examinations of professional concerns, thoroughly researched destination reports, and columns by industry experts *$50.00*

Annual
Circulation: 60,000

7266 HCEA Directory of Healthcare Meetings and Conventions
Healthcare Convention & Exhibitors Association
5775 Peachtree Dunwoody Road NE
Building G, Suite 500
Atlanta, GA 30342-1542
404-252-3663
FAX: 404-252-0774
hcea@kellencompany.com
www.hcea.org

Eric Allen, Executive Director
Carol Wilson, Director Meetings

Information on 6,000 health care meetings.

500 pages Founded: 1930

7267 IAFE Directory
International Association of Fairs & Expositions
Box 985
Springfield, MO 65801
417-862-5771
FAX: 417-862-0156
www.fairsandexpos.com

Jim Tucker, President
Max Willis, COO/CFO

Annual

7268 IEG Sponsorship Sourcebook
IEG
640 N La Salle Drive
Suite 600
Chicago, IL 60610-3777
312-944-1727
FAX: 312-944-1897 800-834-4850
ieg@sponsorship.com
www.sponsorship.com

Lesa Ukman, Editor
John Ukman, Publisher
Alicia Fidler, Product Manager

A directory of sponsors, properties, agencies and suppliers from th most active sponsors to the hottest sponsorship opportunities. Contains the critical data you need to make smart sponsorship connections. *$299.00*

468 pages Annual ISBN 0-944807-43-7
Printed in on glossy stock : Floppy

7269 MPI Membership Directory
Meeting Professionals International
3030 LBJ Freeway
Suite 1700
Dallas, TX 75234
972-023-3000
FAX: 972-702-3070
feedback@mpiweb.org
www.mpiweb.org

Colin C Rorrie, Jr PhD CAE, President/CEO

Annual

7270 Meetings and Conventions: Gavel International Directory Issue
Reed Travel Group
500 Plaza Drive
Suite C
Secaucus, NJ 07094-3685
201-902-1960
FAX: 207-319-1628

Alina Dalmau, Editor
Lori Cioffi, Manager

Lists over 4,000 convention halls and hotels in the United States, suitable for meetings. *$35.00*

Annual
Circulation: 80,000

7271 NCEE Membership Directory
National Catholic Educational Exhibitors
2621 Dryden Road
Suite 300
Dayton, OH 45439
937-293-1415
FAX: 937-293-1310 888-555-8512

Bret Thomas, Executive Director

Annual

7272 Nationwide Directory of Corporate Meeting Planners
Reed Reference Publishing RR Bowker
121 Chanlon Road
New Providence, NJ 07974-1541
908-665-2834
FAX: 908-464-3553
info@bowker.com www.bowker

Offers valuable information on over 12,000 corporations that hold regular, off-site meetings arranged by over 18,000 corporate meeting planners. *$297.00*

1140 pages Annual

7273 Official Meeting Facilities Guide
Reed Travel Group
500 Plaza Drive
Suite C
Secaucus, NJ 07094-3685
201-902-1960
FAX: 201-902-2053

Virginia Nonneman, Editor
Lori Cioffi, Manager

One thousand national and international meeting facilities, primarily hotels in the US. *$45.00*

SemiAnnual
Circulation: 18,500

7274 Protocol
Protocol Directory
101 W 12th Street
Suite PH-H
New York, NY 10011-8142
212-336-6934
FAX: 212-633-6934 copeorg@aol.com

Edna Greenbaum, Editor

Approximately 4,000 suppliers of products and services used by planners of executive meetings, special events and other entertainment. *$60.00*

1 issue Founded: 1989
Printed in on matte stock

7275 Trade Show Exhibitors Association: Membership Directory
Trade Show Exhibitors Association
2301 S Lane Shore Drive
Suite 1005
Chicago, IL 60616
312-842-8732
FAX: 312-842-8744
tsea@tsea.org www.tsea.org

Steve Schuldenfrei, President
Michael J Bandy, VP

About 1,900 members of the Trade Show Exhibitors Association. *$55.00*

Annual February

7276 TradeShow & Exhibit Manager's Buyer's Guide
1150 Yale Street
Suite 12
Santa Monica, CA 90403-4734
310-828-1309
FAX: 310-829-1169

Steve Goldstein, Owner

Over 1,000 suppliers of products and services to the trade show industry are profiled. *$60.00*

150 pages Annual
Circulation: 12,000

7277 TradeShow Manager's Major Exhibit Hall Directory
ESP Publishing
5200 S Jules Verne
Tampa, FL 33611

FAX: 813-837-1043
www.espbooks.com

Directory of services and supplies to the industry. *$50.00*

300 pages Annual

7278 Tradeshow Week Exhibit Manager
Goldstein & Associates
1150 Yale Street
Suite 12
Santa Monica, CA 90403-4734
310-828-1309
FAX: 310-829-1169 sgold@lainet.com

Steve Goldstein, Publisher

For exhibit managers. *$80.00*

Bi-Monthly Founded: 1983

7279 Tradeshow Week's Tradeshow Services Directory
Business Information Publication
5700 Wilshire Boulevard
Suite 120
Los Angeles, CA 90036
310-595-5711
FAX: 323-965-2407
tgeorgereyes@tsweek.com
www.tradeshowweek.com

Tina George-Reyes, Editor
Adam Schaffer, Publisher

Offers information on designers, builders, carriers and decorators involved in tradeshow and convention industries. *$95.00*

300 pages Annual

7280 VSA Membership Directory
Visitor Studies Association
8175-A Sheridan Boulevard
Suite 362
Arvada, CO 80003-1928
303-467-2200
FAX: 303-467-0064
info@visitorstudies.org
www.visitorstudies.org

Alan Friedman, President
Ellen Cox, Manager

Annual

7281 Who's Who in Exposition Management
International Assn for Exhibition Management
PO Box 802425
Dallas, TX 75380-2425
972-216-1511
FAX: 972-458-8119

Over 1,500 show manager members and 1,500 associate members. *$225.00*

Annual June

7282 Worldwide Tradeshow Schedule
1700 K Street NW
Suite 403
Washington, DC 20006-3810
202-463-4088

Over 110 international trade fairs are listed in all major industrial sectors.

10 pages

Industry Web Sites

7283 **www.aacei.org**
Association for Advancement of Cost Engineering

Association for Advancement of Cost Engineering provides its members with the resources they need to enhance their performance and ensure continued grouth and success. Serves cost management professionals: cost management and engineers, project managers, planners and schedulers, estimators and bidders, and value engineers.

7284 **www.acced-i.colostate.edu**
Colorado State University

Members are college and university conference and special events directors, profesionals and others who design, market and coordinate conferences and special events.

7285 **www.acmenet.org**
Association for Convention Marketing Executives

Annual meetings for marketing and sales executives.

7286 **www.cimpa.org**
Connected Int'l Meeting Professionals Association

Members are conference and convention planners with a certificate in convention management. Specializes in planning meetings events, incentives, using the internet.

7287 **www.clc.org**
Convention Liaison Council

Members are associations which are directly involved in the convention, exposition, trade show and meeting industry.

7288 **www.edpa.com**
Exhibit Designers & Producers Association

Exhibit Designers and Producers Association is an internationally recognized national trade association with more than 370 corporate members from 18 countries that are engaged in the design, manufacture, transport, installation and service of display and exhibits primarily for the trade show industry

7289 **www.edsc.org**
Electronic Distribution Show Corporation

Attendees are manufacturers of electronic components who sell their products through electronics distributors.

7290 **www.esca.org**
Exposition Service Contractors Association

Guide to exposition service is distributed annually and lists safety regulations and building rules in major US convention centers.

7291 **www.greyhouse.com**
Grey House Publishing

Selected Grey House directories in the fields of business, health and education are available online. Users can search our online databases by several different search criteria, such as product categories, geographic area, sales volume and much, much more. Full Grey House catalog and online ordering also available.

7292 **www.hcea.org**
Healthcare Convention & Exhibitors Association

Trade association of over 700 organizations involved in health care exhibiting or providing services to health care conventions, exhibitions and/or meetings.

7293 **www.iaam.org**
International Association of Assembly Managers

Members are managers of auditoriums, arenas, convention centers, stadiums and performing arts centers.

7294 **www.iacc.online.org**
International Association of Conference Centers

A facilities-based organization which advances the understanding and awareness of conference centers as distinct within the training, education, hospitality and travel fields.

7295 **www.iaem.org**
Int'l Association for Exposition Management

Members are managers of shows, exhibits and expositions; associate members are industry suppliers.

7296 **www.moderndisplay.com**
Modern Display

Members are distributors of display equipment.

7297 **www.mpiweb.org**
Meeting Planners International

Meeting industry professionals who plan and/or manage meetings, trade shows and conferences for corporations, educational institutions and associations.

7298 **www.naca.org**
National Association for Campus Activities

Largest collegiate organization for campus activities.

7299 **www.pcma.org**
Professional Convention Management Association

Features emphasize solutions of practical and logistical problems concerning business travel, the hospitality/hotel industry, and related event planning topics

7300 **www.psmashows.org**
Professional Show Managers Association

7301 **www.publicshows.com**
National Association of Consumer Shows

Non-profit organization dedicated to furthering the interests of consumer show producers and suppliers.

7302 **www.rcmaweb.org**
Religious Conference Management Association

7303 **www.sgmp.org**
Society of Government Meeting Planners

Trade association for government meeting planners and exhibitors.

7304 **www.siso.org**
Society of Independent Show Organizers

7305 **www.tsea.org**
Trade Show Exhibitors Association

Provides knowledge to marketing and management professionals.

Associations

7306 **AACE International**
209 Prairie Avenue
Suite 100
Morgantown, WV 26501
304-296-8444
FAX: 304-291-5728 800-858-2678
info@aacei.org www.aacei.org

Andrew S Dowd, Interim Executive Director
Christian Heller, Staff Director Technical
Charla Miller, Staff Director Education
Carol S Rogers, Manager Finance

A professional society of individuals interested in applying scientific principles to the solution of problems of cost management, engineering, estimating, cost control, planning and scheduling, project management, and profitability.
5500 Members Founded: 1956

7307 **ACA International**
PO Box 390106
Minneapolis, MN 55439
952-926-6547
FAX: 952-926-1624
aca@acainternational.org
www.acainternational.org

Gary D Rippentrop CAE, CEO
Toni Nuernberg CAE, COO

International trade organization of over 5,300 credit and collection professionals providing a variety of accounts receivable management services to over 1,000,000 credit grantors.

7308 **Alliance of Merger and Acquisition Advisor s**
150 N Michigan Avenue
Suite 2700
Chicago, IL 60601
312-856-9590
FAX: 312-729-9800 877-844-2535

Kevin Carlie, President
Karin Gale, Conference Committee
Michael Nall, Manager

A national organization serving the educational and resource needs of the M&A profession.
200 Members Founded: 1999

7309 **Allied Financial Adjusters Conference**
PO Box 20708
Chicago, IL 60620

800-621-3016
alliedhmoff@aol.com
www.alliedfinancialadjusters.com

James R Kickliter, Chairman
Carl Purvis, Executive Secretary

Membership is composed of professsional liquidators, repossessors and skip tracers. Membership fee varies with size of populations of the city served.
200 Members Founded: 1936

7310 **American Association of Healthcare Administrative Management**
11240 Waples Mill Road
Suite 200
Fairfax, VA 22030
703-340-0164
FAX: 703-359-7562
aaham#statmarketing.com
www.aaham.org

Sharon Galler, CMP, Executive Director

To promote patient account management as an integral part of financial management in the health care industry. Provides educational and professional development for its members.
3500 Members Founded: 1968

7311 **American Association of Individual Investors**
625 N Michigan Avenue
Chicago, IL 60611
312-280-0170
FAX: 312-280-9883 800-428-2244
members@aaii.com www.aaii.com

James B Cloonan, Chairman
John Markese, President

An independent, nonprofit corporation formed in 1978 for the purpose of assisting individuals in becoming effective managers of their own assets through programs of education, information and research.
15000 Members Founded: 1978

7312 **American Association of Residential Mortgage Regulators**
1255 23rd Street NW
Suite 200
Washington, DC 20037
202-521-3999
FAX: 202-833-3636
egundersen@aarmr.org
www.aarmr.org

David Saunders, Executive Director
Erika Gundersen, Meeting/Membership Coordinator

Members are state employees responsible for administration or residential mortgage oversight. Primary members include model legislation and best practices.
100 Members Founded: 1989

7313 **American Bankers Association**
1120 Connecticut Avenue NW
Washington, DC 20036
202-635-5000
FAX: 202-828-4540 800-Ban-kers
custserv@aba.com www.aba.com

Elizabeth A Duke, Chairman
Earl D McVicker, Vice Chairman
Donald G Ogilvie, President/CEO

Brings together all categories of banking institutions to best represent the interests of this rapidly changing industry. Its membership — which includes community, regional and money center banks and holding companies, as well as savings associations, trust companies and savings banks — makes ABA one of the largest banking trade associations in the country.
Founded: 1875

7314 **American Bankruptcy Institute**
44 Canal Center Plaza
Suite 404
Alexandria, VA 22314
703-739-0800
FAX: 703-739-1060
info@abiworld.org www.abiworld.org

Keith J Shapiro, Chairman
Samuel J Gerdano, Executive Director
Kathy Sheehan, Director Administration
Caroline Milani, Director Special Projects
Melissa Lanning-Trumpower, Director Communications

Multidisiplinary, nonpartisan organization dedicated to research and education on matters related to insovency. Engaged in numerous educational and research activities as well as the production of a number of publications both for the insolvency practitioner and the public.

7315 **American Cash Flow Association**
255 S Orange Avenue
#600
Orlando, FL 32801
407-843-2032
FAX: 407-648-9470
info@americancashflow.com
www.acfa-cashflow.org

Fred Rewey, President
Debbie Bracknell, Executive Director

7316 **American Collectors Association**
PO Box 39106
Minneapolis, MN 55439-106
952-926-6547
FAX: 612-926-1624
pr@acainternational.org
www.collector.com
Promoting professional and ethical conduct in the global market place.

7317 **American Council of Life Insurance**
101 Constitution NW
Suite 700
Washington, DC 20001
202-242-2000
FAX: 202-624-2319

Frank Keating, President

Works to advance the interests of the life insurance industry and to provide effective government relations. Conducts investment and social research programs.
631 Members Founded: 1976

7318 **American Education Finance Association**
8365 S Armadillo Trail
Evergreen, CO 80439
303-674-0857
FAX: 303-670-8986 www.aefa.cc

Ed Steinbecher, Executive Director

AEFA encourages communications among groups and individuals in the education finance field, including academicians, researchers, policy makers and practitioners. Serving as a forum for a broad range of issues and concerns, AEFA concerns include traditional school finance concepts, issues of public policy, and teaching school finance.
650 Members Founded: 1975

7319 **American Finance Association**
University of California
Haas School of Business
Berkley, CA 94720-1900
510-426-6000
FAX: 510-525-6246
pyle@haas.berkley.edu
www.afajof.org

David Pyle, Executive Secretary/Treasurer
David H Pyle, Executive Secretary/Treasurer

Seeks to improve public understanding of financial problems and to provide for exchange of ideas.
8000+ Members Founded: 1939

7320 American Financial Services Association
919 18th Street NW
Suite 300
Washington, DC 20006
202-296-5544
FAX: 202-223-0321
afsa@afsaonline.org
www.afsaonline.org

Tom Hallman, Chairperson
Randy Lively, President/CEO
Lynne B Strang, VP/Communication

Established in 1916 and based in Washington D.C., the American Financial Services Association is the national trade association for market funded providers of financial services to consumers and small business. These providers offer an array of financial services, including unsecured personal loans, automotive loans, home equity loans and credit cards through specialized bank institutions
400 Members

7321 American Society of Appraisers
555 Herdon Parkway
Herndon, VA 20170
703-478-2228
FAX: 703-742-8471 800-272-8258
info@appraisers.org
www.appraisers.org

Edwin W Baker, Executive VP
Eugene G Kaczkowski, President
Donna J Walker, Secretary/Treasurer

Professional association of appraisers of all kinds.
6500 Members Founded: 1936

7322 American Society of Military Comptrollers
415 N Alfred Street
Alexandria, VA 22314-4650
703-549-0360
FAX: 703-549-3181 800-462-5637

James F McCall, Executive Director

ASMC is the successor to the Society of Military Accountants and Statisticians.
18000 Members Founded: 1949

7323 Association for Entrepreneurial Growth
PO Box 875
Merrimack, NH 03054
603-429-1631
FAX: 603-424-8641 gouldnc@aol.com

Neil C Gould, Executive Director

7324 Association for Financial Counseling and Planning Education
1500 W. Thrid Avenue
Suite 223
Coloumbus, OH 43212
614-485-9650
FAX: 614-485-9621
sburns@afcpe.org www.afcpe.org

Sharon Burns, PhD, Executive Director

AFCPE is a non-profit professional organization created to promote the education and training of the professional in financial management.
810 Members Founded: 1983

7325 Association for Financial Professionals
7315 Wisconsin Avenue
Suite 600 West
Bethesda, MD 20814
301-907-2862
FAX: 301-907-2864
afp@afponline.org www.afponline.org

Sally M Smedal, Chairman
James A Kaitz, President
Kevin R Keller, Senior VP/COO

Association of 12,000 financial professionals. Please call for our publication listings or visit us online.
14000 Members Founded: 1979

7326 Association for Financial Technology
34 North High Street
New Albany, OH 43054-8057
614-895-1208
FAX: 614-895-3466
aft@aftweb.com www.aftweb.com

James R Bannister, Executive Director

Trade association for companies providing services to the financial industry. Our members provide systems, applications and outsourcing services to 90% of America's banks. Vendors of computer hardware, software and ancilliary products and services are also welcome.
52 Members Founded: 1975

7327 Association for Management Information in Financial Services
3895 Fairfax Court
Atlanta, GA 30339
770-444-3557
FAX: 770-444-9084
ami@amifs.org www.amifs.org

Kevin Link, Executive Director

Membership open to individuals employed by any commerical bank, trust company, Federal Reserve bank, bank holding company, credit union or thrift institution.
600 Members Founded: 1980

7328 Association of Commercial Finance Attorneys
Kennedy Covington Lobdell & Hickman, LLP
214 North Tryon Street, Hearst Tower
43rd Floor
Charlotte, NC 28202
704-331-7403

info@acfa.cc www.acfa.cc

Nancy A Kagan, President
Richard K Brown, Secretary

ACF members are attorneys specializing in commercial finance and bankruptcy law. ACFA provides continuing education and publishes material relevant to the field for its members.
350 Members Founded: 1958

7329 Association of Finance and Insurance Professionals
5100 Thompson Terrance
Suite B
Colleyville, TX 76034
817-428-2434
FAX: 817-428-2534
david.robertson@afip.com
www.afip.com

David N Robertson, Executive Director

AFIP supports finance/insurance personnel and the finance/insurance industry for franchised automobile dealers in the U.S. and 13 foreign countries.
3500 Members Founded: 1989

7330 Association of Government Accountants
2208 Mount Vernon Avenue
Alexandria, VA 22301
703-684-6931
FAX: 703-548-9367 800-242-7211
rvandaniker@agacgfm.org
www.agacgfm.org

Relmond P Van Daniker, Executive Director
Marie S Force, Director Communications
Susan Fritzlen, Deputy Executive Director

AGA is an educaitonal organization dedicated to the enhancement of public financial management. AGA serves the professional interests of govermental financial managers and public accounting firms.
18000 Members Founded: 1950

7331 Avancement of Cost Engineering
209 Prairie Avenue
Suite 100
Morgantown, WV 26501
304-296-8444
FAX: 304-291-5728 800-858-2678
info@aacei.org www.aacei.org

Ozzie F Belcher, President
Dr James E Rowings, VP Administrator

Association for those interested in the financial aspects of engineering and all aspects of cost management.
5500+ Members Founded: 1956

7332 BKD
901 E St. Louis Street, Suite 1800
PO Box 1900
Springfield, MO 65806
417-698-8588
FAX: 417-831-4763
mail@bkd.com www.bkd.com

William E Fingland Jr, Managing Partner
Wade Clark, Director Sales/Marketing
Jennifer Ailor, Director Communications
Steve Blumreich, President

Provides solutions for success to thousands of individuals; closely held and publicly trade business in the health care, manufacturing, distribution, financial institutions, construction, real estate, retail and other industries; not-for-profit organizations; and governmental entities.
Founded: 1923

7333 Broadcast Cable Credit Association
555 Frontage Road
Suite 3600
Northfield, IL 60093
847-960-0200
FAX: 847-784-8059
info@bccacredit.com
www.bccacredit.com

Mary Collins, President/CEO
Founded: 1972

7334 Broadcast Cable Financial Management Association
550 W Frontage Rd
Ste 3600
Northfield, IL 60093-1243
847-716-7000
FAX: 847-716-7004
info@bcfm.com www.bcfm.com

Mary M Collins, President/CEO
Jamie Smith, Operations Manager
Mary Teister, Meetings Manager

Professional society of over 1,200 of television, radio and cable TV's top financial,

MIS and HR executives, plus associates in auditing, data processing, software development, credit and collections.
1200 Members Founded: 1961
Mailing list available for rent 1100 names $495 per M.

7335 Bureau of Business Practice
1185 Avenue of the Americas
New York, NY 10036
212-597-0333
FAX: 212-597-0338 800-638-8437
alicia.pierce@aspenpubl.com
www.aspenpublishers.com
Robert Becker, CEO
Gustavo Dobles, VP Operations
Jeanmarie Smith, VP HR
Kevin Entricken, CFO
Supports all those needing information on a specific business, or general business practice information.
200 Members Founded: 1974

7336 Coalition of Higher Education Assistance Organizations
1101 Vermont Avenue NW
Suite 400
Washington, DC 20005-3586
202-289-3910
FAX: 202-371-0197
hwadsworth@wpllc.net
www.coheao.com
Alisa Abadinsky, President
Harrison Wadsworth, Executive Director
Focus is on legislative and regulatory advocacy for Federal Perkins and other campus based student loan programs.
365 Members Founded: 1980

7337 Coalition of Publicly Traded Partnerships
1801 K St Nw
Ste 500
Washington, DC 20006-1320
202-197-7000
FAX: 202-371-6601
www.ptpcoalition.org
Letitia Chambers, Owner
Mary Lyman, Director
CPTP is a trade association representing pubicly traded partnerships, corporations which are general partners of PTP's and attorneys, accountants and investment bankers who work with them.
Founded: 1983

7338 Commercial Finance Association
225 W 34th Street
New York, NY 10122
212-594-3490
FAX: 212-564-6053
postmaster@cfa.com www.cfa.com
Richard P Palmieri, Chairman
Bruce H Jones, Executive Director/Secretary
Terrence Ullrich, VP
Michael Sharkey, President
Theodore Kompa, VP
Trade group of the asset based financial services industry, with members throughout the US, Canada and around the world. Members include the asset based lending arms of domestic and foreign commercial banks, small and large independent finance companies, floor plan financing organizations, factoring organizations and financing subsidiaries of major industrial corporations. CFA membership is by organization, not by individual.

7339 Commercial Mortgage Securities Association
30 Broad Street
28th Floor
New York, NY 10004-2304
212-509-1844
FAX: 212-509-1895
info@cmbs.org www.cmbs.org
Dottie Cunningham, CEO
Jane Gelfand, Managing Director Finance/Admin
Marcu Henderson, Coordinator Membership/Facilities
Trish Madonia, Director Meetings
International trade organization for the commercial real estate capital markets. Also represents and promotes an orderly ans ethical global institutional secondary market for the sale of commercial mortgage loans and equity investments.
309 Members Founded: 1994

7340 Commerical Mortgage Securities Association
30 Broad Street
New York, NY 10004-2304
212-509-1844
FAX: 212-509-1895
info@cmbs.org www.cmbs.org
Dottie Cunningham, CEO
Jane Gelfand, Director of Finance
Marcus Henderson, Coordinator Membership/Facilities
Trish Madonia, Director Meetings
Mission is to promote the strength, liquidity and viability of commercial real estate capital market finance worldwide. CMSA is an international trade organization that additionally addresses the non-availability of terrorism insurance by working with other associations throughout the Congressional session to create a federal backstop.
Founded: 1994

7341 Community Development Venture Capital Alliance
424 West 33rd Street
Suite 320
New York, NY 10001
212-594-6747
FAX: 212-594-6717
cdvca@cdvca.org www.cdvca.org
Kerwin Tesdell, President
Gary Brooks, Managing Director
The Community Development Venture Capital Alliance is the network for the rapidly growing field of community development venture capital investing.
Founded: 1995

7342 Conference on Consumer Finance Law
Oklahoma City University School of Law
2501 N Blackwelder
Oklahoma City, OK 73106
405-521-5363
FAX: 405-521-5089
info@theccfl.com www.theccfl.com
Alvin C Harrell, Executive Director
Ann P Fortney, President
The objects of teh Conference are to encourage research in the commercial law, banking, and consumer finance fields, to promote by discussion and publication the improvement of legal procedures affecting credit law and installment finance, and to afford a forum at which lawyers may meet and exchange opinions.
1400 Members Founded: 1926

7343 Construction Financial Management Association
29 Emmons Drive
Princeton, NJ 08540
609-452-8000
FAX: 609-452-0474
info@cfma.org www.cfma.org
Henry Waggoner, Treasurer
Anthony Stagliano, Secretary
Herbert Brownett, Chairman
William Schwab, President
Financial managers and CPAs concerned with financial management in the construction industry.
7000 Members Founded: 1981

7344 Consumer Data Industry Association
1090 Vermont Avenue NW
Suite 200
Washington, DC 20005-4905

FAX: 202-371-0134
bbyrnes@cdiaonline.org
www.cdiaonline.org
Stuart Pratt, President/CEO
Betty Byrnes, Member Services
Represents consumer information companies that provide fraud prevention and risk management products, credit and mortgage reports, tenant and employment screening services, check fraud and verification services, and collection services.
500 Members Founded: 1906

7345 Corporate Facility Advisors
2000 N 15th Street
Suite 101
Arlington, VA 22201
703-528-3500
FAX: 703-528-0113
tom@corfac.com www.corfac.com
Thomas P Bennett, Executive Director
Provide a full spectrum of coordinated commercial real estate services, including brokerage, counseling valuation, finance, project management and asset management.
805 Members

7346 Council for International Tax Education
PO Box 1012
White Plains, NY 10602
914-949-5656
FAX: 914-328-5757
info@citeusa.org www.citeusa.org
The only organization operating on a national level devoted to educational interests of companies that have set up a foreign sales corporation.
300 Members Founded: 1982

7347 Council of Development Finance Agencies
301 NW 63rd Avenue
Suite 500
Oklahoma City, OK 73116
405-848-6059
FAX: 405-842-3299
info@cdfa.net www.cdfa.net
Stan Provus, Training Director
Don Conkle, Manager
CDFA members are state, city and county public agencies and special authorities whose primary purpose is the provision of economic development financing. Offers a Newsletter online.
Founded: 1984

7348 **Council of Infrastructure Financing Authorities**
1801 K St Nw
Ste 500
Washington, DC 20006-1320
202-973-3100
FAX: 202-973-3101
cifa@navigantconsulting.com
www.cifanet.org

Anna Miller, President
Joe Freeman, VP

CIFA is an organization of state and local agencies that have authority to assist and facilitate the issuance of debt financing for public infrastructure purposes. It is the only national organization dedicated exclusively to the service and representation of public environmental financing authorities, many of which issue debt, manage state loan funds, and provide various mechanisms to enhance credit arrangement and generally facilitate public financing.
Founded: 1988

7349 **Council of Institutional Investors**
1730 Rhode Island Avenue NW
Washington, DC 20036
202-822-0800
FAX: 202-822-0801
info@cii.org www.cii.org

Sarah Teslik, Executive Director

Members include employee benefit plans, nonprofit foundations and endowment funds.
75 Members

7350 **Credit Research Foundation**
8840 Columbia Parkway
Suit 100
Columbia, MD 21045-2117
410-740-5499
FAX: 410-740-4620
crf_info@crfonline.org
www.crfonline.org

William T Callahan, CCE CRF, President

CRF is a membership organization dedicated to developing and enhancing the skills, talents and knowledge of credit professionals. Members are cash managers, credit executives, treasurers, and other responsible for any portion of the credit function in an organization.
Founded: 1949

7351 **Credit Union Executives Society**
5510 Research Park Drive
Madison, WI 53711-5377
608-271-2664
FAX: 608-271-2303 800-252-2664
cues@cues.org www.cues.org

Fred Johnson, President/CEO
Mary Arnold, VP Publications
George Hofheimer, VP Professional Development
Barbara Kachelski, CAE, SVP/CIO
Dennis Porter, VP Finance/Administration

Members are credit union CEOs and other senior management personnel. CUES divisions include Directors Educational Forum and Financial Suppliers Forum. Offers a FYI Management Memo Weekly by Email and Credit Union Directory online.
3500 Members Founded: 1962

7352 **Credit Union National Association**
5710 Mineral Point Road
Madison, WI 53705
608-314-4000
FAX: 608-231-4263
dorothy@cuna.coop www.cuna.org

Daniel Mica, President
Guy Hood, Director
Dick Ensweiler, Chairman

With its network of affiliated state credit union leagues, CUNA serves more than 90 percent of America's 10,000 credit unions, which are owned by more than 83 million consumer members. Based in Washington, DC and Madison, Wisconsin, this nonprofit group is governed by volunteer directors who are elected by their credit union peers.
52 Members Founded: 1970

7353 **Defense Credit Union Council**
601 Pennsylvania Avenue NW
Suite 600
Washington, DC 20004-2601
202-829-9110
FAX: 202-638-3410
ducl@cuna.com www.dcuc.org

Roland Arty Arteaga, President/CEO

Organizations of credit unions whose membership consists wholly or in part of personnel of the US Department of Defense, both military and civilians.
300 Members Founded: 1963

7354 **EMTA - Trade Association for the Emerging Markets**
360 Madison Avenue
18th Floor
New York, NY 10017
646-637-9100
FAX: 646-637-9128
awerner@emta.org www.emta.org

Michael M Chamberlin, President
Aviva Werner, General Counsel

EMTA is the principal trade group for the Emerging Markets trading and investment community and is dedicated to promoting the orderly development of fair, efficient, and transparent trading markets for Emerging Markets into the global capital markets.
Founded: 1990

7355 **Evangelical Council for Financial Accountability**
440 W Jubal Early Drive
Suite 130
Winchester, VA 22601
540-535-0103
FAX: 540-535-0533 800-323-9473
info@ecfa.org www.ecfa.org

Paul Nelson, President
Dan Busby, VP

Accreditation agency for religious charities. Seal granted to members who meet ECFA's Seven Standards of Responsible Stewardship.
1200 Members Founded: 1979

7356 **FSC/DISC Tax Association**
1 Barker Avenue
White Plains, NY 10601-1517
914-997-0615
FAX: 914-328-5757

Robert Ross, Executive Director

The only organization operating on a national level devoted to educational interests of companies that have set up a foreign sales corporation.
300 Members Founded: 1982

7357 **Fiduciary and Risk Management Association**
PO Box 48297
Athens, GA 30604
706-354-0083
FAX: 706-353-3994
info@thefirma.org www.thefirma.org

Hale Mast, Executive Director

Members are audit and compliance professionals.
820 Members Founded: 1989

7358 **Finacial Services Coordinating Council**
901 7th Street NW
2nd Floor
Washington, DC 20001
202-315-5100
FAX: 202-315-5010 www.fscnews.com

Phil Anderson, Executive Director

Formed by the four principal trade associations representing the major finacial sectors of the US economy to address issues of common concern at both the federal and state levels. Its members are the American Bankers Association, American Council of Life Insurers, American Insurance Association, and Securities Industry Association. These organizations represent thousands of financial firms that, taken together, serve nearly every household in America.

7359 **Finacial Services Technology Consortium**
44 Wall Street
12th Floor
New York, NY 10005
212-461-7116
FAX: 646-349-3629
fstcadmin@fstc.org www.fstc.org

Zachary Tumin, Executive Director
Jim Salters, Technology Initiatives
Deb Karl, Business Manager

Association of leading North American-based financial institutions, technology vendors, independent research organizations and government agencies. Goal is to promote interoperable, open-standard technologies that provide critical infrastructures for the finacial services industry.

7360 **Financial & Security Products Association (FSPA)**
Plaza Ladera
5300 Sequoia Road NW, Suite 205
Albuquerque, NM 87120
505-839-7958
FAX: 505-839-0017 800-843-6082
info@fspal.com www.fspal.com

John M Vrabec, Executive Director
Elizabeth Vrabec, General Manager

Promotes growth of the security equipment industry. Professional business association representing companies involved in the manufacturing, selling, installing and servicing products sold primarily to financial institutions.
Founded: 1973

7361 **Financial Executives International**
200 Campus Drive
PO Box 674
Florham Park, NJ 07932-674
973-360-0177
FAX: 973-765-1018 www.fei.org

Colleen S Cunningham, President
Barbara Chanes, Manager
Paul Chase, CFO
Grace Hinchman, Senior VP
Jeffrey Marshall, Director/Publications

A professional organization of individuals performing the duties of CFO, Controller, Treasurer or VP of Finance. Has an annual budget of $6.5 million.

15M Members Founded: 1931

7362 Financial Management Association International
University of South Florida
College of Business Admin, #3331
Tampa, FL 33620
813-974-2084
FAX: 813-974-3318
kwright@fma.org www.fma.org
Jack S Rader, Executive Director
Karen Wright, Special Events Coordinator
Members are college professors of financial management and corporate and organizational financial officers.
12000 Members Founded: 1970

7363 Financial Managers Society
100 W Monroe
Suite 810
Chicago, IL 60603
312-578-1300
FAX: 312-578-1308 800-275-4367
info@fmsinc.org
www.fmsinc.org/cms
Richard Yingst, President/CEO
Diane Walter, VP/Professional Development
Jennifer Doak, Director Marketing
Is the only individual membership society exclusively serving the technical and professional needs of today's bank, thrift and credit union financial officers.
1600 Members Founded: 1949

7364 Financial Markets Association
PO Box 156
Parlin, NJ 08859
732-316-0384

info@fma-usa.org www.fma-usa.org
Robert J Tum-Suden, Administrator
Members are foreign exchange and money market traders and brokers.
300 Members Founded: 1958

7365 Financial Planning Association
4100 E Mississippi Avenue
Suite 400
Denver, CO 80246
303-759-4900
FAX: 303-759-0749 800-322-4237
fpa@fpanet.org www.fpanet.org
Marvin W Tuttle, CAE, Executive Director/CEO
Al Hockwalt, Director Career Development
Ian McKenzie, Director Publications
Terry Monrad, Director Communications
Curt Niepoth, CFO
Accepts members who have qualified for the CFP (Certified Financial Planner) designation.
29000 Members Founded: 2000

7366 Financial Services Roundtable
1001 Pennsylvania Avenue NW
Suite 500 South
Washington, DC 20004
202-289-4322
FAX: 202-289-1903 www.fsround.org
Richard M Whiting, Executive Director/General Counsel
Steve Bartlett, President/CEO
Lisa McGreevy, EVP External Affairs
Founded: 1993

7367 Financial Services Technology Consortium
44 Wall Street
12th Floor
New York, NY 10005
212-711-1400
FAX: 646-349-3629
fstcadmin@fstc.org www.fstc.org
J Andrew Spindler, President
Zachary Tumin, Executive Director
FSTC sponsors product testing, development programs, and other projects to ensure the continued viability of new technologies in the financial sector.
Founded: 1993

7368 Financial Services Technology Network
8 S Michigan Avenue
Chicago, IL 60603
312-782-4951
FAX: 312-580-0165 fstn@gss.net
Kathleen Luleasile, Executive Director
Dale Smith, President
Kathy Johnson, Secretary/Treasurer

7369 Financial Women International
1027 W Roselawn Avenue
Roseville, MN 55113
703-696-4444
FAX: 651-489-1322
info@fwi.org www.fwi.org
Ann Dvaal, FWI Management Services
Judy Rogers, President
Nancy Kinder, Treasurer
Rilla Dath, Secretary

7370 Fraud & Theft Information Bureau
9770 S Military Trail
Suite 380
Boynton Beach, FL 33436
561-737-8700
FAX: 561-737-5800
sales@fraudandtheftinfo.com
www.fraudandtheftinfo.com
Larry Schwartz, Founder/Director
Pearl Sax, Founder/Director
A leading consultant on credit card and check fraud control and loss prevention, and the publisher of related manuals and fraud-blocker data bases.
Founded: 1982

7371 Futures Industry Association
2001 Pennsylvania Avenue Northwest
Suite 600
Washington, DC 20006-1823
202-466-5460
FAX: 202-296-3184
info@futuresindustry.org
www.futuresindustry.org
John M Damgard, President
Barbara Wierzynski, Executive VP
Jeffrey D Morgan, COO
Representative of all organizations that have an interest in the futures market.
180 Members Founded: 1955

7372 Global Association of Risk Professionals
100 Pavonia Avenue
Suite 405
Jersey City, NJ 07310
201-222-0054
FAX: 201-222-5022
rich.apostolik@garp.com
ww.garp.com
Richard Apostolik, President/CEO
Carolin Statman, Sales/Marketing
GARP's international membership includes a varity of professionals from the finance industry who share a common interest in financial risk management practice and research.
52330 Members Founded: 2000

7373 Government Finance Officers Association
203 N LaSalle Street
Suite 2700
Chicago, IL 60601-1210
312-977-9700
FAX: 312-977-4806
inquiry@gfoa.org www.gfoa.org
Edward Harrington, President
Tammy E Clayton, Director Finance
Catherine McClary, Treasurer
Susan Gaffney, Director
Jeffery Esser, Executive Director/CEO
Association for the management level executive in the financial community.
15500 Members Founded: 1906

7374 Healthcare Billing and Management Association
1540 South Coast Highway
Suite 203
Laguna Beach, CA 92651

877-640-4262
Members are companies providing third-party medical billing services.
500 Members Founded: 1992

7375 Institute for Divorce Financial Analysts
24901 Northwestern Highway
Suite 710
Southfield, MI 48075
989-631-3605
FAX: 248-223-0199 800-875-1760
shar@institutedfa.com
www.institutedfa.com
Shar Lockley, Client Service Manager

7376 Institute for Responsible Housing Preservation
401 Ninth Street NW
Suite 900
Washington, DC 20004
202-858-8000
FAX: 202-585-8080
info@housingpreservation.org
www.housingpreservation.org
Linda D Kirk, Executive Director
IRHP members are owners and managers of Low Income Housing Preservation and Resident Housing Act housing and ELIHPA housing and concerned professionals.
Founded: 1989

7377 Institute for Supply Management Association
2055 E Centennial Circle
PO Box 22160
Tempe, AZ 85285-2160
480-752-6276
FAX: 480-752-7890 800-888-6276
Paul Novak, CPM, CEO
Holly LaCroix Johnson, SVP
Deborah Webber, SVP
The mission os ISM is lead supply management.
43000 Members Founded: 1915

7378 Institute of Industrial Engineerings
3577 Parkway Lane
Suite 200
Norcross, GA 30092-2928
770-490-0461
FAX: 770-441-3295 800-494-0460
cs@iienet.org www.iienet.org
John Powers, Executive Director

7379 Institute of Internal Auditors
247 Maitland Avenue
Altamonte Springs, FL 32701-4201
407-937-1100
FAX: 407-937-1101
iia@theiia.org www.theiia.org
David Richards, President
Betty L McPhilimy, Chair
Patricia E. Scipio, Treasurer
Gerald D. Cox, Secretary
Independent, objective assurance and consulting activity designed to add value to an organization's operations. It helps an organization accomplish its objectives by bringing a systematic, disciplined approach to evaluate and improve the effectiveness of risk management, control and governance processes. Representation from more than 100 countries.
100M Members Founded: 1941

7380 Institute of International Finance
1333 H St NW
Suite 800 E
Washington, DC 20005-4770
202-857-3600
FAX: 202-775-1430
info@iif.com www.iif.com
Josef Ackermann, Chairman
Roberto E Setubal, Vice Chairman
Cees Maas, Vice Chairman/Treasurer
Charles Dallara, Managing Director
Members are primarily international, commercial banks that focus on middle-income countries by communicating with the debtor countries, international financial institutions and regulatory agencies in order to improve the process of international lending.
320 Members Founded: 1983

7381 Institute of Management & Administration
3 Park Avenue
30th Floor
New York, NY 10016
212-244-0360
FAX: 212-564-0465
subserve@ioma.com www.ioma.com
Joe Bremner, President
Supports all those involved in international sales looking for new distribution channels and how to reduce exports costs and risks. Publishes newsletter.

7382 Institute of Management Accountants
10 Paragon Drive
Montvale, NJ 07645-1760
201-573-9000
FAX: 201-474-1600 800-638-4427
ima@imanet.org www.imanet.org
Paul Sharman, President/CEO
IMA is the only U.S. association representing the interests of all management accounting and finance professionals-those who work inside organizations. IMA develops and advances accounting professionals through certification, cutting-edge professional research; and development of standards, best practices and tools supporting effective decision support, planning, and control. *$145.00*
65000 Members Monthly Founded: 1919

7383 Institutional Shareholder Services
2099 Gaither Road
Rockville, MD 20850-4045
202-833-0700
FAX: 202-833-3555
ISSmarketing@issproxy.com
www.irrc.org
John Connolly, President/CEO
Donald Cassidy, Vice Chair
Maryellen F Andersen, VP
Gwenn L Carr, VP/Secretary to Board
Leading provider of independent and impartial research on coporations and their shareholders.
500 Members Founded: 1972

7384 International Association of Financial Engineers
560 Lexington Avenue
9th Floor
New York, NY 10022
212-317-7479
FAX: 212-527-2927
main@iafe.org www.iafe.org
Richard Lindsey, Chairman
Mack Gill, Treasurer
The IAFE is a not-for-profit, professional society dedicated to fostering the profession of quantitative finance by providing platforms to discuss cutting-edge and pivotal issues in the field. Founded in 1992, the IAFE is composed of individual academic and practioners from banks, broker dealers, hedge funds, pension funds, asset managers, technology firms, regulators, accounting, consulting and law firms and universities worldwide.
Founded: 1992

7385 International Association of Purchasing Managers
45 Woodside W
Patchogue, NY 11772
631-654-2384
FAX: 516-475-2754
A professional organization dedicated to the advancement of world trade. Membership is open to buyers, purchasing managers, executives and all individuals that may be involved or have an interest in the important function of buying goods and services on the global market. A nonprofit organization.
1600 Members Founded: 1985

7386 International Business Affairs Corporation
4938 Hampden Lane
Bethesda, MD 20814
301-907-8647
FAX: 301-907-8650
editor@exportsourcebook.com
www.exportsourcebook.com
Richard Barovick, Editor/Publisher
Founded: 1979

7387 International Newspaper Financial Executives
21525 Ridgetop Circle
Suite 200
Sterling, VA 20166
703-421-4060
FAX: 703-421-4068
infehq@infe.org
www.infesecure.org/newsite/extranet/
Robert J Kasabian, Executive Director/VP
The international newspaper association for financial accounting and business management. Offers a Email Newsletter.
1000 Members Founded: 1947

7388 International Probate Research Association
c/o Josh Butler & Company
201 E Commerce Street, Suite 150
Youngstown, OH 44503-1640
330-747-3000
FAX: 330-747-3006
www.lostheir.com/ipa.htm
Josh Butler, President
IPRA members are probate research companies.
Founded: 1989

7389 International Society of Financiers
PO Box 398
Naples, NC 28760
828-698-7805
FAX: 828-698-7806 www.insofin.com
Ronald I Gershen, Chairman/President
A professional society of brokers, consultants, investors and corporate lenders active in financial projects and transactions. ISF provides an exclusive and confidential forum for member-to-member exchange and business networking.
300 Members Founded: 1979

7390 International Swaps and Derivatives Association
360 Madison Avenue
16th Floor
New York, NY 10017
212-901-6000
FAX: 212-901-6001
isda@isda.org www.isda.org
Robert Pickel, CEO
Louise Marshall, Director Communications
Corrine Greasley, Director Administration
Represents firms, primarily financial institutions, corporations and government entities who deal in privately-negoiated derivatives, as well as firms who provide services to such institutions. ISDA's, mission is to encourage the productive development of interest rate, currency, commodity, and equity swaps as financial products.
Founded: 1985

7391 International Union of Housing Finance
111 E Wacker Drive
Chicago, IL 60601
312-946-8200
FAX: 312-946-8202
info.iuhf@housingfinance.org
www.houisingfinance.org
Dale Bottom, Secretary General
Disseminates information in housing finance policies and techniques worldwide.
370 Members Founded: 1914

7392 Investment Company Institute
1401 H Street NW
Washington, DC 20005
202-169-9866
FAX: 202-326-5874
collins@ici.org www.ici.org
Matthew P Fink, President
Paul G Haaga Jr, Chairman
Julie Domenick, Executive VP
Lawrence Maffia, Executive VP/COO
Dan Crowley, Chief Government Affairs Officer

Acts to represent members in matters of legislation, taxation, regulation, economic research and marketing and public information regarding investments and mutual funds.
9400+ Members Founded: 1940

7393 Investment Recovery Association
638 W 39th Street
Kansas City, MO 64111
816-561-5323
FAX: 816-561-1991
ira@invrecovery.org
www.invrecovery.org

Jane Male, Exec Director

Association for manufacturers of services and supplies to the industry.
350+ Members Founded: 1994

7394 Managed Futures Association
1200 19th Street N
Washington, DC 20036
202-671-1140
FAX: 650-325-4944 800-425-4532

John Gaine, Manager

Members are individuals involved in commodity futures trading. Represents the industry to regulatory and legislative governing bodies and to the investing public.

7395 Mortgage Bankers Association of America
1919 Pennsylvania Avenue NW
Washington, DC 20006-3404
202-557-2700
FAX: 202-721-0198 800-793-6222
membership@mbaa.org
www.mortgagebankers.org

Robert M Couch, Chairman
Regina Lowrie, Vice Chairwoman
Jonathan L Kempner, President/CEO
Dan Thoms, VP

Association for all state and local MBA officers.
2700 Members Founded: 1914

7396 Municipal Treasurers Association
2601 Fourth Avenue
Suite 800
Seattle,, WA 98121-1280
202-833-1017

Mission is to promote the profession of municipal treasurers through education, mutual support, professional recognition, and legislative advocacy.
Founded: Was

7397 Mutual Fund Education Alliance
NW Englewood Road
Suite 130
Kansas City, MO 64118
816-454-9422
FAX: 816-454-9322
webservices@mfea.com
www.mfea.com

Michelle Smith, Managing Director

Conducts public education and public relation activities in an effort to acquaint investors, industry organizations and government agencies with direct market funds.
55 Members Founded: 1971

7398 Mutual Fund Investors Association
20 William Street
Wellesley, MA 02481
617-369-2000
FAX: 617-369-2510 800-456-2736

Eric Kobren, Publisher

Association for those interested in information and rates for mutual funds, investments, stocks and bonds.

7399 NACHA - Electronic Payments Association
13665 Dulles Technology Drive
Suite 300
Herndon, VA 20171
703-561-1100
FAX: 703-787-0996
info@nacha.org www.nacha.org

Elliott C McEntee, President/CEO
Deb Evans-Doyle, Senior Director Conference Mktg
Julie Hedlund, Senior Director Electronic Commerce
Michael Herd, Director Public Relations
Priscilla Holland, AAP, Senior Director Corporate Pymts

NACHA is a trade association that forms the cooperative foundation for the automated clearing house (ACH) payments system through a network of 21 ACH associations nationwide. It also provides marketing and educational members through direct memberships and a network of regional payment associations.
Founded: 1974

7400 National Accounting and Finance Council
2200 Mill Road
Alexandria, VA 22314
703-838-1915
FAX: 703-836-0751
atamembership@truckingline.com
www.nafc.truckline.com

Patrick E Quinn, Chairman of the Board
Ray Kuntz, First Vice Chairman

NAFC is a member organization of chief financial officers within the trucking industry and is a part of the American Trucking Association.
1000 Members Founded: 1941

7401 National Aircraft Finance Association
PO Box 85
Poolesville, MD 20837
301-349-2070
FAX: 301-972-7727
info@nafa-us.org www.nafa-us.org

Karen C Griggs, Executive Director

Members are lending institutions involved in aircraft financing.
95 Members Founded: 1969

7402 National Association for Treasurers of Religious Institutes
8824 Cameron Street
Silver Spring, MD 20910
301-587-7776
FAX: 301-589-2897
lelcock@natri.org www.natri.org

Laura Reicks, Executive Director
Lorele Elcock, Associate Director Finance

NATRI's mission is to address the fiscal, legal and administrative responsibilities specific to religious institutes in the U.S. membership.
600 Members Founded: 1981

7403 National Association of Affordable Housing Lenders
1300 Connecticut Avenue NW
Suite 905
Washington, DC 20036
202-293-9850
FAX: 202-293-9852 naahl@naahl.org

Judith A Kennedy, President/CEO

Is the only association devoted to increasing private capital lending and investment in low and moderate income communities.
800 Members Founded: 1988

7404 National Association of Bankruptcy Trustees
One Windsor Cove
Suite 305
Columbia, SC 29223
803-252-5646
FAX: 803-765-0860 800-445-8629
info@nabt.com www.nabt.com

Carol H Webster, Executive Director

The majority of the members of the NABT are Chapter 7 trustees who primarily liquidate nonexempt assets for the benefit of creditors.
1200 Members Founded: 1981

7405 National Association of Certified Valuation Analysts
1111 Brickyard Road
Suite 200
Salt Lake City, UT 84106-5401
801-486-0600
FAX: 801-486-7500
nacva1@nacva.com www.navca.com

Pamela R Bailey, Executive Director
Parnell Black, MBA CPA CVA, CEO
Roberto Castro, Director Business Development
Dean Dinas, Director Economic Research
Brien K Jones, General Manager Conferences

NACVA memberes are professionals, primarily certified public accountants, who provide business valuation services.
5500 Members Founded: 1990

7406 National Association of Corporate Treasurers
12100 Sunset Hills Road
Suite 130
Reston, VA 20190
703-437-4377
FAX: 703-435-4390
nact@nact.org www.nact.org

Karen Treadwell, Chairman
Irina Simmons, President
William Mekrut, Executive VP
William Van Lopik, Secretary
Brent Callinicos, VP/Treasurer

Members are corporate chief financial officers, treasurers or assistant treasurers.
825 Members Founded: 1982

7407 National Association of Development
6764 Old McLean Village Dr
McLean, VA 22101
703-748-2575
FAX: 703-748-2582
merril@nadco.org www.nadco.org

Zola Finch, Chairperson
David King, Region 1 Director
Ira Lutsky, Chairman
Kurt Chilcott, Chairman
Chris Crawford, President

Provides long term, fixed asset financing to small businesses.

135 Members Founded: 1981

7408 National Association of Division Order Analysts
2805 Oak Trail Court
Suite 6312
Arlington, TX 76016
972-715-4489

nadoa_org@hotmail.com
www.nadoa.org

Lynn S McCord, Administrator

Division order analysts are petroleum and gas company employees or independent consultants responsible for royalty working interest and overiding royalty payments. Offers a certification program providing education, training and testing for qualified applicants desiring to attain Certified Divison Order Analyst credentials.
900 Members 4 Founded: 197

7409 National Association of Equipment Leasing Brokers
304 W Liberty Street
Suite 201
Louisville, KY 40202

800-996-2352
info@naelb.org www.naelb.org

Carol Davis, Administrator

Broker-oriented association.
450 Members Founded: 1990

7410 National Association of Federal Credit
3138 10th Street N
Arlington, VA 22201-2149
703-224-4770
FAX: 703-524-1082 800-336-4644
jbruce@nafcu.org www.nafcu.org

Fred R Becker, Jr, President/CEO
Joseph Boyle, Director

Trade association exclusively represents the interests of federal credit unions before the federal government and the public. Provides members with representation, information, education and assistance to meet the challenges that cooperative financial institutions face in today's economic environment. Stands as a national forum for the federal credit union community where new ideas, issues, concerns and trends can be identified, discussed and resolved.

7411 National Association of Independent Public Finance Advisors
PO Box 304
Montgomery, IL 60538-0304
630-896-1292
FAX: 209-633-6265 800-624-7321

Roseanne M Hoban, Executive Director

NAIPFA members are independent firms specializing in providing financial advice to public agencies regarding infrastructure financing, long-term capital improvement, marketing of debt issues, and other financial advisory engagements.
71 Members Founded: 1989

7412 National Association of Investors
1515 E 11 Mile Road
Royal Oak, MI 48067-2027
248-583-6242
800-331-9525
service@better-investing.org
www.better-investing.org

Kenneth Janke, Chairman
Richard Holphaus, President/CEO
Robert O'Hara, VP Business Development

Strives to counsel and teach investing techniques and sound investment procedures to interested people.
23000 Members Founded: 1950

7413 National Association of Local Housing Finance Agencies
2025 M Street NW
Suite 800
Washington, DC 20036-3309
202-367-1197
FAX: 202-367-2197
john_murphy@nalhfa.org
www.nalhfa.org

John C Murphy, Executive Director
Scott Lynch, Association Manager
Kim McKinon, Coordinator Membership

Regular memebers of NALHFA are primarily county and city agencies which finance, directly or indirectly, affordable housing through a variety of means: tax-exempt and taxable bonds, federal grant programs, and state and local subsidies. Affiliate members are organizations providing technical assistance to local agencies.
Founded: 1982

7414 National Association of Mortgage Brokers
7900 Westpark Dr
Ste T309
Mc Lean, VA 22102-4264
703-425-5900
FAX: 703-610-9005 www.namb.org

Michael J Nizankiewicz, PhD CAE, Executive Vice President
Roy DeLoach, VP Legislative
Rebecca Dopkin, VP Meetings

Formed to provide a focal point for mortgage brokers and a communications link with mortgage bankers and underwriters. Only national trade association representing the mortgage broker industry.
5300 Members Founded: 1973

7415 National Association of Personal Financial Advisors
3250 N Arlington Heights Road
Suite 109
Arlington Heights, IL 60004
847-483-5400
FAX: 847-483-5415 800-366-2732
wassermanm@napfa.org
www.napfa.org

Ellen Turf, CEO
Margery Wasserman, Director Conferences

Members are financial planners who are compensated only by fees. NAPFA members are prohibited from receiving any type of product-related compensation, such as sales commissions. Members do not sell products nor do they direct sales to parties with whom they have financial interests.
1050 Members Founded: 1983

7416 National Association of Review Appraisers & Mortgage Underwriters
1224 N Nokomis NE
Alexandria, MN 56308-5072
320-763-6870
FAX: 320-763-9290
nara@iami.org www.iami.org

Robert G Johnson, Executive Director

Association for professionals who review real estate appraisals and underwrite real estate mortgages. The association offers the CRA, Certified Review Appraiser and RMU, Registered Mortgage Underwriter, professional designation.
2852 Members Founded: 1969
Mailing list available for rent 3500 names $75 per M.

7417 National Association of Securities Dealers
1735 K Street NW
Washington, DC 20006-1516
202-288-8000
FAX: 202-728-8882

Robert Glauber, Chief Executive Officer

7418 National Association of Settlement Purchasers
8300 N Hayden Road
Suite 207
Scottsdale, AZ 85258
480-951-4311
FAX: 480-626-4436 877-800-7192
info@nasp.com www.nasp.com

Aaron Bare, President

Members are companies who purchase structured settlements, lottery annuities, and similar periodic payment plans from their beneficiaries.
Founded: 1995

7419 National Association of Small Businesses
666 11th Street NW
Suite 750
Washington, DC 20001
202-628-5055
FAX: 202-628-5080
nasbic@nasbic.org www.nasbic.org

Lee W Mercer, President
Jeanette D Paschal, VP/Executive Director
Jamie G Blake, Director Member Services
Dawna S Kasper, Director Finance
Sam Freedenberg, Director Communications

Trade association representing federally licensed venture capital firms, email, and business investment companies.
400 Members Founded: 1958

7420 National Association of State Budget Officers
444 North Capitol Street NW
Suite 642
Washington, DC 20001
202-624-5382
FAX: 202-624-7745
spattison@nasbo.org www.nasbo.org

Scott Pattison, Executive Director
Lauren Cummings, Manager Member Relations

Membership limited to three budget officers per state. Affiliated with the National Governors Association.
160 Members Founded: 1945

7421 National Association of Tax Professionals
720 Association Drive
Appleton, WI 54912
920-491-1040
FAX: 800-747-0001 800-588-3402
natp@natptax.com www.natptax.com
The National Association of Tax Professionals (NATP) is a nonprofit professional association founded in 1979 and is committed to excellence in the tax profession. Our national headquarters is located in Appleton, Wisconsin and employs 39 professionals and 25 instructors. NATP was formed to serve professionals who work in

all areas of tax practice and has more than 16,000 members nationwide.
17000 Members Founded: 1979

7422 National Association of Trade Exchanges
8836 Tyler Road
Mentor, OH 44060
440-205-5378
FAX: 440-205-5379
bartertrainer@aol.com www.nate.org
Thomas H McDowell, Executive Director
Ron Hollowell, Marketing Director
NATE offers their members additional benefits such national and regional meetings and accreditation opportunities.
80 Members Founded: 1984

7423 National Automotive Finance Association
7250 Parkway Drive,
Suite 510
Hanover, MD 21076-1343
410-712-4036
FAX: 410-712-4038 800-463-8955
information@nafassociation.com
www.nafassociation.com
Jack Tracey, Executive Director
NAF Association serves companies and professionals in the non-prime auto lending industry.
85 Members Founded: 1996

7424 National Bankers Association
1513 P Street NW
Washington, DC 20005
202-588-5432
FAX: 202-588-5443
webmaster@nationalbankers.org
www.nationalbankers.org
Norma Alexan Hart, President
James E Young, Chairman
Association for banks owned or controlled by minority group persons or women.
15000 Members Founded: 1927

7425 National Center on Financial Education
PO Box 34070
San Diego, CA 92163-4070
619-232-8811
FAX: 619-234-3944

7426 National Committee on Planned Giving
233 McCrea Street
Suite 400
Indianapolis, IN 46206-6222
317-269-6274
FAX: 317-269-6276
kramsey@ncpg.org www.ncpg.org
Tanya Howe-Johnson, CAE, President/CEO
Sandra Kerr, Director Government Education
Barbara Owens, Director Membership/Manager HR
Kathryn J Ramsey, Director Meetings
Kurt Reusze, Manager Education/Technology
Members are professionals involved in the process of planning and cultivating charitable gifts.
11500 Members Founded: 1988

7427 National Community Capital Association
Public Ledger Building, 620 Chestnut Street
Suite 572
Philadelphia, PA 19106
215-923-4754
FAX: 215-923-4755
ncca@communitycapital.org
www.communitycapital.org
Mark Pinsky, President/CEO
Provides support for nonprofit, revolving loan funds that lend capital and offer technical assistance in distressed and disenfranchised communities.
52 Members Founded: 1986

7428 National Council of Health Facilities
PO Box 15128
Lansing, MI 48901-5128
517-373-7249
FAX: 517-334-6686
To serve the common interests and enhance the effectiveness of member Authorities through communication, education and advocacy.

7429 National Credit Union Administration
1775 Duke Street
Alexandria, VA 22314
703-518-6300
FAX: 703-518-6319 www.ncua.gov
JoAnn Johnson, Chairperson
Governed by a three member board appointed by the President and confirmed by the US Senate, this independent federal agency charters and supervises federal credit unions. NCUA, with the backing of the full faith and credit of the US government, operates the National Credit Union Share Insurance Fund, insuring the savings of 80 million account holders in all federal credit unions and many state chartered credit unions.

7430 National Defined Contribution Council
714 Hopmeadow Street
Suite 3
Simsbury, CT 06070
860-658-5058
FAX: 860-658-5068
glenna@sparkinstitute.org
www.ndcconline.org
Al Brust, Executive Vice President
Charles E Vieth, President
NDCC is dedicated to the promotion and protection of the defined contribution industry and the public it serves. The Council specifically addresses the legislative needs of the defined contribution industry's plan service providers.
300 Members Founded: 1995

7431 National Federation of Municipal Credit Analysts
PO Box 14893
Pittsburgh, PA 15234
412-341-4898
FAX: 412-341-4894
lgood@nfma.org www.nfma.org
Lisa S Good, Executive Director
Promotes the profession of municipal credit analysts through educational programs, industry, communications and related programming.
1000 Members Founded: 1983

7432 National Finance Adjusters
PO Box 3855
Baltimore, MD 21217-0855
410-728-2400
FAX: 410-523-8336
info@nfa.org www.nfa.org
Burton Greenwood Jr, President
Jack S Barnes, Executive Director
Members are collateral recovery specialists.

7433 National Futures Association
200 W Madison Street
#1600
Chicago, IL 60606-3447
312-781-1300
FAX: 312-781-1457
information@nfa.futures.org
www.nfa.future.org
Michael R Schaefer, Chairman
Douglas O Kitchen, Vice Chairman
Dan Roth, President
Association for corporations and firms that are registered with the Commodity Futures Trading Commission.

7434 National Home Equity Mortgage Association
1301 Pennsylvania Avenue NW
Suite 500
Washington, DC 20049-0001
202-347-1210
FAX: 202-347-1171 800-342-1121
Debbie Rosen, Chairman
Jeffrey Zeltzer, President
Mission is to promote the growth and recognition of the home equity lending industry.
300 Members Founded: 1974

7435 National Institute of Pension Plans
401 N Michigan Avenue
#2200
Chicago, IL 60611-4267
800-999-6472
FAX: 312-245-1085
nipa@nipa.org www.nipa.org
Laura J Rudzinski, Executive Director
Susan Heckman, Operations Manager
The mission is to enhance professionalism in the retirement plan industry
1000 Members Founded: 1983

7436 National Institute of Pension Admini- strators
401 N Michigan Avenue
Suite 2200
Chicago, IL 60611-4267

800-999-6272
nipa@nipa.org www.nipa.org
Laura J Rudzinski, Executive Director
The Institute is responsible for the formation Of professional standards, an ongoing education program consisting of workshops and home study courses, and awards of the APA and the APR designations by examination and experience.
1000 Members Founded: 1983

7437 National Investment Company Service Association
2 Mount Royal Avenue
Suite 320
Marlborough, MA 01752
508-485-1500
FAX: 508-485-1560
info@nicsa.org www.nicsa.org
Barbara V Weidlich, President
Keith Dropkin, VP
Doris Jaimes, Registrar
Sheila Kobaly, Events Manager
Chris Ludent, IT Manager
NICSA works to facilitate and promote leadership and innovation within the operations sector of the mutual fund industry.
10000 Members Founded: 1962

7438 National Pawnbrokers Association
PO Box 1040
Roanoke, TX 76262
817-491-4554
FAX: 817-491-8770
bob@nationalpawnbrokers.org
www.nationalpawnbrokers.org
Bob Benedict, CAE, Executive Director
NPA was founded to unite all pawnbrokers in their common efforts to improve the image of the industry, educate the public, adn disseminate professional information and assistance.
2000 Members Founded: 1988

7439 National Reverse Mortgage Lenders Association
1625 Massachusetts Avenue NW
Suite 601
Washington, DC 20036-2244
202-939-1760
FAX: 202-265-4435
www.reversemortgage.org
Peter H Bell, Executive Director
Glenn Petherick, Director Communications
Is the national voice for lenders and investors engaged in the reverse mortgage business.
Founded: 1997

7440 National Vehicle Leasing Association
100 North 20th Street
4th Floor
Philadelphia, PA 19103
215-564-3484
FAX: 215-963-9785
info@nvla.org www.nvla.org
Dale Davis, President
David Blassingame, First VP
Fosters education, publishing, conferences, legal services, advancement and industry relations certification.
500 Members Founded: 1965

7441 National Venture Capital Association
1655 N Fort Myer Drive
Suite 850
Arlington, VA 22209
703-524-2549
FAX: 703-524-3940
lturner@nvca.org www.nvca.org
Mark Heesen, President
Molly M Myers, VP
National trade association that represents venture capital firms. Activities include advocacy, professional development, networking and research.
450 Members Founded: 1973

7442 Neighborhood Reinvestment Corporation
92 Argonaut
Suite 255
Aliso Viejo, CA 92656-3100
949-770-2000
FAX: 949-770-2157 800-808-3372
sales@federalregister.com
www.federalregister.com
Supplies training, grants, developmental assistance, and a range of other technical services designed to help the local partnerships achieve substantially self-reliant neighborhoods. The goal is to improve a neighborhood's housing and physical conditions, build a positive community image, and establish a healthy real estate market and a core of neighbors capable of managing the continued health of their neighborhood.
Founded: 1978

7443 RMA - Risk Management Association
1650 Market Street
Suite 2300
Philadelphia, PA 19103
215-446-4000
FAX: 215-446-4101 800-677-7621
Maurice H Hartigan, II, President/CEO
William F Githens, Director Member Relations
Dwight Overturf, CFO/Information Technology Officer
Florence J Wetzel, COO/Administration Officer
Seeks to improve the risk management capabilities and principles of commercial lending and credit functions, loan administration and asset management in commercial banks and other financial industries.
17500 Members Founded: 1914

7444 Retirement Industry Trust Association
424 Montgomery Avenue
Suite 102
Bethesda, MD 20814
301-652-5066
FAX: 301-577-6476 obryonco@aol.com
David S O'Bryon, CAE, Executive Director

7445 Securities Industry Association
1425 K Street NW
7th Floor
Washington, DC 20005-3500
202-898-8731
FAX: 202-216-2119
info@sia.com www.sia.com
Marc E Lackritz, President
Marilyn Skiles, Executive Director
Steve Judge, Senior VP
Investment bankers, brokers, dealers, mutual funds and others accounting for about 95 percent of the securities business in North America. Missin is to build and maintain public trust and confidence in the securities market.
700 Members Founded: 1972

7446 Security Traders Association
420 Lexington Avenue
Suite 2334
New York, NY 10170
212-240-0484
FAX: 212-867-7030
traders@securitytraders.org
www.securitytraders.org
John C Giesea, President/CEO
Walter V Dolengo, VP
Bill Yancey, Treasurer
Lisa Utasi, Secretary
Members involved in the securities industry.
7000 Members Founded: 1934

7447 Society for Information Management
401 N Michigan Avenue
Chicago, IL 60611
312-527-6734
SIM@simnet.org www.simnet.org
Robert Keefe, President
SIM was formed to enhance international recognition of information as a basic organizational resource and to promote the effective utilization and management of this resource towards the improvement of management performance. It attempts to enhance communications between IS executives and the senior executives responsible for management of the business enterprise.
3000 Members Founded: 1969

7448 Society of Financial Examiners
174 Grace Boulevard
Altamonte Springs, FL 32714
407-682-4930
FAX: 407-682-3175 800-787-7633
info@sofe.org www.sofe.org
Paula Keyes, Executive Director
Is a professional society for examiners of insurance companies, banks, savings and loans, and credit unions.
1600 Members Founded: 1973

7449 Society of Quantitative Analysts
PO Box 539
Webster, NY 14580
585-545-6925
FAX: 585-545-6927
sqa@sqa-us.org www.sqa-us.org
David Carleton, Executive Director
SQA is concerned with the application of new and innovative techniques for finance, with particular emphasis on the use of quantitative techniques in investment management.
300 Members Founded: 1989

7450 Stable Value Investment Association
2121 K Street NW
Suite 800
Washington, DC 20037
202-261-6530
FAX: 202-261-6527 800-327-2270
Gina Mitchell, President
Members are firms and individuals with a professional interest in savings for retirement.
Founded: 1990

7451 State Debt Management Networking
444 N Capital Street
Suite 400
Washington, DC 20001
202-624-8595
FAX: 202-624-8677
nast@csg.org
www.nast.net/debtnet/index.htm
Dan DeSimone, Director
Anne Gavin, Manager
SDMN members are state officials concerned with the insurance or management of

state debt. The purpose is to enhance debt management practices throough training, development of educational materials, and data collection and dissemination
50 Members Founded: 1991

7452 **State Risk and Insurance Management Association**
PO Box 809
Jefferson City, MO 65102
573-751-4044
FAX: 573-751-7819 www.strima.org
Janice Steenburgen, Risk Manager
STRIMA members are state government risk and insurance managers.
50 Members

7453 **Tax Executives Institute**
1200 G Street NW
Suite 300
Washington, DC 20005-3814
202-638-5601
FAX: 202-638-5607 www.tei.org
Timothy J McCormally, Executive Director
Deborah K Gaffney, Director Conference Planning
Deborah C Giesey, Director Administration
Karina Horesky, Coordinator Membership
Fred F Murphy, General Counsel/Dir Tax Affairs
A professional organization of corporate tax executives. Membership is open to corporate officers and employees chargesd with administering their company's tax affairs.
5400 Members Founded: 1944

7454 **Urban Homesteading Assistance Board**
120 Wall Street
20th Floor
New York, NY 10005
212-479-3300

info@uhab.org www.uhab.org
Charles Laven, Board President
Ingrid Kaminsky, Senior VP
Andrew Reicher, Executive Director
The oldest provider of technical assistance to homesteading and sweat equity groups in the country. Promotes homesteading as an important component of comprehensive self-help housing programs. Provides technical assistance and training in self-help housing rehabilitation and managment to low income tenants, cooperative shareholders and homesteaders.
8 Members Founded: 1973

7455 **Wall Street Technology Association**

241 Maple Avenue
Red Bank, NJ 07701
732-530-8808
FAX: 732-530-0020
rvendola@mpiscon.com
www.wsta.org
Richard Mendola, General Manager
Ivett Ortiz, Communications
Phyllis Lampell, Manager
Nonprofit organization for technology professionals working in the finacial world. Seminars, magazine and web site with the latest information and white papers are featured.

Newsletters

7456 **AARMR Newsletter**
American Association of Residential Mortgage
1255 23rd Street NW
Suite 200
Washington, DC 20037
202-521-3999
FAX: 202-833-3636
cmurphy@aarmr.org www.aarmr.org
David Saunders, Executive Director
Quarterly

7457 **AEFA Newsletter**
American Education Finance Association
8365 S Armadillo Trail
Evergreen, CO 80439
303-674-0857
FAX: 303-670-8986 www.aefa.cc
Ed Steinbacher, Executive Director
Quarterly

7458 **AFCPE Newsletter**
Association for Financial Counseling and Planning
2112 Arlington Avenue
Suite H
Upper Arlington, OH 43221
614-485-9650
FAX: 614-485-9621
sburns@finsolve.com www.afcpe.org
Sharon Burns, PhD, Executive Director
Quarterly

7459 **AMI Bulletin**
Association for Management Information in
3895 Fairfax Court
Atlanta, GA 30339
770-444-3557
FAX: 770-444-9084
ami@amifs.org www.amifs.org
Kevin Link, Executive Director
Quarterly

7460 **Airline Financial News**
PBI Media
1201 Seven Locks Road
Suite 300
Potomac, MD 20854-2931
301-354-1400
FAX: 301-309-3847 800-777-5006
Richard Koulbanis, Publisher
Provides information for CEO's financial directors, operations managers, engine aircraft manufacturers and suppliers on financial, market development, buying, leasing and aircraft transactions. *$697.00*
Weekly
Circulation: 1850

7461 **Annual Statement Studies**
RMA - Risk Management Association
1650 Market Street
Suite 2300
Philadelphia, PA 19103
215-446-4000
FAX: 215-446-4101 800-677-7621
Maurice H Hartigan, II, President/CEO
William F Githens, Director Member Relations
Dwight Overturf, CFO/Information Technology Officer
Florence J Wetzel, COO/Administrative Officer
John Rumm, Executive Director
Annual

7462 **Annual Update Proceedings**
Association of Commercial Finance Attorneys
25 Hook Lane
Suite 302
Baltimore, MD 21208-1302
410-486-2600
FAX: 410-486-8438
Jeremy Friedberg, Secretary
Annual

7463 **Asset-Backed Alert**
Harrison Scott Publications
5 Marine View Plaza
Suite 301
Hoboken, NJ 07030-5722
201-659-1700
FAX: 201-659-4141
info@hspnews.com
http://www.abalert.com
Andrew Albert, Publisher
Tom Ferris, Editor
Daniel Cowles, CEO/President
Barbara Bannace, Marketing
Joan Tassie, Circulation Manager
A weekly newsletter on the securitization of consumer and corporate receivables.
$2297.00
10 pages Weekly Founded: 1988
Circulation: 2178 500 names $400 per M.
Printed in 4 colors on matte stock

7464 **BNA Pension & Benefits Reporter**
Bureau of National Affairs
1231 25th Street NW
Washington, DC 20037
202-452-4200
800-372-1033
customercare@bna.com
http://www.bna.com/
Sarah Stevens, Managing Editor
Covers latest pension developments stemming from the passage of ERISA and its amendments, plus pension and welfare benefit regulations, standards, enforcement actions, court decisions, legislative and administrative actions, agency options, and employee benefit trust fund requirements. *$1448.00*
Weekly Founded: 1929
Printed in on matte stock
Computerized version available

7465 **Back-Office Bulletin**
United Communications Group
11300 Rockville Pike
Suite 1100
Rockville, MD 20852-3030
301-816-8950
FAX: 301-816-8945
webmaster@ucg.com
http://www.ucg.com
Daniel Brown, Publisher
Brian Crotty, President/CEO
For financial operations professionals.
Founded: 1970

7466 **Bandwidth Investor**
Kagan World Media
1 Lower Ragsgale Drive
Building 1 3130
Monterey, CA 93940-8746
831-624-1536
FAX: 831-625-3225
info@kagan.com
http://www.kagan.com
George Niesen, Editor
Harvey Kraft, Marketing Manager
Tim Baskerville, CEO

Harvey Kraft, Circulation Manager
$1195.00
Monthly Founded: 1969

7467 Bank 13D Dictionary
SNL Securities
PO Box 2124
Charlottesvle, VA 22902-2124
434-977-1600
FAX: 434-977-4466
subscriptions@snlnet.com
http://www.snl.com
Todd Davenport, Editor
Reid Nagle, Publisher
For banks, thrifts, investors, investment bankers, law firms, consultants and regulatory agencies. Contains all active 13D filings and related filings for every public traded bank in the country, including those which trade on the 'pink sheets.'
Quarterly Founded: 1987

7468 Barron's National Business and Financial News
Dow Jones & Company
200 Liberty Street
New York, NY 10281-1003
212-416-2000
FAX: 212-416-2829
Kalin House, Publisher
Paul Tigot, Editor
Edwin Finn Jr, President
Jubarry Parry, Marketing Manager
Offers readers in-depth sophisticated news reports and analyses on the financial markets in the United States and around the world. Accepts advertising. *$109.00*

7469 Benefax
SNL Securities
PO Box 2124
Charlottesvle, VA 22902-2124
434-977-1600
FAX: 434-977-4466
subscriptions@snlnet.com
http://www.snl.com
Keith Davis, Editor
Reid Nagle, Publisher
For bank and thrift executives. Contains only summaries of available information.
1 pages Monthly Founded: 1987

7470 Bondweek
Institutional Investor
225 Park Avenue S
7th Floor
New York, NY 10003
212-224-3300
FAX: 212-224-3171
ideas@institutionalinvestor.com
http://www.institutionalinvestor.com
Chris Brown, President
Erik Kolk, Publisher
Deirdre Brennan, Managing Editor
Nick Ferris, Group Marketing Director
Coverage of stocks, bonds and investments for the financial professional and consumer, information includes rates. *$2245.00*
51 issues per y Founded: 1967

7471 Broadcast Banker/Broker
Kagan World Media
One Lower Ragsdale Drive
Building One,Suite 130
Monterey, CA 93940-8746
831-624-1536
FAX: 831-625-3225 800-307-2529
info@kagan.com
http://www.kagan.com
George Niesen, Editor
Tom Johnson, Marketing Manager
A readers guide to equity deals and debt financing for radio and TV Station buying and selling analyzed. Key details on station trades with critical yardsticks of value. Three month trial is available. *$925.00*
Monthly

7472 Broadcast Investor
Kagan World Media
126 Clock Tower Place
Carmel, CA 93923-8746
831-624-1536
FAX: 831-624-5882
info@kagan.com www.kagan.com
George Niesen, Editor
Tom Johnson, Marketing Manager
The newsletter on investments in radio and TV stations and publicly held companies. Comprehensive analysis of cash flow multiples and trends that impact value. Three month trial available. *$895.00*
Monthly

7473 Broker Magazine
Thomson Media
1 State Street Plaza
27th Floor
New York, NY 10004
212-258-8445
FAX: 800-235-5552 800-221-1809
Timothy Murphy, Publisher
James Malkin, Chairman/CEO
Features on training, motivation, technology, legislation and marketing
Monthly
Circulation: 750000

7474 Budget Processors in the States
National Association of State Budge Officers
444 North Capitol Street NW
Suite 642
Washington, DC 20001
202-624-5382
FAX: 202-624-7745
spattison@nasbo.org www.nasbo.org
Scott Pattison, Executive Director
Lauren Cummings, Manager Member Relations
Bi-Ennial

7475 Bull & Bear Financial Report
PO Bo 917179
Longwood, FL 32791
954-781-3455
FAX: 954-781-5865 800-336-2855
David J Robinson, Publisher/Editor
Dozens of original articles by leading investment pros with investment information on precious metals, commodities, mutual funds, currencies, economic trends and monetary survival.
Circulation: 55000

7476 Bulletin Newsletter
EMTA - Trade Association for the Emerging Markets
360 Madison Avenue
18th Floor
New York, NY 10017
646-637-9100
FAX: 646-637-9128
awerner@emta.org www.emta.org
Michael M Chamberlin, Executive Director
Aviva Werner, General Counsel
Quarterly

7477 CFMA Building Profits
Construction Financial Management Association
29 Emmons Drive
Princeton, NJ 08540
609-452-8000
FAX: 609-452-0474 www.cfma.org
Paula Wristen, Editor
Sarah Patt, Sales/Advertising Director
William Schwab, President
The leading source of education and information about financial management within the construction industry. The only magazine dedicated to helping financial managers in the construction business find practical solutions to emerging issues in the industry. Accepts advertising.
32 pages
Circulation: 6500

7478 CIPFA Newsletter
National Association of Independent Public Finance
PO Box 304
Montgomery, IL 60538-0304
630-896-1292
FAX: 209-633-6265 www.naipfa.com
Roseanne M Hoban, Executive Director
Quarterly

7479 CRA/HMDA Update
Inside Mortgage Finance Publishers
7910 Woodmont Avenue
Suite 1010
Bethesda, MD 20814
301-951-1240
FAX: 301-915-0143
service@imfpubs.com
www.imfpubs.com
Guy D Cecala, Publisher/Editor
John Lewis, Managing Editor
Complete coverage of Community Reinvestment Act and Home Mortgage Disclosure Act developments and other affordable housing and community development issues. *$395.00*
Monthly
Circulation: 450

7480 Cable Program Investor
Kagan World Media
126 Clock Tower Place
Carmel, CA 93923-8746
831-624-1536
FAX: 831-624-5882
info@kagan.com www.kagan.com
George Niesen, Editor
Tom Johnson, Marketing Manager
Covers the economics of basic cable programming networks. Numbers, perspective unavailable from any other source. Programmers applaud its accuracy. Three month trial available. *$845.00*
Monthly

7481 Cable TV Finance
Kagan World Media
126 Clock Tower Place
Carmel, CA 93923-8746
831-624-1536
FAX: 831-624-5882 800-307-2529
info@kagan.com
http://www.kagan.com
George Niesen, Editor
Tom Johnson, Marketing Manager
Tim Baskerville, CEO/President
Cable's financial bible. Analyzes sources of funding for cable TV. Selling and buying of cable systems. Financing strategies and trends. Exclusive surveys of capital

sources. Three month trial available. *$995.00*
Monthly Founded: 1969

7482 Cable TV Investor
Kagan World Media
One Lower Ragsdale Drive
Building One, Suite 130
Monterey, CA 93940-8746
831-624-1536
FAX: 831-625-3225 800-307-2529
info@kagan.com www.kagan.com
George Niesen, Editor
Tom Johnson, Marketing Manager
Readers road map to cable stock trends. Chart service tracking stock price movements of 37 publicly held cable TV companies. Each graph shows two years of stock price activity. Three month trial available. *$945.00*
Monthly

7483 Capital Access Millennia
Association for Entrepreneurial Growth
PO Box 875
Merrimack, NH 03054
603-429-1631
FAX: 603-424-8641
gouldcapital@aol.com
Neil C Gould, Executive Director
Provides access to the private capital markets.

7484 Card News
Phillips Publishing
7811 Montrose Road
Suite 2
Potomac, MD 20854-3394
301-340-2100
FAX: 301-424-4297
Ellen Hamm, Publisher
John Seidenber, Editor
Covering the financial card marketplace.

7485 Client Information Bulletin
WPI Communications
55 Morris Avenue
Suite 312
Springfield, NJ 07081-1496
973-678-8700
FAX: 800-677-9742
info@wpicomm.com
www.apidigital.com
Steven Klinghoffer, Publisher
Marilyn Lang, Circulation Manager
Bulletin for lawyers and CPAs to distribute to clients to keep them informed on tax matters. This original publication which has been helping accountants build their practices since 1952, has been redesigned. Covers important new tax developments, general business principals, financial planning, estate planning and other related topics.

7486 Collection Agency Report
First Detroit Corporation
PO Box 5025
Warren, MI 48090-5025
586-573-0045
FAX: 586-573-9219 800-366-5995
info@firstdetroit.com
http://www.firstdetroit.com
Albert Scace, President
Petricia Herrick, Marketing Manager
Provides financially oriented news on the collection agency and bad debt buying industries worldwide. *$289.00*
8 pages Monthly
Mailing list available for rent 5000 names $110 per M.

7487 Commercial Mortgage Alert
Harrison Scott Publications
5 Marine View Plaza
Suite 301
Hoboken, NJ 07030-5722
201-659-1700
FAX: 201-659-4141
info@hspnews.com
http://www.abalert.com
Andrew Albert, Publisher
Tom Ferris, Editor
A weekly newsletter on the securitization of consumer and corporate receivables. *$1497.00*
10 pages Weekly
Circulation: 500 500 names $400 per M.
Printed in 4 colors on matte stock

7488 Conference Executive Summaries
Society for Information Management
401 N Michigan Avenue
Chicago, IL 60611
312-215-5190
FAX: 312-245-1081 www.simnet.org
Jim Luisi, Executive Director
Semi-Annual

7489 Conversion Candidates List
SNL Securities
PO Box 2124
Charlottesvle, VA 22902-2124
434-977-1600
FAX: 434-977-4466
subscriptions@snlnet.com
http://www.snl.com
Chris Smith, Editor
Reid Nagle, Publisher
For thrift executives, individual investors and institutional investors. Lists mutual thrifts that are in a position to convert to stock ownership by offering shares for sale.
Monthly Founded: 1987

7490 Conversion Watch
SNL Securities
PO Box 2124
Charlottesvle, VA 22902-2124
434-977-1600
FAX: 434-977-4466
subscriptions@snlnet.com
http://www.snl.com
Chris Smith, Editor
Delivered via fax whenever new activity is announced, including rumored, pending, announced and completed activity. Provides relevant data from conversion-related filings, including eligible record dates, offering size, Pro Formas, opening and closing dates for the subscription, asset size, net worth and rating of the thrift. *$1200.00*
5 pages Annual+ Founded: 1987

7491 Corporate EFT Report
Phillips Publishing
PO Box 60037
Potomac, MD 20859-0037
301-208-6787
FAX: 301-424-2098
Heather Treat, Publisher
Technologies used by companies to effect sound cash and treasury management.
BiWeekly
Circulation: 1500

7492 Corporate Financing Week
American Publishing
PO Box 11546
Albuquerque, NM 87108-1382
505-265-6121
FAX: 505-265-0632
customerservice@iinews.com
http://www.corporatefinancingweek.com
Elayne Glick, Publisher
Peter Thompson, Executive Editor
Tool for professionals to access knowledgeable attorneys, accountants, brokers, investment bankers and commercial/business leaders on issues from leasing equipment to restructuring and securing capital. *$2395.00*
Weekly Founded: 1980
Circulation: 31,000

7493 Corporate Venture Report
Asset Alternatives
170 Linden Street
Wellesley, MA 02482
781-304-1400
FAX: 781-304-1440 800-257-2947
customerservice@privateequityanalyst.co m http://www.corporateventuring.com
Dave Barry, Senior Editor
Barbara Bissonnette, VP Marketing/Sales
Gives you the latest news and hard-to-find facts about the most effective and innovative corporate venturing organizations...what they look for in investments...and the strategic benefits they expect to gain. *$895.00*
Monthly
Printed in on matte stock

7494 Cost Control News
Siefer Consultants
PO Box 1384
Storm Lake, IA 50588-1384
712-732-7340
FAX: 712-732-7906
info@siefer.com
http://www.siefer.com/
Dan Siefer, Publisher
Cost cutting opportunities for financial institutions. *$297.00*
8 pages Founded: 1981

7495 Credit Collections News
SourceMedia
550 W Van Buren
Ste 1100
Chicago, IL 60607-6680
312-913-1334
FAX: 312-913-1340
www.sourcemedia.com
John Stewart, Publisher
Analysis of the global economy, current industry trends and policies, as well as problems commonly encountered in credit collections.
Monthly

7496 Credit Risk Management Report
Phillips Publishing
9420 Key West Ave
Rockville, MD 20850-2931
301-279-4200
FAX: 301-424-2098 866-279-1930
information@phillips.com
http://www.phillips.com
Heather Treat, Publisher
Thomas L Phillips, Chairman
John J Coyle, President

Information on risk management, trends, forecasts and legislation in the credit consumer credit industry.
Monthly Founded: 1974

7497 Credit Union Journal
SourceMedia
224 Datura Street
Suite 615
West Palm Beach, FL 33401
561-832-2929
FAX: 561-832-2939 www.cujournal.com

Frank J Dierkmann, Publisher/Editor
Tim O'Hara, Co-Publisher

JournalScan to review recent credit union developments, industry news articles, an agenda of upcoming meetings, deadlines and events and Washington Watch covering the latest news in Washington DC.
Weekly
Circulation: 5300

7498 Credit Union Management
Credit Union Executives Society
PO Box 14167
Madison, WI 53714-167
608-271-2664
FAX: 608-271-2303 800-252-2664
cues@cues.org http://www.cues.org

Mary Arnold, Publisher
Theresa Sweeney, Editor
Fred Johnson, CEO/President *$93.00*
Monthly
Printed in 4 colors on glossy stock

7499 Credit and Collection Manager's Letter
Bureau of Business Practice
1185 Avenue of the Americas
New York, NY 10036
212-597-0333
FAX: 800-901-9075 800-638-8437
alicia.pierce@aspenpubl.com
www.bbpnews.com

Alicia Pierce, Operations

Hands-on information for improving the credit and collection departments in both commercial and consumer markets.
SemiMonthly
Circulation: 9380

7500 DC Plan Investing
Institute of Management & Administration

3 Park Avenue
30th Floor
New York, NY 10016
212-244-0360
FAX: 212-564-0465
subserve@ioma.com
http://www.ioma.com

Sheldon Barkoff, President

Covers confirmed searches, hirings and firings, reports on sponsors and changing providers. Rates the leading money managers and bundled service providers, with risk/return benchmarks. Identifies trends in exclusive asset allocation profiles. Shows what new offerings are being launched by providers. Covers mutual funds, GIC/BIC yields, poled funds and contract yields, composite stocks and separate accounts. *$1199.00*

Circulation: 180000

7501 Daily Tax Report
Bureau of National Affairs
1231 25th Street NW
Washington, DC 20037-1197
202-452-4200
800-372-1033
customercare@bna.com www.bna.com

Gregory C McCaffery, Publisher
Rebecca McCracken, Managing Editor

A daily tax notification service that covers legislative, regulatory, judicial and policy developments on a national basis, designed to give tax professionals rapid notification and comprehensive coverage of those developments. *$3215.00*
Daily

7502 Debit Card News
SourceMedia
224 Datura Street
Suite 615
West Palm Beach, FL 33401
561-832-2929
FAX: 561-832-2939 www.cujournal.com

Don Davis, Editor

Marketing, pricing, different card applications, smart cards, point-of-sale and other electronic banking activities.
SemiMonthly

7503 Declined Contribution Market Insights
National Defined Contribution Council
9101 E Kenyon
Suite 300
Denver, CO 80237-0467
303-770-5353
FAX: 303-770-1812
info@ndcconline.org
www.ndcconline.org

Al Brust, Executive Vice President
Annual

7504 Equipment Leasing Today
Equipment Leasing Association
4301 N Fairfax Drive
Suite 550
Arlington, VA 22203-1627
703-527-8655
FAX: 703-527-2649
http://www.elaonline.com

Amy Miller, Publisher/CAE
Mike Fleming, President
Matt Philbin, Director-Editorial Servic

Information of funding sources, portfolio management, sales and marketing strategy, large ticket leasing, transportation leasing, the computer leasing market, remarketing equipment, and the role of the equipment manager and securitization.
Monthly Founded: 1961
Circulation: 10000 10,000 names
Printed in 4 colors on glossy stock

7505 Executive Brief
Society for Information Management
401 N Michigan Avenue
Chicago, IL 60611
312-215-5190
FAX: 312-245-1081 www.simnet.org

Jim Luisi, Executive Director
Quarterly

7506 Executive Compensation Review for Commercial Banks
SNL Securities
PO Box 2124
Charlottesvle, VA 22902-2124
434-977-1600
FAX: 434-977-4466
subscriptions@snlnet.com
www.snlnet.com

Keith Davis, Editor
Reid Nagle, Publisher
Mark Outlaw, Advertising Director

For banks, regulatory agencies and executive recruiters. Includes detailed compensation and benefit information for the top 5 officers of all publicly traded banks, thrifts, REITs and insurance companies.
550 pages Annual Founded: 1988

7507 Executive Compensation Review for Insurance Companies
SNL Securities
PO Box 2124
Charlottesvle, VA 22902-2124
434-977-1600
FAX: 434-977-4466
subscriptions@snlnet.com
www.snlnet.com

Keith Davis, Editor
Reid Nagle, Publisher
Mark Outlaw, Advertising Director
Pat LaBua, Subscription Manager

For insurance companies, investment analysts, service providers to the insurance industry and regulators. Includes detailed compensation and benefit information for the top 5 officers of all publicly traded banks, thrifts, REITs and insurance companies.
200 pages Annual Founded: 1997

7508 Executive Compensation Review for REITs
SNL Securities
PO Box 2124
Charlottesvle, VA 22902-2124
434-977-1600
FAX: 434-977-4466
subscriptions@snlnet.com
http://www.snl.com

Keith Davis, Editor
Chandler Spears, Editor

For REITs, REIT service providers, investment companies, executive recruiters and regulators. Annual data digests that include detailed compensation and benefit information for the top 5 officers of all publicly traded banks, thrifts, REITs and insurance companies. *$495.00*
Monthly Founded: 1987

7509 Executive Compensation Review for Thrift Institutions
SNL Securities
PO Box 2124
Charlottesvle, VA 22902-2124
434-977-1600
FAX: 434-977-4466
subscriptions@snlnet.com
http://www.snl.com

Keith Davis, Editor

For thrifts, regulatory agencies and executive recruiters. Annual data digests that include detailed compensation and benefit information for the top 5 officers of all publicly traded banks, thrifts, REITs and insurance companies. *$495.00*
Monthly Founded: 1987

7510 **Export Finance Letter**
International Business Affairs Corporation
5523 Brite Drive
#346
Bethesda, MD 20817
301-907-8647
FAX: 301-907-8650
editor@exportsourcebook.com
http://www.exportsourcebook.com

Richard Barovick, Publisher/Editor

A report on government and private resources in US Export & Import Finance, Payments and Risk Management.
40 pages Quarterly Founded: 1979
Circulation: 148
Printed in 2 colors

7511 **FEI Briefing**
Financial Executives Institute
200 Campus Drive
PO Box 674
Forham Park, NJ 07932
973-360-0177
FAX: 973-765-1023
ceallen@fei.org http://www.fei.org

P Norman Roy, Publisher
Christopher Allen, Editor
Colleen Sayther Cunningham, CEO/President
Christopher Allen, Marketing

Up-to-date news for treasurers and controllers of large corporations.
Founded: 1931
Circulation: 14000

7512 **FSR Newsletter**
Financial Services Roundtable
1001 Pennsylvania Avenue NW
Suite 500 South
Washington, DC 20004
202-289-4322
FAX: 202-289-1903 www.fsround.org

Richard M Whiting, Executive Director/General Counsel
Steve Bartlett, President/CEO
Lisa McGreevy, EVP External Affairs

Monthly

7513 **Federal Securities Act**
Matthew Bender and Company
744 Broad Street
nawark, NJ 07102
973-820-2000
FAX: 937-865-1284 800-227-9597
international@bender.com
http://www.lexisnexis.com

Dona Hart, Editor

A comprehensive, up-to-date treatise on the Securities Act of 1933 and all amendments thereto, as well as the application of the Trust Indenture Act of 1939.

7514 **Fee Income Report**
Siefer Consultants
PO Box 1384
Storm Lake, IA 50588-1384
712-732-7340
FAX: 712-732-7906
info@siefer.com
http://www.siefer.com

Dan Siefer, Publisher

Fee income news and opportunities for financial institutions. *$297.00*
8 pages Monthly Founded: 1981

7515 **Fidelity Insight**
Mutual Fund Investors Association
20 William Street
Suite 310
Wellesley, MA 02481-9513
617-369-2000
FAX: 617-369-2510 800-444-6342

Eric Kobren, Publisher/CEO

Offers information and rates for mutual funds, investments, stocks and bonds. *$127.00*
8 pages Monthly Founded: 1985

7516 **Finance Company Weekly**
SNL Securities
PO Box 2124
Charlottesvle, VA 22902-2124
434-977-1600
FAX: 434-977-4466
subscriptions@snlnet.com
http://www.snl.com

David Meadors, Editor

Weekly news on publicly and privately traded finance companies. Includes consumer, commercial, credit card companies, pawn shops and leasing companies. Summarizes recent industry earnings announcement, trends, registration statements and performance rankings. *$396.00*
10 pages Weekly Founded: 1987

7517 **Financial Management Association**

College of Business Administration
4202 East Fowler Avenue
Tampa, FL 33620-5500
813-974-2084
FAX: 813-974-3318
fma@coba.usf.edu
http://www.fma.org

Lemma Senbet, Executive Editor
Jack Rader, Executive Director
James Seward, Editor

Financial books, textbooks, databases, newspapers, research services, software and related products and services. *$220.00*

Quarterly Founded: 1970

7518 **Financial Managers Update**
Financial Managers Society
100 W Monroe
Suite 810
Chicago, IL 60603
312-578-1300
FAX: 312-578-1308 800-275-4367
info@fmsinc.org
http://www.fmsinc.org/

Tom Lanning, Editor
Dick Yingst, President/CEO
Diane Walter, VP
Jennifer Doak, Marketing
Aletha Galloway, Office Coordinator

The latest accounting and regulatory information related to financial institutions, as well as news and trends. Includes a regulatory check list.
8 pages
Circulation: 1400
Printed in 1 color

7519 **Financial NetNews**
Institutional Investor
488 Madison Avenue
15th Floor
New York, NY 10022-5702
212-243-3300
FAX: 212-224-3491 800-115-9196
ideas@institutionalinvester.com
http://www.institutionalinvestor.com

Dahlia Weinman, Publisher
Deirdre Brennan, Editor
Nick Ferris, Marketing Manager
Chris Brown, CEO/President

Businesses and their Web sites, providing up-to-date information on networkings and assessment of industry trends and mistakes.
Weekly

7520 **Financial News**
Financial News Corporation
10 N Newnan Street
Jacksonville, FL 32202-3322
904-356-2466
FAX: 904-353-2628

James Bailey Jr, Publisher

Business and legal information for financial institutions. *$89.00*
Daily

7521 **Financial Planning Advisory**
WPI Communications
55 Morris Avenue
Suite 312
Springfield, NJ 07081-1496
973-678-8700
FAX: 800-677-9742 800-323-4995
info@wpicomm.com
http://www.wpicomm.com

Steven Klinghoffer, Publisher
Marilyn Lang, Circulation Manager

Offers institutions and businesses information on financial planning and campaigns.
Founded: 1952

7522 **Financial Services**
8180 Corporate Park Drive
Suite 305
Cincinnati, OH 45242-3309
513-591-0149
FAX: 513-527-3141

Linda Niesz, Publisher

National and regional news for members. *$7.00*
6 pages Monthly

7523 **Financial Services Daily**
SNL Securities
PO Box 2124
Charlottesvle, VA 22902-2124
434-977-1600
FAX: 434-977-4466
CustomerService@snl.com
http://www.snl.com

David Meadors, Editor

Daily fax of news headlines on finance companies, mortgage banks, investment advisors and brokers/dealers, plus divident and earnings announcements, stock highlights and index values, registration statements and ownership filings.
6 pages Daily Founded: 1987

7524 **Financial Services M&A Insider**
SNL Securities
PO Box 2124
Charlottesvle, VA 22902-2124
434-977-1600
FAX: 434-977-4466
subscriptions@snlnet.com
http://www.snl.com

L Vencil, Editor
Reid Nagle, Publisher

Fax newsletter featuring in-depth articles and the latest financial information on financial services M&A activity. Covers mortgage banks, finance companies, investment advisors and broker/dealers. Analyzes industry trends and specific market

and ownership changes to identify potential consolidation activity. *$695.00*
10 pages Monthly Founded: 1987

7525 Financial Women Today
Financial Women International
1027 West Roselawn Avenue
Roseville, MN 55113
651-487-7632
FAX: 651-489-1322
foundation@fwi.org
http://www.fwifoundation.org/
Megan L Eisu, Editor
Gale Wood, Executive Director
Regina Barr, President
Melissa Curzon, VP
Nancy Kinder, SVP/Regional Operations Mgr
Covers financial services industry trends, as well as women's issues and association news.
Founded: 1973
Circulation: 10,000

7526 First Friday
ASCU
PO Box 5488
Madison, WI 53705-0488
608-238-2646
FAX: 608-238-2646
C Barle, Publisher
Market research and statistics. *$35.00*
6 pages Monthly Founded: 1973
Mailing list available for rent 11,000 names $60 per M.
Printed in on matte stock

7527 Fiscal Survey of the States
National Association of State Budget Officers
444 North Capitol Street NW
Suite 642
Washington, DC 20001
202-624-5382
FAX: 202-624-7745
spattison@nasbo.org www.nasbo.org
Scott Pattison, Executive Director
Lauren Cummings, Manager Member Relations
Semi-Annual

7528 Fisheries - A Bulletin of the AFS
American Fisheries Society
5410 Grosvenor Lane
Suite 110
Besthesda, MD 20814-2199
301-897-8616
FAX: 301-897-8096
main@fisheries.org www.fisheries.org
Gus Rassam, Executive Director
Betsy Fritz, Director Administration/Finance
Monthly

7529 Forecaster
Forecaster Publishing Company
19623 Ventura Boulevard
Tarzana, CA 91356-2999
818-345-4421
FAX: 818-345-0468
John Kamin, Publisher
Brian Kamin, CEO/President
Analyzes lucrative speculations in unusual areas. Researches gold, silver, coins, gems, property, antiques, interest rates, business cycles, economic advice, tax strategies, wine, guns, collector cars and more. *$180.00*
8 pages Weekly Founded: 1962
Mailing list available for rent $170 per M.
Printed in 2 colors on matte stock

7530 Fund Directions
Financial Communications Company
225 Park Avenue S
New York, NY 10003
212-953-3500
FAX: 212-224-3699 800-715-9195
customerservice@iinews.com
http://www.funddirections.com
Colin Minnihan, Publisher
Wendy Connett, Executive Editor
Amy Cohen, Managing Editor
Kevin Francella, Plant Manager
Kim Lemmonds, Marketing Director
Trends in the rapidly changing fund environment and analysis of key issues in fund governance.
Monthly
Circulation: 2500

7531 Futures Market Alert
Robbins Trading Company
8700 W Bryn Mawr
Seventh Floor, S Tower
Chicago, IL 60631-3507
773-714-9000
FAX: 773-714-0900 800-453-4444
info@robbinstrading.com
http://www.robbinstrading.com
Reginald Rabjohns, Manager
Covers futures trading.

7532 Genomics Investing
Asset Alternatives
170 Linden Street
Wellesley, MA 02482
781-304-1400
FAX: 781-304-1440
www.assetnews.com
Tom Salemi, Senior Editor
Brian Gormley, Editor
Lisa Hughes, Circulation Manager
Barbara Bissonnette, VP Marketing/Sales
The genomics market offers a wealth of public and pivate investment opportunities. Genomics Investing helps you determine which are likely to be winners by identifying the most attractive companies and industry sub-sectors, and uncovering hot trends in genomics investing. Every monthly issue puts you intouch with the investment analysts, mutual fund managers, venture capitalists, and industry executives who are shaping the marketplace. *$1195.00*
Monthly
Printed in on matte stock

7533 Global Money Management
Institutional Investor
225 S
7th Floor
New York, NY 10003-5782
212-224-3300
FAX: 212-224-3952 800-543-4444
info@iipremium.com
http://www.institutionalinvestor.com/
Mark fortune, Publisher
Deirdre Brennan, Managing Editor
Chris Brown, President
Stuart Wise, Senior Editor
Nick Ferris, Group Marketing Director
Money management news. Accepts advertising. *$11.95*
Fortnightly Founded: 1967

7534 Gold Newsletter
Blanchard and Company
2400 Jefferson Highway
Suite 600
Jefferson, LA 70121
504-319-9310
FAX: 504-837-4884 800-877-8847
gnlmail@jeffersoncompanies.com
http://www.goldnewsletter.com/
James Blanchard, Publisher
Brien Lundin, CEO
Offers information and news for the financial community on stocks, bonds and investment opportunities. *$198.00*
Monthly Founded: 1971

7535 Government Affairs Bulletin
Financial Services Roundtable
1001 Pennsylvania Avenue NW
Suite 500 South
Washington, DC 20004
202-289-4322
FAX: 202-289-1903 www.fsround.org
Richard M Whiting, Executive Director/General Counsel
Steve Bartlett, President/CEO
Lisa McGreevy, EVP External Affairs
Monthly

7536 Government Finance Officers Association Newsletter
Government Finance Officers Association
203 N LaSalle Street
Suite 2700
Chicago, IL 60601-1210
312-977-9700
FAX: 312-977-4806
Inquiry@gfoa.org http://www.gfoa.org
Karen Utterback, Publisher
Nancy Zielke, President
Jeffrey Esser, Executive Director
Federal information, legislation and more for the management level executive in the financial community. *$4.50*
4 pages Monthly Founded: 1906

7537 HBMA Newsletter
Healthcare Billing and Management Association
1540 South Coast Highway
Suite 203
Laguna Beach, CA 92651
877-640-4262
Monthly

7538 Hedge Fund Alert
Harrison Scott Publications
5 Marine View Plaza
Suite 301
Hoboken, NJ 07030-5722
201-659-1700
FAX: 201-659-4141
info@hspnews.com
http://www.hfalert.com
Andrew Albert, Publisher
Tom Ferris, Editor
Howard Kapiloff, Managing Editor
Barbara Eannace, Marketing Manager
A weekly newsletter on the securitization of consumer and corporate receivables. *$2097.00*
10 pages Weekly
Circulation: 500 500 names $400 per M.
Printed in 4 colors on matte stock

7539 **High Yield Report**
American Banker-Bond Buyer
1 State Street Plaza
27th Floor
New York, NY 10004-1505
212-631-1271
FAX: 212-843-9624 800-367-3989

Gerald D Mintz, President
Mario DiUbaldi, Publisher

The only financial publication dealing exclusively with high yield corporate debt and distressed bank debt. *$795.00*

Weekly
Circulation: 350

7540 **Housing Finance Report**
National Assn. of Local Housing Finance Agencies
2050 M Street NW
Suite 800
Washington, DC 20036
202-367-1197
FAX: 202-857-1111 www.nalhfa.org

Greg Brown, Editor
Karen Thompson, Production Manager
Henry Hibery, President

This newsletter covers major developments in housing finance in the Congress, federal agencies and private sector. It also gives highlights new and innovative activities of ALHFA members.

Founded: 1982
Circulation: 450

7541 **IBC's Money Fund Report**
IBC Financial Data
1 Research Drive
West Borough, MA 01581
508-616-6600
FAX: 508-616-5511
info@imoneynet.com
http://www.imoneynet.com/

Kenneth Bohlin, Publisher
Peter Crane, Editor
Randy Wood, CEO
Claudia Missert, marketin

Compiles yield, average maturity and portfolio data for each money fund along with summary information for more than a dozen categories. *$3125.00*

Weekly Founded: 1975
Circulation: 200
Printed in 2 colors on matte stock

7542 **IE News: Financial Services**
Institute of Industrial Engineers
25 Technology Parkway S
Norcross, GA 30092-2928
770-417-1788
FAX: 770-263-8532

Offers full coverage of the financial community pertaining to engineering and industrial corporations.

7543 **IHS Haystack Standard Standards IEL IEEE**
Information Handling Services
15 Inverness Way E
Englewood, CO 80112
303-790-0600
FAX: 303-754-3940 800-525-7052
custvc@ihs.com http://www.ihs.com

Tim Stack, Corporate Communications Director
Charles Pacassl, CEO/President

Daily

7544 **IOMA's Report on Defined Contribution Plan Investing**
Institute of Management & Administration
3 Park Avenue
30th Floor
New York, NY 10016-2221
212-244-0360
FAX: 212-564-0465
subserve@ioma.com
http://www.ioma.com

Sean Hanna, Publisher
Perry Patterson, Editor
David Foster, CEO

Provides information on DC plan investments. *$795.00*

20 pages Monthly Founded: 1984

7545 **IPO Reporter**
Securities Data Publishing
1290 6th Avenue
36th Floor
New York, NY 10104-0101
212-765-5311
FAX: 212-957-0420 ipo@iddis.com

Ted Weissberg, Group Publisher

Reliable news, data and analysis. Provides the most comprehensive coverage available, including a detailed calendar of upcoming deals; new IPOs filled with the SEC; valuation information; comaparison data; company name and locationas well as names of underwriters, auditors and counsels.

Weekly

7546 **IRA Reporter**
Universal Pensions
PO Box 979
Brainerd, MN 56401-0979
218-855-0565
FAX: 218-829-4814 800-346-3860

Thomas G Anderson, President
Jennifer M Norquist, Editor

Discusses IRS rulings, regulations, legislation and other industry news and trends relating to IRA's. *$115.00*

8 pages Monthly
Printed in on glossy stock

7547 **ISDA Newsletter**
International Swaps and Derivatives Association
360 Madison Avenue
16th Floor
New York, NY 10017
212-901-6000
FAX: 212-901-6001
isda@isda.org www.isda.org

Robert Pickel, CEO
Ruth Ainslie, Director Communications
Corrine Gerasley, Director Administration

5/year

7548 **Inside Financial Services Marketing**
Hoke Communications
224 7th Street
Garden City, NY 11530-5771
516-746-6700
FAX: 516-294-8141 800-229-6700

Irwin Lowen, Publisher

Dedicated to the art and science of database marketing financial services; insurance, banking, investments and credit cards. *$ 195.00*

4 pages BiWeekly

7549 **Inside Mortgage Profitability**
Inside Mortgage Finance Publishers
7910 Woodmont Avenue
Suite 1010
Bethesda, MD 20814
301-951-1240
FAX: 301-656-1709
service@imfpubs.com
www.imfpubs.com

Guy Cecala, Publisher
John Bancroft, Managing Editor

Focuses exclusively on the bottom line: earning profits in the mortgage business. Just one cost-saving idea or one lead on a new angle could increase profitability for a firm by many times the cost of this subscription. *$6.86*

14 pages 400 names
Printed in 2 colors on matte stock

7550 **Inside Mortgage Technology**
Inside Mortgage Finance Publishers
7910 Woodmont Avenue
Suite 1010
Bethesda, MD 20814
301-951-1240
FAX: 301-656-1709
service@imfpubs.com
www.imfpubs.com

Guy Cecala, Publisher
Francis Solomon, Editor

Focuses on the evolving technology developments that are changing the mortgage business. Covers internet strategies, what's new and whats working, automated systems and e-commerce businesses. *$556.00*

13 pages 900 names

7551 **Insurance M&A Newsletter**
SNL Securities
One SNL Plaza
PO Box 2124
Charlottesville, VA 22902
434-977-1600
FAX: 434-977-4466
subscriptions@snl.com
http://www.snl.com

L Todd Vencil, Editor
Reid Nagle, Publisher

For investment bankers, analysts, insurance investors, insurance company executives and insurance regulators. Features in-depth articles and the latest financial information on insurance mergers and acquisitions activity. *$998.00*

15 pages Fortnightly Founded: 1987

7552 **Interactive Mobile Investor**
Kagan World Media
126 Clock Tower Place
Carmel, CA 93923-8746
831-624-1536
FAX: 831-625-3225
info@kagan.com www.kagan.com

George Niesen, Editor
Tom Johnson, Marketing Manager

$945.00

Monthly

7553 **Interactive TV Investor**
Kagan World Media
126 Clock Tower Place
Carmel, CA 93923-8746
831-624-1536
FAX: 831-625-3225
info@kagan.com www.kagan.com

George Niesen, Editor
Tom Johnson, Marketing Manager

$895.00

Monthly

7554 International Financier Newsletter
International Society of Financiers
PO Box 398
Naples, NC 28760
828-698-7805
FAX: 828-698-7806 www.insofin.com
Ronald I Gershen, Chairman/President
Monthly

7555 International Securitization & Structured Finance
WorldTrade Executive
2250 Main Street Suite 100
PO Box 761
Concord, MA 01742-761
978-287-0301
FAX: 978-287-0302
info@wtexec.com
http://www.wtexec.com
Jill McKenna, Production Manager
Gary Brown, CEO
Scott stutbar, Editor
John Margel, Marketing
Heather Margel, Circulation Manager
A twice monthly report devoted exclusively to asset-backed securities in international markets. Covers all aspects of international asset-backed securitization, including innovative product trends, issuer considerations, regulatory matters, and tax and accounting considerations. Examines what is working in emerging markets and spotlights unique US transactions. *$1333.00*

7556 International Wealth Success
PO Box 1866
Merrick, NY 11566
516-378-3922
FAX: 516-766-5919 800-323-0548
Tyler G Hicks, Publisher
Monthly newsletter giving sources and techniques for financing a variety of small businesses - import-export, mail order, real estate, home-based activities, etc. Gives specific, hands-on methods for beginners to start and own a successful business of their own. *$24.00*
16 pages Monthly
Mailing list available for rent 100 M names
$75 per M.
Printed in 2 colors on matte stock

7557 Internet Media Investor
Kagan World Media
126 Clock Tower Place
Carmel, CA 93923-8746
831-624-1536
FAX: 831-625-3225
info@kagan.com www.kagan.com
George Niesen, Editor
Tom Johnson, Marketing Manager
$945.00
Monthly

7558 Investing in Crisis
KCI Communications
1750 Old Meadow Road
Suite 301
McLean, VA 22102
703-905-8000
FAX: 703-905-8100 800-832-2330
service@kci-com.com
www.2.kci-com.com
Allie Ash Jr, Publisher
Offers information on investments, low-risk bonds, stocks and campaigns for businesses in times of economic survival. *$195.00*
80 pages

7559 Investment Dealers' Digest
Thomson Financial Publishing
195 Broadway
8th Floor
New York, NY 10007
646-222-2000
FAX: 646-822-3220
http://www.thomson.com
Ron Cooper, Editor-in-Chief
Corporation financing, market conditions, financial techniques and organizational strategies.
Weekly
Circulation: 6255

7560 Investment News
Crain Communications
711 3rd Avenue
New York, NY 10017
212-210-0100
FAX: 212-210-0465 888-446-1422
info@crain.com
http://www.investmentnews.com
William Bisson, Publisher
Rance E Crain, President
Robert C. Adams, Circulation Manager
Information on mutual funds, variable annuities, life and long term care insurance, tax issues, estate planning, market and investing, banks and money management. *$38.00*
Weekly Founded: 1916
Circulation: 59400

7561 Investment Quality Trends
IQ Trends
6450 Lusk Boulverd
Suite 104
La Jolla, CA 92121-5192
858-459-3818
FAX: 858-459-3819
info@iqtrends.com
http://www.iqtrends.com
Geraldine Weiss, Publisher
Kelly Writht, Editor
Joseph Pettrick, Marketing Manager
Stocks, bonds and investment rates and campaigns. *$310.00*
12 pages Bi-monthly Founded: 1966

7562 Investment Recovery Association
638 W 39th Street
Kansas City, MO 64111
816-561-5323
FAX: 816-561-1991
ira@invrecovery.org
http://www.invrecovery.org
Jane Male, Executive Director
Association for manufacturers of services and supplies to the industry. *$300.00*
16 pages Monthly Founded: 1980
Circulation: 900

7563 Investor Relations Newsletter
Kennedy Information
1 Pheonix Mill Lane
5th Floor
Petersborough, NH 03458
603-924-1006
FAX: 603-924-4460 800-531-0007
bookstore@kennedyinfo.com
http://www.kennedyinfo.com
Gerald Murray, Editor
Provides practical, hands on strategy and tactics for the investor relations professional. *$295.00*
Monthly Founded: 1970

7564 Jumbo Rate News
Bauer Financial
2655 LeJeune Road
Penthouse 1-A
Coral Gables, FL 33114
305-445-9500
FAX: 305-445-6775 800-388-6686
customerservice@bauerfinancial.com
http://www.bauerfinancial.com
Paul Bauer, Founder
Karen Dorway, President
Caroline Jervey, Editor
Each issue contains over 1,000 separate Jumbo CD rates in seven categories from over 200 creditworthy banks and thrifts nationwide. Includes star ratings, wire transfer fees, deposit requirements and financial highlights for each institution. *$445.00*
Weekly Founded: 1983
Printed in 2 colors on matte stock

7565 Kagan Media Investor
Kagan World Media
126 Clock Tower Place
Carmel, CA 93923-8746
831-624-1536
FAX: 831-625-3225 800-307-2529
info@kagan.com
http://www.kagan.com
George Niesen, Editor
Tom Johnson, Marketing Manager
Robin Flynn, Senior VP
News of the Kagan Media Investor. Three month trial available. *$1195.00*
Monthly Founded: 1969

7566 Kagan Media Money
Kagan World Media
1 Lower Ragsdale Drive
Bldg 1 3130
Monterui, CA 93940-8746
831-624-1536
FAX: 831-625-3225
info@kagan.com
http://www.kagan.com
George Niesen, Editor
Harvey Kraft, Marketing Manager
Tim Baskerville, CEO
Harvey Kraft, Circulation Manager
Sandy Borthwick, Communications Manager
Analysts dissect deals, anticipate trends, project revenues, track financings and value the debt and equity of hundreds of privately held and publicly traded advertising, broadcasting, cable TV, digital TV, home video, Internet media, motion picture, newspaper, pay TV, professional sports and wireless telecommunications companies in the US and abroad. *$1245.00*
Monthly Founded: 1969

7567 Kagan Music Investor
Kagan World Media
126 Clock Tower Place
Carmel, CA 93923-8746
831-624-1536
FAX: 831-625-3225
info@kagan.com www.kagan.com
George Niesen, Editor
Tom Johnson, Marketing Manager
News and analysis for investors in the music industry. *$945.00*
Monthly

7568 Kiplinger Tax Letter
Kiplinger Washington Editors
1729 H Street NW
Washington, DC 20006-3925
202-887-6400
FAX: 202-872-8977 800-544-0155

Austin H Kiplinger, Publisher
Steven D Ivins, Editor

Biweekly tax letter for investors, business owners and managers. Covers current developments in Congress, IRS and the courts. *$ 54.00*

4 pages
Circulation: 125000
Mailing list available for rent
Printed in 1 color

7569 Latin American Finance & Capital Markets
WorldTrade Executive
PO Box 761
Concord, MA 01742-0761
978-287-0301
FAX: 978-287-0302 www.wtexec.com

Alison French, Production Manager

An action-oriented report on treasury management, tax, legal, accounting and other operational issues that impact doing business in Latin America. Provides an independent assessment of local capital markets. *$595.00*

Twice monthly

7570 Long Term Investing
Concept Publishing
5202 Humphreys Road
Lake Park, GA 31636
229-257-0367
FAX: 229-219-1097
http://www.newconceptspublishing.com

Jim Dovan, Publisher
David Coleman, Editor
Madris Gutierrez, Editor-in-Chief
Andrea DePasture, Senior Editor

Offers full coverage of long term stocks, bonds and investments. *$98.00*

12 pages Monthly Founded: 1998
Circulation: 600 Audited
Printed in 1 color on matte stock

7571 MAR/Hedge
Managed Account Reports
1250 Broadway
26th Floor
New York, NY 10001
212-213-6202
FAX: 212-213-1870 800-638-2525
subs@marhedge.com
http://www.marhedge.com

Greg Newton, Publisher
Randall Devere, Editor-in-Chief
Lisa McErlane, Director of Marketing
Gary Lynch, President/Publisher

The first newsletter to cover the field of hedge funds in its entirety with industry news, in-depth articles and reviews of hedge fund managers and fund of funds and rankings of these managers and fund of funds. *$1195.00*

16 pages Monthly Founded: 1994
Circulation: 300 Audited
Printed in 2 colors on matte stock

7572 Managing 401(k) Plans
Institute of Management & Administration
33 Park Av
33th Floor
New York, NY 10016-5902
212-244-0360
FAX: 212-564-0465
subserve@ioma.com
http://www.ioma.com

David Foster, CEO/President
Rebbeca Morrow, Editor
Perry Paterson, Publisher
Jim Bo, Marketing
Paul Moriss, Circulation Manager

How to provide the best plan for 401 (k) participants, while keeping the lid on costs. Shows how to administer your plan with less effort and how to limit your fiduciary liability. *$279.00*

Monthly Founded: 1984
Circulation: 10000

7573 Managing Credit, Receivable & Collections
Institute of Management & Administration
29 W 35th Street
5th Floor
New York, NY 10001-2299
212-244-0360
FAX: 212-564-0465
subserve@ioma.com
http://www.ioma.com/

Mary Schaeffer, Editor

Accelerate receivables and learn what technology and techniques are working best. *$269.00*

Monthly

7574 Media Mergers & Acquisitions
Kagan World Media
126 Clock Tower Place
Carmel, CA 93923-8746
831-624-1536
FAX: 831-624-5882
info@kagan.com www.kagan.com

George Niesen, Editor
Tom Johnson, Marketing Manager

Where it all comes together. Exclusive scorecard of deals done by media companies. Dollar amounts, multiples paid, trends captured in succinct summaries of complex transactions. Three month trial available. *$795.00*

Monthly

7575 Merger Strategy Report
SNL Securities
PO Box 2124
Charlottesvle, VA 22902-2124
434-977-1600
FAX: 434-977-4466
subscriptions@snlnet.com
www.snlnet.com

Erik Winthrow, Editor
John Minor, Editor
Reid Nagle, Publisher
Mark Outlaw, Advertising Director

For bank and thrift executives, with a regional M&A recap; list of deals; ranking of advisors and lawyers.

5 pages Quarterly Founded: 1995

7576 Mergers & Acquisitions Executive Compensation Review
SNL Securities
One SNL Plaza
PO Box 2124
Charlottesvle, VA 22902-2124
434-977-1600
FAX: 434-977-4466
subscriptions@snlnet.com
http://www.snl.com

John Minor, Editor
Michael Spears, Advertising
Mike Scott, Mergers/Acquisitions

For banks, thrifts, investment banks, law firms that advise on mergers, executives at banks expecting to merge and personnel and compensation specialists. Provides compensation information on the executives of banks that have entered into agreements to be acquired. *$495.00*

10 pages Monthly Founded: 1987

7577 Micro Ticker Report
Waters Information Services
PO Box 2248
Binghamton, NY 13902-2248
607-770-8535
FAX: 607-723-7151

Dennis Waters, Publisher
Andrew Delaney, Editor

Covers the financial quotation industry.

7578 Money Management Letter
Institutional Investor
225 Park Avenue
12th Floor
New York, NY 10022-5782
212-224-3300
FAX: 212-224-3353
edit@imagazine.com
http://www.imagazine.com

Walker Jacob, Publisher
Tom Lamont, Editor

This newsletter offers businesses information on investments, stocks, bonds, low-risk campaigns and financial planning opportunities.

7579 Mortgaged Backed Securities Letter
American Banker-Bond Buyer
1 State Street
26th Floor
New York, NY 10004-1505
212-631-1271
FAX: 212-635-0232
mbs@iddis.com http://www.iddis.com

Michael Fisk, Editor

Provides coverage of structured finance and includes comprehensive listings of asset backed securities.

Weekly
Circulation: 4200

7580 Motion Picture Investor
Kagan World Media
126 Clock Tower Place
Carmel, CA 93923-8746
831-624-1536
FAX: 831-625-3225
info@kagan.com
http://www.kagan.com/

George Niesen, Editor
Tom Johnson, Marketing Manager
$845.00

Monthly Founded: 1969

7581 NACHA Operating Rules & Guidelines
NACHA: Electronic Payments Association
13665 Dulles Technology Drive
Suite 300
Herndon, VA 20171
703-561-1100
FAX: 703-787-0996
info@nacha.org www.nacha.org

Elliott C McEntee, President/CEO
Deb Evans-Doyle, Senior Director Conference Mktg
Julie Hedlund, Senior Director Electronic Commerce
Michael Herd, Director Public Relations
Priscilla Holland, AAP, Senior Director Corporate Pymts

Annual

7582 **NADOA Newsletter**
National Association of Division Order Analysts
2805 Oak Trail Court
Suite 6312
Arlington, TX 76016
972-715-4489

nadoa_org@hotmail.com
www.nadoa.org
Lynn S McCord, Administrator
Bi-Monthly

7583 **NALHFA Conference Program**
National Association of Local Housing Finance
2025 M Street NW
Suite 800
Washington, DC 20036-3309
202-367-1197
FAX: 202-367-2197
john_murphy@nalhfa.org
www.nalhfa.org
John C Murphy, Executive Director
Scott Lynch, Association Manager
Kim McKinon, Coordinator Membership
Semi-Annual

7584 **NALHFA Newsletter**
National Association of Local Housing Finance
2025 M Street NW
Suite 800
Washington, DC 20036-3309
202-367-1197
FAX: 202-367-2197
john_murphy@nalhfa.org
www.nalhfa.org
John C Murphy, Executive Director
Scott Lynch, Association Manager
Kim McKinon, Coordinator Membership
Bi-Monthly

7585 **NAPFA Newslink**
National Association of Personal Financial Advisor
3250 N Arlington Heights Road
Suite 109
Arlington Heights, IL 60004
847-483-5400
FAX: 847-483-5415 800-366-2732
wassermanm@napfa.org
www.napfa.org
Ellen Turf, CEO
Margery Wasserman, Director Conference

Quarterly

7586 **NASD Manual**
CCH
2700 Lake Cook Road
Riverwoods, IL 60015-3867
847-267-7000
FAX: 773-866-3608 800-835-5224
Wendy Albertson, PGL
Gene Landoe, CEO
Officials, members, by-laws and rules of NASD.
Founded: 1913

7587 **NASDAQ Subscriber Bulletin**
National Association of Securities Dealers
1212newyork anenue
suite950
Washington, DC 20005-1516
202-371-5535
FAX: 202-371-5536
Margo Porter, Publisher
Richard DeLouise, Editor
Pamela Anderson, Executive
Developments in the NASDAQ market.

7588 **NATRI Newsletter**
National Association for Treasurers of Religious
8824 Cameron Street
Silver Springs, MD 20910
301-587-7776
FAX: 301-589-2897
lelcock@natri.org www.natri.org
Laura Reicks, Executive Director
Lorelle Elcock, Associate Director Finance
Bi-Monthly

7589 **NCFE Motivator**
National Center on Financial Education
PO Box 34070
San Diego, CA 92163-4070
619-232-8811
FAX: 616-236-1401
Loren Dunton, Publisher
Paul Richard, Editor
Regular features include Spend Yourself Rich! and $pend $mart-$ave More! Plus questions and answers and financial wisdom. *$10.00*
8 pages
Circulation: 16000 Audited Est. Pass-Along Circ: 8000
Printed in 1 color on matte stock

7590 **NICSA News**
National Investment Company Service Association
36 Washington Street
Suite 70
Wellesley Hills, MA 02481
781-416-7200
FAX: 781-416-7065
info@nicsa.org www.nicsa.org
Barbara V Weidlich, President
Keith Dropkin, Director Operations
Doris Jaimes, Registrar
Sheila Kobaly, Events Manager
Chris Ludent, IT Manager
Quarterly

7591 **National Mortgage News**
Thomson Financial Publishing
One State Street Plaza
27th Floor
New York, NY 10004
212-258-8445
FAX: 212-292-5216 800-235-5552
custserv@thomsonmedia.com
http://www.nationalmortgagenews.com/
Timothy Murphy, Group Publisher
Mark Fogarty, Editorial Director
Paul Muolo, M&A/Data Editor
Timothy Reifschneider, Advertising Director
Jose Thomas, Manager
Mortgage information, legislation and news. *$228.00*
Weekly
Circulation: 5000
Printed in 2 colors on newsprint stock

7592 **Network Newsletter**
Society for Information Management
401 N Michigan Avenue
Chicago, IL 60611
312-215-5190
FAX: 312-245-1081 www.simnet.org
Jim Luisi, Executive Director
Bi-Monthly

7593 **Newspaper Investor**
Kagan World Media
One Lower Ragsdale Drive
Building One, Suite 130
Monterey, CA 93940
831-624-1536
FAX: 831-625-3225 831-625-3225
info@kagan.com www.kagan.com
George Niesen, Editor
Tom Johnson, Marketing Manager
$845.00
Monthly Founded: 1969

7594 **Notice to Members**
National Association of Securities Dealers
1735 K Street NW
Washington, DC 20006-1516
202-288-8000
FAX: 202-728-8882
info@nasphq.com
http://www.nasphq.org
Jean Robinson Curtis, Editor
Kimberly Moore, Production Manager
Porter Bingham, CEO/President
Rules, regulations and qualifications for members.
Quarterly Founded: 1985
Circulation: 1000

7595 **OTC Chart Manual**
Standard & Poor's Corporation
55 Water Street
New York, NY 10041
212-382-2000
www.standardandpoors.com
KW Lutz, Publisher
Charts on over 800 OTC stocks.

7596 **Origination News**
Thomson Financial Publishing
One State Street Plaza
27th Floor
New York, NY 10004
212-258-8445
FAX: 800-235-5552 888-321-3373
customerservice@tfp.com
http://www.tfp.com/
Timothy Murphy, Group Publisher
Mark Fogarty, Editorial Director
Jose Thomas, Manager
Information for mortgage industry executives on mortgage brokers, mortgage bankers and mortgage executives in commercial banks, savings banks, savings and loan associations and credit unions. *$78.00*
Monthly

7597 **Pawnbroker News**
National Pawnbrokers Association
PO Box 1040
Roanoke, TX 76262
817-491-4554
FAX: 817-491-8770
bob@nationalpawnbrokers.org
www.nationalpawnbrokers.org
Bob Benedict, CAE, Executive Director
8/year

7598 **Pink Comparison Report**
SNL Securities
PO Box 2124
Charlottesvle, VA 22902-2124
434-977-1600
FAX: 434-977-4466
subscriptions@snlnet.com
www.snlnet.com
Maria Moyer, Editor
Reid Nagle, Publisher
Mark LaBua, Subscription Manager
Mark Outlaw, Advertising Director

For CEOs, CFOs and IRCs of banks. Compares a subscribing bank or thrift's consolidated financial and market performance to other banks and thrifts chosen by the subscriber and banks and thrifts of similar asset size and location.
40 pages Quarterly

7599 Private Equity Week
Securities Data Publishing
40 W 57th Street
New York, NY 10019
212-844-4701
FAX: 212-956-0112
pew@iddis.com
http://www.sdponline.com

Jennifer Reed, Editor-in-Chief
Edward Cortese, Marketing Executive

News of the past week and forecast of the weeks to come for investors. *$780.00*
Weekly

7600 Private Placement Letter
Securities Data Publishing
1290 6th Avenue
36th Floor
New York, NY 10104-101
212-765-5311
FAX: 212-957-0420
custserv@sourcemedia.com
http://www.privateplacementletter.com/

John Toth, Publisher
Ronald Cooper, Editor-in-Chief
Lauren Klopacs, Marketing Manager
Mark Cialdella, Circulation Manager
David Harkey, Advertising Manager

Highly sophisticated information on the debt private placement market including senior and mezzanine level debt. *$1395.00*

7601 Proceedings of the National Conference on Planned Giving
National Committee on Planned Giving
233 McCera Street
Suite 400
Indianapolis, IN 46225-1030
317-269-6274
FAX: 317-269-6276
kramsey@ncpg.org www.ncpg.org

Tanya Howe Johnson, President/CEO
Sandra Kerr, Director Government Education
Barbara Owens, Director Membership/Manager HR
Kathryn J Ramsey, Director Meetings
Kurt Reusze, Manager Education/Technology

Annual

7602 Professional Tape Reader
Information Forecast
13715 Burbank Boulevard
Sherman Oaks, CA 91401-5040
818-908-3050
FAX: 818-902-5401
informationforecast.com

William Meier, Publisher

Covers issues in the project finance industry, interviews of major endeavors in the field, also industry ratings, and personnel news. *$245.00*
Monthly
Circulation: 700

7603 Quality Performance Report
Managed Account Reports
220 5th Avenue
19th Floor
New York, NY 10001-7708
212-213-6202
FAX: 212-213-6273 800-638-2525
rdevere@marhedge.com
http://www.marhedge.com

Randall Devere, Editor-in-Chief
Lois Peltz, Editor
Gary Lynch, President
Lisa McErlane, Marketing

The pre-eminent source of qualitative and quantitative information on global managed derivatives. Delivers in-depth analysis on the performance of the trading advisors in MAR's qualified database. Now covering over 500 trading advisors and programs. *$299.00*
Quarterly Founded: 1913
Circulation: 400 Audited
Printed in 2 colors on matte stock

7604 REIT Daily Fax
SNL Securities
One SNL Plaza
PO Box 2124
Charlottesvle, VA 22902-2124
434-977-1600
FAX: 434-293-0407
subscriptions@snlnet.com
http://www.snl.com

Amy Woolard, Editor
Michael Chinn, President
Alan Zimmerman, Publisher
Pat LaBua, Customer Service Director

Newsletter designed specifically for REIT industry professionals and investors. Features important industry events, condensed news stories, recent capital offerings and the latest market information.
4 pages Daily Founded: 1987

7605 REIT Performance Graph
SNL Securities
One SNL Plaza
PO Box 2124
Charlottesvle, VA 22902-2124
434-977-1600
FAX: 434-977-4466
subscriptions@snl.com
http://www.snl.com

Steve Arnold, Publisher
Chandler Spears, Editor
Keven Lindemann, Real Estate
Gregg Amonette, General Media

For publicly traded REITs and REIT service providers. Compares the investment performance of a publicly traded REIT to a specific SNL index or to a selected peer group and the appropriate broad multi-industry index. Covers a 5-year period or the period beginning with the IPO date. *$399.00*
1 pages Founded: 1987

7606 Real Estate Alert
Harrison Scott Publications
5 Marine View Plaza
#301
Hoboken, NJ 07030-5795
201-659-1700
FAX: 201-659-4141
info@hspnews.com
http://www.abalert.com

Andrew Albert, President/Publisher
Bob Mura, Editor
Barbara Eannaci, Marketing Manager

Information on investment opportunities in institutional grade commercial real estate, includes sales acquisitions and personnel changes. *$1597.00*
Weekly Founded: 1989
Circulation: 650

7607 Real Estate Finance Today
Mortgage Bankers Association of America
1919 Pennsylvania Avenue NW
Washington, DC 20006-3438
202-557-2700
FAX: 202-721-0167
crene@mortgagebankers.org
http://www.mbaa.org

Jennet Hewitt, Editor
Jonathan Kempner, CEO/President

Information on anticipating industry trends, regulatory changes, economic outlook, federal and state legislation and trends in the secondary mortgage industry. *$100.00*
Monthly Founded: 1939
Circulation: 1500

7608 Real-Estate Alert
Harrison Scott Publications
5 Marine View Plaza
Suite 301
Hoboken, NJ 07030-5722
201-659-1700
FAX: 201-659-4141
info@hspnews.com
http://www.abalert.com

Andrew Albert, Publisher
Tom Ferris, Editor/CEO

A weekly newsletter on the securitization of consumer and corporate receivables. *$1497.00*
10 pages Weekly
Circulation: 600 500 names $400 per M.
Printed in 4 colors on matte stock

7609 Reducing Benefits Costs
Institute of Management & Administration
29 W 35th Street
5th Floor
New York, NY 10001-2299
212-244-0360
FAX: 212-564-0465
subserve@ioma.com
http://www.ioma.com/

Rebecca Morrow, Publisher
Perry Patterson, Editor

Provides information on controlling benefit costs. *$245.00*
16 pages Monthly

7610 Regional Economic Digest
Federal Reserve Bank of Kansas City
925 Grand Avenue
Kansas City, MO 64198-0001
816-881-2970
FAX: 816-881-2569 800-333-1010

Thomas Davis, Publisher
Bob Regan, Editor

A review of financial and economic conditions in the Tenth District. Includes articles of regional interest, statistics on District commercial banks and the area economy and results of a survey of agricultural credit conditions.
32 pages

7611 Regulatory Risk Monitor
United Communications Group
11300 Rockville Pike
Rockville, MD 20852
301-287-2700
FAX: 301-816-8945
webmaster@ucg.com
http://www.ucg.com

Dennis Sullivan, Publisher
Sherry Keramidas, Executive Director

Updates banking officials, credit union, compliance officers, attorneys and auditors with current independent news and guidance.

Founded: 1970

7612 Report on Financial Analysis, Planning & Reporting
Institute of Management & Administration

3 Park Avenue
30th Floor
New York, NY 10016-2299
212-244-0360
FAX: 212-564-0465
subserve@ioma.com
http://www.ioma.com/

Andy Dzamba, Editor
Jonathan Wentworth-Ping, Director Corporate Licensing

FARP regularly covers performance measurements effective use of new FASB, IRS and SEC financial and accounting requirements for all industries, shows managers the best way to evaluate business opportunities, how to read and evaluate capital budgets, earbug reports and analysts see the big picture through the use of new financial tools such as Economic Value Assets and Shareholder Valuations models. *$269.00*

Monthly

7613 Retirement Plans Bulletin
Universal Pensions
PO Box 979
Brainerd, MN 56401
218-855-0565
FAX: 218-829-4814 800-346-3860

Thomas G Anderson, President
Jennifer M Norquist, Editor

Digests IRS technical jargon on IRA's and qualified plans and translates it into understandable articles and advice for financial organizations. *$89.00*

10 pages Monthly
Printed in 2 colors on glossy stock

7614 SNL Bank M&A DataSource
SNL Securities
One SNL Plaza
PO Box 2124
Charlottesvle, VA 22902-2124
434-977-1600
FAX: 434-977-4466
subscriptions@snl.com
http://www.snl.com

John Minor, Publisher
Eric Hoffer, Editor
John McCune, Banks/Thrifts Manager
Michael Spears, Advertising
Mike Chinn, President

For investment bankers, investment companies, banks, thrifts, consultants and broker/dealers. Includes all merger and acquisition activity involving a bank or thrift as a buyer or seller.

Founded: 1987

7615 SNL Branch Migration DataSource
SNL Securities
PO Box 2124
Charlottesvle, VA 22902-2124
434-977-1600
FAX: 434-977-4466
subscriptions@snlnet.com
www.snlnet.com

Melissa Hobson, Editor
John Minor, Editor
Reid Nagle, Publisher
Mark Outlaw, Advertising Director

For investment bankers, investment companies, banks, thrifts, consultants and regulatory agencies. Re-assigns bank and thrift branch deposits to account for all M&A activity that has occurred since the last regulatory release.

Annual Founded: 1991

7616 SNL Corporate Performance Graphs for Banks
SNL Securities
One SNL Plaza
PO Box 2124
Charlottesvle, VA 22902-2124
434-977-1600
FAX: 434-977-4466
subscriptions@snl.com
http://www.snl.com

Will Wick, Editor
James Record, Editor
John McCune, Banks/Thrifts Manager
Michael Spears, Advertising
Mike Chinn, President

For publicly traded banks, law firms, accountants and consulting firms. Includes a 5-year comparison of an institution's stock to both a selected peer group index and a broad multi-industry index.

1 pages Founded: 1987

7617 SNL Financial DataSource
SNL Securities
One SNL Plaza
PO Box 2124
Charlottesvle, VA 22902-2124
434-977-1600
FAX: 434-977-4466
subscriptions@snl.com
http://www.snl.com

Steve Tomasi, Editor
Steve Ferguson, Editor
Edward Metz, Financial
Michael Spears, Advertising
Mike Chinn, President

For investment bankers, investment companies, banks, thrifts, institutional investors, consultants and broker/dealers. Available in six separate interactive modules that contain data for equity research, industry trend analysis, peer group comparisons and identification of investment and acquisition opportunities.

Founded: 1987

7618 SNL Mutual Thrift Conversion Investors Kit
SNL Securities
One SNL Plaza
PO Box 2124
Charlottesvle, VA 22902-2124
434-977-1600
FAX: 434-977-4466
subscriptions@snl.com
http://www.snl.com

Chris Smith, Editor
Reid Nagle, Publisher
John McCune, Banks/Thrifts Manager
Michael Spears, Advertising
Mike Chinn, President

For thrift executives, individual investors and institutional investors. Contains a set of articles explaining the mechanics of mutual-to-stock conversion and the 'how-to' of investing, reviewing profitability of conversion investments and outlining regulatory issues that affect conversions. *$495.00*

100 pages Monthly Founded: 1987

7619 SNL Pink Quarterly
SNL Securities
PO Box 2124
Charlottesvle, VA 22902-2124
434-977-1600
FAX: 434-977-4466
subscriptions@snlnet.com
www.snlnet.com

Maria Moyer, Editor
Reid Nagle, Publisher
Mark Outlaw, Advertising Director
Pat LaBua, Subscription Manager

For investment companies, banks and thrifts, broker/dealers and individual investors. Contains detailed financial and market information on all banks and thrifts traded on the OTC bulletin boards and by market makers, as well as in-depth analysis of this sector.

240 pages Quarterly Founded: 1995

7620 SNL Securities Thrift Performance Graph
SNL Financial
PO Box 2124
Charlottesvle, VA 22902-2124
434-977-1600
FAX: 434-977-4466
subscriptions@snlnet.com
www.snlnet.com

Reid Nagle, Publisher
John Racine, Editor
Mark Outlaw, Advertising Director
Pat Labua, Subscription Manager
Jeff Sternberg, Production Editor

SNL Securities is a research and publishing company that focuses on banks, thrifts, REITs insurance companies, and specialized, financial service companies. Founded in 1987, SNL securities has become the authority for information on financial institutions.

7621 SNL Securities Bank Comparison Report
SNL Securities
PO Box 2124
Charlottesvle, VA 22902-2124
434-977-1600
FAX: 434-977-4466
subscriptions@snlnet.com
www.snlnet.com

Mona Thompson, Editor
Dan Oakey, Editor
Keith Davis, Editor
Reid Nagle, Publisher

For CEOs, CFOs and IRCs of banks. Compares a subscribing bank's consolidated financial and market performance to that of banks and thrifts of similar asset size and location.

40 pages Quarterly Founded: 1987

7622 SNL Securities Thrift Comparison Report
SNL Securities
PO Box 2124
Charlottesvle, VA 22902-2124
434-977-1600
FAX: 434-977-4466
subscriptions@snlnet.com
www.snlnet.com

Dave Spence, Editor
Reid Nagle, Publisher
Mark Outlaw, Advertising Director
Pat LaBua, Subscripton Manager

Report for CEOs, CFOs and IRCs of thrifts and major corporate stockholders. Illustrates and compares a subscribing thrift's consolidated financial and market perfor-

mance to thrifts of similar asset size and location.
40 pages Quarterly Founded: 1988

7623 Secured Leader
Commercial Finance Association
225 W 34th Street
Suite 1815
New York, NY 10122-1899
212-594-3490
FAX: 212-564-6053
postmaster@cfa.com
http://www.cfa.com

Bruce H Jones, Publisher

Only publication devoted exclusively to the asset-based financial services industry. Editorial matter is directed toward practitioners of asset-based financing. Accepts advertising. *$56.00*
76 pages Founded: 1944
Circulation: 5000

7624 Securities Industry News
American Banker
1 State Street Plaza
27th floor
New York, NY 10004-1505
212-038-8350
FAX: 212-803-1556 800-221-1809
scott.dattoli@sourcemedia.com
http://www.securitiesindustry.com

Stuart Arnold, Publisher
Collin Brayton, Editor-in-Chief
Bruce Morris, President
Scott Dattoli, Publisher
Barbara Heltzel, Marketing Coordinator

Coverage of the latest financial technology, the internet, and who is purchasing what productsto better enhance their bottom line. *$575.00*
Bi-monthly

7625 Securities Week
McGraw Hill
PO Box 182604
Columbus, OH 43272
614-304-4000
FAX: 614-759-3759 877-833-5524
customer.service@mcgraw-hill.com
http://www.mcgraw-hill.com

Michael Ocrant, Managing Editor
Harold McGraw, CEO

Information on firms and exchanges strategy plans, new hires, events and issues, as well as legislation and legal rulings impacting the securities industry.
Weekly Founded: 1884

7626 Seller/Service Update
Inside Mortgage Finance Publishers
7910 Woodmont Avenue
Suite 1010
Bethesda, MD 20814
301-951-1240
FAX: 301-656-1709
service@imfpubs.com
www.imfpubs.com

Guy D Cecala, Publisher
John Bancroft, Managing Editor
Mary Lou Probka, Director of Marketing
Mary Lou Probka, Director of Circulation

Complete coverage of underwriting and servicing, changes occurring in the mortgage market. Focuses on Fannie Mae, Freddie Mac, HUD, FHA, VA, private mortgage insurers and private conduits. *$395.00*
Monthly Founded: 1984
Circulation: 500

7627 Shareholder Satisfaction Survey
National Investment Company Service
36 Washington Avenue
Suite 70
Wellesley Hills, MA 02481
781-416-7200
FAX: 781-416-7065
info@nicsa.org www.nicsa.org

Barbara V Weidlich, President
Keith Dropkin, Director Operations
Doris Jaimes, Registrar
Sheila Kobaly, Events Manager
Chris Ludent, IT Manager

Annual

7628 Special Stock Report
Wall Street Transcript
67 Wall Street
9th Floor
New York, NY 10005-3701
212-952-7400
FAX: 212-668-9842 800-246-7673
pickup@twst.com
http://www.twst.com

Andrew Pickup, President/CEO
Doug Estadt, Online Editor
Andrew Pickup, Publisher
Jason Flatt, Marketing

Monthly stock pick based on research, interviews, and data contained in the wall st. transcript. *$399.00*
Monthly Founded: 1963
Circulation: 7274 525 names

7629 Specialty Lender
SNL Securities
PO Box 2124
Charlottesvle, VA 22902-2124
434-977-1600
FAX: 434-977-4466
subscriptions@snlnet.com
www.snlnet.com

Dave Meadors, Editor
Jim Allen, Editor
L Todd Vencil, Editor
Reid Nagle, Publisher

For executives of specialty lending companies, banks and thrifts which have specialty lending operations, heads of captive finance companies, investors, investment bankers and equity analysts. Provides news, analysis and financial and market information about specialty lenders, focusing on credit management and access to capital.
40 pages Monthly Founded: 1996

7630 Specialty Lender Performance Graph
SNL Securities
PO Box 2124
Charlottesvle, VA 22902-2124
434-977-1600
FAX: 434-977-4466
subscriptions@snlnet.com
www.snlnet.com

David Meadors, Editor
Reid Nagle, Publisher
Mark Outlaw, Advertising Director
Pat LaBua, Subscription Manager

For publicly traded specialty lenders and specialty lender service providers. Compares the investment performance of a specialty lender to a specific SNL index or to a selected peer group and the appropriate broad multi-industry index. Covers a 5-year period or the period beginning with the IPO date.
By request Founded: 1997

7631 Statistical Report of Defense Credit Unions
Defense Credit Union Council
601 Pennsylvania Avenue NW
Suite 600
Washington, DC 20004-2601
202-829-9110
FAX: 202-638-3410
dcucl@cuna.org www.dcuc.org

William Archey, Chief Executive Officer

Annual

7632 Streaming Media Investor
Kagan World Media
126 Clock Tower Place
Carmel, CA 93923-8746
831-624-1536
FAX: 831-624-5882
info@kagan.com www.kagan.com

George Niesen, Editor
Tom Johnson, Marketing Manager

News of the Streaming Media Investor. Three month trial available. *$895.00*
Monthly

7633 TV Program Investor
Kagan World Media
126 Clock Tower Place
Carmel, CA 93923-8746
831-624-1536
FAX: 831-625-3225 800-307-2529
info@kagan.com
http://www.kagan.com

George Niesen, Editor
Harvy Kraft, Marketing Manager
Tim Baerville, CEO/President
Robert Naylor, Circulation Manager
$895.00
Monthly Founded: 1969

7634 Tax Management Compensation Planning
1250 23rd Street NW
Washington, DC 20037-1164
202-337-7240
FAX: 202-496-6013 800-223-7270

David McFarland, President
Glenn Davis, Managing Editor

Nearly 40 portfolios, each focusing on specific tax, labor and other aspects of qualified and non-qualified retirement plans, employee welfare benefit plans, executive compensation, employment taxes and accounting for deferred compensation. Offers practitioner-authored articles, analysis of recent developments and decisions, and insightful comments from leading practitioners on the latest planning strategies. *$837.00*
Monthly

7635 Taxpractice
Tax Analysts
6830 North
Fairfax Drive
Arlington, VA 22213-1001
703-533-4400
FAX: 703-533-4444 800-955-2444
webmaster@tax.org
http://www.tax.org

Thomas F Field, Publisher

Contains comprehensive coverage of IRS rulings, court decisions, tax law changes and other topics of interest. *$749.00*
Weekly Founded: 1970
Circulation: 2200

7636 Thestreet.Com
Two Rector Street
14th Floor
New York, NY 10006-1819
212-321-5000
FAX: 212-321-5016
letters@thestreet.com
www.thestreet.com

Dave Kansas, Editor-in-Chief

Information on what is happening on Wall Street, along with mutual fund and economic news, stock quotes, market summaries, and analyses of key indicators. *$69.95*
Daily

7637 Thrift 13D Dictionary
SNL Securities
PO Box 2124
Charlottesvle, VA 22902-2124
434-977-1600
FAX: 434-977-4466
subscriptions@snlnet.com
www.snlnet.com

Todd L Davenport, Editor
Reid Nagle, Publisher
Mark Outlaw, Advertising Director
Pat LaBua, Subscription Manager

Contains all active 13D filings and related filings for every publicly traded bank in the country, including those which trade on the pink sheets.
250 pages Quarterly

7638 Thrift Performance Graph
SNL Securities
One SNL Plaza
PO Box 2124
Charlottesvle, VA 22902-2124
434-977-1600
FAX: 434-977-4466
subscriptions@snl.com
http://www.snl.com

Will Wick, Editor
James Record, Editor
John McCune, Banks/Thrifts Manager
Michael Spears, Advertising

Compares investment performance of a publicly traded Thrift company to a specific SNL index or to a selected peer group and the appropriate broad multi-industry index. Graph covers a 5-year period or the period beginning with the IPO date. For publicly traded thrifts, law firms, accountants and consulting firms.
1 pages Founded: 1987

7639 Tower Investor
Kagan World Media
One Lower Ragsdale Drive
Building One Suite 130
Monterey, CA 93940
831-624-1536
FAX: 831-624-5882 800-307-2529
info@kagan.com
http://www.kagan.com

George Niesen, Editor
Tom Johnson, Marketing Manager

News of the Tower Investor. Three month trail available. *$1045.00*
Monthly Founded: 1969

7640 Tower Program Investor
Kagan World Media
One Lower Ragsdale Drive
Building One Suite 130
Monterey, CA 93940
831-624-1536
FAX: 831-625-3225 800-307-2529
info@kagan.com
http://www.kagan.com/

George Niesen, Editor
Tom Johnson, Marketing Manager
$1045.00
Monthly Founded: 1969

7641 Trading Technology Week
Waters Information Services
270 Lafayette Street
Suite 700
New York, NY 10012
212-130-0711
FAX: 212-925-7585
eugene.grygo@incisivemedia.com
http://www.dealingwithtechnology.com

Tim Weller, CEO
Eugene Grygo, Editor
Adrian Goulbourn, Publisher
Lillian Lopez, Production Manager

Information covering the latest applications, platforms and strategies in trading room systems and proprietary execution. *$2025.00*
Weekly Founded: 2000

7642 Transactions
AACE International
209 Prairie Avenue
Suite 100
Morgantown, WV 26501-5949
304-296-8444
FAX: 304-291-5728
info@aacei.org http://www.aacei.org

James R Dexter, Executive Director
Malvin Gelhouser, Editor
Jenny Alms, Marketing Manager *$65.00*

Monthly Founded: 1956
Circulation: 5000

7643 Turning Points
Concept Publishing
PO Box 500
York, NY 14592-500
800-836-4575
FAX: 585-243-3148 800-836-4575
publishing@conceptpub.com
http://www.conceptpub.com

Jim Dovan, Publisher
David Coleman, Editor

Economic news. *$198.00*
2 pages Founded: 1974
Circulation: 600 Audited
Printed in 1 color on matte stock

7644 VOD Investor
Kagan World Media
126 Clock Tower Place
Carmel, CA 93923-8746
831-624-1536
FAX: 831-625-3225 800-307-2529
info@kagan.com
http://www.kagan.com

George Niesen, Editor
Tom Johnson, Marketing Manager
Robin Flynn, Senior VP

News of the VOD Investor. Three month trial available. *$1045.00*
Monthly Founded: 1969

7645 Venture Capital & Health Care
Asset Alternatives
170 Linden Street
Wellesley, MA 02482-7919
781-304-1400
FAX: 781-304-1440
www.assetnews.com

Tom Salemi, Senior Editor
Lisa Hughes, Circulation Manager

Explores the business of health care investing in the trillion dollar health care market. Provides insight into the deals, deal makers, and portfolio companies in all sectors of health care, including services, biotechnology, medical devices, and 'infomedics.' *$795.00*
Monthly

7646 Venture Capital Information Technology
Asset Alternatives
170 Linden Street
Wellesley, MA 02482-7919
781-304-1400
FAX: 781-304-1440
info@PrivateEquityAnalyst.com
http://www.assetnews.com

Lisa Hughes, Circulation Manager
Barbara Bissonnette, Vice President Marketing/Sales

Delivers information an insight into the fast-moving world of venture investing in technology. Every month, it brings readers the IT deals, fund formations, exits, and personnel news at the venture firms and corporate venturing groups they need to stay abreast of venture investing in IT. *$795.00*
Monthly

7647 Video Investor
Kagan World Media
126 Clock Tower Place
Carmel, CA 93923-8746
831-624-1536
FAX: 831-624-5882
info@kagan.com
http://www.kagan.com

George Niesen, Editor
Tom Johnson, Marketing Manager

Authoritative look inside the business of renting and selling video cassettes. Exclusive estimates of retail and wholesale transactions and inventories. Tracking movies into the home. Three month trial is available. *$795.00*
Monthly

7648 Water Investment Newsletter
US Water News
230 Main Street
Halstead, KS 67056-1913
316-835-2222
FAX: 316-835-2223 800-251-0046
editor@uswaternews.com
http://www.uswaternews.com

Thomas Bell, Publisher
Toni Young, Circulation Manager

News, features and profiles of shareholder owned water supply and treatment companies. General news on water-related investment opportunities with stock portfolio. *$140.00*
8 pages Monthly
Printed in 1 color on matte stock

7649 Wireless Market Stats
Kagan World Media
One Lower Ragsdale Drive
Building One, Suite 130
Monterey, CA 93940-8746
831-624-1536
FAX: 831-625-3225 800-307-2529
info@kagan.com
http://www.kagan.com

George Niesen, Editor
Tom Johnson, Marketing Manager

News of the Wireless Market Stats. Three month trial available. *$1095.00*
Monthly Founded: 1969

7650 **Wireless Telecom Investor**
Kagan World Media
1 Lower Ragscale
Bldg 1, Suite 130
Monterey, CA 93940
831-624-1536
FAX: 831-625-3225 800-307-2529
info@kagan.com
http://www.kagan.com
Tim Baskerville, President
Harvey Kraft, Director of Marketing
George Niesen, Editor
Robert Naylor, Circulation Manager
Sandie Borthwick, Publisher
Exclusive analysis of private and public values of wireless telecommunications companies, including cellular telephone, ESMR and PCS. Exclusive databases of subscribers, market penetrations, market potential, industry growth. Catching super-fast growth in a capsule. Three month trial available. *$1095.00*
Monthly Founded: 1970

7651 **Wireless/Private Cable Investor**
Kagan World Media
126 Clock Tower Place
Carmel, CA 93923-8746
831-624-1536
FAX: 831-624-5882
info@kagan.com
http://www.kagan.com
George Niesen, Editor
Tom Johnson, Marketing Manager
The original bible of the wireless cable, multipoint distribution pay TV industry. Published continuously since 1972, this newsletter is the window on cable competition. Three month trial available.

Magazines & Journals

7652 **AAII Journal**
American Association of Individual Investors
625 N Michigan Avenue
Chicago, IL 60611-3110
312-280-0170
FAX: 312-280-9883 800-428-2244
members@aaii.com
http://www.aaii.com
John Markese, President
Maria Crawford Scott, Editor
James Cloonan, Founder
Journal focusing on personal finance, specifically investing in stocks and mutual funds and portfolio management. *$29.00*
40 pages Founded: 1978
Circulation: 170000

7653 **AG Lender**
Doane Agricultural Services
11701 Borman Drive
Suite 300
Saint Louis, MO 63146-4193
314-569-2700
FAX: 314-569-1083
aglender@doane.com
http://www.doane.com
Rob Wiley, Editorial Director
Shanon Weaver, Customer Service
Darlene Pitts, Production Manager
Provides articles on credit planning and analysis, legal briefs, news from Washington and lender profiles. *$159.00*
16 pages Monthly Founded: 1923
Circulation: 1700
Printed in 2 colors

7654 **AGA Today**
Association of Government Accountants
2208 Mount Vernon Avenue
Alexandria, VA 22301
703-684-6931
800-242-7211
cculkin@agacgfm.org
www.agacgfm.org
Relmond P Van Daniker, Executive Director
Marie S Force, Director Communications
Susan Fritzlen, Deputy Executive Director
Bi-Weekly

7655 **Accounting and Business Review World**
Scientific Publishing Company
1060 Main Street
River Edge, NJ 07661-2013
201-487-9655
FAX: 201-487-9656
Ed Yang Hoong Pang
Aims to provide a forum for the publication of accounting and business research papers which are of interest to educators, students and practitioners. *$60.00*

7656 **Affiliate Forum**
NACHA: Electronic Payments Association
13665 Dulles Technology Drive
Suite 300
Herndon, VA 20171
703-561-1100
FAX: 703-787-0996
info@nacha.org www.nacha.org
Elliott C McEntee, President/CEO
Deb Evans-Doyle, Senior Director Conference Mktg
Julie Hedlund, Senior Director Electronic Commerce
Michael Herd, Director Public Relations
Priscilla Holland, AAP, Senior Director Corporate Pymts
3/year

7657 **Alert**
Defense Credit Union Council
601 Pennsylvania Avenue NW
Suite 600
Washington, DC 20004-2601
202-829-9110
FAX: 202-638-3410
dcucl@cuna.com www.dcuc.org
William Archey, Chief Executive Officer
Monthly

7658 **American Cash Flow Journal**
American Cash Flow Association
255 S Orange Avenue #624
PO Box 2668
Orlando, FL 32801-3428
407-843-2032
FAX: 407-648-9470 800-253-1294
info@americancashflow.com
http://www.acfa-cashflow.org
Judy Arndt, Editor
Debbie Bracknell, Executive Director
Issues cover factoring accounts receivable and dealing with privately held mortgages, along with thirty income streams. Offering updates on the legal and regulatory aspects of handling debt instruments and reports on new technology.
Monthly
Circulation: 25,000

7659 **Annual Institute Journal**
National Association of Division Order Analysts
2805 Oak Trail Court
Suite 6312
Arlington, TX 76016
972-715-4489
nadoa_org@hotmail.com
www.nadoa.org
Lynn S McCord, Administrator
Annual

7660 **Armed Forces Comptroller**
American Society of Military Comptrollers
415 N Alfred Street
Alexandria, VA 22314-4650
703-549-0360
FAX: 703-549-3181 800-462-5637
James F McCall, Executive Director
Quarterly

7661 **Asset Management**
ASMC
170 Avenue at the Common
PO Box 7930
Shrewsbury, NJ 07702-4803
732-389-8700
FAX: 732-389-8701
www.djassetmanagement.com
Barry Vinocur, Publisher
Departments include a mutual fund snapshot, a variable annuity databank, asset allocation, a journal watch and much more. Also offering topical features of interest to industry professionals.
Bi-Monthly
Circulation: 30,000

7662 **Asset Protection: Offshore Tax Reports**
Offshore Press
4500 W 72nd Terrace
Prairie Village, KS 66208-2824
913-362-9667
FAX: 913-432-7174
jacobs@offshorepress.com
http://www.offshorepress.com
Vernon Jacobs, President *$120.00*
Weekly Founded: 1981

7663 **Barter News**
PO Box 3024
Mission Viejo, CA 92690-1024
949-831-0607
FAX: 949-831-9378
bmeyer@barternews.com
http://www.barternews.com
Bob Meyer, Publisher/Editor
Industry news is covered including listings of CEO's and CFO's and editorials. An in-depth look into the changes and evolution of barter, and shows how-to profitability use barter to increase the bottom line. *$40.00*
96 pages Quarterly Founded: 1980
Circulation: 30,000
Printed in 4 colors on glossy stock

7664 **Business Credit**
National Association of Credit Management
8840 Columbia 100 Parkway
Columbia, MD 21045-2107
410-740-5560
FAX: 410-740-5574
bcm@nacm.org http://www.nacm.org

Norma J Heim, Editor-in-Chief
Norma Heim, Marketing Director
Robin Schauseil, CEO/President

For professionals responsible for extending credit and collecting receivables. Topics include business law, lein law, technology, credit management, collections, deductions, fraud, credit risk, credit scoring, outsourcing, information services, trade finance and more. *$54.00*

72 pages Founded: 1896
Circulation: 32000
Printed in 4 colors on matte stock

7665 Business Finance
Duke Communications International
221 E 29th Street
PO Box 3438
Loveland, CO 80539-3438
970-634-4700
FAX: 970-593-1050
info@businessfinancemag.com
http://www.businessfinancemag.com

David Blansfield, Publisher
Laurie Brannen, Editor-in-Chief
Meg Waters, Managing Editor
Matthew Weiner, Associate Publisher

Articles cover a broad range of topics from accounting to the Internet, from benchmarking to best practices, and cost management to career management.

Monthly
Circulation: 50000

7666 CEIR - Quarterly National Economic Reports
National Association of Certified Valuation
1111 Brickyard Road
Suite 200
Salt Lake City, UT 84106-5401
303-698-1883
800-677-2009
sherril@nacva.com www.navca.com

Pamela R Bailey, Executive Director
Parnell Black, MBA CPA CVA, CEO
Roberto Castro, Director Business Development
Dean Dinas, Director Economic Research
Brien K Jones, General Manager Conferences

Quarterly

7667 CMBA World
Commerical Mortgage Securities Association
30 Broad Street
28th Floor
New York, NY 10004-2304
212-509-1844
FAX: 212-509-1895
info@cmbs.org www.cmbs.org

Dottie Cunningham, CEO
Jane Gelfand, Managing Director Finance
Marcus Henderson, Coordinator Membership/Facilities
Trish Madonia, Director Meetings

Quarterly

7668 Capitol Comment
National Association of Mortgage Brokers
8201 Greensboro Drive
Suite 300
McLean, VA 22102
703-610-9009
FAX: 703-610-9005 www.namb.org

Michael J Nazankiewicz, Executive Vice President
Roy DeLoach, VP Legislative
Rebecca Dopkin, VP Meetings

Monthly

7669 Certified Government Financial Management Topics
Association of Government Accountants
2208 Mount Vernon Avenue
Alexandria, VA 22301
703-684-6931
800-242-7211
cculkin@agacgfm.org
www.agacgfm.org

Relmond P Van Daniker, Executive Director
Marie S Force, Director Communications
Susan Fritzlen, Deputy Executive Director

Quarterly

7670 Collections & Credit Risk
Thomson Financial Publishing
One State Street Plaza
27th Floor
New York, NY 10004
212-258-8445
FAX: 212-803-1592 800-221-1809
custserv@thomsonmedia.com
http://www.creditcollectionsworld.com

Sharon Rowlands, President/CEO
Louis Eccleston, Marketing Director
Catherine Ladwig, Editor
Darren Waggoner, Executive Editor
Jose Thomas, Manager

Focuses on news and trends of strategic and competitive importance to collections and credit policy executives. Covers the credit risk industry's growth, diversification and technology in both commercial and consumer credit. *$98.00*

66 pages Monthly Founded: 1961
Circulation: 25000
Printed in 4 colors on glossy stock

7671 Collector Magazine
ACA International
4040 W 70th Street
PO Box 390106
Minneapolis, MN 55439-106
952-926-6547
FAX: 952-926-1624
pr@acainternational.org
http://www.collector.com

Timothy Dressen, Editor/Director Comm
Gary Rippentrop, Chief Executive Officer
Anne Rosso, Associate Editor

Brings you vital, up to the minute information on industry trends, regulations and legislation each month. *$70.00*

Monthly Founded: 1939
Circulation: 6000

7672 Commercial Mortgage Insight
Zackin Publications
PO Box 2180
Waterbury, CT 06722-2180
203-755-0158
FAX: 203-755-3480 800-325-6745
info@cmi-online.com
http://www.cmi-online.com

Joe Caton, Editor
Paul Zackin, Publisher
June Han, Marketing

For desicion making executives in commercial mortgage banking and brokerage firms, commercial banks and community/savings institutions. Provides professionals with timely and comprehensive market news, trends and know-how needed to make informed decisions and choices. *$48.00*

32 pages Monthly Founded: 1969
Circulation: 18000 17505 names $100 per M.
Printed in 4 colors

7673 Computerized Investing
American Association of Individual Investors
625 N Michigan Avenue
Chicago, IL 60611-3110
312-280-0170
FAX: 312-280-9883 800-428-2244
journal@aaii.com http://www.aaii.com

John Markese, CEO
Maria Scott, Editor

Offers information on computed investing, stocks and bonds. *$40.00*

Founded: 1978

7674 Conference Abstract
American Education Finance Association
8365 S Armadillo Trail
Evergreen, CO 80439
303-674-0857
FAX: 303-670-8986 www.afea.cc

Ed Steinbecher, Executive Director

Annual

7675 Consumer Finance Law Bulletin
American Financial Services Association
919 Eighteenth Street NW
Suite 300
Washington, DC 20006-5503
202-296-5544
FAX: 202-223-0321
afsa@afsamail.org
http://www.afsaonline.com

Randy Lively, President/CEO
Robert Mekew, Editor

Legislative information on the financial industry.

Monthly Founded: 1916

7676 Consumer Finance Law Quarterly Report
Conference on Consumer Finance Law
Oklahoma City University School of Law
2501 N Blackwelder
Oklahoma City, OK 73106
405-521-5363
FAX: 405-521-5089
ccflqr@lec.okcu.edu www.theccfl.com

Alvin C Harrell, Executive Director

Quarterly

7677 Contingency Planning & Management
Witter Publishing Corporation
84 Park Avenue
Flemington, NJ 08822
908-788-0343
FAX: 908-788-3782
www.WitterPublishing.com

Steve Biggers, Publisher
Andy Hagg, Editor
Andrew Witter, President

Serves the fields of financial/banking, manufacturing industrial, transportation, utilities, telecommunications, health care, government, insurance and other allied fields.

8 per year Founded: 1996

7678 Contoller
National Accounting and Finance Council
2200 Mill Road
Alexandria, VA 22314
703-838-1915
FAX: 703-836-0751
rcurtis@trucking.org
www.nafc.truckline.com

Rich Curtis, Executive Director

Monthly

7679 Controller's Quarterly
Institute of Management Accountants
10 Paragon Drive
Montvale, NJ 07645-1718
201-573-9000
FAX: 201-474-1600 800-638-4427
ima@imanet.org www.imanet.org
Paul Sherman, Interim Executive Director
Monthly

7680 Corporate Controller
RIA Group
395 Hudson Street
New York, NY 10014-3669
212-367-6300
FAX: 212-367-6305 www.riahome.com
Andrew W Boden, Publisher
Omer Karabey, Owner
Includes health care costs, cash management, executive compensation and environmental insurance as well as regular columns on tax planning, technology advances, and innovative business trends.
Bi-Monthly
Circulation: 3500

7681 Corporate Risk Management
Oster Communications
219 Parkade
Cedar Falls, IA 50613-2752
319-277-1271
FAX: 319-277-7481
Written for financial decision makers.
48 pages Monthly Founded: 1989

7682 Cost Engineering
AACE International
209 Prairie Avenue
Suite 100
Morgantown, WV 26501
304-296-8444
FAX: 304-291-5728 800-858-2678
info@aacei.org www.aacei.org
Andrew S Dowd, Interim Executive Director
Christian Heller, Staff Director Technical
Charla Miller, Staff Director Education
Carol S Rogers, Manager Finance
Monthly

7683 Cost Engineering Journal
AACE International
209 Prairie Avenue
Suite 100
Morgantown, WV 26501-5949
304-296-8444
FAX: 304-291-5728 800-858-3678
info@aacei.org http://www.aacei.org
Clive D Francis, President
Marvin Gelhausen, Editor
Cost engineering topics include latest news on estimation, cost control and management science. *$65.00*
Monthly Founded: 1956
Circulation: 5000
Mailing list available for rent

7684 Cost Management Update
Institute of Management Accountants
10 Paragon Drive
Montvale, NJ 07645-1718
201-573-9000
FAX: 201-474-1600 800-638-4427
ima@imanet.org www.imanet.org
Paul Sherman, Interim Executive Director
Monthly

7685 Credit Card Management
Thomson Financial Publishing
One State Street Plaza
27th Floor
New York, NY 10004
212-258-8445
FAX: 800-235-5552 800-535-8403
custserv@sourcemedia.com
http://www.cardforum.com
James Daly, Editor
Sharon Rowlands, President/CEO
Louis Eccleston, Marketing Director
Jose Thomas, Manager
Information on the major developments in the credit card industry. *$98.00*
74 pages Monthly Founded: 1962
Circulation: 19000
Printed in 4 colors on glossy stock

7686 Credit Scoring
Credit Research Foundation
8840 Columbia Parkway
Suite 100
Columbia, MD 21045-2117
410-740-5499
FAX: 410-740-4620
crf_info@crfonline.org
www.crfonline.org
William T Callahan, CCE CRF, President

7687 Credit Union Executive Journal
Credit Union National Association
5710 Mineral Point Road
Madison, WI 53705-4454
608-231-4000
FAX: 608-231-4370 800-348-3646
slanphear@cuna.com
http://www.cuna.org
James Hanson, Publisher
Kathryn Kuehn, Editor
Techniques and concepts available in management, finance, marketing, lending, human resources and technology for credit unions. *$ 202.00*
Founded: 1930
Circulation: 2400

7688 Credit Union Magazine
Credit Union National Association
5710 Mineral Point Road
Madison, WI 53705-4454
608-314-4000
FAX: 608-231-4263 800-356-9655
dorothy@cuna.org
http://www.cuna.org
N Mica, President
Cathy Kuehn, Editor
Bill Merrick, Managing Editor
The role and operations of modern credit unions. *$50.00*
100 pages Monthly Founded: 1981
Circulation: 32776
Printed in 4 colors on glossy stock

7689 Credit Union Management Magazine
Credit Union Executives Society
5510 Research Park Drive
Madison, WI 53711-5377
608-271-2664
FAX: 608-271-2303
cues@cues.org www.cues.org
Fred Johnson, President/CEO
Mary Arnold, VP Publications
George Hofheimer, VP Professional Development
Barbara Kachelski, CAE, SVP/CIO
Dennis Porter, VP Finance/Administration

Monthly

7690 Credit Union Technology
Credit Union Technology
110-64 Queens Boulevard
#106
Forest Hills, NY 11375-6347
718-793-9400
FAX: 718-793-9414
pr@cutmag.com www.cutmag.com
Andrew Mallon, Publisher
Information on improving customer service through technological advances. *$36.00*
24 pages Bi-Monthly Founded: 1991
Circulation: 6000 2500 names $500 per M.
Printed in 4 colors on glossy stock

7691 Credit and Collection Survey
Broadcast Cable Credit Association
550 Frontage Road
Suite 3600
Northfield, IL 60093
847-960-0200
FAX: 847-784-8059
info@bccacredit.com
www.bccacredit.com
Mary Collins, President/CEo
Bi-Ennial

7692 DC Advocate
National Defined Contribution Council
9101 E Kenyon
Suite 300
Denver, CO 80237-0467
303-770-5353
FAX: 303-770-1812
info@ndcconline.org
www.ndcconline.org
Al Brust, Executive Vice President
Quarterly

7693 Directions in Affordable Housing Finance
National Association of Affordable Housing Lenders
1300 Connecticut Avenue NW
Suite 905
Washington, DC 20036
202-293-9850
FAX: 202-293-9852 naahl@naahl.org
Judith A Kennedy, President/CEO
Quarterly

7694 Disclosure Record
Newsfeatures
8511 249th Street
Jamaica, NY 11426-2105
Jack Lotto, Editor
Full texts of corporate and financial news reports. *$50.00*
8 pages Monthly Founded: 1973

7695 Economic Outlook
America's Community Bankers
900 19th Street NW
Suite 400
Washington, DC 20006
202-857-3100
FAX: 202-296-8716 888-872-0275
info@acbankers.org
http://www.americascommunitybankers.com
Nancy Feig, Editor
Debra Cope, Publisher
Diane Casey-Landry, President/CEO
A first rate resource for strategically countering the hanging economic winds of the financial world. *$315.00*

4 pages Monthly Founded: 1992

7696 Electronics Payment Journal
NACHA: Electronic Payments Association

13665 Dulles Technology Drive
Suite 300
Herndon, VA 20171
703-561-1100
FAX: 703-787-0996
info@nacha.org www.nacha.org
Elliott C McEntee, President/CEO
Deb Evans-Doyle, Senior Director Conference Mktg
Julie Hedlund, Senior Director Electronic Commerce
Michael Herd, Director Public Relations
Priscilla Holland, AAP, Senior Director Corporate Pymts
Bi-Monthly

7697 Estate Planning Review
2700 Lake Cook Road
Riverwoods, IL 60015-3867
847-267-7000
FAX: 800-224-8299 800-224-8299
Robert Becker, President and Ceo
$275.00
Monthly Founded: 1913

7698 Examiner
Society of Financial Examiners
174 Grace Boulevard
Altamonte Springs, FL 32714
407-682-4930
FAX: 407-382-3175 800-787-7633
info@sofe.org www.sofe.org
Paula Keyes, Executive Director
Quarterly

7699 F & I Management Technology
Association of Finance and Insurance Professionals
4112 Southwood E
Colleyville, TX 76034
817-428-2434
FAX: 817-428-2534
afip@aol.com www.afip.com
David N Robertson, Executive Director

7700 Federal Credit Union Magazine
National Association of Federal Credit Unions
3138 10th Street
North Arlington, VA 22201-2149
703-522-4770
FAX: 703-524-1082 800-336-4644
jbruce@nafcu.org
http://www.nafcu.org
Peter Taylor, Marketing Director
Fred R Becker Jr, President/CEO
Written for CEO's, senior staff and volunteers of Federal Credit Unions. Offers legislative and regulatory news, as well as technology and operational issues. Call for rates.
50 pages Founded: 1967
Circulation: 1500
Printed in 4 colors on glossy stock

7701 Financial Analysts Journal
Association for Investment Management & Research
PO Box 3668
Charlottesville, VA 22903-668
434-951-5499
FAX: 434-951-5370
faj@aimr.org
http://www.cfapubs.org/faj/home.html
Robert D Arnott, Editor
Bette Collins, Managing Editor
Jeffrey J Diermeier, President/CEO
Elizabeth Collins, Editorial Manager
Jenine A. Kaznowski, Corporate Sales Manager
Articles on securities analysis, portfolio management, accounting, economics, securities law, regulation and ethics. *$235.00*
88 pages Founded: 1945
Circulation: 40,000 40,000 names $150 per M.

7702 Financial Executive
Financial Executives International
200 Campus Drive
Suite 8
Florham Park, NJ 07932
973-360-0177
FAX: 973-765-1018 800-336-0773
jstankard@fei.org http://www.fei.org
Jeffrey Marshall, Editor-in-Chief
Ellen Heffes, Managing Editor
Colleen S Cunningham, President
Maria O'Grady, Marketing Manager
Addresses accounting and treasury subjects, as well as overall strategies in corporate financial mangement. *$74.39*
72 pages Monthly Founded: 1931
Circulation: 16500
Printed in 4 colors on glossy stock : web

7703 Financial Management
Financial Management Association International
University of South Florida
College of Business Admin, #3331
Tampa, FL 33620
813-974-2084
FAX: 813-974-3318
kwright@fma.org www.fma.org
Jack S Rader, Executive Director
Karen Wright, Special Events Coordinator

Quarterly

7704 Financial Manager
Broadcast Cable Financial Management Association
550 Frontage Road
Suite 3600
Northfield, IL 60093
847-960-0200
FAX: 847-716-7004
info@bcfm.com http://www.bcfm.com

Mary M Collins, President/CEO
Jamie Smith, Operations Manager
Stewart Schley, Editor
A bi-monthly magazine published by the Broadcast Cable Financial Management Association. *$69.00*
36 pages
Circulation: 300
Mailing list available for rent 1100 names $495 per M.

7705 Financial Manager/Credit Topics
Broadcast Cable Credit Association
550 Frontage Road
Suite 3600
Northfield, IL 60093
847-960-0200
FAX: 847-784-8059
info@bccacredit.com
www.bccacredit.com
Mary Collins, President/CEO
Bi-Monthly

7706 Financial Planning & Counseling Journal
Association for Financial Counseling and Planning
2112 Arlington Avenue
Suite H
Upper Arlington, OH 43221
614-485-9650
FAX: 614-485-9621 www.afcpe.org
Sharon Burns, PhD, Executive Director
Semi-Annual

7707 Financial Planning Digest
Harcourt Brace Professional Publishing
6277 Sea Harbor Drive
Orlando, FL 32887
407-345-2000
FAX: 407-345-3016
webmaster@harcourt.com
http://www.harcourt.com
Angelita Streeter, Editor
Paul Amidei, Managing Editor
Estate, retirement, insurance planning tips and strategies, practice management insight, book reviews and legislation updates.
$ 99.00
Monthly

7708 Financial Review Magazine
NFR Communications
4948 Washburn Avenue S
Minneapolis, MN 55410
612-929-8110
FAX: 612-929-8146
nfr@nfr.net www.nfrcom.com
Tom Bengtson, Editor
Jackie Hilgert, Production Manager
Trade publication covering the commercial banking industry in the upper midwest. Designed for the decision-maker in the bank.
25 per year

7709 Financial Services Quarterly
SNL Securities
One SNL Plaza
PO Box 2124
Charlottesvle, VA 22902-2124
434-977-1600
FAX: 434-977-4466
subscriptions@snl.com
http://www.snl.com
Pam Askea, Editor
Dan Oakey, Editor
Michael Spears, Advertising
Edward Metz, Financial Services
Comprehensive reference guide available on finance companies, mortgage banks, investment advisors and securities brokers/dealers. In-depth company profiles and financial data on these publicly traded companies and summary financials on thousands of non-public financial services companies. *$696.00*
400 pages Quarterly Founded: 1987

7710 Financier
Bank Administration Institute
1 N Franklin Street
Chicago, IL 60606-3421
312-553-4600
FAX: 312-683-2426 www.bai.org
R Gerald Fox, Publisher
Willard Rappleye Jr, Editor
Forum of ideas for the private sector. *$5.00*

Circulation: 32,000

7711 Focus on Accountability
Evangelical Council for Financial Accountability
440 W Jubal Early Drive
Suite 130
Winchester, VA 22601
540-535-0103
FAX: 540-535-0533 800-323-9473
info@ecfa.org www.ecfa.org

Paul D Nelson, President
Dan Busby, VP

Quarterly

7712 Forbes Global
Forbes
90 5th Avenue
New York, NY 10011-8882
212-202-2200
FAX: 212-366-8804 212-620-2200
readers@forbes.com
http://www.forbes.com

Timothy C Forbes, Chairman
Jim Spanfeller, CEO
Paul Maidment, Executive Editor
Michael Smith Maidment, VP, GM Operations
Bruce Rogers, VP Marketing

A magazine giving detailed information about business and finance.
Monthly

7713 Forbes Magazine
Forbes
28 W 23rd Street
11th Floor
New York, NY 10011-8882
212-673-3540
FAX: 212-366-8804
http://www.forbes.com

Bill Baldwin, Editor
Jim Spanfeller, Chief Executive Officer

A magazine giving detailed information about business and finance. *$4.95*
304 pages Founded: 1917

7714 Futures Industry
Futures Industry Association
2001 Pennsylvania Avenue NW
#600
Washington, DC 20006-1850
202-466-5460
FAX: 202-296-3184
lensslin@futureindustry.org
http://www.futuresindustry.org

Mary Ann Burns, Publisher
John M Damgard, President
Will Acworth, Editor

Front and back office operations, marketing, research, money management, regulatory and brokerage issues from a domestic and international perspective.
Founded: 1955
Circulation: 15000

7715 Futures Magazine
Oster Communications
219 Parkgate Road
#6
Cedar Falls, IA 50613-1953
319-277-1271
FAX: 319-277-7481
pdjuvik@futuresmag.com
http://www.futuresmag.com

James T Holter, Editor
Ginger Szala, Publisher

News, analysis, and strategies for futures, options and derivatives traders. Descriptions include annual sourcebook directory of exchange, contract, company and product information. *$39.00*
Monthly Founded: 1972
Circulation: 60000

7716 Global Custodian
Asset International
125 Greenwich Avenue
Greenwich, CT 06830
203-295-5015
FAX: 203-629-5024
office@assetpub.com
http://www.globalcustodian.com

Dominic Hobson, Editor-in-Chief
Charles Ruffel, Executive Editor
Meredith Hughes, Publisher
Alix Hughes, Sales Director

An in-depth perspective on the business of international investing, custody and clearing, and directory-type data on industry participants and trends. Provides investment professionals with an analysis of the strength and weaknessed of the players and systems that underlie international investing. *$185.00*
Founded: 1989
Circulation: 30,488

7717 Global Investment Magazine
Global Investment Technology
820 2nd Avenue
4th Floor
New York, NY 10017
212-370-3700
FAX: 212-370-4606 globalinv.com

Michael Horton, Publisher

Portfolio management, trading and global asset services, and a wide range of issues pertaining to institutional portfolio management strategies and decision making in the US and cross-border markets.
Quarterly
Circulation: 15000

7718 Global Investment Technology
Global Investment Technology
820 2nd Avenue
4th Floor
New York, NY 10017
212-370-3700
FAX: 212-370-4606
info@globalinv.com
http://www.globalinv.com

Michael Horton, Publisher
Pavan Sehgal, Editor

The strategic business interests of top-level decision makers as well as their operations and systems professionals. *$695.00*
Founded: 1990
Circulation: 1800

7719 Government Finance Review
Government Finance Officers Association

203 N LaSalle Street
Suite 2700
Chicago, IL 60601-1210
312-977-9700
FAX: 312-977-4806
pchristensen@gfoa.org
http://www.gfoa.org

Karen Utterback, Editor
Peter Christensen, Managing Editor

Finance and financial management for state and local governors. *$30.00*
Founded: 1906
Circulation: 16000

7720 Healthcare Financial Management
Healthcare Financial Management Association
Two Westbrook Corporate Center
Suite 700
Westchester, IL 60154-5700
708-319-9600
FAX: 708-531-0032 800-252-4362
kgallagher@hfma.org
http://www.hfma.org

Richard L Clarke, President/CEO
Gina Cavelle, Marketing Manager
Rob Fromberg, Editor-in-Chief
Carole Bolster, Senior Editor
Richard Dunckley, Sales Representative

Serves hospitals, medical clinics, nursing homes, extended care facilities, multi-hospital corporations, accounting, consulting firms, government, professional and academic institutions, consultants and others allied to the field. *$110.00*
94 pages Monthly Founded: 1946
Circulation: 32900 32900 names $750 per M.
Printed in 4 colors on matte stock

7721 IBIS Review
Charles D Spencer
250 S Wacker Drive
#600
Chicago, IL 60606-5800
312-993-7900
FAX: 312-993-7910
ibisnet@mindspring.com
www.ibisnews.com

Charles D Spencer, Publisher
Celia Cruz, Owner

For the individual responsible for the compensation and benefits of employees working abroad. Topics include pensions and profit-sharing plans, stock purchase and savings plans, death and disability benefits, health care coverage, termination indemnities, executive renumeration plans, investments, and expatriate plans.
Monthly
Circulation: 1500

7722 IMA Focus
Institute of Management Accountants
10 Paragon Drive
Montvale, NJ 07645-1718
201-573-9000
FAX: 201-474-1600 800-638-4427
imaQimanet.org www.imanet.org

Paul Sharman, President

Bi-Monthly

7723 INSIGHT
Society of Financial Examiners
174 Grace Boulevard
Altamonte Springs, FL 32714
407-682-4930
FAX: 407-682-3175 800-787-7633
info@sofe.org www.sofe.org

Paula Keyes, Executive Director

Monthly

7724 ISM Info Edge
Institute for Supply Management
2055 E Centennial Circle
PO Box 22160
Tempe, AZ 85285-2160
480-752-6276
FAX: 480-752-7890 800-888-6276

Paul Novak, CPM, CEO
Holly LaCroix Johnson, SVP
Deborah Webber, SVP

Quarterly

7725 **Inside Mortgage Finance**
Inside Mortgage Finance Publishers
7910 Woodmont Avenue
Suite 1010
Bethesda, MD 20814-987
301-951-1240
FAX: 301-656-1709
service@imfpubs.com
http://www.imfpubs.com
Guy Cecala, Publisher
John Bancroft, Managing Editor
Mary Lou Probka, Director of Marketing/Cir
John Bancroft, Editor
Tony Cecala, Production Manager
Industry news and related trade literature. Includes extensive market data, from rankings of top originators to the leading private mortgage insurers. *$889.00*
12 pages Founded: 1984
Printed in 2 colors on matte stock

7726 **Inside Mortgage Update**
Inside Mortgage Finance Publishers
7910 Woodmont Avenue
Suite 1010
Bethesda, MD 20814
301-951-1240
FAX: 301-656-1709
service@imfpubs.com
http://www.imfpubs.com
Guy Cecala, Publisher
John Bancroft, Managing Editor
Covers this dynamic market of lending to borrowers with less than perfect credit with news, analysis and truly useful market intelligence. *$659.00*
14 pages Founded: 1996
Circulation: 1000 1,150 names
Printed in 2 colors on matte stock

7727 **Inside Supply Management**
Insitute for Supply Management
2055 E Centennial Circle
PO Box 22160
Tempe, AZ 85285-2160
480-752-6276
FAX: 480-752-7890 800-888-6276
Paul Novak, CPM, CEO
Holly LaCroix Johnson, SVP
Deborah Webber, SVP
Monthly

7728 **Institute of Management & Administration Newsletter**
3 Park Avenue
30th Floor
New York, NY 10016
212-244-0360
FAX: 212-564-0465
subserve@ioma.com www.ioma.com
Joe Bremner, President
Information for those involved in international sales. Regular monthly features.

7729 **Institutional Investor Magazine**
Institutional Investor
488 Madison Avenue
New York, NY 10022
212-224-3300
FAX: 212-224-3491
info@iijournals.com
http://www.institutionalinvestoronline.com
Chris Brown, President
Deirdre Brennan, Managing Editor
Stuart Wise, Senior Editor
Erik Vander Kolk, CEO/Publisher
Institutional Investor serves corporations; non-profit institutions, charitable organizations, associations and foundations pension fund management; union pension fund management; government; educational institutions and endowments fund management. *$445.00*
182 pages Monthly Founded: 1967
Circulation: 103639
Printed in 4 colors on glossy stock

7730 **International Journal of Supply Chain Management**
Institute for Supply Management
2055 E Centennial Circle
PO Box 22160
Tempe, AZ 85285-2160
480-752-6276
FAX: 480-752-7890 800-888-6276
Paul Nocak, CPM, CEO
Holly LaCroix Johnson, SVP
Deborah Webber, SVP
Quarterly

7731 **Investor Relations Business**
Securities Data Publishing
40 W 57th Street
New York, NY 10019
212-844-4701
FAX: 212-956-0112 sdp@tfn.com
Matthew Greco, Editor
Edward Cortese, Marketing Executive
News updates, career opportunities and personnel announcements for CEO's, CFO's, treasurers and directors of corporations. *$415.00*
Bi-Monthly

7732 **Journal of Applied Finance**
Financial Management Association International
University of South Florida
College of Business Admin, #3331
Tampa, FL 33620
813-974-2084
FAX: 813-974-3318
kwright@fma.org www.fma.org
Jack S Rader, Executive Director
Karen Wright, Special Events Coordinator
Bi-Annual

7733 **Journal of Aquatic Animal Health**
American Fisheries Society
5410 Grosvenor Lane
Suite 110
Bethesda, MD 20814-2199
301-897-8616
FAX: 301-897-8096
main@fisheries.org www.fisheries.org
Gus Rassam, Executive Director
Betsy Fritz, Director Administration/Finance
Quarterly

7734 **Journal of Asset Protection**
Warren, Gorham & Lamont
395 Hudson Street
New York, NY 10014-3669
212-367-6300
FAX: 212-367-6718 800-742-3348
Dick O'Donnel, Managing Editor
Information on shielding personal and business assets from creditors, third party attachments and government claims. *$195.00*
Bi-Monthly
Circulation: 2,000

7735 **Journal of Cost Management**
RIA Group
395 Hudson Street
New York, NY 10014-3669
212-367-6300
FAX: 212-367-6305
RIA.editorialquestions@Thomson.com
http://www.riahome.com
Information on cost management techniques and manufacturing technology. Provides essays and or research papers by professionals and educators. *$210.00*
Monthly Founded: 1940
Circulation: 5000

7736 **Journal of Education Finance**
American Education Finance Association
5249 Cape Leyte Drive
Sarasota, FL 34242-1805
941-349-7580
Information and news to educational organizations on financial investing and prospecting.
150 pages Quarterly Founded: 1978
Circulation: 700

7737 **Journal of Finance**
American Finance Association
Haas School of Business
Berkley, CA 94720-1900
510-642-2397
FAX: 510-525-6246
pyle@haas.berkley.edu
www.afajof.org
Robert F. Stambaugh, Editor
Anat R Admati, Associate Editors
Wendy Washburn, Editorial Assistant
David H Pyle, Business Manager
Covers theory and practice in the field of finance.
Bi-Monthly Founded: 1939
Circulation: 10000+

7738 **Journal of Financial Planning**
4100 E Mississippi Avenue
Suite 400
Denver, CO 80246
303-759-4900
FAX: 303-759-0749 800-322-4237
journal@fpanet.org
http://www.fpanet.org/
Lynn Hopewell, Publisher, Editor
Maureen Peck, Managing Editor
Bruce W. Most, Senior Editor
Bob Haddad, National Advertising Sales Director
A comprehensive financial publication offering information and news on financial planning, investing and prospecting. *$90.00*
Monthly Founded: 1979
Circulation: 50,000

7739 **Journal of Fixed Income**
Institutional Investor
488 Madison Avenue
16th Floor
New York, NY 10022-5702
212-243-3300
FAX: 212-224-3491 800-945-2034
info@iipremium.com
http://www.institutionalinvestor.com/
Allison Adams, Publisher
Brian Bruce, Editor
Anne O'Brien, Marketing
Reporting on analysis of theories and ideas involving fixed income. *$370.00*
Quarterly Founded: 1967
Circulation: 2500

7740 Journal of Gift Planning
National Committee on Planned Giving
233 McCrea Street
Suite 400
Indianapolis, IN 46225-1030
317-269-6274
FAX: 317-269-6276
kramsey@ncpg.org www.ncpg.org
Tanya Howe Johnson, CAE, President/CEO
Sandra Kerr, Director Government Education
Barbara Owens, Director Membership Manager
Kathryn J Ramsey, Director Meetings
Kurt Reusze, Manager Education/Technology
Quarterly

7741 Journal of Government Financial Manage- ment
Association of Government Accountants
2208 Mount Vernon Avenue
Alexandria, VA 22301
703-684-6931
800-242-7211
cculkin@agacgfm.org
www.agacgfm.org
Relmond P Van Daniker, Executive Director
Marie S Force, Director Communications
Susan Fritzlen, Deputy Executive Director
Quarterly

7742 Journal of Healthcare Administrative Management
American Association of Healthcare Administrative
11240 Waples Mill Road
Suite 200
Fairfax, VA 22030
703-340-0164
FAX: 703-359-7562
aaham@statmarketing.org
www.aaham.org
Sharon Galler, CMP, Executive Director
Quarterly

7743 Journal of Investing
Institutional Investor
1900 Preston Road
#267-310
Plano, TX 75093-5175
214-495-9533
FAX: 212-224-3491
info@iijournals.com
http://www.iijournals.com
Brian Bruce, Editor-in-Chief
Allison Adams, Publisher
Anne O'Brien, Director of Marketing
Features equity investments, fixed income investing, security valuation and related investment vehicles. *$360.00*
Quarterly Founded: 1967
Circulation: 2500

7744 Journal of Mutual Fund Services
Securities Data Publishing
600 Atlantic Avenue
Boston, MA 02210-2211
617-723-6400
FAX: 617-624-7200 www.dalbar.com
Ken Heath, Publisher
Focuses on backroom operations of the mutual fund industry, with directories featuring transfer assets, fund accountants, custodians, attorneys and other service personnel. *$795.00*
8 per year

7745 Journal of Performance Management
Association for Management Information in
3895 Fairfax Court
Atlanta, GA 30339
770-444-3557
FAX: 770-444-9084 www.amifs.org
Kevin Link, Executive Director
3/year

7746 Journal of Portfolio Management
Institutional Investor
488 Madison Avenue
16th Floor
New York, NY 10022-5702
212-243-3300
FAX: 212-224-3491 800-437-9997
info@iijournals.com
http://www.institutionalinvestor.com/
Allison Adams, Publisher
Peter Bernstein, Editor
Anne O'Brien, Marketing Manager
Ideas and concepts in the practice and theory of portfolio management. *$430.00*
Quarterly Founded: 1975
Circulation: 5000

7747 Journal of Taxation
RIA Group
1325 G Street NW
Suite #910
Washington, DC 20005
202-393-6449
FAX: 202-393-6502 800-431-9025
RIA.CustomerServices@Thomson.com
http://www.ria.thomson.com
Joseph Graf, Editor
Terry Storholm, Advertising Sales Manager
Paul Muolo, Manager
Information on tax developments and trends, revenue rulings, court decisions and legislative and administrative actions of significance to the sophisticated tax professional. *$315.00*
Monthly Founded: 1984
Circulation: 12000
Printed in on glossy stock

7748 Legislative Currents
American Association of Healthcare Administrative
11240 Waples Mill Road
Suite 200
Fairfax, VA 22030
703-340-0164
FAX: 703-359-7562
aaham@statmarketing.org
www.aaham.org
Sharon Galler, CMP, Executive Director
Bi-Monthly

7749 MS Quarterly Journal
Society for Information Management
401 N Michigan Avenue
Chicago, IL 60611
312-215-5190
FAX: 312-245-1081 www.simnet.org
Jim Luisi, Executive Director
Quarterly

7750 Management Accounting Quarterly
Institute of Management Accountants
10 Paragon Drive
Montvale, NJ 07645-1718
201-573-9000
FAX: 201-474-1600 800-638-4427
ima@imanet.org www.imanet.org
Paul Sherman, Interim Executive Director
Quarterly

7751 Management and Technology
Association of Finance and Insurance Professionals
412 Southwood E
Colleyville, TX 76034
817-428-2434
FAX: 817-428-2534
afip@aol.com www.afip.com
David N Robertson, Executive Director

7752 Market Survey
International Swaps and Derivatives Association
360 Madison Avenue
16th Floor
New York, NY 10017
212-901-6000
FAX: 212-901-6001
isda@isda.org www.isda.org
Robert Pickel, CEO
Ruth Ainslie, Director Communications
Corrine Greasley, Director Administration
Semi-Annual

7753 Money
1271 Avenue of the Americas
32nd Floor
New York, NY 10020-1300
212-759-4094
FAX: 212-522-0773

7754 Mortgage Originator
Pfingsten Publishing
3990 Oldtown Avenue
Suite A203
San Diego, CA 92110
619-223-9989
FAX: 619-223-9943 800-995-2090
drobinson@pfpublish.com
http://www.mortgageoriginator.com
Chuck Hirsch, Publisher
David Robinson, Editor
Andy Strasser, Marketing Manager
Sue Burns, Circulation Director
Information on sales and marketing issues, correspondent management, retail mortgage, bankers and wholesale originators. *$58.00*
Founded: 1998
Circulation: 19,500
Printed in 4 colors on glossy stock

7755 Mortgage Servicing News
Thomson Financial Publishing
One State Street Plaza
27th floor
New York, NY 10004
212-258-8445
FAX: 212-292-5216 800-221-1809
custserv@thomsonmedia.com
http://www.mortgageservicingnews.com
Timothy Murphy, Publisher
Mark Fogarty, Editorial Director
Robert Cullen, CEO
Information on cross serving techniques, legislative decisions, management strategies, and professional profiles. *$98.00*
Monthly
Circulation: 20000

7756 **NAPFA Advisor Magazine**
National Association of Personal Financial Advisor
3250 N Arlington Heights Road
Suite 109
Arlington Heights, IL 60004
847-483-5400
FAX: 847-483-5415 800-366-2732
wassermanm@napfa.org
www.napfa.org
Ellen Turf, CEO
Margery Wasserman, Director Conferences
Monthly

7757 **NATE Update**
National Association of Trade Exchange
8836 Tyler Road
Mentor, OH 44060
440-205-5378
FAX: 440-205-5379
bartertrainer@aol.org www.nate.org
Thomas H McDowell, Executive Director

7758 **NBATalk**
National Association of Bankruptcy Trustees
One Windsor Cove
Suite 305
Columbia, SC 29233
803-252-5646
FAX: 803-765-0860 800-445-8629
info@nabt.com www.nabt.com
Carol H Webber, Executive Director
Quarterly

7759 **Natinal Pawnbroker Magazine**
National Pawnbrokers Association
PO Box 1040
Roanoke, TX 76262
817-491-4554
FAX: 817-481-8770
bob@nationalpawnbrokers.org
www.nationalpawnbrokers.org
Bob Benedict, CAE, Executive Director
Quarterly

7760 **National Association of Investors Corporation**
711 N 13 Mile Road
Madison Heights, MI 48071
248-352-5649
FAX: 248-583-4880 887-ASK-NAIC
Richard Holthaus, President/CEO
Adam Ritt, Editor
Articles on counseling and teaching investing techniques. Magazine is included with membership.
100 pages Monthly Founded: 1951
Circulation: 250,000
Printed in 4 colors on glossy stock

7761 **National Mortgage Broker**
National Association of Mortgage Brokers
23425 N 39th Drive
104-193
Glendale, AZ 85310
623-516-2723
FAX: 623-516-7738
mollie@banatcommunications.com
www.namb.org
Jon Ruzan, Publisher/Editorial Director
Bob Armbruster, President
Mollie Regan, Editor
Michael Nizankiewicz, Executive Vice President/CEO
Information on the National Association of mortgage Brokers including regulatory activities, education and certification, and building consumer awareness. *$59.95*
Monthly Founded: 1973
Circulation: 7500

7762 **Nelson's Quarterly Performance Monitor**
Nelson Publishing
2500 Tamiami Trail N
Nokomis, FL 34275
941-966-9521
FAX: 941-966-2590
webmaster@nelsonpub.com
www.nelsonpub.com
A Verner Nelson, Owner
George G Lindsey, COO
Kevin T Black, VP Database
Up-to-date performance information for pension officers, pension consultants, trustees and money managers. *$975.00*
200 pages Quarterly

7763 **Nelson's World's Best Money Managers**
Nelson Publishing
2500 Tamiami Trail N
Nokomis, FL 34275
941-966-9521
FAX: 941-966-2590
webmaster@nelsonpub.com
www.nelsonpub.com
A Verner Nelson, Owner
George G Lindsey, COO
Kevin T Black, VP Database
A special quarterly report extracted from the Nelson Investment Manager Database which ranks the top investment managers by performance results in each of 200 categories. *$245.00*
200 pages Quarterly

7764 **North American Journal of Fisheries Managment**
American Fisheries Society
5410 Grosvenor Lane
Suite 110
Bethesda, MD 20814-2199
301-897-8616
FAX: 301-897-8096
main@fisheries.org www.fisheries.org
Gus Rassam, Executive Director
Betsy Fritz, Director Administration/Finance
Quarterly

7765 **OCC Quarterly Journal**
Comptroller of the Currency Communications Division
250 E Street SW
Washington, DC 20219-1
202-874-4700
FAX: 202-874-5263 800-613-6743
Mark Nishan, Chief of Staff
Nancy K Jones, Executive Assistant
Significant actions and policies of the Office of Comptroller of the Currency, the agency that regulates national banks. Legal interpretations, merger decisions, speeches and testimony and statistical and structural data on national banks are included. *$100.00*
132 pages Quarterly Founded: 1863
Circulation: 6500 : pdf

7766 **Pensions & Investments**
Crain Communications
360 N. Michigan Ave
Chicago, IL 60601
312-495-5231
FAX: 312-649-7937
info@crain.com http://www.crain.com
William T Bisson Jr, Publisher
Nancy K Webman, Editor
Michael J Clowes, Editorial Director
$239.00
Monthly Founded: 1916
Circulation: 50000

7767 **Plan Horizons**
National Institute of Pension Administrators
401 N Michigan Avenue
Suite 2200
Chicago, IL 60611-4267
800-999-6472
nipa@nipa.org www.nipa.org
Laura J Rudzinski, Executive Director
Quarterly

7768 **Private Equity Analyst**
Asset Alternatives
888 Worcester Street
3rd Floor
Wellesley, MA 02482
781-304-1400
FAX: 781-304-1440 800-257-2947
CustomerService@PrivateEquityAnalyst.com http://www.assetnews.com
David Toll, Managing Editor
Lisa Hughes, Circulation Manager
Insider contacts and timely reports on the latest in venture capital, mezzanine, LBO and turn around financing. Original research and in-depth feature articles helps you understand critical trends and issues in the market. *$1495.00*
Monthly

7769 **Professional Collector**
Pohly & Partners
27 Melcher Street
2nd Floor
Boston, MA 02210
617-451-1700
FAX: 617-338-7767
procollector@pohlypartners.com
http://www.pohlypartners.com
Karen English, Editor
Piania Pohly, CEO/President
Annie Swearingven, Marketing Manager
Information on the latest technology, legislation and other issues affecting the debt collections industry. *$24.95*
Quarterly
Circulation: 148000
Printed in 4 colors

7770 **Purchasing**
Reed Business Information
225 Wyman Street
Waltham, MA 02451
617-643-3030
FAX: 781-290-3201 800-446-6551
subsmail@reedbusiness.com
http://www.purchasing.com
Paul Teague, Editor-in-Chief
Kathy Doyle, Publisher
Information for purchasing personnel in industry.
bi-monthly Founded: 1915
Circulation: 95,078
Printed in 4 colors on glossy stock

7771 **REIT Securities Monthly**
SNL Securities
PO Box 2124
Charlottesvle, VA 22902-2124
434-977-1600
FAX: 434-977-4466
subscriptions@snlnet.com
http://www.snlnet.com

Eden Rood, Editor
Reid Naglews, Publisher

Features sector analysis and interviews with industry leaders, as well as coverage of REIT investing and capital raising. The source for REIT and real estate investors, analysts and executives.

50 pages Monthly

7772 **RMA Journal**
RMA - Risk Management Association
1650 Market Street
Suite 2300
Philadelphia, PA 19103
215-446-4000
FAX: 215-446-4101 800-677-7621

Maurice H Hartigan, II, President/CEO
William F Githens, Director Member Relations
Dwightce J Overturf, CFO/Information Technology Officer
Florence J Wetzel, COO/Administrative Officer

Monthly

7773 **Regional Review**
Federal Reserve Bank of Boston
600 Atlantic Avenue
Boston, MA 02210
617-973-3000
FAX: 617-973-3957 800-248-0168
boston.library@bos.frb.org
http://www.bos.frb.org

Steven Sass, Editor
Cathy E Minehan, President/CEO
Jane Katz, Editor

Reliable and balanced discussions of economic issues. It is addressed to the opinion leaders of New England's business and government community.

Quarterly Founded: 1913
Circulation: 21000

7774 **Registered Representative**
Primedia
9800 Metcalf Avenue
Overland Park, KS 66212
913-341-1300
FAX: 913-967-1898 866-505-7173
rgcs@pbsub.com
http://www.rmag.com

Dan Jamieson, Editor-in-Chief
Rich Santos, Group Publisher

Magazine for retail stockbrokers that presents highly focused career-oriented editorials. Accepts advertising. *$59.00*

Monthly Founded: 1976
Circulation: 108067
Printed in 4 colors on glossy stock

7775 **Report on Business**
Institute for Supply Management
2055 E Centennial Circle
PO Box 22160
Tempe, AZ 85285-2160
480-752-6276
FAX: 480-752-7890 800-888-6276

Paul Novak, CFM, CEO
Holly LaCroix Johnson, SVP
Deborah Webber, SVP

Monthly

7776 **Research**
Financial Communications Company
PO Box 7588
San Francisco, CA 94120
415-621-0220
FAX: 415-621-0735
www.researchmag.com

Robert Tyndall, Publisher
Bill Nieder, Owner

Corporate profiles, investment information, and reports on building and keeping client base. *$35.00*

Monthly
Circulation: 65,227

7777 **Responsible Owner**
Institute for Responsible Housing Preservation
401 Ninth Street NW
Suite 900
Washington, DC 20004
202-858-8000
FAX: 202-585-8080
info@housingpreservation.org
www.housingpreservation.org

Linda D Kirk, Executive Director

Monthly

7778 **Reverse Mortgage Advisor**
National Reverse Mortgage Lenders Association
1625 Massachusetts Avenue NW
Suite 601
Washington, DC 20036-2244
202-939-1760
FAX: 202-265-4435
www.reversemortgage.org

Peter H Bell, Executive Director
Glenn Petherick, Director Communications

Quarterly

7779 **Secondary Marketing Executive**
LDJ Corporation
PO Box 2180
Waterbury, CT 06722-2330
203-755-0158
FAX: 203-755-3480 800-325-6745
info@sme-online.com
http://www.sme-online.com

Paul Zackin, Publisher
Mike Kling, Editor
June Han, Marketing

Delivers news, analysis and how-to advice to people involved in the buying and selling of mortgage loans and servicing rights nationwide. *$48.00*

44 pages Monthly Founded: 1986
Circulation: 21000

7780 **Secured Lender**
Commercial Finance Association
225 W 34th Street
Suite 1815
New York, NY 10122
212-594-3490
FAX: 212-564-6053
postmaster@cfa.com
http://www.cfa.com

Bruce H Jones, Editor-in-Chief
Michele A Ocejo, Executive Editor
Eileen M. Wubbe, Assistant Editor
Edward R. Fallon, Editorial Consultant
Linda C. Mohr, Production Manager

Provides in-depth reporting on federal and state legislation affecting the industry, legal notes on a wide range of issues, a full caladar year of industry workshops, meetings and seminars, personnel shifts, industry news and reviews of publications covering the industry. Discouted subscription rates for members. *$56.00*

6 issues per ye Founded: 1944
Circulation: 27000
Printed in 4 colors on glossy stock

7781 **Small Business Update**
Institute of Management Accountants
10 Paragon Drive
Montvale, NJ 07645-1718
201-573-9000
FAX: 201-474-1600 800-638-4427
ima@imanet.org www.imanet.org

Paul Sherman, Interim Executive Director

Monthly

7782 **Stable Times**
Stable Value Investment Association
2121 K Street NW
Suite 800
Washington, DC 20037
202-261-6530
FAX: 202-261-6527 800-327-2270

Gina Mitchell, President

Quarterly

7783 **Strategic Finance**
Institute of Management Accountants
10 Paragon Drive
Montvale, NJ 07645-1718
201-573-9000
FAX: 201-474-1600 800-638-4427
ima@imanet.org www.imanet.org

Paul Sherman, Interim Executive Director

Monthly

7784 **Takeover Targets**
High Tech Publishing Company
PO Box 1275
Amherst, MA 01004-1275
413-534-4500
FAX: 413-256-6378

Philip T DiPeri, Editor

Analyzes, evaluates and reports on situations, industries and individual enterprises throughout the world which may provide takeover investment opportunities. *$1200.00*

Monthly

7785 **Tax Executive**
Tax Executives Institute
1200 G Street NW
Suite 300
Washington, DC 20005-3814
202-638-5601
FAX: 202-638-5607 www.tei.org

Timothy J McNormally, Executive Director
Deborah K Gaffney, Director Conference Planning
Deborah C Giesey, Director Administration
Karina Horesky, Coordinator Membership
Fred F Murray, General Counsel/Dir Tax Affairs

Bi-Monthly

7786 **Tax Lawyer**
American Bar Association
750 N Lake Shore Drive, 7th Floor
Taxation Section
Chicago, IL 60611-4497
312-988-5000
FAX: 312-988-6281
Journal of scholarly articles written by highly respected attorneys in the field and a thought-provoking student notes and comments section. *$53.00*

Quarterly

7787 Taxes: the Tax Magazine
CCH
2700 Lake Cook Road
Riverwoods, IL 60015-3867
847-267-7000
FAX: 773-866-3095 800-449-8114
taxes@cch.com
http://www.tax.cch.com

Kevin Robert, President and CEO

Information on legal, accounting and economic aspects of federal and state taxes. *$245.00*

Monthly Founded: 1913
Circulation: 10000

7788 ThriftInvestor
SNL Securities
One SNL Plaza
PO Box 2124
Charlottesvle, VA 22902
434-977-1600
FAX: 434-977-4466
customerservice@snl.com
http://www.snl.com

Mark Saunders, Editor
Pat LaBua, Customer Service
Michael Spears, Advertising Sales Directo

Timely articles by industry experts on topics such as conversions, investment opportunities and government regulations. Source for important financial news, investor filings, conversion data and current financial and market information on all publicly traded thrifts. *$495.00*

80 pages Monthly Founded: 1987

7789 Trader's World Magazine
Halliker's
2508 W Graylock Drive
Springfield, MO 65810-2165
417-882-9697
FAX: 417-886-5180 1 8-0 2-8 42
publisher@tradersworld.com
http://www.tradersworld.com

Larry Jacobs, Publisher

Information on stock indexes, techniques of trading, exchange activities and current developments. *$19.95*

64 pages Quarterly Founded: 1989
Circulation: 12000
Printed in 4 colors on glossy stock

7790 Traders Magazine
Securities Data Publishing
40 W 57th Street
11th Floor
New York, NY 10019-4001
212-484-4701
FAX: 212-956-0112

Ken Heath, Publisher
Edward Cortese, Marketing Executive

Focuses on industry news, market and regulatory trends and the firms and individuals who shape the equities market.

Monthly
Circulation: 6,000

7791 Treasury & Risk Management
Wicks Business Information
52 Vanderbilt Avenue
Suite 514
New York, NY 10017-3808
212-557-7480
FAX: 212-557-7653
http://www.wicksbusinessinfo.com

John Whelan, VP/Group Publisher
Bob Raidt, Publisher
Pat Wechsler, Editorial Director

Provides information on areas such as pension funds, insurance, money manager selection, leasing and employee benefits. *$80.00*

Monthly Founded: 1991
Circulation: 44,000

7792 Trusts and Estates
PRIMEDIA Intertec-Marketing & Professional Service
9800 Metcalf Ave
Overland Park, KS 66212-2941
913-341-1300
FAX: 913-967-1898
treddy@primediabusiness.com
http://www.trustsandestates.com

Geoffrey Lewis, Group Editorial Director
Rorie Sherman, Editor in Chief
Thrupthi Reddy, Editor
Rich Santos, Group Publisher

Features updates on trust department operations, estates and life insurance, wills, federal tax notes and current literature. *$ 199.00*

Monthly Founded: 1886
Circulation: 14730

7793 US Fast Food and Multi-Unit Restaurants
Business Trend Analysts/Industry Reports
2171 Jericho Tpke
Suite 200
Commack, NY 11725-2937
631-462-5454
FAX: 631-462-1842 800-866-4648
sales@bta-ler.com
http://www.businesstrendanalysts.com

Charles J Ritchie, Executive VP
Donna Priani, General Manager

This survey offers information on the fast food industry, including chains and franchises. *$1995.00*

Founded: 1986
Computerized version available: Disc

7794 US Liquor Industry
Business Trend Analysts/Industry Reports
2171 Jericho Turnpike
Suite 200
Commack, NY 11725-2900
631-462-5454
FAX: 631-462-1842
sales@bta-ler.com
http://www.businesstrendanalysts.com

Charles J Ritchie, Executive VP
Donna Priani, Marketing Director

A survey summarizing the past, current and future markets and trends in the liquor industry. *$1495.00*

Founded: 1999
Computerized version available: Disc

7795 US Market for Bakery Products
Business Trend Analysts/Industry Reports
2171 Jericho Turnpike
Suite 200
Commack, NY 11725-2937
631-462-5454
FAX: 631-462-1842 800-866-4648
mkt@bta-ler.com
http://www.businesstrendanalysts.com/

Charles J Ritchie, Executive VP
Donna Priani, General Manager

Profiles markets for bread, rolls, cakes, pies, cookies, crackers, other sweets and pretzels; provides information on consumption patterns, distribution trends, pricing, new products, and advertising strategies. *$1495.00*

Annual+ Founded: 1978
Computerized version available: Disk

7796 Value Examiner
National Association of Certified Valuation
1111 Brickyard Road
Suite 200
Salt Lake City, UT 84106-5401
303-698-1883
FAX: 801-486-7500 800-677-2009
sherril@navca.com www.navca.com

Pamela R Bailey, Executive Director
Parnell Black, MBA CPA CVA, CEO
Roberto Castro, Director Business Development
Dean Dinas, Director Economic Research
Brien K Jones, General Manager Conferences

Bi-Monthly

7797 Venture Capital Journal
Securities Data Publishing
40 W 57th Street
New York, NY 10019
212-844-4701
FAX: 212-956-0112 sdp@tfn.com

Merry Logan, Associate Publisher
Edward Cortese, Marketing Executive

Provides information on recent issues, monitors current companies and looks at companies who have recently gone public. *$1025.00*

Monthly
Circulation: 1500

7798 Wall Street Computer Review
Miller Freeman Publications
1199 S Belt Line Road
Suite 100
Coppell, TX 75019-4667
972-906-6500
FAX: 972-419-7825

Elizabeth Katz, Publisher
Pavan Sahgal, Editor

For financial and investment professionals and individual investors. *$5.00*

Circulation: 34,000

7799 Washington Alert
Institute for Responsible Housing Preservation
401 Ninth Street NW
Suite 900
Washington, DC 20004
202-858-8000
FAX: 202-585-8080
info@housingpreservation.org
www.housingpreservation.org

Linda D Kirk, Executive Director

Irregular

7800 Washington Update
National Association of Affordable Housing Lenders
1300 Connecticut Avenue NW
Suite 905
Washington, DC 20036
202-293-9850
FAX: 202-293-9852 naahl@naahl.org

Judith A Kennedy, President/CEO

Monthly

Trade Shows

7801 **AACE Annual Meeting**
AACE International
209 Prairie Avenue
Suite 100
Morgantown, WV 26501
304-296-8444
FAX: 304-291-5728 800-858-2678
info@aacei.org www.aacei.org
Andrew S Dowd, Interim Executive Director
Christian Heller, Staff Director Technical
Charla Miller, Staff Director Education
Carol S Rogers, Manager Finance
July, Tennessee

7802 **AACE International Annual Meeting & Exposition**
AACE International
209 Prairie Avenue
Suite 100
Morgantown, WV 26507
304-296-8444
FAX: 304-291-5728 800-858-2678
info@aacei.org www.aacei.org
Jennie Cunningham Amos, Meetings Coordinator
Andy Dowd, Executive Director
Offers a unique opportunity to learn, network, and expand your professional horizons in a cost-effective manner. Our goal is to provide cost professionals with the knowledge necessary for survival in today's incredibly fast-changing marketplace. AACE's technical presentations, skills and knowledge track, exhibitors, transactions, certification program and social events combine to create an experience you can't afford to miss.
800 Attendees June 5000+ names $100 per M.

7803 **AAHAM Annual Meeting**
American Association of Healthcare Administrative
11240 Waples Mill Road
Suite 200
Fairfax, VA 22030
703-340-0164
FAX: 703-359-7562
aaham@statmarketing.com
www.aaham.org
Sharon Galler, CMP, Executive Director
October

7804 **AARMR Annual Meeting**
American Association of Residential Mortgage
1255 23rd Street NW
Suite 200
Washington, DC 20037
202-521-3999
FAX: 202-883-3636
cmurphy@aarmr.org www.aarmr.org
Christopher Murphy, Executive Director
Fall

7805 **ACA Annual International Convention & Exposition**
ACA International
PO Box 390106
Minneapolis, MN 55439
952-926-6547
FAX: 952-926-1624
meetings@acainternational.org
www.acainternational.com
Gary D Rippentorp CAE, CEO
Cathy Berg, Director Meetings
Annual international convention and exposition for credit and collection professionals.
July

7806 **AEFA Annual Meeting**
American Education Finance Association
8365 S Armadillo Trail
Evergreen, CO 80439
303-674-0857
FAX: 303-670-8986 www.aefa.cc
Ed Steinbecher, Executive Director
March

7807 **AFS Annual Meeting**
American Fisheries Society
5410 Grosvenor Lane
Suite 110
Bethesda, MD 20814-2199
301-897-8616
FAX: 301-897-8096
main@fisheries.org
www.fisheries.org
Gus Rassam, Executive Director
Betsy Fritz, Director Administration/Finance
September

7808 **AGA Annual Meeting**
Association of Government Accountants
2208 Mount Vernon Avenue
Alexandria, VA 22301
703-684-6931
800-242-7211
cculkin@agacgfm.org
www.agacgfm.org
Relmond P Van Daniker, Executive Director
Marie S Force, Director Communications
Susan Fritzlen, Deputy Exeucutive Director
July

7809 **AMIFS Annual Meeting**
Association for Management Information
3895 Fairfax Court
Atlanta, GA 30339
770-444-3557
FAX: 770-444-9084
ami@amifs.org www.amifs.org
Kevin Link, Executive Director
May

7810 **ASMC Annual Meeting**
American Society of Military Comptrollers
415 N Alfred Street
Alexandria, VA 22314-4650
703-549-0360
FAX: 703-549-3181 800-462-5637
James F McCall, Executive Director
May

7811 **American Bankers Association Annual Convention & Banking Industry Forum**
American Bankers Association
1120 Connecticut Avenue NW
Washington, DC 20036-3902
202-635-5000
FAX: 202-663-5210
Edward Yingling, President/CEO
Annual convention and 200 exhibitors of systems and products for the banking industry.
5000 Attendees

7812 **American Bankers Association National Agricultural Bankers Conference**
1120 Connecticut Avenue NW
Washington, DC 20036-3902
202-635-5000
Edward Yingling, President/CEO
Lucille Davis, Marketing Manager
Four thousand booths.
1M Attendees November/December

7813 **American Bankers Association: Bank Operations & Technology Conference**
American Bankers Association
1120 Connecticut Avenue NW
Washington, DC 20036-3902
202-635-5000
FAX: 202-663-5210
Edward Yingling, President
Annual conference and exhibits of automation, operating, data processing and related equipment, supplies and services.
2600 Attendees

7814 **American Bankers Association: Fiduciary and Securities Conference**
1120 Connecticut Avenue NW
Washington, DC 20036-3902
202-635-5000
800-338-0626
Edward Yingling, President/CEO
Betsy Love, Marketing Services
Seventy booths of financial equipment and supplies.
Annual

7815 **American Bankers Association: National Bank Card Conference**
American Bankers Association
1120 Connecticut Avenue NW
Washington, DC 20036-3902
202-635-5000
FAX: 202-663-5210
Edward Yingling

7816 **American League of Financial Institutions Annual Conference**
900 19th Street NW
Suite 400
Washington, DC 20006
202-857-3100
FAX: 202-296-8716
Diane Casey-Landry, President
Exhibits for financial institutions, federal and state chartered minority savings and loan associations in 25 states and DC.
Annual

7817 **Appraisers Association of America National Conference**
386 Park Avenue S
Suite 2000
New York, NY 10016-8804
212-889-5404
FAX: 212-889-5503
aaa1@ven.com
www.appraisersassoc.org
Aleya Lehmann, Executive Director
Angelina Ebreo, Associate Director
Linde Marke, Membership Associate
Exhibits of interest to appraisers.
Founded: 1949

7818 Association for Financial Professionals Annual Conference
Association for Financial Professionals
7315 Wisconsin Avenue
Suite 600 W
Bethesda, MD 20814
301-907-2862
FAX: 301-907-2864
AFP@AFPonline.org
www.AFPonline.org
Laurie R Kelly, Show Manager
Stephanie Clark, Sales Director
Karen E Ball, Marketing Director
Workshop and 642 exhibits of lockboxes, check processing systems, computers, investments, pensions, foreign exchange, consulting, mergers, aquistions and more information of interest to finacial professionals.
6000 Attendees November Founded: 1979

7819 BCCA Annual Meeting
Broadcast Cable Credit Association
550 Frontage Road
Suite 3600
Northfield, IL 60093
847-960-0200
FAX: 847-784-8059
info@bccacredit.com
www.bccacredit.com
Mary Collins, President/CEO
May

7820 Bond Market Association Fixed Income Summit & Expo
Flagg Management
353 Lexington Avenue
New York, NY 10016
212-286-0333
FAX: 212-286-0086
flaggmgmnt@msn.com
www.flaggmgmt.com/DM
Russell Flagg, President
1M Attendees December Founded: 1994

7821 CCFL Semi-Annual Meetings
Conference on Consumer Finance Law
Oklahoma City University School of Law
2501 N Blackwelder
Oklahoma City, OK 73106
405-521-5363
FAX: 405-521-5089
ccflqr@lec.okcu.edu www.theccfl.com
Alvin C Harrell, Executive Director
Held with American Bar Association.
Spring, Summer

7822 CDFA Annual Meeting
Council of Development Finance Agencies
301 NW 63rd Avenue
Suite 500
Oklahoma City, OK 73116
405-848-6059
FAX: 405-842-3299
info@cdfa.net www.cdfa.net
Stan Provus, Training Director
Don Conkle, Manager
Fall

7823 CDVCA Annual Meeting
Community Development Venture Capital Alliance
330 Seventh Avenue
19th Floor
New York, NY 10001
212-594-6747
FAX: 212-594-6717
cdvca@cdvca.org www.cdvca.org
Kerwin Tesdell, President
Kelly Williams, Director Program Development
Winter

7824 CIFA Semi-Annual Meetings
Council of Infrastructure Financing Authorities
805 15th Street NW
Suite 500
Washington, DC 20005
202-371-9694
FAX: 202-371-6601
cifa@chambersinc.org
www.cifanet.org
Richard T Farrell, Executive Director
Richard T Farrell, Executive Director
Letitia Chambers, Owner
Legislative Conference, Spring & Workshop, Fall

7825 CMSA Annual Meeting
Commercial Mortgage Securities Association
30 Broad Street
28th Floor
New York, NY 10004-2304
212-509-1844
FAX: 212-509-1895
info@cmbs.org www.cmbs.org
Dottie Cunningham, CEO
Marcus Henderson, Coordinator Membership/Facilities
Trish Madonia, Director Meetings
Winter

7826 CORFAC Semi-Annual Meetings
Corporate Facility Advisors
2000 N 15th Street
Suite 101
Arlington, VA 22201
703-528-3500
FAX: 703-528-0113
tom@corfac.com www.corfac.com
Thomas P Bennett, Executive Director
February, September

7827 CPTP Meeting/Conference
Coalition of Publicly Traded Partnerships
805 15th Street NW
Suite 500
Washington, DC 20005
202-719-9694
FAX: 202-371-6601
www.ptpcoalition.org
Letitia Chambers, Owner
Mary Lyman, Director
February

7828 CRF Annual Meeting
Credit Research Foundation
8840 Columbia Parkway
Suite 100
Columbia, MD 21045-2117
410-740-5499
FAX: 410-740-4620
crf_info@crfonline.org
www.crfonline.org
William T Callahan, CCE CRF, President
May

7829 CUES Annual Meeting
Credit Union Executives Society
5510 Research Park Drive
Madison, WI 53711-5377
608-271-2664
FAX: 608-271-2303
cues@cues.org www.cues.org
Fred Johnson, President/CEO
Mary Arnold, VP Publications
George Hofheimer, VP Professional Development
Barbara Kachelski, CAE, SVP/CIO
Dennis Porter, VP Finance/Administration
June

7830 California Accounting & Business Show
Flagg Management
353 Lexington Avenue
New York, NY 10016
212-286-0333
FAX: 212-286-0086
flaggmgmnt@msn.com
www.flaggmgmt.com
Russell Flagg, President
One hundred fifty exhibitors of investment management systems, databases, real-time and on-line systems. Global and US markets, Windows, PC and client/server systems.
2M Attendees September

7831 Credit Union Executives Expo
Credit Union Executives Society
5510 Research Park Drive
Madison, WI 53711-5377
608-712-2664
FAX: 608-271-2303
cues@cues.org www.cues.org
Fred Johnson, President
Linda Stemper, SVP/COO
Barbara Kachelski, SVP/CIO
Expo is held in conjunction with CUES Marketing, Operations and Technology Conference, where the top marketers and operations professionals in the industry gather.
500 Attendees May Founded: 1962

7832 DCUC Annual Meeting
Defense Credit Union Council
601 Pennsylvania Avenue NW
Suite 600
Washington, DC 20004-2601
202-829-9110
FAX: 202-638-3410
dcucl@cuna.com www.dcuc.org
William Archey, Chief Executive Officer
August

7833 EMTA Annual Meeting
EMTA - Trade Association for the Emerging Markets
360 Madison Avenue
18th Floor
New York, NY 10017
646-637-9100
FAX: 646-637-9128
awerner@emta.org www.emta.org
Michael M Chamberlin, President
Aviva Werner, General Counsel
December

7834 FMA Annual Meeting
Financial Markets Association
PO Box 156
Parlin, NJ 08859
732-316-0384
info@fma-usa.org www.fma-usa.org
Robert J Tum-Suden, Administrator
June

7835 FMAI Annual Meeting
Financial Management Association International
University of South Florida
College of Business Admin, #3331
Tampa, FL 33620
813-974-2084
FAX: 813-974-3318
kwright@fma.org www.fma.org
Jack S Rader, Executive Director
Karen Wright, Special Events Coordinator
200 Attendees October

7836 FMS Annual Meeting
Financial Managers Society
100 W Monroe Street
Suite 810
Chicago, IL 60603-1959
312-781-1300
FAX: 312-578-1308 800-275-4367
diane@fmsinc.org www.fmsinc.org
Richard A Yingst, President/CEO
Jennifer Doak, Director Marketing
Diane Walter, VP/Director Professional Developmnt
June

7837 FPA Annual Meeting
Financial Planning Association
4100 E Mississippi Avenue
Suite 400
Denver, CO 80246
303-759-4900
FAX: 303-759-0749 800-322-4237
fpa@fpanet.org www.fpanet.org
Martin W Tuttle, CAE, Executive Director/CEO
Al Hockwalt, Director Career Development
Ian McKenzie, Director Publications
Terry Monrad, Director Communications
Curt Niepoth, CFO
Fall

7838 FSR Semi-Annual Meetings
Financial Services Roundtable
1001 Pennsylvania Avenue NW
Suite 500 South
Washington, DC 20004
202-289-4322
FAX: 202-289-1903 www.fsround.org
Richard M Whiting, Executive Director/General Counsel
Steve Bartlett, President/CEO
Lisa McGreevy, EVP External Affairs
Spring, Fall

7839 FSTC Annual Meeting
Financial Services Technology
44 Wall Street
12th Floor
New York, NY 10005
212-711-1400
FAX: 646-349-3629
fstcadmin@fstc.org www.fstc.org
Zachary Tumin, Executive Director
Spring

7840 Fiduciary and Risk Management Association Annual Meeting
Fiduciary and Risk Management Association
PO Box 48297
Athens, GA 30604
706-354-0083
FAX: 706-353-3994
info@thefirma.org www.thefirma.org
Hale Mast, Executive Director
Deborah A Austin, VP

To educate, support and promote risk management professionals and improve the effectiveness of risk management for the fiduciary and investment service industry.
Spring

7841 FinEXPO
Miller Freeman Publications
1975 W El Camino Real
Suite 307
Mountain View, CA 94040-2218

FAX: 650-966-8934
Sixty exhibitors of full range of systems, software, service and solutions that financial and information system decision makers need to meet the challenges of today and the future.
2000 Attendees

7842 Financial Institute Marketing Association
111 E Wacker Drive
Chicago, IL 60601-3713
312-814-2000

Michele Latz, Manager
130 booths.
1M Attendees February

7843 Financial Management Association Meeting
Financial Management Association
University South Florida
Tampa, FL 33620
813-974-2084
FAX: 813-974-3318
Jack Rader, Executive Director
Annual meeting and exhibits of financial management related equipment, supplies and services.
October, Honolulu

7844 Financial Women International
1027 West Roselawn Avenue
Roseville, MN 55113
651-487-7632
FAX: 651-489-1322
info@fwi.org www.fwi.org
Ann Kvaal, FWI Management Services
Judy Rogers, President
Annual show and exhibits geared toward women officers and managers in the financial industry.
1000 Attendees September Founded: 1921

7845 HBMA Annual Meeting
Healthcare Billing and Management Association
1540 South Coast Highway
Suite 203
Laguna Beach, CA 92651

877-640-4262
March

7846 IMA Annual Meeting
Institute of Management Accountants
10 Paragon Drive
Montvale, NJ 07645-1718
201-573-9000
FAX: 201-474-1600 800-638-4427
ima@imanet.org www.imanet.org
Paul Sharman, President
1500 Attendees July

7847 INFE Annual Meeting
International Newspaper Financial Executives
21525 Ridgetop Circle
Suite 200
Sterling, VA 20166
703-421-4060
FAX: 703-421-4068
infehq@infe.org
www.infesure.org/newsite/extranet/
Robert J Kasabian, Executive Director/VP
June

7848 IRHP Meeting/Conference
Institute for Responsible Housing Preservation
401 Ninth Street NW
Suite 900
Washington, DC 20004
202-858-8000
FAX: 202-585-8080
info@housingpreservation.org
www.housingpreservation.org
Linda D Kirk, Executive Director
January

7849 ISM Annual Meeting
Institute for Supply Management
2055 E Centennial Circle
PO Box 22160
Tempe, AZ 85285-2160
480-752-6276
FAX: 480-752-7890 800-888-6276
Paul Novak, CPM, CEO
Holly LaCroix Johnson, SVP
Deborah Webber, SVP
3000 Attendees May

7850 International Association Financial Planning
2 Concourse Parkway NE
Suite 800
Atlanta, GA 30328-5588
770-351-9600

Jimmie Sue Schillecti, Show Manager
J Patrick Tinley, Chief Executive Officer
Five hundred booths.
4.6M Attendees October

7851 NAAHL Annual Meetings
National Association of Affordable Housing Lenders
1300 Connecticut Avenue NW
Suite 905
Washington, DC 20036
202-293-9850
FAX: 202-293-9852 naahl@naahl.org
Judith A Kennedy, President/CEO
Winter, Spring

7852 NABT Semi-Annual Meetings
National Association of Bankruptcy Trustees
One Windsor Cove
Suite 305
Columbia, SC 29233
803-252-5646
FAX: 803-765-0860 800-445-8629
info@nabt.com www.nabt.com
Carol H Webster, Executive Director
August

7853 NACHA Annual Meeting
NACHA: Electronic Payments Association

13665 Dulles Technology Drive
Suite 300
Herndon, VA 20171
703-561-1100
FAX: 703-787-0996
info@nacha.org www.nacha.org

Elliott C McEntee, President/CEO
Deb Evans-Doyle, Senior Director Conference Mktg
Julie Hedlund, Senior Director Electronic Commerce
Michael Herd, Director Public Relations
Priscilla Holland, AAP, Senior Director Corporate Pymts

1000 Attendees April

7854 NACM's Credit Congress and Exposition
National Association of Credit Management
8840 Columbia 100 Parkway
Columbia, MD 21045-2282
410-740-5560
FAX: 410-740-5574
lynnev@nacm.org www.nacm.org

Lynne Valentio, Director of Meetings
Robin Schauseil, President

Annual exhibits of relevance to credit and financial executives.

2500 Attendees June

7855 NACVA Annual Consultants' Conference
Nat'l Association of Certified Valuation Analysts
1111 Brickyard Road
Suite 200
Salt Lake City, UT 84106-5401
801-486-0600
FAX: 801-486-7500 800-677-2009
sheilat1@nacva.com www.navca.com

Sheila Travis, Director Member Services

750 Attendees June

7856 NADOA Annual Meeting
National Association of Division Order Analyst
2805 Oak Trail Court
Suite 6312
Arlington, TX 76016
972-715-4489

nadoa_org@hotmail.com
www.nadoa.org

Lynn S McCord, Administrator

September

7857 NAELB Annual Meeting
National Association of Equipment Leasing Brokers
304 W Liberty Street
Suite 201
Louisville, KY 40202

800-996-2352

Carol Davis, Administrator

May

7858 NAFC Annual Meeting
National Accounting and Finance Council
2200 Mill Road
Alexandria, VA 22314
703-838-1915
FAX: 703-836-0751
rcurtis@trucking.com
www.nafc.truckline.com

David Hershey, Executive Director

500 Attendees June

7859 NAFCU Annual Conference and Exhibition
National Association of Federal Credit Unions
3138 10th Street N
Suite 300
Arlington, VA 22201-2149
703-224-4770
FAX: 703-524-1082 800-336-4644
jbruce@nafcu.org www.nafcut.org

Jerome Bruce, Exhibits/Advertising Manager
Fred Becker, President

Annual show of 150 manufacturers and suppliers of complete range of financial products and services. 175 booths.

7860 NAIPFA Semi-Annual Meetings
National Association of Independent Public Finance
PO Box 304
Montgomery, IL 60538-0304
630-896-1292
FAX: 209-633-6265 www.naipfa.com

Roseanne M Hoban, Executive Director

Spring, Fall

7861 NALHFA Semi-Annual Meetings
National Association of Local Housing Finance
2025 M Street NW
Suite 800
Washington, DC 20036-3309
202-367-1197
FAX: 202-367-2197
john_murphy@nalhfa.org
www.nalhfa.org

John C Murphy, Executive Director
Scott Lynch, Association Manager
Kim McKinon, Coordinator Membership

Spring, Fall

7862 NAMB Annual Meeting
National Association of Mortgage Brokers
8201 Greensboro Drive
Suite 300
McLean, VA 22102
703-610-9009
FAX: 703-610-9005 www.namb.org

Michael J Nizankiewicz, PhD CAE, Executive VP/CEO
Roy DeLoach, VP Legislative
Rebecca Dopkin, VP Meetings

June

7863 NAPFA Annual Meeting
National Association of Personal Financial Advisor
3250 N Arlington Heights Road
Suite 109
Arlington Heights, IL 60004
847-483-5400
FAX: 847-483-5414 800-366-2732
wassermanm@napfa.org
www.napfa.org

Ellen Turf, CEO
Margery Wasserman, Director Conferences

800 Attendees May

7864 NASBO Annual Meeting
National Association of State Budget Officers
444 North Capitol Street NW
Suite 642
Washington, DC 20001
202-624-5382
FAX: 202-624-7745
spattison@nasbo.org www.nasbo.org

Scott Pattison, Executive Director
Lauren Cummings, Manager Member Relations

Summer

7865 NATE Semi-Annual Meetings
National Association of Trade Exchange
8836 Tyler Road
Mentor, OH 40060
440-205-5378
FAX: 440-205-5379
bartertrainer@aol.com www.nate.org

Thomas H McDowell, Executive Director

800 Attendees Spring, Fall

7866 NATRI Annual Meeting
National Association for Treasurers of Religious
8824 Cameron Street
Silver Springs, MD 20910
301-587-7776
FAX: 301-589-2897
lelcock@natri.org www.natri.org

Laura Reicks, Executive Director
Lorelle Elcock, Associate Director Finance

600 Attendees Fall

7867 NCPG Annual Meeting
National Committee on Planned Giving
233 McCre Street
Suite 400
Indianapolis, IN 46225-1030
317-269-6274
FAX: 317-269-6276
kramsey@ncpg.org www.ncpg.org

Tanya Howe Johnson, President/CEO
Sandra Kerr, Director Government Education
Barbara Owens, Director Membership/Manager HR
Kathryn J Ramsey, Director Meetings
Kurt Reusze, Manager Education/Technology

1700 Attendees

7868 NDCC Semi-Annual Meetings
National Defined Contribution Council
9101 E Kenyon
Suite 300
Denver, CO 80237-0467
303-770-5353
FAX: 303-770-1812
info@ndcconline.org
www.ndcconline.org

Al Brust, Executive Vice President

Spring, Fall

7869 NICSA Annual Meeting
National Investment Company Service Association
36 Washingtn Street
Suite 70
Wessesley Hills, MA 02481
781-416-7200
FAX: 781-416-7065
info@nisca.org www.nisca.org

Barbara V Weidlich, President
Keith Dropkin, Director Operations
Doris Jaimes, Registrar
Sheila Kobaly, Events Manager
Chris Ludent, IT Manager

February

7870 **NIPA Semi-Annual Meetings**
National Institute of Pension Administrators
401 N Michigan Avenue
Suite 2200
Chicago, IL 60611-4267

800-999-6472
nipa@nipa.org www.nipa.org
Laura J Rudzinski, Executive Director
Winter, Spring

7871 **NPA Annual Meeting**
National Pawnbrokers Association
PO Box 1040
Roanoke, TX 76262
817-491-4554
FAX: 817-491-8770
bob@nationalpawnbrokers.org
www.nationalpawnbrokers.org
Bob Benedict, CAE, Executive Director
1000 Attendees Summer

7872 **National Association of Review Appraisers & Mortgage Underwriters Convention**
National Assn of Review Appraisers/Mortgage Under.
1224 N Nokomis NE
Alexandria, MN 56308
320-763-7626
FAX: 320-763-9290
nara@iami.org www.iami.org
Robert G Johnson, Executive Director
Annual convention of real estate related information and services. Containing 50-75 booths, as well as environmental, home inspection, and construction inspection.
450 Attendees October Founded: 1962
Mailing list available for rent 2500 names $75 per M.

7873 **National Association of Tax Professionals Conference**
National Association of Tax Professionals

720 Association Drive
PO Box 8002
Appleton, WI 54912-8002
920-491-1040
FAX: 800-747-0001 800-558-3402
ingridl@natptax.com
www.natptax.com
Ingrid Lynd, Expo Coordinator
Annual conference and exhibits of computer hardware, tax accounting and planning software, tax research information, tax forms, one-write accounting, financial planning information, office products and business equipment.
1000 Attendees July, August

7874 **National Corporate Cash Management Association**
52 Church Hill Road
Newtown, CT 06470-1622
203-256-1191

Laura Stark, Show Manager
Two hundred seventy five booths exhibiting treasury management services and products.
5M Attendees October

7875 **Private Equity Analyst Conference**
Asset Alternatives
170 Linden Street
2nd Floor
Wellesley, MA 02482-7919
781-304-1400
FAX: 781-304-1440
www.assetnews.com
Lisa Hughs, Production Manager
The industry's premiere gathering of more than 1000 institutional investors, venture capitalists, buyout specialists, deal originators, and senior and mezzanine lenders. Three specialized tracks focus on institutional, venture capital, and LBO investing.

7876 **Private Equity Analyst Global Investing Conference**
Asset Alternatives
170 Linden Street
2nd Floor
Wellesley, MA 02482-7919
781-235-4565
FAX: 781-304-1440 www.assetalt.com
Lisa Hughs, Production Manager
Hundreds of institutional investors, private equity managers, and deal sources to debate the merits of funds of funds and regional funds for investing in Western and Eastern Europe, Latin America, Asia, the Middle East, and elsewhere.
May

7877 **Risk Management Association's Annual Conference**
Risk Management Association
1801 Market St
Ste 300
Philadelphia, PA 19103-1613
215-635-5398
FAX: 215-446-4101
jgermanotta@rmahg.org
www.rmahq.org
Jennifer Germanotta, Exhibits/Sponsors
Maurice Hartigan, President/CEO
Educates and helps risk management professionals develop new techniques and learn about new innovative products at different stages of their careers.
800 Attendees September/October

7878 **SFE Annual Meeting**
Society of Financial Examiners
174 Grace Boulevard
Altamonte Springs, FL 32714
407-682-4930
FAX: 407-682-3175 800-787-7633
info@sofe.org www.sofe.org
Paula Keyes, Executive Director
500 Attendees

7879 **SIM Annual Meeting**
Society for Information Management
401 N Michigan Avenue
Chicago, IL
312-215-5190
FAX: 312-245-1081 www.simnet.org
Jim Luisi, Executive Director
Fall

7880 **SQA Annual Meeting**
Society of Quantitative Analysts
151 Herricks Road
Suite 1
Garden City Park, NY 11040-5200
516-739-2510
FAX: 513-739-3803 800-284-6228
sqa@sqa-us.org www.sqa-us.org
Harry A Hansen, Executive Director
May

7881 **Security Traders Association**
420 Lexington Avenue
Suite 2334
New York, NY 10170
212-524-0484
FAX: 212-867-7030
traders@securitytraders.org
www.securitytraders.org
John C Giesea, President
Walter V Dolengo, VP
Members involved in the securities industry, 25 booths.
1.7M Attendees October

7882 **Southern Finance Association**
University of Florida
Mowry Road, Building 116
PO Box 110811
Gainesville, FL 32611-0811
352-392-5930
FAX: 352-392-7902
ace@mail.ifas.edu www.aceweb.org
Dr. Robert Radcliffe, Show Manager
Twenty five ooths.
1.4M Attendees November

7883 **Success Forum**
International Association for Financial Planning
2 Concourse Parkway NE
Suite 800
Atlanta, GA 30328-5588
770-351-9600
FAX: 770-668-7758 800-945-IAFP
J Patrick Tinley, Chief Executive Officer
Annual show and exhibits of financial services equipment, supplies and services.
2500 Attendees

7884 **TEI Annual Meeting**
Tax Executives Institute
1200 G Street NW
Suite 300
Washington, DC 20005-3814
202-638-5601
FAX: 202-638-5607 www.tei.org
Timothy J McNormally, Executive Director
Deborah K Gaffney, Director Conference Planning
Deborah C Giesey, Director Administration
Karina Horesky, Coordinator Membership
Fred F Murray, General Counsel/Dir Tax Affairs
April

7885 **Venture Capital & Health Care Conference**
Asset Alternatives
170 Linden Street
2nd Floor
Wellesley, MA 02482-7919
781-235-4565
FAX: 781-304-1440 www.assetalt.com
Lisa Hughs, Production Manager
This annual gathering of top investors, deal sources, entrepreneurs, Wall Street analysts, and senior health care executives explores the latest trends in health care services, devices, and medical information systems.

7886 Wall Street Technology Association Spring Conference & Exhibition
Wall Street Technology Association
241 Maple Avenue
Red Bank, NJ 07701
732-530-8808
FAX: 732-530-0020
ilazar@mpsicon.com www.wsta.org
Irwin Lazar, Conference Director
Ivett Ortiz, Communications
Richard Vendola, General Manager
Phyllis Lampell, Manager
Technologies, solutions and trends for the financial industry. Attendees are carriers and service providers for major finacial institutions.
May

Directories & Databases

7887 AACE Directory
AACE International
209 Prairie Avenue
Suite 100
Morgantown, WV 26501
304-296-8444
FAX: 304-291-5728 800-858-2678
info@aacei.org www.aacei.org
Andrew S Dowd, Interim Executive Director
Christian Heller, Staff Director Technical
Charla Miller, Staff Director Education
Carol S Rogers, Manager Finance
Annual

7888 AEFA Membership Directory
American Education Finance Association
8365 S Armadillo Trail
Evergreen, CO 80439
303-674-0857
FAX: 303-670-8986 www.afea.cc
Ed Steinbecher, Executive Director
Annual

7889 ALERT
AuTex Systems
11 Farnsworth Street
Boston, MA 02210-1210
617-345-2000
A database offering all available information on securities and securities trading information.
Numeric

7890 ATLAS
Technical Data
11 Farnsworth Street
Boston, MA 02210-1210
617-345-2000
Contains a variety of financial data and analyses of 7 major government bond markets.
Numeric

7891 All-Quotes
545 Madison Avenue
Suite 1400
New York, NY 10022-4219
FAX: 212-425-6895
Offers real-time and delayed quotes, and price and volume history for about 100,000 stocks, options and commodities.
Numeric

7892 Almanac of Business and Industrial Financial Ratios
Pearson Education
1 Lake Street
Upper Saddle River, NJ 07458-1813
201-236-7000
FAX: 201-236-3381 800-947-7700
Profiles corporate performance in two analytical tables for a variety of industries.
$69.95
Annual

7893 American Banker On-Line
American Banker-Bond Buyer
1 State Street Plaza
27th Floor
New York, NY 10004-1505
212-631-1271
FAX: 207-581-3015 207-581-3042
Gerald D Mintz, President
Mario DiUbaldi, Publisher
Phil Roosevelt, Editor
Carole Lambert, Sales/Marketing Director
Stacy Weinstein, Production Director
World wide web edition of daily financial services newspaper. Journal available.

7894 American Financial Directory
TFP
4709 Golf Road
6th Floor
Skokie, IL 60076
847-676-9600
FAX: 847-933-8101 800-321-3373
customerservice@tfp.com
www.tfp.com
Marideth Johnson, Manager, Marketing/Communications *$523.00*
January/July ISBN 1-563103-47-8
Circulation: 41300 : Hardcover

7895 American Society of Appraisers Directory
American Society of Appraisers
555 Herndon Parkway
Suite 125
Herndon, VA 20170-5248
703-782-2228
FAX: 703-742-8471 800-272-8258
asainfo@apppraisers.org
www.appraisers.org
Jerry F Larkins, Executive VP
Directory of association members who are accredited appraisers. *$12.50*
Circulation: 8,000
Mailing list available for rent 5,000 names $200 per M.

7896 American Stock Exchange Fact Book
Publications Department
86 Trinity Pl
New York, NY 10006-1817
212-308-0046
FAX: 212-306-2160
Neal Wolkoff, Chief Executive Officer
Lists addresses, telephone and fax numbers and ticker symbols of every listed company. Historical statistics and all-time trading records for equities, with a list of every stock option, index option and derivative security traded on the American Stock Exchange.
$20.00
Annual Founded: 1994
Circulation: 10,000

7897 American Stock Exchange Guide
CCH
2700 Lake Cook Road
Riverwoods, IL 60015-3867
847-267-7000
FAX: 773-866-3608 800-835-5224
Volume 1 lists a directory of officials, members, organizations and securities; Volume 2 lists by-laws and rules of the exchange.
$570.00

7898 Arthur D Little: Online
Decision Resources
6120 SW 132rd Street
Miami, FL 33156
305-666-0476
This database offers interpreted information on business trends, emerging technologies, strategic planning and company assessments.
Bibliographic

7899 Asia Pacific Securities Handbook
Reference Press
6448 E Highway 290
Suite E104
Austin, TX 78723-1041
512-331-1815
FAX: 512-374-4501
Dan Capper, President
Offers stock information on the exchanges in Australia, Bangladesh, China, Hong Kong, India, Indonesia, Japan, Malaysia, Nepal, New Zealand, Pakistan, Taiwan, Sri Lanka, and Thailand. *$99.95*
250 pages Founded: 1993

7900 Bank Mergers & Acquisitions Yearbook
SNL Securities
PO Box 2124
Charlottesvle, VA 22902-2124
434-977-1600
FAX: 434-977-4466
subscriptions@snlnet.com
www.snlnet.com
John Minor, Editor
Christie Atkinson, Editor
Reid Nagle, Publisher
Mark Outlaw, Advertising Director
For bank and thrift CEOs, CFOs, investment banks, merger and acquisition advisors, law firms, accounting firms and individual investors. Covers all bank and thrift merger activity from the previous year, state-by-state reviews of all private sector whole-bank and whole-thrift transactions, branch sales, merger conversions and government-assisted transactions announced in that year.
150 pages Annual Founded: 1994

7901 Bloomberg Business News
499 Park Avenue
New York, NY 10022-1240
212-315-5000
FAX: 609-497-6577
Michael Bloomberg, Publisher
Matthew Winkler, Editor
A 24-hour global news service available exclusively on The Bloomberg. All stories are fully integrated into The Bloomberg's newsminder which instantly alerts you to developments in all stock and bond markets.

7902 **Bloomberg Financial Markets Commodities News**
PO Box 888
Princeton, NJ 08542-0888
609-279-3000
FAX: 609-279-2028
Michael Bloomberg, Publisher
Matthew Winkler, Editor
Beth Mazzeo, Global Products
A leading multimedia distributor of news, information, data and analysis, providing information on everything from capital markets and airline schedules to employment opportunities and luxury goods. *$795.00*
Monthly

7903 **Blue List Corporate Bond Service**
Kenny S&P Information Services
65 Broadway
New York, NY 10006-2503
212-739-9870
FAX: 646-471-2609
warren_hirschhorn@standardpoors.com
www.standardandpoors.com
This database provides real-time data on corporate bond offerings and price information as well as corporate and municipal bond offerings, evaluations and commentary.
Numeric

7904 **Blue List Retrieval**
Kenny S&P Information Services
65 Broadway
New York, NY 10006-2503
212-739-9870
FAX: 646-471-2609
warren_hirschhorn@standardandpoors.com www.standardandpoors.com
Richard Chalme, Manager
This database contains data on current municipal and corporate bond offerings.
Numeric

7905 **Bond Buyer's Municipal Marketplace**
Thomson Financial Publishing
4709 Golf Road
6th Floor
Skokie, IL 60076-1231
847-778-8037
James L Nowell, Editor
Offers information on firms and personnel in the municipal bond industry, including municipal bond dealers, chief finance officers of municipalities which issue bonds, and attorneys specializing in the field of municipal finance. *$185.00*
937 pages Semiannual

7906 **Bonds Data Base**
ADP Data Services
42 Broadway
Suite 1730
New York, NY 10004-1617
212-406-2820
This database, update daily, contains historical prices and trading volumes for more than 33,000 corporate, government and agency bonds.
Numeric

7907 **Bowser Directory of Small Stocks**
Bowser Report
PO Box 6278
Newport News, VA 23606-0278
757-877-5979
FAX: 757-595-0622
Ministocks@aol.com
www.thebowsersreport.com
Cindy Bowser, Editor
Lists 14 fields of information on over 700 low-priced stocks. *$89.00*
35 pages Monthly

7908 **Bridge Information System**
717 Office Parkway
Saint Louis, MO 63141-7115
314-567-8100
FAX: 314-432-5391 800-325-3282
Tony Bridge, Manager
This large database contains real-time, last sale and quote data on all listed and unlisted stocks, options, futures and foreign securities.
Numeric

7909 **Bull and Bear's Directory of Investment Advisory Newsletters**
Bull & Bear Financial Report
PO Box 917179
Longwood, FL 32791-7179
407-682-6170
thebullandbear.com
www.thebullandbear.com
David J Robinson, President
Advice from investment advisory newsletters on various investment areas, small-cap stocks, global and domestic stock markets, mutual funds, precious metals and economy. *$29.00*
48 pages Annual Founded: 1974
Circulation: 55,000 100,000 names $125 per M.

7910 **Business & Finance Career Directory**
Gale Research
27500 Drake Road
Farmington Hills, MI 48331
248-699-4253
FAX: 248-699-8214 800-877-4253
galeord@gale.com www.gale.com
Bradley J Morgan, Editor
Accounting, banking, investment banking, stock brokerage, and insurance companies are listed in this directory, offering entry-level positions and internships. *$34.00*
400 pages Cloth Founded: 1992

7911 **Business Week North America**
McGraw Hill
1221 Avenue of the Americas
43 Floor
New York, NY 10020-1095
212-512-2000
www.mcgraw-hill.com
Mia Fowler, Editor
William Kupper Jr, Chief Executive Officer *$3.00*
Annual April

7912 **Business and Financial News Media**
Larriston Communications
PO Box 20229
New York, NY 10025-1518
310-871-0563
Sheila Gordon, Editor
Lists over 300 daily newspapers with at least 50,000 in circulation and a business or finance correspondent; television stations and all-news radio stations in the largest 40 markets. *$89.00*
175 pages Annual

7913 **CDA/Wiesenberger Investment Companies Service**
CDA Investment
1355 Piccard Drive
Suite 200
Rockville, MD 20850-4300
Jay Nadler, Editor
Lists 5,000 open and closed mutual funds, unit trusts and investment companies listing policies and objectives, history, and statistical information of the company.
1500 pages Annual

7914 **CIN: Corporation Index System**
Office of Applications & Reports Services
450 5th Street NW
Washington, DC 20001-2739
202-942-0020
David Weiss, Manager
Lists 1,580 active companies registered under the Investment Company Act of 1940. Information is extend to include related underwriters and advisers and 800 number. *$90.00*
Monthly

7915 **CISCO**
CISCO
170 W Tasman Drive
San Jose, CA 95134
408-526-4000
805-553-6387
John Chambers, Chief Executive Officer
Contains technical analyses and prices of commodities futures, and currencies.
Numeric

7916 **CUSIP Master Directory**
Standard & Poor's Corporation
55 Water Street
New York, NY 10041
212-382-2000
FAX: 212-438-6578
Official listings of numbers and descriptions for more than 1,500,000 stocks, bonds and warrants of 100,000 issuers, including corporations and municipalities of the United States and Canada. *$1900.00*
Annual

7917 **Commodity Futures Trading Commission Geographic Directory**
Three Lafayette Centre
1155 21st Street NW
Washington, DC 20581
202-418-5000
FAX: 202-418-5521
opa@cftc.org www.cftc.org
Offers information on corporations and firms that are registered with the Commodity Futures Trading Commission. *$25.00*

7918 **Corporate Finance Sourcebook**
Reed Reference Publishing RR Bowker
121 Chanlon Road
New Providence, NJ 07974-1541
908-665-2834
FAX: 908-464-3553
info@bowker.com www.bowker.com

Tom Bachmann, Editor
Christine Kerwin, Editor

Contains a variety of information on the financial services industry. Listings include securities research analysts, major private lenders, mergers and acquisitions, commercial finance firms, pension managers and leasing companies. *$425.00*

1600 pages Annual

7919 Corporate Venturing Directory & Yearbook
Asset Alternatives
170 Linden Street
Wellesley, MA 02482
781-304-1400
FAX: 781-304-1440
www.corporateventuring.com

Dave Barry, Senior Editor
Barbara Bissonnette, VP Marketink/Sales

Features the most comprehensive data ever assembled on corporations participating in venture-backet deals, and the young companies they're financing. *$495.00*

Annual
Printed in on matte stock

7920 Corporate Yellow Book
Leadership Directories
104 5th Avenue
New York, NY 10011-6901
212-627-4140
FAX: 212-645-0931
corporate@leadershipdirectories.com
www.leadershipdirectories.com

Vonessa Ruffin, Editor

Contact information for over 48,000 executives at over 1,000 companies and more than 9,000 board members and their outside affiliations. *$360.00*

1,400 pages Quarterly Founded: 1986
50,000 names $105 per M. : CD-Rom

7921 Cost Engineers Notebook
AACE International
209 Prairie Avenue
Suite 100
Morgantown, WV 26501
304-296-8444
FAX: 304-291-5727 800-858-2678
info@aacei.org www.aacei.org

Andrew S Dowd, Interim Executive Director
Christian Heller, Staff Director Technical
Charla Miller, Staff Director Education
Carol S Rogers, Manager Finance

Irregular

7922 Credit Decisioning Study
Credit Research Foundation
8840 Columbia Parkway
Suite 100
Columbia, MD 21045-2117
410-740-5499
FAX: 410-740-4620
crf_info@crfonline.org
www.crfonline.org

William T Callahan, CCE CRF, President

7923 Current Market Snapshot
CompuServe Information Service
PO Box 20212
Columbus, OH 43220-0212
614-457-8600

Offers information on up-to-date stock prices foreign currency data, and general market statistics.

Numeric

7924 DIAL/DATA
Track Data Corporation
95 Rockwell Place
Brooklyn, NY 11217
718-522-7373
FAX: 718-923-3137 www.trackdata.com

This database contains current and historical data on securities, options and commodities.

Numeric

7925 DRI Commodities
DRI/McGraw-Hill
11000 Regency Parkway
Suite 400
Cary, NC 27511
919-462-8600
FAX: 919-468-9890 www.profound.com

This database contains more than 51,000 daily time series of price and trading data for major commodities traded on makrets in the US, Canada, London and Singapore.

7926 DRI Transportation
DRI/McGraw-Hill
11000 Regency Parkway
Suite 400
Cary, NC 27511
919-462-8600
FAX: 919-468-9890 www.profound.com

This large database contains over 15,000 weekly, monthly, and annual time series on commodity traffic by mode, carrier operations and financial data.

7927 DRI US Bonds
DRI/McGraw-Hill
11000 Regency Parkway
Suite 400
Cary, NC 27511
919-462-8600
FAX: 919-468-9890 www.profound.com

This financial database contains daily time series of current and historical prices, yields and fundamental financial information for more than 60,000 dealer-priced debt issues.

7928 Daily Foreign Exchange Analysis & Updates
Technical Data
11 Farnsworth Street
Boston, MA 02210-1210
617-345-2000

This database offers daily reports from major world financial centers including, currency forecasts, analysis of the US bond and money markets, currency reports and the trends of the New York foreign exchange market.

Full-text

7929 Dick Davis Digest
Dick Davis Publishing
PO Box 26774
Fort Lauderdale, FL 33320-6774
954-733-3996
FAX: 954-733-8559
editorial@dickdavis.com
www.dickdavis.com

Steven Halpern, Publisher/Editor
Lorianne Kiesl, Marketing Director
Donald Hanrahan, Owner

The digest excerpts over 400 newsletters and the research reports from leading Wall Street analysts and compiles this information into a 12 page compendium of what leading financial advisors currently recommend. *$165.00*

BiWeekly

7930 Directory of Alternative Investment Programs
Asset Alternatives
170 Linden Street
2nd Floor
Wellesley, MA 02482-7919
781-304-1400
FAX: 781-304-1440
www.assetnews.com

David Toll, Managing Editor

The private equity programs of more than 500 leading pension funds, endowments and other institutions, plus their advisors. *$ 595.00*

7931 Directory of Buyout Financing Sources
Securities Data Publishing
40 W 57th Street
New York, NY 10019
212-484-4701
FAX: 212-956-0112
sdp@tfn.com www.sdponline.com

Ted Weissberg, Editor-in-Chief
Deborah Chieglis, Advertising Manager
Edward Cortese, Marketing Executive

Over 700 sources of financing, including senior lenders, equity and mezzanine providers in the United States and international avenues, with detailed information on industry, geographic and invetment size preferances and recent activity for each firm.

7932 Directory of Defense Credit Union
Defense Credit Union Council
601 Pennsylvania Avenue NW
Suite 600
Washington, DC 20004-2601
202-829-9110
FAX: 202-638-3410
dcucl@cuna.com www.dcuc.org

William Archey, Chief Executive Officer

Bi-Ennial

7933 Directory of M+A Intermediaries
Securities Data Publishing
40 W 57th Street
11th Floor
New York, NY 10019-4001
212-484-4701
FAX: 212-956-0112
sdp@tfn.com www.sdponline.com

Ted Weissberg, Editor-in-Chief
Deborah Chieglis, Advertising Manager
Edward Cortese, Marketing Executive

Over 700 firms listed, including accounting firms, business brokers, banks, consulting firms, advisory executive recruiters, law firms, and valuation firms, all involved in mergers and acquisitions.

7934 Directory of Manufacturers' Sales
Manufacturers' Agents National Association
PO Box 3467
Laguna Hills, CA 92654-3467
949-859-4040
FAX: 949-855-2973
www.manaonline.org

Joseph Miller, President

Association for independent agents and firms representing manufacturers and other businesses in specified territories on a commission basis, including consultants and associate member firms interested in the manufacturer/agency method of marketing. *$129.00*
Annual
Circulation: 25,000

7935 Directory of Mastercard and Visa Credit Cards
Todd Publications
PO Box 635
Nyack, NY 10960-0635
845-358-6213
FAX: 845-358-1059
toodpub@aol.com
toddpublications.com

Barry Klein, Editor

Offers information on 500 credit cards from 200 banks across the country. *$50.00*
1000 pages Biennial Founded: 1994
Circulation: 5,000
Mailing list available for rent 200 names $50 per M. : Mac

7936 Directory of Mutual Funds
Investment Company Institute
1600 M Street NW
Suite 600
Washington, DC 20036-3215
202-169-9866

Sue Duncan, Editor *$5.00*
247 pages Annual

7937 Directory of Venture Capital and Private Equity Firms
Grey House Publishing
185 Millerton Road
PO Box 860
Millerton, NY 12546
518-890-0526
FAX: 518-789-0545 800-562-2139
books@greyhouse.com
www.greyhouse.com

Leslie Mackenzie, Publisher
Richard Gottlieb, Editor

Offers access to over 3,000 domestic and international venture capital and private equity firms, including detailed contact information and extensive data on investments and funds. *$450.00*
1,200 pages Annual ISBN 1-592370-62-4

7938 Dow Jones Business and Finance Report
Dow Jones & Company
PO Box 300
Princeton, NJ 08543-0300
609-520-4000

This large database offers financial news and inforamtion on developments in business and industry, domestic and international economies, and the stock market.
Full-text

7939 Dow Jones Futures and Index Quotes
Dow Jones & Company
PO Box 300
Princeton, NJ 08543-0300
609-520-4000

This database, updated continuously, offers current and historial stock quotations for more than 80 contracts from major North American stock exchanges.
Numeric

7940 Dow Jones Text Library
Dow Jones & Company
PO Box 300
Princeton, NJ 08543-0300
609-520-4000

This large database offers business and financial news covering more than 6,000 US companies, 700 Canadian companies and 50 industries.
Full-text

7941 E-Z Telephone Directory of Brokers and Banks
106 7th Street
Garden City, NY 11530-5796
516-294-0350
FAX: 516-294-0356

MJ Gentile, Editor

Security brokers, banks, and financial organizations in the New York area are listed in this directory. *$90.00*
200 pages SemiAnnual
Circulation: 10,000
Printed in on matte stock

7942 ECFA Member List
Evangelical Council for Financial Accountability
440 W Jubal Early Drive
Suite 130
Winchester, VA 22601
540-535-0103
FAX: 540-535-0533 800-323-9473
info@ecfa.org www.ecfa.org

Paul D Nelson, President
Dan Busby, VP

Annual

7943 EMARKET
International Financial Corporation
2121 Pennsylvania Avenue NW
Washington, DC 20433-0001
202-473-1000
FAX: 202-477-6391
Webmaster@ifc.org www.ifc.org

This database offers over 1,000 weekly, annual and monthly time series on company stocks from over 18 developing countries.

7944 Evans Economics Analysis and Commentary
Evans Economics
1660 L Street NW
Suite 207
Washington, DC 20036-5603

This database reports on changes in economic activity to all major financial markets. Over 20 files are listed that provide the forecasts and reports on the effect of economic variables on debt and equity markets.
Full-text

7945 Financial Ratios for Manufacturing Corporations Database
US Department of Commerce
Herbert Rm 4885
Washington, DC 20230-0001
202-690-7650
FAX: 202-482-0325
pnacci@doc.gov www.access.gpo.gov

Pam Nacci

This database provides 20 quarterly seasonally adjusted financial and operating ratios for selected two- and three-digit SIC groups in the manufacturing sector. *$85.00*
Series

7946 Financial Yellow Book
Leadership Directories
104 5th Avenue
New York, NY 10011-6901
212-627-4140
FAX: 212-645-0931
financial@leadershipdirectories.com
www.leadershipdirectories.com

Don Doyle, Editor
James M Petrie, Associate Publisher

Contact information for over 26,000 executives at public and private financial institutions, and over 5,000 board members and their outside affiliations. *$245.00*
900 pages Semiannual Founded: 1987
Mailing list available for rent 20,000 names $95 per M.
Computerized version available: CD-ROM

7947 Financing Your Business in Eastern Europe
WorldTrade Executive
PO Box 761
Concord, MA 01742-0761
978-287-0301
FAX: 978-287-0302 www.wtexec.com

Alison French, Production Manager

Provides reliable information on financing sources, including local and international banks, capital markets, venture capital funds, and government sources *$135.00*

7948 FirstList
Vision Quest Publishing
PO Box 27963
Prescott Valley, AZ 86312
928-772-4165
FAX: 928-774-4074
mergers@firstlist.com

A Robert Weicherding, President

Information is offered in this directory covering companies that are candidates for merger or acquisition, buyers seeking acquisitions, sources of financinf, equity or debt financing and joint venture and licensing opportunities. Also available on-line and the Internet. *$350.00*
120 pages 8 per year

7949 Ford Data Base
Ford Investor Services
11722 Sorrento Valley Road
Suite 1
San Diego, CA 92121-1021
858-755-1327
FAX: 858-455-6316

Tim Alward, President

This database offers 80 financial data items for each of 2,000 leading common stocks.
Numeric

7950 Futures Magazine Sourcebook
Oster Communications
219 Parkade
#6
Cedar Falls, IA 50613-2752
319-277-1271

Kristin Beane, Editor

This issue deals with exchanges in futures and options contracts, including commodities, foreign currencies, stock indexes and international financial coverage. *$22.00*
130 pages Annual
Circulation: 60,000

7951 Galante's Venture Capital & Private Equity Directory
Asset Alternatives
170 Linden Street
Wellesley, MA 02482-7919
781-304-1400
FAX: 781-304-1440
www.assetnews.com
David Toll, Managing Editor
Complete investment criteria of venture capital, buyout, and mezzanine firms into one complete reference. *$395.00*

7952 Guide to Life, Health and Annuity Insurers
Weiss Ratings
PO Box 109665
Palm Beach Gardens, FL 33410-9665

FAX: 561-625-6685 800-291-8545
wr@weissinc.com
www.weissratings.com
Martin D Weiss PhD, Editor
Melissa Gannon, VP
David Lackey, President
Weiss Ratings evaluates the financial solvency risk of over 1,400 insurance companies offering life insurance, health insurance, and annuities. *$219.00*
350 pages Every 4 Years ISBN 1-889499-45-5

7953 Guide to Stock Mutual Funds
Weiss Ratings
PO Box 109665
Palm Beach Gardens, FL 33410-9665

FAX: 561-625-6685 800-291-8545
wr@weissinc.com
www.weissratings.com
Martin D Weiss PhD, Editor
Melissa Gannon, VP
David Lackey, President
Covering over 5,000 equity mutual funds, Weiss Ratings consumer-oriented mutual fund ratings combine both risk and reward measures into a single evaluation to make mutual fund investing safer and easier. *$219.00*
300 pages Quqrterly ISBN 1-889499-49-8

7954 How To Pay For Your Degree In Agriculture & Related Fields
Reference Service Press
5000 Windplay Drive
Suite 4
El Dorado Hills, CA 95762-9600
916-939-9620
FAX: 916-939-9626
info@rspfunding.com
www.rspfunding.com
Gail Schlachter, Editor
R David Weber, Editor
Contains detailed descriptions of the more than 600 scholarships, fellowships, loans, grants and awards established specifically for students working on a 2 year, 4 year, master's or doctoral degree in business fields. No other directory comes close to providing the kind of comprehensive coverage offered here. *$30.00*
320 pages Biennial ISBN 1-588411-03-6 : database

7955 How To Pay For Your Degree In Business & Related Fields
Reference Service Press
5000 Windplay Drive
Suite 4
El Dorado Hills, CA 95762-9600
916-939-9620
FAX: 916-939-9626
info@rspfunding.com
www.rspfunding.com
Gail Schlachter, Editor
R David Weber, Editor
Information on nearly a billion dollars set aside specifically for students working on a 2 year, 4 year, master's or doctoral degree in agricultural science, animal science, apiculture, ranching, cooperative extension, dairy science, agricultural economics, crops or soils science, enology/viticulture, horticulture and many other related fields. *$30.00*
300 pages Biennial ISBN 1-588411-04-4 : database

7956 Hulbert Guide to Financial Newsletters
Dearborn Financial Publishing
155 Wacker Avenue
Chicago, IL 60606
312-836-4400

Matt Schiff, Owner
Kathleen A Welton, VP
Lists over 100 financial newsletters offering descriptions and evaluation of model portfolios. *$27.95*
574 pages Biennial

7957 IBC/Donoghue's Money Fund Report/ Electronic
290 Eliot Street
#9104
Ashland, MA 01721-2351

This valuable database offers information and analyses of trends and developments in the money market mutual funds industry.
Full-text

7958 IBC/Donoghue's Mutual Funds Almanac
290 Eliot Street
#9104
Ashland, MA 01721-2351

Ann V Needle, Editor
Over 2,400 load and no load mutual funds, including equity, bond and municipal funds. *$39.95*

Circulation: 25,000

7959 IVCI Directory of Domestic and International Venture Groups
International Venture Capital Institute
PO Box 1333
Stamford, CT 06904-1333
203-323-3143
$9.95
25 pages Annual

7960 Insider Trading Monitor Database
CDA Investment
3265 Meridian Parkway
Suite 130
Fort Lauderdale, FL 33331-3506
954-384-1500

More than 12,500 companies and all insider security transactions reported to the US Securities and Exchange Commission, FDIC, Toronto Stock Exchange and OTS.
Daily

7961 Insiders' Chronicle
CDA Investment
3265 Meridian Parkway
Suite 130
Fort Lauderdale, FL 33331-3506
954-384-1500

Robert Gabele, Editor
Publicly held companies in whose securities there has been significant buying or selling by executive officers, directors, and those who hold 10% or more of its shares.
15 pages

7962 International Financial Statistics
International Monetary Fund
700 19th Street NW
Washington, DC 20431-0002
202-623-7000
FAX: 202-623-7201
publications@imf.org www.imf.org
Cathy Willis, Deputy Chief, Publication Services
Kathleen Tilmans, Publications Officer
Offers informaiton on more than 23,000 annual, quarterly and monthly time series of economic and dinancial statistics on over 200 countries.

7963 International Investor's Directory
Asset International
125 Greenwich Avenue
Suite 5
Greenwich, CT 06830-5512
203-629-5015
FAX: 203-629-5024
Eric Laursen, Editor
Directory of services and supplies to the industry. *$235.00*
735 pages Annual

7964 Investment Blue Book
Securities Investigations
PO Box 888
Woodstock, NY 12498-0888
845-679-2300

Lists over 6,000 brokers and dealers in tax shelter plans; 2,000 sponsors of tax shelter products and suppliers of service to the industry and mututal funds information. *$145.00*
350 pages Irergular
Circulation: 10,000

7965 Investment Recovery Association Directory
Investment Recovery Association
5800 Foxridge Drive
Suite 115
Mission, KS 66202-2338
913-624-4597
FAX: 913-262-0174
Jane Male, Editor
Directory of services and supplies to the industry. *$250.00*
Annual
Circulation: 400

7966 **Investor Relations Resource Guide**
National Investor Relations Institute
8045 Leesburg Pike
Suite 600
Vienna, VA 22182
571-633-0532
FAX: 703-506-3571
info@niri.org www.niri.org
Melissa Jones, Editor
Lists about 110 investment counseling firms, 50 financial investment associations and 40 financial investment service firms such as publishers of magazines and newsletters. *$50.00*
83 pages Annual

7967 **Japanese Investment in the Midwest**
Japan-America Society of Greater Cincinnati
300 Carew Tower
441 Vine Street
Cincinnati, OH 45202

FAX: 513-579-3102
A list of more than 400 Japanese manufacturing firms in the states of Illinois, Indiana, Kentucky, Michigan, Ohio, and Tennessee. *$40.00*
30 pages Annual

7968 **Loan Broker: Annual Directory**
Ben Campbell, Publisher
917 S Park Street
Owosso, MI 48867-4422

Lists approximately 800 loan brokers, private funding sources and business financing services operating in the continental United States. *$59.95*
Annual
Circulation: 3,000

7969 **MJK Commodities Database**
MJK Associates
1289 S Park Victoria Drive
Suite 205
Milpitas, CA 95035-6974

FAX: 408-941-3404
Offers information on United States and Canadian commodities; internatinal monetary markets; futures indexes and stock index futures.

7970 **Manufacturers Representatives of America: Yearbook and Directory of Members**
Manufacturers Representatives of America
PO Box 150229
Arlington, TX 76015-6229
817-465-5511
FAX: 817-561-7275
WR Bess, Executive Director
Several hundred independent manufacturers' representatives in paper, plastic, packaging and sanitary supplies. *$250.00*
Annual Fall
Circulation: 1,200

7971 **Manufacturing USA: Industry Analyses, Statistics & Leading Companies**
Gale Research
27500 Drake Road
Farmington Hills, MI 48331
248-699-4253
FAX: 248-699-8214 800-877-4253
galeord@gale.com www.gale.com
Arsen J Darnay, Editor
Lists of up to 75 leading companies for each manufacturing industry, selected on the basis of annual sales. *$205.00*

7972 **Market Scope**
Trade Dimensions
45 Danbury Road
Wilton, CT 06897-4445
203-563-3000
FAX: 203-563-3131
info@tradedimensions.com
www.tradedimensions.com
Lynda Gutierrez, Managing Editor
The definitive source of market share and category sales data for supermarkets. The book configures the information in Trade Dimensions' database to determine market share by Nielsen, DMA, MSA and IRI definitions - over 300 markets in all. Market Scope also provides extensive category sales data as reported by Nielsen and IRI. *$325.00*
Annual

7973 **Mentor Support Group Directory**
National Association of Certified Valuation
1111 Brickyard Road
Suite 200
Salt Lake City, UT 84106-5401
303-698-1883
FAX: 801-486-7500 800-677-2009
sherril@nacva.com www.navca.com
Pamela R Bailey, Executive Director
Parnell Black, MBA CPA CVA, CEO
Roberto Castro, Director Business Development
Dean Dinas, Director Economic Research
Brien K Jones, General Manager Conferences
Annual

7974 **Merger & Acquisition Sourcebook Edition**
Quality Services Company
5290 Overpass Road
Suite 126
Santa Barbara, CA 93111-3009
805-964-7841
FAX: 805-964-1073
Walter Jurek, Editor
Nancy Rothlein, Production Manager
Contains complete information on the previous years' merger and acquisitions actuary. *$350.00*

7975 **Merger Yearbook**
Securities Data Publishing
40 W 57th Street
11th Floor
New York, NY 10019-4001
212-484-4701
FAX: 212-956-0112
sdp@tfn.com www.sdponline.com
Ted Weissberg, Editor-in-Chief
Deborah Chieglis, Advertising Manager
Edward Cortese, Marketing Executive
Information on tens of thousands of announces and completed deals plus charts giving awards information on industry rankings and transactions.

7976 **Merger and Corporate Transactions Database**
Securities Data Publishing
1180 Raymond Boulevard
Suite 5
Newark, NJ 07102-4107

This database contains more than 85,000 records on transactions involving mergers, acquisitions, divestitures leveraged buyouts and stock repurchases.
Full-text

7977 **Mergers & Acquisitions Yearbook**
American Banker-Bond Buyer
1 State Street Plaza
27th Floor
New York, NY 10004-1505
212-631-1271
FAX: 212-843-9624 800-367-3989
Gerald D Mintz, President
Mario DiUbaldi, Publisher
Phil Roosevelt, Editor
Carole Lambert, Sales/Marketing Director
Stacy Weinstein, Production Director
Annual yearbook detailing all bank merger and acquisition activity for the previous year. Includes sale price, financial and legal advisors and governmental information. *$175.00*
Annual

7978 **Mergers and Acquisitions Handbook**
National Association of Division Order Analysts
2805 Oak Trail Court
Suite 6312
Arlington, TX 76016
972-715-4489

nadoa_org@hotmail.com
www.nadoa.org
Lynn S McCord, Administrator
Annual

7979 **Money Market Directory of Pension Funds and their Investment Managers**
Money Market Directories
320 E Main Street
Charlottesville, VA 22902-5234
434-977-1450
FAX: 434-979-9962 800-446-2810
sdthrusto@standardandpeeps.com
www.mmdwebaccess.com
Jesse Noel, Editor Manager
John Martin, Production Manager
Dennis Thurston, Publications
Tom Lupo, President
Over 44,000 tax-exempt funds with over $1,000,000 in assets, and about 1,800 investment management services including bank trust departments and insurance companies, each handling at least $25,000,000 in tax-exempt funds. *$1150.00*
2000 pages Annual January Founded: 1970 ISBN 0-939712-31-8
Circulation: 8,500

7980 **Money Source Book**
Business Information Network
15851 Dallas Parkway
Suite 600
Dallas, TX 75248
972-982-8686

Over 1,500 traditional and non-traditional sources of business capital with an empha-

sis on the south-central United States. *$24.95*
200 pages Annual
Circulation: 20,000

7981 Money for Graduate Students in the Social & Behavioral Sciences
Reference Service Press
5000 Windplay Drive
Suite 4
El Dorado Hills, CA 95762-9600
916-939-9620
FAX: 916-939-9626
info@rspfunding.com
www.rspfunding.com
Gail Schlachter, Editor
R David Weber, Editor
For graduate students working on a master's or doctoral degree in a social science, this book provides 1,100 fellowships, forgivable loans, grants and awards to support their work. *$42.50*
332 pages Biennial ISBN 1-588410-78-1 : database

7982 MoneyData
Technical Data
11 Farnsworth Street
Boston, MA 02210-1210
617-345-2000
This database offers a full line of information on money markets.
Numeric

7983 MoneyWatch
McCarthy, Crisanti & Maffei
71 Broadway
New York, NY 10006-2601
212-675-5880
FAX: 212-509-7389
This database offers valuable information on the money market, including economic indicators.
Full-text

7984 Morningstar Closed-End Funds
Morningstar
53 W Jackson Boulevard
Chicago, IL 60604-3606
312-351-1050
FAX: 312-696-6001
www.morningstar.com
Catherine Gillis, Editor
Offers an abundance of financial information on closed-end investment companies. *$195.00*
300 pages BiWeekly

7985 Mutual Fund Encyclopedia
Dearborn Financial Publishing
155 Wacker Drive
Chicago, IL 60606
312-836-4400
Gerald W Perritt, Author
Directory of services and supplies to the industry. *$35.95*
600 pages Annual

7986 Mutual Fund Sourcebook
Morningstar
225 W Wacker Drive
Chicago, IL 60606-1224
312-696-6000
Patty Dutile, Editor
Michael Laszuk, Editor
Offers all types of information including fund name, address, charges and fees and more for over 2,500 mutual funds. *$225.00*
3100 pages 2 Volumes

7987 Mutual Fund/Municipal Bond
Interactive Data Corporation
Post Office Square
39th Floor
Boston, MA 02109
617-428-1600
This database contains over 3,000 time series of price data for municipal bonds held in the portfolios of selected mutual funds.

7988 NADOA Directory
National Association of Division Order Analysts
2805 Oak Trail Court
Suite 6312
Arlington, TX 76016
972-715-4489
nadoa_org@hotmail.com
www.nadoa.org
Lynn S McCord, Administrator
Annual

7989 NAIPFA Directory
National Association of Independent Public Finance
PO Box 304
Montgomery, IL 60538-0304
630-896-1292
FAX: 209-633-6265 www.naipfa.com
Roseanne M Hoban, Executive Director
Annual

7990 NALHFA Membership Directory
National Associatin of Local Housing Finance
2025 M Street NW
Suite 800
Washington, DC 20036-3309
202-367-1197
FAX: 202-367-2197
john_murphy@nalhfa.org
www.nalhfa.org
John C Murphy, Executive Director
Scott Lynch, Association Manager
Kim McKinon, Coordinator Membership
Annual

7991 NASBO Newsletter
National Association of State Budget Officers
444 North Capitol Street NW
Suite 642
Washington, DC 20001
202-624-5382
FAX: 202-624-7745
spattison@nasbo.org www.nasbo.org
Scott Pattison, Executive Director
Lauern Cummings, Manager Member Relations

7992 NATRI Membership Directory
National Association for Treasurers of Religious
8824 Cameron Street
Silver Springs, MD 20910
301-587-7776
FAX: 301-589-2897
lelcock@natri.org www.natri.org
Laura Reicks, Executive Director
Lorelle Elcock, Associate Director Finance
Annual

7993 National Bankers Association: Roster of Minority Banking Institutions
National Bankers Association
1513 P Street NW
Washington, DC 20005-1909
202-588-5432
FAX: 202-588-5443
nahart@nationalbankers.org
www.nationalbankers.org
Norma Hart, President
About 140 banks owned or controlled by minority group persons or women. *$5.00*
Annual October

7994 National Credit Union Administration Directory
National Credit Union Administration
1775 Duke Street
Alexandria, VA 22314
703-518-6300
FAX: 703-518-6319 www.ncua.gov
JoAnn Johnson, Chairperson
Directory of credit unions governed by a three member board appointed by the President and confirmed by the US Senate, by the independent federal agency that charters and supervises federal credit unions. NCUA, with the backing of the full faith and credit of the US government, operates the National Credit Union Share Insurance Fund, insuring the savings of 80 million account holders in all federal credit unions and many state chartered credit unions.

7995 National Directory of Investment Newsletters
GPS
PO Box 372
Morrisville, PA 19067-8372
215-295-8700
George T Scilieber, Editor
Lists over 800 newsletters dealing with investments and financial planning and their publishers. *$49.95*
60 pages Biennial

7996 Nelson's Catalog of Institutional Research Reports
Nelson Publications
1455 Research Boulevard
Rockville, MD 20850
FAX: 301-545-4964 800-333-6357
George G Lindsey, COO
Kevin T Black, VP Database
Catalogs the 12,000 research reports published each month by virtually every investment research firm worldwide. *$1.55*
120 pages

7997 Nelson's Directory of Investment Managers
Nelson Publications
1455 Research Boulevard
Rockville, MD 20850
FAX: 301-545-4964 800-333-6357
Dan Ragusa, Editor
Over 2,600 worldwide institutional investment management firms. *$575.00*
Annual April

7998 **Nelson's Directory of Investment Research**
Nelson Publications
1455 Research Boulevard
Rockville, MD 20850

FAX: 301-545-4964 800-333-6357

George G Lindsey, COO
Kevin T Black, VP Database

Complete analyst coverage assignments of over 500 research firms - over 6,000 security analyses. *$620.00*
3,700 pages Annual

7999 **Nelson's Directory of Plan Sponsors**
Nelson Publications
1455 Research Boulevard
Rockville, MD 20850

FAX: 301-545-4964 800-333-6357

George G Lindsey, COO
Kevin T Black, VP Database

The best reference on the pension and foundation industry, giving comprehensive data on all funds with assets over $10 million. *$ 620.00*
4,000 pages Annual

8000 **Nelson's Financial Mailing Lists/Custom Databases**
Nelson Publications
1455 Research Boulevard
Rockville, MD 20850

FAX: 301-545-4964 800-333-6357

George G Lindsey, COO
Kevin T Black, VP Database

Offers the most comprehensive and accurate information on the global institutional investment market. Updated daily, this database contains over 200,000 of the world's most important institutional investment executives and more than 35,000 organizations.

8001 **Nelson's Guide to Pension Fund Consultants**
Nelson Publications
1455 Research Boulevard
Rockville, MD 20850

FAX: 301-545-4964 800-333-6357

George G Lindsey, COO
Kevin T Black, VP Database

This guide delivers up-to-date profiles of over 300 consulting firms, more than 1,800 professional consultants at 750 offices, with names, phone numbers, services provided and a client cross-section. *$365.00*
500 pages Annual

8002 **Nelson's Institutional Market Place for Windows**
Nelson Publications
1455 Research Boulevard
Rockville, MD 20850

FAX: 301-545-4964 800-333-6357

George G Lindsey, COO
Kevin T Black, VP Database

A powerful relational database that provides the most accurate and current information on the 13,000 largest plan sponsors, 2,500 institutional money managers, 300 pension fund consultants and 60,000 key business executives that run those organizations.
Quarterly

8003 **North American Financial Institutions Directory**
TFP
4709 Golf Road
6th Floor
Skokie, IL 60076
847-676-9600
FAX: 847-933-8101 800-321-3373
customerservice@tfp.com
www.tfp.com

Marideth Johnson, Manager, Marketing/Communications *$460.00*

Circulation: 31850

8004 **O'Dwyer's Directory of Corporate Communications**
JR O'Dwyer Company
271 Madison Avenue
New York, NY 10016
212-791-1032
FAX: 212-683-2750
jack@odwyerpr.com
www.odwyerpr.com

Jack O'Dwyer, Publisher

Public relations departments are profiled that represent the United States companies that are listed on the New York Stock Exchange. *$110.00*
400 pages Annual

8005 **PC Bridge**
Bridge Information Systems
717 Office Parkway
Saint Louis, MO 63141-7115
314-567-8100
FAX: 314-432-5391

Tony Bridge, Manager

This database delivers real-time market information, monitoring up to 100 symbols per page on 10 available pages.
Numeric

8006 **Pacific Stock Exchange Guide**
CCH
2700 Lake Cook Road
Riverwoods, IL 60015-3867
847-267-7000
FAX: 773-866-3608 800-835-5224

James Rooney, Editor

Lists officials, members, member organizations; by-laws and rules of the Pacific Stock Exchange. *$405.00*

8007 **Pensions & Investments: Investment Managers**
Crain Communications
711 3rd Avenue
New York, NY 10017
212-210-0100
FAX: 212-210-0465
jmurphy@crain.com

Jeff Murphy, Editor
Chris Battaglia, Publisher

List of over 1,050 banks, insurance companies, investment advisors and other investment management organizations. *$40.00*
Annual May
Circulation: 41,000

8008 **Pensions & Investments: Master Trust, Custody and Global Custody Banks**
Crain Communications
711 3rd Avenue
New York, NY 10017
212-210-0100
FAX: 212-210-0465
jmurphy@crain.com

Jeff Murphy, Editor
Chris Battaglia, Publisher

List of banks with master trust/master custodial assets and global custody assets. *$10.00*
Annual October
Circulation: 41,000

8009 **Philadelphia Stock Exchange Guide**
CCH
2700 Lake Cook Road
Riverwoods, IL 60015-3867
847-267-7000
FAX: 773-866-3608 800-835-5224

Wendy Albertson, PGL

Lists officials, members, member organizations, securities; by-laws and rules of the Exchange. *$350.00*
Monthly

8010 **Pratt's Guide to Venture Capital Sources**
Securities Data Publishing
195 Broadway
10th Floor
New York, NY 10007
646-822-2000
FAX: 646-822-3230
www.sdponline.com

Steve Pratt, Editor
Dan Bokser, Editor

Offers information on over 900 venture capital firms in the United States and small investment corporations. Also included in the directory are listings of corporate venture groups, consultants and providers of professional services to venture capitalists. *$385.00*
1050 pages Annual Founded: 1970 ISBN 0-914470-93-0 : CD

8011 **Professional Investor Report**
Dow Jones & Company
PO Box 300
Princeton, NJ 08543-0300
609-520-4000

Offers information on unusual stock trading activity taking place on the New York and American stock exchanges and the National Market System portion of the OTC market.
Numeric

8012 **Quarterly Financial Report**
GE Information Services
401 N Washington Street
Rockville, MD 20850-1707
301-388-8284
FAX: 301-294-5501

Cathy Ge, Owner

This unique database offers information on financial estimates for US enterprises within 31 industry classifications.

8013 RSP Funding for Nursing Students and Nurses
Reference Service Press
5000 Windplay Drive
Suite 4
El Dorado Hills, CA 95762-9600
916-939-9620
FAX: 916-939-9626
info@respfunding.com
www.rspfunding.com

Gail Schlachter, Editor
R David Weber, Editor

You can find out about the more than 600 scholarships, fellowships, loans, loan repayment programs, forgivable loans, grants, awards, prizes and interships set aside specifically to support study, research, creative activities, past accomplishments, future projects, professional development and traineeships. This is more than twice the number of nursing related funding programs covered in any other source. *$30.00*

210 pages Biennial Founded: 1998 ISBN 1-588410-95-1 : database

8014 Registry of Financial Planning Practitioners
International Association for Financial Planning
2 Concourse Parkway NE
Suite 800
Atlanta, GA 30328-5588
770-351-9600

J Patrick Tinley, Chief Executive Officer

Directory of services and supplies to the industry.

80 pages Annual

8015 Research Reports
National Committee on Planned Giving
233 McCrea Street
Suite 400
Indianapolis, IN 46225-1030
317-269-6274
FAX: 317-269-6276
kramsey@ncpg.org www.ncpg.org

Tanya Howe Johnson, President/CEO
Sandra Kerr, Director Government Education
Barbara Owens, Director Membership/Manager HR
Kathryn J Ramsey, Director Meetings
Kurt Reusze, Manager Education/Technology

Irregular

8016 Roster of Minority Financial Institutions
US Department of the Treasury
401 14th Street SW
Room 523C
Washington, DC 20024-2106
202-874-5740
FAX: 202-874-6907

Robert Jones, Editor

About 170 commercial, minority-owned and controlled financial institutions participating in the Department of the Treasury's Minority Bank Deposit program.

Biennial

8017 S&P MarketScope Database
Standard & Poor's Corporation
55 Water Street
New York, NY 10041
212-382-2000

Over 5,000 companies are listed in the Reference Section of Standard and Poors database offering names, addresses, background information and current and historical financial information.

8018 S&P Marketplace
Standard & Poor's Corporation
55 Water Street
New York, NY 10041
212-382-2000
800-823-3209

This comprehensive database offers all types of information in the areas of finance, business and investments.

Numeric

8019 Secondary Marketing Executive Directory of Mortgage Technology
LDJ Corporation
PO Box 2330
Waterbury, CT 06722-2330
203-755-0158
FAX: 203-755-3480

David Zackin, Publisher
John Florian, Editor

A who's who directory of technology products and services to the real estate finance industry. *$5.00*

Annual
Circulation: 21,000

8020 Securities Industry Association Buyer's Guide
Securities Industry Association
1801 K Street NW
Suite 1203L
Washington, DC 20006-1301
202-898-8731
FAX: 202-408-1918 www.sia.com

Marc E Lackritz, President
Donald D Kittell, Executive VP

Directory of services and supplies to the industry. *$100.00*

150 pages Annual

8021 Securities Industry Data Bank
Securities Industry Association
120 Broadway
35th Floor
New York, NY 10271-3599
212-608-1500

Don Kittell, Executive Vice President

This comprehensive database offers information on acquisitions, mergers, and securities in the financial world.

8022 Securities Industry Yearbook
Securities Industry Association
120 Broadway
New York, NY 10271-0002
212-608-1500
FAX: 202-408-1918

James D Spellman, VP Communications

Represents business interests of over 750 member securities firms. *$125.00*

900 pages Annual

8023 Service Directory
National Association for Treasurers of Religious
8824 Cameron Street
Silver Springs, MD 20910
301-587-7776
FAX: 301-589-2897
lelcock@natri.org www.natri.org

Laura Reicks, Executive Director
Lorelle Elcock, Associate Director Finance

Annual

8024 Sheshunoff Banking Organization Quarterly
Sheshunoff Information Services
505 Barton Springs Road
Suite 1200
Austin, TX 78704
512-472-2244
FAX: 512-305-6575 800-456-2340

Gabrielle Sheshunoff, Chief Executive Officer

Offers ownership structure for all bank holding companies and overview and ratings for bank holding companies and their brinking subs. *$499.00*

Quarterly

8025 Small Business Investment Company Directory and Handbook
International Wealth Success
PO Box 186
Merrick, NY 11566-0186
516-766-5850
FAX: 516-766-5919 800-323-0548
admin@iwsmoney.com
www.iwsmoney.com

Tyler G Hicks, President

Lists more than 400 small business investment companies that invest in small businesses to help them prosper. Also gives tips on financial management in business. *$15.00*

135 pages Annual Founded: 1975 ISBN 1-561503-12-6

8026 Speakers Bureau Directory
National Association of Certified Valuation
1111 Brickyard Road
Suite 200
Salt Lake City, UT 84106-5401
303-698-1883
FAX: 801-486-7500 800-677-2009
sherril@nacva.com www.nacva.com

Pamela R Bailey, Executive Director
Parnell Black, MBA CPA CVA, CEO
Roberto Castro, Director Business Development
Dean Dinas, Director Economic Research
Brien K Jones, General Manager Conferences

Annual

8027 Standard & Poor's Directory of Bond Agents
Standard & Poor's Corporation
55 Water Street
New York, NY 10041
212-382-2000

Terry McGraw, Chief Executive Officer

A list of paying agents, registrars, co-registrars and conversion agents for 30,000 corporate and municipal bonds are included. *$ 1250.00*

8028 Standard & Poor's Security Dealers of North America
Standard & Poor's Corporation
55 Water Street
New York, NY 10041-1010
212-382-2000
800-221-5277

Terry McGraw, Chief Executive Officer

Directory of services and supplies to the industry. *$498.00*

1700 pages Semiannual

8029 Standard & Poor's Stock Reports
Standard & Poor's Corporation
55 Water Street
New York, NY 10041-1010
212-382-2000
800-221-5277
Terry McGraw, Chief Executive Officer
All companies whose securities are traded on the American Stock Exchange are listed. *$1260.00*

8030 Standard & Poor's Stock Reports: Nasdaq and Regional Exchanges
Standard & Poor's Corporation
25 Broadway
New York, NY 10004-1010
212-382-2000

Stuart Parr, Owner
Directory of services and supplies to the industry. *$1260.00*
1600 pages

8031 Standard & Poor's Stock Reports: New York Stock Exchange
Standard & Poor's Corporation
25 Broadway
New York, NY 10004-1010
212-382-2000

Stuart Parr, Owner
Directory of services and supplies to the industry. *$1465.00*

8032 State Expenditure Report
National Association of State Budget Officers
444 North Capitol Street NW
Suite 642
Washington, DC 20001
202-624-5382
FAX: 202-624-7745
spattison@nasbo.org www.nasbo.org
Scott Pattison, Executive Director
Lauren Cummings, Manager Member Relations
Annual

8033 TA Guide & Checklist
National Investment Company Service Association
36 Washington Street
Suite 70
Wellesley Hills, MA 02481
781-416-7200
FAX: 781-416-7065
info@nisca.org www.nisca.org
Barbara V Weidlich, President
Keith Dropkin, Director Operations
Doris Jaimes, Registrar
Sheila Kobaly, Events Manager
Chris Ludent, IT Manager
Annual

8034 TRW Trade Payment Guide
TRW Business Credit Services
505 City Parkway W
Orange, CA 92868-2912
714-385-7000
FAX: 714-938-2586 800-344-0603
Approximately 2,500,000 credit active business locations.
Quarterly

8035 Tax Directory
Tax Analysts
6830 N Fairfax Drive
Arlington, VA 22213-1001
703-533-4400
FAX: 703-533-4664 800-955-3444
taxdir@tax.org www.tax.org
Amie Chant, Editor
Thomas F Field, Publisher
A reference tool that provides users with comprehensive listings of federal, state and private sector tax professionals. Now in three sections - Government Officials, Corporate Tax Managers and International Officials. *$399.00*
960 pages Quarterly
Circulation: 2,000

8036 Tax Free Trade Zones of the World

Matthew Bender and Company
11 Penn Plaza
New York, NY 10001-2006
212-448-2000

Walter H Diamond, Editor
Covers over 450 free trade zones, transit zones, free perimeters and free ports. The emphasis is placed on tax advantages of each. *$280.00*
1000 pages

8037 Technical Resources Handbook
National Association of Certified Valuation
1111 Brickyard Road
Suite 200
Salt Lake City, UT 84106-5401
303-698-1883
FAX: 801-486-7500 800-677-2009
sherril@nacva.com www.navca.com
Pamela R Bailey, Executive Director
Parnell Black, MBA CPA CVA, CEO
Roberto Castro, Director Business Development
Dean Dinas, Director Economic Research
Brien K Jones, General Manager Conferences
Annual

8038 Top Mortgage Market Players Directory
Inside Mortgage Finance Publishers
7910 Woodmont Avenue
Suite 1010
Bethesda, MD 20814-0987
301-951-1240
FAX: 301-656-1709
service@imfpubs.com
www.imfpubs.com
Guy D Cecala, Publisher
John Bancroft, Managing Editor
Didi Parks, Marketing/Advertising
Listing of over 4,500 residential mortgage lenders. *$375.00*
Annual 300 names $1 m per M. : diskette

8039 Trading Volume Survey
EMTA - Trade Association for the Emerging Markets
360 Madison Avenue
18th Floor
New York, NY 10017
646-637-9100
FAX: 646-637-9128
awerner@emta.org www.emta.org
Michael M Chamberlin, Executive Director
Aviva Werner, General Counsel
Quarterly

8040 Trusts & Estates: Directory of Trust Institutions Issue
Primedia
9800 Metcalf Avenue
Overland Park, KS 66212
913-341-1300
FAX: 913-967-1898
www.primediabusiness.com
Mike Klim, Editor
Offers a list of about 5,000 trust departments in the United States and Canadian banks. *$82.00*
Annual January
Circulation: 12,200

8041 Valuation Compilation
National Association of Certified Valuation
1111 Brickyard Road
Suite 200
Salt Lake City, UT 84106-5401
303-698-1883
FAX: 801-486-7500 800-677-2009
info@nacva.com www.nacva.com
Pamela R Bailey, Executive Director
Parnell Black, MBA CPA CVA, CEO
Roberto Castro, Director Business Development
Dean Dinas, Director Economic Research
Brien K Jones, General Manager Conferences
Bi-Ennial

8042 Venture Capital Directory: Small Business Administration
Forum Publishing Company
383 E Main Street
Centerport, NY 11721-1538
631-754-5000
www.forum123.com
Raymond Lawrence, Editor
Lists over 500 members of the Small Business Administration and the Small Business Investment Company that provide funding for small and minority businesses. *$12.95*
50 pages Annual

8043 Venture Capital: Where to Find it
National Association of Small Business Investment
1199 N Fairfax Street
Suite 200
Alexandria, VA 22314-1437
703-549-2100

Jeanette D Smith, Editor
Directory of services and supplies to the industry.
Annual

8044 Who's Who in Economic Development Directory
International Economic Development Council (IEDC)
734 15th Street NW
Suite 900
Washington, DC 20005
202-223-7800
FAX: 202-223-4745 www.iedc.org
Jeff Finkle, President
A listing of over 2,500 Council members and other certified individuals. Directory is limited to international coverage.
200 pages Annual

8045 Who's Who in Venture Capital
Grey House Publishing
185 Millerton Road
PO Box 860
Millerton, NY 12546
518-890-0526
FAX: 518-789-0545 800-562-2139
books@greyhouse.com
www.greyhouse.com
Leslie Mackenzie, Publisher
Richard Gottlieb, Editor
Provides immediate access to nearly 10,000 principals, partners and managing directors heading the world's Venture Capital and Private Equity firms.
Annual

8046 World Emerging Stock Markets
Probus Publishing Company
1333 Burbridge Parkway
Burbridge, IL 60521

Directories of stock markets in Central and South America, Middle East and Europe.
$59.95

8047 Yearbook of Education Finance
American Education Finance Association
8365 S Armadillo Trail
Evergreen, CO 80439
303-674-0857
FAX: 303-670-8986 www.aefa.cc
Ed Steinbecher, Executive Director
Information and updates for educational institutions and organizations regarding financial investing, prospecting and fundraising.
Annual

Industry Web Sites

8048 www.aacei.org
Association for Advancement of Cost Engineering

Association for those interested in the financial aspects of engineering all aspects of cost management.

8049 www.aaii.com
American Association of Individual Investors

An independent nonprofit corporation formed in 1978 for the purpose of assisting individuals in becoming effective managers of their own assets through programs of education, information and research.

8050 www.abiworld.org
American Bankruptcy Institute

Provides a multi-disiplinary, non-partisan organization dedicated to research and education on matters related to insolvency. Provides a forum for the exchange of ideas and information. ABI is engaged in numerous educational and research activities, as well as the production of a number of publications both for the insolvency practitioner and the public.

8051 www.acainternational.org
ACA International

Formerly know as the American Collectors Association, is the association of credit and collection professionals. Founded in 1939, it has over 5,300 members, including third party collection agencies, attorneys, credit grantors and vendor affiliates. Headquartered in Minneapolis, ACA serves members in the US and Canada plus 58 other countries worldwide.

8052 www.aefa.org
American Education Finance Association

Encourages communications among groups and individuals in education financial fields.

8053 www.afponline.org
Association for Financial Professionals

Association of 12,000 financial professionals.

8054 www.afsaonline.com
American Financial Services Association

National trade association for market funded providers of financial services to consumers and small businesses. These providers offer an array of finacial services, including unsecured personal loans, automobile loans, home equity loans and credit cards through specialized bank institutions.

8055 www.appraisalinstitute.org
Appraisal Institute

Promotes a code of ethics and uniform standards of the real estate appraisal practice. Publishes periodicals, books and appraisal-related materials, and sponsors courses and seminars.

8056 www.appraisers.org
American Society of Appraisers

Professional association of appraisers of all kinds.

8057 www.bcfm.com
Broadcast Cable Financial Management Association

Professional association for TV, radio and cable CEOs, bueinss managers, HR, MIS controllers and financial personnel, as well as associate members in legal, audit and related fields.

8058 www.bma.net.org
Bank Marketing Association

Association for suppliers of industry related products and services.

8059 www.ccthomas.com
Charles C Thomas

Producing a strong list of specialty titles and textbooks in medicine, dentistry,nursing, and veterinary medicine. Very active in publishing bio- logical sciences and social sciences. Thomas also is one of the largest producers of books in all areas of criminal justice

8060 www.communitycapital.org
National Community Capital Association

Provides support for non-profit revolving loan funds that lend capital and offer technical assistance in distressed and disenfranchised communities.

8061 www.dbcams.com
FCSI Industry Web Sites

A resource for the financial industry, including stock exchanges, news, pricing services, research, information and more.

8062 www.federalregister.com
Neighborhood Reinvestment Corporation

Supplies training, grants, developmental assistance, and a range of other technical services designed to help the local partnerships achieve substantially self-reliant neighborhoods. The goal is to improve a neighborhood's housing and physical conditions, build a positive community image, and establish a healthy real estate market and a core of neighbors capable of managing the continued health of their neighborhood.

8063 www.fei.org
Financial Executives International

A professional organization of individuals performing the duties of C.F.O., Controller, Treasurer or Vice President of Finance.

8064 www.fma.org
Financial Management Association

Strives to facilitate exchanges of ideas among persons in financial management.

8065 www.fmsinc.org
Financial Managers Society

Provides technical information and education to financial officers in banks, thrifts and credit unions.

8066 **www.globalpurchasing.org**
International Association of Purchasing Managers

A professional organization dedicated to the advancement of world trade, membership is open to buyers, purchasing managers, executives and all individuals that may be involved or have an interest in the important function of buying goods and services on the global market. A NON-PROFIT organization..

8067 **www.greenwood.com**
Greenwood Publishing Group

Business and professional publishing, academic books in Business, Finance, Business Law, and Applied Economics management.

8068 **www.greyhouse.com**
Grey House Publishing

Selected Grey House directories in the fields of business, health and education are available online. Users can search our online databases by several different search criteria, such as product categories, geographic area, sales volume and much, much more. Full Grey House catalog and online ordering also available.

8069 **www.houisingfinance.org**
Int'l Union of Housing Finance Institutions

Disseminates information in housing finance policies and techniques worldwide.

8070 **www.iami.org**
National Association of Review Appraisers &

Association for professionals who review real estate appraisals and underwrite real estate mortgagers. The association offers the CRA, Certified Review Appraiser and RMU, Registered Mortgage Underwriter, professional designation.

8071 **www.ici.org**
Investment Company Institute

Acts to represent members in matters of legislation, taxation, regulation, economic research and marketing and public information regarding investments and mutual funds.

8072 **www.investavenue.com**
Invest Avenue

Online magazine featuring articles from leading professionals in the finacial world, current news and analysis. Newsletter can be e-mailed on request.

8073 **www.invrecovery.org**
Investment Recovery Association

Association for manufacturers of services and supplies to the industry.

8074 **www.irrc.org**
Investor Responsibility Research Center

Acts to publish reports and analyses of social issues and public policy affecting corporation and investors.

8075 **www.kobren.com**
Mutual Fund Investors Association

Association for those interested in information and rates for mutual funds, investments, stocks and bonds.

8076 **www.marketresearch.com**
Research Reports

Search financial services reports from over 350 sources. Updated daily.

8077 **www.mfea.com**
Mutual Fund Education Alliance

Conducts public education and public relation activities in an effort to acquaint industry, organizations and government agencies with direct market funds.

8078 **www.mortgagepress.com**
National Mortgage Professional

Information on new products, industry news, personnel announcements and calendar of events.

8079 **www.nact.org**
National Association of Corporate Treasurers

Members are corporate chief financial officers, treasurers or assistant treasurers.

8080 **www.nadco.org**
National Association of Development Companies

Provides long-term fixed asset financing to small businesses.

8081 **www.nafa-us.org**
National Aircraft Finance Association

Members are lending institutions involved in aircraft financing.

8082 **www.nafcunet.org**
National Association of Federal Credit Unions

Association for manufacturers and suppliers of complete range of financial products and services.

8083 **www.nasbic.org**
Nat'l Assn of Small Business Investment Companies

Trade Association representing federally licensed ventures capital firms, Email, and business investment companies.

8084 **www.natptax.com**
National Association of Tax Professionals

The National Association of Tax Professionals (NATP) is a nonprofit association dedicated to excellence in taxation and related financial services. NATP was formed to serve professionals who work in all areas of tax practice. Members include Enrolled Agents, Certified Public Accountants, individual practitioners, accountants, attorneys, and financial planners.

8085 **www.nchffa.com**
National Council of Health Facilities Finance

To serve the common interests and enhance the effectiveness of member Authorities through communication, education and advocacy.

8086 **www.nfa.future.org**
National Futures Association

Association for corporations and firms that are registered with the Commodity Futures Trading Commission.

8087 **www.nfa.org**
National Finance Adjusters

Members are collateral recovery specialists.

8088 **www.nfma.org**
National Federation of Municipal Analysts

Promotes the profession of municipal credit analysts through educational programs, industry, communications and related programming.

8089 **www.nibesa.com**
National Independent Bank Equipment & Systems Assn

Association of financial security equipment nationwide. Annual convention and showcase and monthly newsletter.

8090 www.nipa.org
National Institute of Pension Administrators

Enhancing professionalism in the retirement plan industry through education.

8091 www.nvca.org
National Venture Capital Association

Corporations, corporate financiers and private individuals who invest private capital in young companies on a professional basis.

8092 www.nvla.org
National Vehicle Leasing Association

Fosters education, publishing, conferences, legal services, advancement and industry relations certification.

8093 www.plunkettresearch.com/finance/index.htm
Plunkett Research

Free section of company web site provides an synopsis of trends in the finacial industry and a glossary of terms.

8094 www.securitytraders.org
Security Traders Association

Members involved in the securities industry.

8095 www.snl.com
SNL Securities

News articles on banks and thrifts, insurance and other financial services. Also features vital company information.

8096 www.theiia.org
Institute of Internal Auditors

International organization composed of internal auditors, corporate executives and board members. Contact and current development information.

8097 www.uhab.org
Urban Homesteading Assistance Board

Information on affordable housing and self reliance. Activities include advocacy, organizing, classroom and on-site training, direct technical assistance, development consulting, development and sponsorship of new co-ops and services to member co-ops that include bookkeeping, insurance, legal services, bulk purchasing, newsletters and IT services.

8098 www.wsta.org
Wall Street Technology Association

White papers on the latest in technology for IT professionals working in the finacial field. Resource guide for industry products and services and information on seminars and conferences included.

Associations

8099 **American Crappie Association**
125 Ruth Avenue
Benton, KY 42025
270-395-4204

lcrecel@earthlink.net
www.crappieusa.com
Darrell VanVactor, President
Charles Rogers, VP
Larry Crecelius, Public Relations Director
For all crappie anglers, from weekend fishermen to tournament pros. Influencing national manufacturers to produce more and better crappie fishing products, establishing a voice and lobby for crappie anglers everywhere and elevating the sport of crappie fishing to its rightful place in the limelight. *$20.00*
Individual Membership

8100 **American Fisheries Society**
5410 Grosvenor Lane
Suite 110
Bethesda, MD 20814-2199
301-897-8616
FAX: 301-897-8096
main@fisheries.org
www.fisheries.org
Chris Kohler, President
Jennifer Nielsen, President-Elect
Gus Rassam, Executive Director
AFS promotes scientific research and enlightened management of resources for optimum use and enjoyment by the public. It also encourages a comprehensive education for fisheries scientists and continuing on-the-job training *$100.00*
8500 Members Membership Fee Founded: 1870

8101 **American Fly Fishing Trade Association**
800 NE Tenney Road
Suite 110
Vancouver, WA 98685
706-355-3804
FAX: 706-353-2390
robert@affta.com www.affta.com
Robert Ramsay, President
Rori Homme, Managing Director
A sole trade organization for the fly fishing industry. The mission is to promote the sustained growth of the fly fishing industry.
400 Members Founded: 2003

8102 **American Institute of Fishery Research Biologists**
205 Blades Road
Havelock, NC 28532

feeshdr@starfishnet.com
www.aifrb.org
Linda Jones, President
Barbara Warkentine, Secretary
Founded to promote conservation and proper utilization of fishery resources through application of fishery science.
1000 Members Founded: 1956

8103 **American Littoral Society**
Building 18
Sandy Hook Highlands, NJ 07732
732-291-0055
FAX: 732-291-3551 www.alsnyc.org
Eilleen Kennedy, Director of Communications/Dev.
Mary Ann Griesbach, Membership Director
Dedicated to the environmental well-being of coastal habitat.
5000+ Members Membership Fee: $30-$35
Founded: 1961

8104 **American Sportfishing Association**
225 Reinekers Lane
Suite 420
Alexandria, VA 22314
703-519-9691
FAX: 703-519-1872
info@asafishing.org
www.asafishing.org
Mike Nussman, President/CEO
Diane Carpenter, CFO
Gordon Robertson, VP
Ric Ice, Membership Director
Promotes the enduring social, economic, and conservation values of sportfishing
650+ Members Founded: 1962

8105 **American Zoo and Aquarium Association**
8403 Colesville Road
Suite 710
Silver Spring, MD 20910
301-562-0777
FAX: 301-562-0888
membership@aza.org www.aza.org
Jim Maddy, Executive Director
Laura Benson, Director Finance/Administration
Kris Vehrs, JD, Deputy Director
Dedicated to excellent in animal care and welfare, conservation, education, and research that collectively inspire respect for animals and nature.
5500+ Members Founded: 1924

8106 **Association of Fish and Wildlife Agencies**
444 North Capitol Street NW
Suite 544
Washington, DC 20001
202-624-7890
FAX: 202-624-7891
info@iafwa.org www.iafwa.org
John Baughman, Executive Vice President
Rachel Brittin, Public Relations
Represents the government agencies responsible for North America's fish and wildlife resources.
300 Members Founded: 1902

8107 **Association of Smoked Fish Processors**
c/o Shuster Labs
85 John Road
Canton, MA 02120
781-821-2200
FAX: 781-821-9266
Dr George W Bierman, Technical Director
Members are food processors with an interest in smoked fish.
Founded: 1963

8108 **At-Sea Processors Association**
4039 21st Avenue West
Suite 400
Seattle, WA 98199
206-285-5139
FAX: 206-285-1841
apa@atsea.org www.atsea.org
Kevin C Duffy, Executive Director
James L Gilmore, Public Affairs Director
Represents U.S. flag catcher/processor vessels that participate in the healthy and abundant groundfish fisheries of the Bering Sea/Aleutian Islands management areas and in the west coast Pacific whiting fishery. *$500.00*
7 Members Membership Fees Vary
Founded: 1985

8109 **Atlantic States Marine Fisheries Commission**
1444 Eye Street NW
6th Floor
Washington, DC 20005
202-289-6400
FAX: 202-289-6051
comments@asmfc.org
www.asmfc.org
Preston Pate, Chair
George LaPointe, Vice-Chair
John O'Shea, Executive Director
The commission was formed by the fifteen Atlantic coast states. It serves as a deliberative body, coordinating the conservation and management of the states shared near shore fishery resources.
45 Members Founded: 1942 2000 names

8110 **Bass Anglers Sportsman Society**
Po Box 17900
Montgomery, AL 36141
334-272-9530
FAX: 334-279-7148
customerservice@bassmaster.com
www.bassmaster.com
Dean Kassel, President
Chris Horton, Associate Director
A service organization for bass fishermen. Its primary aim is to help anglers get the most out of bass fishing - whether it's by protecting and preserving the fishing environment, reporting on the newest products and techniques, telling them about the latest hot spots or providing an arena for professional and amateur fishing competitions. *$14.95*
600M Members Annual Membership Fee
Founded: 1972

8111 **Blue Water Fisherman's Association**
PO Box 398
Barnegat Light, NJ 08006-0398
609-361-9229

bwfa@usa.net www.bwfa.org
Nelson R Beideman, Executive Director
Non-profit organization of companies and individuals representing fishermen, Captains, vessel owners, docks, dealers, suppliers and related service businesses.
Founded: 1990

8112 **California Fisheries & Seafood Institute**
1521 I Street
Sacramento, CA 95814
916-441-5560
FAX: 916-446-1063
fishead123@aol.com
www.calseafood.net
Robert E Ross, Executive Director
Jane Townsend, Administrative Director
Regional trade organization representing members of the consumer seafood supply industry.
130+ Members Founded: 1954

8113 **California Salmon Council**
PO Box 2255
Folsom, CA 95763-2255
916-933-7050
FAX: 916-933-7055
info@calkingsalmon.org
www.calkingsalmon.org
Represents the marketing interests of California's commercial salmon fishermen. It creates consumer awareness and demand for California King Salmon.
Founded: 1989

8114 **Carteret County Fishermen's Association**
PO Box 152
Atlantic, NC 28511
252-225-6101

Buster Salter, President

8115 **Catfish Farmers of America**
1100 Highway 82 East
Suite 202
Indianola, MS 38751
662-887-2699
FAX: 662-887-6857
info@catfishfarmersamerica.com
www.catfishfarmersamerica.com
Hugh Warren, III, President
The largest aquaculture industry in the United States. CFA has represented the interests of the farm-raised catfish industry *$ 40.00*
Membership Fee Founded: 1968

8116 **Fishermen's Marketing Association**
320 2nd Street
Suite 2B
Eureka, CA 95501
707-442-3789
FAX: 707-442-9166
fma@trawl.org www.trawl.org
Peter Leipzig, Executive Director
Represents commercial groundfish and shrimp fishermen from San Pedro, California to Bellingham, Washington. The mission is to engage in activities which promote stable prices and an orderly flow of wholesome seafood to the consumer
60 Members Founded: 1952

8117 **Fishing Vessel Owners Association**
4005 20th Avenue W
Room 232, West Wall Bldg
Seattle, WA 98199
206-284-4720
FAX: 206-283-3341 www.fvoa.org
Robert D Alverson, Manager
Carol Batteen, Executive Assistant
Trade association of longline vessel operators which promotes safety at sea, habitat-friendly gear with minimum bycatch and ensures competitive pricing.
Founded: 1914

8118 **Garden State Seafood Association**
212 West State Street
Trenton, NJ 08608
609-898-1100
FAX: 609-898-6070
gregdi@voicenet.com
www.fishingnj.org
Greg DiDomenico, Executive Director
Nils Stolpe, Communications Director
Dedicated to assure that New Jersey's marine resources are managed responsibly and are able to be enjoyed by anglers and seafood consumers for generations.

8119 **Great Lakes Fishery Commission**
2100 Commonwealth Boulevard
Suite 100
Ann Arbor, MI 48105
734-662-3209
FAX: 734-741-2010
info@glfc.org www.glfc.org
Chris Goddard, Executive Secretary
Barbara Staples, Administrative Officer
The commission has two major responsibilities; to develop coordinated programs of research on the Great Lakes and to formulate and implement a program to eradicate or minimize sea lamprey populations in the Great Lakes.
Founded: 1955

8120 **Gulf and Caribbean Fisheries Institute (GCCFI)**
C/O Florida Fish and Wildlife Conservation
2796 Overseas Highway, Suite 119
Marathon, FL 33050
305-289-2330
FAX: 305-289-2334
leroy.creswell@gcfi.org www.gcfi.org
Leroy Creswell, Executive Secretary
Bob Glazer, Chair
Provides information exchange among governmental, non-governmental, academic and commerical users of marine resources in the Gulf and Carribean Region
950 Members Founded: 1947

8121 **Gulf of Mexico Fishery Management Council**
2203 N Lois Avenue
Suite 1100
Tampa, FL 33607
813-282-2815
FAX: 813-348-1711 888-833-1844
gulfcouncil@gulfcouncil.org
www.gulfcouncil.org
Wayne Swingle, Executive Director
Rick Leard, Deputy Executive Director
The council preserves fishery plans which are designed to manage fishery resources from where state waters end out to the 200 mile limit of the Gulf of Mexico.
Founded: 1976

8122 **Hunting Creek Fisheries**
PO Box 308
Thurmont, MD 21788
301-271-7475
FAX: 301-271-7059
info@ornamentalfish.com
www.ornamentalfish.com
Drusilla Tresselt, President
A family owned, professionally managed company growing quality goldfish, koi and golden orfe. We are a specialized business focused on providing outstanding products and service to our customers. Our market includes pet shops, garden centers, pond specialists and fish distributors.
Founded: 1924

8123 **International Coalition of Fisheries Association**
7918 Jones Branch Drive
Suite 700
McLean, VA 22102
703-752-8880

contact@icfa.net www.icfa.net
A coalition of the national fish and seafood industry trade associations from the world's major fishing nations. ICFA members represent countries harvesting more than 85% of the globe's fish.
15 Members Founded: 1988

8124 **International Institute of Fisheries Economics and Trade**
Dept of Agricultural & Resource Economic
Oregon State University
Corvallis, OR 97331-3601
541-737-1416
FAX: 541-737-2563
iifet@oregonstate.edu
www.oregonstate.edu/dept/iifet
Ann L Shriver, Executive Director
Mahfuzuddin Ahmed, President
IIFET is organized to promote the discussion of factors which affect international trade in seafoods, and fisheries policy questions. Designed to be attractive to individuals from governments, industries, and universities from all over the world, a major goal of the organization is to facilitate cooperative research and data exchange. *$50.00*
400 Members Regular Membership Fee
Founded: 1982

8125 **Meat Industry Suppliers Alliance**
200 Daingerfield Road
Alexandria, VA 22314
703-684-1080
FAX: 703-548-6563
info@fpmamail.com
www.fpsa.org/MISA06
George O Melnykovich, PhD, President
Cheryl Clark, Member Services Director
Sponsored by the Food Processing Machinery Association, is your key to better access and visibility in the meat industry. MISA offers its members an opportunity to project a common and uniform stance on important industry issues, particularly in the regulatory and machinery safety and hygienic standards area
Founded: 1948

8126 **National Fisheries Institute**
7918 Jones Branch Drive
Suite 700
McLean, VA 22201
703-752-8880
FAX: 703-752-7583
www.aboutseafood.com
John P Connelly, President
Bob Collette, VP Science & Technology
Judy Dashiell, VP Membership/Marketing
Margaret Black, VP Government Affairs
Advocacy organization for the seafood industry. Its member companies represent every element of the industry from the fishing vessels at sea to the national seafood restaurant chains
380 Members Founded: 1946

8127 **National Party Boat Owners Alliance**
181 Thames Street
Groton, CT 06340
860-535-2066
FAX: 860-535-8389
Bradley J Glas, President/Executive Director
NPBOA members are Coast Guard licensed Operators or Masters of passenger-for-hire charter/party boats. NPBOA's principal activity is monitoring proposed and new laws or regulations that might be determined to its segment of the maritime industry.
500 Members Founded: 1952

8128 National Seafood Educators
PO Box 60006
Richmond Beach, WA 98160
206-546-6410
FAX: 206-546-6411 800-348-0010
christanse@aol.com
www.seafoodeducators.com

Evie Hansen, Founder
Oscar Hansen, President

The goal is to educate and inform the public about the many health benefits of a seafood diet. National Seafood Educators has also consulted with many seafood retail businesses on how to sell, store and prepare wholesome seafood.
Founded: 1982

8129 National Shellfisheries Association
C/O US EPA, Atlantic Ecology Division
27 Tazewell Drive
Narragansett, RI 02880
401-782-3155
FAX: 401-782-3030
news@shellfish.org
www.shellfish.org

Dr Lou D'Abramo, President
Dr Chris Davis, Treasurer

An international organization of scientists, management officials and members of industry that is deeply concerned and dedicated to the formulation of ideas and promotion of knowledge pertinent to the biology, ecology, production, economics and management of shellfish resources.
$85.00
1000 Members Membership Fee Founded: 1908

8130 National Shrimp Industry Association
c/o Beth Dancy
1520 Berkeley Road
Highland Park, IL 60035
847-831-2030
FAX: 847-831-2343
info@nsiaonline.org
www.nsiaonline.org

Beth Dancy, Membership Coordinator
Travis Larkin, President

Our focus is on providing leadership in resource management, food safety, education and market development.
Founded: 1957

8131 North Carolina Fisheries Association
PO Box 12303
New Bern, NC 28561
252-633-2288
FAX: 252-633-9616
karen@ncfish.org www.ncfish.org

Sean McKeon, President
Karen Fothergill, Bookkeeper

Non-profit trade organization created to facilitate the promotion of North Carolina families, heritage and seafood through accessible data about the commercial fishing industry. NCFA lobbies Local, State, and Federal legislators and engages in a wide scope of public awareness projects.
Founded: 1952

8132 Pacific Coast Federation of Fishermen
Building 991, Marine Drive
Po Box 29370
San Francisco, CA 94129-0370
415-561-5080
FAX: 415-561-5464
fish1ifr@aol.com www.pcffa.org

Zeke Grader, Executive Director
Chuck Wise, President

Commercial fishermen's organizations from California to Alaska. Works to prevent and improve the resources of the commercial fishing industry, protect rivers from herbicide and pesticide applications that may threaten salmon populations, maintain activity within the industry, regain local control over fisheries management.
22 Members Founded: 1976

8133 Pacific Seafood Processors Association
1900 W Emerson Place
Suite 205
Seattle, WA 98119
206-281-1667
FAX: 206-283-2387
info@pspafish.net www.pspafish.net

Glenn E Reed, President

Trade association for the onshore processors in Oregon, Washington and Alaska.
25 Members Founded: 1914

8134 Recreational Fishing Alliance
Po Box 3080
New Gretna, NJ 08224
609-404-1060
FAX: 609-404-1968 888-564-6732
rfa@joinrfa.org www.savefish.com

James Donofrio, Executive Director
Gary Caputi, Corporate Relations Director
Courtney Howell Thompson, Marketing Coordinator/PR

An organization that supports and fights back against federal government state legislatures impose unreasonable restrictions on our ability to enjoy recreational fishing.

$35/Membership

8135 Southeastern Fisheries Association
1118 Thomasville Road
Tallahassee, FL 32303
850-224-0612
FAX: 850-222-3663
bobfish@aol.com
www.southeasternfish.org

Bob Gill, President
Bob Jones, Executive Director

To defend, preserve and enhance the commercial fishing industry in the southeastern United States for present participants as well as future generations through all legal means.
Founded: 1952

8136 United Tuna Cooperative
2535 Kettern Boulevard
Suite 3-C1
San Diego, CA 92101
619-238-1838
FAX: 619-238-1708
krampepaul@aol.com

Paul Krampe, Executive Director

Members are U.S. flag purse seiner owners that operate their fishing vessels in the Western Pacific ocean
20 Members Founded: 1921

8137 West Coast Seafood Processors Association
1618 SW First Avenue
Suite 318
Portland, OR 97201
503-227-5076
FAX: 503-227-0237
seafood@integraonline.com
www.wcspa.com

Rod Moore, Executive Director

Serves the needs of the shore-based seafood processors in California, Oregon and Washington, helping them to face and survive economic, environmental and regulatory challenges.
13 Members

8138 Wholesale Seafood Merchants
7 Dey Street
Suite 805
New York, NY 10007
212-732-4340
FAX: 212-732-6444

Albert Altesman, Executive Secretary

The credit exchange for US and Canadian wholesale seafood merchants.
400 Members Founded: 1933

8139 Women's Fisheries Network
2422 NW Market Square
Suite 199
Seattle, WA 98107
206-789-1987
FAX: 206-789-1987 www.fis.com

Stephanie Madsen, President

Men and women dedicated to education of issues confronting the fishing and seafood industry.
2000 Members Founded: 1983

Newsletters

8140 ASA Newsletter
American Sportfishing Association
225 Reinekers Lane
Suite 420
Alexandria, VA 22314
703-519-9691
FAX: 703-519-1872
bfisher@asafishing.org
www.asafishing.org

Mary Jane Williamson, Editor
Brad Fisher, Assistant Editor
Gordon Robertson, VP

Represents the recreational sport fishing community.
Bi-Monthly

8141 Briefs
American Institute of Fishery Research Biologists
205 Blades Road
Havelock, NC 28532

feeshdr@starfishnet.com
www.aifrb.org

Gene Huntsman, Editor
John Merriner, Production Editor

It is intended to communicate the professional activities and accomplishments of the Institute, its District, and Members; the results of research; the effects of management; unusual biological events; matters affecting the profession; political problems and other matters of importance to the fishery community.

Bi-Monthly

8142 **Crow's Nest**
Casamar Group/Holdings
8082 Firethorn Lane
Las Vegas, NV 89123
702-792-6868
FAX: 702-792-6668
casamarholdings@casamarintl.com

Malu Marigomen, Executive Director

An in-depth report on the status of the Tuna Industry
Monthly

8143 **Currents**
Women's Fisheries Network
2422 NW Market Square
Seattle, WA 98107
206-789-1987
FAX: 206-789-1987
sndslotvig@juno.com
www.fis.com/wfn

Debbie Slotivg, Editor
Ron Gawith, Owner

Features current topics in fisheries, members'activities, upcoming events and chapter reports.
Monthly

8144 **IAFWA Newsletter**
Association of Fish and Wildlife Agencies
444 North Capitol Street NW
Suite 544
Washington, DC 20001
202-624-7890
FAX: 202-624-7891
rbrittin@iafwa.org www.iafwa.org

Eric Schwaab, Resource Director
Rachel Brittin, Public Affairs Director
John Baughman, Executive VP

Provides state fish and wildlife agencies with legal counsel, national surveys and information on the fish industry
Monthly

8145 **IIFET Newsletter**
International Institute of Fisheries Economics
Dept of Agricultural & Resource Economic
Oregon State University
Corvallis, OR 97331-3601
541-737-1416
FAX: 541-737-2563
iifet@oregonstate.edu
www.oregonstate.edu/dept/iifet

Kara Keenan, Editoral Assistant

Provides conference listings, news items, and information on new publications and the activities of members.
20 pages Semi-Annual

8146 **Littorally Speaking**
American Littoral Society Northeast Chapter
28 West 9th Road
Broad Channel, NY 11693
718-318-9344
www.alsnyc.org

Barbara Toborg, Editor
Don Riepe, Chapter Director

A digest of environmental concerns

8147 **NSA Newsletter**
National Shellfisheries Association
C/O US EPA, Atlantic Ecology Division
27 Tazewell Drive
Narragansett, RI 02880
401-782-3155
FAX: 401-782-3030
news@shellfish.org www.shellfish.org

Dr Evan Ward, Editor

Current issues and concerns in shellfish research and in the shellfish industry, including details regarding upcoming meetings, employment listings, and gossip items for our Metamorphoses column.
Quarterly

8148 **Northern Aquaculture**
Capemara Communications
4623 William Head Road
Victoria, BC 1244
250-478-3973
FAX: 250-478-3979 800-661-0368
editor@naqua.com www.naqua.com

Peter Chetteburgh, Editor-in-Chief
Jeremy Thain, Sales Manager
James Lewis, Production Department

A trade publication devoted to the growth of a strong, economically viable and environmentally conscious cold water aquaculture industry in North America. It covers the latest news in finfish and shellfish culture from both coasts as well as the central regions of North America. Species covered include salmon, trout, arctic charr, halibut and shellfish. *$27.95*
Bi-monthly Founded: 1985
Circulation: 3600

8149 **Wheel Watch**
Fishing Vessel Owners Association
4005 20th Avenue W
Room 232, West Wall Bldg
Seattle, WA 98199-1290
206-284-4720
FAX: 206-283-3341 www.fvoa.org

Robert D Alverson, Manager
Quarterly

Magazines & Journals

8150 **American Seafood Institute Report**
American Seafood Institute
25 Fairway Circle
Hope Valley, RI 02832
401-491-9017
FAX: 401-491-9024
www.americanseafood.org
A trade magazine of the seafood industry.
Monthly

8151 **Aquaculture Magazine**
Aquaculture Magazine
Po Box 1409
Arden, NC 28704
828-547-7334
FAX: 828-681-0601 877-687-0011
circulations@aquaculturemag.com
www.aquaculturemag.com

Gregory J Gallagher, Editor/Publisher
Rebekah Craig, Circulation Manager
Brenda Jo McManama, Advertising/Sales

Focus emphasizes the production, processing, and marketing of aquatic organisms and plant life. *$24.00*
96 pages Annually/Summer Founded: 1968
Circulation: 5000

8152 **Atlantic Fisherman**
Advocate Media Publishing
181 Brown's Point Road
Nova Scotia B0K-1H0
902-485-1990
FAX: 902-485-6353 800-236-9526
editorial@advocatemediaink.com
www.advocateprinting.com

Susan Purdy, Publications Manager

Provides news for the commercial fisherman in the four Atlantic provinces of Canada. Includes prespectives from the unions, the government and the fishermen themselves. *$16.00*
Monthly
Circulation: 9950

8153 **Catfish Journal**
Catfish Farmers of America
Po Box 55648
Jackson, MS 39296
601-206-1600
FAX: 601-977-9632
info@catfishfarmersamerica.com
www.catfishfarmersamerica.org

Mike McCall, Editor
Sandra Goff, Production Manager

News on catfish production, processing, feed manufacturing and research
Monthly

8154 **Commercial Fisheries News**
Compass Publications
PO Box 37
Stonington, ME 04681
207-367-2396
FAX: 207-367-2490 800-989-5253
comfish@fish-news.com
www.fish-news.com

Richard W Martin, Publisher
Susan Jones, Editor

Commercial Fisheries News is the Atlantic fishing industry newspaper, covering: waterfront news, new boats, gear, technology, market and fish handling developments. and fish and lobster prices. *$21.95*
72 pages Monthly Founded: 1978
Circulation: 9223
Printed in 4 colors on n stock

8155 **Communique**
American Zoo and Aquarium Association
8403 Colesville Road
Suite 710
Silver Spring, MD 20910
301-562-0777
FAX: 301-562-0888 www.aza.org

Tim Lewthwaite, Editor/Publications Manager
Kristin L Vehrs, Deputy Director
Ian Litmans, Membership Coordinator
Jim Maddy, Executive Director

A benefit with your membership this publication provides the latest news about our members
Monthly

8156 **Esox Angler**
Esox Angler
Po Box 895
Hayward, WI 54843
715-638-2311

info@esoxangler.com
www.esoxangler.com

Jack Burns, Senior Editor
Rob Kimm, Editor

A muskie and pike magazine for the world's muskie and pike anglers. Articles focusing on proven techniques and new ideas from

top name anglers, as well as regular guys who are catching lots of fish. *$22.00*
4x/year

8157 Fish Farming News
Compass Publications
PO Box 37
Stonington, ME 04681
207-367-2396
FAX: 207-367-2490 800-989-5253
comfish@fish-news.com
http://www.fish-news.com
Richard W Martin, Publisher
Susan Jones, Editor
Stephen Rappaport, Managing Editor
Fish Farming News is aquaculture's business newspaper. *$14.95*
24 pages Founded: 1993
Circulation: 7500
Printed in 4 colors on n stock

8158 Fish Sniffer
3201 Eastwood Road
Sacramento, CA 95821
916-685-2245
FAX: 916-685-1498
danielbacher@fishsniffer.com
www.fishsniffer.com
Dan Bacher, Editor
Cal Kellogg, Associate Editor
Current fishing reports, weather conditions, fishing news, photos, boats for sale, what and where to fish and much more. *$29.00*
Bi-Weekly

8159 Fisheries
American Fisheries Society
5410 Grosvenor Lane
Bethesda, MD 20814-2199
301-897-8616
FAX: 301-897-8096
main@fisheries.org
http://www.fisheries.org
Beth Beard, Managing Editor
Aaron Lerner, Publications Director
Cherie Worth, Production Editor
Peer reviewed articles that address contemporary issues and problems, techniques, philosophies and other areas of interest to the general fisheries profession. Monthly features include letters, meeting notices, book listings and reviews, environmental essays and organization profiles. *$106.00*
50 pages Monthly Founded: 1870
Circulation: 9800
Mailing list available for rent 8500 names $250 per M.

8160 Fisherman
326 12th Street
1st Floor
New Westminster, BC V3M-4H6
604-669-5569
FAX: 604-688-1142
fisherman@ufawu.org
www.thefisherman.ca
Sean Griffin, Editor
Suzanne Thomson, Advertising Manager
News and information for the commercial fisherman in British Columbia. Also features article of interest to shore plant workers, tendermen and others involved in the fishing industry.
Monthly
Circulation: 8000

8161 Fishermen's News
Philips Publishing Group
2201 W Commodore Way
Seattle, WA 98199-1298
206-284-8285
FAX: 206-284-0391
circulation@rhppublishing.com
http://www.fishermensnews.com
Peter Philips, Publisher
Lisa Albers, Editor
Maggie Cheung, Circulatiom Manager
Covers commercial fishing activity, market trends, gear and boat building news, political news and financial matters related to the industry. *$21.00*
Monthly Founded: 1945
Circulation: 8000 $200 per M.
Printed in 4 colors on n stock

8162 Fly Fisherman
Primedia
745 Fifth Avenue
New York, NY 10151
212-745-0100
FAX: 212-745-0121
lindaw@flyfisherman.com
www.primediamags.com/www.flyfisherman.com
John Randolph, Editor/Publisher
Linda Wood, Associate Publisher
Jay Nichols, Managing Editor
Each issue provides expert advice on the latest fly fishing techniques, the newest tackle and the hottest new fly patterns. Through informative articles, it highlights the best destinations for trout, salmon, steelhead, bass and saltwater species around the world. *$19.95*
Annually Founded: 1969

8163 IAfWA Proceedings
International Association of Fish and Wildlife
444 North Capitol Street NW
Suite 725
Washington, DC 20001
202-624-7890
FAX: 202-624-7891
info@iafwa.org www.iafwa.org
John Baughman, Executive Vice President
Wayne Muhlstein, VP
Eric Schwaab, Resource Director
Reports on the business transacted by the Association at its March meeting held in conjunction with the North American Wildlife and Natural Resources Conference and at its September annual conference. *$20.00*
Annual

8164 In-Fisherman
Primedia
745 Fifth Avenue
New York, NY 10151
212-745-0100
FAX: 212-745-0121
information@primedia.com
www.primediamags.com/www.in-fisherman.com
Doug Stange, Editor-in-Chief
Dave Csanda, Editor
Rob Neumann, Managing Editor
Written for the avid freshwater angler. In each issue, you'll find detailed instructions and demonstrations on catching, cleaning, and eating your favorite species of fish, and reports on the latest scientific studies concerning fish and habitat conservation. *$12.00*
8x/year Founded: 1975

8165 Island Fisherman
1004 Bellevue Road
Parksville, BC V9P-2C2
250-248-4730
FAX: 250-248-4734
info@islandfishermanmagazine.com
www.islandfishermanmagazine.com
Larry E Stefanyk, Founder/Publisher
Bob Jones, Editor
Covering the west coast of British Columbia from the Queen Charlottes to Victoria on Vancouver Island. Covering saltwater and freshwater fishing with how to and where to tips to help you find the big one or just experience what the west coast of British Columbia has to offer. *$40.00*
Monthly Founded: 2001

8166 Marlin
World Publications
460 N Orlando Avenue
Suite 200
Winter Park, FL 32789
407-628-4802
FAX: 407-628-7061
editor@marlinmag.com/info@worldpub.net
www.marlinmag.com/www.worldpub.net
Dave Ferrell, Editor
Glen Hughes, Group Publisher
Terry Snow, Owner
The bible for big-game fishermen. It is written for the most affluent anglers who need to know what is happening around the world regarding offshore fishing. It is the who's who of the sport, written in the voice of the sportfisherman, one-on-one to a peer, as a member of this elite fraternity. Marlin magazine will continue to be the No. 1 buy in big-game fishing by delivering the best targeted edit to the wealthiest boat-owning saltwater fishermen in the world. *$24.95*
8x/year
Circulation: 40,000

8167 National Fisherman
Diversified Business Communications
121 Free Street
Portland, ME 04101-7438
207-842-5500
FAX: 207-842-5609
editor@nationalfisherman.com
http://www.nationalfisherman.com
Jerry Fraser, Editor-in-Chief/Publisher
Lincoln Bedrosian, Senior Editor
Nancy Hasselback, President
Regional coverage of boats, fishing gear, environmental developments, technology, new products, and fishery resource information *$19.95*
Monthly Founded: 1903
Circulation: 38,000

8168 North American Journal of Aquaculture
American Fisheries Society
5410 Grosvenor Lane
Bethesda, MD 20814-2199
301-897-8616
FAX: 301-897-8096
main@fisheries.org
www.fisheries.org
Bruce A Barton, Editor
William L Shelton, Editor
Christopher C Kohler, Development Editor
Formerly published as The Progressive Fish-Culturist. The focus is on culture of all aquatic organisms that are of importance to North American culturists. Topics

include, but are not limited to, nutrition and feeding, broodstock selection and spawning, drugs and chemicals, health and water quality, and testing new techniques and equipment for the management and rearing of aquatic species *$38.00*
Quarterly

8169 Pacific Fishing
Pacific Fishing
1710 South Norman Street
Seattle, WA 98144
206-245-5644
FAX: 206-324-8939
pfmag@salmonbay.com
http://www.pfmag.com

Peter Hurme, Group Publishing Director
Jon Holland, Editor
Duane Brady, Sales & Marketing Manager
Michael Daigle, Manager

Serving owners and operators of commercial fishing boats throughout the world's most productive ocean, from Alaska to the tropical Pacific. Our readers also include crew members, processors, fisheries managers, suppliers, seafood brokers and distributors, educators, and others who want serious information about the business of hauling up food from the Pacific. *$15.00*
Monthly Founded: 1980
Circulation: 7160

8170 SaltWater
Time, Inc.
2 Park Avenue
New York, NY 10016
212-221-1212
FAX: 212-779-5999
editor@saltwatersportsman.com
www.saltwatersportsman.com

David DiBenedetto, Editor
Gerald Bethge, Executive Editor
Jason Y Wood, Managing Editor
Karl Anderson, Senior Editor

A publication on salt-water sport fishing. Each monthly issue contains exciting feature stories, columns, award-winning color photos covering both big- and small-game fishing, the newest techniques, tackle, boats and equipment, and the latest developments in conservation and fishery management. *$20.00*
Monthly Founded: 1939
Circulation: 165,000

8171 Sea Technology
Compass Publications
1501 Wilson Boulevard
Suite 1001
Arlington, VA 22209
703-524-3136
FAX: 703-841-0852
oceanbiz@sea-technology.com
www.sea-technology.com

Michele Umansky, Managing Editor
Travis Talent, Assistant Editor
Richard F Burns, Associate Editor
Russell Conward, Production Manager

Read worldwide in more than 100 countries by management, engineers, scientists and technical personnel working in industry, government and educational research institutions. Readers are involved with oceanographic research, fisheries management, offshore oil & gas exploration and production, undersea defense including antisubmarine warfare, ocean mining and commercial diving. *$45.00*
Monthly Founded: 1960
Circulation: 20.5M
Mailing list available for rent 20.5mil names $40 per M.

8172 Seafood Business
Diversified Business Communications
121 Free Street
PO Box 7438
Portland, ME 04112-7437
207-425-5500
FAX: 207-842-5505
www.divbusiness.com/www.seafoodbusiness.com

Bill Springer, Publisher
Fiona Robinson, Editor

Provides its readers in-depth, relevant information to help them make the best buying decisions and stay on top of trends in their industry.
Monthly Founded: 1982
Circulation: 15,000

8173 Sport Fishing
World Publications
460 N Orlando Avenue
Winter Park, FL 32789
407-628-4802
FAX: 407-628-7061
editor@sportfishingmag.com
www.sportfishingmag.com/www.worldpub.net

Glenn Hughes, Group Publisher
Bruce Miller, Circulation VP
Terry Snow, Owner

Written for the passionate angler who must have in-depth, cutting-edge information on the latest techniques, the hottest locations and the newest equipment to maximize his day on the water, Sport Fishing magazine is the source for saltwater fishing information. *$19.97*
10x/year Founded: 2001
Circulation: 150,000

8174 Transactions of the American Fisheries Society
American Fisheries Society
5410 Grosvenor Lane
Bethesda, MD 20814-2199
301-897-8616
FAX: 301-897-8096
main@fisheries.org www.fisheries.org

Richard J Beamish, Editor
Dennis R DeVries, Editor
Fred M Utter, Editor

The Society's highly regarded international journal of fisheries science features results of basic and applied research in genetics, physiology, biology, ecology, population dynamics, economics, health, culture, and other topics germane to marine and freshwater finfish and shellfish and their respective fisheries and environments *$43.00*
Bi-Monthly Founded: 1872

8175 Underwater Naturalist
American Littoral Society Northeast Chapter
28 West 9th Road
Broad Channel, NY 11693
718-318-9344

driepe@nyc.rr.com www.alsnyc.org

Don Riepe, Chapter Director

A publication providing news and analysis of animals and wildlife such as fish,
Quarterly

8176 Washington Report
National Ocean Industries Association
1120 G Street NW
Suite 900
Washington, DC 20005
202-347-6900
FAX: 202-347-8650
noia@noia.org www.noia.org

Thomas A Fry, III, President
Kim Harb, Director Government Affairs
Franki K Stuntz, Director Administration
Nolty J Thuriot, Director Congressional Affairs

Bi-Weekly

Trade Shows

8177 AFS Annual Meeting
American Fisheries Society
5410 Grosvenor Lane
Bethesda, MD 20814
301-897-8616
FAX: 301-897-8096
thechair@afslakeplacid.org
www.fisheries.org

Ed Woltmann, Conference Chair
Doug Stang, Conference Program Chair
Gus Rassam, Executive Director

Held in conjunction with American Institute of Fishery Research Biologists. Explore the interrelation between fish, aquatic habitats and man; highlight challenges facing aquatic resource professionals and the methods that have been employed to resolve conflicts between those that use or have an interest in our aquatic resources. *$295.00*
Annual/September

8178 ASA Sportfishing Summit
American Sportfishing Association
225 Reinekers Lane
Suite 420
Alexandria, VA 22314
703-519-9691
FAX: 703-519-1872
info@asafishing.org
www.asafishing.org

Mary Jane Williamson, Communications Director
Deanna Eastman, Administrative Services Manager
Gordon Robertson, VP

The association's annual membership meeting that provides the Board of Directors, committees, members and ASA's partners the best opportunity for networking and strategic planning. Focusing their efforts on issues surrounding angling participation, the federal excise tax on sportfishing equipment and the future of the industry.
125 Attendees October

8179 AZAA Regional Meeting
American Zoo and Aquarium Association
8403 Colesville Road
Suite 710
Silver Spring, MD 20910
301-562-0777
FAX: 301-562-0888
bstrelitz@aza.org www.aza.org

Beth Strelitz, Meetings Manager
Jim Maddy, Executive Director
Kris Vehrs, JD, Deputy Director

Exhibits, workshops and discussions about the industry.
500 Attendees March/April

8180 **CFA Fish Farming Trade Show**
Catfish Farmers of America
100 Highway 82 East
Suite 202
Indianola, MS 38751
662-887-2699
FAX: 662-887-6857
www.catfishjournal.com
Hugh Warren, III, Executive Director
America's largest fish farming equipment expo.
February

8181 **Eastern Fishing & Outdoor Expo**
Eastern Fishing & Outdoor Expositions
Po Box 4720
Portsmouth, NH 00380
603-431-4315
FAX: 603-431-1971
info@sportshows.com
www.sportshows.com
Paul Fuller, President/Show Director
Judy L Chapman, Assistant Show Director
Partnership with American Sportfishing Association. Exhibitors representing the entire spectrum of saltwater sportfishing. This includes inshore to offshore, light tackle to big-game tackle, and everything in between. Fishermen will see and touch the latest from major tackle manufacturers and buy the latest tackle from local retailers at special show prices.
Feb/Mar

8182 **Fish Expo Workboat Atlantic**
National Fisherman/Diversified Bus. Communications
121 Free Street
PO Box 7437
Portland, ME 04112
207-425-5608
FAX: 207-842-5509
fewa@divcom.com
www.fishexpoatlantic.com
Bob Callahan, Show Director
Heather Palmeter, Show Coordinator
Now held in the spring time, this expo for commerical vessel owners presents new products and services for the industry. *$20.00*
6,000 Attendees April

8183 **Fly-Fishing Retailer World Trade Expo**
VNU Expositions/Business Media
770 Broadway
New York, NY 10003
646-545-5100

atompkins@vnuexpo.com
www.fly-fishing-retailer.com/www.vnubusinessmedia.com
Andy Tompkins, Show Director
Peter Devin, Group Show Director
Where brands are launched, innovations are unveiled and connections are made. Designed for the specialty fly-fishing industry, Fly-Fishing Retailer World Trade Expo connects a targeted audience to conduct business in a professional yet friendly atmosphere. *$200.00*
August Founded: 1998

8184 **IAFWA Annual Meeting**
International Association of Fish and Wildlife
444 North Capitol Street NW
Suite 725
Washington, DC 20001
202-624-7890
FAX: 202-624-7891
rbrittin@iafwa.org www.iafwa.org
Gary T Myers, Executive Director
Cindy Delaney, Meetings Coordinator
Wayne Muhlstein, VP
Providing many opportunities to hear from our nation's wildlife conservation leaders, partners, and management experts. The meeting is our response to the need for national consensus on state-by-state fish and wildlife management issues. *$300.00*
250 Attendees September

8185 **ICAST**
American Sportfishing Association
225 Reinekers Lane
Suite 420
Alexandria, VA 22314
703-519-9691
FAX: 703-519-1872
mdelvalle@asafishing.org
www.asafishing.org
Maria del Valle, ICAST Director
Kelly Camirand, ICAST Coordinator
A showcase of all the new products and gear for the fishing industry
7,000 Attendees July

8186 **IIFET Biennial Conference/Meeting**
Int'l Institute of Fisheries Economics and Trade
Dept. of Agricultural and Resources Economics
Oregon State University
Corvallis, OR 97331
541-737-1439
FAX: 541-737-2563
Ann.L.Shrivor@oregonstate.edu
www.osu.orst.edu/dept/iifet
Ann L Shriver, Executive Director
Kara Keenan, Assistant Executive Director
An important forum for members and others to learn about important research developments in seafood trade, aquaculture, and fisheries management issues. Attended by fisheries social scientists, managers, and industry members from all of the world's fishing areas.
July

8187 **International Boston Seafood Show**

Diversified Business Communications
PO Box 7437
Portland, ME 04112-7437
207-842-5504
FAX: 207-842-5505
customerservice@divcom.com
www.bostonseafood.com
Diane Vassar, Promotions Director
David Lowell, President
This event attracts top-tier buyers and sellers of seafood. You will find exhibit categories representing every aspect of seafood including; seafood, seafood equipment, services and organizations and seafood packaging. *$495.00*
20M Attendees March/Silver Pkg $250

8188 **International West Coast Seafood Show**
Diversified Business Communications
PO Box 7437
Portland, ME 04112-7437
207-842-5500
FAX: 207-842-5503
mlarkin@divcom.com
www.westcoastseafood.com
Mary Larkin, VP Seafood Expositions
A total resource for seafood industry leaders; showcases the latest seafood products and equipment from the US, Pacific Rim and beyond.
October Founded: 1996

8189 **NSA Annual Meeting**
National Shellfisheries Association
C/O US EPA, Atlantic Ecology Division
27 Tazewell Drive
Narragansett, RI 02880
401-782-3155
FAX: 401-782-3030
news@shellfish.org
www.shellfish.org
Dr Lou D'Abramo, President
Christopher Davis, Treasurer
A time and place to interact with other associations and industry people. *$295.00*
Spring

8190 **Pacific Marine Expo**
Diversified Business Communications
121 Free Street
PO Box 7437
Portland, ME 04112
207-425-5608
FAX: 207-842-5509
pme@divcom.com
www.pacificmarineexpo.com
Bob Callahan, Show Director
Heather Palmeter, Show Coordinator
A trade show dedicated to the pacific maritime industry that provides a gathering of marine products and services. With nearly 500 manufacturers and distributors showcasing the latest technologies and thousands of products for all commercial vessels, tugs, barges, boat building, marine construction, passenger vessels, seafood processing plants and more, PME is the best source for all marine business needs. *$20.00*
6,000 Attendees November

Directories & Databases

8191 **AZA Membership Directory**
American Zoo and Aquarium Association
8403 Colesville Road
Suite 710
Silver Spring, MD 20910
301-562-0777
FAX: 301-562-0888
ilitmans@aza.org www.aza.org
Tim Lewthwaite, Publications Coordinator
Ian Litmans, Membership Coordinator
Institutional statistics, species and specimen charts and conservation program information. *$125.00*
Biennial/$50 for Members

8192 **Angling America Database**
Po Box 22567
Alexandria, VA 22304

info@anglingamerica.com
www.anglingamerica.com

Stephen Aaron, Director
Austin Ducworth, Director

The most searchable database for fishing charters and guides across America.

8193 **IIFET Membership Directory**
International Institute of Fisheries Economics
Dept of Agricultural & Resource Economic
Oregon State University
Corvallis, OR 97331-3601
541-737-1416
FAX: 541-737-2563
iifet@oregonstate.edu
www.orst.edu/dept/iifet

Ann L Shriver, Executive Director
Kara Kennan, Assistant Executive Director

This handbook lists all members with complete contact information, including an e-mail directory, plus areas of interest. Regular updates are provided with the newsletter.
Biennial

8194 **Who's Who in the Fish Industry**
Urner Barry Publications
PO Box 389
Toms River, NJ 08754-0389
732-240-5330
FAX: 732-341-0891 800-932-0617
sales@urnerbarry.com
www.urnerbarry.com

Jay Bailey, Sales Manager
Janice Brown, Advertising Manager

The source for buying and selling contacts in the North American Seafood Industry. This 2006-2007 edition is fully updated and verified, boasting over 6,000 listings of seafood companies in the US and Canada. The directory boasts detailed information about each company listed such as products handled, contact names, product forms, product origin, sales volume, company website and much more. *$199.00*
800 pages Softcover Founded: 1979

Industry Web Sites

8195 **www.asafishing.org**
American Sportfishing Association

Manufacturers and importers of fishing tackle and allied products. Promotes fishing for children and adults. Compiles statistics. Sponsors National Fishing Week.

8196 **www.fish307.com/links.htm**

This site provides links to Lake George Regional Web Sites, Fishing Charters, International Web Sites related to fishing.

8197 **www.fishhoo.com**

Fishhoo search Index for Fishermen. The internet's best fishing resources. There are 2991 links to choose from and translate to: French, German and Spanish.

8198 **www.greyhouse.com**
Grey House Publishing

Selected Grey House directories in the fields of business, health and education are available online. Users can search our online databases by several different search criteria, such as product categories, geographic area, sales volume and much, much more. Full Grey House catalog and online ordering also available.

8199 **www.internets.com/sfishing.htm**

Fishing Databases Search Engines.

8200 **www.nauticalworld.com**

Dedicated to bringing all related web sites within easy access to watersports enthusiasts. This search engine has been designed to locate advertiser's information within Nautical World but will also offer access to other watersport related web sites as well. Offers sections on marine electronics and hardware, sailing, boats, dock supplies, fishing accessories, diving accessories, industry news, watersports, weather forecasting and more.

8201 **www.nfi.org**
National Fishing Institute

Promotes the shipping and production of fishery products in international trade.

8202 **www.ospafish.net**
Pacific Seafood Processors Association

Trade association for the onshore processors in Oregon, Washington and Alaska.

8203 **www.pcffa.org**
Pacific Coast Federation of Fishermen's Assoc

Commercial fishermen's organizations from California to Alaska. Works to prevent and improve the resources of the commercial fishing industry, protect rivers from herbicide and pesticide applications that may threaten salmon populations, maintain activity within the industry, regain local control over fisheries management.

8204 **www.web.mit.edu/seagrant/www/wfn.html**
Women's Fisheries Network

Men and women dedicated to education of issues confronting the fishing and seafood industry. Conducts educational programs.

Associations

8205 APICS: Association for Operations Management
5301 Shawnee Road
Alexandria, VA 22312-2317
703-354-8851
FAX: 703-354-8106 800-444-2742
service@apicshq.org www.apics.org
Nicholas M Testa, President
Joseph F Shedlawski, President-Elect
Robert Vokurka, Secretary/Treasurer
Douglas Kelly, Publisher
Provides lifelong learning for lifetime success. APICS certification programs, training tools and networking opportunities increase workplace performance. The society supports 20,000 manufacturing and service industry companies worldwide. *$110.00*
60000 Members Membership/Professional
Founded: 1957

8206 ASI Food Safety Consultants
7625 Page Boulevard
St. Louis, MO 63133
314-725-2555
FAX: 314-727-2563 800-477-0778
asi@asifood.com www.asifood.com
Jeanette Huge, Sales Director
Cheryl Rich, Sales
A full service provider of food safety audits, GMP audits, seminars and HACCP setups, as well as HACCP verification. Thoroughly addresses every vital concern of your valuable facility including food safety, pest control, employee practices and facility conditions.
Founded: 1930

8207 ASMC Foodservice
Grocery Manufactures Association
2401 Pennsylvania Ave, NW 2nd Floor
Washington, DC 20037
202-337-9400
FAX: 202-337-4508
info@gmabrands.com www.asmc.org
Rick Abraham, President
Advances the interests of the food, beverage and consumer products industry on key issues that effect the ability of brand manufacturers their products profitably and deliver superior value to the consumer.
250 Members Founded: 1995

8208 Agricultural Communicators of Tomorrow
Oklahoma State University
435 Ag Hall
Stillwater, OK 74078-0180
405-446-6630

shelly.sitton@okstate.edu
www.nact.okstate.edu
Julie Wetmore, President
Ashley Woodward, First VP
Kathryn Bolay, Second VP
Megan Knight, Secretary/Treasurer
The Mission of National ACT is to build relationships among agricultural communication professionals and college students and faculty, to provide professional and academic development for members and to promote agriculture through communications efforts.
Founded: 1970

8209 Agricultural History Society
University of Arkansas Little Rock
2801 S University Avenue
Little Rock, AR 72204-1099
501-693-3000
FAX: 501-569-3059
www.usi.edu/libarts/history/AHS
Hal S Barron, President
Donald J Pisani, President-Elect
C Fred Williams, Executive Secretary/Treasurer
Larry Poldrack, Executive Director
Organized to stimulate interest in and promote the study of the history of agriculture.
915 Members Founded: 1919

8210 Agricultural Research Institute
9650 Rockville Pike
Bethesda, MD 20814-3998
301-530-7122
FAX: 301-530-7007 ari@nal.usda.gov
Richard A Herrett, Executive Director
One hundred and twenty-five member institutions concerned with environmental issues, pest control, agricultural meteorology, biotechnology, food irradiation, agricultural policy, research and development, food safety, technology transfer and remote sensing. *$50.00*

8211 Agricultural Retailers Association
1156 15th Street NW
Suite 302
Washington, DC 20005
202-457-0825
FAX: 202-457-0864 800-844-4900
ara@aradc.org www.aradc.org
Jack Eberspacher, President/CEO
Stacy Mayuga, Marketing/Communications Director
Alida Malcom, Membership Director
Jim Thrift, VP Regulatory
Richard Gupton, Director Legislative Policy
Nonprofit trade organization representing the interests of retailers across the United States on legislative and regulatory issues on Capitol Hill.
1200 Members Membership Dues Vary
Founded: 1993

8212 Agricultural and Industrial Manufacturers Representatives Association
7500 Flying Cloud Drive
Suite 900
Eden Prairie, MN 55344
952-253-6230
FAX: 952-835-4774
jrmanke@associationsolutionsinc.com
www.aimrareps.org
Jim Manke, Executive Director
Rob L Neal, President
Association of industrial manufacturers who sell equipment into light industrial, agricultural, lawn and garden markets. *$275.00*
125 Members Membership Dues

8213 Agriculture Council of America
11020 King Street
Suite 205
Overland Park, KS 66210-1201
913-491-1895
FAX: 913-491-6502
info@agday.org www.agday.org
Kendal Frazier, Chairman
Jim Bone, Vice-Chairman
Gerald Tumbleson, Secretary/Treasurer
Eldin White, President
An organization uniquely composed of leaders in the agriculture, food and fiber communities dedicated to increasing the public awareness of agriculture's vital role in our society.

8214 Alfalfa Processors Council
8810 Craig Drive
Overland Park, KS 66212
913-648-6800
FAX: 913-648-2648
aapa@cysource.com
www.aapausa.org
Wanda L Cobb, Contact Person
In May of 2001, the AAPA merged with the American Feed Industry Association and became the Alfalfa Processors Council. This association is for operators and suppliers of alfalfa processing farms.
130 Members Founded: 1941

8215 Alliance for Bio-Integrity
2040 Pearl Lane
#2
Fairfield, IA 52556
206-888-4852

info@biointegrity.org
www.biointegrity.org
Steven M Druker, Executive Director
A nonprofit organization dedicated to the advancement of human and environmental health through sustainable and safe technologies.

8216 Allied Purchasing
PO Box 1249
Mason City, IA 50402
641-231-1824
FAX: 800-635-3775
kbamrick@alliedpurchasing.com
www.alliedpurchasing.com
Carol Peterson, CEO
Brian Janssen, CFO
Dennis Bodoh, Executive VP
Kim Bamrick, Executive Secretary
A member owned not-for-profit buying organization established to negotiate favorable purchasing programs in part because we offer quantity purchases and prompt payment to suppliers. *$50.00*
1200 Members Membership: 1 Share Stock
Founded: 1937

8217 Allied Trades of the Baking Industry
C/O Cereal Food Processors
2001 Shawnee Mission Parkway
Mission Woods, KS 66205
913-890-6300

t.miller@cerealfood.com
www.atbi.org
Gary Cain, President
Mike Gude, First VP
Brad Burris, Second VP
Tim Miller, Secretary/Treasurer
A fraternal organization of equipment manufacturers, ingredient suppliers and affiliated service providers that support the commercial baking industry through service, scholarship and industry participation. *$50.00*
Annual Dues Founded: 1920

8218 Aluminum Foil Container Manufacturers Association
10 Vecilla Lane
Hot Springs Village, AR 71909
501-922-7425
FAX: 501-922-0383
eddoyle@cox-internet.com
www.afcma.org

CB Richardson, Executive Secretary

Represents leading manufacturers of aluminum foil containers in the United States and Canada. The Association has worked to promote aluminum foil as a superior packaging material since the beginning.
13 Members Founded: 1955

8219 American Agricultural Economics Association
415 S Duff Avenue
Suite C
Ames, IA 50010-6600
515-233-3202
FAX: 575-233-3101
info@aaea.org www.aaea.org

Yvonne Bennett, Executive Director
Terri Haffner, Membership/Association Manager
Tami Kuhn, Communications Coordinator

The professional association for agricultural economists and related fields. *$150.00*

4M Members Regular Membership Fee Founded: 1910

8220 American Agricultural Law Association
American Agricultural Economics Association
2585 Bowmont Drive
PO Box 2025
Eugene, OR 97402-2025
541-021-1958
FAX: 541-302-1958
roberta@aglaw-assn.org
www.aglaw-assn.org

Robert Achenbach, Executive Director

Non-profit association devoted to education about agricultural law.
600 Members Founded: 1980

8221 American Agriculture Movement Inc.
24800 Sage Creek Road
Scenic, SD 57780-6706
605-993-6201
FAX: 605-993-6185
parity79@hotmail.com
www.aaminc.org

Larry Matlack, President
Arthur Chaney, Director
Wayne Allen, VP
Ed Fashing, Communications VP

An umbrella organization composed of state organizations representing family farm producers. *$100.00*
35 Members Membership Fee Founded: 1977

8222 American Angus Association
3201 Frederick Avenue
Saint Joseph, MO 64506
816-383-5100
FAX: 816-233-9703
angus@angus.org www.angus.org

Ben Eggers, President
John R Crouch, Executive VP
Jot Hartley, VP
Paul H Hill, Treasurer

Beef breed organization. Our goal is to serve the beef cattle industry, and increase the production of consistent, high quality beef that will better satisfy consumers throughout the world. *$80.00*
30+M Members Membership Fees Vary Founded: 1883

8223 American Association of Candy Technologist
175 Rock Road
Glen Rock, NJ 07452
201-652-2655
FAX: 201-652-3419
acctinfo@gomc.com
www.aactcandy.org

Bob Huzinec, President
Bill Dryer, First VP
Eric Schmoyer, Second VP
Patrick Hurley, Secretary

A premier professional group of individual technologists, operations personnel, educators, students, business staff and others dedicated to the advancement of the confectionery industry. *$60.00*
Membership Fee Founded: 1947

8224 American Association of Cereal Chemists
3340 Pilot Knob Road
Saint Paul, MN 55121-2097
651-454-7250
FAX: 651-454-0766
aacc@scisoc.org www.aaccnet.org

Rob J Hamer, President
George Lookhart, Chairperson
Elizabeth Knight, Treasurer
Steven Nelson, VP

An international organization of scientists and other professionals studying the chemistry of cereal grains and their products or working in related fields. *$128.00*
4000 Members Regular Membership Fee Founded: 1915

8225 American Association of Crop Insurers
One Massachusetts Avenue NW
Suite 800
Washington, DC 20001-1401
202-789-4100
FAX: 202-408-7763
aaci@mwmlaw.com
www.cropinsurers.com

Steve Harms, Chairman
Sam Scheef, Vice-Chairman
Michael McLeod, General Counsel/Executive Director
Kim Siebecker, Association Coordinator

Nonprofit, industry service organization representing the interests of insurance companies, agents, and adjusters involved in the Federal Crop Insurance Program.
15 Members Membership Fee

8226 American Association of Exporters and Importers
1050 17th Street NW
Suite 810
Washington, DC 20005
202-857-8009
FAX: 202-857-7843
hq@aaei.org www.aaei.org

Charlene Stocker, Chairman
Katie Terricciano, Vice Chair, Education/Confrences
Lori Goldberg, Vice Chair Membership/Communication
Tim Van Oost, Chair Elect
Tom Hughes, Secretary/Treasurer

Association advocating free trade among nations, with members consisting of firms engaged in international trade who interact with US customs and the FDA.
Membership Fees Vary Founded: 1921

8227 American Association of Grain Inspection and Weighing Agencies
1390 Channel Avenue
Po Box 13302
Memphis, TN 38113
901-942-3216
FAX: 901-774-9651
mphsgrain@aol.com www.aagiwa.org

Tom Dahl, President
Larry Kitchen, VP
Barry Hibbets, Director/Secretary/Treasurer

Established to provide a liaison between the Federal Grain Inspection Service and designated agencies.
50 Members Founded: 1964

8228 American Association of Meat Processors
One Meating Place
PO Box 269
Elizabethtown, PA 17022-0269
717-367-1168
FAX: 717-367-9096
aamp@aamp.com www.aamp.com

Mark P Schad, President
David A Sutton, First VP
Dwight Ely, Second VP
Philip E Berntha, Third VP
Stephen Krut, Executive Director

Membership consists of small to medium sized meat, poultry and food businesses including, slaughterers, processors, wholesalers, home food service businesses, deli and catering operators and suppliers to the industry. AAMP is affliated with 33 state, regional and provincial associations. *$100.00*
1700 Members Membership Fee Founded: 1939

8229 American Association of Nutritional Consultants
401 Kings Highway
Winona Lake, IN 46590
574-696-6165
FAX: 574-268-2120 888-828-2262
registrar@aanc.net www.aanc.net

Wendell Whitman, Owner

Promotes ethical standards in the field of nutrition consultants, and those who hold bachelor's degrees in the health related fields. *$60.00*
Annual Membership Fee

8230 American Bakers Association
1350 I Street NW
Suite 1290
Washington, DC 20005-3300
202-789-0300
FAX: 202-898-1164
info@americanbakers.org
www.americanbakers.org

Gary Prince, Chairman
Renato G Turano, First Vice-Chairman
Kenneth Klosterman Jr, Second Vice-Chairman
Albert Lepage, Treasurer
Paul Abenante, President

A long and dedicated history of representing the interests of the wholesale baking industry before the U.S. Congress, federal agencies, state legislatures and agencies, and international regulatory authorities.
300 Members Membership Dues Vary Founded: 1897

8231 American Beekeeping Federation
115 Morning Glory Circle
Po Box 1337
Jesup, GA 31546
912-427-4233
FAX: 912-427-8447
info@abfnet.org www.abfnet.org

Daniel Weaver, President
Zac Browning, VP
Troy Fore, Executive Director

A national association that makes a difference in the beekeeping industry. Members include honey producers, packers, suppliers and shippers of honey products. *$35.00*

1300 Members Membership Fees Vary Founded: 1943

8232 American Berkshire Association
1769 US 52 West
West Lafayette, IN 47996-2346
765-497-3618
FAX: 765-497-2959
berkshire@nationalswine.com
www.americanberkshire.com

Dr M Peter Hoffman, President
Amy Smith, Manager

The official national registry for the Berkshire breed of pigs.
300+ Members Founded: 1875

8233 American Beverage Licensees Association
5101 River Road
Suite 108
Bethesda, MD 20816-1560
301-656-1494
FAX: 301-656-7539
rogers@ablusa.org www.ablusa.org

Kevin O'Laughlin, President
Harry G Wiles, Executive Director
John Bodnovich, Communications/PR Coordinator

An association representing off-premise licensees in the open or license states and on-premise proprietors in markets across the nation. ABL was created after the merger of the National Association of Beverage Retailers (NABR) and the National Licensed Beverage Association (NLBA).
17000 Members Founded: 2002

8234 American Brahman Breeders Association
3003 S Loop West
Suite 140
Houston, TX 77054-1301
713-349-0854
FAX: 713-349-9795
abba@brahman.org
www.brahman.org

James C Chapman, President
Chris Shivers, Executive VP

The first beef breed developed in the US, has played an important role not only in crossbreeding programs throughout the US and beyond, but also has become a common thread connecting other American breeds developed in the last century.
Founded: 1924

8235 American Butter Institute
2101 Wilson Boulevard
Suite 400
Arlington, VA 22201
703-243-5630
FAX: 703-841-9328
AMiner@nmpf.org
www.butterinstitute.org

Jim Bleick, President
Rich Stammer, First VP
Deborah Van Dyke, Second VP
Anjua Miner, Membership Services Director

Represents manufacturers, handlers and brokers of butter and butter products. Originally established as the National Association of Creamery Manufacturers in 1908, ABI's mission is to promote and protect the interests and welfare of the industry.
31 Members Founded: 1908

8236 American Center for Wine, Food & the Arts
500 First Street
Napa, CA 94559
707-259-1600
FAX: 707-257-8601 888-512-6742
info@copia.org www.copia.org

Arthur Jacobus, President
Kurt Nystrom, COO
Larry Tsai, Chief Marketing Officer

A non-profit discovery center whose mission is to explore and celebrate the cultural significance of wine, food and the arts. *$ 60.00*
Membership Fees Vary

8237 American Cheese Society
304 West Liberty Street
Suite 201
Louisville, KY 40202
502-583-3783
FAX: 502-589-3602
acs@hqtrs.com
www.cheesesociety.org

Bill McKenna, Chairman
Cathy Strange, President
Allison R Hooper, VP
Mary Keehn, Secretary
Paula Lambert, Treasurer

The Society's membership includes farmstead, artisanal and specialty cheesemakers; academicians and enthusiasts; marketing and distribution specialists; food writers and cookbook authors and specialty foods retailers from the United States, Canada and Europe.
800 Members Founded: 1982

8238 American Correctional Food Service
4248 Park Glen Road
Minneapolis, MN 55416
952-928-4658
FAX: 952-929-1318
info@acfsa.org www.acfsa.org

Ellen L White, President
Richard C Wyckoff, VP
Ricky Clark, VP-Elect
Linda Shear, Secretary
Richard B Dansdill, Treasurer

A national non-profit organization dedicated to the professional growth of our nation's correctional foodservice employees. Association members are foodservice professionals employed in correctional facilities and agencies within federal, state and municipal prison/jail systems. Members are employed within government and commercially operated facilities within the United States, Canada and an expanding international market. *$50.00*
1300 Members Dues up to $150 Founded: 1969

8239 American Council on Science & Health
1995 Broadway
2nd Floor
New York, NY 10023
212-362-7044
FAX: 212-362-4919
acsh@acsh.org www.acsh.org

Elizabeth M Whelan, President
Jeff Stier, Associate Director
Gilbert Ross MD, Executive/Medical Director
Judy D'Agostino, Administrative Assistant

A nonprofit, consumer education organization concerned with issues related to food, nutrition, chemicals, pharmaceuticals, lifestyles, the environment and health. *$50.00*
350 Members Membership Fees Vary Founded: 1978

8240 American Culinary Federation
180 Center Place Way
St. Augustine, FL 32095
904-824-4468
FAX: 904-825-4758 800-624-9458
acf@acfchefs.net www.acfchefs.org

John Kinsella, President
Dawn Jantsch, Managing Director
Laura Howell, Communications Coordinator
Michael Baskette, Executive Director

A professional, not-for-profit organization for chefs and cooks. The principal goal of the founding chefs remains true to ACF today_to promote the professional image of American chefs worldwide through education among culinarians at all levels, from apprentices to the most accomplished certified master chefs.
19000 Members Founded: 1929 19,000 names $150 per M.

8241 American Dairy Association Diary Council Mid East
5950 Sharon Woods Boulevard
Columbus, OH 43229
614-890-1800
FAX: 614-890-1636 800-292-6455

Scott Higgins, President/CEO
Dave Arter, Operations VP
Mary Drennan, Administrative Assistant

We represent dairy farmers and serve as the local affiliate for the American Dairy Association and the National Dairy Council. We work closely with Dairy Management Inc. and the Milk Processors Education Program to extend national dairy promotion programs to the local level.
3800 Members

8242 American Dairy Council
219 SW Street
Suite 100
Syracuse, NY 13202-1287
315-472-9143
FAX: 315-472-0506

Richard Naczi, Director

This organization promotes milk and milk products.

8243 American Dairy Products Institute
116 N York Street
Elmhurst, IL 60126-1704
630-530-8700
FAX: 630-530-8707
info@adpi.org www.adpi.org

Jim Page, CEO
Beth Sutton, Member Communications Director

An association for manufactured dairy products. ADPI's main purpose is to effectively communicate the many positive attributes and benefits of our members' products. Additionally, we serve our membership by offering the most current industry information available and by collaborating with dairy associations to represent members' interests before state and federal regulatory agencies.

85 Members Founded: 1986

8244 **American Dairy Science Association**
1111 N Dunlap Avenue
Savoy, IL 61874-9604
217-565-5146
FAX: 217-398-4119 www.adsa.org

Steve Nickerson, Editor in Chief
Breda Carlson, Executive Director

Organization of professional researchers. Publishes journals and holds annual member meetings.

4000 Members Founded: 1896

8245 **American Dietetic Association**
120 S Riverside Plaza
Suite 2000
Chicago, IL 60606
312-990-0040
800-877-1600
media@eatright.org www.eatright.org

Ronald S Moen, CEO
Patricia M Babjak, Executive VP

This association is a promoter of optimal health and nutritional status of the population advancing the science of food and nutrition by offering food and nutrition referrals and information.

65000 Members Founded: 1917

8246 **American Egg Board**
1460 Renaissance Drive
Park Ridge, IL 60068
847-296-7043
FAX: 847-296-7007
aeb@aeb.org www.aeb.org

Louis Raffel, President
Joanne C Ivy, Industry Relations Sr. VP
Elisa Maloberti, Consumer Information Coordinator

U.S. egg producer's link to the consumer in communicating the value of the incredible egg. As the egg industry's promotion arm, AEB's foremost challenge is to convince the American public that the egg is still one of nature's most nearly perfect foods. AEB's basic task is to improve the demand for shell eggs, egg products, as well as spent fowl throughout the United States.

300 Members Founded: 1976

8247 **American Emu Association**
PO Box 2502
San Angelo, TX 76902
541-332-0675

info@aea-emu.org www.aea-emu.org

Charles Ramey, President
Martha Hendricks, VP
Marcia Huddleston, Secretary
Deitra McCleery, Treasurer

Trade association that develops and promotes programs and services to benefit the emu industry. *$100.00*

1,700 Members Membership Fee Founded: 1989

8248 **American Farm Bureau Federation**
600 Maryland Avenue SW
Suite 800
Washington, DC 20024
202-406-3600
FAX: 202-406-3602
mls@fb.org www.fb.com

Bob Stallman, President
Richard Newpher, Chief Administrative Officer
Don Lipton, Public Relations Director
Michael L Stanton, Member Services Coordinator

An independent, non-governmental, voluntary organization governed by and representing farm and ranch families united for the purpose of analyzing their problems and formulating action to achieve educational improvement, economic opportunity and social advancement and, thereby, to promote the national well-being.

3MM Members Founded: 1919

8249 **American Fisheries Society**
5410 Grosvenor Lane
Suite 110
Bethesda, MD 20814-2199
301-897-8616
FAX: 301-897-8096
main@fisheries.org www.fisheries.org

Chris Kohler, President
Jennifer Nielsen, President-Elect
Gus Rassam, Executive Director

Representing fisheries scientists. AFS promotes scientific research and enlightened management of resources for optimum use and enjoyment by the public. It also encourages a comprehensive education for fisheries scientists and continuing on-the-job training. *$76.00*

Membership Fee Founded: 1870

8250 **American Forage and Grassland Council**
350 Poplar Avenue
Elmhurst, IL 60126
630-941-3240
FAX: 630-359-4274 800-944-2342
info@afgc.org www.afgc.org

Bill Talley, President
Gary Pederson, Senior VP
Ray Smith, Secretary

Provides the following member services concerning federal and state legislation and regulation: information on industry developments; assistance in efficient operations; and cooperation on projects of mutual interest with other organizations. *$30.00*

3,000 Members Annual Dues

8251 **American Frozen Food Institute**
2000 Corporate Ridge
Suite 1000
McLean, VA 22102
703-821-0770
FAX: 703-821-1350
info@affi.com www.affi.com

Leslie G Sarasin, President/CEO

National trade association representing all aspects of the frozen food industry supply chain, from manufacturers to distributors to suppliers to packagers; the Institute is industry's voice on issues crucial to future growth and progress.

500 Members Annual Dues Vary Founded: 1942

8252 **American Guernsey Association**
7614 Slate Ridge Boulevard
Reynoldsburg, OH 43068
614-864-2409
FAX: 614-864-5614
info@usguernsey.com
www.usguernsey.com

Seth Johnson, Executive Secretary/Treasurer
Josey Morris, Programs Coordinator
Ida Albert, Records Director

Provides and promotes programs and services to enhance the value and profitability of the Guernsey breed for members, owners and the dairy industry worldwide. Registers and delivers Guernsey cattle throughout the US.

36 Members

8253 **American Herb Association**
PO Box 1673
Nevada City, CA 95959-1673
530-265-9552
FAX: 530-274-3140 www.ahaherb.com

Kathi Keville, Director
Robert Brucia, Co-Director
Marion Wyckoff, Secretary

An association of Medical Herbalists. Membership is open to anyone interested in herbs and includes the AHA Quarterly. The goals of the AHA are to promote the understanding, acceptance and ecological use of herbs. *$20.00*

Membership Fee Founded: 1981

8254 **American Herbal Products Association**
8484 Georgia Avenue
Suite 370
Silver Spring, MD 20910
301-881-1171
FAX: 301-588-1174
ahpa@ahpa.org www.ahpa.org

Michael McGuffin, President
Karen Robin, Communications Director
Devon Powell, Administration Director

The national trade association which represents manufacturers, importers and distributors of herbs and herbal products. AHPA seeks self-regulation, establishment of standards and rules of ethical conduct, member enrichment and public outreach. *$1000.00*

300 Members Membership Fees Vary Founded: 1983

8255 **American Hereford Association**
PO Box 014059
Kansas City, MO 64101
816-182-2250
FAX: 816-842-6931
aha@hereford.org www.hereford.org

Craig Huffhines, Executive VP
Joe Rickabaugh, Communications Director
Leslie Mathews, Treasurer

Association for people in the Hereford cattle industry.

8M Members

8256 **American Honey Producers Association**
3307 Sanger Creek Way
Waxahachie, TX 75165-0368
972-937-2002
FAX: 972-937-2002
pegbrady55@msn.com
www.americanhoneyproducers.org

Steve Park, President
Mark Brady, VP
Jerry Brown, Executive Secretary

Represents the interests of major US honey producers and pollinators. *$150.00*
700 Members Membership Fees Vary
Founded: 1969

8257 American Institute for Cancer Research
1759 R Street NW
Washington, DC 20009
202-328-7744
FAX: 202-328-7226 800-843-8114
aicrweb@aicr.org www.aicr.org
Marilyn Gentry, President
Kelly B Browning, Executive VP
A cancer charity that fosters research on diet and cancer prevention and educates the public about the results.
Founded: 1982

8258 American Institute of Baking
1213 Bakers Way
PO Box 3999
Manhattan, KS 66505-3999
785-537-4750
FAX: 785-537-1493 800-633-5137
info@aibonline.org
www.aibonline.org
James Munyon, President/CEO
Paul Klover, Administration VP
Brian Soddy, Marketing/Sales VP
This organization provides research, education, training and consulting for the baking and food industries worldwide.
900 Members Founded: 1919

8259 American Institute of Food Distribution
1 Broadway
Elmwood Park, NJ 07407
201-791-5570
FAX: 201-791-5222
food1@foodinstitute.com
www.foodinstitute.com
Mike Slattery, Chairman
Joe Crocker, Vice-Chairman
Donna George, Treasurer
Brian Todd, President
Serves as a central information service for food trades. Issues reports, studies and statistical data. Member companies throughout the US and over 40 foreign countries.
$725.00
2700 Members Annual Membership Fee
Founded: 1928

8260 American Institute of Wine & Food
304 W Liberty Street
Suite 201
Louisville, KY 40202
502-992-1022
FAX: 502-589-3602 800-274-2493
aiwf@hqtrs.com www.aiwf.org
Susan Walter, Chairman
Peter Ventura, Vice Chairman
The American Institute of Wine & Food is one of the few national organizations with the unique combination membership of dedicated wine and food enthusiasts and professionals. Wine and food enthusiasts get to meet and learn from reowned chefs, winemakers, authors, culinary historians, and food producers, while industry professionals have the opportunity to know and understand their core consumers *$75.00*
6000+ Members Memberships Vary
Founded: 1981

8261 American Jersey Cattle Association
6486 E Main Street
Reynoldsburg, OH 43068-2362
614-861-3636
FAX: 614-861-8040 www.usjersey.com
Donald Sherman, President
Neal Smith, Executive Secretary/CEO
The most profitable, adaptable and responsive dairy producers in the world.
Founded: 1868

8262 American Livestock Breeds Conservancy
PO Box 477
Pittsboro, NC 27312-0477
919-542-5704
FAX: 919-545-0022
albc@albc-usa.org www.albc-usa.org
Charles R Bassett, Executive Director
Don T Schrider, Communications Director
Marjorie Bender, Research/Technical Program Manager
Anneke Jakes, Office Manager
A clearinghouse for information on livestock and genetic diversity. The only organization in the U.S. working to conserve rare breeds and genetic diversity in livestock. *$30.00*
Membership Fee Founded: 1977

8263 American Logistics Association
1133 15th Street NW
Suite 640
Washington, DC 20005-2708
202-466-2520
FAX: 202-296-4419
membership@ala-national.org
www.ala-national.org
John Molino, President
Maurice Branch, Operations VP
Tracey Durand, Office Manager
Organization that represents the private industry to promote food sales to commissaries on military bases. *$828.00*
400 Members Membership Dues Vary
Founded: 1972

8264 American Meat Institute
1150 Connecticut Avenue NW
12th Floor
Washington, DC 20036
202-587-4200
FAX: 202-587-4300
memberservices@meatami.com
www.meatami.com
J Patrick Boyle, President/CEO
Robert Manly, Chairman
Dave Miniat, Treasurer
Rod Brenneman, Secretary
Works to improve operating methods and products, worker safety, legislation and education.
300 Members Membership Fees Vary
Founded: 1906

8265 American Meat Science Association
1111 N Dunlap Avenue
Savoy, IL 61874
217-356-5368
FAX: 217-398-4119
information@meatscience.org
www.meatscience.org
Dennis R Buege, President
Daniel S Hale, President-Elect
C Ann Hollingsworth, Secretary/Treasurer
Thomas Powell, Executive Director
A broad-reaching organization of individuals that develops and disseminates its collective food and animal science knowledge to provide meat science education and professional development. *$145.00*
Membership Dues Founded: 1964

8266 American Mushroom Institute
One Massachusetts Avenue NW
Suite 800
Washington, DC 20001
202-842-4344
FAX: 202-408-7763
ami@mwmlaw.com
www.americanmushroom.org
Donna Silvestri Fecondo, Chairman
Laura Phelps, President
Peter Gray, Vice-Chair/Treasurer
This organization is comprised of mushroom growers, associate businesses and suppliers who represent growers and coordinate industry research.
Founded: 1955

8267 American Oil Chemists' Society
2211 W Bradley Avenue
PO Box 3489
Champaign, IL 61821-1827
217-359-2344
FAX: 217-351-8091
general@aocs.org www.aocs.org
Jean Willis, Executive VP
Gloria Cook, Finance/Operations VP
Greg Reed, Manager
Largest international society focused on the science and technology of fats, oils, lipids and related substances. *$10.00*
5400 Members Membership Dues Vary
Founded: 1909 6000 names

8268 American Ostrich Association
PO Box 166
Ranger, TX 76470
254-647-1645
FAX: 254-647-1645
aoa@ostriches.org www.ostriches.org
Carole A Price, President
Dianna Westmoreland, VP
Glinda Cunningham, Secretary/Treasurer
Organization that provides leadership for the ostrich industry and its future through the promotion of ostrich products. *$150.00*
Membership Fee Founded: 1988

8269 American Peanut Council
1500 King Street
Suite 301
Alexandria, VA 22314-2737
703-838-9500
FAX: 703-838-9508
peanutsusa@aol.com
www.peanutsusa.com
Patrick Archer, President
The council was formed through a merger of the National Peanut Council and the National Peanut Council of America. Serving as a forum for all segments of the peanut industry to discuss issues which impact the production, utilization and marketing of peanuts and peanut products worldwide.
Founded: 1997

8270 American Peanut Research and Education Society
Oklahoma State University
376 Ag Hall
Stillwater, OK 74078
405-372-3052
FAX: 405-624-6718
nickeli@provalue.net
www.apres.okstate.edu

Dr J Ronald Sholar, Executive Officer
Irene Nickels, Administrative Assistant

The purpose of the Society is to instruct and educate the public on the properties, production, and use of the peanut through the organization and promotion of public discussion groups, forums, lectures, and other programs or presentations to the interested public. *$80.00*

550 Members Organizational Fee: $100 Founded: 1968

8271 American Pomological Society
103 Tyson Building
University Park, PA 16802-4200
814-863-6163
FAX: 814-237-3407
aps@psu.edu
www.americanpomological.org

Ed Stover, President
Desmond Layne, VP
Kirk Pomper, Secretary
Robert Crassweller, Treasurer

The oldest fruit organization in North America, to foster the science and practice of fruit growing and variety development. *$ 40.00*

1000 Members Annual Membership Fee Founded: 1848

8272 American Poultry Association
5830 Sheits Rd
Cincinnati, OH 45252-2144
817-379-6475

slbrush@verizon.net
www.amerpoultryassn.com

Dave Anderson, President
Sam Brush, VP/Internet Contact
Ric Ashcraft, Secretary/Treasurer

The mission of the association is to promote and protect the standard bred poultry industry in all its phases. To encourage and protect poultry shows as being the show window of the industry, an education for both breeders and the public and a means of interesting young future breeders. *$25.00*

Annual Membership

8273 American Seafood Institute
25 Fairway Circle
Hope Valley, RI 02832
401-491-9017
FAX: 401-491-9024
www.americanseafood.org

8274 American Seed Trade Association
225 Reinekers Lane
Suite 650
Alexandria, VA 22314-2875
703-837-8140
FAX: 703-837-9365 www.amseed.com

Richard T Crowder, CEO
Sonny Beck, First VP

Producers of seeds for planting purposes. Consists of companies involved in seed production and distribution, plant breeding and related industries in North America.

850 Members Membership Fees Vary Founded: 1883

8275 American Sheep Industry Association
9785 Maroon Circle
Suite 360
Englewood, CO 80112
303-771-3500
FAX: 303-771-8200
info@sheepusa.org www.sheepusa.org

Paul Frischknecht, President
Peter Orwick, Executive Director
Judy Malone, Industry Information Director
Burdell Johnson, VP

A federation of state associations dedicated to the welfare and profitability of the sheep industry. *$25.00*

64000 Members Monthly Founded: 1865 Circulation: Mbrshp

8276 American Shrimp Processors Association
PO Box 50774
New Orleans, LA 70150
504-368-1571
FAX: 504-368-1573
chauvin@shrimpcom.com
www.americanshrimpprocessorsassociation.org

William Chauvin, Managing Director
Allene M Scoma, Coordinator

Represents shrimp processors, as well as promoting shrimp consumption.

56 Members Founded: 1960

8277 American Society for Enology and Viticulture
PO Box 1855
Davis, CA 95617-1855
530-753-3142
FAX: 530-753-3318
society@asev.org www.asev.org

Dr. Robert Wample, President
Patricia Howe, First VP
Lyndie Boulton, Executive Director

A non-profit, scientific organization dedicated to the interests of enologists, viticulturists, and others in the fields of wine and grape research and production throughout the world. Our membership includes professionals from wineries, vineyards, academic institutions and organizations.

2400 Members Membership Fees Founded: 1950

8278 American Society for Horticultural Science
113 S West Street
Suite 200
Alexandria, VA 22314-2851
703-836-4606
FAX: 703-836-2024
mwneff@ashs.org www.ashs.org

Frederick S Davies, Chair
William R Woodson, President
Michael W Neff, Executive Director

A cornerstone of research and education in horticulture and an agenet for active promotion of horticultural science.

Membership Fees Vary Founded: 1903

8279 American Society of Agricultural Consultants
950 S Cherry Street
Suite 508
Denver, CO 80246-2664
303-583-3513
FAX: 303-758-0190
asac@agri-associations.org
www.agconsultants.org

Fred Hepler, President
Sam Bartee, President-Elect
Richard Edmounds, VP/Secretary
Hope Evans, Membership Coordinator

An association representing the full range of agricultural consultants which serves as an information, resource, and networking base for its members. *$350.00*

181 Members Membership Dues Founded: 1963

8280 American Society of Agronomy
677 S Segoe Road
Madison, WI 53711
608-273-8080
FAX: 608-273-2021
headquarters@agronomy.org
www.agronomy.org

David A Sleper, President
Jerry L Hatfield, President-Elect
Ellen Bergfeld, Executive VP

Supports educators and scientists interested in the impacts of environmental perturbations on the biological and physical sciences.

11000 Members Founded: 1907

8281 American Society of Animal Science
1111 N Dunlap Avenue
Savoy, IL 61874
217-356-9050
FAX: 217-398-4119
meghanwr@assochq.org www.asas.org

Dr David Buchanan, President
Dr Maynard Hogberg, President-Elect
Jerome Baker, CEO
Christina Tomlinson, Executive Secretary

A professional organization for animal scientists designed to help members provide effective leadership through research, extension, teaching and service for the dynamic and rapidly changing livestock and meat industries.

Founded: 1908

8282 American Society of Baking
27 E Napa Street, Suite G
PO Box 1853
Somoma, CA 95476
707-935-0103
FAX: 707-935-0174
asbe@asbe.org www.asbe.org

Thomas J Kuk, President
Tammi Matthias, Membership Coordinator

Formerly known as the American Society of Bakery Engineers, a professional society comprised of members in either engaged in, involved with, or interested in wholesale or large scale bakery production. The purpose is to promoted the advancement of baking science technology through the exchange of information and interaction among baking industry professionals. *$135.00*

2900 Members Membership Fee Founded: 1924

8283 American Society of Brewing Chemists
3340 Pilot Knob Road
St. Paul, MN 55121-2097
651-454-7250
FAX: 651-454-0766 800-328-7560
asbc@scisoc.org www.asbcnet.org

Steven C Nelson, Executive Officer
Amy Hope, Operations VP
Susan Kohn, Membership/Communications Director

Improve and bring uniformity to the brewing industry on a technical level. ASBC can provide you with; analytical, scientific process control methods to ensure high quality and safety standards, problem solving, scientific support and professional development opportunities. *$ 233.00*

750+ Members Membership Fee Founded: 1934

8284 American Society of Farm Managers
950 S Cherry Street
Suite 508
Denver, CO 80246
303-758-3513
FAX: 303-758-0190
hevans@asfmra.org www.asfmra.org

Brian Stockman, Executive VP
Cheryl Cooley, PR/Communications Manager
Hope Evans, Membership Coordinator

Founded by a group of dedicated farmers whose basic objective is to create and maintain a professionally trained group of farm managers, rural appraisers, review appraisers and accredited agricultural consultants capable of providing expert guidance and assistance to farmland owners, farmers and other groups which have caretaking responsibilities for farm lands and rural properties. *$175.00*

Membership Fees Vary Founded: 1929

8285 American Soybean Association
12125 Woodcrest Executive Drive
Suite 100
Saint Louis, MO 63141-5009
314-576-1770
FAX: 314-576-2786 800-688-7692
sderscheid@soy.org
www.soygrowers.com

Neal Bredehoeft, Chairman
Bob Metz, President
Richard Ostlie, First VP
Steve Censky, Chief Executive Officer
Sue Derschied, Membership Director

A primary focus of the American Soybean Association is policy development and implementation and to improve US soybean farmer profitability. *$110.00*

27000 Members Membership Fees Vary Founded: 1920

8286 American Spice Trade Association
2025 M Street NW
Suite 800
Washington, DC 20036
202-367-1127
FAX: 202-367-2127
info@astaspice.org
www.astaspice.org

Lou Sanna, President
Dan Cooper, VP/Secretary
Cheryl Deem, Manager

Protects the interests and welfare of the spice industry; also sponsors chili cookoff competitions.

Membership Dues Vary Founded: 1907

8287 American Sugar Alliance
2111 Wilson Boulevard
Suite 600
Arlington, VA 22201
703-351-5055
FAX: 703-351-6698
info@sugaralliance.org
www.sugaralliance.org

Vickie Myers, Executive Director
Phillip Hayes, Media Relations Director
Kendra Lockhart, Project Coordinator
Jack Roney, Manager

A national coalition of cane, beet and corn farmers, processors, suppliers, workers and others dedicated to preserving a strong domestic sweetener industry.

Membership Fee Founded: 1983

8288 American Sugar Beet Growers Association
1156 15th Street NW
Suite 101
Washington, DC 20005-1704
202-833-2398
FAX: 202-833-2962
info@americansugarbeet.org
www.americansugarbeet.org

Luther Markwart, Executive VP
Ruthann Geib, VP
James Creek, Executive Assistant
Pam Alther, Office/Financial Manager

The purpose of the organization is to unite sugarbeet growers in the United States and promote the common interest of state and regional beet grower associations, which include legislative and international representation and public relations.

10000 Members

8289 American Veal Association
1500 Fulling Mill Road
Middletown, PA 17057-3116
717-859-9125
FAX: 717-546-0055
info@vealfarm.com
www.vealfarm.com

Dick Dennis, President
Paul Slayton, Executive Director

Provides information on veal production practices, industry facts, a tour of a modern veal barn and educational materials.

1300 Members Founded: 1984

8290 American Wholesale Marketers Association
2750 Prosperity Avenue
Suite 530
Fairfax, VA 22031
703-208-3358
FAX: 703-573-5738 800-482-2962
info@awmanet.org www.awmanet.org

Scott Ramminger, President/CEO
Robert Pignato, VP Mktg/Membership/Affairs
Jennifer Moulton, Administration/Information Director
Anne Holloway, Director Government Affairs

An organization supporting the confectionery, tobacco and allied products industries through programs and services. Members include wholesale distributors, manufacturers and others allied to the industry.

800 Members Membership Dues Founded: 1942

8291 American Wine Society
PO Box 3330
Durham, NC 27702
919-403-2002
FAX: 919-403-0392
dautlick@americanwinesociety.org
www.americanwinesociety.com

Janice Cobett, President
Albert L Guber Jr, VP
Tania Dautlick, Executive Director

A non-profit, educational, consumer-oriented organization for those interested in learning more about all aspects of wine. *$52.00*

5000 Members Membership Dues Vary Founded: 1967 3000 names

8292 Animal Agriculture Alliance
PO Box 9522
Arlington, VA 22209-2403
703-562-5160
FAX: 703-524-1921
info@animalagalliance.org
animalagalliance.org

Kay N Johnson, VP

Supports and promotes animal agriculture practices that provide for farm animal well being through sound science and public education. Its goal is to bring truthful, science based information to consumers so the role of animal agriculture in improving consumers' quality of life is better understood and appreciated.

Membership/Donation Founded: 1987

8293 Apple Processors Association
1100 17th Street NW
10th Floor
Washington, DC 20036
202-856-6715
FAX: 202-331-4212
pweller@agriwashington.org
www.appleprocessors.org

Kenneth Guise, Chairman
Paul S Weller Jr, President
Tim Proctor, Secretary/Treasurer

Organization consisting of processors and suppliers which provides a forum for discussion regarding legislation, regulations and new technology.

25 Members Founded: 1987

8294 Apple Products Research & Education Council
5775 Peachtree-Dunwoody Road
Building G, Suite 500
Atlanta, GA 30342-1542
404-252-3663
FAX: 404-252-0774
info@appleproducts.org
www.appleproducts.org

Sue Taylor, Communications Director

Formerly known as The Processed Apples Institute. We are producers of processed apple products; suppliers of equipment, packaging or ingredients to the industry and brokers and concentrate manufacturers.

80 Members Founded: 1951

8295 Associated Corporation for Citrus Growers
495 E Summerlin Street
Bartow, FL 33830-4732
863-533-4114
FAX: 863-534-1758
svickers@barpr.com

Ernie Ness, Editor

Association for citrus grower organizations and other trade associations within the industry.

8296 Association for Dressings and Sauces
1100 Johnson Ferry Road
Suite 300
Atlanta, GA 30342
404-252-3663
FAX: 404-252-0774
ads@kellencompany.com
www.dressings-sauces.org

Pam Chumley, President
Jeannie Milewski, Executive Director
Jacque Knight, Membership/Administration Manager
Jana Wright, Communications Specialist

This association is comprised of manufacturers of mayonnaise, salad dressings and condiment sauces, as well as industry suppliers. *$1168.00*
184 Members Membership Dues Vary
Founded: 1926

8297 Association of American Feed Control
Purdue University
Office of the Indiana State Chemist
175 S University Street
West Lafayette, IN 47907-2063
765-944-4600
FAX: 765-494-4331 www.aafco.org
Judy Thompson, President
Eric Nelson, President-Elect
Rodney J Noel, Secretary/Treasurer
Officials of government agencies at the state and federal levels engaged in the regulation and distribution of products, animal feeds and livestock remedies.
54 Members Founded: 1909

8298 Association of American Seed Control Officials
Utah Department of Agriculture and Food
350 N Redwood Road
PO Box 146500
Salt Lake City, UT 84116-3087
801-965-4574
www.seedcontrol.org
Mary Smith, President
Joe Garvey, First VP
David Buckingam, Second VP
An organization of seed regulatory officials from the United States and Canada. The members meet annually to discuss mutual concerns of seed law enforcement, to be updated on new developments in the seed industry, and to update the Recommended Uniform State Seed Law (RUSSL) which the organization developed and maintains as a model law for states and federal programs.
Founded: 1949

8299 Association of Food Industries
3301 Route 66
Building C, Suite 205
Neptune, NJ 07753
732-922-3008
FAX: 732-922-3590
info@afius.org www.afius.org
Howard Schreiber, Chairman
Barbara Harloe, First Vice-Chairman
Dee Bartlett, Second Vice-Chairman
Robert Bauer, President
Vincent Arguimbau, Secretary
Promotes free trade and commerce in the food industry. Offers information and education on customs and usage of trade in the food markets and represents member interests in government. *$1040.00*
800 Members Membership Dues Vary
Founded: 1906

8300 Association of Food and Drug Officials
2550 Kingston Road
Suite 311
York, PA 17402
717-757-2888
FAX: 717-755-8089
afdo@afdo.org www.afdo.org
Marion Aller, President
Charlene Bruce, President-Elect
Denise Rooney, Executive Director
Promotes the enforcement of laws and regulations at all levels of government. Fosters understanding and cooperation between industry and regulators. Develops model laws and regulations and seeks their adoption.
800 Members Membership Dues Vary
Founded: 1896

8301 Association of Sale Marketing Companies
1010 Wisconsin Avenue NW
Suite 900
Washington, DC 20007
202-337-9351
FAX: 202-337-4508
info@asmc.org www.asmc.org
Mark Baum, President/CEO
Karen Connell, Contact
Provides referral service and other methods of assistance in locating sales and marketing companies.
250 Members Founded: 1995

8302 Association of Seafood Importers
Empress International
10 Harbor Park Drive
Port Washington, NY 11050
516-621-5900
FAX: 516-621-8318 800-645-6244
Membership is comprised of seafood importers focusing on problems facing the industry.

8303 Association of Smoked Fish Processors
85 John Road
Canton, MA 02021
781-821-2200
FAX: 781-821-9266 800-444-8705
gerald.kelly@shusterlabs.com
www.shusterlabs.com
Gerry Kelly, Account Manager
This association provides technical consulation and services to the smoked fish and seafood industry. Services include recall manuals, plant audits, product evaluations, process evaluation, process evaluation, microbiological testing, analytical testing. HACCP plan development and plan ventilation.

8304 At-Sea Processors Association
4039 21st Avenue West
Suite 400
Seattle, WA 98199-1252
206-285-5139
FAX: 206-285-1841
apa@atsea.org www.atsea.org
Trevor McCabe, Executive Director
James L Gilmore, Public Affairs Director
Represents U.S. flag catcher/processor vessels that participate in the healthy and abundant groundfish fisheries of the Bering Sea/Aleutian Islands management areas and in the west coast Pacific whiting fishery. *$500.00*
7 Members Membership Max. $2,000
Founded: 1985

8305 BEMA: Baking Industry Suppliers Association
7101 College Boulevard
Suite 1505
Overland Park, KS 66210
913-338-1300
FAX: 913-338-1327
info@bema.org www.bema.org
Kerwin Brown, President/CEO
Michael Gude, Chairman
Non-profit trade association representing leading bakery and food equipment manufacturers and suppliers, whose combined efforts in research and development have led to the continual improvement of the baking and food industries. *$1250.00*
Annual Membership Dues Founded: 1918

8306 Baking Industry Sanitation Standards Committee
PO Box 3999
Manhattan, KS 66505-3999
785-537-4750
FAX: 785-565-6060
bissc@bissc.org www.bissc.org
Jon Anderson, Executive Director/Secretary
Sigismondo De Tora, Chairman
Develops and promotes sanitation standards for the design and construction of bakery equipment. Offers self certification and third party certification programs for the member companies whose equipment conforms to the BISSC standards. *$350.00*
125 Members Annual/Regristration Fee
Founded: 1949

8307 Beef Industry Council
National Cattlemen's Beef Association
444 N Michigan Avenue
Suite 1700B
Chicago, IL 60611
312-467-5520
FAX: 312-670-9414
Members are beef producers and live stock farmers.

8308 Beer Institute
Beer Institute
122 C Street NW
Suite 350
Washington, DC 20001-2109
202-737-2337
FAX: 202-737-7004 800-379-2739
info@beerinstitute.org
www.beerinstitute.org
Jeff Becker, President
Art DeCelle, Executive VP/General Council
The national trade association for the brewing industry. Representing both big and small brewers as well as importers and industry suppliers.
Founded: 1986

8309 Beet Sugar Development Foundation
800 Grant Street
Suite 300
Denver, CO 80203-2987
303-832-4460
FAX: 303-832-4468
Tom@bsdf-assbt.org
www.bsdf-assbt.org
Robert W Strickland, President
Victor J Jaro, First VP
Jeffrey L Carlson, Second VP
Thomas K Schwartz, Executive VP
Association specializing in beet sugar research and the advertisement of seed companies. *$100.00*
13 Members Membership Fee/Max. $450

8310 Biodynamic Farming & Gardening Association
PO Box 29135
San Francisco, CA 94129-0135

FAX: 415-561-7796 888-516-7797
biodynamic@aol.com
www.biodynamics.com
Charles Beedy, Contact

Supporting biodynamic growers and processors in North America and acts to safeguard and promote the biodynamic method of agriculture. *$45.00*

6 per year
Circulation: 1000+

8311 Biscuit & Cracker Manufacturers Association
6325 Woodside Court
Suite 125
Columbia, MD 21046-5619
443-545-1645
FAX: 410-290-8585
ssullivan@thebcma.org
www.thebcma.org

Francis Rooney, President
Stacey Sharpless, Marketing Director

B&CMA has sought to serve the interests of the biscuit and cracker industry through combined membership efforts. This includes working in the areas of education and government, encouraging pooled resources. B&CMA is the leading cookie and cracker baking association, providing important advantages for members and significant contributions to this multibillion dollar industry.
250 Members Founded: 2001

8312 Blue Diamond Growers
1802 C Street
PO Box 17068
Sacramento, CA 95814
916-442-0771
FAX: 916-446-8461
feedback@bdgrowers.com
www.bluediamondgrowers.com

Douglas Youngdahl, Chief Executive Officer

8313 Board of Trade of Wholesale Seafood Merchants
7 Dey Street
Room 801
New York, NY 10007-3201
212-732-4340
FAX: 212-732-6644

Albert Altesmao, Executive Secretary

Credit exchange and collection agency for wholesale seafood merchants and producers, in the US and Canada.
Founded: 1930

8314 Bread Bakers Guild of America
3203 Maryland Avenue
North Versailles, PA 15137
412-823-2080
FAX: 412-823-2495
info@bbga.org www.bbga.org

Gina Renee Piccolino, Director Activities Membership

1300 Members Founded: 1993
Mailing list available for rent 1000 names

8315 Brewers Association
736 Pearl Street
Boulder, CO 80302
303-447-0816
FAX: 303-447-2825 888-822-6273
info@brewersassociation.org
www.brewersassociation.org

Charlie Papazian, President
Bob Pease, VP
Cindy Jones, Sales/Marketing Director

A merger of the Association of Brewers and the Brewers Association of America became Brewers Association. The goal is to unify the combined 88-year history of service and to promote and protect the U.S. craft brewing community's interests.
11000 Members Founded: 1978

8316 Brewers' Association of America
736 Pearl Street
Boulder, CO 80302-3814
303-447-0816
FAX: 303-447-2825

Henry King, Editor/Author

Brewers Association members receive regular updates on industry growth, including fact sheets and state-by-state and province-by-province brewery lists.
150 Members Founded: 1941

8317 Brown Swiss Cattle Breeders' Association
800 Pleasant Street
Beloit, WI 53511
608-365-4474
FAX: 608-365-5577
info@brownswissusa.com
www.brownswissusa.com

Adam Barbee, Editor
David Kendall, Manager

8318 Calorie Control Council
5775 Peachtree Dunwoody Road
Atlanta, GA 30342
404-252-3663
FAX: 404-252-0774
ccc@kellencompany.com
www.caloriecontrol.org

Lyn Nabors, VP
Beth Hubrich, VP
John Foreyt, Director Nutrition

60 Members Founded: 1966

8319 Can Manufacturers Institute
1730 Rhode Island Avenue NW
Washington, DC 20036-2212
202-232-4677
FAX: 202-232-5756
clee@cancentral.com
www.cancentral.com

Robert Budway, President

Serves can manufacturers and can industry suppliers
35 Members Founded: 1939

8320 Canned Vegetable Council
PO Box 5258
Madison, WI 53705-0258
608-231-2250
FAX: 608-231-6952
gene@cannedveggies.org
www.cannedveggies.org

Gene Kroupa, Executive Director

An educational and promotional organization of vegetable canners whose goals are to raise the awareness of consumer and food service buyers regarding canned vegetables.
80 Members Founded: 1977

8321 Cape Cod Cranberry Growers Association
266 Main Street
Wareham, MA 02571
508-295-4132
FAX: 508-759-6294
info@cranberries.com
www.cranberries.org

8322 Catfish Farmers of America
1100 Highway 82 E
Suite 202
Indianola, MS 38751-2330
662-887-2699
FAX: 662-887-6857
hmmcall1@jam.rr.com
www.catfishjournal.com

Hugh Warren, Executive VP

2000 Members Founded: 1986

8323 Center for Food Safety & Applied Nutrition
5100 Paint Branch Parkway
College Park, MD 20740-3835
301-995-5996

laurence.dusold@fda.hhs.gov
www.cfsan.fda.gov

Frances Korbly-Canter, Owner

8324 Cheese Importers Association of America
488 Madison Avenue
New York, NY 10022
212-356-6020
FAX: 212-688-2870
150 Members Founded: 1942

8325 Cherry Marketing Institute
PO Box 30285
Lansing, MI 48909-7785
517-731-1636
FAX: 517-669-3354
www.usacherries.com

Fred Tubbs, Chairman
Robert Underwood, Vice Chairman
Philip J Korson, President
David Hackert, Chairman/Sweet Cherry Member
Deborah Cherry, Manager

Association representing the cherry industry. Provides promotional material to food service operators, brokers, retailers and manufacturers.
Founded: 1988

8326 Chocolate Manufacturers Association
8320 Old Courthouse Road
Suite 300
Vienna, VA 22182
703-790-5011
FAX: 703-790-5752
keranss@fleishman.com
www.chocolateusa.org

Lynn Bragg, President
Susan Snyder-Smith, Public Relations Sr. VP
Stacey Kerans, Media Relations Director

The trade group for manufacturers and distributors of cocoa and chocolate products in the United States. The association was founded to fund and administer research, promote chocolate to the general public and serve as an advocate of the industry before Congress and government agencies.
9 Members Founded: 1923

8327 Club Managers Association of America
1733 King Street
Alexandria, VA 22314
703-739-9500
FAX: 703-739-0124
cmaa@cmaa.org www.cmaa.org

James B Singerling, CEO
Gordon Welch, Senior VP
Kathi Driggs, Senior VP

8328 Coca-Cola Bottlers Association
3290 N Side Park Way
Suite 300
Atlanta, GA 30327
404-489-9798
FAX: 404-872-2869

Michael Coco, President
Thomas Haynes, Executive Director

8329 Coffee, Sugar and Cocoa Exchange
New York Board of Trade
1 N End Avenue
New York, NY 10282-1101
212-748-4000
FAX: 212-748-4039 www.csce.com
Acts as a financial exchange where futures and options are traded, the CSCE provides hedging and investing, opportunities in the coffee, sugar, cocoa and dairy markets.

8330 Colombia Coffee Federation
140 E 57th Street
New York, NY 10022
212-421-8300
FAX: 212-758-3816
judyb@juynvald.com

John Boden, Manager

Founded: 1964

8331 Commercial Food Equipment Service
2211 W Meadowview Road
Suite 20
Greensboro, NC 27407
336-346-4700
FAX: 336-346-4745
info@cfesa.com www.cfesa.com

Roger Kauffman, President
Tina Reese, First VP
Jean Choquette, Second VP
Todd Maxwell, Treasurer
Carla Strickland, Executive Director

Sponsors audiovisual technical training programs, surveys and maintains library.
450 Members Founded: 1963

8332 Commercial Refrigerator Manufacturers Association
Commercial Refrigerator Manufacturer Division
4100 North Fairfax Drive
Arlington, VA 22203
703-524-8800
FAX: 703-524-9011
crm@ari.org www.ari.org/crm

William G Sutton, President
Robert Wilkin, Chairman

Provides information, instruction, education to members in technical and business areas; also specializes in solving common problems and stimulating growth within the industry.

8333 Communicating for Agriculture
112 E Lincoln Avenue
Fergus Falls, MN 56537
218-739-3241
FAX: 218-739-3832 caep@cainc.org

Patty Strickland, Board Secretary
Milton Smebsrud, President

Strives to promote health, well-being and advancement of people in agriculture and agribusiness.
40M Members Founded: 1972

8334 Composite Can and Tube Institute
50 S Pickett Street
Suite 110
Alexandria, VA 22304-7206
703-823-7234
FAX: 703-823-7237
ccti@cctiwdc.org www.cctiwdc.org

Kristine Garland, Executive Vice President
Wayne Vance, Association Counsel
Jack Sanders, Treasurer
Lloyd Anderson, VP

Serving the composite cans and tube industry.

8335 Concord Grape Association
112 North Portage Street
PO Box 399
Westfield, NY 14787-1542
716-326-3161

info@concordgrape.org
www.concordgrape.com

Pam Chumley, Executive Director
Linda Whitley, Contact

The Concord Grape Association represents processors of Concord grapes and manufacturers of products derived from them. The organization operates as the Concord Grape Section under the umbrella of the Juice Products Association (JPA), which represents the juice and juice products industry in the U.S. and overseas. Members handle more than the majority of the Concord grapes processed annually in the United States.

8336 Consultants Association for the Natural Products Industry (CANI)
PO Box 689
Clovis, CA 93613-0689
559-325-7192
FAX: 559-325-7195
info@caniconsultants.com
www.cani-consultants.com

Karena K Dillon, President

Committed to working individually and collectively, to enhance the growth and integrity of the natural products industry by providing professional expertise and objective counsel to our clients. These specialized services contribute to the prosperity and values of the individual business as well as the industry as a whole.

8337 Contract Manufacturing and Packaging
1601 North Bond Street
Naperville, IL 60563
630-544-5053
FAX: 630-544-5055
info@contractpackaging.org
www.contractpackaging.org

William Pflaum, Executive Director/President

National trade association handling outsourced production projects on a contract basis.
100 Members Founded: 1992

8338 Cookware Manufacturers Association
PO Box 531335
Mountain Brook, AL 35253-1335
205-823-3448
FAX: 205-823-3449
hrushing@usit.net www.cookware.org

Steve Fraser, President
Scott Mayer, VP
Hugh J Rushing, Executive VP

Represents manufactures of cookware and bakeware in the US and Canada. Publishes consumer guides to cookware and engineering standards for industry.
21 Members Founded: 1922

8339 Corn Refiners Association
1701 Pennsylvania Avenue
Suite 950
Washington, DC 22203
202-331-1634
FAX: 202-331-2054
details@corn.org www.corn.org

Audrae Erickson, President/Managing Director
Jennifer Snyder, Senior Director Regulatory Affairs
Bob Adams, Director Public Affairs
Pat Saks, Assistant Director

Supports carbohydrate research programs through grants to colleges, government laboratories and private research centers.
8 Members Founded: 1913

8340 Council for Agricultural Science
4420 W Lincoln Way
Ames, IA 50014-3447
515-292-2125
FAX: 515-292-4512
cast@cast-science.org
www.cast-science.org

Teresa A Gruber, Executive VP
Dale M Maronek, President
Martin A Massengale, Treasurer

Identifies food, fiber, environmental and other agricultural issues for all stake holders.
2500 Members Founded: 1972

8341 Council for Biotechnology Information
PO Box 34380
Washington, DC 20043-0380
202-467-6565
FAX: 202-467-5777
cbi@whybiotech.com
www.whybiotech.com

Linda Thrane, Executive Director

8342 Council for Responsible Nutrition
1828 L Street NW
Suite 900
Washington, DC 20036-5114
202-776-7929
FAX: 202-204-7980
webmaster@crnusa.com
www.crnusa.org

Annette Dickinson, President
John Hathcock, VP International Affairs
Verna Breland, Director Administration
Elly Flippen, Controller/Director Finance
Mike Greene, Director Government Relations

Dietary supplement association for manufacturers and suppliers.
115 Members Founded: 1973

8343 Council of Food Processors Association
1401 New York Avenue NW
Washington, DC 20005-2124
202-328-9451
FAX: 202-639-5932

8344 Council of Supply Chain Management Professionals
333 East Butterfield Road
Suite 140
Lombard, IL 60148
630-574-0985
FAX: 630-574-0989
cscmpadmin@cscmp.org
www.cscmp.org

Rick Blasgen, President
Sue Paulson, Executive Assistant
James Schulze, Director Operations

CSCMP's mission is to lead the evolving supply chain management profession by developing, advancing, and disseminating supply chain knowledge and research.
10000 Members Founded: 1963

8345 Council on Hotel and Restaurant Industries
2810 N Parham Road
Suite 230
Richmond, VA 23294
804-346-4800
FAX: 804-346-5009
info@chrie.org www.chrie.org

Kathy McCarty, Executive VP/CEO
Michael Zema, President
Cynthia Mayo, Secretary
Arun Upneja, Treasurer

Enhances professionalism at all levels of the hospitality and tourism industry through education and training.
1400 Members Founded: 1946

8346 Council on Packaging in the Environment
1255 23rd Street NW
Suite 850
Washington, DC 20037-1152
202-331-0099
FAX: 202-833-3636
info@incpen.org www.incpen.org

Steve Young, President

Serving the soft drink bottlers industry.

8347 Cranberry Institute
3203-B Cranberry Highway
East Wareham, MA 02538
508-954-4132
FAX: 508-759-6294 800-295-4132
cinews@earthlink.net
www.cranberryinstitute.org

Jere D Downing, Executive Director
Bill Cutts, Chairman
Jeff Kapell, Vice Chairman

A nonprofit organization founded to further the success of US and Canadian cranberry growers through health, agricultural and environmental stewardship research as well as cranberry promotion and education.

8348 Crop Insurance Research Bureau
9200 Indian Creek Parkway
Suite 220
Overland Park, KS 66210-2008
913-338-0470
FAX: 913-661-1640
denicec@cropinsurance.org
www.cropinsurance.org

Paul L Horel, President
W Kurt Henke, Legal Counsel
Jane Shey, Federal Affairs Representative

National trade association made up of insurance providers and related organizations that provide a variety of insurance products for our nation's farmers.
Founded: 1964

8349 Crop Life America
1156 15th St NW
Suite 400
Washington, DC 20005
202-296-1585
FAX: 202-463-0474
webmaster@croplifeamerica.org
www.croplifeamerica.org

Jay Vroom, President
Rich Nolan, VP

A trade association of manufacturers and distributors of agriculture crop protection and pest control products.
74 Members Founded: 1933

8350 Crop Science Society of America
677 S Segoe Road
Madison, WI 53711
608-738-8086
FAX: 608-273-2021
headquarters@crops.org
www.crops.org

Steven L Fales, President
Henry L Shands, President-Elect
Ellen Berfeld, Executive VP

An educational and scientific organization comprised of memebers who advance the discipline of crop science by acquiring and disseminating information about crops in relation to seed genetics and lant breeding; crop physiology; crop production, quality and ecology; crop germplasm resources; and environmentality.
4700 Members Founded: 1955

8351 Culinary Institute of America
1946 Campus Drive
Hyde Park, NY 12538
845-529-9600
FAX: 845-452-8692
marketing@culinary.edu
www.ciachef.edu
Private, nonprofit college dedicated to providing the world's best professional culinary education.
Founded: 1946

8352 D/FW Grocers Association
1720 S Edmonds Lane
Suite 29
Lewisville, TX 75067-5863
972-353-5885
FAX: 972-353-5886 valeries@flash.net

Valerie A Schenewerk, Executive Director
200 Members Founded: 1906

8353 Dairy Farmers of America
10220 N Ambassador Drive
Kansas City, MO 64153
816-016-6455
FAX: 816-801-6456 888-332-6455
webmail@dfamilk.com
www.dfamilk.com

Harold Papen, Corporate VP Human Resources
Gary E Hanman, President/CEO
Donald H Schriver, Executive VP

Supports dairy farms and production of cheese, milk, butter and dehydrated products
Founded: 1998

8354 Dairy and Nutrition Council
9360 Castlegate Drive
Indianapolis, IN 46256
317-842-3060
FAX: 317-842-3065
hardin@mpsiinc.com
www.indianadairycouncil.org

Don Gurtner, President
Paul Mills, VP
Sue Brames, Manager

8355 Diamond Walnut Growers
1050 S Diamond Street
Stockton, CA 95201-1727
209-467-6000
FAX: 209-467-6788
wfoster@dcpubs.com
www.diamondnuts.com

Michael Mendes, President/CEO
John J Gilbert, Chairman
Jeff J Colombini, Director
Gary E Hester, Director
1900 Members Founded: 1912

8356 Distilled Spirits Council of the United States
1250 I Street NW
Suite 400
Washington, DC 20005
202-628-3544
FAX: 202-628-8888
tibig@americaneagle.com
www.discus.org

Peter H Cressy, President/CEO
Frank Coleman, Sr VP/Govt Relations
Lynne J Omlie, Sr.VP/General Counsel/Corp Secy

Serves as a public information source, represents producers and marketers of liquor.
32 Members Founded: 1973

8357 Distillers Grains Technology Council
University of Louisville
Lutz Hall Room 435
Louisville, KY 40292
502-525-5442
FAX: 502-852-1577
distillergrains@louisville.edu
www.distillersgrains.org

Charles Staff, President

Members are beverage and fuel ethenal distillers.
7 Members Founded: 1945

8358 Dr. Pepper Bottlers Association
PO Box 906
Rowlett, TX 75030
972-475-7397
FAX: 972-717-9031

Bob Berssong, Secretary

Represents 430 bottlers for the Dr. Pepper Company.

8359 Drug, Chemical & Associated Technologies Association
1 Washington Boulevard
Suite 7
Robbinsville, NJ 08691
609-448-1000
FAX: 609-448-1944
info@dcat.org www.dcat.org

Patrick Vazquez, President
Lynda M Doyle, Senior VP
Margaret Timony, Executive Director

Members include more than 350 companies, in the US and abroad, who manufacture, distribute or provide services to the chemical, pharmaceutical, nutritional and related industries. Services, programs and activities are designed to support business development objectives. These programs and events provide opportunities for member representatives to make important contacts, learn new industry information, dialogue with counterparts in other companies and build relationships with customers.

Founded: 1890

8360 Eastern Dairy Perishable Products
411 Route 17 S
Hasbrouck Heights, NJ 07604
201-288-5454
FAX: 201-288-5422
eppa@eppainc.org www.eppainc.org
Lorraine Hoytne, Executive Director
Robert F Policano, President
This association encourages growth and education regarding perishable products. It promotes the sales of perishable products through supermarkets and specialty stores and acts as a resource and information center for the industry.
350 Members Founded: 1971

8361 Eastern Dairy, Deli, Bakery Association
411 Route 17 S
Hasbrouck Heights, NJ 07604
201-288-5454
FAX: 201-288-5422
Members include retailers, brokers, manufacturers and distributors of dairy, deli, seafood, meat, and bakery products located in the New York metropolitan area.

8362 Eastern Frosted Foods Association
17 Park Street
Wanaque, NJ 07465
973-835-1710
FAX: 973-835-1708
mryan@bellatlantic.net
Mike Ryan, Executive Director
Ron Kamin, President
This organization is comprised of manufacturers, distributors, refrigerated warehouses and retailers in the frozen food market.
65 Members Founded: 1930

8363 Eastern Milk Producers Cooperative
PO Box 6966
Syracuse, NY 13217-6966

FAX: 315-437-1225
Communicates to members of the association dairy issues, farm issues, association events and policy.

8364 Eastern Perishable Products Association
Route 411 S
Hasbrouck Heights, NJ 07604
201-288-5454
FAX: 201-288-5422
eppa@eppainc.org www.eppainc.org
Lorraine Hoyt, Executive Director
John Ruane, President
Robert F Policano, Executive VP
Steve Migliara, Administrative VP
Stan Futoron, Operations VP

8365 Energy Foodservice Council
115 1st Street
Clayton, NC 27520
919-553-5800
FAX: 919-553-2499
khatch@mindspring.com
www.foodservicecouncil.org

8366 Enteral Nutrition Council
5775 Peachtree Dunwoody Road NE
Atlanta, GA 30342-1556
770-531-7060
FAX: 404-252-0774
Encourages communication between marketers and manufacturers of enteral nutrition products, especially research and new development.
7 Members Founded: 1983

8367 Entomological Society of America
10001 Derekwood Lane
Suite 100
Lanham, MD 20706-4876
301-731-4535
FAX: 301-731-4538
esa@entsoc.org www.entsoc.org
Paula G Lettice, Executive Director
Chris Stelzig, Director Membership
Judy Miller, Director Meetings
Alan Kahan, Director Communications
Serves the professional and scientific needs of entomologists and people in related disciplines.
6000 Members Founded: 1889

8368 FEWA
PO Box 1347
Iowa City, IA 52244
319-354-5156
FAX: 319-354-5157
info@fewa.org www.fewa.org
Pat Collins, Executive VP
Chris Ford, President
International trade association of wholesale/distributors of agricultural equipment and related products.
190 Members Founded: 1945

8369 Farm Equipment Manufacturers Association
1000 Executive Parkway
Suite 100
Saint Louis, MO 63141-6369
314-878-2304
FAX: 314-878-1742
info@farmequip.org
www.farmequip.org
Robert K Schnell, Executive VP
Vernon F Schmidt, VP Operations
Hannah Hamontree, Membership Services
Sarah Stevener, Special Programs
An information gathering and distributing organization for farm equipment manufacturers and suppliers.
340 Members

8370 Farmer Direct Foods
511 Commercial
PO Box 326
Atchison, KS 66002
913-367-4422
FAX: 913-367-4443 800-370-4422
info@farmerdirectfoods.com
www.farmerdirectfoods.com
Kent Symns, President
125 Members Founded: 1988

8371 Fertilizer Institute
Union Center Plaza, 820 1st Street NE
Suite 430
Washington, DC 20002
202-623-3956
FAX: 202-962-0577
information@tfi.org www.tfi.org
Kraig R Naasz, President
Kathy Mathers, VP
Harry L Vroomen, VP
Pamela D Guffain, Director
Members include brokers, producers, importers, dealers and manufacturers of fertilizer and fertilizer-related equipment.
325 Members Founded: 1970

8372 Flavor & Extract Manufacturers Association
1620 I Street NW
Suite 925
Washington, DC 20006
202-293-5800
FAX: 202-463-8998
kjones@therobertsgroup.net
www.femaflavor.org
Glenn Roberts, President
Locates suppliers and manufacturers of rare chemicals and oils used in the flavor and fragrance industry.
75 Members Founded: 1969

8373 Flexible Packaging Association
971 Corporate Boulevard
Linthicum, MD 21090
410-694-0800
FAX: 410-694-0900
fpa@flexpack.org www.flexpack.org
Marla Donahue, President
Ram Singhal, Director Regulatory & Gov't Affairs
Bob Zaborowski, Director Economic Research

8374 Food & Nutrition Service
3101 Park Center Drive
Room 926
Alexandria, VA 22302
703-305-2286
FAX: 703-305-2312
webmaster@tns.usda.gov
www.fns.usda.gov
Steven Christensen, Director
Kathie Klass, Deputy Director
Alberta Frost, Staff Office Director
Rich Lucas, Assistant to the Director
Don Arnette, Deputy Administrator
Agency that administers federal programs including School Lunch, Food Stamps, WIC and the Child/Adult Care Food Program.
Founded: 1969

8375 Food Allergy & Anaphylaxis Network
11781 Lee Jackson Highway
Suite 160
Fairfax, VA 22033-3309
703-913-3179
FAX: 703-691-2713
faan@foodallergy.org
www.foodallergy.org
Anne Munoz-Furlong, President
The only nonprofit organization in the United States devoted soely to patient education for food allergies. Mission is to create public awareness about food allergies and anaphylaxis, to provide education, and to advance research on behalf of all those affected by food allergy. *$30.00*

26000 Members 6 per year Founded: 1991

8376 Food Distribution Research Society

Silesia Companies
PO Box 441110
Fort Washington, MD 20749
301-292-1970
FAX: 301-292-1787
james.7@osu.edu fdrs.ag.utk.edu

Dr Randy James, President
R Wes Harrison, VP Education
James Ahern, VP Programs
Roger Hinson, VP Communications
Delmy Salin, VP-Research

Food distribution research society encourages research, serves as an information clearinghouse and encourages implementation of research. The Society organizes conferences and meetings for industry, academic and government leaders within the food industry sector.
Founded: 1967

8377 Food Distributors International
201 Park Washington Court
Falls Church, VA 22046
703-532-9400
FAX: 703-538-4673
mallen@ifdaonline.org
www.ifdaonline.org

Mark Allen, President
Steve Potter, VP

Trade association comprised of food distribution companies that supply and service independent grocers and food service operations throughout the US, Canada and 19 other countries.
Founded: 2003

8378 Food Export USA
150 S Independence Mall West
Suite 1036, Public Ledger Building
Philadelphia, PA 19106
215-829-9111
FAX: 215-829-9777
info@foodexportusa.org
www.foodexportusa.org

Tim F Hamilton, Executive Director
Daleen D Richmond, Deputy Director

A non-profit organization that promotes the export of food and agricultural products from the northeast region of the United States. The organization has been helping exporters of northeast food and agricultural products sell their products overseas since it was first organized.
Founded: 1973

8379 Food Industry Association Executives
PO Box 2510
Flemington, NJ 08822
908-782-7833
FAX: 908-782-6907
bmcconnell@fiae.net www.fiae.net

Barbara McConnell, President
Linda Gobler, Chairman
Jim Hopper, Vice Chairman
Nancy Christensen, Secretary/Treasurer
Matt Echols, Director State Government Relations

125 Members Founded: 1927

8380 Food Industry Suppliers Association
1207 Sunset Drive
Greensboro, NC 27408
336-274-6311
FAX: 336-691-1839
stella@fisanet.org www.fisanet.org

Stella Jones, Executive Director
Jeffrey Hennessey, President
Hank Brink, VP

Members are distributors and suppliers to the food processing industry.
245 Members Founded: 1968

8381 Food Information Service Center
21050 SW 93rd Lane Road
Dunnellon, FL 34431
352-489-8919
FAX: 352-489-8919 800-443-5820

James Allen Mixon, Owner

Founded: 1985

8382 Food Institute
One Broadway
Elmwood Park, NJ 07407
201-791-5570
FAX: 201-791-5222
www.foodinstitute.com
The institute is depended upon by industry professionals. Serves the food industry in many aspects.
Founded: 1928

8383 Food Marketing Institute
655 15th Street NW
Washington, DC 20005
202-220-0600
FAX: 202-220-0884
fmi@fmi.org www.fmi.org

Tim Hammomds, President/CEO
Beth Watt, Director Membership

Infomation about retail and wholesale firms in the food retailing and food wholesaling industries that use computer technology.
2600 Members Founded: 1977

8384 Food Processing Suppliers Association
1451 Dolley Madison Blvd
Ste 200
McLean, VA 22101-3847
703-761-2600
FAX: 703-761-4334 800-331-8816
info@fpmamail.com
www.foodprocessingmachinery.com

George Melnykovich, President
Nancy Janssen, Executive Director
Sacha Carey, Executive Director/Membership Serv

Trade association for food and beverage processing suppliers.
350 Members Founded: 1885

8385 Food Processors Institute
1350 I Street NW
Suite 300
Washington, DC 20005
202-393-0890
FAX: 202-639-5932 800-355-0983
fpi@nfpa-food.org www.fpi-food.org

Lisa Weddig, Executive Director

Founded: 1973

8386 Food Products Association
1350 1 Street NW
Suite 300
Washington, DC 20005
202-639-5900
FAX: 202-639-5932 800-355-0983
nfpa@nfpa-food.org
www.fpa-food.org

Cal Dooley, President/CEO
Bradley J Taylor, Executive Director
Timothy Willard, Communications VP
Carla Mitchell, Human Resources Senior Director

A principal scientific and technical trade association representing the food products industry. With two laboratory centers in Washington, DC, and Seattle, WA, FPA is the industry's leading authority on food science and food safety.
400 Members Membership Dues Founded: 1907

8387 Food Safety Consortium
110 Agriculture Building
University of Arkansas
Fayetteville, AR 72701
479-575-5647
FAX: 479-575-7531
fsc@cavern.uark.edu
www.fsconsortium.net

Dave Edmark, Communications Manager

Food safety research alliance of University of Arkansas, Iowa State University and Kansas State University.
Founded: 1988

8388 Food Service Distributors
201 Park Washington Court
Falls Church, VA 22046-4521
703-532-9400
FAX: 703-538-4673
mallen@ifdaonline.org
www.ifdaonline.org

Mark Allen, President/CEO
Stan Barret, Membership Director
David French, Senior VP
Steve Potter, Senior VP
Chris Caldwell, Director Communications

An association of wholesale grocers and food service distributors providing research, assistance and educational services for all aspects of the grocery industry.
135 Members Founded: 2003

8389 Food and Dairy Research Association
214 Homer Street
Box 608
Commerce, GA 30529-1861
706-335-9703
FAX: 706-335-9704

Ann Green, President

8390 Foodservice & Packaging Institute
150 S Washington Street
Suite 204
Falls Church, VA 22046
703-538-2800
FAX: 703-538-2187
fpi@fpi.org www.fpi.org

John R Burke, President
Lynn Rosseth, Market Development Director
Elizabeth T Phillips, Director Member Services

A national association comprised of manufacturers and suppliers of single-use foodservice packaging products.
25 Members Founded: 1933

8391 Foodservice Consultants Society
304 West Liberty Street
Suite 201
Louisville, KY 40202
502-583-3783
FAX: 502-589-3602
info@fcsi.org www.fcsi.org

Albert Dacosta, President
Kenneth W Winch, Secretary/Treasurer
Greg Hobby, Executive VP
Gerhard Kuehnel, Director

This organization offers a professional exchange of ideas between consultants working in the food service industry.
300 Members

8392 Foodservice Equipment Distributors
2250 Point Blvd
Ste 200
Elgin, IL 60123-7887
224-293-6500
FAX: 224-293-6505 800-677-9605
feda@feda.com www.feda.com
Rick Ellingson, President
Bruce Gulbas, VP
Jim Hanson, Treasurer
Kimberley Gill-Rimsza, Secretary
Raymond Herrick, Executive Director
Dealers and distributors of food service equipment and supplies.
300 Members Founded: 1933

8393 Foodservice Group, Inc (The)
630 Village Trace, Building 15
Suite A
Marietta, GA 30067
770-989-0049
FAX: 770-956-7498
info@fsgroup.com www.fsgroup.com
Kenneth W Reynolds, Executive Director
This organization is comprised of food service brokerage companies meeting the needs and offering a national exchange of ideas and information of food service sales professionals.
42 Members Founded: 1978

8394 Foodservice Marketplace
Machalek Communications
603 W Travelers Trail
Burnsville, MN 55337
952-736-8000
FAX: 952-736-0234 800-846-5520
info@machalek.com
www.foodservicecards.com
Andrea McChalek, President/CEO
Tammy Earley, VP/Sales/Marketing
Meghan Largley, Marketing Coordinator
25 Members Founded: 1987

8395 Foodservice Sales & Marketing Association
C/O:Grocery Manufacturers Association
2401 Pennsylvania Avenue
2nd Floor
Washington, DC 20037
202-379-9400

info@fsmaonline.com
www.fsmaonline.com
Andy Wilson, Chair
Rick Abraham, Executive Director
Specializes in selling food and related products to retail companies.

Mailing list available for rent

8396 Fresh Produce Association of the Americas
30 N Hudgins Street
PO Box 848
Nogales, AZ 85628
520-287-2707
FAX: 520-287-2948
info@fpaota.org www.fpaota.org
Chuck Ciruli, Chairman
William Sykes, Vice Chairman
Rod Sbragia, Director
Alicia Bon Martin, Director
Lee Frankel, President
Represents more than 125 member companies involved in growing, harvesting, marketing and importing of Mexican produce entering the US at Nogales, Arizona.
125 Members Founded: 1962

8397 Fresh Produce and Floral Council
16700 Valley View Ave
Ste 130
La Mirada, CA 90638-5844
714-739-0177
FAX: 714-739-0226
fpfc@aol.com www.fpfc.org
Linda Stine, President
Emily Marlphanskul, VP
Pauleen Yoshikane, Director Operations
Promotes through communication and education, fresh fruit, vegetable and floral products. Acts as a trade organization providing an environment for better communication within the industry.
500 Members Founded: 1965

8398 Fresh-Cut Produce Association
1600 Duke Street
Suite 440
Alexandria, VA 22314-3400
703-299-6282
FAX: 703-299-6288
info@fresh-cuts.org
www.fresh-cuts.org
Ken Silveira, Chairman
Bob Whitaker, Vice Chairman
Jarry Welcome, President
Founded: 1987

8399 Frozen & Refrigerated Association of the Northeast
38 Mill Street
Arlington, MA 02476-4700
781-641-4669
FAX: 781-641-3379
ffane@ffane.org www.ffane.org
Harold Lombardi, Executive Director
Promotes the frozen food industry.
135 Members Founded: 1955

8400 Frozen Potato Products Institute
2000 Corporate Ridge
Suite 1000
McLean, VA 22102-7844
703-821-0770
FAX: 703-821-1350
info@affi.com
www.affi.com/www.healthyfood.org
Leslie G Sarasin, President/CEO
Robert L Garfield, Senior VP Public Policy
This organization is made up of processors of frozen potato products.

8401 Future Food
220 Bay Street
4th Floor
Toronto, ON M5J 2
416-955-0375
FAX: 416-955-0380
rebeccan@marcusevans.com
www.marcusevans.com
European events and publications for food industry.

8402 Ginseng Board of Wisconsin
555 N 72nd Ave
2
Wausau, WI 54401-9038
715-845-7300
FAX: 715-845-8006
ginseng@ginsengboard.com
www.ginsengboard.com
Joe Heil, President/Contact
Testing of ginseng's active ingredients.

8403 Glass Packaging Institute
515 King Street
Suite 420
Alexandria, VA 22314
703-684-6359
FAX: 703-684-6048
jcattaneo@gpi.org www.gpi.org
Joseph J Cattaneo, President
Kerrin McKillop, Director Member Services
Serves the glass container suppliers for the beer, juice, tea, liquor, wine and dairy businesses.
Founded: 1945

8404 Glutamate Association: US
PO Box 14266
Washington, DC 20044-1426
202-637-6800
FAX: 202-637-5910 www.msgfacts.com
Marting J Hahn, Executive Director
Members are manufacturers, distributors and processed food users of glutamate, glutamate acid and its salts in the food industry.

12 Members Founded: 1977

8405 Grocery Manufacturers Association

2401 Pennsylvania Avenue NW
2nd Floor
Washington, DC 20037
202-337-9400
FAX: 202-337-4508
info@gmabrands.com
www.gmabrands.com
C Manly Molpus, President/CEO
Richard H Lenny, Chairman
Stephanie Childs, Communications Director
Troy Beeler, Membership Development Manager
Advances the interests of the food, beverage and consumer products industry on key issues that affect the ability of brand manufacturers to market their products profitably and deliver superior value to the consumer.
43 Members Membership Dues Vary
Founded: 1908

8406 Hand in Hand Foundation
200 Helen Court
Santa Cruz, CA 95065
831-476-1866
FAX: 717-567-9997
fredbarnes@handinhandfoundation.com
www.handinhandfoundation.com
Fred Barnes, Director
Not for profit that solicits food and donations for the needy.
Founded: 1971

8407 Hazelnut Council
Harborside Financial Center, Plaza V
25th Floor, Suite 2500
Jersey City, NJ 07311
201-633-8686
FAX: 201-633-8687
hazelnutcouncil@hazelnutcouncil.org
www.hazelnutcouncil.org

Greg Eckhardt, Contact
David Tourville, Marketing Director

The Hazenut Council represents the world's leading hazelnut producers, importers and distributors. The Council is made up of the Oregon Hazelnut Marketing Board, the Black Sea and Istanbul Exporters Unions and the Association of Food Industries.

8408 Healthy Water Association
PO Box 1417
Patterson, CA 95363
408-897-3023
FAX: 408-897-3028
magnesum@ix.netcom.com
www.mgwater.com

Paul Mason, President

Serves the bottled water industry.

8409 Herb Growing and Marketing Network
PO Box 245
Silver Spring, PA 17575-0245

FAX: 717-393-9261
herbworld@aol.com
www.herbnet.com, www.herbworld.com
$48.00

8410 Herb Research Foundation
4140 15th Street
Boulder, CO 80304
303-449-2265
FAX: 303-449-7849
rmccaleb@herbs.org www.herbs.org

Rob McCaleb, President
Maureen DeCoursey, Director Sustainable Development

Provides scientific based and traditional information about use and safety of herbs for health. Fee based hotline, information packs and literature are available to all.
Founded: 1983

8411 Herb Society of America
9019 Kirtland Chardon Road
Kirtland, OH 44094
440-256-0514
FAX: 440-256-0541
herbs@herbsociety.org
www.herbsociety.org

Wendy Daugherty, Executive Administrator
Michele Meyers, Director Education
Robin Siktberg, Editor/Horticulturist

This association maintains herb gardens, establishes gardens for the blind, and provides a speaker's bureau for people located in the herb industry.
Founded: 1933

8412 Home Baking Association
10841 S Crossroads Drive
Suite 105
Parker, CO 80135
303-840-8787
FAX: 303-840-6877
hbadavis@wamego.net
www.homebaking.org

8413 Home Wine and Beer Trade Association
PO Box 1373
Valrico, FL 33595-1373
813-685-4261
FAX: 813-681-5625
dee@hubta.org www.hwbta.org

Dee Roberson, Executive Director

Manufacturers, wholesalers, retailers, authors and editors having a commercial interest in the beer and wine trade. Offers publications to members only.
200+ Members Founded: 1976

8414 Hospitality Link
866 SE 14th Terrace
Suite 128
Deerfield Beach, FL 33441
954-579-1802
FAX: 954-421-1046
info@hospitalitylink.com
www.hospitalitylink.com
Provides consulting for food technology.

8415 Hydroponic Society of America
PO Box 1183
El Cerrito, CA 94530
510-232-2323
FAX: 510-232-2384
hydrolist@hydroponics.org
hsa.hydroponics.org

Gene Brisbon, Executive Director

Promotes the development of hydroponics.

8416 Independent Bakers Association
PO Box 3731
Washington, DC 20007
202-333-8190
FAX: 202-337-3809
independentbaker@yahoo.com
www.mindspring.com/independentbaker

Nicholas Pyle, President
Alexis Fobes, Administration
Rachel Retrum, Press Relations

Mostly family owned wholesale bakeries and allied industry trades. Established to protect the interests of independent wholesale bakers from antitrust and anti-competitive mergers and acquisitions; pressure Congress to support market oriented farm commodity programs; seek representation to consider federal labor, tax and environmental law. *$475.00*
400 Members Membership Dues Vary
Founded: 1968

8417 Institute of Food Science and Engineering
1500 Research Parkway
Suite A220
College Station, TX 77840
979-862-2036
FAX: 979-458-3405
ifse@tamu.edu ifse.tamu.edu

Dr Mark McLellan, Director
Dr Suresh Pillai, Assistant Director Research
Dr Andy Vestal, Assistant Director Outreach

8418 Institute of Food Technologists
525 W Van Buren Street
Suite 1000
Chicago, IL 60607
312-782-8424
FAX: 312-416-7921
info@ift.org www.ift.org

Barbara Byrd Keenan, Executive VP
Tekla Syers, VP Membership Experiences
Stan V Butler, Director Meetings/Expositions

Serves all management levels of firms engaged in research, promotion, production, processing, packaging, distribution, preparation and utilization of foods as well as university, government, and independent laboratories and consulting firms providing services to the foods industry.
21000 Members Founded: 1939

8419 Institute of Food and Agricultural Sciences
University of Florida
Building 116 Annex, Mowry Road
PO Box 110810
Gainesville, FL 32611-0811
352-392-5930
FAX: 358-392-7902
ace@mail.ifas.ufl.edu
www.aceweb.org

Melanie Mercer, Program Assistant
Ashley M Wood, Communications Director
Mary Anne Gularte, Human Resources Director

A federal-state-county partnership throughout Florida, dedicated to improving your life by developing and providing knowledge in agriculture, natural resources, and life sciences.
Founded: 1906

8420 Institute of Packaging Professionals
1601 N Bond Street
Suite 101
Naperville, IL 60563
630-544-5050
FAX: 630-544-5005 800-432-4085
elandon@iopp.org www.iopp.org

Edwin Landon, Executive Director
Patrick Farrey, General Manager
Stan Zelesnik, Director Education
Robert DePauw, Finance Manager
Kelly Staley, Member Services Manager

Information regarding the packaging industry internationally.

8421 Institute of Shortening & Edible Oils
1750 New York Avenue NW
Suite 120
Washington, DC 20006
202-783-7960
FAX: 202-393-1367
info@iseo.org www.iseo.org

Robert M Reeves, President

21 Members Founded: 1936

8422 International Association for Color

1620 I Street NW
Suite 925
Washington, DC 20006
202-293-5800
FAX: 202-463-8998
info@iacmcolor.org
www.iacmcolor.org

Glenn Roberts, Owner

Members are makers of certified colors for food, drugs and cosmetics.

8423 International Association for Food Protection
6200 Aurora Avenue
Suite 200W
Des Moines, IA 50322-2864
515-276-3344
FAX: 515-276-8655 800-369-6337
info@foodprotection.org
www.foodprotection.org

Kathy Glass, President
Jeffrey Farber, VP
David Tharp, Executive Director
Frank Yiannas, Secretary

A nonprofit association of food protection professionals. The association is dedicated to the education and service of its members, specifically, as well as industry personnel.
3000 Members Founded: 1911

8424 International Association of Culinary Professionals
304 W Liberty Street
Suite 201
Louisville, KY 40202
502-877-7953
FAX: 502-589-3602 800-928-4227
iacp@hqtrs.com www.iacp.com

Martha Johnson, President
Sarah Labensky, VP
William K Wallace, Secretary/Treasurer
Trina Gribbins, Manager

A not-for-profit organization whose members represent virtually every profession in the culinary universe: teachers, cooking school owners, caterers, writers, chefs, media cooking personalities, editors, publishers, food stylists, food photographers, restauranteurs, leaders of major food corporations and vintners. Literally a who's who of the food world.
4000 Members Founded: 1978

8425 International Association of Food Industrial Services
1451 Dolly Madison Boulevard
McLean, VA 22101-3850
703-761-2600
FAX: 703-761-4334
info@iafis.org www.iafis.org

Stephen C Schlegel, President/CEO
Annette Damey, Director Clinical Services
Andrew Drennan, Director/Business Development
Robyn Roche, VP/Finance & Admin
Jan Rogers, Manager/Membership

Members are manufacturers and distributors of dairy and food industry machinery, equipment, ingredients and supplies.
500+ Members Founded: 1912

8426 International Association of Ice Cream
1900 Arch Street
Philadelphia, PA 19103
215-564-3484
FAX: 215-564-2175
iaicv@fernley.com www.iaicv.org

Allan Barish, President
Nick Nikbakht, VP
Joshua L Waldorf, Executive Director

Members are manufacturers and distributors of ice cream novelties and street vendors.
122 Members Founded: 1969

8427 International Association of Milk Control Agencies
Department of Agriculture
Division of Dairy Industry Services
Albany, NY 12235-0001
518-457-3880
FAX: 518-485-5816

Lyle Newcomb, Secretary/Treasurer
Charles Huff, Manager

26 Members Founded: 1935

8428 International Association of Operative Millers
5001 College Boulevard
Suite 104
Leawood, KS 66211-1618
913-338-3377
FAX: 913-338-3553
info@iaom.info www.aomillers.org

Steve Curran, President
Gary A Anderson, Executive VP
Keith Horton

An international organization, comprised of flour millers, cereal grain and seed processors and allied trades representatives and companies devoted to the advancement of technology in the flour milling, cereal grain processing industries.
1500 Members Founded: 1896

8429 International Association of Refrigerated Warehousing
1500 King Street
Suite 201
Alexandria, VA 22314
703-373-4300
FAX: 703-373-4301
email@iarw.org www.iarw.org

J William Hudson, President/CEO
Benjamin Milk, VP/Secretary
Lorien Onderdonk, Members/Communications Coordinator
Susan Shores, Administration Director

Trade association of public refrigerated warehouse storing of all types of perishable products.
900 Members Membership Dues Vary Founded: 1891

8430 International Banana Association
727 N Washington Street
Alexandria, VA 22314
703-836-5499
FAX: 703-836-2049

8431 International Beverage Dispensing Association
4145 Amos Avenue
Baltimore, MD 21215
410-764-0616
FAX: 410-764-6799
ibdea@cornerstoneassoc.com
www.ibdea.org

Marvin Howard, Executive Director

Serves independent purveyors of equipment, service and products for the food and beverage industry.
250+ Members Founded: 1971

8432 International Bottled Water Association
1700 Diagonal Road
Suite 650
Alexandria, VA 22314
703-683-5213
FAX: 703-683-4074
ibwainfo@bottledwater.org
www.bottledwater.org

Joseph K Doss, President
Stephen Kay, VP Communications
Max Busetti, Manager Publications
Susan Frate, Director Conventions
Jerry Hayes, Director Government Relations

8433 International Dairy Equipment Associates
44 S Broad Street
Nazareth, PA 18064
610-759-1228
FAX: 610-759-3195 ideainc1@aol.com

Barry Morris, Sales Contact
Aida Negron, Sales Contact

Processing equipment; batch control systems, butter processing equipment, centrifuges, fillers, heat exchangers, plate, homogenizers, ice cream equipment, ice equipment, ice builders, margarine processing equipment.

8434 International Dairy Foods Association
1250 H Street NW
Suite 900
Washington, DC 20005
202-737-4332
FAX: 202-331-7820
membership@idfa.org www.idfa.org

Lou Gentine, Chair
Geoff Covert, Vice Chair
Paul Kruse, Secretary/Treasurer
Constance Tipton, President

IDFA's members— over 500 companies— represent approximately 83 percent of all dairy foods processed in the US, as well as the industry's leading supplier companies.
300 Members Founded: 1990

8435 International Dairy-Deli-Bakery Association
PO Box 5528
Madison, WI 53705-0528
608-310-5000
FAX: 608-238-6330 www.iddbanet.org

Carol Christison, Executive Director

IDDBA members meet the challenges of today's business world by exchanging information and ideas, participating in educational programs and networking.
Founded: 1964

8436 International Food Additives Council
5775 Peachtree Dunwoody Road
Building G, Suite 500
Atlanta, GA 30342
404-252-3663
FAX: 404-252-0774
jrogers@kellencompany.com

8437 International Food Information Council
1100 Connecticut Avenue NW
Suite 430
Washington, DC 20036
202-296-6540
FAX: 202-296-6547
foodinfo@ific.org www.ific.org

Nick Alexander, Senior Director Media Relations
Jennifer Schleman, Associate Director Media Relations
Sylvia Rowe, President

Mission is to communicate science-based information on food safety and nutrition to health and nutrition professionals, educators, government officals, journalists and others providing information to consumers.

Primarily supported by the broad-based food, beverage and agricultural industries.
33 Members Founded: 1985

8438 **International Food Processors Association**
200 Daingerfield Road
Suite 100
Alexandria, VA 22314-2884
703-299-5001
FAX: 703-299-5100

8439 **International Food Service Brokers Association**
2100 Reston Parkway
Suite 400
Reston, VA 20191-1240
703-758-7790
FAX: 703-758-7787
info@asmc.org www.asmc.org
About 1,300 broker members and 150 associate members and their subsidiaries.
265 Members Founded: 1956

8440 **International Food Service Editorial Executives**
PO Box 491
Hyde Park, NY 12538-491
845-229-6973
FAX: 845-229-6993
ifec@aol.com www.ifec-is-us.com
Carol Allly, Executive Director
Gail Bellamy, Secretary
Suzanne Finne, Treasurer
An association comprised of food service journalists and public relations executives representing food service companies.
265 Members Founded: 1956

8441 **International Food Service Executives**
2609 Surfwood Drive
Las Vegas, NV 89128
702-838-8821
FAX: 702-838-8853
hq@ifsea.com www.ifsea.com
Larry Brown, Chairman
Robin Keys, Treasurer
Ed Manley, President
Provides education and community service to the food service industry.
3000 Members Founded: 1901

8442 **International Food Service Manufacturers**
180 N Stetson Avenue
Suite 4400
Chicago, IL 60601
312-540-4400
FAX: 312-540-4401
ifma@ifmaworld.com
www.ifmaworld.com
Dave Pfanzelter, Chairman
Allan Lutz, First Vice Chairman
William Lovette, Treasurer
Michael Licata, President
Cathy Clark, Communications Coordinator
Trade association for food, beverage, equipment and supply manufacturers and ancillary service companies serving the food service industry.
650 Members Founded: 1952

8443 **International Foodservice Distributors Association**
201 Park Washington Court
Falls Church, VA 22046-4521
703-532-9400
FAX: 703-538-4673
sbarrett@ifdaonline.org
www.ifdaonline.org
Mark Allen, President/CEO
Stan Barrett, Director Membership
Advocates the interests of the foodservice distribution community and industry affairs through research, education and communication. Represents distrubutors throughout the US and internationally. Members include broadline and specialty foodservice distributors that supply food and related products to restaurants, institutions and other food away from home operations.
135 Members Founded: 2003

8444 **International Fresh-Cut Produce Association**
1600 Duke Street
Suite 440
Alexandria, VA 22314-3400
703-996-6282
FAX: 703-299-6288
jwelcome@fresh-cuts.org
www.fresh-cuts.org
Jerry Welcome, President
Mark Miller, Secretary/Treasurer
Ken Silveira, Chairman
Bob Whitaker, Vice Chairman
Advances the fresh-cut produce industry by supporting members with technical information, representation and knowledge to provide convenient, safe and wholesome food. Members are processor companies, suppliers and researchers.
600 Members Founded: 1987

8445 **International Frozen Food Association**
2000 Corporate Ridge
Suite 1000
McLean, VA 22102-7844
703-821-0770
FAX: 703-821-1350
info@affi.com
www.affi.com/www.healthyfood.org
Leslie G Sarasin, President/CEO
Robert L Garfield, Senior VP Public Policy
Members are companies and associations that are engaged in some aspect of the production, distribution or marketing of frozen food.

8446 **International Glutamate Technical Committee**
5775 Peachtree Dunwoody Road
Building G, Suite 500
Atlanta, GA 30342-1181
404-252-3663
FAX: 404-252-0774
Andrew Ebert PhD, Chairman
Judy Rogers, Contact
Members are associations that are engaged in the manufacture, sale and commercial use of glutamates.
8 Members Founded: 1969

8447 **International Herb Association**
PO Box 5667
Jacksonville, FL 32247-5667
904-399-3241
FAX: 904-396-9467
wor@poncacity.net www.iherb.org
Tina M Wilcox, Board President
Marge Powell, Treasurer
Supports herb businesses and educates the public.
Founded: 1986

8448 **International Ice Cream Association**
1250 H Street NW
Suite 900
Washington, DC 20005
202-737-4332
FAX: 202-331-7820
membership@idfa.org www.idfa.org
Constance Tipton, President
Cindy Cazallo, Membership Senior Manager
Represents manufacturers, distributors and marketers of ice cream, frozen yogurt and other frozen desserts. Provides regulatory advocacy market research, industry training. Part of the International Dairy Food Association.
175 Members Founded: 2000

8449 **International Inflight Food Service Association**
5775 Peachtree-Dunwoody Road, Building G
Suite 500
Atlanta, GA 30342
404-252-3663
FAX: 404-252-0774
ifsa@kellencompany.com
www.ifsanet.com
Sandra Pineau, President
Ken Samara, VP
Represents the $14 billion inflight and travel catering industry. Activities include annual conferences, trade shows, seminars and training events around the world.
400 Members Founded: 1965

8450 **International Institute of Ammonia**
1110 N Glebe Road
Suite 250
Arlington, VA 22201
703-312-4200
FAX: 703-312-0065
iiarinfo@iiar.org www.iiar.org
Jeff Welch, Treasurer
Lawrence J Basel, Chair
David Grong, Vice Chair
Kent Anderson, President
Promotes the safe use of ammonia as a refrigerant. Offers educational, promotional and standards development programs and legislative/regulatory support to manufacturers, contractors, consulting engineers, wholesalers and end users.
1200 Members Founded: 1971

8451 **International Institute of Fisheries Economics and Trade**
213 Ballard Hall
Corvallis, OR 97331-3601
541-737-1000
FAX: 541-737-2563
osuweb@lists.orst.edu
www.osu.orst.edu/dept/iifet
Ann Shriver, Executive Director
Claire Renard, Assistant
Promotes discussion, research projects and sponsors educational courses. Publications available.
400 Members Founded: 1982

8452 International Institute of Foods
2742 N Paulina
Chicago, IL 60614
773-404-5300

Rim Yurkus, Partner/Executive VP

Marketing and public relations arm of the International Natural Sausage Canning Association.

8453 International Jelly and Preserves
5775 Peachtree-Dunwoody Road,
Building G
Suite 500
Atlanta, GA 30342
404-252-3663
FAX: 404-252-0774
lwhitley@kellencompany.com
www.jelly.org

Linda Whitley, Member Services

Members are producers of fruit jams, preserves, and related products and suppliers of packaging materials or equipment.
78 Members Founded: 1918

8454 International Maple Syrup Institute

W 10010 Givens Road
Hortonville, WI 54944
802-524-4966
FAX: 920-779-6672

Members are producers, processors, industry suppliers and others interested in promoting the industry.
15M Members Founded: 1975

8455 International Natural Sausage Casing Association
12100 Sunset Hills Road
Suite 130
Reston, VA 20190
703-234-4112
FAX: 703-435-4390
insca@aol.com www.insca.org

Manfred Grundt, Chairman
Mounir Shehfe, Vice Chairman
Michael Mayo, Treasurer
Christian Billon, Director
Yozo Kawamura, Director

265+ Members Founded: 1965

8456 International Olive Oil Council
515 E 71st Street
Suite 904
New York, NY 10021

FAX: 212-746-8310 800-232-6548

Meg Lundsager, Contact

8457 International Packaged Ice Association
PO Box 1199
Tampa, FL 33601-1199
813-258-1690
FAX: 919-787-4916 800-742-0627

Roger Breisch, Chairman
Ben Key, Vice-Chair/Treasurer
Jerry Counsell, Secretary/Assistant Treasurer

A trade association representing manufacturers and distributors of packaged ice and manufacturers of ice making equipment.
400 Members Call For Membership Info
Founded: 1917

8458 International Sanitary Supply Association
7373 N Lincoln Avenue
Lincolnwood, IL 60712-1799
847-821-1012
FAX: 847-982-1012 800-225-4772
info@issa.org www.issa.org

Randal A Brame, President
Mattie Chinks, VP
Robert J Stahurski Jr, Treasurer
Anne-Marie Samson, European Board Chair
John Garfinkel, Executive Director

4700+ Members Founded: 1923

8459 International Warehouse Logistics Association
2800 South River Road
Suite 260
Des Plaines, IL 60018
847-813-4699
FAX: 847-813-0115
email@iwla.com www.iwla.com

Joel Anderson, President/CEO
Alex Glann, VP/COO
Carrie Gremer, Marketing/Communications VP

The Association is a result of the merger of the nearly 80 year old Canadian Association of Warehousing and Distribution Services (CAWDS) with the American Warehouse Association (AWAA). A trade association of warehouse logistics providers that helps members run high-quality, profitable businesses.
Founded: 1891

8460 Interstate Professional Applicators Association
International Pesticide Applicators Association
20057 Ballinger Road NE
Seattle, WA 98060
425-747-1200
FAX: 206-367-7625 www.ippa.net

Dianna Tovoli, Publisher

Provides education and information for the professional horticultural applicator. Legislative work involves the states of Washington, Oregon, Idaho in the area of laws and regulations.

8461 Iowa Meat Processors Association
Po Box 334
Clarence, IA 52216-0334
515-972-4478
nanajo@dodgenet.com

Nancy Henning, Executive Director

8462 Italian Trade Commission
33 E 67th Street
New York, NY 10022-1240
212-480-0300
FAX: 212-758-1050
newyork@newyork.ice.it
www.italtrade.com/ice

Robert Luongo, Executive Director
Aniello Musella, Manager

8463 Italian Wine and Food Institute
Lincoln Building, 60 East 42nd Street
Suite 1341
New York, NY 10165
212-867-4111
FAX: 212-867-4114
iwfi@aol.com
www.italianwineandfoodinstitute.com

Lucio Caputo, President

Members are producers, distributors and marketers of Italian wines and foods.
Founded: 1974

8464 Juice Products Association
1156 15th Street, N.W.
Suite 900
Washington, DC 20005
202-785-3232
FAX: 202-223-9741
jpa@kellencompany.com
www.juiceproducts.org

Carol Freysinger, Executive Director

The trade association for the fruit and juice products industry, including juice processors, packers, extractors, brokers as well as marketers of fruit juices and vegetable juices, juice beverages, fruit jams, jellies and preserves and similar products. JPA also represents juice industry suppliers and food testing laboratories and includes firms engaged in the trading of frozen concentrated orange juice futures and/or options on behalf of JPA processor members.
120 Members Founded: 1957

8465 LaSalle Food Processing Association
108 S Broadway
PO Box 97
La Salle, MN 56056-0097
507-375-3408
FAX: 507-642-3077

Pat Thiner, Manager

A meat packers trade association.

8466 Label Printing Industries of America
200 Deer Run Road
Sewickleya, PA 15143
412-259-1802
FAX: 412-741-2311
gain@printing.org www.gain.net

Laurie Reynolds, Executive Director
Ben Cooper, Executive VP for Public Affairs
Wendy Lechner, Senior Director
Jim Kyger, Director

Members are companies printing labels for food or consumer products.
40 Members

8467 Leafy Greens Council
33 Pheasant Lane
Saint Paul, MN 55127
651-484-3321
FAX: 651-484-1098
www.leafy-greens.org

Ray Clark, Executive Director
Robert Strube, President

Made up of growers and shippers. This association promotes the consumption of leafy greens and vegetables for battling diseases like cancer.
117 Members Founded: 1974

8468 Les Amis D'Escoffier
1230 Main Street
Leicester, MA 01524-1351
508-892-9090
FAX: 508-892-3620
castlerestaurant.com

Dr. Stanley Nicas, Director

An educational organization of professionals in the food and wine industries.
Founded: 1936

8469 **Livestock Marketing Association**
10510 NW Ambassador Drive
Kansas City, MO 64153
816-891-0502
FAX: 816-891-7926 800-821-2048
lmainfo@imaweb.com
www.imaweb.com

Ivan Harder, President
Mike Samples, Manager
Jake Jacobson, Yard Foreman

8470 **Maraschino Cherry and Glace Fruit Processors**
5 Ravine Drive
#776
Matawan, NJ 07747-3106

FAX: 732-583-0798

Richard Sullivan, Executive VP

8471 **Material Handling Industry of America**
8720 Red Oak Boulevard
Suite 201
Charlotte, NC 28217-3992
704-676-1190
FAX: 704-676-1199
vwheeler@mhia.org www.mhia.org

John B Nofsinger, CEO
F Hal Vandiver, Executive VP Business Development
Dr Richard E Ward, Executive VP
Dr Michael Ogle, Director Engineering Services

8472 **Meat & Livestock Australia**
1401 K Street NW
Suite 602
Washington, DC 20005
202-521-2551
FAX: 202-521-2699
dpalmer@mlana.com
www.mla.com.au

David Crombie, Chairman
Mark Spurr, Managing Director
Arthur Don Heatley, Director
Christopher Hudson, Director
Peter Milliken, Director

Promotes consumption of Australian beef, lamb, mutton and goat in Canada, US and Mexico. The company is funded by Australian producers. They key focus is to increase access for Australian meat producers to the North American market and to raise awareness of its nutritional value, quality and safety.

30000 Members Founded: 1998

8473 **Meat & Wool New Zealand**
PO Box 121
Wellington, NZ 60152
703-821-1040
FAX: 703-821-3795
help@meatnz.co.nz
www.meatnz.co.nz

Andrew Burtt, Contact

Meat & Wool New Zealand is funded by livestock producers through levies on all beef, sheep and goats slaughtered and on all wool sold. This income is used primarily to market New Zealand wool and meat worldwide, to maintain and extend trade access for New Zealand wool and meat, to provide solutions that will help improve New Zealand farm returns, and to provide technology to the this wool industry.

8474 **Meat Importers Council of America**
1901 N Fort Meyer Drive
Arlington, VA 22209
703-522-1910
FAX: 703-524-6039 800-522-1910
lauriebryant@micausa.org
www.micausa.org

Laurie Bryant, Executive Director
Stuart Leifer, Chairman
David Rind, Vice Chairman

To foster the trade, commerce and interests of importers and exporters of fresh and/or frozen and/or cured and/or cooked and/or canned meats.

181 Members Founded: 1962

8475 **Meat Industry Suppliers Association**
200 Daingerfield Road
Alexandria, VA 22314-4513
703-684-1080
FAX: 703-548-6563
info@fpmamail.com www.fpma.org

Cheryl Clark, Director Membership

Trade association for those businesses that supply services or products to the meat industry.

317 Members Founded: 1885

8476 **Meat Trade Institute**
186 North Avenue E
Suite 101
Cranford, NJ 07016
908-276-5111
FAX: 212-279-4016
sflannagan@sprintmail.com
www.spcnetwork.com

John Calcangno, President

8477 **Mexican Restaurant & Cantina Association**
909 S 8th Street
Suite 200
Louisville, KY 40203
502-736-9530
FAX: 502-736-9531 800-489-8324
jstraughan@mexrca.com
www.mexrca.com

Joe Straughan, Executive Director
Pete Lachapelle, President

Representing America's $16.9 billion dollar mexican style segment of foodservice. A trade association forstering relationships between 12,000 independent mexican restaurants and 618 chain operations with five or more units. We support professional enhancement of our members through informational and educational programs.

8478 **Mid-Atlantic Canners Association**
316 S Front Street
Hamburg, PA 19526
610-562-3061
FAX: 610-562-0281

Robert Crosswell, Crosswell
D Seibert, VP Finance

Mid Atlantic Canners Association is a cooperative soft drink canning facility for the Coca-Cola system. All of the national Coca-Cola Company brands are canned, packaged and shipped by truck to various Coca-Cola franchised distributors located throughout the northeast United States.

8479 **Mid-Atlantic Dairy Association**
325 Chesnut Street
Suite 600
Philadelphia, PA 19106
215-627-8800
FAX: 215-627-8887
www.dairyspot.com

Patricia S Purcell, CEO

8480 **Mid-States Meat Association**
3280 Riverside Drive
Suite 10
Columbus, OH 43221
614-459-5188
FAX: 614-442-5516
kristin@ohiogrowers.org

Kristin Mullins, Executive Director

100 Members

8481 **Midwest Dairy Association**
2015 Rice Street
Rosevillel, MN 55113
651-488-0261
FAX: 651-488-0265
info@midwestdairy.com
www.midwestdairy.com

Michael Kruger, Chief Executive Officer
Bev Stark, Administrator

Conducts advertising, campaigns on a nonbrand basis.

210M Members Founded: 1940

8482 **Midwest Food Processors Association**
Naylor Publications
502 E Main Street
PO Box 1297
Madison, WI 53701-1297
608-255-9946
FAX: 608-255-9838
info@mwfpa.org www.mwfpa.org

Nickolas C George, Jr, President
Judy Meyer, Director Admin/Member Svcs Manager

This association offers food processing member companies information on legislation and industry matters.

200 Members Founded: 1904

8483 **Milk Industry Foundation**
1250 H Street NW
Suite 900
Washington, DC 20005
202-737-4332
FAX: 202-331-7820
membership@idfa.org www.idfa.org

Geoff Covert, Chair
Miriam Brown, Vice Chair
Scott Charlton, Secretary
Mike Krueger, Treasurer
Constance Tipton, President

Part of the International Dairy Food Association.

8484 **Mobile Industrial Caterers' Association**
304 W Liberty
Suite 201
Louisville, KY 40202
502-583-3783
FAX: 714-632-5405
mica@hqtrs.com
www.mobilecaterers.com

Kelly Ramirez, Executive Director

Aids with problems common within the industry through exchange of ideas, advice on legal problems, safety standards and licensing regulations.

185 Members Founded: 1964

8485 Mushroom Council
11875 Dublin Boulevard
Suite D-262
Dublin, CA 94568
925-556-5970
FAX: 925-556-5979
info@mushroomcouncil.com
www.mushroomcouncil.com

Bart Minor, President

8486 National Agri-Marketing Association
11020 King Street
Suite 205
Overland Park, KS 66210-1201
913-491-6500
FAX: 913-491-6502
arc@nama.org www.nama.org/arc

Tom Smull, President
Stephanie Gable, President-Elect
Ken Anderson, VP
Eldon White, Chief Executive Officer

A national association where members involved in agricultural public relations can connect with other leading industry professionals; in marketing, advertising, public relations, media and more; to gain a unique perspective you simply can't find elsewhere. *$170.00*

3500 Members Membership Dues Founded: 1957

8487 National Alcohol Beverage Control
4216 King Street W
Alexandria, VA 22302
703-784-4201
FAX: 703-820-3551
jsgueo@nabca.org www.nabca.org

James M Sgueo, President/CEO
Jerome J Janicki, Operations Sr. VP/COO
Patricia K LaCava, Administration Sr. VP/CFO

It is the mission of the National Alcohol Beverage Control Association to support and benefit alcohol control systems by providing research, fostering relationships, and managing resources to address policy for the responsible sale and consumption of alcohol beverages. Members include control jurisdictions, supplier members and industry trade associations. *$750.00*

175 Members Membership Dues Vary Founded: 1938

8488 National Alliance of Independent Crop Consultants
349 E Nolley Drive
Collierville, TN 38017
901-861-0511
FAX: 901-861-0512
jonesnaicc@aol.com www.naicc.org

Dan Easton, President
Robert Glodt, President-Elect
Orvin Bontrager, Secretary
Dennis Hattermann, Treasurer
Allison Jones, Executive Vice President

Represents individual crop consultants and contract researchers. *$225.00*

500+ Members Membership Dues Founded: 1978

8489 National Association for the Specialty Food Trade
120 Wall Street
27th Floor
New York, NY 10005-4001
212-482-6440
FAX: 212-482-6459
custserv@fancyfoodshows.com
www.fancyfoodshows.com

John Roberts, President
Ann G Daw, President-Elect

A business trade association to foster trade, commerce and interest in the specialty food industry. Composed of domestic and foreign manufacturers, importers, distributors, brokers, retailers, restaurateurs, caterers and others in the specialty foods business.

2100 Members Founded: 1952

8490 National Association of Agricultural Educators
University of Kentucky
300 Garrigus Building
Lexington, KY 40546-215
859-257-2224
FAX: 859-323-3919 800-509-0204
naae@uky.edu www.naae.org

Allan Sulser, President
Lee James, President-Elect
Dr Wm Jay Jackman, Executive Director
Samantha Alvis, Associate Executive Director

A federation of 50 affiliated state vocational agricultural teacher associations. The mission is to provide agricultural education for the global community through visionary leadership, advocacy and service.

7600 Members Membership Dues:$35-$60 Founded: 1948

8491 National Association of Animal Breeders
PO Box 1033
Columbia, MO 65205-1033
573-445-4406
FAX: 573-446-2279
naab-css@naab-css.org
www.naab-css.org

Dr Denny Funk, Chairman
Al Kuck, Vice-Chairman
Dr Gordon A Doak, President

Unite those individuals and organizations engaged in the artificial insemination of cattle and other livestock into an affiliated federation operating under self-imposed standards of performance and to conduct and promote the mutual interest and ideals of its members. Members are farmer co-ops and others interested in livestock improvement. *$100.00*

22 Members Membership Fee: Max. $125 Founded: 1946

8492 National Association of Beverage Importers
932 Hungerford Drive
Unit 12-A
Rockville, MD 20850
240-453-9998
FAX: 240-453-9358
beverageimporters@nabi-inc.org
www.nabi-inc.org

Robert J Maxwell, President
Bernadeen P Emamali, VP
John A Scribner, Chairman

Representing the interests of beer, wine and spirit importers at state and federal levels. We will inform you of fast changing U.S. import rules and regulations, as well as the maze of international policies that affect importers.

100 Members Founded: 1934

8493 National Association of Chewing Gum
17000 Commerce Parkway
Suite C
Mount Laurel, NJ 08054
856-439-0500
FAX: 856-439-0525
ah@ahint.com www.nacgm.org

William Macmillan, CEO
Lisa A Long, CFO
Dominick Pagone, VP Operations
Susan J Nelson, Senior VP

8494 National Association of Concessionaires
35 E Wacker Drive
Suite 1816
Chicago, IL 60601
312-236-3858
FAX: 312-236-7809
info@naconline.org
www.naconline.org

Charles A Winans, Executive Director
Susan M Cross, Communications Director
Barbara Aslan, Membership Services Manager

This association works to professionalize the concession industry by providing information services and training programs for concession managers and employees. Holds conventions, seminars, trade shows, and certification programs for the leisure time food and beverage industry. Produces newsletters and magazines for its international membership.

800 Members Membership Dues Vary Founded: 1944

8495 National Association of Conservation Districts
509 Capitol Court NE
Washington, DC 20002-4937
202-547-6223
FAX: 202-547-6450
Bill-Wilson@nacdnet.org
www.nacdnet.org

Bill Wilson, President
Olin Sims, President-Elect
Steve Robinson, Second VP
John Redding, Secretary/Treasurer
Krysta Harden, CEO

NACD develops national conservation policies, influences lawmakers and builds partnerships with other agencies and organizations. NACD also provides services to its districts to help them share ideas in order to better serve their local communities. *$35.00*

17000 Members Membership Fee:Max. $100 Founded: 1946

8496 National Association of Convenience Stores
1600 Duke Street
Alexandria, VA 22314
703-684-3600
FAX: 703-836-4564
nacs@nacsonline.com
www.nacsonline.com

Henry Armour, President/CEO
Brian Kimmel, Senior VP/CFO
Jeff Lenard, Communciations Director
Carolyn Schnare, Member Relations Coordinator

Providing news, information and resources to the convenience and petroleum retail stores.

4000 Members Founded: 1961

8497 National Association of County Agricultural Agents
252 N Park Street
Decatur, IL 62523
217-424-5144
FAX: 217-424-5115
execdir@nacaa.com www.nacaa.com

Mickey Cummings, President
Chuck Otte, President-Elect
Fred Miller, VP
Leon Church, Secretary
Chuck Schwartau, Treasurer

A professional organization of 3,850 agents focusing on educational programs for the youth of the community.

3850 Members Founded: 1917
Mailing list available for rent 3850 names $125 per M.

8498 National Association of Flavors and Food- Ingredient Systems
3301 Route 66
Building C, Suite 205
Neptune, NJ 07753
732-220-0500
FAX: 732-922-3590
info@naffs.org www.naffs.org

Mike Bloom, President
Paula Boudjouk, President-Elect
Phil Parisi, VP
Bill Becker, Secretary
Bob Bauer, Executive Director

A broad-based trade association of manufacturers, processors and suppliers of fruits, flavors, syrups, stabilizers, emulsifiers, colors, sweeteners, cocoa and related food ingredients. Its associate membership is open to all companies that provide products and services to the food industry. *$400.00*

120 Members Membership Dues

8499 National Association of Pizzeria Operators
909 S 8th Street
Suite 200
Louisville, KY 40203
502-736-9532
FAX: 502-736-9502
jstraughan@pizzatoday.com
www.pizzatoday.com

Joe Straughan, President
Mary Sullivan, Membership Coordinator

Trade association representing America's $33 billion dollar pizza sement of foodservice. Fosters relationships between foodservice operations and their suppliers of goods and services specific to the segment. NAPO supports professional enhancement through information and educational programs.

1100+ Members Founded: 1984
Mailing list available for rent 25000 names

8500 National Association of State Departments of Agriculture
1156 15th Street NW
Suite 1020
Washington, DC 20005
202-235-5454
FAX: 202-296-9686
nasda@nasda.org www.nasda.org

J Carlton Courter III, President
Valoria Loveland, President-Elect
Roger Johnson, VP
Douglas Gillespie, Secretary/Treasurer
Richard W Kirchoff, Executive VP/CEO

Our mission is to represent the state departments of agriculture in the development, implementation, and communication of sound public policy and programs which support and promote the American agricultural industry, while protecting consumers.

8501 National Association of Wheat Growers
415 2nd Street NE
Washington, DC 20002-4993
202-547-7800
FAX: 202-546-2638
wheatworld@wheatworld.org
www.wheatworld.org

Dale Schuler, President
Daren Coppock, CEO
Melissa George, Communications Director

A nonprofit partnership of U.S. wheat growers who formed this association to solve common problems and make decisions for the future of America's wheat producers. *$100.00*

35000 Members Annual/Membership Dues
Founded: 1950

8502 National Association of Wholesaler Distributors
1725 K Street NW
Washington, DC 20006
202-872-0885
FAX: 202-785-0586
naw@nawd.org www.naw.org

Dirk Van Dongen, President
Ed an Jones, Chief Information Officer
John Anderson, Government Relations VP
Joy Goldman, Administration Director
Ruth Stadius, Communications Director

Representing the wholesale distributor industry. NAW is active in these areas: government relations and political action; research and education; and group purchasing. In addition the association operates the Wholesaler-Distributor Political Action Committee, the Distribution Research & Education Foundation, and the NAW Service Corporation.

Membership Dues Vary

8503 National Automatic Merchandising

20 North Wacker Drive
Suite 3500
Chicago, IL 60606-3102
312-346-0370
FAX: 312-704-4140 800-331-8816
saizenberg@vending.org
www.vending.org

James H Terry, Chairman
Richard L Wyckoff, Sr. Vice-Chairman
Jim Brinton, Vice-Chairman
Rich Geerdes, President/CEO
Mark Walkie, Membership Service Manager

Serves merchandising, vending, contract foodservice management and office coffee service industries.

Membership Dues Vary Founded: 1936

8504 National Bar and Restaurant Association
307 W Jackson Avenue
Oxford, MS 38655
662-236-5510
FAX: 662-513-3989
join@bar-restaurant.com
www.bar-restaurant.com

Jennifer Robinson, COO
Laura Speakes, Financial Affairs VP

Founded by Nightclub and Bar magazine, the association's mission is to provide discounts, services and networking opportunities enabling restaurant, bar and hospitality professionals to increase revenues and profits through innovative promotions, marketing and management.

Founded: 1924

8505 National Barbecue Association
1306-A W.Anderson Lane
Austin, TX 78757
512-454-8626
FAX: 512-454-3036 888-909-2121
nbbqa@assnmgmt.com
www.nbbqa.org

Trey Dishner, President
Howard Miller, President-Elect
Don McCullough, Executive VP
Ed Wilson, Secretary/Membership Director

The mission is to provide the barbecue related industry and enthusiasts with a visionary, beneficial, and responsive association. *$50.00*

Membership Fees Vary Founded: 1991

8506 National Beer Wholesalers Association
1101 King Street
Suite 600
Alexandria, VA 22314-2944
703-390-0591
FAX: 703-683-8965
info@nbwa.org www.nbwa.org

Craig Purser, President
Michelle Semones, Public Affairs VP

Trade association for beer wholesalers. Provides government and public affairs outreach as well as education and training for its wholesaler members.

2400 Members Membership Fees Vary
Founded: 1938

8507 National Beverage Packaging Association
200 Daingerfield Road
Alexandria, VA 22314-2884
703-299-5001
FAX: 703-548-6563

Wesley J Trochil

Represents over 600 individuals involved in the beverage packaging industry with 11 chapters throughout the US.

650 Members Founded: 1947

8508 National Bison Association
1400 W 122nd Avenue
Suite 106
Westminster, CO 80234
303-292-2833
FAX: 303-292-2564
info@bisoncentral.com
www.bisoncentral.com

Mike Duncan, President
Steve Wilson, Chairman
Gail Griffin, VP
John Flocchini, Secretary/Treasurer
Dave Carter, Executive Director

This association was formed to promote the production, marketing and preservation of bison. *$150.00*

2400 Members Membership Fee Founded: 1995

8509 National Bulk Vendors Association
191 N Walker Drive
Suite 1800
Chicago, IL 60606-1615
312-521-2400
FAX: 312-521-2300
nbva@muchshelist.com
www.nbva.org

Daniel Case, President
Peter Becker, VP

An organization comprised of manufacturers, distributors and operators of bulk vending merchandise and equipment. *$400.00*
350 Members Membership Dues Vary
Founded: 1950

8510 National Cattlemen's Beef Association
9110 E Nichols Avenue
Suite 300
Centennial, CO 80112
303-694-0305
FAX: 303-694-2851
customerservice@beef.org
www.beefusa.org

Mike John, President
John M Queen III, President-Elect
Terry Stokes, Chief Executive Officer
Paul Hitch, VP

Consumer focused, producer directed organization representing the largest segment of the nation's food and fiber industry.
25000 Members Founded: 1898

8511 National Cheese Institute
1250 H Street NW
Suite 900
Washington, DC 20005
202-737-4332
FAX: 202-331-7820 www.idfa.org

Mike Reidy, Chairman
Kevin Ponticelli, Vice-Chairman
Gary Vanic, Secretary
Mark Leddy, Treasurer
Constance Tipton, President

A constituent organization of the International Dairy Foods Association. NCI's members manufacture, process and distribute all types of natural and imitation cheese and cheese products, representing approximately 80 percent of the U.S. cheese industry.
70 Members Founded: 1927

8512 National Chicken Council
1015 15th Street NW
Suite 930
Washington, DC 20005-2622
202-081-1339
FAX: 202-293-4005
ncc@chickenusa.org
www.nationalchickencouncil.com

George Watts, President
William P Roeniqk, Senior VP
Richard L Lobb, Communications Director

A full-service trade association that promotes and protects the interests of the chicken industry and is the industry's voice before Congress and federal agencies. Members include chicken producer/processors, poultry distributors and allied industry firms.
Membership Fee Founded: 1954

8513 National Coffee Association
15 Maiden Lane
Suite 1405
New York, NY 10038
212-766-4007
FAX: 212-766-5815
info@ncausa.org www.ncausa.org

Robert F Nelson, President/CEO
Joseph F DeRupo, Communications/PR Director
Steven M Wolfe, Membership/Marketing Director

Established on the behalf of the coffee companies in the United States. Respond to external issues and represent the coffee industry before the legislative and executive branches of government.
200 Members Membership Dues Vary
Founded: 1911

8514 National Confectioners Association
8320 Old Courthouse Road
Suite 300
Vienna, VA 22182
703-790-5750
FAX: 703-790-5752
info@CandyUSA.org
www.ecandy.com

Lawrence T Graham, President
Susan Fussell, Communications Senior Director
Susan S Smith, Public Affairs Senior VP

Representing the entire confection industry, offering education and leadership in manufacturing, technical research, public relations, retailing practices, government relations, and statistical analyses.
Membership Dues Vary Founded: 1884

8515 National Confectionery Sales Association
10225 Berea Road
Suite B
Cleveland, OH 44102
216-631-8200
FAX: 216-631-8210
ttarantino@mail.propressinc.com
www.candyhalloffame.com

Tony Rufrano, Chairman
Douglas E Taylor, President
Bill Stoelker, First VP
Michael F Gilmore, Second VP
Morton B Gleit, Treasurer

Dedicated to furthering positive growth and acceptance of confectionery and allied products by education, open and frank dialogue and recognition of peers' notable accomplishments. *$75.00*
375 Members Annual/Membership Dues
Founded: 1899

8516 National Conference of State Liquor Administrators
6183 Beau Douglas Avenue
Gonzales, LA 70737
225-473-7209

pamsalario@cox.net www.ncsla.org

Lynn Walding, President
Pamela D Salario, Executive Director
Lou Bright, First VP
Jack Cordrey, Second VP
Matt Cook, Third VP

To provide opportunities for state-licensed administrators to meet and exchange ideas and information and to formulate uniform regulations, statue and laws affecting the sales of alcholic beverages.
Membership Fees

8517 National Conference on Interstate Milk Shipments
123 Buena Vista Drive
Frankfort, KY 40601
502-695-0253
FAX: 502-695-0253
ltownsend@ncims.org www.ncims.org

Leon Townsend, Executive Secretary
Marlena G Bordson, Chair
Don M Breiner, Vice-Chair

The goal is to assure the safest possible milk supply for all the people. The NCIMS is governed by an executive board comprised of representatives from state and local regulatory agencies from three geographical regions; FDA, USDA, industry and laboratories and academia.
Founded: 1940

8518 National Convenience Store Advisory Group
3331 Street Road
Suite 410
Bensalem, PA 19020
215-245-4555
FAX: 215-245-4060
jhowton@nag-net.com
www.nag-net.com

Joseph Howton, Executive VP/COO

National organization that provides support and services to managers, owners and suppliers of convenience stores nationwide.

8519 National Cooperative Business Association
1401 New York Avenue NW
Suite 1100
Washington, DC 20005
202-638-6222
FAX: 202-638-1374
ncba@ncba.coop www.ncba.coop

Paul Hazen, President/CEO
Jane Hoffman, CFO
Adam Schwartz, Member Services/Public Affairs VP
Art Jaeger, Communications Director

Representing cooperatives of all types and in all industries. We are democratically organized and operate according to internationally recognized cooperative principles.
50000 Members Membership Dues
Founded: 1916

8520 National Corn Growers Association

632 Cepi Drive
Chesterfield, MO 63005
636-733-9004
FAX: 636-733-9005
corninfo@ncga.com www.ncga.com

Rick Tolman, CEO
Kathy Baker, Executive Assistant
Rodger Mansfield, Administration Director

Our mission is to create and increase opportunities for corn growers across the country.

32300 Members Founded: 1957

8521 National Cotton Council of America
1918 N Parkway
PO Box 820285
Memphis, TN 38112-5000
901-274-9030
FAX: 901-725-0510
info@natbat.com www.natbat.com

Allen B Helms, Chairman
Dr Mark D Lange, President/CEO
John Gibson, Member Services Director
Marjory L Walker, Communication Services Director

The council serves as the central forum for consensus-building among producers, ginners, warehousers, merchants, cottonseed processors/dealers, cooperatives and textile manufacturers.

8522 National Cottonseed Products Association
104 Timber Creek Drive
Suite 200
Cordova, TN 38018
901-682-0800
FAX: 901-682-2856
info@cottonseed.com
www.cottonseed.com

Danny W Brown, President
David Johnson, VP
Ben Morgan, VP

A trade association for the cottonseed processing industry. Products include cottonseed vegetable oil for cooking; cottonseed meal, a high protein supplement for livestock and poultry; hulls, a roughage for cattle feed; and linters, a cellulose feed stock for many industrial and consumer products. *$300.00*
Annual/Membership Dues Founded: 1897

8523 National Council of Agricultural Employers
1112 16th Street NW
Suite 920
Washington, DC 20036
202-728-0300
FAX: 202-728-0303
webmaster@ncaeonline.org
www.ncaeonline.org

Sharon M Hughes, Executive VP
Jason Rios, Administration Manager

Members are growers and producers who employ agricultural laborers, as well as processors and organizations related to the agriculture business. *$400.00*
250 Members Membership Fees Vary
Founded: 1964

8524 National Council of Chain Restaurants
325 7th Street NW
Suite 1100
Washington, DC 20004
202-626-8183
FAX: 202-626-8185
purviss@nrf.com www.nccr.net

Scott Vinson, Government Relations VP
Shawna Purvis, Executive Assistant

Formed by a group of foodservice and restaurant executives who felt that they were not receiving adequate government relations representation from existing organizations. The NCCR helps shape federal legislative and regulatory issues that are of uniform significance to our member companies.
Inquire For Membership Founded: 1965

8525 National Country Ham Association
PO Box 948
Conover, NC 28613
828-466-2760
FAX: 828-466-2770 800-820-4426
eatham@countryham.org
www.countryham.org

Sam Edwards, President
Keith Fletcher, VP
Brian Harper, Treasurer

Encourages promotion, development and improvement of the businesses of country ham carvers and encourages the use of country carved meats through co-operative methods of production, promotion, education and advertisement. *$150.00*
53 Members Membership Fees Vary
Founded: 1992

8526 National Dairy Council
10255 W Higgins Road
Suite 900
Rosemont, IL 60018-5616
847-803-2000
FAX: 847-803-2077
transf.tovm
www.nationaldairycouncil.org

Ron Stoner, VP Information Services
Tab Forgac, Contact

This association operates under the auspices of the United Dairy Industry Association. NDC provides timely, scientifically sound nutrition information to the media, physicians, dietitians, nurses, educators, consumers and others concerned about fostering a healthier society.
Founded: 1915

8527 National Dairy Herd Improvement Association
421 S Nine Mound Road
PO Box 930399
Verona, WI 53593-0399
608-848-6455
FAX: 608-848-7675
dwboyke@requestltd.com
www.dhia.org

Jay Mattison, CEO
Mark Adam, President
Dan Sheldon, VP

The objective is to promote accuracy, credibility and uniformity of DHI records. To represent the DHI system on issues involving other National and international organizations.
65M Members

8528 National Educational Foundation
175 W Jackson Boulevard
Suite 1500
Chicago, IL 60604
312-715-1010
FAX: 312-583-9767 800-765-2122
info@foodtrain.org www.nraef.org

Mary Adolf, President

Advances professional standards in the industry through education.
40 Members Founded: 1971

8529 National Federation of Coffee Growers of Colombia
140 E 57th Street
New York, NY 10022-2703
212-421-8301
FAX: 212-371-3489
juan@juanvaldez.com
www.juanvaldez.com
This organization is comprised of coffee growers from Colombia whose goal is to promote Colombian coffee in the US.

8530 National Fisheries Institute
7918 Jones Branch Drive
Suite 700
McLean, VA 22101
703-524-8880
FAX: 703-524-4619
tressler@nfi.org www.nfi.org

Linda Candler, VP Communications
Antony Purcell, Member Manager
Wally Pereyra, Chairman
John Connelly, President
Tony Pelegrin, Director Finance

An organization promoting and advancing the interests of the seafood industry.
750 Members Founded: 1946

8531 National Frozen & Refrigerated Foods Association
4755 Linglestown Road, Suite 300
PO Box 6069
Harrisburg, PA 17112
717-657-8601
FAX: 717-657-9862
info@nfraweb.org www.nfraweb.org

Nevin Montgomery, President/CEO
H V Skip Shaw Jr, Executive VP/COO
Marlene Redden, VP Membership

Non profit trade association representing all segments of the frozen and refrigerated foods industry. NFRA's mission is to promote the sales and consumption of frozen & refrigerated foods through: education, training, sales planning and menu development and providing a forum for industry dialogue. NFRA is also the sponsor of the March National Frozen Food Month, June Dairy Month, End-oof-Summer Back to Cool and October Frozen Foods Festival promotions.
400 Members Founded: 1945

8532 National Frozen Dessert and Fast Food Association
PO Box 1116
Millbrook, NY 12545
845-677-9301
FAX: 845-677-3387 800-535-7748
nfd-ffa@juno.com www.nfdffa.org

David Roberts, Executive Director

This association is made up of small, independent owners and operators of ice cream and fast food establishments.
500 Members Bi-Monthly Founded: 1950

8533 National Grain Feed Association
1250 Eye Street NW
Suite 1003
Washington, DC 20005-3922
202-289-0873
FAX: 202-289-5388 ngfa@ngfa.org

Kendell W Keith, President
Randall C Gordon, VP Communications
Todd E Kemp, Director
Marketing/Treasurer

8534 National Grange Association
1616 H Street NW
Washington, DC 20006
202-628-3507
FAX: 202-347-1091 888-447-2643
info@nationalgrange.org
www.nationalgrange.org

William Steel, President
Robert Clouse, Chairman
Bruce Croucher, Secretary

Promotes general welfare and agriculture through local organizations. Presides over the advancement and promotion of the farming and agriculture industry.
30000 Members Founded: 1867

8535 National Grape Growers Association
1223 Potomac Street NW
Washington, DC 20007-3212
202-333-8190
FAX: 202-337-3809
npyle@attglobal.net

Nicholas A Pyle, DC Representative

8536 National Grocers Association
1005 N Glebe Road Drive
Suite 250
Arlington, VA 22201-5758
703-516-0700
FAX: 703-316-0115
info@nationalgrocers.org
www.nationalgrocers.org

Thomas Zaucha, President
Larry Gibson, Member Services Director

Purposes are handling government affairs regarding the operation of retail groceries, developing educational programs and literature regarding the industry and supporting women in the retail distribution industry.

Mailing list available for rent

8537 National Honey Board
390 Lashley Street
Longmont, CO 80501
303-776-2337
FAX: 303-776-1177 800-553-7162
webmaster@nhb.org www.nhb.org

Lee Heine, Chair/Producer Region 4
Bob Coyle, Vice-Chair/Importer 2
Clint Walker III,
Secretary/Treasurer/Producer Reg. 5
Bruce Boynton, Chief Executive Officer

Conducts research, advertising and promotion programs to help maintain and expand domestic and foreign markets for honey.
12 Members Founded: 1987

8538 National Honey Packers and Dealers Association
3301 Route 66
Suite 205, Building C
Neptune, NJ 07753
732-922-3008
FAX: 732-922-3590
info@nhpda.org nhpda.org.org

Bob Bauer, Executive Vice President
Greg Eckhardt, Administrative Assistant

Comprises cooperative and independent processors, packers and dealers of honey at wholesale or retail levels.
34 Members

8539 National Hot Pepper Association
400 NW 20th Street
Fort Lauderdale, FL 33311-3818
954-565-4972
FAX: 954-566-2208
peppergal@mindspring.com
Networking among industry and private members. Education and information sharing. *$20.00*

8540 National Ice Cream Mix Association
2101 Wilson Boulevard
Suite 400
Arlington, VA 22201
703-435-5630
FAX: 703-841-9328

Thomas M Balmer, Executive Director

This group is made up of manufacturers of soft-serve ice cream, ice milk, shakes and other dessert mixes.

8541 National Ice Cream Retailers Association
1028 West Devon Avenue
Elk Grove Village, IL 60007
847-301-7500
FAX: 847-301-8402
info@nicra.org www.nicyra.org

Mark Leichtman, President
Rich Johnson, VP
Mark Leichtman, Secretary/Treasurer

The National Ice Cream Retailers association is a trade organization for ice cream and frozen dessert retailers, wholesalers and distributors . The members of NICRA are located all across the country, Cadana, and several other countries.
500 Members Founded: 1933

8542 National Institute for Animal Agriculture
1910 Lyda Avenue
Bowling Green, KY 42104
270-782-9798
FAX: 270-782-0188
niaa@animalagriculture.org
www.animalagriculture.org

Glenn Slack, President/CEO
Michelle Vise-Brown, Director Member Relations
Dr Rick Sibbel, Chairman
Scott Stuart, Vice Chairman
James Fraley, Secretary

202 Members

8543 National Juice Products Association

400 N Tampa Street
Suite 2300
Tampa, FL 33602-4708
813-273-6572
FAX: 813-273-4397
aw@macfar.com www.njpa.com

Ansley Watson Jr, Executive Director
Tammy Andis, Executive Secretary

108 Members Founded: 1957

8544 National Live Stock and Meat Board
444 N Michigan Avenue
Chicago, IL 60611
312-467-5520
FAX: 312-467-9729

8545 National Meat Association
1970 Broadway Avenue
Suite 825
Oakland, CA 94612
510-763-1533
FAX: 510-763-6186
staff@nmaonline.org
www.nmaonline.org

Kiran Kernell, Communications Manager
Rosemary Mucklow, Executive Director
Jen Kempis, Operations Manager

National Meat Association is a nonprofit association with over 600 members throughout the United States, as well as internationaly. For its members, NMA is a vanguard, an associate, a lifesaver and a friend.
600 Members Founded: 1946

8546 National Meat Canners Association
1150 Connecticut Avenue, NW, 12th Floor
Washington, DC 20036
202-587-4200
FAX: 202-587-4300
webmaster@meatami.com
www.meatami.org

J. Patrick Boyle, President
Susan Hogan, Executive Assistant To President

AMI is the national trade association representing companies that process 70 percent of U.S. meat and their suppliers throughout America.

35 Members

8547 National Milk Producers Federation
2101 Wilson Boulevard
Suite 400
Arlington, VA 22201
703-436-6113
FAX: 703-841-9328
info@nmpf.org www.nmpf.org

Jerry Kozak, President/CEO
Tom Balmer, Senior VP

30 Members Founded: 1916

8548 National Nutritional Foods Association
2112 E 4th St
Ste 200
Santa Ana, CA 92705-3816
714-460-7732
FAX: 714-460-7444 800-966-6632
nnfa@nnfa.org www.nnfa.org

David Seckman, Executive Director/CEO
Adam Finney, Membership Director
Tracy Taylor, Director Public Affairs

Promotes consumption of nutritional foods as a way of life.
90M Members

8549 National Oilseed Processors Association
1300 L Street NW
Suite 1020
Washington, DC 20005
202-420-0400
FAX: 202-842-9126
nopa@nopa.org www.nopa.org

Thomas A Hammer, President
David J Hovermale, Executive VP
David C Ailor, Director Regulatory Affairs
Julia J Kinnaird, Manager

13 Members Founded: 1929

8550 National Onion Association
822 7th Street
Suite 510
Greeley, CO 80631
970-353-5895
FAX: 970-353-5897
tfell@onions-usa.org
www.onions-usa.org

Bob Sakata, President
Wayne Mininger, Executive VP

Represents interests of US onion producers. Informational lobbying and general promotional headquarters for fresh dry bulb onion growers. Provides connections for networking and education exchange.
600 Members Founded: 1913

8551 National Pasta Association
1156 15th Street NW
Suite 900
Washington, DC 20005
202-375-5888
FAX: 202-223-9741
www.hqcyberservices.com

Rick Cristol, VP

8552 National Peanut Board
2839 Paces Ferry Rd Se
Ste 210
Atlanta, GA 30339-5769
678-424-5750
FAX: 678-424-5751
peanuts@nationalpeanutboard.org
www.nationalpeanutboard.org

Raffaela M Fenn, President/Managing Director

Dee Dee Darden, Chairperson
Larry Ford, Vice Chairperson
Donnie White, Treasurer
Richard Robbins, Secretary

8553 National Pecan Shellers Association
1100 Johnson Ferry Road
Suite 300
Atlanta, GA 30342
404-252-3663

info@ilovepecans.org
www.pecans.org

Jon Krueger, Contact

An association aimed at promoting the pecan shelling and processing industry.
60 Members

8554 National Pork Producers Council
122 C Street NW
Suite 875
Washington, DC 20001
202-347-3600
FAX: 202-347-5265
flynnk@nppc.org www.nppc.org

Neil Dierks, Chief Executive Officer
Kirk Ferrell, VP Public Policy
Dave Warner, Director Communications

8555 National Potato Council
1300 L Street NW
Suite 910
Washington, DC 20005-4107
202-682-9456
FAX: 202-682-0333
spudinfo@nationalpotatocouncil.org
www.npcspud.com

John Keeling, Executive VP/CEO
Hollee Stubblebrue, Director Industry Communications

Represents US potato growers on federal legislative and regulatory issues.
6000 Members Founded: 1949

8556 National Potato Promotion Board
7555 E Hampden Avenue
#412
Denver, CO 80231
303-696-6420
FAX: 303-369-7718
info@uspotatoes.com
www.uspotatoes.com

Tim O'Connor, President/CEO
Meredith Meyers, Manager Industry Communications
Diana LeDoux, VP Finance
Pamela Lee, Compliance Coordinator
John Toaspern, VP International Marketing

Also known as the US Potato Board. Organized to operate a national marketing program to position potatoes as low calorie, nutritious vegetables and to facilitate market expansion into domestic and export sales.
109 Members Founded: 1971

8557 National Poultry & Food Distributors
958 McEver Road Ext
Unit B-8
Gainesville, GA 30504
770-535-9901
FAX: 770-535-7385 877-845-1545
info@npfda.org www.npfda.org

Kristin McWhorter, Executive Director
Russell Maltbie, President
Jeff Highlander, VP

A nationwide association that serves the needs of the poultry and food distribution and processing industries.
220 Members Founded: 1967

8558 National Renderers Association
801 N Fairfax St
Ste 205
Alexandria, VA 22314-1776
703-683-0155
FAX: 703-683-2626
renders@nationalrenders.com
www.renderers.org

Tom Cook, President

Members recycle animal by products only, also provide services to renderers.

8559 National Restaurant Association
1200 17th Street NW
Washington, DC 20036-3097
202-331-5900
FAX: 202-331-2429 800-424-5156
info@dineout.org www.restaurant.org

Craig S Miller, Chairman
Edward R Tinsley, Vice-Chairman
Steven C Anderson, President/CEO

Supports the food service industry with programs in education, promotion and government relations.
60000 Members Founded: 1919

8560 National Seafood Educators
PO Box 60006
Richmond Beach, WA 98160
206-546-6410
FAX: 206-546-6411

Evie Hansen, Market Director

Seafood publishing, marketing, and sales company.
Founded: 1977

8561 National Seasoning Manufacturers Association
8905 Maxwell Drive
Potomac, MD 20854-3125
301-765-9675
FAX: 301-299-7523

Dick Alsmeyer, Executive Director

8562 National Shellfisheries Association
National Marine Fisheries Service Laboratory
Oxford, MD 21654
631-283-4000
FAX: 631-287-8054
webmaster@shellfish.org
www.shellfish.org

Sandra Shumway, Editor
J Evan Ward, President
Carolyn S Friedman, Secretary

Organization comprised of scientists, public health workers, shellfish producers and fishery administrators to promote and advance shellfisheries research and the application of results to the shellfish industry.
1M Members Founded: 1908

8563 National Society on Health Care Food Service
204 E Street NE
Washington, DC 20002
202-546-7236
FAX: 202-547-6348
hfm@hfm.org www.hfm.org
This organization provides services for independent health care food service operators and their suppliers.

8564 National Soft Drink Association
1101 16th Street NW
Washington, DC 20036
202-463-6732
FAX: 202-659-5349
info@ameribev.org
www.ameribev.org

Ralph D Crowley Jr, Chairman
Susan K Neely, President
John E Pelo, Vice-Chairman
Patricia M Vaughn, Secretary

A trade association for America's non-alcoholic refreshment beverage industry. ABA provides a neutral forum in which members convene to discuss common issues while maintaining their tradition of spirited competition in the American marketplace. The Association also serves as liaison between the industry, government and the public, and provides a unified voice in legislative and regulatory matters.
18300 Members Founded: 1919

8565 National Sunflower Association
4023 State Street
Bismarck, ND 58503-690
701-328-5100
FAX: 701-328-5101 888-718-7033
klgrtnr@sunflowernsa.com
www.sunflowernsa.com

Larry Kleingartner, Executive Director
John Sandbakken, International Marketing Director
Lerrene Kroh, Meeting Planner/Sales
Tina Mittelsteadt, Business/Office Manager

Trade association for the sunflower industry.
200 Members Founded: 1981

8566 National Turkey Federation
1225 New York Avenue NW
Suite 400
Washington, DC 20005-6404
202-898-0100
FAX: 202-898-0203
info@turkeyfed.org
www.eatturkey.com

Alice L Johnson, President
Brie Wilson, Memberhip/Convention Services Mgr.

Advocate for all segments of the US turkey industry, providing services and conducting activities that increase demand for its members' products. The federation also protects and enhances its members' ability to effectively and profitably provide wholesome, high quality, nutritious turkey products.
600 Members Founded: 1939

8567 National WIC Association
2001 S Street NW
Suite 580
Washington, DC 20009-1042
202-232-5492
FAX: 202-387-5281
nawdexdir@aol.com www.nwica.org

Douglas Greenaway, Executive Director
Cecilia Richardson, Nutrition Programs

Members are geographic state, Native American state and local agency directors of the Special Supplement nutrition program for women, infants and children.
800 Members Founded: 1983

8568 National Wheat Growers Association
415 2nd Street NE
Washington, DC 20002-4993
202-547-7800
FAX: 202-546-2638
wheatworld@wheatworld.org
www.wheatworld.org

Darren Coppock, CEO
June Silverberg, Director Business Development
Mark Gage, President
Sherman Reese, First VP
Dale Schuler, Second VP

8569 National Young Farmers Association
1410 King Street
Suite 400
Alexandria, VA 22314

FAX: 703-838-5888 888-332-2668

Dr Larry Case, CEO
Coleman Harris, Executive Secretary

8570 Natural Marketing Institute
272 Ruth Road
Harleysville, PA 19438
215-513-7300
FAX: 215-513-1713
info@nmisolutions.com
www.nmisolutions.com

Maryellen Molyneaux, President/Managing Partner
Steven French, Managing Partner
Nancy White, Marketing Director

NMI is a strategic consulting, market research and business development company specializing in the health and wellness marketplace. Our dynamic capabilities focus on the well being of people and products and the environmental and social responsibility of the planet.
Founded: 1989

8571 New England Equipment Dealers Association
PO Box 895
Concord, NH 03302-0895
603-225-5510
FAX: 603-225-5510

George M Becker, Managing Director

The New England Equipmént Association serve equipment manufacturing companies who provide products and services to the food and beverage industry.

8572 New England Meat and Food Processors
Nodines Smokehouse
Torrington, CT 06790
860-489-3309
FAX: 860-496-9787 nodines@snet.net

Ronald Nodine, VP

35 Members Founded: 1999

8573 New York Apple Association
7645 Main Street
PO Box 350
Fishers, NY 14453-0350
585-924-2171
FAX: 585-924-1629
www.nyapplecountry.com

Jim Allen, President
David McClurg, VP

A nonprofit trade association representing commercial apple growers in New York State.
600 Members

8574 North American Association of Food Equipme nt Manufacturers
161 North Clark Street
Suite 2020
Chicago, IL 60601-4255
312-821-0201
FAX: 312-821-0202
info@nafem.org www.nafem.org

Lee Couture, Executive Secretary
Deidre Flynn, VP

The North American Association of Food Equipment Manacturers (NAFEM) is a trade association of more than 625 food preparation, cooking, storage and table service providers. NAFEM's biennial trade show attrcacts 19,000 foodservice professionals and features more than 600 North American manufacturers.
625 Members

8575 North American Blueberry Council

2390 East Bidwell Street
Suite 300
Folsom, CA 95630
916-983-2279
FAX: 916-983-9370
info@nabcblues.org
www.nabcblues.org

Mark Villata, Executive Director
Mary Nezbeth, Compliance Coordinator

A non-profit association with the important role of acting as a voice for the highbush blueberry industry.

8576 North American Deer Farmers Association
1215 N 7th St
Ste 104
Lake City, MN 55041-1266
651-345-5600
FAX: 651-345-5603
info@nadefa.org www.nadefa.org

Frederick Huebnerh, President
Dave Mc Quaig, First VP
David King, Second VP
Dr J Bradley Thurston, Treasurer
John Behrmann, Director

A nonprofit organization that offers representation of US and Canadian breeders and producers of venison. Velvet and trophy stock.
Founded: 1983

8577 North American Farm Show Council
590 Woody Hayes Drive
Room 232
Columbus, OH 43210
614-292-4278
FAX: 614-292-9448
fendrick@osu.edu
www.ag.ohio-state.edu

Craig Fendrick, Executive Coordinator
Bob Oberheim, President
Scott Grigor, First VP
Patrick Kennedy, Second VP

Members are agriculture trade show sponsors and suppliers of services to these shows. Provides members with education, communication and evaluation. Offers the best possible marketing showcase for exhibitors and related products to the farmer, rancher, producer and customer.
46 Members Founded: 1972

8578 North American Limousin Foundation
7383 S Alton Way
Suite 100
Englewood, CO 80112-2302
303-220-1693
FAX: 303-220-1884
kent@nalf.or www.nalf.org

Kent Anderson, Executive VP

Registers, promotes and develops Limousin beef cattle.
9600 Members Founded: 1968

8579 North American Meat Processors Association
1910 Association Drive
Reston, VA 20191
703-758-1900
FAX: 703-758-8001
info@namp.com www.namp.com

Joseph A Miller, Executive VP
Sabrina Moore, Accounting/Meetings Manager
Ann Rasor, Director Scientific Affairs
Jane Jacobs, Communications Director

Represents processors and distributors of meat, poultry, seafood and game to the food service industry.
400 Members Founded: 1942

8580 North American Millers' Association
600 Maryland Avenue SW
Suite 825 W
Washington, DC 20024-2573
202-484-2200
FAX: 202-488-7416
generalinfo@namamillers.org
www.namamillers.org

Betsy Faga, President
James Bair, VP

Trade association representing the wheat, corn, oat and rye milling industry. NAMA members operate one hundred and seventy mills in thirrty-eight states and Canada. Their aggregate production of more than one hundred and sixty million pounds per day is approximately ninety-five percent of the industry capacity.
46m Members Monthly Founded: 1902
Circulation: Newslett

8581 North American Natural Casing Association
494 Eight Avenue
Suite 805
New York, NY 10001
212-695-4980
FAX: 212-695-7153
info@nanca.org www.nanca.org

Barbara Negron, President
Michael Mayo, VP
Shirley Coffield, Secretary/Executive VP
Phil Schwartz, Treasurer

To obtain legislation favorable to the industry's interests and prevent or change legistation deemed harmful at the local, state and federal levels, including protection from unfair trade practices by foreign countries, and working with member governments to ease trade. Also addresses common industry problems encountered by management in the production, distribution and financial function of the naturasl casing industry.

8582 North American Olive Oil Association
3301 Route 66
Suite 205, Building C
Neptune, NJ 07753
732-922-3008
FAX: 732-922-3590
info@afius.org www.afius.org

Bob Bauer, President

Committed to supplying North American consumers with quality products in a fair and competitive environment; to fostering a clear understanding of the different grades of olive oil; and to expounding the benefits of olive oil in nutrition, health, and the culinary arts.

Founded: 1989

8583 Northeast Fresh Foods Alliance
1189R N Main Street
Randolph, MA 02368
781-963-9726
FAX: 781-963-5829
neffa@neffa.com www.neffa.com

Brian Long, President
Bob Ogan, Executive VP
Chris Bruhn, First VP
Paul Sullivan, Secretary
Paul Palumbo, Treasurer

350 Members Founded: 1979

8584 Northwest Agricultural Congress
4672 Drift Creek Road SE
Sublimity, OR 97385-9764
503-769-7120
FAX: 503-769-3549

Jim Heater, Manager

8585 Northwest Cherry Briners
1105 NW 31st Street
Corvallis, OR 97330-4449
541-753-8508

Carl Payne, VP Tech Services

Association of briners of sweet cherries in the northwestern US. The organization works to inform briners of regulatory decisions and current practices affecting brining operations.

8 Members Founded: 1936

8586 Northwest Cherry Growers
105 S 18th Street 205
Yakima, WA 98901
509-453-4837
FAX: 509-453-4880
info@wastatefruit.com
www.nwcherries.com

BJ Thurlby, President
Idell Dunn, Assessment Supervisor
David Severn, Marketing/Promotion
JoAnne Daniels, Teasurer
Peggy Palmer, Accounts Payable

Founded: 1946

8587 Northwest Food Processors Association
9700 SW Capitol Highway
Suite 250
Portland, OR 97219
503-327-2200
FAX: 503-327-2201
nwfpa@nwfpa.org www.nwfpa.org

David Zepponi, President
David C Klick, Executive VP
Kenneth M Yates, VP Government Affairs
Connie Kirby, Director Scientific Affairs
Pam Barrow, Energy Affairs Manager

An organization that aims to develop and promote the food processing industry located in Oregon, Idaho and Washington.

486 Members Founded: 1914

8588 Northwest Meat Processors Association
Hays Management
2380 NW Roosevelt Street
Portland, OR 97210
503-226-2758
FAX: 503-224-0947
haysmgmt@pipeline.com

Dennis Hays, Executive Director

250 Members Founded: 1962

8589 Organic Alliance
400 Selby Avenue
Suite T
Saint Paul, MN 55102
651-265-3678
FAX: 651-265-3679
contactus@organicalliance.org
www.organicalliance.org

Angela Sterns, Executive Director

A national non-profit organization that creates marketing, promotional, and educational programs for retailers to increase the organic market share. The Alliance offers merchandising and training materials to help retailers educate their employees and boost organic sales.

8590 Organic Crop Improvement Association International (OCIA)
6400 Cornhusker Highway
Suite 125
Lincoln, NE 68507-3160
402-477-2323
FAX: 402-477-4325
info@ocia.org www.ocia.org

Jeff See, Executive Director
Colleen Schroeder, Membership Services

An accredited world leader in the certified organic industry, provides certification, education and research services to thousands of organic farmers, processors and handlers from 20 countries in North, Central and South America and Asia. *$75.00*

3500 Members Membership Fee Founded: 1985

Mailing list available for rent 3500 names $50 per M.

8591 Organic Trade Association
60 Wells Street
PO Box 547
Greenfield, MA 01302
413-774-7511
FAX: 413-774-6432
info@ota.com www.ota.com

Phil Margolis, President
Linda Lutz, Membership Manager
Holly Given, Communications Director

A business association for the organic industry in North America. OTA's mission is to encourage global sustainability through promoting and protecting the growth of diverse organic trade. *$300.00*

1600 Members Membership Dues Vary
Founded: 1985

8592 Orthodox Union
11 Broadway
New York, NY 10004
212-563-4000
FAX: 212-564-9058
info@ou.org www.ou.org

Dr Tzvi Hers Weinreb, Executive VP
Eliezer Eliezer, Executive Director Operations
Rabbi Moshe D Krupka, Executive Director Programming
David Olivestone, Director Communications
Susan Borger, Director Human Resources

8593 Ozark Empire Grocers Association

315 N Ken Avenue
#10223
Springfield, MO 65802-321
417-831-6662
FAX: 417-831-3907

John Morrison, Executive Director

8594 Ozark Food Processors Association

2650 N Young Avenue
Fayetteville, AR 72704-5585
479-575-4607
FAX: 479-575-2165
ofpa@mail.uark.edu
www.uark.edu/depts/ifse/ofpa

Steve Crider, President
Earl Wells, VP
Dr Justin Morris, Executive VP
Dr Renee Threlfal, Secretary
Mike Heilman, Treasurer

This association is comprised of regional food processors and national suppliers for the food service industry. *$175.00*

100 Members Membership Fees Vary
Founded: 1906

8595 Pacific Coast Shellfish Growers
509 12th Avenue SE, Suite 15
120 State Avenue NE, PO Box 142
Olympia, WA 98501
360-754-2744
FAX: 360-754-2743
pcsga@pcsga.org www.pcsga.org

Robin Downey, Executive Director
Connie Smith, Projects Coordinator

Representing the local, state and federal interests of oyster, clam, mussel, scallop and geoduck growers from Alaska, Washington, Oregon, California and Hawaii. We're involved in everything from environmental protection, shellfish safety and health issues and technological advances to international marketing and research.

Membership Dues Vary

8596 Packaging Education Forum
Packaging Machinery Manufacturers Institute
4350 N Fairfax Drive
Suite 600
Arlington, VA 22203
703-243-8555
FAX: 703-243-8556
pmmi@pmmi.org www.pmmi.org

Charles Yuska, President
Corinne Mulligan, Executive Assistant
Matt Croson, Member Services/Communications VP
Ben Miyares, Industry Relations VP

Members manufacture packaging and packaging-related converting machinery in the United States and Canada. PMMI's vision is to be the leading global resource for packaging. Its mission is to improve and promote members' abilities to meet the needs of their customers. *$1500.00*

500+ Members Membership Dues Vary

8597 Packaging Machinery Manufacturers
3141 Fairview Park Drive
#550
Falls Church, VA 22042
703-205-0923
FAX: 703-205-6409 888-275-7664
info@packexpo.com
www.packexpo.com

Mary Ann Japour, COO
Betsy McBride, VP Business Operations
Ellen Crupi, Director
Denise Bell, Account Manager
Erwin Stierle, Senior Account Manager

Members are manufacturers of packaging and packaging related coconverting machinery in the US and Canada. Offers meetings, an inquiry service, statistics and surveys and a business-to-business service on its website. Also sponsors Pack Expo International and Pack Expo Las Vegas tradeshows.
500 Members Founded: 1933

8598 Paperboard Packaging Council
201 N Union Street
Suite 220
Alexandria, VA 22314
703-836-3300
FAX: 703-836-3290
paperboardpackaging@ppcnet.org
www.ppcnet.org

Jerome T Van de Water, President
James Brown, Executive Director
Steve Smith, Operations Manager
Melissa Teates, Industry Information Director

Trade association serving converters and suppliers of all forms of paperboard packaging, including folding cartons, rigid boxes, paper cylinders, and laminated small flute containers.
Founded: 1929

8599 Peanut Advisory Board
1025 Sugar Pike Way
Canton, GA 30115
770-998-7311

lpwagner@comcast.net
www.peanutbutterlovers.com

Leslie Wagner, Executive Director

Representing peanut farmers in Georgia, Alabama and Florida. Formed to educate American consumers about the U.S. peanut industry and its products.
6000 Members Founded: 1980

8600 Peanut and Tree Nut Processors Association
PO Box 59811
Potomac, MD 20859-9811
301-365-2521
FAX: 301-365-7705
rbarker@ptnpa.org ptnpa.org

Russell Barker, President

The mission is to provide a common forum for the processors and manufacturers of peanuts, tree nuts and related products and the suppliers of goods and services in order to further the advancement of the industry.
$1150.00
Membership Dues Vary

8601 Pear Bureau Northwest
4382 SE International Way
Suite A
Milwaukie, OR 97222-4635
503-652-9720
FAX: 503-652-9721
info@usapears.com www.usapears.org

Kevin Moffitt, President/CEO
Laura Wieking, Public Relations Manager

A non-profit marketing organization that promotes, advertises and develops markets for fresh pears grown in Oregon and Washington. Through professional representatives in the U.S. and around the world, the Bureau coordinates activities designed to increase awareness and consumption of fresh USA Pears, facilitating research on behalf of the Northwest pear industry relative to consumer awareness and preferences, nutritional benefits and emerging global markets.
1755 Members Founded: 1931

8602 Pepsi-Cola Bottlers Association
251 Oconnor Ridge Boulevard
Irving, TX 75038
972-717-1049
FAX: 972-717-9031

John Gabriel, President

8603 Pickle Packers International
1620 I Street NW
Suite 925
Washington, DC 20006
202-312-2859
FAX: 202-463-8998
bbursiek@therobertsgroup.net
www.ilovepickles.org

Richard Hentschell, Executive VP
Yaron Deckel, Manager

Addresses the concerns of pickle packers, shippers and manufacturers. *$1500.00*
100+ Members Membership Dues Founded: 2000

8604 Popcorn Board
401 North Michigan Avenue
Chicago, IL 60611-4267
312-644-6610
FAX: 312-321-5150
gbertalmio@smithbucklin.com
www.popcorn.org

Deirdre Flynn, Executive Director
Genny Bertalmio, Manager

A trade association representing the popcorn industry. Institute activites include trade management as well as government relations for the popcorn processing industry.
28 Members Founded: 1943

8605 Private Label Manufacturers Association
369 Lexington Avenue
New York, NY 10017-6506
212-972-3131
FAX: 212-983-1382
info@plma.com www.plma.com

Brian Sharoff, President
Myra Rosen, VP

Trade association promoting the private label industry.
3200+ Members Founded: 1979

8606 Produce Marketing Association
1500 Casho Mill Road
PO Box 6036
Newark, DE 19714-6036
302-738-7100
FAX: 302-731-2409
solutionsctr@mail.pma.com
www.pma.com

Bryan Silbermann, President
Duane Eaton, Association Services Sr. VP
Lorna Christie, Industry Products/Services Sr. VP

A not-for-profit trade association serving members who market fresh fruits, vegetables, and floral products worldwide. Its members are involved in the production, distribution, retail and foodservice sectors of the industry. *$925.00*
100 Members Membership Dues Vary
Founded: 1949

8607 Professional Farmers of America
219 Parkade
Cedar Falls, IA 50613
319-277-1278
FAX: 319-827-1792 800-772-0023

Mike Walsten, VP
Merrill Oster, Executive Director

Provides farmers with marketing strategies and market-trend data, as well as seminars and home study courses.
25M Members Founded: 1972

8608 Quality Bakers of America Cooperative
1055 Parsippany Boulevard
Suite 201
Parsippany, NJ 07054
973-263-6970
FAX: 973-263-0937
info@qba.com www.qba.com

Ernie Stolzer, Executive VP
Norm Trapp, Membership Director

Owned by leading U.S. wholesale bakers. Sunbeam is the brand name and trademark licensed by QBA to our members who also manufacture and market bakery products under their own brand names. We offer expertise in product development, marketing and training.
40 Members Founded: 1922

8609 Quality Checked Dairies
1733 Park Street
Naperville, IL 60563-8478
630-717-1110
FAX: 630-717-1126
mmurphy@qcheked.com
www.qchekd.com

Peter Horvath, Managing Director
Molly Murphy, Marketing & Sales Director

A cooperative of dairy foods processors who use the Quality Checked trademark on their products and engage in group purchasing of ingredients and supplies.
40 Members Founded: 1944

8610 RMA Annual Convention
USA Rice Millers Association/Federation
4301 Fairfax Drive
Suite 425
Arlington, VA 22203-1627
703-518-8161
FAX: 703-236-2301
jdavis@usarice.com
www.riceprocessing.com

Jeanette Davis, Convention Coordinator

Exhibits, seminars on the advances in products, technologies and services, keynote

speakers from the industry and fun activities. *$400.00*
June/Non-Members:$550 Founded: 1900

8611 Raisin Administration Committee
3445 N 1st Street, Suite 101
PO Box 5217
Fresno, CA 93726
559-225-0520
FAX: 559-225-0652
info@raisins.org www.raisins.org
Ron Worthley, General Manager
Debbie Pilloud, Operations/Human Resources VP
Jerry Stiavelli, Compliance Director
John Beck, Manager
Administrative board of growers and packers of raisins.

8612 Red Angus Association of America
4201 N Interstate 35
Denton, TX 76207
940-387-3502
FAX: 940-383-4036
info@redangus1.org
www.redangus1.org
Dr Bob Hough, Executive Secretary
Betty Grimshaw, Association Admin Director
Ben Spitzer, Member Services/Communications Dir
Judy Edwards, Manager
Dedicated to providing its members with excellence and innovation in leadership, service, information and education. An association for breeders of Red Angus cattle. *$60.00*
2000 Members Annual/Membership Dues
Founded: 1954

8613 Refrigerated Foods Association
2971 Flowers Road S
Suite 266
Atlanta, GA 30341
770-452-0660
FAX: 770-455-3879
info@refrigeratedfoods.org
www.refrigeratedfoods.org
Terry Dougherty, Executive Director
Stephanie Cooke, Communications Director
Judy Stokes, Founding Executive Director
Formerly known as the Salad Manufacturers Association, the RFA is an international organization comprised of manufacturers and suppliers of prepared, refrigerated, ready-to-eat food products. *$700.00*
200+ Members Membership Dues Vary
Founded: 1980

8614 Refrigerating Engineers & Technicians Association
PO Box 1819
Salinas, CA 93902
831-455-8783
FAX: 831-455-7856
info@reta.com www.reta.com
Dave Murphy, President
Doug Sweet, Chairman
Stephan L Shaub, Executive VP
Edward Seffens, VP
Seeks to upgrade the skills and knowledge of experienced members. Offers home-study courses on refrigeration and air conditioning. *$115.00*
2300+ Members Membership Fees Vary
Founded: 1910

8615 Research & Development Associates for Military Food
16607 Blanco Road
Suite 1506
San Antonio, TX 78232-1945
210-493-8024
FAX: 210-493-8036
rda50@flash.net
www.militaryfood.org
Joe Marinacci, Chairman
Bob Williams, President
Bob Ripp, Executive VP
Lewis Marshall, Treasurer
James Fagan, Executive Director
To provide the safest and highest food service to the US Armed Forces by linking industry, government and academics. *$400.00*
700 Members Dues/For 2 Members
Founded: 1946

8616 RestaurantChains.net
1 Bridge Street
Suite 44
Irvington, NY 10533
914-915-5399
FAX: 914-591-4293
info@restaurantchains.net
www.RestaurantChains.net
Keith Gellman, Publisher
James Sanro, President
Market research company that provides contact information for companies in the foodservice industry. Our two primary brands are RestaurantChains.net, a directory of company profiles and sales leads for US restaurant chains, and FoodserviceReport.com; a weekly bulletin on new US restaurant openings and changes of ownership.
3600 Members Founded: 1996
Mailing list available for rent 80000 names

8617 Retail Bakers of America
8201 Greenboro Drive
Suite 500
McLean, VA 22102
703-610-9055
FAX: 703-610-9005 800-638-0924
Bill Mihu, President
Michael Kalupa, First VP
Lynn Schurman, Second VP
Mark Faber, Treasurer
Susan Nicolais, Secretary/Executive VP
Comprised of retail bakeries, allied suppliers and other industry members. The purpose is to offer our members knowledge and resources to enhance business operations through learning opportunities, shared best practices, networking and industry communication. *$500.00*
2000 Members Membership Fees Vary
Founded: 1918

8618 Retail Confectioners International
1807 Glenview Road
Glenview, IL 60025-2968
847-724-6120
FAX: 847-724-2719 800-545-5381
van@retailconfectioners.org
www.retailconfectioners.org
Van Billington, Executive Director
Michelle May, Executive Assistant
Providing education, promotion and legislative services to our members who are manufacturing retailers of quality boxed chocolate and other confectionery products throughout the U.S., Canada and overseas.
600 Members Founded: 1917

8619 Rice Millers' Association
4301 Fairfax Drive
Suite 425
Arlington, VA 22203-1627
703-518-8161
FAX: 703-236-2301
riceinfo@usarice.com
www.riceprocessing.com
Stuart Proctor, President/CEO
Reece Langley, Government Affairs Sr. VP
John King, Chairman
A national association representing producers, millers and allied businesses advancing the use and consumption of U.S. grown rice.
Founded: 1899

8620 Rocky Mountain Bean Dealers Association
11178 Huron Street
Suite 200
Northglenn, CO 80734-3343
303-280-5208
FAX: 303-457-2097
Vickie Root, Executive Director
This organization is dedicated to advancing the general interest of its members and the industry.

8621 Rocky Mountain Food Industry Association
8795 Ralston Road
Suite 103
Arvada, CO 80002
303-830-7001
FAX: 303-830-7040
Mary Lou Chapman, President
This organization was established to provide information and support to retail grocers, convenience stores, manufacturers and other suppliers
500 Members Founded: 1917

8622 Roundtable of Food Professionals
4363 Larwin Avenue
Cypress, CA 90630
714-562-5088
FAX: 714-670-2965
info@rfporg.org www.rfporg.org
Barb Colucci, President
Jenny Rosoff, President-Emeritus
David Stennes, VP
Stephany Rosenthal, Membership Co-Chair
Provide opportunities for development and career expansion within the whole spectrum of the food industry. *$250.00*
50 Members Membership Fees Vary
Founded: 2002

8623 Royal Crown Bottlers Associations
515 Eline Avenue
Louisville, KY 40207-3655
502-896-0861
FAX: 502-896-0861
rcba2@hotmail.com
Stephanie Garling, Executive Director
Represents francised Royal Crown bottlers.
100 Members Founded: 1964

8624 Salt Institute
700 N Fairfax Street
Suite 600
Alexandria, VA 22314-2040
703-549-4648
FAX: 703-548-2194
info@saltinstitute.org
www.saltinstitute.org

Dick Hanneman, President
Tammy Goodwin, Administrative Director

A source of authoritative information about salt and its more than 14,000 known users. Provides public information and advocates on behalf of its members, including use of the website.
36 Members Membership Dues Vary
Founded: 1914

8625 Santa Gertrudis Breeders International
PO Box 1257
Kingsville, TX 78364
361-592-9357
FAX: 361-592-8572
sgbi@sbcglobal.net
www.santagertrudis.ws
Ervin Kaatz, Executive Director
Patti L Manak, Membership/Association Director
The original American beef breed. Custom built for the range and market, these cattle have proven themselves worldwide to be a hardy and profitable breed from the mountains of Montana and Mexico to the tropics and deserts of Argentina and Australia. Worldwide, cattlemen are getting results using Santa Gertrudis genetics.
Founded: 1950

8626 School Nutrition Association
700 S Washington Street
Suite 300
Alexandria, VA 22314
703-739-3900
FAX: 703-739-3915 800-877-8822
servicecenter@schoolnutrition.org
www.schoolnutrition.org
Ruth Jonen, President
Janey Thorton, President-Elect
Mary Hill, VP
Linda Godfrey, Secretary/Treasurer
Formerly the American School Food Service Association, this is a national, nonprofit professional organization representing members who provide high quality, low-cost meals to students across the country.
55000 Members Membership Fees Vary
Founded: 1946

8627 Sioux Honey Association
301 Lewis Boulevard
PO Box 388
Sioux City, IA 51101
712-258-0638
FAX: 712-258-1332
www.suebeehoney.com
David Allibone, President/CEO
Established by five beekeepers so that they could market their honey at greater profit through sharing services and equipment, processing and packing facilities and complete marketing and sales organizations.
315 Members Founded: 1921

8628 Snack Food Association
1600 Wilson Blvd
Suite 650
Arlington, VA 22209
703-836-4500
FAX: 703-836-8262 800-628-1334
sfa@sfa.org www.sfa.org
James A McCarthy, President/CEO
Chris Clark, Operations/Membership VP
Representing snack manufacturers and suppliers worldwide. Serving as the voice for the snack industry before government, researches and compiles annual snack sales and consumer data, educates manufacturers on technological advances in equipment and raw ingredients and provides technical support to its members through direct assistance, videos, seminars and publications.
800 Members Founded: 1937

8629 Society for Biomolecular Sciences
36 Tamarack Avenue
Suite 348
Danbury, CT 06811
203-788-8828
FAX: 203-748-7557
email@sbsonline.org
www.sbsonline.org
Al Kolb, President
Ricardo Macarron, President-Elect
Christine Giordano, Executive Director
Supports research and discovery in pharmaceutical biotechnology and the agrichemical industry that utilize biomolecular screening procedures.
$150.00
2000+ Members Membership Fee Founded: 1994

8630 Society of Commercial Seed Technologists
101 E State Street
Suite 214
Ithaca, NY 14850
607-256-3313
FAX: 607-256-3313
scst@twcny.rr.com
www.seedtechnology.net
Diane Mesa, President
Gil Waibel, VP
Anita Hall, Executive Director
A organization comprised of commercial, independent and government seed technologists. Developed over the years into a progressive organization that trains and provides accreditation of technologists, conducts research studies and proposes rule changes, and serves as an important resource to the seed industry. *$75.00*
Membership Dues Vary Founded: 1922

8631 Southeast United Dairy Industry Association
5340 W Fayetteville Road
Atlanta, GA 30349-5416
770-996-6085
FAX: 770-996-6925 800-343-4693
info@sudiainc.com
www.southeastdairy.org
Cheryl Hayne, Executive Director
Bob Earle, General Manager
Provides a wealth of information for milk and dairy consumers, media, school and health professionals and dairy farmers.
6000 Members Founded: 1971

8632 Southeastern Association of Fish and Wildlife Agencies
8005 Freshwater Farms Road
Tallahassee, FL 32309-9009
850-770-0007
FAX: 850-893-6204
seafwa@aol.com www.seafwa.org
Robert Cook, President
Robert M Brantly, Executive Secretary
Kenneth Haddad, VP
John D Hoskins, Secretary/Treasurer
Darrell Smith, Manager
An organization whose members are the state agencies with primary responsibility for management and protection of the fish and wildlife resources in 16 states, Puerto Rico and the US Virgin Islands.
18 Members Founded: 1947

8633 Southeastern Dairy Foods Research Center
NCSU Department of Food Science
PO Box 7624
Raleigh, NC 27695
919-515-4197
FAX: 919-513-0014
sdfrc@ncsu.edu www.cals.ncsu.edu
Dr Todd Klaenhammer, Director
Paula Pharr, Program Assistant
One of six National Centers funded and managed by Dairy Management Incorporated. The mission is to conduct research to develop and apply new technologies for value-added processing of fluid milk and its components into dairy products and ingredients with improved safety, quality or expanded functionalities.
Founded: 1988

8634 Southern US Trade Association
2 Canal Street
Suite 2515
New Orleans, LA 70130
504-568-5986
FAX: 504-568-6010
susta@susta.org www.susta.org
Mary Beth Wesdock, Marketing Manager
Troy Rosamond, Financial Director
Bernadette Wiltz, Deputy Director/Generic Prog. Dir.
Nonprofit organization was designed to promote the sales of US agricultural products produced in the south.
Founded: 1973

8635 Southwestern Peanut Growers Association
304 S E Lubbock
PO Box 338
Gorman, TX 76454
254-734-2222
FAX: 254-734-2288
info@swpga.com www.swpga.com
Dan Hunter, Manager
Dale Curb, Assistant Manager
Carries out numerous functions for its members. SWPGA also represents the interest of peanut producers nation wide in issues that are important to maintaining optimal marketing options for all peanut producers.
$10.00
Annual Dues/Requirements Founded: 1937

8636 Soy Protein Council
1255 23rd Street NW
Washington, DC 20037-1174
202-467-6610
FAX: 202-466-4949
spinfo@spcouncil.org
www.spcouncil.org
David A Saunders, Executive VP
Elroy Wolff, General Counsel
Members of this association include persons, firms and corporations regularly engaged within the US in the processing and sale of vegetable proteins or vegetable protein products derived from agricultural services.
3 Members Founded: 1971

8637 Soyfoods Association of North America
1001 Connecticut Avenue NW
Suite 1120
Washington, DC 20036
202-659-3520

info@soyfoods.org
www.soyfoods.org

Geri Berdak, President
Ted Nordquist, VP
Neil Widlak, Treasurer

A resource in providing and disseminating information about the health benefits related to soy consumption. We encourage sustainability, integrity and growth of the soyfoods industry through our members, by promoting the benefits of soy-based foods in diets. SANA is committed to providing focus and leadership on governmental policy related issues which benefit the use of soy in food products. *$500.00*

50+ Members Membership Fees Vary
Founded: 1978

8638 Specialty Coffee Association of America
330 Golden Shore
Suite 50
Long Beach, CA 90802
562-624-4100
FAX: 562-624-4101
coffee@scaa.org www.scaa.org

Rick Peyser, President
Rob Stephen, First VP
Mary Petitt, Second VP
Jeff Vojta, Secretary/Treasurer
Ted Lingle, Executive Director

One of the primary functions is to set the industry's standards for growing, roasting and brewing. Members of the SCAA include coffee retailers, roasters, producers, exporters and importers, as well as manufacturers of coffee equipment and related products. *$175.00*

2500+ Members Membership Dues Vary
Founded: 1982

8639 Sugar Association
1101 15th Street NW
Suite 600
Washington, DC 20005
202-785-1122
FAX: 202-785-5019
sugar@sugar.org www.sugar.org

Andrew Briscoe, President/CEO
Charles W Baker, Executive VP/Chief Science Officer
Melanie Miller, Media Relations VP

Represents processors and refiners of beet and cane sugar in nutrition and health matters.

16 Members Founded: 1943

8640 Switzerland Cheese Association
704 Executive Boulevard
Valley Cottage, NY 10989
845-268-2460
FAX: 845-268-2480 800-628-2460

Paul Schilt, Executive Vice President

8641 Tea Association of the USA
420 Lexington Avenue
Suite 825
New York, NY 10170
212-986-9415
FAX: 212-697-8658
info@teausa.com www.teausa.com

Joe Simrany, President

Association of companies dedicated to the interests and growth of the US tea industry.

100 Members Membership Dues Vary
Founded: 1899

8642 Tea Board of India
350 5th Avenue
Suite 1124
New York, NY 10118
212-563-5261
FAX: 212-563-5650
teaboardny@yahoo.com
www.teaindia.org

Kumar Sanjay Krishana, Director

This association promotes Indian tea and develops new markets for tea in the US and Canada.

1 Members Founded: 1953

8643 The Vegetarian Resource Group
PO Box 1463
Baltimore, MD 21203
410-366-8343
FAX: 410-366-8804
vrg@vrg.org www.vrg.org

Debra Wasserman, Co-Director
Charles Stahler, Co-Director

An organization dedicated to educating the public on vegetarianism and the interrelated issues of health, nutrition, ecology, ethics, and world hunger. *$20.00*

15000 Members Membership Fee Founded: 1982

8644 Tortilla Industry Association
8201 Greensboro Drive
Suite 300
McLean, VA 22102
703-610-9036
FAX: 703-610-9005
info@tortilla-info.com
www.tortilla-info.com

Marcelino Solis, President
Ricardo Baez, VP
Ann M Rolow, Second VP/Membership Chair
Jose Angulo, Treasurer
Roberto Quinones, Executive Director

Members include companies engaged in manufacturing tortillas and suppliers, food brokers and Mexican restaurant owners. *$500.00*

175 Members Membership Fees Vary
Founded: 1990

8645 Transportation Intermediaries Association
1625 Prince Street
Suite 200
Alexandria, VA 22314
703-172-2140
FAX: 703-836-0123
info@tianet.org www.tianet.org

Robert Voltman, President/CEO
Kelly Scott, Member Services Director
Peggy Douglas, Communications Manager

TIA is the premiere organization for third-party logistics professionals doing business in North America, providing resources, education, information, advocacy and connections to establish, maintain and expand ethical, profitable and growing businesses in the industry.

700 Members Membership Dues Vary
Founded: 1977

8646 US Animal Health Association
8100 Three Chopt Road
Suite 203, PO Box K227
Richmond, VA 23288
804-285-3210
FAX: 804-285-3367
usaha.@usaha.org www.usaha.org

Dr Bret Marsh, President
Dr Lee Myers, President-Elect
James Leafstedt, First VP
Dr Don Hoenig, Second VP

Seeks to prevent, control and eliminate livestock diseases. *$110.00*

1400 Members Membership Dues Founded: 1897

8647 US Apple Association
8233 Old Courthouse Road
Suite 200
Vienna, VA 22182
703-442-8850
FAX: 703-790-0845 www.usapple.org

Nancy Foster, President/CEO
Shannon Schaffer, Membership/Communications Manager

Mission is to provide to all segments of the U.S. apple industry the means to profitably produce and market apples and apple products. *$500.00*

440 Members Membership Fees Vary
Founded: 1970

8648 US Beet Sugar Association
1156 15th Street NW
Suite 1019
Washington, DC 20005
202-296-4820
FAX: 202-331-2065
usbsa@beetsugar.org
www.beetsugar.org

James Johnson, President
Elin Peltz, VP
Claudia Tidwell, Administration Director

Beet sugar processing companies make up the membership of this association.

9 Members Founded: 1911

8649 US Canola Association
600 Pennsylvania SE
Suite 320
Washington, DC 20003
202-969-7040
FAX: 202-969-7036
jgordley@gordley.com
www.uscanola.com

John Haas, President
Steve Kakela, First VP
John Gordley, Executive Director

Producers, companies and associations that advertise and promote US canola and rapeseed industries comprise the membership of this association.

50 Members Membership Fees Apply
Founded: 1989

8650 US Grains Council
1400 K Street NW
Suite 1200
Washington, DC 20005
202-789-0789
FAX: 202-898-0522
grains@grains.org www.grains.org

Kenneth Hobbie, President/CEO
Andrew Pepito, Operations VP
Erick Erickson, Special Assistant
Kim Karst, Executive Assistant

Motivated by the grain sorghum, barley and corn producer associations and representatives of the agricultural community.

Provides commodity export market development.
100 Members Founded: 1960

8651 US Meat Export Federation
1050 17th Street
Suite 2200
Denver, CO 80265
303-623-6328
FAX: 303-623-0297
info@usmef.org www.usmef.org
Phil Seng, President/CEO
John Hinners, Industry Relations Asst. VP
Lynn Heinze, Information Services VP
A trade association working to create new opportunities and develop existing international markets for U.S. beef, pork, lamb and veal.
160 Members Founded: 1975

8652 US Poultry & Egg Association
1530 Cooledge Road
Tucker, GA 30084-7303
770-493-9401
FAX: 770-493-9257
chanson@poultryegg.org
www.poultryegg.org
Dr Ron Prestage, Chairman
Don Dalton, President
Carol Hanson, Executive Assistant
Representing the entire industry as an All Feather association. Membership includes producers and processors of broilers, turkeys, ducks, eggs, and breeding stock, as well as allied companies. *$300.00*
600 Members Membership Dues Founded: 1947

8653 USA Rice Federation
4301 N Fairfax Drive
Suite42 5
Arlington, VA 22203
703-518-8161
FAX: 703-236-2301
riceinfo@usarice.com
www.usarice.com
Lee Adams, Chairman
Stuart E Proctor Jr, President/CEO
Patricia Alderson, Member Services VP
Sarah Castleberry, Communications Coordinator
National advocate for all segments of the rice industry, conducting activities to influence government programs, developing and initiating programs to increase worldwide demand for U.S. rice, and providing other services to increase profitability for all industry segments.
Membership Dues

8654 Unipro Food Service Companies
2500 Cumberland Parkway
Suite 600
Atlanta, GA 30339
770-952-0871
FAX: 770-952-0872
info@uniprofoodservice.com
www.uniprofoodservice.com
Mike Roacher, Chairman
Roger Toomey, Chief Executive Officer
Richard Pineda, VP
Kristin Poggio, Divisional VP
Jim Zeck, Divisional VP
Secures reputable manufacturers' and processors' products. Conducts sales training seminars and offers field sales assistance to salesmen.
300 Members Founded: 1985

8655 United Dairy Industry Association
O'Hare International Center
10255 W Higgins Road
#900
Rosemont, IL 60018
847-906-6640
FAX: 847-803-2077 www.dairyinfo.com
Thomas Galaghar, CEO
This association aims to provide the sale and consumption of milk and milk products in the US.
75 Members Founded: 1980

8656 United Egg Producers
1720 Windward Concourse
Suite 320
Alpharetta, GA 30005
770-360-9220
FAX: 770-360-7058
info@unitedegg.org
www.unitedegg.org
Al Pope, President/CEO
Gene Gregory, Senior VP
Chad Gregory, VP
The largest federation of regional cooperatives in the egg industry.
5 Members Founded: 1968

8657 United Food and Commercial Workers
1775 K Street NW
Washington, DC 20006
202-223-3111
FAX: 202-466-1562 www.ufcw.org
Joseph T Hansen, President
Anthony M Perrone, Secretary
William T McDonough, Executive VP
This association offers support and representation of its members.
1.4 M Members Founded: 1979

8658 United Fresh Fruit and Vegetable
1901 Pennsylvania Avenue NW
Suite 1100
Washington, DC 20006
202-624-4989
FAX: 202-303-3433
info@uffva.org www.uffva.org
Tom Stenzel, President
Sandy Nguyen, Finance/Operations Sr. Director
Ginny Pugh, Membership Information Manager
Equipment, supplies, cartons, packaging machinery, computers, sorting and sizing equipment, harvesting equipment, film wrap manufacturing and commodity organizations.
110 Members Founded: 1904

8659 United Soybean Board
16640 Chesterfield Grove Road
Suite 130
Chesterfield, MO 63005
636-530-1777
FAX: 636-530-1560 800-989-8721
ydock@unitedsoybean.com
www.unitedsoybean.org
John Becherer, CEO
Yvonne Dock, Executive Director
Teresa Lee, Internal Communications Manager
National soybean checkoff farmer led organization. USB invests in research and marketing activities for US soybeans and soy products.
Founded: 1972

8660 United States Cane Sugar Refiners
1730 Rhode Island Avenue NW
Washington, DC 20036
202-754-4399
FAX: 202-785-5110
Joseph Cox, President

8661 United States Tuna Foundation
1101 17th Street NW
Suite 609
Washington, DC 20036
202-857-0610
info@tunafacts.com
www.tunafacts.com
David Burney, Executive Director
Serves as an umbrella organization representing the various interests of the U.S. canned tuna industry. Representing the internationaln and domestic interests to federal and state regulations, to national legislation, to domestic marketing.
7 Members Founded: 1976

8662 Vegetarian Awareness Network
National Headquarters
PO Box 321
Knoxville, TN 37901-0321
865-558-8343
FAX: 877-329-8343 800-872-8343
Lige Weill, President
A.L. Bourdonnay, VP
An all-volunteer, nonsectarian, nonpartisan, not-for-profit, educational, social service organization. Networks nationally with consumers, communities and companies to: encourage eco-friendliness for products, people and the planet through informed eating; advance public awareness of the benefits of a vegetarian lifestyle; assist consumers in making informed dietary decisions.
Founded: 1980

8663 Vidalia Onion Committee
100 Vidalia Sweet Onion Drive
PO Box 1609
Vidalia, GA 30475
912-537-1918
FAX: 912-537-2166
info@vidaliaonion.org
www.vidaliaonion.org
Wendy Brannen, Executive Director
Promote growth, distribution and awareness of this one of a kind crop.
225 Members Founded: 1931

8664 Vinegar Institute
5775 Peachtree-Dunwoody Road
Building G, Suite 500
Atlanta, GA 30342
404-252-3663
FAX: 404-252-0774
1whitley@kellencompany.com
www.versatilevinegar.org
Pamela A Chumley, President
Jeannie Milewski, Executive Director
Manufacturers and bottlers of vinegar and suppliers to the industry are the members of this association. Publications available only to members.
28 Members Membership Fees Vary Founded: 1967

8665 Walnut Council
Wright Forestry Center
1011 N 725 West
West Lafayette, IN 47906-9431
765-583-3501
FAX: 765-583-3512
www.walnutcouncil.org

Larry Frye, President
Liz Jackson, Executive Director
Barbara Luchsinger, VP

Representing woodland owners, foresters, forest scientists and wood producing industry representatives. The purpose is to assist in the technical transfer of forest research to field applications, help build and maintain bettermarkets for wood products and nut crops. *$25.00*

1000 Members Membership Dues Founded: 1970

8666 Walnut Marketing Board
1540 River Park Drive
Suite 203
Sacramento, CA 95815-4609
916-922-5888
FAX: 916-923-2548 800-982-8345
wmbcwc@walnuts.org
www.walnuts.org

Dennis Balint, CEO/Executive Director
Amy Myrdal, Marketing Director
David Ramos, Research Director

Established to represent walnut growers and handlers. The board promotes usage of walnuts in the U.S. through publicity, product promotions and production research and education programs.

Founded: 1933

8667 Weed Science Society of America
PO Box 7050
Lawrence, KS 66044-8897
785-429-9622
FAX: 785-843-1274 800-627-0629
wssa@allenpress.com www.wssa.net

Dale Shaner, President
Jeff Derr, VP

Promotes research, education, and extension outreach activities related to weeds; provides science-based information to the public and policy makers; and fosters awareness of weeds and their impacts on managed and natural ecosystem. *$155.00*

2000 Members Membership Fee Founded: 1956

8668 Western Dairy Council
12000 N Washington Street
Suite 200
Thornton, CO 80241
303-451-7711
FAX: 303-451-0411 800-274-6455
info@wdairycouncil.com
www.wdairycouncil.com

Stephanie Smith, Communications Director
Tom Jenkinson, Executive Director

An affiliate of National Dairy Council, WDC is funded by dairy farmers and processors. Serving as a nutrition education resource to health professionals, educators, community leaders, the media and consumers in Colorado, Montana and Wyoming.

8669 Western Fairs Association
1776 Tribute Road
Suite 210
Sacramento, CA 95815-4495
916-927-3100
FAX: 916-927-6397
wfa@fairsnet.org
www.westernfairs.org

Bill Blair, President
Stephen J Chambers, Executive Director

National association for fairground owners, managers and workers. Also includes government regulations, fair vendors and service providers.

2000 Members Founded: 1922

8670 Western Growers Association
17620 Fitch Street
PO Box 2130
Newport Beach, CA 92658-8944
949-863-1000
FAX: 949-863-9028
rhause@wga.com www.wga.com

Tom Nassif, President
David Zanze, Sr. VP/CIO
Randy Hause, Member Relations VP
Lynne Ross, Sales Operations VP

Association for growers, shippers, packers, brokers and distributors of fruits and vegetables in California and Arizona.

3000 Members Founded: 1926

8671 Western United States Agricultural Trade
4601 NE 77th Avenue
Suite 200
Vancouver, WA 98662
360-693-3373
FAX: 360-693-3464
andy@wusata.org www.wusata.org

Andy Anderson, Executive Director
Eliza Lane, Outreach Coordinator
Scotty Frederick, Office Coordinator

This organization offers information and support to increase exports of US agricultural products.

200 Members Founded: 1980

8672 Wheat Foods Council
10841 S Crossroads Drive
Suite 105
Parker, CO 80138
303-840-8787
FAX: 303-840-6877
wfc@wheatfoods.org
www.wheatfoods.org

Marcia Scheideman, President
Lynne E Holly, Communications Director
Vikki Berry, Manager

A national nonprofit organization formed to help increase awareness of dietary grains as an essential component to a healthy diet. The WFC consists of grain producers, millers, bakers, baking suppliers, life science companies and cereal, tortilla, and pasta manufacturers.

48 Members Membership Fees Vary Founded: 1972

8673 Wild Blueberry Association of North America
PO Box 1130
Kennebunkport, ME 04046
207-967-5024
FAX: 207-967-5023 800-233-9453
wildblueberries@gwi.net
www.wildblueberries.com

John M Sauve, Executive Director

Represents processors and growers of wild blueberries in Eastern Canada and Maine. The Association is focused on the generic promotion of wild blueberries around the world. It offers promotional materials, joint funding, product development, assistance, seminars, newsletters, supplier lists and ongoing support to users of wild blueberries in all retail, manufacturing, food service and bakery trade segments.

Founded: 1981

8674 Wine Appreciation Guild
360 Swift Avenue
Unit 30-40
South San Francisco, CA 94080
650-866-3020
800-239-9463
info@wineappreciation.com
www.wineappreciation.com

Alex Shaw, Contact Person
Jason Simon, Manager

Formed as the official successor in the distribution of wine accessories, and the publication and distribution of books and educational materials.

1500 Members Founded: 1973

8675 Wine Institute
425 Market Street
Suite 1000
San Francisco, CA 94105
415-512-0151
FAX: 415-442-0742
webmaster@wineinstitute.org
www.wineinstitute.org

Robert Koch, President
Kaye Clement, Executive Assistant
Britta Purcell, Member Relations Coordinator
Nancy Light, Communications Director
John DeLuca, Manager

Dedicated to initiating and advocating state, federal and international public policy to enhance the environment for the responsible consumption and enjoyment of wine. *$180.00*

887 Members Annual/Min. Dues Founded: 1934

8676 Wine and Spirits Shippers Association
11800 Sunrise Valley Drive
Suite 332
Reston, VA 20191-5396
703-860-2300
FAX: 703-860-2422
info@wssa.com www.wssa.com

James V Andretta Jr, Chairman
Louis Healey, President
Howard Jacobs, VP
Geoffrey Giovanetti, Executive Director

A non-profit shippers association composed of importers and exporters of beverages and allied products. Provides members, importers and exporters with efficient and economical ocean transportation and other logestic services. *$100.00*

400 Members Annual/Membership Fee Founded: 1976

8677 Wine and Spirits Wholesalers of America
805 15th Street NW
Suite 430
Washington, DC 20005
202-371-9792
FAX: 202-789-2405
stephanie.shafer@wswa.org
www.wswa.org

Juanita D Duggan, President/CEO
Karen Elliot, Sr VP Communications/PR
Rae Ann Bevington, Sr VP Convetions/Meetings

This association is comprised of wholesale distributors of domestic and imported wine and distilled spirits. *$1000.00*
450 Members Fee/Max. $10,000 Founded: 1943

8678 Women in Flavor & Fragrance Commerce
Association of Food Industries
3301 Route 66
Suite 205, Building C
Neptune, NJ 07753
732-922-3008
FAX: 732-922-0560
info@wffc.org www.wffc.org
Pia Henzi, President
Nancy Poulos, VP/Membership Services
Joanne Kennedy, Public Relations
Bob Bauer, Executive Director
Provides a center of education, camaraderie, support and networking opportunities for women in our industry. Our membership encompasses women involved is sales, purchasing, customer service as well as technical and laboratory careers. WFFC has timely seminars as well as social and networking opportunities for our members and the industry as a whole. *$85.00*
300 Members Membership Fee Founded: 1982

8679 World Food Logistics Organization
1500 King Street
Suite 201
Alexandria, VA 22314
703-373-4300
FAX: 703-373-4301
email@iarw.org www.wflo.org
J William Hudson, President/CEO
Benjamin Milk, VP/Secretary
Susan Shores, Administration Director
A non-profit and research foundation organized by members of the International Association of Refrigerated Warehouses to promote the proper handling and storage of temperature sensitive commodities. *$390.00*
300 Members Membership Fees Vary Founded: 1943

Newsletters

8680 AAMPlifier
American Association of Meat Processors
One Meating Place
PO Box 269
Elizabethtown, PA 17022-269
717-367-1168
FAX: 717-367-9096
info@aamp.com http://www.aamp.com
Steve Krut, Executive Director
Debbie Sinex, Convention Manager
The American Association of Meat Processors is North America's largest meat trade organization. AAMP represents small to medium-sized businesses including packers, processors, wholesalers, home food service businesses, meat retailers, deli and catering operators, and industry suppliers. AAMP offers information/services for: Food Safety, HACCP, State & Federal Meat & Poultry Inspection Issues, BSE, CWD, Equipment & Supplies Trade Show and National Cured Meats Competition. *$50.00*
4 pages Founded: 1939
Circulation: 2500

8681 AAPA Bulletin
American Alfalfa Processors Association
8810 Craig Drive,
Overland Park, KS 66212
913-648-6800
FAX: 913-648-2648
aapa@cysource.com www.aapausa.org
Wanda Cobb, Executive VP
Information for the processors and suppliers in the alfalfa industry.
Founded: 1941

8682 ABA Bulletin
1350 I Street NW
Suite 1290
Washington, DC 20005-3305
202-789-0300
FAX: 202-898-1164
kkotche@americanbakers.org
www.americanbakers.org
Kelly Kotche,
Communications/Membership Manager
Paul Abenante, President/CEO
The association's newsletter that covers the conventions.
Monthly

8683 AHA Quarterly
American Herb Association
PO Box 1673
Nevada City, CA 95959-1673
530-265-9552
FAX: 530-274-3140 www.ahaherb.com
Kathi Keville, Director
Robert Brucia, Co-Director
Marion Wyckoff, Secretary
Reports on the latest scientific studies, new herb, aromatherapy, cooking and gardening books, international herb news, legal and environmental issues, herb-related events and conferences. *$20.00*
20 pages w/Membership Founded: 1981

8684 AICR Newsletter
American Institute for Cancer Research
1759 R Street NW
Washington, DC 20009
202-328-7744
FAX: 202-328-7226 800-843-8114
aicrweb@aicr.org www.aicr.org
Marilyn Gentry, Editor
Explains current cancer research, provides recipes and menu ideas for healthy eating, and offers practical advice to lower cancer risk.
Quarterly Founded: 1982
Circulation: 1.6MM

8685 ALBC News
American Livestock Breeds Conservancy
15 Hillsboro Street
PO Box 477
Pittsboro, NC 27312
919-542-5704
FAX: 919-545-0022
albc@albc-usa.org
http://www.albc-usa.org
Marjorie Bender, Prog. Coord./Research
Don Schrider, Communication Director
Charles Bassett, Executive Director
Breeders directory; annual conference; catalog of publications available. *$30.00*
20 pages Founded: 1977
Circulation: 3000
Printed in 1 color on matte stock

8686 APIS
CITA International
3464 W Earll Drive
Suites E & F
Phoenix, AZ 85017
602-447-0480
FAX: 602-447-0305
esam@citainternational.com
www.citainternational.com
EM Morsy, Editor
PE Pederson, Advertising/Sales
The international bulletin for specialty livestock, pet animal and ag-chem product developments.
Quarterly Founded: 1988

8687 ASBC Newsletter
American Society of Brewing Chemists
3340 Pilot Knob Road
Saint Paul, MN 55121-2055
651-454-7250
FAX: 651-454-0766 800-328-7560
asbc@scisoc.org www.asbcnet.org
Karen Cummings, Publications Director
Steven Nelson, VP
Provides news items and technical reports on brewing and related matters. *$20.00*
Quarterly Founded: 1934

8688 Agri Times Northwest
Sterling Ag
PO Box 189
Pendleton, OR 97801
541-276-7845
FAX: 541-276-7964
info@agritimes.com
http://www.agritimes.com/
Virgil Rupp, CEO/President
Sterling Allen, Publisher/Marketing Director
Regional agricultural newspaper. *$20.00*
16 pages
Circulation: 3700
Printed in 4 colors on newsprint stock

8689 Agweek
Grand Forks Herald
375 2nd Avenue
PO Box 6008
Grand Forks, ND 58206-6008
701-780-1100
FAX: 701-780-1211 800-811-2580
feedback@gfherald.com
http://www.gfherald.com
Mike Jacobs, Publisher
Kim Deats, Editor
Offers information to professionals working in the field of agriculture, from farmers to equipment manufacturers. *$32.00*
80 pages Weekly Founded: 1879
Circulation: 26,000
Printed in on newsprint stock

8690 Alcoholic Beverage Control: From the State Capitals
Wakeman Walworth
PO BOX 7376
Alexandria, VA 22307-7376
703-768-9600
FAX: 703-768-9690
newsletters@statecapitals.com
http://statecapitals.com
Keyes Walworth, Publisher
Allen Klein, Editor
Christine Ryan, Marketing Manager/Circula
Tommy Broyles, Manager
Reports on state-by-state liquor regulatory activities. Gives an accurate picture on how states are governing liquor advertising, liquor taxes, and bottle bills, Sunday sales

laws, liquor shop liability, license regulation, drunken driving laws, legal drinking ages and other state endeavors affecting liquor. *$265.00*
4 pages Weekly Founded: 1962
Printed in 1 color on matte stock
Computerized version available

8691 Alcoholic Beverage Executives' Newsletter International
Patricia Kennedy
PO Box 3188
Omaha, NE 68103-1088
402-397-5514
FAX: 402-397-3843
pats2410@aol.com
Patricia Kennedy, Editor
Current news of the wine, beer, and distilled spirits marketplace, and provides information and ideas for the marketing and advertising campaigns of these beverages. *$275.00*
Weekly

8692 American Agriculturist
Farm Progress Companies
191 S Gary Avenue
Carol Stream, IL 60188-2095
630-690-5600
FAX: 630-462-4656 800-441-1410
wvogt@farmprogress.com
http://www.farmprogress.com
Jeffrey Apin, CEO/President
Sarah Hess, Circulation Director
Kim Smith, Director, Marketing Servi
Jeffrey E. Tennant, manager- custom publishing
Agricultural magazine serving New York farmers and agri-businesses. *$23.00*
Monthly Founded: 1905
Circulation: 20000

8693 American Beekeeping Federation Newsletter
American Beekeeping Federation
115 Morning Glory Circle
PO Box 1337
Jesup, GA 31598-1337
912-427-4233
FAX: 912-427-8447
info@abfnet.org
http://www.abfnet.org
Troy H Fore Jr, Executive Director/Chief Executive
Troy Fore, Advertising/Sales Manager
Newsletter for members of the American Beekeeping Federation. *$35.00*
24 pages Founded: 1943
Circulation: 1,200 Audited
Printed in on newsprint stock

8694 American Institute of Baking Technical Bulletin
American Institute of Baking
PO Box 3999
Manhattan, KS 66505-3999
785-537-4750
FAX: 785-537-1493 800-633-5137
info@aibonline.org
http://www.aibonline.org
Janette Goroth, Editor
Martin Puntney, Production Manager
James Munyon, President/CEO
Developed to keep the baking and allied trades apprised of current trends in ingredients, products, equipment, processing, packaging, nutrition and research. *$50.00*
Monthly Founded: 1919

8695 American Meat Institute: Newsletter
1150 Connecticut Avenue
NW 12th floor
Washington, DC 20036
202-587-4200
FAX: 202-587-4300
http://www.meatami.com
J Patrick Boyle, President/CEO
Janet Riley, Editor
Ayoka Blandford, Marketing Manager
Subscription includes news of legislative and government regulations and actions relevant to the meat industry.
Quarterly Founded: 1906
Circulation: 3000

8696 American Society of Agricultural Consultants News
American Society of Agricultural Consultants
950 S Cherry Street
Suite 508
Denver, CO 80246-2664
303-758-3514
FAX: 303-758-0190
asac@agr-associations.org
www.agconsultants.org
Deborah Wiig, Editor
Informs ASAC members of news regarding members, events, education and government issues.
8-12 pages Quarterly Founded: 1963
Circulation: 200
Printed in on newsprint stock

8697 American Soybean Association Newsletter
12125 Woodcrest Executive Drive
Suite 100
Saint Louis, MO 63141-5009
314-576-1770
FAX: 314-576-2786 800-688-7692
bcallanan@soy.org
http://www.soygrowers.com
Ron Heck, Chairman
Neal Bredehoeft, President
Bob Metz, VP
Steve Censky, Chief Executive Officer
Mission is to improve US soybean farmer profitability.
Monthly Founded: 1920
Printed in 4 colors on glossy stock

8698 Association of American Seed Control Officials Bulletin
Utah Department of Agriculture
350 N Redwood Road
Salt Lake City, UT 84116-3087
801-965-4574
Steve Burningham
Seed laws in the US and Canada.
Annual

8699 Association of Food Industries Newsletter
Association of Food Industries
3301 Route 66
Suite 205, Building C
Neptune, NJ 07753
732-922-3008
FAX: 732-922-3590
afi@afius.org http://www.afius.org/
Bob Bauer, President
Offers information & education on customs and usage of trade in the food industry and current events in the business.
Founded: 1906

8700 BEMA Newsletter
BEMA, the Baking Industry Suppliers Association
825 Green Bay Road
Suite 120
Wilmette, IL 60091
847-920-1230
FAX: 847-920-1253
office@bema.org www.bema.org
Quarterly

8701 Beer Institute
122 C Street NW
Suite 750
Washington, DC 20001-2109
202-737-2337
FAX: 202-737-7004 800-379-2739
info@beerinstitute.org
www.beerinstitute.org
Jeff Becker, President
Art DeCelle, Executive VP
The national trade association for the brewing industry, representing both big and small brewers as well as importers and industry suppliers.
6 pages Quarterly
Circulation: 2500

8702 Beer Marketer's Insights Newsletter
Beer Marketer's Insights
PO Box 264
West Nyack, NY 10994
845-624-2337
FAX: 845-624-2340
www.beerinsights.com
Benj Steinman, President
Reports on the competitive battle among brewers for a share of the beer market. Analyzes recent legislation and factors that affect the industry.
Monthly

8703 Beer Perspectives
National Beer Wholesalers Association
1101 King Street
Suite 600
Alexandria, VA 22314-2944
703-390-0591
FAX: 703-683-8965
info@nbwa.org www.nbwa.org
Erin Rutherford, Editor
Lindsay Blankenship, Membership Development Manager
NBWA's newsletter reporting legislative, regulatory and industry news of importance to beer distributors.
Bi-Weekly/Members Only

8704 Beer Statistics News
Beer Marketer's Insights
PO Box 264
West Nyack, NY 10994
845-624-2337
FAX: 845-624-2340
http://www.beerinsights.com
Benj Steinnan, CEO/President
Jerry Curley, Circulation Manager
Supplies data for major brewers' shipments in 39 reporting states. *$450.00*
Annual+

8705 Beverage Digest
2 Depot Plaza
Suite 101A
Bedford Hills, NY 10507
914-244-0700
FAX: 914-244-0774
order@beverage-digest.com
http://www.beverage-digest.com

John Sicher, Editor/Publisher
Tom Fine, Managing Editor

Authoritative publication covering the non-alcoholic beverages industry. *$675.00*

22 issues per y Founded: 1982

8706 Beverage World Periscope
Keller International Publishing Corporation
150 Great Neck Road
Great Neck, NY 11021
516-829-9722
FAX: 516-829-5414
http://www.kellerpubs.com

Terry Beirne, Publisher
Bryan DeLuca, Editor
Jerry Keller, President

Analysis of developments as they occur in the beverage marketplace, presented in a tightly-written, four-color tabloid format, makes this a unique newsletter. This publication limits advertising to tabloid or standard pages.

Monthly Founded: 1882
Circulation: 33000

8707 Bison Connection
National Bison Association
1400 W. 122nd Ave
Suite 106
Westminster, CO 80234-2140
303-292-2833
FAX: 303-292-2564
laurie@bisoncentral.com
www.bisoncentral.com

Laurie Dineen, Editor/Advertising Director
Dave Carter, Manager

Timely information important to buffalo producers around the country.

Monthly Founded: 1975

8708 Bottled Water Reporter
Bottled Water Association
1700 Diagonal Road
Suite 650
Alexandria, VA 22314-2844
703-683-5213
FAX: 703-683-4074
mbusetti@bottledwater.org
http://www.bottledwater.org

Max Busetti, Editor

Trade news.

8709 Brewers Bulletin
PO Box 677
Thiensville, WI 53092
262-242-6105
FAX: 262-242-5133
bulletindigest@milwpc.com

Thomas Volke, President

Brewing industry newspaper. *$53.00*

Founded: 1907
Circulation: 550

8710 Business of Herbs
Northwind Farm Publications
439 Ponderosa Way
Jemez Springs, NM 87025-8036
505-829-3448
FAX: 505-829-3449
northwind@sulphercanyon.com
www.herb-biz.com

David Oliver, Publisher
Paula Oliver, Editor

News of interest for herb growers and marketers. Covers all aspects of the herb industry and offers book reviews, events calendar, new products, business profiles, sources, resources, networking and more. Geared to small businesses. *$24.00*

48 pages Bi-Monthly
Circulation: 2,500
Printed in 1 color on matte stock

8711 Cameron's Foodservice Marketing Reporter
Cameron's Publications
5423 Sheridan Drive
PO Box 676
Williamsville, NY 14231
519-586-8785
FAX: 519-586-8816
mail@cameronpub.com
www.cameronpub.com
Successful promotion and advertising case histories for the restaurant and hotel industry.

100.00 names

8712 Can Shipments Report
1730 Rhde Island Avenue NW
Suite 1000
Washington, DC 20036-2212
202-232-4677
FAX: 202-232-5756
clee@cancentral.com
http://www.cancentral.com

Robert Budway, CEO/President
Shawn Relly, Editor/Publisher *$265.00*

Quarterly Founded: 1938

8713 Capitol Line-Up
American Association of Meat Processors
One Meeting Place
PO Box 269
Elizabeth town, PA 17022
717-367-1168
FAX: 717-367-9096
aamp@aamp.com
http://www.aamp.com

Jey Wenther, Editor
Steve Krut, CEO/President

Features news and information on meat products and issues brought up by the US Department of Agriculture and its Food Safety and Inspection Service. *$50.00*

Monthly Founded: 1939
Circulation: 12000
Printed in 1 color

8714 Catering Service Idea Newsletter
Prosperity & Profits Unlimited
PO Box 416
Denver, CO 80201
303-573-5564
http://

A Doyle, Editor

Catering service business ideas and possibilities. *$5.00*

4 pages
Circulation: 1750 Audited
Printed in 1 color on matte stock

8715 Center of the Plate
American Culinary Federation
180 Center Place Way
Saint Augustine, FL 32095
904-824-4468
FAX: 904-825-4758 800-624-9458
acf@acfchefs.net
http://www.acfchefs.org

Brent Frei, Director Marketing
Kay Orde, Editor
Joachim Buchner, CEO

Official membership newsletter of the American Culinary Federation. *$50.00*

Monthly Founded: 1956
Circulation: 25,000

8716 Champagne Wines Information Bureau
KCSA
800 2nd Avenue
5th Floor
New York, NY 10017-4709
212-682-6300
FAX: 212-697-0910 800-642-4267
info@champagnes.com
http://www.champagnes.com

Jean-Louis Carbonnier, Editor
Herbert L Corbin, President/CEO

Representative of Comite Interprofessionnel duVinde Champagne, Epernay, France.

4 pages
Circulation: 10000
Printed in 1 color on matte stock

8717 Cheese Reporter
Cheese Reporter Publishing Company
2810 Crossroads Drive
Suite 3000
Madison, WI 53718
608-246-8430
FAX: 608-246-8431
info@cheesereporter.com
http://www.cheesereporter.com

Richard D Groves, Publisher/Editor
Kevin Thome, Marketing Director
Betty Mertes, Circulation Manager

Leading weekly publication serving manufacturers and marketers of cheese, butter, ice cream, yogurt and other fermented milk foods, whey and other dairy processors. *$150.00*

16 pages Weekly Founded: 1876
Circulation: 2000
Printed in 4 colors on n stock

8718 Coffee Reporter
National Coffee Association
15 Maiden Lane
Suite 1405
New York, NY 10038
212-766-4007
FAX: 212-766-5815
info@ncausa.org www.ncausa.org

Steven M Wolfe, Membership/Marketing Director
Joseph F DeRupo, Communications/PR Director

Contains news of NCA activities and programs, new product development and market trends in both the U.S. and global coffee industry, regulatory action affecting the U.S. coffee industry and statistical data on ICO prices and U.S. retail prices. A single copy subscription is supplied free of charge to members, non-eligible parties for membership the cost is $40.00 *$65.00*

Quarterly

8719 Coffee, Sugar and Cocoa Exchange Daily Market Report
New York Board of Trade
1 North End Avenue
New York, NY 10282-1101
212-748-4000
FAX: 212-748-4039 877-877-8890
webmaster@nybot.com
http://www.nybot.com

Leonel Fernández, President

Offers market reports on the stock market exchange covering foods and specific food investing.

8720 **Concessionworks Newsletter**
National Association of Concessionaires
35 E Wacker Drive
Suite 1816
Chicago, IL 60601-2270
312-236-3858
FAX: 312-236-7809
scross@naconline.org
www.naconline.org

Susan Cross, Communications Director

For members with updates on association happenings, feature articles, new member listings, product news and industry updates.
Bi-Annually Founded: 1944
Printed in 4 colors

8721 **Council for Agricultural Science and Technology Newsletter**
4420 Lincoln Way
Ames, IA 50014-3447
515-292-2125
FAX: 515-292-4512
cast@cast-science.org
www.cast-science.org

John M Bonner, Executive VP
Donna Freeman, Membership/Marketing Director
Lynette Allen, Assistant Editor

Identifies food, fiber, environmental and other agricultural issues for all stake holders. *$60.00*
Quarterly Founded: 1972
Printed in 2 colors

8722 **Country World Newspaper**
Echo Publishing Company
401 Church Street
PO Box 596
Sulphur Springs, TX 75483
903-885-8663
FAX: 903-885-8768 800-245-2149
lori@countryworldnews.com
http://www.countryworldnews.com

Scott Keys, Publisher
Lori Cope, Editor
Jim Horton, Manager

A newspaper offering agricultural information to farmers, ranchers, dairyfarmers, and agribusinesses. *$24.00*
36 pages Weekly Founded: 1981
Circulation: 16200
Printed in 4 colors on newsprint stock

8723 **Crop Protection Management**
2892 Crescent Avenue
Eugene, OR 97408
541-343-5641
FAX: 541-686-0248 800-874-3276

Jeff Powell, Publisher

This newsletter covers all aspects of crop management and protection, including pesticides, agricultural chemicals and legislation.
5 per year

8724 **Daily Advocate**
Thomson Newspapers
PO Box 220
Greenville, OH 45331-220
937-548-3151
FAX: 937-548-3913
info@dailyadvocate.com
http://www.dailyadvocate.com

Gary Lamberg, Publisher
Bob Robinson, Editor
Ken Bowen, Circulation Manager

Farming interests, grain, livestock. Sections on senior citizens, farmers, builders, religion, sports, as well as special sections on agriculture and home improvement. *$117.00*
Daily Founded: 1883

8725 **Dairy Industry Newsletter**
Eden Publishing Company
2714 Crawford Avenue
Evanston, IL 60201-4924
847-803-2000
FAX: 847-803-2077
www.dairyindustrynewsletter.com

Barry Wilson, Publisher

Resource serving all sectors of the dairy industry. Reports on commercial, trade, political and market information. *$400.00*
8 pages 25 per year
Printed in 2 colors on glossy stock

8726 **Dairy Profit Weekly**
DairyBusiness Communications
6437 Collamer Road
East Syracuse, NY 13057-1031
315-703-7979
FAX: 315-703-7988 800-334-1904
smiller@dairybusiness.com
http://www.dairybusiness.com

Dave Natzke, Editorial Director
Joel Hastings, Publisher
Eleanor Jacobs, Regional Editor

Latest information, tips, and trends. *$179.00*
4 pages Weekly
Circulation: 1700
Printed in 2 colors on newsprint stock

8727 **Doane's Agricultural Report**
Doane Agricultural Services
11701 Borman Drive
Suite 300
Saint Louis, MO 63146-4193
314-569-2700
FAX: 314-569-1083 800-535-2342
adever@doane.com
http://www.doane.com

Dan Manternach, Publisher/Editor
Kathy Topping, Managing Editor
Allen Dever, Market Analyst

Marketing and management information for farmers and agribusiness professionals. *$118.00*
Weekly Founded: 1925
Circulation: 26000

8728 **Farm Managers & Rural Appraisers News**
Amer. Society of Farm Managers & Rural Appraisers
950 S Cherry Street
Suite 508
Denver, CO 80246-2664
303-758-3513
FAX: 303-758-0190
Info@agri-associations.org
http://www.asfmra.org

Cheryl L Cooley, Manager Communications
Tamela White, Marketing Manager

Published by the American Society of Farm Managers and Rural Appraisers. *$24.00*
Founded: 1929
Mailing list available for rent 2500 names $1M per M.
Printed in 2 colors on glossy stock

8729 **Farm and Ranch Guide**
4023 N State Street
Bismarck, ND 58503-620
701-255-4905
FAX: 701-255-2312
http://www.farmandranchguide.com

Brian Kroshus, Publisher
Mark Conlon, Editor
Becky Lensegrav, Circulation Manager

A leading agriculture publication in the upper Midwest, distributed to 38,000 qualified farmers and ranchers in North Dakota, Minnesota, northern South Dakota and eastern Montana. Our readers requalify every year so our database is up-to-date with their farming information. *$32.95*
107 pages
Circulation: 34000+
Printed in 4 colors on newsprint stock : online

8730 **Farm and Ranch Living**
Reiman Publications
5400 S 60th Street
Greendale, WI 53129-1404
414-423-0100
FAX: 414-423-1143 800-344-6913
subscriberservices@reimanpub.com
http://www.reimanpub.com/

Roy Reiman, Publisher

Newspaper for farmers. *$14.98*
68 pages Founded: 1965

8731 **Farmer's Friend**
116 Main Street
Suite 4
Towanda, PA 18848
570-265-2151
FAX: 570-265-1647 800-253-3662
review@epix.net
http://www.farmers-friend.com

Kathy Thomas, Managing Editor
Ronald W Hosie, Editor
Jim Towner, Publisher
Debbie Fero, Circulation Manager

Farming news.
Weekly Founded: 1977

8732 **Fence Post**
423 Main Street
Windsor, CO 80550-5129
970-686-5691
FAX: 970-686-5694 800-275-5646
shill@thefencepost.com
http://www.thefencepost.com

Jim Eisberry, President
Gary Sweeney, Publisher
Luke Gonzales, Business Manager

Farming news and reports. *$39.00*
Weekly

8733 **Food & Fiber Letter**
Sparks Companies
6862 Elm Street
McLean, VA 22101
703-484-4700
FAX: 703-556-7865
Legislative updates, news and information on agricultural policy, environment and conservation industry.
Weekly
Printed in 2 colors on matte stock
Computerized version available

8734 **Food Allergy News**
Food Allergy & Anaphlaxis Network
11781 Lee Jackson Hwy
Suite 160
Fairfax, VA 22033-2208
703-691-3179
FAX: 703-691-2713 800-929-4040
faan@foodallergy.org
http://www.foodallergy.org

Anne Munoz-Furlong, Publisher
Andreia MIller, Editor

Allergy newsletter with two pages of allergy-free recipes, coping strategies, research and studies. *$30.00*
12 pages Founded: 1991
Circulation: 28000
Printed in 2 colors on glossy stock

8735 Food Industry Futures: A Strategy Service
CRS
PO Box 430
Fayetteville, NC 28302
910-486-9059
FAX: 910-486-9058
Ian Cuthill, Publisher, Editor
Includes new developments concerning management or marketing practices, mergers and acquisitions, economics, trade policies, etc. It covers the industry from farm and retail stores, mostly in the US but also internationally. Accepts advertising. *$150.00*
4 pages

8736 Food Industry Newsletter
Newsletters
PO Box 342730
Bethesda, MD 20827-2730
301-469-8507
FAX: 301-469-7271 foodltr@aol.com
Ellis Meredith, Publisher
Ray Marsili, Editor
Alice Corcoran, Circulation Manager
Concise, objective report for busy food executives, covering major food industry developments, including mergers and acquisitions, new trends and products, corporate and marketing strategies, etc. In addition to 22 regular issues a year, subscription also includes Special Food Marketing Reports on timely matters. *$245.00*
twice monthly except Aug. Founded: 1972

8737 Food Insight
International Food Information Council
1100 Connecticut Avenue NW
Suite 430
Washington, DC 20036-4120
202-296-6540
FAX: 202-296-6547
foodinfo@ific.org http://ific.org
Ann Bouchoux, Editor
Nick Alexander, Associate Editor
Michael Hayes, Copy Editor
Joe Trento, President
8 pages 6 issues per ye
Circulation: 45000
Printed in 4 colors on glossy stock
Computerized version available

8738 Food Institute Report
Food Institute
1 Broadway
Elmwood Park, NJ 07407
201-791-5570
FAX: 201-791-5222
food1@foodinstitute.com
http://www.foodinstitute.com
Brian Todd, President
Sue Antisti, Marketing
Serves as a central information service for food trades. Issues reports, studies and statistical data. Member companies throughout the US over 40 foreign countries. *$695.00*
Weekly Founded: 1928
Circulation: 3000

8739 Food Merchants Advocate
New York State Food Merchant
130 Washington Avenue
Albany, NY 12210-2219
518-463-5315
FAX: 518-434-9962
Christopher Pellnat, Editor
A tabloid newspaper for food retailers. *$10.00*
Monthly

8740 Food Safety Consortium Newsletter
Food Safety Consortium
110 Agriculture Building
University of Arkansas
Fayetteville, AR 72701
479-575-5647
FAX: 479-575-7531
fsc@cavern.uark.edu
http://www.fsconsortium.net
David Edmark, Editor
Gregory Weidemann, CEO
A quarterly newsletter published by the Food Safety Consortium.
Quarterly Founded: 1988
Circulation: 700

8741 Food Safety Professional
Carpe Diem
208 Floral Vale Boulevard
Yardley, PA 19067
215-860-7800
FAX: 215-860-7900
staff@carpediemcomm.com
www.foodquality.com
The Food Safety Professional is a quarterly publication of The antional Registry of Food Safety Professionals. Practical hands on article and advice form the experts will keep you informed of the latest technique an technologies in food safety.' *$20.00*
Quarterly
Circulation: 30,000

8742 Food Trade News
Best-Met Publishing
5537 Twin Knolls Road
Suite 438
Columbia, MD 21045
410-730-5013
FAX: 410-740-4680
office@best-met.com
http://www.best-met.com
Nina Weiland, Vice-President
Jeffrey W Metzger, Publisher
Terri Maloney, Editor
Beth Pripstein, Circulation Manager
$63.00
Monthly
Printed in 1 color on matte stock

8743 Food World Information Services
Best-Met Publishing Company
5537 Twin Knolls Road
Suite 438
Columbia, MD 21045
410-730-5013
FAX: 410-740-4680
tmaloney@best-met.com
http://www.best-met.com
Jeffrey W Metzger, Publisher
Terri Maloney, Editor
Beth Pripstein, Circulation Manager
Richard J. Bestany, President
Provides market data for Baltimore, Washington, Central Pennsylvania and Philadelphia
Monthly
Printed in on newsprint stock

8744 FoodTalk
Pike & Fischer
109 North Henry Street
Alexandria, VA 22314
703-548-3146
FAX: 703-548-3017 800-255-8131
info@setantapublishing.com
http://www.setantapublishing.com
Declan Couroy, Editor
John Pike, Executive Director
Sanitation tips for food workers. *$120.00*
Quarterly Founded: 1939
Circulation: 5000
Printed in 2 colors on matte stock

8745 Global Dairy Update
DairyBusiness Communications
6437 Collamer Road
East Syracuse, NY 13057-1031
315-703-7979
FAX: 315-703-7988 800-334-1904
dgarno@dairybusiness.com
www.dairybusiness.com
Focuses on dairy developments throughout the world. *$197.00*
4 pages Monthly Founded: 1904
Printed in 2 colors on newsprint stock

8746 Grayson Report
Grayson Associates
30728 Paseo Elegancia
San Juan Capistrano, CA 92675
949-487-9970
FAX: 949-487-9975
webmaster@graysonassociates.com
http://www.graysonassociates.com
Suzanne Grayson, Publisher
Robert Grayson, Marketing Manager
Marketing analysis of the packaged goods industry.
Founded: 1970

8747 Greenhouse Grower
Meister Publishing Company
37733 Euclid Avenue
Willoughby, OH 44094-5992
440-942-2000
FAX: 440-942-0662 800-572-7740
donofrey@meistermedia.com
http://www.meistermedia.com
Richard Meister, Chairman
Gary Fitzgerald, President
Don Keating, Circulation Manager
Delilah Onofrey, Group Editor
Association news offering articles of information on crops, farming and nursery news.
Monthly Founded: 1983
Circulation: 21834

8748 Greenhouse Product News
Scranton Gillette Communications
380 E NW Highway
Suite 200
Des Plaines, IL 60016
847-298-6622
FAX: 847-390-0408
http://www.onhort.com
Bridget White, Editor
For owners and managers of commercial floricultural growing facilities. *$30.00*
Monthly
Circulation: 19000
Mailing list available for rent 19,000 names

8749 **Grocery Manufacturers of America: Executive Update**
2401 Pennsylvania Avenue NW
2nd Floor
Washington, DC 20037
202-337-9400
FAX: 202-337-4508
info@gmabrands.com
http://www.gmabrands.com
C Manly Molpus, President/Publisher
Jeff Nedelman, VP Communications
Focuses on the productivity and public policy issues affecting our industry.
6 pages Monthly Founded: 1908

8750 **Hay Market News**
US Department of Agriculture
1400 Independence Ave
S.W
Washington, DC 20250
202-907-7650
FAX: 509-457-7132
shessman2@kda.state.ks.us
http://www.usda.gov
Abraham Lincoln, President
Federal newsletter offering information and updates on crops and farming. *$40.00*
8 pages Founded: 1862
Circulation: 180 Audited

8751 **Hot Sheet**
Fresh-Cut Produce Association
1600 Duke Street
Suite 440
Alexandria, VA 22314
530-756-8900
FAX: 530-756-8901
jgorny@fresh-cuts.org
http://www.fresh-cuts.org
Jerry Gorny, President
Sean Handerhan, Marketing Director
A newsletter containing technical information, marketing news and exhibit information on the produce trade. Serves over 500 members. *$35.00*
Monthly Founded: 1987
Circulation: 23,000

8752 **Hotel, Restaurant, Institutional Buyers Guide**
Urner Barry Publications
PO Box 389
Toms River, NJ 08754
732-240-5330
FAX: 732-341-0891 800-932-0617
mail@urnerbarry.com
http://www.urnerbarry.com/
Paul B Brown Jr, President
Sheila M Deane, Marketing Manager
Richard A. Brown, VP
Reports on perishable food prices, meat, seafood, fruits, vegetables and others compiled for the metropolitan New York, New Jersey and Connecticut markets. *$86.00*
4 pages Weekly Founded: 1858
Circulation: 120

8753 **Hotel, Restaurant, Institutional Meat Price Report**
Urner Barry Publications
PO Box 389
Toms River, NJ 08754-2741
732-240-5330
FAX: 732-341-0891 800-932-0617
mail@urnerbarry.com
http://www.urnerbarry.com
Paul B Brown Jr, President
Karen Mick, Circulation Director
Current meat and poultry pricing for the hotel, restaurant and institutional buyers. *$174.00*
Weekly Founded: 1858
Circulation: 200

8754 **IAFIS Global Food MegaTrends**
International Assn. of Food Industry Suppliers
1451 Dolley Madison Boulevard
Mc Lean, VA 22101-3847
703-761-2600
FAX: 703-761-4334
info@iafis.org www.iafis.org
Stephanie Webb, Editor
A quarterly bulletin covering international news and its effect on the food processing and packaging industries.
Circulation: 1,500

8755 **Ice Cream Reporter**
Ice Cream Reporter
Hilton Terrace
Willsboro, NY 12996
518-963-4333
FAX: 518-963-4999
hwaxman55@msn.com
Howard Waxman, Publisher/Editor
News for ice cream executives. *$395.00*
Monthly Founded: 1987

8756 **Insight**
Retailer's Bakery Association
14239 Park Central Drive
Laurel, MD 20707-5261
301-725-2149
FAX: 301-725-2187 800-638-0924
rba@rbanet.com
http://www.rbanet.com
Bernard Reynolds, Executive VP
Stewart Taylor, Convention Director
Ed Fraser, President
Katrina Cooley, Marketing & Communications Director
Member newsletter for baking industry professionals.
8 pages Monthly Founded: 1918
Printed in 2 colors on matte stock

8757 **International Association of Food Industry Suppliers**
1451 Dolly Madison Boulevard
McLean, VA 22101-3850
703-761-2600
FAX: 703-761-4334
info@iafis.org http://www.iafis.org/
Stephen C Schlegel, President
Annette Damey, Client Services
Andrew Drennan, Business Development
Dairy food and beverage industries, and related sanitary processing industries addressing the marketing and business information needs of the food supply channel. *$250.00*
Monthly Founded: 1983

8758 **Italian Trade Commission**
33 E 67th Street
New York, NY 10022-1240
212-480-0300
FAX: 212-758-1050
newyork@newyork.ice.it
www.italtrade.com/ice
Robert Luongo, Executive Director
Aniello Musella, Manager
Developments in the Italian wine industry and market, as well as reviews of imported wines from Italy.

8759 **Kane's Beverage Week**
Whitaker Newsletters
313 S Avenue
#340
Fanwood, NJ 07023-1364
FAX: 908-889-6339 800-359-6049
Joel Whitaker, Publisher
News on marketing, economic and regulatory factors affecting the alcohol beverage industry. *$499.00*
6 pages Quarterly

8760 **Kashrus Magazine**
Yeshiva Birkas Revuen
PO Box 204
Brooklyn, NY 11230
718-336-8544
FAX: 718-336-8550
info@kashrusmagazine.com
http://www.kashrusmagazine.com
Rabbi Yosef Wikler, Editor
Regular, complete update on Kosher food mislabelings, dairy/nondairy status, kosher supervision standards, newly certified products and food technology, travel and Jewish life. *$18.00*
88 pages Founded: 1980
Circulation: 10000
Printed in 4 colors on glossy stock

8761 **Kettle Talk**
Retail Confectioners International
1807 Glenview Road
Suite 204
Glenview, IL 60025-2968
847-724-6120
FAX: 847-724-2719 800-545-5381
sales@makinbatch.com
http://www.retailconfectioners.org
Terry Craft, President
Terry Hickling, Chairman of Marketing
Dan Malley, VP
Membership newsletter, including confection recipes. Also regional meetings.
Monthly Founded: 1917
Circulation: 550
Printed in on matte stock

8762 **Kiplinger Agricultural Letter**
Kiplinger Washington Editors
1729 H Street NW
Washington, DC 20006-3938
202-887-6400
FAX: 202-785-3648 800-544-0155
sub.services@kiplinger.com
http://www.kiplinger.com
Austin Kiplinger, Chairman
Kevin McCormally, Editorial Director
Fred Frailey, Editor
David Harrison, Manager
Forecasts and judgments on wages, income, food packaging, processing and marketing techniques. *$56.00*
Founded: 1923

8763 **Kitchen Times**
Howard Wilson and Company
555 W Taft Drive
South Holland, IL 60473
708-339-5111
FAX: 708-210-2069 800-245-7224
Howard Wilson, Publisher, Editor
News on food and cooking. *$33.00*
8 pages Monthly Founded: 1959

8764 Lean Trimmings
National Meat Association
1970 Broadway
Suite 825
Oakland, CA 94612-2299
510-763-1533
FAX: 510-763-6186
staff@nmaonline.org
http://www.nmaonline.org

Jeremy Russell, Editor
Jen Kempis, Operations Manager

Deals with the latest regulatory and business news on the meat industry.
Weekly Founded: 1946
Circulation: 1350
Printed in 1 color on matte stock

8765 Legislative Onion Outlet
822 7th Street
Suite 510
Greeley, CO 80631-3941
970-353-5895
FAX: 970-353-5897
tfell@onions-usa.org
http://www.onions-usa.org

Wayne Mininger, Executive VP
Tanya Fell, Public/Industry Relations

An annual bulletin published by the National Onion Association.
Founded: 1913
Circulation: 600
Mailing list available for rent 600 names

8766 Legislative Update
Independent Bakers Association
1223 Potomac Street NW
PO Box 3731
Washington, DC 20007-3212
202-333-8190
FAX: 202-337-3809
bpyle@independencebaker.com
www.indepencebaker.com
Monthly

8767 Link Newsletter
R&D Associates
16607 Blanco Road
Suite 1506
San Antonio, TX 78232-1940
210-493-8024
FAX: 210-493-8036
hqs@militaryfood.org
www.militaryfood.or

David Dee, Editor

Of interest to the food, food packaging, food processing and foodservice industry.
300 pages Quarterly

8768 Loan Trimmings & Herd on the Hill
1970 Broadway Avenue
Suite 825
Oakland, CA 94612-2299
510-763-1533
FAX: 510-763-6186
staff@amaonline.org
Weekly
Circulation: 600

8769 Make It Tasty
Prosperity & Profits Unlimited
PO Box 416
Denver, CO 80201-0416
303-573-5564

AC Doyle, Publisher

Spice company blends food business newsletter with salt-free, herb and spice blend recipes. *$25.00*
8 pages Annual Founded: 1996
Circulation: 2,500 Audited
Printed in on matte stock

8770 NCA Annual Convention
National Coffee Association
15 Maiden Lane
Suite 1405
New York, NY 10038
212-766-4007
FAX: 212-766-5815
info@ncausa.org www.ncausa.org

Ernesto Alvarez, Convention Committee Chairman
Steven M Wolfe, Membership/Marketing Director
Robert Nelson, President

The coffee event of the year, industry executives from all over the world get together to learn from the most current educational sessions, see old friends and meet new ones.
Annual/March Founded: 1911

8771 National Automatic Merchandising Association
20 N Wacker Drive
Suite 3500
Chicago, IL 60606-3102
312-346-0370
FAX: 312-704-4140 800-331-8816
rgeerdes@vending.org
http://www.vending.org

Richard M Geerdes, President/CEO
Steve DeGrave, VP Sales/Marketing

Serves merchandising, vending, contract foodservice management and office coffee service industries.
Founded: 1946

8772 National Chicken Council
National Chicken Council
1015 15th Street NW
Suite 930
Washington, DC 20005-2605
202-408-1339
FAX: 202-293-4005
rlobb@chickenusa.org
http://www.eatchicken.com

George Watts, President
Richard L Lobb, Communications Director

News on the chicken production and processing industry. Free subscription with membership to the National Chicken Council.
Weekly Founded: 1950
Circulation: 400

8773 National Conference on Interstate Milk Shipments
National Conference on Interstate Milk
123 Buena Vista Drive
Frankfort, KY 40601-8770
502-695-0253
FAX: 502-695-0253
ltownsend@ncims.org
http://www.ncims.org

Leon Townsend, Executive Secretary
Marlena Bordson, Chair

Founded: 1946

8774 National Cottonseed Products Association Newsletter
National Cottonseed Products Association
104 Timber Creek Drive
Suite 200
Cordova, TN 38018-2267
901-682-0800
FAX: 901-682-2856
info@cottonseed.com
http://www.cottonseed.com

Ben Morgan, Publisher
Dave Johnson, President
Robert Lacy, VP
Ben Morgan, Editor

Current events.
Founded: 1897
Circulation: 400

8775 National Fertilizer Solutions Association Newsletter
339 Consort Drive
Manchester, MO 63011-4439
636-256-6650
FAX: 636-256-4901

Kelly O'Brien-Wray, Publisher
Fred Speckmann, Editor

Accepts advertising.
90 pages

8776 National Honey Market News
US Department of Agriculture
21 N 1st Avenue
#224
Yakima, WA 98902-2663
509-575-2494
FAX: 509-457-7132
lverstrate@usda.gov
www.ams.usda.gov/fv/mncs

Linda Verstrate, Publisher

Current honey market information and colony conditions in the US. *$24.00*
10-12 pages Monthly

8777 National Hot Pepper Association
400 NW 20th Street
Fort Lauderdale, FL 33311-3818
954-565-4972
FAX: 954-566-2208
peppergal@mindspring.com
http://www.inter-linked.com/org/nhpa

Robert J Payton, Publisher
Betty Payton, Editor

Networking among industry and private members. Education and information sharing. *$20.00*
28 pages Quarterly
Printed in on matte stock

8778 National Nutritional Foods Association Today
National Nutritional Foods Association
2112 E 4th St
Ste 200
Santa Ana, CA 92705-3816
949-622-6272
FAX: 949-622-6266 800-966-6632
nnfa@nnfa.org http://www.nnfa.org

Amanda Thomason, Editor/Publications Manager
Paul Bennett, CEO/President
Paul Bennett, CEO/President

Nonprofit trade organization dedicated to protecting and advancing the natural products industry for both retailers and suppliers. *$48.00*
Monthly Founded: 1936
Circulation: 8000

8779 National Onion Association Newsletter
822 7th Street
Suite 510
Greeley, CO 80631-3941
970-353-5895
FAX: 970-353-5897
kreddin@onions-usa.org
http://www.onions-usa.org

Wayne Mininger, Executive VP
Kim Reddin, Public/Industry Relation

Newsletter published by and only for the National Onion Association.
Monthly Founded: 1913
Circulation: 600
Mailing list available for rent 600 names

8780 National Shellfisheries Association News
Long Island University/Southampton College
Natural Sciences Division
Southampton, NY 11968
631-283-4000
FAX: 631-287-8054
Sandra Shumway, Production Manager
Eric Lang, Owner
Newsletter focusing on information for public health workers, shellfish producers and fishery administrators. *$125.00*

Circulation: 1000
Mailing list available for rent 1M names
Printed in 1 color on matte stock

8781 National Young Farmer Educational News
PO Box 68960
6060 FFA Drive
Alexandria, VA 22309-160
317-802-6060
FAX: 800-366-6556 888-332-2668
aboutffa@ffa.org http://www.ffa.org
Wayne Sprick, Publisher
Larry Case, Chief Executive Officer
Tabloid which receives articles and information from state associations as well as information from the National Association.
12 pages Founded: 1928

8782 No-Till Farmer
Lessiter Publications
225 Regency Court
Suite 200
Brookfield, WI 53008
262-782-4480
FAX: 262-782-1252 800-645-8455
info@lesspub.com
http://www.no-tillfarmer.com
Erin Weileder, Marketing Director
Frank Lessiter, Editor/Publisher
Management information for farmers interested in conservation tillage. *$37.95*
16 pages Monthly Founded: 1984
Circulation: 5500
Mailing list available for rent 5,000 names $90m per M.
Printed in 2 colors on glossy stock

8783 Organic Business News
Hotline Printing & Publishing
PO Box 161132
Atamonte Springs, FL 32716-1132
407-628-1377
FAX: 407-628-9935
dnnsblnk@cs.com
http://www.hotlineprinting.com/obn.html

Dennis Blank, Publisher/Editor
Christine Blank, Senior Editor
Leading industry publication that tracks the latest government actions, policy trends and financial development in development in the organic food business. *$110.00*
12 pages
Printed in 2 colors

8784 Organic Trade Association Newsletter
Organic Trade Association
60 Wells Street
Greenfield, MA 01301
413-774-7511
FAX: 413-774-6432
info@ota.com http://www.ota.com/
Katherine DiMatteo, Executive Director
Holly Givens, Editor
Members are businesses involved in the organic agriculture and products industry. Seeks to promote the industry and establish production and marketing standards. Also publishes The Organic Page: North American Resource Directory *$100.00*
24 pages Quarterly Founded: 1985
Circulation: 2500
Printed in 2 colors

8785 Packer
Vance Publishing
1901 W 84th Terrace
Suite 200
Lenexa, KS 66214
913-438-8700
FAX: 913-438-0695
rbertels@vancepublishing.com
http://www.thepacker.com
Robb Bertels, VP/Director Publishing
Ben Wood, Editor
Leanne Ball, Manager
Newspaper about produce marketing available in print and online. Includes articles, classifieds and accepts advertising. *$65.00*

Weekly

8786 Peterson Patriot
Peterson Patriot Printers-Publishers
202 Main Street
Peterson, IA 51047
712-295-7711
FAX: 712-295-7711
patriot@iowatelecom.net
Roger Stoner, Publisher
Jane Stoner, Editor
Jane Stoner, Production/Circulation Ma
Agricultural news. *$18.00*
12 pages Weekly
Circulation: 549

8787 Practical Gourmet
Linick Group
7 Putter Lane
PO Box 102
Middle Island, NY 11953
631-924-3888
FAX: 631-924-3890
linickgrp@att.net
http://www.lgroup.addr.com
Gaylen Andrews, Publisher/Editor
Roger Dextor, Production
Barbara Deal, Marketing Manager
Andrew Linick, Manager
The focus of this publication is light, healthy gourmet dining; includes reports on wine tastings, food festivals, contests, celebrations, cooking schools and other events. *$48.00*
36 pages Monthly Founded: 1975
Circulation: 210,000 Controlled
Mailing list available for rent 210 M names $110 per M.
Printed in 4 colors on glossy stock
Computerized version available

8788 Press Release
Independent Bakers Association
1223 Potomac Street NW
PO Box 3731
Wasington, DC 20007-3212
202-333-8190
FAX: 202-337-3809
bpyle@independencebakers.com
http://www.mindspring.com/~independentbaker/
Nick Pyle, President
Ann Parnow, Editor
Monthly Founded: 1964
Circulation: 400

8789 Produce Merchandiser
United Fresh Fruit & Vegetable Association
1901 Pennsylvania Avenue NW
Suite 1100
Washington, DC 20006
202-624-4989
FAX: 202-303-3433
united@uffva.org www.uffva.org
Information on promotion and consumer issues.

8790 Product Alert
Marketing Intelligence Service
6473D State Route 64
Naples, NY 14512-9726
585-374-6326
FAX: 585-374-5217 800-836-5710
mi@productscan.com
www.productscan.com
Christine Dengler, Marketing/Sales Manager
A twice-monthly briefing on new packaged goods introduced in North America. Featuring product pictures and descriptions with indexing provided in two convenient formats. Also available in a twice monthly, international version. *$795.00*
Fortnightly

8791 SIGNALS Newsletter
Agricultural Communicators in Education

Building 116 Mowry Road
PO Box 110810
Gainesville, FL 32611
352-392-9588
FAX: 352-392-7902
ace@ifas.ufl.edu
http://www.aceweb.org
Judy Winn, President
Amanda Chambliss, Editor
Offers news and information to communications professionals in the agricultural and farming industry. *$75.00*
six issues per

8792 Salad Special
Refrigerated Foods Association
2971 Flowers Road S
Suite 266
Atlanta, GA 30341-5403
770-452-0660
FAX: 770-455-3879
info@refrigeratedfoods.org
http://www.refrigeratedfoods.org
Gene Graves, President
A newsletters covering technical and marketing aspects of the industry, including news of projects, conventions and expositions.
Monthly Founded: 1980

8793 Salt & Trace Mineral Newsletter
Salt Institute
700 N Fairfax Street
Suite 600
Alexandria, VA 22314-2040
703-549-4648
FAX: 703-548-2194
info@saltinstitute.org
http://www.saltinstitute.org

Dick Hanneman, President,/Editor
Martina Moran, Administrative Assistant

Information on animal nutrition.
Founded: 1940
Circulation: 3000
Printed in on glossy stock

8794 Seafood Price-Current
Urner Barry Publications
PO Box 389
Toms River, NJ 08754-389
732-240-5330
FAX: 732-341-0891 800-932-0617
mail@urnerbarry.com
http://www.urnerbarry.com

Paul B Brown Jr, President
Karen Mick, Circulation Director

Spot market prices of the most widely traded fresh and frozen fin and shellfish items. *$383.00*
8 pages Weekly Founded: 1858
Circulation: 1500

8795 Seafood Trend Newsletter
8227 Ashworth Avenue N
Seattle, WA 98103-4434
206-523-2280
FAX: 206-526-8719
seafoodtrend@aol.com

Ken Talley, Editor/publisher

Provides information, statistics and economic facts and figures pertaining to the seafood market. *$235.00*
4 pages Founded: 1984
Circulation: 400
Printed in 2 colors on matte stock

8796 Seed Midden
Abundant Life Seed Foundation
PO Box 772
Port Townsend, WA 98368
360-385-5660
FAX: 360-385-7455
http://www.abundantlifeseeds.com

Forest Shomer, Publisher

Information covering events, seminars and meetings. *$8.00*
8 pages Quarterly

8797 Shelby Report of the Southeast
Shelby Publishing Company
517 Green Street NW
Gainesville, GA 30501-3300
770-534-8380
FAX: 770-535-0110
shelbpub@bellsouth.net
http://www.shelbypublishing.com

Ron Johnston, President/Publisher
Chuck Gilmer, Editor
Carol Tomaseski, Circulation Manager
Ileen Bloch, VP Publishing

A newsletter offering information on the retail and wholesale food trade. *$36.00*
Monthly Founded: 1966
Circulation: 25,201
Printed in on newsprint stock

8798 Shelby Report of the Southwest
Shelby Publishing Company
517 Green Street NW
Gainesville, GA 30501-3300
770-534-8380
FAX: 770-535-0110
shelbyedt@aol.com
http://www.shelbypublishing.com

Ron Johnston, President
Chuck Gilmer, Editor

A newsletter offering information on the retail and wholesale food trade. *$36.00*
Monthly Founded: 1966
Circulation: 23,380
Printed in on newsprint stock

8799 Shrimp News International
Aquaculture Digest
9450 Mira Mesa Boulevard
#B562
San Diego, CA 92126-4850

FAX: 858-271-0324

Robert Rosenberry, Editor

Publishes reports and directories on the world's shrimp industry. *$95.00*
24 pages Biweekly
Mailing list available for rent
Printed in 1 color on matte stock

8800 Soft Drink Letter
Whitaker Newsletters
313 S Avenue
#203
Fanwood, NJ 07023-1364
908-889-6336
FAX: 908-889-6339 800-359-6049
bevnews@att.net http://www.att.net

Joel Whitaker, Editor

For managers and owners of bottling and soft drink and water companies. *$349.00*

Printed in 1 color

8801 Spiceletter
American Spice Trade Association
2025 M Street NW
Washington, DC 20036
202-367-1127
FAX: 202-367-2127 www.astaspice.org
Bi-Monthly

8802 Spirited Living: Dave Steadman's Restaurant Scene
5301 Towne Woods Rd
Coram, NY 11727-2808
631-736-0436
FAX: 631-736-0436
spiritedliving@aol.com

Dave Steadman, Editor

Newsletter published biweekly except January, July, and August. *$75.00*

8803 Supermarket News
Fairchild Publications
750 3rd Ave
New York, NY 10017-2703
212-304-4274
FAX: 212-630-4760 180- 22- 472
orgeld@fairchildpub.com
http://www.fairchildpub.com

Mary Berner, President/CEO
David Merrefield, VP, Editorial Director
David Orgel, Editor-in-Chief
Dan Bagan, Publishing Director

A weekly guide aimed at retailers, wholesalers, manufacturers and others in the food industry. *$23.00*
Weekly Founded: 1892
Circulation: 36346

8804 TecAgri News
Clark Consulting International
435 Root
St. PO Box 68
Park Ridge, IL 60068-3347
847-836-5100
FAX: 847-792-7565
warren.clark@ccimarketing.com
http://www.tecagrinews.com

Warren E Clark, President/CEO

News on new technology in agriculture reaching large computerized family farmers. *$1200.00*
Weekly Founded: 1986
Circulation: 100,000 Audited
Mailing list available for rent 2.1M names
$250 per M.
Computerized version available

8805 The Business of Herbs
Herb Growing and Marketing Network
PO Box 245
Silver Spring, PA 17575-0245

FAX: 717-393-9261
herbworld@aol.com
www.herbnet.com, www.herbworld.com

Maureena Rogers, Editor

Information on commercial cultivation of herbs and marketing. Also regulatory information, calender of events, business notes.
40 pages Monthly Founded: 1990
Circulation: 2,000

8806 Today's Grocer
Florida Grocer Publications
PO Box 430760
S Miami, FL 33243
305-661-0792
FAX: 305-661-6720 800-440-3067
todaysgr@bellsouth.net
http://www.todaysgrocer.com

Jack Nobles, Publisher
Dennis Kane, Editor

Provides the latest food industry news and trends to Florida, Georgia, Alabama, Louisiana, Mississippi and the Carolinas. *$29.00*

24 pages Monthly Founded: 1968
Circulation: 19500
Printed in 4 colors on newsprint stock

8807 US Beer Market
Business Trend Analysts/Industry Reports
2171 Jericho Turnpike
Suite 200
Commack, NY 11725-2937
631-462-5454
FAX: 631-462-1842 800-866-4648
sales@bta-ler.com
http://www.bta-ler.com

Charles J Ritchie, Executive VP
Donna Priani, Marketing Director

Profiles markets for premium, superpremium, popular and light beers. *$1495.00*
Founded: 1978 $150 per M.
Computerized version available: Disk

8808 Uncorked
California Wine Club
2175 Goodyear Ave Suite 102
PO Box 3699
Ventura, CA 93006-3699
805-504-4330
FAX: 800-700-1599 800-777-4443
info@cawineclub.com
http://www.cawineclub.com

Bruce Boring, Publisher
Judy Reynolds, Editor

8 page newsletter that describes featured winery. It provides an upclose and personal look at a small boutique California winery.

Founded: 1990
Circulation: 10000

8809 Urner Barry's Price-Current
Urner Barry Publications
PO Box 389
Toms River, NJ 08754-0389
732-240-5330
FAX: 732-341-0891 800-932-0617
mail@urnerbarry.com
www.urnerbarry.com

Paul B Brown Jr, President
Sheila M Deane, Marketing Manager

Daily market price report serving the poultry and egg industries. *$415.00*

8 pages Daily
Circulation: 3,000

8810 Urner Barry's Price-Current West Coast Edition
Urner Barry Publications
PO Box 389
Toms River, NJ 08754
732-240-5330
FAX: 732-341-0891 800-932-0617
mail@urnerbarry.com
http://www.urnerbarry.com/

Paul Brown Jr, President
Sheila M Deane, Marketing Manager
Richard A. Brown, VP

Reports changes in price and market conditions of poultry and eggs on the West Coast. *$444.00*

8 pages Daily Founded: 1858
Circulation: 3000

8811 Urner Barry's Yellow Sheet
Urner Barry Publications
PO Box 389
Toms River, NJ 08754
732-240-5330
FAX: 732-341-0891 800-932-0617
mail@urnerbarry.com
http://www.urnerbarry.com

Paul B Brown Jr, President
Richard A Brown, VP/Treasurer

Market price report of timely unbiased meat quotes to help pinpoint the latest trading levels of beef, pork, lamb, veal, meat by-products, carcasses and boxed cuts. *$559.00*

8 pages Daily Founded: 1858
Circulation: 1500

8812 Vinegar Institute Newsletter
5775 Peachtree Dunwoody Road NE
Suite G500
Atlanta, GA 30342-1542
404-252-3663
FAX: 404-252-0774
info@versatilevinegar.com
http://www.versatilevinegar.org

Pam Chumley, Executive Director

Manufacturers and bottlers of vinegar and suppliers to the industry are the members of this association. Publications available only to members.

42 pages Quarterly
Circulation: 60

8813 Vinotizie Italian Wine Newsletter
Italian Trade Commission
499 Park Avenue
6th Floor
New York, NY 10022-1279
212-980-1500
FAX: 212-758-1050
www.italtrade.com/ice

Michelle Jones, Editor

This newsletter discusses developments in the Italian wine industry and market, as well as reviews of imported wines from Italy.

Bi-Monthly

8814 WSSA Newsletter
Weed Science Society of America
PO Box 7050
Lawrence, KS 66044-8897
785-429-9622
FAX: 785-843-1274 800-627-0629
wssa@allenpress.com www.wssa.net

David Shaw, Editor
Michael E Foley, Publications Director

Subscription is included in the annual dues. *$5.00*

Quarterly/Non-Member Fee

8815 Washington Association of Wine Grape Growers
PO Box 716
Cashmere, WA 98815
509-782-8234
FAX: 509-782-1203
info@wawgg.org
http://www.wawgg.org

Vicky Scharlau, Executive Director
Paul Champoux, Chairman

Guidance in research and education, and maintaining leadership in local, state and national wine grape issues. *$115.00*

Founded: 1983 500 names

8816 Webster Agricultural Letter
Webster Communications Corporation
3835 N 9th Street
Suite 401W
Arlington, VA 22203
703-525-4512
FAX: 703-852-3534
agletter@aol.com
http://www.agletter.com

James C Webster, Editor/CEO

Agricultural politics and policy issues. *$397.00*

6 pages Fortnightly Founded: 1980
Printed in 1 color on matte stock

8817 Weekly Insiders Dairy & Egg Letter
Urner Barry Publications
PO Box 389
Toms River, NJ 08754
732-240-5330
FAX: 732-341-0891 800-932-0617
mail@urnerbarry.com
http://www.urnerbarry.com

Paul B Brown Jr, President
Randy Pesciotta, Editor
Janice Brown, Advertising

Statistical newsletter of storage stocks of whole, liquid and dried eggs, slaughter and consumption figures and retail selling prices as well as critical data on butter, margarine and cheese. *$24.00*

4 pages Weekly Founded: 1858
Circulation: 10000

8818 Weekly Insiders Poultry Report
Urner Barry Publications
PO Box 389
Toms River, NJ 08754-389
732-240-5330
FAX: 732-341-0891 800-932-0617
mail@urnerbarry.com
http://www.urnerbarry.com

Paul B Brown Jr, President
Sheila M Deane, Marketing Manager

Statistical news of broiler eggs set and hatched, current chicken and fowl slaughter, storage holdings and competing red meat availability. *$190.00*

4 pages Weekly Founded: 1858
Circulation: 230

8819 Weekly Insiders Turkey Report
Urner Barry Publications
PO Box 389
Toms River, NJ 08754-389
732-240-5330
FAX: 732-341-0891 800-932-0617
mail@urnerbarry.com
http://www.urnerbarry.com

Paul B Brown Jr, President
Sheila M Deane, Marketing Manager
Richard A. Brown, VP Treasurer
Michael W. O'Shaughnessy, Secretary

Statistical report containing slaughter figures, consumption patterns, US Storage Stock Estimates and comparative weekly prices. *$173.00*

4 pages Weekly Founded: 1858
Circulation: 230

8820 Weekly Livestock Reporter
120 North Rayner
Fort Worth, TX 76111
817-838-0106
FAX: 817-831-3117
service@weeklylivestock.com
http://weeklylivestock.com

Ted Gouldy, Publisher
Phil Stoll, Editor

Offers comprehensive weekly information for cattle farmers and livestock agricultural professionals. *$18.00*

Weekly Founded: 1897
Circulation: 10000

8821 Weekly Weather and Crop Bulletin

NOAA/USDA Joint Agricultural Weather Facility
U.S Department of Commerce
14th Street & Constitution Avenue N
Washington, DC 20230-3800
202-206-6633
FAX: 202-482-3154
jawfweb@oce.usda.gov
http://www.noaa.gov

Douglas LeComte, Publisher
David Miscus, Managing Editor

Text and tables describing the weekly weather over the US and other major crop producing countries. *$60.00*

Weekly Founded: 1807
Circulation: 1500

8822 Western Hemisphere Agriculture and Trade Report
US Department of Agriculture
Room 112-A
US Department of Agriculture
Washington, DC 20250-3810
202-012-2000
FAX: 202-690-4915
webmaster@usda.gov
http://www.usda.gov

Miriam Stuart, Publisher
Abraham Lincoln, President

Information on current and projected agricultural production and trade trends for North, Central, South America and the Caribbean. Includes information on trade agreements and blocks in the Hemisphere.
Founded: 1862

8823 Wine on Line Food and Wine Review
Enterprise Publishing
138 N 16th Street
Blair, NE 68008
402-426-2121
FAX: 402-426-2227
www.enterprisepub.com

J Waman, Publisher

Reviews, feature articles and information on all areas of food and wine, including restaurants, hotels, trains and airlines. Accepts advertising. *$100.00*
10 pages Monthly

Magazines & Journals

8824 AHA Quarterly
American Herb Association
PO Box 1673
Nevada City, CA 9595-1673
530-265-9552
FAX: 530-274-3140
LFCecil@aol.com
http://www.ahaherb.com

Kathi Keville, Editor/Director
Mindy Green, Associate Editor

Contains news bulletins, scientific studies, book reviews, research in the field and networking between members. Also offers directories of herb education and mail order sources of herbs. *$20.00*
20 pages Quarterly Founded: 1981
Circulation: 1000
Printed in on matte stock

8825 ASMC Sales & Marketing Magazine
Association of Sales & Marketing Companies
1010 Wisconsin Avenue NW, #900
9th Floor
Washington, DC 20007
202-337-9351
FAX: 202-337-4508
info@asmc.org www.asmc.org

Jamie DeSimone, Dir, Marketing/Member Services

Reports on the progress and change in the food broker profession. *$25.00*
450 pages Bi-Annual Founded: 1904
Printed in 4 colors

8826 Acreage Magazine
Malheur Publishing Company
PO Box 130
Ontario, OR 97914-130
541-889-5387
FAX: 541-889-3347
SteveK@argusobserver.com
http://www.argusobserver.com

Stever Krehl, Publisher
Pat Caldwell, Editor
Tom Hooton, Circulation Manager
John Dillon, Marketing

Cultural news and features edited for rural farm producers magazine. *$5.00*
40 pages Monthly Founded: 1897

8827 Acres USA
5321 Industrial Oaks Boulevard
Suite 128
Austin, TX 78735
512-892-4446
FAX: 512-892-4448 800-355-5315
info@acresusa.com
http://www.acresusa.com

Fred C Walters, Publisher/Editor
Paula Buchalla, Circulation Director

Articles of exposition and analysis in biologically sound farming. *$27.00*
48 pages Monthly Founded: 1970
Circulation: 12500
Printed in on newsprint stock

8828 Ag Retailer
Doane Agricultural Services
11701 Borman Drive
Suite 300
Saint Louis, MO 63146-4193
314-569-2700
FAX: 314-569-1083
agretailer@doane.com
http://www.doane.com

Lynn Henderson, CEO/President
Den Gardner, Editorial Director
Michael Stanly, Marketing Manager
Mike Perine, Advertising Manager

Serves retailers/dealers and distributors of fertilizers and pesticides. *$40.00*
80 pages Monthly Founded: 1959
Circulation: 28500
Printed in 4 colors on glossy stock

8829 AgBiotech Reporter
Andrew Apel
2302 W 1st Street
PO Box 7
Cedar Falls, IA 50613-1879
319-277-3599
FAX: 319-277-3783 800-959-3276
informa@cfu.net
http://www.bioreporter.com

William H Feldman, Publisher
David Acord, Managing Editor
Stephen Clapp, Associate Editor

Offers a complete overview of information in the area of biotechnology as it relates to and affects agriculture. *$524.00*
24 pages Monthly
Circulation: 500 $100 per M.

8830 Agri Marketing Magazine
Doane Agricultural Services
11701 Borman Drive
Suite 300
Saint Louis, MO 63146-4193
314-569-2700
FAX: 314-569-1083
info@agrimarketing.com
http://www.agrimarketing.com

Bill Schuermann, VP/Group Publisher
Stephanie Wobbe, News Editor
Bill Schuermann, Publisher/Editorial Direc

Agri Marketing Magazine is the premier publication of the agriculture Industry, reaching over 9,000 sales, marketing and advertising executives in the US and Canada. The Marketing Services Guide lists companies, advertising agencies, direct marketing, market research, print media, broadcast media, e-business and associations. *$30.00*
88 pages Founded: 1963 9,227 names
$105 per M.
Printed in on matte stock : Web

8831 Agribusiness Council
1312 18th Street NW
Suite 300
Washington, DC 20036
202-296-4563
FAX: 202-887-9178
info@agribusinesscouncil.org
www.agribusinesscouncil.org

Nicholas E Hollis, President

Council news, information and calendar.

8832 Agribusiness Fieldman
Western Agricultural Publishing Company

4969 E Clinton Way
Suite 104
Fresno, CA 93727-1549
559-252-7000
FAX: 559-252-7387 888-382-9772
westag@psnw.com
www.westagpubco.com

Paul Baltimore, Publisher
Jim Baltimore, Publisher
Randy Bailey, Editor
Robert Fujimoto, Assistant Director

For the professional agricultural consultant, featuring the latest information on chemical regulation, pest control techniques and feature stories on PCA and PCO community.
Monthly

8833 Agribusiness Fresh Fruit and Business News
Agribusiness Publications
PO Box 669
Sanger, CA 93657-669
559-875-4585
FAX: 559-875-4587 800-364-4894
editor@agribusinesspublisher.com
http://www.agribusinesspublisher.com

John Van Nortwick, Publisher
Michelle Cox, Editor

Keeps subscribers abreast of business news for the fruit growing and producing industry. *$36.00*
Monthly Founded: 1980
Circulation: 10000

8834 Agrichemical Age
Farm Progress Publishers
191 S Gary Avenue
Carol Stream, IL 60188-2089
630-690-5600
FAX: 630-462-2869
transf.tovm www.farmprogress.com

Bill Edy, Editor

Information for fertilizer/pesticide dealers, distributors, commercial applicators and crop consultants. *$20.00*
Monthly

8835 Agricultural Engineering
American Society of Agricultural Engineers
2950 Niles Road
Saint Joseph, MI 49085-8607
269-429-0300
FAX: 269-429-3852 800-371-2723
miller@asae.org http://www.asae.org

Donna Hull, Director of Publications
Melissa Miller, Editor

Focus is on agricultural equipment, farm buildings, electrification, soil conservation, irrigation and food engineering. *$119.00*
26 pages Monthly Founded: 1907
Circulation: 9000

8836 Agriculture Research Magazine
Agricultural Research Service
USDA ARS 5601 Sunnyside Avenue
Beltsville, MD 20705-5130
301-504-1651
FAX: 301-504-1641
rsowers@ars.usda.gov
http://www.ars.usda.gov/ar
Robert Sowers, Editor/Circulation Manager
William Johnson, Art Director
Edward Knipling, CEO *$50.00*
27 pages Monthly Founded: 1954
Circulation: 45000

8837 Agronomy Journal
American Society of Agronomy
677 S Segoe Road
Madison, WI 53711
608-273-8080
FAX: 608-273-2021
fkatzagronomy.org
www.agronomy.org
Matt Nilsson, Managing Editor
Susan Ernst, Managing Editor
Frances Katz, Publications Director
Ellen Bergfeld, Executive Vice President
An international journal of agriculture and natural resource sciences with articles relating to original research in soil science, crop science, agroclimatology and agronomic modeling, production agriculture, and computer software. *$100.00*
Bi-Monthly/Per Issue Fee

8838 Agweek
Grand Forks Herald
375 2nd Avenue
PO Box 6008
Grand Forks, ND 58206-6008
701-780-1100
FAX: 701-780-1211 800-811-2580
feedback@gfherald.com
http://www.gfherald.com
Michael Jacobs, Publisher/Editor
Kim Deats, Editor
Weekly magazine of agriculture which emphasizes market trends and the people making them happen. *$32.00*
80 pages Weekly

8839 Alaska Fisherman's Journal
Diversified Business Communications
121 Free Street
Portland, ME 04101-7437
207-425-5500
FAX: 207-842-5609
editor@afjournal.com
http://www.afjournal.com
John Van Amerongen, Editor
Randy Le Shane, Production Manager
Mike Lodato, Publisher
Neil Casey, Advertising Coordinator
Stephanie Wendel, Audience Development Manager
Primary publication serving the North Pacific commercial fishing fleet in the world's healthiest and most lucrative commercial fishing region. *$21.00*
Monthly
Circulation: 10,000 10,000 names $110 per M.

8840 Alimentos Balanceados Para Animales
WATT Publishing Company
122 S Wesley Avenue
Mount Morris, IL 61054-1497
815-734-4171
FAX: 815-734-4201
gill@wattmm.com
http://www.wattnet.com/
Clayton Gill, Editorial Director
James Watt, Owner
For feed industry professionals in Latin America. *$42.00*
Founded: 1917
Circulation: 9471 9,471 names $225 per M.

Printed in 4 colors on glossy stock

8841 Alimentos Procesados
Steve Slakis
1350 E Touhy Aenue
Des Plains, IL 60018
630-320-7406
FAX: 630-320-7470
s.slakis@cahners.com
www.alimentosprocesados.com
International food processing magazine that provides information on food development, processing and packaging technologies to Latin American food and beverage manufacturers.
Monthly
Circulation: 20,500

8842 All About Beer
501-H Washington Street
Durham, NC 27701
800-977-2337
FAX: 919-530-8160 800-999-9718
editor@allaboutbeer.com
http://www.allaboutbeer.com
Daniel Bradford, Publisher
Julie Bradford, Editor
Natalie Abernethy, Circulation Manager
Quality beers, breweries and restaurants. *$19.99*

8843 Allied Tradesman
Allied Trades of the Baking Industry
2001 Shawnee Mission Pkwy
Mission Woods, KS 62205
707-935-0103
FAX: 707-935-0174
atbi@atbi.org www.atbi.org
Gary Cain, President
Tim Miller, Secretary/Treasurer
Monthly Founded: 1920
Circulation: 500

8844 Almond Facts
Blue Diamond Growers
1802 C Street
PO Box 1768
Sacramento, CA 95814
916-442-0771
FAX: 916-325-2880
feedback@bdgrowers.com
http://www.bluediamond.com
Susan Brauner, Editor
Douglas D Youngdahl, CEO/President
For food brokers and members producers of Blue Diamond. *$25.00*
Founded: 1910
Printed in 4 colors

8845 American Bee Journal
Dadant and Sons
51 S 2nd Street
Stop 2
Hamilton, IL 62341-1397
217-847-3324
FAX: 217-847-3660
abj@dadant.com
http://www.dadant.com
Joe Graham, Editor
Dianne Behnke, Publishing Department
Marta Menn, Advertising Manager
Timothy Dadant, Owner
Read by commercial and hobby beekeepers and entomologists. *$22.95*
80 pages Monthly Founded: 1905
Circulation: 13000
Printed in 4 colors on glossy stock

8846 American Beefalo World Registry
30 Stevenson Road
#5
Laramie, WY 82070
307-745-3505
FAX: 307-745-3505 866-374-2297
Offers information for beef and cattle farmers.

8847 American Brewer
1049 B Street
PO Box 510
Hayward, CA 94543-510
510-886-7418
FAX: 510-538-7644
info@ambrew.com
http://www.ambrew.com
Bill Owens, Publisher
Greg Kitsock, Editor
A magazine covering the business of beer. *$50.00*
Quarterly Founded: 1979

8848 American Fruit Grower
Meister Publishing Company
37733 Euclid Avenue
Willoughby, OH 44094-5992
440-942-2000
FAX: 440-942-0662 800-572-7740
afg.circ@meistermedia.com
http://www.meisterpro.com
Richard T Meister, Chairman
Joe Monahan, Group Publisher
Fran Mihalik, Circulation Manager
Specialized production and marketing information and industry-wide support for fruit growers. *$19.95*
66 pages Monthly Founded: 1931
Circulation: 37,000

8849 American Journal of Agricultural Economics
Blackwell Publishing
350 Main Street
Malden, MA 02148
781-888-8250
800-835-6770
Christopher Barrett, Editor
B Wade Brorsen, Editor
Stephen K Swallow, Editor
Ian M Sheldon, Editor
Its content covers the economics of agriculture, natural resources and the environment, and rural and community development.
5x/year

8850 American Journal of Enology and Viticulture
American Society for Enology and Vinticulture
PO Box 1855
Davis, CA 95617
530-753-3142
FAX: 530-753-3318
editor@asev.org www.asev.org
Linda F Bisson, Science Editor
Judith McKibben, Managing Editor
Judy Sams, Publications Coordinator
Full-length research papers, literature reviews, research notes and technical briefs on various aspects of enology and viticulture, including wine chemistry, sensory science, process engineering, wine quality

assessments, microbiology, methods development, plant pathogenesis, diseases and pests of grape, rootstock and clonal evaluation, effect of field practices and grape genetics and breeding.
Quarterly
Mailing list available for rent

8851 American Small Farm Magazine
560 Sunbury Rd
Ste 6
Delaware, OH 43015-8692
740-363-2395
FAX: 740-369-9526
sales@smallfarm.com
http://www.smallfarm.com

Marti Smith, Information/Producti
Andy Stevens, Editor

Published for the owner/operator of farms from five to three hundred acres. Focuses on production agriculture including alternative and sustainable farming ideas and technology, case studies, small farm lifestyle and tradition. *$18.00*
71M names

8852 American Vegetable Grower
Meister Media Worldwide
3773 Euclid Avenue
Willoughby, OH 44094-5925
440-942-2000
FAX: 440-942-0662 800-572-7740
avg.circ@meistermedia.com
http://www.meistermedia.com

Rosemary Gordon, Managing Editor
Ken Hall, Communications Manager
Josep W Monahan, Publisher
Fran Mihalik, Circulation manager

Information source for commercial vegetable growers. *$19.95*
Monthly Founded: 1931
Circulation: 34772

8853 American Wine Society Journal
American Wine Society
PO Box 3330
Durham, NC 27702
919-403-2002
FAX: 919-403-0392
jhmoulton@aol.com
www.americanwinesociety.com

Jane Moulton, Editor-in-Chief
Angel E Nardone, Publisher
Jim Rink, Assistant Editor

A publication that reflects AWS members' diverse interests in the many facets of wine. Definitely it is a publication geared to the Society but for the most part covers what interests the members about the favored beverage rather than about the organization itself. *$4.00*
Quarterly Founded: 1967 3000 names

8854 Aquaculture Magazine
Achill River Corporation
PO Box 2329
Asheville, NC 28802-2329
828-687-0011
FAX: 828-681-0601
info@aquaculturemag.com
http://www.aquaculturemag.com

Gregory J Gallagher, Editor/Publisher
Doinita Cociovei, Circulation Manager
Joseth Strickland, Advertisement Manager

Focus emphasizes the production, processing, and marketing of aquatic organisms and plant life. *$24.00*
96 pages Founded: 1968
Circulation: 5000
Printed in 4 colors on glossy stock

8855 Arbor Age
Adams Business Media
833 West Jackson Blvd.
7th Floor
Chicago, IL 60607
312-846-4600
FAX: 312-846-4634
jkmitta@aip.com
http://www.arborage.com

John Kmitta, Editor
Mark Adams, President
Joanne Juda, Circulation Manager
Steve Brackett, Group Publisher

Serves the urban industry including tree service companies/arborists, railroads, utilities, etc. *$40.00*
43 pages Monthly Founded: 1981
Printed in 4 colors on glossy stock

8856 Atlantic Control States Beverage Journal
Club & Tavern
3 12th Street
Wheeling, WV 26003-3276
304-232-7620
FAX: 304-233-1236
wvbevjournal@aol.com

Arnold Lazarus, Editor

A magazine for the alcoholic beverage industry. Serving bars, restaurants, clubs and industry personnel with West Virginia, Virginia, and North Carolina state editions. Includes states' liquor price lists.

8857 Automatic Merchandiser
Cygnus Publishing
1233 Janesville Avenue
Fort Atkinson, WI 53538-803
920-563-6388
FAX: 920-328-9029 800-547-7377
info@Amonline.com
http://www.amonline.com

Gloria Cosby, Publisher
Elliot Maras, Editor
Wendy Chady, Circulation Manager
Monique Terrazas, Regional Sales Manager

The AM Vending Publications Group is comprised of three magazines - Automatic Merchandiser, Route Driver and Service Technician and AM Show Days; and the group website www.AMonline.com - all serving the information and communication needs of the vending and office coffee service industry. *$66.00*
84 pages Monthly Founded: 1937
Circulation: 15000
Mailing list available for rent 16004 names $150 per M.
Printed in 4 colors on newsprint stock

8858 Bagel Bits
Independent Bakers Association
Post Office Box 3731
Washington, DC 20027-3212
202-333-8190
FAX: 202-337-3809
independentbakers@yahoo.com
http://www.independencebaker.org

Nicholas Pyle, CEO/President

Founded: 1965
Circulation: 100

8859 Bakers Way
American Institute of Baking
1213 Bakers Way
PO Box 3999
Manhattan, KS 66505-3999
785-537-4750
FAX: 785-537-1493 800-633-5137
info@aibonline.org
http://www.aibonline.org

Janette Gelroth, Associate Editor
Maureen Olewnik, VP Tech Services
Paul Abenante, President / CEO

12 pages Quarterly Founded: 1919
Circulation: 2900

8860 Bakery Production and Marketing
245 W 17th Street
1350 E Toughy Avenue
New York, NY 10011
212-414-1160
FAX: 212-337-7198
plachapelle@cahners.com
www.cahners.com

Doug Krumrei, Editor

Dedicated to delivering sensible ideas for profitable baking with editorial that addresses solutions and opportunities found within retail, instore, food service and intermediate wholesale bakeries. *$70.00*
Monthly
Circulation: 31,000

8861 Baking Buyer
Sosland Publishing Company
4800 Main Street
Suite 100
Kansas City, MO 64112
816-756-1000
FAX: 816-756-0494
junrein@sosland.com
http://www.bakingbusiness.com

John Sonderegger, Publisher
John Unrein, Editor
Tarre Beach, Managing Editor

This publication offers information on state-of-the-art baked foods and ingredients.
Founded: 1922
Circulation: 31000

8862 Baking and Snack
Paul Lattan
4800 Main Street
Suite 100
Kansas City, MO 64112-2504
816-756-1000
FAX: 816-756-0494
bbcservice@sosland.com
http://www.bakingbusiness.com

Steve Barne, Editor
Laurie Gorton, Executive Editor

A magazine offering information on baking equipment and ingredients for the commercial baker.
Monthly Founded: 1922
Circulation: 12,494

8863 Bar & Beverage Business Magazine

Mercury Publications
1839 Inkster Boulevard
Winnipeg, Ma 0
204-954-2085
FAX: 204-954-2057
mp@mercury.mb.ca
http://www.mercury.mb.ca/

Frank Yeo, Publisher
Robert Thompson, National Account Manager
Kelly Gray, Editor
Angie Finnbogason, Circulation Manager

Carly Peters, Editorial Production Manager

The buying and selling of beverages, operator profiles, new products, product merchandising and trends. *$35.00*

Quarterly Founded: 1948
Circulation: 16923
Mailing list available for rent

8864 **Bartender Magazine**
Foley Publishing Corporation
PO Box 158
Liberty Corner, NJ 07938-158
908-766-6006
FAX: 908-766-6607 800-463-7465
info@bartender.com
http://www.bartender.com

Raymond Foley, Publisher
Jaclyn Wilson Foley, Circulation Director

Serves all full-service drinking establishments, including individual restaurants, hotels, motels, bars, taverns, lounges and all other full service on premise licenses. Subscription price is $40 for Canada, and $55 for all other foriegn countries. *$30.00*

76 pages Founded: 1980
Circulation: 150000 150000 names $125 per M.
Printed in 4 colors on glossy stock

8865 **Bee Culture**
AI Root Company
623 W Liberty Street
Medina, OH 44256-2225
330-725-6677
FAX: 330-725-5624 800-289-7668
kim@beeculture.com
http://www.beeculture.com

Kim Flottum, Editor
Kathy Summers, Production Manager
John Root, President

Honey bees and their keeping for beginners and experienced apiculturists. Accepts advertising, press releases, new products, and book reviews. *$21.50*

64 pages Founded: 1863
Circulation: 12000 20000 names $45 per M.
Printed in 4 colors on matte stock

8866 **Beer, Wine & Spirits Beverage Retailer**
Oxford Publishing
307 W Jackson Avenue
Oxford, MS 38655
662-236-5510
FAX: 662-236-5541 800-247-3881
ncb@nightclub.com
http://www.nightclub.com

Ed Meek, Publisher
Michael Harrelson, Editor
Jennifer Parsons, Marketing
Jennifer Robinson, COO

Beverage Retailer serves retail establishments in the beer, wine and spirits industries, including liquor, package and wine stores and others allied to the field. *$30.00*

52 pages Monthly Founded: 1997
Circulation: 19985
Printed in 4 colors on glossy stock

8867 **Belt Pulley**
Belt Pulley Pub Company
PO Box 58
Jefferson, WI 53549-1341
920-674-9732
http://www.beltpulley.com

Katie Elmore, Publisher
Jane Aumann, Managing Editor

Covers antique tractors and farm machinery of all makes and models. *$20.00*

Monthly Founded: 1987
Circulation: 3500

8868 **Beverage & Dynamics**
Adams Business Media
257 Park Avenue S
3rd Floor
New York, NY 10011
646-542-2015
FAX: 646-654-2099
jlenorad@aip.com
www.beveropes.com

John Pennacchio, Publisher

All beverage catergories including distilled spirits, beer, wine, juices, soft drinks, etc., as well as the compatability of beverage and food. Regularly covers the application of new products and store equipment, industry news, and the development of new merchandising techniques. *$35.00*

9 per year
Circulation: 65,000

8869 **Beverage Industry**
Stagnito Communications
155 Pfingster Road
Suite 205
Deerfield, IL 60015
847-205-5660
FAX: 847-205-5680
info@stagnito.com
http://www.stagnito.com

Tom Bachmann, Publisher
Joan Holleran, Editor
Harry Stagnito, President

Provides the most in-depth information about the beverage market including production, technology and distribution. The changing industry demands a change leader and BI fills that role by reporting behind the scenes of the gigantic 65 billion market. *$40.00*

Monthly Founded: 1946
Circulation: 28000

8870 **Beverage Journal**
Michigan Licensed Beverage Association
920 North Fairview
Lansing, MI 48912
517-749-9611
FAX: 517-374-1165 877-292-2896
info@mlba.org http://www.mlba.org

Amy Shock, Editor/Advertising Director
Catherine Pavick, Executive Director

Offers information on the alcoholic beverage industry/retail sales *$52.00*

Monthly
Printed in on glossy stock

8871 **Beverage Media**
161 Avenue of the Americas
New York, NY 10013-1205
212-571-3232
FAX: 212-571-4443

Anita Rosepka, Editor
William Sloane, Owner

Journal offering information on the liquor, wine and beer trade.

Monthly

8872 **Beverage Network**
4437 Concord Lane
Skokie, IL 60076-2605
617-497-0062
FAX: 617-812-7740 www.bevnet.com
Organization of beverage distributors dealing with specialty, nonalcoholic products.

8873 **Beverage Retailer Magazine**
Oxford Publishing
307 Jackson Avenue W
Oxford, MS 38655-2154
662-236-5510
FAX: 662-236-5541 800-247-3881
br@beverage.retailer.com
http://www.beverage-retailer.com

Ed Meek, Publisher
Brenda Owen, Editor
Ruth Ann Wolfe, Circualtion Manager

A magazine covering the off-premise market for retailers in the wine, beer and spirits business. *$30.00*

Monthly Founded: 1920
Circulation: 25000
Printed in 4 colors on glossy stock

8874 **Bison World Magazine**
National Bison Association
1400 W. 122nd Ave
Suite 106
Westminster, CO 80234-2140
303-292-2833
FAX: 303-292-2564
laurie@bisoncentral.com
www.bisoncentral.com

Laurie Dineen, Editor/Advertising Director
Dave Carter, Executive Editor

Featured articles and regular departments cover all aspects of raising bison and what's happening in this exciting industry. Available with all levels of membership with the association.

Quarterly
Circulation: 1500

8875 **Body, Mind & Spirit Magazine**
PO Box 95
Dogsland, SK 0
306-356-4634
FAX: 306-356-4634
jenim@sasktel.net
http://www.saskworld.com/bodymindspirit

Jeni Mayer, Publisher
Adele Azar-Rucquoi, Contributing Writers

Quarterly

8876 **Bottled Water Reporter**
International Bottled Water Association
1700 Diagonal Road
Suite 650
Alexandria, VA 22314-2973
703-683-5213
FAX: 703-683-4074 1 8-0 9-8 37
ibwainfo@bottledwater.org
http://www.bottledwater.org

Max Busetti, Editor
Joseph Doss, Publisher/President

Covers IBWA events and programs while highlighting new technologies and equipment within the industry, taking notice of personnel changes and reporting on the latest industry statistical data. It also features useful articles on management, operations and marketing specific to the bottled water industry. *$50.00*

74 pages Founded: 1958
Circulation: 2500
Printed in 4 colors on glossy stock

8877 **Brahman Journal**
American Brahman Breeders Association
1037 Austin Street
Hempstead, TX 77445
979-826-4347
FAX: 979-826-2007
subscriptions@brahmanjournal.com
www.brahmanjournal.com

Chris Shivers, Executive VP

This publication provides timely and useful information about one of the largest and most dynamic breeds of beef cattle in the world. In each issue the Brahman Journal reports on Brahman shows, events, and sales as well as technical articles and the latest research as it pertains to the Brahman Breed. *$25.00*

Monthly Founded: 1971

8878 Brandpackaging

Independent Publishing Company
46 W. St. George Blvd
Suite C
St George, UT 84770-2700
435-656-1555
FAX: 435-656-1511 800-808-7449
comments@independentpublishing.com
http://www.independentpublishing.com

Josh Warburton, President/Publisher

Founded: 1996
Circulation: 5500

8879 Brewers Digest

Siebel Publishing Company
Business Office
PO Box 677
Thiensville, WI 53092-6026
915-877-3319
FAX: 915-877-3319

Thomas Volke, Publisher
Dori Whitney, Editor

The gamut of operational, production, buying, engineering, and packaging issues affecting brewing companies and enterprises. *$ 20.00*

70 pages Monthly Founded: 1926
Circulation: 3000
Printed in 4 colors on glossy stock

8880 Business of Herbs

Northwind Farm Publications
439 Ponderosa Way
Jemez Springs, NM 87025-8036
505-829-3448
FAX: 505-829-3449
northwind@sulphercanyon.com
www.herb-biz.com

Paula Oliver, Publisher
David Oliver, Editor

Primarily for herb businesses and those keenly interested in herbs and botanicals. *$4.00*

8881 CRC Press

2000 NW Corporate Boulevard
Boca Raton, FL 33431
561-994-0555
FAX: 772-998-0876 800-272-7737
info@crcpress.com www.crcpress.com

Eleanor Riemer, Publisher
Emmett Dages, Chief Executive Officer

Publisher in science, medicine, environmental science, forensic, engineering, business, technology, mathematics, and statistics. Our food science and nutrition books and our journal, Critical Reviews in Food and Nutrition, are well established and respected publications in the food science industry.

8882 Calf News (Cattle Feeder Magazine)

1531 Kensington Blvd
Garden City, KS 67846
620-276-7844
FAX: 620-275-7333
steve@calfnews.com
http://www.calfnews.com

Betty Jo Gigot, Editor & Publisher
Patti Wilson, Sales Manager
Larisa Willrett, Copy Editor/Circulation M

This magazine offers the latest information to cattle breeders and feeders. *$33.00*

Founded: 1964
Circulation: 6,352

8883 Candy Industry

Stagnito Communications
155 Pfingsten Road
Suite 205
Deerfield, IL 60015
847-205-5660
FAX: 847-205-5680
info@stagnito.com
http://www.stagnito.com

Harry Stagnito, President
Korry Stagnito, Publishing Director
Sue Ravenscraft, VP Circulation

Magazine serving chocolate and confectionary manufacturers. *$59.00*

Monthly Founded: 1944
Printed in 4 colors on glossy stock

8884 Capital Press

Press Publishing Company
PO Box 2048
Salem, OR 97308-2048
503-364-4431
FAX: 503-370-4383 800-882-6789
eshein@capitalpress.com
http://www.capitalpress.com

Carl Sampson, Managing Editor
Elaine Shein, Editor/Publisher
Mike O'Brien, Circulation/General Manager

For the agricultural and forest community of the Pacific Northwest. *$44.00*

60 pages Weekly Founded: 1928
Circulation: 37000
Printed in 4 colors on newsprint stock

8885 Carnetec

1415 N Dayton
Chicago, IL 60622
312-266-3311
FAX: 312-266-3363
annica@meatingplace.com
http://www.carnetec.com

Spanish language magazine reaching executives in the Latin American meat and poultry processing industry. Helps improve the manufacturing process, equipment, sanitation, safety and technology.

8886 Carrot Country

Columbia Publishing
413-b N 20th Avenue
Yakima, WA 98902
509-248-2452
FAX: 509-248-4056 800-900-2452
columbia@columbiapublications.com
http://www.columbiapublications.com

Mike Stoker, Publisher
Brent Clement, Editor

Includes information on carrot production, grower and shipper feature stories, carrot research, new varieties, market reports, spot reports on overseas production and marketing and other key issues and trends of interest to US and Canadian carrot growers. *$8.00*

Quarterly Founded: 1975
Circulation: 2700 2400 names $200 per M.
Printed in 4 colors on glossy stock

8887 Cattle Guard

Colorado Cattlemen's Agricultrual Land Trust
8833 Ralston Road
Arvada, CO 80002
303-431-6422
FAX: 303-431-6446
ccaglt@aol.com http://cca.beef.org/

Todd Inglee, Publisher
Terry R Fankhauser, Executive VP
Jan Ammon, Executive Admin Assistant
Robert Farnam, Media Relations

A full overview of information is given through this magazine for cattle farmers and breeders.

Founded: 1867

8888 Cattleman

Texas & Southwestern Cattle Raisers Association
1301 W 7th Street
Fort Worth, TX 76102-2660
817-327-7064
FAX: 817-332-5446 800-242-7820
lionel@thecattlemanmagazine.com
http://www.texascattleraisers.org

Lionel Chambers, Editor
Ellen Humphries, Assistant Editor
Matt Brockman, Manager

A full overview of information for the cattle producer in Texas and Oklahoma. *$25.00*

130 pages Monthly Founded: 1914
Circulation: 17000
Printed in 4 colors on glossy stock

8889 Cereal Chemistry

American Association of Cereal Chemists
3340 Pilot Knob Road
Saint Paul, MN 55121-2097
651-454-7250
FAX: 651-454-0766 800-328-7560
aacc@scisoc.org www.aaccnet.org

Steven C Nelson, Publisher
R Carl Hoseney, Editor-in-Chief
Dawn Wuest, Circulation Coordinator
Karen Cummings, Publication Production Director

An international archival journal in cereal science. Research presented in this journal explores raw materials, processes, products utilizing cereal, oilseeds and pulses, as well as analytical procedures, technological tests and fundamental research in the cereal area. *$79.00*

Bi-Monthly Founded: 1915
Circulation: 3539

8890 Cereal Foods World

American Association of Cereal Chemists
3340 Pilot Knob Road
Saint Paul, MN 55121-2055
651-454-7250
FAX: 651-454-0766 800-328-7560
aacc@scisoc.org www.aaccnet.org

Jody Grider, Executive Editor
Jordana Anker, Managing Editor
Dawn Wuest, Circulation Coordinator
Steven Nelson, VP

A source of information on grain-based food science, technology, and new product development. CFW includes feature and original research articles that focus on advances in grain-based food science and the application of these advances to product development and current food production practices. *$48.00*

Bi-Monthly Founded: 1956
Circulation: 4500

8891 Cheers
Jobson Publishing Corporation
100 Avenue of the Americas
New York, NY 10013-1678
212-274-7000
FAX: 212-431-0500 www.jobson.com
Every issue is designed to help on-premise operators enhance the profitability of their beverage operations.

8892 Cheese Market News
Quarne Publishing
PO Box 620244
Middleton, WI 53562
608-831-6002
FAX: 608-831-1004
squarne@cheesemarketnews.com
http://www.cheesemarketnews.com
Susan Quarne, Publisher
Kate Sander, Editorial Director
Weekly trade news for the nation's cheese and dairy/deli business *$105.00*
16 pages Weekly Founded: 1981
Circulation: 2200 Audited
Mailing list available for rent 2200 names $500 per M.
Printed in 4 colors on newsprint stock

8893 Chef
Talcott Communications Corporation
20 W Kinzie
Suite 1200
Chicago, IL 60610
312-849-2220
FAX: 312-849-2174 800-229-1967
rbenes@talcott.com
http://www.chefmagazine.com
Daniel Von Rabenau, Publisher
Robert S Benes, Senior Editor
Information on food production and presentation, includes chef profiles, trend studies, marketing information and restaurant profiles. *$32.00*
Founded: 1956
Circulation: 40,000 1000 names $125 per M.
Printed in 4 colors on glossy stock

8894 Chemical and Pharmaceutical Press
C&P Press
90 william strret
5th Floor
New York, NY 10106-2899
212-326-6760
FAX: 646-733-6010 800-544-7377
cpp@cppress.com
http://www.cppress.com
Dr. Mary Conway, Executive Editor
Bron Zienkiewicz, Sales/Marketing
Sonia Tighe, Publisher
Supplies chemical information to professionals involved with the sale, application, storage or regulations of agricultural or ornamental and turf pesticides. Information is available in either reference book form or on computer disc. Complete product labels, MSDS's and indexes are included.
Founded: 1984

8895 Choices
American Agricultural Economics Association
415 S Duff Avenue
Suite C
Ames, IA 50010-6600
515-233-3202
FAX: 515-233-3101
info@aaea.org http://www.aaea.org
Joe Outlaw, Editor
Betty Eckerbrecht, Information Contact
Laurian Unnevehr, President
The magazine of food, farm and resource issues.
Quarterly Founded: 1910
Circulation: 6000 6000 names
Printed in 4 colors on glossy stock

8896 Citograph
Western Agricultural Publishing Company
4969 E Clinton Way
#104
Fresno, CA 93727-1549
559-252-7000
FAX: 559-252-7387
westag@psn.com www.westapub.com
Paul Baltimore, Publisher
Jim Baltimore, Publisher
The oldest continuous citrus-specific publication in the world. Stories centering on all aspects of citrus production from planting to harvest and all maintenance in between. Lemons, limes, oranges, avocados — all citrus is included.
Monthly

8897 Citrus & Vegetable Magazine
16057 Tampa Palms Boulevard
PMB 416
West Tampa, FL 33647-1376
813-975-8377
FAX: 352-463-1376
cvmscott@compuserve.com
http://www.citrusandvegetable.com
Scott Emerson, Editor
Jina Martin, Associate Editor
Monthly Founded: 1937
Circulation: 12003 $125 per M.
Printed in 4 colors on glossy stock

8898 Citrus Industry
Associated Publishing Corporation
495 E Summerlin Street
Bartow, FL 33830-4732
863-533-4114
FAX: 863-534-1758
eneff@barpr.com
http://www.citrusindustry.net
Ernie Neff, Editor
Mariann Holland, Publisher
News, facts and data of interest to citrus growers, processors and shippers. *$24.00*
64 pages Founded: 1920
Circulation: 9851
Printed in 4 colors on glossy stock

8899 CleanRooms Magazine
PennWell Publishing Company
98 Spit Brook Road
Suite 100
Nashua, NH 03062-5723
603-891-0123
FAX: 603-891-9200
info@pennwell.com
http://www.cleanrooms.com
John Haystead, Editorial Director
James Enos, Publisher
Adam Japker, CEO
Serves the contamination control and ultrapure materials and process industries. Written for readers in the microelectronics, pharmaceutical, biotech, health care, food processing and other user industries. Provides technology and business news and new product listings.
Monthly Founded: 1987
Circulation: 30000

8900 Communications in Soil Science and Plant Analysis
Marcel Dekker
270 Madison Avenue
New York, NY 10016
212-696-9000
FAX: 212-685-4540 800-228-1160
journals@dekker.com
http://www.dekker.com
Harry A Mills, Editor
Marcel Dekker, President
All aspects of soil science and crop production in all climates. *$567.00*
120 pages Founded: 1963
Circulation: 23500

8901 Concession Professsion
National Association of Concessionaires
35 E Wacker Drive
Suite 1816
Chicago, IL 60601-2270
312-236-3858
FAX: 312-236-7809
scross@NAConline.org
www.naconline.org
Susan Cross, Communications Director
Devoted to the recreational and leisuretime food and beverage concessions industry, featuring news briefs, feature articles, association news and advertising opportunities.
Bi-Annual
Printed in 4 colors

8902 Consultant
Food Service Consultants Society International
304 W Liberty Street
Suite 201
Louisville, KY 40202-3011
502-583-3783
FAX: 502-589-3602
info@fcsi.org http://www.fcsi.org
David Drain, Executive Vice President
Cindy O'Brien, Director Marketing/Programs
Dori Sacksteder, Membership/Marketing Mana
Travis Doster, Director Public Relations/Editor
George Stinson, Owner
Professional publication for FCSI members and the food service industry. *$40.00*
150 pages Quarterly
Circulation: 4500
Printed in 4 colors on glossy stock

8903 Convenience Store Decisions
Donohue/Meehan Publishing
1300 E 9th Street
Cleveland, OH 44114
216-696-7000
FAX: 216-696-1752
information@penton.com
http://www.c-storedecisions.com
David B Nussbaum, CEO
Jay Gordon, Editor
For buyers, directors, field managers, owners and executives in the convenience store business. Free to qualified subscribers.

180 pages Monthly Founded: 1892
Circulation: 41716

8904 Cooking for Profit
CP Publishing
PO Box 267
Fond du Lac, WI 54936
920-923-3700
FAX: 920-923-6805
comments@cookingforprofit.com
http://www.cookingforprofit.com

Colleen Phalen, Editor-in-Chief/Publisher

Paid subscription trade magazine targeted to foodservice owners, managers and chefs. Each month features current trends in food preparation with step-by-step recipes and photographs; effective management techniques; and the latest in foodservice equipment — all written by industry experts. Also features in-depth profiles of a successful foodservice operation. *$26.00*
28 pages Monthly Founded: 1932
Circulation: 75000
Printed in 4 colors on glossy stock

8905 Cooperative Business Journal
National Cooperative Business Association

1401 New York Avenue NW
Suite 1100
Washington, DC 20005
202-638-6222
FAX: 202-638-1374
jstevenson@ncba.coop
www.ncba.coop

Jill Stevenson, Subscription Coordinator
Jeannine Kenney, Editor

Your one-stop source for the latest in cooperative news and information. CBJ is the only national publication covering co-op happenings across all industries. *$25.00*
Bi-Monthly Founded: 2004

8906 Cooperative Grocer
361 East College Street
Iowa City, IA 52240-267
319-466-9029
FAX: 866-600-4588
dave@cooperativegrocer.com
http://cooperativegrocer.coop

Dave Gutknecht, Editor
Dan Nordley, Publisher
Don McLemore, CEO

Trade magazine by and for people working with consumer cooperative grocery stores. *$25.00*
36 pages Founded: 1999
Circulation: 2400
Printed in 4 colors on matte stock

8907 Cotton Farming
Vance Publishing
5050 Poplar Avenue
Suite 2000
Memphis, TN 38157-2099
901-767-4020
FAX: 901-767-4026
throton@vancepublishing.com
http://www.cottonfarming.com

Adam Ballinger, Publisher
Tommy Horton, Editor
Benjamin Potter, Assistant Editor
Lia Guthrie, Sales Manager
Gary Taylor, President

For commercial cotton growers across the US Cotton Belt. *$12.00*
52 pages Founded: 1937
Circulation: 36,297

8908 Country Folks
Lee Publications
6113 State Highway 5
PO Box 121
Palatine Bridge, NY 13428-121
518-673-2269
FAX: 518-673-3245 800-218-5586
subscriptions@leepub.com
http://www.countryfolks.com

Frederick Lee, Publisher
Marjorie Struckle, Editor
Bruce Button, President
Janet Button, Marketing Manager
Tom Mahoney, Sales Manager

Agricultural news from national, state and local levels. Some features on farm and agricultural industry, rural interest, etc. *$ 12.00*
75 pages Weekly
Circulation: 27000

8909 Country Living
Arens Corporation
395 S High Street
Covington, OH 45318-1121
937-473-2028
FAX: 937-473-2500
garyg@arenspub.com
http://www.arenspub.com

Jean Devlin, Editor
Garry Godfrey, Publisher/CEO
Connie Didier, Circulation Manager

Current news and features devoted to the agricultural industry. *$1395.00*
Monthly Founded: 1950
Circulation: 17500

8910 Country Woman
Reiman Publications
5400 S 60th Street
Greendale, WI 53129-1404
414-423-0100
FAX: 414-423-1143 800-344-6913
subscriberservices@reimanpub.com
http://www.countrywomanmagazine.com

Kathy Pohl, Managing Editor
Ann Kaiser, Editor

Offers recipes, stories, profiles and articles pertaining to the country woman. *$14.98*
68 pages Founded: 1965

8911 County Agents
National Association of County Agricultural Agents
252 N Park Street
Decatur, IL 62523
217-876-1220
FAX: 217-877-5382
nacaaemail@aol.com
http://www.nacaa.com

Scott Hawbaker, Editor
Frank L FitzSimons, III, President

Members receive professional improvement, news of association activities, shared education efforts from other states and reports from NACAA leadership and member states. *$10.00*
Founded: 1916
Circulation: 5000
Mailing list available for rent 3850 names $125 per M.
Printed in 4 colors on matte stock

8912 Critical Reviews in Food and Nutrition
CRC Press
6000 Broken Sound Parkway NW
(Suite 300)
Boca Raton, FL 33487
561-994-0555
FAX: 561-989-9732 800-272-7737
info@crcpress.com
http://www.crcpress.com

Mr. Rudolf, Publisher
Emmett Dages, Chief Executive Officer
Susan Lee, Editor

Founded: 1913

8913 Crop Decisions
Doane Agricultural Services
11701 Borman Drive
Suite 100
Saint Louis, MO 63146-4199
314-569-2700
FAX: 314-569-1083
info@cropdecisions.com
www.cropdecisions.com

Lynn Henderson, President
Holly Bollinger, Managing Editor
Robert Wiley, Publisher/Editorial Director

Published to serve employees of professional farm management firms, crop consulting firms, farm suppliers, contract research firms, financial institutions and other agricultural related businesses. *$7.00*

48 pages 8 per year Founded: 1997
Circulation: 16,500
Printed in 4 colors

8914 Crop Insurance Today
National Crop Insurance Services
8900 Indian Creek Parkway
Suite 600
Overland Park, KS 66210
913-685-2767
FAX: 913-685-3080 800-951-6247
webmaster@ag-risk.org
http://www.ag-risk.org

Robert W Parkerson, President
Laurie Langstraat, Editor

A quarterly magazine published by the National Crop Insurance Services. *$13.00*
Quarterly Founded: 1915
Circulation: 18000
Printed in 4 colors on glossy stock

8915 Culinary Trends
Culinary Trends Publications
6285 Spring St
Number 107
Long Beach, CA 90808
714-826-9188
FAX: 714-826-0333
info@culinarytrends.net
http://www.culinarytrends.net

Fred Mensigna, Publisher

Information for food and beverage managers along with managers of hotels and restaurants. *$21.00*
Quarterly Founded: 1993
Circulation: 10000

8916 Cygns Business Media
445 Broad Hollow Road
Melville, NY 11747-3669
631-845-2700
FAX: 631-845-2723 800-308-6397
micheal.schiavetta@cysnuspub.com
www.healthproductsbusiness.com

Micheal Scharetta, Editor
Chris Biscuiti, Assistant Editor

Cover news and trends in the natural health products industry vitamins, herbs, dietary supplements and other products. Publishes annual raw materials directory and purchasing guide.
Monthly Founded: 1954

8917 DDBC News
Dairy, Deli, Bakery Council of Southern California
PO Box 1872
Whittier, CA 90609
562-947-7016
FAX: 562-947-7872
delicouncil@earthlink.net
http://www.ddbcsc.com
Bob Dreffler, CEO
Dave Daniel, Editor
Susan Steele, Circulation Manager
Serves the deli, dairy, bakery and meat industry. *$25.00*
Monthly Founded: 1960
Circulation: 5000
Printed in 4 colors on glossy stock

8918 Dairy Field
Stagnito Communications
155 Pfingsten Road
Suite 205
Deerfield, IL 60015
847-205-5660
FAX: 847-205-5680
kollinstagnito@stagnito.com
http://www.stagnito.com
Allison Bardic, Editor
Rose Weiss, Production Manager
Matthew O'Shea, Publisher
Mary Mazur, Circulation Manager
Helping processors manage the changing industry.
Monthly Founded: 1919
Circulation: 20970
Mailing list available for rent 17.5M names
Printed in 4 colors on matte stock

8919 Dairy Foods Magazine
Business News Publishing
1050 Illinois Route 83
Suite 200
Bensenville, IL 60106
630-694-4353
FAX: 630-227-0527
phillipsd@bnp.com
http://www.dairyfoods.com
Joel Iverson, Publisher
David Phillips, Editor
Dairy Foods serves the dairy industry by analyzing and reporting on technologies trends and issues and how they affest North America's processors of milk, cheese, frozen deserts and cultured products. Current issues and qualification forms for free subsciptions will be available to attendees. Dairy Foods is part of BNP Food Group.
Weekly Founded: 1926
Circulation: 20000
Printed in 4 colors on glossy stock

8920 Dairy Today
AgWeb.com
1501 Market Street
Centre Square W, 28th Floor
Philadelphia, PA 19102-2181
507-664-9151
800-331-9310
DairyToday@farmjournal.com
http://www.agweb.com
Allen Moczygemba, Publisher
Wayne Bollum, National Sales Manager
Jim Dickrell, Editor
Marv Hoekema, Marketing Manager
Award-winning editorial covers the broad spectrum of production, nutrition and marketing information. It serves dairy producers who milk 40+ cows or are members of the Dairy Herd Improvement Association.
Monthly Founded: 1989
Circulation: 65000

8921 Dairy, Food and Environmental Sanitation
International Association for Food Protection
6200 Aurora Avenue
Suite 200W
Des Moines, IA 50322-2864
515-276-3344
FAX: 515-276-8655 800-369-6337
info@foodprotection.org
http://www.foodprotection.org
David W Tharp, Executive Director
Kathleen A Glass, President
Published as the general membership publication by the International Association for Food Protection, each issue contains referred articles on applied research, applications of current technology and general interest subjects for food safety professionals. Regular features include industry and association news, an industry related product section and a calendar of meetings, seminars and workshops.Updates of government regulations and sanitary design is also featured. All members receive DFES. *$227.00*
Monthly Founded: 1980
Circulation: 3000
Mailing list available for rent 3000+ names $150 per M.
Printed in 4 colors

8922 Dealer & Applicator
50 Poplar Avenue
Suite 2000
Memphis, TN 38157-2099
913-638-0708
FAX: 913-438-0697
gvincent@vancepublishing.com
http://www.dealerandapplicator.com
John Sowell, Publisher
Greg Vincent, Editor
Serves as the reader's business partner to provide full-service dealers with management and business strategies to increase profitability.
Founded: 1937
Circulation: 22,002

8923 Deli Digest
National Live Stock and Meat Board
444 N Michigan Avenue
Chicago, IL 60611
312-467-5520
FAX: 312-467-9729
Sharlet R Brown, Editor
Provides information on the activities of the Board's Deli/Prepared Meats Committee.
Monthly

8924 Design Handbook for Easily Cleanable Equipment
Baking Industry Sanitation Standards Committee
PO Box 3999
Manhattan, KS 66505-3999
785-537-4750
FAX: 785-565-6060 866-342-4772
bissc@bissc.org www.bissc.org
Rosalie Wagner, Administrative Assistant
Jon Anderson, Executive Director/Secretary
The purpose of this handbook is to give the design engineer and field installer a quick and ready reference on the design and installation of bakery equipment so that it may comply with sanitation standards set forth by ANSI/BISSC/Z50.2-2003.
Founded: 1949

8925 Dietitian's Edge
Rodman Publications
70 Hilltop Road
Ramsey, NJ 07446
201-825-2552
FAX: 201-825-0553
dietitiansedpe@rodpub.com
www.dietitiansedge.com

8926 Distribution Channels
American Wholesale Marketers Association
2750 Prosperity Avenue
Suite 530
Fairfax, VA 22031
703-208-3358
FAX: 703-573-5738 800-482-2962
info@awmanet.org www.awmanet.org
Traci Carneal, Editor-in-Chief
Joan Fay, Associate Publisher
A magazine specifically targeted toward convenience distributors. Our readers are involved in the purchase and sale of candy, tobacco, snacks, beverages, health and beauty care items, general merchandise, foodservice, groceries and more. *$36.00*
Monthly/Non-Members Fee
Circulation: 11,000
Printed in 4 colors on glossy stock

8927 Down to Earth
DowElanco/Dow AgroSciences
9330 Zionsville Road
Indianapolis, IN 46268-1054
317-337-3000
FAX: 317-337-4256 800-905-7326
subscribe@downtoearth.org.in
http://www.dowapro.com
Sunita Narain, Editor
Offers international reviews of agricultural research and practice. *$48.00*
32 pages Monthly Founded: 1989

8928 Drovers Journal
Vance Publishing
10901 W 84th Terrace
Terrace
Lenexa, KS 66214-1631
913-438-8700
FAX: 913-438-0695 800-255-5113
jgerke@drovers.com
http://www.vancepublishing.com
Angela Pishney, Publisher
Greg Henderson, Editor
Farming news.
Monthly Founded: 1937
Circulation: 1500

8929 Eastern Milk Producer
Eastern Milk Producers Cooperative Association
PO Box 6966
Syracuse, NY 13217-6966
315-437-1225
Bob Stronach, Editor
Trish Stokes, Production Manager
Communicates to members of the association dairy issues, farm issues, association events and policy. *$13.00*
20 pages Monthly

8930 Egg Industry
WATT Publishing Company
122 S Wesley Avenue
Mount Morris, IL 61054-1497
815-734-4171
FAX: 815-734-5649
tuten@wattmm.com
http://www.wattnet.com

Charles Olentine Jr, Publisher/VP
Chris Wright, Editor
James Watt, Owner

For executives and managers of egg operations. *$36.00*
Monthly Founded: 1917
Circulation: 1553

8931 El Restaurante Mexicano
Maiden Name Press
106 S Oak Park Avenue Suite 204
PO Box 2249
Oak Park, IL 60303
708-445-8330
FAX: 708-445-9477 800-407-5845
brussell@restmex.com
http://www.restmex.com

Brenda Russell, Publisher
Kathleen Furore, Editor

A bilingual magazine featuring industry specific food news, features restaurant profiles and new product information for personnel of restaurants serving mexican/southwestern menu items nationwide. *$108.00*
Founded: 1997
Circulation: 27000
Printed in 4 colors on glossy stock

8932 Europe Agriculture and Trade Report
USDA Economic Research Service
1800 M Street NW
Washington, DC 20036-5831
202-203-3935
800-999-6779
service@ers.usda.gov
http://www.ers.usda.gov

Susan Offutt, Administrator
Leslee Lowstuter, Central Operations Staff Director
Thomas McDonald, Publishing/Communications
Suchada Langley, Global Agricultural Markets Branch

An important resource for agribusiness and researchers.

Circulation: 2000

8933 Executive Guide
WATT Publishing Company
122 S Wesley Avenue
Mount Morris, IL 61054-1497
815-734-4171
FAX: 815-734-4201
http://www.wattnet.com

James Watt, Owner

A statistical review of the poultry industry, including supply and demand charts, egg layer numbers and chicken meat producer rankings.

8934 FEDA News & Views
Foodservice Equipment Distributors Association
223 W Jackson Boulevard
Suite 620
Chicago, IL 60606-6911
312-427-9605
FAX: 312-427-9607
feda@feda.com http://www.feda.com

Ray Herrick, Editor/Publisher/Ceo

Focus is on sales, technology, new products and other areas of benefit to dealers, as well as industry trends and news. *$145.00*
Founded: 1933
Circulation: 1300

8935 Fancy Foods & Culinary Products
Talcott Communications Corporation
20 West Kinzie
12th Floor
Chicago, IL 60610
312-849-2220
FAX: 312-849-2174 888-545-3676
fancyfood@talcott.com
http://www.talcott.com

Daniel Von Rabenau, Publisher
Natalie Hamm Noblitt, Editor

Specialty food stores, department store specialty food departments, gift departments, confection stores, independent groceries and supermarket chains, gift basket retailers, cookware and kitchen stores, cooking school gift stores, cheese stores, coffee and tea stores brokers/represenatives/manufacturers/importers/wholesalers/distributors and others allied to the field. *$26.00*
Monthly Founded: 1983
Circulation: 23,000

8936 Farm Chemicals International
Meister Publishing Company
37733 Euclid Avenue
Willoughby, OH 44094-5925
440-942-2000
FAX: 440-942-0662 800-572-7740

Alan Strohmaier, Publisher
James Sulecki, Group Editor
Gary Fitzgerald, President

Information on production, marketing and application of crop protection chemicals and fertilizers.
Founded: 1932
Circulation: 8551

8937 Farm Equipment
Cygnus Publishing
1233 Janesville Avenue
Fort Atkinson, WI 53538
920-563-6388
FAX: 920-563-1702 800-547-7377
cheri.johnson@cygnuspub.com
www.farm-equipment.com

Daniel Newman, Publisher
Grant Dunham, Editor

An industry-wide information and product news curriculum for farm equipment dealers that enhances their knowledge of business management principles. *$40.00*
Founded: 1970 10,000 names
Printed in on glossy stock

8938 Farm Equipment Guide
Heartland Communications
1003 Central Avenue
PO Box 1115
Fort Dodge, IA 50501-1115
515-551-1600
FAX: 515-574-2182 800-247-2000
aginfo@AgDeal.com
http://www.agdeal.com

Tony Smith, Publisher
Sandra Simonson, Group Publisher, Guide & Subscripti

A subscription that includes an annual blue book of specifications, serial numbers and average pricing on farm machinery with monthly updates that list thousands of pieces for sale and thousands of actual auction values. *$49.95*
120 pages Annual+ Founded: 1981
Circulation: 320,100 1.5MM names
Printed in 4 colors on glossy stock : internet

8939 Farm Impact
314 E Church Street
Mascoutah, IL 62258-2100
618-566-8282
FAX: 618-566-8283

Greg Hoskins, Publisher
Michael King, Advertising Manager

Offers information to farmers.
Monthly

8940 Farm Journal
1818 Market Street
31st Floor
Philadelphia, PA 19103
215-578-8900
FAX: 215-568-4221 800-523-1538
kherzog@farmjournal.com
http://www.farmjournalmedia.com

Roger Randall, President
Earl Ainsworth, Publisher
Kandy Herzog, Market Intelligence Manager
Andrew Weber Jr, Chief Executive Officer

Published for operators and owners of commercial farms and ranches. Provides timely, useful marketing and management information to help them produce more efficiently, buy more wisely, sell their products at the highest possible prices, and retain as much of their income as possible. *$12.00*
182 pages Monthly Founded: 1880
Circulation: 685000

8941 Farm Reporter
Meridian Star
814 22nd Avenue
Meridian, MS 39301-5023
601-693-1551
FAX: 601-485-1210 800-232-2525
Reports on every phase of farming including timber, cattle, poultry and all growing crops. *$2.00*
Monthly

8942 Farm Review
Lynden Tribune
PO Box 153
Lynden, WA 98264-153
360-354-4444
FAX: 360-354-4445
editor@lyndentrib.com
http://www.lyndentrib.com

Kelvin Bratt, Editor
Michael Lewis, President

Offers a review of farming techniques and trends nationwide. *$30.00*
Monthly Founded: 1888
Circulation: 11,150

8943 Farm Show Magazine
Farm Show Publishing
PO Box 1029
Lakeville, MN 55044-5404
952-469-5572
FAX: 952-469-5575 800-834-9665
mark@farmshow.com
http://www.farmshow.com

Mark Newhall, Publisher/CEO

Focuses on latest agricultural products, and product evaluation. Contains no advertising. *$19.95*
Founded: 1977
Circulation: 200000

8944 Farm Talk
Farm Talk
1801 S US Highway 59
#601
Parsons, KS 67357-4900
620-421-9450
FAX: 620-421-9473
farmtalk@terraworld.net
http://www.farmtalknewspaper.com

Mark Parker, Publisher/Editor/CEO
Ted Gum, Manager

Agriculture for Eastern Kansas, Western Missouri, Northeast Oklahoma and Northwest Arkansas. *$30.00*
60 pages Weekly Founded: 1974
Circulation: 10000

8945 Farm and Dairy
Lyle Printing and Publishing Company
185 E State Street
PO Box 38
Salem, OH 44460
330-337-3419
FAX: 330-337-9550 800-837-3419
advertising@farmanddairy.com
http://www.farmanddairy.com

Susan Crowell, Editor
Scot Darling, Production Manager
Howard Marsh, Circulation Manager

Briefs of research reports from experiment stations in agriculture,success stories concerning farmers of Ohio, Pennsylvania and West Virginia, saleand livestock market reports, auctions and more. Accepts advertising. *$38.00*
132 pages Weekly Founded: 1915
Circulation: 13500 $20 per M.
Printed in 4 colors on newsprint stock

8946 FarmWorld
DMG World Media
27 N Jefferson Street
PO Box 90
Knightstown, IN 46148-1242
765-345-5133
FAX: 765-345-5133 800-876-5133
mkuhn@farmworldonline.com
http://www.farmworldonline.com

Richard Lewis, Publisher
David Blower Jr, Editor
Megan Kuhn, Assistant Editor
Toni Hodson, Advertising Manager

Agriculture, farming, and related areas in Indiana, Ohio and Kentucky. Accepts advertising. *$38.95*
84 pages Weekly Founded: 1955
Printed in 4 colors on newsprint stock

8947 Farmer's Friend
116 Main Street
Suite 503
Towanda, PA 18848-1832
570-265-2151
FAX: 570-265-1647
http://www.farmersfriend.com

Kathy Thomas, Editor
Jim Cowner, Publisher

Farming news. *$30.00*
Weekly
Circulation: 11,000

8948 Farmers Digest
Heartland Communications
PO Box 1115
Fort Dodge, IA 50501-1115
515-955-1600
FAX: 515-574-2182 800-247-2000
dgsupport@agbusinessgroup.com
www.agdeal.com
A subscription that in includes an annual blue book of specifications, serial numbers and average pricing on farm machinery with monthly updates that list thousands of pieces for sale and thousands of actual auction values. *$69.95*
120 pages Monthly Founded: 1981 ISBN 0-970241-10-0
Circulation: 20000 1.4 M names $65 per M.
Printed in 4 colors on glossy stock

8949 Farmers Hot Line
Heartland Communications
1003 Central Avenue
PO Box 1115
Fort Dodge, IA 50501
515-551-1600
FAX: 515-574-2182 800-673-4763
aginfo@AgDeal.com
http://www.agdeal.com

Patti Woodall, Publisher
Andrea Peterson, Circulation Manager

Distributed to manufacturers, farmers, auctioneers and service companies nationwide. Designed to help buyers and sellers of new and used farm machinery, auctions, farm real estate, services and supplies. *$29.00*

Circulation: 75000

8950 Farmers' Advance
331 E Bell Street
PO Box 130
Camden, MI 49232-9613
517-368-0365
FAX: 517-368-5131
transfer@ca.homecomm.net
http://www.farmersadvance.com

Kurt Greenhoe, Publisher
Deb Fink, Circulation Manager
Erin Robinstine, Editor
Julia Hite, Production Manager

Farming technology magazine. *$27.95*
Weekly Founded: 1898
Circulation: 17,500

8951 Farmers' Exchange
Exchange
PO Box 490
Fayetteville, TN 37334
931-433-9737
FAX: 931-433-0053
exchange@vallnet.com
http://www.fexonline.com

William Thomas, Publisher/Editor/CEO
Jim Bowers, Sales/Marketing Manager

Magazine offers a forum for the exchange of farming ideas and information country-wide.
56 pages Monthly Founded: 1987
Circulation: 30000

8952 Farmshine
Dieter Krieg
State and Main Streets
PO Box 219
Brownstown, PA 17508
717-656-8050
FAX: 717-656-8188 866-724-6455
advertise@farmshine.com
http://www.farmshine.com

Dieter Krieg, Publisher/Editor
Tammy Krieg, Ad Sales

Information pertaining to the farming community. *$12.00*
Weekly Founded: 1979
Printed in on newsprint stock

8953 Fastline Productions
4900 Fox Run Rd.
Buckner, KY 40010-248
502-222-0146
FAX: 502-222-0615 800-626-6409
custcare@fastline.com
http://www.fastlinepub.com

William Howard, President
Crysten Minzenberger, Marketing Director

Nationwide and regional picture buying guides for the farming industry. *$144.00*
Monthly Founded: 1978

8954 Feed Additive Compendium
Miller Publishing Company
12400 Whitewater Drive
Suite 160
Minnetonka, MN 55343-2524
952-931-0211
FAX: 952-938-1832
smuirhead@feedstuffs.com
http://www.feedstuffs.com

Sarah Muirhead, Publisher
Michael Howie, Managing Editor
Mike Miller, Manager

This magazine takes a closer look at the food additives and agriculture industries. *$52.00*
Weekly Founded: 1931

8955 Feed International
WATT Publishing Company
122 S Wesley Avenue
Mount Morris, IL 61054-1497
815-734-4171
FAX: 815-734-5649
schreiber@wattmm.com
http://www.wattnet.com

Clay Schreiber, Publisher
Clayton Gill, Editor
Greg Watt, Ceo

A magazine for feed manufacturers outside North America. Provides vital information on the efficient, profitable and safe manufacture and distribution of animal feed products. *$54.00*
Monthly Founded: 1980
Circulation: 16843
Mailing list available for rent 19,191 names $225 per M.
Printed in 4 colors

8956 Feed Management
WATT Publishing Company
122 S Wesley Avenue
Mount Morris, IL 61054-1497
815-734-4171
FAX: 815-734-4201
http://www.wattnet.com

Clay Schreiber, Publisher
Philip Lobo, Editor

A magazine for feed manufacturers in North America providing vital information on the efficient, profitable and safe manufacture and distribution of animal feed products. Helps identify and develop market opportunities for the feed manufacturer. *$48.00*
Monthly Founded: 1950
Circulation: 20249
Mailing list available for rent 20,249 names $155 per M.
Printed in 4 colors on glossy stock

8957 **Feed and Grain**
Cygnus Publishing
1233 Janesville Avenue
Fort Atkinson, WI 53538
920-563-6388
FAX: 920-563-1702 800-547-7377
arlette.sambs@cygnuspub.com
http://www.feedandgrain.com

Arlette Sambs, Publisher
Jean Van Dyke, Editor
Paul Mackler, President
Julie Nachtigal, Circulation Manager

Trade magazine serving feed manufacturers and firms involved in handling and processing grain commodities including feed mixers/dealers, country and terminal elevators and allied grain processors. *$48.00*
Founded: 1966
Circulation: 16600
Mailing list available for rent 16,505 names $100 per M.
Printed in 4 colors on glossy stock

8958 **Fine Foods Magazine**
Griffin Publishing Group
201 Oak Street
Suite A
Pembroke, MA 02359
781-294-4700
FAX: 781-829-0134
griffinbooks@earthlink.com
http://www.griffenpublishing.com

Stephen Griffin, President

A magazine offering information on the Northeast specialty, ethnic and prepared foods business.
Monthly

8959 **Fisheries**
American Fisheries Society
5410 Grosvenor Lane
Bethesda, MD 20814-2199
301-897-8616
FAX: 301-897-8096
main@fisheries.org
http://www.fisheries.org

Beth Beard, Managing Editor
Aaron Lerner, Publications Director
Cherie Worth, Production Editor

Peer reviewed articles that address contemporary issues and problems, techniques, philosophies and other areas of interest to the general fisheries profession. Monthly features include letters, meeting notices, book listings and reviews, environmental essays and organization profiles. *$106.00*
50 pages Monthly Founded: 1870
Circulation: 9800
Mailing list available for rent 8500 names $250 per M.

8960 **Food & Drug Packaging**
Stagnito Communications
210 S 5th Street
Suite 202
Saint Charles, IL 60174
847-205-5660
FAX: 630-377-1678
szelesnik@stagnito.com
http://www.fdp.com

Edwin Landon, Publisher

Food and Drug Packaging serves industries engaged in packaging food, beverages, pharmaceuticals, cosmetics and consulting/engineering firms.
Monthly Founded: 1959
Circulation: 75140

8961 **Food Aid Needs Assessment**
US Department of Agriculture
14th & Independence Avenue SW
Washington, DC 20250
202-690-7650
FAX: 202-219-0942

Gene Mathia, Branch Chief

This annual report assesses the food situation in 60 developing countries. Most of the data are presented by region; crisis countries are covered individually.

8962 **Food Arts Magazine**
M Shanken Communications
387 Park Avenue S
8th Floor
New York, NY 10016
212-684-4224
FAX: 212-779-3383

Marvin R Shanken, Chairman
Julie Mautner, Editor

A publication serving the fine food service industry is edited for restauranteurs, chefs, food and beverage directors and caterers.
Monthly Founded: 1972
Circulation: 50000
Printed in 4 colors on glossy stock

8963 **Food Businesses: Snack Shops, Specialty Food Restaurants & Other Ideas**
Prosperity & Profits Unlimited
PO Box 416
Denver, CO 80201
303-573-5564

A Doyle, Editor

Ideas and possibilities for food businesses, snack shops, restaurants. *$29.95*
82 pages Founded: 1990 ISBN 0-911569-69-3
Circulation: 8000
Printed in on matte stock

8964 **Food Channel Trend Wire**
Noble & Associates
2155 W Chesterfield
Springfield, MO 65807
417-755-5000
FAX: 417-875-5051 800-545-4087
art.siemering@noble.net
www.foodchannel.com

Art Siemering, Editor
Robert Noble, Chief Executive Officer

Designed to make the food industry professionals food trend experts. Encapsulates trend information from more than 125 food and consumer publications each month. Provides insights into emerging food trends. *$195.00*

Circulation: 2000

8965 **Food Distribution Research Society News**
Silesia Companies
PO Box 441110
Fort Washington, MD 20749-1110
301-292-1970
FAX: 301-292-1787
http://www.fdrs.ag.utk.edu/journal.html

John Strovinsky, Publisher
Wojciech Florkowski, Editor
Dixie Watts Reaves, President

Food distribution research society encourages research, serves as an information clearinghouse and encourages implementation of research. The Society organizes conferences, and meetings for industry, academic and government leaders within the food industry sector. *$65.00*
16 pages Founded: 1960
Circulation: 150 Audited
Mailing list available for rent 150 names

8966 **Food Engineering**
Business News Publishing Company
2401W Big Beaver
Suite700
Troy, MI 48084
248-362-3700
FAX: 248-362-0317
fasslj@bnpmedia.com
http://www.foodengineeringmag.com

Joyce Fassl, Editor in Chief
Patrick Young, Publisher
Handerson Taggart, CEO
Kevin T. Higgins, Senior Editor
Karen Schweizer, Associate Managing Editor

A publication offering information on all facets of the food industry, from ingredients to food packaging and processing. *$64.00*
Monthly Founded: 1926
Circulation: 15000

8967 **Food Engineering & Ingredients**
Reed Europe
2000 Clearwter Drive
Oak Brook, IL 60523
630-320-7000
FAX: 630-288-8282 800-446-6551
mschechter@reedbusiness.com
http://www.fesmag.com

Maureen Slocum, Publisher
Mitchell Schechter, Editor-in-Chief

Edited for readers outside the US who are employed in firms that manufacture food and beverage products.
Monthly Founded: 1948
Circulation: 22,719

8968 **Food Engineering International**
Reed Business Information
360 Park Avenue S
New York, NY 10010
212-450-0067
FAX: 646-746-7433
corporatecommunications@reedbusiness.com www.reedbusiness.com

Joyce Fassl, Editor
Peter Havens, Publisher
James Reed, Owner

A publication offering information on all facets of the food industry, from ingredients to food packaging and processing.
Bi-Monthly
Circulation: 15,000

8969 **Food Management**
Penton Publishing Company
1300 E 9th Street
Cleveland, OH 44114-1503
216-967-7000
FAX: 216-696-0836
information@penton.com
www.food-management.com

David B Nussbaum, Chief Executive Officer
Preston L Vice, Chief Financial Officer

Combines the industry's most comprehensive circulation package with an editorial mix that emphasizes business management strategies and ideas, food trends and recipes and in-depth news analysis in a contemporary feature magazine.
90 pages Monthly Founded: 1892
Circulation: 47899
Printed in 4 colors on glossy stock

8970 Food Processing
555 W Pierce Road
Suite 301
Itasca, IL 60143
630-467-1300
FAX: 630-467-1124
sennen@putnam.net
http://www.foodprocessing.com
Lily Modjeski, Sales Manager
Patricia Donatiu, Circulation Manager
Dave Fusaro, Editor-in-Chief
Steve Slankis, Group Publisher
Information on food equipment, packaging material and other supplies and services.
Monthly Founded: 1938
Circulation: 65000

8971 Food Production/Management Magazine
CTI Publications
2 Oakway Road
Timonium, MD 21093
410-308-2080
FAX: 410-308-2079
books@ctipubs.com
http://www.ctipubs.com
Randy Gerstmyer, Publisher/Editor
Serves those in the canning, glasspacking, freezing and aseptic packaged food industries. Readers include corporate executives and staff personnel responsible for direction of management, operations, production, engineering, packaging, research and development. Accepts advertising. *$40.00*
32 pages Monthly Founded: 1878
Circulation: 4482
Mailing list available for rent 4500 names
$675 per M.
Printed in 4 colors on glossy stock

8972 Food Protection Trends
International Association for Food Protection
6200 Aurora Avenue
Suite 200W
Des Moines, IA 50322-2864
515-276-3344
FAX: 515-276-8655 800-369-6337
info@foodprotection.org
http://www.foodprotection.org
David Tharp, Executive Director
Bev Brannen, Administrative Editor
Kathleen Glass, President
Donna Bahun, Production Editor
Edmund Zottola, Scientific Editor
Each issue contains refereed articles on applied research, applications of current technology and general interest subjects for food safety professionals. *$227.00*
Monthly Founded: 1980 ISSN 0362-028X
Circulation: 9000
Mailing list available for rent 3000+ names
$150 per M.
Printed in 4 colors on glossy stock

8973 Food Quality
Carpe Diem Communications
208 Floral Vale Boulevard
Yardley, PA 19067
215-860-7800
FAX: 215-860-7900
staff@carpediemcomm.com
http://www.foodquality.com
Rick Biros, Publisher
Norma Jean DeVico, Chief Editor
Written to keep the food and beverage industry informed about the very latest technologies, techniques and legislation in food quality assurance and control. *$195.00*
66 pages Fortnightly Founded: 1994
Circulation: 21000
Mailing list available for rent 15,000 names
$195 per M.
Printed in 4 colors on glossy stock

8974 Food Safety Magazine
Target Group
1945 W Mountain Street
Glendale, CA 91201
818-842-4777
FAX: 818-769-2939
info@foodsafetymagazine.com
http://www.foodsafteymagazine.com
Stacey Atchison, Publisher
Don Meeker, CEO
Julie Larson Bricher, Editorial Director
Rita Stanley, Circulation Manager
Publicaton is for food safety and quality assurance/control professionals at food and beverage processors, food service companies and agri-food laboratories worldwide. These decision makers implement science-based food safety strategies and systems to prevent, control, test and verify that chemical, microbiological and physical hazards do not enter the food supply. *$19.00*
Monthly Founded: 1980
Circulation: 20,000 $130 per M.

8975 Food Service Equipment & Supplies Specialist
Reed Business Information
2000 Clearwater Drive
Oak Brook, IL 60523
630-740-0825
FAX: 630-288-8686
mschechter@reedbusiness.com
http://www.reedbusiness.com
Mitchell Schechter, Editor-in-Chief
Maureen Slocum, Publisher
Judy Erickson, Group Circulation Manager
Magazine for professionals who specify, sell and distribute food service equipment, supplies and furnishings. *$69.95*
Monthly Founded: 1948
Circulation: 22,740
Printed in 4 colors on glossy stock : web site

8976 Food Technology
Institute of Food Technologists
525 W Van Buren Street
Suite 1000
Chicago, IL 60607
312-782-8424
FAX: 312-782-8348
myift@ift.org http://www.ift.org
Barbara Byrd Keenan, Executive Vice President
Bob Swientek, Editor-in-Chief
Neil H Mermelstein, Executive Editor
News and analysis of current trends in the food industry. Presents information regarding new and improved food sources, products and processes, their proper utilization by industry and the consumer and their effective regulation by government agencies. *$145.00*
Monthly Founded: 1947

8977 Food Trade News
Best-Met Publishing
5537 Twin Knolls Road
Suite 438
Columbia, MD 21045
410-730-5013
FAX: 410-740-4680
jmetzger@best-met.com
http://www.best-met.com
Jeffrey W Metzger, Publisher
Terri Maloney, Editor
Nina Weiland, Vice-President/General Ma
Beth Pripstein,, Circulation Manager
Richard J. Bestany, Advertising Director
A magazine aimed at the players in the food distribution industry.

8978 Food World
Best-Met Publishing Company
5537 Twin Knolls Road
Suite 438
Columbia, MD 21045
410-730-5013
FAX: 410-740-4680
jmetzger@best-met.com
http://www.best-met.com
Terri Maloney, Editor
Jeffrey W. Metzger, Publisher
Beth Pripstein, Circulation Manager
Richard J. Bestany, President
Regional food trade newspaper covering the Mid-Atlantic market
Monthly
Printed in on newsprint stock

8979 Food for Thought
D/FW Grocers Association
1720 S Edmonds Lane
Suite 29
Lewisville, TX 75067-5863
972-353-5885
FAX: 972-353-5886 valeries@flash.net
Valerie A Schenewerk, Executive Director/Editor
Offers information on grocery retailing and items of interest to members of the Grocers Association. *$20.00*
8 pages Quarterly Founded: 1947
Circulation: 1,000
Printed in 1 color on matte stock

8980 FoodService and Hospitality
Kostuch Publications
Two City Place Drive
Suite 200 PMB 2004
Saint Louis ario, MO 63141-3P6
314-812-2565
FAX: 314-835-0044
wgilchri@ix.netcom.com
www.foodserviceworld.com
Mitch Kostuch, President
Rosanna Caira, Publisher/Editor
Wendy Gilchrist, Director Business Development
Canada's only national specialty business magazine reaching owners,managers and buyers in all sections of the foodservice industry. *$50.00*
Monthly
Circulation: 25,000
Printed in on glossy stock

8981 FoodTalk
Pike & Fischer
109 North Henry Street
Alexandria, VA 22314
703-548-3146
FAX: 703-548-3017
minfo@setantapublishing.com
http://www.setantapublishing.com
Declan Couroy, Editor
John Pike, Executive Director
Sanitation tips for food workers. *$120.00*
Quarterly
Circulation: 5000
Printed in 2 colors

8982 For Fish Farmers
Mississippi Cooperative Extension Service

PO Box 9690
Mississippi State, MS 39762-9690
662-325-3174
FAX: 601-857-2358

Martin W Bunson, Editor

A magazine offering information that addresses the concerns of fish farmers.
Quarterly

8983 Fresh Cup Magazine
Fresh Cup Publishing Company
537 SE Ash Street Suite 300
PO Box 14827
Portland, OR 97293
503-236-2587
FAX: 503-236-3165 800-868-5866
freshcup@freshcup.com
http://www.freshcup.com

Ward Barbee, Publisher
Jan Weigel, President
Julie Beals, Marketing
Bill Berninger, Circulation Manager
$60.00

80 pages Monthly Founded: 1992
Circulation: 15000
Printed in 4 colors on glossy stock : Website

8984 Fresh Cut Magazine
Columbia Publishing
417 N 20th Avenue
Yokima, WA 98902
509-248-2452
FAX: 509-248-4056 800-900-2452
ken@freshcut.com
http://www.freshcut.com

Ken Hodge, Managing Director
Loren Queen, Advertising Manager

Features all aspects of fresh-cut fruits and vegetables, from processors who cut, package and handle them to retail and food service outlets where consumers buy or consume them. Readership includes processors, wholesalers, distributors, brokers, retailers, food service operators and chains.
$25.00

40 pages Monthly Founded: 1993 18,464 names $200 per M.
Printed in 4 colors on glossy stock

8985 Frozen Food Digest
271 Madison Avenue
Suite 805
New York, NY 10016
212-557-8600
FAX: 212-986-9868
saulbeckffqdff@aol.com

Saul Beck, Editorial Director /CEO
$45.00

Founded: 1985
Circulation: 16000

8986 Fruit Country
Clintron Publishing
PO Box 30998
Spokane, WA 99223-3016
509-248-2452
FAX: 509-458-3547 800-869-7923
info@agpowermag.com
http://www.agpowermag.com

Clintke Withers, Publisher
John M Dahlin, Editor
Tyson Graff, Circualtion Manager

Written for and about growers, their operations and their needs. Stories on growers and shippers, developments and trends in the fruit industry, human interest stories and politics, new products, chemicals and supplies, avant garde management techniques, cultural practices and tips on profitability. Advertising equipment and services to the fruit industry and distribution system.
$12.00

Monthly Founded: 1976
Circulation: 11500

8987 Futures Magazine
Futures Magazine
833 W. Jackson
7th Floor
Chicago, IL 60607
312-770-0999
FAX: 312-846-4638
dcollins@futuresmag.com
http://www.futuresmag.com

Ginger Szala, Group Publisher
Daniel P Collins, Editor
Gabby Mouizerh, Production Manager
Steve Lown, Manager

Agriculture commodities charted by various technical studies, plus analysis. *$39.00*

24 pages Monthly Founded: 1972
Circulation: 60,000

8988 Game Bird Gazette
Allen Publishing
970 East
3300 South
Salt Lake City, UT 84106
801-485-1299

gamebird@gamebird.com
http://www.gamebird.com

George Allen, Editor

All about keeping, breeding and raising pheasants, quails, partridges, peacocks, doves, pigeons, waterfowl and gamebirds of all kinds. *$23.95*

45 pages Monthly Founded: 1940

8989 Gourmet Business
Gourmet Business Magazine
3300 N Central Avenue
Suite 2500
Phoenix, AZ 85012
480-990-1101
FAX: 480-990-0819
peggyj@vpico.com
http://www.vpico.com/

Heather Granato, Editor
Jenny Bolton, CEO/President
Amy Sharman, Marketing
Karen McAulliffe, Circulation Manager

Founded: 1986
Circulation: 25005

8990 Gourmet News
United Publications
106 Lafayette Street
PO Box 1056
Yarmouth, ME 04096-1600
207-846-0600
FAX: 207-846-0657
info@gourmetnews.com
http://www.gourmetnews.com

Anna Wolfe, Editor
Rick Rector, Publisher
Mario Alves, Managing Editor
Brenda Boothby, Circulation Director

The business newspaper for the gourmet industry. *$65.00*

40 pages Monthly Founded: 1991
Circulation: 23100
Mailing list available for rent $125 per M.
Printed in 4 colors on glossy stock

8991 Gourmet Retailer Magazine
3301 Ponce De Leon Boulevard
Suite 300
Coral Gables, FL 33134
305-446-3388
FAX: 305-446-2868 800-765-9797
info@gourmetretailer.com
http://www.gourmetretailer.com

Edward Loeb, Publisher
Michael Keighley, Editorial Director
Laura Everage, Managing Editor

Monthly Founded: 1979
Circulation: 25000

8992 Grape Grower
Western Agricultural Publishing Company

4969 E Clinton Way
#104
Fresno, CA 93727-1549
559-252-7000
FAX: 559-252-7387 888-382-9772
westag@westagpubco.com
www.westagpubco.com

Paul Baltimore, Publisher
Jim Baltimore, Publisher
Randy Bailey, Editor
Robert Fujimoto, Assistant Editor

The West's most widely read authority on the cultivation of table grapes, raising grapes and wine grapes. All aspects of production are covered with the most current university, government and private research. *$19.95*

Monthly
Circulation: 11,276

8993 Griffin Report: Market Studies
Griffin Publishing Company
201 Oak Street
Pembroke, MA 02359
781-829-4700
FAX: 781-829-0134
mberger@griffinreport.com
www.griffinreport.com

Mike Berger, Editor
Kevin Griffin, Publisher

This report offers statistics on the leading chain and multi-store independent grocers in the northeast. *$42.00*

Monthly Founded: 1966
Mailing list available for rent 10,000 names $350 per M.
Printed in on newsprint stock

8994 Grocers Report
Super Markets Productions
PO Box 6124
San Rafael, CA 94903-124
415-479-0211
FAX: 415-479-0211

Lori Abrams, CEO
JM Adlman, Publisher
Joan Adams, Circulation Manager

Offers information on the retail grocery industry. *$10.00*

Quarterly Founded: 1978
Circulation: 18000
Printed in 4 colors on glossy stock

8995 Grower
Vance Publishing
10901 W 84th
Terrace
lenexa, KS 66214
913-388-8700
FAX: 847-634-4350 847-634-2600
vlboyd@worldnet.att.net
http://www.vancepublishing.com

Sonia Tighe, Publishing Director
Vicky Boyd, Editor
Michael Ross, CEO/President

Food safety, new technology, growing equipment, legislation.
Monthly Founded: 1937
Circulation: 22,004 22000 names $125 per M.
Printed in 4 colors on glossy stock

8996 Growertalks Magazine
Ball Publishing
335 N River Street
Batavia, IL 60510-9
630-208-9080
FAX: 630-208-9350 800-456-5380
info@ballpublishing.com
http://www.ballpublishing.com
Diane Blazek, President/Publisher
Chris Beytes, Editor
Specializes in the publishing of horticulture information, primarily related to floriculture production and marketing. *$29.00*
Monthly Founded: 1937
Circulation: 12000

8997 Growing for Market
Fairplain Publications
PO Box 3747
Lawrence, KS 66046
785-748-0605
FAX: 785-748-0609 800-307-8949
growing4market@earthlink.net
http://www.growingformarket.com
Lynn Byczynski, Editor/Publisher
Roger Yepsen, Author
A monthly periodical for small-scale farmers, market gardeners, and grower of vegetables, fruits, herbs and flowers. Offers news and ideas about organic production, pest control, tools and equipment and direct marketing. *$30.00*
20 pages Monthly Founded: 1992
Circulation: 4000

8998 Guernsey Breeders' Journal
American Guernsey Association
7614 Slate Ridge Boulevard
Reynoldsburg, OH 43068-3126
614-864-2409
FAX: 614-864-5614
info@usguernsey.com
http://www.usguernsey.com
Lynnette Wright, Editor
Seth Johnson, Executive Secretary-Treasurer *$20.00*

8999 HSR: Health Supplement Retailer
Virgo Publishing
3300 N Central Avenue, Suite 300
Phoenix, AZ 85012
480-990-1101
FAX: 480-675-8154
asharman@vpico.com
www.hsrmagazine.com
Peggy Jackson, Publisher
Heather Granato, Editor
Publication for the dietary supplement industry, focusing on the latest news, products and trend analysis to keep retailers informed and ahead of the competition.
50 pages Monthly + Buyer's Guide
Founded: 1995
Circulation: 17000+
Mailing list available for rent 17000+ names $var per M.
Printed in 4 colors on glossy stock

9000 Health Products Business
Cygnus Publishing
445 Braod Hollow Road
Melville, NY 11747-3669
631-845-2700
FAX: 631-845-2723 800-308-6397
micheal.schiavitz@cygnuspub.com
www.healthproducts.com
Bruce Ceftakes, Publisher/Sales
Micheal Schiavetta, Editor
Christian Biscuiti, Assistant Editor
This is a trade magazine that covers news and trends in the natural health products industry including vitamins, herbs, dietary supplements and other products. Publishes annual raw materials directory and purchasing guide, as well as other speciality issues. Targets natural products retail store owners, buyers and managers. Qualified subsciption only.

9001 Herb Quarterly
EGW Publishing Company
4075 Papazian Way
208
Fremont, CA 94538-4300
510-668-0269
FAX: 510-668-0280
info@egw.com
www.herbquarterly.com
Chris Slaughter, Circulation Director
Jennifer Barrett, Editor
Each issue introduces readers to new herbs and fascinating herbal lore; provides tips on hard to grow varieties and medicinals; showcases gardens from around the world; and tempts the palate with seasonal menus and tantalizing recipes built around herbs and edible flowers. *$19.97*
68 pages Quarterly Founded: 1978
Circulation: 36753
Printed in 4 colors on matte stock

9002 Hereford World
PO Box 014059
Kansas City, MO 64101
816-842-3757
FAX: 816-842-6931
aha@hereford.org
http://www.hereford.org
Amy Cowan, Communications Coordinator
Craig Huffhines, Executive VP
Kelly Hale, Assistant Editor
Caryn Vaught, Production Manager
Trade magazine for breeders of registered Hereford cattle.
Monthly Founded: 1742
Circulation: 9500

9003 High Country News
119 Grand Avenue
Paonia, CO 81428-9905
970-527-4898
FAX: 970-527-4897
emarston@hcn.org
http://www.hcn.org
Paul Larmer, Publisher
Greg Hanscom, Editor
Covers environmental and public lands issues. *$32.00*
Monthly Founded: 1970
Circulation: 24000 22,000 names

9004 High Plains Journal
High Plains Publishing Company
PO Box 760
Dodge City, KS 67801
620-227-1834
FAX: 620-227-7173 800-452-7171
journal@hpj.com http://www.hpj.com
Terry Frisbic, Production Manager
Holly Martin, Editor
Duane Ross, President
Farming news for the central states. *$46.00*
52 Issues a Yea
Circulation: 50000

9005 Honey Producer
American Honey Producers Association
PO Box 107
Rocky Ford, CO 81067-0368
719-254-6321
FAX: 719-254-6331
www.americanhoneyproducers.org
Lyle Johnston, Editor
Highlights current industry news, publishes submitted articles from the scientific community, informs you of legal battles being fought in Washington, DC and provides convention details. *$20.00*
Annual Subscription Fee

9006 HortScience
American Society for Horticultural Science
113 S West Street
Suite 200
Alexandria, VA 22314-2851
703-836-4606
FAX: 703-836-2024
hortscience@ashs.org www.ashs.org
M LeRon Robbins, Editor-in-Chief
Michael W Neff, Publisher
Nancy Hubbell, Managing Editor
A journal concentrating on significant research, education, extension findings and methods. *$55.00*
7x/Year/Members Rate Founded: 1903
Circulation: 2500
Mailing list available for rent 2500 names $100 per M.

9007 Hospitality News Featuring Coffee Talk
PO Box 21027
Salem, OR 97307-1027
503-390-8343
FAX: 503-390-8344 800-685-1932
eds@hospnews.com
http://www.hospnews.com
Kerri R Goodman-Small, Publisher
Miles Small, Editor-in-Chief
Serves restaurants, lodges, health care facilities, schools, clubs,casinos, caterers, and culinary and beverage marketplaces nationally.
Founded: 1988
Circulation: 30000
Printed in on newsprint stock

9008 IAFIS Reporter
International Assn. of Food Industry Suppliers
1451 Dolley Madison Boulevard
Mc Lean, VA 22101-3850
703-761-2600
FAX: 703-761-4334
info@iafis.org http://www.iafis.org/
Jennifer Korolishih, Editor
Stephen C. Schlegel, President
Happenings and trends in the food and dairy industry.

12 pages Founded: 1983
Circulation: 3000
Printed in 4 colors on glossy stock

9009 IGA Grocergram
Pace Communications
1301 Carolina Street
Greensboro, NC 27401-1022
336-378-6065
FAX: 336-273-4808
info@pacecommunications.com
www.pacecommunications.com

Bill Hayes, Editor-in-Chief
Wes Isley, Managing Editor

Edited for IGA retailers and wholesalers throughout the US. Focuses on training, merchandising, display, promotion, and advertising and marketing techniques. Also addresses financial and personnel management and innovations in store engineering and development. *$24.00*
Monthly

9010 Import Statistics
Association of Food Industries
3301 Route 66
Suite 205, Building C
Neptune, NJ 07753
732-922-3008
FAX: 732-922-3590
info@afius.org http://www.afius.org

Bob Bauer, President *$40.00*
Annual+ Founded: 1906
Circulation: 1200

9011 In Good Taste
Specialty Coffee Association of America
302 5th Avenue
5th Floor
New York, NY 10001
646-733-6000
FAX: 646-733-6010 800-544-7377
cpp@cppress.com www.cppress.com

Ted R Lingle, Editor

This periodical offers business, promotional and educational advice in the areas of cultivation, processing, preparation and marketing of specialty coffee.
Monthly

9012 Industria Alimenticia
Stagnito Communications
155 Pfingster Road
Suite 205
Deerfield, IL 60015
847-205-5660
FAX: 847-205-5680
info@stagnito.com
http://www.stagnito.com

Harry Stagnito, President
Elsa Rico, Director/Editor
Mary Mazur, Circulation

Information source for Latin American food and beverage processors *$85.00*

Printed in 4 colors on glossy stock

9013 Insider Magazine
American Correctional Food Service Association
4248 Park Glen Road
Minneapolis, MN 55416-4758
952-928-4658
FAX: 952-929-1318
hcook@acfsa.org www.acfsa.org

Hope Cook, Advertising Director
Joseph W. Montgomery, President
Ellen L. White, Vice-President
Karen Wesloh, Executive Director

Magazine of the correctional food service industry.

56 pages Quarterly Founded: 1969
Circulation: 1500 900 names $200 per M.
Printed in 4 colors on glossy stock

9014 Institute of Food and Nutrition
HealthComm International
9770 44th Ave
N.W. Suite 100
Gig Harbor, WA 98332
253-851-3943
FAX: 253-851-9749 800-692-9400
client_services@metagenics.com
http://www.metagenics.com

Jeffrey Bland, President/Chief Science Officer
Jeffrey Katke, Chairman of the Board/CEO
Carl Mickey Moore, Co-Chief Operating Office
Janice Moore, Co-Chief Operating Officer
Matthew Tripp, VP of Research & Development

Founded: 1983

9015 Intermountain Retailer
Utah Food Industry Association
1578 W 1700 S
Suite 100
Salt Lake City, UT 84104-3470
801-973-9517
FAX: 801-972-8712 800-423-6636
mrapp@utfood.com
http://www.utfood.com

James V Olsen, President
Meik Rapp, Editor

This annual guide offers information on brokers in Utah that are serving the retail food industry. *$25.00*
48 pages Annual+ Founded: 1896
Circulation: 1200

9016 International Poultry Exposition Guide
WATT Publishing Company
122 S Wesley Avenue
Mount Morris, IL 61054-1497
815-734-4171
FAX: 815-734-5649
schreiber@wattmm.com
http://www.wattpoultry.com

Chris Wright, Editor
Clay Schreiber, Publisher
Jim Wessel, Circulation Director
James Watt, Owner

Monthly
Circulation: 20,059

9017 International Product Alert
Marketing Intelligence Service
6473D Route 64
Naples, NY 14512-9726
585-374-6326
FAX: 585-374-5217 800-836-5710
mi@productscan.com
http://www.productscan.com

Tom Vierhile, Executive Editor
Sherry Meeker-Barton, Editor-in-Chief

Reports the introduction of new food, beverage, health & beauty aides, household & pet products outside of North America. Reports include full product descriptions and selected illustrations of products and advertising backup. *$700.00*

9018 Italian Cooking and Living
Italian Culinary Institute
302 5th Avenue
9th Floor
New York, NY 10001
212-899-9057
FAX: 212-889-3907 888-742-2373
irene@italiancookingandliving.com
http://www.italiancookingandliving.com

Paolo Villoresi, Publisher
Irene De Gasparis, Associate Publisher
Charles Pennino, Owner

American magazine devoted to Italian cuisine/culture/travel *$18.00*
112 pages Founded: 2001
Circulation: 75000 20,000 names $400 per M.
Printed in 4 colors on glossy stock

9019 JAOCS: Journal of the American Oil Chemists' Society
American Oil Chemists' Society
2211 W Bradley Avenue
PO Box 3489
Champaign, IL 61821-1827
217-359-2344
FAX: 217-351-8091
plandman@aocs.org www.aocs.org

John P Cherry, Editor-in-Chief
Pam Landman, Production Editor

A peer-reviewed journal devoted to fundamental and practical research, production, processing, packaging, and distribution in the field of fats, oils, proteins, and other related substances.
Monthly Founded: 1947 6000 names

9020 Journal of Animal Science
American Society of Animal Science
1111 N Dunlap Avenue
Savoy, IL 61874
217-356-9050
FAX: 217-398-4119
susanp@assochq.org www.asas.org

Larry Reynolds, Editor-in-Chief
Susan Pollack, Managing Editor/Editorial Director

The official journal of the American Society of Animal Science, JAS publishes results of original research in Genetics, Growth and Physiology, Nutrition, Production, Products, and Special Topics. JAS consistently ranks in the top tier in the category of Agriculture, Dairy, and Animal Sciences
Monthly Founded: 1908
Circulation: 3500 3000 names $100 per M.
Printed in on glossy stock

9021 Journal of Dairy Science
American Dairy Science Association
1111 N Dunlap Avenue
Savoy, IL 6187-9604
217-356-5146
FAX: 217-398-4119
adsa@assochq.org
http://www.adsa.org

Michael Mangino, Senior Editor
Sharon Frick, Journal Support Coordinator

Research in dairy cattle production and dairy food products. *$110.00*
Monthly Founded: 1990

9022 Journal of Food Protection
International Association for Food Protection
6200 Aurora Avenue
Suite 200W
Des Moines, IA 50322-2864
515-276-3344
FAX: 515-276-8655 800-369-6337
info@foodprotection.org
http://www.foodprotection.org

Bev Corron, Public Relations
Bev Brannen, Marketing Manager
Kathleen A Glass, President

Each issue contains scientific research and authoritative review articles reporting on a variety of topics in food science pertaining to food safety and quality. *$335.00*

Monthly Founded: 1911 ISSN 0362-028X
Circulation: 11,000
Mailing list available for rent 3000+ names $150 per M.
Printed in 4 colors on glossy stock

9023 Journal of Food Science
Institute of Food Technologists
525 W Van Buren Street
Suite 1000
Chicago, IL 60607
312-782-8424
FAX: 312-782-8348
info@ift.org http://www.ift.org

Barbara Byrd-Keenan, Publisher
Daryl B Lund, Editor-in-Chief

Food science journal containing peer-reviewed reports of original research and critical reviews of all aspects of food science for food professionals. Publishes more than 500 papers per year to help food technologists stay informed and keep current.

Founded: 1936

9024 Journal of Foodservice Business Research
Haworth Press
10 Alice Street
Binghamton, NY 13904-1580
607-722-5857
FAX: 607-771-0012 800-429-6784
getinfo@haworthpress.com
http://www.haworthpress.com

David A Cranage, Editor
H G Parsa, Editor-in-Chief

Articles from international experts in various desciplines, including management, marketing, finance, law, food technology, nutrition, psychology, and more. *$45.00*

Quarterly Founded: 1978 553 names $495 per M.
Printed in on matte stock

9025 Journal of Sugar Beet Research
800 Grant Street
Suite 300
Denver, CO 80203-2987
303-832-4460
FAX: 303-832-4468
aa@bsdf-assbt.org
www.bsdf-assbt.org

Robert W Strickland, President
Thomas Schwartz, Executive VP

Fosters all phases of sugarbeet and beet sugar research, promotes the dissemination of relevant scientific knowledge, and strives to maintain high standards of ethics, and to cooperate with other organizations having objectives beneficial to the beet sugar industry.

Quarterly

9026 Journal of Sustainable Agriculture
Haworth Press
10 Alice Street
Binghamton, NY 13904-1580
607-722-5857
FAX: 607-722-6362 1 8-0 4-9 67
getinfo@haworthpress.com
http://www.haworthpress.com

Raymond P Poincelot, Editor
Bill Cohen, Publisher

Professional journal is specifically devoted to the rapidly growing field of sustainable agriculture, and is aimed at increasing professional and public awareness and gaining support for necessary changes in agricultural industry. *$60.00*

Founded: 1978

9027 Journal of Vegetable Crop Production
Haworth Press
10 Alice Street
Binghamton, NY 13904-1580
607-722-5857
FAX: 607-722-6362 800-429-6784
getinfo@haworthpress.com
http://www.haworthpress.com

Amarjit S Basra, Editor
Bill Cohen, Publisher

Journal aimed at those specialists and professionals who labor with the problems of vegetable crop management from land preparation to seeding and consumption. *$80.00*

9028 Journal of the American Dietetic Association
Elsevier Health Publishing
1600 John F Kennedy Boulevard
Suite 1800
Philadelphia, PA 19106-2899
215-239-3900
FAX: 215-239-3990
journal@eatright.org/elspcs@elsevier.com
www.eatright.org/www.us.elsevierhealth.com

Jennifer Herendeen, Editorial Director
Jason Swift, Editor
Ryan Lipscomb, Department Editor
Linda Van Horn, Editor-in-Chief

A premier source for the practice and science of food, nutrition, and dietetics. The Journal focuses on advancing professional knowledge across the range of research and practice issues such as: nutritional science, medical nutrition therapy, public health nutrition, food science and biotechnology, foodservice systems, leadership and management and dietetics education. *$229.00*

Monthly/Subscription

9029 Journal of the American Pomological Society
103 Tyson Building
University Park, PA 16802-4200
814-863-6163
FAX: 814-237-3407
bardenja@vt.edu
www.americanpomological.org

Dr John Barden, Editor

The Journal contains refereed technical articles and a wide variety of applied articles relating to fruit varieties.

Quarterly/Free to Members

9030 Journal of the American Society for Horticultural Science
American Society for Horticultural Science
113 S West Street
Suite 200
Alexandria, VA 22314-2851
703-836-4606
FAX: 703-836-2024
journal@ashs.org www.ashs.org

Neal E De Vos, Editor-in-Chief
Michael W Neff, Publisher
Katharine J Lewis, Managing Editor

A peer-reviewed publication of results of orginal research on horticultural plants and their products or directly related research areas. Its prime function is communication of mission-oriented, fundamental research to other researchers. *$55.00*

Bi-Monthly/Members Rate Founded: 1903
Mailing list available for rent 2500 names $100 per M.

9031 Journal of the Association of Food and Drug Officials
Association of Food and Drug Officials
2550 Kingston Road
Suite 311
York, PA 17402-425
717-757-2888
FAX: 717-755-8089
afdo@afdo.org www.afdo.org

Denise Rooney, Executive Director

News and the latest legislation for the Food and Drug Association. *$80.00*

4x/year Founded: 1937

9032 Kosher Today
1428 36th street
219
Brooklyn, NY 11218
718-854-4460
FAX: 718-854-4474
info@koshertoday.com
http://www.koshertoday.com/

Menachem Lubinsky, CEO
Bill Springer, Publisher

Covers the kosher food industry.

28 pages Weekly Founded: 1984
Circulation: 20000
Printed in 4 colors on newsprint stock

9033 Land
Free Press Company
418 S. 2nd Street
Mankato, MN 56001-3784
507-446-6395
FAX: 507-345-1027 800-657-4665
theland@the-land.com
http://www.the-land.com

Kevin Schulz, Editor
Vail Belgard, Office Manager
Kim Henrickson, Advertising Manager
Ken Lingen, Manager

Agricultural news. *$20.00*

48 pages Monthly Founded: 1887
Circulation: 39000 39000 names
Printed in on newsprint stock

9034 Logistics Journal
Transportation Intermediaries Association

1625 Prince Street
Suite 200
Alexandria, VA 22314
703-172-2140
FAX: 703-836-0123
info@tianet.org www.tianet.org

Robert A Voltmann, President/CEO
Nancy King, Marketing Manager

Education and policy organization for North American transportation intermediaries. The only national association representing the interests of all third party transportation service providers. Members include logistics management firms, property brokers, perishable commodities brokers, freight forwarders, intermodal marketers and ocean and air forwarders.
700 pages Monthly Founded: 1978
Circulation: 1000 700 names

9035 Manufacturing Confectioner
MC Publishing
175 Rock Road
Glen Rock, NJ 07452-1700
201-652-2655
FAX: 201-652-3419
themc@gomc.com
http://www.gomc.com
Rachel Beck, Editor
Magazine devoted exclusively to the confectionery market of the food industry. *$50.00*
Monthly Founded: 1921

9036 Meat Marketing and Technology
Marketing & Technology Group
1415 N Dayton Street
Chicago, IL 60622
312-266-3311
FAX: 312-266-3363
bill@meatingplace.com
http://www.meatingplace.com
Mark Lafens, Publisher
Dan Allen, Editor-at-Large
Jim Goldberg, VP Sales/Marketing
John Gregerson, Editor
Deborah Silver, Managing Editor
Provides information on meat processing, retail, slaughtering and fabricating and rendering. *$40.00*
Monthly Founded: 1993
Circulation: 20,009
Printed in 4 colors on glossy stock

9037 Meat Processing: North American Edition
122 S Wesley Avenue
Mount Morris, IL 31054-1497
815-734-4171
FAX: 815-734-5631
stevebjerklie@yahoo.com
http://www.meatnews.com
Steve Bjerklie, Editor
Gregg Watt, President/COO
Monthly magazine for the meat and poultry processing industries. Edited to provide new product technology, regulatory, marketing and industry newsto primary and further processors of meat products with business locations in the US and Canada.
Monthly
Circulation: 21057 21057 names $150 per M.

9038 Meat and Poultry
Sosland Publishing Company
4800 Main Street
Suite 100
Kansas City, MO 64112-2513
816-756-1000
FAX: 816-756-0494
meat&poultry@sosland.com
http://www.meatpoultry.com
Keith Nunes, Executive Editor
Mark Sabo, President
Joel Crews, Editor
Serves meat, poultry and seafood processors, wholesalers-distrubuters, slaughterers, fabricators, cutters, meat buyers, and rendering and pet food manufacturers. Subscription: $42. *$42.00*
Monthly Founded: 1955
Circulation: 21,000
Printed in 4 colors on glossy stock

9039 Mid-American Farmer Grower
19 N Main Street
PO Box 323
Perryville, MO 63775-1337
573-547-2244
FAX: 573-547-5663 877-489-6997
editor@mafg.net http://www.mafg.net
John LaRose, Publisher
Barbara Galeski, Editor
Jack R Thompson II, Marketing Director
Offers farming news for the middle states.
$19.00
Weekly

9040 Midwest Food Service News
Pinnacle Publishing
316 N Michigan Avenue
Suite 300
Chicago, IL 60601
312-272-2401
FAX: 312-960-4106 800-493-4867
pinpub@ragan.com
www.midwestfoodservicenews.com
Keith Hadley, Publisher
Joanne Cooper, Editor
Communicates directly and exclusively with restaurant and food service operations in Indiana, Kentucky, Michigan, Ohio, Pennsylvania and West Virginia.
52 pages Bi-Monthly Founded: 1982
Circulation: 40,000
Printed in 4 colors on newsprint stock

9041 Military Grocer
Downey Communications
4800 Montgomery Lane
Suite 710
Bethesda, MD 20814-3461
301-718-7600
FAX: 301-718-7604
Richard T Carroll, Publisher
Loretta M Downey, CEO
Serves defense commissary employees worldwide.
5 per year
Printed in 4 colors on glossy stock

9042 Milk and Liquid Food Transporter
Glen Street Publications
W4652 Glen Street
Appletone, WI 54913
920-749-4880
FAX: 920-749-4877
jplout@glenstreet.com
http://www.glenstreet.com
Jane Plout, Publisher
Information for owners, operators and managers of companies that haul milk or other liquid foods in sanitary or food grade tankers. Publication covers maintenance, association news, state of the industry, business management, and activities of independent haulers.
16 pages Monthly Founded: 1960
Circulation: 4768
Printed in 4 colors on glossy stock

9043 Milling Journal
3065 Pershing Court
Decatur, IL 62526
217-877-9660
FAX: 217-877-6647 800-728-7511
mark@grainnet.com
http://www.grainnet.com
Jim Camillo, Editor
Mark Avery, Publisher
Kay Merryfield, Circulation Manager
Jody Sexton, Editorial Assistant
Deb Coontz, Sales Manager
Mailed to all active AOM members in the US, Canada, and internationally, including wheat flour/corn mills and corn/oilseed processors in US and Canada.
Quarterly
Circulation: 1217

9044 Milling and Baking News
Sosland Publishing Company
4800 Main Street
Suite 100
Kansas City, MO 64112
816-756-1000
FAX: 816-756-0494
gdavidson@sosland.com
http://www.bakingbusiness.com/
Mike Gude, Associate Publisher
El Joshua Sosland, Editor
Neil N Sosland, Executive Editor
Eric Schroeder, Managing Editor
Jeff Gelski, Associate Editor
This magazine is aimed at baking, milling and food processing industries. *$52.00*
Monthly
Circulation: 4032

9045 Modern Baking
Donohue/Meehan Publishing
2700 River Road
Suite 303
Des Plaines, IL 60018
847-299-4430
FAX: 847-296-1968
http://www.bakery-net.com
Jerry Rymond, Publisher
Heather Brown, Editor
Articles about and directed to the retail bakery foods industry. Free to qualified subscribers. $60.00 per year for others. *$75.00*

112 pages Monthly Founded: 1987
Circulation: 27000
Mailing list available for rent 27,000 names
Printed in 4 colors on glossy stock

9046 Modern Brewery Age
Business Journals
50 Day Street
S Norwalk, CT 06854-3100
203-853-6015
FAX: 203-852-8175
pete@breweryage.com
http://www.breweryage.com
Peter VK Reid, Editor
Britton Jones, President
Arthur Heilman, Circulation Manager
A magazine for the wholesale and brewing industry. *$95.00*
Quarterly Founded: 1933

9047 Modern Brewery Age: Tabloid Edition
Business Journals
50 Day Street
#5550
Norwalk, CT 06854-3100
203-853-6015
FAX: 203-852-8175
Peter VK Reid, Editor
Brewery industry tabloid. *$85.00*
Weekly

9048 Monthly Price Review
Urner Barry Publications
PO Box 389
Toms River, NJ 08754
732-240-5330
FAX: 732-341-0891 800-932-0617
mail@urnerbarry.com
http://www.urnerbarry.com
Paul B Brown Jr, President
Karen Mick, Circulation Director
Lists price of eggs, turkeys, chickens, fowl, butter, margarine, cheese and concentrated milk products for the month and compares the monthly average to the previous year. *$149.00*
Monthly Founded: 1858
Circulation: 310

9049 Mushroom News
American Mushroom Institute
1284 Gap Newport Pike
Suite 2
Avondale, PA 19311-1030
610-268-7483
FAX: 610-268-8015
mushroomnews@kennett.net
http://www.americanmushroom.org
Dr. Peter Romaine, Editor-in-Chief
Mark Wach, Chairman
Laura Phelps, President
Bill Barber, Publisher
For growers and scientists in mushroom production. *$275.00*
Monthly Founded: 1956

9050 NACS Magazine
National Association of Convenience Stores
1600 Duke Street
Alexandria, VA 22314
703-684-3600
FAX: 703-836-4564
bmoyer@nacsonline.com
www.nacsmagazine.com
Gina Veazy, Publisher
Ben Moyer, Advertising Manager
Delivered to all members, this magazine reaches a majority of the convenience and petroleum marketing channel of trade.
Monthly
Circulation: 27,632

9051 NAEDA Equipment Dealer
NAEDA
1195 Smizer Mill Road
Fenton, MO 63026
636-349-5000
FAX: 636-349-5443
webmaster@naeda.com
www.naeda.com
Mike Kraemer, Managing Editor
Larry Krueger, Advertising Manager
$40.00
Monthly Founded: 1900
Circulation: 9,500
Printed in 4 colors on glossy stock

9052 NWAC News: Thad Cochran National Warmwater Aquaculture Center
127 Experiment Station Road
Stoneville, MS 38776-197
662-686-3273
FAX: 662-686-3320
http://www.msstate.edu/dept/tcnwac
Jimmy Avery, Editor
J Lee, CEO/President
Monthly Founded: 1998
Circulation: 1200
Printed in 3 colors on matte stock

9053 Nation's Restaurant News
Lebhar-Friedman
425 Park Avenue
New York, NY 10022-3506
212-756-5000
FAX: 212-756-5215
info@lf.com http://www.lf.com
Alan Gould, Publisher
Michael Cardillo, VP Sales
Serves commercial and onsite food service and lodging establishments including restaurants, schools, universities, hospitals, nursing homes and other health and welfare facilities, hotels and motels with food service, government installations, clubs and other related firms. *$ 44.95*
Founded: 1925
Circulation: 85999
Mailing list available for rent 100,000 names $100 per M.
Printed in 4 colors on matte stock

9054 National Confectionery Sales Association Annual Journal
Teresa Tarantino
10225 Berea Road, Suite B
Cleveland, OH 44102
216-631-8200
FAX: 216-631-8210
ttarantino@mail.propressinc.com
http://www.candyhalloffame.com
Tony Rufrano, President
Steve Foster, Executive Director
Annual membership listing and biographies of Candy Hall of Fame industees. *$25.00*
76 pages Founded: 1997 350 names $75 per M.
Printed in 4 colors on matte stock

9055 National Culinary Review
American Culinary Federation
180 Center Place Way
Saint Augustine, FL 32095
904-824-4468
FAX: 904-825-4758 800-624-9458
acf@acfchefs.net www.acfchefs.org
Kay Orde, Editor
Heidi Cramb, Membership Director
Michael Baskette, Executive Director
A monthly magazine that is circulated by paid subscription. ACF members receive this publication as a benefit of membership in the American Culinary Federation. The National Culinary Review contains chef-tested recipes, industry news, and culinary techniques and is an educational resource for everyone interested in food preparation. *$50.00*
Monthly Founded: 1932
Circulation: 25,000

9056 National Farmers Union News
National Farmers Union
11900 E Cornell Avenue
Aurora, CO 80014-3194
303-337-5500
FAX: 303-368-1390 800-347-1961
info@nfu.org http://www.nfu.org
David Frederickson, President
Rae Price, Publications Editor
A grass roots structure in which policy positions are initiated locally. The goal is to sustain and strengthen family farm and ranch agriculture. *$30.00*
Monthly Founded: 1902

9057 National Fisherman
Diversified Business Communications
PO Box 7437
121 Free Street
Portland, ME 04112-7438
207-842-5500
FAX: 207-842-5503
info@divcom.com
http://www.nationalfisherman.com/
Jerry Frazier, Editor-in-Chief
Randy Le Shane, Production Manager
Nancy Hasselback, President
Stephnie Wendel, Circulation Manager
The most widely read commercial fishing magazine and the only commercial fishing publication providing national coverage and national circulation. *$22.95*
Monthly Founded: 1949
Circulation: 38000

9058 National Food Processors Association State Legislative Report
National Food Processors Association
1350 I Street NW
Suite 300
Washington, DC 20005-2102
202-930-0890
FAX: 202-639-5932 800-355-0983
custserv@nfpa-food.org
http://www.nfpa-food.org
Cal Dooley, President/CEO
Lisa Weddig, Executive Director
Tammy Morgan, Contact
Monthly Founded: 1901
Circulation: 345

9059 National Grocer
National Grocers Association
1005 N Glebe Road
Suite 250
Arlington, VA 22201-5758
703-516-0700
FAX: 703-516-0115
info@naionalgrocers.org
http://www.nationalgrocers.org
Thomas Zaucha, CEO
Jen Teel, Communications Coordinator
Source of information on all aspects of the retail/wholesale grocery industry. *$5.00*
Quarterly Founded: 1992
Circulation: 7000

9060 National Hog Farmer
7900 International Drive
Suite 300
Minneapolis, MN 55425-1576
952-514-4710
FAX: 952-851-4601
nhf@primediabusiness.com
http://nationalhogfarmer.com/
Steve May, Publisher
Dale Miller, Editor
JoAnn DeSmet, Marketing
Robert Moraczewski, Senior Vice President
Offers production information for hog farming business managers.
Monthly Founded: 1960
Circulation: 84000
Mailing list available for rent 84M names
Printed in 4 colors on glossy stock

9061 National Provisioner
Stagnito Communications
155 Pfingster Road
Suite 205
Deerfield, IL 60015
847-205-5660
FAX: 847-205-5680
info@stagnito.com
http://www.nationalprovisioner.com

Ned Bardic, Publisher
Barbara Young, Editor
Tommy Howell, Marketing

Magazine for meat, poultry, prepared food processors. *$85.00*
Monthly Founded: 1912
Circulation: 25000

9062 National Wheat Growers Journal
National Wheat Growers Association
415 2nd Street NE
Suite 300
Washington, DC 20002-4900
202-547-7800
FAX: 202-546-2638
www.wheatworld.org

Darren Coppock, CEO
June Silverberg, Director Corporate Relations

Accepts advertising.

9063 Natural Foods Merchandiser
New Hope Natural Media
1401 Pearl Street
Suite 200
Boulder, CO 80302
303-939-8440
FAX: 303-939-9886 800-431-1255
info@newhope.com
http://www.newhope.com

Maurice Lluch, Group Publisher
Marty Traynor, Editor
Lynne Brenner, Human Resources Executive

Natural Foods Merchandiser features a comprehensive overview of the industry, the latest reports on new ingredients and formulations, market news, new product releases and many other features specifically designed for the retailmarket. It offers the information and the products retailers require to succeed in the competitive natural products marketplace.
65 pages Monthly Founded: 1979
Circulation: 15,000 15,000 names $125 per M.
Printed in 4 colors on glossy stock

9064 Natural Products INSIDER
Virgo Publishing
3300 N Central Avenue, Suite 300
Phoenix, AZ 85012
480-990-1101
FAX: 480-675-8154
asharman@vpico.com
www.naturalproductsinsider.com

Peggy Jackson, Publisher
Heather Granato, Editor

Official magazine for SupplySide. Provides timely information and news for marketers, manufacturers and formulators of dietary supplements, functional foods and personal care. The website also offers exclusive resources and offers, free weekly e-newsletters and a searchable news archive.
80 pages 13/Yr + 2 Buyer's Guides
Founded: 1996
Circulation: 12000
Mailing list available for rent 15000+ names $var per M.
Printed in 4 colors on glossy stock : digital

9065 Nightclub & Bar Magazine
Oxford Publishing
307 W Jackson Avenue
Oxford, MS 38655-2154
662-236-5510
FAX: 662-236-5541 800-247-3881
ed@oxpub.com
http://www.nightclub.com

Ed Meek, Publisher
Taylor Rau, Editor
Jennifer Parsons, Marketing
Jennifer Robinson, CEO/President

A monthly publication covering the nightclub and bar hospitality industry. *$30.00*
Monthly
Circulation: 30000
Printed in 4 colors on glossy stock

9066 North Africa and Middle East International Agricultural and Trade Report
US Department of Agriculture
1301 New York Avenue NW
#612
Washington, DC 20005-4701
202-219-0724
FAX: 202-219-0942

Michael Kurrzig, Editor

Information on current and projected agriculture production and trade in North Africa and the Middle East. Reports include trade and production data and highlight US and European trade with the region.
Annual

9067 North American Deer Farmers Magazine
North American Deer Farmers Association

1215 N 7th St
Ste 104
Lake City, MN 55041-1266
651-345-5600
FAX: 651-345-5603
info@nadefa.org
http://www.nadefa.org

Phyllis Menden, Executive Director
Suzanne Folts, Administrative Assistant
Gary Nelson, President

National association of deer farming and ranching. Membership dues are $75-195 which include this quarterly magazine.
Quarterly Founded: 1983
Circulation: 1000
Mailing list available for rent
Printed in on glossy stock

9068 North American Journal of Aquaculture
American Fisheries Society
5410 Grosvenor Lane
Bethesda, MD 20814-2199
301-897-8616
FAX: 301-897-8096
main@fisheries.org www.fisheries.org

Bruce A Barton, Editor
William L Shelton, Editor
Christopher C Kohler, Development Editor

Formerly published as The Progressive Fish-Culturist. The focus is on culture of all aquatic organisms that are of importance to North American culturists. Topics include, but are not limited to, nutrition and feeding, broodstock selection and spawning, drugs and chemicals, health and water quality, and testing new techniques and equipment for the management and rearing of aquatic species *$38.00*
Quarterly

9069 Northeast DairyBusiness
DairyBusiness Communications
6437 Collamer Road
East Syracuse, NY 13057-1031
315-703-7979
FAX: 315-703-7988 800-334-1904
smiller@dairybusiness.com
http://www.dairybusiness.com

Eleanor Jacobs, Editor
Susan Harlow, Managing Editor

Business resource for successful milk producers. Devoted exclusively to the business and dairy management needs of milk producers in the 12 northeastern states. *$38.95*
51 pages Monthly Founded: 1904
Circulation: 17,500
Printed in 4 colors on glossy stock

9070 Northwest Palate Magazine
Pacifica Publishing
PO Box 10860
Portland, OR 97296
503-224-6039
FAX: 503-222-5312 800-398-7842
editorial@nwpalate.com
http://www.nwpalate.com

Cameron Nagel, Publisher/Editor
Angie Jabine, Managing Editor
Cameron Nagel, CEO

Regional magazine that focuses on food, wine and travel. Coverage includes restaurants, destinations and the wines of the Pacific Northwest states and British Columbia. *$15.00*
56 pages 6 issues per ye Founded: 1987
Circulation: 45000 Audited 4M names $100 per M.
Printed in 4 colors on glossy stock

9071 Nut Grower
Western Agricultural Publishing Company

4969 E Clinton Way
Suite 104
Fresno, CA 93727-1549
559-252-7000
FAX: 559-252-7387 888-382-9772
editorial@westgpubco.com
www.westagpubco.com

Paul Baltimore, Publisher
Jim Baltimore, Publisher
Randy Bailey, Editor
Robert Fujimoto, Assistant Editor

Covers production topics, the latest in research developments, and crop news on almonds, walnuts, pistachios, pecans and chestnuts. *$19.95*
Monthly
Circulation: 11,993

9072 Nutraceuticals World
Rodman Publications
70 Hilltop Road
Ramsey, NJ 07446
201-825-2552
FAX: 201-825-0553
nutraceuticals@rodpub.com
http://www.nutraceuticalsworld.com/

Rebecca Madley-Wright, Editor
Rodman J Zilenziger Jr, President
Matthew J Montgomery, Publisher/Executive VP
Tom Branna, Editorial Director
Ellen Pfister, Circulation Manager

Monthly
Circulation: 12010

9073 Nutrition Action Healthletter
Center for Science in the Public Interest
1875 Connecticut Avenue NW
Suite 300
Washington, DC 20009
202-332-9110
FAX: 202-265-4954
cspi@cspinet.org
http://www.cspinet.org

Stephen B Schmidt, Editor-in-Chief
Chris Schmidt, Circulation Manager
Michael Jacobson, Executive Director

A magazine covering food and nutrition, the food industry, and relevant government regulations. *$32.00*
16 pages Founded: 1971
Circulation: 800000
Mailing list available for rent 700,000 names $90 per M.
Printed in 4 colors on matte stock

9074 OEM Off-Highway
1233 Janesville Avenue
PO Box 803
Fort Atkinson, WI 53538-803
920-563-6388
FAX: 920-328-9029 800-547-7377
Leslie.Shalabi@cygnuspub.com
http://www.oemoff-highway.com
Richard Reiff, Executive VP
Leslie Shalabi, Publisher/Editor
Paul Mackler, President/CEO
Barb Hesse, Circulation Manager
Offers information on off-road machinery and farm equipment.
Founded: 1965

9075 On-Campus Hospitality
Executive Business Media
825 Old Country Road
PO Box 1500
Westbury, NY 11590
516-334-3030
FAX: 516-334-8959
ebm-mail@ebmpubs.com
http://www.ebmpubs.com
Murry H Greenwald, President/Publisher
Paul Ragusa, Managing Editor
College and university food service operations and outlets and related purchasing and administrative offices. *$30.00*
Founded: 1979
Circulation: 9,445
Printed in 4 colors

9076 Onboard Services
International Publishing Company of America
664 La Villa Drive
Miami, FL 33166-6095
305-887-1700
FAX: 305-885-1923 800-525-2015
onboard@ipca.com
www.onboard-services.com
Alexander C Morton, Publisher
George Hulcher, Contributing Editor
Keeps airline, cruise ships, railroad, and terminal concessions management and purchasing departments up-to-date on all phases of passenger services. *$25.00*
24 pages Founded: 1968
Printed in 4 colors on glossy stock

9077 Organic WORLD
John Pappenheimer
3939 Leary Way NW
Seattle, WA 98107-5043
206-781-3347
FAX: 206-632-7055
Covers the news of organic gardening. *$15.00*
Quarterly

9078 Organic and Natural News
Virgo Publishing
3300 N Central Avenue, Suite 2500
PO Box 40079
Phoenix, AZ 85067-0079
480-990-1101
FAX: 480-675-8151
jonb@vpico.com www.vpico.ocm
Jon Benninger, Group Publisher
Susan Warner, Publisher
Heather Granato, Editor
Trade magazine dedicated to the organic and natural products market.
Monthly Founded: 1998
Circulation: 20,741
Printed in 4 colors on glossy stock

9079 Pacific Farmer-Stockman
999 West Riverside Avenue
PO Box 2160
Spokane, WA 99201-1006
509-595-5385
FAX: 509-459-3929 800-624-6618
information@spokane.net
http://www.nmv.pointshop.com
Barry Roach, Ad Director
Shaun Higgins, President
Colleen Striegel, Operations Manager
Mike Craigen, Marketing Executive
Offers farming news and information for farmers and herdsmen located in the Pacific states. *$29.95*
Monthly

9080 Packer: Produce Services Sourcebook
Vance Publishing
10901 W 84th Terrace
Lenexa, KS 66214
913-438-8700
FAX: 913-438-0691 800-255-5113
online@thepacker.com
http://www.thepacker.com
Robert Bertels, Group Publisher
Ben Wood, Editor
Leanne Ball, Manager
Annual reference offering information on produce packers, processers and handlers. *$65.00*
Weekly Founded: 1937
Circulation: 13000
Printed in on glossy stock

9081 Peanut Farmer
Specialized Agricultural Publications
5808 Faringdon Place
Suite 200
Raleigh, NC 27609
919-872-5040
FAX: 919-876-6531
publisher@peanutfarmer.com
http://www.peanutfarmer.com
Dayton H Matlick, President
Mary Evans, Publisher
Mary Cornwall, Chief Copy Editor
Jeanne Sherman, Director of Circulation
Offers peanut farmers profitable methods of raising, marketing and promoting peanuts, plus key related issues. *$15.00*
24 pages Monthly Founded: 1965
Circulation: 18500 18,500 names $80 per M.
Printed in 4 colors on glossy stock

9082 Peanut Grower
Vance Publishing
38 Peace Drive
Bronson, FL 32621
352-486-7006
FAX: 352-486-7009
ahuber@svic.net
http://www.peanutgrower.com
Amanda Huber, Editor
Lia Guthrie, Sales
Written for the largest 24,000 US peanut farmers. Covers disease, weed and insect control, legislation, farm equipment, marketing and new research.
Monthly Founded: 1937
Circulation: 17700

9083 Peanut Science
American Peanut Research and Education Society
Oklahoma State University
376 Ag Hall
Stillwater, OK 74078-6025
405-372-3052
FAX: 405-624-6718
nickeli@provalue.net
www.apres.okstate.edu
Dr J Ronald Sholar, Executive Officer
A professional journal with current research results. *$9.00*
Bi-annually/Fee Per Issue Founded: 1979

9084 Pesticide Chemical News Guide
Food Chemical News
1725 K Street NW
Suite 506
Washington, DC 20006-1401
202-887-6320
FAX: 202-887-6339
newsdiv@crcpress.com
http://www.foodregulation.com
Margie Weiner, Publisher
Patrick Duggan, Editor
William Feldman, CEO
Tamara Yeldell, Circulation Manager
Tracks changes to existing and pending regulations for the use of over 1,100 chemicals on approximately 360 crops and foodstuffs. Compiled from the CFR and the Federal Register, the Guide is conveniently organized. *$975.00*
Monthly Founded: 1960

9085 PetroMart Business
Virgo Publishing
3300 N Central Avenue, Suite 2500
PO Box 40079
Phoenix, AZ 85067-0079
480-990-1101
FAX: 480-675-8146
www.petromartbusiness.com
Magazine for owners of gas stations, convenience stores, and their managers.

9086 Pig International
WATT Publishing Company
122 S Wesley Avenue
Mount Morris, IL 61054-1497
815-734-4171
FAX: 815-734-5649
schreiber@wattmm.com
http://www.wattnet.com
Clay Schreiber, Publisher
Peter Best, Editor
James Watt, Owner
Edited for pig producers and others allied to the field in Asia, Europe, Africa and the US. Provides information to the commercial pig industry on the efficient and profitable production and processing of pig meat. *$50.00*
Monthly Founded: 1971
Circulation: 17642
Printed in 4 colors on glossy stock

9087 Pizza Today
National Association of Pizzeria Operators
908 S 8th Street
Suite 200
Louisville, KY 40203
502-736-9500
FAX: 502-736-9502 800-489-8324
plachapelle@pizzatoday.com
http://www.pizzatoday.com
Pete Lachapelle, Publisher/President
Jeremy White, Editor-in-Chief

Mandy Detwiler, Managing Editor
Pat Cravens, Editorial Coordinator

Up-to-date information on pizza restaurant management, pizza equipment for sale, a vendor directory and more.

130 pages Monthly Founded: 1983
Circulation: 47,000 25000 names
Printed in 4 colors on glossy stock

9088 **Pork**
10901 W. 84th Terrace
Parkway
Lenexa, IL 66214
913-438-8700
FAX: 913-438-0674 800-255-5113
mmiller@vancepublishing.com
http://www.vancepublishing.com

Marlys Miller, Editor
Jane Messenger, Associate Editor
Cliff Becker, Group Publisher
Bill Raufer, Contributing Editor

A magazine specifically designed for the professional pork producer. *$59.88*

Monthly Founded: 1981
Circulation: 21,464
Mailing list available for rent

9089 **Potato Country**
Columbia Publishing
413-b N 20th Avenue
Yakima, WA 98902-2504
509-248-2452
FAX: 509-248-4056 800-900-2452
columbia@columbiapublications.com
http://www.columbiapublications.com

D Brent Clement, Editor/Publisher
Mike Stoker, Publisher/Advertising Sales Manager
Carol Kieffer, Production Manager

Edited for potato growers and allied industry people throughout the Western fall-production states. Editorial material covers production, seed, disease forecast, equipment, fertilizer, irrigation, pest/weed management, crop reports and annual buyers guide. *$15.00*

32 pages Founded: 1975
Circulation: 6300
Printed in 4 colors on glossy stock

9090 **Potato Grower**
Harris Publishing Company
360 B Street
Idaho Falls, ID 83402
208-524-4217
FAX: 208-522-5241
jason@potatogrower.com
http://www.potatogrower.com

Jason Harris, Publisher
Gary Rawlings, Editor
Nancy Butler, Staff Writer
Rob Erickson, Marketing
Eula Endecott, Circulation

Current news on growing potatoes, market trends, technology. *$20.95*

48 pages Monthly Founded: 1965 ISBN
m-ountai-n -w ² names
Printed in 4 colors on glossy stock

9091 **Poultry**
Marketing and Technology Group
1415 N Dayton Street
Chicago, IL 60622-2643
312-266-3311
FAX: 312-266-3363
bill@meatingplace.com
http://www.meatingplace.com

Mark Lefens, Editor-in-Chief
Tom Cosgrove, Editor

Serves companies who deal with poultry slaughter, rendering or processing.

Monthly Founded: 1993
Circulation: 20,000
Printed in 4 colors on glossy stock

9092 **Poultry Digest**
WATT Publishing Company
122 S Wesley Avenue
Mount Morris, IL 61054-1497
815-734-4171
FAX: 815-734-4201
olentine@wattmm.com
http://www.wattnet.com

James W Watt, President
Charles G Olentine Jr, PhD, Publisher

A magazine serving the production side of the entire poultry industry. *$15.00*

Monthly Founded: 1917
Circulation: 19000

9093 **Poultry International**
WATT Publishing Company
122 S Wesley Avenue
Mount Morris, IL 61054-1497
815-734-4171
FAX: 815-734-5679
olentine@wattmm.com
http://www.wattnet.com

David Martin, Editor
James Watt, Owner

Poultry International serves the poultry industry worldwide. *$63.00*

68 pages Founded: 1962
Circulation: 23427
Printed in 4 colors

9094 **Poultry Times**
Poultry & Egg News
345 Green Street
PO Box 1388
Gainesville, GA 30503-1338
770-536-2476
FAX: 770-532-4894
editorial@poultryandeggnews.com
http://www.poultryandeggnews.com

Christopher Hill, Publisher/Editor
Cindy Wellborn, Advertising Director
Chris Hill, CEO
Barbara L. Olejnik, Associate Editor
Kyle Hatcher, National Sales Representative

A annual resource offering information on companies that market poultry and egg products. *$12.00*

Founded: 1954
Circulation: 10500
Printed in on glossy stock

9095 **Poultry USA**
WATT Publishing Company
122 S Wesley Avenue
Mount Morris, IL 61054-1497
815-734-4171
FAX: 815-734-5679
gthornton@bellsouth.net
http://www.wattnet.com

Gary Thornton, Editor
Clay Schreiber, Publisher
James Watt, Owner
Pam Ballard, Regional Sales Manager
Jeff Swanson, Production Director

Poultry USA serves individuals and firms engaged in the production, processing and marketing of broilers.

60 pages Monthly Founded: 1917
Circulation: 15,092
Printed in 4 colors on glossy stock

9096 **Practical Winery & Vineyard**
58-D Paul Drive
Suite D
San Rafael, CA 94903-1534
415-479-5819
FAX: 415-492-9325
editor@practicalwinery.com
http://www.practicalwinery.com

Don Neel, Publisher
Tina L Vierra, Associate Publisher

Journal of grape grown and wine production in North America. *$33.86*

6 issues per ye Founded: 1985
Circulation: 7,500

9097 **Prairie Farmer**
1100 N Broadway Street
Carlinville, IL 62626
217-854-2547
FAX: 217-854-6426
icebox@prairiefarms.com
www.prairiefarms.com

Tom Budd, Publisher
Mike Wilson, Editor
Roger Capps, Chief Executive Officer

Agricultural news.

9098 **Prepared Foods**
Business News Publishing
2401 W Big Weaver Road
Suite 700
Troy, MI 48084
248-893-3500
FAX: 630-227-0527
robertsw@bnp.com
http://www.bnpmedia.com/

William Roberts, Editor-in-Chief
Kathy Travis, Art Director

About 600 food and beverage companies. *$95.00*

109 pages Founded: 1926
Circulation: 70100
Printed in 4 colors on glossy stock

9099 **Private Label Buyer**
Stagnito Communications
155 Pfingsten Road
Suite 205
Deerfield, IL 60015
847-205-5660
FAX: 847-205-5680
info@stagnito.com
http://www.stagnito.com

Steven T Lichtenstein, Publisher
Jill Bruss, Editor

Serves the private label industry, including retailers, voluntaries, wholesalers, manufacturers and others allied to the field.

Monthly Founded: 1986
Circulation: 30021

9100 **Process Cooling & Equipment**
BNP Publications
1050 IL Route 83
Suite 200
Bensonville, IL 60106
630-616-0200
FAX: 630-694-4002
GlennD@bnpmedia.com
www.process-cooling.com

Linda Becker, Publisher
Doug Glenn, Publishing Director

Written for manufacturing engineers who use cooling equipment, components, materials and supplies. refrigerated engineers and technicians assoc

9101 Progressive Farmer
2100 Lakeshore Drive
Birmingham, AL 35209-6721
205-877-6333
FAX: 205-877-6860 800-357-4466
ProgressiveFarmer@timeinc.com
http://www.progressivefarmer.com
Ed Dickinsen, Publisher
Jack Odle, Editor
Farming news with regional focus on the midwest, midsouth and southwest. *$84.00*
106 pages Monthly
Circulation: 610000

9102 Progressive Grocer's Marketing Guidebook
Trade Dimensions
770 Broadway
New York, NY 10003
847-763-9050
FAX: 203-563-3131
info@progressivegrocer.com
http://www.progressivegrocer.com
Jenny McTaggart, Senior Editor
Olivia Wilson, Publisher
Over 800 retailer chains and wholesalers in the US and Canada. Also includes over 20,000 key executives. Plus, over 1,700 speciality distributors including C-Store and smaller food store wholesalers, food brokers, and candy, tobacco, and media distributors. *$380.00*
Founded: 1970

9103 QSR Magazine
4905 Pine Cone Drive
Suite 2
Durham, NC 27707
919-489-1916
FAX: 919-489-4767 800-638-0776
katherine@journalistic.com
http://www.qsrmagazine.com
Sherri Daye Scott, Editor
Eugene Drezner, Sales Manager
Monthly

9104 RCI Magazine
Retail Confectioners International
1807 Glenview Road
Suite 204
Glenview, IL 60025-2968
847-724-6120
FAX: 847-724-2719 800-545-5381
Evans Billington, Executive Director
Covers the retail confection industry.
Monthly Founded: 1917
Circulation: 800

9105 RF Design
131 E Main Street
Bellevue, OH 44811-1449
419- 48- 741
FAX: 419-483-3617
pmay@primediabusiness.com
http://www.rfdesign.com/
David Morrison, Editor
Pete May, President
Comprehensive source of rural agricultural news and information for farmers and the general public.
Monthly Founded: 2000

9106 Refrigerated & Frozen Foods
Stagnito Communications
155 Pfingsten Road
Suite 205
Deerfield, IL 60015
847-205-5660
FAX: 847-205-5680
info@stagnito.com
http://www.refrigeratedfrozenfood.com
Jeff Plaster, Publisher
Geneine Esquibel, Editor
Features on leading refrigerated and frozen food processors. Current and future trends in processing, packaging, new product development, food safety and logistics. Serves the dairy, meat, vegetable, fruit, bakery, deli, ingredient, snack, ethnic and other food industry related organizations. Free to qualified subscribers. *$65.00*
64 pages Monthly Founded: 1919
Circulation: 20500
Printed in 4 colors on glossy stock

9107 Restaurant Digest
Panagos Publishing
7913 Westpark Drive
Suite 305
McLean, VA 22102
703-917-6420
FAX: 703-917-6408
www.restaurantdigest.com
Bruce Panagos, Publisher
Developments and news of interest to owners, managers, and operators of dining and entertainment establishments in the region.
$ 24.00
Monthly
Circulation: 20,000

9108 Restaurant Hospitality
Penton Media
1300 E 9th Street
Cleveland, OH 44114-1503
216-696-7000
FAX: 216-696-0836
information@penton.com
http://www.foodservicesearch.com
Jess Grossberg, Publisher
Mike Sanson, Editor-in-Chief
A national trade publication that covers the full-service restaurant industry. It offers cover story features, an extensive food section with recipes, a multi-page news section and a variety of one page profiles on rising stars, equipment, food safety, beverages, design and more. *$70.00*
130 pages Monthly Founded: 1892
Circulation: 117,721
Mailing list available for rent $165 per M.
Printed in 4 colors on glossy stock

9109 Restaurant Marketing
Oxford Publishing
307 W Jackson Avenue
Oxford, MS 38655-9979
662-236-5510
FAX: 662-236-5541 800-247-3881
ed@oxpub.com
http://www.nightclub.com
Ed Meek, Publisher
Taylor Rau, Editor
Jennifer Parsons, Marketing Director
Amy Dierks, V.P. of Advertising
Michael Harrelson, Executive Editor
A trade magazine providing marketing information and promotional ideas for restaurant owners, hotel and casino operators and caterers. *$30.00*
Monthly Founded: 1985
Circulation: 30000

9110 Restaurant Wine
Wine Profits
PO Box 222
Napa, CA 94559-222
707-224-4777
FAX: 707-224-6740
restwine@tastetour.com
http://www.restaurantwine.com
Zelma Long, President
Ronn R Wiegand, Publisher
Sandy Flanders, Director of Marketing/Pub
Information on the marketing of wine in restaurants, hotels and clubs, wine and food pairing ideas and review of wines. *$99.00*
Circulation: 3000
Printed in 2 colors on matte stock

9111 Restaurants & Institutions
Reed Business Information
2000 Clearwater Drive
Oak Brook, IL 60523
630-740-0825
FAX: 630-288-8686 800-446-6551
subsmail@reedbusiness.com
http://www.rimag.com
Patricia B Dailey, Editor-in-Chief
Scott Hume, Managing Editor
Commercial and noncommercial food service establishments including restaurant, hotels, motels, fast-food chains, coffee shops and food stores with food service.
Monthly Founded: 1937
Circulation: 154110
Printed in 4 colors on glossy stock

9112 Restaurants USA
National Restaurant Association
1200 17th Street NW
Washington, DC 20036-3006
202-331-5900
FAX: 202-331-2429 800-424-5156
info@dineout.org www.restaurant.org
Jennifer Batty, Editor
Sarah Smith-Hamaker, Managing Editor
A trade magazine offering information for restaurant owners and managers, including industry trends, operational pointers, management principles and association activities. *$125.00*
48 pages Monthly Founded: 1980
Circulation: 44,000
Printed in 4 colors

9113 Restaurants and Institutions Marketplace Magazine
2000 Clearwater Drive
Oak Brook, IL 60523
FAX: 630-288-8225

9114 Rice Farming
Vance Publishing
5050 Poplar Avenue
Suite 200
Memphis, TN 38157-2099
901-767-4020
FAX: 901-767-4026 800-888-9784
vlboyd@worldnet.att.net
http://www.ricefarming.com
John Sowell, Publisher
Marci Deshores, Editor
Barbara Johnson, Manager
Profitable production strategies for commercial rice growers.
Monthly Founded: 1937
Circulation: 9000
Printed in 4 colors on glossy stock

9115 Rice Journal
Specialized Agricultural Publications
3000 Highwoods Boulevard
Suite 300
Raleigh, NC 27604-1029
919-878-0540
FAX: 919-876-6531
publisher@ricejournal.com
www.ricejournal.com

Dayton H Matlick, President
Mary Evans, Publisher

Offers rice growers profitable methods of producing, marketing and promoting rice, plus key related issues. *$15.00*

24 pages Monthly January-July Founded: 1897
Circulation: 11,600 $80 per M.
Printed in 4 colors on glossy stock

9116 Ristorante!
Maiden Name Press
804 Harrison Street Suite E2
PO Box 2249
Oak Park, IL 60303
708-483-3200
FAX: 708-445-9477 800-407-5845
brussell@maidennamepress.com
http://www.ristorantemag.com

Kathleen Furore, Editor
Brenda Russell, Publisher

A magazine featuring industry specific food news, features, restaurant profiles and new product information for personnel of restaurants serving Italian menu items nationwide. *$15.00*

Quarterly Founded: 2003
Circulation: 24200
Printed in 4 colors on glossy stock

9117 Rural Heritage
Allan Damerow
281 Dean Ridge Lane
Gainesboro, TN 38562-5039
931-268-0655
FAX: 931-268-5884
RuralHeritge@InfoAve.Net
http://www.ruralheritage.com

Gail Damerow, Editor
Allan Damerow, Publisher

Publication for people who farm and log with horses and other draft animals. *$28.00*

100 pages Founded: 1976
Printed in 4 colors on glossy stock

9118 Rural Living
Michigan Farm Bureau
7373 W Saginaw Highway
PO Box 30960
Lansing, MI 48909-8460
517-237-7000
FAX: 517-323-6793 800-292-2680

Dennis Rudat, Editor
Sue Snyder, Editor

Editorial emphasis on consumer food news, travel information and issue analysis.

24 pages Quarterly

9119 School Foodservice & Nutrition
School Nutrition Association
700 S Washington Street
Suite 300
Alexandria, VA 22314
703-739-3900
FAX: 703-739-3915 800-877-8822
sfn@asfsa.org
www.schoolnutrition.org

Patricia Fitzgerald, Editor
Martin Tubridy, Advertising Director

This is the official publication of the School Nutrition Association which contains the latest information on a host of items that affect the successful operation of a school foodservice program. *$75.00*

Fee/Non-Members
Circulation: 57,000 55,000 names

9120 Seafood Business
Diversified Business Communications
121 Free Street
PO Box 7437
Portland, ME 04112-7437
207-842-5500
FAX: 207-842-5503
bspringer@divcom.com
http://www.seafoodbusiness.com

Fiona Robinson, Editor
Bill Springer, Publisher
Nancy Hasselback, CEO
Linda Skinner, Managing Editor

Current, comprehensive news on the rapidly expanding seafood industry.

Monthly Founded: 1949
Circulation: 15,000

9121 Seed Industry Journal
Freiberg Publishing Company
PO Box 7
Cedar Falls, IA 50613-0007
319-530-0642
FAX: 319-277-3783 800-959-3276

Bill Freiberg, Publisher
Carol Cutler, Editor

International seed industry news.

9122 Seed Technologist Training Manual
Society of Commercial Seed Technologists

101 E State Street
Suite 214
Ithaca, NY 14850
607-256-3313
FAX: 607-256-3313
scst@twcny.rr.com
www.seedtechnology.net

Anita Hall, Executive Director
Dr Wayne Guerke, Editor

This manual represents the most comprehensive treatment of seed testing technology anywhere. *$175.00*

450 pages Bi-Annually Founded: 1922
Circulation: 500

9123 Seed Technology Journal
Society of Commerical Seed Technologists

101 E State Street
Suite 214
Ithaca, NY 14850
607-256-3313
FAX: 607-256-3313
scst@twcny.rr.com
www.seedtechnology.net

Anita Hall, Executive Director
Dr Wayne Guerke, Editor

Published jointly with the Association of Official Seed Analysts. an international journal containing scientific and technological papers in all areas of seed science and technology. The emphasis is on applied and basic research in seed physiology, pathology and biology that may relate to seed development, maturation, germination, dormancy and deterioration. *$125.00*

Members Cost: $75.00 Founded: 1922

9124 Seed World
Scranton Gillette Communications
380 E Northwest Highway
Suite 200
Des Plaines, IL 60016-2282
847-986-6622
FAX: 847-390-0408
egillette@sgcmail.com
http://www.seedworld.com/

Angela Dansby, Editor
Jim Sivicek, Sales Representative

Seed marketers. *$30.00*

48 pages Monthly Founded: 1915
Circulation: 5000

9125 Seed and Crops Industry
Freiberg Publishing Company
2302 W 1st Street
Cedar Falls, IA 50613-1879
319-530-0642
FAX: 319-277-3783 800-959-3276

Bill Freiberg, Publisher

Offers information for farmers related to crop protection.

Monthly

9126 Sheep!
Duck Creek Publications
PO Box 10
Lake Mills, WI 53551-0010
920-648-8285
FAX: 920-648-3770
www.sheepmagazine.com

Dave Thompson, Publisher/Editor
Doris Thompson, Publisher

For individuals interested in sheep, wool and woolcrafts. *$20.00*

Circulation: 12,090

9127 Shorthorn Country
Durham Management Company
8288 Hascall Street
Omaha, NE 68124-3234
402-393-7051
FAX: 402-393-7080
durham@shorthorn.com
www.beefshorthornusa.com

Deb Hostert, Editor
Pat Cloutier, Production Manager

Magazine published for cattle producers who breed and sell registered Shorthorn and Polled Shorthorn cattle. *$24.00*

11 per year
Circulation: 3,000

9128 Simply Seafood
1553 NW Ballard Way
Seattle, WA 98107-4633
360-706-4022
FAX: 206-789-0504 877-706-4022

Peter Redmayne, Editor

A publication offering information on seafood, chefs, wine, nutrition and recipes.

Quarterly
Circulation: 131,257

9129 Snack Food & Wholesale Bakery
Stagnito Communications
155 Pfingster Road
Suite 205
Deerfield, IL 60015
847-205-5660
FAX: 847-205-5680
info@stagnito.com
http://www.stagnito.com

Ron Bean, Publisher
Harry Stagnito, Publishing Director
Dan Malovany, Editor
Bernard Pacyniak, Editorial Director
Andy Hanacek, Managing Editor

Covers topics and products in the snack and wholesale bakery market *$85.00*

Monthly Founded: 1912
Circulation: 14,854
Printed in 4 colors on glossy stock

9130 Snack World
Snack Food Association
1233 Janesville Avenue
Fort Atkinson, WI 53538-2738
703-836-4500
FAX: 920-563-1702 800-547-7377

Gloria Cosby, Publisher
Tracey McMahon, Editor

The official international publication of the Snack Food Association covering trends in the snack food industry, including new products and services, industry news and supplier services.

10 per year
Circulation: 14,000

9131 Soil Science of America Journal
Soil Science Society of America
677 S Segoe Road
Madison, WI 53711-1048
608-273-8095
FAX: 608-273-2021
cczerwonka@agronomy.org
http://www.agronomy.org

Lloyd Hossner, Editor
Nick Rhamel, Managing Editor
Ellen Bergfeld, Executive VP

For those involved in research, teaching and extension activities in physics, chemistry, minrology, microbiology, soil fertility and plant nutrition. *$117.00*

Founded: 1936
Circulation: 8290

9132 Southeast Farm Press
14920 US Highway 61
Clarksdale, MS 38614
662-624-8503
FAX: 662-627-1977 866-505-7173
dparker@primediabusiness.com
http://www.southeastfarmpress.com

Grey Frey, Publisher
Paul Hollis, Editor

Offers farming news for the southeastern states.

Founded: 1989

9133 Southeastern Peanut Farmer
Southern Peanut Farmer's Federation
110 E 4th Street
Tifton, GA 31794
229-386-3470
FAX: 229-386-3501 800-346-4993
info@gapeanuts.com
http://www.gapeanuts.com/

Don Koehler, Executive Director
Joy Carter, Communications Specialist

Offers information to peanut farmers. *$25.00*

20 pages Monthly Founded: 1961
Circulation: 8400
Printed in 4 colors on glossy stock

9134 Southern Beverage Journal
14337 SW 119th Avenue
Miami, FL 33186-6006
305-233-7230
FAX: 305-252-2580
info@bevmedia.com
http://www.bevmedia.com

Wanda Rowe, Editor
William Slone, Publisher
Sharon Mijares, Manager

A magazine for the alcoholic beverage industry. *$35.00*

Monthly
Circulation: 10000

9135 Southwest Farm Press
Farm Press Publications
745 Fifth Avenue
New York, Ne 10151
212-745-0100
FAX: 212-745-0121 866-505-7173
information@primedia.com
http://www.primedia.com

Hembree Brandon, Editorial Director
Kevin Hudson, Sales Representative
Forrest Laws, Executive Editor
Ron Smith, Editor
Grey Frey, Publisher

Farming news. *$40.00*

Founded: 1974

9136 Soybean Digest
Primedia Business
7900 International Drive
Suite 300
Minneapolis, MN 55425
952-851-9329
FAX: 952-851-4601 800-722-5334
csd@primediabusiness.com
http://www.cornandsoybeandigest.com

Greg Lamp, Editor
Ron Sorensen, Publisher
Kelly Conlin Conlin, President/CEO

Leading publication in the soybean market. Offers in-depth coverage for wise management decisions dealing with production of soybeans, corn, wheat, sorghum and cotton. *$25.00*

Monthly Founded: 1940
Circulation: 147000

9137 Soybean South
6263 Poplar Avenue
Suite 540
Memphis, TN 38119-4736
901-385-0595
FAX: 901-767-4026

John Sowell, Publisher
Jeff Kehl, Circulation Director

Profitable prediction strategies for soybean farmers.

5 per year
Printed in 4 colors on glossy stock

9138 Specialty Food Magazine
National Association for the Specialty Food Trade
120 Wall Street
27th Floor
New York, NY 10005-4001
212-482-6440
FAX: 212-482-6459
www.fancyfoodshows.com

Cynthia Eisenmann, Product Listings/Media Services
Kathy Clark, Advertising Materials Coordinator

Provides comprehensive planning information for each Show and aggressive on-site bonus distribution, as well as the industry's most in-depth pre-Show, on-site, and post-Show coverage. *$30.00*

Monthly Founded: 1952
Circulation: 30100

9139 Speedy Bee
Fore's Honey Farms
PO Box 998
Jesup, GA 31598
912-427-4018
FAX: 912-427-8447
donna@abfnet.com

Troy Fore, Editor

Honey and beekeeping industry news. *$17.25*

16 pages Monthly Founded: 1972
Circulation: 4000
Printed in on newsprint stock

9140 Spudman Magazine
75 Applewood Drive
Sparta, MI 49435
616-887-9008
FAX: 616-887-2666
spud@iserv.net
http://www.spudman.com

Matt McCallum, Publisher
Greg Brown, Managing Editor
Erica Bernard, Circulation Manager

Information for potato farming and marketing.

9 issues per ye Founded: 1964
Circulation: 15500

9141 Stagnito Communications
155 Pfingsten Road
Suite 205
Deerfield, IL 60015-5354
847-205-5660
FAX: 847-205-5680
info@stagnito.com
http://www.stagnito.com

Harry Stagnito, President
Sue Ravenscraft, VP Circulation
Korry Stagnito, Publishing Director
Tom Vierhile, Executive Editor
Bill Mcilwaine, Senior Marketing Manager

Publisher of food, beverage and packaging information and magazines, including Dairy Field, National Provisioner, Snack Food & Wholesale Bakery, Beverage Industry, Candy Industry, Refrigerated & Frozen Foods, Confectioner and Industria Alimenticia, Private Label Buyer and Food and Drug Packaging. *$895.00*

9142 Standard & Poor's Industry Surveys
Standard & Poor's Corporation
55 Water Street
New York, NY 10041
212-382-2000

michaelzelkind@standardandpoors.com
http://www.standardandpoors.com

Terry McGraw, Chief Executive Officer

A two-volume book that examines the prospects for specific industries, including the beer and beverage industry. Also provides analyses of trends and problems, statistical tables and charts, and comparative company analyses. *$1475.00*

9143 Standards for the Design and Construction of Bakery Equipment

Baking Industry Sanitation Standards Committee
PO Box 3999
Manhattan, KS 66505-3999
785-537-4750
FAX: 785-565-6060 866-342-4772
bissc@bissc.org www.bissc.org

Jon Anderson, Executive Director/Secretary
Rosalie Wagner, Administrative Assistant

Provides the requirements of this standard apply to the design , construction , and cleaning of various items and groups of items of bakery equipment as specifically set forth herein. This standard applies equally to accessory equipment where applicable. *$15.00*

125 pages Quarterly Founded: 1949

9144 StateWays
Adams Business Media
17 High Street
2nd Floor
Norwalk, CT 06851
203-855-8499
FAX: 203-855-9446
mminor@aip.com
http://www.beveragenet.net
Marion Minor, President/CEO
Charles Forman, Publisher
Richard Brandes, Editor
Trade magazine addressing the subjects that are important to the Control State System of government owned liquor stores.

Circulation: 8500

9145 Successful Farming
Tom Davis
1716 Locust Street
Des Moines, IA 50309-3023
515-284-2818
FAX: 515-284-3563 800-678-2659
tom.davis@meredith.com
http://www.agriculture.com
Loren Kruse, Editor-in-Chief
Sandy Williams, Production Manager
William Kerr, CEO
Jon Backstrom, Editor
James Cornick, Publisher
US commercial farmers, ranchers and those employed in those operations or a directly related occupation. *$15.95*
Monthly Founded: 1902
Circulation: 442000
Mailing list available for rent 500M names $75 per M.
Printed in 4 colors on glossy stock

9146 Sugar: The Sugar Producer Magazine
Idaho Golf Harris Publishing
520 Park Avenue
Idaho Falls, ID 83402
208-523-1500
FAX: 208-522-5241 800-638-0135
customerservice@harrispublishing.com
http://www.sugarproducer.com
Jason Harris, Publisher
David FairBourn, Editor
Eula Endecott, Circulation Manager
Rob Erickson, Marketing Manager
Sugar beet industry information. *$15.95*
Monthly Founded: 1975
Circulation: 16000

9147 Sunbelt Food Service
Shelby Publishing Company
517 Green Street
Gainsville, GA 30501
770-534-8380
FAX: 770-535-0110
shelbyfs@bellsouth.net
http://www.shelbypublishing.com
Stormie Ellwanger, Foodservice Manager
Penny Smith, Account Manager
Sales and promotion of products and services sold through food service establishments across the sunbelt. *$36.00*
Monthly Founded: 1965
Circulation: 30090
Printed in on newsprint stock

9148 Sunflower Magazine
National Sunflower Association
4023 State Street
Bismarck, ND 58503
701-328-5100
FAX: 701-328-5101 888-718-7033
lkroh@sunflowernsa.com
http://www.sunflowernsa.com
Larry Kleingartner, Editor
Lerrene Kroh, Circulation Director
Magazine geared to sunflower products. *$9.00*
Monthly Founded: 1981
Circulation: 29,300 $150 per M.
Printed in 4 colors

9149 Sunflower and Grain Marketing Magazine
Sunflower World Publishers
3307 Northland Drive
Suite 130
Austin, TX 78731-4964
512-407-3434
FAX: 512-323-5118
Ed Randall Allen
Offers news and information on the sunflower and grain industries.

Circulation: 15,000

9150 Supermarket News: Center Store
Fairchild Publications
7 W 34th Street
New York, NY 10001
212-630-3880
FAX: 212-630-4201 800-204-4515
david.merrefield@fairchildpub.com
http://www.supermarketnews.com
David Merrefield, Editorial Director
Dan Bagan, Publisher *$195.00*
Weekly

9151 Supermarket News: Retail/Financial
Fairchild Publications
7 W 34th Street
New York, NY 10001
212-630-3880
FAX: 212-630-4201 800-204-4515
customerservice@fairchildpub.com
http://www.supermarketnews.com
David Merrefield, Editorial Director
David Orgel, Editor-in-Chief
Mark Hamstra, Editor
Dan Bagan, Publishing Director
Mary Berner, President and CEO
Monthly Founded: 1892
Circulation: 36346

9152 Supermarket News: Technology Solutions
Fairchild Publications
7 W 34th Street
New York, NY 10001
212-630-3880
FAX: 818-487-4550 800-424-8698
David Dreyer, Publisher
David Merrefield, Editorial Director
Christina Veiders, Managing Editor
David Orgel, Editor-In-Chief
Dan Bagan, Publishing Director *$45.00*
Founded: 1892

9153 Swine Practitioner
Vance Publishing
10901 W 84th Terrace
3 Pine Ridge Plaza
Lenexa, KS 66214-1649
913-438-8700
FAX: 913-438-0695 800-255-5113
cbecker@vancepublishing.com
http://www.vancepublishing.com
Jim Carlton, Editor
Cliff Becker, Group Publisher
William C Vance, Chairman
Offers technical information, primarily on swine health and related production areas, to veterinarians and related industry professionals.
Monthly Founded: 1937
Circulation: 2540
Mailing list available for rent

9154 Tea & Coffee Trade Journal
Lockwood Publications
26 Broadway
Floor 9M
New York, NY 10004
212-697-7053
FAX: 212-827-0945 845-267-3489
info@teaandcoffee.net
http://www.teaandcoffee.net
Jane McCabe, Editor/Co-Publisher
Premiere magazine for tea and coffee industry. *$49.00*
Monthly Founded: 1901
Circulation: 12
Printed in 4 colors on glossy stock

9155 Today's Farmer
MFA
201 Ray Young Dr
Columbia, MO 65201
573-874-5111
FAX: 573-876-5430 800-359-7893
todaysfarmer@mfa-inc.com
http://www.mfa-inc.com
Chuck Lay, Editor
Don Copenhaver, President
Bruce Hanson, VP Distribution
Management and marketing news. *$12.00*

9156 Today's Grocers
Florida Grocer Publications
PO Box 430760
S Miami, FL 33246
305-661-0792
FAX: 305-661-6720 800-440-3067
Jack Nobles, Publisher
Dennis Kane, Editor
Provides the latest food industry news and trends to Florida, Georgia, Alabama, Louisiana, Mississippi and the Carolinas. *$29.00*

24 pages Monthly Founded: 1956
Circulation: 19,000
Printed in on newsprint stock

9157 Tomato Country
Columbia Publishing
417 N 20th Avenue
Yakima, WA 98902-7008
509-248-2452
FAX: 509-248-4056 800-900-2452
chris@freshcut.com
http://www.freshcut.com
Matt McCallum, Publisher
Kimberly Warren, Managing Editor
Includes information on tomato production and marketing, grower and shipper feature stories, tomato research, from herbicide and pesticide studies to new varieties, market reports, feedback from major tomato meet-

ings and conventions, along with other key issues and points of interest for US and Canada tomato growers. *$25.00*
Monthly Founded: 1993

9158 Trading Rules
National Oilseed Processors Association
1300 L Streeet NW
Suite 1020
Washington, DC 20005-4168
202-420-0400
FAX: 202-842-9126
nopa@nopa.org http://www.nopa.org
Thomas Hammer, President
David J Hovermale, Executive VP
Karri L Moore, Project Manager
Julia Kinnaird, Manager *$50.00*
Founded: 1929

9159 Transactions of the American Fisheries Society
American Fisheries Society
5410 Grosvenor Lane
Bethesda, MD 20814-2199
301-897-8616
FAX: 301-897-8096
main@fisheries.org
www.fisheries.org
Richard J Beamish, Editor
Dennis R DeVries, Editor
Fred M Utter, Editor
The Society's highly regarded international journal of fisheries science features results of basic and applied research in genetics, physiology, biology, ecology, population dynamics, economics, health, culture, and other topics germane to marine and freshwater finfish and shellfish and their respective fisheries and environments *$43.00*
Bi-Monthly Founded: 1872

9160 Tree Farmer Magazine
American Forest Foundation
1111 19th Street NW
Suite 800
Washington, DC 20036-3603
202-632-2700
FAX: 202-463-2785 800-878-8878
info@afandpa.ccm
http://www.afandpa.org
Lawrence Wiseman, President
Practical information on a number of tree farming-related topics, including sustainable forestry, private landowners, professional forests, wildlife, recreation, as well as water and soil conservation.
Founded: 1993
Circulation: 20000

9161 Tree Fruit
Western Agricultural Publishing Company
4969 E Clinton Way
#104
Fresno, CA 93727-1546
559-252-7000
FAX: 559-252-7387 888-382-9772
Paul Baltimore, Publisher
Jim Baltimore, Publisher
Randy Bailey, Editor
Robert Fujimoto, Assistant Editor
For tree fruit growers in California. *$19.95*
8 per year
Circulation: 7,470

9162 US Beer Market: Impact Databank Review and Forecast
M Shanken Communications
387 Park Avenue S
8th Floor
New York, NY 10016-8872
212-844-4224
FAX: 212-779-3366
impact@mshanken.com
http://www.winespectator.com
Marvin Shanken, CEO/President
$895.00
Annual+ Founded: 1972

9163 US Distribution Journal
BMT Commodity Corporation
530 5th Avenue
24th Floor
New York, NY 10036-5101
212-302-4200
FAX: 212-302-0007
info@BMTNY.com www.bmtny.com
Kevin Francecca, Editor
This periodical offers information for tobacco, candy, grocery, and convenience store distributors and wholesalers. *$48.00*
Founded: 1922

9164 Valley Potato Grower
Ola Highway 2 E
East Grand Forks, MN 56721
218-773-7783
FAX: 218-773-6227
communication@nppga.org
http://www.rrvpotatoes.org
Duane W Maatz, President
Ted Kreis, Marketing
Information on potato farming. *$17.95*
Monthly Founded: 1946

9165 Vegetable
US Department of Agriculture
PO Box 1258
Sacramento, CA 95812-1258
http://www.usda.gov
Historic information relating to various types of vegetable crops.

9166 Vegetable Growers News
Great American Publishing
75 Applewood Dr. Ste. A
PO Box 128
Sparta, MI 49345-1531
616-887-9008
FAX: 616-887-2666
http://www.vegetablegrowersnews.com
Kimberly Warren, Managing Editor
Matt McCallum, Executive Publisher
Erica Bernard, Circulation Manager
Market and marketing news. *$12.00*
Monthly Founded: 1970
Circulation: 14000

9167 Vegetables
Western Agricultural Publishing Company
4969 E Clinton Way
#104
Fresno, CA 93727-1549
559-252-7000
FAX: 559-252-7387 888-382-9772
Paul Baltimore, Publisher
Jim Baltimore, Publisher
Randy Bailey, Editor
Robert Fujimoto, Assistant Editor
The definitive source for information on all aspects of western vegetable production.
Monthly

9168 Vegetarian Journal
Vegetarian Resource Group
PO Box 1463
Baltimore, MD 21203
410-366-8343
FAX: 410-366-8804
vrg@vrg.org www.vrg.org
Michael Vogel, Senior Editor
Informative articles, recipes, book reviews, notices about vegetarian events, product evaluations, where to find vegetarian products and services. All nutrition information based on scientific studies. *$25.00*
36 pages Quarterly/Membership Founded: 1982
Circulation: 18000 Audited
Mailing list available for rent

9169 Vegetarian Times
Active Interest Media
300 N Continental Blvd
Ste 650
El Segundo, CA 90245
310-356-4100
FAX: 310-356-4110
editor@vegetariantimes.com
http://www.vegetariantimes.com
M Margaret Chappell, Editor-in-Chief
John Robles, Marketing Manager
$19.95
Monthly Founded: 1999

9170 Veggie Life Magazine
EGW
4075 Papazian Way
208
Fremont, CA 94538-4300
510-668-0269
FAX: 510-668-0280
info@egw.com www.veggielife.com
Chris Slaughter, Circulation Director
Shanna Masters, Editor
The modem voice on seasonal vegetarian cooking, optimum nutrition, and natural healing for today's health-conscious consumer features vaulable tips techniques, recipes, and remedies from dietcians, herbalists, doctors and other health experts on new ways to prpare creative plant-based cuisine, implement diet programs, and use natural remedies for an improved and vibrant lifestyle. *$19.96*
68 pages Quarterly Founded: 1980
Circulation: 80000

9171 Vending Times
Vending Times
1375 Broadway
6th Floor
New York, NY 10018
212-302-4700
FAX: 212-221-3311
subscriptions@vendingtimes.net
http://www.vendingtimes.com
Tim Sanford, Editor-in-Chief
Alicia Lavay-Kertes, President/Publisher
Jenny Dumerve, Director of Advertising
Tanya Street, Circulation Administrator
Vending Times serves the automatic merchandising and coffee service industries. This includes music and game operations, vending operations, mobile catering operations, consultants and associations. *$35.00*
Monthly Founded: 1961
Circulation: 17755

9172 Views of the Metropolitan Food Brokers
Association of Food Industries
PO Box 545
Matawan, NJ 07747-0545
732-583-8272
FAX: 732-583-0798
Monthly

9173 Vineyard and Winery Management
Vineyard & Winery Services
PO Box 231
Watkins Glen, NY 14891
607-535-7133
FAX: 607-535-2998 800-535-5670
Tom Loid, Executive Editor
Graham Parnell, Managing Editor
Bottom line resource for growers and vintners. Keeps readers tuned and primed for profit. *$37.00*
100 pages Bi-monthly Founded: 1975
Circulation: 4500
Printed in 4 colors on glossy stock

9174 WATT Poultry Magazine
122 S Wesley Avenue
WATT PoultryUSA
Mount Morris, IL 61054-1451
815-734-4171
FAX: 815-734-4201
watt@wattmm.com
http://www.wattnet.com/
James Watt, President
Charles Olentine, Publisher
Gary Thornton, Editor
Dedicated to supporting every phase of the turkey industry by providing information for decision-makers on breeding, production, management, processing and marketing. *$8.00*
Monthly
Circulation: 10500

9175 WD Hoard and Sons Company
28 Milwaukee Avenue W
Fort Atkinson, WI 53538
920-563-5551
FAX: 920-563-7298
hoards@hoards.com
http://www.hoards.com
W D Knox, Publisher
Gary L Vorpahl, Marketing Director
News aimed at the dairy farmer. *$16.00*
Monthly Founded: 1871
Circulation: 85,564
Printed in 4 colors on glossy stock

9176 Wallaces Farmer
Farm Progress Publishers
191 S Gary Avenue
Carol Stream, IL 60188-2095
630-690-5600
800-441-1410
rswoboda@farmprogress.com
http://www.farmprogress.com
Fran O'Leary, Publisher
Teresa Hebda, Circulation Manager
Rod Swoboda, Editor
Farm management and agricultural news serving midwest farmers. *$23.95*
1 Year 13 Issue Founded: 1859

9177 Washington Wire
National Food Processors Association
13501 Street NW
Suite 300
Washington, DC 20005-2102
202-639-5900
FAX: 202-639-5932
http://www.nfpa-food.org
Monthly

9178 Western Dairy Business
DairyBusiness Communications
6437 Collamer Road
East Syracuse, NY 13057-1031
315-703-7979
FAX: 315-703-7988 866-520-2880
circ@dairybusiness.com
http://www.dairybusiness.com
Ron Goble, Associate Publisher
Cecilia Parsons, Associate Editor
Scott A Smith, CEO
Business resource for successful milk producers. Covers 13 Western states. Provides information and news that is helpful in the daily operations of dairymen. *$38.95*
67 pages Monthly Founded: 1904
Circulation: 14000
Printed in 4 colors on glossy stock

9179 Western Farm Press
Primedia
2104 Harvell Circle
Bellevue, NE 68005
913-341-1300
FAX: 913-967-1898 866-505-7173
wfcs@pbsub.com
http://www.westernfarmpress.com
Robert Fraser, Managing Editor
Harry Cline, Editor
Greg Frey, Publisher
Darrah Parker, Marketing Director
Founded: 1989
Circulation: 16,000

9180 Western Fruit Grower
Meister Media Worldwide
37733 Euclid Avenue
Willoughby, OH 44094-5925
440-942-2000
FAX: 440-942-0662 800-572-7740
afg.edit@meistermedia.com
http://www.americanfruitgrower.com
Brian Sparks, Production Manager
Gary Fitzgerald, President
Brian Sparks, Editor
Terry Doak, Circulation Manager
Edited for commercial growers of deciduous crops and citrus fruit, nut grape crops in the Western US. *$20.00*
66 pages Monthly
Circulation: 36,000

9181 Western Grocery News
80 Willow Road
Menlo Park, CA 94025-3661
650-321-3600
FAX: 650-327-7537 800-227-7346
Bi-Monthly
Circulation: 9,187

9182 Western Growers & Shippers
Western Growers Association
PO Box 2130
Newport Beach, CA 92658-8944
949-863-1000
FAX: 949-863-9028
tnassif@wga.com http://www.wga.com
Tom Nassif, President
Tim Linden, Editor
Listing over 3,000 growers, shippers, packers, brokers and distributors of fruits and vegetables in California and Arizona.
32 pages Monthly Founded: 1926
Circulation: 5000
Printed in 4 colors on glossy stock

9183 Western Livestock Journal
650 S Lipan Street
Denver, CO 80223-2307
303-722-7600
FAX: 303-722-0155
pete@wlj.net http://www.wlj.net
Pete Crow, Publisher
Michele Michele McRae, Circulation Manager
Valuable information for cattle breeders and farmers. *$35.00*
Weekly Founded: 1922
Circulation: 17378

9184 Wheat Grower
415 2nd Street NE
Suite 300
Washington, DC 20002-4900
202-547-7800
FAX: 202-546-2638
www.wheatworld.org
Darren Coppock, CEO
June Silverberg, Director Corporate Relations
Offers valuable information aimed at the farmer of wheat.

9185 Who's Who
WATT Publishing Company
122 S Wesley Avenue
Mount Morris, IL 61054-1497
815-734-4171
FAX: 815-734-4201
olentine@wattmm.com
www.wattnet.com
James Watt, Owner

9186 Who's Who International
WATT Publishing Company
122 S Wesley Avenue
Mount Morris, IL 61054-1497
815-734-4171
FAX: 815-734-4201
olentine@wattmm.com
www.wattnet.com
James Watt, Owner
Founded: 1917

9187 Whole Foods Magazine
WFC
4041 G Hadley Road
#101
South Plainfield, NJ 07080
908-769-1160
FAX: 908-769-1171
info@wfcinc.com
http://www.wfcinc.com/
Heather Wainer, Publisher
Alan Richman, Editor
Howard Wainer, President
Sandra Wainer, Circulation
Jaclyn Hirschorn, Assistant Editor
Serves the natural/health products industry. *$70.00*
Monthly Founded: 1979
Circulation: 16332 16,000 names $125 per M.
Printed in on glossy stock

9188 Wine Advocate
Robert M Parker Jr
PO Box 311
Monkton, MD 21111
410-329-6477
FAX: 410-357-4504
wineadvocate@erobertparker.com
http://www.erobertparker.com
Robert M Parker Jr, Editor/CEO
Daniel Thomases, Partner

An independent magazine covering reviews of wine. *$60.00*
64 pages Bi-monthly Founded: 1978
Circulation: 40000

9189 **Wine Enthusiast**
103 Fairview Park Drive
Elmsford, NY 10523
914-345-9463
FAX: 914-345-3129 800-356-8466
cutserv@wineenthusiast.com
http://www.wineenthusiast.com
Tim Moriarty, Managing Editor
Sybil Strum, President/CEO *$26.95*
Founded: 1979
Circulation: 500,000

9190 **Wine World**
Wine World Publishing
6433 Topanga Canyon Boulevard
#412
Canoga Park, CA 91303-2621

Dee Snidt, Editor
For the wine consumer and industry. *$16.00*
48 pages Monthly Founded: 1971

9191 **Wines & Vines**
1800 Lincoln Avenue
San Rafael, CA 94901-1298
415-453-9700
FAX: 415-453-2517
geninfo@winesandvines.com
http://www.winesandvines.com
David F Bayard, Advertising Representative
Chet Klingensmith, Publisher
Tina Caputo, Editor
Voice of the grape and wine industry. *$32.50*
Monthly Founded: 1919
Circulation: 3200 1900 names $425 per M.
Printed in 4 colors on matte stock

9192 **Yankee Food Service**
201 Oak Street
Suite A
Pembroke, MA 02359
781-829-4700
FAX: 781-829-0134 866-677-4700
Stephen M Griffin, President
Jack Walsh, Marketing Director
Reports news and happenings of the food service industry in New England. *$47.00*
48 pages Monthly Founded: 1970
Circulation: 22,111

Trade Shows

9193 **A Year of Enchantment**
Int'l Council on Hotel, Restaurant Institute Edu.
1200 17th Street NW
Washington, DC 20036-3006
202-467-6300

alliance@digex.net www.chrie.org
Susan Gould, Manager
Containing over 70 booths and over 50 exhibits.
750 Attendees August Founded: 1946

9194 **AACC Annual Meeting**
American Association of Cereal Chemists

3340 Pilot Knob Road
Saint Paul, MN 55121-2055
651-454-7250
FAX: 651-454-0766
bford@scisoc.org www.aaccnet.org
Betty Ford, Meetings Director
Sue Casey, Meetings Coordinator
This event brings together experts from around the world to discuss evolving products, ingredients, advancing technologies, scientific and technological progress, and the future of the grain-based foods and beverages industries. A showcase products and services to professionals in the cereal/foods science.
2M Attendees Sept/Oct

9195 **AACT Technical Conference**
American Association of Candy Technologists
175 Rock Road
Glen Rock, NJ 07452
201-652-2655
FAX: 201-652-3419
aactinfo@gomc.com
www.aactcandy.org
Bob Huzinec, President
Bill Dyer, First VP
An audience of technologists in the sweet goods industry. These talks range from basics to innovations, providing the industry with practical information to help in understanding processes and ingredients used by their companies.
300 Attendees September/2006

9196 **AAEA Annual Meeting**
American Agricultural Economics Association
1110 Buckeye Avenue
Ames, IA 50010-8063
515-233-9087
FAX: 575-233-3101
nknight@iastate.edu
Nancy Knight, Manager Meetings
Annual meeting and trade show of 25 exhibitors.
1700 Attendees

9197 **ABI/ADPI Joint Annual Meeting**
American Butter Institute
2101 Wilson Boulevard
Suite 400
Arlington, VA 22201
703-243-5630
FAX: 703-841-9328
AMiner@nmpf.org
www.butterinstitute.org
Jerome J Kozak, Executive Director
Chris Galen, Communications VP
This event is co-sponsored by The American Dairy Products Institute for manufacturers, marketers and suppliers of manufactured dairy products.
600+ Attendees April

9198 **ACS Annual Conference and Competition**
American Cheese Society
304 W Liberty Street
Suite 201
Louisville, KY 40202
502-583-3783
FAX: 502-589-3602
mwilson@hqtrs.com
www.cheesesociety.org
Marci Wilson, Executive Director
Carlos Scrivener, Manager
This Conference and Competition offers a unique opportunity to learn the latest about cheese in America and indulge your cheese fantasies by tasting more than 700 American artisan and specialty cheeses. *$90.00*
Associate Fee

9199 **AEA National Convention**
American Emu Association
PO Box 2502
San Angelo, TX 76902
541-332-0675

info@aea-emu.org www.aea-emu.org
Charles Ramey, President
Martha Hendricks, VP
This convention provides a chance for the AEA Board of Directors (AEA-BOD) to meet, face to face, during the week prior to the actual convention. It is a place for members to gather to learn the latest information and research about the emu industry, see the latest new products and network with other emu growers from across the U.S. and around the world. *$175.00*
July/Non-Member $230

9200 **AFS Annual Meeting**
American Fisheries Society
5410 Grosvenor Lane
Bethesda, MD 20814
301-897-8616
FAX: 301-897-8096
thechair@afslakeplacid.org
www.fisheries.org
Ed Woltmann, Conference Chair
Doug Stang, Conference Program Chair
Gus Rassam, Executive Director
Held in conjunction with American Institute of Fishery Research Biologists. Explore the interrelation between fish, aquatic habitats and man; highlight challenges facing aquatic resource professionals and the methods that have been employed to resolve conflicts between those that use or have an interest in our aquatic resources. *$295.00*
Annual/September

9201 **AMI International Meat, Poultry & Seafood Convention and Exposition**
Convention Mangement Group
10472 Armstrong Street
Fairfax, VA 22031
703-934-4700
FAX: 703-934-4899
exhibitsales@worldwidefood.com
www.worldwidefood.com
Anne Halal, Convention/Member Services VP
Anne Nuttall, Convention/Members Director
Katie Brannan, Convention/Members Sr. Manager
Sponsored by the American Meat Institute it features exhibits featuring the latest innovations in processing and packaging equipment, business and processing software systems, supplies, services and formulations.
25000 Attendees October/2007

9202 **APA Annual Meeting**
Apple Processors Association
1100 17th Street NW
10th Floor
Washington, DC 20036
202-856-6715
FAX: 202-331-4212
aball@agriwashington.org
www.appleprocessors.org

Andrea Ball, Meetings Director
Niaz Mian, Manager

Industry and consumer experts together for a dialogue on timely issues. These include marketing tips, packaging trends, consumer research, and media reports and reaction to industry initiatives. APA members also share industry ideas and experiences. *$795.00*

June/Non-Member Fee Founded: 1987

9203 APS/CPS/MSA Annual Joint Meeting
American Phytopathological Society
3340 Pilot Knob Road
Saint Paul, MN 55121-2097
651-454-7250
FAX: 651-454-0766 800-328-7560
scasey@scisoc.org
www.meeting.apsnet.org

Jan Leach, President
Sue Casey, Meetings Coordinator
Steven Nelson, VP

A joint meeting between the American Phytopathological Society, Canadian Phytopathological Society and the Mycological Society of America. Featuring; over 18 state-of-the-art education sessions daily, over 700 poster presentations, one-of-a-kind preconvention tours and workshops and exhibits from leading suppliers.

July/August

9204 ASA/CSSA/SSSA International Annual Meeting
American Society of Agronomy
677 S Segoe Road
Madison, WI 53711
608-273-8080
FAX: 608-273-2021 www.agronomy.org

Keith R Schlesinger, Meetings/Convention Director
Stacey Phelps, Exhibit/Meetings Assistant
Linda Nelson, Meetings Specialist
Ellen Bergfeld, Executive Vice President

Co-sponsored with Crop Science Society of America and with the Soil Science Society of America. This event is a unique convergence of the leading agronomy, crops, soils and environmental sciences professionals from around the world. A blend of technical sessions, poster sessions, social functions, career networking and exhibits draw a growing number of prominent professionals and students.

3,500 Attendees November Founded: 1907

9205 ASABE Annual International Meeting
American Society of Agricultural & Biological Eng.
950 S Cherry Street
Suite 508
Denver, CO 80246-2664
303-759-5091
FAX: 303-758-0190
chesser@asabe.org www.asabe.org

Michael Chesser, Meetings/Conference Director
Sharon McKnight, Meetings Support Staff

100 and more diverse technical sessions, 11 continuing professional development sessions, 5 technical tours, an industry exhibit hall and a keynote address from Dr. Lowell B. Catlett; this year's meeting is full of must attend events.

July

9206 ASAS Annual Meeting
American Society of Animal Science
1111 N Dunlap Avenue
Savoy, IL 61874
217-356-9050
FAX: 217-398-4119
paulas@assochq@org www.asas.org

Paula Schultz, Meetings Coordinator
Lorena Nicholas, General Meeting Information
Kim Surles, Exhibits/Advertising
Jerry Baker, Executive Director

This meeting serves as an international forum to gather vital information for the future of the animal agriculture industry. A cutting-edge scientific program in food science, animal health, dairy production, beef nutrition, swine nutrition, reproduction, companion animals, and many other diverse interests. *$625.00*

3500 Attendees July/Non-Members Fee Founded: 1908

9207 ASBC Annual Meeting
American Society of Brewing Chemists
3340 Pilot Knob Road
Saint Paul, MN 55121-2055
651-454-7250
FAX: 651-454-0766 800-328-7560
bford@scisoc.org
www.meeting.asbcnet.org

Betty Ford, Meetings Director
Sue Casey, Meetings Coordinator
Steven Nelson, VP

An opportunity to network, learn, build business relationships and hear first-hand the latest brewing science and related research. Contains exhibits, technical and keynote presentations and workshops. *$625.00*

300 Attendees June/Non-Members Fee Founded: 1934

9208 ASHS Annual Conference
American Society for Horticultural Science
113 S West Street
Suite 200
Alexandria, VA 22314-2851
703-836-4606
FAX: 703-836-2024
meetings@ashs.org. www.ashs.org

Michael W Neff, Executive Director
Tracy Shawn, Assistant Executive Director

A place to meet with colleagues, talk with exhibitors and view over 400 posters. *$375.00*

1,200 Attendees July/Members Rate

9209 ASME Business Forum & Expo
Associaton of Sales and Marketing Companies
2100 Reston Parkway
Suite 400
Reston, VA 20191
703-758-7790
FAX: 703-758-7787
info@asmc.org www.asmc.org

Julie Casson, Sales Manager

Seminar and 75 exhibits of food manufacturers, computer equipment and services, food product services, foreign trade, incentive displays, shelf space management and related information.

7000 Attendees Annual Founded: 1985

9210 ASTA/CSTA Joint Annual Convention
American Seed Trade Association
225 Reinekers Lane
Suite 650
Alexandria, VA 22314-2875
703-837-8140
FAX: 703-837-9365 www.amseed.com

Jennifer Lord, Meetings Director
Jason Laney, Meetings Associate Director

Includes meetings of all divisions of ASTA and CSTA and several joint meetings of both organizations, exhibits, prominent keynote speakers relevant to both associations, sessions that include representatives discussing how seed moves through the pipelines of our industry to the end user and those whose roles affect the regulation and administration of the framework.

800 Attendees July/Fee $129-$799

9211 AWMA Real Deal Expo
American Wholesale Marketers Association
1128 16th Street NW
Washington, DC 20036
202-449-6418
FAX: 202-467-0559 800-482-2962
awmaregistration@jspargo.com
www.realdealexpo.com

Marcia Barker, Public Affairs Manager
Nate Wills, Exhibit Information

The only trade show geared to convenience distributors. Exhibitors include purveyors of tobacco products, candy, beverages, snacks, foodservice, health and beauty care items, general merchandise, warehouse equipment, computer systems and much more.

2,500 Attendees February

9212 AWS Annual National Conference
American Wine Society
PO Box 3330
Durham, NC 27702
919-403-2002
FAX: 919-403-0392
dautlick@americanwinesociety.org
www.americanwinesociety.com

Tania Dautlick, Executive Director

The annual conference brings professional, serious amateurs and novices together to discover what is new in wine. Seminars and lectures on all aspects of wine appreciation, wine production, grape growing and cuisine. Attendees must be a member of the society. *$385.00*

November/Members Only Founded: 1976
3000 names

9213 Ag Progress Days
Penn State University Agricultural Sciences
420 Agricultural Administration Building
University Park, PA 16802
814-865-2081
FAX: 814-865-1677
agprogressdays@psu.edu
www.apd.cas.psu.edu

Bob Oberheim, Manager

Agricultural trade show focusing on the innovations and progress made in the agricultural industry.

50M Attendees August 15-17, 2006
Founded: 1976

9214 Agri News Farm Show
Agri News
18 1st Avenue SE
Rochester, MN 55904-3722
507-857-7707
FAX: 507-281-7474 800-633-1727
rallen@agrinews.com
www.agrinews.com
Rosie Allen, Show Manager
John Losness, Publisher
Annual show of 160 exhibitors of farming equipment, supplies and services.
8000 Attendees March

9215 Agricultural Communicators in Education Summer Meeting
PO Box 35
Evinston, FL 32633-0035
352-392-1582
Agricultural communications.
400 Attendees Summer

9216 Agricultural Horticulture Congress and Show Northwest
4672 Drift Creek Road SE
Sublimity, OR 97385-9764
503-769-7120
FAX: 503-769-3549
James Heater, Manager
Features educational meetings, seminars and exhibits of agricultural equipment.
26M Attendees January

9217 Agricultural Retailers Association Convention and Expo
Agricultural Retailers Association
11701 Borman Drive
Suite 110
Saint Louis, MO 63146-4193
314-676-6655
FAX: 314-567-6888 800-844-4900
Annual show of 120 manufacturers, suppliers and distributors of agricultural chemicals and fertilizers.
1200 Attendees December, St. Louis

9218 Agro-International Trade Fair for Agricultural Machinery & Equipment
Glahe International
PO Box 2460
Germantown, MD 20875-2460
301-515-0012
FAX: 301-515-0016 glahe@glahe.com
Biennial show of agricultural machinery and equipment.

9219 All Candy Expo
National Confectioners Association
8320 Old Courthouse Road
Suite 300
Vienna, VA 22182
703-790-5750
FAX: 703-790-5752
AllCandyExpo@CandyUSA.com
allcandyexpo.com
Theresa Delaney, Expo/Membership Director
Daria Moore, Exhibits Manager
A trade show offering exhibits of confectionery industry supplies.
5000+ Attendees June

9220 All Things Organic Conference and Trade Show
Organic Trade Association
60 Wells Street
PO Box 547
Greenfield, MA 01301
413-774-7511
FAX: 413-774-6432
info@ota.com www.ota.com
David Gagnon, Conference/Special Projects Coord.
May 1-4, 2004 in Chicago, Illinois. More than 300 booths.
1000+ Attendees May

9221 America's Supermarket Showcase
National Grocer's Association
1825 Samuel Morse Drive
Reston, VA 20190
703-437-5300
FAX: 703-437-7768 neasc@alo.com
Dan Rudt
350 exhibits of food and non food consumer goods and services, fixtures and equipment for supermarket operations. Workshop, conference, banquet, luncheon and tours.
5000 Attendees Annual Founded: 1983

9222 American Agri-Women
1005 Highway 92
Keota, IA 52248-9110
641-636-2293
Sandy Greiner, President
Tradeshow consisting of products of interest to women in agriculture.
350 Attendees November

9223 American Bakery Expo
eShow2000
5 Executive Court
Suite 2
South Barrington, IL 60010
610-667-9600
FAX: 610-667-1475
info@americanbakeryexpo.com
www.americanbakeryexpo.com
Mark Gedris, Membership Manager
Sponsored by Retail Bakers of America and New York/New Jersey Bakers Association. A trade show, creative decorating competition, bakery arts and cakes display, industry chats, tips and trends demonstrations and seminars. *$60.00*
8000 Attendees Oct 21-23/Fees Vary

9224 American Beverage Licensees Annual Convention & Trade Show
American Beverage Licensees
5101 River Road
Suite 108
Bethesda, MD 20816-1560
301-656-1494
FAX: 301-656-7539
nabr@nabronline.org
www.nabronline.org
Harry Wiles, Executive Director
Susan Day Pirieda, Office Manager
Annual show of 75 manufacturers, suppliers and distributors of alcoholic beverages.
700 Attendees March

9225 American Butter Institute Annual Conference
2101 Wilson Boulevard
Suite 400
Arlington, VA 22201
703-243-5630
FAX: 703-841-9328
AMiner@nmpf.org
www.butterinstitute.org
Jim Bleick, President
Chris Galen, VP Communications
Anuja Miner, Director of Membership Services
The annual conference and meeting is a joint project between the American Butter Institute and the American Diary Products Institute. Over 600 manufacturers, marketers and suppliers of butter and dairy products are represented at the convention which offers the opportunity to network with industry professionals.

9226 American Convention of Meat Processors
American Association of Meat Processors
One Meating Place
PO Box 269
Elizabethtown, PA 17022-0269
717-367-1168
888-888-8889
aamp@aamp.com www.aamp.com
Debbie Sinex, Convention Manager
Jane Frey, Exhibit Booth Contact
The convention consists of educational programs, a trade show, the American Cured Meat Championships, as well as numerous social invents to interact with other meat processors.
1200+ Attendees July

9227 American Correctional Food Service Association Conference
ACFSA
4248 Park Glen Road
Minneapolis, MN 55416-4758
952-928-4658
FAX: 952-929-1318
info@acfsa.org www.acfsa.org
Karen Wesloh, Executive Director
Hope Cook, Assistant Director Exhibits
Gloria Grove, Assistant Director Atendees
Annual exhibit of 200 exhibitors of food products, kitchen equipment, food processing equipment, dining facility equipment, tableware and related food service equipment.
450 Attendees August Founded: 1999 $200 per M.

9228 American Culinary Federation National Convention
10 San Bartola Drive
Saint Augustine, FL 32086
904-824-4468
FAX: 904-825-4758 800-624-9458
acf@acfchefs.net www.acfchefs.org
Debra Bulak, Show Manager
Michael Baskette, Executive Director
Two-hundred booths of products and foodstuffs for the food service industry. Seminars, workshops, cooking demos, more.
2000 Attendees July

9229 **American Dairy Products Institute Trade Show**
300 W Washginton Street
Suite 400
Chicago, IL 60606-1704
312-782-4888
FAX: 312-782-5299
adpi@flash.net
www.americandairyproducts.com

Jim Page

Fifty exhibits of equipment and supplies for condensed milk, dry and evaporated milk and whey products, plus conference, seminar, workshop and banquet.
675 Attendees April

9230 **American Farm Bureau Federation Annual Convention**
600 Maryland Avenue SW
Ste 1000
Washington, DC 20024
202-406-3600
FAX: 202-406-3602 www.fb.com

Bob Stallman, President

One hundred booths featuring exhibits of farm equipment, chemical fertilizers and agricultural equipment and supplies.
6M Attendees January

9231 **American Frozen Foods Institute Western Frozen Food Convention**
2000 Corporate Ridge
Suite 1000
McLean, VA 22102-7844
703-821-0770
FAX: 703-821-1350
info@affi.com
www.affi.com/www.healthyfood.org

Leslie G Sarasin, President/CEO
Robert L Garfield, Senior VP Public Policy

National trade association representing the interests of the frozen food industry for more than 60 years. Its 540 corporate members account for more than 90 percent of the frozen food production in the US.

9232 **American Frozen Foods Institute: Government Action Summit**
2000 Corporate Ridge
Suite 1000
McLean, VA 22102-7844
703-821-0770
FAX: 703-821-1350
info@affi.com
www.affi.com/www.healthyfood.org

Leslie G Sarasin, President/CEO
Robert L Garfield, Senior VP Public Policy

National trade association representing the interests of the frozen food industry for more than 60 years. Its 540 corporate members account for more than 90 percent of the frozen food production in the US.

9233 **American Meat Institute**
PO Box 3556
Washington, DC 20007-0056
202-874-4200
FAX: 703-527-0938

Dinah Sprouse, Show Manager
J Patrick Boyle, President

400 booths for equipment, supplies and services to the meat-packaging industry.
12M Attendees September

9234 **American Mushroom Institute**
North American Mushroom Conference
1 Massachusetts Avenue, Suite 800
Washington, DC 20001
202-842-4344
FAX: 202-408-7763

Laura Phelps, President

9235 **American Oil Chemists Society Annual Meeting & Exposition**
American Oil Chemists Society
2211 W Bradley Avenue
Champaign, IL 61821-1827
217-359-2344
FAX: 217-359-8091
general@aocs.org www.aocs.org

Jeffry Newman, Meetings Manager
Greg Reed, Manager

184 booths displaying fat and oil processing equipment, instrumentation and related services. Seminar, banquet, luncheon and dinner.
2000 Attendees

9236 **American Peanut Research and Education Society Annual Meeting**
American Peanut Research and Education Society
Oklahoma State University
376 Ag Hall
Stillwater, OK 74078
405-372-3052
FAX: 405-624-6718
nickeli@provalue.net
www.apres.okstate.edu

Ron Sholar, Executive Officer

Annual meetings of the Society are held for the presentation of papers and/or discussion, and for the transaction of business. At least one general business session will be held during regular annual meetings at which reports from the executive officer and all standing committees will be given to such other matters as the Board of Directors may determine.
300 Attendees July Founded: 1957

9237 **American Society for Enology and Vinticulture Annual Meeting**
American Society for Enology and Vinticulture
PO Box 1855
Davis, CA 95617
530-753-3142
FAX: 530-753-3318
society@asev.org www.asev.org

Lyndie Boulton, Executive Director

Two hundred and fifty exhibits of equipment, supplies and services to the wine and grape industries, as well as a seminar.
$30.00
2400 Attendees June Founded: 1951
Mailing list available for rent

9238 **American Society of Baking**
533 1st St E
Sonoma, CA 95476-6703
707-935-0103
FAX: 707-935-0174 866-920-9885

Tom Kuk, President

9239 **American Spice Trade Association Annual Meeting**
2025 M Street NW
Washington, DC 20036
202-367-1127
FAX: 202-367-2127 www.astaspice.org

Cheryl Deem, Manager

9240 **American Sugarbeet Growers Asscociation Annual Meeting**
American SugarBeet
1156 15th Street NW
Suite 101
Washington, DC 20005-1704
202-833-2398
FAX: 202-833-2962
RGeib@americansugarbeet.org
www.americansugarbeet.org

Ruthann Geib, Meetings Director/VP
Luther Markwart, Executive VP
James Creek, Executive Assistant
Pam Alther, Office/Financial Manager

Attendees are primarily the officers and board members of these local associations and their spouses, as well as representatives of seed, chemical, and other supplier companies. The purpose of the Annual Meeting is to bring members up-to-date on legislative and international issues that affect the domestic sugar industry, and to determine future policy and strategies.
350 Attendees July/November Founded: 1983

9241 **American Wine Society**
3006 Latta Road
Rochester, NY 14612-3298
585-225-7613
FAX: 585-225-7613
angel910@aol.com
americanwinesociety.com

Angel E Nardone, Executive Director

Twelve booths.
600 Attendees November Founded: 1967
3000 names

9242 **Animal Transportation Association**
PO Box 797095
Dallas, TX 75379-7095

FAX: 214-769-2867

Cherie Derouin, Administrator
Sherry Lynne Boone, Administrative Assistant

An international association promoting the humane handling and transportation of animals. 10-15 booths.
150 Attendees Spring

9243 **Annual Hotel, Motel and Restaurant Supply Show of the Southeast**
Leisure Time Unlimited
708 Main Street
PO Box 332
Myrtle Beach, SC 29577
843-448-9483
FAX: 843-626-1513 800-261-5991
hmrss@sc.rr.com www.hmrsss.com

Linda Cremer, Show Director

Trade show for the hospitality industry.
23000 Attendees January Founded: 1975

9244 **Annual Organic Products Tradshow and Conference**
Organic Trade Association
60 Wells Street
PO Box 547
Greenfield, MA 01301
413-774-7511
FAX: 413-774-6432
info@ota.com
www.theorganicreport.com
May

9245 **Asia Food Processing & Packaging Technology Exhibition**
Reed Exhibition Companies
383 Main Avenue
PO Box 6059
Norwalk, CT 06851
203-840-4800
FAX: 203-840-9628
One hundred and seventy four exhibitors for an audience of manufacturers, packaging design and development professionals.

Biennial

9246 **Associated Food Dealers Annual Trade Show**
Associated Food Dealers of Michigan
18470 W Ten Mile
Southfield, MI 48075
248-557-9600
FAX: 248-557-9610
gbennettafd@pop.net www.afdom.org

Ginny Bennett, Show Manager
September

9247 **Association for Dressing and Sauces Annual Meeting**
5775 Peachtree Dunwoody Road NE
Building G, Suite 500
Atlanta, GA 30342
404-252-3663
FAX: 404-252-0774
ads@kellencompany.com
www.dressings-sauces.org
Jacque Knight, Manager Membership/Administration
Open to members only. Sponsored for manufacturers of commercial dressings and sauces and the suppliers to that industry.
150 Attendees October Founded: 1926

9248 **Association of College Unions International Prof Conference**
120 W 7th Street
Suite 200
Bloomington, IN
812-855-8550
FAX: 812-855-0162
marcanne@indiana.edu
www.indiana.edu/nacui
Mary Ann Cannon, Member Services
Marsha Herman-Betzen, Executive Director
International conference with 100 exhibits of graphic supplies, recreation equipment, computer hardware & software, furnishings, entertainment and speaker bureau information, food service equipment, and more related information and supplies.
1000 Attendees Annual Founded: 1951

9249 **Atlantic Coast Exposition: Showcasing the Vending and Food Service Industry**
InfoMarketing
PO Box 3159
Durham, NC 27715-3159
919-383-0044
FAX: 919-383-0035 877-831-3824
info@atlanticcoastexpo.com
www.atlanticcoastexpo.com
Steven Hughes, Convention Director
This convention offers exhibits of vending machines, office coffee service products, commissary equipment, food and beverage products for the institututional market, as well as accountability systems and security devices.
3M Attendees May

9250 **Beer, Wine & Spirits Industry Trade Show**
Indiana Association of Beverage
200 S Meridian Street
Suite 350
Indianapolis, IN 46225
317-684-7580
FAX: 317-673-4210
Teresa Koch, Show Manager
Annual show of 125 exhibitors of alcohol beverage distillers brewers that are recognized primary sources in the state of Indiana as supplies for retailers.
2500 Attendees

9251 **Beltwide Cotton Conference**
National Cotton Council of America
PO Box 820285
Memphis, TN 38182-0285
901-274-9030
FAX: 901-725-0510
info@natbat.com www.natbat.com
Fred W Middleton, Executive Secretary
Tony Wolf, President
Alan Posner, VP
Offers a forum for agricultural professionals.

9252 **Big Iron Farm Show and Exhibition**
Red River Valley Fair Association
PO Box 797
West Fargo, ND 58078-0797
701-282-2200
FAX: 701-282-6909 800-456-6408
Bruce A Olson, Manager
Annual show of 500 manufacturers of agricultural machinery and related products.
67M Attendees September, West Fargo

9253 **Branding ID: Strategies to Drive Sales**
Association of Sales & Marketing Companies
1010 Wisconsin Avenue NW #900
Washington, DC 20007
202-337-9351
FAX: 202-337-4508 info@asmc.org
Mark Baum, President
Karen Connell, Executive VP
Rick Abraham, VP/COO Foodservice
Jamie DeSimone, Director Marketing/Member Services
March

9254 **California League of Food Processors Expo & Showcase of Processed Foods**
980 Ninth Street
Sacremento, CA 95814
916-444-9260
FAX: 916-444-2746
ed@clfp.org www.clfp.com
Robert Graf, President/CEO
Ed Yates, Senior VP
Nora Basrai, Meetings/Members Services

Information, networking and displays of processed food from apricots to zucchini in every package type imaginable.
January Founded: 1905

9255 **Canola Council of Canada**
167 Lombard Avenue, Suite 400
Winnipeg, Manitoba
Canada R3B 0T6
204-982-2100
FAX: 204-942-1841
admin@canola-council.org
www.canola-council.org
Jennifer Dyek, Convention Coordinator
Annual meeting and convention.
200 Attendees March

9256 **CaterSource**
PO Box 14776
Chicago, IL 60614
773-525-6800
FAX: 800-387-4744 800-932-3632
Micheal Roman, President

9257 **Citrus Expo**
Associated Publishing Corporation
495 E Summerlin Street
Bartow, FL 33830
863-533-4114
FAX: 863-533-6924
lbrickey@barpr.com
www.citrusindustry.net
Laura Brickey, Show Manager
Citrus Trade Show with seminars, containing 150 exhibits.
1500 Attendees August

9258 **Club Managers Association of America**
World Conference on Club Management
1733 King Street
Alexandria, VA 22314
703-739-9500
FAX: 703-739-0124
cmaa@cmaa.org www.cmaa.org
Guy Doria, Show Manager
Jim Singerling, Executive VP
3000 Attendees February

9259 **Commodity Classic**
American Soybean Association
12125 Woodcrest Executive Drive
Suite 100
Saint Louis, MO 63141-5009
314-576-1770
FAX: 314-576-2786 800-688-7692
bcallanan@soy.org
www.soygrowers.com
Steve Censky, CEO
Meeting and exhibits of soybean industry related equipment and information.

9260 **Conference on New Food & Beverage Concepts Innovators**
NorthStar Conferences
1211 Avenue of the Americas
New York, NY 10036
212-596-6006
FAX: 212-596-6092
cservice@northstarconferences.com
www.northstarconferences.com
Cheryl Callahan, Marketing Director

9261 **Council of Food Processors Association Annual Convention**
1401 New York Avenue NW
Suite 400
Washington, DC 20005-2124
202-471-1835
FAX: 202-639-5932
John Cady, President
Barbara Arnwine, Executive Director

9262 Craft Brewers Conference and Brew Expo America
Association of Brewers
736 Pearl Street
Boulder, CO 80302
303-447-0816
FAX: 303-447-2825 888-822-6273
info@brewersassociation.org
www.beertown.org
Nancy Johnson, Show Manager
Cindy Jones, Director Sales/Marketing
Charlie Papazian, President
1200 Attendees April

9263 Crop Science Society of America Meeting and Exhibits
Crop Science Society of America
677 S Segoe Road
Madison, WI 53711-1048
608-273-8086
FAX: 608-273-2021
tmoeller@agronomy.org
www.crops.org
John Nicholiadis, Managing Editor
David M Kral, Associate Executive VP
Ellen Bergfeld, Executive VP
Annual exhibits of agricultural equipment, supplies and services.
October

9264 Dairy and Food Industries Supply Association
1451 Dolley Madison Boulevard
Mc Lean, VA 22101-3847
703-883-0515
FAX: 703-761-4334
info@iafis.org www.iafis.org

9265 Dairy-Deli-Bake
International Dairy-Deli-Bakery Association
636 Science Drive
Madison, WI 53711-1073
608-238-7908
FAX: 608-238-6330
iddba@iddba.org www.iddba.org
Judy Valaskey, Membership Coordinator
7000 Attendees June

9266 Dixie Classic Fair
City of Winston-Salem
PO Box 7525
Winston-Salem, NC 27109
336-727-2236
FAX: 336-727-2236
David Sparks, Executive Director

9267 EastPack
Cannon Communications
11444 W Olympic Boulevard
Los Angeles, CA 90064-1549
323-755-7646
FAX: 310-996-9499
www.eastpackshow.com

9268 Eastern Perishable Products Association Trade Show
Eastern Perishable Products Association
411 S State Route 17
Hasbrouck Heights, NJ 07604-1002

FAX: 201-288-5422
eppa@eppainc.org www.eppainc.org
Lorraine Hoyt, Show Manager
For the perishable food industry, including dairy, deli, bakery, seafood, food service, meat ect. Exhibitors are manufacturers and services of perishable food products. Attendees are buyers, executives, managers and supervisors of supermarket chains, independents and specialty stores. 400 Booths
8M Attendees April Founded: 1971

9269 El Foro
WATT Publishing Company
122 S Wesley Avenue
Mount Morris, IL 61054-1497
815-734-4171
FAX: 815-734-7727
olentine@wattmm.com
www.wattnet.com
James Watt, Owner
A trade show and technical symposium for the Latin American poultry, pig and feed industries. Containing 50 booths and 150 exhibits.
275 Attendees July

9270 Electric Power & Farm Equipment Show
Midwest Equipment Dealers Association
13 Odana Center
#44364
Madison, WI 53719-1109
608-240-4700
FAX: 608-276-6719
Annual show of 300 exhibitors of farm machinery, including tractors, field equipment, minimum tillage, no-till harvesting equipment and farm supplies, lawn, garden and outdoor power equipment, irrigation equipment, farmstead mechanization equipment and dairy equipment.
18M Attendees

9271 Entomological Society of America
9301 Annapolis Road
Lanham, MD 20706-3115
301-731-4535
FAX: 301-731-4538
esa@entsoc.org www.entsoc.org
Judy Miller, Show Manager
50 booths of scientific equipment, supplies and services relevant to entomology.
3M Attendees December 3k names $125 per M.

9272 Executive Conference
Association of Sales & Marketing Companies
1010 Wisconsin Avenue NW
#900
Washington, DC 20007
202-337-9351
FAX: 202-337-4508 info@asmc.org
Mark Baum, President
Karen Connell, Executive VP
Rick Abraham, VP/COO Foodservice
Jamie DeSimone, Director Marketing/Member Services
July

9273 Expo of the Americas
EJ Krause & Associates
6550 Rock Spring Drive
Suite 500
Bethesda, MD 20817-1126
301-493-5500
FAX: 301-493-5705
ejkinfo@ejkrause.com
www.ejkrause.com
Ned Krause, President
Annual show and exhibits of hotel and restaurant food and beverages.

9274 FEWA's Industry Showcase
Farm Equipment Wholesalers Association
PO Box 1347
Iowa City, IA 52244
319-354-5156
FAX: 319-354-5157
info@fewa.org www.fewa.org
Patricia A Collins, Executive VP
Annual convention and 130 exhibits of equipment, supplies and services for independent wholesalers of shortline and specialty farm equipment, light industrial tractors, lawn and garden tractors, turf care equipment, estate and park maintenance equipment and power vehicles for outdoor recreation and sports.
800 Attendees November

9275 FFA National Agricultural Career Show
5632 Mount Vernon Memorial Highway
Alexandria, VA 22309-1502

FAX: 800-366-6556 888-332-2668
jack-pitzer@ffa.org www.ffa.org
Jack Pitzer, Show Manager
Eight hundred and fifty booths encouraging high school youth to select careers in the agricultural industry.
45M Attendees November

9276 Farm Progress Show
Farm Progress Companies
191 South Gary Avenue
Carol Stream, IL 60188
630-905-5600
FAX: 630-462-2869 866-264-7469
info@farmprogress.com
www.farmprogressshow.com
Dottie Rovner, National Sales/Shows Coordinator
Annual farm show of 400 exhibitors representing various types of agricultural products and services for farmers and agribusiness, including small operations to top producers. The 2006 show is scheduled for August 29th to August 31st.

9277 Farm Science Review
Ohio State University
590 Woody Hayes Drive
Agricultural Engr. Building- Rm 232
Columbus, OH 43210
614-292-3671
FAX: 614-292-9448 800-644-6377
fendrick.1@osu.edu fsr.osu.edu
Craig Fendrick, Manager
Annual show of 625 exhibitors of agricultural equipment, supplies and services.
140M Attendees September

9278 Farmfest
Farm Fairs
PO Box 731
Lake Crystal, MN 56055-0731
507-726-6863
FAX: 507-726-6750 800-347-5863
Annual show of 450 manufacturers, suppliers and distributors of farm equipment and machinery, computers and software products, chemicals, seeds and crops, and techniques of planting, tillage and harvesting.
50M Attendees

9279 **Fish Expo Workboat Northwest**
National Fisherman Magazine
121 Free Street
PO Box 7437
Portland, ME 04112
207-842-5608
FAX: 207-842-5509
cmmarketing@divcom.com
www.fishexposeattle.com
Jane Bogual, Director
West Coast trade show attracting thousands of visitors from the fields of commercial fishing, workboat, port/harbor, boatbuilding, seafood processing, and other marine industries. *$5.00*
6,000 Attendees November

9280 **Food & Nutrition Conference & Expo**
American Dietetic Association
120 South Riverside Plaza
Suite 2000
Chicago, IL 60606-6995
312-899-4741
FAX: 312-899-0008 800-877-1600
gandruch@eatright.org
www.eatright.org
Greg Andruch, Exhibition Manager
More than 8,000 professionals come to the Food & Nutrition Conference & Expo for the latest technological and nutritional advancements. This is the premier selling opportunity in the fields of nutrition and food service management. The event continues to expand-attracting a wider audience of professionals, including hotel and restaurant managers, sports, health and nutrition professionals and executive chefs. *$ 150.00*
8000 Attendees 9/29-10/2, 2006 PA
Founded: 1917
Circulation: 65000

9281 **Food Marketing Institute: Annual Meat Marketing Conference**
Adams Mark Hotel
655 15th Street NW, Suite 700
Washington, DC 20005
202-220-0600
FAX: 202-492-4519
Laurel Kelly, Manager Education
Beth Watt, Contact
Tim Hammonds, Chief Executive Officer

9282 **Food Processing Suppliers Association**
Food Processing Machinery Association
1451 Dolley Madison Blvd
Ste 200
Mc Lean, VA 22101-3847
703-761-2600
FAX: 703-761-4334 800-331-8816
info@fpmamail.com
www.foodprocessingmachinery.com
October

9283 **Food Safety Summit: Chicago**
Eaton Hall Exhibitions
256 Columbia Turnpike
Florham Park, NJ 07932
973-514-5900
FAX: 973-514-5977 800-746-9646
sgoldman@eatonhall.com
www.foodsafetysummit.com
Scott Goldman, President
Michael Pesick, Exhibits/Sponsors
Amy Reimer, Registration
Food safety, quality assurance, microbiology and plant sanitation.
1500 Attendees October

9284 **Food Safety Summit: Washington**
Eaton Hall Exhibitions
256 Columbia Turnpike
Florham Park, NJ 07932
973-514-5900
FAX: 973-514-5977 800-746-9646
sgoldman@eatonhall.com
www.foodsafetysummit.com
Scott Goldman, President
Michael Pesick, Exhibits/Sponsors
Amy Reimer, Registration
Held in Washington DC. Food safety, quality assurance, microbiology and plant sanitation.
1500 Attendees March

9285 **Food Tech**
Glahe International
PO Box 6009
Sun City Center, FL 33571
813-633-6335
FAX: 813-633-6355 glahe@glahe.com
Iye Boyd, President
Annual exhibits of food technology.

9286 **Gourmet Products Show**
George Little Management
577 Airport Boulevard
Suite 440
Burlingame, CA 94010
650-344-5171
FAX: 650-344-5270 800-272-SHOW
Susan Corwin, VP
Cookware, tabletop, gadgets, cutlery, specialtry electric appliances, home textiles, home contemporary lifestyle, furnishings, garden and travel accessories, home storage items, personal care, coffee and teas and specialty foods. Contains 950 exhibitors. 2700 booths
9000 Attendees April

9287 **Grape Grower Magazine Farm Show**
Western Agricultural Publishing Company
4974 E Clinton Way
Suite 123
Fresno, CA 93727-1520
559-261-0396
FAX: 559-252-7387
Phill Rhoads, Manager
Seminars, exhibits and prizes for grape growers. Contianing 80 booths and exhibits.
1000 Attendees March/November

9288 **Great American Beer Festival**
Association of Brewers
736 Pearl Street
Boulder, CO 80302
303-447-0816
FAX: 303-447-2825 888-822-6273
info@brewersassociation.org
www.beertown.org
Bob Pease, VP
September

9289 **GrowerExpo**
Ball Publishing
PO Box 9
Batavia, IL 60510-0009
630-208-9080
FAX: 630-456-0132 800-456-5380
John Martens, President
A trade show devoted to horticulture and floriculture production and marketing. 175 booths.
2M Attendees January

9290 **HMAA Food & New Products Show**
Pacific Expositions
1580 Makaola Street
Suite 1200
Honolulu, HI 92814
808-945-3594
FAX: 808-946-6399
Pat Shine, General Sales Manager
Kimalar K Carroll, Show Director/Coordinator
This popular event, featuring the Food Show in the arena and New Products Show in the exhibition hall, is the original new products expo. Local and mainland exhibitors gather each year to present electronic, household, recreational and food products and service— often unvailed for the first time in Hawaii.
96000 Attendees

9291 **Hawkeye Farm Show**
Midwest Shows
PO Box 737
Austin, MN 55912
507-437-7969
FAX: 507-437-7752
www.farmshowsusa.com
Penny Swank, Show Manager
18000 Attendees March

9292 **Health & Nutrition Product Development Start to Finish**
New Hope Natural Media
1401 Pearl Street
Suite 200
Boulder, CO 80302
303-998-9399
rdebarros@newhope.com
Rob DeBarros, Marketing Manager
March 8-11 2007 Anaheim

9293 **Heart of America Hospitality Expo**
Bartle Hall Convention & Entertainment Center
301 W 13th Street, Suite 100
Kansas City, MO 64105
816-513-5000
FAX: 816-513-5001 800-821-7060
Charles Hart II, President
Pat Bergaur, Regional Director

9294 **Home Baking Association Annual Conference**
10841 S Crossroads Drive
Suite 105
Parker, CO 80135
303-840-8787
FAX: 303-840-6877
hbadavis@wamego.net
www.homebaking.org
Sharon Davis, Show Manager

9295 **Hospitality Food Service Expo**
Reed Business Information
275 Washington Street
Boston, MA 02458
617-261-1166
FAX: 630-288-8686
www.reedbusiness.com
Patrick Paleno, Show Manager
Barry Reed Jr, Manager

Four hundred booths featuring educational seminars, culinary salon, and exhibits of products and services.
12M Attendees October

9296 Hydroponic Society of America
PO Box 6067
Concord, CA 94524-1067

FAX: 510-232-2323
Gene Brisbon, Executive Director
Thirty five booths featuring the latest in hydroponic equipment.
500 Attendees April

9297 IBA Messe Duesseldorf North America
150 N Michigan Avenue
Suite 2920
Chicago, IL 60601
312-621-5800
FAX: 312-781-5188
info@mdna.com www.mdna.com
Frank Thorwirth, President
Pyon Klemon, Senior Project Manager
100 T Attendees October

9298 IBIE Bakery Expo
BEMA: Baking Industry Suppliers Association
7101 College Boulevard
Suite 1505
Overland Park, KS 66210
913-338-1300
FAX: 913-338-1327
info@bema.org www.ibie2007.org
Matt Zielsdorf, Convention Chairman
Co-sponsored with the American Bakers Association. event that offers complete equipment, ingredient and supply solutions to serious baking professionals. Directors and managers from every segment of the grain-based food industry count on IBIE for the new technology, products, strategies and information they need to stay competitive in all aspects of their operation.
20000 Attendees October, 2007

9299 IBWA Convention & Trade Show International Bottled Water Assn
International Bottled Water Association
1700 Diagonal Road
Suite 650
Alexandria, VA 22314
703-683-5213
FAX: 703-683-4074 800-WAT-ER11
ibwainfo@bottledwater.org
www.bottledwater.org
Susan Frate
Trade association representing the bottled water industry. IBWA's member companies produce and distribute 80 percent of the bottled water sold in the US. Our membership includes US and international bottlers, distributors and suppliers.
3250 Attendees October 3-6, 2006 Founded: 1958

9300 IS/LD Conference
2401 Pennsylvania Avenue NW
2nd Floor
Washington, DC 20037
202-337-9400
FAX: 202-337-4508
cbaker@gmabrands.com
www.gmabrands.com
Cindy Baker, Meetings/Conference Sr. Manager
A place where senior logistics and information technology executives from CPG manufacturers and leading retailers come together to study and seek solutions to the pressing issues affecting today's global supply chain.
April Founded: 1908

9301 Institute of Food Technologists Annual Meeting & Food Expo
Institute of Food Technologists
525 W Van Buren Street
Suite 1000
Chicago, IL 60607-3814
312-782-8424
FAX: 312-782-0045 800-438-3663
info@ift.org www.ift.org
Stan Butler, Director Meetings
Roy Hlavacek, Sales Director
Susan Audronowitz, Meetings Manager
Barbara Byrd Keenan, VP
Technical exposition directed to the $302 billion food industry. Offering person-to-person marketplace and technical forum for suppliers of food ingredients. 2,400 booths.
24M Attendees July
Mailing list available for rent

9302 International Air Conditioning, Heating & Refrigerating Expo
ASHRAE
Chicago McCormick Place
1791 Tulie Circle
Atlanta, GA 30329
404-636-8400
FAX: 404-321-5478
leggling@ashrae.org www.ashrae.org
Irene Eggling, Advertising Production Manager
Heating, Ventilating, Air Conditioning, Refrigeration show for engineers, contractors, consultants and wholesalers.
30000 Attendees January

9303 International Assoc. of Operative Millers Technical Conference/Trade Show
Assocaiton of Operative Millers
5001 College Boulevard
Suite 104
Leawood, KS 66211
913-338-3377
FAX: 913-338-3553
info@iaom.info www.iaom.org
James Doyle, President
Gary Anderson, Executive VP
Conference, banquet and over 100 exhibits of cereal milling equipment, ancillary equipment, supplies and information.
May

9304 International Beverage Industry Exposition
1101 16th Street NW
Washington, DC 20036-4803
202-857-4722

Lisa Feldman, Show Manager
450 booths.
16M Attendees October

9305 International Boston Seafood Show
National Fishermans Expositions
PO Box 7437
Portland, ME 04112-7437
207-842-5500
FAX: 207-842-5505
Diane Vassar, Promotions Director
David Lowell, President
Nine hundred and seventy booths. Annual trade show for the seafood industry. *$20.00*
20M Attendees March

9306 International Exposition for Food Processors
Food Processing Machinery Association
200 Dangerfield Road
Alexandria, VA 22314-2800
703-684-1080
FAX: 703-548-6563 800-331-8816
info@fpmamail.com
www.foodprocessingmachinery.com
Nancy Janssen, Show Manager
Show with more than 1,600 exhibitors, up-to-the-minute technology, fast-track educational sessions. Great source for solutions and networking with industry peers. Colocated with Pack Expo International. McCormick Place, Chicago, IL.
50000 Attendees September
Mailing list available for rent

9307 International Food Processors Association Expo
200 Daingerfield Road
Suite 100
Alexandria, VA 22314-2884
703-299-5001
FAX: 703-299-5100
George Melnykozich, Show Manager
Four hundred and twenty five booths of food processing and supplies.
16M Attendees January

9308 International Food Service Exposition
Florida Restaurant Association
230 S Adams Street
Tallahassee, FL 32301
850-224-2250
FAX: 850-224-9213 www.flra.com
Hosting the third largest food service show in the country with over 1,200 booths and over 23,000 qualified buyers and attendees.

22000 Attendees

9309 International Foodservice Distributors: Pr oductivity Convention & Exposition
201 Park Washington Court
Falls Church, VA 22046-4521
703-532-9400
FAX: 703-538-4673
sbarrett@ifdaonline.org
www.ifdaonline.org
Mark Allen, President/CEO
Stan Barrett, Director Membership
Workshops, assemblies, facility tours and an exposition are featured. Educational programming features many practitioners who sahre knowledge to be applied to various operations. Practical information for transportation, information technology, human resources and more.
October Founded: 2003

9310 International Institute of Foods and Family Living Annual Meeting
225 W Ohio Street
Chicago, IL 60610-4198
312-527-3860
FAX: 312-670-0824
Phyllis Favelman, President

9311 International Pizza Expo
MacFadden Protech
137 E Market Street
New Albany, IN 47150
812-949-0909
FAX: 812-949-1867 800-489-8324
boakley@pizzatoday.com
www.pizzaexpo.com
William T Oakley, Senior VP Expositions
Linda Keith, VP Meetings/Conferences
One thousand booths featuring exhibits of equipment for pizza industry and restaurants.
6000 Attendees February/March

9312 International Poultry Expo
US Poultry & Egg Association/American Feed Assoc.
1530 Cooledge Road
Tucker, GA 30084-7303
770-493-9401
FAX: 770-493-9257
colentine@poultryegg.org
www.internationalpoultryexposition.com
Charles Olentine, Executive VP
Pennie Howard-Stathes, Expo Coordinator
A world large trade show for the poultry and feed sectors.
15000 Attendees January

9313 Interpack
150 N Michigan Avenue
Suite 2920
Chicago, IL 60601
312-781-5180
FAX: 312-781-5188
info@mdna.com www.mdna.com
Ryan Klemm, Senior Project Manager
April 24-30, 2008

9314 KFYR Radio Agri International Stock & Trade Show
KFYR Radio
PO Box 1658
Bismarck, ND 58502-1738
701-224-9393
FAX: 701-255-8155 800-472-2170
mwall@clearchannel.com
www.kfyr.com
Syd Stewart, General Manager
Michelle J Wall, Sales Manager
Annual show of 250 exhibitors of agricultural equipment, supplies, livestock and services.
15000 Attendees February

9315 Keystone Farm Show
Lee Publications
PO Box 121
Palatine Bridge, NY 13428-0121
518-673-2269
FAX: 518-673-2699 www.leepub.com
Ken Maning, Show Manager
Tom Mahoney, Sales Manager

9316 MWR Expo
American Logistics Association
1133 15th Street NW
Suite 640
Washington, DC 20005-2708
202-466-2520
FAX: 202-296-4419
membership@ala-national.org
www.ala-national.org
Cologne Hunter, Meetings/Expo Director
Maurice Branch, Operations VP
A gathering of MWR professionals and brings together the many components of the Morale, Welfare and Recreation industry. The event features products and services that are sold to military and government agencies for use in community support activities on military installations throughout the world.
Biennial/August 2006 Founded: 1972

9317 Maraschino Cherry and Glace Fruit Processors Annual Convention
5 Ravine Drive
#776
Matawan, NJ 07747-3106

FAX: 732-583-0798
Richard Sullivan, Executive VP
April/May

9318 Marketechnics
Food Marketing Institute
800 Connecticut Avenue NW
Washington, DC 20006
202-220-0600
FAX: 202-429-4519
Beth Watt, Contact
6000 Attendees

9319 Material Handling Industry of America
Promat
8720 Red Oak Boulevard
Suite 201
Charlotte, NC 28217-3992
704-676-1190
FAX: 704-676-1199
Carol Miller, Director Marketing
John Nofsinger, Chief Executive Officer

9320 Meatxpo
National Meat Association
1970 Broadway
Suite 825
Oakland, CA 94612
510-763-1533
FAX: 510-763-6186
March

9321 Mid-America Farm Show
Salina Area Chamber of Commerce
120 W Ash Street
PO Box 586
Salina, KS 67401
785-827-9301
FAX: 785-827-9758
chamber@informatics.net
www.salinakansas.org
Don Weiser, Show Manager
Annual show of 325 exhibitors of agricultural equipment, supplies and services, including irrigation equipment, fertilizer, farm implements, hybrid seed, agricultural chemicals, tractors, feed, farrowing crates and equipment, silos and bins, storage equipment and farm buildings.
13M Attendees March 20, 21, 22

9322 Mid-America Horticultural Trade Show
1000 N Rand Road
Suite 214
Wauconda, IL 60084-1188
847-526-2010
FAX: 847-526-3993 www.midam.org
Rand A Baldwin CAE, Managing Director
Suzanne Spohr, Show Manager
Mid-Am is the premier event featuring more than 650 leading suppliers offering countless products, equipment, and services for the horticulture industry. Mid-Am also offers a variety of educational seminars featuring the best and the brightest in the horticultural and business communities to help keep you informed of the latest trends.
January

9323 Mid-America Resturant, Soft Serve & Pizza Exposition
Exhibition Productions
PO Box 81845
Wellesley, MA 02481

FAX: 617-431-2662 800-909-7469
17000 Attendees

9324 Mid-Atlantic Food, Beverage & Lodging Expo
Restaurant Association of Maryland
6301 Hillside Court
Columbia, MD 21046
410-290-6800
FAX: 410-290-7898 800-874-1313
dimbessi@marylandrestaurants.com
www.midatlanticexpo.com
Dennis Imbessi, Director Expo/Membership Sales
Licia Spinelli, Director Marketing/Special Events
Valerie Maione, Owner
Annual Mid-Atlantic regional trade show of products and services for the restaurant and hospitality industry. Exhibitors include food manufacturers, equipment, beverages and services providers. Open to food service professionals, taking place annually during the month of September with 500 exhibitors and 600 booths.
15000 Attendees October
Mailing list available for rent 29000 names

9325 Midway USA Food Service and Hospitality Exposition
Kansas Restaurant and Hospitality Association
359 S Hydraulic Street
Wichita, KS 67211-1908
316-267-8383
FAX: 316-267-8400
Dennis Carpenter, CEO
Annual show of 35 food service, beverage, suppliers.
6000 Attendees

9326 Midwest Agri Industries Expo
Illinois Fertilizer & Chemical Association

PO Box 186
Saint Anne, IL 60964-0186
815-427-6644
FAX: 815-427-6573 800-892-7122
Annual show of 130 manufacturers, suppliers and distributors of agricultural chemical and fertilizer application equipment, supplies and services.
2500 Attendees August, Danville

9327 Midwest Farm Show
North Country Enterprises
PO Box 1
Chippewa Falls, WI 54729-0001
715-723-5061

Steve Henry, President
Top farm show exhibiting dairy and Wisconsin's tillage equipment, feed and seed. 20 booths.
11M+ Attendees January

9328 Midwest Food Processors Association
502 E Main Street
PO Box 1297
Madison, WI 53701-1297
608-255-9946
FAX: 608-255-9838
info@mwfpa.org www.mwfpa.org
Nickolas C George, Jr, President
Judy Meyer, Director Admin/Member Svs Mgr
Approximately one hundred and fifty booths including food processing equipment and suppliers to the industry.
1M Attendees November 29-30, 2006
Founded: 1999

9329 Midwest Gourmet Exposition
Fairchild Urban Expositions
1395 S Marietta Parkway
Building 400, Suite 210
Marietta, GA 30067
678-901-1700
FAX: 770-956-9644
Robert Collins, President

9330 Midwest Leadership Conference
Indiana Retail Grocers Association
115 W Washington Street
Suite 1364
Indianapolis, IN 46204
317-220-0033
FAX: 317-231-7858

9331 Midwest Regional Grape & Wine Conference
Missouri Grape and Wine Board
1616 Missouri Boulevard
Jefferson City, MO 65109-0630
573-751-3374
FAX: 573-751-2868 800-392-WINE
sue.berendzen@mda.mo.gov
www.missouriwine.org
Jim Anderson, Executive Director
Denise Kottwitz, Assistant
A major national conference for hundreds of vintners, growers and wine industry executives throughout the US Conference includes speakers, trade show, workshops and wine dinners. Over 45 booths.
400+ Attendees February Founded: 1985

9332 Midwestern Food Service and Equipment Exposition
Missouri Restaurant Association
9233 Ward Parkway
Suite 123
Kansas City, MO 64114
816-753-5222
FAX: 816-753-6993
www.morestaurants.org
Chad Treaster, President
Annual show of 200 suppliers of food service and hospitality industries equipment, supplies and services.
12M Attendees

9333 NAAB Annual Convention
National Association of Animal Breeders
PO Box 1033
Columbia, MO 65205
573-445-4406
FAX: 573-446-2279
mderby@naab-css.org
www.naab-css.org
Mary Derby, Convention/Conference Coordinator
A welcomer reception, election of directors, consideration of Bylaw Amendments, resolutions and other association business and a award recognitions presentation.
Sept 13-14, 2006

9334 NAAE Annual Convention
National Association of Agricultural Educators
University of Kentucky
300 Garrigus Building
Lexington, KY 40546-215
859-257-2224
FAX: 859-323-3919 800-509-0204
JJackman.NAAE@uky.edu
www.naae.org
Wm Jay Jackman, Executive Director
Samantha Alvis, Associate Executive Director
Featuring a meet and greet, professional development workshops, meetings, tours and a career tech expo. *$305.00*
Nov 28-Dec 2/Fees Vary Founded: 1948

9335 NABCA Annual Conference
National Alcohol Beverage Control Association
4216 King Street
Alexandria, VA 22302-1507
703-784-4201
FAX: 703-820-3551
info@nabca.org www.nabca.org
James M Goldberg, General Counsel
Lorrie Belford, Meeting Planner
James Sgueo, Executive Director
An event to provides its members opportunities to interact and conduct business. Featuring nationally known speakers, informative seminars, interact workshops and suppliers and vendors demonstrating their products.
800+ Attendees May

9336 NABR Tasting & Display Event Annual Convention
American Beverage Licensees
5101 River Road
Suite 108
Bethesda, MD 20816-1560
301-656-1494
FAX: 301-656-7539
nabr@nabronlline.org
www.nabronline.org
Harry Wiles, Executive Director
Shawn Ross, Office Manager
Offers exhibits on spirits, beer and wine industry supplies, equipment, bar accessories and computers. The NABR Annual Convention is a gathering of alcohol beverage retailers and proprietors for networking and educational opportunities. An exclusive trade display and tasting event is held to promote brands and services of use to retailers and proprietors. There are 25-75 booths.
500+ Attendees March 15M names

9337 NAC Annual Convention & Trade Show
35 E Wacker Drive
Suite 1816
Chicago, IL 60601-2103
312-236-3858
FAX: 312-236-7809
cwinans@NAConline.org
www.naconline.org
Charles Winans, Executive Director
Barbara Aslan, Membership Services Manager
Bringing together the top food and beverage concession leaders in the recreation and leisure-time industry at this annual event. *$495.00*
3M Attendees Aug 5-8/Non-Members:$695
Founded: 1982

9338 NACD Annual Meeting
National Association of Conservation Districts
509 Capitol Court NE
Washington, DC 20002-4937
202-547-6223
FAX: 202-547-6450
krysta-harden@nacdnet.org
www.nacdnet.org
Krysta Harden, Meeting Coordinator
Discussions with agency leaders on priorities for the coming years, training sessions, key leaders in agricultural, conservation and wildlife discussing their perspectives on the future Farm Bill, highlighted challenges and addressing areas of common interest.
Feb 4-8, 2007 Founded: 1946

9339 NACS Show
National Association of Convenience Stores
1600 Duke Street
Alexandria, VA 22314
703-684-3600
FAX: 703-836-4564
sromello@nacsonline.com
www.nacsshow.com
Sherri Romello, Conventions/Meeting Director
Bob Hughes, Expo/Advertising Director
Access thousands of new profit centers on the expo floor, discover insights on issues facing convenience and petroleum retailers in educational sessions and network with industry peers. *$375.00*
24000 Attendees Oct 8-11/Non-Members:$525

9340 NAFFS Annual Convention
3301 Route 66
Suite 205, Building C
Neptune, NJ 07753
732-223-3218
FAX: 732-922-3590
info@naffs.org www.naffs.org
Bob Bauer, Executive Director
Offering innovative programs presented by industry experts on the latest issues, an opportunity to learn about the products, services, ideas and trends that will influence tomorrow's success, meet and network with industry peers, education, guest activities and social events.
October 12-15, 2006

9341 NAMA National Expo
National Automatic Merchandising Association
20 N Wacker Drive
Suite 3500
Chicago, IL 60606-3102
312-346-0370
FAX: 312-704-4140 800-331-8816
saizenberg@vending.org
www.namaexpo.org
Richard Geerdes, President
Stuart Aizenberg, CEM, Trade Show Director
This event features an impressive array of the industry's newest products and hottest technology, educational sessions and unmatched networking opportunities.
5000+ Attendees Oct 25-27, 2006 Founded: 1936

9342 NAPO International Pizza Expo
National Association of Pizzeria Operators
908 S 8th Street
Suite 200
Louisville, KY 40203
502-736-9500
FAX: 502-736-9501 800-489-8324
bmacintosh@pizzatoday.com
www.pizzatoday.com

Bobbie MacIntosh, Booth/Sponsorship Sales Director

The trade show for the pizza industry that includes; pizzeria owners, operators, managers, distributors and food brokers. Workshops, seminars and exhibits.
5400 Attendees March

9343 NASFT Fancy Food Shows
National Association for the Specialty Food Trade
120 Wall Street
27th Floor
New York, NY 10005-4001
212-482-6440
FAX: 212-482-6459
custserv@fancyfoodshows.com
www.fancyfoodshows.com

Chris Nemcher, Manager

Held three times a year; winter, spring and summer time. Over 350 domestic exhibitors from around the country, presentations of exotic new specialty foods from all over the world, tastings, seminars and workshops. These shows are a chance to learn about each product first-hand and do business directly with the decision makers onsite.
30000 Attendees Spring/Summer/Winter
Founded: 1955

9344 NBBQA Annual Convention
National Barbecue Association
1306-AW Anderson Lane
Austin, TX 78757
512-454-8626
FAX: 512-454-3036
wholysmokebbq@optonline.net
www.nbbqa.org

Trey Dishner, President
Howard Miller, President-Elect
Don McCullough, Executive VP
Ed Wilson, Secretary/Membership Director

Learn and network with a group of BBQ folks on how to better prepare and utilize grills, smokers, fuels, sauces, marinades, rubs and all the necessary utensils. Barbeque presentations, programming, demonstrations, contests, sampling and contacts and leads. *$355.00*
February/Fees Vary Founded: 1991

9345 NBVA Annual Convention
National Bulk Vendors Association
191 N Walker Drive
Suite 1800
Chicago, IL 60606-1615
312-521-2400
FAX: 312-521-2300
nbva@muchshelist.com
www.nbva.org

Steve Siegel, Convention Seminar Chairman
Daniel Case, President

Each spring the leading manufacturers and suppliers of bulk vending machines and products display their merchandise. Featuring workshops and seminars to discuss current industry problems and interchange ideas.
530 Attendees Spring

9346 NBWA Annual Convention
National Beer Wholesalers Association
1101 King Street
Suite 600
Alexandria, VA 22314
703-390-0591
FAX: 703-863-8965
info@nbwa.org www.nbwa.org

Patti Rouzie, Membership/Meetings Director
Tracey Anderson, Meetings Manager
Diane Mahoney, Registration Manager
Craig A Purser, President

Designed to provide valuable education programs and important networking opportunities for the beer industry. Featuring speakers and seminars on a number of topics of importance to beer distributors.
2500 Attendees Fall/Sept 17-20, 2006

9347 NCBA Annual Convention & Trade Show
National Cattlemen's Beef Association
9110 E Nichols Avenue
Suite 300
Centennial, CO 80112
303-694-0305
FAX: 303-694-2851
DKaylor@beef.org www.beefusa.org

Debbie Kaylor, Convention/Meetings Executive Dir.
Meghan Kavanaugh, Registration Manager
Kristin Torres, Trade Show Coordinator
Terry Stokes, Chief Executive Officer

The meeting will feature joint and individual meetings by five industry organizations. Over 250 companies will offer attendees a chance to see the latest products and services while networking with other cattle producers.
Jan-Feb 2007

9348 NCIMS Conference
National Conference on Interstate Milk Shipments
123 Buena Vista Drive
Frankfort, KY 40601
502-695-0253
FAX: 502-695-0253
ltownsend@ncims.org
www.ncims.org

Leon Townsend, Executive Secretary

Bringing together the people in the dairy industry to discuss laws that directly involve the dairy industry.
Biennially/May, 2007 Founded: 1950

9349 NCSLA Annual Conference
National Conference of State Liquor Administrators
C/O Massachusetts ABCC
239 Causeway Street, 1st Floor
Boston, MA 02114
617-727-3040
FAX: 617-727-1510
cmarshall@tre.state.ma.us
www.ncsla.org

Cheryl Marshall, Conference Coordinator

Provide opportunities for state-licensed administrators to meet and exchange ideas and information and to formulate uniform regulations, statue and laws affecting the sales of alcholic beverages. *$325.00*
June/Fee Varies

9350 NW Food Manufacturing & Packaging Expo
Northwest Food Processors Association
9700 SW Capitol Highway
Suuite 250
Portland, OR 97219
503-327-2200
FAX: 503-327-2201
nwfpa@nwfpa.org www.nwfpa.org

Teonna Embelton, Events Coordinator
Stephanie Kennedy, Events Consultant

Provides comprehensive programs encompassing topics ranging from food sciences and technologies to energy efficiencies.
Jan Oregon

9351 National Agri-Marketing Association Conference
National Agri-Marketing Association
11020 King Street
Suite 205
Overland Park, KS 66210-1201
913-491-6500
FAX: 913-492-6502
agrimktg@nama.org www.nama.org

Eldon White, Executive VP/CEO
Jenny Pickett, Director/Communications/Operations
Dawn Foster, Contact

Annual show of 60 exhibitors of marketing and communication suppliers, including trade publications, radio and television broadcast sales organizations, premium/incentive manufacturers, printers, marketing research firms and photographers.
1100 Attendees

9352 National Agricultural Plastics Congress
American Society for Plasticulture
526 Brittany Drive
State College, PA 16803-1420
814-238-7045
FAX: 814-238-7051
info@plasticulture.org
www.plasticulture.org

Patricia Heuser, Executive Director

Congress of research presentations, with exhibit area of equipment, supplies and services relating to greenhouse production and mulch film production of agricultural and horticultural crops.
225 Attendees September

9353 National Association Extension 4-H Agents Convention
University of Georgia
Hoke Smith Annex
Athens, GA 30602
706-542-3000
FAX: 706-542-2115

Peggy Adkins, Show Manager

Fifty booths for young people, youth staff and volunteers involved in 4-H.
1.2M Attendees November

9354 National Association for the Specialty Food Trade
International Fancy Food & Convention Show
120 Wall Street, 27th Floor
New York, NY 10005
212-482-6440
FAX: 212-482-6459
custserv@fancyfoodshows.com
www.specialtyfood.com

Betsy Krobot, Director International Sales
Phyllis Maritz, Director Domestic Sales
John Roberts, Owner

21000 Attendees January

9355 **National Association of College and University Food Services Convention**
Michigan State University-Manly Miles Building
1405 S Harrison Road
Suite 305
East Lansing, MI 48823-5245
517-332-2494
FAX: 517-332-8144
www.nacufs.org/nacufs
Joseph Spina, Executive Director
Annual convention and exhibits of equipment, supplies and services for food preparation and service on college and university campuses.

9356 **National Association of County Agricultural Agents Conference**
National Association of County Agricultural Agents
Courthouse-Room 217
5th & Main Street
Ellensburg, WA 98926

FAX: 509-627-74
Annual conference and exhibits for county agricultural agents and extension workers.

9357 **National Association of Fruits, Flavors and Syrups Annual Convention**
5 Ravine Drive
#776
Matawan, NJ 07747-3106
732-988-4800
FAX: 732-583-0798
Bob Bauer, Director
September

9358 **National Confectioners Association Education Exposition**
National Confectioners Association
7900 Westpar Drive
Suite A-320
McLean, VA 22102
703-790-5750
FAX: 730-790-5752
Linda Jamie, Finance Executive
600 Attendees

9359 **National Confectioners Association Expo**
8320 Old Courthouse Road
Suite 300
Vienna, VA 22182
703-790-5750
FAX: 703-790-5752
info@candyusa.org
www.allcandyexpo.com
Larry Graham, President
Libby Taylor, VP
Confectionery trade show featuring more chocolate, candy and gum than one can imagine. Held annually in June at Chicago's McCormick Place. 1200 booths.
15 M Attendees June

9360 **National Conservation Association District Annual Convention**
9150 W Jewell Avenue
Suite 113
Lakewood, CO 80232-6469
303-839-1852

Robert Raschke, Regional Representative
Eighty booths including companies who manufacture, service or who are otherwise involved with equipment used in agricultural production.
2M Attendees February

9361 **National Convenience Store Advisory Group Convention**
2063 Oak Street
Jacksonville, FL 32204
904-845-5989
FAX: 904-387-3362
jhowton@nag-net.com
www.nag-net.com
Joseph Howton, Executive VP/COO
One-hundred booths.
500 Attendees January

9362 **National Corn Growers Association**

1000 Executive Parkway Drive
Suite 105
Creve Cocur, MO 63141-6397
314-275-9915
FAX: 314-275-7061
Peggy Findley, Director of Conventions
Five hundred and fifty booths of equipment, seed and chemicals.
4000 Attendees February

9363 **National Country Ham Association Annual Meeting**
PO Box 948
Conover, NC 28613
828-466-2760
FAX: 828-466-2770 800-820-4426
eatham@countryham.org
www.countryham.org
Candace Cansler, Executive Director
Providing an array of speakers, discussion topics and activities. *$150.00*
Non-Members:$300

9364 **National Farm Machinery Show and Championship Tractor Pull**
Kentucky Fair and Exposition Center
PO Box 37130
Louisville, KY 40233
502-367-5000
FAX: 502-367-5299
harold.workman@mail.state.ky.us
www.farmmachineryshow.org
Harold Workman, Show Manager
Annual show of 800 plus exhibitors of agricultural products, equipment, supplies and services.
280M Attendees February

9365 **National Food Processors Association Convention**
National Food Processors Association
1350 I Street NW
Suite 300
Washington, DC 20005-3377
202-930-0890
FAX: 202-639-5932
John Cady, President
Lisa Weddig, Executive Director
Annual convention and exhibits of equipment, supplies and services for food processing quality control measures, spoilage prevention, frozen food technology, sanitation techniques and waste treatment techniques.

9366 **National Frozen and Refrigerated Foods Convention**
National Frozen & Refrigerated Foods Association
4755 Linglestown Road, Suite 300
PO Box 6069
Harrisburg, PA 17112
717-657-8601
FAX: 717-657-9862
info@nfraweb.org www.nfraweb.org
Skip Shaw, Executive VP/COO/Show Manager
Kim Smith, Director Member Services
The National Frozen and Refrigerated Foods Convention is an opportunity for you to meet with hundreds of frozen and refrigerated food decision makers. This premier business event brings representatives from all segments of our industry together to conduct business and build relationships. It is structured around one-on-one business appointments, with ample opportunity to network.
1,200 Attendees October 8-12, 2005

9367 **National Grange Annual Meeting**
1616 H Street NW
Washington, DC 20006
202-628-3507
FAX: 202-347-1091
Robert Barrow, Program Director
Agricultural forum.
3M Attendees November

9368 **National Grocers Association Annual Convenience & Supermarket Showcase**
National Grocers Association
1825 Samuel Morse Drive
Reston, VA 22090
703-437-5300
FAX: 703-437-7768
2800 Attendees

9369 **National Honey Packers and Dealers Association Annual Meeting**
3301 Route 66
Suite 205, Building C
Neptune, NJ 07753
732-922-0500
FAX: 732-922-3590
afi@afius.org www.afius.org
Bob Bauer, President
Speakers, two full day meetings and a dinner are arranged.

9370 **National Ice Cream Retailers Association Annual Convention**
1841 Hicks Road
Suite C
Rolling Meadows, IL 60008
847-202-4770
FAX: 847-202-4791
info@nicra.org www.nicra.org
Lynda Utterback, Executive Director
A major national convention for those in the retail ice ceam and frozen dessert business. Attendees are mostly independent operators/owners and vendors that sell to the retail/wholesale trade. Thirty-five to forty booths.
300 Attendees November

9371 **National Nutritional Foods Association**
2112 E 4th St
Ste 200
Santa Ana, CA 92705-3816
714-460-7732
FAX: 714-460-7444 800-966-6632
nnfa@nnfa.org www.nnfa.org
Sheldon Metz, Show Director
David Seckman, Executive Director
Brent Weickert, COO
Six hundred booths including educational seminars and exhibits of health and natural foods.
7.5M Attendees June Founded: 1936

9372 **National Orange Show**
PO Box 5749
San Bernardino, CA 92412-5749
909-888-6788
FAX: 909-889-7666
Esther Armstrong, Executive Director
Brad Randall, Manager
Agricultural forum.
262M Attendees May

9373 **National Pest Management Association Annual Eastern Conference**
9300 Lee Hwy
Ste 301
Fairfax, VA 22031-6051
703-352-6762
FAX: 703-352-3031 800-678-6722
Cindy Mannes, Executive Director
Robert Lederer, Executive VP
Patty McKnight, Director Marketing Convention
Two hundred forty booths.
2M Attendees October

9374 **National Potato Council's Annual Meeting**
National Potato Council
5690 Dtc Boulevard
Greenwood Village, CO 80111-3232
303-773-9295
FAX: 303-773-9296
npcspud@ix.netcom.com
www.npcspod.com
Annual meeting and exhibits of potato growing equipment, supplies and services.

9375 **National Poultry & Food Distributors: Poultry Suppliers Showcase (NPFDA)**
958 McEver Road Extension
Suite B8
Gainesville, GA 30506
770-535-9901
FAX: 770-535-7385
info@npfda.org www.npfda.org
Kristin McWhorter, Show Manager/Executive Director
C C Hill, President
Melanie Taylor, Executive Assistant
Annual convention and poultry suppliers showcase. Three day convention and trade show.
900 Attendees January Founded: 1967

9376 **National Restaurant Association Convention**
National Restaurant Association
150 N Michigan Avenue
Suite 2000
Chicago, IL 60601
312-853-2525
FAX: 312-853-2548
Mary Heftman, Senior Vice President
80000 Attendees May

9377 **National Seasoning Manufacturers Association Annual Meeting**
National Seasoning Manufacturers Association
8905 Maxwell Drive
Potomac, MD 20854-3125
301-765-9675
FAX: 301-299-7523
Dick Alsmeyer, Executive Director
28 Attendees June Founded: 1973

9378 **National Soft Drink Association Show**
1101 16th Street NW
Suite 700
Washington, DC 20036-4877
202-463-6732
FAX: 202-463-8178
Susan K Neely, President
Patricia M Vaughan, Secretary
Jim L Turner, Treasurer
Annual show of 300 members of soft drink makers and their suppliers.
25M Attendees Annual Fall Founded: 1919

9379 **National Turkey Federation**
1225 New York Avenue NW
Suite 400
Washington, DC 20005-6404
202-898-0100
FAX: 202-898-0203
info@turkeyfed.org
www.eatturkey.com
Stuart E Proctor Jr, President
Kelley Moss, Member Services Assistant
Annual meeting advocates for all segments of the US turkey industry, providing services and conducting activities that increase demand for its members' products. The federation also protects and enhances its members' ability to effectively and profitably provide wholesome, high quality, nutritious turkey products.
600 Attendees February

9380 **National Watermelon Association**
Annual Meeting
406 Railroad Street
Morven, GA 31638
229-775-2130
FAX: 229-775-2344
Nacy Childers, Contact

9381 **National Wheat Growers Association Convention**
415 2nd Street NE
Suite 300
Washington, DC 20002-4900
202-547-7800
FAX: 202-546-2638
www.wheatworld.org
Darren Coppock, CEO
June Silverberg, Director Corporate Relations
Major agri business exhibits including farm equipment and services. 100 booths.

9382 **Natural Products Exposition East**
New Hope Natural Media
1301 Spruce Street
Boulder, CO 80302
303-939-8440
FAX: 303-939-9559
20000 Attendees

9383 **Natural Products Exposition West**
New Hope Communications
1301 Spruce Street
Boulder, CO 80302
303-939-8440
FAX: 303-939-9559
31000 Attendees

9384 **New England Equipment Dealers Association**
PO Box 895
Concord, NH 03302-0895
603-225-5510
FAX: 603-225-5510
George M Becker, Managing Director
Annual convention and trade show held the first weekend in December for farm, industrial and outdoor equipment dealers in the six New England states. 95 booths.
300 Attendees December

9385 **Nightclub & Bar Beverage Retailer Beverage & Food Convention and Trade Show**
Oxford Publishing
307 West Jackson Avenue
Oxford, MS 38655
662-236-5510
FAX: 662-513-3990 888-966-2727
registration@oxpub.com
www.nightclub.com

9386 **Nightclub & Bar/Beverage Retailer Food & Beverage Trade Show**
Oxford Publishing
307 W Jackson Avenue
Oxford, MS 38655-2154
662-236-5510
FAX: 662-513-3990 888-966-2727
jrobinson@oxpub.com
www.nightclub.com
Jennifer Robinson, Show Manager
Fastest growing food, beverage and hospitality show in the US. This show is for both on-premise and off-premise.
20M Attendees March/July/November

9387 **Nightclub and Bar/Beverage Retailer Convention and Trade Show**
National Bar and Restaurant Association
307 Jackson Avenue W
Oxford, MS 38655
662-236-5510
FAX: 662-236-5541 800-247-3881
br@beverage-retailer.com
www.beverage-retailer.com
Jennifer Robinson, Senior VP
Hollis Green, Trade Show Director
Kaytee Hazlewood, VP Marketing
The industry's first national conference and trade show devoted to business basics, promotions and marketing for liquor stores, nightclubs and bars. More than 2,500 exhibits.
38800 Attendees March 40,000+ names $150 per M.

9388 **North American Deer Farmers Association Annual Conference & Exhibit**
North American Deer Farmers Association
1215 N 7th St
Ste 104
Lake City, MN 55041-1266
651-345-5600
FAX: 651-345-5603
info@nadefa.org www.nadefa.org
Phyllis Menden, Show Manager

Annual show of more than 30 exhibitors of deer farming equipment, supplies and services. *$15.00*
550+ Attendees Quarterly Founded: 1984
Circulation: 1,000

9389 North American Farm and Power Show
Tradexpos
811 W Oakland Avenue
PO Box 1067
Austin, MN 55912
507-437-4697
FAX: 507-437-8917 800-949-3976
steve@tradexpos.com
www.tradexpos.com
Steve Guenthner, Show Director
Agri-business farm show for the 5-state region. Free admission and parking.
28M Attendees March

9390 North American Meat Processors Association Exposition
1910 Association Drive
Reston, VA 20191-1545
703-758-1900
FAX: 703-758-8001
Sharon Ritchey, Special Projects Manager
30 booths.
250 Attendees March

9391 North American Olive Oil Association Mid- Year Meeting
North American Olive Oil Association
3301 Route 66
Suite 205, Building C
Neptune, NJ 07753
732-922-0500
FAX: 732-922-3590
info@aboutoliveoil.com
www.aboutoliveoil.org
Bob Bauer, President
Olive growers and oil processors group for legislative advocacy and trade networking.

9392 North American Specialty Coffee Retailers' Expo
PO Box 14827
Portland, OR 97293
503-236-2587
FAX: 503-236-3165 800-548-0551
jan@nascore.net www.nascore.net
Jan Weigel, Director
Founded: 1995

9393 Northeast Food Service and Lodging Expo and Conference
Reed Exhibition Companies
383 Main Avenue
Norwalk, CT 06851
203-840-4800
FAX: 203-840-4824
Linda Karpowich, Customer Service Manager
Annual show of 600 exhibitors of food services, operating equipment and services for the hospitality and institutional foodservice industry.
29000 Attendees

9394 Northeast Pizza Expo
MacFadden Protech
137 E Market Street
New Albany, IN 47150
812-949-0909
FAX: 812-949-1867 800-489-8324
lkeith@pizzatoday.com
www.pizzaexpo.com
William T Oakley, Senior VP Expositions
Linda F Keith, VP Meetings/Conferences
Manufacturers, food purveyors and service representatives from pizza or related industries.

9395 Northwest Agricultural Show
Northwest Agricultural Congress
4672 Drift Creek Road SE
Sublimity, OR 97385-9764
503-769-7120
FAX: 503-769-3549
James Heater, Exhibits Director
Annual show and exhibits of agricultural equipment and services.
27M Attendees

9396 Northwest Food Manufacturing & Packaging Association
Northwest Food Processors Association
6950 SW Hampton Street
Suite 340
Portland, OR 98223-8332
503-639-7676
FAX: 503-639-7007
mwpfa@nwpfa.org
www.nwpfa@nwpfa.org
Stephanie Green, Show Manager
Mindy Todd, Marketing Coordinator
Containing 450 booths.
3000 Attendees Janurary

9397 Nut Grower Magazine Farm Show
Western Agricultural Publishing Company
4974 E Clinton Way
Suite 123
Fresno, CA 93727-1520
559-261-0396
FAX: 559-252-7387
Phill Rhoads, Manager
Productions seminars, guest speakers, prizes and exhibits for nut growers. Containing 80 booths and exhibits.
1000 Attendees March

9398 Nut Grower Magazine Harvest Show
Western Agricultural Publishing Company
4974 E Clinton Way
Suite 123
Fresno, CA 93727-1520
559-261-0396
FAX: 559-252-7387
Phill Rhoads, Manager
Productions seminars, guest speakers, prizes and exhibits for nut growers. Containing 80 booths and exhibits.
1000 Attendees November

9399 OFPA Annual Convention
Ozark Food Processors Association
2650 N Young Avenue
Fayetteville, AR 72704
479-575-4607
FAX: 479-575-2165
ewells@allencanning.com
www.uark.edu/depts/ifse/ofpa
Earl Wells, Convention Committee Chairman
Keynote speakers, informative sessions, exhibits, food samples and much more.
$50.00
March

9400 Oklahoma Restaurant Convention & Expo
Oklahoma Restaurant Association
3800 N Portland Avenue
Oklahoma City, OK 73112-2948
405-942-8181
FAX: 405-942-0541 800-375-8181
Lori@okrestaurants.com
www.okrestaurants.com
Lori Culver, Convention Manager
Annual show of 450 manufacturers, suppliers and distributors. Exhibits of providers of food service and hospitality products, services and equipment. Held at the Myriad Convention Center in Oklahoma City, Oklahoma.
9M Attendees April Founded: 1938

9401 PACK International Expo
Packaging Machinery Manufacturers Institute
4350 N Fairfax Drive
Suite 600
Arlington, VA 22203
703-243-8555
FAX: 703-243-8556
expo@pmmi.org
www.pei2006.packexpo.com
Jim Pittas, Trade Show VP
Dinah Sprouse, Trade Show Operations Director
Kim Beaulieu, Exhibitor Services Manager
Browse more than 2,000 packaging and processing exhibitors covering virtually the entire packaging supply chain. Network with others in the industry, attend specialized education sessions led by industry experts and evaluate the latest advances while experiencing hands on demonstrations of the latest technologies in the industry. *$50.00*
1600 Attendees Oct-Nov

9402 PACex International
Packaging, Food Process and Logistics Exhibition
2255 Sheppard Avenue E
Suite E330
Toronto Ontario M2J-4YI
416-490-7860
FAX: 416-490-7844
info@pacexinternational.com
www.pacexinternational.com
Maria Tavares, Expositions Manager
15000 Attendees September-October

9403 PLMA Trade Show
Private Label Manufacturers Association
369 Lexington Avenue
New York, NY 10017-6506
212-972-3131
FAX: 212-983-1382
info@plma.com www.plma.com
Brian Sharoff, President
A show that is devoted entirely to store brands for manufacturers, retailers, wholesalers, brokers and trade suppliers.
10000 Attendees Nov 12-14 Founded: 1979

9404 PMA Foodservice Conference & Exposition
Produce Marketing Association
1500 Casho Mill Road
PO Box 6036
Newark, DE 19711-3547
302-738-7100
FAX: 302-731-2409
showmanagement@pma.com
www.pma.com
Jamie Hillegas, Show Manager
Susan Eller, Trade Show Planner

Join the who's-who of chefs, menu developers, restaurant operators, grower-shippers, distributors and foodservice suppliers to see and sample the newest products and services, learn about the latest consumer trends and tastes, see old colleagues or make new contacts. *$895.00*

July 2006/Fees Vary Founded: 1981

9405 PMA Fresh Summit International Convention & Exposition

Produce Marketing Association
1500 Casho Mill Road
PO Box 6036
Newark, DE 19711-3547
302-387-7100
FAX: 302-731-2409
showmanagement@pma.com
www.pma.com/freshsummit

Don Harris, Summit Chairman
Jamie Hillegas, Show Manager
Susan Eller, Trade Show Planner
Sheli Parlier, Exhibits Sales Manager
Bryan Silbermann, President

An event that attracts buyers and suppliers from the produce and floral industries; from the retail and foodservice channels and from more than 70 counties. *$775.00*

17000 Attendees Oct 20-24/Members Fee

9406 PTNPA Annual Convention

Peanut & Tree Nut Processors Association
PO Box 59811
Potomac, MD 20859-9811
301-365-2521
FAX: 301-365-7705
ptnpa@mindspring.com
www.ptnpa.org

Russ Barker, President

General meeting sessions, keynote speakers, exhibitors from the industry.

400 Attendees January 13-17, 2007
Mailing list available for rent

9407 Pan-American International Livestock Exposition

State Fair of Texas
PO Box 150009
Dallas, TX 75315-0009
214-565-9931
FAX: 214-421-8792
livestock@greatstatefair.com
www.bigtex.com

Benny Clark, Director

Annual show and exhibits of livestock, livestock equipment, agricultural technology and consumer products.

3.5M Attendees September/October

9408 Pickle Packers International Pickle Fair

1620 i St Nw
Ste 925
Washington, DC 20006-4035
202-312-2859
FAX: 630-584-0759 staff@ppii.org

Richard Hentschell, Executive VP

Fifty booths, seminars and programs held in odd numbered years.

300+ Attendees October

9409 Prairie Farmer Farm Progress Show

Farm Progress Companies
1301 E Mound Road
Decatur, IL 62526-9394
217-877-9070
FAX: 217-877-9695

Mike Wilson, Editor
Jerry Lucht, Advertising
Sherry Stout, Manager

One of the largest farm shows in the country.

9410 Private Label Manufacturers Association Trade Show

369 Lexington Avenue
3rd Floor
New York, NY 10017
212-972-3131
FAX: 212-983-1382 www.plma.com

Brian Sharoff, President

A private label trade show.

November

9411 Produce Marketing Association

1500 Casho Mill Road
PO Box 6036
Newark, DE 19711-3547
302-738-7100
FAX: 302-731-2409
bsilbermann@mail.pma.com
www.pma.com

Bryan Silbermann, President
Dan Henderaon, Marketing

Largest convention and exposition for the fresh fruit, vegetable and floral industries. More than 12,000 people and 1,500 booths.

12M Attendees October

9412 Productivity Conference and Distribution/ Transportation Exposition

Food Distributors International
201 Park Washington Court
Falls Church, VA 22046-4519
703-532-9400
FAX: 703-538-4673

Michael McCarthy, Director/Education

A conference exhibiting services and supplies geared toward the grocery industry. Containing 200 booths and 200 exhibits.

2400 Attendees October

9413 R&DA Annual Spring & Fall Meeting and Exhibition

R&D Associates
16607 Blanco Road
Suite 305
San Antonio, TX 78232-1940
210-682-4302
FAX: 830-493-8036
jfagan@militaryfood.org

Jim Fagan, Meeting Coordinator

Hear presentations by key officials, network with decision makers, get updates on key issues and gain a competitive edge within the industry. *$999.99*

300 Attendees Apr/Oct/Non-Members:$1099

9414 RFA Annual Conference & Exhibition

Refrigerated Foods Association
2971 Flowers Road S
Suite 266
Atlanta, GA 30341-5403
770-452-0660
FAX: 770-455-3879
info@refrigeratedfoods.org
www.refrigeratedfoods.org

Terry Dougherty, Executive Director

Suppliers displaying the latest offerings in equipment, packaging, ingredients and services for the industry. A great way to network and gain important new information affecting the industry, including technical innovations, sales and marketing tips, consumer trends, distribution solutions, new product and packaging development and food safety issues.

April, 2007

9415 Retail Confectioners International Annual Convention and Exposition

Retail Confectioners International
1807 Glenview Road
Suite 204
Glenview, IL 60025-2968
847-724-6120
FAX: 847-724-2719

Van Billington, Director
Michelle May, Contact

Annual exhibition offering exhibits of confectionery equipment, supplies, finished products and packaging materials.

1.5M Attendees Annual

9416 SANA/USB Annual Soy Symposium

Soyfoods Association of North America
1001 Connecticut Avenue NW
Suite 1120
Washington, DC 20036
202-659-3520

info@soyfoods.org
www.soyfoods.org

Nancy Chapman, Executive Director
Anne Chambers, Membership Coordinator

Co-sponsored with United Soybean Board, see the latest innovative designs and products from industry representatives. *$795.00*

Apr/Non-Members:$995 Founded: 1978

9417 SBS Annual Conference & Exhibition

Society for Biomolecular Sciences
36 Tamarack Avenue
Suite 348
Danbury, CT 06811
203-788-8828
FAX: 203-748-7557
email@sbsonline.org
www.sbsonline.org

Agnes Amos, Exhibitions/Meetings Director
Marietta Manoni, Exhibitions/Meetings Manager

This event brings together leaders in the pharmaceutical, biotech and agrochemical industries from around the world. Highlighting the impact of screening and technology applications on drug discovery. *$1265.00*

Sept/Non-Members $1,445 Founded: 1995

9418 SCAA Annual Conference & Exhibition

Specialty Coffee Association of America
330 Golden Shore
Suite 50
Long Beach, CA 90802
562-624-4100
FAX: 562-624-4101
coffee@scaa.org www.scaa.org

Ted Lingle, Executive Director
Scott Welker, Administrative Director

The country's premier coffee event, attracting coffee professionals from more than 40 countries. Attendees include coffee producers, exporters and importers, roasters, manufacturers, brew masters, and consumer enthusiasts. *$485.00*

8000 Attendees April/Non-Members:$585
Founded: 1982

9419 SCST Annual Meeting
Society of Commerical Seed Technologists

101 E State Street
Suite 214
Ithaca, NY 14850
607-256-3313
FAX: 607-256-3313
scst@twcny.rr.com
www.seedtechnology.net

Anita Hall, Executive Director

A joint meeting with the Association of Official Seed Analysts and the Association of Official Seed Certifying Agencies. Workshops, Exhibits, speakers and more regarding the seed industry.
June Founded: 1922

9420 SEAFWA Annual Convention
Southeast Association of Fish & Wildlife Agencies
8005 Freshwater Farms Road
Tallahassee, FL 32309-9009
850-893-1204
FAX: 850-893-6204
SEAFWA2006@dgif.virginia.gov
www.seafwa2006.org/www.seafwa.org

Robert M Brantly, Executive Secretary
Dianne Waller, Conference Coordinator

Providing a forum for presentation of information and exchange of ideas regarding the management and protection of fish and wildlife resources throughout the nation but emphasis on the southeast.
Oct/Nov Founded: 1947

9421 SNAXPO: Snack Food Association
1600 Wilson Blvd
Ste 650
Arlington, VA 22209-2510
703-836-4500
FAX: 703-836-8262 800-628-1334
sfa@sfa.org www.sfa.org

Judi Barth, VP Marketing
Ann Wilkes, VP Communications

2000 Attendees February/March Founded: 1938

9422 School Nutrition Association Annual National Conference
School Nutrition Association
700 S Washington Street
Suite 300
Alexandria, VA 22314
703-739-3900
FAX: 703-739-3915 800-877-8822
ANC2006@schoolnutrition.org
www.schoolnutrition.org

Barb Dunlavey CMP, Director Meetings/Exhibits
Barbara Belmont, Executive Director

Learn, grow and exchange ideas with others committed to the healthful feeding of our children. With over 400 exhibitors and more than 90 quality education sessions, ANC gives you the opportunity to learn about the top trends and issues in school nutrition.
July/Fee $259-$700 55,000 names

9423 Southern Convenience Store & Petroleum Show
GA Ass'n of Convenience Stores/Petroleum Retailers
PO Box 855
Snellville, GA 30078
770-736-9723
FAX: 770-736-9725 877-294-1885
jtudor@aol.com www.gacs.com

Jim Tudor, President

Contains 250 exhibits.
2000 Attendees October

9424 Southwest Foodservice Exposition
Texas Restaurant Association
PO Box 1429
Austin, TX 78767
512-472-8990
FAX: 512-472-2777
31000 Attendees

9425 Special Event
Special Event Corporation
PO Box 8987
Malibu, CA 90265-8987
310-317-4522
FAX: 310-317-9644
4300 Attendees

9426 Sugar Association Annual Meeting
1101 15th Street NW
Suite 600
Washington, DC 20005-5076
202-785-1122
FAX: 202-785-5019 www.sugar.org

Andrew Briscoe, President/CEO
Evelyn Brewster, Contact

9427 Sunbelt Agricultural Exposition
PO Box 28
Tifton, GA 31793-0028
229-985-1968
FAX: 229-387-7503
sunexpo@surfsouth.com

Dr. Edward White, Director

The latest agricultural technology in products and equipment plus harvesting and tillage demonstrations in the field. Largest farm show in North America. 4,000 booths.
October

9428 Supermarket Industry Convention and Educational Exposition
Food Marketing Institute
800 Connecticut Avenue NW
Washington, DC 20006
202-220-0600
FAX: 202-429-4519
fmi@fmi.org www.fmi.org

Brian Tully, Show Manager
Matt Olmsted, Consumer Goods Exhibiting
Allyson Samuel, Technolgy/Equip/Packaging Exhibit
Carrie Anderson, Attending

Features over 1,500 exhibitors, over 30 educational workshops and unique pavilions as well as the presentation of the Food Marketing Institute's annual state of the industry research. Attended by a worldwide audience of professionals with an interest in the food distribution industry from CEOs through store level management.
36000 Attendees May

9429 SupplySide East
Virgo Publishing
3300 N Central Avenue, Suite 300
Phoenix, AZ 85012
480-990-1101
FAX: 480-281-6744 800-454-5760
asharman@vpico.com
www.supplysideshow.com

Dana Hicks, Show Manager

Tradeshow that brings global dietary supplement, food and personal care companies together with healthy and innovative ingredient suppliers. Meadowlands Exposition Center, Secaucus, NJ. More than 340 booths.
3600 Attendees April-May 2007 Founded: 1998
Mailing list available for rent 10000+ names $var per M.

9430 SupplySide West
Virgo Publishing
3300 N Central Avenue, Suite 300
Phoenix, AZ 85012
480-990-1101
FAX: 480-281-6744 800-454-5760
asharman@vpico.com
www.supplysideshow.com

Dana Hicks, Show Manager

Tradeshow that brings global dietary supplement, food and personal care companies together with healthy and innovative ingredient supplier. More than 850 booths.
6000 Attendees October Founded: 1997
Mailing list available for rent 10000 names $var per M.

9431 Top-to-Top Conference
Association of Sales & Marketing Companies
1010 Wisconsin Avenue NW
#900
Washington, DC 20007
202-337-9351
FAX: 202-337-4508 info@asmc.org

Mark Baum, President
Karen Connell, Executive VP
Rick Abraham, VP/COO Foodservice
Jamie DeSimone, Director Marketing/Member Services

February

9432 Tortilla Industry Annual Convention and Trade Exposition
Tortilla Industry Association
8201 Greensboro Drive
Suite 300
McLean, VA 22102
703-610-9036
FAX: 703-610-9005
info@tortilla-info.com
www.tortilla-info.com

Roberto Quinones, Executive Director

A growing event for tortilla producers and suppliers that provides the only annual trade show featuring materials, equipment, and services exclusively for the Tortilla industry, plus business lectures to assist in improving your business and personal knowledge.
900 Attendees September

9433 Tree Fruit Expo
Western Agricultural Publishing Company

4974 E Clinton Way
Suite 123
Fresno, CA 93727-1520
559-261-0396
FAX: 559-252-7387

Phill Rhoads, Manager

Productions seminars, dessert contest, guest speakers, prizes and exhibits for tree fruit growers. Containing 80 booths and exhibits.
1000 Attendees October

9434 UP Show
Minneapolis Convention Center
305 E Roselawn
Saint Paul, MN 55117
651-778-2400
FAX: 651-778-2424
susan@hospitalitymn.com
www.upshowonline.com

Susan Larson, Trade Show Development Director

8000 Attendees February Founded: 1958

9435 US Apple Association Annual Apple Crop Outlook & Marketing Conference
8233 Old Courthouse Road
Suite 200
Vienna, VA 22182
703-442-8850
FAX: 703-790-0845
sschaffer@usapple.org
www.usapple.org

Shannon Schaffer, Membership/Communications Manager
Nancy Foster, Manager

Provides up to the minute apple market analysis and premier networking opportunities. *$395.00*

300+ Attendees April/Non-Members:$595 Founded: 1970

9436 US Meat Export Federation
1050 17th Street
Suite 2200
Denver, CO 80265-2077
303-623-6328
FAX: 303-623-0297
info@usmef.org www.usmef.org

Jackie Boubin, Show Manager
Phil Seng, President

A convention of meat packers, grain, cattle and hog producers, trade officials and agribusiness and a trade show offering exhibits of beef, pork, veal, lamb products and more for foreign buyers. Trade show in May, convention in November.

300 Attendees

9437 Unified Wine and Grape Symposium
PO Box 1855
Davis, CA 95617-1855
530-753-3142
FAX: 530-753-3318

Lyndie Boulton

Over five hundred booths displaying products and technology for the wine and grape industry.

January

9438 Unipro Food Service Companies Association
Unipro Food Service
PO Box 724945
Atlanta, GA 31139-1945
770-952-0871
FAX: 770-952-0872

Donna Campbell, Show Manager
Roger Toomey, Chief Executive Officer

250 tables.

1.3M Attendees

9439 United Produce Show
United Fresh Fruit & Vegetable Association
1901 Pennsylvania Avenue NW
Suite 1100
Washington, DC 20006
202-624-4989
FAX: 202-303-3433 www.uffva.org

Mark Lemke, Convention Co-Chair
Mark Hilton, Convention Co-Chair

Access to the best and newest products from the entire retail supply continuum, make new contacts, learn what your competition is bringing to the table and much more.

30000 Attendees May

9440 Upper Midwest Hospitality Restaurant & Lodging Show
Corcoran Expositions
33 N Dearborn Street
Suite 505
Chicago, IL 60602
312-541-0567
FAX: 312-541-0573

33000 Attendees

9441 WFLO/IARW Annual Convention & Trade Show
World Food Logistics Organization
1500 King Street
Suite 201
Alexandria, VA 22314
703-373-4300
FAX: 707-373-4301
mkalaski@iarw.org www.wflo.org

Megan Kalaski, Trade Show Coordinator
Lorien Onderdonk, Member Services Coordinator

offers a singular opportunity to present product and service information to the largest concentration of public refrigerated warehouse executives in the world.

Annual/April 21-26, 2007

9442 WSSA Annual Meeting
Weed Science Society of America
PO Box 7050
Lawrence, KS 66044
785-429-9622
FAX: 785-843-1274 800-627-0629
vblanton@allenpress.com
www.wssa.net

Rhonda Green, Registration Coordinator

Usually held during the first full week of February in the United States or Canada. These Meetings provide a venue for the exchange of research and educational ideas and for discussion and activity on society business.

1M Attendees February Founded: 1956

9443 WSWA Annual Convention
Wine and Spirits Wholesalers of America
805 15th Street NW
Suite 430
Washington, DC 20005
202-719-9792
FAX: 202-789-2405
Kari.Mazanec@wswa.org
www.wswa.org

Rae Ann Bevington, Convention Manager
Kari Mazanec, Exhibit Manager
Juanita Duggan, Chief Executive Officer

Get the latest information for wholesale wine distributors, exhibits and speakers from the industry.

April-May Founded: 1943

9444 Waldbaum International Food Nutrition Show
80 Town Line Road
Rocky Hill, CT 06067-1249
860-529-1416
FAX: 860-721-6258

John Masterson, Manager

A wide variety of new and existing food products and services. 225 booths.

25M Attendees March

9445 Walnut Council Annual Meeting
Walnut Council
Wright Forestry Center
1011 N 725 West
West Lafayette, IN 47906-9431
765-583-3501
FAX: 765-583-3512
jackson@purdue.edu
www.walnutcouncil.org

Liz Jackson, Exhibits Coordinator

Exhibits of equipment, supplies and services for walnut growing. *$135.00*

July/Non-Members:$160

9446 West Coast Seafood Show
Diversified Expositions
121 Free Street
Portland, ME 04112
207-842-5500
FAX: 207-842-5505
food@divcom.com
www.westcoastseafood.com

Karen Butland, Show Manager
Brian Perkins, Executive Director

November, 2002

9447 Western Fairs Association Annual Trade Show
Western Fairs Association
1776 Tribute Road
Suite 210
Sacramento, CA 95815-4495
916-927-3100
FAX: 916-927-6397
sarahr@fairsnet.org
www.westernfairs.org

Sarah Ruzanov, Trade Show Coordinator
Stephen J Chambers, Executive Director

Meet face to face with buyers from the Fair and Festival Industry across the Western United States. Acts, attractions, services, supplies, commericial exhibitors and more.

1000+ Attendees Annual/Jan 14-17

9448 Western Farm Show
Southwestern Association
638 W 39th Street
PO Box 419264-64141
Kansas City, MO 64111
816-561-5323
FAX: 816-561-1249 800-762-5616
donnah@swassn.com
www.westernfarmshow.com

Donna Haughenberry, Show Administrator

Annual show of 700 manufacturers, suppliers and distributors of equipment, supplies and services relating to the agricultural industry.

35M Attendees February

9449 Western Food Industry Exposition
555 Capitol Mall
Suite 235
Sacramento, CA 95814-4557

FAX: 703-876-0904
cga@cmgexpo.com

Keith Biersner, Account Executive

Retailers from 13 western states and suppliers from around the world. Relevant education sessions, vibrant exhibits and excellent social events are all designed to create the best form to enhance your companies bottom line. 400 booths.

3500 Attendees October Founded: 1998

9450 **Western Food Service and Hospitality Expo**
California Restaurant Association
383 Main Avenue
PO Box 6059
Norwalk, CT 06851
203-840-5612
FAX: 203-840-9612 800-840-5612
comments@westernfoodexpo.com
www.westernfoodexpo.com
Chris Tatulli, Sales Manager
Steve Kalman, Industry VP
Showcases food products, food service equipment and allied services for the restaurant, food service and hospitality industries, as well as gourmet and prepared foods. Located on the West Coast, the show alternates annually between the Moscone Center in San Francisco and the LA Convention Center.
20M Attendees August 20,000 names $140 per M.

9451 **Western Restaurant Show**
California Restaurant Association
1011 10th St
Sacramento, CA 95814-3501
916-447-5793
FAX: 213-384-1723
A trade show of food service equipment, supplies and services. 2,000 booths.
35M Attendees August

9452 **Wine and Spirits Wholesalers of America**
805 15th Street NW
Suite 430
Washington, DC 20005
202-371-9792
FAX: 202-789-2405
wswa@wswa.org www.wswa.org
Juanita Duggan, President/CEO
Megan McIntire, Director Convention/Meetings
Karen Gravois, VP Public Relations/Communications
Suppliers of alcoholic beverages from around the world. 300 booths plus educational sessions.
3M Attendees April

9453 **Wineries Unlimited**
Vineyard & Winery Services
PO Box 231
Watkins Glen, NY 14891
607-535-7133
FAX: 607-535-2998 800-535-5670
Richard Leahy, Show Manager
Bob Mignarri, Program Trade Show Sales
2000 Attendees March

9454 **Wisconsin Restaurant Expo**
Wisconsin Restaurant Association
2801 Fish Hatchery Road
Madison, WI 53703-3197
608-270-9950
FAX: 608-270-9960 800-589-3211
dfaris@wirestaurant.org
www.wirestaurant.org
Dawn Renz-Faris, Exposition Director
Comprehensive foodservice trade show featuring hundreds of exhibits, free educational seminars and exciting floor show events.
10000 Attendees March Founded: 1933
Mailing list available for rent

9455 **World Conference & Exhibition on Oil Seed and Vegetable Oil Utilization**
American Oil Chemists Society
Po Box 3489
Champaign, IL 61826-3489
217-359-2344
FAX: 217-351-8091
general@aocs.org www.aocs.org
Sevim Erhan, Committee Chairperson
Aug 14-16 2006 Istanbul

9456 **World Dairy Expo**
3310 Latham
Madison, WI 53713
608-224-6455
FAX: 608-224-0300
wde@wdexpo.com
www.worlddairyexpo.com
Tom McKittrick, Manager
Lisa Behnke, Marketing Manager
65M Attendees October, Annually Founded: 1966

9457 **World Pork Exposition**
National Pork Producers Council
PO Box 10383
Des Moines, IA 50306-9960
515-788-8012
FAX: 847-838-1941
wrigleyj@nppc.org
www.worldpork.org
John Wrigley, General Manager
Alice Vinsand, Trade Show Manager
More than 450 companies show the newest technology, information, products and services for pork producers. Activities include breed shows and sales, business district, environmental education center, pork product showcase, big grill, pork 101, educational seminars and activities.
40000 Attendees June

9458 **World Wine Market**
775 E Blithedale Avenue
#370
Mill Valley, CA 94941
415-383-1226
FAX: 415-383-0858
sclarke@world-wine-market.com
www.world-wine-market.com
Stephanie Clarke, VP Sales/Marketing

9459 **World of Food and Fuel EXPO**
Tennessee Grocers Association
1838 Elm Hill Pike
Suite 136
Nashville, TN 37210-3726
615-889-0136
FAX: 615-889-2877 800-238-8742
tga@tngrocer.org www.tngrocer.org
Jarron Springer, President
Cyndi Randle, Exhibits Coordinator
8000 Attendees April

9460 **Worldwide Food Expo**
Dairy and Food Industries Supply Association
1451 Dolley Madison Boulevard
Mc Lean, VA 22101-3847
703-883-0515
FAX: 703-761-4334
info@iafis.org www.iafis.org
Liz Overstreet, Show Manager
Trade show and education forum for the food, dairy, beverage and technologically related industries, featuring equipment, services and ingredients that highlight new development and technologies in processing and packaging. 350,000 square feet.
October Founded: 1999

Directories & Databases

9461 **2006 Soya & Oilseed Bluebook**
Soyatech Inc
1369 State Hwy 102
Bar Harbor, ME 04609
207-288-4969
FAX: 207-288-5264 800-424-7692
subscribe@soyatech.com
www.soyatech.com
Provides the world with information on the processing industry that supports development and value creation along each step of the supply chain.

9462 **ACFSA Directory**
American Correctional Food Service Association
4248 Park Glen Road
Minneapolis, MN 55416-4758
952-928-4658
FAX: 952-929-1318
info@acfsa.org www.acfsa.org
Gloria Grove, Membership Coordinator
Hope Cook, Advertising Coordinator
Directory of ACFSA members and the services provided by vender members. *$5.00*
235 pages Annually
Circulation: 1,500 900 names $200 per M.
Printed in 4 colors on glossy stock

9463 **AFI Annual Convention**
Association of Food Industries
3301 Route 66
Suite 205, Building C
Neptune, NJ 07753
732-922-3008
FAX: 732-922-3590
bobbauer@afius.org www.afius.org
Bob Bauer, President
Keeping members abreast of critical issues affecting their businesses. It provides an opportunity to learn about current and future initiatives and regulations and meet and network with industry peers to exchange knowledge and insights.
2500 pages Annual

9464 **AGRICOLA**
US National Agricultural Library
10301 Baltimore Avenue
Room 13
Beltsville, MD 20705-2326
301-504-5755
FAX: 301-504-7473
Gary K McCone, Associate Director
A database containing more than 3.2 million citations to journal literature, government reports, proceedings, books, periodicals, theses, patents, audiovisuals, electronic information, and other materials related to agriculture and its allied sciences.

Bibliographic

9465 **ARI Network**
330 E Kilbourn Avenue
Suite 200
Milwaukee, WI 53202-3166
414-209-9100
FAX: 414-283-4357 800-558-9044
Jeff Joerres, VP Marketing
Lawrence Shindell, Owner
Offers current information on agricultural business, financial and weather information

as well as statistical information for farmers.
Numeric

9466 Ag Ed Network
ARI Network Services
330 E Kilbourn Avenue
Suite 200
Milwaukee, WI 53202-3166
414-209-9100
FAX: 414-283-4357 800-558-9044
Offers access to more than 1,500 educational agriculture lessons covering farm business management and farm production.
Full-text

9467 Agri Marketing: Marketing Services Guide Issue
Doane Agricultural Services
11701 Borman Drive
Suite 300
Saint Louis, MO 63146-4139
314-569-2700
FAX: 314-569-1083
info@agrimarketing.comn
www.agrimarketing.com
Bill Schuermann, Editorial Director/Publisher
Judy Knoll, Group Manager Sales/Services
Offers lists of top agricultural companies in the US, top agricultural advertisers and marketing services firms, as well as network programmers related to the agriculture industry. *$30.00*
Annual December Founded: 1969
Circulation: 8,700

9468 Agribusiness Worldwide International Buyer's Guide Issue
Keller International Publishing Corporation
150 Great Neck Road
Great Neck, NY 11021-3309
516-829-9722
FAX: 516-829-5414
Jerry Keller, President
A list of companies that supply, manufacture or distribute agricultural products and services. *$42.00*
Annual

9469 Agricultural Research Institute: Membership Directory
Agricultural Research Institute
9650 Rockville Pike
Bethesda, MD 20814-3998
301-530-7122
FAX: 301-530-7007 ari@nal.usda.gov
Richard A Herrett, Executive Director
One hundred and twenty-five member institutions; also lists study panels and committees interested in environmental issues, pest control, agricultural meteorology, biotechnology, food irradiation, agricultural policy, research and development, food safety, technology transfer and remote sensing. *$50.00*
Annual

9470 Airline, Ship & Catering: Onboard Service Buyer's Guide & Directory
International Publishing Company of America
664 La Villa Drive
Miami Springs, FL 33166-6095
305-887-1700
FAX: 305-885-1923
Offers information on over 6,000 airlines, railroads, ship lines and terminal restaurants. *$125.00*
Annual
Circulation: 6,000

9471 Almanac of Food Regulations and Statistical Information
Edward E Judge & Sons
PO Box 866
Westminster, MD 21158-0866
410-876-2052
FAX: 410-848-2034 800-729-5517
info@eejudge.com www.eejudge.com
Includes labeling law and FDA regulations, HACCP requirements for seafood, FDA current good manufacturing practice regulations, USDA canning regulations, frozen food handling code, FDA standards of identity, quality and fill of container, USDA quality grade standards, frozen fruit and vegetable pack statistics, agricultural statistics, and census of manufacturing. *$71.00*
824 pages Annual Founded: 1916 ISBN 1-880821-19-2
Circulation: 3,000

9472 American Butter Institute: Membership Directory
American Butter Institute
2101 Wilson Boulevard
Suite 400
Arlington, VA 22201
703-243-5630
FAX: 703-841-9328
AMiner@nmpf.org
www.butterinstitute.org
Cindy Cazallo, Editor
This directory offers a comprehensive list of over 35 processors, distributors and packagers of butter in the US and suppliers to the industry. *$250.00*
25 pages Annual

9473 American Fruit Grower
Meister Media Worldwide
37733 Euclid Avenue
Willoughby, OH 44094-5925
440-942-2000
FAX: 440-942-0662 800-572-7740
jwmonahan@meistermedia.com
www.americanfruitgrower.com
Joe Monahan, Group Publisher
Sue Stearns, Assistant Circulation Manager
JoAnne Mauer, Sales Assistant
Offers a list of manufacturers and distributors of equipment and supplies for the commercial fruit growing industry. *$19.95*
66 pages 10x Founded: 1880
Circulation: 35,849

9474 American Meat Science Association Directory of Members
American Meat Science Association
1111 N Dunlap Avenue
Savoy, IL 61874
217-356-5368
FAX: 217-398-4119
www.meatscience.org
Thomas Powell, Executive Director
Sharon Frick, Administrative Assistant
Offers information on over 900 persons that are engaged in meat research, extension and education in industry, government and other organizations. *$20.00*
230 pages Biennial

9475 American Red Angus: Breeders Directory
Red Angus Association of America
4201 N Interstate 35
Denton, TX 76207-3415
940-387-3502
FAX: 940-383-4036
info@redangus1.org
www.redangus.org
Ann Holsinger, Managing Editor
Judy Edwards, Manager
This directory is a list of over 1,800 breeders of Red Angus cattle.
Annual
Circulation: 8,000

9476 American Society of Consulting Arborists: Membership Directory
American Society of Consulting Arborists
15245 Shady Grove Road
Rockville, MD 20850-3222
301-947-0483
Beth Palys, Executive Director
About 270 persons specializing in the growth and care of urban shade and ornamental trees; includes expert witnesses and monetary appraisals.
Annual March

9477 American Spice Trade Association Membership Roster
American Spice Trade Association
2025 M Street NW
Washington, DC 20036
202-367-1127
FAX: 202-367-2127 www.astaspice.org
Cheryl Deem, Manager
Annual

9478 Association of Seafood Importers
Empress International
10 Harbor Park Drive
Port Washington, NY 11050-4681
516-621-5900
FAX: 516-621-8318 800-645-6244
Burt C Faure
Membership is comprised of seafood importers focusing on problems facing the industry.

9479 Automatic Merchandiser Blue Book Buyer's Guide Issue
Cygnus Publishing
1233 Janesville Avenue
Fort Atkinson, WI 53538
920-563-6388
FAX: 920-563-1701 800-547-7377
Thousands of suppliers are profiled that offer products, services and equipment to the merchandise vending, food service and office coffee service industries. *$35.00*
Annual

9480 Bakery Materials and Methods
Elsevier Science
655 Avenue of the Americas
New York, NY 10010-5107
212-989-5800
FAX: 212-633-3680
AR Daniel *$41.50*
Founded: 1978

9481 Bakery Production and Marketing Buyers Guide Issue
Delta Communications
11617 W Bluemound Road
Wauwatosa, WI 53226
414-774-7270
FAX: 414-777-7277
www.deltacommunications.com
delta@deltacommunications.com

Pat Reynolds, Editor

This publication offers a list of over 1,800 manufacturers of equipment, ingredients, and supplies for bakeries. Enteries offer company names, addresses, phones, faxes and name and title of contract.

9482 Bakery Production and Marketing Red Book Issue
Delta Communications
N6w23673 Bluemond Road
Waukesha, WI 53188
262-542-9111
FAX: 262-542-8820
delta@deltacommunications.com
www.deltacommunications.com
Offers a list of over 2,500 wholesale, multi-unit retail, grocery chain and co-op bakery companies and plants in the US and Canada that manufacture bread, cakes, cookies, crackers, pretzels, snack foods, and frozen bakery products. *$255.00*
Annual

9483 Baking Buyer Yearbook Issue
Sosland Publishing Company
4800 Main Street
Suite 100
Kansas City, MO 64112-2513
816-756-1000
FAX: 816-756-0494 www.sosland.com

Charles Sosland, President

Over 1,000 distributors and manufacturers of products and equipment for the baking industry are profiled in this comprehensive directory. *$75.00*
Annual

9484 Baking Industry Suppliers Association: Bakery Equipment Guide
Baking Industry Suppliers Association
7101 College Blvd
Ste 1505
Overland Park, KS 66210-2087
913-338-1300
FAX: 913-338-1327
office@bema.org www.bema.org

Richard I Hoskins III, Chairman
Dennis Gunnell, First VP

220 pages Founded: 1918

9485 Baking/Snack Directory and Buyer's Guide
Sosland Publishing Company
4800 Main Street
Suite 100
Kansas City, MO 64112-2513
816-756-1000
FAX: 816-756-0494 www.sosland.com

Charles Sosland, President

Wholesalers of bread and baked goods, as well as snacks and frozen dough are listed in this directory. *$90.00*
Annual
Circulation: 8,000

9486 Beef Sire Directory
American Breeders Service/Customer Service
6908 River Road
#459
De Forest, WI 53532-2430
608-837-9616
FAX: 608-846-6443
A directory listing beef cattle associations in the US and Canada.
Annual

9487 Beverage Digest Fact Book
Beverage Digest
2 Depot Plaza
Suite 101A
Bedford Hills, NY 10507
914-244-0700
FAX: 914-244-0774
order@beverage-digest.com
www.beverage-digest.com

John Sicher, Owner

This book is a complete portrait of the global non-alcoholic beverage business.

9488 Beverage Digest Soft Drink Atlas
Beverage Digest
2 Depot Plaza
Suite 101A
Bedford Hills, NY 10507
914-244-0700
FAX: 914-244-0774
order@beverage-digest.com
www.beverage-digest.com

John Sicher, Owner

Book of US maps related to soft drink bottler territories. This book offers a geographic portrait of the US carbonated beverage bottling business.

9489 Beverage Marketing Directory
Beverage Marketing Corporation
2670 Commercial Avenue
Mingo Junction, OH 43938
740-598-4133
FAX: 740-598-3977 800-332-6222

Andrew Standardi, Director Operations
Kathy Smurthwaite, Editor
Terry Welling, VP

Publication is available in Print Copy (Price-$1,095), PDF Format (Price-$1,995), CD-ROM Format (For pricing, call number listed for details or visit our website), and Online. *$1095.00*
1080 pages Annual $995 per M.

9490 Biological & Agricultural Index
HW Wilson Company
950 University Avenue
Bronx, NY 10452-4224
718-888-8405
FAX: 718-590-1617 800-367-6770
custserv@hwwilson.com
www.hwwilson.com
Provides fast access to core literature. In addition to citations to research and feature articles, users finding indexing of reports of symposia and conferences, and citations to current book reviews. Available on Web and disc.

9491 Blue Book Buyer's Guide
Food Processing Machinery Association
200 Dangerfield Road
Alexandria, VA 22314-2800
703-684-1080
FAX: 703-548-6563
info@fpmamail.com
www.foodprocessingmachinery.com

Donna Bolyard, Editor

A buyers guide offering information on over 500 member food and beverage industry firms. Entries are cross-referenced with both a product and commodity locator. *$50.00*
200 pages
Circulation: 30,000

9492 Blue Book: Fruit and Vegetable Credit and Marketing Service
Produce Reporter Company
845 E Geneva Road
Carol Stream, IL 60188-3520
630-668-3500
FAX: 630-668-0303
info@bluebookprco.com
www.bluebookprco.com

CJ Carr, President/CEO

A directory offering information on over 15,000 produce growers, wholesalers, shippers and retailers in the US. *$575.00*
1275 pages Semiannual Founded: 1901

9493 Bottled Water Market
MarketResearch.com
641 Avenue of the Americas
3rd Floor
New York, NY 10011
212-807-2629
FAX: 212-807-2676 800-298-6699
The report provides descriptions and coverage of market size and growth, market comppsition, leading marketers, the competitive situation, new product trends, advertising and promotion, and more. *$2750.00*
139 pages

9494 Brahman Journal: American Brahman Breeders Association Directory
American Brahman Breeders Association
3003 South Loop W
Suite 140
Houston, TX 77054
713-349-0854
FAX: 713-349-9795
abba@brahman.org www.braham.org

Chris Shivers, Executive Vice President
Jim Reeves, Executive Director

Annual issue offering information on over 1,000 member breeders. *$15.00*
30 pages Annual

9495 Brand Directory
Vance Publishing
10901 W 84th Terrace
Lenexa, KS 66214-1649
913-438-8700
FAX: 913-438-0695 800-255-5113

Darla Amstien, Managing Editor
Dan Woods, Editor

A composite of major fresh fruit and vegetable brands and suppliers. It is divided into three sections and contains 66 commodities. *$10.00*

9496 Brewers Digest: Buyers Guide and Brewery Directory
Ammark Publishing
4049 W Peterson Avenue
Chicago, IL 60646-6001

Lists all breweries in the Western Hemisphere, suppliers, associations and importers. *$30.00*

Annual
Circulation: 3,000

9497 Brewers Resource Directory
Association of Brewers
736 Pearl Street
Boulder, CO 80302
303-447-0816
FAX: 303-447-2825 888-822-6273
info@brewersassociation.org
www.beertown.org

Paul Gatza, Director
Ray Daniels, Editor
Charlie Papazian, President

Various categories of listees are included that have a direct relation to the beer and liquor industry.

Mailing list available for rent

9498 Brown Swiss Cattle Breeders' Association Directory
Brown Swiss Cattle Breeders' Association

800 Pleasant Street
Beloit, WI 53511-5456
608-365-4474
FAX: 608-365-5577
info@brownswissusa.com
www.brownswissusa.com

Adam Barbee, Editor
David Kendall, Manager

9499 CID Service
US Department of Agriculture
1400 Indepencence Avenue SW
Washington, DC 20250
202-690-7650

This database contains 467 categories of information prepared by the US Department of Agriculture and its agencies.
Full-text

9500 CRC Press
2000 NW Corporate Boulevard
Boca Raton, FL 33431
561-994-0555
FAX: 561-998-0876 800-272-7737
info@crcpress.com
www.crcpress.com

Eleanor Riemer, Publisher
Emmett Dages, Chief Executive Officer

Publisher in science, medicine, environmental science, forensic, engineering, business, technology, mathematics, and statistics. Our food science and nutrition books and our journal, Critical Reviews in Food and Nutrition, are well established and respected publications in the food science industry.

9501 CRIS/USDA Database
Current Research Information System
1400 Independence Avenue SW
Suite 2270
Washington, DC 20250
202-690-0119
FAX: 202-690-0634
cris@csrees.usda.gov
http://cris.csrees.usda.gov

Ellen A Terpstra, Chief Executive Officer

Offers over 35,000 ongoing and recently completed agricultural, food and nutrition and forestry research projects sponsored by the US Department of Agriculture.

9502 California League of Food Processors Annual Directory of Members
980 Ninth Street
Sacremento, CA 95814
916-444-9260
FAX: 916-444-2746
ed@clfp.org www.clfp.com

Robert Graf, President/CEO
Ed Yates, Senior VP
Nora Basrai, Meetings/Members Services

Contains listings of all members, including plant locations and products produced. Over 800 industry leaders are listed.
200 pages Founded: 1905

9503 Candy Marketer: Candy, Snack and Tobacco Buyers' Guide
Stagnito Communications
155 Pfingster Road
Suite 205
Deerfield, IL 60015
847-205-5660
FAX: 847-205-5680

Linda Stagnito, President

A publication that includes a list of suppliers to the confectionery, snack and tobacco products industries. Entries include company names, addresses, key personnel, warehouse locations and firms represented. *$25.00*
Annual

9504 Canned Food Pack Statistics
National Food Processors Association
13501 I Street NW
Suite 300
Washington, DC 20005
202-639-5900
FAX: 202-639-5932
Annual

9505 Chain Restaurant Operators Directory
Chain Store Guide
3922 Coconut Palm Drive
Tampa, FL 33616
813-276-6700
FAX: 813-627-6882 800-972-9202
info@csgis.com www.csgis.com

Arthur Sciarrotta, Senior Vice President
Chris Leedy, Advertising Sales

Discover more than 5,600 listings and more than 26,000 unique personnel within the Restaurant Chain, Foodservice Management, and Hotel/Motel Operator markets in the U.S. and Canada. Each company must have at least $1 million in annual sales either system wide or industry and have two or more units/accounts. *$335.00*
Annual

9506 Cheese Market News: Annual
Quarne Publishing
PO 628254
Middleton, WI 53562
608-831-6002
FAX: 608-831-1004
www.cheesemarketnews.com

Susan Quarne, Publisher

Comprehensive listings include the companies that manufacture the latest styles and varieties of cheese as well as the industry's key suppliers of cheese equipment, packaging equipment, materials and supplies and services. *$30.00*
Annual
Circulation: 3,000

9507 Citrus & Vegetable Magazine: Farm Equipment Directory Issue
Vance Publishing
10901 W 84th Terrace
Lenexa, KS 66214
913-438-8700
FAX: 913-438-0695
cvmscott@compuserve.com
www.vancepublishing.com
Offers information on a list of manufacturers of produce and citrus growing, handling, picking and packaging equipment.
$25.00
48 pages Annual Founded: 1938
Circulation: 12,000

9508 Coffee Anyone???
9616 Thunderbird Drive
Suite 215
San Ramon, CA 94583
925-829-4022
FAX: 925-829-4025 800-347-9687
coffee@coffee-anyone.com
www.coffee-anyone.com
This database contains descriptions of gourmet, regular, decaffenated and flavored coffees, including a chart summarizing the strength and taste of each coffee.

9509 Coffee, Sugar and Cocoa Exchange Guide
Commerce Clearing House
2700 Lake Cook Road
Riverwoods, IL 60015-3888
847-267-7000
FAX: 847-779-1535

Karen Clanton, Managing Editor

Offers information on member and member organizations of the Exchange.
$240.00
170 pages Monthly

9510 Commercial Food Equipment Service Association Directory
Commercial Food Equipment Service Association
2211 W Meadowview Road
Suite 20
Greensboro, NC 27407
336-346-4700
FAX: 336-346-4745
info@cfesa.com www.cfesa.com
Independent food service companies that repair commercial food equipment.
Annual

9511 Complete Directory of Concessions & Equipment
Sutton Family Communications & Publishing Company
155 Sutton Lane
Fordsville, KY 42343
270-740-0870

jlsutton@apex.net
www.fleamarketeer.net

Theresa Sutton, Editor
Lee Sutton, General Manager

Printout from database of wholesalers, manufacturers, distributors, importers and close-out houses; updated daily to guarantee the most current and up-to-date sources available. *$27.90*
100+ pages

9512 Complete Directory of Food Products
Sutton Family Communications & Publishing Company
155 Sutton Lane
Fordsville, KY 42343
270-740-0870

jlsutton@apex.net
www.fleamarketeer.net

Theresa Sutton, Editor
Lee Sutton, General Manager

Printout from database of wholesalers, manufacturers, distributors, importers and close-out houses. Database is updated daily to guarantee the most current and up-to-date sources available. *$27.90*
100+ pages

9513 Consumer's Guide to Fruits & Vegetables & Other Farm Fresh Products
Missouri Cooperative Extension Service
PO Box 29
Jefferson City, MO 65102-0029
573-681-5301
FAX: 573-635-2314

David N Sasseville, Editor

A directory covering over 400 fruit and vegetable farm markets in Missouri.
124 pages Annual

9514 Contemporary World Issues: Agricultural Crisis in America
ABC-CLIO
PO Box 1911
Santa Barbara, CA 93116-1911
805-705-9339
FAX: 805-685-9685 800-422-2546

Barbara McEwan, Editor

List of agencies and organizations in the US concerned with agricultural issues. *$39.50*

9515 Convenience Store News: Buyers Guide Issue
BMT Commodity Corporation
530 5th Avenue
24th Floor
New York, NY 10036-5101
212-302-4200
FAX: 212-302-0007 bmt@bmtny.com

Maureen Azzato, Editor

A directory offering information on firms and organizations that supply the convenience store industry. *$95.00*
Annual

9516 Cookies Market
MarketResearch.com
641 Avenue of the Americas
3rd Floor
New York, NY 10011
212-807-2629
FAX: 212-807-2676 800-298-6699
This report uncovers trends in its in-depth investigation of US retail sales of packaged and fresh-baked cookies. The analysis covers packaged cookie retail sales by distribution channel, marketer, and product line. The leading marketers are profiled in order to review growth-and-profit-oriented strategies. The data information is analyzed in order for users to uncover growing product lines, target key demographics, pinpoint distribution channel sales opportunities, and profitable strategies. *$2250.00*
169 pages

9517 Corn Annual
Corn Refiners Association
1701 Pennsylvania Avenue
Suite 950
Washington, DC 20006
202-331-1634
FAX: 202-331-2054

Audrae Erickson, President

Report featuring articles on the state of the industry. Includes statistical report on corn shipments, supply and consumption in the US and abroad.

Circulation: 8,000

9518 Crop Protection Reference
C&P Press
302 5th Avenue
5th Floor
New York, NY 10001
212-326-6760
FAX: 646-733-6010
cpp@cppress.com www.cppress.com
A single comprehensive source of up-to-date label information of crop protection products marketed in the US by basic manufacturers and formulators. Extensive product indexing helps to locate products by brand name, manufacturer, crop site, mode of action, disease, insect, week, product category, common name and tank mix.
$170.00
Annual

9519 Culinary Collection Directory
International Association/Culinary Professionals
304 W Liberty Street
Suite 201
Louisville, KY 40202
502-587-7953
FAX: 502-589-3602 800-928-4227
iacp@hqtrs.com www.iacp.com

Kerry Edwards, Sr Member Services Representative
Trina Gribbins, Manager

Teachers, cooking school owners, caterers, writers, chefs, media cooking personalities, editors, publishers, food stylists, food photographers, restauranteurs, leaders of major food corporations and vintners. Literally a who's who of the food world.

9520 Dairy Foods Market Guide
Delta Communications
455 N Cityfront Plaza Drive
Chicago, IL 60611-5503
312-836-2000
FAX: 312-222-2026
A guide including a list of 1,600 manufacturers of dairy processing equipment and over 900 distributors of dairy processing equipment. *$99.00*
Annual

9521 Directory & Products Guide
Vineyard & Winery Services
PO Box 2358
Windsor, CA 95492
707-836-6820
FAX: 707-836-6825 800-535-5670

Jennifer Merietti, Sales/Marketing Manager

A must have reference book that belongs on the desk of every wine professional. Whether it's tracking down a particular vendor, shopping for the best deal on oak barrels or searching for out-of-state winery contacts, the DPG is a powerhouse of information. Over 2,300 supplier listings and 2,700 winery/vineyard listings, it is a reliable resource that saves time and money.
$95.00
450+ pages Annually

9522 Directory of AFFI Member Companies
American Frozen Food Institute
2000 Corporate Road
Suite 1000
McLean, VA 22102-7844
703-821-0770
FAX: 703-821-1350
info@affi.com
www.affi.com/www.healthyfood.org

Leslie G Sarasin, President/CEO
Robert L Garfield, Senior VP Public Policy *$100.00*
Annual
Circulation: 5000

9523 Directory of American Agriculture
Agricultural Resources & Communications

301 Broadway
Belvue, KS 66407
785-456-9705
FAX: 785-456-1654
chris@agresources.com
www.agresources.com

Christina Wilson, President

This directory lists over 7,000 state and national associations involved in providing products and services related to food and fiber industries, in 27 categories. There are categorical indexes as well. Includes guide to Washington, DC offices, USDA listings, and guide to ag commodity commissions. Available on CD for $99. *$64.95*
350 pages Founded: 1988
Printed in on matte stock : CD

9524 Directory of Convenience Stores
Trade Dimensions
45 Danbury Road
Wilton, CT 06897-4445
203-563-3000
FAX: 860-563-3131
info@tradedimensions.com
www.tradedimensions.com

Jennifer Gillbert, Editor
Lynda Guticulez, Managing Editor

The directory comprises nearly 1,500 detailed profiles on the companies you need to do business with. Extensive dependable information on the grocery industry's most volatile segment. *$245.00*
Annual

9525 Directory of Custom Food Processors and Formulators
Delphi Marketing Services
400 E 89th Street
Apartment 2J
New York, NY 10128-6728

Covers formulators and processors of custom food products. *$260.00*
Annual

9526 Directory of Food Information Sources
Food Information Service Center
21050 SW 93rd Lane Road
Dunnellon, FL 34431-5802
352-489-8919
FAX: 352-489-8919
FCSGROUP@ARTDC.net

James Mixon, Editor/Author
Bob Jacobs, Contact *$75.00*

575 pages Bi-Annual Founded: 1985
35000 names
Printed in 1 color on matte stock

9527 Directory of State Departments of Agriculture
US Department of Agriculture
14 Independence
Room 3964
Washington, DC 20250-0001
202-690-7650

Offer valuable information on all the state departments of agriculture, including their officials.
73 pages Biennial

9528 Directory of the Canning, Freezing, Preserving Industries
Edward E Judge & Sons
PO Box 866
Westminster, MD 21158-0866
410-876-2052
FAX: 410-848-2034
info@eejudge.com www.eejudge.com

Daniel P Judge, Publisher
This directory offers extensive company profiles including over 10,000 managers, over 3,000 North American Food plants that are involved in canning, freezing and preserving fruits, vegetables, dinners, specialties and more. Published in standard edition, 768 pages, and special deluxe edition 1,408 pages. *$175.00*
768 pages Biennial Founded: 1966 ISBN 1-880821-20-6
Computerized version available: CD-Rom

9529 Diversified Business Communications
121 Free Street
Portland, ME 04101
207-842-5500
FAX: 207-842-5505
www.divbusiness.com
Nancy Hasselback, Chief Executive Officer
A producer of international trade expositions for the seafood and commercial marine industries.

9530 Eastern Dairy, Deli, Bakery Association Membership Directory

411 Route 17 S
Hasbrouck Heights, NJ 07604
201-288-5454
FAX: 201-288-5422
eppa@eppainc.org www.eppainc.org
John R Fugazzie, Editor
This guide offers information on members in the areas of retailers, brokers, manufacturers and distributors of dairy, deli, seafood, meat, and bakery products located in New York metropolitan area.
35 pages Annual

9531 Electronic Pesticide Reference: EPR II
C&P Press
212-326-6760
FAX: 646-733-6010
cpp@cppress.com www.cppress.com
Complete electronic reference to our 1,500 crop protection products; a full range of product information: full text labels and supplemental labels, full text MSDS's, product summaries, list of labeled tank mixes, worker protection information, DOT shipping information, SARA Title III reporting information. Search by brand name, manufacturer, common name crop, plant, site, weed, disease, insect plus much more. All versions of EPR II are provided on CD-ROM for windows.

9532 Food & Beverage Market Place
Grey House Publishing
185 Millerton Road
PO Box 860
Millerton, NY 12546
518-890-0526
FAX: 518-789-0545 800-562-2139
books@greyhouse.com
www.foodmp.com
Leslie Mackenzie, Publisher
Richard Gottlieb, Editor
This information packed three-volume set is the most powerful buying and marketing guide for the US food and beverage industry. Includes thousands of industry and transportation listings. *$595.00*
6500 pages Annual

9533 Food Channel Database
Noble Communications
500 N Michigan Avenue
Chicago, IL 60611-3764
312-670-4470
FAX: 312-670-7410
This database reports industry news and developments of interest to decision-makers in food processing, grocery, and c-store retailing distribution.

9534 Food Engineering Directory
Business News Publishing
3817 Timothy Lane
Bethlehem, PA 18020
610-317-6180
FAX: 610-317-0378 miskog@bnp.com
George Misko
Hardbound reference book listing of all food and beverage companies with 20 or more employees throughout the US. *$395.00*

9535 Food Master
BNP Media
2401 W Big Beaver Road
Suite 700
Troy, MI 48084
248-362-3700
FAX: 248-362-0317
kalbr@bnpmedia.com
www.foodmaster.com
Peter Havens, Group Publisher
Founded: 1978

9536 Food Processing Guide & Directory
555 W Pierce Road
Suite 301
Itasca, IL 60143
773-252-7891
FAX: 630-467-1108
Lily Modjeski, Sales Manager
Presents advertising opportunities that will generate quality sales leads, incerase market share, identify market opportunities and increase exposure through our website.

Annual

9537 Food Production Management: Advertisers Buyers Guide Issue
CTI Publications
2 Oakway Road
Timonium, MD 21093-4247
410-308-2080
FAX: 410-308-2079
books@ctipubs.com
www.ctipubs.com
W Randall Gerstmyer, Publisher *$15.00*

48 pages Annual Founded: 1878
Circulation: 5,000

9538 Food Service Industry
MarketResearch.com
641 Avenue of the Americas
3rd Floor
New York, NY 10011
212-807-2629
FAX: 212-807-2676 800-298-6699
The report analyzes sales and profit trends of full-service restaurants, limited-service restaurants, cafeterias, snack bars, in-plant contractors, caterers, mobile food services and drinking places. *$2250.00*
240 pages

9539 Food and Agricultural Export Directory
US Department of Agriculture
PO Box 2022
Washington, DC 20250-0001
202-690-7650
FAX: 202-512-2250
www.access.gpo.gov
Offers valuable information on federal and state agencies, trade associations and others willing to assist the US firms that wish to export food and agricultural products overseas.
100 pages Annual

9540 Food, Beverages & Tobacco in US Industrial Outlook
Superintendent of Documents
US Government Printing Office
Washington, DC 20402-0001

FAX: 202-512-2250
Contains industry reviews and forecasts; coverage includes bakery products. *$34.00*

Annual

9541 Food, Hunger, Agribusiness: A Directory of Resources
Third World Resources
218 E 21st Street
Oakland, CA 94606
510-533-7583
FAX: 510-533-0923
Offers information on organizations and publishers of books and other materials on food, hunger and agribusiness overseas. *$12.95*
160 pages

9542 FoodService Distributors Database

Chain Store Guide
3922 Coconut Palm Drive
Tampa, FL 33616-3506
813-276-6700
FAX: 813-627-6882 800-778-9794
info@csgis.com www.csgis.com
Chris Leedy, Advertising Sales
Shami Choon, Manager
Over 4,900 distributors of food, equipment and supplies to restaurants and institutions are reviewed in this directory for the food service industry. The names of more than

23,000 key executives are included, along with each company's distribution centers. *$335.00*
800 pages

9543 Foods ADLIBRA
Foods ADLIBRA Publications
9000 Plymouth Avenue N
Minneapolis, MN 55427-3870
763-764-4759
FAX: 763-764-3166
oxcon002@mailigenmills.com
Judith O'Connell, Editor
This database offers over 287,000 citations, with abstracts to journal literature on research and development in food technology and packaging. Seafood, food service, snacks and beverage monthly current awareness are also available. *$200.00*
Bibliographic

9544 Foodservice Yearbook International/Global Foodservice
150 Great Neck Road
Great Neck, NY 11021
516-829-9210
FAX: 516-829-5414
jryan@globalfoodservice.com

9545 Foreign Countries and Plants Certified to Export Meat and Poultry to the US
US Department of Agriculture
Food Safety & Inspection Services
Washington, DC 20250-0001
202-690-7650
800-535-4555
A comprehensive list of over 1,000 meat and poultry plants in foreign countries.
150 pages Annual

9546 Fortified Foods Market
MarketResearch.com
641 Avenue of the Americas
3rd Floor
New York, NY 10011
212-807-2629
FAX: 212-807-2676 800-298-6699
This new study examines the regulatory environment, analyzes the growth and product trends shaping the fortified foods market and inspects the changing retail picture. It also unveils the marketing and promotional strategies of major players such as Kellogg's, General Mills, PepsiCo, Coca-Cola, Novartis, Heinz and many others. Finally, the study takes a look at differences and commonalities among consumers of fortified cereals, breads, juice drinks, baby foods and snacks. *$2750.00*
234 pages

9547 Frozen Dinners and Entrees
Leading Edge Reports/Industry Reports
2171 Jericho Turnpike
Suite 200
Commack, NY 11725-2937
631-462-5454
FAX: 631-462-1842
bta@li.net
www.businesstrendanalysts.com
Charles J Ritchie, Executive VP
Donna Priani, Marketing Director
Linda Sherman, Production Manager
Jennifer Wichert, Research Director
A product-by-product analysis of the markets for frozen dinners and entrees, including traditional as well as low-calorie and health oriented products. *$1995.00*
170 pages Founded: 1996
Computerized version available: Disk

9548 Getaways for Gourmets in the Northeast
Wood Pond Press
365 Ridgewood Road
W Hartford, CT 06107-3517
860-521-0389
FAX: 860-313-0185
Directory of services and supplies to the industry. *$14.95*
514 pages

9549 Gold Book: AAMP
American Association of Meat Processors
One Meating Place
PO Box 269
Elizabethtown, PA 17022-0269
717-367-1168
FAX: 717-367-9096
aamp@aamp.com www.aamp.com
Nancy Matako, Publisher
Debbie Sinex, Editor
Consists of AAMP members, including: honorary members, associates, operators/wholesalers, home food service companies, suppliers, distributors, allied and affiliated state/regional/provincial associations. A powerful source for meat business buyers seeking products/services. *$300.00*
170 pages Every 2 Years
Circulation: 2,000

9550 Grain & Milling Annual
Sosland Publishing Company
4800 Main Street
Suite 100
Kansas City, MO 64112-2513
816-756-1000
FAX: 816-756-0494
web@sosland.com www.sosland.com
Offers a list of milling companies, mills, grain companies and cooperatives. *$90.00*
Annual
Circulation: 6,000

9551 Grain Journal
Country Journal Publishing Company
2490 N Water Street
Decatur, IL 62526-4251
217-877-9660
FAX: 217-877-6647 800-728-7511
mark@grainnet.com
www.grainnet.com
Mark Avery, Publisher
Ed Zdrojewski, Editor
Deb Coontz, Advertising Sales
Jeff Miller, Advertising Sales
Provides a list of over 700 equipment manufacturers, suppliers and system designers, as well as offering useful information on governmental agencies relevant to the grain industry. *$40.00*
254 pages Bi-Monthly Founded: 1972
Circulation: 13,000
Mailing list available for rent 10,000 names $600 per M.
Printed in 4 colors on glossy stock

9552 Great Lakes Vegetable Growers News
PO Box 128
Sparta, MI 49345-0128
616-887-9008
FAX: 616-887-2666
Barry Brand, Editor

9553 Guernsey Breeders' Journal: Convention Directory Issue
American Guernsey Association
7614 Slate Ridge Boulevard
Reynoldsburg, OH 43068-3126
614-864-2409
FAX: 614-864-5614
info@usguernsey.com
www.usguernsey.com
Seth Johnson, Manager
A convention directory offering a list of officers and national members of the American Guernsey Cattle Association. *$15.00*
Annual

9554 Guide to Poultry Associations
Poultry & Egg News
PO Box 1338
Gainesville, GA 30503-1338
770-536-2476
FAX: 770-532-4894
ptedit@mindspring.com
Randall Smalladod, Publisher
Chris Hill, Editor
This directory offers information on national, regional and state poultry associations. *$25.00*
24 pages Annual
Circulation: 11,500

9555 Health and Natural Foods Market
MarketResearch.com
641 Avenue of the Americas
3rd Floor
New York, NY 10011
212-807-2629
FAX: 212-807-2676 800-298-6699
The report covers six product categories: packaged groceries, bulk groceries, frozen, refrigerated, produce and other/miscellaneous. The major players in the market are profiled, including Gardenburger, Hain Food Group, Horizon Organic Dairy, Small Planet Foods and others. The report details which types of new products have been recently introduced and reports on consumer attitudes and behavior. *$2750.00*
289 pages

9556 Health and Natural Foods Market: Past Performance, Current Trends & More
Business Trend Analysts/Industry Reports
2171 Jericho Turnpike
Suite 200
Commack, NY 11725-2900
631-462-5454
FAX: 631-462-1842
sales@bta-ler.com
www.businesstrendanalysts.com
Charles J Ritchie, Executive VP
Vincent Seeno, Editor
Donna Priani, General Manager
Linda Holm, Production Manager
A statistical summary and analysis offering historical, current and projected sales data for the natural foods market. *$2195.00*
335 pages Founded: 1986
Computerized version available: Disk

9557 Herbal Green Pages
Herb Growing and Marketing Network
PO Box 245
Silver Spring, PA 17575-0245
FAX: 717-393-9261
herbworld@aol.com www.herbnet.com
Maureen Rogers, Editor

This annual guide offers information on 5,000 companies involved in herbal marketing and growing. *$25.00*
Annual
Printed in 1 color on matte stock

9558 High Volume Independent Restaurants Database
Chain Store Guide
3922 Coconut Palm Drive
Tampa, FL 33616-3506
813-276-6700
FAX: 813-627-6882 800-778-9794
info@csgis.com www.csgis.com
Chris Leedy, Advertising Sales
Shami Choon, Manager
Covers this growing niche through its nearly 5,900 listings featuring casual dining, family restaurants and fine dining establishments. Plus, access to over 15,000 key personnel names puts you in contact with key decision makers. *$335.00*
1,000 pages Annual

9559 Hort Expo Northwest
Mt Adams Publishing and Design
14161 Fort Road
White Swan, WA 98552-9786
509-948-2706
FAX: 509-848-3896 800-554-0860
hortexponw@aol.com
www.hortexponw.com
Vee Graves, Editor
Julie LaForge, Advertising Manager
Besides being mailed to it's family of subscribers it is also available complimentary at horticulture shows in the Northwest.
32 pages Annually Founded: 1989
Circulation: 11,000 10,200 names $200 per M.
Printed in 4 colors on glossy stock

9560 IFT's Classified Guide to Food Industry Services
Institute of Food Technologists
525 W Van Buren Street
Suite 1000
Chicago, IL 60607-3814
312-782-8424
FAX: 312-416-7921
info@ift.org www.ift.org
Barbara Byrd-Keenan, Publisher
Roy G Hlavacek, VP Communications
Offers information on over 180 independent food testing laboratories, government agencies, and educational institutions pertaining to the food industry. *$15.00*
70 pages Annual
Circulation: 23,000

9561 Ice Cream and Frozen Desserts
Business Trend Analysts/Industry Reports
2171 Jericho Turnpike
Commack, NY 11725-2937
631-462-5454
FAX: 631-462-1842
bta@li.net
www.businesstrendanalysts.com
Charles J Ritchie, Executive VP
Donna Priani, Marketing Director
Linda Sherman, Production Manager
Jennifer Wichert, Research Director
A survey of the ice cream and frozen dessert market, including low-calorie, low-fat and gourmet ice creams and frozen desserts. *$ 1295.00*
Founded: 2000
Computerized version available: Disk

9562 Illinois Beverage Guide
Indiana Beverage Life, Inc
7379 Fox Hollow Ridge
PO Box 5067
Zionsville, IN 46077
317-733-0527
FAX: 317-733-0528
ibjzstew@indy.rr.com
Stewart Baxter, Publisher/Editor

9563 Impact International Directory: Leading Spirits, Wine and Beer Companies
M Shanken Communications
387 Park Avenue S
8th Floor
New York, NY 10016-8872
212-684-4224
FAX: 212-684-5424
Marvin R Shanken, Editor
A directory offering information on the major players of the alcoholic beverage industry. *$295.00*

9564 Impact Yearbook: Directory of the US Wine, Spirits & Beer Industry
M Shanken Communications
387 Park Avenue S
8th Floor
New York, NY 10016-8872
212-684-4224
FAX: 212-684-5424
Marvin Shanken, Owner
A directory offering information on the top 40 American distributors and profiles of companies. *$170.00*
Annual

9565 International Association of Food Industry Suppliers
1451 Dolley Madison Boulevard
McLean, VA 22101-3847
703-761-2600
FAX: 703-761-4334 info@iafis.org
Stephen C Schlegel, President/CEO
Stephen M Perry, Executive VP
John Lyons, Director Marketing/Communications
George Melnykovich, President/COO
A directory offering information on member manufacturers and suppliers of equipment, ingredients and services to the food and dairy industry.
700 pages Founded: 1911

9566 International Dairy Foods Association: IDFA Membership Directory
IDFA Membership Directory
1250 H Street NW
Suite 900
Washington, DC 20005
202-737-4332
FAX: 202-331-7820
membership@idfa.org www.idfa.org
Cindy Cazallo, Editor
Ellen Brophy, Editor
Constance Tipton, President
The directory provides a complete listing of IDFA's members— over 500 companies— representing approximately 83 percent of all dairy foods processed in the US, as well as the industry's leading supplier companies. Information about locations, products and contacts is included. *$495.00*
250 pages

9567 International Directory of Refrigerated Warehouse & Distribution Centers
Int'l Association of Refrigerated Warehouses
1500 King Street
Suite 201
Alexandria, VA 22314
301-652-5674
FAX: 703-373-4301
email@iarw.org www.iarw.org
A complete listing of public refrigerated warehouses available to the food industry. *$18.00*

9568 International Green Front Report
Friends of the Trees
PO Box 1064
Tonasket, WA 98855-1064
FAX: 509-485-2705
Michael Pilarski, Editor
Organizations and periodicals concerned with sustainable forestry and agriculture and related fields. *$7.00*
Irregular

9569 International Jelly and Preserve Association Directory
5775 Peachtree Dunwoody Road NE
Suite G500
Atlanta, GA 30342-1542
404-252-3663
FAX: 404-252-0774
Annual

9570 International Soil Tillage Research Organization
International Soil Tillage Research
1680 Madison Avenue
Wooster, OH 44691-4114
330-263-3700
FAX: 330-263-3658
More than 750 individuals and institutions in 72 countries involved in the research or application of soil tilage and related subjects. *$100.00*
Semiannual

9571 Kosher Directory: Directory of Kosher Products & Services
Union of Orthodox Jewish Congregations of America
333 7th Avenue
18th Floor
New York, NY 10001-5004
212-563-4122
FAX: 212-564-9058
Shelly Sharf, Editor
A directory covering over 10,000 consumer, institutional and industrial products and services.

9572 Landscape & Irrigation: Product Source Guide
Adams Business Media
68-860 Perez Road
Suite J
Cathedral City, CA 92234-7248
312-846-4600
FAX: 312-846-4638
mdavis@aip.com
www.americanbusinessmedia.com
Lonny Adams, Owner
Offers information on suppliers, distributors and manufacturers serving the professional agriculture and landscaping community. *$ 6.00*

Circulation: 37,000

9573 LifeWise Ingredients
350 Telser Road
Lake Zurich, IL 60047-6701
847-550-8270
FAX: 847-550-8272 www.lifewise1.com

Millie Galey, Manager
Carol Bender, Manager
Richard Share, Owner

Manufacture industrial food ingredients.

9574 MISA Buyer's Guide on CD
Meat Industry Suppliers Alliance
200 Daingerfield Road
Alexandria, VA 22314
703-684-1080
FAX: 703-548-6563 800-331-8816
misahq@aol.com
www.foodprocessingmachinery.com

George O Melnkovich, PhD, President
Cheryl Clark, Director Member Services

Annual

9575 Manufacturing Confectioner: Directory of Ingredients, Equipment & Packaging
Manufacturing Confectioner Publishing Company
175 Rock Road
Glen Rock, NJ 07452-1724
201-652-2655
FAX: 201-652-3419

Kate Allured, Editor

Publication offers suppliers of machinery, equipment, raw materials, and supplies to the confectionery industry. *$25.00*

Annual

9576 Market for Nutraceutical Foods & Beverages
Frost & Sullivan Market Intelligence
2525 Charleston Road
Mountain View, CA 94043-1626
650-961-1000
FAX: 650-961-5042

Analyzes the nutraceutical market and offers information on ongoing laboratory research and forecasts for this particular industry. *$1850.00*

9577 Material Safety Data Sheet Reference
C&P Press
302 5th Avenue
5th Floor
New York, NY 10001
212-326-6760
FAX: 646-733-6010
cpp@cppress.com www.cppress.com

Regulatory and product safety requirements. Contains full text MSDS's for products listed in the 1999 15th Edition Crop Protection Reference plus additional safety information such as DOT shipping information, SARA Title III regulations, Hazardous Chemical inventory reporting information plus much more.

9578 Meat Buyer's Guide
North American Meat Processors Association
1920 Association Drive
Suite 400
Reston, VA 20191-1545
703-758-1900
FAX: 703-758-8001

A pictorial directory depicting the food service cuts of beef, lamb, pork, and veal, along with their corresponding IMPS numbers (Institutional Meat Purchase Specification) numbers, instituted by USDA. The Guide is used by chefs, meat processors, and purveyors, food service personnel in institutions, hotels and restaurants.

9579 Meat Price Book
Urner Barry Publications
PO Box 389
Toms River, NJ 08754-0389
732-240-5330
FAX: 732-341-0891 800-932-0617
mail@urnerbarry.com
www.urnerbarry.com

Paul B Brown Jr, President
Sheila M Deane, Marketing Manager

Seven year price history of selected beef, lamb and veal cuts as quoted in Urner Barry's Yellow Sheet. *$95.00*

Annual
Circulation: 400

9580 Meat and Poultry Inspection Directory
US Department of Agriculture
Administration Building
Room 344
Washington, DC 20250-0001
202-690-7650
FAX: 202-512-2250
www.access.gpo.gov

Offers valuable information on all meat and poultry plants that ship meat interstate and therefore come under the US Department of Agriculture inspection. *$16.00*

600 pages Semiannual

9581 Membership Directory & Buyers Guide: AFFI
American Frozen Food Institute
2000 Corporate Road
Suite 1000
Mc Lean, VA 22102-7844
703-821-0770
FAX: 703-821-1350

Traci Carneal, Communications VP

This directory offers information on over 500 members located within the processing, supplying, brokerage, and distributing ends of the frozen food industry. *$100.00*

150 pages Annual

9582 Membership Directory of the Retail Confectioners International
1807 Glenview Road
Suite 204
Glenview, IL 60025-2968
847-724-6120
FAX: 847-724-2719

Annual

9583 Mid-Atlantic Retail Food Industry Buyers' Guide
Mid-Atlantic Food Dealers Services
Dundalk Center
14 Commerce Street
Baltimore, MD 21222
410-226-6924
FAX: 410-377-7137

Robert Mead, Executive Director

Offers extensive coverage of retail food stores and suppliers to the food industry in the states of Delaware, Maryland, New Jersey, Virginia and Washington, DC. *$15.00*

130 pages Annual
Circulation: 5,000

9584 Missouri Grocers Association Annual Convention & Food Trade Show
Missouri Grocers Association
PO Box 10223
Springfield, MO 65808
417-831-6667
FAX: 417-831-3907

1300 pages

9585 NABCA Contacts Director
National Alcohol Beverage Control Association
4216 King Street
Alexandria, VA 22302-1507
703-784-4201
FAX: 703-820-3551
info@nabca.org www.nabca.org

Patricia K LaCava, Administration Sr VP/CFO
William W Hindman, Data Manager
James Sgueo, Executive Director

A compilation of the names and addresses of every member organization and its top officials. Also included are non-member trade associations and license state, Federal and Canadian agencies. *$295.00*

Non-Members Price

9586 NAMA Directory of Members
National Automatic Merchandising Association
20 N Wacker Drive
Suite 3500
Chicago, IL 60606-3102
312-346-0370
FAX: 312-704-4140 800-331-8816
sgraf@vending.org www.vending.org

Susi Graf, Membership Services Coordinator
Ricahrd Geerdes, President

Listings of over 2,200 vending, coffee service and foodservice management firms that are NAMA members, including independent firms and branches of national operating companies. Listed by state and city, identifies products vending by each firm and other services provided. Includes listing of machine manufacturer and product supplier firms that are members as well as brokers and distributors and sustaining. *$25.00*

Annual Founded: 1936

9587 NASDA Directory
National Association of State Dept of Agriculture
1156 15th Street NW
Suite 1020
Washington, DC 20005-1711
202-235-5454
FAX: 202-296-9686
nasda@patriot.net www.nasda.org

Richard Kirchoff, CEO

Top agricultural officials in 50 states and four territories. *$100.00*

Annual

9588 National Agri-Marketing Association Directory
11020 King Street
Suite 205
Overland Park, KS 66210-1201
913-491-6500
FAX: 913-491-6502
agrimktg@nama.org www.nama.org

Eldon White, Chief Executive Officer
Dawn Foster, Contact *$150.00*

2500 pages Annual Spring Founded: 1956

9589 National Association of Specialty Food and Confection Brokers
11004 Wood Elves Way
Columbia, MD 21044-1085
410-969-3663
FAX: 410-740-2958

Judi Epstein, Secretary

Lists members by state of residence and by states covered. Code of ethics and articles describing the function of a 'specialty' food broker in the marketplace.
86 pages

9590 National Coffee Service Association: Membership Directory
8201 Greensboro Drive
Suite 300
McLean, VA 22102-3814
703-610-9000
FAX: 703-273-9011 800-221-3196
A directory covering over 800 member operators and suppliers of office coffee service products.
Annual

9591 National Meat Association: Membership Directory
1970 Broadway
Suite 825
Oakland, CA 94612-2299
510-763-1533
FAX: 510-768-6186
staff@nmaonline.org
www.nmaonline.org

Etta D Reyes, Editor
Rosemary Mucklow, Executive Director

This annual guide offers information on over 250 meat packers, processors and jobbers in 19 western states.
100 pages Annual

9592 National Organic Directory
Community Alliance with Family Farmers

PO Box 464
Davis, CA 95617-0464
916-786-5155
FAX: 530-756-7857 800-852-3832
Annual directory offering information on over 1,000 growers and wholesalers of organically grown produce and organic products. The new edition includes information on regulations and resources for the industry. *$34.95*
288 pages Annual
Circulation: 2,500

9593 New Product News
Delta Communications
N6W23673 W Bluemound Road
Wauwatosa, WI 53188
262-542-9111
FAX: 414-777-7277
delta@deltacommunications.com
www.deltacommunications.com

Lynn Dornblaser, Publisher
Martin Friedman, Editor
Diane McBride, Circulation Manager

Offers food and drug manufacturers up-to-date information on products sold in supermarkets, drug stores, gourmet stores and natural food stores. Includes in-depth analysis of new product trends. *$359.00*
65 pages Monthly
Mailing list available for rent $300 per M.
Printed in 1 color on matte stock

9594 Organic Food Mail Order Suppliers
Center for Science in the Public Interest
1875 Connecticut Avenue NW
Suite 300
Washington, DC 20009-5736
202-332-9110
FAX: 202-265-4954 www.cspinet.org

Michael Jacobson, Executive Director

A directory of organic-food growers and suppliers who make their products available by mail-order.
Founded: 1992

9595 Organic Pages
OTA Press
60 Wells Street
PO Box 547
Greenfield, MA 01302-0547
413-774-7511
FAX: 413-774-6432
dpratt@ota.com www.ota.com
The most comprehensive resource directory of businesses involved in organic trade in North America. Only available online. *$50.95*
346 pages Annual Founded: 1984 ISBN 1-881427-90-0
Circulation: 3500
Printed in 4 colors on matte stock

9596 PMMI Packaging Machinery Directory
Packaging Machinery Manufacturers Institute (PMMI)
4350 N Fairfax Drive
Suite 600
Arlington, VA 22203
703-243-8555
FAX: 703-243-8556
maria@pmmi.org www.pmmi.org

Maria Ferrante, Editorial/Workforce Director
Alaina Sacramo, Services Coordinator
Chuck Yuska, President

Contains information on all 500+ member companies, who are committed to producing quality products and providing world class service to their customers. *$5.00*
Non-Members Fee

9597 Packer: Produce Availability and Merchandising Guide
Vance Publishing
10901 W 84th Terrace
Lenexa, KS 66214
913-438-8700
FAX: 913-438-0695 800-255-5113
subscription@thepacker.com
www.thepacker.com

Robb Bertels, Publisher
Ben Wood, Editor
Lance Jungmeyer, Managing Editor
Leanne Ball, Manager

Publication of about 6,000 fruit and vegetable suppliers and sales agents. *$35.00*
Annual

9598 Parity Corp
11812 N Creek Parkway N
Suite 204
Bothell, WA 98011-8202
425-487-0997

info@paritycorp.com
www.paritycorp.com

Amy Loges, Marketing Communications Manager
Arvid Tellevik, Owner

Integrated business information system and services designed specifically for the food industry.
Founded: 1985

9599 Pasta Industry Directory
National Pasta Association
1156 15th Street NW
Suite 900
Washington, DC 20005
202-637-5888
FAX: 202-223-9741
www.ilovepasta.org

Cecelia Leavitt, Editor

Lists by category pasta manufacturers and industry suppliers, including contact names. *$25.00*
Annual
Circulation: 1,000

9600 Pickle Packers International Directory
1620 i St Nw
Ste 925
Washington, DC 20006-4035
202-312-2859
FAX: 630-584-0759
www.ilovepickles.org

Richard Hentschell, Executive VP
Annual

9601 Pizza Today: Pizza Industry Buyer's Guide
National Association of Pizzeria Operators (NAPO)
908 S 8th Street
Suite 200
Louisville, KY 40203
502-736-9530
FAX: 502-736-9531 800-489-8324
jstraughan@napo.com
www.pizzatoday.com

Pete Lachapelle, Publisher
Joe Straughan, Association Executive Director

A directory listing over 3,000 manufacturers and suppliers of products, equipment and services to the pizza industry. *$25.00*
Annual Founded: 1984
Circulation: 40000

9602 Pork Guide to Hero Health Issue
Vance Publishing
1901 W 84th Terrace
Suite 200
Lenexa, KS 66214
913-438-8700
FAX: 913-438-0695

Bill Newham, Publisher

This comprehensive directory offers a list of manufacturers of swine health products.
$25.00
Annual
Circulation: 77,000

9603 Poultry Digest: Buyer's Guide Issue
WATT Publishing Company
122 S Wesley Avenue
Mount Morris, IL 61054-1497
815-734-4171
FAX: 815-734-7727
olentine@wattmm.com
www.wattnet.com

Charles Perry, Editor
James Watt, Owner

A list of suppliers to the poultry industry of the US and Canada are listed. *$6.00*
Annual
Circulation: 20,000

9604 Poultry International: Who's Who International
WATT Publishing Company
122 S Wesley Avenue
Mount Morris, IL 61054-1497
815-734-4171
FAX: 815-734-7727
olentine@wattmm.com
www.wattnet.com

David Martin, Editor
James Watt, Owner

A guide offering information on over 2,500 manufacturers and suppliers of poultry equipment, services and products. *$15.00*
Annual
Circulation: 20,000

9605 Poultry Price Book
Urner Barry Publications
PO Box 389
Toms River, NJ 08754-0389
732-240-5330
FAX: 732-341-0891 800-932-0617
mail@urnerbarry.com
www.urnerbarry.com

Paul B Brown Jr, President
Sheila M Deane, Marketing Manager

Seven year price history of selected turkey and chicken items as quoted in Urner Barry's Price— Current. *$55.00*
Annual
Circulation: 400

9606 Poultry Processing: Buyer's Guide Issue
WATT Publishing Company
122 S Wesley Avenue
Mount Morris, IL 61054-1497
815-734-4171
FAX: 815-734-7727
olentine@wattmm.com
www.wattnet.com

Virginia Lazar, Editor
James Watt, Owner

Annual reference offering information on over 800 manufacturers and suppliers of equipment, machinery and raw materials for the poultry packing industry. *$27.50*
Annual
Circulation: 11,000

9607 Prepared Foods
Delta Communications
455 N Cityfront Plaza Drive
Chicago, IL 60611-5503
312-836-2000
FAX: 312-222-2026
This database offers information of interest to the processed food industry.
Full-text

9608 Proceedings
Flavor & Extract Manufacturers Assn of the US
1620 I Street NW
Suite 925
Washington, DC 20006-4005
202-293-5800
FAX: 202-463-8998

Glenn Roberts, President
Kim Earle, Contact

Updates and reports on the proceedings of the association.
Annual

9609 Produce Marketing Association Membership Directory & Buyer's Guide
Produce Marketing Association
1500 Casho Mill Road
PO Box 6036
Newark, DE 19711-3547
302-738-7100
FAX: 302-731-2409

Kathy Means, VP Membership
Dan Henderson, Marketing
Bryan Silbermann, President

A directory offering information on over 2,000 members involved in retail grocery and food service marketing. *$70.00*
280 pages Annual

9610 Produce Services Sourcebook
Vance Publishing
10901 W 84th Terrace
Lenexa, KS 66214-1649
913-438-8700
FAX: 913-438-0695 800-255-5113

Erica Shafser, Special Projects

The produce industry's directory of allied services and products. Content is a balance between practical reference information, allied trends and supplier or source listings. *$20.00*

9611 Professional Workers in State Agricultural Experiment Stations
US Department of Agriculture
PO Box 2022
Washington, DC 20250-0001
202-690-7650
FAX: 202-512-2250
www.access.gpo.gov
This directory offers information on academic and research personnel in all agricultural, forestry, aquaculture and home economics industries. *$15.00*
289 pages Annual

9612 Purebred Picture: Breeders Directory Issue
American Berkshire Association
PO Box 2346
W Lafayette, IN 47996-2346
765-497-3618
FAX: 765-497-2959

Lois Wall, Managing Editor

Annual guide offering information on cattle and hog breeders in the US. *$12.00*
Annual
Circulation: 4,000

9613 Quick Frozen Foods Annual Processors Directory & Buyer's Guide
Frozen Food Digest, Saul Beck Publications
271 Madison Avenue
Suite 1107
New York, NY 10016-1082
212-557-8600
FAX: 212-986-9868

Saul Beck, Publisher
Audrey Beck, General Manager

A buyer's guide listing over 10,000 frozen food processors, associations, equipment manufacturers and suppliers, and public refrigerated warehouses, transportation, freezing & refrigerated equipment, manufacturers, packagers and railroad lines, brokers, etc. *$140.00*
400 pages Annual
Circulation: 5,000

9614 Refrigerated Transporter: Warehouse Directory Issue
Tunnell Publications
PO Box 66010
Houston, TX 77266
713-523-8124
FAX: 713-523-8384

Gary Macklin, Editor

Listing of approximately 265 refrigerated warehouses in the US and Canada.

9615 Restaurant Hospitality: Hospitality 500 Issue
Penton Media
1300 E 9th Street
Cleveland, OH 44114-1503
216-696-7000
FAX: 216-696-0836
information@penton.com
www.penton.com

Michael P Keefe, Publisher

500 independent restaurants selected on basis of sales. *$25.00*
Annual June
Circulation: 123,000

9616 Restaurants and Institutions: Annual 400 Issue
Reed Business Information
1350 E Touhy Avenue
Suite 200E
Des Plaines, IL 60018-3358
847-962-2200
FAX: 630-288-8686
www.reedbusiness.com

Roland Dietz, Chief Executive Officer
$25.00
Annual
Circulation: 16,000

9617 Santa Gertrudis Breeders International Membership Directory
PO Box 1257
Kingsville, TX 78364-1257
361-592-9357
FAX: 361-592-8572
www.strangertrudis.ws

Ervin Kaatz, Executive Director

Annual guide offering information on over 4,5000 producers of Santa Gertrudis beef and cattle throughout the world.

9618 Santa Gertrudis USA
Santa Gertrudis Breeders International
PO Box 1257
Kingsville, TX 78364-1257
361-592-9357
FAX: 361-592-8572
www.santagertrudis.ws

Ervin Kaatz, Executive Director

Monthly publication offering information on over 1,000 producers of Santa Gertrudis beef cattle throughout the United States. *$ 30.00*
125 pages Monthly Founded: 1998
Circulation: 2,500
Printed in on glossy stock

9619 Sauces and Gravies
MarketResearch.com
641 Avenue of the Americas
3rd Floor
New York, NY 10011
212-807-2629
FAX: 212-807-2676 800-298-6699
This market profile analyzes US shipments, retail sales, consumer demographics, and

food service and food processor purchases for 22 product lines. Also analyzes the sauce and gravy product line, retail sales, brand share, and customer demographics for 16 major marketers. *$ 2250.00*
250 pages

9620 Seafood Buyer's Handbook
Diversified Business Communications
PO Box 7438
Portland, ME 04112-7438
207-842-5500
FAX: 207-842-5505
www.divbusiness.com
This comprehensive directory lists about 1,200 North American fish and shellfish suppliers, distributors and suppliers of related services and equipment to the seafood industry. *$18.00*
250 pages Annual
Circulation: 15,000

9621 Seafood Price Book
Urner Barry Publications
PO Box 389
Toms River, NJ 08754-0389
732-240-5330
FAX: 732-341-0891 800-932-0617
mail@urnerbarry.com
www.urnerbarry.com
Paul B Brown Jr, President
Sheila M Deane, Marketing Manager
Seven year price history of selected fresh/frozen seafood items as quoted in Urner Barry's Seafood Price— Current. *$95.00*
Annual
Circulation: 400

9622 Seafood Shippers' Guide
American Seafood Institute
25 Fairway Circle
Hope Valley, RI 02832
401-491-9017
FAX: 401-491-9024
www.americanseafood.org
Trucking, freight and cold storage companies that directly affect the seafood packing and shipping industry. *$29.95*
100 pages
Circulation: 2,000

9623 Single Unit Supermarkets Operators Directory
Chain Store Guide
3922 Coconut Palm Drive
Tampa, FL 33616-3506
813-276-6700
FAX: 813-627-6882 800-778-9794
info@csgis.com www.csgis.com
Chris Leedy, Advertising Sales
Shami Choon, Manager
Discover more than 7,100 single-unit supermarkets with annual sales topping $500,000 dollars. This comprehensive desktop reference makes it easy to reach our compiled list of 21,000 key executives and buyers, plus their primary wholesalers. *$335.00*
725 pages Annual

9624 Supermarket News Distribution Study of Grocery Store Sales
Fairchild Publications
7 W 34th Street
3rd Floor
New York, NY 10001-8100
212-304-4000
FAX: 212-630-3768
Directory of services and supplies to the industry. *$75.00*
Annual

9625 Supermarket News Retailers & Wholesalers Directory
Fairchild Publications
7 W 34th Street
New York, NY 10001-8100
212-630-3880
FAX: 212-630-3768 800-360-1700
Over 2,200 US and Canadian retailers, including supermarkets, discount department stores, membership clubs, drug stores, plus voluntary, cooperative and nonsponsoring wholesalers.

9626 Supermarket, Grocery & Convenience Stores
Chain Store Guide
3922 Coconut Palm Drive
Tampa, FL 33616-3506
813-276-6700
FAX: 813-627-6882 800-778-9794
info@csgis.com www.csgis.com
Chris Leedy, Advertising Sales
Shami Choon, Manager
Contains information on close to 3,400 U.S. and Canadian supermarket chains, each with at least $2 million in annual sales - one of the most profitable segments in this sector of the economy. The companies in this database operate over 41,000 individual supermarket, superstore, club store, gourmet supermarkets and combo-store units. A special convenience store section profiles 1,700 convenience store chains operating over 85,000 stores. *$335.00*
Annual 700 names

9627 The Organic Pages Online
OTA Press
60 Wells Street
PO Box 547
Greenfield, MA 01302-0547
413-774-7511
FAX: 413-774-6432
dpratt@ota.com
www.theorganicpages.com
Dan Pratt, Directory Coordinator
Online searchable directory of over 1600 businesses involved in the organic industry.
Annual Founded: 1984 ISBN 1-881427-90-0
Printed in 4 colors on matte stock

9628 Trade Dimensions
45 Danbury Road
Wilton, CT 06897
203-563-3000
FAX: 203-563-3131
info@tradedimensions.com
www.tradedimensions.com
Hal Clark, Owner
Trade Dimensions has over 30 years of experience and innovation in developing some of the most sophisticated, reliable and widely used directories and retail site data bases available.

9629 US Agriculture
WEFA Group
800 Baldwin Tower Boulevard
Eddystone, PA 19022-1368
610-490-4000
FAX: 610-490-2770
info@wefa.com www.wefa.com
Harry Baurnes
This large database offers information on US macroeconomic farm crop and related agricultural data.

9630 US Alcohol Beverage Industry Category CD
Beverage Marketing Corporation
2670 Commercial Avenue
Mingo Junction, OH 43938
740-598-4133
FAX: 740-598-3977 800-332-6222
Andrew Standardi, Director Operations
Kathy Smurthwaite, Editor *$3386.00*
Annual

9631 US Bagel Industry
Leading Edge Reports/Industry Reports
2171 Jericho Turnpike
Suite 200
Commack, NY 11725-2937
631-462-5454
FAX: 631-462-1842
bta@li.net
www.businesstrendanalysts.com
Charles J Ritchie, Executive VP
Donna Priani, Marketing Director
Linda Sherman, Production Manager
Vincent Seeno, Research Director
A comprehensive investigation of the dynamics of the US Bagel Industry. Both historical and current market data is presented. *$ 1995.00*
150 pages Founded: 2000
Computerized version available: Disk

9632 US Beer Distributors: A Delivery Fleet Profile
Beverage Marketing Corporation
850 3rd Avenue
New York, NY 10022-6222
212-688-7640
FAX: 212-826-1255 800-275-4630
Over 3,200 beer distributors. *$895.00*

9633 US Beer Distributors: A Sales Profile
Beverage Marketing Corporation
850 3rd Avenue
New York, NY 10022-6222
212-688-7640
FAX: 212-826-1255 800-275-4630
Over 3,200 US beer distributors. *$895.00*
Annual

9634 US Beer Market Sales Survey
Beverage Marketing Corporation
850 3rd Avenue
New York, NY 10022-6222
212-688-7640
FAX: 212-826-1255 800-275-4630
List of approximately 3,200 beer wholesalers in the US. *$725.00*
Annual

9635 US Beer Wholesalers Category CD
Beverage Marketing Corporation
2670 Commercial Avenue
Mingo Junction, OH 43938
740-598-4133
FAX: 740-598-3977 800-332-6222
Andrew Standardi, Director Operations
Kathy Smurthwaite, Editor
A who's who directory of wholesale services and supplies to the industry. *$2302.00*
Annual

9636 US Beverage Distribution Landscape Category CD
Beverage Marketing Corporation
2670 Commercial Avenue
Mingo Junction, OH 43938
740-598-4133
FAX: 740-598-3977 800-332-6222

Andrew Standardi, Director Operations
Kathy Smurthwaite, Editor *$4190.00*

Annual

9637 US Bottled Water Industry
Business Trend Analysts/Industry Reports
2171 Jericho Turnpike
Suite 200
Commack, NY 11725-2937
631-462-5454
FAX: 631-462-1842
bta@li.net
www.businesstrendanalysts.com

Charles J Ritchie, Executive VP
Donna Priani, Marketing Director
Linda Sherman, Production Manager
Vincent Seeno, Research Director

BTA continues its pioneering coverage of the bottled water industry with this updated and dramatically expanded edition. *$1550.00*

Founded: 1997
Computerized version available: Disc

9638 US Bottled Water Operations Category CD
Beverage Marketing Corporation
2670 Commercial Avenue
Mingo Junction, OH 43938
740-598-4133
FAX: 740-598-3977 800-332-6222

Andrew Standardi, Director Operations
Kathy Smurthwaite, Editor *$2910.00*

Annual

9639 US Bread Market
MarketResearch.com
641 Avenue of the Americas
3rd Floor
New York, NY 10011
212-807-2629
FAX: 212-807-2676 800-298-6699
This study covers packaged, fresh and frozen bread products, including a growing number of specialty bread products. Major marketing, retailing and demographic trends are all explored in-depth. Special attention is given to the in-store bakery phenomenon. *$2750.00*

197 pages

9640 US Candy and Gum Market
MarketResearch.com
641 Avenue of the Americas
3rd Floor
New York, NY 10011
212-807-2629
FAX: 212-807-2676 800-298-6699
This report dissects the 23.5 billion market for chocolate candy, hard candy, soft candy, mints and gum, covering both the mass-market and gourmet levels. Market size, growth and composition are tabulated, with sales projections through 2004. Competition at the retail level as a major impetus to market growth is covered in full, as are consumer demographics by product type, brand and usage levels. *$2750.00*

351 pages

9641 US Cheese Market
Business Trend Analysts/Industry Reports
2171 Jericho Turnpike
Suite 200
Commack, NY 11725-2937
631-462-5454
FAX: 631-462-1842 800-866-4648
sales@bta-ler.com www.bta-ler.com

Charles J Ritchie, Executive VP
Donna Priani, Marketing Director
Linda Holm, Production Manager
Jennifer Wichert, Research Director

Survey offering the size and growth of markets for natural, process, cottage and substitute cheeses. *$1395.00*

480 pages Founded: 2001
Computerized version available: Disk

9642 US Confectionary Market
Business Trend Analysts/Industry Reports
2171 Jericho Turnpike
Suite 200
Commack, NY 11725-2937
631-462-5454
FAX: 631-462-1842
bta@li.net
www.businesstrendanalysts.com

Charles J Ritchie, Executive VP
Donna Priani, Marketing Director
Linda Sherman, Production Manager
Vincent Seeno, Research Director

Profiles markets for chocolate and nonchocolate candies, gum, snack nuts, and seeds, as well as providing information on distribution, trends and future opportunities. *$1250.00*

760 pages Founded: 1996
Computerized version available: Disc

9643 US Date Code Directory for Product Labeling
Danis Research
1 Gothic Plaza
Fairfield, NJ 07004-2411
973-575-3509
FAX: 973-575-5366
Over 500 companies using date code labeling on their food products; over 500 quality control managers and consumer affairs managers from companies that produce snack foods, baked goods, confectioneries and other food products. *$295.00*

9644 US Ethnic Foods Market
Business Trend Analysts/Industry Reports
2171 Jericho Turnpike
Suite 200
Commack, NY 11725-2937
631-462-5454
FAX: 631-462-1842
bta@li.net
www.businesstrendanalysts.com

Charles J Ritchie, Executive VP
Donna Priani, Marketing Director
Linda Sherman, Production Manager
Vincent Seeno, Research Director

A detailed analysis of the expanding US markets for Italian, Hispanic/Mexican, Oriental, Indian and Kosher foods. *$995.00*

Founded: 1995
Computerized version available: Disk

9645 US Hot Beverage Market
Business Trend Analysts/Industry Reports
2171 Jericho Turnpike
Suite 200
Commack, NY 11725-2937
631-462-5454
FAX: 631-462-1842
bta@li.net
www.businesstrendanalysts.com

Charles J Ritchie, Executive VP
Donna Priani, Marketing Director
Linda Sherman, Production Manager
Vincent Seeno, Research Director

A survey offering profiles of the coffee, tea and cocoa products market. *$1995.00*

330 pages Founded: 1998
Computerized version available: Disk

9646 US Market for Cereal & Other Breakfast Foods
Business Trend Analysts/Industry Reports
2171 Jericho Turnpike
Suite 200
Commack, NY 11725-2937
631-462-5454
FAX: 631-462-1842 800-866-4648
mkt@bta-ler.com
www.businesstrendanalysts.com

Charles J Ritchie, Executive VP
Donna Praini, General Manager
Linda Sherman, Production Manager
Jennifer Wichert, Research Director

Provides up-to-date information on consumer attitudes and buying patterns, new product development, marketing strategies and current and projected sales trends for all types of hot and cold cereals, baked breakfast foods and frozen breakfast products. *$1495.00*

396 pages Founded: 1986
Computerized version available: Disk

9647 US Market for Fats & Oils
Business Trend Analysts/Industry Reports
2171 Jericho Turnpike
Suite 200
Commack, NY 11725-2937
631-462-5454
FAX: 631-462-1842
bta@li.net
www.businesstrendanalysts.com

Charles J Ritchie, Executive VP
Donna Priani, Marketing Director
Linda Sherman, Production Manager
Vincent Seeno, Research Director

Analyzes the markets for different oils (corn, soybean, peanut, canola, linseed, cottonseed, fish and others), edible and inedible tallow, grease and lard. *$1295.00*

540 pages Founded: 1998
Computerized version available: Disc

9648 US Market for Fruit and Vegetable Based Beverages
MarketResearch.com
641 Avenue of the Americas
3rd Floor
New York, NY 10011
212-807-2629
FAX: 212-807-2676 800-298-6699
This new study covers refrigerated juices and juice drinks, aseptic juices, frozen and unfrozen concentrates, shelf-stable juices and juice drinks in bottles and cans. It provides the latest available sales and volume by category and retail outlet, as well as detailed marketer/brand shares. The report unveils the competitive strategies, advertising and promotional campaigns and new product launches of major players; tracks trends in packaging, flavor-blending, health drinks, and other niches. *$2750.00*

258 pages

9649 US Market for Juices, Aides & Noncarbonated Drinks
Business Trend Analysts/Industry Reports

2171 Jericho Turnpike
Suite 200
Commack, NY 11725-2937
631-462-5454
FAX: 631-462-1842
bta@li.net
www.businesstrendanalysts.com

Charles J Ritchie, Executive VP
Donna Priani, Marketing Director
Linda Sherman, Production Manager
Vincent Seeno, Research Director

A comprehensive market analysis covering all types of fresh and frozen fruit juices, fruit drinks, vegetable juices and canned ades. *$1195.00*

810 pages Founded: 1998
Computerized version available: Disc

9650 US Market for Pizza
Leading Edge Reports/Industry Reports
2171 Jericho Turnpike
Suite 200
Commack, NY 11725-2937
631-462-5454
FAX: 631-462-1842
bta@li.net
www.businesstrendanalysts.com

Charles J Ritchie, Executive VP
Donna Priani, Marketing Director
Linda Sherman, Production Manager
Vincent Seeno, Research Director

This report examines the size and growth of the US Pizza market through all channels. *$1995.00*

225 pages Founded: 1999
Computerized version available: Disk

9651 US Market for Salted Snacks
MarketResearch.com
641 Avenue of the Americas
3rd Floor
New York, NY 10011
212-807-2629
FAX: 212-807-2676 800-298-6699

This new study provides a coherent view of the market as well as its individual segments: potato chips, tortilla chips, corn chips, pretzels, popcorn, snack nuts and extruded snacks. It explains not only what the industry does, but how it works: how shelf life shapes the entire industry; how hundreds of smaller companies manage to thrive in a market dominated by Frito-Lay. This study profiles the giant companies and regional players. *$2750.00*

263 pages

9652 US Non-Alcoholic Beverage Industry Category CD
Beverage Marketing Corporation
2670 Commercial Avenue
Mingo Junction, OH 43938
740-598-4133
FAX: 740-598-3977 800-332-6222

Kathy Smurthwaite, Editor
Andrew Standardi, Director of Operations *$3969.00*

Annual

9653 US Organic Food Market
MarketResearch.com
641 Avenue of the Americas
3rd Floor
New York, NY 10011
212-807-2629
FAX: 212-807-2676 800-298-6699

This report covers the booming organic market as it expands into mainstream and gains increased public awareness. The report covers the market size and composition, important trends, and projections for future growth. The information contained in this report will help players in the organic arena make informed decisions to complete successfully in this exciting market. *$2750.00*

275 pages

9654 US Pasta Market
Business Trend Analysts/Industry Reports

2171 Jericho Turnpike
Suite 200
Commack, NY 11725-2937
631-462-5454
FAX: 631-462-1842
bta@li.net
www.businesstrendanalysts.com

Charles J Ritchie, Executive VP
Donna Priani, Marketing Director
Linda Sherman, Production Manager
Vincent Seeno, Research Director

Quantifies historial, current and projected sales trends in the ever-expanding market for pasta products. Covers all typed of dry, canned, frozen and fresh pasta, as well as shelf-stable noodle dishes and pasta meals. *$1395.00*

380 pages Founded: 2000
Computerized version available: Disc

9655 US Poultry and Small Game Market
Business Trend Analysts/Industry Reports

2171 Jericho Turnpike
Suite 200
Commack, NY 11725-2937
631-462-5454
FAX: 631-462-1842
bta@li.net
www.businesstrendanalysts.com

Charles J Ritchie, Executive VP
Donna Priani, Marketing Director
Linda Sherman, Production Manager
Vincent Seeno, Research Director

Profiles market for poultry and small game products and provides information on pricing, foreign trade, and advertising and promotion. *$1995.00*

280 pages Founded: 1999
Computerized version available: Disc

9656 US Processed Fruits & Vegetables Market
Business Trend Analysts/Industry Reports

2171 Jericho Turnpike
Suite 200
Commack, NY 11725-2937
631-462-5454
FAX: 631-462-1842
bta@li.net
www.businesstrendanalysts.com

Charles J Ritchie, Executive VP
Donna Priani, Marketing Director
Linda Sherman, Production Manager
Vincent Seeno, Research Director

A comprehensive marketing, economic and financial analysis of the processed fruits and vegetables industry, covering all types of canned, frozen, dried and dehydrated fruits and vegetables. *$1195.00*

815 pages Founded: 1997
Computerized version available: Disc

9657 US Processed Meat Market
Business Trend Analysts/Industry Reports

2171 Jericho Turnpike
Suite 200
Commack, NY 11725-2937
631-462-5454
FAX: 631-462-1842
bta@li.net
www.businesstrendanalysts.com

Charles J Ritchie, Executive VP
Donna Praini, Marketing Director
Linda Sherman, Production Manager
Vincent Seeno, Research Director

Profiles markets for processed meat products, including sausage, processed pork products, canned meats, and meat snacks. *$1295.00*

800 pages Founded: 2000
Computerized version available: Disc

9658 US Snack Food Market
Business Trend Analysts/Industry Reports

2171 Jericho Turnpike
Suite 200
Commack, NY 11725-2937
631-462-5454
FAX: 631-462-1842
bta@#li.net
www.businesstrendanalysts.com

Charles J Ritchie, Executive VP
Donna Priani, Marketing Director
Linda Sherman, Production Manager
Vincent Seeno, Research Director

A product-by-product analysis of the intensely competitive US snack food industry. *$1495.00*

860 pages Founded: 1999
Computerized version available: Disc

9659 US Soyfoods Market
MarketResearch.com
641 Avenue of the Americas
3rd Floor
New York, NY 10011
212-807-2629
FAX: 212-807-2676 800-298-6699

This report covers five product categories: meat alternatives, dairy alternatives, snacks, cereals, breads, bulk soybeans, meal replacements/protein powders and other soyfoods including soy sauce and miso. It profiles leading soyfoods producers such as Kellog's, White Wave and Lightlife Foods. The report projects sales trends through 2005 and provides insight into the factors shaping this market. Distributor trends and consumer attitudes and behaviors are also covered in detail. *$2750.00*

150 pages

9660 US Sweeteners Market
Business Trend Analysts/Industry Reports

2171 Jericho Turnpike
Suite 200
Commack, NY 11725-2937
631-462-5454
FAX: 631-462-1842
bta@li.net
www.businesstrendanalysts.com

Charles J Ritchie, Executive VP
Donna Priani, Marketing Director
Linda Sherman, Production Manager
Vincent Seeno, Research Director

In-depth coverage of the continually evolving sweetener industry, providing up-to-date information on the latest product developments. *$1995.00*

375 pages Founded: 1998
Computerized version available: Disc

9661 US Vitamins & Nutrients Market
Business Trend Analysts/Industry Reports
2171 Jericho Turnpike
Suite 200
Commack, NY 11725-2937
631-462-5454
FAX: 631-462-1842
bta@li.net
www.businesstrendanalysts.com
Charles J Ritchie, Executive VP
Donna Priani, Marketing Director
Linda Sherman, Production Manager
Vincent Seeno, Research Director
Statistical report on the vitamin and health food industries. *$1995.00*
410 pages Founded: 1999
Computerized version available: Disk

9662 US Wine Market
Business Trend Analysts/Industry Reports
2171 Jericho Turnpike
Suite 200
Commack, NY 11725-2937
631-462-5454
FAX: 631-462-1842
mkt@cbta-ler.com
www.businesstrendanalysts.com
Charles J Ritchie, Executive VP
Donna Priani, Marketing Director
Linda Sherman, Production Manager
Jennifer Wichert, Research Director
An analysis of the wine industry, domestic and imported. *$1295.00*
470 pages Founded: 1996
Computerized version available: Disk

9663 Uker's International Tea and Coffee Buyer's Guide & Directory
Lockwood Trade Journal
130 W 42nd Street
Suite 1050
New York, NY 10036-7804
212-697-7053
FAX: 212-827-0945 teacof@aol.com
Robert Lockwood, Publisher
Jane McCabe, Editor
A directory covering firms that are involved in importing and exporting coffee and tea; manufacturers, suppliers and retailers to the industry; and specialty roasters and their suppliers. *$48.00*
Annual
Printed in 4 colors on glossy stock

9664 Urner Barry's Meat & Poultry Directory
Urner Barry Publications
PO Box 389
Toms River, NJ 08754-0389
732-240-5330
FAX: 732-341-0891 800-932-0617
mail@urnerbarry.com
www.urnerbarry.com
Paul B Brown Jr, President
Karen Mick, Circulation Director
National business directory of traders in the meat and poultry industry. *$95.00*
760 pages Annual
Circulation: 2,000

9665 Vinegar Institute Directory
Vinegar Institute
5775 Peachtree Dunwoody Road NE
Suite G500
Atlanta, GA 30342-1542

FAX: 404-252-0774
Membership directory including manufacturers index, bottlers index and name index of active and associate members.
Annual

9666 Vinegar Institute: Basic Reference Manual
Vinegar Institute
5775 Peachtree Dunwoody Road NE
Suite G500
Atlanta, GA 30342-1542

FAX: 404-252-0774
Looseleaf service guide to vinegar products for technical personnel such as shop foremen and production managers. *$250.00*

9667 Vineyard & Winery Management Magazine
Vineyard & Winery Services
PO Box 2358
Windsor, CA 95492
707-836-6820
FAX: 707-836-6825 800-535-5670
Robert Merletti, President
Jennifer Merletti, Sales/Marketing Manager
A leading technical trade publication serving the North American Wine Industry and designed for today's serious wine business professional. *$37.00*
100+ pages Bi-Monthly Founded: 1975
Circulation: 6,000

9668 Warehouses Licensed Under US Warehouse Act
Farm Service Agency-US Dept. of Agriculture
PO Box 2415
Washington, DC 20013-2415

FAX: 202-690-0014
Agricultural warehouses voluntarily licensed under the US Warehouse Act governing public storage facilities.
Annual

9669 Western Fruit Grower: Source Book Issue Agriculture
Meister Publishing Company
37733 Euclid Avenue
Willoughby, OH 44094-5925
440-942-2000
FAX: 440-942-0662 800-572-7740
This annual resource offers information on manufacturers and distributors of suppliers and supplies for the fruit growing industry. *$5.00*
Annual
Circulation: 57,000

9670 Western Growers Export Dirctory
Western Growers Association
PO Box 2130
Newport Beach, CA 92658-8944
949-863-1000
FAX: 949-863-9028 www.wga.com
Heather Flower, Editor
A directory offering information on shippers of fresh produce and fruit in the states of California and Arizona.
32 pages Annual

9671 Who is Who: A Directory of Agricultural Engineers Available for Work
American Society of Agricultural Engineers
2950 Niles Road
Saint Joseph, MI 49085-8607
269-429-0300
FAX: 269-429-3852
This directory pertains to the availability of agricultural engineers to work in developing countries. The directory lists over 650 individuals from 60 countries, primarily engineers, available for work in land or water management, farm structures and other aspects of the field. *$27.50*
210 pages

9672 Who's Who in Beer Wholesaling Directory
National Beer Wholesalers Association
1101 King Street
Suite 600
Alexandria, VA 22314-2944
703-390-0591
FAX: 703-683-8965
info@nbwa.org www.nbwa.org
Erin Rutherford, Communications Manager
Marcia S Jones, Design/Production Manager
A listing of more than 3,000 beer distributors and suppliers in the industry. *$50.00*
Biennially/1st Copy Free Founded: 1938

9673 Who's Who in the Egg & Poultry Industries
WATT Publishing Company
122 S Wesley Avenue
Mount Morris, IL 61054-1497
815-734-4171
FAX: 815-734-7727
olentine@wattmm.com
www.wattnet.com
Robert Tuten, Editor
James Watt, Owner
Annual directory offering information on producers, processors, and distributors of poultry meat and eggs in the US. *$75.00*
170 pages Annual
Circulation: 10,000

9674 Who's Who in the Fish Industry
Urner Barry Publications
PO Box 389
Toms River, NJ 08754-0389
732-240-5330
FAX: 732-341-0891 800-932-0617
mail@urnerbarry.com
www.urnerbarry.com
Paul B Brown Jr, President
Sheila M Deane, Marketing Manager
A business directory of Canadian traders in the seafood industry. *$125.00*
Annual
Circulation: 2,000

9675 Whole Foods Annual Source Book
Wainer Finest Communications
3000 Hadley Road
2nd Floor
South Plainfield, NJ 07080-1183
908-769-1160
FAX: 908-769-1171
info@wfcinc.com www.wfcinc.com
Howard Wainer, Publisher
Alan Richman, Editor
Heather Wainer, Associate Publisher
$75.00
135 pages Monthly Founded: 1979
Circulation: 16,000

Mailing list available for rent 16000 names $125 per M.

9676 **Wholesale Beer Association Executives of America Directory**
Wholesale Beer Association Executives of America
2805 E Washington Avenue
Madison, WI 53704-5165
608-255-6464
FAX: 608-255-6466
7 pages Annual

9677 **Wholesale Grocers Directory**
Chain Store Guide
3922 Coconut Palm Drive
Tampa, FL 33616-3506
813-276-6700
FAX: 813-627-6882 800-972-0292
info@csgis.com www.csgis.com
Chris Leedy, Advertising Sales
Shami Choon, Manager
We have uncovered the facts on more than 1,900 grocery suppliers in the U.S. and Canada in this database. This targeted database allows you to reach food wholesalers, cooperatives and voluntary group wholesalers, non-sponsoring wholesalers, and cash and carry operators who serve grocery, convenience, discount and drug stores. You will also find information regarding company headquarters, divisions, branches, and over 11,000 key executives and buyers. *$335.00*
Annual 700 names

9678 **Wine & Spirits Industry Marketing**
Jobson Publishing Corporation
100 Avenue of the Americas
9th Floor
New York, NY 10013-1678
212-274-7000
FAX: 212-431-0500
Nicolas Furlotte, Editor
List of about 300 wine and liquor firms including wineries, producers, distillers and importers. *$150.00*
Annual April

9679 **Wines and Vines Directory of the Wine Industry in North America Issue**
Hiaring Company
1800 Lincoln Avenue
San Rafael, CA 94901-1221
415-453-9700
FAX: 415-453-2517
geninfo@winesandvines.com
www.winesandvines.com
Dorthy Kubota-Cordery, Editor
Phil Hiaring, Publisher
Debbie Hennessy, Editor
Renee Skiadas, Circulation Direct
Chet Klingensmith, Owner
Annual guide offering listings of wineries and wine industry suppliers in the US, Canada and Mexico. *$85.00*
505 pages Annual
Circulation: 5000 1800 names $850 per M.

9680 **World Databases in Agriculture**
National Register Publishing
121 Chanlon Road
New Providence, NJ 07974-1541
908-464-6800
FAX: 908-464-3553 800-473-7020
CJ Armstrong, Editor
Agricultural information on databases, including CD-ROM, magnetic tape, diskette, online, fax or databroadcast worldwide. *$165.00*

9681 **Yogurt Market**
MarketResearch.com
641 Avenue of the Americas
3rd Floor
New York, NY 10011
212-807-2629
FAX: 212-807-2676 800-298-6699
Brand share and brand consumer profiles are supplemented with profiles of major US manufacturers and new product information in order to provide the reader with competitor intelligence. *$2250.00*
140 pages

9682 **Zagat.Com Restaurant Guides**
Zagat Survey
4 Columbus Circle
New York, NY 10019-1100
212-977-6000
FAX: 212-977-6488
customerservice@zagat.com
www.zagat.com
Tim Zagat, President
Zagat.com was launched in May of 1999 and contains the most trusted and authoritive dining information online for over 20,000 restaurants in twenty-eight cities worldwide, with 17 more cities to be added shortly. Based in New York City, the Zagat survey was founded in 1979 by Tim and Nina Zagat.

Industry Web Sites

9683 **www.aaccnet.org**
American Association of Cereal Chemists

Non profit international organization of nearly 4,000 members who are specialists in the use of cereal grains in foods. AACC has been an innovative leader in gathering and disseminating scientific and technical information to professionals in the grain-based foods indusrty wordwide for over 85 years. We know it's hard to keep up with the latest technology, that's why AACC is here to help you. We're a tool unlike any other in your lab or office. Industry leaders turn to and trust AACC.

9684 **www.aaea.org**
American Agricultural Economics Association

The professional association for agricultural economists and related fields.

9685 **www.aaicc.org**
National Alliance of Independent Crop Consultants

Represents individual crop consultants and contract researchers.

9686 **www.aaminc.org**
American Agriculture Movement

An umbrella organization composed of state organizations representing family farm producers.

9687 **www.aamp.com**
American Association of Meat Processors

Membership consists of small to medium sized meat, poultry and food businesses including: packers, processors, wholesalers, home food service businesses, retailers, deli and catering operators and suppliers to the industry. AAMP is also affiliated with 34 states, regional and provincial organizations which represent meat and poultry businesses.

9688 **www.aanc.net**
American Association of Nutritional Consultants

An association combating public ignorance and adverse legislation.

9689 **www.aapausa.org**
American Alfalfa Processors Association

Information for the processors and suppliers in the alfalfa industry.

9690 **www.abfnet.org**
American Beekeeping Federation

For honey producers, packers, suppliers and shippers of honey products.

9691 **www.aceweb.org**
Agricultural Communicators in Education

For writers, editors, broadcasters and communicators who are involved in the dissemination of agricultural, food sciences and natural resource information in land-grant colleges, federal and state agencies, international agencies and other private communications work.

9692 **www.acfsa.org**
American Correctional Food Service Association

International, professional association created to serve the needs and interests of food service personnel in the correctional environments. The association brings together highly skilled food service workers and their vendors who are interested in the common goal of providing nutritious, cost-efficient meal service for confined populations.

9693 **www.acsh.org**
American Council on Science and Health

A nonprofit, consumer education organization concerned with issues related to food, nutrition, chemicals, pharmaceuticals, lifestyles, the environment and health.

9694 www.adsa.uiuc.edu
American Dairy Science Association

Publications, information, etc.

9695 www.aeb.org
American Egg Board

Facts, recipes, industry and nutrition information.

9696 www.afco.org
Association of American Feed Control Officials

Officials of government agencies at the state and federal levels engaged in the regulation and distribution of products, animal feeds and livestock remedies.

9697 www.affi.com
American Frozen Food Institute

News and events, facts, tips, and recipes, etc.

9698 www.afia.org
Animal Industry Foundation

Works to improve animal production practices in the US, to dispel misconceptions that a diet containing meat, milk and eggs is unhealthy and that animals raised for foods in the US are mistreated.

9699 www.afius.org
Association of Food Industries

The association is a trade association serving the food import trade.

9700 www.ag.ohio-state.edu/~farmshow
North American Farm Show Council

Agriculture trade shows and suppliers of services to these shows. Strives to improve education, communication and evaluation and provide the best possible marketing showcase for exhibitors and related products to the farmer/rancher/producer customer.

9701 www.agnic.org/

Access to experts in various fields of agriculture as well as links to agricultural databases. Find out about conferences, meetings and seminars in your area.

9702 www.agribsuiness.com
National Agri-Marketing Association

Industry information, member directory and links to member sites.

9703 www.agriwashington.org
Apple Processors Association

Organization consisting of processors and suppliers which provides a forum for discussion regarding legislation, regulations and new technology.

9704 www.agriwashington.org/aagiwa.html
American Association of Grain Inspection

Established to provide a liaison between the Federal Grain Inspection Service and designated agencies.

9705 www.agview.com/

All aspects of agriculture: Usenet groups, Web resources, archives, mailing lists, etc.

9706 www.ahpa.org
American Herbal Products Association

For manufacturers, importers and distributors of herbs and herbal products. AHPA seeks self-regulation, establishment of standards and rules of ethical conduct, member enrichment and public outreach.

9707 www.aibonline.org
American Institute of Baking Technical Bulletin

This organization provides research, education, training and consulting for the baking and food industries worldwide.

9708 www.aiccbox.org
International Corrugated Packaging Foundation

Videos, promotional materials, demonstrating support of the corrugated packaging industry worldwide. Place corrugated equipment into universities and technical colleges to provide students with corrugated industry skills.

9709 www.aicr.org
American Institute for Cancer Research

Third largest cancer charity in the US, focusing exclusively on research and education in regard to diet and cancer.

9710 www.aiwf.org
American Institute of Wine & Food

A non-profit educational organization devoted to improving the appreciation, understanding and accessibility of food and drink.

9711 www.ala-national.org
American Logistics Association

A nonprofit trade organization supporting the Military Resale and Morale, Welfare & Recreation industry.

9712 www.alaskaseafood.org
Alaska Seafood Marketing Institute

Organization of private industry and government fishing. Markets only Alaskan seafood. This association also offers educational and promotional materials on fresh and frozen seafood.

9713 www.allied-purchasing.com
Allied Purchasing

A group of ice cream plants, soft drink bottlers, dairies, brewries and water companies collaborating to obtain group purchasing rates on equipment, services, ingredients and supplies.

9714 www.almond-growers.com
California Independent Almond Growers

Association for almond growers, processors, packers and shippers

9715 www.almondsarein.com
Almond Board of California

This association provides production research, mandatory inspection and marketing promotion statistics for the almond/nut industry.

9716 www.americanbakers.org
American Bakers Association

Association comprised of wholesale bakers.

9717 www.americanberkshire.com
American Berkshire Association

Association for cattle and hog breeders in the US.

9718 www.americandairyproducts.com
American Dairy Products Institute

A national trade association representing the processed dairy products industry.

9719 www.americanhoneyproducers.org
American Honey Producers Association

Represents the interests of major USA honey producers and pollinators.

9720 **www.americanwineries.org**
American Vintners Association

9721 **www.amif.org**
American Meat Institute Foundation

9722 **www.amseed.com**
American Seed Trade Association

Producers of seeds for planting purposes.

9723 **www.amsey.org**
American Soybean Association

To improve US soybean farmer profitability. Publishes a monthly newsletter

9724 **www.angus.org**
American Angus Association

Industry and member links, information, etc.

9725 **www.animalagriculture.org**
National Institute for Annual Agriculture

9726 **www.aob.org**
Association of Brewers

Membership, publications, news, events, etc.

9727 **www.apics.org**
APICS Association for Operations Management

The primary purpose of this specific industry group is to educate food and beverage manufacturers on effective marketing strategies, market trends and material management.

9728 **www.applejuice.org**
Processed Apples Institute

Producers of processed apple products; suppliers of equipment, packaging or ingredients to the industry and brokers and concentrate manufacturers.

9729 **www.appleproducts.org**
Processed Apples Institute

Links to related industry sites.

9730 **www.apricotproducers.com**
Apricot Producers of California

9731 **www.ari.org/crm**
Commercial Refrigerator Manufacturers Division

Provides information, instruction, education to members in technical and business areas; also specializes in solving common problems and stimulating growth within the industry.

9732 **www.asac.org**
American Society of Agricultural Consultants

For agricultural consultants acting as an information base for members.

9733 **www.asae.org**
American Society of Agricultural Engineers

Information on agricultural engineering, biological engineering and food process engineering.

9734 **www.asas.org**
American Society of Animal Society

For professional researchers, publishes journals and holds seminars in the Animal Science field.

9735 **www.asbe.org**
American Society of Baking

Research and development of machinery for baking applications.

9736 **www.asfsa.org**
American School Food Service Association

An association focused on good nutrition for all children.

9737 **www.ashrae.org**
American Society of Heating, Refrigerating and Air Conditioning

An international membership organization of engineers who create the worlds we live in.

9738 **www.asifood.com**
ASI Food Safety Consultants

ASI Food Safety Consultants is a full service provider of food safety audits, seminars and HACCP programs.

9739 **www.asmc.org**
Association of Sales & Marketing Companies

Members are representatives for producers of food, packaged goods, and other consumer products.

9740 **www.astaspice.org**
American Spice Trade Association

United States based organization whose worldwide membership is comprised of the leading firms in the spice industry.

9741 **www.atsea.org**
AT-SEA Processors Association

The At-sea Association represents US flag catcher/processor vessels that participate in the healthy and abundant ground fish fisheries of the Bering Sea.

9742 **www.australian-beef.com**
Meat & Livestock Australia

Promotes comsumption of Australian beef, lamb, mutton and goat in Canada, US and Mexico. The company is funded by Australian producers. They key focus is to increase access for Australian meat producers to the North American market and to raise awareness of its nutritional value, quality and safety.

9743 **www.australian-lamb.com**
Meat & Livestock Australia

Promotes comsumption of Australian beef, lamb, mutton and goat in Canada, US and Mexico. The company is funded by Australian producers. They key focus is to increase access for Australian meat producers to the North American market and to raise awareness of its nutritional value, quality and safety.

9744 **www.australianmeatsafety.com**
Meat & Livestock Australia

Promotes comsumption of Australian beef, lamb, mutton and goat in Canada, US and Mexico. The company is funded by Australian producers. They key focus is to increase access for Australian meat producers to the North American market and to raise awareness of its nutritional value, quality and safety.

9745 **www.avocado.org**
California Avacado Commission

A resource for the California avocado industry.

9746 **www.awmanet.org**
American Wholesale Marketers Association

An international trade organization working on behalf of convenience distributors in the United States.

9747 **www.awwpa.com**
American White Wheat Producers Association

Organization of white wheat producers promoting and introducing new white wheat products.

9748 **www.bakeryonline.com**
Bakery Online

A database for bakers, food scientists, food engineers, process engineers, plant managers, business managers, executives and other professionals involved in the bakery industry. Features a comprehensive buyer's guide, interactive discussion forums and daily news updates and reports on business, regulatory and technology trends vital to the industry.

9749 **www.bbga.org**
Bread Bakers Guild of America

Links to member sites.

9750 **www.beef.org**
National Cattlemen's Beef Association

Related industry information.

9751 **www.beerinstitute.org**
Beer Institute

National trade association for the malt beverage industry. Represents the diversity of brewers and suppliers.

9752 **www.beertown.org**
American Homebrewers Association

Devoted to the education of home-brewed beer. Publishes magazine devoted exclusively to education, art and science of homebrewing. Services include: Beer Judge Certification Program, Sanctioned Competitions, World's Largest Homebrew Competition.

9753 **www.bema.org**
Bakery Equipment Manufacturers Association

An international nonprofit association representing leading bakery and food equipment manufacturers and suppliers whose combined efforts in research and development have led to the continual improvement of the baking and food industries.

9754 **www.bestapples.com**
Washington Apple Commission

Marketing professionals promote apples through retail marketing, advertising, public relations, health and food communications.

9755 **www.beverageonline.com**
Beverage Online

A database for beverage chemists, food scientists, food technologists, process engineers, plant managers, business managers, executives and other professionals involved in the beverage processing industry.

9756 **www.biodynamics.com**
Bio-Dynamic Farming and Gardening Association

Supporting biodynamic growers and processors in North America and acts to safeguard and promote the biodynamic method of agriculture.

9757 **www.bisoncentral.com**
National Bison Association

The National Bison Association was formed to promote the production, marketing and preservation of bison.

9758 **www.bissc.org**
Baking Industry Sanitation Standards Committee

Develops and promotes sanitation standards for the design and construction of bakery equipment. Offers self certification and third party certification programs for the member companies whose equipment conforms to the BISSC standards.

9759 **www.blueberry.org**
North American Blueberry Council

History, crop information, products, international markets and berry sites.

9760 **www.bottledwater.org**
Bottled Water Association

9761 **www.bsdf-assbt.org**
Beet Sugar Development Foundation

Association specializing in beet sugar research and the advertisement of seed companies.

9762 **www.butterinstitute.org**
American Butter Institute

Represents butter manufacturers and conducts research.

9763 **www.ca-seafood.org**
California Seafood Council

9764 **www.caa-aqua.org**
California Aquaculture Association

9765 **www.cacheeseandbutter.org**
California Cheese & Butter Association

Membership directory along with links.

9766 **www.calbeef.org**
California Beef Council

9767 **www.californiadates.org**
California Date Commission

9768 **www.californiafigs.com**
California Fig Advisory Board

History and facts, nutritional information, recipes and contests.

9769 **www.calolive.org**
California Olive Committee

9770 **www.caloriecontrol.org**
Calorie Control Council

9771 **www.calpear.com**
California Pear Association

Consumer information, research reports, marketing and promo information.

9772 **www.calstrawberry.com**
California Strawberry Commission

Health and nutrition, contests, recipes, news, etc.

9773 **www.cancentral.com**
Can Manufacturers Institute

Serves can manufacturers and can industry suppliers

9774 **www.candyhalloffame.com**
National Confectionery Sales Association

Association of salespersons, brokers, sales managers, wholesalers and manufacturers in the confectionery industry.

9775 **www.candyusa.org**
National Confectioners Association

Association news, candy stats, health information, and candy history.

9776 **www.cannedveggies.org**
Canned Vegetable Council

An educational and promotional organization of vegetable canners whose goals are to raise the awareness of consumer and food service buyers regarding canned vegetables.

9777 **www.canonline.org**
Composite Can & Tube Institute

Serving the composite cans and tube industry.

9778 **www.cast-science.org**
Council for Agricultural Science and Technology

Identifies food, fiber, environmental and other agricultural issues for all stake holders.

9779 **www.cawineclub.com**
California Wine Club

A wine of the month club that features only California's small boutique wineries. Each month members receive two bottles of award-winning wine.

9780 **www.ccpgab.com**
California Cling Peach Advisory Board

9781 **www.cdfa.ca.gov**
North American Agricultural Marketing

For state and provincial officials responsible for agricultural products marketing programs in the US, Canada and ultimately Mexico.

9782 **www.cemanet.org**
Conveyor Equipment Manufacturers Association

9783 **www.cheesesociety.org**
American Cheese Society

Promotes cheese industry. Holds cheese tasting and workshops on cheesemaking. Sponsors competition.

9784 **www.cherrymkt.org**
Cherry Marketing Institute

Association representing the cherry industry. Provides promotional material to food service operators, brokers, retailers and manufacturers.

9785 **www.chicagomidwestmeatasso.com**
Chicago-Midwest Meat Association

The CMMA conducts its activities as a not-for-profit trade association for meat companies in the midwest. Its purpose is to support and promote the meat industry

9786 **www.chocolateandcocoa.org**
American Cocoa Research Institute

9787 **www.chowbaby.com**

This web site is a search engine for restaurants. Provides help in finding the perfect eatery close to your home or travel destination. Online reservations, maps, menus and more. Can be searched by International Location, US Location, US Map or Cuisine type.

9788 **www.chrie.org**
Int'l Council on Hotel, Restaurant Institute Edu.

To enhance professionalism at all levels of the hospitality and tourism industry through education and training.

9789 **www.christree.org**
National Christmas Tree Association

Provides industry leaders a chance to work directly with their suppliers and distributors.

9790 **www.ciachef.edu**
Culinary Institute of America

9791 **www.clm1.org**
Council of Logistics Management

9792 **www.coffeeindustry.org**
Specialty Coffee Association of America

Association offering business, professional, promotional and educational assistance in the areas of cultivation, processing, and marketing of specialty coffees. The association also hosts the largest event in the world dedicated to coffee, the SCAA Annual Conference and exhibition.

9793 **www.colborne.com/apc/home.htm**
American Pie Council

Membership, recipes, coupons, etc.

9794 **www.corn.org**
Corn Refiners Association

Stats, career opportunities, publications and newsbriefs.

9795 **www.cosmos.com.mx:80**
Index of Food

Manufacturers indexed by industry, company name, products and brands.

9796 **www.cottonseed.com**
National Cottonseed Products Association

National association of cottonseed products.

9797 **www.countryham.org**
National Country Ham Association

The NCHA encourages promotion, development, and improvement at the businesses of country ham carvers and encourages the use of country carved meats through cooperative methods of production, promotion, education and advertisement.

9798 **www.cpif.org**
California Poultry Industry Federation

Links to other associations.

9799 **www.cpma.ca**
Canadian Produce Marketing Association

Profile and services, links, technical resources, etc.

9800 **www.cranberries.org**
Cranberry Institute

Association which gathers and disseminates information about cranberry growing, horticultural and environmental issues to cranberry growers and handlers in the US and Canada.

9801 **www.crnusa.org**
Council for Responsible Nutrition

Vitamin manufacturers.

9802 **www.cropinsurance.org**
Crop Insurance Research Bureau

Crop insurance trade organization.

9803 www.croplifeamerica.org
CropLife America

Information on protecting crops and environmentally fragile agriculture.

9804 www.crops.org
Crop Science Society of America

Seeks to advance research, extension and teaching of all basic and applied phases of the crop sciences.

9805 www.csce.com
Coffee, Sugar and Cocoa Exchange

Acts as a financial exchange where futures and options are traded, the CSCE provides hedging and investing, opportunities in the coffee, sugar, cocoa and dairy markets.

9806 www.css.orst.edu/weeds/iwss
International Weed Science Society

For institutions and individuals concerned with the study of weeds and their control.

9807 www.culinary.com
Louisiana Sweet Potato Commission

Links to member sites.

9808 www.dairyinfo.com
Dairy Management

Links to related associations.

9809 www.dairynetwork.com
Dairy Network

Searchable database of food industry related items.

9810 www.delianet.com
Deli Associates

Association for manufacturers or suppliers of confectionary, candy and bakery products.

9811 www.delicouncil.com
Dairy, Deli-Bakery Council of Southern California

9812 www.dhia.org
National Dairy Herd Improvement Association

Sets policies, holds meetings and offers seminars for dairymen.

9813 www.diamondwalnut.com
Diamond Walnut Growers

9814 www.doitwithdairy.com

Dairy Management — American Dairy Association, National Dairy Council, US Dairy Export Council

9815 www.dressings-sauces.org
Association for Dressings and Sauces

This association is comprised of manufacturers of mayonnaise, salad dressings and condiment sauces, as well as industry suppliers.

9816 www.duckling.org
Duckling Council

Consortium of duckling producers located coast-to-coast, whose goal is to increase consumption of duckling nationwide and increase awareness of duckling's nutritionally improved profile.

9817 www.eatchicken.com
National Broiler Council

Recipes, industry information and statistics.

9818 www.eatright.org
American Dietetic Association

Nutrition resources, hot topics, FAQ's.

9819 www.eatturkey.com
National Turkey Federation

Advocate for all segments of the US turkey industry, providing services and conducting activities that increase demand for its members' products. The federation also protects and enhances its members' ability to effectively and profitably provide wholesome, high quality, nutritious turkey products.

9820 www.eddal.com
Eastern Dairy Deli Bakery Association

This association encourages growth and education regarding dairy, deli and bakery industries. It promotes the sales of Dairy, Deli and Bakery products through supermarkets and specialty stores and acts as a resource and information center for the industry.

9821 www.eggs.org
Egg Clearing House

Links to related members and associations.

9822 www.ejkrause.com
EJ Krause & Associates

Association for suppliers of hotel and restaurant food and beverages.

9823 www.elettric80.com
Electric 80

Supports automated material handling systems, robotic palletizers and laser-guided vehicles.

9824 www.eppainc.org
Eastern Dairy Perishable Products Association

This association encourages growth and education regarding perishable products. It promotes the sales of perishable products through supermarkets and specialty stores and acts as a resource and information center for the industry.

9825 www.fancyfoodshows.com
Nat'l Association for the Specialty Food Trade

Members are manufacturers, importers, distributors and retailers of specialty gourmet and fancy foods. Has an annual budget of approximately $15 million.

9826 www.fb.com
American Farm Bureau Federation

For state Farm Bureaus in the 50 states and Puerto Rico.

9827 www.fbminet.ca/agnews.htm

Agricultural news releases.

9828 www.fcsi.org
Food Service Consultants Society International

Membership, publications, industry links etc.

9829 www.fda.gov
Food and Drug Administration

The official website of FDA.

9830 www.fdi.org
Food Service Distributors International

9831 www.fdrs.ag.utk.edu/
Food Distribution Research Society

Investigates how food is distributed and traded.

9832 **www.feda.com**
Food Service Equipment Distributors Association

Dealers and distributors of foodservice equipment and supplies.

9833 **www.femaflavor.org**
Flavor & Extract Manufacturers Assn of the US

9834 **www.fewa.org**
Farm Equipment Wholesalers Association

For wholesale/distributors of ag equipment and related products.

9835 **www.ffane.org**
Frozen Food Association of New England

Promotes the frozen food industry.

9836 **www.fiae.com**
Food Industry Association Executives

9837 **www.fightbac.org**
Fight Bac

Sound advice for better food safety.

9838 **www.fl-citrus-mutual.com**
Florida Citrus Mutual

History and mission, member information.

9839 **www.foodallergy.org**
Food Allergy & Anaphylaxis Network

The only nonprofit organization in the US devoted solely to patient education for food allergies. Mission is to create public awareness about food allergies and anaphylaxis to provide education, and to advance research on behalf of all those affected by food allergy.

9840 **www.foodcontact.com**
Food Contact

Searchable directory of food and beverage processors and exporters.

9841 **www.foodexplorer.com**
Food Explorer

Database of industry related materials.

9842 **www.foodfront.com**
Internet Foodfront

Searchable database of food industry related items and resources.

9843 **www.foodindustry.com**
Industry Guides.net

Link directory for related industry.

9844 **www.foodingredientsonline.com**
Food Ingredients Online

International forum where buyers and sellers connect. Highly targeted and focused site offers original material, daily news updates, a product showcase, projects for bid, employment opportunities, downloadbale software, and a free interactive buyers guide which produces instant leads.

9845 **www.foodinstitute.com**
American Institute of Food Distribution

Serves as a central information service for food trades. Issues, reports, studies and statistical data and maintains a library. Member companies throughout the US and over 40 foreign countries.

9846 **www.foodnet.gr**
FoodNet

Searchable database of food industry related items and resources.

9847 **www.foodonline.com**
Food Online

Searchable database of food industry related items.

9848 **www.foodproductdesign.com**

Food product design magazine

9849 **www.foodprotection.org**
International Association for Food Protection

The International Association for Food Protection, founded in 1911, is a nonprofit educational association with a mission to provide food safety professional worldwide with a forum to exchange information on protecting the food supply. The Association is comprised of over 3,000 members from 50 nations. Affiliate chapters are located in the US, Canada, Mexico and South Korea.

9850 **www.foodservice.com/doorway.htm**

Foodservice.com

Database of information and resources for food industry buyers and sellers.

9851 **www.foodserviceworld.com**
Food Service World

Food associations, suppliers and events.

9852 **www.foodshow.com**
Foodshow

Electronic food show with booths for manufacturers.

9853 **www.foodweb.com**
Foodweb

Links to suppliers of food and equipment, distributors, unions, etc.

9854 **www.foodwine.com/digest**
Netfood Directory (The BLUE Directory)

List of relevant food and food service internet sites.

9855 **www.fourhcouncil.edu**
National 4-H Council

Focuses on diverse groups of young people in a variety of urban and suburban locales while continuing to serve youth in rural areas. Helps provide hands-on co-educational programs and activities to young people nationwide.

9856 **www.fpaota.org**
Fresh Produce Association of the Americas

Trade association for Mexican produce. Formerly known as West Mexico Vegetable Distributors Association.

9857 **www.fpfc.org**
Fresh Produce and Floral Council

Promotes through communication and education, fresh fruit, vegetable and floral products.

9858 **www.fpi.org**
Food Service & Packaging Institute

A national association comprised of manufacturers and suppliers of disposables for the food service industry.

9859 **www.fpmsa.org (or www.iefp.org)**
Food Processing Machinery Association

List of exhibitors from IEFP (links included).

9860 **www.fresh-cuts.org**
International Fresh-Cut Produce Association

IFPA advances the fresh-cut produce industry by supporting members with technical information, representation, and knowledge to provide convenient safe and wholesome food. Members are processor companies, suppliers and researchers.

9861 **www.freshcut.com**
Columbia Publishing

Information on carrot production, growers and shippers.

9862 **www.frozenfoodcouncil.com**
Frozen Food Council of Northern California

Coupons, promotions, contests, member information and events.

9863 **www.fsgroup.com**
Food Service Group

This organization is comprised of food service brokerage companies meeting the needs and offering a national exchange of ideas and information of food service sales professionals.

9864 **www.fspronet.com**
Food Service Professionals Network

Database of food industry related items including directories, etc.

9865 **www.georgiapecans.org**
Georgia Pecan Commission

9866 **www.gmabrands.com**
Grocery Manufacturers of America

Government affairs, industry regulations, news, etc.

9867 **www.gpi.org**
Glass Packaging Institute

Serves the glass container suppliers for the beer, juice, RTD tea, liquor, wine and dairy businesses.

9868 **www.grains.org**
US Feed Grains Council

For grain sorghum, barley and corn producer associations and representatives of the agricultural community. Provides commodity export market development.

9869 **www.greyhouse.com**
Grey House Publishing

Selected Grey House directories in the fields of business, health and education are available online. Users can search our online databases by several different search criteria, such as product categories, geographic area, sales volume and much, much more. Full Grey House catalog and online ordering also available.

9870 **www.hazelnut.com**
Hazelnut Growers of Oregon

Recipes, health and ingredient information, etc.

9871 **www.hazelnutcouncil.org**
Hazelnut Council

Promotion to commercial information exhibiting ingredient users and recipies, formulas and food service

9872 **www.healthfinder.gov**
Association of Food and Drug Officials

Promotes the enforcement of laws and regulations at all levels of government. Fosters understanding and cooperation between industry and regulators. Develops model laws and regulations and seeks their adoption.

9873 **www.herbnet.com/, www.herbworld.com**
Herb Growing and Marketing Network

Trade assocation information services for herb related businesses. Hosts national conference for those in the herb industry with seminars covering commercial production, medicinal herbs and general business topics.

9874 **www.herbs.org**
Herb Research Foundation

Provides scientific-based and traditional information about use and safety of herbs for health. Fee-based hotline, information packs and literature are available to members.

9875 **www.herbsociety.org**
Herb Society of America

This association maintains herb gardens, establishes gardens for the blind, and provides a speakers bureau for people located in the herb industry.

9876 **www.hereford.org**
American Hereford Association

For people in the Hereford cattle industry.

9877 **www.holsteinusa.com**
Holstein Association

For people with strong interests in breeding, raising and milking Holstein cattle.

9878 **www.iacp.com**
International Association of Culinary

A not-for-profit organization whose members represent virtually every profession in the culinary universe: teachers, cooking school owners, caterers, writers, chefs, media cooking personalities, editors, publishers, food stylists, food photographers, restauranteurs, leaders of major food corporations and vintners. Literally a who's who of the food world. Founded in 1978.

9879 **www.iacsc.org**
International Association of Cold Storage

9880 **www.iafenet.org**
International Association of Fairs & Expositions

Membership consists of individual agricultural fairs and regional associations of agricultural fairs.

9881 **www.iaff.ttu.edu/aals**
Association for Arid Land Studies

9882 **www.iafis.org**
Int'l Association of Food Industry Suppliers

Serves the dairy food and beverage industries, and related sanitary processing industries addressing the marketing and business information needs of the food supply channel.

9883 **www.iaicv.org**
International Association of Ice Cream Vendors

Members are manufacturers and distributors of ice cream novelties and street vendors.

9884 **www.iarw.org**
International Association of Refrigerated

Trade association of public refrigerated warehouse storing of all types of perishable products.

9885 **www.ibdea.org**
International Beverage Dispensing Equipment

Serves independent purveyors of equipment, service and products for the food and beverage industry.

9886 **www.iddanet.org**
International Dairy-Deli-Bakery Association

Newsletter, training information, publications, member list and FQA's.

9887 **www.iddba.org**
International Dairy-Deli-Bakery Association

Furthers relationship between manufacturing, production, marketing used in delivery of goods to marketplace. Presents awards and maintains a hall of fame.

9888 **www.idfa.org**
American Butter Institute

Represents butter manufacturers and conducts research.

9889 **www.ifas.ufl.edu**
Agricultural Communicators of Tomorrow

For college students professionally interested in communications related to agriculture, food, natural resources and allied fields.

9890 **www.ific.org**
International Food Information Council

Food safety and nutritional information, press releases and publications.

9891 **www.ifmaworld.com**
International Foodservice Manufacturers

Trade association for food, beverage, equipment and supply manufacturers and ancillary service companies serving the food service industry.

9892 **www.ifse.tamu.edu/sma.html**
Southwest Meat Association

Newsletter, member information and links.

9893 **www.ifsea.org**
International Food Service Executives

Provides education and community service to the foodservice industry.

9894 **www.ift.org**
Institute of Food Technologists

Member information, publications, calender of expos and meetings.

9895 **www.iherb.org**
International Herb Association

Supports the herb businesses and educates the public.

9896 **www.iiar.org**
International Institute of Ammonia Refrigeration

Promotes the safe use of ammonia as a refrigerant. Offers educational, promotional and standards development programs and legislative/regulatory support to manufacturers, contractors, consulting engineers, wholesalers and end users.

9897 **www.ilovepasta.org**
National Pasta Association

List of members, FAQ's, pasta nutrition and recipes.

9898 **www.ilovepickles.org**
Pickle Packers International

Addresses the concerns of pickle packers, shippers and manufacturers.

9899 **www.ilsi.org**
International Life Sciences Institute

Scientific institution that supports research on nutrition, food safety and toxicology.

9900 **www.independentbaker.org**
Independent Bakers Association

Organization of member bakers.

9901 **www.insca.org**
International Natural Sausage Casing Association

9902 **www.iopp.org**
Institute of Packaging Professionals

9903 **www.ipmwww.ncsu.edu/cernag/**

All aspects of agriculture: Usenet groups, Web resources, archives, mailing lists, etc.

9904 **www.irrigation.org**
Irrigation Association

Irrigation industry information.

9905 **www.iseo.org**
Institute of Shortening & Edible Oils

9906 **www.jps.net/ahaherb**
American Herb Association

Membership is comprised of professional herablists and herbal enthusiasts. The goal is to increase knowledge and offer updated scientific information on herbs.

9907 **www.juanvaldez.com**
National Federation of Coffee Growers of Colombia

This organization is comprised of coffee growers from Colombia whose goal is to promote Colombian coffee in the US.

9908 **www.kab.org**
Keep America Beautiful

National nonprofit education organization whose corporate members include packagers, retailers, bottlers, and makers of chemical, steel, glass, paper and aluminum products.

9909 **www.kiwifruit.org**
California Kiwifruit Commission

News, recipes, export information, etc.

9910 **www.kla.org**
Kansas Livestock Association

9911 **www.lambchef.com**
American Lamb Council

9912 **www.larw.org**
Refrigeration Research and Education Foundation

Sponsors graduate-level scientific research on the refrigeration of perishable commodities. Offers annual training institute for public refrigerated warehouse personnel.

9913 **www.leafy-greens.org**
Leafy Greens Council

Made up of growers and shippers. This association promotes the consumption of leafy greens and vegetables for battling diseases like cancer.

9914 **www.llovepecans.org**
National Pecan Shellers Association

An association aimed at promoting the pecan shelling and processing industry.

9915 **www.mainelobsterpromo.com**
Maine Lobster Promotion Council

9916 **www.mainpotatoes.com**
Maine Potato Board

9917 **www.meatami.com**
American Meat Institute

A leading trade association for the meat processing industry.

9918 **www.meatandpoultryonline.com**
Meat and Poultry Online

Searchable database of food industry related items.

9919 **www.meatnz.co.nz**
Meat New Zealnd

9920 **www.meatpoultry.com**

Meat and poultry magazine

9921 **www.mhia.org**
Material Handling Industry

9922 **www.micausa.org**
Meat Importers Council of America

9923 **www.michiganapples.dcom**
Michigan Apple Committee

9924 **www.militaryfood.org**
Research and Development Associates for Military

Founded as a forum for the interchange of technical data on food products, feeding systems, food and feeding equipment and food packaging between industry and professors of Food Science and Technology and the US Armed Forces and Government.

9925 **www.mindspring.com/~independent baker**
Independent Bakers Association

Links, issue papers, etc.

9926 **www.msgfacts.com**
Glutamate Association— US

Members are manufacturers, distributors and processed food users of glutamate, glutamate acid and its salts in the food industry.

9927 **www.mtgplace.com**

Source of information for food product developers

9928 **www.mushroomcouncil.com**
Mushroom Council

9929 **www.mwfpa.org**
Midwest Food Processors Association

This association offers member companies information on legislation and industry matters.

9930 **www.naab-css.org**
National Association of Animal Breeders

For farmer co-ops and others interested in livestock improvement.

9931 **www.nabi-inc.gpg.com**
National Association of Beverage Importers

Members hold a Federal Basic Importer's permit.

9932 **www.nabronline.org**
National Association of Beverage Retailers

Represents over 15,000 off-premise licensees in the 'open' or 'license' states and on-premise proprietors in markets across the nation. Offers members information on legislation and industry matters.

9933 **www.nacaa.com**
National Association County Agricultural Agents

For agents focusing on educational programs for the youth of the community.

9934 **www.naconline.org**
National Association of Concessionaires

This association works to professionalize the concession industry by providing information services and training programs for concession managers and employees. Holds conventions, seminars, trade shows, and certification programs for the leisure time food and beverage industry. Produces newsletters and magazines for its international membership.

9935 **www.nacufs.org**
National Assn of College & University Food Service

Educational programs, conferences, publications, etc.

9936 **www.nadefa.org**
North American Deer Farmers Association

A nonprofit organization that offers representation of US and Canadian breeders and producers of venison. Velvet and trophy stock.

9937 **www.nafem.org**
Food Equipment Manufacturers Association

9938 **www.naffs.org**
National Association of Fruits, Flavors & Syrups

Industry information, member directory and links to member sites.

9939 **www.nama.org**
National Agri-Marketing Association

Marketing and communication suppliers, including trade publications, radio and television broadcast sales organizations, premium/incentive manufacturers, printers, marketing research firms, photographers and related professionals.

9940 **www.namamillers.org**
North American Millers' Association

9941 **www.namp.com**
North American Meat Processors Association

Represents processors and distributors of meat, poultry, seafood and game to the food service industry.

9942 **www.nanca.org**
North American Natural Casing Association

The NANCA responds to issues and service needs that are unique to the North American segment of the industry.

9943 **www.nas.edu**
National Research Council/National Academy

9944 **www.nasda-hq.org**
National Association of State Departments of Agriculture

9945 **www.nationalgrange.org**
National Grange

Promotes general welfare and agriculture through local organizations. Presides over the advancement and promotion of the farming and agriculture industry.

9946 **www.nationalgrocers.org**
National Grocers of America

This association services as the information network to the National Grocers Association. Purposes of this organization: handling government affairs regarding the operation of retail groceries; developing educational programs and literature regarding the industry; and supports women in the retail distribution industry.

9947 **www.navigator.tufts.edu**
Tufts University Nutrition Navigator

A rating guide for more than 300 nutrition websites.

9948 **www.nbva.org**
National Bulk Vendors Association

An organization comprised of manufacturers, distributors and operators of bulk vending merchandise and equipment.

9949 **www.nbwa.org**
National Beer Wholesalers Association

Research and development, quality control and ingredients.

9950 **www.nca-cna.org**
National Confectioners Association

Manufacturers of confectionary products and services.

9951 **www.ncausa.org and www.coffeescience.org**
National Coffee Association of USA

This association promotes business relations among members of the trade. Also collects and publishes information on the coffee industry, maintaining a library of 1000 science and medical books and literature about coffee and caffeine.

9952 **www.ncga.com**
National Corn Growers Association

9953 **www.neffa.com**
Northeast Fresh Foods Alliance

9954 **www.nfdffa.org**
National Frozen Dessert and Fast Food Association

This association is made up of small, independent owners and operators of ice cream and fast food establishments.

9955 **www.nffa.org**
National Frozen Food Association

Training, research, networking services, etc.

9956 **www.nfi.org**
National Aquaculture Council

For farmers, food processors and food distributors with an interest in aquaculture.

9957 **www.nfo.org**
National Farmers Union

Promotes educational, cooperative and legislative activities of farm families in 44 states.

9958 **www.nfpa-food.org**
National Food Processors Association

A leading food industry trade association.

9959 **www.nfraweb.org**
National Frozen & Refrigerated Foods Association

Nonprofit trade association comprised of 650 member companies representing all segments of the frozen and refrigerated food industry. NFRA has been serving the frozen food industry since 1945 and just recently in 2001 began serving the refrigerated foods industry. The mission of NFRA is to promote the sales and consumption of frozen and refrigerated foods through: educations, training, research, sales planning and menu development and providing a forum for industry dialogue.

9960 **www.nhb.org**
National Honey Board

This organization offers information and support to members in the honey producing industry.

9961 **www.nims.com**
Network of Ingredient Marketing Specialists

This organization has established a network of ingredient manufacturers' representatives that offers ingredient manufacturers the most cost effective access to US, Canadian and European markets.

9962 **www.njpa.com**
National Juice Products Association

9963 **www.nmaonline.org**
National Meat Association

Events, publications and resource library.

9964 **www.nmpf.org**
National Milk Producers Federation

9965 **www.noble.net**
Noble & Associates

Advertising agency for food industry professionals.

9966 **www.nopa.org**
National Oilseed Processors Association

9967 **www.npcspud.com**
National Potato Council

Represents US potato growers on federal legislative and regulatory issues.

9968 **www.nppc.org**
National Pork Producers Council

Nutrition information, educational resources and research results.

9969 **www.nsda.org**
National Soft Drink Association

Industry, product and recycling information, issues and events.

9970 **www.nwcherries.com**
Northwest Cherry Growers

9971 **www.nwfpa.com**
Northwest Food Processors Association

Conventions and exhibits, member listings and links.

9972 **www.nwfpa.org**
Northwest Food Processors Association

An organization that aims to develop and promote the food processing industry located in Oregon, Idaho, and Washington.

9973 **www.nyapplecounty.com**
New York Apple/New York Cherry Growers

9974 **www.oamp.org**
Ohio Association of Meat Processors

9975 **www.ocia.org**
Organic Crop Improvement Association

For farmers, processors, manufacturers and traders of organic crops.

9976 **www.oilseeds.org**
American Soybean Association

Consumption statistics, related associations.

9977 **www.onions-usa.org**
National Onion Association

Recipes, member information and allied industry and export information.

9978 **www.opensecrets.org**
Cheese Association of America

The Center for Responsive Politics is a nonpartisan, nonprofit research group based in Washington, DC that tracks money in politics, and its effect on campaign finance issues for the news media, academics, activists and the public at large.

9979 **www.oregon-berries.com**
Oregon Rasberry & Blackberry Commission

Supports the rasberries, blackberries, marionberries and boysenberries industries.

9980 **www.oregonhazelnuts.org**
Hazelnut Marketing Board

This organization was established to promote and provide for the Oregon hazelnut industry.

9981 **www.organic.org**
Organic Alliance

9982 **www.ostriches.org**
American Ostrich Association

Organization that provides leadership for the ostrich industry and its future through the promotion of ostrich products.

9983 **www.osu.orst.edu/dept/iifet**
International Institute of Fisheries Economics

Promotes discussion, research projects and sponsors educational courses. Publications available.

9984 **www.ota.org**
Organic Trade Association

For businesses involved in the organic agriculture and products industry. Seeks to promote the industry and establish production and marketing standards.

9985 **www.ou.org**
Orthodox Union

9986 **www.pabeef.org**
Pennsylvania Cattlemen's Association

9987 **www.packagingeducation.org**
Packaging Education Forum

A membership organization through which industry guides the development of, establishes quality standards for, and provides financial assistance to packaging education programs, curricula and students at the university.

9988 **www.packagingnetwork.com**
Packaging Network

Searchable database of food industry related items.

9989 **www.packexpo.com**
Packging Machinery Manufacturers Institute

Members are manufacturers of packaging and packaging related coconverting machinery in the US and Canada. PMMI offers meetings, an inquiry service, statistics and surveys and a business to business service on it's website. PMMI also sponsors several Pack Expos (packaging related tradeshows).

9990 **www.packinfo-world.com**
World Packaging Organization

Information regarding the packaging industry internationally.

9991 **www.packinfo-world.org**
Contract Packaging and Manufacturing Association

Information on major packaging associations.

9992 **www.peanutbutterlovers.com**
Peanut Advisory Board

This organization conducts the marketing and promotion of peanut and peanut butter products.

9993 **www.peanutsusa.com**
American Peanut Council

Association members include growers and manufacturers of peanuts and peanut products.

9994 **www.pigglywiggly.com**
National Piggly Wiggly Operators Association

An association of independent grocers operating under Piggly Wiggly franchises in 24 states. Includes both small operators of one to five supermarkets as well as multiple store organizations of as many as 90 or more supermarkets.

9995 **www.pistachios.org**
California Pistachio Commission

Commodity board representing California pistachio growers.

9996 **www.pizzatoday.com**
National Association of Pizza Operators

The membership of this organization is independent and franchised pizza operators, manufacturers and suppliers of pizza equipment.

9997 **www.plma.com**
Private Label Manufacturers Association (PLMA)

Trade Association promoting the private label industry.

9998 www.pma.com
Produce Marketing Association

For those who market fresh fruits, vegetables, and floral products worldwide; involved in the production, distribution, retail, and food service sectors of the industry.

9999 www.popcorn.org
Popcorn Institute

A trade association representing the popcorn industry. Institute activites include projects to improve popcorn growing and processing technology, serving as a liasion with several government regulatory agencies and a generic marketing program to promote product awareness and consumption.

10000 www.poultryegg.org
US Poultry & Egg Association

10001 www.ppws.vt.edu/newss/society.htm
Northeastern Weed Science Society

10002 www.processfood.com
Food Processing Machinery & Supplies Association

10003 www.prunes.org
California Prune Board

10004 www.ptnpa.org
Peanut and Tree Nut Processors Association

10005 www.qba.com
Quality Bakers of America Cooperative

Members are independent wholesale bakeries and their suppliers.

10006 www.qchekd.com
Quality Checked Dairies

A cooperative of Dairy foods processors who use the Quality Checked trademark on their products and engage in group purchasing of ingredients and supplies.

10007 www.raisins.org
California Raisin Marketing Food Tech. Program

10008 www.rbanet.com
Retail Bakers Association

Links to other associations.

10009 www.realbutter.com
American Dairy Association

Recipes, media information, celebrity chefs and industry news.

10010 www.redangus1.org
Red Angus Association of America

Association for breeders of Red Angus cattle.

10011 www.redraspberry.com
Washington Red Raspberry Commisson

10012 www.refrigeratedfoods.com
Refrigerated Foods Association

Formerly called the Salad Manufacturers Association, the Refrigerated Foods Association is an international organization comprised of manufacturers and suppliers of prepared, refrigerated, ready-to-eat food products.

10013 www.register.com/food
Food Institute

Member and industry links.

10014 www.renderers.org
National Renderers Association

Members recycle animal by-products only, also provide services to renderers.

10015 www.restaurant.org
National Restaurant Association

Trends, government affairs, training, research, dining guides and links.

10016 www.reta.com
Refrigerating Engineers & Technicians Association

10017 www.retailconfectioners.org
Retail Confectioners International

Provides education, promotion and legislative services. Holds courses and bestows awards.

10018 www.saltinstitute.org
Salt Institute

Industry information and member businesses.

10019 www.sbsonline.org
Society for Biomolecular Screening

Supports research and discovery in pharmaceutical biotechnology and the agrichemical industry that utilize biomolecular screening procedures.

10020 www.scaa.com
Specialty Coffee Association of America

Training programs, newsletter, member websites, etc.

10021 www.scisoc.org/asbc
American Society of Brewing Chemists

Annual scientific meeting for professionals in the brewing industry.

10022 www.seafwa.org
Southeastern Association of Fish and Wildlife

The Southeastern Association of Fish and Wildlife Agencies is an organization whose members are the state agencies with primary responsibility for management and protection of the fish and wildlife resources in 16 states, Puerto Rico and the US Virgin Islands.

10023 www.seedtechnology.net
Society of Commercial Seed Technologists

Professionals involved in the testing and analysis of seeds, including research, production and handling based on botanical and agricultural sciences.

10024 www.sheepusa.org
American Sheep Industry Association

For state associations dedicated to the welfare and profitability of the sheep industry.

10025 www.shellfish.org
National Shellfisheries Association

Organization comprised of scientists, public health workers, shellfish producers and fishery administrators. To promote and advance shellfisheries research and the application of results to the shellfish industry

10026 www.snax.com
Snack Food Association

Facts, stats and trivia about snack food industry.

10027 www.southeastdairy.org
Southeast United Dairy Industry Association

Promotes milk and milk products in the southeastern states.

10028 www.southerncottonginners.org
Southern Cotton Ginners Association

Operates in a five state area as an information center covering safety and governmental regulations.

10029 www.soyfoods.com
US Soy Food Directory

Searchable database of soy food processors, suppliers, and industry information.

10030 www.soyfoods.org
Soyfoods Association of North America

Sponsors April as soy foods month. Conducts annual seminar on soy foods in fall.

10031 www.spcouncil.org
Soy Protein Council

Members of this association include persons, firms and corporations regularly engaged within the US in the processing and sale of vegetable proteins or vegetable protein products derived from agricultural services.

10032 www.specialityfoods.org
Speciality Food Distributors & Manufacturers

10033 www.state.id.us/bean
Idaho Bean Commission

Directory of dealers, recipes, nutritional values and research.

10034 www.steel.org
American Iron and Steel Institute

Develops and implements market development programs for appropriate food and beverage packaging applications.

10035 www.suebeehoney.com
Sioux Honey Association

10036 www.sugar.org
Sugar Association

Represents processors and refiners of beet and cane sugar in nutrition and health matters.

10037 www.sugaralliance.org
American Sugar Alliance

For domestic producers, processors, suppliers and labor organizations in the sugar and sugarcane industry.

10038 www.sunflowernsa.com
National Sunflower Association

For companies associated with sunflower products.

10039 www.sunmaid.com
Sun-Maid Growers of California

10040 www.susta.org
Southern US Trade Association

This nonprofit organization was designed to promote the sales of US agricultural products produced in the south.

10041 www.teausa.com
Tea Council of the USA

International companies and governments interested in cultivating and expanding the demand for the sale and consumption of tea in the US.

10042 www.teleport.com/~hazelnut
Hazelnut Marketing Board

This organization was established to promote and provide for the Oregon hazelnut industry.

10043 www.tfi.org
Fertilizer Institute

For brokers, producers, importers, dealers and manufacturers of fertilizer and fertilizer-related equipment.

10044 www.tfir.com
Grey House Publishing

Using this comprehensive online database you can access information on over 40,000 food and beverage companies, products, key executives, corporate, facility information and more.

10045 www.theamericancenter.org
American Center for Wine, Food & the Arts

10046 www.thebcma.org
Biscuit & Cracker Manufacturers Association

An organization that represents and promotes the cookie and cracker manufacturing industry.

10047 www.therestaurantfinder.com

This search engine help to find restaurants by type or location.

10048 www.tianet.org
Transportation Intermediaries Association

Education and policy organization for North American transportation intermediaries representing the interests of all third party transportation service providers. Members include logistics management firms, property brokers, perishable commodities brokers, freight forwarders, intermodal marketers, ocean and air forwarders, and NVOCC's.

10049 www.tortilla-info.com
Tortilla Industry Association

News, trade information, 'where to buy' and recipes.

10050 www.turkeyfed.org
National Turkey Federation

Member site links and industry information.

10051 www.txbeef.com
Texas Beef Council

Recipes, ranching information, tips and links.

10052 www.uark.edu/depts/ifse/ofpa
Ozark Food Processors Association

This association is comprised of regional food processors and national suppliers for the food service industry. Hosts an annual convention in the spring which includes at attendence of over 700 and over 100 exhibitors.

10053 www.uffva.org
United Fresh Fruit & Vegetable Association

Equipment, supplies, cartons, packaging machinery, computers, sorting and sizing equipment, harvesting equipment, film wrap manufacturing and commodity organizations.

10054 www.usapears.com
Pear Bureau Northwest

Promotes fresh pears grown in the Pacific Northwest area.

10055 www.usapple.org
US Apple Association

Members are US and foreign firms, other than retailers, that handle apples.

10056 www.usarice.com
USA Rice Federation

10057 www.usda.gov
US Department of Agriculture

The official website of USDA.

10058 www.usda.gov/fcs/fcs.html
Food & Nutrition Service

10059 www.usguernsey.com
American Guernsey Association

Register and deliver guernsey cattle throughout the US.

10060 www.usmef.org
US Meat Export Federation

10061 www.uspastry.org
US Pastry Alliance

10062 www.uspotatoes.com
National Potato Promotion Board

Also known as the potato board. Organized to operate a national promotion plan to position potatoes as low calorie, nutritious vegetables and to facilitate market expansion into domestic and export sales.

10063 www.vealfarm.com
American Veal Association

For veal producers and processors.

10064 www.vending.org
National Automatic Merchandising Association

Serves merchandising, vending, contract foodservice management and office coffee service industries.

10065 www.versatilevinegar.org
Vinegar Institute

Manufacturers and bottlers of vinegar and suppliers to the industry are the members of this association. Publications available only to members.

10066 www.vrg.org
Vegetarian Resource Group

10067 www.vtcheese.com
Vermont Cheese Council

10068 www.walnut.org
Walnut Marketing Board

History, statistics, supplier listings, etc.

10069 www.warehouselogistics.org
American Warehouse Association

10070 www.watermelon.org
National Watermelon Promotional Board

10071 www.wawgg.org
Washington Association of Wine Grape Growers

Guidance in research and education, and maintaining leadership in local, state and national wine grape issues.

10072 www.wdairycouncil.com
Western Dairyfarmers' Promotion Association

Promotes dairy products for the dairy farmer.

10073 www.westernassn.com
Western Retail Implement and Hardware Association

For manufacturers, suppliers and distributors of equipment, supplies and services relating to the agricultural industry.

10074 www.wflo.com
World Food Logistics Organization

The activities of the WFLO include improving the application of refrigeration technology for the preservation and distribution of food and other commodities, stimulating and supporting research in the science of food refrigeration through grants, training and educating industry personnel, growing its bank of scientific information on the storage and distribution of perishable goods, and developing and supporting national associations.

10075 www.wga.com
Western Growers Association

Links and news, safety and legal information.

10076 www.wheatfoods.org
Wheat Foods Council

Links, nutrition and product information, news and tips.

10077 www.wheatworld.org
National Association of Wheat Growers

Member information, government agencies, research information, etc.

10078 www.whybiotech.com
Council for Biotechnology Information

Our vision and mission is to improve understanding and acceptance of biotechnology by collecting balanced, credible and science based information, then communicating this information through a variety of channels. Plant biotechnology has the potential to provide more and better food for a growing world population while helping steward the environment.

10079 www.wicdirectors.org
National Association of WIC Directors

Members are geographic state, Native American state and local agency directors of the special supplement nutrition program for women, infants and children.

10080 www.wildblueberries.com
Wild Blueberry Association of North America

Sources, recipes, news and product ideas.

10081 www.wineinstitute.org
Wine Institute

Organization that represents the wine and spirit industry to state and federal lawmaking bodies.

10082 www.wislink.org
Wisconsin Milk Marketing Board

10083 www.worldfoodnet.com

Source of information for food product developers

10084 www.wssa.com
Wine and Spirits Shippers Association

Provides members, importers and exporters with efficient and economical ocean transportation and other logistic services.

10085 www.wusata.org
Western US Agricultural Trade Association

This organization offers information and support to increase exports of US agricultural products.

Associations

10086 A Philanthropic Partnership for Black Communities
55 Exchange Place
New York, NY 10005
212-982-6925
FAX: 212-982-6886 www.abfe.org

Judy Ford, Chair
Dwayne Proctor, Vice Chair
Kenneth W. Austin, President
Wenda Weeks Moore, Secretary
Dr Ricardo A. Millet, Treasurer

Encourages blacks in the grantmaking field and helps members improve their job effectiveness.
Founded: 1971

10087 American Association of Fund-Raising
4700 W Lake Avenue
Glenview, IL 60025
847-375-4709
FAX: 866-263-2491 800-462-2372
info@aafrc.org www.aafrc.org

C. Ray Clements, Chair
George C. Ruotolo, Vice Chair
Carl Hefton, Vice Chair
David C. Spilman, Treasurer
Rita J. Galowich, Secretary

To promote ethical practice and professional standards in the fund-raising consultant field.
30 Members Founded: 1935

10088 American Society of Association Executives
1575 I Street NW
Washington, DC 20005
202-626-2723
FAX: 202-371-8825
service@asaenet.org www.asaenet.org

Thomas R. Kuhn, Chairman
Paulette V. Maehara, Chair Elect
John H. Graham IV, President/CEO

The society is dedicated to advancing the value of voluntary associations to society and supporting the professionalism of the individuals who lead them.
25000 Members Founded: 1920

10089 Association for Healthcare Philanthropy
313 Park Avenue
Suite 400
Falls Church, VA 22046
703-532-6243
FAX: 703-532-7170
ahp@ahp.org www.ahp.org
Represents health care fundraising professionals through education and eventually bestows the credentials upon them.
$395.00
4100 Members Individual Membership Fee
Founded: 1967
Mailing list available for rent

10090 Association of Fund Raising Distributors & Suppliers
1100 Johnson Ferry Road
Suite 300
Atlanta, GA 30342
404-252-3663
FAX: 404-252-0774
afrds@kellencompany.com
www.afrds.org

Russell Lemieux, Executive Director
Vickie Mabry, Associate Director

Association for manufacturers or suppliers of fundraising products, supplies and services. Its members manufacturer, supply or distribute products that are resold by not-for-profit organizations for fundraising purposes.
700+ Members

10091 Association of Fund-Raising Professionals
1101 King Street
Suite 700
Alexandria, VA 22314
703-684-0410
FAX: 703-684-0540
mbrship@afpnet.org www.afpnet.org

Alphonce J Brown Jr, Chair
Timothy R Burcham, Chair Elect
Paulette V. Maehara, President/CEO
Scott C. Staub, Secretary
Philip G. Schumacher, Treasurer

Supports all involved in the fundraising profession. Publishes monthly newsletter.
26000 Members Founded: 1965

10092 Association of Small Foundations
4905 Del Ray Avenue
Suite 200
Bethesda, MD 20814
301-907-3337
FAX: 301-907-0980 888-212-9922
asf@smallfoundations.org
www.smallfoundations.org

Landon B. Lane, Chair
Christyne Hamilton, Secretary
Thomas Blaney, Treasurer
Tim Walter, Chief Executive Officer

Committed to building and strengthening small foundation philanthropy by providing quality programs, products and services to foundations with few or no staff.
$400.00
2900 Members Annual Membership Fee

10093 BBB Wise Giving Alliance
4200 Wilson Boulevard
Suite 800
Arlington, VA 22203
703-276-0100
FAX: 703-525-8277
give@cbbb.bbb.org www.give.org

H. Art Taylor, President/CEO
Bennett Weiner, Chief Operating Officer

The alliance collects and distributes information on hundreds of nonprofit organizations that solicit nationally or have national or international program services. It routinely asks such organizations for information about their programs, governance, fund raising practices, and finances when the charities have been the subject of inquiries.
Founded: 2001

10094 BoardSource
1828 L Street NW
Suite 900
Washington, DC 20036-5114
202-452-6262
FAX: 202-452-6299 800-883-6262
mail@boardsource.org
www.boardsource.org

Lorie A Slutsky, Chair
Phyllis J Campbell, Vice Chair
Deborah S. Hechinger, President/CEO
Barry D. Gaberman, Secretary
Peter A. Kirsch, Treasurer

Formerly the National Center for Nonprofit Boards, is the premier resource for practical information, tools and best practices, training, and leadership development for board members of nonprofit organizations worldwide.
7000 Members Founded: 1988

10095 Center for Effective Philanthropy
675 Massachusetts Avenue
7th Floor
Cambridge, MA 02139
617-760-0859
FAX: 617-492-0888
alysed@effectivephilanthropy.org
www.effectivephilanthropy.com

Ron Gallo, President/CEO
Phil Buchanan, Executive Director

The center's mission is to advance the practice of philanthropy by providing management and governance tools to define, assess and improve overall foundation performance.

10096 Christopher Reeve Paralysis Foundation
636 Morris Tpke
Ste 3A
Short Hills, NJ 07078-2608
973-379-2690
FAX: 973-379-1448 800-225-0292
info@crpf.org
www.christopherreeve.org

Peter G Kiernan III, Chairperson
Henry G Stifel, Vice Chairperson
John M. Hughes, Vice Chairman
Executive Committee
Kathy Lewis, President/CEO
Robert L. Guyett, Chairman Executive Committee

Committed to funding research that develops treatments and cures for paralysis caused by spinal cord injury and other central nervous system disorders. The Foundation also vigorously works to improve the quality of life for people living with disabilities through its grants program, paralysis resource center and advocacy efforts.
Founded: 1982

10097 Council for Advancement & Support of Campus Fund Raising
1307 New York Avenue NW
Suite 1000
Washington, DC 20005-4701
202-285-5900
FAX: 202-387-4973
memberservicecenter@case.org
www.case.org

John Lippincott, President/CEO
Lekan Adesioye, Membership Development Coordinator
Rae Goldsmith, VP Communications

Supports all those involved in campus fund raising, public relations,and alumni administration. Publishes monthly magazine.

10098 Council on Foundations
1828 L Street NW
Washington, DC 20036
202-466-6512
FAX: 202-785-3926
info@cof.org www.cof.org

Emmett D Carson, Chair
Dorothy S Ridings, President/CEO
Sarah Thompson, Executive Assistant
Robert Shalett, Marketing & Publications Director
Jeff Martin, Media Relations Director

Supports all those involved in the foundation business. Publishes monthly magazine. We provide leadership expertise, legal services and networking opportuni-

ties among other services to our members and to the general public.
2000 Members

10099 Foundation Center
79 Fifth Avenue/16th Street
New York, NY 10003-3076
212-204-4230
FAX: 212-807-3677 800-424-9836
communications@fdncenter.org
www.fdncenter.org
Sara Engelhardt, President
Cheryl Loe, Communications Director
Alyson Tufts, VP Development
A national association for those interested in fund raising related to government agencies.
Founded: 1956

10100 Independent Sector
1200 18th Street NW
Suite 200
Washington, DC 20036
202-467-6100
FAX: 202-467-6101 888-860-8118
info@independentsector.org
www.independentsector.org
William E Trueheart, Chair
Gary L Yates, Vice Chair
Diana Aviv, President/CEO
Paula Van Ness, Treasurer
Hilary Pennington, Secretary
The leadership forum for charities, foundations, and corporate giving programs committed to advancing the common good in America and around the world.
700 Members Founded: 1980

10101 MacArthur Foundation
140 S. Dearborn Street
Chicago, IL 60603-5285
312-726-8000
FAX: 312-920-6258
4answers@macfound.org
www.macfound.org
Sara Lawrence-Lightfoot, Chair
Lloyd Axworthy, President
Rebecca Koman, Manager
A private, independent grantmaking institution dedicated to helping groups and individuals foster lasting improvement in the human condition.
Founded: 1978

10102 Music Performance Fund
1501 Broadway
Suite 518
New York, NY 10036
212-391-3950
FAX: 212-221-2604
info@MusicPF.org www.musicpf.org
Noel Berman, Trustee
Elby Schneidman, Manager
John Hall, Manager
Foundation allocates money for the promotion of live music for the general public. The concerts must be free of charge and have no admittance restrictions.
15 Members Founded: 1948

10103 National Association of Counties
440 1st Street NW
Washington, DC 20001-2028
202-393-6226
FAX: 202-393-2630
agoldsch@naco.org www.naco.org
Colleen Landkamer, President
Andrew Goldschmidt, Membership/Marketing Director
Larry Naake, Chief Executive Officer
We ensure that the nation's 3066 counties are heard and understood in the White House and the halls of Congress. NACo's membership totals more than 2,000 counties, representing over 80 percent of the nation's population. provides an extensive line of services including legislative, research, technical, and public affairs assistance, as well as enterprise services to its members.
Founded: 1935

10104 National Catholic Development Conference
86 Front Street
Hempstead, NY 11550-3667
516-481-6000
FAX: 516-489-9287 888-879-6232
glehmuth@ncdcusa.org
www.ncdcusa.org
Sr. Kathleen Lunsmann, Chair
Andrew W Rivers, Vice Chair
Georgette Lehmuth, President/CEO
Frances A. MacAllister, Secretary
Richard L. Heist, Treasurer
Members include development officers and key fund raisers of charitable institutions and agencies.
400 Members Founded: 1968

10105 National Committee for Responsive Philanthropy
2001 S Street NW
Suite 620
Washington, DC 20009
202-387-9177
FAX: 202-332-5084
info@ncrp.org www.ncrp.org
Rick Cohen, Executive Director
Jeff Krehely, Deputy Director
Supports all those involved in the philanthropy field. Publishes quarterly newsletter.
Founded: 1976

10106 National Committee on Planned Giving
233 McCrea Street
Suite 400
Indianapolis, IN 46225
317-269-6274
FAX: 317-269-6276
ncpg@ncpg.org www.ncpg.org
Joseph O Bull, Chair
Wallace Munro, Chair Elect
Tanya Howe Johnson, President/CEO
Jan S. Adams, Senior Vice President
Andrea M. Latchem, Secretary
A professional association for people whose work includes developing, marketing, and administering charitable planned gifts. Those people include fund raisers for nonprofit institutions and consultants and donor advisors working in a variety of for-profit settings.
112 Members Founded: 1988

10107 North American Association of State and Provincial Lotteries
2775 Bishop Road
Suite B
Willoughby Hills, OH 44092
216-241-2310
FAX: 216-241-4350
nasplhq@aol.com www.naspl.org
Thomas Shaheen, President
Gerald Aubin, First VP
Clint Harris, Second VP
Ernie Passailaigue, Secretary
David Gale, Manager
Represents 47 lottery organizations throughout North America. Provides information and benefits of state and provincial lottery organizations.
50 Members Founded: 1971

10108 Northwest Development Officers Association
2150 N 107th Street
Suite 205
Seattle, WA 98133-9009
206-367-8704
FAX: 206-367-8777
office@ndoa.org www.ndoa.org
Joann Marshall, President
Tara Morgan, Secretary
Reidun Crowley, Treasurer
NDOA provides fellowship and a sounding board for development officers, volunteers, board members, students, nonprofit managers and others who are committed to fund raising and philanthropy. *$95.00*
800+ Members Annual Membership Fee
Founded: 1978

10109 Society for Nonprofit Organizations
5820 Canton Center Road
Suite 165
Canton, MI 48187
734-451-3582
FAX: 734-451-5935 www.snpo.org
Katie Burnham, Co-Founder/President/CEO
Dedicated to bringing together those who serve in the nonprofit world in order to build a strong network of professionals throughout the country. *$59.00*
Individual Membership Fee Founded: 1983

10110 The Grantsmanship Center
1125 W. 6th Street, 5th Floor
PO Box 17220
Los Angeles, CA 90017
213-482-9860
FAX: 213-482-9863 800-421-9512
info@tgci.com www.tgci.com
Cathleen E Kiritz, President
Formed to offer grantsmanship training and low cost publications to nonprofit organizations and government agencies. *$375.00*
Membership Fee Founded: 1972

Newsletters

10111 AID for Education
CD Publications
8204 Fenton Street
Silver Spring, MD 20910
301-588-0519
FAX: 301-588-6385 800-666-6380
info@cdpublications.com
http://www.cdpublications.com
Mike Gerecht, Publisher
Frank Kalimko, Editor
Private and federal funding opportunities and news for all levels of education including grants for bilingual education, special education, literacy, minorities and more. *$419.00*
18 pages Founded: 1991
Mailing list available for rent 2,000 names $160 per M.

10112 Board Source
1828 L Street NW
Suite 900
Washington, DC 20036-5114
202-452-6262
FAX: 202-452-6299 800-883-6262
boardsource@boardsource.org
http://www.boardsource.org

Deborah S Hechinger, President/CEO
Betsy Rosenblatt, Senior Editor

National newsletter for board members and staff leaders of nonprofit organizations includes strategies for building effective nonprofit boards. Comentaries from nonprofit leaders, case studies, and nonprofit governance news. *$139.00*

Founded: 1988

10113 Chronicle of Philanthropy
1255 23rd Street N.W.
Suite 700
Washington, DC 20037-1125
202-466-1200
FAX: 202-466-2078 800-728-2819
press@philanthropy.com
http://www.philanthropy.com/

Robin Ross, Publisher
Phil Semas, Editor
Michael Solomon, Manager of External Commu

A newspaper providing news and information for executives of nonprofit, tax-exempt organizations in health, education, religion, the arts, social services and other fields, as well as fund raisers, professional employees of foundation, and corporate grant makers. Features news, lists of grants, fundraising ideas and techniques, statistics, updates on regulations, reports on tax and court rulings, book summaries, calendar of events. *$72.00*

Fortnightly Founded: 1997
Circulation: 100000

10114 Community Health Funding Report
CD Publications
8204 Fenton Street
Silver Spring, MD 20910
301-588-0519
FAX: 301-588-6385 800-666-6380
hmr@cdpublications.com
http://www.cdpublications.com

Mike Gerecht, Publisher
Amy Bernstein, Editor
Jessica Cha, Owner

Highlights sources of funding for healthcare ranging from AIDS education to teen pregnancy to minority health care. Plus national and local community health news. *$339.00*

Mailing list available for rent 2,000 names
$160 per M.

10115 Contributions
PO Box 338
Medfield, MA 02052
508-359-0019
FAX: 508-359-2703
info@contributionsmagazine.com
http://www.contributionsmagazine.com

Jerry Cianciolo, Editor
Kathleen Brennan, Publisher

Offers full coverage of fund raising campaigns. *$40.00*

Founded: 1987
Circulation: 22,000

10116 Corporate Giving Watch
Gale Research
27500 Drake Road
Farmington Hills, MI 48331
248-699-4253
FAX: 800-414-5043
galeord@gale.com www.gale.com
News and ideas for nonprofit organizations seeking corporate funds. *$127.00*

16 pages Monthly Founded: 1981

10117 Corporate Philanthropy Report
LRP Publications
360 Hiatt Drive
Palm Beach Gardens, FL 33418
561-226-6520
FAX: 516-622-0757
webmaster@lrp.com
http://www.lrp.com

Craig Smith, Publisher
Eileen Banashek, Editor

A report for both the corporate and nonprofit communities, spotlighting a different field or industry in each issue. *$235.00*

Monthly Founded: 1977

10118 Development and Alumni Relations Report
LRP Publications
747 Dresher Road Suite 500
PO Box 980
Horsham, PA 19044-980
215-784-0912
FAX: 215-784-9639 800-341-7874
custserve@lrp.com
http://www.lrp.com

Anne Checkosky, Editor
Dionne Ellis, Marketing

Gives innovative ideas for improving annual giving, endowment and capital campaigns, planned giving, and alumni relations. Offers suggestions on new ways to spur participation and increase total contributions from alumni, corporate donors and foundations. *$185.00*

Monthly Founded: 1977

10119 Dimensions
NCDC
86 Front Street
Hempstead, NY 11550-3617
516-481-6000
FAX: 516-489-9287 888-879-6232
glehmuth@ncdcusa.org
http://www.ncdcusa.org

Rachel Donofrio, Editor
Richard Reale, Director Membership
Georgette Lehmuth, CEO

Offers information on development and fund raising including direct mail, planned giving and major gifts and capitol campaigns. *$ 1000.00*

16 pages Founded: 1968
Circulation: 550
Printed in 2 colors on matte stock

10120 Disability Funding News
CD Publications
8204 Fenton Street
Silver Spring, MD 20910
301-588-0519
FAX: 301-588-6385 800-666-6380
info@cdpublications.com
http://www.cdpublications.com

Mike Gerecht, Publisher
Martha McPartlin, Editor

Alerts the reader to funding for programs for the disabled, including housing, transportation, rehabilitation, research and special education. Plus advice on successful grantseeking and news updated on national and local developments. *$419.00*

Founded: 1993
Mailing list available for rent 2,000 names
$160 per M.
Computerized version available: On-line

10121 FRI Monthly Portfolio
Gale Research
27500 Drake Road
Farmington Hills, MI 48331
248-699-4253
FAX: 800-414-5043
galeord@gale.com www.gale.com
Provides practical advice through articles written by fundraisers and nonprofit managers. *$75.00*

Monthly Founded: 1962

10122 FRM Weekly: Fund Raising Management
Hoke Communications
224 7th Street
Garden City, NY 11530-5771
516-746-6700
FAX: 516-294-8141 800-229-6700

Henry R Hoke III, Publisher
William Olcott, Editor

Offers the latest news to fund raisers on what's happening in the nonprofit field. *$115.00*

6 pages Weekly
Mailing list available for rent
Printed in 1 color on matte stock

10123 Foundation Giving Watch
Gale Research
27500 Drake Road
Farmington Hills, MI 48331
248-699-4253
FAX: 800-414-5043
galeord@gale.com www.gale.com
Reports current information on future funding opportunities, funding decisions, trends in giving and changes in private foundations. *$139.00*

16 pages Daily
Computerized version available

10124 Giving USA Update
American Association of Fund-Raising Counsel
4700 W Lake Avenue
Glenview, IL 60025
847-375-4709
FAX: 866-263-2491 800-462-2372
info@aafrc.org http://www.aafrc.org

Ann Kaplan, Publisher
John J Glier, Chair

Contains analysis, data and comments on charitable giving. *$125.00*

Quarterly Founded: 1935

10125 Health Grants Funding Alert
Health Resources Publishing
1913 Atlantic Avenue
Suite F4
Manasquan, NJ 08736
732-292-1100
FAX: 732-292-1111 888-843-6242
hrp@healthrespubs.com
http://www.healthrespubs.com

Bob Jenkins, President/
Barbara Brown, Marketing Assistant

Monthly report sharing news of critical federal and foundation funding opportunities and trends, read by development directors and grants officers. *$495.00*

8 pages Monthly Founded: 1978

10126 National Center for Nonprofit Boards: Board Member Newsletter
1828 L Street NW
Washington, DC 20036
202-452-6262
FAX: 202-452-6299 800-883-6262
ncnb@ncnb.org http://www.ncnb.org
Larry Slesinger, Acting President
Richard L Moyers, Editor
Monthly newsletter for board members and staff leaders of nonprofit organizations includes news updates, case studies, checklists, interviews and opinion pieces to increase the effectiveness of nonprofit boards. *$99.00*
Monthly
Circulation: 6800
Printed in 2 colors on matte stock

10127 Planned Gifts Counselor
Gale Research
27500 Drake Road
Farmington Hills, MI 48331
248-699-4253
FAX: 248-699-8061 800-877-4253
Robert Elster, Publisher
Veine Thompson, Editor
Lisa Bracken, CEO
Donna Coleman, Marketing Manager
Donna Coleman, Circulation Manager
Articles on developing the planned giving function in an organization, as well as articles on marketing planned giving to potential donors. *$150.00*
8 pages Monthly Founded: 1980

10128 Responsive Philanthropy
National Committee for Responsive Philanthropy
2001 S Street NW
Suite 620
Washington, DC 20009-1125
202-387-9177
FAX: 202-332-5084
info@ncrp.org http://www.ncrp.org
Rick Cohen, Director
Naomi Tacuyan, Editor
With news and feature articles about philanthropy, fund raising and social justice, covering issues often unreported in mainstream philanthropic publications. *$25.00*
16 pages Quarterly Founded: 1976
Circulation: 5000 Audited Est. Pass-Along Circ: 5000
Mailing list available for rent 10000 names
Printed in 2 colors on matte stock

10129 Smith Funding Report
SFR
20 O'Neill Circle
Monroe, NY 10950-3210
914-774-4449
Melanie Smith, President
Quarterly guide to private foundation research/project grant opportunities for education and health institutions. *$195.00*
40 pages Quarterly
Printed in 1 color on matte stock

10130 Substance Abuse Funding News
CD Publications
8204 Fenton Street
Silver Spring, MD 20910
301-588-0519
FAX: 301-588-6385 800-666-6380
hmr@cdpublications.com
http://www.cdpublications.com
Mike Gerecht, Publisher
Joseph Smith, Editor
Detailed coverage of private and federal funding opportunities nationwide for alcohol and substance abuse programs. Advice on successful grantmaking strategies and roundup of national news. *$419.00*
Founded: 1992
Mailing list available for rent 2,000 names $160 per M.

Magazines & Journals

10131 Association Management
American Society of Association Executives
1575 I Street NW
Washington, DC 20005
202-626-2723
FAX: 202-408-9635
service@asaenet.org
http://www.asaenet.org
Keith C Skillman, Editor
Karl Ely, Publisher
Association Management strives to provide timely, practical information to help association executives succeed in their dual role as manager and visionary. *$50.00*
106 pages Monthly Founded: 1920
Circulation: 24678
Printed in 4 colors on glossy stock

10132 Association for Healthcare Philanthropy Journal
313 Park Avenue
Suite 400
Falls Church, VA 22046-3303
703-532-6243
FAX: 703-532-7170
ahp@ahp.org http://www.ahp.org
Kathy Renzetti, Marketing Manager/Editor
William C McGinly, CEO/President
Yvette Banks, Membership Manager
Terence J Rainey, Executive Vice President
Alison Shaffer, Administrative Assistant
Written for development professionals, fundraisers, trustees, public relations professionals and executives in health care fundraising. Provides timely information on fundraising, career enhancement, planned giving, donor relations, organizational strategies and the effect of health care reform on philanthropy. *$50.00*
Bi-annually Founded: 1967
Circulation: 4100 3000 names $200 per M.
Printed in on glossy stock : TXT

10133 Currents
Council for Advancement & Support of Education
1307 New York Avenue NW
Suite 1000
Washington, DC 20005-4701
202-285-5900
FAX: 202-387-4973
currents@case.org
http://www.case.org
John Lippincott, President
Deborah Bangiorno, Editor-in-Chief
Andrea Gabrick, Senior Editor
Toni Lewis-Bennett, Director of Membership
Anne Brown, Executive Director, Integrated Mark
Offers information on campus fund raising, public relations,and alumni administration. *$115.00*
Founded: 1994
Circulation: 15,000

10134 Foundation News & Commentary
Council on Foundations
1828 L Street NW
Washington, DC 20036-5104
202-466-6512
webmaster@cof.org www.cof.org
Offers news and information for foundations, legislation news and fundraising campaign reviews. *$24.00*
Monthly

10135 Fund Raising Management
Hoke Communications
224 7th Street
Garden City, NY 11530-5771
516-746-6700
FAX: 516-294-8141 800-229-6700
Henry R Hoke Jr, Publisher
William Olcott, Editor
Offers the latest in news and trends, case studies and features, new products/services, personnel changes, campaigns, legislation, tax rulings and special conference reports. Accepts advertising. *$50.00*
74 pages Monthly

10136 Fundraising: Hands on Tactics for Nonprofit Groups
McGraw-Hill Trade
2 Penn Plaza
New York, NY 10121-2298
212-042-2000
FAX: 614-759-3749 877-833-5524
Philip_Ruppel@mcgraw-hill.com
www.books.mcgraw-hill.com
L Peter Edles, Editor
Philip Ruppel, VP & Group Publisher
Jeffrey Krames, Publisher & Editor-in-Chief
This hands-on operations manual remedies the funding crisis by showing nonprofit professionals and volunteers how to design and run successful fundraising campaigns for their organizations. Combines sound, cost-effective strategies for building better organizational, management, sales, and marketing practices. *$19.95*
288 pages Founded: 1992 ISBN 0-070189-28-5

10137 Giving USA
American Association of Fund-Raising Counsel
4700 W Lake Ave
Glenview, IL 60025-7406
847-375-4709
FAX: 866-263-2491 800-462-2372
info@aafrc.org http://www.aafrc.org/
Ann Kaplan, Editor
An annual report on charitable giving in the United States, tracking total charitable giving from four categories of sources to seven kinds of organizations. *$125.00*
Quarterly Founded: 1935
Circulation: 9000

10138 Grant Funding for Elderly Health Services: 4th Edition
Health Resources Publishing
1913 Atlantic Avenue
Suite F4
Manasquan, NJ 08736
732-292-1100
FAX: 732-292-1111 888-843-6242
hrp@healthrespubs.com
http://www.healthresourcesonline.com

Bob Jenkins, President
Lisa Mansfield, Marketing Assistant
Caroline Pense, Editor

This report will give insight into which proposals will get funds for which organization. Lists the organizations that will recieve the most funds from grantmakers during this decade and beyond. Also studies different case histories of successful grant proposals. *$95.00*

Monthly Founded: 1978 ISBN 1-882364-46-5

10139 Grants Magazine
Plenum Publishing Corporation
233 Spring Street
New York, NY 10013-1522
212-421-1490
FAX: 212-463-0742
info@plenum.com www.plenum.com

Ricot Paillent, Manager

A magazine listing sources for grants, offering legislative news for the fundraising community, and foundation listings.

Monthly Founded: 1946

10140 International Journal of Educational Advancement
Association of Fundraising Professionals
Henry Stewart Publications
PO Box 10812
Birmingham, AL 35202-0812
205-995-1567
FAX: 205-995-1588 800-633-4931
brenda@hspublications.co.uk
www.afpnet.org / www.henrystewart.com

Joyce O'Brien, VP of Communications & Marketing
Brenda Rouse, Publisher

Features new ideas, shares examples of best practices and develops a body of knowledge in educational advancement. *$250.00*

4x/year

10141 Journal of Gift Planning
National Committee on Planned Giving
233 McCrea Street
Suite 400
Indianpolis, IN 46225
317-269-6274
FAX: 317-269-6276
ncpg@ncpg.org www.ncpg.org

Barbara Yeager, Editor/Operations Director

Provides in-depth analysis of issues of daily concern to both nonprofit planners and for-profit donor advisors. Each issue provides an orientation to national issues and trends affecting the profession, such as the release of major research related to planned gift fundraising or the debate over professional certification for gift planners. *$45.00*

Quarterly

10142 Nonprofit World
Society for Nonprofit Organizations
5820 Canton Center Road
Suite 165
Canton, MI 48187
734-513-3582
FAX: 734-451-5935
info@snpo.org http://www.snpo.org

Jill Muehrcke, Editor
Jason Chmura, Membership Director
Katie Burnham Laverty, President

Contains original articles and departments on all aspects of running an effective nonprofit organization. Accepts advertising. Now includes the Directory of Service and Product Providers and the Resource Center Catalog with discounted resources for nonprofit organizations. *$ 79.00*

40 pages Founded: 1983
Circulation: 4000 4,000 names $110 per M.

Printed in 2 colors

10143 Philanthropy Monthly
Non-Profit Report
PO Box 989
New Milford, CT 06776
860-354-7132
FAX: 860-354-7132 860-354-7132

Henry Suhrke, Publisher

Editorial range covers concerns of nonprofits; legislative, economic, fund raising, nonprofit accounting, litigation, etc. *$84.00*

Circulation: 6208

Trade Shows

10144 AFP International Conference on Fundraising
Association of Fundraising Professionals
1101 King Street
Suite 700
Alexandria, VA 22314-2944
703-684-0410
FAX: 703-684-0540 800-666-3863

Shannon Watson, Director Meetings & Expositions
Myrlin Young, Conferences Coordinator
Paulette Maehara, President

The largest gathering of fundraisers in the profession. The Conference has become the premier resource for fundraisers to network, learn, and discover new products and services.

April Founded: 1962

10145 Council on Foundations Annual Conference
Council on Foundations
1828 L Street NW
Washington, DC 20036-5104
202-466-6512
FAX: 202-785-3926
jonee@cof.org www.cof.org

Edward Jones, Program Director
Heidi Lyn Capati, Conference Logistics
Michelle Dunston, Registration
Dorothy Ridings, President

Annual conference and exhibits relating to trends and legislation in the field of philanthropy.

April

10146 Independent Sector Annual Conference
Independent Sector
1200 18th Street NW
Suite 200
Washington, DC 20036
202-467-6100
FAX: 202-467-6101 888-860-8118
info@independentsector.org
www.independentsector.org

Angelia Bland, Conference & Meetings Director
Keith Greenidge, Meeting Planning Assist Director
Diana Aviv, President

The conference focuses on the social compact of the charitable community's role.

1000 Attendees Annual/October

10147 NACo's Annual Conference and Exposition
National Association of Counties
440 1st Street NW
Washington, DC 20001-2028
202-393-6226
FAX: 202-393-2630
kstruble@naco.org www.naco.org

Amanda Clark, Conference & Meetings Associate
Kim Struble, Conference & Meetings Director
Larry Naake, Chief Executive Officer

The place for elected and appointed county officials to network, attend educational sessions and meet with companies that sell products to counties. It includes a variety of activities designed to meet the needs of all delegates. In addition to strong educational sessions, the conference includes affiliate, steering and subcommittee meetings, state association meetings and social events.

4000 Attendees Annual

10148 National Conference on Planned Giving
National Committee on Planned Giving
233 McCrea Street
Suite 400
Indianapolis, IN 46225-1030
317-269-6274
FAX: 317-269-6276
smcmahon@ncpg.org www.ncpg.org

Shana McMahon, Meetings Manager
Kathryn J Ramsey, Meetings Director
Tanya Howe Johnson, President

Annual conference and exhibits of fundraising equipment, supplies and services.

September-October

Directories & Databases

10149 Annual Register of Grant Support: A Directory of Funding Services
Information Today
143 Old Marlton Pike
Medford, NJ 08055-8750
609-654-6266
FAX: 609-654-4309
custserv@infotoday.com
www.infotoday.com

Thomas H Hogan, Publisher/President
John Bryans, Publisher/Editor-in-Chief Books
Lauree Padgett, Editorial Services Manager
Inge Coffey, Circulation Manager
Pat Palatucci, Assistant to the President

Contains more that 3,500 grant giving organziations. IS also the definitive resource for researching and uncovering a full range of available grant sources.Also directs you to traditional corporate, private, and public funding programs, it also shows you the way to little known, nontraditional grant sources such as educational associations and unions. *$240.00*

1476 pages ISBN 1-573872-04-0

10150 Charitable Trust Directory
Office of the Secretary of State
Charitable Trust Program
801 Capitol Way South
Olympia, WA 98504-0234
360-753-0863
800-332-GIVE
charities@secstate.wa.gov
www.secstate.wa.gov/charities

Sam Reed, Chairman/Secretary of State
Linda Vallegos Bremer, Director of General Administration

Directory of charitable trusts regulations in the State of Washington. *$27.00*

290 pages CD-ROM Available

10151 Corporate Giving Directory
Taft Group/Thompson Gale
27500 Drake Road
PO Box 9187
Farmington Hills, MI 48331-9187
248-699-4253
FAX: 800-414-5043 800-877-GALE
gale.galeord@thomson.com
www.gale.com

Dennis Poupard, Executive VP Editorial & Production
Rich Foley, Executive VP Sales & Marketing

In this directory you will find 331 email addresses for company giving programs, as well as web addresses for 462 corporate foundations and 1,129 corporate headquarters. *$595.00*

1900 pages Annual Founded: 2004 ISBN 1-569954-67-4

10152 Directory of Research Grants
Greenwood Publishing Group
88 Post Road W
Westport, CT 06881
203-226-3571

webmaster@greenwood.com
www.greenwood.com

James Lingle, Publicity & Advertising Manager

A treasure chest of information on more than 5,100 current programs from 1,880 sponsors, including U.S. and foreign foundations, corporations, government agencies, and other organizations. Find grants for basic research, equipment acquisition, building construction/renovation, fellowships, and 23 other program types *$145.00*

Annual ISBN 1-573566-19-5 : web

10153 Environmental Grantmaking Foundations Directory
Resources for Global Sustainability
PO Box 3665
Cary North, NC 27519-3665

FAX: 919-363-9841 800-724-1857
rgs@environmentalgrants.com
www.environmentalgrants.com

Corrine Szymko, President

Over 900 private foundations, community foundations and corporate giving programs that provide funding for environmental interests. *$115.00*

Annual ISBN 0-976788-00-4

10154 Financial Aid for African Americans
Reference Service Press
El Dorado Business Park
5000 Windplay Drive, Suite 4
El Dorado Hills, CA 95762-9600
916-939-9620
FAX: 916-939-9626
findaid@aol.com
www.rspfunding.com

R David Weber, Editor
Gail A Schlachter, Editor

This directory describes nearly 1,450 scholarships, fellowships, loans, grants, awards and internships for African Americans *$ 40.00*

522 pages Biennial Founded: 1997 ISBN 1-588410-68-5 : database

10155 Financial Aid for Asian Americans
Reference Service Press
El Dorado Business Park
5000 Windplay Drive, Suite 4
El Dorado Hills, CA 95762-9600
916-939-9620
FAX: 916-939-9626
findaid@aol.com
www.rspfunding.com

R David Weber, Editor
Gail A Schlachter, Editor

Use this source to find funding for Americans of Chinese, Japanese, Korean, Vietnamese, Filipino, or other Asian origins. Nearly 1,000 funding opportunities are described. *$37.50*

346 pages Biennial Founded: 1997 ISBN 1-588410-69-2
Printed in on matte stock : database

10156 Financial Aid for Hispanic Americans
Reference Service Press
El Dorado Business Park
5000 Windplay Drive, Suite 4
El Dorado Hills, CA 95762-9600
916-939-9620
FAX: 916-939-9626
findaid@aol.com
www.rspfunding.com

R David Weber, Editor
Gail A Schlachter, Editor

This directory describes nearly 1,300 funding opportunities open to Americans of Mexican, Puerto Rican, Central American, or other Latin American heritage. *$30.00*

402 pages Biennial Founded: 1997 ISBN 1-588410-70-6
Printed in on matte stock : database

10157 Financial Aid for Native Americans

Reference Service Press
El Dorado Business Park
5000 Windplay Drive, Suite 4
El Dorado Hills, CA 95762-9600
916-939-9620
FAX: 916-939-9626
findaid@aol.com
www.rspfunding.com

R David Weber, Editor
Gail A Schlachter, Editor

In this directory you will find 1,500 funding opportunities set aside just for American Indians, Native Alaskans, and Native Pacific Islanders. *$40.00*

546 pages Founded: 1997 ISBN 1-588410-71-4 : database

10158 Financial Aid for Veterans, Military Personnel and their Dependents
Reference Service Press
El Dorado Business Park
5000 Windplay Drive, Suite 4
El Dorado Hills, CA 95762-9600
916-939-9620
FAX: 916-939-9626
findaid@aol.com
www.rspfunding.com

R David Weber, Editor
Gail A Schlachter, Editor

This one-stop directory identifies 1,200 scholarships, fellowships, loans, awards, grants and internships. *$40.00*

418 pages Biennial Founded: 1988 ISBN 1-588410-97-8
Printed in on matte stock : database

10159 Financial Aid for the Disabled and their Families
Reference Service Press
El Dorado Business Park
5000 Windplay Drive, Suite 4
El Dorado Hills, CA 95762-9600
916-939-9620
FAX: 916-939-9626
findaid@aol.com
www.rspfunding.com

R David Weber, Editor
Gail A Schlachter, Editor

A comprehensive directory identifies 1,200 scholarships, fellowships, loans, internships, awards, and grants for these groups. *$ 40.00*

502 pages Biennial ISBN 0-918276-65-9

10160 Foundation Directory
Foundation Center
79 5th Avenue/16th Street
New York, NY 10003-3076
212-620-4230
FAX: 212-807-3677 800-424-9836
customerservice@fdncenter.org
www.gtionline.fdncenter.org

Cheryl Loe, Director of Communications
Laura Cascio, Fulfillment Manager

Key facts on the nation's top 10,000 foundations by total giving. And, with over 46,000 descriptions of selected grants, the Directory provides fundraisers with unique insight into foundation giving priorities. *$215.00*

2,533 pages ISBN 1-595420-18-5

10161 Foundation Directory Online Database
Foundation Center
79 5th Avenue/16th Street
New York, NY 10003-3076
212-620-4230
FAX: 212-807-3677 800-424-9836
customerservice@fdncenter.org
www.fdncenter.org

Cheryl Loe, Director of Communications
Laura Cascio, Fulfillment Manager

Search our databases online to get detailed information on up to nearly 80,000 foundations, links to current foundation 990-PF returns, crucial facts on more than half a million grants, including the purpose of grants. *$19.95*

Monthly

10162 Foundation Directory Supplement
Foundation Center
79 5th Avenue/16th Street
New York, NY 10003-3076
212-620-4230
FAX: 212-807-3677 800-424-9836
customerservice@fdncenter.org
www.fdncenter.org

Cheryl Loe, Director of Communications
Laura Cascio, Fulfillment Manager

Provides revised entries for hundreds of foundations in The Foundation Directory and The Foundation Directory Part 2. Any alterations in giving interests, or updates on staff, financial data, contact information, and more, will be reflected in the Supplement. *$125.00*
1000 pages ISBN 1-931923-89-2

10163 Foundation Grants Index
Foundation Center
79 5th Avenue/16th Street
New York, NY 10003-3076
212-620-4230
FAX: 212-807-3677 800-424-9836
customerservice@fdncenter.org
www.fdncenter.org

Cheryl Loe, Director Communications
Laura Cascio, Fulfillment Manager
Michael Seltver, President

Covers the grants of over 1,000 of the largest independent, corporate, and community foundations in the U.S. and features approximately 125,000 grant descriptions in all. *$175.00*
CD-ROM ISBN 1-595420-09-6

10164 Foundation Grants to Individuals
Foundation Center
79 5th Avenue/16th Street
New York, NY 10003-3076
212-620-4230
FAX: 212-691-1828 800-424-9836
customerservice@fdncenter.org
www.fdncenter.org

Cheryl Loe, Director Communications
Laura Cascio, Fulfillment Manager
Michael Seltver, President

Featuring over 6,200 entries packed with current information for individual grantseekers. *$65.00*
1,117 pages Biennial ISBN 1-595420-42-8

10165 Foundation Reporter
Taft Group/Thompson Gale
27500 Drake Road
PO Box 9187
Farmington Hills, MI 48331
248-699-4253

gale.galeord@thomson.com
www.gale.com

Dennis Poupard, Executive VP Editorial & Production
Rich Foley, Executive VP Sales & Marketing

Provides all the important contact, financial and grant information you'll need. This comprehensive resource covers the top 1,000 private foundations in the United States that have at least $10 million in assets or have made $500,000 in charitable giving. *$590.00*
Founded: 2005 ISBN 1-569954-95-X

10166 Funding for Persons with Visual Impairments
Reference Service Press
El Dorado Business Park
5000 Windplay Drive, Suite 4
El Dorado Hills, CA 95762-9600
916-939-9620
FAX: 916-939-9626
info@rspfunding.com
www.rspfunding.com

R David Weber, Editor-in-Chief
Sandy Perez, Business Manager

For low-vision readers, we have prepared a large-print listing of the scholarships, fellowships, loans, grants-in-aid, awards, and internships that are set aside just for persons with visual impairments (from high school seniors through professionals and others). Nearly 270 funding opportunities are described in detail here. *$30.00*
274 pages Annual Founded: 1997 ISBN 1-588411-29-X : Disk

10167 Grants for Foreign and International Programs
Foundation Center
79 5th Avenue/16th Street
New York, NY 10003-3076
212-620-4230
FAX: 212-807-3677 800-424-9836
orders@fdncenter.org
www.fdncenter.org

Laura Cascio, Fulfillment Manager
Michael Seltver, President

A customized list of thousands of recent grants of $10,000 or more that have been awarded to organizations in foreign countries and to domestic recipients for international activities in such areas as: development and relief, peace and security, arms control, human rights, conferences and research, and more. *$75.00*
436 pages ISBN 1-595420-23-1

10168 Grants: Corporate Grantmaking for Racial and Ethnic Minorities
Moyer Bell
549 Old North Road
Kingston, RI 02881-1220
401-783-5480
FAX: 401-284-0959
contact@moyerbellbooks.com
www.miyerbellbooks.com

Britt Bell, Publisher

This is the only comprehensive listing of 124 coroporations and the over ten thousand grants they offer each year to benefit minorities. African-American, Hispanics, and Latinos, Native Americans and Asian Pacific Americans. A unique and important reference tool for grant givers as well as grant seekers. *$89.95*
736 pages ISBN 1-559212-80-2

10169 Guide to Funding for International and Foreign Programs
Foundation Center
79 5th Avenue/16th Street
New York, NY 10003-3076
212-620-4230
FAX: 212-807-3677 800-424-9836
orders@fdncenter.org
www.fdncenter.org

Laura Cascio, Fulfillment Manager

Includes up-to-date information on over 1,000 foundations and corporate givers that have supported a wide range of projects with an international focus both in the U.S. and in foreign countries. *$125.00*
358 pages ISBN 1-931923-95-7

10170 Guide to US Foundations, Their Trustees, Officers and Donors
Foundation Center
79 5th Avenue/16th Street
New York, NY 10003-3076
212-620-4230
FAX: 212-807-3677 800-424-9836
orders@fdncenter.org
www.fdncenter.org

Laura Cascio, Fulfillment Manager

The only published source of data on all active grantmaking foundations and the individuals who run them, provides current information on over 68,000 foundations. Featuring a master list of the decision-makers who direct America's foundations, the Guide is a powerful fundraising reference tool. *$350.00*
4,235 pages Annual ISBN 1-595420-35-5

10171 Matching Gift Details
Council for Advancement & Support of Education
1307 New York Avenue NW
Suite 1000
Washington, DC 20005-4701
202-285-5900
FAX: 202-387-4973
matchinggifts@case.org
www.case.org

Silvia France, Matching Gifts Coordinator
Linda Jackson, Matching Gifts Associate

Compiled and maintained by the Matching Gifts Clearinghouse, a comprehensive annual directory of more than 8,600 companies that match employee charitable gifts. *$100.00*
286 pages ISBN 0-899643-83-3

10172 National Directory of Corporate Giving
Foundation Center
79 5th Avenue/16th Street
New York, NY 10003-3076
212-620-4230
FAX: 212-807-2426 800-424-9836
orders@fdncenter.org
www.fdncenter.org

Laura Cascio, Fulfillment Manager

This comprehensive directory features up-to-date information that helps fundraisers tap into their share of grant money earmarked by companies for nonprofit support. Detailed portraits of close to 2,500 corporate foundations and some 1,400 direct giving programs feature essential information. *$195.00*
1,165 pages Annual ISBN 1-595420-04-5

10173 New Foundation Guidebook
Association of Small Foundation
4905 Del Ray Avenue
Suite 200
Bethesda, MD 20814
301-073-3337
FAX: 301-907-0980 888-212-9922
asf@smallfoundations.org
www.smallfoundations.org

Carmen Wong, Director of Communications
Deborah Brody Hamilton, Director Member Services

Contains articles and advice from over 40 foundation respresentatives and experts included in the Association of Small Foundations' newsletters and publications. *$40.00*
86 pages

10174 New Nonprofit Almanac & Desk Reference
Independent Sector
1200 18th Street NW
Suite 200
Washington, DC 20036
202-467-6100
FAX: 202-467-6101 888-860-8118
info@independentsector.org
www.independentsector.org
Patricia Nash Christel, VP Communications & Marketing
Bill Wright, Associate Director Communications
Diana Aviv, President

Provides managers, researchers, volunteers, and the press with the essential facts and figures needed to understand the size, scope, and nature of the nonprofit sector and its contributions to American society.
$38.00

Industry Web Sites

10175 www.aafrc.org
American Association of Fund-Raising Counsel

To promote ethical practice and professional standards in the fund-raising consultant field.

10176 www.ahp.org
Association for Healthcare Philanthropy

Represents health care fundraising professionals through education and eventually bestows the credentials upon them.

10177 www.boardsource.org
BoardSource

Formerly the National Center for Nonprofit Boards, is the premier resource for practical information, tools and best practices, training, and leadership development for board members of nonprofit organizations worldwide.

10178 www.cof.org
Council on Foundations

Supports all those involved in the foundation business. Publishes monthly magazine. We provide leadership expertise, legal services and networking opportunities among other services to our members and to the general public.

10179 www.grantsmart.org
Grantsmart

An online resource database that contains 96,337 private foundations and charitable trusts.

10180 www.greyhouse.com
Grey House Publishing

Selected Grey House directories in the fields of business, health and education are available online. Users can search our online databases by several different search criteria, such as product categories, geographic area, sales volume and much, much more. Full Grey House catalog and online ordering also available.

10181 www.guidestar.org
GuideStar

A database of more than 1 million nonprofit organizations in the United States. It's the world's most comprehensive source of information about American nonprofit organizations.

10182 www.idealist.org
Action Without Borders

Over 45,000 nonprofit and community organizations in 165 countries, which you can search or browse by name, location or mission.

10183 www.independentsector.org
Independent Sector

The leadership forum for charities, foundations, and corporate giving programs committed to advancing the common good in America and around the world.

10184 www.naspl.org
North American Assn of State & Provincial Lottery

Represents 47 lottery organizations throughout North America. Provides information and benefits of state and provincial lottery organizations.

10185 www.ncdcusa.org
National Catholic Development Conference

Members include development officers and key fund raisers of charitable institutions and agencies.

10186 www.philathropy.org
A Philanthropic Partnership for Black Communities

Providing information on innovative vehicles for the black communities.

10187 www.snpo.orgorg/snpo
Society for Nonprofit Organizations

Dedicated to bringing together those who serve in the nonprofit world in order to build a strong network of professional throughout the country.

10188 www.uwex.edu/li
Learning Institute

The Center provides you with a number of resources on the web that could provide you with assistance in a variety of nonprofit management and leadership issues. In the nonprofit web sites section you will find a number of useful annotated resources organized by topic.

Associations

10189 Adhesive Manufacturers Association
2300 N Barrington Road
Hoffman Estates, IL 60195
847-490-5377
FAX: 847-884-9423
Association for the packaging industry.

10190 Air Freight Association of America
1710 Rhode Island Avenue NW
2nd Floor
Washington, DC 20036
202-296-0509

Stephen A Alterman, Executive VP
Promotes interests of firms engaged in domestic and international airfreight forwarding.
27 Members Founded: 1948

10191 Association of Independent Corrugated Packaging
PO Box 25708
Alexandria, VA 22313
703-836-2422
FAX: 703-836-2795 877-836-2422
info@aiccbox.org www.aiccbox.org
A Steven Young, President
Zell Murphy, Director Operations
David Core, Director Education
Taryn Pyle, Director Member Services
Provides a forum for discussion of problems and offers educational programs and seminars.
1100 Members Founded: 1974

10192 Center for Packaging Education
537 Riverdale Drive
Yonkers, NY 10705
914-963-0426
FAX: 914-276-0428
Advances packaging and structural design, conducts seminars in professional management, bestows awards and compiles statistics, expert in warning labels on products and packages.
Founded: 1971

10193 Composite Can and Tube Institute
50 South Pickett Street
Suite 110
Alexandria, VA 22304-7206
703-823-7234
FAX: 703-823-7237
ccti@cctiwdc.org www.cctiwdc.org
Kristine Garland, Executive VP
Wayne Vance, Association Counsel
Andrea Edwards, Associate Manager Events
Represents the composite can and tube industry.
Founded: 1934

10194 Containerization Institute
195 Fairfield Avenue
West Caldwell, NJ 07006-6417
732-179-9131
FAX: 973-364-1212 cii@bsya.com
Barbara Yeninas, Executive Director
Disseminates information on intermodal transportation. Maintains speakers' bureau and bestows awards.
8 Members Founded: 1960

10195 Corrugated Packaging Council
2850 Golf Road
Rolling Meadows, IL 60008
847-364-9600
FAX: 847-364-9639
hmarshall@fibrebox.org
www.corrugated.org
Rachel K Kenyon, Chairman
Stephanie Maegdlin, Comm/Marketing Coordinator
Develops and coordinates industry-wide programs to address corrugated packaging issues. The Council's mission is to inform consumers, manufacturers, retailers and government officials of corrugated packaging's performance and environmental attributes.
Founded: 1994

10196 Express Carriers Association
PO Box 4376
Allentown, PA 18105-4376

FAX: 866-322-3299 866-322-7447
eca@expresscarriers.com
www.expresscarriers.com
Cheryl Williamson, Executive Director
Tim Bergin, Board of Directors
Bruce Birtwell, Board of Directors
Develops business between carriers, shippers and vendors of products and services to the transportation industry.

10197 Fibre Box Association
2850 Golf Road
Rolling Meadows, IL 60008
847-364-9600
FAX: 847-364-9639
fba@fibrebox.org www.fibrebox.org
Represents 90 percent of the US corrugated paper board, packaging, manufacturing industry.
141 Members Founded: 1940

10198 Flexible Intermediate Bulk Container
PO Box 26068
Macon, GA 31221-6068
478-757-1006
FAX: 478-757-9444
info@fibca.org www.fibca.com
Steve Russell, President
Mary Ellen Henry, VP
Brad Eisenbarth, Treasurer
Gale Simmons, Secretary
Works to develop minimum standards of testing and performance for FIBC. Acts as a forum through seminars and other programs and serves as an advocate for the industry.
50 Members Founded: 1983

10199 Foodservice & Packaging Institute
150 S Washington Street
Suite 204
Falls Church, VA 22046
703-538-2800
FAX: 703-538-2187
fpi@fpi.org www.fpi.org
John R Burke, President
Elizabeth T Phillips, Director Member Services
Lynn Rosseth, Director Market Development
Manufacturers, suppliers and distributors of one-time use products used for food service, as well as packaging products made from paper, plastic, aluminum and other materials. Membership dues based on sales.
37 Members Founded: 1933

10200 Gemini Shippers Group National Fashion Accessories Assoc
350 5th Avenue
Suite 2030
New York, NY 10118
212-947-3424
FAX: 212-629-0361
smayes@geminishippers.com
www.geminishippers.com
Harold Sachs, Executive Director
Sara Mayes, President
Arlena Blocker, Director Membership
Shippers association with global contracts for all commodities.
200 Members Founded: 1916

10201 Glass Packaging Institute
515 King Street
Suite 420
Alexandria, VA 22314
703-684-6359
FAX: 703-684-6048
jcattaneo@gpi.org www.gpi.org
Joseph J Cattaneo, President
Kerrin McKillop, Director Member Services
Jung Weil, Director Communications
Andy Bopp, Director Public Affairs
Bryan J Vickers, Legislative Affairs
Develops and evaluates testing procedures and equipment, conducts advertising campaigns for generic products.
40 Members Founded: 1945

10202 Healthcare Compliance Packaging Council
131 E Broad Street
Suite 206
Falls Church, VA 22046
703-538-4030
FAX: 703-538-6305
kshemming@aol.com
www.unitdose.org
Renard Jackson, Chairman
Sandra Luciano, Vice Chairman
Peter G Mayberry, Executive Director
Walter Berghahn, Treasurer
A nonprofit trade association that was established in 1990 to promote the many benefits of unit dose blister and strip packaging, especially its ability to be designed in compliance, promoting formats that help people take their medications properly.
Founded: 1990

10203 Institute of International Container Leasing
555 Pleasantville Road
Suite 140
South Briarcliff Manor, NY 10510
914-747-9100
FAX: 914-747-4600
info@iicl.org www.iicl.org
Henry F White Jr, President
Gary Danback, Director Technical Services
Brian Sondey, Chairman
Represents international container and chassis leasing industry in technical, governmental and legal matters. Publishes leading worldwide manuals on inspection and repair of containers and inspector and maintenance of chassis. Sponsors container and chassis inspection examination once a year in over 40 countries and chassis examination in North America.
13 Members Founded: 1971

10204 Institute of Packaging Professionals

1601 North Bond Street
Suite 101
Naperville, IL 60563
703-438-7518
FAX: 630-544-5055 800-432-4085
info@iopp.org www.iopp.org

Edwin Landon, Executive Director
Patrick Farrey, General Manager
Stan Zelesnik, Director Education
Kelly Staley, Member Services Manager
Chris Barry, Communications Manager

Packaging consultants in the US.

10205 International Molded Pulp Environmental Professionals Assocation

1425 W Mequon Road
Suite A
Mequon, WI 53092
262-241-0522
FAX: 262-241-3766
info@impepa.org www.impepa.org

Joseph Grygny, Chairman
Hub Ranger, Executive Director

Founded: 1996

10206 Lake Carriers Association

614 W Superior Avenue
Suite 915
Cleveland, OH 44113-1383
216-811-1173
FAX: 216-241-8262
ggn@lcaships.com www.lcaships.com

James H I Weakley, President
Richard W Harkins, VP Operations
Glen Nekvasil, VP Corporate Communications
Carol Ann Lane, Secretary/Treasurer

Members are US- Flag Great Lakes vessel operators engaged in transporting iron ore, coal, grain, limestone, cement and petroleum products.

12 Members Founded: 1880

10207 National Customs Brokers and Forwarders

1200 18th Street NW
#901
Washington, DC 20036
202-466-0222
FAX: 202-466-0266
staff@ncbfaa.org www.ncbfaa.org

Barbara Reilly, Executive VP
Federico C Zuniga, President
Mary Jo Muoio, VP
Jeffrey C Coppersmith, Treasurer
Peter H Powell Sr, Chairman

Learn about new business leads, stay on top of Customs Service and other agency regulations that will impact your operations and provide invaluable professional development resources for your employees.

600+ Members

10208 National Highway and Airway Carriers

PO Box 6099
Buffalo Grove, IL 60089-6099
847-634-0606
FAX: 847-634-1026
www.national-highway.com

Pam W Ferreira, President

Businesses or people involved with merchandise distribution throughout the U.S. and Canada.

Founded: 1942 5000 names

10209 National Institute of Packaging and Handling Engineers

6902 Lyle Street
Lanham, MD 20706-3454
301-459-9105
FAX: 301-459-4925 niphle@erols.com

Originally the DC chapter of the Society of Packaging and Handling engineers, the Institute became independent in an effort to give more emphasis on the governmental responsibilities of its members.

600 Members Founded: 1956

10210 National Paperbox Association

113 S West Street
Third Floor
Alexandria, VA 22314
703-684-2212
FAX: 703-683-6920
npahq@paperbox.org
www.paperbox.org

Scott Miller, VP

Represents industry before legislative and regulatory bodies. Conducts technical seminars on sales, marketing, costs and management methods. Publishes a quarterly newsletter.

100 Members Founded: 1918

10211 Paperboard Packaging Council

201 N Union Street
Suite 220
Alexandria, VA 22314
703-836-3300
FAX: 703-836-3290
paperboardpackaging@ppcnet.org
www.ppcnet.org

Jerome T Van De Water, President
James Brown, Director Business Services
Melissa Teates, Director Industry Information
Heather Neese, Director Marketing

Members are companies making folding cartons. Provides publications and instructional materials on the paper industry and recycling.

Founded: 1967

10212 Petroleum Packaging Council

ATD Management Inc.
1219 Ganado
San Clemente, CA 92673
949-369-7102
FAX: 949-498-6496
PPC@ATDmanagement.com
www.ppcouncil.org

John Kirk, President
Andy Rapp, VP

Provides technical leadership and education to the petroleum packaging industry.

400 Members Founded: 1950

10213 Polystyrene Packaging Council

1300 Wilson Boulevard
8th Floor
Arlington, VA 22209
703-741-5649
FAX: 703-741-5651
pspc@americanplasticscouncil.org
www.polystyrene.org

Michael H Levy, Executive Director
Annie F Walton, Office Manager

Promotes effective use of recycling of polystyrene. Works to provide effective information about waste disposal and offers technical assistance.

9 Members Founded: 1988

10214 Pressure Sensitive Tape Council

2514 Stonebridge Lane
PO Box 609
Northbrook, IL 60062
847-562-2630
FAX: 847-562-2631
contactus@pstc.org www.pstc.org

Glen R Anderson, Executive VP
Sharon M Belter, Director Membership & Meetings
Lynn Valastyan, Director Communications
Chris Wisniewski, Director Meetings
Pamela Jones, Audio Visual Consultant

Members are manufacturers of pressure sensitive tape.

Founded: 1953

10215 Recycled Paperboard Technical Association

920 Davis Road
Suite 306
Elgin, IL 60123-1352
847-622-2544
FAX: 847-622-2546 rpta@rpta.org

Phillip Forsyth, Executive Director

An association of US, Canadian and overseas companies interested in cooperative research and development in the industry.

33 Members Founded: 1953

10216 Technical Association of the Pulp & Paper Industry

15 Technology Parkway S
Norcross, GA 30092
770-446-1400
FAX: 770-446-6947
tj@tappi.org www.tappi.org

Wayne H Gross, President

To engage the people and resources of our association in providing technically sound solutions to the workplace problems and opportunities that challenge our current and future members.

12000 Members Founded: 1915

10217 Transportation Intermediaries Association

1625 Prince Street
Suite 200
Alexandria, VA 22314
703-317-2140
FAX: 703-836-0123
info@tianet.org www.tianet.org

David Gee, Chairman
Daniel Yoest, First Vice Chairman
Alec Gizzi, Treasurer
Doug Clark, Secretary
Robert Voltmann, President

Education and policy organization for North American transportation intermediaries. The only national association representing the interests of all third party transportation service providers. Members include logistics management firms, property brokers, perishable commodities brokers, freight forwarders, intermodal marketers and ocean and air forwarders.

700 Members Founded: 1977

Newsletters

10218 Air Cargo Report
Phillips Publishing
1201 Seven Locks Road
Potomac, MD 20854-2931
301-541-1400
FAX: 301-424-2098
information@phillips.com
http://www.accessintel.com
Richard Koulbanis, Publisher
Donald Pazour, CEO/President
Reports on emerging trends and business strategies for airline cargo, integrator, freight forwarding and all-cargo carrier operations.
Founded: 1974
Circulation: 1430

10219 Composite Can and Tube Institute Newsletter
50 South Pickett St
Suite 110
Alexandria, VA 22304-7206
703-823-7234
FAX: 703-549-4912
ccti@cctiwdc.org
http://www.cctiwdc.org
Kristine Garland, President
Andrea Edwards, Publisher
International trade association representing the composite can and tube industry. Accepts advertising. *$50.00*
Founded: 1933

10220 Mail Center Management Report
Institute of Management & Administration
29 W 35th Street
5th Floor
New York, NY 10001-2299
212-244-0360
FAX: 212-564-0465
subserve@ioma.com www.ioma.com
Shows you how to improve mail center productivity, reduce costs, and get you the recognition you deserve through buying and leasing new equipment, negotiating rates with carriers, and much more. Shows proven techniques to improve relations with the USPS and other service vendors. You'll find tactics for improving your dealing with senior management, purchasing, marketing and logistics.

10221 National Paperbox Association
113 S West Street
3rd Floor, Suite 211
Alexandria, VA 22313
703-684-2212
FAX: 703-683-6920
boxmaker@paperbox.org
http://www.paperbox.org
Scott Miller, Executive VP
Represents industry before legislative and regulatory bodies. Conducts technical seminars on sales, marketing, costs and management methods. *$103.50*
Quarterly Founded: 1918

10222 Packaging Strategies
Packaging Strategies
901 S Bolmar Street
Suite P
West Chester, PA 19382-4550
610-436-4220
FAX: 610-436-6277 800-524-7225
packinfo@packstrat.com
http://www.packstrat.com
Shaun Riley, Managing Editor
Janet Martinelly, Circulation Manager
A subscription newsletter focusing on news and analysis of technology and business issues in the packaging industry. *$497.00*
8 pages Founded: 1983
Printed in 2 colors on matte stock

10223 Packet Magazine
National Paperbox Association
113 South W Street
Third Floor
Alexandria, VA 22314-1420
703-684-2212
FAX: 703-683-6920
npahq@paperbox.org
http://www.paperbox.org
Scott Miller, Publisher/Editor
Trade news for independent rigid box and folding carton manufacturers. Accepts advertising.
32 pages Founded: 1918
Circulation: 500

10224 Postal Link
Johnson & Hayward
500 Route 46 E
Clifton, NJ 07011-1800
973-253-2323
FAX: 973-253-2313 800-521-0080
postallink@jhinc.com www.jhinc.com
John P Michell, President
A newsletter for the international mailer.

10225 Techpak
Market Search
2727 Holland Sylvania Road
#A
Toledo, OH 43615-1800
419-535-7899
FAX: 419-535-1243 jb@sbries.biz
James Best, Editor
James Best, President
Newsletter that covers packaging materials and markets. Features new product reviews, industry news and an overview of current trends. *$397.00*

10226 Transportation Intermediaries Update
Transportation Intermediaries Association
3601 Eisenhower Avenue
Suite 110
Alexandria, VA 22304
703-317-2140
FAX: 703-329-1898
info@tianet.org www.tianet.org
Robert A Voltmann, Executive Director/CEO
Kelly Scott, Contact
Education and policy organization for North American transportation intermediaries. TIA is the only national association representing the interests of all third party transportation service providers. The members of TIA include logistics management firms, property brokers, perishable commodities brokers, freight forwarders, intermodal marketers, ocean and air forwarders, and NVOCC's.
700 pages Monthly Founded: 1977

Magazines & Journals

10227 Advanced Packaging
PennWell Publishing Company
98 Spit Brooke
Nashua, NH 03060
603-891-0123
FAX: 603-897-9297
lwilliam@pennwell.com
http://www.pennwell.com
J. Regan, Group Publisher
Gail Flower, Editor
Focuses on materials, assembly, design and reliability issues facing the global packaging community. *$88.00*
Monthly Founded: 1910
Circulation: 22,000

10228 Air Cargo News
PO Box 98
Portage, MI 49081-98
718-479-0716
FAX: 718-740-0761
judy@aircargonews.com
http://www.aircargonews.com
Geoffrey Arend, Publisher
CAB regulations, and other news of interest to those in the air cargo industry. *$39.95*
Monthly Founded: 1975
Circulation: 100,000

10229 American Shipper
Howard Publications
300 W Adams Street Suite 600
PO Box 4728
Jacksonville, FL 32201-4728
904-355-2601
FAX: 904-791-8836 800-874-6422
nbarry@shippers.com
http://www.americanshipper.com
Hayes H Howard, Publisher
Gary G. Burrows, Managing Editor
Provides those involved in domestic and global supply chain management with news and information of a strategic nature, useful in the formation of logistics polices and partnerships. *$30.00*
100 pages Monthly Founded: 1951
Circulation: 13487
Printed in 4 colors on glossy stock

10230 CNS Focus
Cargo Network Services Corporation
300 Garden City Plaza
Suite 312
Garden City, NY 11530
516-747-3312
FAX: 516-747-3431
cns@cnsc.us http://www.cnsc.net
Richard Malkin, Editor
Anthony F. Calabrese, President
A forum for professionals involved in the sale , marketing, services and movement of air cargo.
Quarterly Founded: 1986
Circulation: 8000

10231 Cargo Facts
Air Cargo Managment Group
520 Pike Street
Suite 1010
Seattle, WA 98101-1662
206-587-6537
FAX: 206-587-6540
news@cargofacts.com
http://www.cargofacts.com

Edwin C Laird, Publisher
David Harris, Editor
Jackie Edinger, Circulation Manager

Includes fiscal reports, freighter aircraft transactions, short segments, international perspectives, and industry updates. *$ 395.00*

24 pages Monthly Founded: 1980
Circulation: 7500

10232 Cosmetic Personal Care Packaging
O&B Communications
11444 W. Olympic Blvd
Los Angeles, CA 90064-1303
310-445-4200
FAX: 310-445-4299
info@cpcpkg.com
http://www.cpcpkg.com

Patricia Spinner, Publisher
John Bethune, Editorial Director
Jennifer Kwok, Managing Editor

Provides information on new packaging containers, materials, equipment and services that are involved with the cosmetic industry. *$60.00*

Monthly Founded: 1996
Circulation: 12,500

10233 Courier Times
Courier Times
27-16 168th Street
Flushing, NY 11358-1130
718-291-1253
FAX: 718-359-1959
mrcourier@couriertimes.com
http://www.couriertimes.com

Bill Goodman, Editor
C Tsamis, Owner

New products vital to the industry, discusses insurance and technology updates, also offers customer service guidelines. *$39.00*

Monthly
Circulation: 1100

10234 Electronic Packaging & Production
Reed Business Information
360 Park Avenue S
New York, NY 10014
212-450-0067
FAX: 630-288-8686
corporatecommunications@reedbusiness.c om http://www.reedbusiness.com

Vicky Steen, Publisher
Michael Sweeney, Editorial Director
James Reed, Owner

Edited for engineers and managers who are involved in packaging design, printed circuit board fabrication and assembly, and production testing of electronic circuits, systems, products and equipment.

Founded: 1960

10235 Food & Drug Packaging
Stagnito Publishing Group
210 S 5th Street
Suite 202
Saint Charles, IL 60174
847-205-5660
FAX: 630-377-1678

Edwin O Landon, Publisher

Food and Drug Packaging serves industries engaged in packaging food, beverages, pharmaceuticals, cosmetics and consulting/engineering firms.

Monthly Founded: 1959
Circulation: 75140

10236 Harbour & Shipping
Progress Publishing Company, Ltd
1489 Marine Drive
Suite 510,
West Vancouver, BC V7 T1
604-922-6717
FAX: 604-922-1739
harbour&shipping@telus.net

Allison Smith, Editor
Murray McLellan, Publisher
Murray McLellan, CEO/President
Murray McLellan, Circulation Manager
Murray McLellan, Marketing Manager

Serves the deep sea and coastal shipping, and ship building, repair and supply industries of Canada and worldwide. Accepts advertising. *$60.00*

Monthly Founded: 1918
Circulation: 2200
Printed in 4 colors on glossy stock

10237 Hazmat Packager & Shipper
Packaging Research International
404 Price Street
West Chester, PA 19382
610-436-8292
FAX: 610-436-9422 877-429-7447
dmazzone1@verizon.net
http://www.hazmatship.com

Vincent Vitollo, CEO/President

Published for the chemical, cosmetics, and pharmaceutical industries, transportation of hazardous materials, as well as industrial packaging industries. *$209.00*

Founded: 1990
Circulation: 1000
Printed in 4 colors on matte stock

10238 International Paper Board Industry

Brunton Publications & NV Public
43 Main Street
Avon By The Sea, NJ 07717-1051
732-502-0500
FAX: 732-502-9606
jcurley@NVPublications.com
http://nvpublications.com

Mike Brunton, Publisher
Jim Curley, Editor
Tom Vilardi, President

Information on corrugated paper and converting industry, encompassing news and production worldwide. *$60.00*

Monthly
Circulation: 6500

10239 Label & Narrow Web Industry
Rodman Publications
70 Hilltop Rd
Ramsey, NJ 07446
201-825-2552
FAX: 201-825-0553
label@rodpub.com
www.labelandnarrowweb.com/

Rodman J Zilenziger, President
Kathleen Scully, Publisher
Jack Kenny, Editor

Information source for label printers and manufacturers of narrow web packaging.

8 issues per ye Founded: 1996
Circulation: 10000

10240 Mail Magazine
1 Elmcoft Road
Stamford, CT 06926-700
203-356-5000
FAX: 203-739-3488 800-672-6937

Meg Reiley, President
Ina Steiner, Publisher

Manages change and positions customers for both tactical and long-term success with innovative, cost-effective, end-to-end messaging solutions.

10241 Milk & Liquid Food Transporter
Brady Company
N 80 W
12878 Fond du Lac Avenue
Menomonee Falls, WI 53051-4474
262-255-0100
FAX: 262-255-3388
lmittag@bradyco.co

Linda Mittag, Publisher

Information for owners, operators and managers of companies that haul milk or other liquid foods in sanitary or food grade tankers. Publication covers maintenance, association news, state of the industry, business management, and activities of independent haulers. *$12.00*

Monthly
Circulation: 4,100

10242 Modern Bulk Transporter
Tunnell Publications
PO Box 66010
Houston, TX 77266
713-523-8124
FAX: 713-523-8384
cwilson@primediabusiness.com
http://www.bulktransporter.com/

Charles Wilson, Editor
Martine Ewing, Advertising Director
Mary Davis, Associate Editor

Serves the truck industry that transports petroleum and petroleum products. Accepts advertising.

Monthly Founded: 1905
Circulation: 15000

10243 Mover Magazine
Virgo Publishing
3300 N Central Avenue, Suite 2500
PO Box 40079
Phoenix, AZ 85067-0079
480-990-1101
FAX: 480-675-8146
For the moving and storage industry.

10244 PARCEL Shipping & Distribution
RB Publishing
2901 International Lane
Suite 200
Madison, WI 53704-3102
608-778-8785
FAX: 608-241-8666 800-536-1992
rbpub@rbpub.com
http://www.rbpub.com

Marll Thriede, President
Ron Brent, Publisher
Dan Rourke, Editor

Founded: 1988
Circulation: 30000

10245 Packaging Digest Magazine
Reed Business Information
360 Park Avenue S
New York, NY 10010
212-450-0067
FAX: 630-288-8686
http://www.reedbusiness.com

Robert Heitzman, Editor
John Kimler, Publisher
James Reed, Owner

Serves the manufacturing, wholesale and service industries. *$75.00*

Monthly Founded: 1963

10246 Packaging Technology & Engineering

North American Publishing Company
401 N Broad Street
Philadelphia, PA 19108-1001
215-238-5300
FAX: 215-238-5429 800-777-8074
customerservice@napco.com
http://www.napco.com

Jim Harvey, Publisher
Richard Soloway, CEO/President
Glen Rreynolds, Circulation Manager
Nolle Skodzinski, Editor

Reports on evironmental concerns, legislation and regulation, product design, material availability, and economic trends. *$69.00*

Monthly Founded: 1958
Circulation: 20271

10247 Packaging World

Summit Publishing Company
One IBM Plaza Suite 2401
330 N Wabash Avenue
Chicago, IL 60611
312-222-1010
FAX: 312-222-1310
info@packworld.com
http://www.packworld.com

Lloyd Ferguson, President
Joseph Angel, VP/Publisher
Patrick Reynolds, VP/Editor
Timothy Hammack, Circulation Director
Jim George, Marketing & Design Editor

Serves the manufacturing, wholesaling, and service industries.

Monthly Founded: 1994
Circulation: 92547 90,000 names $135 per M.
Printed in 4 colors on matte stock

10248 Paper, Film, Foil Converter

Primedia
330 N. Wabash Avenue
Suite 2300
Chicago, IL 60611
312-595-1080
FAX: 312-595-0295
mderda@primediabusiness.com
http://www.pffc-online.com

Claudia Hine, Managing Editor
Scott Bieda, Publisher

Serves the field which fabricates paper, paperboard, plastic films and foil materials into packaging and other products.

94 pages Monthly Founded: 1927

10249 Paperboard Packaging

Advanstar Communications
545 Boylston Street
Boston, MA 02116
617-514-4600
FAX: 617-267-6900
info@advanstar.com
www.advanstar.com

Jackie Schultz, Editor

Publication edited for management and other key personnel involved in the manufacturing and marketing segments of the paperboard packaging industry. *$39.00*

Monthly

10250 Pharmaceutical & Medical Packaging News

Canon Communications
11444 W Olympic Boulevard
Suite 700
Los Angeles, CA 90064
310-445-4200
FAX: 310-445-4269
sales@devicelink.com
http://www.devicelink.com

Bill Cobert, CEO
Daphne Allen, Editor

Information and news on events, new technology, industry trends, regulatory matters, and health care trade associations for professionals involved in the pharmaceutical and medical product packaging industry. *$150.00*

Monthly Founded: 1978
Circulation: 20000

10251 Refrigerated Transporter

Primedia
9800 Metcalf Avenue
Overland Park, KS 66212
913-341-1300
FAX: 913-967-1898
gmacklin@primediabusiness.com
http://www.primediabusiness.com

Raymond Anderson, Publisher
Gary Macklin, Editor

Monthly Founded: 1905
Circulation: 15023

10252 TAPPI Journal

Technical Association of the Pulp & Paper Industry
15 Technology Parkway South
Norcross, GA 30092
770-446-1400
FAX: 770-446-6947 800-332-8686
tj@tappi.org http://www.tappi.org

Mary Beth O Bennett, Publishing Director
Donald G Meadows, Editor
Willis Potts, Chairman

Serves domestic and international pulp, paper, paperboard, packaging and converting industries; manufacturers and suppliers of machinery, equipment, chemicals and other material. *$350.00*

130 pages Monthly Founded: 1949
Circulation: 5300
Printed in 4 colors on glossy stock

10253 Trucker's Connection

Megan Cullingford
5960 Crooked Creek Road
Suite 15
Norcross, GA 30092
770-416-0927
FAX: 770-416-1734
dan@truckersconnection.com
http://www.truckersconnection.com

Megan Cullingford, General Manager
Dan Barnhill, Editor
Reid Ramsay, Production Manager

Published for the use of long haul, over-the-road truck drivers, owner operators, small trucking company fleet owners, safety and recruiting of personnel for trucking companies in the US and Canada.

Monthly Founded: 1986
Circulation: 165000
Printed in 4 colors on glossy stock

10254 World Wide Shipping (WWS)

World Wide Shipping Guide
16302 Byrnwyck Lane
Odessa, FL 33556-2807
813-920-4788
FAX: 813-920-8268
lee@wwship.com
http://www.wwship.com

Lee Di Paci, Publisher
Barbara Edwards, Editor

Dedicated to the interests of North American exporters, importers, distributors, freight forwarders, NVOCC's and customs brokers requiring freight tranportation services and equipment. *$32.00*

32 pages Fortnightly Founded: 1919
Circulation: 9000 32 names $200 per M.
Printed in 4 colors on glossy stock

Trade Shows

10255 Asia Food Processing & Packaging Technology Exhibition

Reed Exhibition Companies
383 Main Avenue
PO Box 6059
Norwalk, CT 06851
203-840-4800
FAX: 203-840-9628

One hundred and seventy four exhibitors for an audience of manufacturers, packaging design and development professionals.

Biennial

10256 International Packaging Exchange

Reed Business Information
2000 Clearwater Drive
Oak Brook, IL 60523
630-740-0825
FAX: 630-288-8686
www.reedbusiness.com

Carol Armbrust, Show Manager

One thousand three hundred and fourteen booths.

40M Attendees June

10257 LabelExpo

Tarsus Group
9501 W Devon Avenue
Rosemont, IL 60018-4811
847-292-3700
FAX: 847-318-1506
www.labelresource.com

Steve Krogulski, Manager

13700 Attendees September

10258 NORPACK

333 Trapelo Road
Belmont, MA 02478-1856
781-489-3400
FAX: 781-489-5534 800-543-5259

Packaging and material handling exposition with 200 exhibitors and booths.

3000 Attendees April

10259 National Paperbox and Packaging Association Annual Conference

National Paperbox Association
113 S West Street
3rd Floor
Alexandria, VA 22313
703-684-2212
FAX: 703-683-6920
boxmaker@paperbox.org
www.paperbox.org

Scott Miller, Executive VP

Annual conference for rigid box and folding carton manufacturers. Thirty booths.
325 Attendees June

10260 Transportation Intermediaries Annual Convention & Trade Show
Transportation Intermediaries Association
3601 Eisenhower Avenue
Suite 110
Alexandria, VA 22304
703-317-2140
FAX: 703-329-1898
info@tianet.org www.tianet.org
Robert Voltmann, President
Nancy King, Contact
Education and policy organization for North American transportation intermediaries. TIA is the only national association representing the interests of all third party transportation service providers. The members of TIA include logistics management firms, property brokers, perishable commodities brokers, freight forwarders, intermodal marketers, ocean and air forwarders, and NVOCC's.
700 Attendees Founded: 1977

Directories & Databases

10261 ABS International Directory of Offices
American Bureau of Shipping
16855 N Chase Drive
Houston, TX 77060
281-877-5800
FAX: 281-877-5801
www.abs-group.com
Over 175 operations offices of the bureau worldwide are listed.
122 pages Semiannual

10262 Air Freight Directory
Air Cargo
1819 Bay Ridge Avenue
Suite 1
Annapolis, MD 21403-2899
410-805-5578
FAX: 410-268-3154 800-747-6505
Debbi Mayes
Lists more than 500 motor carriers contracting with Air Cargo for delivery or pick up of freight. *$84.00*
Bi-Monthly

10263 American Drop-Shippers Directory
World Wide Trade Service
PO Box 283
Medina, WA 98039-0283
206-236-4795

Over 200 firms are listed that are willing to drop ship single item orders at wholesale prices for mail order and other direct marketers. *$15.00*
36 pages Biennial
Circulation: 5,000

10264 American Motor Carrier Directory
PRIMEDIA Information
745 5th Avenue
New York, NY 10151
212-745-0100
FAX: 212-745-0121 www.primedia.com
John Capers III, Publisher
Amy Middlebrook, Editor
Lists all licensed Less Than Truckload general commodity carriers in the US; includes specialized motor carriers and related services, refrigerated carriers, heavy haulers, bulk haulers, riggers and specified commodity carriers, state and federal regulatory bodies governing the trucking industry, tariff publishing bureaus, freight claim councils, industry associations, etc. *$595.00*
1000 pages Annual Founded: 1952
Circulation: 5,100 $150 per M.

10265 Commercial Carrier Journal: Buyers' Guide Issue
Reed Business Information
1 Chilton Way
Wayne, PA 19089-0002
646-746-6400
FAX: 646-746-7433
cheavens@chilton.net
www.reedbusiness.com
Gerald F Standley, Editor
List of vehicles, components and accessories suppliers for the truck and bus fleet markets. *$10.00*
Annual October
Circulation: 85,000

10266 Commercial Carrier Journal: Top 100 Issue
Reed Business Information
360 Park Avenue
New York, NY 10010
212-450-0067
FAX: 646-746-7433
jstandle@chilton.net
www.reedbusiness.com
Gerald F Standley, Editor
James Reed, Owner
List of top 100 for-hire motor carriers, ranked by gross revenues; also the next 200 carriers in gross revenue. *$10.00*
Annual August
Circulation: 85,000

10267 Directory of Contract Packagers and their Facilities
Institute of Packaging Professionals
1601 N Bond Street
Suite 101
Naperville, IL 60563
630-544-5050
FAX: 630-544-5055
info@iopp.org www.iopp.org
More than 400 contract packagers in the US and abroad.
Biennial

10268 Directory of Corrugated Plants
Fibre Box Association
2850 Golf Road
Suite 412
Rolling Meadows, IL 60008-4040
847-364-9600
FAX: 847-364-9639
fba@fibrebox.org www.fibrebox.org
Amy Turner
Stephanie Maegdlin, Comm/ Marketing Coordinator
Over 1,600 manufacturing facilities in the North American corrugated and solid fibre industry. Distributed in microsoft excel spreadsheet. *$200.00*

10269 Directory of Freight Forwarders and Custom House Brokers
International Wealth Success
PO Box 186
Merrick, NY 11566-0186
516-766-5850
FAX: 516-766-5919 800-323-0548
admin@iwsmoney.com
www.iwsmoney.com
Tyler G Hicks, President
Lists hundreds of these firms throughout the U.S. who help in the export/import business. *$17.50*
106 pages Annual Founded: 1980 ISBN 1-561503-46-0

10270 Directory of Packaging Consultants

Institute of Packaging Professionals
1601 N Bond Street
Suite 101
Naperville, IL 60563
630-544-5050
FAX: 630-544-5055
infor@iopp.org www.iopp.org
Packaging consultants in the US. *$25.00*
Annual

10271 Directory of Packaging Sources
JPC Directories
PO Box 488
Plainview, NY 11803-0488
516-822-6861

Joel J Shulman, Editor
Offers information on narrow web and wide web printer/converters and suppliers to the printing industry.
125 pages Annual
Circulation: 50,000

10272 Flexible Packaging Association Membership Directory
Hearst Business Communications
645 Stewart Avenue
Garden City, NY 11530-4709
516-227-1300

Over 200 member companies that manufacture flexible packaging and supplies used in this industry are profiled. *$28.00*
Annual
Circulation: 20,000

10273 Food & Beverage Market Place
Grey House Publishing
185 Millerton Road
PO Box 860
Millerton, NY 12546
518-890-0526
FAX: 518-789-0545 800-562-2139
books@greyhouse.com
www.foodmp.com
Leslie Mackenzie, Publisher
Richard Gottlieb, Editor
This information packed three-volume set is the most powerful buying and marketing guide for the US food and beverage industry. Includes thousands of industry and transportation listings. *$595.00*
6500 pages Annual

10274 Modern Bulk Transporter: Buyers Guide
Tunnell Publications
PO Box 66010
Houston, TX 77266
713-523-8124
FAX: 713-523-8384
Charles Wilson, Editor
Directory of suppliers of products or services for companies operating tank trucks.
Annual October
Circulation: 16,000

10275 National Customs Brokers and Forwarders Association of America
National Customs Brokers & Forwarders Association
1200 18th Street NW
#901
Washington, DC 20036
202-466-0222
FAX: 202-466-0226
staff@ncbfaa.org www.ncbfaa.org
Greg Pitkoff, Editor
Barbara Reilly, Executive VP
About 600 customs brokers, international air cargo agents, and freight forwarders in the United States. *$24.00*
Annual

10276 National Highway and Airway Carriers Directory
National Highway Carriers Directory
PO Box 6099
Buffalo Grove, IL 60089-6099
847-634-0606
FAX: 847-634-1026
www.national-highway.com
Pam W Ferreira, President/Editor
Provides information on: LTL motor freight carriers - with over 250,000 detailed routing points and terminals for US and Canada, contract carriers (truckload), airline cargo companies, transportation brokers, intermodel trucking companies, freight forwarders, warehousing companies, Canadian carriers, refrigerated carriers, railroads and ocean carriers. *$195.00*
1400 pages Spring & Fall Founded: 1942
Circulation: 5000
Printed in 2 colors on newsprint stock

10277 National Motor Carrier Directory and Additional Products
Transportation Technical Services
500 Lafayette Boulevard
Fredericksburg, VA 22401-6070
540-899-9872
FAX: 540-899-1948 888-665-9887
truckinfo@ttstrucks.com
www.ttstrucks.com/www.fleetseek.com
Ronald D Roth, Executive VP
Over 46,000 motor carriers with revenues of $100,000 or more. *$495.00*
1781 pages Annual November Founded: 1989 21000 names
Printed in on matte stock

10278 Official Container Directory
Advanstar Communications
545 Boylston Street
Boston, MA 02116
617-514-4600
FAX: 617-267-6900
info@advanstar.com
www.advanstar.com
Directory of services and supplies to the industry.
200 pages 4500
Circulation: 5,000

10279 Official Motor Carrier Directory
Official Motor Freight Guides
1700 W Cortland Street
Chicago, IL 60622-1121
773-342-1000
FAX: 773-489-0482 800-621-4650
Edward K Koch, Editor
Approximately 2,100 general and specialized motor carriers and air cargo carriers; federal and state agencies concerned with the trucking industry; tariff publishing bureaus, US and Canadian port authorities; state associations. *$59.50*
SemiAnnual
Circulation: 6,000

10280 Official Motor Freight Guide
C&C Publishing Company
1700 W Cortland Street
Chicago, IL 60622-1121
773-536-2050
This directory is published in over 21 regional editions that list air and water freight transportation, motor carriers and warehouse facilities for the metropolitan areas of Baltimore, Boston, Chicago, Cincinnati, Cleveland, Denver, Detroit, Evansville, Ft. Wayne, Indianapolis, Kansas City, Philadelphia, Pittsburgh, Quad Cities and Toledo. *$45.00*
500 pages Semiannual

10281 Official Shippers Guide
Official Motor Freight Guides
1700 W Cortland Street
Chicago, IL 60622-1121
773-342-1000
FAX: 773-489-0482 800-621-4650
E Koch, Editor
Eric J Robison, Editor
Major air, rail, water and motor carriers published in three local editions covering Chicago, New York and St. Louis. *$55.00*
Annual

10282 PMMI Packaging Machinery Directory
Packaging Machinery Manufacturers Institute (PMMI)
4350 N Fairfax Drive
Suite 600
Arlington, VA 22203
703-243-8555
FAX: 703-243-8556
pmmiwebhelp@pmmi.org
www.pmmi.org, www.packexpo.com
Matt Croson, Director Member Services
Sara Kryder, Manager Communications
Chuck Yuska, President
Contains information on all 500+ member companies, who are committed to producing quality products and providing world class service to their customers.

10283 Packaging Digest: Machinery Materials Guide Issue
Delta Communications
N6W23673 Bluemont Road
Waukesha, WI 53188
262-429-9111
FAX: 262-546-8820
delta@deltacommunications.com
www.deltacommunicatons.com
Barbara McDonough, Editor
List of more than 3,100 manufacturers of machinery and materials for the packaging industry, and about 260 contract packagers. *$ 6.00*
Annual

10284 Rauch Guide to the US Packaging Industry
Impact Marketing Consultants
PO Box 1226
Manchester Center, VT 05255
802-362-2325
802-362-3693
comments@impactmarket.com
www.impactmarket.com
Donald R Dykes, Editor
C Verbanic, Editor
Analyzes the US packaging industry, with data on industry economics, raw materials, major products, and unique profiles of 50% producers. *$495.00*
Triennial

10285 Service Directory
Express Carriers Association
PO Box 4307
Bethlehem, PA 18018
610-740-5857
FAX: 610-740-3174 866-322-7447
eca@expresscarriers.com
www.expresscarriers.com
Cheryle Williamson, Executive Director
An annual directory published by the Express Carriers Association.
Annual
Circulation: 1250

10286 Transportation Telephone Tickler
Commonwealth Business Media
50 Millstone Road
Building 400, Suite 200
East Windsor, NJ 08520
609-371-7700
FAX: 609-371-7883 800-215-6084
customerservice@cbizmedia.com
www.cbizmedia.com,
www.tickleronline.com
Ann Bednarik-Smith, Publisher
Edith Chaudoin-Stahlberger, Editor
Provides vital contact information for 24,000 suppliers of 160 types of transportation services in the US, Canada, Caribbean and parts of Latin America. *$124.95*
2425 pages Annual Founded: 1949

10287 Who's Who & What's What in Packaging
481 Carlisle Drive
Herndon, VA 20170-4830
703-471-8922
Offers information on members of the Institute of Packaging Professionals, including placement firms, colleges that offer packaging curricula, and related organizations. *$125.00*
240 pages Annual

Industry Web Sites

10288 www.adhesive.org
Adhesive Manufacturers Association
Association for the packaging industry.

10289 www.aiccbox.org
Association of Independent Corrugated Converters
Provides a forum for discussion of problems and offers educational programs and seminars.

10290 www.corrugated.org
Corrugated Packaging Council
Develops and coordinates industry-wide programs to address corrugated packaging issues. The Council's mission is to inform consumers, manufacturers, retailers and government officials of corrugated pack-

aging's performance and environmental attributes.

10291 www.fibca.com
Flexible Intermediate Bulk Container Association

Works to develop minimum standards of testing and performance for FIBC. Acts as a forum through seminars and other programs and serves as an advocate for the industry.

10292 www.fibrebox.org
Fibre Box Association

Represents 90 percent of the US corrugated paper board, packaging, manufacturing industry.

10293 www.flexpack.org
Flexible Packaging Association

Trade association of manufacturers, converters and suppliers of paper, metal foil and plastic or cellulose film.

10294 www.fpi.org
Foodservice & Packaging Institute

Sanitation and environmental information, plus programs and services.

10295 www.ftdassociation.org
Florists' Transworld Delivery Association

Has an annual budget of approximately $140 million.

10296 www.geminishippers.com
Gemini Shippers Group

Shippers association with global contracts for all commodities.

10297 www.graysonassociates.com
Grayson Associates

Association for those interested in marketing analysis of the package goods industry.

10298 www.greyhouse.com
Grey House Publishing

Selected Grey House directories in the fields of business, health and education are available online. Users can search our online databases by several different search criteria, such as product categories, geographic area, sales volume and much, much more. Full Grey House catalog and online ordering also available.

10299 www.homefair.com

Offers comprehensive content and services for people moving to a new home or relocating to another community.

10300 www.iicl.org
Institute of International Container Lessors

Represents international container and chassis leasing industry in technical, governmental and legal matters. Publishes leading worldwide manuals on inspection and repair of containers and inspector and maintenance of chassis. Sponsors container and chassis inspection examination once a year in over 40 countries and chassis examination in North America.

10301 www.lcaships.com
Lake Carriers Association

Members are US- Flag Great Lakes vessel operators engaged in transporting iron ore, coal, grain, limestone, cement and petroleum products.

10302 www.masa.org
Mailing & Fulfillment Service Association

For over 80 years, this national trade association has been serving the mailing and fulfillment services industry by providing opportunities for learning and professional development of the managers of these companies.

10303 www.mfsanet.org
Mailing & Fulfillment Service Association

80 year old trade association which provides education/training, information, surveys and industry representation for companies which offer 3rd party mailing and fulfillment services.

10304 www.niphle.com
National Institute of Packaging, Handling and

Originally the DC chapter of the Society of Packaging and Handling engineers, the Institute became independent in an effort to give more emphasis on the governmental responsibilities of its members.

10305 www.nmaonline.org
National Meat Association

Association for meat packers, processors and jobbers through out the USA.

10306 www.nwpca.org
National Wooden Pallet & Container Association

Membership roster, tech talk, publications and industry watch.

10307 www.packagingnetwork.com
Packaging Network

Searchable database of food industry related items.

10308 www.packexpo.com
Packaging Machinery Manufacturers Institute (PMMI)

For manufacturers of packaging and packaging-related converting equipment.

10309 www.paperbox.org
National Paperbox Association

Represents industry before legislative and regulatory bodies. Conducts technical seminars on sales, marketing, costs and management methods. Publishes a quarterly newsletter

10310 www.polysort.com
Polysort.com

Links to related companies.

10311 www.polystyrene.org
Polystyrene Packaging Council

Links to other associations.

10312 www.ppcouncil.org
Petroleum Packaging Council

Provides technical leadership and education to the petroleum packaging industry.

10313 www.tianet.org
Transportation Intermediaries Association

Education and policy organization for North American transportation intermediaries. TIA is the only national association representing the interests of all third party transportation service providers. The members of TIA include logistics management firms, property brokers, perishable commodities brokers, freight forwarders, intermodal marketers, ocean and air forwarders, and NVOCC's.

10314 www.uffva.org
United Fresh Fruit & Vegetable Association

Equipment, supplies, cartons, packaging machinery, computers, sorting and sizing equipment, harvesting equipment, film wrap manufacturing and commodity organizations.

10315 www.unitdose.org
Healthcare Compliance Packaging Council

A not-for-profit trade association that was established in 1990 to promote the many benefits of unit dose blister and ship packaging - especially its ability to be designed in compliance-promoting formats that help people take their medications properly.

Associations

10316 American Association of Family and Consumer Sciences
400 N Columbus Street
Suite 202
Alexandria, VA 22314
703-706-4600
FAX: 703-706-4663 800-424-8080
Don Bower, President
Karen Tucker, Manager
An association dedicated to Family & Consumer Sciences professionals. AAFCS strives to improve the quality and standards of individual and family life by providing educational programs, influencing public policy, and through communication.
10000 Members

10317 American Home Furnishings Alliance
PO Box HP-7
High Point, NC 27261
336-884-5000
FAX: 336-884-5303
furninfo@ahfa.us www.ahta.us
Robert Maricich, Chairman
Paul B Toms, First Vice Chairman
Andy Counts, Chief Executive Officer
A who's who in the furniture industry, supplying information on over 500 furniture manufacturers and their suppliers.
450 Members Founded: 1984

10318 American Innerspring Manufacturers Association
1918 N Parkway
Memphis, TN 38112
901-749-9030
800-882-5604
aimy@aiminfo.org www.aiminfo.org
Arthur Grehan, Manager
Members make and sell innerspring units and box springs to mattress manufacturers. Also conducts year round public relations program directed at consumers, encouraging purchase of innerspring mattresses.
12 Members Founded: 1966

10319 American Society of Furniture Designers
144 Woodland Drive
New London, NC 28127
910-576-1273
FAX: 910-576-1573
info@asfd.com www.asfd.com
James Dipersia, President
Christine Evans, Executive Director
An international non-profit professional organization dedicated to advancing, improving, and supporting the profession of furniture design and its positive impact in the marketplace.
Founded: 1981

10320 Association of Progressive Rental Dealers
1504 Robin Hood Trail
Austin, TX 78703
512-794-0095
FAX: 512-794-0097
cmay@apro-rto.com
www.aprovision.org
Shannon Strunk, President
John C Cleekk, First VP
Jeannie Hutchinson, Program Coordinator
Kevin Quinn, Secretary
Bill Keese, Manager
Members include television, appliance and furniture dealers who rent merchandise with an option to purchase.
5500+ Members Founded: 1980

10321 Association of Woodworking & Furnishings
5733 Rickenbacker Road
Commerce, CA 90040
323-838-9440
FAX: 323-838-9443 800-946-2937
awfsofc@aol.com www.awfs.org
Barry Howerton, President
Skip Hem, VP
Joan Kemp, Secretary/Treasurer
Organization for furniture and accessories manufacturers and suppliers.
Founded: 1979

10322 Business and Institutional Furniture Manufacturers Association
2680 Horizon Drive SE
Suite A-1
Grand Rapids, MI 49546-7500
616-285-3963
FAX: 616-285-3765
email@bifma.org www.bifma.org
P Daniel Miller, President
Thomas Reardon, Executive Director
BIFMA is a not-for-profit trade association of furniture manufacturers and suppliers, addressing issues of common concern.
245+ Members Founded: 1973

10323 Furniture Rental Association of America
5008 Pine Creek Drive
#6
Westerville, OH 43081-4848
614-755-3910
800-367-7368
Furniture rental companies.

10324 Futon Association International
PO Box 6548
Chico, CA 95927-6548
530-534-7833
FAX: 530-534-7875 800-327-3262
Tom Tedesco, President
Patricia MacMillen, VP
Richard Arnovitz, Treasurer
Mark Bello, Secretary
Dan Neenan, Director
Assists retailers in marketing product and keeps members informed of codes, laws, regulations.
400 Members Founded: 1984

10325 Home Furnishings International Association
PO Box 420807
Dallas, TX 75342
214-741-7632
FAX: 214-742-9103
info@hfia.com www.hfia.com
Mary Frye, President
Ken Allred, Vice Chairman
Bobby Leon, Chairman
Stan Pickett, Secretary/Treasurer
Commited to strengthening the home furnishing industry trhough collective support, services, and leadership.
Founded: 1923

10326 Illuminating Engineering Society of North America
120 Wall Street
Room 17
New York, NY 10005-4001
212-248-5000
FAX: 212-248-5017 www.iesna.org
William Hanley, Manager
To advance knowledge and disseminate information for the improvement of the lighted environment to the benefit of society. Publishes a monthly magazine.
Mailing list available for rent 8,500 names $120 per M.

10327 International Furniture Suppliers Associat ion
PO Box 2482
High Point, NC 27261
336-884-1566
FAX: 336-884-1350
info@ifsa-info.com
www.ifsa-info.com
Gary Chase, Chairman
David Kuluva, President
Joe Blazar, First VP
Ron Paddock, Secretary/Treasurer
Phyllis Tuttle, Director
Nonprofit trade association of wholesale distributors, importers and manufacturers of finished goods. Supports furniture retailers by continuous improvement of our industry through advocacy, research and the exchange of ideas. Membership is open to any legitimate furniture wholesaler, importer, manufacturer, agent or any other firm operating within the supply chain of finished goods.
150 Members Founded: 1928

10328 International Furniture Transportation and Logistics Council
PO Box 889
Gardner, MA 01440-0889
978-632-1913
FAX: 978-630-2917
jsears@iftlc.org www.iftlc.org
Raynard F Bohman Jr, Managing Director
Members are furniture manufacturers, retailers, carriers, wholesalers and warehouses of allied products.
150 Members

10329 International Housewares Association
6400 Shafer Court
Suite 650
Rosemont, IL 60018
847-292-4200
mkulik@housewares.org
www.housewares.org
Douglas J Bradshaw, Chairman
Linda S Graebner, Vice Chairman/Chairman Elect
Philip J Brandl, President
Jennifer Lamberg, Executive Assistant
A full-service trade association dedicated to promoting the sales and marketing of housewares.
Founded: 1938

10330 International Sleep Products Association
501 Wythe Street
Alexandria, VA 22314-1917
703-683-8371
FAX: 703-683-4503
www.sleepproducts.org

Debi Sutton, VP, Marketing Member Services

Maintains a strong organization to influence government actions, inform and educate the membership and act on industry issues to enhance the growth, profitability and stature of the sleep products industry. Provides members with information and services to manage their business more effectively and efficiently. Publishes a magazine devoted exclusively to the mattress industry, BEDtimes covers a broad range of issue and news important to the industry.
$65.00
650 Members Monthly Founded: 1915
Circulation: 3,500

10331 Juvenile Products Manufacturers Association
15000 Commerce Parkway
Suite C
Mt. Laurel, NJ 08054
856-638-0420
FAX: 856-439-0525 jpma@ahint.com

William MacMillan, Show Manager
Robert Waller Jr., President

Home accessories and products for children's rooms.

10332 National Association of Casual Furniture
214 N Hale Street
Wheaton, IL 60187
630-510-4562
FAX: 630-510-4501 800-956-2237

Janet Svazas, Executive Director

Members are retailers; associate members are manufacturers and sales representatives.
270 Members Founded: 1981

10333 National Association of Display Industries
3595 Sheridan Street
Suite 200
Hollywood, FL 33021
954-893-7300
FAX: 954-893-7500
nasfm@nasfm.org www.nasfm.org

Klein Merriman, Executive Director
Tracy Dillon, Director Communications
Karen Doodeman, Director Sales & Marketing
Shawn Pariaug, Manager Member Services
Pamela Presley, Director Administration & Meetings

Sponsors seminars and annual contests. Conducts research programs and maintains placement services.
400 Members Founded: 1937

10334 National Cotton Batting Institute
41 S Walnut Bend Road
Cordova, TN 38018
901-624-1200
FAX: 901-624-1200
info@natbat.com www.natbat.com

Alan Posners, President
Fred Middleton, Executive Secretary
Alan Posner, VP

Association representing members of the cotton batting industry.
27 Members Founded: 1954

10335 National Home Furnishings Association
3910 Tinsley Drive
Suite 101
High Point, NC 27265-3610
336-886-6100
FAX: 336-801-6102 800-888-9590
info@nhfa.org www.nhfa.org

Mary Ann Levitt, President
Steve De Haan, Executive VP

The nation's largest organization devoted specifically to the needs and interests of home furnishings retailers. Also to provide members with the information, education, products and services they need to remain successful. *$7.95*
2600 Members Monthly Founded: 1920
Circulation: 14,000

10336 National Unfinished Furniture Institute
1850 Oak Street
Northfield, IL 60093-3042
847-784-1225
FAX: 847-446-3523

Ray Passis, Executive Director

Provides publicity and insurance for industry, offers educational seminars and bestows awards.
1.2M Members Founded: 1979

10337 National Waterbed Retailers Association
2 Greetree Center
Suit 225
Marlton, NJ 08053-3102
312-236-6662
FAX: 312-232-6114 800-832-3553

Promotes industry through educational seminars, sells educational materials on waterbeds, health care and conducts surveys.
500 Members Founded: 1972

10338 Paint & Decorating Retailers Association
403 Axminister Drive
Fenton, MO 63026-2941
636-326-2636
FAX: 636-326-1823 www.pdra.org

David Garland, President
Louie Frazier, VP/Treasurer
Larry DeWitt, Marketin & Senior Art Director
Dan Simon, Manager

To provide members with the tools they need and prosper such as information, sales training, and business operations programs.
1500 Members Founded: 1947

10339 Quarters Furniture Manufacturers

1211 Popes Head Drive
Fairfax, VA 22030
703-381-2222
www.house.gov

Represents companies who produce furniture for military markets. Monitors federal procurement policy as it relates to prison industries.
20 Members Founded: 1995

10340 Retail Office Furniture Forum
301 N Fairfax Street
Alexandria, VA 22314-2633
703-362-2770
FAX: 703-683-7552

Encourages competition and aims to help dealers take advantage of growth in market. Sponsors seminars.
220 Members Founded: 1984

10341 Society of Glass & Ceramic Decorators
47 N 4th Street
PO Box 2489
Zanesville, OH 43702
740-588-9882
FAX: 740-588-0245
sgcd@sgcd.org www.sgcd.org

Randall Van Hise, President
Julie Butterfield, VP
Nancy Klinefelter, Secretary/Treasurer

Provides decorating professionals with a competitive edge in business by providing opporotunities for networking to learn about new decorating technologies and techniques.
525 Members

10342 Summer and Casual Furniture Manufacturers
PO Box HP-7
High Point, NC 27261
336-884-5000
FAX: 336-884-5303
jlogan@afma4u.org www.afma4u.org

Robert Spilman, President
Rob Sligh, First VP
Robert Maricich, Second VP
Steve Kincaid, Chairman

Sponsors the International Casual Furniture and Accessories Market in Chicago, the Apollo Awards, recognizing excellence in casual furniture retailing and the Casual Furniture Design Excellence Awards.
500+ Members Founded: 1959

10343 Unfinished Furniture Association
1500 Commerce Parkway
Suite C
Mt. Laurel, NJ 08054
800-487-8321
FAX: 856-439-0525
ufa@ahint.com
www.unfinishedfurniture.org

Sylvia Thompson, President
Dave Sommer, VP
Thomas Habers, Treasurer
Charles Blakenship, Director
Joe Hutchens, Director

Our mission is to promote the common business interests of the unfinished furniture industry, encourage the most efficient and professional organization and administration of firms in the unfinished furniture industry; and to conduct meetings and educational programs, and to collect and publish information about the unfinished furniture industry.
600 Members Founded: 1990

10344 Upholstered Furniture Action Council
PO Box 2436
High Point, NC 27261
336-885-5065
FAX: 336-885-5072
info@ufac.org
www.homefurnish.com/ufac

Joe Ziolkowski, Executive Director

Conducts research and disseminates information about adoption of guidelines for cigarette-resistant furniture. Educates public about safe use of smoking materials.

Founded: 1972

10345 Woodworking & Furnishings Suppliers
5733 Rickenbacker Road
Commerce, CA 90040
562-921-6970
FAX: 323-838-9443 800-946-2937
info@awfs.org www.awfs.org

Barry Howerton, President
Skip Hem, VP
Joan Kemp, Secretary/Treasurer
Dale Silverman, Executive Director

A national trade association in the U.S. representing the interests of the broad array of companies that supply the home and commercial furnishings industry.

10346 World Floor Covering Association
2211 E Howell Avenue
Anaheim, CA 92806
714-978-6440
FAX: 714-978-6066 800-624-6880
wfca@wfca.org www.wfca.org

Christopher Davis, CEO
Terry Hearne, Director of Operations
Cammie Weitzel, Director of Finance/Administration
Donna Archambault, Membership Operations Manager

Shapes and defines public policy through agressive, national legislative advocacy on behalf of our members. Provides continuing professional educational programming through educational forums and the Regional Installation and Training Education (RITE) program.

45 Members Founded: 1973

Newsletters

10347 American Furniture Manufacturers Association Newsletter
American Furniture Manufacturers Association
317 W High Avenue
PO Box HP-7
High Point, NC 27261
336-884-5000
FAX: 336-884-5303
info@afma4u.org
http://www.afma4u.org

Andy Counts, CEO
Jaclyn C Hirschhaut, VP Marketing

Information for the AFMA memberrship regarding the Association programs and services.

6 pages Monthly Founded: 1905
Circulation: 2000
Printed in g colors on 3 stock

10348 Architectural Lighting
Miller Freeman Publications
600 Harrison Street
Suite 400
San Francisco, CA 94107-1391

FAX: 415-905-2239

Art Golden, Publisher
David Malman, Owner

Covers design specifications and application of electrical lighting and daylighting systems.

Circulation: 54,000

10349 National Association of Display Industries
3595 Sheridan Street
Suite 200
Hollywood, FL 33021
954-893-7300
FAX: 954-893-7500
nasfm@nasfm.org
http://www.nasfm.org

Klein Merriman, Executive Director
Tracy Dillon, Director Communications
Betty Jo Bass, Advertising/Sponsorship Manager
Monica Jenkins, Graphics & Production Coordinator

Accepts advertising. *$45.00*

16 pages Founded: 1956
Circulation: 8000

10350 Square Yard
American Floorcovering Association
2211 E Howell Avenue
Anaheim, CA 92806-6009
714-572-8370
FAX: 714-780-0488

Edward Korczak, Publisher

Offers full coverage of interior design in association with floor coverings, carpets and rug manufacturers.

8 pages Monthly

Magazines & Journals

10351 Accessory Merchandising
Vance Publishing
400 Knightsbridge Parkway
Lincolnshire, IL 60069
847-634-2600
FAX: 847-634-4379
http://www.vancepublishing.com

Laura Van Zeyl, Editor
Michael R Reckling, Group Publisher
Steven J. Kulikowski, Marketing Manager
Douglas A. Riemer, Circulation Director

Monthly Founded: 1937
Circulation: 21,000

10352 BEDtimes Magazine
International Sleep Products Association
501 Wythe Street
Alexandria, VA 22314-1917
703-683-8371
FAX: 703-683-4503
bedtimes@sleepproducts.org
http://www.sleepproducts.org

Julie Palm, Editor
Kerri Bellias, Sales Director

A magazine covering the bedding industry. Target audience as mattress suppliers and manufacturers. *$50.00*

Monthly Founded: 1915
Circulation: 3000
Printed in 4 colors on glossy stock

10353 Designer
HDC Publications
429 Montague Avenue
Caro, MI 48723
989-673-4121
FAX: 989-673-2031 800-843-6394
info@hdc-caro.org www.hdc-caro.org
A magazine offering information on interior design.
Monthly

10354 Draperies and Window Coverings
840 US Highway One
Suite 330
North Palm Beach, FL 33408
561-627-3393
FAX: 561-694-6578 847-548-3900
hshingle@lcclark.com
http://www.dwcdesignet.com

Carolyn Silberman, Publisher
Howard Shingle, Editor
Sarah Christy, Associate Editor

Covers trends and specific industry topics.
$33.00

160 pages Monthly Founded: 1981
Circulation: 28,000

10355 Eastern Floors Magazine
Specialist Publications
22801 Ventura Boulevard
Suite 115
Woodland Hills, CA 91364-1230
818-224-8035
FAX: 818-224-8042 800-835-4398
johnsonp@bnpmedia.com
http://www.icsmag.com

Howard Olansky, Editor
Phil Johnson, Group Publisher
Evan Kessler, Publisher

Serving the floor covering and tile industry.
$140.00

Monthly Founded: 1990

10356 Furniture Design and Manufacturing
Delta Solutions
400 N Michigan Avenue
Chicago, IL 60611-4104
312-163-3439
312-616-6005
vderon@deltasi.com
http://www.deltasi.com

Michael Chazin, Editor
Sandy Berliner, Publisher

News and information for the furniture supplier and manufacturer. *$25.00*

Monthly Founded: 1996

10357 Furniture Today
Reed Business Information
7025 Albert Pick Road
Greensboro, NC 27409
336-605-1000
FAX: 336-605-1143 800-395-2329
rallegrezza@reedbusiness.com
http://www.furnituretoday.com

Joseph Carroll, Publisher
Ray Allegeeza, Editor-in-Chief
Helene Checinski, Circulation Manager
Kim Bashford, Production Manager
Delaney Rudd, Ower

Business and fashion newspaper of the furniture industry, edited for retail furniture executives in furniture stores, department stores, mass merchants, furniture specialty stores and catalog showrooms, as well as manufacturing executives at all levels. Focus is on the business and fashion news that these executives need at key decision times in their merchandising and marketing cycles. *$159.97*

Weekly Founded: 1976
Circulation: 21212
Printed in on glossy stock

10358 Home Accents Today
Reed Business Information
360 Park Avenue S
New York, NY 10010
212-450-0067
FAX: 646-746-7433
bbsmith@reedbusiness.com
http://www.reedbusiness.com

Cindy Sheaffer, Editor
Marion Kelly, Publisher
Gerard Van de Aast, CEO
Becky Boswell Smith, Editor-in-Chief
James Reed, Owner

Enables home furnishing retailers to develop merchandising programs, define new style statements, make buying decisions, and create retail strategies. Editorially covers the broad fashion mix of home accent products. *$24.94*

Monthly
Circulation: 21300

10359 Home Furnishing Retailer
National Home Furnishings Association
3910 Tinsley Drive Suite 101
PO Box 2396
Highpoint, NC 27265-3610
336-886-6100
FAX: 336-801-6102 800-888-9590
hfr@nhfa.org http://www.nhfa.org

Trisha Kemerly, Editor
Mike Pierce, Publisher
Steve DeHaan, Executive VP

Official journal of the National Home Furnishings Association, is dedicated to serving home furnishings retailers by providing comprehensive, in-depth, how-to business information designed to help retailers run their businesses more profitably. Dedicated to serving manufacturers and suppliers to home furnishings retailers by providing an editorial environment that offers the best forum for their marketing message and a qualified readership. *$60.00*

48 pages Monthly Founded: 1919
Circulation: 14000

10360 Home Lighting & Accessories
Doctorow Communications
1011 Clifton Avenue
Clifton, NJ 07013
973-779-1600
FAX: 973-779-3242
email@homelighting.com
http://www.homelighting.com

Linda Longo, Editor-in-Chief
Jeff Doctorow, Publisher
Jon Doctorow, Circulation Director

Home Lighting & Accessories is a magazine of lamps, lighting fixtures, shades and decorative home accessories. Articles cover marketing and retailing aspects applied to portable lamps, lamps shades, residential lighting fixtures and decorative home accessories - customer relations, sales training, trends, lighting showroom laycut, design and operations. Plus industry and company news, new promotions, appointments, literature, patents *$15.00*

Founded: 1953

10361 ICS Cleaning Specialist
Business News Publishing Company
22801 Ventura Boulevard
Suite 115
Woodland Hills, CA 91364-1230
818-224-8035
FAX: 818-224-8042 800-835-4398

Phil Johnson, Group Publisher
Evan Kessler, Publisher
Jeffrey Stouffer, Editor
Amy Levin, Production Manager

For carpet cleaning, restoration and floor care service providers.

68 pages Monthly Founded: 1963
Circulation: 24250 $120 per M.
Printed in 4 colors on glossy stock

10362 Laminating Design & Technology
Cygnus Publishing
1233 Janesville Avenue
Fort Atkinson, WI 53538-2738
920-563-6388
FAX: 920-563-1707
www.laminateonline.com

Kenn Busch, Publisher

Global design and color trends, as well as surfacing solutions for furniture architecture and interior design. Focuses on surface design, performance and application. *$30.00*

44 pages Bi-Monthly Founded: 1996
Circulation: 40,006

10363 Metropolis
Bellerophon Publications
61 W 23rd St. Fl. 4
New York, NY 10010-3100
212-627-9977
FAX: 212-627-9988
edit@metropolismag.com
http://www.metropolismag.com

Horace Havemeyer III, Publisher
Susan Szenasy, Editor in Chief
Julie Taraska, Editor
Denise Csaky, Marketing Director

The only magazine that covers all facets of design: architecture, interiors, furniture, preservation, urban design, graphics and crafts. *$27.95*

Founded: 1981
Circulation: 51000

10364 Plywood and Panel World
Hatton-Brown Publishers
PO Box 2268
Montgomery, AL 36102-2268
334-834-1170
FAX: 334-834-4525 800-665-4793
mail@hattonbrown.com
http://www.hattonbrown.com/

D K Knight, Editor-in-chief
Rich Donnell, Editor
David Ramsey, President
Rhonda Thomas, Marketing

A magazine covering the interior design community. *$40.00*

Monthly
Circulation: 12000 $145 per M.
Printed in 4 colors on matte stock

Trade Shows

10365 AAFCS Annual Conference & Exposition
American Association of Family & Consumer Sciences
400 N Columbus Street
Suite 202
Alexandria, VA 22314
703-706-4600
FAX: 703-706-4663
connect@aafcs.org www.aafcs.org
Informative speakers, cutting-edge workshops, and a panel discussion.

Annual/June

10366 Association of College Unions International Prof Conference
120 W 7th Street
Suite 200
Bloomington, IN
812-855-8550
FAX: 812-855-0162
marcanne@indiana.edu
www.indiana.edu/nacui

Mary Ann Cannon, Member Services
Marsha Herman-Betzen, Executive Director

One hundred exhibits of graphic supplies, recreation equipment, computer hardware and software, furnishings, entertainment and speaker bureau information, food service equipment, and more related information and supplies.

1000 Attendees Annual Founded: 1951

10367 Association of Progressive Rental Organizations Convention
1504 Robin Hood Trail
Austin, TX 78703
512-794-0095
FAX: 512-794-0097
rmay@aprovison.org
www.apro-rto.com

Shannon Strunk, President
John C Cleek, First VP
Jeannie Hutchison, Program Coordinator
Bill Keese, Manager

Seminar, reception and tours, plus 280 exhibits of products and services of interest to rent to own dealers: stereos, televisions, furniture, fabric protection and more.

2000 Attendees Annual Founded: 1980

10368 Builders Home, Flower and Furniture Show
Builders Association of Southeastern Michigan
30375 Northwestern Highway
Farmington Hills, MI 48334-3233
248-737-4477
FAX: 313-862-1051
bia@builders.org www.builders.org

Susan Alder Shanteau, Editor

Annual show of 350 exhibitors of home modernization, energy conservation and leisure living equipment, supplies and services; garden materials and home and garden equipment.

10369 Canyon County Home & Garden Show
Spectra Productions
837 E State Street
PO Box 333
Eagle, ID 83616
208-939-6426
FAX: 208-939-6437
www.spectraproductions.com

David Beale, Show Manager

150 Attendees April

10370 Evergreen Home Show
Westlake Promotions
6020 Seaview Avenue NW
Seattle, WA 98107
206-783-5957
FAX: 206-782-6250
www.westlakepromo.com

Bill Bradley, VP

See what's new and what you can do for your home. Fresh ideas and practical advice from our remodeling and construction specialists. See demonstrations on how to make dramatic improvements to your home.

7500 Attendees

10371 Fall Home and Garden Expo
Mid-America Expositions, Inc
7015 Spring Street
Omaha, NE 68106
402-346-8003
FAX: 402-346-5412 800-475-7469
info@showofficeonline.com
www.showofficeonline.com

Robert P Mancuso, CEO
Mike Mancuso, VP/Manager

Displays on everything for the home including kitchens, room additions, bathrooms, interior decorating, fireplaces, outdoor equipment, heating and air conditioning, remodeling contractors, security, siding, appliances, windows, doors, fencing, roofing, fitness equipment, spas and much more.
October

10372 Furniture Expo
Glahe International
PO Box 2460
Germantown, MD 20875-2460
301-515-0012
FAX: 301-515-0016 glahe@glahe.com
Annual show and exhibits of furniture making.

10373 Glass & Ceramic Decorators Annual Seminar & Exposition
Society of Glass & Ceramic Decorators
47 N 4th Street
PO Box 2489
Zanesville, OH 43702
202-298-8660
FAX: 740-588-0245 www.sgcd.org

Myra Warne, Exhibit

The SGCD show attracts major suppliers to the decorating industry, including several firms from overseas. With a full seminar program and first step program that attracts attendees on their own merits.
525 Attendees

10374 Home World Home & Garden Show
Show Biz Productions
16520 Harbor Blouevard
Fountain Valley, CA 92708
714-418-2000
FAX: 714-418-2009
marlene@sbhomeshow.com
www.sbhomeshow.com

Marlene Thorne, VP

Featuring vendors of window, doors, painting, heating, air conditioning, kitchens and baths, flooring, furniture, remodeling services and more.
40000 Attendees Founded: 1991

10375 Home and Outdoor Living Expo
Tower Show Productions
800 Roosevelt Road
Building A, Suite 109
Glen Ellyn, IL 60137
630-469-4611
FAX: 630-469-4811 800-946-4611
jaylake20@towershow.com
www.towershow.com

J Lake, VP Home Shows

The largest and longest running home improvement show.
15000 Attendees January Founded: 1977

10376 ICFF International Contemporary Furniture
George Little Management
10 Bank Street
White Plains, NY 10606-1933
914-486-6070
FAX: 914-948-6180 800-272-7469
icff@glmshow.com www.icff.com

Troy Hansen, Show Manager
Alex Cabat, Show Coordinator
George Little II, President

More than 500 exhibitors will display contemporary furniture, seating, lighting, carpet and flooring, wall coverings, textiles, accessories, kitchen and bath, outdoor furniture, and materials for residential and commercial interiors. The combination of domestic and international exhibitors provides easy access to the best and hippest home and contract products.
12000 Attendees

10377 International Bedding Exposition
International Sleep Products Association
501 Wythe Street
Alexandria, VA 22314-1917
703-683-8371
FAX: 703-683-4503
sperry@sleepproducts.org
www.sleepproducts.org

Susan Perry, Executive VP, Business Development

200 booths, net 120,000 square feet with 200 exhibitors participating.
4M Attendees March

10378 International Home Furnishings Market
International Home Furnishings Market Authority
101 S Main Street
High Point, NC 27262
336-691-1000
FAX: 336-889-6999
www.highpointmarket.org

Judy Mendenhall, President

Large home furnishings trade show with a variety of new opportunities to make your visit easy, cost effective and productive. Ten million square seet of exhibition space with 2,500 manufacturers represented.
75000 Attendees April & October Founded: 1921

10379 International Housewares Show
National Housewares Manufacturers Association
6400 Shafer Court
Suite 650
Rosemont, IL 60018
708-292-4200
FAX: 847-292-4211
www.housewares.org

Mia Rampersad, VP Trade Show & Meetings

58000 Attendees

10380 International Woodworking Machinery and Furniture Supply Fair: USA
Reed Exhibition Companies
1350 E Touhy Avenue
Des Plaines, IL 60018-3303
847-294-0300
FAX: 847-635-1571

Paul Pajor, National Marketing Manager

The largest woodworking machinery and furniture supply manufacturing exposition held in the Western Hemisphere. Exhibitors interface with North American furniture, cabinet, and woodworking manufacturers. One thousand booths.
37M Attendees August/Biennial

10381 Juvenile Products Manufacturers Association Trade Show
PO Box 955
Marlton, NJ 08053-0955
856-231-8500
FAX: 856-985-2878

William Macmillan, Show Manager

Home accessories and products for children's rooms.
2.5M Attendees October

10382 Kitchen & Bath Industry Show
National Kitchen & Bath Association
687 Willow Grove Street
Hackettstown, NJ 07840
908-520-0033
FAX: 908-852-1695 800-843-6522
kbiscustomerservice@vnuexpo.com
www.kbis.com

Lee Hershberg, Sales Manager
Grayson Lutz, Operations Manager

Targeting dealers, designers, distributors, retailers, consumers, home centers and many other high-quality kitchen and bath professionals. Showcasing the latest products and cutting-edge design ideas of the kitchen and bath industry.
40000 Attendees April

10383 Kitchen/Bath Industry Show & Multi-Housing World Conference
VNU Expositions
1145 Sanctuary Parkway
Suite 355
Alpharetta, GA 30004
770-691-1540
FAX: 770-777-8700 800-933-8735

Lee Hershberg, Sales Manager

The latest products and technologies, industry and consumer trends, design and business tools and more to stay ahead of your competitors.
35000 Attendees

10384 LightFair
AMC
120 Wall Street
17th Floor
New York, NY 10005
212-843-8358
FAX: 212-248-5017 www.iesna.org

Pamela R Weess, Circulation Director
Nini Schwenk, Manager

A major lighting trade show in North America featuring architectural lighting products from all spectrons of the industry. Containing 600 booths and 400 exhibits.
17M Attendees June
Mailing list available for rent 10M names $100 per M.
Printed in 4 colors on glossy stock

10385 Mid-Atlantic Industrial Woodworking Expo Supply Show
Trade Shows
PO Box 2000
Claremont, NC 28610-2000
828-459-9894
FAX: 828-459-1312
tsi@tsishows.com www.tsishows.com

Keith Eidson, Show Manager

Annual show of 300 manufacturers of woodworking and furniture industry equipment, supplies and services.
4500 Attendees April

10386 National Association of Display Industries
3595 Sheridan Street
Suite 200
Hollywood, FL 33021
954-893-7300
FAX: 954-473-8268
Klein Merriman, Executive Director
Denise Rich, Manager Programs & Events
Yajayra Saunders, Education & Meetings Assistant
Four booths.
200 Attendees October

10387 National City Home & Garden Show
Expositions
PO Box 550
Edgewater Branch
Cleveland, OH 44107-0550
216-529-1300
FAX: 216-529-0311
expoinc@expoinc.com
www.expoinc.com
Featuring showcases on how to make your dream home a reality. Create the garden oasis, backyard retreat or a relaxing sanctuary.
35000 Attendees Feb

10388 National Hardware Show
Reed Exhibition Companies
383 Main Avenue
Norwalk, CT 06851
203-840-4800
FAX: 203-840-4824
70000 Attendees

10389 Northeast Home and Leisure Expo
Osborne/Jenks Productions
936 Silas Deane Highway
Wethersfield, CT 06109-4273
860-563-2111
FAX: 860-563-3472 800-955-7469
Susan Osborne, Executive Producer
Two hundred and fifty booths.
25M Attendees

10390 Old House New House Home Show
Kennedy Productions
1208 Lisle Place
Lisle, IL 60532-2262
630-515-1160
FAX: 630-515-1165
kp@corecomm.net
www.kennedyproductions.com
Laura McNamara, Event Producer
Over 300 home improvement exhibitors displaying cutting-edge home enhancements for kitchens, baths, home and garden including landscape, interior remodeling, pools, spas, floors, doors and more.
8000 Attendees Feb/Sept Founded: 1984

10391 PDRA Paint & Decorating Show
Paint & Decorating Retailers Association
403 Axminister Drive
Fenton, MO 63026
636-326-2636
FAX: 636-326-1823 800-737-0107
tina@pdra.org www.pdra.org
Dan Simon, Manager
Retailers from the paint and decorating products industry to discuss a variety of business topics. Gain insight from retailers who face the same problems that you do everyday.
1000 Attendees May

10392 Remodeling and Decorating Expo
893 N Jan Mar Ct
Olathe, KS 66061-3693
913-768-8148
FAX: 785-780-4777
Tom Reno, VP
Mary Jo Doherty, Executive Director
Four hundred booths of the latest products and services related to remodeling and decorating. Also a presentation of How-To stage presentations on remodeling, decorating and home repair.
40M Attendees February

10393 Southern Home & Garden Show
Home Builders Association
702 E McBee Avenue
Greensville, SC 29601
864-229-7722
FAX: 864-232-3541
40000 Attendees

10394 Spring Home & Patio Show
Industrial Expositions
PO Box 480084
Denver, CO 80248-0084
303-892-6800
FAX: 303-892-6322 800-457-2434
info@iei-expos.com
www.bigasalloutdoors.com
Linda Card, Show Manager
Dianne Seymour, Asst Show Manager
Jeff Houghton, Owner
23000 Attendees March

10395 Spring Home Show
Osborne/Jenks Productions
936 Silas Deane Highway
Wethersfield, CT 06109
860-563-2111
FAX: 860-563-3472

10396 Spring Home and Garden Show
International Exhibitions
1635 W Alabama
Houston, TX 77006
713-295-5366
FAX: 713-529-0936

10397 Surfaces Conference
World Floor Covering Association
2211 E Howell Avenue
Anaheim, CA 92806
714-978-6440
FAX: 714-978-6066 800-624-6880
casey@wbma.org www.wfca.org
Casey Voorhees, Executive Director
Tina Krulich, Administrative Assistant
The event for the floor covering industry with the latest trends to keep your business competitive, proven strategies to increase sales and profitability and all the critical industry information you need to make the right decisions.
40000 Attendees January-February

10398 West Week
Pacific Design Center
8687 Melrose Avenue
West Hollywood, CA 90069
310-652-6992
FAX: 310-652-9576

10399 Woodworking and Furniture Expo
Glahe International
PO Box 2460
Germantown, MD 20875-2460
301-515-0012
FAX: 301-515-0016 glahe@glahe.com
Annual show and exhibits of woodworking and furniture making.

Directories & Databases

10400 American Furniture Manufacturers Association Membership Directory
PO Box HP-7
High Point, NC 27261
336-884-5000
FAX: 336-884-5303 www.afma4u.org
Andy Counts, Executive VP
A who's who in the furniture industry, supplying information on over 500 furniture manufacturers and their suppliers.
80 pages Founded: 1966

10401 American Society of Furniture Designers
144 Woodland Drive
New London, NC 28127
910-576-1273
FAX: 910-576-1573 www.asfd.com
Judith Reagan, Executive Administrator
Christine Evans, Executive Director
Promotes the profession of furniture design and educates members of the furniture industry.
262 pages Founded: 1981

10402 Casual Living: Casual Outdoor Furniture and Accessory Directory Issue
Reed Business Information
360 Park Avenue S
New York, NY 10010
212-450-0067
Laura Christian, Editor
Toni Agpar, Editor
James Reed, Owner
List of manufacturers, manufacturers' trepresentatives, and suppliers of outdoor furniture, wicker and rattan furniture, and backyard accessories such as barbecue grills, picnic accessories, outdoor lighting cushions, pads, patio umbrellas, vinyl refinishing, and maintenance, products.
$10.00
Annual October
Circulation: 13,000

10403 Complete Directory of Discount & Catalog Merchandisers
Sutton Family Communications & Publishing Company
155 Sutton Lane
Fordsville, KY 42343
270-740-0870
jlsutton@apex.net
www.fleamarketeer.net
Theresa Sutton, Publisher
Lee Sutton, Editor
Print-out from database of wholesalers, manufacturers, distributors, importers and close-out houses. Database is updated daily to guarantee the most current and up-to-date sources available. *$125.00*
100 pages

10404 Complete Directory of Home Furnishings
Sutton Family Communications & Publishing Company
155 Sutton Lane
Fordsville, KY 42343
270-740-0870

jlsutton@apex.net
www.fleamarketeer.net
Theresa Sutton, Publisher
Lee Sutton, Editor

Print-out from database of wholesalers, manufacturers, distributors, importers and close-out houses. Database is updated daily to guarantee the most current and up-to-date sources available. *$44.50*
100 pages

10405 Complete Directory of Kitchen Accessories
Sutton Family Communications & Publishing Company
155 Sutton Lane
Fordsville, KY 42343
270-740-0870

jlsutton@apex.net
www.fleamarketeer.net
Theresa Sutton, Editor
Lee Sutton, General Manager

Print-out from database of wholesalers, manufacturers, distributors, importers and close-out houses. Database is updated daily to guarantee the most current and up-to-date sources available. *$49.50*
100+ pages

10406 Complete Directory of Lamps, Lamp Shades & Lamp Parts
Sutton Family Communications & Publishing Company
155 Sutton Lane
Fordsville, KY 42343
270-740-0870

jlsutton@apex.net
www.fleamarketeer.net
Theresa Sutton, Editor
Lee Sutton, General Manager

Print-out from database of wholesalers, manufacturers, distributors, importers and close-out houses. Database is updated daily to guarantee the most current and up-to-date sources available. *$39.50*
100+ pages

10407 Complete Directory of Serving Ware
Sutton Family Communications & Publishing Company
155 Sutton Lane
Fordsville, KY 42343
270-740-0870

jlsutton@apex.net
www.fleamarketeer.net
Theresa Sutton, Editor
Lee Sutton, General Manager

Print-out from database of wholesalers, manufacturers, distributors, importers and close-out houses. Database is updated daily to guarantee the most current and up-to-date sources available. *$39.50*
100+ pages

10408 Complete Directory of Showroom Fixtures and Equipment
Sutton Family Communications & Publishing Company
155 Sutton Lane
Fordsville, KY 42343
270-740-0870

jlsutton@apex.net
www.fleamarketeer.net
Theresa Sutton, Publisher
Lee Sutton, Editor

Print-out from database of wholesalers, manufacturers, distributors, importers and close-out houses. Database is updated daily to guarantee the most current and up-to-date sources available. *$39.50*
100 pages

10409 Complete Directory of Small Furniture
Sutton Family Communications & Publishing Company
155 Sutton Lane
Fordsville, KY 42343
270-740-0870

jlsutton@apex.net
www.fleamarketeer.net
Theresa Sutton, Publisher
Lee Sutton, Editor

Print-out from database of wholesalers, manufacturers, distributors, importers and close-out houses. Database is updated daily to guarantee the most current and up-to-date sources available. *$39.50*
100 pages

10410 Complete Directory of Upholstery Materials Supplies and Equipment
Sutton Family Communications & Publishing Company
155 Sutton Lane
Fordsville, KY 42343
270-740-0870

jlsutton@apex.net
www.fleamarketeer.net
Theresa Sutton, Publisher
Lee Sutton, Editor

Print-out from database of wholesalers, manufacturers, distributors, importers and close-out houses. Database is updated daily to guarantee the most current and up-to-date sources available. Over 600 American wholesale direct supplies in 3-ring binder. *$67.50*
100 pages

10411 Form-Buyer's Guide Issue
National Business Forms Association
433 E Monroe Avenue
Alexandria, VA 22301-1693
703-836-6225
FAX: 703-836-2241 800-336-4641
Brad Holt, Editor

This directory is a compiled list of more than 600 suppliers of business forms, labels, commercial printing, ad specialties and other business printing. *$49.00*
Annual Fall
Circulation: 13,000

10412 Furniture Rental Association of America: Membership Directory
Furniture Rental Association of America
5008 Pine Creek Drive
#6
Westerville, OH 43081-4848
614-755-3910
800-367-7368

About 100 member furniture rental companies.

10413 Furniture Retailer: Official Directory of Industry Suppliers
Pace Communications
1301 Carolina Street
Suite 100
Greensboro, NC 27401-1022
336-378-6065

Directory of services and supplies to the industry. *$20.00*
Annual;
Circulation: 16,000

10414 Hearth & Home: Furnishings Issue
Village West Publishing
PO Box 1288
Laconia, NH 03247-2008
603-528-4285
FAX: 603-524-0643 800-258-3772
Richard Wright, Publisher/Editor
Jackie Avignone, Advertising Director
Karen Dipietro, Owner

Trade journal for hearth, barbecue and patio retailing. July issue is Buyer's Guide for the three industries, available separately for $15. *$6.00*
Monthly
Circulation: 17,000

10415 Home Furnishing Retailers
Chain Store Guide
3922 Coconut Palm Drive
Tampa, FL 33619
813-276-6700
FAX: 813-627-6882 800-972-0292
info@csgis.com www.csgis.com
Chris Leedy, Advertising Sales
Shami Choon, Manager

This database features detailed information on over 2700 companies in the U.S. and Canada, with contact information for over 8600 key executives and buyers. *$275.00*
Annual

10416 Lighting Dimensions: Directory Issue
32 W 18th Street
New York, NY 10011-4612
212-462-0100

A list of over 2,000 manufacturers, suppliers and consultants of lighting and related equipment and supplies. *$15.00*
Annual
Circulation: 13,000

10417 Market Resource Guide
International Home Furnishings Center
210 E Commerce Avenue
High Point, NC 27260-5238
336-888-3700
FAX: 336-882-1873
marketing@ihfc.com www.ihfc.com
Tom Loney, VP Marketing

Two-volume directory offers over 1,500 manufacturers and distributors in the furniture industry with exhibits at the International Home Furnishings Market. *$25.00*
624 pages Semiannual Founded: 1974
Printed in 4 colors on glossy stock

10418 National Directory of Specialized Furniture Carriers
National Furniture Traffic Conference
PO Box 889
Gardner, MA 01440-0889
978-632-1913
FAX: 978-630-2917

Ray Bohman, Editor

Nearly 200 trucking firms specializing in transportation of new furniture, not including household moving firms. *$39.95*

10419 Who's Who in Furniture Distribution

International Furniture Supplies Association
PO Box 2482
High Point, NC 21261
336-884-1566
FAX: 336-884-1350 www.isa-info.com

Phyllis Tuttle, Editor

Trade directory for members and business associates. *$39.00*
Annual, July

Industry Web Sites

10420 www.afma4u.org

Summer & Casual Furniture Manufacturers Assn

Sponsors the International Casual Furniture and Accessories Market in Chicago, the Apollo Awards recognizing excellence in casual furniture retailing and the Casual Furniture Design Excellence Awards.

10421 www.apro-rto.com

Association of Progressive Rental Organizations

Members include television, appliance and furniture dealers who rent merchandise with an option to purchase.

10422 www.awfs.org

Association of Woodworking & Furnishing Supplies

Organization for furniture and accessories manufacturers and suppliers that are covered in this comprehensive journal.

10423 www.bifma.org

Business and Institutional Furniture Manufacturers

The voice of the office furniture industry, BIFMA members are manufacturers and suppliers of goods and services to the industry.

10424 www.casualfurniture.org

National Association of Casual Furniture Retailers

Members are retailers; associate members are manufacturers and sales representatives.

10425 www.furnituremarketing.org

Int'l Home Furnishings Marketing Association

Product categories include residential casegoods, upholstery, gift and decorative accessories, lighting and area floor coverings and beddings.

10426 www.greyhouse.com

Grey House Publishing

Selected Grey House directories in the fields of business, health and education are available online. Users can search our online databases by several different search criteria, such as product categories, geographic area, sales volume and much, much more. Full Grey House catalog and online ordering also available.

10427 www.natbat.com

National Cotton Batting Institute

Association representing members of the cotton batting industry.

10428 www.nhfa.org

National Home Furnishings Association

Trade association of furniture retailers which works to improve retailer's business opportunities and management practices.

10429 www.ofdanet.org

Contract Furnishings Forum

Explores the effect of office environment on productivity and uses contract sales staff to anticipate changes in market.

10430 www.unfinishedfurniture.org

Unfinished Furniture Association

Associations

10431 American Horticultural Society
7931 E Boulevard Drive
Alexandria, VA 22308
703-768-5700
FAX: 703-768-8700 800-777-7931
sdick@ahs.org www.ahs.org
Katy Moss Warner, President
Kristen K Gedeon, Membership Coordinator
Dr H Marc Cathey, President Emeritus
Joe Lamoglia, Director Business Operations
Educates and inspires people of all ages to become successful and environmentally responsible gardeners by advancing the art and science of hoticulture. It is an education, nonprofit, 501 organization that recognizes and promotes best practices in American horticulture. AHS is known for its educational programs and the dissemination of horticultural information.
27M Members Founded: 1922

10432 American Horticultural Therapy Association
3570 E 12th Ave
Ste 206
Denver, CO 80206-3447
303-222-2482
FAX: 303-331-5776 800-634-1603
joy@ahta.org www.ahta.org
Nancy Easterling, President
John Paul Breault, VP
Dave Wilber, Treasurer
Wally Szyndler, Secretary
Joy Harrison, Manager
Professional therapists, rehabilitation specialists and others using horticulture as a medium of rehabilitation.
700 Members Founded: 1973

10433 American Institute of Floral Designers
720 Light Street
Baltimore, MD 21230
410-752-3318
FAX: 410-752-8295
aifd@assnhqtrs.com www.aifd.org
Michael O'Neill, President
Brian Smith, VP
David Siders, Secretary
Tim Farrell, Treasurer
Tom Shaner, Executive Director
Nonprofit association to support the floral design industry.
1300 Members Founded: 1962

10434 American Nursery & Landscape Association
1000 Vermont Avenue NW
Suite 300
Washington, DC 20005-4914
202-789-2900
FAX: 202-789-1893 www.anla.org
Dale L Bachman, President
Bob Dolibois, Executive VP
Gary E Briggs, VP/Region IV Director
Buzz Bertolero, Treasurer/Region IV Director
Joanne C Kostecky, Region Director
The American Nursery and Landscape Association serves firms who grow, sell or use plants. ANLA advocates the industry's interests before government and provides its members with unique business knowledge essential to long-term growth and profitability.
2200 Members Founded: 1876

10435 American Rose Society
PO Box 30000
8877 Jefferson Paige Road
Shreveport, LA 71130-30
318-938-5402
FAX: 318-938-5405
ars@ars-hq.org www.ars.org
Marilyn Wellan, President
Steve Jones, VP
Mike Kromer, Executive Director
Clif Jeter, Treasurer
Ellen Trice, Associate Editor
Striving to provide educational services to encourage the greater use of our national flower in private and public gardens throughout the country.
24000 Members Founded: 1892

10436 American Society of Consulting Arborists
15245 Shady Grove Road
Rockville, MD 20850-3222
301-947-0483
FAX: 301-990-9771
Beth Palys, Executive Director
About 270 persons specializing in the growth and care of urban shade and ornamental trees.

10437 American Society of Irrigation Consultants
125 Paradise Lane
Po Box 426
Rochester, MA 02770
508-763-8140
FAX: 508-763-8102
info@asic.org www.asic.org
Norman F Bartlett, Executive Director
Kathleen A Bartlett, Executive Secretary
Jeffrey Bruce, Director
Rick Davis, Director
Steven Sisler, Director
Promotes education skills for data exchange landscape irrigation. Members are irrigation consultants, suppliers and manufacturers.

10438 American Society of Landscape Architects
636 Eye Street NW
Washington, DC 20001-3736
202-898-2444
FAX: 202-898-1185 800-787-2752
webmaster-b@asla.org www.asla.org
Gerald Beaulieu, Managing Director/CFO
Victor Akinnagbe, Network Administrator
Nancy Somerville, Executive VP
JoAnn Brown, Manager Meetings
Residential and commercial real estate developers, federal and state agencies, city planning commissions and individual property owners are all among the thousands of people and organizations in America and Canada that will retain the services of landscape architect this year.
13500 Members Founded: 1899

10439 Associated Landscape Contractors of America
The Professional Landcare Network
950 Herndon Parkway
Suite 450
Herndon, VA 20170
703-736-9666
FAX: 703-736-9668 800-395-2522
webmaster@alca.org www.alca.org
Jim Martin, President
Jason Cupp, President-Elect
Debra Holder, CEO
The ALCA cultivates and safeguards opportunities for their members and dedicated professionals and companies who create and enhance the world's landscapes.
2500 Members Founded: 1961

10440 Association of Specialty Cut Flower Growers
PO Box 268
Oberlin, OH 44074
440-774-2887
FAX: 440-774-2435
ascfg@oberlin.net www.ascfg.org
Bob Wollam, President
Tom Wikstrom, VP
Ray Gray, Secretary
Betsy Hitt, Treasurer
Judy M Laushman, Executive Director
Trade association that provides cultural and marketing information to specialty cut flower growers.
700 Members Founded: 1988

10441 Farm Equipment Wholesalers Association
PO Box 1347
Iowa City, IA 52244
319-354-5156
FAX: 319-354-5157
info@fewa.org www.fewa.org
Brad Stout, President
Chris Ford, First VP
Bradley W Stout, Second VP
Patricia A Collins, Executive VP
David C Rankin, Secretary/Treasurer
International trade association of wholesale/distributors of agricultural equipment and related products.
190 Members Founded: 1945

10442 Floral Trade Council
PO Box 228
Haslett, MI 48840-228
989-341-1322
FAX: 517-339-1393
William Carlton, Executive Director
Association of US fresh cut flower growers.
70 Members Founded: 1988

10443 Garden Council
2024 McCormick Boulevard
Evanston, IL 60201
847-864-5781
FAX: 847-448-8805
Composed of six local garden clubs. Promotes community service and beautification projects throughout Evanston.

10444 Garden Writers Association of America
12210 Leatherleaf Court
Manassas, VA 20111
703-257-1032
FAX: 703-257-0213
webmaster@gardenwriters.org
www.gwaa.org
Cathy Wilkin Barash, President
Steven Dobbs, VP
Anne Marie Van Nest, Treasurer
Janel Leatherman, Secretary
Robert LaGasse, Executive Director
A organization with materials of interest to garden writers and news on members of the Association.

10445 International Society of Arboriculture
1400 W Anthony Drive
PO Box 3129
Champaign, IL 61826-3129
217-355-9411
FAX: 217-355-9516
isa@isa-arbor.com
www.isa-arbor.com

Mike Neal, President
Bob Tate, President
Lauren Lanphear, VP
Terrence P Flanagan, VP
Pius Floris, VP

A worldwide professional organization dedicated to fostering a greater appreciation for trees and to promoting research, technology, and the professional practice of arboriculture.

10446 Lawn & Garden Marketing & Distribution Association
2105 Laurel Bush Road
Ste 200
Bel Air, MD 21015
443-640-1080
FAX: 443-640-1031
lgmda@ksgroup.org www.lgmda.org

Steven T King, Executive VP
Marci L Hickey, Director Meetings/Member Services
Amy Chetelat, Financial Manager

Promotes industry, provides sales training, holds competitions and bestows awards.
550 Members Founded: 1970

10447 Mailorder Gardening Association
5836 Rockburn Woods Way
Elkridge, MD 21075
410-540-9830
FAX: 410-540-9827
consumer@mailordergardening.com
www.mailordergardening.com

Camille Cimino, Executive Director
Jim Bryant, First VP/Program Chair
Magaret Koogle, Second VP
Roberta Simpson, Executive Secretary
Jean Vivlamore, Treasurer

Mail-order suppliers of gardening and nursery stock and supplies.
210 Members Founded: 1934

10448 National Council of Commercial Plant Breeders
225 Reinekers Lane
Suite 650
Alexandria, VA 22314
202-546-8000
FAX: 202-296-7698

Dean Urmston, Executive VP

A non-profit organization to promote the achievement and interest of American plant breeders both in the United States and abroad.

10449 National Landscape Association
1250 I Street NW
Suite 500
Washington, DC 20005

Daivd Peiffer, Administrator

Managers of firms offering maintenance services, design and planting services for landscape sites.
900 Members Founded: 1939

10450 National Pest Management Association
9300 Lee Hwy
Ste 301
Fairfax, VA 22031-6051
703-352-6762
FAX: 703-352-3031 800-678-6722
gharrington@pestworld.org
www.pestworld.org

Rob Lederer, Executive VP
Cindy Mannes, Director Public Affairs
Gary McKenzie, Director Finance
Bob Rosenberg, Director Government Affairs
Gene Harrington, Manager Government Affairs

Represents the interests of its members and the structural pest control industry.
4600 Members Founded: 1933

10451 North American Horticultural Supply
1900 Arch Street
Philadelphia, PA 19103-1498
215-564-3484
FAX: 215-963-9784
nahsa@fernley.com www.nahsa.org

Ronald R Eberly, President
Jim Smith, VP
James D Harkins, Treasurer
Jim Franklin, Director
Lynn John, Director

Promotes full service distributors in the greenhouse and nursery hard good supply market.
120 Members Founded: 1988

10452 PLANET/Professional Landcare Network
1000 Johnson Ferry Rd
Ste B255
Marietta, GA 30068-2182
770-977-5222
FAX: 770-578-6071 800-458-3466
info@landcarenetwork.org
www.landcarenetwork.org

John Gibson, President
Tanya Tolpegin, COO
Betsy Demoret, Events & Product Manager
James Garnett, Director Membership
Sherry MacDonald, Director Marketing

PLANET emerged from the joining of the PLCAA and the ALCA in 2005. It is an educational, professional resource for landcare, exterior maintenance and interiorscape professionals and the lawn and landscape industry.
1200 Members Founded: 1979

10453 Plants for Clean Air Council
3458 Godspeed Road
Davidsonville, MD 21035-1303
410-956-9299
FAX: 301-459-9625
Supports and promotes the benefits of plants including research on how plants clean indoor air.

10454 Professional Grounds Management Society
720 Light Street
Baltimore, MD 21230
410-232-2861
FAX: 410-752-8295 800-609-7467
pgms@assnhqtrs.com www.pgms.org

Todd Cochran, President
Ellen Newell, VP
Michael Mongon, Treasurer
Andy Nicholson, Director
Tom Shaner, Executive Director

Members are professionals involved in the care and maintenance of public and private sites.
1400 Members Founded: 1911

10455 Roses Association
PO Box 99
Haslett, MI 48840-99

FAX: 517-339-3760
Greenhouse rose growers in the United States and Canada are members.
400 Members Founded: 1930

10456 Society of American Florists
1601 Duke Street
Alexandria, VA 22314
703-999-9216
FAX: 703-836-8705 800-336-4743
memberinfo@safnow.org
www.safnow.org

Chuck Gainan, Chairman
Terril A Nell, President
Peter J Moran, Executive VP/CEO
Robert P Billings, Treasurer

Originally was organized as the Center for Commerical Floriculture.
18M Members Founded: 1884

10457 Turf Grass Producers International
2 East Main Street
East Dundee, IL 60118
847-649-5555
FAX: 847-649-5678
info@turfgrasssod.org
www.turfgrasssod.org

Warren Bell, President
Arthur Milberger, VP
Kirk T Hunter, Executive Director
James J Novak, Public Relations Manager

An organization featuring business news and updates on legislation and agronomics concerning the turf industry.
1000 Members Founded: 1967

Newsletters

10458 Action Letter
Associated Landscape Contractors of America
950 Herndon Parkway
Suite 450
Herndon, VA 20170
703-736-9666
FAX: 703-736-9668 800-395-2522
info@actionletter.com
http://www.alca.org

Dan Foley, President

News and information of the gardening and landscaping industries.
16 pages Monthly Founded: 1961

10459 American Society for Horticultural Science
113 SW Street
#200
Alexandria, VA 22314-2851
703-836-4606
FAX: 703-836-2024
ashs@ashs.org http://www.ashs.org

Micheal W Neff, Executive Director
Fred Davis, President

The purpose of the American Society for Horticultural Science is to promote and encourage interest in scietific research and

education in all branches of horticulture.
$400.00
36 pages Monthly Founded: 1903
Circulation: 5000 Audited
Mailing list available for rent 5000 names
Printed in 2 colors on matte stock

10460 Cut Flower Quarterly
Association of Specialty Cut Flower Growers
PO Box 268
Oberlin, OH 44074
440-774-2887
FAX: 440-774-2435
http://www.ascfg.org

Judy Laushman, Manager

Newsletter *$175.00*
Quarterly
Circulation: 1200

10461 Garden Club of America
598 Madison Avenue
New York, NY 10022-1614
212-721-1000
FAX: 212-753-0134

Marion White, Publisher

Includes feature articles and legislative news. *$8.00*
8 pages Monthly

10462 Landscape Architect and Specifier News
George Schmok
14771 Plaza Drive
Suite M
Tustin, CA 92780
714-979-5276
FAX: 714-979-3543
circulation@landscapeonline.com
http://www.landscapeonline.com/

George Schmok, Publisher/Editor-in-Chief
Jim Lipot, Circulation Manager
Leslie McGuire, Managing Editor

A photographically oriented professional journal featuring topics of concern and state of the art projects designed or influenced by registered landscape architects worldwide.
Monthly
Circulation: 29162
Printed in 4 colors on glossy stock

10463 Penntalk
Penntech Papers
100 Center Street
Johnsonburg, PA 15845-1301
814-965-2521
FAX: 814-965-6231

Mella Chirillo, Publisher

Coverage of landscaping and gardening industries.
6 pages Monthly

10464 Quill and Trowel
Garden Writers Association of America
10210 Leatherleaf Court
Manassas, VA 20111
703-257-1032
FAX: 703-257-0213
info@gwaa.org
http://www.gardenwriters.com

Robert Lagassa, Publisher/CEO
Carol Ledbetter, Editor
Seymour Jordan, President

Material of interest to garden writers and news of members of the Association.
12 pages Monthly Founded: 1848
Circulation: 1800

Magazines & Journals

10465 American Nurseryman
American Nurseryman Publishing Company
223 W Jackson Boulevard
Suite 500
Chicago, IL 60606
312-277-7318
FAX: 312-427-7346 800-621-5727
editors@amerinursery.com
http://www.amerinursery.com

Allen W Seidel, President/Publisher
Sally Benson, Editor

Focuses on topics relevant to professional growers, landscapers and retail garden center operators. *$48.00*
100 pages Fortnightly Founded: 1904
Circulation: 16000
Printed in 4 colors on glossy stock

10466 American Rose Magazine
American Rose Society
PO Box 30000
Shreveport, LA 71130
318-221-5026
FAX: 318-938-5405 800-637-6534
ars@ars-hq.com http://www.ars.org

Mike Kromer, Executive Director
Beth Smiley, Editor
Benny Ellerbe, Executive Director & Edit
Marny Fife, Marketing Director

Publication focusing on rose growing, culture and enjoyment. Accepts advertising. *$37.00*
Monthly Founded: 1894
Circulation: 21000

10467 Casual Living
Reed Business Information
7025 Albert Pick Road
Suite 200
Greensboro, NC 27409
336-051-1000
FAX: 336-605-1143 800-652-2948
bbsmith@reedbusiness.com
http://www.reedbusiness.com

Kevin Castellani, Group Publisher
Becky B Smith, Editor-in-Chief
Delaney Rudd, Owner

Monthly Founded: 1958
Circulation: 10000

10468 Farm Press Publications
PO Box 14920
Clarksdale, MS 38614-1420
662-624-8503
FAX: 662-627-1137
information@primedia.com
http://www.primedia.com

Elton Robinson, Editor
Greg Frey, Publisher
Dennis Miner, Sales Manager

Covers the sunbelt farm market. *$25.00*
Weekly Founded: 1942
Printed in 4 colors

10469 Fine Gardening
Taunton Press
63 South Main St
PO Box 5506
Newtown, CT 06470-5506
203-706-6206
FAX: 203-426-3434 800-888-8286
fg@taunton.com
http://www.taunton.com

LeeAnne White, Editor
Cathy Austermann, Advertising Manager
Todd Meier, Publisher

Landscaping and ornamental gardening are the magazine's primary editorial focus. Step-by-step in-depth information for the country. Articles written by gardening experts and enthusiasts. *$29.95*
83 pages Founded: 1988
Circulation: 202163

10470 Floral Retailing
Vance Publishing
10901 W 84th Terrace
Lenexa, KS 66214
913-438-8700
FAX: 913-438-0691
www.vacnepublishing.com

Carolyn Hathaway, Editor

Monthly slick-stock magazine for high-volume floral retailers, including supermarket floral buyers, mass marketers, garden centers, craft stores and high-volume tranditional florists. Information on product care and handling, new products, industry news and issues, management merchandising and more.
Monthly
Circulation: 15000

10471 Florists' Review
PO Box 4368
Topeka, KS 66604
785-266-0888
FAX: 785-266-0333 800-367-4708
frsub@floristsreview.com
http://www.floristsreview.com

Frances Dudley, President / Publisher
David L. Coake, Editorial Director
Heather Kline, Circulation Coordinator

For wholesalers and retailers and desingers of fresh and dried flowers. *$42.00*
Monthly Founded: 1897
Circulation: 28000

10472 Flowers and Magazine
Richard Salvaggio
11444 W Olympic Boulevard
Los Angeles, CA 90064-1549
310-966-3518
FAX: 310-966-3610 800-321-2665
flowersand@teleflora.com
http://www.flowersandmagazine.com

Bruce Wright, Editor
Jill Fox, Circulation Manager
Richard Salvaggio, Publisher

Business information and tips for the retail florist. *$54.00*
Monthly Founded: 1985
Circulation: 30,000
Printed in 4 colors on glossy stock

10473 Garden Center Merchandising & Management
Branch-Smith Publishing
120 St. Louis Ave
PO Box 1868
Fort Worth, TX 76101
817-882-4120
FAX: 817-882-4121 800-433-5612
kneal@branchsmith.com
http://www.greenbeam.com

Carol Miller, Editor
Patricia Kuhl, Publisher
Tiffany O'Kelley, Media Manager
Mike Branch, President

Monthly

10474 Garden Center Products & Supplies
Branch-Smith Publishing
120 Saint Louise Avenue
Fort Worth, TX 76104
817-882-4100
FAX: 817-882-4121 800-433-5612
greenbeam@branchsmith.com
http://www.greenbeam.com

Yale Youngblood, Editor
Mike Branch, President *$90.00*

Monthly
Circulation: 16249

10475 Garden Style
Krause Publications
700 E State Street
Iola, WI 54990-1
715-445-2214
FAX: 715-445-4087 800-258-0929

Joel Toner, Publisher
Trish Wesley Umbrell, Editor

The ultimate, single-subject resource for experienced and up-and-coming gardeners. Individual issues cover such popular subjects as container plantings, vegetables, rose care, shade plants, and selecting a design. With accessible, expert-instruction and gorgeous, detailed photography, this magazine encourages gardeners of all levels to explore their favorite gardening pursuits.

84 pages Bi-annually Founded: 1952
Circulation: 150000

10476 Greenhouse Management & Production
Branch-Smith Printing
120 Saint Louis
PO Box 1868
Fort Worth, TX 76104
817-824-4100
FAX: 817-882-4111 800-315-4110

Mike Branch, President
Ken Tichelbaut, Publisher
Stephen Gent, Marketing Director
Terri Smith, Circulation Director
Regina Carter, Production Manager

National magazine for commercial greenhouse growers. Accepts advertising. *$24.00*

150 pages Monthly Founded: 1982
Circulation: 15,000

10477 Grounds Maintenance
Primedia
9800 Metcalf Avenue
Overland Park, KS 66212
913-341-1300
FAX: 913-967-1898 866-505-7173
inquiries@primediabusiness.com
http://www.primediabusiness.com

Jack Condon, Chief Operating Officer
John French, Executive VP
Brian Aanes, Publisher
Cindy Ratcliff, Editor

Provides technical and management guidance for practical, problem-solving applications in landscape design, construction and maintenance at the professional level.

96 pages Monthly Founded: 1966
Circulation: 50597

10478 Hearth & Home
Village West Publishing
PO Box 1288
Laconia, NH 03247
603-284-4285
FAX: 603-524-0643 800-258-3772

Richard Wright, Editor
Jackie Avignone, Advertising Director

Magazine for retailers, including specialty, hardware, patio and barbecue.

Monthly
Circulation: 17,000

10479 Horticulture
Krause Publications
700 E State Street
Iola, WI 54990
715-445-2214
FAX: 715-445-4087
info@krause.com www.krause.com

Joel Toner, Publisher
Tom Fischer, Editor

The premier source of ideas and information about gardening for active, sophisticated gardeners seeking information and inspiration on plants and design. The world's top gardeners provide authoritative information in lively text and stunning photographs. Each issue contains the latest gardening news and discoveries, regional planting secrets and pest control plans to help make your garden experiences as rewarding as possible. *$28.00*

88 pages Founded: 1952
Circulation: 245889

10480 Journal of Aboriculture
International Society of Arboriculture
PO Box 3129
Champaign, IL 61826-3129
217-355-9411
FAX: 217-355-9516
isa@isa-arbor.com
http://www.isa-arbor.com

Dr. Bob Miller, Editor
Peggy Currid, Editorial/Production

Scientific journal about trade and ornamental trees. *$105.00*

Founded: 1924
Circulation: 17000
Printed in 1 color on glossy stock

10481 Landscape & Irrigation
Adams Business Media
833 West Jackson Blvd. 7th Floor
Chicago, IL 60607
312-846-4600
FAX: 312-977-1042
jkmitta@aip.com
http://www.adamsbusinessmedia.com

John Kmitta, Editor
Steve Brackett, VP/Group Publisher
Joanne Juda, Circulation Manager

Monthly

10482 Landscape Management
Advanstar Landscape Group
7500 Old Oak Boulevard
Cleveland, OH 44130-3343
440-243-8100
FAX: 440-819-2651 800-225-4569
ncapra@advanstar.com
http://www.landscapegroup.com

Tony D Avino, General Manager
Kevin Stoltman, Publisher
Michael Harris, Sales Manager
Stephanie Ricca, Managing Editor
Ron Hall, Editor In Chief

Covers news, market trends, business and operations management, technical information on horticulture and agronomy for 51,000 professional landscape contractors, lawncare operators and inhouse grounds managers. *$46.00*

Monthly Founded: 1965
Circulation: 60,000
Printed in 4 colors on glossy stock

10483 Lawn & Landscape
Gie Publishing
4012 Bridge Avenue
Cleveland, OH 44113
216-961-4130
FAX: 216-961-0364 800-456-0707

Ron Lowy, Publisher

National trade magazine for the landscape professional. Accepts advertising.

120 pages Monthly Founded: 1980
Circulation: 73000

10484 Nursery Business Grower
Brantwood Publications
3023 Eastland Boulevard
Suite 103
Clearwater, FL 33761-4106
727-786-9771
FAX: 722-786-9772

Jeffrey A Morey, Editor

Articles of interest to the nursery grower. *$15.00*

Monthly Founded: 1955

10485 Nursery Business Retailer
Brentwood Publications
3023 Eastland Boulevard
Clearwater, FL 33761-4106
727-786-9771
FAX: 727-791-4126

Jeffrey A Morey, Editor

News of retail growers. *$15.00*

Bi-Monthly Founded: 1955

10486 Nursery Management & Production
Branch-Smith Publishing
120 St. Louis
PO Box 1868
Fort Worth, TX 76104
817-824-4100
FAX: 817-882-4111 800-315-4711
dbranch@branchsmith.com
http://www.branchsmithprinting.com

David Branch, Chairman/ President
Daniel Hanson, VP/GM

Nurserymen, landscapers and garden centers. Accepts advertising. *$24.00*

136 pages Monthly Founded: 1910

10487 Outdoor Power Equipment
Adams Business Media
833 West Jackson
7th Floor
Chicago, IL 60607
312-846-4600
FAX: 312-977-1042
webmaster@adamsbusinessmedia.com
http://www.adamsbusinessmedia.com

Joanne Juda, Circulation Manager
Steve Noe, Editor

Serves retailers and distributors who sell and service outdoor power equipment products, including retailers, lawn and garden supply retailers, farm supply retailers, hardware store retailers, home centers, and building supply retailers.

Monthly Founded: 1959
Circulation: 21,000

10488 PRO Magazine
Cygnus Publishing
1233 Janesville Avenue
Fort Atkinson, WI 53538
920-563-6388
FAX: 920-563-1702 800-547-7377
Grant.Dunham@cygnuspub.com
http://www.promagazine.com

Noël Amerpohl, Editor-in-Chief
Rich Reiff, President

Dan Newman, Group Publisher
Grant Dunham, Managing Editor
Rick Monogue, National Sales Manager

Contains information for lawn care professionals.

Monthly Founded: 1937
Circulation: 55000

10489 Pacific Coast Nurseryman and Garden Supply Dealer
Cox Publishing Company
PO Box 1477
Glendora, CA 91740-1477
626-914-3916
FAX: 626-914-3751 800-577-5225
hyoungpcn@aol.com
http://www.pacificcoastnurseryman.com

Jan Groot, CEO
John Humes, Associate Editor

Edited for those who work in the environmental horticulture industry. News magazine for the green industry on the West Coast. *$ 30.00*

Monthly Founded: 1941
Circulation: 6000
Printed in 4 colors on glossy stock

10490 Power Equipment Trade
Hatton-Brown Publishers
225 Hanrick Street
PO Box 2268
Montgomery, AL 36102-2268
334-834-1170
FAX: 334-834-4525 800-669-5613
rich@hattonbrown.com
http://www.poweret.com

David H Ramsey, Co-Publisher
DK Knight, CEO
Rich Donnell, Editor

Leading publication in the power equipment community. Articles include profiles on successful power equipment retailers (dealers) and manufacturers and accounts pertaining to technology, market trends and timely issues.

Founded: 1952
Circulation: 21788 21,465 names $145 per M.
Printed in on glossy stock

10491 ProSource
Professional Lawn Care Association of America
1000 Johnson Ferry Road NE
Suite C135
Marietta, GA 30068-2112
770-977-5222
FAX: 770-578-6071 800-458-3466
plcaa@plcaa.orgt www.plcaa.org

Tom Delaney, Executive VP
Karen Weber, Communications Director/Editor

Association news and industry information for lawn and landscape professionals. Subscription available with association membership.

12-16 pages BiMonthley Founded: 1980
Circulation: 2,000

10492 Southern Nursery Digest
Betrock Information Systems
7770 Davie Road Ext
Hollywood, FL 33024-2516
954-810-0300
FAX: 954-438-2632

Irv Betrock, Editor
Sean Patrick, Manager

This comprehensive magazine covers the gardening and nursery business in the south.

Monthly

10493 Tomato Country
Columbia Publishing
417 N 20th Avenue
PO Box 9036
Yakima, WA 98902
509-248-2452
FAX: 509-248-4056 800-900-2452

J Stoker, Publisher

Includes information on tomato production and marketing, grower and shipper feature stories, tomato research, from herbicide and pesticide studies to new varieties, market reports, feedback from major tomato meetings and conventions, along with other key issues and points of interest for USA and Canada tomato growers.

10494 Turf News
Turfgrass Producers International
1855-A Hicks Road
Rolling Meadows, IL 60008-1215
847-705-9898
FAX: 847-705-8347 800-405-8873
info@turfgrasssod.org
http://www.turfgrasssod.org

Kirk Hunter, Publisher
Bob O'Quinn, Editor

Business news and updates on legislation concerning the turf industry. Subscription included with membership to Turfgrass Producers International.

Founded: 1977
Circulation: 1200

10495 Yard and Garden
Cygnus Publishing
1233 Janesville Avenue
Fort Atkinson, WI 53538
920-563-6388
FAX: 920-563-1702 800-547-7377
noel.brown@cygnuspub.com
http://www.yardngarden.com

Noel Brown, Editor-in-Chief
Dan Newman, Publisher

Contains information for retailers of outdoor power equipment. *$60.00*

8 issues per ye Founded: 1977
Circulation: 17504
Mailing list available for rent 2.7M names
Printed in 4 colors on glossy stock

Trade Shows

10496 American Nursery & Landscape Association Convention
American Nursery & Landscape Association
1000 Vermont Avenue NW
Suite 300
Washington, DC 20005-3922
202-789-2900
FAX: 202-789-1893 www.anla.org

Robert J Dolibois, Executive Director

Serves firms who grow, sell or use plants. ANLA advocates the industry's interests before government and provides its members with unique business knowledge essential to long-term growth and profitability.

July

10497 American Society of Irrigation Consultants Conference
PO Box 426
Byron, CA 94514-0426
925-516-1124
FAX: 925-516-1301

Wanda M Sarsfield, Secretary

Irrigation design equipment, supplies, services and seminar.

Annual Founded: 1970

10498 American Society of Landscape Architects Annual Meeting & Educational Expo
636 Eye Street NW
Washington, DC 20001-3736
202-898-2444
FAX: 202-898-1185 800-787-2752

Nancy Somerville, Executive VP
Gerald Beaulieu, CFO/Director Business Operations

Landscape architect ecucational session and workshop plus 500 exibits of outdoor lighting, playground and park equipment, landscape maintanence equipment, computer hardware and software and much more.

4700 Attendees

10499 Andry Montgomery and Associates Show
550 S 4th Avenue
#200
Louisville, KY 40202-2504

FAX: 502-473-1999

Warren Sellers, Show Manager

A show for lawn and garden products and equipment. 560 booths.

10500 Annual Convention of the International Lilac Society
9500 Sperry Road
Kirtland, OH 44094
440-946-4400
FAX: 216-256-1655

Exhibits on lilacs, including innovative cultivation and the use of lilacs in public and private landscaping.

Annual

10501 Annual Gulf Coast Home & Garden Show
Exposition Enterprises of Alabama
PO Box 430
Pinson, AL 35126
205-680-0234
FAX: 205-680-0615

12000 Attendees

10502 Annual Spring Fort Worth Home & Garden Show
International Exhibitions
1635 W Alabama
Houston, TX 77006
713-295-5366
FAX: 713-529-0936

40000 Attendees

10503 Arizona Fall Home & Garden Show

Dmg World Media
301 E Bethany Home Road
#C-298
Phoenix, AZ 85012
602-277-4748
FAX: 602-265-3024 800-439-7550
jodi.shepperd@us.dmgworldmedia.com
www.arizonahomeshown.com

Jessica Boweak, Show Manager

Quality products and services for interior design, home remodeling, redecorating, landscaping.
32000 Attendees October

10504 Bonsai and Orchid Expo
Bonsai & Orchid Association International
26 Pine Street
Dover, DE 19901-4452
302-736-6781
FAX: 302-736-6763
bonsai@boaint.com www.boaint.com
Leroy Rench, Manager
There are 75 booths and 50 exhibits that include bonsai trees, pots, tools and supplies, orchids, live plants and supplies for orchids and more.
500+ Attendees April

10505 Central Environment Nursery Trade Show
Ohio Nursery & Landscape Association
72 Dorchester Square
Westerville, OH 43081-3350
614-991-1195
FAX: 800-860-1713 800-825-5062
info@onla.org www.onla.org/cents
Runs concurrently with the nationally acclaimed Ohio State University short course.
January

10506 FEWA's Industry Showcase
Farm Equipment Wholesalers Association
PO Box 1347
Iowa City, IA 52244
319-354-5156
FAX: 319-354-5157
info@fewa.org www.fewa.org
Patricia A Collins, Executive VP
Annual convention and 130 exhibits of equipment, supplies and services for independent wholesalers of shortline and specialty farm equipment, light industrial tractors, lawn and garden tractors, turf care equipment, estate and park maintenance equipment and power vehicles for outdoor recreation and sports.
800 Attendees November

10507 Farwest Show Oregon Association of Nurserymen
2780 SE Harrison Street
Suite 102
Milwaukie, OR 97222-7574
FAX: 503-653-1528 800-342-6401
Geoff Horning, Trade Show Manager
870 booths.
13K Attendees August

10508 Floral & Garden Accessories
George Little Management
10 Bank Street
Suite 1200
White Plains, NY 10606-1954
914-486-6070
FAX: 914-948-6180 800-272-SHOW
George Little II, President
Semi-annual show presenting silk flowers, dried flowers, vases, plant stands, ribbons, outdoor and garden room furniture, decorative tabletop and stationery products with floral motifs and much more, to floral buyers.
SemiAnnual

10509 Green Industry Expo
Professional Lawn Care Association of America
1000 Johnson Ferry Road NE
Suite C-135
Marietta, GA 30068-2112
770-977-5222
FAX: 770-578-6071 800-458-3466
info@gieonline.com
www.gieonline.com
Anna Demoret, Trade Show Coordinator
Annual show of 400 manufacturers, suppliers and distributors of lawn care equipment, supplies and services, including fertilizers, weed control materials, insurance information and power equipment. Six-hundred and fifty booths.
6,000 Attendees November

10510 Green Profit's Retail Experience
Green Profit Magazine
335 N River Street
Batavia, IL 60510
630-208-9080
FAX: 630-208-9350 888-888-0013
info@ballpublishing.com
www.ballpublishing.com/conferences
Michelle Mazza, Show Manager
Educational event and tradeshow dedicated exclusively to garden center retailing. Covers topics from store layout and design to merchandising strategies and business management. 20 booths
300 Attendees September Founded: 2006

10511 Home World Home & Garden Show
Show Biz Productions
16600 Harbor Blouevard
Suite F
Fountain Valley, CA 92708
714-418-2000
FAX: 714-418-2009 877-418-2001
Rachel Perry, President
Marlene Thorne, VP
Featuring vendors of window, doors, painting, heating, air conditioning, kitchens and baths, flooring, furniture, remodeling services and more.
30000 Attendees Founded: 1991

10512 International Accessories Tradeshow
PO Box 499
Fresh Meadows, NY 11365-0499
718-997-1212
George Birne, Show Manager
Seminars, contests, educational information and exhibits of products by manufacturers and suppliers. 2,000 booths.
40M Attendees July

10513 International Azalea Festival
220 Boush Street
PO Box 3595
Norfolk, VA 23514
757-822-2800
FAX: 757-282-2787
amcleod@azaleafestival.org
www.azaleafestival.org
Rob Cross, Owner
Ashley McLeod, Executive Director
A salute to the NATO's Allied Command Atlantic forces in order to create new friendships, provide a basis for cultural exchange, recognize the military's role in maintaining peace in the world and pursue new lines of trade between Norfolk and the world.
5M Attendees 2006 Canada Founded: 1953

10514 International Florist Accessories Tradeshow
Trade Show Bookings
PO Box 499
Fresh Meadows, NY 11365-0499
George Birne, Show Manager
2,000 booths.
40M Attendees August

10515 International Lawn Garden Power Equipment Exposition
Andry Montgomery and Associates
550 S 4th Avenue
#200
Louisville, KY 40202-2504
FAX: 502-473-1999
Warren Sellers, Show Manager
Lawn and garden products and equipment. 560 booths.
25M Attendees July

10516 Lawn & Garden Marketing & Distribution Summit Conference
2105 Laurel Bush Road
Ste 200
Bel Air, MD 21015
443-640-1080
FAX: 443-640-1031
lgmda@ksgroup.org www.lgmda.org
Steven T King, Executive VP
Marci L Hickey, Director Meetings/Member Services
Amy Chetelat, Financial Manager
Lawn and garden products. 120 booths.
500 Attendees July

10517 Lawn, Flower and Patio Show
Mid-America Expositions, Inc
7015 Spring Street
Omaha, NE 68106
402-346-8003
FAX: 402-346-5412 800-475-7469
info@showofficeonline.com
www.showofficeonline.com
Robert P Mancuso, CEO
Mike Mancuso, VP/Manager
Annual show and exhibits of equipment, supplies and services for the lawn, flower and patio.
February 1-4, 2007

10518 Mid-Atlantic Nurserymen's Trade
Mid Atlantic Nurserymen's Trade Shows
PO Box 11739
Baltimore, MD 21206-0339
410-226-6924
FAX: 410-256-2268
Carville Akenurst, VP Show Manager
Robert Mead, Executive Director
350 booths.
3.4M Attendees

10519 Midwest Garden and Food Fair
PO Box 3434
Omaha, NE 68103-0434
Jane Booth, Show Manager
100 booths.
15M Attendees February

10520 Midwest Trade Fair and Design School
PO Box 20189
Indianapolis, IN 46220-0189
317-253-0500

Pat Cronin, Executive Secretary

Design and business contests, new products and sales information for the retail florist. 200 booths.

4M Attendees September

10521 National City Home & Garden Show
Expositions
PO Box 550
Edgewater Branch
Cleveland, OH 44107-0550
216-529-1300
FAX: 216-529-0311
expoinc@expoinc.com
www.expoinc.com
Featuring showcases on how to make your dream home a reality. Create the garden oasis, backyard retreat or a relaxing sanctuary.

35000 Attendees Feb

10522 National Lawn & Garden Trade Show
Great American Exhibitions
112 Main Street
Norwalk, CT 06851
203-498-8735
FAX: 203-845-9183

Ronald Gratt, Manager

5000 Attendees

10523 National Lawn and Garden Show
Controlled Marketing Conferences
PO Box 1771
Monument, CO 80132
719-488-0226
FAX: 719-488-8168 888-316-0226
info@nlgshow.com www.nlgshow.com

Linda Botkin, Show Manager

This is the lawn and gardens premier headlines event and features both a pre-set scheduled appointment division and a traditional booth division.

300 Attendees June

10524 National Pest Management Association Annual Eastern Conference
9300 Lee Hwy
Ste 301
Fairfax, VA 22031-6051
703-352-6762
FAX: 703-352-3031 www.pestworld.org

Cindy Mannes, Executive Director
Robert Lederer, Executive VP

January

10525 Novi Expo Backyard, Pool and Spa Show
Show Span
1400 28th Street SW
Grand Rapids, MI 48509
616-530-1919
FAX: 616-530-2122 800-328-6550
events@showspan.com
www.showspan.com

Melissa Moore
Mike Wilbraham

Held at the Novi Expo Center in Novi, Michigan.

10526 Nursery Garden Supply Show Farwest
2780 SE Harrison Street
Suite 102
Milwaukie, OR 97222-7574

FAX: 503-653-1528

Clayton Hannon, Executive Director

775 booths promoting the sale and exchange of nursery/landscape products and services.

13M Attendees August

10527 Nursery Trade Show Mid Atlantic Summer Show
PO Box 11739
Baltimore, MD 21206-0339
410-882-5300

Caryville Akehurst, Executive VP

Landscaping materials and horticultural tools. 750 booths, nursery stock, garden center and greenhouse supplies. 750 booths.

7.1M Attendees January

10528 Nursery Trade Show Mid Atlantic Winter Show
PO Box 11739
Baltimore, MD 21206-0339
410-882-5300

Carville M Akehurst, Executive VP

750 booths of landscaping materials and equipment.

7M Attendees January

10529 Nursery/Landscape Expo
Texas Nursery & Landscape Association
7730 S IH-35
Austin, TX 78745-6698
512-280-5182
FAX: 512-280-3012 800-880-0343
info@txnla.org www.txnla.org

Ed Edmonson, Show Manager
Amy Prenger, Exhibits Coordinator

Containing 1,600 booths and 750 exhibits of plant materials including foliage, bedding plants, cut flowers, woody ornamentals and palms. Allied products include machinery, equipment and supplies for the horticultural industry.

11M Attendees August

10530 Old House New House Home Show
Kennedy Productions
1208 Lisle Place
Lisle, IL 60532
630-515-1160
FAX: 630-515-1165
kp@corecomm.net
www.kennedyproductions.com

Laura McNamara, Event Producer

Over 300 home improvement exhibitors displaying cutting-edge home enhancements for kitchens, baths, home and garden including landscape, interior remodeling, pools, spas, floors, doors and more.

8000 Attendees Feb/Sept 2007 Founded: 1984

10531 PLCAA Annual Conference and the GIE
Professional Lawn Care Association of America
1000 Johnson Ferry Road NE
Suite C-135
Marietta, GA 30068-2112
770-977-5222
FAX: 770-578-6071 800-458-3466
plcaa@plcaa.org
www.plcaa.org/conference
National conference in conjunction with the Green Industry Expo for the lawn and landscape industry.

November

10532 Perennial Production Conference
Grower Talk Magazine
335 N River Street
Batavia, IL 60510
630-208-9080
FAX: 630-208-9350 888-888-0013
info@ballpublishing.com
www.ballpublishing.com/conferences

Michelle Mazza, Show Manager

Designed for perennial producers of all levels, from beginner to advanced. This conference and tradeshow offers in-depth seminars, tours, and workshops on everything needed to know about perennial production. 60-80 booths.

600 Attendees September Founded: 2003

10533 Tropical Plant Industry Exhibition
Florida Nursery Growers Landscape Association
1533 Park Center Drive
Orlando, FL 32835
407-295-7994
FAX: 407-295-1619 800-375-3642
info@fngla.org www.fngla.org

Linda Adams, Show Manager
Sabrina Haines, Trade Show Coordinator

An international interior foliage show featuring 500 plus exhibitors in more than 1,000 booths showing interior foliage and tropical plants as well as horticulturally related supplies.

8,000 Attendees January 18-20, 2007

Directories & Databases

10534 Buyer's Guide
Bonsai & Orchid Association International

26 Pine Street
Dover, DE 19901-4452
302-736-6781
FAX: 302-736-6763
bonsai@boaint.com www.boaint.com

Leroy Rench, Chairman

Grower's, exporter's, importer's, manufacturers, suppliers, trade magazine, of bonsai, orchids, pots, tools, and supplies. *$12.00*

500+ pages

10535 Complete Directory of Home Gardening Products
Sutton Family Communications & Publishing Company
155 Sutton Lane
Fordsville, KY 42343
270-740-0870

jlsutton@apex.net
www.fleamarketeer.net

Theresa Sutton, Editor
Lee Sutton, General Manager

Print-out from database of wholesalers, manufacturers, distributors, importers and close-out houses. Database is updated daily to guarantee the most current and up-to-date sources available. *$39.50*
100+ pages

10536 Complete Directory of Horticulture

Sutton Family Communications & Publishing Company
155 Sutton Lane
Fordsville, KY 42343
270-740-0870

jlsutton@apex.net
www.fleamarketeer.net
Theresa Sutton, Editor
Lee Sutton, General Manager

Print-out from database of wholesalers, manufacturers, distributors, importers and close-out houses. Database is updated daily to guarantee the most current and up-to-date sources available. *$39.50*
100+ pages

10537 Complete Guide to Gardening and Landscaping by Mail
Mailorder Gardening Association
5836 Rockburn Woods Way
Elkridge, MD 21075
410-409-9830
FAX: 410-540-9827
www.mailordergardening.com
Camille Cimino, Executive Director

Member catalogers who sell gardening and nursery stock and supplies to consumers.
$2.00
Annual

10538 Yard and Garden
Cygnus Publishing
1233 Janesville Avenue
Fort Atkinson, WI 53538
920-563-6388
FAX: 405-275-3101   800-547-7377
Over 33,000 dealers, retailers and distributors of lawn and garden power equipment are profiled. *$40.00*

Industry Web Sites

10539 www.abatflowers.com
Society of American Florists

Originally was organized as the Center for Commerical Floriculture.

10540 www.ahs.org
American Horticultural Society

Individuals, institutions and businesses interested in a wide range of horticultural concerns.

10541 www.ahta.org
American Horticultural Therapy Association

Professional therapists, rehabilitation specialists and others using horticulture as a medium of rehabilitation.

10542 www.aisd.org
American Institute of Floral Designers

Non-profit association to support the floral design industry.

10543 www.anla.org
American Nursery & Landscape Association

The American Nursery and Landscape Association serves firms who grow, sell or use plants. ANLA advocates the industry's interests before government and provides its members with unique business knowledge essential to long-term growth and profitability.

10544 www.ascfg.org
Association of Specialty Cut Flower Growers

Trade association that provides cultural and marketing information to specialty cut flower growers.

10545 www.asla.org
American Society of Landscape Architects

Landscape architects.

10546 www.fewa.org
Farm Equipment Wholesalers Association

International trade association of wholesale/distributors of ag equipment and related products.

10547 www.gardenseek.com

Garden Seek.Com is a search engine for the gardener, landscaper, nurseries and garden in general.

10548 www.gcamerica.org
Garden Club of America

Bestows awards, maintains a library and more.

10549 www.greyhouse.com
Grey House Publishing

Selected Grey House directories in the fields of business, health and education are available online. Users can search our online databases by several different search criteria, such as product categories, geographic area, sales volume and much, much more. Full Grey House catalog and online ordering also available.

10550 www.gwaa.org
Garden Writers Association of America

A organization with materials of interest to garden writers and news on members of the Association.

10551 www.lgmda.org
Lawn and Garden Marketing & Distribution

Promotes industry, provides sales training, holds competitions and bestows awards.

10552 www.mailordergardening.com
Mailorder Gardening Association

Mail-order suppliers of gardening and nursery stock and supplies.

10553 www.nahsa.org
North American Horticultural Supply Association

Promotes full service distributors in the greenhouse and nursery hard good supply market.

10554 www.pgms.com
Professional Grounds Management Society

Members are professionals involved in the care and maintenance of public and private sites.

10555 www.plcaa.org
Professional Lawn Care Association of America

Lawn care companies, manufacturers/suppliers, ground managers and university personnel comprise membership of PLCAA. PLCAA is an educational, professional resource for the lawn and landscape industry.

10556 www.turfgrasssod.org
Turf Grass Producers International

An organization featuring business news and updates on legislation and agronomics concerning the turf industry.

10557 www.turfzone.com/equipment
Turf Zone

Includes, commerical lawn care, consumer lawn care, irrigation equipment, fertilizer and other turf products.

Associations

10558 Museum Store Association
4100 E Mississippi Avenue
Suite 800
Denver, CO 80246-3055
303-504-9223
FAX: 303-504-9585
www.museumdistrict.com

Beverly Barsook, Executive Director
Stacey Woldt, Assistant Director Programs

Providing member representatives with the professional opportunities and educational resources they need to operate effectively and ethically.

2500 Members April, Annually Founded: 1955

10559 National Association of Gifts & Collectibles
332 Hurst Mill N
Bremen, GA 30110
505-798-0375
800-446-2533
webmaster@naled.org www.naled.org

Ken Shirley, President

Trade association for the gift and collectibles industry. Offers once yearly expositions, a newsletter, software, low cost credit card processing, telephone service discounts and more to help you run your business profitably.

350 Members

10560 National Specialty Gift Association
7238 Bucks Ford Drive
Riverview, FL 33569
813-671-4757
FAX: 813-677-5075
nsga@giftprofessionals.com
www.nsgaonline.com

Joni Damico, Executive Director

Specialty gift resource center for retailers, wholesale vendors and related professionals. *$29.95*

400 Members Founded: 1998

10561 Organization of Associated Salespeople in the Southwest
1250 E Missouri Avenue
Phoenix, AZ 85014
602-952-2050
FAX: 602-952-2244 800-424-9519
information@oasis.org www.oasis.org
A gift trade association which represents the manufacturing, sales and distribution side of the giftware industry.
Founded: 1976

Magazines & Journals

10562 Gift Basket Review
Festivities Publications
815 Haines Street
Jacksonville, FL 32206-6025
904-634-1902
FAX: 904-633-8764 800-729-6338
info@festivities-pub.com
http://www.festivities-pub.com

Debra Paulk, Publisher
Kathy Horak, Managing Editor

Magazine devoted to issues relating to the gift basket and gift packing industries. *$29.94*

Monthly Founded: 1990
Circulation: 15000

10563 Gifts & Decorative Accessories
Reed Business Information
360 Park Avenue South
4th Floor
New York, NY 10010
212-450-0067
FAX: 646-746-7692
corporatecommunications@reedbusiness.com http://www.reedbusiness.com

Lawrence Rotondi, Publisher
Quinn Halford, Editor-in-Chief
James Reed, Owner

Serves retailers of stationery, greeting cards, collectibles, china, glass, lamps, and accessories. *$49.95*

Monthly Founded: 1946
Circulation: 23737
Printed in 4 colors on glossy stock

10564 Giftware News
Talcott Communications Corporation
20 West Kinzie
12TH FLOOR
Chicago, IL 60610
312-849-2220
FAX: 312-849-2174 800-229-1967

Daniel von Rabenau, Publisher
Claire Weingarden, Associate Editor
John Saxtan, Editor in Chief

Edited for gift, stationery and department stores. *$39.00*

18 issues per y Founded: 1982
Circulation: 60000

10565 Souvenirs, Gifts & Novelties Magazine
Kane Communications
7000 Terminal Square
Suite 210
Upper Darby, PA 19082-2330
610-734-2420
FAX: 610-734-2423
sgnta@aol.com www.souvmag.com

Scott Borowsky, President
Mary Anne Peacocti, Director Circulation
Caroline Burns, Managing Editor
Larry White, VP Marketing

Trade magazine for the resort gift and souvenir industry. Accepts advertising. *$30.00*

140 pages 7 per year Founded: 1962
Circulation: 34,000
Printed in 4 colors on glossy stock

Trade Shows

10566 ASD/AMD National Trade Show
ASD/AMD Merchandise Group
2950 31st Street
Suite 100
Santa Monica, CA 90405
310-255-4633
FAX: 310-396-8476
10000 Attendees

10567 ASD/AMD Trade Show, Jewelry Show & Gift Expo
ASD/AMD Merchandise Group
2950 31st Street
Suite 100
Santa Monica, CA 90405
310-396-6006
FAX: 310-399-2662 800-421-4511

Julie Ichiba, Show Director

A general merchandise event which attracts over 50,000 buyers to Las Vegas. Tens of thousands of unique products in hundreds of popular consumer product categories are on display at this event.

55000 Attendees March/August

10568 Accent on Design
George Little Management
10 Bank Street
Suite 1200
White Plains, NY 10606-1954
914-486-6070
FAX: 914-948-2867 800-272-7469
elizabeth_murphy@glmshows.com
www.nyigf.com

Elizabeth Murphy, Manager
George Little II, President

370 booths of the latest and most innovative gift lines such as decorative accessories and home furnishings.

50M Attendees August Founded: 1999

10569 Annual Dickens Christmas Show and Festival
Leisure Time Unlimited
708 Main Street
Myrtle Beach, SC 29577
843-448-9483
FAX: 843-626-1513 800-261-5991
dickensshow@sc.rr.com
www.dickenschristmasshow.com

Linda Cremer, Show Director

Victorian craft and gift show.

28000 Attendees November Founded: 1981

10570 Annual Spring New Products Show
Pacific Expositions
1580 Makaola Street
Suite 1200
Honnolulu, HI 96814-3801
808-945-3594
FAX: 808-946-6399

Pat Shine, General Sales Manager
Kimalar K Carrol, Show Director/Coordinator

Over 200 New Products Booth Displays featuring for the entire family. All categories of consumer products and service are presented: roofing, siding, jewerly, cosmetics, cars, boats, home improvement products. Over 75 Food & Crafts displays, Sportscards & memorabilia displays.

18000 Attendees Annual, April Founded: 1974

10571 At Home
George Little Management
10 Bank Street
Suite 1200
White Plains, NY 10606-1954
914-486-6070
FAX: 914-948-6180 800-272-7469

Deborah Hilfman, Division Manager
George Little II, President

Semi annual show includes manufacturers of products that beautify a home including small furniture, lighting and lamps, decorative accessories, artwork and floor coverings.

SemiAnnual

10572 Dickens Christmas Show & Festival

Leisure Time Unlimited
708 Main Street
PO Box 332
Mytrtle Beach, SC 29578
843-489-9483
FAX: 803-626-1513

26000 Attendees

10573 East Coast Gift Exposition
Fairchild Urban Expositions
5500 Interstate N Parkway
Suite 520
Atlanta, GA
770-952-6444
FAX: 770-956-9644
4000 Attendees

10574 Eureka Springs Gift Show
Miracle Marketing
436 SW 102 Street
Oklahoma City, OK 73139
405-353-3357
FAX: 405-799-4685
Features the broadest possible diversity of domestic and imported giftware, souvenirs, fashion, gourmet, floral, jewelry, country, and seasonal products.
3500 Attendees

10575 General Gifts: A Division of the New York International Gift Fair
George Little Management
10 Bank Street
White Plains, NY 10606-1954
914-486-6070
FAX: 914-948-6180 800-272-7469
George Little II, President
SemiAnnual

10576 Gift and Variety Show
Norton Shows
PO Box 265
Gatlinburg, TN 37738
865-436-6151
FAX: 865-436-6152
nortonshows@aol.com
www.nortonshows.com
Norton Johnston, Owner
Wholesale only, cash-and-carry gifts from around the world including candles, gourmet food, gift baskets, and holiday gifts.
20M+ Attendees March/June/Sept/Nov
Founded: 1987
Mailing list available for rent 79,000 names

10577 Grand Strand Gift and Resort Merchandise Show
Fairchild Urban Expositions
5500 Interstate N Parkway
Suite 520
Atlanta, GA 30328
770-952-6444
FAX: 770-956-9644
300 Attendees

10578 Handmade in the USA
Gerorge Little Management
10 Bank Street
Suite 1200
White Plains, NY 10606

FAX: 914-948-2918 800-272-7469
45000 Attendees

10579 Holiday Jubilee!
Festivities Publications
815 Haines Street
Jacksonville, FL 32204
904-634-1902
FAX: 904-633-8764
reader@festivities-pub.com
www.festivities-pub.com
Ange Scarbrough, Manager/Meeting Plan

Join progressive and sucessful gift basket professionals at Jubilee! and Holiday Jubilee!, the industry's national convention and trade show. Participate in important seminars and workshop sessions and negotiate with motivated sellers at the Jubilee! and Holiday Jubilee! trade show.
4000 Attendees April

10580 Holiday Market
Gilmore Enterprises
3514 Drawbridge Pkwy
Ste A
Greensboro, NC 27410-8584
336-282-5550
FAX: 336-282-0555
contact@gilmoreshows.com
www.gilmoreshows.com
Terri Lambert, Show Manager
Celebrate the season at Holiday Market, a true feast for all the senses. Of course there is shopping with a capital SHOP. Enjoy the singing of the Victorian-costumed strolling carolers and let the children visit with Santa. You'll come away with ideas, recipes, samples, beauty makeovers and lots of holiday gifts and ideas.
35000 Attendees November

10581 Immediate Delivery Show: Fall
AMC Trade Shows/DMC Expositions
240 Peachtree Street NW
Suite 2200
Atlanta, GA 30303
404-220-2000
FAX: 404-220-2442
Mary Ellen Jackson, Show Manger
Jeff Portman, Chief Executive Officer
A trade show that allows you to move discontinued merchandise, overstocked inventory, samples and one of a kind items.
9000 Attendees November

10582 Indoor/Outdoor Home Show
True Value
PO Box 17
Bethel Park, PA 15102
412-276-6292
FAX: 412-851-6975
EllenDiOrio@aol.com
www.pitthomeshow.com
61000 Attendees

10583 International Gift Show
New Angle Trade Shows
7200 E Hampden Avenue
Suite 209
Denver, CO 80224
303-757-5969
FAX: 303-757-5987
2500 Attendees

10584 International Jewelry Fair/General Merchandise Show-Fall
Helen Brett Enterprises
5111 Academy Drive
Lisle, IL 60532
630-241-9865
FAX: 630-241-9870 800-541-8171
dharrington@helenbrett.com
www.gift2jewelry.com
Dave Harrington, Show Manager
Containing 1500 booths during the fall show and 800 booths during the spring show. Tradeshow open to wholesale buyers only (credentials required to attend).
44000 Attendees October 2007

10585 International Licensing and Merchandising Conference and Expo
Expocon Management Associates
363 Reef Road
#915
Fairfield, CT 06430-6550
203-256-4730
FAX: 203-256-4730
ecv@expocon.com
www.expocon.com
Annual show of 220 exhibitors of logos, corporate trademarks, characters, designs and other advertising techniques that require licensing.
7000 Attendees

10586 Jubilee!
Gift Basket Review
815 Haines Street
Jacksonville, FL 32204
904-634-1902
FAX: 904-633-8764
reader@festivities-pub.com
www.festivities-pub.com
David L Paulk, Manager/Meeting Plan
Join progressive and sucessful gift basket professionals at Jubilee! and Holiday Jubilee!, the industry's national convention and trade show. Participate in important seminars and workshop sessions and negotiate with motivated sellers at the Jubilee! and Holiday Jubilee! trade show.
4000 Attendees September

10587 Just Kidstuff New York International Gift Fair
George Little Management
10 Bank Street
White Plains, NY 10606-1954
914-486-6070
FAX: 914-948-6180 800-272-7469
B Wilson, PR Administration
George Little II, President
Semi annual show presenting a wide variety of upscale products for children of all ages, including bedding, furniture, dolls, toys and games, gifts, clothes, books and educational products and accessories.
SemiAnnual

10588 Just Kidstuff West: A Division of the San Francisco International Gift Fair
George Little Management
10 Bank Street
White Plains, NY 10606-1954
914-486-6070
FAX: 914-948-6180 800-272-7469
George Little II, President
SemiAnnual

10589 Memphis Gift & Jewelry Show-Fall
Helen Brett Enterprises
5111 Academy Drive
Lisle, IL 60532
630-241-9865
FAX: 630-241-9870 800-541-8171
dharrington@helenbrett.com
www.gift2jewelry.com
Dave Harrington, Show Manager
Containing over 350 booths during the fall show and 350 booths during the spring show. Tradeshow open to wholesale buyers only (credentials required to attend).
9000 Attendees August

10590 Memphis Gift & Jewelry Show-Spring
Helen Brett Enterprises
5111 Academy Drive
Lisle, IL 60532
630-241-9865
FAX: 630-241-9870 800-541-8171
dharrington@helenbrett.com
www.gift2jewelry.com
Dave Harrington, Show Manager
Containing over 350 booths during the spring show and 350 booths during the fall show. Tradeshow open to wholesale buyers only (credentials required to attend).
9000 Attendees February

10591 Mid-South Jewelry & Accessories Fair -Spring
Helen Brett Enterprises
5111 Academy Drive
Lisle, IL 60532
630-241-9865
FAX: 630-241-9870 800-541-8171
dharrington@helenbrett.com
www.gift2jewelry.com
Dave Harrington, Show Manager
Containing over 300 booths during the spring show and 500 booths during the fall show. Tradeshow open to wholesale buyers only (credentials required to attend).
8500 Attendees May 2007

10592 Mid-South Jewelry & Accessories Fair-Fall
Helen Brett Enterprises
5111 Academy Drive
Lisle, IL 60532
630-241-9865
FAX: 630-241-9870 800-541-8171
dharrington@helenbrett.com
www.gift2jewelry.com
Dave Harrington, Show Manager
Containing 500 booths during the fall show and over 300 booths during the spring show. Tradeshow open to wholesale buyers only (credentials required to attend).
16000 Attendees November 2007

10593 Museum Source
George Little Management
10 Bank Street
Suite 1200
White Plains, NY 10606-2867
914-486-6070
FAX: 914-948-6180 800-272-7469
chelsea_weinert@glmshows.com
www.glmshows.com/nyigf
Chelsea A Weinert, Divisional Manager
George Little II, President
Semi-annual show devoted to manufacturers, importers and publishers whose products are appropriate for museum gift shops, bookshores, specialty shops, zoos, aquariums and galleries. Items displayed include calendars, novelties, ethnic and craft items, historical interpretational products, art objects, children's educational items and posters.
SemiAnnual

10594 Museum Source: West
George Little Management
10 Bank Street
Suite 1200
White Plains, NY 10606-1954
914-486-6070
FAX: 914-948-6180 800-272-7469
Elizabeth Murphy, Division Manager
George Little II, President
Semi-annual show devoted to manufacturers, importers and publishers whose products are appropriate for museum gift shops, bookshores, specialty shops, zoos, aquariums and galleries. Items displayed include calendars, novelties, ethnic and craft items, historical interpretational products, art objects, children's educational items and posters.
SemiAnnual

10595 Museum Store Association Trade Show
Museum Store Association
4100 E Mississippi Avenue
Suite 800
Denver, CO 80246
303-504-9223
FAX: 303-504-8585
www.museumdistrict.com
Beverly Barsook, Executive Director
Stacey Woldt, Assistant Director Programs
2500 Attendees April Founded: 1955

10596 National Halloween Show
Transworld Exhibits
1850 Oak Street
Northfield, IL 60093
847-784-6905
FAX: 847-446-3523 800-323-5462
This once a year event is where over 10,000 attendees will converge on Chicago from all across the US and over 50 foreign countries to see what over 700 manufacturers and distributors are showcasing as new and exciting for parties, shops and haunted houses. Free educational seminars and workshops.
March

10597 National Merchandise Show
Miller Freeman Publications
One Plaza
PO Box 2549
New York, NY 10116
212-714-1300
FAX: 212-714-1313
16000 Attendees

10598 National Premium/Incentive Show
Hall-Erickson
98 E Naperville Road
Westmont, IL 60559
630-963-9185
FAX: 630-434-1216 800-752-6312
moti@heiexpo.com
www.motivationshow.com
Nancy A Petitti, Show Director
24000 Attendees September Founded: 1929

10599 National Stationery Show
Gerorge Little Management
10 Bank Street
Suite 1200
White Plains, NY 10606
741-421-3200
FAX: 914-948-2918 800-272-7469
nationalstationeryshow@gmshows.com
www.nationalstationeryshow.com
Lori Robinson, Show Manager
The National Stationery Show is the premiere market for stationery resources in the Unite States. The National Stationery Show presents more than 1,400 exhibitors and product in five distinctive sections; Presents, Celebrate, Take Note, HomeWork, and Indulgences. The show draws 15,000 domestic and international retailers representing department, chain and specialty stores, museum shops, galler and craft retailers, boutiques, stationery, greeting card and gift shops, bookstores, bridal shops
15000 Attendees May

10600 New & Distinctive Resources: A Division of the NY International Gift Fair
George Little Management
10 Bank Street
White Plains, NY 10606-1954
914-486-6070
FAX: 914-948-6180 800-272-7469
George Little II, President
SemiAnnual

10601 New Orleans Gift & Jewelry Show-Fall
Helen Brett Enterprises
5111 Academy Drive
Lisle, IL 60532
630-241-9865
FAX: 630-241-9870 800-541-8171
dharrington@helenbrett.com
www.gift2jewelry.com
Dave Harrington, Show Manager
Containing 850 booths during the fall show and 750 booths during the spring show. Tradeshow open to wholesale buyers only (credentials required to attend).
27000 Attendees August

10602 New Orleans Gift & Jewelry Show-Spring
Helen Brett Enterprises
5111 Academy Drive
Lisle, IL 60532
630-241-9865
FAX: 630-241-9870 800-541-8171
dharrington@helenbrett.com
www.gift2jewelry.com
Dave Harrington, Show Manager
Containing 750 booths during the spring show and 850 booths during the fall show. Tradeshow open to wholesale buyers only (credentials required to attend).
20000 Attendees January

10603 OASIS Gift Show
Organization of Assn Salespeople in the Southwest
1250 E Missouri Avenue
Phoenix, AZ 85014
602-952-2050
FAX: 602-952-2244 800-424-9519
information@oasis.org www.oasis.org
250,000 square feet of contiguous exhibit space representing thousands of product lines of manufacturing, sales and distribution of the giftware industry.
6000+ Attendees

10604 Offinger's Handcrafted Martketplace
Offinger Management Company
1100-H Brandywine Boulevard
PO Box 3388
Zanesville, OH 43702-3388
740-452-4541
FAX: 740-452-2552 888-878-4438
gift@offinger.com
www.offinger.com/handcrafted
Gayla Fleming, Event Manager
Wholesale market for country, primitive, folkart products. Held in January, March, August and November.
3300 Attendees

10605 Personal Accessories
George Little Management
10 Bank Street
Suite 1200
White Plains, NY 10606-1954
914-486-6070
FAX: 914-948-6180 800-272-7469
George Little II, President

Semi-annual show features people products such as men's gifts, fashion accessories, jewelry, travelware, perfume and personal care items, including health products and grooming aids.
SemiAnnual

10606 Smoky Mountain Gift Show: Fall
Smoky Mountain Gift Show
PO Box 50
Gatlinburg, TN 37738
865-436-4418
FAX: 865-436-2878 800-441-7889
Eva Havlicek, Owner
Geared to the gift and souvenier market. Wholesale trade show open only to buyers in the retail industry. Buyers must present credentials upon registration.
3000 Attendees November Founded: 1966

10607 Smoky Mountain Gift Show: Spring
Smoky Mountain Gift Show
PO Box 50
Gatlinburg, TN 37738
865-436-4418
FAX: 865-436-2878 800-441-7889
Eva Havlicek, Owner
Geared to the gift and souvenier market. Wholesale trade show open only to buyers in the retail industry. Buyers must present credentials upon registration.
12000 Attendees March

10608 Southern Christmas Show
Southern Shows
PO Box 36859
Charlotte, NC 28236
704-566-1898
FAX: 703-376-6345
13200 Attendees

10609 Southern Ideal Home Show: Fall
Southern Shows
PO Box 36859
Charlotte, NC 28236
704-566-1898
FAX: 704-676-6345 800-849-0248
dzimmerman@southernshows.com
www.southershows.com
David Zimmerman, Show Manager
Brenda Crofts, Assistant Show Manager
Gardens, designer rooms, seminars, exhibitors, and experts on remodeling, decorating, home improvement and landscaping
20000 Attendees September

10610 Souvenir & Novelty Trade Gift Show
Multi Expo
920 Honeysuckle Lane
Wynnewood, PA 19096
305-448-7976
7000 Attendees

10611 Toy Fair
Toy Industry Association
1115 Broadway
Suite 400
New York, NY 10010
212-675-1141
FAX: 212-645-3246
toyfairs@toy-tia.org www.toy-tia.org
Thomas Conley, President
Diane Cardinale, Public Information Manager
Products include: games, toys, puzzles, dolls, science and hobby craft kits, books, bicycles and ride-ons, computer and video games and software, playground and sporting equipment, costumes and holiday decorations.
22000 Attendees February

10612 Tropical Plant Industry Exhibition
Florida Nursery Growers Landscape Association
1533 Park Center Drive
Orlando, FL 32835
407-295-7994
FAX: 407-295-1619 800-375-3642
info@fngla.org www.fngla.org
Linda Adams, Show Manager
Sabrina Haines, Trade Show Coordinator
An international interior foliage show featuring 500 plus exhibitors in more than 1,000 booths showing interior foliage and tropical plants as well as horticulturally related supplies.
8,000 Attendees January

10613 Variety Merchandise Show
Miller Freeman Publications
One Penn Plaza
PO Box 2549
New York, NY 10116
212-714-1300
FAX: 212-714-1313
20000 Attendees

10614 Western States Toy and Hobby Show
Western Toy and Hobby Representative Association
9397 Reserve Drive
Corona, CA 92883
951-771-1598
FAX: 909-277-1599
info@wthra.com www.wthra.com
Phylis St. John, Manager
If it's for kids, it's here. Show is for trade members only, not open to the public.
3000 Attendees March

Directories & Databases

10615 AR100 Award Show Guide
Black Book Marketing Group
10 Aston Place
6th Floor
New York, NY 10003
212-956-1425
FAX: 212-539-9801
H Huntington Stehli, President/Publisher
Lists of winners at the AR100 Award Show, which recognizes excellence in the field of annual reports; includes photographers, design firms, illustrators, printers and paper companies; includes listings and ads for winners of past shows. *$60.00*
Annual, September
Circulation: 10,000

10616 Complete Directory of Giftware Items
Sutton Family Communications & Publishing Company
155 Sutton Lane
Fordsville, KY 42343
270-740-0870
jlsutton@apex.net
www.fleamarketeer.net
Theresa Sutton, Publisher
Lee Sutton, Editor
Print-out from database of wholesalers, manufacturers, distributors, importers and close-out houses. Database is updated daily to guarantee the most current and up-to-date sources available. Approximately 1,500 American direct wholesale sources in a three-ring binder. *$107.50*
100 pages

10617 Complete Directory of Tabletop Items
Sutton Family Communications & Publishing Company
155 Sutton Lane
Fordsville, KY 42343
270-740-0870
jlsutton@apex.net
www.fleamarketeer.net
Theresa Sutton, Editor
Lee Sutton, General Manager
Print-out from database of wholesalers, manufacturers, distributors, importers and close-out houses. Database is updated daily to guarantee the most current and up-to-date sources available. *$54.50*
100+ pages

10618 Giftware Associates Interchange
1100 Main Street
Buffalo, NY 14209
716-885-4444
FAX: 716-878-2866
J Warren Wright, Secretary
An online credit interchange database.
240 pages Founded: 1974

10619 Giftware Manufacturers Credit Interchange
1100 Main Street
Buffalo, NY 14209-2356
716-885-4444
FAX: 716-878-2866
linda.montes@amegagroup.com
www.gaingroup.com
J Warren Wright, Executive Secretary
Manufacturers and importers of giftware and china.
60 pages

Industry Web Sites

10620 www.catalogcity.com
Altura International
CatalogCity.com is a powerful and flexible e-commerce technology. This site includes recognized brand names such as Blair, Bombay, Chef's Catalog, Fisher-Price, Gump's by Mail, Hammacher Schlemmer, Ross-Simmons, The Sharper Image, and many more.

10621 www.giftprofessionals.com
TeleGift Network
Directory lists professional designers who make it their business to create just the right gift. One that matches the event as well as the specific tastes of the person who will recieve the gift.

10622 www.greyhouse.com
Grey House Publishing
Selected Grey House directories in the fields of business, health and education are

available online. Users can search our online databases by several different search criteria, such as product categories, geographic area, sales volume and much, much more. Full Grey House catalog and online ordering also available.

10623 www.museumdistrict.com
Museum Store Association

Providing member representatives with the professional opportunities and educational resources they need to operate effectively and ethically.

10624 www.naled.org
National Association of Gifts & Collectibles

Trade association for the gift and collectibles industry. Offers once yearly expositions, a newsletter, software, low cost credit card processing, telephone service discounts and more to help you run your business profitably.
350 pages

10625 www.nsgaonline.com
National Specialty Gift Association

Specialty gift resource center for retailers, wholesale vendors and related professionals.

10626 www.oasis.org
Organization of Associated Salespeople Southwest

A gift trade association which represents the manufacturing, sales and distribution side of the giftware industry.

Associations

10627 American Ceramic Society
735 Ceramic Pl
Ste 100
Westerville, OH 43081-8728
614-890-4700
FAX: 614-899-6109
info@ceramics.org www.ceramics.org

John E Marra, President
John A Kaniuk, Treasurer
Glenn F Harvey, Secretary/Executive Director
David W Johnson Jr, Parliamentarian

The National Institute of Ceramic Engineers, the Ceramic Manufacturing Council and the Ceramic Education Council are affiliated groups. All are leading organizations dedicated to the advancement of ceramics.
10000 Members Founded: 1898

10628 American Cut Glass Association
PO Box 482
Ramona, CA 92065-0482
760-789-2715
FAX: 760-789-7112
acgakathy@aol.com
www.cutglass.org

Kathy Emmerson, Executive Secretary

An organization with annual shows and exhibits of American brilliant period cut glass and related articles.
1500 Members Founded: 1978

10629 American Flint Glass Workers Union
1440 S Byrne Road
Toledo, OH 43614-2363
419-385-6687
FAX: 419-385-8839 ljs@primenet.com

Timothy Tuttle, President

Organized as the United Flint Glass Workers.
21.7M Members

10630 American Scientific Glassblowers Society
PO Box 778
Madison, NC 27025
336-427-2406
FAX: 336-427-2496
natl-office@asgs-glass.org
www.asgs-glass.org

Amy Collins, National Office Manager
Stephanie Stevens, Assistant Office Manager
James Hodgson, Treasurer
David Daenzer, Executive Secretary

A not for profit organization that is dedicated to sharing the knowedge,techniques, and skills of scientific glassblowing to its worldwide membership.
680 Members Founded: 1954

10631 Art Glass Association
1100-H Brandywine Boulevard
PO Box 3388
Zanesville, OH 43702-3388
740-452-4541
FAX: 740-452-2552 888-866-2472
randyw@artglassassociation.com
www.artglassassociation.com

Randy Wardell, Chairman

International, nonprofit organization whose purpose is to create awareness, knowledge and involvement for the growth and prosperity of the art glass industry. Programs include an annual conference, group health insurance, marchant listings on our website and more.

10632 Ceramic Tile Distributors Association
800 Roosevelt Road, Building C
Suite 312
Glen Ellyn, IL 60137
630-459-9415
FAX: 630-790-3095
questions@ctdahome.org
www.ctdahome.org

Cindy Bell, President
Mark Carlson, VP
Rick Church, Manager

Promotes the sales of ceramic tile and similar products.
500 Members Founded: 1978

10633 Ceramic Tile Institute
12061 Jefferson Boulevard
Culver City, CA 90230-6219
310-574-7800
FAX: 310-821-4655 www.ctioa.org

Judy Williams, Manager

This organization has over 500 member manufacturers of ceramic tile in the western United States.

10634 China Clay Producers Association
113 Arkwright Lndg
Macon, GA 31210-1364
478-571-1252
FAX: 478-757-1949
info@georgiamining.org
www.kaolin.com

Lee Lemke, Executive VP

Educates producers of china clay concerning federal and state governmental activities that affect industry.
6 Members Founded: 1978

10635 China Clay Products Trade Association
4885 Riverside Drive
Suite 108
Macon, GA 31210
478-757-1211
FAX: 478-757-1949
info@georgiamining.org
www.kaolin.com

Lee Lemke, Executive VPresident

Educates producers of china clay concerning federal and state governmental activities that affect industry.
6 Members Founded: 1978

10636 Dame Associates
100 Lincoln Street
Boston, MA 02135
617-783-4777
FAX: 617-783-4787 800-843-3263
dame@dameassoc.com
www.dameassoc.com

Douglas A Dame, President

An organization with an biennial show with 250 manufacturers and suppliers of windows, doors, sun enclosures, windshields, mirrors, glass machinery, hardware, insulating units, sealants, adhesives, mastic, security glazing, thermal barriers, aluminum, curtain wall computers and trucks.
9 Members Founded: 1966

10637 Glass Art Society
3131 Western Avenue
Suite 414
Seattle, WA 98121
206-382-1305
FAX: 206-382-2630
info@glassart.org www.glassart.org

Shane Fero, President
Pamela Koss, Executive Director

An international non-profit organization founded in 1971 whose purpose is to encourage excellence, to advance education, to promote the appreciation and development of the glass arts, and to support the worldwide community of artists who work with glass. GAS members are artists, students, educators, collectors, gallery and museum personnel, writers, and critics, among others. Membership is open to anyone interested in glass art.
3100 Members 24000 names $115 per M.

10638 Glass Association of North America
2495 SW Wanamaker Drive
Suite A
Topeka, KS 66614-5621
785-271-0208
FAX: 785-271-0166
gana@glasswebsite.com
www.glasswebsite.com

Stanley L Smith, Executive VP
Ashley M Charest, Account Executive
C Gregory Carney, Technical Director
Brian K Pitman, Director Marketing

Offers education on blueprint reading, labor and glass estimating and analysis; manuals on glazing guidelines, sealant compatibility and labor hours and a quarterly newsletter. Serves distributors, installers and fabricators of glass for use in the construction automotive and industrial industries.
250 Members Founded: 1994

10639 Glass, Molders, Pottery and Plastics Association
608 E Baltimore Pike
PO Box 607
Media, PA 19063-607
610-565-5051
FAX: 610-565-0983
gmpiu@ix.netcom.com
www.gmpiu.org

John Ryan, International President
Bruce R Smith, International VP
Ignacio de la Fuente, International VP
David Doyle, International VP
Richard Kline, Director Communications

Supports their own political action committee.
51000 Members Founded: 1842

10640 Glazing Industry Code Committee
2945 SW Wanamaker Drive, Suite A
Topeka, KS 66614-5321
785-271-0208
FAX: 785-271-0166
gicc@glazingcodes.org
www.glazingcodes.org

Stanley L Smith, Administrator
Bill Koffel, Technical Consultant

Protects the glass and glazing interests by monitoring, testifying and developing code proposals at the model building and energy codes.

10641 Insulating Glass Certification Council
PO Box 9
Henderson Harbor, NY 13651
315-646-2234
FAX: 315-646-2297
jgkent@gisco.net www.igcc.org
Mark Cody, President
John G Kent, Program Administrator
Sponsors and directs a program of laboratory testing and unannounced plant inspection to ensure continuing product information.
48 Members Founded: 1977

10642 National Glass Association
8200 Greensboro Drive
McLean, VA 22102
703-442-4890
FAX: 703-442-0630
nga@glass.org www.glass.org
Elizabeth Messner, Member Services Manager
Founded in 1948, the National Glass Association is the largest trade association representing the flat (architectural and automotive) glass industy. More than 4,900 member companies and locations reflect the entire vertical flat glass market. To support this ever changing industry, NGA produces products and services specifically for the industry.
4900 Members Founded: 1948

10643 National Industrial Sand Association
2011 Pennsylvania Avenue
Suite 301
Washington, DC 20705
202-457-0200
FAX: 202-457-0287
info@sand.org www.sand.org
Darrel Smith, VP
Serves producers of industrial sand for glass manufacturers and distributors.
24 Members Founded: 1936

10644 Porcelain Enamel Institute
PO Box 920220
Norcross, GA 30010
770-281-8980
FAX: 770-281-8981
penamel@aol.com
www.porcelainenamel.com
Tom Sanford, Exec VP
Patricia Melton, Executive Secretary
Members include suppliers and makers of porcelain enamel products and raw materials.
85 Members Founded: 1930

10645 Refractory Ceramic Fiber Coalition
1133 Connecticut Avenue NW
Suite 1200
Washington, DC 20036
202-937-7150
FAX: 202-833-8491
rcfc@buffnet.net www.rcfc.net
William P Kelly, President
An association of the leading U.S. producers of refactory ceramic fibers.
Founded: 1992

10646 Safety Glazing Certification Council
PO Box 9
Henderson Harbor, NY 13651
315-646-2234
FAX: 315-646-2297 www.sgcc.org
John C Kent, Administrative Staff
Christine Flitcroft, Administrative Staff
Nonprofit corporation that provides for the certifacation of safety glazing materials, comprised of safety glazing manufacturers and other parties concerned with public safety. SGCC is managed by a board of directors comprised of representatives from the safety glazing industry and the public interest sector.
105 Members Founded: 1971

10647 Society of Glass & Ceramic Decorators
47 N 4th Street
PO Box 2489
Zanesville, OH 43702
740-588-9882
FAX: 740-588-0245
sgcd@sgcd.org www.sgcd.org
Randall Van Hise, President
Julie Butterfield, VP
Nancy Klinefelter, Secretary/Treasurer
Provides decorating professionals with a competitive edge in business by providing opporotunities for networking to learn about new decorating technologies and techniques.
525 Members

10648 Stained Glass Professionals Association
PO Box 557
Jensen Beach, FL 34958-0557
772-334-8844
Jay Petersen, Executive Director
Seeks to upgrade the services of retailers and studios by promoting teacher certification in studios. Offers advertising and public relations program.
Founded: 1983

10649 Technical Ceramics Manufacturers Association
25 N Broadway
Tarrytown, NY 10591-3221
914-332-0040
FAX: 914-332-1541
Rich Byrne, Executive Director
A organization of manufacturers of custom and standard technical ceramic products for use in commercial, residential or industrial applications.

10650 United States Advanced Ceramics Association
1800 M Street NW
Suite 300
Washington, DC 20036-5802
202-293-6253
FAX: 202-223-5537
usaca@ttcrop.com
www.advancedceramics.org
Doug Freitag, Acting Government Affairs Chairman
Arvid Pasto, Membership Committee Chairman
Jeff Serfass, President
The premier association that champions the common business interests of the advanced ceramic producer and end user industries.
8 Members Founded: 1985

Newsletters

10651 American Ceramic Society Bulletin
The American Ceramic Society
735 Ceramic Place
Suite 100
Westerville, OH 43081
614-890-4700
FAX: 614-794-5892
info@ceramics.org
http://www.ceramicbulletin.org
Glenn Harvey, Executive Director
Marcus Bailey, Publisher
Patricia Janeway, Editor
Jeff Calvert, Marketing Manager
Magazine for ceramic technology, engineering and manufacturing. *$75.00*
Monthly Founded: 1898
Circulation: 10,000
Printed in 4 colors on glossy stock

Magazines & Journals

10652 AGRR Magazine
Key Communications
PO Box 569
Garrisonville, VA 22463
540-577-7174
FAX: 540-720-5687
agrr@glass.com
http://www.agrrmag.com
Debra Levy, Publisher
Megan Headley, Assistant Editor
Source of unbiased, accurate information about auto glass repair and replacement industry. *$49.95*
6 issues per ye Founded: 1993
Circulation: 10000+

10653 American Flint Magazine
American Flint Glass Workers Union
1440 S Byrne Road
Toledo, OH 43614-2363
419-385-6687
FAX: 419-385-8839
Timothy Tuttle, President
Union news and information for the glass industry.
Monthly

10654 American Glass Review
Doctorow Communications
1011 Clifton Avenue
PO Box 2147
Clifton, NM 07015-2147
973-779-1600
FAX: 973-779-3242
info@homelighting.com
Jon Doctorow, Publisher
Editorial content covers energy efficiency, emerging technologies, glass recycling, emission standards, and applications of finished glass products. *$25.00*
Bi-Monthly
Circulation: 1,150

10655 Ceramic Bulletin
American Ceramic Society
735 Ceramic Place
Suite 100
Westerville, OH 43081
614-890-4700
FAX: 614-794-5822
pjaneway@acers.org
http://www.ceramicbulletin.org

Patricia A Janeway, Editor
Marcus A. Bailey, Publisher

Written for ceramic and materials engineers and production management teams involved in industrial ceramics manufacturing. Topics covered include government relations, environmental issues, developing technology, industry statistics, cutting-edge manufacturing processes and technology. *$75.00*

Monthly Founded: 1953
Circulation: 50000
Printed in 4 colors on glossy stock

10656 Ceramic Industry
Business News Publishing Company
755 W Big Beaver Road
Suite 1000
Troy, MI 48084-4900
248-362-3700
FAX: 248-244-6439
loves@bnpmedia.com
http://www.ceramicindustry.com

Sue Love, Publisher
Christine L Grahl, Editor

Highlights include case histories, new plants, plant expansion, developments in manufacturing processes, testing and quality control, research reports and management techniques as well as energy saving ideas.

Monthly Founded: 1926
Circulation: 10000

10657 Ceramics Monthly
American Ceramic Society
735 Ceramic Pl
Ste 100
Westerville, OH 43081-8728
614-895-4213
FAX: 614-891-8960
editorial@ceramicsmonthly.org
http://www.ceramicsmonthly.org

Sherman Hall, Editor
Rich Guerrein, Publisher
Jennifer Poellot, Assistant editor
Susan Enderle, Marketing Manager

An internationally distributed magazine covering ceramic arts and crafts. Includes lists of conferences, exhibitions, festivals, fairs, sales and workshops for crafts people. *$32.00*

Monthly Founded: 1953
Circulation: 35000
Printed in on glossy stock

10658 Fired Arts and Crafts
Jones Publishing
N7450 Aanstad Road
PO Box 5000
Iola, WI 54945-5000
715-445-5000
FAX: 715-445-4053 800-331-0038
jonespub@jonespublishing.com
http://www.jonespublishing.com

Joe Jones, CEO/President
Mick Harbridge, Editor
Branden Hardy, Marketing

Features on projects and patterns, celebrity clips, new products, show listings, industry news and book reviews. *$32.95*

Monthly
Circulation: 15000

10659 Fusion
American Scientific Glassblowers Society

PO Box 778
Madison, NC 27025
336-427-2406
FAX: 336-427-2496
natl-office@asgs-glass.org
http://www.asgs-glass.org

Marylin Brown, Editor
Marylin Brown, Publisher
Scott Bankroff, President

Unique publication covering information and news for glassblowers. *$40.00*

Quarterly Founded: 1954
Circulation: 850

10660 Glass Craftsman
Arts & Media
10 Canal Street
Suite 300
Bristol, PA 19007
215-826-1799
FAX: 215-826-1788
info@glasscraftsman.com
www.artglassworld.com

Joe Porcelli, Publisher

Contains features on all types of artistic glass, glass restoration, design, and applications. *$25.00*

Circulation: 12000

10661 Glass Digest
Ashlee Publishing
18 E 41st Street
21st Floor
New York, NY 10017-6222
212-376-7722
FAX: 212-376-7723
glassdgst@aol.com
www.ashleepub.aol.com

Jordan Wright, Publisher

Regular issue features include coverage of industry trends and developments, new products, marketing ideas and new installation methods. *$40.00*

Monthly
Circulation: 11,376

10662 Glass Magazine
Nicole Harris
8200 Greensboro Drive
Suite 302
Mc Lean, VA 22102-3881
866-342-5642
FAX: 703-442-0630
editorialinfo@glass.org
http://www.glassmagazine.net

Nicole Harris, VP
Nancy Davis, Editor in Chief
Sahely Mukerji, Managing Editor

These publications cover all facets of the glass industry. *$34.95*

Monthly Founded: 1948
Circulation: 27098

10663 Hobstar
American Cut Glass Association
PO Box 482
Ramona, CA 92065-482
760-789-2715
FAX: 760-789-7112
algakathy@aol.com
http://www.cutglass.org

Verle Davison, Editor
Kathy Emmerson, Executive Secretary

Published by the American Cut Glass Association.

Founded: 1876
Printed in 2 colors on glossy stock

10664 Journal of the American Ceramic Society
American Ceramic Society
735 Ceramic Pl
Ste 100
Westerville, OH 43081-8728
614-890-4700
FAX: 614-899-6109
info@ceramics.org
http://www.ceramics.org

W Paul Holbrook, Publisher
Warren W Wolf, President
Sherman Hall, Editor

Topics covered include glass, electronics, waste management, nuclear, engineered materials, structural materials, and powders processing and fabrication. Appeals to materials research scientists and developers, academics and primary corporate research and development units. *$1190.00*

Monthly Founded: 1905

10665 Popular Ceramics
Jones Publishing
N7450 Aanstad Road
PO Box 5000
Iola, WI 54945-5000
715-445-5000
FAX: 715-445-4053 800-331-0038
jonespub@jonespublishing.com
http://www.jonespublishing.com/

Joe Jones, President/Publisher
Brandan Hardie, Circulation Manager
Julie Maher, Advertising Manager

For individuals interested in creative fired arts. Features and columns are designed for ceramists, manufacturers, studio owners, teachers and students. Includes ceramics projects for all ability levels, the business of operating a successful studio, current industry events, trends and educational products, guest editorials, reader feedback, questions and answers and much more. *$27.95*

Monthly

10666 Pottery Making Illustrated
American Ceramic Society
735 Ceramic Pl
Ste 100
Westerville, OH 43081-8728
614-890-4700
FAX: 614-891-8960
info@ceramics.org
www.potterymaking.org

Bill Jones, Editor/Publisher
Glenn Harvey, CEO

Content includes articles and information from professionals and teachers, how-to instructions for featured projects, updates on new techniques, processes and materials, and related information on the ceramics industry. *$22.00*

Fortnightly Founded: 1905
Circulation: 20000

10667 US Glass, Metal & Glazing
Key Communications
PO Box 569
Garrisonville, VA 22463
540-577-7174
FAX: 540-720-5687
scarpenter@glass.com
http://www.usglassmag.com

Penny Stacey, Advertising Coordinator
Ellen Giard Chilcoat, Editor
Debra Levy, President

Serves manufactures/fabricators, contract glaziers, distributors and wholesalers,

retailors/dealers of glass/metal and/or glass/metal products and others allied to the field.
Monthly Founded: 1965
Circulation: 25572
Printed in 4 colors on glossy stock

Trade Shows

10668 American Ceramic Society Annual Meeting and Expo
735 Ceramic Place
Westerville, OH 43081
614-890-4700
FAX: 614-794-5882
customersrvc@acess.org
www.ceramics.org
Christine Schnitzer, Director Membership/Meetings/Expo
Glenn Harvey, Executive Director
Three-hundred booths of ceramic materials, products manufacturing, testing, processing, research, components and software. Technical conference on ceramic materials research and development with over 1000 papers presented in more than 25 topical areas.
2,500 Attendees April 3500 names $120 per M.

10669 Annual Exposition American Ceramic Society
American Ceramic Society
735 Ceramic Place
Westerville, OH 43081
614-890-4700
FAX: 614-899-6109
Annual

10670 Annual International Conference on Advanced Ceramics
American Ceramic Society
614-890-4700
FAX: 614-899-6109
customersrvc@acers.org
www.ceramics.org
January

10671 Art Glass Show
Offinger Management Company
1100-H Brandywine Boulevard
PO Box 3388
Zanesville, OH 43702-3388
740-452-4541
FAX: 740-452-2552 888-866-2472
info@asga.org www.asga.org
June

10672 DECO
Society of Glass & Ceramic Decorators
4340 E West Highway
Suite 200
Bethesda, MD 20814
301-986-9800
FAX: 301-951-3801
sgcd@sgcd.org www.sgcd.org
Focusing on technical and regulatory issues affecting glass and ceramic decorators.

10673 Dealers Show of the American Cut Glass Association
American Cut Glass Association
PO Box 482
Ramona, CA 92065-0482
760-789-2715
FAX: 760-789-7112
algakathy@aol.com www.cutglass.org
Kathy Emmerson, Executive Secretary
Annual show and exhibits of American brilliant period cut glass and related articles. Attendees at show are members only except saturday afternoon 1-5pm. Containing approximately 10 booths and 10 exhibits.

10674 Glass & Ceramic Decorators Annual Seminar & Exposition
Society of Glass & Ceramic Decorators
47 N 4th Street
PO Box 2489
Zanesville, OH 43702
202-298-8660
FAX: 740-588-0245
myrawarne@sgcd.org www.sgcd.org
Myra Warne, Exhibit
The SGCD show attracts major suppliers to the decorating industry, including several firms from overseas. With a full seminar program and first step program that attracts attendees on their own merits.
525 Attendees

10675 Glass Art Society Conference
Glass Art Society
3131 Western Avenue
Suite 414
Seattle, WA 98121
206-382-1305
FAX: 206-382-2630
info@glassart.org www.glassart.org
Pamela Koss, Executive Director
Sarah Bak, Executive Assistant
Annual conference and exhibits for those who make, collect, exhibit and appreciate objects made with glass. Glass Art Society 36th Annual Conference - Glass Gateways/Meet in the Middle; and 37th Annual Conference - Transformational Matter.
2000 Attendees June

10676 Glass Craft Exposition
Las Vegas Management
2408 Chapman Drive
Las Vegas, NV 89104
702-734-0070
FAX: 702-734-0636 800-217-4527
Shirley Harvey, Director
3500 Attendees March

10677 Glass Expo
Appliance Manufacturer
5900 Harper Road
Suite 105
Solon, OH 44139-1935
440-349-3060
FAX: 440-498-9121
www.usglassmag.com
Mitch Henderson, Group Publisher
Joe Jancsurak, Editor
January

10678 Glass Expo Hawaii
Appliance Manufacturer
5900 Harper Road
Suite 105
Solon, OH 44139-1935
440-349-3060
FAX: 440-498-9121
www.usglassmaqg.com
Mitch Henderson, Group Publisher
Joe Jancsurak, Editor
February

10679 Glass Expo Midwest
US Glass Magazine
PO Box 569
Garrisonville, VA 22463
540-720-5584
FAX: 540-720-5687
expos@glass.com
www.glassexpos.com/
Patrick Smith, Marketing Manager
Annual show and exhibits of flat, container, heavy insulated and tempered glass, architectural sealants and hardware, mirror products and windows and doors.
800 Attendees August

10680 Glass Show
Dame Associates
100 Lincoln Street
Brighton, MA 02135-1407
617-783-4777
FAX: 617-426-8019 800-843-3263
Annual show of 115 manufacturers and suppliers of windows, doors, sun enclosures, windshields and mirrors, glass, machinery, hardware and insulating units, sealants, adhesives, mastic, security glazing and thermal barriers, aluminum, curtain wall computers and trucks.
2500 Attendees

10681 Glass TEXpo
US Glass Magazine
PO Box 569
Garrisonville, VA 22463-0569
540-720-5584
FAX: 540-720-5687
expos@glass.com
www.glassexpos.com
Patrick Smith, Marketing Manager
Annual show and exhibits of flat, container, heavy insulated and tempered glass, architectural sealants and hardware, mirror products and windows and doors. Hosted in Dallas, TX.
700 Attendees October

10682 Innovative Material Solutions
814-863-8735
FAX: 814-667-2813
rgc@imspowder.com
www.imspowder.com/pim2002
March

10683 International Window Film Conference and Expo
Window Film Magazine
PO Box 569
Garrisonville, VA 22463-0569
540-720-5584
FAX: 540-720-5687
expos@glass.com
www.glassexpos.com
Patrick Smith, Marketing Manager
Numerous opportunities to network, socialize, and learn from others in the window film industry.
March

10684 Porcelain Enamel Institute Technical Forum & Suppliers Mart
4004 Hillsboro Pike
Suite B224
Nashville, TN 37215-2722
615-385-5357
FAX: 615-385-5463
penamel@aol.com
www.porcelainenamel.com
Cullen Hackler, Executive VP
Patricia Melton, Executive Secretary
Members include suppliers and makers of porcelain enamel products and raw materi-

als. Attendees of the PEI conference and workshops attend this show. There will be 20 booths.

250 Attendees Founded: 1989

10685 Society of Glass & Ceramic Decorators
SGCD 4340 E - W Highway
Suite 200
Bethesda, MD 20814
301-986-9800
FAX: 301-951-3801
sgcd@sgcd.org www.sgcd.org

Andrew Bopp, Executive Director

75 booths of materials equipment and services for commercial decorators of glass and ceramicware.

500 Attendees February

10686 Surface Engineering Exposition
ASM International
9639 Kinsman Road
Materials Park, OH 44073
440-338-5151
FAX: 440-338-4634
asmexpos@asminternational.org
www.asminternational.org
Focus on the practical application and science of surface engineering.

October

10687 Washington Gift Show
George Little Management
10 Bank Street
Suite 1200
White Plains, NY 10606
914-486-6070
FAX: 914-948-2918 800-272-7469
louise_seeber@glmshows.com
www.washingtongiftshow.com

Louise Seeber, Show Manager
Laura Scott, Exhibit Sales Manager
George Little II, President

The Mid Atlantic's premier gift market featuring 300 exhibitors and 6000 buyers.

6000 Attendees January/July

Directories & Databases

10688 Ceramic Abstracts
American Ceramic Society
735 Ceramic Place
Westerville, OH 43081-8719
614-890-4700
FAX: 614-794-5812

Christine Schnitzer, Product Manager
Linda Lakemacher, Publications Director

Abstracting/indexing publication covering ceramic materials-related literature. 15,000 entries published annually.

Bi-Monthly
Circulation: 2,500

10689 CeramicSOURCE
American Ceramic Society
735 Ceramic Pl
Ste 100
Westerville, OH 43081-8728
614-904-4700
FAX: 614-794-5892
info@ceramics.org
www.ceramicsource.org

Patricia Janeway, Editor
Marc Bailey, Director Global Marketing

Annual buyer's guide/directory of equipment and materials' suppliers to the industrial ceramic manufacturing market. *$25.00*

1 issue Founded: 1985
Circulation: 14,500
Printed in 4 colors on glossy stock : on-line

10690 Complete Directory of Glassware & Glass Items
Sutton Family Communications & Publishing Company
155 Sutton Lane
Fordsville, KY 42343
270-740-0870

jlsutton@apex.net
www.fleamarketeer.net

Theresa Sutton, Publisher
Lee Sutton, Editor

Print-out from database of wholesalers, manufacturers, distributors, importers and close-out houses. Database is updated daily to guarantee the most current and up-to-date sources available. Over 800 American firms which sell direct to small retailers, in three-ring binder format. *$94.50*

100 pages

10691 Complete Guide: US Advanced Ceramic Industry
Business Communications Company
25 Van Zant Street
Suite 113
Norwalk, CT 06855-1713
203-853-4266
FAX: 203-853-0348
saes@bccresearch.com
www.bccresearch.com

Louis Naturman, Publisher

Approximately 450 companies and institutions involved in the advanced ceramic industry in the US. *$2750.00*

10692 Data Book and Buyers' Guide
Ceramic Industry
2540 Billingsley Road
Business News Publishing Company
Columbus, OH 43235-1990

FAX: 440-498-9121
List of over 1300 suppliers of equipment and materials for the advanced and traditional ceramics and heavy clay products. *$25.00*

10693 Glass Factory Directory of North America
Glass News
PO Box 2267
Hempstead, NY 11551-2267
516-481-2188

Liz Scott, Editor

Over 600 glass manufacturers and plants in the US, Canada and Mexico. *$25.00*

Annual Fall
Circulation: 1,500

10694 International Glass and Metal Catalog
Glass Digest
18 E 41st Street
New York, NY 10017
212-376-7722
FAX: 212-376-7723
publisher@ashlee.com
www.glassdigestmagazine.com
Importers, manufacturers and other suppliers who furnish products and services used by distributors and retailers of flat glass and related products are the focus of this directory. *$30.00*

85 pages Annual
Circulation: 12,000

10695 Popular Ceramics
Jones Publishing
N7 450 Aanstad Road
PO Box 5000
Iola, WI 54945-5000
715-445-5000
FAX: 715-445-4053 800-331-0038
jonespub@jonespublishing.com
www.jonespublishing.com

Mary Kay Berg, Editor

List of 500 manufacturers. *$12.95*

Annual

10696 Porcelain Enamel Institute Source List
4004 Hillsboro Pike
Suite B224
Nashville, TN 37215-2722
615-385-5357
FAX: 615-385-5463
penamel@aol.com
www.porcelainenamel.com

Tom Sanford, Executive VP
Patricia Melton, Executive Secretary

Members include suppliers and makers of porcelain enamel products and raw materials.

Annual Fall Founded: 1930

10697 Society of Glass & Ceramic Decorators Directory
Society of Glass & Ceramic Decorators
1701 K Street
Washington, DC 20006-1702
202-728-4132
FAX: 202-728-4133
sgcd@sgcd.org www.sgcd.org

Andy Bopp, Executive Director
Caroline Struggs, Communications Associate

Directory of more than 700 member manufacturers, suppliers, decorators and designers of glass and ceramics; international coverage indexed by product type and decorating technology. *$250.00*

172 pages Annual Founded: 1964
Circulation: 800

10698 Technical Ceramics Manufacturers Associati on Directory
Technical Ceramics Manufacturers Association
25 N Broadway
Tarrytown, NY 10591-3221
914-332-0040
FAX: 914-332-1541
Manufacturers of custom and standard technical ceramic products for use in commercial, residential or industrial applications.

10699 US Glass, Metal & Glazing: Buyers Guide
Key Communications
PO Box 569
Garrisonville, VA 22463-0569
540-577-7174
FAX: 540-720-5687
usglass@aol.com www.usglass.com

Debra A Levy, Publisher

About 3,000 suppliers of glass and glazing supplies for the glass, metal and glazing industry. *$20.00*

Annual December
Circulation: 21,000

Industry Web Sites

10700 **www.acers.org**
American Ceramic Society

The National Institute of Ceramic Engineers, the Ceramic Manufacturing Council and the Ceramic Education Council are affiliated classes.

10701 **www.asgs-glass.org**
American Scientific Glassblowers Society

Encourages the free exchange of knowledge and the broadening of scientific glassblowing skills to assist scientists, educators and the industry by designing and constructing glass components and scientific apparatus.

10702 **www.ceramics.org**
American Ceramic Society

The National Institute of Ceramic Engineers, the Ceramic Manufacturing Council and the Ceramic Education Council are affiliated groups.

10703 **www.ctdahome.org**
Ceramic Tile Distributors Association

Promotes the sales of ceramic tile and similar products.

10704 **www.ctioa.org**
Ceramic Tile Institute

This organization has over 500 member manufacturers of ceramic tile in the western United States.

10705 **www.cutglass.org**
American Cut Glass Association

An organization with annual shows and exhibits of American brilliant period cut glass and related articles.

10706 **www.dameassoc.org**
Dame Associates

An organization with an biennial show w/250 manufacturers and suppliers of windows, doors, sun enclosures, windshields, mirrors, glass machinery, hardware, insulating units, sealants, adhesives, mastic, security glazing, thermal barriers, aluminum, curtain wall computers and trucks.

10707 **www.glass.org**
National Glass Association

An organization with an annual show of 325 manufacturers, suppliers and distributors of glass and glass-related products, supplies, equipment, tools and machinery, automotive glazing, equipment/machinery, curtain wall, store front systems, doors/hardware, windows, mirrors, shower/tub enclosures and tools.

10708 **www.glasswebsite.com**
Glass Assoication of North America

Offers educational on blueprint reading, labor, and glass estimating and analysis; manuals on glazing guidelines, sealant compatibility and labor hours; and a quarterly newsletter. Serves distributors, installers, fabircators of glass for use in the construction automotive and industrial industries.

10709 **www.glasswebsite.com/gicc**
Glazing Industry Code Committee

Protects the glass and glazing interests by monitoring, testifying and developing code proposals at the model building and energy codes.

10710 **www.greyhouse.com**
Grey House Publishing

Selected Grey House directories in the fields of business, health and education are available online. Users can search our online databases by several different search criteria, such as product categories, geographic area, sales volume and much, much more. Full Grey House catalog and online ordering also available.

10711 **www.igcc.org**
Insulating Glass Certification Council

Sponsors and directs a program of laboratory testing and unannounced plant inspection to ensure continuing product information.

10712 **www.porcelainenamel.com**
Porcelain Enamel Institute

Members include suppliers and makers of porcelain enamel products and raw materials.

10713 **www.sgcc.org**
Safety Glazing Certification Council

Information center for this nonprofit corporation that provides for the certification of safety glazing materials.

10714 **www.sigmaonline.org/sigma**
Sealed Insulating Glass Manufacturers Association

10715 **www.ttcrop.com/usaca/**
United States Advanced Ceramics Association

Associations

10716 Academy for State and Local Government
Hall of States
444 N Capitol Street NW
Washington, DC 20001-1512
202-083-3860
FAX: 202-434-4851
The policy center for the national organizations for the chief elected and appointed officials for state and local governments, functioning as their joint technical assistance, training and research organization. Its mission is to promote cooperation among federal, state and local governments.

10717 American Association of Access Professionals
7910 Woodmont Avenue
Bethesda, MD 20814-3002

FAX: 301-913-0001
Claire E Shanley, Executive Director
Christine DeVries, Manager
Members include government lawyers, employees, journalists and others concerned with access to government data.
350 Members

10718 American Association of State Highway and
444 North Capitol Street NW
Suite 249
Washington, DC 20001
202-245-5800
FAX: 202-624-5806
info@aashto.org www.aashto.org
Trindal S Aboud, Deputy Director Meetings
Jose Aldayuz, Project Manager
Shane Artim, Communications Coordinator
John Horsley, Executive Director
Jack Basso, Director Business Development
Membership is composed of highway and transportation departments in the 50 states, the District of Columbia, and Puerto Rico.
52 Members

10719 American Conference of Governmental
1330 Kemper Meadow Drive
Cincinnati, OH 45240
513-742-2020
FAX: 513-742-3355
mail@acgih.org www.acgih.org
Vickie L Wells, Chairman
Cindy Laseter, Vice Chairman
David G Taylor, Secretary/Treasurer
A professional society of government and university employees engaged in a full program of industrial hygiene.
4.5M Members

10720 American Correctional Association

206 N Washington St
Ste 200
Alexandria, VA 22314-2528
703-224-0000
FAX: 703-224-0010 800-222-5646
jeffw@aca.org www.aca.org
Charles J Kehoe, President
Terry L Stewart, VP
Harold W Clark, Treasurer
James A Gondles, Executive Director
For individuals involved in the correctional field.
20000 Members Founded: 1870

10721 American Federation of Government
80 F Street NW
Washington, DC 20001
202-737-8700
FAX: 202-639-6490
comments@afge.org www.afge.org
John Gage, President
Jim Davis, Secretary/Treasurer
Andrea E Brooks, VP Women's/Fair Practices
Michael Beatley, Chief Engineer Building Operations
Enid Doggett, Director Communications Department
The largest federal employee union representing 600,000 workers nationwide and overseas.
Founded: 1932

10722 American Federation of School
1101 17th St NW
Ste 408
Washington, DC 20036-4720
202-986-4209
FAX: 202-986-4211
afsa@admin.org www.admin.org
Joe Greene, President
Linda Chavez-Thompson, Executive VP
Richard L Trumka, Secretary/Treasurer
National education union providing professional, labor and leadership services to public school principals, assistant principals, administrators and supervisors.
18500 Members Founded: 1973

10723 American Federation of State, County and Municipal Employees
1625 L Street NW
Washington, DC 20036-5687
202-452-4800
FAX: 202-429-1293 www.afscase.org
Gerald W McEntee, President
Sponsors their own Political Action Committee.

10724 American Foreign Service Association
2101 E Street NW
Washington, DC 20037
202-338-4045
FAX: 202-338-6820
member@afsa.org www.afsa.org
Anthony Holmes, President
Susan K Reardon, Executive Director
Cory Nishi, Membership Representative
Janet Hedrick, Director
Acts as the elected representative of all Foreign Service personnel and professional association of Foreign Service personnel in the AID, State Department, USIA, FAS & FCS.
11M Members Founded: 1924

10725 American Judges Association
National Center for State Courts
300 Newport Avenue
Williamsburg, VA 23185-4147
757-259-1841
FAX: 757-259-1520
aja@ncsc.dni.cs aja.ncsc.dni.us
Shelley Rockwell, Account Executive
An independent organization of judges in all jurisdictions in Canada, Mexico and the US.
2500 Members Founded: 1959

10726 American League of Lobbyists
PO Box 30005
Alexandria, VA 22310
703-960-3011

alldc.org@erols.com www.alldc.org
Patti Jo Baber, Executive Director
National association dedicated to serving government relations and public affairs professionals. Provides programs and conferences of interest to lobbyists.
600+ Members Founded: 1979

10727 American National Standards Institute
1819 L Street NW
6th Floor
Washington, DC 20036
202-293-8020
FAX: 202-293-9287
info@ansi.org www.ansi.org
Mark W Hurwitz, President/CEO
Stacy M Leistner, Communications/PR Director
Promotes the knowledge for approved standards for industry, engineering and safety design.
1000 Members Founded: 1918

10728 American Public Human Services Association
810 1st Street NE
Suite 500
Washington, DC 20002
202-682-0100
FAX: 202-289-6555 www.aphsa.org
Karl Kurtz, President
Dan Engstrom, VP
John Cuddy, Treasurer
Jerry Friedman, Executive Director
Nonprofit, bipartisan organization of individuals and agencies concerned with human services. Members include all state and many territorial human service agencies, more than 1,200 local agencies, and several thousand individuals.
Founded: 1930

10729 American Society for Public Administration
1120 G Street NW
Suite 700
Washington, DC 20005
202-393-7878
FAX: 202-638-4952
pyearwood@aspanet.org
www.aspanet.org
Mary Hamilton, Executive Director
Erik Bergrud, Senior Director Chapter
Karen Pane, CAP Director
Offers a wide range of services and membership options for individuals in public administration careers. Sponsors 127 local chapters and 16 sections on specific areas of governments, such as the Section of Natural Resources and Environmental Administration and the Section on Human Resource Administration.
15M Members Founded: 1939

10730 American Society of Access Professionals
1444 I Street NW
Suite 700
Washington, DC 20005-6542
202-712-9054
FAX: 202-212-9054
ASAP@bostromdc.com
www.accesspro.org

Claire Shanley, Executive Director

Members are government employees, lawyers, journalists and others concerned with access to government data under current personal privacy and public informaiton statues.

10731 Americans for Democratic Action

1625 K Street NW
Suite 210
Washington, DC 20006
202-785-5980
FAX: 202-785-5969
adaction@ix.netcom.com
www.adaction.org

Jim McDermott, President
Joel Cohen, Executive Committee Chair
Amy Isaacs, Executive Director
Maria Wilkinson, Secretary
Jack Blum, Counsel

Liberal lobbying group.

10732 Associated Business Publications

317 Madison Avenue
New York, NY 10017
212-903-3999
FAX: 212-986-7864 www.abptuf.org
Association for purchasers of laser/optical products.

10733 Association for Federal Information

OC&R
1616 N Fountain Myer Drive
Arlington, VA 22209
202-298-5233

webmaster@affirm.org
www.affirm.org

Scott Hastings, President
Michael S Sade, VP
Michelle Heffner, Co VP

Seeks to improve the management of information systems and resources of the Federal Government.
350 Members Founded: 1979

10734 Association for Governmental Leasing and

1255 23rd Street NW
Washington, DC 20037-1174
202-742-2453
FAX: 202-833-3636
info@aglf.org www.aglf.org

Graham Hauck, Executive Director

Provides an exchange of information among tax-exempt issuers, investment banking firms and party lease brokers.
260 Members Founded: 1981

10735 Association for Postal Commerce

1901 N Fort Myer Drive
Suite 401
Arlington, VA 22209-1609
703-524-0096
FAX: 703-524-1871
info@postcom.org www.postcom.org

Gene A Del Polito, President
Kate Muth, VP
Caroline Miller, Director Administrative Services
Joseph V DeSantis, VP Distribution/Postal Affairs
Paul Imbierowicz, VP Product Management

National organization representing those who use, or who support, the use of mail as a medium for communication and commerce. Publishes a weekly newsletter covering postal policy and operational issues.
231 Members Founded: 1947

10736 Association of Boards of Certification

208 5th Street
Ames, IA 50010-6259
515-232-3623
FAX: 515-232-3778
abc@abccert.org www.abccert.org

Kim Dyches, President
Margaret Doss, VP
James Holeva, Treasurer
Stephen Ballou, Executive Director

The Association of Boards of Certification is dedicated to protecting public health and the environment by advancing the quality and integrity of environmental certification programs through innovative technical support services, effective information exchange, professional and cost-effective examination services, and other progressive services for certifying members.
Founded: 1972

10737 Association of Civilian Technicians

12620 Lake Ridge Drive
Lake Ridge, VA 22192
703-494-4845
FAX: 703-494-0961
actnat@actnat.com www.actnat.com

Thomas G Bastas, President
Dwain Reynolds, VP
Leon J Cich, Executive VP
Michael Vasko, Treasurer
Norman Smith, Secretary

Union of civilian employees of the Army and National Guard and Air Reserve.
12M Members

10738 Association of Food and Drug Officials

2550 Kingston
Suite 311
York, PA 17402-0425
717-757-2888
FAX: 717-755-8089
afdo3425@aol.com
www.healthfinder.gov

Denise Rooney, Executive Director

Promotes the enforcement of laws and regulations at all levels of government. Fosters understanding and cooperation between industry and regulators. Develops model laws and regulations and seeks their adoption.
800 Members Founded: 1986 1000+ names

10739 Association of Former Agents of the US Secret Service

525 SW 5th Street
Suite A
Des Moines, IW 50309-0848
515-282-8192
FAX: 515-282-9117 www.oldstar.org

Kathy Rinkenberger, Executive Director

Association of the Former Agents of the United States Secret Services, is a nonprofit organization eligible to recieve tax deductible charitable donations under section 501 of the Internal Revenue Code.
950 Members

10740 Association of Labor Relations Agencies

Illinois Relations Board
160 N LaSalle Street
Suite S400
Chicago, IL 60601
312-936-6400
FAX: 312-793-6989 www.alra.org

Dan Nielsen, President
Jackie Gallagher, Manager

Members are at the federal, local and state levels in the US.
75 Members

10741 Association of Local Air Pollution

444 North Capitol Street NW
Suite 307
Washington, DC 20001
202-624-7864
FAX: 202-624-7863
4clnair@4cleanair.org
www.cleanairworld.org

Cory R Chadwick, President
Dennis J McLerran, VP
Brian L Jennison, Treasurer
Gary Young, Director
S William Becker, Executive Director

Represents air pollution control officials from over 150 major metropolitan areas across the US.

10742 Center for the Study of the Presidency

1020 Nineteenth Street NW
Suite 250
Washington, DC 20036
202-872-9800
FAX: 202-872-9811
Center@thePresidency.org
www.thepresidency.org

David Abshire, President/CEO
Thomas Kirlin, COO/Program Director

The center seeks to futher the understanding and functioning of the American Presidency and its related institutions and, thereby, to educate, illuminate and inspire leaders of tomorrow.

10743 Citizens Against Government Waste

1301 Connecticut Avenue Northwest
Suite 400
Washington, DC 20036
202-467-5300
FAX: 202-467-4253
membership@cagw.org www.cagw.org

Thomas Schatz, President
Ariane Sweeney, VP Membership & Development
David Williams, VP Policy

Seeks to educate the public, individuals in public administration and congress on eliminating waste, mis-management and inefficiency in government spending.
1MM+ Members Founded: 1984
Mailing list available for rent

10744 Coalition for Government Procurement

1990 M Street NW
Suite 400
Washington, DC 20036-3420
202-331-0975
FAX: 202-695-5754
www.coalgovpro.org

Larry Allen, Executive VP
Bruce McLellan, Executive Director

Members are firms who provide commercial goods to the federal government.
350 Members Founded: 1979

10745 Commissioned Officers Association of the United States Public Health Service
8201 Corporate Drive
Suite 560
Landover, MD 20785
301-731-9080
FAX: 301-731-9084
Jerry Farrell, Executive Director
7M Members

10746 Community Leadership Association
1240 S Lumpkin Street
Athens, GA 30602
706-542-0301
FAX: 706-542-7007
info@communityleadership.org
www.communityleadership.org
Gene A Honn, Executive Director
Founded by 40 community leadership organizations.
2M Members

10747 Conference of Minority Public Administrators
9717 Summit Circle
Suite 3E
Largo, MD 20774
301-333-5282
FAX: 202-638-4952
Joanne E Dunne, Director
Section of American Society for Public Administration.
500 Members

10748 Contract Services Association of America
1000 Wilson Boulevard
Suite 1800
Arlington, VA 22209
703-243-2020
FAX: 703-243-3601
info@csa-dc.org www.csa-dc.org
Jenny Adlakha, Marketing Specialist
Cathy Garman, Senior VP
Ron Mueller, Director
Membership/Marketing
Scot Munro, Executive Editor
Chris Jahn, President
Represents the government services contracting industry. Membership ranges from small businesses and corporations servicing federal and state government in numerous capacities. CSA acts to foster the effective implementation of the government's policy of reliance on the private sector for support services.
650 Members Founded: 1965

10749 Council for Excellence in Government
1301 K Street NW
Suite 450 W
Washington, DC 20005
202-728-0418
FAX: 202-728-0422
ceg@excelgov.org www.excelgov.org
Patricia McGinnis, President/CEO
Joseph E Kasputys, Treasurer
J T Smith II, Secretary
Nonprofit, non-partisan agency that works to improve the performance of government.

10750 Council for State Community Development
1825 K Street
Suite 515
Washington, DC 20006
202-935-5820
FAX: 202-293-2820
dtaylor@coscda.org www.coscda.org
Dianne Taylor, Executive Director
Marcia J Sigal, Director
Employees of state community affairs agencies.
48 Members

10751 Council of Governors Policy Advisors
400 North Capitol Street, Hall of the States
Suite 390
Washington, DC 20001
202-247-7806
FAX: 202-624-7846
Matthew Chase, Executive Director
170 Members

10752 Council of Governors' Policy Advisors
400 N Capitol Street NW
Washington, DC 20001-1511
202-624-1512
FAX: 202-624-7846
Alice Tetelman, Executive Director
Comprised of planning and policy executives.
170 Members

10753 Council of State Community Affairs Agencies
Hall of States
444 N Capitol Street NW
Suite 251
Washington, DC 20001-1512
202-083-3860
John Horsley, Executive Director
Promotes national common interests in housing, infrastructure, community development, local economic development and government relations. Provides information, education and technical assistance.

10754 Council of State Governments
2760 Research Park Drive
PO Box 11910
Lexington, KY 40578-1910
859-244-8000
FAX: 859-244-8001 800-800-1910
web_editor@csg.org www.csg.org
Daniel Sprague, Executive Director
Laura Williams, Deputy Director
C B Baize, Administration Director
Research and service agency for state governments and state officials.
Founded: 1933

10755 Council on Licensure, Enforcement and Regulation
403 Marquis Avenue
Suite 100
Lexington, KY 40502-2104
859-269-1289
FAX: 859-231-1943
clear@uky.campuscw.net
www.clearhq.org
Pamela Brinegar, Executive Director
Members include occupational and professional licensing boards and agencies and private interests in the 50 states, territories and Canada.
380 Members Founded: 1980

10756 Digital Government Institute
6213 Crathie Lane
Bethesda, MD 20816
301-320-4397
FAX: 301-320-0268
www.digitalgovernment.com
DGI is a network of public sector practitioners and leaders that provides education on new business practices and how to recognize and implement them in this era of constant change.

10757 Energy Bar Association
1020 19th Street NW
Suite 525
Washington, DC 20036
202-223-5625
FAX: 202-833-5596
admin@eba-net.org www.eba-net.org
Frederic G Berner Jr, President
Lorna Johnson Wilson, Public Relations
John E McCaffrey, Secretary
Lawyers engaged in promoting excellence in the administration of laws relating to the production, development, conservation, delivery and economic regulation of energy and non-attorney professionals employed in a professional capacity in an energy company/trade association, federal, state or local government organization having jurisdiction over energy companies; employed in a professional capacity in firms providing professional services to energy COS/government organization.
2300 Members Founded: 1946

10758 Federal Bar Association
2215 M Street NW
Washington, DC 20037
202-785-1614
FAX: 202-785-1568
fba@fedbar.org www.fedbar.org
Thomas Shuck, President
Robyn J Spalter, VP
William N LaForge, Treasurer
Members are attorneys in the Federal Government or who have interest in federal law.
16000 Members Founded: 1920

10759 Federal Facilities Council
2001 Wisconsin Anenue NW
Harris Building, Suite 274
Washington, DC 20007-0007
202-334-3374
FAX: 202-334-3370
Lynda Stanley, Director
Members are professional employees of federal agencies and members of the Board on Infrastructure and the Constructed Environment of the National Research Council. Encourages cooperation among sponsoring federal agencies.
130 Members Founded: 1952

10760 Federal Investigators Association
935 Pennsylvania Avenue NW
Room 7972
Washington, DC 20535
FAX: 202-324-4705 www.fbi.gov
Ernest Alexander, National President
Formerly the United States Treasury Agents.
5M Members

10761 Federal Law Enforcement Officers Association
PO Box 508
Lewisberry, NY 17339
717-938-2300
FAX: 717-932-2262
services@fleoa.org www.fleoa.org
Art Gordon, President
John D Amat, VP Operations
John Adler, National Executive VP
Represents federal law enforcement officers and criminal investigators.
23000 Members Founded: 1977

10762 Federal Managers Association
1641 Prince Street
Alexandria, VA 22314-2818
703-683-8700
FAX: 703-683-8707
info@fedmanagers.org
www.fedmanagers.org
Michael Styles, President
Darryl A Perkinson, VP
Didier-Kim Q Trinh, Executive Director
Richard J Oppedisano, Secretary
Membership includes managers and supervisorss in all federal agencies.
15M Members Founded: 1913

10763 Federal Physicians Association
12427 Hedges Run Drive
Suite 1
Lakeridge, VA 22192
703-426-8100
FAX: 703-426-8400 800-403-3374
info@fedphy.org www.fedphy.org
Dennis Boyd, Manager
The purpose of the Federal Physicians Association is to improve the practice of medicine within the federal government; and to improve the working conditions and benefits of Federal Civil Service Physicians.
400 Members Founded: 1979

10764 Federation of Tax Administrators
444 North Capitol Street NW
Suite 348
Washington, DC 20001-1512
202-624-5890
FAX: 202-624-7888 www.taxadmin.org
Harley Duncan, Executive Director
Members are the tax agencies of the 50 state governments, the District of Columbia & New York City.

10765 Fund for Constitutional Government
122 Maryland Avenue NE
Washington, DC 20002
202-546-3799
FAX: 202-543-3156
funcongov@aol.com www.epic.org/fcg
Anne Zill, President
Russell D Hemenway, Chairperson
James Abourezk, Advisory Board
Conrad Martin, Executive Director
Tracy L Glisson, Secretary
Seeks to expose and correct illegal activities, corruption, and lack of accountability in the federal government.
Founded: 1974

10766 Fund for Open Information and Accountability
PO Box 22397
Brooklyn, NY 11202-2397
Adele Ottman, Acting Director
Maintains speakers bureaus and archives of news clippings and scholastic articles on a number of topics relating to the implementations and uses of the Freedom of Information Act, Intelligence Agency abuses and the right to know laws.

10767 Government Finance Officers Association
203 N LaSalle Street
Suite 2700
Chicago, IL 60601-1210
312-977-9700
FAX: 312-977-4806 www.gfoa.org
Jeffrey Esser, Executive Director
GFOA is the professional association of state/provincial and local finance officers in the United States and Canada, and has served the public finance profession.
15500 Members Founded: 1906

10768 Government National Mortgage Association - Ginnie Mae
Department of Housing and Urban Development
451 7th Street SW
Room 6151
Washington, DC 20410-0001
202-863-2800
FAX: 202-708-4117
www.ginniemae.gov/about/contract.htm
Susan M Taylor
Supports government housing objectives by establishing secondary markets for residential mortgages. Through its mortgage-backed securities programs, Ginnie Mae creates a vehicle for channeling funds from the securities markets into the mortgage market and helps to increase the supply of credit available for housing.
Founded: 1968

10769 Hispanic Elected Local Officials
National League of Cities
1301 Pennsylvania Avenue NW
6th Floor
Washington, DC 20004-1763
202-393-4230
FAX: 202-626-3043
Mary Gordon, Staff Liaison
Serves as a forum for communication and exchange among Hispanic local government officials within the framework of the National League of Cities.
100+ Members Founded: 1976

10770 Housing Assistance Council
1025 Vermont Avenue NW
Suite 606
Washington, DC 20005
202-842-8600
FAX: 202-347-3441
hac@ruralhome.org
www.ruralhome.org
Moises Loza, Executive Director
Joe Belden, Deputy Executive Director
Lilla Sutton, Executive Coordinator
Karin Klusmann, Director Loan Fund Division
Theodore J Russell, Director Finance
Expands the pool of decent housing available to the rural poor. Creates and sustains interest and action from all levels of government concerning rural housing for low-income people and helps rural housing organizations become more productive and professional.
30 Members Founded: 1971

10771 Interagency Council on the Homeless
US Department of Housing and Urban Development
451 7th Street SW
Suite 7274
Washington, DC 20410-0001
202-708-1480
www.ich.gov
Anthony Principi, Chairman/Secretary
Seeks to evaluate and monitor federal activities for the homeless, collect information, study problems related to homelessness and disseminate information. Provides technical and professional assistance to the State and local governments and other public and private organizations to maximize resources and develop innovative programs to help the homeless.
Founded: 1987

10772 International Association for Food Protection
6200 Aurora Avenue
Suite 200W
Des Moines, IA 50322-2864
515-276-3344
FAX: 515-276-8655 800-369-6337
info@foodprotection.org
www.foodprotection.org
Kathy Glass, President
Jeffrey M Farber, VP
Frank Yiannas, Secretary
David W T Tharp, Executive Director
A nonprofit educational association of food protection professionals. The association is dedicated to the education and service of its members, specifically, as well as industry personnel.
3000 Members Founded: 1911

10773 International Association of Chiefs
515 N Washington Street
Alexandria, VA 22314
703-836-6767
FAX: 703-836-4543 800-843-4227
information@theiacp.org
www.theiacp.org
Mary Ann Viverette, President
Daniel N Rosenblatt, Executive Director
Supports law enforcement professionals with a wide variety of services, including conducting management and operational services, presenting training programs and materials, establishing law enforcement policies and procedures, publishing a professional monthly magazine and research.
$25.00
20000 Members Monthly Founded: 1893

10774 International Association of Correctional Officers
PO Box 81826
Lincoln, NE 68501
312-341-6340
www.acsp.uic.edu/iaco
James Clark, President
Correctional officers and juvenile administrators.
9.5M Members

10775 International Association of Fire Chiefs
4025 Fair Ridge Drive
Suite 300
Fairfax, VA 22033-2868
703-273-0911
FAX: 703-273-9363 www.iafc.org
Gary L Briese, Executive Director
Ernie Mitchell, President
Bob DiPoli, First VP

William D Killen, Second VP
Julian Taliaferro, Treasurer

Members are chief fire officers, equipment manufacturers and others concerned with fire prevention, protection and emergency services management.

12000 Members Founded: 1873

10776 International Association of Fish & Wildlife Agencies
444 N Capitol Street NW
Suite 544
Washington, DC 20001
202-624-7890
FAX: 202-624-7891
iafwa@sso.org www.sso.org/iafwa

C Thomas Bennett, President
Terry Crawforth, VP
John Baughman, Executive VP

Established as the National Association of Game Commissioners. State plus some Canadian and Mexican fish and wildlife resources.

425 Members Founded: 1902

10777 International Association of Milk Control Agencies
Department of Agriculture
Division of Dairy Industry Services
Albany, NY 12235-0001
518-457-3880
FAX: 518-485-5816

Lyle Newcomb, Secretary/Treasurer
Charles Huff, Manager

26 Members Founded: 1935

10778 International Association of Official
444 N Capitol Street NW
Suite 536
Washington, DC 20001
202-624-5410
FAX: 202-624-8185
iaohra@sso.org www.sso.org

James Stowe, President
Rodney Braxton, VP
Paula Haley, Secretary
Homer Floyd, Treasurer
Shannon Bennett, Manager

Members are state and local government human rights and human relations agencies.

200 Members

10779 International Code Council
4051 W Flossmoor Road
Country Club Hills, IL 60478
708-799-2300
FAX: 800-799-4981 800-214-4321

Paul K Heilstedt, President

A nonprofit membership association dedicated to preserving the public health, safety and welfare in the built environment through the promulgation of model codes suitable for adoption by governmental entities and assisting code enforcement officials, design professionals, builders, manufacturers and others involved in the design, construction and regulatory processes.

16M Members Founded: 1915 16 K names

10780 International Downtown Association
1250 H Street NW 10th Floor
Washington, DC 20005-2603
202-393-6801
FAX: 202-393-6869
ida@atlantech.net
www.ida-downtown.org

Elizabeth Jackson, President

Founded in 1954, the International Downtown Association has more than 650 member organizations worldwide in North America, Europe, Asia and Africa. Through a network of committed individuals, a rich body of knowledge and unique capacity to nurture community-building partnerships, IDA is a guiding force in creating healthy and dynamic centers that anchor the well being of towns, cities and regions of the world.

600 Members Founded: 1954
Mailing list available for rent 600 names

10781 International Municipal Signal Association
165 E Union Street
PO Box 539
Newark, NY 14513-539
315-331-2182
FAX: 315-331-8205 800-723-4672
info@imsasafety.org
www.imsasafety.org

Don Fullerton, President
Marilyn Lawrence, Executive Director
Gregory Bothwell, First VP
Norm Akin, Second VP
Lenny Addair, Third VP

The leading international resource for information, education and certification for public safety.

10000 Members Founded: 1896

10782 Interstate Council on Water Policy
51 Monroe Street
Suite PE-08A
Rockville, MD 20850
301-984-1908
FAX: 301-984-5841
icwp2005@yahoo.com www.icwp.org

Joe Hoffman, Past Chairman
Peter Evans, Executive Director
Steven Oltmans, Secretary/Treasurer

The ICWP is the national organization of state and regional water resources management agencies. It provides a means for memebers to exchange information, ideas and experience to work with federal agencies which share water management responsibilities.

70 Members

10783 Interstate Oil and Gas Compact Commission
PO Box 53127
Oklahoma City, OK 73152-3127
405-525-3556
FAX: 405-525-3592 800-822-4015
iogcc@iogcc.state.ok.us
www.iogcc.state.ok.us

Gov Frank Murkowski, Chairman
John Norman, Vice Chairman
Christine A Hansen, Executive Director

A multi-state government agency that champions the conservation and efficient recovery of domestic oil and natural gas resources.

700 Members Founded: 1935

10784 National Academy of Public Administration
1100 New York Avenue NW
1090 East
Washington, DC 20005
202-347-3190
FAX: 202-393-0993
roneill@napawash.org
www.napawash.org

C Morgan Kinghorn, President
Terry Buss, Director International Programs

An independent, non-profit organization chartered by Congress to improve governance at all levels- local, regional, state, national and international.

500 Members Founded: 1967

10785 National Affordable Housing Management
400 N Columbus Street
Suite 203
Alexandria, VA 22314
703-683-8630
FAX: 703-683-8634 www.nahma.org

Kris C Cook Cae, Executive Director
Daria Jakubowski, Deputy Director
Michelle Kitchen, Director Government Affairs
Jessica L Allen, Program Manager

Trade association representing individuals involved in the management of affordable multifamily housing.

3000 Members Founded: 1989

10786 National Alliance of State and Territorial
444 N Capitol Street NW
Suite 339
Washington, DC 20001
202-434-8090
FAX: 202-434-8092
nastad@nastad.org www.nastad.org

Chris Aldridge, Prevention Program Specialist
Deepa Bhat, Evaluation Specialist
Julie Scofield, Executive Director

Provides support to the directors of the state and territorial health departments.

59 Members Founded: 1992

10787 National Assembly of State Arts Agencies
1029 Vermont Avenue NW
2nd Floor
Washington, DC 20005
202-347-6352
FAX: 202-737-0526
nasaa@nasaa-arts.org
www.nasaa-arts.org

Anthony Gittens, Executive Director
Dorothy McSweeny, Chairman
Jose Dominguez, Public Information
Dennis Dewey, Manager

NASAA's mission is to advance and promote a meaningful role for the arts in the lives of individuals, families and communities throughout the United States. We empower state art agencies through strategic assistance that fosters leadership, enhances planning and decision making, and increases resources.

56 Members Founded: 1968

10788 National Association County Information Officers
440 1st Street NW
Washington, DC 20001-2028
202-936-6226
FAX: 202-393-2630 www.naco.org

G Thomas Goodman, Staff Liason
Anthony Giancola, Executive Director

Members are county public information officers and staff.

300 Members Founded: 1965

10789 National Association for County Community and Economic Development
2025 M Street NW
Suite 800
Washington, DC 20036-3309
202-367-1224
FAX: 202-367-2149 www.nacced.org

John C Murphy, Executive Director
Carmel McGuire, Coordinator
Tracy McCrimmon, Aministrative Coordinator

Members are directors and staff members of county, community and economic development agencies.

135 Members Founded: 1989

10790 National Association for Search and Rescue
PO Box 232020
Centreville, VA 20120-8020
703-222-6277
FAX: 703-222-6283 877-893-0702
jackig@nasar.org www.nasar.org

Randy Servis, President
Jim Stumpf, Secretary
Larry Pugh, Treasurer
Cole Brown, External Affairs
Norm Rooker, Technical Programs

Members belong to various emergency medical, fire or survival rescue services.

3M Members

10791 National Association for State Community Service Programs
609 H Street NE
5th Floor
Washington, DC 20002
202-723-0800
FAX: 202-727-6881

Marjorie J Witherspoon, Executive Director

Members are state administrators of federal Community Service Block Grant and Low Income Weaterization Assistance programs. Monthly newsletter poverty issues such as welfare reform and upcoming conferences

100 Members Founded: 1968

10792 National Association of
Alexandria Group
10366 Democracy Lane
Suite B
Fairfax, VA 22030
703-691-0377

info@nagc.com www.nagc.com
A merger of Federal Editors Association, the Government Information Organization, and the Armed Forces Writers League.

10793 National Association of Attorneys General
750 1st Street NE
Suite 1100
Washington, DC 20002
202-897-7484
FAX: 202-408-7014 www.naag.org

Lynne Ross, Executive Director
William H Sorrell, President
Steve Carter, VP

Fosters interstate cooperation on legal and law enforcement issues, conducts policy research and analysis, provides advocacy.

56 Members Founded: 1907
Mailing list available for rent 56 names

10794 National Association of Conservation Districts (NACD)
509 Capitol Court Northeast
Washington, DC 20002-4937
202-547-6223
FAX: 202-547-6450
Bill-Wilson@nacdnet.org
www.nacdnet.org/

Bill Wilson, President
Krysta Harden, Chief Executive Officer
John Redding, Secretary/Treasurer
Arthur Ganta, Director Finance & Administration
Keira Franz, Director Government Affairs

NACD develops national conservation policies, influences lawmakers and builds partnerships with other agencies and organizations. NACD also provides services to its districts to help them share ideas in order to better serve their local communities.

17000 Members Founded: 1946

10795 National Association of Counties
440 1st Street NW
Washington, DC 20001-2028
202-393-6226
FAX: 202-393-2630
agoldsch@naco.org www.naco.org

Tom Sweet, Corporate Relations Director
Andrew Goldschmidt, Membership/Marketing Director
Larry Naake, Chief Executive Officer

We ensure that the nation's 3066 counties are heard and understood in the White House and the halls of Congress. NACo's membership totals more than 2,000 counties, representing over 80 percent of the nation's population. provides an extensive line of services including legislative, research, technical, and public affairs assistance, as well as enterprise services to its members.

Founded: 1935

10796 National Association of County Engineers
440 1st Street NW
Washington, DC 20001-2028
202-393-5041
FAX: 202-393-2630
nace@naco.org
www.countyengineers.org

Anthony R Giancola, Executive Director
Bonnie M West, Assistant Executive Director

Members are county engineering professionals or road management authorities.

1700 Members Founded: 1956

10797 National Association of County Health Facility Administrators
440 1st Street NW
Washington, DC 20001-2028
202-393-6226
FAX: 202-942-4281

Jennifer Wilson, Staff Liaison
Anthony Giancola, Executive Director

Works to improve the quality of health care available from county nursing homes and other long-term care institutions. An affiliate organization of The National Association of Counties.

240 Members Founded: 1978

10798 National Association of County Information Technology Administrators
440 1st Street NW
Washington, DC 20001-2028
202-393-6226
FAX: 202-393-2630 www.naco.org

Anne Powell, Staff Liason
Larry Naake, Chief Executive Officer

Founded: 1935

10799 National Association of County and City Health Officials
1100 17th Street NW
2nd Floor
Washington, DC 20036
202-265-7546
FAX: 202-783-1583

Patrick Libbey, Executive Director

Non-profit organization membership organization serving health departments nationwide in cities, counties, townships and districts. Provides education information, research and technical assistance; facilitates partnerships among local and state and federal agencies.

3000 Members Founded: 1966

10800 National Association of Government Archives and Records Administrators
90 State Street
Suite 1009
Albany, NY 12207
518-463-8644
FAX: 518-463-8656
nagara@caphill.com www.nagara.org

Mary Beth Herkert, President
Tracey Berezansky, VP

Local, state, and federal records administrators and others concerned with improving administration of government records.

10801 National Association of Housing
1707 H Street NW
Suite 201
Washington, DC 20006
202-737-0797
FAX: 202-783-7869
info@coophousing.org
www.coophousing.org

Barbara Meskunas, Chair
Bill Magee, President
Albert F Pennisi, Executive VP
Mark Shernicoff, Treasurer
Douglas Kleine, Executive Director

Provides up to date information on issues of interest to the cooperative housing community.

10 Members Founded: 1960

10802 National Association of Housing and
630 Eye Street NW
Washington, DC 20001
202-289-3500
FAX: 202-289-8181 877-866-2476
nahro@nahro.org www.nahro.org

James M Inglis, President
Donald J Cameron, Senior VP
Joseph E Gray Jr, VP
Elizabeth C Morris, VP Housing
Saul Ramirez, Manager

A professional membership association representing local housing authorities, community development agencies and individual professionals in the housing, community development and redevelopment fields.

700 Members Founded: 1933

10803 National Association of Local Housing Finance Agencies
2025 M Street NW
Suite 800
Washington, DC 20036-3309
202-367-1197
FAX: 202-367-2197
john_murphy@nalhfa.org
www.nalhfa.org

John C Murphy, Executive Director
Scott Lynch, Association Manager
Kim McKinon, Coordinator Membership

Regular memebers of NALHFA are primarily county and city agencies which finance, directly or indirectly, affordable housing through a variety of means: tax-exempt and taxable bonds, federal grant programs, and state and local subsidies. Affiliate members are organizations providing technical assistance to local agencies.
Founded: 1982

10804 National Association of Neighborhoods
1300 Pennsylvania Avenue NW
Suite 700
Washington, DC 20004
202-332-7766
FAX: 202-332-2314
staff@nanworld.org
www.nanworld.org

Cleta Winslow, Chairperson
Sam Thompson Jr, Board Member
Richard Adams, Board Member
Frances Walker, Board Member
Essie Wiggins, Board Member

A national umbrella organization to provide a policy voice for 40 neighborhood groups. NAN operates as an information resource, lobbyist and project director for neighborhood organizations and coalitions. The projects work to develop and improve skills of community-based organizations to negotiate and execute service delivery contracts with local governments.

2500 Members Founded: 1975

10805 National Association of Postmasters of the United States
8 Herbert Street
Alexandria, VA 22305-2600
703-683-9027
FAX: 703-683-6820
napusinfo@napus.org www.napus.org

Dale Goff, President
Robert J Rapoza, Secretary/Treasurer
Charlie Moser, Executive Director
Bob Levi, Director of Government Relations
Gerri Swarm, Executive Assistant

Sponsors and supports the Political Education for Postmasters Political Action Committee.
41M Members

10806 National Association of Regional Councils
1666 Connecticut Avenue NW
Suite 300
Washington, DC 20009
202-457-0710
FAX: 202-986-1038
rsoko@narc.org www.narc.org

F Wayne Hill, President
Randall Morris, VP
Kenneth J Sweet, Second VP

State of regional repositories of instructional materials or services.
250 Members

10807 National Association of Regulatory Utility Commissioners (NARUC)
1101 Vermont NW
Suite 200
Washington, DC 20005
202-898-2200
FAX: 202-898-2213
admin@naruc.org www.naruc.org

Diane Munns, President
James Y Kerr III, First VP
Marsha Smith, Second VP

NARUC is a nonprofit organization whose members include the government agencies that are engaged in the regulation of utilities and carriers in the fifty states, the District of Columbia, Puerto Rico & the Virgin Islands.

10808 National Association of State Development
12884 Harbor Drive
Woodbridge, VA 22192
703-490-6777
FAX: 703-492-4404
spope@nasda.com www.nasda.com

Miles Friedman, President/CEO
Sally Pope, Director Finance
Pofen Salem, Project Manager

Established to provide a forum for directors of state economic development agencies to exchange information, compare programs, and establish an organizational base to approach the Federal Government on issues of mutual interest.
250 Members Founded: 1946

10809 National Association of State Facilities
2760 Research Park Drive
PO Box 11910
Lexington, KY 40578-1910
859-244-8000
FAX: 859-244-8001 800-800-1910
web_editor@csg.org www.csg.org

Daniel Sprague, Executive Director/CEO
Laura Williams, Director Membership/Marketing
CB Baize, Director Finance/Administration
John Ruffin, President

State administrators of facilities and property.

10810 National Association of Towns and Townships
4855 Woodland Dr
Enola, PA 17025-1262
202-624-3550
FAX: 202-624-3554
natat@sso.org www.natat.org

Bryan Smith, President
Michael Cochran, VP
Keith Hite, Secretary/Treasurer

A nonprofit membership organization offering technical assistance, educational services and public policy support to local officials from more than 13,000 town and township governments across the country. The purpose is to strengthen the effectiveness of town and township governments and promote their interests in the public and private sectors.
13M Members

10811 National Association of WIC Directors
2001 S Street NW
Washington, DC 20009
202-232-5492
FAX: 202-387-5281
khummons@nwica.org
www.nwica.org

Betsy Clarke, President
Douglas Greenaway, Executive Director

Members are geographic state, Native American state and local agency directors of the Special Supplement nutrition program for women, infants and children.
800 Members Founded: 1983

10812 National Border Patrol Council
7320 N La Cholla Boulevard
#154-534
Tucson, AZ 85741-2354
520-219-5152
FAX: 520-219-5154
president@local2544.org
www.borderpatrol1613.org

TJ Bonner, President
Rich Pierce, Executive VP

Labor union representing employees of the US border patrol.
69000 Members Founded: 1965

10813 National Center for Neighborhood
1625 K. Street NW
Suite 1200
Washington, DC 20006
202-518-6500
FAX: 202-588-0314 866-518-6500
info@ncne.com www.ncne.com

Robert L Woodson Sr, President

The Center's mission is to empower neighborhood leaderbohood leaders to promote solutions that reduce crime and violence, restore families, revitalize low-income communities, and create economic enterprise.
Founded: 1981

10814 National Community Development Association
522 21st Street NW
Suite 120
Washington, DC 20006-5012
202-293-7587
FAX: 202-887-5546
www.nedaonline.org

Shandra Western, Editor

A national nonprofit membership organization representing local governments that implement community development programs. The members administer federally supported community development, housing and human services programs. NCDA provides counsel at the federal level on new program design and current program implementation and advocates on behalf of responsive community development.
503 Members Founded: 1970

10815 National Conference of Black Mayors
1151 Cleveland Avenue
Building D
East Point, GA 30344
404-765-6444
FAX: 404-765-6430
info@ncbm.org
www.blackmayors.org

Roosevelt F Dorn, President
Robert L Bowser, First VP
L Grace George, Treasurer
Vanessa Williams, Executive Director

An outgrowth of the Southern Conference of Black Mayors. One of the principal functions is to provide management and technical assistance to its members, many of whom represent small rural towns that do not have professional management or community development staffs.

542 Members Founded: 1974

10816 National Conference of State Legislatures

7700 East First Place
Denver, CO 80230
303-364-7700
FAX: 303-364-7800
deana.blackwood@ncsl.org
www.ncsl.org

William T Pound, Executive Director
Leticia Van de Putte, President
Steven Rauschenberger, VP
Max Arinder, Staff Chair

Bipartisan organization dedicated to serving the lawmakers and staffs of the nation's 50 states, its commonwealths and territories.

13M+ Members Founded: 1975

10817 National Conference on Weights and

15245 Shady Grove Road
Suite 130
Rockville, MD 20850
240-632-9454
FAX: 301-990-9771
ncwm@mgmtsol.com www.ncwm.net

H Oppermann, Executive Secretary
D Ehrhart, Chairman
Beth Palys, President
Arden Bement Jr, Honorary President
Beth Palys, Executive Director

Members are weights and measures enforcement officials from Federal, state, county, and local governments; associate members from industry.

10818 National Council State Emergency Medical

201 Park Washington Court
Falls Church, VA 22046

FAX: 703-241-5603 888-240-4696
info@ncsemstc.org www.nscemstc.org

Dwight Corning, Chairman
Steve Mercer, Vice Chairman
John Gosford, Secretary
Kay Hollingsworth, Treasurer
Larry Weber, Parliamentarian

Members are supervisors or coordinators of state EMS training programs (limited to three members from each state.).

10819 National Council for Urban Economic Development

1730 K Street NW
Suite 700
Washington, DC 20006-3834
202-081-1047
FAX: 202-223-4745
mail@urbandevelopment.com
www.cued.org

Jeff Sinkle, President
Jeff Stone, VP

A national membership organization serving public and private participants in economic development across the United States and in international settings. CUED provides information to its members who build local economies through the tools used for job creation, attraction and retention. CUED members include public economic development directors, chamber of commerce staff, utility executives and academicians, plus the many other professionals who help design and implement development programs

1.8M Members Founded: 1967

10820 National Council of State Housing Agencies

Hall of States
444 N Capitol Street NW
Suite 438
Washington, DC 20001
202-083-3860
FAX: 202-624-5899
bthompson@ncsha.org www.ncsha.org

Robert Strickland, President
Richard H Godfrey Jr, VP
Kim Herman, Secretary
Susan F Dewey, Treasurer
Barbara Thompson, Executive Director

Represents the views of state housing finance agencies in 48 states. A high priority for the Council is promoting the views of state housing agencies on the issue of delivery of housing financing for low and moderate income people. Other priorities include increasing the stock of affordable rental units and generating innovative approaches to providing public housing acceptable to residents and communities.

350 Members Founded: 1974

10821 National Distric Attorneys Association

National District Attorneys Association
99 Canal Center Plaza
Suite 510
Alexandria, VA 22314
703-549-9222
FAX: 703-836-3195
hr@ndaa.org www.ndaa-apri.org

Mathia H Heck Jr, President
M David Barber, VP
Jerry M Blair, VP
Thomas Charron, Executive Director
Dino Amoroso, Associate Director

Voice of America's prosecutors and to support their efforts to protect the rights and safety of the people.

7000 Members Founded: 1950

10822 National Emergency Management

PO Box 11910
Lexington, KY 40578
859-244-8175
FAX: 859-244-8239
nemaadmin@csg.org
www.nemaweb.org

Trina Hembree, Executive Director
Karen Cobuluis, Meeting/Marketing Coordinator
Amy Hughes, Policy Analyst
Emily DeMers, Executive Director

Members include federal agencies, local emergency management representatives and interested individuals, associations and corporations.

263 Members Founded: 1970

10823 National Forum for Black Public Administrators

ICMA Publications
777 N Capitol Street NE
Suite 807
Washington, DC 20002-4239
202-624-4600
FAX: 202-408-8558
nfbpa@erols.com www.nfbpa.org

James Wright, Executive Director

An association for public administrators.

2.8M Members Founded: 1983

10824 National Governors' Association

Hall of States
444 N Capitol Street NW
Suite 250
Washington, DC 20001-1512
202-508-3860

Ray Scheppach, Executive Director

Coordinates the formulation of state policies by governors, and works to ensure consideration of these positions in the development of national policies and programs. The governors belong to seven standing committees: agriculture; community and economic development; justice and public protection; energy and environment; human resources; international trade; and foreign relations.

10825 National Housing Law Project

614 Grand Avenue
Suite 320
Oakland, CA 94610
510-251-9400
FAX: 510-451-2300
nhlp@nhlp.org www.nhlp.org

Gideon Anders, Executive Director
Elaine Beale, Development Consultant
Sylvia Brennan, Staff Attorney
Louis Briones, Controller
Maeve Elise Brown, Staff Attorney

A nonprofit corporation that provides assistance on public and private housing and community development matters to Legal Services attorneys and housing specialists throughout the country. The project's goals are to produce, maintain and conserve low and moderate income housing and protect and expand the rights of lower income persons to decent and affordable housing.

Founded: 1968

10826 National Institute of Governmental Purchasing

151 Spring Street
Suite 300
Herndon, VA 20170-5223
703-736-8900
FAX: 703-736-9644 www.nigp.org

Provides its members with education, research, technical assistance and networking opportunities in public purchasing.

10827 National Labor Relations Board of

1617 Duke Street
Alexandria, VA 22314
703-836-9626
FAX: 703-836-9628 800-296-2230
info@npelra.org www.npelra.org

Matthew W Iarocci, President
Michael D Suppan, Executive VP
Denyce L Holsey, VPs
James Richter, Labor Relations Manager
Teresa Rotschafer, Secretary-Treasurer

Represents members in contract negotiations and grievance laws.

Founded: 1935

10828 National League of Cities

1301 Pennsylvania Avenue NW
Suite 550
Washington, DC 20004
202-263-3169
FAX: 202-626-3043
inet@nlc.org www.nlc.org

Melissa Assion, Manager Program Development
William Barnes, Director Research
Katherine Barnes, Manager Policy Analysis
David Bean, Director Information Technology
Christine Becker, Deputy Executive Director

Advocates on behalf of cities and regularly monitors all three branches of the Federal Government. Promotes the National Municpal Policy developed and adopted by member cities at the annual Congress of Cities.

1700 Members Founded: 1924

10829 National Public Employer Labor
1617 Duke Street
Alexandria, VA 22314

FAX: 703-836-9628 800-296-2230
info@npelra.org www.npelra.org

Roger E Dahl, Executive Director
Michael D Suppan, Executive VP
Denyce L Holsey, VP
James J Pendergast, President
Denyce L Holsey, VP

Members are federal, state, county and municipal labor and employee relations professionals.

10830 National Rural Housing Coalition
1250 I Street NW
Suite 902
Washington, DC 20005
202-393-5229
FAX: 202-393-3034
nrhc@nrhcweb.org www.nrhcweb.org

Peter Carey, President
Bob Rapoza, Legislative Director
Karen Spenkman, First VP

A national membership organization that advocates improved housing for low income rural families and works to increase public awareness of rural housing problems. The Coalition works with a network of state coalitions and nonprofit organizations to promote federal housing policy that benefits both rural housing and community development programs.

300 Members Founded: 1969

10831 North American Gaming Regulators
26 E Exchange Street
Suite 500
St. Paul, MN 55101
651-203-7244
FAX: 651-290-2266
info@nagra.org www.nagra.org

Dale Fuga, President
Kay Gaines, VP
Kathy Baertsch, Western US Regional Director
Jim Logue, Eastern US Regional Director
Bob Blessing, Secretary

Members are government entities involved in local, state, federal and provincial regulation of gambling activities.

120 Members Founded: 1984

10832 North American Securities Administrators
10 G Street NE
Suite 710
Washington, DC 20002
202-370-0900
FAX: 202-783-3571
info@nasaa.org www.nasaa.org

Ralph Lambiase, President
John H Lynch, Deputy Executive Director
Craig A Goettsch, Treasurer
Scott P Borchert, Director
Donald G Murray, Director

NASAA is the international organization representing 66 securities administrators from all 50 states, the District of Columbia, Canada, Mexico and Puerto Rico, and is responsible for investor protection and education. NASAA recommends national policies in the securities industry and provides model legislation for state securities agencies to adopt affecting the regulation of broker/dealers and investment advisers. Consumers can contact NASAA to get phone numbers of state securities regulators.

66 Members Founded: 1919

10833 Patent and Trademark Office Society
PO Box 2089
Arlington, VA 22202-0089
703-305-8340
www.ptos.org

Judy Swann, Administration/Communication

Members are examiners in the US Patent & Trademark Office, registered patent attorneys and agents, agencies, judges and other patent professionals.

1800 Members Founded: 1917

10834 Procurement Round Table
1464 Nieman Road
Shady Side, MD 20764
301-261-9918

Dr. John F Magnotti Jr, Secretary

Members provide advice on federal procurement policy.

40 Members Founded: 1984

10835 Prosecutor
National District Attorneys Association
99 Canal Center Plaza
Suite 510
Alexandria, VA 22314-1588
703-549-9222
FAX: 703-836-3195
jean.holt@ndaa-apri.org
www.ndaa-apri.org

Jean Holt, Director of Publication

To be the voice of America's prosecutors and to support their efforts to protect the rights and safety of the people.

7000 Members Founded: 1950 7000 names

10836 Public Employees Roundtable
500 N Capitol Street
Suite 1204
Washington, DC 20001
202-927-4926
FAX: 202-927-4920
info@theroundtable.org
www.patriot.net/users/permail

Adam Bratton, COO
Kirke Harper, Chairman
William Bransford, Vice Chairman
Dan C Galvan, Director at Large
Kevin Simpson, Director at Large

Demonstrates the value of government employees. Develops an 'espirit de corps' among public service employees and encourages public service careers.

20000 Members Founded: 1986

10837 Public Housing Authorities Directors Association
511 Capitol Center NE
Washington, DC 20002-4947
202-546-5445
FAX: 202-546-2280 www.phada.org

Larry Martin, Director Communication
Timothy Kaiser, Executive Director

Represents and serves the needs of executive directors of housing authorities of all sizes, in all regions of the nation. In pursuing the Association's goal of improving assisted housing, the corporation works with Congress and federal agencies as well as with all interested groups to improve the nation's housing programs.

1.6M Members Founded: 1979

10838 Republican Communications Association
PO Box 550
Washington, DC 20515-0001

David Redmond, Executive Director

Sponsors professional development and networking programs. Conducts seminars, briefings, and tours.

165 Members Founded: 1970

10839 Society of Government Economists
10371 Painted Cup
Columbia, MD 21044
877-743-3266

sge@sge-econ.org www.sge-econ.org

Nabeel Alsalam, Ex-Officio

Membership benefits economists employed in the public sector or who are interested in the economic aspects of government policies.

500 Members Founded: 1970

10840 State Governmental Affairs Council
1255 23rd Street NW
Suite 200
Washington, DC 20037-1174
202-742-2453
FAX: 202-833-3636
stategov@sgac.org www.sgac.org

HC Pete Poynter, President
Elizabeth Loudy, Executive Director

Seeks to improve the state legislative process through interaction with major state governmental conferences. Conducts educational programs on public policies to further understanding between private sector businesses and state legislations.

10841 State Higher Education Executive Officers
3035 Center Green Dr
Ste 100
Boulder, CO 80301-2205
303-541-1600
FAX: 303-541-1639
sheeo@sheeo.org www.sheeo.org

Dr. Paul E Lingenfelter, Executive Director

Members are the full-time chief executive officers serving statewide coordinating or governing boards of postsecondary education.

56 Members Founded: 1954

10842 Trust for Public Land
116 New Montgomery Street
San Francisco, CA 94105
415-954-4014
FAX: 415-495-4103
info@tpl.org www.tpl.org

John W Baird, Chairman
Brian M Beitner, Managing Director
James S Hoyte, Associate VP
Alex Tolkach, Manager

A nonprofit land acquisition and conservation organization, working with community groups, landowners, public land management agencies and rural groups to preserve open space lands and to pioneer methods of community ownership of land. Through its Investment Lands Program, the Trust for Public Land also acquires underutilized properties by gift or bargain sales.
Founded: 1972

10843 U.S. Chamber of Commerce
1615 H Street NW
Washington, DC 20062-2000
202-659-6000
800-638-6582

Thomas Donohue, President/CEO
Jeffrey Crowe, Chairman
John Bachmann, Vice Chairman

Provides a voice of experience and influence in Washington, DC and around the globe.

10844 US House Of Representatives
US House of Representatives
Washington, DC 20515
202-224-3121

info.clerkweb@mail.house.gov
www.house.gov
Sponsors professional development and networking programs. Conducts seminars, briefings, and tours.
165 Members Founded: 1970

10845 United States Conference of Mayors

1620 Eye Street NW
Washington, DC 20006
202-630-0999
FAX: 202-293-2352
info@usmayors.org
www.usmayors.org/uscm

Michael Guido, President
Donald L Plusquellic, VP
Beverly O'Neill, Chair Advisory Board

An organization of city government officials.
30000 Members Founded: 1987

10846 Urban Land Institute
1025 Thomas Jefferson Street
Washington, DC 20007
202-624-7000
FAX: 202-624-7140
ulifoundation@uli.org www.uli.org

Harry H Frampton III, Chairman
Richard Rosan, President
Joan Campbell, Manager

Founded to provide a land-use information resource for both the professionals and the public. ULI conducts seminars, workshops, semiannual meetings, research programs and publishes books on all aspects of land use and development issues. ULI offers an advisory service, and gives annual Awards for Excellence.
14M Members Founded: 1936

10847 Urban and Regional Information Systems
1460 Renaissance Drive
Suite 305
Park Ridge, IL 60068
847-824-6300
FAX: 847-824-6363
info@urisa.org www.urisa.org

Wendy Francis, CEO/Director Marketing
Christine Dionne, COO
Barbara Hirsch, CFO/Director Finance
Michele Meng, Membership Manager
Scott Grams, Education Certification Manager

Concerned with the effective use of information systems technology at the state, regional and local levels. Members informed of current developments in the information systems field. Its goal is to stimulate and encourage the advancement of an interdisciplinary professional approach to planning, designing and operating information systems.
3000 Members Founded: 1963

10848 World Federalist Association
418 7th Street SE
Washington, DC 20003
202-546-3950
FAX: 202-546-3749
info@globalsolutions.org

Aaron M Knight, Interim CEO
Don Kraus, Executive VP
Scott Hoffman, Director
Heather B Hamilton, VP Programs
Angela Kim, Development Manager

Nonprofit, tax deductible memebership organization of over 11,000, organized in approximately 50 chapters and groups throghout the United States. We work to educate policy-makers and the American public on issues of global governance, international law and grassroots activism.
34 Members Founded: 1978

Newsletters

10849 ADA Today
Americans for Democratic Action
1625 K Street NW
Suite 210
Washington, DC 20006-1611
202-785-5980
FAX: 202-785-5969
adaction@ix.netcom.com
www.kogod-b9.battelle1american

Valerie Dulk-Jacobs, Editor
Amy Isaacs, Executive Director

The nation's oldest liberal lobbying group. This newsletter describes national and local chapter activities and updates federal legislative action. *$20.00*
Quarterly
Circulation: 65000 Audited
Mailing list available for rent 65000 names
Printed in 2 colors on matte stock

10850 ADAction News and Notes
Americans for Democratic Action
1625 K Street NW
Suite 210
Washington, DC 20006-1611
202-785-5980
FAX: 202-785-5969
adaction@ix.netcom.com
http://www.adaction.com

Amy Isaacs, Editor
Jim McDermott, CEO
Don Kufler, Circulation Manager

Offers information on legislative issues and lobbying. *$20.00*
Weekly Founded: 1948
Circulation: 3000 Audited
Mailing list available for rent 3000 names
Printed in 1 color on matte stock

10851 American Independent
William Shearer
8158 Palm Street
Lemon Grove, CA 91945-3028
619-604-4484

William Shearer, Publisher

Discusses the activities and history of the American Independent party. *$15.00*
4 pages Monthly
Circulation: 800 Est. Pass-Along Circ: 800
Printed in 1 color

10852 American Planning Association
1776 Massachusetts Avenue NW
Suite 400
Washington, DC 20036-1904
202-872-0611
FAX: 202-872-0643
CustomerService@planning.org
http://www.planning.org/

Paul Farmer, Executive Director
Israel Stollman, Publisher
Raquel Lavin, Editor
Jeri Parish, Circulation Manager

Serves the field of city and regional planning. Accepts advertising. *$645.00*
Monthly Founded: 1917

10853 Assisted Housing Accounts & Audits Insider
Brownstone Publishers
149 5th Avenue
16th Floor
New York, NY 10010-6801
212-738-8200
FAX: 212-473-8786 800-643-8095
vendomecs@qualitycustomercare.com
http://www.vendomegrp.com

David B Klein, Editor
John M Striker, Publisher

Explains how to comply with regulatory STET requirements for accounting and auditing for HUD-assisted housing. Includes accounting control policies, audit preparation checklists, model accounting book entries, forms, staff memos and model letters.
$195.00
Monthly Founded: 1980
Printed in 2 colors on matte stock

10854 Assisted Housing Management Issue
Brownstone Publishers
149 5th Avenue
16th Floor
New York, NY 10010-6801
212-473-8200
FAX: 212-473-8786 800-643-8095
info@hcmarketplace.com
http://www.hcmarketplace.com

John Striker, Owner

Explains HUD regulatory requirements for federally-assisted housing, and gives advice on how to stay in compliance. Includes sample copies of model leases, clauses, letters, eviction notices, authorization forms, checklists and signs.

Printed in 2 colors on matte stock

10855 BMD Monitor
Pasha Publications
1616 N Fort Myer Dr
Suite 1000
Arlington, VA 22209-3107
703-528-1244
FAX: 703-528-1253 800-424-2908
bmdmon@pasha.com
http://www.newsletteraccess.com

Harry Baisden, Group Publisher
Anne Roosevelt, Editor

This newsletter is the only source available on the ballistic missile defense initiative. Contractors and scientists in the field look to BMD Monitor for a first alert to trends in the government's program to provide a defense against ballistic missiles. *$787.00*

10856 BNA's Eastern Europe Reporter
Bureau of National Affairs
1231 25th Street NW
Washington, DC 20037-1197
202-452-4200
800-372-1033
customercare@bna.com
http://www.bna.com

Gregory C McCaffery, Publisher
Basco Eszeki, Managing Editor

A biweekly notification service covering legislative, regulatory and legal developments affecting business, trade and investment in Eastern Europe and the former Soviet Union. *$1750.00*
Bi-annually

10857 CLEAR News
Council on Licensure, Enforcement and Regulation
PO Box 11910
Lexington, KY 40578-1910
859-244-8203
FAX: 859-244-8053

Lisa Smith-Peters, Editor

Provides timely information relative to the occupational and professional regulation and to CLEAR. Accepts advertising.
11 pages Quarterly
Circulation: 5,000
Mailing list available for rent
Printed in 2 colors on matte stock

10858 Census and You
Census Bureau
4700 Silver Hill Road
Washington, DC 20233
301-763-4748

genealogy@census.gov
http://www.census.gov

Neil Tillman, Editor

Highlights data products and program of the US Census Bureau. Shows which reports, CD-ROMs, tapes, etc. to choose and also highlights releases on the Internet. *$21.00*
12 pages Monthly Founded: 1790
Circulation: 11000 Audited
Printed in 2 colors on matte stock
Computerized version available

10859 Civil Rights-From the State Capitals
Wakeman Walworth
po box 7376
Suite 204
Alexandria, VA 22307-7276
703-768-9600
FAX: 703-768-9690
newsletters@statecapitals.com
http://www.statecapitals.com/civilrights.html

Keyes Walworth, Publisher/CEO
Allen Kelin, Editor
Christine Ryan, Marketing/Circulation Man

Covers civil rights and affirmative action legislation across the country, including ethic, race and sex discrimination, judicial decisions regarding desegregation, discrimination compensation, gay rights and civil rights of the disabled. *$275.00*
4 pages Weekly Founded: 1962
Printed in 1 color on matte stock
Computerized version available

10860 Collected Legislation of Russia
Oceana Publications
75 Main Street
Dobbs Ferry, NY 10522-1632
914-938-8100
FAX: 914-693-0402
marketing@oceanalaw.com
http://www.oceanalaw.com

William Butler, Publisher
Nancy Maron, Editor-in-chief

Monthly Founded: 1948

10861 Congressional Monitor Daily
Congressional Quarterly
1414 22nd Street NW
Washington, DC 20037-1003
202-887-8500

Offers information on House and Senate committee hearings scheduled for up to two months from publication date. *$1299.00*

10862 Cooperative Housing Bulletin
National Association of Housing Cooperatives
1707 H Street NW
Suite 201
Washington, DC 20006
202-737-0797
FAX: 202-783-7869
info@coophousing.org
http://www.coophousing.org

Alporia Ross, Director Publication
Boughlas Kleine, Head
Alporia Ross, Editor
Rejinad Becham, Marketing/Circulation Manager

Provides up-to-date information on issues of interest to the cooperative housing community. Accepts advertising.
Monthly
Circulation: 2500
Printed in 2 colors on matte stock

10863 Defense Acquisition Report
Callahan Publications
PO Box 1173
Mc Lean, VA 22101-1173
703-356-1925
FAX: 703-356-9614

Vincent F Callahan Jr, Editor

Covers opportunities and legislative initiatives for military procurement, acquisition, and research, development, test and evaluation. This report combines the Missile/Ordinance Letter and the Military research Letter. *$225.00*
8 pages BiWeekly
Printed in 1 color

10864 Democratic Communique
Union for Democratic Conventions
1016 61st Street
Oakland, CA 94608-2355

Janet Wasko, Publisher

News of Democratic and grassroots communications projects, issues and publications. *$20.00*
12 pages BiWeekly

10865 Downtown Idea Exchange
Alexander Communications Group
28 W 25th Street
8th Floor
New York, NY 10003-1600
212-280-0246
FAX: 212-228-1343 800-232-4317
info@downtowndevelopment.com
http://www.downtowndevelopment.com

Laurence Alexander, Owner
Nadine Harris, Marketing Manager

News of downtown revitalization for downtown leaders and officials in local and state government. *$167.00*
8 pages Monthly

10866 Downtown Promotion Reporter
Alexander Communications Group
28 W 25th Street
8th Floor
New York, NY 10010-1600
212-228-0246
FAX: 212-228-0376 800-232-4317
info@downtowndevelopment.com
http://www.downtowndevelopment.com

Margaret Dewitt, Marketing Manager
Laurence Alexander, CEO
Sarah Benardos, Production Manager
Paul Felt, Editor

Proven promotion ideas and methods to bring shoppers to downtown stores. *$189.00*
12 pages Monthly Founded: 1954
Circulation: 1000

10867 Economic Development: From the State Capitals
Wakeman Walworth
PO BOX 7376
Alexandria, VA 22307
703-768-9600
FAX: 703-768-9690
newsletters@statecapitals.com
http://www.statecapitals.com

Keyes Walworth, Publisher
Keyes Walworth, Editor
C Rayan, Marketing Manager

Covers the highly competitive efforts of states across the nation to attract new income, which includes new industry, new jobs, commerce and tourism. Also reports on a wide range of economic incentives and disincentives, including environmental requirements, mass transportation policies, highway construction plans, utility rates, changes in labor laws, tax policies and enterprise zones. *$275.00*
8 pages Weekly Founded: 1963
Printed in 1 color on Y stock

10868 Employee Policy for the Public and Private Sector - From the State Capitals
Wakeman Walworth
300 N Washington Street
Suite 204
Alexandria, VA 22314-2530
703-768-9600
FAX: 703-549-1372
newsletters@statecapitals.com
http://statecapitals.com/employeepolicy.html

Keyes Walworth, Publisher

Devoted to state labor laws, regulations and court decisions affecting employees in both the private sector and the public sector. Reports on working conditions, collective bargaining, dismissal practices and minimum wages, AIDS disclosure regulations, drug testing, workplace restrictions such as smoking bans, job discrimination, migrant and child labor, wage taxes, unemployment and workers compensation. *$235.00*

4 pages Monthly
Printed in 1 color on matte stock
Computerized version available

10869 EuroWatch
WorldTrade Executive
PO Box 761
Concord, MA 01742
978-287-0301
FAX: 978-287-0302 www.wtexec.com

Alison French, Production Manager

Analyzes the most recent EU judicial and legislative developments. Covers EU trade issues, labor issues, single market and currency issues, EU and individual country business law, trademark issues. *$797.00*

10870 Federal Action Affecting the States-From the State Capitals
Wakeman Walworth
P O Box 7376
Suite 204
Alexandria, VA 22307-2530
703-768-9600
FAX: 703-768-9690
newsletters@statecapitals.com
http://statecapitals.com/fedaction.html

Keyes Walworth, Publisher

Reports on key developments in Washington that impact on the states. Included are Federal court rulings, overseer programs, changes in state jurisdiction, federal funds for state programs including highway, drug abuse control, disaster and emergency programs. *$245.00*

4 pages Annual+ Founded: 1955
Printed in 1 color on matte stock
Computerized version available

10871 Federal Assistance Monitor
CD Publications
8204 Fenton Street
Silver Spring, MD 20910
301-588-0519
FAX: 301-588-6385 800-666-6380
hmr@cdpublications.com
http://www.cdpublications.com

Mike Gerecht, Publisher
Dave Kittross, Editor

Comprehensive review of federal funding announcements, private grants, rule changes and legislative actions affecting the community programs. *$419.00*

Monthly Founded: 1961
Mailing list available for rent 2,000 names $160 per M.

10872 Federal Employees News Digest
1850 Centennial Park Drive
Suite 520
Reston, VA 20191
703-648-9551
FAX: 703-648-0265 800-989-3363

Publishes weekly newsletter and self-help books for federal and postal employees on retirement and pay, as well as other benefit-related topics. Accepts advertising. *$49.00*

4 pages 5 per year Founded: 1951

10873 Federal Veterinarian
National Association of Federal Veterinarians
1101 Vermont Avenue NW
Suite 710
Washington, DC 20005-6308
202-289-6334
FAX: 202-842-4360
dboyle@nafv.org
http://users.erols.com/nafv/fedvet.htm

Joe Yearous, President
Michael Gilsdorf, VP
Dale Boyle, Editor

Association and legislative news related to public health, food safety, food animal disease control and federal veterinary employment. *$45.00*

12 pages Monthly Founded: 1922
Circulation: 2000
Printed in on matte stock

10874 Friday Flash
Coalition for Government Procurement
1990 M Street NW
Suite 400
Washington, DC 20036
202-331-0975
FAX: 202-822-9788
info@thecgp.org
http://www.thecgp.org

Larry Allen, Editor
Bruce McLellan, Executive Director

A weekly newsletter published by the Coalition for Government Procurement.

38387 pages Weekly Founded: 1979
Circulation: 1200

10875 From the State Capitals
Wakeman Walworth
PO BOX 7376
Alexandria, VA 22307-7376
703-768-9600
FAX: 703-768-9690
newsletters@statecapitals.com
http://statecapitals.com/

Keyes Walworth, Publisher

Keeps readers informed of national trends in domestic lawmaking. Issues dealing with taxes, the environment, economic development, drug abuse, abortion and education.

Founded: 1955

10876 Government Employee Relations Report
Bureau of National Affairs
1231 25th Street NW
Washington, DC 20037-1197
202-452-4200
800-372-1033
customercare@bna.com www.bna.com

Gregory C McCaffery, Publisher
James F Fitzpatrick, Managing Editor

A notification service that covers federal, state and municipal government employee relations. *$1479.00*

Weekly

10877 Government Report
American Advertising Federation
1101 Vermont Avenue NW
Suite 500
Washington, DC 20005-6306
202-898-0089
FAX: 202-898-0159
aaf@aaf.org http://www.aaf.org

Wallice Snyder, CEO
Robert Kohlmeyer, Editor

An exclusive bulletin detailing advertising-related legislative developments on the federal state and local level-and the AAF response.

Weekly Founded: 1905
Circulation: 1000

10878 Government Waste Watch Newspaper
Citizens Against Government Waste
1301 Connecticut Avenue NW
Suite 400
Washington, DC 20036
202-467-5300
FAX: 202-467-4253
membership@cagw.org
http://www.cagw.org

Thomas Schatz, President
Ariane C Sweeney, VP Development
Tom Finnigan, Marketing Manager
Mark Fennel, Membership Services Manager
Lauren Cook, Media Associate

A quarterly newspaper published by Citizens Against Government Waste. *$25.00*

Quarterly Founded: 1984
Circulation: 108000
Mailing list available for rent

10879 HAC News
Housing Assistance Council
1025 Vermont Avenue NW
Suite 606
Washington, DC 20005-3516
202-842-8600
FAX: 202-347-3441
hac@ruralhome.org
http://www.ruralhome.org

Leslie Strauss, Communications Direc
Moises Loza, CEO/President

Newsletter publishing issues of rural and low-income housing. Free.

10880 HOTLINE
National Journal
1501 M Street NW
#300
Washington, DC 20005
202-739-8400
FAX: 202-833-8069 1 8-0 2-7 80
memberships@nationaljournal.com
http://nationaljournal.com/

Charles Green, Marketing

Online daily newsletter offers information on US national, state and local political campaigns and issues.

Weekly Founded: 1987

10881 Highway Financing and Construction-From the State Capitals
Wakeman Walworth
PO BOX 7376
Alexandria, VA 22307-7376
703-768-9600
FAX: 703-768-9690
newsletters@statecapitals.com
http://statecapitals.com/

Keyes Walworth, Publisher

Provides weekly intelligence on allocation of funds for highway, street and bridge construction, extension, repair, renovation, replacement, and truck weight limits and fees, impact fees, new toll roads and highway privatization, bonding practices and other revenue sources. *$235.00*

4 pages Weekly Founded: 1955
Printed in 1 color on matte stock
Computerized version available

10882 Inside Energy
Platts, McGraw Hill Companies
1221 Avenue of the Americas
New York, NY 10020-1095
212-122-2000
FAX: 212-904-6030
support@platts.com
http://www.mcgraw-hill.com
Bill Loveless, Editor
Georgia Safos, Circulation Director
Harold McGraw III, President/CEO
Covers the Department of Energy including energy, science/technology, and environmental management programs as well as energy programs at the Interior Department. *$1395.00*
16 pages Weekly Founded: 1884

10883 International Association of Emergency Managers
201 Park Washington Court
Falls Church, VA 22046-4513
703-538-1795
FAX: 703-241-5603
info@iaem.com http://www.iaem.com
Elizabeth B Armstrong, Executive Director
Sharon L Kelly, Member Director
Elizabeth B Armstrong, CEO
Karen Thompson, Editor
Dawn Shiley, Communication Manager
Representatives of city and county government departments responsible for emergency management and disaster preparedness. *$160.00*
20 pages Monthly Founded: 1952
Circulation: 2700 2,500 names $600 per M.
Printed in 2 colors on matte stock

10884 Internet Connection
Innovation Groups
PO Box 16645
Tampa, FL 33687-6645
813-622-8484
FAX: 813-664-0051
shastings@mindspring.com
Shawn Hastings, Production Manager
Features innovative on-line and Internet services. It targets local government professionals who are getting connected and want to know more about what their on-line services can do. Accepts advertising. *$19.00*
8 pages Quarterly
Circulation: 5000 Audited Est. Pass-Along Circ: 9000
Printed in 1 color on matte stock

10885 Local Health Officers News
US Conference of Local Health Officers
1620 I Street NW
Washington, DC 20006-4005
202-887-6120
FAX: 202-293-2352
Alan Campbell, Publisher
Stephen Horn, Editor
The official publication of the US conference of local health officers. Accepts advertising. *$35.00*
12 pages BiWeekly

10886 Lottery, Parimutuel & Casino Regulations - From the State Capitals
Wakeman Walworth
PO BOX 7376
Alexandria, VA 22307-7376
703-768-9600
FAX: 703-768-9690 800-876-2545
newsletters@statecapitals.com
http://www.statecapitals.com
Keyes Walworth, Publisher
Allen Klein, Editor
Christine Ryan, Marketing Manager
Newsletter covers regulation and development of state lottery programs, including prize structures, ticket marketing policies, distribution of revenues, new games and equipment. Regulations and taxation of casinos, parimutuel wagering operations and other forms of legalized wagering including horse racing, dog racing, jai alai, riverboat gambling and bingo. *$345.00*
4 pages Weekly Founded: 1962
Printed in 1 color on matte stock
Computerized version available

10887 Majority Rules
Jenkins Hill Publishing Company
324 Old Beech Road
PO Box 607
Grove City, PA 16127-6722
814-786-9085
FAX: 814-786-8209 866-641-7141
Myron Struck, Publisher
Political newsletter for women. *$51.00*
24 pages Monthly
Circulation: 300 Audited
Printed in 2 colors

10888 Managing Today's Federal Employees
LRP Publications
747 Dresher Road
Suite 500
Horsham, PA 19044-2247
215-840-0912
FAX: 215-784-9639 800-341-7874
custserve@lrp.com
http://www.lrp.com
Dionne Ellis, Managing Editor
Patrick Byrne, Editor
Chris Donohue, Legal Editor
Keeping supervisors informed of their personnel management responsibilities has always been one of the most difficult tasks facing federal agency personnel officers. This newsletter is a working resource as well as a comprehensive training tool. Gives sensible solutions to common management challenges and covers controversial issues such as sexual harassment, contracting out of federal jobs, alternative dispute resolutions and more. *$155.00*
8 pages Monthly Founded: 1977
Printed in 2 colors on matte stock
Computerized version available: Internet

10889 McGraw-Hill's Federal Technology Report
McGraw Hill
1200 G Street NW
Suite 1200
Washington, DC 20005-3814
202-383-2350
FAX: 202-383-2125 800-223-6180
Bill Loveless, Chief Editor
Georgia Safos, Circulation Director
Brings readers inside those areas of the federal government where federal technology policy and legislation is made; also identifies commercial opportunities at federal labs. *$1015.00*
16 pages Weekly

10890 Memo to Mailers
US Postal Service
475 Lenfant Plaza SW
Room 10523
Washington, DC 20260-0004
202-268-2900
Jim Quirk, Editor
Carries information and news about the Postal Service as well as value added information about using the mail effectively and efficiently. Also offers information to mail center managers on ways to cut costs.
8 pages Daily
Circulation: 100,000

10891 Monitor
Center for Democratic Renewal
PO Box 50469
Atlanta, GA 30302
404-221-0025
FAX: 404-221-0045
info@thecdr.org
http://www.thecdr.org
Loretta Ross, Editor
Lynora Williams, CEO/President
Articles on current white supremacist, neo-Nazi and far-right activities, and on community responses to specific incursions by hate groups, as well as to hate violence, bigotry and institutionalized racism within the community.
Founded: 1979
Circulation: 3000 Audited Est. Pass-Along Circ: 15000
Printed in 1 color on glossy stock

10892 Motor Vehicle Regulation-From the State Capitals
Wakeman Walworth
PO Box 7376
Alexandria, VA 22307
703-768-9600
FAX: 703-768-9690
newsletters@statecapitals.com
http://www.statecapitals.com/motorreg.html
Keyes Walworth, President
Allen Klein, Editor
Christine Ryan, Marketing Manager
State laws and regulations regarding vehicle safety, inspections, tags, fees, taxes, emissions standards, drunken driving laws, motorist licensing, insurance, education and school bus regulations. *$275.00*
4 pages Weekly Founded: 1962
Printed in 1 color on matte stock
Computerized version available

10893 NATAT's Reporter
National Association of Towns and Townships
444 N Capitol Stree NW
Suite 397
Washington, DC 20001-1202
202-289-0777
FAX: 202-624-3554
natat@sso.org www.natat.org
Ronnie J Kweller, Editor
Covers federal legislation and regulation that pertain to local governments, with emphasis on compact or small towns (under 50,000; many under 1,000); also includes case studies of exemplary, creative local government, programs and association news from the National Association of Towns & Townships. *$36.00*
24 pages BiWeekly
Circulation: 15,200 Audited
Mailing list available for rent 11700 names

$85 per M.
Printed in 2 colors on newsprint stock

10894 Nation's Cities Weekly
National League of Cities
1301 Pennsylvania Avenue NW Suite 550
6th Floor
Washington, DC 20004-1763
202-263-3169
FAX: 202-626-3043
info@nlc.org http://www.nlc.org
Donald J Borut, Executive Director
Cyndy Hogan, Managing Editor
News for and about cities. *$96.00*
Weekly
Circulation: 30000

10895 National Affordable Housing Management Association
National Affordable Housing Management Association
526 King Street
Suite 511
Alexandria, VA 22314-3143
703-683-8630
FAX: 703-683-8634 www.nahma.org
Kris C Cook CAE, Executive Director
Daria Jakubowski, Deputy Director
Trade association for professional property managers of federally assisted housing. Publishes a newsletter. *$95.00*

Circulation: 3000

10896 National Assisted Housing Management Association News
National Affordable Housing Management Association
526 King Street
Suite 511
Alexandria, VA 22314-3143
703-683-8630
FAX: 703-683-8634 www.nahma.org
Kris C Cook CAE, Executive Director
Daria Jakubowski, Deputy Director
Offers information for the housing management executives.

10897 National Association of County Executives
440 1st Street NW
8th Floor
Washington, DC 20001-2028
202-936-6226
FAX: 202-393-2630 www.naco.org
Dotty Byars, Staff Liason
Larry Naake, Chief Executive Officer

10898 National Association of Development Companies
6764 Old McLean Village Drive
Mc Lean, VA 22101-3906
703-748-2575
FAX: 703-748-2582
http://www.nadco.org
Christopher Crawford, President
Merril Ferber, Editor
Provides long-term fixed asset financing to small businesses. Publishes newsletter.
Monthly Founded: 1981
Circulation: 244

10899 National Association of State Facilities Administrators
2760 Research Park Drive
PO Box 11910
Lexington, KY 40578-1910
859-311-1877
FAX: 859-244-8001 800-800-1910
nasfa@nasfa.net http://www.nasfa.net/

Marcia Stone, Associate Manager/Editor
Michael Kenig, Membership Committee Executive
Sheldon Greenberg, Special Projects Committe
John Ruffin, President
State administrators of facilities and property. A newsletter is published for members.
$1800.00
Quarterly Founded: 1987
Circulation: 2000

10900 National Community Development Association
522 21st Street NW
Suite 120
Washington, DC 20006-5012
202-293-7587
FAX: 202-887-5546
info@nedaonline.org
http://www.nedaonline.org
Shandra Western, Editor
A national nonprofit membership organization representing local governments that implement community development programs. The members administer federally supported community development, housing and human services programs. NCDA provides counsel at the federal level on new program design and current program implementation and advocates on behalf of responsive community development.
13 pages

10901 Navy News and Undersea Technology
Pasha Publications
1616 N Fort Myer Drive
Suite 1000
Arlington, VA 22209-3107
703-528-1244
FAX: 703-528-1253 800-424-2908
Harry Baisden, Group Publisher
Thomas Jandl, Editor
Tod Sedgwick, Publisher
This report on the Navy, as well as the Marine Corps and naval developments overseas. Frequently cited by experts in the field as the source for breaking developments in submarine and anti-submarine warfare technology, this newsletter sets the standard for Navy reporting. *$545.00*
Weekly

10902 Outlook-From the State Capitals
Wakeman Walworth
300 N Washington Street
Suite 204
Alexandria, VA 22314-2530
703-768-9600
FAX: 703-549-1372
newsletters@statecapitals.com
http://statecapitals.com/theoutlook.html
Keyes Walworth, Publisher
Weekly newsletter reporting trends in state law making. Reports on the challenges of taxes and revenues, economic development, drug abuse, abortion, environmental issues and teacher salaries. It includes developments in all areas of state government action which may be indicators of important changes in public policy. *$235.00*
4 pages Weekly
Printed in 1 color on matte stock
Computerized version available

10903 Phyllis Schlafly Report
Eagle Trust Fund
PO Box 618
Alton, IL 62002
618-462-5415
FAX: 618-462-8909
www.eagleforum.org
Phyllis Schafly, Editor
Conservative political newsletter. *$20.00*
Monthly

10904 Public Assistance and Welfare Trends - From the State Capitals
Wakeman Walworth
300 N Washington Street
Suite 204
Alexandria, VA 22314-2530
703-768-9600
FAX: 703-549-1372
newletters@statecapitals.com
http://statecapitals.com/publicassist.html
Keyes Walworth, Publisher
Weekly summary of trends and developments concerning state welfare, including AFDC and Medicaid programs, AIDS legislation, services for the elderly and disabled, special tax breaks, health plans, respite care, and specialized assistance to indigents including utility bill and housing subsidies.
$235.00
4 pages Weekly
Printed in 1 color on matte stock
Computerized version available

10905 Public Health-From the State Capitals
Wakeman Walworth
300 N Washington Street
Suite 204
Alexandria, VA 22314-2530
703-768-9600
FAX: 703-549-1372
newslwtters@statecapitals.com
http://statecapitals.com
Keyes Walworth, Publisher
Devoted to all state issues affecting public health including Medicaid legislation, AIDS disclosure and testing, drug programs, abortion rulings, cancer prevention such as smoking restrictions in public places, asbestos removal, mental health and disability programs, disease control, regulation of hospitals and nursing homes as well as clinics. *$235.00*
4 pages Weekly
Printed in 1 color on matte stock
Computerized version available

10906 Public Risk
Public Risk Management Association (PRIMA)
500 Montgomery Street
Suite 750
Alexandria, VA 22314
703-528-7701
FAX: 703-739-0200
info@primacentral.org
http://www.primacentral.org/
Jim Hirt, Executive Director
Jon Ruzan, Director of Communication
Articles on public risk management and risk management professionalism in the public sector. *$130.00*
40 pages Monthly Founded: 1978
Circulation: 8,250

10907 Public Risk Management Association
500 Montgomery Street
Suite 750
Alexandria, VA 22314
703-528-7701
FAX: 703-739-0200
info@primacentral.org
http://www.primacentral.org

Jim Hirt, Executive Director
Jon Ruzan, Director Communications

Supports all risk management professionalism in the public sector. Publishes magazine.

10908 Public Safety and Justice Policies-From the State Capitals
Wakeman Walworth
300 N Washington Street
Suite 204
Alexandria, VA 22314-7376
703-768-9600
FAX: 703-768-9690 800- 87- 254
newsletters@statecapitals.com
http://statecapitals.com/publicsafety.html

Keyes Walworth, Publisher

Covers police and fire department administrations, gun control laws, law enforcement regulations, firefighting, curfews, arrest procedures, community right-to-know laws. On the justice side it includes prison overcrowding, judicial selection process, sentencing guidelines, parole programs, public defender systems, court financing and fees, prisoner drug and AIDS testing, new evidence such as DNA, inmate work programs, living conditions, security and staffing, punishment and penalties. *$235.00*
4 pages Weekly
Printed in 1 color on matte stock
Computerized version available

10909 Riskwatch
Public Risk Management Association
500 Montgomery Street
Suite 750
Alexandria, VA 22314-1805
703-528-7701
FAX: 703-739-0200
info@primacentral.org
http://www.primacentral.org

Jim Hirt, Executive Director
Jon Ruzan, Publisher
Tony D'Alba, Director of Business Deve
Senga Howat, Membership C ordinator
Heather Ripley, Education and Training Manager

This monthly 8-page newsletter covers current news and events of interest to risk managers practicing in the public sector; professors and students; and service providers. Relevant Court cases, insurance market and employee benefits news and PRIMA chapter activities are included. The 'Government Affairs' section features legislative and regulatory developments. Job listings cost $50 for 70 words. *$130.00*

Monthly Founded: 1978
Circulation: 2000

10910 Roads and Bridges
Scranton Gillette Communications
380 E Northwest Highway
Suite 200
Des Plaines, IL 60016-2282
847-298-6622
FAX: 847-390-0408
hgillette@sgcmail.com
http://www.spcpubs.com

Larry Flynn, Editor

For highway contractors, design/engineering firms, state DOT's and municipal employees with road jurisdiction. *$40.00*
92 pages Monthly Founded: 1905
Circulation: 70000

10911 Society of Government Economists
10371 Painted Cup
Columbia, MD 21044
301-497-6174
www.sge-econ.org

Harvey Bronstein, President

Economists employed in the public sector or who are interested in the aspects of government policies. Newsletter is available.
Monthly Founded: 1970

10912 Surveillant: Acquisitions & Commentary for Security/Intelligence Professionals
National Intelligence Book Center
2020 Pennsylvania Avenue NW
#165
Washington, DC 20006-1811
202-296-4426
FAX: 202-296-4319

Cameron LaClair, VP Marketing
Elizabeth Bancroft, Editor
Bagley Fordyce, Advertising/Sales

Newsletter offering reviews of books and other media on the subject of intelligence and national security. *$96.00*
48 pages Bi-Monthly
Circulation: 7,800 Audited Est. Pass-Along Circ: 10500
Mailing list available for rent 14M names $190 per M.
Printed in 1 color on matte stock

10913 Tax Administrators News
Federation of Tax Administrators
444 N Capitol Street NW
Washington, DC 20001-1512
202-624-5890
FAX: 202-624-7888
http://www.taxadmin.org

Harley Duncan, Executive Director
Rian Turruss, Editor

Covers state and federal legislation, US Supreme Court and state court cases, and developments relating to state tax administration. *$40.00*
12 pages Monthly Founded: 1930
Circulation: 2000 Audited Est. Pass-Along Circ: 250
Printed in 1 color on matte stock

10914 Taxes/Property-From the State Capitals
Wakeman Walworth
300 N Washington Street
Suite 204
Alexandria, VA 22314-2530
703-689-9600
FAX: 703-549-1372

Keyes Walworth, Publisher

Weekly perspective on laws and regulations regarding property taxes including assessment programs, exemptions, incentives, and collection methods. Includes court decisions and other regulatory rulings. Also includes special emphasis on school financing including referenda, state aid formulas, alternative school financing methods, budgetary issues related to teacher pay, class sizes and drug testing programs. *$235.00*
4 pages Weekly
Printed in 1 color on matte stock
Computerized version available

10915 US Mayor
US Conference of Mayors
1620 Eye Street NW
Washington, DC 20006-4005
202-640-0790
FAX: 202-293-2352
info@usmayors.org
http://www.usmayors.org/

Don Plusquellic, President
Tom Cochan, EdItor
Guy Smith, Managing Editor
Michael Guido, Chair Advisory Board
J Thomas Cochran, CEO

Federal government and congressional activities. *$35.00*
16 pages Founded: 1933
Circulation: 6000

10916 United Nations Jobs Newsletter
Thomas F Burola & Associates
6477 Telephone Road
Suite 7R
Ventura, CA 93003-4459
805- 64- 725
FAX: 805-654-1708 tburola@alf.tel.hr

Thomas F Burola, Publisher

Focus of this newsletter is employment conditions within the United Nations System and vacancy notices. *$145.00*
Founded: 1994
Circulation: 3,500 Audited Est. Pass-Along Circ: 10000
Printed in 2 colors on matte stock
Computerized version available

10917 United States Conference of Mayors
16201 Street NW
Washington, DC 20006-4005
202-635-6325
FAX: 202-293-2352
info@usmayors.org
http://www.usmayors.org/uscm/

J Thomas Cochran, President
William Fay, Chief Executive Officer

City government officials. Newsletter is available for members.
Founded: 1932
Circulation: 30000

10918 Urban and Regional Information Systems Association
1460 Renaissance Drive
Suite 305
Park Ridge, IL 60068
847-824-6300
FAX: 847-824-6363
info@urisa.org http://www.urisa.org

Nancy Tosta, President
Wendy Francis, Director Marketing

Effective use of information systems technology at the state, regional and local levels Newsletter is published.
Monthly Founded: 1963

10919 Washington Remote Sensing Letter
Dr. Murray Felsher
1057B National Press Building
Washington, DC 20045-2001
202-393-3640
felsher@encul.msn.com

Dr. Murray Felsher, Publisher
Murray Felsher, Editor
Dr. Murray Felsher, Publisher
Dr. Murray Felsher, Marketing
Dr. Murray Felsher, Circulation Manager

The recognized leader in reporting and analysis of US and international news dealing with all phases and applications of satellite remote sensing of the earth and global analyses research, including imagery, photography, surveillance and monitoring the Earth from space. *$ 1100.00*

4 pages Founded: 1980
Printed in 2 colors on matte stock
Computerized version available

10920 Washington Spectator
Public Concern Foundation
PO Box 20065
New York, NY 10011
212-741-2365

subscriptions@washingtonspectator.com
http://www.washingtonspectator.com/

Kevin Walter, Publisher
Ben A Franklin, Editor
Lisa Vandepaer, Associate Editor
Marvin Shanken, Owner

News, comment and analysis on current national and international affairs; politics, economics, environment and social issues. *$ 15.00*

4 pages Founded: 1974
Circulation: 60,000 Audited
Mailing list available for rent 60000 names $75 per M.
Printed in 1 color on matte stock

10921 Washington Trade Daily
Trade Reports International Group
PO Box 1802
Wheaton, MD 20915-1802
301-946-0817
FAX: 301-946-2631
trigtrig@aol.com
http://www.washingtontradedaily.com/

Jim Berger, CEO
D Kanth, Editor

The only faxed daily newsletters of its kind that covers the goings-on in the nation's Capital related to imports, exports and foreign investment. It reports daily to readers on the Executive Branch - including the US Trade Representative's office and the Commerce Department - as well as Congress. Readers can gain insight every morning on what are likely to be new laws and regulations governing international business tomorrow. *$650.00*

16 pages Daily Founded: 1991
Printed in 1 color
Computerized version available: Fax

10922 Worldwide Government Report
Worldwide Government Directories
7979 Old Georgetown Road
Suite 900
Bethesda, MD 20814-2429
301-258-2677
FAX: 301-718-8494 800-332-3535

Jonathan Hixon, Publisher

Each issue provides detailed reports of elections, government and military turnover. Events covered include ousted heads of state, reshuffled governments, changes in ruling majorities, analyses of recent elections, outlooks for upcoming elections, and senior military appointments. *$247.00*

Monthly

Magazines & Journals

10923 APWA Reporter
American Public Works Association
2345 Grand Boulevard
Suite 500
Kansas City, MO 64108-2641
816-472-6100
FAX: 816-472-1610
reporter@apwa.net
http://www.apwa.net/reporter

R Kevin Clark, Managing Editor
Jon Dilley, Marketing Manager
Connie Hartline, Publisher
Kaye Sullivan, Chief Executive Officer

Prime communication link uniting the community of public works professionals that make up APWA. *$100.00*

Monthly Founded: 1937
Circulation: 25000
Mailing list available for rent

10924 Army Magazine
2425 Wison Boulevard
Arlington, VA 22201-3326
703-841-4300
FAX: 703-525-9039 800-336-4570
ausa-info@ausa.org
http://www.ausa.org

Gen. Gordon Sullivan, President
Mary Blake French, Editor
Millie Hurlbut, Marketing Manager

Founded: 1950

10925 Army Reserve
1421 Jefferson Davis Highway
Suite 12300
Arlington, VA 22202
703-601-0854
FAX: 703-601-0833

10926 Army Times
Army Times Publishing Company
6883 Commercial Drive
Springfield, VA 22159-500
703-509-9000
FAX: 703-750-8129 800-368-5718
jmccoy@atpco.com
http://www.armytimes.com

Elaine Howard, President/CEO
Judy McCoy, Associate Publisher
Tobias Naegele, Executive Editor
David Smith, Marketing Manager *$52.00*

Weekly

10927 Certifier
Association of Boards of Certification
208 5th Street
Ames, IA 50010-6259
515-232-3623
FAX: 515-232-3778
abc@abccert.org
http://www.abccert.org

Stephen W Ballou, Executive Director
Suzanne De la Cruz, Manager of Testing and Certificatio
Cheryl Bergener, President
Kathy Cook, VP

Association news.

Monthly Founded: 1972

10928 Classifiers Column
Classification and Compensation Society
1730 K Street NW
Suite 713
Washington, DC 20006-3834
202-408-9333
FAX: 301-567-9325

Richard Bell, President

10929 Code Official
International Code Council
4051 Flossmoor Road
Country Club Hills, IL 60478-5795
800-423-6587
FAX: 708-799-0310 800-214-4321
magazine@bocai.org
http://www.bocai.org

Paul K Myers, CEO
Margaret M Leddin, Managing Editor

Serves a wide-ranging readership of professionals who are interested in the development, maintenance and enforcement of progressive and reponsive building regulations. *$30.00*

Monthly Founded: 1994
Circulation: 16000 15,000 names $90 per M.
Printed in on glossy stock

10930 Congressional Digest
Congressional Digest Corporation
4416 East-West Highway
Suite 400
Bethesda, DC 20814-3389
301-634-3113
FAX: 301-634-3189 800-638-8380
griff.thomas@congressionaldigest.com
http://www.congestionaldigest.com

Griff Thomas, President
Page Robinson, Publisher
Kathy Thorne, Circulation Manager
Sarah Orrick, Editor

The only publication about Congress that concentrates each month on a single legislative issue in a unique Pro and Con format. It is an indispensable education tool for students of national and world affairs. *$62.00*

36 pages Founded: 1921
Printed in 2 colors on glossy stock

10931 Contingency Planning & Management
Witter Publishing Corporation
20 Commerce Street
Flemington, NJ 08822
908-788-0343
FAX: 908-788-3782
cpmmagazine@witterpublishing.com
http://www.witterpublishing.com

Bob Joudanin, Publisher
Paul Kirvan, Editor
Courtney Witter, Circulation Manager
Andrew Witter, President

Serves the fields of financial/banking, manufacturing industrial, transportation, utilities, telecommunications, health care, government, insurance and other allied fields. *$275.00*

Monthly Founded: 1987

10932 Contract Management
National Contract Management Association
8260 Greensboro Drive
Suite 200
McLean, VA 22102-3728
571-382-0082
FAX: 703-448-0939 800-344-8096
cm@ncmahq.org
http://www.ncmahg.org

Neal J Couture, Executive Director
Kathryn Mullan, Assistant Editor

It covers the myriad aspects of government and commercial contract management. News and features provide information on such topics as procurement policy, on-the-job techniques, regulations, case law, ethics, contract administration, electronic commerce, international and small business matters, education and career development. *$178.00*

80 pages Monthly Founded: 1959
Circulation: 22000
Printed in 4 colors on glossy stock

10933 Corrections Today
4380 Forbes Boulevard
Lanham, MD 20706-4322
301-918-1890
FAX: 301-918-1886 800-222-5646
susanc@aca.org http://www.aca.org

Susan Clayton, Managing Editor
Gabriella Daley, Director of Publication/Communicati

Published by the American Correctional Association. *$25.00*

200 pages Founded: 1870
Circulation: 21000
Mailing list available for rent

10934 Defense News
6883 Commercial Drive
Springfield, VA 22151
703-642-7300
FAX: 703-658-8412 800-424-9335
armylet@atpco.com
http://www.armytimes.com

Tobias Naegele, Publisher
Elaine Howard, President/CEO
Alex Neill, Managing Editor
Jim Tice, Senior Writer
David Smith, Marketing *$55.00*

Weekly
Circulation: 1 millio

10935 Family Magazine
51 Atlantic Avenue
Suite 200
Floral Park, NY 11001-2721
516-616-1930
FAX: 516-616-1936

10936 Federal Criminal Investigator
888 18th Street NW
Suite 600
Washington, DC 20006-3502

This comprehensive publication covers legislation and federal information for the police official and officer.
Quarterly

10937 Federal Managers Magazine
1641 Prince Street
Alexandria, VA 22314-2818
703-683-8700
FAX: 703-683-8707
info@fedmanagers.org
http://www.fedmanagers.org

Michael B Styles, Publisher
Susan Holliday, Editor
Michael B. Styles, President
Didier Trinh, Executive Director

Association and legislative news. *$25.00*
Quarterly

10938 Federation Bulletin
Federation of State Medical Boards of the US
400 Fuller Wiser Road
Suite 300
Euless, TX 76039-3855
817-868-4000
FAX: 817-868-4098

News and legislation for the medical profession.
Quarterly

10939 Food Protection Trends
International Association for Food Protection
6200 Aurora Avenue
Suite 200W
Des Moines, IA 50322-2864
515-276-3344
FAX: 515-276-8655 800-369-6337
info@foodprotection.org
http://www.foodprotection.org

Bev Corron, Public Relations
David W. Tharp, Executive Director
Donna Gronstal, Marketing

Each issue contains refereed articles on applied research, applications of current technology and general interest subjects for food safety professionals. *$227.00*

Monthly Founded: 1911 ISSN 0362-028X
Circulation: 9000+
Mailing list available for rent 3000+ names $150 per M.
Printed in 4 colors on glossy stock

10940 Foreign Service Journal
American Foreign Service Association
2101 E Street NW
Washington, DC 20037
202-338-4045
FAX: 202-338-6820 800-704-2572
member@afsa.org
http://www.afsa.org

Steve Honley, Editor
Susan Maitra, Senior Editor
Ed Miltenberger, Advertising Manager
John Limbert, President

Written for members of the US Foreign Service. Journal readers include: diplomats, congresspersons and other foreign affairs professionals. Our readers are influential decision-makers and in the examples they set in the United States and abroad. They spend one-third of their working lives in the US and the balance at diplomatic posts in more than 135 countries. It's a lifeline to products and services that meet their needs. *$40.00*

68 pages Monthly Founded: 1924
Circulation: 12500
Printed in on glossy stock

10941 Government Executive
National Journal
4th Floor Receiving
600 New Hampshire Ave NW
Washington, DC 20037
202-739-8400
FAX: 202-739-8460
webmaster@govexec.com
http://www.govexec.com

Fred Kuhn, National Sales Manager
Shane Harris, Editor

Management solutions written for senior federal executives and presented in the context of government. *$48.00*

72 pages Fortnightly Founded: 1970
Circulation: 75,000

10942 Government PROcurement
Penton Media
The Penton Media Building
1300 E 9th Street
Cleveland, OH 44114
216-696-7000
FAX: 216-931-9799
ldrahos@penton.com
http://www.govpro.com

Kate Friseh, Editor-in-Chief
Kristin M Atwater, Managing Editor
Kay Ross Baker, Publisher

Specifically for the public sector purchasing professional.

58 pages Founded: 1892
Circulation: 20000
Printed in 4 colors on glossy stock

10943 Government Product News
Penton Media
The Penton Media Building
1300 E 9th Street
Cleveland, OH 44114-1503
216-696-7000
FAX: 216-696-1752
vrockhold@penton.com
http://www.gpnews.com

Leslie A Drahos, Editor-in-Chief
Kristin M Atwater, Managing Editor
Vaughn Rockhold, Group Publisher
Kay Ross-Baker, Publisher
Sarah Arnold, Marketing Director

Serves officials in the executive, legislative, administrative, engineering, purchasing, financial and other operational departments, within government agencies.

40 pages Monthly Founded: 1962
Circulation: 85000
Printed in 4 colors on glossy stock

10944 Government Recreation & Fitness
Executive Business Media
825 Old Country Road
PO Box 1500
Westbury, NY 11590
516-334-3030
FAX: 516-334-3059
ebmpubs2@aol.com
http://www.ebmpubs.com

Murry Greenwald, Publisher
Paul Ragnoz, Managing Editor

Government Recreation and Fitness reaches recreation and fitness professionals in every department and agency of the federal government, goes directly to the people who purchase your products, with deep market penetration, and covers both appropriated and nonappropriated fund budgets. *$35.00*

42 pages 15 issues per y Founded: 1996
Circulation: 9250
Printed in 4 colors on glossy stock

10945 Government Technology
GT Publications
150 Almaden Boulevard
Suite 600
San Jose, CA 95113
408-275-9000
FAX: 408-275-0582
http://www.grantthornton.com

Jeffrey S Pera, Managing Partner
Sherese Graves, Advertising Director
Dennis McKenna, Publisher
Micki Gerardi, Manager

Devoted exclusively to covering information technology in state and local government. Provides public sector executives with the new tools required to manage government in the Information Age. Features articles highlighting unique computer and

telecommunications technology applications that are solving public sector problems. Accepts advertising.
56 pages Monthly Founded: 1980

10946 International Municipal Signal Association Journal
165 E Union Street
PO Box 539
Newark, NY 14513-539
315-331-2182
FAX: 315-331-8205 800-723-4672
info@imsasafety.org
http://www.imsasafety.org
Marilyn E Lawrence, Executive Director
Sharon Earl, Executive Assistant
Marilyn E Lawrence, Editor
Articles on information, education, and certification for public safety. *$60.00*
80 pages Founded: 1896
Circulation: 10,000 8800+ names
Printed in 4 colors on glossy stock

10947 Journal of Food Protection
International Association for Food Protection
6200 Aurora Avenue
Suite 200W
Des Moines, IA 50322-2864
515-276-3344
FAX: 515-276-8655 800-369-6337
info@foodprotection.org
http://www.foodprotection.org
Bev Brannen, Editor
David W. Tharp, Executive Director
Each issue contains scientific research and authoritative review articles reporting on a variety of topics in food science pertaining to food safety and quality. *$335.00*
Monthly Founded: 1911 ISSN 0362-028X
Circulation: 11000
Mailing list available for rent 3000+ names $150 per M.
Printed in 4 colors on glossy stock

10948 Journal of Housing
Nat'l Assn of Housing & Redevelopment Officials
630 Eye Street NW
Suite 500
Washington, DC 20001-3736
202-289-3500
FAX: 202-289-8181 877-866-2476
nahro@nahro.org
http://www.nahro.org
James M Inglis, President
Donald J Cameron, CEO
Manufacturers, distributors and consultants of products for the housing and community development field are presented in this comprehensive and valuable buyer's guide.
$33.00
Founded: 1933

10949 Journal of the Association of Food and Drug Officials
2550 Kingston Road
Suite 311
York, PA 17402
717-757-2888
FAX: 717-755-8089
afdo@afdo.org http://www.afdo.org
News and the latest legislation for the Food and Drug Association. *$80.00*
Quarterly Founded: 1896

10950 Legislative Update
1250 Eye Street NW
Suite 902
Washington, DC 20005
202-393-5229
FAX: 202-393-3034
nrhc@nrhcweb.org
http://www.nrhcweb.org
Peter Carey, President
Bob Rapoza, Publisher/Executive Director
Published by the National Rural Housing Coalition. *$250.00*
25 issues per y Founded: 1969
Circulation: 300

10951 Military Grocer
Downey Communications
4800 Montgomery Lane
Suite 710
Bethesda, MD 20814-3461
301-718-7600
FAX: 301-718-7604
Richard T Carroll, Publisher
Loretta M Downey, CEO
Serves defense commisionary employees worldwide.
5 per year
Printed in 4 colors on glossy stock

10952 NCOA Journal
Todays NCOA
10635 IH 35 N
San Antonio, TX 78233-6627
210-653-6161
FAX: 210-637-3337 800-662-2620
membsvc@ncoausa.org
http://www.ncoausa.org
Tina Kish, Editor
Jene Overstreet, CEO
Cathy John, Advertising Manager
Quarterly Founded: 1960
Circulation: 60000

10953 NDIS Reports
Council on Licensure, Enforcement and Regulation
PO Box 11910
Lexington, KY 40578-1910
859-244-8203
FAX: 859-244-8053
Bi-Monthly

10954 NIST Update
High Tech Publishing Company
PO Box 1275
Amherst, MA 01004-1275
413-534-4500
FAX: 413-256-6378
I Justin DiPeri, Editor
A guide to recent activities of the United States National Institute of Standards and Technology. NIST is the nation's physical sciences and engineering measurement laboratory. *$125.00*

10955 Nation's Cities Weekly
National League of Cities
1301 Pennsylvania Avenue NW
6th Floor
Washington, DC 20004-1763
202-626-3000
FAX: 202-626-3043
info@nlc.org http://www.nlc.org
Jeff Fletcher, Editor
Cyndy Hogan, Managing Editor
Articles cover municipal management news as well as federal legislation of interest to cities and towns. *$96.00*
12 pages Weekly Founded: 1978
Circulation: 27000

10956 National Journal
National Journal
The Watergate
600 New Hampshire Ave NW
Washington, DC 20037-1702
202-398-8400
FAX: 202-833-8069 800-207-8001
John Fox Sullivan, President *$1799.00*
Founded: 1969

10957 Navy Times
6883 Commercial Drive
Springfield, VA 22159-500
703-750-7400
FAX: 703-750-8622 800-368-5718
tnaegele@atpco.com
http://www.navytimes.com
Elaine Howard, President
Judy McCoy, Associate Publisher
David Smith, VP Marketing/Business Dev
Dick Howlett, AVP Circulation Operations
Tobias Naegele, Executive Editor
$143.00
Weekly

10958 Off the Shelf
Coalition for Government Procurement
1990 M Street NW
Suite 400
Washington, DC 20036-3420
202-331-0975
FAX: 202-822-9788
info@coalgovpro.org
http://www.coalgovpro.com
Larry Allen, Executive VP
Bruce McLellan, Executive Director
Paul Caggiano, President
Monthly Founded: 1979

10959 Parameters: US Army War College Quarterly
US Army War College
122 Forbes Avenue
Carlisle, PA 17013-5238
717-453-3131
parameters@carlisle.army.mil
http://www.carlisle.army.mil
Robert Taylor, Editor
Robert Ivany, Manager *$26.00*
Quarterly
Circulation: 1300

10960 Police Chief
International Association of Chiefs of Police
515 N Washington Street
Alexandria, VA 22314-2357
703-836-6767
FAX: 703-836-4543 800-843-4227
information@theiacp.org
http://www.theiacp.org
Joseph G. Estey, President
Jayme Walker Holcomb, Associate Chief Counsel
A monthly magazine published by the International Association of Chiefs of Police.
$25.00
80 pages Monthly Founded: 1893
Circulation: 21300

10961 Public Risk
Public Risk Management Association
500 Montgomery Street
Suite 750
Alexandria, VA 22314
703-528-7701
FAX: 703-739-0200
info@primacentral.org
http://www.primacentral.org

Jim Hirt, Executive Director
Jon Ruzan, Director Communications

Features substantive articles on issues facing risk management professionals working in public agencies and examines in detail the approaches they take to meet today's challenges. Articles accepted. Also includes book reviews, pooling issues, innovations and a calendar of events. *$130.00*
32 pages Founded: 1978
Circulation: 2,400

10962 Pull Together
1306 Dahlgren Ave SE
Washington Navy Yard, DC 20374-5055
202-678-4333
FAX: 202-889-3565
nhfwny@navyhistory.org
http://www.navyhistory.org

CAPT Charles Creekman, Executive Director
Robert F Dunn, President *$25.00*
Founded: 1926

10963 Rural Housing Reporter
1250 Eye Street NW
Suite 902
Washington, DC 20005
202-393-5229
FAX: 202-393-3034 800-424-9540
nrhc@nrhcweb.org
http://www.nrhcweb.org

Peter Carey, President
Robert Rapoza, Publisher/Executive Director

Published by the National Rural Housing Coalition. *$250.00*
Monthly Founded: 1969

10964 Rural Voices
Housing Assistance Council
1025 Vermont Avenue NW
Suite 606
Washington, DC 20005-3516
202-842-8600
FAX: 202-347-3441
hac@ruralhome.org
http://www.ruralhome.org

Moises Loza, Executive Director
Ali Alad Hab, Publisher

Magazine publishing issues of rural and low-income housing. Free.
Quarterly Founded: 1971

10965 Society of Cost Estimating and Analysis Journal
Society of Cost Estimating and Analysis
101 S Whiting Street
Suite 201
Alexandria, VA 22304-3416
703-751-8069
FAX: 703-461-7328
scea@erols.com
http://www.erols.com

LeRoy Baseman, Executive Director
Leonard Cheshire, Manager

Subscribers are professionals engaged primarily in the field of government contract estimating and pricing. *$40.00*
Annual+ Founded: 1984
Circulation: 4500

10966 State Government News
Council of State Governments
2760 Research Park Drive
PO Box 11910
Lexington, KY 40578-1910
859-244-8000
FAX: 859-244-8001 800-800-1910
sales@csg.org http://www.csg.org

Daniel M Sprague, CEO/President
Kelley Arnold, Sales and Publications Manager
Sacha Pruitt, Associate Editor

Source of information on current developments in all state government.
40 pages Founded: 1933 $150 per M.
Printed in 4 colors on glossy stock

10967 State Legislatures
National Conference of State Legislatures
7700 E First Place
Denver, CO 80230
303-364-7700
FAX: 303-364-7800
pubs-info@ncsl.org
http://www.ncsl.org

Karen Hansen, Editor
Sharon Randal, Managing Editor

The national magazine of state government and policy. *$49.00*
Founded: 1975
Circulation: 18000 18,385 names $85 per M.
Printed in 4 colors

10968 Supreme Court Debates
Congressional Digest Corporation
4416 E West Hwy
Ste 400
Bethesda, MD 20814-4568
301-634-3113
FAX: 301-634-3189 800-637-9915
info@congressionaldigest.com
http://www.pro-and-con.org/

Griff Thomas, President
Page Robinson, Publisher

Monthly publications provide in-depth, unibased analysis of cases before the US Supreme Court. Each single-topic issue explains the facts in plain English through oral arguments, briefs, related speeches and expert analysis. *$57.00*
Monthly Founded: 1921
Printed in 2 colors on matte stock

10969 Translog
200 Stovall Street
Hoffman Building Room 11N57
Alexandria, VA 22332-5000
703-428-3207
FAX: 703-428-3312

10970 Washington Law & Politics
100 W Harrison N Tower
Suite 340
Seattle, WA 98119
206-282-9527
FAX: 206-282-9601
http://www.lawandpolitics.com

Keith Goben, Associate Publisher
Beth Taylor, Editor
Paul Englund, Circulation Manager

48 pages 6 issues per ye Founded: 1977
Circulation: 18000
Printed in 4 colors on glossy stock

10971 Western City Magazine
League of California Cities
1400 K Street
4th Floor
Sacramento, CA 95814
916-658-8256
FAX: 916-658-8289 800-262-1801
info@westerncity.com
http://www.westerncity.com

Jude Hudson, Editor
Pam M Blodgett, Advertising Manager
Megan Taylor, Managing Editor
Chris McKenzie, Executive Director

The magazine of the League of California Cities. *$39.00*
Monthly Founded: 1924
Circulation: 10500
Printed in 4 colors on glossy stock

Trade Shows

10972 American Association of Port Authorities Annual Convention
1010 Duke Street
Alexandria, VA 22314-3589
703-684-5700
FAX: 703-684-6321
info@aapa-ports.org
www.aapa-ports.org

Kurt Nagle, President/CEO

60 booths.
700 Attendees September Founded: 1912

10973 American Compensation Association National Conference
14040 N Northsight Boulevard
Scottsdale, AZ 85260-3627
480-970-4268
FAX: 480-483-8352

Lorraine Bergstrom, Marketing Planner

75 booths.
900 Attendees May

10974 American Inns of Court Foundation
1120 G Street NW
Suite 700
Washington, DC 20005
202-393-7878
FAX: 202-638-4952 www.aspanet.org

Michael Daigneault, Executive Director

30 booths.
550 Attendees May

10975 American Political Science Association Annual Meeting
1527 New Hampshire Avenue NW
Washington, DC 20036
202-483-2512
FAX: 202-483-2657
apsa@apsanet.org www.apsanet.org

Jenn Gorne, Meetings/Conventions Manager
Michael Brintnall, Executive Director

Workshop, luncheon and 150 plus exhibits of publications and software relating to political science.
6500 Attendees Annual Founded: 1903

10976 American Society Public Administration
1120 G Street NW
Suite 500
Washington, DC 20005-3897
202-393-7878

Joanne Dunne, Show Manager

40 booths offering exhibits of publications, consulting, training and computer companies.
1.5M Attendees July

10977 Annual National Conference of the Enlisted Association of US National Guard
Exhibit Promotions Plus
11620 Vixens Path
Ellicott City, MD 21042
301-596-3028
FAX: 410-997-0764
exhibits@epponline.com
www.epponline.com
Harve C Horowitz, President
Kevin M Horowitz, Director Business Development
EANGUS attendees are "end-users" or in mid-management within the National Guard community.
1500 Attendees August 21-23, 2005
Founded: 1971

10978 Civilian Congress Annual Conference
Civilian Congress
2361 Mission Street
Room 238
San Francisco, CA 94110-1813
415-695-1597
Jack Fitch, Secretary
Annual conference and exhibits relating to the acquisition and dissemination of biographical data on the current military affiliations of congressmen which cannot be obtained from standard government or private directories.

10979 Congress of Cities & Exposition
National League of Cities
11208 Waples Mill Road
Suite 112
Fairfax, VA 22030
703-631-6200
FAX: 703-654-6931 800-564-4220
nlc@jspargo.com www.nlc.org
Nathan Wills, Account Manager
Serves as NLC's annual convention and offers a broad range of learning opportunities combined with conducting organizational business. This conference is unique in that it partners with the hosting city to develop educational programs which allow the city to display its accomplishments. This is the only NLC conference with an exposition. Containing 270 booths and 200 exhibits.
4200 Attendees December Founded: 1924

10980 Council State Governments-WEST, Western Legislative Conference
1107 9th Street
Suite 650
Sacramento, CA 95814
916-553-4423
FAX: 916-446-5760
csgw@csg.org www.csgwest.org
Kent Briggs, Executive Director
Cheryl Lee Duvauchelle, Deputy Director
500 Attendees July Founded: 1933

10981 Council of State Governments Annual State Trends and Leadership Forum
Council of State Governments
2760 Research Park Drive
PO Box 11910
Lexington, KY 40578-1910
859-244-8000
FAX: 859-244-8001 800-800-1910
Daniel Sprague, Executive Director
Laura Williams, Deputy Director
1000+ Attendees October

10982 Energy - Exhibit Promotions Plus
US Dept. of Energy/US Dept. of Defense/GSA
11620 Vixens Path
Ellicott City, MD 21042
301-596-3028
FAX: 410-997-0764
energy@epponline.com
www.energy2003.ee.doe.gov
Harve Horowitz, President
Kevin Horowitz, Senior Association Manager
Energy is an exclusive Federal Grant sponsored annual educational forum and exhibition.
1000+ Attendees August 1,000+ names

10983 FOSE
National Trade Productions
313 S Patrick Street
Alexandria, VA 22314-3501
703-683-8500
800-638-8510
Sylvia Griffiths, Customer Supervisor
1,800 booths offering exhibits of computers and information systems. This show is America's leading computer conference and exposition.
80M Attendees April

10984 Federal Imaging, the Document Management Conference for the Government
National Trade Productions
313 S Patrick Street
Alexandria, VA 22314-3501
703-683-8500
FAX: 703-706-8208 800-638-8510
Pam Nazaruk, Public Relations
Jayne Leifert, Exposition Manager
Dedicated to demonstrating imaging products and services to the federal government. The comprehensive conference program, with more than 30 sessions, covers crucial industry issues such as the benefits and challenges in utilizing a UNIX-based imaging system, imaging in Department of Defense, legality of optical storage, and integration of document imaging and multimedia.
8M Attendees November Founded: 1992

10985 Federally Employed Women Training Program
1400 I Street NW
Washington, DC 20005-2208
202-898-0994
Karen Scott, Show Manager
Patricia Wolfe, President
100 booths.
2.5M Attendees July

10986 Fish Wildlife Agencies Association Southeast
8005 Freshwater Farms Road
Tallahassee, FL 32309
850-893-1204
FAX: 850-893-6204
seafwa@aol.com www.seafwa.org
Robert Brently, Executive Secretary
Fifteen booths.
1,000 Attendees October

10987 Government Finance Officers Association Annual Conference
180 N Michigan Avenue
Suite 800
Chicago, IL 60601-7476
312-413-3605
FAX: 312-977-4806 www.gfoa.org
Dan Zielinski, Show Manager
Steven Grant, Owner
250 booths with 200 exhibitors.
7000 Attendees June 15000 names $250 per M.

10988 IAEM Conference and Exhibit
International Association of Emergency Managers
201 Park Washington Court
Falls Church, VA 22046
703-538-1795
FAX: 703-241-5603 www.iaem.com or www.emex.com
Clay Tyeryar, Show Manager
Elizabeth Armstrong, Executive Director
Containing 200 booths.
1000 Attendees November

10989 ITLG: Information Technology for Local Government
Reed Exhibition Companies
255 Washington Street
Newton, MA 02458-1637
617-584-4900
FAX: 617-630-2222
Elizabeth Hitchcock, International Sales
Information technology for local government exhibition and conference.
450 Attendees May

10990 International Association Personnel Employment Security
1801 Louisville Road
Frankfort, KY 40601-3922
502-223-4459
FAX: 502-223-3695
Michael Stone, Show Manager
Mary Riddell, Manager
20 booths including workshops and exhibits of employment security equipment and services.
2M Attendees June

10991 International City Management Association
777 N Capitol Street NE
Suite 500
Washington, DC 20002-4239
202-289-4262
FAX: 312-541-0573
barry@corcexpo.com www.icma.org
Barry Sacks, Show Manager
200 booths by the suppliers of products to the municipal market.
3.5M Attendees September

10992 International City/County Management Association
ICMA Publications
777 N Capitol Street NE
Suite 500
Washington, DC 20002
202-624-4600
FAX: 202-962-3500 800-745-8780
amahoney@icma.org www.icma.org
Pat Phillips, Show Manager
Bill Hansell, Executive Director
200 booths of suppliers to the municipal market.
3.5M Attendees

10993 Long Island Business Trade Show & Conferen ce
Hauppauge Industrial Association
225 Wireless Blvd
Hauppauge, NY 11788
631-543-5355
FAX: 631-543-5380 www.hia-li.org

10994 Marine West Exposition
VNU Expositions
PO Box 17413
Washington, DC 20041
703-318-0300
FAX: 703-318-8833
dchirles@vnuexpo.com
www.marinecorpsexposistion.com
Denis Chirles, Marketing Manager
Jeff McQuilhin, Sales Director
80 Attendees January

10995 Massachusetts Municipal Association
Hynes Convention Center
900 Boylston
Boston, MA 07115
617-954-2000
FAX: 617-954-2125
info@mccahome.com
www.mccahome.com
Geoffrey Beckwith, Executive Director
1000 Attendees January

10996 Micro, Microcomputer Conference and Exposition for the Government
National Trade Productions
313 S Patrick Street
Alexandria, VA 22314-3501
703-683-8500
FAX: 703-706-8208 800-638-8510
Pam Nazaruk, Public Relations
Enables top executives and senior IRM officials, system integrators and VARs, mid-level managers, and advanced users of microcomputers in the government to come together with vendors and developers to share information and preview the latest microcomputer related products and services.
55M+ Attendees August/September

10997 NACo's Annual Conference and Exposition
National Association of Counties
440 1st Street NW
Washington, DC 20001-2028
202-393-6226
FAX: 202-393-2630
kstruble@naco.org www.naco.org
Amanda Clark, Conference & Meetings Associate
Kim Struble, Conference & Meetings Director
Larry Naake, Chief Executive Officer
The place for elected and appointed county officials to network, attend educational sessions and meet with companies that sell products to counties. It includes a variety of activities designed to meet the needs of all delegates. In addition to strong educational sessions, the conference includes affiliate, steering and subcommittee meetings, state association meetings and social events.
4000 Attendees Annual

10998 National Association Consumer Agency Administrators
1010 Vermont Avenue NW
Suite 514
Washington, DC 20005-4969
202-347-7395
FAX: 202-347-2563
nacaa@erols.com www.nacaanet.org
Anna Flores, Executive Director
20 booths.
600 Attendees October

10999 National Association County Engineers
440 1st Street NW
Washington, DC 20001-2028
202-393-5041
FAX: 202-393-2630
Anthony Giancola, Executive Director
50 booths of equipment and shop supplies.
450 Attendees January

11000 National Association Regional Councils
1700 K Street NW
Suite 1300
Washington, DC 20006-3822
202-628-1558
Shawn Sample, Show Manager
80 booths.
1.2M Attendees June

11001 National Association Superintendents/ Public Residential Facilities
1400 W Pickard Street
Mount Pleasant, MI 48858-1364
989-773-7921
FAX: 989-772-5093
Charla Miller
10 booths.
200 Attendees February

11002 National Association Towns/Township
444 N Capitol Street NW
Suite 294
Washington, DC 20001-1512
202-624-3550
FAX: 202-289-7996
Bruce G Rosenthal, Communications Director
20 booths displaying products and services sold to local governments.
1M Attendees September

11003 National Civic League Conference on Governance
1445 Market Street
Suite 300
Denver, CO 80202-1717
303-571-4343
FAX: 303-571-4404 800-223-6004
Leslie Koretz, Marketing Coordinator
Christopher Gates, President
25 booths appealing to the government and chamber of commerce policy and decision makers.
350 Attendees November

11004 National Conference and Exhibition
Nat'l Assn of Housing & Redevelopment Officials
630 I Street NW
Washington, DC 20001-3736
202-289-3500
FAX: 202-289-8181 877-866-2476
nahro@nahro.org www.nahro.org
A wide array of products and services needed by the housing and community development field.
3M Attendees October

11005 National Conference of State Legislatures Annual Meeting & Exhibition
National Conference of State Legislatures
1560 Broadway
Suite 700
Denver, CO 80202-5140
303-830-2200
FAX: 303-863-8003 www.ncsi.org
Peg Coniglio, Manager
Deana Blackwood, Circulation Director
Containing 450 booths and 250 exhibits.
6700 Attendees July

11006 National Council State Housing Agencies Annual Convention
444 N Capitol Street NW
Washington, DC 20001-1512
202-624-5400
FAX: 202-624-7719
Louise Moors, Membership Coordinator
William Pound, Executive Director
30 booths.
700 Attendees October

11007 National Forum for Black Public Administrators
ICMA Publications
777 N Capitol Street NE
Washington, DC 20002-4239
202-289-5851
FAX: 202-962-3500 800-745-8780
Quentin Lawson, Show Manager
James Wright, Executive Director
50 booths.
1.4M Attendees April

11008 National League of Postmasters Convention
Exhibit Promotions Plus
11620 Vixens Path
Ellicott City, MD 21042
301-596-3028
FAX: 410-997-0764
exhibit@epponline.com
www.epponline.com
Harve C Horowitz, President
Kevin M Horowitz, Director Business Development
Expect to access over 1,400 active Postmasters, Office in Charge, influential US Postal Service officals, customers and business associates.
1400 Attendees August Founded: 1903

11009 National Postal Forum
3998 Fair Ridge Drive
Suite 300
Fairfax, VA 22033
703-218-5015
FAX: 703-218-5020
info@npf.org www.npf.org

Mary Guthrie, Director, Marketing & Exhibits
Laurie Woodhams, Exhibits Assistant

Attend to recieve a complete education in the 'Business of Mail'
March Washington

11010 **National Public Relations Labor Relations Association**
1620 I Street NW
4th Floor
Washington, DC 20006-4005
202-591-1190
FAX: 202-293-2352

Tony Wang

12 booths.
350 Attendees April

11011 **National State Legislatures Conference and Expo**
1560 Broadway
Denver, CO 80202
303-830-2200

Linda Worrell, Show Manager

300 booths consisting of businesses, associations and government agencies.
8M Attendees

11012 **Public Housing Authorities Directors Association**
511 Capitol Ct NE
Washington, DC 20002-4947
202-546-5445
FAX: 202-546-2280

Larry Beach, Conference Director
Timothy Kaiser, Executive Director

60 booths.
800 Attendees May/June

11013 **State Emergency Management Agencies**
PO Box 116
Jefferson City, MO 65102-0116
573-751-9500
FAX: 573-751-9746

Cathy Andres

30 booths for all local emergency management directors for counties and cities.
225 Attendees April

11014 **Supervisors County Legislators Association**
132 State Street
Albany, NY 12207-1610
518-477-7117

Mary L Hanak, Executive Director
William Conboy, Manager

30 booths. This show informs and educates delegates exhibiting various goods and services available to them.
350 Attendees June

11015 **Transforming Local Government**
Innovation Groups
6604 Harney Road, Suite L
PO Box 16645
Tampa, FL 33687-6645
813-622-8484
FAX: 813-664-0051
shastings@mindspring.com

Madeline Havlick, Manager
Jim

City managers and staff from around the country will meet in clearwater to discuss transformation and change in local government. Containing 100 booths and 100 exhibits.
800 Attendees May
Printed in 1 color on matte stock

11016 **UDT: Undersea Defense Technology Conference and Exhibition**
Reed Exhibition Companies
255 Washington Street
Newton, MA 02458-1637
617-584-4900
FAX: 617-630-2222

Elizabeth Hitchcock, International Sales

An international conference and exhibition concerned with the research and development of equipment and services for undersea defense environment.
June

11017 **United Nations Association USA**
801 2nd Avenue
New York, NY 10017
212-697-3232
FAX: 212-682-9185 www.unausa.org

Carol Christian, Director

Government forum.
400 Attendees November

11018 **Winter Workshop**
Association of University Research Parks
c/o Wachovia Bank
Po Box 758936
Baltimore, MD 21275-8936
703-234-4088
FAX: 703-435-4390
info@aurp.net www.aurp.net

Lora Lee Martin, Chiar

Annual

Directories & Databases

11019 **ACT Directory**
Americans Combatting Terrorism
PO Box 635
Kingshill, VA 00851-0635

Information is given on corporate, nonprofit, media and government members that maintain specialized information on policies and activities concerning terrorism.
Annual

11020 **AP Political Service**
Associated Press
50 Rockefeller Plaza
6th Floor
New York, NY 10020-1666
212-621-1500
FAX: 212-621-5488
Covers local, state, and national political news and statistics with an emphasis on political campaigns.
Full-text

11021 **Almanac of American Politics**
National Journal
1730 M Street NW
Suite 1100
Washington, DC 20036-4500
202-828-0355

Ambassador Kattouf, President

Offers information on governors, US senators and members of the US House of Representatives. *$59.95*
1500 pages Biennial

11022 **Almanac of the Federal Judiciary**
Prentice Hall Law & Business
270 Sylvan Avenue
Englewood Cliffs, NJ 07632-2521
201-569-0006

Offers biographical information and anonymous lawyer evaluations of all federal judges.
1000 pages SemiAnnual

11023 **American Bench**
Forster-Long
3280 Ramos Circle
Sacramento, CA 95827-2513
916-362-3276
FAX: 916-362-5643 800-328-5091
clientrelations@forster-long.com
www.americanbench.com

Mary Bliss, Editor
Jason Long, VP/Marketing

Over 19,000 judges who sit in local, state and federal courts are profiled. The definitive biographical reference to the American judiciary. *$405.00*
2,700 pages Annual

11024 **American Lobbyists Directory**
Gale Research
27500 Drake Road
Farmington Hills, MI 48331
248-699-4253
FAX: 248-699-8214 800-877-4253
galeord@gale.com www.gale.com
Organizations that employ over 65,000 registered federal and state government lobbyists are listed. *$175.00*
1500 pages

11025 **Billcast Archive**
George Mason University, Public Choice Center
4400 University Drive
Fairfax, VA 22030-4444
703-931-1120

This database contains information on public bills introduced in the US House of Representatives and Senate during the preceding session of Congress.
Bibliographic

11026 **Book of the States**
Council of State Governments
2760 Research Park Drive
PO Box 11910
Lexington, KY 40578-1910
859-244-8000
FAX: 859-244-8001 800-800-1910

Daniel Sprague, Executive Director
Laura Williams, Dir. Membership/Marketing/Comm.

This base edition serves as the foundation for three supplements containing directory data on statistics related to governments of various states. *$99.00*

11027 **CSG State Directories**
Council of State Governments
2760 Research Park Drive
PO Box 11910
Lexington, KY 40578-1910
859-244-8000
FAX: 859-244-8001 800-800-1910

Daniel Sprague, Executive Director
Laura Williams, Dir. Membership/Marketing/Comm.

A set of three directories with the names, addresses, e-mail, fax and telephone numbers of key executive branch officials, members of the house and senate. Legislative administrators in state government.

11028 Capital Guide
Savings & Community Bankers of America
900 19th Street NW
Suite 400
Washington, DC 20006-2105
202-857-3100

Diane Casey-Landry, President

Offers valuable information on presidential cabinet members, members of Congress, Senate and House committees. *$10.00*
340 pages Annual

11029 Capital Source
National Journal
The Watergate
600 New Hampshire Avenue, NW
Washington, DC 20037
202-739-8400
FAX: 202-833-8069
capitalsource@nationaljournal.com

Katherine Burrow, Manager/Public Relations

Who's who, what and where in Washington. *$29.95*
160 pages Annujal

11030 Capitol Advantage
Capitol Advantage
2731-A Prosperity Avenue
Fairfax, VA 22031
703-289-9636
FAX: 703-289-4678
capitoladvantage.com

Robert Hansan, President
Sherri Stanley, VP, Sales

Provides the essential information to access political institutions, current members of congress, addresses, telephones, faxes and addresses. *$8.95*
190 pages Annual Founded: 1986

11031 Carroll's County Directory
Carroll Publishing
4701 Sangamore Road
Suite S-155
Bethesda, MD 20816
301-263-9800
FAX: 301-263-9801 800-336-4240
customersvc@carrollpub.com
www.carrollpub.com

Thomas E Carroll, President
William Wade, Director, Editorial Operations *$350.00*

11032 Carroll's Federal Advisory Directory
Carroll Publishing
4701 Sangamore Road
Suite 155S
Bethesda, MD 20816-2508
301-639-9800
FAX: 202-337-7020 800-336-4240

Tracey Ryan, Editor
Thomas Carroll, President

Profiles over 900 federal advisory committees and the 19,000 members who serve on them. Information offers committee name, purpose, type and authorization, and contacts for each. *$150.00*
725 pages Annual

11033 Carroll's Federal Directory
Carroll Publishing
4701 Sangamore Road
Suite 155S
Bethesda, MD 20816-2508
301-639-9800
FAX: 202-337-7020 800-336-4240

Albert Ruffin, Editor
Thomas Carroll, President

Updated six times a year, the Federal Directory is the only source for contact information on over 35,000 key decision makers in all three branches of the federal government. *$230.00*
450 pages Bi-Monthly

11034 Carroll's Federal Regional Directory
Carroll Publishing
4701 Sangamore Road
Suite 155S
Bethesda, MD 20816-2508
301-639-9800
FAX: 202-337-7020 800-336-4240

Lela Harris, Editor
Thomas Carroll, President

Instant access to key federal officials located outside Washington, DC. Complete contact information for over 20,000 non-Washington-based executives in Cabinet departments, Congress, the courts, administrative agencies, and military bases. Dozens of maps detailing agency jurisdictions are included. *$170.00*
370 pages 2 per year

11035 Carroll's Municipal Directory
Carroll Publishing
4701 Sangamore Road
Suite 155S
Bethesda, MD 20816-2508
301-639-9800
FAX: 202-337-7020 800-336-4240

Lela Harris, Editor
Thomas Carroll, President

Provides information access to more than 35,000 elected, appointed and career officials in 7,800 cities, towns and villages across the country. *$170.00*
550 pages 2 per year

11036 Carroll's State Directory
Carroll Publishing
4701 Sangamore Road
Suite 155S
Bethesda, MD 20816-2508
301-639-9800
FAX: 202-337-7020 800-336-4240

Lela Harris, Editor
Thomas Carroll, President

Provides complete contact information for over 20,000 key officials in all 50 states, plus the District of Columbia, Puerto Rico and the American Territories. *$210.00*
530 pages TriAnnual

11037 Committee Votes
Mead Data Central
PO Box 933
Dayton, OH 45401-0933

FAX: 518-487-3584 888-223-6337
Database in directory format listing information on legislation voted upon by full, joint and select committees of the US Congress.
Directory

11038 Communications Services/Writer's Military Market
US Department of the Army, Public Affairs
1500 Army Pentagon
Washington, DC 20310-1500
703-695-4436

Offers information on periodicals which accept unsolicited manuscripts and whose editorial content is geared toward the military.
40 pages

11039 Compensation: An Annual Report on Local Government Executive Salaries
ICMA Publications
777 N Capitol Street NE
Suite 500
Washington, DC 20002-4239
202-624-4600
FAX: 202-962-3500 800-745-8780
Reports on compensation and benefits for 19 managerial positions. *$125.00*
279 pages Annual

11040 Complete Guide to Public Employment
Impact Publishers
PO Box 6016
Atascadero, CA 93423-6016
805-665-5917
FAX: 805-466-5919 800-246-7228
A list of state, federal and local government agencies and departments, trade and professional associations and other organizations offering public service career opportunities. *$34.95*
Triennial

11041 Congress at Your Fingertips: Congressional Directory
Capitol Advantage
2751 Prosperity Avenue
Suite 600
Fairfax, VA 22031
703-899-9636
FAX: 703-289-4678 800-659-8708
sales@capitoladvantage.com
www.capitoladvantage.com

Dr. John Hansan, Production Manager

100 current senators and 440 House of Representative members. Complete with photo, bio, e-mail, staff, communities, district offices and more. *$13.95*
Annual

11042 Congressional Handbook
US Chamber of Commerce
1615 H Street NW
Washington, DC 20062-0001
202-659-6000
FAX: 202-463-3190 800-638-6582
$10.00
150 pages Annual

11043 Congressional Quarterly Almanac
Congressional Quarterly
1414 22nd Street NW
Washington, DC 20037-1003
202-887-8500
FAX: 800-380-3810 800-432-2250

Robert Merry, President

All legislative actions and information for the year. *$315.00*
Quarterly

11044 Congressional Staff Directory
Staff Directories
1414 22nd Street NW
Washington, DC 20037

FAX: 800-380-3810 800-638-1710
Cq@cqpress.com www.cqpress.com
Directory of services and supplies to the industry. *$69.00*
1200 pages SemiAnnual

11045 Congressional Yellow Book
Leadership Directories
104 5th Avenue
New York, NY 10011-6901
212-627-4140
FAX: 212-645-0931
congressional@leadershipdirectories.com
www.leadershipdirectories.com
Eric L Birkholz, Editor
James M Petrie, Associate Publisher
Contact information for US Senators and Representatives, as well as Senate and House committee and subcommittee staffs, and leadership and party organizations. *$325.00*
1,200 pages Quarterly Founded: 1975
Mailing list available for rent 12,000 names $125 per M.
Computerized version available: CD-ROM

11046 Cooperative Housing Bulletin
National Association of Housing Cooperatives
1614 King Street
Alexandria, VA 22314-2719
703-549-5201
FAX: 703-549-5204
coophousing@usa.net
www.coophousing.org

Printed in 2 colors on matte stock

11047 Current World Leaders
International Academy at Santa Barbara
5385 Hollister Avenue
Suite 210
Santa Barbara, CA 93111-2392
805-683-8889
FAX: 805-964-0890
info@iasb.org www.iasb.org
Thomas S Garrison, Editorial Director
Joanne St.John, Publisher
An up-to-date and reliable directory to key officials of 193 independet nations, 31 colonies and dependent territories, and some 38 international organizations and alliances. Contains information and listings from several sources: directly from embassies and information offices of the countries, colonies and dependent territories, international organizations, and alliances covered. *$215.00*
300 pages 3 per year Founded: 1998
Circulation: 1000 : online

11048 Daily Defense News Capsules
United Communications Group
11300 Rockville Pike
Suite 1100
Rockville, MD 20852-3030
301-816-8950
FAX: 301-816-8945
Greg Beaudoin, Editor
This database offers the complete text of Periscope - Daily Defense News Capsules, that provide abstracts of international press coverage of military and defense news.
Bibliographic

11049 Defense Industry Charts
Carroll Publishing
4701 Sangamore Road
Suite 155S
Bethesda, MD 20816-2508
301-639-9800
FAX: 202-337-7020 800-336-4240
Mary Maloof, Editor
Thomas Carroll, President
Offers information on over 170 organization charts detailing the structure of the top 100 defense contractors and their subsidiaries. Puts you in direct contact with over 9,000 key personnel in more than 1,900 top US defense contractors. *$960.00*
Quarterly

11050 Defense Organization Charts
Carroll Publishing
4701 Sangamore Road
Suite 155S
Bethesda, MD 20816-2508
301-639-9800
FAX: 202-337-7020 800-336-4240
Monique Davis, Editor
Thomas Carroll, President
More than 200 organization charts that detail structure of Headquarters, major commands and important research facilities for DoD agencies, Army, Navy, and Air Force. *$1160.00*
185 pages 8 per year

11051 Defense Programs
Carroll Publishing
4701 Sangamore Road
Suite 155S
Bethesda, MD 20816-2508
301-639-9800
FAX: 202-337-7020 800-336-4240
Thomas Carroll, President
Detailed description of more than 2,000 military research, development, test and evaluation programs and projects. *$1060.00*
Quarterly

11052 Defense and Foreign Affairs Handbook
International Strategic Studies Association
PO Box 19289
Alexandria, VA 22320-0289
703-548-1070
FAX: 703-684-7476
dfa@strategicstudies.org
www.strategicstudies.org
Gregory Copley, Editor
Important global reference encyclopedia for most world leaders .Comprehensive chapters on 238 countries and territories worldwide, with each chapter giving full cabinet and leadership listings, history, recent developments, demographics, economic statistics, political and constitutional data, news media,defense overview, defense structure. *$297.00*
2000+ pages Annual Founded: 1976 ISBN 1-892998-06-8
Circulation: 4,000

11053 Department of Defense Directory of Contract Administration Services
Contract Mgmt. Command/Defense Logistics Agency
Caremon Station
Alexandria, VA 22304
703-781-9807

Directory of services to the industry.
110 pages SemiAnnual

11054 Department of Defense Telephone Directory
US Department of Defense
The Pentagon
Washington, DC 20301-0001
703-695-4436
$19.00

11055 Directory of Department of Veterans Affairs Facilities
Analysis & Reports Service
810 Vermont Avenue NW
Washington, DC 20420-0001
202-273-5400

Offers information on over 350 facilities, medical centers and regional offices with associated outpatient clinics and veterans outreach centers.
40 pages Annual

11056 Directory of Legislative Leaders
National Conference of State Legislatures
1560 Broadway
Suite 700
Denver, CO 80202-5140
303-830-2200
$15.00
110 pages Annual

11057 Directory of US Government Datafiles for Mainframes and Microcomputers
US National Technical Information Service
5285 Port Royal Road
Springfield, VA 22161-0001
703-487-4724
$65.00
352 pages Annual

11058 Directory of the Governors of the American States and Territories
National Governors' Association
444 N Capitol Street NW
Suite 250
Washington, DC 20001-1512
202-624-5300
$7.50
60 pages Annual

11059 Directory of the US Association of Former Members of Congress
1775 Massachusetts Avenue NW
#422
Washington, DC 20036-2188

Over 600 congressional alumni are profiled. *$50.00*
80 pages Biennial

11060 Encyclopedia of Governmental Advisory Organizations
Gale Research
27500 Drake Road
Farmington Hills, MI 48331
248-699-4253
FAX: 248-699-8214 800-877-4253
donna_batten@gale.com
www.gale.com
Donna Batten, Editor
Approximately 7,000 boards, panels, commissions, committees, presidential conferences and other groups that advise the President, Congress and departments and agencies of federal government. *$530.00*
Annual

11061 FDA Electronic Bulletin Board
US Food & Drug Administration
5600 Fishers Lane
Rockville, MD 20852-1750
301-443-1544

Thomas Cunningham, Manager

This government database offers the complete text of reports, press releases and articles issued by the FDA.
Full-text

11062 Federal Benefits for Veterans and Dependents
US Department of Veterans Affairs
810 Vermont Avenue NW
Washington, DC 20420-0001
202-273-5400
FAX: 202-225-5396

Joseph Thompson, Manager

List of VA offices, assistance centers and national comentaries. *$3.25*
Annual

11063 Federal Buyers Guide
Gold Crest
650 Ward Drive
Santa Barbara, CA 93111-2337
805-683-9000
FAX: 805-683-7661 800-922-3233
sales@goldcrestinc.com
www.goldcrestinc.com

Perry Hambright, Marketing
Gunnar Sundstrom, OPS Manager

Companies that serve or wish to serve as vendors to the federal government. Reading specialty lights, giftware, manufacturer, distributor, Mighty Bright brand.
170 pages Quarterly Founded: 1979

11064 Federal Career Opportunities
Federal Research Service
370 Maple Avenue W
Suite 5
Vienna, VA 22180-5615
703-281-0200
FAX: 703-281-7639
Current federal job vacancies in the United States and overseas. *$160.00*
64 pages BiWeekly

11065 Federal Communications Commission Telephone Directory
International Transcription Services
4455 12 SW
Washington, DC 20037-1207
202-314-3070

Key contact information. *$2.50*
35 pages

11066 Federal DataBase Finder
Gale Research
27500 Drake Road
Farmington Hills, MI 48331
248-699-4253
FAX: 248-699-8214 800-877-4253
galeord@gale.com www.gale.com
Approximately 4,200 databases and data files that are available to the public from the US government. *$125.00*
Biennial

11067 Federal Directory Library Edition
Carroll Publishing
4701 Sangamore Road
Suite 155S
Bethesda, MD 20816-2508
301-639-9800
FAX: 202-337-7020 800-336-4240

Thomas Carroll, President

35,000 federal government and 17,000 federal regional government officials.
$150.00
Annual July

11068 Federal Government Certification Programs
US National Institute of Standards & Technology
Administration Building
Room 629
Gaithersburg, MD 20899-0001
301-975-2281
FAX: 301-963-2871
A directory available certification programs. *$18.95*
229 pages

11069 Federal Organization Charts
Carroll Publishing
4701 Sangamore Road
Suite 155S
Bethesda, MD 20816-2508
301-639-9800
FAX: 202-337-7020 800-336-4240

Albert Ruffin, Editor
Thomas Carroll, President

Personnel in more than 2,100 departments, bureaus and agencies. *$700.00*

11070 Federal Organization Service
Carroll Publishing
4701 Sangamore Road
Suite 155S
Bethesda, MD 20816-2508
301-639-9800
FAX: 202-337-7020 800-336-4240

Albert Ruffin, Editor
Thomas Carroll, President

Over 200 uniform fold-out organization charts that show the reader who's who and where in more than 2,100 departments and offices with over 11,000 key decision makers listed. *$760.00*
240 pages 8 per year

11071 Federal Regional Yellow Book
Leadership Directories
104 5th Avenue
New York, NY 10011-6901
212-627-4140
FAX: 212-645-0931
info@leadershipdirectories.com
www.leadershipdirectories.com

Mark Nensel, Editor
James M Petrie, Associate Publisher

Contact information for over 37,000 federal officials located outside of Washington, DC in government departments, agencies, military installations, diplomatic missions and service academies. *$245.00*
1,100 pages SemiAnnual Founded: 1992
Mailing list available for rent 31,000 names $125 per M.
Computerized version available: CD-ROM

11072 Federal Regulatory Directory
Congressional Quarterly
1255 22nd Street NW
Washington, DC 20037
202-878-8500
FAX: 800-380-3810 800-432-2250
A directory of regulatory agencies within the federal government. *$139.95*
950 pages Quadrennial

11073 Federal Staff Directory
Staff Directories
1255 22nd Street NW
Suite 400
Washington, DC 20037
202-729-1800
FAX: 800-380-3810 www.fsd.cq.com
Offers information on persons in the federal government offices and independent agencies, with bibliographies given of over 2,500 key personnel. *$79.00*
1500 pages 2 per year

11074 Federal Technology Source
Government Executive- National Journal Group
600 New Hampshire Avenue NW
Washington, DC 20037
202-739-8500
FAX: 202-739-8511 800-356-4838
mailbag@govexec.com
www.govexec.com

Timothy B Clark, President/Editor
Sue Fourney, Managing Editor

Who's who in government technology. Contact information for almost 2,400 key political officials, chief information officers and strategic information technology staff in the White House, Cabinet departments, independent agencies and Congress. Corporate section covers corporations, trade associations, education and media. Includes a section with a conference/show calendar and indexes. *$9.95*
168 pages Annual
Circulation: 73,500
Printed in 4 colors on glossy stock

11075 Federal Yellow Book
Leadership Directories
104 5th Avenue
New York, NY 10011-6901
212-627-4140
FAX: 212-645-0931
federal@leadershipdirectories.com
www.leadershipdirectories.com

Forrest Fisanich, Editor
James M Petrie, Associate Publisher

Contact information for over 38,000 government officials in the Executive Office of the President, Cabinet level departments, and more than 70 federal agencies. *$325.00*
1,100 pages Quarterly Founded: 1975
Mailing list available for rent 33,000 names $125 per M.
Computerized version available: CD-ROM

11076 Foreign Consular Offices in the United States
Bureau of Public Affairs/US Department of State
2201 C Street NW
Washington, DC 20520-0001
202-647-6141

A directory of foreign consulates in the US. *$4.00*
290 pages Annual

11077 Foreign Counsel Directory
American Corporate Counsel Association
1025 Connecticut Avenue NW
Suite 200
Washington, DC 20036
202-318-8327
FAX: 202-293-4701 www.acca.com
Information is given on lawyers practicing in over 90 foreign countries and translators and translating firms.
50 pages

11078 Foreign Representatives in the US Yellow Book
Leadership Directories
104 5th Avenue
New York, NY 10011-6901
212-627-4140
FAX: 212-645-0931
info@leadershipdirectories.com
www.leadershipdirectories.com

Seth Zupnik, Editor
James M Petrie, Associate Publisher

Contact information for foreign representatives of over 187 nations at embassies, consulates, and intergovernmental organizations in the US, US executives of over 1,100 foreign corporations, over 275 foreign financial institutions with offices in the US, and over 300 international media outlets with bureaus in the US. *$245.00*
1,000 pages SemiAnnual Founded: 1997
Mailing list available for rent 12,000 names $125 per M.
Computerized version available: CD-ROM

11079 Getting Started in Federal Contracting: A Guide Through the Federal Maze
Panoptic Enterprises
6055 Ridge Ford Drive
Burke, VA 22015-3653
703-451-5953
FAX: 703-451-5953 800-594-4766
blmcvay@erols.com
fedgovcontracts.com

Vivina Mcvay, President
Barry L McVay, Editor

Information is given on over 65 government procurement offices, Department of Labor offices, General Services Administration business services and Small Business Administration regional and branch offices. *$39.95*
395 pages Founded: 1984 ISBN 0-912481-24-2

11080 Government Activity Report
Dun & Bradstreet Information Service
1 Diamond Hill Road
New Providence, NJ 07974-1218
908-665-5000
800-362-3425
This database offers current information on businesses, universities and foundations that have received contracts, loans or grants from US federal agencies.
Numeric

11081 Government Affairs Yellow Book
Leadership Directories
104 5th Avenue
New York, NY 10011-6901
212-627-4140
FAX: 212-645-0931
info@leadershipdirectories.com
www.leadershipdirectories.comm

Martha David, Editor
James M Petrie, Associate Publisher

Contact information for government affairs specialists employed by corporations, financial institutions, associations, labor unions, interest groups, lobbying firms, and federal, state and city governments agencies. *$245.00*
1,200 pages SemiAnnual Founded: 1994
Mailing list available for rent 15,000 names $125 per M.
Computerized version available: Internet

11082 Government Assistance Almanac: Guide to all Federal Financial Programs
Omnigraphics
615 Griswold
Detroit, MI 48226
313-961-1340
FAX: 313-961-1383 800-234-1340
editorial@omnigraphics.com
www.omnigraphics.com

Robert Dumouchel, Editor

Provides updated information on all 1,613 federal domestic assistance programs available. These programs represent $1.675 trillion worth of federal assistance earmarked for distribution to consumers, children, parents, veterans, senior citizens, students, businesses, civic groups, state and local agencies, and others. *$240.00*
1,000 pages Annual ISBN 0-780807-00-6

11083 Government Job Finder: Where Jobs are in Local, State & Federal Government
Planning/Communications
7215 Oak Avenue
River Forest, IL 60305-1935
708-366-5200
FAX: 708-366-5280 888-366-5200
dl@planningcommunications.com
www.jobfindersonline.com

Daniel Lauber, President

This new fourth edition describes in detail over 2,000 online and print sources of jobs in local, state and federal government; including online job and resume databases, periodicals, online email job alerts, job hotlines, online and print directories, and salary surveys. *$19.95*
325 pages Founded: 1989 ISBN 1-884587-05-4
Circulation: 6,000
Printed in 1 color on matte stock

11084 Government Phone Book USA
Omnigraphics
615 Griswold Street
Detroit, MI 48226
313-961-1340
FAX: 313-961-1383 800-234-1340
editorial@omnigraphics.com
www.omnigraphics.com

David Bianco, Marketing Director

Key federal, state and local government offices in the US are profiled. More than 270,000 listings with complete contact data. *$ 275.00*
2,700 pages Annual Founded: 1992 ISBN 0-780806-93-X

11085 Government Research Directory
Gale Research
27500 Drake Road
Farmington Hills, MI 48331
248-699-4253
FAX: 248-699-8214 800-877-4253
galeord@gale.com www.gale.com
Research and development facilities operated or sponsored by the US or Canadian governments. *$405.00*
1200 pages Biennial

11086 Grey House Safety & Security Directory
Grey House Publishing
185 Millerton Road
PO Box 860
Millerton, NY 12546
518-890-0526
FAX: 518-789-0545 800-562-2139
books@greyhouse.com
www.greyhouse.com

Leslie Mackenzie, Publisher
Richard Gottlieb, Editor

Two-volume guide to the safety and security industry, including articles, checklists, OSHA regulations and product listings. The 16 chapters focus on creating and maintaing a safe and secure enviroment, and deal specifically with hazardous materials, noise and vibration, workplace preparation and maintenance, electrical and lighting safety, fire and rescue and more. Accepts advertising. *$225.00*
1500 pages Annual ISBN 1-592370-67-5

11087 Guide to Management Improvement Projects in Local Government
ICMA Publications
777 N Capitol Street NE
Suite 500
Washington, DC 20002-4239
202-624-4600
FAX: 202-962-3500 800-745-8780
Projects conducted by municipal governments that have resulted in improvements in efficiency or cost reductions are listed. *$65.00*
50 pages Quarterly

11088 IAEM Directory
International Association of Emergency Managers
111 Park Pl
Falls Church, VA 22046-4513
703-538-1795
FAX: 703-241-5603
iaem@aol.com www.iaem.com

Shan Coffin, Editor
Sharon L Kelly, Circulation Director
$100.00

Circulation: 8,000

11089 Immediate Need Resource Directory
Gold Crest
650 Ward Avenue
Santa Barbara, CA 93111
805-683-9000
FAX: 805-683-7661 800-922-3233
sales@goldcrestinc.com
www.goldcrestinc.com

Perry Hambright, Marketing
Gunnar Sundstrom, OPS Manager

A directory catering to the immediate needs of Federal government purchasing agents. Reading and speciality lights, giftware, manufacturer, distributor, Mighty Bright brand. *$20.00*
50 pages Monthly Founded: 1990

11090 Internet Blue Pages
Information Today
143 Old Marlton Pike
Medford, NJ 08055-8750
609-654-6266
FAX: 609-654-4309
custserv@infotoday.com
www.infotoday.com

Thomas H Hogan, Publisher/President
John Bryans, Publisher/Editor-in-Chief Books
Lauree Padgett, Editorial Services Manager
Igne Coffey, Circualtion Manager

The Guide to Federal Government Web Sites is the leading guide to federal government information on the web. Includes over 1,800 annotated agency listings, arranged in the US Government Manual style to help you find the information you need. *$34.95*

464 pages ISBN 0-910965-43-9

11091 Judicial Yellow Book
Leadership Directories
104 5th Avenue
New York, NY 10011-6901
212-627-4140
FAX: 212-645-0931
judicial@leadershipdirectories.com
www.leadershipdirectories.com

Imogene Akins, Editor
James M Petrie, Associate Publisher

Contact information for over 3,250 federal and state judges in federal and state appellate courts, including staff and law clerks, and the law schools they attended. *$245.00*

1,100 pages SemiAnnual Founded: 1995
Mailing list available for rent 13,000 names $125 per M.
Computerized version available: CD-ROM

11092 Kaleidoscope: Current World Data

ABC-CLIO
130 Cremona Drive
#1911
Santa Barbara, CA 93117-5599
805-681-1911
FAX: 805-685-9685

This comprehensive database takes a look at all aspects of the American culture. Listings of information include statistics and factual information on the population, culture, economy, military forces, government, and political systems of countries around the world, the US States and Canadian provinces.
Full-text

11093 Leadership Directories
104 5th Avenue
New York, NY 10011
212-627-4140
FAX: 212-645-0931
info@leadershipdirectories.com
www.leadershipdirectories.com

David J Hurvitz, President/Publisher
Barry Graubart, Executive VP/CMO

The mission of Leadership Directories is to compile, produce and offer subscribers, in all media and in easily usable form, the most current and accurate directories of leaders in the major categories of American activity, including government, business, the professions, and the nonprofits.
Founded: 1969

11094 Leadership Library in Print
Leadership Directories
104 5th Avenue
New York, NY 10011
212-627-4140
FAX: 212-645-0931
info@leadershipdirectories.com
www.leadershipdirectories.com

James M Petrie, Associate Publisher
David Hurvitz, Chief Executive Officer

Complete set of all 14 leadership directories. Provides subscribers with complete contact information for the 400,000 individuals who constitute the institutional leadership of the US. *$2300.00*

Five directories quarterly, nine directories semiannually

Semiannually Founded: 1996
Computerized version available: CD-ROM

11095 Leadership Library on Internet and CD-ROM
Leadership Directories
104 5th Avenue
New York, NY 10011
212-627-4140
FAX: 212-645-0931
info@leadershipdirectories.com
www.leadershipdirectories.com

James M Petrie, Associate Publisher
David Hurvitz, Chief Executive Officer

Makes all 14 leadership directories available over the Internet and on CD-ROM in one integrated directory. They provide subscribers with complete contact information, in one database. Subscription includes Internet access and four CD-ROM editions quarterly. *$3065.00*
Updated Daily Founded: 1999
Mailing list available for rent
Printed in A colors on B stock

11096 Local Court & County Record Retrievers
BRB Publications
PO Box 27869
Tempe, AZ 85285
480-677-7200
FAX: 480-829-8505 800-929-3811
brb@brb.com www.brbpub.com

Mark Sankey, President

Who's who of the public record retrieval industry. Over 2,700 companies profiled and indexed, can search alphabetically and by location. *$39.95*
632 pages Annual Founded: 1994 ISBN 1-879792-76-1 2600 names

11097 Member Data Disk
CQ Staff Directories
815 Slaters Lane
Alexandria, VA 22314-1219

FAX: 703-739-0234 800-252-1722

Bruce B Brownson, Editor

Covers all members of the US Congress and their key staff members in Washington, DC and principal district offices. *$395.00*
Quarterly

11098 Military Biographical Profiles
CTB/McGraw Hill
20 Ryan Ranch Road
Monterey, CA 93940
831-498-8400
FAX: 800-282-0266 800-538-9547

Offers valuable information on US military officers and Department of Defense officials.
Full-text

11099 Municipal Year Book
ICMA Publications
777 N Capitol Street NE
Suite 500
Washington, DC 20002-4239
202-624-4600
FAX: 202-962-3500 800-745-8780

Directory of services and supplies to the industry. *$79.95*
416 pages Annual

11100 Municipal Yellow Book
Leadership Directories
104 5th Avenue
New York, NY 10011-6901
212-627-4140
FAX: 212-645-0931
municipal@leadershipdirectories.com
www.leadershipdirectories.com

Brian Combs, Editor
James M Petrie, Associate Publisher

Contact information for over 33,000 elected and administrative officials of US cities, counties, and local authorities. *$245.00*
1,200 pages SemiAnnual Founded: 1991
Mailing list available for rent 30,000 names $125 per M.
Computerized version available: CD-ROM

11101 National Directory of Corporate Public Affairs
Columbia Books
PO Box 251
Annapolis Junction, MD 20701-0251

FAX: 240-646-7020 888-265-0600
info@columbiabooks.com
www.columbiabooks.com

J Valerie Steele, Senior Editor

Tracks the public/government affairs programs of about 1,900 major US corporations and lists the 14,00 people who run them, Also lists: Washington area offices, corporate PACs, federal and state lobbyists, outside contract lobbyists. Indexed by subject and geographic area. Includes membership directory of the Public Affairs Council. *$109.00*
Annual January 14,000 names $10 per M.

11102 National Directory of Women Elected Officials
National Women's Political Caucus
1630 Connecticut Avenue NW
Suite 201
Washington, DC 20009
202-785-1100
FAX: 202-785-3605
info@nwpc.org www.nwpc.org

Directory of services and supplies to the industry.
230 pages Biennial

11103 National and Federal Employment Report
Federal Reports
1010 Vermont Avenue NW
Suite 408
Washington, DC 20005-4947
202-933-3311
FAX: 202-393-1553

Richard Herman, Owner

Over 600 current attorney and law-related job opportunities with the US government are listed. *$111.20*
Monthly

11104 New York State Directory
Grey House Publishing
185 Millerton Road
PO Box 860
Millerton, NY 12543
518-789-8700
FAX: 518-789-0545 800-562-2139
books@greyhouse.com
ww.greyhouse.com

Richard Gottlieb, President
Leslie Mackenzie, Publisher

A comprehensive and easy-to-use guide to accessing public officials and private sector organizations and individuals who influence public policy in the state of New York. *$145.00*
1008 pages Annually Founded: 1983

11105 Politics in America
Congressional Digest
4416 East West Highway
Suite 400
Bethesda, MD 20814-4568
301-634-3113
FAX: 301-634-3189 800-637-9915
griff.thomas@pro-and-con.org
www.pro-and-con.org
Offers information on United States senators and representatives. *$89.95*
1700 pages Biennial

11106 Profiles of Worldwide Government Leaders
Worldwide Government Directories
7979 Old Georgetown Road
Suite 900
Bethesda, MD 20814-2429
301-258-2677
FAX: 301-718-8494 800-332-3535
Jonathan Hixon, Publisher
Spanning 195 countries, includes comprehensive biographical snapshots of as many as 30 or more ministers from each country. The material is obtained from primary and secondary sources including embassies, government ministries, offices of the United States government and proprietary global network of correspondents. *$297.00*
850+ pages Annual

11107 Public Record Research System
BRB Publications
PO Box 27869
Tempe, AZ 85285
480-677-7200
FAX: 480-829-8505 800-929-3811
brb@brbpub.com
www.publicrecordsources.com
Mark Sankey, President
Comprehensive public records locator, over 26,000 government agencies and institutions profiled. *$119.00*

11108 Public Records Online
BRB Publications
PO Box 27869
Tempe, AZ 85285-7869
480-677-7200
FAX: 800-929-4981 800-929-3811
Mark Sankey, President
Comprehensive listing of government agencies that have placed public records online, both free and fee based. *$20.95*
520 pages Founded: 2000 ISBN 1-889150-21-5

11109 Public Risk Management Association Membership Directory
500 Montgomery Street
Suite 750
Alexandria, VA 22314
703-528-7701
FAX: 703-739-0200
info@primacentral.org
www.primacentral.org
Jim Hirt, Executive Director
Jon Ruzan, Director Communications
Lists all members alphabetically; by state/country; by category; government; private; associate. Yellow pages give vender and service provider 50-wind thumbnail descriptions. Advertising sold.
Circulation: 2,000

11110 Register of Foreign Consulates and Associated Government Offices
NYC Commission for the UN Consular Corps
2 United Nations Plaza
27th Floor
New York, NY 10017-4403
212-319-9300
FAX: 212-319-3430
www.nyc.gov/unccp/html/contact/main.shtml
Marjorie Bloomburg-Tiven, Commissioner
Directory of 106 foreign consulates, staff offices and services. *$13.00*
175 pages Annual

11111 Research Services Directory
Grey House Publishing
185 Millerton Road
PO Box 860
Millerton, NY 12546
518-890-0526
FAX: 518-789-0545 800-562-2139
books@greyhouse.com
www.greyhouse.com
Leslie Mackenzie, Publisher
Richard Gottlieb, Editor
This Ninth Edition provides access to well over 7,700 independent Commercial Research Firms, Corporate Research Centers and Laboratories offering contract services for hands-on, basic or applied research. *$550.00*
992 pages Annual ISBN 1-592370-03-9

11112 State Government Mailing Lists
Council of State Governments
2760 Research Park Drive
PO Box 11910
Lexington, KY 40578-1910
859-244-8000
FAX: 859-244-8001 800-800-1910
Daniel Sprague, Executive Director
Laura Williams, Dir. Membership/Marketing/Comm.
The lists include leaders in all three branches of state government, committee chairs, administrative officials, key officers in each chamber and directors of more than 150 departments and agencies.

11113 State Government Research Directory
Gale Research
27500 Drake Road
Farmington Hills, MI 48331
248-699-4253
FAX: 248-699-8214 800-877-4253
galeord@gale.com www.gale.com
Directory of services and supplies to the industry. *$175.00*
350 pages

11114 State Yellow Book
Leadership Directories
104 5th Avenue
New York, NY 10011-6901
212-627-4140
FAX: 212-645-0931
info@leadershipdirectories.com
www.leadershipdirectories.com
Howard Hammermann, Editor
James M Petrie, Associate Publisher
Contact information for state officials in the executive and legislative branches of the 50 state governments and the US territories, as well as intergovernmental organizations. *$325.00*
1,400 pages Quarterly Founded: 1987
Mailing list available for rent 38,000 names
$125 per M.
Computerized version available: CD-ROM

11115 US Government Purchasing and Sales Directory
Office of Procurement Assistance/Small Business Ad
409 3rd Street SW
Washington, DC 20024-3212
202-712-1500
FAX: 202-216-3056 877-486-2046
osdbu@usaid.gov www.usaid.gov
A directory of government purchasing offices. *$5.50*
190 pages

11116 Union Recognition in the Federal Government
Office of Labor Relations & Workforce Performance
1900 E Street NW
Room 7429
Washington, DC 20415-0001
202-606-2820
FAX: 202-606-2613
A directory of government unions. *$36.00*
525 pages Biennial

11117 United States Government Manual
Office of the Federal Register
National Archives Administration
Washington, DC 20408-0001
202-564-2480
FAX: 202-501-0599
The official handbook of the United States government; includes descriptions and lists of principal personnel of agencies and government bodies. *$30.00*
935 pages Annual

11118 University of Missouri School of Journalis m: Freedom of Information Center
University of Missouri
133 Neff Annex
Columbia, MO 65210-0012
573-882-7539
FAX: 573-884-6204
www.missouri.edu/~foiwww
Charles N Davis, Executive Director
Kathleen M Edwards, Center Manager
Reference and research library serving the public and media regarding access to government information. The center has a collection of over a million articles and documents concerning access to information at state, federal and local levels and offers a wide variety of online documents through its webpage.

11119 Washington Information Directory
Congressional Quarterly
1414 22nd Street NW
Washington, DC 20037-1003
202-887-8500
FAX: 202-822-6583
Paul McClure, Editor
Will Gardner, Associate Editor
5,000 governmental agencies, congressional committees and non-governmental associations considered competent sources of specialized information. *$105.00*
Annual June

11120 Washington: Comprehensive Directory of the Key Institutions and Leaders
Columbia Books
1212 New York Avenue NW
Suite 330
Washington, DC 20005-3969
202-641-1662
FAX: 202-898-0775 888-265-0600
info@columbiabooks.com
www.columbiabooks.com
Buck Downs, Senior Editor
Over 5,000 federal and district government offices, businesses, associations, publications, radio and television stations, labor organizations, religious and cultural institutions, health care facilities and community organizations in the District of Columbia area. *$75.00*
Annual May 25,000 names $10 per M.

11121 Who's Who in Local Government
ICMA Publications
777 N Capitol Street NE
Suite 500
Washington, DC 20002-4239
202-624-4600
FAX: 202-962-3500 800-745-8780
Over 8,000 appointed administrators of cities, counties and councils of governments.
450 pages Annual

11122 Who's Who in the Federal Executive Branch
Congressional Quarterly
1414 22nd Street NW
Washington, DC 20037-1003
202-887-8500
FAX: 202-822-6583
Members of the executive branch of the US federal government. *$15.95*
Annual March

11123 Worldwide Directory of Defense Attorneys
Worldwide Government Directories
7979 Old Georgetown Road
Suite 900
Bethesda, MD 20814-2429
301-258-2677
FAX: 301-718-8494 800-332-3535
Jonathan Hixon, Publisher
One-of-a-kind resource covering military and civilian defense and national security agencies from the ministry of defense down to service branches in 195 countries worldwide. *$647.00*
1,100 pages Annual

11124 Worldwide Government Directory
Worldwide Government Directories
7979 Old Georgetown Road
Suite 900
Bethesda, MD 20814-2429
301-258-2677
FAX: 301-718-8494 800-332-3535
Jonathan Hixon, Publisher
Offers valuable information on every senior government official in the executive, legislative, and judicial branches as well as the diplomatic and defense communities of 195 countries worldwide. Plus senior officials in over 100 international organizations. Each entry includes name, address, title, telephone, telex, facsimile number, and more. Also included are current state agencies and corporations, official forms of address, international dialing codes and central bank information. *$347.00*
1,400 pages Annual

Industry Web Sites

11125 www.aashto.org
American Association of State Highway and
Transportation

Membership is composed of highway and transportation departments in the 50 states, the District of Columbia, and Puerto Rico.

11126 www.abccert.org
Association of Boards of Certification

The Association of Boards of Certification is dedicated to protecting public health and the environment by advancing the quality and integrity of environmental certification programs through innovative technical support services, effective information exchange, professional and cost-effective examination services, and other progressive services for certifying members.

11127 www.access.digex.net/fedbar
Federal Bar Association

Members are attorneys in the Federal Government or who have interest in federal law.

11128 www.accesspro.org
American Society of Access Professionals

Members are government employees, lawyers, journalists and others concerned with access to government data under current personal privacy and public informaiton statues.

11129 www.acsp.uic.edu/iaco
International Association of Correctional Officers

Correctional officers and juvenile administrators.

11130 www.actnat.com
Association of Civilian Technicians

Union of civilian employees of the Army and National Guard and Air Reserve.

11131 www.admin.org
American Federation of School Administrators

Established in 1971 as the school administrators and supervisors organizing committee. Information of interest to those in public education.

11132 www.affirm.org
Associ for Federal Information Resources Mngt

Seeks to improve the management of information systems and resources of the Federal Government.

11133 www.afge.org
American Federation of Government Employees

The largest federal employee union representing 700,000 workers nationwide and overseas.

11134 www.afscase.org
American Federation of State, County and

Municipal Employees

Sponsors their own Political Action Committee.

11135 www.aglf.org/
Association for Governmental Leasing and Finance

Provides an exchange of information among tax-exempt issuers, investment banking firms and party lease brokers.

11136 www.aja.ncsc.dni.cs
American Judges Association

An independent organization of judges in all jurisdictions in Canada, Mexico and the United States.

11137 www.alexandriagroup.com
National Association of Government Communicators

A merger of Federal Editors association, the Government Information Organization, and the Armed Forces Writers League.

11138 www.alldc.org
American League of Lobbyists

National association dedicated to serving government relations and public affairs professionals. Provides programs and conferences of interest to lobbyists.

11139 www.ansi.org
American National Standards Institute

Promotes the knowledge for approved standards for industry, engineering and safety design.

11140 www.aphf.org
National Association of Chiefs of Police

Operates the American police Academy as its educational arm. Maintains the American Police Hall of Fame & Museum in Miami, Florida.

11141 www.aspanet.org
American Society for Public Administration

Offers a wide range of services and membership options for individuals in public administration careers. Sponsors 127 local chapters and 16 sections on specific areas of governments, such as the Section of Natural Resources and Environmental Administration and the Section on Human Resource Administration.

11142 www.aspehhs.gov
Interagency Council on the Homeless

Seeks to evaluate and monitor federal activities for the homeless, collect information, study problems related to homelessness and disseminate information. Provides technical and professional assistance to the State and local governments and other public and private organizations to maximize resources and develop innovative programs to help the homeless.

11143 www.brbpub.com
BRB Publications

Over 700 reviewers are indexed and profiled by county of expertise. Includes the membership of The Public Record Retriever Network, links to hundreds of sites with free public records and you may order research books online.

11144 www.cagw.convio.com
Citizens Against Government Waste

Seeks to educate the public, individuals in public administration and Congress on eliminating waste, mismanagement, and inefficiency in government spending.

11145 www.clearhq.org
Council on Licensure, Enforcement and Regulation

Members include occupational and professional licensing boards and agencies and private interests in the 50 states, territories and Canada.

11146 www.communityleadership.org
Community Leadership Association

Founded by 40 community leadership organizations.

11147 www.coscda.org
Council for State Community Development Agencies

Employees of state community affairs agencies.

11148 www.csa-dc.org
Contract Services Association of America

Represents the government services contracting industry in Washington, DC. Members range from small businesses to large corporations servicing federal and state government in numerous capacities. CSA acts to foster effective implementation of the government's policy of reliance on the private sector for support services.

11149 www.cued.org
National Council for Urban Economic Development

National membership organization serving public and private participants in economic development across the United States and in international settings. CUED provides information to its members who build local economies through the tools used for job creation, attraction and retention. Members include public economic development directors, chamber of commerce staff, utility executives and academicians, plus the many other professionals who help design and implement development programs.

11150 www.eba-net.org
Energy Bar Association

Lawyers engaged in promoting proper administration of federal laws relating to the production, development and economic regulation of energy.

11151 www.epic.org
Fund for Constitutional Government

Seeks to expose and correct illegal activities, corruption, and lack of accountability in the federal government.

11152 www.fbi.gov
Federal Investigators Association

Formerly the United States Treasury Agents.

11153 www.fedphy.org
Federal Physicians Association

The purpose of the Federal Physicians Association is to improve the practice of medicine within the federal government; and to improve the working conditions and benefits of Federal Civil Service Physicians.

11154 www.foodprotection.org
International Association for Food Protection

The International Association for Food Protection founded in 1911, is a nonprofit educational association with a mission to provide food safety professional worldwide with a forum to exchange information on protecting the food supply. The Association is comprised of a cross-section of over 3,000 members from 50 nations. Affiliate chapters are located in the United States, Canada and South Korea.

11155 www.ginniemae.gov/about/contract.htm
Government National Mortgage Association -
Ginnie Mae

Supports government housing objectives by establishing secondary markets for residential mortgages. Through its mortgage-backed securities programs, Ginnie Mae creates a vehicle for channeling funds from the securities markets into the mortgage market and helps to increase the supply of credit available for housing.

11156 www.govexec.com
National Journal

The website of Government Executive Magazine.

11157 www.greyhouse.com
Grey House Publishing

Selected Grey House directories in the fields of business, health and education are available online. Users can search our online databases by several different search criteria, such as product categories, geographic area, sales volume and much, much more. Full Grey House catalog and online ordering also available.

11158 www.healthfinder.gov
Association of Food and Drug Officials

Promotes the enforcement of laws and regulations at all levels of government. Fosters understanding and cooperation between industry and regulators. Develops model laws and regulations and seeks their adoption.

11159 www.ida-downtown.org
International Downtown Association

Represents organizations and individuals involved in downtown development. Members include city center redevelopment organizations and local officials, businesses, property owners, financiers, planners, university and foundation representatives, and legal and accounting professionals. Offers conferences, technical assistance, consulting services and extensive information services.

11160 **www.ihs.com**
International Code Council

Nonprofit membership association with more than 16,000 members who span the building community, from code enforcement officials to materials manufacturers. Dedicated to preserving the public health, safety and welfare in the built environment through the effective use and enforcement of model codes.

11161 **www.imsasafety.org**
International Municipal Signal Association

International resource for information, education and certification for public safety.

11162 **www.iogcc.state.ok.us**
Interstate Oil and Gas Compact Commission

Represents the governors of 37 states that produce virtually all the domestic oil and natural gas in the United States.

11163 **www.leadershipdirectories.com**
Leadership Directories

Offers free online directory of Presidential Transition Team, free online roster of newly elected congressman and subscription information.

11164 **www.liberty.uc.wlu.edu**
Journalism Resources

Lists of newspapers, film resources, jobs and internships and political advocacy groups.

11165 **www.nacced.org**
National Association for County Community and
Economic Development

Members are directors and staff members of county, community and economic development agencies.

11166 **www.naco.org**
Nat'l Assn of County Information Technology Admin

11167 **www.nagra.org**
North American Gaming Regulators Association

Members are government entities involved in local, state, federal and provincial regulation of gambling activities.

11168 **www.nahma.org**
National Affordable Housing Management Association

Trade association representing companies and individuals involved in the management of affordable multifamily housing.

11169 **www.nahro.org**
Ntl Assoc of Housing & Redevelopment Officials

A professional membership association representing local housing authorities, community development agencies, and individual professionals in the housing, community development, and redevelopment fields.

11170 **www.nalhfa.org**
National Assn. of Local Housing Finance Agencies

County and city agencies which finance affordable housing using tax-exempt annual tools such as the low income housing tax credit and private activity bonds.

11171 **www.napawash.org**
National Academy of Public Administration

An independent, non-profit organization chartered by Congress to improve governance at all levels- local, regional, state, national and international.

11172 **www.napus.org**
National Association of Postmasters of the US

Sponsors and supports the Political Education for Postmasters Political Action Committee.

11173 **www.narc.org**
National Association of Regional Councils

State of regional repositories of instructional materials or services.

11174 **www.nasaa-arts.org**
National Assembly of State Arts Agencies

NASAA's mission is to advance and promote a meaningful role for the arts in the lives of individuals, families and communities throughout the United States. We empower state art agencies through strategic assistance that fosters leadership, enhances planning and decision making, and increases resources. TTD 202-347-5948.

11175 **www.nasaa.org**
North American Securities Administrators Assoc

NASAA is the international organization representing 66 securities administrators from all 50 states, the District of Columbia, Canada, Mexico and Puerto Rico, and is responsible for investor protection and education. NASAA recommends national policies in the securities industry and provides model legislation for state securities agencies to adopt affecting the regulation of broker/dealers and investment advisers. Consumers can contact NASAA to get phone numbers of state securities regulators.

11176 **www.nasar.org**
National Association for Search and Rescue

Members belong to various emergency medical, fire or survival rescue services.

11177 **www.nasda.com**
National Association of State Development Agencies

Established to provide a forum for directors of state economic development agencies to exchange information, compare programs, and establish an organizational base to approach the Federal Government on issues of mutual interest.

11178 **www.nast.net**
Ntl Assoc of State Facilities Administrators

State administrators of facilities and property.

11179 **www.natat.org**
National Association of Towns and Townships

A nonprofit membership organization offering technical assistance, educational services and public policy support to local officials from more than 13,000 town and township governments across the country. The purpose is to strengthen the effectiveness of town and township governments and promote their interests in the public and private sectors.

11180 **www.nbpc.net**
National Border Patrol Council

A labor union representing employees of the US border patrol.

11181 **www.ncne.com**
National Center for Neighborhood Enterprise

A research demonstration and development organization providing support and technical assistance to grassroots organizations who are working toward revitalization of urban communities. The Center accomplishes this goal by promoting, and explaining alternative approaches to community development; identifies successful transferable program principles, strategies and techniques; and encouraging policy recommendations to assist neighborhood revitalization.

11182 **www.ncsha.org**
National Council of State Housing Agencies

Represents the views of state housing finance agencies in 48 states. A high priority for the Council is promoting the views of state housing agencies on the issue of delivery of housing financing for low and moderate income people. Other priorities include increasing the stock of affordable rental units and generating innovative approaches to providing public housing acceptable to residents and communities.

11183 **www.ncsl.org**
National Conference of State Legislatures

A bipartisan organization dedicated to serving the lawmakers and staffs of the nations 50 states, its commonwealths and territories.

11184 **www.ndaa-apri.org**
Prosecutor

To be the voice of America's prosecutors and to support their efforts to protect the rights and safety of the people.

11185 **www.nedaonline.org**
National Community Development Association

A national nonprofit membership organization representing local governments that implement community development programs. The members administer federally supported community development, housing and human services programs. NCDA provides counsel at the federal level on new program design and current program implementation and advocates on behalf of responsive community development.

11186 **www.nemaweb.org**
National Emergency Management Association

Members include federal agencies, local emergency management representatives and interested individuals, associations and corporations.

11187 **www.nfbpa.org**
National Forum for Black Public Administrators

An association for public administrators.

11188 **www.nhlp.org**
National Housing Law Project

A nonprofit corporation that provides assistance on public and private housing and community development matters to Legal Services attorneys and housing specialists throughout the country. The project's goals are to produce, maintain and conserve low and moderate income housing and protect and expand the rights of lower income persons to decent and affordable housing.

11189 **www.nlc.org**
National League of Cities

Advocates on behalf of cities and regularly monitors all three branches of the federal government. Promotes the National Municipal Policy developed and adopted by member cities at the annual Congress of Cities.

11190 **www.npelra.org**
National Labor Relations Board of Professionals

Represents members in contract negotiations and grievance laws.

11191 **www.nrhcweb.org**
National Rural Housing Coalition

A national membership organization that advocates improved housing for low-income rural families and works to increase public awareness of rural housing problems. The Coalition works with a network of state coalitions and nonprofit organizations to promote federal housing policy that benefits both rural housing and community development programs.

11192 **www.patriot.net/users/permail**
Public Employees Roundtable

Demonstrates the value of government employees. Develop an 'espirit de corps' among public service employees and encourages public service careers.

11193 **www.phada.org**
Public Housing Authorities Directors Association

Represents and serves the needs of executive directors of housing authorities of all sizes, in all regions of the nation. In pursuing the Association's goal of improving assisted housing, the corporation works with Congress and federal agencies as well as with all interested groups to improve the nation's housing programs.

11194 **www.postcom.org**
Association for Postal Commerce

National Organization representing those who use, or support the use, of mail as a medium for communication and commerce. Postcom publishes a weekly newsletter covering postal policy and operational issues.

11195 **www.ptos.org**
Patent and Trademark Office Society

Members are examiners in the US Patent & Trademark Office, registered patent attorneys and agents, agencies, judges and other patent professionals.

11196 **www.publicrecordsources.com**
BRB Publications

The BRB Public Record Vendor search tool indexes and categorizes: Over 450 search firms, gateways, proprietary database managers and online public record vendors, over 250 pre employment and tenant screening companies, has links to free public sites, and locates industry trade associations.

11197 **www.ruralhome.org**
Housing Assistance Council

Expands the pool of decent housing available to the rural poor. Creates and sustains interest and action from all levels of government concerning rural housing for low-income people and helps rural housing organizatins become more productive and professional.

11198 **www.sgac.org**
State Government Affairs Council

Seeks to improve the state legislative process through interaction with major state governmental conferences. Conducts educational programs on public policies to further understanding between private sector businesses and state legislations.

11199 **www.sge-econ.org**
Society of Government Economists

Membership benefits economists employed in the public sector or who are interested in the economic aspects of government policies.

11200 **www.sheeo.org**
State Higher Education Executive Officers

Members are the full-time chief executive officers serving statewide coordinating or governing boards of postsecondary education.

11201 **www.sso.org**
Intl Assoc of Official Human Rights Agencies

Members are state and local government human rights and human relations agencies.

11202 **www.sso.org/iafwa**
Intl Assoc of Fish and Wildlife Agencies

Established as the National Association of Game Commissioners.

11203 www.statenews.org
Council of State Governments

Research and service agency for state governments and state officials.

11204 www.theiacp.org
International Association of Chiefs of Police

Has an annual budget of approximately $7 million.

11205 www.urisa.org
Urban & Regional Information Systems Association

Concerned with the effective use of information systems technology at the state, regional and local levels. Members informed of current developments in the information systems field. Its goal is to stimulate and encourage the advancement of an interdisciplinary professional approach to planning, designing and operating information systems.

11206 www.usmayors.org/uscm/
United States Conference of Mayors

An organization of city government officials.

11207 www.water.dnr.state.sc.us/water/icwp
Interstate Council on Water Policy

Members are state and regional agencies concerned with conservation and environmental issues.

11208 www.wicdirectors.org
National Association of WIC Directors

Members are geographic state, Native American state and local agency directors of the Special Supplement nutrition program for woman,infants and children.

Associations

11209 American Institute of Graphic Arts
164 5th Avenue
New York, NY 10010
212-554-4004
FAX: 212-807-1799
comments@aiga.org www.aiga.org

George Fernandez, Membership Director
David Hall, Membership Associate
Gabriela Mirensky, Director Competitions & Exhibits
Michelle Stanek, Events Project Manager
Ric Grefe, Executive Director

To further excellence in design as a broadly defined discipline, strategic tool for business and cultural force. A professional association committed to stimulating thinking about design through the exchange of ideas and information, the encouragement of critical analysis and research and the advancement of education and ethical practice.
18575 Members Founded: 1922

11210 Association of Graphic Communications
330 7th Avenue
9th Floor
New York, NY 10001-5010
212-279-2100
FAX: 212-279-5381
susie@agcomm.org www.agcomm.org

Susan Greenwood, President/CEO
Vicki Keenan, Executive VP
Diane Chavan, VP Education/Training

A provider of graphic arts education and training, a vehicle for industry promotion and marketing, and an advocate on legislative and environmental issues.
560 Members Founded: 1865

11211 Communications Roundtable
1250 24th Street NW
Suite 250
Washington, DC 20037
202-755-5180
FAX: 202-466-0544
michael@SolutionsWebDesign.net
www.roundtable.org

Michael Reichgut, Chairman
Shawn Dolley, Chief Executive Officer

Association of 24 public relations, marketing, graphics, advertising, training, information technology and other communications and organizations. Goals include furthering professionalism, cooperation between member organizations, career and employment support, employer assistance, and membership services and benefits. The largest organization of its type.
12000 Members Founded: 1991

11212 Electrostatic Discharge Association
7900 Turin Road
Building 3
Rome, NY 13440-2069
315-339-6937
FAX: 315-339-6793
info@esda.org www.esda.org/

Kay Adams, President
Dave Swenson, Senior VP
Donn Bellmore, Treasurer
Michele McSwain, Secretary
Lisa Pimpinella, Operations Manager

Professional voluntary association dedicated to advancing the theory and practice of electrostatic discharge avoidance. Initial emphasis on the effects of ESD on electronic components has broadened to include textiles, plastics, web processing, clean rooms, and graphic arts. Expands ESD awareness through educational programs, development of standards, tutorials, publications, local chapters, symposia and certification.
2000+ Members Founded: 1982

11213 Graphic Artists Guild
90 John Street
Suite 403
New York, NY 10038-3202
212-910-0330
800-500-2672
webcomments@gag.org www.gag.org

John Schmelzer, President
Lara Kisielewska, Secretary
Patricia McKiernan, Administrative Director
Barbara Pannone, Membership & Database

Promotes and protects the economic interests of member artists and is committed to improving conditions for all ceators of graphic arts and raising standards for the enitre industry.
4M Members Founded: 1967

11214 Graphic Arts Association
1210 Northbrook Drive
Suite 250
Trevose, PA 19053
215-396-2300
FAX: 215-396-9890
gaa@gaa1900.com www.gaa1900.com

Margaret Baumhauer, President
Melissa Jones, Director Membership
Maria Allen, Education Coordinator
Bill Scotese, Director Credit/Collections
Barbara Boorse, Assistant Director Credit

To be the leading resource for the printing and graphic communications industry in advocacy,education, and information to enhance the strength and profitability of its members.
400 Members Founded: 1886

11215 Graphic Arts Sales Foundation
845 West Chester Pike
West Chester, PA 19382
610-436-9778
FAX: 610-436-5238

Dick Gorelick, President Graphic Arts Sales

Training organization in the graphic arts industry offering one-day, five-day, and custom in-house programs for chief executive officers, sales managers, marketing professionals, sales people, production supervisors, estimators, manufacturing managers and customer service representatives.
1.5M Members Founded: 1988

11216 Graphic Communications International Union
1900 L Street NW
Washington, DC 20036
202-462-1400
FAX: 202-721-0600
webmessenger@gciu.org
www.gciu.org

George Tedeschi, President
Gerald H Deneau, Secretary/Treasurer

Represents U.S. and Canadian workers in all craft and skills areas in the printing and publishing industry. Members are also journalists, graphic artists, typesetters, sales people, and support staff.
100,0 Members Founded: 1983

11217 Graphic Products Association/Graphics Pro
4709 N. El Captain Avenue
Suite 103
Fresno, CA 93722
559-276-8494
FAX: 559-276-8494 800-276-8428
info@graphicspro.org
www.graphicspro.org

Michael R Neer, Executive Director
Steven V Neer, Associate Executive Director

Worldwide membership organization for businesses that produce and sell custom graphic products such as awards,custom gifts, decorated apparel, promotional items, signs, or stamps. Also represents manufacturers and other companies who supply products to industry producers.
82000 Members Founded: 1994

11218 Guild of Natural Science Illustrators
PO Box 652
Ben Franklin Station
Washington, DC 20044-0652
301-309-1514
FAX: 301-309-1514
gnsihome@his.com www.gnsi.org
Non-profit organization that sets high professional standards, provides opportunities for professional and scholarly development, encourages and assists member networking, and promotes itself to potential clients and the general public.
1.1M Members Founded: 1968

11219 International Digital Enterprise Alliance
100 Daingerfield Road
4th Floor
Alexandria, VA 22314
703-837-1070
FAX: 703-837-1072
info@idealliance.org
www.idealliance.org

Chuck Myers, Chair
Anne Marie Bushell, Vice Chair
David J. Steinhardt, President/CEO
Dan Minnick, Secretary/Treasurer

Enables publishers and other information-driven enterprisers to strategize, innovate, standardize and implement information technology solutions in an open and cooperative crops industry environment.
300+ Members Founded: 1966

11220 International Reprographic Association
401 N Michigan Avenue
Chicago, IL 60611-1929
312-245-1026
FAX: 312-527-6705 800-833-4742
sbova@irga.com www.irga.com

Chuck Gremillion, President
Michael Shaw, VP
Mike Carter, Secretary/Treasurer
Steve Bova, Executive Director

Represents entrepreneurial businesses serving the wide-format imaging needs of graphic arts, architectural, engineering, manufacturing, corporate, legal, retail, and POP industries.

Founded: 1927

11221 National Association for Printing Leadership (NAPL)
75 West Century Road
Paramus, NJ 07652-1408
201-634-9600
FAX: 201-634-0325 800-642-6275
info@napl.org www.napl.org
John B Davidson, Chairman
Stephen Johnson, Vice Chairman
Joseph P Truncale CAE, President/CEO
Joan Kasper, Senior Director Corporate Planning
A not-for-profit national trade association serving companies in the $100 billion+ graphic communications industry. NAPL offers a comprehensive slate of business and building solutions that provides company leaders with the strategies, insights, and guidance they can use to make informed business decisions, minimize risk, anticipate change, and profitably grow their business.
2000 Members Founded: 1933

11222 North American Graphic Arts Suppliers Association
POBox 934483
Margate, FL 33093
954-971-1383
FAX: 954-971-4362
nagasa4info@nagasa.org
www.nagasa.org
Don Harvey, Chairman
The association for the channel that distributes printing and imaging technologies.
362 Members Founded: 1993

11223 PIA/GATF (Electronic Prepress Section)
200 Deer Run Road
Sewickley, PA 15143-2311
412-741-6860
FAX: 412-741-2311 800-742-2666
piagatf@piagatf.org www.piagatf.org
Michael Makin, President/CEO
Dee Gentile
Mary Garnett, VP
Jusy Allen, Executive Secretary
Delivers products and services that enhance the growth,efficiency and profitability of its members and the industry through advocacy, education,research and technical information.
13000 Members Founded: 1887

11224 Pacific Printing & Imaging Association
1400 SW 5th Avenue
Suite 815
Portland, OR 97201
503-297-3328
FAX: 800-824-1911 877-762-7742
info@pacprinting.org
www.pacprinting.org
Marcus Sassaman, Executive Director
David Katz, VP
Amy Wagner, Marketing Program Administrator
Angie Khong, Marketing/Program Administer
Provides programs, services and promotes an environment which assists members to see and adapt to the future, while continuing to improve and profit in the present.
200 Members Founded: 1948

11225 Printing Industries of America/Graphics Arts Technical Foundation
200 Deer Run Road
Sewickley, PA 15143-2600
412-741-6860
FAX: 412-741-3227
piagatf@piagatf.org www.gain.net
Jim Mayes, Chairman
Dave DeLana, Secretary
A graphic arts trade association representing our members in this industry. PIA/GATF, along with its affiliates, delivers products and services that enhance the growth, efficiency and profitability of its members and the industry through advocacy, education, research and technical information.
12000 Members Founded: 1887

11226 Society for Environmental Graphic Design
1000 Vermont Avenue
Suite 400
Washington, DC 20005
202-638-5555
FAX: 202-638-0891
segd@segd.org www.segd.org
Peter Dixon, President
Leslie Dilworth, Executive Director
Ann Makowski, Director Membership
Craig M Berger, Director Education
International non-profit educational foundation that provides resources for design specialists in the field of environmental graphic design, architecture, and landscape, interior, and industrial design. Members are leading designers of directional and attraction sign systems, destination grpahics, identityprograms, exhibits and themed environments.
1000+ Members Founded: 1973

11227 Society of Publication Designers
17 E 47th St
Rm 600
New York, NY 10017-7923
212-838-8585
FAX: 212-268-1867 spdnyc@aol.com
Bride Whelan, Executive Director
A professional organization which includes art directors, designers, illustrators, photographers, printers and publishers. Serves the needs of editorial designers and art directors by sponsoring annual competitions, speakers evenings, exhibitions and other activities.
550 Members Founded: 1964

11228 Special Interest Group on Computers
Association for Computing Machinery
1515 Broadway
New York, NY 10036
212-697-7440
FAX: 212-302-5826 800-342-6626
webmaster@acm.org
www.siggraph.org
Alain Chesnais, President
Barb Helfer, VP
Anthony Baylis, Treasurer
A forum for the promotion and distribution of current computer graphics research and technology.
6367 Members Founded: 1947

11229 Technical Association of the Graphic Arts
68 Lomb Memorial Drive
Rochester, NY 14623-5604
858-475-7470
FAX: 858-475-2250
tagaofc@aol.com www.taga.org
William Ray, President
Karen E Lawrence, Managing Director
Richard Goodman, Executive VP
Provides a worldwide forum for sharing and disseminating theoretical,functional and practical information on current and emerging technologies for Graphic Arts print production and related processes
900+ Members Founded: 1948

11230 Urban Art International
PO Box 868
Tiburon, CA 94920
415-435-4767
FAX: 415-435-4240
uai@hansenarchitects.com
www.imagesite.com
Fani Hansen, President
Provides a forum for a creative exchange of ideas and information.
150 Members Founded: 1980

Newsletters

11231 Board Report for Graphic Artists
Board Report Publishing Company
900 Lincoln Street
#300789
Denver, CO 80203-2712
303-839-9058
FAX: 303-839-1272
Drew Miller, Publisher
Mabel Frazier, Editor
Information and ideas on market design and trends in the graphic art field. *$96.00*
18 pages Monthly Founded: 1978

11232 Comics/Animation Forum
CompuServe Information Service
5000 Arlington Centre Boulevard
Columbus, OH 43220-5439
614-457-8600
FAX: 614-457-0348
76703.3041@compserve.com
http://www.compuserve.com
Bob Massey, President
Offers information of interest to collectors of comic books and animation art. *$199.00*
Monthly Founded: 1969

11233 Document Image Automation
Phillips Business Information
7811 Montrose Road
Potomac, MD 20854-3363
301-340-2100
FAX: 301- 34- 054
http://www.phillips.com
John Coyle, President
Thomas Avedon, VP
Alan Meckler, Publisher
Don Burne, Editor
This quarterly newsletter offers information and coverage on events in optical storage and electronic document imaging fields. *$ 59.00*
10 pages Quarterly Founded: 1974

11234 Graphic News
Printing Industry of Minnesota
2829 University Avenue SE
Suite 750
Minneappolis, MN 55414-3222
612-379-3360
FAX: 618-379-6030 800-448-756

David Radziej, President
Arlene Roth, Director Public Relations/Marketin
John Connelly, Director of Membership Se
Carla Steuck, Director of Education Services

For the printing and graphic arts industries.

16 pages Monthly Founded: 1955
Circulation: 12000

11235 Graphics Update
Printing Association of Florida
6095 NW 167 Street
Suite D-7
Miami, FL 33015
305-558-4855
FAX: 305-823-8965 800-331-0461
printpaf@ix.netcom.com
http://www.pafgraf.org

Gene Strul, Editor
Michael H Streibig, Staff Executive
Ron Davis, Chief Economist

A monthly newsletter to the members of the Printing Association of Florida. Full color publication with attractive advertising purchases and a focused buying circulation.
$200.00
Monthly

11236 Guild News
Graphic Artists Guild
90 John Street
Suite 403
New York, NY 10038-3202
212-910-0330
FAX: 212-791-0333 800-500-2672
info@gag.org
http://www.gag.org/news

Steven Schubert, Executive Director
Molly Knappen, President
Sara Love, Communications Chair
Patricia McKiernan, Administrative Director
Barbara Pannone, Membership and Database Director

Information on contracts for artists.
$115.00
Monthly Founded: 1973

11237 Guild of Natural Science Illustration
Guild of Natural Science Illustrators
PO Box 652
Ben Franklin Station
Washington, DC 20044-652
301-309-1514
FAX: 301-309-1514
gnsihome@his.com
http://www.gnsi.org/

Steve Buchanan, Editor
Elaine Hodges, President/VP

Non-profit organization for those interested in the field of natural science illustrations. Newsletter is published 10 times a year.
$75.00
Monthly Founded: 1968
Circulation: 1000

11238 Holography News
Reconnaissance International Consulting
PO Box 40976
Denver, CO 80204
303-628-5568
FAX: 303-628-5594
adminamericas@reconnaisance-intl.co
http://www.reconnaissance-intl.com

Ian Lancaster, Director
Jon Senft, VP
Lewis Kontnik, Publisher

The international business newsletter reporting on the holography industry.
$774.00
Monthly

11239 In House Graphics
United Communications Group
11300 Rockville Pike
Suite 1100
Rockville, MD 20852-3030
301-816-8950
FAX: 301-816-8945
webmaster@ucg.com www.ucg.com

Ronnie Lipton, Publisher

For graphics and desktop publishing professionals with large needs and small resources.
Monthly

11240 Messages
Society of Environmental Graphic Designers
100 Vermont Avenue NW
Suite 400
Washington, DC 20005
202-638-5555
FAX: 202-638-0891
sedgofice@aol.com www.segd.org

Sarah Speare, Publisher
V Shetty, Owner

News of interest for graphic designers.

Magazines & Journals

11241 Animation Magazine
Animation Magazine
30941 W Agoura Road
suite 102
Westlake Village, CA 91361
818-991-2884
FAX: 818-991-3773
info@animationmagazine.net
http://www.animationmagazine.net

Jean Thoren, President

Covers the animation industry trends, technology, new products, historical perspectives coverage of current animated programming and features, and general news. *$65.07*
Monthly Founded: 1985 $165 per M.
Printed in 4 colors on glossy stock

11242 Around the Bargaining Loop
Graphic Arts Employers of America
100 Daingerfield Road
Alexandria, VA 22314-2886
703-519-8100
FAX: 703-548-3227 www.gain.org

Joy Johnson

Employers guide, information and news for professionals working in the graphic arts industry.
Monthly

11243 Art & Design News
Boyd Publishing Company
5783 Park Plaza Ct
Indianapolis, IN 46220-3914
317-841-9940
FAX: 765-576-5859

Jeanne Pulliam, Publisher/Advertising Director
Rebecca Tapley, Editor

Features developments in graphic arts, design and related topics.

Circulation: 48,278

11244 Art Direction
Advertising Trade Publications
10 E 39th Street
6th Floor
New York, NY 10016-111
212-683-8905
FAX: 212-889-6504

Dan Barron, Editor/Publisher
Tom Davis, Advertising/Sales Manager

For visual professionals; reports events, people, shows, awards, new techniques, products, and services. Accepts advertising. *$ 27.50*
128 pages Monthly

11245 Art of Production
QBC Publishing Systems
1223 Hemlock Farms
Hawley, PA 18428-9064
570-775-6856
FAX: 570-775-7907
qbcsystems@aol.com
http://www.webpdf.com/aop/

Richard Sasso, Publisher

News and features address the technological advances in the industry, provide reviews of books, newsletters and events, and keep industry professionals updated on talent, training and business operations affecting management. *$49.00*
Fortnightly Founded: 1989
Circulation: 5000

11246 Artes Graficas Magazine
CC International Publishing
1680 SW Bayshore Boulevard
Port Saint Lucie, FL 34984-3500
772-337-1250
FAX: 772-879-7388

Holger Hilkinger, Circulation Manager

A Spanish-language magazine distributed to the printing, packaging, newspaper and graphic arts professionals throughout Latin America. Accepts advertising.

Circulation: 23,837

11247 Before & After: How to Design Cool Stuff
Pagelab
323 Lincoln Street
Roseville, CA 95678-2229
956-78 -229
FAX: 916-784-3995 800-266-5783
contact@bamagazine.com
http://www.bamagazine.com

John McWade, Publisher
Gaye McWade, Editor

Teaches graphic design to desktop publishers. Topica include newsletter and brochure design, advertising and logo design, typography, illustration, color and more. *$36.00*
Founded: 1990
Circulation: 26000

11248 Cadalyst
Advanstar Communications
545 Boylston Street
Boston, MA 02116
617-514-4600
FAX: 617-267-6900 888-527-7008
editors@cadalyst.com
http://www.cadalyst.com/

Sara Ferris, Editor-in-Chief
Lara Sheridan, Managing Editor

For computer-aided design and visualization hardware and software. It proivides practical solutions, time-saving tips, and product reviews for users of CDD software for AEC mechanical and manufacturing applications. *$39.95*

100 pages Monthly Founded: 1987
Circulation: 90000
Printed in 4 colors

11249 Communication Arts
Coyne & Blanchard
110 Constitution Drive
Menlo Park, CA 94025
650-326-6040
FAX: 650-326-1648
editorial@commarts.com
http://www.commarts.com

Jean A Coyne, Executive Editor
Ernie Schenck, Advertising Manager
Mike Krigel, Marketing Executive

Features profile individuals, studios and agencies with examples of their work. Includes reviews of software, books and products, as well as discussing the latest in digital and broadcast design. *$53.00*

8 issues per ye Founded: 1959
Circulation: 71927
Printed in 4 colors

11250 Computer Graphics World
PennWell Publishing Company
98 Spit Brook
Nashua, NH 03062
603-891-0123
FAX: 603-891-0574
http://www.cgw.com

Bill LoPiccolo, Editor
Mark Finkelstein, Publisher

Covers specific applications of computer graphics, written by users and vendors of equipment and services to the industry. The magazine of 3D computer graphics for engineering and animation professionals. *$55.00*

Monthly Founded: 1977
Circulation: 40597
Printed in 4 colors on glossy stock

11251 Computers in Graphics
Virgo Publishing
3300 N Central Avenue, Suite 2500
PO Box 40079
Phoenix, AZ 85067-0079
480-990-1101
FAX: 480-675-8146

Jennifer Lutener, Editor

Explores the use of computer technology in the graphics industries. *$35.00*

Monthly Founded: 1990

11252 Critique
Neumeier Design Team
120 Hawthorne Avenue
#102
Palo Alto, CA 94301-1000
650-326-4396
FAX: 650-323-3298
editor@critiquemag.com
http://www.critiquemag.com

Marty Neumeier, Editor

Features include methods and products to increase the creativity and technological advance of graphic artwork. *$60.00*

Quarterly
Circulation: 10000

11253 Desktop Publishers Journal
Desktop Publishing Institute
462 Boston Street
Topsfield, MA 01983-1200

FAX: 978-887-9245

Thomas Tetreault, Publisher
Barry Harrigan, Editor

Desktop publishing topics and issues and association information.

Weekly
Circulation: 60000

11254 Digital Imaging
Cygnus Publishing
3 Huntington Quadrangle
Suite 301N
Melville, NY 11747
631-845-2700
FAX: 631-845-2798 800-308-6397
info@digitalimagingmag.com
http://www.cygnuspub.com

Laureen Delaney, Associate Publisher
Kathy Schneider, Group Publisher
Andrew Darlow, Editorial Director
Liz Vickers, Advertising Sales Manager

For the imaging professional. Dedicated to bridging the digital imaging gap between graphics and photography while providing in-depth solutions.

Founded: 1966
Circulation: 30,000

11255 Dynamic Graphics
Dynamic Graphics
6000 N Forest Park Drive
Peoria, IL 61614-3592
309-888-8851
FAX: 800-488-3492 888-698-8542
info@dynamicgraphics.com
http://www.dynamicgraphics.com

Alan Meckler, President, JupiterMedia
David Moffly, President/CEO
Marcy Slane, Managing Editor

Encourages users to take their electronic tools to the next level of productivity and creativity. Emphasizes practical and real-world solutions. *$36.00*

72 pages 6 Founded: 1964
Circulation: 66143 40,000 names $130 per M.
Printed in on glossy stock

11256 Electronic Publishing
PennWell Publishing Company
98 Spit Brook Road
Nashua, NH 03062-5737
603-891-0123

keithh@pennwell.com
http://www.pennwell.com

Keith V Hevenor, Editor
Nancy A Hitchcock, Senior Associate Editor

News magazine for owners, managers and production executives of electronic printing and publishing sites. *$61.44*

Monthly Founded: 1910

11257 GATFWORLD Magazine
Graphic Arts Technical Foundation Association
200 Deer Run Road
Sewickley, PA 15143-2324
412-741-6860
FAX: 412-741-2311 800-910-4283
gatf@piagatf.org http://www.gain.net

George Ryan, Executive VP/COO
Michael Makin, President/CEO
Deanna Gentile, Editor

A bi-monthly magazine for GATF members and subscribers that reports on research and technical trends in the graphic arts (printing) industry, environmental and safety news, developments in graphic communications education and news of emerging products, programs and services. *$ 75.00*

Founded: 1924
Circulation: 18000

11258 Gasp Report
GASP Engineering
234 Benjamin W Avenue
Swarthmore, PA 19081-1421
610-543-5194
FAX: 610-328-1358 800-256-4282
hannaford@gaspnet.com
http://www.gaspnet.com

Steve Hannaford, Publisher

Covers new technology, financing, marketing and other business concerns of the printing, graphics and publishing industries. In-depth articles highlight strategies for industry professionals. *$195.00*

Monthly
Circulation: 400

11259 Graphic Arts Monthly
360 Park Avenue S
New York, NY 10010
212-636-6834
FAX: 646-746-7422 800-217-7874
psaran@reedbusiness.com
http://www.worldleadersinprint.com

Phil Saran, Publisher
Roger Ynostroza, Editorial Director

The magazine of the printing industry including commercial, in-plant and related operations, such as color separations, composition, binding and pre-press service bureaus.

Monthly
Circulation: 75,000

11260 Graphic Communications World
Hayzlett & Associates
3133 South Western Avenue
Sioux Falls, SD 57106
605-336-3335
FAX: 605-275-2087
www.hayzlett.com/index.htm

Jeanette Clinkunbroomer, Editor-in-Chief
Jeff Hayzlett, Owner

Created to inform senior printing and publishing management with regards to new technology and top management news, as well as a calendar of industry events and meetings. *$347.00*

4 pages BiWeekly Founded: 1968
Circulation: 4,000

11261 Graphic Communicator
Graphic Communications International Union
1900 L Street NW
Washington, DC 20036-5002
202-462-1400
FAX: 202-721-0600
http://www.gciu.org

James Harff, Owner
George Teddeschi, CEO

Coverage ranges from printing and publishing news to information from the international union, as well as local members. *$12.00*

Founded: 1983
Circulation: 140000

11262 Graphic Design: USA
Kaye Publishing Corporation
79 Madison Avenue
Suite 1202
New York, NY 10016-4503
212-696-4380
FAX: 212-696-4564
gkaye@gdusa.com
http://www.gdusa.com

Susan Benson, Editor
Maria Mohamed, Circualtion Manager
Gordon D. Kaye, Publisher

A publication for the graphic designer, offering information and news of the industry. *$60.00*

120 pages Monthly Founded: 1965

11263 Graphic Impressions
Pioneer Communications
6th & Walnut Street
Fleming Building, Suite 610
Des Moines, IA 50309
515-246-0402
FAX: 515-246-0398
rthomas@thepioneergroup.com
www.pioneercommunicationsinc.com

Richard C Thomas, President/Publisher

Provides providing industry news and information including in-depth coverage of PIM, and PIAMS association news and events. Features cover technology, legal, environmental, niche printing, education, new products, marketing, distribution, finance and insurance. *$20.00*

32 pages 10 per year Founded: 1995
Circulation: 7,000
Printed in 4 colors on glossy stock

11264 Graphics Pro
Graphic Products Association
4709 N EI Capitan
Suite 103
Fresno, CA 93722
559-276-8494
FAX: 559-276-8496 800-276-8428
info@graphicspro.org
http://www.graphicspro.org

Michael R Neer, Publisher
Steven V Neer, Associate Publisher
Damara Torres, Owner

A bi-monthly journal published by the Graphic Products Association. *$55.00*

Founded: 1994
Circulation: 7500
Printed in on glossy stock

11265 Graphis
Graphis Press
307 Fifth Avenue
10th Floor
New York, NY 10016-8191
212-329-9387
FAX: 212-213-3229 866-648-2915
info@graphis.com
http://www.graphis.com

B Martin Pedersen, Publisher
Walter Herdeg, Editor

Graphis is an international journal of design and visual communication, covering graphic arts, design, photography, architecture and related topics. The targeted readership includes professionals in these disciplines as well as all creative visual communicators. *$90.00*

Founded: 1944
Circulation: 22000

11266 HOW Magazine
F&W Publications
4700 E Galbraith Road
Cincinnati, OH 45236
513-312-2222

editorial@howdesign.com
http://www.fwpublications.com

Jeffry M Lapin, Publisher
Bryn Mooth, Editor
William R. Reed, President
David Stewart, Chairman/CEO

Business and creative resource for graphic designers. Latest business, technological and creative information. *$49.00*

194 pages Founded: 1900
Circulation: 39946
Printed in 4 colors on glossy stock

11267 ID Magazine
1507 Dana Avenue
Cincinnati, OH 45207
513-396-6160
idedit@fwpubs.com

Kelly N Kofron, Executive Editor
Dave Richmond, Executive Editor

Leading critical magazine covering the art, business and culture of design.

8 per year

11268 Industrial Relations Reporter
Graphic Arts Employers of America
100 Daingerfield Road
Alexandria, VA 22314-2886
703-519-8100
FAX: 703-548-3227 www.gain.org

Joy Johnson

Quarterly

11269 PC Graphics & Video
Advanstar Communications
201 Sandpointe Avenue
Suite 600
Santa Ana, CA 92707-8700
714-513-8400
FAX: 714-513-8481
info@advanstar.com
www.advanstar.com

Michael Forcillo, Publisher
Gene Smarte, Editor

Covers graphics and video for personal computers. *$5.00*

Circulation: 10,699

11270 Print Magazine
RC Publications
38 E 29th Street
3rd Floor
New York, NY 10016
212-447-1400
FAX: 212-447-5231
info@printmag.com
http://www.printmag.com

Joyce Rutter Kay, Editor in Chief
Joel Toner, Publisher
Stephany Skirvin, Art Director
Steven Kent, CEO
William Reed, President

News and information for the graphic design industry. *$53.00*

160 pages Founded: 1940
Circulation: 45000 45,000 names $125 per M.
Printed in 4 colors on glossy stock

11271 Print-Equip News
Pen Publications
215 Allen Avenue
PO Box 5540
Glendale, CA 91221-5540
818-954-9495
FAX: 818-954-0452

Jeff Jutras, Advertising Manager

Articles include features on education, technological advances, and manufacturers news.

Monthly
Circulation: 25000

11272 Printer's Northwest Trader
Eagle Newspapers
650 N 1st Street
PO Box 96
Woodburn, OR 97071-450
503-981-3441
FAX: 503-981-1253
http://www.eaglenewspapers.com

Rod Stollery, Publisher
Sandy Hubbard, Editor

Reviews new equipment and techniques and highlights industry leaders of note. Serves the northwestern portion of the United States. *$10.00*

Monthly Founded: 1933
Circulation: 16000

11273 Publication Design Annual #39
Society of Publication Designers
475 Park Avenue S
Suite 2200
New York, NY 10016
212-838-8585
FAX: 212-268-1867
mail@spd.org http://wwww.spd.org

Bride M Whelan, Executive Director

A compendium of the best designed magazine/trade and consumer newspapers. Annual reports of the year as judged by a panel. Also includes web and interactive design sites and annual reports. *$195.00*

Monthly Founded: 1969 ISBN 1-564966-21-6
Circulation: 15000 272 names
Printed in 4 colors on matte stock

11274 Publish How-to Magazine
MacWorld Communications
501 2nd Street
Suite 310
San Francisco, CA 94107-1469
415-243-3500
FAX: 415-442-0766

Gordon Haight, Publisher
Susan Gubemat, Editor

The definitive source on how to use personal computers to integrate text and graphics into printed communication. *$4.00*

Circulation: 98,819

11275 SEGD Design
Society for Environmental Graphic Design

1000 Vermont Avenue
Suite 400
Washington, DC 20005
202-638-5555
FAX: 202-638-0891
segd@segd.org www.segd.org

Leslie Gallery Dilworth, Executive Director
Ann Makowski, Manager

A magazine published to target the designers and firms for environmental graphics, exhibit and industrial design, architecture

interiors, landscapearchitecture and communication arts. *$200.00*
Quarterly

11276 Screen & Display Graphics
National Business Media
2800 W Midway Boulevard
PO Box 1416
Broomfield, CO 80038-1416
303-469-0424
FAX: 303-469-5730 800-870-0904
greditor@nbm.com
http://www.nbm.com
Mike Musselman, Publisher
Robert H Wieber, President
Covers the latest industry news and technology. Includes product and literature reviews, provides managerial advice, and keeps abreast of government regulations.
$30.00
Monthly
Circulation: 12000

11277 Southern Graphics
PTN Publishing Company
445 Broadhollow Road
Suite 21
Melville, NY 11747-3601

FAX: 631-845-7109
Rob Schweiger, Publisher
KJ Moran, Editor
Edited for those in the graphic arts industry throughout the southeastern US and the Caribbean. *$5.00*

Circulation: 21,000

11278 Trade Show Times
Fichera Communications
441 S State Road
Suite 14
Margate, FL 33063
954-971-4360
FAX: 954-971-4362 800-327-8999
rickktst@aol.com
http://www.tradeshowtimes.com
Orazio Fichera, Publisher
Rick Kelly, Contact
Hand distributed to attendees at major graphic arts trade shows. Accepts advertising.
32 pages Monthly Founded: 1974

11279 Visual Communications Journal
Graphic Arts Technical Foundation Association
200 Deer Run Road
Sewickley, PA 15143-2324
412-741-6860
FAX: 412-741-2311 800-910-4283
info@gatf.org www.gain.net
George Ryan, Executive VP/COO
Michael Makin, President/CEO
Peter Oresick, VP Publishing
Educational guide and news for scholars and students studying the graphic arts industry.

Trade Shows

11280 3D Design & Animation Conference & Expo
Miller Freeman Publications
525 Market Street
Suite 500
San Francisco, CA 94110
415-955-5533
FAX: 415-278-5341
mthompson@mfi.com www.mfi.com
For animators and digital content creators, exibits include equipment supplies and services for the 3D design and animation industry. Conferences, reception and publications. Space rental available.
Annual

11281 Annual Automated Imaging Associates Business Conference
Appliance Manufacturer
5900 Harper Road
Suite 105
Solon, OH 44139-1935
440-349-3060
FAX: 440-498-9121
jburnstein@robotics.org
www.machinevisiononline.org
Jeff Burnstein, Executive Director
The industry's leading conference and networking event. This conference gathers over 150 top industry executives to do business with their peers and hear presentations on issues affecting the global economy in general and the machine vision industry specifically.
Annual,February

11282 Grafix
Conference Management Corporation
200 Connecticut Avenue
Norwalk, CT 06854-1940

FAX: 203-831-8446 800-342-3238
Annual show of 200 exhibitors of computer hardware and software for graphic design and computer publishing, paper supplies, typesetting equipment and services, stock photography, clip art service and related equipment, supplies and services.
4000 Attendees

11283 Graph Expo & Converting Expo
Graphic Arts Show Company
1189 Preston White Drive
Reston, VA 20191-5435
703-264-7200
FAX: 703-620-9187
info@gasc.org www.gasc.org
Chris Thiel, VP
Kelly Kilga, Director Operations
David Poulos, Director Communications
Largest, most comprehensive prepess, printing,converting and digital equipment trade show and conference in America.
40000 Attendees Annual Founded: 1976
Mailing list available for rent

11284 Graph Expo West
Graphic Arts Show Company
1899 Preston White Drive
Reston, VA 20191
703-264-7200
FAX: 703-620-9187
info@gasc.org www.gasc.org
Lilly Kinney, Conference Manager
Chris Theil, VP
Two hundred booths for the graphics industry.
13M Attendees November Founded: 1982

11285 Graphics Trade Show Expo Southwest
910 W Mockingbird Lane
Dallas, TX 75247-5182

Jim Weinstein, Show Manager
Six hundred and fifty booths.
13M Attendees June

11286 Graphics of the Americas
Printing Association of Florida
6275 Hazeltine National Drive
Orlando, FL 32822
407-240-8009
FAX: 407-240-8333
oprice@patgraf.org www.pafgraf.org
Holly Price, Booth Sales & Marketing
Michelle Torres, Attendee Info.
Largest annual international graphic commincations education and exhibit showplace. Over 450 exhibitors in 500,000 square feet.
22000 Attendees February

11287 Gutenberg & Digital Outlook
Graphic Arts Show Company
1189 Preston White Drive
Reston, VA 22091
703-264-7200
FAX: 703-620-9187
info@gasc.org www.gasc.org
Chris Thiel, VP
Kelly Kilga, Director Operations
Largest graphic design, digital prepress, printing, publishing, and converting trade show in the Westen United States. Over 100 exhibitors with the widest selection of vendors.
8000 Attendees Annual,June

11288 Printing Expo Conference Mid America
Graphics Arts Show Company
1899 Preston White Drive
Reston, VA 20191
703-264-7200
FAX: 703-620-9187
info@gasc.org www.gasc.org
Paul Kaplan, Show Manager
Exhibits by manufacturers and dealers of the latest graphics equipment and services.

3000 Attendees June Founded: 1982

11289 Sunbelt Computer and Graphics
Printing Industry Association of Georgia
5020 Highlands Parkway
Smyrna, GA 30082
770-433-3050
FAX: 770-433-3062 800-288-1894
info@sunbeltshow.org
www.sunbeltshow.org
Dianne McPherson, Trade Show Director
Denise Holland, VP Communications
Two hundred and fifty exhibitors of current printing technology.
18M Attendees

Directories & Databases

11290 **365: AIGA Year In Design**
American Institute of Graphic Arts
164 5th Avenue
New York, NY 10010
212-554-4004
FAX: 212-807-1799
publications@aiga.org www.aiga.org
About 500 works of graphic designers that have been cited for outstanding design by the American Institute of Graphic Arts.
$45.00
Annual

11291 **Graphic Artist's Guide to Marketing and Self-Promotion**
North Light Books
1557 Dana Avenue
Cincinnati, OH 45207-1005

FAX: 513-531-4082
A list of publishers of resources about marketing for the graphic artist. *$19.95*

11292 **Graphic Arts Blue Book**
AF Lewis & Company
245 5th Avenue
New York, NY 10016-8728
212-828-8448
FAX: 212-545-7963
gartsbb@village.ios.lom
www.d-net.com/graphartsbb
Doris Reyes, Editor
Timothy Lewis, Editor
Offers information on printing plants, bookbinders, imagesetters, platemakers, paper merchants, paper manufacturers, printing machinery manufacturers and dealers and others serving the graphic arts industry.
$85.00
8 Annual Editions
Circulation: 51500

11293 **Graphic Arts Monthly Sourcebook**
Reed Business Information
2000 Clearwater Drive
Oak Brook, IL 60523
630-740-0825
FAX: 630-288-8540
psaran@reedbusiness.com
Phil Saran, Publisher
Bill Esler, Editor-in_Chief
Roger Ynostroza, Editorial Director
About 1,400 manufacturers and distributors of graphic arts equipment, supplies and services, as well as over 700 graphic arts dealers. *$50.00*
Annual March
Circulation: 85,000

11294 **Graphic Communications Association Bar Code Reporter**
International Digital Enterprise Alliance
100 Daingerfield Road
4th Floor
Alexandria, VA 22314-2886
703-837-1070
FAX: 703-837-1072
info@idealliance.org
www.idealliance.org
Alan Kotok, Editor
The authoritative quarterly journal of bar codes, electronic data interchange, and related electronic commerce technologies in the publishing, printing, and paper industries. *$95.00*
Quarterly
Circulation: 150

11295 **Graphic Support Forum**
CompuServe Information Service
PO Box 20212
Columbus, OH 43220-0212
614-457-8600
FAX: 614-457-0348
This database offers a forum for the discussion of Graphics Interchange Format hardware and software support issues.
Bulletin Board

11296 **RSVP: Directory of Illustration and Design**
RSVP
PO Box 050314
Brooklyn, NY 11205
718-857-9267

info@rsvpdirectory.com
www.rsvpdirectory.com
Kathleen Creighton, Co-Publisher/Co-Editor
Richard Lebenson, Co-Publisher/Co-Editor
Fully illustrated resource book for the graphic arts/media industry. Showcases work of illustrators and designers, nationwide.

Circulation: 18,000

Industry Web Sites

11297 **www.agcomm.org**
Association of Graphic Communications

Promtes the interest of graphic communication professionals.

11298 **www.aiga.org**
American Institute of Graphic Arts

The purpose of the AIGA is to further excellence in a communication design as a broadly defined discipline, as a strategic tool for business and as a cultural force. The AIGA is the place design professionals turn first to exchange ideas and information, participate in critical analysis and research and advance education and ethical practice.

11299 **www.gaa1900.com**
Graphic Arts Association

Promotes the interests of graphic art professionals. Members consist of suppliers and distributors of graphic arts equipment.

11300 **www.gatf.org**
Graphic Arts Technical Foundation Association

To serve the graphic comunications community as the leading source for the technical information and services through research and education.

11301 **www.greyhouse.com**
Grey House Publishing

Selected Grey House directories in the fields of business, health and education are available online. Users can search our online databases by several different search criteria, such as product categories, geographic area, sales volume and much, much more. Full Grey House catalog and online ordering also available.

11302 **www.idealliance.org**
International Digital Enterprise Alliance

Provides the opportunity for those who create, produce, manage, and deliver content to interface with those who develop the software tools to facilitate these functions.

11303 **www.myfonts.com**
MyFonts.com

Allows a user to find fonts with simple keywords. The user can test a font. The site also offers a MyFonts forum, where users can ask the experts

11304 **www.nagasa.org**
North American Graphic Arts Suppliers Association

The association for the channel that distributes printing and imaging technologies.

11305 **www.napl.org**
National Association for Printing Leadership

NAPL publishes industry specific books and periodicals for the graphic arts community. Topics cover management in the areas of sales, marketing, human resources, finance and operations technology.

11306 **www.ppi-assoc.org**
Pacific Printing & Imaging Association

To provide programs, offer services, and promote an environment, which assists members to see and adapt to the future, while continuing to improve and profit in the present.

11307 **www.recouncil.org**
Research and Engineering Council of the National
Association for Printing Leadership

A technical trade association established to identify graphic arts industry problems, coordinate graphic arts technical activities and develop industry associated technical/education programs, conference and seminars.

11308 **www.siggraph.org**
Special Interest Group on Computer Graphics

A forum for the promotion and distribution of current computer graphics research and technology.

11309 **www.taga.org**
Technical Association of the Graphic Arts

Organized to advance the science and technology of graphic arts. Disseminates graphic arts research internationally via annual technical conference and proceedings.

Associations

11310 American Hardware Manufacturers Association
3500 Easy Street
Schaumburg, IL 75247-4977
847-605-1025
FAX: 847-605-1030 800-532-2562
info@AHMA.org www.ahma.org
William P Farrell, Vice Chairman
Timothy S Farrell, President/CEO
John W. Hasemann, International Programs
Eileen Hoblit, Membership/Member Services
Provides a broad spectrum of programs for its members and the entire industry, including educational opportunities, legislative representation, domestic and international marketing support, technology initiatives, a menu of cost-containment offerings, targeted publications, and many other industry-directes services. Members include U.S. hardware producers, manufacturers' agents and industry trade publications.
500+ Members Founded: 1901

11311 Associated Locksmiths of America
3500 Easy Street
Dallas, TX 75204
214-199-9733
FAX: 214-827-1810 800-532-2562
webmaster@aloa.org www.aloa.org
William Young, President
John Soderland, Secretary
Robert E. Mock, Director
Peter Sarailian, Director
Mark E. Blum, Director
International professional organization of highly qualified security professionals engaged in consulting,sales,installation and maintenance of locks,keys,safes,premises security,access controls,alarms, and other secutriy relates endeavors.
10000 Members

11312 Builders' Hardware Manufacturers Association
355 Lexington Avenue
17th Floor
New York, NY 10017
212-297-2122
FAX: 212-370-9047
www.buildershardware.com
Anthony Mudford, President
Helen Rose, First VP
Paul Dauphin, Second VP
Ed Pilatowicz, Third VP
Represents products that are mounted onto moving parts of buildings such as doors, windows, etc, in order to move, fasten or protect them. Examples are locks,latches, cabinet hardware, hinges, door hardware, door closers, exit devices, power doors, sliding and folding doors.
Founded: 1925

11313 Door and Hardware Institute
14150 Newbrook Drive
Suite 200
Chantilly, VA 20151
703-222-2010
FAX: 703-222-2410
bjohnson@dhi.org www.dhi.org
Neal Frazier, VP
Bill Johnson, Managing Director
Gerald S. Heppes, Sr, Secretary, EVP
To deliver education which enables members of the architectural openings industry to overcome the threats and challenges facing our channel of distribution at the local level.
5000 Members Founded: 1934

11314 Equipment Leasing Association
4301 N Fairfax Drive
Suite 550
Arlington, VA 22203-1627
703-527-8655
FAX: 703-527-2649
rpetta@elamail.com
www.elaonline.com
Michael Fleming, President
Don Ethier, VP Marketing/Communications
Ralph Petta, VP Industry Services
Companies lease equipment to other users
780 Members Founded: 1961

11315 Garrett Metal Detectors
1881 West State Street
Garland, TX 75042-6797
972-494-6151
FAX: 972-494-1881 800-234-6151
sales@garrett.com www.garrett.com
Jim Dobrei, Director of Sales
Vaughn Garrett, Director Marketing/Communications
Global leader of walk-through, hand-held and ground search metal detection products and training for security and law enforcement.
4 Members Founded: 1964

11316 Hand Tools Institute
25 N Broadway
Tarrytown, NY 10591-3221
914-332-0040
FAX: 914-332-1541
info@hti.org www.hti.org
Richard Byrne, Executive Director
Trade association of North American manufacturers of non-powered hand tools and tool boxes. Objectives of the institute is to promote and further the interests of its members relative to manufacturing,safety,standardization,international trade and government relations.
70 Members Founded: 1935

11317 Hardware Implement Association
4629 Mark Iv Parkway
Fort Worth, TX 76106-2213
817-625-5562
FAX: 817-626-5333
Allen Murfin, Executive VP
Supports all those in the hardware implement industry. Hosts annual trade show.

11318 International Door Association
PO Box 246
West Milton, OH 45383-0246
937-698-8042
FAX: 937-698-6153 800-355-4432
info@longmgt.com www.doors.org
Garry Stewart, President
Chris Long, Managing Director
Roe Long, Meetings Manager
Supports all those in the door and door operator industry, especially garage doors, installation hardware, roller shades and garage door openers. Publishes bimonthly magazine.
12 Members Founded: 1996

11319 Mid-America Lumbermen's Assocation
638 W 39th Street
Kansas City, MO 64111
816-561-5323
FAX: 816-561-1991
mail@themla.com www.themla.com
Jeff Flora, Executive Vice President
A organization which holds an annual show of 150 manufacturers, suppliers and distributors of building materials and hardware products.
Founded: 1889

11320 North American Retail Hardware Association
5822 W 74th Street
Indianapolis, IN 46278-1787
317-290-0338
FAX: 317-328-4354 800-772-4424
contact@nrha.org www.nrha.org
Kevin Nyberg, Chairman
Rick Cossey, Vice Chairman
John Hammond, Executive Director
To help independent home improvement retailers become better and more profitable merchants.
Founded: 1805

11321 Service Specialists Association
4015 Marks Road
Suite 2B
Medina, OH 44256-8316
330-725-7160
FAX: 330-722-5638 800-763-5717
trucksvc@aol.com
www.truckservice.org
Mark Broehm, Director
Toni Nastali, President
Don Jones, VP
Neil Middleton, Secretary
Howard Siegel, Treasurer
Suports all the specialists in the truck repair industry. Members exchange ideas, share technical information, and network with other repair shops and suppliers.
200 Members Founded: 1981

Newsletters

11322 American Hardware Manufacturers Association Newsletter
801 Norht Plaza Drive
Schaumburg, IL 60173-4977
847-605-1025
FAX: 847-605-1030
info@ahma.org http://www.ahma.org
William Farrell, CEO
Charles Hermes, Chairman
Industry association news.
36 pages Monthly Founded: 1900

11323 Builders' Hardware Manufacturers Association Newsletter
355 Lexington Avenue
17th Floor
New York, NY 10017-6603
212-297-2122
FAX: 212-370-9047
www.buildershardware.com
Peter Rush, President
Adam Curley, Editor
Information on manufacturing, distributing and supplying of hardware and construction materials.

2 pages Monthly

11324 Service Specialists Newsletter
Service Specialists Association
4015 Marks Road
Suite 2B
Medina, OH 44256-8316
330-725-7160
FAX: 330-722-5638 800-763-5717
trucksvc@aol.com
http://www.truckservice.org

Cara R Giebner, Editor
Don Jones, President

Monthly Founded: 1981

Magazines & Journals

11325 Asian Sources Hardwares
Asian Sources
PO Box 2118
Santa Fe Springs, CA 90670
562-945-4612
FAX: 562-906-2420
us-circ@globalsources.com
http://www.globalsources.com

Dianna Corriero, US Circulation Manager

The leading publication providing the latest product and market information on home center/DIY, lighting, security and safety, auto parts and accessories, and machinery and industrial supplies from around the world for volume buyers worldwide. *$75.00*

Monthly Founded: 1976
Computerized version available: On-line

11326 Brushware
Centaur Company
5515 Dundee Road
Huddleston, VA 24104-3070
540-297-1517
FAX: 540-297-1519

Carl H Wurzer, Publisher
Tom Goldberg, Editor

Accepts advertising. *$35.00*

88 pages
Circulation: 1200

11327 Building Material Dealer
National Lumbermans Publishing Corporation
1405 Lilac Drive N
Suite 130
Minneapolis, MN 55422-4528
763-544-6822
FAX: 763-595-4060 800-328-9125
bmr@bmrmag.com
http://www.dealer.org

Gary Donnelly, Publisher
Gary Smith, President

Content focuses on a mixture of regional and national news relating to governmental regulations, dealer and supplier news, meetings and seminars affecting the independent building retailer.

Monthly
Circulation: 24647

11328 Do-It-Yourself Retailing
National Retail Hardware Association
5822 W 74th Street
Indianapolis, IN 46278-1787
317-290-0338
FAX: 317-328-4354 800-772-4424
contact@nrha.org
http://www.nrha.org

Richard Jarrett, Circulation Manager
Kevin Hohman, Publisher
John Hammond, Executive Director

News and information for hardware retailers. *$50.00*

Monthly Founded: 1901
Circulation: 48000

11329 Doors and Hardware
Door and Hardware Institute
14150 Newbrook Drive
Suite 200
Chantilly, VA 20151-2223
703-222-2010
FAX: 703-222-2410
info@dhi.org http://www.dhi.org

Jennifer Rosso, Managing Editor
Wendy Felt, Publication Director
Jesse Madden, Editor
Molly Long, Advertising Manager
Gerald Heppes Sr, Executive Director

Manufacturers, distributors and specifiers of commercial and wholesale door hardware. *$69.00*

88 pages Monthly Founded: 1934
Circulation: 13000

11330 Hearth & Home
Village West Publishing
PO Box 2008
Laconia, NH 03247

FAX: 603-524-0643 800-258-3772

Richard Wright, Editor

Magazine for retailers, including specialty, hardware, patio and barbecue.

11331 Home Channel News
Lebhar-Friedman
425 Park Avenue
6th Floor
New York, NY 10022
212-756-5000
FAX: 212-754-6897
info@lf.com http://www.lf.com/

Jeff Arlen, Publisher
Terry Evans, Editor
J.Roger Friedman, CEO

Merchandising, marketing, management, and product trends that are important to owners, managers, and buyers. *$120.00*

50 issues per y Founded: 1925
Circulation: 50,000

11332 International Door & Operator Industry
International Door Association
PO Box 246
West Milton, OH 45383-246
937-698-8042
FAX: 937-698-6153 800-355-4432
info@longmgt.com
http://www.doors.org

Christopher Long, Editor
Jim Lett, President
Art Komorowski, Publisher

Analyzes new products in this industry, including garage doors, installation hardware, roller shades and garage door openers.

Founded: 1996
Circulation: 14000

11333 Keynotes
Associated Locksmiths of America
3003 Live Oak Street
Dallas, TX 75204-6189
214-827-1701
FAX: 214-827-1810 800-532-2562
betty@aloa.org http://www.aloa.org

Betty Handerson, Editor
Charles Gibson, CEO

Technical magazine for locksmiths.

Monthly Founded: 1956
Circulation: 8000

11334 Modern Paint & Coatings
110 William Street
New York, NY 10038
212-621-4900
FAX: 212-621-4800 800-774-5733
wkch@kable.com
http://www.chemweek.com

Nella Veldran, Publisher
Joseph Mennella, National Sales Manager
Nicholos P Chopey, Editor-in-Chief
Suzanne A Shelley, Managing Editor
William C Graham, Production Manager
$59.00

Monthly

11335 Outdoor Power Equipment
Adams Business Media
833 West Jackson
7th Floor
Chicago, IL 60607
312-846-4600
FAX: 312-846-4634
webmaster@adamsbusinessmedia.com
http://www.adamsbusinessmedia.com/

Joanne Juda, Circulation Manager
Steve Brackett, VP/Group Publisher
Steve Noe, Editor

Serves retailers and distributors who sell and service outdoor power equipment products, including retailers, lawn and garden supply retailers, farm supply retailers, hardware store retailers, home centers, and building supply retailers.

11336 Power Equipment Trade
Hatton-Brown Publishers
PO Box 2268
Montgomery, AL 36102-2268
334-834-1170
FAX: 334-834-4525
petnet@powerequipmenttrade.com
http://www.powerequipmenttrade.com

David Knight, Co-Owner/Editor-in-Chief
Dan Shell, Managing Editor
Rich Donnell, Editor
Dianne Sullivan, General Manager
Dave Ramsey, Co-Owner Advertising Sales Manager

Service-oriented and technical articles, product evaluations, industry news, dealer surveys and business management information. *$55.00*

Founded: 1952
Circulation: 21441 21,465 names $145 per M.
Printed in on glossy stock

Trade Shows

11337 Ace Hardware Fall Convention and Exhibit
Ace Hardware Corporation
2200 Kensington Court
Oak Brook, IL 60521
630-990-6600
FAX: 708-990-0278

David Myer, Senior Vice President

Over 950 exhibitors with hardware related products for Ace Hardware dealers. Seminar and dinner are part of the event.

17000 Attendees Annual

11338 Ace Hardware Spring Convention and Exhibit
Ace Hardware Corporation
2200 Kensington Court
Oak Brook, IL 60521
630-990-6600
FAX: 708-990-0278
David Myer, Senior Vice President
Over 900 exhibitors with hardware related products for Ace Hardware dealers.
8000 Attendees Annual

11339 Door & Hardware Exposition & Convention
Door & Hardware Institute
14170 Newbrook Drive
Chantilly, VA 20151
703-222-2010
FAX: 703-222-2410
stevehildebrand@paonline.com
www.dhi.org
Stephen R Hildebrand, Director Business Development
Garld Heppes Sr, Executive Director
Over 150 exhibitors bringing the latest in industry trends, education and developments to safely secure the built environment.
4200 Attendees Annual

11340 Equipment Leasing Association Annual Meeting
4301 N Fairfax Drive
Suite 550
Arlington, VA 22203-1608
703-527-8655
FAX: 703-522-6741
Sally Maloney, Meeting Manager
Michael Fleming, President
25 booths.
1,200 Attendees October

11341 FBMA Show
Florida Building Materials Association
1303 Limit Avenue
Mount Dora, FL 32757
352-383-0366
FAX: 352-383-8756
mail@fbma.org www.fbma.org
Bill Tucker, President
Kari Hebrank, VP Government Relations
Betty Askew, Director of Operations
A place for members of the Building Supply Industry to gather. It provides an affordable opportunity to learn about new and innovative equipment and products.
3000 Attendees Annual Founded: 1920

11342 Florida Building Products and Design Show
Florida Lumber & Building Material Dealers
1303 Limit Avenue
Mount Dora, FL 32757
352-383-0366
FAX: 352-383-8756
mail@fbma.org www.fbma.org
Bill Tucker, President
Kair Hebrank, VP Government Relations
Betty Askew, Director of Operations
A place for members of the Building Supply Industry to gather. It provides an affordable opportunity to learn about new and innovative equipment and products.
3000 Attendees Annual Founded: 1920

11343 Gemstate Industrial and Construction Show
Trade Shows West
360 S Fort Ln
Ste 2C
Layton, UT 84041-5708
801-485-0176
FAX: 801-485-0241 800-794-3706
jeffwfredericks@hotmail.com
www.facetofacemarketing.net
Exhibit focusing on the needs of the industrial, construction, and plant maintenance industries.
6049 Attendees Annual/November

11344 Hardware Wholesalers: Merchandise Mart
Hardware Wholesalers
Nelson Road
Box 868
Ft.Wayne, IN 46801
260-748-5300
FAX: 260-496-1245
11500 Attendees

11345 International Hardware Week
American Hardware Manufacturers Association
801 N Plaza Drive
Schaumburg, IL 60173-4977
847-605-1025
FAX: 847-605-1030
info@ahma.org www.ahma.org
Tim Farrell, President/CEO
Charles Hermes, Chairman
3,000 exhibitors.
62.5M Attendees August Founded: 2001

11346 Iowa Lumber Convention
Northwestern Lumber Association
1405 Lilac Drive N
Suite 130
Minneapolis, MN 55422
763-544-6822
FAX: 612-544-0820 800-331-0193
nlassn@nlassn.org www.nlassn.org
Joan Sutton, Board Chair
Gary Smith, President/Secretary
Dennis Meillier, First VP
Jeff Gallagher, Treasurer
Hosts educational seminars and held a silent auction for the first time.
1286 Attendees Annual,March

11347 Lumber and Hardware Show Mid-America
PO Box 1828
Columbus, OH 43216
614-460-6000
FAX: 614-833-6983
Joe Bailey, Show Manager
300 booths for retail lumber yard stores.
7M Attendees February

11348 National Building Products Exposition & Conference
American Hardware Manufacturers Association
801 N Plaza Drive
Schaumburg, IL 60173-4977
847-605-1025
FAX: 847-605-1093
info@ahma.org www.ahma.org
Time Farrell, President/CEO
70000 Attendees

11349 National Hardware Show
Association Expositions & Services
383 Main Avenue
Norwalk, CT 06851
203-840-5622
FAX: 203-840-4824 888-425-9377
inquiry@hardware.reedexpo.com
www.nationalhardwareshow.com
Timothy Farrell, Executive VP
Martin O'Rourke, Membership Manager
Held in conjunction with International Hardware Week, this is the industry's leading hardware/home improvement event, with products from over 2,000 manufacturers from around the world. Includes hardware and allied lines, plumbing, paint and home decorating, lawn and garden, building products and housewares. Also international pavilions.
70000 Attendees August Founded: 1945

11350 National Hardware Show/National Building Products Exposition & Conference
Reed Exhibition Companies
383 Main Avenue
Norwalk, CT 06851
203-840-4800
FAX: 203-840-4801
inquiry@reedexpo.com
www.reedexpo.com

11351 Rocky Mountain Industrial and Machine Tool Show
Trade Shows West
360 S Fort Ln
Ste 2C
Layton, UT 84041-5708
801-485-0176
FAX: 801-485-0241
www.facetofacemarketing.net
A three day exhibit focusing on the needs of the industrial, manufacturing and plant maintenance industries.
8463 Attendees Annual/May

11352 Salt Lake Machine Tool & Manufacturing Exposition
Trade Shows West
2880 S Main Street
Suite 110
Salt Lake City, UT 84115
801-485-0176
FAX: 801-485-0241
jeffwfredericks@hotmail.com
www.facetofacemarketing.net

11353 Service Specialists Association Annual Convention
Service Specialists Association
4015 Marks Road
Apartment 2B
Medina, OH 44256-8316
330-725-7160
FAX: 330-722-5638 800-763-5717
trucksvc@aol.com
www.truckservice.org
Cara R Giebner, Manager
Containing 70 booths and 70 exhibits.
400 Attendees

11354 Servistar Corporation Lumber & Home Center: Fall
Servistar Corporation
PO Box 1510
Butler, PA 16001
773-695-5000
FAX: 773-695-5172
1500 Attendees

11355 Servistar Corporation Lumber & Home Center : Spring
Servistar Corporation
8600 W Bryn Mawr Avenue
Chicago, IL 60631-3505
773-695-5000
FAX: 773-695-5172
1500 Attendees

11356 Servistar Market
Truserv Corporation
8600 W Bryn Mawr Avenue
Chicago, IL 60631-3505
773-695-5000
FAX: 773-695-5172
Johnathan Mills, Show Manager
Hardware manufacturers, suppliers and distributors.
5M Attendees September

Directories & Databases

11357 Complete Directory of Hardware Items
Sutton Family Communications & Publishing Company
155 Sutton Lane
Fordsville, KY 42343
270-740-0870

jlsutton@apex.net
www.fleamarketeer.net
Theresa Sutton, Editor
Lee Sutton, General Manager
Print-out from database of wholesale distributors,importers,manufacturers,close-out houses, and liquidators. Database is updated daily to guarantee the most current and up-to-date sources available. *$109.00*
100+ pages

11358 Complete Directory of Household Items
Sutton Family Communications & Publishing Company
155 Sutton Lane
Fordsville, KY 42343
270-740-0870

jlsutton@apex.net
www.fleamarketeer.net
Theresa Sutton, Editor
Lee Sutton, General Manager
Print-out from database of wholesalers, manufacturers, distributors, importers and close-out houses. Database is updated daily to guarantee the most current and up-to-date sources available. *$109.00*
100+ pages

11359 Directory and Buyer's Guide of the Door and Hardware Institute
Door and Hardware Institute
14170 Newbrook Drive
Suite 200
Chantilly, VA 20151-2232
703-222-2010
FAX: 703-222-2410
Jerry S. Heppes Sr., Executive Director
More than 700 firms which supply doors, hinges, locks, cabinets and closet hardware, door motors, smoke clothing and detection devices.
Annual

11360 Door and Hardware Institute: Membership Directory
Door and Hardware Institute
14170 Newbrook Drive
Suite 200
Chantilly, VA 20151-2232
703-222-2010
FAX: 703-222-2410 www.dhi.org
Christine Umbrell, Editor
Gerald Heppes Sr, Executive Director
Includes names and addresses of more than 5,000 members, including 700 manufacturing firms. Excellent resource for networking and staying in touch with your colleagues. Advertising is available.
Annually Founded: 1999

11361 Home Center Operators & Hardware Chains
Lebhar-Friedman
425 Park Avenue
New York, NY 10022
212-756-5000
FAX: 813-627-6882
info@lf.com www.lf.com
J Roger Friedman, President
Directory of major buying groups, sales category leaders, statistical analysis of the home improvement sector. *$335.00*

11362 Homecenter Operators & Hardware Chains
Chain Store Guide
3922 Coconut Palm Drive
Tampa, FL 33619
813-276-6700
FAX: 813-627-6800 800-927-9292
info@csgis.com www.csgis.com
William Lamed, Publisher
Arthur Rosenberg, Editor
Shami Choon, Manager
The facts on more than 4,600 company headquarters and subsidiaries operating almost 23,500 units in the vast Home Improvement Building Material Industry. Also included are 19 major buying/marketing groups and coops that contribute approximately $30 billion and serve 103,243 accounts. *$30.00*
Annual, Paperback

Industry Web Sites

11363 www.ahma.org
American Hardware Manufacturers Association

Over 280 manufacturer representatives in the hardware industry.

11364 www.aloa.org
Associated Locksmiths of America

Strives to educate and provide information to industry. Maintains referral service and offers insurance and bonding programs. Holds technical training.

11365 www.americanladderinstitute.org
American Ladder Institute

Members include manufacturers of wood, metal and fiberglass ladders. Represents US companies engaged in the research, development, manufacture and safety ladders.

11366 www.greyhouse.com
Grey House Publishing

Selected Grey House directories in the fields of business, health and education are available online. Users can search our online databases by several different search criteria, such as product categories, geographic area, sales volume and much, much more. Full Grey House catalog and online ordering also available.

11367 www.hti.org
Hand Tools Institute

Provides safety education and concerned with product standards.

11368 www.nrha.org
National Retail Hardware Association

An organization which features news and information for hardware retailers.

Associations

11369 Academy of Dental Materials
520 North 12th Street
PO Box 980566
Richmond, VA 23298
804-828-9184
FAX: 804-828-6072
admabstr@vcu.edu
www.academydentalmaterials.org
Susanne Scherrer, President
Dorin Ruse, VP
Ann Marie Neme, Secretary
Mike Bagby, Treasurer
Formerly known as American Academy for Plastics Research in Dentistry.
Founded: 1941

11370 Academy of General Dentistry
211 E Chicago Avenue
Suite 900
Chicago, IL 60611-1999
312-404-4300
FAX: 312-440-0559 888-243-3368
msc@agd.org www.agd.org
Elizabeth A Clemente, Foundation President
Russell A Secter, VP Sales/Marketing
Jay Donohue, Executive Director
Mark Buczko, VP
Desi Nuckolls, Associate Director
37000 Members Founded: 1952

11371 Academy of Osseointegration
85 W Algonquin Road
Suite 550
Arlington Heights, IL 60005
847-439-1919
FAX: 847-439-1569
academy@osseo.org www.osseo.org
Established to provide a focus for the rapidly advancing biotechnology involving the natural bond between bone and certain alloplastic reconstructive materials.
5200 Members Founded: 1982

11372 Adenna
12216 McCann Drive
Sante Fe Springs, CA 90670
562-777-8026
FAX: 562-777-8905 888-323-3662
info@adenna.com www.adenna.com
Maxwell Lee, President
We market and distribute a variety of hand protection and healthcare products including: examination gloves and disposable gloves to medical, dental, laboratory, veterinary, food, auto and other industries through authorized dealers and distributors.
Founded: 1997

11373 Advanced Medical Technology Association
1200 G Street NW
Suite 400
Washington, DC 20005-3814
202-783-8700
FAX: 202-783-8750
info@advamed.org www.advamed.org
Pamela G Bailey, President
Carol A Kelly, Executive VP Health Care Systems
Stephen J Ubl, Executive VP
Blair Childs, Executive VP Strategic Planning
Kristen M Bogenrief, Executive VP Finance/Operations
Former Health Industry Manufacturers Association, or HIMA, AdvaMed represents more than 1,100 innovators and manufacturers of medical devices, diagnostic products and medical information systems. Our members manufacture 90 percent of the $71 billion of health care technology purchased annually in the United States and more than 50 percent of the health care technology products purchased around the world. We represent our members with advocacy, information and education.
1100 Members Founded: 1980

11374 Aerospace Medical Association
320 S Henry Street
Alexandria, VA 22314-3579
703-739-2240
FAX: 703-739-9652
gcarter@asma.org www.asma.org
David Schroeder, President
Russell B Rayman, Executive Director
Aerospace medical association offers valuable information on the technological advances in medicine, pertaining to the aviation and aerospace industry.
3500+ Members Founded: 1929

11375 American Academy for Cerebral Palsy and Developmental Medicine
555 E Wells St
Ste 1100
Milwaukee, WI 53202-3800
414-918-3014
FAX: 414-276-2146 www.aacpdm.org
Sheril King, Executive Director
Luciano S Dias, Second VP
Virginia S Nelson, Secretary
Henry G Chambers, Treasurer
1500 Members Founded: 1947

11376 American Academy of Allergy, Asthma and Immunology
555 E Wells Street
Suite 1100
Milwaukee, WI 53202
414-272-6071
FAX: 414-272-6070
info@aaaai.org www.aaaai.org
Kay A Whalen, Executive VP
Eric Lanke, Asscociate Executive VP
The largest professional medical specialty organization in the United States, representing allergists, asthma specialists, clinical immunologists, allied health professionals, and others with a special interest in the research and treatment of allergic disease.
6000+ Members Founded: 1943
Mailing list available for rent 6000+ names $120 per M.

11377 American Academy of Child & Adolescent Psychiatry
3615 Wisconsin Avenue NW
Washington, DC 20016-3007
202-966-7300
FAX: 202-966-2891 www.aacap.org
Eva Brown, Manager
The mission of the AACAP is to promote mentally healthy children, adolescents and families through research, training, advocacy, prevention, comprehensive diagnosis and treatment.

11378 American Academy of Dermatology
PO Box 4014
Shaumburg, IL 60168-4014
847-240-1280
FAX: 847-240-1859 800-503-7546
jbarnes@aad.org www.aad.org
John Barnes, Associate Executive Director
Paul Bonta, Assistant Director Federal Affairs
Laura Saul Edwards, Assistant Director Federal Affairs
Jorge Martinez, Manager Political Affairs
Robert Bohannon, Specialist Political Affairs
An association of doctors specializing in dermatology, provides pamphlets and general information about skin cancers, contact allergies (like poison ivy), shingles (herpes zoster), and other skin conditions.
13700 Members Founded: 1938

11379 American Academy of Fixed Prosthodontics
1930 Sea Way
PO Box 1409
Bodega Bay, CA 94923-1409
800-860-5633
800-785-9188
ttaylor@nso.uchc.edu
www.prosthodontics.org
600 Members Founded: 1991

11380 American Academy of Forensic Sciences
410 N 21st Street
Colorado Springs, CO 80904-2798
719-636-1100
FAX: 719-636-1993
awarren@aafs.org www.aafs.org
Anne Warren, Executive Director
Jim Hurley, Director Development
Charlene Albertson, Finance Manager
Nancy Jackson, Meetings/Expositions Manager
Kathy Reynolds, Publications Coordinator
5000+ Members Founded: 1948

11381 American Academy of Implant Dentistry
211 E Chicago Avenue
Chicago, IL 60611
312-335-1550
FAX: 312-335-9090
aaid@aaid-implant.org
www.aaid-implant.org
John Rutkauskas, Executive Director
Joyce Sigmon, Director Administrative Activities
Laurie Storen, Director Communications/Meeting
Afshin Alavi, Director Finance/Business
Latasha Bryant, Assistant- Finance Edu/Exams
2700 Members Founded: 1951

11382 American Academy of Medical Administrators
701 Lee Street
Suite 600
Des Plaines, IL 60016-4516
847-759-8601
FAX: 847-759-8602
info@aameda.org www.aameda.org
Holly Estal, Director Education
Renee S Schleicher, President/CEO
Nancy L Anderson, VP Finance/Administration
Individuals involved in medical administration at the executive or middle-management levels. Promotes educational courses for the training of persons in medical administration. Conducts research and offers placement service.
3000 Members Founded: 1957

11383 American Academy of Neurology
1080 Montreal Avenue
Saint Paul, MN 55116
651-695-2717
FAX: 651-695-2791 800-879-1960
memberservices@aan.com
www.aan.com
An association of doctors specializing in disorders of the brain and central nervous system.
18000 Members Founded: 1948

11384 American Academy of Ophthalmology
PO Box 7424
San Francisco, CA 94120-7424
415-561-8500
FAX: 415-561-8533 800-222-3937
customer_service@aao.org
www.aao.org
Allan D Jensen, President
H Dunbar Hoskins Jr, Executive VP
Malcolm L Mazow, Chair
John R Stechschulte, Vice Chair
An association of doctors specializing in eye diseases.
7000 Members Founded: 1896

11385 American Academy of Optometry
6110 Executive Boulevard
Suite 506
Rockville, MD 20852
301-984-1441
FAX: 301-984-4737
aaoptom@aol.com www.aaopt.org
Dr Thomas L Lewis, President
Lois Schoenbrun, Executive Director
Christine L Armstrong, Foundation Director
Deborah K Brandt, Director Membership
Joni Hoskie, Finance Director

11386 American Academy of Oral and Maxillofacial
PO Box 55722
Jackson, MS 39296
601-984-6060
FAX: 601-984-6086
Founded: 1949

11387 American Academy of Orofacial Pain
19 Mantua Road
Mount Royal, NJ 08061
856-233-3629
FAX: 856-423-3420
aaopco@talley.com www.aaop.org
Peter M Baragona, President
Reny de Leeuw, President-Elect
Donald R Tanenbaum, Secretary
Kenneth Cleveland, Executive Director

11388 American Academy of Orthopedic Surgeons
6300 N River Road
Rosemont, IL 60018-4262
847-823-7186
FAX: 847-823-8125 800-346-2267
ustserv@aaos.org www.aaos.org
Stuart L Weinstein, President
Richard F Kyle, First VP
Edward A Toriello, Treasurer
Karen Hackett, Chief Executive Officer
Non-profit organization of doctors specializing in bones, joints, muscles, ligaments, and tendons.
28000 Members Founded: 1933

11389 American Academy of Otolaryngology
1 Prince Street
Alexandria, VA 22314-3357
703-836-4444
FAX: 703-683-5100
membership@entnet.org
www.entnet.org
Khatereh Calleja, Director Board Governors
Gerry Keegan, Manager State Legislative Affairs
LaKisha Hill, Administrative Coordinator
Tom Harlow, Finance Executive
International association of scientists and physicians dedicated to scientific exploration among all of the disiplines in the field of otolaryngology. Research efforts involve the ear, nose, head and neck and related functions including balnce, hearing, taste and smell, among others. The primary scientific meeting is the Mid-Winter Meeting held annually in February.
Founded: 1896

11390 American Academy of Pain Medicine
4700 W Lake
Glenview, IL 60025
847-375-4731
FAX: 877-734-8750
aapm@amctec.com www.painmed.org
Samuel J Hassenbusch, President
Frederick W Burgess, Treasurer
Daniel B Carr, Secretary

11391 American Academy of Pediatric Dentistry
211 E Chicago Avenue
#700
Chicago, IL 60611-2663
312-337-2169
FAX: 312-337-6329
info@aapd.org www.aapd.org
Stephen Wilson, President
Constance M Killian, VP
Arthur Nowak, Executive Director
David L Good, VP
John Rutkauskas, Executive Director
Founded: 1948

11392 American Academy of Periodontology
737 N Michigan Avenue
Suite 800
Chicago, IL 60611-2690
312-787-5518
FAX: 312-787-3670
rethman@hotmail.com www.perio.org
Michael P Rethman, President
Kenneth A Krebs, VP
Preston D Miller, Secretary/Treasurer
Alice Deforest, Executive Director
Founded: 1914

11393 American Academy of Physical Medicine and Dentistry
One IBM Plaza
Suite 2500
Chicago, IL 60611-3604
312-464-9700
FAX: 312-464-0227
info@aapmr.org www.aapmr.org
Ronald Henrichs, Executive Director
Founded: 1938

11394 American Academy of Physical Medicine and Rehabilitation (AAPMR)
300 N Wabash Avenue
Suite 2500
Chicago, IL 60611
312-464-9700
FAX: 312-464-0227 www.aapmr.org
Organization of physicians who treat people with disabilities.

11395 American Academy of Physician Assistants
222 S Westmonte Dr
Ste 101
Altamonte Springs, FL 32714-4268
703-836-2272
FAX: 703-684-1924
aapa@aapa.org www.aapa.org
Pamela Scott, President
Robert L Wooten, Secretary

11396 American Academy of Professional Coders
2480 South 3850 West
Suite B
Salt Lake City, UT 84120

FAX: 801-236-2258 800-626-2633
info@aapc.com www.aapc.com
Traci Wood, Marketing Coordinator
Founded in an effort to raise the professional standards of medical coders by providing on-going education, networking, recognition, and certification.
45000 Members

11397 American Alliance for Health, Phys Ed, and Recreation
1900 Association Drive
Reston, VA 20191-1598
703-476-3400
800-213-7193
ginfo@aahperd.org www.aahperd.org
Shirley Ann Holt/Hale, President
Harve Horowitz, Show Manager
Michael Davis, Manager
Organization of professionals supporting and assisting those involved in physical education, leisure, fitness, dance, health promotion and education and all specialties related to having a healthy lifestyle.
2600 Members Founded: 1885

11398 American Association for Clinical Chemistry
1850 K St NW
Ste 625
Washington, DC 20006-2215
800-892-1400
FAX: 202-887-5093 800-892-1400
jrhame@aacc.org www.aacc.org
Thomas P Moyer, President
Larry A Broussard, Treasurer
Robert H Christenson, Secretary
Thomas M Annesley, Director
An international scientific/medical society of clinical laboratory professionals, physicians, research scientists and other individuals with clinical chemistry, molecular diagnostics and other clinical laboratory related disciplines.
10000 Members Founded: 1948

11399 **American Association for Continuity of Care**
PO Box 532
Dunedin, FL 34697
800-816-1575
FAX: 727-738-8099
phudsonsommers@ij.net
www.continuityofcare.com
Pat Hudson-Sommers, President
Jan White, Secretary
Florence Miller, Treasurer/Finance Chairman
Founded: 1982

11400 **American Association for Laboratory Systems**
9190 Crestwyn Hills Drive
Memphis, TN 38125-8538
901-754-8620
FAX: 901-753-0046
info@aalas.org www.aalas.org
Ann Turner, Executive Director
11300 Members Founded: 1950

11401 **American Association for Marriage and Fami ly Therapy (AAMFT)**
112 S Alfred Street
Alexandria, VA 22314
703-838-9808
FAX: 703-838-9805 www.aamft.org
Professional association of qualified marriagae and family therapists.

11402 **American Association for Medical Technology**
100 Sycamore Avenue
Modesto, CA 95354-550
209-527-9620
FAX: 209-527-9633 800-982-2182
aamt@aamt.org www.aamt.org
Jefferson Howe, President
Vallie Piloian, Secretary
Beth Tribelhorn, Treasurer
April L Martin, Director
Founded: 1978

11403 **American Association for Respiratory Care**
9425 N MacArthur Boulevard
Suite 100
Irving, TX 75063-4706
972-243-2272
FAX: 972-484-2720
info@aarc.org www.aarc.org
Michael T Amato, Chairman
Neil MacIntyre, Vice Chairman
Sam P Giordano, Executive VP
Gary A Smith, Secretary/Treasurer
Professional society for respiratory therapists in hospitals and with home care companies, managers of respiratory and cardiopulmonary services and educators who provide respiratory care training.
35000 Members Founded: 1947

11404 **American Association for Thoracic Surgery**
900 Cummings Center
Suite 221-U
Beverly, MA 01915
978-927-8330
FAX: 978-524-8890
aats@prri.com www.aats.org
Dr Bruce W Lytle, President
Dr Irving L Kron, Secretary
Encourages and stimulates education and investigation into the areas of intrathoracic physiology, pathology and therapy. Members include surgeons representing 34 countries around the world.
1160 Members Founded: 1917

11405 **American Association for the Study of Headaches**
19 Mantua Road
Mount Royal, NJ 08061
609-845-0322
FAX: 609-384-5811
Founded: 1958

11406 **American Association of Nurse Anesthetists**
222 S Prospect Avenue
Park Ridge, IL 60068-4001
847-927-7055
FAX: 847-692-6968
info@aana.com www.aana.com
Jeffery M Beutler, Executive Director
Rita Rupp, Special Assistant to Exec. Director
Lorraine M Jordan, Director Research
John A Fetcho, Director AANA Insurance Services

11407 **American Association of Bioanalysts**
917 Locust Street
Suite 1100
Saint Louis, MO 63101-1419
314-241-1445
FAX: 314-241-1449
aab@aab.org www.aab.org

11408 **American Association of Blood Banks**
8101 Glenbrook Road
Bethesda, MD 20814-2749
301-907-6977
FAX: 301-907-6895
aabb@aabb.org www.aabb.org
Karen Lipton, Chief Executive Officer
Promoting the highest standard of care for patents and donors in all aspects of blood banking and transfusion medicine.
Founded: 1947

11409 **American Association of Cardiovascular & Pulmonary Rehabilitation**
401 N Michigan Avenue
Suite 2200
Chicago, IL 60611
312-321-5146
FAX: 321-527-6635
aacvpr@sba.com www.aacvpr.org
Angela Wilson, Association Manager
Marie Bass, Executive Director
An organization of certified heart, lung, and blood specialists that provides information on diagnosis, treatment, and disease prevention.
Founded: 1985

11410 **American Association of Clinical Endocrinology**
1000 Riverside Avenue
Suite 205
Jacksonville, FL 32204
904-353-7878
FAX: 904-353-8185
info@aace.com www.aace.com
Carlos R Hamilton Jr, President
Steven M Petak, VP
Richard Hellman, Treasurer
Donald Jones, Chief Executive Officer
Professional medical organization devoted to the enhancement of the practice of clinical endocrinology. Maintains high standards in a society of qualified medical, pediatric, reproductive and surgical endocrinologists to futher the practice through advocacy and education.
4200 Members Founded: 1991

11411 **American Association of Critical-Care Nurs es**
101 Columbia
Aliso Viejo, CA 92656-4109
949-362-2000
FAX: 949-362-2020 800-899-2226
info@aacn.org www.aacn.org
Non-profit professional association dedicated to meeting the needs of its members who care for acutely and critically ill patients and their families.

11412 **American Association of Diabetes Educators**
100 W Monroe Street
Suite 400
Chicago, IL 60603
312-242-2426
FAX: 312-424-2427 800-338-3633
aade@aadenet.org
www.diabeteseducator.org
Christopher Laxton, Executive Director
10000 Members Founded: 1973

11413 **American Association of Electrodiagnostic Medicine**
421 1st Avenue SW
Suite 300 E
Rochester, MN 55902
507-288-0100
FAX: 507-288-1225
aaem@aaem.net www.aaem.net
Shirlyn A Adkins, Executive Director
Shelly D Hansen, Member Services Manager
Ginny Jeche, Project Specialist
Ryan C Mahannah, Education Specialist
Tiffany Schmidt, Director Policy
1000 Members

11414 **American Association of Forensic Dentists**
1000 N Avenue
Waukegan, IL 60085
847-223-5077
info@andent.net www.andent.net
Bringing forensic dental knowledge not only to dentists and their staff, but also to anthropologists, attorneys and law enforcement personnel. A quarterly journal is published.
3000 Members Founded: 1978

11415 **American Association of Health Plans**
1129 20th Street NW
Washington, DC 20036-3421
202-783-3200
FAX: 202-331-7487
webmaster@ahip.net www.aahp.org
Trade group that represents managed care companies. The group advocates against regulations of the managed care industry.

11416 **American Association of Healthcare Managers**
11240 Waples Mill Road
Suite 200
Fairfax, VA 22030
703-340-0164
FAX: 703-359-7562
debra@statmarketing.com
www.aaham.org

Steven M Markesich, Chairman
Linda S Sheaffer, President
Jim Grigsby, First National VP
Bob DeBiase, Second VP
Linda Kruszewski, Treasurer

Business offices, credit and collection managers, admitting officers for hospitals, clinics and other health care organizaitons. Our mission is to educate members, exchange information and techniques, and keep members abreast of new regulations relating to their field. Seeks proper recognition for the financial aspect of hospital and clinic managememnt.

2500 Members Founded: 1968

11417 American Association of Homes and Services
2519 Connecticut Avenue NW
Washington, DC 20008
202-783-2242
FAX: 202-783-2255
info@aahsa.org www.aahsa.org

William Minnux, President/CEO

National, non-profit organization providing older people with services and information on housing, health care, and community involvement.

5600 Members Founded: 1980

11418 American Association of Immunologists
9650 Rockville Pike
Bethesda, MD 20814
301-634-7178
FAX: 301-571-1816
infoaai@aai.faceb.org www.aai.org

Laurie H Hogan, President
Susan L Swain, VP
Steven J Burakoff, Secretary/Treasurer

Founded: 1913

11419 American Association of Integrated Health Care
4435 Waterfront Drive
Suite 101
Glen Allen, VA 23060
804-747-5823
FAX: 804-747-5316
sreed@aaihds.org www.aaihds.org

Doug Chaet, Chairman
W C Williams III, President
Matthew Prins, VP Membership
Sloane Reed, VP Sales/Marketing
Katie Eads, VP Education

Nonprofit organization dedicated to the educational advancement of provider based, managed care professionals involved in integrated health care delivery.

1000 Members Founded: 1993

11420 American Association of Managed Care
4435 Waterfront Drive
Suite 101
Glen Allen, VA 23060
804-747-9698
FAX: 804-747-5316
northbod@aamcn.org www.aamcn.org

William C Williams III, Senior VP
Katie Eads, VP Education
Matthew Prins, VP Membership
Sloane Reed, VP Sales/Marketing

200 Members Founded: 1994

11421 American Association of Medical Assistants
20 N Wacker Drive
Suite 1575
Chicago, IL 60606-2963
312-899-1500
FAX: 312-899-1259 800-228-2262
dknight@aama-ntl.org
www.aama-ntl.org

Don Balasa, Executive Director

To enable medical assisting professionals to enhance and demostrate the knowledge, skills and professionalism required by employers and patients; protect medical assistants' right to practice; and promote effective, efficient health care delivery through optimal use of multiskilled Certified Medical Assistants.

11422 American Association of Naturopathic Medicine
3201 New Mexico Avenue NW
Suite 350
Washington, DC 20016
202-895-1392
FAX: 202-274-1992
member.services@naturopathic.org
www.naturopathic.org

1800+ Members Founded: 1985

11423 American Association of Neurological Sciences
5550 Meadowbrook Drive
Rolling Meadows, IL 60008
847-378-0500
FAX: 847-378-0600
info@aans.org www.aans.org

Thomas A Marshall, Executive Director
Ronald W Engelbreit, Deputy Executive Director
Kathleen T Craig, Director Marketing
Heather L Monroe, Director Communications
Kenneth L Nolan, Director Information Systems

6500+ Members Founded: 1931

11424 American Association of Neuroscience
4700 W Lake Avenue
Glenview, IL 60025
847-754-4712
FAX: 877-734-8677 800-477-2266
info@aann.org www.aann.org

Andrea Strayer, President
Diane Simmons, Chief Executive Officer
Susan Fowler, Secretary/Treasurer

3000 Members Founded: 1968

11425 American Association of Office Nurses
52 Park Avenue
Suite B-4
Park Ridge, NJ 07656
201-391-2600
FAX: 201-573-8543 800-457-7504
aaonmail@aaon.org www.aaon.org

Michelle Aronowitz, Managing Director
Sherry Levy, Associate Managing Director
Teresa Holbrook, Secretary
Revenia J Buck, Treasurer

Commited to the continuing education and long-term welfare of healthcare office professionals.

1100 Members Founded: 1988

11426 American Association of Oral & Maxillofacial Surgeons
9700 W Bryn Mawr Avenue
Rosemont, IL 60018-5701
847-678-6200
FAX: 847-678-6286 800-822-6637
inquiries@aaoms.org www.aaoms.org

Robert Rinaldi, Executive Director
Kim Peterman, Manager

Professional association serving the professional and public needs of the specialty of oral and maxillofacial surgery. Major activities include a monthly publication, annual meeting and numerous educational and research activities.

7000 Members Founded: 1918

11427 American Association of Orthodontists
401 N Lindbergh Boulevard
Saint Louis, MO 63141-7816
314-931-1700
FAX: 314-997-1745
info@aaortho.org www.aaortho.org

James J Caveney, President
Chris Varanas, Manager

14600 Members Founded: 1900

11428 American Association of Pharmaceutical Scientists
2107 Wilson Boulevard
Suite 700
Arlington, VA 22201-3042
703-243-2800
FAX: 703-243-9650
aaps@aaps.org www.aaps.org

John Lisack, Jr, Executive Director
Maureen Downs, Director Finance
Peter Inchauteguiz, Director Marketing/Members Svcs
James Greif, Communcations Specialist
Jerry Skelly, President

Aims to advance science through the open exchange of scientific knowledge, serve as an information resource and contribute to human health through pharmaceutical research and development.

11000 Members Founded: 1986
Mailing list available for rent

11429 American Association of Physician Specialists
2296 Henderson Mill Road
Suite 206
Atlanta, GA 30345
770-939-8555
FAX: 770-939-8559
jhansen@aapsga.org
www.aapsga.com

William J Carbone, CEO
Jennifer Hansen, Director Development
Spencer Elrod, Director Finance/Operations
Eric E Grier, Director Governmental Affairs
Stanley J Kalisch, Director Certification

2000+ Members Founded: 1950

11430 American Association of Retired Persons (A ARP)
601 E Street NW
Washington, DC 20049

888-687-2277

Non-profit organization that advocates for older American's health, rights, and life choices.

11431 American Association of Suicidology
5221 Wisconsin Avenue NW
Washington, DC 20015
202-237-2280
FAX: 202-237-2282
info@suicidology.org
www.suicidology.org

M David Rudd, President
Jack Herrmann, Secretary
Michael Hendricks, Treasurer
Alan Berman, Executive Director

AAS, a not-for-profit organization, encourage and welcomes both individual and organization members.
1003 Members Founded: 1969

11432 American Association of Tissue Banks
1320 Old Chain Bridge Road
Suite 450
Mc Lean, VA 22101
703-827-9582
FAX: 703-356-2198
aatb@aatb.org www.aatb.org

Duke Kasprisin, President
Robert Rigdy, Chief Executive Officer

11433 American Association on Mental Retardation
444 N Capitol Street NW
Suite 846
Washington, DC 20001-1512
202-387-1968
FAX: 202-387-2193 800-424-3688
dcroser@aamr.org www.aamr.org

Ann P Turnbull, President
Valerie J Bradley, VP
Joanna L Pierson, Secretary/Treasurer
M Doreen Croser, Executive Director
9500 Members Founded: 1876

11434 American Brain Tumor Association (ABTA)
2720 River Road
Des Plaines, IL 60018
847-827-9910
FAX: 847-827-9918 800-886-2282
info@abta.org www.abta.org

John Hipchen, President

Non-profit organization, offering free social work consultations, a nationwide database of established support groups, mentorship for people who want to start a support group, a resource listing of specialist physicians, and referrals to organizations providing services for brain tumor patients.

11435 American Burn Association
625 N Michigan Avenue
Suite 1530
Chicago, IL 60611
312-642-9260
FAX: 312-642-9130
info@ameriburn.org
www.ameriburn.org

Richard L Gamelli, President
David Greenhalgh, First VP
Roger W Yurt, Second VP
Richard J Kagan, Secretary
John Krichbaum, Executive Director

Committed to study and research in acute care, rehabilitation and prevention of burns. We support educational opportunities for burn care providers and encourage pubications within the burn care field.
3500+ Members Founded: 1967

11436 American Chiropractic Association
1701 Clarendon Boulevard
Arlington, VA 22209
703-276-8800
FAX: 703-243-2593
memberinfo@amerchiro.org
www.acatoday.com

Kevin P Corcoran CAE, Executive VP
Richard G Brassard DC, President
16000 Members Founded: 1963

11437 American Cleft Palate Craniofacial Association
1504 E Franklin Street
Suite 102
Chapel Hill, NC 27514-2820
919-933-9044
FAX: 919-933-9604
info@acpa-cpf.org www.acpa-cpf.org

Marilyn A Cohen, President
Peter M Spalding, VP
Nancy Smythe, Executive Director

Organization of plastic surgeons, dentists, orthodontists, speech pathologists, geneticists, social workers and others.
Founded: 1943

11438 American Clinical Neurophysiology Society
PO Box 30
Bloomfield, CT 06002
860-243-3977
FAX: 860-286-0787
acns@ssmgt.com www.acns.org

Charles Epstein, President
Ronald Emerson, First VP
Richard Brenner, Second VP
Ivo Drury, Secretary
Peter Kaplan, Treasurer
Founded: 1946

11439 American College Health Association
PO Box 28937
Baltimore, MD 21240-8937
410-859-1500
FAX: 410-859-1510
contact@acha.org www.acha.org

Doreen A Perez, President
Patsy Huff, Treasurer
Lesley Sacher, VP
P J Godwin, Executive Assistant

The American College Health Association (ACHA) is the principal advocate and leadership organization for college and university health. The association provides advocacy, education, communications, products, and services, as well as promoting research and culturally competent practices to enhance its members' ability to advance the health of all students and the campus community.
2600 Members Founded: 1920

11440 American College of Allergy, Asthma and Immunology
85 West Algonquin Road
#550
Arlington Heights, IL 60005-4460
847-427-1200
FAX: 847-427-1294
mail@acaai.org www.acaai.org

Michael S Blaiss, President
William K Dolen, VP
Founded: 1942

11441 American College of Angiology
295 Northern Boulevard
Suite 104
Great Neck, NY 11021-4701
516-466-4055
FAX: 516-466-4099
aca@collegeofangiology.org
www.collegeofangiology.org

Joan Shaffer, Executive Director
Founded: 1954

11442 American College of Cardiology
9111 Old Georgetown Road
Bethesda, MD 20814-1699
301-897-5400
FAX: 301-897-9745 800-253-4636
resource@acc.org www.acc.org

Michael J Wolk, President
Steven E Nissen, VP
Christine W McEntee, CEO

11443 American College of Cardiovascular Administrators (ACCA)
American Academy of Medical Administrators
701 Lee Street
Suite 600
Des Plaines, IL 60016-4516
847-759-8601
FAX: 847-759-8602
info@aameda.org www.aameda.org

Renee S Schleicher, President/CEO

ACCA is the organization of choice for the nation's cardiovascular/respiratory administrators. Its mission is to promote excellence in cardiovascular leadership. Through information exchange, two annual conferences, a peer-reviewed journal, recognized credential (FACCA) and networking opportunities, ACCA keeps members up-to-date with significant developments, as well as the broad multi-disciplined healthcare environment. ACCA is a specialty group of the AAMA.
900 Members Founded: 1986

11444 American College of Emergency Physicians
1125 Executive Circle
Irving, TX 75038-2522
972-550-0911
FAX: 972-580-2816 800-798-1822
customerservice@acep.org
www.acep.org

Frederick C Blum, MD, FACEP, President
Brian F Keaton, MD, FACEP, President-Elect
Nicholas J Jouriles, MD, FACEP, Secretary/Treasurer
Michael Gallery, Executive Director

Exists to support quality emergency medical care, and to promote the interests of emergency physicians.
23000 Members Founded: 1968
Mailing list available for rent 25000 names

11445 American College of Healthcare Executives
1 N Franklin Street
Suite 1700
Chicago, IL 60606-4425
312-424-2800
FAX: 312-424-0023
geninfo@ache.org www.ache.org

Richard A Henault, Chairman
Thomas C Dolan, President/CEO

International professional society of more than 30,000 health care executives. Credentialing and educational programs, Congress

on Healthcare Management. ACHE's publishing division, Health Administration Press, is one of the largest publishers of books.
30000 Members Founded: 1933

11446 American College of Healthcare Information Administrators (ACHIA)
701 Lee Street
Suite 600
Des Plaines, IL 60016-4516
847-759-8601
FAX: 847-759-8602
info@aameda.org www.aameda.org
Von Yetzer, Director/Membership/Communications
Renee Schleicher, President/CEO
Health care leaders serving in a management position in the information field. Works to promote the advancement of members' knowledge, professional standing credentialing, and personal achievements in information technology, management, and strategic planning. Conducts employment referral and education programs. A specialty group of the American Academy of Medical Administrators.
300 Members Founded: 1991

11447 American College of Home Health Care
Thomas R ODonovan
Southfield, MI 48076
248-540-4310
FAX: 248-645-0590
Home health administrators, executives, and managers at all levels. Promotes professional identification within the home health care field and seeks to facilitate the career and professional development of members. Represents the interests of the home health care industry within the medical community and before government agencies and the public; makes available to members discounts on educational programs conducted by the ACHHA; offers professional referral services; holds examiniations.
3500 Members Founded: 1957

11448 American College of Medical Practice
104 Inverness Terrace E
Englewood, CO 80112-5306
303-799-1111
FAX: 303-643-4439
acmpe@mgma.com www.mgma.com
Norma J Plante, Chairman
Alan M Stoll, Vice Chair
Betsy McEldowney, Secretary/Treasurer
Professional credentialing organization. Works to encourage medical group practice administrators to improve and maintain their proficiency and to provide appropriate recognition; to establish a program with uniform standards of admission, advancement, certification and fellowship in order to achieve the highest possible standards in the profession of medical group practice administration; to participate in the development of educational and research programs.
3000 Members Founded: 1956

11449 American College of Medical Quality
4334 Montgomerey Avenue
Bethesda, MD 20814
301-913-9149
FAX: 301-913-9142 800-924-2149
acmq@acmq.org www.acmq.org
Paul Gitman, President
Bridget Brodie, Executive VP
Robert F Pendrak, Secretary
Mark Granoff, Treasurer
Founded: 1973

11450 American College of Obstetricians and Gynecologists
409 12th Street SW
PO Box 96920
Washington, DC 20090-6920
202-638-5577
FAX: 202-484-5107
resources@acog.org www.acog.org
John M Gibbons, President
William P Dillon, VP
William J Peters, Treasurer
Michael T Mennuti, Secretary
45000 Members Founded: 1951

11451 American College of Oncology Administrator (ACDA)
701 Lee Street
Suite 600
Des Plaines, IL 60016-4516
847-759-8601
FAX: 847-759-8602
info@aameda.org www.aameda.org
Von Yetzer, Director/Membership/Communication
Renee S Schleicher, President/CEO
Oncology administrators, managers and consultants. Brings together all components of oncology management to develop creative strategies, quality programs, and sound evaluation mechanisms. Promotes advancement of members through continuing education and research in oncology management. Conducts educational programs.
300 Members Founded: 1991

11452 American College of Oral and Maxillofacial Surgeons
100 NW Loop 410
Suite 420
San Antonio, TX 78213-6676
210-344-5674
FAX: 210-344-9754 800-522-6676
director@acoms.org/admin@acoms.org
www.acoms.org
Daniel A Lanka, Executive Director
Katrina Rohrmaier, Administrative Assistant
2331 Members Founded: 1975
Mailing list available for rent 2331 names $250 per M.

11453 American College of Osteopathic Family Practice
330 E Algonquin Avenue
Suite 1
Arlington Heights, IL 60005
847-286-6090
FAX: 847-228-9755 800-323-0794
Glenn G Miller, President
Thomas N Told, President-Elect
Ronnie B Martin, Secretary/Treasurer
Emily Kalata, Communications/Marketing Manager
Peter Schmelzer, Executive Director
23173 Members Founded: 1950

11454 American College of Osteopathic Medicine
2615 Merrick Street
Fort Worth, TX 76107-3365
817-377-0421
FAX: 817-377-0439 800-875-6360
acoog@acoog.com www.acoog.com
Paul M Krueger, Chairman
Sheryl A Bushman, Vice Chairman
W Lee Irving, Secretary/Treasurer
ACOOG is passionately committed to exellence in women's health. Offers education and support for osteopathic health care professionals to improve the quality of lifes for woman.
Founded: 1934

11455 American College of Osteopathic Surgeons
123 N Henry Street
Alexandria, VA 22314-2903
703-684-0416
FAX: 703-684-3280
info@theacos.org www.facos.org
Guy Beaumont, Executive Director
Judith T Mangum, Director Finance
Founded: 1926

11456 American College of Physician Executives
4890 W Kennedy Boulevard
Suite 200
Tampa, FL 33609
813-287-2000
FAX: 813-287-8993 800-562-8088
acpe@acpe.org www.acpe.org
Roger Schenke, Executive Vice President
Tina Ramsey, Advertising
Bill Steiger, Editor/Journal & Leading Edge
Robin Doty, Finance & General Counsel
Luke Barnes, Systems Administrator
Physicians whose primary professional responsibility is the management of health care organizations. Provides for continuing education and certification of the physician executive and the profession. Offers specialized career planning, counseling, recruitment and placement services, research and information data on physican managers.
1200 Members Founded: 1974

11457 American College of Physicians
190 N Independence Mall West
Philadelphia, PA 19106-1572
215-512-2400

archives@acponline.org
www.acponline.org
Charles K Francis, President
John Tooker, Chief Executive Officer
Eric B Larson, Chair, Board of Regents
Founded: 1956

11458 American College of Rheumatology
1800 Century Place
Suite 250
Atlanta, GA 30345-4300
404-633-3777
FAX: 404-633-1870
www.rheumatology.org
David Wofsy, President
Mark Andrejeski, Executive VP
Founded: 1934

11459 American College of Sports Medicine
401 W Michigan Street
PO Box 1440
Indianapolis, IN 46202-3233
317-637-9200
FAX: 317-634-7817
publicinfo@acsm.org www.acsm.org
Lynn Walters, Director/Meetings
David Hillery, Treasurer
James R Whitehead, Secretary

Promotes and integrates scientific research, education, and practical applications of sports medicine and exercise science to maintain and enhance physical performance, fitness, health, and quality of life.
50000 Members Founded: 1954

11460 American College of Surgeons
633 N Saint Clair Street
Chicago, IL 60611
312-202-5000
FAX: 312-440-7143
postmaster@facs.org www.facs.org
Thomas Russell, Executive Director
Founded: 1914

11461 American Congress of Rehabilitation Medicine
6801 Lake Plaza Drive
Suite B- 205
Indianapolis, IN 46220
317-915-2250
FAX: 317-915-2245
acrm@acrm.org www.acrm.org
Richard D Morgan, Executive Director
Jean Ball, Director Finance
900 Members Founded: 1923 900 names

11462 American Counseling Association (ACA)
5999 Stevenson Avenue
Alexandria, VA 22304
800-347-6647
FAX: 800-473-2329
www.counseling.org
Marie Wakefield, President
Offers information to older people on adult psychological development and aging.

11463 American Dental Association
211 E Chicago Avenue
20th Floor
Chicago, IL 60611-2637
312-440-2500
FAX: 312-440-2800 www.ada.org
James Bramson, CEO
R Barkley Payne, Senior Director
Serves the dental profession and dental industry.
Founded: 1913

11464 American Dental Education Association
1625 Massachusetts Avenue NW
Suite 600
Washington, DC 20036-2212
202-299-9267
FAX: 202-667-0642
webmaster@adea.org www.adea.org
Kenneth L Kalkwarf, President
Candy B Ross, VP
Richard W Valachovic, Executive Director
The mission of the American Dental Education Assocation is to lead individuals and institutions of the dental education community to address contemporary issues influencing education, research, and the delivery of oral health care for the improvement of the health of the public.
Founded: 1983

11465 American Dental Hygenists Association
444 N Michigan Avenue
Suite 3400
Chicago, IL 60611
312-440-8900
FAX: 312-440-8929
mail@adha.org www.adha.org
Kathy Madryk, Manager Marketing
Isaac Carpenter, Executive Director
Founded: 1993

11466 American Dental Society of Anesthesiology
211 E Chicago Avenue
Suite 780
Chicago, IL 60611
312-664-8270
800-722-7788
adsahome@cs.com
www.adsahome.org
Robert Campbell, President
Joseph E Carlisle, VP
R Knight Charlton, Executive Director
Founded: 1954

11467 American Diabetes Association
1701 N Beauregard Street
Alexandria, VA 22311
703-549-1500
FAX: 703-683-1351 800-342-2383
meetings@diabetes.org diabetes.org
Lynn B Nicholas, CEO
Vaneeda Bennett, Chief Development Officer
Tom Bognanno, Chief Field Officer
John Courtney, CFO
Richard Kahn, Chief Scientific/Med Officer
Provides information and educational materials on preventing, treating, and living with diabetes.
250 Members Founded: 1940

11468 American Dietetic Association
120 S Riverside Plaza
Suite 2000
Chicago, IL 60606
312-990-0040
800-877-1600
marketing@eatright.org
www.eatright.org
Al Cassady, Chairman
Margaret L Bogle, Vice Chair
B Thomas Malone, Financial Officer
Mary Ellen Collins, Directors at Large
This association is a promoter of optimal health and nutritional status of the population advancing the science of food and nutrition by offering food and nutrition referrals and information.
70000 Members Founded: 1917

11469 American Gastroentological Society
6900 Grove Road
Thorofare, NJ 08086
856-848-1000
FAX: 856-848-1881

11470 American Head and Neck Society
11300 W Olympic Boulevard
Suite 600
Los Angeles, CA 90064
310-437-0559
FAX: 310-437-0585
admin@ahns.info
www.headandneckcancer.org
Jonas T Johnson, President
John J Coleman, VP
John C O'Brien, Treasurer
Wayne M Koch, Secretary
Founded: 1998

11471 American Health Care Association
1201 L Street NW
Washington, DC 20005
202-842-4444
FAX: 202-842-3860
webmaster@ahca.org www.ahca.org
Dave Kyllo, VP
12000 Members Founded: 1949

11472 American Health Information
233 N Michigan Avenue
Suite 2150
Chicago, IL 60601-5800
312-233-1100
FAX: 312-233-1090
info@ahima.org www.ahima.org
Melanie Brodnik, President
Linda L Kloss, Executive VP/CEO
Katherine E Byrd, Privacy Office/Director
46000 Members Founded: 1928

11473 American Health Quality Association
1155 21st Street NW
Washington, DC 20036
202-331-5790
FAX: 202-331-9334
info@ahqa.org www.ahqa.org
David Schulke, Executive VP
Marc Bennett, CEO
Dave Adler, Associate Director
Charlie McBride, President
Patricia Riley, Treasurer
The American Health Quality Association is an educational, not-for-profit national membership association dedicated to promoting and facilitating fndamental change that improves the quality of health care in America.

11474 American Healthcare Radiology
490-B Boston Post Road
#101
Sudbury, MA 01776
978-443-7591
FAX: 978-443-8046 800-334-2472
info@ahraonline.org www.ahra.com
Judy A Dye, Chair
Elizabeth D McKnight, Vice Chair
Mel L Allen, Secretary/Treasurer
Michael J Albertina, Director
Edward Cronin, Executive Director
Professional association of radiology administrators from the US, Canada and several other countries. AHRA is a resource and catalyst for the development of professional leaders in imaging sciences and other health care disciplines. Publications available to members. Dues are $140 per year.
4000 Members Founded: 1972

11475 American Heart Association
7272 Greenville Avenue
Dallas, TX 75231
214-736-6300
FAX: 214-570-5930 800-242-8721
siebelprod@heart.org
www.americanheart.org
M Cass Wheeler, CEO
A non-profit organization funding research and providing information on the diagnosis, treatment, and prevention of heart diseases and stroke.

11476 American Horticultural Therapy Association (AHTA)
3570 E 12th Avenue
Denver, CO 80206
303-322-2482
FAX: 303-322-2485 800-634-1630
Joy Harrison, Administrative Director
A non-profit, membership organization that promotes and advances horticultural therapy as a therapeutic intervention and rehabilitation option.
ISBN s-uite 2-06-

11477 American Hospital Association
1 N Franklin Street
Chicago, IL 60606-3421
312-422-3000
FAX: 312-422-4591
ddavidson@aha.org www.aha.org
David L Bernd, Chairman
Richard J Davidson, President
Jeanette Harlow, Executive Director
National organization that represents and serves all types of hospitals, health care networks, and their patients and communities. AHA ensures that members' perspectives and needs are heard and addressed in national health policy development, legislative and regulatory debates, and judicial matters. AHA provides education for health care leaders and is a source of information on health care issues and trends.
37000 Members Founded: 1898

11478 American Industrial Hygiene Association
2700 Prosperity Avenue
Suite 250
Fairfax, VA 22031
703-498-8267
FAX: 703-207-3561
infonet@aiha.org www.aiha.org
Steven Davis, Executive Director
Organization of professionals in the science of occupational and environmental health and safety.
12000 Members Founded: 1939

11479 American Institute of Ultrasound Medicine
14750 Sweitzer Lane
Suite 100
Laurel, MD 20707-5906
301-984-4392
FAX: 301-498-4450 800-638-5352
membership@aium.org
www.aium.org
Carmine Valente, CEO
Diane Eberle, CFO
Mary Ann Hann, Accounting Manager
Jennifer Morse, Human Resources/Operations Manager
Paula Woletz, Director Accreditation
Multidisciplinary organization dedicated to advancing the art and science of ultrasound in medicine and research through its educational, scientific and professional activities.
85000 Members Founded: 1952

11480 American Lung Association
61 Broadway
6th Floor
New York, NY 10006
212-315-8700
FAX: 212-315-8874
cheaden@lungusa.org
www.lungusa.org
Charles A Heinrich, Chairman
John Kirkwood, Chief Executive Officer
John F Sutter, Vice Chair
Imajean Hetherington, Secretary
Dedicated to the prevention, cure, and control of lung diseases such as asthma, emphysema, tuberculosis, and lung cancer. The Association offers community service, public health education, advocacy, and research.
100 Members Founded: 1904

11481 American Medical Association
515 N State Street
Chicago, IL 60610-4320
312-464-5000
FAX: 312-464-4184 800-262-3211
robin_rusell@ama-assn.org
www.ama-assn.org
Dr Donald J Palmisano MD JD, President
William G Plested III MD, Chairman
Herman I Abromowitz MD, Secretary
Partnership of physicians and their professional associations dedicated to promoting the art and science of medicine and the betterment of the public health. Serves physicians and their patients by establishing and promoting ethical, educational and clinical standards for the medical profession and by advocating for the highest principle of all — the integrity of the physician/patient relationship.

11482 American Medical Directors Association
10480 Little Patuxent Parkway
Suite 760
Columbia, MD 21044
410-740-9743
FAX: 410-740-4572 800-876-2632
info@amda.com www.amda.com
Lorraine Tarnove, Executive Director
Jacqueline Vance, Director Clinical Affairs
Lisa Marlow, Project Coordinator
Meg LaPorte, Director Government Affairs
7400 Members Founded: 1978

11483 American Medical Group Association
1422 Duke Street
Alexandria, VA 22314-3430
703-838-0033
FAX: 703-548-1890
roconnor@amga.org www.amga.org
Donald W Fisher, President/CEO
Ryan O'Connor, VP of Membership
A trade association that represents, the nation's leading medical groups. *$95.00*
300 Members Monthly Founded: 1949
Circulation: 65000

11484 American Medical Informatics Association
4915 Street Elmo Avenue
Suite 401
Bethesda, MD 20814
301-657-1291
FAX: 301-657-1296
eberner@uab.edu www.amia.org
Charles Safran, President
Eta S Berner, Secretary
Justin B Starren, Treasurer
Karen Greenwood, Manager
3200 Members Founded: 1990

11485 American Medical Network/Occupational Association
PO Box 604
Hendersonville, NC 28793
704-896-3312
Practicing physicians. Represents doctors' concerns for their patients; establishes a national quality database for use in negotiating managed care contracts; educates laymen and policy makers on quality of care issues; and influences health care policy.
Founded: 1996

11486 American Medical Student Association
1902 Association Drive
Reston, VA 20191
703-620-6600
FAX: 703-620-5873 800-767-2266
amsa@www.amsa.org www.amsa.org
Paul R Wright, Executive Director
Lauren Oshman, President
Braden Hexom, Executive Associate
40000 Members Founded: 1950

11487 American Medical Technologists
10700 West Higgins Road
Rosemont, IL 60018
847-823-5169
FAX: 847-823-0458 800-275-1268
Christopher Damen, Executive Director
Michelle Vahlkamp, Director Marketing/Membership
35000 Members Founded: 1939

11488 American Medical Women's Association
801 N Fairfax Street
Suite 400
Alexandria, VA 22314
703-838-0500
FAX: 703-549-3864
info@amwa-doc.org
www.awma-doc.org
10000 Members Founded: 1915

11489 American Music Therapy Association
8455 Colesville Road
Suite 1000
Silver Spring, MD 20910
301-589-3300
FAX: 301-589-5175
info@musictherapy.org
www.musictherapy.org
Non-profit organization that advocates, promotes, and provides resources and information on the uses and benefits of music therapy.

11490 American Nephrology Nurses Association
E Holly Avenue
Box 56
Pittman, NJ 08071-56
856-256-2320
FAX: 856-256-7463 anna@ajj.com
Lesley C Dinwiddie, President
JoAnne Gilmore, Treasurer
Glenda M Payne, Secretary
Mike Cunningham, Manager
12000 Members Annual Founded: 1969

11491 American Nurses Association
8515 Georgia Avenue
Suite 400
Silver Spring, MD 20910
301-628-5000
FAX: 301-628-5001 800-274-4262
webmaster@ana.org
www.nursingworld.org

William L Holzemer, President
Linda Gobis, VP
Barbara Reck, Secretary
Janice E Bussert, Treasurer

Serves registered nurses in North America.

11492 American Occupation Therapy Association
4720 Montgomery Lane
PO Box 31220
Bethesda, MD 20824-1220
301-652-2682
FAX: 301-652-7711
aotapresident@aol.com www.aota.org

Barbara L Kornblau, President, VP
Aimee J Luebben, Secretary
Melanie T Ellexson, Treasurer

11493 American Occupational Health
6900 Grove Road
Thorofare, NJ 08086
856-848-1000
FAX: 856-848-3522
bkehler@slackinc.com
www.slackinc.com

Betty Kehler, Exhibit Manager
Nancy Kay Olson, Conference Meeting Manager

4500 Members

11494 American Occupational Therapy Association
4720 Montgomery Lane
Bethesda, MD 20824-1220
301-652-2682
FAX: 301-652-7711 www.aota.org

Frederick P Somers, Executive Director

Offers information on the role of occupational therapy in promoting functional independence, preventing disability, and maintaining health.

11495 American Optometric Association
243 N Lindbergh Boulevard
1st Floor
Saint Louis, MO 63141
314-991-4100
FAX: 314-991-4101 800-365-2219
mdjones@aoa.org www.aoanet.org

Dr. Michale Jones, Exective Director

National organization of optometrists, evaluates ophthalmic products and sponsors continuing education programs.

32000 Members Founded: 1898

11496 American Optometric Student Association
243 N Lindbergh Boulevard
St. Louis, MO 63141
314-991-4100

esheckmann@aoa.org www.aoanet.org

Michael Jones, Executive Director

11497 American Orthopsychiatric Association
2001 N Beauregard
12th Floor
Alexandria, VA 22311
703-797-2584
FAX: 703-684-5968
amerortho@aol.com
www.amerortho.org

Lisa Shuger Hublitz, Executive Director
Ellen Olshansky, Treasurer
Gary B Melton, President

700 Members Annual Founded: 1923

11498 American Orthotic & Prosthetic Association
330 John Carlyle Street
Suite 200
Alexandria, VA 22314
703-367-7116
FAX: 571-431-0899
info@aopanet.org www.aopanet.org

Keith D Cornell, President
Walter L Racette, VP
Tyler Wilson, Executive Director

1783 Members Founded: 1917

11499 American Osteopathic Association
142 E Ontario Street
Chicago, IL 60611
312-202-8000
FAX: 312-202-8200 800-621-1773
info@osteotech.org
www.osteopathic.org

John Crosby, Executive Director

Promotes public health, encourages scientific research, and is the accrediting agency for all osteopathic medical schools and health care facilities.

52000 Members Founded: 1897

11500 American Pain Society
4700 W Lake Avenue
Glenview, IL 60025
847-375-4715
FAX: 877-734-8758
info@ampainsoc.org
www.ampainsoc.org

Richard Payne, President
Patricia McGrath, Treasurer
Judith A Paice, Secretary
Cathy Underwood, Manager

11501 American Parkinsons' Disease Association
135 Parkinson Avenue
Staten Island, NY 10305
718-981-8001
FAX: 718-981-4399 800-223-2732
apda@apdaparkinson.org
www.apdaparkinson.org

Vincent N Gattullo, President
Joel A Miele, First VP

Funds research to find a cure for Parkinson's disease.

11502 American Pediatric Society
3400 Research Forest Drive
The Woodlands, TX 77381
281-419-0052
FAX: 281-419-0082
info@aps-spr.org www.aps-spr.org

Debbie Anagnostelis, Executive Director
Kathy Cannon, Associate Executive Director
Debbie Atwood, Information Services Director
Kate Culliton, Accounting Manager

11503 American Pharmaceutical Association
1100 15th Street NW
Suite 400
Washington, DC 20005-1707
202-628-4410
FAX: 202-783-2351 800-237-2742

Linda K Gainey, Director Executive Office Oper.

National society of licensed pharmacists providing public health information and referrals to resources on medicine and public policy.

11504 American Physical Therapy Association
1111 N Fairfax Street
Alexandria, VA 22314
703-684-2782
FAX: 703-684-7343
svcctr@apta.org www.apta.org

Ben F Massey, President
Frank Mallon, CEO
Janet Bezner, VP
Randy Roesch, Secretary
Francis J Welk, Treasurer

Organization of physical therapists providing referrals to APTA geraitric-certified therapists and information on debilitating ailments like arthritis, stroke, scoliosis, and sudden onset of illness.

11505 American Physiological Society
9650 Rockville Pike
Bethesda, MD 20814
301-634-7164
FAX: 301-634-7241
webmaster@the-aps.org
www.the-aps.org

Dr Martin Frank, Executive Director
Kevin Chian, Financial Analyst
Santa Vadala, Secretary
Robert Price, Director Finance

A nonprofit devoted to fostering education scientific research and dissemination of information in the physiological sciences. A member of the Federation of American Societies for Experimental Biology (FASEB) a coalition of 18 independent societies that plays an active role in lobbying for the interests of biomedical scientists.

10163 Members Founded: 1887

11506 American Podiatric Medical Association
9312 Old Georgetown Road
Bethesda, MD 20814
301-571-9200
FAX: 301-530-2752
jescherer@apma.org www.apma.org

Glenn B Gastwirth DPM, Executive Director
Jay Levrio PhD, Deputy Executive Director

An association of podiatrists providing services and information on foot problems and foot health.

11000 Members Founded: 1912

11507 American Psychiatric Association
1000 Wilson Boulevard
Suite 1825
Arlington, VA 22209-3901
703-077-7300
FAX: 703-907-1085
apa@psych.org www.psych.org

James Scully, Manager

Association for manufacturers, suppliers, distributors, publishers, state/federal agencies and psychiatric facilities.

11508 American Psychological Association
750 1st Street NE
Washington, DC 20002-4242
202-336-5500
FAX: 202-336-5568 800-374-2721
pracmarket@apa.org www.apa.org

Diane F Halpern, President
Norman Anderson, VP
Gerald P Koocher, Treasurer

A professional society of psychologists that provides assistance and information on mental, emotional, and behavioral disorders.

15000 Members Founded: 1892

11509 American Public Human Services Association
810 1st Street NE
Suite 500
Washington, DC 20002
202-682-0100
FAX: 202-289-6555
memberserviceshelpdesk@aphsa.org
www.aphsa.org

Jerry W Friedman, Executive Director
Anita Light, Director Human Resources

Nonprofit, bipartisan organization of individuals and agencies concerned with human services. Members include all state and many territorial human service agencies, more than 1,200 local agencies, and several thousand individuals.

Founded: 1930

11510 American School Health Association
7263 State Route 43
PO Box 708
Kent, OH 44240
330-678-1601
FAX: 330-678-4526 800-445-2742
asha@ashaweb.org www.ashaweb.org

Susan Wooley, Executive Director
Thomas Reed, Director of Editoral Services

We unite the many professionals working in schools who are committed to safeguarding the health of school-aged children. The Association is a multidisciplinary organization of administrators, counselors, health educators, physical educators, psychologists, school health coordinators, school nurses, school physicians, and social workers. *$110.00*

2000 Members Annual Membership Fee Founded: 1927

11511 American Society for Aesthetic Plastic Surgery
36 W 44th Street
New York, NY 10036
212-921-0500
FAX: 212-921-0011
media@surgery.org www.surgery.org

Robert Stanton, Executive Director

Organization of plastic surgeons certified by the American Board of Plastic Surgery who specialize in cosmetic surgery of the face and body.

11512 American Society for Bone and Mineral Research
2025 M Street NW
Suite 800
Washington, DC 20036-3309
202-367-1161
FAX: 202-367-2161
asbmr@smithbucklin.com
www.asbmr.org

Joan Goldberg, Executive Director

3600 Members Founded: 1977

11513 American Society for Cell Biology
8120 Woodmont Avenue
Suite 750
Bethesda, MD 20814
301-530-7153
FAX: 301-347-9310
ascbinfo@ascb.org www.ascb.org

11514 American Society for Clinical Nutrition
9650 Rockville Pike
Bethesda, MD 20814-3998
301-711-1825
FAX: 301-571-1863
routzahn@ascn.faseb.org
www.asns.org

Dale A Schoeller, President
Samuel Klein, VP
Richard J Deckelbaum, Treasurer
Janet C King, Secretary
Elaine Strass, Executive Director

11515 American Society for Dermatologic Surgery
5550 Meadowbrook Drive
Suite 120
Rolling Meadows, IL 60008
847-956-0900
FAX: 847-956-0999
info@asds.net www.asds-net.org

Alastair Carruthers, President
Kimberly Butterwick, Board of Directors

To promote optimal quality care for patients as well as support and develop investigative knowledge in the field of dermatologic surgery.

800 Members Founded: 1973

11516 American Society for Histocompatability
17000 Commerce Parkway
Suite C
Mt. Laurel, NJ 08054
913-541-0009
FAX: 856-439-0525
info@ashi-hla.org www.ashi-hla.org

Steve Echard, Executive Director
Kimberly Glenn, Assistant Executive Director

11517 American Society for Laser Medicine
2100 Stewart Avenue
Suite 240
Wausau, WI 54401-1709
715-845-9283
FAX: 715-848-2493
information@aslms.org
www.aslms.org

Dianne Dalsky, Executive Director
Ken Day, Director of Organization Developmen

Promotes excellence in patient care by advancing biomedical application of lasers and other related technologies worldwide.

11518 American Society for Medicine and Science
875 Providence Highway
Dedham, MA 02026-6868
781-326-7800
FAX: 781-326-2921 800-972-7777

Organizes medical and scientific conventions worldwide for nonprofit organizations.

11519 American Society for Microbiology
1752 N Street NW
Washington, DC 20036-2904
202-373-3600
FAX: 202-942-9333
webmaster@asmusa.org
www.asm.org

Thomas Shenk, President
Judy A Daly, Secretary
Michael Goldberg, Executive Director

11520 American Society for Pharmacology
9650 Rockville Pike
Bethesda, MD 20814-3995
301-347-7060
FAX: 301-530-7061
webmaster@faseb.org www.faseb.org

Christine Carrico, Executive Director

11521 American Society for Surgery of the Hand
6300 N River Road
Suite 600
Rosemont, IL 60018
847-384-8300
FAX: 847-384-1435
info@assh.org www.assh.org

Roy A Meals, President
David M Lichtman, VP
L Andrew Koman, Secretary
Mark Anderson, Executive Director

2000 Members Founded: 1946

11522 American Society for Therapeutic Radiology And Oncology
12500 Fair Lakes Circle
Suite 375
Fairfax, VA 22033
703-502-1550
FAX: 703-502-7852 800-962-7876
meetings@astro.org www.astro.org

Theodore S Lawrence, President
Joel E Tepper, Chairman
Laura Mulay, ASTRO Meetings Manager

10000 Members October/Annual Founded: 1958
Mailing list available for rent

11523 American Society of Anesthesiologists
520 N Northwest Highway
Park Ridge, IL 60068-2573
847-825-5586
FAX: 847-825-1692
mail@asahq.org www.asahq.org

Ronald A Bruns, Executive Director
Denise M Jones, Assistant Executive Director
Michael Scott, Director Governmental Affairs
Jill A Formeister, Director Scientific Affairs

Janice L Plack, Director Information Services
39000 Members Founded: 1905

11524 American Society of Bariatric Physicians
2821 S. Parker Rd.
Aurora, CO 80014-5234
303-770-2526
FAX: 303-779-4834 877-266-6834
info@asbp.org www.asbp.org
Gary Albertson, President
Mary C Vernon, VP
Arthur T Davidson, Chairman
Russell Pavich, Secretary/Treasurer
Beth Little, Manager
ASBP is a non profit international professional medical association headquartered in Aurora, Colorado. In 2000, the ASBP was awarded a seat in the House of Delegates of American Medical Association. The American Society of Bariatric Physicians has members worldwide.

11525 American Society of Cataract & Refractive Medicine
4000 Legato Road
Suite 850
Fairfax, VA 22033
703-591-2220
FAX: 703-591-0614 800-451-1339
Stephen S Lane, President
Priscilla Perry Arnold, VP
Roger F Steinert, CFO
David Karcher, Executive Director
Manus C Kraff, Chair Program Committee

11526 American Society of Clinical Oncology
1900 Duke Street
Alexandria, VA 22314
703-299-0150
FAX: 703-299-1044
asco@asco.org www.asco.org
Margaret A Tempero, President
David R Gandara, Secretary/Treasurer
Charles Balch, Executive Director
World's leading professional society representing physicians from nearly one hundred countries who treat people with cancer. ASCO's 18,000 members set the standard for patient care worldwide and lead the fight for more effective cancer treatments, increase funding for clinical and translational research and ultimately, cures for the many different cancers that strike 12 million Americans every year.
20000 Members Founded: 1964

11527 American Society of Clinical Pathologists
2100 W Harrison Street
Chicago, IL 60612-3798
312-738-1336
FAX: 312-738-1619
info@ascp.org www.ascp.org
John Ball, Executive VP
Fred Rodriguez, VP

11528 American Society of Colon & Rectal Medicine
85 W Algonquin Road
Suite 550
Arlington Heights, IL 60005
847-290-9184
FAX: 847-290-9203 800-791-0001
ascrs@fascrs.org www.fascrs.org

David J Schoetz, President
Leela M Prasad, VP
Ann C Lowry, Treasurer
2300 Members Founded: 1899

11529 American Society of Contemporary Healthcare
820 N Orleans
Chicago, IL 60610
847-779-9093
FAX: 312-440-0580 800-621-4002
Randall Bellows MD, Director
Educational, nonprofit organization dedicated to improving the quality of health care delivered to the patient by the physician. We provide seminars, conferences and small group discussions, a journal and consultation to this end.
2000 Members Founded: 1969

11530 American Society of Cytopathology
400 W 9th Street
Suite 201
Wilmington, DE 19801
302-429-8802
FAX: 302-429-8807
asc@cytopathology.org
www.cytopathology.org
Elizabeth Jenkins, Director
David B Kaminsky, Secretary/Treasurer
Elizabeth Jenkins, Manager
3,000 Members Founded: 1951

11531 American Society of Directors of American Hospital Association
1 N Franklin 27th Floor
Chicago, IL 60606
312-223-3937
FAX: 312-422-4505
storeservice@aha.org
www.ahaonlinestore.com
David L Bernd, Chairman
Richard J Davidson, President
Audrey Harris, Executive Director
37000 Members Founded: 1898

11532 American Society of Electroneurodiagnostic Technologists
6501 East Commerce Avenue
Suite 120
Kansas City, MO 64120
816-931-1120
FAX: 816-931-1145
info@aset.org www.aset.org
Gail P. Hayden, President
L. Elizabeth Mullikin, President-Elect
ASET is the largest national professional association for individuals involved in the study and recording of electrical activity in the brain and nervous system. Organized in 1959 as a not-for-profit society, ASET's mission is to provide leadership, advocacy and professional excellence for members, creating greater awareness of the profession and establishing standards and best practices to ensure quality patient care.
Founded: 1959

11533 American Society of Extra-Corporeal Activities
503 Carlisle Drive
Suite 125
Herndon, VA 20170
703-435-8556
FAX: 703-435-0056
judyr@amsect.org www.amsect.org
George M Cate, Executive Director
Judy Luther, Deputy Executive Director
Enhancing the quality of extra-corporeal (involving heart and lung machines) rendered to the public by engaging in the programmatic activities that will further the knowledge, skills, abilities and general proficiency of practitioners.
1700 Members Founded: 1968

11534 American Society of Health Care Marketing
1 N Franklin Street
Chicago, IL 60606-3421
773-327-1064
FAX: 312-422-4579

11535 American Society of Health-Systems Pharmacists
7272 Wisconsin Avenue
Bethesda, MD 20814-4836
301-657-3000
FAX: 301-657-1641
custserv@ashp.org www.ashp.org
Jill E Martin, President
Henri R Manasse, Executive VP
Marianne F Ivey, Treasurer
31000 Members Founded: 1936

11536 American Society of Hematology
1900 M Street NW
Suite 200
Washington, DC 20036
202-776-0544
FAX: 202-776-0545
ash@hematology.org
www.hematology.org
Stanley L Schrier, President
Kanti R Rai, VP
Nancy Berliner, Secretary
J Evan Sadler, Treasurer
Martha Liggett, Executive Director
10000 Members Founded: 1958

11537 American Society of Human Genetics
9650 Rockville Pike
Bethesda, MD 20814
301-571-1825
FAX: 301-530-7079 866-486-4363
webmaster@faseb.org www.faseb.org
Geri Swindle, Director
Jean Lash, Exhibit Manager
Mary Grocki, Meeting Manager
Elaine Strass, Executive Director

11538 American Society of Interventional and Therapeutic Neuroradiology
3975 Fair Ridge Dr
400
Fairfax, VA 22033-2911
703-605-5560
FAX: 703-691-1855
marie@asitn.org www.asitn.org
Charles M Strother, President
Patricia A Hudgins, VP
3000 Members Founded: 1962

11539 American Society of Nephrology
1725 I Street NW
Washington, DC 20006
202-160-0640
FAX: 202-659-0709
email@asn-online.org
www.asn-online.org
William E Mitch, President
Alan M Krensky, Secretary/Treasurer
Karen Campbell, Executive Director

11540 American Society of Neuroradiology
2210 Midwest Road
Suite 207
Oak Brook, IL 60523-8205
630-574-0220
FAX: 630-574-0661
cstrother@tmh.tmc.edu www.asnr.org

Robert I Grossman, VP
John R Hesselink, Secretary

Active members must devote approximately one half or more of their professional practice to nueroradiology. Publishes a monthly journal and holds an annual meeting.
3000 Members Founded: 1962

11541 American Society of Ophthalmic Professionals
4000 Legato Road
#850
Fairfax, VA 22033
703-591-2220
FAX: 703-591-0614 800-451-1339
ascrs@ascrs.org www.ascrs.org

Lucy Santiago, Executive Director

Division of the American Society of Cataract and Retractive Surgery. People involved with the administration of an ophthalmic office or clinic can be members. Facilitates the exchange of ideas and information in order to improve management practices and working conditions. Offers placement services.
1900 Members Founded: 1986

11542 American Society of Plastic Surgeons
444 E Algonquin Road
Arlington Heights, IL 60005
847-228-9900
FAX: 847-228-9131 888-475-2784
webmaster@plasticsurgery.org
www.plasticsurgery.org

Scott Stear, President

Promotes the specialty of plastic surgery and supports the highest quality patient care, professionalism and ethical standards through our role as patient and physician advocates.
4559 Members Founded: 1931
Mailing list available for rent $750 per M.

11543 American Speech-Language-Hearing Association
10801 Rockville Pike
Rockville, MD 20852
301-897-5700
FAX: 877-541-5035 800-638-8255
actioncenter@asha.org www.asha.org

Arlene Pietranton, Executive Director

Represents the interests of medical specialists in speech, language, and hearing science and advocates for people with communication-related disorders.

11544 American Stroke Association
7272 Greenville Avenue
Dallas, TX 75231
800-242-8721
FAX: 214-570-5930 888-478-7653
Toll-free information and referral service offering lists of certified doctors who are stroke specialists and volunteer stroke survivors or family members.

11545 American Tinnitus Association
PO Box 5
Portland, OR 97207
503-248-9985
FAX: 503-248-0024 800-634-8978
Volunteer organization supporting research and providing information on tinnitus, a constant buzzing or ringing in the ears or head.

11546 American Urological Association Foundation
1000 Corporate Boulevard
Suite 410
Linthicum, MD 21090
410-689-3700
FAX: 410-689-3998 866-746-4282
Works toward the prevention and cure of urologic disease in part by keeping patients, family members, and friends informed about these disorders, treatment options, and recent research findings.

11547 Arthroscopy Association of North America
6300 N River Road
Suite 104
Rosemont, IL 60018
847-292-2262
FAX: 847-292-2268
moreinfo@aana.org www.aana.org

Brian Day, President
James C Y Chow, Second VP
David A McGuire, Treasurer
Edward Goss, Executive Director

11548 Association for Applied Psychophysiology and Biofeedback

10200 W 44th Avenue
Suite 304
Wheat Ridge, CO 80033-2840
303-422-8436
FAX: 303-422-8894 800-477-8892
resourcenter.com www.aapb.org

Steven M Baskin, President
Jay Gunkelman, Treasurer
Francine Butler, Executive Director

Founded: 1969

11549 Association for Gerontology in Higher Educ ation
1030 15th Street NW
Suite 240
Washington, DC 20005
202-289-9806
FAX: 202-289-9824 www.aghe.org
Seeks to advance gerontology as a field of study at institutions of higher education.

11550 Association for Professionals in Infection Control and Epidemiology
1275 K Street NW
Suite 1000
Washington, DC 20005-4006
202-789-1890
FAX: 202-789-1899
apicinfo@apic.org www.apic.org

Jeanne A Pfieffer, President
Patti Grant, Secretary
Jim Maslend, Executive Director

10000 Members Founded: 1972

11551 Association for Worksite Health Promotion
60 Revere Drive
Northbrook, IL 60062-1577
847-480-9574
FAX: 847-480-9282 www.awhp.org
Exists to advance the profession of worksite health promotion and the career development of its practitioners and to improve the performance of the programs they administer. Represents a variety of disciplines and worksites, for decision makers in the areas of health promotion/disease prevention and health care cost management.
3000 Members

11552 Association for the Advancement of Medical Instumentation
1110 N Glebe Road
Suite 220
Arilington, VA 22201-4595
703-525-4890
FAX: 703-276-0793 800-332-2264
webmaster@aami.org www.aami.com

Michale Miller, President
Betsy Bridgmen, Executive VP

6000 Members Founded: 1967

11553 Association for the Advancement of Medical Instrumentation
1110 North Glebe Road
Suite 220
Arlington, VA 22201-4795

The Association for the Advancement of Medical Instrumentation (AAMI), founded in 1967, is a unique alliance of over 6,000 members united by the coommon goal of increasing the understaning and use of medical instrumentation. AAMI is the primary source of consensus and timely information on medical instrumentation and technology for the industry, professionals, and the government for national and intemational standrards.

11554 Association of Academic Chairmen of Plastic Surgery
444 E Algonquin Road
Arlington Heights, IL 60005-4654
847-228-8375
FAX: 847-228-6509

Catherine May, Contact

Seeks to advance the study and teaching of plastic and reconstructive surgery. Facilitates establishment of graduate medical education and residency programs in plastic and reconstructive surgery. Conducts educational programs.
270 Members Founded: 1985

11555 Association of Air Medical Services

526 King Street
Suite 415
Alexandria, VA 22314-3143
703-836-8732
FAX: 703-836-8920
information@aams.org www.aams.org

Tom Judge, President
Ed Eroe, VP
Blair Beggan,
Communications/Marketing Manager
Dawn Mancuso, Executive Director

Voluntary, nonprofit organization, encourages and supports its members in maintaining a standard of performance reflecting

safe operations and efficient, high quality patient care. Built on the idea that representation from a variety of medical transport services and businesses can be brought together to share information, collectively resolve problems and provide leadership in the medical transport community.
581 Members Founded: 1980

11556 Association of American Physicians & Surgeons
1601 N Tucson Boulevard
Suite 9
Tucson, AZ 85716-3450

800-635-1196
AAPS is a nonpartisan professional association of physicans in all types of practices and specialties across the country.
Founded: 1943

11557 Association of Behavioral Healthcare
12300 Twinbrook Parkway
Suite 320
Rockville, MD 20852
847-480-9626
FAX: 301-881-7159
dklatzker@riverbendcmhc.org
www.nccbh.org

11558 Association of Family Medicine Administration
11400 Tomahawk Creek Parkway
Leawood, KS 66211-2672
734-998-7122
FAX: 913-906-6092 800-274-2237
dsexton@aafp.org www.afpa.net/
Elizabeth Gregg, President
Dawn Sexton, Executive Secretary
Promotes professionalism in family practice administration. Serves as a network for sharing information and fellowship among members. Provides technical assistance to members, functions as a liaison to related professional organizations.
370+ Members

11559 Association of Family Practice Residency
11400 Tomahawk Creek Parkway
Suite 670
Leawood, KS 66211-2672
913-906-6000
FAX: 913-906-6105 800-274-2237
afprd@aafp.org www.afprd.org
Robin O Winte, President
Timothy A Munzing, Secretary/Treasurer
Joetta Melton, Publisher
Provides representation for residency directors at a national level and provides a political voice for them to appropriate arenas. Promotes cooperation and communication between residency programs and different branches of the family practice specialty. Dedicated to improving education of family physicians. Provides a network for mutual assistance among Family Practice, residency directors.
410 Members

11560 Association of Healthcare Internal Auditors
PO Box 10
Adrian, MI 49221-10
517-467-7729
FAX: 517-467-6104
ahia@ahia.org www.ahia.org
Pat Bogusz, Executive Director
Mark Eddy, Director
Karen Young, Secretary/Treasurer
Promotes cost containment and increased productivity in health care institutions through internal auditing. Serves as a forum for the exchange of experience, ideas, and information among members, provides continuing professional education courses and informs members of developments in health care internal auditing. Offers employment clearinghouse services.
1000 Members Founded: 1981

11561 Association of Otolaryngology
1844 Ardmore Boulevard
Pittsburgh, PA 15221
412-243-5156
FAX: 412-243-5160
AOA@oto-online.org
www.oto-online.org
Jean Aldrich, President/CEO
Robert Martin, Secretary/Treasurer
Seeks to promote the concept of professional management in otolaryngology, provide a forum for interaction and exchange of information between otolaryngological managers and present educational programs. Maintains data exchange service for members researching specific topics.
1000 Members Founded: 1983
Mailing list available for rent $500 per M.

11562 Association of Pediatric Oncology Nurses
4700 W Lake Avenue
Glenview, IL 60025-1485
847-375-4724
FAX: 877-734-8755
info@apon.org www.apon.org
Karla Wilson, President
Janine Primomo, Treasurer
2000 Members Founded: 1976

11563 Association of Perioperative Registered Nurses
2170 S Parker Road
Suite 300
Denver, CO 80231-5711
303-755-6304
FAX: 303-755-3211 800-755-2676
custserv@aorn.org www.aorn.org
William J Duffy, President
Lorraine J Butler, VP
Paula R Graling, Treasurer
Charlotte L Guglielmi, Secretary
41000 Members Founded: 1954

11564 Biomedical Marketing Association
10293 N Meridian Street
Suite 175
Indianapolis, IN 46290
317-816-1640
FAX: 317-816-1633
info@bmaonline.org
www.bmaonline.org
Michael L Boner, President
Steve Hamburger, Treasurer
Stewart Marsden, Secretary
Builds diagnostic industry leadership by providing market education, professional development and a forum for fellowship and the exchange of ideas.

11565 Case Management Society of America
8201 Cantrell Road
Suite 230
Little Rock, AR 72227-2448
501-225-2229
FAX: 501-221-9068
cmsa@cmsa.org www.cmsa.org
Jeanne Boling, Executive Director
Lisa Wilder, Director Finance
Randall Van Den Berghe, Senior Director Operations
Exclusively for the case management profession.
70+ Members Founded: 1990

11566 Catholic Health Association
4455 Woodson Road
Saint Louis, MO 63134-3797
314-427-2500
FAX: 314-427-0029
khewitt@chausa.org www.chausa.org
Richard J Statuto, Chairperson
Carol Keehan, Vice Chairperson
John J Finan Jr, Secretary/Treasurer
Edward E Dolejsi, Executive Director
2000+ Members Founded: 1915

11567 Christopher & Dana Reeve Paralysis Resourc e Center
636 Morris Tpke
Ste 3A
Short Hills, NJ 07078-1020
973-467-8270
FAX: 973-467-9745 800-539-7309
info@crpf.org www.paralysis.org
Joseph cenose, VP Quality of Life/Program Director
Angela Carter, Associate Director of Operations
The Christopher & Dana Reeve Paralysis Resource Center (PRC) promotes the health and well-being of people living with paralysis and their families by providing comprehensive information resources and referral services.
Founded: 2001

11568 Clinical Laboratory Management Association
989 Old Eagle School Road
Suite 815
Wayne, PA 19087
610-995-9580
FAX: 610-995-9568
website@clma.org www.clma.org
C Anne Pontius, President
Dana Procsal, VP
John R Snyder, Dean/Director
Anne T Daley, Consultant

11569 Consumer Healthcare Manufacturers Association
900 19th Street, NW
Suite 700
Washington, DC 20006
202-429-9260
FAX: 202-223-6835
eassey@chpa-info.org
www.chpa-info.org
Linda A Suydam, President
Priya Samuel, Executive Assistant
Promotes industry growth through consumer understanding, appreciation, and acceptance of responsible self-care in America's health care system by developing and sustaining a climate that provides consumers with convienient access to safe and effective nonprescription medicines and other self-care products marketed without undue restrictions.

11570 Consumer Healthcare Products Association
900 19th Street NW
Suite 700
Washington, DC 20006
202-429-9260
FAX: 202-223-6835
lsuydam@chpa-info.org
www.chpa-info.org

Linda Suydam, President
Elizabeth Assey, Director
Timothy Hayes, Senior VP

Consumer education about responsible medicine use has been a long standing priority for CHPA and the industry, especially as over-the-counter medicines and nutritional supplements play such a vital role in today's society.
Founded: 1981

11571 Cremation Association of North America
401 N Michigan Avenue
Chicago, IL 60611
775-831-6555
FAX: 312-321-4098
cana@smithbucklin.com
www.cremationassociation.org

11572 Dental Group Management Association
North Point Dental Group
7040 N Port Washington
Glendale, WI 53217
262-251-6148
FAX: 262-251-6148
200 Members Founded: 1951

11573 Emergency Nurses Association
915 Lee Street
Des Plaines, IL 60016-6569
847-460-4100
FAX: 847-460-4001 800-900-9659

David Westman, Chief Executive Officer

11574 Federated Ambulatory Surgery Association Meeting
1012 Cameron St
Alexandria, VA 22314-2427
703-836-8808
FAX: 703-549-0976
fasa@fasa.org www.fasa.org

Kathy Bryant, Executive Vice President
Sarah Siberstein, Deputy Executive Director

11575 Federation of American Health Systems
801 Pennsylvania Avenue NW
Suite 245
Washington, DC 20004-2604
202-624-1500
FAX: 202-737-6462
info@fah.org www.fahs.com

Michael Parsons, Chairman
Mike Bromberg, Vice Chairman
Bruce Gilbert, Treasurer
Barry Schochet, Secretary
Charles Kahn, President

11576 Gerantological Society of America
1030 15th Street NW
Suite 250
Washington, DC 20005
202-842-1275
FAX: 202-842-1150
geron@geron.org www.geron.org

Carol Ann Schutz, Executive Director
Jennifer Campi, Director Publications
800+ Members Founded: 1939

11577 Health Industry Distributors Association
310 Montgomery Street
Alexandria, VA 22314
703-549-4432
FAX: 703-549-6495
rowan@hida.org www.hida.org

Matthew Rowan, President/CEO
Lyn Rawdon, CFO
Seth Aidoo, Director MIS

11578 Health Industry Manufacturers Association
1200 G Street NW
Washington, DC 20005-3814

FAX: 202-783-8750
Established as the Wholesale Surgical Trade Association. Represents manufacturers of health care technology, including medical devices, diagnostic products, and health care information systems.

11579 Healthcare Compliance Packaging Council
131 E Broad Street
Suite 206
Falls Church, va 22046
703-538-4030
FAX: 703-538-6305
pgmayberry@aol.com
www.unitdose.org

Peter G Mayberry, Executive Director
Kathleen Hemming, Staff Consultant

Nonprofit trade association promoting the benefits of unit dose blister and strip packaging — especially its ability to be designed in compliance prompting formats that help people take their medications properly.
Founded: 1990

11580 Healthcare Convention & Exhibitors Association
1100 Johnson Ferry Road
Suite 300
Atlanta, GA 30342
404-252-3663
FAX: 404-252-0774
hcea@kellencompany.com
www.hcea.org

Eric Allen, VP
Jackie Beaulieu, Associate Director

Trade association of over 700 organizations involved in health care exhibiting or providing services to health care conventions, exhibitions and/or meetings.
700 Members Founded: 1930

11581 Healthcare Distribution Management Association
900 N Glebe Road
Suite 1000
Arlington, VA 22203
703-787-0000
FAX: 703-935-3200
www.healthcaredistribution.org

John M Gray, President/CEO
Nancy E Hanagan, Executive VP/COO
Susan Mirvis, Senior VP Marketing/Communications

An organization representing all major constituents of healthcare product distribution management.

11582 Healthcare Financial Management Association
2 Westbrook Corporate Financial Center
Suite 700
Westchester, IL 60154
708-531-9600
FAX: 708-531-0032 800-252-4362
webmaster@hfma.org www.hfma.org

Richard L Clarke, President/CEO
David P Canfield, Chairman
Richard Rodriguez, Secretary/Treasurer

Brings perspective and clarity to the industry's complex issues for the purpose of preparing our members to succeed. Through our programs, publications and partnerships we enhance the capabilities that strengthen not only individual careers, but also the organizations from which our members come.
34000 Members Founded: 1946

11583 Healthcare Marketing & Communications Council
1525 Valley Center Parkway
Bethlehem, PA 18017
610-868-8299
FAX: 610-868-8387
info@hmc-council.org
www.hmc-council.org

Janis Cohen, President/CEO
Gary J Gyss, Founder

Enhancing the professional development of its members by providing continuing education and career development opportunities. The council also works toward a better understanding of the role of marketing, education, and communications in health care.

11584 Institute of Certified Healthcare
307 N Michigan Avenue
Suite 800
Chicago, IL 60601-5309
312-360-0384
FAX: 312-360-0388 800-447-1684
info@ichbc.org www.ichbc.org

Barbara Boden, Executive Director
Paul D Haynes, Secretary/Treasurer

Maintains code of ethics, rules of professional conducts, and certification program; administers exams and conduct certification course. Membership by successful completion of certification examination only.
350 Members Founded: 1975

11585 International Anesthesia Research Society
2 Summit Park Drive
Suite 140
Cleveland, OH 44131
216-642-1124
FAX: 216-642-1127

Anne Maggiore, Executive Director

11586 International Association for Healthcare Security and Safety
PO Box 5038
Glendale Heights, IL 60139
630-871-9936
FAX: 630-871-9938 888-353-0990
info@iahss.org www.iahss.org

Frederick G Roll, President
William A Farnsworth, Vice-President/Treasurer
Evelyn F Meserve, VP Secretary
Jim Balija, Executive Director

The International Association for Healthcare Security and Safety, (IAHSS) is an organization dedicated to professionals involved in managing and directing security and safety programs in healthcare institutions. Its members have joined together to develop educational and credentialing programs and create a body of knowledge that meets the needs of today's fast paced and ever changing environment.

1,700 Members Founded: 1968 1700 names $200 per M.

11587 International Oxygen Manufacturers Association
1255 23rd Street NW
Suite 200
Washington, DC 20037
202-521-9300
FAX: 202-833-3636
ioma@iomaweb.org
www.iomaweb.org

The International Oxygen Manufacturers Association is the truly worldwide trade association of companies in the industrial and medical gas business

190 Members Founded: 1943

11588 International Sleep Products Association
501 Wythe Street
Alexandria, VA 22314-1917
703-683-8371
FAX: 703-683-4503
bedtimes@sleepproducts.org
www.sleepproducts.org

Debi Sutton, VP, Marketing & Member Services

Maintains a strong organization to influence government actions, inform and educate the membership and act on industry issues to enhance the growth, profitability and stature of the sleep products industry. Provides members with information and services to manage their business more effectively and efficiently. Publishes a magazine devoted exclusively to the mattress industry, BEDtimes covers a broad range of issue and news important to the industry.

$65.00
650 Members Monthly Founded: 1915
Circulation: 3,500

11589 International Society for Quality-of-Life Research
2056 Pamplin
Virginia Tech
Blacksburg, VA 24061-0236
540-231-5110
FAX: 540-231-3076
sirgy@vt.edu marketl.cobvt.edu/sqols

M Joseph Sirgy, Executive Director/Secretary

Was founded to stimulate interdisciplincary research in quality-of-life studies and closer cooperation among scholars. Members are academic and government social/behavioral science researchers drawn from such fields as marketing, management, applied psychology, applies sociology, political science, economics, public administration, educational administration family/child development leisure/recreation studies and technology development.

Founded: 1995

11590 Interstate Postgraduate Medical Association
PO Box 5474
Madison, WI 52705
608-231-9045
FAX: 608-231-9045

Mary Ales, Executive Director

11591 Intravenous Nurses Society
315 Norwood Park South
Norwood, MA 02062
781-440-9408
FAX: 781-440-9409 www.ins1.org

Lynn Czaplewski, President
Mary Alexander, Cheif Executive Officer

The INS is committed to bringing innovative new resources and opportunities to a wide range of healthcare professionals who are involved with the specialty practice of infusion therapy.

11592 Medical Group Management Association
104 Inverness Terrace E
Englewood, CO 80112-5306
303-799-1111
FAX: 303-643-4439 888-608-5601

William F Jessee MD, President/CEO
Patricia L Brewster, Chair
Jyl D Bradley, Chair
Warren C White Jr, Chair
Nicholas H Kupferle III, Chair

Members are actively engaged in the business management of medical groups consisting of three or more physicians in medical practice with centralized business functions. Sponsors educational training programs, provides placement and information services, also compiles statistics.

19000 Members Founded: 1926

11593 Medical Library Association
65 E Wacker Place
Suite 1900
Chicago, IL 60601-7246
312-419-9094
FAX: 312-419-8950
info@mlahq.org www.mlanet.org / www.marketing.mlanet.org

Lynanne Feilen, Director Publications
Carla J Funk, Executive Director

A nonprofit, educational organization that is a leading advocate for health sciences information professionals worldwide. Through it's programs and services, we provide lifelong educational opportunities, supports a knowledgebase of health information research and works with a global network of partners to promote the importance of quality information for improved health to the health care community and the public.

4500 Members Founded: 1898
Mailing list available for rent

11594 NAMDRC-Physician Advocacy for Excellance in Delivery Pulmonary/Critical Care
5454 Wisconsin Avenue
Suite 1270
Chevy Chase, MD 20815
301-718-0202
FAX: 301-718-2976
namdrc@erols.com www.namdrc.org

Phillip Porte, Executive Director

Improves access to quality care for patients with respiratory disease by removing regulatory and legislative barriers to appropriate treatment. It advises on coding issues and federal reimbursement policies; provides economic and regulatory updates; and offers unique educational opportunities.

700 Members Founded: 1977

11595 National Association Medical Staff Service
2025 M St Nw
Ste 800
Washington, DC 20036-2422
202-571-1196
FAX: 512-381-3036
namss@namss.org www.namss.org

Becky Nichols, CEO
Stefanie Kisamore, Information Management Director
Carl Dodd, Director Edu/Certification
Sarah Green, Certification Coordinator
Tracie Harris, Director Publications

Individuals involved in the management and administration of health care provider services. Seeks to: enhance the knowledge and experience of medical staff services professionals; promote the certification of those involved in the profession.

4000 Members Founded: 1978

11596 National Association for Healthcare Recruitment
PO Box 531107
Orlando, FL 32853
407-843-6981
FAX: 407-423-4648
catlaya@fha.org www.naher.com

Karen A Hart, Executive Director

Individuals employed directly by hospitals and other health care organizations which are involved in the practice of professional health care recruitment. Promotes sound principles of professionals health care recruitment. Provides financial assistance to aid members in planning and implementing regional educational programs. Offers technical assistance and consultation services. Compiles statistics.

800 Members Founded: 1975

11597 National Association for Home Care
228 7th Street SE
Washington, DC 20003
202-547-7424
FAX: 202-547-3540 www.nahc.org

Val Halamandaris, Executive Director

11598 National Association of County Health Facility Administrators
440 1st Street NW, 8th Floor
Washington, DC 20001
202-936-6226
FAX: 202-393-2630

Tom Joseph, Staff Liaison
Larry Naake, Chief Executive Officer

Administrators of freestanding and hospital-based long-term care facilities owned and operated by county governments or city-county consolidations; elected local officials. Promotes interests of county long-term care facilities; offers guidance in relevant legislative and regulatory areas. Provides technical assistance; conducts training workshops. Compiles statistics on public policy changes, such as changes in the Medicaid program, which affect long-term care facilities.

250 Members Founded: 1977

11599 National Association of State Medicaid Directors
810 1st Street NE
Suite 500
Washington, DC 20002-4267
202-682-0100
FAX: 202-682-3706
sfarrell@aphsa.org www.athfa.org

Nancy Atkins, Chair
Mary Kennedy, Director
Michael Deily, Director
Jason Cooke, Director
Jerry Friedman, Executive Director

Promotes effective Medicaid policy and program administration; works with the federal government on issues through technical advisory groups. Conducts forums on policy and technical issues.

Founded: 1979

11600 National Athletic Trainers Association
2952 Stemmons Freeway
Dallas, TX 75247
214-637-6282
FAX: 214-637-2206
webdude@nata.org www.nata.org

Eve B Doyle, Executive Director
Julie Max, President

32000 Members Founded: 1950

11601 National Cancer Institute
6116 Executive Boulevard
Room 3036A
Bethesda, MD 20892-8322

800-422-6237
cancergovstaff@mail.nih.gov
www.cancer.gov

Andrew C Eschenbach, Director
Michelle Gaye, Manager

Conducts and supports research, training, health information dissemination and otherprograms with respect to the cause, diagnosis, prevention and treatment of cancer, rehabilition from cancer and the continuing care of cancer patients.

11602 National Council on the Aging
300 D Street SW
Suite 801
Washington, DC 20024
202-479-1200
FAX: 202-479-0735
info@ncoa.org www.ncoa.org

James Firman, President/CEO
Wanda R Baker, Director for Human Resources
Lynn Beattie, Assistant VP Research
Howard Bedlin, VP

11603 National Environmental Health Association
720 S Colorado Boulevard
Suite 970-S
Denver, CO 80246-1925
303-756-9090
FAX: 303-691-9490
staff@neha.org www.neha.org

Jim Balsamo, President
Ron Grimes, First VP
Rick Collins, 2nd VP

NEHA offers a variety of programs that are all in keeping with the association's mission which is as relevant today as it was when the organization was founded. The mission of NEHA is to advance the environmental health and protection professional for the purpose of providing a healthful environment for all.

5000 Members

11604 National Managed Health Care Congress
71 2nd Avenue
3rd Floor
Waltham, MA 02154

FAX: 941-365-0157 888-882-2500

11605 National Medical Association
1012 Tenth Street NW
Washington, DC 20001
202-347-1895
FAX: 202-898-2510 800-257-8290
cme@nmanet.org www.nmanet.org

Willarda V Edwards, Chair
Randall W Maxey, President
Nelson L Adams, VP
Guthrie L Turner, Treasurer
James Barnes, Executive Director

Founded: 1895

11606 National Renal Administrators Association
1904 Naomi Place
Prescott, AZ 86303-5061
928-717-2772
FAX: 928-441-3857
nraa@nraa.org www.nraa.org/renal/

Michael Paget, Executive Director
Karin Gosney, Administrative Assistant

Administrative personnel involved with dialysis programs for patients suffering from kidney failure. Provides a vehicle for the development of educational and informational services for members. Maintains contact with health care facilities and government agencies. Operates placement serve; compiles statistics; conducts political action committee.

475 Members Founded: 1977

11607 National Rural Health Association
1 W Armour Boulevard
Suite 203
Kansas City, MO 64111-2087
816-756-3140

mail@NRHArural.org
www.nrharural.org

Rob McVay, Manager

A national membership organization, whose mission is to improve the health care of rural Americans and to provide leadership on rural issues through advocacy, communications, education and research.

11608 National Society for Histotechnology
4201 Northview Drive
Suite 502
Bowie, MD 20716-2604
301-262-6221
FAX: 301-262-9188
histo@nsh.org www.nsh.org

Vincent Della Speranza, President
Janet Tunnicliffe, VP
Carrie Diamond, Executive Director

Committed to quality health care by the constant pursuit of excellence, the advancement of histotechnology and professional representation of the medical community, government agencies and the public whom we serve.

Founded: 1974 4400 names $150 per M.

11609 New England Medical Equipment Dealers Assn
509 Kempton Street
New Bedford, MA 03302
508-993-0700
FAX: 508-993-0797
Karyn@nemed.org www.nemed.org

Karyn Estrella, Executive Director
Brian Simonds, President
Jim Greatorex, VP
Rebecca Godley, Secretary
Paula Finamore, Treasurer

Works together supporting the common goals and interests of the home medical equipment, respiratory, and rehab/assistive techology and home infusion therapy industry.

15 Members Founded: 1988

11610 Northwest Urological Society
2033 6th Avenue
Suite 1100
Seattle, WA 98121
206-441-9762

11611 OMA: Optical Industry Association
6055A Arlington Boulevard
Falls Church, VA 22044-2721
703-237-8433
FAX: 703-237-0643

Members are makers and importers of spectacle frames, and related products.

57 Members Founded: 1916

11612 Optical Society of America
2010 Massachusetts Avenue NW
Washington, DC 20036-1023
202-223-8130
FAX: 202-223-1096
info@osa.org www.osa.org

Elizabeth Rogan, Executive Director
Tony Keane, COO
John Childs, Sr Director

OSA was organized to increase and diffuse the knowledge of optics, pure and applied; to promote the common interests of investigators of optical problems, of designers and of users of optical apparatus of all kinds; and to encourage cooperation among them.

Founded: 1916

11613 Orthopedic Surgical Manufacturers Association
BioMet
PO Box 587
Warsaw, IN 46581-0587
574-267-6639
FAX: 574-372-1790

Lonnie Witham, President

Members are manufacturers of orthopedic surgical items. Sponsors research, information and ethics programs.

25 Members Founded: 1955

11614 Pacific Dermatological Association
100 Meadowcreek Drive
Suite 150
Corte Madera, CA 94925
415-927-5729
FAX: 415-927-5726
pda@hp-assoc.org
www.pacificderm.org

Julie Hodge, President

Provides opportunitites for exchange of information and advancement of knowledge of dermatology among physicians within the membership area. Execlusively for education, scientific and charitable purposes.

11615 Pacific Northwest Radiological Society
2033 6th Avenue
Seattle, WA 98121
206-441-9762
FAX: 206-441-5863
Jan Larson, Manager

11616 Professional Association of Health Care
461 E Ten Mile Road
Pensacola, FL 32534
850-749-9460
FAX: 850-474-6352 800-451-9311
pahcom@pahcom.com
www.pahcom.com
Kim Rape, Professional Dev Coordinator
Roger Landers, Executive Director
Allison Villarreal, Business Manager
Amanda Brown, Membership Coordinator
Karen Williams, Conference Coordinator
Office managers of small groups and solo medical practices. Operates certification program for health care office managers.
Founded: 1988

11617 Radiological Society of North America
820 Jorie Boulevard
Oak Brook, IL 60523-2251
630-571-2670
FAX: 603-571-7837 800-381-6660
The mission is to promote and develop the highest standards of radiology and related sciences through education and research. The society seeks to provide radiologists and allied health scientists with educational programs and materials of the highest quality and to constantly improve the content and value of these educational activities.

11618 Radiology Business Management Association
RBMA, 8001 Irvine Center Drive
Suite 1060
Irvine, CA 92618
949-340-5000
FAX: 949-340-5001 888-224-7262
info@rbma.org www.rbma.org
Sharon Urch, Executive Director
Daphne Brown, Marketing Director
Robin Hopkins, Meetings Department
Business managers for private radiology groups. Corporate members include vendors of equipment, services, or supplies. Purposes is to improve business administration of radiologists' practices to better serve patients and the medical profession; and to provide opportunities for professional development and recognition. Offers extensive educational and networking opportunities and informal placement service. Maintains information services emphasizing those aspects unique to the business.
1600 Members Founded: 1968

11619 Sisters Network: National Headquarters
8787 Woodway Drive
Suite 4206
Houston, TX 77063
713-781-0255
FAX: 713-780-8998 866-781-1808
sisnet4@aol.com sisnetworkinc.org
Karen Jackson, National President/Founder
Erie Calloway, Executive Director
Committed to increasing local and national attention to the devastating impact that breast cancer has in the African American community. *$10.00*
3000 Members Founded: 1994

11620 Society for Computer Applications in Medical Imaging
10105 Cottesmore Court
Great Falls, VA 22066-3540
703-757-0054
FAX: 703-757-0454
info@scarnet.org www.scarnet.org
Bruce I Reiner, Chairman
Bradley J Erickson, Treasurer
Mary Shaw, Director
Curtis P Langlotz, Director
Devoted to advance computer applications and information technology in medical imaging through education and research. Provides an open environment for imaging information professionals to access expert and cutting edge resources in a collegial and practical atmosphere.

11621 Society of Critical Care Medicine
701 Lee Street
Des Plaines, IL 60016
847-827-6869
FAX: 847-827-6886
info@sccm.org www.sccm.org
David Julian Martin, Executive VP
Diane Scott, Technology Manager
Brian Schramm, Director Business Affairs
Professional organization devoted exclusively to the advancement of multidisciplinary, multiprofessional intensive care through excellence in patient care, education, research, and advocacy.
11000 Members Founded: 1972

11622 Society of Medical-Dental Management
125 Strafford Avenue
Suite 300
Wayne, PA 19087-3318
FAX: 610-687-7702 800-826-2264
patricia01@aol.com www.smdmc.org
Joseph Cobo, President
Richard G Bock, Regional Director/Coordinator
Rex Stanley, Secretary/Treasurer
Professional medical and/or dental management consultants associated for educational and information sharing purposes. Objectives are to: advance the profession; share management techniques; improve individual skills; provide clients with competent and capable business management. Provides information on insurance and income tax. Conducts surveys; compiles statistics.
60+ Members Founded: 1968

11623 Society of Nuclear Medicine
1850 Samuel Morse Drive
Reston, VA 20190-5316
703-708-9000
FAX: 703-708-9015
volunteer@snm.org www.snm.org
Virginia Pappas, Executive Director
Kathy Bates, Director
Setha Golds, Senior Educational Manager
Laura Myers, Controller
International scientific and professional organization that promotes the science, technology and practical applications of nuclear medicine.
15000 Members Founded: 1954

11624 Southern Medical Association
35 Lakeshore Drive
Birmingham, AL 35209
205-945-1840
FAX: 205-945-1830 800-423-4992
webmast@sma.org www.sma.org
T Rudolph Howell, President
Ed J Waldron, Executive
Physician's choice for education and support to enhance practice and performance and career development.
88 Members Founded: 1906

11625 Textile Rental Services Association
1800 Diagonal Road
Suite 200
Alexandria, VA 22314
703-519-0029
FAX: 703-519-0026
trsa@trsa.org www.trsa.org
Roger Cocivera, Executive Director/President
George Ferencz, VP
Covers the uniform, linen supply, health care and dust control service markets.
1300 Members Founded: 1917

11626 US Medicine Association
2021 L Street NW
Suite 400
Washington, DC 20036
202-463-6000
FAX: 202-223-2849
usmedicine@usmedicine.com
www.usmedicine.com
Frank M Best, Chairman
Ann O Cannon Finch, Publisher
Matt Pueschel, Editor
Nancy Tomich, Co-Managing Director
James F Breuning, Director Advertising
9 Members Founded: 1964

Newsletters

11627 AOA News
American Optometric Association
243 N Lindbergh Boulevard
Saint Louis, MO 63141
314-991-4100
FAX: 314-991-4101 800-365-2219
amoptnews@aoa.org
http://www.aoa.org
Bob Foster, Editor-in-Chief
Sean Hickson, Assistant Editor
Michael Jones, CEO
Official newspaper of the American Optometric Association *$93.50*
Founded: 1896
Circulation: 30000 22,500 names $70 per M.
Printed in 4 colors on glossy stock

11628 Adult Day Services Letter
Health Resources Publishing
1913 Atlantic Avenue
Suite F4
Manasquan, NJ 08736
732-292-1100
FAX: 732-292-1111
info@healthrespubs.com
http://www.healthrespubs.com
Robert F Jenkins, CEO
A monthly newsletter that contains management information, reports on trends and

new developments and information about other adult day care programs across the country. *$147.00*
38574 pages Monthly Founded: 1985

11629 Association Alert
Healthcare Convention & Exhibitors Association
5775 Peachtree Dunwoody Road
Building G, Suite 500
Atlanta, GA 30342-1542
404-252-3663
FAX: 404-252-0774
hcea@assnhq.com
http://www.hcea.org/
Frank Corcoran, President
Carol Wilson, Meetings Director
Eric Allen, Executive VP
Information needs of health care associations.
Founded: 1930

11630 BNA's Health Law Reporter
Bureau of National Affairs
1231 25th Street NW
Washington, DC 20037-1157
202-452-4200
800-372-1033
customercare@bna.com
www.bna.com
Gregory C McCaffery, Publisher
Susan Webster, Managing Editor
Contains information on health care policy, bankruptcy, antitrust, insurance and state developments, employment issues as well as a congressional and a regulatory calendar. *$1782.00*
Weekly

11631 Biomedical Market Newsletter
3237 Idaho Place
Costa Mesa, CA 92626-2207
714-434-9500
FAX: 714-434-9755 800-875-8181
info@biomedical-market-news.com
http://www.biomedical-market-news.com
Dave.G Anast, Publisher
Steve Baker, Director of Marketing/Sales
Richard Guiss, Senior Editor
George Anast, CFO
New business development, FDA, regulatory, financial, and marketing NL on medical equipment, device, diagnostic test and instrument industries worldwide. *$199.00*
Monthly Founded: 1991 150,000 names
Printed in 4 colors on matte stock : PDF

11632 Bulletin on Long-Term Care Law
Health Resources Publishing
1913 Atlantic Avenue
Suite F4
Manasquan, NJ 08736
732-292-1100
FAX: 732-292-1111
hrp@healthrespubs.com
http://www.healthrespubs.com/
Bob Jenkins, President
Lisa Mansfield, Marketing Assistant
A newsletter that covers compliance problems, Medicaid and Medicare overhauls, charges of abuse, fraud, negligence, needless litigation and other concerns of those involved in long-term health care. *$227.00*
Monthly Founded: 1978

11633 Diagnostic Testing & Technology Report
Institute of Management & Administration
29 W 35th Street
5th Floor
New York, NY 10001-2299
212-244-0360
FAX: 212-564-0465
subserve@ioma.com www.ioma.com
Generally covers: new product development, stock and financial performance for major medical device manufacturers, how to use new instruments, trends in genetic or esoteric testing, the cost of outsourcing lab work to third party vendors, the FDA position on the use of new devices and the effect approval may have on the company's stock.

11634 Directions: Looking Ahead in Healthcare
Health Resources Publishing
1913 Atlantic Avenue
Suite F4
Manasquan, NJ 08736
732-292-1100
FAX: 732-292-1111 888-843-6242
hrp@healthrespubs.com
http://www.healthrespubs.com
Bob Jenkins, President
Lisa Mansfield, Marketing Assistant
Carolin Pense, Publisher
Robert Jenkins, Circulation Manager
Provides management news on such topics as alerts, trends, forecasts, profitable innovations, facts and statistics. *$127.00*
Monthly Founded: 1978

11635 Elderly Health Services Letter
Health Resources Publishing
1913 Atlantic Avenue
Suite F4
Manasquan, NJ 08736
732-292-1100
FAX: 732-292-1111 888-843-6242
info@themcic.com
www.themcic.com/www.healthresources
Bob Jenkins, President
Lisa Mansfield, Marketing Assistant
A newsletter on projections and trends for health services provided for the elderly. Subjects include inpatient care, long-term care, outpatient, home care, primary care, ambulatory care, day care, health promotion, disease prevention, support groups, health education and residental care. *$227.00*
Monthly

11636 Emergency Department Law
Business Publishers
8737 Colesville Road
Suite 1100
Silver Spring, MD 20910-3928
301-876-6300
FAX: 301-589-8493 800-274-6737
custserv@bpinews.com
http://www.bpinews.com
Leonard A Eiserer, Publisher
James Lawlor, Editor
Devoted entirely to legal issues pertinent to emergency medicine, and covers monthly the latest case law, legal trends, risk management, tort reform and explains how they could impact your emergency care facility. *$357.00*
Monthly

11637 Employee Assistance Program Management Letter
Health Resources Publishing
1913 Atlantic Avenue
Suite F4
Manasquan, NJ 08736
732-292-1100
FAX: 732-292-1111 888-843-6242
info@themcic.com
http://www.healthrespubs.com/
Bob Jenkins, President
Lisa Mansfield, Marketing Assistant
A briefing published monthly on the range of influences surrounding your employee assistance program. *$237.00*
Monthly Founded: 1978

11638 Executive Report on Integrated Care & Capitation
Managed Care Information Center
1913 Atlantic Avenue
Suite F4
Manasquan, NJ 08736
732-921-1100
FAX: 888-329-6242 888-843-6242
info@themcic.com
http://www.themcic.com
Robert Jenkins, Publisher
Joseph Schmidt, Editor
A newsletter published twice a month to keep readers informed of the competitive market. Gives facts on strategic issues, mergers and acquisitions, market facts, economics, network alliances and plan affiliations. *$447.00*
Monthly

11639 Executive Report on Managed Care
Managed Care Information Center
1913 Atlantic Avenue
Suite F4
Manasquan, NJ 08736
732-921-1100
FAX: 888-329-6242 888-843-6242
info@themcic.com
http://www.themcic.com
Robert F Jenkins, Publisher
A monthly report that gives news of how major employers are implementing their managed care programs. The report also aids companies in preparing to evaluate and monitor different managed care proposals to determine cost effectiveness, quality and liability to the employer. *$ 437.00*

11640 Executive Report on Physician Organizations
Managed Care Information Center
1913 Atlantic Avenue
Suite F4
Manasquan, NJ 08736
732-921-1100
FAX: 888-329-6242 888-843-6242
info@themcic.com www.themcic.com
Robert K Jenkins, Publisher
The newsletter covers mergers, acquisitions, practice management agreements and strategic planes implemented in the physician marketplace. Also provides information about the ways that managed care and goverment regulations affect the physician marketplace. *$257.00*
8-10 pages 12 per year Founded: 1998 : PDF/HTML

11641 G-2 Compliance Report
Institute of Management & Administration

3 Park Avenuel
30th Floor
New York, NY 10016
212-244-0360
FAX: 212-564-0465
subserve@ioma.com
http://www.ioma.com

David Foster, President
Kim Scott, Editor
Perry Paterson, Publisher
Janet Goris, Manager

Eash issue of GRC covers key information to lab managers and hospital compliance officers that need to satisfy government requirements and avoid legal pitfalls and can help managers insure their billing and coding practice are compliant, stay on top of fast-changing federal mandates, prevent violations when entering new business arrangements, and reduce their facilities' exposure to whistleblower of lawsuits. *$359.00*
Monthly

11642 Health Care Reimbursement Monitor
Health Resources Publishing
1913 Atlantic Avenue
Suite F4
Manasquan, NJ 08736
732-292-1100
FAX: 732-292-1111 888-843-6242
info@themcic.com
http://www.themcic.com

Bob Jenkins, President
Lisa Mansfield, Marketing Assistant

A monthly newsletter that covers the latest details of actions taken or proposals in Washington concerning changes to the BBA; updates on Medicaid and Medicare budget and reimbursement issues; reimbursement news for hospital operations executives as well as top financial management. Reimbursement briefings cover hospitals, home health care, long-term care, hospice, ambulatory care and physician payment. *$257.00*
Monthly : PDF/HTML

11643 Healthcare Market Reporter
Managed Care Information Center
1913 Atlantic Avenue
Suite F4
Manasquan, NJ 08736
732-292-1100
FAX: 732-292-1111 888-843-6242
info@themcic.com
http://www.themcic.com

Robert K Jenkins, Publisher

Twice-a-month newsletter to help you abreast of the fiercely competitive market. Get the facts and details you'll need on strategies issues, market facts, mergers and acquisitions, economics, network alliances and plan affiliations. *$457.00*
10 pages : PDF/HTML

11644 Healthcare Marketers Executive Briefing
Health Resources Publishing
1913 Atlantic Avenue
Suite F4
Manasquan, NJ 08736
732-292-1100
FAX: 732-292-1111
hrp@healthrespubs.com
www.healthrespubs.com

Bob Jenkins, President
Lisa Mansfield, Marketing Assistant

Helps managers stay informed of the latest innovations and changes in the health care field. Gives contact information for other community relations, publication practioners, administrators and marketing and advertising professionals. *$237.00*
Monthly

11645 Healthcare e-Business Manager
Managed Care Information Center
1913 Atlantic Avenue
Suite F4
Manasquan, NJ 08736
732-292-1100
FAX: 732-292-1111 888-843-5242
info@healthrespubs.com
http://www.healthresourcesonline.com

Robert K Jenkins, Publisher

Monthly executive briefing on the latest developments in the proliferation of electronic commerce among healthcare and managed care organization. Focuses on the internet marketplace, reports on trends in the industry and predictions of where the market seems to be heading. *$ 477.00*
10 pages

11646 Hospice Letter
Health Resources Publishing
1913 Atlantic Avenue
Suite F4
Manasquan, NJ 08736
732-292-1100
FAX: 732-292-1111 888-843-6242
info@themcic.com
http://www.healthrespubs.com/

Bob Jenkins, President
Lisa Mansfield, Editor

Monthly newsletter reporting the latest development in the rapidly hospice concept of caring for the terminally ill. Ready by administrators and directors who follow Medicare reimbursement and hospice accreditation. How hospices are raising money and staging community events; new legislation and regulations and the latest on nursing care, volunteers and counseling programs. Delivery options: via mail or e-mail (indicate PDF or HTML format) *$227.00*
10 pages Monthly Founded: 1978 : PDF/HTML

11647 Journal of the American Association of For ensic Dentists
1000 N Avenue
Waukegan, IL 60085
847-244-0292

info@andent.net www.andent.net
Quarterly journal that brings forensic dental knowledge not only to dentists and their staff, but also to anthropologists, attorneys and law enforcement personnel.
3000 pages Founded: 1978

11648 Medical Group Management Update
Medical Group Management Association
104 Inverness Ter E
Englewood, CO 80112-5313
303-991-1111
FAX: 303-643-4427

Brenda Hull, Publisher
Eileen Barker, Editor
William Jessee, Manager

Monthly association newspaper offering up-to-the-minute articles on current legislation, practical management, health care trends, association activities and other timely subjects.
Monthly

11649 National Intelligence Report
Institute of Management & Administration

29 W 35th Street
5th Floor
New York, NY 10001-2299
212-244-0360
FAX: 212-564-0465
subserve@ioma.com
http://www.ioma.com

Mr. Foter, CEO
Bowman Cox, Editor

NIR regularly tracks Medicare payment and claims processing policy, billing and coding guidelines for diagnostic testing and payment actions by managed care and third party payers. *$389.00*
Annual+

11650 Nephrology News and Issues
Nephrology News and Issues
13880 N Northsight Boulevard
Suite 101
Scottsdale, AZ 85260
480-443-4635
FAX: 480-443-4528
info@nephnews.com
http://www.nephnews.com

Lawrence Coutts, CEO
Mark Neumann, Editor
Marcia Coutts, Circulation Manager
$55.00
Monthly Founded: 1986
Circulation: 22000

11651 Nurses' Notes
American Association of Managed Care Nurses
4435 Waterfront Drive
Suite 101
Glen Allen, VA 23060
804-747-9698
FAX: 804-747-5316
amason@aamcn.org www.aamcn.org

Andrea Mason, Executive Administra
Katie Eads, VP Education

A quarterly newsletter published by the American Association of Managed Care Nurses. Available to members only.

Circulation: 2000

11652 Nursing News Update
American Association of Managed Care Nurses
4435 Waterfront Drive
Suite 101
Glen Allen, VA 23060
804-747-9698
FAX: 804-747-5316
amason@aamcn.org www.aamcn.org

Andrea Mason, Executive Administrator
Katie Eads, VP Education

A weekly electronic newsletter published by the American Association of Managed Care Nurses. Available to members only.

Circulation: 2000

11653 Physician's News Digest
Physician's New Digest
230 Windsor Avenue
Suite 212
Narberth, PA 19072
610-668-1040
FAX: 610-668-9177 800-220-6109
jbarg@physiciansnews.com
http://www.physiciansnews.com

Jeffrey Barg, Publisher
Christopher Gaudagnino, Managing

Editor
Jeffrey Barg, CEO/President *$35.00*
Monthly Founded: 1987
Circulation: 40000 40,000 names $50 per M.
Printed in 4 colors on newsprint stock

11654 Public Health
State Capitals Newsletters
PO Box 7376
Alexandria, VA 22307-7376
703-768-9600
FAX: 703-768-9690
legistate@statecapitals.com
http://statecapitals.com *$245.00*
Weekly

11655 Sisters Network/National Newsletter
Sisters Network
8787 Woodway Drive
Suite 4206
Houston, TX 77063
713-781-0255
FAX: 866-781-1808
sisnet4@aol.com
http://www.sistersnetworkinc.org/
Karen Jackson, National President/CEO
Erie Calloway, Executive Director
Caleen Burtonalleen, Public Relations Manager
Cherlyn K Latham, Project Director
Publication of the group committed to awareness of the impact that breast cancer has on the African American community, with the latest information, medical research and news about events taking place within the Sisters National Network of affiliate chapters.
Monthly Founded: 1994

11656 Today's School Psychologist
LRP Publications
747 Dresher Road
PO Box 980
Horsham, PA 19044-2247
215-784-0912
FAX: 215-784-9639 800-341-7874
custserve@lrp.com www.lrp.com
Caroline Miller, Editor
In-depth guide to a school psychologists job, offering proactive strategies and tips for handling day-to-day tasks and responsibilities, encouraging change and improving professional standing and performance. *$135.00*
Monthly

11657 Walking Tomorrow
Christopher Reeve Paralysis Foundation
500 Morris Avenue
Springfield, NJ 07081-1020
973-379-2690
FAX: 973-912-9433 800-225-0292
circle@crpf.org
http://www.christopherreeve.org/
Julie Kwon, Director of Marketing
Kathy Lewis, CEO/President
Newsletter of the Christopher Reeve Paralysis Foundation.
Monthly Founded: 1982

11658 Wellness Program Management Advisor
Health Resources Publishing
1913 Atlantic Avenue
Suite F4
Manasquan, NJ 08736
732-292-1100
FAX: 732-292-1111 888-843-6242
info@themcic.com
http://www.healthresources.com
Bob Jenkins, President
Lisa Mansfield, Marketing Assistant
A newsletter that is designed to help professionals manage their organization's health promotion and wellness programs. Gives information about how other wellness programs are doing in such areas as strategies adopted, expenses and return on investments. Also included are in depth profiles of wellness programs around the country that list the problems that they encountered and the steps that they took to alter them. *$ 247.00*
Monthly

Magazines & Journals

11659 24 X 7
HealthTech Publishing Company
6100 Center Drive
Suite 1000
Los Angeles, CA 90045
310-642-4400
FAX: 310-641-4444
tantikadjian@medpubs.com
http://www.24x7mag.com
Tony Ramos, Publisher
Kelly Stephens, Editor
Jennifer Bezahler, Circulation Manager
News and business magazine for the healthcare service support and technology management industry.
Monthly Founded: 1996
Circulation: 15000
Printed in 4 colors on glossy stock

11660 AAMA Executive
American Academy of Medical Administrators
701 Lee Street
Suite 600
Des Plaines, IL 60016-4516
847-759-8601
FAX: 847-759-8602 800-621-6902
info@aameda.org
http://www.aameda.org
Renee S Schleicher, President/CEO
Nancy L Anderson, VP, Finance & Administration *$90.00*
Quarterly Founded: 1957

11661 AAPS Newsmagazine
American Association of Pharmaceutical Scientists
2107 Wilson Boulevard
Suite 700
Arlington, VA 22201-3046
703-243-2800
FAX: 703-243-9054
aaps@aaps.org www.aaps.org
Jake Harris, Publications Associate Director
Rebecca Jensen, Managing Director
Janelle Kihlstrom, Editorial Assistant
Exclusive to AAPS members. Features expanded coverage of the industry, complete with expert information on marketplace trends, regulatory matters, and career opportunities.

Mailing list available for rent

11662 AAPS PharmSciTech Journal
American Association of Pharmaceutical Scientists
2107 Wilson Boulevard
Suite 700
Arlington, VA 22201-3046
703-243-2800
FAX: 703-243-9054
pharmscitech-edoffice@aaps.org
www.aapspharmaceutica.com
Patrick P DeLuca, Editor-in-Chief
James Greif, Communications Specialist
An online-only journal published and owned by the American Association of Pharmaceutical Scientists. The journal's mission is to disseminate scientific and technical information on drug product design, development, evaluation and processing to the global pharmaceutical research community, taking full advantage of web-based publishing by presenting innovative text with 3-D graphics, interactive figures and databases, video and audio files.

Mailing list available for rent

11663 ACSM's Health & Fitness Journal
Lippincott Williams & Wilkins
351 W Camden Street
Baltimore, MD 21201-2436
410-284-4000
FAX: 410-528-4452 800-222-3790
cchapman@lww.com
http://www.acsm.org
Cathy Chapman, National Sales Manager
Michael Hargrett, Publisher
Edward Howley, Editor-in-Chief
The Journal strives to help health and fitness practitioners improve their knowledge and experience through reports and recommendations from experts, CEC offerings, opportunities to question the experts, listings of job openings and more. *$40.00*
Fortnightly Founded: 1997
Circulation: 11144 200 names
Printed in 4 colors on matte stock

11664 ADA Courier
American Dietetic Association
120 South Riverside Plaza
Suite 2000
Chicago, IL 60606-6995
312-990-0040
FAX: 312-899-4757 800-877-1600
affiliate@eatright.org
http://www.eatright.org
Susan H Laramee, President
Ronald S Moen, CEO
Patricia M. Babjak, Executive VP
Jennifer Herendeen, Editorial Director
Jason Switt, Editor
Readers look to the Courier for current association activities, membership news, updates on continuing education opportunities, ADA policies and coverage of the Associations' lobbying efforts in Washington. *$315.00*
10 pages Monthly Founded: 1917
Circulation: 80000
Printed in 4 colors on glossy stock

11665 ADA News
American Dental Association
211 E Chicago Avenue
Chicago, IL 60611-2678
312-440-2500
FAX: 312-440-3538 http://www.ada.org

Judy Jakush, Editor
Jill Philbein, Circulation Manager

James Bramson, Chief Executive Officer
$64.00
Founded: 1859

11666 **AHA News**
1 N Franklin Street 27th Floor
Suite 700
Chicago, IL 60606-3421
312-952-2500
FAX: 312-422-4796 800-242-2626
storeservice@aha.org
http://www.aha.org
Harry Baisdeu, Editor
Anthony Burke, Chief Executive Officer
Provides extensive coverage of regulatory, judicial and legislative developments while also providing news and information from the AHA. *$45.00*
Weekly Founded: 1917
Circulation: 40000

11667 **AMA Alliance Today**
515 N State Street
Chicago, IL 60610-4325
312-464-4470
FAX: 312-464-5020
amaa@ama-assn.org
http://www.ama-assn.org/go/alliance
Maryann Homer, President
Megan Pellegrini, Editor
Hazel Lewis, Executive Director
Founded: 1922
Circulation: 30,000

11668 **Advance for Health Information Executives**
Advance Newsmagazines/Merion Publications
2900 Horizon Drive
King of Prussia, PA 19406-4025
610-265-8249
FAX: 610-278-1421 800-355-5627
FIrving@merion.com
http://www.advanceforhie.com
Frank Irving, Editor
Maryann Kurkowski, Circulation Manager

Coverage of emerging e-health and computer-based patient record technologies.
Monthly Founded: 1997

11669 **Aesthetic Plastic Surgery**
6277 Sea Harbor Drive
Orlando Florida
Orlando, Fl 32887-7703
407-345-4000
FAX: 407-363-9661 800-364-2147
elspcs@elsevier.com
http://www.surgery.org/
Elizabeth Sadati, Executive Editor
Paul Bernstein, Scientific Forum Editor
Stanley A Klatsky, Managing Director
$196.00
Monthly Founded: 1996

11670 **Air Medical Journal**
Mosby
11830 Westline Industrial Drive
Saint Louis, MO 63146-3318
314-453-4307
FAX: 314-872-9164 800-325-4307
elspcs@elsevier.com
http://www.mosby.com/airmedj
David Dries, Editor
Liz Bennett-Bailey, Publisher
Eric Ferguson, Issue Manager *$85.00*
bi-monthly Founded: 1986

11671 **American Clinical Laboratory**
International Scientific Communications
30 Controls Drive
PO Box 870
Shelton, CT 06484-870
203-926-9300
FAX: 203-926-9310
webmaster@iscpubs.com
http://www.iscpubs.com
Brian Howard, Editor
Kim Kelly Rubin, Publisher
Jane Deyoe, Marketing Manager
Steven J. Morris, President
Paul Rossage, Circulation Manager
American Clinical Laboratory serves independent and hospital clinical laboratories, private laboratories, physicians' office laboratories and their personnel.
Monthly Founded: 1982
Circulation: 39995
Printed in 4 colors on glossy stock

11672 **American Family Physician**
American Academy of Family Physicians
11400 Tomahawk Creek Parkway
Leawood, KS 66211-2672
913-906-6000
FAX: 913-906-6080 800-274-2237
fp@aafp.org http://www.aafp.org
Jay Siwek, Editor
Janis Wright, Managing Editor
Dan Gowan, Director Advertising Sales
Joetta Melton, Publisher
AFP serves family physicians, general practitioners, selected office and hospital based physicians who are general internists and family practice and general practice osteopaths. *$240.00*
Monthly Founded: 1947

11673 **American Health Line**
600 New Hampshire Avenue NW
Washington, DC 20037
202-295-5381
FAX: 202-266-5700 800-717-3245
ahl@advisory.com
http://www.americanhealthline.com
Joshua Perin, Editor-in-Chief
Josh Kotzman, Editors
Weekly Founded: 1992

11674 **American Imago: Studies In Psychoanalysis And Culture**
Johns Hopkins University Press
2715 N Charles Street
Baltimore, MD 21218-4363
410-516-6900
FAX: 410-516-6968 800-548-1784
webmaster@jhupress.jhu.edu
http://www.press.jhu.edu/journals
Peter Rudnytsky, Editor
Kathleen Keane, Director
William M. Breichner, Publisher
Founded: 1878

11675 **American Journal of Cosmetic Surgery**
737 N Michigan Avenue
Suite 820
Chicago, IL 60611
312-981-6760

Jeffrey Knezovich, Executive Vice President

11676 **American Journal of Hypertension**
148 Madison Avenue
Fifth Floor
New York, NY 10016
212-320-0537
FAX: 212-696-0711
journal@ash-us.org
http://www.ash-us.org
John H Laragh, Editor In Chief
Ellen Twyne, Managing Editor *$246.00*
Monthly Founded: 1985

11677 **American Journal of Managed Care**
American Medical Publishing
241 Forsgate Drive
Jamesburg, NJ 08831
732-656-1006
FAX: 732-656-0818
info@ajmc.com http://www.ajmc.com
Jim King, Publisher
Lyn Beamesderfer, Editor
The American Journal of Managed Care is an independent, peer-reviewed forum for the publication of clinical research and opinion related to quality, value, and policy in health care delivery. The Journal delivers original research on patient outcomes, clinical effectiveness, cost effectiveness, quality management, and health policy to managed care decision makers.
Monthly Founded: 1995
Circulation: 53000

11678 **American Journal of Neuroradiology**
2210 Midwest Road
Suite 207
Oak Brook, IL 60523
630-574-0220
FAX: 630-574-0661 800-783-4903
info@asnr.org http://www.asnr.org
Charles M Strother MD, President
Victor M Haughton MD, VP
Relays news and schedules of events for members. *$235.00*
Founded: 1937
Circulation: 7000

11679 **American Journal of Roetgenology**
American Roentgen Ray Society
44211 Slatestone Court
Leesburg, VA 20176-5109
703-729-3353
FAX: 703-729-4839 800-438-2777
info@arrs.org http://www.arrs.org
R. B. Merritt Christopher, President
Connie Wolfe, Publications Assistant
Fran Schuweiler, Managing Editor
A monthly journal published by the American Roentgen Ray Society. *$275.00*
Monthly Founded: 1900
Circulation: 25,000
Mailing list available for rent 10000 names $160 per M.

11680 **American Medical News**
American Medical Association
515 N. State Street
9th Floor
Chicago, IL 60610-4320
312-464-4429
FAX: 312-464-4445 800-621-8335
ben_mindell@ama-assn.org
http://www.amednews.com
Benjamin Mindell, Editor
John Nelson, CEO/President
Kathryn Trombatore, Manager
Intended to serve as an impartial forum for information affecting physicians and their practices. The views expressed in AMNews

are not necessarily endorsed by the American Medical Association. *$95.00*
Weekly Founded: 1847
Circulation: 230,000

11681 American Nurse
American Nurses Association
600 Maryland Avenue SW
Washington, DC 20024-2571
202-651-7000
FAX: 202-651-7003
www.NursingWorld.org
Serves registered nurses in North America.

6 per year
Printed in 4 colors on glossy stock

11682 Anesthesiology News
545 W 45th Street
8th Floor
New York, NY 10011-1916
212-957-5300
FAX: 212-957-7230
marsap@mcmahonmed.com
http://www.anesthesiologynews.com
John H. Dreyfuss, Editor
Raymond E. McMahon, Publisher
Marsha Radebaugh, Circulation Coordinator *$65.00*
Monthly Founded: 1975
Circulation: 39720

11683 Annals of Emergency Medicine
Elsevier Publishing
6277 Sea Harbor Drive
Orlando, FL 32887-4800

FAX: 407-363-1354 877-839-7126
customerservice@acep.org
www.acep.org
Nancy B Medina, CAE, Editorial Director
Tracy Napper, Managing Editor
Michael L Callaham, MD, Editor-in-Chief
An international, peer-reviewed journal dedicated to improving the quality of care by publishing the highest quality science for emergency medicine and related medical specialties.
Monthly
Circulation: 30000

11684 Annals of Opthalmology
Am. Society of Cont. Medicine, Surgery & Opth.
North Cisero Avenue
Suite 208
Chicago, IL 60712
847-677-9093
FAX: 847-677-9094 800-621-4002
iaos@aol.com
http://www.medlit.ru/medeng/vof5.htm
Mikhail Krasnov, Editor-in-Chief
Randall Bellows MD, CEO/President
Exclusive articles written and peer-reviewed by doctors.
bi-monthly Founded: 1884

11685 Annals of Periodontology
737 N Michigan Avenue
Suite 800
Chicago, IL 60611-2690
312-787-5518
FAX: 312-787-3670
rjgenco@buffalo.edu
http://www.perio.org
Robert Genco, Editor
Julie Daw, Managing Editor
Vincent J. Iacono, President
Alice Deforest, Executive Director
$365.00
Monthly

11686 Annals of Plastic Surgery
530 Walnut st.
Philadelphia, PA 19106-3713
215-521-8300
FAX: 215-521-8902
http://www.lww.com
William D Morain, Editor-in-Chief
$375.00
Monthly

11687 Applied Clinical Trials
Advanstar Communications
One Park Avenue
New York, NY 10016
212-797-7631
FAX: 212-951-6793 888-527-7008
info@advanstar.com
http://www.advanstar.com
Rob Davidson, Managing Editor
Wayne K Blow, Publisher
Mike Kiley, President
Practical information for clinical research professionals in industry and academia who develop, execute and manage clinical trials worldwide. Regular topics include regulatory affairs, protocol development, data management and harmonization updates.
Monthly Founded: 1987
Circulation: 16255

11688 Archives of Physical Medicine and Rehabilitation
American Congress of Rehabilitation Medicine
6801 Lake Plaza Drive
Suite B- 205
Indianapolis, IN 46220
317-915-2250
FAX: 317-915-2245
acrm@acrm.org http://www.acrm.org
Richard D Morgan, Executive Director
Jean Ball, Director Finance
Judy Reuter, Publications & Web Develo
Available with membership to American Congress of Rehabilitation Medicine.
Monthly Founded: 1923
Circulation: 900 900 names

11689 Arthritis Hotline
2824 Swift Avenue
Dallas, TX 75204
972-286-6664
FAX: 214-363-2817

11690 Assisted Living Expo
VNU Expositions
Dulles International Airport
PO Box 17413
Washington, DC 20041
703-318-0300
FAX: 703-318-8833 800-765-7616
Displays of assisted living information and equipment.

11691 Assisted Living Success
3300 N Central Avenue Suite 2500
PO Box 40079
Phoenix, AZ 85067-79
480-990-1101
FAX: 480-990-0819
alsuccess@vpico.com
http://www.alsuccess.com
Susan Kavanaugh, Associate Publisher
Lori Chervenak, Managing Editor
Donna Briggs, Publisher
Emphasis on various aspects of the assisted-living profession, including regulatory updates, customer service, equipment and technology, staff training and design, financial issues and remodeling ideas.
$45.00
Monthly Founded: 1986
Circulation: 15,000

11692 BNA's Health Care Policy Report
1231 25th Street NW Building 3
5th Floor
Washington, DC 20037
202-452-4107
FAX: 202-452-4084 800-372-1033
customercare@bna.com
http://www.bna.com
Scott R Falk, Managing Editor
Paul N Wojcik, President
Weekly Founded: 1929

11693 Behavioral Health Management
MEDQUEST Communications
3800 Lakeside Avenue E
Suite 201
Cleveland, OH 44114-3857
216-391-9100
FAX: 216-391-9200
editor@behavioral.net
http://www.behavioral.net
Douglas J Edwards, Managing Editor
Monica E Oss, Editor-in-Chief
Largest publication reporting on the cutting edge trends and management practices in the behavioral health field. *$94.00*
52 pages
Circulation: 21615
Printed in 4 colors on glossy stock

11694 Behavioral Neuroscience
750 1st Street NE
Washington, DC 20002-4242
202-365-5920
FAX: 202-336-5549 800-374-2721
journals@apa.org
http://www.apa.org/journals/bne/submission.html
John Disterhoft, Editor
Ronald Levant, President
Barbara Wanchisen, Manager *$235.00*
Founded: 1988
Circulation: 200,000

11695 Biomedical Safety & Standards
Aspen Publishers
280 Orchard Ridge Drive
Suite 200
Gaithersburg, MD 20878-1978
301-417-7591

Jack Bruggeman, Publisher

11696 Birth-Issues in Perinatal Care
350 Main Street
6th Floor
Malden, MA 02148-5023
781-388-8200
FAX: 781-388-8210 800-759-6102
books@blackwellpublishingasia.com
http://www.blackwellpublishing.com
Diony Young, Editor
Gordon Tibbitts III, President
Robert Campbell, Publisher
Ginny Foley, Communications Manager
$36.00
Quarterly Founded: 1897
Circulation: 1709

11697 Body Positive
19 Fulton Street
Suite 308 B
New York, NY 10038-2100
212-566-7333
FAX: 212-566-4539 800-566-6599
bodypositive@bodypos.org
http://www.bodypos.org/

Raymond A Smith, Editor
Eric Rodriguez, Executive Director
$40.00

Quarterly Founded: 1987
Circulation: 10000

11698 Business and Health
Medical Economics Publishing
131 West First Street
Duluth, Mi 55802-2065
218-723-9200
FAX: 218-723-9437 888-346-0085
info@advanstar.com
http://www.advanstar.com

Tracey Walker, Senior Editor
Julie Miller, Managing Editor
Daniel Corcoran, Publisher

Provides the business and industry fields with information on manufacturing, wholesale, retail and financial, insurance companies, law/accounting firms, hospitals, HMO/PPOs, labor unions, consulting firms, and Medicare/Medicade. *$64.00*

Monthly Founded: 1987
Circulation: 39736
Printed in 4 colors on glossy stock

11699 CA: A Cancer Journal for Clinicians
1599 Clifton Road NE
Atlanta, GA 30329-4251
404-929-6902
FAX: 404-325-9341
journals@cancer.org
http://caonline.amcancersoc.org

Harmon J Eyre, Editor
Vickie Thaw, Publisher
John R. Seffrin, CEO

Founded: 1913
Circulation: 90,000

11700 CVS InStep with Healthy Living
Drug Store News Consumer Health Publications
Drug Store News
425 Park Avenue
New York, NY 10022
212-565-5220
845-426-7612
jtanzola@lf.com
http://www.consumerhealthpubs.com

Terry Nicosia, Marketing
John Tanzola, National Sales Manager

Helps educate and inform over 25 millions 45+ shoppers that visit CVS every month. Topics include health, nutrition, fitness, lifestyle, travel, coupons and CVS programs and events.

Quarterly Founded: 2002
Circulation: 950000

11701 Cancer Case Presentations: Tumor Board
530 Walnut Street
Philadelphia, PA 19106
215-521-8783
FAX: 215-521-8485

11702 Case Manager
Mosby
10801 Executive Center Drive
Suite 509
Little Rock, AR 72211
501-223-5165
FAX: 501-220-0519
nataniasawyer@mosby.com
www.mosby.com

Catherine Mullahy, Editor
Tom Strickland, Editor-in-Chief
Cheri Lattimer, Executive Director

Exclusively for the case management profession. *$52.00*

80 pages Bi-Monthly Founded: 1990
Circulation: 20M
Printed in 4 colors on glossy stock

11703 Circulation Research
PO Box 1620
Suite 230
Hagerstown, MD 21741
301-223-2300
FAX: 301-223-2400 800-638-3030
educsales@lww.com
http://www.lww.com

Eduardo Marbán, Editor *$377.00*

Founded: 1792

11704 CleanRooms Magazine
PennWell Publishing Company
98 Spit Brook Road
Nashua, NH 03062-5723
603-891-0123
FAX: 603-891-9200
georgem@pennwell.com
http://www.cleanrooms.com

George Miller, Editorial Director
John Haystead, Editor
James Enos, Publisher
Adam Japko, President
Heidi Barnes, Circulation Manager

Serves the contamination control and ultrapure materials and process industries. Written for readers in the microelectronics, pharmaceutical, biotech, health care, food processing and other user industries. Provides technology and business news and new product listings.

Founded: 1910
Circulation: 34019

11705 Clinical Lab Products
MWC Allied Healthcare Group
6100 Center Drive
Suite 1000
Los Angeles, CA 90045
310-642-4400
FAX: 310-641-4444
tantikadjian@ascendmedia.com
http://www.clpmag.com

Scott Anderson, Publisher
Carol Andrews, Editor
Sharon Marsee, Production Manager
Tony Ramos, President
Jennifer Bezahler, Circulation Director

CLP is the leading monthly product news magazine on key decision makers in the clinical diagnostic laboratory. New product annoucements and editorial features assist lab professionals in providing cost effective timely and accurate patient diagnostic information. *$ 125.00*

Monthly Founded: 1976
Circulation: 45000
Printed in 4 colors on glossy stock

11706 Clinical Pulmonary Medicine
530 Walnut St.
Philadelphia, PA 19106-3621
215-521-8300
FAX: 215-521-8902 800-638-6423

Barry Morrill, Publisher
Michael S Niederman MD, Editor-in-Chief
Jay Lippincott, President

Provides a forum for the discussion of important new knowledge in the field of pulmonary medicine that is of interest and relevance to the practitioner.

11707 Clinical Strategies: Psychotherapy in Mana ged Care
10 Alice Street
Binghamton, NY 13904-1580
607-722-5857
FAX: 607-721-0012 800-429-6784
getinfo@haworthpress.com
http://www.haworthpressinc.com

Frank De Piano, Editor
Sandra J Stickles, Marketing
Bill Cohen, CEO

Resource for innovative and effective approches to clinical practice in relation to managed care. *$35.00*

Founded: 1978

11708 Computers and Biomedical Research
525 B Street
Suite 1900
San Diego, CA 92101-4401
619-231-6616
FAX: 619-699-6422 800-321-5068
t.decarlo@elsevier.com
http://www.elsevier.com

Gilbert Laporte, Editor

Monthly Founded: 1974

11709 Computers, Informatics, Nursing
Lippincott Williams & Wilkins
10 A Beech Street
Suite 2
Portland, ME 04101
207-553-7750
FAX: 207-553-7751
edit@medesk.com
http://www.nursingcenter.com

Leslie H. Nicoll, Editor
Lippin Cott, Publisher/President

Computer and informatics applications and product selection in nursing and education for nurse managers, patient care executives, nurses in direct patient care, nurse educators and researchers. *$63.00*

Founded: 1985
Circulation: 4112

11710 Consultant Pharmacist
American Society of Consultant Pharmacists
1321 Duke Street
Alexandria, VA 22314-3563
703-739-1300
FAX: 703-739-1321 800-355-2727
info@ascp.com http://www.ascp.com/

Ed Davidson, Senior Editor
Patti Thompson, Production Manager
Marlene Bloom, Editor
John Feather, CEO
Debbie Furman, Circulation

Official peer reviewed journal of the American Society of Consultant Pharmacists. Editorial deals with geriatric pharmacotherapy. *$210.00*

76 pages Monthly
Circulation: 11000
Printed in 4 colors on glossy stock

11711 Contemporary Urology
Medical Economics Publishing
5 Paragon Drive
Montvale, NJ 07645-1742
973-447-7777
FAX: 218-723-9477 888-581-8052
ccc@advanstar.com
http://www.contemporaryurology.com

Nancy Lucas, Editor
Culley C Carson MD, Editor-in-Chief
Matthew J Holland, Publisher

Comtemporary Urology serves medical and osteopathic physicians specializing in urology. *$120.00*
Monthly Founded: 1992
Circulation: 4276
Printed in 4 colors on glossy stock

11712 Contingency Planning & Management
Witter Publishing Corporation
20 Commerce Street
Flemington, NJ 08822
908-788-0343
FAX: 908-788-3782
CPMmagazine@WitterPublishing.com
http://www.witterpublishing.com

Bob Joudanin, Publisher
Paul Kirvan, Editor-in-Chief
Mike Viscel, Production Manager
Andrew Witter, President

Serves the fields of financial/banking, manufacturing industrial, transportation, utilities, telecommunications, health care, government, insurance and other allied fields. *$195.00*
Monthly Founded: 1987

11713 Continuing Care
Stevens Publishing Corporation
5151 Beltline Road
10th Floor
Dallas, TX 75254
972-687-6700
FAX: 972-687-6770
custserv@stevenspublishing.com
http://www.stevenspublishing.com

Susan Stilwill, Publisher
Dana Cornett, President
Craig Stevens, CEO
Angela Neville, Editor

To provide case management and discharge planning professions with practical and professional information to ensure quality patient services at a cost-effective price. *$119.00*
Founded: 1925

11714 Coping with Allergies and Asthma
Media America
PO Box 682268
Franklin, TN 37068-2268
615-790-2400
FAX: 615-794-0179
info@copingmag.com
http://www.copingmag.com

Michael D Holt, Publisher
Julie McKenna, Editor
Michael D Holt, CEO

Information, tips and news for sufferers of allergies or asthma. *$13.95*
36 pages Founded: 1998
Circulation: 30,000

11715 Coping with Cancer
Media America
PO Box 682268
Franklin, TN 37068-2268
615-790-2400
FAX: 615-794-0179
info@copingmag.com
http://www.copingmag.com

Michael D Holt, Publisher
Julie McKenna, Editor

A magazine for people whose lives have been touched by cancer. Provides knowledge, hope and inspiration to its readers including cancer patients (survivors) and their families, caregivers, healthcare teams and support group leaders. *$19.00*
Founded: 1987
Circulation: 572,000

11716 Cosmetic Surgery Times
Advanstar Communications
Cosmetic Surgery Times
7500 Old Oak Boulevard
Cleveland, Oh 44130
440-243-8100
FAX: 440-891-2683 888-527-7008
magazines@superfill.com
www.cosmeticsurgerytimes.com
/www.advanstar.com

Claudia Shayne-Ferguson, Group Publisher
Maureen Hrehocik, Editor-in-Chief
Michelle Tackla, Senior Editor
Ray Lender, General Manager
Carol Bessick, Manager

Provides cosmetic surgeons with the most current clinical news available. Covers latest surgical techniques, medicolegal issues, updates on new technologies, and suggestions for practice management. *$95.00*
10x/yr Founded: 1987
Circulation: 10,003

11717 Cost Reengineering Report
National Health Information
PO Box 15429
Atlanta, GA 30333-0429
404-607-9500
FAX: 404-607-0095 800-597-6300
nhinfo@aol.com www.nhionline.com

David Schwartz, President

Contains strategies for reengineering clinical and operational functions, and cutting costs while maintaining or improving quality. *$299.00*
Monthly

11718 Critical Strategies: Psychotherapy in Managed Care
Bill Cohen
10 Alice Street
Binghamton, NY 13904-1580
607-722-5857
FAX: 607-722-6362 800-342-9678
getinfo@haworthpressinc.com
www.haworthpressinc.com

Frank DePiano, Editor
Sandra J Sickels, Marketing VP
William Cohen, Owner

Resource for innovative and effective approaches to clinical practice in relation to managed care. *$35.00*
2 per year

11719 Data Strategies & Benchmarks
National Health Information
PO Box 15429
Atlanta, GA 30333-429
404-607-9500
FAX: 404-607-0095 800-597-6300
nhi@nhionline.net
http://www.nhionline.net

David Schwartz, Publisher
Steve Larose, Editor
David Schwartz, CEO

Provides insightful guidance and how-to advice to help them meet all the key challenges faced under managed care. *$339.00*
Monthly Founded: 1994

11720 Dental Economics
PennWell Publishing Company
1421 S Sheridan Road
Tulsa, OK 74112
918-835-3161
800-331-4463
joeb@pennwell.com
http://www.pennwell.com

Joseph A Blaes DDS, Editor
Lyle Hoyt, Publisher
Robert Bolchini, President *$105.76*
Monthly Founded: 1911

11721 Dental Lab Products
MEDEC Dental Communications
2 Northfield Plaza
Suite 300
Northfield, IL 60093-1219
847-441-3700
FAX: 847-441-3702 800-225-4569
kschaefer@advanstar.com
http://www.dentalproducts.net

Bob Kehoe, Editorial Director
Gail Weisman, Editor
Fran Martin, Managing Editor
Richard Fischer, Publisher
Tom Delaney, National Sales Manager

Serves the dental profession and the dental industry, list rentals, classifieds and other services to complete your marketing plan.$35 subscription per year
35 pages Founded: 1967
Circulation: 19,000
Printed in 4 colors on glossy stock

11722 Dental Practice
MEDEC Dental Communications
2 Northfield Plaza
Suite 300
Northfield, IL 60093-1219
847-441-3700
FAX: 440-826-2865 800-225-4569
practicereport@medec.com
http://www.dentalproducts.net

Richard Fischer, Publisher
Bob Kehoe, Editorial Director
Steven Diogo, Editor
Daniel McCann, Senior Editor
Tom Delaney, National Sales Manager

Serves the dental industry. Subscription,
75 pages
Circulation: 120,000
Printed in 4 colors on glossy stock

11723 Dental Products Report
MEDEC Dental Communications
2 Northfield Plaza
Suite 300
Northfield, IL 60093-1219
847-441-3700
FAX: 847-441-3702
www.dentalproducts.net

Dolph Sharp, Publisher
Gail Weisman, Editor
Matthew LaFleur, Illustrator

Serves the dental profession and the dental industry. $120 subscription per year
141 pages 12 per year Founded: 1967
Printed in 4 colors on glossy stock

11724 Dental Products Report Europe
MEDEC Dental Communications
Two Northfield Plaza
Suite 300
Northfield, IL 60093-1219
847-441-3700
FAX: 847-441-3702
kschaefer@advanstar.com
http://www.dentalproducts.net

Richard Fisher, Publisher
Pam Johnson, Editor
Keith Easty, Circulation Director
Dennis Spaeth, Editor
Bob Kehoe, Editorial Director

Designed to inform dentists in Europe and selected Middle Eastern and North African countries and dental distributors and depot personnel worldwide of new developments and ongoing trends in the dental market. *$40.00*
Founded: 1987
Circulation: 50000

11725 Dentistry Today
100 Passaic Avenue
Fairfield, NJ 07004-3520
973-882-4700
FAX: 973-882-3622
pradcliffe@dentistrytoday.net
http://www.dentistrytoday.com/

Paul F Radcliffe, Publisher
Phillip Bonner, Editor
Susan Oettinger, Circulation Manager

The nation's leading clinical news magazine for dentists *$65.00*
122 pages Monthly Founded: 1981
Circulation: 150,000
Printed in 4 colors on glossy stock

11726 Devices and Diagnostics Letter
300 N Washington Street
Suite 200
Falls Church, VA 22046-3431
703-538-7600
FAX: 703-538-7676 888-838-5578
customerservice@fdanews.com
http://www.fdanews.com

Robert Barton, Editorial Director
Matt Salt, Publisher
Maritza Lizama, Marketing Director
Cynthia Carter, President *$987.00*
Weekly
Circulation: 3300

11727 Diabetes Care
1701 North Beauregard Street
Alexandria, VA 22311
703-549-1500
FAX: 703-549-6995 800-342-2383
askada@diabetes.org
http://www.diabetes.org

Lynn Nicholas, CEO
Joseph Scheffer, Editor
Peter Banks, Publisher
Joe Herget, Marketing Manager *$314.00*

Monthly Founded: 1940
Circulation: 13637

11728 Diabetes Digest Family
Drug Store News Consumer Health Publications
425 Park Avenue
New York, NY 10022
212-565-5220
www.consumerhealthpubs.com
Contains health news of importance to those with diabetes.
Annual
Circulation: 6.8mm

11729 Diabetes Educator
American Association of Diabetes Educators
100 W Monroe Street
Suite 400
Chicago, IL 60603
312-424-2426
FAX: 312-424-2427 800-338-3633
aade@aadenet.org
http://www.diabeteseducator.org

James Sain, Editor
Chris Laxton, CEO
Michael Warner, Marketing Director

Published by the American Association of Diabetes Educators.
Founded: 1973
Mailing list available for rent 10000 names $160 per M.

11730 Diabetes Interview
6 School Street
Suite: 160
Fairfax, CA 94930-1650
415-258-2828
FAX: 415-258-2822 800-234-1218

Nadia Al-Samarrie, Publisher
Scott King, Editorial
Daniel Trecroci, Managing Editor
Dick Young, Production *$12.00*
Monthly Founded: 1989
Circulation: 120,000

11731 Diagnostic Imaging
Miller Freeman Publications
600 Harrison Street
San Francisco, CA 94107
415-947-6478
FAX: 415-947-6099
jhayes@cmp.com
http://www.diagnosticimaging.com

John C. Hayes, Editor
Gary Marshall, President
Suzanne Johnston, Publisher
Kathy Mischak, Associate Publisher

The news magazine of imaging innovation and economics. *$113.00*
90 pages Monthly Founded: 1984
Circulation: 31240
Printed in 4 colors on glossy stock

11732 Diagnostic Imaging America Latina

Miller Freeman Publications
600 Harrison Street
San Francisco, CA 94107
415-947-6478
FAX: 415-947-6099
jhayes@cmp.com
http://www.diagnosticimaging.com

Suzanne Johnston, Editor/Publisher
John Hayes, Editorial
Buckley Dement, Circulation
Heidi Torpey, Marketing *$113.00*
Monthly Founded: 1996

11733 Diagnostic Imaging Asia Pacific
Miller Freeman Publications
600 Harrison Street
San Francisco, CA 94107
415-947-6491
FAX: 415-947-6099
diedit@mfi.com
www.diagnosticimaging.com

Philip Ward, Editor
David E Lese, Publisher

A newsmagazine aimed at radiologists and allied medical professionals involved in the practice of diagnostic imaging, and provides timely articles on new diagnostic and technical developments in the field mixed with extensive coverage of important political, commercial and economic trends in the specialty. *$120.00*
42 pages Quarterly
Circulation: 10,000
Printed in 4 colors on glossy stock

11734 Diagnostic Imaging Europe
Miller Freeman Publications
600 Harrison Street
San Francisco, CA 94107
415-947-6478
FAX: 415-947-6099
jhayes@cmp.com
http://www.diagnosticimaging.com

Philip Ward, Editor
Suzanne Johnston, Publisher
Jose Joaquin, Circulation
Kim Spinoso, National Sales Manager

A newsmagazine aimed at radiologists and allied medical professionals involved in the practice of diagnostic imaging. Provides a balanced mix of timely articles on new diagnostic and technical developments in the field mixed with extensive coverage of important political, commercial and economic trends in the specialty. *$125.00*
58 pages Founded: 1996
Circulation: 10062
Printed in 4 colors on glossy stock

11735 Diagnostic Insight
Biomedical Marketing Association
10293 N Meridian Street
Suite 175
Indianapolis, IN 46290-1130
317-816-1640
FAX: 317-816-1633 1 8-0 2-8 78
info@bmaonline.org
http://www.bmaonline.org

Michael F Ward, Executive Director/Editor

A quarterly magazine published by Biomedical Marketing Association.
24 pages Quarterly Founded: 1978

11736 Dialysis and Transplantation
Creative Age Publications
7628 Densmore Avenue
Van Nuys, CA 91406-2042
818-782-7328
FAX: 818-782-7450 800-442-5667
dnpcs@magserv.com
http://www.eneph.com

Deborah Carver, Publisher/CEO
Joseph G Herman, Executive Editor
Carlos Benskin, Circulation Manager

Serves the renal care community. Subscription: $17.50. *$35.00*
Monthly Founded: 1975
Printed in 4 colors on glossy stock

11737 Dietitian's Edge
Rodman Publications
70 Hilltop Road
Ramsey, NJ 07446
201-825-2552
FAX: 201-825-0553
dietitian@rodpub.com
www.dietitiansedge.com

11738 Director
NFDA Services
13625 Bishop's Drive
Brookfield, WI 53005
262-789-1880
FAX: 262-789-6977 800-228-6332
nfda@nfda.org http://www.nfda.org

Chris Raymond, Editor
Barb Gamez, Marketing Manager
Christine Pepper, CEO
Benjamin Lund, Assistant Editor

Melinda Mueller, Marketing Communications Specialist

Coverage concentrates on funeral service education and licensure, community service and public relations as well as public health concerns and legal, ethical and moral issues. *$45.00*

84 pages Monthly Founded: 1882
Circulation: 13906
Printed in 4 colors on glossy stock

11739 Diseases of the Colon & Rectum
American Society of Colon & Rectal Surgeons
85 W Algonquin Road
Suite 550
Arlington Heights, IL 60005
847-427-1200
FAX: 847-290-9203 www.fascrw.org

Stella Zedalis, Associate Executive Director

A monthly journal published by the American Society of Colon & Rectal Surgeons.

143+ pages
Mailing list available for rent 2300 names $250 per M.

11740 Drug Store News
Lebhar-Friedman
425 Park Avenue
New York, NY 10022
212-756-5000
FAX: 212-756-5176 800-216-7117
jkenlon@drugstorenews.com
http://www.lf.com

John Kenlon, Publisher
Tony Lisanti, Editor/Associate Publisher
Terry Nicosia, Senior Production Manager
K Dement, Circulation Manager
Wayne Bennett, Advertising Manager

Publication consists of merchandising trends and pharmacy developments. Provides extensive coverage of every major segment of chain drug retailing and combination stores.

Monthly Founded: 1925
Circulation: 44372

11741 Emergency Medicine
7 Century Drive
Siute 302
Parsippany, NJ 07051
973-206-3434
FAX: 973-206-9251
emergencymedicine@qhc.com
http://www.emedmag.com

Steven Stoneburn, CEO
Michael Pepper, Publisher
Martin Dicarlantonio, Editor
Donna Sickles, Circulation Manager
Kathleen Corbett, Advertising Coordinator *$90.00*

Monthly Founded: 1967
Circulation: 158000

11742 Emerging Trends
Trends Analysis Group
1 N Franklin
29th Floor
Chicago, IL 60606-3421
312-422-3990
FAX: 312-422-4569

Marcia Foley, Editor

Published as a community hospital trends which focuses on financial performance, personnel, utilization and facilities. *$135.00*

Quarterly
Circulation: 1,700

11743 EndoNurse
Virgo Publishing
3300 N Central Avenue, Suite 300
Phoenix, AZ 85012
480-990-1101
FAX: 480-675-8154
asharman@vpico.com
www.endonurse.com

Peggy Jackson, Publisher
Kelly Pyrek, Editor

For the continuing advancement of nurses and technicians in endoscopy and other minimally invasive procedures, providing practical education and updated protocol information for hospitals and freestanding facility practices. Articles address medical treatment options, surgical procedures, pharmaceuticals, new products and technologies, infection control, occupational health and endoscopy suite management.

40 pages Bi-Monthly Founded: 2001
Circulation: 13000+
Mailing list available for rent 13000+ names $var per M.
Printed in 4 colors on glossy stock

11744 Endocrine
505 NW 185th Avenue
Beaverton, OR 97006-3448
503-690-5350
FAX: 503-690-5245
journals@ohsu.edu
http://www.bioscience.org

P Michael Conn, Editor-in-Chief
Peter O Kohler, President *$365.00*

Founded: 1867

11745 Endocrine Reviews
The Endocrine Society
8401 Connecticut Avenue
Suite 900
Chevy Chase, MD 20815-5817
301-410-0200
FAX: 301-941-0257 888-363-6274
endoreviews@endo-society.org
http://www.endo-society.org

Dr. E. Brad Thompson, Editor-in-Chief
Anthony R. Means, President
Scott Hunt, Executive Director *$252.00*

Founded: 1916
Circulation: 5907

11746 European Medical Device Manufacturer
Canon Communications
1144 W Olympic Boulevard
Los Angeles, CA 90064
310-445-4200
FAX: 310-445-4269
feedback@cancom.com
http://www.cancom.com

William F. Cobert, CEO/President *$150.00*

Founded: 1978
Circulation: 15,048

11747 Exercise and Sport Sience Reviews
Lippincott Williams & Wilkins
530 Walnut Street
Philadelphia, PA 19106-3621
215-521-8300
FAX: 215-521-8902
support@ovid.com
http://www.acsm-essr.org

Douglas R. Seals, Editor-in-Chief
Lori A Tish, Editorial Assistant
Michael A. Hargrett, Associate Publisher

This Journal provides premier reviews of the most contemporary scientific, medical and research-based topics emerging in the field of sports medicine and exercise science, targeted to students, professors, clinicians, scientists and professionals for practical and research applications.

192 pages Quarterly Founded: 1998 200 names
Printed in 4 colors on matte stock

11748 Extended Care Product News
HMP Communications
83 General Warren Boulevard
Suite 100
Malvern, PA 19355
610-560-0500
FAX: 610-560-0501 800-237-7285
pnorris@hmpcommunications.com
http://www.extendedcarenews.com

Peter Norris, Publisher
Elizabeth Klumpp, Executive Editor
Peter Treaill, CEO/President
Michelle Cook, Marketing Manager
Michelle Koch, Circulation Manager

Serves purchasing professionals in acute, long term, and home care, offering product information, reimbursement updates, legislative news, industry trends, and a health care business focus.

24 pages Founded: 1989
Circulation: 100000
Printed in 4 colors on glossy stock

11749 Family Medicine
11400 Tomahawk Creek Parkway
Leawood, KS 66211
913-906-6000
FAX: 913-906-6096 800-274-2237
stfmoffice@stfm.org
http://www.stfm.org

Joetta K. Melton, Publisher
Kurt C. Stange, Editor
Claire Zimmerman, Managing Editor
Jeannette E. South-Paul, President
Roger Sherwood, Executive Director

Founded: 1967
Circulation: 6000

11750 General Dentistry
211 E Chicago Avenue
Suite 900
Chicago, IL 60611-1999
312-404-4300
FAX: 312-440-0559 888-243-3368
drudt@townsend-group.com
http://www.agd.org

Thomas A. Howley, President
Roger Winland, Editor
Jay Donohue, Executive Director

Founded: 1951
Circulation: 37,000

11751 General Surgery News
545 W 45th Street
8th Floor
New York, NY 10036
212-957-5300
FAX: 212-957-7230
cdahnke@mcmahonmed.com
http://www.mcmahonmed.com

Ray Mcmahon, Publisher
Van Velle, President *$60.00*

Monthly Founded: 1974
Circulation: 37,268

11752 Geriatric Nursing
11830 Westline Industrial Drive
Little Rock, AR 63146-3318
501-223-5165
FAX: 501-223-0519 800-325-4177

11753 Grant Funding for Elderly Health Services
Health Resources Publishing
1913 Atlantic Avenue
Suite F4
Manasquan, NJ 08736
732-292-1100
FAX: 732-292-1111 888-843-6242
hrp@healthrespubs.com
http://www.healthrepubs.com

Bob Jenkins, President/Managing E
Lisa Mansfield, Marketing Assistant
Robert Jenkins, Editor
Robert Jenkins, Circulation Manager

This report will give insight into which proposals will get funds for which organization. Lists the organizations that will recieve the most funds from grantmakers during this decade and beyond. Also studies different case histories of successful grant proposals. *$147.00*

Monthly Founded: 1969 ISBN 1-882364-46-5

11754 Group Practice Data Management
SourceMedia
550 W Van Buren
Ste 1100
Chicago, IL 60607-6680
312-913-1334
FAX: 312-913-1959
www.sourcemedia.com

Howard Anderson, Publisher/Editor

Analyses of trends, insights on technology and practice advice from automation pioneers for executive and physician administrators of medical groups in charge of making decisions about information technology investments. Profiles on practices, new software development updates, and ideas on plans for implementing information technology.

Semiannual
Circulation: 15M

11755 Gynecologic Oncology
525 B Street
Suite 1900
San Diego, CA 92101-4401
619-231-6616
FAX: 619-699-6700 800-321-5063

11756 Harvard Mental Health Letter
Harvard Health Publcations
10 Shattuck Street
Boston, MA 02115
617-432-1485
FAX: 617-432-1506 877-649-9457
hhp_info@hms.harvard.edu
http://www.health.harvard.edu

Michael Crai Miller, Editor in Chief
Edward H Coburn, Publishing Director
$59.00

Monthly Founded: 1985

11757 Harvard Public Health Review
Harvard School of Public Health
665 Huntington Avenue
Boston, MA 02115
617-321-1184
FAX: 617-384-8989
editor@hsph.harvard.edu
http://www.hsph.harvard.edu/review

Alexandra Molloy, Editor
Barry R. Bloom, Dean of the School
Martha Cassin, Manager

Flagship magazine of the Harvard School of Public Health.

60 pages Bi-annually Founded: 1922
Circulation: 10000
Printed in 4 colors on glossy stock

11758 Health Care Strategic Management
Business Word
1211 E Arapahoe Road
Suite 101
Centennial, CO 80112-3851
303-290-8500
FAX: 303-290-9025 800-328-3211
hcsm/businessword@businessword.com
http://www.businessword.com

Donald E. L Johnson, Publisher/Editor
Donald E. L Johnson, Chief Executive Officer

Articles emphasize on evaluating hospital lines and services for positioning in the marketplace, and interviews with key health care leaders. *$284.00*

20 pages Monthly Founded: 1982
Circulation: 1300 $450 per M.
Printed in on matte stock

11759 Health Data Management
SourceMedia
550 W Van Buren
Ste 1100
Chicago, IL 60607-6680
312-913-1334
FAX: 312-913-1959
hlthdata@aol.com
http://www.healthdatamanagement.com/

Howard J Anderson, Publisher
Bill Siwicki, Editorial Director
Greg Gillespie, Managing Editor
Bill Briggs, Senior Editor
Jim Siebert, Sales/Marketing Manager

Reporting on important information technology issues in health care with emphasis on computerization trends that improve health care efficiency.

Monthly Founded: 1994
Circulation: 41116

11760 Health Facilities Management
American Hospital Publishing
1 N Franklin
29th Floor
Chicago, IL 60606
312-222-2000
FAX: 312-422-4500 800-821-2039
hfcustsvc@healthforum.com
http://www.hfmmagazine.com

Mary Grayson, Publisher
Mike Hrickiewicz, Managing Editor
Gary A. Mecklenburg, Chairman
Neil J. Jesuele, Director

Reflects their highly specialized needs such as changes in codes and standards, industry news, new products and technical developments of suppliers. *$30.00*

Monthly Founded: 1998
Circulation: 28160 28,000 names

11761 Health Management Technology
Nelson Publishing
2500 Tamiami Trail N
Nokomis, FL 34275
941-966-9521
FAX: 941-966-2590
rblair@healthmgttech.com
http://www.healthmgttech.com

Michael E Hilts, Publisher/Editorial Director
Robin Blair, Editor

Serves the health care industry including hospitals/multi-hospital systems, managed care organizations and others allied to the field. *$60.00*

66 pages Monthly Founded: 1965
Circulation: 45751
Printed in 4 colors on glossy stock

11762 Health Progress
Catholic Health Association
4455 Woodson Road
Saint Louis, MO 63134
314-427-2500
FAX: 314-427-0029
http://www.chausa.org

Michael Rogers, Publisher/Interim President
Monica Heaton, Editor
Martha Slover, Circulation Manager

Focuses on management concepts, ethical issues, legislative trends, and theological issues. *$50.00*

Monthly Founded: 1914
Circulation: 12000

11763 Healthcare Advertising Review
11211 E. Arapahoe Rd.
Suite 101
Centennial, CO 80112-3851
303-290-8500
FAX: 303-290-9025 800-328-3211
har/businessword@businessword.com
http://www.businessword.com/

Donald E Johnson, Chairman/CEO
Tom Rees, Editor
Richard J. Rhinehart, Circulation Manager *$314.00*

Founded: 1986

11764 Healthcare Executive
American College of Healthcare Executives
1 N Franklin Street
Chicago, IL 60606
312-422-3840
FAX: 312-454-0023
GenInfo@ache.org www.ache.org

Ann C Bartling, Publisher
Deborah A Labb, Editor-in-Chief
Michael C Waters, Chairman
Deborah Sprindzunas, Executive Director

Serves members of the American College of Health care executives, whose primary business/industries include hospitals, managed care organizations, long-term care facilities and others allied to the field. *$65.00*

Bi-Monthly
Printed in 4 colors on glossy stock

11765 Healthcare Financial Management
Healthcare Financial Management Association
2 Westbrook Corporate Center
Suite 700
Westchester, IL 60154-5700
708-319-9600
FAX: 708-531-0032 800-252-4362
taary@hfma.org http://www.hfma.org

Cheryl T Stachura, Publisher
Marilyn Ferdinand, Editor
Sharon Malik, Advertising Coordinator
Kathleen Gallagher, Sales Manager
Richard Clarke, President

Serves hospitals, medical clinics, nursing homes, extended care facilities, multi-hospital corporations, accounting, consulting firms, government, professional and academic institutions, consultants and others allied to the field. *$110.00*

94 pages Monthly Founded: 1946
Circulation: 32900
Printed in 4 colors on glossy stock

11766 Healthcare Foodservice Magazine
International Publishing Company of America
664 La Villa Drive
Miami, FL 33166-6095
305-887-1700
FAX: 305-885-1923 800-525-2015
health@ipca.com
www.healthcare-services.com

Alexander C Morton, Publisher
Melora Grattan, Assistant Editor

Devoted to foodservice topics for foodservice directors, foodservice managers, dieticians, foodservice supervisors, chefs, purchasing managers, purchasing agents, administrators and others. *$25.00*

24 pages Quarterly
Printed in 4 colors on glossy stock

11767 Healthcare Informatics
McGraw Hill
4530 W 77th Street
Suite 350
Minneapolis, MN 55435
952-928-4872
FAX: 952-835-3460

Jim Dougherty, Publisher

11768 Healthcare Purchasing News
Nelson Publishing
7650 So. Tamiami Trail N
Suite 10
Sarasota, FL 34275
941-927-9345
FAX: 941-927-9588
jgehring@hpnonline.com
http://www.hpnonline.com

Rick Dana Barlow, Senior Editor
Jeannie Akridge, New Products Editor
Kristine Russell, Publisher
Julie Williamson, Features Editor
Susan Cantrell, Infection Control Editor

Serves the field of hospital materials management, purchasing, central services and administration. *$63.00*

27 pages Monthly Founded: 1965
Circulation: 33000
Printed in 4 colors on glossy stock

11769 Healthplan
American Association of Health Plans
601 Pennsylvania Avenue
Suite 500
Washington, DC 20004-3421
202-778-3200
FAX: 202-778-8508
ahip@ahip.org http://www.ahip.org

Kebin New, Editor
Karen Ignagni, CEO

A magazine of trends, insights and best practices. *$60.00*

Founded: 2004
Circulation: 19000

11770 Home Health Products
Stevens Publishing Corporation
5151 Beltline Road 10th Floor
Dallas, TX 75254
972-687-6700
FAX: 972-687-6770
Sbienkowski@stevenspublishing.com
http://www.stevenspublishing.com

Craig Stevens, CEO
Dana Cornett, President/COO
Randy Dye, Publisher
Sandra Bienkowski, Editor *$119.00*

Founded: 1925
Circulation: 20000

11771 Home Medical Equipment News
United Publications
106 Lafayette Street
PO Box 998
Yarmouth, ME 04096
207-846-0600
FAX: 207-846-0657
hmenews@hmenews.com
http://www.hmenews.com

Rick Rector, Publisher
Brook Taliaferro, Editorial Director
Brenda Boothby, Circulation Director
James G. Taliaferro, President
Jim Sullivan, Editor

Serves home medical equipment providers. *$84.00*

Monthly Founded: 1995
Circulation: 17100

11772 HomeCare
Primedia
745 Fifth Avenue
Overland Park
New York, NY 10151
212-745-0100
FAX: 212-745-0121 866-505-7173
information@primedia.com
http://www.homecaremag.com

Gregg Herring, Publisher
Gail Walker, Editor-in-Chief
Tim Heston, Associate Editor
Rebecca Grilliot, Staff Writer
Kent Peterson, National Sales Manager

Monthly Founded: 1989

11773 Hospital Law Manual
Publishers
111 Eighth Avenue
7th Floor
New York, NY 10011-1978
212-771-0600
FAX: 212-771-0885 800-234-1660
customer.service@aspenpubl.com
http://www.aspenpub.com

Robert Becker, CEO
Stacey Caywood, Publisher
Richard H Kravitz, VP

Hospital law. *$1325.00*

Quarterly Founded: 1965

11774 Hospital Outlook
801 Pennsylvania Avenue NW
Suite 245
Washington, DC 20004-2604
202-783-1555
FAX: 202-737-6462 202-624-1500
info@fah.org
http://www.fahs.com/publications/hospital_outlook/

Charles N. Kahn III, President
LaQuanda Washington, Editor Asst.
Richard P Coorsh, Publisher

Founded: 1966

11775 Hypertension
1516 Jefferson Highway
BH 514
New Orleans, LA 70121
504-842-3700
FAX: 504-842-3258

11776 ICT: Infection Control Today
Virgo Publishing
3300 N Central Avenue, Suite 300
Phoenix, AZ 85012
480-990-1101
FAX: 480-675-8154
asharman@vpico.com
www.infectioncontroltoday.com

Peggy Jackson, Publisher
Kelly Pyrek, Editor

Science-based articles for the general ward, operating room, sterile processing and environmental services departments of healthcare facilities, as well as for the public-health community. Articles are in-depth, comprehensively researched and explore important trends, legislative events, new guidelines and technologies impacting the areas of infection control, patient safety, occupational health, epidemiology, risk management and healthcare purchasing.

60 pages Monthly + Buyer's Guide
Founded: 1996
Circulation: 30000+
Mailing list available for rent 30000+ names $var per M.
Printed in 4 colors on glossy stock
Computerized version available: website

11777 Imprint
555 W 57th Street
Suite 1327
New York, NY 10019-2925
212-645-5477
FAX: 212-581-2368

Sara Seagull, Owner

11778 In Touch
48 S Service Road
Melville, NY 11747
631-777-3800
FAX: 631-777-8700 877-468-6824

11779 Infection and Immunity
1752 N Street NW
Washington, DC 20036
202-737-3600
FAX: 202-942-9355

11780 Insight
Healthcare Convention & Exhibitors Association
5775-G Peachtree Dunwoody Road NE
Building G, Suite 500
Atlanta, GA 30342
404-252-3663
FAX: 404-252-0774
hcea@kellencompany.com
http://www.hcea.org

Eric Allen, President/Director
Jennifer Palcher, Editor
Jennifer Palcher, Communications Manager

Providing health care convention education and news. *$29.00*

Quarterly Founded: 1930

11781 International Journal of Trauma Nursing
Mosby/Professional Opportunities
11830 Westline Industrial Drive
St Louis, MO 63146-3318
314-453-4338
FAX: 314-872-9164 800-237-9851
c.kilzer@elsevier.com
http://www.mosby.com/trauma

Judith Stoner Halpern, Editor
Sarah Papke Kalamazoo, EDITORIAL ASSISTANT
Carol Kilzer, Advertising Sales Service

Reaches today's trauma nurses, coordinators,and managers who direct the nursing aspects of patient care. The journal's multidisciplinary and collaborative approach to the unique needs of the trauma patient represents the vision and clinical expertise of each nursing specialty. These professionals influence the purchase of

supplies and equipment for use in emergency and trauma departments. *$42.00*
Quarterly Founded: 1995
Circulation: 1298

11782 Internet Healthcare Strategies
Dean Anderson
PO Box 50507
Santa Barbara, CA 93150
805-564-2177
FAX: 805-564-2146
info@corhealth.com
http://www.corhealth.com

11783 JAAPA
Medical Economics Publishing
131 W 1st Street
Duluth, MN 55802-2065
877-922-2022
FAX: 218-723-9437
aapa@aapa.org http://www.jaapa.com
Leslie A Kole, Editor-in-Chief
Tanya Gregory, Editor
Dominic Barone, Publisher
Miguel Van Brakle, Circulation manager
Lee Maniscalco, CEO
Official journal of the American Academy of Physican Assistants.
92 pages Monthly
Circulation: 52500

11784 Journal Of Oncology Management
Alliance Communications Group
810 E 10th Street
Lawrence, KS 66044-368
785-843-1235
FAX: 785-843-1244 800-627-0932
jhallett@allenpress.com
http://www.allenpress.com
Darlene Johnson, Editor-in-Chief
Jorgene Hallett, Publishing Manager
Bi-monthly, peer-reviewed journal. Includes original research, case studies and other features pertinent to improving performance of oncology administrators. *$87.00*
32 pages Founded: 1935
Circulation: 10000
Printed in 4 colors on glossy stock

11785 Journal Watch
860 Winter Street
Waltham, MA 02154
781-893-3800
FAX: 781-893-3914 800-843-6356
jwatch@mms.org
http://www.jwatch.org
Allan S Brett, Editor In Chief
Alberta L Fitzpatrick, Publisher
Founded: 1987

11786 Journal of Allergy and Clinical Immunology
American Academy of Allergy, Asthma and Immunology
555 E Wells Street
Suite 1100
Milwaukee, WI 53202
414-272-6071
FAX: 414-272-6070
info@aaaai.org www.aaaai.org
Donald Y M Leung, MD,PhD, Editor-In-Chief
Harold S Nelson, MD, Deputy Editor
Andrea J Apter, MD, Associate Editor
Nancy T Hopper, Managing Editor
Kay Whalen, Executive Vice President
The official scientific journal of the American Academy of Allergy, Asthma and Immunology and the premiere journal in the field. Each issue features the very latest and best research in the allergy/immunology specialty.
Monthly

11787 Journal of American Dietetic Association
American Dietetic Association
120 South Riverside Plaza
Suite 2000
Chicago, IL 60606-6995
312-990-0040
FAX: 312-899-4757 800-877-1600
elspcs@elsevier.com
http://www.adajournal.org
Linda Van Horn, Editor-in-Chief
Jason T Switt, Editors:
The Journal of American Dietetic Association serves the dietetic field. *$220.00*
Monthly Founded: 1925
Circulation: 65000
Printed in 4 colors on glossy stock

11788 Journal of Cardiovascular Management
Alliance Communications Group
810 E 10th Street
Lawrence, KS 66044
785-843-1235
FAX: 785-843-1853 800-627-0932
info@aameda.org
http://www.aameda.org
Christopher LaCoe, Editor-in-Chief
Jorgene Hallett, Publishing Manager
Renee S Schleicher, CEO/President
Bi-monthly, peer-reviewed journal of articles pertinent to cardiovascular administration. *$87.00*
32 pages Founded: 1957
Circulation: 12,500
Mailing list available for rent 400 names $350 per M.
Printed in 4 colors on glossy stock

11789 Journal of Clinical Endocrinology & Metabolism
630 W 168th Street
New York, NY 10032
301-941-0210
FAX: 301-941-0257
jcen@endo-society.org
http://jcem.endojournals.org/
Paul Ladenson, Editor-in-Chief
Lenne Miller, Journal Publications
Steve Hamburger, Advertising Manager
Monthly

11790 Journal of Clinical Epidemiology
Elsevier Publishing
11830 Westline Industrial Drive
St. Louis, MO 63146
314-534-4100
FAX: 800-535-9935 800-545-2522

11791 Journal of Clinical Investigation
11830 Westline Industrial Drive
St Louis, MO 63146
314-453-7010
FAX: 314-453-7095 800-460-3110
authorssupport@elsevier.com
http://www.elsevier.com
A Knottnerus, Editor
P Tugwell, Editor
Laurence Zipson, Group Advertisement Manag
Karlyn Messinger, Communications Manager *$274.00*
Monthly Founded: 1955

11792 Journal of Craniofacial Surgery
Lippencott Williams & Wilkins
16522 Hunters Green Parkway
Hagerstown, MD 21740
301-223-2300
FAX: 301-223-2398 800-638-3030
service@lww.com
http://www.lww.com
Mutaz B Habal MD, Editor
Jay Lippioctt, CEO
An international journal dedicated to the art and science essential to the practice of craniofacial surgery. Online version available. *$586.00*
Founded: 1998

11793 Journal of Emergency Nursing
Mosby/Professional Opportunities
PO Box 1510
Clearwater, FL 33757-1510
727-443-3047
FAX: 727-445-9380 800-237-9851
Presents original, peer-reviewed clinical articles as well as the annual ENA Scientific Assembly program.

Circulation: 27240

11794 Journal of Environmental Health
720 S Colorado Boulevard
South Tower, Suite 970
Denver, CO 80246-1925
303-756-9090
FAX: 303-691-9490

11795 Journal of Extra-Corporeal Technology
503 Carlisle Drive
Suite 125
Hendon, VA 20170
703-435-8556
FAX: 703-435-0056
judy@amsect.org
http://www.amsect.org
Alfred H Stammers, Editor
Ron Richards, President
Dedicated to the study and practice of extra-corporeal (relating to heart and lung machines) circulation and perfusion technologies. The journal also covers a broad range of topics on the physical sciences as they are related to fluid dynamics. *$100.00*
Quarterly Founded: 1967

11796 Journal of Forensic Neuropsychology
10 Alice Street
Binghamton, NY 13904-1580
607-722-5857
FAX: 607-722-6362 800-342-9678
getinfo@haworthpressinc.com
www.haworthpressinc.com
Features articles conveying current research and studies in the field of forensic neuropsychology. *$45.00*
Quarterly
Circulation: 700

11797 Journal of Forensic Psychology Practice
Bill Cohen
10 Alice Street
Binghamton, NY 13904-1580
607-225-5857
FAX: 607-771-0012 607-722-5857
getinfo@haworthpress.com
http://www.haworthpressinc.com
Bill Cohen, President/Publisher
Jim Hom, Editor

Provides the forensic psychology practicioner and professional with timely information and regional research that examines the impact of new knowledge in the field as it relates to their practice. *$60.00*
Quarterly Founded: 1978
Circulation: 700

11798 Journal of Healthcare Quality
National Association for Healthcare Quality
4700 W Lake Avenue
Glenview, IL 60025-1485
847-375-4720
FAX: 888-576-4349 800-966-9392
jhq@nahq.org http://www.nahq.org
Luc R Pelletier, Editor-in-Chief
John D Hartley, President
Professional forum that advances quality in a diverse and changing health care environment. Health care professionals worldwide depend upon the Journal for its creative solutions and scientific konwledge in the pursuit of quality. *$115.00*
54 pages Founded: 1976
Printed in 4 colors on glossy stock

11799 Journal of Magnetic Resonance
525 B Street
Suite 1900
San Diego, CA 92101-4401
619-231-6616
FAX: 619-699-6280 800-321-5068
S.J. Opella, Editor
JJH Ackerman, Associate Editor
L Frydman, Associate Editor
W.S. Brey, Founding Editor
Founded: 1880

11800 Journal of Midwifery & Women's Health
American College of Nurse-Midwives
8403 Colesville Road,Suite 1550
Silver Spring, MD 20910
240-485-1815
FAX: 240-485-1817
jmwh@acnm.org
http://www.jmwh.org/
tekoa king, Editor
Tekoa King, Publisher *$130.00*
Circulation: 8000

11801 Journal of Neurotherapy
Bill Cohen
10 Alice Street
Binghamton, NY 13904-1580
607-722-5857
FAX: 800-895-0582 800-429-6784
getinfo@haworthpressinc.com
http://www.haworthpressinc.com/
David L Trudeau, Editor
Bill Cohen, President/Publisher
Darlene Nelson, Managing Editor
Andrew Cary, VP
Roger Hall, Senior Vice President
Provides an integrated, multidisiplinary perspective on clinically relevant research, treatment, and public policy for neurotherapy. *$60.00*
Monthly Founded: 1978

11802 Journal of Occupational and Environmental Hygiene
American Industrial Hygiene Association
2700 Prosperity Avenue
Suite 250
Fairfax, VA 22031
703-498-8267
FAX: 703-207-3561
infonet@aiha.org http://www.aiha.org
Lisa Junker, Sr Editor
Rachel Parsons, Communications Assistant
Sheila Brown, Editor
Essential source of information on occupational and environmental health and safety issues. Available in print and online. *$530.00*
Monthly Founded: 1939
Circulation: 15000

11803 Journal of Prosthetics and Orthotics
351 W Camden Street
Baltimore, MD 21201-2436
410-528-4000
FAX: 410-528-8596 800-638-6423
webmaster@lww.com
http://www.lww.com
Jeffrey A Nemeth, Editor *$91.00*
Quarterly Founded: 1792

11804 Journal of School Nursing
Alliance Communications Group
1416 Park Street
Suite A
Castle Rock, CO 80109
303-663-2329
FAX: 303-663-0403 866-627-6767
nasn@nasn.org http://www.nasn.org
Wanda Miller, Executive Director
Janice Denehy, Executive Editor
Founded: 1968

11805 Journal of Social Behavior & Personality
Drawer 37
Corte Madera, CA 94976
415-209-9838
FAX: 415-209-6719
selectpress@cello.com
http://www.rickcrandall.com
Rick Crandall, CEO/President
Rick Crandall, Editor *$70.00*
Quarterly Founded: 1985

11806 Journal of Trauma & Dissociation
Bill Cohen
10 Alice Street
Binghamton, NY 13904-1580
607-722-5857
FAX: 800-895-0582 800-429-6784
getinfo@haworthpressinc.com
http://www.haworthpressinc.com
James A Chu, Co-Editors
Jennifer J Freyd, Co-Editors
Etzel Cardeña, Associate Editor
S. Singh, Managing Editor
William Cohen, Owner
Contains scientific literature on dissociation, the dissociative disorders, post traumatic stess disorder, psycholgical trauma, and on aspects of memory associated with trauma and dissociation. *$60.00*
Quarterly Founded: 1978

11807 Journal of Ultrasound in Medicine
American Institute of Ultrasound in Medicine
14750 Sweitzer Lane
Suite 100
Laurel, MD 20707-5906
301-984-4392
FAX: 301-498-4450 800-638-5352
subscriptions@aium.org
http://www.aium.org
Dr Beryl R Benacenraf, Editor-in-Chief
Bruce Totaro, Director of Publications
Thomas R. Nelson, Deputy Editor
Dedicated to the rapid, accurate publication of original articles dealing with all aspects of diagnostic ultrasound, particularly its direct application to patient care, but also relevant basic science, advances in instrumentation and biologic effects. Research papers, case reports, review articles, technical notes and letters to the editor are published. *$265.00*
Monthly Founded: 1952
Circulation: 8200
Mailing list available for rent
Printed in 4 colors on glossy stock

11808 Journal of the American College of Surgeons
633 N St. Clair Street
Chicago, IL 60611
312-202-5136
FAX: 312-202-5027 800-440-5227

11809 Journal of the American Dental Association
American Dental Association
211 East Chicago Ave
Chicago, IL 60611-2678
312-440-2500
FAX: 312-440-2800 http://www.ada.org
Lawrence H Meskin, Editor
Daniel M Castagna, Editorial Board
Serves the dental profession and dental industry. *$95.00*
Monthly Founded: 1859
Circulation: 135361
Printed in 4 colors on glossy stock

11810 Journal of the American Health Information Management Association
American Health Information Management Association
633 N St. Clair Street
Chicago, IL 60611-3211
312-202-5000
FAX: 312-202-5001 800-621-4111
postmaster@facs.org
http://www.facs.org/
Barry M. Manuel, Editor-in-chief
Paul F. Nora, Editor
Provides information in the field of health information and medical record management in all health care settings. Subscription: non-members $72, *$25.00*
Monthly Founded: 1913
Printed in 4 colors on glossy stock

11811 Journal of the Medical Library Association
Medical Library Association
65 E Wacker Drive
Suite 1900
Chicago, IL 60601-7246
312-419-9094
FAX: 312-419-8950
info@mlahq.org
http://www.mlanet.org

Lynanne Feilen, Director Publication
Carla J Funk, Executive Officer
Susan Talmage, Editorial Assistant
Bleu Caldwell, Production Assistant
Scott Plutchak, Editor *$163.00*

Quarterly Founded: 1898
Circulation: 5000
Mailing list available for rent

11812 Journal of the National Medical Association
1012 10th Street NW
Washington, DC 20001
856-848-1000
FAX: 856-853-5991 800-257-8290

11813 MS Connection
Lippincott Williams & Wilkins
351 W Camden
Baltimore, MD 21201
410-528-4000
FAX: 800-787-8982 800-787-8981

Dainel Schwartz, Publisher
Michael Levin-Epstein, Managing Editor
Michele Swain, Marketing Manager

11814 Managed Healthcare
Advanstar Communications
7500 Old Oak Boulevard
Cleveland, OH 44130
440-243-8100
FAX: 440-891-2727
info@advanstar.com
http://www.advanstar.com

Daniel J. Corcoran, Publisher
Michael T. McCue, Editor-In-Chief
Craig Roth, Group Publisher
Tracey L. Walker, Senior Editor
Julie Miller, Managing Editor

Valuable resource for managers charged with controlling health care costs and quality. *$64.00*

Monthly Founded: 1987
Circulation: 40000

11815 McKnight's Long-Term Care News
McKnight Medical Communications
2 Northfield Plaza
Suite 300
Northfield, IL 60093-1219
847-441-3700
FAX: 847-441-3703 800-558-1703
ltcn-webmaster@mltcn.com
http://www.mcknightsonline.com

Curtis Allen, President/CEO
Lee Maniscalco, Executive VP
Jim Berklan, Editor
Jeff Hartford, Circulation Director

Serves the field of long term care including nursing homes, senior housing centers, assisted living facilities, hospitals with LTC units, continuing care retirement communities, nursing home chains and other allied organizations in the field.

35 pages Weekly
Circulation: 46000
Printed in 4 colors on glossy stock

11816 Medical Abbreviations: 24,000
Niel M Davis Associates
2049 Stout Drive
B-3
Warminster, PA 18974-3861
215-427-7430
FAX: 888-333-4915
med@neilmdavis.com
http://www.neilmdavis.com

Neil M. Davis, Editor

This current edition paperback pocket book contains 16,000 medical related abbreviations and 24,000 of their possible meanings. It is current, comprehensive, and formatted so that it is easy to use. It also contains a cross-referenced listing of 3,300 generic and trade drug names. *$24.95*

Monthly Founded: 1981 ISBN 0-931431-09-3

11817 Medical Economics
Advanstar Communications
5 Paragon Drive
Montvale, NJ 07645-1742
973-944-7777
FAX: 973-944-7778
dazevedo@advanstar.com
http://www.memag.com

Joseph Loggia, CEO, Advanstar Communications
Marianne Dekker Mattera, Editor-in-Chief
Mike Graziani, Publisher
Sean Keating, Managing Editor
Laura Wagner, VP Operations

Medical Economics guides physicians in the business of practicing by giving advice about malpractice, third-party reimbursement, managed care, tax strategies, legal information and counseling, fraud, abuse and anti-trust strategies. It helps them manage their practice more efficiently so they can be more effective in delivering patient care. *$109.00*

Monthly Founded: 1987
Circulation: 154897

11818 Medical Meetings
Primedia
745 Fifth Avenue
NY, NY 10151
212-745-0100
FAX: 212-745-0121
information@primedia.com
http://www.meetingsnet.com

Melissa Fromento, Publisher
Tamar Hosansky, Editor
Kelly P. Conlin, CEO

International guide for health care and meeting planners. *$57.00*

106 pages Founded: 1989
Circulation: 12000
Printed in 4 colors on glossy stock

11819 Medical Reference Services Quarterly
Haworth Press
10 Alice St
Binghamton, NY 13904
607-722-5857
FAX: 607-771-0012 800-429-6784
getinfo@haworthpress.com
http://www.haworthpress.com

M Sandra Wood, Editor
Bill Cohen, Publisher

Providing a wealth of exciting and instructive material, Science & Technology Libraries is prepared specifically for the science and technology librarian. This exciting journal represents the viewpoints, concerns and perspectives of the sci-tech librarianship community in a lively and professional style that makes every issue an item to be read and referred to often. Each issue centers on a specialized theme around which the major articles are focused, allowing for in-depth explorations. *$60.00*

Quarterly Founded: 1978

11820 Medical Research Funding Bulletin
PO Box 7507
New York, NY 10150-7507
212-371-3398
FAX: 801-761-4200
grants-one@nyc.rr.com

John Connolly, CEO
Carroll Gordon, Circulation Manager
$75.00

Fortnightly Founded: 1972
Circulation: 4500

11821 Modern Healthcare
Crain Communications
360 N Michigan Avenue
Chicago, IL 60601
312-649-5231
FAX: 312-649-5331 800-678-9595
mheditorial@crain.com
http://www.modernhealthcare.com/

David Burda, Editor
Fawn Lopez, Publisher
Neil McLaughlin, Managing Editor
Charles S. Lauer, VP Publishing/Editorial Director
Brenda Stewart, Director Marketing
$149.00

Founded: 1916
Circulation: 71000

11822 Molecular Endocrinology
Molecular Society Journals
8401 Connecticut Avenue
Suite 900
Chevy Chase, MD 20815-4410
301-941-0200
FAX: 301-941-0259 888-363-6274
molendo@endo-society.org
http://www.endo-society.org

John A Cidlowski, Editor-in-chief
Scott Hunt, Executive Director
Maggie Haworth, Managing Editor
Jessica Peterson, Marketing Manager
$376.00

Weekly Founded: 1916
Circulation: 11000

11823 NASN Newsletter
163 US Route 1
PO Box 1300
Scarborough, ME 04074-9060
207-883-2117
FAX: 207-883-2683 877-627-6476
nasn@nasn.org http://www.nasn.org

Devin Dinkel, Editor
Wanda Miller, Executive Director
Donna Mazyck, President
Gloria Durgin, Administrator/Sponsorship
$2.00

Founded: 1968

11824 New England Journal of Medicine
10 Shattuck Street
Boston, MA 02115-6094
617-734-9800
FAX: 617-739-9864
comments@nejm.org
http://www.nejm.org

Charles Welch, President
Jeffrey M Drazen, Editor-in-Chief
Christopher R. Lynch, VP Public Affairs

General medicine journal that publishes new medical research findings, review articles, and editorial opinion on a wide variety of topics of importance to biomedical science and clinical practice. Published with an emphasis on internal medicine and specialty areas including allergy/immunology, cardiology, endocrinology, gastroenterology, hematology, kidney disease, oncology, pulmonary disease, rheumatology, HIV, and infectous diseases.
$149.00

Weekly

11825 **Nursing**
Ambler Office of Lippincott Williams and Wilkins
323 Norrstown Rd
Suite 200
Ambler, PA 19002
215-646-8700
FAX: 215-646-4399 800-346-7844
Jay Lippincott, President
Cheryl Mee, Publisher & Editor
Keith Sollweiler, Marketing *$34.00*
Monthly Founded: 1971
Circulation: 300000

11826 **Nursing News**
48 W Street
Concord, NH 03301-3595
603-225-3783
FAX: 603-228-6672
Sue@NHNurses.org
http://www.nhnurses.org
Bob Desc, CEO
Susan Fetzer, President *$26.00*
Quarterly Founded: 1906
Circulation: 18000

11827 **Nursing Outlook**
1111 Middle Drive
Indiana, IN 46202
317-274-1486
FAX: 317-278-1842
mbroome@iupui.edu
http://www.nursiniupui.edu
Marion Broome, Editor
Adam Herberg, President, Circulation Manager

11828 **Nutrition Business Journal**
4452 Park Boulevard
Suite 306
San Diego, CA 92116
619-295-7685
FAX: 619-295-5743
info@nutritionbusiness.com
http://www.nutritionbusiness.com
David Nussbaum, Chief Executive Officer
Preston Vice, Chief Financial Officer
$995.00
Monthly Founded: 1892

11829 **O&P Almanac**
American Orthotic & Prosthetic Association
330 John Carlyle Street
Suite 200
Alexandria, VA 22314
703-367-7116
FAX: 571-431-0899
info@aopanet.org
http://www.aopanet.org
Lisa Gough, Editor-in-Chief
Amy Clontz, Director Advertising
Michael E Hamontree, President
Brian Walrath, Membership Manager
Malissa Bennett, Director of Membership & Communicat *$59.00*
84 pages Monthly Founded: 1951
Circulation: 13000
Printed in 4 colors on glossy stock

11830 **Occupational Health & Safety**
Stevens Publishing Corporation
5151 Beltline Road
10th Floor
Dallas, TX 75254
972-687-6700
FAX: 972-687-6770
jlaws@stevenspublishing.com
http://www.stevenspublishing.com
Susan Stilwill, Publisher
Jerry Laws, Editor
Dana Cornett, President/Chief Operating
Craig Stevens, Chief Executive Officer
Margaret Perry, Circulation Director
Practical advice on workplace safety and compliance with laws and regulations. Feature articles and product information.
Monthly Founded: 1925
Circulation: 84000

11831 **Oncology**
48 S Service Road
Suite 310
Melville, NY 11747-2335
631-777-3800
FAX: 631-777-8700 800-777-0965

11832 **Oncology Times**
333 7th Avenue
19th Floor
New York, NY 10001
646-674-6544
FAX: 645-674-6500 800-933-6525
ot@lww.com http://www.lww.com
Serena Stockwell, Editor
Ken Senerth, Publisher
Frank Cox, Advertising Manager
Larry Klein, Director *$189.00*
Founded: 1972
Circulation: 45000

11833 **Optometry: Journal of the American Optometric Association**
American Optometric Association
243 N Lindbergh Boulevard
Saint Louis, MO 63141
314-991-4100
FAX: 314-991-4101
aoa@aoa.org http://www.aoa.org
Paul B Freeman, Editor
Michael Gekones, Executive
Eddy Heckmann, Marketing
Stevin Wasserman, Circulation Manager
Michael Jones, Executive Director
Most widely circulated scholarly optometry journal, provides a forum for research that advances the art and science of the practice of primary care optometry. *$95.00*
68 pages Monthly Founded: 1898
Circulation: 20000
Printed in 4 colors on glossy stock

11834 **Ostomy Wound Management**
HMP Communications
83 General Warren Blvd
Suite 100
Malvern, PA 19355
610-560-0500
FAX: 610-560-0501 800-237-7285
subscriptions@hmpcommunications.com
http://www.o-wm.com
Beth McTamney, Production Editor
Barbara Zieger, Editor
Jeremy Bowden, Publisher
Michelle Koch, Circulation Manager
Information on the diciplines of ostomy care, wound care, incontinence care, and related skin and nutritional issues. *$39.95*
Monthly Founded: 1980
Circulation: 25,400
Printed in 4 colors on glossy stock

11835 **Patient Care**
Medical Economics Publishing
5 Paragon Drive
Montvale, NJ 07645-1742
973-447-7777
FAX: 973-847-5330
dkaplan@advanstar.com
http://www.patientcareonline.com/
Deborah Kaplan, Editor
Stuart Williams, Publisher
Christine Shappell, Circulation Manager
Patient care serves selected medical and osteopathic physicians. *$51.50*
Monthly Founded: 1967
Printed in 4 colors

11836 **Physicians & Computers**
Moorhead Publications
810 S Waukegan Road
#200
Lake Forest, IL 60045-2672
847-615-8333
FAX: 847-615-8345
physcomp@aol.com
www.physicians-computers.com
Tom Moorhead, Publisher
Provides physicians with information on computer advances helpful in the private practice of medicine. Practice management, current medical and non-medical software, computer diagnostics, etc.
$40.00
Monthly
Circulation: 90M

11837 **Pneumogram**
1961 Main Street
#246
Sacremento, CA 95076
916-441-2222
FAX: 916-442-4182 888-730-2772
Janyth Bolden, President
Abbie Rosenberg, Publisher
Quarterly Founded: 1968

11838 **Psychoanalytic Psychology**
211 E 70th Street
Suite 17 H
New York, NY 10021
212-633-9162
FAX: 212-628-8453
Lori Sloan, Executive Director

11839 **Psychology of Addictive Behaviors**
University of South Florida
BEH 339
Department of Psychology
Tampa, FL 33620
813-974-4826
FAX: 202-336-5568 800-374-2721

11840 **Public Health Nursing**
350 Main Street
6th Floor
Malden, MA 02148
781-388-8200
FAX: 781-388-8210
mspencer@bos.blackwellpublishing.com
http://www.blackwellpublishing.com/
Sarah E Abrams, Editor
Judith C Hays, Editor
Otis Dean, Publisher
Alice Meadows, Senior Manager, Circulation
Paige Larkin, Sr. Marketing Manager
$149.00
Founded: 1922

11841 Quality Matters
385 Highland Colony Parkway
Suite 120
Ridgeland, MS 39157
601-957-1575
FAX: 601-956-1713 800-844-0500

11842 RDH
PennWell Publishing Company
1421 S Sheridan Road
Tulsa, OK 74112
918-835-3161
FAX: 918-831-9497

Mark Hartley, Editor

National magazine for dental hygiene professionals. *$48.00*
60 pages Monthly

11843 RN
Medical Economics Publishing
5 Paragon Drive
Montvale, NJ 07645-1742
973-944-7777
FAX: 973-847-5390 888-581-8052
rnmagazine@advanstar.com
http://www.rnweb.com

Thomas Pizor, VP/Group Publisher
Wendy Raupers, Associate Publisher
Joy Puzzo, Marketing/Circulation Man

Published to serve professional nurses in hospitals, physician's offices, extended care facilities, schools of nursing, occupational and community health agencies and other professional nurses. *$35.00*
Monthly Founded: 1937
Circulation: 2500

11844 RN Magazine
5 Paragon Drive
Montvale, NJ 07645-1742
201-587-7500
FAX: 201-358-7450 800-284-8945
RNMagazine@advanstar.com
http://www.rnweb.com

Matthew J Holland, Group Publisher
Marya Ostrowski, Editor
Ray Lender, VP
Erin Riley, Production Manager
Steve Morris, Vice President, Market Development *$24.97*
Monthly Founded: 1992
Circulation: 250000

11845 Radiology
820 Jorie Boulevard
Oak Brook, IL 60523-2251
630-571-2670
FAX: 630-571-7837 800-381-6660
radiolog@rsna.org
http://www.rsna.org

Anthony V. Proto, Editor
Michael Ulezlo, Senior Marketing Manager *$250.00*
Monthly Founded: 1915
Circulation: 35000

11846 Radiology Management
American Healthcare Radiology Administrators
490-B Boston Post Road
Suite 101
Sudbury, MA 01776
978-443-7591
FAX: 978-443-8046 800-334-2472
info@ahraonline.org
http://www.ahraonline.org

Roberta M Edge, President
Kathy Delaney, Publications Editor
Karen Guy, Communications Director

A peer reviewed journal with an editorial review board of AHRA members. *$65.00*
64 pages Founded: 1978
Circulation: 4,000
Printed in 4 colors on glossy stock

11847 Remington Report
Remington Report
30100 Town Center Drive
Suite 421
Laguna Niguel, CA 92677
800-247-4781
FAX: 949-715-1797 800-247-4781
remrptedit@aol.com
http://www.remingtonreport.com

Lisa Remington, Publisher *$44.50*
Founded: 1993

11848 Renal Business Today
Virgo Publishing
3300 N Central Avenue, Suite 300
Phoenix, AZ 85012
480-990-1101
FAX: 480-675-8154
asharman@vpico.com
www.renalbusiness.com

Peggy Jackson, Publisher
Keith Chartier, Editor

Offers renal practice/management news, information and resources. Editorials include the latest business and technology trends in renal care, expert advice, strategic business solutions written by industry leaders and human-interest articles.
40 pages Monthly Founded: 2006
Circulation: 20000
Printed in 4 colors on glossy stock

11849 Research Quarterly for Exercise and Sport
Am. Alliance for Health, Phys. Ed., Rec. & Dance
1900 Association Drive
Reston, VA 20191-1598
703-476-3400
FAX: 703-476-9527 800-213-7193
rqes@aahperd.org
http://www.aahperd.org

Linda Topper, Managing Editor
Stephen Silverman, Editor-in-Chief

RQES is a well respected, comprehensive professional journal, publishing the latest research in the art and science of human movement studies. *$175.00*
128 pages Quarterly Founded: 1930
Circulation: 6000
Printed in 1 color on glossy stock

11850 Respiratory Care
9425 N. MacArthur Blvd
Suite 100
Irving, TX 75063-4706
972-432-2272
FAX: 206-223-0563
info@aarc.org
http://www.rcjournal.com

Charles G Durbin, Editor
Sam P Giordano, Publisher

Journal for the professional respiratory care therapist. Member publication of the American Association for Respiratory Care. *$ 89.95*
Monthly Founded: 1947

11851 Review of Optometry
11 Campus Boulevard
Newton Square, PA 19073
610-492-1000
FAX: 610-492-1039
reviewofoptometry@jobson.com
http://www.revoptom.com

Amy Hellem, Editor-in-Chief
Jeffrey S Eisenberg, Managing Editor
Monthly

11852 Risk Management Handbook
NACHA: Electronic Payments Association

13665 Dulles Technology Drive
Suite 300
Herndon, VA 20171
703-561-1100
FAX: 703-787-0996 800-487-9180
info@nacha.org http://www.nacha.org

Elliott McEntee, President/CEO
William B Nelson, Executive VP

Published by NACHA. *$65.00*
Monthly Founded: 1991

11853 Rite Aid Be Healthy & Beatiful
Drug Store News Consumer Health Publications
425 Park Avenue
New York, NY 10022
212-565-5220

jtanzola@lf.com
http://www.consumerhealthpubs.com

John Tanzola, Marketing

Provides health and beauty tips to millions of women who visit Rite Aid stores.
Quarterly Founded: 2002
Circulation: 950,000

11854 Scrip Magazine
270 Madison Avenue
New York, NY 10016
212-262-8230
FAX: 212-262-8234
pharmabooks@pharmabooks.com
http://www.pjbpubs.com

Jenny Hone, Editor
Alice Dunmore, Circulation Manager
Jenefer Trevena, Marketing Manager
Phillip Every, Worldwide Advertising Sales

An in-depth view of the issues and challenges facing all sectors of the pharmaceutical industry worldwide. Analytical features are written by pharmaceutical experts and opinion leaders as well as specialist journalists. *$1190.00*

11855 Sports Medicine Digest
351 W Camden Street
Baltimore, MD 21201
410-528-4068
FAX: 800-787-8982 800-787-8981

Daniel Schwartz, Publisher
Michael Levin-Epstein, Managing Editor
$125.00
12 pages Monthly Founded: 1978
Printed in 1 color on matte stock

11856 Surgical Products
Reed Business Information
100 Enterprise Drive
Suite 600
Rockaway, NJ 07866-912
973-920-7000
FAX: 630-288-8686
rritsma@reedbusiness.com
http://www.surgprodmag.com/

Noreen Costelloe, Group VP/Publisher
Richard Ritsma, Editor-in-Chief
James Reed, Owner
Sabrina Crow, Managing Director
Steve Koppelman, Circulation Manager

Surgical products provides surgeons, OR supervisors and OR materials managers

working in hospitals and surgi-centers with new product technology and equipment.
Monthly Founded: 1946
Circulation: 71000

11857 Synergist
American Industrial Hygiene Association
2700 Prosperity Avenue
Suite 250
Fairfax, VA 22031
703-849-8267
FAX: 703-207-3561
infonet@aiha.org http://www.aiha.org

Donna M Doganiero, Director
Amanda Kramer, Editor
Connie Paradise, Marketing Manager
$72.00
Monthly Founded: 1939

11858 Transplantation
351 W Camden Street
Baltimore, MD 21201-2436
410-361-1083
FAX: 410-528-4452 800-222-3790
J. Andrew Bradley, Editor
Mark A Hardy, Editor
Jim Mulligan, Publisher
Taron Buttler, National Sales Manager
Jeff Hargrove, Manager *$657.00*

Circulation: 2556

11859 Urologic Nursing
Society of Urologic Nurses and Associates
East Holly Avenue
PO Box 56
Pitman, NJ 08071
856-256-2300
FAX: 856-589-7463
uronsg@ajj.com http://www.suna.org
Nancy Mueller, President
Robert McIlvaine, Circulation Manager
Mike Cunningham, Marketing
Jane Hokanson Hawks, Editor
Anthony Jannetti, Publisher *$40.00*
Founded: 1981
Circulation: 4500 2,700 names $600 per M.

Printed in 4 colors on glossy stock

11860 Virology
125 Park Avenue
23rd Floor
New York, NY 10017
212-309-5498
FAX: 212-309-5480 800-821-5068
d.weerd@elsevier.com
http://www.reed-elsevier.com/
A Pinczuk, Editor-in-Chief
Karlyn Messinger, Communications Manager *$139.00*
Monthly Founded: 1993
Circulation: 280

11861 Volunteer
119 W 24th Street
9th Floor
New York, NY 10011-1913
212-870-4940
FAX: 212-367-1236
Esperanza Jorge-Garcia, Executive Director

11862 Walgreens Diabetes & You
Drug Store News Consumer Health Publications
425 Park Avenue
New York, NY 10022
212-565-5220

jtanzola@lf.com
http://www.consumerhealthpubs.com
John Tanzola, National Sales Manager
Edward H King, Director
Contains health news of importance to those with diabetes.

Circulation: 1.1 mill

11863 World Disease Weekly
2900 Paces Ferry Road
Bldg D 2nd Floor
Atlanta, GA 30339
770-507-7777
FAX: 770-435-6800 800-726-4550
$2329.00
Weekly Founded: 1984

11864 today's surgicenter
Virgo Publishing
3300 N Central Avenue, Suite 300
Phoenix, AZ 85012
480-990-1101
FAX: 480-675-8154
asharman@vpico.com
www.surgicenteronline.com
Peggy Jackson, Publisher
Kelly Pyrek, Editor
Business and clinical solutions for ambulatory surgery centers. It covers the industry-altering shift from inpatient care to outpatient care, documents trends in development and operations of such centers, shortstay facilities, surgical hospitals and hospital outpatient facilities.
50 pages Monthly Founded: 2001
Circulation: 22000+
Mailing list available for rent 22000+ names $var per M.
Printed in 4 colors on glossy stock

Trade Shows

11865 AAAAI Annual Conference and Exhibition
American Academy Allergy, Asthma, and Immunology
555 E Wells Street
Suite 100
Milwaukee, WI 53202
414-272-6071
FAX: 414-272-6070 800-822-2762
info@aaaai.org www.aaaai.org
Katie Ferguson, Sr. Meetings Manager
Exhibits, pharmaceuticals, medical supplies and books.
7000 Attendees Annual/Feb 23-27 7987 names $N/A per M.

11866 AAHP Institute & Display Forum
American Association of Health Plans
1129 20th Street NW
Washington, DC 20036
202-778-3200
FAX: 202-778-8506

11867 AARC International Respiratory Congress
American Association for Respiratory Care
9425 N MacArthur Boulevard
Suite 100
Irving, TX 75063
972-243-2272
FAX: 972-484-2720
info@aarc.org www.aarc.org
Annette Phillips, Exhibits Coordinator
Sam Giordano, Executive Director
Largest respiratory care meeting in the world. Offers the latest information in all aspects of respiratory care. The congress offers you an opportunity to earn all the continuing education hours required for your state license annually.
7000 Attendees December Founded: 1947

11868 ABRF
FASEB/OSMC
9650 Rockville Pike
Bethesda, MD 20814
301-634-7100
FAX: 301-634-7014
www.faseb.org/meetings
Jean Lash, Exhibit Manager
Marcella Jackson, Show Manager
900 Attendees March

11869 ACOFP Convention & Scientific Seminar
American College of Osteopathic Family Physicians
330 E Algonquin Road
Arlington Heights, IL 60005
847-228-6090
FAX: 800-323-0794
2500 Attendees

11870 AMGA's Annual Conference
American Medical Group Association
1422 Duke Street
Alexandria, VA 22314
703-838-0033
FAX: 703-548-1890
fhaag@amga.org www.amga.org
Fred Haag, VP
Brings together physician and nonphysician executives from the nation's leading health care organizations, medical groups and physician owned and operated IPAs. It offers both an interactive exhibit area and a relaxed environment for meeting one-on-one with management from the nation's leading health care organizations. National conference dedicated to leadership development in multispecialty medical groups.
1100+ Attendees March 1-3, Arizona
Founded: 1949
Mailing list available for rent 600 names

11871 AORN Congress
Association of PeriOperative Registered Nurses
2170 S Parker Road
Suite 300
Denver, CO 80231-5711
303-755-6300
FAX: 303-755-4511 800-755-2676
clindmar@aorn.com www.aorn.org
Garth Jordan, VP Marketing/Business
Lori Ropa, Manager
Surgical tradeshow featuring medical devices and supplies for the operating room and facilities recruiting for open OR nursing positions.
7000 Attendees Annual Founded: 1954
4,500 names $750 per M.

11872 AORN World Conference of Perioperative Nurses
2170 S Parker Road
Suite 300
Denver, CO 80231-5711
303-755-6300
FAX: 303-755-5411 www.aorn.org
Christine Lindmark, Exhibits Director
Lori Ropa, Manager
Seminar and 82 equipment & supplies displays used in operating room suites, and pre-surgical areas.
2500 Attendees Biennial Founded: 1978

11873 APTA Scientific Meeting & Exposition
American Physical Therapy Association
1111 N Fairfax Street
Alexandria, VA 22314
703-684-2782
FAX: 703-706-3396
Frank Mallon, Chief Executive Officer

11874 ARVO
FASEB/OSMC
9650 Rockville Pike
Bethesda, MD 20814
301-634-7100
FAX: 301-634-7014
www.faseb.org/meetings

11875 ASCRS Symposium & ASOA Congress
American Society of Cataract & Refractive Surgery
American Society of Opthalmic Administrators
4000 Legato Road, # 850
Fairfax, VA 22033-4003
703-912-2220
FAX: 703-591-0614 800-451-1339
ascrs@ascrs.org www.ascrs.org
Jane Krause, Show Manager
Seminar and 700 exhibits of opthalmic related intruments of interest to opthalmologists, administrators, nurses and technicians.
7000 Attendees June Founded: 1986 30000 names $24 per M.

11876 ASHCSP Annual Conference: American Society for Heathcare Central Servi
American Hospital Association
One N Franklin
Chicago, IL 60601
312-422-2000
FAX: 312-422-4572
Conference and exhibition of health care administration supplies and services.

11877 ASHHRA'S Annual Conference & Exposition American Soc'ty Healthcare Hum.Res.
Corcoran Expositions, Inc
100 W Monroe Street
Suite 1001
Chicago, IL 60603
312-541-0567
FAX: 312-541-0573
ricky@corcexpo.com www.ashhra.org
Ricky Iovino, Exhibit Manager
ASHHRA's Annual Conference & Exposition is the opportunity to connect face-to-face with the top human resource executives and decision-makers in the healthcare field. The attendees come from hospital, hospital system, ambulatory care, long-term care and hospice organizations. Attendee job titles include: Chief Human Reosurce Officer; Vice President/Director of Human Resources; Director/Manager of Recruitment, Compensation, Benefits, Organizational Development or Employee Relations
500 Attendees September, Disneyland

11878 ASHP Midyear Clinical Meeting
American Society of Health-System Pharmacists
7272 Wisconsin Avenue
Bethesda, MD 20814-4836
301-657-3000
FAX: 301-657-1641
ipa@ashp.org www.ashp.org
Containing 1,160 booths and 320 exhibits.

11879 ASPRS/PSEF/ASMS Annual Scientific Meeting
American Society of Plastic Surgeons
444 E Algonquin Road
Arlington Heights, IL 60005
847-228-9900
FAX: 847-228-9131 888-475-2784
webmaster@plasticsurgery.org
www.plasticsurgery.org
Bonnie Burkoth, Exhibit Manager
Close to four hundred exhibits of plastic surgery products, patient education and software to assist plastic surgeons, nurses and paramedical staff.
4000 Attendees October 6-11, 2006
Mailing list available for rent $750 per M.

11880 ASRA Annual Fall Meeting on Pain
Amer. Soc. of Regional Anesthesia & Pain Medicine
2209 Dickens Road
PO Box 11086
Richmond, VA 23116
804-532-2323
FAX: 804-282-0090
exhibits@societyhq.com
www.societyhq.com/exhibitors
Matt Van Wie, Show Manager
Nidal Amro, Manager
Exhibits of anethesia and pain equipment, information, supplies and services, conference, meals, breaks, sponsorships available.
400 Attendees November 7,000 names $1M per M.

11881 ASRA Annual Spring Meeting and Workshops
Amer. Soc. of Regional Anesthesia & Pain Medicine
2209 Dickens Road
PO Box 11086
Richmond, VA 23116
804-532-2323
FAX: 804-282-0090
exhibits@societyhq.com
www.societyhq.com/exhibitors
Matt Van Wie, Show Manager
Nidal Amro, Manager
Exhibits of anethesia and pain equipment, information, supplies and services, conference, meals, breaks, sponsorships available.
400 Attendees March 7,000 names $1M per M.

11882 Academy of General Dentistry Annual Meeting
Academy of General Dentistry
211 E Chicago Avenue
Suite 900
Chicago, IL 60611
312-440-4300
FAX: 312-440-0559 888-243-3368
agd.dented@aol.com www.agd.org
Heather Nash CMP, Director Meetings
Jay Donohue, Executive Director
Educational session and over 225 dental manufacturers and supplier exhibits. Attended by dentists and the general public.
5000 Attendees Annual Founded: 1954

11883 Academy of Osseointegration Convention
Smith, Bucklin and Associates
401 N Michigan Avenue
Chicago, IL 60611-4267
312-644-6610
FAX: 312-245-1082
Sandy Reynolds, Convention Manager
Osseointegration medical exhibition.

11884 Adult Day Services Exposition
VNU Expositions
Dulles International Airport
PO Box 17413
Washington, DC 20041
703-318-0300
FAX: 703-318-8833 800-765-7616
lhoffman@billexpo.com
www.vnuexpo.com
Luellen Hoffman, Show Director
Adult/geriatric health care professionals gather to see exhibits of equipment, supplies, services and consulting for those who represent senior centers, adult day centers, nursing homes, hospitals and other health care markets.
300 Attendees Annual

11885 Aerospace Medical Association Annual Scientific Meeting
Aerospace Medical Association
320 S Henry Street
Alexandria, VA 22314-3579
703-739-2240
FAX: 703-739-9652 www.asma.org
Russell B Rayman MD, Executive Director
Gloria Carter, Membership Director
Pamela Day, Managing Editor
Annual show of 50-90 exhibitors for aviation medical examiners, scientists and bioengineers engaged in biomedical research, physicians and nurses of Aerospace Medical Association.

Mailing list available for rent 3000 names

11886 Air Medical Transport Conference
Association of Air Medical Services
526 King Street
Sutie 415
Alexandria, VA 22314-3143
703-836-8732
FAX: 703-836-8920
information@aams.org www.aams.org
Johanna VanArsdall, Education/Meetings Manager
Blair Marie Kelly, Commuications/Marketing Director
Andy Papovie, Member Serives Coordinator
Annual exhibit of air medical transport equipment, supplies and services.

1500 Attendees November

11887 AmSECT International Conference
American Society of Extra-Corporeal Technology
503 Carlise Drive
Suite 125
Herndon, VA 20170
703-435-8556
FAX: 703-435-0056 www.amsect.org
Heart and lung machine technology.
1200 Attendees

11888 American Academy for Cerebral Palsy and Developmental Medicine Meeting
Amer. Academy for Cerebral Palsy/Dev. Medicine
555 E Wells St
Ste 1100
Milwaukee, WI 53202-3800
414-918-3014
FAX: 414-276-2146
king@aaos.org www.aacpdm.org
Mary Gebhardt, Society Coordinator
Seminar, luncheon and 35 exhibitors with publications, wheelchairs, rehabilitation products and communication aids.
800 Attendees September-October

11889 American Academy of Dermatology Annual Meeting
American Academy of Dermatology
930 N Meacham Road
PO Box 4014
Shaumburg, IL 60168-4014
708-330-1090
FAX: 708-330-1090
Seven hundred exhibits from 300 technical companies relating to skin care, professional and scientific organizations.
Annual Founded: 1940

11890 American Academy of Environmental Medicine Conference
American Academy of Environmental Medicine
7701 E Kellog
Suite 625
Wichita, KS 67207-1705
316-684-5500
FAX: 316-684-5709
centraloffice@aaem.com
www.aaem.com
D E Rodgers, Executive Director
Environmental medicine equipment, supplies and services of interest to physicans.
175 Attendees October

11891 American Academy of Family Physicians Scientific Assembly
American Academy of Family Physicians
11400 Tomahawk Creek Parkway
Leawood, KS 66211-2672
913-906-6000
FAX: 913-906-6082 800-274-2237
sbiggs@aafp.org www.aafp.org
Sondra Biggs CMP, Meetings/Convention Director
20000 Attendees Annual

11892 American Academy of Fixed Prosthodontics Scientific Session
American Academy of Fixed Prosthodontics
PO Box 1409
Bodega Bay, CA 94923
707-875-3040
FAX: 707-875-2927 800-860-5633
secaafp@comcast.net
www.fixedprosthodontics.org
Dr. Robert Staffanou, Secretary
Dr. Don Garver, Treasurer/Meeting Site Director
Thirty-two exhibits of prosthodontics equipment, supplies and services. Luncheon and meeting.
800 Attendees Annual Feb. 23-24 Founded: 1951

11893 American Academy of Forensic Sciences Annual Meeting
American Academy of Forensic Sciences
410 N 21st St
Colorado Springs, CO 80904-2712
719-636-1100
FAX: 719-636-1993
membship@aafs.org www.aafs.org
Anne Warren, Executive Director
Kemberly Wrasse, Membership Services
Professionals in the forensic science field attend meeting and see 120 exhibits of scientific instruments.
2300 Attendees Annual

11894 American Academy of Implant Dentistry Annual Meeting
American Academy of Implant Dentistry
211 E Chicago Avenue
Suite 750
Chicago, IL 60611
312-335-1550
FAX: 312-335-9090
aaid@aaid-implant.org
www.aaid-implant.org
J Vincent Shock, Executive Director
Eighty exhibitors with dental equipment, supplies and services. Dental professionals attend free seminar, conference and workshop.
600 Attendees Annual Founded: 1955

11895 American Academy of Neurology: Annual Meeting
American Academy of Neurology
1080 Montreal Avenue
Suite 335
Saint Paul, MN 55116-2325
651-951-1940
FAX: 651-695-2791 800-879-1960
aan@aan.com www.aanos.org
Judy Larson
One hundred and seventy-four publishers, pharmaceutical companies, and related suppliers have exibits, along with the seminar, workshop, banquet and reception.
6500 Attendees Annual, August

11896 American Academy of Ophthalmology Annual Meeting
American Academy of Ophthalmology
655 Beach Street
San Francisco, CA 94109
415-618-8500
FAX: 415-561-8576
meetings@aao.org www.aao.org
Karen Cristello, Promotions Coordinator
Dunbar Hoskins, Executive VP
25000 Attendees November Founded: 1896

11897 American Academy of Optometry Annual Meeting
American Academy of Optometry
6110 Executive Boulevard
Suite 506
Rockville, MD 20910
301-984-1441
FAX: 301-984-4737 aaoptom@aol.com
Lisa M Watson CMP, Director Education
Two hundred exhibits focusing on the latest patient treatment and research. Workshop and banquet.
4000 Attendees Annual

11898 American Academy of Oral and Maxillofacial Radiology Annual Session
American Academy of Oral & Maxillofacial Radiology
PO Box 55722
Jackson, MS 39296
601-984-6060
FAX: 601-984-6086
mocarroll@sod.umsmed.edu
www.aaomr.org
Dr M Kevin O'Carroll, Executive Secretary
Over 20 exhibits relating to dental radiology, equipment, software and accessories.
120 Attendees November Founded: 1949

11899 American Academy of Orofacial Pain Annual Scientific Meeting
American Academy of Orofacial Pain
19 Mantua Road
Mount Royal, NJ 00861
856-233-3629
FAX: 856-423-3420
dblackmore@tmg.smarthub.com
Donna Blackmore, Manager Meetings
Bob Talley, President
Ten exhibits relating to orofacial pain and temporomandibular disorders. Medical and dental doctors attend meeting, luncheon, tours and a reception.
350 Attendees Annual

11900 American Academy of Orthopedic Surgeons Annual Meeting
American Academy of Orthopedic Surgeons
6300 N River Road
Rosemont, IL 60018-4262
847-823-7186
FAX: 847-323-8031
tomala@aaos.org www.aaos.org
Stuart L Weinstein, President
Richard F Kyle, First VP
Karen Hackett, Chief Executive Officer
Three hundred and fifty-five exhibits of surgical equipment, supplies and services used by the orthopedic professional.
28000 Attendees Annual Founded: 1933

11901 American Academy of Otolaryngology Mid-Winter Meeting
American Academy of Otolaryngology-Head & Neck
19 Mantua Road
Mt. Royal, NJ 08061
856-423-0041
headquarters@aro.org www.aro.org
Darla Dobson, Executive Director
Over 300 exhibits of otolaryngology, diseases of the ear, nose and throat, head and neck surgery equipment, supplies and services plus seminar.

9000+ Attendees February Founded: 1896

11902 American Academy of Pain Medicine Annual Conference and Review Course
American Academy of Pain Medicine
4700 Lake Avenue
Glenview, IL 60025
847-375-4731
FAX: 847-375-4777
aapm@amctec.com www.painmed.org
Meeting and exhibits relating to pain medicine, particularly related socioeconomic and governmental issues.
Annual

11903 American Academy of Pediatric Dentistry Annual Meeting
American Academy of Pediatric Dentistry
211 E Chicago Avenue
Suite 700
Chicago, IL 60611
312-337-2169
FAX: 312-337-6329
aapoinfo@aapd.org www.aapo.org
Catherine Hay, Meetings & Program Manager
Gauri Patel, Meeting Associate
John Rutkauskas, Executive Director
Seventy-five to 100 displays of dental products and publications.
2500 Attendees May Founded: 1948

11904 American Academy of Pediatrics Annual Meeting
American Academy of Pediatrics
141 NW Point Boulevard
Elk Grove Village, IL 60009
847-434-4000
FAX: 847-434-8000
kidsdocs@aap.org www.aap.org
E Stephen Edwards MD FAAP, President
Joe M Sanders Jr, MD FAAP, Executive Director
Joann Barbour, Manager
Three hundred and fifty exhibits relating to prescription and over the counter drugs, infant formulas medical equipment and publications. Reception, tours and meeting.
10000 Attendees Annual

11905 American Academy of Periodontology Annual Meeting & Exhibition
American Academy of Periodontology
737 N Michigan Avenue
Suite 800
Chicago, IL 60611
312-787-5518
FAX: 312-573-3225 www.perio.org
Melody Anderson, Meetings Manager
Alice Deforest, Executive Director
Two hundred and seventy-five exhibits of products and services relating to periodontics, including dental instruments, literature, X-ray equipment, furniture, software and more.
5800 Attendees Annual Founded: 1914

11906 American Academy of Physical Medicine and Rehabilitation Annual Meeting
American Academy of Physical Medicine & Rehab
1 IBM Plaza
Suite 2500
Chicago, IL 60611-3514
312-464-9700
FAX: 312-464-0227
cmason@aapmr.org www.aapmr.org
Cathy Mason, Director Meetings
Ronald Henrichs, Executive Director
One hundred and twenty-five exhibitors representing pharmceutical companies, diagnostics, rehabilitation equipment manufacturers and more.
2500 Attendees Annual, November Founded: 1938

11907 American Academy of Professional Coders The Spirit of Coding
2480 South 3850 West
Suite B
Salt Lake City, UT 84120
FAX: 801-236-2258 800-626-2633
traci.wood@aapc.com www.aapc.com
Traci Wood, Marketing Coordinator
April 15-18, Seattle

11908 American Alliance for Health, Phys Ed, Rec reation & Dance Conference & Expo
American Alliance for Hlth. Phys. Edu. Rec. Dance
1900 Association Drive
Reston, VA 20191-1599
703-476-3400
FAX: 703-476-9527 800-213-7193
conv@aahperd.org www.aah-perd.org
Harve Horowitz, Show Manager
Michael Davis, Manager
Two hundred and eighty exhibits concerning physical education, sporting goods, supplies, equipment, service and organization representatives.
7000 Attendees Annual

11909 American Ambulance Association Annual Conference & Trade Show
Executive Management Services
1255 23rd Street NWrd
Suite 200
Washington, DC 20037
202-213-3999
FAX: 202-452-0005 800-523-4447
aaa911@the-aaa.org www.the-aaa.org
David Saunders, Executive Director
6100 Attendees Annual, October

11910 American Association for Continuity of Care Annual Conference
American Association for Continuity of Care
638 Prospect Avenue
Hartford, CT 06105-4250
860-867-7525
FAX: 203-586-7550
Ipiorek@csunet.ctstateu.edu
Seminar, reception and 35 exhibits of suppliers of health care delivery resources, products and services.
Annual Founded: 1982

11911 American Association for Laboratory Animal Science National Meeting
American Association for Laboratory Animal Science
9190 Crestwyn Hills Drive
Memphis, TN 38125
901-754-8620
FAX: 901-753-0046
info@aalas.org www.aalas.org
Ann Turner, Executive Director
Two-hundred and seventy exhibits of pharmaceuticals and laboratory animal supplies.
4,500 Attendees October

11912 American Association for Medical Transcription Annual Meeting
PO Box 576187
Modesto, CA 95357-6187
209-551-0883
FAX: 209-551-9317 800-982-2182
aamt@sns.com www.aamt.org
Daryl Ochs, Director Marketing
Exhibitors are medical transcription businesses, hardware, software, publishers and services.
750 Attendees Annual Founded: 1978

11913 American Association for Thoracic Surgery Annual Meeting
American Association for Thoracic Surgery
900 Cummings Center
Suite 221-U
Beverly, MA 01915
978-526-8330
FAX: 978-524-8890
aats@prri.com www.aats.org
Bob Jones, Executive Director
Yvonne Grunebaum, Director Exhibits
Scientific meeting.
5000 Attendees Annual Founded: 1917

11914 American Association for the Study of Headache Meeting
19 Mantua Road
Mount Royal, NJ 08061
609-845-0322
FAX: 609-384-5811
Twenty-five exhibits of research equipment supplies, and services related to headache study.
650 Attendees Annual Founded: 1958

11915 American Association of Nurse Anesthetists Midyear Assembly
222 S Prospect Avenue
Park Ridge, IL 60068-4001
847-927-7055
FAX: 847-692-6968
meetings@aana.com www.aana.com
Exhibits relating to nurse anesthetists.
350 Attendees

11916 American Association of Bioanalysts Annual Meeting & Conference
American Association of Bioanalysts
917 Locust Street
Suite 1100
Saint Louis, MO 63101-1419
314-241-1445
FAX: 314-241-1449 aab@aab.org
Mark S Biernbaum PhD, Show Manager
Assembles clinical laboratory directors, managers, supervisors, medical laboratory technologists, technicans for technical and managerial educational sessions and workshops. 5-10 booths.
350 Attendees April

11917 American Association of Blood Banks Annual Meeting
American Association of Blood Banks
8101 Glenbrook Road
Bethesda, MD 20814-2749
301-907-6977
FAX: 301-951-3425
meeting@aabb.org www.aabb.org
Phyllis Brashears, Manager Meetings
Four hundred and eighty-nine exhibits relating to blood banking and transfusion medicine, gloves, donor coaches, chairs and

equipment. Seminar, workshop and banquet.
7500 Attendees November Founded: 1947

11918 **American Association of Cardiovascular & Pulmonary Rehabilitation Conf.**
American Assoc of Cardiovascular & Pulmonary Rehab
7611 Elmwood Avenue
Suite 201
Middleton, WI 53562
608-316-6989
FAX: 608-831-5122
aacvpr@tmahq.com www.aacvpr.org
Sheil Kirshbaum, Director Meetings
Seminar and workshop, plus 70 exhibits of cardiovascular and pulmonary rehabilitation equipment, supplies and services.
1800 Attendees Annual Founded: 1985

11919 **American Association of Clinical Endocrino logists Congress**
American Association of Clinical Endocrinologists
1000 Riverside Avenue
Suite 205
Jacksonville, FL 32204
904-353-7878
FAX: 904-353-8185 www.aace.com
Hossein Gharib MD, President
Donald Jones, Chief Executive Officer
John B Tourtelot MD, Membership Chairman
Clinical endocrinologists and endocrine surgeons gather for meeting and exhibits of equipment, supplies and services.
May

11920 **American Association of Diabetes Educators Annual Meeting & Educational Prog.**
American Association of Diabetes Educators
100 W Monroe
Chicago, IL 60603
312-424-2426
FAX: 312-424-2427 800-338-3633
Christopher Laxton, Executive Director
Six hundred exhibits of dietary food and beverages, testing and screening tools, educational programs and publications. Banquet and reception available.

Mailing list available for rent 10000 names $160 per M.

11921 **American Association of Electrodiagnostic Medicine Meeting**
American Association of Electrodiagnostic Medicine
421 1st Avenue SW
Suite 300E
Rochester, MN 55902-3018
507-288-0100
FAX: 507-288-1225
aaem@aaem.net www.aaem.net
Kathy Smith, Meeting Operator
Shirlyn Adkins, Executive Director
Forty exhibits of electromyographic and electrodiagnosis equipment and accessories. Seminar, workshop and breakfast.
1000 Attendees

11922 **American Association of Homes and Services for the Aging Convention**
American Association of Homes and Services/Aging
901 E Street NW
Suite 500
Washington, DC 20004-2037
202-661-5700
FAX: 202-783-2255
mraynor@aahsa.org www.aahsa.org
Daniel Smith, VP
Mary-Louise Raynor, Director
One thousand eight hundred exhibitors of equipment, supplies and services for housing and long term care facilities for the aged, conference and tours.
4000 Attendees Annual Founded: 1980

11923 **American Association of Immunologists Annual Meeting**
American Association of Immunologists
9650 Rockville Pike
Bethesda, MD 20814
301-530-7178
FAX: 301-571-1816
infoaai@aai.faseb.org www.aai.org
Exhibits related to immunological research, equipment and supplies.
10000 Attendees April 6000 names

11924 **American Association of Managed Care Nurses Annual Conference**
American Association of Managed Care Nurses
4435 Waterfront Drive
Suite 101
Glen Allen, VA 23060
804-747-9698
FAX: 804-747-5316
amason@aamcn.org www.aamcn.org
Andrea Mason, Executive Administrator
Katie Eads, VP Education
William Williams, Manager
The AAMCN Annual Conference is designed to provide registered nurses, licensed practical nurses, advanced practice, executive nurses and other healthcare professionals with current information they can use to influence their marketplace.

11925 **American Association of Medical Assistants National Convention**
American Association of Medical Assistants
20 N Wacker Drive
Suite 1575
Chicago, IL 60606-2963
312-899-1500
FAX: 312-899-1259 800-228-2262
dknight@aama-ntl.org
www.aama-ntl.org
Don Balasa, Executive Director
David V Knight, Director
Main exhibits, data processing equipment, pharmaceuticals, publications, insurance services, text books, coding system reference guides, health care services and more.

500 Attendees Annual

11926 **American Association of Naturopathic Physicians Convention**
601 Valley Street
Suite 105
Seattle, WA 98109
206-298-0126
FAX: 206-298-0129
www.naturopathic.org
One hundred and twenty exhibits of Naturopathic medicine, supplies and services plus conference and banquet.
750 Attendees Annual Founded: 1986

11927 **American Association of Neurological Surgeons Annual Meeting**
American Association of Neurologists
22 S Washington Street
Park Ridge, IL 60068
847-378-0500
FAX: 847-692-2589
info@aans.org www.aans.org
Two hundred manufacturers and suppliers have 500 booths of equipment, publications and supplies.
2400 Attendees Annual

11928 **American Association of Neuroscience Nurses Convention**
224 N Des Plaines
#601
Chicago, IL 60661
312-258-1200
FAX: 312-993-0362 800-477-2266
tjodowd@aol.com www.aann.org
Thomas O'Dowd, Manager Meetings
Sixty exhibits of nuerological and neurosurgical supplies, services and industry related recruiters.
900 Attendees Annual Founded: 1968

11929 **American Association of Nurse Anesthetists Annual Meeting**
222 S Prospect Avenue
Park Ridge, IL 60068-4001
847-985-5400
FAX: 847-692-6968
meetings@aana.com www.aana.com
Cindy Wood, Director Programs
325 exhibits of equipment, supplies, publications and recruiters. Seminar and workshop, as well as a banquet.
3500 Attendees

11930 **American Association of Nurse Anesthetists Assembly of School Faculty**
222 S Prospect Avenue
Park Ridge, IL 60068-4001
847-927-7055
FAX: 847-692-6968
meetings@aana.com www.aana.com
Nurse anesthetist related exhibits
250 Attendees Annual

11931 **American Association of Office Nurses Annual Meeting & Convention**
52 Park Avenue
Suite B4
Park Ridge, NJ 07656
201-391-2600
FAX: 201-573-8543 800-457-7504
aanonmail@aanon.org
www.aanon.org
Michelle Aronowitz, Managing Director
Sherry Levy, Associate Managing Director
American Association of Office Nurses annual meeting and convention at the Eden Roc Hotel in Miami Beach, Florida.
150 Attendees Sept 29-Oct 2, 2005
Founded: 1988

11932 American Association of Oral & Maxillofaci al Surgeons Scientific Meeting
American Assn. of Oral & Maxillofacial Surgeons
9700 W Bryn Mawr Avenue
Rosemont, IL 60018-5701
847-678-6200
FAX: 847-678-6286 800-822-6637
inquiries@aaoms.org www.aaoms.org
Teri Jarrie, Manager
Kim Peterman, Manager
Educational session, reception, tours. Over 275 exhibits relating to the profession.
4000 Attendees Annual Founded: 1918

11933 American Association of Orthodontists Trade Show and Scientific Session
401 N Lindbergh Boulevard
Saint Louis, MO 63141-7816
314-993-1700
FAX: 314-997-1745
aao@worldnet.att.net
www.aaortho.org
Chris Varanas, Manager
Five hundred and fifty exhibits of orthodontic equipment, publications, supplies and services.
9000 Attendees Annual

11934 American Association of Physician Speciali sts Annual Scientific Meeting
2296 Henderson Mill Road
Suite 206
Atlanta, GA 30345
770-939-8555
FAX: 770-939-8559
khaouhton@aapsga.org
www.aapsga.com
Kimberly Haughton, Director/Programs/CME
Sharita Morse, Programs/CME Coordinator
William Carbone, Manager
Conference, banquet and luncheon plus pharmaceutical, medical and equipment exhibits.
1000 Attendees

11935 American Association of Suicidology Conference
4201 Connecticut Avenue NW
Suite 408
Washington, DC 20008
202-237-2280
FAX: 202-237-2282
www.suicidology.org
Alan Berman PhD, Executive Director
Exhibits relating to the advancement of studies to prevent suicide and life threatening behavior.
Annual Founded: 1969

11936 American Association of Tissue Banks Meeting
1350 Beverly Road
Suite 220-A
Mc Lean, VA 22101-2198
703-442-8088
FAX: 703-356-2198
Exhibits for the revival, preservation, storage, and distribution of tissues for transplantation.

11937 American Association on Mental Retardation Annual Meeting
444 N Capitol Street
Suite 846
Washington, DC 20001-1512
202-387-1968
FAX: 202-387-2193 800-424-3688
aamr@aamr.org www.aamr.org
Doreen Croser, Executive Director
Paula A Hirt, Programs Director
2000 Attendees Founded: 1876

11938 American Chiropractic Association Annual Convention and Exhibition
1701 Clarendon Boulevard
Arlington, VA 22209
703-276-8800
FAX: 703-243-2593 800-986-4636
Kevin Corcoran, VP
Fifty displays of chiropractic tables and products, mattress companies, nutritional supplements, computer software, services and supplies.
500 Attendees Annual Founded: 1963

11939 American Cleft Palate Craniofacial Association Annual Meeting
104 S Estes Drive
Suite 204
Chapel Hill, NC 27514
919-933-9044
FAX: 919-933-9604
meetings@acpa-cpf.org
www.acpa-cpf.org
Kathy Bogie, Manager Meetings
Nancy Smythe, Executive Director
Scientific meeting.
600 Attendees March Founded: 1943

11940 American Clinical Neurophysiology Society Convention
1 Regency Drive
PO Box 30
Bloomfield, CT 06002
860-447-9408
FAX: 860-286-0787
Jacquelyn Coleman, Executive Director
Over 40 exhibits of electroencephalographic and neurophysiology equipment, seminar, workshop and conference.
400 Attendees Annual Founded: 1946

11941 American College Health Association Trade Show
American College Health Association
PO Box 28937
Baltimore, MD 21240
410-859-1500
FAX: 410-859-1510
cperez@acha.org www.acha.org
Cynthia Perez, Trade Show Program Coordinator
Doreen A Perez, President
Over 85 exhibits of pharmaceuticals, insurance plans, laboratory services, medical equipment, publications and more. Tours and breakfast.
1800 Attendees Annual Founded: 1922

11942 American College of Allergy, Asthma and Immunology Annual Meeting
85 West Algonquin Road
#550
Arlington Heights, IL 60005-4460
847-427-1200
FAX: 847-427-1294
diannekubis@acaai.org www.acaai.org
Dianne K Kubis, Exhibition Manager
2006 Annual Meeting will be held November 9-15 in Philadelpia, Pennsylvania
November Founded: 1942
Mailing list available for rent 4500 names $100 per M.

11943 American College of Angiology Conference
295 Northern Boulevard
Suite 104
Great Neck, NY 11021-4701
516-466-4055
FAX: 516-466-4099
joan.shaffer@collegeangiology.org
www.collegeofangiology.org
Joan Shaffer, Executive Director
CME Seminars and 50 exhibits from commercial and scientific suppliers.
300 Attendees October Founded: 1954

11944 American College of Cardiology Annual Scientific Session
American College of Cardiology
9111 Old Georgetown Road
Bethesda, MD 20814-1699
301-897-5400
FAX: 301-897-9745 800-253-4636
jmiller@acc.org www.acc.org
Christine McEntee, Chief Executive Officer
Julie Miller, Assistant Professor of Medicine
Seminar, workshop, dinner and 385 exhibits of products, supplies and services related to cardiovascular medicine.
30000 Attendees

11945 American College of Cardiovascular Adminis trators Leadership Conference
American Academy of Medical Administrators
701 Lee Street
Suite 600
Des Plaines, IL 60016
847-759-8601
FAX: 847-759-8602
info@aameda.org www.ammeda.org
Holly Estal Ed M, Director Education
Gen Hedland, Manager of Exhibits
Featuring keynote and concurrent sessions on human relations, finance and business developments, CV program development technology plus exhibitors that include the latest technological and innovative systems and products in cardiovascular health care. There are 30-40 booths.
300 Attendees March
Mailing list available for rent 3,000 names $150 per M.

11946 American College of Emergency Physicians Scientific Assembly
American College of Emergency Physicians
PO Box 619911
Dallas, TX 75261-9911
972-550-0911
FAX: 972-580-2816 800-798-1822
dbellantone@acep.org www.acep.org
Dana Bellantone, Manager Meetings
Five hundred and twenty-five exhibits of products and services related to emergency medicine.
4400 Attendees Annual Founded: 1972

11947 **American College of Medical Quality Annual Meeting**
4334 Montgomerey Avenue
2nd Floor
Bethesda, MD 20814-4402
301-913-9149
FAX: 301-913-9142 800-924-2149
acmq@aol.com www.acmq.org
Bridget Brodie, Executive Director
Seminar, reception and exhibits of computer hardware and software, publications, phamaceuticals and supplies. Medical professionals and others involved in quality assurance and utilization review and risk management attend.
150 Attendees Founded: 1973

11948 **American College of Nurse Practitioners**
J Spargo & Associates
11208 Waples Mill Road
Suite 112
Fairfax, VA 22030
703-631-6200
FAX: 703-654-6931 800-564-4220
acnp@jspargo.com www.afcea.org
June LaMountain, Exhibit Sales Account Manager
The premier educational offering for nurse practitioners. It offers the opportunity to earn a full scope of continuing education contact hours at sessions led by top clinical experts in many areas.
1200 Attendees October

11949 **American College of Obstetricians and Gynecologists Clinical Meeting/Expo**
American College of Obstetricians
409 12th Street SW
Washington, DC 20024
202-857-3288
FAX: 202-484-3933
Prioffessionally related exhibits.

11950 **American College of Oral and Maxillofacial Surgeons Annual Conference**
100 NW Loop 410
Suite 420
San Antonio, TX 78213
210-344-5674
FAX: 210-344-9754 800-522-6676
director@acoms.org or
admin@acoms.org www.acoms.org
Daniel A Lanka, Executive Director ACOMS
Katrina Rohrmeier, Administrative Assistant
Fifty exhibits for oral and maxillofacial surgery.
250 Attendees Annual 2,331 names $250 per M.

11951 **American College of Physicians Annual Convention**
American College of Physicians
Independence Mall W
6th Street & Race
Philadelphia, PA 19106
215-351-2400
John Tooker, Chief Executive Officer
Five hundred exhibits of medical supplies and services, as well as a seminar.
8000 Attendees

11952 **American College of Rheumatology Scientific Meeting**
Slack
6900 Grove Road
Thorofare, NJ 08086
856-848-1000
FAX: 856-848-3522
Peter Slack, President
Two hundred and ten exhibits of diagnostic testing kits, pharmaceuticals, equipment and supplies, of interest to professionals in Rheumatology.
4500 Attendees Annual Founded: 1934

11953 **American College of Surgeons Annual Clinical Congress**
American College of Surgeons
633 N Saint Clair Street
Chicago, IL 60611
312-202-5000
FAX: 312-440-7143
postmaster@facs.org www.facs.org
Felix P Niespodziewanski, Conventions Manager
Thomas Russell, Executive Director
One thousand one hundred exhibits of medical and patient care products, equipment and supplies. Conference, seminar and workshop, as well as luncheon and tours.
10000 Attendees Annual Founded: 1914

11954 **American College of Surgeons Annual Spring Meeting**
American College of Surgeons
55 E Erie
Chicago, IL 60611
312-202-5000
FAX: 312-440-7143
2000 Attendees

11955 **American Congress of Rehabilitation Medicine Annual Meeting**
6801 Lake Plaza Drive
Suite B- 205
Indianapolis, IN 46220
317-915-2250
FAX: 317-915-2245
acrm@acrm.org www.acrm.org
Richard D Morgan, Executive Director
Seminar, workshop and conference with 20 exhibits of rehabilitation supplies and equipment.
250 Attendees September/October Founded: 1923
Mailing list available for rent 750 names $275 per M.

11956 **American Dental Association Annual Session & Technical Exhibition**
211 E Chicago Avenue
Suite 200
Chicago, IL 60611-2678
312-440-2500
FAX: 312-440-2707
donovanj@ada.org www.ada.org
James P Donovan, Exhibit Manager
Patricia A Johnson, Manager Program Development
Vicki Guinta, Director
James Bramson, Chief Executive Officer
The annual session scientific program consists of over 180 programs, including science of dentistry, practice of dentistry, dental technology and general insterest programs as well as participation workshops. The leading suppliers will showcase their products and services. Dental professionals can compare products, see demonstrations, and make decisions about applying the latest technology. Attendees visiting the Technical Exhibition can also look for the ADA Seal which has long been recognizd
30000 Attendees October

11957 **American Dental Education Association Annual Session and Exposition**
American Dental Education Association
1625 Massachusetts Avenue NW
Washington, DC 20036
202-667-9433
FAX: 202-667-0642 www.adea.org
Kenneth L Kalwarf, President
One hundred commercial and educational exhibits of supplies, video equipment, publications and more.
3000 Attendees Annual Founded: 1983

11958 **American Dental Hygenists Association Conference**
444 N Michigan Avenue
Suite 3400
Chicago, IL 60611
312-440-8900
FAX: 312-440-8929
mail@adha.org www.adha.org
Isaac Carpenter, Executive Director
Kathy Madryk, Marketing Manager
Educational session and 120 exhibits of dental products.
1500 Attendees Annual Founded: 1993

11959 **American Dental Society of Anesthesiology Scientific Meeting**
211 E Chicago Avenue
Suite 948
Chicago, IL 60611
312-664-8270
FAX: 312-642-9713 800-722-7788
R Knight Charlton, Executive Director
Meeting and over 15 exhibits of anesthetics and monitoring equipment.
200 Attendees Annual Founded: 1954

11960 **American Diabetes Association Annual Meeting and Scientific Sessions**
1701 N Beauregard Street
PO Box 25757
Alexandria, VA 22311
703-549-1500
FAX: 703-683-1351 800-676-4065
meetings@diabetes.org
www.afassano.com/ada
Anna Fassano, Director Exhibits
Lynn Nicholas, Chief Executive Officer
Three hundred and fifty exhibits of medical and dietary products and services, seminar and workshop.
June Founded: 1940

11961 **American Health Care Association Annual Convention and Exhibition**
1201 L Street NW
Washington, DC 20005
202-842-4444
FAX: 202-842-3860
abradem@ahca.org www.ahca.org
Dave Kyllo, VP
Three hundred and fifty exhibits of supplies and information for the long term health care industry, banquet, luncheon and tours.
5000 Attendees Annual

11962 **American Health Information Management Association National Convention**
American Health Information Management Association
233 N Michigan Avenue
Suite 2150
Chicago, IL 60601
312-233-1100
FAX: 312-233-1090
wrint@ahima.org www.ahima.org
Erin Toth, Exhibition Manager
Linda Kloss, Executive Director
Five hundred exhibits of interest to health information management professionals, reception.
3500 Attendees Annual Founded: 1928

11963 **American Health Quality Association Annual Session**
1140 Connecticut Avenue NW
Washington, DC 20036
202-331-5790

info@ahqa.org www.ahqa.org
David Thomas MD, President
David Adler, Public Affairs Associate
Quality Improvement Organizations (QIOs) and professionals working to improve the quality of health care in communities across America gather for educational sessions and networking.
March

11964 **American Healthcare Radiology Administrato rs Annual Meeting and Exposition**
490B Boston Post Road
#101
Sudbury, MA 01776
978-443-7591
FAX: 978-443-8046 800-334-2472
info@ahraonline.org www.ahra.com
Edward Cronin, Executive Director
One-hundred and sixty-five exhibits of radiology equipment, supplies and services, including software. Conference, seminar and workshop.
3000 Attendees Annual 7800 names

11965 **American Heart Association Scientific Sessions**
American Heart Association
7272 Greenville Avenue
Dallas, TX 75231
214-736-6300
FAX: 214-373-3406 www.amhrt.org
M Cass Wheeler, Chief Executive Officer
Conference, seminar and tours, plus 325 exhibits relating to exercise, equipment, pharmceuticals and services related to cardiovascular health care.
29000 Attendees

11966 **American Hospital Association Convention**
1 N Franklin Street
Chicago, IL 60606
312-222-2000
FAX: 312-422-4579 www.aha.org
Jeanette Harlow, Executive Director
Lauren Barnett, Director
Exhibits of equipment supplies, and services for the medical, hospital industry.

11967 **American Industrial Hygiene Association Conference and Exposition**
American Industrial Hygiene Association
2700 Prosperity Avenue
Suite 250
Fairfax, VA 22031
703-849-8267
FAX: 703-207-3561
infonet@aiha.org www.aiha.org
Caroline Lacey, Expo Manager
Conference for occupational and environmental health and safety professionals around the globe.
4,000 Attendees Annual

11968 **American Lung Association/American Thoracic Society Int Conference**
1740 Broadway
New York, NY 10019-4374
212-315-8700
FAX: 212-265-5642
John Kirkwood, Chief Executive Officer
Two hundred and fifty exhibits of pharmaceuticals, equipment and books.
8500 Attendees Annual Founded: 1904

11969 **American Medical Directors Association Annual Symposium**
American Medical Directors Association
10480 Little Patuxent Parkway
Suite 760
Columbia, MD 21044
410-951-1240
FAX: 410-740-4572 800-876-2632
mbrey@amda.com www.amda.com
Megan Brey, Director Meetings
Lorraine Tarnove, Manager
Exhibits relating to geriatrics, pharmaceuticals and medical administration of long term care facilities. Long term health care physicians and professionals attend educational sessions, receptions and special events. Spouse/guest program offered.
1400 Attendees April

11970 **American Medical Informatics Association Fall Symposium**
American Medical Informatics Association

4915 Saint Elmo
Suite 401
Bethesda, MD 20814
301-657-1291
FAX: 301-657-1296
Megan Brey, Meeting Coordinator
Karen Greenwood, Manager
One hundred ten commercial and scientific medical informatics software and hardware, supplies and service dealers. Attended by medical professionals and the general public.
2500 Attendees Annual Founded: 1977

11971 **American Medical Student Association Convention**
American Medical Student Association
1902 Association Drive
Reston, VA 20191
703-620-6600
FAX: 703-620-5873 800-767-2266
amsa@amsa.org www.amsa.org
One hundred exhibits relating to medical supplies and equipment, residency programs, physician recruitment and professional associations.
1500 Attendees

11972 **American Medical Technologists Convention**
American Medical Technologists
10700 West Higgins Road
Rosemont, IL 60018
847-823-5169
FAX: 847-823-0458 800-275-1268
dianepowell.amt@juno.com amtc.com
Diane Powell, Show Manager
Forty eight exhibits of clinical laboratory books, supplies and equipment, seminar, workshop, banquet and tours.
600 Attendees Annual Founded: 1939

11973 **American Medical Women's Association Annual Meeting**
801 N Fairfax Street
Suite 400
Alexandria, VA 22314
703-838-0500
FAX: 703-549-3864
gmiller@awma-doc.org
www.awma-doc.org
Gwenn Miller, Meeting Consultant
Seminar, banquet, tours and 60 exhibits of medical equipment, supplies and services.
1000 Attendees Annual Founded: 1915

11974 **American Nephrology Nurses Association Symposium**
Society of Urologic Nurses and Associates

E Holly Avenue
Box 56
Pittman, NJ 08071
856-256-2350
FAX: 609-589-7463
Mike Cunningham, Manager
One hundred fifteen companies have exhibits of equipment, supplies, pharmaceuticals and services for nephrology.
2000 Attendees Annual Founded: 1970

11975 **American Nurses Association Convention**
600 Maryland Avenue SW
Suite 100
Washington, DC 20024-2571
202-651-7000
FAX: 202-651-7003
exhibits@ana.org
www.nursingworld.org
Exhibits of nursing professional equipment, supplies and services.
Annual

11976 **American Occupational Health Conference & Exhibits**
Slack
6900 Grove Road
Thorofare, NJ 08086
856-848-1000
FAX: 856-848-3522
Peter Slack, President
Four hundred exhibits of pharmaceuticals, equipment, software and supplies for health professionals, offices and labs.
4500 Attendees

11977 **American Occupational Therapy Association Annual Conference**
American Occupation Therapy Association

4720 Montgomery Lane
PO Box 31220
Bethesda, MD 20824-1220
301-652-2682
FAX: 301-652-7711
cynthia@aota.org www.aota.org

M Carolyn Baum, President
Lizette Rosales, Manager

7000 Attendees May Founded: 1919

11978 American Optometric Student Association Annual Meeting
243 N Lindbergh Boulevard
Saint Louis, MO 63141
314-991-4100
FAX: 314-991-4101

Michael Jones, Executive Director

Optometry equipment, supplies and services.
Annual

11979 American Organization of Nurse Executives Meeting and Exposition

American Hospital Association
1 N Franklin
Suite 27
Chicago, IL 60606
312-222-2000
312-422-4519
aone@aha.org www.aha.org

Pamela Thompson, Chief Executive Officer

One hundred fifty exhibits of patient care equipment and supplies, computer hardware and software, communications systems and information for the professional in health care.
Annual

11980 American Orthopsychiatric Association Annual Meeting
330 7th Avenue
18th Floor
New York, NY 10001
212-564-5930
FAX: 212-564-6180
amerortho@aol.com

Rachel L MacAulay, Program Associate

Meeting and exhibits by social service agencies, publications, computer software companies and more.
700 Attendees Annual Founded: 1923

11981 American Orthotic & Prosthetic Association on National Assembly
American Orthotic & Prosthetic Association
330 John Carlyle Street
Suite 200
Alexandria, VA 22314
703-367-7116
FAX: 571-431-0899
info@aopanet.org aopanet.org

Tina Moran, Director Meetings and Conventions
Tyler Wilson, Executive Director
Sheila Pasquini, Administrative Assistant

2200 Attendees Annual Founded: 1917

11982 American Osteopathic Association Meeting & Exhibits
American Osteopathic Hospital Association
142 E Ontario Street
Chicago, IL 60611
312-587-3709
FAX: 312-202-8212

John Crosby, Executive Director

Over 25 exhibits of products and services relating to the osteopathic health care industry, including building and finacing, marketing and operations.
500 Attendees Founded: 1983

11983 American Pain Society Scientific Meeting
4700 W Lake Avenue
Glenview, IL 60025
847-375-4715
FAX: 847-975-4777
info@ampainsoc.org
www.ampainsoc.org

Kathryn Checea, Sales Manager
Cathy Underwood, Manager

Seminar, banquet, luncheon, breakfast and 100 exhibits of pharmceutical and medical insturments, medical equipment, products, supplies, services, and alternative delivery systems.
1700 Attendees Annual Founded: 1978

11984 American Physical Therapy Association Annual Conference
American Physical Therapy Association
1111 N Fairfax Street
Alexandria, VA 22314
703-684-2782
FAX: 703-706-8575 800-999-2782
kellyglascoe@apta.org www.apta.org

Kelly Glascoe, Director/Exposition
Frank Mallon, Chief Executive Officer

450 exhibits of physical therapy equipment, supplies and services.
4000 Attendees Annual

11985 American Physical Therapy Association: Private Practice Session
1111 N Fairfax Street
Alexandria, VA 22314
703-684-2782
FAX: 703-706-8575 800-999-2782

Frank Mallon, Chief Executive Officer

Seminar, workshop, dinner and 120 exhibits of physical therapy and rehabilitation equipment, supplies and services.
1200 Attendees Annual Founded: 1983

11986 American Podiatric Medical Association Annual Meeting
9312 Old Georgetown Road
Bethesda, MD 20814
301-719-9200
FAX: 301-530-2752

Anne Martinez CMP, Meetings Administrator

One-hundred and fifty exhibits of medical and laser equipment, supplies and podiatric services.
1,500 Attendees August

11987 American Psychiatric Association Annual Meeting
1400 K Street NW
Washington, DC 20005
202-682-6100
FAX: 202-682-6132
gank@psych.org www.psych.org

Ken Robinson, Manager Meetings

Conference, seminar, workshop and 850 exhibits of computer online service and software, media products, criminal justice, dianostic tools and much more.
18000 Attendees Annual Founded: 1844

11988 American Psychological Association Annual Meeting
American Psychological Association
750 1st Street NE
Washington, DC 20002-4242
202-336-5500
FAX: 202-336-5568 800-374-2721

Norman Anderson, Chief Exceutive Officer

12000 Attendees Annual, August

11989 American Public Health Association Annual Exhibition
American Public Health Association
800 I Street NW
Washington, DC 20001
202-777-2742
FAX: 202-777-2534
lynn.schoen@apha.org www.apha.org

Lynn Schoen, Exhibition Manager
Georges Benjamin, Executive Director

Five-hundred seventy exhibits of medical interest, pharmaceuticals, publishers, educational, governmental, software and more. Seminar and banquet available.
13000 Attendees November

11990 American Roentgen Ray Society Meeting
American Roentgen Ray Society
44211 Slatestone Court
Leesburg, VA 20176
703-729-3353
FAX: 703-729-4839 800-438-2777
info@arrs.org www.arrs.org

Maureen Robertson, Show Manager
Noel Montesa, Manager

Forty-one and a half hours of Category ICME credits available; Categorical course on Body CT; 30 commercial exhibits; 300 scientific exhibits; scientific paper presentations.
2,500 Attendees April-May

11991 American School Health's Annual School Health Conference
American School Health Association
7263 State Route 43
PO Box 708
Kent, OH 44240
330-678-1601
FAX: 330-678-4526 800-445-2742
mbramsier@ashaweb.org
www.ashaweb.org

Mary Bamer Ramsier, Meeting Planner
Thomas Reed, Manager

Join school health professionals who will come together to learn, share perspectives and resources, and network during the more than 120 educational sessions and workshops. General Sessions, multiple break-outs, and exhibits.
800 Attendees Annual Founded: 1927
Mailing list available for rent 650 names

11992 American Society for Aesthetic Plastic Surgery Conference
American Society for Aesthetic Plastic Surgery
36 W 44th Street
Suite 630
New York, NY 10036
212-921-0500
FAX: 212-921-0011
media@surgery.org www.surgery.org
Educational sessions and displays of the latest prdoducts and developments.
2500 Attendees May

11993 American Society for Artificial Internal Organs Meeting and Exhibits
PO Box C
Boca Raton, FL 33429-8589
561-391-8589
FAX: 561-368-9153
info@asaio.org www.asaio.org
Workshop, and over 30 exhibits of interest to physicians, nurses, engineers, perfusionists and technicians.

1000 Attendees Annual Founded: 1954

11994 American Society for Bone and Mineral Research Congress
1200 19th Street NW
Suite 300
Washington, DC 20036
202-289-5900
FAX: 202-857-1880
asbmr@dc.sba.com www.asbmr.org
Joan Goldberg, Executive Director
Exhibits for the research of bone and mineral diseases.
Annual Founded: 1977

11995 American Society for Cell Biology Annual Meeting
9650 Rockville Pike
Bethesda, MD 20814
301-530-7153
FAX: 301-530-7139
enewman@ascb.org
www.ascb.org/ascb
Edward Newman, Director Marketing
Conference and 425 exhibits of interest to biomedical researchers, scientists, and related trade professionals.
8000 Attendees Annual Founded: 1961

11996 American Society for Clinical Nutrition Annual Meeting
9650 Rockville Pike
Bethesda, MD 20814-3998
301-571-1825
FAX: 301-571-1863
secretar@ascn.faseb.edu
www.faseb.org
Elaine Strass, Executive Director
Exhibits relating to clinical nutrition of interest to physicians and scientists.
Annual

11997 American Society for Dermatologic Surgery Annual Meeting
American Society for Dermatologic Surgery
5550 Meadowbrook Drive
Suite 120
Rolling Meadows, IL 60008
847-956-0900
FAX: 847-956-0999
info@asds.net www.asds-net.org
Alastair Carruthers, President
Kimberly Butterwick, Board of Directors
Educational session, banquet and tours plus 80 exhibits of surgical instruments, dressings, closure materials and dermatologic pharmceuticals.
800 Attendees Founded: 1973

11998 American Society for Health Care Human Resources Administration Meeting
American Hospital Association
1 N Franklin
Chicago, IL 60606
312-222-2000
FAX: 312-422-4519 www.aha.org
Human resources administration in health care exhibition.

11999 American Society for Healthcare Management Convention
Corcoran Expositions
100 W Monroe Street
Suite 1001
Chicago, IL 60603
312-541-0567
FAX: 312-541-0573

12000 American Society for Histocompatability and Immunogenetics
PO Box 15804
Lexana, KS 66285-5804
913-541-0009
FAX: 913-541-0156 ashiamp@aol.com
Michael P Flanigan CAE, Executive Director
Fifty exhibits from medical suppliers relating to tissue typing.
1000 Attendees Annual Founded: 1974

12001 American Society for Laser Medicine and Surgery Conference
2100 Stewart Ave
Ste 240
Wausau, WI 54401-1709
715-845-9283
FAX: 715-848-2493
information@aslms.org
www.aslms.org
Richard O Gregory MD, Board Secretary
Dianne Dalsky, Manager
Seventy five exhibits of laser medicine and supplies of interest to physicians, physicists, nurses, veterinarians, dentists, podiatrists and technicians.
Annual Founded: 1980

12002 American Society for Microbiology: General Meeting
1325 Massachusetts Anvenue NW
Washington, DC 20005
202-942-9252
FAX: 202-942-9340
Professionally related exhibits.

12003 American Society for Pharmacology & Experi mental Theraputics Annual Meeting
9650 Rockville Pike
Bethesda, MD 20814
301-347-7060
FAX: 301-634-7061
info@aspet.org www.aspet.org
Jean Lash, Exhibit Manager
Christine Carrico, Executive Director
Four-hundred exhibits of pharmacology and toxicology equipment, supplies and services.
13000 Attendees April

12004 American Society for Surgery of the Hand Annual Meeting
American Society for Surgery of the Hand
6300 N River Road
Suite 600
Rosemont, IL 60018
847-384-8300
FAX: 847-384-1435
info@assh.org www.assh.org
Carissa Wehrman, Meetings/Exhibits Coordinator
Mark Anderson, Executive Director
Meeting plus exhibits of microsurgical instruments, finger splinting devices, surgical telescopes, trauma products, external fixation systems and more.
2,000 Attendees September 2,000 names

12005 American Society for Therapeutic Radiology and Oncology Annual Meeting
American Society for Therapeutic Radiology & Onc.
12500 Fairlakes Circle
Suite 375
Fairfax, VA 22033
703-502-1550
FAX: 703-502-7852 800-962-7876
meetings@astro.org www.astro.org
Laura Mulay, ASTRO Meetings Manager
Eight-hundred exhibits of products, supplies and services for the treatment of cancer.
10000 Attendees October 6,500 names

12006 American Society of Aesthetic Plastic Surgery Meeting
11081 Winners Circle
Suite 200
Los Alamitos, CA 90720-2813
562-799-2356
FAX: 310-427-2234
Robert Stanton, Manager
Meeting and 100 exhibits of plastic surgery medical instruments and equipment.
Annual

12007 American Society of Anesthesiologists Annual Meeting
American Society of Anesthesiologists
520 N Northwest Highway
Park Ridge, IL 60068-2573
847-825-5586
FAX: 847-825-1692
mail@asahq.org www.asahq.org
Ronald Bruns, Executive Director
18000 Attendees Annual, October

12008 American Society of Clinical Oncology Annual Convention
J Spargo & Associates
11212 Waples Mill Road
Suite 104
Fairfax, VA 22030
703-631-6200
FAX: 703-818-9177 800-564-4220
info@jspargo.com www.jspargo.com
John Spargo, President
Three hundred exhibits of medical equipment, supplies and services used in the practice of clinical oncology.
20000 Attendees Annual Founded: 1964

12009 American Society of Clinical Pathologists and College of American Pathologist
American Society of Clinical Pathologists
2100 W Harrison Street
Chicago, IL 60612
312-738-1336
FAX: 312-738-1619
John Ball, Executive Vice President
4500 Attendees

12010 American Society of Colon & Rectal Surgeons
American Society of Colon & Rectal Surgeons
85 W Algonquin Road
Suite 550
Arlington Heights, IL 60005
847-427-1200
FAX: 847-290-9203 www.fascrw.org
Stella Zedalis, Associate Executive Director

2300 Attendees Founded: 1899
Mailing list available for rent 2300 names
$250 per M.

12011 American Society of Cytopathology Annual Scientific Meeting
400 W 9th Street
Suite 201
Wilmington, DE 19801
302-429-8802
FAX: 302-429-8807
asc@cytopathology.org
www.cytopathology.org

Christy Myers, Meetings Manager
Elizabeth Jenkins, Manager

Premier event in the field of cytopathology. The objectives of the Annual Meeting are to update cytologists on the current practice of cytopathology, foster research in early diagnosis and effective treatment of human disease and provide a forum for advocacy on behalf of cytologists and their patients.
850 Attendees November Founded: 1951

12012 American Society of Directors of Volunteer Services Leadership Training Conf
1 N Franklin
Chicago, IL 60606
312-223-3937
FAX: 312-442-4575

Audrey Harris, Executive Director

Workshop, banquet, luncheon and 55 exhibits of health care administration equipment, supplies and services.
700 Attendees Annual Founded: 1964

12013 American Society of Electroneurodiagnostic Technologists Convention
204 W 7th Street
Carroll, IA 51401
712-792-2978
FAX: 712-792-6962
info@aset.org www.aset.org

Renee Yhredehal, Marketing Director

Seminar, reception and 60 exhibits of insturmentation, books, supplies and services in EEG, EP, polysomnography, nerve conduction, and intraoperative monitoring.
700 Attendees Annual Founded: 1959

12014 American Society of Extra-Corporeal Techno logy International Conference
503 Carlisle Drive
Suite 125
Herndon, VA 20170-4838
703-435-8556
FAX: 703-435-0056
webmaster@amsect.org
www.amsect.org

Judy Luther, Deputy Executive Director

Seminar, workshop, conference and 75 exhibits relating to the practice of extra-corporeal technology (involving heart and lung machines).
Annual

12015 American Society of Hand Therapists Convention
Smith, Bucklin and Associates
401 N Michigan Avenue
Chicago, IL 60611-4267
312-644-6610
FAX: 312-245-1082

Lisa Keckich, Manager

Workshop and 40 - 60 exhibits of books, and hand therapy equipment.
800 Attendees Annual Founded: 1977

12016 American Society of Health Care Marketing & Public Relations
1 N Franklin Street
31st Floor
Chicago, IL 60606-3421
773-327-1064
FAX: 312-422-4579

Lauren Barnett, Executive Director

Sixty booths of communications, printing, computer equipment, public relations and fund raising consultants in the health care profession.
600 Attendees September

12017 American Society of Hematology Annual Meeting & Exposition
1200 19th Street NW
Suite 300
Washington, DC 24226
202-857-1118
FAX: 202-847-1164 ash@sba.com

Gail Sparks

Four hundred fifty exhibits of equipment and supplies of interest to hematologists and related professionals.
15000 Attendees Founded: 1958

12018 American Society of Human Genetics Convention
American Society of Human Genetics
9650 Rockville Pike
Bethesda, MD 20814
301-571-1825
FAX: 301-530-7079 866-486-4363
mryan@genetics.faseb.org
www.faseb.org

Marsha Ryan, Senior Meetings & Exhibits Manager
Elaine Strass, Executive Director
6,000 Attendees November 7,000 names

12019 American Society of Nephrology
American Society of Nephrology
1200 19th Street NW
Suite 300
Washington, DC 20036
202-857-1190
FAX: 202-429-5112
13000 Attendees

12020 American Society of PERI Anesthesia Nurses
American Gastroenterological Association

4930 Del Ray Avenue
Bethesda, MD 20814
301-654-2055
FAX: 301-654-5920
member@gastro.org www.gastro.org

12021 American Society of Post Anesthesia Nurses Meeting
Slack
6900 Grove Road
Thorofare, NJ 08086
856-848-1000
FAX: 856-848-3522

Peter Slack, President

One hundred seventy exhibits of pharmaceuticals and recovery room supplies.
1700 Attendees Annual Founded: 1981

12022 American Society of Psychoprophylaxis in Obstetrics/Lamaze Conference
Smith, Bucklin and Associates
1200 19th Street NW
Suite 300
Washington, DC 20036-2412
202-861-6416
FAX: 202-429-5112

Leigh McMillan, Senior Convention Director

One hundred exhibitors of educational materials for Lamaze method of prepared childbirth, obstetric equipment and supplies, infant products, breast pumps and more.
500 Attendees Annual Founded: 1960

12023 American Society of Transplant Physicians Scientific Meeting
Slack
6900 Grove Road
Thorofare, NJ 08086
856-848-1000
FAX: 856-848-3522

Peter Slack, President

Fifty exhibits of medical supplies and services of interest to physicans and others actively involved with transplantaion.
800 Attendees Annual Founded: 1981

12024 American Society of Transplant Surgeons Annual Meeting
Wright Organization
716 Lee Street
Des Plaines, IL 60016-4515
847-245-5700
FAX: 708-824-0394
Sixty exhibitors of medical equipment, supplies and services relating to renal and cardiac transplants.
750 Attendees Founded: 1974

12025 American Society of Tropical Medicine and Hygiene Annual Scientific Meeting
60 Revere Drive
Suite 500
Northbrook, IL 60062
847-480-9592
FAX: 847-480-9282
astmh@astmh.org www.astmh.org

Madhuri Carson, Conference Administrator

Reception and over 20 exhibits related to tropical medicine and hygiene, including the areas of arboviology, entomology, medicine, nursing and parasitology.
1500 Attendees November Founded: 1951

12026 American Speech-Language-Hearing Association Annual Convention
American Speech- Language Hearing Association
10801 Rockville Pike
Rockville, MD 20852
301-897-5700
FAX: 301-571-0454 800-498-2071
convention@asha.org www.asha.org

Mary Harding, Exhibition Manager
Arlene Pietranton, Executive Director

Four hundred exhibits of medical, educational and testing equipment, plus publications.
12000 Attendees

12027 American Urological Association Convention
1120 N Charles Street
Baltimore, 21
410-727-1100
FAX: 410-244-8752
Eight hundred ten exhibits of publications, equipment and supplies for the field of urology.
1650 Attendees Annual

12028 Anesthesia in the XXI Century
College of Physicians & Surgeons, Columbia Univ.
2209 Dickens Road
PO Box 11086
Richmond, VA 23116
804-565-6310
FAX: 804-282-0090
exhibits@societyhq.com
www.societyhq.com/exhibitors
Matt Van Wie, Show Manager
Exhibits of anesthesia equipment, information, supplies and services, conference, meals, breaks, sponsorships available.
100 Attendees February

12029 Annual Clinical Assembly of Osteopathic Specialists
American College of Osteopathic Surgeons
123 N Henery Street
Alexandria, VA 22314
703-684-0416
FAX: 703-684-3280
Annual

12030 Annual Conference on Healthcare Marketing
Alliance for Healthcare Strategy & Marketing
11 S LaSalle Street
Suite 2300
Chicago, IL 60603
312-704-9700
FAX: 312-704-9709
www.alliancehlth.org/hlthmktg
Workshop and social events plus 50 exhibits of marketing communications, health care information lines, strategic planning and more.
600 Attendees Annual Founded: 1984

12031 Annual Contact Lens and Primary Care Seminar, MOA
Michigan Optometric Association
530 W Ionia Street
Suite A
Lansing, MI 48933-1062
517-482-0616
FAX: 517-482-1611
mioptoassn@aol.com www.themoa.org
William D Dansby CAE, Executive VP
Continuing education program and trade show for optometrists and optometric technicians/assistants.
1100 Attendees October, Annually Founded: 1968

12032 Annual Convention of American Institute of Ultrasound in Medicine
American Institute of Ultrasound in Medicine
14750 Sweitzer Lane
Suite 100
Laurel, MD 20707
301-498-4392
FAX: 301-498-4450 800-638-5352
conv_edu@aium.org www.aium.org
Jenny Clark, Show Manager
Brenda Kinney, Meeting Coordinator
Lisa Shendan, Sales Manager
June

12033 Annual Convention of the American College of Osteopathic Obstetricians
American College Of Osteopathic Obstetricians
900 Auburn Road
Pontiac, MI 48342
248-332-6360
FAX: 248-332-4607 800-875-6360
jbritton@acoog.com www.acoog.com
Jaki Britton, Administrator
Workshop, reception and banquet as well as exhibits relating to women's health, medical equipment and supplies.
350 Attendees Annual Founded: 1934

12034 Annual Critical Care Update
National Professional Education Institute
2525 Ossen Fort Road
PO Box 118
Glencoe, MO 63068-1107
636-735-5570
FAX: 561-743-9596 800-575-5575
JJMcDaid@aol.com
www.npeinursing.com
Judie McDaid, Exhibitor Relations Manager
Leslie Brock, Registration Manager
The Annual Critical Care Update and Nurse Managers Conference/EXPO provides a fully integrated program dedicated to the continuing education of critical care nurses, nurse managers and other healthcare professionals. Exhibitors showcase their latest healthcare products, pharmaceuticals, services, research and facilities. Knowledge gained in the informative, entertaining EXPO Hall, will influence these nurses' purchasing decisions throughout the year.
1500 Attendees Annual, April Founded: 1973

12035 Annual Disease Management Congress: Innnovative Strategies
National Managed Health Care Congress
71 2nd Avenue
3rd Floor
Waltham, MA 02154
FAX: 941-365-0157 888-882-2500
register@nmhcc.org www.nmhcc.org
Frances Pratt, Director/Marketing
One hundred exhibits of targeted disease management and services.
1700 Attendees Annual Founded: 1996

12036 Annual Educational Conference and Exhibits
Society for Healthcare Strategy & Market Dev.
One N Franklin
Chicago, IL 60606
312-422-3840
FAX: 312-422-4579
stratsoc@aha.org www.stratsociety.org
September

12037 Annual Meeting & Clinical Lab Exposition
American Association for Clinical Chemistry
1850 K St NW
Ste 625
Washington, DC 20006-2215
202-857-0717
FAX: 202-887-5093 800-892-1400
jrhame@aacc.org www.aacc.org
Jean Rhame, Director Professional Affairs
Six hundred exhibitors of clincal laboratory equipment, supplies and services for lab automation, information, robotics and OEM products. Seminar, worhshop and conference.
20000 Attendees Annual
Mailing list available for rent 11000 names $150 per M.

12038 Annual Meeting of the American Association on Mental Retardation
American Association on Mental Retardation
444 N Capitol Street NW
Suite 846
Washington, DC 20001-1512
202-387-1968
FAX: 202-387-2193 800-424-3688
Doreen Croser, Executive Director
2000 Attendees Annual, May

12039 Annual Meeting of the American Society of Human Genetics
9650 Rockville Pike
Bethesda, MD 20814
301-571-1825
FAX: 301-530-7079 866-486-4363
society@genetics.faseb,org/genetics
www.faseb.org/genetics
Marsha Ryan, Senior Meetings & Exhibits Manager
Reception and 250 exhibits of lab equipment, computer software, information resources, laboratory services and publishers.
6,000 Attendees November 7,000 names

12040 Annual Meeting of the Microscopy Society of America
Bostrom Corporation
230 E Ohio
Suite 400
Chicago, IL 60611-3265
312-644-1527
FAX: 312-644-8557 800-538-3672
BusinessOffices@MSA.Microscopy.com
www.msa.microscopy.com
Judy Janes, Manager
Microscopes and related supplies of interest to medical, biological, metalurgical, and polymer research scientists, technicians and physicists interested in instrument design and improvement.
Annual, August

12041 Annual National Managed Health Care Congress
71 2nd Avenue
3rd Floor
Waltham, MA 02154
FAX: 941-365-0157 888-882-2500
register@mnhcc.com www.nmhcc.org
Seminar, workshop, conference, and 600 exhibits of services and products dedicated to improving the quality of health care.
10000 Attendees Annual Founded: 1989

12042 Annual PPO Forum
American Assn of Preferred Provider Organizations
222 South First Street
Suite 303
Louisville, KY 40202

FAX: 502-403-1129
mcox@aappo.org www.aappo.org
Melissa Cox, Event Coordinator
San Diego Founded: 2003

12043 Annual Physician Assistant Conference
American Academy of Physician Assistants
950 N Washington Street
Alexandria, VA 22314
703-836-2272
FAX: 703-684-1924
aapa@aapa.org www.aapa.org
Amy Phillips, Conference/Education/Meetings
Germaine Schaefer, Exhibits/Registration
Lauren Brillante, Meetings
Stephen Crane, Executive Vice President
For PAs across the nation in all specialties. 250 educational sessions, plus 225 exhibits of medical software, books, pharmaceuticals, equipment and supplies, as well as sponsored symposia and adjuncts.
8000 Attendees June 2M-5M names $500 per M.

12044 Annual Scientific Meeting of the Gerontological Society of America
Gerontological Society of America
1030 15th Street NW
Suite 250
Washington, DC 20005
202-842-1275
FAX: 202-842-1150 www.geron.org
Carol Schutz, Executive Director

12045 Applied Ergonomics Conference
Institute of Industrial Engineers
3597 Parkway Lane
Suite 200
Norcross, GA 30097
770-449-0461
FAX: 770-263-8532 800-494-0460
Carol LeBlanc, Conference Manager
An exclusive event for ergonomists, engineers, and safety professionals. The conference focuses on how companies have successfully implemented programs that provide excellent return on their ergonomics investment.
800 Attendees March Founded: 1998

12046 Arthroscopy Association of North America Annual Meeting
6300 N River Road
#104
Rosemont, IL 60018
847-292-2262
FAX: 847-292-2268
holly@aana.org www.aana.org
Holly Albert, Meetings Manager
Edward Goss, Executive Director
Seminar, reception and 100 exhibits of video and arthroscopy equipment, braces, books and more.
1000 Attendees

12047 Association for Applied Psychophysiology & Biofeedback Annual Meeting
Association for Applied Psychophysiology
10200 W 44th Avenue
Suite 304
Wheat Ridge, CO 80033
303-228-8436
FAX: 303-422-8894 800-477-8892
aapb@resorcecenter.com
www.aapb.org
Tina Watkins, Meetings Manager
Francine Butler, Executive Director
Exhibits of biofeedback equipment, supplies, and training programs, medical supplies and software, as well as annual meeting.
500 Attendees March Founded: 1969

12048 Association for Healthcare Philanthropy Annual Int'l Educational Conference
Association for Healthcare Philanthropy
313 Park Avenue
Suite 400
Falls Church, VA 22046
703-532-6243
FAX: 703-532-7170
ahp@ahp.org www.ahp.org
Conference and 120 exhibits with information about equipment and services for the fundraising and helatcare development community, including computer software, recognition gifts, direct mail companies, executive recriuters, special events and more.
900 Attendees September 3,100 names $200 per M.

12049 Association for Professionals in Infection Control & Epidemiology
Association for Professionals in Infection Control
1275 K Street NW
Suite 1000
Washington, DC 20005
202-789-1890
FAX: 202-789-1899
nicoleguy@mindspring.com
wwwapic.com
Nicole Guy, Show Manager
Jim Maslend, Executive Director
Workshop, banquet, reception and 150 exhibits of infection control products, pharmaceuticals, disinfectants, soaps, dataprocessing software, housekeeping equipment and supplies.
2700 Attendees Annual Founded: 1974

12050 Association for Worksite Health Promotion Annual International Conference
60 Revere Drive
Suite 500
Northbrook, IL 60062-1577
847-480-9574
FAX: 847-480-9282
awhp@awhp.org www.awhp.org
Liz Freyn, Conference Manager
One hundred twenty two booths of information and supplies to promote and develop quality programs of health and fitness in business and industry. Seminar, workshop, conference, tours and luncheon.

950 Attendees Founded: 1974

12051 Association for the Advancement of Medical Instrumentation Meeting and Exhibit
Association for the Advancement of Medical Inst
3330 Washington Boulevard
Suite 400
Arilington, VA 22201-4598
703-525-4890
FAX: 703-276-0793 800-332-2264
education@aami.com www.aami.com
Suzanne Stone, VP Communications
Seminar, conference, educational session, reception and 200 exhibits of biomedical equipment, medical device technologies, products and services.
2500 Attendees Annual

12052 Association of Behavioral Healthcare Management Convention
60 Revere Drive
Suite 500
Northbrook, IL 60062
847-480-9626
FAX: 847-480-9282
Exhibits related to the administration of services for the emotionally disturbed, mentally ill, mentally retarded, developmentally disabled, and those with substance abuse problems.
Annual

12053 Association of Healthcare Internal Auditors Conference
PO Box 449
Onstead, MI 49265-0449
517-467-7729
FAX: 517-467-6104
ahia@ahia.org www.ahia.org
Thomas Monahan, Executive Director
Exhibits concerning cost containment and increased productivity in health care institutions through internal auditing.
1000 Attendees Founded: 1981

12054 Association of Pediatric Oncology Nurses Annual Conference
Association of Pediatric Nurses
4700 W Lake Avenue
Glenview, IL 60025-1485
847-375-4724
FAX: 847-375-4777
info@apon.org www.apon.org
Exhibits on caring for children who have cancer.

12055 Association of Rehabilitation Nurses Annual Educational Conference
4700 W Lake Avenue
Glenview, IL 60025-1485
847-375-4710
FAX: 847-375-4777 800-229-7530
Conference, educational session, workshop and 225 exhibits of rehabilitational aids and supplies, medical equipment, hospitals and rehbilitation facilities and publications of interest to rehabilitation nurses.
2300 Attendees Founded: 1974

12056 Benefits New York Show
Flagg Management
353 Lexington Avenue
New York, NY 10016
212-286-0333
FAX: 212-286-0086
flaggmgmnt@msn.com
www.flaggmgmt.com
Russell Flagg, President

Human resources, personnel, administration and training marketplace. HRMS, systems and services 250 exhibits.
3000 Attendees

12057 Building Bridges VII
American Association of Health Plans
1129 20th Street NW
Washington, DC 20036
202-778-3200
FAX: 202-778-8506

12058 Center for School Mental Health Assistance National Convention
Exhibit Promotions Plus
11620 Vixens Path
Ellicott City, MD 21042
301-596-3028
FAX: 410-997-0764 exhibit@erols.com
Harve C Horowitz, President
Supports school health, mental health professionals by offering ongoing consutation to address administrative, clinical and systems issues relevant to school health services.
October

12059 Clinical Laboratory Expo
AACC; c/o Scherago International
11 Penn Plaza
Suite 1003
New York, NY 10001
212-643-1750
FAX: 212-643-1758
tonym@scherago.com
www.scherago.com/AACC
Tony Maiorino, Exhibits Manager
20000 Attendees July-August

12060 Clinical Laboratory Management Association Annual Conference & Exhibition
Clinical Laboratory Management Association
989 Old Eagle School Road
Suite 815
Wayne, PA 19087
610-995-9580
FAX: 610-995-9568 www.clma.org
Dana Procsal, VP
CLMA-ASCP have combined forces to offer the largest, most comprehensive laboratory conference and exhibition ever, specifically designed for laboratory professionals at all levels.
4800 Attendees June

12061 Clinical and Scientific Congress of the Int'l Anesthesia Research Society
International Anesthesia Research Society
2 Summit Park Drive
Suite 140
Cleveland, OH 44131
216-642-1124
FAX: 216-642-1127
iarshq@iars.org www.iars.org
1200 Attendees March

12062 Congress on Invitro Biology
Society for Invitro Biology
9315 Lango Drive W
Suite 255
Lango, MD 20774
301-324-5054
FAX: 301-324-5057 800-741-7476
sivb@sivb.org www.sivb.org
Marietta Ellis, Show Manager
Focus on issues pertinent to the Vertebrate, Invertebrate, and Cellular Toxicology Sections and will give participants a unique learning experience on animal cell culture and biotechnology.
1,000 Attendees June

12063 Consumer Directed Health Care Conference
Po Box 448, East Cary Street
Suite 102
Richmond, VA 23219
804-266-7422
FAX: 804-225-7458 www.cdhcc.com or www.consumerhealthworld.com
Carlotta Farmer, Director of Programming
December, Washington

12064 Digestive Disease Week Meeting & Exhibition
American Gastroenterological Association
4930 Del Ray Avenue
Bethesda, MD 20814
301-654-2055
FAX: 301-652-3890
member@gastro.org www.gastro.org
14000 Attendees March

12065 Distribution Management Conference & Expo
Healthcare Distribution Management Association
900 N Glebe Road
Suite 1000
Arlington, VA 22203
703-787-0000
FAX: 703-935-3200
lburke@hdmanet.org
www.healthcaredistribution.org
Lori Burke, Director Meetings/Conferences
Denise Woodson, Meerings Coordinator
Provides the latest information on the most important topics affecting healthcare distribution.
June

12066 Drug Discovery Technology
Hynes Convention Center
900 Boylston Street
Boston, MA 02115
617-954-2000
FAX: 617-954-2125 800-845-8800
info@mccahome.com
www.mccahome.com
2000 Attendees August

12067 Eastern Pain Association Annual Meeting
2209 Dickens Road
PO Box 11086
Richmond, VA 23116
804-565-6310
FAX: 804-282-0090
exhibits@societyhq.com
www.societyhq.com/exhibitors
Matt Van Wie, Show Manager
Exhibits of pain equipment, information, supplies and services, conference, meals, breaks, sponsorships available.
150 Attendees September 300 names

12068 Emergency Nurses Association Scientific Assembly & Exhibits
Emergency Nurses Association
915 Lee Street
Des Plaines, IL 60016-6569
847-460-4100
FAX: 847-460-4001 800-900-9659
David Westman, Chief Executive Officer
3500 Attendees Annual, September

12069 Endocrine Society Annual Meeting
Scherago International
11 Penn Plaza
Suite 1003
New York, NY 10001
212-643-1750
FAX: 212-643-1758
6500 Attendees

12070 Experimental Biology
FASEB/OSMC
9650 Rockville Pike
Bethesda, MD 20814
301-634-7100
FAX: 301-634-7014
www.faseb.org/meetings
Pauline Minhinnett, Meeting Manager
Jean Lash, Exhibit Manager
12M Attendees April

12071 Fall Symposium
American College of Emergency Physicians
PO Box 619911
Dallas, TX 75261
972-550-0911
FAX: 972-580-2816
325 Attendees

12072 Federated Ambulatory Surgery Association
Federated Ambulatory Surgery Assocation
1012 Cameron St
Alexandria, VA 22314-2427
703-836-8808
FAX: 703-549-0976
fasa@fasa.org www.fasa.org
Kathy Bryant, Executive Vice President
Sarah Siberstein, Deputy Executive Director
71000 Attendees April 3800 names $350 per M.

12073 Federation of Hospitals Public Policy Conference & Business Exposition
Federation of American Health Systems
801 Pennsylvania Avenue NW
Suite 245
Washington, DC 20004-2604
202-624-1500
FAX: 202-737-6462
info@fah.org www.fah.org
Bonnie Moneypenny, Senior VP Administrative Services
The conference brings together hospital executives and leading policymakers each Spring for important discussions. It also affords an important opportunity for suppliers to meet face-to-face with hospital managers and buyers.
Annual, March Founded: 1966

12074 Fire-Rescue International
International Association of Fire Chiefs
4025 Fair Ridge Drive
Fairfax, VA 22033
703-273-0911
FAX: 703-273-9363
www.iafc.org/conference.shtml
Conference and exposition of the fire service industry.
16000 Attendees August

12075 Food & Nutrition Conference & Expo
American Dietetic Association
120 South Riverside Plaza
Suite 2000
Chicago, IL 60606
312-899-4741
FAX: 312-899-0008 800-877-1600
gandruch@eatright.org
www.eatright.org
Greg Andruch, Exhibits Manager
More than 8,000 professionals come to the Food & Nutrition Conference & Expo for the latest technological and nutritional advancements. This is the premier selling opportunity in the fields of nutrition and food service management. The event continues to expand-attracting a wider audience of professionals, including hotel and restarurant managers, sports, health and nutrition professionals and executive chefs. *$ 150.00*
8000 Attendees September, Pennsylvania
Circulation: 65000

12076 HDMA Annual Meeting
Healthcare Distribution Management Association
900 N Glebe Road
Suite 1000
Arlington, VA 22203
703-787-0000
FAX: 703-935-3200
lburke@hdmanet.org
www.healthcaredistribution.org
Lori Burke, Director Meetings/Conferences
Denise Woodson, Meetings Coordinator
Provides a unique opportunity for senior-level retailer and supplier member executives to interact and discuss strategic issues.
October

12077 Health Industry Distributors Association Trade Show & Education Forum
Health Industry Distributors Association
66 Canal Center Plaza
Suite 520
Alexandria, VA 22314-1591
703-549-4432
FAX: 703-549-4695
mail@hida.org www.heida.org
Matt Rowan, Chief Executive Officer
8000 Attendees

12078 Healthcare Financial Management Association Idea Exchange
Corcoran Expositions
100 W Monroe Street
Suite 1001
Chicago, IL 60603
312-541-0567
FAX: 312-541-0573

12079 Healthcare Information and Management Systems Society
HIMSS/Healthcare Information and Management
230 E Ohio
Suite 500
Chicago, IL 60611
312-664-4467
FAX: 312-664-6143

12080 INTERPHEX - The World's Forum for the Pharmaceutical Industry
Reed Exhibition Companies
383 Main Avenue
Norwalk, CT 06851
203-840-4800
FAX: 203-840-4804
Chet Burchett, President
11000 Attendees

12081 Infusion Nurses Society Annual Meeting and Industrial Exhibition
Infusion Nurses Society
220 Norwood Park S
Norwood, MA 02062
781-440-9408
FAX: 781-440-9409
jason.beal@ins1.org www.ins1.org
Jason Beal, Marketing Manager
Mary Alexander, Chief Executive Officer
1000 Attendees Annual $200 per M.

12082 International Conference on Head and Neck Cancer
American Head and Neck Society
1805 Ardmore Boulevard
Pittsburgh, PA 15221
412-243-5156
FAX: 412-243-5160
rwagnercme@aol.com
www.headandneckcancer.org
Robin Wagner, Show Manager
Sixty exhibits of equipment and supplies, conference, luncheon and reception.
2,500 Attendees August

12083 International Congress on Ambulatory Surgery Conference
Hynes Convention Center
900 Boylston Street
Boston, MA 02115
617-954-2000
FAX: 617-954-2125
info@mccahome.com
www.mccahome.com
1500 Attendees May

12084 International Society for Magnetic Resonance in Medicine
International Society for Magnetic Resonance
2118 Milvia Street
Suite 201
Berkeley, CA 94704
510-841-1899
FAX: 510-841-2340
info@ismrm.org www.ismrm.org
May

12085 International Vision Exposition & Conference
Association Expositions & Services
383 Main Avenue
Norwalk, CT 06851
203-840-4820
FAX: 203-840-4824 800-811-7151
Eileen Baird
Ed Gallo, Sales Manager
Tracy Flacherty, Marketing Director
As the most comprehensive vision care show and conference in the US, International Vision Expo is where today's eye care professionals meet, learn and conduct business. International vision expo draws optical professionals from all career path including: Ophthalmologist, Optometrist, Opticians, Lab Personnel, Practice managers, Ophthalmic Medical Personnel, Retailers, Manufacturing Executives, Import Export buyers, Ophthalmic Assistants, Optical Interns and more.
15000 Attendees March/September

12086 Managed Care Institute & Display Forum
American Association of Health Plans
1129 20th Street NW
Suite 600
Washington, DC 20036
202-783-3200
FAX: 202-955-4395 877-291-2247
aahp@aahp.org www.aahp.org
Two hundred exhibits by suppliers to the managed health care industry, conference and reception.
2000 Attendees Annual Founded: 1986

12087 Managed Care Law Conference
American Association of Health Plans
1129 20th Street NW
Washington, DC 20036
202-778-3200
FAX: 202-778-8506

12088 Medical Design & Manufacturing Conference & Exhibition West
Canon Communications
11444 W Olympic Boulevard
Los Angeles, CA 90064
310-445-4200
FAX: 310-996-9499
register@cancom.com
www.cancom.com
Diane O'Conner, Trade Show Director
Dan Cutrone, Show Marketing Manager
Devoted to the design, development, and manufacture of medical products. Visitors can preview the latest advances in medical-grade materials, assembly components, machinery, electronics, systems, software, services and more. Held at the Anaheim Convention Center in Anaheim, California.
8,500 Attendees January

12089 Medical Design and Manufacturing Minneapolis Conference
Canon Communications
11444 W Olympic Boulevard
Los Angeles, CA 90064
310-445-4200
FAX: 310-996-9499
exhibit@cancom.com.com
www.mdm-minneapolis.com
Diane O'Connor, Trade Show Director
Dan Cutrone, Show Marketing Manager
Four hundred thirty three exhibitors in 52,500 square feet of the Minneapolis Convention Center. Medical supplies and information promotional opportunities in show directory, web site advertising, conference program, sponsorships and product previews. *$45.00*
3374 Attendees October Founded: 1994

12090 Medical Equipment Design & Technology Exhibition & Conference
Canon Communications
11444 W Olympic Boulevard
Los Angeles, CA 90064-1549
310-445-4200
FAX: 310-445-4299
exhibit@cancom.com
www.medtecshow.com
Diane O'Conner, Trade Show Director
Dan Cutrone, Show Marketing Manager
Devoted to the design, development and manufacture of medical products. Visitors

can preview the latest advances in medical-grade materials, assembly components, electronics, machinery, software, systems, services and more. Held at the RAI International Exhibition and Congress Center in Amsterdam, Netherlands.
2231 Attendees October

12091 Medical Group Management Association
Medical Group Management Association
104 Inverness Terrace E
Englewood, CO 80112-5306
303-991-1111
FAX: 877-329-6462 800-275-6462
William Jessee, Manager
3800 Attendees Annual, October

12092 Medicare and Medicaid Conference
American Association of Health Plans
1129 20th Street NW
Washington, DC 20036
202-778-3200
FAX: 202-778-8506

12093 Medtrade West
VNU Expositions
Dallas International Airport
PO Box 17413
Washington, DC 20041
703-318-0300
FAX: 703-318-8833

12094 Medtrade/Comtrade
VNU Communications
1130 Hightower Trail
Atlanta, GA 30350
770-569-1540
FAX: 703-318-8833

12095 NCPA Rx Exposition
NCPA
100 Daingerfield Road
Alexandria, VA 22314
703-683-8200
FAX: 703-683-3619 800-544-7447
info@ncpanet.org www.ncpanet.org
2000 Attendees Annual, October

12096 NEPA Annual Winter Conference
New England Pain Association
2209 Dickens Road
PO Box 11086
Richmond, VA 23116
804-565-6310
FAX: 804-282-0090
exhjbits@societyhq.com
www.societyhq.com/exhibitors
Matt Van Wie, Show Manager
Exhibits of pain equipment, information, supplies and services, conference, meals, breaks, sponsorships available.
150 Attendees February 300 names

12097 National Association for Home Care & Hospi ce Annual Meeting & Homecare Expo
National Association for Home Care and Hospice
228 7th Street SE
Washington, DC 20003
202-547-7424
FAX: 202-547-3540
ree@nahc.org www.nahc.org
Ron Everly, VP NAAC Expo
Val Halamandaris, Executive Director
Gathering of Home Care and Hospice professionals.
4000 Attendees October

12098 National Athletic Trainers Association
National Athletic Trainers
2952 Stemmons Freeway
Dallas, TX 75247
214-637-6282
FAX: 214-637-2206
Eve Becker-Doyle, Executive Director

12099 National Convention: Opticians Association of America
Opticians Association of America
10341 Democracy Lane
Fairfax, VA 22030
703-916-8856
FAX: 703-691-8929

12100 National Council on the Aging Annual Conference
National Council on the Aging
100 3rd Street SW
Washington, DC 20024
202-479-1200
FAX: 202-479-0735
James Firman, Chief Exceutive Officer

12101 National Managed Healthcare Congress
Po Box 3685
Boston, MA 02441-3685

FAX: 941-365-2507 888-670-8200
March 5-7 2007 Atlanta

12102 National Medical Association Annual Convention & Scientific Assembly
J Spargo & Associates
11208 Waples Mill Road
Suite 112
Fairfax, VA 22030
703-631-6200
FAX: 703-654-6931 800-564-4220
nma@jspargo.com www.nmanet.org
June LaMountain, Exhibit Sales Account Manager
Promotes the collective interests of physicians and patients of African descent. NMA carries out this mission by serving the collective voice of physicians of African descent and a leading force for purity in medicine, elimination of health disparities and optimal health.
3000 Attendees August

12103 National Safety Council Congress Expo
National Safety Council
1121 Spring Lake Drive
Itasca, IL 60143
630-775-2213
FAX: 630-285-0798 800-621-7619
customerservice@nsc.org
www.congress.nsc.org
Nancy Gavin, Expo Manager
Christine Paplaczyk, Exhibit Sales
Alan McMillan, Chief Executive Officer
Annual event for safety, health and the environment.
16000 Attendees September

12104 National Society for Histotechnology Symposium/Convention
4201 Northview Drive
Suite 502
Bowie, MD 20716
301-262-6221
FAX: 301-262-9188
histo@nsh.org www.nsh.org
Aubrey Wanner, Meeting Manager
Carrie Diamond, Executive Director
National gathering for all chapters, advancing professional growth through educational sessions and the exchange of ideas.
1500 Attendees October 1500 names $35 per M.

12105 Neocon South
Designfest/NeoCon South
200 World Trade Center Chicago
Chicago, IL 60654
312-527-7999
FAX: 312-527-7782
Chris Kennedy, President

12106 Neocon West
Designfest/Neocon South
200 World Trade Center
Chicago, IL 60654
312-527-7999
FAX: 312-527-7782
Chris Kennedy, President

12107 Neocon's World Trade Fair
Design/Neocon South
200 World Trade Center
Chicago, IL 60654
312-527-7999
FAX: 312-527-7782
Chris Kennedy, President

12108 New England Grows
Hynes Convention Center
900 Boylston
Boston, MA 07115
617-954-2000
FAX: 617-954-2125
info@mccahome.com
www.mccahome.com
1500 Attendees February

12109 Northwest Urological Society
Northwest Urological Society
2033 6th Avenue
Suite 1100
Seattle, WA 98121
206-441-9762

180 Attendees

12110 Nurse Managers Update
National Professional Education Institute
2525 Ossen Fort Road
PO Box 118
Glencoe, MO 63068-1107
636-735-5570
FAX: 561-743-9596 800-575-5575
JJMcDaid@aol.com
www.npeinursing.com
Judie McDaid, Exhibitor Relations Manager
Leslie Brock, Registration Manager
The Nurse Managers Update and Critical Care Conference/EXPO provides a fully integrated program dedicated to the continuing education of critical care nurses, nurse managers and other healthcare professionals. Exhibitors showcase their latest

healthcare products, pharmaceuticals, services, research and facilities. Knowledge gained in the informative, entertaining EXPO Hall, will influence these nurses' purchasing decisions throughout the year.
1500 Attendees Annual, April Founded: 1989

12111 Obesity and Associated Conditions Symposium
American Society of Bariatric Physicians/ASBP
5453 E Evans Place
Denver, CO 80222
303-794-4833
FAX: 303-779-4834
info@asbp.org www.asbp.org
Cathy Suski, Communications
Learn about the latest research in obesity treatment and how to use it in your practice.
500 Attendees Annual 1,000 names $300 per M.

12112 Optometry's Meeting
American Optometric Association
243 N Lindbergh Boulevard
Saint Louis, MO 63141
314-991-4100
FAX: 314-991-4101
www.acanet.org/acanet
Main exhibits: optometric equipment, supplies and services.
8000 Attendees June

12113 Osteopathic Physicians & Surgeons Annual Convention
Osteopathic Physicians & Surgeons of California
455 Capitol Mall
Suite 230
Sacramento, CA 95814
916-561-0724
Kathleen Creason, Executive Director

12114 Pacific Dermatological Association
Pacific Dermatological Association
100 Meadowcreek Drive
Suite 150
Corte Madera, CA 94925
415-927-5729
FAX: 415-927-5726
pda@hp-assoc.com
www.pacificderm.org
Julie Hodge, President
Exclusively for education, scientific and charitable purposes. Provides opportunities for exchange of information and advancement of knowledge of dermatology among physicians within the membership area.
August

12115 Pacific Northwest Radiological Society
Pacific Northwest Radiological Society
2033 6th Avenue
Suite 1100
Seattle, WA 98121
206-441-9762
FAX: 206-441-5863
Jan Larson, Manager

12116 Pediatric Academic Societies Annual Meeting
American Pediatric Society & Society for Pediatric
3400 Research Forest Drive
Suite B7
The Woodlands, TX 77381
281-419-0052
FAX: 281-419-0082
info@pas-meeting.org
www.pas-meeting.org
Debbie Anagnostelis, Meeting Director
Kathy Cannon, Associate Director
4500 Attendees May

12117 Policy Conference
American Association of Health Plans
1129 20th Street NW
Washington, DC 20036
202-778-3200
FAX: 202-778-8506

12118 Postgraduate Assembly in Anesthesiology
New York State Society of Anesthesiologists
85 5th Avenue
8th Floor
New York, NY 10003
212-867-7140
FAX: 212-867-7153
kurt@nyssa-pga.org
www.nyssa-pga.org
Kurt G Becker, Executive Director
Annual conference for anesthesia professionals, held each December in New York City.
7000 Attendees December

12119 Primary Care Update
Interstate Postgraduate Medical Association
PO Box 5474
Madison, WI 52705
608-231-9045
FAX: 608-231-9045
info@ipmameded.org
www.ipmameded.org
Mary W Ales, Executive Director
1000 Attendees October

12120 Radiological Society of North America's Scientific Assembly
Radiological Society of North America
2021 Spring Road
Suite 600
Oak Brook, IL 60521
630-571-5424
62000 Attendees

12121 SABM Annual Symposium
Society for the Advancement of Blood Management
2209 Dickens Road
PO Box 11086
Richmond, VA 23116
804-565-6310
FAX: 804-282-0090
exhibits@societyhq.com
www.societyhq.com/exhibitors
Matt Van Wie, Show Manager
Exhibits of blood management equipment, information, supplies and services, conference, meals, breaks, sponsorships available.
300 Attendees September 400 names

12122 SCA Annual Meeting and Workshops
Society of Cardiovascular Anesthesiologists
2209 Dickens Road
PO Box 11086
Richmond, VA 23116
804-820-0084
FAX: 804-282-0090
exhibits@societyhq.com
www.societyhq.com/exhibitors
Matt Van Wie, Show Manager
Exhibits of cardiac anesthesia and pain equipment, information, supplies and services, conference, meals, breaks, sponsorships available.
1,000 Attendees April 6,500 names $1M per M.

12123 SCA Annual Update on Cardiopolmonary Bypass
Society of Cardiovascular Anesthesiologists
2209 Dickens Road
PO Box 11086
Richmond, VA 23116
804-820-0084
FAX: 804-282-0090
exhibits@societyhq.com
www.societyhq.com/exhibitors
Matt Van Wie, Show Manager
Exhibits of cardio, anesthesia equipment, information, supplies and services, conference, meals, breaks, sponsorships available. Fifty-eight percent anesthesiologists, 28 percent perfusionists, eight percent surgeons and six percent other.
300 Attendees March 6,500 names $1M per M.

12124 SCA Comprehensive Review of Interoperative Echo
Society of Cardiovascular Anesthesiologists
2209 Dickens Road
PO Box 11086
Richmond, VA 23116
804-820-0084
FAX: 804-282-0090
exhibits@societyhq.com
www.societyhq.com/exhibitors
Matt Van Wie, Show Manager
Exhibits of anesthesia and echo equipment, information, supplies and services, conference, meals, breaks, sponsorships available.
800 Attendees February 6,500 names $1M per M.

12125 SCCM Educational & Scientific Symposium
Society of Critical Care Medicine
8101 E Kaiser Blouevard
Anaheim, CA 92808
714-282-6000
2500 Attendees

12126 SIIM 2007
Society for Imaging Informatics in Medicine
19440 Golf Vista Drive
Suite 330
Leesburg, VA 20176
703-757-0054
FAX: 703-757-0454
info@scarnet.org www.scarnet.org
Janice Honeyman-Buck Ph.D, Editor-in-Chief
The SIIM is an annual meeting and conference for members that is a comprehensive

educational and scientific program unmatched in the field. SIIM provides an open environment for imaging information professionals to access expert, unbiased, and cutting-edge resources in a collegial and practical atmosphere.
June

12127 SNACC Annual Meeting
Society of Neurological Anesthesia & Critical Care
2209 Dickens Road
PO Box 11086
Richmond, VA 23116
804-565-6310
FAX: 804-282-0090
exhibits@societyhq.com
www.societyhq.com/exhibitors
Matt Van Wie, Show Manager
Exhibits of Anesthesia equipment, information, supplies and services, conference, meals, breaks, sponsorship available.
300 Attendees October

12128 SOAP Annual Meeting
Society for Obstetric Anesthesia and Perinatology
2209 Dickens Road
PO Box 11086
Richmond, VA 23116
804-825-5051
FAX: 804-282-0090
exhibits@societyhq.com
www.societyhq.com/exhibitors
Matt Van Wie, Show Manager
Exhibits of anesthesia and obstetric equipment, information, supplies and services, conference, meals, breaks, sponsorships available.
500 Attendees May 1,000 names

12129 SPA Annual Meeting
Society for Pediatric Anesthesia
2209 Dickens Road
PO Box 11086
Richmond, VA 23116
804-565-6310
FAX: 804-282-0090
exhibits@societyhq.com
www.societyhq.com/exhibitors
Matt Van Wie, Show Manager
Exhibits of anethesia equipment, information, supplies and services, conference, meals, breaks, sponsorships available.
600 Attendees October 4,000 names

12130 SPA Winter Meeting, Pediatric Anesthesiology
Society for Pediatric Anesthesia
2209 Dickens Road
PO Box 11086
Richmond, VA 23116
804-565-6310
FAX: 804-282-0090
exhibits@societyhq.com
www.societyhq.com/exhibitors
Matt Van Wie, Show Manager
Exhibits of anethesia equipment, information, supplies and services, conference, meals, breaks, sponsorships available.
350 Attendees March 4,000 names

12131 Society for Computer Applications in Radio logy Annual Meeting
10105 Cottesmore Court
Great Falls, VA 22066-3540
703-757-0054
FAX: 703-757-0454
info@scarnet.org www.scarnet.org
Anna Marie Mason, Executive Director
Devoted to advance computer applications and information technology in medical imaging through education and research. Provides an open environment for imaging information professionals to access expert and cutting edge resources in a collegial and practical atmosphere.
1400 Attendees June

12132 Society for Disability Studies Annual Meeting
Exhibit Promotions Plus
11630 Vixens Path
Ellicott City, MD 21042
301-596-3028
FAX: 410-997-0764
exhibits@erols.com
www.epponline.com
Harve C Horowitz, President
June

12133 Society for Neuroscience
Herlitz Company
1890 Palmer Avenue
Suite 202 A
Larchmont, NY 10538
914-833-1979
FAX: 914-833-0920
Bruce Herlitz, President

12134 Society of Nuclear Medicine Annual Meeting
Society of Nuclear Medicine
1850 Samuel Morse Drive
Reston, VA 20190
703-708-9000
Virginia Pappas, Executive Director
7000 Attendees

12135 Society of Thoracic Surgeons Annual Meeting
Society of Thoracic Surgeons Annual Meeting
401 N Michigan Avenue
Chicago, IL 60611
312-644-6610
4200 Attendees

12136 Society of Toxicology Annual Meeting
Society of Toxicology
1767 Business Center Drive
Suite 302
Reston, VA 20190
703-438-3115
FAX: 703-438-3113
clarissa@toxicology.org
www.toxicology.org
Shawn Lamb, Executive Director
Clarissa Russell Wilson, Contact
Professional and scholarly organization meeting of scientists from academic institutions, government and industry representing the great variety of scientists who practice toxicology in the US and abroad.
5000 Attendees March

12137 Southeastern Surgical Congress Annual Assembly
South Med. Associates
PO Box 330
Pelham, AL 35124
205-991-3552
FAX: 205-991-6771

12138 Southern Association for Primary Care
Southern Medical Association
PO Box 190088
Birmingham, AL 35219
205-945-1840
FAX: 205-945-1830

12139 Southern Medical Association Meeting
Southern Medical Association
PO Box 190088
Birmingham, AL 35219
205-451-1840
FAX: 205-945-1830 800-423-4992
Ed Waldron, Chief Executive Officer
2500 Attendees

12140 Symposium of the Protein Society
FASEB
9650 Rockville Pike
Bethesda, MD 20814
301-634-7100
FAX: 301-530-7001 www.faseb.org

12141 United States and Canadian Academy of Pathology
Herlitz Company
1890 Palmer Avenue
Suite 202A
Larchmont, NY 10538
914-833-1979
FAX: 914-833-0929
kris@herlitz.com www.herlitz.com
Kris Herlitz, Show Manager
3000 Attendees March

12142 Vision New England
Hynes Convention Center
900 Boylston Street
Boston, MA 07115
617-954-2000
FAX: 617-954-2125
info@mccahome.com
www.mccahome.com
24000 Attendees January

12143 World Congress on Pediatric & Intensive Care
Hynes Convention Center
900 Boylston Street
Boston, MA 02115
617-954-2000
FAX: 617-954-2125 800-845-8800
info@mccahome.com
www.mccahome.com
2500 Attendees June

12144 Yankee Dental Congress
Hynes Convention Center
900 Boylston Street
Boston, MA 07115
617-954-2000
FAX: 617-954-2125
info@mccahome.com
www.mccahome.com
2400 Attendees January

12145 today's surgicenter conference
Virgo Publishing
3300 N Central Avenue, Suite 300
Phoenix, AZ 85012
480-990-1101
FAX: 480-281-6744 800-454-5760
asharman@vpico.com
www.surgicenterconference.com
Dana Hicks, Show Manager
Offers owners and operators of ambulatory surgery centers high-caliber instructive seminars by leading industry veterans, ex-

hibits, and networking opportunities. Decision makers attend to learn more about construction and design, technology, equipment, legal and regulatory issues, marketing and finance and development. Approximately 50 booths.
200+ Attendees September Founded: 2004 Mailing list available for rent 15000+ names $var per M.

Directories & Databases

12146 American Academy of Forensic Sciences Membership Directory
410 N 21st St
Colorado Springs, CO 80904-2712
719-636-1100
FAX: 719-636-1993
membership@aafs.org www.aafs.org
Anne Warren, Executive Director
Offers valuable information on over 5,000 persons qualified in forensic sciences including law, anthropology and psychiatry. *$ 50.00*
250 pages Annual 5000 names $295 per M.

12147 Catalog of Professional Testing Resources
Psychological Assessment Resources
PO Box 998
Odessa, FL 33556

FAX: 800-727-9329 800-331-8378

12148 Comparitive Guide to American Hospitals
Grey House Publishing
185 Millerton Road
PO Box 860
Millerton, NY 12546
518-789-8700
FAX: 518-789-0545 800-562-2139
books@greyhouse.com
www.greyhouse.com
Richard Gottlieb, President
Leslie Mackenzie, Publisher
Compares all of the nation's hospitals by 19 measures of quality in the treatment of heart attack, heart failure, pneumonia, and surgical procedures. *$2.25*
2500 pages Annual

12149 Complete Directory for Pediatric Disorders
Grey House Publishing
185 Millerton Road
PO Box 860
Millerton, NY 12546
518-890-0526
FAX: 518-789-0545 800-562-2139
books@greyhouse.com
www.greyhouse.com
Leslie Mackenzie, Publisher
Richard Gottlieb, Editor
Provides parents and caregivers with information about pediatric conditions, disorders, diseases and disabilities. Contains understandable descriptions of 16 major bodily systems, descriptions of more than 200 disorders and a resource section. *$165.00*
1,120 pages Annual

12150 Complete Directory for People with Disabilities
Grey House Publishing
185 Millerton Road
PO Box 860
Millerton, NY 12546
518-890-0526
FAX: 518-789-0545 800-562-2139
books@greyhouse.com
www.greyhouse.com
Leslie Mackenzie, Publisher
Richard Gottlieb, Editor
Comprehensive resource for people with disabilities, detailing independent living centers, rehabilitation facilities, state and federal agencies, associations and support groups. This one-stop resource also provides immediate access to the latest products and services for people with disabilities, such as periodicals and books, assistive devices, employment and education programs and travel groups. *$165.00*
1,139 pages Annual

12151 Complete Directory for People with Chronic Illness
Grey House Publishing
185 Millerton Road
PO Box 860
Millerton, NY 12546
518-890-0526
FAX: 518-789-0545 800-562-2139
books@greyhouse.com
www.greyhouse.com
Leslie Mackenzie, Publisher
Richard Gottlieb, Editor
This widely-hailed directory is structured around the 90 most prevelent chronic illness — from asthma to cancer to Wilson's Disease — and provides a comprehensive overview of the support services and information resources available for people diagnosed with a chronic illness. Each chronic illness has its own chapter and contains a brief description in layman's language, followed by important resources for national and local organizations. *$165.00*
1,200 pages Annual

12152 Complete Learning Disabilities Directory
Grey House Publishing
185 Millerton Road
PO Box 860
Millerton, NY 12546
518-890-0526
FAX: 518-789-0545 800-562-2139
books@greyhouse.com
www.greyhouse.com
Leslie Mackenzie, Publisher
Richard Gottlieb, Editor
The most comprehensive database of programs, services, curriculum materials, professional meetings and resources, camps, newsletters and support groups for teachers, students and families concerned with learning disabilities. Includes information about associations and organizations, schools, colleges and testing materials, government agencies, legal resources and more. *$145.00*
848 pages Annual

12153 Complete Mental Health Directory
Grey House Publishing
185 Millerton Road
PO Box 860
Millerton, NY 12546
518-890-0526
FAX: 518-789-0545 800-562-2139
books@greyhouse.com
www.greyhouse.com
Leslie Mackenzie, Publisher
Richard Gottlieb, Editor
Comprehensive information covering the field of behavioral health, with critical information for both the layman and mental health professional. Provides the layman with understandable descriptions of 25 mental health disorders, as well as detailed information on associations, media, support groups and mental health facilities. Offers the professional critical and comprehensive information on managed care organizations, information systems, government agencies and provider organizations. *$165.00*
687 pages Annual

12154 Detwiler's Directory of Health and Medical Resources
Information Today
143 Old Marlton Pike
Medford, NJ 08055-8750
609-654-6266
FAX: 609-654-4309
custserv@infotoday.com
www.infotoday.com
Thomas H Hogan, Publisher/President
John Bryans, Publisher/Editor-in-Chief Books
Lauree Padgett, Editorial Services Manager
Inge Coffey, Circulation Manager
Pat Palatucci, Assistant to the President
A comprehensive guide to over 2,000 health and medical corporations,associations, state and federal agencies, helathcare market research firms, foundations, institutes, and more. *$195.00*
ISBN 1-573871-55-9

12155 Directory of Health Care Group Purchasing Organizations
Grey House Publishing
185 Millerton Road
PO Box 860
Millerton, NY 12546
518-890-0526
FAX: 518-789-0545 800-562-2139
books@greyhouse.com
www.greyhouse.com
Leslie Mackenzie, Publisher
Richard Gottlieb, Editor
This comprehensive directory provides the important data you need to get in touch with over 1,000 Group Purchasing Organizations. *$325.00*
1,000 pages

12156 Directory of Hospital Personnel
Grey House Publishing
185 Millerton Road
PO Box 860
Millerton, NY 12546
518-890-0526
FAX: 518-789-0545 800-562-2139
books@greyhouse.com
www.greyhouse.com
Leslie Mackenzie, Publisher
Richard Gottlieb, Editor
The Directory of Hospital Personnel is the best resource you can have at your fingertips when researching or marketing a product or service to the hospital industry. You're in touch with over 80,000 key decision-makers from over 6,500 hospitals. *$275.00*
2,500 pages

12157 Employee Assistance Program Management Yearbook
Health Resources Publishing
1913 Atlantic Avenue
Suite F4
Manasquan, NJ 08736
732-292-1100
FAX: 732-292-1111 888-843-6242
info@themcic.com
www.themcic.com/www.healthresourcesonline.com

Bob Jenkins, President/Managing Editor
Lisa Mansfield, Marketing Assistant

Explore major areas of involvement for EAPS. Investigate tools for effectively managing your EAP. Learn how screening tools for mental illness can help EAPS manage care. Learn how to help families deal with workplace changes. Learn how to identify potentially violent situations in the workplace and much more. *$149.00*
ISBN 1-882364-25-2

12158 HCEA Directory of Healthcare Meetings and Conventions
Healthcare Convention & Exhibitors Association
5775 Peachtree Dunwoody Road NE
Building G, Suite 500
Atlanta, GA 30342-1542
404-252-3663
FAX: 404-252-0774
hcea@assnhq.com www.hcea.org

Frank Corcoran, President/Director
Carol Wilson, Meetings Director

Information on 6,000 health care meetings.
500 pages Founded: 1930

12159 HMO/PPO Directory
Grey House Publishing
185 Millerton Road
PO Box 860
Millerton, NY 12546
518-890-0526
FAX: 518-789-0545 800-562-2139
books@greyhouse.com
www.greyhouse.com

Leslie Mackenzie, Publisher
Richard Gottlieb, Editor

The HMO/PPO Directory is a comprehensive source that provides detailed information about Health Maintenance Organizations and Preferred Provider Organizations nationwide. *$275.00*
500 pages

12160 Health Funds Grants Resources Yearbook
Health Resources Publishing
1913 Atlantic Avenue
Suite F5
Manasquan, NJ 08736
732-292-1100
FAX: 732-292-1111 888-843-6242
info@themcic.com
www.themcic.com/www.healthresourcesonline.com

Bob Jenkins, President/Managing Editor
Judy Granholm, Marketing Director

A resource book that gives dollar amounts, descriptions of previous grant recipients and programs that attract funding and details of future funding trends. *$165.00*
ISBN 1-882364-30-9

12161 Managed Care Yearbook
Health Resources Publishing
1913 Atlantic Avenue
Suite F4
Manasquan, NJ 08736
732-292-1100
FAX: 732-292-1111 888-843-6242
info@themcic.com
www.themcic.com/www.healthresourcesonline.com

Bob Jenkins, President/Managing Editor
Judy Granholm, Marketing Director

Resource book that includes critical facts, statistics cost, analysis, comparisions, enrollment and trends studies on managed care. Topics also include member retention, international markets and disease management. *$29.00*
608 pages ISBN 1-882364-26-0

12162 Medical Device Register
Grey House Publishing
185 Millerton Road
PO Box 860
Millerton, NY 12546
518-789-8700
FAX: 518-789-0545 800-562-2139
books@greyhouse.com
www.greyhouse.com

Richard Gottlieb, President
Leslie Mackenzie, Publisher

The one-stop source for locating suppliers and products; looking for nre manufacturers of hard-to-find medical devices; comparing products and companies; knowing who's selling what and who to buy from cost effectively. *$325.00*
3000 pages Annual

12163 National Directory of Integrated Healthcare Delivery Systems
Health Resources Publishing
1913 Atlantic Avenue
Suite F4
Manasquan, NJ 08736
732-292-1100
FAX: 732-292-1111 888-843-6242
info@themcic.com
www.themcic.com/www.healthresourcesonline.com

Bob Jenkins, President/Managing Editor
Lisa Mansfield, Marketing Assistant

Gives facts and stastics on more than 850 health care delivery systems and affiliations. Includes profiles of IHDSs by state and by alphabetical order. Also includes a directory of health care associations, a ranking of systems by revenues and an analysis of IHDSs growth projections. *$995.00*
ISBN 1-882364-31-7

12164 National Directory of Physician Organizations Database On Cd-Rom
Health Resources Publishing
1913 Atlantic Avenue
Suite F5
Manasquan, NJ 08736
732-292-1100
FAX: 732-292-1111 888-843-6242
info@themcic.com
www.themcic.com/www.healthresourcesonline.com

Bob Jenkins, President/Managing Editor
Judy Granholm, Marketing Director

Detailed profiles on over 1,800 physician organizations. Listings include physician hospitals organizations (PHOs), independent practice associations, management services organizations and physician practice management companies. Key elements of the data profile include: executive officers; year founded; profits status, statue of incorporation; numbers of associates physician; market area; market analysis; affiliated/participating hospital; management service organizations used. *$995.00*
ISBN 1-882364-18-X : CD-ROM

12165 Older Americans Information Directory
Grey House Publishing
185 Millerton Road
PO Box 860
Millerton, NY 12546
518-890-0526
FAX: 518-789-0545 800-562-2139
books@greyhouse.com
www.greyhouse.com

Leslie Mackenzie, Publisher
Richard Gottlieb, Editor

Important resources for older americans, including national, regional, state and local organizations, government agencies, research centers, legal resources, discount travel information, continuing education programs, disability aids and assistive devices, health, print media and electronic media. *$165.00*
1200 pages ISBN 1-592370-53-5

12166 Wellness Program Management Yearbook: 2nd Edition
Health Resources Publishing
1913 Atlantic Avenue
Suite F4
Manasquan, NJ 08736
732-292-1100
FAX: 732-292-1111 888-843-6242
info@themcic.com
www.themcic.com/www.healthresourcesonline.com

Bob Jenkins, President/Managing Editor
Lisa Mansfield, Marketing Assistant

This yearbook highlights such issues as obtaining senior management support, encouraging employment participation in programs, finding, funding and developing different programs. Also helps in planning initiatives by providing details of the components that will be important to include about the programs that will help you to meet your goals. *$155.00*
ISBN 1-882364-39-2

Industry Web Sites

12167 www.aaham.org
American Association of Healthcare Administrative
Management

Business offices, credit and collection managers, and admitting officers for hospitals, clincis and other health care organizaitons. To educate members, exchange information and techniques, and keep members abreast of new regulations relating to their field. Seeks proper recognition for the financial aspect of hospital and clinic managememnt.

12168 www.aahperd.org
American Alliance for Hlth, Phys. Edu. Rec. Dance
Recreation & Dance

12169 **www.aaihds.org**
American Association of Integrated Healthcare
Delivery Systems

Physicians, hospital executives and board members, health plan executives, and other key entities and professionals employed by all forms of IDDSs including PHOS, IPA POSOS, and MSOS. Seeks to provide advocacy for issues related to integrated health care through research, education, and communication. Conducts educational and research programs; maintains speakers' bureau and information clearinghouse.

12170 **www.aameda.org**
American Academy of Medical Administrators

Individuals involved in medical administration at the executive- or midele-management levels. Promotes educational courses for the training of persons in medical administration. Conducts research. Offers placement service.

12171 **www.aaos.org**
American Academy for Cerebral Palsy and
Developmental Medicine

12172 **www.aap.org**
American Academy of Pediatrics

12173 **www.academydentalmaterials.org**
Academy of Dental Materials

Formerly known as American Academy for Plastics Research in Dentistry.

12174 **www.ache.org**
American College of Healthcare Executives

International professional society of more than 30,000 healthcare executives. Credentialing and educational programs, Congress on Healthcare Management. ACHE's publishing division, Health Administration Press, is one of the largest publishers of books.

12175 **www.acpe.org**
American College of Physician Executives

Physicians whose primary professional responsibility is the management of health care organizations. Provides for continuing education and certification of the physician executive and the profession. Offers specialized career planning, counseling, recruitment and placement services, and research and information data on physican managers.

12176 **www.acrm.org**
American Congress of Rehabilitation Medicine

12177 **www.acsm.org**
American College of Sports Medicine

The ACSM promotes and integrates scientific research, education, and practical applications of sports medicine and exercise science to maintain and enhance physical performance, fitness, health, and quality of life.

12178 **www.afprd.org**
Association of Family Practice Residency Directors

Provides representation for residency directors at a national level and provides a political voice for them to approprite arenas. Promotes cooperation and communication between residency programs and different branches of the family practice specialty. Dedicated to improving of education of family physicians. Provides a network for mutual assistance among FP, residency directors.

12179 **www.aha.org**
American Hospital Association

12180 **www.ahia.org**
Association of Healthcare Internal Auditors

Promotes cost containment and increased productivity in health care institutions through internal auditing. Serves as a forum for the exchange of experience, ideas, and information among members; provides continuing professional education courses and informs members of developments in health care internal auditing. Offers employment clearinghouse services.

12181 **www.ahqa.org**
American Health Quality Association

Central news area for the group that represents quality inprovement organizations and professionals working to improve the quality of health care in communities across America.

12182 **www.ahraonline.org**
Radiology Administrators

For radiology administrators from the US, Canada, and several other countries.

12183 **www.ama-assn.org**
American Medical Association

A partnership of physicians and their professional associations dedicated to promoting the art and science of medicine and the betterment of the public health. To serve physicians and their patients by establishing and promoting ethical, educational, and clinical standards for the medical profession and by advocating for the highest principle of all - the integrity of the physician/patient relationship.

12184 **www.amga.org**
American Medical Group Association

12185 **www.arrs.org**
American Roentgen Ray Society

102 years strong radiological association for all subspecialties.

12186 **www.ascrs.org**
American Society of Ophthalmic Administrators

A division of the American Society of Cataract and Retractive Surgery. Persons involved with the administration of an ophthalmic office or clinic. Facilitates the exchange of idease and information in order to improve management practices and working conditions. Offers placement services.

12187 **www.asnr.org**
American Society of Neuroradiology

12188 **www.asrm.org**
American Society for Reproductive Medicine

Organization devoted to advancing knowledge and expertise in reproductive medicine and biology. Members of this voluntary nonprofit organization must demonstrate the high ethical principals of the medical profession, evince an interest in reproductive medicine and biotechnology, and adhere to the objectives of the Society.

12189 **www.awhp.org**
Association for Worksite Health Promotion

Exists to advance the profession of worksite health promotion and the career development of its practitioners and to improve the performance of the programs they administer. Represents a variety of disciplines and worksites, for decision-makers in the areas of health promotion/disease prevention and health-care cost management.

12190 **www.cdc.gov**
Centers for Disease Control and Prevention

The official website of CDC, the government's public health agency.

12191 **www.chpa-info.org**
Consumer Healthcare Products Association

Members are producers of nonprescription medicines and dietary supplements for self-care. Has an annual budget of approximately $10 million.

12192 **www.cleftline.org**
American Cleft Palate Craniofacial Association

Organization of plastic surgeons, dentists, orthodontists, speech pathologists, geneticists, social workers and others.

12193 **www.cmsa.org**
Case Management Society of America

Exclusively for the case management profession.

12194 **www.crnusa.com**
Council for Responsible Nutrition

Government relations, scientific and regulatory affairs, publications.

12195 **www.docinfo.org**

A national data bank of disciplinary histories on US licensed physicians from the Federation of State Medical Boards; charges $9.95 per report

12196 **www.entnet.org**
American Academy of Otolarygngology-Head & Neck

12197 **www.fascrw.org**
American Society of Colon & Rectal Surgeons

12198 **www.foodallergy.org**
Food Allergy & Anaphylaxis Network

Facts, common questions, resources and news.

12199 **www.gretmar.com/webdoctor/**

General medical information.

12200 **www.greyhouse.com**
Grey House Publishing

Selected Grey House directories in the fields of business, health and education are available online. Users can search our online databases by several different search criteria, such as product categories, geographic area, sales volume and much, much more. Full Grey House catalog and online ordering also available.

12201 **www.hcea.org**
Healthcare Convention & Exhibitors Association

Trade association of over 650 organizations involved in health care exhibiting or providing services to health care conventions, exhibitions and/or meetings.

12202 **www.healthfinder.gov**

A comprehensive guide to resources for health information from the federal government and related agencies

12203 **www.hfma.org**
Healthcare Financial Management Association

Brings perspective and clarity to the industry's complex issues for the purpose of preparing our members to succeed. Through our programs, publications and partnerships, we enhance the capabilities that strengthen not only individuals careers, but also the organizations from which our members come.

12204 **www.ichbc.org**
Institute of Healthcare Business Consultants

Maintains code of ethics, rules of professional conducts, and certification program, administers examination and conducts certification course. Membership by successful completion of certification examination only.

12205 **www.jamesbeard.org**
James Beard Foundation

Not-for-profit organization dedicated to preserving the country's culinary heritage and fostering the appreciation and development of gastronomy by recognizing and promoting excellence in all aspects of the culinary arts.

12206 **www.managedcaremarketplace.com**

Managed Care Information Center

An online yellow pages for companies providing services to MCOs, hospitals and physicians groups. There are more than three dozen targeted categories, offering information on vendors from claims processing to transportation services to health care compliance.

12207 **www.medicaid.apwa.org**
National Association of Medicaid Directors

Promotes effective Medicaid policy and program administration; works with the federal government on issues through technical advisory groups. Conducts forums on policy and technical issues.

12208 **www.mgma.com**
American College of Medical Practice Executives

Professional credentialing organization. Works to encourage medical group practice administrators to improve and maintain their proficiency and to provide appropriate recognition; to establish a program with uniform standards of admission, advancement, certification and fellowship in order to achieve the highest possible standards in the profession of medical group practice administration; to participate in the development of educational and research programs.

12209 **www.mwsearch.com/**

Medical world search.

12210 **www.mywebmd.com**

The largest commercial health site, offers easy - to read information on health and wellness issues and latest medical news

12211 **www.naher.com**
National Association for Healthcare Recruitment

Individuals employed directly by hospitals and other health care organizations which are involved in the practice of professional health care recruitment. Promotes sound principles of professionals health care recruitment. Provides financial assistance to aid members in planning and implementing regional educational programs. Offers technical assistance and consultation services. Compiles statistics.

12212 **www.namdrc.org**
National Association of Medical Directors for
Respiratory Care

Works to provide educational opportunities to fit the needs of medical directors of respiratory care and represents the interests of members to regulatory agencies to ensure that the needs of respiratory patients are not overlooked. Offers educational programs; maintains speakers' bureau.

12213 **www.namss.org**
National Association Medical Staff Service

Individuals involved in the management and administration of health care provider services. Seeks to enhance the knowledge and experience of medical staff services professionals and promote the certification of those involved in the profession.

12214 **www.nerf.org**
National Eye Research Center

Improving your vision through eyecare, education and research.

12215 **www.nlm.nih.gov/databases/medline.html**

Vast bibliographic database maintained by the US National Library of Medicine. Medline contains citations and abstracts from several thousand biomedical journals, covering medicine, nursing, dentistry, vetinary medicine and other fields.

12216 **www.nraa.org/renal/**
National Renal Administrators Association

Administrative personnel involved with dialysis programs for patients suffering from kidney failure. Provides a vehicle for the development of educational and informational services for members. Maintains contact with health care facilities and government agencies. Operates placement serve; compiles statistics; conducts political action committee.

12217 **www.oncolink.com**

Founded by specialist at the University of Pennsylvania, provides information on wide range of childhood and adult cancers

12218 **www.pahcom.com**
Professional Association of Health Care Office
Management

Office managers of small group and solo medical practices. Operates certification program for health care office managers.

12219 **www.paralysis.org**
Christopher Reeve Paralysis Foundation

Our mission is to raise money to help fing spinal cord injury research.

12220 **www.quackwatch.com**

A nonprofit corporation whose purpose is to combat health - related frauds, myths, fads, and fallacies and investigate phony medical news

12221 **www.rbma.org**
Radiology Business Management Association

Business managers for private radiology groups; corporate members include: vendors of equipment, services, or supplies. Purposes are to improve business administration of radiologists' practices to better serve patients and the medical profession; and to provide opportunities for professional development and recognition. Offers extensive educational and networking opportunities and informal placement service. Maintains information services emphasizing those aspects unique to the business.

12222 **www.sleepproducts.org**
International Sleep Products Association

Maintains a strong organization to influence government actions, inform and educate the membership and act on industry issues to enhance the growth,profitability and stature of the sleep products industry. Provides members with information and services to manage their business more effectively and efficiently. Publishes a magazine devoted exclusively to the mattress industry, BEDtimes covers a broad range of issue and news important to the industry.

12223 **www.smamc.org**
Society of Medical-Dental Management Consultants

Professionals medical and/or dental management consultants associated for educational and information sharing purposes. Objectives are to: advance the profession; share management techniques; improve individual skills; provide clients with competent and capable business management. Provides information on insurance and income tax. Conducts surveys; compiles statistics.

12224 **www.themcic.com**
Healthcare IS/IT Yearbook

The Health care IS/IT Market Yearbook is a unique and valuable sales and marketing reference tool for IT companies selling into the health and managed care industries. Great for sales and marketing research; developing reports or preparing presentations. Now, it's easy to identify what hospitals are contracting for, get information on hundreds of millions of dollars in healthcare. IT contract deals, discover what other companies are doing.

12225 **www.toxicology.org**
Society Of Toxicology

Members are scientists concerned with the effects of chemicals on man and the environment. Promotes the aquisition and utilization of knowledge in toxicology, aids in the protection of public health and facilitates disiplines. The society has a strong commitment to education in toxicology and to the recruitment of students and new members into the profession.

12226 **www.uams.edu/afpa/**
Association of Family Practice Administrators

Promotes professionalism in family practice administration. Serves as a network for sharing of information and fellowship among network for sharing of information and fellowship among members. Provides technical assistance to members; functions as a liaison to related professional organizations.

Associations

12227 Air Balance Consultants
4207 Maycrest Avenue
Los Angeles, CA 90032

FAX: 408-437-7590 800-429-6880
Members are engineers specializing in the balancing of air conditioning systems.
35 Members

12228 Air Conditioning & Refrigeration Institute
4100 N Fairfax Drive
Suite 200
Arlington, VA 22203
703-524-8800
FAX: 703-528-3816
ari@ari.org www.ari.org
William G Sutton, President
Kathryn Alexander, Director Administration/Membership
Becky Lyon, Director Budget/Accounting
Dave Martz, VP Administration/Statistics
Ed Dooley, VP Communications/Education
Trade association representing manufacturers of more than 90% of North American produced central air-conditioning and commercial refrigeration equipment.
250 Members Founded: 1953

12229 Air Conditioning Contractors of America
2800 Shirlington Road
Suite 300
Arlington, VA 22206
703-575-4477
FAX: 703-575-4449
info@acca.org www.acca.org
Paul Stalknecht, President/CEO
Michael Honeycutt, Senior VP/Chief of Staff
Kevin Holland, VP for Communications
Larry Kaplan, VP for Finance
Hilary Atkins, Corporate Counsel
Represents HVAC contractors and holds annual meetings and exhibits for heating, air conditioning and refrigeration equipment, supplies and services.

12230 Air Diffusion Council
1901 North Roselle Road
Suite 800
Schaumburg, IL 60195
847-706-6750
FAX: 847-706-6751
info@flexibleduct.org
www.flexibleduct.org
Jack Lagershausen, President
The purpose of the Air Diffusion Council is to promote and further the interests of the manufacturers of air distribution equipment, more specifically, flexible air ducts and related products, and the interests of the general public in the areas of safety, quality, efficiency and energy conservation. Also, to develop programs approved and supported by the membership that legally promote and futher these interests.
40 Members Founded: 1961

12231 American Boiler Manufacturers Association
8221 Old Courthouse Rd
Ste 207
Vienna, VA 22182-3839
703-356-7172
FAX: 703-356-4543
randy@abma.com www.abma.com
W Randall Rawson, President
Geoffrey Halley, Director Technical Affairs
David Mort, Director Information Technology
Cheryl Jamall, Director Meetings
Manufacturers' trade association representing companies involved in utility, industrial and commercial steam generation. Includes associate memberships for companies who sell to or work with these companies and those who own boilers. Holds technical and production conferences and publishes technical guideline publications.
115 Members Founded: 1888

12232 American Society of Heating, Refrigerating
1791 Tullie Circle NE
Atlanta, GA 30329
404-636-8400
FAX: 404-321-5478
ashrae@ashrae.org www.ashrae.org
Lee Burgett, President
Frank Coda, Executive VP
Sponsors research, writes standards, publishes technical literature and offers development seminars. *$8.00*
55M Members Monthly Founded: 1894

12233 American Supply Association
222 Merchandise Mart Plaza
Chicago, IL 60654
312-464-0090
FAX: 312-464-0091
info@asaef.org www.asa.net
H Steve Anderson, Chairman
Chris Murin, Managing Director
Dottie Ramsey, Director
Joel Becker, VP
The national association of full-service plumbing, heating, cooling, and piping products for wholesalers, manufacturers, and distributors.
4000 Members Founded: 1969

12234 Cooling Technology Institute
2611 FM 1960 West Road
Suite A-101
Houston, TX 77068
281-583-4087
FAX: 281-537-1721
vmanser@cti.org www.cti.org
James Baker, President
Bill Howard, VP
Steven Chaloupka, Treasurer
Virginia Manser, Administrator
Charles W Foster, Director
Seeks to improve technology, design and performance of water conservation apparatus. Provides inspection services and conducts research.
400 Members Founded: 1950

12235 Gas Appliance Manufacturers Association
2107 Wilson Boulevard
Arlington, VA 22209-1718
703-257-7060
FAX: 703-525-0718
Jack Klimp, President
Represents manufacturers of residential, commercial and industrial gas and oil fired appliances, associated controls and accessories, as well as equipment used in the production, transmission and distribution of fuel gases.
262 Members Founded: 1935

12236 Heating, Air Conditioning & Refrigeration Distributors International
1389 Dublin Road
Columbus, OH 43215
614-488-1835
FAX: 614-488-0482
hardimail@hardinet.org
www.hardinet.org
Donald Frendberg, Executive VP/COO
Eileen Mantel, Senior Administrator
Mark Faessler, Secretary/Treasurer
Nonprofit organization dedicated to advancing the science of wholesale distribution in the HVACR industry.
1200 Members Founded: 1947

12237 International District Energy Association (IDEA)
125 Turnpike Roa
Suite 4
Westborough, MA 01581-2841
508-366-9339
FAX: 508-366-0019
idea@dc.sba.com
www.districtenergy.org
John L Fiegel, Director
IDEA fosters the success of its members as leaders in providing reliable, economical, and environmentally sound district energy services.
800 Members Founded: 1909

12238 International Microwave Power Institute
7076 Drinkard Way
Mechanicsville, VA 23111-5007
804-596-6667
FAX: 540-961-1463
info@impi.org www.impi.org
Kimberly D Thies, Executive Director
O Risman, President
David Baron, Treasurer
IMPI's members include scientists, researchers, lab technicians, product developers, marketing managers and a variety of other professionals in the microwave industry. The Institute serves the information needs of all specialists working with dielectric (microwave and RF) heating systems, and was expanded in 1977 to meet the information needs relating to consumer microwave ovens and related products.
700 Members Founded: 1966

12239 Masonry Heater Association of North America
1252 Stock Farm Road
Randolph, VT 05060
802-728-5896
FAX: 802-728-6004
bmarois@sovernet.com
www.mha-net.org
Jerry Frisch, President
Tim Seaton, VP
Rod Zander, Treasurer
Beverly Marois, Administrator
Promotes use of masonry heaters, increases public awareness and encourages reasonable governmental regulation.
115 Members Founded: 1989

12240 Mechanical Contractors Association of America
1385 Piccard Drive
Rockville, MD 20850
301-869-5800
FAX: 301-990-9690
John Gentille, Executive Vice President

Represents heating, piping and air conditioning professionals.
1.4M Members

12241 Mobile Air Conditioning Society Worldwide
225 S Broad Street
Lansdale, PA 19446
215-631-7020
FAX: 215-631-7017
info@macsw.org www.macsw.org
Elvis Hoffpauir, President/COO
Marion Posen, VP Sales and Marketing
Non-profit organization provides technical training, information and communication for the professionals in the automotive air-conditioning industry.
1600 Members Founded: 1981

12242 National Air Duct Cleaners Association
1518 K Street Northwest
Suite 503
Washington, DC 20005
202-372-2926
FAX: 202-347-8847
info@nadca.com www.nadca.com
John Schulte, Executive Director
Kenneth M Sufka, Executive VP
Leanne Murray, Director Membership
Jess Madden, Director Publications
Adam Garrison, Director Meetings
The trade association of the HVAC/Heating-Ventilation-Air Conditioning industry.
1000 Members Founded: 1989

12243 National Association of Plumbing, Heating
180 S Washington Street
PO Box 6808
Falls Church, VA 22040
703-237-8100
FAX: 703-237-7442 800-533-7694
naphcc@naphcc.org
www.phccweb.org
Steve Carder, President
Jim Stack, VP
Ike Casey, Executive VP
Lake A Coulson, VP Government Relations
Darrence Adams, Staff Accountant
National organization designed for suppliers of equipment, supplies and services for the plumbing, heating and cooling industries.
3700 Members Founded: 1883

12244 National Association of Power Engineers
1 Springfield Street
Chicopee, MA 01013
413-926-6273

napenatl@verizon.net
www.powerengineers.com
Michael Morin, President
Charles D Bayer, VP
David H Nolle, National Education Chairman
William Judd, Manager
Members include power plant operators and maintenance personnel who supply the industry with process power and related building and plant services.

12245 Solar Energy Industries Association
805 15th Street, NW
Suite 510
Washington, DC 20005
202-682-0556
FAX: 202-628-7779
info@seia.org www.seia.org
Glenn Hamer, Executive Director
Membership consists of companies, universities and utilities concerned with the development of the sun as an energy source.
150 Members Founded: 1974

12246 Wholesalers Association of the Northeast
111 Center Street
Middleboro, MA 02346
508-947-7100
FAX: 508-923-1044 www.wane5.org
Presently comprised of the leading wholesale distributors of pluming, heating, cooling and industrial pipe supplies, located throughout the northeast states.
Founded: 1932

Newsletters

12247 HVACR News
Trade News International
4444 Riverside Drive
Suite 202
Burbank, CA 91505
818-848-6397
FAX: 818-848-1306
news@hvacrnews.com
http://www.hvacrnews.com
Gary McCarty, Editor-in -Chief
Mark Deitch, Publisher
Jordan Tolila, Associate Publisher
A monthly national trade newspaper serving contractors, technicians, mechanical engineers, manufactures, manufacturer representatives, wholesalers, distributors, trade associations, government representatives, schools, students and other in the heating, ventilating, air conditioning, refrigarating, hydronics, sheet metals, solar, and allied trades.
Monthly Founded: 1981
Circulation: 50000
Printed in 4 colors on n stock

12248 Heating/Combustion and Equipment News
Business Communications Company
1 Penn Plaza
New York, NY 10119-0002

800-685-4488
Equipment, materials and supplies for the heating and air conditioning industry.
$12.00
Monthly

12249 Impact Compressor/Turbines News And Patents
Impact Publishers
PO Box 3113
Ketchum, ID 83340-3113
208-726-2332
FAX: 208-726-2115
Mary Jo Helmeke, Publisher
Regular features include new product announcements, patent information and up-to-date industry news and information on current books, brochures, software, seminars and meetings. *$60.00*
30 pages Annual

12250 Impact Pump News and Patents
Impact Publishers
PO Box 3113
Ketchum, ID 83340-3113
208-720-4876
FAX: 208-726-2115
Mary Jo Helmeke, Publisher
Regular features include new product announcements, patent information and up-to-date industry news and information on current books, brochures software, seminars and meetings. *$100.00*
25 pages

12251 Indoor Air Quality Update
Cutter Information Corporation
37 Broadway
Arlington, MA 02474-5552
781-641-2886
FAX: 781-648-8707 800-888-8939
Karen Fine Coburn, Publisher
Carlton Vogt, Editor
Practical control of indoor air problems.
$287.00
Monthly

12252 MACS Action!
Mobile Air Conditioning Society Worldwide
225 S Broad Street
PO Box 88
Lansdale, PA 19446
215-631-7020
FAX: 215-631-7017
jt@macsw.org http://www.macsw.org
Elvis Hoffpauir, Editor-in-Chief
Jim Taylor, Editor
Marion Posen, Marketing Manager
Maria Whipworth, Circulation Manager
Industry informational newsletter of Mobile Air Conditioning Society Worldwide.
8 pages Monthly
Circulation: 12000 Audited 80000 names
Printed in 4 colors on glossy stock

12253 MACS Service Reports
Mobile Air Conditioning Society Worldwide
PO Box 100
East Greenville, PA 18041
215-679-2220
FAX: 215-541-4635
http://www.macsw.org
Elvis Hoffpauir, Editor
Paul DeGuiseppi, Manager of Service
Amy Anderson, Production Designer
Technical newsletter for mobile air conditioning industry.
Monthly Founded: 1981
Circulation: 1600

12254 Residential Heat Recovery Ventilators Directory
Cutter Information Corporation
37 Broadway
Arlington, MA 02474-5552
781-641-2886
FAX: 781-648-8707 800-888-8939
Kim Leonard, Editor
A comprehensive comparative guide and product directory to heat exchangers and ventilators. *$75.00*

12255 Superinsulated House Design and Construction Workbook
Cutter Information Corporation
37 Broadway
Arlington, MA 02474-5552
781-641-2886
FAX: 781-648-8707 800-888-8939

Kim Leonard, Editor

Detailed, graphic information to design and build superior houses. *$85.00*

Magazines & Journals

12256 ASHRAE Journal
1791 Tullie Circle NE
Atlanta, GA 30329-2305
404-636-8400
FAX: 404-321-5478 800-527-4723
ashrae@ashrae.org
http://www.ashrae.org

Ronald Vallort, President

A publication by the American Society of Heating, Refrigeration and Air Conditioning Society, and articles with practical applications. *$59.00*
80 pages Monthly Founded: 1885
Circulation: 56000 55000 names
Printed in 4 colors on matte stock

12257 Air Conditioning Today
PO Box 311776
New Braunfels, TX 78131
830-627-0605
FAX: 830-627-0614 877-669-4228
info@ac-today.com
http://ac-today.com

Joe Eaton, Editor

Updates readers on the latest products, materials and technologies available.
Monthly Founded: 1986
Circulation: 19000

12258 Air Conditioning, Heating & Refrigeration News
Business News Publishing Company
755 W Big Beaver Road
Suite 1000
Troy, MI 48084
248-362-3700
FAX: 248-362-0317
kathyjanes@achrnews.com
http://www.achrnews.com

Mark Skaer, Editor
John Conrad, Publisher

Timely information to contractors, wholesalers, distributors, manufacturers, owner/operators and consulting engineers. Features technical, marketing, design, engineering, installation, management, governmental and labor aspects of the heating and cooling industry. Regular columns highlight new products and literature, legal rulings, manufacturer announcements, industry events and the latest hvac/r patents. *$49.00*
Weekly Founded: 1926
Circulation: 32854
Mailing list available for rent 35M names
Printed in 4 colors on glossy stock

12259 American Supply Association News
222 Merchandise Mart Plaza
Suite 1400
Chicago, IL 60654-1203
312-464-0090
FAX: 312-464-0091
info@asa.net http://www.asa.net

Inge Calderon, Executive VP
Bob Christian, Director
Kevin Neupert, Marketing
Joel Becker, Editor

Articles on plumbing, heating, cooling, and piping products.
50 pages Monthly Founded: 1969
Circulation: 2500
Mailing list available for rent 4,000 names
Printed in 4 colors on matte stock

12260 Automotive Cooling Journal
National Automotive Radiator Service Association
15000 Commerce Parkway
Suite C
Mount Laurel, PA 8054
856-439-1575
FAX: 856-439-9596 800-551-3232
acj@narsa.org http://www.narsa.org

Mike Dwyer, Executive Director
Sarah Lerow, Associate Editor
Lauren Petracci, Advertising Coordinator

Auto cooling system service data. Free to members. *$30.00*
60 pages Monthly Founded: 1954
Circulation: 10,000

12261 Contracting Business
Penton Media
1300 E 9th Street
Cleveland, OH 44114
216-696-7000
FAX: 216-696-1752
information@penton.com
http://www.contractingbusiness.com

David B Nussbaum, CEO
Michael S Weil, Editor-in-Chief
Gwen Hostnik, Marketing Manager

Directed to the residential, commercial and industrial mechanical systems contracting marketplace. HVAC mechanical systems and Design/Build/Maintain contractors, wholesalers and commercial/industrial in-house service organizations. *$75.00*
120 pages Monthly Founded: 1944
Circulation: 49,001
Printed in 4 colors on glossy stock

12262 Contractor Magazine
Penton Media
1300 E 9th Street
Cleveland, OH 44114
216-696-7000
FAX: 216-696-1752
information@penton.com
http://www.pentonmedia.com

Bob Miodonski, Editorial Director/Publisher
Bob Mader, Managing Editor
David B. Nussbaum, CEO

For contractors who sell, install, service air conditioning, heating, piping, plumbing, air handling, heat transfer and fluid controls equipment. Accepts advertising.
70 pages Monthly Founded: 1892
Circulation: 50000

12263 Die Casting Engineer Magazine
North American Die Casting Association
241 Holbrook Drive
Wheeling, IL 60090
847-279-0001
FAX: 847-279-0002
peterson@diecasting.org
www.nadca.org/

Donna Peterson, Editor
Norwin A Merens, Managing Director

Provides members with the latest industry information, technology innovation and state-of-the-art developments. Each issue presents readers with up to date die casting news topics, opinion features of interest, and an editorial theme. *$150.00*
1000 pages Bi-Monthly Founded: 1989

12264 Energy Engineering
Association of Energy Engineers
4025 Pleasantdale Rd
Suite 420
Atlanta, GA 30340
770-447-5083
FAX: 770-446-3969
webmaster@AEEcenter.org
http://www.aeecenter.org

Wayne Turner, Editor-in-Chief
Albert Thumann, Executive Director
Patricia Ardavin, Membership Director

Engineering solutions to cost efficiency problems and mechanical contractors who design, specify, install, maintain, and purchase non-residential heating, ventilating, air conditioning and refrigeration equipment and components. *$40.00*

Circulation: 8000

12265 Engineered Systems
Business News Publishing Company
755 W Big Beaver Road
Suite 100
Troy, MI 48084-4900
248-362-3700
FAX: 248-362-0317
beverlyr@bnpmedia.com
http://www.esmagazine.com

Peter Moran, Publisher
Robert Beverly, Editor
Nikki Smith, Marketing
Janel Webster, Circulation
Carrie Streling, Manager

Research conducted by us shows that endusers, consulting engineeers, and contractors work together closely on the specification and selection of engineered hvacr systems and componenents.We give this receptive audience solid editorial information about real-world solutions to the everyday situations faced in the industry.
72 pages Monthly Founded: 1985
Circulation: 57515
Mailing list available for rent 57.5M names
Printed in 4 colors on glossy stock

12266 Fuel Oil News
Hunter Publishing Limited
833 W. Jackson Blvd
7th Floor
Chicago, IL 60607
312-846-4600
FAX: 312-846-4632
kkenny@aip.com
http://www.fueloilnews.com

George M Schultz, Editor
Joanne Juda, Circulation Director
Kate Kenny, Publisher
Chris Traczek, Editor-in-Chief
Patricia McCartney, Associate Editor

For home heating oil retailers. *$28.00*
70 pages Monthly Founded: 1935
Circulation: 15200 18 M names
Printed in 4 colors on glossy stock

12267 HVAC Insider
Retailing Newspapers
PO Box 81489
Conveyors, GA 30013
770-787-0115
FAX: 770-787-1213
insider@mindsprin.com
http://www.mindspring.com/~insider/insider

Jerry M Lawson, Publisher

Up to date information on technical tips, product reviews, commercial and industrial industry new, a job bulletin, new businesses and promotions, and a calendar of events. Retailing Newspapers issues a monthly publication for the Appliance and Electronics trade. Insiders Newspapers issues a quarterly national and 14 monthly regionals for the HVAC trade and a monthly regional publication for the plumbing trade.
Monthly Founded: 1969
Circulation: 118740
Printed in 4 colors on newsprint stock

12268 HVAC/R Distribution Today
HARDI
1389 Dublin Road
Columbus, OH 43215-1084
614-488-1835
FAX: 614-488-0482 888-253-2128
hardimail@hardinet.org
http://www.hardinet.org
Donald Frendberg, Executive VP/COO
David Kellough, Executive Editor
Randy Tice, President
Official publication of Heating, Air Conditioning and Refrigeration International. Uniting world class distribution.
Quarterly Founded: 1960

12269 HVACR & Plumbing Distribution
Penton Media
The Penton Media Building
1300 E 9th Street
Cleveland, OH 44114
216-696-7000
FAX: 216-696-1752
information@penton.com
http://www.penton.com
Robert Korte, Editor
Perry Clark, Publisher
Exclusively for plumbing and heating equipment distributors.
Founded: 1890
Circulation: 10,000

12270 Hearth & Home
Village West Publishing
PO Box 1288
Laconia, NH 00
603-528-4285
FAX: 603-524-0643 800-258-3772
info@hearthnhome.com
http://villagewest.com
Richard Wright, Editor
Susan Salls, Publisher
Magazine for retailers, including specialty, hardware, patio and barbecue. *$36.00*
Monthly
Circulation: 18000

12271 Industrial Heating
Business News Publishing Company
1910 Cochran Road
Manor Oak One, Suite 450
Pittsburgh, PA 15220
412-531-3370
FAX: 412-531-3375
jhdkp@aol.com
http://www.industrialheating.com
Ed Kubel, Editor
Beth McClelland, Production Manager
Doug Glenn, Publisher
Kathy Pisano, Advertising Director
Patrick Connolly, Sales Representative
We have been applying the latest advances in thermal technology to practical use since 1931. With over 22,000 BPA audited circulation comprised of mostly thermal processing engineeers, technical articles cover heat treatments, brazing, sintering, melting, process control, instrumentation, refractories, burners, heating elements, and other thermal processes typically in excess of 1000 degrees. *$55.00*
70 pages Founded: 1931
Circulation: 22100
Printed in 4 colors on glossy stock

12272 International District Energy Association (IDEA)
125 Turnpike Road
Suite 4
Westborough, MA 01581-2841
508-366-9339
FAX: 508-366-0019
idea@districtenergy.org
http://www.districtenergy.org
John L Fiegel, Director
Rob Thornton, President
Monica Westerlund, Editor
Journal of district heating and cooling industry, congeneration, physical plants and energy efficiency. Accepts advertising. *$ 50.00*
Quarterly Founded: 1909

12273 Oilheating
Industry Publications
3621 Hill Road
Parsippany, NJ 07054-1001
973-331-9545
FAX: 973-331-9547
info@oilheating.com
http://www.oilheating.com
Donald J. Farrell, Publisher
Michael L. SanGiovanni, Editor
Addresses issues on dispatching and delivery efficiency, residential and commercial fuel oil use, as well as sales and services of oilfired equipment. *$42.00*
Monthly Founded: 1922
Circulation: 13280

12274 PM Engineer
Business News Publishing Company
755 W Big Beaver Road
Suite 1000
Troy, MI 48084
248-362-3700
FAX: 248-244-6439
wrdwzrd@aol.com
http://www.pmengineer.com
Scott Reimer, Publisher
Julius Ballanco, Editorial Director
Tim Fausch, Publishing Director
Provides technical sheets, manufacturer product brochures, news features and analysis of useful industry information on the engineering and design of plumbing, piping, hydronics, cooling/heating, and fire protection/sprinkler systems. Free to trade engineers. *$64.00*
80 pages Monthly Founded: 1926
Circulation: 25000
Printed in 4 colors on glossy stock

12275 Reeves Journal
23421 S Pointe Dr. Suite no280
Laguna Hills, CA 92654
949-830-0881
FAX: 949-859-7845
ReevesJrnl@aol.com
http://www.reevesjournal.com
Ellyn Fishman, Publisher
John Fultz, Editor
Tagg Henderson, CEO
An invaluable tool for western plumbing contractors and industry professionals for more than 80 years.
Monthly Founded: 1926
Circulation: 13545

12276 Refrigerated Transporter
Primedia
4200 S. Shepherd Drive
Suite 200
Houston, TX 77098
713-233-3826
FAX: 713-523-8384
inquiries@primediabusiness.com
http://www.refrigeratedtrans.com/
Gary Macklin, Editor-in-Chief
Tom Rogers, CEO
Monthly
Circulation: 15,023

12277 Refrigeration
John W Yopp Publications
73 Sen Island Parkway Suite 21
PO Box 1147
Beaufort, SC 29901-1147
843-521-0239
FAX: 843-521-1398 800-849-9667
cgraffo@jwyopp.com
http://www.refrigeration-magazine.com
John W Yopp, Chairman
Joe Cronley, Publisher
Mary Yopp Cronley, Associate Publsiher
Cheryl Graffo, Editor
About the plants and processes used in ice manufacture, marketing and merchandising information, news of associations, meetings and new products available. *$20.00*
Monthly Founded: 1919
Circulation: 3200
Printed in 4 colors on glossy stock

12278 Snips
Business News Publishing Company
2401 W. Big Beaver
Suite 700
Troy, MI 48084
248-362-3700
FAX: 248-362-0317
http://www.snipsmag.com/
Sally Fraser, Publisher
Michael McConnell, Editor
Lisa Cooper, Market research
Kari Rowe, Subscriptions
Magazine directed to the heating, air conditioning, sheet metal and ventilation industry. Accepts advertising. *$18.00*
120 pages Monthly Founded: 1926
Circulation: 22000
Printed in 4 colors on glossy stock

12279 Tab Journal
Associated Air Balance Council
1518 K Street NW
Washington, DC 20005-1203
202-737-0202
FAX: 202-638-4833
info@aabcdirect.com
http://www.aabchq.com/
Kenneth M Sufka, Publisher
Mike Young, President
Case studies, industry updates, as well as other news of importance to engineers. *$24.00*
Quarterly Founded: 1965
Circulation: 12000

12280 Todays A/C and Refrigeration News
Todays Trade Publications
PO Box 521247
130 W Pine Ave
Longwood, FL 32750-1247
407-332-4959
FAX: 407-332-5319 866-320-2773
nick@todayspubs.com
http://www.todays-ac.com

Thomas Fatchell, Editor

Covers industry legislation, building codes, licensing requirements and continuing educations. New product reviews and personnel changes are also included.

Monthly Founded: 1988
Circulation: 20000

Trade Shows

12281 ABMA Annual Meeting
American Boiler Manufacturers Association
4001 N 9th Street
Suite 226
Arlington, VA 22203-1900
703-522-7350
FAX: 703-522-2665
cheryl@abma.com www.abma.com

Cheryl Jamall, Meetings Director
W Randall Rawson, President

Learn about developments and trends, both inside and outside the industry, that are likely to influence their business, members are also afforded the opportunity, through committee and product/market group meetings, to focus on issues and concerns of specific relevance to their product and market segments.

2x year/January & June

12282 ABMA Manufacturers Conference
American Boiler Manufacturers Association
4001 N 9th Street
Suite 226
Arlington, VA 22203-1900
703-522-7350
FAX: 703-522-2665
cheryl@abma.com www.abma.com

Cheryl Jamall, Meetings Director
W Randall Rawson, President

Bringing together manufacturing plant, office and others concerned with the design, fabrication, sales and distribution of ABMA products and services to network, discuss trends and developments, and problems solve with others in the industry and with outside experts.

Annual/April

12283 ASA Convention and ISH North America Trade Show
American Supply Association
222 Merchandise Mart Plaza
Suite 1400
Chicago, IL 60654
312-640-0090
FAX: 312-464-0091
info@asa.net www.asa.net or www.ish-na.com

Ruth Mitchell, Manager/Convention Director
Bob Jarvie, Show Manager

Annual conference for wholesalers, distributors and manufacturers of plumbing and heating pipes, valves and fittings.

1800 Attendees September-October

12284 AeroMat Conference and Exposition
ASM International
9639 Kinsman Road
Materials Park, OH 44073-0002
440-385-5151
FAX: 440-338-4634
asmexpos@asminternational.org
www.asminternational.org

Annual event focusing on affordable structures and low-cost manufacturing, titanium alloy technology, advanced intermetallics and refractory metal alloys, materials and processes for space applications, aging systems, high strength steel, NDT evaluation, light alloy technology, welding and joining, and engineering technology.

900 Attendees June

12285 Air Conditioning Contractors of America Annual Conference
Air Conditioning Contractors of America
1712 New Hampshire Avenue NW
Washington, DC 20009-2502
202-518-3236
FAX: 202-332-5293
choelzel@acca.org www.acca.org

Christopher Holelzel, Director Marketing

Annual meeting and exhibits of heating, air conditioning and refrigeration equipment, supplies and services. Over 140 exhibitors, plus seminar, workshop and banquet.

1000 Attendees

12286 Air Conditioning Heating & Refrigeration Expo Mexico - AHR
Industrial Shows of America
164 Lake Front Drive
Hunt Valley, MD 21030-2215
410-771-1445
FAX: 410-771-1158 800-638-6396
pmckay@penton.com www.isoa.com

Bryan Mayes, President
Phillip McKay, Managing Director

300 exhibitors with air conditioning, heating and refridgerating equipment, supplies and information. Attended by professionals.

5000 Attendees Annual

12287 Hearth Products Association
1555 Wilson Boulevard
Suite 300
Arlington, VA 22209-2405
703-522-0086
FAX: 703-812-8875

Joan Letch Worth, Show Manager

900 booths of products related to the residential alternative fuel heating industry.

8M Attendees March

12288 Heating, Air Conditioning & Refrigeration Distributors International
1389 Dublin Road
Columbus, OH 43215-1084
614-488-1835
FAX: 614-488-0482
hardimail@hardinet.org
www.hardinet.org

Donald L Frendberg, Executive VP/COO
Eileen Mantel, Senior Administrator

Annual show of 200 exhibitors of heating and air conditioning equipment, supplies and services.

1200 Attendees Founded: 2003

12289 International Air Conditioning, Heating, & Refrigerating Expo
ASHRAE
Chicago McCormick Place
1791 Tulie Circle
Atlanta, GA 30329
404-636-8400
FAX: 404-321-5478
leggling@ashrae.org www.ashrae.org

Irene Eggling, Advertising Production Manager

Annual show and exhibits of industrial, commercial and residential heating, refrigeration, air conditioning and ventilation equipment and components. Containing 386,000 sq. ft. of booths and 1300 exhibits.

30000 Attendees January

12290 International District Energy Association (IDEA) Show
1200 19th Street NW
Suite 300
Washington, DC 20036-2428
202-429-5131
FAX: 202-429-5113
idea@sba.com
www.energy.rochester.edu/idea

John L Fiegel, Editor
Tammie Jackson, Advertising Manager

Show of the district heating and cooling industry, cogeneration, physical plants, energy efficiency. 40 booths.

450 Attendees June

12291 International Institute Ammonia Refrigeration
1101 Connecticut Avenue NW
Washington, DC 20036-4303
202-463-8777
FAX: 202-857-1104

Denise Rodgers, Membership Director
Joe Trento, President

70 booths.

750 Attendees March

12292 International Thermal Spray Conference and Exposition
ASM International
9639 Kinsman Road
Materials Park, OH 44073-0002
440-385-5151
FAX: 440-338-4634
jdirosa@asminternational.org

Jan DiRosa, Expositions Sales

Global annual event attracting professionals interested in thermal spray technology focusing on advances in HVOF, plasma and detonation gun, flame spray and wire arc spray processes; performance of coatings; future trends. Westing-Stamford Hotel, Singapore.

1,000 Attendees May

12293 Midwest Contractors Expo
Kansas Assn of Plumbing, Heating & Cooling Contr
320 Laura Street
Wichita, KS 67211-1517
316-262-8860
FAX: 316-262-2782

Ray Katzenmeier, Owner

Annual show and exhibits of plumbing, heating and cooling equipment, supplies and services.

12294 Mobile Air Conditioning Society Worldwide Convention and Trade Show
Mobile Air Conditioning Society Worldwide
225 S Broad Street
PO Box 88
Lansdale, PA 19446
215-631-7020
FAX: 215-631-7017
info@macsw.org www.macsw.org

Wendy Moyer, Trade Show Manager
Marion Posen, VP

MACS Convention and Trade Show will be held in Orlando, Florida.

2000 Attendees January 2,000 names

12295 National Plumbing, Heating, Cooling and piping Products Exposition
Nat'l Assn of Plumbing-Heating-Cooling Contractors
180 S Washington Street
Falls Church, VA 22046-2900
703-237-8100
FAX: 703-237-7442 800-533-7694
Annual show of 500 manufacturers and suppliers of equipment, supplies and services for the plumbing, heating and cooling industries.
15M Attendees October, Philadelphia

12296 North American Thermal Analysis Society
Complete Conference
1540 River Park Drive
Suite 111
Sacramento, CA 95815-4608
916-922-7032
FAX: 916-922-7379
Marilyn Hauck, President
30 booths.
300 Attendees September

12297 Oil Heat Business and Industry Expo
20 Summer Street
#9137
Watertown, MA 02472-3468

FAX: 781-924-1022
Bernard A Smith, Executive VP
Nancy Spinney, Expo Manager
This show provides a marketplace for prime purchasers of heating oil; oil heating, and air conditioning, as well as accessory equipment; fuel oil distribution equipment, trucks, transports, service and salesmen's vehicles; computers, office equipment; insurance programs and more.
8.5M Attendees June

12298 Refrigeration Service Engineers Society Show
Refrigeration Service Engineers Society
1666 Rand Road
Des Plaines, IL 60016-3552
847-297-6464
800-297-5660
general@rses.org www.rses.org
Kim Heselbarth, Marketing Director
Robb Isaacs, Executive VP
80 booths consisting primarily of products and services.

12299 Sheet Metal Air Conditioning Contractors National Association Show
4201 Lafayette Center Drive
Chantilly, VA 20151-1209
703-032-2980

Mary Lou Taylor, Convention Director
John Sroka, Executive VP
250 booths.
2.3M Attendees October

12300 Southwestern Ice Association Show

823 Congress Avenue
1300
Austin, TX 78701
512-479-0425
FAX: 512-495-9031 swia@tarei.com
Andrea Barnard, Executive Director
30 booths.
200 Attendees February

Directories & Databases

12301 AGA GasNet
American Gas Association
1515 Wilson Boulevard
Suite 100
Arlington, VA 22209-2469
703-841-8400
FAX: 703-841-8406
Offers access to news and information on and about the natural gas industry.
Bibliographic

12302 Air Conditioning Contractors of America Membership Directory
172 New Hampshire Avenue NW
Washington, DC 20009

FAX: 202-234-4721
230 pages Annual
Circulation: 2,700

12303 Air Conditioning, Heating & Refrigeration News Directory Issue

Business News Publishing
755 W Big Beaver Road
Suite 100
Troy, MI 48084-4900
248-362-3700
FAX: 248-362-0317
Mary Wray, Publisher
This issue offers a list of over 2,000 manufacturers, 5,000 wholesalers and factory outlets. Over 10,000 HVAC/R products, exporters and related trade organizations are also covered. *$32.50*
618 pages Annual
Circulation: 38,000
Printed in 4 colors on glossy stock

12304 Annual Member Directory
Air Conditioning & Heating Contractors of America
1712 New Hampshire Avenue NW
Washington, DC 20009-2502
202-483-9370
FAX: 202-234-4721
Rae Dorsey, Production Manager
A publication for the members of the Air Conditioning and Heating Contractors of America.

Circulation: 5,000

12305 Directory of Certified Applied Air-Conditioning Products
Air-Conditioning & Refrigeration Institute
4301 Fairfax Drive
Suite 425
Arlington, VA 22203-1634
703-248-8800

A list of 50 manufacturers of air conditioning and heating products. *$8.50*
Semiannual

12306 Directory of Certified Unitary Air-Conditioners & Heat Pumps
Air-Conditioning & Refrigeration Institute
4301 Fairfax Drive
Suite 425
Arlington, VA 22203-1634
703-248-8800

Air and coil heating and cooling units and air-to-air heat pumps manufacturers are profiled. *$13.00*
Semiannual

12307 HPAC Engineering Information
Penton Media
1300 E 9th Street
Cleveland, OH 44114
216-696-7000
FAX: 216-696-1752
information@penton.com
www.hpac.com
Terry Tanker, Publisher *$30.00*
300 pages Annual
Circulation: 56,000 54000 names $125 per M.
Printed in 4 colors on glossy stock

12308 Industrial Heating Buyers Guide and Reference Handbook
Business News Publishing
755 W Big Beaver Road
Suite 100
Troy, MI 48084-4900
248-362-3700
FAX: 248-362-0317
Companies are profiled that have over 1,200 heating products, and heat treating, and other services in the worldwide industrial heating market. *$25.00*
250 pages
Circulation: 20,000

12309 LP/Gas: Industry Buying Guide Issue
Advanstar Communications
131 W 1st Street
Duluth, MN 55802-2065
218-723-9200
FAX: 218-723-9122 800-346-0085
info@advanstar.com
www.advanstar.com
List of about 1,000 liquid propane gas equipment manufacturers and suppliers; list of about 700 distributors of gas appliances and equipment. *$50.00*
Annual
Circulation: 16,000
Printed in 4 colors on glossy stock

12310 PM Directory & Reference Issue
Business News Publishing
755 W Big Beaver Road
Suite 100
Troy, MI 48084-4900
248-362-3700
FAX: 248-362-0317 800-837-7370
Steve Smith, Editor
Manufacturers, wholesalers, exporters, associations, products, consultants and manufacturers' representatives in the industries of plumbing, piping and hydronic heating. *$30.00*
Annual December
Circulation: 42,000

12311 Refrigeration: Ice Industry's Buyer's Guide Issue

John W Yopp Publications
PO Box 1147
Beaufort, SC 29901-1147
843-521-0239
FAX: 800-849-8418 800-849-9677

Joe Cronley

Directory of services and supplies to the industry. *$3.00*

Annual
Circulation: 3,000

Industry Web Sites

12312 www.abma.com
American Boiler Manufacturers Association

Manufacturers trade association representing companies involved in utility, industrial and commercial steam generation. Includes associate memberships for companies who sell to or work with these companies and those who own boilers. Holds technical and production conferences, and publishes technical guideline publications.

12313 www.achrnews.com
BNP Media

News, tips and a calendar of events for the heating & cooling industry.

12314 www.aga.com
American Gas Association

Events, publications, information, etc.

12315 www.ari.org
Air Conditioning & Refrigeration Institute

Trade association representing manufacturers of more than 90% of North American produced air-conditioning and commercial refrigeration equipment.

12316 www.asa.net
American Supply Association

The National association of full-service plumbing, heating, cooling, and piping products for wholesalers, manufacturers, and distributors.

12317 www.ashrae.org
American Society of Heating, Refrigeration, AC

Research, activities, education and publications.

12318 www.districtenergy.org
International District Energy Association

Journal of district heating and cooling industry, congeneration, physical plants and energy efficiency. Accepts advertising.

12319 www.gamanet.org
Gas Appliance Manufacturers Association

Represents manufacturers of residential, commercial and industrial gas and oil fired appliances, associated controls and accessories, as well as equipment used in the production, transmission and distribution of fuel gases.

12320 www.greyhouse.com
Grey House Publishing

Selected Grey House directories in the fields of business, health and education are available online. Users can search our online databases by several different search criteria, such as product categories, geographic area, sales volume and much, much more. Full Grey House catalog and online ordering also available.

12321 www.impi.org
International Microwave Power Institute

IMPI's members include scientists, researchers, lab technicians, product developers, marketing managers and a variety of other professionals in the microwave industry. The Institute serves the information needs of all specialists working with dielectric (microwave and RF) heating sytems, and was expanded in 1977 to meet the information needs relating to consumer microwave ovens and related products.

12322 www.macsw.org
Mobile Air Conditioning Society Worldwide

Information on technical training for professionals in the automotive air-conditioning industry.

12323 www.mha-net.org
Masonry Heater Association of North America

Promotes use of masonry heaters, increases public awareness and encourages reasonable governmental regulation.

Associations

12324 American Camping Association
5000 State Road 67 N
Martinsville, IN 46151
765-342-8456
FAX: 765-342-2065 800-428-2267
shallway@aca-camps.org
www.aca-camps.org
Marla Coleman, President
Peg Smith, Chief Executive Officer
6600+ Members Founded: 1910

12325 American Craft Council
72 Spring Street
New York, NY 10012
212-274-0630
FAX: 212-274-0650
council@craftcouncil.org
www.craftcouncil.org
Carmine Branagan, Executive Director
Hope O'Reilly, Director Development
Lois Moran, Manager
Reed J McMillan, Director Marketing
Salvatore Chiarelli, Manager Show Operations
National nonprofit, educational organization dedicated to promotion, understanding and appreciation of contemporary American craft. Sponsors annual wholesale and retail shows, a magazine, a library and seminars.
Founded: 1943

12326 American Home Sewing and Craft Association
1350 Broadway
Suite 1601
New York, NY 10018
212-714-1633
FAX: 212-714-1655
info@sewing.org www.sewing.org

12327 American Philatelic Society
100 Match Factory Place
Bellefonte, PA 16823
814-933-3803
FAX: 814-933-6128
apsinfo@stamps.org www.stamps.org
Janet Klug, President
Ken Martin, Company Contact
National organization for stamp collectors, monthly magazine, the American Philatelist; lending library; insurance for philatelic materials; sales division, seminars and annual conventions open to the public.
46000 Members Founded: 1886

12328 American Quilt Study Group
1610 L St
Lincoln, NE 68508-2509
402-477-1181
FAX: 402-477-1183
aqsg2@alltel.net
www.h-net.org/~aqsg/
Bettina Havig, President
Bobbi Finley, VP
Bunnie Jordan, VP
Jennifer Goldsborough, Secretary
Linda Pumphrey, Treasurer
Organization that holds annual seminars and exhibits of quilt-related articles.
1000 Members Founded: 1980

12329 American Specialty Toy Industry
4700 W Lake Avenue
Glenview, IL 60025
847-375-4727
FAX: 888-840-2650
info@astratoy.org www.astratoy.org
Kathleen McHugh, Executive Director
Providing a unified voice for the specialty toy industry, and opportunities to exchange information and ideas with counterparts. Membership benefits include workshops and seminars, vendor representative roundtables, membership directory and annual convention.

12330 American Stamp Dealers Association
3 School Street
Suite 205
Glen Cove, NY 11542
516-759-7000
FAX: 516-759-7014
asdashows@erols.com
www.asdaonline.com
Elizabeth Pope, President
Joseph B Savarese, Executive VP
Dr Ray Ameen, VP
Edward Hines, Treasurer
Arthur Morowitz, Secretary
800 Members Founded: 1914

12331 Archery Trade Association
860 E 4500 S
Suite 310
Salt Lake City, UT 84107
801-261-2380
FAX: 801-261-2389
jaymcaninch@archerytrade.org
www.archerytrade.org
Jay McAninch, President/CEO
Denise Parker, VP/Director Marketing
Jay Barrs, Director Promotions
Cindy Brophy, Tradeshow/Membership Services
Former Archery Manufacturers and Merchants Association. Provides core funding and direction for two new foundations critical to the future of archery and bowhunting: Arrow Sport and the Bowhunting Preservation Alliance. In addition the ATA continues to direct the industry's annual archery and bowhunting trade show.
Founded: 1956

12332 Association of Traditional Hooking Artists
600 1/2 Maple Street
Endicott, NY 13760

jcahill29@aol.com
www.rughookersnetwork.com
Joan Cahill, Membership Chairperson
Karen Balon, Guild Secretary
Mary Henck, President
Provides educational material about rug hooking, free patterns, supplies information, chapter/rug camp meetings and teacher information that is not available through any other source. Membership includes all 50 states, England, Japan and Australia.

12333 Game Manufacturers Association
280 N High Street
Suite 230
Columbus, OH 43215
303-469-3277
FAX: 303-991-3583
president@gama.org www.gama.org
Chris Wiese, President
John Kaufeld, VP
Brian Darymple, Secretary
Bruce Neidlinger, Treasurer
Chris Watson, Finance Director
A non-profit trade association dedicated to the advancement of the hobby game business.

12334 Hobby Industry Association
319 E 54th Street
Elmwood Park, NJ 07407
201-794-1133
FAX: 201-797-0657
hia@hobby.org www.hobby.org
James Bremer, President
Ron LaRosa, VP Finance
Jane Anne Davis, VP Member Programs/Services
Michael McCooey, VP New Business Development
Steve Berger, Executive Director
Trade association in the craft and hobby market. The group produces an international trade show open to qualified professionals and is the industry's only market research show.
4000 Members Founded: 1940

12335 Miniatures Association of America
PO Box 3388
Zanesville, OH 43702-3388
740-452-4541
FAX: 740-452-2552 888-360-2224
miaa.info@offinger.com
www.miaa.com

12336 Model Railroad Division of Hobby Manufactu rers Association
PO Box 315
Butler, NJ 07405-0315
973-283-9088
FAX: 973-838-7124
pat.koziol@hmahobby.org
www.hmahobby.org
Zana Ireland, President
Bill McClung, VP
Henry Carsten, Secretary/Treasurer
Patricia S Koziol, Executive Director
Bob Hayden, Assoc. Ex. Dir
Originally MRIA/Model Railroad Industry Association. Works to publicize the hobby and to keep members informed on the industry. Assists clubs and retailers in their shows.
153 Members Founded: 1967

12337 Museum Store Association
4100 E Mississippi Avenue
Suite 800
Denver, CO 80246-3055
303-504-9223
FAX: 303-504-9585
www.museumdistrict.com
Beverly Barsook, Executive Director
Stacey Woldt, Assistant Director Programs
Providing member representatives with the professional opportunities and educational resources they need to operate effectively and ethically.

2500 Members April, Annually Founded: 1955

12338 National School Supply Equipment
8380 Colesville Road
Suite 250
Silver Spring, MD 20910
301-495-0240
FAX: 301-495-3330 800-395-2123
nssea@nssea.org www.nssea.org

Lorraine Moore, Chairman
Jim Meharry, First Vice Chair
Brian Roberts, Second Vice Chair
Dennis Gosney, Treasurer
Tim Holt, President

1400+ Members Founded: 1995

12339 Radio Control Hobby Trade Association
PO Box 315
Butler, NJ 07405-315
973-283-9088
FAX: 973-838-7124
pkoziol@rchta.org www.rchta.org

Mark Schwing, President
Mike MacDowell, VP
Ed Stevens, Treasurer
Janet Ottmers, Secretary
Pat Koziol, Executive Director

Holds an annual show of 400 manufacturers and distributors of model hobby kits and hobby equipment, supplies and services. Products are usually associated with retail hobby stores.

Founded: 1983

12340 Society of Creative Designers
PO Box 3388
Zanesville, OH 43702-3388
740-452-4541
FAX: 740-452-2552
scd@offinger.com
www.creativedesigners.org

Julie Stephani, President
Vicki Schrechen, Secretary/Treasurer
Mark Bennett, Executive Director
Barbara Matthiessen, Director
Andrea Rothenberg, Director

Professional organization for those who believe that quality craft design is the basis of a strong and viable craft industry. It is the only membership organization exclusively serving those who design for the consumer craft industry.

500 Members Founded: 1975

12341 Toy Industry Association
1115 Broadway
Suite 400
New York, NY 10010
212-675-1141
FAX: 212-633-1429
toyfairs@toy-tia.org www.toy-tia.org

Arnie Rubin, Chairman
Thomas P Conley, President
Norman Walker, Member of Board of Directors
Barry Shapiro, Member of Board of Directors
Michael J Johnston, Member of Board of Directors

National organization with over 300 toy, game and holiday decoration manufacturers and their representatives, as well as toy designers, testing laboratories, licensors, sales representatives and trade magazines.

400+ Members Founded: 1916

12342 Western Toy & Hobby Representatives Association
9397 Reserve Drive
Corona, CA 92883
951-277-1598
FAX: 951-277-1599
info@wthra.com www.wthra.com

Phylis St John, Show Director

A nonprofit association organization. For the last 40 years we have produced and promoted the Western States Toy & Hobby Show.

Founded: 1961

Newsletters

12343 ATHA Newsletter
Association of Traditional Hooking Artists

63 Robinson Drive
Rochester, VT 05767
802-767-9024

arikera@sover.net
http://www.atharugs.org

BJ Andreas, Editor
Nancy Martin, Membership

Provides educational material about rug hooking, free patterns, supplies information, chapter/rug camp meetings and teacher information that is not available through any other source. Membership includes all 50 states, England, Japan and Australia.

Founded: 1980

12344 American Stamp Dealers Association Newsletter
3 School Street
Suite 205
Glen Cove, NY 11542-2548
516-759-7000
FAX: 516-759-7014
jsavarese@erds.com
http://www.asdaonline.com

Joseph Savarese, Executive Director
Elizabeth Pope, President

Association news.

Monthly Founded: 1914
Circulation: 810
Printed in on matte stock

12345 Bill Nelson Newsletter
Nelson Newsletter Publishing Corporation
PO Box 41630
Tucson, AZ 85717-1630
520-629-0868
FAX: 520-629-0387 800-368-8434
sales@pinsbymail.com
http://www.billnelsonnewsletter.com/

Bill Nelson, Publisher

Features news on the pin collecting hobby. *$20.00*

8 pages Monthly
Printed in 1 color on matte stock

12346 This Time
Homeworkers Organized for More Employment
PO Box 10
Orland, ME 04472
207-469-7961
FAX: 207-469-1023
info@homecoop.net
http://www.homecoop.net/

Lucy Toulin, President
J Ralph, Editor
F Eldridge, Volunteer Coordinator

Home community newsletter, part of the world Emmaus movement, offering information on craft store items and antiques. Member of rural coalition , Washington D.C.. *$5.00*

16 pages Quarterly Founded: 1970
Circulation: 300

Magazines & Journals

12347 ABCs of Retailing
Hobby Industry Association
319 E 54th Street
#348
Elmwood Park, NJ 07407-2712
201-794-1133
FAX: 201-797-0657
afliss@rfcp.com
http://www.hobby.org/

Guide to opening and maintaining a craft/hobby retail store.

20 pages Founded: 1940

12348 American Craft Magazine
72 Spring Street
New York, NY 10012
212-274-0630
FAX: 212-274-0650
council@craftcouncil.org
http://www.craftcouncil.org

Elena Averoff, President
John Gourlay, Publisher
Lois Moran, Editor-in-Chief

Celebrates the excellence of contemporary craft, focusing on masterful achievements in the craft media — clay, fiber, metal, glass, wood and other materials — with the goal to create intellectual and visual interest for the reader on today's craft. *$40.00*

Founded: 1943

12349 American Philatelist
American Philatelic Society
100 Match Factory Place
Bellefonte, PA 16823-8000
814-373-3803
FAX: 814-933-6128
kpmartin@stamps.org
http://www.stamps.org/

Charles Peterson, President
Kim Martin, Administrator
Barbara Boal, Editor
Bonny Farmer, Manuscript Editor
Dana Guyer, Public Relations Manager

One hundred page monthly magazine for stamp collectors. *$35.00*

100 pages Monthly Founded: 1886
Circulation: 50000 47000 names $50 per M.

12350 Antiques and Collecting Hobbies
Lightner Publishing Corporation
1006 S Michigan Avenue
Chicago, IL 60605-2254
312-939-4767
FAX: 312-939-0053
lightnerpub@aol.com

Fran Graham, Editor
Dale K Graham, Publisher

Antiques and collectible news articles. *$32.00*

88 pages Monthly Founded: 1931
Circulation: 18,000

12351 Bank Note Reporter
Krause Publications
700 E State Street
Iola, WI 54990-1
715-445-2214
FAX: 715-445-4087 800-258-0929
mike@iolaoldcarshow.com
http://www.krause.com
Bill Bright, Publisher
Dave Harper, Editor
Buddy Redling, Manager
Recognized as the finest publication for paper money collectors available. Contains news on market values, 'Bank Note Clinic' (a collector Q&A), an up-to-date foreign exchange chart, 'Fun Notes' (interesting, odd & unusual notes), a price guide, a world currency section, historical features on paper money worldwide (emphasizing US issues), & hundreds of display & classified ads offering to buy, sell, & trade bank notes of all kinds. Contributors include some of the top experts in the field. *$37.00*
84 pages Monthly Founded: 1952
Circulation: 8072

12352 Big Reel
Krause Publications
700 E State Street
Iola, WI 54990-1
715-445-2214
FAX: 715-445-4087
http://www.krause.com
Greg Smith, Publisher
Claire Fliess, Editor
Your ticket to Hollywood collectibles. Since 1974, Big Reel has been bringing collectors and fans together to buy, sell, and trade Hollywood memorabilia. Films, videos, posters, and autographs are listed 'For Sale' or 'Wanted' each month. Articles on Hollywood and television are always included - from feature stories on performers of the golden era to the stars of today as well as a show calendar. *$37.00*
84 pages Monthly Founded: 1974
Circulation: 5602

12353 Blade
Krause Publications
700 E State Street
Iola, WI 54990
715-445-2214
FAX: 715-445-4087 www.krause.com
Hugh McAloon, Publisher
Steve Shackleford, Editor
Provides knifemakers, collectors, and knife enthusiasts with information concerning new knife-making techniques and processes, field tests, and the latest news and features on knives and their makers. Also includes a Q&A section, letters to the editor, features about individual knifemakers, an extensive listing of upcoming knife shows, and a reader feature entitled, 'The Knife I Carry.' *$25.98*
140 pages Monthly Founded: 1973
Circulation: 38068

12354 Blade Trade
Krause Publications
700 E State Street
Iola, WI 54990
715-445-2214
FAX: 715-445-4087
blade@krause.com
http://www.fwpublications.com
William F Reilly, Chairman
William R Reed, President
Includes reviews of specific types of knives, new product information and trade show information. Annual issue sent free to qualified cutlery retailers. *$5.95*
68 pages Annual+ Founded: 1989
Circulation: 2,484

12355 Card Trade
Krause Publications
700 E State Street
Iola, WI 54990-1
715-445-2214
FAX: 715-445-4087 800-258-0929
info@krause.com
http://www.krause.com
Dean Listle, Publisher
Scott Kelnhofer, Editor
The official trade journal of the sports collectible industry. Card Trade touches a wide range of topics pertinent to the sports hobby professional, including new products, marketing strategies, retailer advice, late-breaking hobby news, market reports (sales reports and trends from all regions of the country), annual dealer surveys, product release calendars, hobby happenings, industry news, and product analysis.
44 pages Monthly Founded: 1995
Circulation: 5752

12356 Coin Prices
Krause Publications
700 E State Street
Iola, WI 54990-1
715-445-2214
FAX: 715-445-4087
info@krause.com
http://www.krause.com
Bill Bright, Publisher
Bob Van Ryzin, Editor
Coin Prices is a complete guide to retail values for collectible US coins. A market update section (value guide) by market editor Joel Edler beings each issue. Rotating special sections provide values for Canadian and Mexican coins, Colonial coins, territorial coins, errors and varieties and selected issues of US paper money. Regular departments include a guide to grading US coins. *$18.98*
96 pages Founded: 1952
Circulation: 56611

12357 Coins
Krause Publications
700 E State Street
Iola, WI 54990
715-445-2214
FAX: 715-445-4087
info@krause.com
http://www.krause.com
Bill Bright, Publisher
Bob Van Ryzin, Editor
Covers market trends, buying tips, and historical perspectives on all aspects of numismatics. The news section, 'Bits and Pieces,' wraps up the latest happenings in numismatics. Regular columns and departments include 'Basics& Beyond,' 'Budget Buyer,' 'Coin Clinic' (Q&A), the editor's column, coin finds, a calendar of upcoming shows nationwide, 'Coin Values Guide' and 'Market Watch.' *$20.98*
120 pages Monthly Founded: 1955
Circulation: 52660

12358 Collector Magazine & Price Guide
Krause Publications
700 E State Street
Iola, WI 54990-1
715-445-2214
FAX: 715-445-4087
mike@iolaoldcarshow.com
http://www.krause.com
Patricia DuChene, Associate Editor
Provides information to collectors and dealers interested in a wide variety of antiques and collectibles. Each issue features stories on collectibles - from antique to contemporary, auction results, show calendar, 20-page price guide on a variety of collectibles, antique Q&A, and directories (show, specialty, wanted, travel, Internet, and service) covering a multitude of collecting interests. *$35.00*
72 pages Monthly Founded: 1952
Circulation: 21374

12359 Collector's Mart
Krause Publications
700 E State Street
Iola, WI 54990-1
715-445-2214
FAX: 715-445-4087
info@krause.com
http://www.krause.com
Greg Smith, Publisher
Mary Sieber, Editor
A magazine devoted to contemporary collectibles, gifts & home decor. Coverage has expanded to include gifts, holiday/special occasion decor & functional intems. Covers collectible figurines, cottages, plates, ornaments, dolls, bells, steins & prints. Each issue offers columns written by hobby experts, interviews with popular artists, and profiles of the world's top producers of collectibles and home decor. Also features hobby news, secondary market trends, new release announcements. *$35.00*
60 pages Quarterly Founded: 1976
Circulation: 46715

12360 Comics & Games Retailer
Krause Publications
700 E State Street
Iola, WI 54990-6025
715-445-2214
FAX: 715-445-2214
info@krause.com www.krause.com
Mark Williams, Publisher
John Miller, Editor
Norma Jean Fochs, Ad Manager
Provides information to retailers about marketing, industry news, and practical how-to tips on selling comics and games at the retail level. Regular columns include 'Suggested for Mature Retailers,' 'Small Store Strategy,' 'Trade Show Calendar,' 'Retailer News,' and 'Distributor News.' Special issue focus on the comic book industry, trade shows, trading cards, gaming, display racks, and other retail store supplies. 'Market Beat' gives a national overview of the comics market. *$29.95*
72 pages Monthly Founded: 1992
Circulation: 5,201

12361 Comics Buyer's Guide
Krause Publications
700 E State Street
Iola, WI 54990-1
715-445-2214
FAX: 715-445-4087
info@krause.com
http://www.krause.com
Mark Williams, Publisher
Maggie Thompson, Editor
The longest-running magazine about comic books. Each 200+ page monthly issue features new comic reviews, nostalgic retroviews, interviews and the largest monthly price guide. Aslo included is the latest convention news, opinion pieces from celebrity columnists and expanded

coverage of anime, manga and other comics-related auctions. *$38.95*

244 pages Monthly Founded: 1952
Circulation: 30,000

12362 Craftrends
Primedia Enthusiast Group Publishing
741 Corporate Circle
Suite A
Golden, CO 80401
303-278-1010
FAX: 303-277-0370 800-881-6634
craftrends@primedia.com
http://www.craftrends.com

Bill Gardner, Editorial Director
Beth Hess, Managing Editor
Dave O'Neil, VP Group Publishing
Kelly P. Conlin, President/CEO

Includes new products, coverage of industry trade shows, merchandising and promotion ideas. Also has timely information to operate a craft business and stay on top of a rapidly changing retail environment. *$26.00*

Monthly Founded: 1989
Circulation: 22000

12363 Crafts Magazine
Primedia Enthusiast Group Publishing
PO Box 420494
Palm Coast, FL 32142-9524
800-727-2387
FAX: 386-447-2321
papercrafts@palmcoastd.com
http://www.craftsmag.com

Valerie Pingree, Editor-in-Chief
Mike Irish, Associate Publisher
Kelly P Conlin, CEO/President

Monthly craft consumer magazine reaching the crafting enthusiast. *$15.97*

112 pages Founded: 1989
Circulation: 300272
Printed in 4 colors on glossy stock

12364 Crafts Report
Crafts Reports Publishing
100 Rogers Road
Wilmington, DE 19801
302-656-2209
FAX: 302-656-4894 800-777-7098
theeditor@craftsreport.com
http://www.craftsreport.com

Lammot Copeland Jr, Publisher
Heather Skelly, Editor
Stewart Abowitz, Marketing Director
Deborah Copeland, Co-Publisher

Monthly business magazine for the crafts professional, providing information on marketing, growing your craft business, time management, studio safety, retail relationships, artist/retailer profiles, show listings and more. *$29.00*

Monthly Founded: 1975
Circulation: 30000 $100 per M.
Printed in 4 colors on glossy stock

12365 Doll Artisan
Jones Publishing
N7 450 Aanstad Road
PO Box 5000
Iola, WI 54945-5000
715-445-5000
FAX: 715-445-4053
joejones@jonespublishing.com
www.dollmakingartisian.com
Edited to entertain, fascinate and educate the doll maker in reproduction of antique porcelain dolls. Encourages and promotes efforts to make porcelain doll making easier, safer and more accessible to a growing number of enthusiasts. *$5.95*

Bi-Monthly

12366 Doll World
Jones Publishing
N7 450 Aanstad Road
PO Box 5000
Iola, WI 54945-5000
715-445-5000
FAX: 715-445-4053 800-331-0038
jonespub@jonespublishing.com
http://www.jonespublishing.com

Joe Jones, President
Nayda Rondon, Editor
Trina Laube, Assistant Editor
Virginia Adams, Marketing
Brandan Hardie, Circulation Manager
$32.95

Monthly

12367 Dollmaking
Jones Publishing
N7 450 Aanstad Road
PO Box 5000
Iola, WI 54945-5000
715-445-5000
FAX: 715-445-4053
jonespub@jonespublishing.com
www.Dollmaking/Artisan.com
Resource for makers of porcelain and sculpted modern dolls, is edited for the serious costume and doll maker. *$4.95*

Bi-Monthly

12368 Embroidery Business News
Virgo Publishing
3300 N Central Avenue, Suite 2500
PO Box 40079
Phoenix, AZ 85012
480-990-1101
FAX: 480-675-8146
http://www.ebnmag.com
Business resource for commercial embroiderers.

Founded: 1993
Circulation: 18937

12369 Family Tree
B&W Publications
1507 Dana Avenue
Cincinnati, OH 45207-1056
513-943-9464
FAX: 513-531-1843
Ideas and advice for discovering, preserving and celebrating family history.

12370 Family Tree Magazine
Krause Publications
700 E State Street
Iola, WI 54990-1
715-445-2214
FAX: 715-445-4087
info@krause.com
http://www.krause.com

Bill Reed, CEO/President
Allison Stacy, Editor
Kelly Klener, Marketing

America's most popular family history magazine. It covers all areas of potential interest to family history enthusiasts, reaching beyond strict genealogy research to include ethnic heritage, family reunions, memoirs, oral history, scrapbooking, historical travel and other ways that families connect with their pasts. Each issue features the latest tools, how-to tips and expert advice to guide readers through the journey of discovering, preserving and celebrating their roots. *$27.00*

84 pages Founded: 1952
Circulation: 80050

12371 Fine Woodworking
Taunton Press
63 S Main Street
PO Box 5506
Newtown, CT 06470-5506
203-270-6206
FAX: 203-426-3434 800-926-8776
fw@taunton.com
http://www.taunton.com

David Grey, Publisher
Linda Abbett, Advertising Manager
Anatole Burkin, Editor

Published since 1975, written by woodworkers for woodworkers regularly shows the finest work in wood being done today. *$34.95*

120 pages Founded: 1975
Circulation: 295000
Mailing list available for rent 185M names
Printed in 4 colors on glossy stock

12372 Gun List
Krause Publications
700 E State Street
Iola, WI 54990
715-445-2214
FAX: 715-445-4087
info@krause.com
http://www.krause.com

Hugh McAloon, Publisher
Steve Hudziak, Marketing

An all-advertising, nationwide marketplace for buyers and sellers of new, used and antique firearms. Display advertising from the nation's top dealers, manufacturers, distributors, and suppliers is found in each bi-weekly issue, along with thousands of classified word ads, organized alphabetically, from collectors all over the world. The nation's leading indexed firearms paper. Hundreds of gun show listings and knife show listings are included to help readers schedule their show attendance. *$37.98*

136 pages Founded: 1952
Circulation: 81120

12373 Gun-Knife Show Calendar
Krause Publications
700 E State Street
Iola, WI 54990-1
715-445-2214
FAX: 715-445-4087
http://www.krause.com

Hugh McAloon, Publisher
Bruce Wolberg, Ad Manager
John Koenig, Editor'

A compilation of gun shows and knife shows held throughout the country, and is intended to be used as a complete guide for anyone who attends or displays at these shows. Regular listings include the dates of the show, the address, the city, state, number of tables, and the cost of tables. For attendees, the show hours and the cost of admission are listed. Shows are listed for a full year ahead and there is no charge to list a show. *$15.95*

88 pages Quarterly Founded: 1952
Circulation: 5758

12374 HIA Craft/Hobby Consumer Study
Hobby Industry Association
319 E 54th Street
Elmwood Park, NJ 07407-2712
201-794-1133
FAX: 201-797-0657
info@craftandhobby.org
http://www.hobby.org

Susan Brandt, Assistant Executive
Steve Berger, Associate director

An extensive study of consumer behavior and buying habits relevant to the hobby/craft/creative industry. Executive summary is available on-line. *$400.00*
Founded: 2004
Circulation: 5000

12375 Hobby Merchandiser
Hobby Publications
207 Commercial Court
PO Box 102
Morganville, NJ 07751-102
732-536-5160
FAX: 732-536-5761 800-969-7176
info@hobbymerchandiser.com
http://www.hobbymerchandiser.com/
Robert Gherman, Publisher
Jeff Troy, Editor
Patrick Sarver, Associate Publisher
Trade magazine for the model hobby industry, available to professionals only. *$20.00*
96 pages Monthly Founded: 1947
Circulation: 7000
Mailing list available for rent 8,300 names $241 per M.
Printed in 4 colors on glossy stock

12376 Hobby Rocketry
California Rocketry Publishing
PO Box 1242
Claremont, CA 91711-1242
760-389-2233
FAX: 661-824-0868
01rocket@gte.net
www.v-serv.com/crp
Jerry Irvine, Publisher
Covers consumer rocket products which are available in hobby, toy and retail outlets. Product reviews, manufacturers notes, consumer feedback and more. Back issues available. *$16.00*
16 pages Quarterly Founded: 1992
Circulation: 8M
Printed in on newsprint stock

12377 Horizons
Hobby Industry Association
319 E 54th Street
Elmwood Park, NJ 07407-2712
201-794-1133
FAX: 201-797-0657
hia@hobby.org www.hobby.org
Available only to members of the Hobby Association of America. This magazine offers information and updates on what is happening in the industry.
6 pages Quarterly

12378 Knitting World
House of White Birches
House of White Birches
306 East Parr Road
Berne, IN 46711
260-898-8741
FAX: 260-589-8093 800-829-5865
customer_service@drgbooks.com
http://www.whitebirches.com
John Robinson, CEO
John Boggs, Advertising Sales Director
Carl Musselman, Editor
David J McKee, Publishing Director
Greg Deily, Marketing Director
Serves the knitting industry. *$13.00*
64 pages Monthly Founded: 1947

12379 Military Trader
Krause Publications
700 E State Street
Iola, WI 54990
715-445-2214
FAX: 715-445-4087 800-258-0929
info@krause.com
http://www.krause.com
Rick Groth, Publisher
John Adams-Graf, Editor
For military collectors, the best monthly source of news, features, collecting advice, shows, and events. Each issue offers thousands of 'For Sale' and 'Wanted' mlitary collectibles from hundreds of dealers and collectors. This is where to go when you are trying to buy or sell vintage military uniforms, pins, medals, helmets, ammunition, firearms, flags, and other militaria. *$19.00*
56 pages Monthly Founded: 1975
Circulation: 9414

12380 Military Vehicles
Krause Publications
700 E State Street
Iola, WI 54990-1
715-445-2214
FAX: 715-445-4087
http://www.krause.com
Bill Reed, President
John Adams-Graf, Editor
Each issue includes news, vintage military photos, collecting advice, market information, show listings, and extensive display and classified advertising sections offering to buy and sell hundreds of jeeps, tanks, trucks, vehicle parts, and accessories from dealers and enthusiasts all over the world. Other regular features include book and media reviews, letters to the editor, tech topics, weapons & replicas, models & toys, and internet sightings. *$23.98*
176 pages Founded: 1952
Circulation: 19,000

12381 Model Retailer
Kalmbach Publishing Company
21027 Crossroads Circle
PO Box 1612
Waukesha, WI 53187
262-796-8776
FAX: 262-796-8776 800-533-6644
hmiller@modelretailer.com
http://www.modelretailer.com
Kevin Keefe, Publisher
Hal Miller, Editor
Rick Albers, Advertising Sales Manager
Jim Meinhardt, Circulation Manager
The business of hobbies, from financial and shop management issues to industry news and trends, as well as the latest in product releases. Provides hobby shop entreprenuers with the information, ideas and examples they need in order to be successful retailers.
Monthly Founded: 1934
Circulation: 6350

12382 Needlework Retailer
Yarn Tree Designs
117 Alexander Avenue
PO Box 2438
Ames, IA 50010-2438
515-232-3121
FAX: 515-232-0789 800-247-3952
info@needleworkretailer.com
http://www.needleworkretailer.com
Larry Johnson, VP
Megan Chriswisser, Editor
Highlights a variety of new products and designs in needlework. Includes infornation on upcoming needlework trade shows and association news. *$12.00*
Circulation: 11000

12383 Numismatic News
Krause Publications
700 E State Street
Iola, WI 54990-1
715-445-2214
FAX: 715-445-4087 800-942-0673
info@krause.com
http://www.krause.com
Bill Bright, Publisher
Dave Harper, Editor
Provides timely reports on market happenings and news concerning collectible coins. 'Coin Clinic' is a very popular weekly Q&A column that gives readers a chance to learn all about numismatics. The 'Coin Market' section provides comprehensive pricing monthly. Each issue also includes columns with practical how-to advice and historical features by some of the top experts in the field including 'Making the Grade' and 'Facts about Fakes.' Sponsors the annual Mid-America Coin Convention. *$35.99*
72 pages Weekly Founded: 1952
Circulation: 34392

12384 Play Meter
Skybird Publishing Company
PO Box 337
Metairie, LA 70004-0337
504-488-7003
FAX: 504-488-7083 888-473-2376
news@playmeter.com
http://www.playmeter.com
Valerie Cognevich, Editor
Renee Pierson, Circulation Director
About 500 firms that manufacture and distribute coin-operated video and electronic games and other amusement machines; 300 firms that supply the industry; state and national trade associations; exporters and importers foreign manufacturers and distributors. *$60.00*
Monthly Founded: 1974

12385 Playthings
Reed Business Information
360 Park Avenue S
4th Floor
New York, NY 10010
212-450-0067
FAX: 646-746-7433 800-309-3332
mlaporte@reedbusiness.com
http://www.playthings.com
Maria Weiskott, Editor-in-Chief
Larry Oliver, VP/Group Publisher
Micki LaPorte, Circulation Director
James Reed, Owner
Emphasizes a merchandising approach for improving sales and promotional techniques. Features include new product listings, market reports, licensing updates and general industry trends. *$33.95*
80 pages Monthly Founded: 1903
Printed in 4 colors on glossy stock

12386 SCRYE
Krause Publications
700 E State Street
Iola, WI 54990-1
715-445-2214
FAX: 715-445-4087
http://www.krause.com
Mark Williams, Publisher
Joyce Greenholdt, Editor
The most respected price guide in the industry for collectible card games and col-

lectible miniatures. SCRYE also provides collectors and players the latest news, checklists, player strategies, deck building tips and tricks for collectible card games. The latest collectible card games are reviewed in each issue in addition to related role-playing and board games. *$29.98*

160 pages Monthly Founded: 1994

Circulation: 47000

12387 Snapshot Memories

PRIMEDIA Consumer Magazine & Internet Group
2 News Plaza
PO Box 1790
Peoria, IL 61656-1790
309-682-6626
FAX: 309-679-5057
snapshotsales@primediasi.com

Mike Irish, Associate Publisher
Miram Olson, Editor-in-Chief

Scrapbook page idea magazine. *$16.98*

92 pages Quarterly Founded: 1998

Circulation: 90,000

Printed in 4 colors on glossy stock

12388 Sports Collectors Digest

Krause Publications
700 E State Street
Iola, WI 54990-1
715-445-2214
FAX: 715-445-4087 800-258-0929

Dean Listle, Publisher
TS O'Connell, Editor

The Bible of Hobby covers every aspect of modern sports collecting, including cards, memorabilia, equipment, lithographs, figurines, and autographed material. Online collecting, graded cards, memorabilia and auction news are covered each week in specially designed sections that complement columns from some of the most respected experts in the hobby and up-to-date card pricing checklisting data from expert analysts, along with display advertisements from all the major dealers in the country. *$49.95*

96 pages Weekly Founded: 1973

Circulation: 23356

12389 Stamp Collector

Krause Publications
700 E State Street
Iola, WI 54990
715-445-2214
FAX: 715-445-4087 www.krause.com

Wayne Youngblood, Publisher
Jill Ruesch, Ad Manager

Covers a wide variety of US & foreign stamp news. Sepcial inserts cover topicals, errors, postal history, and many others. Regular columns and features include 'Decoding the Catalog,' 'Q&A,' 'Meet the Designer,' 'Postal History,' 'New Stamps of the World,' 'Stamp Values Today,' an auction guide and the most extensive stamp show calendar in the hobby. The first issue each month cotains Stamp Wholesaler - stamp dealer info that is used as a 'philatelic phone book' by the entire industry. *$32.98*

60 pages Founded: 1931

Circulation: 13251

12390 Tole World

EGW.com
4075 Papazian Way
208
Fremont, CA 94538-4300
510-668-0269
FAX: 510-668-0280
editor@toleworld.com
http://www.toleworld.com

Chris Slaughter, Circulation Director
Rickie Wilson, Advertisement Manager

Serving crafters in the decorative painting field; each issue features 10 to 12 projects complete with full color photographs, step-by-step instructions and line art patterns. Project designs come from the nation's leading decorative artists, many of whom are also teachers in the field. *$35.94*

84 pages Quarterly Founded: 1977

Circulation: 85956

12391 Toy Book

Adventure Publishing Group
1107 Broadway
Suite 1204
New York, NY 10010
212-575-4510
FAX: 212-575-4521
nlombardi@toybook.com
http://www.adventurepub.com

Owen Shorts, Owner
Nelson Lombardi, Editor
A Schwartz, Marketing

Keeps readers abreast of new products and marketing information related to the industry. *$48.00*

Monthly Founded: 1980

Circulation: 18000

12392 Toy Shop

Krause Publications
700 E State Street
Iola, WI 54990-1
715-445-2214
FAX: 715-445-4087
http://www.fwpublications.com

Mark Williams, Publisher
Tom Bartsch, Editor
Stephen J Kent, CEO/President

A complete marketplace for buyers and sellers of toys, action figures, Barbie, Hot Wheels, character toys, and more. Offers thousands of easy-to-read, categorized classified ads, display ads, and a complete editorial package covering baby-boomer toys, vintage collectibles, TV toys, action figures, and many helpful Q&A columns. Also contains up-to-date market trends as well as thorough auction updates and reports from toy shows nationwide. *$33.98*

76 pages Founded: 1988

Circulation: 11577

12393 Trapper & Predator

Krause Publications
700 E State Street
Iola, WI 54990-1
715-445-2214
FAX: 715-445-4087
http://www.krause.com

Hugh McAloon, Publisher
Paul Wait, Editor

Contains news, in-depth features, and how-to tips on trapping, the art of predator calling, and animal damage control. Contributors include the top names in the business. Regular columns and departments include 'The Fure Shed,' 'Let's Swap Ideas,' 'Q&A,' and news from state trapping associations nationwide. *$18.95*

80 pages Founded: 1975

Circulation: 38260

12394 Tuff Stuff

Krause Publications
700 E State Street
Iola, WI 54990-1
715-445-2214
FAX: 715-445-4087
http://www.krause.com

Dean Listle, Publisher
Rocky Landsverk, Editor

A guide to the sports card and collectibles hobby. Coverage of sports cards includes the latest prices on baseball, football, basketball, hockey, racing, and more. Each issue lists pricing information on Hall of Fame baseball and football memorabilia, autographed items, and commentary on the sports card industry. Columns and opinion pieces include a Q&A section, directories to professional teams, geographical and product directories, and hobby dealer listings for the US and Canada. *$29.95*

Monthly Founded: 1983

Circulation: 175,682

12395 Turkey & Turkey Hunting

Krause Publications
700 E State Street
Iola, WI 54990
715-445-2214
FAX: 715-445-4087 800-258-0929
info@krause.com
http://www.krause.com

Hugh McAloon, Publisher
James Schlender, Editor

Edited for serious, technical, year-round, gun and bow turkey hunters. Features emphasize success and enjoyment of the sport. Articles focus on hunting, scouting, turkey behavior and biology, hunting ethics, new equipment, methodologies, turkey management, and current research. Columns include 'Tree Call,' 'Mail Pouch,' 'Turkey Biology,' a Q&A column, 'Hunter's Library,' 'Turkey Gear,' and 'Last Call.' *$15.95*

72 pages Founded: 1975

Circulation: 68962

12396 Weekend Woodcrafts

EGW.com
1041 Shary Circle
Concord, CA 94518-2407
925-671-9852
FAX: 925-671-0692
info@egw.com
http://www.weekendwoodcrafts.com

Chris Slaughter, Circulation Director
Rickie Wilson, Advertising

Wide selection of easy-to-finish wood projects ranging from craft fair novelties and decorative home-accents to useful housewares and wooden toys. *$35.94*

68 pages Monthly Founded: 1980

12397 Wisconsin Outdoor Journal

Krause Publications
700 E State Street
Iola, WI 54990-0001
715-445-2214
FAX: 715-445-4087 www.krause.com

Hugh McAloon, Publisher
Paul Wait, Editor
Brad Rucks, Ad Manager

An exclusively in-state publication for hunters and anglers is edited for the active Wisconsin outdoors enthusiast who enjoys a year-round hunting and fishing lifestyle. Covers Wisconsin hunting and fishing through how-to features and informational features, a state news section, reports from seven different regional field editors, historical features about the state, and features on Wisconsin's flora, fauna, and geography. *$17.97*

72 pages 8 Per Year Founded: 1987

Circulation: 30,390

12398 **Wood Strokes**
EGW.com
1041 Shary Circle
Concord, CA 94518-2407
925-671-9852
FAX: 925-671-0692
info@egw.com http://www.egw.com

Chris Slaughter, Circulation Manager

Wide selection of easy-to-finish decorative wood painting projects ranging from craft fair novelties and decorative home accents to useful housewares and wooden toys. *$5.99*

76 pages
Circulation: 110437

12399 **World Coin News**
Krause Publications
700 E State Street
Iola, WI 54990
715-445-2214
FAX: 715-445-4087
info@krause.com
http://www.krause.com

Bill Bright, Publisher
Dave Harper, Editor

Recognized as the leading authority on world coins. It regularly reports on new issues, auctions and other coin news from around the world. Features by some of the top experts in the field provide in-depth historical information on coins and the countries that issue them. Regular features include "World Coin Clinic" (Q&A), "World Coin Roundup" (newly issued coins), "Rule Britannia," "Nautical Numismatics," "Mexican Potpourri," and "Coin Critters." Each issue provides a calendar of shows. *$30.99*

84 pages Monthly Founded: 1952
Circulation: 8729

Trade Shows

12400 **ACC Craft Show**
American Craft Council
21 S Eltings Corner Road
Highland, NY 12528
845-883-6100
FAX: 845-883-6130 800-836-3670
shows@craftcouncil.org
www.craftcouncil.org
Craft fair.
Annual

12401 **APS Stampshow**
American Philatelic Society
100 Match Factory Place
Ballefonte, PA 16823
814-373-3803
FAX: 814-933-6128
stampshow@stamps.org
www.stamps.org

Ken Martin, Director Shows/Exhibitions
Robert Lamb, Executive Director

Annual show for postage stamp collectors. Includes 150 dealers buying and selling material, more than 100 seminars, and 10,000 pages of stamps in collection. *$45.00*

6,000 Attendees Annual Founded: 1886
Circulation: 45,000

12402 **ASD/AMD Group**
Flectcher
2950 31st Street
Suite 100
Santa Monica, CA 90405
310-255-4633
FAX: 310-396-8476
15000 Attendees

12403 **AmeriStamp Expo**
American Philatelic Society
100 Match Factory Place
Bellafonte, PA 16823
814-373-3803
FAX: 814-933-6128
stampshow@stamps.org
www.stamps.org

Ken Martin, Director Shows/Exhibitions

Annual event for postage stamp collectors, featuring 75 dealers, 50 meetings and services, auction, 5,000 pages of exhibits and beginner actions. *$45.00*

2,500 Attendees Annual Founded: 1998
Circulation: 45,000

12404 **American Camping Association Conference & Exhibits**
5000 State Road 67 N
Martinsville, IN 46151-7902
765-342-8456
FAX: 765-342-2065 800-428-2267
bwilliems@aca-camps.org
www.aca-camps.org

Peg Smith, Chief Executive Officer
Bill Willems, Director Business

One hundred fifty booths of arts and crafts, computer software, sporting goods, waterfront equipment and more plus a seminar and workshop.

1,200 Attendees Annual Founded: 1943

12405 **American Craft Council Fairs**
ACC
21 S Elting Corners Road
Highland, NY 12528-2805
845-883-6100
FAX: 845-883-6130 800-836-3470
shows@craftcouncil.org
www.craftcouncil.org
Nine fairs nationwide each year. Each show incorporates crafts from the ceramics, wood, metal, mixed media, fiber, glass, jewelry, accessories and related industries. Most fairs include retail portion (public sales); some fairs also have wholesale (trade) component.

12406 **American International Toy Fair**
Toy Industry Association
1115 Broadway
Suite 400
New York, NY 10010
212-675-1141
FAX: 212-675-3246
toyfairs@toy-tma.org
www.toy-tia.org

Laura Green, VP Trade Shows/Meetings
Diane Cardinale, Public Information Manager

1,800-2,000 booths for producers of all types of toys and games, party and holiday items, models, hobby products, as well as collectibles, dolls, plush and miniatures. Attendees are retail buyers and trade professionals. Seminar and program.

20000 Attendees Annual Founded: 1903

12407 **American Needlepoint Guild Show**
3410 Valley Creek Circle
Middleton, WI 53562-1990
608-831-3328
FAX: 608-831-0651
seminars@needlepoint.org
www.needlepoint.org

Estelle Kelley, Seminars Director

Two hundred exhibits of needlework pieces, banquet and luncheon.

830 Attendees Annual Founded: 1972

12408 **American Numismatic Association Trade Show**
8181 N Cascade Avenue
Colorado Springs, CO 80903
719-632-2646

anacvn@money.org www.money.org

Brenda Bishop, Show Manager
Nancy Green, Manager

Four hundred twenty five booths of coins, medals and paper money.

15M Attendees August

12409 **American Quilt Study Group Seminar**
American Quilt Study Group
1610 L St
Lincoln, NE 68508-2509
402-477-1181
FAX: 402-477-1183
aqsg2@alltel.net
www.h0net.org/~aqsg/
Annual seminar and presentation of quilt-related articles.

October, Kansas Founded: 1980

12410 **American Stamp Dealers Association Stamp Shows**
3 School Street
Suite 201
Glen Cove, NY 11542-2548
516-759-7000

Joseph Savarese, Show Manager/Executive VP

Two hundred booths.

12.5M Attendees

12411 **Americover**
American First Day Cover Society
PO Box 1335
Maplewood, NJ 07040
973-762-2012
FAX: 973-762-7916
americover@aol.com www.afdcs.org

Steve Ripley, Show Manager

US and international first day postal covers, USPS first day ceremonies at most shows, 50 stamp dealers, cover dealers, cachetmalchers philatelic suppliers.

1500 Attendees Annual

12412 **Annual Spring-Easter Arts & Crafts Show & Sale**
Finger Lakes Craftsmen Shows
1 Freshour Road
Shortsville, NY 14548
585-289-9439
FAX: 585-289-9440

Ronald L Johnson, President

Annual show of 150 exhibitirs of arts and crafts manufacturers. Exhibits include handcrafted arts and crafts, including photos and prints.

9000 Attendees March Founded: 1999

12413 Antique Arms Show
PO Box 2231
Palm Springs, CA 92263-2231

Wallace Beinfield

Public show with 850 booths of antiques and collectibles.

4M Attendees January

12414 Association of Crafts and Creative Industries Show: ACCI Show
Offinger Management Company
1100-H Brandywine Boulevard
PO Box 3388
Zanesville, OH 43702
740-452-4541
FAX: 740-452-2552 888-360-2224
accishow@offinger.com
www.accicrafts.org

Marrijane Jones, Executive Director
Erica McKenzie, ACCI Communications Manager

The ACCI Show is sponsored by the Association of Crafts and Creative Industries. Over 1,300 booths are represented, featuring general crafts, softcrafts, art materials and framing, scrapbooking materials and floral, home and garden items.

8000+ Attendees Annual

12415 Christmas Gift & Hobby Show
HSI Show Productions
PO Box 502797
Indianapolis, IN 46250
317-576-9933
FAX: 317-576-9955 800-215-1700
info@hsishows.com
www.hsishows.com

Donell Hebererwalton, Sales Director
Todd Jameson, Show Manager

45000 Attendees

12416 Christmas Gift and Hobby Show
HSI Show Productions
PO Box 502797
Indianapolis, IN 46250-7797
317-576-9933
FAX: 317-576-9955 800-215-1700
info@hsishows.com
www.hsishows.com

Donell Hebererwalton, Sales Director
Todd Jameson, Show Manager

Annual show of 360 exhibitors of arts, crafts and giftware.

70M Attendees

12417 Coin and Stamp Exposition
Bick International
PO Box 854
Van Nuys, CA 91408
818-997-6496
FAX: 818-988-4337
iibick@sbcglobal.net www.bick.net

Israel I Bick, Managing Director

5000 Attendees Annual/December/May, NV
13,000 names $125 per M.

12418 Coin and Stamp Exposition: San Francisco
Bick International
PO Box 854
Van Nuys, CA 91408
818-997-6496
FAX: 818-988-4337
iibick@sbcglobal.net www.bick.net

Israel I Bick, Managing Director

5000 Attendees June/September, Annually
30,000 names $100 per M.

12419 Doll, Teddy Bear & Toy Show & Sale
Jones Publishing
9572 Forest Hills Lodge & Route 173
Rockford, IL 54945-5000
715-445-5000
chujorey@essex1.com

JoAnn Reynolds, Contact

Great assortment of toys featuring teddy bears of all kinds.

12420 Eastern States Doll, Toy, and Teddy Bear Show and Sale
Maven Company
PO Box 937
Plandome, NY 11030
914-248-4646
FAX: 914-248-0800
www.mavencompany.com

N Chittenden, VP

Wide variety of dolls, toys and teddy bears. Largest show of its kind in the northeast.

5000 Attendees November/April Founded: 1982

12421 Ed Expo
National School Supply and Equipment Association
8380 Colesville Road
Suite 250
Silver Spring, MD 20910
301-495-0240
FAX: 301-495-3330 800-395-5550
nssea@nssea.org www.nssea.org

Adrienne West, VP Marketing

Educational products including games and toys.

April

12422 HIA: Hobby Industries of America Trade Show
Hobby Industries of America
319 E 54th Street
PO Box 348
Elmwood Park, NJ 07407
201-794-1133
FAX: 201-798-0657 www.hobby.org

Steve Berger, Executive Director

International trade show open to qualified professionals and is the industry's only market research show.

10000 Attendees

12423 Halloween Costume and Party Show
TransWorld Exhibits
1850 Oak Street
Northfield, IL 60093
847-784-6905
FAX: 847-446-3523 800-323-5462

12424 International Gift and Collectible Expo
Krause Publications
700 E State Street
Iola, WI 54990
715-445-2214
FAX: 715-445-4087 877-746-9757

Claude Chmiel, Show Producer

17000 Attendees June

12425 International JPMA Show
Juvenile Products Manufacturers Association
15000 Commerce Parkway
Suite C
Mt Laurel, NJ 08054
856-439-0500
FAX: 856-439-0525
lstill@ahinf.com www.jpma.org

Linda Still, Director of Trade Show

Items of interest to retailers of children's apparel and toys.

3000 Attendees Annual

12426 International Miniature Collectibles Trade Show
Offinger Management Company
PO Box 3388
Zanesville, OH 43702-3388
740-452-4541
FAX: 740-452-2552
miaa.info@offinger.com
www.miaa.com

August

12427 Just Kidstuff & The Museum Source
George Little Management
10 Bank Street
Suite 1200
White Plains, NY 10606
914-486-6070
FAX: 914-948-2918 800-272-7469

George Little II, President

45000 Attendees

12428 National Dollhouse & Miniatures Trade Show & Convention
Miniatures Association of America
1100-H Brandywine Boulevard
PO Box 3388
Zanesville, OH 43702-3388
740-452-4541
FAX: 740-452-2552 888-360-2224

1400 Attendees

12429 National Merchandise Show
Miller Freeman Publications
One Penn Plaza
PO Box 2549
New York, NY 10119
212-714-1300
FAX: 212-714-1313

16000 Attendees

12430 National Model and Hobby Show
Radio Control Hobby Trade Association
PO Box 315
Butter, NJ 07405-0315
973-283-9088
FAX: 973-838-7124 www.rchta.org

Annual show of 400 manufacturers and distributors of model kits and hobby equipment, supplies and services. Radio controlled cars, planes, boats, model trains, plastic kits, games, rockets, die cash, collectibles, and accessories. Containing 400 booths and 2000 exhibits.

20M Attendees October

12431 National NeedleArts Association Trade Show
National Needlework Association
PO Box 3388
Zanesville, OH 43702-3388
740-452-4541
FAX: 740-452-2552 800-889-8662
tnna.info@offinger.com www.tnna.org

Rise Fulmer, Trade Show Manager
Patty Parrish, Executive Director

January Founded: 1974

12432 **National Sewing Show: Home Sewing Association**
American Home Sewing and Craft Association
1350 Broadway
Suite 1601
New York, NY 10018
212-714-1633
FAX: 212-714-1655
info@sewing.org www.sewing.org
Pat Kobishyn, Show Manager
Two hundred exhibits of fabric, notions, patterns, sewing and trimmings. Attended by professionals from major chain stores, independent retailers, wholesalers and manufacturers.
3000 Attendees Annual

12433 **SHOPA**
SHOPA
3131 Elbee Road
Dayton, OH 45439-1900
937-297-2250
FAX: 937-297-2254 800-854-7467
info@shopa.org www.shopa.org
Steven Jacober, President
Doris Condron, Director of Communications
7500 Attendees November

12434 **Souvenirs Gifts & Novelties Trade Association**
Kane Communications
7000 Terminal Square
Suite 210
Upper Darby, PA 19082-2330
610-734-2420
FAX: 610-734-2423
sgnta@aol.com www.souvmag.com
Al Barry, Show Manager
Larry White, VP Marketing
Trade show serving amusements, museums, zoos, entertainment, bowling, and retailers. Seminars and networking party.
5000 Attendees July

12435 **Variety Merchandise Show**
Miller Freeman Publications
One Penn Plaza
PO Box 2549
New York, NY 10119
212-714-1300
FAX: 212-714-1313
20000 Attendees

12436 **Western States Toy and Hobby Show**
Western Toy and Hobby Representative Association
9397 Reserve Drive
Corona, CA 92883
951-771-1598
FAX: 909-277-1599
info@wthra.com www.wthra.com
Phylis St. John, Contact
If it's for kids, it's here. Show is for trade members only, not open to the public.
3000 Attendees March

Directories & Databases

12437 **American International Toy Fair Official Directory of Showrooms & Exhibits**
Toy Industry Association
1115 Broadway
Suite 400
New York, NY 10010
212-675-1141
FAX: 212-645-3246
info@toy-tia.org www.toy-tia.org
Thomas Conley, President
Diane Cardinale, Public Information Manager
Over 1,500 toy, game and hobby decoration manufacturers and their representatives are profiled. *$50.00*
400 pages Annual
Circulation: 12,000

12438 **Complete Directory of Collectibles**
Sutton Family Communications & Publishing Company
155 Sutton Lane
Fordsville, KY 42343
270-740-0870

jlsutton@apex.net
www.fleamarketeer.net
Theresa Sutton, Publisher
Lee Sutton, Editor
Print-out from database of wholesalers, manufacturers, distributors, importers and close-out houses. Database is updated daily to guarantee the most current and up-to-date sources available. *$67.50*
100 pages

12439 **Complete Directory of Crafts and Hobbies**
Sutton Family Communications & Publishing Company
155 Sutton Lane
Fordsville, KY 42343
270-740-0870

jlsutton@apex.net
www.fleamarketeer.net
Theresa Sutton, Editor
Lee Sutton, General Manager
Print-out from database of wholesalers, manufacturers, distributors, importers and close-out houses. Database is updated daily to guarantee the most current and up-to-date sources available. *$54.50*
100+ pages

12440 **Complete Directory of Figurines**
Sutton Family Communications & Publishing Company
155 Sutton Lane
Fordsville, KY 42343
270-740-0870

jlsutton@apex.net
www.fleamarketeer.net
Theresa Sutton, Publisher
Lee Sutton, Editor
Print-out from database of wholesalers, manufacturers, distributors, importers and close-out houses. Database is updated daily to guarantee the most current and up-to-date sources available. *$44.50*
100 pages

12441 **Complete Directory of Games**
Sutton Family Communications & Publishing Company
155 Sutton Lane
Fordsville, KY 42343
270-740-0870

jlsutton@apex.net
www.fleamarketeer.net
Theresa Sutton, Publisher
Lee Sutton, Editor
Print-out from database of wholesalers, manufacturers, distributors, importers and close-out houses. Database is updated daily to guarantee the most current and up-to-date sources available. *$39.50*
100 pages

12442 **Complete Directory of Novelties**
Sutton Family Communications & Publishing Company
155 Sutton Lane
Fordsville, KY 42343
270-740-0870

jlsutton@apex.net
www.fleamarketeer.net
Theresa Sutton, Publisher
Lee Sutton, Editor
Print-out from database of wholesalers, manufacturers, distributors, importers and close-out houses. Database is updated daily to guarantee the most current and up-to-date sources available. *$79.50*
100 pages

12443 **Complete Directory of Pewter Items**
Sutton Family Communications & Publishing Company
155 Sutton Lane
Fordsville, KY 42343
270-740-0870

jlsutton@apex.net
www.fleamarketeer.net
Theresa Sutton, Publisher
Lee Sutton, Editor
Print-out from database of wholesalers, manufacturers, distributors, importers and close-out houses. Database is updated daily to guarantee the most current and up-to-date sources available. *$39.50*
100 pages

12444 **Complete Directory of Plush and Stuffed Toys and Dolls**
Sutton Family Communications & Publishing Company
155 Sutton Lane
Fordsville, KY 42343
270-740-0870

jlsutton@apex.net
www.fleamarketeer.net
Theresa Sutton, Editor
Lee Sutton, General Manager
Print-out from database of wholesalers, manufacturers, distributors, importers and close-out houses. Database is updated daily to guarantee the most current and up-to-date sources available. *$39.50*
100+ pages

12445 Complete Directory of Posters, Buttons and Novelties
Sutton Family Communications & Publishing Company
155 Sutton Lane
Fordsville, KY 42343
270-740-0870

jlsutton@apex.net
www.fleamarketeer.net

Theresa Sutton, Editor
Lee Sutton, General Manager

Print-out from database of wholesalers, manufacturers, distributors, importers and close-out houses. Database is updated daily to guarantee the most current and up-to-date sources available. *$39.50*
100+ pages

12446 Complete Directory of Toys and Games
Sutton Family Communications & Publishing Company
155 Sutton Lane
Fordsville, KY 42343
270-740-0870

jlsutton@apex.net
www.fleamarketeer.net

Theresa Sutton, Editor
Lee Sutton, General Manager

Print-out from database of wholesalers, manufacturers, distributors, importers and close-out houses. Database is updated daily to guarantee the most current and up-to-date sources available. *$44.50*
100+ pages

12447 Directory of Manufacturer Representatives Service Suppliers
Hobby Industry Association
319 E 54th Street
Elmwood Park, NJ 07407-2712
201-794-1133
FAX: 201-797-0657
Two hundred manufacturers representatives and 105 trade show booth demonstrators working in the hobby equipment industry. *$25.00*
Biennial

12448 Game Manufacturers Association Membership Directory
Game Manufacturers Association
280 N High Street
Suite 230
Columbus, OH 43215
614-255-4500
FAX: 614-255-4499 www.gama.org
Approximately 350 member manufacturers and distributors of adventure games. *$30.00*
Annual

12449 Games and Entertainment on CD-ROM
Mecklermedia Corporation
20 Ketchum Street
Westport, CT 06880-5908
203-341-2806
FAX: 203-454-5840
Over 1,300 multimedia encyclopedias, children's educational software and interactive 'board games'. *$29.95*

12450 Hobby Industries of America Trade Show Program and Buyers Guide
Hobby Industry Association
319 E 54th Street
Elmwood Park, NJ 07407-2712
201-794-1133
FAX: 201-797-0657
hia@ihobby.org www.hobby.org

Steve Berger, Executive Director

Over 1000 manufacturers are listed that exhibit at the HIA trade show. *$25.00*
170 pages Annual Founded: 1940

12451 Hobby Merchandiser Annual Trade Directory
Hobby Publications
207 Commercial Court
Morganville, NJ 07751
732-536-5160
FAX: 732-536-5761
hobbypub@injersey.com
www.hobbymerchandiser.com

Robert Gherman, Publisher
Jeff Troy, Editor
Ellen Gherman, Circulation Director
Tracey Decesure, Production Manager

Offers valuable information on manufacturers, wholesalers, industry suppliers and publishers of books and periodicals in the hobby trade industry. *$35.00*
140 pages Annual Founded: 1945
Circulation: 7,000
Mailing list available for rent 8M names
Printed in 4 colors on glossy stock

12452 Hobby RoundTable
GE Information Services
401 N Washington Street
Rockville, MD 20850-1707
301-388-8284

Cathy Ge, Owner

This database offers a forum enabling participants to share information on hobby-related topics, the hobby industry and hobby-related software.
Bulletin Board

12453 Radio Control Hobby Membership Directory
Radio Control Hobby Trade Association
31632 N Ellis Avenue
Unit 111
Volo, IL 60073
847-740-1111
FAX: 847-740-1111 www.rchta.org
Members and manufacturers of radio control products.
Founded: 1983

Industry Web Sites

12454 www.amo-archery.org
Archery Manufacturers & Merchants Organization

Members are producers and sellers to the archery consumer.

12455 www.asdaonline.com
American Stamp Dealers Association

Holds annual International Philatelic Exhibition Interpex. Sponsors the annual International Dealers course. Postage stamp mega event twice a year (spring and fall).

12456 www.craftdesigners.org
Society of Craft Designers

The Society of Craft Designers (SCD), founded in 1975, is a professional organization for those who believe that quality craft design is the basis of a strong and viable craft industry. It is the only membership organization exclusively serving those who design for the consumer craft industry.

12457 www.greyhouse.com
Grey House Publishing

Selected Grey House directories in the fields of business, health and education are available online. Users can search our online databases by several different search criteria, such as product categories, geographic area, sales volume and much, much more. Full Grey House catalog and online ordering also available.

12458 www.hobby.org
Hobby Industry Association

The world's largest trade association in the craft and hobby market. The group produces an International Trade Show open to qualified professionals and is the industrys only market research show.

12459 www.mria.org
Model Railroad Industry Association

Works to publicize the hobby and to keep members informed on the industry. Assists clubs and retailers in their shows.

12460 www.rchta.org
Radio Control Hobby Trade Association

For manufacturers and distributors of model hobby kits and hobby equipment, supplies and services and products associated with retail hobby stores.

12461 www.stamps.org
American Philatelic Society

National organization for stamp collectors; lending library; insurance for philatelic materials; sales division, seminars and annual conventions open to the public.

12462 www.tnna.org
National Needlework Association

For maufacturers, suppliers and distributers of needlework and related equipment, supplies and services.

12463 www.toy-tia.org
Toy Industry Association

National organization with over 300 toy, game and holiday decoration manufacturers and their representatives, as well as toy designers, testing laboratories, licensors, sales representatives and trade magazines.

12464 www.wccwis.gr.jp/home.html
World Craft Council

A national organization for Handicraft

Associations

12465 **American Hotel & Lodging Association**
1201 New York Avenue NW
Suite 600
Washington, DC 20005-3931
202-289-3100
FAX: 202-289-3199
info@ahla.com www.ahla.com
Pedro Mandoki, Chairman
Joseph A. McInerney, President/CEO
Joseph R. Kane, Jr, Vice Chair
Supports all those involved in managing or franchising properties worldwide. Publishes annual directory.
10000 Members Founded: 1910

12466 **American Hotel & Lodging Educational Foundation**
1201 New York Avenue NW
Suite 600
Washington, DC 20005-3931
202-289-3100
FAX: 202-289-3199
chammond@ahlef.org www.ahma.com
Michelle Poinelli, VP Foundation Program
Crystal Hammond, Manager Foundation Program
Jada Smith, Development Coordinator
Joseph McInerney, President
Fosters education, research programming, and information regarding operating techniques in the lodging industry.
11000 Members Founded: 1910

12467 **American Hotel & Motel Association**
1201 New York Avenue NW
Washington, DC 20005
202-289-3100
FAX: 202-289-3199 800-252-2462
info@ahma.com www.ahma.com
Pedro Mandoki, Chairman
Joseph McInerney, President
Trade association covering news, issues and activities of related industry groups.
11000 Members Founded: 1910

12468 **American Resort Development Association Annual Convention**
1201 15th Street NW
Suite 400
Washington, DC 20005-2842
202-371-6700
FAX: 202-289-8544
webmaster@arda.org www.arda.org
John M Burlingame, Chairman
Howard C Nusbaum, President
Robert J Webb, Treasurer
William B Ingersoll, General Counsel/Secretary
Supports all those involved in the development of resorts nationwide. Hosts annual trade show.
1000 Members Founded: 1969

12469 **Arizona Hotel & Lodging Association**
1240 E Missouri Avenue
Phoenix, AZ 85014
602-604-0729
FAX: 602-604-0769 800-707-3921
info@azhla.com www.azhla.com
Debbie Johnson, President/CEO
David Nance, Director Of Membership
Linda Schneider, Administrative Coordinator
Michelle Wade, Director Of Marketing
AZHLA is the leading public policy advocate for the Statewide Lodging Industry. The mission is to enhance, unite and protect the interests of the Arizona lodging industry.
450 Members Founded: 1938

12470 **Arkansas Hospitality Association**
603 S Pulaski
PO Box 3866
Little Rock, AR 72203
501-376-2323
FAX: 501-376-6517
www.arhospitality.org
Montine McNulty, Executive Director
Rita Walker, Executive Assistant
Janelle Powell, Director, Membership Services
Kristy Seago, Director, Communications
Dee Carroll, Director,Education
The association is the official voice of the Arkansas Restaurant, the Arkansas Lodging Association, and the Arkansas Travel Council. Membership is open to any business interested in obtaining the services, information, and benefits provided by the Association. Sponsors the largest annual trade show. Also publishes a monthly newsletter and quarterly magazine.

12471 **Asian/American Hotel Owners Association**
66 Lenox Pointe NE
Atlanta, GA 30324
404-816-5759
FAX: 404-816-6260
info@aahoa.com www.aahoa.com
Manhar Rama, Chairman
Mukesh Mowji, Vice Chair
Fred Schwartz, President
Ashwin Patel, Treasurer
Dilipkumar Patel, Secretary
Supports Asian/American hotel and motel owners and operators.
8,700 Members Founded: 1989

12472 **Associated Luxury Hotels**
1000 Connecticut Avenue NW
Suite 603
Washington, DC 20036
202-887-7020
FAX: 202-887-0085
meetings@alhi.com www.alhi.com
John F. Metcalfe, Chairman
David G. Gabri, President/CEO
Ed Simon, Regional VP
Laura Arth, VP Sales/Marketing
Helaine Metcalfe, VP Finance
Provided a National Sales Network to associations and corporations in America for the distinguished hotels and resorts now in 26 states, Canada, Mexico, and the Caribbean.
Founded: 1987

12473 **Bed and Breakfast League**
PO Box 9490
Washington, DC 20016-9490
202-363-7767
FAX: 202-363-8396
bedandbreakfast/washingtondc@erols.com
Millie Groobey, Director
A reservation service for bed and breakfasts in Washington, DC, that welcome selected travelers into their homes.
Founded: 1976

12474 **California Hotel & Lodging Association**
PO Box 160405
414 29th Street
Sacramento, CA 95816-3211
916-444-5780
FAX: 916-444-5848
service@calodging.com
www.chma.com
James Abrams, President/CEO
Lynn Mohrfeld, VP, Marketing & Business Develop
Jennifer Flohr, Membership Manager
Debra Kurtti, Membership Manager
The resource for communicating and protecting the rights and interests of the California lodging industry, for providing educational training and cost-saving programs for all segments of the industry, and for supporting alliances to promote the value of California tourism and travel.
1597 Members Founded: 1893

12475 **Central Florida Hotel & Lodging Association**
7380 Sand Lake Road
Suite 300
Orlando, FL 32819
407-313-5000
FAX: 407-313-5050 www.cfhla.org
Pat Engfer, Chairperson
Greg Hauenstein, Vice Chairperson
Rich Maladecki, President
Serves as both an industry leader in governmental affairs and community service to enhance the success of tourism in the region. Also one of Central Florida's largest and most influential trade groups.

12476 **Distinguished Inns of North America**
501 E. Michigan Avenue
POBox 150
Marshall, MI 49068
269-789-0393
FAX: 269-789-0970 800-344-5244
maincontact@selectregistry.com
www.innbook.com
Keith Kehlbeck, Executive Director
Represents the finest country inns, B&Bs, and unique small hotels from California to Nova-Scotia. The very best the travel industry has to offer.
400 Members Founded: 1968

12477 **Educational Institute of the American Hotel & Lodging Association**
2113 N High Street
Lansing, MI 48906
517-372-8800
FAX: 517-372-5141
info@ei-ahla.org www.ei-ahla.org
Anthony G Marshall, President
Anthony Farris, Chairman
Thomas J. Corcoran Jr., Vice Chair
George Glazer, Manager
A nonprofit educational foundation of the American Hotel & Lodging Association and the world's largest provider of hospitality education training resources, videos, books, workbooks, seminars, management courses, complete training systems and professional certification programs.
120 Members Founded: 1953

12478 Greater Miami & Beaches Hotel Association
407 Lincoln Road
Suite 10G
Miami Beach, FL 33139
305-531-3553
FAX: 305-531-8954 800-531-3553
info@gmbha.org www.gmbha.org

Juan Romero, Chairperson
Stuart L. Blumberg, President/CEO
Charlie Hines, Vice Chairperson
Spero Canton, Secretary
Stephen Nostrand, Treasurer

The mission is to unify the industry countywide and to provide through education and proactive leadership, an enhanced visitor experience that compliments other efforts currently designed to make greater Miami a prime worldwide destination. Membership is a cross section of hotels and a partnership with member businesses, corporations and individuals.

12479 Hospitality Financial & Technology Professionals
11709 Boulder Lane
Suite 110
Austin, TX 78726-1832
512-249-5333
FAX: 512-249-1533 800-646-4387
membership@hftp.org www.hftp.org

Frank Wolfe, Executive VP/CEO
Frank A. Agnello Jr., President
Yvonne Lane, Staff VP,Conferences&Communications
Lance Peterson, Director Marketing
Shelley Brand, Membership Marketing Manager

Professional society for those in the financial segment of the hospitality industry.
4300 Members Founded: 1952

12480 Hotel Association of New York City
320 Park Avenue
22nd Floor
New York, NY 10022-6838
212-754-6700
FAX: 212-754-0243
ramato@hanyc.org www.hanyc.org

Vijay Dandapani, Chair
John Fitzpatrick, Vice Chair
Joseph E Spinnato, President/CEO
Mike Stengel, Secretary
Jospeh Gelchion, Treasurer

One of the oldest professional trade associations in the nation.
200+ Members Founded: 1878

12481 Hotel Employees and Restaurant Employees
275 7th Avenue
New York, NY 10001-6708
212-265-7000
www.uniterhere.org

Bruce S Raynor, General President
John W Wihelm, President,Hospitality Industry

Formed upon the merge of Union of Needletrades, Textiles and Industrial Employees and the Hotel Employees and Restaurant Employees International Union. Hosts a diverse membership, comprised largely of immigrants and including high percentages of African-American, Latino, and Asia-American workers. The majority of members are women.
850m Members Founded: 1891

12482 International Council on Hotel, Restaurant and Institutional Education
2810 North Parham Road
Suite 230
Richmond, VA 23294
804-346-4800
FAX: 804-346-5009
webmaster@chrie.org www.chrie.org

Mike Zema, President
Bob Bosselman, VP
Kathy McCarty, Executive Vice P
Cynthia Mayp, Secretary
Lea Dopson, Treasurer

A nonprofit professional association which provides programs and services to continually improve the quality of global education, research, service, and business operations in the hospitality and tourism industry.
Founded: 1946

12483 International Executive Housekeepers Association
1001 Eastwind Drive
Suite 301
Westerville, OH 43081-3361
614-895-7166
FAX: 614-895-1248 800-200-6342
excel@ieha.org www.ieha.org

Hazel Reese, President
J. Darrel Hicks, President-Elect
Donna Prater, Secretary/Treasurer
Beth Risinger, Chief Executive Officer

An organization for persons working in the housekeeping area of the lodging industry.
4000 Members Founded: 1930

12484 International Facility Management Association
1 E Greenway Plaza
Suite 1100
Houston, TX 77046-0194
713-623-4362
FAX: 713-623-6124
ifma@ifma.org www.ifma.org

Joseph M. Dawson, Chair
Teena G. Shouse, First Vice Chair
Garyp. Broersma, Second Vice Chair
David Brady, President
John McGee, CEO

Sponsors tradeshows, seminars and exhibitions for those in facility management.
17300 Members Founded: 1990

12485 Massachusetts Lodging Association
7 Liberty Square
Suite 200
Boston, MA 02109
617-720-1776
FAX: 617-720-1305
info@masslodging.com
www.masslodging.com
Trade association representing and promoting the lodging industry in Massachusetts. Members include hotels, motels, resorts, inns, bed and breakfasts.
400+ Members

12486 National Bed & Breakfast Association
148 E Rocks Road
Norwalk, CT 06851-1723
203-431-0005
www.nbba.com
An organization of services and supplies to the industry offering a list of the best in bed and breakfast accommodations in the USA, Canada and the Carribbean.
Founded: 1981

12487 New Mexico Lodging Association
811 St Michael's Drive
Suite 107
Santa Fe, NM 87505
505-983-4554
FAX: 505-982-9359
information@nmlodging.org
www.nmhotels.com

Art Bouffard, President
Jeff Mahan, Chair
Bob Gansfuss, Vice Chair
Mike Coy, Secretary/Treasurer
Karla A Romero, Deputy Director

New Mexico's trade association representing the lodging industry. Represents individual hotels, motels, resorts, and bed & breakfast inns, comprising over 29,000 transient rooms or approximately 64% of the total room inventory in New Mexico.
300+ Members Founded: 1934

12488 New York State Hospitality & Tourism Association
80 Wolf Road
Albany, NY 12205
518-465-2300
FAX: 518-465-4025
andy@nyshta.org www.nyshta.org

Daniel C Murphy, President
Jan Marie Chesterton, VP
Nancy S Sykes, Executive Assistant

The oldest lodging association in the country. Includes members from nearly all segments of the tourism industry.
1600 Members Founded: 1887

12489 Preferred Hotels and Resorts Worldwide
311 S Wacker Drive
Suite 1900
Chicago, IL 60606-6620
312-913-0400
FAX: 312-913-0444
info@preferredhotels.com
www.preferredhotels.com

John Ueberroth, President/CEO
Nora Gainer, Director Marketing

Independently owned luxury hotels and resorts. Each provides the highest standards of quality and extraordinary service.
120 Members Founded: 1968

12490 Professional Association of Innkeepers International
207 White Horse Pike
Haddon Heights, NJ 08035-1703
856-310-1102
FAX: 856-310-1105 800-468-7244
membership@paii.org www.paii.org

Pam Horovitz, President/CEO
Jeanine Zeman, Director of Meetings & Events

Serving bed and breakfast/country inn owners, aspiring innkeepers, inn sitters, vendors with educational and consultative services. International conference.
3500 Members Founded: 1988

12491 Small Luxury Hotels
14673 Midway Road
Suite 201
Addison, TX 75001
972-866-8010

lanny.grossman@slh.com
www.slh.com
Members are independent owners and managers of deluxe hotels with fewer than 200 rooms.
233 Members Founded: 1991

12492 **Small Luxury Hotels of the World**
370 Lexigton Avenue
Suite 1506
New York, NY 10017
212-953-2064
FAX: 212-953-0576 800-525-4800
lanny.grossman@slh.com
www.slh.com

Lanny Grossman, Marketing
Johnathan Slater, Chairman
Ed Donaldson, Manager

Collection of 300 independently owned exclusive hotels in more than 50 countries. Selected for style and comfort, properties include spas, country houses, golf resorts, island retreats, city sanctuaries, game and wilderness lodges. Publishes directory.

300 Members Founded: 1991

12493 **Tennessee Hotel & Lodging Association**
644 West Iris Drive
Nashville, TN 37204-9131
615-385-9970
FAX: 615-385-9957
admin@thla.net www.thla.net

Pam Inman, CEO
Karen R Belcher, Director Administrative Services
Stacie Hindman, Director Member Services
Jennifer W Montgomery, Communications Director

The source for information, education and the advocacy voice for the hotel/lodging industry in Tennessee.

Newsletters

12494 **AH & MA Register**
American Hotel & Motel Association
1201 New York Avenue NW
6th Floor
Washington, DC 20005-3917
202-289-3100
FAX: 202-289-3138

Kathryn Potter, Publisher
Cathy Pippin, Circulation Manager

Newsletter covers association news, as well as issues and activities of related industry groups.

8 pages Annual
Circulation: 12,000 Audited
Mailing list available for rent 12000 names $135 per M.
Printed in 2 colors

12495 **AHF Developments**
American Hotel Foundation
1201 New York Avenue NW
Suite 600
Washington, DC 20005-3917
202-289-3100
FAX: 202-289-3199
AHF@ahma.com
www.ahma.com/ahf.htm

Douglas Viehland, Publisher
Michelle Poinelli, Program Director
Joseph McInerney, President

AHF Developments is published three times a year with circulation to donors, scholarship recipients and members of the American Hotel and Motel association.

Quarterly Founded: 1910

12496 **Cameron's Foodservice Marketing Reporter**
Cameron's Publications
5423 Sheridan Drive
PO Box 676
Williamsville, NY 14231
519-586-8785
FAX: 519-586-8816
mail@cameronpub.com
http://www.cameronpub.com

Bob McClelland, CEO
Nina Cameron, Editor

Successful promotion and advertising case histories for the restaurant and hotel industry.

100.00 names

12497 **Epicurean Revue**
PO Box 35128
Sarasota, FL 34242-5128

FAX: 941-349-4370

Jean-Noel Prade, Publisher
Georgia Brown, Editor
JN Prade, Circulation Manager

The publication for the jetsetters exclusive recommendations on top class hotels and restaurants. Total analysis of the various issues of the Michelin Guide and results of the wine auctions. *$79.00*

8 pages Monthly
Circulation: 5,000 Audited Est. Pass-Along Circ: 2000
Printed in 1 color on matte stock
Computerized version available

12498 **Hospitality Law**
LRP Publications
360 Hiatt Drive
Palm Beach Gardens, FL 33418
561-622-6520
FAX: 561-622-2423 800-341-7874
custserve@lrp.com
http://www.lrp.com

Kenneth Kuhn, Publisher
Dave Light, Editor

Details and analyzes significant cases in the hospitality industry so you can learn from the mistakes that landed other properties in court. You receive summaries of the latest court cases - without legalese - involving hotels, inns, resorts and restaurants. *$229.00*

12 pages Monthly
Circulation: 1400 8000 names $145 per M.

12499 **Hotel Technology Newsletter**
Chervenak, Keane and Company
307 E 44th Street
New York, NY 10017
212-986-8230
FAX: 212-983-5275
www.e-hospitality.com.storefronts/ckchoteltech.html

J Christmas, Publisher
L Chervenak, Editor

Covers hotel information processing, telecommunications, security, fire safety, energy and audio-visual systems. *$180.00*

Annual

12500 **Hotel and Casino Law Letter**
William F Harrah College of Hotel Administration
4505 Maryland Parkway
Box 456013
Las Vegas, NV 89154-6013
702-895-3161
FAX: 702-895-4109
hoaadvise@ccmail.nevada.edu
http://hotel.unlv.edu/

Annette Kannenberg, Business Manager
Stuart H Mann, Dean
Alice Baker, Administrative Assistant
Pat Merl, Management Assistant
Sherri Theriault, Director

Legislative news for executive level management of hotels and motels.

12501 **Hyatt Overseas**
Hyatt International Corporation
71 south wacker
Chicago, IL 60606-3414
312-750-1234
FAX: 312-750-8578

Kristin Sandberg, Publisher
Thomas Pritzker, Chief Executive Officer

A summary of news, packages and events happening at Hyatt Hotels.

2 pages

12502 **Inn Side Issues**
Hotel and Motel Brokers of America
10220 N Executive Boulevard
Suite 610
Kansas City, MO 64153
816-891-8776
FAX: 816-891-7071

Robert Kralicek, Editor

News of hotel owners and investors with articles about hospitality real estate.

Magazines & Journals

12503 **Bed & Breakfast**
Virgo Publishing
3300 N Central Avenue Suite 2500
PO Box 40079
Phoenix, AZ 85067-79
480-990-1101
FAX: 480-990-0819
http://www.vpico.com

Troy Bix, Publisher

Contains interesting and vital topics such as marketing, improving guest service, and suggests business strategies designed to increase workload. Provides profiles on unique inns from around the world and their owners. *$14.95*

Founded: 1986
Circulation: 15000

12504 **Bottomline**
Hospitality Financial & Technology Professionals
11709 Boulder Lane
Suite 110
Austin, TX 78726-1832
512-249-5333
FAX: 512-249-1533 800-646-4387
thebottomline@hftp.org www.hftp.org

Jen Gonzales, Communications Manager
Theresa Pulley, Advertising Director

Official publication of the international association for individuals employed as controllers and financial officers in the hospitality industry. Articles include topics such as technology, personnel management, financial analysis, ethics and financial controls. *$ 200.00*

Founded: 1952
Circulation: 4300
Printed in on glossy stock

12505 Cameron's Worldwide Hospitality Marketing Reporter
53256 Sheridan Drive
Williamsville, NY 14221-3503
416-636-5666
FAX: 416-636-5026

12506 Cheers
257 Park Avenue S
3rd Floor, Suite 303
New York, NY 10010
212-967-1551
FAX: 646-654-2099

John Eastman, Owner

Every issue is designed to help on-premise operators enhance the profitability of their beverage operations.

12507 Club Management Magazine
Finan Publishing Company
107 W Pacific
Saint Louis, MO 63119-3776
314-961-6644
FAX: 314-961-4809
dkaplan@finan.com
http://www.club-mgmt.com

Thomas J Finan, IV, Managing Editor
Dee Kaplan, Publisher
Dianne Dierkes, Circulation Manager

The resource for successful club operations. *$26.95*
150 pages Founded: 1921
Mailing list available for rent 21,000 names
Printed in 4 colors on glossy stock

12508 Consortium of Hospitality Research Information Services
Quanta Press
1313 5th Street SE
Suite 223A
Minneapolis, MN 55414

Consists of academic and industry groups which together have produced a comprehensive index of hospitality literature in CD-ROM format. Over 47,000 bibliographic records with abstracts from over 50 journals serving the hospitality industry.

12509 Cornell Hotel & Restaurant Administration Quarterly
Elsevier Science Publishing Company
415 Horsham Road
Horsham, PA 19044
212-633-3730
FAX: 212-633-3680 888-437-4636
nicole@leonardmedia.com
http://www.hotelschool.cornell.edu/

Glenn Withiam, Executive Editor
Dr. Michael Sturman, Editor
Thomas Cullen, Associate Professor

A journal devoted to the development and exchange of management ideas for the hospitality industry. *$113.00*
Quarterly Founded: 1960
Circulation: 4500

12510 Executive Housekeeping Today (EHT)
International Executive Housekeepers Association
1001 Eastwind Drive
Suite 301
Westerville, OH 43081-3361
614-895-7166
FAX: 614-895-1248 800-200-6342
excel@ieha.org http://www.ieha.org

Beth B Risinger, Publisher
Andi Vance, Advertising/Sales/Ed
Hazel Reese, President

Magazine for management personnel in the institutional housekeeping industry. Highlighting products, services, association news and industry trends. *$40.00*
30 pages Monthly Founded: 1930
Circulation: 4130

12511 Foodservice Equipment & Supplies Specialist
Reed Business Information
2000 Clearwater Drive
Oak Brook, IL 60523-3358
630-740-0825
FAX: 630-288-8225
411_webmaster@reedbusiness.com
http://www.foodservice411.com

Joseph M. Carbonara, Editor-in-Chief
Maureen Slocum, Publisher
Paulette Cortopassi, Managing Editor
Victoria Jones, Production Manager

Magazine for professionals who specify, sell and distribute foodservice equipment, supplies and furnishings.
Monthly Founded: 1948
Circulation: 22719
Printed in 4 colors on glossy stock : web site

12512 Hospitality News
PO Box 11960
Prescott, AZ 86304-1960
206-686-7378
FAX: 206-463-0090 800-685-1932
lindas@hospnes.com
http://www.hospnews.com

Linda Sanders, Publisher
Miles Small, Editor-in-Chief

Serves restaurants, lodges, health care facilities, schools, clubs, casino's, caterers, and culinary and beverage marketplaces.
Founded: 1988
Circulation: 105000

12513 Hospitality Product News
Advanstar Communications
One Park Avenue
New York, NY 10016
212-797-7631
FAX: 212-951-6793 888-527-7008
info@advanstar.com
http://www.advanstar.com/

Doug Ferguson, Group Publisher
Helen Gardner, General Manager
Georgiann Decenzo, Director of Corporate mar
Joseph Loggia, Chief Executive Officer

Contains ADA compliance, maintenance and cleaning, fitness, leisure and entertainment, food and beverage, foodservice equipment and supplies, furnishings and fixtures, guest amenities, tabletop, technology, uniforms, and bedding and linens. *$35.00*
Founded: 1987
Circulation: 30019

12514 Hospitality Technology
Edgell Communications
4 Middlebury Boulevard
Randolph, NJ 07869
973-252-0100
FAX: 973-252-9020
rpaul@edgellmail.com
http://www.htmagazine.com

Lenore O'Meara, Associate Publisher
Reid Paul, Editor
Gerald Ryerson, President

Aimed at owners/operators, franchise and chain executives, and managers in operations, finance, sales/marketing and information systems. Emphasis on applications, new products, industry news and trade show highlights.
Founded: 1984
Circulation: 16000
Printed in 4 colors on glossy stock

12515 Hotel & Motel Management
Advanstar Communications
757 3rd Ave
New York, NY 10017-2013
212-951-6600
FAX: 212-951-6793
info@advanstar.com
http://www.advanstar.com

Scott E Pierce, President
Mike Malley, Publisher
Jeff Higley, Editor-in-Chief
Mary M. Malloy, National Sales Manager

Publication reaching more than 57,000 management personnel in hotels, motels, motor inns and other related businesses.
Founded: 1875
Circulation: 53058

12516 Hotels
Reed Business Information
2000 clear water drive
Oakerook, IL 60523
630-740-0825
FAX: 630-288-8265
hotels_webmaster@reedbusiness.com
http://www.hotelsmag.com

Dan Hogan, Publisher
Jim Caseolla, CEO
Jeff Weinstein, Editor

The magazine for the worldwide hotel industry *$125.90*
Monthly
Circulation: 62000
Printed in 4 colors on glossy stock

12517 Infoline
Hospitality Financial & Technology Professionals
11709 Boulder Lane
Suite 110
Austin, TX 78726-1832
512-249-5333
FAX: 512-249-1533 800-646-4387
eliza.selig@hftp.org
http://www.hftp.org

Eliza Selig, Editor
Lance Peterson, Director Marketing
Frank Wolfe, Executive ViP

Chapter and officer activities.
Monthly Founded: 1952
Circulation: 4000

12518 Journal of Quality Assurance in Hospitality & Tourism
Bill Cohen
10 Alice Street
Binghamton, NY 13904-1580
607-722-5857
FAX: 607-722-6362 800-342-9678
getinfo@haworthpressinc.com
http://www.haworthpressinc.com

Timothy R Hinkin, Editor
Pyo Sungsoo, Editor
William Cohen, Owner

Serves as a medium to share and disseminate information coming from new research findings and superior practices in tourisim and hospitality; covers planning, development, management and marketing.
$50.00

Quarterly Founded: 1978

12519 Journal of Teaching in Travel & Tourism
Bill Cohen
10 Alice Street
Binghamton, NY 13904-1580
607-722-5857
FAX: 607-722-6362 800-342-9678
getinfo@haworthpress.com
www.haworthpressinc.com

Timothy R Hinkin, Editor
Pyo Sungsoo, Editor
Cathy HC Hsu, Editor
William Cohen, Owner

Serves as an international interdisiplinary forum and reference source for travel and tourisim education at professional schools and universities.

Founded: 1978

12520 Lodging
American Hotel & Motel Association
1201 New York Avenue NW
6th Floor
Washington, DC 20005-3931
202-289-3100
FAX: 202-289-3129
lwilhelm@ahlaonline.com
http://www.lodgingmagazine.com

Joseph A McInerney, CEO/President
Kristy Freeman, Associate Publisher
Philip Hayward, Editor
Jessica Downey, Managing Editor
Bob Ryan, Publisher

News of the hotel, motel, and association news industry. Covers management procedures, changes, general industry news, new products, national trends, legislative developments, and trade shows. *$65.00*

100 pages Monthly Founded: 1975
Circulation: 34500

12521 Lodging Hospitality
Penton Media
1300 E 9th Street
Cleveland, OH 44114-1503
216-696-7000
FAX: 216-931-9706
ewatkins@penton.com
http://www.lhonline.com

Gary Dietz, Publisher
Edward Watkins, Editor
David B. Nussbaum, CEO
Preston L. Vice, Chief Financial Officer & Corporate

Serving the US hotel, motel and resort industry. Published 16 times per year, LH provides owners and operators with the latest trends and information on the development, operations and marketing of lodging properties

Monthly Founded: 1892
Circulation: 50,976
Printed in 4 colors on glossy stock

12522 Market Watch
M Shanken Communications
387 Park Avenue S
Floor 8
New York, NY 10016-8872
212-844-4224
FAX: 212-779-3383

Marvin R Shanken, Editor
Felicia Bedoya, Circulation Manager

Up-to-date information for individuals and businesses working in the beverage and alcohol industry. *$75.42*

200 pages Founded: 1981
Circulation: 65000
Printed in 4 colors

12523 Nation's Restaurant News
Lebhar-Friedman Publications
425 Park Avenue
New York, NY 10022-3506
212-756-5000
FAX: 212-756-5215
info@lf.com http://www.lf.com

Alan Gould, Publisher
Michael Cardillo, VP Sales
Ellen Koteff, Editor

Serves commercial and onsite food service and lodging establishments including restaurants, schools, universities, hospitals, nursing homes and other health and welfare facilities, hotels and motels with food service, government installations, clubs and other related firms. *$ 44.95*

Founded: 1925
Circulation: 85,999
Mailing list available for rent 100,000 names $100 per M.
Printed in 4 colors on matte stock

12524 National Culinary Review
American Culinary Federation
180 center place way
Saint Augustine, FL 32095
904-824-4468
FAX: 904-825-4758 800-624-9458
acf@acfchefs.net
http://www.acfchefs.org

Brent Frei, Director Marketing
Kay Orde, Editor
Edward Leonard, Presient
Michael Baskette, Executive Director

Accepts advertising. *$50.00*

Monthly Founded: 1929
Circulation: 20000

12525 Restaurant Hospitality
Penton Media
1300 E 9th Street
Cleveland, OH 44114-1503
216-696-7000
FAX: 216-696-0836
information@penton.com
http://www.penton.com

David B. Nussbaum, CEO
Jennifer Daugherty, Communications Manager

A national trade publication that covers the full-service restaurant industry. If offers cover story features, an extensive food section with recipes, a multi-page news section and a variety of one page profiles on rising stars, equipment, food safety, beverages, design and more.

130 pages Monthly Founded: 1892
Circulation: 117721
Printed in 4 colors on glossy stock

12526 Restaurants & Institutions
Reed Business Information
1350 E Touhy Avenue
Des Plains, IL 60018
630-320-7000
FAX: 630-288-8686
privacymanager@reedbusiness.com
http://www.reedbusiness.com

Patricia B Dailey, Editor-in-Chief
Scott Hume, Managing Editor
Jim Casella, CEO
Brion Palmer, Publisher

Commercial and noncommercial foodservice establishments including restaurant, hotels, motels, fast-food chains,coffee shops, food stores with foodservice *$477.00*

Monthly Founded: 1937
Circulation: 154,110
Printed in 4 colors on glossy stock

12527 Ritz Carlton Magazine
3930 E Ray Road
Suite 150
Phoenix, AZ 85044
480-682-2050
FAX: 480-706-4801

12528 Ski Area Management
Beardsley Publishing Corporation
PO Box 644
Woodbury, CT 06798-644
203-263-0888
FAX: 203-266-0452
sam@saminfo.com
http://www.saminfo.com

Jennifer Rowan, Publisher
Rick Kahl, Editor
Donna Jacobs, Production Manager

Content includes technologies of skilifts, snowmaking and slope grooming, at year-round resort operations. Other features include product and supplier directories, resort architecture and design, new products, marketing, real estate and rental.

$42.00
Monthly
Circulation: 3100
Printed in 4 colors on glossy stock

Trade Shows

12529 American Hotel & Motel Association Annual Conference/Leadership Forum
1201 New York Avenue NW
Suite 600
Washington, DC 20005-3931
202-289-3100
FAX: 202-289-3158 800-252-2462
kwaslsh@ahma.com www.ahma.com

Ken Walsh, Manager Meetings
Jeanne Traugot, Contact
Joseph McInerney, President

189 exhibits of hotel supplies, equipment and information, conference and workshop.

1500 Attendees Annual Founded: 1910

12530 American Hotel & Motel Association Annual Convention
1201 New York Avenue NW
Suite 600
Washington, DC 20005-3917
202-289-3100
FAX: 202-289-3158
conventions@ahla.com
www.ahma.com

Jeanne Traugot, Contact
Kimberly Miles, VP Conventions&Events
Joseph McInerney, President

125 booths consisting of telecommunication systems, supplies and equipment for the hotel and motel industry.

1.5M Attendees April

12531 American Resort Development Association Convention
1201 15th Street NW
Suite 400
Washington, DC 20005
202-371-6700
FAX: 202-289-8544
clacey@arda.org www.arda.org

Howard C Nusbaum, President/CEO
Catherine Lacey, VP Meetings&Conferences

One hundred fifty booths.

3600 Attendees April

12532 Annual Council on Hotel, Restaurant and Institutional Education Conference
Int'l Council on Hotel & Restaurant Education
2810 North Parham Roaf
Suite 230
Richmond, VA 23294
804-346-4800
FAX: 804-346-5009
info@chrie.org www.chrie.org
Kathy McCarty, Executive VP/CEO
Bill Shoemaker, Conference&Exposition Manager
Terrific opportunity to gain knowledge, exchange ideas, and enjoy the camaraderie and fellowship of colleagues in the hospitality industry
6MM Attendees July

12533 Annual Hotel, Motel and Restaurant Supply Show of the Southeast
Leisure Time Unlimited
708 Main Street
PO Box 332
Myrtle Beach, SC 29577
843-448-9483
FAX: 843-626-1513 800-261-5991
hmrss@sc.rr.com www.hmrsss.com
Brooke P Baker, Show Director
Trade show for the hospitality industry.
23000 Attendees January Founded: 1975

12534 Arizona Hospitality Expo
2400 North Central Avenue
Suite 109
Phoenix, AZ 85004-1300
602-277-6290
FAX: 602-277-6350
info@azhospialityexpo.org
www.azhospitalityexpo.com
John Mathern, Contact
Largest gathering of hospitality professionals in the Southwest.For 18 years there was a joint show of Arizona Restaurant and Hospitality Association. They held separate shows for 30 years before combining.
3000 Attendees

12535 Fall Conference for Hospitality Supply Man agement
Institute for Supply Management
Po Box 22160
Tempe, AZ 85285-2160
480-752-6276
FAX: 480-752-7890 800-888-6276
Oct 17-19 Dallas, TX

12536 Great Southwest Lodging & Restaurant Show
Arizona Hotel and Lodging Association
1240 East Missouri Avenue
Phoenix, AZ 85014
602-604-0729
FAX: 520-604-0769 800-788-2462
info@azhla.com www.azhla.com
Britt Kimball, Show Manager
Seminars, workshops and 450+ exhibits of food service and lodging equipment, marketing, decorations, berverage services (alcoholic and non), cleaning services and pest control, furnishings, lighting, insurance, transportation and more.
5000 Attendees Annual Founded: 1970

12537 IEHA's Association Convention/in Conjunction with ISSA Interclean
International Executive Housekeepers Association
1001 Eastwind Drive
Suite 301
Westerville, OH 43081-3361
614-895-7166
FAX: 614-895-1248 800-200-6342
excel@ieha.org www.ieha.org
Beth Risinger, CEO
Educational seminars and exhibits by firms engaged in manufacturing, marketing and distribution of cleaning and maintenance suppliers. Containing 750 exhibits.
15M Attendees Oct 23-26 Orlando Florida

12538 Innkeeping
PAII
Box 97010
Santa Barbara, CA 93190
805-965-4525

JoAnn Bell, Publisher
Offers a forum for innkeepers, hotel and motel managers, owners and operators.
500 Attendees March/April

12539 International Hotel/Motel & Restaurant Show
George Little Management
10 Bank Street
Suite 1200
White Plains, NY 10606-1954
914-486-6070
FAX: 914-948-6180 800-272-7469
ihmrs@glmshows.com
www.ihmrs.com
Christian Falkemberg, Show Manager
George Little II, President
Products and services for lodging and food service properties organized in 12 categories: Technology; Uniforms, Linens and Bedding; Tabletop; Guest amenities and services; Food and Beverage; Cleaning and Maintenance; Food Service Equipment and Supplies; Franchise, Finance and Management; Furnishings and Fixturtes; Fitness, Leisure and Entertainment; The Environment; Advertising and Promotion
45000 Attendees Early November

12540 Marine Hotel Catering Duty Free Conference
PO Box 1659
Sausalito, CA 94966
415-332-1903
FAX: 415-332-9457
mha@mhaweb.org www.mhaweb.org
Caroline Prichard, Administrator
100 booths.
700 Attendees April

12541 NYSH&TA Annual Conference
New York State Hospitality & Tourism Association
80 Wolf Road
Albany, NY
518-465-2300
FAX: 518-465-4025
info@nyshta.org www.nyshta.org
Debra Trulli-Cassale, Events Director
Conference where members can mix business with pleasure and allowed to conduct Association business in addition to enjoying fun-filled entertainment.

12542 National Restaurant Association: Restaurant, Hotel-Motel Show
Convention Office
150 North Michigan Avenue
Suite 2000
Chicago, IL 60601
312-853-2525

mheftman@dineout.org
www.restaurant.org
Mary Pat Heftman, Sr Vice President Conventions
Jamie Schaefer, Exhibitor Services Specalist
1,800 booths.
Annual,May

12543 Pacific Hospitality Expo Convention Center
1801 Kalakaua Avenue
Honolulu, HI 96815-2558
808-973-9790

Joanie Gribbin, Director
220 booths.
2.5M Attendees June

12544 Rocky Mountain Hospitality Convention and Expo
899 Logan Street
Suite 300
Denver, CO 80203-3155
303-792-9621

Bruce Whiticker, Convention Director
413 booths.
7M Attendees June

Directories & Databases

12545 All Suite Hotel Guide
Ten Speed Press
PO Box 7123
Berkley, CA 94707
510-559-1600
FAX: 510-559-1629 800-841-2665
order@tenspeed.com
www.tenspeedpress.com
Pamela Lanier, President
Over 1,600 hotels are offered which have suites available consisting of two or more rooms for rent. *$14.95*
336 pages Annual ISBN 1-580080-91-

12546 America's Wonderful Little Hotels & Inns
St. Martin's Press
175 5th Avenue
4th Floor
New York, NY 10010
212-674-5151
FAX: 212-674-3179
Sandra W Soule, Editor
A directory listing hotels and inns that are located throughout the United States and Canada in various volumes. Prices vary per region, per volume.
Founded: 1952 ISBN 0-312081-30-8

12547 Bed & Breakfast Home Directory: Homes Away from Home, West Coast
Knighttime Publications
890 Calabasas Road
Watsonville, CA 95076-0418

Diane Knight, Author
Suzy Blackaby, Author
Kevin McElvain, Author

Over 250 bed and breakfast homes are listed that are located in the areas of California, Oregon, Washington and British Columbia, Canada. *$12.95*

203 pages Biennial ISBN 0-942902-03-3

12548 Bed and Breakfast Guest Houses and Inns of America
PO Box 38066
Germantown, TN 38183-0066
901-946-1902
FAX: 901-758-0816

Directory of services and supplies to the industry. *$45.00*

350 pages Annual

12549 Cabin Guide to Wilderness Lodging

Hammond Publishing
1500 E Tropicana Avenue
Suite 110
Las Vegas, NV 89119-8333

Information is given on over 500 cabins in national and state forests, preserves and other wildlife areas. *$14.95*

250 pages Annual

12550 Complete Guide to Bed & Breakfasts, Inns & Guesthouses in US & Canada
Lanier Publishing International
PO Drawer D
Petaluma, CA 94953
707-763-0271
FAX: 707-763-5762
lanier@travelguides.com
www.travelguides.com

Pamela Lanier, President

Directory of services and supplies to the industry. *$16.95*

536 pages Annual

12551 Country Inns and Back Roads, North America
HarperCollins
10 E 53rd Street
Cellar 1 Floor
New York, NY 10022-5299
212-207-7000

Over 200 country inns in the United States and Canada are listed. *$13.00*

450 pages Annual

12552 Directory of Hotel & Lodging Companies
American Hotel & Lodging Association
1201 New York Avenue NW
Suite 600
Washington, DC 20005-3931
202-289-3100
FAX: 202-289-3199
directory@ahla.com www.ahla.com

Richard Turner, Publisher/Editor
Joseph McInerney, President

Lists over 1,000 companies that own, manage or franchise properties worldwide. Also lists, in 7 sections: companies by type, company/brand web site, company listings, geographical, company rankings, hotel brokers, and vendors. *$100.00*

Annual Founded: 1931 1150 names $260 per M. : CD-Rom

12553 Hotel Development Guide
Hospitality Media
17950 Preston Road
Suite 710
Dallas, TX 75252
972-934-2040
FAX: 972-934-2040

Offers a list of suppliers of equipment, fixtures and services needed for new motels. *$100.00*

12554 Hotel and Travel Index
Reed Travel Group
PO Bxo 5820
Subscription Department
Cherry Hill, NJ 08034

800-442-0900

Over 45,000 hotels worldwide are profiled in this travel directory. *$125.00*

2000 pages Quarterly
Circulation: 60,000

12555 Inspected, Rated and Approved Bed and Breakfast Country Inns
American Bed & Breakfast Association
10800 Midlothian Tpke
Suite 254
Richmond, VA 23235-4700

www.abba.com

Beth Burgreen Stuhlman, Editor

Information on over 500 overnight accommodations in North American bed and breakfast locations are listed. *$17.95*

350 pages Founded: 1996 ISBN 0-934473-27-7

12556 National Directory of Budget Motels
Pilot Books
127 Sterling Avenue
#2102
Greenport, NY 11944-1439
631-477-0978
FAX: 631-477-0978 800-79 -ILOT

Guide to the best in economy-priced chain motel accommodations in the United States and Canada. *$12.95*

346 pages Annual

12557 National Trust Guide to Historic Bed & Breakfasts, Inns & Small Hotels
Preservation Press
1785 Massachusetts Avenue NW
Washington, DC 20036-2117
202-588-6083
FAX: 202-588-6299

Directory of services and supplies to the industry. *$13.95*

416 pages Biennial

12558 Official Bed and Breakfast Guide
National Bed & Breakfast Association
148 E Rocks Road
Norwalk, CT 06851
203-847-6196
FAX: 203-847-0469 www.nbba.com

Phyllis Featherston, President

A who's who directory of services and supplies to the industry offering a list of the best in bed and breakfast accommodations in USA, Canada and the Carribbean. *$17.95*

560 pages

12559 Official Hotel Guide
Reed Hotel Directories Network
500 Plaza Drive
Secaucus, NJ 07094-3619
201-902-1960
FAX: 201-319-1628

Wilma Goldenberg, Editor

3 volumes of 25,000 hotels, motels and resorts worldwide. *$385.00*

Annual
Circulation: 20,000

12560 Pelican's Select Guide to American Bed and Breakfast
Pelican Publishing Company
1000 Burmaster Street
Gretna, LA 70053-2246
504-368-1175
FAX: 504-368-1195
sales@pelicanpub.com
bedandbreakfastguide.com

Judi Russell, Editor
Milburn Calhoun, Owner

Independent guest houses, inns and bed and breakfast accommodations are profiled. *$14.95*

216 pages ISBN 1-589800-61-8
Printed in 2 colors on matte stock

12561 Preferred Hotels Directory
Preferred Hotels & Resorts Worldwide
311 S Wacker Drive
Suite 1900
Chicago, IL 60606-6676
312-913-0400
FAX: 407-679-3361 800-323-7500

John Ueberroth, Chief Executive Officer

80 pages Annual
Circulation: 25,000

12562 Recommended Country Inns
Globe Pequot Press
246 Goose Lane
PO Box 480
Guilford, CT 06437
203-458-4500
FAX: 800-820-2329 888-249-7586
info@glbepequot.com
www.globepequot.com

Elizabeth Squier
Elenor Berman

This series of directories offers information on country inns located in certain parts of the United States. *$18.95*

416 pages Biennial · ISBN 0-762728-48-5

12563 Where to Stay USA
Prentice Hall Law & Business
1 Lake Street
Saddle River, NJ 07458-1813
201-236-7000
FAX: 201-236-3381

Information is given on over 1,200 places to stay and eat from $4 to $35 a night. *$16.00*

350 pages Biennial

Industry Web Sites

12564 www.abba.com
American Bed & Breakfast Association

National organization with information on over 500 overnight accomodations in North American bed and breakfast locations.

12565 www.ahma.com
American Hotel & Lodging Foundation

Trade association covering news, issues and activities of related industry groups.

12566 www.biztravel.com
Biztravel.com

Internet travel service offering discounts on flights, hotels, car rentals, packages and cruises.

12567 www.chrie.org
Int'l Council on Hotel & Restaurant Education

To enhance professionalism at all levels of the hospitality and tourism industry through education and training.

12568 www.ei-ahla.org
American Hotel&Lodging Educational Foundation

A non-profit educational foundation of the American Hotel & Lodging Association and the world's largest provider of hospitality education training resources, videos, books, workbooks, seminars, management courses, complete training systems and professional certification programs.

12569 www.expedia.com
Expedia.com

Internet travel service offers access to airlines, hotels, car rentals, vacation packages, cruises and corporate travel.

12570 www.goworldnet.com/cgi-bin
Worldnet USA

A database of states with hotels, theaters and museums.

12571 www.greyhouse.com
Grey House Publishing

Selected Grey House directories in the fields of business, health and education are available online. Users can search our online databases by several different search criteria, such as product categories, geographic area, sales volume and much, much more. Full Grey House catalog and online ordering also available.

12572 www.hanyc.org
Hotel Association of New York City

One of the oldest professional trade associations in the nation.

12573 www.hotels.com
Hotels.com

Provides discount accommodations worldwide.

12574 www.hotwire.com
Hotwire.com

Internet travel service offering discounts on flights, hotels, car rentals, packages and cruises.

12575 www.ieha.org
International Executive Housekeepers Association

An organization for persons working in the housekeeping area of the lodging industry.

12576 www.innbook.com
Bed and Breakfast Inns & Small Luxury Hotels

Includes the finest inns, B&Bs, and getaway retreats in Canada and the Us, carefully chosen and inspected to maintain the highest standards.

12577 www.masslodging.com
Massachusetts Lodging Association

A trade association representing and promoting the lodging industryin Massachusetts.

12578 www.nmhotels.com
New Mexico Lodging Association

New Mexico's trade association representing the lodging industry.

12579 www.orbitz.com
Orbitz.com

Internet travel service offering discounts on flights, hotels, car rentals, packages and cruises.

12580 www.paii.org
Professional Association of Innkeepers International

Serving bed and breakfast/country inn owners, aspiring innkeepers, inn sitters, vendors with educational and consultative services. International conference.

12581 www.preferredhotels.com
The Luxury Hotels of Preferred Hotels & Resorts Worldwide

An exclusive group of independent luxury hotels in the United States.

12582 www.travel.lycos.com
Lycos.com

Internet travel service offering discounts on flights, hotels, car rentals, packages and cruises.

12583 www.travel.yahoo.com
Yahoo.com

Internet travel service providing access to flights, hotels, car rentals, vacation packages and cruises.

12584 www.travelocity.com
Sabre Holdings

Travel service offering consumers access to hundreds of airlines and thousands of hotels, as well as cruises, last-minute and vacation packages and best-in-class car rental companies.

12585 www.travelweb.com
Travelweb.com

Internet provider of hotel accommodations.

Associations

12586 American Composites Manufacturers Association
1010 N Glebe Road
Suite 450
Arlington, VA 22201
703-525-0511
FAX: 703-524-2303
info@acmanet.org www.acmanet.org

Missy Henriksen, Executive Director
Sabeena Hickman, Deputy Director
Jeanne McCormack, Conferences/Meetings Director
Shaine Anderson, Membership/Marketing Director

Membership is open to any person, firm or corporation performing the hand layup or sprayup method of fiberglass fabrication.
1100 Members Founded: 1979

12587 American Electroplaters Surface Finishers Society
1155 Fifteenth Street, NW
Suite 500
Washington, DC 20005
202-457-8401
FAX: 202-530-0659
info@aesf.org www.aesf.org

Tracey Kohler, Executive Director
Alison Ashe, Membership/Bookstore/Education

AESF is an international society that advances the science of surface finishing to benefit industry and society through education, information and social involvement, as well as those who provide services, supplies and support to the industry.
5000 Members Founded: 1909

12588 American Society of Industrial Security
1625 Prince Street
Alexandria, VA 22314-2818
703-519-6200
FAX: 703-519-6299
asis@asisonline.org
www.asisonline.org

Jeff M Spivey, CPP/PSP, President
Michael J Stack, Executive Director

The largest international organization for professionals who are responsible for security, including managers and directors of security.
33000 Members Founded: 1955

12589 Asphalt Recycling and Reclaiming
#3 Church Circle
Suite 250
Annapolis, MD 21401
410-267-0023
FAX: 410-267-7546
krissoff@arra.org www.arra.org

Tom Johnson, President
Michael Krissoff, Executive Director

Promotes the interest of owners and manufacturers of recycling equipment, engineers, suppliers and businesses involved in the asphalt recycling industry. Newsletter published quarterly.
200 Members Founded: 1976

12590 Associated Equipment Distributors
615 W 22nd Street
Oak Brook, IL 60523
630-574-0650
FAX: 630-574-0132 800-388-0650
info@aednet.org www.aednet.org

Toby Mack, President
Marcia Arge, conventions/Meetings Manager

Membership organization of 1,200 independent distributors, manufacturers and other organizations involved in the distribution of construction equipment and related products and services in North America and throughout the world.
1200 Members Founded: 1919

12591 Association of Equipment Manufacturers
6737 W Washington Street
Suite 2400
Milwaukee, WI 53214-5647
414-272-0943
FAX: 414-272-1170 866-236-0943
aem@aem.org www.aem.org

Dennis Slater, President

Formed from the merging of Construction Industry Manufacturers Association and Equipment Manufacturers Institute. Also the trade and business development resource for companies that maufacture equipment, products and services used worldwide in the construction, agricultural, mining, forestry, and utility fields.
Founded: 2002

12592 Association of Machinery and Equipment
315 South Patrick Street
Alexandria, VA 22314
703-836-7900
FAX: 703-836-9303 800-537-8629
amea@amea.org www.amea.org

Mary Flynn, Executive Director
Lorna Lindsey, Manager

Certifies and accredits the most qualified capital equipment appraisers in the appraisal industry through promotion of standards of professional practice, ethical conduct, and marketing based experience.
300 Members Founded: 1983

12593 Casting Industry Suppliers Association
14175 W Indian School Road
Suite B4-504
Goodyear, AZ 85338
623-547-0920
FAX: 623-536-1486
info@cisa.org www.cisa.org

Sara Joyce, President
Roger A Hayes, Executive Director

Fosters better trade practices. Serves as industry representative before the government and public. Encourages member research into new processes and methods of foundry operation. Association of suppliers to the worldwide metal casting industry.
70 Members Founded: 1986

12594 Composite Can and Tube Institute
50 S Pickett Street
Suite 110
Alexandria, VA 22304-7206
703-823-7234
FAX: 703-823-7237
ccti@cctiwdc.org www.cctiwdc.org

Kristine Garland, Executive VP
Dale Ann Rader, Assoc Manager/Events/Publications
Andrea Edwards, Associate Manager Events

Represents the interests of manufacturers of compsite paperboard cans, containers, canisters, tubes, cores cones, spools, fiber drums, and related items as well as suppliers of paperboard, equipment, and other materials and services.
Founded: 1933

12595 Equipment Leasing Association
4301 N Fairfax Drive
Suite 550
Arlington, VA 22203-1627
703-527-8655
FAX: 703-527-2649
dbrown@elamail.com
www.elaonline.com

Michael Fleming, President
Kenneth E Bensten Jr, Incoming President
Donald Ethier, Vp Marketing/Communications

Represents companies involved in the dynamic equipment leasing and finance industry to the business community, government and media.
850+ Members Founded: 1961

12596 Federation of Societies for Coatings
492 Norristown Road
Blue Bell, PA 19422-2350
610-940-0777
FAX: 610-940-0292
fsct@coatingstech.org
www.coatingstech.org

David Jack, President
Frederick Walker, Secretary/Treasurer

Provides technical education and professional development to its members and to the global industry through its multinational Constituent Societies and collectively as a Federation
Founded: 1922

12597 Fluid Controls Institute
1300 Sumner Avenue
Cleveland, OH 44115
216-241-7333
FAX: 216-241-0105
fci@fluidcontrolsinstitute.org
www.fluidcontrolsinstitute.org

John H Addington, Executive Secretary

Manufacturers of equipment for fluid (liquid or gas) control and conditioning. This institute is organized into product specific sections which address issues that are relevant to particular products and or/or technologies.
68 Members Founded: 1921

12598 Fluid Sealing Association
994 Old Eagle School Road
#1019
Wayne, PA 19087-1866
610-971-4850
FAX: 610-971-4859
info@fluidsealing.com
www.fluidsealing.com

Robert Ecker, Executive Director
Hope Silverman, Administrative Director

An international association of manufacturers of mechanical packings, sealing devices, gaskets, rubber expansion joints and allied products.
57 Members Founded: 1933

12599 Hoist Manufacturers Institute
8720 Red Oak Boulevard
Suite 201
Charlotte, NC 28217
704-676-1190
FAX: 704-676-1199 hmi@mhia.org

Hal Vandiver, Managing Director
John B Nofsinger, CEO

An affiliate of Material Handling Industry, also a trade association of maufacturers of overhead handling hoists. The products of member companies include hand chain hoists, ratchet lever hoists, trolleys, air chain and air rope hoists, and electric chain and electric wire rope hoists.

12600 Independent Lubricant Manufacturers Association
400 N Columbus Street
Suite 201
Alexandria, VA 22314
703-684-5574
FAX: 703-836-8503
ilma@ilma.org www.ilma.org

Celeste Powers, CAE, Executive Director
Martha Jolkovksi, Publications/Advertising Director
Carla Mangone, Meetings/Communications Director

Independent blenders and compounders of lubricants.

320 Members Founded: 1948
Mailing list available for rent 2000 names $750 per M.

12601 Industrial Diamond Association of America
PO Box 29460
Columbus, OH 43229
614-797-2265
FAX: 614-797-2264
tkane-ida@insight.rr.com
www.superabrasives.org

Terry M Kane, Executive Director

Trade association for those in the superabrasives industry. Products and services provided and used in most manufacturing and constuction industries such as: stone processing, glass, construction, woodworking, electronics, medical, etc.

Founded: 1946

12602 Industrial Heating Equipment Association
PO Box 54172
Cincinnati, OH 45254
513-231-5613
FAX: 513-624-0601
ihea@ihea.org www.ihea.org

Steve W Furth, President
Anne Goyer, VP
Brian Russell, First VP

Provides services to member companies that will enhance member company capabilities to serve end users in the industrial heat processing industry and improve the member company's business performance as well.

Founded: 1929

12603 Industrial Supply Association
100 North 20th Street, 4th Floor
Philadelphia, PA 19103
215-320-3862
FAX: 215-564-2175 866-460-2360
info@isapartners.org
www.ida-assoc.org

John Buckley, Executive VPresident
Mary Ritchie, Director
Steve Short, Treasurer

ISA goal is to help members increase sales, reduce expenses and improve profitability.

600 Members Founded: 1988

12604 Industrial Supply Manufacturers' Association
1300 Sumner Avenue
Cleveland, OH 44115-2851
216-241-7333
FAX: 216-241-0105

Charles Stockinger, Executive Director

Manufacturers of industrial machinery and supplies.

550 Members Founded: 1905

12605 Institute for Supply Management
PO Box 22160
Tempe, AZ 85285-2160
480-752-6276
FAX: 480-752-7890 800-888-6276
sdelabio@ism.ws www.ism.ws

Paul Novak, CEO
Debbie Webber, Senior VP/Corporate Treasurer
Holly LaCroix Johnson, Senior VP/Corporate Secretary
Nora Neibergall, CPM, Senior VP
Cindy Urbaytis, VP Marketing/Sales

The largest supply management association in the world as well as one of the most respected. Their mission is to lead the supply management profession through its standards of excellence, research, promotional activities, and education.

40000 Members Founded: 1915

12606 Institute of Industrial Engineers
3577 Parkway Lane
Suite 200
Norcross, GA 30092
770-490-0461
FAX: 770-441-3295 800-494-0460
cs@iienet.org www.iienet.org

Don Greene, Executive Director
Elaine Fuerst, Marketing Director

The world's largest professional society dedicated solely to the support of the industrial engineering profession and individuals involved with improving quality and productivity. IIE is also an international, non profit association that provides leadership for the application, education, training, research, and development of industrial engineering.

15000 Members Founded: 1948

12607 International Staple, Nail and Tool
512 West Burlington Avenue
Suite 203
La Grange, IL 60525-2245
708-482-8138
FAX: 708-482-8186
isanta@ameritech.net www.isanta.org

John Kurtz, Executive Vice President
David Rapp, Codes/Technical Services

An international organization of premier power fastening companies involved in the design, manufacturing, and sales of cordless tools and the fasteners they drive.

19 Members Founded: 1966

12608 Machinery Dealers National Association
315 S Patrick Street
Alexandria, VA 22314
703-836-9300
FAX: 703-836-9303 800-872-7807
office@mdna.org www.mdna.org

Joseph R Kraemer, Jr, CEA, President
Mark Robinson, Executive VP

Dedicated to the promotion of the used machinery industry.

400+ Members Founded: 1941

12609 NIBA - The Belting Association
N19W24400 Riverwood Drive
Waukesha, WI 53188
262-523-9090
FAX: 262-523-9091 800-488-4845
support@niba.org www.niba.org

Randall E Rakow, Executive Vice President/CEO
Cie Motelet, Manager Association Services

Promotes the common business interests of all distribution/fabricators and manufacturers of conveyor and flat power transmission belting and material that enhances/changes belt.

Founded: 1927

12610 National Association of Industrial Technology
3300 Washtenaw Avenue
Suite 220
Ann Arbor, MI 48104
734-677-0720
FAX: 734-677-2407
nait@nait.org www.nait.org

Rick Coscarelli, Executive Director
Dave Monforton, Associate Director
Mary Lee, Association Manager
Keith Bretzius, Publications Coordinator

Provides support to all those involved in the industrial technology industry. Hosts trade shows and publishes various materials.

12611 National Corrugated Steel Pipe Association
14070 Proton Road
Suite 100, LB 9
Dallas, TX 75244
972-850-1907
FAX: 972-490-4219
info@ncspa.org www.ncspa.org

Brian C Roberts PE, Executive Director

Seeks to promote sound public policy relating to the use of corrugated steel drainage structures in private and public construction.

60 Members Founded: 1956

12612 National Spray Equipment Manufacturers
PO Box 2147
Skokie, IL 60076
440-366-6808
FAX: 847-763-9538
ipp@halldata.com
www.ippmagazine.com

Bruce Bryan, Advertising Director
Ted Klaiber, Sales Manager

Serves as a technical forum for safety and environmental matters pertaining to the spray finishing industry.

16 Members Founded: 1922

12613 North American Equipment Dealers
1195 Smizer Mill Road
Fenton, MO 63026-3480
636-349-5000
FAX: 636-349-5443
webmaster@naeda.com
www.naeda.com

Bob Frazee, Chairman
Paul Kindinger, President/CEO
Dennis Booth, First Vice Chairman
F M (Mike) Kraemer, Communications Director

NAEDA and its affiliates provides a variety of educational, financial and legislative

services to equipment dealers in the United States and Canada.
Founded: 1900

12614 North American Sawing Association
1300 Sumner Avenue
Cleveland, OH 44115-2851
216-241-7333
FAX: 216-241-0105
nasa@sawing association.com
www.sawingassociation.com

Charles M Stockinger, Secretary/Treasurer

The purpose of this association is to improve the band sawing and power tool accessoried industries.
8 Members Founded: 1959

12615 Society of Tribologists & Lubrication Engineers
840 Busse Highway
Park Ridge, IL 60068
847-825-5536
FAX: 847-825-1456
information@stle.org www.stle.org

Edward Salek, CAE, Executive Director
Judy Enbolm, Administrative Assistant
Beth Weinstein, Membership Marketing Director

Purpose is to advance the science of tribology and the practice of lubrication engineering in order to foster innovation, improve the performance of equipment and products, conserve resources and protect the environment.
4000 Members Founded: 1944

12616 ToolBase Services
c/o NAHB Research Center
400 Prince George's Boulevard
Upper Marlboro, MD 20774
301-494-4000
800-898-2842
toolbase@nahbrc.org
www.toolbase.org
The housing industry's resource for technical information on building products, materials, new technologies, business management, and housing systems.

12617 Unified Abrasive Manufacturers' Association
30200 Detroit Road
Cleveland, OH 44145-1967
440-899-0010
FAX: 440-892-1404
contact@uama.org www.uama.org

J Jeffery Wherry, Executive Director

The purpose is to undertake those activties that can be pursued more effectively by an association than individual companies in order to enable the industry to freely create and market safe, productive abrasive products throughout the world.
30 Members Founded: 1999

Newsletters

12618 Asphalt Recycling and Reclaiming Association
3 Church Circle
PMB Box 250
Annapolis, MD 21401-1933
410-267-0023
FAX: 410-267-7546 http://www.arra.org

Michael Krissoff, Executive Director

Promotes the interest of owners and manufacturers of recycling equipment, engineers suppliers and businesses involved in the asphalt recycling industry.
Quarterly Founded: 1976
Circulation: 1200

12619 Can Tube Bulletin
Composite Can & Tube Institute
50 South Pickett Street
Suite 110
Alexandria, VA 22304-7206
703-823-7234
FAX: 703-823-7237
ccti@cctiwdc.org www.cctiwdc.org

Andrea Ball, Editor
Kristine Garland, Executive VP
Andrea Edwards, Publisher
Wayne Vance, Association Counsel

For members only, is an excellent source of information about issues affecting this industry, as well as updates on CCTI activities. *$350.00*
Bi-monthly
Circulation: 500

12620 Fastener Industry News
Business Information Services
5028 Dumont Place
Woodland Hills, CA 91364-2407
818-248-5023
FAX: 818-249-1169 800-929-5586
info@biscomputer.com
http://www.biscomputer.com

Richard Callahan, Publisher
John Wolz, Editor
Miro Macho, CEO/President

Publication written for executives and administrators in the fastener industry. Focuses on providing readers with business and financial news from within the industry. Includes personnel notices, management ideas and related materials. *$200.00*
8 pages Monthly Founded: 1971
Mailing list available for rent
Printed in 2 colors on matte stock

12621 Industrial Building & Complexes:E-Mail News & Analysis
Forecast International
22 Commerce Road
Newtown, CT 06470-1643
203-426-0800
FAX: 203-426-0223 800-451-4975
info@forecast1.com
www.forecastinternational.com

Elsie Luciano, Production Manager
Monty Nebinger, Circulation Director
Ed Nebinger, CEO

An electronic information/data service sourced from thousands of worldwide publications, in 15 languages. Provides concise summaries, news, trends and contract information with hyper-links to the source or a related website. Delivered 100 times a year. *$425.00*
Founded: 1973

12622 Instrumentation and Automation News
Chilton Company
201 King of Prussia Road
Radnor, PA 19087-5197
610-964-4007
FAX: 610-964-1888 800-274-2207

Matt DeJulio, Publisher

The control technology/instrumentation market's only product news tabloid.

12623 Journal of the National Spray Equipment Manufacturers Association
550 Randall Road
Elyria, OH 44035-2974
440-366-6808
FAX: 440-892-2018

Don R Scarbrough, Executive Secretary

Includes editorial on safety and environmental matters pertaining to the spray finishing industry. Regular monthly features.
16 pages Founded: 1922

12624 Manufacturing Automation
Vital Information Publications
321 Carrera Drive
Mill Valley, CA 94941-3995
413-662-3700
FAX: 650-345-7018 800-774-4410

Naimisha Patel, Industrial, Market Development Mana
Patricia Primmer, Communications/Technology Director
Sharon Oakes, Market Development Direct
Arik Keller, President

Detailed information on key industrial automation markets, technologies, applications, and products. *$395.00*
Monthly Founded: 1991

12625 Sensor Business Digest
Vital Information Publications
321 Carrera Drive
Mill Valley, CA 94941-3995
413-662-3700
FAX: 650-345-7018 800-774-4410

Sarah Collins, Publisher
Peter Adrian, Editor
Naimisha Patel, Market Development Manage
Patricia Primmer, Communications and Technology

Provides indepth information on key established and emerging sensor and instrumentation markets, products, applications and technologies. *$395.00*
Monthly Founded: 1991

12626 Sensor Technology
John Wiley & Sons
111 River Street
Hoboken, NJ 07030
201-748-6000
FAX: 201-748-5915 800-825-7550
subinfo@wiley.com
http://www.wiley.com

Angelo Depalma, Editor
William J Pesce, President

Written for companies and enterprises involved in a broad range of industrial disciplines. Publication follows advances in sensor technologies and their applications, along with opportunities for their use in the industrial marketplace. *$565.00*
10 pages Daily Founded: 1807
Mailing list available for rent 25000 names $180 per M.
Printed in 2 colors on newsprint stock

Magazines & Journals

12627 American Industry
Publications for Industry
21 Russell Woods Road
Great Neck, NY 11021-4644
516-487-0990
FAX: 516-487-0809
ai@publicationsforindustry.com
http://www.publicationsforindustry.com
Jack S Panes, Publisher
Created for those executives responsible for overall plant operations and maintenance. Editorial focus is on new products and related services. *$25.00*
Founded: 1946
Circulation: 300000 30000 names $96 per M.
Printed in 4 colors on newsprint stock

12628 American Tool, Die & Stamping News
Eagle Publications
42400 Grand River Avenue
Suite 103
Novi, MI 48375-2572
248-473-3487
FAX: 248-347-3492 800-783-3491
sales@ameritooldie.com
http://www.ameritooldie.com/
Gail Dawson, Marketing
Joan Oakley, Circulation Director
Arthur Brown, Editor
Applications, techniques, equipment and accessories of metal stamping, moldmaking, electric discharge machining; and new product information relating to the tool and die industry. Accepts advertising.
70 pages Monthly Founded: 1971
Circulation: 30000
Printed in 5 colors on glossy stock

12629 Asian Industrial Report
Keller International Publishing Corporation
150 Great Neck Road
Great Neck, NY 11021
516-299-9722
FAX: 516-829-5414
info@kellerpubs.com
http://www.kellerpubs.com
Gerald E Keller, President
Bryan DeLuca, Editorial Director
Terry Beirne, Publisher
Bob Herlihy, Sales manager
English language tabloid presenting new products, equipment and services.
36 pages Founded: 1882
Circulation: 37107
Printed in 4 colors on glossy stock

12630 Business & Industry
Business Magazines
1720 28th Street
Suite B
West Des Moines, IA 50266-1400
515-225-2545
FAX: 515-225-2318
busindmag@aol.com
www.busindmag.com
James V Snyder, Publisher
RJ Balch, Editor
Industrial news publication *$24.00*
56 pages Monthly Founded: 1946
Circulation: 14M
Printed in 4 colors on glossy stock

12631 Cleaner
COLE Publishing
PO Box 220
Three Lakes, WI 54562-0220
715-546-3346
FAX: 715-546-3786 800-257-7222
cleaner@cleaner.com
www.cleaner.com
Jeff Bruss, President
Winnie May, Advertising Sales/Subscriptions
Ted Rulseh, Editor
Bob Kendall, Co-founder
The latest tools and equipment promoting safety and efficiency, employment and enviromental concerns, as well as industry profiles. *$15.50*
Monthly Founded: 1979
Circulation: 22780

12632 Filtration News
Eagle Publishers
42400 Grand River Avenue
Suite 103
Novi, MI 48375-2572
248-473-3487
FAX: 248-347-3079 800-783-3491
joan@filtnews.com
www.filtnews.com
Arthur E Brown, Publisher
Carol Brown, CEO/Editor
Laurie Rosario, Marketing
Joan Oakley, Circulation Manager
New products and events on the special aspects of filtraion ranging from new equipment applications to new trends in the filtraion industry. *$58.00*
Bi-Monthly Founded: 1985
Circulation: 28500

12633 Finer Points Magazine
Industrial Diamond Association of America
PO Box 29460
Columbus, OH 43229
614-797-2265
FAX: 614-797-2264
tkane-ida@insight.rr.com
http://www.superabrasives.org
Terry Kane, Publisher/Editor
Joe Tabling, President
Information for people who are involved in superabrasives or superabrasive products in some way. *$35.00*
Quarterly Founded: 1946
Circulation: 7,500

12634 Flow Control
Witter Publishing Corporation
200 Croft Street
Suite 1
Birmingham, AL 35242
908-788-0343
FAX: 908-788-3782
flowcontrol@witterpublishing.com
http://www.flowcontrolnetwork.com
John Harris, Publisher
Matt Migliore, Editor
Three primary disciplines are addressed: operations, system design, and maintenance. Control, measurement and containment catergories are organized in the product flow sections whitch include photos and discriptions of components representing the entire fluid handling systems plus overviews literature available. *$19.95*
Monthly
Circulation: 40100 40100 names $230 per M.
Printed in 4 colors on glossy stock

12635 Hart's Lubricants World
Hart Publications
4545 Post Oak Place
#210
Houston, TX 77027-3105
713-993-9320
FAX: 713-840-8585 www.hartpub.com
Diane Green, Publisher
Rich Eichler, President
Magazine for producers and users of lubricants and related products. *$65.00*
Monthly
Circulation: 13,120

12636 I&CS-Instrumentation & Control Systems
PennWell Publishing Company
1421 S Sheridan Road
Tulsa, OK 74112
918-835-3161
FAX: 918-831-9497 800-331-4463
headquarters@pennwell.com
www.pennwell.com
Dick Coleman, Publisher
Regular issue features include new systems analyses, new products listings, application ideas, and tutorial technology features. *$65.00*
Monthly
Circulation: 92,618

12637 ICS Cleaning Specialist
22801 Ventura Boulevard
#115
Woodland Hills, CA 91364
818-224-8035
FAX: 818-224-8042 800-835-4398
kesslere@bnpmedia.com
http://www.icsmag.com
Evan Kessler, Publisher
Jeffrey Stouffer, Editor
Phil Johnson, Group Publisher
Amy Levin, Production Manager
Annual+

12638 Industrial Distribution
225 Wyman Street
Waltham, MA 02451
781-734-8000
FAX: 781-734-8070
www.manufacturing.net/ind
Jack Keough, Associate Publisher/Editor
Victoria Fraza Kickham, Managaing Editor
Kimberly Griffiths, Associate Editor
Mary Ann Gajewski, Production Manager

Provides current, comprehensive, issues-oriented editorial unique to the distribution industry including news, product updates, profitable product selection, management techniques, features on distribution-manufacturer relationships, legal issues and sales improvement. *$ 89.90*
Monthly
Circulation: 38000+

12639 Industrial Equipment News
Thomas Publishing Company
5 Penn Plaza
Manhattan, NY 10001
212-695-0500
FAX: 212-290-7206 800-733-1127
dmaskin@tpmgnet.com
www.ienonline.com
Mark Maskin, Editorial Director
Deborah Maskin, Managing Editor
Ciro Buttacavoli, Publisher
Marie Urbanowicz, Marketing Director
Serves the industrial field including manufacturing, mining, utilities, construction,

transportation,governmental establishments, and educational services.
Monthly Founded: 1898
Circulation: 205,000+

12640 Industrial Laser Solutions
PennWell Publishing Company
1421 S Sheridan Road
Tulsa, OK 74112
918-835-3161
800-331-4463
headquarters@pennwell.com
http://ils.pennnet.com

David Belforte, Publisher/Editor-in-Chief
Laureen Belleville, Managing Editor

Devoted exclusively to global coverage of industrial laser applications, technology, and the people and companies who participate in this, the largest commercial portion of the global laser market.
45 pages Monthly Founded: 1986
Circulation: 10000

12641 Industrial Literature Review
Thomas Publishing Company
5 Penn Plaza
12th Floor
New York, NY 10001-1860
212-290-7341
FAX: 212-629-1585
businesslists@thomaspublishing.com
http://www.thomaspublishing.com/

Deborah Maskin, Editor

Created to provide the dissemination of manufacturer catalogs and literature and mailed to buyers and specifies at plants with more than twenty employees.
Founded: 1976

12642 Industrial Maintenance & Plant Operation
Reed Business Information
100 Enterprise Drive, Suite 600
Box 912
Rockaway, NJ 07866-0912
973-207-7000
FAX: 973-920-7531 www.impomag.com

Rick Carter, Editor-in-Chief
Nancy Syverson, Managing Editor
Kyle Orr, Senior Circulation Manager
Hank Pendrak, Marketing Director
R Reed, Owner

New product listings, industry news new literature and plant maintenance procedures.
$70.00
Monthly Founded: 1940
Circulation: 107052

12643 Industrial Management
Institute of Industrial Engineers
3577 Parkway Lane Suite 200
Norcross, GA 30092-2928
770-490-0461
FAX: 770-441-3295 800-494-0460
cs@iienet.org http://www.iienet.org

Cliff Cary, Publisher
Monica Elliott, Managing Editor

Directed to the full range of management issues including adapting and evaluating new technologies, improving productivity and quality, and motivating employees. *$35.00*
Monthly Founded: 1948
Circulation: 8500

12644 Industrial Market Place
Wineberg Publications
7842 Lincoln Avenue
Skokie, IL 60077
847-676-1900
FAX: 847-676-0063 800-323-1818
info@industrialmktpl.com
www.industrialmktpl.com

Joel Wineberg, President
Jakie Bitensky, Editor

Has advertisements on machinery, industrial and plant equipment, services and industrial auctions in each issue. *$175.00*
Bi-Weekly Founded: 1951
Circulation: 100,000
Mailing list available for rent 120 names
$70 per M.
Printed in 4 colors on glossy stock

12645 Industrial Process Products & Technology
Swan Erickson Publishing
1011 Upper Middle Road E
#1235
Oakville, CA 68529
905-845-1347
FAX: 905-845-5521
erickson@ippt.com
http://www.ippt.com

Michael Swan, Publisher
Bob Erickson, Editor
Robert Erickson, CEO/President
Michael Swan, Marketing Manager
Michael Swan, Circulation Manager

Aimed at purchasers of these products who use chemical materials and chemical processes in their manufacturing operations.
$47.00
56 pages Founded: 1987
Circulation: 24524
Mailing list available for rent 23,500 names
$220 per M.
Printed in on glossy stock
Computerized version available: Web Site

12646 Industrial Purchasing Agent
Publications for Industry
21 Russell Woods Road
Great Neck, NY 11021-4644
516-487-0990
FAX: 516-487-0809
http://www.PublicationsforIndustry.com

Jack Panes, Publisher
Pearl Shaine, Editor

New products publication for industrial purchasing agent executives in largest plants in the United States. Contains new releases on products, brochures, materials handling, etc. *$25.00*
Monthly Founded: 1958
Circulation: 27000 27M names $96 per M.
Printed in 4 colors on newsprint stock

12647 International Journal of Purchasing & Materials Management
National Association of Purchasing Management
2055 E Centennial Circle
PO Box 22160
Tempe, AZ 85285-2160
480-752-2277
FAX: 480-491-7885
www.capsresearch.com

Phillip L Carter, CEO/President

Publishes articles dealing with concepts from business, economics, operations management, information systems, the behavioral sciences, and other disciplines which contribute to the advancement of knowledge in the various areas of purchasing, materials management, and related fields.
$59.00
Quarterly Founded: 1986
Circulation: 2800

12648 Journal of Coatings Technology
Federation of Societies for Coatings Technology
492 Norristown Road
Ste 100
Blue Bell, PA 19422-2350
610-940-0777
FAX: 610-940-0292
fsct@coatingstech.com
http://www.coatingstech.org

Robert Ziegler, Publisher
Patricia D Ziegler, Senior Editor
Frederick Walker, President
Audrey Boozer, Circulation Manager

Provides a major service to the coatings industry, serves as a link between users and supplies of raw materials, production equipment, coatings, adhesives, inks, sealants, testing equipment, containers and laboratory apparatus. Each issue contains peer-reviewed technical articles as well as informative feature articles, special departments and news of the Constituent Societies of the Federation. *$400.00*
Quarterly
Circulation: 9500

12649 Journal of Materials Engineering and Performance
9639 Kinsman Road
Materials Park, OH 44073-0002
440-338-5151
FAX: 440-338-4634 800-336-5152
customerservice@asminternational.org
www.asminternational.org
Peer-reviewed journal which publishes contributions on all aspects of materials selection, design, characterization, processing and performance testing. The scope includes all materials used in engineering applications: those that typically result in components for larger systems. *$1243.00*
Bi-Monthly Founded: 1913
Circulation: 645

12650 Journal of Protective Coatings & Linings
Technology Publishing Company
2100 Wharton Street
Suite 300
Pittsburgh, PA 15203-1951
412-431-8300
FAX: 412-431-5428 800-837-8303
webmaster@paintsquare.com
www.protectivecoatings.com

Bernadette Landon, Publisher
Karen Kapsanis, Editor
Milissa Bogats, Production Director

Focuses on good practice in the use of protective coatings for steel and concrete surfaces. Features articles on such topics as coatings selection for specific service environments, surface preparation, coating application, quality control, cost-effectiveness in maintenance programs, safety issues, and environmental regulations. *$80.00*
Monthly
Circulation: 15000

12651 Lift Equipment
Group III Communications
204 W Kansas Street
Suite 103
Independence, MO 64050
816-254-8735
FAX: 816-254-2128
kebbes@liftlink.com

Terry Ford, President
Michael Scheibach, Publisher

Tracy L Bennett, Editor/Associate Publisher

The buyer's source for equipment, technology and trends. Free to qualified subscribers. *$24.00*

80 pages 10 per year
Circulation: 18,000
Printed in 4 colors on glossy stock

12652 Lubes-N-Greases
LNG Publishing Company
6105 G Arlington Boulevard
Falls Church, VA 22044
703-536-0800
FAX: 703-536-0803
info@LNGpublishing.com
www.lngpublishing.com

Nancy J DeMarco, Publisher
Lisa Tocci, Managing Editor
Deborah Wessmiller, Circulation Manager
Gloria Steinberg Briskin, Advertising Director

Features an exciting mix of news and feature stories covering automotive and industrial lubricants, metalworking fluids, greases, base stocks, lube additives, packaging, biodegradeable and synthetic products. Print edition is free to qualified subscribers in the U.S. and Canada, and available on a paid subscription basis elsewhere.

Monthly Founded: 1995
Circulation: 16000
Printed in 4 colors

12653 Lubricating Engineering
Society of Tribologists & Lubrication Engineers
840 Busse Highway
Park Ridge, IL 60068
847-825-5536
FAX: 847-825-1456
information@stle.org www.stle.org

Edward Salek, Executive Director
Karl Phipps, Associate Managing Editor
Tracy Nicholas, National Sales Manager

Technical papers and news articles with up to date developments in the lubrication industry.

Monthly
Circulation: 6000

12654 MRO Today
Pfingsten Publishing
730 Madison Avenue
Fort Atkinson, WI 53538-606
920-563-5225
FAX: 920-563-4269 800-932-7732
IGwebeditor@pfpublish.com
http://www.mrotoday.com

Todd Rank, VP
Tom Hammel, Associate Publisher/Editorial Direc
John Mansavage, Circulation and Research
Jill Sheppard, Marketing Manager

Provides best practices for industrial maintanence, production, MRO purchasing, quality and safety personnel. MRO Today helps these pros do their jobs cheaper, better, faster and smarter.

Founded: 1996
Circulation: 120,000 104,743 names $125 per M.
Printed in on glossy stock

12655 Maintenance Technology
Applied Technology Publications
1300 S Grove Avenue
Suite 105
Barrington, IL 60010
847-382-8100
FAX: 847-304-8603
www.mt-online.com

Tom Madding, Group Publisher
Terry Wireman, Editorial Director
Jane Alexander, Managing Editor
Nancy Williams, Production Manager

The premier business and technical information source for managers, engineers and supervisors responsible for plant and equipment maintenance and reliability, and asset management.

Monthly
Circulation: 50,000
Printed in 4 colors on glossy stock

12656 Measurements & Control
100 Wallace Avenue
Suite 100
Sarasota, FL 34237
941-954-8405
FAX: 941-366-5743 800-883-8894

12657 Modern Paint & Coatings
Cygnus Publishing
445 Broad Hollow Road
Melville, NY 11747-3601
631-845-2700
FAX: 631-845-2723
www.cygnuspub.com

Esther D'Amico, Editor

The latest technology and news including chemical innovations, new production equipment,new trends and coverage of regulatory affairs. *$45.00*

Monthly
Circulation: 14,000

12658 NAEDA Equipment Dealer
North American Equipment Dealers Association
1195 Smizer Road
Fenton, MO 63026-3480
636-349-5000
FAX: 636-349-5443
kraemerm@naeda.com
www.naeda.com

Larry Krueger, Advertising Manager
Mike Kraemer, Communications Director

A monthly management and merchandising magazine features articles about successful dealers, new products, new technology, industry news, insurance loss control solutions, and top management tips. *$45.00*

32 pages Monthly Founded: 1900
Printed in 4 colors on glossy stock

12659 New Equipment Digest
Penton Media
1300 E 9th Street
Cleveland, OH 44114-1503
216-696-7000
FAX: 216-696-1752
information@penton.com
www.newequipment.com

Robert F King, Editor-in-Chief
Diane Madzelonka, Production Manager
Bobbie Macy, Circulation Manager
John DiPaola, VP/Group Publisher
Steven R Bush, Administrative Editor

Serves the general industrial field which includes manufacturing, processing, engineering services, construction, transportation, mining, public utilities, wholesale distributors, educational services, libraries, and governmental establishments.

Monthly Founded: 1936
Circulation: 206154

12660 Plant
Rogers Media Publishing
777 Bay Street
Toronto, Ontario M5W1A
416-596-5729
FAX: 416-596-5552 www.plant.ca

Dan Bordun, Group Publisher
Joe Terrett, Editor
Daryl Way, Production Supervisor

PLANT serves manufacturing and processing industries in Canada. *$125.00*

14 per year Founded: 1941

12661 Purchasing Magazine's Buying Strategy Forecast
Reed Business Information
257 Washington Street
Newton, MA 02458-1646
617-964-3030
FAX: 617-558-4327
kbecker@reedbusiness.com
http://www.purchasing.com

Kathy Doyle, Publisher
Paul Teague, Chief Editor
Kathy Becker, Publisher's Assistant

Provides insight and forecasts of numerous industrial and commercial raw materials products.

Founded: 1960
Circulation: 95,095

12662 Rental Product News
Cygnus Publishing
3 Huntington Quadrangle
Suite 301N
Melville, NY 11747-3669
631-845-2700
FAX: 631-845-2798 800-308-6397

Dave Davel, Group Publisher
Kris Flitcroft, Associate Publisher
Jenny Lescohier, Editor
Lisa Cleaver, Managing Editor

The complete guide to new equipment and major changes in existing models. Also provides insight on how leaders in the equipment rental field are getting the best return from their assets through better equipment selection, application, maintenance and safety techniques.

Founded: 1966
Circulation: 20000

12663 Robotics World
Douglas Publications
2807 N Parham Road
Suite 200
Richmond, VA 23294
804-762-9600
FAX: 804-217-8999
info@douglaspublications.com
www.douglaspublications.com

Jack Browne, Editor
Andrew Dwyer, Publisher

Covers key developments in the field of flexible automation and intelligent machines for an audience of management level automation professionals.

Monthly Founded: 1985
Circulation: 87000

12664 Twin Plant News
Nibbe Hernandez and Associates
725 S Mesa Hills
Building 1, Suite 2
El Paso, TX 79912
915-532-1567
FAX: 915-544-7556
tpn@twinplantnews.com
www.twinplantnews.com

Rosa Maria Nibbe, President/Publisher
Mike Patten, Managing Editor
Kimberley Pannell-Davis, Production

This publication focuses on the Mexican fiscal and labor laws, culture and taxes as well as economics and trends of the industry. This is a monthly publication covering the maquila & mexican industry *$85.00*

Monthly Founded: 1985
Circulation: 10000

12665 UnderWater
Doyle Publishing Company
607 Mason
Tomball, TX 77375
281-516-0350
FAX: 281-516-0391
www.underwater.com

William H Doyle III, Publisher
Ross Saxon, Executive Editor
Daron Jones, Managing Editor

The official publication of The Association of Diving Marine Contractors International. This magazine covers marine technology and underwater vehicles. Subscriptions are free to qualified applicants in the U.S., and subscriptions outside the U.S. are $50.00

Quarterly Founded: 1993
Circulation: 45,000

12666 World Industrial Reporter
Keller International Publishing Corporation
150 Great Neck Road
Great Neck, NY 11021-3309
516-829-9722
FAX: 516-829-5414
info@kellerpubs.com
http://www.kellerpubs.com

Bryan DeLuca, Editor
Terry Beirne, Publisher
Jerry Keller, President

New equipment, machinery and techniques for the industry.

34 pages Founded: 1882
Circulation: 37,107

Trade Shows

12667 American Society of Industrial Security: Annual Seminar and Exhibits
1625 Prince Street
Alexandria, VA 22314-2818
703-519-6200
FAX: 703-276-3043 703-519-6299
asis@asisonline.org
www.asisonline.org

Michael Stack, Executive Director
Lewis C Schneider CAE, Director

More than 1,300 exhibit booths displaying the latest in products and services including security systems and consultation services, as well as more than 120 educational sessions.

14M Attendees September

12668 Association of Machinery and Equipment Appraisers Annual Conference
315 S Patrick Street
Alexandria, VA 22314-3501
703-836-7900
FAX: 703-836-9303 800-537-8629
amea@amea.org www.amea.org

Lorna Lindsey, Manager

Exhibits of interest to machinery and equipment appraisers.

Founded: 1982

12669 Capital Industrial Show
Industiral Shows of America
1794 The Alameda
San Jose, CA 95126-1729
408-947-0233
FAX: 408-286-8836
Annual show and exhibits of industrial equipment, supplies and services.

4000 Attendees

12670 FABFORM
Industrial Shows of America
164 Lake Front Drive
Hunt Valley, MD 21030-2215
410-771-1445
FAX: 410-771-1158 800-638-6396
This is the most effective way to reach forming, fabricating and welding equipment buyers in the Northern California area.

3000 Attendees April

12671 Federation of Societies for Coatings Technology
Federation of Societies for Coatings Technology
492 Norristown Road
Blue Bell, PA 19422-2350
610-940-0777
FAX: 610-940-0292
fsct@coatingstech.com
www.coatingstech.com

Robert Ziegler, Publisher
Patricia D Ziegler, Semior Editor
Ray Dickie, Editor

Provides a major service to the coatings industry, serves as a link between users and supplies of raw materials, production equipment, coatings, adhesives, inks, sealants, testing equipment, containers and laboratory apparatus.International Coating Expo November, Georgia World Congress Center in Atlanta, Georgia.

12672 Great Lakes Industrial Show
North American Expositions Company
33 Rutherford Avenue
Boston, MA 02129
617-242-6092
FAX: 617-242-1817 800-225-1577
dnovack@naexpo.com
www.naexpo.com

Denise Novack, Contact

With over 300 companies exhibiting, showcases the latest technology, products, services and solutions for your manufacturing needs.

14319 Attendees November Founded: 1972

12673 ISMA/IDA Spring & Fall Conventions
Industrial Distribution Association
1277 Lenox Park Boulevard, Suite 275
PO Box 49088
Atlanta, GA 30359
404-266-3991
FAX: 404-266-8311 877-591-6210
idainc@mindspring.com ida-assoc.org

Mary R Ritchie, Meetings/Convention Director

Semi-annual conventions for distributors and manufacturers of industrial (MROP) supplies.

12674 In-Tech Syracuse
Professional Program Management
3494 Delaware Avenue
Buffalo, NY 14217-1230
716-688-6641
FAX: 716-871-9638 800-222-4465

Bill Hedrick, Sales Director

200+ booths displaying industrial products and equipment.

4M Attendees October

12675 Industrial Marketing Expo
Lobos Services
16016 Perkins Road
Baton Rouge, LA 70810
225-751-5626

Debbie Balough, Show Manager

250 booths.

6M Attendees April

12676 Industrial Products Expo and Conference
Key Productions
94 Murphy Road
Hartford, CT 06114-2121
860-247-8363
FAX: 860-947-6900 880-753-9776
webadmin@keypro.com
www.keypro.com

Maura Lewis, Show Manager

This show features exhibits and/or services used in manufacturing, management and warehousing.

6M Attendees September

12677 Industrial Show Pacific Coast
Industrial Shows of America
164 Lake Front Drive
Hunt Valley, MD 21030-2215
410-771-1445
FAX: 410-771-1158 800-638-6396

James K Donahue, President

Four hundred booths.

11M Attendees November

12678 International Fastener and Precision Formed Parts Manufacturing Expo
Pemco
383 Main Avenue
Norwalk, CT 06851-1543
203-840-7700
FAX: 630-260-0395 800-323-5155
Biennial show and exhibits of cold headers and header tooling, tools and dies, forming machines, parts feeding and handling equipment and test equipment for the industrial fastener and precision formed parts manufacturing industry.

12679 International Off-Highway and Power Plant Meeting and Exposition
Society of Automotive Engineers
400 Commonwealth Drive
Warrendale, PA 15096-0001
724-776-4841
FAX: 724-776-4026
advertising@sae.org www.sae.org

Diane Rogne, Show Manager
Sam Barill, Student Design Competition

Annual show of 270 suppliers of parts, components, materials and systems utilized in farm and industrial machinery and off-road and recreational vehicles.
5000 Attendees
Circulation: 84,000

12680 Mid South Industrial, Material Handling and Distribution Expo
Industrial Shows of America
164 Lake Front Drive
Hunt Valley, MD 21030-2215
410-771-1445
FAX: 410-771-1158 800-638-6396
James K Donahue, President
300 booths of industrial and business related products and services.
8M Attendees June

12681 National Association of Industrial Technology Convention
National Association of Industrial Technology
3300 Washtenaw Avenue
Suite 220
Ann Arbor, MI 48104-4294
734-677-0720
FAX: 734-677-2407
nait@nait.org www.nait.org
Dr. Alvin Thadisill, Show Manager
Dave Monporan, Exhibit Manager
Rick Coscarelli, Executive Director
Annual convention of National Association of Industrial Technology, professional association of two and four year Industrial Technology program, faculty, standards and professionals in industry. Exhibitors desired in textbooks, training manuals, software and video; testing and training equipment, computer hardware and software, ISP's and distance learning hosts; CAD/CAM; Rapid Protyping; PC's. There are 25 booths. Next show is in Pittsburgh, Pennsylvania.
500 Attendees November 500 names

12682 Pacific Coast Industrial and Machine Tool Show
ISOA
1794 The Alameda
San Jose, CA 95126-1729
408-947-0233
FAX: 408-286-8836 800-286-2882
Annual show of 260 exhibitors of industrial equipment, machine tools, business services, hand tools and related equipment, supplies and services.
12M Attendees November, Santa Clara

12683 Tidewater Industrial & Manufacturing Technology Show
Industrial Shows of America
164 Lake Front Drive
Hunt Valley, MD 21030-2215
410-771-1445
FAX: 410-771-1158 800-638-6396
info@isoa.com www.isoa.com
Annual show of 250 suppliers and distributors of industrial and marine equipment, machine and hand tools, business services and related equipment, supplies and services.
September, VA Beach

12684 Tri-State Industrial & Machine Tools Show
Industrial Shows of America
164 Lake Front Drive
Hunt Valley, MD 21030-2215
410-771-1445
FAX: 410-771-1158 800-638-6396
This show will bring together exhibitors and customers to preview products and discuss new technologies for the metalworking and manufacturing industries. The show will feature machine tools, metalworking equipment, services for manufacturing industrial products and supplies. Thousands of qualified decision-makers involved in management, engineering, purchasing and manufacturing will attend.
April

12685 USA/Mexico Industrial Expo
Industrial Shows of America
164 Lake Front Drive
Hunt Valley, MD 21030-2215
410-771-1445
FAX: 410-771-1158 800-638-6396
This event draws attendees from avariety of manufacturing and assembly companies. Product categories include material handling, safety equipment, compressors, maintenance equipment, industrial water products, hydraulic/pneumatics, tools and many more. On average, attendees spend over $100,000 per year obn these products.

9000 Attendees June

Directories & Databases

12686 Capital Cities Regional Industrial Buying Guide
Thomas Publishing Company
5 Penn Plaza
New York, NY 10001-1810
212-950-0500

A who's who directory of supplies to the industry. *$65.00*
1200 pages Annual

12687 Complete Directory of Tools, All Types
Sutton Family Communications & Publishing Company
155 Sutton Lane
Fordsville, KY 42343
270-740-0870

jlsutton@apex.net
www.fleamarketeer.net
Theresa Sutton, Editor
Lee Sutton, General Manager
Includes names, addresses, phone & fax numbers, and product descriptions from wholesale distributors, importers, manufacturers, close-out houses and liquidators. Updated daily to guarantee the most current and up to date information. *$55.20*
100+ pages

12688 Directory of the Association of Machinery and Equipment Appraisers
Association of Machinery and Equipment Appraisers
315 S Patrick Street
Alexandria, VA 22314-3501
703-836-7900
FAX: 703-836-9303 800-537-8629
Nearly 300 member certified machinery appraisers.
Annual January

12689 High-Performance Composites
Ray Publishing
4891 Independence Street
Suite 270
Wheat Ridge, CO 80033
303-467-1776
FAX: 303-467-1777
info@raypubs.com
www.compositesworld.com
Judith R Hazen, Publisher
Mike Mussleman, Managing Editor
Donna K Dawson, Senior Editor
Distributed free of charge to people who need information about composites.
60 pages 6/Year Founded: 1993
Circulation: 20,000
Printed in 4 colors on glossy stock

12690 Industrial Machinery Digest
Cygnus Publishing
2100 Riverchase Center
Suite 307
Birmingham, AL 35244
205-988-9708
FAX: 205-987-3237 800-366-0676
william.strickland@cygnusb2b.com
www.indmacdig.com
William Strickland, Publisher
Adrienne Gallender, National Sales Industrial Pub
A leader among industrial trade publications distributed to machine shops, job shops, fabricating shops, gear manufacturers, industrial warehouses & distribution centers, large industrial facilities & manufacturing plants, material handling, retro & rebuilding machine maintenance, pipe & tube manufacturers and manchinery dealers and wholesalers.
18 Per Year Founded: 1986
Circulation: 226,8000
Printed in 4 colors on glossy stock

12691 SBC Industrial Purchasing Guide
100 E Big Beaver Road
Suite 700E
Troy, MI 48083-1204
248-524-4800
FAX: 248-524-4849 800-331-1385
industrial@smartpages.com/industrial
www.smartpages.com
Susan Wright, Industrial Operations Manager
Nicole Howard-Combs, Director
Providers of industrial products and services; seperate regional editions cover Illinois, Wisconsin, Indiana, Michigan, and Ohio.

12692 Sweets Directory
Sweets Group/Division of The McGraw-Hill Companies

800-442-2258
sweets_customerservice@mcgraw-hill.com www.sweets.construction.com
Annual reference for architects, engineers and contractors since 1906. Lists more than 10,000 building product manufacturers and their products. Design and construction professionals can select, evaluate, compare and specify buiding products. *$59.00*
Annual Founded: 1906

12693 US Distribution Journal: Source Book
BMT Commodity Corporation
530 5th Avenue
24th Floor
New York, NY 10036
212-302-4200
FAX: 212-302-0007 bmt@bmtny.com
Kevin Francella, Editor
Approximately 2,500 manufacturers, suppliers and importers of grocery, food, tobacco, confectionery, health and beauty aids, general merchandise products; material handling, warehouse and transport equipment. *$95.00*
Annual December
Circulation: 15,000

12694 World Industrial Reporter: Directory of Distributors Issue
Keller International Publishing Corporation
150 Great Neck Road
Great Neck, NY 11021-3309
516-829-9722

Jerry Keller, President
A list of over 3,000 international advertisers and their distributors with product line related to the industrial supplies and equipment industry. *$45.00*
Annual

12695 World Industrial Reporter: International Buyer's Guide Issue
Keller International Publishing Corporation
150 Great Neck Road
Great Neck, NY 11021-3309
516-829-9722

Jerry Keller, President
Over 275 international advertisers are listed that offer industrial supplies and equipment for export. *$5.00*
Annual
Circulation: 40,000

Industry Web Sites

12696 www.amea.org
Association of Machinery and Equipment Appraisers

An organization for certified machinery appraisers of the metalworking industry.

12697 www.arra.org
Asphalt Recycling and Reclaiming Association

Promotes the interest of owners and manufacturers of recycling equipment, engineers suppliers and businesses involved in the asphalt recycling industry.

12698 www.greyhouse.com
Grey House Publishing

Selected Grey House directories in the fields of business, health and education are available online. Users can search our online databases by several different search criteria, such as product categories, geographic area, sales volume and much, much more. Full Grey House catalog and online ordering also available.

12699 www.ida-assoc.org
Industrial Distribution Association

Trade association for distributors of industrial MROP supplies.

12700 www.mdna.org
Machinery Dealers National Association

Represents dealers of used industrial equipment.

12701 www.nait.org
National Association of Industrial Technology

For faculty, students and professionals in industry.

12702 www.polysort.com
Polysort.com

Includes materials, machinery and equipment, processors and industry services.

12703 www.sweets.construction.com McGraw Hill Construction

In depth product information that lets you find, compare, select,s pecify and make purchase decisions in the industrial product marketplace.

12704 www.thomasregister.com Thomas Register

Comprehensive online resource for defining companies and products manufactured in North America. Use it for placing orders, downloading computer-aided design drawings, and viewing thousands of online company catalogs and websites.

Associations

12705 **Alliance of Claim Assistance Professionals**
873 Brentwood Drive
West Chicago, IL 60185-3743
630-562-1000
FAX: 630-562-1448
askacap@charter.net www.claims.org
Susan A Dressler, President
Professionals dedicated to the effective management of health insurance claims. Our members are claims assistance professionals who work for patients. Membership fee of $75.00.
40 Members Founded: 1998

12706 **Alliance of Insurance Agents and Brokers**
1768 Arrow Highway
Suite 105
La Verne, CA 91750
909-392-0836
FAX: 909-392-0892
memberinfo@agentsalliance.com
www.agentsalliance.com
David Nielson, President
Ken Nigohosian, Executive Director
Mary Ann Legaspi, Administrative Assistant
Judy Corathers, Member Service Manager
Ricardo Meraz, Sales/Marketing Manager
Formerly known as American Agents Alliance, but with the inherent and necessary changes in the industry, the Alliance has grown and adapted , to best serve our members, and to become what it is now. This organization is a member driven organization that is dedicated to protect and serve independent insurance producers and consumers.

12707 **America's Health Insurance Plans**
601 Pennsylvania Avenue NW
South Building, Suite 500
Washington, DC 20004
202-778-3200
FAX: 202-331-7487 877-291-2247
webmaster@ship.org www.ahip.org
Karen M Ignagni, President/CEO
Carmella Bocchino, Senior VP Medical Affairs
Robert O Borchardt, VP of Finance & Operations
Diana Dennett, Executive VP of Government Affairs
Dan Leonard, Chief Administrative Officer
As the voice of America's health insurers, our member companies offer medical expense coverage, long-term care insurance, disability income insurance, dental insurance, supplemental insurance, stop-loss insurance and reinsurance to consumers, employers, and public purchasers.
1300 Members Founded: 2003

12708 **American Academy of Actuaries**
1100 17th Street NW
7th Floor
Washington, DC 20036
202-223-8196
FAX: 202-872-1948
webmaster@actuary.org
www.actuary.org
Kevin Cronin, Executive Director
Joanne B Anderson, Finance/Administration Director
Lauren M Bloom, Professionalism Dir/General Counsel
Noel Card, Communications Director
Craig Hanna, Public Policy Director
The AAA is a public policy organization for actuaries within the US. The Academy acts as the public information organization for the profession. Assisting public policy process through the presentation of clear actuarial analysis, the Academy regularly prepares testimony for Congress, provides information to federal elected officials, regulators and congressional staff, comments on proposed federal regulations, and works closely with state officials on issues related to insurance.
Founded: 1965

12709 **American Academy of Insurance Medicine**
174 Colonnade Road
Unit 25
Ottawa, K2E 7J5, ON
613-226-9601
FAX: 613-721-3581 888-211-3204
info@aaimedicine.org
www.aaimedicine.org
Robert Watson, President
Jacki Goldstein, President-Elect
Patrick Snow, VP Finance
Founded as the Association of Life Insurance Medical Directors of America. This organization offers information and legislative updates for people in the medical insurance field.
460 Members Founded: 1889

12710 **American Agents Association**
PO Box 7079
Hilton Head Island, SC 29938
843-785-2808
FAX: 843-785-9068
akaamerican@hargray.com
James Fitzpatrick, President
AAA members are licensed insurance agents. *$25.00*
250 Members Membership Fee

12711 **American Association of Cooperative/ Mutual Insurance Society**
1 W Nationwide Boulevard
Columbus, OH 43215-2220
614-228-6377
FAX: 614-249-9071
Bill Leffel, Director
Formerly the North American Association of the International Cooperative Insurance Federation.

12712 **American Association of Crop Insurers**
1 Massachusetts Avenue NW
Suite 800
Washington, DC 20001-1401
202-789-4100
FAX: 202-408-7763
aaci@mwmlaw.com
www.aginsurance.org
Steve Harms, Chairman
Sam Scheef, Vice Chairman
David Graves, Secretary/Treasurer
Michael Mcleod, General Counsel/Executive Director
David Graves, Manager/Sr Gov't Relations Rep
Nonprofit industry service organization representing the interests of insurance companies, agents, and adjusters involved in the federal crop insurance program.
25 Members

12713 **American Association of Dental Consultants**
10032 Wind Hill Drive
Greenville, IN 47124
812-923-2600
FAX: 812-923-2900 800-896-0707
info@aadc.org www.aadc.org
Dr Jerry Blum, President
Dr Robert Laurenzano, Secretary/Treasurer
Judith K Salisbury, Executive Director
Members are dentists, insurance consultants, benefits programs administrators and other dental professionals. *$100.00*
450 Members Membership Fee Founded: 1977

12714 **American Association of Insurance Management Consultants**
Eaglemark Consulting Group
PO Box 20
Lemoyne, PA 17043
717-763-7717
FAX: 717-763-7989
nmallouf@mrcgroup.ws
www.aaimco.com
Nick Mallouf, President
Al Diamond, Executive Director
THe premier association of consultants to the insurance industry: insurance companies, agents, brokers, and their consumers. Also dedicated to helping the insurance industry operate more efficiently and more profitably, thus enabling improved service to the buying public.
35 Members

12715 **American Association of Managing General Agents**
150 South Warner Road
Suite 156
King of Prussia, PA 19406
610-225-1999
FAX: 610-225-1996
bernie.heinze@aamga.org
www.aamga.org
Bernd Heinze, Esq, Executive Director
Martin W Bair, Accolade CFO
Jennifer Bair, Administrative Assistant
Barb Dziengelski, Comptroller
Martha Heinze, Operations/Meetings Manager
A trade association of the premier wholesale property and casualty agents and companies in the insurance industry, committed to fostering the business partnerships, networking, professionalism, trusted expertise and exchange of knowledge among its members.
Founded: 1926

12716 **American Association of Retired Persons**
601 E Street NW
Washington, DC 20049
202-342-2277
www.aarp.org
Marie Smith, President
Erik Olsen, President-Elect
Bill Novelli, CEO
Dawn Sweeney, Services President
The leading nonproft, nonpartisan membership organization for people age 50 and over in the United States. Dedicated to enhancing quality of life for all as we age. WE lead positive social change and deliver value to members through information, advocacy and service. Membership is open to anyone over the age of 50.

35Mil Members Founded: 1958

12717 American Bail Coalition
1725 Desales Street NW
Suite 800
Washington, DC 20036
202-596-6540
FAX: 202-296-8702 800-375-8390
dnabic@aol.com
www.americanbailcoalition.com

Jerry Watson, President
Thomas Ritchey, Treasurer

Dedicated to the long term growth and continuation of the surety bail bond industry.
5 Members Founded: 1992

12718 American Cargo War Risk Reinsurance
30 Broad Street
7th floor
New York, NY 10004
212-405-2835
FAX: 212-344-1664
amich@amich.org www.amich.org

TD Montgomery, Chairman
RJ Decker, Vice Chairman
TA Haig Dick, Secretary/Director
Warren C Dietz, Treasurer

Reinsurance pool of member companies.
Founded: 1939

12719 American Council of Life Insurance

101 Constitution NW
Suite 700
Washington, DC 20001
202-242-2000
FAX: 202-624-2319

Frank Keating, President/CEO

Works to advance the interests of the life insurance industry and to provide effective government relations. Conducts investment and social research programs.
631 Members Founded: 1976

12720 American Institute for Chartered Property Casualty Underwriters
720 Providence Road
PO Box 3016
Malvern, PA 19355-0716
610-512-2728
FAX: 610-640-9576 800-644-2101
cserv@cpcuiia.org www.aicpcu.org

Karen Burger CPCU CPIW, Director PR/Advertising
Terrie E Troxel CPCP, President/CEO
Jim Marks, Executive Director

An independent, nonprofit organization offering educational programs and professional certification to people in all segments of the property and liability insurance business. More than 150,000 insurance practitioners around the world are involved in Institute programs.

12721 American Institute of Marine Underwriters
14 Wall Street
New York, NY 10005
212-233-0550
FAX: 212-227-5102
aimu@aimu.org www.aimu.org

James M Craig, President
David S French, Chairman
Robert V Huffert, Vice Chairman
Richard J Decker, Director Finance

Provides information of interest to marine underwriters and promotes their interests.

12722 American Insurance Association
1130 Connecticut Avenue NW
Suite 1000
Washington, DC 20036
202-828-7100
FAX: 202-293-1219
info@aiadc.org www.aiadc.org

Marc Racicot, President/CEO

The leading property and casualty insurance trade organization. Member companies offer all types of property and casualty insurance, as well as personal and commercial auto insurance, commercial property and liability coverage for small businesses, worker's compensation, homeowners' insurance, medical malpractice coverage, and product liability insurance.
Founded: 1964

12723 American Insurance Marketing & Sales Society
PO Box 35718
Richmond, VA 23235
804-674-6466
FAX: 804-915-9435 877-674-2742
kitty.ambers@att.net www.cpia.com

Kitty Ambers, Executive Director
Donna M Gray, Staff Liaison

Provides training, information and networking services designed to increase the personal and agency sales production of property and casualty insurance agents. Membership is open to any individual engaged in sales and marketing in property and casualty insurance business.
Founded: 1968

12724 American Nuclear Insurers
95 Glastonbury Boulevard
Glastonbury, CT 06033
860-682-1301
FAX: 860-659-0002
antion@attglobal.net
www.amnucins.com

George Turner, President
John Quatrocchi, Senior VP

A joint underwriting association, and and organization created by some of the largest stock insurance companies in the United States. The purpose is to pool the financial assets pledged by these member companies to provide significant amount of property and liability insurance we make available to nuclear power plants and related facilities throughout the world.
60 Members Founded: 1957

12725 American Prepaid Legal Services Institute
321 N Clark Street
Chicago, IL 60610
312-988-5751
FAX: 312-988-5032
tucker2@staff.abanet.org
www.aplsi.org

Alec Schwartz, Executive Director

Professional trade organization representing the legal services plan industry. The members include lawyers, sponsor representatives, administrators and marketers of legal service plans. These people have invested their time, money and organizational resources to build legal service plans into the premier mechanism for supplying affordable legal services.

12726 American Risk and Insurance Association
716 Providence Road
Malvern, PA 19355-3402
610-640-1997
FAX: 610-725-1007
aria@cpcuiia.org www.aria.org

James Garven, President

The premier professional association of insurance scholars and other thoughtful risk management and insurance professionals. Through this association members receive many valuable tools and opportunities for enlightenment, growth and education. Membership is made up of academics, individual insurance industry representatives, and institutional sponsors.
500 Members Quarterly Founded: 1932

12727 American Society for Healthcare Risk Management
1 N Franklin Street
Chicago, IL 60606
312-223-3840
FAX: 312-422-4580
ashrm@aha.org
www.hospitalconnect.com/ashrm

Deborah Sprindzunas, Executive Director
Grecelda Buchanan, Administrative Assistant
Diane Farina White, Associate Executive Director

National organization for the health care industry risk management equipment, supplies and services.
4400+ Members Founded: 1980

12728 American Society of Law, Medicine and Ethics
765 Commonwealth Avenue
Suite 1634
Boston, MA 02215
617-262-4990
FAX: 617-437-7596
info@aslme.org www.aslme.org

Benjamin W Moulton, Executive VP/Executive Director
Danielle Dombkowski, Membership/Subscription Srvcs Dir

An outgrowth of two founding organizations; the Massachusetts Society of Examining Physicians and the Massachusetts Society of Law and Medicine. Formerly American Society of Law and Medicine. Multi-disciplinary membership of professionals concerned with the interrelation of law, medicine and health care. *$200.00*
4500 Members Membership Fee Founded: 1972

12729 American Society of Pension Professionals and Actuaries
4245 N Fairfax Drive
Suite 750
Arlington, VA 22203
703-160-0512
FAX: 703-516-9308
asppa@asppa.org www.asppa.org

Sarah E Simoneaux, President
Chris Stroud, President-Elect
Brian H Graff, Esq, Executive Director/CEO
Tom Hopkins, CFO

The premier national organization for career retirement plan professionals. The membership is comprised of the many disciplines supporting retirement income management and benefits policy. Members are part of the diversified, technical, and highly regulated benefits industry.

5400+ Members Founded: 1966

12730 American Society of Safety Engineers
1800 E Oakton Street
Des Plaines, IL 60018
847-699-2929
FAX: 847-768-3434
customerservice@asse.org
www.asse.org

Fred Fortman, Executive Director
Jim Drzewiecki, Finance/Controller Director
Kelly Fanella, Marketing/Communications Director

Nonprofit, global organization that works to advance the technical, scientific, managerial and ethical knowledge and skills of occupational safety, heath and envionmental professionals, and is committed to protecting people, property and the envionnment. Offers education, technical publications, involvement in safety standards development, annual conferences and more.
30000 Members Founded: 1911

12731 Appraisers Association of America
386 Park Avenue S
Suite 2000
New York, NY 10016
212-889-5404
FAX: 212-889-5503
aaa@appraisersassoc.org
www.appraisersassoc.org

Aleya Lehmann, Executive Director
Angelina Ebreo, Associate Director
Linda Marke, Membership Associate

The oldest non-profit professional association of personal property appraisers. This association has also been a leader in the field by ensuring that appraisers with the AAA credential continue to be a consistently trustworthy source known for the highest standards of ethics, conduct and professionalism.
900 Members Founded: 1949

12732 Arbitration Forums
3350 Buschwood Park, Drive 3
Suite 295
Tampa, FL 33618
813-314-4004
FAX: 813-931-4618 888-272-3453

Geoffrey K Engert, Director
D Kay Smith, President/CEO
Tom VonBraunsberg, Director
Paul Bonds, Director
Ken Butler, Director

Arbitration Forums is a not-for-profit provider of intercompany insurance dispute resolution services. More than 2,000 insurers and self-insurers participate in AF's programs. AF resolves over 250,000 disputes with a claim value approaching one billion dollars.
Founded: 1943

12733 Associated Risk Managers International
702 Colorado Street
Suite 200
Austin, TX 78745
512-479-6886
FAX: 512-479-0577 www.arminet.com

John Atkinson, Executive Director
James Sanders, International Executive Director

Develops specialized insurance/risk management services for trade associations, professional groups and other industry organizations. Conducts seminars and sponsors competitions.
505 Members Founded: 1970

12734 Association of Advanced Life Underwriters
1922 F Street NW
Washington, DC 20006-4302
202-331-6099
FAX: 202-331-2164

Karen Keating, Communications Director

Offers services in complex fields of estate analysis, business, insurance, pension planning, employee benefit plans.
1.4M Members Founded: 1957

12735 Association of Average Adjusters of the U.S.
79 Palmer Drive
Livingston, NJ 07039-1314
973-597-0824

averageadjusters@aol.com
www.usaverageadjusters.org

Jay McGuire, Chairman
Richard P Carney, Executive Chairman
Eileen M Fellin

Marine insurance and general average adjusters, ship and cargo surveyors and admiralty lawyers. Has no paid staff. Membership principally in New York area.

700+ Members Founded: 1879

12736 Association of California Insurance Companies
1121 L Street
Suite 406
Sacramento, CA 95814
916-442-4581
FAX: 916-444-3872 www.acic-1.org

Samuel Sorich, President
Jeffrey Fuller, Executive VP

The mission is to successfully advocate a financially sound, competitive insurance marketplace which promotes the availability and affordability of insurance essential to the business and personal needs of the people of California.

12737 Association of Finance and Insurance Professionals
4112 Southwood E
Colleyville, TX 76034
817-428-2434
FAX: 817-428-2534
afip@aol.com www.afip.com

David N Robertson, Executive Director
Tarrah Lett, Sr VP
Heather M Barnett, Communications Director

A nonprofit educational foundation that serves the needs of in-dealership finance and insurance personnel for the automobile, RV, commercial truck and equipment, motorcycle, and motorized sports industries while assisting the lenders, vendors, and independent general agents who support the F&I function. *$95.00*
3500 Members $2,500 for Company's Founded: 1989

12738 Association of Financial Guaranty Insurers
TowersGroup
15 W 39th Street, 14th Floor
New York, NY 10018
212-354-5020
FAX: 212-391-6920
margarettowers@towerspr.com
www.afgi.org

Robert E Mackin, Executive Director
Margaret Towers, Contact Person

The trade association of the insurers and reinsurers of municipal bonds and asset-backed securities.
10 Members Founded: 1986

12739 Association of Home Office Underwriters
22300 Windy Ridge Parkway
Suite 600
Atlanta, GA 30339-8443
770-984-3715
FAX: 770-984-6418 www.ahou.org

Sharon Smith, President
Nazir Damji, Executive VP

Founded when the Home Office Life Underwriters Association and Institute of Homes Office Underwriters joined forces to provide one unified underwriting voice. The mission is to advance the knowledge of sound underwriting of life and disability insurance risks, toward which end it holds meetings, publishes papers and discussions, and promotes educational programs.
$100.00
1400 Members Membership Fee Founded: 2002

12740 Association of Insurance Compliance Professionals
12100 Sunset Hills Road
Suite 130
Reston, VA 20190
703-234-4074
FAX: 703-435-4390
aicp@aicp.net www.aicp.net

Richard A Guggolz, Executive Director

Formerly the Society of State Filers. AICP represents individuals involved or interested in statutes, state filing methods, and/or regulatory requirements. Associate members are consultants, attorneys, association managers, education/service organizations and other interested individuals.
$175.00
1200 Members Membership Fee Founded: 1985

12741 Association of Professional Ins. Agents
400 N Washington Street
Alexandria, VA 22314
703-836-9340
FAX: 703-836-1279
piainfo@pianet.org www.pianet.com

Leonard Brevik, Executive VP
Ted Besesparis, VP Communications/Public Relations
Alexi Papandon, Marketing Director
Loan Nguyen, VP Finance

Represents professional independent insurance agents in all 50 states, Puerto Rico and the District of Columbia. Our members are local Main Street Agents who serve their communities throughout America
Founded: 1931

12742 Association of Professional Insurance Women
551 5th Avenue
Suite 1625
New York, NY 10176
212-867-0228
FAX: 212-867-2544
info@apiw.org www.apiw.org
Laurie Kamaiko, President
Provides women in the insurance insudtry with opportunities for professional development and assistance in advancing their careers. Our membership consists of professional insurance women, highly regarded, decision makers with primary insurers, reinsurers, insurance brokers, risk management, professional services firms and other industry related organizations.
135 Members Founded: 1976

12743 Automobile Insurance Plans Service Office
302 Central Avenue
Johnston, RI 02919-4932
401-946-2310
FAX: 401-528-1350
David Kohlhammer, President
Develops and files rates and provides services for auto insurance plans.

12744 Aviation Insurance Association
14 W 3rd Street
Suite 200
Kansas City, MO 64105
816-221-8488
FAX: 816-472-7765
gary@aiaweb.org www.aiaweb.org
Tom Thornton, President
Gary Hicks, Executive Director
A nonprofit association dedicated to expanding the knowledge of an d promoting the general welfare of the aviation insurance industry through numerous educational programs and events. WElcomes members of all facets of the aviation insurance industry, including such professionals as; agents/brokers, claims professionals, underwriters, attorneys, associates and college students interested in the business.
900 Members Founded: 1976

12745 Blue Cross and Blue Shield Association
225 N Michigan Avenue
Chicago, IL 60601
312-297-6000
FAX: 312-297-6609 www.bluecares.com
Scott Serota, President
Formerly Blue Cross Association and National Association of Blue Shield Plans. Members must be medical and/or hospital plans and operate according to established standards. Offers information, consulting, representation and operation services to members. Member plans represent over 68.1 million health care consumers.
55 Members Founded: 1946

12746 Captive Insurance Companies Association
4248 Park Glen Road
Minneapolis, MN 55416
952-928-4655
FAX: 952-929-1318
cica@harringtoncompany.com
www.captiveassociation.com
Dennis P Harwick, President
An organization dedicated to networking, educating, and promoting the captive insurance industry. Its mission is to be the first and best source of unbiased information, knowledge, and leadership for captive insurance decision makers.
Founded: 1972

12747 Casualty Actuarial Society
4350 N Fairfax Drive
Suite 250
Arlington, VA 22203
703-276-3100
FAX: 703-276-3108
office@casact.org www.casact.org
Cynthia R Ziegler, Executive Director
J Michael Boa, Communications/Research Director
Todd P Rogers, Finance/Operations Director
The purpose is to advance the body of knowledge of actuarial science applied to property, casualty and similar risk exposures, to establish and maintain standards of qualification for membership, to promote and maintain highstandards of conduct and competence for the members, and to increase the awareness of actuarial science.
3400+ Members Founded: 1914

12748 Certified Claims Professional Accreditation Council
PO Box 441110
Fort Washington, MD 20749-1110
301-292-1988
FAX: 301-292-1787
animag@lattmag.com
www.lattmag.com
A nonprofit organization that seeks to raise the professional standards of individuals who specialize in the administration and negotiation of freight claims. Specifically it seeks to give recognition to those who have acquired the necessary degree of experience, education, and expertise in domestic and international freight claims to warrant acknowledgment of their professional stature.

12749 Chartered Property Casualty Underwriters
720 Providence Road
Malvern, PA 19355
610-251-2728
FAX: 610-251-2780 800-932-2728
membercenter@cpcusociety.org
www.cpcusociety.org
James R Marks, Executive VP
Pi-Lan S Hsu, VP Communications/Marketing
Cathy Karch, VP Finance/Administration
Dedicated to meeting the career development needs of a diverse membership of professionals who have earned the CPCU designation, so that they may serve others in a competent and ethical manner.
28000 Members Founded: 1944

12750 Conference of Consulting Actuaries
1110 W Lake Cook Road
Suite 235
Buffalo Grove, IL 60089-1968
847-999-9088
FAX: 847-419-9091
conference@ccactuaries.org
www.ccactuaries.org
Rita K DeGraaf, Executive Director
Keith G Stewart, Operations Director
Patricia D Johnson, Project Manager
Matthew D Noncek, Member Services Manager
The Conference advances the quality of consulting practice, supports the needs of consulting actuaries, and represents their interests.
1100+ Members Founded: 1950

12751 Conference of Insurance Legislators
PO Box 217
Brookfield, WI 53008-0217
262-419-9794
FAX: 262-782-9607
Charles Davis, Executive Director
Organization of chairmen of state legislative committees concerned with insurance-related matters.

12752 Consumer Credit Insurance Association
542 S Dearborn
Suite 400
Chicago, IL 60605
312-394-4371
FAX: 312-939-8287
ccia@cciaonline.com
www.cciaonline.com
Jeff Boszor, Chair
Elizabeth Kastigar, President
Barbara Hollonquest, VP
William F Burfeind, Executive VP/Treasurer
Larry Diehl, VP Government Relations
Preserves, promotes and enhances the availability, utility and integrity of insurance and related products and services delivered in connection with financial transactions.
140+ Members Founded: 1951

12753 Council of Insurance Agents and Brokers
701 Pennsylvania Avenue Northwest
Suite 750
Washington, DC 20004-2608
202-783-4400
FAX: 202-783-4410
ciab@ciab.com www.ciab.com
Ken A Crerar, President
Gerry Van De Velde, CFO
Maura M Nelson, VP Marketing/Communications
Alison E Bowman, ARM, VP Member Services
Joel Wood, Sr VP/Government Affairs
Formerly the National Association of Casualty and Surety agents. The council represents the nation's largest commercial property and casualty insurance agencies and brokerage firms. Council members annually place some 80% of the commercial property/casualty insurance premiums in the United States. Council members who operate both nationally and internationally, specialize in a wide range of insurance products and risk management services for business, industry, government and the public.
300 Members Founded: 1913

12754 Council of Insurance Company Executives
701 Pennsylvania Avenue NW
Suite 750
Washington, DC 20004-2608
202-783-4400
FAX: 202-783-4410
ciab@ciab.com www.ciab.com
Ken A Crerar, President
Alison Bowman, VP Member Services
Barbara Haugen, Senior VP
Coletta I Kemper, VP Industry Affairs
Gerry Van DeVelde, CFO

Formerly the National Association of Casualty and Surety Executives. The object and purpose of CICE is to afford insurance companies an opportunity to discuss industry problems with insurance agents and brokers so the insurance business may better serve the insuring public. A standing committee of the Council of Insurance Agents and Brokers, CICE co-hosts the annual insurance Leadership forum.

67 Members Founded: 1996

12755 Council on Employee Benefits
4910 Moorland Lane
Bethesda, MD 20814
301-664-5940
FAX: 301-664-5944
vschieber@ceb.org www.ceb.org

Vicki A Schieber, Executive Director

Stimulates the development and improves the administration of sound, progressive employee benefit plans among its members. Also provides an excellent medium for the exchange of ideas, thought and information on the design, operation and financing of such plans. *$1500.00*

225 Members Membership Fee Founded: 1946

12756 Crop Insurance Research Bureau
10800 Farley
Suite 330
Overland Park, KS 66210
913-338-0470
FAX: 913-339-9336 888-274-2472
denicec@cropinsurance.org
www.cropinsurance.org

Paul Horel, President
Denice Cajigas, Executive Assistant
Michael Torrey, Federal Affairs Representative
W Kurt Henke, Legal Council

National trade association made up of insurance providers and related organization who provide a variety of insurance products for our Nation's Farmers.

Founded: 1964

12757 Eastern Claims Conference
PO Box 2730
Stamford, CT 06906
212-615-7424
FAX: 212-615-7345
Stan.brozowski@pfsfhg.com
www.easternclaimsconference.com

John Healy, Executive Director

Provides education and training to examiners, managers, and officers who review medical and disability claims. Holds seminars for life, health and disability clinics.

Founded: 1977

12758 Employee Benefit Research Institute
2121 K Street NW
Suite 600
Washington, DC 20037-1896
202-659-0670
FAX: 202-775-6312
info@ebri.org www.ebri.org

Dallas L Salisbury, President/CEO
Stephen Blakely, Communications Dir/Managing Editor
John MacDonald, Media Relations Director

Contribute to, to encourage, and to enhance the development of sound employee benefit programs and sound public policy through objective research and education.

50 Members $1,500-$15,000/Membership Founded: 1978

12759 Federal Insurance Administration
500 C Street SW
Washington, DC 20472-2110
202-646-3535
FAX: 202-646-4320

Bud Schaurte, Administrator

Administers the federal flood insurance and crime insurance programs.

12760 Federation of Defense & Corporate Counsel
11812-A N 56th Street
Tampa, FL 33617
813-983-0022
FAX: 813-988-5837
mstreeper@thefederation.org
www.thefederation.org

Lewis F Collins Jr, President
Martha J Streeper, Executive Director

The objectives and purposes of this Federation are to establish and maintain an organization consisting of members of the bar who are actively engaged in the legal aspects of the insurance business, executives of insurance companies and associations and corporate counsel engaged in the defense of claims; to assist in establishing standards for providing competent, efficient and economical legal services; to encourage and provide for legal education of the members of this Federation.

1400+ Members Founded: 1936

12761 Financial & Insurance Conference Planners
401 N Michigan Avenue
22nd Floor
Chicago, IL 60611
312-245-1023
FAX: 312-321-5150
info@icpanet.com www.icpanet.com

Michael Burke, CMP, President
Steve Bova, CAE, Executive Director
Jeff DeVine, CMP, Events Director
Jennifer Harmon, Membership Coordinator

Formerly the Insurance Conference Planners Association. FICP is and assocition whose membership is comprised of Meeting, Convention and Conference Planning Professionals who work for or under contract to Insurance or Financial Services Companies. *$150.00*

400 Members Membership Fee Founded: 1957

12762 Florida Association of Insurance Agents
3159 Shamrock S
PO Box 12129
Tallahassee, FL 32317-2129
850-893-4155
FAX: 850-668-2852 893-415-5

Jeff Grady, President/CEO
Larry Thompson, VP/CFO
Anita Burchnell, Membership Coordinator
Scott Johnson, Executive VP

Dedicated to enhancing the independent agency system through education, legislation, communication and FAIA member services. A nonprofit state trade association of insurance agencies affiliated with the Independent Insurance Agents of America.

1300 Members Founded: 1941

12763 Foreign Credit Insurance Association
125 Park Avenue
14th Floor
New York, NY 10017
212-885-1500
FAX: 212-885-1535
service@fcia.com www.fcia.com

Ken Cavanagh, Senior Vice President

To provide credit insurance covering teh risk of non-payment on foreign and,in certain cases, domestic receivables.

12764 Fraternal Field Managers' Association
Concordia Mutual Life
3020 Woodcreek Drive
Downers Grove, IL 60515
630-971-8000
FAX: 630-971-9332 www.ffma.info

William J. Murray, President
Jay Schenk, VP

FFMA is dedicated to the promotion of higher ethical standards and the professional development of the fraternal field force, fostering harmony, unity of purpose and the exchange of ideas among the member societies.

70 Members Founded: 1935

12765 GAMA International
2901 Telestar Court
Suite 140
Falls Church, VA 22042-1205
703-770-8184
FAX: 703-770-8182 800-345-2687
gamamail@gama.naifa.org
www.gamaweb.com

Michael Condry, VP
Edward G Deutschlander, President
Jeff Hughes, CEO

The only association dedicated to promoting the professional development needs of managers in the insurance and financial services industry. Also the only volunteer organization that focuses on the agency building tasks and skills of successful career agenices and firms. *$ 300.00*

5500 Members Membership Fee

12766 General Agents and Managers Conference of NALU
1922 F Street NW
Washington, DC 20006-4302
202-331-6099
FAX: 202-785-5612

Dennis Stork, Executive Director

Seeks to improve quality of management and life insurance selling through educational programs, code of ethical practices, and research programs.

7.2M Members Founded: 1951

12767 Health Insurance Association of America
1025 Connecticut Avenue NW
Washington, DC 20036-5405
202-824-0609
FAX: 202-223-7897

Carl Schramm, President

Promotes development of voluntary insurance against loss of income and financial burdens resulting from accident and sickness. Holds individual insurance for UMS.

340 Members Founded: 1956

12768 Highway Loss Data Institute
1005 N Glebe Road
Suite 800
Arlington, VA 22201-5759
703-247-1600
FAX: 703-247-1595 www.hwsafety.org

Brian O'Neill, President

Provides the public with insurance industry data concerning human and economic loss resulting from crashes.
12 Members Founded: 1972

12769 Home Office Life Underwriters Association
Minnesota Mutual Life
400 Robert Street N
Suite A
Saint Paul, MN 55101-2098
651-665-3500
FAX: 651-665-4488
www.ontherisk.org/houla/

Darrell Trenary, Executive Director

Offers educational programs through the Academy Life Underwriting designed for professional home office underwriters.
560 Members Founded: 1930

12770 I-Car
5125 Trillium Boulevard
Hoffman Estates, IL 60192
847-901-1198
FAX: 800-590-1215 800-422-7872
tom.mcgee@i-car.com www.i-car.com

Tom McGee, President/CEO
Margaret Knell, Corporate Administration Director
Shirley Pincus, Human Resources Director
Krista Flanagan, Marketing Executive

Mission is to research, develop, and deliver quality technical educational programs related to collision repair; to raise the level of available knowledge and recognize professional achievement; and to thereby improve communication throughout the collsion repair, insurance, and related industries for the ultimate benefit of the consumer
$500.00
100 Members Individual Membership Fee Founded: 1979

12771 IMCA Annual Meeting
Insurance Marketing Communications Association
4916 Pt. Fosdick Drive Nw
#180
Gig Harbor, WA 98335
206-219-9811
FAX: 866-210-2481
tseibert@imcanet.com
www.imcanet.com

September J Seibert, Executive Director
Temie Seibert, Executive Director

To promote education and development of its members. *$795.00*
Registration Fee

12772 Independent Automotive Damage Appraisers Association
PO Box 12291
Columbus, GA 31917-2291

FAX: 888-IDA-NOW 800-369-IADA

Wayne T Marsden, President
Jerry Cain, First VP
Mike Didonato, Secretary/Treasurer

A nationwide network of appraiser specialists with the knowledge and experience to assess vehicle damage and to make unbiased repair decisions based on the manufacturer's specifications, accepted industry procedures, and safety concerns.
731 Members Founded: 1947

12773 Independent Insurance Agents & Brokers of America
127 S Peyton Street
Alexandria, VA 22314
703-834-4422
FAX: 703-683-7556 800-221-7917
info@iiaa.org www.iiaa.org

Ronald Tubertini, Chairman
Robert Rusbuldt, Chief Executive Officer

A national alliance of business owners and their employees who offer all types of insurance and financial services products. IIABA agents and brokers not only advise clients about insurance, they recommend loss-prevention ideas that can cut costs.
300M+ Members Founded: 1896

12774 Independent Insurance Agents of America
127 S Peyton Street
Alexandria, VA 22314-2803
703-683-4422
FAX: 703-683-7556 800-221-7917

Jeffrey Yates, Executive VP
Robert Rusbuldt, Chief Executive Officer

Trade association of independent insurance agents.
28M Members

12775 Information, Incorporated
7700 Old Georgetown Road
Suite 700
Bethesda, MD 20814-6100
301-215-4688
FAX: 301-215-4600
acarr@mail.infoinc.com
www.infojnc.com

Alain Carr, Manager

Organization offers evaluations of companies on their claims-paying ability. Association news services.
Founded: 1979

12776 Inland Marine Underwriters Association
14 Wall Street
8th Floor
New York, NY 10005
212-233-0550
FAX: 212-227-5102
rthronton@imua.org www.imua.org

Ronald Thornton, President
Lillian Colson, Assistant VP

Serves as the collective voice of the U.S. inland marine insurance industry. Also provides its members with education, research and communications services that support the inland marine underwriting discipline.
$1750.00
400+ Members Membership Fee Founded: 1930

12777 Institute of Home Office Underwriters
General American Life Insurance Company
13045 Tesson Ferry Road
Saint Louis, MO 63128-3499
314-843-8880
FAX: 314-525-5491

Paul E McDaniel, President

Goals are to increase underwriting knowledge of members through educational programs. Prepares program and examinations leading to Fellowship in Academy of Life Underwriting.
425 Members Founded: 1937

12778 Insurance Accounting Systems Association
3511 Shannon Road
Suite 160, PO Box 51340
Durham, NC 27707
919-489-0991
FAX: 919-489-1994
info@iasa.org www.iasa.org

J Stephen Meziere, President
Joseph Pomilia, Executive Director
Howard Norwick, CFO
John Bauer, VP Membership

Membership includes insurance companies of all types, as well as companies that serve the insurance industry, regulators and also organizations more broadly representative of the financial services industry, including banks and investment brokerage firms.
1.7M Members Founded: 1928

12779 Insurance Committee for Arson Control
3601 Vincennes Road
Indianapolis, IN 46268
317-575-5601
FAX: 317-879-8408
info@arsoncontrol.org
www.arsoncontrol.org

Don J Hancock, Executive Director
Larry Baile, Event Manager

Serves as a national resource, education and communications organization. ICAC works to increase public awareness of the arson problem, what can be done and how the industry is responding on both the national and local levels.

12780 Insurance Consumer Affairs Exchange
PO Box 746
Lake Zurich, IL 60047
847-997-8454

info@icae.com www.icae.com

John Cloyd, President

Promotes professionalism and to shape the standardsof behavior in relationships between insurance organizations, regulators and customers through proactive dialogue, research, communication and education.
$150.00
110 Members Individual Membership Fee Founded: 1976

12781 Insurance Cost Containment Service
330 S Wells
Chicago, IL 60606-4701
312-427-2520
FAX: 312-368-8336

Robert Kissane, President

Assists insurance companies with property claims adjustment and arson and fraud claims investigation.

12782 Insurance Information Institute
110 William Street
New York, NY 10038-3901
212-346-5500
FAX: 212-732-1916 800-942-4242

Gordon Stewart, President
Jeanne M Salvatore, Sr VP Public Affairs
Gary Johnson, Executive Director

A factfinding communication and media organization for all lines of insurance except life and health insurance. Affiliated with Western Insurance Information Services of-

fering consumer information services to 10 western states. Also offers a national insurance consumer helpline.
250 Members Founded: 1959

12783 Insurance Institute for Highway Safety
1005 N Glebe Road
Suite 800
Arlington, VA 22201-5718
703-247-1500
FAX: 703-247-1678
webmaster@iihs.org
www.highwaysafety.org

Adrian Loud, President

Traffic and motor vehicle safety organization supported by auto insurers.

12784 Insurance Institute of America
720 Providence Road
PO Box 3016
Malvern, PA 19355-716
800-644-2101
FAX: 610-640-9576 800-644-2101
cserv@cpcuiia.org www.aicpcu.org

Terrie Troxel, President/CEO
Peter L Miller, Executive VP
Kenneth R Dauscher, Senior VP
Christine L Lewis, Senior VP/Secretary
Elizabeth A Sprinkel, Senior VP

Independent, nonprofit organization offering educational programs, professional certification and research to people who practice or have an interest in risk management and/or property casualty insurance.
Founded: 1942

12785 Insurance Loss Control Association
3601 Vincennes Road
Indianapolis, IN 46268
317-875-5250
FAX: 317-879-8408
ccarson@namic.org
www.insurancelosscontrol.org

Daniel Finn, President
Brock Bell, VP
Pat McIntire, Secretary

Supports loss control professionals. Publishes quarterly newsletter.
Founded: 1931

12786 Insurance Marketing Communications Association
4916 Pt. Fosdick Drive NW
Suite 180
Gig Harbor, WA 98335
206-219-9811
FAX: 866-210-2481
tseibert@imcanet.com
www.imcanet.com

Cora Barren, President
Temie Seibert, Executive Director

An international organization of insurance communications professionals who specialize in marketing, marketing communications, advertising, sales promotion, and public relations. *$500.00*
180 Members Annual Membership Fee Founded: 1923

12787 Insurance Premium Finance Association
1520 Sheridan Drive
Buffalo, NY 14217-1212
716-874-1644
FAX: 716-695-8757

Sullivan Bemak, Executive Director

Firms licensed by New York State to finance property and casualty insurance premiums.
16 Members Founded: 1961

12788 Insurance Research Council
718 Providence Road
PO Box 3025
Malvern, PA 19355-0725
610-644-2212
FAX: 610-640-5388
irc@cpcuiia.org www.ircweb.org

Robert K Yass, Chairman
Kevin Kelso, Treasurer
Elizabeth A Sprinkel, Secretary

Non profit division of the American Institute for Chartered Property Casualty Underwriters and the Insurance Institute of America. Addresses subjects relating to all lines of property-casualty insurance, including coverages of automobiles, homes, businesses, municipalities, and professionals.
Founded: 1977

12789 Insurance Value Added Network Services
1455 E Putnam Avenue
Old Greenwich, CT 06870-1307
203-698-1900
FAX: 203-698-7299 800-288-4826
ivans.info@ivans.com
www.ivans.com

Clare DeNicola, President/CEO
Jeffery K Dobish, Sr VP/CFO
Linda Welsh, CAO

Industry-sponsored organization offering value added data communications network linking agencies, companies and healthcare providers to the insurance industry.
Founded: 1983

12790 Intermediaries and Reinsurance Underwriters Association
971 Rte 202 North
Branchburg, NJ 08876
908-203-0211
FAX: 908-203-0213
info@irua.com www.irua.com

Mary K Clancy, Executive Director
Tony Joseph, President

Promotes professionalism and educational advancement, and to provide a forum for the useful exchange of ideas among member companies.
60 Members Founded: 1967

12791 International Association for Financial
5775 Glenridge Drive NE
Suite B-300
Atlanta, GA 30328-9904
404-845-0011
FAX: 404-845-3660 800-945-4237
marv.tuttle@fpanet.org
www.fpanet.org

Marvin W Tuttle, Executive Director/CEO
Craig Noll, Director Finance
Curtis Niepoth, CFO
Dale Brown, Executive Director
Kim Porto, Director Career Development

Members include accountants, financial planners, lawyers, bankers, stockbrokers, insurance professionals and others who provide financial advice and services to individuals.
15M Members Founded: 1969

12792 International Association for Insurance Law: United States Chapter
Chase Communications
PO Box 3028
Malvern, PA 19355-0728

FAX: 914-699-2025

Stephen C Acunto, VP

Members are attorneys, professors, regulators and others who are interested in international or comparative aspects of insurance law.
700 Members Founded: 1963

12793 International Association of Accident Reconstruction Specialists
1036 Gretchen Lane
Grand Ledge, MI 48837-1873
517-622-3135

brandtb@benchmarktrafficservices.com
www.iaars.org

Dan Lofgren, President
Fred Rice, VP
Bill Brandt, Secretary/Treasurer

Composed of members and associates from 38 states, as well as abroad. Membership comprised of law enforcement officers and civilian personnel.
152 Members Founded: 1980

12794 International Association of Arson Investigators
12770 Boenker Road
Bridgeton, MO 63044
314-739-4224
FAX: 314-739-4219
www.firearson.com

R Kirk Hankins, President
James Whitaker, Executive Director
Thomas J Fee, First VP
Eileen Stauss, Second VP
Marsha Sipes, Manager

Formed at Purdue University by U.S. and Canadian representatives of the insurance, fire services, law enforcement agencies and law firms. *$65.00*
7500 Members $15 Initiation Fee Founded: 1949

12795 International Association of Defense Counsel
One N Franklin
Suite 1205
Chicago, IL 60606
312-368-1494
FAX: 312-368-1854
info@iadclaw.org www.iadclaw.org

Oliver Yandle, Executive Director
Joe Blaszynski, Operations Director
Mary Beth Kurzak, Marketing/Communications Director
Pamela Miczuga, Finance Director

Formerly the International Association of Insurance Counsel. Members are defense attorneys and insurance and corporate counsels, by invitation only. *$580.00*
2400 Members Membership Fee Founded: 1920

12796 International Association of Industrial Accident Boards and Commissions
5610 Medical Circle
Suite 24
Madison, WI 53719
608-663-6355
FAX: 608-663-1546
gkrohm@iaiabc.org www.iaiabc.org

Gregory Krohm, Executive Director
Julie Krautkramer, Membership Services

A not for profit trade association representing government agencies charged with the administration of workers' compensation systems throughout most of the United States and Canada, and other nations and territories.

300+ Members Founded: 1914

12797 International Association of Insurance Receivers
174 Grace Boulevard
Altamonte Springs, FL 32714
407-682-4513
FAX: 407-682-3175
info@iair.org www.iair.org

Paula Keyes, Executive Director

Founded to provide individuals who were involved with insurance receiverships and organization through which they could receive education, exchange information, and enhance the standards followed by those who work in this professional area.

Founded: 1991

12798 International Association of Special Investigation Units
110 William Street
New York, NY 10038-3901
212-442-0632
FAX: 212-791-1807

Larry Henning, President

An association of more than 870 insurance company SIU professionals representing 130 of the largest property and casualty companies in the country.

12799 International Claim Association
1155 15th Street, NW
Suite 500
Washington, DC 20005
202-452-0143
FAX: 202-530-0659
cmurphy@claim.org www.claim.org

Mark A Langenfeld, President
Christopher Murphy, Executive Director
Julie M Kleve, Secretary

Provides a forum for information exchange and a program of education tailored to the needs of its member life and health insurance companies, reinsurers, managed care companies, TPAs, and Blue Cross and Blue Shield organizations worldwide

Founded: 1909

12800 International Foundation of Employee Benefit Plans
18700 W Bluemound Road
Brookfield, WI 53045
262-786-6700
FAX: 262-786-8670 888-334-3327
pr@ifebp.org www.ifebp.org

Michael Wilson, CEO
Dean D Ossanna, Marketing/Membership Sr Director
John W Steinbach, Administrations Sr. Director
Stacy Van Alstyne, PR/Advertising Assistant Director

The largest educational association serving the employees and compensation industry.

$295.00

35000 Members $575/Organization Fee
Founded: 1954

12801 International Insurance Council
900 19th Street NW
Washington, DC 20006-2105
202-682-2345

Robert Gibbons, President

Unites the insurance, reinsurance, and insurance services industries to build trade and investment relations with overseas markets. Promotes trade, educates on international insurance, speaks out on insurance trade and investment issues and champions international business-to-business and business-to-government cooperation.

75 Members Founded: 1985

12802 International Insurance Society
101 Murray Street
New York, NY 10007
212-815-9291
FAX: 212-815-9297
ej@iisonline.org www.iisonline.org

Tonya Wishneski, Finance Director
Colleen McKenna Tacker, Operations Director
Patrick Kenny, President

Provides a world forum for leading insurance executives, academicians and others interested in insurance to share interests and ideas on timely global issues.

1000 Members Founded: 1965

12803 International Risk Management Institute
12222 Merit Drive
Suite 1450
Dallas, TX 75251-2276
972-960-7693
FAX: 972-371-5120
info@irmi.com www.irmi.com

William S McIntyre, Owner/Chairman of the Board
Jack P Gibson, President
Paul D Murray, VP Marketing/Sales
Cathy J Roberts, VP Finance/Administration
Mike Wojcik, VP Information Technology

Provides important risk and insurance information to business, legal, risk management, and insurance professionals

Founded: 1978

12804 Intersure Ltd
Three Hotel Street
Warrenton, VA 20186
540-349-0969
FAX: 540-349-0971
intersure@staffnet.com
www.intersurepartners.com/partners.asp

Millie Curtis, Executive Officer

Formerly the Association of International Insurance Agents. Founded to promote the principles of a free exchange of ideas and mutual cooperation based on the highest standards of intergrity, confidentiality and trust.

45 Members Founded: 1966

12805 LIMRA International
300 Day Hill Road
Windsor, CT 06095-1783
860-688-3358
FAX: 860-298-9555 800-235-4672
customer.service@limra.com
www.limra.com

Richard A Wecker, President/CEO
Howard S Drescher, Public Relations Director

We offer our clients insight in the form of cooperative research and value added marketing and distribution expertise. Insight that helps you identify trends, evaluate options and implement solutions. All of which leads to one clear outcome; the growth of your company.

800 Members Founded: 1916

12806 LOMA: Life Office Management Association
2300 Windy Ridge Parkway
Suite 600
Atlanta, GA 30339-8443
770-951-1770
FAX: 770-984-0441 800-275-5662
askloma@loma.org www.loma.org

Thomas P Donaldson, President/CEO

Insurance worldwide association of insurance companies specializing in research and education.

1200+ Members Founded: 1924

12807 Liability Insurance Research Bureau
3025 Highland Parkway
Suite 800
Downers Grove, IL 60515-1291
630-242-2250
FAX: 630-724-2260 888-711-7572
pdispensa@lirb.org www.lirb.org

Tom Mallin, President
Paul C Despensa, VP/General Counsel

Spun off from Property Loss Research Bureau, we provide legal research, consulting and educational services in auto liablility and CGL lines. Members are stock and mutual insurance companies.

252 Members Founded: 1990

12808 Life Insurers Council
2300 Windy Ridge Parkway
Suite 600
Atlanta, GA 30339-8443
770-984-3724
FAX: 770-984-3780
lic@loma.org
www.loma.org/IndexPage-LIC.asp

Michael H Siris, Executive Director
Rose Hoyt, Administrative Assistant

In 1997, the LIC merged with (LOMA) Life Office Management Association which added extensive benefits for all LIC members. Serving the basic insurance needs of the general public, including the underserved market, through various distribution methods.

62 Members Founded: 1910

12809 Lightning Protection Institute
25475 Magnolia Drive
PO Box 99
Maryville, MO 64468
816-233-0140
FAX: 816-676-0093 800-488-6864
lpi@lightning.org www.lightning.org

Harold "Bud" VanSickle III, Executive Director
Kim Loehr, Media/Marketing Consultant

A not-for-profit organization whose members are dedicated to insuring that today's lightning protection systems are the best possible quality in design, materials and installation, so that precious live and property can be protected from the damaging and costly effects of one of nature's most exciting phenomenons, lightning.

100 Members Founded: 1955

12810 Loss Executives Association
Industrial Risk Insurers
85 Woodland Street
Hartford, CT 06102-3103
860-207-7412
FAX: 860-520-7546
info@lossexecutives.com
www.lossexecutives.com

Thomas N Leidell, President
Donald Nunn, VP

A professional association of property loss executives providing education to the industry.

12811 Mass Marketing Insurance Institute
14 W 3rd Street
Suite 200
Kansas City, MO 64105
816-221-7575
FAX: 816-561-7765
gary@robstan.com www.mi2.org

Jason Krouse, President
Ken Bowman, Executive Director
Jim Barrett, First VP
Mary Walsh, VP Membership
Jennifer Branfort, Associate Director

The oldest not-for-profit membership organization that promotes the voluntary benefits industry by providing a forum for education, business development and fellowship.

300 Members Annual Meeting (Spring) Founded: 1970

12812 Massachusetts Association of Insurance Agents Convention
137 Pennsylvania Avenue
Framingham, MA 01701-8837
508-663-0223
FAX: 508-628-5443
www.massagent.com

Sheron Gagnon, Trade Show Manager

Trade show for everyday use in the insurance agency office.

1800 Members November

12813 Million Dollar Round Table
325 W Touhy Avenue
Park Ridge, IL 60068-4265
847-692-6378
FAX: 874-518-8921
info@mdrt.org www.mdrt.org

Stephen O Rothschild, CLU, ChFC, President
Thomas Ensign, Membership Services Director
John Prast, Executive VP
Stephen P Stahr, Public Relations Director
Jacqueline F Campa, Human Resources Director

The premier association of financial professionals, providing its members with resources to improve their technical knowledge, sales and client service while maintaining a culture of high ethical standards. *$350.00*

28000 Members Membership Fee Founded: 1927

12814 Mortgage Insurance Companies of America
1425 K Street NW
Suite 210
Washington, DC 20005
202-682-2683
FAX: 202-842-9252
www.privatemi.com

Suzanne C Hutchinson, Executive Vice President

Representing the private mortgage insurance industry.

6 Members Founded: 1973

12815 National Alliance for Insurance Education & Research
3630 N Hills Drive
PO Box 27027
Austin, TX 78755-2020
512-457-7932
FAX: 512-349-6194 800-633-2165
alliance@scic.com
www.thenationalalliance.com

William Hold, President

National education providers offering programs for all insurance and risk management professionals in property, liability and life insurance, with a continuing education requirement upon designation.

75000 Members Founded: 1969

12816 National Association of Independent Insurers
2600 S River Road
Des Plaines, IL 60018-3203
847-297-7800
FAX: 847-297-5064

Jack F Ramirez, President

Membership consists of property-liability companies Supports the National Association of Independent Insurers Political Action Committee.

12817 National Association of Bar-Related Title
1430 Lee Street
Des Plaines, IL 60018
847-298-8300
FAX: 847-298-8388
Pjb@atgf.com www.nabrti.com

Peter J Birnbaum, President
David Huffman, VP
Henry L Shulruff, VP

Members are bar-related title insurance companies registered with the US Patent Office.

10 Members Founded: 1965

12818 National Association of Casualty and Surety Agents
316 Pennsylvania Avenue SE
Suite 400
Washington, DC 20003-1172
202-543-7500
FAX: 202-293-1219

Lawrence Zippin, Executive Director

A trade organization of insurance agentswho represent and sell for stock insurers. Its purpose is to foster the growth of its members through cooperation with the insurers its members represent.

12819 National Association of Catastrophe Adjusters
5217 Cloyce Court
North Richland Hills, TX 76180
817-498-3466
FAX: 817-498-0480
nacatadj@aol.com www.nacatadj.org

Pat Plover, President
Lori Ringo, Contact

Provides a professional organization focused on excellence in catastrophe insurance adjusting for members through education, shared resources, and technology.

347 Members Founded: 1976

12820 National Association of Dental Plans
8111 LBJ Freeway
Suite 935
Dallas, TX 75251-1347
972-458-6998
FAX: 972-458-2258
info@nadp.org www.nadp.org

Evelyn F Ireland, CAE, Executive Director
Jerry Berggren, Research/Information Director
Kris Hathaway, Government Relations Director

Non profit trade association representing the entire dental benefits industry; dental HMOs, dental PPOs, discount dental plans and dental indemnity products. Members include major commercial carriers, regional and single state companies, as well as companies organized as Delta and Blue Cross Blue Shield plans.

80 Members Founded: 1989

12821 National Association of Disability Evaluating Professionals
13801 Village Mill Drive
Midlothian, VA 23113
804-378-7275
www.nadep.com

Virgil Robert May III, Executive Director

Members are lawyers, medical doctors and other professionals involved in the evaluation and rehabilitation of persons with disabilities resulting from work or personal injuries. *$150.00*

1000 Members Membership Fee Founded: 1984

12822 National Association of Fire Investigators
857 Tallevast Road
Sarasota, FL 34243
941-359-2800
FAX: 941-351-5849 877-506-6234
info@nafi.org www.nafi.org

Heather Kennedy, Director Membership Services
Christine Kennedy, Director Training Program

Primary purpose of this association is to increase the knowledge and improve the skills of persons engaged in the investigation and analysis of fires, explosions, or in the litigation that ensues from such investigations. The Association also originated and implemented the National Certification Board.

4300 Members Founded: 1961

12823 National Association of Fraternal Insurance
PO Box 357
Sheboygan, WI 53082-0357
920-458-1996
FAX: 920-457-4661

Peter Schmitt, Executive Director

Promotes and educates the sales force in fraternal life insurance. Bestows quality service award and production awards annually.

3.1M Members Founded: 1950

12824 National Association of Health Underwriter s
2000 N 14th Street
Suite 450
Arlington, VA 22201
703-276-0220
FAX: 703-841-7797
info@nahu.org www.nahu.org

Janet Trautwein, Executive VP/CEO
Jennifer B Murphy, CPA, Sr VP/CFO
Illana Maze, VP Membership
Martin Carr, Publisher

The mission is to improve its members' ability to meet the health, financial and retirement security needs of all Americans through education, advocacy and professional development.

18000 Members Founded: 1930
Mailing list available for rent 18000 names $350 per M.

12825 National Association of Independent Insurance Adjusters
825 W State Street
Suite 117-C&B
Geneva, IL 60134
630-397-5012
FAX: 630-397-5013
assist@naiia.com www.naiia.com

David F Mehren, Executive Director

Members are companies and individuals adjusting claims for insurance companies on a fee basis.

300 Members Founded: 1937

12826 National Association of Independent Life Brokerage Agencies
12150 Monument Drive
Suite 125
Fairfax, VA 22033
703-383-3081
FAX: 703-383-6942
jnormandy@nailba.org
www.nailba.org

Joseph M Normandy, Executive Director
John M Phillips, Marketing Director

Influencing the independent life and health brokerage community.

12827 National Association of Insurance Commissioners
2301 McGee Street
Suite 800
Kansas City, MO 64108-2662
816-842-3600
FAX: 816-783-8175
webpost@naic.org www.naic.org

Alessandro A Iuppa, President
Walter Bell, President-Elect
Catherine J Weatherford, Executive VP/CEO
Sandy Praeger, VP
Eric P Serna, Secretary/Treasurer

Assists state insurance regulators, individually and collectively, in serving the public interest and achieving the following fundamental insurance regulatorygoals in a responsive, efficient and cost effective manner, consistent with the wishes of its members.

Founded: 1871

12828 National Association of Insurance Women
6526 E 101st Street
PMB #750
Tulsa, OK 74133
918-445-5195
FAX: 918-743-1968 800-766-6249
joinnaiw@naiw.org www.naiw.org

L King, Executive VP
K O'Bryant, Member Services Director
M Adams, Communications Director/Editor
K Mccolloch, Meetings/Marketing Director

Serves its members by providing professional education, an environment in which to build business alliances and the opportunity to make connections with people of differing career paths and levels of experience within the insurance industry.

2000 Members Founded: 1940

12829 National Association of Insurance and Financial Advisors
2901 Telestar Court
PO Box 12012
Falls Church, VA 22042-1205
703-770-8100
FAX: 703-770-8201
membersupport@naifa.org
www.naifa.org

John A Davidson, President
David F Woods, CEO
Francesca Dea, COO
Jeffrey J Taggart, Secretary

A national nonprofit organization representing the interests of insurance and financial advisors nationwide, through its federation of over 900 state and local associations. NAIFA is the nation's largest financial services membership association.

$100.00
70M+ Members Membership Fee Founded: 1890

12830 National Association of Life Underwriters
1922 F Street NW
Washington, DC 20006-4394
202-331-6099

Seeks to support and maintain the principles of legal reserve life and health insurance. Promotes high ethical standards, informs and promotes public goodwill.

1M Members

12831 National Association of Mortgage Brokers
7900 Westpark Drive
Suite T309
McLean, VA 22102
703-425-5900
FAX: 703-342-5905 www.namb.org

Cathi Eifert, CAE, Sr VP/COO
Roy DeLoach, Sr VP/CFO
Mike Nizankiewicz, Chief Executive Officer
Katie Jones, Membership Manager
Jodi Greenblatt, VP Communications

THe only national trade association representing the mortgage broker industry. Promotes the industry through programs and services such as education, professional certification and government affairs representation.

27000 Members Founded: 1973

12832 National Association of Mutual Insurance Companies
3601 Vincennes
Indianapolis, IN 46268
317-875-5250
FAX: 317-879-8408 www.namic.org

Charles Chamness, President

A full service nationaltrade association with more than 1,400 member companies that underwrite 43 percent of the property/casualty insurance premium in the United States.

1400 Members Founded: 1985

12833 National Association of Professional Surplus Lines Offices
6405 N Cosby Avenue
Suite 201
Kansas City, MO 64151
816-741-3910
FAX: 816-741-5409
info@napslo.org www.napslo.org

Richard M Bouhan, Executive Director
Mike Ardis, Communications/Technology Director
Steve Stephan, Government Relations Director
Cheryl Rupp, Executive Assistant/Office Manager

A national trade association representing the surplus lines industry and the wholesale insurance marketing system. Acting as a source of information, spends a great deal of time identifying and explaining to regulatory, other segments of the insurance industry, the media and the public the vital role surplus lines in the insurance industry.

Founded: 1975

12834 National Association of Public Insurance Adjusters
21165 Whitfield Place
Suite 105
Potomac Falls, VA 20165
703-433-9217
FAX: 703-433-0369
info@napia.com www.napia.com

Richard S Cohen, SPPA, President/Chairman
David W Barrack, Executive Director

Experts on property loss adjustment who are retained by policy holders to assist in preparing, filing and adjusting insurance claims. NAPIA members have joined together for the purpose of professional education, certification, and promotion of a code of professional conduct.

12835 National Association of Surety Bond
1828 L Street NW
Suite 720
Washington, DC 20036-5104
202-686-3700
FAX: 202-686-3656
info@nasbp.org www.nasbp.org

Richard Foss, Executive Vice President
Stephen L Cory, Second VP

International organization of professional surety bond producers and brokers.

500+ Members Founded: 1942

12836 National Cargo Bureau
17 Battery Place
Suite 1232
New York, NY 10004-1110
212-785-8300
FAX: 212-785-8333 www.natcargo.org

James J McNamara, President
Ian J Lennard, VP/General Counsel/Secretary

The Bureau was created to render assistance to the United States Coast Guard in discharging its responsibilities under the 1948 International Convention for Safety of Life at Sea and for other purposes closely related thereto.

Founded: 1952

12837 National Committee for Quality Assurance
2000 L Street NW
Suite 500
Washington, DC 20036
202-556-6428
FAX: 202-955-3599
Customersupport@ncqa.org
www.ncpanet.org

Margaret E O'Kane, President
Esther Emard, COO
Greg Pawlson, Executive VP
Scott Hartranft, CFO
Robert Kaplan, CIO

The premier source for information about the quality of the nation's managed care plans. Our mission is to improve health care quality everywhere.

Founded: 1900

12838 National Conference of Insurance Legislators
385 Jordan Road
Troy, NY 12180
518-687-0178
FAX: 518-687-0401
info@ncoil.org www.ncoil.org

Frank Wald, President
Susan F Nolan, Executive Director
Candace Thorson, Deputy Executive Director

An organization of state legislators whose main area of public policy concern is insurance legislation and regulation.

12839 National Council of Self-Insurers
1253 Springfield Avenue
PMB 345
New Providence, NJ 07974
908-665-2152
FAX: 908-665-4020
natcouncil@aol.com
www.natcouncil.com

George H Nelson, President
Robin R Obetz, VP
Larry Holt, Executive Director

The Council believes that the workers' compensation system, properly administered by the states, is a vital part of the economic and social fabric of the United States. The Council aime to preserve it and protect it as the most effective means of resolving claims for industrial injuries and occupational diseases between employers and employees.

3500 Members Founded: 1946

12840 National Council on Compensation Insurance
901 Pennisula Corporate Circle
Boca Raton, FL 33487
561-893-1000
FAX: 561-917-7025 www.ncci.com

Stephen J Klingel, President/CEO
Alfredo T Guerra, CFO
Cheryl Budd, Chief Communications Officer
Bradley Kitchens, Chief Human Resources Officer
Michael Shawn O'Rouke, Chief Information Officer

Manages the nation's largest database of workers' compensation insurance information. They analyze industry trends, prepares workers compensation insurance rate recommendations, determines the cost of propsed legislation, and provides a variety of services and tools to maintain a healthy workers compensation system.

Founded: 1922

12841 National Fraternal Congress of America (NFCA)
1315 W 22nd Street
Suite 400
Oak Brook, IL 60523
630-522-6322
FAX: 630-522-6326
jbarngrover@nfcante.org
www.nfcanet.org

Fred Grubbe, President/CEO
Joan Barngrover, Dir. Admin. Services

The voice of fraternals, creating our brand and promoting our competitive advantages. Also alert and support our members about regulatory changes that could impact their fraternal uniqueness, including, and perhaps most importantly, the preservation of our tax exempt status.

78 Members Founded: 1886

12842 National Independent Statistical Service
3601 Vincennes Road
PO Box 68950
Indianapolis, IN 46268-0950
317-876-6200
FAX: 317-876-6210
questions@niss-stat.org
www.niss-stat.org

Theresa Szwast, President

A unique resource for the property/casualty insurance industry. Collect and report timely, quality insurance data, and perform other related functions, at a reasonable cost.

Founded: 1966

12843 National Insurance Association
1133 Desert Shale Avenue
Las Vegas, NV 89120
702-269-2445
FAX: 702-269-2446

Josephine King, Executive Director

Organization of about 14 insurance companies owned or controlled by African Americans.

14 Members Founded: 1921

12844 National Insurance Crime Bureau
1111 E Touhy Avenue
Suite 400
Des Plaines, IL 60018

800-447-6282

Robert M Bryant, President/CEO
Robert J Jachnicki, VP/CFO
Frank J Visconi, Sr VP/COO
James E Armstrong, VP Marketing
Bill Schroeder, Membership Director

Not for profit organization that receives support from property/casualty insurance companies. Partners with insurers and law enforcement agaencies to facilitate the identification, detection and prosecution of insurance criminals. Formed from ther merging of the National Automobile Theft Bureau and the Insurance Crime Prevention Institute.

1000 Members Founded: 1992

12845 National Risk Retention Association
4248 Park Glen Road
Minneapolis, MN 55416
952-928-4656
FAX: 952-929-1318
info@nrra-usa.org www.nrra-usa.org

Patrick E Winters, CAE, Executive Director

Promotes Risk Retention Act-authorized group insurance programs as a practical, economical, efficient and financially sound option for distributing the liability risks of member insuerds.

Founded: 1987

12846 National Structured Settlements Trade Association
1800 K Street NW
Suite 718
Washington, DC 20006
202-466-2714
FAX: 202-466-7414 www.nssta.com

Randy Dyer, Executive Director

A trade association that advances the use of structured settlements as a means of using periodic payments to resolve personal injury claims, workers compensation, and other types of claims.

600+ Members

12847 National Underwriter Company
5081 Olympic Boulevard
Erlanger, KY 41018-3164

FAX: 859-692-2246 800-543-0874
webmistress@nuco.com
www.nationalunderwriter.com

James M Keefe III, Senior Vice President
Charlie Smith, Chief Executive Officer

Organization with listings which include companies, brokers and agents in each area handling all lines of insurance.

12848 National Viatical Association
1030 15th Street NW
Washington, DC 20005
202-347-7361
FAX: 202-393-0336 800-741-9465

Charles C Reely, Executive Director

NVA is dedicated to financially assisting and effectively promotingthe needs of people coping with terminal illnesses in a compassionate, professional and ethical manner. The National Viatical Association is further dedicated to educating and informing the public on the viatical settlement processs.

60 Members Founded: 1993

12849 New England Professional Insurance Agents Association
1 Ash Street
Hopkinton, MA 01748-1822
508-497-2590

Stella Di Camilo, Manager

Supports all those in professional agents in the insurance industry in the New England region. Hosts annual trade show.

12850 Nonprofit Risk Management Center
1130 17th Street NW
Suite 210
Washington, DC 20036
202-785-3891
FAX: 202-296-0349
info@nonprofitrisk.org
www.nonprofitrisk.org

Melanie L Herman, Executive Director
Barbara B Oliver, Communications Director
John C Patterson, Sr Program Director

Provides assistance and resources for community serving organizations, and helps nonprofits cope with uncertainty.
Founded: 1990

12851 Patrons Group
769 Hebron Avenue
Glastonbury, CT 06033
860-633-4678
FAX: 860-657-2362 800-800-0863

Bill Siclari, President/CEO
Erin Allendale, VP Claims
Michael F Lyons, VP Finance/Treasurer

Offers personal insurance, as well as commercial and farm insurance, exclusively through independent agents.
Founded: 1833

12852 Physician Insurers Association
2275 Research Boulevard
Suite 250
Rockville, MD 20850
301-479-9090
FAX: 301-947-9090
wchao@thepiaa.org www.thepiaa.org

Lawrence E Smarr, President
Lisa Cole, Commuications Director
Betty P Hong, CPA, Finance/Accounting Director
Ann G Horwich, Business Development/Mktg Director
Michael Stinson, Government Relations Director

An organization of healthcare liability insurance entities which share the common values of its founders to advocate on behalf of physicians, dentists, and other healthcare providers in the areas of legislation, education, risk management and research.
1000 Members Founded: 1977

12853 Professional Insurance Agents of VA & DC
8092 Villa Park Drive
Richmond, VA 23228
804-264-2582
FAX: 804-266-1075
pia@piavadc.com www.piavadc.com

Dennis Yocom, Executive VP
Lori Lohr, Education Manager
Carol Throckmorton, Accounting Manager

Provides effective representation, top quality education and superior membership services.
44M Members Founded: 1931

12854 Professional Insurance Communicators of America
PO Box 68700
Indianapolis, IN 46268-0700
317-875-5250
FAX: 317-879-8408

Janet EH Wright, Secretary/Treasurer

Members are editors of insurance company newsletters.
90 Members Founded: 1955

12855 Professional Insurance Marketing Association
6300 Ridglea Pl
Ste 410
Fort Worth, TX 76116-5706
817-569-7462
FAX: 817-569-7461
mona@pima-assn.org
www.pima-assn.org

Mona Buckley, CEO
Gail Cannon, Sr Driector Membership/Programs
Carol Tierney, Membership Services Director
Ralph Gill, Communications Director

The leading national membership association of third-party administrators, insurance carriers and allied business partners involved in the direct marketing of insurance products. Also provides educational conferences, legislative updates, networking opportunities, publications and manuals to all those whose primary business is insurance marketing.
140 Members Founded: 1975

12856 Professional Insurance Mass-Marketing Association
4733 Bethesda Avenue
Suite 330
Bethesda, MD 20814-5248
301-951-1260
FAX: 301-951-1264

Jean McNeil, Editor

Over 325 member organization of insurance administrators, associates, companies and allied members that market and service insurance lines for trade and professional associations, societies and organizations.

12857 Professional Liability Underwriting Society
5353 Wayzata Boulevard
Suite 600
Minneapolis, MN 55416
952-746-2580
FAX: 952-746-2599 800-845-0778

Derek Hazeltine, Executive Director

Enhances the professionalism of its members through education and other activities and to responsibly address issues related to professional liability.
6000 Members Founded: 1986

12858 Property Casualty Insurers Association of America
2600 South River Road
Des Plaines, IL 60018-3286
847-297-7800
FAX: 847-297-5064
pcinet@pciaa.net www.pciaa.net

Jack Ramirez, President
Jean Demas, Assistant VP Information Services
Joseph Annotti, Sr VP Public Affairs

Established by the Merger of the Alliance of American Insurers and the National Association Association of Independent Insurers. Provides a responsible and effective voice on public policy questions affecting insurance products and services, fosters a competitive insurance marketplace for the benefit of insurers and consumers, and provides members with the highest quality products, information and services at a reasonable cost.
1000 Members Founded: 2004

12859 Property Insurance Loss Register
700 New Brunswick Avenue
Rahway, NJ 07065-3819
732-388-0332
FAX: 732-388-0537

Lawrence Zippin, President

A voluntary nonprofit organization administered by the American Insurance Services Group; maintains a computerized registry of property loss claims which can be used by its subscribers to fight insurance fraud, and provides data for nonactuarial/statistical research.

12860 Property Loss Research Bureau
3025 Highland Parkway
Suite 800
Downers Grove, IL 60515-5506
630-242-2200
FAX: 630-724-2260
whanson@ilrb.org www.plrb.org

Tom Mallin, President

Provides access to legal and technical databases, legal research on property and inland marine coverage issues countrywide, claims education, and daily catastrophe information for a membership of 570 property/casualty insurance companies.
600 Members Founded: 1947

12861 Public Agency Risk Managers Association
PO Box 6810
San Jose, CA 95150

FAX: 888-412-5913 888-907-2762
brenda.reisinger@parma.com
www.parma.com

Steve Martinez, President
David Clovis, ARM, VP
Susan Eldridge, Secretary/Treasurer

A forum promoting, developing and advancing education and leadership in public agency risk management. PARMA is dedicated to facilitating the exchange of ideas and innovative solutions toward risk management in government.
600+ Members Founded: 1974

12862 Registered Mail Insurance Association
100 William Street
New York, NY 10038-4512
212-612-4000
FAX: 212-425-2539 800-969-7462

Cheryl Martinez, Assistant VP

Insurance companies providing insurance for shipments of currency, securities and other valuables. LSTD Instrument Bonds are provided to facilitate the reproduction of lost documents.
3 Members Founded: 1921

12863 Reinsurance Association of America
1301 Pennsylvania Avenue NW
Suite 900
Washington, DC 20004
202-638-3690
FAX: 202-638-0936
infobox@reinsurance.org
www.reinsurance.org

Franklin Nutter, President

Non profit association committed to an activist agenda that represents the interests of reinsurance professionals across the United States.
Founded: 1968

12864 Risk and Insurance Management Society
1065 Avenue of the Americans
13th Floor
New York, NY 10018
212-286-9292
FAX: 212-986-9716 www.rims.org
Mary Roth, Executive Director
Deborah Flam, Human Resoures Manager
Lynn Chambers, CFO
Stephanie Orange, Chief Marketing Officer
Valerie Cammiso, Membership/Chapter Serves Director
Dedicated to advancing the practice of risk management, a professinal discipline that protects physical, financial and human resources.
3900 Members Founded: 1950

12865 SNL Financial
PO Box 2124
Charlottesvle, VA 22902
434-977-1600
FAX: 434-977-4466
customerserviee@snl.com
www.snl.com
Bjorn Turnquist, Director Product Management
Reid Nagle, Chief Executive Officer
This organization offers the most up-to-date information available in the insurance industry featuring the latest news releases, filings and important events. Provides current data on top-performing stocks, insider trades, ownership filings, company news and events and legislative issues.
Founded: 1987

12866 Self Insurance Institute of America
PO Box 1237
Simpsonville, SC 29681
FAX: 864-962-2483 800-851-7789
administration@siia.org www.siia.org
James A Kinder, CEO
Mike Ferguson, Executive Director
Mieka Scholten, Finance Director
Raquel Horton, Marketing Manager
Dedicated to protecting and promoting the self insurance and alternative risk transfer industry.
1500 Members Founded: 1981

12867 Shipowners Claims Bureau
1 Battery Park Plaza,
31st Floor
New York, NY 10004
212-847-4500
FAX: 212-847-4599
info.@american-club.com
www.american-club.com
Joseph Hughes, CEO
Members are claim managers and adjusters for shipping lines and protection and indemnity clubs.
31 Members Founded: 1917

12868 Society of Actuaries
475 N Martingale Road
Suite 600
Schaumburg, IL 60173
847-706-3500
FAX: 847-706-3599
webmaster@soa.org www.soa.org
Sarah Sanford, Executive Director
Cheryl Enderlein, Sr Dir Governance/Volunteer Relat
Joel Albizo, Deputy Executive Director Marketing
Stacy Lin, Sr Director Finance/Facilities
An educational, research and professional organization dedicated to serving the public and Society members. The vision is for actuaries to be recognized as the leading professionals in the modeling and management of finanacial risk and contingent events.
17000 Members Founded: 1949

12869 Society of Certified Insurance Counselors
3630 N Hills Drive
Austin, TX 78731-3028
FAX: 512-343-2167
William Hold, President
National education program in property, liability and life insurance, with a continuing education requirement upon designation.

12870 Society of Financial Examiners
174 Grave Boulevard
Altamonte Springs, FL 32714
407-682-4930
FAX: 407-682-3175 800-787-7633
info@sofe.org www.sofe.org
Paula Keyes, Executive Director
Chris Gerhard, Publications Director
The one organization where financial examiners of inusrance companies, banks, savings and loans, credit unions come together for training and to share exchange information on a formal and informal level.
1600 Members Founded: 1973

12871 Society of Financial Service Professionals
17 Campus Boulevard
Suite 201
Newton Square, PA 19073
610-526-2500
FAX: 610-527-1499
custserv@financialpro.org
www.financialpro.org
Joseph E Frack, CEO
Donna Conrad, CFO
Asha Williams, VP Marketing/Communications
Brian Horn, Chief Information Officer
Beverly Meyers Fox, Human Resources Director
Members are dedicated to the highest standards of competence and service in insurance and financial services.
22000 Members Founded: 1928

12872 Society of Insurance Research
631 Eastpoint Drive
Shelbyville, IN 46176-2291
317-398-3684
FAX: 317-642-0535
sir.mail@comcast.net www.sirnet.org
Ed Budd, Company Contact
Howard Goldstein, Secretary
F Reilly Cobb, VP Marketing
Provides a forum for the free exchange of ideas in all areas of insurance research. The Society includes representation from many different organizations such as insurance and non-insurance companies, government agencies, institutions of higher education, and trade associations.
350 Members Founded: 1970

12873 Society of Insurance Trainers and Educators
2120 Market Street
#108
San Francisco, CA 94114
415-212-2830
FAX: 415-621-0889
ed@insurancetrainers.org
www.insurancetrainers.org
Patricia M McCarthy, President
Lois Markovich, Executive Director
Beth Gamble Riggins, VP Annual Conference
Mary Jo Burfeind, VP Membership Services
Professional organization of trainers and educators in insurance.
600 Members Founded: 1953

12874 Society of Professional Benefit Administrators
2 Wisconsin Circle
Suite 670
Chevy Chase, MD 20815
301-718-7722
FAX: 301-718-9440
spba@erols.com
http://users.erols.com/spba/
Frederick D Hunt Jr, President
The national association of Third Party Administration firms who are contracted to administer employee benefit plans on an ongoing basis. The members are firms, not individuals who are employed within a firm to handle employee benefits and human resources.
400 Members Founded: 1975

12875 Society of Risk Management Consultants
330 S Executive Drive
Suite 301
Brookfield, WI 53005-4275
FAX: 212-572-6499 800-765-7762
Susan Kaufman, Public Relations
The mission is to advance these professions to benefit the consultants themselves, their clients and the public through research, education, the exchange of information, anf the promotion of professional and ethical guidlines.
150 Members Founded: 1984

12876 Sun States Professional Insurance Agents Association
13416 N 32nd Street
Suite 106
Phoenix, AZ 85032-6000
602-482-3333
Maryls M Graser, Executive VP
Supporst all those professional insurance agents who serve the southern region of the country. Hosts annual trade show.

12877 Think Believe Act
21700 Oxnard Street
Suite 1430
Woodland Hills, CA 91367
818-226-2800
FAX: 818-226-2801
losangeles@tbaglobal.com
www.tbaglobal.com
Robert Geddes, President&CEO
TBA is a privately-held company that is now one of the world's leading producers and marketers of brand events and experiences for Fortune 1000 companies

12878 Transportation & Logistics Council
120 Main Street
Huntington, NY 11743
631-549-8988
FAX: 631-549-8962
tlc@transportlaw.com
www.tlcouncil.org

Myrsa Bonet, Membership Secretary
Judy Selvaggio, Administrative Secretary

Formerly the Transportation Consumer Protection Council, a not for profit trade association dedicated to the education of shippers, carriers and others involved in the transportation of goods, the prevention of transit loss and damage, the promulgation of reasonable practices, laws and regulations, and the equitable resolution of disputes invloving frieght claims, freight charges and related maters.
375 Members Founded: 1974

12879 Underwriters Laboratories
333 Pfingsten Road
Northbrook, IL 60062-2096
847-120-0136
FAX: 847-272-8129 www.ul.com

Keith Williams, President/CEO
Stuart Paul, Senior VP Sales/Marketing

An independent, not for profit product safety testing and certification organization. They have also tested products for public safety for more than a century.
Founded: 1894

12880 Vermont Captive Insurance Association
One Lawson Lane
Suite 320
Burlington, VT 05401-8445
802-658-8242
FAX: 802-658-9365
vcia@vcia.com www.vcia.com

Molly Lambert, President/COO
Diane Leach, Education/Program Planning Director
Barbara Casanova LaRock, Membership/Development Director
Elizabeth Halpern, Communications Director

The mission is A) to provide its members with opportunities for education and information sharing. B) to maintain a network of mutual support with others who share its objectives. C) to ensure a favorable regulatory evironment for the captive insurance industry. D) to disseminate relevant information and position statements to key constituencies in support of the US domiciled captive insurance community.
450+ Members Founded: 1985

12881 Women Life Underwriters Confederation
17 S High Street
#1200
Columbus, OH 43215-3413

FAX: 414-142-2585 800-776-3008

Ann Wells, Managing Director

Seeks to advance the life insurance field. Informs women members of opportunities in the profession. Develops education programs and conducts seminars.
1.5M Members Founded: 1987

12882 Workers Compensation Reinsurance Bureau
2 Hudson Place
Hoboken, NJ 07030-5515
201-798-6312
FAX: 201-792-4441

Alfred O Weller, President

An association of insurance companies which pool their workers compensation excess losses as an alternative to purchasing reinsurance.
Founded: 1912

Newsletters

12883 ACTION
Association of Professional Insurance Agents
400 N Washington Street
Alexandria, VA 22314-2312
703-836-9340
FAX: 703-836-1279
piaweb@pianet.org
http://www.pianet.com/

Dan Blum, Publisher

News on the insurance and accounting professions.
14 pages Monthly Founded: 1931

12884 AWCP Newsletter
Association of Workers' Compensation Professionals
One Capitol Mall
Suite 320
Sacramento, CA 95814
916-669-5355
FAX: 916-444-7462
awcp@amgroup.us www.awcp.org

J R Robles, President/Golf Chairman
Joshua Bragg, Membership Chair
Amy Medina, VP
Jim Carmazzi, Secretary/Treasurer

Newsletter written for the members of the Association of Workers' Compensation Professionals, a nonprofit organization for those engaged in the field of workers' compensation, providing members with training and certification. The newsletter features articles and departments that provide tips on controlling workers' compensation costs; how to best work with your insurance company; successful return to work stories; certification and training schedules and more. Nonmembers pay nominal price.
Monthly Founded: 1998
Printed in 2 colors on matte stock

12885 Actuarial Studies in Non-Life Insurance
Astin Bulletin
B641 Locust Walk
Philadelphia, PA 19104-6218
215-898-2741

Jean Lemaire, Chairman

Promotes actuarial research and study and publishes the ASTIN Bulletin.
2.2M pages Founded: 1957

12886 Advanced Underwriting Services
Dearborn Financial Publishing
155 N Wacker Drive
Floor 1
Chicago, IL 60606-6819
312-836-4400
FAX: 312-836-1146

Georgia Mann, Publisher

Information on the law. *$395.00*
Monthly

12887 Agent Newsletter
American Association of Crop Insurers
1 Massachusetts Avenue NW
Washington, DC 20001-1401
202-789-4100
FAX: 202-408-7763
Insurance news for representatives working in the agricultural market.
Quarterly

12888 Best's Agents Guide to Life Insurance Companies
AM Best Company
Ambest Road
Oldwick, NJ 08858-9988
908-439-2200
FAX: 908-439-3296 800-544-2378

Larry G Mayewski, Editor
Art Sneider, CEO

Offers information on over 1,400 life and health insurance companies nationwide.
$150.00
Monthly Founded: 1899

12889 Cibyny Month
Chase Communications
PO Box 3028
Malvern, PA 19355-0728

Carole Acuto, Publisher

Insurance update for brokers. *$20.00*
12 pages Monthly

12890 Community Risk Management and Insurance Newsletter
Nonprofit Risk Management Center
1130 Seventeenth Street, NW
Suite 210
Washington, DC 20036
202-785-3891
FAX: 202-296-0349
info@nonprofitrisk.org
www.nonprofitrisk.org

Melanie Herman, Executive Director

Covers a wide spectrum of issues, showcases the Center's training and workshops and highlights new publications offering risk management advice from a nonprofit perspective.
16 pages 3 times a year
Circulation: 15000
Printed in 1 color on matte stock

12891 Compensation & Benefits for Law Offices
Institute of Management & Administration

3 Park Avenue
30th Floor
New York, NY 10016-5902
212-244-0360
FAX: 212-564-0465
subserve@ioma.com www.ioma.com
An indespensible reference for law firm recruitment, training, compensation, benefits, and HR managers who want and need to keep pace with what it takes to successfully, recruit, retain, train, reward, recognize, and compensatetop legal talent. *$269.00*
Monthly

12892 Crittenden Insurance Markets Newsletter
Crittenden Publishing
PO Box 1150
Novato, CA 94948
415-382-2400
FAX: 415-382-2476 800-421-3483
ins@crittendenonline.com
www.crittendenonline.com
Colleen Pestana, Publisher
Contains concise and pertinent information on commercial lines including worker's comp. You can also stay up to date with informed analysis and inside knowledge of hot markets, new carriers, program information and the competition. *$1167.00*
Monthly Founded: 1975
Circulation: 20000

12893 Disability Eval and Rehab Review
National Association of Disability Evaluating
13801 Village Mill Drive
Midlothian, VA 23113
804-378-7275
www.nadep.com
Virgil Robert May III, Executive Director
This periodical is peer reviewed and addresses issues which are impacting the field of medicine and rehabilitation and which specifically address impairment rating, disability determination, functional capacity evaluation, vocational evaluation and current trends in reimbursement and how the Americans with Disabilities Act of 1990 has changed the practice of medicine and rehabilitation.
Quarterly

12894 HELP Newsletter
Insurance Loss Control Association
PO Box 68700
Indianapolis, IN 46268
317-875-5250
FAX: 317-879-8408
ccarson@namic.org
http://www.insurancelosscontrol.org
Brock Bell, President
Daniel Finn, VP
Stig Ruxlow, Financial Secretary
Association news and activities.
Quarterly Founded: 1931
Circulation: 325
Printed in 2 colors on matte stock

12895 Highlights
American Association of Retired Persons
601 E Street NW
Washington, DC 20049-0002
202-434-2277
FAX: 202-434-6499
Lovola Burgess, Publisher
Offers information and updates on the association, tax information and legal statistics.
4 pages BiWeekly

12896 IOMA's Report on Hourly Compensation
Institute of Management & Administration
3 Park Avenue
30th Floor
New York, NY 10016-5902
212-244-0360
FAX: 212-564-0465
subserve@ioma.com www.ioma.com
RHC is a sister publication for IOMA's Report on Salary Surveys and takes compensation and salary dates from major surveys produced by firms like Watson Wyatt Data Services, the Big Six Accounting firms and local HR groups to show benefits and compensation managers the going rate for hourly workers in a variety of positions.

12897 Insurance Daily
SNL Financial
PO Box 2124
Charlottesvle, VA 22902-2124
434-977-1600
FAX: 434-977-4466
CustomerService@snl.com
www.snl.com
Mike Deane, Editor
Reid Nagle, Publisher
THe most timely and comprehensive news source on the insurance industry, goes beyond simply recapping relevant news from the prior day. This also includes updates on analyst coverage, earnings estimates, new filings, insider trades, ratings changes, dividend announcements, stock highlights, and earnings release and conference call dates.
3 pages Daily Founded: 1987

12898 Insurance Finance & Investment
Institutional Investor
488 Madison Avenue
New York, NY 10022-5702
212-224-3300
FAX: 212-224-3491 800-715-9195
ideas@institutionalinvestor.com
http://www.institutionalinvestor.com
Erik Kolk, Publisher
Chris Brown, CEO/President
Stuard Wise, Senior Editor
Nick Ferris, Marketing Director
Provides reviews of investment performance, financing strategies, overviews of ratings, and highlights of new issues. *$1495.00*
Monthly Founded: 1905

12899 Insurance Performance Graph
SNL Financial
PO Box 2124
Charlottesvle, VA 22902-2124
434-977-1600
FAX: 434-977-4466
subscriptions@snlnet.com
www.snl.com
Mike Deane, Editor
Matt Mueller, Editor
For publicly traded insurance companies and law, accounting and consulting firms. Compares the investment performance of an insurance company to a specific SNL index or to a selected peer group and the appropriate broad multi-industry index. Covers a 5-year period or the period beginning with the IPO date. *$399.00*
1 pages Monthly Founded: 1987

12900 Insurance Regulation
Wakeman Walworth
PO Box 7376
Alexandria, VA 22307-7376
703-768-9600
FAX: 703-768-9690
newsletters@statecapitals.com
http://statecapitals.com
Keyes Walworth, Publisher
The best way to track day to day changes and innovations at the state and level N covers, health insurance including HMOs, CHIP programs and the battle to increase health insurance benefits. Also covers life, automobile, homeowner, unemployment insurance, workers compensation and malpractice. *$245.00*
Weekly

12901 Insurance Weekly
SNL Financial
PO Box 2124
Charlottesville, VA 22902-2124
434-977-1600
FAX: 434-977-4466
subscriptions@snlnet.com
www.snl.com
Mike Deane, Editor
Reid Nagle, Publisher
Available in two forms either Life & Health Edition and Property & Casualty Edition. Provides a complete review of the latest insurance industry activity. Received either by email of fax, this contains industry and company specific news, M&A activity, index values, registration statements and ownerships filing. *$396.00*
15 pages Weekly Founded: 1987

12902 Journal for Insurance Compliance Professionals Newsletter
Association of Insurance Compliance Professionals
12100 Sunset Hills Road
Suite 130
Reston, VA 20190
703-234-4074
FAX: 703-435-4390
aicp@aicp.net www.aicp.net
Richard A Guggolz, Executive Director
Brady Smith, Editor
This Journal includes topical information for members, covering regulatory and industry issues, along with the latest techniques in filing and news from each Association Region and its Chapter.
Quarterly

12903 LIC Newsletter
Life Insurers Council
2300 Windy Ridge Parkway
Suite 600
Atlanta, GA 30339-8443
770-951-1770
FAX: 770-984-0441 188-275-5662
askloma@loma.org www.loma.org
Scott J Cipinko, Executive Director
Rose Hoyt, Administrative Assistant
Includes news and analysis about issues of concern to executives and those involved in operations and compliance in addition to LIC news, personals, and company activities.
Monthly

12904 Mealey's Catastrophic Loss
LexisNexis Mealey's
1018 W Ninth Avenue
Third Avenue
King of Prussia, PA 19406-1225
610-768-7800
FAX: 610-768-0880
mealeyinfo@lexisnexis.com
www.lexisnexis.com/mealeys
Tom Hagy, VP/General Manager
Maureen McGuire, Editorial Director
Gina Cappello, Editor
This report focuses on business interruption insurance claims in the aftermath of the Hurricane Katrina, September 11th, and other catastrophic loss tragedies. Additionally, the report will go beyond these claims and will offer important business interruption insurance coverage news related to computer viruses, computer failures, and natural disasters. *$1075.00*

100 pages Monthly Founded: 2001

12905 Mealey's Emerging Insurance Disputes
LexisNexis Mealey's
1018 W Ninth Avenue
Third Avenue
King of Prussia, PA 19406-1225
610-768-7800
FAX: 610-768-0880
mealeyinfo@lexisnexis.com
www.lexisnexis.com/mealeys

Tom Hagy, VP/General Manager
Maureen McGuire, Editorial Director
Gina Cappello, Editor

The report tracks new areas of coverage liability, novel policy applications, and conflicting policy language interpretations as they arise in insurance litigation. Some areas of coverage featured are: sexual harassment and discrimination, assault and battery, professional liability, patent and trademark infringement, construction defects, directors and officers claims, emotional distress, intentional acts, technology, and insurance business practices. *$1229.00*

100 pages Semi-Monthly Founded: 1996

12906 Mealey's Litigation Report: Asbestos
LexisNexis Mealey's
1018 W Ninth Avenue
Third Avenue
King of Prussia, PA 19406-1225
610-768-7800
FAX: 610-768-0880
mealeyinfo@lexisnexis.com
www.lexisnexis.com/mealeys

Tom Hagy, VP/General Manager
Maureen McGuire, Editorial Director
Bryan Redding, Editor

The report offers unsurpassed coverage of litigation arising from asbestos-related injury and death. Key issues include: massive class action settlements involving present and future claimants, state and federal verdicts, litigation experts, medical monitoring claims, suits against the tobacco industry, discovery battles, discovery rule decisions, insurance coverage rulings, and asbestos property decisions. *$1789.00*
100 pages Semi-Monthly Founded: 1984

12907 Mealey's Litigation Report: California Ins urance
LexisNexis Mealey's
1018 W Ninth Avenue
Third Avenue
King of Prussia, PA 19406-1225
610-768-7800
FAX: 610-768-0880
mealeyinfo@lexisnexis.com
www.lexisnexis.com/mealeys

Tom Hagy, VP/General Manager
Maureen McGuire, Editorial Director
Jennifer Hans, Editor

The Report focuses on ever-changing California and federal Ninth Circuit insurance coverage disputes and developments. Topics include California developments in bad faith litigation, earthquake damage coverage, disability insurance, products liability coverage, environmental insurance coverage, mold coverage. asbestos coverage, aviation litigation coverage, entertainment law and more. *$949.00*
100 pages Monthly Founded: 2001

12908 Mealey's Litigation Report: Disability Ins urance
LexisNexis Mealey's
1018 W Ninth Avenue
Third Avenue
King of Prussia, PA 19406-1225
610-768-7800
FAX: 610-768-0880
mealeyinfo@lexisnexis.com
www.lexisnexis.com/mealeys

Tom Hagy, VP/General Manager
Maureen McGuire, Editorial Director
Karen Miehle, Editor

This report tracks the burgeoning number of disputes involving complex disability coverage claims. Topics covered include: claims for chronic fatigue, chronic pain, stress, psychiatric disabilities, chemical dependency and risk of relapse, plus key issues like total disability, own occupation, bad faith, ERSA, class actions and much more. *$849.00*
100 pages Monthly Founded: 2000

12909 Mealey's Litigation Report: Insurance
LexisNexis Mealey's
1018 W Ninth Avenue
Third Avenue
King of Prussia, PA 19406-1225
610-768-7800
FAX: 610-768-0880
mealeyinfo@lexisnexis.com
www.lexisnexis.com/mealeys

Tom Hagy, VP/General Manager
Maureen McGuire, Editorial Director
Vivi Gorman, Editor
Shawn Rice, Co-Editor

The report tracks declaratory judgment actions regarding coverage for litigation arising from long-tail claims, including environmental contamination and latent damage and injury allegedly caused by asbestos, tox chemicals and fumes, lead, breast implants, medical devices, construction defects, and more. Key issues: allocation, occurrence, policy exclusion, choice of law, discovery, duty to defend, notice, trigger of coverage and known loss. *$2115.00*
100 pages Weekly Founded: 1984

12910 Mealey's Litigation Report: Insurance Frau d
LexisNexis Mealey's
1018 W Ninth Avenue
Third Avenue
King of Prussia, PA 19406-1225
610-768-7800
FAX: 610-768-0880
mealeyinfo@lexisnexis.com
www.lexisnexis.com/mealeys

Tom Hagy, VP/General Manager
Maureen McGuire, Editorial Director
Teresa Kent Zink, Editor

The report reviews civil and criminal cases arising from efforts by policyholders and third parties to defraud insurance carriers. Topics include false and fraudulent claims, arson, reverse bad faith, restitution, RICO, incontestability clauses, material misrepresentation, rescission, qui tam actions and fraud rings. Readers receive reports on schemes involving property & casualty, health care, automobile, life, homeowners, and workers' compensation fraud. *$839.00*
100 pages Monthly Founded: 1994

12911 NACA NEWS
National Association of Catastrophe Adjusters
PO Box 821864
North Richland Hills, TX 76182-1864
817-498-3466
FAX: 817-498-0480
nacatadj@aol.com
http://www.nacatadj.org

Lori Ringo, Executive Administrator

Quarterly Founded: 1976

12912 NFPA Update
National Fire Protection Association
1 Batterymarch Park
Quincy, MA 02169-7471
617-930-0100
FAX: 617-770-0700 800-344-3555

James M Shannon, President

Member newsletter with issues going to every member, providing standards information and association reports on events of interest to the entire membership.
Monthly

12913 Report on Property/Casualty Rates & Ratings
Institute of Management & Administration

3 Park Avenue
30th Floor
New York, NY 10001-2299
212-244-0360
FAX: 212-564-0465
subserve@ioma.com
http://www.ioma.com

Mr. Foster, CEO
Bowman Cox, Editor

Helps agents and brokers get competitive premium rates for their clients. *$389.00*
16 pages Monthly Founded: 1755

12914 Riskwatch
Public Risk Management Association
500 Montgomery Street
Suite 750
Alexandria, VA 22314
703-528-7701
FAX: 703-739-0200
info@primacentral.org
www.primacentral.org

Marshall Davies, Executive Director

Association and chapter news, resources and government affairs and job ads, all of which are relevant to public sector risk management professionals. *$130.00*
2 pages Monthly
Circulation: 2400
Mailing list available for rent
Printed in 2 colors on matte stock

12915 Surety Association of America
1101 Connecticut Avenue NW
Suite 800
Washington, DC 20036-4347
202-463-0600
FAX: 202-463-0606
information@surety.org
http://www.surety.org

Lynn Schubert, President
Mary Scutt, Editor
Mary Scutt, Circulation Manager

Statistical, rating, development and advisory organization for surety companies.
Founded: 1920
Circulation: 500

12916 UPDATE
Insurance Marketing Communications Association
PO Box 473054
Charlotte, NC 28247
704-755-5551
FAX: 704-543-6345
tseibert@imcanet.com
www.imcanet.com

September J Seibert, Executive Director

Contains reviews and previews of meetings, articles on communications issues and techniques, and news of IMCA members.
For Members Only

Magazines & Journals

12917 AHIP Solutions Directory Resource Directory of Health Plans

America's Health Insurance Plans
601 Pennsylvania Avenue NW
South Building, Suite 500
Washington, DC 20004
202-778-3200
FAX: 202-331-7487 877-291-2247
ahip@ahip.org www.ahip.org

Karen M Ignagni, President/CEO
Susan Pisano, VP Communications

More than 3,400 key executives listed, types of products offered such as HMO, PPO, POS, etc., company contact information, national enrollment by type of products, and national and state level enrollment data by company. There is also a CD-ROM availablie for $1,495.00
$492.00

12918 ASPPA Journal
American Society of Pension Professionals & Act
4245 N Fairfax Drive
Suite 750
Arlington, VA 22203
703-160-0512
FAX: 703-516-9308
asppa@asppa.org www.asppa.org

Brian H Graff, Executive Director
Geoff Brehm, Information Services Manager

A technical publication providing critical insight into legislative and regulatory developments. The ASPPA Journal also features technical analyses of benefit plan matters and information regarding ASPPA's education and examination program, membership activities, and conferences and workshops.
Bi-Monthly
Circulation: 5,000

12919 Actuarial Digest
Actuarial Digest Publishing Company
PO Box 1127
Ponte Vedra, FL 32004-1127
904-273-1245

Eric R Hubbard, CEO/President
Gene Hubbard, Editor

Covers fields such as life, group, health, reinsurance, pension/employee benefits, government regulations and educational institutions. *$24.00*
Quarterly Founded: 1982
Circulation: 15000
Printed in 4 colors on glossy stock

12920 Actuarial Studies in Non-Life Insurance
Peeters
3641 Locust Walk
Philadelphia, PA 19104-6218
215-670-0097
FAX: 215-898-0310
lemaire@wharton.upenn.edu
http://www.actuaries.org

Hans Buhlmann, President
Andrew Cairns, Editor
David G Hartman, Chairman

Promotes actuarial research and study and publishes the ASTIN Bulletin. *$65.00*
500 pages Quarterly Founded: 1957
Circulation: 3000

12921 Advisor Toady
2901 Telestar Court
Falls Church, VA 22042
703-770-8202

mleyes@naifa.org
www.advisortoday.com

Ayo Mseka, Editor-In-Chief
Maggie Leyes, Managing Editor
Helen Thompson, Editor
Rhoda Geasland, Production Director

The official publication of the National Association of Insurance and Financial Advisors. The service and advocacy news magazine for insurance agents and financial planners, write with style and authority about life and health insurance, financial advising, tax and legislative issues.
Founded: 1906

12922 American Journal of Law & Medicine
American Society of Law, Medicine and Ethics
765 Commonwealth Avenue
16th Floor
Boston, MA 02215
617-262-4990
FAX: 617-437-7596
info@aslme.org www.aslme.org

Benjamin W Moulton, JD, MPH, Executive VP/Executive Director
Ted Hutchinson, Publications Director

A law review fulfilling the need to improve communication between legal and medical professionals. Issues contain professional articales and case notes-on themes in health la wand policy, and on the legal, ethical, and economic aspects of medical practice, research, and education-and health law court decisions and book reviews.
$140.00
Annual

12923 Annuity Shopper
United States Annuities
8 Talmadge Dr
Monroe Twp, NJ 08831
732-521-5110
FAX: 732-521-5113 877-206-8141

Hersh Stern, CEO/Founder

Helps consumers purchase the safest and most reliable lifetime income annuities for their retirement. *$45.00*
Bi-annually Founded: 1986

12924 Beacon
American Association of Dental Consultants
10032 Wind Hill Drive
Greenville, IN 47124
812-923-2600
FAX: 812-923-2900
info@aadc.org www.aadc.org

Judy Salisbury, Executive Director

Informs members about the latest issues affecting dentistry and dental benefits. *$1.50*

3x/year
Circulation: 500

12925 Benefits & Compensation Solutions Magazine
Field Media Publishing
200 S Main Street
Alpharetta, GA 30004
770-475-9770
FAX: 678-990-5565
www.bcsolutionsmag.com

Doug Field, CEO/Publisher
Steve Milano, Editor

A business magazine that addresses real-world issues by delivering best-practice solutions and information to those involved in benefits and compensation decisions. Free to members.
Monthly

12926 Benefits Quarterly
Int'l Society of Certified Employee Benfit Special
18700 W Bluemound Road
PO Box 209
Brookfield, WI 53008-0209
262-786-8771
FAX: 262-786-8650
iscebs@iscebs.org www.iscebs.org

Daniel W Graham, CEBS, Executive Director
Sandra L Becker, CEBS, Director of Operations
Edith K Biwer, Administrative Manager
Pamela White Wu, CEBS, Chapter Services/Development Dir

Highly respected journal that offers comprehensive coverage of the latest trends and innovations in benefits and compensation. ISCEBS members receive this as a member service. Also available on an annual subscription basis
Quarterly Founded: 1981
Circulation: 15000

12927 Benefits and Compensation Digest
International Foundation of Employee Benefit Plans
18700 W Bluemound Road
Brookfield, WI 53045
262-786-6700
FAX: 262-786-8670 www.ifebp.org

Michael Wilson, CEO

Combines the insightful atricles previously published in the Employee Benefits Journal with monthly news previously published in the Employee Benefits Journal with monthly news previously seen in the Employee Benefits.
Monthly
Circulation: 35000

12928 Best's Review
AM Best Company
Ambest Road
Oldwick, NJ 08858
908-439-2200
FAX: 908-439-3296
editor_br@bestreview.com
www.ambest.com

Marilyn Ostermiller, Editor
Jill Kardor, Advertising Representative

Offers insightful coverage of issues and trends in the industry. A must read for the insurance professional. *$20.00*

150 pages Monthly Founded: 1899
Circulation: 42732

12929 Bestweek

AM Best Company
Ambest Road
Oldwick, NJ 08858
908-439-2200
FAX: 908-439-3363
bestweek@ambest.com
www.ambest.com

Arthur Snyder, Publisher

The industry's leading news publication that includes Best's Rating Monitor and online access to Statistical Studies, Special Reports, and real time and archived news stories. *$665.00*

Weekly

12930 Broker World

Insurance Publications
9404 Reeds Road
PO Box 11310
Overland Park, KS 66207-1010
913-383-9191
FAX: 913-383-1247
info@brokerworldmag.com
www.brokerworldmag.com

Sharon A Chace, Editor
John H Coleman, III, Managing Director
Stephen P Howard, Publisher
Jennifer K Hooker, Marketing Coordinator
Patty L Godfrey, Circulation Director

Founded, focused and edited to specifically address the brokerage marketplace and the unique informational needs of independent life and health producers who select the products best suited to their clients' needs from a variety of companies and marketers. *$6.00*

146 pages Monthly Founded: 1980
Circulation: 29000
Printed in 4 colors on glossy stock

12931 Business Insurance

Crain Communications
360 N Michigan Avenue
Chicago, IL 60601-3806
312-495-5231
FAX: 312-280-3174 800-678-9595
rcoccia@BusinessInsurance.com
www.businessinsurance.com

Martin J Ross, Publisher
Paul D Winston, Editorial Director
Regis Coccia, Editor
Ronnie I Drachman, Communications Director
John Azua, Circulation Manager

Serves business executives who are repsonsible for the purchase and administration of corporate insurance/self insurance programs, encompassing both property and liability insurance and employee benfits programs, including life, health and pensions. *$97.00*

45 pages Weekly Founded: 1967
Circulation: 45700 $89y per M.
Printed in on matte stock

12932 CPCU Journal

Chartered Property Casualty Underwriter Society
720 Providence Road
Malvern, PA 19355
610-512-2728
FAX: 610-251-2780 800-932-2728
membercenter@cpcusociety.org
www.cpcusociety.org

Michele A Ianetti, Editor
James R Marks, President

Articles take an in-depth, practical look at diverse insurance topics including legislative issues, management concerns, financial questions, and key trends in property and casualty insurance coverage. CPCU Journal is an online publication available on our website.

Quarterly
Circulation: 150,000 30,000 names $210 per M.
Printed in 4 colors on matte stock

12933 Contingencies

American Academy of Actuaries
1100 17th Street NW
7th floor
Washington, DC 20036
202-223-8196
FAX: 202-872-1948
webmaster@actuary.org
www.contingencies.org

Steve Sullivan, Editor
Joe Vallina, Mktg/Publications Production Mgr
Peter Perkins, President
Kevin T Cronin, Executive Director

Explores the issues driving the insurance and financial services industries. It is written for actuaries as well as general readers with an interest in a range of financial and social concerns. *$24.00*

Bi-Monthly Founded: 1965
Printed in 4 colors on glossy stock

12934 Contingency Planning & Management

Witter Publishing Corporation
20 Commerce Street
Flemington, NJ 08822
908-788-0343
FAX: 908-788-3782
info@witterpublishing.com
http://www.witterpublishing.com

Bob Joudanin, Publisher
Paul Kirvan, Editor-in-Chief
Mike Viscel, Production Manager
Courtney Witter, Circulation Manager
Andrew Witter, President

Serves the fields of financial/banking, manufacturing industrial, transportation, utilities, telecommunications, health care, government, insurance and other allied fields. *$275.00*

Monthly Founded: 1987
Circulation: 62000

12935 Crittenden Excess & Surplus Insider

Crittenden Publishing
250 Bel Marin Keys Boulevard
PO Box 1150, #A
Novato, CA 94948-1150
415-382-2400
FAX: 415-382-2476
ins@crittendenonline.com
www.crittendenonline.com

Robert Fink, Publisher

Focuses on new products, trade literature, industry news, and personnel changes. *$411.00*

Weekly
Circulation: 20,000

12936 EXAMINER Magazine

Society of Financial Examiners
174 Grace Boulevard
Altamonte Springs, FL 32714
407-682-4930
FAX: 407-682-3175 800-787-7633
info@sofe.org www.sofe.org

Paula Keyes, Executive Director

A quarterly magazine offering association news and information. *$65.00*

Quarterly Founded: 1973
Circulation: 2500
Printed in 2 colors on glossy stock

12937 Fraternal Advantage

National Fraternal Congress of America
1240 Iroquois Avenue
Suite 300
Naperville, IL 60563-8476
630-355-6633
FAX: 630-355-0042
nfca@nfcanet.org www.nfcanet.org

Anthony Snyder, Communications Director

The quarterly publication for the member-societies of the national Fraternal Congress of America.

Quarterly Founded: 2003
Circulation: 2000
Printed in 4 colors on glossy stock

12938 GAMA International Journal

GAMA International
2901 Telestar Court
Suite 140
Falls Church, VA 22042-1205
703-708-8184
FAX: 703-770-8182 800-345-2687
rwolpert@gama.naifa.org
www.gamaweb.com

Rion Wolpert, Managing Editor
Jeff Hughes, CEO
Miriam Hankins, Marketing Director

Devoted to the professional development of leaders in the insurance and financial services industry. *$300.00*

56 pages Founded: 1951
Circulation: 5000
Printed in 4 colors on glossy stock

12939 Health Insurance Underwriters

National Association of Health Underwriters
2000 N 14th Street
Suite 450
Arlington, VA 22201
703-276-0220
FAX: 703-841-7797
editor@nahu.org www.nahu.org

Jim Hostetler, VP Communications/Executive Editor
Martin Carr, Communication Dir/Managing Editor

Covers technology, legislation and product news-everything that affects how health insurance professionals do business *$40.00*

Monthly Founded: 1930
Circulation: 30,000
Mailing list available for rent 19000 names $350 per M.
Printed in 4 colors on glossy stock

12940 Independent Agent Magazine
Independent Insurance Agents & Brokers of America
127 Peyton Street
Alexandria, VA 22314
703-683-4422
FAX: 703-683-7556 800-221-7917
katie.butler@iiaba.net www.iiaa.org

Dave Evans, Publisher
Katie Butler, Editor-in-Chief

Regular issue features include agency managemetn and automation, insurance products and markets, legislative issues, and analysis of industry trends. *$24.00*
Monthly
Circulation: 57,814

12941 Inquiry
1807 Glenview Rd
Ste 100
Glenview, IL 60025-2944
847-724-9280
FAX: 847-729-2199
inquiry@hartleydata.com
www.inquiryjournal.org

Katherine Swartz, Editor
Ronny Frishman, Managing Editor

Seeks to contribute to the continued improvement in the nation's health care system by providing a thoughtful forum for the communication and discussion of relevant public policy issues, innovative concepts, and original research and demonstration in the areas of health care organization, provision, and financing. *$85.00*
Quarterly Founded: 1963
Mailing list available for rent 1000 names $250 per M.

12942 Insurance & Technology
CMP Media
11 West 19th Street
New York, NY 10011
212-928-8400
FAX: 212-600-3045
vporter@cmp.com
www.insurancetech.com

Katherine Burger, Editorial Director
Felicia Aronov, Publisher
Sophie Chan, Production Manager
Les Kovach, Managing Editor

Information on how technology can help life, health, property and casualty and multi-line insurance companies perform more productively, profitably, and competitively. *$65.00*
Monthly
Circulation: 18513

12943 Insurance Advocate
PO Box 14367
Cincinatti, OH 45250-0367
908-859-0893

cluke@nuco.com
http://cms.nationunderwriter.com

Chris Luke, Publisher
Phil Gusman, Editor
Eric V Gilkey, Assistant Editor
Steve Acunto, Associate Publisher

Covers the people and issues affecting the insurance industry in New York, New Jersey, Connecticut and beyond. Also the source for new markets and coverages, financial trends, legislative isssues, M&A, insurance law and industry developments. *$59.00*
Weekly Founded: 1889
Circulation: 7200
Printed in 4 colors on glossy stock

12944 Insurance Conference Planner
Primedia
745 Fifth Avenue
NY, NY 10151
212-745-0100
FAX: 212-745-0121
information@primedia.com
http://primedia.com

Regina Baraban, Editor
Melissa Fromento, Publisher
Kelly P. Conlin, CEO

Meeting and incentive strategies for the financial services industry. *$57.00*
148 pages Founded: 1989
Circulation: 9000
Printed in 4 colors on glossy stock

12945 Insurance Forum
Insurance Forum
PO Box 245
Ellettsville, IN 47429-245
812-876-6502
888-876-9590
help@naic.org
www.theinsuranceforum.com

Joseph M Belth, Editor
Ann I Belth, Business Manager
Jeffrey E Belth, Circulation Manager

A monthly periodical directed at persons with a professional interest in the insurance business. *$90.00*
Monthly Founded: 1974
Printed in on glossy stock

12946 Insurance Insight
Professional Independent Insurance Agents of Ill.
4360 Wabash Avenue
Springfield, IL 62711
217-793-6660
FAX: 217-793-6744 800-628-6436
info@piiai.org www.piiai.org

Laura Richter, VP Communications/Editor
Dennis Garrett, VP Marketing/Membership
Mark Kuchar, CPA, CFO
Mike Tate, CAE, Chief Operating Officer

Features articles that are relevant to the Illinois insurance industry, and includes topics such as industry news, technology, markets and coverages, financial planning, sales and marketing, state and federal issues, agency management, The Middleton Letter, and education. *$65.00*
68 pages Monthly Founded: 1993
Circulation: 2500

12947 Insurance Journal West
3570 Camino Del Rio N
Suite 200
San Diego, CA 92108
619-584-1100
FAX: 619-584-1200 800-897-9965
info@insurancejournal.com
www.insurancejournal.com

Mark Wells, Publisher
Mitch Dunford, Chief Operating Officer
Katie Robley, Circulation Manager
Suzie Song, Marketing Manager
Andrea Ortega-Wells, Editor-In-Chief

Insurance Journal is written for the independent agent and broker. Insurance Journal West covers California and the western states, while Insurance Journal Texas/South Central covers Texas, Arkansas, Oklahoma & Louisiana. We cover legal issues, people, markets, regulations and legistation, the very things that affect our readers. *$58.00*
Founded: 1923
Circulation: 40000
Printed in 4 colors on matte stock

12948 Insurance Loss Control Association Newsletter
3601 Vincennes Rd
Indianapolis, IN 46268
317-875-5250
FAX: 317-879-8408
ccarson@namic.org
http://www.insurancelosscontrol.org

Raquel DeLaRosa, Administrative Assistant
Brock Bell, President
Daniel Finn, VP

Quarterly newsletter offers editorial of interest to loss control professionals. Regular features and departments.
Founded: 1931
Circulation: 250
Printed in 2 colors on matte stock

12949 Insurance Networking
SourceMedia
550 W Van Buren
Suite 1100
Chicago, IL 60607
312-913-1334
FAX: 312-913-1366
frank.cerne@tfn.com
www.insurancenetworking.com

Pat Speer, Editor-In-Chief
Andrew Rowe, Publisher
Therese Rutkowski, Managing Editor
Lisa Tully, Marketing Manager
Joe Madaj, Owner

A trusted source for information on how technology is being implemented to support insurers' strategic business objective, providing insightful analysis of-and case studies on-how technology is being innovatively utilized to automate critical processes. *$65.00*
66 pages Monthly Founded: 1997
Circulation: 25300
Printed in 4 colors on glossy stock

12950 International Insurance Monitor
Shea-Haarman Companies
25-35 Beechwood Avenue
PO Box 9001
Mount Vernon, NY 10552-9001
914-699-2020
FAX: 914-699-2025

Stephen H Acunto, Publisher

Features information regarding trends, statistical reviews, new legislation and market developments. *$25.00*
Quarterly
Circulation: 2,200

12951 Journal of Healthcare Risk Management
American Society for Healthcare Risk Management
1 N Franklin
Chicago, IL 60606
312-422-3840
FAX: 312-422-4580 www.aha.org

Deborah Sprindzunas, Executive Director
$80.00

Circulation: 4500
Mailing list available for rent 4400 names

12952 Journal of Insurance Medicine
American Academy of Insurance Medicine

1290 Broadway
15th Floor
Denver, CO 80203-5699
303-446-8400
FAX: 303-813-2049
info@aaimedicine.org
http://www.aaimedicine.org/

Nina C Smith, President
Richard E Braun, VP
Nigel K Roberts, Editor

Offers information and legislative updates for people in the medical insurance field.
Quarterly Founded: 1889

12953 Journal of Law, Medicine & Ethics
American Society of Law, Medicine and Ethics
765 Commonwealth Avenue
16th Floor
Boston, MA 02215
617-262-4990
FAX: 617-437-7596
info@aslme.org www.aslme.org

Benjamin W Moulton, JD, MPH, Executive VP/Executive Director
Ted Hutchinson, Publications Director

Provides articles on such timely topics as health care quality and access, managed care, pain, relief, genetics, child/maternal health, reproductive health, informed consent, assisted dying, ethics committees, HIV/AIDS, and public health. *$140.00*
Quarterly
Circulation: 4,500+

12954 Journal of Sport and Social Issues
Sage Publications
805-499-9774
FAX: 805-499-0871 800-818-7243
journals@sagepub.com
www.sagepublications.com
Brings together the latest research, discussion, and analysis on contemporary sport issues such as race, media, gender, economics, drugs, recruiting, injuries, and youth sports.
Quarterly

12955 LIMRA Marketfacts
LIMRA International
300 Day Hill Road
PO Box 208
Windsor, CT 06141-208
860-688-3358
FAX: 860-298-9555
bragaglia@limra.com
http://www.limra.com

Brad Ragaglia, Editor
Richard Wecker, Chief Executive Officer

Features in-depth, timeless articles devoted to the critical issues of the day, including such topics as distribution, technology, marketing strategies, retirement, globalization, demographics, financial integration and products and services. *$500.00*

Circulation: 7500

12956 LIMRA Vision
LIMRA International
300 Day Hill Road
Windsor, CT 06095-1783
860-688-3358
FAX: 860-298-9555 800-235-4672

Brad Ragaglia, Managing Editor
Richard Wecker, Chief Executive Officer

Content focuses on leadership styles and concepts, business management concerns and 21st century strategical positioning. Ideas are presented from top business leaders in a variety of industries around the globe, as well as information from today's cutting-edge sales associates. Includes full-length features, regular columns and shorter idea pieces, product reviews, and information on technology. *$59.96*
Founded: 1916
Circulation: 10000

12957 Leader's Edge Magazine
Council of Insurance Agents & Brokers
701 Pennsylvania Avenue NW
Suite 750
Washington, DC 20004-2608
202-783-4400
FAX: 202-783-4410
pat.wade@ciab.com www.ciab.com

Rick Pullen, Editor-in-Chief
Pat Wade, Subscription Services
Ken Crerar, President

Comprised of vital information and news for the industry of insurance agents and brokers. *$100.00*
Bi-Monthly

12958 Leaders Magazine
Insurance Publications
98 Dennis Drive
Lexington, KY 40503-2915
859-277-8059
FAX: 859-277-8059

Fred Kissling Jr, Editor *$12.00*
84 pages Monthly Founded: 1938

12959 Liability & Insurance Week
JR Publishing
PO Box 6654
McLean, VA 22106-6654
703-532-2235
FAX: 703-532-2236
jvreistrup@erols.com

John Reistrup, Publisher

Reports on political, legislative and regulatory actions affecting the insurance and legal industries. *$545.00*
48 per year

12960 Life & Health Advisor
JonHope Communications
71 Emerson Road
PO Box 613
Walpole, MA 02081
508-668-8025
FAX: 508-668-8056 888-578-8025
pkelley@lifehealth.com
www.lifehealth.com

Sally O'Connell, Publisher/Ad Sales Manager
Peter Kelley, Editor
Deb Glynn, Accounting
Liz Kelley, Administration

Provides critical information and news analysis of this rapidly changing marketplace. Represents a broad constituency of advisors from all channels: life agents, brokers, attorneys, CPA's, registered reps and stock brokers who are selling the entire spectrum of financial products, from life insurance, annuities and disability, to long term care insurance, mutual funds and life settlements.
Monthly Founded: 1995
Circulation: 27000

12961 Life Insurance Selling
Pfingsten Publishing
1801 Park 270 Drive
Suite 550
Saint Louis, MO 63146
314-824-5500
FAX: 341-824-5640
lis@pfpublish.com
www.lifeinsuranceselling.com

Charles K Hirsch, CLU, VP Publisher
Gordon Bess, FLMI, Editor
Brian D Baetz, CLU, Associate Editor
Andy Strasser, Marketing Manager
Nancy Leape, Circulation

Designed to help life insurance sellers. *$28.00*
160 pages Monthly Founded: 1926

12962 Life and Health Insurance Sales Magazines
Rough Notes Company
11690 Technology Drive
Carmel, IN 46032-5600
317-821-1600
FAX: 317-816-1055 800-321-1909
rnc@roughnotes.com
www.roughnotes.com

Tom McCoy, Editor-In-Chief
Nancy Doucette, Senior Editor
Elisabeth Boone, CPCU, Associate Editor

For life and health agents, general agents, managers and brokers with prospects to culivate and clients to serve. Accepts advertising.
48 pages Monthly Founded: 1878

12963 Long-Term Care Insurance Sales Strategies
Sales Creators
3835 E Thousand Oaks Boulevard
Suite 336
Westlake Village, CA 91362
818-597-3205
FAX: 818-597-3206 888-599-5997
jslome@ltcsales.com
http://www.ltcsales.com

Jesse Sloame, Publisher/President
Mindy Hartman, Ad Director

Content covers successful sales approaches, new and unexplored marekts, industry trends, and upcoming training seminars. *$24.00*
Quarterly Founded: 1998
Circulation: 7500

12964 Medical Malpractice News
45 Leveroni Court
Suit 204
Navato, CA 94949-5727
415-382-2400
FAX: 415-382-2476 800-421-3483

12965 Momentum
Metropolitan Life Insurance Company
1 Madison Avenue
New York, NY 10010-3687
212-604-4440
www.metlife.com
Magazine covering the Metropolitan Life Insurance Company.
Monthly Founded: 1970

12966 NRRA News
National Risk Retention Association
4248 Park Glen Road
Minneapolis, MN 55416-4758
952-284-4643
FAX: 952-929-1318 800-999-4505
jharrington@harringtoncompany.com
www.captive.com

Judith Harrington, Editor *$195.00*

Quarterly
Circulation: 250,000

12967 National Underwriter Life & Health Financial Services Edition
33-41 Newark Street
2nd Floor
Hoboken, NJ 07030
201-526-1230
FAX: 201-526-1260
spiontek@nuco.com
http://cms.nationalunderwriter.com

Stephen Piontek, Editor-In-Chief
Jim Connolly, Senior Editor

Uniquely positioned to provider producers, brokers, marketers and company executives with timely, insightful information. Each week, identifies, analyzes and comments on the latest trends and developments for their significance to the market-giving our readers the information they need to make critical business decisions.
Weekly

12968 National Underwriter: Life & Health Insurance Edition
National Underwriter Company
5081 Olympic Boulevard
Erlanger, KY 41018
859-922-2100
FAX: 800-874-1916 800-543-0874
nulife@IX.netcom.com
www.nuco.com

Thomas Slattery, Publisher
Charlie Smith, Chief Executive Officer

Offers features on agent activities, stocks and marketing, brokers and financial planners, trade meetings, business trends and outside developments in the industry. *$75.00*
Weekly
Circulation: 48,5070

12969 National Underwriter: Property & Casualty Risk & Benefits Management
National Underwriter Company
5081 Olympic Boulevard
Erlanger, KY 41018
859-922-2100
FAX: 800-874-1916 800-543-0874
webmaster@nuco.com
http://www.nuco.com

Thomas Slattery, Publisher
Charlie Smith, Chief Executive Officer

Covers industry trends, risk management, state and federal legislation, and judicial affairs. *$149.00*
Weekly Founded: 1897
Circulation: 485070

12970 PIA Magazine-Connecticut
25 Chamberlain Street
Glenmont, NY 12077-4835
518-434-3111
FAX: 518-434-2342 800-424-4244
pia@piaonline.org
http://www.piaonline.org

Kenneth Bessette, President/CEO
Lisa Lannon, Managing Editor
Athena Hoesten, Marketing Coordinator

Publication is written for Connecticut independent insurance agents specializing in property and casualty coverage.
Monthly
Circulation: 4000

12971 POA Bulletin/Merritt Risk Management News and Review
POA Publishing
1625 Prince Street
Alexandria, VA 22314-2818
703-519-6200
FAX: 703-519-6299 877-663-4890
asis@asisonline.org
http://www.asisonline.org

Michael E. Knoke, Managing Editor
Sherry Harowitz, Editor-In-Chief
Denny White, Director/Publishing

Editorial content is designed to keep security managers and risk managers abreast of legal, legislative and insurance issues, and contains features that identify security and risk management trends and present analysis of insurance coverage and needs. *$690.00*
Quarterly Founded: 1955
Circulation: 3400

12972 Proceedings
Conference of Consulting Actuaries
1110 W Lake Cook Road
Suite 235
Buffalo Grove, IL 60089-1968
847-999-9088
FAX: 847-419-9091
conference@ccactuaries.org
www.ccactuaries.org

Rita K DeGraaf, Executive Director
Keith G Stewart, Director of Operations
Patricia D Johnson, Project Manager
Matthew D Noncek, Member Services Manager

The professional journal of the Conference of Consulting Actuaries. Promotes the interchange of information among actauries and the various actuarial organizations, and to keep its publics informed of the viewpoints and activities of the professional consulting actuary. *$95.00*
500 pages Founded: 1950
Circulation: 1,200

12973 Professional Agent
Association of Professional Insurance Agents
400 N Washington Street
Alexandria, VA 22314-2312
703-836-9340
FAX: 703-836-1279
piainfo@pianet.org
http://www.pianet.com

Michael P Grace, President
Anne R Grant, Publisher
Leonard Brevik, Executive VP
Alexi Papandon, Marketing Director
Ted Besesparis, Vice President

Magazine for the insurance professional. *$24.00*
65 pages Monthly Founded: 1931
Circulation: 35000

12974 Property/Casualty Insurance
National Association of Mutual Insurance Companies
3601 Vincennes Road
PO Box 68700
Indianapolis, IN 46268
317-875-5250
FAX: 317-879-8408
service@namic.org
http://www.namic.org

Bart Anderson, Publisher
Laura Biddle-Bruckman, Managing Editor
Matt Keating, Editor

Highlights insurance industry news, personnel announcements, industry events, and new products in the field. *$20.00*
Monthly Founded: 1895
Circulation: 2500

12975 Public Risk
Public Risk Management Association
500 Montgomery Street
Suite 750
Alexandria, VA 22314
703-528-7701
FAX: 703-739-0200
info@primacentral.org
www.primacentral.org

Jim Hirt, Executive Director
Jon Ruzan, Editor

Magazine exclusively targeting risk management practitioners in the public sector: state and local governments. *$130.00*
1 Year 10 Issue Founded: 1978
Circulation: 8250

12976 Resource Magazine
Life Office Management Association
2300 Windy Ridge Parkway
Suite 600
Atlanta, GA 30339-8443
770-951-1770
FAX: 770-984-0441 800-275-5662
resource@loma.org www.loma.org

Thomas P Donaldson, President/CEO

Covers every topic of interest to management of insurance and financial services companies.
Monthly

12977 Risk & Insurance
LRP Publications
747 Dresher Road, Suite 500
Dept 640, PO Box 980
Horsham, PA 19044-0980
215-840-0912
FAX: 215-784-0275 800-341-7874
custserv@lrp.com
www.riskandinsurance.com

Matthew Kahn, Publisher
Jack Roberts, Editor-in-Chief
Cyril Tuohy, Managing Editor

Provides business executives and insurance professionals with the insight, information and strategies they need to mitigate challenging business risks. Published monthly and semi-monthly in April when publish two special editions focusing on the Risk and Insurance Management Society's annual RIMS conference.
Monthly Founded: 1977
Circulation: 51541

12978 Risk Management
Risk Management Society Publishing
1065 Avenue Of The Americas
13th Floor
New York, NY 10018-5637
212-214-4556
FAX: 212-922-0716
tdonovan@rims.org www.rims.org

Ted Donovan, Publisher
Bill Coffin, Editor-In-Chief
Morgan O'Rouke, Managing Editor
Jared Wade, Editor
Callie Nelson, Circulation Manager

The premier source of analysis, insight and news for corporate risk managers. RM strives to explore existing and emerging techniques and concepts that address the needs of those who are tasked with protecting the physical, financial, human and intellectual assets of their companies. *$64.00*

Monthly Founded: 1950
Circulation: 17000

12979 Risk Report
International Risk Management Institute
12222 Merit Drive
#1450
Dallas, TX 75251-3205
972-960-7693
FAX: 972-960-6037
info@irmi.com http://www.irmi.com

Robert A Bregman, Editor
Jack P Gibson, President

Helps risk and insurance professionals in both of these areas with analysis and interpretation of the latest innovations in insurance *$219.00*

Monthly Founded: 1987

12980 Rough Notes
Rough Notes Company
11690 Technology Drive
Carmel, IN 46032-5600
317-582-1600
FAX: 317-816-1000 800-428-4384
rnc@roughnotes.com
http://www.roughnotes.com

Tom McCoy, Editor
Evelyn Egan, Production Manager
Thomas A McCoy, Editor-in-Chief
Tina Stemler, Circulation Manager
Walter Gdowski, Chief Executive Officer

Monthly sales and management magazine for property and casualty insurance agents. *$357.00*

120 pages Monthly Founded: 1878 45000 names $150 per M.
Printed in 4 colors on glossy stock

12981 Round the Table Magazine
Million Dollar Round Table
325 W Touhy Avenue
Park Ridge, IL 60068-4265
847-926-6378
FAX: 847-518-8921
editor@mdrt.org www.mdrt.org

Michelle Vallet, Editor
Kathyrn F Keuneke, Associate Editor
John Prast, Executive VP

Productivity ideas, reaching your clients, professional knowledge, motivational stories, all this to share with clients and to help you make the sale. *$14.00*

Bi-Monthly

12982 Standard
Standard Publishing Corporation
155 Federal Street
13th Floor
Boston, MA 02110-1727
617-457-0600
FAX: 617-457-0608
e.ayers@spcpub.com
http://www.standardpublishingcorp.com

Erin Ayers, Editor
John Cross, Publisher
John Cross, President

Content focuses on all aspects involving legislative and regulatory developments at the state and federal levels, court decisions, trade association positions and more. Coverage includes news, feature articles and opinion pieces, with an emphasis on property/casualty insurance. *$80.00*

Weekly Founded: 1870
Circulation: 5000 13,000 names $125 per M.

12983 Today's Insurance Woman
National Association of Insurance Women
1847 E 15th Street
PO Box 4410
Tulsa, OK 74159-0410
918-744-5195
FAX: 918-743-1968 naiw@aol.com

Melissa Carlson, Editor

Focus is on business careers, legislation, leadership, management and social issues facing women in the industry. *$15.00*

Bi-Monthly
Circulation: 12,887

12984 Tort and Insurance Law Journal
American Bar Association
321 north park street
Tort and Insurance Practice Section
Chicago, IL 60610-4497
312-988-5000
FAX: 312-988-6281
http://www.abanet.org

Jenny Gibbs, CFO
Wendy Smith, Editor

Scholarly journal on current or emerging issues of national scope in the fields of tort and insurance law. *$50.00*

Quarterly Founded: 1878

12985 Underwriter's Report
National Underwriter Company
5081 Olympic Boulevard
Erlanger, KY 41018
859-922-2100
FAX: 800-874-1916 800-543-0874

Tom Fowler, VP
Charlie Smith, Chief Executive Officer

12986 Underwriters' Report
National Underwriters Company
5081 Olympic Boulevard
Erlanger, KY 41018
859-922-2100
FAX: 800-874-1916 800-543-0874

Roy Pasini, Editor

Offering complete information on fire, casualty and life insurance every week. *$45.00*

40 pages Weekly
Circulation: 5000

12987 Worker's Compensation Monitor
LRP Publications
360 Hiatt Drive
West Palm Beach Gardens, FL 33418
561-622-6520
FAX: 561-622-0757
custserv@lrp.com http://www.lrp.com

Nancy Grover, Managing Editor
Leslie Lake, Managing Editor
Josh Clifton, Editor

Information on worker's compensation laws. *$210.00*

Monthly Founded: 1977

Trade Shows

12988 AADC Annual Spring Workshop
American Association of Dental Consultants
10032 Wind Hill Drive
Greenville, IN 47124
812-923-2600
FAX: 812-923-2900
info@aadc.org www.aadc.org

Judith K Salisbury, Executive Director

These meetings provide a forum to discuss topical subjects involving the Dental Benefit Industry and Clinical Dentistry as a whole. AADC presenters and lectures are recognized as leaders in the Dental Industry.

300 Attendees Annual/May

12989 AHIP Annual Meeting
America's Health Insurance Plans
601 Pennsylvania Avenue NW
South Building, Suite 500
Washington, DC 20004
202-778-3200
FAX: 202-331-7487 877-291-2247
ahip@ahip.org www.ahip.org

Karen M Ignagni, President/CEO
Susan Pisano, VP Communications

This meeting continues to be the nation's leading health care conference where all segments of the health insurance industry convene to share perspectives on, and analysis of, the most recent developments in health care.

300 Attendees

12990 AHOU Annual Conference
Association of Home Office Underwriters
22300 Windy Ridge Parkway
Suite 600
Atlanta, GA 30339-8443
770-984-3715
FAX: 770-984-6418
ahou@loma.org www.ahou.org

Jennifer Richards, Convention Vice President
Lee Janecek, Convention Assistant VP

Providing career development, underwriting solutions, the latest medical issues and valuable insight to keep you prepared.

Annual/October Founded: 2001

12991 AIA Annual Conference
Aviation Insurance Association
14 W 3rd Street
Suite 200
Kansas City, MO 64105-6301
816-221-8488
FAX: 816-472-7765
shelby@aiaweb.org www.aiaweb.org

Gary Hicks, Executive Director
Shelby Diltz, Conference Director

To help improve the skills and knowledge of industry professionals, forums for discussions, examination and exchange of ideas on issues facing all participants in the aviation insurance business, including purchases, providers and the flying public.

Annual/April-May

12992 AICP Annual Conference
Association of Insurance Compliance Professionals
12100 Sunset Hills Road
Suite 130
Reston, VA 20190
703-234-4074
FAX: 703-435-4390
aicp@aicp.net www.aicp.net

Richard A Guggolz, Executive Director
Elaine Bailey, Conference Chair

Learning opportunities for a broad range of compliance professionals, sessions for beginners and seasoned professionals and networking opportunities with colleagues, peers and state regulators.

680 Attendees Annual/Sept-Oct

12993 ASPPA Annual Conference
American Society of Pension Professionals & Act
4245 N Fairfax Drive
Suite 750
Arlington, VA 22203
703-160-0512
FAX: 703-516-9308
meetings@asppa.org www.asppa.org

Brian H Graff, Executive Director
Joanne Lawrence Smith, Director of

Meetings
Kim Graumann, Meetings Coordinator
Rachel Wallmuller, Meetings Coordinator

Multitude of exhibits, sponsorships marketing opportunities to help grow your business. The conference offers 20 hours of ASPPA continuing education credit.
Annual/November

12994 ASSE Annual Conference & Exposition
American Society of Safety Engineers
1800 E Oakton Street
Des Plaines, IL 60018-2187
847-699-2929
FAX: 847-296-3769
asse@heiexpo.com www.asse.org
Tracy Flaherty, Meetings Coordinator
Featuring more than 200 sessions, an exposition with 300 exhibitors, special pre- and post-conference seminars, conference proceedings on CD, numerous networking events and more! Learn the latest strategies to expand your knowledge base and network with other safety, health and environmental professionals
3500 Attendees Annual/June

12995 Advanced Life Underwriting Association
1922 F Street NW
Washington, DC 20006-4302
202-331-6099
FAX: 202-331-2164
Karen G Keating, Director
22 booths.
1.1M Attendees February

12996 American Association of Managing General Agents Annual Meeting
American Association of Managing General Agents
9140 Ward Parkway
Kansas City, MO 64114-3306
816-444-3500
FAX: 816-444-0330
Jeanne Corlew-Knox, Director Meetings
Annual meeting and exhibits for managing general agents of insurance companies.
1000 Attendees Annual

12997 American Society Pension Actuaries
4245 N Fairfax Drive
Suite 750
Arlington, VA 22203
703-160-0512
FAX: 703-516-9308
aspa@aspa.org www.aspa.org
Becky Panneton, Managing Director
Brian Graff, Executive Director
The nation's leading source of pension industry education, conducts a series of informative conferences and workshops throughout the United States. These conferences and workshops provide pension and retirement professionals with an outstanding source of continuing education, networking, and the ability to inetrface with government and industry leaders.
1M Attendees October

12998 American Society for Healthcare Risk Management Convention
American Society for Healthcare Risk Management
American Hospital Association
1 N Franklin
Chicago, IL 60606
312-422-3840
FAX: 312-422-4580 www.aha.org
Deborah Sprindzunas, Executive Director

Annual convention and exhibits of health care industry risk management equipment, supplies and services.
Annual

12999 American Society of CLU and CHFC Annual Conference
American Society of CLU and CHFC
270 S Bryn Mawr Avenue
Suite 2
Bryn Mawr, PA 19010-2195
215-726-3160
FAX: 610-527-1400
Annual conference and exhibits for insurance agents and financial services professionals who hold Chartered Life Underwriter or Chartered Financial Consultant designations.
October, San Diego

13000 Annual Conference for Public Agencies
Public Risk Management Association
1815 Fort Myer Drive
Suite 1020
Arlington, VA 22209-1805
703-527-5546
FAX: 703-528-7966
info@primacentral.org
www.primacentral.org
James F Coyle, Executive Director
Tony D'Alba, Meetings Manager
Largest conference in North America for state and local government risk managers who purchase insurance, safety and training products, computer software, TPA and consultant services. 150 booths.
2000 Attendees June Founded: 1979
Mailing list available for rent 2000 names

13001 Annual National Association of Insurance Women International
1847 E 15th
PO Box 4410
Tulsa, OK 74159
918-744-5195
FAX: 918-743-1968 800-766-6249
naiw@ionet.net www.naiw.org
Equipment, information and supplies for women in the insurance industry.
900 Attendees Annual

13002 Appraisers Association of America National Conference
386 Park Avenue S
Suite 2000
New York, NY 10016-8804
212-889-5404
FAX: 212-889-5503
appraisers@appraisersassoc.org
www.appraisersassoc.org
Aleya Lehmann, Executive Director
A unique opportunity to connect with fellow appraisers as well as with allied professionals in insurance companies, law firms, government agencies, auction houses, galleries, museums, and libraries to debate and discuss the latest issues impacting the appraisal profession. We'll offer panels, specialist sessions, roundtable discussions, networking, and behind-the-scenes tours.

13003 Association for Advanced Life Underwriting
2901 Telester Court
Falls Church, VA 22042
703-641-9400
888-275-0092
Karen Keating, Communications Director
David Stertzer, Executive VP
Twenty two booths.
1M Attendees March

13004 CEB Spring Conference
Council on Employee Benefits
4910 Moorland Lane
Bethesda, MD 20814
301-664-5940
FAX: 301-664-5944
vschieber@ceb.org www.ceb.org
Vicki A Schieber, Executive Director
Melodee Webb, Conference Committee Chair
An excellent forum for the exchange of ideas, thought and information on the design, operation and financing.
230+ Attendees April

13005 CIRB Annual Meeting
Crop Insurance Research Bureau
10800 Farley
Suite 330
Overland Park, KS 66210-2008
913-338-0470
FAX: 913-339-9336 888-274-2472
denicec@cropinsurance.org
www.cropinsurance.org
Denice Cajigas, Executive Assistant
Jane Shey, Federal Affairs Representative
Paul Horel, President
The purpose of the meeting is to provide speakers and presentations of national repute on subjects of interest to membership.

Annual/January-February

13006 CPCU Annual Meeting & Seminar
Chartered Property Casualty Underwriter Society
720 Providence Road
PO Box 3009
Malvern, PA 19355-0709
610-251-2728
FAX: 610-251-2780 800-932-2728
lrizzo@cpcusociety.org
www.cpcusociety.org
Liliana Rizzo, CMP, Meeting Services Director
Join your fellow society members, new designees and industry leaders for the best in education, networking and leadership the property and casualty insurance industry has to offer.
2600 Attendees Annual/October Founded: 1944

13007 CPCU Conferment Ceremony
American Institute for CPCU
720 Providence Road
PO Box 3016
Malvern, PA 19355
610-251-2733
FAX: 610-640-9576 800-644-2101
cserv@cpcuiia.org www.aicpcu.org
Karen Burger CPCU CPIW, Public Relations
Annual graduation ceremony for people who have earned the Chartered Property

Casualty Underwriter - CPCU - designation.
October

13008 Captive Insurance Companies Association Conference
Captive Insurance Companies Association
4248 Park Glen Road
Minneapolis, MN 55416
952-928-4655
FAX: 952-928-1318
www.captiveassociation.com
Annual conference and exhibits of captive insurance equipment, supplies and services.

13009 Chartered Property Casualty Underwriters Society Fall Seminar
Chartered Property Casualty Underwriter Society
720 Providence Road
Malvern, PA 19355-3402
610-512-2728

Joseph Wisniewski, VP Finance
Jim Marks, Executive Director
Offers a forum for the exchange of ideas between insurance representatives.
3M Attendees October

13010 Employee Benefits Annual Conference
International Foundation of Employee Benefit Plans
18700 W Bluemound Road
Brookfield, WI 53045
262-786-6700
FAX: 262-786-8670 www.ifebp.org
Cheryl Hyslop, Exhibits/Sponsorship
Ronaelle Carlson, Exhibits/Sponsorship
This conference is designed to meet the specific needs of multiemployer and public sector plan trustees and administrators, attorneys, accountants, actuaries, investment managers and others who provide services or who are involved in the overall management and administration of benefit trust funds.
Annual/Nov 4-7

13011 Financial Service Forum
Society of Financial Service Professionals
270 S Bryn Mawr Avenue
Bryn Mawr, PA 19010
610-526-2500
FAX: 610-526-2538 800-392-6900
Amy Johnson CMP, Director Meetings/Travel
G Ronald MacDonald CAE, Managing Director Member Services
Composed of motivational speakers, break-out educational session with continuing education for insurance, CFP, PACE, CLE, CPE, ICB, and EA. Exhibithall includes demo theaters.
3000+ Attendees October

13012 General Agents and Managers Life Agency Management Program
1922 F Street NW
Washington, DC 20006-4302
202-331-6099
FAX: 202-785-5612
Jo Anne Kohler, Show Manager
80 booths including publishers, computer software and hardware manufacturers and office management services.
2.7M Attendees March

13013 I-Car International Annual Meeting
3701 W Algonquin Road
Suite 400
Rolling Meadows, IL 60008
925-961-0393
FAX: 800-590-1215 800-422-7872
pat.perren@i-car.com www.i-car.com
Pat Perren, Meetings Manager
Matt Forpanek, Customer Care Manager
A important event that brings together collision industry leaders from across the United States, Canada and New Zealand to address current trends and issues in the industry. Attendees will have the opportunity to learn about new products and technologies and share ideas with other industry leaders. *$500.00*
Annual/July

13014 IAAI Annual Conference and General Meeting
International Association of Arson Investigators
12770 Boenker Road
Bridgeton, MO 63044
314-739-4224
FAX: 314-739-4219
orders@firearson.com
www.firearson.com
Marsha Sipes, Conference/Meeting Services
Dolores Nelson, Conference/Meeting Services
Provides the means to stay abreast of the latest techniques and theories in the investigation of the crime of arson. *$425.00*
Annual/April

13015 IADC Annual Meeting
International Association of Defense Counsel
One N Franklin
Suite 1205
Chicago, IL 60606-3401
312-368-1494
FAX: 312-368-1854
oyandle@iadclaw.org
www.iadclaw.org
Nancy Chase, Director of Meetings
Oliver Yandle, Executive Director
Offering interests CLE and excellent networking opportunities in family friendly environment.
Annual/July

13016 IAIR Roundtable and Meetings
International Association of Insurance Receivers
174 Grace Boulevard
Altamonte Springs, FL 32714
407-682-4513
FAX: 407-682-3175
info@iair.org www.iair.org
Daniel A Orth III, Meetings VP
Mary Cannon Veed, Meeting Coverage
Quarterly meetings that provides an opportunity to share information about important industry issues and topics in insurance and reinsurance as they relate specifically to insurance receiverships.
June, Sept, December

13017 IASA Annual Conference
Insurance, Accounting & Systems Association
3511 Shannon Road
Suite 160
Durham, NC 27707
919-489-0991
FAX: 919-489-1994
info@iasa.org www.iasa.org
Thom Hoffman, Exhibit Manager
R Iovino, Account Manager
Providing the most comprehensive education program and business show targeted for financial and technology professionals in the industry.
1800 Attendees June

13018 ICAE Annual Fall Exchange
Insurance Consumer Affairs Exchange
PO Box 746
Lake Zurich, IL 60047
614-228-1593

nbrebner@icae.com www.icae.com
Nancy Brebner, Executive Director
Exploring the challenges and opportunities of utilizing advances in information processing and customer service technology to better serve our customers in the future. Meeting the customer service needs of today's insurance buyers.
Annual/October

13019 ICPA Annual Meeting
Insurance Conference Planners Association
401 N Michigan Avenue
Chicago, IL 60611
312-245-1023
FAX: 312-321-5150
jdevine@icpanet.com
www.icpanet.com
Jeff Devine, CMP, Events Director
Steve Bova, CAE, Executive Director
Exhibits, education and networking activities.
Annual/November

13020 Insuromer Services Expo
Property Loss Research Bureau
3025 Highland Parkway
Suite 800
Downers Grove, IL 60515-1291
630-242-2200
FAX: 630-724-2260
expo@pcrb.orgrb.org
www.insuromerserviceexpo.org
Hugh O Strawn, Show Manager
Exhibits by those who provide products and services to the property-casualty claims industry. A variety of insurance industry personnel attend the Claims Conference. The single largest group of attendees is employees of member insurance companies. This group consists of highly experienced claims personnel, claims managers, home office managers and claim vice-presidents. The remainder of the group includes vendors that service the insurance industry.
1700 Attendees April

13021 LAMP Annual Meeting
GAMA International
2901 Telestar Court
Suite 140
Falls Church, VA 22042-1205
703-770-8184
FAX: 703-770-8182
deverett@gama.naifa.org
www.gamaweb.com
Nicole Travers, Meetings/Products Administrator
Delaine Everett, Meetings/Convention Director
The event for field leaders in the insurance and financial services industry. Featuring top-notch main platform speaker presentations, more than 30 leading practices concurrent sessions, resource center with more than 50 exhibitors that will be offering valu-

able products and services and networking opportunities with your peers.
Annual/March
Printed in 4 colors on glossy stock

13022 LIC Annual Meeting
Life Insurers Council
2300 Windy Ridge Parkway
Suite 600
Atlanta, GA 30339-8443
770-984-3724
FAX: 770-984-3780
lic@loma.org
www.loma.org/IndexPage-LIC.asp
Michael H Siris, Executive Director
Rose Hoyt, Administrative Assistant
Designed to educate members about critical issues for competing in today's regulatory, legislative and business climates.
Annual/May

13023 LIRB/PLRB Claims Conference & Insurance Expo
Liability Insurance Research Bureau
3025 Highland Parkway
Suite 800
Downers Grove, IL 60515-1291
630-242-2250
FAX: 630-724-2260 888-711-7572
pdispensa@lirb.org www.lirb.org
Tom Mallin, President
Paul C Despensa, VP/General Counsel
Concept sessions that feature a thorough presentation of a topic by expert panelists. A forum of experts/panels that will discuss controversial topics in response to questions and comments from participants on a range of subjects outlined in the agenda for that forum. Also; workshops that are working sessions. Participants form a small discussion group to reach consensus on hypothetical problems. Each table debates and defends its conclusions with other groups.
April

13024 MDRT Annual Meeting
Million Dollar Round Table
325 W Touhy Avenue
Park Ridge, IL 60068-4265
847-926-6378
FAX: 847-518-8921
meetings@mdrt.org www.mdrt.org
Ray Kopcinski, Meeting Services Director
Jody Egel, Meeting Coordinator
Kathyrn H Pagura, Meeting Coordinator
John Prast, Executive Vice President
Known throughout the industry as the premier meeting for financial professionals. Motivational stories, educational sessions, experienced colleagues, networking opportunities come together at these annual meetings.
Annual/June

13025 MI2 Annual Conference and Expo
Mass Marketing Insurance Institute
14 W 3rd Street
Suite 200
Kansas City, MO 64105
816-221-7575
FAX: 816-561-7765
gary@robstan.com /
jenniferb@robstan.com www.mi2.org
Gary Hicks, Executive Director
Jennifer Branfort, Associate Director
Dirk Moss, Owner
Educational programming, networking and social events. There is a full trade show in conjunction with the educations sessions to keep you abreast of all the latest in the industry.
Annual

13026 Massachusetts Association of Insurance Agents Convention
137 Pennsylvania Avenue
Framingham, MA 01701-8837
508-663-0223
FAX: 508-628-5443
www.massagent.com
Sheron Gagnon, Trade Show Manager
Trade show for everyday use in the insurance agency office.
1800 Attendees November

13027 NACA Convention
National Association of Catastrophe Adjusters
PO Box 821864
North Richland Hills, TX 76182-1864
817-498-3466
FAX: 817-498-0480
nacatadj@aol.com www.nacatadj.org
Lori Ringo, Executive Administrator
Annual convention and business meeting offering continuing education credits for some states; also a vendor show. Convention is held in Las Vegas, NV.
200 Attendees January Founded: 1976

13028 NADP Annual Conference
National Association of Dental Plans
8111 LBJ Freeway
Suite 935
Dallas, TX 75251-1347
972-458-6998
FAX: 972-458-2258
info@nadp.org www.nadp.org
Evelyn F Ireland, CAE, Executive Director
Tim Brown, Deputy Executive Director
Get the greater industry insight, re-energized creativity and influential contacts.
Annual/September

13029 NAIFA Convention and Career Conference
Ntl Association of Insurance & Financial Advisors
2901 Telestar Court
Falls Church, VA 22042-1205
703-770-8100
FAX: 703-770-8201
jboyle@naifa.org, www.naifa.org
Mike Pomponio, Exhibiting/Sponsoring Director
John Boyle, General Sessions Director
David Woods, Chief Executive Officer
One of the largest exhibits of financial services and products. Get answers to your questions and learn about the latest industry issues, trends and products.
Annual/September

13030 NAIIA Annual Conference
National Association of Independent Insurance Adj.
825 W State Street
Suite 117-C&B
Geneva, IL 60134
630-397-5012
FAX: 630-397-5013
assist@naiia.com www.naiia.com
David F Mehren, Executive Director
Brenda Reisenger, Sponsorship Director
Attendance is open to claims handling professionals.
Annual

13031 NAPIA Annual Meeting
National Association of Public Insurance Adjusters
21165 Whitfield Place
Suite 105
Potomac Falls, VA 20165
703-433-9217
FAX: 703-433-0369
info@napia.com www.napia.com
David W Barrack, Executive Director
Education sessions, networking and social events and exhibits by industry suppliers.
Annual/June

13032 National Association of Independent Life Brokerage Agencies Conference
National Assn of Independent Life Brokerage Agents
8201 Greensboro Drive
Suite 300
Mc Lean, VA 22102-3814
703-610-9011
FAX: 703-524-2303
Annual conference and exhibits of equipment, supplies and services for licensed independent life brokerage agencies that represent at least 3 insurance companies, but are not controlled or owned by an underwriting company.
November, San Diego

13033 National Association of Life Underwriters Conference
1922 F Street NW
Washington, DC 20006-4394
202-331-6099
FAX: 202-331-2179
William V Regan III, Executive VP
Teresa Bonnema, Advertising Account
Sales professionals in life and health insurance and other financial services. 110 booths.
3.5M Attendees September

13034 National Association of Mutual Insurance Companies Annual Convention & Expo
National Association of Mutual Insurance Companies
3601 Vincennes Road
#68700
Indianapolis, IN 46268-1154
317-875-5250
FAX: 317-879-8408
bnastally@namic.org www.namic.org
Charles Chamness, President
Barbara Nastally, Manager Vendor Services
Convention and exhibit show for property/casualty insurance executives. Four day event.
1700 Attendees Fall Founded: 1895

13035 New England Professional Insurance Agents Association Conference
1 Ash Street
Hopkinton, MA 01748-1822
508-497-2590
Stella Di Camilo, Show Manager
100 booths of insurance-related products.
1.5M Attendees November

13036 PRIMA Annual Conference Trade Show
500 Montgomery Street
Suite 750
Alexandria, VA 22314
703-480-0875
FAX: 703-739-0200
info@primacentral.org
www.primacentral.org
Tony D'Alba, Business Development Director
N Romanchok, Meetings Manager
Vanna So, Owner
Containing 150 exhibits concerning insuring the public.
2,200 Attendees June Founded: 1976

13037 Physician Insurers Association of America Annual Conference
Physician Insurers Association of America
2275 Research Boulevard
Rockville, MD 20850-3268
301-947-9090
FAX: 301-947-9090
Annual exhibits related to physician liability insurance.

13038 Professional Insurance Agents National Annual Conference & Exhibition
National Association of Prof. Insurance Agents
400 N Washington Street
Alexandria, VA 22314-2312
703-836-9340
FAX: 703-836-1279
Ted Besesparis, VP
Annual conference and exhibits of equipment, supplies and services for independent property and casualty agents.

13039 Public Agency Risk Managers Association Convention
Public Agency Risk Managers Association
PO Box 6810
San Jose, CA 95150-6810
Annual convention and exhibits of risk management equipment, supplies and services.

13040 Public's Health and the Law in the 21st Century Annual Partnership
765 Commonwealth Avenue
16th Floor
Boston, MA 02215
617-262-4990
FAX: 617-437-7596
conferences@aslme.org
www.aslme.org
Katie Kenney, Conference Planner
This conference is for everyone who is active in, or interested in, law as a tool for improved public health. It will focus on innovative legal tools and strategies for improved public health and will give special emphasis to information conference participants can use in their day-to-day practice.
Annual/June

13041 Risk Insurance Management Society
111 W 40th St
Fl 13
New York, NY 10018-2539
212-286-9292
Brian Stevenson, Show Manager
Mary Roth, Executive Director
500 booths of premier insurance companies and associated service companies.
5M Attendees

13042 Society of Financial Service Professionals Financial Service Forum
17 Campus Blvd
Ste 201
Newtown Square, PA 19073-3230
610-526-2500
FAX: 610-527-1499 800-927-2427
custsvc@financialpro.org
www.financialpro.org
Michelle Connor, Exhibit Manager
Show for leading producers and executives in insurance and financial services fields.
750 Attendees October 15-17

13043 Society of Insurance Trainers and Educators Conference
2120 Market Street
Suite 108
San Francisco, CA 94114
415-621-2830
FAX: 415-621-0889
ed@insurancetrainers.org
www.insurancetrainers.org
Lois A Markovich, Executive Director
Forty booths. A major conference for those involved with training and education in the insurance industry.
200 Attendees June-July Founded: 1953

13044 Sun States Professional Insurance Agents Association
13416 N 32nd Street
Suite 106
Phoenix, AZ 85032-6000
602-482-3333
Maryls M Graser, Executive VP
50 booths.
300 Attendees May

13045 Women Life Underwriters Confederation
1126 S 70th Street
Suite S-106
Milwaukee, WI 53214-3151
FAX: 414-475-2585 800-776-3008
Ann Wells, Managing Director
For women insurance agents, their managers and their companies. 20 booths.
100 Attendees September

Directories & Databases

13046 ADP Parts Exchange New
ADP Claims Services Group
2010 Crow Canyon Place
San Ramon, CA 94583
925-866-1100
www.adpclaims.com
Provides an electronic link from your ADP estimating system to comprehensive database of new replacement parts. Data on over three and a half million parts facilitates the writing of complete, cost-effective damage reports.

13047 Adjusters Reference Guide
Bar List Publishing Company
425 Huehl Road
Building 6B
Northbrook, IL 60062-2323
847-498-6133
FAX: 847-498-6695 800-726-1007
info@barlist.com www.barlist.com
Bruce Rodgers, President
Leslie Rodgers, Production Manager
A professional service for anyone who handles insurance claims. It contains a complete set of ISO Policy and Forms and is divided into two major categories; Personal Lines and Commercial Lines.
Annual

13048 Best's Directory of Recommended Insurance Attorneys and Adjusters
AM Best Company
Ambest Road
Oldwick, NJ 08858
908-439-2200
FAX: 908-439-2688
john.czuba@ambest.com
www.ambest.com
John Czuba, Editor
Includes over 5,300 insurance defense law firms and over 1,200 insurance adjusters companies recommended by the insurance industry. Includes a section on expert services providers, insurance company groups or fleets, legal and claims services, officials and a digest of insurance laws. *$1205.00*
5100 pages Annual Founded: 1928
Circulation: 19,000

13049 Best's Insurance Reports
AM Best Company
Ambest Road
Oldwick, NJ 08858
908-439-2200
FAX: 908-439-3363 www.ambest.com
Published in two editions - life-health insurance and property-casualty insurance, United States and Canada. *$570.00*
Annual

13050 Best's Insurance Reports: International Edition
AM Best Company
Ambest Road
Oldwick, NJ 08858
908-439-2200
FAX: 908-439-3363 www.ambest.com
Burton Kellogg, Editor
Offers information on over 800 insurance companies in Canada, Europe, Asia, Africa, Australia, and South America that offer life/health and property/casulaty insurance policies. *$495.00*
1200 pages Annual

13051 Best's Key Rating Guide
AM Best Company
Ambest Road
Oldwick, NJ 08858
908-439-2200
FAX: 908-439-3296 www.ambest.com
Eric Simpson, Editor
Larry Mayewski, Editor
Financial and operating characteristics on over 2,600 major property/casualty insurance companies, over 1,750 major life and health insurance companies. *$95.00*

Annual August

13052 Best's Market Guide
AM Best Company
Ambest Road
Oldwick, NJ 08858
908-439-2200
FAX: 908-439-3363 www.ambest.com
Kenneth J Millroy, Editor
In each volume, separate volumes for corporate stocks, corporate bonds, and municipal bonds, a list of insurance company investment officers are offered. *$1425.00*
3-Volume Set

13053 Business Insurance Directory of Reinsurance Intermediaries
Crain Communications
360 N Michigan Avenue
Chicago, IL 60601
312-495-5231
FAX: 312-649-7801 800-678-9595
Kathryn McIntyre, Publisher
Sandra L Budde, Editor
Lists nearly 100 reinsurance intermediaries in the United States and Bermuda. *$4.00*
Annual
Circulation: 53,000

13054 Business Insurance Directory of Corporate Buyers of Insurance/Benefit Plans
Crain Communications
360 N Michigan Avenue
Chicago, IL 60601
312-495-5231
FAX: 312-649-7801 800-678-9595
Sandra L Budde, Editor
Over 3,000 corporations that are corporate buyers of insurance, benefit plans and risk management services. *$95.00*
508 pages Annual

13055 Business Insurance Directory of Employee Assistance Program Providers
Crain Communications
360 N Michigan Avenue
Chicago, IL 60601
312-495-5231
FAX: 312-649-7801 800-678-9595
This directory lists more than 150 employee assistance providers. *$2.50*
Annual
Circulation: 50,000

13056 Business Insurance Directory of Property Loss Control Consultants
Crain Communications
360 N Michigan Avenue
Chicago, IL 60601
312-495-5231
FAX: 312-649-7801 800-678-9595
Sandra L Budde, Editor
Offers information on 120 companies that provide loss prevention inspection and research, building plan reviews, training seminars and other loss control consulting services. *$4.00*
Annual
Circulation: 53,000

13057 Captive Insurance Company Directory
Tillinghast/Towers Perrin Company
263 Tresser Boulevard
Stamford, CT 06901-3236
203-631-1900
FAX: 203-326-5498
Corinne Ramming, Editor
Lists over 3,000 captive insurance companies and their parent or sponsor companies; management companies and insurance subsidiary investment advisors. *$210.00*
270 pages Annual

13058 Certified Claims Professional Accreditation Council
PO Box 441110
Fort Washington, MD 20749-1110
301-292-1988
FAX: 301-292-1787
animag@lattmag.com
www.lattmag.com
Dale L Anderson, Editor
Offers a variety of information on members of the CCPAC and certified claims professionals.
76 pages
Circulation: 350

13059 Claim Service Guide
Bar List Publishing Company
425 Huehl Road
Building 6B
Northbrook, IL 60062-2323
847-498-6133
FAX: 847-498-6695 800-726-1007
info@barlist.com www.barlist.com
Bruce Rodgers, President
Edna MacMillan, Editor
National Directory of Independent Insurance Adjusters, Appraisers, Expert Consultants and Property Specialists. Distributed to every home and branch office insurance company claims manager. *$80.00*
Annual
Circulation: 13,000

13060 Corporate Yellow Book
Leadership Directories
104 5th Avenue
New York, NY 10011-6901
212-627-4140
FAX: 212-645-0931
corporate@leadershipdirectories.com
www.leadershipdirectories.com
Vonessa Ruffin, Editor
Contact information for over 48,000 executives at over 1,000 companies and more than 9,000 board members and their outside affiliations. *$360.00*
1,400 pages Quarterly Founded: 1986
50,000 names $105 per M. : CD-Rom

13061 Custom Publishing & News Services
Information
7700 Old Georgetown Road
Suite 700
Bethesda, MD 20814-6100
301-215-4688
FAX: 301-215-4600
acarr@mail.infoinc.com
www.infoinc.com
Alain Carr, Publisher
Offers evaluations of companies on their claims-paying ability.

13062 Directory of Specialty Markets Issue
Insurance Journal
9191 Towne Centre Drive
Suite 550
San Diego, CA 92122-1231
619-584-1100
FAX: 619-584-1200
Mark Wells, Editor
Lists about 200 insurance companies and surplus lines brokers offering specialty lines to insurance agents and brokers in California, Arizona, Alaska, Oregon, Hawaii and Washington. *$10.00*
SemiAnnual
Circulation: 10,400

13063 Directory of TPA's & Stop Loss
Society of Professional Benefit Administrators
2 Wisconsin Circle
Suite 670
Chevy Chase, MD 20815-7043
301-718-7722
FAX: 301-718-9440 spba@erolse.com
Directory of third party administration firms and their services, of leading stop-loss vendors, and in-depth analysis of the employee benefits industry and trends.
$395.00

13064 III Data Base Search
Insurance Information Institute
110 William Street
New York, NY 10038-3901
212-669-9200
FAX: 212-732-1916
Provides citations and abstracts of insurance-related literature appearing in magazines, newspapers and trade publications and books.
Bibliographic

13065 III Insurance Daily
Insurance Information Institute
110 William Street
New York, NY 10038-3901
212-669-9200
FAX: 212-732-1916
This insurance database provides summaries of news and articles relating to the property and casualty insurance industry.
Full-text

13066 Independent Insurance
Independent Insurance Agents of America
127 Peyton
Alexandria, VA 22314
703-683-4422
FAX: 703-683-7556
www.independentagent.com
Robert Rusbuldt, Chief Executive Officer
This web site contains information for consumers on property and casualty insurance including homeowner, renter, landlord, and automobile insurance.
Full-text

13067 Insurance Almanac
Underwriter Printing & Publishing Company
50 E Palisade Avenue
Suite C
Englewood, NJ 07631-2929
201-569-8808
Over 3,000 insurance companies that write fire, casualty, accident, health and life insurance policies.
650 pages Annual
Circulation: 10,000

13068 Insurance Bar Directory
Bar List Publishing Company
425 Huehl Road
Building 6B
Northbrook, IL 60062-2323
847-498-6133
FAX: 847-498-6695 800-726-1007
info@barlist.com www.barlist.com

Bruce Rodgers, President
Edna MacMillin, Editor
Leslie Rodgers, Production Manager

National Directory of Insurance Defense Attorneys that is distributed to all insurance company home office and branch office company executives and claims personnel. *$80.00*
Annual
Circulation: 40,000

13069 Insurance Companies' Directory List of Mortgage Directors
Communication Network International
3918 Avenue T
Brooklyn, NY 11234-5028
718-396-6245

Listing of 210 morgage offices of major insurance companies that make real estate mortgages and related investments. *$75.00*
Founded: 1993

13070 Kelly Casualty Insurance Claims Directory
Francis B Kelley & Associates
123 Veteran Avenue
Los Angeles, CA 90024-1900

FAX: 310-472-1290 800-328-4144

Francis B Kelley, Editor

Lists only casualty insurance claims payment offices. Workers' Compensation and Auto Insurance can pay health care providers for their services. Directory covers Casualty Insurance Companies, Independent Claims Companies, Insurance Commissioners with their Web sites. *$150.00*
280 pages Annual

13071 Kirschner's Insurance Directories
National Underwriter Company
PO Box 3930
Citrus Heights, CA 95611-3930

FAX: 800-724-0408 800-984-7170

Richard Gillmeister, Manager

Insurance companies, agents, brokers and adjusters are listed for the western states. Separate editions are available for northern California, southern California and the Pacific Northwest. *$19.95*
350 pages Semiannual
Circulation: 27,500

13072 Kirschner's Insurance Directory: Western States
Kirschner's Insurance Directories
PO Box 1087
Folsom, CA 95763-1087

FAX: 800-724-0408 800-984-7170
Insurance companies, agents, brokers and adjusters are listed for the western states. Separate editions are available for northern California, southern California and the Pacific Northwest. *$14.95*
350 pages Semiannual
Circulation: 27,500

13073 Kirschner's Red Book Directories
National Underwriter Company
5081 Olympic Boulevard
Erlanger, KY 41018
859-692-2100
FAX: 800-874-1916 800-543-0874

Jaclyn Meder Ruzsa, Editor *$49.95*
Semi-Annual

13074 LEXIS Insurance Law Library
Mead Data Central
9443 Springboro Pike
Dayton, OH 45401

FAX: 518-487-3584 888-223-6337

Andrew Prozes, Chief Executive Officer

This full database contains the complete text of the insurance statutes for 50 states, the District of Columbia and Puerto Rico.
Full-text

13075 LOMA's Information Center Database
Life Office Management Association
2300 Windy Ridge Parkway
Suite 600
Atlanta, GA 30339-8443
770-951-1770
FAX: 770-984-0441 800-275-5662
infoctr@loma.org www.loma.org

Thomas P Donaldson, President/CEO

A team of experienced researchers provide current data utilizing our comprehensive database. More than 10,000 documents are maintained and updated. A comprehensive list of Industry Research Links can also be found in this area.
Available to Members

13076 Life Insurance Selling: Sources Issue
Commerce Publishing Company
330 N 4th Street
Suite 200
Saint Louis, MO 63102-2041
314-421-5445
FAX: 314-421-1070

Larry Albright, Editor

Lists life insurance companies, publishers of software used in the insurance field and financial planning corporations. *$7.00*
45000

13077 Life Office Management Association Directory
5770 Powers Ferry Road NW
Atlanta, GA 30327-4350
770-953-6872
FAX: 770-984-0441

Philippa Griffith, Editor

Offers information on life insurance and financial service companies.
190 pages Annual

13078 Morningstar Variable Annuity/Life Sourcebook
Morningstar
53 W Jackson Boulevard
Chicago, IL 60604-3606
312-351-1050

Jennifer Strickland, Editor

Offers variable annuity and variable life contracts offered by insurance and mutual fund companies. *$195.00*
1200 pages Annual

13079 NAIC Database
National Association of Insurance Commissioners
2301 McGee Street
Kansas City, MO 64108
816-842-3600
www.naic.org

Deborah Scott, Manager

13080 National Association of Catastrophe Adjusters Membership Directory
National Association of Catastrophe Adjusters
PO Box 821864
North Richland Hills, TX 76182-1864
817-498-3466
FAX: 817-498-0480
nacatadj@aol.com www.nacatadj.org

Lori Ringo, Executive Administrator

Annual Founded: 1976
Circulation: 2000

13081 National Insurance Law Service/Insource Insurance
NILS Publishing Company
PO Box 2507
Chatsworth, CA 91313-2507
818-998-8830
FAX: 818-718-8482 800-423-5910
creative@nills.com www.nils.com

Jon Fish, Circulation Director
Karen G Beaudoin, VP Marketing
Jonathon K Fish, Production Manager

This insurance database contains the complete text of insurance codes, related laws, regulations, bulletins and selected attorney general opinions for all 50 states and the federal government. Available on CD-ROm and in looseleaf print. The CD-ROM service 'Insource Insurance' is accessible for licensed users on the NILS Publishing Website. *$520.00*
Monthly Updates
Circulation: 5,000

13082 National Underwriter Kirschner's Insurance Directories (Red Book)
National Underwriter Company
5081 Olympic Boulevard
Erlangerer, KY 41018
859-692-2100
FAX: 800-874-1916 www.kirshners.com

Jaclyn Meder Ruzsa, Editor
Charlie Smith, Chief Exceutive Officer

This series of 24 directories are published by state or region. Listings include companies, brokers and agents and services for each state handling property and casualty. *$19.95*
150+ pages Semi-Annual/Annual 150 names
Printed in on matte stock

13083 Profiles: Health Insurance Edition
National Underwriter Company
5081 Olympic Boulevard
Erlanger, KY 41018
859-922-2100
800-543-0874

Edward A Lyon, Editor

Your reliable resource for up-to-date news and information in the life & health insurance/financial services industry. *$39.95*
300 pages Annual

13084 **Profiles: Property and Casualty Insurance Edition**
National Underwriter Company
505 Gest Street
Cincinnati, OH 45203-1716
513-723-0012

Edward A Lyon, Editor

Offers information on more than 1,500 property and liability insurance companies. *$39.95*
852 pages Annual

13085 **Register of North American Insurance Companies**
American Preeminent Registry
PO Box 622
Old Bridge, NJ 08857-0622
732-225-5533

Brian Axelrod, Publisher

Directory of services and supplies to the industry. *$125.00*
450 pages Annual

13086 **Risk Retention Group Directory and Guide**
Insurance Communications
PO Box 50147
Pasadena, CA 91115-0147
626-796-4972
FAX: 626-796-4972

Karen Cutts, Editor

Offers information on over 80 risk retention groups formed under the 1986 Risk Retention Act or the 1981 Product Liability Risk Retention Act through 1990. *$165.00*

144 pages Annual

13087 **Shortcut 2: Insurance Markets Tracking Systems**
National Underwriter Company
505 Gest Street
Cincinnati, OH 45203-1716
513-723-0012

Directory of services and supplies to the industry. *$300.00*

13088 **Statistics of Fraternal Benefit Societies**
1240 Iroquois Avenue
Suite 300
Naperville, IL 60563-8476
630-355-6633
FAX: 630-355-0042
nfca@nfcanet.org www.nfcanet.org

Anthony Snyder, Communications Director

NFCA membership is currently made up of 82 fraternal benefit societies in the United States and Canada. Each of these societies pay annual membership dues to belong to the organization and it is their executives, employees and grassroots members who serve on the NFCA Board of Directors and various NFCA committees and sections. *$11.00*

13089 **WESTLAW Insurance Library**
West Publishing Company
610 Opperman Drive
Eagan, MN 55123-1340
651-687-7327
www.westgroup.com

This database offers information on US state laws relating to the insurance industry.

Full-text

13090 **Yearbook of the Insurance Industry**
American Association of Managing General Agents
150 S Warner Road
#156
King of Prussia, PA 19406
610-225-1999
FAX: 610-225-1996
jerry@mfassoc.com www.aamga.org

Jerry Fogel, Executive VP

250 managing general agents of insurance companies and more than 500 branch offices; coverage includes Canada.
Annual Spring

Industry Web Sites

13091 **www.aaimco.com**
American Association of Insurance Management Consultants

Supports the insurance management industry.

13092 **www.aaimedicine.org**
American Academy of Insurance Medicine

This organization offers information and legislative updates for people in the medical insurance field.

13093 **www.actuary.org**
American Academy of Actuaries

The AAA is a public policy organization for actuaries within the US The Academy acts as the public information organization for the profession. Assisting public policy process through the presentation of clear actuarial analysis, the Academy regularly prepares testimony for Congress, provides information to federal elected officials, regulators and congressional staff, comments on proposed federal regulations, and works closely with state officials on issues related to insurance.

13094 **www.aha.org**
American Society for Healthcare Risk Management

National organization for the health care industry risk management equipment, supplies and services.

13095 **www.aicpcu.org**
Insurance Institute of America

Sponsors programs for property and casualty insurance firms, conducts exams and award certificates. Maintains a library.

13096 **www.aicpeu.org**
American Institute for CPCU

An independent, nonprofit educational organization that confers the Chartered Property Casualty Underwriter professional designation on those individuals who meet its education and ethics requirements.

13097 **www.allianceai.org**
Alliance of American Insurers

Trade association of property and casualty insurers providing educational, legislative and safety services to its members.

13098 **www.apiw.org**
Association of Professional Insurance Women

Promotes cooperation and understanding among members. Maintains high professional standards and provides a network of professional contacts. Encourages women in industry.

13099 **www.arbifile.org**
Arbitration Forums

Arbitration Forums is a not-for-profit provider of intercompany insurance dispute resolution services. More than 2,000 insurers and self-insurers participate in AF's programs. AF resolves over 250,000 disputes with a claim value approaching 1 billion dollars.

13100 **www.arminet.com**
Associated Risk Managers International

Develops specialized insurance/risk management services for trade associations, professional groups and other industry organizations. Conducts seminars and sponsors competitions.

13101 **www.awpc.org**
Association of Workers' Compensation Professionals

A nonprofit organization for those engaged in the field of workers' compensation, providing members with training and certification.

13102 **www.ccactuaries.org**
Conference of Consulting Actuaries

Full-time consulting actuaries.

13103 **www.easternclaimsconference.com**
Eastern Claims Conference

Provides education and training to examiners, managers, and officers who review medical and disability claims. Holds seminars for life, health and disability clinics.

13104 www.financialpro.org
Society of Financial Service Professionals

Members are dedicated to the highest standards of competence and service in insurance and financial services.

13105 www.greyhouse.com
Grey House Publishing

Selected Grey House directories in the fields of business, health and education are available online. Users can search our online databases by several different search criteria, such as product categories, geographic area, sales volume and much, much more. Full Grey House catalog and online ordering also available.

13106 www.highwaysafety.org
Insurance Institute for Highway Safety

Traffic and motor vehicle safety organization supported by auto insurers.

13107 www.hwsafety.org
Highway Loss Data Institute

Provides the public with insurance industry data concerning human and economic loss resulting from crashes.

13108 www.iasa.org
Insurance Accounting Systems Association

Facilitates the exchange of ideas among insurance industry professionals and their industry-related associates.

13109 www.insuranceallnations.com
Allnations Insurance

Provides financial and technical assistance to new and developing cooperative insurance facilities. Promotes and develops all types of cooperative insurance organizations.

13110 www.ivans.com
Insurance Value Added Network Services

Industry-sponsored organization offering value added data communications network linking agencies, companies and providers of data to the insurance industry.

13111 www.nacatadj.org
National Association of Catastrophe Adjusters

Association of Catstrophe Insurance Adjusters and independent adjustment companies.

13112 www.nafi.org
National Association of Fire Investigators

Primary purpose of this association is to increase the knowledge and improve the skills of persons engaged in the investigation and analysis of fires, explosions, or in the litigation that ensues from such investigations. The Association also originated and implemented the National Certification Board.

13113 www.nafi921.org
National Association of Fire Investigators

Primary purpose is to increase the knowledge and improve the skills of persons engaged in the investigation and analysis of fires, explosions, or in the litigation that ensues from such investigations.

13114 www.nahu.org
National Association of Health Underwriters

Sponsors advanced health insurance underwriting and research seminars. Testifies before federal and state committees on pending health insurance legislation. Presents numerous awards.

13115 www.naiw.org
National Association of Insurance Women

Professional membership association for employees in all facets of the insurance industry. The association exists to promote continuing education and networking for the professional advancement of its members, and offers education programs, meetings, publications, services and leadership opportunities for its members' benefits.

13116 www.ncci.com
National Council on Compensation Insurance

Develops and administers rating plans and systems for workers compensation insurance.

13117 www.nfcanet.org
National Fraternal Congress of America

The association of America's Fraternal Benefit Societies, representing more than 80 not-for-profit fraternal organizations providing social, educational and leadership opportunities and insurance protection to their nearly 10 million members.

13118 www.nonprofitrisk.org
Nonprofit Risk Management Center

Publishes materials and delivers workshops and conferences on risk management, liability and insurance issues of special concern to nonprofit organizations.

13119 www.ontherisk.org/houla/
Home Office Life Underwriters Association

Offers educational programs through the Academy Life Underwriting designed for professional home office underwriters.

13120 www.plrb.org
Property Loss Research Bureau

Provides access to legal and technical databases, legal research on property and inland marine coverage issues countrywide, claims education, and daily catastrophe information for a membership of 570 property/casualty insurance companies.

13121 www.sirnet.org
Society of Insurance Research

Members are individuals actively engaged in some form of insurance research.

13122 www.snl.com
SNL Securities

News articles on banks and thrifts, insurance and other financial services. Also features vital company information.

13123 www.snlnet.com
SNL Securities

This organization offers the most up-to-date information available in the insurance industry featuring the latest news releases, filings and important events. Provides current data on top-performing stocks, insider trades, ownership filings, company news and events and legislative issues.

13124 www.soa.org
Society of Actuaries

Nonprofit professional society of 17,000 members involved in the modeling and management of financial risk and contingent events. The mission of the SOA is to advance actuarial knowledge and to enhance the ability of actuaries to provide expert advice and relevant solutions for financial, business and societal problems involving uncertain future events.

13125 www.thefederation.org
Federation of Insurance and Corporate Counsel

For members of the bar who are actively engaged in the legal aspects of the insurance business, executives of insurance companies and associations and corporate counsel engaged in the defense of claims.

13126 www.thepiaa.org
Physician Insurers Association

Represents domestic and international medical malpractice insurance companies which are practioner-owned or controlled.

13127 www.transportlaw.com
Transportation Consumer Protection Council

Dedicated to the reduction of transit losses and the improvement of freight claim and freight charge payment procedures in domestic and international commerce.

13128 www.users.erols.com/spba
Society of Professional Benefit Administrators

Third-party contract administration (TPA) administers employee benefit plans for client employers and unions. It is estimated that 66 percent of US workers with employee benefits are in plans administered by TPA.

Associations

13129 American Floorcovering Alliance
210 West Cuyler Street
Dalton, GA 30720-8209
706-278-4101
FAX: 706-278-5323
afa@americanfloor.org
www.americanfloor.org

Wanda Ellis, Executive Director

Provides marketing services, employee benefit programs and other services to members of the floor covering industry nationwide.

190 Members Founded: 1979

13130 American Lighting Association
PO Box 420288
Dallas, TX 75342-0288

800-274-4484

Tom M Underwood, Chairman
Richard D Upton, President/CEO

A trade association uniting lighting; component manufacturers, showrooms/distributors, manufacturer representatives; industry related companies dedicated to providing quality residential illumination.

700 Members Founded: 1945

13131 American Society of Interior Designers
608 Massachusetts Avenue NE
Washington, DC 20002-6006
202-546-3480
FAX: 202-546-3240
asid@asid.org www.asid.org

Michael Alin, Executive Director
Thom Banks, Deputy Executive Director
Valerie Vaughn, Executive Assistant

This organization provides articles, features and valuable information for interior designers involved in both contract and residential projects, students and design-related companies.

34500 Members Founded: 1975

13132 Association of University Interior Design
1652 Cross Center Drive
Norman, OK 73019-5050

FAX: 405-325-4164
webmaster@auid.org www.auid.org

Cindy Howe, President
Anne Adesso, First VP/Newsletter Editor
Michele Bowlen, Secretary
John Branies, Treasurer

Provides a network for individuals who work within institutions of higher education and to promote activities designed to benefit its members through education, research, and communication.

Founded: 1979

13133 Association of the Wall and Ceiling Industry
513 W Broad Street
Suite 210
Falls Church, VA 22046
703-534-8300
FAX: 703-534-8307
info@awci.org www.awci.org

Steven A Etkin, Executive VP
Marie Batiste, Membership Coordinator/Exec.Assist
Bahman Kheradmand, Director Accounting Services

Offers information on contractors, manufacturers, suppliers and organizations affiliated with the interior design, building and contracting community. Strives to provide services and undertake activities that enhance the members ability to operate a successful business.

Founded: 1918

13134 California Council for Interior Design Certification
1605 Grand Avenue
Suite 4
San Marcos, CA 92078
760-761-4734
FAX: 760-761-4736
office@ccidc.org www.ccidc.org

Donald Chu, President
Ron Lewis, VP
Joann Cleckner, Treasurer

To establish and implement professional standards and educational requirements, educate the public, and facilitate interior design professional's compliance with our standards and codes of ethics in order to provide for the protection, health, safety, and welfare of the public.

Founded: 1992

13135 California Legislative Coalition for Interior Design
13971 Annadale Lane
Rancho Cucamonga, CA 91739
909-899-8211
FAX: 909-899-7129 800-792-5243
office@clcid.org www.clcid.org

Betty Wood, Executive Director
Marie Chan, Secretary
Betty Noll Wood, Executive Director

Serves as the unified voice for the California Interior Design Profession. Effectively monitors legislation and advocates improvement of professional standards of certification by the State of California along with local government agencies through legislative activities that protect public health, safety, and welfare

5000 Members Founded: 1985

13136 Can Manufacturers Institute
1730 Rhode Island Avenue NW
Suite 1000
Washington, DC 20036
202-232-4677
FAX: 202-232-5756
webmaster@cancentral.com
www.cancentral.com

Robert Budway, President

The trade association of the metal and composite can manufacturing industry and its suppliers in the United States. The mission is to foster the prosperity of the industry and bring value to its members in a cost effective way.

35 Members Founded: 1938

13137 Carpet Cushion Council
PO Box 546
Riverside, CT 06878
203-637-1312
FAX: 203-698-1022
carpetcushion@msn.com
www.carpetcushion.org

Jack Lens, President
Steve Drap, VP
Ernest Schorsch, Secretary
John Mitchell, Treasurer

Encourages distribution and use of seperate carpet cushions. Works with regulatory agencies at the national, state and local levels.

31 Members Founded: 1976

13138 Carpet and Rug Institute
730 College Dr
Dalton, GA 30720-3782
706-278-3176
FAX: 706-278-8835 800-882-8846

National association representing the carpet and rug industry. It is also a source of extensive carpet information for consumers, writers, interior designers, specifiers, facility managers, architects, builders, and building owners and managers, installation contractors, and retailers.

150 Members Founded: 1969

13139 Foundation for Interior Design Education
146 Monroe Center NW
Suite 1318
Grand Rapids, MI 49503-2822
616-458-0400
FAX: 616-458-0460
fider@fider.org www.fider.org

Kayem Dunn, Executive Director

Leads the interior design profession to excellence by setting standards and accrediting academic programs.

135 Members Founded: 1970

13140 Foundation for International Design
1950 N Main Street
PO Box 139
Salinas, CA 93906
650-326-1867
FAX: 831-449-7040 www.ffdi.org

Peg Callard, Chairman

The foundation honors those who conceive, design, engineer and develop innovative new products for the Interior and Architectural Design Community and their clients.

150+ Members Founded: 1994

13141 Home Fashion Partners
585 S Duncan Ave
Clearwater, FL 33756-6256
727-443-2702
www.wallpaperguide.com
This organization has a list of wallcovering manufacturers and distributors aimed at the interior design community.

13142 Home Show Management Corporation
1450 Madruga Avenue
Suite 301
Coral Gables, FL 33146-3164
305-667-9299
FAX: 305-667-3266 888-353-3976
info@homeshows.net
www.homeshows.net

Steve Plotkin, Show Director
Larry Perl, Show Director

Organizes four annual south Flordia home design and remodeling shows in Coconut Grove, Ft. Lauderdale and Miami Beach convention centers. Open to the trade and public.

Founded: 1978

13143 Illuminating Engineering Society of North America
120 Wall Street
17th Floor
New York, NY 10005
212-248-5000
FAX: 212-248-5018
iesna@iesna.org www.iesna.org

Craig A Bernecker, President
William H Haney, Executive VP
Alan L Lewis, Senior VP

Boyd Corbett, Treasurer
William Hanley, Manager

To advance knowledge and disseminate information for the improvement of the lighted environment to the benefit of society. Publishes a monthly magazine.

9,000 Members Founded: 1906

13144 Int'l Interior Design Association/CA
1933 S Broadway
Suite 1130
Los Angeles, CA 90007
213-747-2391
FAX: 213-747-2394
office@iida-socal.org
www.iida-socal.org

Judith Wilson FIIDA, Executive Director
Eric Magallon, Associate Executive Director

Strives to enhance the quality of life through excellence in interior design and to advance interior design through knowledge.

10000 Members Founded: 1994

13145 Interior Design Educators Council
7150 Winton Drive
Suite 300
Indianapolis, IN 46268
317-328-4437
FAX: 317-280-8527
info@idec.org www.idec.org

Pamela Evans, President
Eric Weidegreen, President-Elect
Lisa Waxman, Secretary/Treasurer
Anna Marshall-Baker, Past President

Dedicated to the advancement of education and research in interior design. IDEC fosters exchange of information, improvement of educational standards and development of the body of knowledge relative to the quality of life and human performance in the interior environment.

Founded: 1963

13146 Interior Design Society
3910 Tinsley Drive
Suite 101
High Point, NC 27265

FAX: 336-886-6100 800-888-9590
info@interiordesignsociety.org
www.interiordesignsociety.org

Faye Laverty, Executive Director

The largest design organization exclusively dedicated to serving the residential interior design industry. Promote retail interior design, emphasizing education and skills improvement.

3000 Members Founded: 1973

13147 International Furnishings and Design Association
191 Clarksville Road
Princeton Junction, NJ 08550
609-799-3423
FAX: 609-799-7032
info@ifda.com www.ifda.com

Lee K Croggin, President
Mark H Jeross, President-Elect
Jennifer Wagner, Treasurer

The only all-industry association whose members provide services and products to the furnishings and design industry. IFDA is the driving force, through its programs and services, to enhance the professionalism and strature of the industry worlwide.

1400 Members Founded: 1947

13148 International Institute of Carpet and Upholstery Certification
2715 E Mill Plain Boulevard
Vancouver, WA 98661
360-693-5675
FAX: 360-693-4858

Kenway Mead, Executive Director

Sets standards of skill and ethics in fabric restoration industry. Works with regulatory bodies to develop proficiency standards and issues certification.

1.6M Members Founded: 1972

13149 International Interior Design Association/IL
13-500 Merchandise Mart
Chicago, IL 60654-1104
312-467-1950
FAX: 312-467-0779 888-799-4432
iidahq@iida.org www.iida.org

John Lijewski, President
John Mack, VP Communications
Cheryl Durst, Executive VP/CEO
John Scherf, CFO

Members are professionals from various facets of the interior design trade.

10000 Members Founded: 1994

13150 National Association of Decorative Fabric Distributors
One Windsor Cove
Suite 305
Columbia, SC 29223

FAX: 803-765-0860 800-445-8629
info@nadfd.com www.nadfd.com

Harvey Giberson, President
Ted Sargetakis, VP
Joe Governal, Secretary/Treasurer

Comprised of the leading fabric distributors who reach the reupholsterers, made to order drapery and home decorator markets, and more than fifty of their major suppliers, fabric mills, fabric finishers, manufacturers of upholstery and drapery supplies.

75 Members Founded: 1968

13151 National Association of Floor Covering Distributors
401 N Michigan Avenue
Suite 2400
Chicago, IL 60611-4267
312-321-6836
FAX: 312-673-6962
info@nafcd.org www.nafcd.org

Scott Hendricks, President
Stephen Johnson, VP
Mariann B. Gregory, Executive Director
Christophe Freed, Treasurer
Al Maghes, Secretary

Organized to foster trade and commerce for those having a business, financial, or professional interest as wholesale distributors or manufacturers of floor coverings and allied products.

557 Members Founded: 1971

13152 National Council for Interior Design Qualification
1200 18th Street NW
Suite 1001
Washington, DC 20036-2506
202-721-0220
FAX: 202-721-0221
info@ncidq.org www.ncidq.org

Jeffrey F Kenney AIA, Executive Director
Barbara Pallat, President
Kathleen Butler, Director of Administration
Joshua Prentice, Director of Information Technology
Yvonne Lewis, Office Manager

Serves to identify to the public those interior designers who have met the minimum standards for professional practice by passing the NCIDQ examination in addition to protecting the public by identifying those individuals who are competent to practice interior design.

10000 Members Founded: 1974

13153 National Guild of Professional Paperhangers
136 S Keowee Street
Dayton, OH 45402
937-222-6477
FAX: 937-222-5794 800-254-6477
ngpp@ngpp.org
www.thepaperhangers.com

Joseph Parker, President
Dave DiBacco, First VP
Gary Lucas Columbas, Second VP
Patricia Niehaus, Secretary
Lyle Gehrke, Treasurer

Promotes products, upgrades skills of paperhangers and encourages good business ethics. Holds workshops and seminars.

328 Members Founded: 1974

13154 National Home Furnishings Association
3910 Tinsley Drive
Suite 101
High Point, NC 27265-3610
336-886-6100
FAX: 336-801-6102 800-888-9590
info@nhfa.org www.nhfa.org

Steve De Haan, Executive VP
Jerry Baer, President

The nation's largest organization devoted specifically to the needs and interests of home furnishings retailers. Also to provide members with the information, education, products and services they need to remain successful.

10M Members Founded: 1920

13155 National Kitchen and Bath Association
687 Willow Grove Street
Hackettstown, NJ 07840
908-852-0033
FAX: 732-852-1695 800-843-6522

Paul A Kohmescher, Executive Director
Larry Spangler, Chief Executive Officer

Protects the interests of members by fostering a better business climate. Awards certification. Conducts training schools and seminars.

25000 Members Founded: 1965

13156 Paint and Decorating Retailers Association
403 Axminster Drive
Fenton, MO 63026
636-326-2636
FAX: 636-326-1823 800-737-0107
info@pdre.org www.pdra.org

Nicholas R Cicelo, CEO
Cindy Nusbaum, Membership Director
Diane Capuano, Editor
Dan Simon, Manager

This organization lists 1,500 manufacturers, manufacturer's representatives, distributors, and suppliers of decorating merchandise. Also to help focus on the paint, wall and floor coverings products manufacturers.

1500 Members Founded: 1947

13157 Painting and Decorating Contractors of America
11960 Westline Industrial Drive
Suite 201
St. Louis, MO 63146-3209
314-514-7322
FAX: 314-514-9417 800-332-7322
ihoren@pdca.org www.pdca.org

Dr Ian R Horen, CEO
Richard Bright, Director Of Communications
Liz Werle, Director Of Membership
Annette DeLorenzo, Director Of Meetings & Expositions

This organization offers listings of over 3,300 member contractors engaged in painting, decorating and special coatings applications.
10000 Members Founded: 1884

13158 Professional Picture Framers Association
3000 Picture Place
Jackson, MI 49201
517-788-8100
FAX: 517-788-8371
ppfa@ppfa.com www.ppfa.com

Mark Klostermeyer, President
John Pruitt, VP
Fran Gray, Treasurer
Ted Fox, Secretary/Executive Director

An international trade association for the art and framing industry. Supporting a membership of custom picture framers, art galleries, manufacturers, and distributors.
3000+ Members Founded: 1971

13159 Society of Glass & Ceramic Decorators
47 N 4th Street
PO Box 2489
Zanesville, OH 43702
740-588-9882
FAX: 740-588-0245
sgcd@sgcd.org www.sgcd.org

Randall Van Hise, President
Julie Butterfield, VP
Nancy Klinefelter, Secretary/Treasurer

Provides decorating professionals with a competitive edge in business by providing opporotunities for networking to learn about new decorating technologies and techniques.
525 Members

13160 Wholesale Florists and Florist Suppliers of America
147 Old Solomons Island Rd.
Suite 302
Annapolis, MD 21401
410-573-0400
FAX: 410-573-5001 888-289-3372

Billy Hardin Jr., President
Jim Wanko, Executive VP

To provide networking and business opportunities to wholesale distributors and floral suppliers.
1.3M+ Members Founded: 1926

13161 Window Coverings Association of America
3550 McKelvey Road
Suite 202c
Bridgetonis, MO 63044-2523
314-397-7494
FAX: 314-777-0263 888-298-9222
solutions@wcaa.org www.wcaa.org

Beth Hodges, President
Teresa Grysikiewicz, VP
Larry Lariviere, Treasurer
Mark Norman, Executive Director

The only national non-profit trade association dedicated to the retail window covering industry and to the dealers, decorators, and workrooms that are our members.
1200 Members Founded: 1987

Newsletters

13162 Architectural Lighting
1515 Broadway
34th Floor
New York, NY 10036-8901
212-360-0660
FAX: 646-654-4484 847-763-9050
archl@halldata.com
http://www.archlighting.com

Gary Gyss, Group Publisher
Emilie Worth Sommerhoff, Editor-in-Chief
Elizabeth Donoff, Managing Editor
Carolyn Cunningham, Brand Manager
Cliff Smith, Sales Manager

Showcases the application of lighting in architectural and interior design applications.

Founded: 1964
Circulation: 25,000

13163 Mirror News
Market Power
103 2nd Street N
Hopkins, MN 55343-9276

Wil Tiller, Publisher

Offers interior design news and developments for professionals in the industry.
$16.00
24 pages Monthly

13164 National Guild of Professional Paper Hangers
136 S Keowee Street
Dayton, OH 45402
937-222-6477
FAX: 937-222-5794 800-254-6477
ngpp@ngpp.org http://www.ngpp.org

Kim Fantaci, Executive VP
Joseph Parker, President

Accepts advertising.
16 pages Founded: 1974

13165 Professional Designer
American Society of Interior Designers
608 Massachusetts Avenue NE
Washington, DC 20002-6006
202-546-3480
FAX: 202-546-3240
asid@asid.org http://www.asid.org

Julian Warren, Editor
Michelle Alien, Excecutive Director
Micheal Berens, Marketing Manager

Provides articles, features and valuable information for interior designers involved in both contract and residential projects, students and design-related companies.
$100.00
32 pages Quarterly Founded: 1975
Circulation: 40000 Audited
Mailing list available for rent 30500 names $75 per M.
Printed in 4 colors on glossy stock

Magazines & Journals

13166 ASID Icon
American Society of Interior Designers
608 Massachusetts Avenue NE
Washington, DC 20002-6006
202-546-3480
FAX: 202-546-3240
asid@asid.org http://www.asid.org

Julie Warren, Editor
Anita Baltimore, President
Chip DcGrace, Marketing Manger
Erik Henson, Circulation Manager

Monthly Founded: 1975
Circulation: 40,000

13167 ASID Professional Designer
American Homestyle Group
608 Massachusetts Avenue NE
Washington, DC 20002-6006
202-546-3480
FAX: 202-546-3240 http://www.asid.org

Julie Warren, Editor-in-Chief
Michael Alin, Executive Directors

Focuses on issues affecting the industry, including news, trends, technology, leglislation, and educational standards.
Quarterly Founded: 1975
Circulation: 36000

13168 Better Homes and Gardens
Meredith Corporation
1716 Locust Street
Des Moines, IA 50309-3023
515-284-3000
FAX: 515-284-3371 800-678-8091
1716Locust@meredith.com
http://www.meredith.com

Herbert M. Baum, CEO/President
Daniel M. Lagani, V.P./Publisher
Karol DeWulf Nickell, Editor in Chief

Ideas and how-to information on both new and remodeled kitchen and bath. *$11.00*
Monthly Founded: 1902
Circulation: 7.6 mill

13169 Country Home Product Guide
1716 Locust Street
Des Moines, IA 50309-3038
515-842-2015

Candace Manroe, Interiors Editor
David Kahn, Publisher

Offers information on residential projects focusing on innovative design work for homes with a country motif.
Monthly

13170 Decor
Pfingsten Publishing
330 N 5th Street
Saint Louis, MO 63102-2036
314-421-5445
FAX: 314-421-1070 800-867-9285
decor@cpcmags.com
www.decormagazine.com

Gary S Goldman, Publisher
Alice C Gibson, Editor

In the business of furnishing helpful information, education, and marketing services that will assist art and framing retailers, distributors, and wholesalers in the manufacture and sale of their products and services, and in the successful management of their business. Every article of Decor must give art and framing retailers helpful informa-

tion that they can use to make their business stronger. *$20.00*
13 per year
Circulation: 27,000

13171 Design Solutions Magazine
Architectural Woodwork Institute
1952 Isaac Newton Square W
Reston, VA 20190-5001
703-733-0600
FAX: 703-733-0584
awiweb@vt.edu
http://www.awinet.org
David Ritchey, Editor
Judith Durham, Executive VP
Kirsten Ingham, President
Philip Duvic, Director of Marketing
Covers new commercial construction, as well as renovation. Updates on doors, paneling, laminatem plywood, architectural hardware and finishes. *$25.00*
Quarterly
Circulation: 25000

13172 Designers West
Designers World Corporation
8914 Santa Monica Boulevard
Los Angeles, CA 90069-4902
213-748-8291
FAX: 213-748-0039
Carol Soucek King, Editor
Rafael Nadal, President
For interior designers, architects and other design professionals involved in residential, office and hospitality projects. Accepts advertising. *$30.00*
120 pages Monthly Founded: 1953

13173 Designing with Tile and Stone
Tile & Stone
18 E 41st Street
20th Floor
New York, NY 10017-6222
212-376-7722
FAX: 212-376-7723
ashleepub@aol.com www.ashlee.com
Jordan Wright, Publisher
Articles on design, selection, installation and maintenance.
Quarterly
Circulation: 12000

13174 Facilities Design & Management
1515 Broadway
34th Floor
New York, NY 10036-8901
212-840-0595
FAX: 212-302-6273 800-950-1314
Anne Fallucchi, Editor-in-Chief
Covers all aspects of the planning, design and management of facilities for corporate offices and related facilities, health care, government, hospitality and education.
Monthly

13175 Floor Care Professional
Vacuum Dealers Trade Association
2724 2nd Avenue
Des Moines, IA 50313-4933
515-282-9101
FAX: 515-282-4483 800-367-5651
mail@vdta.com http://www.vdta.com/
Judy Patterson, President
Beth Vitiritto, Editor
Offers news and information for the distributers and dealers of vacuum and sewing machines. *$100.00*
Monthly Founded: 1981
Circulation: 18000
Printed in 4 colors on glossy stock

13176 Flora-Line
Berry Hill Press
7336 Berry Hill Drive
Palos Verdes Estates, CA 90275-4404
310-377-7040
Dody Lyness, Editor
Targeted to the home-based business person engaged in dried floral design. Its format keeps readers abreast of the floral trends in herbal growing and the most modern techniques for drying and designing with flowering herbs. Accepts advertising. *$16.95*
20 pages Quarterly Founded: 1981
Circulation: 1,000

13177 Furniture Style
400 Knightsbridge Parkway
Lincolnshire, IL 60069-3613
847-634-4339
FAX: 847-634-4379 800-621-2845
Michael R Reckling, Publisher
Judy Riggs, Director
Steve Chair, Marketing Manager
Douglas A. Riemer, Circulation Manager
William C Vance, Chairman *$49.95*
Monthly Founded: 1937
Circulation: 25000

13178 HOW Design Ideas at Work
F&W Publications
4700 E Galbaith Road
Cincinnati, OH 45236
513-531-2222
FAX: 513-891-7153 800-333-1115
editorial@howdesign.com
http://www.howdesign.com
Jeffry M Lapin, Publisher
Bryn Mooth, Editor
David Stewart, President
HOW reaches visual communicators, including art directors, graphic designers, type designers, typographers, illustrators, advertising and sales promotion managers, and other design-minded executives; also manufacturers and suppliers of graphic arts products and services. *$29.96*
194 pages Monthly Founded: 1990
Circulation: 39946
Printed in 4 colors on glossy stock

13179 Home Furnishings Executive
305 W High Street
Suite 400
High Point, NC 27260-4950
336-820-0130
FAX: 336-801-6100 800-888-9590

13180 Home Lighting & Accessories
Doctorow Communications
1011 Clifton Avenue
Clifton, NJ 07013
973-779-1600
FAX: 973-779-3242
email@homelighting.com
http://www.homelighting.com
Linda Longo, Editor-in-Chief
Jeff Doctorow, Publisher
Jon Doctorow, Circulation Manager
$15.00
Monthly Founded: 1953

13181 Homeworld Business
45 Research Way
Suite 106
East Setauket, NY 11733
631-246-9300
FAX: 631-246-9496
circulation@homeworldbusiness.com
http://www.homeworldbusiness.com
Ian Gittlitz, Publisher/Editor-in-Chief
Peter Giannetti, Editor
Bill McLoughlin, Executive Editor
Peter Chamberlin, Circulation Manager
Hope Rosenzweig, Classified Advertising
$185.00

13182 House Beautiful
959 Eighth Avenue
New York, NY 10019-3737
212-492-2098
FAX: 212-586-3439
mhurley@hearst.com
http://www.hearstcorp.com
Mark Mayfield, Editor-in-Chief
David Arnold, Publisher
Victor F Ganzi, Chief Executive Officer
Bruce Paisner, VP
Michael A Hurley, Marketing Director
$19.97
Monthly Founded: 1887
Circulation: 854627

13183 Interior Design
Reed Business Information
345 Hudson Street
4th Floor
New York, NY 10014
212-959-9550
FAX: 630-288-8686
custserv@espcomp.com
http://www.interiordesignmag.com
Cindy Allen, Editor-in-Chief
Woody Goldfien, Owner
Jim Casella, CEO
Offers information on quality residential and contract design work. Recent issues include corporate offices, remodeling/restoration, kitchen and bath design, health care and hospitality. *$64.95*
250 pages Monthly Founded: 1932
Circulation: 59,000 55M names
Printed in 4 colors on glossy stock

13184 Interiors and Sources
840 US Highway 1
Suite 330
North Pal Beach, FL 33408
561-627-3393
FAX: 561-694-6578
http://www.isdesignet.com
Robert Nieminen, Editor
Guy De Silva, Publisher
Charlotte Vann, Circulation Manager
Offers national commercial and residential design work articles. Emphasizes design solutions and focuses on challenges encountered by designers. *$27.00*
Monthly Founded: 1990
Circulation: 28,000

13185 Kitchen & Bath Design News
Cygnus Publishing
1233 Janesville Avenue
Fort Atkinson, WI 53538-803
920-563-6388
FAX: 920-563-1699
ESefrin@kbdn.net
http://www.cygnusb2b.com
Scott Cravens, VP
Eliot Sefrin, Editorial Director

Offers articles for kitchen and bath dealers, interior designers and architects.
Monthly Founded: 1966
Circulation: 50000

13186 Laminating Design & Technology
Cygnus Publishing
1233 Janesville Avenue
Fort Atkinson, WI 53538-2738
920-563-6388
FAX: 920-563-1707
http://www.laminateonline.com
Kenn Busch, Publisher
Rich Reiff, President
Global design and color trends, as well as surfacing solutions for furniture architecture and interior design. Focuses on surface design, performance and application. *$30.00*
44 pages Monthly Founded: 1937
Circulation: 40006

13187 Lighting Dimensions
Primedia
9800 Metcalf Avenue
Overland, KS 66212
913-341-1300
FAX: 913-967-1898
djohnson@primediabusiness.com
http://www.primediabusiness.com
Jacqueline Tien, Publisher
David Barbour, Editorial Director *$34.97*
Monthly

13188 Metropolis
Bellerophon Publications
61 West
23rd Street
New York, NY 10010
212-627-9977
FAX: 212-627-9988 800-344-3046
jtaraska@metropolismag.com
http://www.metropolismag.com
Horace Havemeyer III, Publisher
Susan S Szenasy, Editor in Chief
Denise Csaky, Marketing Director
Tamara Costa, Advertising Manager
Peter Sangiorgio, Circulation Controller
The only magazine that covers all facets of design: architecture, interiors, furniture, preservation, urban design, graphics and crafts. *$32.95*
Founded: 1980
Circulation: 54000

13189 Michaels Create!
Krause Publications
700 E State Street
Iola, WI 54990
715-445-2214
FAX: 715-445-4087
info@krause.com
http://www.krause.com
Debbie Knauer, Publisher
Jane Beard, Editor
Features contemporary designs reflecting the latest trends with clear instructions. The home decorating, fashion, and gift ideas will inspire experienced crafters as well as seasonal crafters to explore new possibilities. Step-by-step instructions, tips, and techniques will engage crafters of all ages - including kids - with the creative skills of crafting to be enjoyed as a year-round activity. *$21.97*
116 pages Monthly Founded: 1975
Circulation: 24991

13190 Midwest Retailer
8528 Columbus Avenue
South Bloomington, MN 55420-2460
952-854-7610
FAX: 952-854-6460
Joan Thomasberg, President/Publisher
$10.00
38588 pages Founded: 1972
Circulation: 5000
Printed in 2 colors on newsprint stock

13191 National Floor Trends
Business News Publishing Company
22801 Ventura Boulevard
Suite 113
Woodland Hills, CA 91364-1230
818-224-8035
FAX: 818-224-8042
privacy@BNPMedia.com
http://www.bnpmedia.com
Jeff Golden, Publisher/Editorial Director
Phil Johnson, Group Publisher
Rick Arvidson, Marketing Manager
For interior designers.
Monthly Founded: 1952

13192 Panel World
Hatton-Brown Publishers
225 Hanrick Street
PO Box 2268
Montgomery, AL 36102
334-834-1170
FAX: 334-834-4525
rich@hattonbrown.com
http://www.hattonbrown.com
Rich Donnell, Editor
David Knight, Co-Owner
Rhonda Thomas, Circulation Director
$30.00
Monthly Founded: 1948
Circulation: 12754 2,465 names $145 per M,
Printed in on glossy stock : CD

13193 Perspective
13-500 Merchandise Mart
Chicago, IL 60654-1104
312-467-1950
FAX: 312-467-0779 888-799-4432
ahq@iida.org http://www.iida.org
John Lijewski, President
Cheryl Durst, EVP/CEO
Jocelyn Pysarchuk, Managing Director, Commun
Suzanne Murphy, Director, Membership & Chapter Rela
Robert Friedman, Editor
International magazine of IIDA. *$30.00*
Monthly Founded: 1994
Circulation: 10000
Mailing list available for rent 10000 names
Printed in on matte stock

13194 Picture Framing Magazine
Hobby Publications
225 Gordon's Corner Road
PO Box 420
Manalapan, NJ 07726
732-446-4900
FAX: 732-446-5488 800-969-7176
gcoughlin@hobbypub.com
http://www.pictureframingmagazine.com
Bruce Gherman, Executive Publisher
Anne Vazquez, Editor
Deborah Salmon, Circulation Director
Alan Pegler, Production Manager
News and trends in the picture framing trade, marketing strategies, and economic developments. *$20.00*
Monthly Founded: 1995
Circulation: 23000

13195 Progressive Architecture
Progressive Scale
382 S Beach Avenue
Old Greenwich, CT 06870-2223
203-792-2854
FAX: 203-748-2456
Valerie Kanter Sisca, Managing Editor
This magazine has been covering the fields of architecture and interiors for more than 60 years and publishes projects that illustrate both current trends and innovative design solutions. *$48.00*
Monthly
Circulation: 65,000

13196 Wall Paper
Waldman Publishers
570 7th Avenue
New York, NY 10018-1603
212-730-9590
FAX: 212-391-6610
Maurice Murray, Editor
Jeanine LoPresti, Advertising Manager
Ann Waldman Gober, President
Edited for wallcovering retailers and the wallcovering industry. Accepts advertising. *$25.00*
40 pages Monthly Founded: 1980
Circulation: 18,000

13197 Wallcoverings, Windows and Interior Fashion
Cygnus Publishing
445 Broad Hollow Road
Melville, NY 11747-3669
631-845-2700
FAX: 631-845-2723
www.cygnuspub.com

13198 Walls & Ceilings
Business News Publishing Company
2401 West Big Beaver Road
Suite 700
Troy, MI 48084-4900
248-362-3700
FAX: 248-362-5103
mazures@bnp.com
http://www.wconline.com/
Amy Tuttle, Publisher
Nick Moretti, Editor
John Wyatt, Managing Editor
Lyn Sopala, Production Manager
Christine Baloga, Circulation Director
Information regarding management, building methods, technology, government regulations, consumer trends, and product information for the contractor involved in exterior finishes, waterproofing, insulation, metal framing, drywall, fireproofing, partitions, stucco and plaster. *$ 49.00*
140 pages Monthly Founded: 1939
Circulation: 32800
Printed in 4 colors

Trade Shows

13199 Accent on Design
George Little Management
10 Bank Street
Suite 1200
White Plains, NY 10606-1954
914-486-6070
FAX: 914-948-2867 800-272-7469
elizabeth_murphy@glmshows.com
www.nyigf.com

George Little II, President
Elizabeth Murphy, Show Manager

370 booths of the latest and most innovative gift lines such as decorative accessories and home furnishings.

50M Attendees August Founded: 1984

13200 Aidex: Asian International Interior Design Exposition
Reed Exhibition Companies
383 Main Avenue
PO Box 6059
Norwalk, CT 06851
203-840-4800
FAX: 203-840-9628
Audio visual systems, bathroom equipment, supplies and services, plus interior decorations. More than 22 exhibitors, for trade professionals.
Annual

13201 American Society of Interior Designers National Conference
American Society of Interior Designers
608 Massachusetts Avenue NE
Washington, DC 20002-6006
202-546-3480
FAX: 202-546-3240

Michael Alin, Executive Director

Workshop and annual conference with 100 manufacturers and suppliers. Exhibits include interior design merchandise, including wall coverings, laminates, lighting fixtures, plumbing fixtures, carpets, furniture, office systems and fabrics.

3000 Attendees Annual Founded: 1976

13202 Dickens Christmas Show & Festival
Leisure Time Unlimited
708 Main Street
Myrtle Beach, SC 29577
843-448-9483
FAX: 843-362-6153
dickensshow@sc.rr.com
www.dickenschristmasshow.com
Offers a unique blend of craft and gift exhibits presented in a 19th century setting
25000 Attendees Annual November

13203 Evergreen Home Show
Westlake Promotions
6020 Seaview Avenue NW
Seattle, WA 98107
206-783-5957
FAX: 206-782-6250
www.westlakepromo.com

Bill Bradley, VP

See what's new and what you can do for your home. Fresh ideas and practical advice from our remodeling and construction specialists. See demonstrations on how to make dramatic improvements to your home.

7500 Attendees

13204 Fall Decor
Paint & Decorating Retailers Association
403 Axminister Drive
Fenton, MO 63026
636-326-2636
FAX: 314-991-5039
info@ndpa.hygexp.com
www.pdra.org

Tina Sullivan, Show Coordinator
Kathy Witmeyer, Director of Trade Shows

Annual show of 350 manufacturers, suppliers and distributors of decorating and office products and related equipment, supplies and services.

4000 Attendees October

13205 Galeria
Decor Magazine
330 N 4th Street
Saint Louis, MO 63102
314-421-5445
FAX: 314-421-1070
12000 Attendees

13206 Holiday Fair
Textile Hall Corporation
25 Woodslake Road
Greenville, SC 29607
864-331-2277
FAX: 864-293-0619
25000 Attendees

13207 Home Furnishings Summer Market
1355 Market Street
San Francisco, CA 94103-1324
415-934-1380

Donald Preiser, Show Manager

600 booths.

30M Attendees

13208 Home World Home & Garden Show
Show Biz Productions
16600 Harbor Blouevard
Suite F
Fountain Valley, CA 92708
714-418-2000
FAX: 714-418-2009 877-418-2001

Rachel Perry, President
Marlene Thorne, VP

Featuring vendors of window, doors, painting, heating, air conditioning, kitchens and baths, flooring, furniture, remodeling services and more.

30000 Attendees Founded: 1991

13209 Home and Garden Show
Reed Exhibition Companies
255 Washington Street
Newton, MA 02458-1637
617-584-4900
FAX: 617-630-2222

Elizabeth Hitchcock, International Sales

Home products and services.

75M Attendees March

13210 IFAI Expo
Industrial Fabrics Association International
1801 County Road BW
Roseville, MN 55113
651-222-2508
FAX: 651-631-9334
confmgmt@ifai.com
www.ifaiexpo.info

Jennifer Thompson, Director Conference Management

Offers exhibits, educational programs, dynamic speakers, recognition opportunitites, certification testing and many networking opportunities. It's everything that speciality fabrics industry professionals could want or need to develop their business.

8500 Attendees October Founded: 1912

13211 International Home Furnishings Market
International Home Furnishings Market Authority
POBox 5243
High Point, NC 27262
336-888-3794
FAX: 336-889-6999 800-874-6492
Judy@highpointmarket.org
www.highpointmarket.org

Judy Mendenhall, President
G Bruce Miller, Chief Executive Officer
Tammy Covington, Director Operations

Large home furnishings trade show with a variety of new opportunities to make your visit easy, cost effective and productive. Ten million square feet of exhibition space with 2,500 manufacturers represented.

80000 Attendees April & October Founded: 1921

13212 International Silk Flower Accessories Exhibition
Dallas Market Center
2000 N Stemmons Freeway
Dallas, TX 75207
214-655-6100
FAX: 214-655-6238 800-325-6587
8000 Attendees

13213 LightFair
AMC
120 Wall Street
17th Floor
New York, NY 10005
212-843-8358
FAX: 212-248-5017 www.iesna.org

Pamela R Weess, Circulation Director
Nini Schwenk, Manager

A major lighting trade show in North America featuring architectural lighting products from all spectrons of the industry. Containing 600 booths and 400 exhibits.

17M Attendees June
Mailing list available for rent 10M names $100 per M.
Printed in 4 colors on glossy stock

13214 Miami Spring Home Design & Remodeling Show
Home Show Management
1450 Madruga Avenue
Suite 301
Coral Gables, FL 33146
305-667-9299
FAX: 305-667-3266 888-353-3976
info@homeshows.net
www.homeshows.net

Steve Plotkin, Show Manager

Open to both the public and the trade. Over 800 exhibits of residential furniture, accessories, interior design, remodeling, landscaping, home improvement products, and services.

100M Attendees March, 2007 Founded: 1996

13215 Museum Store Association
4100 E Mississippi Avenue
Suite 800
Denver, CO 80246-3055
303-504-9223
FAX: 303-504-9585
expo@msaweb.org
www.museumdistrict.com

Beverly Barsook, Executive Director
Stacey Woldt, Assistant Director Programs
Eric Curtis, Conference & Expo Manager

2500 Attendees April, Annually Founded: 1955

13216 National Decorating Product Show
Paint & Decorating Retailers Association
403 Axminister Drive
Fenton, MO 63026-2941
636-326-2636
FAX: 314-991-5039

James B Savens III, Executive Director

430 booths for home supplies, equipment and services.
10M Attendees November

13217 National Decorating Products Association: Western Show
1050 N Lindbergh Boulevard
Saint Louis, MO 63132-2912
314-432-6001
FAX: 314-991-5039

Ruth Williams, Convention Manager

230 booths of decorating products such as paint, furniture and more.
2.5M Attendees March

13218 National Decorating Products Southern Show
Paint & Decorating Retailers Association
403 Axminister Drive
Fenton, MO 63026-2941
636-326-2636
FAX: 314-991-5039

Ruth Williams, Convention Manager

850 display booths of floor coverings, paint, furniture and various interior decorating products.
4M Attendees February

13219 Needlework Markets
Needlework Markets
PO Box 533
Pine Mountain, GA 31822
706-663-0140
FAX: 706-663-0202
NMItradeesh@aol.com
www.stitching.com

Emily Castleberry, Owner

February

13220 Old House New House Home Show
Kennedy Productions
1208 Lisle Place
Lisle, IL 60532-2262
630-515-1160
FAX: 630-515-1165
kp@corecomm.net
www.kennedyproductions.com

Laura McNamara, Event Producer

Over 300 home improvement exhibitors displaying cutting-edge home enhancements for kitchens, baths, home and garden including landscape, interior remodeling, pools, spas, floors, doors and more.
8000 Attendees Feb/Sept Founded: 1984

13221 Paint & Decorating Show
Paint and Decorating Retailers Association

403 Axminister Drive
Fenton, MO 63026-2941
636-326-2636
FAX: 636-326-1823 800-737-0107
info@pdra.org www.pdra.org

Kathy Witmeyer, Director Trade Shows
Nicholas Cichielo, CEO
Diane Capuane, Senior Contributing Editor
Dan Simon, Manager

Paint and decorating trade show.
2000 Attendees May Founded: 1999

13222 Paint Industries Show
492 Norristown Road
Blue Bell, PA 19422-2355
610-940-0777
FAX: 215-840-0292

Robert F Ziegler, Show Manager

Exhibits of raw materials, production equipment, instrumentation and testing apparatus for the coatings, inks and adhesives manufacturing industries. 920 booths.
3.5M Attendees October

13223 Painting and Decorating Contractors of America National Convention
3913 Old Lee Highway
Suite 301
Fairfax, VA 22030-2433
703-359-0826
FAX: 703-359-2976

Mary S DePersig, Director Meetings

200 booths of painting, wallcoverings, coatings and sundries.
1.2M Attendees March

13224 Surtex
George Little Management
10 Bank Street
Suite 1200
White Plains, NY 10606-1954
914-486-6070
FAX: 914-948-6180 800-272-7469
SURTEX@glmshows.com
www.SURTEX.com

Gina DeLuca, Show Coordinator
Rita Malek, Show Manager
George Little II, President

Annual show of 350 exhibitors featuring prints and patterns for all applications-decorative fabrics, linens, and domestics, apparel and contract textiles, wall and floor coverings, greeting cards, giftwrap and other paper products, tabletop, ceramics and packaging. Available for sale and/or license.
5000 Attendees May

13225 TEXBO
Reed Exhibition Companies
255 Washington Street
Newton, MA 02458-1637
617-584-4900
FAX: 617-630-2222

Elizabeth Hitchcock, International Sales

International trade fair for the interior design industry.
7M Attendees January

13226 Tabletop Market
George Little Management
577 Airport Boulevard
Burlingame, CA 94010-2020
650-548-1200
FAX: 650-344-5270 800-272-SHOW

Susan Corwin, VP

Annual show of 90 exhibitors featuring tableware, table linens, better housewares and decorative accessories.
1500 Attendees October

13227 West Coast Art and Frame
Art Trends/Picture Framing/Digital Fine Arts
PO Box 594
Lynbrook, NY 11563
516-596-3937
FAX: 516-596-3941
3500 Attendees

Directories & Databases

13228 Carpet & Rug Industry Buyers Guide Issue
Rodman Publishing
17 S Franklin Tpke
Ramsey, NJ 07446-2522
201-252-2552

More than 300 suppliers of machinery, equipment and colors and dyes used in the making of carpets and rugs. *$7.00*
Annual
Circulation: 5,500

13229 Carpet Cleaners Institute of the Northwest Membership Roster
Carpet Cleaners Institute of the Northwest
PMB #40 2421 South Union Avenue
Suite L-1
Tacoma, WA 98405
253-759-5762
FAX: 253-761-9134 877-692-2469
info@ccinw.org www.ccinw.org

Lyle Neville, President
Matt O'Haleck, Treasurer
Jim Thomas, Secretary
Mike Elias, Director of Education

Over 330 member companies involved in the carpet cleaning industry in Washington, Oregon, and Montana, USA and Alberta and British Columbia, Canada.
Annual

13230 Decor-Sources Issue
Commerce Publishing Company
330 N 4th Street
Suite 200
Saint Louis, MO 63102-2041
314-421-5445

Over 1,200 wholesale suppliers of pictures, frames, interior accessories and mirrors to art galleries and home accessories retailers are profiled. *$5.00*
Annual
Circulation: 35,000

13231 Decorating Registry
Paint and Decorating Retailers Association

403 Axminister Drive
Fenton, MO 63026-2941
636-326-2636
FAX: 636-326-1823
info@pdra.org www.pdra.org

Diane Capuano, Editor
Mary Paker, Directories Editor
Michael Austin, Managing Editor

List of 1,500 manufacturers, manufacturers' representatives, distributors, and suppiers of decorating merchandise; a comprehensive trademark and brand name directory. *$15.00*
200 pages Annual, Magazine
Printed in on glossy stock

13232 Decorating Retailer's Decorating Registry
National Decorating Products Association
1050 N Lindbergh Boulevard
Saint Louis, MO 63132-2912
314-432-6001
FAX: 314-991-5039 800-737-0107

Ernest Stewart, Executive VP
Cindy Nusbaum, Directories Editor

Trademark and brand name directory covering paint, wallcovering, window covering, floor covering and related sundries. *$9.00*

Annual
Circulation: 30,000
Mailing list available for rent 30,000+ names
Printed in 4 colors on glossy stock

13233 Decorating Retailer: Directory of the Wallcoverings Industry Issue
National Decorating Products Association

1050 N Lindbergh Boulevard
Saint Louis, MO 63132-2912
314-432-6001
FAX: 314-991-5039 800-737-0107

Ernest Stewart, Publisher
Cindy Nusbaum, Editor

Over 1,000 manufacturers and distributors of wallcoverings and related products are listed. *$25.00*
Annual
Circulation: 5,000
Printed in 4 colors

13234 DesignSource: Official Specifying and Buying Directory
PO Box 5059
Hoboken, NJ 07030-1501
201-963-9000

More than 10,000 companies that manufacture or supply products or services for interior designers. *$25.00*
Annual
Circulation: 40,000

13235 Directory of African American Design Firms
San Francisco Redevelopment Agency
770 Golden Gate Avenue
San Francisco, CA 94102
415-749-2400
FAX: 415-749-2526
Over 100 architectural, engineering, planning and landscape design firms.
Annual December

13236 Directory of Decorating Products' Retailers
Paint and Decorating Retailers Association
403 Axminister Drive
Fenton, MO 63026-2941
636-326-2636
FAX: 636-326-1823
info@pdra.org www.pdra.org

Ernest W Stewart, Executive VP

Nearly 2,800 retailers of decorating products, such as wall coverings, paints, window treatments, floor coverings, and household accessories. *$595.00*
Annual May
Computerized version available: Disk

13237 Draperies & Window Coverings: Directory and Buyer's Guide Issue
LC Clark Publishing Company
840 US Highway
Suite 330
North Palm Beach, FL 33408
561-627-3393
FAX: 561-964-6578

Howard K Shingle, Editor
Sarah Christy, Associate Editor
Katie Sosnowchik, Senior Editor
John J Lichty, Senior Editor
John Clark, Owner

Over 2,000 manufacturers and distributors of window coverings and other products used in the window coverings and interior fashions industry. *$15.00*
Annual

13238 ENR Directory of Design Firms
McGraw Hill
PO Box 182604
Columbus, OH 43272
614-304-4000
FAX: 614-759-3759
customer.service@mcgraw-hill.com
www.mcgraw-hill.com

Paul Hermannsfeldt, Editor

Profiles of 88 architects, architectural engineers, consultants and other design firms; limited to advertisers. *$95.00*
Biennial

13239 ENR: Top 500 Design Firms Issue
McGraw Hill
1221 Avenue of the Americas
Suite C3A
New York, NY 10020-1095
212-512-3916
FAX: 212-512-2820
constructioninfo@ecnext.com
www.mcgraw-hill.com

Howard B Stussman, Editor

List of 500 leading architectural, engineering and specialty design firms selected on basis of annual billings. *$35.00*
Annual April
Circulation: 71,000

13240 Flooring: Buying and Resource Guide Issue
Leo Douglas
9609 Gayton Road
Suite 100
Richmond, VA 23233-4904

Lists various manufacturers, workrooms, manufacturers' representatives and distributors of floor, and other interior surfacing products and equipment. *$38.50*
Annual
Circulation: 24,000

13241 Home Lighting & Accessories Suppliers Directory
Doctorow Communications
1011 Clifton Avenue
Clifton, NJ 07013
973-779-1600
FAX: 973-779-3242
info@homelighting.com
www.homelighting.com

Jeff Doctorow, Publisher
Linda Longo, Editor-in-Chief
Susan Grisham, Managing Editor
Dina Tamburro, Associate Publisher

A list of over 1,000 suppliers of lighting fixtures and other products for use in the retail lighting industry are provided. *$6.00*
Semi-Annual
Circulation: 9,690

13242 Interior Decorators Handbook
EW Williams Publications
370 Lexington Avenue
Suite 1409
New York, NY 10017
212-661-1516
FAX: 212-661-1713
philpl@ewwpi.com
www.idhonline.com

Andrew Williams, President
Phillip Russo, Publishing Director
Lynne Lancaster, Advertising Sales Director

Designers resource guide with over 600 product/service categories. 3,000 suppliers are listed with their headquarters, showrooms. Addresses, phone numbers, fax numbers and e-mail. *$36.00*
230 pages Bi-annual Founded: 1922
Circulation: 25,000
Printed in 4 colors on glossy stock

13243 LDB Interior Textiles Annual Buyers' Guide
EW Williams Publications
370 Lexington Avenue
Room 1409
New York, NY 10017-1999
212-661-1516

karenldb@ewwpi.com
ldbinteriortextiles.com

Karen Chambers, Editor-in-Chief
Philippa Hochschild, Publisher

Over 2,000 manufacturers and importers of home accessories and interior design products are listed. *$40.00*
Monthly Founded: 1927
Circulation: 14000

13244 Lighting Dimensions-Directory Issue
32 W 18th Street
New York, NY 10011-4612
212-462-0100

A list of over 2,000 manufacturers, suppliers and consultants of lighting and related equipment and supplies. *$15.00*
Annual
Circulation: 13,000

13245 Market Resource Guide
International Home Furnishings Center
210 E Commerce Avenue
High Point, NC 27260-5238
336-888-3700
FAX: 336-882-1873
marketing@ihfc.com www.ihfc.com

Tom Loney, VP Marketing

Two-volume directory offers over 1,500 manufacturers and distributors in the furniture industry with exhibits at the International Home Furnishings Market. *$25.00*
624 pages Semiannual Founded: 1974
Printed in 4 colors on glossy stock

13246 Painting and Wallcovering Contractor
Painting & Decorating Contractors of America
11960 Wesline Industrial Drive
Suite 201
St Louis, MO 63146-3209
314-514-7322
FAX: 314-514-9417 800-332-7322

Ian R Horen, CEO
Richard Bright, Director Communications

Offers a list of over 3,300 member contractors engaged in painting, decorating and special coatings applications.
Annual
Circulation: 3,500

13247 Rauch Guide to the US Paint Industry
Grey House Publishing
PO Box 860
Millerton, NY 12546
518-789-8700
FAX: 518-789-0545 800-562-2139
books@greyhouse.com
www.greyhouse.com

Leslie Mackenzie, Publisher
Richard Gottlieb, President

Provides industry structure and current market information about the industry. Divided into five major chapters with 90 tables and 20 figures in its 316 pages. There is a profile of 778 industry manufacturers, with sales estimates, products, mergers, and aquisitions, diversities and other information for the 361 largest companies. *$595.00*

Annual ISBN 0-932157-09-2
Computerized version available: CD-ROM

13248 Specifiers' Guide and Directory of Contract Wallcoverings
Wall Publications
570 7th Avenue
New York, NY 10018-1603
212-730-9590

A who's who directory of services and supplies to the industry. *$15.95*
Annual
Circulation: 15,000

13249 Tile & Decorative Surfaces
18 E 41st Street
New York, NY 10017-6222
212-376-7722
FAX: 212-376-7723
publisher@ashlee.com
www.ashlee.com/tile

Jordan M Wright, President/Publisher

The Tile industry including ceramic, natural stone, terrazzo, agglomerated, cement glasstiles and others allied to the field. Architects, designers, importers, retail floor covering dealers, distributors, installers and contractors. Also, firms involved with renovation and restoration of tile. Accepts advertising. *$25.00*
Monthly Founded: 1950
Circulation: 24,000

13250 Wallcovering Pattern Guide and Source Directory
Home Fashion Information Network
557 S Duncan Avenue
Clearwater, FL 33756-6255

A list of wallcovering manufacturers and distributors are offered in this comprehensive directory aimed at the interior design community. *$78.00*
Semiannual
Circulation: 10,000

13251 Western Floors: Buyers Guide & Directory
Specialist Publications
17835 Ventura Boulevard
Suite 312
Encino, CA 91316-3634
818-709-1437

A list of firms which manufacture, import or distribute floor coverings. *$15.00*
Annual
Circulation: 17,000

13252 Who's Who in Floor Covering Distribution
National Association of Floor Covering Distributor
401 N Michigan Avenue
Suite 2400
Chicago, IL 60611-4267
312-321-6836
FAX: 312-673-6962

Offers information on over 400 member distributors and suppliers of floor coverings.
40 pages Annual

Industry Web Sites

13253 www.carpet-rug.com
Carpet and Rug Institute

National association of carpet and rug manufacturers. Source for product information.

13254 www.fider.org
Foundation for Interior Design Education Research

Promotes excellence in interior design education through research and the accreditation of academic programs.

13255 www.greyhouse.com
Grey House Publishing

Selected Grey House directories in the fields of business, health and education are available online. Users can search our online databases by several different search criteria, such as product categories, geographic area, sales volume and much, much more. Full Grey House catalog and online ordering also available.

13256 www.homeshows.net
Home Show Management

Organizes three annual south Flordia home design and remodeling shows in Coconut Grove, Ft. Lauderdale and Miami Beach convention centers. Open to the trade and public.

13257 www.i-d-d.com
Interior Design Directory

Sources and links for the interior designer.

13258 www.iesna.org
Illuminating Engineering Society of North America

To advance knowledge and disseminate information for the improvement of the lighted environment to the benefit of society. Publishes a monthly magazine.

13259 www.iida.org
International Interior Design Association

Members are professionals from various facets of the interior design trade.

13260 www.nadfd.com
National Assn of Decorative Fabric Distributors

Promotes the textile and home furnishings manufacturers and distributors.

13261 www.nafcd.org
National Assn of Floor Covering Distributors

This organization offers information on over 500 member distributors and suppliers of floor coverings. Publications available to members.

13262 www.ncidq.org
National Council for Interior Design Qualification

Serves to identify to the public those interior designers who have met the minimum standards for professional practice by passing the NCIDQ examination.

13263 www.ngpp.org
National Guild of Professional Paperhangers

Promotes products, upgrades skills of paperhangers and encourages good business ethics. Holds workshops and seminars.

13264 www.nhfa.org
National Home Furnishings Association

A federation of local home furnishings representatives association.

13265 www.oikos.com
Oikos

Devoted to serving professionals whose work promotes sustainable design and construction. Oikos is a Greek word meaning house. Oikos serves as the root for two English words: ecology and economy. That may seem contradictory at first, but it makes perfect sense. Ecology is the science of interactions in natural communities. It examines the web of life where plants, animals, rocks and gases all affect one another. Healthy communities, healthy ecosystems exist ina dynamic equilibrium.

13266 www.pdra.org
Paint and Decorating Retailers Association

This organization lists 1,500 manufacturers, manufacturers' representatives, distributors, and suppliers of decorating merchandise.

13267 www.resources.com
Resources

Organized into easy point and click directories under a highly interactive database.

Associations

13268 Academy of International Business
Michigan State University
7 Eppley Center
East Lansing, MI 48824-1121
517-432-1452
FAX: 517-432-1009
aib@aib.msu.edu http://aib.msu.edu
G Tomas M Hult, Executive Director
Tunga Kiyak, Managing Director
Irem Kiyak, Treasurer
Leading association of scholars and specialists in the field of international business. Members include academics, consultants, researchers, and NGO representatives. AIB has chapters worldwide to facilitate networking and information exchange at a local level.
3000 Members Founded: 1959
Mailing list available for rent 3000 names $250 per M.

13269 American Association of Exporters and Importers
1050 17th Street, NW
Suite 810
Washington, DC 20036
202-857-8009
FAX: 202-857-7843
hg@aaei.org www.aaei.org
Hallock Northcott, President/CEO
Kathy Corrigan, Director Meetings & Events
Terri A Lankford, Director Membership & Marketing
David A Potts, Manager Office Administration
Supports those involved in trade development with other countries and conducting business in the United States, as well as developments affecting trade originating from Treasury, Customs, US Courts, Commerce Department, International Trade Commission, Federal Maritime Commission and other regulatory agencies. Hosts annual trade show.
Founded: 1921

13270 American League for Exports and Security Assistance
122 C Street NW
Suite 740
Washington, DC 20001-2109
202-933-3903
FAX: 202-737-4727
David Lewis, President
Encourages and supports the sale of American defense products abroad in agreement with foreign policy, security and economic goals of the nation.
38 Members Founded: 1976

13271 California Council for International Trade
442 Post Street
Suite 800
San Francisco, CA 94102
415-788-4127
FAX: 415-788-5356
info@ccit.net www.ccit.net
David Zuercher, Chairman
Tamsin Randlett, Vice Chair
John Liebman, Vice Chair
Joseph Harrison, President
To facilitate through education, promotion, and advocacy communication between its member companies and policy makers to protect and promote trade policies and programs which advance the global trade investment of California businesses.
Founded: 1960

13272 Distributors & Consolidators of America
2240 Bernays Drive
York, PA 17404

FAX: 717-764-6531 888-519-9195
daca@dacacarriers.com
www.dacacarriers.com
Kevin J Brink, Chairman
Mark Anness, President
Mike Wichert, VP
Rich Eberhart, Treasurer
Rich Brown, Secretary
This organization helps firms and individuals active in the shipping, warehousing, receiving, distribution or consolidation of freight shipments.

13273 FSC/DISC Tax Association
Council for International Tax Education
PO Box 1012
White Plains, NY 10602
914-328-5656
FAX: 914-328-5757
info@citeusa.org www.citeusa.org
Robert Ross, Owner
The only organization operating on a national level devoted to educational interests of companies that have set up a foreign sales corporation.
300 Members Founded: 1984

13274 Gemini Shippers Group National Fashion Accessories Assoc
350 5th Avenue
Suite 2030
New York, NY 10118
212-947-3424
FAX: 212-629-0361
info@Geminishippers.com
www.geminishippers.com
Sara Mayes, President
Harold Sachs, Executive Director
Offers membership to importers and exporters of various products.
200 Members Founded: 1916

13275 Hong Kong Trade Development Council
219 E 46th Street
New York, NY 10017-2951
212-388-8941
FAX: 212-838-8941
hktdc@tdc.org.hk www.tdctrade.com
Louis Ho, Executive Director
Promotes trade between the United States and Hong Kong.

13276 Institute of Management & Administration
3 Park Avenue
30th Floor
New York, NY 10016
212-244-0360
FAX: 212-564-0465
subserve@ioma.com www.ioma.com
Joe Bremner, President
Perry Patterson, VP/Group Publisher
Publishes a broad range of high quality information products for business profesionals. The two purposes of the products are to improve the efficiency of the subscriber and to enhance the financial performance of the firm or organization.
180M Members

13277 International Chamber of Commerce (ICC)

www.iccwbo.org
Yong Sung Park, Chairman
Marcus Wallenberg, Vice Chairman
Maria Livanos Cattaui, Secretary General

The voice of world business championing the global economy as a force for economic growth, job creation and prosperity. Headquartered in Paris. Hosts conferences.
Founded: 1919

13278 International Trade Council
3114 Circle Hill Road
Alexandria, VA 22301
703-548-1234
FAX: 703-548-6216
Dr Peter Nelsen, President
Robert Tedwell, VP
Promotes free trade and eliminates trade barriers and facilitates logistics, research, and marketing for members. Conducts educational programs.
850 Members Founded: 1981

13279 International Warehouse Logistics Association
2800 River Road
Suite 260
Des Plaines, IL 60018
847-813-4699
FAX: 847-813-0115
email@iwla.com www.iwla.com
Robert R Auray Jr, Chairman
Joel Hoiland, CEO
David Pettit, Vice Chairman
John J Zevalkink, Secretary/Treasurer
The unified voice of the global logistics outsourcing industry, representing third party warehousing, transportation and logistics service providers. Our member companies provide the most timely and cost-effective global logistics solutions for their customers and are committed to protecting the free flow of products across international borders.
500 Members Founded: 1997

13280 Latin American Studies Association
University of Pittsburgh
946 William Pitt University
Pittsburgh, PA
412-648-7929
FAX: 412-624-7145
lasa@pitt.edu
lasa.international.pitt.edu/
Sonia E Alvarez, President
Charles R Hale, VP
Marysa Navarro, Past President
To foster intellectual discussion, research, and teaching on Latin America, the Caribbean, and its people throughout the Americas, promote the interests of its diverse membership, and encourage civic engagement through network building and public debate.
5000+ Members
Mailing list available for rent

13281 Matson Navigation Company
555 12th Street
Oakland, CA 94607

800-4MA-TSON
Leader in Pacific shipping, and is closely associated with its longstanding position

as Hawaii's premier carrier, as well as service to Guam and the Mid-Pacific.
Founded: 1882

13282 Meridian IQ
10990 Roe Avenue
Overland Park, KS 66211
913-906-6800
FAX: 913-344-4191 877-246-4909
contact_us@meridianiq.com
www.meridianiq.com
Suzanne Dawson, Public/Media Relations
Plans and coordinates the movement of goods throughout the world.

13283 Monterey Bay International Trade Association
PO Box 523
Santa Cruz, CA 95061-0523
831-335-4780
FAX: 831-335-4822
info@mbita.org www.mbita.org
Tony Livoti, Executive Director
A non-profit international trade association dedicated to promoting business networking, and education in the greater Monterey Bay Region.
60000 Members Founded: 1984

13284 National Association of Export Companies
Grand Central Station
PO Box 3949
New York, NY 10163
877-291-4901

director@nexco.org www.nexco.org
Gerri Cristantiello, Executive Director
Members are import and export trading and import and export management companies, international trade service vendors and other international trade companies.
300 Members Founded: 1965

13285 National Council on International Trade Development (NCITD)
818 Connecticut Avenue NW
12th Floor
Washington, DC 20006
202-872-9280
FAX: 202-872-8324
cu@ncitd.org www.ncitd.org
Mary Fromyer, Executive Director
Non-profit membership organization dedicated to providing direct expertise on a wide range of international trade topics. Our mission is to identify impediments to all aspects of international commerce and to provide solutions to faciliting the global process.
Founded: 1967

13286 Russian Trade Development Association
Palms & Company
515 Lake Street S
Palms Habor Lights Building #3103
Kirkland, WA 98033
425-828-6774

Russia@peterpalms.com
www.PeterPalms.com
Evgenui Kolesnikov, Show Manager
Variety of industrial trade shows by SIC code occuring in the Russian Federation throughout the year. Export services from USA to purchasing agent services in Russia for buyers worldwide.
25000 Members Founded: 1989

13287 US China Business Council
1818 N Street NW
Suite 200
Washington, DC 20036
202-429-0340
FAX: 202-775-2476
info@uschina.org www.uschina.org
John Frisbie, President
Erin Ennis, VP
R Mark Mechem, Director/Business Advisory Services
E Palmer Golson, Director Membership Services
Membership association for US companies doing business with the People's Republic of China. Provides representation, practical assistance, and up-to-date information to members.
Founded: 1973

13288 US Council for International Business
1212 Avenue of the Americas
New York, NY 10036
212-354-4480
FAX: 212-575-0327
info@uscib.org www.uscib.org
William G Parrett, Chairman
Peter M Robinson, President
John E Merow, Secretary
Addresses a broad range of policy issues with the objective of promoting an open system of world trade, finance and investment in which business can flourish and contribute to economic growth, human welfareand protection of the environment.
300 Members Founded: 1945

13289 US Russia Business Council
1701 Pennsylvania Avenue NW
Suite 520
Washington, DC 20006
202-739-9180
FAX: 202-659-5920
info@usrbc.org www.usrbc.org
Eugene K Lawson, President
Z Blake Marshall, Executive VP
Karen Montagne, VP
Jeff Barnett, Program Manager
A Washington based trade association that represents the interests of 300 member companies operating in the Russian market. Their mission is to expand and enhance the US-Russian commercial relationship.
300 Members Founded: 1993

13290 US Vietnam Trade Council
731 Eighth Street SE
Washington, DC 20003
202-547-3800
FAX: 202-546-4784
vfoote@usasean.org www.usvtc.org
Virginia Foote, President/Co-founder
Robert Schiffer, Executive VP
Non-profit membership organization founded under the leadership of Ambassador William H Sullivan and Foreign Minister Nguyen Co Thach with the purpose to build a new future relationship between.
Founded: 1989

Newsletters

13291 AAMA News
Asian American Manufacturers Association
3300 Zanker Road
Maildrop Sj2f8
San Jose, CA 95134
408-955-4505
FAX: 408-955-4516 aama@aamasv.com

Robert M Lee, Executive Director
$30.00
Monthly
Circulation: 1000

13292 AIB Newsletter
Academy of International Business
Michigan State University
7 Eppley Center
East Lansing, MI 48824-1121
517-432-1452
FAX: 517-432-1009
aib@aib.msu.edu http://aib.msu.edu
G Tomas M Hult, Executive Director
Tunga Kiyak, Managing Director
Ireem Kiyak, Treasurer
International trade news. *$85.00*
16 pages Quarterly

13293 Asahi Shimbun Satellite Edition
Japan Access
757 3rd Avenue
Front 3
New York, NY 10017-2013
212-869-7018
FAX: 212-317-3025
Mo Matsuchita, Publisher *$3.00*

Circulation: 12,000

13294 Asian Economic News
Kyodo News International
50 Rockefeller Plaza
Room 803
New York, NY 10020-1605
212-603-6600
FAX: 212-397-3721
kni@kyodonews.com
www.kyodonews.com
Economic business news of Asian countries and regions.

13295 Business Russia
Economist Intelligence Unit
111 W 57th Street
New York, NY 10019-2211
212-586-1115
FAX: 212-586-1181 800-938-4685
newyork@eiu.com www.eiu.com
Hyunkyu Lee, Owner
Monthly newsletter providing financial and market information as well as current business statistics, economic forecasts and political risk analysis for Russia. *$865.00*
12 pages Monthly

13296 Business Africa
Economist Intelligence Unit
111 W 57th Street
New York, NY 10019-2211
212-861-1115
FAX: 212-586-1181 800-938-4685
newyork@eiu.com http://www.eiu.com

Daniel Franklin, Editorial Director
Richard Epstein, Director

Ingersoll Rand, Managing Director
Jane Morley, Senior Editor

Fortnightly newsletter identifying key business issues across Africa; forecasting future developments and trends and analysing their implications on Africa's business environment. *$1095.00*

12 pages Founded: 1946

13297 Business Asia
Economist Intelligence Unit
111 W 57th Street
New York, NY 10019-2211
212-861-1115
FAX: 212-586-1181 800-938-4685
newyork@eiu.com
http://www.eiu.com

Daniel Franklin, Editorial Director
David Butter, Editor
Euan Rellie, Executive Director

Fortnightly newsletter focusing on operating issues and analyzing current political, business and economic developments across Asia. *$1055.00*

12 pages Fortnightly Founded: 1946

13298 Business China
Economist Intelligence Unit
111 W 57th Street
New York, NY 10019-2211
212-586-1115
FAX: 212-586-1181 800-938-4685
newyork@eiu.com
http://www.eiu.com

Daniel Franklin, Editorial Director
Richard Epstein, Advertising Manager

Fortnightly newsletter alerting business executives to the political economic and legal changes that will affect corporate interests. Provides corporate case studies. Analysis financial issues in, and affecting, China. Offers practical, detailed advice. *$895.00*

12 pages 50 issues per y Founded: 1946

13299 Business Eastern Europe
Economist Intelligence Unit
111 W 57th Street
New York, NY 10019-2211
212-861-1115
FAX: 212-586-1181 800-938-4685
newyork@eiu.com
http://www.eiu.com

Daniel Franklin, Editorial Director
Richard Epstein, Advertising Manager

Fortnightly newsletter providing information for business planning on the latest political and economic developments in Eastern Europe on a country-by-country basis. *$1395.00*

12 pages Weekly Founded: 1946

13300 Business Europe
Economist Intelligence Unit
111 W 57th Street
New York, NY 10019-2211
212-861-1115
FAX: 212-586-1181 800-938-4685
newyork@eiu.com
http://www.eiu.com/

Lou Hencken, CEO/President
Paul Lewis, Editor
Nina Andrikian, Marketing

Fortnightly newsletter providing hard facts about changes in the EU's business environment; identifying opportunities for growth and analysing the impact of current issues on business in Europe. *$1435.00*

12 pages 44 issues per y Founded: 1946

13301 Business India Intelligence
Economist Intelligence Unit
111 W 57th Street
New York, NY 10019-2211
212-586-1115
FAX: 212-586-1181 800-938-4685
newyork@eiu.com
http://www.eiu.com

Helen Alexander, CEO
Lou Kelly, Marketing Manager
Louis Ceil, VP

Monthly newsletter tracking the issues and trends in India's business environment; providing information on infrastructure and industries, tariffs, taxes and economic policy and consumer markets. *$660.00*

16 pages Monthly Founded: 1946

13302 Business Latin America
Economist Intelligence Unit
111 W 57th Street
New York, NY 10019-2211
212-861-1115
FAX: 212-586-1181 800-938-4685
newyork@eiu.com
http://www.eiu.com

Daniel Franklin, Editorial Director
Richard Epstein, Director, Business Development

Weekly newsletter covering vital issues affecting business in Latin America, identifying the opportunities, and forecasting the risks to help executives make competetive corporate decisions. *$1370.00*

12 pages Founded: 1946

13303 Caribbean Update
52 Maple Avenue
Maplewood, NJ 07040-2626
973-762-1565
FAX: 973-762-9585
mexcarib@cs.com
http://www.caribbeanupdate.org

Kal Wagenheim, Editor/Publisher

Monthly newsletter focusing on trade and investment opportunities in the Caribbean and Central America. *$267.00*

24 pages Monthly Founded: 1985
Mailing list available for rent 2500 names
Printed in 1 color on newsprint stock

13304 Country Finance
Economist Intelligence Unit
111 W 57th Street
New York, NY 10019-2211
212-861-1115
FAX: 212-586-1181 800-938-4685
newyork@eiu.com
http://www.eiu.com

Daniel Franklin, Editorial Director
Richard Epstein, Director, Business Development

Covering 47 countries, this service is a comprehensive overview of global financial issues and conditions. Provides case studies and resources to help companies find and manage finances in countries around the globe. A weekly alert service highlights changes as they happen. *$ 445.00*

41 issues per y Founded: 1946

13305 Country Forecasts
Economist Intelligence Unit
111 W 57th Street
New York, NY 10019-2211
212-861-1115
FAX: 212-586-1181 800-938-4685
newyork@eiu.com
http://www.eiu.com

Daniel Franklin, Editorial Director

Five-year forecasts of political, economic and business trends in 60 countries. Each quarterly updated forecast focuses on the key factors affecting a country's political and economic outlook and its business environment over the next five years. *$845.00*

36 pages Quarterly

13306 Country Monitor
Economist Intelligence Unit
111 W 57th Street
New York, NY 10019-2211
212-861-1115
FAX: 212-586-1181 800-938-4685
newyork@eiu.com
http://www.eiu.com

Daniel Franklin, Editorial Director
Richard Epstein, Director, Business Development

Weekly newsletter analysing the latest global economic and political events; providing risk assessment in emerging markets and facts on global trends and markets. *$895.00*

12 pages Weekly Founded: 1946

13307 Country Reports
Economist Intelligence Unit
111 W 57th Street
New York, NY 10019-2211
212-861-1115
FAX: 212-586-0248 800-938-4685
newyork@eiu.com
http://www.eiu.com

Daniel Franklin, Editorial Director
Emily Morris, Senior Editor

Quarterly updates on the situation in over 180 countries. Each report includes and analysis of a country's current political and economic climate as well as 12-18 month economic projection. *$425.00*

Founded: 1946

13308 Country Risk Service
Economist Intelligence Unit
111 W 57th Street
New York, NY 10019-2211
212-861-1115
FAX: 212-586-1181 800-938-4685
newyork@eiu.com
http://www.eiu.com

Daniel Franklin, Editorial Director

Information to assist financial risk management in emerging countries. Country Risk Service is an exclusive two-year forecasting service, assessing the solvency of 100 indebted countries. Each report includes projections of GDP, the budget deficit, trade and current account balances, financing requirements and debt-service ratio. *$760.00*

60 pages Quarterly Founded: 1946

13309 Craighead's Country Reports
Craighead Publications
397 Post Road
PO Box 1006
Darien, CT 06820-1006
203-655-1007
FAX: 203-655-0018
scraighead@craighead.com
http://www.craighead.com

Scott Craighead, President

Reports on more than 80 countries focusing on living and working conditions for international business travelers and employees who relocate abroad on business assignments. *$95.00*

50 pages Founded: 1977

13310 East Asian Business Intelligence
International Executive Reports
717 D Street NW
Suite 300
Washington, DC 20004-2812
202-783-2424
FAX: 202-628-6618 execrep@aol.com
William Hearn, Publisher
Twice-a-month newsletter containing business leads and market studies on Far East business. *$345.00*
8 pages 22 per year Founded: 1986
Circulation: 300
Printed in on matte stock

13311 East/West Executive Guide
WorldTrade Executive
PO Box 761
Concord, MA 01742
978-287-0301
FAX: 978-287-0302 www.wtexec.com
Alison French, Production Manager
Provides detailed information on how to do business in Russia, the CIS, and East/Central Europe. Focuses on key mechanical issues such as accounting and tax matters, local sourcing, the due diligence process, labor, finance, permits, environmental issues etc. *$656.00*
Monthly

13312 European Community
US Council for International Business
1212 Avenue of the Americas
Suite 1805
New York, NY 10036-1689
212-544-4480
FAX: 212-575-0327
Cly Wallace, Editor
Newssheet on developments in the European community affecting business on council activities.
Circulation: 2,800

13313 Export Update
Trade Communications
733 15th Street NW
Suite 1100
Washington, DC 20005-2112
202-737-1060
FAX: 202-783-5966
Stephen Pfeiderer, Publisher
Includes significant buying trends, specific sales leads, in-depth country market profiles, latest figures on trade activity, schedules for trade affairs and missions and insight on the affects of international news.

13314 Hong Kong Trade Development Council Newsletter
219 E 46th Street
New York, NY 10017-2951
212-388-8941
FAX: 212-838-8941
new.york.office@tdc.org.hk
http://www.tdctrade.com
Mike Mehta, Coordinator Communications
Pehen Wong, CEO
Elfyweet Rufino, Editor
Will Li, Marketing
Louis Ho, Executive Director
Promotes trade between United States and Hong Kong.
Weekly Founded: 1966

13315 Hong Kong Trader
Hong Kong Trade Development Council
219 E 46th Street
New York, NY 10017-2951
212-388-8941
FAX: 212-838-8941 www.tdctrade.com
Martin Evans, Editor
Louis Ho, Executive Director
8 pages Monthly
Printed in on glossy stock

13316 Indonesia Letter
Asia Letter Group
12508 Whitley Street
Whittier, CA 90601-2729
FAX: 852-526-2950

13317 International Finance & Treasury
WorldTrade Executive
PO Box 761
Concord, MA 01742
978-287-0301
FAX: 978-287-0302 www.wtexec.com
Alison French, CEO
Focus on techniques used by leading firms to manage worldwide financial resources. Topics covered include: tax, accounting and regulatory changes, currency and interest rate risk, cash management techniques, risk management strategies, regional treasury alerts. *$1245.00*
Weekly

13318 International Observer
PO Box 5997
Washington, DC 20016-1597
202-244-7050
FAX: 202-244-5410
J Wagner, Publisher
Informs on world developments in political, diplomatic, government, security, and economic origins. *$240.00*
10 pages Monthly
Printed in 1 color

13319 International Securitization & Structured Finance
WorldTrade Executive
PO Box 761
Concord, MA 01742
978-287-0301
FAX: 978-287-0302
info@wtexec.com
http://www.wtexec.com
Jill McKenna, Production Manager
George Veoger, Editor
Pierre Brown, Publisher
Alleesa Aughas, Marketing Manager
A twice monthly report devoted exclusively to asset-backed securities in international markets. Covers all aspects of international asset-backed securitization, including innovative product trends, issuer considerations, regulatory matters, and tax and accounting considerations. Examines what is working in emerging markets and spotlights unique US transactions. *$1296.00*
Bi-monthly Founded: 1996

13320 International Trade Alert
American Association of Importers and Exporters
1200 G Street NW
Suite 800
Washington, DC 20005
212-944-2230
FAX: 202-661-2185
hg@aaei.org www.aaei.org
Mathew Mermigousis, Production Manager
Stuart Iserber, Editor
Reports on current trade developments and advance notices of changes in rules for conducting business in the United States, as well as developments affecting trade originating from Treasury, Customs, US Courts, Commerce Department, International Trade Commission, Federal Maritime Commission and other regulatory agencies.
10 pages Monthly
Circulation: 2,200

13321 International Trade Reporter Current Reports
Bureau of National Affairs
1231 25th Street NW
Washington, DC 20037-1197
202-452-4200
800-372-1033
customercare@bna.com
http://www.bna.com/
Gregory C McCaffery, Publisher
Alan Stowell, Managing Editor
A comprehensive source that reports and analyzes legislative and regulatory developments as well as private sector activities affecting international trade (both export and import). *$1744.00*
Weekly Founded: 1929

13322 International Trade Reporter Decisions
Bureau of National Affairs
1231 25th Street NW
Washington, DC 20037-1197
202-452-4200
800-372-1033
customercare@bna.com
http://www.bna.com
Gregory C McCaffery, Publisher
Alan Stowell, Managing Editor
Only available source of digested, classified and indexed judicial and administrative decisions dealing with legal issues arising from US trade law (mostly import cases). *$2265.00*

13323 International Trade Reporter Import Reference Manual
Bureau of National Affairs
1231 25th Street NW
Washington, DC 20037-1197
202-452-4200
800-372-1033
customercare@bna.com
http://www.bna.com
Gregory C McCaffery, Publisher
Alan Stowell, Managing Editor
A complete guide to the entire import process with analysis and full text of statutes, regulations, and executive orders on subjects such as customhouse brokers, dumping, countervailing duties, escape clauses, and presidential retaliation. *$1781.00*

13324 Investing, Licensing & Trading
Economist Intelligence Unit
111 W 57th Street
New York, NY 10019-2211
212-586-1115
FAX: 212-586-1181 800-938-4685
newyork@eiu.com www.eiu.com
Updated twice a year, ILT outlines business requirements for operating successfully in the world's major markets. This reference service, shows how the laws work in practice, with case studies of how leading multinationals obtain government approvals, set

up local companies, calculate corporate and personal taxes and overcome restrictions and other legal hurdles in 60 countries and the European Union. *$345.00*

13325 Managing Exports
Institute of Management & Administration
3 Park Avenue
New York, NY 10016
212-244-0360
FAX: 212-564-0465
subserve@ioma.com
http://www.ioma.com/
Chris Horner, Editor
David Foster, CEO
Paul Morris, Circulation
Jim Bell, Marketing
David Solomon, Sub-Editor
Shows how to increase international sales, and find new distribution channels and reduce exports costs and risks. *$311.95*
Monthly Founded: 1982

13326 Market Europe
PRS Group
6320 Fly Road
Suite 102
East Syracuse, NY 13057-9358
315-431-0511
FAX: 315-431-0200
prsgroup@prsgroup.com
http://www.prsgroup.com
Patti Davis, Circulation Manager
Doris Walsh, Editor
Mary Lou Walsh, President
Demographic and lifestyle information about consumers in Europe to help businesses do a better job marketing to those consumers. *$397.00*
Monthly Founded: 1985
Circulation: 325 Audited
Printed in 1 color on matte stock

13327 Mexican Forecast
WorldTrade Executive
2250 Main Street
Suite 100
Concord, MA 01742
978-287-0301
FAX: 978-287-0302
info@wtexec.com
http://www.wtexec.com
Alison French, Production Manager
Provides up-to-date information and forecasts on Mexican business. Includes coverage of foreign trade, currency, major industry sectors, market trends and investment climates. *$535.00*

13328 Middle East Business Intelligence
International Executive Reports
717 D Street NW
Suite 300
Washington, DC 20004-2812
202-783-2424
FAX: 202-628-6618 execrep@aol.com
William Hearn, Publisher
Twice-a-month newsletter containing business leads and market studies on Middle East business. *$345.00*
8 pages
Circulation: 400
Printed in 1 color on matte stock

13329 Middle East Trade Letter
PO Box 472986
Charlotte, NC 28247-2986
704-536-9847
FAX: 704-543-6161
Leslie B Cohen, Publisher
Business in the Middle East. *$139.00*
4 pages Quarterly
Circulation: 500 Audited
Printed in 1 color on newsprint stock

13330 Nielsen's International Investment Letter
Nielsen & Nielsen
PO Box 7532
Olympia, WA 98507-7532
360-542-2663

Thor Nielsen, Publisher
Nancy Nelson, Owner
Tracks domestic and international stock markets and economics, precious metals and other commodities, USA and foreign bonds, interest rates, foreign currencies and real estate; offers clients specific buy and sell recommendations on domestic and international investments for both traders and investors. *$360.00*
10 pages Monthly
Printed in on matte stock

13331 North American Free Trade & Investment
WorldTrade Executive
PO Box 761
Concord, MA 01742
978-287-0301
FAX: 978-287-0302
info@wtexec.com
http://www.wtexec.com
Alison French, Production Manager
Gary Brown, CEO/President
Gary Brown, Editor
Dana Pierce, Marketing Manager
Dana Pierce, Circulation Manager
Covers NAFTA trade and investment developments. Key topics include rules of origin, tariff phaseouts, intellectual property protection, compliance and planning options, and business opportunities. *$734.00*

Annual+ Founded: 1992
Circulation: 100

13332 Pacific Russia Oil & Gas Report
Pacific Russia Information Group
2415 La Honda Drive
Anchorage, AK 99517
907-258-2331
FAX: 907-258-2332
update@russianfareast.com
www.russianfareast.com
Elisa Miller PhD
A quarterly executive briefing for executives and other decision makers covering oil and gas projects of the Russian Far East. *$ 495.00*
Quarterly

13333 Practical Latin American Tax Strategies
WorldTrade Executive
PO Box 761
Concord, MA 01742
978-287-0301
FAX: 978-287-0302 www.wtexec.com
Alison French, Production Manager
A monthly report on how leading companies are reacting to changes and developments in Latin American tax practice. Includes commentary from senior practitioners at major law and accounting firms and case studies from major corporations. *$645.00*
Monthly

13334 Practical US/International Tax Strategies
WorldTrade Executive
PO Box 761
Concord, MA 01742-761
978-287-0301
FAX: 978-287-0302
info@wtexec.com
http://www.wtexec.com
Dana Pierce, Production Manager
Gary Brown, CEO/Publisher
David Cooper, Editor
John Nartel, Marketing Manager
Jay Stanley, Circulation Manager
Analyzes how leading companies are reacting to changes in US-international tax practice. Leading experts provide practical guidance covering every area of international transactions. *$614.00*
Fortnightly Founded: 1992
Circulation: 200

13335 Russian Far East Update
Russian Far East Update
PO Box 22126
Seattle, WA 98122-0126
206-447-2668
FAX: 206-628-0979
update@russianfareast.com
www.russianfareast.com
Trade and economic information plus news analysis of Russia's far east. *$20.00*

Circulation: 1,300

13336 Vietnam Business Info Track
Vietnam Access
PO Box 1210
Port Hueneme, CA 93044-1210

FAX: 805-985-0839
Kahn Le, Editor
Comprehensive coverage of Vietnam market. Focuses on trade, investment and sector reports. Gives you an immediate advantage in evaluating the potential of doing business in Vietnam and operating in a timely and cost effective matter.

13337 Vietnam Market Watch
Vietnam Market Resources
375 Lexington Avenue
New York, NY 10017
212-499-2000
FAX: 203-256-9790
http://www.inc.com/
Khoung Ho, Publisher
For companies and professionals doing business in Vietnam. *$295.00*
Monthly Founded: 2004
Circulation: 500

13338 Weekly International Market Alert

International Business Communications
114 E 32nd Street
#602
New York, NY 10016
212-686-1460

Johnathan Block, Publisher
International trade news.
Monthly

13339 World Trade
Taipan Press
4199 Campus Drive
Suite 230
Irvine, CA 92612-4684
949-410-0980
FAX: 949-725-0306
Will Swaim, Publisher
Articles aim to help companies expand international opportunities. Accepts advertising. *$24.00*
96 pages Monthly

Magazines & Journals

13340 AIB Insights
Academy of International Business
Michigan State University
7 Eppley Center
East Lansing, MI 48824-1121
517-432-1452
FAX: 517-432-1009
aib@aib.msu.edu http://aib.msu.edu
G Tomas M Hult, Executive Director
Tunga Kiyak, Managing Director
Irem Kiyak, Treasurer
The AIB's new publication, provides an outlet for interesting, topical, and thought provoking articles that are relatively short, and don't fit requirements for publication in JIBS, or other existing outlets. Insights provides ideas to stimulate discussion and research, as well as material for classroom use.
Quarterly

13341 Aaonline
Africa-America Institute
420 Lexington Avenue
Graybar Building, Suite 1706
New York, NY 10170-2
212-949-5666
FAX: 212-682-6174
aainy@aaionline.org
http://www.aaionline.org
Margaret Novicki, Editor
Mora McLean, President/CEO
Quarterly Founded: 1953
Circulation: 3000

13342 American Business in China
Caravel
23545 Crenshaw Boulevard
#101E
Torrance, CA 90505
310-325-0100
FAX: 310-325-2583
info@88yp.com
http://www.china4us.com
Davisson Chang, Editor
Sheryl Chang, Production Manager
Directory of US firms operating in China and Hong Kong; Hong Kong: a special administrative region; exporting to China - best US exporting prospects; China's major cities for foreign investments; marketing, advertising and exhibiting in China. *$99.00*
288 pages Founded: 1993 ISBN 0-964432-29-3
Circulation: 10,000
Mailing list available for rent 2,000 names $95 per M. : word

13343 Asian Finance
Asian Finance Publications
14 Davis Drive
Armonk, NY 10504-3005
Focuses on international banking and finance.
Circulation: 13147

13344 Asian Industrial Report
Keller International Publishing Corporation
150 Great Neck Road
Great Neck, NY 11021-3309
516-829-9722
FAX: 516-829-5414
mcamca@rad.net.id
http://www.theasianreport.com
Robert Herihly, Publisher
Brian Deluca, Editor
Jerry Keller, President
New machinery and equipment. *$85.00*
36 pages Monthly Founded: 1882
Circulation: 20000 20000 names
Printed in 4 colors on matte stock

13345 Australia/USA
Australian Information Service
630 5th Avenue
New York, NY 10111-0100
212-332-2540
FAX: 212-265-4917
Tony Miller, Editor
Walter Stern, Manager
Emphasis on the US/Australia relationship between governments and in commerce, industry, welfare, and scientific areas. Circulates to key congress and administration officials, chambers of commerce, business and industry leaders.
Circulation: 40,000

13346 Business America: the Magazine of International Trade
US Department of Commerce
14th Street & Constitution Avenue NW
Washington, DC 20230-0001
202-935-5000
FAX: 202-377-5819
Douglas Carrol, Editor
Designed to help American exporters penetrate overseas markets by providing them with timely information on opportunities for trade and methods of doing business in foreign countries. *$2.00*
Circulation: 13,000

13347 China Business Review
US China Business Council
1818 N Street NW
Suite 200
Washington, DC 20036-2473
202-429-0340
FAX: 202-775-2476
publications@uschina.org
http://www.uschina.org
John Frisbie, President
Ms. Catherin Gelb, Director of Publications
Virginia A. Hulme, Associate Editor
E. Palmer Golson, Director of Membership Services
Covers all aspects of doing business with China and Hong Kong. *$100.00*
Founded: 1973
Circulation: 6000
Printed in on glossy stock

13348 Cross Border
Economist Intelligence Unit
111 W 57th Street
New York, NY 10019-2211
212-586-1115
FAX: 212-586-1181
Debrah Langley, Publisher
Focuses on multinational management issues faced by managers of international businesses.
Circulation: 55,000

13349 East Asian Executive Report
International Executive Reports
717 D Street NW
Suite 300
Washington, DC 20004-2812
202-783-2424
FAX: 202-628-6618 execrep@aol.com
William Hearn, Publisher
Monthly magazine covering the legal and practical requirements of doing business in Far Eastern countries. *$455.00*
28 pages Monthly Founded: 1979
Circulation: 600
Printed in on matte stock

13350 Export
Adams/Hunter Publishing
2101 S Arlington Heights Road
Suite 150
Arlington Heights, IL 60005-4142
FAX: 847-427-2006
David Thayer, Publisher
Covers all aspects of international trade for distributors of consumer durables in 183 countries.
Circulation: 38589

13351 Foreign Affairs
Foreign Affairs
58 E 68th Street
New York, NY 10021-1196
212-349-9522
FAX: 386-447-2321 800-829-5539
order@wshein.com
http://www.foreignaffairs.org
David Kellogg, Publisher
James Hoge Jr, Editor
Michael Pasuit, Marketing Coordinator
Eugnia Chang, Circulation Director
Reviews on events, news, people, and foreign relations. *$44.00*
Founded: 1921

13352 Global Trade
North American Publishing Company
401 N Broad Street
Philadelphia, PA 19108-1001
215-238-5300
FAX: 215-238-5457
Michelle Dalton, Editor
Bennett Zucker, Publisher
Assists international cargo decision makers in planning, financing and documenting goods and commodities in international trade. Accepts advertising. *$45.00*
Monthly Founded: 1934

13353 IGT Magazine
World Trade Winds
610 Old Campbell Road
Suite 108
Richardson, TX 75080-519
972-699-1188
FAX: 972-699-1189 877-861-1188
service@asiatrademart.com
http://www.asiatrademart.com

Daniel Foong, Editor
Melody Lin, Circulation Director

Offers information for exporters to find international buyers.
Founded: 1975

13354 Institute of Management & Administration Newsletter
29 W 35th Street
5th Floor
New York, NY 10001-2299
212-244-0360
FAX: 212-564-0465
subserve@ioma.com
http://www.ioma.com

Joe Bremner, President

Monthly newsletter that offers information for all those involved in international sales, looking for new distribution channels and how to reduce exports costs and risks.

Circulation: 180,000

13355 International Industrial Opportunities
High Tech Publishing Company
PO Box 1275
Amherst, MA 01004-1275
413-534-4500
FAX: 413-256-6378

Philip T DiPeri, Editor

A compendium of selected industrial situations existing in the international arenas. Describes projects and situations requiring additional resources of a specialized nature. *$360.00*
Monthly

13356 Journal of International Business Studies
Academy of International Business
Michigan State University
7 Eppley Center
East Lansing, MI 48824-1121
517-432-1452
FAX: 517-432-1009
aib@aib.msu.edu http://aib.msu.edu

G Tomas K Hult, Executive Director
Tunga Kiyak, Managing Director
Irem Kiyak, Treasurer

The official publication of the American Academy of International Business, publishing papers of significant interest that contribute to the theoretical basis of business and management studies.
Bi-Monthly

13357 LASA Forum
Latin American Studies Association
946 William Pitt Union
University of Pittsburgh
Pittsburgh, PA 15260
412-648-7929
FAX: 412-624-7145
lasa@pitt.edu
http://lasa.international.pitt.edu/

Hane Horowitz, Exhibit Management Head
Arturo Arias, Associate Editor
Sonia E Alvarez, President/Editor
Charles R Hale, VP
Milagros Pereyra-Rojas, Managing Editor

Published by the Latin American Studies Association. *$30.00*
Quarterly Founded: 1969
Mailing list available for rent

13358 Latin Trade
Freedom Latin America
95 Merrick Way
6th Floor
Coral Gables, FL 33134
305-441-0102
FAX: 305-358-9166 800-761-7067
info@latintrade.com
http://www.latintrade.com

Adrian Fletes, Production Manager
Tom Chamberlin, Circulation Director
Mike Selner, Publisher

Comprehensive news coverage and analysis of business issues in Latin America and the Caribbean. *$109.95*
Monthly Founded: 1993
Circulation: 92,319

13359 Middle East Executive Reports
International Executive Reports
717 D Street NW
Suite 300
Washington, DC 20004-2812
202-783-2424
FAX: 202-628-6618 execrep@aol.com

William Hearn, Publisher

Monthly magazine covering the legal and practical requirements of doing business in the Middle East. *$455.00*
28 pages Monthly Founded: 1978
Circulation: 1,000
Printed in 2 colors on matte stock

13360 Showcase USA
Bobit Publishing Company
21061 S Western Avenue
Torrance, CA 90501
310-533-2400
FAX: 310-533-2500 www.bobit.com

Mike Spivak, Editor

International marketing vehicle for American manufacturing. *$12.00*
165 pages Founded: 1979

13361 Trade and Culture Magazine
Key Communications
385 Garrisonville Road
Suite 116
Stafford, Vi 22554
540-577-7174
FAX: 540-720-5687 800-544-5684

Holly Biller, Marketing Director
Kim White, Managing Editor
Penny Stacey, Advertising Coordinator

Published to help executives make their companies competitive worldwide, featuring 22 trade zone presentations in each issue covering every country. Trade and Culture blends cultural insight with practical how-to business information. *$39.95*
96 pages Quarterly Founded: 1993
Circulation: 45000

13362 US Council for International Business
1212 Avenue of the Americas
Suite 1805
New York, NY 10036-1689
212-354-4480
FAX: 212-575-0327
info@uscib.org http://www.uscib.org

Thomas M.T. Niles, President
Peter Robinson, SVP/Chief Operating Officer
Davis Hodge, Marketing & Advertising

Monthly newsletter that supports those involved in the developments in the European community affecting business on council activities.
Monthly Founded: 1945

13363 Understanding Russia Banking
Holland House Publishing
515 Lake Street S
Palms Habor Lights Building #203
Kirkland, WA 98033
425-828-6774
FAX: 425-827-5528
hi@2cupsofjoy.com
http://www.2cupsofjoy.com

Anke Van De Wall, Publisher
Evgenui Kolesnikov, Editor

How Russian banking systems operates. *$50.00*
300 pages Founded: 1997 ISBN 0-964546-42-6

13364 Vietnam Business Journal
VIAM Communications Group
535 W 114th Street
New York, NY 10027
212-854-2271
FAX: 212-854-9099

Kenneth Felderbaum, Publisher

Research and experience based articles and graphics produces by journalists.

13365 World Trade
Freedom Magazine
2401 W Big Beaver Rd
SUITE 700
Troy, MI 48084
248-362-3700
FAX: 248-362-0317
espositot@bnpmedia.com
http://www.worldtrademag.com

Neil Shister, Editorial Director
Thomas Esposito, Group Publisher
Nikki Smith, Marketing Director
Amy Schuler, Circulation Manager
Suzanne Fairman, Production Manager

Articles are aimed at helping companies to expand their international opportunities.
Monthly Founded: 1987
Circulation: 70590

Trade Shows

13366 American-Turkish Council Annual Meeting
Ideea
6233 Nelway Drive
McLean, VA 22101
703-760-0762
FAX: 703-760-0764
qwhiteree@ideea.com
www.ideea.com

Quentin C Whiteeree, President

High level military and government officials and businessmen from Turkey and the United States. Seminar and over 25 exhibits of trade, defense, banking, investments and tourism.
1000 Attendees Annual Founded: 1983

13367 Annual Convention and Trade Show
American Association of Exporters and Importers
1050 17th Street NW
Suite 810
Washington, DC 20036
202-857-8009
FAX: 202-857-7843
hq@aaei.org www.aaei.org

Kathy Corrigan, Director Meetings/Events

Reports on current trade developments and advance notices of changes in rules for conducting business in the United States, as well as developments affecting trade originating from Treasury, Customs, US Courts, Commerce Department, International Trade Commission, Federal Maritime Commission and other regulatory agencies. 50 exhibitors with 50 booths.

550 Attendees May

13368 International Business Expo

Assist International
90 John Street
Room 505
New York, NY 10038
212-442-2074
FAX: 212-725-3312
info@assist-intl.com
www.assist-intl.com

Peter Robinson, Director

This expo has 170 exhibitors with 170 booths.

1800 Attendees April Founded: 1999

13369 Showcase USA Trade Show

Bobit Publishing Company
3520 Challenger Street
Torrance, CA 90503
310-533-2400
FAX: 310-533-2500
webmaster@bobit.com
www.bobit.com

Mike Spivak, Editor
Ty Bobit, Chief Executive Officer

International marketing vehicle for American manufacturing. *$12.00*

165 Attendees Founded: 1979

Directories & Databases

13370 A Basic Guide to Exporting

World Trade Press
1450 Grant Avenue
Suite 204
Novato, CA 94945
415-549-9934
FAX: 415-898-1080 800-833-8586
gm@worldtradepress.com
www.worldtradepress.com

Alexandra Woznick

Includes significant new information on export regulations, customs benefit, and tax incentives. There are also hundreds of new sources of assistance available with updated addresses and telephone numbers.

188 pages Founded: 1999 ISBN 1-885073-83-6

13371 American Business in China

Caravel
23545 Crenshaw Boulevard
Sutie 101E
Torrance, CA 90505
310-325-0100
FAX: 310-325-2583
info@china4us.com
www.china4us.com

Davisson Chang, Editor
Sheryl Chang, Production Manager
Betty Yao, Marketing Manager

Directory of US firms operating in China and Hong Kong; Hong Kong as a special administrative region; exporting to China - best US exporting prospects; China's major cities for foreign investments; marketing, advertising and exhibiting in China. Also contains 1,000+ US contacts and 1,800+ China & Hong Kong contacts *$99.00*

288 pages Annual Founded: 1995 ISBN 0-964432-29-3

Mailing list available for rent 2,000 names $95 per M.

13372 Arthur Andersen North American Business Sourcebook

Triumph Books
601 S LaSalle Street
Suite 500
Chicago, IL 60605
312-939-3330
FAX: 312-663-3557

Mitch Rogatz, President/Publisher
Tom Bast, Editorial Director
Blythe Hurley, Managing Editor
Kelley Thornton, Associate Editor

Government and trade agencies and trade-related databases in the United States, Canada and Mexico are profiled. *$150.00*

Founded: 1994

13373 Brazil Tax, Law, & Business Briefing

WorldTrade Executive
2250 Main Street
Suite 100
Concord, MA 01742
978-287-0301
FAX: 978-287-0302
info@wtexec.com www.wtexec.com

Alison French, Production Manager

Coverage includes economic analysis and risk assessment, new transfer pricing rules, foreign direct investment, labor regulation, environment, privatization, accessing the Mercosur market, litigation, arbitration, and debt collection in Brazil, antitrust concerns for foreign acquisition, securitizing infrastructure projects, foreign investor access to the telecommunications market, and choices in creating Brazilian subsidiaries. *$297.00*

340 pages ISBN 1-893323-57-9

13374 CSI Market Statistics

Commodity Systems
200 West Palmetto Park Road
Suite 200
Boca Raton, FL 33432
561-392-8663
FAX: 561-392-7761 800-274-4727

Bob Pelletier, President

Offers information on daily, weekly and monthly time series of price and trading data for commodity markets worldwide, cash, futures options, index options, US stocks and mutual funds and government instruments.

13375 Chinese Business in America

Caravel
23545 Crenshaw Boulevard
Suite 101E
Torrance, CA 90505
310-325-0100
FAX: 310-325-2583
info@china4us.com
www.china4us.com

Davisson Chang, Editor
Sheryl Chang, Production Manager

Directory of ethnic Chinese importers and exporters in the US; marketing, sourcing and establishing a business in the US; US business laws and immigration regulations; money saving tips and business bargains. *$88.00*

288 pages Annual Founded: 1997 ISBN 0-964432-26-9

Circulation: 5,000 3000 names $95 per M. : word

13376 DACA Directory

Distributors & Consolidators of America
2240 Bernays Drive
York, PA 17404

888-519-9195
daca@dacacarries.com
www.dacacarriers.com

Jim Latta III, Board of Directors
Mark Anness, President

Firms and individuals active in the shipping, warehousing, receiving, distribution or consolidation of freight shipments.

13377 DRI Europe

DRI/McGraw-Hill
24 Hartwell Avenue
Lexington, MA 02421-3158
781-863-5100

Subjects covered in this database include macroeconomic, microeconomic, and financial indicators for the European countries.

13378 DRI Middle East and African Forecast

DRI/McGraw-Hill
24 Hartwell Avenue
Lexington, MA 02421-3158
781-863-5100

This large database offers more than 500 annual historical and forecast time series for 10 Middle Eastern and African economies.

13379 DRI/TBS World Sea Trade Forecast

DRI/McGraw-Hill
24 Hartwell Avenue
Lexington, MA 02421-3158
781-863-5100

This comprehensive database covers cargo movements over major water trade routes worldwide.

13380 DRI/TBS World Trade Forecast

DRI/McGraw-Hill
24 Hartwell Avenue
Lexington, MA 02421-3158
781-863-5100

Offers over 82,000 annual historical and forecast time series on import and export volumes, and prices in current US dollars.

13381 Dictionary of International Trade

World Trade Press
1450 Grant Avenue
Suite 204
Novato, CA 94945
415-549-9934
FAX: 415-898-1080 800-833-8586

Edward G Hinkelman

The most respected and largest-selling dictionary of trade in the world. It is in use in more than 100 countries by importers, exporters, bankers, shippers, logistics professionals, attorneys, economists, and government officials. *$55.00*

688 pages Founded: 2004 ISBN 1-885073-72-0

13382 Directory of US Exporters
Journal of Commerce
33 Washington Street
Floor 13
Newark, NJ 07102
973-848-7000

amiddlebrook@cbizmedia.com
www.cbizmedia.com

Amy Middlebrook, Group Publisher

Provides logistics professionals with active confirmed leads for over 60,000 US companies involved in world trade.
$450.00
Annual

13383 Directory of US Importers
Journal of Commerce
33 Washington Street
13 Floor
Newark, NJ 07102
973-848-7000

amiddlebrook@cbizmedia.com
www.cbizmedia.com

Amy Middlebrook, Group Publisher

Provides logistics professionals with active confirmed leads for over 60,000 US companies involved in world trade.
$450.00

13384 Export Yellow Pages
US West Marketing Resources Group
1101 30th Street NW
Suite 200
Washington, DC 20007-3769
202-934-4584
FAX: 202-944-4680 800-228-2582

David Lee, President

Approximately 16,000 US suppliers distributed worldwide through US commerce department channels.

13385 Foreign Exchange Forecast Data Base
Global Insight
800 Baldwin Tower
Eddystone, PA 19022
610-490-4000
FAX: 610-490-2770
info@wefa.com www.wefa.com

Ben G Hackett, International Trade/Transportation

This large database covers over 130 monthly and 60 quarterly time series of historical and forecast data for foreign exchange rates.

13386 Foreign Representatives in the US Yellow Book
Leadership Directories
104 5th Avenue
New York, NY 10011-6901
212-627-4140
FAX: 212-645-0931
info@leadershipdirectories.com
www.leadershipdirectories.com

Seth Zupnik, Editor
James M Petrie, Associate Publisher

Contact information for foreign representatives of over 187 nations at embassies, consulates, and intergovernmental organizations in the US, US executives of over 1,100 foreign corporations, over 275 foreign financial institutions with offices in the US, and over 300 international media outlets with bureaus in the US. *$245.00*
850+ pages SemiAnnual Founded: 1997
Mailing list available for rent 12,000 names $125 per M.
Computerized version available: CD-ROM

13387 GIN International Database
Global Information Network
146 W 29th Street
Suite 7E
New York, NY 10001
212-443-3123

Lisa Vives, Owner

This large database offers all sorts of information on developing countries, ranging from economics and finance to health and social trends.
Full-text

13388 GLOBAL Vantage
Standard & Poor's Corporation
55 Water Street
New York, NY 10041
212-382-2000
800-525-8640

This database provides corporate financial data covering more than 2,500 US companies and over 1,500 companies in 23 other countries.

13389 Global Report
Citicorp
850 3rd Avenue
New York, NY 10022
212-881-1308

One of the most comprehensive databases in the world offering information on foreign exchange, country reports, money markets, bonds, companies, industries and news.
Full-text

13390 Import Export USA
Gale Research
27500 Drake Road
Farmington Hills, MI 48331
248-699-4253
FAX: 248-699-8214 800-877-4253
galeord@gale.com www.gale.com

Dennis Poupard, Executive VP Editorial & Production
Rich Foley, Executive VP Sales & Marketing

US import and export data on more than 20,000 commodities and 85,000 international importing and exporting companies.
$1695.00

13391 Importers Manual USA
World Trade Press
1450 Grant Avenue
Suite 204
Novato, CA 94945-3142
415-549-9934
FAX: 415-898-1080 800-833-8586
egh@worldtradepress.com
www.worldtradepress.com

Edward Hinkelman, Publisher
James Nolan, Editor
Karla Shippey, Editor

Lists of trade fairs, embassies, chambers of commerce, banks, and other sources of information on various aspects of international trade. *$145.00*
960 pages 2-3 per year Founded: 1993
ISBN 1-885073-93-3
Circulation: 3,000 8500 names $76 per M.

13392 International Business & Trade Directories
Grey House Publishing
185 Millerton Road
PO Box 860
Millerton, NY 12546
518-890-0526
FAX: 518-789-0545 800-562-2139
books@greyhouse.com
www.greyhouse.com

Leslie Mackenzie, Publisher
Richard Gottlieb, Editor

A comprehensive listing of business and trade directories from around the world. Organized by industry, and then by country, this updated resource puts at your fingertips nearly 7,000 world-wide industry-specific business and trade directories. Entries include detailed content description, price, publisher, editorial staff, phone and fax numbers and US distributors. *$225.00*
1,800 pages

13393 International Directory of Importers
1741 Kekamek NW
Poulsbo, WA 98730
360-779-1511
FAX: 360-697-4696 800-818-0140

Esther Camacho, Circulation

Publishes reference guides for worldwide importers, wholesalers, agents, and distributors. *$250.00*
5000 pages Annual Founded: 1978

13394 Japan Economic Daily
Kyodo News International
474 Third Avenue
Suite 1803
New York, NY 10017
212-508-5440
FAX: 212-508-5441
kni@kyodonews.com
www.kyodonews.com

This full coverage database contains news on Japanese business, industry, economics and finance developments.
Full-text

13395 LEXIS International Trade Library
Mead Data Central
9443 Springboro Pike
Dayton, OH 45401

FAX: 518-487-3584 888-223-6337

Andrew Prozes, Chief Executive Officer

This database contains information on international trade regulation decisions handed down from the Supreme Court and other legislative bodies.
Full-text

13396 Local Chambers of Commerce Which Maintain Foreign Trade Services
US Chamber of Commerce-International Division
1615 H Street NW
Washington, DC 20062-0001
202-659-6000
FAX: 202-463-3114 *$15.00*

13397 Mexico Tax, Law,& Business Briefing
WorldTrade Executive
2250 Main Street
Suite 100
Concord, MA 01742
978-287-0301
FAX: 978-287-0302
info@wtexec.com www.wtexec.com
Alison French, Production Manager
A single volume special report that provides guidance on tax and legal issues investors should consider when evaluating a possible company aquisition, starting a business or entering into a joint venture or strategic alliance in Mexico. Also featuring important guidance prepared by major accounting and law firms. *$297.00*
291 pages ISBN 1-893323-67-6

13398 North American Export Pages
US West Marketing Resources Group
1101 30th Street NW
Suite 200
Washington, DC 20007-3769
202-934-4584
FAX: 202-944-4680 800-288-2582
David Lee, President
Approximately 50,000 suppliers from the United States, Canada, and Mexico wishing to export products worldwide. *$39.95*

13399 Official Export Guide
North American Publishing Company
401 N Broad Street
Philadelphia, PA 19108-1001
215-238-5300
FAX: 215-238-5094
Tery Moran-Lever, Editor
Offers information on customs officials, port authorities, embassies and consulates, chambers of commerce and other organizations involved in international trade. *$399.00*
1800 pages Annual

13400 Political Handbook of the World
McGraw Hill
PO Box 182604
Columbus, OH 43272
614-866-5769
FAX: 614-759-3759
customerservice@mcgraw-hill.com
www.mcgraw-hill.com
Arthur S Banks, Editor
Thomas C Muller, Editor
Annual reference book containing separate sections on every country in the world and more than 100 intergovernment organizations. Each edition completely updates political developments over the past year while retaining the extensive background information necessary for researchers to place current events in a comprehensive historical perspective.
1400 pages Founded: 1979

13401 Practical Guide: Doing Business in Ukraine
WorldTrade Executive
PO Box 761
Concord, MA 01742-0761
978-287-0301
FAX: 978-287-0302 www.wtexec.com
Alison French, Production Manager
Topics covered include: common business structures, registration procedures, real property transactions, tax and foreign investment legislation, currency reforms and regulations, privatization programs, intellectual property. *$145.00*

13402 Protecting Intellectual Property in Latin America
WorldTrade Executive
PO Box 761
Concord, MA 01742-0761
978-287-0301
FAX: 978-287-0302 www.wtexec.com
Alison French, Production Manager
A complete guide to the protection of intellectual property in Latin America, including in-depth coverage of copyright law, patents and trademarks, software, pharmaceuticals, etc. Also deals with issues of enforcement and prosecution. *$235.00*

13403 Russian Far East: A Business Reference Guide
Russian Far East Advisory Group
PO Box 22126
Seattle, WA 98122-0126
206-447-2668
FAX: 206-628-0979
update@russianfareast.com
www.russianfareast.com
Elisa Miller, Editor
Alexander Karp, Editor
Sourcebook for business people, travelers, and researchers focusing on trends and economic developments in the Russian Far East. Includes reviews of each of the ten administrative regions and 27 maps *$79.00*
270 pages ISBN 0-964128-63-2

13404 Selling Successfully in Mexico
WorldTrade Executive
PO Box 761
Concord, MA 01742-0761
978-287-0301
FAX: 978-287-0302 www.wtexec.com
Alison French, Production Manager
A detailed guide to market research, advertising, direct marketing, and trade show exhibition in Mexico, written by marketing professionals and supplemented by extensive data and key contracts. *$129.00*

13405 Showcase USA: American Export-Buyers Guide and Membership
Bobit Publishing Company
3623 Artesia Boulevard
Redondo Beach, CA 90278

FAX: 310-376-9043
List of member companies and organizations of Sell Overseas America.

13406 Sourcing Manufactured Products in China
WorldTrade Executive
PO Box 761
Concord, MA 01742-0761
978-287-0301
FAX: 978-287-0302 www.wtexec.com
Alison French, Production Manager
A 10,000 name searchable database (PC compatible) of China's best export manufacturers, presented in both English and Chinese. Includes print version of top 4000 companies with full contact information. *$495.00*

13407 Trade Opportunity
US International Trade Association
14 Street & Constitution Avenue NW
Washington, DC 20230-0001
202-822-2867
FAX: 202-482-4473 800-872-8723
Leads to export opportunities for United States businesses.

13408 Trade Shows Worldwide
Gale Research
27500 Drake Road
Farmington Hills, MI 48331
248-699-4253
FAX: 248-699-8214 800-877-4253
galeord@gale.com www.gale.com
Ketih Jones, Editor
International directory of events, facilities, and suppliers that details entries for more than 6,500 scheduled exhibitions, trade shows and association conventions, and similar events, including 680 newly listed shows. Approximately one-third of the listed shows are based outside the US and Canada. *$220.00*
Annual

13409 US Custom House Guide
Primedia
9800 Metcalf Avenue
Overland Park, KS 66212
913-341-1300
FAX: 913-967-1898
www.primediabusiness.com
List of ports having customs facilities, customs officials, port authorities, chambers of commerce, embassies and consulates, foreign trade zones and other organizations; related trade services. *$399.00*
Annual January

13410 World Trade Almanac
World Trade Press
1450 Grant Avenue
Suite 204
Novato, CA 94945
415-454-9934
415-898-1124
gm@worldtradepress.com
www.worldtradepress.com
Gayle Madison
Peter Jones

Industry Web Sites

13411 www.aib.msu.edu/
Academy of International Business

Members are executives and teachers in the international business field.

13412 www.fancyfoodshows.com
National Association for the Specialty Food Trade

Members are manufacturers, importers, distributors and retailers of specialty gourmet and fancy foods. Has an annual budget of approximately $15 million. Publications available to members.

13413 www.geminishippers.com
Gemini Shippers Group

Shippers association with global contracts for all commodities.

13414 www.getbiz.com
BizNet Internet Solutions

Literature and information sources useful to international advertising researchers and practitioners.

13415 www.greyhouse.com
Grey House Publishing

Selected Grey House directories in the fields of business, health and education are available online. Users can search our online databases by several different search criteria, such as product categories, geographic area, sales volume and much, much more. Full Grey House catalog and online ordering also available.

13416 www.iwla.com
International Warehouse Logistics Association

13417 www.ncitd.org
National Council on Int'l Trade Development

For exporters and importers and other professionals serving the international commerce industry.

13418 www.tdctrade.com
Hong Kong Trade Development Council

Promotes trade between United States and Hong Kong.

13419 www.uschina.org
US China Business Council

Membership association for US companies doing business with the People's Republic of China. Provides representation, practical assistance, and up-to-date information to members.

13420 www.vita.com
VMEbus International Trade Association (VITA)

Association for manufacturers of microcomputer boards, hardware, software, military products, controllers, bus interfaces and other accessories compatible with VMEbus architecture.

International Trade Resources

13421 Albania Mission to the United Nations
320 E 79th Street
New York, NY 10021
212-249-2059

Geronimo Albano, Owner

13422 Austrian Trade Commission
500 N Michigan Avenue
Suite 1950
Chicago, IL 60611
312-644-5556

Peter Athanasiadis, Manager

13423 Azerbaijan Mission to the United Nations
866 United Nations Plaza
Suite 560
New York, NY 10017
212-371-2559

Eldar Kouliev, Manager

13424 Barbados Trade Commission
800 2nd Avenue
2nd Floor
New York, NY 10017
212-867-8435

June Clark, Manager

13425 Belize Mission to the United Nations
800 2nd Avenue
Suite 400 G
New York, NY 10017
212-837-7482

Mohamed Latheef, Manager

13426 Botswana Embassy
1531 New Hampshire Avenue NW
Washington, DC 20036
202-244-4990

Lapolang Caesar Lekoa, President

13427 British Trade and Investment Office
845 3rd Avenue
9th Floor
New York, NY 10022
212-745-0495

13428 Bulgarian General Consulate
121 E 62nd Street
New York, NY 10021
212-935-4646

13429 Business Council for the United Nations
801 2nd Avenue
2nd Floor
New York, NY 10017
212-661-1772

13430 Chile Trade Commission
866 United Nations Plaza
Suite 603
New York, NY 10017
212-980-3366

Oscar Fuentes, Manager

13431 Colombia Government Trade Bureau
277 Park Avenue
47th Floor
New York, NY 10172
212-223-1120

13432 Consulate General of Bahrain
866 2nd Avenue
14th Floor
New York, NY 10017
212-236-6200

Jassim Buallay, Manager

13433 Consulate General of Belgium
235 Peachtree Street NE
N Tower, Suite 850
Atlanta, GA 30303
404-659-9611

Piet Morisse, Manager

13434 Consulate General of Brazil
1185 Avenue of the Americas
21st Floor
New York, NY 10036-2601
917-777-7777

Julio Cesar Gomes Dos Sant, Manager

13435 Consulate General of Costa Rica
80 Wall Street
Suite 718
New York, NY 10005
212-509-3066

Otto Barcas, Manager

13436 Consulate General of Germany
871 United Nations Plaza
New York, NY 10017
212-610-9700

Bernhard Von Der Planit, Manager

13437 Consulate General of Haiti
271 Madison Avenue
17th Floor
New York, NY 10016
212-697-9767

Marie Therese, Manager

13438 Consulate General of Honduras
80 Wall Street
Suite 415
New York, NY 10005
212-490-2722

13439 Consulate General of India
3 E 64th Street
New York, NY 10021
212-774-0600

13440 Consulate General of Indonesia
5 E 68th Street
New York, NY 10021
212-879-0600

13441 Consulate General of Israel
800 2nd Avenue
New York, NY 10017
212-499-5000

13442 Consulate General of Kenya
424 Madison Avenue
Suite 1401
New York, NY 10017
212-538-8191

Rolando Visconti, Manager

13443 Consulate General of Lebanon
9 E 76th Street
New York, NY 10021
212-744-7905

Hassan Saad, Manager

13444 Consulate General of Lithuania
420 5th Avenue
3rd Floor
New York, NY 10018
212-354-7840

Rimantas Morkvenas, Manager

13445 Consulate General of Malta
249 E 35th Street
New York, NY 10016
212-425-2345

13446 Consulate General of Morocco
1821 Jefferson Place NW
Washington, DC 20036
202-736-1000

Ramon Xilotl, Manager

13447 Consulate General of Nigeria
828 2nd Avenue
New York, NY 10017
212-808-0301

13448 Consulate General of Paraguay
211 E 43rd Street
Suite 2101
New York, NY 10017
212-682-9441

Juan Baiardi, Manager

13449 Consulate General of Peru
215 Lexington Avenue
21st Floor
New York, NY 10016
212-481-7410

13450 Consulate General of Qatar
809 United Nations Plaza
4th Floor
New York, NY 10017
212-486-9335

13451 Consulate General of Saudi Arabia
866 United Nations Plaza
Suite 480
New York, NY 10017
212-980-3366

Abdulrahman Gdaia, Execellency

13452 Consulate General of Slovenia
600 3rd Avenue
24th Floor
New York, NY 10016
212-370-3007

Reimo Pettai, Manager

13453 Consulate General of South Africa
333 E 38th Street
9th Floor
New York, NY 10016
917-493-8950

13454 Consulate General of St. Lucia
800 2nd Avenue
9th Floor
New York, NY 10017
212-499-5000

Julian Hunte, Manager

13455 Consulate General of Switzerland
633 3rd Avenue
30th Floor
New York, NY 10017
212-599-5700

Raymond Loretan, Excellency

13456 Consulate General of Trinidad & Tobago
733 3rd Avenue
Suite 1716
New York, NY 10017-3204
212-682-7272

Hon Harold Robertson, Contact

13457 Consulate General of Ukraine
240 E 49th Street
New York, NY 10017
212-371-5690

13458 Consulate General of Uruguay
747 3rd Avenue
21st Floor
New York, NY 10017
212-935-9000

Basil Bryan, Manager

13459 Consulate General of Venezuela
7 E 51st Street
New York, NY 10022
212-826-1660

13460 Consulate General of the Commonwealth of the Bahamas
231 E 46th Street
2nd Floor
New York, NY 10017
212-717-5643

Hon Eldred E Bethel, Contact

13461 Consulate General of the Dominican Republic
1501 Broadway
4th Floor, Suite 410
New York, NY 10036
212-698-8899

13462 Consulate General of the Netherlands
1 Rockefeller Plaza
11th Floor
New York, NY 10020-2094
212-246-1429

Wanda Fleck, Manager

13463 Consulate General of the Principality of Monaco
565 5th Avenue
New York, NY 10017
212-286-0500

Magguy Maccario-Doyle, Manager

13464 Consulate General of the Republic of Croatia
369 Lexington Avenue
11th Floor
New York, NY 10017
212-972-2277

Abdul Seraj, Manager

13465 Consulate General of the Republic of Belarus
708 3rd Avenue
21st Floor
New York, NY 10017
212-682-5392

Sergei Kolos, Manager

13466 Consulate General of the Russian Federation
9 E 91st Street
New York, NY 10128
212-371-8222

13467 Consulate of Guyana
866 United Nations Plaza
New York, NY 10017
212-527-3215

Brentnold Evans, Manager

13468 Consulate of the Republic of Uzbekistan
866 United Nations Plaza
Suite 327-A
New York, NY 10017-7671
212-754-6178

13469 Cyprus Trade Commission
13 E 40th Street
New York, NY 10016
212-213-9100

Klio Demetriou, Manager

13470 Department of Trade- Government of Antigua & Barbuda
610 5th Avenue
Suite 311
New York, NY 10020
212-541-4117

13471 Ecuadorian Consulate
800 2nd Avenue
Suite 600
New York, NY 10017
212-808-0170

13472 Egyptian Consulate Economic & Commercial Office
45 Rockefeller Plaza
Suite 1507
New York, NY 10111
212-332-2570

Ayden Nour, Executive Director

13473 Embassy of Australia
1601 Massachusetts Avenue NW
Washington, DC 20036
202-797-3126

13474 Embassy of Benin
2124 Kalorama Road NW
Washington, DC 20008
202-232-6656

Cyrille Segbe Oguin, President

13475 Embassy of Bosnia and Herzegovina
2109 E Street NW
Washington, DC 20037
202-337-1500

Bisera Turkovic, President

13476 Embassy of Cambodia
4500 16th Street NW
Washington, DC 20011
202-726-7742

Sereyath Ek, President

13477 Embassy of Estonia
2131 Massachusetts Avenue NW
Washington, DC 20008
202-880-0101

Kaleikalev Stoicescu, Manager

13478 Embassy of Ethiopia Trade Affairs
3506 International Drive NW
Washington, DC 20008
202-364-1200

Kassahun Ayele, President

13479 Embassy of Finland
3301 Massachusetts Avenue NE
Washington, DC 20008
202-298-5800

Aukka Valtasaari, President

13480 Embassy of Georgia
1615 New Hampshire Avenue NW
Suite 300
Washington, DC 20009
202-387-2390

Levan Mikeladze, President

13481 Embassy of Jamaica (JAMPRO)
520 New Hampshire Avenue NW
Washington, DC 20036
202-452-0660

Gordon Shirley, President

13482 Embassy of Jordan
3504 International Drive NW
Washington, DC 20008
202-966-2664

Briggeneral Sariah, Chief Executive Officer

13483 Embassy of Mali
2130 R Street NW
Washington, DC 20009
202-322-2249

Abdoulaye Diop, President

13484 Embassy of Mongolia
2833 M Street NW
Washington, DC 20007
202-333-7117

Bold Ravdan, President

13485 Embassy of Panama
2862 McGill Terrace NW
Washington, DC 20008
202-387-6154

Francisco Morales, Manager

13486 Embassy of Tanzania
2139 R Street NW
Washington, DC 20008
202-939-6125

Andrew Mhando Daraja, President

13487 Embassy of Tunisia
1515 Massachusetts Avenue NW
Washington, DC 20005
202-862-1850

Mohamed Hachana, President

13488 Embassy of Uganda
5911 16th Street NW
Washington, DC 20011
202-726-7100

Edith Ssempala, President

13489 Embassy of Vietnam
1233 20th Street NW
Suite 400
Washington, DC 20036
202-861-0737

Nguyen Tam Chien, President

13490 Embassy of Zimbabwe
1608 New Hampshire Avenue NW
Washington, DC 20009
202-332-7100

13491 Embassy of the Lao People's Democratic Republic
2222 S Street NW
Washington, DC 20008
202-332-6416

Phanthong Phommahaxay, President

13492 Embassy of the People's Republic of China
2300 Connecticut Avenue NW
Washington, DC 20008
202-456-6764

Zhou Wenzhoung, President

13493 **Embassy of the Republic of Angola**
1615 M Street NW
Suite 900
Washington, DC 20036
202-785-1156

Josefina Pitra Diakite, President

13494 **Embassy of the Republic of Latvia**
4325 17th Street NW
Washington, DC 20011
202-726-8213

13495 **Embassy of the Republic of Yemen**
2600 Virginia Avenue NW
Suite 705
Washington, DC 20037
202-965-4760

Abdulwahab Al-Hajjri, President

13496 **Embassy of the Republic of the Marshall Islands**
2433 Massachusetts Avenue NW
Washington, DC 20008
202-234-5414

Banny DeBrum, President

13497 **Fiji Mission to United Nations**
630 3rd Avenue
7th Floor
New York, NY 10017
212-687-4130

Isikia Savua, Manager

13498 **French Trade Commission**
1 E Wacker Drive
Suite 3730
Chicago, IL 60601
312-661-1880

13499 **Gambia Mission to the United Nations**
800 2nd Avenue
Suite 400 F
New York, NY 10017
212-949-6640

B Jagne, Manager

13500 **General Consulate of Luxembourg**
17 Beekman Place
New York, NY 10022
212-888-6664

Georges Faber, Manager

13501 **Gibraltar Information Bureau**
1156 15th Street NW
Suite 1100
Washington, DC 20005
202-452-1108

Perry Stieglitz, Executive Director

13502 **Greek Trade Commission**
150 E 58th Street
17th Floor
New York, NY 10155
212-751-2404

Yannis Papadimitriou, Manager

13503 **Grenada Mission (Consulate)**
800 2nd Avenue
Suite 400 K
New York, NY 10017
212-599-0301

Lamuel Stanislaus, Manager

13504 **Hungarian Trade Commission**
150 E 58th Street
33rd Floor
New York, NY 10155-3398
212-355-0240

13505 **Icelandic Consulate General**
800 3rd Avenue
New York, NY 10022
212-593-2700

13506 **International Chamber of Commerce (ICC)**

www.iccwbo.org
Bryce Corbett, Director of Communications
Dawn Bartram, Communications Manager

The voice of world business championing the global economy as a force for economic growth, job creation and prosperity. Headquartered in Paris. Hosts conferences.
Founded: 1919

13507 **Irish Trade Board**
345 Park Avenue
17th Floor
New York, NY 10154
212-180-0800

Jean McCluskey, Marketing Executive

13508 **Japanese External Trade Organization**
1221 Avenue of the Americas
42nd Floor
New York, NY 10020
212-997-0400

13509 **Kazakhstan Mission to the United Nations**
866 United Nations Plaza
Suite 586
New York, NY 10017
212-230-1900

13510 **Korea Trade Promotion Center**
460 Park Avenue
Room 402
New York, NY 10022
212-826-0900

Jae Woo, President

13511 **Kyrgyzstan Mission to the United Nations**
866 United Nations Plaza
Room 477
New York, NY 10017
212-486-4214

13512 **Malaysia Trade Commission**
313 E 43rd Street
3rd Floor
New York, NY 10017
212-986-6310

Mohamad Sadik Gany, Manager

13513 **Mexico Trade Commission**
757 3rd Ave
Ste 2400
New York, NY 10017-2042
212-826-2978

13514 **Moldova Mission to the United Nations**
573-577 3rd Avenue
15th Floor
New York, NY 10016
212-682-3523

13515 **New Zealand Trade Development Board**
780 3rd Avenue
Suite 1904
New York, NY 10017-2024
212-832-7420

13516 **Norwegian Trade Council**
800 3rd Avenue
23rd Floor
New York, NY 10022
212-421-9210

13517 **Pakistan Trade Commission**
12 E 65th Street
4th Floor
New York, NY 10021
212-879-5800

Abbas Zaidi, Manager

13518 **Permanent Mission of Bangladesh to the United Nations**
821 United Nations Plaza
8th Floor
New York, NY 10017
212-786-6300

13519 **Permanent Mission of Bhutan to the United Nations**
2 United Nations Plaza
27th Floor
New York, NY 10017
212-486-9191

Francesco Fulci, Manager

13520 Permanent Mission of Ghana to the United Nations
19 E 47th Street
New York, NY 10017
212-171-1670

13521 Permanent Mission of Myanmar (Formerly Burma)
10 E 77th Street
New York, NY 10021
212-986-6310

Janis Priedkalns, Manager

13522 Permanent Mission of Saint Vincent & the Grenadines to the United Nations
800 2nd Avenue
9th Floor
New York, NY 10017
212-599-0950
FAX: 212-599-1020

Margaret H Ferrari, Permanent Representative

13523 Permanent Mission of the Czech Republic to the United Nations
1109-1111 Madison Avenue
New York, NY 10028
212-288-0830

13524 Permanent Mission of the Republic of Sudan to the United Nations
655 3rd Avenue
Suite 500-10
New York, NY 10017
212-593-0999

Jenine Selson, Manager

13525 Permanent Mission of the Republic of Armenia to the United Nations
119 E 36th Street
New York, NY 10016
212-752-3370

Andrezej Towpik, Manager

13526 Permanent Mission of the Solomon Islands to the United Nations
800 2nd Avenue
Suite 400
New York, NY 10017
212-949-6640

B Jagne, Manager

13527 Philippines Commercial Office
556 5th Avenue
New York, NY 10036
212-764-1330

13528 Poland Trade Commission
675 3rd Avenue
19th Floor
New York, NY 10017
212-351-1713

Phyllis Poland, Owner

13529 Portuguese Trade Commission
590 5th Avenue
3rd Floor
New York, NY 10036
212-544-4610

13530 Romanian Consulate General
200 E 38th Street
New York, NY 10016
212-687-0180

Corina Suteu, Manager

13531 Singapore Trade Commission
55 E 59th Street
Suite 21-B
New York, NY 10022
212-421-2200

Kc Yeoh, Executive Director

13532 Slovak Republic Mission to the United Nations
866 United Nations Plaza
Suite 493
New York, NY 10017
212-980-1558

13533 Swedish Trade Council
150 N Michigan Avenue
Chicago, IL 60601
312-781-6222

Stefam Bergstrom, Manager

13534 Syrian Arab Republic Embassy
2215 Wyoming Avenue NW
Washington, DC 20008
202-232-6313

13535 Taiwan Trade Center
1 Penn Plaza
Suite 3410
New York, NY 10119
212-730-4466

13536 Tajikistan Mission to the United Nations
136 E 67th Street
New York, NY 10021
212-744-2196

Khamrokhon Zaripov, President

13537 Thailand Trade Center- Consulate General of Thailand
401 N Michigan Avenue
Suite 544
Chicago, IL 60611
312-467-0044
FAX: 312-467-1690 ttcc@wwa.com

13538 Trade Commission of Denmark
285 Peachtree Center Avenue NE
Suite 2102
Atlanta, GA 30303
404-588-1588

Henrik Bronner, Manager

13539 Trade Commission of Spain
500 N Michigan Avenue
Suite 1500
Chicago, IL 60611
312-644-1154

13540 Turkish Trade Commission
821 United Nations Plaza
4th Floor
New York, NY 10017
212-687-1530

13541 Turkmenistan Mission to the United Nations
866 United Nations Plaza
Suite 424
New York, NY 10017
212-486-8908

Aksoltan Ataeva, Manager

13542 United Nations Mission to El Salvador
46 Park Avenue
New York, NY 10016
212-759-9444

Antonio Montiero, Manager

Associations

13543 Advanced Network & Services
2600 South Road
Suite 44-193
Poughkeepsie, NY 12601
845-795-2090
FAX: 845-795-2180
contact@advanced.org
www.advanced.org

Dr. James McGroddy, Chairman of the Board
Allan Weis, President/Managing Director

To advance education by accelerating the use of computer network applications and technology.

13544 Alliance for Public Technology
919 18th Street NW
Suite 900
Washington, DC 20006
202-263-2970
FAX: 202-263-2960 ww.apt.org

Sylvia Rosenthal, Executive Director
Matthew Bennett, Policy Director

A nonprofit membership organization based in Washington, DC.

13545 American Public Communications Council
10302 Eaton Place
Suite 340
Fairfax, VA 20030
703-385-5300
FAX: 703-385-5301 800-868-2722
apcc@apcc.net www.apcc.net

Bruce Renard, State Assistant Director
Brad Benge, Additional Director
Michael Bright, At-Large Director
David Cotton, At-Large Director

Aims to protect and expand domestic and foreign markets for public communications and provide business opportunities for members.
Founded: 1988

13546 American Registry for Internet Numbers
3635 Concorde Parkway
Suite 200
Chantilly, VA 20151-1130
703-227-9840
FAX: 703-227-0676
hostmaster@arin.net www.arin.net

John Curran, Chairperson
Lee Howard, Treasurer
David Conrad

Manage the internet numbering resources for North America focused completely on serving our members and the Internet community at large.

13547 Association for the Advancement of Computing in Education
PO Box 3728
Norfolk, VA 23514
757-623-7588
FAX: 703-997-8760
info@aace.org www.aace.org
International, educational and professional nonprofit organization dedicated to the advancement of the knowledge, theory and quality of learning and teaching at all levels with information technology. Encourages scholarly inquiry related to information technology and research results through publications, conferences, societies and chapters plus inter-organizational projects.

13548 Information Security
117 Kendrick Street
Suite 800
Needham, MA 02494
781-255-0200
FAX: 781-657-1100
webmaster@infosecuritymag.com
www.infosecuritymag.com

Andrew L Briney, Editorial Director
Anne Saita, Senior Editor
Neil Roiter, Features Editor

13549 International Computer Security Association
117 Kendrick Street
Suite 800
Needham, MA 02494-5292
888-804-5501
FAX: 781-657-1100
ptippett@icsa.net
www.infosecuritymag.com

Andrew L. Briney, VP

ICSA is the enterprise security and risk managers' leading source of critical, objective information on strategic and practical security issues. Information security teams of veteran security journalists and experts break down the security problems challenging enterprises and provide practical resolutions.

13550 International Society for Technology in
175 W Broadway
Ste 300
Eugene, OR 97401-3042
541-023-3770
FAX: 541-302-3778 800-336-5191
iste@iste.org www.iste.org

Jan Van Dam, President
Kurt Steinhaus, Treasurer
Chuck Chulvick, Secretary
Leslie Conery, Manager

A large nonprofit organization serving the technology-using educator.
12M Members Founded: 1979

13551 Internet Society
1775 Wiehle Avenue
Suite 102
Reston, VA 20190-5108
703-326-9880
FAX: 703-326-9881
info@isoc.org www.isoc.org

Lynn St Amour, President/CEO
Glenn Ricart, Treasurer
Scott Bradner, Secretary

Technologists, developers, educators, researchers, government representatives, and business people.
16000 Members Founded: 1992

Newsletters

13552 Dot.COM
Business Communications Company
25 Van Zant Street
Suite 13
Norwalk, CT 06855-1713
203-853-4266
FAX: 203-853-0348
sales@bccresearch.com
www.bccresearch.com

Louis Naturman, Publisher
C Toenne, Editor

Updates readers on the commercial use of the Internet and related platforms. *$38.00*

13553 E-Healthcare Market Reporter
Health Resources Publishing
1913 Atlantic Avenue
Suite F4
Manasquan, NJ 08736
732-292-1100
FAX: 732-292-1111 888-843-6242
info@themcic.com
http://www.themcic.com

Bob Jenkins, President
Judith Granel, Marketing
John Russel, Editor

A bi-monthly covering strategies, new products, innovation, privacy issue, business solutions, service available, vendor news and comparative for implementing sales and marketing on the internet.
$397.00
Fortnightly Founded: 1988 : PDF/HTML

13554 Ecommerce @lert
ZD Journals
500 Canal View Boulevard
Rochester, NY 14623-2800
585-407-7301
FAX: 585-214-2387
eca@zd.com
www.ecommercealert.com

Bob Artner, Managing Editor

Explores the emerging digital and online technology used in sales management, as well as the companies in the forefront of this change. *$495.00*

13555 Electronic Commerce News
Phillips Publishing
PO Box 60037
Potomac, MD 20859
301-208-6787
FAX: 301-424-2098
htreat@phillips.com
http://www.ectoday.com

Heather Treat, Publisher
Stuart Zipper, Editor
Diane Schwartz, Publisher
Laurie Hofmann, Director of Marketing

Provides business strategies for the extended enterprise with the latest technological development and opportunities.
$597.00
Weekly

13556 Higher Education Technology News
Business Publishers
8737 Colesville Road
Suite 1100
Silver Spring, MD 20910-3928
301-587-6300
FAX: 304-587-4530 800-274-6737
custserv@bpinews.com
http://www.bpinews.com

Leonard A Eiserer, Publisher
Rasheeda Childress, Co-Editor

Provides timely, independent coverage of the issues surrounding technology in a higher educational setting. Offers news from federal and state government, the business world and others educators. *$307.00*

8 pages Founded: 1963

13557 INTRANETS Newsletter
Information Today
143 Old Marlton Pike
Medford, NJ 08055-8750
609-654-6266
FAX: 609-654-4309
custserv@infotoday
www.infotoday.com

Thomas Hogan, Publisher/President
Lauree Padgett, Editorial Services Manager
Inge Coffey, Circulation Manager

Covers strategies, tips, and tools required to help organizations develop, deploy, and manage intranest, extranets, portals, and other knowledge adnd information management initiatives. *$149.95*

Bi Monthly

13558 Information Advisor
Information Today
143 Old Marlton Pike
Medford, NJ 08055-8750
609-654-6266
FAX: 609-654-4309
custserv@infotoday
www.infotoday.com

Robert Berkman, Editor

Provides comprehensive evlauation of research tools, timely and specific information you will use, new sources valuable to researchers and head to head analysis of the most popular information services. *$165.00*

Monthly

13559 Internet Alliance Cyberbrief
Internet Alliance
6399 Wilshire Boulevard
Suite 920
Los Angeles, CA 90048
323-866-2084
FAX: 323-866-2088
richards@internetalliance.org
www.internetalliance.org

Jeff Richards, Executive Director

Coverage of public policy changes in government, enhancing consumer satisfaction in interactive services, and education.

Weekly

13560 Internet Business
Information Gatekeepers
320 Washington Street
Suite 302
Brighton, MA 02135
617-825-5033
FAX: 617-782-5735 800-323-1088
editor@igigroup.com
www.igigroup.com

Paul Polishuk, Publisher
Cathey Mallen, Production Manager
Patricia Hoffman, Managing Editor
Chris Danachek, Circulation Manager
Tony Carmona, Editor

Covers the rapid developments in the industry. *$695.00*

Monthly 20,000 names $150 per M.

13561 Internet Business Advantage
ZD Journals
500 Canal View Boulevard
Rochester, NY 14623-2800
585-407-7301
FAX: 585-214-2387
iba@zdjournals.com
www.zdjournals.com

Bob Artner, Editor-in-Chief

Keeps readers up-to-date of technological advances and new services available on the Internet. Reviews new products and provides tips on businss applications. *$295.00*

13562 Internet Media Investor
Kagan World Media
126 Clock Tower Place
Carmel, CA 93923-8746
831-624-1536
FAX: 831-625-3225 800-307-2529
info@kagan.com
http://www.kagan.com

George Niesen, Editor
Tom Johnson, Marketing Manager

Follows public stocks and private deals, analyzes publicly held interactive multimedia companies, tracks key industry subgroups through Kagan stock averages that relate companies by product lines, projects growth of new TV and data networks, programming and technology. Provides economic modeling of new corporate ventures and interprets announcements and events. Three month trial is available. *$1095.00*

Monthly Founded: 1969

13563 Internet World
Mecklermedia Corporation
20 Ketchum Street
Westport, CT 06880
212-260-0758
FAX: 203-454-5840
bbesch@mecklermedia.com

Bill Besch, Publisher

Internet industry news, product reviews and technical reports, with an emphasis on Internet technology, hardware, management and security. *$160.00*

Weekly
Circulation: 98,947

13564 Internetweek
CMP Media
600 Community Drive
Manhasset, NY 11030-3847
516-562-5000
FAX: 516-562-5554
mazzara@cmp.com
www.internetweek.com

Mike Azzara, Publisher

News and coverage of the latest trends in electronic commerce and intranet application platforms, the effects of high technology on daily production, changing regulations and operating standards, the best tools and practices, and related business and financial news. *$143.00*

Weekly
Circulation: 161264

13565 Marketing Library Services
Information Today
143 Old Marlton Pike
Medford, NJ 08055-8750
609-654-6266
FAX: 609-654-4309
custserv@infotoday
www.infotoday.com

Thomas Hogan, Publisher/President
Lauree Padgett, Editorial Services Manager
Inge Coffey, Circulation Manager

Provides information professional in all types of libraries with specfic ideas for marketing their services. *$79.95*

Bi Monthly

13566 Mass Storage News
Corry Publishing
2840 W 21st Street
Erie, PA 16506
814-838-0025
FAX: 814-838-0035
terryp@corrypub.com
www.corrypub.com

Terry Peterson, Publisher

News on optical disk based imaging and storage systems, new products, technical developments and insdustry developments. *$597.00*

BiWeekly
Circulation: 1,500

13567 Mealey's Litigation Report: Cyber Tech & E -Commerce
LexisNexis Mealey's
1018 W Ninth Avenue
Third Avenue
King of Prussia, PA 19406-1225
610-768-7800
FAX: 610-768-0880
mealeyinfo@lexisnexis.com
www.lexisnexis.com/mealeys

Tom Hagy, VP/General Manager
Maureen McGuire, Editorial Director
Mark Rogers, Editor

The Report covers disputes arising from e-commerce. The report tracks emerging legal issues, including: Internet security, data destruction and/or alteration, defamation on the Web, software errors, hardware failure, electronic theft, e-mail trespass, online privacy, government action, shareholder lawsuits, Internet jurisdiction issues, file sharing (copyright) disputes and much more. *$999.00*

100 pages Monthly Founded: 1999

13568 Mobile Internet
Information Gatekeepers
320 Washington Street
Suite 302
Boston, MA 02135
617-782-5033
FAX: 617-782-5735 800-323-1088
editor@igigroup.com
http://www.igigroup.com

Paul Polishuk, Publisher
Cathey Mallen, Production Manager
Paul Polishuk, CEO
Brian Mark, Newsletter Managing Editor
Bev Wilson, Marketing Manager

Covers worldwide developments in 3G wireless networks, with an emphasis on the worldwide PCS/GSM/CDMA markets. *$695.00*

Monthly Founded: 1977 20,000 names $150 per M.

13569 Multimedia & Internet Training Newsletter
Brandon Hall Resources
6990 W Freemont Avenue
#9C
Sunnyvale, CA 94087
408-736-2335

editor@brandon-hall.com
brandon-hall.com

Brandon Hall, Publisher/Editor

The latest in multimedia news, virtual clasroom reports, insight into web-based training, and technology tutorial. Job bank listings, upcoming events, seminars, and tips and techniques. *$189.00*
Monthly
Circulation: 900

13570 Online & CD-ROM Review
Information Today
1308 W Main
University of Illinois
Urbana, IL 61801
217-333-1074
FAX: 217-762-3956 800-248-8466
custserv@infotoday.com
http://www.infotoday.com/

Martha Williams, Editor
Thomas H Hogan, CEO/President
Heather Rudolph, Marketing
Inge Coffey, Circulation Manager

Covers the use and management of online and CD-ROM services, the training and education of online and CD-ROM users, creation and marketing of databases, and new development in search aids. *$115.00*
Monthly
Circulation: 4745

13571 Online Libraries & Microcomputers
Information Intelligence
PO Box 31098
Phoenix, AZ 31098
602-996-2283

news@infointelligence.com
www.infointelligence.com

George Machovec, Managing Editor

Examines new library online and automation applications with reviews of new software and hardware, industry news and trends, and upcoming related events. *$62.50*
9 pages 10 per year Founded: 1983

13572 Online Newsletter
Information Intelligence
PO Box 31098
Phoenix, AZ 85046-1098
602-996-2283

news@infointelligence.com
wwww.infointelligence.com

Richard S Huleatt, Editor

Covers all aspects of online and CD-ROM developments throughout the world. Regular feature sections include news and events, mergers and acquisitions, people in the news, telecommunications, and networks. Editoral reflects product development and its impact on users, and provides listings of upcoming events related to this industry. *$62.50*
9 pages 10 per year Founded: 1983

13573 Online Reporter
G2 Computer Intelligence
PO Box 7
Glen Head, NY 11545-1616
516-759-7025
FAX: 516-759-7028
news@g2news.com www.g2news.com

Maureen O'Gara, Publisher

Information on recent developments on the Internet through news briefs and a section called Chat Room. Includes information on e-commerce, Java and network security. *$695.00*
Weekly

13574 Privacy Journal
PO Box 28577
Providence, RI 2908
401-274-7861
FAX: 401-274-4747
orders@privacyjournal.net
http://www.privacyjournal.net

Robert Ellis Smith, Publisher
Barbara Green, Circulation Manager

An independent monthly on privacy in a computer age. *$65.00*
Monthly Founded: 1974
Printed in 1 color
Computerized version available

13575 Report on Electronic Commerce
Telecommunications Reports International
1333 H Street NW
#100 E
Washington, DC 20005-4707
202-842-3022
FAX: 202-842-1875 www.tr.com

Jerry Ashworth, Editor

Provides insiths on the latest developments in EDI, EFT, EBT, digital cash, home shopping and baking, value-added networks, and transaction processing. Offers articles, analysis and case studies regarding financial and business transaction over the Internet. *$745.00*
BiWeekly

13576 Sysop News and Cyberworld Report
BBS Press Service
5610 SW 10th Avenue
Topeka, KS 66604-2104
785-286-4272
FAX: 785-271-0192
alanbenchtold@sysop.com
www.sysop.com

Alan R Bechtold, Publisher
Debbie Boos, Owner

Online industry news and updates, Web site reviews, event announcements, Web design basics, Internet-based applicaitons, business solutions and various technical articles of interest. *$59.95*
Weekly
Circulation: 18M

13577 The CyberSkeptic's Guide to Internet Research
Information Today
143 Old Marlton Pike
Medofrd, NJ 08055-8750
609-654-6266
FAX: 609-654-4309
custserv@infotoday.com
www.infotoday.com

A monthly subscription newsletter in print, that explores and evaluates free and low cost Web sites and searcg strategies to help you use the INternet and stay up to date. *$164.95*

13578 Web Review
Miller Freeman Publications
600 Harrison Street
San Francisco, CA 94107
650-573-3210

Veronica Costanza, Publisher

Timely and practical information on the practice of Internet development as well as news on the latest techniques and technologies.
BiWeekly
Circulation: 12M

13579 Webdeveloper.com
Mecklermedia Corporation
23 Old Kings Highway South
Darien, CT 06820
203-662-2800
FAX: 203-655-4686
wdstaff@webdeveloper.com
http://www.webdeveloper.com

David Fiedler, Editor-in-Chief
Alan M Meckler, CEO
Mike Demiot, Marketing Manager

Product reviews, practical techniques, codes, tools and tips for Internet professionals who design, develop and maintain Web sites and Internet services.
Daily

13580 West Side Leader/Green Leader
Leader Publications
3075 Smith Road
Suite 204
Akron, OH 44333
330-665-9595
FAX: 330-665-0908 888-945-9595
editor@leaderpublications.com
http://www.akron.com

Kathryn Core, Editor
Clark Burns, General Manager
Mike Serge, Manager

Weekly newspapers. *$10.00*

Circulation: 53000

Magazines & Journals

13581 Active Server Developer's Journal
ZD Journals
500 Canal View Boulevard
Rochester, NY 14623-2800
585-407-7301
FAX: 585-214-2387
asp@zdjournals.com www.asdj.com

Jon Pyles, Publisher
Taggard Andrews

Addresses such issues as database publishing, creating hack-proof files and getting the most out of server-side components. Special sections focus on client-side solutions, covering the basics and taking an in-depth look at more detailed techniques. *$149.00*
Monthly

13582 B-to-B
Crain Communications
360 N Michigan Avenue
Chicago, IL 60601
312-495-5231
FAX: 312-649-5462
ebooker@crain.com
http://www.btobonline.com

Robert Felsenthal, VP-Publisher
Ellis Booker, Editor
John Obrecht, Managing Editor
Mary E. Morrison, Senior Editor
Ricardo Moraga, Owner *$59.00*

Monthly Founded: 1916
Circulation: 45000

13583 Bio & Software and Internet Report
Mary Ann Liebert
140 Huguenot Street
3rd Floor
New Rochelle, NY 10801-5215
914-343-3100
FAX: 914-740-2101
info@liebertpub.com
http://www.liebertpub.com

Mary Ann Liebert, President/Publisher
Gerry Elman, Editor-in-Chief
Robert A Bohrer, Executive Editor
Judith Gunn Bronson, Managing Editor

News and reviews of all areas of scientific computing, including software, hardware and network products. *$1554.00*
Founded: 1980

13584 Boardwatch Magazine
Penton Media
1300 E 9th Street
Cleveland, OH 44114
216-696-7000
FAX: 216-696-1752
rgoldner@boardwatch.com
www.ispworld.com

Michael Rand Goldner, Publisher
David Icopf, Editorial Director

Editorial coverage for communications service providers. *$72.00*
Monthly Founded: 1987
Circulation: 50,000 50,000 names $250 per M.

13585 CATIA Solutions Magazine
ConnectPress
551 W Cordova Road
Suite 701
Santa Fe, NM 87505-4100
505-474-5000
FAX: 505-474-5001
dbennie@hmp.com
http://www.catiasolutions.com

Dale Bennie, Publisher

CATIA geometry transfer using IGES Step, distributed file systems, and reviews of CATIA/CADAM workstations, 3D printers, and others. *$90.00*

13586 Card Technology
Thomson Financial Publishing
One State Street Plaza
27th Floor
New York, NY 10004
212-825-8445
FAX: 212-843-9622 800-221-1809
custserv@thomsonmedia.com
http://www.cardtechnology.com

Jim Baker, National Advertising Sales Manager
Andrew Rowe, Publisher
Donald Davis, Editor
James Malkin, CEO
Jose Thomas, Manager

Store-value cards, optical-memory cards, biometrics, cards on the Internet, cards for electronic data storage, and devices used with these cards in banking, government, telecommunications, transportation and education. *$98.00*
Monthly
Circulation: 25000
Printed in 4 colors on glossy stock

13587 Computer & Online Industry Litigation Reporter
Andrews Publications
175 Strafford Avenue
Building 4, Suite 140
Wayne, PA 19087-3331
610-225-0510
FAX: 610-225-0501 800-345-1101
editor@andrewspub.com
www.andrewspub.com

John Backe, Publisher

Editorial covers telecommuncations and the Internet for attorneys and professionals in the legal field. *$850.00*

13588 Computer Gaming World
Ziff Davis Publishing Company
101 Second Street
8th Floor
San Francisco, CA 94105
415-547-8778
FAX: 415-547-8777
amy_mishra@ziffdavis.com
http://www.computergaming.com

Sam Kennedy, Editor-in-Chief
Matt Leone, Editor
Paul Fusco, Sales Director
Bobby Markowitz, Marketing Director

Reviews commercially available and on-line games. Features interviews with game designers, as well as strategy tips, contests and news. *$98.88*
Monthly
Circulation: 212783

13589 Computer Journal
Las Vegas Computer Journal
2232 S Nellis Boulevard
#169
Las Vegas, NV 89104-6213
702-270-4656
FAX: 702-432-6204
info@internetsurfer.com
www.internetsurfer.com

Johanna Nezhoda, Publisher

Spotlights Web news, site reviews, interface tools and commentary on the changing face of computing. *$24.95*
Monthly
Circulation: 25M

13590 Computer Music Journal
MIT Press
Five Cambridge Center
Cambridge, MA 02142-1407
617-253-2864
FAX: 617-577-1545
journals-orders@mit.edu
http://www.mitpress.mit.edu/cmj

Douglas Keisler, Editor
Keeril Makan, Managing Editor

Tutorials and research articles, news and reviews of computer music systems, hardware and software for music sound, digital audio, signal processing and multimedia. *$82.00*
120 pages Quarterly Founded: 1926
Circulation: 5000

13591 Computer Service & Repair Magazine
Searle Publishing Company
40 W. Littleton Blvd
#210-110
Littleton, CO 80120-8200
303-730-3006
FAX: 303-797-0276 810-797-8708
csr@searlepub.com
http://searlepub.com

Robert Searle, Editor
Roderick Robles, Associate Publisher

Information on the maintenance and repair of computer systems. Reviews new products and technology.

13592 Corporate Help Desk Solutions
Gartner Group
56 Top Gallant Road
Stamford, CT 06904-2212
203-964-0096
FAX: 866-618-0806
help@gartner.com
http://www.gartner.com/

Check Trendell, Editor
Gene Hall, CEO/President
Carol Carol, Marketing/Circulation Ma

Key technologies, management practices and techniques for the most cost-effective help desk solutions. *$395.00*
Monthly Founded: 1979

13593 Customer Interaction Solutions
Technology Marketing Corporation
One Technology Plaza
Norwalk, CT 06854
203-852-6800
FAX: 203-853-2845 800-243-6002
tmc@tmcnet.com
http://www.tmcnet.com

Nadji Tehrani, Publisher
Tracey Schelmetic, Managing Editor
Erik D Lounsbury, Editorial Director

Magazine devoted to teleservices and e-services outsourcing, marketing and consumer management issues.
Monthly Founded: 1982

13594 Customer Interface
Advanstar Communications
1 Park Avenue
New York, NY 10016
212-797-7631
FAX: 212-951-6793
clong@advanstar.com
http://www.c-interface.com

Larry Tuck, Editor-in-Chief
Catherine Long, Marketing Director
Kerry Gumas, VP

Business management resource for senior and mid-level decision makers who are responsible for call centers, customer contact and customer service initiatives. We are stewards for the industry as we prepare it for continued transformation and growth.
Founded: 1988
Circulation: 50,000

13595 CyberDealer
Meister Publishing Company
37733 Euclid Avenue
Willoughby, OH 44094
440-942-2000
FAX: 440-942-0662 800-572-7740
Helps agricultural dealerships better manage their operations.
6 per year

13596 Desktop Video Communications
BCR Enterprises
950 York Road
#203
Hinsdale, IL 60521-8609
630-789-6700
FAX: 630-323-5324 www.bcr.com

Fred Knight, Publisher/Editor-in-Chief

Useful infomration for communications and informations systems managers, line managers, system developers and integrators, value-added resellers, and software vendors.

Bi-Monthly
Circulation: 30M

13597 Digital Travel
Jupiter Communications Company
627 Broadway
2nd Floor
New York, NY 10012-2612
212-338-8885
FAX: 212-780-6075
eva@jup.com www.jup.com

Eva Papoutsakis, Editor
Marla Kammer, Managing Editor

Editorial includes the latest information and technology in agencies, airlines, lodging, ticketing, mapping, Web advertising, transaction processing, revenue models, demographics, and full-service sites. *$595.00*

Monthly

13598 E-Business Advisor
Advisor Media
4849 Viewridge Avenue
San Diego, CA 92123-1643
858-278-5600
FAX: 858-278-0300 800-336-6060
pr@advisor.com
http://www.e-businessadvisor.com

John L Hawkins, Editorial Director
Jane Falla, Senior Editor
Brian Dunning, Technical Editor

E-Business Advisor is the monthly magazine presenting the best innovation, strategies, and practices for e-business leaders. It is an independent guide for the team of business and technical managers within an enterprise responsible for strategic innovation, planning, design, implementation, and management of e-business and e-commerce solutions. *$49.00*

68 pages Founded: 1983
Circulation: 60000
Mailing list available for rent 60000 names $175 per M.

13599 E-Content
Information Today
143 Old Marlton Pike
Medford, CT 08055-8750
609-654-6266
FAX: 609-654-4309 800-248-8466
custserv@infotoday.com
http://www.infotoday.com/

Michelle Manafy, Editor
Jared Bernstein, Editorial Assistant

Delivers essential research, reporting, news and analysis of content related issues. It is essential reading for executive and professionals involved in content creation, management, acquisition, distribution organization and distribution in both commercial and enterprise environments. *$115.00*

10 issues/yr
Mailing list available for rent 4M names
Printed in 4 colors on glossy stock

13600 ESchool News
IAQ Publications
7920 Norfolk Avenue
Suite 900
Bethesda, MD 20814-2507
301-913-0115
FAX: 301-913-0119
gdowney@eschoolnews.com
http://www.schoolnews.com

Gregg Downey, President/Editor

Guide to buying and updating classroom technology for K-12 educators. Product information listings, industry updates and related reports. Covers grant writing and funding, as well as government legislation regarding education. *$90.00*

13601 Electronic Commerce Advisor
RIA Group
395 Hudson Street
New York, NY 10014-3669
212-367-6300
FAX: 212-367-6305 800-431-9025
ria.customerservices@thomson.com
http://www.riahome.com

Andrew Boden, Publisher

Offers the latestin electronic commerce covering what's available and how to select and employ the best technology without costly trial-and-error mistakes. Information on EDI, e-mail, fax gateways, Internet, encryption, VANs, procurement cards, imaging, voice response, remote computering and other related information. *$155.00*

Founded: 1940
Circulation: 4500

13602 Electronic Mail & Messaging Systems
Business Research Publications
1333 H Street NW
Suite 100 East
Washington, DC 20005-4707
202-364-6473
FAX: 202-842-1875 800-822-6338

Rod Kuckro, Editor-in-Chief

Exclusive biweekly intelligence technology applications, products and market trends in electronic mail, computer fax, wireless messaging and the Internet. *$595.00*

BiWeekly

13603 Electronic Publishing
PennWell Publishing Company
98 Spit Brook Road
Nashua, NH 03062-2880
603-891-0123
FAX: 603-891-0539
genepri@pennwell.com
http://www.electronic-publishing.com

Steve Taneman, Publisher
Keith V. Hevenor, Editor

For those who communicate in print, including service bureaus, printers, prepress houses and desktop publishers, it provides latest products, news and related developments. *$59.00*

Monthly Founded: 1910
Circulation: 68441

13604 Emediaweekly
Mac Publishing
501 2nd Street
San Francisco, CA 94107
415-243-0505
FAX: 415-442-0766 800-288-6848
macworld@macworld.com
http://www.macworld.com

Rick LePage, Publisher

Covers the creation, technologies, applications and hardware for the publishing spectrum, including print, Web, multimedia, CD and digital video. Emphasis on hardware and software products, along with analysis, reviews, and buyer's guides. *$125.00*

Weekly

13605 Explore the Net with Internet Explorer
ZD Journals
500 Canal View Boulevard
Rochester, NY 14623-2800
585-407-7301
FAX: 585-214-2386
etn_editor@zdjournals.com
www.zdjournals.com

Joelle Martin, Publisher

Informs readers of new features and how they may be used; covering such concepts as browser upgrades, compatibility issues, authoring tools and connection utilities. Regular departments showcase the 'site of the month,' in addition to reviewing other sites that have attractive interfaces and are valauble resources. *$49.00*

Monthly

13606 GEOWorld
Adams Business Media
250 S Wacker Drive
Suite 1150
Chicago, IL 60606
773-932-2774
FAX: 312-980-3135
admin@gisworld.com
http://www.geoplace.com

Matt Ball, Publisher
John Hughs, Editor

Reports news, events, business, projects, meetings and conventions, and features analysis, technical tutorials and GIS applications for engineering, natural resources, federal and local government, utilities and business. *$72.00*

Monthly
Circulation: 25000

13607 Genealogical Computing
Ancestry
360 West 4800 North
Provo, UT 84604-476
801-705-7000
FAX: 801-705-7001 800-262-3787
pr@myfamilyinc.com
http://www.ancestry.com

Dick Eastman, Editor
Matthew Wright, Contributing Editor
David C Moon, CEO
Mary-Kay Evans, Director, Public Relations

For readers who use computers and technology to organize and enhance their research into accounts of ancestries and descent. *$ 25.00*

Quarterly

13608 Geospatial Solutions
Advanstar Communications
1 Park Avenue
New York, NY 10016
212-797-7631
FAX: 212-951-6793 888-527-7008
info@advanstar.com
http://www.advanstar.com/

Dave Huisman, Advertising Sales Manager
Scottie Barnes, Editor-in-Chief
Jim Engelhardt, Managing Editor

Practical applications of geographic information systems and technologies for plan-

ning, developing, preserving, analyzing and managing environments.
Monthly Founded: 1987
Circulation: 30000

13609 Harlow Report: Geographic Information Systems
Advanced Information Management Group
905 Thistledown Lane
Birmingham, AL 35244-3361
334-982-9203

chris@geoint.com
http://www.theharlowreport.com/
Chris Harlow, Publisher/Editor

Key management issues and new software highlights, service providers and users for the geographic information systems industry. *$ 190.00*
Monthly Founded: 1982

13610 Heller Report on Internet Strategies for Education Markets
Nelson B Heller & Associates
9933 Lawler Avenue
#502
Skokie, IL 60077-3708
800-525-5811
FAX: 303-209-9444 877-435-5373
info@hellerreports.com
http://www.hellerreports.com
Nelson B Heller, President/Publisher
Emily Garner, Sales/Marketing Director

Covers Internet hardware, software and services for educational use. Discusses the funding and deadlines relevant to the products and services offered through the Internet. *$397.00*
12 pages Monthly Founded: 1981
Circulation: 500
Printed in 2 colors

13611 IEEE Internet Computing
IEEE Computer Society
PO Box 3014
Los Alamitos, CA 90720-1314
714-821-8380
FAX: 714-821-4010 800-272-6657
mloeb@computer.org
http://www.computer.org/internet
Angela Burges, Publisher
Davis Hennage, CEO/President
Steve Woods, Editor
Sandy Brown, Marketing
Steve Woods, Circulation Manager

Provides a technology roadmap for high-end users and applicatoin developers, as well as a venue for standards, case histories, and new ideas. Essays, interview, and roundtable discussions address the Internet's impact on engineering practice. Describes Internet tools, technologies, and application-oriented research. *$28.00*
Quarterly Founded: 1946
Circulation: 11265

13612 IT Cost Management Strategies
Computer Economics
2082 Business Center Dr
Ste 240
Irvine, CA 92612-6500
949-831-8700
FAX: 949-442-7688 800-326-8100
info@compecon.com
http://www.computereconomics.com
Frank Scavo, President
Ed Pasahow, Senior Editor
Jim Miller, Director Sales
Barbara McDonald, Editor

Covers budgeting, financial news, computer programming, marketing and management for management information systems directors as a planning assistant.
Monthly Founded: 1978

13613 ITS World
Advanstar Communications
859 Willamette Street
Eugene, OR 97401-2918
541-431-0026
FAX: 541-344-3514
its@itsworld.com www.itsworld.com
Phillip Arndt, Publisher

Articles on industry news, current issues that affect Intelligent Transportation Systems, practical advice, applications, new and existing technology, and new product information. *$35.00*
9 per year
Circulation: 15,124

13614 Information Display
Palisades Institute for Research Services
2 Shadybrook Lane
Norwalk, CT 06854
203-853-7069
FAX: 203-855-9769
office@sid.org http://www.sid.org
Kenneth I Werner, Editor
Shigeol Mikoshiba, President/Ceo

State-of-the-art developments in electronic, electromechanical and hardcopy display equipment; input and output technologies; storage media; human factors and display standards; entrepreneurship, marketing and management; and manufacturing. *$36.00*
Monthly Founded: 1962
Circulation: 11000
Printed in 4 colors

13615 Information Retrieval & Library Automation
Lomond Publications
PO Box 88
Mount Airy, MD 21771-0088
202-362-1361
FAX: 202-362-6156
Thomas Hattery, Publisher

New technology, products and equipment that improve information systems and library services, for science, social, social science, law, medicine, academic institutions and the public. *$75.00*
Monthly

13616 Information Security
International Computer Security Association
117 Kendrick Street
Suite 800
Needham, MA 02494
781-657-1000
FAX: 781-657-1100
lwalsh@infosecuritymag.com
http://www.infosecuritymag.com
Andrew Briney, VP
Lawrence Walsh, Editor
Michael S Mimoso, Senior Editor
Gabrielle DeRussy, Advertising Sales
Susan Rastellini Smith, Product Management

Articles and analysis of information-security issues such as media, entwork and virus protection, internet security and encryption reports. *$100.00*
Monthly Founded: 1999
Circulation: 60000

13617 Information Systems Security
Auerbach Publications
2494 Bayshore Boulevard
Suite 201
Dunedin, FL 34698
703-891-6781
FAX: 703-891-0782 800-737-8034
institute@isc2.org
http://www.isc2.org
Jim Tiller, Managing Editor
Richard O'Hanley, Publisher
John Colley, Chairman

Facts and experience, expert opinion on directions in security, public policy, computer crime and ethics related to the information security field. *$175.00*
Founded: 2003
Circulation: 1500

13618 Inside the Internet
ZD Journals
500 Canal View Boulevard
Rochester, NY 14623-2800
585-407-7301
FAX: 585-214-2387
int@zdjournals.com
www.zdjournals.com
Joelle Martin, Publisher

Information and hands-on instruction for applicaitons along with some pictorial explanation. *$49.00*
Monthly

13619 Internet & Intranet Business and Technology Report
Computer Technology Research Corporation
6 N Atlantic Wharf
Charleston, SC 29401-2115
843-766-5293
FAX: 843-853-7210
editors@ctrcorp.com
www.ctrcorp.com
Edward Wagner, Publisher

Reports on international news, historial profiles of the impact of various applications, and developing standards and regulations. Topics covered include domain registration, Webcasting and the market for Internet e-mail. *$390.00*
Monthly

13620 Internet Business
Ziff Davis Publishing Company
28 E 28th Street
New York, NY 10016
212-033-3500
steven_thompson@zd.com
Steven K Thompson, Publisher
Adam Gordon, VP

Provides in-depth information and analysis on Internet products, techniques and tools, based on comparative lab testing and real world experience. Feature articles address technology segments that optimize an Internet strategy such as firewalls, authoring tools, etc., and how-to columns look at technical issues surrounding Web site development. *$24.99*
Monthly

13621 Internet Business Strategies
Gartner Group
56 Top Gallant Road
Stamford, CT 06904
203-964-0096
FAX: 203-316-6271
http://www.gartner.com
Chuck Trendell, Editor
Eugene Hall, Chief Executive Officer

Michael W McCarty, Senior VP
John Gardner, President

Helps readers make informed decisions about how to use the Internet to deploy electronic commerce and interactive initiatives. *$ 395.00*

Weekly Founded: 1993
Circulation: 10,000

13622 Internet Reference Service Quarterly
Haworth Press
10 Alice Street
Binghamton, NY 13904-1580
607-722-5857
FAX: 607-722-6362 800-429-6784
getinfo@haworthpress.com
http://www.haworthpress.com

Margaret K Scharf MLS, MBA, Editor
Bill Cohen, Publisher/CEO

Covers topics such as using World Wide Web software for reference and instruction, using the Internet for document delivery, Internet training and advancing reference information systems on the Web. *$40.00*

Quarterly Founded: 1978
Circulation: 3000

13623 Internet Shopper
Mecklermedia Corporation
20 Ketchum Street
Westport, CT 06880-5908
203-662-2800
FAX: 203-454-5840
sleiterstein@internetshopper.com
www.internetshopper.com

Susan Leiterstein, Publisher

Edited for consumers who purchas products and services direct from Interet Web sites. Covers online malls, computers and electronics, stocks, books, home furnishings, music and more. Reviews the best sites within their categoreis and includes tips on how to conduct safe ande effective online transactions.

Daily

13624 Internet Telephony
Technology Marketing Corporation
One Technology Plaza
Norwalk, CT 06854
203-852-6800
FAX: 203-853-2845 800-243-6002
tmc@tmcnet.com
http://www.internettelephonymag.com

Greg Galitzine, Editor
Richard Tehrani, President/Group Publisher
Shirley A. Russo, Circulation Director

News and departments focus on providing readers with information they need to learn about and purchase the equipment, software and services necessary for Internet telephony, through the convergence of voice, video, fax and data.

Monthly Founded: 1972
Circulation: 28024

13625 Internet World
Mecklermedia Corporation
20 Ketchum Street
Westport, CT 06880-5908
203-226-6967
FAX: 203-454-5840

Corey Friedman, Publisher
Michael Neubarth, Editor

For noncommercial and commercial uses of Internet and the National Research and Education Network. *$5.00*

Founded: 1971
Circulation: 256883

13626 Journal of Educational Multimedia & Hypermedia
Association for Advance of Computing in Education
PO Box 3728
Norfolk, VA 23514
757-623-7588
FAX: 703-997-8760
info@aace.org http://www.aace.org

Gary Marks, Editor

Product and book reviews, projects and developer dialogue for international research and applications on multimedia and hypermedia in education.

Quarterly Founded: 1981

13627 Journal of Electronic Imaging
International Society for Optical Engineering
1000 20th Street
Bellingham, WA 98225-10
360-676-3290
FAX: 360-647-1445
journals@spie.org http://www.spie.org

Kristin Lewotsky, Executive Editor
Winn Hardin, Senior Editor
Michael Brownell, Contributing Editors

Timely information about evolving imaging technologies, including image acquistions, image data storage, image data display, image visualization, image processing, image data communciations, hard copy output and multimedia systems. *$135.00*

Quarterly Founded: 1992
Circulation: 1500

13628 Journal of Internet Law
Apen Publishers
400 Hamilton Avenue
Palo Alto, CA 94301-1809
650-328-6561
FAX: 650-327-3699 www.gcfw.com

Mark F Radcliffe, Editor-in-Chief

Discusses strategies utilized by top intellectual property, computer law and information technology industry experts.

Monthly

13629 Journal of Research on Computing in Education
International Society for Technology in Education
480 Charmelton Street
Eugene, OR 97401-2626
541-302-3770
FAX: 541-302-3778 800-336-5191
iste@iste.org http://www.iste.org/

Davis Smith, Editor
Don Knezek, President
Jean Hall, Publication Manager

Covers computer research and developments relating to all levels of education. Articles define the state of current and future use of technology in education. *$79.00*

Quarterly Founded: 1989
Circulation: 4500

13630 Journal of Technology in Human Services
Haworth Press
10 Alice Street
Binghamton, NY 13904-1503
607-722-5857
FAX: 607-722-1424 800-429-6784
getinfo@haworthpress.com
http://www.haworthpress.com

Dick Schoech PhD, Editor
Bill Cohen, Publisher

Contents discuss the future of technology in various fields of human services, including applications, service techniques and developments. *$75.00*

Quarterly Founded: 1978
Mailing list available for rent
Printed in 1 color on matte stock

13631 KM World
Information Today
18 Bayview Street
PO Box 1358
Camden, ME 04843-1358
207-236-8524
FAX: 207-236-6452
editor@kmworld.com
http://www.kmworld.com

Hugh McKellar, Editor in Chief
Sandra Haimila, Managing Editor
Michael V Zarrello, Advertising Director
Andy Moore, Publisher
David Panara, Sales Manager

Serves content, document and knowledge of management market to help improve business performance.

Circulation: 56000 55M names $86 per M.

13632 MacTech
Xplain Corporation
PO Box 5200
Westlake Village, CA 91359-5200
805-494-9797
FAX: 805-494-9798
press-releases@mactech.com
http://www.mactech.com

Neil Ticktin, Publisher
Dave Mark, Editor-in-Chief

Provides web developers and network administrators with the most technically advanced information for them to combat the needs of the industry. How to articles, technically oriented product reviews with a Mac focus. *$19.95*

Monthly Founded: 1984 ISBN 3-212874-88-7 $125 per M.
Printed in on glossy stock

13633 MultiMedia Schools
Information Today
143 Old Marlton Pike
Medford, NJ 08055-8750
609-654-6266
FAX: 609-654-4309
custserv@infotoday.com
http://www.infotoday.com

Thomas Hogan, Publisher/President
David Hoffman, Editor
Inge Coffey, Circulation Manager
Heather Rudolph, Marketing Manager:

Examines the benefits of multimedia, CD-ROM, online and Internet services to educators of K-12. *$39.95*

13634 On the Internet
Rickard Group
10 E Broad Street
#A
Hopewell, NJ 08525-1810
609-466-4343
FAX: 609-466-8892
editor@isoc.org www.isoc.org

Wendy Rickard Bollentin, Publisher

Internet information for technologists, developers, educators, researchers, government representatives, and business people. *$ 22.00*

Bi-Monthly
Circulation: 9M

13635 Optical Technology 21st Century
Frames Data
PO Box 57016
Irvine, CA 92619-7016
949-788-0150
FAX: 949-788-0130
frames@framesdata.com
www.framesdata.com

Skip Johnson, President

Movement of product electronically; computerization of office functions, lab work, testing procedures and equipment; information on the Internet, optical Web sites, and onlines services. *$299.00*
Quarterly
Circulation: 19M

13636 PC Photo
Werner Publishing
12121 Wilshire Boulevard
12th Floor
Los Angeles, CA 90025-1176
310-820-1500
FAX: 310-826-5008
editors@pcphotomag.com
http://www.pcphotomag.com

Steven Werner, Publisher
Rob Shepherd, Editor

Covers the new desktop darkroom or home photo lab technologies, trends and methods. Designed to stimulate desktop photographers through the listing of new products and technologies. *$11.97*
Founded: 1965

13637 PCAI
Knowledge Technology
PO Box 30130
Phoenix, AZ 85046
602-971-1869
FAX: 602-971-2321
info@pcai.com
http://www.pcai.com/pcai

Terry Hengl, Publisher
Daniel W Rasmus, Editorial Advisor
Don Barker, Senior Editor
Robin Okun, VP of Marketing

Information necessary to help managers, programmers, executives and other professionals understand the unfolding realm of artificial intelligence and intelligent applications. *$24.00*
Founded: 1987

13638 PDN's Pix
VNU Business Media
770 Broadway
New York, NY 10003-9595
646-545-5100

bmcomm@vnuinc.com
http://www.vnu.com

Rob van den Bergh, CEO
Rob Ruijter, CFO

Covers the world of electronic digital imaging to help readers use new imaging technology and the Web, digital meda, image capture and transfer. *$19.94*
Founded: 1964
Circulation: 51753

13639 VRML Developer's Journal
SYS-CON Publications
39 E Central Avenue
Pearl River, NY 10965-2306
845-735-1900
FAX: 845-735-3922
fkircaali@sys-conpublications.com
www.vrmldevelopersjournal.com

Fuat Kircaali, Publisher

Timely and insightful coverage of the growing technology for creating virtual worlds on the Web. Technical explanations and commentary related to VRML and its theme of promoting 3D world development. *$49.00*
Bi-Monthly
Circulation: 20M

13640 Virus Bulletin
Virus Bulletin
590 Danbury Road
Ridgefield, CT 06877-2722
203-438-7714
FAX: 203-431-8165

Richard Ford, Editor
Victoria Lammer, Production Manager

An international journal addressing computer viruses, Trojan horses and other malicious programs. Emphasis is placed on providing technical and procedural countermeasures for businesses using computers. *$35.00*

13641 WWWiz Magazine
WWWiz Corporation
8840 Warner Avenue
Suite 200
Fountain Valley, CA 92708
714-848-9600
FAX: 714-375-2493
wiz@wwwiz.com
http://www.wwwiz.com

Don Hamilton, Editor-in-Chief
Vivian Hamilton, Managing Editor

WWWiz is a publication focused on the internet with content aimed entrepenuers and business professionals. We interview people who have found success in internet business along with articles pertaining to legal issues, marketing, technology, travel, and other special interest areas. *$28.00*
Monthly Founded: 1995
Circulation: 120000

13642 Wall Street & Technology
Miller Freeman Publications
11 West 19th Street
New York, NY 10011
212-780-0400
FAX: 212-600-3045
mfrieden@cmp.com
http://www.wallstreetandtech.com

Michael Friedenberg, Group Publisher
Richard Rosenblatt, CEO/President
Kerry Massaro, Editor-in-Chief
Anne Marie Miller, Senior VP/Sales & Marketing

Editoral emphasis on the automation of brokerage houses and money management firms.
Monthly
Circulation: 21226

13643 Web Builder
Fawcette Technical Publications
2600 South El Camino Real
Suite 300
San Mateo, CA 94403-2332
650-378-7100
FAX: 650-570-6307 800-848-5523
customerservice@fawcette.com
http://www.ftponline.com

Paul Spyksma, Publisher
Karen Koenen, Sr Circulation Director
John Sutton, Executive VP
Susan Ogren, Marketing Manager
James Fawcette, President

Highly technical, code-sensitive articles that cover all that goesinto designing interfaces for sophisticated Internet/Intranet applications. Features a case-study approach to finding out who is using which Web sites and how. *$32.96*
Monthly

13644 Web Content Report
Lawrence Ragan Communications
316 N Michigan Avenue
Suite 400
Chicago, IL 60601
312-604-4100
FAX: 312-960-4106 800-493-4867
cservice@ragan.com
http://www.ragan.com

Rebecca Anderson, Editor
Mark Ragan, CEO/President
Kasia Chalko, Marketing Director Events
Frank Bleers, Marketing Director
Publisher

Outlines ways to attract visitors to a Web site, and be able to then monitor and evaluate the traffic on the home page. New developments in Web technology, how products can be sold on sites, budgeting matters and communicaiton with management. *$269.00*
Monthly Founded: 1996
Printed in 2 colors on matte stock

13645 Web Guide Monthly
H&S Media
430 Oak Grove Street
Suite 100
Minneapolis, MN 55403-3234
612-990-3203
FAX: 612-879-1082
wdorn@webguidemag.com
www.webguidemag.com

Dan Beaver, Publisher

Examines and evaluates useful tools that merge the Internet with everyday life, at work and at home. Sites are sorted into categories, and are referenced in an index. *$34.95*
Monthly
Circulation: 120M

13646 Web Techniques
Miller Freeman Publications
411 Borel Avenue
#100
San Mateo, CA 94402-3516
650-573-3210
FAX: 650-655-4250
editors@web-techniques.com
www.webtechniques.com

Manny Sawit, Publisher

Latest information, tips and techniques to Web site developers. Contains information on new products and the latest information about the ever-changing world of Web development. *$34.95*
Monthly
Circulation: 100M

13647 Webserver Online Magazine
Computer Publishing Group
1340 Centre Street
Newton Centre, MA 02459-2499
617-641-9101
FAX: 617-641-9102
editor@cpg.com http://www.cpg.com

S Henry Sacks, CEO/President
Doug Pryor, Editorial Director
Carol Flanagan, Marketing Manager
Tina Jackson, Circulation Manager
S Sacks, Publisher

Source for information Web professionals who need to get the most ot of their Web development and deployment efforts. Technology and industry news, systems and network adminsitration issues, the latest in Web tools, and a guide to new products, services and resources.

Monthly Founded: 1989

13648 WirelessWeek.com
PO Box 266008
Highlands Ranch, CO 80163-6008
303-470-4800
FAX: 303-470-4892
subsmail@reedbusiness.com
http://www.wirelessweek.com

Gerard Van de Aast, CEO
Debby Denton, Publisher
Rhonda Wickham, Editor -in- Chief
Glenn Comar, Marketing Director

Trade Shows

13649 American Public Communications Council Conference & Expo
10302 Eaton Place
Suite 340
Fairfax, VA 22030

FAX: 703-385-5301 800-868-2722

Bruce Renard, President

Conference, luncheon and 100 exhibits of public communications equipment and information including, pay phones, internet, atm, multimedia and more.

Founded: 1988

13650 Info Today Conference
Information Today
143 Old Marlton Pike
Medford, NJ 08055-8758
609-654-6266
FAX: 609-654-4309 800-300-9868
custserv@infotoday.com
www.infotoday.com

Carol Nixon, Manager
Mike Zarrello, Advertising/Sales
Thomas Hogan, President

Users of online information services, electronic databases and the Internet. 200 booths.

6M Attendees May Founded: 1980 5000 names

13651 Internet Communications Exposition
IDG Expositions
1400 Providence Highway
Norwood, MA 02062
508-879-6700

13652 Internet Publishing Expo
401 N Broad Street
5th Floor
Philadelphia, PA 19108

FAX: 215-409-0100 888-627-2630
dmorrishall@napco.com
www.iPubExpo.com

13653 VoIP 2.0
Technology Marketing Corporation
One Technology Plaza
Norwalk, CT 06854
203-852-6800
FAX: 203-853-2845 800-243-6002

October, San Diego

Directories & Databases

13654 Adweek Directories
VNU Business Publications
770 Broadway
7th Floor
New York, NY 10003
646-654-5100
FAX: 646-654-5351
publisher@adweek.com

Wright Ferguson Jr, VP/Magazine Publisher

Publishes directories, all the Adweek Directories are available online. Also publishes magazines about the media, marketing and advertising industry which are also available online.

13655 America Online
8619 Westwood Center Drive
Suite 200
Vienna, VA 22182-2238

FAX: 540-265-2135 800-227-6364

Jack Daggitt, Director
Anne Botsford

This multi-faceted information service provides complete access to a variety of databases and computer services of interest to users of Macintosh and Apple II computers. Databases included in this systems range from Computing & Software to Lifestyles & Interests.

Full-text

13656 Boardwatch Magazine Directory of Internet Service Providers
Penton Media
1300 E 9th Street
Cleveland, OH 44114
216-696-7000
FAX: 216-696-1752
rgolden@boardwatch.com
www.ispworld.com

Michael Rand Goldner, Publisher
Bill McCarthy, Editorial Director

Reviews various Internet providers and lists different programs available through their individual companies who operate in the US and Canada. *$72.00*

Monthly
Circulation: 70,000

13657 Fulltext Sources Online
Information Today
143 Old Marlton Pike
Medford, NJ 08055-8750
609-654-6266
FAX: 609-654-4309
custserv@infotoday.com
www.infotoday.com

Thomas H Hogan, Publisher/President
John Bryans, Publisher/Editor-in-Chief Books
Lauree Padgett, Editorial Services Manager
Inge Coffey, Circulation Manager

A directory of periodicals accessible online in full text through 28 aggregator products. Lists over 22,000 newspapers, journals, newsletters, newswires, and transcripts. *$145.00*

Biannually Jan & July ISBN 1-573872-23-7

13658 IQ Directory
ADWEEK
770 Broadway
7th Floor
New York, NY 10003
646-545-5220
FAX: 646-654-5351
publisher@adweek.com
www.adweek.com

Mitch Tebo, Directory Publisher

Profile of companies at the leading edge of digital marketing, has the specifics you'll need to investigate, launch and/or expand your digital presence. Profiles over 2,200 interactive agencies, web developers, brand marketers, online media, CD-ROM developers, POP/Kiosk designers and multimedia creative companies

13659 Internet Blue Pages
Information Today
143 Old Marlton Pike
Medford, NJ 08055-8750
609-654-6266
FAX: 609-654-4309
custserv@infotoday.com
www.infotoday.com

Thomas H Hogan, Publisher/President
John Bryans, Publisher/Editor-in-Chief Books
Lauree Padgett, Editorial Services Manager
Igne Coffey, Circualtion Manager

The Guide to Federal Government Web Sites is the leading guide to federal government information on the web. Includes over 1,800 annotated agency listings, arranged in the US Government Manual style to help you find the information you need. *$34.95*

464 pages ISBN 0-910965-43-9

13660 Key Guide to Electronic Resources: Art and Art History
Information Today
143 Old Marlton Pike
Medford, NJ 08055-8750
609-654-6266
FAX: 609-654-4309
custserve@infotoday.com
www.infotoday.com

Martin Raish, Editor
Pat Ensor, Series Editor

An evaluative directory of electronic reference in the fields of art and art history. *$39.50*

120 pages ISBN 1-573870-22-6

13661 Key Guide to Electronic Resources:Language and Literature

Information Today
143 Old Marlton Pike
Medford, NJ 08055-8750
609-654-6266
FAX: 609-654-4309
custserve@infotoday.com
www.infotoday.com

Diane K Kovacs, Editor
Pat Ensor, Series Editor

Part of the ongoing topic related series of reference guides is an evaluative directory of electronic reference sources in the fields of language and literature. *$39.50*

120 pages ISBN 1-573870-20-x

13662 On-Line Networks, Databases & Bulletin Boards on Assistive Technology
ERIC Document Reproduction Service
7420 Fullerton Road
Suite 110
Springfield, VA 22153-2852
703-440-1400
FAX: 703-440-1408 800-443-ERIC
Directory of electronic networks that focus on technology-related services.

13663 Supply Chain e-Business
Keller International Publishing Corporation
150 Great Neck Road
Great Neck, NY 11021
516-829-9722
FAX: 516-829-7265 www.glscs.com
Thomas A Foster, Editor-in-Chief
Russel W Goodman, Managing Editor
Jerry Keller, President
Offers a thorough analysis of on-line solutions designed to help corporations achieve greater supply-chain visibility and real-time connections with suppliers and customers
Bi-Monthly
Circulation: 75M
Printed in 4 colors on glossy stock

Industry Web Sites

13664 www.aace.org
Association for the Advancement of Computing in Ed

Promotes the use of computers and the internet in educational settings.

13665 www.adsl.com/adsl_forum.html

Information about ADSL, Asymmetric Digital Subscriber Line, a system that provides high-speed Internet connections

13666 www.apcc.net
American Public Communications Council

APCC Proudly offers a wide array of services to the public communications industry, from Perspectives magazine to our annual trade show to our involvement in legal and regulatory issues. This site is a place for the public to find out about our industry and for our members to learn of legal and regulatory developments, to become aware of APCC programs and events and to have a forum for discussion.

13667 www.cabledatacomnews.com/cmic.htm

Cable modems

13668 www.conferences.calendar.com/

Academic conferences, symposia, courses and workshops.

13669 www.ditiitalmx.com/wires/

Integrated Services Digital Network

13670 www.greyhouse.com
Grey House Publishing

Selected Grey House directories in the fields of business, health and education are available online. Users can search our online databases by several different search criteria, such as product categories, geographic area, sales volume and much, much more. Full Grey House catalog and online ordering also available.

13671 www.hayes.com/prodinfo/adsl/intro.html

Information about ADSl, Asymmetric Digital Subscriber Line, a system that provides high-speed Internet connections

13672 www.internets.com
Internets.com

Searchable database and related industry links.

13673 www.iste.org
International Society for Technology in Education

Nonprofit professional organization with a worldwide membership of leaders and potential leaders in educational technology.

13674 www.spie.org
International Society for Optical Engineering

Serves the international technical community as the premier provider of education, information, and resources covering optics, photonics, and their applications.

Associations

13675 American Gem & Mineral Suppliers
475 Smith Street
Middletown, CT 06457-1529
860-632-2020

13676 American Gem Society
8881 W Sahara Avenue
Las Vegas, NV 89117
702-336-6120
FAX: 702-255-7420 www.ags.org
Ruth Batson, Executive Director
Donna Jolly, Marketing Executive
Seeks to build consumer confidence in the retail jeweler by promoting ethical business standards and professional excellence.
4.4M Members Founded: 1934

13677 American Gem Trade Association
PO Box 420643
Dallas, TX 75342-643
214-742-4367
FAX: 214-742-7334 800-972-1162
info@agta.org www.agta.org
Douglas K Hucker, Executive Director
Eric Braunwart, President
Ashok Sancheti, VP
Barbara Lawrence, Treasurer
Trade association for the colored gemstone industry in North America. Operates a gemological testing laboratory in New York.
750+ Members Founded: 1981

13678 American Jewelry Design Council
119 N 4th Street
Minneapolis, MN 55401-1786
312-726-0225

13679 American Watch Association
1201 Pennsylvania Avenue NW
PO Box 464
Washington, DC 20044-0464
703-759-3377
FAX: 703-759-1639
Emilio Collado, Executive Director
Walter Fischer, Chairman
Trade association for communication among professionals and legislative advocacy.
45 Members Founded: 1933

13680 American Watch Guild
257 Adams Lane
Hewlett, NY 11557
516-295-2516
FAX: 516-374-5060

13681 American Watchmakers Institute
701 Enterprise Drive
Harrison, OH 45030
513-367-9800
FAX: 513-367-1414 www.awi-net.org
James Lubic, Executive Director
Lucy Fuleki, Assistant Executive Director
Examines and certifies master watchmakers and clockmakers. Maintains a placement service. Conducts home study courses.
5000 Members Founded: 1960

13682 American Watchmakers-Clockmakers Institute
701 Enterprise Drive
Harrison, OH 45030-1696
513-367-9800
FAX: 513-367-1414 866-367-2924
Jim Lubic, Executive Director
Lucy Fuleti, Assistant Executive Director
Examines and certifies master watchmakers and clockmakers. Maintains a placement service. Conducts home study courses.
4000 Members Founded: 1892

13683 Appraisers Association of America
386 Park Avenue S
Suite 2000
New York, NY 10016-8804
212-889-5404
FAX: 212-889-5503
aaa1@ven.com
www.appraisersassoc.org
Aleya Lehmann, Executive Director
Trade organization for professional appraisers. Holds an annual conference.
520 Members Founded: 1949

13684 Brotherhood of Traveling Jewelers
Leys, Christie & Company
342 Madison Avenue
New York, NY 10173-1599
212-867-3675
Represents traveling jewelers.
300 Members

13685 Cultured Pearl Information Center
331 E 53rd Street
New York, NY 10022-4923
212-688-5580
FAX: 212-688-5857 www.pearlinfo.com
Devin MacNow, Executive Director
Conference information and buying guide for pearls.

13686 Diamond Council of America
3212 Westend Avenue
Suite 202
Nashville, TN 37203
615-385-5301
FAX: 615-385-4955
www.diamondcouncil.org
Bruce Kenny, Chairman
Terry Chandler, President/CEO
Provides courses in diamontology and gemology to retail jewelers and their employees who are DCA members. Sixty-six retailers representing 1,800 locations.
70 Members Founded: 1941

13687 Diamond Dealers Club
580 5th Avenue
10th Floor
New York, NY 10036-4781
212-790-3600
FAX: 212-869-5164
mhochbaum@ddcny.com nyddc.com
Jacob Banda, President
Dr Martin Hochbaum, Managing Director
Seeks to foster the interest of the diamond industry, promote equitable trade principles and eliminate abuses and unfair trading practices.
Founded: 1931

13688 Diamond Manufacturers and Importers Association of America
PO Box 5297
Rockefeller Center Station
New York, NY 10185
212-944-2066
FAX: 516-482-2749 800-223-2244
benler@aol.com www.dmia.net
Jeffery Fischer, President
Ben Kinzler, General Counsel
Represents and promotes manufacturers and importers of diamonds and rare gems.
150 Members

13689 Diamond Peacock Club
Kebadjian Brothers
333 Washington Street
Boston, MA 02108-5111
617-235-5565

13690 Diamond Promotion Service
466 Lexington Avenue
New York, NY 10017
212-210-7590
FAX: 212-210-8779 800-421-7250
Jay Walter Thompson, Contact
Resource for the tools and strategies to sell more diamonds. Buy marketing materials, train your staff, find the suppliers of advertised jewelry and more.

13691 Eastern Jewelers Travelers Association
5550 77th Center Drive
Charlotte, NC 28217
FAX: 704-504-1333 800-525-3582
Dennis Williams, President

13692 Estate Jewelry Association of America
209 Post Street
Suite 718
San Francisco, CA 94108-5209
415-834-0718
FAX: 415-834-0717 800-584-5522

13693 Fashion Jewelry Association of America
3 Davol Sq Unit 135
Providence, RI 02903-4710
401-528-1147
Al Tribelli, President
Nick Macris
150 Members Founded: 1985

13694 Gem & Lapidary Dealers Association
PO Box 2391
Tucson, AZ 85702
520-792-9431
FAX: 520-882-2836
info@glda.com www.glda.com
Tanna Wyatt, President

13695 Gemological Institute of America
Robert Mouawad Campus
5345 Armada Drive
Carlsbad, CA 92008
760-603-4000
FAX: 760-603-4003 800-421-7250
eduinfo@gia.edu www.gia.edu

William E Boyajian, President
Kathryn Kimmil, VP Marketing/Public Relations
Robert J Buscher, VP/CFO
Leigh Kelly, Advertising Coordinator
Dona Dirlam, Executive Director

Nonprofit institution providing knowledge and professionalism that will maintain long-term stability and integrity while strengthening and securing consumer confidence.

1100 Members Founded: 1931

13696 Gold Prospectors Association of America
43445 Business Park Drive
Temecula, CA 92590
951-994-4749
FAX: 909-699-4062 800-551-9707

Perry Massie, CEO
Tom Massie, Executive VP
Richard Dickson, COO/Counsel

GPAA is the largest recreational gold prospecting club. Owner of The Outdoor Channel, a cable TV channel featuring real outdoors for real people.

35M Members Founded: 1985

13697 Independent Jewelers Organization
25 Seir Hill Road
Norwalk, CT 06850-1322
203-846-4215
FAX: 203-846-8571 800-624-9252
ijo@ijo.com www.ijo.com

Richard Swetz, Chairman
Penny Palmer, Director Member Services

Works to aid independent jewelers in competing in local markets through advertising, promotion and buyers assistance.

850 Members Founded: 1972

13698 Indian Arts & Crafts Association
4010 Carsile NE
Albuquerque, NM 87101
505-265-9149
FAX: 505-265-8251
info@iaca.com www.iaca.com

Vincent P Eysoldt, Chairman/Co-Founder
Stuart Graham, President/CEO/Co-Founder
Vere Spandow, Chief Technology Advisor
Walter Dubowec, Chief Marketing Officer
Debbie Duffy, Manager

Nonprofit trade association. Our mission is to promote, protect and preserve Indian arts.

700 Members Founded: 1974

13699 Industrial Diamond Association of America
PO Box 29460
Columbus, OH 43229
614-797-2265
FAX: 614-797-2264
tkane-ida@insight.rr.com
www.superabrasives.org

Terry Kane, Executive Director
Robert Linares, Secretary/Treasurer
Ion C Benea, Board of Directors

Association of industrial diamond, cvd diamond and polycrystalling supplies, toolmakers. Products and services provided and used in most manufacturing and constuction industries such as: stone processing, glass construction, electronics, medical, woodworking, etc.

190 Members Founded: 1946

13700 International Colored Gemstone Association
19 W 21st Street
Suite 705
New York, NY 10010-6805
212-528-8814
FAX: 212-352-9054
ica@gemstone.org www.gemstone.org

Joseph Menzie, President
Barbara Lipatapanlop, Executive Director
Pat Koziol, Manager

Nonprofit association representing the international gemstone industry. Works to increase the understanding, appreciation and sales of colored gemstones worldwide.

13701 International Gem & Jewelry Show
120 Derwood Circle
Rockville, MD 20850
301-294-1640
FAX: 301-294-0034
info@intergem.com
www.intergem.net

Herb Duke, Owner

Jewelry, gemstones and related equipment, supplies and services.

13702 International Precious Metals Institute
4400 Bayou Boulevard
Suite 18
Pensacola, FL 32503-1908
850-476-1156
FAX: 850-476-1548
mail@ipmi.org www.ipmi.org

Kevin Beirne, President
Fred Saada, VP
Larry Manziek, Executive Director

International association of producers, refiners, fabricators, scientists, users, financial institutions, merchants, private and public sector groups and the general precious metals community created to provide a forum for the exchange of information and technology.

Founded: 1976

13703 International Society of Appraisers
1131 SW 7th St
Suite 105
Renton, WA 98055-2965
206-241-0359
FAX: 206-241-0436
isahq@isa-appraisers.org
www.isa-appraisers.org

Katherine Vandygriff, President
Charles T Cripps, VP
Charles Ellias, Treasurer
Jorge Sever, Executive Director
Joanna Stearns, Director

Nonprofit professional association of personal property appraisers. ISA provides education and organizational support to its members, to serve the public by producing highly qualified and ethical appraisers who are recognized authorities in personal property appraising.

1400+ Members Founded: 1979

13704 Jewelers Board of Trade
95 Jefferson Boulevard
Warwick, RI 02888-1046
401-467-0055
FAX: 401-467-1199
www.jewelersboard.com

Dione Kenyon, President

Trade Association: credit and collection for the jewelry industry.

3300 Members Founded: 1884

13705 Jewelers Vigilance Committee
25 W 45th Street
Suite 400
New York, NY 10036
212-997-2002
FAX: 212-997-9148 www.jvclegal.org

Cecilia Gardner Esq, Executive Director
Laurence R Grunstein, President
Jeffrey H Fischer, Treasurer
William Montalto, First VP
Steven Kaiser, Second VP

Identifies deceptive trade practices and misleading advertising. Provides advice on marketing and assists in prosecution of violations.

2.8M Members Founded: 1912

13706 Jewelers of America
52 Vanderbuilt Avenue
New York, NY 10017
646-580-0255

info@jewelers.org www.jewelers.org

Matt Runci, President

Center of knowledge for the jeweler and an advocate for professionalism and high social, ethical and environmental standards in the jewelry trade. Our mission is to assist all members in improving their business skills and profitability. JA will provide acess to meaningful educational programs and services, leadership in public and industry affairs, and encourage members with common interests to act in the industry's best interest.

13707 Jewelers' Security Bulletin
Jewelers' Security Alliance
6 E 45th Street
Suite 1005
New York, NY 10017-2414
212-687-0328
FAX: 212-808-9168 800-537-0067
jsa2@jewelerssecurity.org
www.jewelerssecurity.org

John J Kennedy, President

Principal activity is providing education and information to jewelers so they can guard against loss through crimes, including burglary, robbery and theft.

19500 Members Founded: 1883

13708 Jewelry Industry Distributors Association
701 Enterprise Drive
Harrison, OH 45030
513-367-2357
FAX: 513-367-1414
info@jida.info www.jida.info

Bill Nagle, President
Harvey Cobrin, First VP
Rick Foster, Secretary/Treasurer

Sets standards of service and facilitates the exchange of information of all types among members in order to improve business, maximize opportunities, and minimize risks.

150 Members Founded: 1946

13709 Jewelry Information Center
52 Vanderbuilt Avenue
19th Floor
New York, NY 10017
646-658-0240
FAX: 646-658-0245 800-459-0130
info@jic.org www.jic.org

Matthews Runzi, Chief Executive Officer
David Lafleur, Executive Director

Identifies deceptive trade practices and misleading advertising. Provides advice on marketing and assists in prosecution of violations. The media side of the Jewelers Vigilance Committee.
1000 Members Founded: 1946

13710 Jewelry Manufacturers Guild
PO Box 46099
Los Angeles, CA 90046-0099
909-769-1082

Promotes and improves conditions in the fine jewelry manufacturing industry.
400 Members

13711 Leading Jewelers Guild
PO Box 64609
Los Angeles, CA 90064
310-820-3386
FAX: 310-820-3530
www.love-story.com

James West, President

13712 Manufacturing Jewelers & Suppliers of America
45 Royal Little Drive
Providence, RI 2904
401-274-3840
FAX: 401-274-0265 800-444-6572
mjsa@mjsainc.com www.mjsainc.com

James Marquart, President/CEO
Paula Esposito, Director Trade Shows/Events
Bruce Coltin, Trade Show Sales Manager
Susan Palmateer, Trade Show Assistant
Rich Youmans, Director Communications

National trade association for the manufacturing jewelers and silversmiths. Sponsors trade shows, expositions and social events.
1.8M Members

13713 Manufacturing Jewelers and Silversmiths
45 Royal Little Drive
Providence, RI 2904
401-274-3840
FAX: 401-274-0265
mjsa@mjsainc.com www.mjsainc.com

James F Marquart, President/CEO
John Green, President
Alan Bell, Director
Curtis A Ley, Chairman

The trade association for all segments of the American jewelry manufacturing and supply industry.
Founded: 1903

13714 National Association of Jewelry Appraisers
PO Box 18
Rego Park, NY 11374
718-896-1536
FAX: 586-314-2442
naja.appraisers@netzero.net
www.najaappraisers.com

Gail B Levine, Executive Director

Purpose is to maintain professional standards and education in the field of jewelry appraising and provide members benefits at lower cost than can be attained individually.
720 Members Founded: 1981

13715 National Cuff Link Society
PO Box 5970
Vernon Hills, IL 60061
847-816-0035
FAX: 847-816-0035
genek@cufflink.com
www.justcufflinks.com

Gena Klompus, President

We are a membership organization for cuff link wearers and collectors. We provide a quarterly publication called The Link and an annual convention.
8000 Members Founded: 1990

13716 Platinum Guild International USA
620 Newport Center Drive
Suite 800
Newport Beach, CA 92660
949-760-8279
FAX: 949-760-8780
info@pgiusa.com
www.preciousplatinum.com

Laurie A Hudson, President

Organization promoting platinum jewelry. Maintains a website where the press and the public can find helpful information.
Founded: 1975

13717 Plumb Club
157 Engle Street
Englewood, NJ 07631
201-816-8881
FAX: 201-816-8882
susan@plumbclub.com
www.plumbclub.org

Susan Lee Cullum, Administrative Director

Exclusive social organization within the jewelry industry holding black tie events for members and their clients and exhibitor shows.

13718 Schneider National
3101 S Packerland Drive
Po Box 2545
Green Bay, WI 54313
920-592-2000
800-558-6767

Don Schneider, Chairman
Christopher Lofgren PhD, President & CEO

A leading provider of transportation and logistics services with a comprehensive reach across North America and a growing presence in Europe and Asia.

13719 Silver Institute
1200 G Street NW
Suite 800
Washington, DC 20005
202-835-0185
FAX: 202-835-0155
info@silverinstitute.org
www.silverinstitute.org

Paul Bateman, Executive Director
Keith Hulley, President

International association of miners, refiners, fabricators and wholesalers of silver and silver products.
Founded: 1971

13720 Silver Users Association
11240 Waples Mill Road
Suite 200
Fairfax, VA 22030
703-934-0219
FAX: 703-359-7562 800-245-6999
silverusers@capitolonellc.com
www.silverusersassociation.org

Mike Merolla, President
John Gannon, VP

Represents manufacturers and distributors of products in which silver is an essential element, such as photographic materials, medical and dental supplies, batteries and electronic and electrical equipment, silverware, mirrors, commemorative art and jewelry.
27 Members Founded: 1947

13721 Society of American Silversmiths
PO Box 72839
Providence, RI 02907
401-567-7800
FAX: 401-567-7801
sas@silversmithing.com
www.silversmithing.com

Jeffrey Herman, Founder/Executive Director

Organization devoted to the preservation and promotion of the silversmithing art and craft.
240 Members Founded: 1989

13722 Society of North American Goldsmiths
1300 Iroquois Avenue
Suite 160
Naperville, IL 60563
630-852-6385
FAX: 630-416-3333
info@snagmetalsmith.org
www.snagmetalsmith.org

Ken Bova, President
Angela Gleason, Treasurer
Ellen Wieske, Secretary

Promotes a favorable and enriching environment in which contemporary metalsmiths practice their art. One aspect of this process is educating the public about the quality and rich diversity within the field of metalsmithing. Exhibitions, public forums, lectures, and published documents are our primary methods of reaching out to the public. SNAG sponsors workshops, seminars, audio-visual services and an annual conference.
Founded: 1969

13723 Tucson Gem & Mineral Society
PO Box 42588
Tucson, AZ 85733
520-322-5773
FAX: 520-322-6031
tgms@tgms.org www.tgms.org

Rose Marques, Administrative Assistant

A non-profit organization dedicated to encouraging the interest and study in geology, mineralogy, lapidary and allied earth sciences. Sponsors the annual Tucson Gem and Mineral Show.
Founded: 1946

13724 Women's Jewelry Association
19 Mantua Road
Mount Royal, NJ 08061
856-423-3126
FAX: 856-423-3420
wjahg@talley.com
www.womensjewelry.org

Amy Rosi, Communications

To empower women to achieve their highest goals in the international jewelry, watch and related businesses.
Founded: 1983

13725 World Gold Council
444 Madison Avenue
New York, NY 10022
212-317-3800
FAX: 212-688-0410 www.gold.org
James E Burton, CEO
Kelvin Williams, Executive Director
John Calnon, Manager
Organization formed and funded by the world's leading gold mining companies with the aim of stimulating and maximizing the demand for, and holding of gold by consumers, investors, industry and the official sector.
23 Members Founded: 1987

Newsletters

13726 Benchmark
Manufacturing Jewelers & Suppliers of America
45 Royal Little Drive
Providence, RI 02904
401-274-3840
FAX: 401-274-0265
James Marguart, President
Offers details of association activities and industry events for members.
4 pages Bi-Monthly

13727 Costume Jewelry Review
Retail Reporting Bureau
302 5th Avenue
11th Floor
New York, NY 10001-3604
212-279-7000
Offers news and information on the costume jewelry industry, suppliers and manufacturers. *$108.00*
Monthly

13728 Diamond Insight
Tryon Mercantile
790 Madison Avenue
New York, NY 10021-6124
212-288-9011
FAX: 212-772-1286
http://www.newsletteraccess.com
Guido Giovannini-Torelli, Editor
Penetrates the multifaceted world of diamonds, giving intelligence on the world's important stones, future price indicators, key individuals behind the trends, jewelry auctions and DeBeers/CSO Activities. *$325.00*
12 pages Monthly
Circulation: 250 Audited Est. Pass-Along Circ: 500
Printed in 1 color on glossy stock

13729 Diamond Registry Bulletin
Diamond Registry
580 5th Avenue
New York, NY 10036-4701
212-575-0444
FAX: 212-575-0722 800-223-7955
diamond58@aol.com
http://www.diamondregistry.com
Joseph Schlussel, President
Monthly newsletter offering the latest trends, prices and forecasts concerning diamonds, diamond jewelry and diamond mining. *$ 97.00*
Monthly Founded: 1961

13730 Jewelers' Security Alliance Newsletter
6 East 45th Street
Suite 1005
New York, NY 10017-2414
212-687-0328
FAX: 212-808-9168 800-537-0067
JSA@polygon.net
http://www.jewelerssecurity.org
John J Kennedy, President
Robert W Frank, VP
Helen M Buck, Manager of Membership Ser
Principal activity is providing education and information to jewelers so they can guard against loss through crimes, including burglary, robbery and theft. *$375.00*
Annual+ Founded: 1883

13731 Jewelry Newsletter International
Newsletters International
2600 S Gessner Road
Houston, TX 77063-3297
713-783-0100
Len Fox, Editor
Informs manufacturers, wholesalers, suppliers, and retailers of jewelry how to stimulate sales, increase profits, and cut costs. *$250.00*
4-8 pages Monthly Founded: 1973
Printed in on matte stock

13732 Spectra
American Gem Society
8881 W. Sahara Avenue
Las Vegas, NV 89117
702-336-6120
FAX: 702-255-7420
AGSwein@aol.com www.ags.org
Charlotte Preston, Publisher
Society news covering all aspects of the jewelry world.
12 pages Quarterly Founded: 1934

Magazines & Journals

13733 AJM Magazine: The Authority on Jewelry Manufacturing
Manufacturing Jewelers & Suppliers of America
45 Royal Little Drive
Providence, RI 2904
401-274-3840
FAX: 401-274-0265
ajm@ajm-magazine.com
http://www.ajm-magazine.com
Tina Wojtkielo, Editor
James F Marquart, Publisher
This is the only magazine dedicated solely to jewelry manufacturers. It delivers the three T's of jewelry manufacturing: trends, technology and techniques. *$47.00*
Monthly Founded: 1903
Printed in 4 colors on glossy stock

13734 Accent Magazine
Larkin Group
485 7th Avenue
#1400
New York, NY 10018-6804
212-594-0880
FAX: 212-594-8556
AJ Larkin, Publisher
Provides trend analysis and market forecasts for buyers and designers, for accessories, clothing, and footwear. Also covers convention and tradeshow news, and new product launches. *$24.00*
Monthly
Circulation: 13,000

13735 Adornment: Newsletter of Jewelry and Related Arts
1333A N Avenue
New Rochelle, NY 10804
914-636-3784
ekarlin@usa.net
Elyse Karlin, Publisher/Editor/CEO
$60.00
Quarterly Founded: 1999
Circulation: 800

13736 Chronos
Golden Bell Press
2403 Champa Street
Denver, CO 80205-2621
303-296-1600
FAX: 303-295-2159
print@goldenbellpress.com
http://www.goldenbellpress.com
Lawrence Bell, Publisher
Lawrence Bell, CEO
Sherry Simpson, Circulation Manager/Marke
Dara Hinshaw, Editor
Editorial material looks at timepieces of the past, present and future, bringing you the latest, the best and the most intriguing creation from the leading international watch and clock makers. The history of timepiece manufacturers and their significant milestones are also reported as well as armchair tours of the world's most prestigious horological museums. *$2250.00*
Quarterly Founded: 1933
Circulation: 20000

13737 Colored Stone
PRIMEDIA
60 Chestnut Avenue
Suite 201
Devon, PA 19333-1312
610-964-6300
FAX: 610-293-1717 610-232-5700
us.editorial@primedia.com
http://www.colored-stone.com
Joseph Breck, Publisher
Morgan Beard, Editor-in-Chief
Contains news and information on the gem and gemstone jewelry industry. *$29.95*
64 pages Founded: 1986
Circulation: 10000

13738 Couture International Jeweler
Miller Freeman Publications
770 Broadway
5th Floor
New York, NY 10003-9595
212-780-0400
FAX: 847-763-9037
ijmag@halldata.com
http://www.couturejeweler.com
Debra De Roo Ballard, Publisher
Lynda Roguso, Marketing Director
Publication features information on hot trends in fine jewelry and fashion. *$60.00*
Founded: 1964
Circulation: 20000

13739 GZ (European Jeweler)
JCK International Publishing Group
360 Park Avenue South
New York, NY 10010
646-466-6400
FAX: 646-746-7131
msmelzer@reedbusiness.com
http://www.jckgroup.com

Mark Smelzer, Publisher
Donna Borrelli, Associate Publisher
Hedda Schupak, Editor-in-Chief
Tracey Peden, Marketing Manager
Nancy Walsh, Senior Vice President
$49.95
Monthly Founded: 1874

13740 Gems & Gemology
Gemological Institute of America
Mail Stop 38

760-603-4561
FAX: 760-603-4595 800-421-7250
gandg@gia.edu
www.gia.edu/gemsandgemology/70/sectio n_main_page.cfm

Laura Simanton, Senior Public Relations Manager
Debbie Ortiz, Subscriptions Coordinator
Leigh Kelley, Advertising Coordinator

As the award-winning quarterly journal of GIA, Gems & Gemology publishes up-to-date technical information about diamonds and colored stones-where they are found, their special characteristics, simulants and synthetics, treatments, and identification techniques. *$74.95*
Quarterly

13741 High-Volume Jeweler
Reed Business Information
201 King of Prussia Road
Radnor, PA 19087-5114
610-889-9577
FAX: 630-288-8686
www.reedbusiness.com

Shawn Mery, Publisher
Lisa Reed, Owner

Provides original market research and in-depth analysis of current news and industry trends affecting this segment of the jewelry and watch market. Features operational strategies and new technological developments that can make and save money for retailers and vendors. *$60.00*
Bi-Monthly
Circulation: 5,000

13742 Horological Times
American Watchmakers-Clockmakers Institute
701 Enterprise Drive
Harrison, OH 45030-1696
513-367-9800
FAX: 513-367-1414 866-367-2924
dbaas@awi-net.org
http://www.awi-net.org

James Lubic, Executive Director
Lucy Fuleki, Assistant Executive Director
Donna Baas, Managing Editor

Provides articles on manufacturers news and the latest in new products for assisting in jewelry repair. The official publication of the American Watchmakers-Clockmakers Institute. *$72.00*
Monthly Founded: 1960
Circulation: 4000

13743 International Wristwatch Magazine USA
International Publishing Corporation
979 Summer Street
PO Box 110204
Stamford, CT 06905
203-259-8100
FAX: 203-295-0847
wristwatch@snet.net
www.intlwristwatch.com

Gary George, Editor-in-Chief
Patricia Russo, General Manager

Editorial content provides a consumer-oriented focus on new, vintage, and collectable watches. *$7.95*
150 pages Bi-Monthly Founded: 1989
ISBN 0-744706-22-2
Circulation: 30,000
Printed in 4 colors on glossy stock

13744 JCK Magazine
JCK International Publishing Group
1018 W. Ninth Ave
King of Prussia, PA 19406-1
610-205-1100
FAX: 610-205-1139 800-305-7759
JCK@pub-serv.com
http://www.jckgroup.com

Nancy Walsh, Senior Vice President
Fran Pennella, Marketing Director
Mark Smelzer, Publisher
Hedda Schupak, Editor-in-chief

Serves retailers, manufacturers, and vendors of fine jewerly and selected upscale gift categories, providing valuable market and design trend information and how-to information about gemology, financial management, employee relations, marketing, advertising, and visual merchandising, e-commerce, and other topics. *$49.95*
Monthly Founded: 1869

13745 JQ Limited Edition
JQ Publishing
585 5th Street W
Sonoma, CA 95476-6831
707-938-1082
FAX: 707-935-6585
pmatthews@aip.com
http://www.retailmerchandising.net

Audrey Bromstad, Publisher
Cynthia Unninayar, Editor
Deborah Rittenberg, Marketing Manager

Issues contain articles presented with illustrations on precious colored gems and diamonds, creative jewelry designs, designers, and luxury watches.
Monthly Founded: 1985
Circulation: 300000

13746 Jewelers' Circular: Keystone
Reed Business Information
360 Park Avenue South
New York, NY 10010
212-450-0067
FAX: 630-288-8686
hschupak@reedbusiness.com
http://www.jckgroup.com

Mark Smelzer, Publisher
Hedda Schupak, Editor

Discusses news of interest mainly to the jewelry shop owner and manager. Covers such topics as; product notices, manufacturer news and tips on operating a successful business. *$49.95*
Monthly Founded: 1874
Circulation: 25000
Printed in on glossy stock

13747 Jewelry Appraiser
National Association of Jewelry Appraisers
64-29 Cromwell Crescent
P. O. Box 18
Rego Park, NY 11374-18
718-896-1536
FAX: 718-997-9057
naja.appraisers@netzero.net
http://www.najaappraisers.com

Gail Brett Levine, Executive Director

An important source for all jewelry appraisers.
Quarterly Founded: 1981

13748 Lapidary Journal
300 Chesterfield Parkway
Suite 100
Malvern, PA 19355-937
610-232-5700
FAX: 610-232-5754 800-676-4336
lj.editorial@primedia.com
http://www.lapidaryjournal.com

Merle White, Editor
Karen Nuckols, Sales Director
Joe Breck, Publisher

This publication focuses fundamentally on the all aspects of the jewelry industry.
$29.95
Monthly Founded: 1947
Circulation: 45000

13749 Link
National Cuff Link Society
PO Box 5970
Vernon Hills, IL 60061-5970
847-816-0035
FAX: 847-816-0035
genek@cufflik.com www.cufflink.com

Gena Klompus, President
Founded: 1990

13750 Lustre
Cygnus Publishing
19 W 44th Street
Suite 1405
New York, NY 10036
212-921-1091
FAX: 212-921-5539
lorraine.depasque@cygnuspub.com
http://www.lustremag.com

Tim Murphy, Publisher
Roy Kim, Sales Director
Lorraine DePasque, Editor In Chief
Barb Hesse, Circulation Manager
Paul Mackler, President/CEO
Founded: 1966
Circulation: 4000

13751 Modern Jeweler
3 Huntington Quadrangle
Suite 301N
Melville, NY 11747-3602
631-845-2700
FAX: 631-845-7109 800-255-5113
tim.murphy@cygnuspub.com
http://www.modernjeweler.com

Matthew Kramer, Managing Editor
Timothy Murphy, Publisher
Cheryl Kremkow, Editor in Chief
Barb Hesse, Circulation Manager

A trade publication serving retail jewelers, wholesalers and manufacturers of jewelry, watches and related items. Accepts advertising. *$66.00*
90 pages Monthly
Circulation: 30000

13752 Monroe Originals
Karen Monroe
14014 Moorpark Street
Apartment 122
Sherman Oaks, CA 91423-3492

FAX: 818-783-5009
Handmade wholesale jewelry designs magazine. *$2.00*
50 pages Monthly

13753 Ornament
PO Box 2349
San Marcos, CA 92079-9806
760-599-0222
FAX: 760-599-0228 800-888-8950
ornament@sbcglobal.net
http://beadwrangler.com/mag-ornament.htm
Robert Liu, Co-Editor
Carolin Denish, Co-Editor
Offers information on contemporary, ethnic, ancient jewelry and costumes. *$26.00*
Quarterly Founded: 1976
Circulation: 38,000

13754 Professional Jeweler
Bond Communications
1500 Walnut Street
Suite 1200
Philadelphia, PA 19102-3523
215-670-0727
FAX: 215-545-9629 888-557-0727
askus@professionaljeweler.com
http://www.professionaljeweler.com
Lee Lawrence, Publisher/President
Peggy Jo Donahue, Editor-in-Chief
Peter James, Circulation Manager
Carole Masciantonio, Marketing Manager

Editorial content provides these professionals with the information they need to meet business objectives and ensure success. Regular departments offer the latest news, trends, technical and practical information on all aspects of the jewelry industry. *$49.95*
105 pages Monthly Founded: 1998
Circulation: 24000 24000 names
Printed in 4 colors on glossy stock

13755 Southern Jewelry News
Mullen Publications
9629 Old Nations Ford Rd.
Charlotte, NC 28273
704-527-5111
FAX: 704-527-5114 800-738-5111
soujew@aol.com
http://www.southernjewelrynews.com
Chip Smith, President/CEO
Bill Newnam, editor-in-chief
Chris Smith, Publisher
Elesa Dillon, Sales Manager
Dedicated to the southern jewelry industry and contains industry news, local and regional events, personnel announcements, and pricing information.
Monthly Founded: 1945
Circulation: 13,431

13756 Watch and Clock Review
Golden Bell Press
2403 Champa Street
Denver, CO 80205
303-296-1600

print@goldenbellpress.com
http://www.goldenbellpress.com
Bertram Kalisher, Editor
Lawrence Dell, CEO/Publisher
Sherri Simpson, Circulation Manager
Offers news and information on fashion accessories and jewelry. *$19.50*
48 pages Founded: 1935

Trade Shows

13757 ASD/AMD National Trade Show
ASD/AMD Merchandise Group
2950 31st Street
Suite 100
Santa Monica, CA 90405
310-255-4633
FAX: 310-396-8476
10000 Attendees

13758 Accent on Design
George Little Management
10 Bank Street
Suite 1200
White Plains, NY 10606-1954
914-486-6070
FAX: 914-948-2867 800-272-7469
elizabeth_murphy@glmshows.com
www.nyigf.com
Elizabeth Murphy, Show Manager
George Little II, President
Three hundred and seventy booths of the latest and most innovative gift lines such as decorative accessories and home furnishings.
50M Attendees August Founded: 1984

13759 American Gem Society Conclave
8881 W Sahara Avenue
Las Vegas, NV 89117
702-255-6500
FAX: 702-255-7420 www.ags.org
Glory Wade, Show Manager
One hundred and sixty booths. Conference and exhibitors.
1M Attendees April

13760 American Gem Trade Association Expo
3030 LBJ Freeway
Suite 840
Dallas, TX 75234
214-742-4367
FAX: 214-742-7334 800-972-1162
info@agta.org www.agta.org
Elizabeth Ross, Marketing Manager
Rick Krementz, President
Two booths featuring exhibits of loose colored gemstones and diamonds.
10.3M Attendees February

13761 Annual Spring New Products Show

Pacific Expositions
1600 Kapiolani Boulevard
Suite 1660
Honnolulu, HI 96814
808-945-3594
FAX: 808-946-6399
48000 Attendees Annual

13762 Bead and Button Show
Offinger Management Company
1100-H Brandywine Boulevard
PO Box 3388
Zanesville, OH 43702-3388
740-452-4541
FAX: 740-452-2552
www.beadandbuttonshow.com
Bill Bird, Show Manager
Rise Fulmer, Assistant Assn. Event Manager
Vicky Barnett, Administrative Coordinator
3500 Attendees

13763 Best Bead Show
Crystal Myths
PO Box 3243
Albuquerque, NM 87190
505-883-9295
FAX: 505-889-9553

13764 Business to Business Gem Trade Show
Gem & Lapidary Wholesalers
Holiday Inn Palo Verde/Holidome
Tucson, AZ
601-879-8832
FAX: 601-879-3282
info@glwshows.com
www.glwshows.com
February

13765 Catalog in Motion
Bell Group
Tucson E Hilton
Tucson, AZ
505-839-3249
FAX: 505-839-3248
www.riogrande.com
February

13766 Columbus Jewelery Show
Ohio Jewelers Association
50 W Broad Street
#2020
Columbus, OH 43215-3301
614-212-2237
FAX: 614-221-7020 800-652-6257
oja@ohioretailmerchants.com
www.ohiojewelers.org
Adriana Sfalcin, Show Manager
Edward Cain, Assistant Show Manager
A jewelry trade show for Ohio and 6 contiguous states - OH, MI, WV, KY, IN, PA and Eastern NY. 180 booths.
3700 Attendees Annual/August Founded: 1942
Mailing list available for rent 7000 names $0 per M.

13767 Fall Pacific Jewelry Show
California Jewelers Association
911 Wilshire Boulevard
Los Angeles, CA 90017-3409
213-235-5722
FAX: 213-623-5742
Pat O'Rourke, Trade Show Director
Annual show and exhibits of jewelry, giftware and related products.
8000 Attendees Los Angeles

13768 Fashion Accessories Expo
Business Journals
50 Day Street
Norwalk, CT 06854
203-853-6015
FAX: 203-852-8175 www.busjour.com
14000 Attendees

13769 Fashion Accessories Expo Accessories to Go
Business Journals
50 Day Street
Norwalk, CT 06854
203-853-6015
FAX: 203-852-8175 www.busjour.com
14000 Attendees

13770 GJX Gem and Jewelry Show
198 S Granada Avenue
Tucson, AZ
520-824-4200
FAX: 520-882-4203
cheryl@gizusa.com www.gjxusa.com

Allan Norville, President
February

13771 GLDA Gem and Jewelry Show
Gem & Lapidary Dealers Association
PO Box 2391
Tucson, AZ 85702
520-792-9431
FAX: 520-882-2836
info@glda.com www.glda.com
Paul Page, Director Marketing
Qualified buyers receive free admission. Buyers are jewelry retailers, manufacturers, wholesalers, gem dealers.
16000 Attendees February

13772 Gatlinburg Apparel & Jewelry Market
Norton Shows
PO Box 265
Gatlinburg, TN 37738
865-436-6151
FAX: 865-436-6152
nortonshows@aol.com
www.nortonshows.com
Tom Norton, Show Manager/Owner
Linda Norton, Owner
Trade show that takes place 4 times per year and has wholesale, cash-and-carry, ladiesa mens, and children's apparel, fashion jewelry, accessories, fine jewelry and gifts from around the world. There are 500-700 booths.
20000 Attendees March/June/Sept/Nov
Founded: 1987
Mailing list available for rent 70,000 names

13773 Gem & Jewelry Show
International Gem & Jewelry Show
120 Derwood Circle
Rockville, MD 20850-1264
301-294-1640
FAX: 301-294-0034
Herb Duke, Owner
Annual show and exhibits of jewelry and gemstones and related equipment, supplies and services.
October, Denver

13774 Gem, Jewelry & Mineral Show
Trade Shows International
PO Box 8862
Tucson, AZ 85738
520-791-2210
FAX: 520-825-9115

13775 Intergam: International Gem & Jewelry Show
International Gem & Jewelry Show
120 Derwood Circle
Rockville, MD 20850
301-294-1640
FAX: 301-294-0034

13776 International Gift Show: The Jewelry & Accessories Expo
Business Journals
50 Day Street
Norwalk, CT 06854
203-853-6015
FAX: 203-852-8175
14000 Attendees

13777 International Jewelry Fair/General Merchandise Show-Spring
Helen Brett Enterprises
5111 Academy Drive
Lisle, IL 60532-2152
630-241-9865
FAX: 630-241-9870 800-541-8171
dharrington@helenbrett.com
www.gift2jewelry.com
Dave Harrington, Show Manager
Containing 800 booths during the spring show and 1500 booths during the fall show. Tradeshow open to wholesale buyers only (credentials required to attend).
24000 Attendees May

13778 International Watch and Jewelry Show
Burley and Olg Bullock
5901-Z Westheimer Road
Houston, TX 77057
713-783-8188
FAX: 281-589-8987 800-554-4992
info@iwjg.com www.iwjg.com
JJ Gilbreath
Christina LeDoux
June-Nov./January-March

13779 JA International Jewelry Show
Jewelers of America
52 Vanderbuilt Avenue
19th Floor
New York, NY 10017
646-580-0255
FAX: 212-768-8087
contactus@jewelers.org
www.jewelers.org
Matthew Runci, President
Showcase of fine jewelry open to the trade only.
11000 Attendees Febuary/July

13780 JCK Orlando International Jewelry Show
Reed Exhibition Companies
383 Manin Avenue
Norwalk, CT 0
203-404-4800
FAX: 203-840-5830 www.jckgroup.com
Conference and exhibition.
2000 Attendees February

13781 Jewelers International Showcase (JIS)
6421 Congress Avenue
Suite 105
Boca Raton, FL 33487-2858
561-998-0205
FAX: 561-998-0209
jisshow@aol.com www.jisshow.com
Michael G Breslow CEM, President
Worldwide manufacturers and wholesalers of jewelry exhibit to trade buyers from Florida, Caribbean, Central and South America, plus other USA states. Exhibits of 1000 suppliers of fine jewelry, fashion jewelry and related products and services. The leading and largest independent Jewelery Trade-Only Show in the Western Hemisphere. *$34.00*
12000 Attendees October, January, April
Founded: 1979
Circulation: 55,000

13782 Memphis Gift & Jewelry Show-Fall
Helen Brett Enterprises
5111 Academy Drive
Lisle, IL 60532
630-241-9865
FAX: 630-241-9870 800-541-8171
dharrington@helenbrett.com
www.gift2jewelry.com
Dave Harrington, Show Manager
Containing over 350 booths during the fall show and 350 booths during the spring show. Tradeshow open to wholesale buyers only (credentials required to attend).
9000 Attendees August

13783 Memphis Gift & Jewelry Show-Spring
Helen Brett Enterprises
5111 Academy Drive
Lisle, IL 60532
630-241-9865
FAX: 630-241-9870 800-541-8171
dharrington@helenbrett.com
www.gift2jewelry.com
Dave Harrington, Show Manager
Containing over 350 booths during the spring show and 350 booths during the fall show. Tradeshow open to wholesale buyers only (credentials required to attend).
9000 Attendees February

13784 Merchandise Mart Gift/Jewelry/ Resort Show
Denver Merchandise Mart
451 E 58th Avenue #470
Suite 4270
Denver, CO 80216
303-292-6278
FAX: 303-298-8473 800-289-6278
Bridget Oakes, Gift Show Exhibit Manager
A wholesale market for retail store buyers for resorts, theme parksand national parks, specialty gift stores and interior designers. Semi - Annual Show.
7000 Attendees February/August

13785 Mid-South Jewelry & Accessories Fair -Spring
Helen Brett Enterprises
5111 Academy Drive
Lisle, IL 60532
630-241-9865
FAX: 630-241-9870 800-541-8171
dharrington@helenbrett.com
www.gift2jewelry.com
Dave Harrington, Show Manager
Containing over 300 booths during the spring show and 500 booths during the fall show. Tradeshow open to wholesale buyers only (credentials required to attend).
8500 Attendees May

13786 Mid-South Jewelry & Accessories Fair-Fall
Helen Brett Enterprises
5111 Academy Drive
Lisle, IL 60532
630-241-9865
FAX: 630-241-9870 800-541-8171
dharrington@helenbrett.com
www.gift2jewelry.com
Dave Harrington, Show Manager
Containing 500 booths during the fall show and over 300 booths during the spring show. Tradeshow open to wholesale buyers only (credentials required to attend).
16000 Attendees November

13787 **Midwest Jewelry Expo**
Wisconsin Jewelry Association
1 East Main Street
Suite 305
Madison, WI 53703
608-257-3541
FAX: 608-257-8755
www.midwestjewelryexpo.com

Mary Kaja, Executive Director

The next jewelry trade show exposition is scheduled for March 24th to March 25th in 2007.

3000 Attendees March

13788 **National Accessory Maintenance Exposition**
240 Peachtree Street NW
Suite 2200
Atlanta, GA 30303-1327
404-203-3000
FAX: 404-607-8682

Jeff Portman, Chief Executive Officer
Charles Sydney, Manager

Offers a forum for the exchange of ideas between manufacturers and suppliers of fashion accessories.

10M Attendees January

13789 **New Orleans Gift & Jewelry Show-Fall**
Helen Brett Enterprises
5111 Academy Drive
Lisle, IL 60532
630-241-9865
FAX: 630-241-9870 800-541-8171
dharrington@helenbrett.com
www.gift2jewelry.com

Dave Harrington, Show Manager

Containing 850 booths during the fall show and 750 booths during the spring show. Tradeshow open to wholesale buyers only (credentials required to attend).

27000 Attendees August

13790 **New Orleans Gift & Jewelry Show-Spring**
Helen Brett Enterprises
5111 Academy Drive
Lisle, IL 60532
630-241-9865
FAX: 630-241-9870 800-541-8171
dharrington@helenbrett.com
www.gift2jewelry.com

Dave Harrington, Show Manager

Containing 750 booths during the spring show and 850 booths during the fall show. Tradeshow open to wholesale buyers only (credentials required to attend).

20000 Attendees January

13791 **Pacific Jewelry Show**
California Jewelers Association
911 Wilshire Boulevard
Suite 1740
Los Angeles, CA 90017-3446
213-235-5722
FAX: 213-623-5742

Richard Trujillo, Owner
Alberta E Hultman, Manager

Annual show of 250 exhibitors of jewelry and related items.

3000 Attendees August Founded: 1999

13792 **Stylemax**
Merchandise Mart Properties
200 World Trade Center
Suite 470
Chicago, IL 60654
312-274-4141
FAX: 312-527-7971

5000 Attendees

13793 **The Whole Bead Show**
PO Box 1100
Nevade City, CA 95959
530-652-2725
FAX: 530-265-2776 800-292-2577
info@wholebead.com
www.wholebead.com

Ava Motherwell, Owner

An international bread trade show that occurs thirteen times per year. Contemporary pieces made from glass, stone, metal, pearl, amber and porcelain. Offering antique beads, handmade, findings, buttons, charms and beaded jewelry. Access merchants, bead makers and importers who are direct suppliers of many professional and novice jewelry makers.

N/A Attendees Jan/Feb/Mar/Apr Founded: 1993

13794 **Trade Show for Jewelry Making**
Manufacturing Jewelers & Suppliers of America
45 Royal Little Drive
Providence, RI 02904
401-274-3840
FAX: 401-274-0265 800-444-6572
bruce@mjsainc.com
www.mjsainc.com

Paula Esposito, Show Manager

New regional trade show designed to service jewelry makers and manufacturers of all sizes throughout New England and surrounding areas. Providing a full range of products that industry professionals need to make their jewelry and operate their business.

1000 Attendees September 27-28

13795 **Transworld's Jewelry, Fashion & Accessories Show**
Transworld Exhibits
1850 Oak Street
Northfield, IL 60093
847-446-8434
FAX: 847-446-3523 800-323-5462

Hundreds of the country's finest exhibitors. Thousands of the best buyers nationwide. The perfect venue for the latest jewelry collections, the most current fashion ideas and new accessories.

25000 Attendees July/October/December

13796 **Tucson Gem and Mineral Show**
Tucson Gem and Mineral Society
PO Box 42588
Tucson, AZ 85733
520-322-5773
FAX: 520-322-6031
tgms@tgms.org www.tgms.org

Rose Marques, Administrative Assistant

Sponsored by the Tucson Gem and Mineral Society. Retail show open to the public at the Tucson Convention Center every February for four days. Over 200 dealers, over 100 exhibitors, children's activities.

25000 Attendees February Founded: 1955

Directories & Databases

13797 **AJM Technology Sourcebook**
Manufacturing Jewelers & Suppliers of America
45 Royal Little Drive
Providence, RI 02904
401-274-3840
FAX: 401-274-0265 800-444-MJSA
ajm@ajm-magazine.com
www.ajm-magazine.com

Rich Youmans, Editor

This publication provides listings and specs on machinery, equipment, raw materials, and software specifically geared to jewelry manufacturing. *$4.50*

Annual
Circulation: 5,000
Printed in 4 colors on glossy stock

13798 **Accent Source Book**
Larkin Group
100 Wells Avenue
Newton, MA 02459-3210
617-326-6525
FAX: 617-964-2752 800-869-7469

Lauren Parker, Editor
Michael Corkin, Owner

Information on over 1,500 manufacturers of jewelry, watches and accessories is available in this comprehensive directory aimed at the gemology and related industries. *$25.00*

200 pages Annual
Circulation: 15,000

13799 **Accessories Resource Directory**
Business Journals
50 Day Street
Norwalk, CT 06854-3100
203-853-6015

Over 1,500 manufacturers, importers and sales representatives that produce accessories are profiled.

Annual
Circulation: 10,000

13800 **Complete Directory of Cubic Zirconia Jewelry**
Sutton Family Communications & Publishing Company
155 Sutton Lane
Fordsville, KY 42343
270-740-0870

jlsutton@apex.net
www.fleamarketeer.net

Theresa Sutton, Editor
Lee Sutton, General Manager

Print-out from database of wholesalers, manufacturers, distributors, importers and close-out houses. Database is updated daily to guarantee the most current and up-to-date sources available. *$39.50*

100+ pages

13801 **Complete Directory of Earrings & Necklaces**
Sutton Family Communications & Publishing Company
155 Sutton Lane
Fordsville, KY 42343
270-740-0870

jlsutton@apex.net
www.fleamarketeer.net

Theresa Sutton, Editor
Lee Sutton, General Manager

Print-out from database of wholesalers, manufacturers, distributors, importers and close-out houses. Database is updated daily to guarantee the most current and up-to-date sources available. *$37.00*
100+ pages

13802 Complete Directory of Jewelry Close-Outs
Sutton Family Communications & Publishing Company
155 Sutton Lane
Fordsville, KY 42343
270-740-0870

jlsutton@apex.net
www.fleamarketeer.net

Theresa Sutton, Editor
Lee Sutton, General Manager

Print-out from database of wholesalers, manufacturers, distributors, importers and close-out houses. Database is updated daily to guarantee the most current and up-to-date sources available. *$34.50*
100+ pages

13803 Complete Directory of Jewelry: General
Sutton Family Communications & Publishing Company
155 Sutton Lane
Fordsville, KY 42343
270-740-0870

jlsutton@apex.net
www.fleamarketeer.net

Theresa Sutton, Editor
Lee Sutton, General Manager

Print-out from database of wholesalers, manufacturers, distributors, importers and close-out houses. Database is updated daily to guarantee the most current and up-to-date sources available. *$54.50*
100+ pages

13804 Complete Directory of Low-Price Jewelry & Souvenirs
Sutton Family Communications & Publishing Company
155 Sutton Lane
Fordsville, KY 42343
270-740-0870

jlsutton@apex.net
www.fleamarketeer.net

Theresa Sutton, Editor
Lee Sutton, General Manager

Print-out from database of wholesalers, manufacturers, distributors, importers and close-out houses. Database is updated daily to guarantee the most current and up-to-date sources available. *$39.50*
100+ pages

13805 Complete Directory of Watches and Watch Bands
Sutton Family Communications & Publishing Company
155 Sutton Lane
Fordsville, KY 42343
270-740-0870

jlsutton@apex.net
www.fleamarketeer.net

Theresa Sutton, Editor
Lee Sutton, General Manager

Print-out from database of wholesalers, manufacturers, distributors, importers and close-out houses. Database is updated daily to guarantee the most current and up-to-date sources available. *$39.50*
100+ pages

13806 Diamond Report
Rapaport Diamond Corporation
15 W 47th Street
Suite 600
New York, NY 10036-3305
212-540-0575
FAX: 212-840-0243
rap@diamonds.net www.diamond.net

Amber Michelle, Editor
Eillene Furrel, Advertising Manager

This large directory database offers background information and current prices for more than 100,000 stores. *$185.00*
Annual

13807 International Society of Appraisers
International Society of Appraisers
16040 Christensen Road
Suite 102
Seattle, WA 98188-2965
206-241-0359
FAX: 206-241-0436 888-472-4732
isahq@isa-appraisers.org
www.isa-appraisers.org

Alice Coleman, Editor

Be Certain of its Value - A Consumer's Guide To Hiring a Competent Personal Property Appraiser is available complimentary to the public. Alphabetical list of appraisers with specialty areas plus indexes: area of expertise, zip code, state and city, company, and related services. *$15.00*
305 pages Annual Founded: 1979
Circulation: 1500
Printed in 2 colors

13808 Jewelers Board of Trade: Confidential Reference Book
Jewelers Board of Trade
95 Jefferson Boulevard
Warwick, RI 02888-1046
401-467-0055
FAX: 401-467-1199
www.jewelersboard.com

Dione D Kenyon, President

Importers, distributors and retailers, close to 45,000, are profiled that are directly related to the jewelry industry.
Semiannual
Circulation: 3,400

13809 Jewelers' Circular/Keystone: Brand Name and Trademark Guide
Chilton Company
1 Chilton Way
Wayne, PA 19089-0002
610-964-4243
FAX: 610-964-4481 800-866-0206

L Roberts, Editor

Over 5,000 manufacturers of jewelry store products. *$49.95*

13810 Jewelers' Circular/Keystone: Jewelers' Directory Issue
Chilton Company
PO Box 2045
Radnor, PA 19089
610-964-4000
FAX: 610-964-4512

Kathleen Ellis, Editor

About 10,000 manufacturers, importers and wholesale jewelers providing merchandise and supplies to the jewelry retailing industry and related trade organizations. *$32.00*
Monthyly
Circulation: 30,000

13811 Lapidary Journal: Annual Buyers' Directory Issue
Lapidary Journal
60 Chestnut Avenue
Suite 201
Devon, PA 19333-1312
610-325-5700
FAX: 610-293-1717 800-676-GEMS

Michele Erazo, Marketing Executive

List of 4,000 suppliers and retailers of gem-cutting and jewelry making and mineral collecting equipment, beads, fossils, minerals and gems, gem and mineral clubs, bead societies, museums, schools and shops. *$6.50*
Annual May
Circulation: 67,000

13812 MJSA Buyers' Guide
Manufacturing Jewelers & Suppliers of America
45 Royal Little Drive
Providence, RI 02908
401-274-3840
FAX: 401-274-0265 800-444-MJSA
mjsa@mjsainc.com www.mjsainc.com

Rich Dumas, Editor

Contains finished jewelry as well as equipment, supplies, and components necessary for jewelry manufacturing. *$45.00*
BiAnnual
Circulation: 5,000

13813 National Jeweler: Industry Yellow Pages
Miller Freeman Publications
1515 Broadway
New York, NY 10036-8901
212-378-0400
FAX: 646-654-4948

Jim Pavia, Editor

Approximately 5,000 companies providing products and services in the jewelry and watch industries. *$10.00*
Annual December
Circulation: 36,000

Industry Web Sites

13814 www.agta.org
American Gem Trade Association

A trade association for the colored gemstone industry in North Africa. Operates gemological testing in New York.

13815 www.awi-net.org
American Watchmakers Institute

Examines and certifies master watchmakers and clockmakers. Maintains a placement service. Conducts home study courses.

13816 www.cufflink.com
National Cuff Link Society

For cuff link wearers and collectors.

13817 www.glda.com
Gem & Lapidary Dealers Association

13818 www.goldinstitue.org
Gold Institute

13819 www.greyhouse.com
Grey House Publishing

Selected Grey House directories in the fields of business, health and education are available online. Users can search our online databases by several different search criteria, such as product categories, geographic area, sales volume and much, much more. Full Grey House catalog and online ordering also available.

13820 www.iaca.com
Indian Arts & Crafts Association

Not for profit trade association. Our mission is to promote, protect and preserve Indian arts.

13821 www.independentjewlers.com
Independent Jewelers

Works to aid independent jewelers in competing in local markets through advertising, promotion, and buyers assistance.

13822 www.isa-appraisers.org
International Society of Appraisers

A not-for-profit professional association of personal property appraisers. ISA provides education and organizational support to its members, to serve the public by producing highley qualified and ethical appraisers who are recognized authorities in personal property appraising.

13823 www.jewelers.org
Jewelers of America

13824 www.jewelersboard.com

Trade association providing credit reporting, collections and marketing services to the US and overseas jewelry industries. Our members are wholesalers, manufacturers and service providers to the jewelry industry.

13825 www.jewelerssecurity.org
Jewelers' Security Alliance

Principal activity is providing education and information to jewelers so they can guard against loss through crimes, including burglary, robbery and theft.

13826 www.jewelryinfo.org
Jewelery Information Center

Identifies deceptive trade practices and misleading advertising. Provides advice on marketing and assists in prosecution of violations. The media side of the Jewelers Vigilance Committee.

13827 www.jvclegal.org
Jewelers Vigilance Committee

Identifies deceptive trade practices and misleading advertising. Provides advice on marketing and assists in prosecution of violations.

13828 www.love-story.com
Leading Jewelers Guild

13829 www.silverinstitute.org
Silver Institute

13830 www.silversmithing.com
Society of American Silversmiths

13831 www.silverusersassociation.org
Silver Users Association

Represents manufacturers and distributors of products in which silver is an essential element, such as photographic materials, medical and dental supplies, batteries and electronic and electrical equipment, silverware, mirrors, commemorative art and jewelry.

13832 www.superabrasives.org
Industrial Diamond Association of America

13833 www.womensjewelry.org
Women's Jewelry Association

For jewelry industry professionals.

Associations

13834 Accrediting Council on Education in Journalism and Mass Communications
1435 Jayhawk Boulevard
Lawrence, KS 66045-7575
785-643-3973
FAX: 785-864-5225
www.ukans.edu/~acejmc
Beth E Barnes, Chairman
Douglas A Anderson, Vice Chair
Karen Brown Dunlap, President
Susanne Shaw, Executive Director
ACEJMC members are journalism and media departments, education associations and professional organizations.

13835 American Association of Sunday & Feature Editors
1921 Gallows Road
Suite 600
Vienna, VA 22182-3900
703-902-1639
FAX: 703-620-4557
nahan@naa.org www.aasfe.org
Chris Beringer, President
Gina Seay, VP
Denise Joyce, VP
Kim Marcum, Secretary-Treasurer
An organization of editors from the United States and Canada dedicated to the quality of features in newspapers and the craft of feature writing.

13836 American Newspaper Representatives
2075 W Big Beaver Road
Suite 310
Troy, MI 48084
248-439-9910
FAX: 248-643-9914 800-550-7557
Hilary Howe, President/National Sales Manager
Robert Sontag, Executive VP/COO
John Jepsen, Controller
Melanie Cox, Regional Sales Manager
Supports those newspaper representatives and distributors in the United States. Hosts annual trade show.

13837 American Society of Journalists and Authors
1501 Broadway
Suite 302
New York, NY 10036
212-997-0947
FAX: 212-768-7414
webeditor@asja.org www.asja.org
Brett Harvey, Executive Director
Lisa Collier Cool, President
Barbara DeMarco Barrett, Newsletter Editor
For freelance nonfiction writers whose bylines appear in periodicals and in books.
1000+ Members Founded: 1948

13838 American Society of Newspaper Editors
11690B Sunrise Valley Drive
Reston, VA 20191-1409
703-453-1122
FAX: 703-453-1133
asne@asne.org www.asne.org
Scott Bosley, Executive Director
Karla G Harshaw, VP
David Zeeck, Treasurer
Diana Mitsu Klos, Senior Project Director
Chris Schmitt, Membership/Finance Manager
Directing editors of daily newspapers who determine editorial and news policy or news gathering operations of daily newspapers.
750 Members Founded: 1922

13839 Associated Press Managing Editors
50 Rockefeller Plaza
New York, NY 10020
212-621-7503
FAX: 212-506-6741
apme@ap.org www.apme.com
Stuart Wilk, President
Deanna Sands, VP
Bill Felber, Treasurer
Mark Mittelstadt, Executive Director
Members are managing editors or executives of Associated Press News Executives.
Founded: 1933

13840 Association for Education in Journalism and Mass Communication (AEJMC)
234 Outlet Pointe Boulevard
Columbia, SC 29210-5667
803-798-0271
FAX: 803-798-3509
aejmchq@aol.com www.aejmc.org/
Jennifer McGill, Executive Director
Felicia Greenlee Brown, Production Manager
Richard Burke, Business Manager
AEJMC promotes the highest possible standards for education in journalism and mass communication, encouraging the widest possible range of communication research and the implementation of a multi-cultural society in the classroom and curriculum, defending and maintaining the freedom of expression in day-to-day living.

13841 Association for Women in Communications
3337 Duke Street
Alexandria, VA 22314
703-370-7436
FAX: 703-370-7437
info@womcom.org www.womcom.org
Amy Carr, VP
Sheryl Liddle, Chair
Nancy Badertscher, Membership Director
Betsy Earley, Director Publications
Elaine Lipczenko, Special Projects Manager
Supporst all those professional women in the fields of journalism, public relations, advertising, marketing, educational communications and film. Hosts annual trade show.

13842 Baptist Communicators Association
PO Box 270187
Nashville, TN 37227
615-329-7543
bca.office@comcast.net
baptistcommunicators.org
Jan Kelley, President
Teresa Dickens, Communications VP
Ele Clay, Missions VP
Jerilynn Armstrong, Treasurer
PR and journalism profesionals.
300 Members Founded: 1953

13843 Collegiate Press Association
330 21st Avenue S
Minneapolis, MN 55455-0480
612-625-3500
FAX: 612-626-0720
Tom Rolnicki, Manager
Supports all those involved in the development and betterment of collegiate press. Hosts annual trade show.

13844 Gay and Lesbian Press Association
PO Box 8185
Universal City, CA 91618-8185
FAX: 818-902-9576
Supports those gay and lesbian professionals in the field of journalism. Publishes quarterly newsletter.

13845 Hollywood Foreign Press Association
646 N Robertson Boulevard
W Hollywood, CA 90069
310-657-1731
FAX: 310-657-5576
info@hfpa.org www.hfpa.org
Dagmar Dunlevy, Chairman
Lorenzo Soria, President
Lawrie Masterson, VP
Chantal Dinnage, Managing Director
Philip Berk, Treasurer
Foreign correspondents covering Hollywood and the entertainment industry.

13846 International American Press Association
1801 SW 3rd Avenue
Miami, FL 33129
305-634-2465
FAX: 305-635-2272
info@sipiapa.org www.sipiapa.com
Jack Fuller, President
Alejo Miro Cisneros, First VP
Diana Daniels, Second VP
Julio E Munoz, Executive Director
Earl Maucker, Treasurer
Supports all those involved in the media and journalism industry. Hosts annual trade show.

13847 International Communications Association
1730 Rhode Island Avenue NW
Suite 300
Washington, DC 20036
202-530-9855
FAX: 202-530-9851
icahdq@icahdq.org www.icahdq.org
Robert Craig, President/Chair
Supports all students and professionals in the international communications industry. Publishes bi-monthly newsletter.
3400 Members Founded: 1950

13848 International Newspaper Financial
21525 Ridgetop Circle
Sterling, VA 20166
703-421-4060
FAX: 703-421-4068
infehq@infe.org www.infesecure.org
Todd Adams, President
Controllers, chief accountants, auditors, business managers, treasurers, secretaries and related newspaper executives, educators and public accountants.

1000 Members Founded: 1947

13849 International Newspaper Marketing
10300 N Central Expressway
Suite 467
Dallas, TX 75231
214-373-9111
FAX: 214-373-9112 972-991-3151
inma@inma.org www.inma.org

Eivind Thomsen, President
Ross McPherson, VP
Scott C Schurz, Treasurer
Earl Wilkinson, Executive Director

Individuals in marketing, circulation, research and public relations of newspapers.
1100 Members Founded: 1930

13850 Investigative Reporters and Editors
138 Neff Annex, Missouri School of Journalism
Columbia, MO 65211
573-882-2042
FAX: 573-882-5431
info@ire.org www.ire.org

Brant Houston, Executive Director
Len Bruzzese, Deputy Director
John Green, Membership Coordinator
Evelyn Ruch-Graham, Conference Coordinator
Heather Feldman, Financial Officer

For individuals involved in investigative journalism.
3300 Members Founded: 1975

13851 National Association of Black Journalists
University of Maryland
8701-A Adelphia Road
Adelphi, MD 20783-1716
301-445-7100
FAX: 301-445-7101 www.nabj.org

Tangie Newborn, Executive Director
Germaine Ashton, Membership Director

An organization of journalists, students and media-related professionals that provides quality programs and services and advocates on behalf of black journalists worldwide.
Founded: 1975

13852 National Newspaper Association
127-129 Neff Annex
Columbia, MO 65211-1200
573-882-5800
FAX: 573-884-5490 800-829-4662
briansteffens@nna.org www.nna.org

Brian Steffens, Executive Director
Lynn Edinger, Associate Director

Representatives of community newspapers. Protects and promotes local newspaper interests via goverment relation programs, advertiser and reader education plus information concerning community newspaper solutions and strategies.
3200 Members Founded: 1885

13853 National Press Club
529 14th Street NW
13th Floor
Washington, DC 20045
202-662-7500
FAX: 202-662-7569 www.press.org

Sylvia Smith, Secretary
John Bloom, Managerer
Sheila R Cherry, President
Rick Dunham, VP
Jerry Zremski, Membership Secretary

A private organization composed of professional journalists who are directly related to the media. Persons must qualify to be admitted.
4.6M Members

13854 National Press Foundation
1211 Connecticut Avenue NW
Suite 310
Washington, DC 20036
202-627-7350
FAX: 202-530-2855
bob@nationalpress.org
www.natpress.org

Jacqueline Thomas, Chairman
George E Condon, Vice Chairman
Walter Wurfel, Treasurer
Bob Meyers, President
Nolan Walters, Director Programs

Supports all those involved with national press and the media. Publishes bi-weekly newsletter.
Founded: 1976

13855 National Scholastic Press Association
2221 University Avenue SE
Suite 121
Minneapolis, MN 55414
612-258-8335
FAX: 612-626-0720
www.studentpress.org

Tom Rolnicki, Executive Director
Ann Akers, Associate Director
Jesse Rinkenberger, Business Manager

Supports all those involved in yearbook printing and photographic services, college journalism departments and video yearbook production services. Hosts annual trade show.

13856 New England Press Association
360 Huntington Avenue 428CP
Boston, MA 02115
617-254-4880
FAX: 617-373-5615
info@nepa.org www.nepa.org

Brenda Reedtani, Executive Director
Lynn Delaney, Second VP
Marlene Switzer, Secretary

This organization offers a publication about the newspaper industry specifically focusing on New England newspapers and the issues that affect them, which goes to every newspaper in New England.
460 Members Founded: 1950

13857 New Jersey Collegiate Press Association
840 Bear Tavern Road
Suite 305
West Trenton, NJ 08628-1019
609-406-0600
FAX: 609-406-0300
foundation@njpa.org
www.njcollegepress.org

Thomas E Engleman, Dir/New Jersey Press Foundation
John Brien, Executive Director

Supports all those involved in the development and betterment of collegiate press. Hosts annual trade show.
49 Members Founded: 1952

13858 Newspaper Association Managers
New England Press Association
70 Washington Street
Salem, MA 01970-3518
978-744-8940
FAX: 978-744-0333

Bob New, Owner
Morley Piper, Executive Director

Executives of state, regional, national and international newspaper associations.
65 Members Founded: 1923

13859 Newspaper Association of America
1921 Gallows Road
Suite 600
Vienna, VA 22182
703-021-1600
FAX: 703-917-0636 www.naa.org

P Anthony Ridder, Chairman
Gregg K Jones, Vice Chairman
Jay R Smith, Secretary
John Sturm, President/CEO
James Abbott, Vice President

Promotes the interests of the newspaper business.

13860 Newspaper Guild: CWA
501 3rd Street NW
Suite 250
Washington, DC 20001
202-341-1254
FAX: 202-434-1472
guild@cwa-union.org
www.newsguild.org

John Clark, President
Bernard J Lunzer, Secretary/Treasurer
Andy Zipser, Guild Reporter
Larkie Gildersleeve, Director Research

Organization covering the newspaper industry, its employment practices, press freedom and labor movement.
Founded: 1937

13861 Overseas Press Club of America
40 W 45th Street
New York, NY 10036
212-626-9220
FAX: 212-626-9210
sonya@opcofamerica.org
www.opcofamerica.org

Sonya K Fry, Executive Director
Marshal Loeb, First VP
Jacqueline Albert-Simon, Treasurer
Alexis Gelber, President
Robert Dowling, Third VP

A media/journalist organization.
630 Members Founded: 1939

13862 Society for News Design
1130 Ten Rod Road
Suite D-202
North Kingstown, RI 02852-4180
401-294-5233
FAX: 401-294-5238 www.snd.org

Christine McNeal, President
Scott Goldman, VP
Elise Burroughs, Executive Director
Gayla Grin, Treasurer/Secretary

An international professional organization comprised of editors, designers, graphic artists, publishers, illustrators, art directors, photographers, advertising artists, Website designers, students and faculty.
2400 Members Founded: 1979

13863 Society of American Travel Writers
1500 Sunday Drive
Suite 102
Raleigh, NC 27607
919-861-5586
FAX: 919-787-4916
satw@satw.org www.satw.org

Marcia Levin, President
June Naylor, VP
Carol Fowler, Secretary
Gerald Breaux, Treasurer

Photographers and 35 associate member representatives of airlines, hotels, resorts, tourist agencies and public relations firms.

13864 Society of Environmental Journalists
PO Box 2492
Jenkintown, PA 19046
215-884-8174
FAX: 215-884-8175
sej@sej.org www.sej.org

Beth Parke, Executive Director
Christine Rigel, Associate Director

The mission is to advance public understanding of environmental issues by improving the quality, accuracy and visibility of environmental reporting.
1450 Members Quarterly Founded: 1990
Circulation: 1600

13865 Society of Professional Journalists
3909 N Meridian Street
Indianapolis, IN 46208
317-927-8000
FAX: 317-920-4789
webmaster@spj.org www.spj.org

Gordon McKerral, President
David E Carlson, Secretary/Treasurer
James Highland, VP

Broad-based journalism organization, dedicated to encouraging the free practice of journalism and stimulating high standards of ethical behavior.
9000 Members Founded: 1909

Newsletters

13866 AEJMC News
234 Outlet Pointe Boulevard
Columbia, SC 29210-5667
803-798-0271
FAX: 803-772-3509
meirick@ou.edu http://www.aejmc.org

Jenniffer Mcgrill, CEO
Kyshra Brown, Editor

Supports all those scholars and educators of journalism and mass communications.
Monthly Founded: 1912
Circulation: 3425

13867 Bulldog Reporter
James Sinkinson/InfoCom Group
15900 Hollis Street
Suite L
Emeryville, CA 94608-2924
510-533-3035
FAX: 510-596-9331
http://www.bulldogreporter.com

Richard Carufel, Administrative Editor
Jim Sinkinson, CEO
Joel Velasquez, Customer Support Head

Journalist contact updates and intelligence on how to successfully place stories with the most influential business media and journalists in the US. *$449.00*
24 issues per y Founded: 1980

13868 Clio Among the Media
Association for Education in Journalism
234 Outlet Pointe Blvd
Columbia, SC 29210-5667
803-798-0271
FAX: 803-772-3509
aejmc@aejmc.org
http://www.aejmc.org

Georgia NeSmith, Assistant Editor
Jennifer McGill, Executive Director

This newsletter is aimed directly at scholars and educators of Journalism and Mass Communications. *$107.50*
24 pages Quarterly Founded: 1966
Circulation: 450

13869 GP Reporter
Star Reporter Publishing Company
PO Box 60193
Staten Island, NY 10306-0193
718-981-5700
FAX: 718-981-5713

RA Lindberg, Publisher

Covers journalism for educational purposes. *$9.00*
20 pages

13870 Guild Reporter
Newspaper Guild: CWA
501 3rd Street NW
Washington, DC 20001-2797
202-341-1254
FAX: 202-434-1472
guild@cwa-union.org
http://www.newsguild.org

Linda Foley, President
Andy Zipser, Editor
Kathy Mulvey, Director, Contract Admini
Tina M. Harrison, Research, Info & Tech/Human Rights/

Covers the newspaper industry, its employment practices, press freedom and labor movement. *$20.00*
6 pages Monthly Founded: 1933

13871 ICA Newsletter
International Communications Association

1730 Rhode Island Avenue NW
Suite 300
Washington, DC 20036
202-530-9855
FAX: 202-530-9851
icahdq@icahdq.org
http://www.icahdq.org

Michael Haley, Executive Director
Barbara Stooksberry, Managing Editor
Wolfgang Donsbach, President
James R. Taylor, Membership Committee Chairman
Mary Beth Oliver, Publications Committee Chairman

Trade association publication for scholars in the field of communication. *$20.00*
10 times a year Founded: 1950
Printed in on matte stock

13872 Journalist and Financial Reporting
TJFR Publishing Company
82 Wall Street
Suite 1105
New York, NY 10005-3600
212-422-2456
FAX: 212-663-3260

Dean Rotbart, Publisher

Financial and business news. *$549.00*
12 pages BiWeekly

13873 Media Reporter
Gay and Lesbian Press Association
PO Box 8185
Universal City, CA 91618-8185

FAX: 818-902-9576

RJ Curry, Publisher

Accepts advertising. *$40.00*
16 pages Quarterly

13874 National Press Foundation Update
National Press Foundation
1211 Connecticut Avenue NW
Suite 310
Washington, DC 20036
202-662-7350
FAX: 202-530-2855
bob@nationalpress.org
www.natpress.org

Bob Meyers, President
Frank Holeman, Editor

News.
4 pages BiWeekly Founded: 1993

13875 New England Press Association Bulletin
New England Press Association
360 Huntington Avenue
428CP
Boston, MA 02115-5005
617-254-4880
FAX: 617-373-5615
info@nepa.org http://www.nepa.org

Brenda Need, Publisher
Linda Conway, Marketing Director
Thomas Guenette, Circulation Manager
Brenda Need, Editor

A monthly publication about the newspaper industry specifically focusing on New England newspapers and the issues that affect them. *$15.00*
Monthly Founded: 1950
Circulation: 1500
Printed in 4 colors on newsprint stock

13876 Overseas Press Club Bulletin
Overseas Press Club of America
40 W 45th Street
New York, NY 10036
212-626-9220
FAX: 212-626-9210
http://www.opcofamerica.org

Sonya Fry, Executive Director
Michael Moran, Chairman of the OPC Board of Govern
Richard Stolley, President

Foreign correspondence news and features.

Monthly Founded: 1939
Circulation: 600

Magazines & Journals

13877 Alternative Press Review
CAL Press
PO Box 6245
Arlington, VA 22206

alternativepressreview@comcast.net
http://www.altpr.org

Jason McQuinn, Editor

Covers alternative press including humor, opinion and art. *$16.00*
Quarterly
Circulation: 7000

13878 American Editor
American Society of Newspaper Editors
11690B Sunrise Valley Drive
Reston, VA 20191-1409
703-453-1122
FAX: 703-453-1133
asne@asne.org http://www.asne.org

Scott Bosley, Executive Director
Suzanne Martin, Assistant/Systems Manager
Freddie Allen, Marketing

A magazine published by the American Society of Newspaper Editors.
30 pages Daily Founded: 1922

13879 American Journalism Review
University of Maryland
1117 Journalism Building
College Park, MD 20742-1
301-405-8803
FAX: 301-405-8323 800-827-0771
editor@ajr.umd.edu
http://www.ajr.org

Tom Kunkel, President
Rem Rieder, Editor
Reese Cleghorn, Publisher
Kathy Darragh, Circulation Manager

Monthly magazine for media professionals. *$24.00*
Founded: 1972
Circulation: 25000

13880 American Prospect
5 Broad Street
Boston, MA 02109
617-570-8030
FAX: 617-570-8028
info@prospect.org
http://www.prospect.org

Robin Hutson, Publisher
Tim Lysler, Associate Publisher
Robert Kuttner, President

Progressive liberal publication *$19.95*
Monthly Founded: 1990
Circulation: 55000
Printed in 4 colors on matte stock

13881 Associated Press Managing Editors Magazine
450 W 33rd St
New York, NY 10020-1666
212-211-1849
FAX: 212-506-6102
apme@ap.org http://www.apme.com

Deanna Sands, President
Ben Post, Editor
Kathleen Carroll, AP Senior VP
Collins Munro, Manager

36 pages Quarterly Founded: 1933
Circulation: 2200
Printed in 4 colors on glossy stock

13882 Brilliant Ideas for Publishers
Creative Brilliance Associates
Mathey Road
PO Box 32
Clam Lake, WI 94517
715-749-2186
FAX: 715-749-2180 800-975-5474

Naomi Shapiro, Editor

Edited and published for the newspaper industry. *$4.00*

Circulation: 17,000

13883 Catholic Journalist
3555 Veterans Memorial Highway
Unit O
Ronkonkoma, NY 11779
631-471-4730
FAX: 631-471-4804
cathjourn@catholicpress.org
http://www.catholicpress.org

Owen McGovern, Executive Director
Helen Osman, President
Mary Lapalucci, Editor
Sheila Alighieri, Catholic Advertising Network Coordi *$12.00*
Quarterly

13884 Columbia Journalism Review
Columbia University
Journalism Building
2950 Broadway
New York, NY 10027
212-541-1754
FAX: 212-854-8580 888-425-7782
subscriptions@cjr.org
http://www.cjr.org

Brent Cunningham, Managing Editor
Evan Cornog, Publisher
Michael Hoyt, Executive Editor

Evaluates all of the media as well as establishes standards for the profession. *$19.95*
72 pages

13885 ESD Technology
Kelvin Publishing
22700 Wood Street
Saint Clair Shores, MI 48080-1762
586-777-0440
FAX: 586-774-3892

John Kelvin, Editor
Kevin Campbell, VP Marketing

Technical articles highlighting new applications and research. *$22.00*
60 pages 10 per year Founded: 1936
Circulation: 8,500

13886 Ideas
International Newspaper Marketing Association
10300 N Central Expressway
Suite 467
Dallas, TX 75231
214-373-9111
FAX: 214-373-9112
inma@inma.org http://www.inma.org

Earl Wilkinson, Executive Director
Marise Trevino, Editor
Earl Wilkinson, CEO/President
Dawn McMullan, Editor

Marketing and promotion ideas for newspaper executives.
32 pages Monthly Founded: 1930
Circulation: 1200

13887 International Communications Association
1730 Rhode Island Avenue NW
Suite 300
Washington, DC 20036
202-530-9855
FAX: 202-530-9851
icahdq@icahdq.org www.icahdq.org

Michael Haley, Executive Director

Bi-monthly newsletter that supports all students and professionals in the international communications industry.

Printed in on matte stock

13888 Journalism & Mass Communication Quarterly (JMC)
234 Outlet Pointe Road
Columbia, SC 29210-5667
803-798-0271
FAX: 803-772-3509
aejmchq@aol.com www.aejmc.org/

Lillian Coleman, JMC Production Manager (AEJMC)
Dan Riffe, Editor (JMCQ Contact)
Patricia A Curtin, Book Manager Editor (JMCQ Contact)
Pamela Price, Membership/Subscription Coordinator

Published by the Association for Education in Journalism and Mass Communication, the JMC Quarterly focuses on research in journalism and mass communication. Each issue features reports of original investigation, presenting the latest developments in theory and methodology of communication, international communication, journalism history, and social and legal problems. Also contains book reviews. Refereed. Four times per year. (est. 1924)
$80.00

Circulation: 4800

13889 Newspaper Financial Executive Journal
International Newspaper Financial Executives
21525 Ridgetop Circle
Suite 200
Sterling, VA 20166
703-421-4060
FAX: 703-421-4068
infohq@infe.org http://www.infe.org

Jane Hermistor, President
Rob Grand, Editor

Trade publication for financial management of newspapers. More than 800 members.
Weekly Founded: 1947
Circulation: 1000

13890 Newspapers & Technology
Conley Magazines
1623 Blake Street
Suite 250
Denver, CO 80202
303-575-9595
FAX: 303-575-9555
letters@newsandtech.com
www.newsandtech.com/

Mary Van Meter, Publisher
Chuck Moozakis, Editor-in-Chief
Tara McMeekin, Editor
Hays Goodman, Associate Editor/Webmaster

Newspapers & Technology is a monthly trade publication for newspaper publishers and department managers involved in applying and integrating technology. Written by industry experts, News & Tech provides regular coverage of the following departments: prepress, press, postpress and new media.

Circulation: 16,874

13891 Overseas Press Club of America Magazine
OPC
40 W 45th Street
New York, NY 10036
212-626-9220
FAX: 212-626-9210
http://www.opcofamerica.org

Sonya K Fry, Executive Director
Michael Serrill, Editor
Richard B Stogley, CEO/President

Benefits of membership.
Annual+ Founded: 1939
Circulation: 600

13892 Presstime
Newspaper Association of America
1921 Gallows Road
Suite 600
Vienna, VA 22182-3900
703-902-1600
FAX: 703-917-0636
Su-Lin.Nichols@naa.org
www.naa.org

Rebecca Albers, VP and Editor
Jeff Lemberg, Managing Editor
A S Berman, Associate Editor
Su-Lin Cheng Nichols, Senior VP

Communications
Pamela Norman Higbie, Art Director

Covers all areas of newspaper fields while addressing important issues within that media. *$175.00*
Monthly
Circulation: 17000

Trade Shows

13893 Association for Education in Journalism and Mass Communication Annual Show
234 Outlet Pointe Boulevard
Suite A
Columbia, SC 29210-5667
803-798-0271
FAX: 803-772-3509
aejmchq@ad.com www.aejmc.org/
Fred Williams, Communications & Convention Manager
Richard Burke, Business Manager/Convention Manager
Jennifer McGill, Executive Director

Annual show of publishers and educational groups. Exhibits include publications, information retrieval services and special programs.
2000 Attendees August Founded: 1912

13894 Collegiate Press Association Trade Show
330 21st Avenue S
Minneapolis, MN 55455-0480
612-625-3500
FAX: 612-626-0720
Tom Rolnicki, Show Manager

20 booths including learning sessions and press conferences.
1.2M Attendees November

13895 International American Press Association T rade Show
2911 NW 39th Street
Miami, FL 33142-5148
305-634-2465

Julio Munoz, Executive Director

12 booths.
500 Attendees September

13896 International Newspaper Marketing Association Central
World-Herald Square
Omaha, NE 68102
402-734-7632
FAX: 402-444-1370
Terry Ausenbaugh

20 booths.
100 Attendees October

13897 National Scholastic Press Association Conference
National Scholastic Press Association
330 21st Avenue S
Suite 620
Minneapolis, MN 55455-0479
612-625-8335
FAX: 612-626-0720
Tom Rolnicki, Executive Director

Annual conference and exhibits of information on yearbook printing and photographic services, college journalism departments and video yearbook production services.
1800 Attendees

13898 Newspaper Association of America/ Circulation Managers International

1921 Gallows Road
Suite 600
Vienna, VA 22182-3995
703-902-1600
FAX: 703-902-1600
James Abbott, VP

Newspaper management forum.
1M Attendees

13899 Women in Communications National Conference
Association for Women in Communications
780 Ritchie Highway
Suite 28-S
Severna Park, MD 21146
410-647-8402
FAX: 410-544-4640
brenda@baymed.com
www.womcom.org
Patricia Troy, Executive Director
Brenda Gracely, Director Marketing

Annual conference and exhibits of journalism, public relations, advertising, marketing, educational communications and film.
500 Attendees

Directories & Databases

13900 1,000 Worldwide Newspapers
Albertsen's
PO Box 339
Nevada City, CA 95959-0339

Over 500 English-language newspapers overseas and in the United States are listed.
$10.00
54 pages Annual

13901 Asian American Journalists Accountants Directory
1182 Market Street
Suite 320
San Francisco, CA 94102
415-346-2051
FAX: 415-346-6343
Renee Astudillo, Executive Director

Student development, job referrals, fellowship and internship reports.
700 pages Founded: 1981

13902 Burrelle's Media Directory
Burrelle's Information Services
75 E Northfield Road
Livingston, NJ 07039-4501
973-992-6600
FAX: 973-992-7675 800-631-1160
Robert Waggoner, Chief Executive Officer

Approximately 60,000 media listings in North America. Listings cover newspapers, magazines (trades and consumer), broadcast, and internet outlets. *$795.00*
Annual

13903 Directory of Selected News Sources Issue
American Journalism Review
8701 Adelphi Road
Suite 310
Adelphi, MD 20783-1716

FAX: 301-405-8323 800-827-0771
Rem Reider, Editor

List of about 400 companies, organizations and associations that provide information to newspapers and freelance reporters. *$2.95*
Annual
Circulation: 28,295

13904 FYI Directory of News Sources and Information
JSC Group
PO Box 868
Severna Park, MD 21146-0868
410-647-1013
FAX: 410-647-9557 www.fyinews.com
Julia Stocks Corneal, Editor

About 400 associations, corporations, individuals and sources for background story gathering for journalists. *$19.95*
Annual
Circulation: 20,000

13905 Journalism Forum
CompuServe Information Service
PO Box 20212
Columbus, OH 43220-0212
614-457-8600

This database provides information on all aspects of professional journalism.
Full-text

13906 National Directory of Community Newspapers
American Newspaper Representatives
1000 Shelard Parkway
Suite 360
Minneapolis, MN 55426-4933
612-545-1116
FAX: 612-545-1116 800-752-6237
Hilary Howe, President

A directory of community and weekly newspapers in the United States offering rates, circulation, etc. *$85.00*
550 pages Annual
Circulation: 2,000

13907 News Media Yellow Book
Leadership Directories
104 5th Avenue
New York, NY 10011-6901
212-627-4140
FAX: 212-645-0931
newsmedia@leadershipdirectories.com
www.leadershipdirectories.com
Laura Gibbons, Editor
James M Petrie, Associate Publisher

Contact information for over 39,000 journalists at over 2,500 new services, networks, newspapers, television, radio stations, as well as independent journalists and syndicated columnists. *$325.00*
1,200 pages Quarterly Founded: 1989
Mailing list available for rent 32,000 names $125 per M.
Computerized version available: CD-ROM

13908 Newswire ASAP
Information Access Company
362 Lakeside Drive
Foster City, CA 94404-1171
650-378-5200
800-227-8431
Provides citations and the complete text of more than 1 million news releases and wire stories from the international news wire agencies. Subjects covered include banking, commodities, companies, currency and economics.
Full-text

13909 Overseas Press Club of America Directory
OPC
40 W 45th Street
New York, NY 10036
212-626-9220
FAX: 212-626-9210
www.pcofamerica.org
Sonya K Fry, Executive Director
Benefits of membership.
Founded: 1939

Industry Web Sites

13910 www.ajr.newslink.org
American Journalism Review

Provides links to sources, journalism organizations, search tools and media newsletters.

13911 www.apme.com
Associated Press Managing Editors

Members are executives of Associated Press News Executives.

13912 www.asja.org
American Society of Journalists and Authors

For freelance nonfiction writers whose bylines appear in periodicals and in books.

13913 www.asne.org
American Society of Newspaper Editors

Directing editors who determine editorial and news policy on daily newspapers and news gathering operations of daily newspapers.

13914 www.cjr.org/resources
Columbia Journalism Review

Contains resource guides and other journalism-related lists.

13915 www.drudgereport.com

Links to international news sources and columnists.

13916 www.greyhouse.com
Grey House Publishing

Selected Grey House directories in the fields of business, health and education are available online. Users can search our online databases by several different search criteria, such as product categories, geographic area, sales volume and much, much more. Full Grey House catalog and online ordering also available.

13917 www.house.gov
Association of House Democratic Press Assistants

Promotes education and professional standards of members through speakers, series, seminars and papers. Offers placement services.

13918 www.infesecure.org
International Newspaper Financial Executives

Controllers, chief accountants, auditors, business managers, treasurers, secretaries and related newspaper executives, educators and public accountants.

13919 www.inma.org
International Newspaper Marketing Association

Individuals in marketing, circulation, research and public relations of newspapers.

13920 www.ire.org
Investigative Reporters and Editors

For individuals involved in investigative journalism.

13921 www.jour.missouri.edu/home.nsf/

Resources at the University of Missouri's School of Journalism and beyond.

13922 www.jrn.columbia.edu/ressources
Columbia University School of Journalism

Access to Columbia University's Journalism School, the library's bibliographies and reference works, job listings and other associations.

13923 www.kausfiles.com

Site for journalists and media specialists.

13924 www.liberty.uc.wlu.edu
Journalism Resources

Lists of newspapers, film resources, jobs and internships and political advocacy groups.

13925 www.naa.org
Newspaper Association of America

This organization covers all areas of newspaper fields while addressing important issues within that media.

13926 www.nepa.org
New England Press Association

This organizatiom offers a publication about the newspaper industry specifically focusing on New England newspapers and the issues that affect them, which goes to every newspaper in New England.

13927 www.nna.org
National Newspaper Association

Representatives of community newspapers. Founded 1885.

13928 www.opcfamerica.org
Overseas Press Club of America

A media/journalist organization.

13929 www.poynter.org

Poynter Institute is dedicated to teaching and inspiring journalists and media leaders. Promotes excellence and integrity in the practice of craft and in the practical leadership of successful businesses.

13930 www.press.org
National Press Club

A private organization composed of professional journalists who are directly related to the media. Persons must qualify to be admitted.

13931 www.ukans.edu/~acejmc/
Accrediting Council on Education in Journalism
and Mass Communications

ACEJMC members are journalism and media departments, education associations and professional organizations.

Associations

13932 Academy of Criminal Justice Science
7319 Hanover Parkway
Suite A
Greenbelt, MD 20770
301-446-6300
FAX: 301-446-2819 800-757-2257
manager@acjs.org www.acjs.org
Mittie Southerland, Executive Director
Cathy Baute, Association Manager

An international association established to foster professional and scholarly activities in the field of criminal justice.
3500 Members Founded: 1963

13933 Air Force Security Police Association
818 Willow Creek Circle
San Marcos, TX 78666-5060
512-396-5444
FAX: 512-396-7328 888-250-9876
Joe Rector, President
Bruce Kilgore, VP

The mission is to bring together all those currently serving in the US Air Force as Security Forces members, past Air Police and Security Police members, as well as future Security forces members.

13934 Airborne Law Enforcement Association
411 Aviation Way
Suite 200
Frederick, MD 21701-4786
301-631-2406
FAX: 301-631-2466
ngentile@alea.org www.alea.org
Daniel B Schwarzbach, President
Kevin R Caffery, VP
Stephen Ingley, Executive Director
Nicole Gentile, Operations Manager
Keith Johnson, Safety Program Director

Members are law enforcement officers who use both fixed and rotary wing air craft, in law enforcement and equipment suppliers.
3500 Members Founded: 1968

13935 American Association of Motor Vehicle
4301 Wilson Boulevard
Suite 400
Arlington, VA 22203
703-522-4200
FAX: 703-522-1553
inquiries@aamva.org www.aamva.org
Linda Lewis, President/CEO
Mike Calvin, Deputy CEO
Jim Magruder, VP

Striving to develop model programs in motor vehicle administration, police traffice services and highway safety. The association also serves as an information clearinghouse in these areas and acts as the international spokesman for these interests.

68 Members Founded: 1933

13936 American Association of Police Officers
1114 W 7th Street
Suite 2
Austin, TX 78703
512-476-1042
FAX: 800-227-1042 www.policeusa.com

Phil LeConte, Executive Officer
David Dierks, Financial Officer

Dedicated to bringing the wisdom of America's law enforcement veterans to the next generation of police officers and citizens. AAPO has provided a national stage for veteran law enforcement officers to share their wisdom and experience. Guided by an advisory council of law enforcement veterans and distinguished citizens, AAPO is committed to tapping into this often overlooked resource - veteran law enforcers both active duty and retired - and putting this unique knowledge to a useful purpose.

13937 American Association of Police Polygraphs
PO Box 657
Waynesville, OH 45068

FAX: 937-488-1046 888-743-5479
NOM@policepolygraph.org
www.policepolygraph.org
Donald Imbordino, President
Elmer Criswell, Quality Control Director

Promote and maintain the highest standards of ethics, integrity, honor and conduct in the polygraph profession; provide an opportunity and forum for the exchange of information regarding polygraph experiences, studies and research; cooperate with other national, regional and state polygraph associations and other professional organizations in matters of mutual interest and benefit to the profession.
900 Members Founded: 1977

13938 American Association of State Highway & Transportation
444 N Capitol Street NW
Suite 249
Washington, DC 20001
202-624-5800
FAX: 202-624-5806
info@aashto.org www.aashto.org
John Horsley, Executive Director
Jack Basso, Management/Business Dev. Director

Representing highway and transportation departments in the 50 states, the District of Columbia, and Puerto Rico. It represents all five transportation modes: air, highways, public transportation, rail ,and water. Its primary goal is to foster the development, operation, and maintenance of an integrated national transportation system.

13939 American Board of Forensic Odontology
C/O Forensic Sciences Foundation
410 N 21st Street
Colorado Springs, CO 80904
719-636-1100
www.abfo.org
Richard Dial, President
Peter Hampi, VP
David Sweet, Chairman of Certification/Examining

The need to identify forensic scientists unequivocally qualified to provide essential professional services for the Nation's judicial and executive branches of government has long been recognized. In response to this professional mandate, The American Board of Forensic Odontology was organized under the auspices of the National Institute of Justice.

13940 American Correctional Association
206 N Washington Street
Suite 200
Alexandria, VA 22314-2528
703-224-0000
FAX: 703-224-0010 800-222-5646
webmaster@aca.org www.aca.org
Gwendolyn C Chunn, President
James A Gondles Jr, Executive Director

Serves all disciplines within the corrections profession and is dedicated to excellence in every aspect of the field. From professional development and certification to standards and accrediation, from the networking and consulting to research and publications, technology and testing.
20000 Members Founded: 1870

13941 American Criminal Justice Association
PO Box 601047
Sacramento, CA 95860-1047
916-484-6553
FAX: 916-488-2227
acjalae@aol.com www.acjalae.org
Abby Schofield, President
Karen Campbell, Executive Secretary

Objectives are to improve criminal justice through educational activities, foster professionalism in law enforcement personnel and agencies, promote professional, academic and public awareness of criminal justice issues and promote high standards of ethical conduct, professional training and higher education within the criminal justice field.

13942 American Federation of Police & Concerned Citizens
6350 Horizon Drive
Titusville, FL 32780
321-264-0911
FAX: 321-264-0033
policeinfo@aphf.org www.aphf.org
Donna Shepherd, Executive Director
Depty Dennis Wise, National President
Jamie Shepherd, Communications Director

Offers benefits and various types of awards to members, magazine, line of duty benefits, film and training library as well as support services, scholarships and financial assistance for police family survivors.

13943 American Jail Association
1135 Professional Court
Hagerstown, MD 21740-5853
301-790-3930

tonycastillo@ongov.net
www.corrections.com/aja
Gwyn Smith-Ingley, Executive Director
Crystal Mann, Jail Manager Program Director

Dedicated to supporting those who work in and operate our nations's jails. AJA is the only national association that focuses exclusively on issues specific to the operations of local correctional facilities.
5000 Members Founded: 1981

13944 American Planning Association
122 S Michigan Avenue
Suite 1600
Chicago, IL 60603
312-431-9100
FAX: 312-431-9985
CustomerService@planning.org
www.planning.org

Paul Farmer, Executive Director/CEO
Kenneth East, Marketing Director
Charlotte McCaskill, COO

A public interest and research organization representing practicing planners, officials, and citizens involved with urban and rural planning issues. APA's objective is to encourage planning that will meet the needs of people and society more effectively.

13945 American Police Hall of Fame
6350 Horizon Drive
Titusville, FL 32780
321-264-0911
FAX: 321-264-0033
dshepherd@aphf.org www.aphf.org

Donna Shepherd, Executive Director
Brent Shepherd, Operations Director
Jamie Shepherd, Communications Director

The nation's first national police museum dedicated to law enforcement officers who have died in the line of duty.
104M Members Founded: 1960

13946 American Polygraph Association
PO Box 8037
Chattanooga, TN 37414-0037
423-892-3992
FAX: 423-894-5435 800-272-8037
manager@polygraph.org
www.polygraph.org

Donald Weinstein, Executive Director
Robbie S Bennett, National Office Manager

Representing experienced polygraph examiners in private business, law enforcement and government. Professional APA polygraph examiners administer hundreds of thousands of polygraph exams each year worldwide. The APA establishes standards of ethical practices, techniques, instrumentation and research, as well as provides advanced training and continuing education programs.
3200 Members Founded: 1966
Mailing list available for rent $125 per M.

13947 American Probation & Parole Association
PO Box 11910
Lexington, KY 40578-1910
859-244-8203
FAX: 859-244-8001
appa@csg.org www.appa-net.org

Carl Wicklund, Executive Director
Mark Carey, President

An international association composed of individuals from the United States and Canada actively involved with probation, parole and community-based corrections, in both adult and juvenile sectors.

13948 American Prosecutors Research Institute
99 Canal Center Plaza
Suite 510
Alexandria, VA 22314
703-549-9222
FAX: 703-836-3195
mediacontact@ndaa.org
www.ndaa-apri.org

Velva Walter, Media Relations Director

Founded by the National District Attorneys Association as a research and program development resource for prosecutors at all levels of government. The Institute is committed to providing interdisciplinary responses to the complex problems of criminal justice. It is also committed to supporting the highest professional standards among officials entrusted with the crucial responsibility for public safety.

13949 American Psychiatric Association
1000 Wilson Boulevard
Suite 1825
Arlington, VA 22209-3901
703-907-7300
FAX: 703-907-1085
apa@psych.org www.psych.org

James Scully, Manager

U.S. and international member physicians work together to ensure humane care and effective treatment for all persons with mental disorder, including mental retardation and substance-related disorders. It is the voice and conscience of modern psychiatry. Its vision is a society that has available, accessible quality psychiatric diagnosis and treatment.
3500 Members

13950 American Society for Law Enforcement Train ing
7611-B Willow Road
Frederick, MD 21702
301-668-9466
FAX: 301-668-9482 www.aslet.org

Robert Bragg, Chairman
Kat Kelly, VP

Promote and enhance the training of peace officers by providing a forum for the dissemination of information, tactics, and technology.

13951 American Society of Criminology
1314 Kinnear Road
Suite 212
Columbus, OH 43212-1156
614-292-9207
FAX: 614-292-6767
asc@osu.edu www.asc41.com

Gary LaFree, President
Michael Tonry, President-Elect
Christopher Uggen, Executive Secretary

Objectives are to encourage the exchange, in a multidisciplinary setting, of those engaged in research, teaching, and practice so as to foster criminological scholarship, and to serve as a forum for the dissemination of criminological knowledge.
Founded: 1941

13952 American Society of Law Enforcement Training
7611-B Willow Road
Frederick, MD 21702
301-668-9466
FAX: 301-668-9482 888-901-3113
info@aslet.org www.aslet.org

Bob Bragg, Chair
Phil Messina, Treasurer
Kat Kelley, Board Member
Nancy Moser, Executive Director

ASLET represents law enforcement trainers, educators and administrators. Dedicated to enhancing and promoting excellence in law enforcement training while increasing the effectiveness of our members to better serve their communitites and society.
5500 Members Founded: 1987

13953 American Society of Safety Engineers
1800 E Oakton Street
Des Plaines, IL 60018
847-699-2929
FAX: 847-768-3434
customerservice@asse.org
www.asse.org

Fred Fortman, Executive Director
Kelly Fanella, Communications/Marketing Director
Michael Thompson, President

Members manage, supervise and consult on safety, health and environmental issues in industry, insurance, government and education.
30000 Members Founded: 1911

13954 American Traffic Safety Services Association
15 Riverside Parkway
Suite 100
Fredericksburg, VA 22406-1022
540-368-1701
FAX: 540-368-1717 800-272-8772

Joe Jeffrey, Traffic Services Director
Kurt Schuldt, Pavement Markings Director
Peter Speer, President

Promotes uniform use of lights, signs, pavement markings and barricades. Distributes technical information and sponsors training courses for worksite traffic supervisors.
Founded: 1966

13955 Americans for Effective Law Enforcement
Legal Center
841 W Touhy Avenue
Park Ridge, IL 60068-3351
847-685-0700
FAX: 847-685-9700
info@aele.org www.aele.org

Wayne Schmidt, Executive Director
Helen Finkel, VP/Business Manager

Incorporated as a not for profit educational organization for the purpose of establishing an organized voice for the law-abiding citizens regarding this country's crime problem, and to lend support to professional law enforcement.
Founded: 1966

13956 Association of Public Safety Communications Officials
351 N Williamson Boulevard
Daytona Beach, FL 32114-1112
386-322-2500
FAX: 386-322-2501 888-272-6911
apco@apco911.org www.apcointl.org

John Ramsey, Executive Director
Tim Ryan, CFO

APCO is a member driven association of communications professionals that provides leadership, influences public safety communications decisions of government and industry, promotes professional development and fosters the development and use of technology for the benefit of the public.
16000 Members Founded: 1935

13957 Association of Public-Safety Communication s Officials-International
351 N Williamson Boulevard
Daytona Beach, FL 32114-1112
386-322-2500
FAX: 386-322-2501 888-272-6911
apco@apco911.org www.apco911.org
George Rice, Executive Director
Tim Ryan, Deputy Executive Director/CFO
International, nonprofit organization fostering the development and progress of the art of public safety communications by means of research, planning, training and education. Promotes cooperation between towns, cities, counties, states and federal, public safety agencies in the area of communications.
15000 Members Founded: 1935

13958 Board of Certified Hazard Control Management
11900 Parklawn Drive
Suite 451
Rockville, MD 20852
301-770-2540
FAX: 301-770-2183
info@chcm-chsp.org
www.chcm-chsp.org
Harold M Gordon, Executive Director
An application of managerial techniques to eliminate or control unsafe and unhealthy conditions, behavior and other factors detrimental to people and property.
2500 Members Founded: 1976

13959 Campus Safety Health and Environmental Management Association
1121 Spring Lake Drive
Itasca, IL 60143-3200
630-752-2291
FAX: 630-285-1315
lewissu@nsc.org www.cshema.org
Susan Lewis, Division Manager
Provides information sharing opportunities, continuing education and professional fellowship to people with environmental health and safety responsibilities in higher education.
936 Members Founded: 1953

13960 Central Station Alarm Association
440 Maple Avenue East
Suite 201
Vienna, VA 22180
703-242-4670
FAX: 703-242-4675
communications@csaaul.org
www.csaaul.org
John A Murphy, President
Stephen P Doyle, Executive VP
Celia Besore, Marketing/Communications Director
Represents companies offering security (alarm) monitoring systems through a central station. It also represents companies that provide services and products to the industry.
Founded: 1950

13961 Commission on Accreditation for Law Enforcement Agencies
10302 Eaton Place
Suite 100
Fairfax, VA 22030-2215
703-352-4225
800-368-3757
calea@calea.org www.calea.org
Sylvester Daughtry Jr, Executive Director
James Brown, Associate Director
Antonio Beatty, Administrative Services Manager
Linda Phillips, Information Technology Coordinator
Established as an independent accrediting authority by the four major law enforcement membership associations: International Association of Chiefs of Police; National Organization of Black Law Enforcement Executives; National Sheriffs' Association; and Police Executive Research Forum.
21 Members Founded: 1979

13962 Concerns of Police Survivors
3096 S State Highway 5
PO Box 3199
Camdenton, MO 65020
573-346-4911
FAX: 573-346-1414
cops@nationalcops.org
www.nationalcops.org
Suzie Sawyer, Executive Director
Denise Wiese, Program Coordinator
Resources are offered in the rebuilding of the lives of surviving families of law enforcement officers killed in the line of duty or determined by federal criteria. Futhermore, COPS provides training to law enforcement agencies on survivor victimizationa issues and educates the public of the need to support the law enforcement profession and its survivors.

13963 Congressional Fire Services Institute
900 Second Street NE
Suite 303
Washington, DC 20002
202-371-1277
FAX: 202-682-3473
update@cfsi.org www.cfsi.org
William M Webb, Executive Director
Dr William Jenaway, President
Designed to educate members of Congress about the needs and challenges of our nation's fire and emergency services so that the federal government provides the types of training and funding needed by our first responders.
Founded: 1989

13964 Criminal Justice Center
Sam Houston State University
PO Box 2296
Huntsville, TX 77341
936-294-1635
FAX: 281-294-1653
icc_www@shsu.edu
Vincent Webb, Director/Dean
Kristi Kreier, Business Office Director
Established to provide an educational program for students seeking careers in law enforcement, cours and corrections and for the development of a continuing education program for professionals working in the field.

13965 D.A.R.E. America
9800 La Cienega Boulevard
Suite 401
Inglewood, CA 90301

FAX: 310-215-0180 800-223-3273
webmaster@dare.com
www.dare-america.com
Frank Pegueros, Executive Director/COO
Charles Parsons, President/CEO
A police officer led series of classroom lessons that teaches children from kindergarten through 12th grad how to resist peer pressure and live productive drug and violence free lives.

13966 Dogs Against Drugs/Dogs Against Crime National Law Enforcement K9 Assn.
4012 W 32nd Street
Anderson, IN 46011
765-642-9447
FAX: 765-643-7781 888-323-3227
office@daddac.com www.daddac.com
Darron Sparks, President/National Director
Dedicated to the betterment of law enforcement K9 operations and to educating the youth on the dangers of drug abuse. DAD/DAC provides grants to officers for purchasing highly trained special purpose dogs and related training equipment and supplies and to provide training for the officer and/or dog. Working/training seminars are offered for K9 officers on numerous topics related to police service dogs.

13967 Evidence Photographers International Council
600 Main Street
Honesdale, PA 18431
570-253-5450
FAX: 570-253-5011 800-356-3742
EPICheadquarters@verizon.net
www.epic-photo.org
Robert F Jennings, Executive Director
Nonprofit scientific/educational organization with a primary purpose of advancement of forensic photography/videography in civil evidence and law enforcement.

13968 FBI National Academy Associates
National Executive Office
FBI Academy
Quantico, VA 22135
703-632-1990
FAX: 703-632-1993
webmaster@fbinna.org
www.fbinaa.org
Mark Willigham, National President
David A Easthon, First VP
Tom Colombell, Executive Director
Liz Seal, Product Manager
Ashley Sutton, Director Of Marketing/Planning
A non-profit international organization of senior law enforcement professionals dedicated to providing communities and profession with the highest degree of law enforcement expertise, training, education and information.
17000 Members Founded: 1935

13969 FEMSA/Fire and Emergency Manufacturers and Services Association
PO Box 147
Lynnfield, MA 01940-0147
781-334-2771
FAX: 781-334-2771
info@femsa.org www.femsa.org
William Swayne, President
Dan Reese, VP
The leading trade association for the Fire and Emergency services industry. Members provide products and services to millions of Fire and EMS professionals throughout the world.

150 Members Founded: 1966

13970 Federal Law Enforcement Officers Association
PO Box 326
Lewisberry, PA 17339
717-938-2300
FAX: 717-932-2262
fleoa@fleoa.org www.fleoa.org
Art Gordon, National President
Jon Adler, National Executive VP
Born out of necessity by a group of concerned agents from Customs, IRS-CI, TIGTA, FBI and INS, FLEOA's primary tenet was and still is, legal assistance and representation are a phone call away.
24000 Members Founded: 1977

13971 Fire Equipment Manufacturers' Association
1300 Sumner Avenue
Cleveland, OH 44115-2851
216-241-7333
FAX: 216-241-0105
fema@taol.com
www.yourfirstdefense.com
John H Addington, Executive Director
Represents the industrys manufacturers of fire protection equipment, products designed to ensure a safe, reliable and effective first defense against fire. The mission is to provide the world with top quality fire equipment and to educate others about the importance of balanced fire protection.
24 Members Founded: 1925

13972 Fire Suppression Systems Association
5024 R Campbell Boulevard
Baltimore, MD 21236-5974
410-931-8100
FAX: 410-931-8111
fssa@clemonsmgmt.com
www.fssa.net
Crista LeGrand, Executive Director
Cal Clemons, Managing Director
Brenda Martin, Association Coordinator
An organization of manufacturers, suppliers, and design-installers, dedicated to providing a higher level of fire protection. Members are specialists in protecting high value special hazardareas from fire.
Founded: 1982

13973 Flight Safety Foundation
601 Madison Street
Suite 300
Alexandria, VA 22314-1756
703-739-6700
FAX: 703-739-6708
www.flightsafety.org
Stuart Matthews, President/CEO
Linda Crowley Horger, Support Services Manager
Robert H Vandel, Executive VP
Independent, nonprofit, international organization engaged in research, auditing, education, advocacy and publishing to improve aviation safety.
Founded: 1947

13974 Grand Lodge Fraternal Order of Police
701 Marriott Drive
Nashville, TN 37214
615-399-0900
FAX: 615-399-0400
webmaster@grandlodgefop.org
www.grandlodgefop.org
Chuck Canterbury, National President
Kenneth Rocks, National VP
Patrick Yoes, National Secretary
Tom Penoza, National Treasurer
This is the world's largest organization of sworn law enforcement officers, with more than 324,000 members in more than 2,100 lodges. It is the voice of those who dedicate their lives to protecting and serving our communities, and is committed to improving the working conditions of law enforcement officers and the safety of those served through education, legislation, information, community involvement,and employeee representation.
324M Members Founded: 1915

13975 Hispanic National Law Enforcement Association
PO Box 6055
Largo, MD 20792
240-508-1967

President@hnlea.zzn.com
www.angelfire.com/md2/hnlea/
Joe Perez, President
Jose Rivera, VP
Mike Cardona, Secretary
Victor Velasquez, Treasurer
Non-profit organization of professionals involved in the administration of justice and dedicated to the advancement of Hispanic(Latino) and minority interests within the law enforcement profession.
Founded: 1988

13976 Institute of Investigative Technology
AccuQuest
6950 Phillips Hwy, #46
Jacksonville, FL 32216-6087
904-296-0212
FAX: 904-296-7385
www.aqonline.com/iitframeset.html
John Ramming, Director
Provides training for law enforcement and corporate clients. Programs can be designed from one-day to multiple week training courses.

13977 Institute of Police Technology and Managem ent
University of North Florida
12000 Alumni Drive
Jacksonville, FL 32224-2678
904-620-4786
FAX: 904-620-2453
info@iptm.org www.iptm.org
Leonard R Jacob, Administrator/Director
Cameron Pucci, Associate Director
Mission of the Institute is to provide the law enforcement community with the highest quality of training at competitive prices. By providing this service, IPTM continues to support law enforcement's efforts in building and maintaining safer communitites.

13978 Insurance Institute for Highway Safety
1005 N Glebe Road
Suite 800
Arlington, VA 22201
703-247-1500
FAX: 703-247-1588
rrader@iihs.org www.iihs.org
Mike Menz, President
Russ Rader, Media Relations Director
Independent, nonprofit, scientific and educational organization dedicated to reducing the losses (deaths, injuries, and property damage) from crashes on the nation's highways.
Founded: 1975

13979 International Association for Property & Evidence
903 N San Fernando Boulevard
Suite 4
Burbank, CA 91504-4327
818-846-2926
FAX: 818-846-4543 800-449-4273
Mail@IAPE.org www.iape.org
Joseph Latta, Executive Director/Lead Instructor
William Kiley, President
Established to further the education, training and professional growth of Law Enforcement Property and Evidence Personnel.

13980 International Association of Arson Investigators
12770 Boenker Road
Bridgeton, MO 63044
314-739-4224
FAX: 314-739-4219
awhitson@firearson.com
www.firearson.com
James Whitaker, Executive Director
Ashley Whitson, Membership Secretary/Receptionist
Fosters, supports and promotes fire and arson awareness through education and training.

13981 International Association of Auto Theft Investigators
PO Box 223
Clinton, NY 13323-0223
315-853-1913
FAX: 315-793-0048
jvabounader@iaati.org www.iaati.org
John V Abounader, Executive Director
Tommy Hansen, President
Improve communications and coordinator among the growing family of professional auto theft investigators. Providing members with an unsurpassed array of experience, training and resources in areas such as technical developments, trends, intelligence information and investigative assistance.
Founded: 1952

13982 International Association of Bomb Technicians and Investigators
PO Box 160
Goldvein, VA 22720-0160
540-752-4533
FAX: 540-752-2796
admin@iabti.org www.iabti.org
Ralph Way, Executive Director
An independent professional association formed for countering the criminal use of explosives. This is sought through the exchange of training, expertise and information among personnel employed in the fields of law enforcement, fire and emergency services, the military, forensic science and other related fields.
4000 Members Founded: 1973

13983 International Association of Campus Law Enforcement Administrators
342 N Main Street
West Hartford, CT 06117-2507
860-586-7517
FAX: 860-586-7550
info@iaclea.org www.iaclea.org
Peter J Berry, Chief Staff Officer
Lynn Sedlak, Membership/Administration Director
Advances public safety for educational institutions by providing educational resources, advocacy and professional development.
Founded: 1958

13984 International Association of Chiefs of Police
515 N Washington Street
Alexandria, VA 22314-2357
703-836-6767
FAX: 703-836-4543 800-THE-IACP
information@theiacp.org
www.theiacp.org
Mary Ann Viverette, President
Daniel N Rosenblatt, Executive Director
The world's oldest and largest nonprofit membership organization of police executives in over 89 countries. IACP's leadership consists of the operating chief executives of international, federal, state and local agencies of all sizes.
20000 Members Founded: 1893

13985 International Association of Directors of Law Enforcement Standards/Training
2521 Country Club Way
Albion, MI 49224
517-857-3828
FAX: 517-857-3826
PJudge@worldnet.att.net
www.iadlest.org
Patrick Judge, Executive Director
Patrick Bradley, President
An international organization of training managers and executives dedicated to the improvement of public safety personnel. The Association serves as the national forum of Peace Officer Standards and Training (POST) agencies, boards and commissions as well as statewide training academies throughout the United States.

13986 International Association of Law Enforceme nt Firearms Instructors
25 Country Club Road 707
Gilford, NH 03249
603-524-8787
FAX: 603-524-8856
ialefi@lr.net www.ialefi.com
R Steven Johnson, President
Robert D Bossey, Executive Director
An independent, non-profit association whose mission is to update and modernize the instruction and teaching techniques used to train the majority of law enforcement officers.
Founded: 1981

13987 International Association of Undercover Officers
142 Banks Drive
Brunswick, GA 31523

FAX: 800-876-5912 800-876-5943
charlie@undercover.org
www.undercover.org
Charlie Fuller, Executive Director
Jean Pierre Maurice, President
Established for the purpose of promoting safety and professionalism among undercover officers. The association continues to foster mutual cooperation, discussion and interests among its members. It provides vast international network of intelligence gathering means for today's undercover officer and sponsors high quality training programs for undercover officers.

13988 International Association of Women Police
PO Box 2710
Phoenix, AZ 85002
602-382-8751
FAX: 602-382-8760
TerrieSwann@aol.com www.iawp.org
Terrie S Swann, President
Amy Ramsey, Executive Director
Glenda Baker, First VP
Michele Lish, Recording Secretary
Jo Ann Acree, Treasurer
To strengthen, unite, and raise the profile of women in criminal justice internationally.
24000 Members Founded: 1915

13989 International Critical Incident Stress Foundation
3290 Pine Orchard Lane
Suite 106
Elliot City, MD 21042
410-750-9600
FAX: 410-750-9601
info@icisf.org www.icisf.org
Donald Howell, President/Executive Director
Lisa Joubert, Finance Director
A foundation dedicated to the prevention and mitigation of disabling stress through the provision of; Education, training and support services for all Emergency Services professions, continuing education and training in Emergency Mental Health Services for Psychologists, Psychiatrists, Social Workers and Licensed Professional Counselors and Consultation in the establishment of Crisis and Disaster Response Programs for varied organizations and communities worldwide.

13990 International Footprint Association
PO Box 1652
Walnut, CA 91788
323-981-1488
FAX: 323-265-4657 877-432-3668
footprint@footprinter.org
www.footprinter.org
Mike Azuela, President
Charles Zigler, First VP
A non-profit association that promotes and encourages fellowship, respect, cooperation, and helpfulness between all arms of law enforcement and all others who are sympathetic with and understanding toward law enforcement and all of its agencies.
4000 Members Founded: 1929

13991 International Law Enforcement Educators & Trainers Association
PO Box 1003
Twin Lakes, WI 53181-1003
262-279-7879
FAX: 262-279-5758
info@ILEETA.org www.ileeta.org
Ed Nowicki, Executive Director
An organization by, for and about instructors and training for the criminal justice professions. Committed to the reduction of law enforcement risk through the enhancement of training for criminal justice practitioners.

13992 International Narcotic Enforcement Officer s Association
112 State Street
Suite 1200
Albany, NY 12207-2079
518-463-6232

ineoa@iopener.net www.ineoa.org
John J Bellizer Jr, Executive Director
Michael Harris, President
Basic purpose is to promote and foster mutual interest in the problems of narcotic control; provide a medium for the exchange of ideas, conduct seminars, conferences and study groups and issue publications.

13993 Law Enforcement & Emergency Services Video Association
PO Box 126156
Fort Worth, TX 76126
817-249-1480
FAX: 817-249-1480
commngr@leva.org www.leva.org
Mike Fergus, President
Shelly Vorce, Communications Manager
Jan Garvin, Training VP
Committed to improving the quality of video training and promoting the use of state-of-the-art, effective equipment in the law enforcement and emergency services community.

13994 Law Enforcement Alliance of America
5538 Port Royal Road
Springfield, VA 22151
703-847-2677
FAX: 703-556-6485
membership@leaa.org www.leaa.org
Jim Fotis, Executive Director
Kevin Watson, Communications Director
Nation's largest nonprofit, non-partisan coalition of law enforcement professionals. Crime victims, and concerned citizens united for justice; with a major focus on public education, LEAA is dedicated to providing hard facts and real world insights into the world of law enforcement and the battle against violent crime. Fighting at every level of government for legislation that reduces violent crime while preserving the rights of honest citizens, particularly the right of self-defense.

13995 Law Enforcement Bloodhound Association
PO Box 190442
Anchorage, AL 99519-0442
720-308-3474

leba@gci.net www.leba98.com
Gerry Nichols, President
LEBA is a professional nonprofit organization dedicated to the promotion of bloodhounds in law enforcement. Also provides beginning, continuing and advanced education to law enforcement professionals and thier bloodhound partners.
Founded: 1998

13996 Law Enforcement Executive Development Association
PO Box 2349
West Chester, PA 19380

FAX: 610-399-1916 877-772-7712
info@leedafbi.org www.leedafbi.org
Tom Stone, Executive Director
Todd R Ackerman, President
Purpose of the association is to advance the Science and Art of Police Management and Administration; to develop and disseminate improved administrative and technical practices; promote the exchange of information and training for executives of law enforcement.

13997 Narcotic Enforcement Officers Association
29 N Plains Highway
Suite 10
Wallingford, CT 06492
203-269-8940
FAX: 203-284-9103 www.neoa.org
Lt. Michael Rinaldi, President
Sgt. Gabriel Lupo, VP
Created to educate, inform and assist both the Law Enforcement community and the public to dangers and growing trends in the world of drug abuse. Bonding together as Law Enforcement and the Public to present a united front in the continuing battle against drug abuse.

13998 National Association School Resource Officers
1951 Woodlane Drive
St. Paul, MN 55125

FAX: 651-457-5665 888-316-2776
kevin.campana@nasro.org
www.nasro.org
Phil Bailey, President
Kevin Campana, Executive Director
A not-for-profit organization for school based law enforcement officers, school administrators, and school security/safety professionals working as partners to protect students, school faculty and staff and the schools they attend.

13999 National Association of Attorneys General
750 1st Street NE
Suite 1100
Washington, DC 20002
202-326-6000
FAX: 202-408-7014 www.naag.org
Lynne Ross, Executive Director
Chris Toth, Deputy Director
Founded to help Attorney's General fulfill the responsibilities of their office and to assist in the delivery of high quality legal services to the states and territorial jurisdictions.
Founded: 1907
Mailing list available for rent 56 names

14000 National Association of Chiefs of Police
6350 Horizon Drive
Titusville, FL 32780-8002
321-264-0911
FAX: 321-264-0033
policeinfo@aphf.org www.aphf.org
Donna Shepherd, Executive Director
Brent Shepherd, Operations Director
The mission is to encourage through the leadership of persons who hold a command law enforcement or security position within the United States and her territories and possessions, educational activities and services to upgrade law enforcement and security on a professional level.
Founded: 1967

14001 National Association of Drug Court Professionals
4900 Seminary Road
Suite 320
Alexandria, VA 22311
703-575-9400
FAX: 703-575-9402 www.nadcp.org
Karen Freeman-Wilson, CEO
Meghan Wheeler, Project Director
Seeks to reduce substance abuse, crime and recidivism by promoting and advocating for the establishment and funding of Drug Courts and providing for collection and dissemination of information, technical assistance, and mutual support to association members.
Founded: 1997

14002 National Association of Field Training Officers
PO Box 3236
Evansville, IN 47731
812-483-6588

director@nafto.org www.nafto.org
Chuck Knoll, Acting Director
Lt. Doug Ninmann, First VP
An educational and professional association concerned with apprenticeship and advance ongoing training for law enforcement, communications, and corrections personnel. Educators, administrators and other criminal justice practitioners are also encouraged to participate.

14003 National Association of Fleet Administrators
100 Wood Avenue S
Suite 310
Iselin, NJ 08830-2709
732-494-8100
FAX: 732-494-6789
info@nafa.org www.nafa.org
Charles A Gibbens, President
Gayle Pratt, Senior VP
Serving the needs of those managing fleets of automobiles, light duty trucks and/or vans for US and Canadian organizations. Offers statistical research, publications, including NAFA's Fleet Executive monthly magazine, regional meetings, government representation, conferences, trade shows and seminars.
2600+ Members

14004 National Association of Police Organizations
750 1st Street NE
Suite 920
Washington, DC 20002
202-842-4420
FAX: 202-842-4396
info@napo.org www.napo.org
Thomas J Nee, President
William Johnson, Executive Director
Coalition of police unions and associations from across the United States that serves to advance the interests of America's law enforcement officers through legislative and legal advocacy, politicalaction and education.
353M Members Founded: 1978

14005 National Association of Police Athletic Activities League
658 W Indiantown Road
Suite 201
Jupiter, FL 33458-4609
561-745-5535
FAX: 561-745-3147
mdillhyon@nationalpal.org
www.nationalpal.org
Brendan R Lee, President
Mike Dillhyon, Executive Director
Exists to prevent juvenile crime and violence by providing civic, athletic, recreational, and educational opportunities and resources to PAL Chapters.
Founded: 1910

14006 National Black Police Association
3251 Mount Pleasant Street NW
2nd Floor
Washington, DC 20010-2103
202-986-2070
FAX: 202-986-0410
nbpanatofc@worldnet.att.net
www.blackpolice.org
Ronald E Hampton, Executive Director
Marcus Jones, Chairperson
Cynthia Parker-Ferguson, Vice Chairperson
Valerie Cummings, Secretary
Law enforcement association to improve the relationship between Police Departments as institutions and the minority.
35000 Members Founded: 1972

14007 National Burglar & Fire Alarm Association
2300 Valley View Lane
Suite 230
Irving, TX 75062-1733
214-260-5970
FAX: 214-260-5979 888-447-1689
MerlinG@alarm.org www.alarm.org
Merlin Guilbeau, Executive Director
Georgia Calaway, Communications/PR Director
Representing, promoting and enhancing the growth and professional development of the electronic life safety, security, and integrated systems industry. In cooperation with a federation of state associations, NBFAA provides government advocacy and delivers timely information, professional development tools, products and services that members use to grow and prosper their businesses.
Founded: 1948

14008 National Constables Association (NCA)
16 Stonybrook Drive
Levittown, PA 19055-2217
215-943-3110
FAX: 215-943-0979 800-292-1775
lefcourtapr@juno.com
www.angelfire.com/la/nationalconstable
Hal Lefcourt APR, Executive Director
John Sindt, President
Leo Bullock, Secretary
Helping to preserve and clearly define the significant role of the constable in the delivery of justice system in the United States; to train, educate and upgrade the quality of performance of the constable; to serve as a clearing house for all positive actions to give a continued rebirth to the dignity, respect, status and duties and responsibilities of the position of constable as the heritage of the law enforcement community.

Founded: 1973 12500 names $55 per M.

14009 National Correctional Industries Association
1202 N Charles Street
Baltimore, MD 21201
410-230-3972
FAX: 410-230-3981
info@nationalcia.org
www.nationalcia.org

Gina Honeycutt, Executive Director/Corp. Secretary
Roger Baysden, President

An affiliate body of the American Correctional Association, the Jail Industries Association and The Workman Fund. The mission is to promote excellence and credibility in correctional industries through professional development and innovative business solutions.
Founded: 1941

14010 National Crime Prevention Council
1000 Connecticut Avenue NW
13th Floor
Washington, DC 20036
202-466-6272
FAX: 202-296-1356
membership@ncpc.org www.ncpc.org

U J Brualdi Jr, Chairman
Alfonso E Lenhardt, President

Enable people to create safer and more caring communitites by addressing the causes of crime and violence and reducing the opportunitites for crimeto occur. NCPC produces tools that communities can use to learn crime prevention strategies, engage community members, and coordinate with local agencies.
136 Members Founded: 1970

14011 National Crime and Punishment Learning Center
623 Sarazen
Gulfport, MS 39507
228-896-5280
FAX: 228-896-8696
Sanford@CrimeAndPunishment.Net
www.crimeandpunishment.net

William H Sanford, President/Founder

Provide free information on the most common crimes and their punishments in each state. The center is unique in its dedicated endeavor to accomplish this task by providing information to bridge the gap between the legal justice system and the American people.

14012 National Criminal Justice Association
720 7th Street NW
3rd Floor
Washington, DC 20001
202-628-8550
FAX: 202-628-0080
info@ncja.org www.ncja.org

Cabell Cropper, Executive Director
Paul Guequierre, Communications Manager

A national voice in shaping and implementing criminal justice policy since its founding. As the representative of state, tribal and local criminal and juvenile justice practitioners, the NCJA works to promote a balanced approach to communities' complex public safety and criminal and juvenile justice system problems.

14013 National Criminal Justice Reference Service
PO Box 6000
Rockville, MD 20849-6000
301-519-5500
FAX: 301-519-5212 800-851-3420

Dolores Kozloski, Executive Director

A federally funded resource offering justice and substance abuse information to support research, policy, and program development worldwide.

14014 National District Attorneys Association
99 Canal Center Plaza
Suite 510
Alexandria, VA 22314
703-549-9222
FAX: 703-836-3195 www.ndaa.org

Thomas J Charron, Executive Director
Mathias H Heck, President

Development resource for prosecutors at all levels of government. APRI has become a vital resource and national clearinghouse for information on the prosecutorial function. The Institute is committed to providing interdisciplinary responses to the complex problems of criminal justice. It is also committed to supporting the highest professional standards among officials entrusted with the crucial responsibility for public safety.

14015 National Drug Court Institute
4900 Seminary Road
Suite 320
Alexandria, VA 22311
703-575-9400
FAX: 703-575-9402
webmaster@nadcp.org www.ndci.org

Lars Levy, President
Milly Merrigan, President-Elect

Promote education, research and scholarship for drug court and other court-based intervention programs.

14016 National Drug Enforcement Officers Association
Drug Enforcement Administration
Office of Training/TRDS
FBI Academy, PO Box 1475
Quantico, VA 22134-1475
202-298-9653

paul.stevens@state.mn.us
www.ndeoa.org

Paul Stevens, President
Steve Peterson, First VP

NDEOA's purpose and objective is to promote the cooperation, education and exchange of information among all Law Enforcement Agencies involved in the enforcement of controlled substance laws.
Founded: 1970

14017 National Fire Protection Association
1 Batterymarch Park
Quincy, MA 02169-7471
617-770-3000
FAX: 617-770-0700 800-844-6058
public_affairs@nfpa.org
www.nfpa.org

James M Shannon, President/CEO

Mission is to reduce the worldwide burden of fire and other hazards on the quality of life by providing and advocating scientifically based concensus codes and standards, research, training, and education. Also serves as the world's leading advocate of fire prevention and is an authoritive source on public safety.
79000 Members Founded: 1896

14018 National Gang Crime Research Center
Research Center
PO Box 990
Peotone, IL 60468-0090
708-258-9111
FAX: 708-258-9546
gangcrime@aol.com www.ngcrc.com

George W Knox, Director

Research on gangs and gang members, disseminate information through publications and reports, and provide training and consulting services.

14019 National Institute Of Justice
US Department Of Justice
810 7th Street NW
Washington, DC 20531
202-664-4000
FAX: 202-307-6394 800-851-3420
askncjrs@ncjrs.org
www.ojp.usdoj.gov

Sarah V Hart, Director
Kirsten Baumgarten Rowe, Chief Of Staff
Sherry Townsend, Administrative Officer

Research, development and evaluation agency of the US department of Justice. Supports all those in the justice industry with education and training, publications and trade shows.

14020 National Insurance Crime Bureau
1111 E Touhy Avenue
Suite 400
Des Plaines, IL 60018

FAX: 847-544-7000 800-447-6282

Robert M Bryant, President/CEO

A not for profit organization that recieves support from approximately 1,000 property/casualty insurance companies. NICB partners with insurers and law enforcement agencies to facilitate the identification, detection and prosecution of insurance criminals.
1000 Members Founded: 1992

14021 National Native American Law Enforcement Association
PO Box 171
Washington, DC 20044

FAX: 202-204-3066 800-948-3863
info@nnalea.org www.nnalea.org

Peter Maybee, President
Gary Edwards, CEO
Dewey Webb, VP
Tracy Crane, Membership Director

NNALEA is a nonprofit organization that promotes and fosters mutual cooperation between American Indian Law Enforcement Officers, Agents and Personnel, their agencies, tribes, private industry and the public.
Founded: 1993

14022 National Organization for Victim Assistance
Court House Square
510 King Street, Suite 424
Alexandria, VA 22314
703-535-6682
FAX: 703-535-5500 800-879-6682
nova@trynova.org www.trynova.org
Carol Lavery, President
Dan Levey, VP Administration
A private, non-profit organization of victim and witness assistance programs and practitioners, criminal justice agencies and professionals, mental health professionals, researchers, former victims and survivors, and others committed to the recognition and implementation of victim rights and services.

14023 National Organization of Black Law Enforce ment Executives
4609-F Pinecrest Office Park Drive
Alexandria, VA 22312
703-658-1529
FAX: 703-658-9479
jlee@noblenational.net
www.noblenational.org
Jimmie Dotson, National President
Jessie Lee, Executive Director
Joseph Akers, Deputy Director
Ensure equity in the administration of justice in the provision of public service to all communities, and to serve as the conscience of law enforcement by being committed to justice by action.

14024 National Police Institute
Central Missouri State University
200 Ming Street
Warrensburg, MO
660-543-4090
FAX: 660-543-4709
wiggins@cmsu.edu
www.cmsu.edu/x4869.xml
Dr Mike Wiggins, Director
An internationally recognized police training center. Provides advanced police training in a number of areas as well as housing the Regional Police Academy.

14025 National Public Safety Information Bureau
PO Box 365
Stevens Point, WI 54481

FAX: 715-345-7288 800-647-7579
info@safetysource.com
www.safetyresource.com
Working hand in hand with law enforcement, fire and emergency departments to develop the most accurate database in the public safety industry with over 70,000 contacts. The result is; the most current and comprehensive reference tools available.

14026 National Public Safety Telecommunications Council
3511 Parkway Center Court
Orlando, FL 32808
407-836-9668
FAX: 407-521-4625 866-907-4755
npstc@highlands-group.com
www.npstc.org
Vincent Stile, Chair
Douglas M Aiken, Vice Chair
Marilyn Ward, Ecexutive Director
NPSTC is a federation of associations representing public safety telecommunications. They follow up on the recommendations of the Public Safety Wireless Advisory Committee.
Founded: 1997

14027 National Reserve Law Officers Association
PO Box 6505
San Antonio, TX 78209
210-805-8917
FAX: 210-804-2463
nrloa01@earthlink.net www.nrlo.net
Capt. Chuck Mantkus, Director of Training
Provides members with training information and services plus the best, most extensive, and lowest cost in-line-of-duty accidental insurance coverage available.

14028 National Sheriff's Association
1450 Duke Street
Alexandria, VA 22314-3490
703-836-7827
FAX: 703-683-6541 800-424-7827
jthompson@sheriffs.org
www.sheriffs.org
Thomas Faust, Executive Director
Sheriff Ted Kamatchus, President
Devoted to helping sheriffs and other law enforcers to execute their duties most effectively and professionally.
21M Members Founded: 1943
Mailing list available for rent 3M names

14029 National Strength & Conditioning Association
1885 Bob Johnson Drive
Colorado Springs, CO 80906
719-632-6722
FAX: 719-632-6367 800-815-6826
nsca@nsca-lift.org www.nsca-lift.org
Bob Jursnick, Executive Director
Kim Dixon, Deputy Executive Director
Tom Hastings, Marketing Director
Develops and presents the most advanced information regarding strength training and conditioning practices, injury prevention, and research findings.
30000 Members Founded: 1978

14030 National Tactical Officers Association
1050 Skyron Drive
Suite D-1
Doylestown, PA 18901

FAX: 215-230-7552 800-279-9127
johngnageyentoa.org www.ntoa.org
John Gnagey, Executive Director
Elaine Crunkleton, Information Coordinator
Established by the Los Angeles County Sheriff's Department to provide a nationwide communication link among SWAT units. Membership is now opened to all sworn active and retired law enforcement personnel, sworn correctional officers, tactical emergency medical personnel, military police and special operations personnel.
Founded: 1983

14031 National Technical Investigators Association
6933 N 26th Street
Falls Church, VA 22046
703-237-9338
FAX: 703-241-0353
NatiaPrez@aol.com www.natia.org
Michael Woods, President
The purpose of NATIA is to further knowledge, develop skills and promote fellowship between those law enforcement and intelligence professionals who support their agencies' and departments' technical surveillance, tactical operations, and forensic activities.

14032 National Traffic Law Center
99 Canal Center Plaza
Suite 510
Alexandria, VA 22314
703-549-4253
FAX: 703-836-3195
trafficlaw@ndaa.org
www.ndaa.org/apri
Marcia Cunningham, Director
A program of the American Prosecutors Research Institute (APRI), the non-profit affiliate of the National District Attorneys Association. NTLC was created in cooperation with the National Highway Traffic Safety Administration (NHTSA) and works closely with NHTSA and the National Association of Prosecutor Coordinators to develop and deliver prosecutor training programs.

14033 National United Law Enforcement Officers
256 E McLemore Avenue
Memphis, TN 38106-2833
901-774-1118
FAX: 901-774-1139
clydevenson@bellsouth.org
Clyde Venson, Executive Director
Samantha Macklin, Secretary
Protects the needs and interests of persons in the law enforcement industry.
5000 Members Founded: 1969

14034 National White Collar Crime Center
10900 Nuckols Road
Suite 325
Glen Allen, VA 23060

www.nw3c.org
Don Brackman, Director
Ken Brooks, Deputy Director
Through a combination of training and critical support services, law enforcement agencies are given the skills and resources they need to tackle emerging economic and cyber crime problems.

14035 Nationwide Bail Bonds
C/O Florida International Associates
430 NE 1st Avenue, Suite D
High Springs, FL 32643
386-454-3573
800-690-0093
DrTimPal@alltel.net
www.nationwidebailbonds.net
Tim Paletti, President/Bondsman
A network of professional and trustworthy local bail bond agents.

14036 Naval Criminal Investigative Services
716 Sicard Street SE
Suite 2000
Washington Navy Yard, DC 20388-5380
202-433-8800
FAX: 202-433-9619 www.ncis.navy.mil

Thomas Betro, Director
Ralph J Blincoes, Operations Deputy Director

Primary law enforcement and counterintelligence arm of the United States Department of the Navy. It works closely with other local, state, federal and foreign agencies to counter and investigate the most serious crimes.

14037 Office of Law Enforcement Standards
100 Bureau Drive
MS 8102
Gaithersburg, MD 20899-8102
301-975-2757
FAX: 301-948-0978
oles@nist.gov www.eeel.nist.gov/oles

Kathleen Higgins, Director
Dereck Orr, Public Safety Communications Mgr.

OLES's mission is to serve as the principal agent for standards development for the criminal justice and public safety communities. Helping criminaal justice and public safety agencies acquire, on a cost-effective basis, the high quality resources they need to do their jobs.

14038 Organized Crime Task Force
101 E Post Road
White Plains, NY 10601-5008
914-422-8710
FAX: 914-422-8835

John C Prather, Deputy Attorney General
Thomas Mullen, Chief Investigator

A forum that brings government, law enforcement and a range of agencies together to set priorities for tackling organized crime.

14039 Police & Firemen's Insurance Association
101 E 116th Street
Carmel, IN 46032
317-581-1913
FAX: 317-571-5946 800-221-7342

Mark Kemp, President
Jeanie Williams, Operations VP

Mission of the association is to create and operate a Supreme Lodge and Subordinate Branches for the purpose of inculcating principles of friendship and brotherhood among police officers and fire fighters. Providing financial assistance to its members through disability certificates and pay final expenses for members with legal reserve life insurance policies.

14040 Police Executive Research Forum
1120 Connecticut Avenue NW
Suite 930
Washington, DC 20036
202-466-7820
FAX: 202-466-7826
www.policeforum.org

Chief Bill Bratton, President
Chief John Timoney, VP

A national membership organization of progressive police executives from the largest city, county and state law enforcement agencies. Dedicated to improving policing and advancing professionalism through research and involvement in public policy debate.

100 Members Founded: 1976

14041 Police Foundation
1201 Connecticut Avenue, NW
Washington, DC 20036-2636
202-833-1460
FAX: 202-659-9149
pfinfo@policefoundation.org
www.policefoundation.org

Hubert Williams, President
Mary Malina, Comm Dir/Special Asst to the Pres

An independent and unique resource for policing, the Police Foundation acts as a catalyst for change and an advocate for new ideas, in restating and reminding ourselves about the fundamental purposes of policing, and in ensuring that an important link remains intact between the police and the public they serve.

14042 Reserve Police Officers Association
105 Fullerton Avenue
Yonkers, NY 10704

800-326-9416

Brooke Webster, President

Dedicated to the support of law enforcement with an emphasis on the role of the reserve and auxiliary law enforcement officer.

Founded: 1996

14043 Texas Department of Public Safety Officer's Association
5821 Airport Boulevard
Austin, TX 78752
512-451-0571
FAX: 512-451-0709 800-933-7762
kim@dpsoa.com www.dpsoa.com

Sgt Henry Brune Jr, President
Sgt Brian Hawthorne, President-Elect
Sgt Gary Chandler, VP
Sr Trooper Mike Smith, Secretary/Treasurer

Offers and executes programs that benefit Texas Troppers and the communitites around them. Also publishes DPSOA a quarterly magazine.

1974 Members Founded: 2500

14044 Transportation Research Board National Research Council
500 Fifth Stret NW
Washington, DC 20001
202-334-2934
FAX: 202-334-2003 www.trb.org

Robert Skinner, Executive Director
Rosa Allen, Administrative Coordinator

A division of the National Research Council, which serves as an independent advisor to the federal government and others on scientific and technical questions of national importance.

14045 Transportation Technology Center
55500 DOT Road
Pueblo, CO 81001
719-584-0750
FAX: 719-584-0711
ttci_marketing@ttci.aar.com
www.ttci.aar.com

Albert J Reinschmidt PhD, Marketing/Bussiness Development VP
Michele Johnson, Administrative Assistant

A wholly owned subsidiary of the Association of American Railroads. TTCI is a world-class transportation research and testing organization, providing emerging technology solutions for the railway industry throughout North America and the world.

14046 United States Conference of Mayors

1620 Eye Street NW
Washington, DC 20006
202-293-7330
FAX: 202-293-2352
info@usmayors.org
www.usmayors.org/uscm

Michael Guido, President
Tom Cochran, Executive Director

An organization of city government officials whose primary roles are to promote the development of effective national urban/suburban policy; strengthen federal-city relationships; ensure that federal policy meets urban needs; provide mayors with leadership and management tools; and create a forum in which mayors can share ideas and information.

Founded: 1987

14047 United States Deputy Sheriff's Association
1304 Langham Creek Drive
Suite 324
Houston, TX 77084
281-782-2630
FAX: 281-578-2073 877-800-8854
usdsa@usdsa.org www.usdsa.com

Steve Van Dyke, Executive Director

Provides needed equipment, free of charge, to the mostly rural, underfunded county law enforcement agencies. All members are given an Emergency Disaster Relief of $2,000, if killed in the line of duty.

Founded: 1995

14048 United States Police Canine Association
PO Box 80
Springboro, OH 45066

800-531-1614

Russ Hess, Executive Director

Nonprofit organization striving for the establishment of minimum standards for Police K-9 dogs through proper methods of training. Police K-9 dogs, properly trained and handled, give Law Enforcement officers one of the finest non-lethal aids in the prevention and detection of crime.

Newsletters

14049 Correctional Education Bulletin
LRP Publications
747 Dresher Road Suite 500
PO Box 980
Horsham, PA 19044
215-784-0912
FAX: 215-784-9639 800-341-7874
custserve@lrp.com
http://www.lrp.com

Kim Yablonski, Editor

Combines and analyzes corrections education issues and management topics. You'll

learn how educators are coping with shrinking budgets and the growing number of youths being sentenced as adults. Expert analysis of current legal issues and the latest regulatory updates given. *$ 125.00*
Monthly Founded: 1977

14050 Corrections Professional
LRP Publications
PO Box 980
Horsham, PA 19044
215-840-0912
FAX: 215-784-9639 800-341-7874
pressroom@lrp.com
http://www.lrp.com
Debi Pelletier, Editor
Kenneth Kahn, President
Tracks innovative strategies, proven techniques and legal developments impacting correction facilities across the country. Gives profiles of other professionals and their institutions, giving an opportunity to learn from their experiences and avoid costly mistakes. Contains Q-A section that addresses difficult situations. *$210.00*
104 issues per Founded: 1977

14051 Criminal Justice Newsletter
Pace Publications
443 Park Avenue S
New York, NY 10016-7322
212-685-5450
FAX: 212-679-4701
Sid Goldstein, Publisher
Craig Fischer, Editor
Peter Kiers, Executive Director
Independent publication providing system-wide perspective of law enforcement. *$219.00*
BiWeekly

14052 Emergency Preparedness News
Business Publishers
8737 Colesville Road
Suite 1100
Silver Spring, MD 20910-3928
301-587-6300
FAX: 301-587-4530 800-274-6737
bpinews@bpinews.com
www.bpinews.com
Leonard A Eiserer, Publisher
Deborah Eby, Editor
Dedicated solely to disaster management: from securing pre-disaster mitigation and counter terrorism funds, to staying prepared for hurricanes, terrorist threats, fires, floods and other natural disasters. *$327.00*

14053 FLEOA Newsletter
Federal Law Enforcement Officers Association
PO Box 326
Lewisberry, PA 17339-2900
717-938-2300
FAX: 717-932-2262
http://www.fleoa.org
Arthur Gordon, CEO
Kate Desch, Editor
Federal newsletter offering information, legislative updates and news for law enforcement officers nationwide.
12 pages Founded: 1976
Circulation: 2400

14054 Journal of the American Association of Forensic Dentists
1000 N Avenue
Waukegan, IL 60085
847-223-5077

info@andent.net
http://www.andent.net
Quarterly journal that brings forensic dental knowledge not only to dentists and their staff, but also to anthropologists, attorneys and law enforcement personnel. *$8.00*
Quarterly Founded: 1978

14055 Keepers' Voice
International Association of Correctional Officers
PO Box 53
Chicago, IL 60690
312-996-5401
FAX: 312-413-0458
Jim Clark, Publisher
Jess Maghan, Editor
Of special interest to correctional officers because it focuses on current developments in the field, including practical, day-to-day training topics, current legislation, resources, conference notices and job openings.

14056 Law Enforcement & Security
Forecast International
22 Commerce Road
Newtown, CT 06470-1643
203-426-0800
FAX: 203-426-1964
www.forecast1.com
Kathy Bertrand, Production Manager
Monty Nebinger, Circulation Director
An electronic information/data service sourced from thousands of worldwide publications in 15 languages. Provides concise summaries,news, trends and contact information with hyperlinks to the source or related website. Delivered 100 times a year. *$235.00*
2 per year

14057 Law Enforcement Legal Publications
421 Ridgewood Avenue
Suite 100
Glen Ellyn, IL 60137-4900
630-858-6392
FAX: 630-858-6392
lelp@xnet.com http://www.lelp.com
James Manak, Publisher/President
Publication for law enforcement, legal professional civil liability, personnel law, labor law, criminal law and law libraries.
Founded: 1970
Printed in 3 colors on newsprint stock

14058 Law Enforcement Legal Review
Law Enforcement Legal Publications
421 Ridgewood Avenue
Suite 100
Glen Ellyn, IL 60137-4900
630-858-6392
FAX: 630-858-6392
lelp@xnet.com http://www.lelp.com/
James Manak, Publisher
Glen Manak, VP Marketing
Case reporter for law enforcement, legal profession and law libraries, covering criminal law, civil liability and personnel law. *$98.00*
16 pages Bi-monthly Founded: 1975
Circulation: 500

14059 Legal Employment Weekly Law Bulletin Publishing Company
415 N State Street
Chicago, IL 60610-4674
312-644-7800
FAX: 312-644-1215
editor@lbpc.com
http://www.lawbulletin.com
Bernard Judge, Publisher
Stephen Brown, Managing Editor
Lanning Macfarland, Chairman
Legal employment opportunities.
Weekly Founded: 1854
Printed in 2 colors on newsprint stock

14060 National Constables Association Newsletter
National Constables Association
PO Box 1172
Haverhill, MA 01831-1572
978-373-5234
FAX: 978-373-1191 800-272-1775
mike@constables.com
http://www.constables.com
Hal Lefcourt, Executive Director
John Sindt, President
A newsletter published for the members of National Constables Association.
4 pages Quarterly $35 per M.
Printed in 1 color on glossy stock

14061 Police Executive Research Forum
1120 Connecticut Avenue NW
Washington, DC 20036
202-466-7820
FAX: 202-466-7826
rneuburger@policeforum.org
http://www.policeforum.org
Chuck Wexler, Executive Director
Rebecca Neuburger, Marketing Specialist
Rebecca Neuburger, Marketing
Chuck Wexler, Head
Members are chief executives of city, county and state police agencies. Membership dues are general $300.00, subscribing $125.00. *$35.00*
Monthly Founded: 1977
Circulation: 1000

14062 Women Police
International Association of Women Police
PO Box 690418
Tulsa, OK 74169
918-234-6445

jvanland@aol.com
http://www.iawp.org/
Mona Moore, Publisher
Accepts advertising. *$25.00*
50 pages Quarterly

Magazines & Journals

14063 Air Beat Magazine
Airborne Law Enforcement Association
411 Aviation Way
Ste 200
Frederick, MD 21701-4786
301-631-2406
FAX: 301-631-2466
airbeat@alea.org http://www.alea.org
Sherry W Hadley, Executive Director
Jennifer Thornton, Marketing Manager
Lisa Wright, Editorial Director
Founded: 1968
Circulation: 6500

14064 Campus Safety Journal
Bricepac
12228 Venice Boulevard
PO Box 66515
Los Angeles, CA 90066
310-390-5277
FAX: 310-390-4777
tnelson@campusjournal.com
http://www.campusjournal.com

John Van Horn, Publisher
Tom Nelson, Managing Editor
Wendy Rackley, Production Manager

Provides a vehicle for communicating campus safety and security issues to all interested parties at the middle, secondary, college and university levels.
40 pages Monthly Founded: 1992
Circulation: 20100
Printed in 4 colors on glossy stock

14065 Contingency Planning & Recovery Journal
Management Advisory Services & Publications
PO Box 81151
Wellesley Hills, MA 02481-1
781-235-2895
FAX: 781-235-5446
jaykmasp@aol.com
http://www.masp.com/

N Lagos, Manager

An independent, subscription supported to all issues of contingency planning, disaster recovery and business continuity. Includes tutorial extensive literature review on the fields of business continuity. *$75.00*

The above price is for North America, $93.00 Asia, $90.00 Europe

Quarterly Founded: 1972
Printed in on glossy stock

14066 Corrections Today
4380 Forbes Boulevard
Lanham, MD 20706
301-918-1800
FAX: 301-918-1900 800-222-5646
jeffw@aca.org
http://www.corrections.com/aca

Susan Clayton, Editor
Gwendolyn C Chunn, President
Harry Wilhelm, Marketing Manager
Alice Heiserman, Publications and Research Manager

Published by the American Correctional Association. *$25.00*
200 pages Founded: 1870
Circulation: 20000
Mailing list available for rent

14067 Credit Card Crime, Law Enforcement Kit
9770 S. Military Trail
Suite 380
Boynton Beach, FL 33436-4011
561-737-8700
FAX: 561-737-5800
sales@fraudandtheftinfo.com
http://www.fraudandtheftinfo.com

Larry Schwartz, Editor

Ways to catch and punish the thieves, including corporate support of police, reverse sting operations, paying informants. Case histories, specific recommendations. *$59.95*
Founded: 1982 ISBN 0-914801-05-8

14068 Crime & Delinquency
Sage Publications
2455 Teller Road
Thousand Oaks, CA 91320-2234
805-499-0721
FAX: 805-499-8096
reprint@sagepub.com
http://www.sagepub.com

Elizabeth Pi Deschenes, Editor
Blaise Simqu, President /CEO
Douglas Rife, President & Publisher
Sara Miller McCune, Chairman

Offers information to probation and parole executives as well as criminologists and lawyers. *$105.00*
Quarterly Founded: 1965
Circulation: 3250

14069 Law Enforcement Legal Review
Law Enforcement Legal Publications
421 Ridgewood Avenue
Suite 100
Glen Ellyn, IL 60137-4900
630-858-6392
FAX: 630-858-6392
lelp@xnet.com
http://home.xnet.com/~lelp

James Manak, President
Glen P Manak, VP Marketing

Civil liability, driminal law and personnel law case reporter for law enforcement, legal professional and law libraries. *$98.00*
Founded: 1970
Circulation: 1000
Printed in on n stock

14070 Law Enforcement Product News
100 Garfield Street
2nd Floor
Denver, CO 80206
303-322-6400
FAX: 303-322-0627 800-291-3911
mgeorge@jhpress.com
http://www.law-enforcement.com

Michael George, Publisher
Jeannine Heinecke, Editor
Paul Mackler, CEO
Chuck Cummings, Sales Manager

Founded: 1966
Circulation: 57000

14071 Law Enforcement Technology
Cygnus Publishing
1233 Janesville Avenue
Fort Atkinson, WI 53538-2738
920-563-6388
FAX: 920-563-1702
Patrick.Bernardo@cygnuspub.com
http://www.letonline.com

Patrick Bernardo, Publisher
Scott Cravens, Circulation Director
Gordon Gavin, VP
Ronnie Garrett, Editor

Covers the innovative products and technology available to the law enforcement manager. Accepts advertising.
64 pages Monthly Founded: 1966
Circulation: 30,000

14072 Law and Order
Hendon
130 Waukegan Rd
Deerfield, IL 60015-5652
847-444-3300
FAX: 847-444-3333 800-843-9764
info@hendonpub.com
http://hendonpub.com

H Scott Kingwill, Publisher
Bruce Cameron, Editor
Pete Kingwill, Circulation Manager

Tailored to the law enforcement officer, the magazine updates professionals on trends, covers new methods and incorporates articles with special focuses. *$24.00*
100 pages Monthly Founded: 1953
Circulation: 32304

14073 Materials Evaluation
American Society for Nondestructive Testing
PO box 28518
1711 Arlingate Lane
Columbus, OH 43228-518
614-274-6003
FAX: 614-274-6899 800-222-2768
kwie@asnt.org http://www.asnt.org

Paul McIntire, Publication Manager
Betsy Blazar, Marketing Manager
Wayne Holliday, Executive Director
Shelby Reeves, Owner

Research, reviews and information of nondestructive testing materials. Provides members and subscribers the latest news and technical information concerning this industry.
Monthly Founded: 1941
Circulation: 10200

14074 National Fire Protection Association Newsletter
1 Batterymarch Park
Quincy, MA 02169-7471
617-930-0100
FAX: 617-770-0700 800-344-3555
service@nfpa.org
http://www.nfpa.org/

Kathleen Robinson, Editorial Director
James M Shannon, President
John Nicolson, Editor
Carol Faber, Circulation
Russ Thibeault, Advertising

Written for various fire safety professionals and covers major topics in fire protection and suppression. The Journal carries investigation reports written by NFPA specialists, special NFPA statistical studies on large-loss fires, multiple deaths, fire fighter deaths and injuries, and others annually and articles on fire protection advances, public education and information of interest to NFPA members. *$135.00*
Founded: 1896
Circulation: 85000

14075 Peace Officer
Dale Corporation
22150 W 9 Mile Road
Southfield, MI 48034
248-204-2244
FAX: 248-204-2240
salesdoctors@ockhamtech.com
www.salesdoctors.com

Dale Jabolonski, President

Covers areas of interest to law enforcement personnel. *$12.00*
40 pages Founded: 1958

14076 Police
Bobit Publishing Company
3520 Challenger St.
Torrance, CA 90503-1542
310-533-2400
FAX: 310-533-2500
webmaster@bobit.com
http://www.bobit.com

Ty Bobit, President

The law officer's magazine. Accepts advertising. *$35.00*
104 pages Monthly Founded: 1961
Circulation: 50000

14077 Police Chief
International Association of Chiefs of Police
515 N Washington Street
Suite 400
Alexandria, VA 22314-2357
703-836-6767
FAX: 703-836-4543 800-843-4227
information@theiacp.org
http://www.theiacp.org

Joseph G. Estey, President
Mark L. Whitman, Chair Commissioner

A monthly magazine published by the International Association of Chiefs of Police.
$25.00
80 pages Monthly Founded: 1893
Circulation: 21300

14078 Police Times
American Federation of Police & Concerned Citizens
3801 Biscayne Boulevard
Miami, FL 33137-3732
321-640-0911
FAX: 305-573-9819
policeinfo@aphf.org

Jim Gordon, Editor

Quarterly publication focusing on law enforcement, security and police survivors.

Circulation: 31,000 82,000 names $60 per M.

14079 Public Safety Communications/APCO Bulletin
Association of Public-Safety Comm Officials Int'l
351 N Williamson Boulevard
Daytona, FL 32114-1112
386-322-2500
FAX: 386-322-2501 888-272-6911
apco@apco911.org
http://www.apco911.org

Toni Edwards, Editor
Gregory Ballentine, President

The world's oldest and largest professional organization dedicated to the enhancement of public safety communications and to serving its more than 15,000 members, the people who use public safety communications systems and services. *$12.00*
Monthly Founded: 1935
Circulation: 13000

14080 Public Safety Product News
Cygnus Publishing
1233 Janesville Avenue
Fort Atkinson, WI 53538-803
920-636-6388
FAX: 920-563-1702 800-547-7377
Patrick.Bernardo@cygnusB2B.com
http://www.publicsafety.com

Patrick Bernardo, Publisher
Sharon Haberkorn, Circulation Manager
Ronnie Garrett, Editor-in-Chief
Paul Mackler, President & CEO

Monthly

14081 Sheriff
National Sherriff's Association
1450 Duke Street
Alexandria, VA 22314-3490
703-836-7827
FAX: 703-836-6541 800-424-7827
nsamail@sheriffs.org
http://www.sheriffs.org

Suzanne Kitts, Editor
Aaron Kennard, President
Thomas N Faust, Executive Director

Published for the law enforcement official.
$25.00
Founded: 1948
Circulation: 20,000

14082 Today's Policeman
Towerhigh Productions
PO Box 875108
Los Angeles, CA 90087-208

Donald Mack, President

General philosophy of the police services.
$9.00
40 pages Founded: 1961

14083 Top 100 Credit Card Crimes and How to Stop Them
PO Box 400
Boynton Beach, FL 33425-4011
561-737-4000
FAX: 561-737-5800
sales@fraudandtheftinfo.com
fraudandtheftinfo.com

Larry Schwartz, Editor

The manual tells you how to identify all of the crimes, how the thieves work and gives you speciic instructions on how to stop the top 100 crimes.
ISBN 0-914801-02-3

14084 Total Chargeback and Fraud Control Manual
9770 S. Military Trail
Suite 380
Boynton Beach, FL 33436-4011
561-737-8700
FAX: 561-737-5800
sales@fraudandtheftinfo.com
http://www.fraudandtheftinfo.com

Pearl Sax, Editor
Larry Schwartz, CEO

All 46 kinds of chargebacks, with countermeasures for each; all the rights you are entitled to despite tough bank contracts. *$ 199.95*
Founded: 1982 ISBN 0-914801-11-2
Circulation: 4000

Trade Shows

14085 Academy of Criminal Justice Sciences Annual Meeting
Academy of Criminal Justice Sciences
7339 Hanover Parkway
Suite A
Greenbelt, MD 20770
301-446-6300
FAX: 301-446-2819 800-757-2257
info@acjs.org www.acjs.org

Mittie Southerland, Executive Director
Cathy Barth, Association Manager

Criminal justice educators, researchers, practicioners, students and the general public visit 45 exhibits and seminars.
2000 Attendees Annual Founded: 1963

14086 Airborne Law Enforcement Annual Conference & Expo
Airborne Law Enforcement Association
411 Aviation Way
Ste 200
Frederick, MD 21701-4786
301-631-2406
FAX: 301-631-2466
execdirector@alea.org www.alea.org

Sherry W Hadley, Executive Director

Containing 157 booths.
1100 Attendees July

14087 American Academy of Forensic Sciences Annual Meeting
American Academy of Forensic Sciences
410 N 21st St
Colorado Springs, CO 80904-2712
719-636-1100
FAX: 719-636-1993
membship@aafs.org www.aafs.org

Nancy Jackson, Meetings & Exposition Manager
Tracie McCray, Exhibit Coordinator
Sondra Bynoe-Doolittle, Assistant Meetings Manager
Addie Arellano, Meetings/Exposition Assistant
Anne Warren, Executive Director

Professionals in the forensic science field attend meeting and see 120 exhibits of scientific instruments.
2300 Attendees Annual,February

14088 American Correctional Association Congress
206 N Washington St
Ste 200
Alexandria, VA 22314-2528
703-224-0000
FAX: 703-224-0010 800-222-5646
jeffw@aca.org www.aca.org

Susan Clayton, Editor

Five hundred booths featuring association whose membership is concerned with correctional services.
3900 Attendees
Mailing list available for rent

14089 American Correctional Association Winter Conference
206 N Washington St
Ste 200
Alexandria, VA 22314-2528
703-224-0000
FAX: 703-224-0010 800-222-5646
jeffw@aca.org www.aca.org

Susan Clayton, Editor

Three hundred and fifty booths.
3M Attendees January Founded: 1935
Mailing list available for rent

14090 American Jail Association Training Conference & Jail Expo
1135 Professional Court
Hagerstown, MD 21740
301-790-3930
FAX: 301-790-2941
dorothyd@aja.org www.aja.org

Dorothy Drass, Marketing Director
Holly Nicarry, Assistant Marketing Director
Stephen Ingley, Executive Director

Brings together more than 2,200 participants from around the world and over 275 companies who provide products and services to jails.
2200 Attendees May Founded: 1981

14091 American Society of Criminology Show
1314 Kinnear Road
Columbus, OH 43212
614-292-9207
FAX: 614-292-6767
asc41@infinet.com www.asc41.com
Twenty-five tables.
1.5M Attendees October

14092 American Society of Safety Engineers Professional Development Conference
American Society of Safety Engineers
1800 E Oakton Street
Des Plaines, IL 60018-2187
847-699-2929
FAX: 847-296-3434
customerservice@asse.org
www.asse.org
Gene Barfield, President
Jack Dobson, President-Elect
Annual conference of 2,000 exhibitors.
3900 Attendees June

14093 Assn. of Public-Safety Commun. Officials International Conference & Expo
351 N Williamson Boulevard
Daytona Beach, FL 32114-1112
386-322-2500
FAX: 386-322-2501 888-272-6911
apco@apcointl.org www.apco911.org

Barbara Myers, Director Conference/Meeting Service
Casey Epton, Conference/Sponsorship Coordinator
Brigid Blaschak, Exhibit Coordinator
John Ramsey, Executive Director
Banquet, breakfast and 200 exhibitors of radio, computer, and supporting equipment companies.
6000 Attendees Annual Founded: 1935

14094 Int'l Assn of Campus Law Enforcement Administrators Annual Conference
International Assn of Campus Law Enforcement Admin
342 North Main Street
West Hartford, CT 06117-2507
860-586-7522
FAX: 860-586-7550
info@iaclea.org www.iaclea.org
Pamela Hayes, Exhibitor Contact
Peter Berry, Executive Director
Offers members an opportunity to attend informative programs to learn more about current issues and developments in campus public safety, network with peers, visit exhibitor booths, and enjoy special events.
Annual

14095 International Association of Chiefs of Police Annual Conference
International Association of Chiefs of Police
515 N Washington Street
Alexandria, VA 22314-2357
703-836-6767
FAX: 703-836-5386 800-843-4227
muwwakkil@theiacp.org
www.theiacp.org
Lia Muwwakkil, Exhibits & Conferences
Colleen Phalen, Exhibits & Sponsorships
Dan Rosenblatt, Executive Director
Enables professionals to examine the state of the police industry through highly rated seminars, forums, and technical workshops. Only open to IACP members and their guests.
Annual,September

14096 International Association of Women Police Annual Show
RR 2
Box 30
Elkhart, IA 50073
515-967-0427
FAX: 515-284-6240
TerrieSwann@aol.com www.iwap.org
Terrie S Swann, President
Amy Ramsay, Executive Director
Fifty booths of law enforcement products of specific interest to women who work in the field of law enforcement.
1M Attendees September/October

14097 National Forensic League
125 Watson Street
PO Box 38
Ripon, WI 54971
920-748-6206
FAX: 920-748-9478
nflsales@centurytel.net
www.nflonline.org
Diane Rasmussen, Associate Secretary
J Scott, Manager
Ten booths.
2.8M Attendees June

14098 National Sheriff's Association
1450 Duke Street
Alexandria, VA 22314-3490
703-836-7827
800-424-7827
kbright@sheriffs.org www.sheriffs.org

Kimberly Bright, Director, Marketing & Exhibits
Thomas Faust, Executive Director
More than 500 exhibits.
3M Attendees June

14099 Spring Conference
American Correctional Food Service Association
4248 Glen Park Road
Minneapolis, MN 55416
952-928-4658
FAX: 952-929-1318
hcook@acfsa.org www.acfsa.org
Hope Cook, Show Manager
Sixty-five exhibits of food products, kitchen and tableware supplies and equipment. Conference, seminar and workshop.
150 Attendees April Founded: 1969

14100 USNI Joint Warfare Atlantic Exposition & Symposium
US Naval Institute
11208 Waples Mill Road
Fairfax, VA 22030
703-631-6200
FAX: 703-654-6931 800-564-4220
usni@jspargo.com www.jspargo.com
Paul doCarmo, Assistant Director/Exhibit Sales
Connie Shaw, Exhibit Sales Account Manager
Each year the US Naval Institute Joint Warfare Exposition & Symposium brings together expert speakers and panelists to examine the most critical issues related to combat, security, operations, personnel and much more.
1000 Attendees October

Directories & Databases

14101 Air Beat Directory
Airborne Law Enforcement Association
PO Box 3683
Tulsa, OK 74101-3683
918-599-0705
FAX: 918-583-2353
sher@webzone.net www.alea.orglalea
Founded: 1968
Circulation: 6,500

14102 American Academy of Forensic Sciences Membership Directory
410 N 21st St
Colorado Springs, CO 80904-2712
719-636-1100
FAX: 709-636-1993
membership@aafs.org www.aafs.org
Kathy Reynolds, Publications Coordinator Editor
Anne Warren, Executive Director
Offers valuable information on over 5,000 persons qualified in forensic sciences including law, anthropology and psychiatry.
$ 50.00
250 pages Annual 5000 names $295 per M.

14103 Directory of Law Enforcement and Criminal Justice Assoc. & Research Centers
Office of Law Enforcement Standards
US National Institute of Standards
100 Bureau Drive M/S 8102
Gaithersburg, MD 20899-8102
301-975-2757
FAX: 301-948-0978
Marilyn Leach, Editor
Ruth Joel, Editor
More than 200 local, national and international organizations involved in the fields of law enforcement, corrections, forensic science and criminal justice in the US.
$4.50

14104 Fire Chief: Equipment and Apparatus Directory Issue
Primedia
9800 Metcalf Avenue
Overland Park, KS 66212
913-341-1300
FAX: 913-967-1898
www.primediabusiness.com
Scott Baltic, Editor
List of approximately 1,000 suppliers of fire protection equipment, including ladder trucks, protective clothing, alarms, alternators and others. *$10.00*
Monthly
Circulation: 52901

14105 Grey House Homeland Security Directory
Grey House Publishing
185 Millerton Road
PO Box 860
Millerton, NY 12546
518-890-0526
FAX: 518-789-0545 800-562-2139
books@greyhouse.com
www.greyhouse.com
Leslie Mackenzie, Publisher
Richard Gottlieb, Editor
Features the latest contact information for government and private organizations involved with Homeland Security along with

the latest product information. The directory provides detailed profiles of nearly 2,000 Federal & State Organizations & Agencies and over 3,000 Officials and Key Executives involved with Homeland Security. *$195.00*
800 pages Annual ISBN 1-592370-56-X

14106 Grey House Safety & Security Directory
Grey House Publishing
185 Millerton Road
PO Box 860
Millerton, NY 12546
518-890-0526
FAX: 518-789-0545 800-562-2139
books@greyhouse.com
www.greyhouse.com
Leslie Mackenzie, Publisher
Richard Gottlieb, Editor
Two-volume guide to the safety and security industry, including articles, checklists, OSHA regulations and product listings. The 16 chapters focus on creating and maintaing a safe and secure enviroment, and deal specifically with hazardous materials, noise and vibration, workplace preparation and maintenance, electrical and lighting safety, fire and rescue and more. Accepts advertising. *$225.00*
1500 pages Annual ISBN 1-592370-67-5

14107 Law Enforcement Technology Directory
Hendon
130 Waukegan Road
Deerfield, IL 60015
847-444-3300
FAX: 847-444-3333 800-843-9764
info@hendonpub.com
www.lawandordermag.com
Bruce Cameron, Editorial Director
Directory of manufacturers and suppliers of one type of law enforcement equipment such as computers, weapons, training, surveillance, forensics and radio and communications equipment. *$60.00*
Annual December

14108 Law and Order Magazine: Police Management Buyer's Guide Issue
Hendon
130 Waukegan Road
2nd Floor
Deerfield, IL 60015
847-444-3300
FAX: 847-444-3333 800-843-9764
esanow@hendonpub.com
www.hendonpub.com
Ed Sanow, Editorial Director
Jennifer Gavigan, Associate Editor
Monthly publication for police managers, covering all aspects of law enforcement including a list of manufacturers, dealers and distributors of products and services for police departments. *$15.00*
Annual February 40,000 names $115 per M.

14109 National Directory of Law Enforcement Administrators Correctional Inst
National Public Safety Information Bureau
PO Box 365
Stevens Point, WI 54481
715-345-2772
FAX: 715-345-7288 800-647-7579
info@safetysource.com
www.safetysource.com
Steve Cywinski, Publisher
Listing of police departments, sheriffs, criminal prosecutors, state law enforcement, criminal investigation agencies, federal law enforcement and homeland security. *$129.00*
924 pages Annual, paperback Founded: 1964 ISBN 1-880245-22-1
Circulation: 9,000 42000 names

14110 National Employment Listing Service Bulletin
Criminal Justice Center
Sam Houston State University
1803 Avenue I
Huntsville, TX 77341
936-295-6371
Kay Billingsley, Editor
Job openings in police departments, sheriff's departments, courts and other law enforcement and security agencies.

14111 Police: Buyer's Guide Issue
Bobit Publishing Company
21061 S Western Avenue
Torrance, CA 90501
310-533-2400
FAX: 310-533-2504 police@bobit.com
Melanie Hamilton, Sr Editor
List of suppliers of police products and services. *$10.00*
Annual August

14112 Transportation Security Directory & Handbook
Grey House Publishing
185 Millerton Road
PO Box 860
Millerton, NY 12546
518-789-8700
FAX: 518-789-0545 800-562-2139
books@greyhouse.com
www.greyhouse.com
Richard Gottlieb, President
Leslie Mackenzie, Publisher
Provides information on everything from Regulatory Authorities to Security Enforcement, this top-flight directory brings together the relevant information necessary for creating and maintaining a security plan for a wide range of transportation facilities. *$195.00*
900 pages Bi-Annual

14113 Who's Who in Jail Management Jail Directory
American Jail Association
1135 Professional Court
Hagerstown, ND 21740-5853
301-790-3930
www.corrections.com/aja
Stephen Ingley, Executive Director
Offers the most current information available on local jails in the US. Also offers an up-to-date listing of all the jails in the US that is available for rent electronically and a valuable resource for sheriffs, jail administrators and vendors. *$85.00*

Industry Web Sites

14114 www.aamva.org
American Assn. of Motor Vehicle Administrators
Nonprofit organization represents state and provincial officials in the US and Canada who administer and enforce motor vehicle laws. Strives to develop model programs in motor vehicle administration, police traffic services and highway safety.

14115 www.aca.org
American Correctional Association
This organization offers information on the correctional field.

14116 www.alea.org
Airborne Law Enforcement Association
Members are law enforcement officers who use both fixed and rotary wing air craft, in law enforcement, and equipment suppliers.

14117 www.apco911.org
Association of Public-Safety Communications
Officials International
The world's oldest and largest professional organization dedicated to the enhancement of public safety communications and to serving its more than 15,000 members, the people who use public safety communications systems and services.

14118 www.aphf.org
American Police Hall of Fame
Offers benefits, and various types of awards to members, magazine, line of duty death benefits, film and training library as well as support services, scholarships and financial assistance for police family survivors.

14119 www.blr.com
Business & Legal Reports
Provides essential tools for safety and environmental compliance and training needs

14120 www.corrections.com/
Corrections Professionals
Information about events, careers, news, legal happenings and newsletters.

14121 www.dpsoa.com
Texas Department of Public Safety Officer's
Association

14122 www.fema.gov
Federal Emergency Management Agency.

14123 www.footprinter.org
International Footprint Association

14124 www.fssa.net
Fire Suppression Systems Association

Designers, suppliers and installers of special hazard fire suppression equipment, gases and detectors.

14125 www.greyhouse.com
Grey House Publishing

Selected Grey House directories in the fields of business, health and education are available online. Users can search our online databases by several different search criteria, such as product categories, geographic area, sales volume and much, much more. Full Grey House catalog and online ordering also available.

14126 www.highwaysafety.org
Insurance Institute for Highway Safety

Traffic and motor vehicle safety organization supported by auto insurers.

14127 www.home.xnet.com/~lelp
Law Enforcement Legal Publications

Publication for law enforcement, legal professional and law libraries.

14128 www.iawp.org
International Association of Women Police

To strengthen, unite and raise the profile of women in criminal justice internationally.

14129 www.ncpc.org
National Crime Prevention Council

14130 www.policeforum.org
Police Executive Research Forum

For chief executives of city, county and state police agencies.

14131 www.polygraph.org
American Polygraph Association

A merger of Academy of Scientific Interrogation, American Academy of Polygraph Examiners and National Board of Polygraph examiners.

14132 www.psa.com
Production Services Associates,Inc.

Dealers and dealer banks who underwrite and trade federal, state and local government securities and mortgage-backed securities.

14133 www.sheriffs.org
National Sherriff's Association

Devoted to helping sheriffs and other law enforcers to execute their duties most effectively and professionally.

14134 www.theiacp.org
International Association of Chiefs of Police

Organization that focuses on topics of interest to professional law enforcers.

14135 www.toxicology.org
Society of Toxicology

Members are scientists concerned with the effects of chemicals on man and the environment. Promotes the aquisition and utilization of knowledge in toxicology, aids in the protection of public health and facilitates disiplines. The society has a strong commitment to education in toxicology and to the recruitment of students and new members into the profession.

Associations

14136 American Apparel & Footwear Association
1061 N Kent Street
Suite 1200
Arlington, VA 22209
703-524-1864
FAX: 703-522-6741 800-520-2262

Kevin Burke, President/CEO
Marti Rust, Executive Administrator

AAFA is a national trade association representing apparel, footwear and other sewn products companies, which compete in the global marketplace.
Founded: 2000

14137 American Leather Chemists Association
1314 50th Street
Suite 103
Lubbock, TX 79412
806-744-1798
FAX: 806-744-1785
alca@leatherchemists.org
www.leatherchemists.org

Carol Adcock, Executive Secretary

Group of leather chemists who are interested in the development of methods that could be utilized to standardize both the supply and application of the tanning agents utilized by the industry.
500 Members Founded: 1903

14138 American Meat Institute
American Meat Institute
1150 Connecticut Avenue, NW
12th Floor
Washington, DC 20036
202-587-4200
FAX: 202-587-4300
webmaster@meatami.com
www.meatami.com

J. Patrick Boyle, President
Susan Hogan, Executive Assistant

AMI is the national trade association representing companies that process 70 percent of U.S. meat and poultry and their suppliers throughout America.
65 Members Founded: 1980

14139 American Saddle Makers Association
12155 Donovan Lane
Black Forest, CO 80908
729-494-2848

info@saddlemakers.org
www.saddlemakers.org

Michael Rifkin, President
Bob Brenner, Executive Director

Representing manufacturers of Western and English saddles in the US.

14140 Association of Restorers
8 Medford Place
New Hartford, NY 13413
315-733-1952
FAX: 315-724-7231 800-260-1829

Andrea Daley, Founder

It is the mission of the AOR, Association of Restorers Inc, to increase the awareness of choice to consere, refurbish or restore historical works of art, household furnishings and architectural constructions
Founded: 1997

14141 International Federation Leather Guild
748 NW Wood Street
Burleson, TX 76028-2619
817-478-2335

Supports all leather craftsmen via eduation, training, publications and trade shows.

14142 Leather Apparel Association
19 W 21st Street
Suite 403
New York, NY 10010
212-727-1210
FAX: 212-727-1218
info@leatherassociation.com
www.leatherassociation.com

Christine Gonzalez, Account Executive

Founded by retailers, manufacturers, tanners, cleaners and suppliers from across the US to unify the industry.
Founded: 1990

14143 Leather Industries of America
3050 K Street NW
Suite 400
Washington, DC 20007
202-342-8497
FAX: 202-342-8583
info@leatherusa.com
www.leatherusa.com

John Wittenborn, President

LIAÆprovides environmental, technical, education, statistical and marketing services-all at the director of its membership and to benefit of the leather industry.
Founded: 1917

14144 Leathercraft Guild
PO Box 734
Artesia, CA 90702-734

Preserves and promotes the art of leather carving and stamping. Seeks to improve skills of members, raise standards of crafts and promote the product.
200 Members Founded: 1949

14145 National Shoe Retailers Association
7150 Columbia Gateway Drive
Suite G
Columbia, MD 21046-1151
410-381-8282
FAX: 410-381-1167 800-673-8446
info@nsra.org www.nsra.org

Ed Habre, Vice Chairman
Phil Wright, Chairman of the Board
Bill Boettge, President

Membership association for independent shoe ratailers. Provides busisness services such as credit-card processing and shipping at special low members only prices. Also provides educational and training programs, consulting and other services.
1400 Members Founded: 1912

14146 Pedorthic Footwear Association
7150 Columbia Gateway Drive
Suite G
Columbia, MD 21046
410-381-7278
FAX: 410-381-1167 800-673-8447
info@pedorthics.org
www.pedorthics.org

Brian Laguna, Executive Director
Nancy Hultquist, Director Communications

Membership organization for individuals and companies involved in the design, manufacture, modification and fit of therapeutic footwear. Provides educational programs, publications, legislative monitoring, marketing materials, professional liason and business operations services. *$55.00*
2000 Members Founded: 1958

14147 Saddle, Harness & Allied Trades Association
Po. Box 818
Harrisonburg, VA 22803
540-434-9845
FAX: 540-434-5298
shoptalk@proleptic.net
www.proleptic.net

Daniel S Preston PhD, Director

A Comprehensive Source for Sewing Machines, Leather working Equipment, Supplies, Tools, Horse Healthcare and Finished Products Repair Shops Rtailers, Crafters, Collectors.
320 Members

14148 Sponge and Chamois Institute
117 Wilmot Cir
Scarsdale, NY 10583-6761

Members are suppliers and dealers of natural sponges and chamois leather.

14149 Travel Goods Association
5 Vaughn Drive
Suite 105
Princeton, NJ 08540
609-720-1200
FAX: 609-720-0620
michele@travel-goods.org
www.travel-goods.org

Michele Marini Pittenger, President/Editor-in-Chief

Trade association that represents manufacturers of luggage, business and computer cases,handbags and accessories. Formerly the Luggage and Leather Goods Association.
450 Members Founded: 1938

14150 Western-English Trade Association

451 East 58th Avenue
Suite 4323
Denver, CO 80216-8468
303-295-2001
FAX: 303-295-6108
weta@netway.net
www.wetaonline.org

Glenda Chipps, Executive Director

Members are manufacturers and retailers of western and english style riding equipment and clothes.
158 Members Founded: 1963

Newsletters

14151 Leather Conservation News
Minnesota Historical Society
345 Kellogg Boulevard W
Saint Paul, MN 55102-1903
651-296-6126
FAX: 651-297-2967
paul.storch@mnhs.org www.mnhs.org

Paul Storch, Editor

Research and advancements in the specialty of leather conservation and preservation; articles on materials science research and treatments; news of conferences and workshops. *$15.00*
24 pages 2 per year
Circulation: 250 Audited Est. Pass-Along Circ: 1000
Printed in on matte stock

14152 Leather Facts
US Hide, Skin & Leather Association
1700 N Moore Street
Suite 1600
Arlington, VA 22209
703-841-2400
FAX: 703-527-0938 www.meatami.com
John Reddington, President
Association news covering the leather and hide industry.

Magazines & Journals

14153 Journal of the American Leather Chemists Association (JALCA)
American Leather Chemists Association
1314 50th Street
Suite 103
Lubbock, TX 79412
806-744-1798
FAX: 806-744-1785
alca@leatherchemists.org
www.leatherchemists.org
Kenneth A Boni, Ph.D, Editor
Carol Adcock, Executive Secretary
Monthly Association journal that discusses the results of research and investigations relevant to the advancement of the knowledge of science and engineering in regard to their application to problems facing leather and leather products industries. *$150.00*
Monthly Founded: 1903
Circulation: 650

14154 Leather Crafters & Saddlers Journal
331 Annette Court
Rhinelander, WI 54501
715-652-2480
FAX: 715-362-5391 888-289-6409
journal@newnorth.net
http://www.leathercraftersjournal.com
Bill Reis, Editor
Publication for crafters. Sponsors several trade shows throughout the year which attract vendors of leather, tools, equipment and supplies. *$29.00*

14155 Pedorthic Footwear Association
7150 Columbia Gateway Drive
Suite G
Columbia, MD 21046-1151
410-381-7278
FAX: 410-381-1167 800-673-8447
info@pedorthics.org
http://www.pedorthics.org/
Brian Lagana, Executive Director
Nancy Hultquist, Director Communication
Membership organization for individuals and companies involved in the design, manufacture, modification and fit of the therapeutcic footwear. Provides educational programs, publications, legislative monitoring, marketing materials, professional liason and business operations services. Dues are $225/595 (individuals/companies). *$185.00*
44 pages Founded: 1958
Circulation: 5000 15,000 names $150 per M.
Printed in 2 colors on glossy stock

Trade Shows

14156 Custom Boot & Saddle Makers' Roundup
Kimmel Boot
2080 County Road 304
Commanche, TX 76442
325-356-3197
FAX: 325-356-2490
www.backattheranch.com
Kathy Kimmel, Coordinator
Eddie Kimmel, Coordinator
Annual trade event for custom boot makers, saddle makers and uphosterers in Wichita Falls, Texas. Professionals only please, not open to the public.
October

14157 International Federation Leather Guild Trade Show
748 NW Wood Street
Burleson, TX 76028-2619
817-478-2335
Open exhibition of leather craftsmen.
400 Attendees

14158 Leather Allied Trade Show
2214 S Brentwood Boulevard
Saint Louis, MO 63144-1804
314-961-2829
Virginia Breen, Secretary
Exhibition of leathers and components.
2.1M Attendees February

14159 Pedorthic Footwear Association Annual Symposium
7150 Columbia Gateway Drive
Drive #G
Columbia, MD 21046-1170
410-381-7278
FAX: 410-381-1167
info@pedorthics.org
www.pedorthics.org
Jeanne Williams, Show Manager
Brian Lagana, Executive Director
Nancy Hultquist, Director Communications
One hundred fifty booths plus educational sessions regarding the design, manufacture or modification and fit of shoes and foot orthoses to alleviate foot problems caused by disease, congenital condition, overuse or injury.
1000 Attendees November 2200 names $75 per M.

Directories & Databases

14160 Complete Directory of Leather Goods & Luggage
Sutton Family Communications & Publishing Company
155 Sutton Lane
Fordsville, KY 42343
270-740-0870
jlsutton@apex.net
www.fleamarketeer.net
Theresa Sutton, Publisher
Lee Sutton, Editor
Print-out from database of wholesalers, manufacturers, distributors, importers and close-out houses. Database is updated daily to guarantee the most current and up-to-date sources available. *$39.50*
100 pages

14161 Leather Industries of America Membership Directory & Buyer's Guide
3050 K Street NW
Washington, DC 20007
202-342-8497
FAX: 202-342-8583
info@leatherusa.com
www.leatherusa.com
John Wittenborn, President
30 pages Annual Founded: 1917

14162 Leather Manufacturer Directory
Shoe Trades Publishing Company
323 Cornelia
Suite 274
Plattsburg, NY 12901
514-457-8787
FAX: 514-457-5832 800-973-7463
info@shoetrades.com
www.shoetrades.com
George McLeish, Group Publisher
Inta Huns, Managing Editor
Classified directory of major leather finishers, tanneries and hide processors in the United States and Canada, and their suppliers. *$61.00*
413 pages Annual
Circulation: 1,200

14163 US Leather Industry Statistics
Leather Industries of America
3050 K Street NW
Washington, DC 20007
202-428-8497
FAX: 202-342-8583
info@leatherusa.com
www.leatherusa.com
Chris Burt, Publisher
John Wittenborn, President *$18.00*
10 pages Annual Founded: 1917

Industry Web Sites

14164 www.greyhouse.com
Grey House Publishing
Selected Grey House directories in the fields of business, health and education are available online. Users can search our online databases by several different search criteria, such as product categories, geographic area, sales volume and much, much

more. Full Grey House catalog and online ordering also available.

14165 www.hidenet.com
Hidenet

Furnishes detailed information on the daily hide market worldwide.

14166 www.leatherusa.com
Leather Industries of America

Works to promote the leather industry through collection of statistics, chemical and technical research and public relations.

14167 www.meatami.org
US Hide, Skin & Leather Association

14168 www.ssia.info
Shoe Service Institute of America

Shop to shop chat room, links and listings of manufacturers and wholesalers plus shoe care tips.

14169 www.travel-goods.org
Travel Goods Association

Manufacturers of luggage and other leather goods.

Associations

14170 Academy of Family Mediators
801 Main Street
Dallas, TX 75202
214-860-2393
FAX: 000-000-0000
currier@dcccd.edu
www.mediationadr.net

Glenn Currier, Director

Produce conflict management specialists who can advance conflict resolution and engagement, as well as a functional approach to conflict within our communities and society.
2M Members

14171 Adjutants General Association of the United States
2001 E Capitol Street
Washington, DC 20003-1719
202-289-6367
FAX: 202-685-9794
douglas.burnett@fl.ngb.army.mil
www.agaus.org

Roger Lempke, VP
David J Rataczak, President
Frank Vavala, Secretary
Claude Williams, Treasurer

Composed of the commander of the National Guard in each state.
55 Members

14172 Alliance for Justice
11 Dupont Circle NW
2nd Floor
Washington, DC 20036
202-822-6070
FAX: 202-822-6068
alliance@afj.org www.afj.org

Nan Aron, President
Greg Wetstone, Treasurer
Jim Weill, Chair
Rita McLennon, Vice Chair

Nonprofit association of public interest advocacy organization. Offers workshops, advocacy projects, legal guides, techinical assistance and public education. Publishes a directory of public interest law centers.
Founded: 1979

14173 American Academy of Psychiatry and the Law
1 Regency Drive
PO Box 30
Bloomfield, CT 06002
860-242-5450
FAX: 860-286-0787
execoff@aapl.org www.aapl.org

Robert Robert Wettstein, President
Stephen Billick, VP
Kenneth L Appelbaum, Treasurer
Jacky Coleman, Executive Director

Members are psychiatrists who have a professional interest in psychiatry and the law.
1500 Members Founded: 1969

14174 American Arbitration Association
335 Madison Avenue
Floor 10
New York, NY 10017-4605
212-716-5800
FAX: 212-716-5905 800-778-7879
websitemail@adr.org www.adr.org

William K Slate, President/CEO
Debi Miller-Moore, VP

Available to resolve a wide range of disputes through mediation, arbitration, elections and other out-of-court settlement procedures.

14175 American Association for Paralegal

407 Wekiva Springs Road
Suite 241
Longwood, FL 32779
407-834-6688
FAX: 407-834-4747
info@aafpe.org www.aafpe.org

Ronald C Goldfarb, President
Susan W Harrell, Secretary
Lise Hunter, Treasurer
William J Mulkeen, Director Certificate Programs

National organization serving paralegal education and institutions which offer paralegal education programs.
Founded: 1981

14176 American Association of Attorney-Certified
24196 Alicia Parkway
Mission Viejo, CA 92691
949-768-0336
FAX: 949-768-7062 800-272-2889
aaacpa@attorney-cpa.com
www.attorney-cpa.com

Ronald Devore, Executive Director

Seeks to safeguard the professional and legal rights of CPA attorneys.
1400 Members Founded: 1964

14177 American Association of Law Libraries
53 W Jackson Boulevard
Suite 940
Chicago, IL 60610
312-939-4764
FAX: 312-431-1097
webmaster@aall.org www.aallnet.org

Ann Fessenden, VP
Steve Ligda, Exec. Director
Heidi Letzmann, Program Coordinator
Stephen M Ligda, Director Finance
Susan Fox, Executive Director

Membership consists of national law library professionals.
5000+ Members Founded: 1906

14178 American Association of Visually Impaired Attorneys
1155 15th Street NW
Suite 1004
Washington, DC 20005-2706
202-467-5081
FAX: 202-467-5085 800-424-8666
info@acb.org www.acb.org

Gary Austin, President
Melanie Brunson, Executive Director

Promotes the interest and skills development of blind or visually impared persons studying or licensed to practice law.
25000 Members Founded: 1961

14179 American Bar Association
321 N Clarke
Chicago, IL 60610-4774
312-988-5000
FAX: 312-988-5177
service@abanet.org www.abanet.org

Dennis W Archer, President
Allan J Joseph, Treasurer
Ellen F Rosenblum, Secretary
Robert A Stein, Executive Director

The largest organization serving lawyers and all professionals involved in the law enforcement and legal industries. Conducts research and educational activities, encourages professional improvement and provides public service.
40000 Members Founded: 1878

14180 American Bar Association Young Lawyers
750 N Lake Shore Drive
Chicago, IL 60611
312-988-5000

legaled@abanet.org www.abanet.org

Dennis Wayne Archer, President
H Thomas Wells Jr, Chair House of Delegates
Allan J Joseph, Treasurer
Robert A Stein, Executive Director

Provides information to lawyers who are beginning their legal careers.
41000 Members Founded: 1878

14181 American Bar Foundation
750 N Lake Shore Drive
Chicago, IL 60611
312-988-6500
FAX: 312-988-6579

BG Garth, Director

Memberships are elected and limited to one third of one percent of the lawyers in the United States.
Founded: 1955

14182 American Bar Retirement Association
541 N Fairbanks Court
Chicago, IL 60611
312-595-1501
FAX: 800-285-2221 800-826-8901
service@abanet.org www.abanet.org

Focuses on the needs and interests of lawyers' retirement and pension plans.

14183 American Civil Liberties Union
125 Broad Street
18th Floor
New York, NY 10004
212-549-2500
FAX: 212-549-2658
membership@aclu.org www.aclu.org

Nadine Strossen, President
Anthony D Romero, Executive Director
Steven Shapiro, Legal Director
Donna McKay, Director Development
Emily Tynes, Communications Director

Protection of civil liberties and constitutional rights through litigation, public education and legislative lobbying.

14184 American College of Legal Medicine
1111 N Plaza Drive
Suite 550
Schaumburg, IL 60173
847-401-1505
FAX: 847-517-7229 800-433-9137
info@aclm.org www.aclm.org

Theodore R LeBlang, President
Wendy J Weiser, Executive Director
Sue O'Sullivan, Associate Director
Bradley Mettson, Manager

Organization related to the field of health law, legal medicine or medical jurisprudence.
1400 Members Founded: 1960

14185 American Corporate Counsel Association
1025 Connecticut Avenue NW
Suite 200
Washington, DC 20036
202-293-4103
FAX: 202-293-4701
webmistress@acca.com
www.acca.com

Fred Krebs, President/CEO
Danielle Boshart, Director Membership Operations
David Barre, Director Communications
Ken Lawrence, Director Publishing
Diane Rusignola, Editoral/Production Coordinator

Lawyers who practice law in a corporation or other private sector entity and do not hold themselves out to the public to practice law.
15000 Members Founded: 1982

14186 American Health Lawyers Association
1025 Connecticut Avenue NW
Suite 600
Washington, DC 20036-5405
202-833-1100
FAX: 202-833-1105
www.healthlawyers.org

Peter Leibold, Executive VP/CEO

Health Lawyers offers numerous services for their members and most are freely available to nonmembers as well.

14187 American Immigration Lawyers Association
918 F Street NW
Washington, DC 20004-1400
202-216-2400
FAX: 202-783-7853 www.aila.org

Palma R Yanni, President
Deborah J Notkin, First VP
Carlina Tapia-Ruano, Second VP
Kathleen C Walker, Treasurer
Andrew Prazuch, Executive Director

Attorneys practicing in the field of immigration and naturalization law.
8500 Members Founded: 1946

14188 American Inns of Court
1229 King Street
2nd Floor
Alexandria, VA 22314
703-684-3590
FAX: 703-684-3607
info@innsofcourt.org
www.innsofcourt.org

Dave Carey, Executive Director
David Akridge, Deputy Executive Director

AIC is designed to improve skills, professionalism and ethics of the bench and bar. The American Inns of Court is an amalgam of judges, lawyers, and in some cases, law professors and law students.

14189 American Institute of Parliamentarians
PO Box 2173
Wilmington, DE 19899-2173
302-762-1811
FAX: 302-762-2170 888-664-0428

Ann Warner, Executive Director
Martha J Haun, Journal Editor

Promotes the use of effective, democratic and parliamentary practices by teaching of parliamentary procedures; training and certification of parliamentarians; promoting the use of parliamentarians; and maintaining a representative, democratic organization.
1.4M Members Founded: 1958

14190 American Intellectual Property Law Association
2001 Jefferson Davis Highway
Arlington, VA 22202-3614
703-415-0780

Margaret A Boulware, President
Michael Kirk, Executive Director

Lawyers whose speciality is trademark, patent or copyright laws.

14191 American Judicature Society
2700 University Avenue
Des Moines, IA 50311
515-271-2281
FAX: 515-279-3090
drichert@ajs.org www.ajs.org

Rachel Caufield, Consultant

Lawyers, judges and educators interested in the effective administration of justice.
7000 Members Founded: 1913

14192 American Law & Economics Association
PO Box 208245
New Haven, CT 06520-8245
203-432-7801
FAX: 203-432-7225
alea@pantheon.yale.edu
www.amlecon.org
Dedicated to the advancement of economic understanding of law and related areas of public policy and regulation.
Founded: 1991

14193 American Law Institute
4025 Chestnut Street
Philadelphia, PA 19104
215-243-1600
FAX: 215-243-1664 800-253-6397
jgiacinto@ali.org www.ali.org

Michael Traynor, President
Conrad K Harper, First VP
Bennett Boskey, Treasurer
Lance Liebman, Director
Joe Mendocino, Manager

A private, nonprofit organization that seeks to promote the clarification and simplification of the law through legal research and reform activities.
Founded: 1923

14194 American Law Institute: American Bar
4025 Chestnut Street
Philadelphia, PA 19104
215-243-1600
FAX: 215-243-1664 800-253-6397
jmendicino@ali-aba.org
www.ali-aba.org

Richard E Carter, Executive Director
Leslie A Belasco, Staff Director
Mark T Carroll, Director
Alexander Hart, Director
Joe Mendicino, Director

Provides continuing legal education courses, books, and periodicals for practicing attorneys and others in the legal profession.
Founded: 1947

14195 American Lawyers Auxiliary
321 North Clark Street
Chicago, IL 60610-4714
312-988-6387
FAX: 312-988-5494
moisantj@staff.abanet.org

Kitty O'Reilley, President
Linda Jarvis, First VP
Bette Rogyom, Second VP

Acts as a clearinghouse for state and local groups throughout the country and suggests educational programs pertaining to the law. Encourages members to volunteer their services.
75M Members Founded: 1958

14196 American Lawyers Newspapers Group
1730 M Street NW
Washington, DC 20036-4513
202-457-0686

Supports all those involved in the reporting of legal issues. Publishes a weekly newsletter.
Founded: 1977

14197 American Society for Legal History

Notre Dame Law School
PO Box R
Notre Dame, IN 46556-780
574-631-6984
FAX: 574-631-3595
walter.f.pratt.1@nd.edu www.aslh.net

Harryt W Scheiber, President
Walter F Pratt Jr, Secretary/Treasurer

Exhibits relating to legal history and its uses in formulating legal policy, decisions and actions; unearthing historical items; and preserving legal and legislative records.
1200 Members Founded: 1956

14198 American Society of Comparative Law
University of California
Law School
Davis, CA 95616
530-752-2580
FAX: 225-388-5935

Kurt Junger, President

60 Members

14199 American Society of International Law
2223 Massachusetts Avenue NW
Washington, DC 20008
202-939-6000
FAX: 202-797-7133
services@asil.org www.asil.org

Lucinda Low, VP
Charlotte Ku, Executive VP/Executive Director
Nancy L Perkins, Treasurer
Frederic L Kirgis, Secretary

Supports all those involved with overseas litigation. Publishes monthly newsletter.
Founded: 1906

14200 American Society of Notaries
PO Box 5707
Tallahassee, FL 32314
850-671-5164
FAX: 850-671-5165

Kathleen Butler, Executive Director

Helps to organize, improve and uphold high standards for notaries public.

21M Members Founded: 1965

14201 American Society of Trial Consultants
Speech and Mass Communications
Towson State University
Towson, MD 21204
410-830-2351
FAX: 410-830-3656

Ronald J Matlon, Executive Secretary

Members are trial consultants from a variety of backgrounds.
375 Members Founded: 1982

14202 Association of American Law Schools
1201 Connecticut Avenue NW
Suite 800
Washington, DC 20036-2605
202-296-8851
FAX: 202-296-8869
aals@aals.org www.aals.org

Mary E Cullen, Meetings Manager
Carl C Monk, Executive VP/Executive Director
Joyce Saltalamachia, Deputy Director
Jane M La Barbera, Associate Director
Vanessa Anderson, Accountant

An association of law schools that serves as the law teachers' learned society.
Founded: 1900

14203 Association of Family and Conciliation
6515 Grand Teton Plaza
Suite 210
Madison, WI 53719-1048
608-664-3750
FAX: 608-664-3751
afcc@afccnet.org www.afccnet.org

George Czutrin, President
Mary M Ferriter, Treasurer
Hugh E Starnes, VP/Secretary

Established to develop and improve the practice of family counseling as a complement to the judicial process.
2000 Members Founded: 1963

14204 Association of Insolvency Advisors
221 Stewart Avenue
Suite 207
Medford, OR 97501
541-858-1665
FAX: 541-858-9187
aira@airacira.org www.airacira.org

James M Lukenda, President
Kenneth H Lefoldt, Chairman
Grant W Newton, Executive Director
Matthew Schwartz, Treasurer

Disseminates judicial and financial information relating to insolvency proceedings as well as offering methods to increase skills needed in these cases. Also administers the (CIRA) Certified Insolvency and Reorganization Account Program.
1250 Members Founded: 1984

14205 Association of Legal Administrators

75 Tri-State International
Suite 222
Lincolnshire, IL 60069-4435
847-671-1252
FAX: 847-267-1329
webmaster@alanet.org
www.alanet.org

Jay Strother, Editor-in-Chief/Associate Publisher
Theresa Rubinas, Publications Assistant
John Michalik, Executive Director

Support for the adminstration of legal firms and businesses.
9500 Members Founded: 1971

14206 Association of Professional Responsibility Lawyers (APRL)
134 N La Salle St
Ste 1600
Chicago, IL 60602-1159
312-782-4396
FAX: 312-782-4725
admin@aprl.net aprl.net

Kirsten Dell, Administrative Assistant

An organization of lawyers who concentrate on professional responsibilities issues.

300 Members Founded: 1990

14207 Association of Trial Lawyers of America
1050 31st Street NW
Washington, DC 20007
202-965-3500
800-424-2725
info@atlahg.org www.atla.org

David S Casey, President
Kenneth M Suggs, VP
Jon Haber, Chief Executive Officer

56000 Members Founded: 1972

14208 Biz Law Association
PO Box 247
Springdale, UT 84767-0247

FAX: 435-635-9817
Suppports all those involved in business law, especially business owners and managers. Publishes newsletter.

14209 Business & Legal Reports
141 Mill Rock Road E
Old Saybrook, CT 06475-6011
203-180-0000
FAX: 860-510-7220
service@blr.com www.blr.com

Robert Brady, President

Provides essential tools for safety and environmental compliance and training needs.
32 Members

14210 CJE Associates
951 Pershing Drive
Silver Spring, MD 20910-4432
301-587-6300

Association for those interested in the latest news from the EPA, Congress, the states, the courts, and private industry.
8 Members

14211 Center for Professional Responsibility
541 N Fairbanks Ct
Chicago, IL 60611-3319
312-595-1501
FAX: 312-988-6281

14212 Center on Children and the Law
740 15th Street NW
Washington, DC 20005
202-621-1720
FAX: 202-662-1755
ctrchildlaw@abanet.org
www.abanet.org

Howard A Davidson, Director
Jonathan J Cole, Chairman

Association for child support prosecutors and those interested in enforcement of child support litigations.

14213 Commercial Law League of America
70 E Lake Street
Suite 630
Chicago, IL 60601
312-781-2000
FAX: 312-781-2010
info@clla.org www.clla.org

Paul I Mendelson, President
Charles R Johanson III, Treasurer
David R Watson, Executive VP

Supports those involved in bankruptcy, collections, debt and insolvency legislation. Publishes bi-monthy newsletter.
4000 Members Founded: 1895

14214 Commission on Mental & Physical Disability Law
American Bar Association
740 15th Street NW
9th Floor
Washington, DC 20005-1022
202-621-1011
FAX: 202-662-1032
hammillj@staff.abanet.org
abanet.org/disability

John Hammill, Subscriptions Coordinator
Lewis Norman, Executive Director

The Commission fulfills the ABA's commitment to justice and the rule of the law for persons with disabilities through publishing the Mental and Physical Disability Law Reporter and various other disability resources. The Commission also offers thorough, yet affordable legal research services.

Founded: 1973

14215 Conference of Chief Justices
National Center for State Courts
300 Newport Avenue
Williamsburg, VA 23185-4147
757-253-2000

Robert Stephens, President

Administration provided by the National Center for State Courts.

14216 Council of State Governments
2760 Research Park Drive
Lexington, KY 40578-1910
859-244-8000
FAX: 859-244-8001 800-800-1910
web_editor@csg.org www.csg.org

Daniel Sprague, Executive Director
Laura Williams, Deputy Director
Sabrenia Baxter, Web Editor
Lisa Eads, Creative Services Manager

14217 Council on Legal Education Opportunity
740 15th Street NW
9th Floor
Washington, DC 20005
202-662-8630
FAX: 202-223-5633

Cassandra Ogden, Exectuive Director

Provides law school preparation assistance for minority and disadvantaged students. Program is six-week summer institute paid for by the program. Scholarship of approximately $16,000 for the three years of law study is granted to selected and certified students, after completion of the summer program.

14218 Council on Licensure, Enforcement and
403 Marquis Avenue
Suite 100
Lexington, KY 40502
859-691-1289
FAX: 859-231-1943
dlaws@ocpinfo.com www.clearhq.org

Deanna Williams, President
Jayne Bunn, Program Manager
Andrew Garipy, Director-General
Pam Prinegar, Executive Director
Kate Nosbisch, Deputy Executive Director

Supports all those involved in occupational and professional testing and credentialing. Publishes bi-annual magazine.

14219 Defense Research Institute
150 N Michigan Avenue
Suite 300
Chicago, IL 60601
312-951-1101
FAX: 312-795-0747
dri@dri.org www.dri.org

Tyler Howes, Deputy Executive Director
John R Kouris, Executive Director
Nancy Parz, Director Administrative Services

Service organization to improve the administration of justice and defense lawyers' skills.

14220 Education Law Association
300 College Park - 0528
Dayton, OH 45469
937-229-3589
FAX: 937-229-3845
ela@educationlaw.org
www.educationlaw.org

Lois F Berlin, President
Mandy Schrank, Executive Director

Brings together educational and legal scholars and practitioners to inform and advance educational policy and practice through knowledge of the law. Together, our professional community anticipates trends in educational law and supports scholarly research through the highest value print and electronic publications, conferences, seminars and professional forums.

1400 Members Founded: 1954 1400 names $600 per M.

14221 Equal Justice Works
2120 L Street NW
Suite 450
Washington, DC 20037-1541
202-466-3686
FAX: 202-429-9766
mail@equaljusticeworks.org
www.napil.org

David Stern, CEO
David Simmons, COO

Founded by law students dedicated to surmounting barriers to equal justice that affect millions of low income individuals and families. Equal Justice organizes, trains and supports public service minded law students, and in creating summer and postgraduate public interest jobs.

Founded: 1986

14222 Federal Bar Association
2215 M Street NW
Washington, DC 20037
202-785-1614
FAX: 202-785-1568
fba@fedbar.org www.fedbar.org

Thomas Shuck, President
Robyn J Spalter, VP
William N LaForge, Treasurer
James S Richardson Sr, Secretary
Juanita S Lee, Deputy Secretary

Members are attorneys in the federal government or who have interest in federal law.

15M Members Founded: 1920

14223 Federal Circuit Bar Association
1620 I Street NW
Suite 900
Washington, DC 20006-3315
202-466-3923
FAX: 202-833-1061 www.fedcirbar.org

Kevin Casey, President

FCBA is a national organization of attorneys who practice before the United States Court of Appeals for the Federal Circuit.

14224 Federal Communications Bar Association
1020 19th Street NW
Suite 325
Washington, DC 20036-6101
202-293-4000
FAX: 202-293-4317
fcba@fcba.org www.fcba.org

Alexandra M Wilson, President
Michele C Farquhar, Secretary
Diane J Cornell, Treasurer
Stanley Zenor, Executive Director

A nonprofit organization of attorneys and other professionals involved in the development, interpretation, implementation and practice of communications law and policy.

3000 Members Founded: 1936

14225 Federation of Defense & Corporate Counsel
11812-A N 56th Street
Tampa, FL 33617
813-983-0022
FAX: 813-988-5837
mstreeper@thefederation.org
www.thefederation.org

Martha Streeper, Executive Director
Robert Dewey, Board Chair
Jack Riley, President
Jean Lawler, VP
Lewis Collins, Jr, Secretary-Treasurer

FDCC members are experienced attorneys in private practice as well as general counsel and insurance claims executive from throughout the world who represent the interests of those who need a defense in civil lawsuits.

14226 First Amendment Lawyers Association
200 S Wacker Drive
Suite 3100
Chicago, IL 60606
312-674-4763
FAX: 312-332-6008 www.fala.org

Wayne Gianpetro, General Counsel

Lawyers concentrating on defending clients under the first amendment of the Constitution.

180 Members Founded: 1972

14227 Hispanic National Bar Association
815 Connecticut Avenue NW
Suite 500
Washington, DC 20006
202-223-4777
FAX: 202-223-2324
webmaster@hnba.com
www.hnba.com

Carlos Singh, President
Lillian Ortiz, VP Membership & Regions
Brigida Benitez, VP External Affairs
María Antill, VP
Dolores Cabrera, Manager

Supports all Hispanic American attorneys with publications and educational conferences.

25000 Members Founded: 1972

14228 Institute for Civil Justice
1700 Main Street
PO Box 2138
Santa Monica, CA 90407-2138
310-393-0411
FAX: 310-451-6979
zakaras@rand.org www.rand.org/icj

James A Greer II, Chairman
Robert T Reville, Director
Stephen Carroll, Senior Economist
Jennifer Gross, Doctoral Fellow
Laura Zakaras, Communications Director

Organization formed within The Rand Corporation to perform independent, objective research and analysis concerning the civil justice system.

14229 Institute of Certified Business Counselors
18615 Willamette Drive
West Linn, OR 97068
503-751-1856
FAX: 323-417-5176 877-422-2674
inquiry@i-cbc.org
www.businesscentre.net/V1cbc.htm

Bob C Ross, President
Jeff Adam, VP/President-Elect
Michael R Coates, Director, Newsletter

Association enhancing the knowledge and professionalism of counselors, brokers and attorneys qualified to act as advisors for persons with business problems.

14230 Institute of Management & Administration
3 Park Avenue
30th Floor
New York, NY 10016
212-244-0360
FAX: 212-564-0465
subserve@ioma.com www.ioma.com

Joe Bremner, President

Supports law office administrators by offering training on how to reduce overhead, improve the firm's profitability and efficiency, get more value for the firm's budget dollar, and improve their own professional standing. Publishes newsletter.

14231 Inter-American Bar Association
1211 Connecticut Avenue NW
Suite #202
Washington, DC 20036
202-466-5944
FAX: 202-466-5946
iaba@iaba.org www.iaba.org

Harry A Inman, Secretary General

The main purposes of this association are to establish and maintain relations among organizations of lawyers, national and local, in the Americas; to provide a forum for the exchange of views; to advance the science of jurisprudence particularly in the study of comparative law; to promote uniformity of the law; to disseminate knowledge of the laws; to promote the Rule of Law and the administration of justice; to preserve and defend human rights and liberties.

3M Members Founded: 1940

14232 International Association of Defense Counsel
One N Franklin
Suite 2400
Chicago, IL 60606-3401
312-368-1494
FAX: 312-368-1854

Oliver Yandle, Executive Director
Richard Hayes, Director

Offers continuing legal education and conducts research projects.
2.5M Members Founded: 1920

14233 International Society of Barristers
2586 E Huron River Drive
Ann Arbor, MI 48104
734-763-0165
FAX: 313-764-8309

John W Reed, Administrative Secretary

Members are trial lawyers interested in encouraging advocacy under the adversary system and presenting trial by jury.
750 Members Founded: 1965

14234 JL Turner Legal Association
PO Box 134002
Dallas, TX 75313-4002
214-761-1707
www.jltla.org

Daryl Washington, President

A nonprofit legal organization.

14235 Japanese American Society for Legal Studies
University of WA Law School-1100 NE Cam.
Seattle, WA 98105
206-233-9292
FAX: 206-685-4469

John Haley, Editor

Association for those interested in Japanese law and legal issues.

14236 Legal Education and Admissions to the Bar
750 N Lake Shore Drive
Chicago, IL 60611-4403
312-944-0575
FAX: 312-988-6281

Association for state bar admission administrators in the United States and its territories.

14237 Maritime Law Association of the United
400 Poydras Street
27th Floor Texaco Center
New Orleans, LA 70130-324
504-680-8433
FAX: 504-561-1932 www.mlaus.org

Raymond P Hayden, President
Thomas S Rue, First VP
Lizabeth L Burrell, Second VP
Patrick J Bonner, Treasurer
Warren J Marwedel, Secretary

256 Members Founded: 1969

14238 Mid-America Association of Law Libraries
53 W Jackson
Suite 940
Chicago, IL 60604
515-265-1208
FAX: 312-431-1097 www.aallnet.org

Kay L Andrus, President
Janet McKinney, VP
Charles J Condon, Secretary
Sharon P Kern, Treasurer

Association for suppliers of law library equipment, supplies and services.

14239 NALS/The Association For Legal Professionals
314 E 3rd Street
#210
Tulsa, OK 74120-2409
918-582-5188
FAX: 918-582-5907 www.nals.org

Tammy Hailey, Executive Director/CAE

Supports all those involved with the technology of the legal profession and the education and training of the legal administrative staff. Publishes quarterly magazine. NALS is dedicated to enhancing the competencies and contributions of members in the legal field.
Founded: 1929
Mailing list available for rent

14240 National Academy of Elder Law Attorneys
1604 N Country Club Road
Tucson, AZ 85716
520-881-4005
FAX: 520-325-7925 www.naela.org

Susan McMahon, Executive Director

Members are private attorneys, law professors and Title III interest in the provision of legal service to the elderly.
3600 Members Founded: 1988 3600 names $500 per M.

14241 National American Indian Court Clerks Association
National Association of Tribal Court Personnel
920 Spring Creek Circle
Green Bay, WI 54311

RMJ143@compuserve.com

Robert Miller, President

Devoted to upgrading the integrity capabilities and management of tribal courts through training, testing and certification of court clerks and court administrators.
257 Members

14242 National American Indian Court Judges
3618 Reder Street
Rapid City, SD 57702
605-342-4804
FAX: 605-719-9357
mail@naicja.org www.naicja.org

Eugene White-Fish, President
Elbridge Coochise, First VP
Roman Duran, Second VP
Chuck Robertson, Executive Director

National voluntary association of tribal court judges. Primarily devoted to the support of the American Indian and Alaska Native justice systems through education, information sharing and advocacy.

14243 National Association for Court Management
300 Newport Avenue
Williamsburg, VA 23185-4147
757-253-2000
FAX: 757-259-1520
nacme@hese.dni.us
www.ascm.vicsc.dni.us

Linda D Perkins, Staff Associate

Members are clerks of court, court administration and others serving in a court management capacity.
2,500 Members Founded: 1989

14244 National Association for Law Placement
1025 Connecticut Avenue
Suite 1110
Washington, DC 20036-5413
202-835-1001
FAX: 202-835-1112
info@nalp.org www.nalp.org

Lisa Dickinson, President
Jose Bahamonde-Gonzalez, VP
Sonia Menon, Treasurer
James Liepold, Executive Director

Deals with issues such as career planning, recruiting and ethics.

14245 National Association of Legal Investigators
1000 Paseo Camarillo
Suite 206
Camarillo, CA 93010
805-445-1997
FAX: 805-445-1427
www.investigativeprofessionals.com

Larry Troxel

NALI was formed with its primary focus to conduct investigations related to litigation. Membership in NALI is open to all professional legal investigators who are actively engaged in negligence investigations for the plaintiff and/or criminal defense, and who are emplyoed by investigative firms, law firms or public defender agencies.

14246 National Association of Attorneys General
750 1st Street NE
Suite 1100
Washington, DC 20002
202-897-7484
FAX: 202-408-7014 www.naag.org

Lynne Ross, Executive Director
William H Sorrell, President

Fosters interstate cooperation on legal and law enforcement issues, conducts policy research and analysis, provides advocacy.
56 Members Founded: 1907
Mailing list available for rent 56 names

14247 National Association of Bar Executives
ABA Division For Bar Services
541 N Fairbanks Ct
Chicago, IL 60611-3319
312-595-1501
FAX: 312-988-6281

Robert Gray, President

Represents top-level executives in law.

14248 National Association of Black Criminal
NC Central University
PO Box 19788
Durham, NC 27707
919-683-1801
FAX: 919-683-1903
office@nabcj.org www.nabcj.org

Matthew B Hamidullah, President
Keith V Branch, Executive Director

Supports all black persons who are involved in the criminal justice system. Hosts annual trade show.

14249 National Association of College and University Attorneys
1 Dupont Circle NW
Suite 620
Washington, DC 20036-1134
202-833-8390
FAX: 202-296-8379

Mary Elizabeth Kurz, President
Kathleen Santora, Chief Executive Officer

Educates attorneys and administrative executives about campus legal issues.

14250 National Association of County Civil Attorneys
440 1st Street NW
Suite 8
Washington, DC 20001-2028
202-936-6226
FAX: 202-393-2630

Lee Ruck, Staff Liaison
Larry Naake, Chief Executive Officer

An affiliate of the National Association of Counties.
240 Members

14251 National Association of Criminal Defense
1150 18th Street NW
Suite 950
Washington, DC 20036
202-872-8600
FAX: 202-872-8690
assist@nacdl.org www.nacdl.org

Ralph Grunewald, Executive Director
Thomas Chambers, Finance Director

Supports all criminal defense lawyers with education, publications and trade shows.
10000 Members Founded: 1958

14252 National Association of Legal Vendors
Juris
5106 Maryland Way
Brentwood, TN 37027-7501
615-377-3740

Mel Goldenburg, Chairman

Trade association of organizations who sell products to the legal community.
100 Members

14253 National Association of Parliamentarians (NAP)
213 South Main Street
Independence, MO 64050-3850
816-833-3892
FAX: 816-833-3893 888-627-2929
hq@nap2.org
www.parliamentarians.org

Jeanette N Williams, President
Connie M Deford, VP
Mary L Randolph, Secretary
Ronald R Stinson, Treasurer
Sarah Nieft, Executive Director

An association for those interested in parliamentary law and procedure, NAP's primary objectives are teaching, promoting, and disseminating the philosophy and principles underlying the rules of deliberative assemblies.
4000+ Members Founded: 1930

14254 National Association of Women Lawyers
321 North Clark Street
Chicago, IL 60610
312-988-6186
FAX: 312-988-5491 nawl@nawl.org

Stacie Strong, Executive Director
Kelly Reese, Project Specialist

Promotes the advancement and welfare of women in the legal profession. NAWL is a professional association of attorneys, judges and law students serving the educational, legal and practical interests of the organized bar and women generally. Founded in 1899, long before most local and national bar associations admitted women.
800 Members Founded: 1899

14255 National Bar Association
1225 11th Street NW
Washington, DC 20001-4217
202-842-3900
FAX: 202-289-6170
headquarters@nationalbar.org
www.nationalbar.org

John L Crump CMP, CAE, Executive Director
Linnes Finney Jr, VP
Rodney G Moore, VP
John Crump, Executive Director

Represents the interests of minority attorneys, offers education and research programs.
18000 Members Founded: 1925

14256 National Center for State Courts
300 Newport Avenue
Williamsburg, VA 23185-4147

FAX: 757-564-2022 800-616-6164
webmaster@ncsc.dni.us
www.ncsconline.org

Ronald M George, Chair
Michael L Buenger, Vice Chair
Charles R Cloud, Director
Gerald T Elliott, Director

Provides a forum for the state courts.
Founded: 1971

14257 National College of District Attorneys
University of Houston Law Center
Houston, TX 77204-0001
713-743-1840
FAX: 713-743-1850

John Jay Douglass, Dean

Provides continuing legal education and training for prosecuting attorneys and their investigators and office administrators through programs specifically tailored to meet their needs. Programs include resident courses held each summer at the University of Houston Law Center, short courses conducted in locations throughout the country, and courses presented cooperatively with state associations and local offices.

14258 National Conference of Bar Examiners
402 W Wilson Street
Madison, WI 53703-3614
608-280-8550
FAX: 608-280-8552

Francis Morrissey, President
Erica Moeser, Manager

Conducts investigations regarding the character of individuals practicing law.

14259 National Conference of Bar Foundations
ABA Division For Bar Services
541 N Fairbanks
Suite 1400
Chicago, IL 60611
312-988-5343
FAX: 312-988-5492
barservices@abanet.org
www.ncbf.org

Linda Thompson, President
Doris Huffman, Secretary
Barbara Bratton, Treasurer

Serves bar foundations in the United States and Canada; conducts biannual conferences; maintains information clearinghouses.
Founded: 1977

14260 National Conference of Bar Presidents
c/o ABA Division for Bar Services
541 N Fairbanks Court
Chicago, IL 60611
312-988-5364
FAX: 312-988-5492
bware@staff.abanet.org
www.ncbp.org

Paul T Moxley, President

Provides a forum for the exchange of ideas and seeks to stimulate work in bar associations.
1M Members Founded: 1950

14261 National Conference of Commissioners on
211 E Ontario Street
Suite 1300
Chicago, IL 60611
312-915-0195
FAX: 312-915-0187
nccusl@nccusl.org www.nccusl.org

Fred Miller, President
Peter Langrock, VP
Robert Stein, Secretary
Carl Lisman, Treasurer
Elizabeth Cotton, Manager

Designed to foster interstate cooperation in legal issues.
Founded: 1892

14262 National Conference of Women's Bar Associations
3223 Lake Avenue
Suite 15C-148
Wilmette, IL 60091-1069
847-256-3303
FAX: 847-853-0498

Juliet Gee, President

Membership organization for women lawyers and associations of women lwayers. Serves as a forum for exchange of information among women's bar association and conducts educational programs.
110 Members Founded: 1981

14263 National Conference of Womens' Bar Associations
PO Box 82366
Portland, OR 97282
503-657-3813
FAX: 503-657-3932
info@ncwba.org www.ncwba.org
Carole V Aciman, President
Lynne T Albert, President - Elect
Pam Nicholson, Executive Director
Supports women who are involved in the legal community and provides a forum for the exchange of ideas, thus stimulating work in bar associations.
30000 Members Founded: 1981

14264 National Court Reporters Association
8224 Old Courthouse Road
Vienna, VA 22182-3808
703-556-6272
FAX: 703-556-6291 800-272-6272
msic@ncrahq.org www.ncraonline.org
Reesa Parker, President
Merilyn Marquardt-Sanchez, Immediate Past President
Mark J Golden, Executive Director/CEO
Supports all those involved in the information/court reporting profession. Publishes a monthly magazine.
2500 Members Founded: 1899

14265 National Criminal Justice
PO Box 6000
Rockville, MD 20849-6000
800-851-3420
Association for correctional institutions constructed since 1985.

14266 National District Attorneys Association
99 Canal Center Plaza
Suite 510
Alexandria, VA 22314
703-549-9222
FAX: 703-836-3195
webmaster@ndaa-apri.org
www.ndaa-apri.org
Robert P McCulloch, President
M David Barber, VP
Jerry M Blair, VP
Thomas Charron, Executive Director
Supports district attorneys nationwide with education, publications, and regular conferences.
Founded: 1960

14267 National Federation of Paralegal Associations
PO Box 2016
Edmonds, WA 98020-9516
425-967-0045
FAX: 425-771-9588
info@paralegals.org
www.paralegals.org
Rich Cantrall, President
Stephen P Imondi, VP
Nonprofit, professional organization comprising state and local paralegal associations throughout the United States and Canada. NFPA affirms the paralegal profession as an independent, self-directed profession which supports increased quality, efficiency and accessibility in the delivery of legal services. NFPA promotes the growth, development and recognition of the profession as a integral partner in the delivery of legal services.
15000 Members Founded: 1974

14268 National Forensic Center
17 Temple Terrace
Lawrenceville, NJ 08648
609-989-8777
800-526-5177
jon@midi.com expertindex.com
Association for those interested in the application of scientific knowledge in litigation.

14269 National Institute for Trial Advocacy
53550 Generations Drive
South Bend, IN 46635-1570
574-271-8370
FAX: 574-271-8375
nita.1@nd.edu www.nita.org
Thomas Hintz, Director Business Development
Peg Hartman, Director Development
Laurence M Rose, Executive Director
Shelly Goethals, Operations Manager
Paula Muhlherr, Owner
60 Members Founded: 1971

14270 National Lawyers Guild
132 Nassau Street
Room 922
New York, NY 10038
212-679-5100
FAX: 212-679-2811
nlgno@nlg.org www.nlg.org
Heidi Boghosian, Executive Director
Ian Head, Administrative and Publications Man
Karen Jo Koonan, President
Edward Elder, Regional VP
Urszula Masny Latos, Executive Director
Dedicated to seeking economic justice, social equality and the right to political dissent.
5000 Members Founded: 1937

14271 National Legal Aid and Defender
1140 Connecticut Avenue NW
Washington, DC 20036
202-452-0620
FAX: 202-872-1031
info@nlada.org www.nlada.org
Harrison D McIver III, Chairperson
Leonard E Noisette, Vice Chairperson
Andrew J Steinberg, Treasurer
Ramon Arias, Board of Directors
Toby Rothschild, Board of Directors
Private, nonprofit association that dedicates all its resources to ensuring the availability of high quality legal assistance for the poor.
3500 Members Founded: 1911

14272 National Notary Association
9350 DeSoto Avenue
Chatsworth, CA 91311-2402
818-394-4000
FAX: 818-700-1830
hotline@nationalnotary.org
www.nationalnotary.org
Milton G Valera, President
Deborah M Thaw, Executive VP
Charles N Faerber, VP Notary Affairs
Tim Reiniger, Executive Director
Mark Valera, Managing Director
Supports all those involved in identity fraud and electronic notarization. Publishes newlsetter.
10000 Members Founded: 1957

14273 National Organizations of Bar Counsel
541 N Fairbanks Ct
Chicago, IL 60611-3314
312-988-5304
FAX: 312-988-5280
armitage@adbmich.org www.nobc.org
Mark A Armitage, President
G Fred Ours, Treasurer
Donald R Lundberg, Director
Association consists of attorneys who represent various bar associations.
Founded: 1965

14274 Native American Rights Fund
1506 Broadway Street
Boulder, CO 80302-6296
303-447-8760
FAX: 303-443-7776
pereira@narf.org www.narf.org
John E Echohawk, Executive Director
Mary LuProsser, Director Development
National legal defense fund. Provides legal services and technical assistance to Indian tribes, organizations and individuals in the areas of preservation of tribal existence, protection of tribal natural resources, promotion of human rights, accountability of governments and development of Indian law.
35000 Members Founded: 1971

14275 People Against Racist Terror
Po Box 1055
Culver City, CA 90232
FAX: 818-848-2680 part2001@usa.net
Michael Novick, Publisher
Association for those interested in anti-racist activism, research and education covering neo-nazi and other racist violence, efforts at conflict resolution and social justic reforms.

14276 Practising Law Institute
810 7th Avenue
New York, NY 10019-5818
212-245-5700
FAX: 212-265-4742 800-260-4754
info@pli.edu www.pli.edu
Victor Rubino, Executive Director
Nonprofit continuing legal education organization chartered by the Regents of the University of the State of New York. Dedicated to providing the legal community and allied professionals with the most up-to-date, revelant information and techniques which are critical to the development of a professional, competitive edge.
Founded: 1933

14277 Rocky Mountain Mineral Law Foundation
9191 Sheridan Boulevard
Suite 203
Denver, CO 80031
303-321-8100
FAX: 303-321-7657
info@rmmlf.org www.rmmlf.org
David Phillips, Executive Director
Mark Holland, Senior Attorney
2000 Members Founded: 1955

14278 Trial Lawyers Marketing
1 Boston Place
Suite 1260
Boston, MA 02108-4471
617-720-5356
FAX: 617-742-5417

James Sokolve, President

Provides education and marketing information to personal injury attorneys.
300 Members Founded: 1986

Newsletters

14279 ALA News
Association of Legal Administrators
75 Tri-State International
Suite 222
Lincolnshire, IL 60069-4435
847-267-1252
FAX: 847-267-1329
media@alanet.org
http://www.ala-gateway.org

David Constantine, President
Rosemary Shiels, Editor-in-Chief
Jay Srother, Publisher
Allison Lagorio, Senior Marketing Specialist
John Michalik, Executive Director

Member magazine focusing on association news and career improvements for administrators in the association. *$36.00*
40 pages Fortnightly Founded: 1971
Circulation: 9000 Controlled Est. Pass-Along Circ: 27000
Mailing list available for rent
Printed in 4 colors on glossy stock
Computerized version available

14280 ATLA Advocate
Association of Trial Lawyers of America
1050 31st Street NW
Washington, DC 20007-4499
202-965-3500
FAX: 202-965-0030 800-424-2725

Rebecca Porter, Editor
Jon Haver, CEO/President
Julie Shoop, Publisher
Filis Woods, Marketing

Keeps association members abreast of association news. Not available by subscription. No advertising or announcements. *$5.00*
Monthly
Printed in 2 colors

14281 Administrative & Regulatory Law News
American Bar Association
740 15th Street NW
8th Floor
Washington, DC 20005-1022
202-621-1000
FAX: 202-662-1669 funk@lclark.edu

William Funk, Editor

Newsletter for section members providing information about section activities and the practice of administrative law.
16 pages Quarterly
Circulation: 6000 Audited
Mailing list available for rent 6000 names
Printed in 2 colors on matte stock

14282 Administrative Judiciary News and Journal
American Bar Association
750 N Lake Shore Drive
Floor 7
Chicago, IL 60611-4497
312-988-5000
FAX: 312-988-6281
Newsletter about Conference activities, work of other organizations concerned with administrative law, and legislative updates on administrative law. *$11.00*
Quarterly

14283 Admiralty Law Newsletter
American Bar Association
750 N Lake Shore Drive
Floor 7
Chicago, IL 60611-4497
312-988-5000
FAX: 312-988-6281
Focuses on summaries of recent case law development, CLE programs in maritime law area, and information and articles on programs and projects. *$15.00*
SemiMonthly

14284 Air and Space Lawyer
American Bar Association
321 N Clark St.
Attn Publishin
Chicago, IL 60610-4497
312-988-5000
FAX: 312-988-6281 800-285-2221

Robert Stein, CEO
Monica Buckley, Marketing Manager

Newsletter of significant developments in the field of air and space law as well as reports of Forum Committee activities. *$40.00*
Bi-monthly Founded: 1878

14285 Allen's Trademark Digest
Congressional Digest Corporation
152413 29th Street NW
Washington, DC 20007-2756
202-333-7332
FAX: 202-625-6670 800-637-9915
ededitor@aol.com
www.trademarkdigest.com

Griff Thomas, President
Page Robinson, Publisher
Brooke Beyer, Editor

Monthly digest of citable and uncitable tradmark decisions issues by the US Patent and Trademark Office. *$695.00*
12 per year Founded: 1989

14286 Alternatives Newsletter
American Bar Association
750 N Lake Shore Drive
Floor 7
Chicago, IL 60611-4497
312-988-5000
FAX: 312-988-6281
Newsletter features editorials on the subject of Alternative Dispute Resolution, articles on young lawyers and ADR programs in operation, as well as Federal and State Case Law updates. *$12.00*

14287 American Association of Visually Impaired Attorneys
American Blind Lawyers Association
1155 15th Street NW
Suite 720
Washington, DC 20005-2706
202-467-5081
FAX: 202-467-5085 800-424-8666
info@acb.org www.acb.org

Gary Austin, President
Melanie Brunson, Executive Director

Audio
Circulation: 150

14288 American Corporate Counsel Association Newsletter
1025 Connecticut Avenue NW
Suite 200
Washington, DC 20036-5425
202-318-8327
FAX: 202-331-7454

Deneen Stambone, Editor

Association news.
16 pages Bi-Monthly
Circulation: 9,700
Printed in 2 colors on matte stock

14289 American Foreign Law Association Newsletter
Forman Law School
140 W 62nd Street
New York, NY 10023
212-636-6844
FAX: 212-636-6899

James Maxelner, Publisher

Reports on programs sponsored by the Association of American Foreign Law. *$20.00*
4 pages Monthly

14290 American Lawyers Newspapers Group
1730 M Street NW
Suite 802
Washington, DC 20036-4513
202-457-0686
FAX: 202-457-0718

Ted Goldman, Manager

Supports all those involved in the reporting of legal issues.
Founded: 1977

14291 American Notary
American Society of Notaries
PO Box 5707
Tallahassee, FL 32314
850-671-5164
FAX: 850-671-5165 800-522-3392
mail@notaries.org www.notaries.org

Lisa K Fisher, Publisher
Joanna Lilly, Editor

Legislation news. *$21.00*
20 pages Quarterly
Circulation: 21000
Printed in 4 colors on glossy stock

14292 American Polygraph Association Newsletter and Polygraph Journal
PO Box 8037
Chattanooga, TN 37414
423-892-3992
FAX: 423-894-5435 800-272-8037

Stuart Senter, Editor
Jack Siconsigly, CEO
Robbie Bennett, Manager

Publishes information on polygraph activities, training, cases, meetings, seminars, laws, legislations, in the United States and abroad. Lists schools accredited by APA under USDOE programs. Provides news of APA state association affiliates and some information on foreign polygraph use and training. Also provides information on new instruments and techniques. *$80.00*
Founded: 1966
Circulation: 2000 Audited Est. Pass-Along Circ: 4000 2,800 names

14293 American Society of International Law Newsletter
2223 Massachusetts Avenue NW
Washington, DC 20008-2847
202-939-6005
FAX: 202-797-7133

Sandra Liebel, Publisher
Charlotte Ku, Executive Director

Association news and updates on overseas litigation.
6 pages Monthly

14294 Antitrust and Trade Regulation Report
Bureau of National Affairs
1231 25th Street NW
Washington, DC 20037-1197
202-452-4200
800-372-1033
customercare@bna.com www.bna.com

Gregory C McCaffery, Publisher
Sheldon B Richman, Managing Editor

Weekly comprehensive coverage of significant competition and deceptive trade practice law developments on the federal, state and international levels. *$1894.00*
Weekly

14295 Arson Reporter: Arson Legislation
American Bar Association
750 N Lake Shore Drive
Floor 7
Chicago, IL 60611-4497
312-988-5000
FAX: 312-988-6281

Reports on court decisions pertaining to arson and legislation at both the state and national level. *$16.00*
Monthly

14296 Attorneys Marketing Report
James Publishing
3505 Cadillac Avenue
Suite H
Costa Mesa, CA 92626-1430
714-755-5450
FAX: 714-556-4133

Kathy McCoy, Publisher
Linda Standke, Editor

The latest practice development tips and news for law firms from Yellow Pages advertising to referral management.

14297 BNA's Bankruptcy Law Reporter
Bureau of National Affairs
1231 25th Street NW
Washington, DC 20037-1197
202-452-4200
800-372-1033
customercare@bna.com www.bna.com

Gregory C McCaffery, Publisher
Mike Moore, Managing Editor

Weekly notification service covering various areas of bankruptcy law. *$1331.00*
Weekly

14298 BNA's Corporate Counsel Weekly Corporate Practice Series
Bureau of National Affairs
1231 25th Street NW
Washington, DC 20037-1197
202-452-4200
800-372-1033
customercare@bna.com www.bna.com

Gregory C McCaffery, Publisher
Michael J Brady, Managing Editor

A weekly roundup of the latest developments in law that affect business, including coverage of the courts, federal regulatory agencies, the executive branch, states and professional associations. *$722.00*
8 pages Weekly
Printed in 1 color on matte stock

14299 BNA's Medicare Report
Bureau of National Affairs
1231 25th Street NW
Washington, DC 20037-1197
202-452-4200
800-372-1033
customercare@bna.com www.bna.com

Gregory C McCaffery, Publisher
Lisa M Rockelli, Managing Editor

Biweekly notification service covering legislative, regulatory and legal developments affecting or pertaining to the Medicare program; also provides information about relevant developments in the Medicaid program that could have implications for Medicare.
$1108.00
Weekly

14300 Bankruptcy Court Decisions
LRP Publications
747 Dresher Road
Suite 500
Horsham, PA 19044-2247
215-840-0912
FAX: 215-784-9639 800-341-7874
custservice@lrp.com
http://www.lrp.com

Joe Fraracci, Editor
Kenneth Khan, CEO

Full-text loose leaf bankruptcy reporting service with an expanded and informative newsletter. *$900.00*
Founded: 1977
Mailing list available for rent
Printed in 1 color on matte stock

14301 Bankruptcy Law Letter
West Group
610 Opperman Drive
Essay-27077
Eagan, MN 55123-1340
651-687-7000
FAX: 800-316-9378 800-328-9352

Charles Tabb, Editor
Peter Warwick, CEO
Michael Suchsland, General Manager
John B. West, Founder Director
William Houston Brown, Author

Highly specialized coverage of case developments in the bankruptcy field. No outside submissions accepted. *$50.00*
Monthly Founded: 1872
Circulation: 3000

14302 Biotechnology Law Report
Mary Ann Liebert
2 Madison Avenue
Larchmont, NY 10538
914-343-3207
FAX: 914-834-3688 800-6 5-3 23

Mary Ann Liebert, President
Gerry J Elman, Editor
Mary Ann Liebert, Publisher
Harry Matisco, Marketing

Legislative news for the world of biotechnology and science. *$1858.00*
96 pages Founded: 1980

14303 Bulletin of Law, Science and Technology
American Bar Association
750 N Lake Shore Drive
Floor 7
Chicago, IL 60611-4497
312-988-5000
FAX: 312-988-6281

News of Section activities, timely developments in the areas of science and technology, and related legal issues and court decisions.

14304 Business Crime: Criminal Liability of the Business Community
Matthew Bender and Company
11 Penn Plaza
New York, NY 10001-2006
212-448-2000
FAX: 212-244-3188

The most complete guide to the many criminal questions that can arise in modern business practice.

14305 Business Information Alert
Alert Publications
401 W Fullerton Parkway
Suite 1403E
Chicago, IL 60614-2801
773-525-7594
FAX: 773-525-7015 866-492-5266
info@alertpub.com
http://www.alertpub.com/

Donna T Heroy, Publisher/Editor
Nina Wendt, Director Marketing

Newsletter for business and law librarians to help them make purchasing decisions for their companies. Includes product reviews and columns on industry news. Discounted price of $99 for non-profit organizations.
$167.00
12 pages Founded: 1981 1.2M names

14306 Business Lawyer Update
American Bar Association
321 North Clark Street
Chicago, IL 60610
312-988-5000
FAX: 312-988-6281

Newsletter on Section activities and recent developments in business and banking law.
Founded: 1878

14307 CLE Guidebook
Law Bulletin Publishing Company
415 N State Street
Chicago, IL 60610-4674
312-644-7800
FAX: 312-644-4255
http://www.lawbulletin.com

Bernard M Judge, Editor
Bernard M Judge, Publisher
Michael Loquercio, Sales Manager
David Loew, President

Lists hundreds of CLE courses by date, subject and provider. *$219.00*
34 pages
Printed in 4 colors on matte stock

14308 Change Exchange: Newsletter of Reduction of Litigation Cost/Delay
American Bar Association
321 north clarck
Floor 7
Chicago, IL 60610-4497
312-988-5000
FAX: 312-988-6281 800-285-2221

Robert Stien, CEO, Marketing

Newsletter on cost and delay reduction programs from state courts. *$14.00*
Quarterly

14309 Chapter 11 Update
Federal Managers Association
1641 Prince Street
Alexandria, VA 22314
703-683-8700
FAX: 703-683-8707
info@fedmanagers.org
http://www.fedmanagers.org
Management issues and concerns.

Monthly

14310 Child Advocacy and Protection Newsletter
American Bar Association
321 N Clark St.
Mailroom
Chicago, IL 60610-4497
312-988-5000
FAX: 312-988-6281
http://www.abanet.org
Robert Stein, CEO
Includes articles on children's rights, information on current services and resources.

14311 Child Protection Report
Business Publishers
8737 Colesville Road
10th floor
Silver Spring, MD 20910-3928
301-587-6300
FAX: 301-587-4530 800-274-6737
bpinews@bpinews.com
http://www.bpinews.com
Quintin Chatman, Editor
Beth Early, Operations Director
Adam Goldstein, Publisher
Marjorie Weiner, Marketing
Pat Maness, Circulation Manager
Reports on changes in legislation, funding and policies affecting children's programs. Tracks federal and state court rulings, new grant and contract opportunities, conferences and resources, and model programs affecting children. *$241.00*
Monthly Founded: 1963

14312 Child Support Prosecutors' Bulletin
Center on Children and the Law
740 15th Street NW
Washington, DC 20005-1019
202-662-1720
FAX: 202-662-1755
ctrchildlaw@abanet.org
http://www.abanet.org/child
Claire Sandt, Editor
Haward Davidson, CEO
Claire Sandt, Publisher
Sally Small Inada, Circulation Manager
Eight-page newsletter focusing on child support prosecutors' best practices and procedures, innovative legislation, and legal issues which arise in the establishment and enforcement of child support litigations. *$219.00*
Weekly Founded: 1975
Circulation: 900

14313 China Law for Foreign Business-Business Regulation
American Bar Association
750 N Lake Shore Drive, 7th Floor
International Law and Practice Sect
Chicago, IL 60611-4497
312-988-5000
FAX: 312-988-6281
Practical journal on issues facing lawyers and scholars who deal with business and law in the People's Republic of China. *$50.00*
Quarterly

14314 Civil RICO Report
LRP Publications
360 Hiatt Drive
Palm Beach Gardens
Florida, FL 33418
561-622-6520
FAX: 561-622-0757 800-341-7874
Thomas G Shack Jr, Publisher
Robert K Latzko, Editor
Weekly report and analysis of litigation under the civil provisions of the Racketeer Influenced and Corrupt Organizations Act as well as legislative developments and state little RICO laws. *$812.00*

Printed in 2 colors on matte stock

14315 Client Counseling Update
American Bar Association
321 North Clark Street
Chicago, IL 60610-4497
312-988-5000
FAX: 312-988-6281 800-526-4902
service@abanet.org
http://www.abanet.org
Robert J Grey, Jr., President
Newsletter contains summaries of publications and news articles concerning client counseling. *$6.00*
Founded: 1878

14316 Collective Bargaining Negotiations and Contracts
Bureau of National Affairs
1231 25th Street NW
Washington, DC 20037-1197
202-452-4200
800-372-1033
customercare@bna.com
http://www.bna.com
Gregory C McCaffery, Publisher
Heather Bodell, Managing Editor
A biweekly notificaiton and reference service containing information designed to help unions and management prepare, negotiate and administer contracts. *$1541.00*

Monthly Founded: 1929

14317 Commercial Law Bulletin
Commercial Law League of America
70 E Lake Street
Suite 630
Chicago, IL 60601-7254
312-781-2000
FAX: 312-781-2010 800-978-2552
info@clla.org http://www.clla.org/
David Watson, Executive VP/editor
Erica Henry, Administrative Director
Provides news and information on bankruptcy, collections, debt and insolvency information, as well as reports from Washington DC and updates on resolutions. *$65.00*
Founded: 1895
Circulation: 5000 3600 names $150 per M.

14318 Commercial Laws of the World
Foreign Tax Law
PO Box 2189
Ormond Beach, FL 32175-2189
386-341-7405

ftlp@foreignlaw.com
http://www.foreignlaw.com
Contains company laws, commercial codes, and related law for over 100 countries. *$100.00*
: int. cdrom

14319 Communications Lawyer
American Bar Association
321 North Coark Street
Chicago, IL 60610-4497
312-988-5000
FAX: 312-988-6281
service@abanet.org
http://www.abanet.org
Janet Gibbs, CEO
Danniel Kim, Editor/Publisher
Diane Vrouhl, Circulation Manager
Newsletter reviews significant activities and developments in communications law and reports on Forum activities. *$45.00*
Quarterly Founded: 1878

14320 Computer & Internet LAWCAST
Vox Juris
PO Box 389
Pennington, NJ 08534
609-737-6543
FAX: 609-737-3860 800-LAW-CAST
INFO@lawcast.com
www.lawcast.com
Jason Meyer, Publisher
Groundbreaking law arising from life and commerce in the digital age...in licensing, torts, intellectual property securities, contracts, privacy, joint ventures, antitrust, content regulation and more. If your clients use email or the internet, have their own websites, produce hardware or software or provide on-line service, listen up here. 60 minute audio and outline twice monthly *$25.00*

14321 Computer Industry Litigation Reporter
Andrews Publications
175 Strafford Avenue
Building 4 Suite 140
Wayne, PA 19087
610-225-0510
FAX: 610-225-0501 800-345-1101
donna.higgins@andrewspub.com
http://www.andrewspub.com
Donna Higgins, Editor
Mary Ellen Fox, Publisher
Jodine Mayberry, Executive Editor
Covers litigation involving copyright, patent, trade secrets, employment, securities, trademark, contracts and other issues related to the computer industry. *$1226.00*
Founded: 1983

14322 Construction Claims Monthly
Business Publishers
8737 Colesville Road
10th floor
Silver Spring, MD 20910-3928
301-587-6300
FAX: 301-587-1081 800-274-6737
bpinews@bpinews.com
http://www.bpinews.com
Adam Goldstein, Publisher
Marjorie Wiener, Marketing
Marjorie Wiener, Circulation Manager
Bruce Jervis, Editor
Adam Goldstein, CEO/President
Contains summaries of important decisions from the federal and state courts, boards of contract appeals, and the Office of Comptroller General on such topics as change orders, design problems, inspection, delay, home office overhead, claims administration, termination, waivers, differing site conditions, subcontractors and insurance. *$244.00*
8 pages Monthly Founded: 1962

14323 Construction Lawyer
American Bar Association
321 North Clark Street
Chicago, IL 60610
312-988-5000
FAX: 312-988-6281 800-285-2221
service@abanet.org
http://www.abanet.org/

Thomas J Campbell, Staff Editor
Charles M Sink, Editor-in-Chief
Robert J. Grey, Jr., CEO/President

Newsletter containing articles on recent developments in the construction industry as well as announcements pertaining to the Forum Committee or to other organizations in the field. *$40.00*

Quarterly Founded: 1879

14324 Construction Litigation Reporter
McGraw Hill
1221 Avenue of the Americas
New York, NY 10020
212-512-2000
800-352-3566

March Schneier, Publisher

Summaries of judicial and agency decisions. *$300.00*

24 pages Monthly

14325 Consumer Financial Services Law Report
LRP Publications
747 Dresher Road
Suite 500
Horsham, PA 19044
215-840-0912
FAX: 215-784-9639 800-341-7874
custserve@lrp.com
http://www.lrp.com/

Julie Kline, Editor
Kenneth Kahn, President

Keeps you up-to-date with the latest changes and developments in the area of consumer financial services litigation. Provides timely coverage of legal developments involving fair lending, debt collection, state UDAP laws and fraud, automobile lending and leasing, damage theories and class actions, and more. *$220.00*

Founded: 1977

14326 Consumer Product Litigation Reporter
Andrews Publications
175 Strafford Avenue
Building 4, Suite 140
Wayne, PA 19087-3331
610-225-0510
FAX: 610-225-0501 800-345-1101
editor@andrewspub.com
http://www.andrewspub.com

Robert Maroldo, Publisher
Eileen Gonyeau, Editor

Covers areas such as strict liability, assumption of risk, insurance coverage, adequacy of warning merchantability, punitive damages, component liability, forseeability and more. *$46.00*

14327 Controlling Law Firm Costs
Institute of Management & Administration

parrt avenue 30th floor
5th Floor
New York, NY 10016-2299
212-244-0360
FAX: 212-564-0465
subserve@ioma.com
http://www.ioma.com

John Curcott, CEO
Perry Paterson, Editor
Perry Paterson, Publisher
Jim Bell, Marketing Manager
Taul Morris, Circulation Manager

Shows law office administrators how to reduce overhead, improve the firm's profitability and efficiency, get more value for the firm's budget dollar, and improve their own professional standing. Includes strategies to control the costs of support staff, insurance, leases, taxes, computers and more. *$300.00*

Annual+

14328 Corporate Counsel LAWCAST
Vox Juris
PO Box 389
Pennington, NJ 08534
609-737-6543
FAX: 609-737-3860 800-LAW-CAST
INFO@lawcast.com www.lawcast.com

Jason Meyer, Publisher

Everything for the in-house counsel in one lively and substantive program. In-house ethics and privileges, the law of the workplace, intellectual property, corporate governance, contracts, regulations, and more...close-ups on how top counsel meet the demands of the in-house practice. 75 minute audio and online, 15 times per year *$25.00*

14329 Corporate Legal Times
Corporate Legal Times
656 West Randolph Street
Suite 500 East
Chicago, IL 60611
312-654-3500
FAX: 312-654-3525
info@cltmag.com
http://www.cltmag.com

Nat Slavin, Publisher
Larry Lannon, Chief Executive Officer

Written for general counsel and other in house corporate attourneys to provide information relevant to strategic planning and day-to-day operation of legal departments including in-house counsel's relationships with outside law firms. *$10.00*

Monthly Founded: 1991
Circulation: 40000

14330 Corporate Practice Series
Bureau of National Affairs
1231
25th Street NW
Washington, DC 20037-1197
202-452-4200
800-372-1033
customercare@bna.com
http://ww.bna.com

Gregory C McCaffery, Publisher
Michael J Brady, Managing Editor

A corporate law reference service organized into a series of portfolios written by legal experts, with a weekly newsletter. Each portfolio covers a different legal subject with detailed analyses, working papers and a bibliography. *$2426.00*

14331 Criminal Law Reporter
Bureau of National Affairs
1231 25th Street NW
Washington, DC 20037-1197
202-452-4200
800-372-1033
customercare@bna.com
http://www.bna.com/

Gregory C McCaffery, Publisher
Hugh Kaplan, Managing Editor

A weekly notification service providing coverage of court decisions, federal legislative activities and administrative developments in the field of criminal law. Fulltext of the cases highlighted in each issue are available free on CrL's web site. Subscribers can also recieve free email notification of Supreme Court decisions. *$1108.00*

Weekly Founded: 1929

14332 DataLaw Report
Clark Boardman Company
155 Pflingsten Road
Deerfield, IL 60015
847-374-0400
FAX: 847-948-7099

Amelia Boss, Editor

Analyzes the changing global legal environment for electronic information.

14333 Death Care Business Advisor
LRP Publications
747 Dresher Road
PO Box 980
Horsham, PA 19044-980
215-784-0912
FAX: 215-784-9639 800-341-7874
custserve@lrp.com
http://www.lrp.com

Jay Kravetz, Editor
Dionne Ellis, Managing Editor

The only twice a month newsletter that offers you in-depth business coverage of memorialization and remembrance issues. You'll recieve news and tips on the latest trends and developments in funeral service, cemetery management and cremation and learn innovative strategies to capture the expanding preneed market and more. *$215.00*

Founded: 1977

14334 Digest of Environmental Law
Strafford Publications
590 Dutch Valley Road NE
Postal Drawer 13729
Atlanta, GA 30324-729
404-881-1141
FAX: 404-881-0074 800-926-7926
custserv@staffordpub.com
http://www.straffordpub.com

Richard Ossoff, Publisher
Jennifer Vaughan, Managing Editor

Monthly digest of nationally significant litigation related to the full range of environmental issues, includes annual index. *$ 547.00*

Monthly Founded: 1984

14335 Disability Compliance for Higher Education
LRP Publications
747 Dresher Road
PO Box 980
Horsham, PA 19044-980
215-784-0912
FAX: 561-622-2423 800-341-7874
custserve@lrp.com
http://www.lrp.com

Marsha Jaquays, Editor
Nancy Grover, Managing Editor

Helps colleges determine if they are complying with the Americans with Disabilities Act (ADA) and section 504 of the Rehabilitation Act. Readers find out how to fulfill legal obligations under the law and save their college from costly litigation. *$198.00*

Monthly Founded: 1977

14336 Dispute Resolution
American Bar Association
321 N CLARK ST
Chicago, IL 60610-4497
312-988-5000
FAX: 312-988-5177
http://www.abanet.org

Professor Fr Sander, Editor
Robert Grey, Jr, President

Compilation of news and updates on events in the field of alternative dispute resolution. *$30.00*

Quarterly Founded: 1978

14337 Document Assembly and Practice Systems Report
American Bar Association
750 N Lake Shore Drive
Floor 7
Chicago, IL 60611-4497
312-988-5000
FAX: 312-988-6281

In addition to document assembly, this newsletter focuses on uses for expert systems, hypertext and other systems that automate substantive practice areas. *$53.00*

Quarterly

14338 ELA Notes
Education Law Association
300 College Park Avenue
Dayton, OH 45469
937-229-3589
FAX: 937-229-3845
ela@educationlaw.org
http://www.educationlaw.org

Mandy Schrank, Executive Director
Jody Thornburg, Publications Editor

ELA is a nonprofit, nonadvocacy, member-based organization found in 1954 to provide an unbiased forum for the dissemination of information about current issues in education law. Membership is open to all individuals and organizations with a special interest in education law. ELA's mission is to bring together educational and legal scholars and practioners to inform and advance educational policy and practice through knowledge of the law. *$125.00*

Quarterly Founded: 1954
Circulation: 1300 1400 names $600 per M.
Printed in 2 colors on matte stock

14339 Employee Benefits Cases
Bureau of National Affairs
1231 25th Street NW
Washington, DC 20037-1197
202-452-4200
800-372-1033
customercare@bna.com
http://www.bna.com

Gregory C McCaffery, Publisher
Sarah Stevens, Managing Editor
Dallas Salisbury, President

A weekly decisional service that reports the full text of federal and state court opinions and selected decisions of arbitrators and the NLRB on employee benefits issues. *$1582.00*

54 pages Weekly Founded: 1929
Circulation: 6000+
Printed in on matte stock

14340 Employment & Labor LAWCAST
Vox Juris
PO Box 389
Pennington, NJ 08534
609-737-6543
FAX: 609-737-3860 180- 52- 227
info@lawcast.com
http://www.lawcast.com

Jason Meyer, Publisher
David Weisenfeld, CEO/President

The newest law and what leading lawyers are doing with it; tips and techniques to strengthen your practice. Our unbiased comprehensive coverage is the favorite of both the plaintiffs' employment bar - and of lawyers in the biggest management firms. 60 minute audio and outline, twice monthly. *$25.00*

14341 Employment Law Report Strategist
Data Research
PO Box 490
Rosemount, MN 55068-0490
952-452-8694
FAX: 952-452-8694 800-365-4900

Covers the latest court cases and late-breaking legislation along with the most recent law review articles affecting employment. *$120.00*

Monthly

14342 Entertainment Law and Finance
345 Park Avenue S
New York, NY 10010-1707
212-779-6611
FAX: 212-696-1848 800-888-8300

Stan Soocher, Editor
Stuart M Wise, Production Manager
Kerry Kyle, Circulation Director

Laws and news in the entertainment field. *$195.00*

8 pages Monthly
Printed in 2 colors
Computerized version available

14343 Entertainment and Sports Lawyer
American Bar Association
321 North Clark Street
Floor 7
Chicago, IL 60610-4497
312-988-5000
FAX: 312-988-6281 800-285-2221
askaba@abanet.org
http://www.abanet.org

Robert G Pimm, Editor
Ray DeLong, Staff Editor

Newsletter on recent developments in the sports and entertainment industries. *$60.00*

Quarterly

14344 Environmental Law
American Bar Association
740 15th Street NW
Washington, DC 20005-1019
202-662-1000
FAX: 202-638-3844 800-285-2221
askaba@aba.net.org
http://www.abanet.org

Elissa Lichtenstein, Publisher
Anne Dunn, Editor

Law and news for the environment featuring articles on current, emerging issues and ABA environmental law activities. *$79.95*

Founded: 1879
Circulation: 6200

14345 Estate Planner's Alert
Research Institute of America
50 Broad Street
Rochester, NY 14594
716-327-2005
FAX: 716-424-5737 800-431-9025
customer-service@riag.com
http://www.riahome.com

Carl Hovgard, Founder

Offers complete coverage of estate planning and law. *$195.00*

Monthly Founded: 1935

14346 Exercise Standards and Malpractice Reporter
PRC Publishing
3976 Fulton Drive NW
Canton, OH 44718-3043
330-492-6063
FAX: 330-492-6176 800-336-0083
prc4926063@aol.com
http://prcpublishingcorp.com

David Herbert, President
Molly Romig, VP
Dr. Doyice Cotton, Publisher
Mary Cotton, Publisher

Designed to cover topics of interest and concern to the exercise professionals. *$39.95*

16 pages Founded: 1997
Circulation: 750
Printed in 2 colors on matte stock

14347 FCBA Newsletter
Federal Communications Bar Association
1020 19th Street NW
Suite 325
Washington, DC 20036-6113
202-293-4000
FAX: 202-293-4317
fcba@fcba.org http://www.fcba.org

Stanley Zenor, Executive Director
Heidi Kurtz, Deputy Director

A non-profit organization of attorneys and other professionals involved in the development, interpretation, implementation and practice of communications law and policy.

Monthly Founded: 1936

14348 Faculty Briefing: A Newsletter for Law Teachers
American Bar Association
750 N Lake Shore Drive
Floor 7
Chicago, IL 60611-4497
312-988-5000

Provides information on ABA programs and resources of special interest to law school teachers.

BiWeekly

14349 Family Law Reporter
Bureau of National Affairs
1231 25th Street NW
Washington, DC 20037-1197
202-452-4200
800-372-1033
customercare@bna.com
http://www.bna.com

Gregory C McCaffery, Publisher
David B Jackson, Managing Editor

A weekly notification and reference service dealing with all significant state and federal developments in the field of family law. *$974.00*

Weekly Founded: 1929

14350 Federal Contract Disputes
Business Publishers
8737 Colesville Road
Suite 1100
Silver Spring, MD 20910-3928
301-587-6300
FAX: 301-587-4530 800-274-6737
bpinews@bpinews.com
www.bpinews.com

Leonard A Eiserer, Publisher
Beth Early, Operations Director

A monthly newsletter designed to help you avoid disputes, and successfully resolve those you can't avoid. Each issue brings you concise synopses of a dozen major decisions, from the courts, the Comptroller

General, and the boards of contract appeals. *$285.00*
Monthly

14351 Federal Contracts Report
Bureau of National Affairs
1231 25th Street NW
Washington, DC 20037-1197
202-452-4200
800-372-1033
customercare@bna.com
http://www.bna.com
Gregory C McCaffery, Publisher
Martha Matthews, Managing Editor
A weekly reporting service providing comprehensive coverage of the latest significant developments affecting federal contracts and grants. *$1887.00*
Weekly Founded: 1929

14352 Federal Discovery News
LRP Publications
747 Dresher Road
PO Box 980
Horsham, PA 19044-980
215-784-0912
FAX: 215-784-9639 800-341-7874
custserve@lrp.com
http://www.lrp.com
John Massaro, Editor
Dionne Ellis, Managing Editor
Each issue covers the whole realm of pretrial case management and discovery, especially the impact of the new civil procedure rules on discovery in federal cases. Provides a timely review of how district developments pertain to your practice. *$275.00*
Monthly Founded: 1977

14353 Federal EEO Advisor
LRP Publications
747 Dresher Road
PO Box 980
Horsham, PA 19044-980
215-784-0912
FAX: 215-784-9639 800-341-7874
custserve@lrp.com
http://www.lrp.com
Allison Uehling, Editor
Clarrisa Spasyk, Staff Writer
One-of-a-kind publication provides readers with essential tips, strategies and news about the constanly changing EEO profession. Each issue includes insightful coverage on topics such as: details on major developments and trends in federal EEO; tips on how to accomplish specific objectives within the EEO program; synopses of decisions by the EEOC and related courts, etc. *$220.00*
Monthly Founded: 1977

14354 Federal Human Resources Week
LRP Publications
747 Dresher Road Suite 500
PO Box 980
Horsham, PA 19044
215-840-0912
FAX: 215-784-9639 800-341-7874
custserve@lrp.com
http://www.feds.com
Daniel J Gephart, Editorial Director
Julie Davidson, Managing Editor
Kathleen Filipczyk, Staff Writer
Federal Human Resources Week helps you stay on top of changes affecting you and your workplace. This revolutionary resource enables you to experience each major development as it occurs. *$365.00*
12 pages Weekly Founded: 1977
Printed in 2 colors on matte stock

14355 Federal Trial News
American Bar Association
750 N Lake Shore Drive
Floor 7
Chicago, IL 60611-4497
312-988-5000
FAX: 312-988-6281
Newsletter provides information to members on Conference activities.

14356 Financial Management Newsletter
Association of Legal Administrators
75 Tri-State International
Suite 222
Lincolnshire, IL 60069-4435
847-267-1252
FAX: 847-267-1329
webmaster@alanet.org
http://www.alanet.org
Jay Strother, Publisher
David P Constantine, President
8 pages Monthly Founded: 1971

14357 Forum
Federal Bar Association
2215 M Street NW
Washington, DC 20037-1483
202-785-1614
FAX: 202-785-1568
fba@fedbar.org http://www.fedbar.org
Thomas R Schuck, President
William N LaForge, VP
A forum for the exchange of ideas, news, updates, and cases for lawyers. *$35.00*
8 pages Monthly Founded: 1924

14358 General Aviation Accident Report
Andrews Communications
175 Stafford Street Building 4
Suite 140
Wayne, PA 19087
610-225-0510
FAX: 610-225-0501 800-345-1101
nick.sullivan@thomson.com
http://www.andrewsonline.com/
Thomson West, Publisher
Nick Sullivan, Editor
General aviation laws. *$99.00*
20 pages Founded: 1872

14359 HRFocus
Institute of Management & Administration
29 W 35th Street
5th Floor
New York, NY 10001-2299
212-244-0360
FAX: 212-564-0465
subserve@ioma.com
http://www.ioma.com
Sue Sandler, Editor
John Turcott, CEO
Covers a variety of HR legal issues, such as avoiding wrongful termination lawsuits, employee handbook language, hot to handle performance reviews, how to set workplace standards and policies that are legal and fair. *$259.00*
Monthly Founded: 1982

14360 Hastings Communications & Entertainment Law Journal
Hastings College of Law
200 McAllister Street
2nd Floor, Room 213
San Francisco, CA 94102-4978
415-654-4600
FAX: 415-565-4863
mailto:traynume@uchastings.edu
http://www.uchastings.edu
Albert Kaba, Public Advertising D
Karen Gibbs, Editor
Mary Kay Kane, Manager
Specializing in a host of legal issues generally grouped under the rubric of communications and entertainment law. Focuses on, but is not limited to, telecommunications, broadcasting, cable and other non-broadcast video, and the print media. *$7.00*
Monthly Founded: 1878
Circulation: 1300

14361 Health Law Week
Strafford Publications
590 Dutch Valley Road NE
Postal Drawer 13729
Atlanta, GA 30324-729
404-881-1141
FAX: 404-881-0074 800-926-7926
custserv@straffordpub.com
http://www.straffordpub.com
Jennifer Vaughan, Executive Editor
Richard Ossoff, President
Case digest of judicial decision affecting all aspects of health care operations. Topics covered include AIPS abortion antitrust, drugs, ERISA, expert testimony, informed consent, amd much more. *$1397.00*
Weekly Founded: 1984
Mailing list available for rent 25M names

14362 Health Lawyer
American Bar Association
321 N Clark street
Chicago, IL 60610
312-988-5000
FAX: 312-988-5528 800-285-2221
askabanet@abanet.org
http://www.abanet.org
Marla Durben Hirsch, Editor
Robert Grey, CEO
Scholarly newsletter on current legal trends in health law; also reports on Forum Committee activities. *$60.00*
Founded: 1878

14363 Hospital Litigation Reporter
Strafford Publications
590 Dutch Valley Road NE
Postal Drawer 13729
Atlanta, GA 30324-729
404-881-1141
FAX: 404-881-0074 800-926-7926
custserv@straffordpub.com
http://www.straffordpub.com
Richard Ossoff, Publisher
Jennifer Vaughan, Editor
Monthly digest of judicial decisions that concern or affect the hospital environment. Cases are screened and selected to provide concise, comprehensive coverage of issues important to hospital attorneys and administrators. *$397.00*
18 pages Monthly Founded: 1984
Mailing list available for rent 11M names
Printed in 1 color

14364 Human Resources Report
Bureau of National Affairs
1231 25th Street NW
Washington, DC 20037-1197
202-452-4200
800-372-1033
customercare@bna.com
http://www.bna.com
Gregory C McCaffery, Publisher
Gail Moorstein, Managing Editor
Covers current developments in every area of human resources; includes in-depth analysis of important events, developments or trends affecting human resource professionals. *$1140.00*

28 pages Weekly Founded: 1929
Printed in 1 color on matte stock

14365 IOMA's Report on Controlling Law Firm Costs
Institute of Management & Administration
3 Park Avenue
30th Floor
New York, NY 10016
212-244-0360
FAX: 212-564-0465
subserve@ioma.com
http://www.ioma.com
Ann Podolske, Editor
Lee Rath, Publisher
Information to control costs of law firms management. *$175.00*
12 pages Monthly

14366 IPC Report
American Bar Association
750 N Lake Shore Drive
Floor 7
Chicago, IL 60611-4497
312-988-5000
FAX: 312-988-6281
Newsletter of the International Procurement Committee of the Public Contract Law Section, deals with questions involving public contracts in countries other than the United States. *$18.00*
Quarterly

14367 IR&R News Report
American Bar Association
321 North Clark Street
Floor 7
Chicago, IL 60610-4497
312-988-5000
FAX: 312-988-6281 800-285-2221
abajournal@abanet.org
http://www.abanet.org
Newsletter reports on ABA resolutions and policy matters by the Individual Rights and Responsibilities Section. *$2.00*

Circulation: 6000

14368 Individual Employment Rights
Bureau of National Affairs
1231 25th Street NW
Washington, DC 20037-1197
202-452-4200
800-372-1033
customercare@bna.com
http://www.bna.com
Gregory C McCaffery, Publisher
Kim Hunter, Managing Editor
Case reference and notification on individual employment rights issues including employment at will, privacy, polygraph testing, and other employee rights issues outside the traditional labor-management relations context. *$1227.00*
Monthly Founded: 1929

14369 Intellectual Property LAWCAST
Vox Juris
PO Box 389
Pennington, NJ 08534-389
609-737-6543
FAX: 609-737-3860
INFO@lawcast.com
http://www.lawcast.com
Jason Meyer, Publisher
US legal news in patents, trademarks, copyrights, trade secrets, unfair trade, etc. including comprehensive coverage of PTO policies and a regular Listening Post on legal issues in the digital age. The buzz for thousands of IP lawyers, nationwide. 60 minute audio and online, twice monthly. *$488.00*

14370 Intellectual Property Law Review
Clark Boardman Company
375 Hudson Street
Room 201
New York, NY 10014-3685
585-546-5530
800-323-1336
David Doughty, Publisher
Compilation of the best law review articles.
Monthly Founded: 1916

14371 Intellectual Property Litigation Reporter
Andrews Publications
175 Strafford Avenue
Building 4 Suite 140
Wayne, PA 19087-3331
610-225-0510
FAX: 610-225-0501 800-345-1101
editor@andrewspub.com
http://www.andrewspub.com
Robert Maroldo, Publisher
Jodine Mayberry, Editor
Covers litigation and regulation of intellectual property issues including patents, copyrights, and tradeworks. *$83.00*

14372 Intellectual Property Today
Omega Communications
29 E Maryland St.
Indianapolis, IN 46204-7258
317-264-4010
FAX: 317-264-4020
planet@iptoday.com
http://www.omegac.com
Douglas Dean, Editor
Steve Barnes, Advertising Sales
Emphasizes developments in leading edge technology, including multimedia, genetic engineering and computer software, and how they effect disciplines of law. *$96.00*
Monthly Founded: 1971
Circulation: 20000

14373 Inter-American Bar Association Newsletter
1211 Connecticut Avenue, NW
Suite 202
Washington, DC 20036
202-466-5944
FAX: 202-466-5946
iaba@iaba.org www.iaba.org
Harry Inman, Manager *$60.00*
Quarterly

14374 International Law News
American Bar Association
321 North Clark Street
Chicago, IL 60610
312-988-5000
FAX: 312-988-6281
askaba@abanet.org
http://www.abanet.org/
Robert J. Grey Jr., President
Whitney Ward, Staff Editor
Newsletter reports on Committee activities and other current matters of interest to Section members.
Quarterly Founded: 1879
Circulation: 15000

14375 Internet Lawyer
GoAhead Productions
123 7th Avenue
#137
Brooklyn, NY 11215-1301
718-399-6136
FAX: 718-499-6039
editor@internetlawyer.com
http://www.internetlawyer.com
Tatia L Gordon-Troy, Editor-in-Chief
Christopher Eddings, Publisher
Gives legal advice and examines how to use the Net for research, marketing and communications purposes. Includes book reviews as well as information on current law office technology. *$149.00*
Monthly

14376 Iolta Update
American Bar Association
541 Fairbanks Court
Chicago, IL 60611-4497
312-988-5000
FAX: 312-988-6281 www.abanet.org
Robert Grey Jr., President
Discusses trends in lawyers' trust accounts nationwide.
Quarterly Founded: 1878

14377 JAD News
American Bar Association
321 North Clark Street
Floor 7
Chicago, IL 60611-4714
312-988-5000
FAX: 312-988-6281
http://www.abanet.org
Robert Grey Jr., President
Timothy Brandhorst, Editor
Catherine Kruse, Marketing Manager
A tabloid type newspaper published after ABA midyear and annual meetings featuring stories about JAD programs, policy developments and human interest matters.
Monthly Founded: 1878

14378 Labor Arbitration and Dispute Settlements
Bureau of National Affairs
1231 25th Street NW
Washington, DC 20037-1197
202-452-4200
800-372-1033
customercare@bna.com
http://www.bna.com
Gregory C McCaffery, Publisher
Kim Hunter, Managing Editor
Contains the full-text of arbitration cases, and digests of court decisions involving arbitration. *$1686.00*
Weekly Founded: 1929

14379 Labor Arbitration in Government
LRP Publications
747 Dresher Road
Horsham, PA 19044-2247
215-784-0912
FAX: 215-784-9639 800-341-7874
custserve@lrp.com
http://www.lrp.com
Brian Greenlee, Editor
Dionne Ellis, Marketing
Selected awards involving city, state, and federal employers (other than those employed by schools) are covered by this reporting service. Some of the issues arbitrated include: absenteeism, smoking policies, layoffs, and substance abuse. *$120.00*

Monthly Founded: 1977
Printed in 2 colors on glossy stock

14380 Labor Lawyer
American Bar Association
321 North Clark Street
Floor 7
Chicago, IL 60610-4497
312-988-5000
FAX: 312-988-6281 800-285-2221
abanews@abanet.org http://abanet.org
Substantive articles on developments in labor and employment law. *$45.00*
Quarterly Founded: 1878
Circulation: 2300

14381 Labor Relations Reporter
Bureau of National Affairs
1231 25th Street NW
Washington, DC 20037-1197
202-452-4200
800-372-1033
customercare@bna.com
http://www.bna.com/
Gregory C McCaffery, Publisher
Kim Hunter, Managing Editor
A multi-part notification and reference service covering labor-management relations, wages and hours, labor arbitration, fair employment practices, individual employment rights and more. *$6175.00*
Weekly Founded: 1929

14382 Labor Relations Week
Bureau of National Affairs
1231 25th Street NW
Washington, DC 20037-1197
202-452-4200
800-372-1033
customercare@bna.com
http://www.bna.com
Gregory C McCaffery, Publisher
Susan Sala, Managing Editor
A weekly reporting service that provides a comprehensive overview of developments influencing labor relations in the private sector. *$1472.00*
Weekly Founded: 1929

14383 Labor and Employment Law
American Bar Association
750 N Lake Shore Drive
Floor 7
Chicago, IL 60611-4497
312-988-5000
FAX: 312-988-6281
Offers news items of interest to members and information on the latest developments in the labor field.
Quarterly

14384 Labor and Employment Law News
American Bar Association
541 N Fairbanks Center
321 North Clark Street
Chicago, IL 60610-4714
312-988-5000
FAX: 312-988-6281 800-285-2221
krusec@staff.abanet.org
http://www.abanet.org/
Whitney Ward, Staff Editor
Victoria Bor, Co-Editor
Legal trends of interest to labor lawyers. *$40.00*
8 pages Monthly
Circulation: 22000

14385 Labor and Employment Law Newsletter
Matthew Bender and Company
321 North Clark Street
Chicago, IL 60610
312-988-5000
FAX: 312-988-6281
http://www.abanet.org
Whitney Ward, Staff Editor
Victoria Bor, Co-editor
A monthly newsletter covering major judicial, legislative and regulatory developments in all areas of labor and employment law.
Quarterly Founded: 1968
Circulation: 22,000

14386 Labor-Management Relations
Bureau of National Affairs
1231 25th Street NW
Washington, DC 20037-1197
202-452-4200
800-372-1033
customercare@bna.com
http://www.bna.com
Gregory C McCaffery, Publisher
Kim Hunter, Managing Editor
Contains a table of cases, digest-summaries of all published NLRB decisions and full-text of opinions of the US Supreme Court, US Courts of Appeals and other courts, in one bound volume, issued several times a year. *$1776.00*
Monthly Founded: 1929

14387 Labor-Management Relations Analysis/News and Background Information
Bureau of National Affairs
1231 25th Street NW
Washington, DC 20037-1197
202-452-4200
800-372-1033
customercare@bna.com
http://www.bna.com
Gregory C McCaffery, Publisher
Kim Hunter, Managing Editor
This weekly section of the Labor Relations Reporter summarizes developments and rulings in the field of labor law, covers major non-decisional developments and recent significant arbitration awards, and provides in-depth analysis and evaluation of the week's labor news. *$ 507.00*
Weekly Founded: 1929

14388 Lamplighter
American Bar Association
321 North Clark Street
Chicago, IL 60611
312-988-5000
FAX: 312-988-6281 800-285-2221
askaba@abanet.org
http://www.abanet.org/
Robert J Grey, Jr., President
Provides useful information to armed forces legal assistance officers and other interested parties.
Quarterly Founded: 1879

14389 Land Use Law Report
Business Publishers
8737 Colesville Road
10th Floor
Silver Spring, MD 20910-3928
301-876-6300
FAX: 301-589-8493 800-274-6737
custserv@bpinews.com
http://www.bpinews.com/
Leonard Eiserer, Publisher
James Esq, Editor
Zoning and land use decisions at all levels of government; impact on business community and environment. *$397.00*
Founded: 1963

14390 Latin America Law and Business Report
WorldTrade Executive
2250 Main Street
Suite 100
Concord, MA 01742
978-287-0301
FAX: 978-287-0302
info@wtexec.com
http://www.wtexec.com
Allison French, Production Manager
Provides practical, current information on how to do business in Latin America. Covers areas such as capital markets, accounting matters, labor issues, privatization, project finance techniques, joint venture regulation, local sourcing, export/import, taxation, intellectual property, environment. *$893.00*
Monthly

14391 Law Bulletin
Andrews Publications
175 Strafford Avenue
Building 4, Suite 140
Wayne, PA 19087-3331
610-225-0510
FAX: 610-225-0501 800-345-1101
editor@adrewspub.com
http://www.andrewspub.com
Donna Higgins, Editor
Rose MacDonald, Production Manager
Newsletter covering the legal issues raided by the Millenium. Bug along with insightful commentary from attorneys and other experts. *$25.00*
Monthly Founded: 1872

14392 Law Firm Profit Report
James Publishing
3505 Cadillac Avenue
Suite H
Costa Mesa, CA 92626-1430
714-755-5450
FAX: 714-751-2709
customer-service@jamespublishing.com
http://www.jamespublishing.com
Kathy McCoy, Publisher
Lorraine Thinnes, Editor
How to manage a small to medium-sized law firm profitably, with tips on cost-cutting, managing automation, personnel and more.
Founded: 1981

14393 Law Office Management & Administration Report
Institute of Management & Administration
29 W 35th Street
5th Floor
New York, NY 10001-2299
212-244-0360
FAX: 212-564-0465
subserve@ioma.com
http://www.ioma.com
Lisa Isom-Rodriguez, Editor
Shows how to operate your law firm at peak efficiency, improve firm profitability, cut costs, update staffing ratios, market and compete for effectiveness. *$299.00*
Monthly Founded: 1983

14394 Law Practice Today
American Bar Association
321 N Clark St
Chicago, IL 60610-4497
312-988-5000
FAX: 312-988-5571
http://www.abanet.org/
Robert Grey, President
Focuses on how lawyers can improve their personal productivity in the hands-on practice of law. *$50.00*

14395 Law Report
American Bar Association
541 N Fairbanks Center
16th Floor
Chicago, IL 60611-3375
312-988-5000
Jack Wolowic, Publisher
Offers legislative information from the American Bar Association.
16 pages Monthly

14396 Law and Society Association Newsletter
Denver College of Law
1900 Olive Street
Denver, CO 80220-1857
303-871-6306
Joyce Sterling, Publisher
Legal updates and information on the Society.
Monthly

14397 Lawyer Referral Network
American Bar Association
321 North Clark Street
Chicago, IL 60610-4497
312-988-5000
FAX: 312-988-6281
abajobs@abanet.org
http://www.abanet.org
Michael Greco, President
Robert Stein, Executive Director
News briefs on activities of the LRIS Committee and state and local lawyer referral services.
Quarterly Founded: 1878

14398 Lawyer's PC
West Group
50 Broad Street E
Rochester, NY 14694
585-549-9585
FAX: 585-258-3707 800-327-2665
lpc@netside.com
http://www.west.thomson.com
Dan Harmon, Editor
Computer and electronics information aimed at the legal profession. *$299.00*
16 pages Founded: 1872
Circulation: 4000
Printed in 1 color

14399 Lawyering Skills Bulletin
American Bar Association
321 North Clark Street
Chicago, IL 60610-4497
312-988-5000
FAX: 312-988-6281
askaba@abanet.org
http://www.abanet.org
Laura Letvger, Marketing
Gordon Kerr, CIO
Focuses on negotiating, research, time management, advocacy, marketing and communications. *$50.00*
Quarterly Founded: 1878

14400 Lawyering Tools and Techniques
American Bar Association
750 N Lake Shore Drive
Floor 7
Chicago, IL 60611-4497
312-988-5000
FAX: 312-988-6281
Focuses on specific tools lawyers can use to improve the productivity of their work including electronic communications, laptops, desk publishing and resources. *$50.00*
Quarterly

14401 Lawyers Tax Alert
Research Institute of America
90 5th Avenue
2nd Floor
New York, NY 10011-7696
212-367-6300
Peter Grean, Manager
Tax laws and news.
Monthly

14402 Lawyers for the Arts Newsletter
American Bar Association
750 N Lake Shore Drive
Floor 7
Chicago, IL 60611-4497
312-988-5000
FAX: 312-988-6281
Contains articles by lawyers on issues in art law, summaries of recent cases and legislation in the area, and reviews of new publications. *$10.00*
SemiMonthly

14403 Lawyers' Apple Systems Report
American Bar Association
750 N Lake Shore Drive
Floor 7
Chicago, IL 60611-4497
312-988-5000
FAX: 312-988-6281
Reports to lawyers using Apple computers. Practicing lawyers review hardware and software products and report on the applications they have developed. *$50.00*
Quarterly

14404 Lawyers' Letter
American Bar Association
321 North Clark Street
Chicago, IL 60610-4497
312-988-5000
FAX: 312-988-6281 800-285-2221
askaba@abanet.org
http://www.abanet.org
Robert Grey, Jr, President
Newsletter informing lawyers of new developments in court improvement and reports on Conference activities. *$13.00*
Founded: 1878

14405 Lawyers' Title Guaranty Funds Newsletter
American Bar Association
750 N Lake Shore Drive
Floor 7
Chicago, IL 60611-4497
312-988-5000
FAX: 312-988-6281
Information on bar-related title insurance funds for bar groups and bar associations.

14406 Legal Advisory
WPI Communications
55 Morris Avenue
Suite 312
Springfield, NJ 07081-1496
973-678-8700
FAX: 800-677-9742 800-323-4995
info@wpicomm.com
http://www.wpicomm.com
Steven Klinghoffer, Publisher
Marilyn Lang, Circulation Manager
Offers updates, news and the latest legislation for lawyers.
Monthly Founded: 1952

14407 Legal Assistant Today Magazine
James Publishing
3505 Cadillac Avenue
Suite H
Costa Mesa, CA 92626-1419
714-755-5450
FAX: 714-751-5508 800-394-2626
editorlat@jamespublishing.com
http://www.legalassistanttoday.com
Jim Pawell, Publisher
Rod Hughes, Managing Editor
Written exclusively for paralegals and legal assistants. Each issue includes coverage if industry news and trends, how-to articles as well as colorful and informative pieces on unique areas and persons in the profession and sound advice for becoming more efficient in the workplace., buy wisely and use their investments to maximize productivity and profitability. *$47.98*
56 pages Founded: 1983
Circulation: 13000 49M names $120 per M.

14408 Legal Review
Native American Rights Fund
1506 Broadway Street
Boulder, CO 80302-6296
303-447-8760
FAX: 303-443-7776
pereira@narf.org http://www.narf.org
John E Echohawk, Executive Director
Mary LuProsser, Director Development
A bi-annual case update published by the Native American Rights Fund.
Bi-annually Founded: 1970

14409 Legal, Bowne Digest for Corporate and Securities Lawyers
Brumberg Publications
124 Harvard Street
Suite 9
Brookline, MA 02446-6454
617-734-1979
FAX: 617-734-1989
editors@mystockoptions.com
http://www.mystockoptions.com/
Bruce Brumberg, Editor/publisher/CEO
Summaries of articles on corporate finance, mergers acquisitions, intial public offerings (ipos) and restructuring. Selects articles from hundreds of publications focusing on articles trends, strategies and advice on deal sturturing.

14410 Litigation Applications
American Bar Association
321 North Clark Street
Chicago, IL 60610
312-885-5000
FAX: 312-988-6281 800-285-2221
service@abanet.org
http://www.abanet.org

Robert Grey, President
Charles D Tobin, Editor-in-Chief

Includes updates on more effective computer use in litigation practice and news about the activities of the Litigation Application User Group. *$45.00*

Quarterly Founded: 1878
Circulation: 60000

14411 Litigation Committee Newsletter
American Bar Association
750 N Lake Shore Drive
Floor 7
Chicago, IL 60611-4497
312-988-5000
FAX: 312-988-6281

Each issue contains 8-10 articles on the subjects of interest to young litigators as well as book reviews, case updates and information on meeting agendas, programs and Litigation Section News. *$15.00*

Quarterly

14412 Litigation LAWCAST
Vox Juris
PO Box 389
Pennington, NJ 08534
609-737-6543
FAX: 609-737-3860 800-529-2278
info@lawcast.com
http://www.lawcast.com

Jason Meyer, Editor & Publisher
Linda Delp, General Manager

Analysis of legal departments and advanced strategic ideas for the most demanding litigators - whatever the subject of your litigation. Stay up to date on substance and tactics in evidence, discovery, advocacy, damages, client management and selection, settlement, ADR, and ethics, plus coverage of groudbreaking decisions affecting personal injury, commercial, and employment law. 60 min./monthly *$399.00*

Monthly Founded: 1994

14413 Litigation News
American Bar Association
321 North Clark Street
Chicago, IL 60610-4497
312-988-5000
FAX: 312-988-6281 800-285-2221
service@abanet.org
http://www.abanet.org

Robert Grey, President
Charles D Tobin, Editor-in-Chief
Annemarie Micklo, Staff Editor

Newsletter of council and committee activities, upcoming meetings and conferences, legislative activities of interest to trial attorneys, and Section publications list.

Quarterly Founded: 1878
Circulation: 60000

14414 Marketing for Lawyers
Leader Publications
345 Park Avenue S
New York, NY 10010-1707
212-799-9200
FAX: 212-696-1848

Sam Adler, Editor
Kerry Kyle, Circulation Director

Helps lawyers expand their practice through marketing. *$17.50*

14415 Mealey's Asbestos Bankruptcy Report
LexisNexis Mealey's
1018 W Ninth Avenue
Third Avenue
King of Prussia, PA 19406-1225
610-768-7800
FAX: 610-768-0880
mealeyinfo@lexisnexis.com
www.lexisnexis.com/mealeys

Tom Hagy, VP/General Manager
Maureen McGuire, Editorial Director
Lisa Schaeffer, Editor

The report provides in-depth news and analysis of asbestos bankruptcy law and the progress of bankrupt asbestos companies through the ever-evolving Chapter 11 process. Topics include: insurance issues, impacts on settlements, how asbestos bankruptcies are affecting the landscape of the litigation and which companies may be forced to file for Chapter 11 protection in the future. *$475.00*

100 pages Quarterly Founded: 2000

14416 Mealey's California Section 17200 Report
LexisNexis Mealey's
1018 W Ninth Avenue
Third Avenue
King of Prussia, PA 19406-1225
610-768-7800
FAX: 610-768-0880
mealeyinfo@lexisnexis.com
www.lexisnexis.com/mealeys

Tom Hagy, VP/General Manager
Maureen McGuire, Editorial Director
Bryan Redding, Editor

Monitors litigation and provides legislative updates on California's Unfair Competition Law. This monthly report will offer readers hard-to-find filings and briefs, new complaints, breaking news, concise case summaries, and trial updates. All major cases involving Section 17200 of the state's Business and Professions Code will be reported, including those dealings with insurance, employment, consumer law, the Internet, telecommunications, securities, fraud, product liability and many more. *$959.00*

100 pages Monthly Founded: 2002

14417 Mealey's Catastrophic Loss
LexisNexis Mealey's
1018 W Ninth Avenue
Third Avenue
King of Prussia, PA 19406-1225
610-768-7800
FAX: 610-768-0880
mealeyinfo@lexisnexis.com
www.lexisnexis.com/mealeys

Tom Hagy, VP/General Manager
Maureen McGuire, Editorial Director
Gina Cappello, Editor

This report focuses on business interruption insurance claims in the aftermath of the Hurricane Katrina, September 11th, and other catastrophic loss tragedies. Additionally, the report will go beyond these claims and will offer important business interruption insurance coverage news related to computer viruses, computer failures, and natural disasters. *$1075.00*

100 pages Monthly Founded: 2001

14418 Mealey's Daubert Report
LexisNexis Mealey's
1018 W Ninth Avenue
Third Avenue
King of Prussia, PA 19406-1225
610-768-7800
FAX: 610-768-0880
mealeyinfo@lexisnexis.com
www.lexisnexis.com/mealeys

Tom Hagy, VP/General Manager
Maureen McGuire, Editorial Director
Kristin Casler, Editor

This newsletter covers the interpretation, adoption and/or rejection of the Supreme Court's landmark expert admissibility ruling, Daubert v. Merrell Dow Pharmaceutical Inc. As the nation's jurisdictions grapple with so called junk science testimony, this monthly newsletter offers subscribers the latest key rulings in this contentious components of civil and criminal litigation. *$735.00*

100 pages Monthly Founded: 1997

14419 Mealey's Emerging Drugs & Devices
LexisNexis Mealey's
1018 W Ninth Avenue
Third Avenue
King of Prussia, PA 19406-1225
610-768-7800
FAX: 610-768-0880
mealeyinfo@lexisnexis.com
www.lexisnexis.com/mealeys

Tom Hagy, VP/General Manager
Maureen McGuire, Editorial Director
Tom Moylan, Editor

The report covers cases involving a variety of prescription drug vaccines, implants and devices. Duract, Parlodel, Accutane, fen-phen, Rezulin, Propulsid, dietary supplements and blood products are among the topics tracked. Medical devices covered include heart catheters, breast implants, heart valves, intraocular lenses, jaw implants, joint replacements, latex gloves, pacemakers, pedicle screws, penile implants, and surgical lasers. *$1249.00*

100 pages Semi-Monthly Founded: 1996

14420 Mealey's Emerging Insurance Disputes
LexisNexis Mealey's
1018 W Ninth Avenue
Third Avenue
King of Prussia, PA 19406-1225
610-768-7800
FAX: 610-768-0880
mealeyinfo@lexisnexis.com
www.lexisnexis.com/mealeys

Tom Hagy, VP/General Manager
Maureen McGuire, Editorial Director
Gina Cappello, Editor

The report tracks new areas of coverage liability, novel policy applications, and conflicting policy language interpretations as they arise in insurance litigation. Some areas of coverage featured are: sexual harassment and discrimination, assault and battery, professional liability, patent and trademark infringement, construction defects, directors and officers claims, emotional distress, intentional acts, technology, and insurance business practices. *$1229.00*

100 pages Semi-Monthly Founded: 1996

14421 Mealey's Emerging Securities Litigation
LexisNexis Mealey's
1018 W Ninth Avenue
Third Avenue
King of Prussia, PA 19406-1225
610-768-7800
FAX: 610-768-0880
mealeyinfo@lexisnexis.com
www.lexisnexis.com/mealeys

Tom Hagy, VP/General Manager
Maureen McGuire, Editorial Director
Mike Lello, Editor

The report covers fiduciary duties to shareholders, 401k and pension implications, class actions, damage calculations, causation questions. Daubert issues, debt bondholder implications, bankruptcy issues and accountant liability in the securities law context. *$875.00*
100 pages Monthly Founded: 2002

14422 Mealey's Emerging Toxic Torts
LexisNexis Mealey's
1018 W Ninth Avenue
Third Avenue
King of Prussia, PA 19406-1225
610-768-7800
FAX: 610-768-0880
mealeyinfo@lexisnexis.com
www.lexisnexis.com/mealeys

Tom Hagy, VP/General Manager
Maureen McGuire, Editorial Director
Bill Lowe, Editor

The report focuses on the hottest areas of toxic tort litigation including: chemical sensitivity; indoor air quality; groundwater, soil and air contamination; radiation; workplace exposure; pesticides; solvents; latex gloves; EMF's; MTBE; endocrine disruptors, and more. The report provides in-depth coverage of medical monitoring; fear of cancer/disease; stigma damages; expert admissibility; federal preemption; class actions; punitive damages and market share theory. *$1539.00*
100 pages Semi-Monthly Founded: 1992

14423 Mealey's International Arbitration Quarter ly Law Review
LexisNexis Mealey's
1018 W Ninth Avenue
Third Avenue
King of Prussia, PA 19406-1225
610-768-7800
FAX: 610-768-0880
mealeyinfo@lexisnexis.com
www.lexisnexis.com/mealeys

Tom Hagy, VP/General Manager
Maureen McGuire, Editorial Director
Edie Scott, Editor

The report provides thought-provoking commentary articles authored by aribitrators, scholars and attorneys with first-hand knowledge of the complex field of commercial dispute resolution. Each issue contains analytical discussions and practical insights on current case law, new treaties and statues, arbitration principles, dispute resolution techniques, and more from our prestigious international authors. *$475.00*
100 pages Quarterly Founded: 2000

14424 Mealey's International Arbritation Report
LexisNexis Mealey's
1018 W Ninth Avenue
Third Avenue
King of Prussia, PA 19406-1225
610-768-7800
FAX: 610-768-0880
mealeyinfo@lexisnexis.com
www.lexisnexis.com/mealeys

Tom Hagy, VP/General Manager
Maureen McGuire, Editorial Director
Edie Scott, Editor

The report examines arbitration and related litigation in courts world-wide. Covers enforcement, jurisdictional disputes, forum selection, use of experts by arbitral parties, enforcement, judicial supervision, the Iran-US Claims Tribunal, the United Nations Compensation Commission, and events of interest at arbitration institutions around the globe. *$2049.00*
100 pages Monthly Founded: 1986

14425 Mealey's International Asbestos Liability Report
LexisNexis Mealey's
1018 W Ninth Avenue
Third Avenue
King of Prussia, PA 19406-1225
610-768-7800
FAX: 610-768-0880
mealeyinfo@lexisnexis.com
www.lexisnexis.com/mealeys

Tom Hagy, VP/General Manager
Maureen McGuire, Editorial Director
Lisa Schaeffer, Editor

The report covers the latest litigation, regulatory, and medical news related to worldwide asbestos exposure - including the emerging issue of subsidiary liability and the question of US jurisdiction - with in-depth case summaries and news of medical findings, full-text court documents, and exclusive expert commentary articles. *$959.00*
100 pages Monthly Founded: 2003

14426 Mealey's Litigation Report: Asbestos
LexisNexis Mealey's
1018 W Ninth Avenue
Third Avenue
King of Prussia, PA 19406-1225
610-768-7800
FAX: 610-768-0880
mealeyinfo@lexisnexis.com
www.lexisnexis.com/mealeys

Tom Hagy, VP/General Manager
Maureen McGuire, Editorial Director
Bryan Redding, Editor

The report offers unsurpassed coverage of litigation arising from asbestos-related injury and death. Key issues include: massive class action settlements involving present and future claimants, state and federal verdicts, litigation experts, medical monitoring claims, suits against the tobacco industry, discovery battles, discovery rule decisions, insurance coverage rulings, and asbestos property decisions. *$1789.00*
100 pages Semi-Monthly Founded: 1984

14427 Mealey's Litigation Report: BaycolØ
LexisNexis Mealey's
1018 W Ninth Avenue
Third Avenue
King of Prussia, PA 19406-1225
610-768-7800
FAX: 610-768-0880
mealeyinfo@lexisnexis.com
www.lexisnexis.com/mealeys

Tom Hagy, VP/General Manager
Maureen McGuire, Editorial Director
Dylan McGuire, Editor

This report tracks the litigation surrounding BaycolØ and other statin-based anti-cholesterol drug cases. Since the voluntary withdrawl of Bayer's BaycolØ) and Lipobay brand cerivastatin anti-cholesterol drugs, numerous complaints have been filed. The report will cover hard-to-find filings, new complaints, class actions, MDL developments, trial updates and more. *$950.00*
100 pages Monthly Founded: 2002

14428 Mealey's Litigation Report: California Ins urance
LexisNexis Mealey's
1018 W Ninth Avenue
Third Avenue
King of Prussia, PA 19406-1225
610-768-7800
FAX: 610-768-0880
mealeyinfo@lexisnexis.com
www.lexisnexis.com/mealeys

Tom Hagy, VP/General Manager
Maureen McGuire, Editorial Director
Jennifer Hans, Editor

The Report focuses on ever-changing California and federal Ninth Circuit insurance coverage disputes and developments. Topics include California developments in bad faith litigation, earthquake damage coverage, disability insurance, products liability coverage, environmental insurance coverage, mold coverage, asbestos coverage, aviation litigation coverage, entertainment law and more. *$949.00*
100 pages Monthly Founded: 2001

14429 Mealey's Litigation Report: Class Actions
LexisNexis Mealey's
1018 W Ninth Avenue
Third Avenue
King of Prussia, PA 19406-1225
610-768-7800
FAX: 610-768-0880
mealeyinfo@lexisnexis.com
www.lexisnexis.com/mealeys

Tom Hagy, VP/General Manager
Maureen McGuire, Editorial Director
David Elreth, Editor

This report will provide in-depth coverage of class action litigation involving mass torts and beyond - including consumer law, employment law, securities litigation and e-commerce disputes. Get the latest on: hard-to-find filings, notice plans, fairness hearings, class certification rulings, settlements, trial news and verdicts, attorney fee news, appeals, breaking news stories, new complaints, Supreme Court battles, and much more. *$1195.00*
100 pages Semi-Monthly Founded: 1997

14430 Mealey's Litigation Report: Construction D efects
LexisNexis Mealey's
1018 W Ninth Avenue
Third Avenue
King of Prussia, PA 19406-1225
610-768-7800
FAX: 610-768-0880
mealeyinfo@lexisnexis.com
www.lexisnexis.com/mealeys

Tom Hagy, VP/General Manager
Maureen McGuire, Editorial Director
Gerry Matics, Editor

The Report tracks the growing area of construction defect litigation, including cases involving water intrusion, building settlement, concrete corrosion, mold and other defects. Topics covered include: recovery of damages, warranty issues, contractor liability, sub-contractor liability, developer liability, architect liability and related insurance cover actions. *$979.00*
100 pages Monthly Founded: 2000

14431 Mealey's Litigation Report: Copyright
LexisNexis Mealey's
1018 W Ninth Avenue
Third Avenue
King of Prussia, PA 19406-1225
610-768-7800
FAX: 610-768-0880
mealeyinfo@lexisnexis.com
www.lexisnexis.com/mealeys

Tom Hagy, VP/General Manager
Maureen McGuire, Editorial Director
Melissa Ritti, Editor

The report offers timely and practical analysis on the hot issues in the field. Also features in-depth reporting of copyright law, including court decisions, new suits, settlements, and trials, plus full-text court documents. *$849.00*
100 pages Monthly Founded: 2002

14432 Mealey's Litigation Report: Cyber Tech & E -Commerce
LexisNexis Mealey's
1018 W Ninth Avenue
Third Avenue
King of Prussia, PA 19406-1225
610-768-7800
FAX: 610-768-0880
mealeyinfo@lexisnexis.com
www.lexisnexis.com/mealeys

Tom Hagy, VP/General Manager
Maureen McGuire, Editorial Director
Mark Rogers, Editor

The Report covers disputes arising from e-commerce. The report tracks emerging legal issues, including: Internet security, data destruction and/or alteration, defamation on the Web, software errors, hardware failure, electronic theft, e-mail trespass, online privacy, government action, shareholder lawsuits, Internet jurisdiction issues, file sharing (copyright) disputes and much more. *$999.00*
100 pages Monthly Founded: 1999

14433 Mealey's Litigation Report: Disability Ins urance
LexisNexis Mealey's
1018 W Ninth Avenue
Third Avenue
King of Prussia, PA 19406-1225
610-768-7800
FAX: 610-768-0880
mealeyinfo@lexisnexis.com
www.lexisnexis.com/mealeys

Tom Hagy, VP/General Manager
Maureen McGuire, Editorial Director
Karen Miehle, Editor

This report tracks the burgeoning number of disputes involving complex disability coverage claims. Topics covered include: claims for chronic fatigue, chronic pain, stress, psychiatric disabilities, chemical dependency and risk of relapse, plus key issues like total disability, own occupation, bad faith, ERSA, class actions and much more. *$849.00*
100 pages Monthly Founded: 2000

14434 Mealey's Litigation Report: Discovery
LexisNexis Mealey's
1018 W Ninth Avenue
Third Avenue
King of Prussia, PA 19406-1225
610-768-7800
FAX: 610-768-0880
mealeyinfo@lexisnexis.com
www.lexisnexis.com/mealeys

Tom Hagy, VP/General Manager
Maureen McGuire, Editorial Director
Shane Dilworth, Editor

This report covers all of the discovery litigation essentials, including how different districts and judges interpret federal discovery rules, procedural changes, the work product, attorney-client and common interest privileges, and discovery abuse. *$785.00*
100 pages Monthly Founded: 2003

14435 Mealey's Litigation Report: ERISA
LexisNexis Mealey's
1018 W Ninth Avenue
Third Avenue
King of Prussia, PA 19406-1225
610-768-7800
FAX: 610-768-0880
mealeyinfo@lexisnexis.com
www.lexisnexis.com/mealeys

Tom Hagy, VP/General Manager
Maureen McGuire, Editorial Director
Joan Grossman, Editor

The report focuses on the hottest areas of ERISA litigation, including preemption, health plan actions, exhaustion of administrative remedies, contingent worker litigation, class actions 401k plans, attorney's fees, breach of fiduciary duty, what courts consider to be equitable relief, downsizing and benefit cutbacks, blackout periods and bad faith claims against disability insurers. *$875.00*
100 pages Monthly Founded: 2002

14436 Mealey's Litigation Report: Ephedra/PPA
LexisNexis Mealey's
1018 W Ninth Avenue
Third Avenue
King of Prussia, PA 19406-1225
610-768-7800
FAX: 610-768-0880
mealeyinfo@lexisnexis.com
www.lexisnexis.com/mealeys

Tom Hagy, VP/General Manager
Maureen McGuire, Editorial Director
Dylan McGuire, Editor

The report tracks every facet of the growing area of litigation resulting from injuries and deaths associated with over-the-counter decongestant and appetite suppressant, phenylpropanolamine (PPA), and the chemically similar weight-loss herb, ephedra. The report offers true litigation reporting of new complaints, answers, discovery motions, appeals, trials, verdicts, settlements, plus covers the latest regulatory news. *$995.00*
100 pages Monthly Founded: 2001

14437 Mealey's Litigation Report: Fen-Phen/Redux
LexisNexis Mealey's
1018 W Ninth Avenue
Third Avenue
King of Prussia, PA 19406-1225
610-768-7800
FAX: 610-768-0880
mealeyinfo@lexisnexis.com
www.lexisnexis.com/mealeys

Tom Hagy, VP/General Manager
Maureen McGuire, Editorial Director
Michael Lefkowitz, Editor

The report provides detailed coverage of the litigation surrounding fen-phen, Redux and other diet drugs. The report covers new filings, class actions, MDL proceedings, trials, settlements, rulings, medical studies, FDA activity and more. *$995.00*
100 pages Monthly Founded: 1997

14438 Mealey's Litigation Report: Insurance
LexisNexis Mealey's
1018 W Ninth Avenue
Third Avenue
King of Prussia, PA 19406-1225
610-768-7800
FAX: 610-768-0880
mealeyinfo@lexisnexis.com
www.lexisnexis.com/mealeys

Tom Hagy, VP/General Manager
Maureen McGuire, Editorial Director
Vivi Gorman, Editor
Shawn Rice, Co-Editor

The report tracks declaratory judgment actions regarding coverage for litigation arising from long-tail claims, including environmental contamination and latent damage and injury allegedly caused by asbestos, tox chemicals and fumes, lead, breast implants, medical devices, construction defects, and more. Key issues: allocation, occurrence, policy exclusion, choice of law, discovery, duty to defend, notice, trigger of coverage and known loss. *$2115.00*
100 pages Weekly Founded: 1984

14439 Mealey's Litigation Report: Insurance Bad Faith
LexisNexis Mealey's
1018 W Ninth Avenue
Third Avenue
King of Prussia, PA 19406-1225
610-768-7800
FAX: 610-768-0880
mealeyinfo@lexisnexis.com
www.lexisnexis.com/mealeys

Tom Hagy, VP/General Manager
Maureen McGuire, Editorial Director
Jennifer Hans, Editor

The report details insurance coverage disputes arising from alleged breaches of the implied covenant of good faith and fair dealing. The topics covered involve third-party and first-party actions, statutory suits, punitive damage claims, coverage denials and delays, the definition of bad faith, relevant legislation, verdicts, and discovery disputes. *$1325.00*
100 pages Semi-Monthly Founded: 1987

14440 Mealey's Litigation Report: Insurance Frau d
LexisNexis Mealey's
1018 W Ninth Avenue
Third Avenue
King of Prussia, PA 19406-1225
610-768-7800
FAX: 610-768-0880
mealeyinfo@lexisnexis.com
www.lexisnexis.com/mealeys

Tom Hagy, VP/General Manager
Maureen McGuire, Editorial Director
Teresa Kent Zink, Editor

The report reviews civil and criminal cases arising from efforts by policyholders and third parties to defraud insurance carriers. Topics include false and fraudulent claims, arson, reverse bad faith, restitution, RICO, incontestability clauses, material misrepresentation, rescission, qui tam actions and fraud rings. Readers receive reports on schemes involving property & casualty, health care, automobile, life, homeowners, and workers' compensation fraud. *$839.00*
100 pages Monthly Founded: 1994

14441 Medical Liability Advisory Service
Business Publishers
8737 Colesville Road
10th Floor
Silver Spring, MD 20910-3928
301-876-6300
FAX: 301-589-8493 800-274-6737
custserv@bpinews.com
http://www.bpinews.com

Eric Easton, Publisher
Bonita Becker, Editor

Gives you practical information on just what triggers a lawsuit. Information you can pass on to your staff to claim-proof your procedures.
Founded: 1963

14442 Medical Malpractice Reports
Matthew Bender and Company
11 Penn Plaza
New York, NY 10001-2006
212-448-2000
FAX: 212-244-3188
All the facts, background information and expert analysis you need to keep on top of new legislation, new theories of liability, the impact of new medical technology and more.

14443 Mergers & Acquisitions Litigation Reporter
Andrews Publications
610 Opperman Drive
Eagan, MN 55123-1396
651-687-7000
FAX: 651-687-5581 866-590-1337
editor@andrewspub.com
http://west.thomson.com

Robert Maroldo, Publisher
Linda H Coady, Editor

Provides summaries and fulltext documents in key litigation concerning mergers and acquisitions. Offers general buyout and acquisition coverage as well as cases related to leveraged buyouts. *$83.00*
Monthly Founded: 1872

14444 Money Laundering Alert
Alert Global Media
1101 Brickell Avenue
Suite #601, South Tower
Miami, FL 33131-3105
305-530-0500
FAX: 305-530-9434 800-232-3652
customerservice@moneylaundering.com
http://www.moneylaundering.com

Charles Intriago, President

Covers legal issues, including new laws, regulations and cases related to money laundering and the bank secrecy act in the US and worldwide. Provides practical guidance and analysis and serves as a training tool. Also full text on the internet. *$945.00*
15 pages Monthly Founded: 1989

14445 Multimedia Strategist
Leader Publications
345 Park Avenue South
New York, NY 10010-1707
212-779-9200
FAX: 212-696-1848 800-888-8300

Stuart M Wise, Editor
Kerry Kyle, Circulation Director
William L Pollak, CEO/President
Aric Press, Editorial Director
Kevin Vermeulen, Vice President, Group Publisher *$175.00*
Monthly Founded: 1997

14446 Municipal Litigation Reporter
Strafford Publications
590 Dutch Valley Road NE
Postal Drawer 13729
Atlanta, GA 30324-729
404-881-1141
FAX: 404-881-0074 800-926-7926
custserv@straffordpub.com
http://www.straffordpub.com

Richard Ossoff, Publisher
Jennifer Vaughan, Managing Editor

Monthly digest of key court decisions on litigation involving local governments. Cases are screened and selected to provide concise, comprehensive coverage of issues important to municipal attorneys and others involved with the local government. *$497.00*
16 pages Founded: 1984
Mailing list available for rent 7.4M names
Printed in 1 color

14447 NARF Legal Review
Native American Rights Fund
1506 Broadway
Boulder, CO 80302-6296
303-447-8760
FAX: 303-443-7776
ramirez@narf.org http://www.narf.org

Ray Ramirez, Editor
John E Echohawk, Executive Director

Law articles and updates on cases of major significance to American Indian tribes and people.
Founded: 1970
Circulation: 30000
Printed in 4 colors on matte stock

14448 National Bankruptcy Reporter
Andrews Communications
175 Stafford, Building 4
Suite 140
Wayne, PA 19087
610-225-0510
FAX: 610-225-0501 800-345-1101
editor@andrewspub.com
www.andrewspub.com

Robert Maroldo, Publisher

Commercial bankruptcy news.
Monthly

14449 National Bar Bulletin
National Bar Association
1225 11th Street NW
Washington, DC 20001-4217
202-842-3900
FAX: 202-289-6170
jcrumpnba@aol.com
http://nationalbar.org

John Crump, Executive Director
Kim M Keenan, President

Association news and activities, legislative updates and information for lawyers.
$20.00
8 pages Monthly Founded: 1925

14450 National Financing Law Digest
Strafford Publications
590 Dutch Valley Road NE
Postal Drawer 13729
Atlanta, GA 30324-729
404-881-1141
FAX: 404-881-0074 800-926-7926
custserv@straffordpub.com
http://www.straffordpub.com

Richard Ossoff, Publisher
Jennifer Vaughan, Managing Editor

Monthly digest of nationally significant litigation concerning secured and unsecured financing transactions, including bonds, bankruptcy collection, and lender liability. *$597.00*
Monthly Founded: 1984

14451 National Notary
National Notary Association
9350 DeSoto Avenue
PO Box 2402
Chatsworth, CA 91311-2402
818-394-4000
FAX: 800-833-1211 800-876-6827
publications@nationalnotary.org
http://www.nationalnotary.org

Deborah Thaw, Executive Vice President
Armando Aguirre, Editor

Contents range from indentity fraud and electronic notarization, to legislation and practicing tips. Also includes human interest stories involving notaries.
Founded: 1957
Circulation: 250,000
Printed in 4 colors on glossy stock

14452 National On-Campus Report
Magna Publications
2718 Dryden Drive
Madison, WI 53704-3086
608-246-3590
FAX: 608-246-3597 800-433-0499
custserv@magnapubs.com
http://www.magnapubs.com

William Haight, President
Jody Glynn Patrick, VP
Therese Kattner, Editor
David Burns, Publisher

The campus legal monthly. *$169.00*
8 pages Founded: 1972
Printed in 2 colors on matte stock

14453 National Paralegal Reporter
National Federation of Paralegal Associations
2517 Eastlake Avenue East
Suite 200
Seattle, WA 98102
206-652-4120
FAX: 206-652-4122
info@paralegals.org
http://www.paralegals.org

Bryan Stevenson, VP Marketing
Rich Cantrall, President
Jane Kennedy, Managing Director
$21.00
Founded: 1974
Circulation: 17000
Mailing list available for rent 23M names

14454 National Property Law Digests
Strafford Publications
590 Dutch Valley Road NE
Postal Drawer 13729
Atlanta, GA 30324-729
404-881-1141
FAX: 404-881-0074 800-926-7926
custserv@straffordpub.com
http://www.straffordpub.com
Jennifer Vaughan, Executive Editor
Case digests of national significant court decisions affecting the acquisition, development, management, transfer and financing of real property. *$697.00*
Monthly Founded: 1984
Mailing list available for rent 25M names

14455 National Report on Substance Abuse
Natioal Retail Federation
325 7th Street NW 1100
Washington, DC 20004
202-837-7971
FAX: 202-737-2849 800-673-4692
Thomas G Shack Jr, Publisher
Terry Peters, Editor
Biweekly review of federal and state laws, regulations and court cases involving alcohol and drug abuse, with an emphasis on workplace drug testing. Also covers treatment and prevention, EAPs, ADA, local laws and policies. *$377.00*
Founded: 1981
Circulation: 36000 Audited
Printed in 2 colors on matte stock

14456 National Report on Work & Family
Business Publishers
8737 Colesville Road
Suite 1100
Silver Spring, MD 20910-3928
301-587-6300
FAX: 301-587-4530 800-274-6737
bpinews@bpinews.com
www.bpinews.com
Leonard A Eiserer, Publisher
Beth Early, Operations Director
Independent, authoritative resource covering the latest federal and state legislative, legal and regulatory developments concerning work/family issues. Includes case studies of organizations that have implemented family-friendly policies. *$497.00*
25 per year

14457 National Security Law Report
American Bar Association
740 15th Street
Washington, DC 20005-1019
202-662-1000
orders@abanet.org
http://www.abanet.org/natsecurity
Mathew Foley, Editor
Holly McMahon, Publishing
Cases, articles, legislation, regulations and other materials concerning national security.
Monthly Founded: 1842
Circulation: 4000

14458 Natural Resources Law Newsletter
American Bar Association
321 North Clark Street
Chicago, IL 60610-4714
312-988-5000
FAX: 312-988-6281 800-285-2221
service@abanet.org
http://www.abanet.org/
Lori T King, Staff Editor
Teresa Salamone, Editor
Amelia Stone, Marketer
Robert J. Grey, President
Legislative developments in natural resources law, Section news and calendar of events. *$60.00*
Quarterly

14459 Nolo News: Legal Self-Help Newspaper
Nolo Press
950 Parker Street
Berkeley, CA 94710-2524
510-704-2248
FAX: 510-548-5902
LibraryCS@nolo.com
http://www.nolo.com
Ralph Warner, Publisher
Mary Randolph, Editor
Jim Bruce, Manager
Self-help legal newspaper. *$39.99*
Weekly Founded: 1971
Circulation: 120000

14460 On the Line: Union Labor Reports Guide
Bureau of National Affairs
1231 25th Street NW
Washington, DC 20037-1197
202-452-4200
800-372-1033
customercare@bna.com
http://www.bna.com
Gregory C McCaffery, Publisher
Leslie Goldman, Managing Editor
Reports on shopfloor issues affecting union stewards. Includes summaries of arbitration awards and court cases. $4.00 per year each subscription. *$4.00*
Founded: 1929

14461 Parascope
American Bar Association
750 N Lake Shore Drive
Floor 7
Chicago, IL 60611-4497
312-988-5000
FAX: 312-988-6281
Newsletter for nation's appellate staff attorneys. Contains book reviews and articles on matters concerning appellate courts. *$ 19.00*
Quarterly

14462 Partner's Report: Monthly Brief for Law Firm Owners
Institute of Management & Administration
3 Park Avenue
30th Floor
New York, NY 10016-2299
212-244-0360
FAX: 212-564-0465
subserve@ioma.com
http://www.ioma.com
Lisa I. Rodriguez, Editor
David Foster, CEO
Management advice for law firm partners to help them improve distributions and ensure they're getting their fair share. *$289.00*
Monthly Founded: 1984
Circulation: 100000

14463 Patent/Trade/Copyright Newsletter
American Bar Association
750 N Lake Shore Drive
Chicago, IL 60611-4497
312-988-5000
FAX: 312-988-6281 800-285-2221
Robert J. Grey, President
Daniel Kim, Editor
Activities of the Section, recent developments in intellectual property law and calendar of events.
Quarterly Founded: 1878

14464 People and Programs
American Bar Association
321 north clarke street
Chicago, IL 60610-4497
312-988-5000
FAX: 312-988-5568 800-285-2221
askaba@abanet.org
http://www.abanet.org
Robert J. Grey, President
Daniel Kim, Editor
A newsletter for donors and volunteers for the ABA fund for Justice and Education, which supports over 150 public service and law-related education programs.
Founded: 1878

14465 People-to-People Newsletter
Association of Legal Administrators
75 Tri-State International
Suite 222
Lincolnshire, IL 60069-4435
847-267-1252
FAX: 847-267-1329 800-526-4902
Paul Morton, Publisher
Offers the newest information and legislative updates for legal administrators.
Monthly Founded: 1971

14466 Personal Injury Verdict Reviews
LRP Publications
747 Dresher Road
Suite 500 POB 980
Horsham, PA 19044-2247
215-840-0912
FAX: 215-784-9639 800-341-7874
custserve@lrp.com
http://www.lrp.com
Robert Stricklin, Editor
David Light, Managing Editor
Brooke Doran, Research Associate
Each twice-monthly issue contains a statistically based feature article backed by nationwide personal injury case summaries. Each case summary includes description of the incident, names and locations of counsel and expert witnesses, verdict or settlement amount, amount of medical expense and wage loss and date and docket number. *$375.00*
Founded: 1977

14467 Personnel Legal Alert
Alexander Hamilton Institute
70 Hilltop Road
Ramsey, NJ 07446-1119
201-825-3377
FAX: 201-825-8696 800-879-2441
editorial@ahipubs.com
http://www.ahipubs.com
Gloria Ju, Editor
Schuyler Jaenks, C.E.O
Deals with legal aspects of personnel. *$97.00*
4 pages Fortnightly Founded: 1989
Circulation: 4000 Audited

Mailing list available for rent 7,000 names
$125 per M.
Printed in 2 colors on matte stock
Computerized version available: Acrobat

14468 Personnel Manager's Legal Letter
Institute of Management & Administration
29 W 35th Street
5th Floor
New York, NY 10001-2299
212-244-0360
FAX: 212-564-0465
subserve@ioma.com www.ioma.com
PMLL regularly covers title VII, the Americans with Disabilities Act, ERISA, the Family and Medical Leave Act, and human resources legal issues around hiring, teminations, compensation and much more.

14469 Practical Law Books Reviews
Library Managemental Services
5914 Highland Hills Drive
Austin, TX 78731-4057
512-320-0320

Judith Helburn, Publisher

Reference book separated by field specification.

14470 Premises Liability Report
Strafford Publications
590 Dutch Valley Road NE
Postal Drawer 13729
Atlanta, GA 30324-729
404-881-1141
FAX: 404-881-0074 800-926-7926
custserv@staffordpub.com
http://www.straffordpub.com

Richard Ossoff, Publisher
Jennifer Vaughan, Managing Editor
Lianna G. Wolff, President

Digest of legal developments offering liability of property owners and managers. Warning system for potential lawsuits for injuries resulting from conditions on or near premises. *$287.00*
Monthly Founded: 1984

14471 Preservation Law Reporter
National Trust for Historic Preservation
1785 Massachusetts Avenue NW
Washington, DC 20036-2117
202-588-6295
800-944-6847
members@nthp.org
http://www.nationaltrust.org

Julia Miller, Editor
Andrew Carroll, Production Manager
Bob Barron, Publisher

The definitive source on preservation law. It provides informative and reliable reports on recent court decisions, tax rulings, new publications and new legislation. *$95.00*
Monthly Founded: 1949
Circulation: 400

14472 Preview of US Supreme Court Cases
American Bar Association
541 N Fairbanks Court
16th Floor
Chicago, IL 60611-3375
312-988-5000
FAX: 312-988-5494
www.abanet.org/publiced

Charles Williams, Editor

Previews cases coming before the US Supreme Court. *$130.00*
Annual

14473 Private Security Case Law Reporter
Strattford Publishers
590 Dutch Valley Road NE
Atlanta, GA 30324-729
404-881-1141
FAX: 404-881-0074 800-926-7926
custserv@straffordpub.com
http://www.straffordpub.com

Richard Ossoff, Publisher
Albert J Pucciarelli, VP

Monthly digest decisions on litigation involving private security operations; includes insights and trend analysis by nations leading security expert. *$347.00*
Monthly Founded: 1984

14474 Probate and Property
American Bar Association
321 North Clark Street
Chicago, IL 60610-4497
312-988-5000
FAX: 312-988-5522 800-285-2221
service@abanet.org
http://www.abanet.org

Robert Grey, President
Edward T Brading, Editor

Aimed at lawyers who devote a large part of their practice to real estate law and laws dealing with wills, trusts and estates. *$ 60.00*
Founded: 1978

14475 Public Contract Newsletter
American Bar Association
321 N Clark
Chicago, IL 60610-4497
312-988-5000
FAX: 312-988-6281 800-285-2221
services@abanet.org
http://www.abanet.org

Robert J Grey Jr, President
Chathrine Mikkelson, Editor

Contains informative articles on a wide range of timely topics including current developments in federal and grant law, recent developments in state and local public contract law, upcoming educational programs and legislative developments. *$60.00*
Quarterly

14476 Purchasing Law Report
Institute of Management & Administration
29 W 35th Street
5th Floor
New York, NY 10001-2299
212-244-0360
FAX: 212-564-0465
subserve@ioma.com www.ioma.com
Purchasing Law Report is the most practical, least expensive and quickest way to understand and apply new purchasing laws and regulations in your day-to-day operations without wasting time sorting through hundreds of legal documents.

14477 Report on Disability Programs
Business Publishers
8737 Colesville Road
Suite 1100
Silver Spring, MD 20910-3928
301-876-6300
FAX: 301-589-8493 800-274-6737
custserv@bpinews.com
http://www.bpinews.com

Leonard A Eiserer, Publisher

Follows legislation, regulations, legal actions and funding in areas import to all persons with disabilities including health care, employment, civil rights, housing, and transportation. *$227.00*
8 pages Monthly Founded: 1963
Printed in on matte stock : Newsletter

14478 Report to Legal Management
Altman Weil
Two Campus Boulevard
Suite 200
Newtown Square, PA 19073
610-886-2000
FAX: 610-359-0467 888-782-7297
info@altmanweil.com
http://www.altmanweil.com

James Wilber, Editor

A management aid to law offices covering the full range of management issues including strategic planning, client and business development, marketing, economic and firms. *$249.00*
Founded: 1970
Circulation: 1000

14479 School Law Reporter
Education Law Association
300 College Park Avenue
Dayton, OH 45469
937-229-3589
FAX: 937-229-3845
ela@educationlaw.org
www.educationlaw.org

M David Alexander, VP
Mandy Schrank, Executive Director

Member association for those with an iunterest in school law issues, such as attorneys, law professors, education professors, school administrators, and teachers.
Monthly Founded: 1954 1400 names $600 per M.

14480 Search and Seizure Law Report
Clark Boardman Company
375 Hudson Street
Room 201
New York, NY 10014-3685
585-546-5530
800-323-1336

Robert Bouchard, Publisher
Elizabeth Brooks, Editor

Provides detailed, current coverage of the law, procedure, trends, and developments evolving in search and seizure law. *$175.00*
8 pages Monthly
Circulation: 2,000
Printed in 2 colors on matte stock

14481 Section of Taxation Newsletter
American Bar Association
750 N Lake Shore Drive
Floor 7
Chicago, IL 60611-4497
312-988-5000
FAX: 312-988-6281
Update on current tax developments, committee projects, meeting information and order forms. *$15.00*
Quarterly

14482 Security Law
Strafford Publications
590 Dutch Valley Road NE
Postal Drawer 13729
Atlanta, GA 30324-729
404-881-1141
FAX: 404-881-0074 800-926-7926
custserv@straffordpub.com
http://www.straffordpub.com

Richard Ossoff, Publisher

Monthly updates on security law without all the legal jargon. *$297.00*

Monthly Founded: 1984
Mailing list available for rent 31.6M names
Printed in 1 color

14483 Sexual Harassment Litigation Reporter
Andrews Publications
175 Strafford Avenue
Building 4 Suite 140
Wayne, PA 19087-3317
610-225-0510
FAX: 610-225-0501 800-345-1101
editor@andrewspub.com
http://www.andrewspub.com
Robert Maroldo, Publisher
Linda Coady, Editor *$49.00*
Monthly

14484 Small Firm Profit Report: Attorney Edition
Professional Newsletters
770-819-4151

Robert Palmer, Publisher
Practice management and marketing help for small law firms and solo practioners.

14485 Software Law Bulletin
Andrews Publications
1735 Market Street
Suite 1600
Wayne, PA 19087
610-225-0510
FAX: 610-225-0501 800-345-1101
donnah@andrewspub.com
http://www.andrewspub.com
Donna Higgins, Editor
As pantenting becomes the predominant method of protecting software, and as cases involving technological copy protection measures wind through the court system, Andrews' Software Law Bulletin provides coverage of decisions and opinions in the key cases. Detailed articles put individual developments into the big picture of the changing law landscape. *$588.00*
Monthly Founded: 1972

14486 Special Court News
American Bar Association
750 N Lake Shore Drive
Floor 7
Chicago, IL 60611-4497
312-988-5000
FAX: 312-988-6281
Newsletter apprises members of the current activities and plans of the Conference. Also provides active, continual contact with members and solicits more active participation. *$11.00*
Quarterly

14487 Special Education Law Monthly
LRP Publications
747 Dresher Road Suite 500
PO Box 980
Horsham, PA 19044-980
215-784-0912
FAX: 215-784-9639 800-341-7874
custserve@lrp.com
http://www.lrp.com
Jessyca Harrington, Editor
Dionne Ellis, Managing Editor
Covers court decisions and administrative rulings affecting the education of students with disabilities. Each issue begins with a brief overview of the case summaries covered allowing you to quickly focus on the decisions and hearings that affect you most. *$140.00*
Monthly Founded: 1977

14488 Sports & Entertainment Litigation Reporter
Andrews Publications
175 Strafford Avenue
Building 4 Suite 140
Wayne, PA 19087-3317
610-225-0510
FAX: 610-225-0501 800-345-1101
editor@andrewspub.com
http://www.andrewspub.com
Robert Maroldo, Publisher
Robert Sullivan, Editor
Covers the latest news in the fast-changing world of entertainment litigation. *$775.00*
Monthly Founded: 1960

14489 Sports Medicine Standards and Malpractice Reporter
PRC Publishing
3976 Fulton Drive NW
Canton, OH 44718-3043
330-492-6063
FAX: 330-492-6176 800-336-0083
prc4926063@aol.com
http://www.prcpublishingcorp.com
David Herbert, President
Molly Romig, Marketing
Designed to keep sports medicine professionals informed about current trends in their challenging professions. Accepts advertising. *$29.95*
16 pages Quarterly Founded: 1984
Circulation: 500
Printed in 2 colors on matte stock

14490 Sports, Parks and Recreation Law Reporter
PRC Publishing
3976 Fulton Drive NW
Canton, OH 44718-3043
330-492-6063
FAX: 330-492-6176 800-336-0083
Sales@PRCPublishingCorp.com
http://www.prcpublishingcorp.com
David L Herbert, Publisher
For those professionals in the sports, parks and recreational law. Accepts advertising. *$39.95*
16 pages Quarterly Founded: 1997
Circulation: 500
Printed in 2 colors on matte stock

14491 State Legislative Report
American Bar Association
1800 M Street NW
#450S
Washington, DC 20036-5802
202-662-1000
FAX: 202-331-2220
Patrick Sheehan, Publisher
Diane Gibson, Editor
A summary of key legislative developments of interest to attorneys. *$50.00*
4 pages
Circulation: 800

14492 State and Local Law News
American Bar Association
750 N Lake Shore Drive
Floor 7
Chicago, IL 60611-4497
312-988-5000
FAX: 312-988-6081
service@abanet.org
http://www.abanet.org
Justina Cint Perino, Editor
Robert Grey, Jr, President
Richard W. Bright, Staff Editor
Informs members regarding Section activities and important issues of law. *$40.00*
Quarterly Founded: 1878
Circulation: 6000

14493 Summary and Reports
American Bar Association
750 N Lake Shore Drive
Floor 7
Chicago, IL 60611-4497
312-988-5000
FAX: 312-988-6281
Contains recommendations and informational reports to the ABA House of Delegates.

14494 Summary of Labor Arbitration Awards
LRP Publications
747 Dresher Road
Suite 500
Horsham, PA 19044-2247
215-840-0912
FAX: 215-784-9639 800-341-7874
webmaster@lrp.com
http://www.lrp.com
Brian Greenlee, Editor
Ken Kahn, CEO
Dana Eynon, Marketing Director
Claude Werder, VP
Marcy Witt, Marketing Director
Since 1959, the summary has been providing digests of private-sector labor arbitration decisions, covering the latest topics in collective bargaining with non-governmental employers. *$120.00*
16 pages Monthly Founded: 1977
Printed in 2 colors on glossy stock

14495 Syllabus
American Bar Association
750 N Lake Shore Drive
Floor 7
Chicago, IL 60611-4497
312-988-5000
FAX: 312-988-6281
aba@net.org http://www.abanet.org
Robert Grey, President
Danniel Kim, Editor
Newspaper describing and commenting on developments in legal education. *$15.00*
Quarterly Founded: 1978

14496 Tax Laws of the World
Foreign Tax Law
PO Box 2189
Ormond Beach, FL 32175-2189
386-253-5785
FAX: 386-257-3003
ftlp@foreignlaw.com
www.foreignlaw.com
Income, corporate and related tax laws for over 100 countries. Many full text translations. *$100.00*

14497 Testifying Expert
LRP Publications
747 Dresher Road
PO Box 980
Horsham, PA 19044-2247
215-784-0912
FAX: 215-784-9639 800-341-7874
custserve@lrp.com
http://www.lrp.com
Patrick Byrne, Editor
Gary Bagin, Circulation Manager
A newsletter designed to help experts develop a reputation or improve their present standing as an expert. Each monthly issue contains relevant decisions affecting the ex-

pert, book reviews and seminar listings. *$140.00*
Monthly Founded: 1977

14498 Tobacco Products Litigation Reporter
TPLR
PO Box 1162
Back Bay Annex
Boston, MA 02117-1162
617-373-2026
FAX: 617-373-3672
info@tplr.com http://www.tplr.com
Lissy Friedman, Publisher
Richard Daynard, Editor
Tobacco industry news. *$995.00*
Founded: 1975

14499 Transnational Bulletin
Lewis, D'Amato, Brisbois & Bisgaard
221 N Figueroa Street
Suite 1200
Los Angeles, CA 90012-2646
213-501-1800
H Bennett Arnberger, Editor
Legal information for the international business community written by lawyers of the firm.

14500 Trial Judges News
American Bar Association
321 North Clark Street
Chicago, IL 60610
312-988-5000
FAX: 312-988-6281 800-285-2221
abajd@abanet.org
http://www.abanet.org
Robert Grey, President
Aimee Skrzekut-Torres, Director
This newsletter informs membership of the National Conference of State Trial Judges of the activities and programs of that conference.
Quarterly Founded: 1978

14501 Turning the Tide
People Against Racist Terror
PO Box 1990
Burbank, CA 91507-1990
FAX: 818-848-2680
Michael Novick, Publisher
Bimonthly newsletter of anti-racist activism, research and education covering neo-nazi and other racist violence, efforts at conflict resolution and social justic reforms. *$10.00*
24 pages BiWeekly
Circulation: 7,500
Printed in 2 colors on newsprint stock

14502 Urban Lawyer
American Bar Association
321 North Clark Street
Chicago, IL 60610
312-988-5000
FAX: 312-988-6081
abanews@abanet.org
http://www.abanet.org
Robert J Grey, President
Richard W Bright, Editor
Articles on various areas of urban, state and local government law. *$49.95*
Quarterly Founded: 1879
Circulation: 6000

14503 Utility Section Newsletter
American Bar Association
321 North Clark Street
Chicago, IL 60610
312-988-5000
FAX: 312-988-6281 800-285-2221
askaba@aba.org
http://www.abanet.org/
Robert J Grey Jr, President
Articles pertaining to the field of public utility law.
Quarterly Founded: 1878

14504 Washington Employment Law Letter
M Lee Smith Publishers
PO Box 5094
Brentwood, TN 37219-2407
615-737-7517
FAX: 615-256-6601 800-274-6774
custserv@mleesmith.com
http://www.mleesmith.com
M Lee Smith, Publisher
Michael Reynvaan, Editor
Reviews of employment laws. *$157.55*
8 pages Monthly Founded: 1975
Circulation: 54,000 Audited
Mailing list available for rent
Printed in 2 colors on matte stock

14505 Washington Letter
American Bar Association
750 N Lake Shore Drive
Floor 7
Chicago, IL 60611-4497
312-988-5000
FAX: 312-988-6281 800-285-2221
service@abanet.org
http://www.abanet.org
Robert J Grey, President
Newsletter reports on congressional activity affecting legislation of interest to lawyers and the organized bar. *$30.00*
Monthly Founded: 1878

14506 Washington Summary
American Bar Association
740 15th Street NW
Floor 7
Washington, DC 20005
202-621-1011
FAX: 202-662-1032
askaba@abanet.org
http://www.abanet.org
Robert J Grey, President
Tracks legislation and federal regulations of interest to lawyers by abstracting the Congressional Record and Federal Register. *$ 55.00*
Daily Founded: 1878

14507 White-Collar Crime Reporter
Andrews Publications
175 Strafford Avenue
Building 4, Suite 140
Wayne, PA 19087-3317
610-225-0510
FAX: 610-225-0501 800-345-1101
editor@andrewspub.com
http://www.andrewspub.com
Robert Maroldo, Publisher
Edith McFail, Editor
Major articles guest written by practitioners in the area of white collar crame and covering such topics as sentencing guidelines, corporate liability, banking and securities fraud and government contract fraud. *$66.00*
Monthly Founded: 1872

14508 Word Progress
American Bar Association
750 N Lake Shore Drive
Floor 7
Chicago, IL 60611-4497
312-988-5000
FAX: 312-988-6281
Newsletter of the Word Processing User Group, includes updates on more effective word processing in the law office. *$50.00*
Quarterly

14509 World Jurist
World Jurist Assn of the World Peace Through Law
1000 Connecticut Avenue NW
Suite 202
Washington, DC 20036
202-466-5428
FAX: 202-452-8540
wja@worldjurist.org
http://www.worldjurist.org
Sona Pancholy, Editor
M Henneberry, Executive VP
Research for international development as a basis for future world peace. *$80.00*
Fortnightly Founded: 1963
Circulation: 6000
Printed in on glossy stock

14510 Your School and the Law
LRP Publications
747 Dresher Road Suite 500
PO Box 980
Horsham, PA 19044-2247
215-840-0912
FAX: 215-784-9639 800-341-7874
custserve@lrp.com
http://www.lrp.com
Stephen Bekiiacqwa, Editor
A monthly newsletter providing practical information on current judicial decisions affecting schools. *$190.00*
Founded: 1977
Mailing list available for rent
Printed in 1 color on matte stock

Magazines & Journals

14511 ABA Journal
American Bar Association
321 N Clark Street
6th Floor
Chicago, IL 60610
312-885-5000
FAX: 312-988-6014 800-285-2221
abajournal@abanet.org
http://www.abanet.org/journal
Danial Kim, Publisher/Editor
Robert Brouwer, Associate Publisher
Elizabeth Sullivan, Marketing Manager
Robert Grey Jr, President
Its editorial materials include news of interest to members of the legal profession. Editorial highlights include reviews of general interest and legal books, a US Supreme Court Digest section, a section listing significant rulings of other courts and news from government agencies. *$75.00*
Monthly Founded: 1878
Circulation: 389420

14512 ABA/BNA Lawyers' Manual on Professional Conduct
Bureau of National Affairs
1231 25th Street NW
Washington, DC 20037-1197
202-452-4200
800-372-1033

Gregory C McCaffery, Publisher
Kirk Swanson, Managing Editor

A notification and reference service covering a broad range of issues dealing with legal ethics and professional responsibility. *$1281.00*

Monthly Founded: 1929

14513 ACCA Docket
1025 Connecticut Avenue NW
Suite 200
Washington, DC 20036-2604
202-293-4103
FAX: 202-293-4701
bracken@acca.com
http://www.acca.com

Anne Bracken, Senior Vice President
Ken Lawrence, Director of Publishing
Breena Jacobs, Marketing Manager
Jennifer Alvey, Editor-in-Chief
Frederick J Krebs, President

Legal magazine covering corporation law. *$25.00*

Founded: 1982
Circulation: 75,000

14514 ATLA Professional Negligence Law Reporter
Assocociation of Trial Lawyers of America
1050 31st Street NW
Washington, DC 20007
202-965-3500
FAX: 202-342-5484 800-424-2725
membership@atlahq.org
http://www.atla.org

Liane Leshne, Editor
Jon Haber, Chief Executive Officer

Abstracts of verdicts, settlements, and opinions in the areas Of product liability. Reports on agency actions, product recalls, and other news in the product field. *$195.00*

Circulation: 2200

14515 Administrative Law Review
American University Washington College of Law
4801 Massachusetts Avenue NW
Washington, DC 20016-5151
202-640-0274
FAX: 202-274-4130
alr-editor-in-chief@wcl.american.edu
http://www.wcl.american.edu

Heather E Kilgore, Editor-in-Chief
Carl E Tugberk, Executive Editor
Chris Thatch, Managing Editor

Scholarly legal journal on developments in the field of administrative law and regulatory practice. *$40.00*

Quarterly Founded: 1898

14516 Advance Sheet
150 Lincoln Street
Boston, MA 02111
617-695-3660
FAX: 617-695-3656

14517 AmLaw Tech
American Lawyer Media
345 Park Avenue S
New York, NY 10010
212-799-9434
FAX: 212-972-6258 800-888-8300
customersvc@amlaw.com
http://www.americanlawyermedia.com

William L Pollak, President
Aric Press, Editorial Director
Kevin Vermeulen, VP Group Publishing

Annual+ Founded: 1997
Circulation: 16,500

14518 American Bankruptcy Law Journal

American Bankruptcy Institute
235 Secret Cove
Lexington, SC 29072
803-576-6225
FAX: 703-739-1060
info@abiworld.org
http://www.abiworld.org

Christine Molick, Executive Director
Marilyn Shea-Stonum, Editor-in-Chief
J Rich Leonard, Associate Editor

Offers information on bankruptcy, legislation and financial information. *$65.00*

Quarterly Founded: 1982

14519 American Judicature Society Magazine
American Judicature Society
The Opperman Center at Drake University
2700 University Avenue
Des Moines, IA 50311
515-271-2281
FAX: 515-279-3090 888-287-2513
llieurance@ajs.org http://www.ajs.org

David Richert, Publication Director
Allen Sobel, CEO

Magazine pulblished by the American Judicature Society. *$24.00*

48 pages Monthly Founded: 1917
Circulation: 10000
Printed in on matte stock

14520 American Lawyer
American Lawyer Corporation
105 Madison Ave
New York, NY 10016-1707
917-562-2000
FAX: 212-696-1845 800-603-6571
lawcatalog@amlaw.com
http://www.americanlawyermedia.com

Barbara Eskin, Circulation Director

Issues affecting lawyers and the legal profession, with an emphasis on the business aspect of law firms. *$349.00*

102 pages Monthly

14521 American Lawyers Quarterly
American Lawyers Company
853 Westpoint Parkway
Suite 710
Cleveland, OH 44145-1546
440-871-8700
FAX: 440-871-9997 800-843-4000
alq@alqlist.com
http://www.alqlist.com

Thomas Hamilton, CEO

Quarterly Founded: 1899

14522 American Polygraph Association Newsletter and Polygraph Journal
PO Box 8037
Chattanooga, TN 37414-37
423-892-3992
FAX: 423-894-5435 800-272-8037
editor@polygraph.org
http://www.polygraph.org

Stuart Senter, Editor
John E. Consigli, President
Robbie Bennett, Manager

Publishes information on polygraph activities, training, cases, meetings, seminars, laws, legislations, in the United States and abroad. Lists schools accredited by APA under USDOE programs. Provides news of APA state association affiliates and some information on foreign polygraph use and training. Also provides information on new instruments and techniques. *$80.00*

Quarterly Founded: 1966
Circulation: 2000 Audited Est. Pass-Along Circ: 4000 2,800 names

14523 Animal Law Report
American Bar Association
750 N Lake Shore Drive, 7th Floor
Young Lawyers Division
Chicago, IL 60611-4497
312-988-5000
FAX: 312-988-6281

Summarizes recent legislation, case decisions and literature. *$10.00*

SemiAnnual

14524 AntiShyster
AntiShyster
PO Box 540786
Dallas, TX 75354-786

FAX: 972-386-8604

Alfred Adask, Editor

Critical examination of the American legal system.

Circulation: 10000

14525 Antitrust Law Journal
American Bar Association
321 North Clark Street
Antitrust Law Sect
Chicago, IL 60611-4497
312-988-5000
FAX: 312-988-6281
mdadisman@staff.abanet.org
http://www.abanet.org

J Grey, President
Tina Miller, Executive Editor
MaryAnn Dadisman, Staff Editor

Covers proceedings of Section meetings, Section reports and positions on legislation, as well as content of National Institutes on antitrust law. *$120.00*

Founded: 1878
Circulation: 10,000

14526 Arbitration Journal
American Arbitration Association
1633 Broadway
Floor 10
New York, NY 10019
212-843-3266
FAX: 212-246-7274 800-778-7879
aaainternational@adr.org;
MartinezL@adr. http://www.adr.org/

William Slate, President/Chief Executive Officer *$30.00*

Quarterly Founded: 1926

14527 Association of Legal Administrators

75 Tri-State International
Suite 222
Lincolnshire, IL 60069-4435
847-267-1252
FAX: 847-267-1329
http://www.alanet.org

Jay Strother, Editor-in-Chief/Associate Publisher
Bob Abramson, Director Marketing
John Michalik, Executive Director
Theresa Rubinas, Publications Assistant
Ann Leffler, Production Assistant

Support for the adminstration of legal firms and businesses. *$10.00*

Founded: 1971
Printed in 4 colors on glossy stock
Computerized version available

14528 Attorney/CPA
3921 Old Lee Highway
Suite71A
Fairfax, VA 22030-3926
703-352-8064
FAX: 703-352-8073
cmulligan@attorney-cpa.com
http://www.attorney-cpa.com

Bernard Eizen, President
Clark Mulligan, Executive Director

Promotes high ethical standards of dual licensed professionals. *$44.37*
Founded: 1964

14529 BNA's Patent, Trademark and Copyright Journal
Bureau of National Affairs
1231 25th Street NW
Washington, DC 20037-1197
202-452-4200
800-372-1033
cuatomercare@bna.com
www.bna.com

Gregory C McCaffery, Publisher
Carol Oberdorfer, Managing Editor

Provides an in-depth review of significant current developments in the intellectual property field. Covers congressional activity, court decisions, relevant conferences, professional associations, international developments, plus actions of the Patent and Trademark Office and the Copyright Office. *$1968.00*
Weekly

14530 Barrister
American Bar Association
750 N Lake Shore Drive
Floor 8
Chicago, IL 60611-4497
312-988-5000
FAX: 312-988-6030
service@abanet.org www.abanet.org
Magazine containing general articles about the profession, the law and society in general. *$19.95*
5 per year

14531 Brief
American Bar Association
321 North Clark Street
Chicago, IL 60610-4497
312-988-5000
800-285-2221
service@abanet.org
http://www.abanet.org

Jane Harper-Alport,, Staff Editor
Robert Grey Jr., CEO
John Warren-May, Editor

Articles and practice tips on insurance and law. *$50.00*
56 pages Quarterly Founded: 1978
Circulation: 30000

14532 Broadcasting and the Law
One SE 3rd Avenue
#1450
Miami, FL 33131-1714
305-530-1322
FAX: 305-539-0013
broadlaw@aol.com

Matthew L Leibowitz

Addresses legal issues within the broadcasting industry.
Monthly
Circulation: 400

14533 Business Law Today
American Bar Association
321 North Clark Street
Chicago, IL 60610-4714
312-988-5000
FAX: 312-988-6081
service@abanet.org
http://www.abanet.org/

Ray DeLong, Editor
Robert Grey Jr, President

Examines issues relating to business law or practice-oriented topics. *$28.00*
Founded: 1879
Circulation: 55000

14534 Business Lawyer
American Bar Association
750 N Lake Shore Drive
Floor 7s Law Section
Chicago, IL 60611-4497
312-988-5000
FAX: 312-988-6281
service@abanet.org
http://www.abanet.org

Roger J.Grey, President
Robert Stain, CEO

Journal of business and financial law, with articles on current legal topics and substantive section programs. *$20.00*
Quarterly Founded: 1915
Circulation: 60000

14535 Business Lawyer's Computer News

American Bar Association
750 N Lake Shore Drive, 7th Floor
Law Practice Management Section
Chicago, IL 60611-4497
312-988-5000
FAX: 312-988-6281
http://www.abanet.org
Information on new developments in technology for the business lawyer and news on how business lawyers are applying technology in their practices. *$50.00*
Quarterly

14536 Champion
National Association of Criminal Defense Lawyers
1150 18th Street NW
#950
Washington, DC 20036-5418
202-872-8600
FAX: 202-872-8690
assist@nacdl.org
http://www.nacdl.org

Richard Bing, Publication Director/Editor
Barry C. Scheck, President
Ralph Grunewald, Executive Director

Of benefit to criminal defnse lawyers. Furthers the association's scientific and educational aim. *$90.00*
68 pages Founded: 1958
Circulation: 10500 $110 per M.
Printed in 4 colors on glossy stock

14537 Chinese Law and Government
ME Sharpe
80 Business Park Drive
Suite 202
Armonk, NY 10504-1715
914-273-1800
FAX: 914-273-2106 800-541-6563
tong@polisci.sscnet.ucla.edu
http://www.mesharpe.com

Myron Sharpe, Publisher
James Tong, Editor

Translations of significant works and policy documents, primarily from the Peoples Republic of China. *$144.00*
1 Year 6 Issues

14538 Clearinghouse Reference Guide
American Bar Association
1800 M Street NW
Washington, DC 20036-5802
202-662-1000
FAX: 202-331-2220

Patrick Sheehan, Editor
Diane Gibson, Publications Coordinator

A summary of key state legislative developments of interest to attorneys.
Annual
Circulation: 800

14539 Commercial Law Journal
Commercial Law League of America
70 E Lake Street
Suite 630
Chicago, IL 60601-7524
312-781-2000
FAX: 312-781-2010
clla@clla.org http://www.clla.org

Mary K Whitmer, President
Mark Matz, Director Marketing
David Watson, Editor

Law review journal covering such issues as credit, debt, insolvency, banking and the Uniform Commercial Code.
Quarterly Founded: 1895
Circulation: 6000

14540 Communications and the Law
Fred B Rotham Company
10368 W Cenntenial Road
Littleton, CO 80127-4205

FAX: 716-883-8100 800-828-7971

Theodore Kupfeman, Publisher

Features articles and book reviews on communications law, new technologies and law. *$25.00*

Circulation: 585

14541 Complete Lawyer
American Bar Association
750 N Lake Shore Drive, 7th Floor
General Practice Sect
Chicago, IL 60611-4497
312-988-5000
FAX: 312-988-6281
http://www.abanet.org/genpractice/lawyers/

Rachel Schick-Siegel, Editor

Magazine provides practical articles directed to general practitioners, on substantive areas of law, news of council and committee activities. *$23.00*
Quarterly
Circulation: 16743

14542 Computer Industry Litigation Reporter
Andrews Publications
175 Strafford Avenue
Building 4, Suite 140
Wayne, PA 19087-3331
610-225-0510
FAX: 610-225-0501 800-345-1101
editor@andrewspub.com
www.andrewspub.com

Robert Maroldo, Publisher

Legal issues as they relate to hardware, software electronic databaes and the computer industry in general. *$875.00*

14543 Computer Law Strategist
Leader Publications
345 Park Avenue S
New York, NY 10010-1707
212-799-9200
FAX: 212-696-1848 leader@ijx.com
Stuart Wise, Publisher
For lawyers operating in the area of computer law and intellectual property.
Monthly

14544 Corporate Control Alert
Daily Deal
105 Madison Avenue
New York, NY 10016
212-313-9200
888-667-3325
dlopenzina@thedeal.com
http://www.thedeal.com
Ed Paisley, Editor
Robert Teitelman, Editor-in-Chief
Bruce Wasserstein, Chairman
Kevin Worth, President & Publisher
Monthly

14545 Corporate Counsel
American Lawyer Media
345 Park Avenue S
New York, NY 10010
212-779-9434
FAX: 212-696-1845 800-234-4256
aweiss@amlaw.com
www.americanlawyermedia.com

14546 Court Review
American Judges Association
300 Newport Avenue
Williamsburg, VA 23185-4147
757-259-1841
FAX: 757-259-1520
aja@ncsc.dni.us
http://www.americanjudgesassociation.us
Judge Gayle Nachtigal, President
Judge Steve Leben, Editor
Highlights court decicions and precedents through articles written by US jurists and legal scholars. *$35.00*
Quarterly
Circulation: 2000

14547 Criminal Justice
American Bar Association
321 Northclock street
Chicago, IL 60610-4497
312-988-5000
FAX: 312-988-6281 800-285-2221
askaba@abanet.org
http://www.abanet.org
Maryann Dadisman, Editor
Roger J Grey, President
Magazine providing practical treatment of aspects of the criminal law and reporting on legislative, policy-making and educational activities of the ABA Criminal Justice Section. *$38.00*
Quarterly Founded: 1915
Circulation: 9000

14548 Cyber Esq.
Daily Journal Corporation
915 E 1st Street
Los Angeles, CA 90012
213-229-5300
FAX: 213-680-3682
Katrina Dewey, Editor
Cyber Esq. is a guide for lawyers who use technology and whose practices are affected by the impact on the latest hardware and software and analysis of cutting-edge legal issues.
52 pages Quarterly
Printed in 4 colors on n stock

14549 Daily Journal
Daily Journal Corporation
915 E. First Street
Los Angeles, CA 90012
213-229-5300
FAX: 213-625-0945
http://www.dailyjournal.com
Caterina Dewey, Editor
Ray Chagolla, Circulation Manager
Gerald Salzman, Chief Executive Officer
The Daily Journal Corporation provides lawyers with concise, comprehensive and intelligent coverage of legal news throughout the city, state, and nation. Through our family of publications we are able to serve the nation's largest legal markets. *$628.00*
28 pages Daily Founded: 1888
Circulation: 11000
Printed in on n stock

14550 Decisions & Developments
PO Box 98
Bolton, MA 01740-0098
781-890-5678
FAX: 781-890-1150

14551 Dispute Resolution Journal
206 Hulston Hall
University of Missouri
Columbia, MO 65211
573-823-3645
FAX: 212-716-5906
umclawcdr@missouri.edu
http://www.law.missouri.edu
Jonathan R Bunch, Editor-in-Chief
Cassandra A Rogers, Managing Editor
Leonard Riskin, Manager *$21.00*
Founded: 1984

14552 Docket
150 Lincoln Street
Boston, MA 02111
617-695-3660
FAX: 617-695-3656

14553 EEOC Compliance Manual
Bureau of National Affairs
1231 25th Street NW
Washington, DC 20037-1197
202-452-4200
800-372-1033
customercare@bna.com www.bna.com
Gregory C McCaffery, Publisher
Heather Bodell, Managing Editor
A two-binder monthly service containing the complete text of the EEOC Compliance Manual, as issued by the EEOC, with monthly notification to related developments. *$410.00*

14554 Education Law Association
300 College Park Avenue
Dayton, OH 45469-0001
937-229-3589
FAX: 937-229-3845
ela@educationlaw.org
www.educationlaw.org
Mandy Schrank, Executive Director
Brings together educational and legal scholars and practitioners to inform and advance educational policy and practice through knowledge of the law. Together, our professional community anticipates trends in educational law and supports scholarly research through the highest value print and electronic publications, conferences, seminars and professional forums. *$125.00*
1400 pages Monthly Founded: 1954
Circulation: 1200 1200 names $600 per M.

14555 Electromagnetic News Report
Seven Mountains Scientific
913 Tressler Street
PO Box 650
Boalsburg, PA 16827
814-466-6559
FAX: 814-466-2777
enr@7ms.com http://www.7ms.com
Josephine Chesworth, Managing Editor
E Thomas Chesworth, Technical Editor
Patrick D. Elliott, Circulation Manager
Offers industry news and technical articles of interest to readers as well as a calendar of events, product news and EMI publications. *$90.00*
40 pages Founded: 1972
Circulation: 1000
Printed in 4 colors on matte stock

14556 Energy Law Journal
Federal Energy Bar Association
1020 19th St. NW
Suite 525
Washington, DC 20036
202-223-5625
FAX: 202-833-5596
admin@eba-net.org
http://www.eba-net.org
Lorna Wilson, Administrator
Clinton A. Vince, Editor-in-Chief,
Stephen Huntoon, CEO/President,
Lawyers and consultants engaged in energy and public utility law. *$35.00*
Monthly Founded: 1946
Circulation: 2600
Printed in 2 colors on matte stock

14557 Environmental Forum
Environmental Law Institute
2000 L Street NW
Suite 620
Washington, DC 20036-1493
202-939-3800
FAX: 202-939-3868 800-433-5120
law@eli.org http://www.eli.org
Leslie Corothers, President
Stephen R. Dujack, Editor
Linda Ellis, Manager Customer Service
Carolyn Fischer, Editorial Associate
Uses diverse points of view to stimulate the exchange of ideas and foster solutions for pressing environmental issues. *$115.00*
60 pages Founded: 1985
Circulation: 2100 1200 names $350 per M.
Printed in 4 colors on matte stock

14558 Environmental Law Journal
State Bar of Texas
1515 S. Capitol of Texas Hwy
Suite 415
Austin, TX 78746-6544
512-322-5800
FAX: 512-478-7750 info@texenrls.org
Jimmy Alan Hall, Editor-in-Chief
Charles Jordan, Chairman
Provides members with current legal activities, recent developments and information pertaining to environmental and natural resource law, as well as section activities and other events pertaining to this area of the law. *$10.00*
68 pages Monthly Founded: 1969

14559 Experience
American Bar Association
750 N Lake Shore Drive
Floor 7
Chicago, IL 60611-4497
312-988-5000
FAX: 312-988-6281 800-285-2221
service@abanet.org
http://www.abanet.org

Thomas J Campbell, Editor
Michael S Greco, President

News magazine for one of the fastest-growing sections in the ABA. Articles cover elderlaw, Council relationships, aspects of retirement including housing and health, and other topics of interest to lawyers pre- and post retirement. *$45.00*
Quarterly Founded: 1878

14560 Expert and the Law
National Forensic Center
17 Temple Terrace
Lawrenceville, NJ 08648-3254

800-562-5177
forenexperts@att.net
http://www.nfstc.org/

Betty Lipscher, Publisher

Appilcation of scientific, medical and technical knowledge to litigation.

14561 Fair Employment Practices/Labor Relations Reporter
Bureau of National Affairs
1231 25th Street NW
Washington, DC 20037-1197
202-452-4200
800-372-1033
customercare@bna.com
http://www.bna.com

Gregory C McCaffery, Publisher
Kim Hunter, Managing Editor

A guide to the regulation of fair employment practices, including federal laws, orders and regulations; policy guides and ground rules; and state and local fair employment practice laws. *$1576.00*
Weekly Founded: 1929

14562 Family Advocate
American Bar Association
321 North Clark Street
Chicago, IL 60610
312-988-5000
FAX: 312-988-6030 800-285-2221
service@abanet.org
http://www.abanet.org

Debby Eisel, Editor
Nicole Maggio, Manager Copyrights & Contracts
Amelia Stone, Marketer
Adrienne Cook, Development Editor

A practical journal in magazine format, containing information on divorce, mental health, juveniles, custody, support and problems of the aging as well as current trends, recent court decisions and new legislation. *$39.50*
Quarterly Founded: 1984
Circulation: 11000

14563 Family Law Quarterly
American Bar Association
321 North Clark Street
Chicago, IL 60610
312-988-5000
FAX: 312-988-6081 800-285-2221
familylaw@abanet.org
http://www.abanet.org

Linda D Elrod, Editor
Deborah Eisel, Managing Editor
Robert J Grey, President

A scholarly journal, including regular coverage of judicial decisions, legislation, taxation, summaries of state and local bar association projects and book reviews. *$79.95*
Quarterly Founded: 1998
Circulation: 11000

14564 Federal Communications Law Journal
University of California-Los Angeles
Box 951476
Los Angeles, CA 90095-1476
310-825-7768
FAX: 310-206-6489
editorinchief@lawtechjournal.com
http://www.law.ucla.edu

John Alden, Editor in Chief
David Matheson, Advertising Director

Articles on legal issues relating to the communications industry. *$10.00*

Circulation: 2500

14565 Federal Lawyer
Federal Bar Association
2215 M Street NW
Washington, DC 20037
202-785-1614
FAX: 202-785-1568
fba@fedbar.org
http://www.fedbar.org

Thomas R. Schuck, President
Stacy Bernstien, Managing Editor
Lisa Sidletsky, Director Membership

Chronicles the news of the association and its members as well as providing practical coverage of issues affecting federal attorneys. *$35.00*
Founded: 1931
Circulation: 15200

14566 Fidelity and Surety News
American Bar Association
321 North Clark Street
Chicago, IL 60610-4497
312-988-5000
FAX: 312-988-6281
service@abanet.org
http://www.abanet.org

Whitney Ward,, Staff Editor
James A. Knox, Jr., Editor

Summarizes selected recent cases on fidelity and surety law for professionals and lawyers. *$165.00*
Quarterly Founded: 1878
Circulation: 1000

14567 Firestation Lawyer
Quinlan Publishing Company
23 Drydock Avenue
Boston, MA 02215-2336
617-542-0048
FAX: 617-345-9646
info@quinlan.com
http://www.quinlan.com

E Michael Quinlan, Publisher
Hoss Homaier, President/CEO

Case summaries of recent lawsuits involving fire departments. Discusses residency requirements of firefighters, worker's compensation, pensions, discrimination, and fire department rules and regulations.
Monthly Founded: 1950

14568 Florida Worker's Compensation Law Bulletin
LRP Publications
360 Hiatt Drive
Palm Beach Garden, FL 33418
561-622-6520
FAX: 561-622-2423 800-341-7874
custserv@lrp.com http://www.lrp.com

Jack Roberts, Editor-in-Chief

Concise analytical summaries of the most significant Judge of Compensation Claims, final merit orders, all appeals of JCC orders to the First District Court of Appeal and the Florida Supreme Court and noteworthy worker's compensation-related cases. *$275.00*
Founded: 1977

14569 Franchise Law Journal
American Bar Association
321 North Clark Street
Chicago, IL 60610-4497
312-988-5000
FAX: 312-988-6081 800-285-2221
service@abanet.org
http://www.abanet.org

William L Killion, Editor-in-Chief
Wendy J Smith, Staff Editor
Robert Grey Jr, President
Robert A Stein, Executive Director

Journal in newsletter format primarily on current legal trends in franchising; also reports on activities of the Forum. *$50.00*
Quarterly

14570 Health Law Litigation Reporter
Andrews Publications
175 Strafford Avenue
Building 4, Suite 140
Wayne, PA 19087-3331
610-225-0510
FAX: 610-225-0501 800-345-1101
editor@andrewspub.com
http://www.andrewspub.com/

John E Backe, Publisher

Focus on cases involving ERSA, experimental insurance coverage, patient dumping, Medicare and Medicaid, medical devices, and federal and state legislation.
Monthly
Circulation: 4100

14571 Hospital Law Manual
Publishers
200 Orchard Ridge Drive
Gaithersburg, MD 20878-1978
301-417-7500
FAX: 301-698-7931 800-234-1660
customer.service@aspenpubl.com
http://www.aspenpub.com

Patricia Younger, Director

Hospital law. *$1325.00*
Quarterly Founded: 1959

14572 Human Rights
American Bar Association
750 N Lake Shore Drive
Floor 7
Chicago, IL 60611-4497
312-988-5000
FAX: 312-988-6281
service@abanet.org
http://www.aba.org

Margaret Thompson, Editor
Robert Grey Jr, President
Ray Luna, Manager

Magazine containing news articles, features and commentary with relevance to human rights and individual rights and responsibilities. *$17.00*

Quarterly Founded: 1878
Circulation: 6000

14573 IP Worldwide
American Lawyer Media
345 Park Avenue S
New York, NY 10010
212-779-9434
FAX: 212-592-4900
aweiss@amlaw.com
http://www.americanlawyermedia.com

Steve Pressman, Editor
William L Pollak, CEO/President
Kevin Vermeulen, Publisher

Quarterly Founded: 1997
Circulation: 8000

14574 Institute of Certified Business Counselors
18615 Willamette Drive
West Linn, OR 97068
503-751-1856
FAX: 503-292-8237 877-422-2674
inquiry@i-cbc.org
http://www.i-cbc.org/

Bob C Ross, President
Jeff Adam, VP/President-Elect
Bud Sandberg, Second VP Membership
Michael R Coates, Director, Newsletter

Monthly newsletter for counselors, brokers and attorneys qualified to act as advisors for persons with business problems. Regular editorial features.
Monthly

14575 Institute of Management & Administration N ewsletter
3 Park Avenue
30th Floor
New York, NY 10001-2299
212-244-0360
FAX: 212-564-0465
subserve@ioma.com
http://www.ioma.com

Joe Bremner, President
Perry Patterson, VP/Group Publisher

Monthly newsletter that supports law office administrators by offering training on how to reduce overhead, improve the firm's profitability and efficiency, get more value for the firm's budget dollar, and improve their own professional standing.
Monthly

14576 International Commercial Litigation
Euromoney Publications
173 W 81st Street
New York, NY 10024-7227
212-874-4265
FAX: 212-501-8926
International litigation and dispute resolution news and developments in commercial law.

14577 International Lawyer
American Bar Association
750 N Lake Shore Drive
Floor 7
Chicago, IL 60611-4497
312-988-5000
FAX: 312-988-6030

Marla Hillery, Editor
Nora Whitford, Advertising Director

Practical issues facing lawyers engaged in an international practice. *$7.00*

Circulation: 11000

14578 Journal of Court Reporting
National Court Reporters
8224 Old Courthouse Road
Vienna, VA 22182-3808
703-556-6272
FAX: 703-556-6291 800-272-6272
msic@ncralhq.org
http://www.ncraonline.org

Brian E Cartier, Publisher
Duane Smith, President

Diverse information and views on matters related to the information/court reporting profession.
Founded: 1905
Circulation: 34000

14579 Journal of Internet Law
Apen Publishers
111 Eighth Avenue
7th Floor
New York, NY 10011
212-771-0600
FAX: 212-771-0885 800-638-8437

Mark F Radcliffe, Editor-in-Chief
Stacey Caywood, VP/Publisher
Mark Radcliffe, Editor
Gerry Centrowitz, VP Marketing and Commu
Robert Becker, CEO

Discusses strategies utilized by top intellectual property, computer law and information technology industry experts. *$380.00*
Monthly

14580 Journal of Paralegal Education and Practice
American Association for Paralegal Education
407 Wekiva Springs Road
Suite 241
Longwood, FL 32779
407-834-6688
FAX: 407-834-4747
info@aafpe.org www.aafpe.org
A journal offering news and information, pertaining to paralegal education.
Annual

14581 Judges' Journal
American Bar Association
321 North Clark Street
Chicago, IL 60610-4497
312-988-5000
FAX: 312-988-6281
askaba@abanet.org
http://www.abanet.org

Robert J Grey Jr, President

Created to help judges and lawyers improve the administration of justice. *$23.00*
Quarterly Founded: 1878

14582 Judicature
American Judicature Society
180 N Michigan Avenue
#600
Chicago, IL 60601-7401
312-558-6900
FAX: 312-558-9175
webmastr@ajs.org http://www.ajs.org

David Richert, Editor
Patricia Frey, Production Manager
Mary-Ann Lupa, Designer
Larry A. Hammond, CEO/President

A forum for fact and opinion relating to all aspects of the administration of justice and its improvement. *$11.00*
Founded: 1917
Circulation: 12000

14583 Jurimetrics: Journal of Law, Science and Technology
American Bar Association
750 N Lake Shore Drive, 7th Floor
Science And Technology Section
Chicago, IL 60611-4497
312-988-5000
FAX: 312-988-6281
Covers a wide range of topics on legal issues in science and technology. *$29.00*
Quarterly

14584 Juvenile and Child Welfare Law Reporter
American Bar Association
750 N Lake Shore Drive, 7th Floor
National Legal Resource Center For
Chicago, IL 60611-4497
312-988-5000
FAX: 312-988-6281
Contains abstracts of case law on juvenile delinquency, abuse and neglect, adoption, termination of parental rights and other topics on child welfare. *$145.00*
Monthly

14585 Law
National Association of Legal Professionals
314 E 3rd Street
Suite 210
Tulsa, OK 74120-2409
918-582-5188
FAX: 918-582-5907
moore@nals.org http://www.nals.org

Jay Moore, Editor
Tammy Hailey, Publisher
Jay Moore, Communications Manager
Tammy Hailey, Executive Director
Cindy Rosser, Executive Assistant

Published content focuses on new products, technology and items of interest to the administrative staff within the legal profession. *$40.00*
Quarterly Founded: 1929
Circulation: 7000

14586 Law Office Computing Magazine Services Section
James Publishing
3505 Cadillac Avenue
Suite H
Costa Mesa, CA 92626-1419
714-755-5450
FAX: 714-751-2709 800-394-2626
editorloc@jamespublishing.com
http://www.lawofficecomputing.com

Amanda Flatten, Editor & Publisher
Tina Dhamija, Assistant Editor
Adrianne Choi, Production Manager
Jim Pawell, Marketing and Circulation Director

Focuses on law office automation. Issues contain independent reviews of legal software with side-by-side comparisons of the top programs, plus how-to articles and expert columns. Targeted editorial attracts legal technology buyers and helps them plan effectively for their purchases, buy wisely and use their investments to maximize productivity and profitability. *$49.00*
96 pages Founded: 1981 31M names $120 per M.

14587 Law Practice Management
American Bar Association
321 N Clark Street
Floor 7
Chicago, IL 60610-4497
312-988-5000
FAX: 312-988-6281 800-285-2221
askaba@educationlaw.org
http://www.abanet.org

Robert J Grey, President
Mandy Schrank, Executive Director
Jody Thornburg, Publications Editor

The pre-eminent magazine on all phases of law office management. Includes feature articles, book reviews, reports on technical innovations and announcements of forthcoming events. *$40.00*

Founded: 1878

14588 Law Reporter
Association of Trial Lawyers of America
1050 31st Street NW
Washington, DC 20007
202-965-3500
FAX: 202-965-0030
law.reporter@atlahq.org
http://www.atlanet.org

Peter Quinn, Editor-in-Chief
John Haber, CEO

Covers civil law, including automobile ,civil rights, insurance, commercial, employment and family law, medical negligence, premises liability and products liability, and workplace safety. *$135.00*

40 pages Founded: 1947
Circulation: 53000
Printed in 2 colors

14589 Law Technology News
American Lawyer Media
345 Park Avenue S
New York, NY 10010
212-779-9434
FAX: 212-592-4900
subscribe@lawtechnews.com
http://www.americanlawyermedia.com

Kevin Vermuellen, Publisher
Monica Bay, Editor
William L Pollak, President/CEO

Covers the use of technology in the law profession. *$99.00*

Monthly Founded: 1997
Circulation: 40000

14590 Law and Social Inquiry: Journal of the American Bar Foundation
American Bar Association
541 N Fairbanks Court
Chicago, IL 60611
312-988-5000
FAX: 312-988-5522
OMaleyA@staff.abanet.org
http://www.abanet.org

Robert J. Grey, President

An academic and legal journal containing a wide range of research reports relating to the law, the profession and legal institutions.

Weekly Founded: 1878
Circulation: 4,00,000

14591 Law in Japan
Japanese American Society for Legal Studies
University of WA Law School-1100 NE Cam.
Seattle, WA 98105
206-233-9292
FAX: 206-685-4469

John Haley, Editor

Academic journal with translation, original articles, comments and case notes on Japanese law and legal issues. *$13.00*

Circulation: 1,400

14592 Lawyers Weekly USA
Lawyers Weekly Publications
41 W Street
Boston, MA 02111-1203
617-451-7300
FAX: 617-451-1466 800-444-5297
comments@lawyersweekly.com
http://www.lawyersweeklyusa.com/

Henry Pildner, Circulatlon Manager
Susan Bocamazo, Editor
Christopher Eddings, CEO

Features profiles, practice tips, technology, marketing, management and other topics related to law practice *$179.00*

Annual+ Founded: 1972
Circulation: 6000

14593 Lawyers' Professional Liability Update
American Bar Association
321 North Clark Street
Chicago, IL 60611-4497
312-988-5000
FAX: 312-988-6281
http://www.abanet.org

Margaret Thompson, Staff Editor
Robert Rabin, Editor

Current reports and articles on legal malpractice insurance marketplace and other aspects of legal malpractice. *$45.00*

Circulation: 23,000

14594 Leadership and Management Directions
American Bar Association
750 N Lake Shore Drive, 7th Floor
Law Practice Management Section
Chicago, IL 60611-4497
312-988-5000
FAX: 312-988-6281

Focuses on trends, principles, and practices in law office management including financial matters, marketing, human resources, facilities and technology. *$50.00*

Quarterly

14595 Legal Management: Journal of the Association of Legal Administrators
Association of Legal Administrators
75 Tri State International
suite 222
Lincolnshire, IL 60069-4435
847-267-1252
FAX: 847-267-1329
editorial@alanet.org
http://www.alanet.org

Jay D Strother, Editor
Theresa Rubinas, Publications Assistant
Rich Murowski, Advertising Representativ
David P. Constantine, President

Covers personnel management, finance, strategic planning, the legal industry, business software, technology. leadership, interpersonal communication, time and stress management, and disaster planning.

Founded: 1971
Circulation: 25000

14596 Legal Tech
Leader Publications
345 Park Avenue S
New York, NY 10010-1707
212-799-9200
FAX: 212-696-1848 800-888-8300

Stuart Wise, Publisher

Monthly

14597 Legal Times
American Lawyers Newspapers Group
1730 M Street NW
Suite 802
Washington, DC 20036-4513
202-457-0686
FAX: 202-457-0718
legaltimes@legaltimes.com
http://www.legaltimes.com

Peter Scheer, Editor
Ann Pelham, Publisher
Eva Rodriguev, Editor-in-Chief
Gwen Jones, Circulation Manager
Rose Mahoney, Sales Manager

Covers law, lobbying and politics. *$349.00*

36 pages Weekly Founded: 1977
Circulation: 6200

14598 Lender Liability Litigation Reporter
Andrews Communications
175 Stafford Building 4
Suite 140
Wayne, PA 19087
610-225-0510
FAX: 610-225-0501 800-328-4880

Robert Maroldo, Publisher

Journal of record, of litigation proceedings involving lender liability issues. *$650.00*

Monthly

14599 License
1 Park Avenue
2nd Floor
New York, NY 10016
212-951-6600
FAX: 212-951-6714 888-527-7008
info@advanstar.com
http://www.licensemag.com

Joyceann Cooney, Editor-in-Chief
Lorri Freifeld, Managing Editor
Steven Ekstract, Publisher

Patents, trademarks and copyrights

Monthly Founded: 1987
Circulation: 25000

14600 Litigation
American Bar Association
321 North Clark Street
Chicago, IL 60610-4497
312-988-5000
FAX: 312-988-6281
http://www.abanet.org

Robert J Grey, JR., President

A journal for trial lawyers and judges, each issue of which focuses on a particular topic involving trial practice. *$39.50*

Quarterly

14601 M and A Lawyer
Glasser LegalWorks
150 Clove Road
Little Falls, NJ 07424-2138
973-890-0008
FAX: 973-890-0042
orders@glasserlegalworks.com
http://www.legalwks.com

Steven E Bochner, Editor
Stephen W Seemer, President

News affecting all types of mergers and acquisitions transactions, including securities law, state law, international, taxation, accounting and practice areas like intellectual property, employee benefits/compensation, antitrust and environmental. *$317.00*

Founded: 1995
Circulation: 500

14602 Mental & Physical Disability Law Digest
American Bar Association
740 15th Street NW
9th Floor
Washington, DC 20005-1022
202-621-1011
FAX: 202-662-1032
khans@staff.abanet.org
abanet.org/disability

Sarina Khan, Subscriptions Coordinator
John Parry, Executive Director

A concise, expert explanation of disability law in 22 subject areas with citations and references.

14603 Mental & Physical Disability Law Reporter
American Bar Association
740 15th Street NW
9th Floor
Washington, DC 20005-1022
202-621-1011
FAX: 202-662-1032
cmpdl@abanet.org
http://www.abanet.org

Sarina Khan, Subscriptions Coordinator
Robert Grey Jr., President
John Parry, Executive Director

A bi-monthly journal published by the Commission on Mental and Physical Disability Law, containing timely summaries of reported legal developments in 22 disability subject areas - over 1600 summaries annually. *$384.00*

Founded: 1878
Circulation: 571

14604 Mental Health Law Reporter
Business Publishers
8737 Colesville Road
10th Floor
Silver Spring, MD 20910-3928
301-587-6300
FAX: 301-587-4530 800-274-6737
custserv@bpinews.com
http://www.bpinews.com

Leonard Eiserer, Publisher

Court decisions affecting mental health professionals. *$277.00*

Monthly Founded: 1963

14605 Midwest Alternative Dispute Resolution Guide
Law Bulletin Publishing Company
415 N State Street
Chicago, IL 60610-4674
312-644-7800
FAX: 312-644-1215
http://www.lawbulletin.com

Bernard M. Judge, Editor & Publisher
Lanning MacFarland Jr, Chairman

Profiles of midwest attorneys. *$219.00*

156 pages Monthly Founded: 1854

14606 Midwest Legal Staffing Guide
Law Bulletin Publishing Company
415 N State Street
Chicago, IL 60610-4674
312-644-7800
FAX: 312-644-1215
editor@lbpc.com
http://www.lawbulletin.com

Scott C Anderson, Director Sales
Bernard Judge, Editor
Stephen E Brown, Publisher

Monthly magazine about law, people and opportunity.

Daily Founded: 1854
Printed in 4 colors

14607 Midwest Legal Technology Guide
Law Bulletin Publishing Company
415 N State Street
Chicago, IL 60610-4674
312-447-7800
FAX: 312-644-1215
www.lawbulletin.com

Scott C Anderson, Director Sales

Supplement to the Chicago Daily Law Bulletin and Chicago Lawyer. Eliminates the confusion arising from the many new technological service and product providers.

60 pages

14608 National Bar Association Magazine
National Bar Association
1225 11th Street NW
Washington, DC 20001
202-842-3900
FAX: 202-289-6170
headquarters@nationalbar.org
www.nationalbar.org *$32.00*

Circulation: 25,000

14609 National Jurist
Jack Crittenden
PO Box 939039
Sandy, CA 92193
858-503-7786
FAX: 858-503-7588
jurist@clark.net
http://www.nationaljurist.com

Jack Crittenden, Editor-in-Chief
Keith Carter, Managing Editor
Rebecca Luczycki, Editor

Information, advice, news and entertainment for law and pre-law students to help them succeed in law school. *$30.00*

Founded: 1996
Circulation: 100000

14610 National Notary
National Notary Association
9350 Desoto Avenue
Post Office Box 2402
Chatsworth, CA 91313-2402
818-739-4000
FAX: 800-833-1211 800-876-6827
publications@nationalnotary.org
http://www.nationalnotary.org

Deborah M. Thaw, Publisher/Executive Vice President
Milton Valera, President
Mark Valera, Managing Director

Focuses on the importance of notaries as public servants and updates readers on related news.

Founded: 1957

14611 National Paralegal Reporter
National Federation of Paralegal Association
2517 Eastlake Avenue E
Suite 200
Seattle, WA 98102
206-652-4120
FAX: 206-652-4122
info@paralegals.org
http://www.paralegals.org

Lu Hangley, Managing Editor
Jane Kennedy, Managing Director
Rich Cantrall, President

Paralegal's professional magazine that offers information on issues relevant to the profession and articles on how to perform paralegal tasks. *$21.00*

Founded: 1960
Circulation: 17,000

14612 National Parliamentarian Magazine

National Association of Parliamentarians
213 South Main Street
Independence, MO 64050-3850
816-833-3892
FAX: 816-833-3893 888-627-2929
aguiberson@gmail.com
www.parliamentarians.org/np.php

A Guiberson, NP Magazine Editor
Chris Dickey, NP Magazine Communications Chairman
Loretta E Santagata, Membership Coordinator
Sarah Nieft, Executive Director

The National Parliamentarian is the official publication of the National Association of Parliamentarians, the largest non-profit association of professional parliamentarians in the world. Each issue of the NP provides readers with insightful, up-to-date information on parliamentary procedure and how it is applied to a variety of situations and needs. *$26.00*

4000 pages Quarterly

14613 Natural Resources and Environment
American Bar Association
740 15th Street NW
Washington, DC 20005-1019
202-662-1000
800-285-2221
service@abanet.org
http://www.abanet.org

Stephen Gidiere, CEO
Lori T King, Staff Editor

Practical magazine on the latest developments in the field of natural resources law. *$60.00*

Quarterly
Circulation: 12000

14614 Negotiation Journal
Plenum Publishing Corporation
513 Pound Hall
Cambridge, MA 02138
617-495-1684
FAX: 617-495-7818
nlawton@law.harvard.edu
http://www.pon.harvard.edu

Michael Wheeler, Editor
Nancy Waters, Managing Editor

Investigates theoretical and practical developments in the conflict resolution field. *$79.00*

Quarterly Founded: 1998

14615 Older Americans Report
Business Publishers
8737 Colesville Road
Suite 1100
Silver Spring, MD 20910-3928
301-876-6300
FAX: 301-589-8493 800-274-6737
custserv@bpinews.com
http://www.bpinews.com

Leonard A Eiserer, Publisher
Beth Early, Operations Director
Mark Sherman, Editor

Covers every issue and program that affects your decision-making: Older Americans Act, long term care, Social Security & SSI, nutrition, nursing home regulation, housing, retirement/pension issues, all block grants for the aged, and more. *$427.00*

Weekly Founded: 1963

14616 Payroll Administration Guide
Bureau of National Affairs
1231 25th Street NW
Washington, DC 20037-1197
202-452-4200
800-372-1033
customercare@bna.com
http://www.bna.com

Gregory C McCaffery, Publisher
Michael Baer, Managing Editor

A notification and reference service for payroll professionals. Covers federal and state employment tax, wage-hour and wage-payment laws. *$896.00*
Bi-Weekly Founded: 1929

14617 Polygraph
American Polygraph Association
PO Box 8037
Chattanooga, TN 37411-37
423-892-3992
FAX: 423-894-5435 800-272-8037

Janet K Pumphrey, Managing Editor
John E Consigli, President *$80.00*

Quarterly Founded: 1964
Circulation: 2600

14618 Practical Lawyer
American Law Institute - American Bar Association
4025 Chestnut Street
Philadelphia, PA 19104
215-243-1600
FAX: 215-243-1664
publications@ali-aba.org
http://www.ali-aba.org

Kathleen Lawner, Executive Director
Leslie A Belasco, Staff Director
Mark T Carroll, Editor

Covers all major areas of law, including bankruptcy, business and commercial law, criminal defense, estate planning, and pension and profit sharing plans. Also highlights real estate law, taxation, and trusts. *$49.00*
64 pages Founded: 1947
Circulation: 3200 $650 per M.
Printed in 1 color on matte stock

14619 Practical Real Estate Lawyer
American Law Institute - American Bar Association
4025 Chestnut Street
Philadelphia, PA 19104
215-243-1600
FAX: 215-243-1664
publications@ali-aba.org
http://www.ali.aba.org

Mark T Carroll, Editor
Michael Traynor, President

Covers news and information regarding pending or proposed real estate law. Gives practical advice in relating to clients. *$49.00*
Founded: 1923
Circulation: 5000

14620 Preview of United States Supreme Court Cases
American Bar Association
541 N Fairbanks Court
Chicago, IL 60611
312-988-5000
FAX: 312-988-5522
info@abanet.org www.abanet.org

L Anita Richardson, Editor

Advance analysis by legal experts of the issues, facts and significance of each case being argued before the Supreme Court, plus special summer issue with all court decisions. *$340.00*
10-12 issues

14621 Probate Lawyer
3415 S Sepulveda Boulevard
Suite 460
Los Angeles, CA 90034-6014
310-478-4454

Offers legislative news for probate courts.
Annual

14622 Professional Lawyer
American Bar Association
321 north clarke st
Center For Professional Responsibil
Chicago, IL 60610-4497
312-988-5000
FAX: 312-988-6281 800-285-2221
service@abanet.org
http://www.abanet.org

Arc Darwin, Editor
Robert Grey, President

A magazine providing a forum for exchange of views and ideas on professionalism issues for bar leaders, lawyers, law school education and others interested in professionalism. *$40.00*
Founded: 1878

14623 Prosecutor
National District Attorneys Association
99 Canal Center Plaza
Suite 510
Alexandria, VA 22314-1588
703-549-9222
FAX: 703-836-3195
jean.holt@ndaa-apri.org
http://www.ndaa-apri.org

Jean Holt, Director Publication/Editor
Paul F Walsh Jr, President

Covers a variety of criminal justice topics including child abuse, telemarketing fraud, violence against women, vehicular crime, DNA, juvenile justice and community prosecution.
48 pages Founded: 1977
Circulation: 7000
Mailing list available for rent 6,500 names
Printed in 4 colors on glossy stock

14624 Public Contract Law Journal
American Bar Association
321 North Clark Street
Public Contract Law Section
Chicago, IL 60611-4497
312-988-5000
FAX: 312-988-6281
wjsmith@staff.abanet.org
http://www.abanet.org

Wendy Smith, Staff Editor
Carl Vacketta, Editor

Contains articles on all phases of federal, state and local procurement and grant law by leading authoritiies. *$60.00*
Annual+

14625 Real Property, Property and Trust Journal
American Bar Association
740 15th Street NW
Washington, DC 20005-1019
202-621-1011
FAX: 312-988-6281 800-285-2221
collinsj@staff.abanet.org
http://www.abanet.org

Robert J Grey Jr, President
Adrienne Cook, Development Editor
Catherine Kruse, Director of Marketing
Sarah Rice, Marketing Specialist
Jennifer Collins, Advertising Sales Coordinator

Scholarly articles in the fields of estate planning, trust law and real property law. *$60.00*
Quarterly

14626 Review of Banking and Financial Services
Standard & Poor's Corporation
55 Water Street
New York, NY 10041
212-382-2000

clientsupport@standardandpoors.com
http://www.standardandpoors.com

Michael Ocrant, Managing Editor
Kathleen Corbet, President
Hendrik Kranenburg, Executive VP

Focuses on laws and regulations affecting the banking and related industries.
Founded: 1941

14627 Review of Securities & Commodities Regulation
Standard & Poor's Corporation
52 Water Street
44th Floor
New York, NY 10041
212-382-2000
FAX: 212-412-0240

Rusty Jacobs, Editor

Information on the laws and regulations affecting the securities and future industries. *$8.55*
22 per year
Printed in on newsprint stock

14628 Right of Way
19750 S Vermont Avenue
Suite 220
Torrance, CA 90502-1144
310-538-0233
FAX: 310-538-1471
info@irwaonline.org
http://www.irwaonline.org

Barbara Billitzer, Editor
Barbara Billitzer, Publisher
Dennis G Stork, Executive VP *$425.00*

Founded: 1985

14629 Specialization Update
American Bar Association
321 N Clark Street
Chicago, IL 60610
312-988-5000
800-285-2221
askaba@abanet.org
http://www.abanet.org

Alec M Schwartz, Staff Director
Robert Grey, President

A compilation of current news briefs and articles of interest on lawyer specialization and related topics.
Founded: 1878
Circulation: 4,00,000

14630 Student Lawyer
American Bar Association
321 N. Clark St
Chicago, IL 60611
312-988-5000
FAX: 312-988-5522
studentlawyer@abanet.org
http://www.abanet.org/lsd/stulawyer

Ira Pilchen, Editor
Roger Grey, President

Magazine for law students featuring articles on legal, political, social issues, law school and the profession. *$20.00*
Monthly Founded: 1972
Printed in 4 colors on glossy stock

14631 Tax Lawyer
American Bar Association
750 N Lake Shore Drive, 7th Floor
Taxation Section
Chicago, IL 60611-4497
312-988-5000
FAX: 312-988-6281
Journal of scholarly articles written by highly respected attorneys in the field and a thought-provoking student notes and comments section. *$53.00*
Quarterly

14632 Technology and Practice Guide
ABA Publishing
750 N Lake Shore Drive
Chicago, IL 60611-4403
312-988-5000
FAX: 312-988-6081 www.abanet.org
Mary Kay Rockwell, Publisher
Helps law professionals of general practice in making decisions about legal information management and technology. *$18.00*
SemiAnnual
Circulation: 13,477

14633 Tort and Insurance Law Journal
American Bar Association
740 15th Street NW
Washington, DC 20005-1019
202-621-1011
FAX: 312-988-6281 800-285-2221
collinsj@staff.abanet.org
http://www.abanet.org
Robert J Grey Jr, President
Catherine Kruse, Director of Marketing
Rick Paszkiet, Development Editor
Jennifer Collins, Advertising Sales Coordinator
Jill Nuppenau, Marketing
Scholarly journal on current or emerging issues of national scope in the fields of tort and insurance law. *$23.00*
Quarterly

14634 Trial
Association of Trial Lawyers of America
1050 31st Street NW
Washington, DC 20007-4409
202-965-3500
FAX: 202-965-0030 800-424-2725
trial@atlahq.org http://www.atla.org
Jon Haber, CEO/President
Julie Shoop, Editor
Judy Lewis, Circulation Manager
In depth articles by experts on socio-legal issues. Evaluates legal practices, points of law, civil law and recent developments in law. *$79.00*
Monthly Founded: 1946
Circulation: 60000

14635 Utilities Law Review
John Wiley & Sons
111 River Street
Hoboken, NJ 07030
201-748-6000
FAX: 201-748-6088 800-825-7550
customer@wiley.com
http://www.wiley.com
William J Pesce, CEO/President
Leigh Hancher, Editor
David Wilson, Publisher
Edited by a team of specialist UK and European lawyers, it is the leading journal in this fast-changing field. Providing detailed coverage of electricity, gas, telecommunications, transport, water and broadcasting.
Founded: 1807

14636 Verdicts & Settlement
Daily Journal Corporation
915 E 1st Street
Los Angeles, CA 90012
213-229-5300
FAX: 213-680-3682
http://www.dailyjournal.com
Gerald Salzman, CEO/President
Malisha Anderson, Editor
Gerald Salzman, Publisher
Ray Chagolla, Marketing Head
Ama Sanchev, Circulation Manager
Weekly Founded: 1888
Circulation: 11000

14637 Women Lawyers Journal
National Association of Women Lawyers
American Bar Center 15.2
321 North Clark Street
Chicago, IL 60610-4403
312-988-6186
FAX: 312-988-5491
nawl@nawl.org
http://www.abanet.org/nawl/journal/wlj.html
Janice Sperow, Editor
Peggy Golden, Managing Editor
Stephanie Scharf, President
Published since 1911 as a forum for the exchange of ideas and information of interest to women lawyers. Unsolicited articles and press releases about non members will not be published. *$45.00*
Founded: 1899
Circulation: 1200

14638 Young Lawyers Division Newsletter

104 Marietta St NW
Suite 100
Atlanta, GA 30303-2934
404-527-8700
FAX: 404-527-8717 800-334-6865
scottlawoffice@mindspring.com
http://www.gabar.org
Damon E Elmore, President
Bryan Scott, Editor
Cliff Brashier, Executive Director
Quarterly Founded: 1978
Circulation: 21000

Trade Shows

14639 AIRA Annual Bankruptcy & Restructuring Conference
Association of Insolvency & Restructuring Advisors
221 Stewart Avenue
Suite 207
Medford, OR 97501
541-858-1665
FAX: 541-858-9187
aira@airacira.org www.airacira.org
Grant Newton, Executive Director
Beverly Huard, Public Relations Director
Exhibits for professionals involved in insolvency and restructuring.
Annual/June 6-9 Founded: 1984

14640 ALA Annual Educational Conference and Exposition
Association of Legal Administrators
175 E Hawthorn Parkway
Suite 325
Vernon Hills, IL 60061
847-816-1212
FAX: 847-816-1213 www.alanet.org
Patty Thurlby, Exhibits Manager
Kathleen Rossell, Director Conferences/Meetings
Seminar, luncheon, tours and 200 exhibitors of information about computer hardware and software, facilities management, publications, printers, suppliers, litigation support, travel consultants and more.
2000 Attendees May

14641 Academy of Criminal Justice Sciences
Northern Kentucky University
402 Nunn Hall
Highland Heights, KY 41099
859-572-5100
FAX: 859-572-6665 800-757-ACJS
Patricia Delancey, Executive Director
Exhibits of publications pertaining to criminal justice and related areas. 45 booths.
1.8M Attendees March

14642 Academy of Legal Studies in Business Annual Meeting
School of Business-Forsyth
Western Carolina University
Cullowhee, NC 28723

Daniel Hebron, Executive Secretary
15 booths.
300 Attendees August

14643 Adjutants General Association of the United States Annual Meeting
1 Massachusetts Avenue NW
Washington, DC 20001-1401
202-289-6367
FAX: 202-682-9558
Government legislation.
300 Attendees Spring

14644 American Association for Paralegal Education Convention
American Association for Paralegal Education
2965 Flowers Road S
Suite 105
Atlanta, GA 30341-5520
770-909-9000
FAX: 913-381-9308
David Scharf, Executive Director
Annual convention of 20 exhibitors of computer hardware and software, paralegal publications and educational materials and related supplies.
200 Attendees Founded: 1984

14645 American Association of Attorney-Certified Public Accountants Convention
American Association of Attorney-CPAs
24196 Alicia Parkway
Suite K
Mission Viejo, CA 92961
949-768-0336
FAX: 949-768-7062 800-272-2889
aaacpa@attorney-cpa.com
www.attorney-cpa.com
Ronald DeVore, Executive Director
Exhibits for persons licensed both as attorneys and CPAs.
Annual

14646 American Association of Law Libraries Meeting & Conference
American Association of Law Libraries
53 W Jackson Boulevard
Suite 940
Chicago, IL 60604-3668
312-939-4764
FAX: 312-431-1097
aallhq@aall.com www.aallnet.org
Paul Graller, Exhibits Manager
Susan Fox, Executive Director
Annual show of 200 booths and 175 exhibitors of library equipment, supplies and services, including computer hardware and software/publishers of legal materials/information.
2000 Attendees July 2000 names $500 per M.

14647 American Bar Association Annual Meeting/ ABA Expo
American Bar Association
750 N Lake Shore Drive
Floor 11
Chicago, IL 60611-4497
312-988-5000
FAX: 312-988-6338 800-238-2667
Andre Burke, Show Manager
Dennis Archer, President
Annual meeting and 200 exhibits of legal technology, law books, computers, data processing equipment and other products and services related to the legal profession.
15000 Attendees August Founded: 1887 $95 per M.

14648 American Corporate Counsel Association Conference
1025 Connecticut Avenue NW
Suite 200
Washington, DC 20036-5425
202-318-8327
FAX: 202-331-7454
Frederick J Krebs, Executive Director
Corporate law.
600 Attendees November

14649 American Immigration Lawyers Association Trade Show
1400 I Street NW
Suite 1200
Washington, DC 20005-6531
202-216-2400
FAX: 202-371-9449
Warren Leiden, Executive Director
628 booths.
600 Attendees June

14650 American Society for Legal History Annual Meeting
American Society for Legal History
Notre Dame Law School
PO Box R
Notre Dame, IN 46556-0780
574-631-6627
FAX: 574-631-3595
pratt.1@nd.edu www.aslh.net
Walter F Pratt Jr, Secretary/Treasurer
Annual meeting of scholarly presses. Exhibits relating to legal history and its uses in formulating legal policy, decisions and actions; unearthing historical items; and preserving legal and legislative records.
1200 Attendees Annual Founded: 1956

14651 American Society of International Law Conference
2223 Massachusetts Avenue NW
Washington, DC 20008-2847
202-939-6005
FAX: 202-797-7133
Rosemarie Rauzino-Heller, Show Manager
Charlotte Ku, Executive Director
30 tables.
1M Attendees

14652 Annual Conference on Legal Medicine
American College of Legal Medicine
611 E Wells Street
Milwaukee, WI 53202-3816
414-276-1881
FAX: 414-276-3349 800-433-9137
info@aclm.org www.aclm.org
Laura Morrone, Meeting/Project Manager
Annual conference and exhibits related to the field of legal medicine or health care related issues.
225 Attendees
Mailing list available for rent 1400 names $150 per M.

14653 Annual Education Conference & Resource Center Exhibition
National Association for Law Placement
1666 Connecticut Avenue NW
Suite 1110
Washington, DC 20009
202-835-1001
FAX: 202-835-1112
info@nalp.org www.nalp.org
Fred Thrasher, Deputy Director
Mark Weber, Northeast Director
Annual conference and exhibits relating to recruitment and placement of lawyers.
800 Attendees Annual

14654 Association of American Law Schools Annual Meeting
Association of American Law Schools
1201 Connecticut Avenue NW
Suite 800
Washington, DC 20036-2605
202-296-8851
FAX: 202-296-8869
aals@aals.org www.aals.org
Mary E Cullen, Director Meetings
Carl Monk, Executive Director
Annual meeting of 51 book publishers, suppliers and distributors, computer software suppliers.
4100 Attendees Founded: 1896

14655 Association of Family and Conciliation Courts Annual Conference
Association of Family and Conciliation Courts
6515 Girard Tenton Plaza
Suite 210
Madison, WI 53719
608-664-3750
FAX: 608-251-2331
Ann Milne
Over 20 exhibits relating to family judicial issues, including child custody and marriage, family, and divorce counseling. Attended by judges, couselors, attorneys, court personnel, mediators, teachers and researchers.
Annual

14656 Association of Trial Lawyers Annual Summer Meeting
1050 31st Street NW
Washington, DC 20007-4499
202-965-3500
FAX: 202-625-7313 800-424-2725
Jon Haber, Chief Executive Officer
Barbara Kohl, Manager
45 booths.
3M Attendees July/August

14657 Association of Trial Lawyers Mid Winter Meeting
1050 31st Street NW
Suite 100
Washington, DC 20007-4499
202-965-3500
FAX: 202-625-7313 800-424-2725
Jon Haber, Chief Executive Officer
Barbara Kohl, Manager
55 booths.
1.5M Attendees January/Febuary

14658 Association of Trial Lawyers of America Convention/Exposition
Association of Trial Lawyers of America
1050 31st Street NW
Washington, DC 20007-4499
202-965-3500
FAX: 202-625-7313 800-424-2725
angela.kocken@atlahq.org
www.atla.org
Angela Kocken, Exhibits Manager
Jon Haber, Chief Executive Officer
Semi-annual convention and exhibits of 130 manufacturers, suppliers and distributors of legal products/service, including computer animation videos, computer software/hardware, demonstrative evidence products, expert witness services and marketing firms, as well as high end consumer gifts.
3000 Attendees July Founded: 1946

14659 Education Law Association Annual Conference
Education Law Association
300 College Park Avenue
Dayton, OH 45469
937-229-3589
FAX: 937-229-3845
ela@educationlaw.org
www.educationlaw.org
Mandy Schrank, Executive Director
Annual conference with over 100 presenters giving presentations on current education law issues. Ten to twelve exhibitors of education law resources.
350 Attendees November

14660 Federal Bar Association Convention
Federal Bar Association
1815 H Street NW
Washington, DC 20006-3604
202-785-1614
FAX: 202-785-1568
Thomas Shuck, President
Annual convention and exhibits of legal publications, computer software and insurance information.
300 Attendees

14661 Federal Taxation Institute
11 W 42nd Street
New York, NY 10036-8002
212-921-2300
Lorrie Ann England, Show Manager
11 booths.

1M Attendees November

14662 Institute of Federal Taxation
USC Law Center
University Park
Suite 124
Los Angeles, CA 90089-0001

FAX: 213-740-9442

Karen Sprague, Director

10 booths.
1M Attendees January

14663 Law and Society Association Annual Meeting
University of Massachusetts
Hampshire House
Amherst, MA 01003
413-545-0111
FAX: 413-545-1640
lsa@lawandsociety.org
www.lawandsociety.org

Ronald Pipkin, Executive Officer
Lissa Ganter, Administrative Coord

The annual meeting brings together 800-1000 scholars from the US and around the world to present research in the field of socio-legal studies. This includes the place of law in relation to other social institutions, legal decision making, legal systems, and operations, and a variety of research methods and modes of analysis. 50 booths including publishers exhibit, mainly academic, in the fiels of legal studies, and social science.
May 2600 names $300 per M.

14664 Legal Administrators Association
Association of Legal Administrators
175 E Hawthorn Parkway
Suite 325
Vernon Hills, IL 60061
847-816-1212
FAX: 847-816-1213 www.alanet.org

Nancy Guthrie, Show Manager

350 booths of products and services related to the legal industry.
2M Attendees April

14665 Mid-America Association of Law Libraries Convention
Mid-America Association of Law Libraries
Drake University Law Library
Opperman Hall
Des Moines, IA 50311
515-265-1208
FAX: 515-271-2530
Annual show and exhibits of law library equipment, supplies and services.
October, Omaha

14666 National Association of Black Criminal Justice
1900 N Loop W
Suite 255
Houston, TX 77018-8116
713-681-3700
FAX: 713-956-8664

Keith Branch Esq, Chairman
Howard Thompson, Owner

60 booths.
700 Attendees July

14667 National Association of Parliamentarians (NAP) Conference
National Association of Parliamentarians
213 South Main Street
Independence, MO 64050-3850
816-833-3892
FAX: 816-833-3893 888-627-2929
hq@nap2.org
www.parliamentarians.org

Jeanette N Williams, President
Connie M Deford, VP
Mary L Randolph, Secretary
Ronald R Stinson, Treasurer
Sarah Nieft, Executive Director

The NAP sponsors a conference and exhibit relating to parliamentary law and procedure on a biennial basis. In addition, the Association also holds a national event once each year, providing the opportunities for members, prospective members, and guests to learn more about effective meetings, how to help others learn the fundamentals of parliamentary procedure, and how to be an effective parliamentarian.

14668 National Bar Association Annual Convention
National Bar Association
1225 11th Street NW
Washington, DC 20001-4217
202-842-3900
FAX: 202-289-6170

Maurice Foster, Director Special Projects
Reese Marshall, Coordinator Special Projects
John Crump, Executive Director

Annual convention and exhibits of computers and legal software, office products, accounting services, financial planners, temporary employment agencies, legal publications, travel agencies, luggage and leather goods, fine arts and jewelry. Containing 50 booths.
2500 Attendees July-August Founded: 1925

14669 National Federation Paralegal Associations
PO Box 33108
Kansas City, MO 64114
816-421-5989
FAX: 816-941-2725
info@paralegals.org
www.paralegals.org

Tena Nichols, Assistant Managing Director

Thirty-five booths.
300 Attendees April 30000 names $100 per M.

14670 National Forensic Center Trade Show
National Forensic Center
17 Temple Ter
Lawrenceville, NJ 08648-3254
609-883-0550
FAX: 609-883-7622 800-526-5177
ForenExpts@att.net expertindex.com

Betty Lipschner, Director

Coverage of the application of scientific, medical and technical knowledge to litigation.
200 Attendees
Printed in 1 color on matte stock

14671 National Judges Association
42 Little Horn Road
Westcliffe, CO 81252-9693

Whitney Sullivan, Executive Director

10 booths.
150 Attendees May

Directories & Databases

14672 ABA Journal Directory of Legal Software and Hardware
American Bar Association
750 N Lake Shore Drive
Floor 7
Chicago, IL 60611-4497
312-988-5000
FAX: 312-988-6281

Dennis Archer, President

Directory of supplies to the industry. *$7.00*
Annual
Circulation: 400,000

14673 Agricultural Law Update
American Agricultural Law Association
University of Arkansas Law Programs Building
Fayetteville, AR 72701
479-575-4671
FAX: 479-575-5830
aala@law.uark.edu
www.aglan-assn.org

Susan Williams, Admininstrative Assistant
Linda McGormic, Editor

Monthly update of legal issues concerning the agricultural industry(members only)
Biennial
Circulation: 1,500

14674 American Association of Attorney-Certified Public Accountants Directory
24196 Alicia Parkway
Suite K
Mission Viejo, CA 92691-3926
949-768-0336

aaacpa@attorney-cpa.com
www.attorney-cpa.com

Ronald De Vore, Executive Director

Offers names, addresses and biographical data on 1,400 individuals licensed as both attorneys and CPAs. *$175.00*
100 pages Annual

14675 American Bar Association Legal Education Database
American Bar Association
750 N Lake Shore Drive
Floor 7
Chicago, IL 60611-4497
312-988-5000
FAX: 312-988-6281 800-242-6005

Dennis Archer, President

Contains the complete text of the Third Tenative Draft of Law School Library Accreditation Standards.
Full-text

14676 American College of Legal Medicine Membership Directory
611 E Wells Street
Milwaukee, WI 53202-3816
414-276-1881
FAX: 414-276-3349 800-433-9137
info@aclm.org www.aclm.org

Janet L Haynes, Director

Lists members alphabetically, specialty or area(s) of expertise, and geographic location. *$75.00*

1400 pages Founded: 1960
Circulation: 1,425

14677 American Law Reports Library
Lawyers Co-operative Publishing Company
50 Broad Street E
Rochester, NY 14694-0001
585-719-9760

A database, updated periodically, that contains the complete text of analyses of state and federal case law.
Full-text

14678 BNA Criminal Practice Manual
Pike & Fischer
1010 Wayne Avenue
Suite 1400
Silver Spring, MD 20910-5600
301-621-1530
FAX: 301-562-1521 800-255-8131

14679 BNA's Directory of State and Federal Courts, Judges and Clerks
BNA Books
1231 25th Street NW
Washington, DC 20037-1164
732-346-0089
FAX: 732-346-1624 800-960-1220
books@bna.com www.bnabooks.com
Margaret Hullinger, Executive Editor
Lois Smith, Marketing Manager
Janie Meidhof, Media Specialist
Complete contact information including e-mail addresses on the nation's judges and clerks, as well as comprehensive details on the structure of federal, state, and territorial courts. Includes 2,201 state courts, 214 federal courts, 14,432 judges, and 5,303 clerks, list of nominations for federal judgeships, federal appellate court jurisdiction map and list, state court structure charts, reports of judicial decisions, directory of electronic public-access services, and personal name index.
714 pages Annual Founded: 1986 ISBN 1-570184-11-9
Circulation: 1,300 1,300 names

14680 Best Lawyers in America
Woodward/White
129 1st Avenue
Aiken, SC 29801-4862
803-648-0300
FAX: 803-641-1709
Kimberly Woodward, Owner
Over 11,000 attorneys who are selected as the best in their specialities by a survey of over 150,000 lawyers are profiled. *$110.00*

1000 pages Biennial

14681 Business Litigation Database
Trans Union Credit Information Company

20 Constance Center
Hauppauge, NY 11788-4200
631-582-2767
FAX: 516-582-2767
Over 8 million court records on companies from New York and New Jersey are included in this database.
Directory

14682 CEMC/ENR Directory of Law Firms
Construction Education Management Corporation
8133 Leesburg Pike
Suite 700
Vienna, VA 22182-2730
703-734-2399

Harvey Kornbluh, Owner
Over 70 construction-oriented law firms located nationwide and overseas are listed.
$75.00
Annual

14683 Common Market Law Review
Kluwer Law and Taxation Publishers
101 Philip Drive
Assinippi Park
Norwell, MA 02061
781-871-6600
FAX: 781-681-9045 866-269-9527
Serves as a medium for the dissemination of legal thinking on community law matters, meeting the need of both the academic and the practitioner.

14684 Comprehensive Guide to Bar Admission Requirements
Legal Education and Admissions to the Bar
750 N Lake Shore Drive
Chicago, IL 60611-4403
312-944-0575
FAX: 312-988-6281
Offers a list of state bar admission administrators in the United States and its territories. *$5.00*
Annual

14685 Corporate Counsel's Law Library
LexisNexis Matthew Bender
1275 Broadway
Albany, NY 12204
518-873-3385
FAX: 518-462-3788 888-223-1940
Matthew Bender, Publisher
This database contains court decisions covering statutory and common law concepts related to the formation, maintenance and dissolution of corporations. *$2484.00*

14686 Criminal Justice Information Exchange Directory
US National Criminal Justice Reference Service
1600 Research Boulevard
#6000
Rockville, MD 20850-3129

Over 100 criminal justice-related organizations are listed.
95 pages Annual

14687 Criminal Justice Periodical Index
University Microfilms International
125 Chapman Hall
1219 University of Oregon
Eugine, OR 97403-1219
541-346-5129
FAX: 541-346-2804
Mary Ann Gilbert, Editor
Offers information on more than 180,000 citations to articles in 145 magazines, journals, newsletters and law reporting periodicals on the administration of justice and law enforcement. *$315.00*
TriAnnual

14688 Current Index to Legal Periodicals
Marian Gould Gallagher Law Library-Univ. of Wash.
William H Gates Hall
Box 353025
Seattle, WA 98195-3025
206-543-4089
FAX: 206-685-2165
clip@u-washington.edu
lib.law.washington.edu/clip/cilp.html
Susan M Sorensen, Editor
Muriel Quick, Information Specialist
List of publishers of titles indexed in the database. *$192.00*
52 issues Founded: 1948
Printed in on matte stock

14689 Deskbook Encyclopedia of Employment Law
Data Research
PO Box 490
Rosemount, MN 55068-0490
952-452-8694
FAX: 952-452-8694 800-365-4900
An up-to-date compilation of summarized federal and state appellate court decisions which affect employment. The full legal citation is supplied for each case. A brief introductory note on the American judicial system is provided along with updated appendices of recent US Supreme Court cases and recently published law review articles. Also included are portions of the US Constitution which are most frequently cited in employment cases. *$85.75*
500 pages Annual Founded: 1996 ISBN 0-939675-55-2

14690 Deskbook Encyclopedia of Public Employment Law
Data Research
PO Box 490
Rosemount, MN 55068-0490
952-452-8694
FAX: 952-452-8694 800-365-4900
An up-to-datre compilation of summarized federal and state appellate court decisions which affect public employment. The full legal citation is cupplied for each case. A brief introductory note on the American judicial system is provided along with updated appendices of recent US Supreme Court cases and recently published law review articles. *$987.54*
531 pages Annual Founded: 1996 ISBN 0-939675-56-0

14691 Directory of Bar Associations
American Bar Association
541 N Fairbanks Court
16th Floor
Chicago, IL 60611-3375
312-988-5000

Offers information on more than 57 state bar associations, local bar associations and other local associations represented in the American Bar Association House of Delegates. *$95.00*
40 pages Annual

14692 Directory of Certified Business Counselors
Institute of Certified Business Counselors
18615 Willamette Drive
West Linn, OR 97068
503-751-1856
FAX: 323-417-5176
Wally Stabbert, Editor
125 member counselors, brokers and attorneys qualified to act as advisors for persons with business problems.

14693 Directory of Courthouses, Abstract and Title Companies of the USA
Harbors International
7020 S Yale Avenue
Suite 206
Tulsa, OK 74136-5744
918-496-3232
FAX: 918-496-8905
A who's who directory of counties, parishes and boroughs with a section on abstract and title companies. *$95.00*
368 pages

14694 Directory of Law-Related CD-ROMs
Infosource Publishing
140 Norma Road
Teaneck, NJ 07666-4234
201-836-7072

Arlene Eis, Editor
A who's who directory of supplies to the industry. *$64.00*
200 pages Annual

14695 Directory of Lawyer Disciplinary Agencies & Lawyers' Funds/Client Protection
Center for Professional Responsibility
541 N Fairbanks Court
Chicago, IL 60611-3319
312-595-1501
FAX: 312-988-6281 *$12.95*
35 pages Annual

14696 Directory of Lawyer Referral Services
American Bar Association
541 N Fairbanks Court
16th Floor
Chicago, IL 60611-3375
312-988-5000

Names of services, sponsoring organizations, phones and names of the directors are listed for over 330 services. *$10.00*
40 pages Annual

14697 Directory of Legal Aid & Defender Offices in the United States & Territories
National Legal Aid and Defender Association
1625 K Street NW
8th Floor
Washington, DC 20006-1617
202-520-0620
FAX: 202-872-1031 info@nlada.org
Steve Kemp, Circulation Director *$70.00*

14698 Directory of Opportunities in International Law
John Bassett Moore Society of International Law
School of Law: University of VA
Charlottesville, VA 22901

Offers hundreds of possible employers in international law. *$10.00*
204 pages

14699 Directory of Private Bar Involvement Programs
American Bar Association
750 N Lake Shore Drive
Floor 7
Chicago, IL 60611-4497
312-988-5000
FAX: 312-988-6281
A list of over 900 programs that provide free or low-cost legal services. *$7.50*
210 pages Annual

14700 Directory of Public Interest Law Centers
Alliance for Justice
11 Dupont Circle NW
2nd Floor
Washington, DC 20036
202-822-6070
FAX: 202-822-6068
alliance@afj.org www.afj.org
Nonprofit association of public interest advocacy organization. Offers workshops, advocacy projects, legal guides, techinical assistance and public education. Lists addresses, branch offices and directors of 200 public interest law centers around the country. Indexed by state and subject area. *$10.00*
48 pages Founded: 1996

14701 Directory of State Court Clerks & County Courthouses
WANT Publishing Company
420 Lexington Avenue
Room 300
New York, NY 10170-0399
212-687-3774
FAX: 212-687-3779
rwant@msn.com www.courts.com
Robert S Want, President
Allows easy access to vital information including court decisions, real estate records, UCC and tax liens, and other important documents maintained by State appellate and trial courts and county courthouses nationwide. *$75.00*
380 pages Annual ISBN 0-970122-91-8

14702 Encyclopedia of Legal Information Sources
Gale Research
27500 Drake Road
Farmington Hills, MI 48331
248-699-4253
FAX: 248-699-8214 800-877-4253
galeord@gale.com www.gale.com
Books, periodicals and newsletters for law and legal professions are listed. *$165.00*
1000 pages

14703 FCBA Directory
Federal Communications Bar Association
1020 19th Street NW
Suite 325
Washington, DC 20036-6113
202-293-4000
FAX: 202-293-4317
fcba@fcba.org www.fcba.org
Stanley Zenor, Executive Director
A nonprofit organization of attorneys and other professionals involved in the development, interpretation, implementation and practice of communications law and policy.

Founded: 1936

14704 Federal Careers for Attorneys
Federal Reports
1010 Vermont Avenue NW
Suite 408
Washington, DC 20005-4947
202-933-3311

Linda Sutherland, President
United States government general counsel and other legal offices throughout the federal system. *$23.95*
150 pages

14705 Federal Law-Related Careers Directory
Federal Reports
1010 Vermont Avenue NW
Suite 408
Washington, DC 20005-4947
202-933-3311
FAX: 202-393-1553 800-296-9611
Linda P Sutherland, Editor
Richard L Hermann, Editor
Listings of over 1,000 federal government recruiting offices. *$16.95*

14706 General Bar Law Directory
General Bar
25000 Center Ridge Road
Suite 3
Cleveland, OH 44145-4108
440-835-2000
FAX: 440-835-3636 800-533-2500
generalbar@aol.com
www.generalbar.com
Charles J Sonnhalter, President
700 pages Founded: 1941
Circulation: 10000 : CD-ROM

14707 Insider's Guide to Law Firms
Mobius Press
PO Box 3339
Boulder, CO 80307
303-188-8205
FAX: 303-499-5389 800-529-5627
Directory of services and supplies to the industry. *$28.95*
740 pages Annual

14708 Judicial Yellow Book
Leadership Directories
104 5th Avenue
New York, NY 10011-6901
212-627-4140
FAX: 212-645-0931
judicial@leadershipdirectories.com
www.leadershipdirectories.com
Imogene Akins, Editor
James M Petrie, Associate Publisher
Contact information for over 3,250 federal and state judges in federal and state appellate courts, including staff and law clerks, and the law schools they attended. *$245.00*
1,100 pages SemiAnnual Founded: 1995
Mailing list available for rent 13,000 names $125 per M.
Computerized version available: CD-ROM

14709 Latin American Labor Law Handbook
WorldTrade Executive
PO Box 761
Concord, MA 01742-0761
978-287-0301
FAX: 978-287-0302 www.wtexec.com
Alison French, Production Manager
Designed to give firms doing business in Latin America some basic knowledge of labor and employment law in the region. Covers countries where US and foreign in-

vestment is particularly high: Argentina, Brazil, Venezuela, Colombia, Costa Rica and Chili - providing an overview of the complex network of laws, regulations, and customs affecting social security, wages, employment security, and labor organizing. *$185.00*

14710 Law Books and Serials in Print
RR Bowker
121 Chanlon Road
New Providence, NJ 07974-1544
908-286-1090
FAX: 908-464-3553 800-521-8110
info@howker.com www.reedref.com
D Gravesande, Editor
L Yuster-Freeman, Editor
List of publishers and producers of over 60,000 legal reference publications, periodicals, software, audio cassette titles under 6,608 headings and video cassettes. *$690.00*

14711 Law Books in Print
Glanville Publishers
75 Main Street
Dobbs Ferry, NY 10522-1601
914-693-1320
Publishers of law books in English are listed. *$750.00*
Base Edition

14712 Law Firms Yellow Book
Leadership Directories
104 5th Avenue
New York, NY 10011-6901
212-627-4140
FAX: 212-645-0931
lawfirms@leadershipdirectories.com
www.leadershipdirectories.com
Janet Nelson-Henry, Editor
James M Petrie, Associate Publisher
Contact information for over 24,000 attorneys and administrators who make the business decisions and manage the practice areas in over 800 of the nation's leading law firms. *$245.00*
1,100 pages SemiAnnual Founded: 1991
Mailing list available for rent 19,000 names $125 per M.
Computerized version available: CD-ROM

14713 Law Office Computing Directory
James Publishing
3520 Cadillac Avenue
Suite E
Costa Mesa, CA 92626-1419
714-755-5450
FAX: 714-751-5508
Lorraine A Thinnes, Editor
Approximately 25 computer products and services designed for use by the legal profession. *$49.95*
Bi-Monthly
Circulation: 9,000

14714 Law Office Economics & Management: Directory of Law Office Software
Clark Boardman Callaghan
155 Pfingsten Road
Deerfield, IL 60015
847-374-0400
FAX: 847-948-9340 800-323-1336
Paul S Hoffman, Editor
List of about 100 suppliers of data processing equipment and software. *$15.00*
Annual June

14715 Law and Legal Information Directory
Gale Research
27500 Drake Road
Farmington Hills, MI 48331
248-699-4253
FAX: 248-699-8214 800-877-4253
galeord@gale.com www.gale.com
National and international organizations, bar associations, federal and highest state courts and federal regulatory agencies are listed.
2000 pages Biennial

14716 Lawyers Referral Directory
PO Box 40335
Cleveland, OH 44140-0335
440-899-8660
FAX: 440-899-1005 800-LAW-LIST
ILlaw@rampant.com
www.lawlistil.com
Ted M McManamon, Editor
Richard T Ostovitz, Production Manager
Bonded reference guide to lawyers specializing in commercial law, creditors' rights and collection litigation. Free to users registering referrals sent.
700 pages Annual

14717 Lawyers' List
Commercial Publishing Company
PO Box 2430
Easton, MD 21601-2430
410-820-4494
FAX: 410-820-4474 800-824-9911
DA Schwartz, President
A listing of law offices engaged in general, corporation and trial practice or patent, trademark and copyright practice.
1700 pages Annual

14718 Legal Information Alert
Alert Publications
401 W Fullerton Parkway
Apartment 1403E
Chicago, IL 60614-2805
773-525-7594
Donna Tuke-Heroy, President
Publishers of books, databases, CD-ROM products and looseleaf services for the legal profession are listed. *$149.00*

14719 Legal Looseleafs in Print
Infosource Publishing
140 Norma Road
Teaneck, NJ 07666-4234
201-836-7072
aeis@carroll.com
www.infosourcespub.com
Over 230 publishers offering 3,600 looseleaf legal information services. *$106.00*
400 pages Annual March Founded: 1981

14720 Legal Newsletters in Print
Infosource Publishing
140 Norma Road
Teaneck, NJ 07666-4234
201-836-7072
Arlene Eis, Editor
Directory of services and supplies to the industry. *$90.00*
400 pages Annual

14721 Legal Researcher's Desk Reference
Infosource Publishing
140 Norma Road
Teaneck, NJ 07666-4234
201-836-7072
Arlene Eis, Editor
Information is provided on federal and state government officials and departments are listed, as well as publishers and law book dealers and much more. *$58.00*
416 pages Biennial

14722 Legal Resource Directory
McFarland & Company Publishers
PO Box 611
Jefferson, NC 28640-0611
336-246-4460
Information is given on national, state and local organizations providing free or inexpensive legal advice to low-income families. *$30.95*
148 pages

14723 Legal Resources Index
Information Access Company
362 Lakeside Drive
Foster City, CA 94404-1171
650-378-5200
800-227-8431
This database contains more than 500,000 citations, with selected abstracts, to articles published in more than 800 key law journals, bar association publications and legal newspapers.
Bibliographic

14724 Martindale-Hubbell Law Directory
Martindale-Hubbell/Reed Reference Publishing
121 Chanlon Road
New Providence, NJ 07974-1541
908-646-6800
FAX: 908-771-8704 800-526-4902
info@martindale.com
www.martindale.com
Paul Johnson, Manager
Directory of services and supplies to the industry. *$690.00*
50000 pages 26 Volumes

14725 NAFTA Handbook
WorldTrade Executive
PO Box 761
Concord, MA 01742-0761
978-287-0301
FAX: 978-287-0302 www.wtexec.com
Alison French, Production Manager
A concise, chapter-by-chapter summary of the NAFTA provisions, providing both a short overview of each chapter and a detailed description and analysis of the chapter's provisions and their impact on doing business in North America. *$125.00*

14726 NAFTA Law Reporter
WorldTrade Executive
PO Box 761
Concord, MA 01742-0761
978-287-0301
FAX: 978-287-0302 www.wtexec.com
Alison French, Production Manager
Contains the full NAFTA text and annexes, plus member-country implementing legislation and the labor and environmental side agreements. *$135.00*

14727 **NALP Directory of Legal Employers**
National Association for Law Placement
1025 Connecticut Avenue NW
Suite 1110
Washington, DC 20036-5413
202-835-1001
FAX: 202-835-1112
info@nalp.org www.nalp.org
James Liepold, Executive Director
Fred Thrasher, Deputy Director
Information on more than 1,700 employers nationwide and is an invaluable tool for job searchers, career counselors, and legal recruiters alike. Published both on-line and in print, this directory includes indexes by location and by practice area keyword. *$75.00*
Annual Founded: 1971
Mailing list available for rent CBC names

14728 **NLADA Directory of Legal Aid and Defender Offices in the US & Territories**
National Legal Aid and Defender Association
1625 K Street NW
Washington, DC 20006-1604
202-520-0620
FAX: 202-872-1031 www.lnada.org
Steven C Kemp, Membership/Training
About 3,600 civil legal aid and indigent defense organizations in the US. *$70.00*
Biennial

14729 **NSA Directory**
National Sherriff's Association
1450 Duke Street
Alexandria, VA 22314-3490
703-836-7827
Suzanne B Litts, Editor
David Strigel, Advertising Manager
Sheriffs of the US address phone and fax. *$50.00*
94 pages Annual

14730 **National Directory of Corrections Construction**
National Institute of Justice
PO Box 6000
Rockville, MD 20849-6000
301-251-5500
Offers valuable information on over 150 correctional institutions constructed since 1985. *$32.00*
354 pages

14731 **National Directory of Courts of Law**
Information Resources
1110 N Glebe Road
Suite 550
Arlington, VA 22201-5762
703-525-4750
Directory of services and supplies to the industry. *$95.00*
888 pages Biennial

14732 **National Directory of Prosecuting Attorneys**
National District Attorneys Association
99 Canal Center Plaza
Suite 510
Alexandria, VA 22314-1588
703-549-9222
Thomas Charron, Executive Director
$15.00
100 pages Biennial
Circulation: 7,000

14733 **National Employment Listing Service Bulletin**
Criminal Justice Center
Sam Houston State University
Huntsville, TX 77341
936-295-6371
FAX: 281-294-1653
Kay Billingsley, Editor
Job openings in police departments, sheriff's departments, courts and other law enforcement and security agencies.

14734 **National Hispanic American Attorney Directory**
Hispanic National Bar Association
100 Seaview Drive
Secaucus, NJ 07094-1800
201-348-4900
FAX: 201-348-6609
Carlos G Ortiz
National directory listing Hispanic American Attorneys. *$65.00*
Circulation: 4,000

14735 **National Law Journal: Directory of Current Law & Law-Related Books**
New York Law Publishing Company
345 Park Avenue S
8th Floor
New York, NY 10010-1700
212-799-9434
FAX: 212-696-1875
nljeds@ljextra.com www.ljextra.com
Ben Gerson, Editor
Bill Pollak, President
Lists over 70 publishers of law and law-related books. *$124.00*
Annual January

14736 **National List**
PO Box 2486
Bismark, ND 58502-2486
701-237-7202
FAX: 701-223-5634 800-227-1675
results@nationallist.com
www.nationallist.com
Randy Nicola, VP
Gerry Cowgill, Manager
A list of lawyers and law firms handling collections and general practice in the United States, Canada, and most foreign countries.
550 pages Annual

14737 **National Trial and Deposition Directory**
321 W Franklin Street
Boise, ID 83702
208-344-3191
FAX: 208-345-8800 *$39.95*
490 pages
Circulation: 2,000

14738 **National and Federal Legal Employment Report**
Federal Reports
1010 Vermont Avenue NW
Suite 408
Washington, DC 20005-4947
202-933-3311
FAX: 202-393-1553 800-296-9611
Linda P Sutherland, Editor
Richard L Hermann, Editor
Listings of approximately 600 current attorney and law-related job opportunities with the US government and other public and private employers in Washington DC, nationwide and abroad. *$35.80*
Monthly

14739 **Nelson's Law Office Directory**
Nelson Company
PO Box 309
Hopkins, MN 55343-0309
952-359-9092
Robert J Nelson, Publisher/Editor
A directory of the top rated law firms in the United States. Rated on legal ability, integrity and diligence by the leading lawyers in each state. *$23.00*
210 pages Annual Founded: 1968

14740 **Now Hiring: Government Jobs for Lawyers**
American Bar Association
750 N Lake Shore Drive
Floor 7
Chicago, IL 60611-4497
312-988-5000
Federal, quasi- and independent government agency jobs for lawyers. *$17.95*
170 pages

14741 **Parole and Probation Compact Administrator Association Mailing List**
Council of State Governments
2760 Research Park Drive
PO Box 11910
Lexington, KY 40578-1910
859-244-8000
FAX: 859-244-8001 800-800-1910
Carl Wicklund, Executive Director
Laura Williams, Duputy Director

14742 **Preview of United States Supreme Court Cases**
American Bar Association
750 N Lake Shore Drive
Floor 7
Chicago, IL 60611-4497
312-988-5000
FAX: 312-988-6281 800-242-6005
This database contains full-text reviews of cases orally argued before the US Supreme Court.
Full-text

14743 **Representative Offices in the Russian Federation**
WorldTrade Executive
PO Box 761
Concord, MA 01742-0761
978-287-0301
FAX: 978-287-0302 www.wtexec.com
Alison French, Production Manager
Combines detailed information on the legal structure within which representative offices must operate, including tax and other requirements, with a user-friendly guide to the accreditation and registration process. *$135.00*

14744 **Russell Law List**
Commercial Publishing Company
PO Box 2430
Easton, MD 21601-2430
410-820-4494
FAX: 410-820-4474 800-824-9911
DA Schwartz, President

A listing of law offices in general practice worldwide.
147 pages Annual

14745 Russia Business & Legal Briefing
WorldTrade Executive
PO Box 761
Concord, MA 01742-0761
978-287-0301
FAX: 978-287-0302 www.wtexec.com
Alison French, Production Manager
Topics include: economic analysis; hard currency regulations; investment legislation in St. Petersburg; enforcing foreign judgements in Russia; new laws on limited liability companies and bankruptcy; new commercial arbitration court in St. Petersburg; changes in tax legislation; managing the Russian tax burden. *$265.00*

14746 Sourcebook of Local Court and County Records Retrievers
BRP Publications
200 E Eager Street
Baltimore, MD 21202-3704
202-312-6060
FAX: - - 047 800-822-6338
Offers information on firms that specialize in finding court and county records, including civil, criminal, probate and bankruptcy files. *$45.00*
432 pages

14747 Summer Legal Employment Guide
Federal Reports
1010 Vermont Avenue NW
Suite 408
Washington, DC 20005-4947
202-933-3311

Linda Sutherland, President
Directory of services and supplies to the industry. *$170.00*
36 pages Annual

14748 US Supreme Court Employment Cases
Data Research
PO Box 490
Rosemount, MN 55068-0490
952-452-8694
FAX: 952-452-8694 800-365-4900
A compilation of summarized US Supreme Court decisions which affect employment. The full legal citation is supplied for each case. *$64.70*
288 pages Annual Founded: 1995 ISBN 0-939675-51-0

14749 United States Probation and Pretrial Services Officers Directory

Probation Div./Admin. Office of US Courts
1 Columbus Circle NE
Suite 4-300
Washington, DC 20544-0001

FAX: 202-273-1603
Federal probation offices and pretrial services offices.
Annual

14750 WESTLAW International Law Library
West Publishing Company
610 Opperman Drive
Eagan, MN 55123-1340
651-687-7327
www.westgroup.com
Database containing the complete information of international and US federal court decisions.
Full-text

14751 WESTLAW Legal Services Library
West Publishing Company
610 Opperman Drive
Eagan, MN 55123-1340
651-687-7327
www.westgroup.com
This database offers the complete text of US federal and state court decisions, statutes and regulations.
Bibliographic

14752 WESTLAW Litigation Library
West Publishing Company
610 Opperman Drive
Eagan, MN 55123-1340
651-687-7327
www.westgroup.com
Offers information on law reviews, bar association journals and law-related texts.
Full-text

14753 Want's Federal-State Court Directory
WANT Publishing Company
420 Lexington Avenue
Room 300
New York, NY 10170-0399
212-687-3774
FAX: 212-687-3779
rwant@msn.com www.courts.com
Robert S Want, President
The nation's number one court reference source, offering comprehensive information on the nation's federal, state and county courts. *$35.00*
235 pages Softcover

14754 Who's Who in American Law
Marquis Who's Who/Reed Reference Publishing
121 Chanlon Road
New Providence, NJ 07974-1544
908-673-1000
FAX: 908-464-3553
Information is given on lawyers, judges and law school deans. *$249.95*
1100 pages Biennial

Industry Web Sites

14755 www.aallnet.org
American Association of Law Libraries

Membership consists of national law library professionals.

14756 www.abanet.org
American Bar Association

The largest organization serving lawyers and all professionals involved in the law enforcement and legal industries. Conducts research and educational activities, encourages professional improvement and provides public service.

14757 www.aclm.org
American College of Legal Medicine

Organization related to the field of health law, legal medicine or medical jurisprudence.

14758 www.aclu.org
American Civil Liberties Union

Protection of civil liberties and constitutional rights through litigation, public education and legislative lobbying.

14759 www.afj.org
Alliance for Justice

Nonprofit association of public interest advocacy organization. Offers workshops, advocacy projects, legal guides, techinical assistance and public education. Publishes a directory of public interest law centers.

14760 www.ajs.org
American Judicature Society

Lawyers, judges and educators interested in the effective administration of justice.

14761 www.ali-aba.org
American Law Institute - American Bar Association

Provides continuing legal education courses, books, and periodicals for practicing attorneys and others in the legal profession.

14762 www.ascm.vicsc.dni.us
National Association for Court Management

Members are clerks of court, court administration and others serving in a court management capacity.

14763 www.atlanet.org
Association of Trial Lawyers of America

14764 www.attorney-cpa.com
American Association of Attorney-CPAs

Seeks to safeguard the professional and legal rights of CPA attorneys.

14765 www.blr.com
Business & Legal Reports

Provides essential tools for safety and environmental compliance and training needs

14766 www.educationlaw.org
Education Law Association

Association for manufacturers or suppliers of law education equipment, supplies and services.

14767 www.fala.org
First Amendment Lawyers Association

Lawyers concentrating on defending clients under the first amendment of the Constitution.

14768 www.fcba.org
Federal Communications Bar Association

A non-profit organization of attorneys and other professionals involved in the development, interpretation, implementation and practice of communications law and policy.

14769 www.findlaw.com

Online Legal Resources. Legal, Professionals, Students, Business, Legal News, etc.

14770 www.greyhouse.com
Grey House Publishing

Selected Grey House directories in the fields of business, health and education are available online. Users can search our online databases by several different search criteria, such as product categories, geographic area, sales volume and much, much more. Full Grey House catalog and online ordering also available.

14771 www.honet.msu.edu/~law
American Society for Legal History

Exhibits relating to legal history and its uses in formulating legal policy, decisions and actions; unearthing historical items; and preserving legal and legislative records.

14772 www.lexis-nexis.com
Mead Data Central

Contains the Lexis-Nexis Source Locator, a powerful new tool for retrieving targeted information about the more 31,000 Lexi-Nexis sources.

14773 www.naela.org
National Academy of Elder Law Attorneys

Members are private attorneys, law professors and Title III interest in the provision of legal service to the elderly.

14774 www.narf.org
Native American Rights Fund

Provides legal services to Indian tribes, organizations and individuals in the areas of preservation of tribal existence, protection of tribal natural resources, promotion of human rights , accoutability of governments, development of Indian law.

14775 www.paralegals.org
National Federation of Paralegal Association

For state and local paralegal associations throughout the United States and Canada.

14776 www.rmmlf.org
Rocky Mountain Mineral Law Foundation

14777 www.romingerlegal.com

Is a Search Engine dedicated to Legal Links, Legal Research Page, Case Law and Professional Directories for Law, etc.

14778 www.searchcrawl.com/legal/justice.html
Searchcrawl

List of legal resources.

14779 www.usfca.edu/law/globaljustice

Web site for the Center for Law and Global Justice. Focus on legal education, judicial training, free and fair elections, and the protection of human rights. The Center is an integral part of the University of San Francisco School of Law.

14780 www.westlaw.com

Westlaw is the premier legal and business research tool on the Internet.

14781 www.worldjurist.org
World Jurist Association of the World Peace
Through Law

Association for those interested in future world peace.

Associations

14782 ARMA International
Ass. for Information Management Professionals
13725 West 109th Street
Suite 101
Lenexa, KS 66215
913-341-3808
FAX: 913-341-3742 800-422-2762
hq@arma.org www.arma.org/
Peter Hermann, Executive Director/CEO
Susan Avery, Senior Strategic Advisor
An international not-for-profit association and the leading authority on managing records and information, paper and electric.
10000 Members Founded: 1955

14783 Africana Librarians Council/African Studies Association
Library of Congress
202-707-0371
FAX: 202-707-4445
olson@pobox.upenn.edu
www.loc.gov/rr/amed/afs/alc
Lauris Olson, Chairperson
Esmeralda Kale, Secretary
Members consist of librarians, archivists or documentalists working with materials from and about Africa or scholars interested in the preseravtionof or access to Africana.
Founded: 1957

14784 American Association of Law Libraries
53 West Jackson
Suite 940
Chicago, IL 60604
312-939-4764
FAX: 312-431-1097
webmaster@aall.org www.aallnet.org/
Susan E. Fox, Executive Director
Kim Rundle, Executive Assistant
Promotes and enhances the value of law libraries to the legal and public communities and rs the profession of law librarianship in addition to providing leadership in the field of legal information.
5000 Members Founded: 1906

14785 American Association of School Librarians
50 E Huron Street
Chicago, IL 60611
312-944-6780
800-545-2433
ala@ala.org www.ala.org/aasl
Julie A Walker, Executive Director
Nichole Gilbert, Program Officer
Jennifer Locke, Deputy Executive Director
Andrea Parker, Program Officer Marketing/Comm
Karla Hayden, President
Works to ensure that all members of the school library media field collaborate to provide leadership in the total education program, participate as active partners in the teaching and learning process, connect learners with ideas and information and prepare students for life long learning, informed decision making, a love of reading and the use of information technologies.
60000 Members

14786 American Indian Library Association
Harris County Public Library
50 E Huron
Chicago, IL 60611
312-280-4386
FAX: 312-664-7459 aaso@ala.org
David Ongley, President
Kelly Webster, VP
Sara Harris, Manager
Association for Native Americans and Native Alaskans libraries and librarians.
10000 Members Founded: 1949

14787 American Library Association
50 E Huron Street
Chicago, IL 60611
312-944-6780
800-545-2433
library@ala.org www.ala.org
John W Berry, President
Association for librarians, libraries, trustees, students and academics, encompassing all aspects of librarianship.

14788 American Society for Information Science
1320 Fenwick Lane
Suite 510
Silver Spring, MD 20910
301-495-0900
FAX: 301-495-0810
asis@asis.org www.asis.org
Samantha K Hastings, President
Andrew Dillon, Director
Cecilia M Preston, Treasurer
Richard Hill, Executive Director
4000 Members Founded: 1937

14789 American Society of Indexers
10200 W 44th Avenue
Suite 304
Wheat Ridge, CO 80033
303-463-2887
FAX: 303-422-8894
info@asindexing.org
www.asindexing.org
Francine Butler, Executive Director
Anne Leech, Editor/Key Words
Kathy Caldwell, Administrative Assistant
A national association with international membership and interests. A nonprofit charitable organization for indexers, librarians, abstractors, editors, publishers, database producers, and organizations concerned with indexing, seeking cooperation and membership of all persons, groups or institutions interested in indexing. Founded in 1968 to promote excellence in indexing and increase awareness of the value of well-written indexes.
1M Members Founded: 1968

14790 American Theological Library Association
250 S Wacker Drive
Suite 1600
Chicago, IL 60606-5889
312-454-5100
FAX: 312-454-5505 888-665-2852
atla@atla.com www.atla.com
Paul Schrodt, President
Paul F Stuehrenberg, VP
Anne Womack, Secretary
Sharon Taylor, Director
Dennis Norlin, Executive Director
Provides indexing services in these formats: online database, CD-ROM versions, magnetic tape for OPAC tapeload and print publications. ATLA Religion indexes in print include Religious Index One: Periodicals, Religion Index Two: Multi-Author Works, Index to Book Reviews, Research in Ministry an Index to D. Min. Project Reports and Theses.
800 Members Founded: 1946

14791 Americans For Libraries Council
27 Union Square West
Suite 204
New York, NY 10003
646-336-6236
FAX: 646-336-6318 800-542-1918
alc@americansforlibraries.org
www.lff.org
Miantha Schull, President
C. Mathews Dick Jr., Chairman
Americans for Libraries Council (ALC) is a national non-profit organization that advocates for libraries at the national level and develops and promotes programs aimed at realizing the potential of libraries in the 21st century.

14792 Art Libraries Society of North America
329 March Road
Suite 232, Box 11
Kanata, ON K2K-2E1
613-599-3074
FAX: 613-599-7027 800-817-0621
clarkassoc@igs.net www.arlisna.org
Elizabeth Clarke, Executive Director
Membership organization for art libraries in the US and Canada.

14793 Asian/Pacific American Librarians
Los Gatos Public Library 110, East Main Street
Los Gatos, CA 95030
408-354-6894
swee@losgatoca.gov
www.apalaweb.org
Yvonne Chen, President
Heawon Paick, VP
Librarians and information specialists of Asian Pacific descent and those interested in APA librarianship.
310 Members Founded: 1980

14794 Association for Library & Information Science Education
65 East Wacker Place
Suite 1900
Chicago, IL 60601-7246
312-795-0996
FAX: 312-419-8950
contact@alise.org
www.alise.org/index.shtml
John Budd, President
Connie Van Fleet, VP/President-Elect
Deborah York, Executive Director
Jeremy Uthank, Information Management
Provides a forum for library educators to share ideas, discuss issues and seek solutions to common problems.

14795 Association for Library Collections & Technical Services
American Library Association
50 E Huron Street
Chicago, IL 60611
312-545-5038
FAX: 312-280-5033
alcts@ala.org www.ala.org/alcts

Charles Wilt, Executive Director

Division of the American Library Association.

5M Members Founded: 1957

14796 Association for Library Service to Children
American Library Association
50 E Huron Street
Chicago, IL 60611
312-280-2163
FAX: 312-944-7671
alsc@ala.org www.ala.org

Diane Foote, Executive Director
Aimee Stritlmatter, Deputy Director
Laura Schulte-Cooper, Program Officer
Marsha P Durrett, Program Coordinator

A network of more than 4,000 children's and youth librarians, children's literature experts, publishers, education and library school faculty members, and other adults committed to improving and ensuring the future of the nation through exemplary library service to children, their families, and others who work with children.

3500 Members

14797 Association for Population/Family Planning
Family Health International Library
PO Box 13950
Research Triangle Park, NC 27709
919-447-7040
FAX: 215-898-2124
gcox@fhi.org www.aplici.org

Ann K Ilaqua, President
Nykia M Perez, VP
Gretl Cox, Membership Secretary

Global network of communication, information and resource professionals dedicated to providing assistance and support to members and to other population and reproductive health colleagues, especially in developing nations.

Founded: 1968

14798 Association for Recorded Sound Collections
PO Box 543
Annapolis, MD 21404
440-564-9340

shambarger@sprynet.com
www.arsc-audio.org

Brenda Nelson-Strauss, President
Jim Farrington, First VP
Louise Spear, Second VP/Program Chair
Esther Gillie, Secretary/Editor

Persons in broadcasting and recording industries, librarians, sound archivists, curators, private collectors and reviewers.
$40.00
1000 Members 2 Per Year Founded: 1966
Circulation: 1000

14799 Association of Christian Librarians
PO Box 4
Cedarville, OH 45314-0004
937-766-2255
FAX: 937-766-2337
info@acl.org www.acl.org

Janice M Bosma, Director Operations

Membership is composed of over 400 evangelical Christian librarians representing primarily evangelical institutions of higher education.

446 Members Founded: 1954

14800 Association of College and Research Libraries
American Library Association
50 E Huron Street
Chicago, IL 60611
800-545-2433
FAX: 312-280-2520 800-545-2433
acrl@ala.org www.ala.org

Camila Alire, President
Susan M Kroll, Budget/Finance Committee Chair
Patricia A Wand, Councilor

13M Members Founded: 1938

14801 Association of Independent Information Professionals (AAIP)
8550 United Plaza Blvd.
Suite 1001
Baton Rouge, LA 70809
225-408-4400
FAX: 225-922-4611
info@aiip.org
www.aiip.org/index.html

Crystal Sharp, President
Mark Goldstein, Secretary

Provides a forum for information professionals to meet and exchange views.

700 Members Founded: 1987

14802 Association of Jewish Libraries
15 E 26th Street
Room 1034
New York, NY 10010
212-725-5359

ajl@jewishbooks.org
www.jewishlibraries.org/ajlweb/home.htm

Yossi Galron, Membership

Promotes the advancement of the interests of Jewish libraries and publications of Jewish biographical interest.

900 Members Founded: 1966

14803 Association of Mental Health Librarians
Cedarcrest Regional Hospital, Medical Libary
525 Russell Road
Newington, CT 06111-1538
860-666-4613
FAX: 860-666-7642

Mary L Conlon

Provides a forum for the introduction of new audiovisual and printed materials in the field of mental health.

140 Members Founded: 1964

14804 Association of Moving Archivists
1313 North Vine Street
Hollywood, CA 0028
323-463-1500
FAX: 323-463-1506
amia@amianet.org www.amianet.org

Keith Laqua, Executive Director

AMIA is a non-profit professional association established to advance the field of moving image archiving by fostering cooperation among individuals and organizations concerned with the collection, description, preservation, exhibition and use of moving image materials.

750 Members Founded: 1991

14805 Association of Research Libraries
21 Dupont Circle NW
Washington, DC 20036
202-296-2296
FAX: 202-872-0884
arlhq@arl.org www.arl.org

Sarah Thomas, President
Camila Alire, Dean Library Services
Joseph Branin, Director Libraries
Duane Webster, Executive Director

Nonprofit organization striving to shape and influence forces affecting the future of research libraries in the process of scholarly communication.

950 Members Founded: 1984

14806 Beta Phi Mu
University of South Florida
4202 East Fowler Avenue
Tampa, FL 33620-7800
813-748-8804
FAX: 813-974-6840
perrault@luna.cas.usf.edu
www.beta-phi-mu.org/

Dr. Anna Perrault, Faculty Representative
Ellen Habib, Secretary

Beta Phi Mu is an organization that recognizes and encourages scholastic achievement among library and information studies students.

Founded: 1948

14807 Black Caucus of ALA
Gladys Smiley Bell
Associate Professor and Reference Librarian
Lib. Med. Serv., Rm 161, Kent State
Kent, OH 44242-0001
330-672-3045
FAX: 330-672-3964
gladysb@lms.kent.edu www.bcala.org

Gladys Smiley Bell, President

Association that supports black librarians. Holds annual meeting in conjunction with the American Library Association conference.

14808 Catholic Library Association
100 North Street
Suite 224
Pittsfield, MA 01201-5109
413-443-2252
FAX: 413-442-2252
cla@cathla.org www.cathla.org

Rev Kenneth O'Malley, President
Catherine Bennett, VP
Jean R Bostley, Executive Director

International membership organization, providing its members professional development through educational and networking experiences, publications, scholarships and other services.

Founded: 1921

14809 Center for Children's Books
501 E Daniel Street
Champaign, IL 61820
217-244-9331
FAX: 217-333-5603

Betsy Heame, Director

A crossroads for critical inquiry, professional training and educational outreach related to literature for youth from birth through adolescence. In partnership with The Bulletin of the Center for Children's Books, it aims to inspire and inform adults who connect young people with resources in person, in print, and online.

14810 Center for Childrens Books
1512 N Fremont Street
Chicago, IL 60622-2567
312-255-8686
FAX: 773-944-0629

14811 Chief Officers of State Library Agencies
201 Eatst Main Street
Suite 1405
Lexington, KY 40507
859-514-9151
FAX: 859-514-9166
gary.nichols@maine.gov
www.cosla.org
J Gary Nichols, President
Susan Mc Vey, VP
Suzanne Miller, Secretary
Association for directors of state libraries.

14812 Chinese-American Librarians Association
UCI Libraries
PO Box 19557
Irvine, CA 92623-9557
949-824-6836
FAX: 949-857-1988
sctseng@uci.edu www.cala-web.org
Sally C Tseng, Executive Director

14813 Church and Synagogue Library Association
2920 SW Dolphin Court
Suite 3A
Portland, OR 97219
503-244-6919
FAX: 503-977-3734 800-542-2752
csla@worldaccessnet.com
www.cslainfo.org
Judith Janzen, Administrator
Religious groups interested in promoting church or synagogue libraries comprise the membership.
1500 Members Founded: 1967

14814 Coalition for Networked Information
21 Dupont Circle
Washington, DC 0036
202-296-5098
FAX: 202-872-0884
info@cni.org www.cni.org
Clifford A. Lynch, Executive Director
Joan K. Lippincott, Asociate Executive Director
The Coalition for Networked Information is an organization dedicated to supporting the transformative promise of networked information technology for the advancement of scholarly communication and the enrichment of intellectual productivity.
202 Members Founded: 1990

14815 Connecticut Library Association
Po Box 75
Middletown, CT 06457
860-346-2444
FAX: 860-344-9199
cla@ctlibrarians.org
www.ctlibraryassociation.org
Pamela Najarian, CLA Coordinator
Professional organization committed to improving library service in Connecticut and increasing public awareness of libraries and library services.
1000+ Members Founded: 1891

14816 Council of Planning Librarians
1313 E 60th Street
Chicago, IL 60637-2830
630-256-2900

14817 Council on Library and Information Resources
1755 Massachusetts Avenue, NW
Suite 500
Washington, DC 0036
202-939-4750
FAX: 202-939-4765
gromero@clir.org www.clir.org
Charles Henry, President
Gary Romero, Administrative Manager
The mission of the Council on Library and Information Resources is to expand access to information, however recorded and preserved, as a public good.
Founded: 1956

14818 Council on Library/Media Technicians
PO Box 256
Oxon Hill, MD 20748

pmcquitt@coin.org
www.library.ucr.edu/COLT
Patricia McQuitty, President
Supports library and media techicians by offering publications, training, networking and annual conference in conjunction with the American Library Association conference.

14819 Ethnic Employees of the Library of Congress
6100 Eastview Street
Bethesda, MD 20817-6004

George E Perry, President
Promotes and strengthens brotherhood among ethnic employees and ethnic members of society.
Founded: 1973

14820 Federal Library and Information Center
Library of Congress
101 Independence Avenue SE
Washington, DC 20540
202-075-5852
FAX: 202-707-4818 www.loc.gov/flicc
Roberta Shaffer, Executive Director
Robin Hatziyannis, Editor-in-Chief/Education
Joseph S Banks, Business Manager
Ruby J Thomas, Head, Member Services
Representatives of departments and agencies of the federal government.
40 Members Founded: 1965

14821 Federal and Armed Forces Libraries Roundtable
American Library Association
1301 Pennsylvania Avenue NW
Suite 403
Washington, DC 20004-1733
202-288-8410

Emily Sheketoff, Executive Director
Association for libraries and information services.

14822 Friends of Libraries (FOLUSA)
1420 Walnut Street
Suite 450
Philadelphia, PA 19102
215-790-1674
FAX: 215-545-3821
folusa@folusa.org www.folusa.com
Laura Bush, Chair
Sally Reed, Executive Director
Lana Porter, President
Susan J Schmidt, VP
Bette M Kozlowski, Treasurer
Encourages the development of excellent library service to all residents of the US. Aids in forming local and state, friends branches in academic and special libraries.

1.8M Members Founded: 1979

14823 Herbert Hoover Presidential Library Association
310 Park Side Drive
Po Box 696
West Branch, IA 52358
319-643-5327
FAX: 319-643-2391 800-828-0475
info@hooverassociation.org
www.hooverassoiation.org
Robert Sierk, President
Ruby Triplett, VP

14824 Insurance Library Association of Boston
156 State Street
Boston, MA 02109
617-227-2087
FAX: 617-723-8524
jlucey@insurancelibrary.org
www.insurancelibrary.org
Jean Lucey, Library Director
Meagan Stefanow, Reference Librarian/Education
Resource for and provider of literature, information services and quality professional education for the insurance industry and related interests.
760+ Members Founded: 1887

14825 Interagency Council on Information
American Nurses Association Library
8515 Georgia Avenue
Suite 400
Silver Spring, MD 20910-2571
301-628-5143
FAX: 301-628-5008
jlevy@cinahl.com www.icirn.org
Richard G Barry, Chair Publicity Committee
June Levy, President
Warren Hawkes, VP
Wanda Hiestand, Treasurer
Jane Root, Secretary
To esablish an effective use of information resources available to the nursing community, and to advance the profession through the promotion and use of its literature.
26 Members Founded: 1960

14826 International Association of Aquatic & Marine Science Libraries
Harbor Branch Oceanographic Institution
5600 Old Dixie Highway
Fort Pierce, FL 34946-7303
772-460-9977

Encourages members to exchange scientific and technical information and explore

issues of mutual concern. Conducts workshops about on line databases.
200 Members Founded: 1975

14827 International Association of School Librarianship
1903 W 8th Street
PMB 292
Erie, PA 16505
814-474-1115
www.iasl-slo.org
Peter Genco, President
IASL provides an international forum for those people interested in promoting effective school library media programs as viable instruments in the educational process.

14828 Law Library Association of St. Louis
1300 Civil Courts Building
10 N Tucker Boulevard
St Louis, MO 63101
314-622-4386
FAX: 314-241-0911 www.tlc.library.net
Jean Moorleghen, Library Director
The law library has remained in continuous operation by the Association since 1838 and is one of the oldest libraries west of the Mississippi River.

14829 Library Administration and Management
American Library Association
50 E Huron Street
Chicago, IL 60611
312-280-5038
FAX: 312-280-5033
lama@ala.org www.ala.org
Lorraine Olley, Executive Director
Paul Anderson, President
Arawa McClendon, Communications Officer
Dollester Thorn Hawkins, Events Manager
Works to improve and develop all aspects and levels of administration in all types of libraries.
5M Members Founded: 1957

14830 Library Binding Institute
4300 S. U.S. Highway One
Suite 203-296
Jupiter, FL 33477
561-745-6821

dnolan@1bibinders.org
www.hardcoverbinders.org
Debra S Nolan, Executive Director
Jay B Fairfield, President
Members are firms binding books for libraries and their suppliers.

14831 Major Orchestra Librarians' Association
MOLA
1530 Locust Street
PMB 154
Philadelphia, PA 19102

admin@mola-inc.org
www.mola-inc.org
Karen Schnackenberg, President
Patrick McGinn, Administrative Officer
Gordon Rowley, Treasurer
International organization whose objectives include: to improve communication among orchestra librarians; present a unified voice in publisher relations; and assist librarians in providing better service to their orchestras.
630 Members Founded: 1983

14832 Medical Library Association
65 E Wacker Place
Suite 1900
Chicago, IL 60601-7246
312-419-9094
FAX: 312-419-8950
info@mlahq.org www.mlanet.org / www.marketing.mlanet.org
Lynanne Feilen, Director Publications
Carla J Funk, Executive Director
Mary M. Langman, Manager Information Issues
Raymond S. Naegele, Director Finance
Kate E. Corcoran, Director Research
A nonprofit, educational organization that is a leading advocate for health sciences information professionals worldwide. Through it's programs and services, we provide lifelong educational opportunities, supports a knowledgebase of health information research and works with a global network of partners to promote the importance of quality information for improved health to the health care community and the public.
4500 Members Founded: 1898

14833 Mid-America Association of Law Libraries
666 Walnut
Suite 2500
Des Moines, IA 50309
515-288-2500
FAX: 515-243-0654
sharon.kern@lawiowa.com
Kay L Andrus, President
Janet McKinney, VP
Sharon P Kern, Treasurer
Charles J Condon, Secretary
David Sokol, Chief Executive Officer
Association for suppliers of law library equipment, supplies and services.
Founded: 1973

14834 Middle East Librarians' Association
University of California
Main Library
Santa Barbara, CA 93106
805-637-7749

Andras Riedlmayer, Secretary
Interested in aspects of librarianship that support the study or dissemination of information about the Middle East. Publishes a bulletin (semi-annually) that is distributed to members and subscriber institutions in North America, Europe, the Middle East, Asia and Africa.
150 Members Founded: 1972

14835 Mountain Plains Library Association
University of SD-I D Weeks Library
414 E Clark Street
Vermillion, SD 57069-2390
605-677-6082
FAX: 605-677-5488
jedelen@usd.edu www.usd.edu/mpla
Carol Hammond, President
Beth Avery, VP
Joe Edelen, Executive Secretary
1600+ Members Founded: 1948

14836 Music Library Association
8551 Research Way
Suite 180
Middleton, WI 53562
608-836-5825
FAX: 608-831-8200
mla@areditions.com
www.musiclibraryassoc.org
Laura Dankner, President
Promotes growth and establishment in the use of music libraries, musical instruments and musical literature.

14837 NYLA: New York Library Association
252 Hudson Avenue
Albany, NY 12210-1802
518-432-6952
FAX: 518-427-1697 800-252-6952
info@nyla.org www.nyla.org
Michael J Borges, Executive Director
Lois A Powell, Membership Coordinator
Works for the development and improvement of librarianship and library and information services, in order to enhance quality of life, learning and equal opportunity for all New Yorkers. *$25.00*
Founded: 1890

14838 National Association of Media & Technology Centers (NAMTC)
PO Box 9844
Cedar Rapics 52409-9844
319-654-0608
FAX: 319-654-0609
bettyge@mchsi.com www.namtc.org/
Ricki Chowning, President
The National Association of Media & Technology Centers is an organization committed to promoting leadership among its membership through networking, advacacy, and support activities that will enhance the equitable access to media, technology, and information services to educational committees. Current membership is over 20 million students.
Founded: 1984

14839 National Center for Information Media & Technology
University of Hertfordshire, College Lane
Chicago, IL 60611
773-846-7300
www.ala.org

14840 National Church Library Association
275 South 3rd Street
Suite 101A
Stillwater, MN 55082
651-430-0770

info@churchlibraries.org
www.churchlibraries.org
Barbara Livdahl, President
Sue Benish, Executive Director
Non-profit support organization that endeavours to further the gospel through church libraries. New resources and support programs are always under development to serve the ever changing needs of the church librarian. Membership is open to individuals, churches or libraries of any denomination or size.
Founded: 1958

14841 National Information Standards Organization
4733 Bethesda Avenue
Suite 300
Bethesda, MD 20814
301-654-2512
FAX: 301-654-1721
nisohq@niso.org www.niso.org
Patricia R. Harris, Executive Director/Secretary
Jan Peterson, Chair
The National Information Standards Organization identifies, develops, maintains, and publishes technical standards to manage information in our changing and ever-more digital environment.
70 Members Founded: 1939

14842 National Library Service for the Blind &
1291 Taylor Street NW
Washington, DC 20542
202-707-5100
FAX: 202-707-0712
nls@loc.gov www.loc.gov/nls
Frank Kurt Cylke, Director
Marvine R Wanamaker, Assistant to the Director
Martinez Majors, IT Specialist
Alice G Freeman, Program Management Assistant
Michael M Moodie, Research/Development Officer

14843 National Media Market
PO Box 87410
Tucson, AZ 85754-7410
520-743-7735
FAX: 520-743-7643
director@nmm.net www.nmm.net
Ursula Schwarz, Executive Director
John Sirabella, Chair
Mission of the National Media Market is to bring media buyers and vendors together in an easy working environment filled with many opportunities for screening quality educational motion media, professional development, and networking.
55 Members Founded: 1978

14844 New England Library Association
14 Pleasant Street
Gloucester, MA 01930
978-282-0787
FAX: 978-282-1304
info@nelib.org www.nelib.org
Mary Ann Rupert, Conference Manager
Barry Blaisdell, Executive Secretary
David Bryan, Newsletter Editor/Webmaster
Barbara Kohl, Exhibits Manager
Promotes excellence in library services to the people of New England and advances the leadership role of it's members. Holds an annual conference.

14845 Reference and User Services Association
50 East Huron Street
Chicago, IL 60611
FAX: 312-944-8085 800-545-2433
rusa@ala.org www.ala.org/RUSA
Cathleen Bourdon, Executive Director
Eileen Hardy, Marketing Specialist
Reference and User Services Association is responsible for stimulating and supporting excellence in the delivery of general library services and materials to adults, and the provision of reference and information services, collection development, and resource sharing for all ages, in every type of library.
5000 Members Founded: 1876

14846 Society of American Archivists
527 S Wells Street
5th Floor
Chicago, IL 60607-3922
312-922-0140
FAX: 312-347-1452
info@archivists.org
www.archivists.org
Susan Fox, Executive Director
Association for those interested in archival theory and practice in North America.
3400 Members Founded: 1936

14847 Southeastern Library Association
1438 W Peachtree Street
Suite 200
Atlanta, GA 30309
845-739-7500
lfallon@solinet.net sela.lib.ucf.edu
Ann Hamilton, President
Judith A Gibbons, VP
Faith A Line, Secretary
Diane N Baird, Treasurer

14848 Special Libraries Association
331 South Patrick Street
Alexandria, VA 22314
703-647-4900
FAX: 703-647-4901
sla@sla.org www.sla.org
Rebecca Vargha, President
International association of information professionals who work in special libraries serving business, research, government and institutions that produce specialized information.
13M Members

14849 State University of New York Librarians Association
Office of Library & Information Services
SUNY Plaza
Albany, NY 12246
518-443-5577
FAX: 518-443-5358
drewwe@morrisville.edu
www.sunyla.org
Wilfred Drew, President
Maureen Zajkowski, Project Manager, SUNYConnect
Statewide professional librarian organization.
348 Members Founded: 1968

14850 Substance Abuse Librarians and Information
PO Box 9513
Berkeley, CA 94709-0513
510-642-5208
FAX: 510-642-7175
salis@arg.org www.salis.org
Andrea Mitchell, Executive Director
Thomas A Mikolyzk, Chair
Provides professional development and exchange of information and concerns about access to and dissemination of information on substance abuse.
160 Members Founded: 1978

14851 Theatre Library Association
New York Public Library for the Performing Arts
40 Lincoln Center Plaza
New York, NY 10023
212-701-1630
FAX: 212-944-4139
nef4@columbia.edu
Martha S LoMonaco, President
Kenneth Schlesinger, VP
The Theatre Library Association is a non-profit, educational organization that promotes the collection, preservation, and use of theatrical and performing arts materials.
Founded: 1937

14852 U.S. National Commission on Libraries and Information Science (NCLIS)
1800 M Street, N.W.
Suite 350 North Tower
Washington, DC 20036-5841
FAX: 202-606-9203
info@nclis.gov www.nclis.gov/
Trudi Bellardo Hahn, Executive Director
C. Beth Fitzsimmons, Chairperson
The U.S. National Commission on Libraries and Information Science is a permanent, independent agency of the federal government charged with advising the executive and legislative branches and other public and private organizations on national library and information policies and plans.
Founded: 1970

14853 Urban Libraries Council
1603 Orrington Avenue
Suite 1080
Evanston, IL 60201
847-866-9999
FAX: 847-866-9989
info@urbanlibraries.org
www.urbanlibraries.org
Eleanor Jo Rodger, President/CEO
Public libraries in cities with over 100,000 people.
150+ Members Founded: 1971

14854 Washington Library Association
4016 1st Avenue NE
Seattle, WA 98105
206-545-1529
FAX: 206-545-1543
nslote@kcls.org www.wla.org
Carolynne Myall, President
Nancy Slote, Secretary
Provides the leadership needed to promote, develop and improve library services to all Washington residents. The only membership requirement is an interest in libraries and the association's goal.
1339 Members

14855 Washington Medical Librarians Association
Attn: Julie Parker
Amgen/4403 NE 1st Place
Renton, WA 98059-5235
wmla@wmla.org www.wmla.org
Janette Schueller, President
Julia Parker, Membership Secretary
The goal of WMLA is to improve the quality of health sciences library service in the State of Washington and provide opportunities for professional growth by interaction and continuing education for

members. Membership is open to all librarians and staffers affiliated with the state's health care centers, hospitals or institutions involved with medicine or health care. *$15.00*

Newsletters

14856 AASL Presidential Hotline
American Library Association
50 E Huron Street
Chicago, IL 60611
312-944-6780
FAX: 312-440-9374 800-545-2433
ala@ala.org http://www.ala.org/aasl
Julie Walker, Executive Director
Andrea Parker, Marketing Specialist
School library media association news.
Monthly Founded: 1951

14857 Church & Synagogue Libraries Newsletter
Po Box 19357
Portland, OR 97280-0357
503-244-6919
FAX: 503-977-3734 800-LIB-CSLA
csla@worldaccessnet.com
www.csla.info
Karen Bota, Publications Editor/Webmaster *$35.00*
Bi-Monthly

14858 Corporate Library Update
Reed Business Information
360 Park Avenue S
New York, NY 10014
212-450-0067
FAX: 646-746-6734
sdimattia@reedbusiness.com
http://www.reedbusiness.com
James Reed, Owner
Lynn Blumenstein, Senior Editor
Susan DiMattia, Editor *$69.95*
Fortnightly
Circulation: 2500

14859 Libraries Alive
National Church Library Association
275 South 3rd Street
Suite 101A
Stillwater, MN 55082
651-430-0770

news@churchlibraries.org
www.churchlibraries.org
Sandra Burrowes, Editor
Features informative articles, reviews of books and other media, a sharing of ideas, Internet resources, chapter news, news of authors and upcoming regional and national workshops.
Quarterly

14860 Library Hotline
Library Journal/School Library Journal
360 Park Avenue South
New York, NY 10010
646-746-6819
FAX: 646-746-6734 800-446-6551
lblumenstein@reedbusiness.com
http://www.libraryjournal.com
Francesca Mazzucca, Manager
Justin Torres, Production Manager
Lynn Blumenstein, Senior Editor
$115.00
Weekly Founded: 1876

14861 MLA News
Medical Library Association
65 E Wacker Place
Suite 1900
Chicago, IL 60601-7298
312-419-9094
FAX: 312-419-8950
info@mlahq.org
http://www.mlanet.org
Lynanne Fielen, Director Publications
Carla Funk, Editor
Lynanne Fielen, Circulation Manager
Covers MLA programs and services as well as the medical librarian profession in general. *$58.00*
Monthly Founded: 1898
Mailing list available for rent

14862 Marcato
MOLA/Editor
Kennedy Center
2700 F Street NW
Washington, DC 20566
202-416-8131
FAX: 202-416-8132
sfriedman@kennedy-center.org
www.mola-inc.org
Shelley Friedman, Editor
Gordon Rowley, Treasurer
Newsletter of Major Orchestra Librarians' Association. *$20.00*
Quarterly

14863 Marketing Treasures
Chris Olson & Associates
857 Twin Harbor Drive
Arnold, MD 21012-1027
410-647-6708
FAX: 410-647-0415
info@chrisolson.com
http://www.chrisolson.com
Christine Olson, Publisher
Provinding creative ideas, helpful hints and insights on how libraries can promote thier services
6 pages Monthly Founded: 1987
Circulation: 1000
Printed in 2 colors on matte stock

14864 Report on Literacy Programs
Business Publishers
8737 Colesville Road
Suite 1100
Silver Spring, MD 20910-3928
301-876-6300
FAX: 301-589-8493 800-274-6737
bpinews@bpinews.com
http://www.bpinews.com
Dave Speights, Editor
Leonard A Eiserer, Publisher
Beth Early, Operations Director
Covers all aspects of literacy including legislation, funding, training programs, important conferences, job skills and much more. *$317.00*
Founded: 1963

14865 State University of New York Librarians Association
Office of Library & Information Services
SUNY Plaza
Albany, NY 12246
518-443-5577
FAX: 518-443-5358
drewwe@morrisville.edu
www.sunyla.org
Wilfred Drew, President
John Schumacher, Electronic Resources Coordinator
Provides news, notes and information from SUNY campus libraries.
2-3/Year

14866 Technicalities
Westport Publishing
802 Broadway Street
Kansas City, MO 64105
816-842-0641

Brian Alley, Editor
A professional journal presenting discussion, opinions, and reviews on library-management topics. Typical issues include articles ranging from computer applications, on-line public access catalogs, library budgets, collection building, book reviews, automation, software, library marketplace trends, and the Library of Congress. Articles are indexed in Library Literature and LISA: Library Information Science Abstracts and are available on microfilm from UMI. *$47.00*
16 pages Monthly
Circulation: 700 Audited
Mailing list available for rent
Printed in 1 color on matte stock

14867 Urban Libraries Council Exchange Letter
1603 Orrington Avenue
Suite 1080
Evanston, IL 60201
847-866-9999
FAX: 847-866-9989
info@urbanlibraries.org
http://www.urbanlibraries.org/
Eleanor Rodger, President/CEO
Linda Crismond, Editor
Newsletter for public libraries in cities with over 100,000 people. Free to members, also available without membership. *$50.00*
150 pages Founded: 1971
Circulation: 6000

Magazines & Journals

14868 ALKI: The Washington Library Association Journal
Washington Library Association/Editor
Everett Public Library
2702 Hoyt Avenue
Everett, WA 98201
425-257-7640
FAX: 425-257-8016
alkieditor@wla.org
www.wla.org/publications/alki
Cameron Johnson, Editor
Margaret Thomas, Assistant Editor
Its purpose is to communicate substantial and philosophical analyses of current and ongoing issues involving Washington libraries, personnel and advocates in order to facilitate the exchange of research, opinion and information. *$20.00*
March/July/December

14869 Advanced Technology/Libraries
GK Hall & Company
1633 Broadway
7th Floor
New York, NY 10019-6708
212-892-2086
FAX: 212-654-4751
peter_jaskowiak@prenhall.com
Peter Jaskowiak, Editor
Audrey Ismal, Owner
Concise, practical information on the advances in development, implementation and use of library automation. Articles

cover new products, new services, legislation and grant information. *$95.00*
Monthly

14870 American Archivist
Society of American Archivists
527 S Wells Street
5th Floor
Chicago, IL 60607-3922
312-922-0140
FAX: 312-347-1452
info@archivists.org
http://www.archivists.org

Susan Fox, Executive Director
Philip B Eppard, Editor
Teresa Brinati, Director of Publications

Offers information and essays on archival theory and practice in North America. *$85.00*
Founded: 1936
Circulation: 4800+

14871 American Libraries
American Library Association
50 E Huron Street
Chicago, IL 60611
312-944-6780
FAX: 312-440-9374 800-545-2433
aasl@ala.org http://www.ala.org

Julie A Walker, Executive Director
Andrea Parker, Marketing Head
Carla D Hayden, President

Library development news. *$60.00*
Monthly Founded: 1876

14872 Book Report: Magazine for Secondary School Librarians
Linworth Publishing
480 East Wilson Bridge Road
Suite L
Worthington, OH 43085
614-436-7107
FAX: 614-436-9490 800-786-5017
linworth@linworthpublishing.com
http://www.linworth.com

Marlene Woo-Lun, Publisher
Amy Robinson, Marketing Manager

In-depth articles, helpful hints, and reviews on books, software, videos, and CD-Roms for secondary school librarians. *$49.00*
105 pages Founded: 1981
Circulation: 15000
Printed in 4 colors on glossy stock

14873 Booklist
American Library Association
50 E Huron Street
Chicago, IL 60611
312-944-6780
FAX: 312-440-9374 800-545-2433
library@ala.org
http://www.ala.org/aasl

Keith Michael Fiels, Executive Director

To provide a guide to current library materials in many formats appropriate for use in public libraries and school library media centers. *$89.95*
Founded: 1876
Circulation: 25000

14874 Bulletin of Bibliography
Greenwood Publishing Group
88 Post Road W
P O Box 5007
Westport, CT 06881-5007
203-226-3571
FAX: 203-226-6009
sales@greenwood.com
http://www.greenwood.com

Bernard McTigue, Editor-in-Chief
Gerry Katz, Executive Editor
Naomi Caldwell Wood, Author

Offers bibliographies in humanities and social sciences. *$125.00*
100 pages Quarterly Founded: 1944
Circulation: 1000
Printed in 2 colors on matte stock

14875 Bulletin of the Center for Children's Books
501 E Daniel Street
MC-493
Champaign, IL 61820
217-244-0324
FAX: 217-244-3302
bbc@alexia.lis.uiuc.edu
http://alexia.lis.uiuc.edu

Deborah Stevenson, Editor
Marlow Welshon, Dean

Reviews of children's books for librarians, teachers, booksellers and parents. *$50.00*
34 pages Monthly Founded: 1893
Circulation: 6500

14876 CD-ROM Librarian
Mecklermedia Corporation
11 Ferry Lane W
Westport, CT 06880-5808

FAX: 203-454-5840

Alan Meckler, Editor

A periodical intended for the library professional. *$80.00*
Monthly Founded: 1986

14877 Catholic Library World
Catholic Library Association
100 N Street
Suite 224
Pittfield, MA 01201-5109
413-443-2252
FAX: 413-442-2252
cla@cathla.org http://www.cathla.org

Mary E Gallagher SSJ, General Editor
Allen Gruenke, Production Editor
Jean Bostley, CEO

Religious, theology, library science, and reference books for young adult and children. *$60.00*
98 pages Quarterly Founded: 1921
Circulation: 1000
Printed in on matte stock

14878 Choice
American Library Association
50 East Huron Street
Chicago, IL 60611-2795
773-261-1600
FAX: 312-280-2520 800-545-2433
acrl@ala.org http://www.acrl.org

Francine Graf, Managing Editor
Irving Rockwood, Publisher
Mary Allen Davis, Executive Director
Ann Christe Galloway, Production Editor
Mary Jane Petrowski, Associate Director

Publishes reviews of books, internet sites, and microcomputer software suitable for college and university libraries. *$280.00*
Monthly Founded: 1938
Circulation: 5000

14879 Church and Synagogue Library Association
2920 SW Dolph Ct
Ste 3A
Portland, OR 97219-4055
503-244-6919
FAX: 503-977-3734 800-542-2752
csla@worldaccessnet.com
www.worldaccessnet.com/ncsla

Judith Janzen, Administrator

Bi-monthly newsletter for groups interested in promoting church or synagogue libraries.
Founded: 1967

14880 Computers in Libraries
Information Today
143 Old Marlton Pike
Medford, NJ 08055-8750
609-654-6266
FAX: 609-654-4309
custserv@infotoday.com
http://www.infotoday.com

Kathleen L Dempsey, Editor in Chief
Thomas H Hogan, President/CEO
Bob Fernekees, Group Publisher
Thomas Hogan, Jr., Marketing Director
Inge Coffey, Circulation Manager

Complete coverage of news and issues in the evolving field of library information technology. Emphasis on practical application of technology in public, school, academic, and special libraries. *$99.95*
Founded: 1985

14881 Information Retrieval & Library Automation
Lomond Publications
PO Box 88
Mount Airy, MD 21771-0088
202-362-1361
FAX: 202-362-6156

Thomas Hattery, Publisher

New technology, products and equipment that improve information systems and library services, for science, social, social science, law, medicine, academic institutions and the public. *$75.00*
Monthly

14882 Journal of the Medical Library Association
Medical Library Association
65 E Wacker Drive
Suite 1900
Chicago, IL 60601-7298
312-419-9094
FAX: 312-419-8950 800-462-6420
info@mlahq.org
http://www.mlanet.org

Lynanne Feilen, Director Publication
Carla J Funk, Executive Director
Susan C Talmage, Editorial Assistant
Bleu caldwell, Production Assistant
Barbara Redmond, Advertising Coordinator *$163.00*

Quarterly
Mailing list available for rent

14883 Knowledge Quest
American Library Association
50 E Huron Street
Chicago, IL 60611
312-944-6780
FAX: 312-440-9374 800-545-2433
library@ala.org
http://www.ala.org/aasl

Keith Michael Fiels, Executive Director
Debby Abilock, Editor
Andria Parker, Marketing
Vickie William, Circulation Manager

Articles on teaching, learning process, ideas and information to prepare students for life long learning. *$40.00*
Founded: 1879
Circulation: 5000
Printed in 4 colors on matte stock

14884 Library Bookseller
PO Box 9544
Berkeley, CA 94709-544

Scott Saifer, Publisher
Gail Russin, Editor

A journal focusing on suppliers to libraries. *$100.00*
36 pages

14885 Library Journal
Reed Business Information
360 Park Avenue South
New York, NY 10010-5300
212-450-0067
FAX: 646-746-6734
rshank@reedbusiness.com
http://www.libraryjournal.com

Francine Fialkoff, Editor
John Berry, Editor-in-Chief
Evan St Lifer, President

Reviews that are edited and written specifically to assess the value of a book. *$141.00*
Founded: 1876
Circulation: 17936
Printed in 4 colors on glossy stock

14886 Library Resources & Technical Services
American Library Association
50 E Huron Street
Chicago, IL 60611
312-944-6780
FAX: 312-440-9374 800-545-2433
library@ala.org
http://www.ala.org/aasl

Keith Michael Fiels, Executive Director
Julie A.Walker, CEO
Steven L Hofman, Circulation Manager
Andrea Parker Parker, Marketing Head

Offers articles to technical service librarians on acquisitions, cataloging and classification. *$30.00*
Bi-annually Founded: 1951
Circulation: 60000

14887 Library Software Review
Sage Publications
Vanderbilt University
419 21st Avenue S
Nashville, TN 37240-0001
615-343-6094
FAX: 615-343-8834
info@sagepub.com www.sagepub.com

Marshall Breeding, Editor

Provides the library professional with information necessary to make intelligent software evaluation, procurement, integration and installation decisions. Issues review software and software books and periodicals. *$52.00*
Quarterly
Circulation: 1M

14888 Library Talk: Magazine for Elementary School Librarians
Linworth Publishing
480 E Wilson Bridge Road
Suite L
Worthington, OH 43085-2372
614-436-7107
FAX: 614-436-9490 800-786-5017
linworth@linworthpublishing.com
http://www.linworth.com

Marlene Woo-Lun, Publisher
Amy Robinson, Marketing Manager
Carol Simpson, Consulting Editor

In-depth articles, helpful hints, and reviews on books, software, and CD-ROMS for elementary school library media and technology specialist. *$49.00*
68 pages Founded: 1988
Circulation: 10000 10,000 names
Printed in 4 colors on glossy stock

14889 Library Trends
University of Illinois Press
1325 S Oak Street
Champaign, IL 61820-6903
217-333-0950
FAX: 217-244-9910 866-244-0626
journals@uillinois.edu
http://www.press.uillinois.edu/

F. W. Lancaster, Editor
Ann Lowry, Journals Manager
Willis G Regier, Director
Cheryl Jestis, Circulation Manager
Pat Hoefling, Marketing and Sales Director

A journal which offers a medium for current thought and information in the library field. *$75.00*
Quarterly Founded: 1918 ISBN 0-252725-23-9
Circulation: 2600

14890 Medical Reference Services Quarterly
Haworth Press
10 Alice Street
Binghamton, NY 13904-1580
607-722-5857
FAX: 607-771-0012 800-429-6784
getinfo@haworthpress.com
http://www.haworthpress.com/web/mrsq/

Bill Cohen, Publisher
M Sandra Wood, Editor

Providing a wealth of exciting and instructive material, Science & Technology Libraries is prepared specifically for the science and technology librarian. This exciting journal represents the viewpoints, concerns and perspectives of the sci-tech librarianship community in a lively and professional style that makes every issue an item to be read and referred to often. Each issue centers on a specialized theme around which the major articles are focused, allowing for in-depth explorations. *$60.00*
Quarterly Founded: 1975

14891 MultiMedia & Internet @Schools
Information Today
143 Old Marlton Pike
Medford, CT 08055-8750
609-654-6266
FAX: 609-654-4309 800-248-8466
custserv@infotoday.com
http://www.infotoday.com/

David Hoffman, Editor

A practical guide for K-12 library media specialists, technology coordinators and other educators with information on how to get high-performance learning from technology-based school products, services and resources. *$39.95*
6 issues/yr
Mailing list available for rent 4M names
Printed in 4 colors on glossy stock

14892 New Equipment Digest
Penton Media
1300 East 9th Street
Cleveland, OH 44114-1503
216-696-7000
FAX: 216-696-1752
information@pentonmedia.com
http://www.newequipment.com

John DiPaola, VP
Robert F King, Editor
Sarah Hughes, Production Manager
Bobbie Macy, Circulation Manager
Morsene F. Hill, Editorial Assistant

Serves the general industrial field which includes manufacturing, processing, engineering services, construction, transportation, mining, public utilities, wholesale distributors, educational services, libraries, and governmental establishments.
Monthly Founded: 1949
Circulation: 206,067

14893 Reference and User Services Quarterly (RUSQ)
American Library Association
50 E Huron Street
Chicago, IL 60611
312-280-4382
FAX: 312-664-7459 800-545-2433
aasl@ala.org www.ala.org

Julie A. Walker, Executive Director
Andrea Parker, Marketing Specialist
Steven L Hofmann, Manager, Communications
Connie Van Fleet, Editor in Chief

News of interest to reference and adult services librarians. *$60.00*
Quarterly Founded: 1951
Circulation: 6,246

14894 School Library Journal
Reed Business Information
360 Park Avenue South
New York, NY 10010
212-450-0067
FAX: 646-746-6689
slj@reedbusiness.com
http://www.reedbusiness.com

Evan St. Lifer, Editor
Phyllis Levy Mandell, Managing Editor
Demetrius Watson, Administrative Coordinato
Ron Shank, Associate Publisher
Wendy Wels, Marketing Director
$124.00
Monthly Founded: 1954
Circulation: 100000

14895 School Library Media Research
American Library Association
50 E Huron Street
Chicago, IL 60611
312-944-6780
FAX: 312-440-9374 800-545-2433
library@ala.org www.ala.org/aasl

Keith Michael Fiels, Executive Director

Available online only. Current developments in the media and library field. Evaluates the most currently available print and nonprint materials for library media centers.

14896 Science and Technology Libraries
Haworth Press
10 Alice Street
Binghamton, NY 13904-1580
607-722-5857
FAX: 607-771-0012 800-429-6784
getinfo@haworthpress.com
http://www.haworthpress.com

Julie M Hurd PhD, Editor
Bill Cohen, Publisher

Providing a wealth of exciting and instructive material, Science & Technology Libraries is prepared specifically for the science and technology librarian. This excitng journal represents the viewpoints, concerns, and perspectives of the sci-tech librarianship community in a lively and professional style that makes every issue an item to be read and reffered to often. Each

issue of Science & Technology Libraries centers on a specialized theme around which the major articles are focused.
$60.00
Quarterly Founded: 1978

14897 Today's Librarian
Virgo Publishing
3300 N Central Avenue, Suite 2500
PO Box 40079
Phoenix, AZ 85067-0079
480-990-1101
FAX: 480-675-8146
www.todayslibrarian.com
Of interest to librarians and media professionals.

14898 Video Librarian
Video Librarian
8705 Honeycomb Court NW
Seabeck, WA 98380
360-309-9345
FAX: 360-830-9346 800-265-7965
vidlib@videolibrarian.com
http://www.videolibrarian.com
Jazza Williams, Editor
Anne Williams, Marketing Director
Randy Pitman, Publisher
Offers video reviews and news for public, school, academic and special libraries.
$64.00
56 pages Founded: 1986
Circulation: 2000
Printed in 4 colors on glossy stock

Trade Shows

14899 ALA National Conference on Asian Pacific American Librarians
American Library Association
50 E Huron Street
Chicago, IL 60611
312-944-6780
FAX: 312-440-9374 800-545-2433
library@ala.org www.ala.org/aasl
Keith Michael Fiels, Executive Director

14900 American Association of School Librarians National Conference & Exhibition
American Association of School Librarians
50 E Huron Street
Chicago, IL 60611-5295
312-280-4386
FAX: 312-664-7459 800-545-2433
aasl@ala.org www.ala.org/aasl
Judy King, Director Program Development
Lissa Salvatierra, Meeting Planner
Biennial continuing education conference and 300-500 exhibits of equipment, supplies and services for school library media centers, including print and nonprint materials and other equipment.
3500 Attendees October Founded: 1876

14901 American Indian Library Association Conference
American Indian Library Assn Univ. of Pittsburgh
207 Hillman Library
Pittsburgh, PA 15260
412-621-4470
FAX: 412-648-1245
Lisa A Mitten
Annual conference and exhibits relating to the development, maintenance and cultural information services on reservations and in communities of Native Americans and Native Alaskans.
Founded: 1979

14902 American Library Association Annual Conference
American Library Association
50 E Huron Street
Chicago, IL 60611
312-944-6780
FAX: 312-440-9374 800-545-2433
library@ala.org www.ala.org/aasl
Keith Michael Fiels, Executive Director
Annual meeting and exhibits of books, periodicals, reference works, audio visual equipment, films, data processing services, computer hardware and software, library equipment and supplies.

14903 American Library Association Midwinter Meeting
American Library Association
50 E Huron Street
Chicago, IL 60611
312-944-6780
FAX: 312-440-9374 800-545-2433
library@ala.org www.ala.org/aasl
Keith Michael Fiels, Executive Director
Annual meeting and 418 exhibits of books, periodicals, reference works, audio visual equipment, films, data processing services, computer hardware and software, library equipment and supplies.

14904 Art Libraries Society of North America Annual Conference
Art Libraries Society of North America
4101 Lake Boone Trail
Suite 201
Raleigh, NC 27607-7506
919-518-1919
FAX: 919-787-4916 800-892-7547
Annual conference and show of publishers, book dealers, library suppliers and visual resources suppliers.
500 Attendees Founded: 1977

14905 Association for Library & Information Science Education Annual Conference
11250 Roger Bacon Drive
Suite 8
Reston, VA 20190-5202
703-360-0500
FAX: 703-435-4390
alise@drohanmgmt.com
www.alise.org/index.shtml
John Budd, President
Deborah York, Executive Director
January

14906 Association for Population/Family Planning Libraries & Information Centers
Assn for Population Family Planning Libraries
Surgical Contraception-79 Madison
New York, NY 10016
212-780-2687
FAX: 212-779-9439
William Record
Annual conference and exhibits for effective documentation, information systems and services in the field of population/family planning.

14907 Association of College and Research Libraries
American Library Association
50 E Huron Street
Chicago, IL 60611-5295
312-280-2511
FAX: 312-280-2520 800-545-2433
acrl@ala.org www.ala.org/acrl
Mary Ellen Davis, Executive Director
Two hundred exhibitors with computers and web products, audiovisual products, furniture and library equipment.
3000 Attendees Biennial Founded: 1978
Mailing list available for rent

14908 Black Caucus of ALA
Gladys Smiley Bell
Associate Professor and Reference Librarian
Lib. Med. Serv., Rm 161, Kent State
Kent, OH 44242-0001
330-672-3045
FAX: 330-672-3964
gladysb@lms.kent.edu www.bcala.org
Gladys Smiley Bell, President
Meets annually in conjunction with the American Library Association.
August

14909 Church and Synagogue Library Association Conference
Church and Synagogue Library Association
2920 SW Dolph Ct
Ste 3A
Portland, OR 97219-4055
503-244-6919
FAX: 503-977-3734 800-542-2752
csla@worldaccessnet.com
www.cslainfo.org
Judith Janzen, Administrator
200 Attendees July/August

14910 Council on Library/Media Technicians
PO Box 256
Oxon Hill, MD 20748
pmcquitt@coin.org
library.ucr.edu/COLT
Patricia McQuitty, President
Meets annually in conjunction with the American Library Association.
August

14911 Culture Keepers: Making Global Connections
Black Caucus of the American Library Association
Newark Public Library
5 Washington Street
Newark, NJ 07101
973-961-2540
FAX: 973-522-4827
wfbbb@cunyvm.cung.edu
Dr. Alex Boyd
Biennial show and exhibits of books, journals and library products.

14912 Federal and Armed Forces Libraries Roundtable Conference
American Library Association
1301 Pennsylvania Avenue NW
Suite 403
Washington, DC 20004-1733
202-288-8410

Emily Sheketoff, Executive Director

Annual conference and exhibits of equipment, supplies and services for libraries and information services.

14913 International Association of Aquatic & Marine Science Libraries Conference
Harbor Branch Oceanographic Institution
5600 US 1 N
Fort Pierce, FL 34946

FAX: 772-465-2446 800-333-4264

Annual conference and exhibits of equipment, supplies and services for marine-related libraries and information centers.
October, Charleston

14914 Mid-Atlantic Regional Library Federation
South Maryland Regional Library
37 606 New Market Road
Charlotte Hall, MD 20622
301-884-0436

Katharine Hurrey, President

Offers exhibits by vendors who provide services and products useful to libraries and information brokers.
1M Attendees March

14915 Mountain Plains Library Association Annual Conference
Mountain Plains Library Association
University of SD-I D Weeks Library
Vermillion, SD 57069

FAX: 605-677-5488

Annual conference and exhibits of publications and library equipment, supplies and services.
600 Attendees

14916 NYLA Annual Conference & Trade Show
New York Library Association
252 Hudson Avenue
Albany, NY 12210-1802
518-432-6952
FAX: 518-427-1697 800-252-6952
marketing@nyla.org www.nyla.org

Deidre Bruce, Marketing Coordinator
April Fernandez, Membership Coordinator

Showcases where to purchase the best products and services within specific budgets, the introduction of new products and services, vendor spotlight sessions, and helps to establish and strengthen business relationships.
1000+ Attendees November Founded: 1935

14917 New England Library Association Annual Conference
New England Library Association
14 Main Street
Gloucester, MA 03031
978-820-0787
FAX: 978-282-1304
info@nelib.org www.nelib.org

Mary Ann Rupert, Show Manager
Barry Blaisdell, Manager

Annual show of publishers, distributors and suppliers of books, media, supplies, furniture, equipment, hardware, software and services used by libraries. Containing 160 booths and 130 exhibits.
1,000 Attendees October

14918 Public Library Association National Conference
Public Library Association
50 E Huron Street
Chicago, IL 60611-5295
312-280-5752
FAX: 312-280-5029 800-545-2433

Barb Macikas, Show Manager

Biennial show of 200 exhibitors of books and other equipment, supplies and services for libraries.
3500 Attendees March

14919 Southeastern Library Association
Combined Book Exhibit
277 White Street
Buchanan, NY 10511-1607
914-739-7500

This biennial conference, offers attendees from over 12 states. The convention offers exhibits, meetings and an open reception in the exhibit hall. The three biggest states, Georgia, North Carolina and South Carolina spend twice as much of expenditures on CD-ROM and 8% more on books than the national average, which makes this the perfect exhibition for sellers.
2.1M+ Attendees Fall

14920 Special Libraries Association
1700 18th Street NW
Washington, DC 20009-2514
202-234-4700

James Mears, Conference Manager

An international professional association of people working in special libraries serving institutions and organizations that use or produce specialized information.
6M Attendees June

14921 Vermont Library Conference
Vermont Educational Media Association
St Johnsbury Academy
Po Box 906
St Johnsbury, VT 05819
802-879-0334
www.vermontlibraryconference.org

Marjorie Shane, Co-Chair
Joanne Bertrand, Treasurer

Offers an opportunity to interact with librarians, media specialists, and library trustees from nearly every library in Vermont.
500 Attendees

14922 WLA Conference
Washington Library Association
State Library
PO Box 42460
Olympia, WA 98504-2460
360-704-5202
FAX: 360-586-7575
lred@secstate.wa.gov
www.wla.org/conferences/wla2006

Lynn Red, Exhibits Chair
400 Attendees April

Directories & Databases

14923 Address List, Regional and Subregional Libraries for the Handicapped
Ntn'l Library Svcs. for the Blind/Physically Hand.
1291 Taylor Street NW
Washington, DC 20542
202-707-5100
FAX: 202-707-0712
nls@loc.gov www.loc.gov/nls

Kurt Cykle, Director
25 pages Semi-Annual

14924 American Library Association Handbook
American Library Association
50 E Huron Street
Chicago, IL 60611
312-944-6780
FAX: 312-440-9374 800-545-2433
library@ala.org www.ala.org/aasl

Keith Michael Fiels, Executive Director

Offers 56 regional groups comprised of libraries, trustees, librarians and others interested in the responsibilities of libraries in the educational and cultural needs of society.

14925 American Library Directory
Information Today
143 Old Marlton Pike
Medford, NJ 08055-8750
609-654-6266
FAX: 609-654-4309
custserv@infotoday.com
www.infotoday.com

Thomas H Hogan, Publisher/President
John Bryans, Publisher/Editor-in-Chief Books
Lauree Padgett, Editorial Services Manager
Inge Coffey, Circulation Manager
Pat Patalucci, Assistant to the President

Profiles for more than 35,00 public, academic, special, and government libraries and library-related organizations in the US and Canada. These include addresses, phone and fax numbers, e-mail addresses, network participation, expenditures, holdings and special collections, key personnel, special services, and more than 40 categories of library information in all. A two volume set. *$299.00*
4000 pages ISBN 1-573872-15-6

14926 Association of Jewish Libraries Membership List
Ramaz Upper School Library
60 E 78th Street
New York, NY 10021-1809
212-172-2103
$100.00
100 pages Annual

14927 Book Reviews Data Base
Cineman Syndicate
7 Charles Ct
Middletown, NY 10941-2003
845-692-4572
FAX: 845-692-8311
cineman@frontiernet.net
www.frontiernet.net/cinema
This database provides brief critiques of new and forthcoming books.

Full-text

14928 BookQuest
ABACIS
135 Village Queen Drive
Owings Mills, MD 21117-4470

FAX: 410-581-0398
This database offers descriptions of book dealers' offerings and books being sought by libraries, dealers and collectors.
Full-text

14929 Chief Officers of State Library Agencies Directory
Chief Officers of State Library Agencies
201 East Main Street
Suite 1405
Lexington, KY 40507
859-514-9151
FAX: 859-514-9166 www.cosla.org
Directors, staff and consultants of state libraries. *$25.00*
Annual April

14930 Computers in Libraries: Buyer's Guide & Consultants Directory Issue
Mecklermedia Corporation
11 Ferry Lane W
Westport, CT 06880-5808

This comprehensive directory offers a list of suppliers of computer products and services for use in libraries. *$30.00*
Annual

14931 CyberHound's Guide to Internet Libraries
Gale Research
27500 Drake Road
Farmington Hills, MI 48331
248-699-4253
FAX: 248-699-8214 800-877-4253
galeord@gale.com www.gale.com
Two thousand academic, public, corporate, nonprofit and special libraries.
Annual

14932 DataLinx
Faxon Company
1001 W Pines Road
Oregon, IL 61061-9507
815-732-9001
FAX: 815-732-2132 800-732-9001
This online system was established to provide technical support to libraries for serials acquisition and control.
Bibliographic

14933 Directory of Federal Libraries
Oryx Press
361 Hanover Street
Portsmouth, NH 03801

FAX: 603-431-2214 800-225-5800
info@oryxpress.com
www.oryxpress.com
Wayne Smith, Executive Director
Offers valuable information on over 3,000 libraries serving branches of the federal government. *$99.95*
392 pages ISBN 1-573560-48-0 $85 per M.

14934 Directory of Library Automation Software, Systems & Services
Information Today
143 Old Marlton Pike
Medford, NJ 08055-8758
609-654-6266
FAX: 609-654-4309
custserv@infotoday.com
www.infotoday.com
Thomas H Hogan, Publisher/President
John Bryans, Publisher/Editor-in-Chief Books
Lauree Padgett, Editorial Services Manager
Inge Coffey, Circulation Manager
Pat Palatucci, Assistant to the President
Recognized as the primary source for software packages used in automating libraries. This entirely new expanded edition provides detailed descriptions of hundreds of currently available microcomputer, minicomputer, and mainframe software packages and services. *$89.00*
351 pages Biannually Founded: 1983
ISBN 1-573872-00-8

14935 Directory of Planning and Urban Affairs Libraries in the US and Canada
Council of Planning Librarians
1313 E 60th Street
Chicago, IL 60637-2830
630-256-2900

Lists over 200 planning and urban affairs libraries in the United States and Canada. *$35.00*
100 pages

14936 Directory of Special Libraries and Information Centers
Gale Research
27500 Drake Road
Farmington Hills, MI 48331
248-699-4253
FAX: 248-699-8214 800-877-4253
galeord@gale.com www.gale.com
Over 20,000 special libraries and information centers are listed in this two volume directory.
3600 pages Annual

14937 Directory of US Government: Depository Libraries
Joint Committee on Printing, US Congress
1309 Longworth
Washington, DC 20515
202-225-8281
FAX: 202-225-9957
Directory of federal depository libraries, regional and select throughout the United States. Includes list of GPO bookstores.
91pp pages Annual

14938 EBSCONET
EBSCO Publishing
10 Estes Street
Lpswich, MA 01938
978-356-6500
FAX: 978-356-6565 800-653-2726
This database provides technical support to libraries, information centers and purchasing departments for serials acquisitions and control.
Bibliographic

14939 Employment Sources in the Library and Information Professions
National Center for Information Media & Technology
University of Hertfordshire, College Lane
Chicago, IL 60611
773-846-7300
www.ala.org
Directory of services to the industry.
140 pages Annual

14940 Film & Video Finder
Information Today
143 Old Marlton Pike
Medford, NJ 08055-8750
609-654-6266
FAX: 609-654-4309
custserv@infotoday.com
www.infotoday.com
Thomas H Hogan, Publisher/President
John Bryans, Publisher/Editor-in-Chief Books
Lauree Padgett, Editorial Serices Manager
Inge Coffey, Circulation Manager
Pat Palatucci, Assistant to the President
Contains information on 130,000 films and videos 25,00 new sine the 4th edition. The most comprehensive reference available to educational films and videos. A three volume hardbound set. *$295.00*
6434 pages Annaul ISBN 0-937548-29-4

14941 Fulltext Sources Online
Information Today
143 Old Marlton Pike
Medford, NJ 08055-8750
609-654-6266
FAX: 609-654-4309
custserv@infotoday.com
www.infotoday.com
Thomas H Hogan, Publisher/President
John Bryans, Publisher/Editor-in-Chief Books
Lauree Padgett, Editorial Services Manager
Inge Coffey, Circulation Manager
A directory of periodicals accessible online in full text through 28 aggregator products. Lists over 22,000 newspapers, journals, magazines, newswires, and transcripts. *$136.50*
Biannually Jan & July ISBN 1-573872-06-7

14942 Gale Directory of Databases
Gale Research
27500 Drake Road
Farmington Hills, MI 48331
248-699-4253
FAX: 248-699-8214 800-877-4253
galeord@gale.com www.gale.com
Allen Paschal, Chief Executive Officer
Over 9,000 publicly available electronic databases are offered in these two volumes.
$290.00

14943 Interlibrary Loan Policies Directory
Neal-Schuman Publishers
100 Varick Street
New York, NY 10013-1506
212-925-8650
800-584-2414
A brand new edition of the standard source of current information about the policies of over 1,425 academic, public and other libraries that offer books through interli-

brary loans in the United States, Canada and Puerto Rico. Updated to include all the members of the Association of Research Libraries, Internet addresses, Ariel addresses and libraries that loan periodicals, government documents, microfilms, software, newspapers, media and foreign countries.
$119.95
800 pages

14944 International Literary Market Place
Information Today
143 Old Marlton Pike
Medford, NJ 08055-8750
609-654-6266
FAX: 609-654-4309
custserv@infotoday.com
www.infotoday.com
Thomas H Hogan, Publisher/President
John Bryans, Publisher/Editor-in-Chief Books
Lauree Padgett, Editorial Services Manager
Inge Coffey, Circulation Manager
The directory of the international book publishing industry with 16,500 book related concerns. Contains 10,500 publishers and literary agents, 1,100 major booksellers and book clubs, 1,520 major libraries and library associations and thousands of other book related concerns. *$ 240.00*
1800 pages ISBN 1-573871-75-3

14945 Librarian's Yellow Pages
Garance
PO Box 179
Larchmont, NY 10538-0179

A database offering information on products and services intended for use by libraries and information centers in the United States.

14946 Library Fax/Ariel Directory
CBR Consulting Services
PO Box 22421
Kansas City, MO 64113-0421

Over 10,500 libraries with telefacsimile services in the United States and Canada and worldwide. *$49.50*
475 pages Annual

14947 Library Journal Sourcebook
Bowker-Saur
249 W 17th Street
New York, NY 10011-5300
212-645-0067

Over 500 suppliers of products and services used by libraries from abstracting to word processing equipment. *$5.75*
Annual

14948 Library Literature & Information Science
HW Wilson Company
950 University Avenue
Bronx, NY 10452-4224
718-888-8405
FAX: 718-590-1617
custserv@hwwilson.com
www.hwwilson.com
Comprehensive listings are offered in this database on more than 25,000 citations to articles and reviews of books, periodicals and audiovisual materials in the library and information science areas.
Bibliographic

14949 Library Periodicals: An Annual Guide for Subscribers, Authors and Publicists
Periodical Guides Publishing
1633 Pearl Street
Alameda, CA 94501-3065
510-865-7439

Over 150 journals and newsletters in the United States and Canada of national or international scope devoted to library science. *$18.00*
55 pages Annual

14950 Literary Market Place
Information Today
143 Old Marlton Pike
Medford, NJ 08055-8750
609-654-6266
FAX: 609-654-4309
custserv@infotoday.com
www.infotoday.com
Thomas H Hogan, Publisher/President
John Bryans, Publisher/Editor-in-Chief
Lauree Padgett, Editorial Services Manager
Inge Coffey, Circulation Manager
The ultimate insider's guide to US book publishing industry with over 14,000 listings in all.

14951 One Hundred and One Software Packages to Use in Your Library
American Library Association
50 E Huron Street
Chicago, IL 60611
312-944-6780
FAX: 312-440-9374 800-545-2433
library@ala.org www.ala.org/aasl
Keith Michael Fiels, Executive Director
Directory of services and supplies to the industry.

14952 Subject Directory of Special Libraries & Information Centers
Gale Research
27500 Drake Road
Farmington Hills, MI 48331
248-699-4253
FAX: 248-699-8214 800-877-4253
galeord@gale.com www.gale.com
This directory listed in three volumes lists over 14,000 special and research libraries, information centers and data centers maintained by government agencies and industry. *$725.00*
5000+ pages Set

14953 The Bowker Annual Library & Book Trade Almanac
Information Today
143 Old Marlton Pike
Medford, NJ 08055-8750
609-654-6266
FAX: 609-654-4309
custserv@infotoday.com
www.infotoday.com
Thomas H Hogan, Publisher/President
John Bryans, Publisher/Editor-in-Chief Books
Lauree Padgett, Editorial Services Manager
Inge Coffey, Circulation Manager
Pat Palatucci, Assistant to the President

The acclaimed must have resource that provides expert reviews of the key trends, events, and developments that will influence your work in 2004 and the years to come. Also has clear explanations of new legislation and changes in funding programs and how it will affect libraries.
$199.00
832 pages May ISBN 1-573871-93-1

14954 University of Missouri School of Journalis m: Freedom of Information Center
University of Missouri
133 Neff Annex
Columbia, MO 65210-0012
573-882-7539
FAX: 573-884-6204
www.missouri.edu/~foiwww
Charles N Davis, Executive Director
Kathleen M Edwards, Center Manager
Reference and research library serving the public and media regarding access to government information. The center has a collection of over a million articles and documents concerning access to information at state, federal and local levels and offers a wide variety of online documents through its webpage.

14955 Who's Who in Special Libraries
Special Libraries Association
1700 18th Street NW
Washington, DC 20009-2514
202-234-4700

Directory of services and supplies to the industry. *$50.00*
364 pages Annual

Industry Web Sites

14956 www.aallnet.org
American Association of Law Libraries

14957 www.acl.org
Association of Christian Librarians

Membership is composed of over 400 evangelical Christian librarians representing primarily evangelical institutions of higher education.

14958 www.aiip.org
Association Independent Information Professionals

14959 www.akla.org
Alaska Library Association

14960 www.ala.org
American Library Association

Association for librarians, libraries, trustees, students and academics, encompassing all aspects of librarianship.

14961 **www.ala.org./alcts**
Assn for Library Collections & Technical Services

A division of the American Library Association.

14962 **www.ala.org/aasl**
American Association of School Librarians

Works to ensure that all members of the school library media field collaborate to: provide leadership in the total eduction program; participate as active partners in the teaching/learning process; connect learners with ideas and information; and prepare students for life-long learning. The American Association of School Librarians is a division of the American Library Association.

14963 **www.ala.org/acrl**
Association of College and Research Libraries

A division of the American Library Association. Represents academic and research librarians.

14964 **www.ala.org/alsc**
Association for Library Service to Children

A division of the American Library Association. For persons interested in the improvement and extension of library services to children.

14965 **www.ala.org/lama**
Library Administrative Management Association

Works to improve and develop all aspects and levels of administration in all types of libraries. The Library Administrative Management Association is a division of the Young Adult Library Services Association, which is part of the American Library Association.

14966 **www.ala.org/yalsa**
The Young Adult Library Services Association

Responsible for the evaluation and selection of books and nonbook materials and the interpretation and use of materials for teenagers and young adults. The Young Adult Library Services Association is a division of the American Library Association.

14967 **www.alise.org/index.shtml**
Association for Library & Information Science
Education

14968 **www.allanet.org**
Alabama Library Association

14969 **www.amianet.org**
Association of Moving Image Archivists

14970 **www.arl.org**
Association of Research Libraries

Non profit organization striving to shape and influence forces affecting the future of research libraries in the process of scholarly communication.

14971 **www.arlib.org**
Arkansas Library Association

Includes constitution and bylaws, conference information, publication, membership, and links to the Arkansas State Library.

14972 **www.arlisna.org**
Art Libraries Society of North America

Membership organization for art libraries in the US and Canada.

14973 **www.arma.org**
Assoc. for Information Management Professionals

14974 **www.arsc-audio.org**
Association for Recorded Sound Collections

Persons in broadcasting and recording industries, librarians, sound archivists, curators, private collectors and reviewers.

14975 **www.asindexing.org**
American Society of Indexers

A national association with international membership and interests. A nonprofit charitable organization for indexers, librarians, abstractors, editors, publishers, database producers, and organizations concerned with indexing, seeking cooperation and membership of all persons, groups or institutions interested in indexing. Founded in 1968 to promote excellence in indexing and increase awareness of the value of well-written indexes.

14976 **www.atla.com/home.html**
American Theological Library Association

Provides indexing services in these formats: online database, CD-ROM versions, magnetic tape for OPAC tapeload and print publications. ATLA Religion indexes in print include Religious Index One: Periodicals, Religion Index Two: Multi-Author Works, Index to Book Reviews, Research in Ministry: an Index to D. Min. Project Reports and Theses. ETHICS Index, a new ATLA interdisciplinary index on CD-ROM, contains indexing from polygraphs, articles, journals and newspapers.

14977 **www.azla.org**
Arizona Library Association

14978 **www.bcala.org**
Black Caucus of the American Library Association

Meets annually in conjunction with the American Library Association in August.

14979 **www.beta-phi-mu-org**
Beta Phi Mu

14980 **www.cal-webs.org/aboutus.html**
Colorado Association Of Libraries

14981 **www.cala-web.org**
Chinese-American Librarians Association

14982 **www.cla-net.org**
California Library Association

14983 **www.cla.uconn.edu**
Connecticut Library Association

14984 **www.clir.org**
Council on Library & Information Resources

14985 **www.cni.org**
Coalition for Networked Information

14986 **www.dla.lib.de.us**
Delaware Library Association

14987 **www.flalib.org**
Florida Library Association

14988 **www.floridamedia.org**
Florida Library Association

14989 **www.folgers.edu**
Independent Research Libraries Association

Seeks to provide consultation to members concerning mutual problems.

14990 **www.folusa.com**
Friends of Libraries (FOLUSA)

Encourages the development of excellent library service to all residents of the US Aids in forming local and state friends branches in academic and special libraries.

14991 **www.glma-inc.org/**
Georgia Media Library Association

14992 **www.greyhouse.com**
Grey House Publishing

Selected Grey House directories in the fields of business, health and education are available online. Users can search our online databases by several different search criteria, such as product categories, geographic area, sales volume and much, much more. Full Grey House catalog and online ordering also available.

14993 **www.hlaweb.org**
Hawaii Library Association

14994 **www.idaholibaries.org**
Idaho Library Association

14995 **www.idaholibraries.org**
Idaho Library Association

14996 **www.ifla.org**
International Federation of Library Associations

14997 **www.ila.org**
Illinois Library Association

14998 **www.ilfonline.org**
Indiana Library Federation

14999 **www.iowalibraryassociation.org**
Iowa Library Association

15000 **www.kylibasn.org**
Kentucky Library Association

15001 **www.lff.org**
Americans for Libraries Council

15002 **www.library.ucr.edu/COLT**
Council on Library/Media Technicians

Meets annually in conjunction with the American Library Association in August.

15003 **www.lita.org**
Library and Information Technology Association

Concerned with information dissemination in the areas of library information technology and automation. The Library and Information Technology Association is a division of the American Library Association.

15004 **www.llaonline.org**
Louisiana Library Association

15005 **www.mainelibraries.org**
Maine Library Association

15006 **www.masslib.org**
Massachusetts Library Association

15007 **www.mdlib.org**
Maryland Library Association

15008 **www.misslib.org**
Mississippi Library Association

15009 **www.mla.lib.mi.us**
Michigan Library Association

15010 **www.mlanet.org**
Medical Library Association

MLA is dedicated to the dissemination of quality health sciences information for use in education, research, and patient care.

15011 **www.mnlibraryassociation.org**
Minnesota Library Association

15012 **www.molib.org**
Missouri Library Association

15013 **www.mtlib.org**
Montana Library Association

The mission of the Montana Library Association is to develop, promote, and improve library and information services and the profession of librarianship in order to enhance learning and ensure accesss to information to all.

15014 **www.musiclibraryassoc.org**
Music Library Association

Promotes growth and establishment in the use of music libraries, musical instruments and musical literature.

15015 **www.namtc.org**
National Association of Media & Technology Centers

15016 **www.nativeculture.com/lisamitten/aila.html**
American Indian Library Association

Association for Native Americans and Native Alaskans libraries and librarians.

15017 **www.nclaonline.org**
North Carolina Library Association

15018 **www.nclis.gov**
U.S. National Commission On Libraries &

Information Science

15019 **www.ndsl.lib.state.nd.usndla**
North Dakota Library Association

15020 **www.nelib.org**
New England Library Association

15021 **www.nevadalibraries.org**
Nevada Library Association

15022 **www.niso.org**
National Information Standards Organization

15023 **www.njla.org**
New Jersey Library Association

15024 **www.nmla.org**
New Mexico Library Association

15025 **www.nmm.net**
National Media Market

15026 **www.nol.org/home/nla**
Nebraska Library Association

15027 **www.nursingworld.org/icirn/indate.htm**
Library American Journal of Nursing Compliance

Comprised of representatives from agencies and organizations concerned with library needs of nurses.

15028 **www.nyla.org**
New York Library Association

15029 **www.oelma.org**
Ohio Educational Library Media Association

15030 **www.oema.net**
Oregon Educational Media Association

15031 **www.oklibs.org**
Oklahoma Library Association

15032 **www.olaweb.org**
Oregon Library Association

15033 **www.olc.org**
Ohio Library Council

15034 **www.palibraries.org**
Pennsylvania Library Association

15035 **www.pla.org**
Public Library Association

Plans programs on current public library issues and concerns, develops publications for public librarians and disseminates statistics on public libraries. The Public Library Association is a division of the American Library Association.

15036 **www.pnla.org**
Pacific Northwest Library Association

15037 **www.rig.org**
Research Libraries Group

15038 **www.rusa.org**
Reference & User Services Association

15039 **www.salis.org**
Substance Abuse Librarians & Info. Specialists

Provides professional development and exchange of information and concerns about access to and dissemination of information on substance abuse.

15040 **www.scla.org**
South Carolina Library Association

15041 **www.seflin.org/seflin/aboutsef.cfm**
Southeast Florida Library Information Network

15042 **www.skyways.lib.ks.us/kla**
Kansas Library Association

15043 **www.sla.org**
Special Libraries Association

International association of information professionals who work in special libraries serving business, research, government and institutions that produce specialized information.

15044 **www.state.nh.us/nhla**
New Hampshire Library Association

15045 **www.taet.org**
Texas Association for Educational Technology

15046 **www.tla.library.unt.edu/default.asp**

Theatre Library Association

15047 **www.tnla.org/**
Tennessee Library Association

15048 **www.txla.org**
Texas Library Association

15049 **www.ublib.buffalo.edu/libraries/units/cts**
University of North Florida, Carpenter Library

For catalogers of audiovisual materials and electronic resources. Provides information exchange, continuing education, and works toward a common understanding of practices and standards.

15050 **www.uic.edu/depts/lib/projects/resources**
Asian/Pacific American Librarians Association

Librarians and information specialists of Asian Pacific descent working in the United States.

15051 **www.ula.org**
Utah Library Assocation

15052 **www.urbanlibraries.org**
Urban Libraries Council

Public libraries in cities with over 100,000 people.

15053 **www.uri.edu/library/rila/rila.html**
Rhode Island Library Association

15054 **www.usd.edu/mpla**
Mountain Plains Library Association

15055 **www.usd.edu/sdla**
South Dakota Library Association

15056 **www.vermontlibraries.org**
Vermont Library Association

15057 **www.vla.org**
Virginia Library Association

15058 **www.wla.lib.wi.us**
Wisconsin Library Association

15059 **www.wla.org**
Washington Library Association

15060 **www.worldaccessnet.com/nesla**
Church and Synagogue Library Association

Religious groups interested in promoting church or synagogue libraries comprise the membership. This association also offers a bi-monthly newsletter to all its members.

15061 **www.worldaccessnet.com/netsa**
Church and Synagogue Library Association

Religious groups interested in promoting church or synagogue libraries comprise the membership. This association also offers a bi-monthly newsletter to all its members.

15062 **www.wvla.org**
West Virginia Library Association

15063 **www.wyla.org**
Wyoming Library Association

Associations

15064 American Agricultural Editors' Association
PO Box 156
New Prague, MN 56071
952-758-9135
FAX: 952-758-5813
ageditors@aol.com
www.ageditors.com

15065 American Medical Writers' Association
9650 Rockville Pike
Bethesda, MD 20814-3998
301-530-7178

Lillian Sablack, President

Concerned with the advancement and improvement of medical communications.
3.4M Members Founded: 1940

15066 American Society of Journalists and Authors
1501 Broadway
Suite 302
New York, NY 10036
212-997-0947
FAX: 212-768-7414 www.asja.org

Brett Harvey, Executive Director
Lisa Collier Cool, President

Association for journalists and authors.
1000+ Members Founded: 1948

15067 American Translators Association
225 Reinekers Lane
Suite 590
Alexandria, VA 22314
703-683-6100
FAX: 703-683-6122
ata@atanet.org www.atanet.org

Scott Bren, President
Phil Bacak, Executive Director

ATA membership is open to anyone with an interest in translation and interpreting as a profession or as a scholarly pursuit.

15068 Association of American Collegiate Literary Societies
Philomathean Society
College Hall
Box G
Philadelphia, PA 19104

Andrew Smith, Governor

Works with literary societies in the United States to promote the creation of new societies, existing socities and reviving old societies.
400 Members Founded: 1978

15069 Association of Professional Writing

3924 S Troost Avenue
Tulsa, OK 74105-3329
918-743-4793

Lee C Johns, President

Organization founded to establish standards for writing consultants. Other goals are to draw new members into the writing consulting field. Also offers a referral system for companies looking for writing consultants.
400+ Members Founded: 1983

15070 Before Columbus Foundation
655 13th Street
Oakland, CA 94612
510-268-9775
www.literature-awards.com

Gundars Strads, Executive Director

Participants are individuals interested in promoting contemporary American multicultural literature.
Founded: 1976

15071 Center for the Book
Library of Congress
101 Independence Avenue SE
Washington, DC 20540
202-075-5852
FAX: 202-707-0269
cfbook@loc.gov
www.loc.gov/loc/cfbook

John Y Cole, Director
Anne Boni, Program Specialist

This organization strives to stimulate consumer interest in books and reading.
Founded: 1977

15072 Council of Biology Editors
111 E Wacker Drive
Suite 200
Chicago, IL 60601-4206
312-540-1410

Cynthia Clark

Represents those members in life sciences who write for journals, medical science publications, and textbooks.
1.1M Members Founded: 1957

15073 Council on National Literatures
68-02 Metropolitan Avenue
Middle Village, NY 11379
718-821-3916

Provides a forum for scholars concerned with comparative study of literature.
Founded: 1976

15074 Dramatists Guild of America
1501 Broadway
New York, NY 10036
212-398-9366
FAX: 212-944-0420
igor@dramaguild.com
www.dramaguild.com

Marsha Norman, VP
John Weidman, President
Arthur Kopit, Secretary

Protects the rights of its international membership of playwrights, composers and lyricists. Supports fair royalty, maintenance of subsidiary rights, artistic control and ownership of copyright.
6M+ Members Founded: 1920

15075 Editorial Freelancers Association
71 W 23rd Street
Suite 1910
New York, NY 10010
212-929-5400
FAX: 212-929-5439 866-929-5400
info@the-efa.org www.the-efa.org

Martha Schuenman, Executive Director

National nonprofit, professional organization of self-employed workers in the publishing and communications industries.
Founded: 1970

15076 Education Writers Association
2122 P Street, NW
Suite 201
Washington, DC 20037
202-452-9830
FAX: 202-452-9837
ewa@ewa.org www.ewa.org

Lisa J. Walker, Executive Director
Lori Crouch, Assistant Director
Lesley Dahlkemper, VP
Linda Lenz, Secretary
Lisa Walker, Executive Director

The Education Writers Association is the national professional organization of education reporters and intent of improving education reporting to the public.
800 Members Founded: 1947

15077 Freelance Editorial Association
PO Box 380835
Cambridge, MA 02238-0835
617-643-8626

freelanc@tiac.net
www.freelancepubs.com

Eileen Kramer, President

Offers editorial services that include editing, writing, proofreading, graphic design, desktop publishing, and project managemant.
500 Members Founded: 1983

15078 International Food, Wine and Travel
5310 Dubois Avenue
Woodland Hills
Calabasas, CA 91372
818-999-9959
FAX: 818-347-7545
ifwtwa@aol.com www.ifwtwa.org

Mel Greenberg, Executive Director
Lillian Africano, President
Andrea Rademan, VP Media Trips
Nick Anis, Secretary/Treasurer

Staff and/or freelance writers in the food, wine and travel field. Also includes other media professionals and industry associate members in 28 countries worldwide.
300 Members Founded: 1956

15079 Literacy & Creative Artists
3543 Albemarle Street NW
Washington, DC 20008-4213
202-362-4688
FAX: 202-362-8875
Lca9643@lcadc.com www.lcadc.com

Muriel Nellis, Founder

LCA is a literacy agency in the Washington area that specializes in adult trade fiction and non-fiction.
Founded: 1981

15080 Mystery Writers of America
17 E 47th Street
New York, NY 10017
212-888-8171
FAX: 212-888-8107
mwa@mysterywriters.org
www.mysterywriters.org
Professional writers of crime and mystery stories and novels. Unpublished writers are affiliate members. MWA annually gives the Edgar Awards for excellence in the mystery genre.
2600 Members Founded: 1945

15081 National Association of Hispanic
1000 National Press Building
Washington, DC 20045-2001
202-662-7145
FAX: 202-662-7144
nahj@nahj.org www.nahj.org
Juan D Gonzalez, President
Art Rascon, VP Broadcast
Jonathan J Higuera, VP Print
Javier J Aldape, Financial Officer
Evan Roman, Executive Director
Works to increase educational and career opportunities in journalism for Hispanic Americans.
2300 Members Founded: 1984

15082 National Federation of Press Women
PO Box 5556
Arlington, VA 22205
703-129-9487
FAX: 703-534-5751 800-780-2715
presswomen@aol.com www.nfpw.org
Ella Wright, President
Carol Pierce, Executive Director
Members are writers, editors and other communication professionals for newspapers, magazines, wire services, agencies and freelance.
2000 Members Founded: 1932
Mailing list available for rent 1700 names $40 per M.

15083 National Writers Club
3140 S Peoria Street
#295PMB
Aurora, CO 80014
303-841-0246
FAX: 303-841-2607
agentquestions@nationalwriters.com
www.nationalwriters.com
Sandy Whelchel, Executive Director
Membership organization for writers.
Founded: 1998

15084 Newspaper Features Council
22 Byfield Lane
Greenwich, CT 06830
203-438-3685
www.nfc.council.com
A forum for editors, writers, columnists, cartoonists and syndicates to exchange views and improve the content of newspapers.
130 Members Founded: 1955

15085 Outdoor Writers Association of America
121 Hickory Street
Suite 1
Missoula, MT 59801
406-728-7434
FAX: 406-728-7445
owaa@montana.com www.owaa.org
Kevin Rhoades, Executive Director
Eileen King, Conference/Contests
Lisa Draeger, Member Services
Nonprofit, international organization representing over 2,000 professional outdoor communicators who report on diverse interests in the outdoors.
2.4M Members Founded: 1927

15086 Self-Employed Writers and Artists Network
PO Box 175
Towaco, NJ 07082
www.swan-net.com
Stan Cohen, President
Liz Kassler, First VP
George Kamper, Membership Director
Dave McCoy, Program Director

15087 Society of American Business Editors and
Missouri School of Journalism
134 Neff Annex
Columbia, MO 65211-1200
573-822-2042
FAX: 573-884-1372
sabew@missouri.edu www.sabew.org
Kathy Kristof, President
Rex Seline, VP
Jon Lansner, Secretary/Treasurer
Brant Houston, Executive Director
Members are financial and economic news writers and editors for print and broadcast outlets.
3200 Members Founded: 1964

15088 Society of American Travel Writers
1500 Sunday Drive
Suite 102
Raleigh, NC 27607
919-861-5586
FAX: 919-787-4916
satw@satw.org www.satw.org
Marcia Levin, President
June Naylor, VP
Carol Fowler, Secretary
Gerald Breaux, Treasurer
Photographers and 35 associate member representatives of airlines, hotels, resorts, tourist agencies and public relations firms.

15089 Space Coast Writers Guild
PO Box 262
Melbourne, FL 32902-0262
SCWG02@aol.com www.scwg.org
Nonprofit, tax-exempt organization of writers of all genres. *$35.00*
Annual Founded: 1982

15090 Washington Independent Writers
220 Woodward Building, 733 15th Street NW,
Suite 220
Washington, DC 20005
202-381-1948
FAX: 202-638-7800
info@washwriter.org
www.washwriter.org
Joseph Barbato, President
Lisa Daniel, VP
Kenneth D Ackerman, Secretary
Alan C Portner, Treasurer
Donald O Graul Jr, Executive Director
Largest regional writer's organization in the country.
1800 Members Founded: 1975

15091 Writers Alliance
12 Skylark Lane
Stony Brook, NY 11790-3121
516-751-7080
Writers' organization.

15092 Writers Guild of America: East
555 W 57th Street
Suite 1230
New York, NY 10019
212-767-7800
FAX: 212-582-1909
info@wgaeast.org www.wgaeast.org
Mona Mangan, Executive Director
James H Kaye, Assistant Executive Director
Uma Sarada, Administrative Director
An independent labor union representing writers in motion pictures, television and radio in the east.
Founded: 1922

15093 Writers Guild of America: West
7000 W 3rd Street
Los Angeles, CA 90048
323-951-4000
FAX: 323-782-4800 www.wga.org
Charles Holland, President
Patric Verrone, Secretary/Treasurer
Ron Bass, Director
Elias Davis, Director
Dennis Feldman, Director
An independent labor union representing writers in motion pictures, television and radio in the west.
9500 Members Founded: 1912

Newsletters

15094 AGENDA
National Federation of Press Women
PO Box 5556
Arlington, VA 22205
703-129-9487
FAX: 703-534-5751 800-780-2715
presswomen@aol.com
http://www.nfpw.org
Tonda Rush, President
Carol Pierce, Executive Director
A quarterly newletter published by the National Federation of Press Women. *$51.50*
4 pages Quarterly Founded: 1937
Circulation: 2000
Mailing list available for rent 1700 names $40 per M.

15095 ASJA Newsletter
American Society of Journalists and Authors
1501 Broadway
Suite 302
New York, NY 10036-5501
212-997-0947
FAX: 212-768-7414
staff@asja.org http://www.asja.org
Brett Harvey, Executive Director
Lisa Collier Coloradool, President
Barbara Barrett, Newsletter Editor
Confidential news for journalists and authors, available only to members of the Society.
Monthly Founded: 1948

15096 Copy Editor
McMurry
1010 E Missouri Ave
Phoenix, AZ 85014
602-955-5850
888-626-8779
marybeth@copyeditor.com
http://www.copyeditor.com
Mary Beth Protomastro, Publisher
Barbara Wallraff, Editor
Chris McMurry, Chief Executive Officer
Helps editors stay up-to-date with the changing language. Articles discuss new words, changes in usage and reference books. Each issue contains interviews with copy editors. *$69.00*

8 pages Founded: 1990
Circulation: 2000 Audited
Printed in 1 color

15097 EFA Newsletter
Editorial Freelancers Association
71 W 23rd Street
Suite 1910
New York, NY 10010-4181
212-929-5400
FAX: 212-929-5439 866-929-5400
info@the-efa.org
http://www.the-efa.org

Anita Mondello, Publisher
J P Partland, CEO
Mary Ratcliffe, Editor
Martha Schuenman, Executive Director

Book reviews, news, features and reports on matters of interest to writers, indexers and editors. *$20.00*

6 issues/year Founded: 1970

15098 Editorial Eye
Editorial Experts
66 Canal Center Plaza
Suite 200
Alexandria, VA 22314
703-683-0683
FAX: 703-683-4915 800-683-8380
info@eeicommunications.com
http://www.eeicommunications.com

Claire Kincaid, Publisher
Candee Wilson, Director
Robin Cormier, VP Publications
Linda B Jorgensen, Editor
Keith C. Ivey, Technical Editor

Professional standards and practices for editors, writers and publication managers. *$139.00*

12 pages Monthly Founded: 1972
Circulation: 3,000

15099 Fillers for Publications
9201 Preston Trail NE
Albuquerque, NM 87111-6421
505-821-7033
FAX: 505-888-0477

Chris Vranas, Senior VP Meetings
John Raydell, Editor
Sarah Flores, Manager

Publish editorial copy, cartoons, clip art and puzzles for editors of all types of publications. All material is camera-ready and timely. *$83.00*

8 pages Monthly
Printed in 1 color on glossy stock

15100 Flash Market News
National Writers Association
10940 s parker rd
#508
parker, CO 80134
303-841-0246
FAX: 303-841-2607
Comments@nationalwriters.com
http://www.nationalwriters.com

Sandy Whelchel, Editor
Sandy Whelchel, CEO

Marketing information for members of The National Writers Association. *$20.00*

Monthly Founded: 1937
Circulation: 3000

15101 Freelance Writer's Report
CNW Publishing
PO Box A
North Stratford, NH 03590
603-922-8338
FAX: 603-922-8339 800-351-9278
info@writers-editors.com
http://www.writers-editors.com

Dana K Cassell, Executive Director

News and marketing information for freelance writers. *$39.00*

Monthly
Circulation: 1200

15102 IDEAS Unlimited for Editors
Omniprint
9700 Philadelphia Court
Lanham Seabrook, MD 20706-4405
301-731-7000
FAX: 301-731-7001 800-774-6809
info@omniprint.net
http://www.omniprint.net

Michael Nagan, President
Ken Kaufman, Chairman / CEO

Editorial ideas and graphics for editors of in-house, corporate newsletters. Provides 16 pages of fresh, ready-to-use items and ideas editors can use to fill out their publications. *$5.00*

16 pages Monthly Founded: 1978
Circulation: 6310 Controlled
Printed in 1 color on matte stock

15103 KEYSTROKES
Writers Alliance
12 Skylark Lane
Stony Brook, NY 11790-3121
516-751-7080

Kiel Stuart, Publisher
Howard Austerlitz, Editor
Charles Spataro, Circulation Manager

A writers newsletter containing marketing, how-to and computer information. *$10.00*

16 pages TriAnnual
Circulation: 250 Audited
Mailing list available for rent 250 names
Printed in 1 color on matte stock

15104 Linington Lineup
1223 Glen Ter
Glassboro, NJ 08028-1315
856-589-1571

Rinehart S Potts, Editor

Editing, publishing, police procedural. *$12.00*

16 pages Bi-Monthly Founded: 1984
Circulation: 400 Audited Est. Pass-Along Circ: 400
Printed in 1 color on matte stock

15105 Speechwriter's Newsletter
Ragan Communications
316 N Michigan Avenue
Suite 400
Chicago, IL 60601-3702
312-960-4100
FAX: 312-960-4105 800-493-4867
cservice@ragan.com
http://www.ragan.com

Mark Ragan, CEO/President
David Murray, Editor
Jim Ylisela, Group Publisher
Rebecca Anderson, Managing Editor

Offers speechwriting tips, examples and criticism. *$307.00*

4 pages Monthly Founded: 1980

15106 Story Bag: National Storytelling Newsletter
5361 Javier Street
San Diego, CA 92117-3215
858-569-9399
FAX: 858-569-0205
storybag@juno.com

Harlynne Geisler, Publisher

Professional storytellers, whether freelance or working for a school or library, will find this newsletter stuffed full of tips on techniques, suggestions for handling the business, reviews of storytelling books and tapes, listings of events nationwide, bibliographies of suggested materials, and discussion of issues such as censorship. Note: Above phone is used on e-mail, if busy try again. *$15.00*

8 pages Bi-Monthly
Circulation: 300 Audited Est. Pass-Along Circ: 700
Printed in 1 color on matte stock

15107 Strategic Employee Publications
Lawrence Ragan Communications
316 N Michigan Avenue
Suite 400
Chicago, IL 60601
312-604-4100
FAX: 312-960-4106 800-878-5331
publicrelations@ragan.com
http://www.ragan.com

Mark Ragan, CEO
David Murray, Editor
Diane Tillman, Marketing Manager

Designed to help organizational editors produce their company publications. *$139.00*

8 pages Monthly Founded: 1970
Circulation: 2500 $125 per M.
Printed in 2 colors on matte stock

15108 Washington Writer
Washington Independent Writers
220 Woodward Building
733 15th Street NW
Washington, DC 20005
202-381-1948
FAX: 202-638-7800
info@washwriter.org
http://www.washwriter.org

Joseph A Barbato, President
Donald O Graul Jr, Executive Director
Callie Rucker Oettinger, Managing Editor
Nicci Yang, Membership Manager

News and information for freelance writers. *$160.00*

8 pages Monthly Founded: 1975

15109 Writers Connection
Writers Connection
1826 Crossover Roade
PMB 108
Fayetteville, AR 72703

www.thewritersconnection.com
Provides how-to information for writers, plus listings of markets, contests and events. Accepts advertising. *$45.00*

16 pages Monthly

Magazines & Journals

15110 Latinos in the US: A Resource Guide for Journalists
National Association of Hispanic Journalists
1000 National Press Building
Washington, DC 20045-2100
202-627-7145
FAX: 202-662-7144

Anna Lopez, Executive Director
Joseph Torres, Communications Director
Rex Nutting, Manager

Purposes are to increase educational and career opportunities in journalism for Hispanic Americans. *$8.50*

Mailing list available for rent $500 per M.

15111 Modernism/Modernity
2715 N Charles Street
Baltimore, MD 21218-4319
410-516-6900
FAX: 410-516-6968 800-548-1784
claity@drew.edu
http://www.press.ghu.edu/journals
Jeffrey T Schnapp, Editor
Becky Brasington Clark, Marketing Director
Tom Lovett, Circulation Manager
Ken Sabol, Production Manager
Focuses systematically on the methodological, archival, and theoretical exigencies particular to modermist studies. It encourages and interdisciplinary approach linking music, architecture, the visual arts, literature, and social and intellectual history. *$40.00*
Quarterly Founded: 1994

Trade Shows

15112 Agricultural Publications Summit
American Agricultural Editors' Association
PO Box 156
New Prague, MN 56071
952-758-9135
FAX: 952-758-5813
ageditors@aol.com
www.ageditors.com
Held at the Renaissance Cleveland Hotel in Cleveland, Ohio.
July

15113 American Society of Journalists and Authors Conference
1501 Broadway
Suite 302
New York, NY 10036-5501
212-997-0947
www.asja.org
Brett Harvey, Executive Director
Michelle Aucoin, Director Alumni Affairs
A forum for the exchange of ideas between journalists.
700 Attendees May

Directories & Databases

15114 AWP Official Guide to Writing Programs
Association of Writers & Writing Programs
Mail Stop 1E3
Fairfax, VA 22030
703-993-4301
FAX: 703-993-4302
awp@awpwriter.org
Supriya Bhatngar, Director of Publications
About 300 colleges and universities offering workshops and degree programs in creative writing; approximately 100 writers' conferences, colonies and centers; coverage includes Canada and the United Kingdom. *$24.95*
400 pages Biennial

15115 American Book Trade Directory
Information Today
143 Old Marlton Pike
Medford, NJ 08055-8750
609-654-6266
FAX: 609-654-4309
custserv@infotoday.com
www.infotoday.com
Thomas H Hogan, Publisher/President
John Bryans, Publisher/Editor-in-Chief,Books
Lauree Padgett, Editorial Services Manager
Inge Coffey, Circulations Manager
Pat Palatucci, Assistant to the President
The US book trade community. Profiles 25,500 retail and antiquarian book dealers, plus 1,200 book and magazine wholesalers, distributors, and jobbers in al 50 states and US territories. *$299.00*
1800 pages ISBN 1-573872-12-1

15116 American Directory of Writer's Guidelines
Dustbooks
PO Box 100
Paradise, CA 95967-0100
530-877-6110
FAX: 530-877-0222 800-477-6110
directories@dustbooks.com
www.dustbooks.com
Brigitte M Phillips, Editor
Susan D Klassen, Editor
Doris Hall, Editor
These guidelines help writers target their submissions to the exact needs of the individual publisher. A compilation of information for freelancers from more than 1,500 magazine editors and book publishers. *$29.95*
752 pages ISBN 1-884956-40-8

15117 American Library Directory
Information Today
143 Old Marlton Pike
Medford, NJ 08055-8750
609-654-6266
FAX: 609-654-4309
custserv@infotoday.com
www.infotoday.com
Thomas H Hogan, Publisher/President
John Bryans, Publisher/Editor-in-Chief Books
Lauree Padgett, Editorial Services Manager
Inge Coffey, Circulation Manager
Pat Palatucci, Assistant to the President
Detailed profiles for more than 35,000 public, academic, special, and government libraries and library related organizations in the US and Canada. These include addresses, phone and fax numbers, e-mail addresses, network participation, expenditures, holdings and special collections, key personnel, special services and more than 40 categories of library information in all. A two volume set. *$299.00*
4000 pages ISBN 1-573872-04-0

15118 American Society of Journalists and Authors Directory
1501 Broadway
Suite 302
New York, NY 10036-5501
212-997-0947
www.asja.org
Brett Harvey, Executive Director
Lists over 800 member freelance nonfiction writers. *$75.00*
90 pages

15119 Applied Science & Technology Index
HW Wilson Company
950 University Avenue
Bronx, NY 10452-4297
718-888-8405
FAX: 718-590-1617 800-367-6770
custserv@hwwilson.com
www.hwwilson.com
Fast, convenient access to the cover-to-cover content of leading trade and industrial publications, journals issued by professional and technical societies, specialized subject periodicals, as well as buyers' guides, directories, and conference proceedings.
Monthly on WlisonDisc : Web & Disc

15120 Association of Professional Writing Consultants Membership Directory
Northwestern University
1902 Sheridan Road
Evanston, IL 60208-0845
847-915-5500
Barbara Shwom *$75.00*
Annual

15121 Authors and Artists for Young Adults
Gale Research
27500 Drake Road
Farmington Hills, MI 48331
248-699-4253
FAX: 248-699-8214 800-877-4253
galeord@gale.com www.gale.com
Offers valuable information on authors and artists who create books, movies and television programs that are of interest to young adults. *$67.00*
250 pages Semiannual

15122 Children's Writer's and Illustrator's Market
Writer's Market
1507 Dana Avenue
Cincinnati, OH 45207-1005
513-396-6160
FAX: 513-531-4082 800-289-0963
Offers valuable information about book and magazine publishers that publish works by authors and illustrators for young audiences. *$22.99*
256 pages Annual

15123 Complete Guide to Self-Publishing
Writer's Market
1507 Dana Avenue
Cincinnati, OH 45207-1005
513-396-6160
FAX: 513-531-4082 800-289-0963
Offers, in appendixes, a list of contacts and companies that help see to publication of a book at the author's expense. *$18.95*

15124 Contemporary Authors
Gale Research
27500 Drake Road
Farmington Hills, MI 48331
248-699-4253
FAX: 248-699-8214 800-877-4253
galeord@gale.com www.gale.com
Covers a wide array of information on over 100,000 authors who are currently active in the industry. *$119.00*
500 pages

15125 Directory of Literary Magazines
Council of Literary Magazines and Presses
154 Christopher Street
Suite 3C
New York, NY 10014-2840
212-419-9110
FAX: 212-741-9112
info@clmp.org www.clmp.org
Contains names, addresses and phone numbers of nearly 600 magazines in the US and abroad that publish poetry, fiction, essays, literary reviews and more. *$17.00*
Annual

15126 Directory of Poetry Publishers
Dustbooks
PO Box 100
Paradise, CA 95967-0100
530-877-6110
FAX: 530-877-0222 800-477-6110
directories@dustbooks.com
www.dustbooks.com
Len Fulton, Editor
Over 2,100 magazines, small and commercial presses and university presses that accept poetry for publication. *$25.95*
300 pages Annual ISBN 0-916685-47-0
Circulation: 2,000

15127 Directory of Small Magazines Press Magazine Editors & Publishers
Dustbooks
PO Box 100
Paradise, CA 95967-0100
530-877-6110
FAX: 530-877-0222 800-477-6110
directories@dustbooks.com
www.dustbooks.com
Len Fulton, Editor
This directory contains more than 7,500 listings of editors and publishers in alphabetical order, along with their associated publishing companies, their addresses, phones, e-mail addresses and Web pages. Includes self publishers. *$25.95*
460 pages Annual Founded: 1967 ISBN 0-913218-28-6
Circulation: 1,000
Mailing list available for rent

15128 Editor & Publisher International Year Book
Editor & Publisher Company
11 W 19th Street
10th Floor
New York, NY 10011-4209
212-929-1259

Michael Parker, President
Ian Anderson, Editor
Offers valuable information on daily and Sunday newspapers in the United States and Canada. *$125.00*
600 pages Annual

15129 Editor & Publisher: Directory of Syndicated Services Issue
Editor & Publisher Company
11 W 19th Street
10th Floor
New York, NY 10011-4209
212-929-1259

Michael Parker, President
A directory of several hundred syndicates serving newspapers in the United States and abroad with news, features and comic strips. *$7.00*
Annual

15130 Editorial Freelancers Association: Membership Directory
Editorial Freelancers Association
71 W Street
Suite 1504
New York, NY 10006-1704
212-929-5400
FAX: 212-929-5439
David R Hall, Editor
Martha Schuenman, Executive Director
1,100 member editorial freelancers. *$25.00*
Annual Spring

15131 Guide to Literary Agents
Writer's Market
1507 Dana Avenue
Cincinnati, OH 45207-1005
513-396-6160
FAX: 513-531-4082 800-289-0963
Agents and representatives for professional writers. *$18.95*
240 pages Annual

15132 Guide to Writers Conferences & Workshops
Shaw Guides
PO Box 231295
New York, NY 10023
212-799-6464
FAX: 212-724-9287
info@shawguides.com
www.shawguides.com
Conferences, workshops, and seminars for amateur and professional writers. *$19.95*
272 pages

15133 Key Guide to Electronic Resources:Language and Literature
Information Today
143 Old Marlton Pike
Medford, NJ 08055-8750
609-654-6266
FAX: 609-654-4309
custserve@infotoday.com
www.infotoday.com
Diane K Kovacs, Editor
Pat Ensor, Series Editor
Part of the ongoing topic related series of reference guides is an evaluative directory of electronic reference sources in the fields of language and literature. *$39.50*
120 pages ISBN 1-573870-20-x

15134 Literary Agents of North America
Author Aid/Research Associates International
340 E 52nd Street
New York, NY 10022-6728
212-758-2344

Arthur Orrmont, Editor
Leonie Rosenstiel, Editor
More than 1,00 US and Canadian literary agencies. *$33.00*

15135 Literary Forum
CompuServe Information Service
PO Box 20212
Columbus, OH 43220-0212
614-457-8600

This database covers literature, including books and poetry, writing, stage and screen, journalism and comic books.
Bulletin Board

15136 Literary Market Place
Information Today
143 Old Marlton Pike
Medford, NJ 08055-8750
609-654-6266
FAX: 609-654-4309
custserv@infotoday.com
www.infotoday.com
Thomas H Hogan, Publisher/President
John Bryans, Publisher/Editor-in-Chief
Lauree Padgett, Editorial Services Manager
Inge Coffey, Circulation Manager
The ultimate insider's guide to US book publishing industry with over 14,000 listings in all.

15137 Market Guide for Young Writers: Where and How to Sell What You Write
Writer's Market
1507 Dana Avenue
Cincinnati, OH 45207-1005
513-396-6160
FAX: 513-531-4082 800-289-0963
A list of over 150 magazines and writers contests are profiles that all accept work from young writers for publishing purposes. *$ 16.95*

15138 Mystery Writer's Market Place and Sourcebook
Writer's Market
1507 Dana Avenue
Cincinnati, OH 45207-1005
513-396-6160
FAX: 513-531-4082 800-289-0963
Offers various profiles of about 50 publishers of mystery and crime books. *$17.95*

15139 Novel & Short Story Writer's Market
Writer's Market
1507 Dana Avenue
Cincinnati, OH 45207-1005
513-396-6160
FAX: 513-531-4082 800-289-0963
More than 2,000 literary magazines, publishers, agents and writer's organizations are profiled. *$19.95*
Annual

15140 Poet's Market
Writer's Market
1507 Dana Avenue
Cincinnati, OH 45207-1005
513-396-6160
FAX: 513-531-4082 800-289-0963
Over 1,500 publishers, periodicals and other markets that accept poetry for publication are profiled. *$22.99*
528 pages Annual

15141 Professional Freelance Writers Directory
National Writers Club
314 Peoria
Suite 290
Aurora, CO 80014
303-841-0246

Over 200 professional members selected from the total membership on the basis of significant articles books or movies published. *$12.50*
75 pages Annual

15142 Science Fiction and Fantasy Writers of America Membership Directory
PO Box 877
Chestertown, MD 21620

exedir@sfwa.org www.sfwa.org
Directory of services and supplies to the industry. *$60.00*
40 pages Annual

15143 Self-Employed Writers and Artists Network Directory
PO Box 440
Paramus, NJ 07653-0440

www.swan-net.com
Phil Cantor, President
Wayne Rousck, VP Marketing
Over 140 freelance writers and graphic designers, as well as illustrators, photographers and more in northern New Jersey and Metropolitan New York City are profiled.
20 pages Annual

15144 Self-Publishing Manual: How to Write, Print and Sell Your Own Book
Para Publishing
PO Box 8206
Santa Barbara, CA 93118-8206
805-968-7277
FAX: 805-968-1379 800-727-2782
info@ParaPub.com ParaPub.com
Dan Poynter, Publisher
A list of wholesalers, reviewers and exporters, etc, are profiled. *$19.95*
900 pages Biennial Founded: 1979 ISBN 1-568600-73-9
Printed in 1 color on matte stock : online

15145 Space Coast Writers Guild: Organization, Activities and Membership
PO Box 262
Melbourne, FL 32902-0262

jehwriter@cfl.rr.com www.scwg.org
A who's who directory of professional writing services and training to the media industry.
25 pages Annual

15146 The Bowker Annual Library & Book Trade Almanac
Information Today
143 Old Marlton Pike
Medford, NJ 08055-8750
609-654-6266
FAX: 609-654-4309
custserv@infotoday.com
www.infotoday.com
Thomas H Hogan, Publisher/President
John Bryans, Publisher/Editor-in-Chief Books
Lauree Padgett, Editorial Services Manager
Inge Coffey, Circulation Manager
Pat Palatucci, Assistant to the President

This acclaimed must have resource provides expert reviews of key trends, events,and developments that will influence your work in 2004 and the years to come. Also provides clear explanations of new legislation and changes in funding programs and how it will affect libraries. *$ 199.00*
832 pages May ISBN 1-573871-93-1

15147 Twentieth-Century Romance and Historical Writers
St. James Press/Gale Research
27500 Drake Road
Farmington Hills, MI 48331
248-699-4253
FAX: 313-961-6741 800-877-GALE
Over 500 authors are profiled that are directly involved in romantic and historical novel writing. *$128.00*
1000 pages

15148 Twentieth-Century Science Fiction Writers
St. James Press/Gale Research
27500 Drake Road
Farmington Hills, MI 48331
248-699-4253
FAX: 313-961-6741 800-877-GALE
Directory of services and supplies to the industry. *$132.00*
1000 pages

15149 Twentieth-Century Western Writers
St. James Press/Gale Research
27500 Drake Road
Farmington Hills, MI 48331
248-699-4253
FAX: 313-961-6741 800-877-GALE
Directory of services and supplies to the industry. *$132.00*
848 pages

15150 Twentieth-Century Young Adult Writers
Gale Research
27500 Drake Road
Farmington Hills, MI 48331
248-699-4253
FAX: 248-699-8214 800-877-4253
galeord@gale.com www.gale.com
Approximately 400 authors of literature for young adults. *$132.00*

15151 Who's Who in Writers, Editors and Poets: US and Canada
December Press
PO Box 302
Highland Park, IL 60035-0302
847-940-4122

Curt Johnson, President
Directory of writers and editors. *$99.00*
700 pages Biennial

15152 Writer's Digest: Writers Conference Issue
F&W Publications
1507 Dana Avenue
Cincinnati, OH 45207-1005
513-531-2222
FAX: 513-531-1843
Directory of services and supplies to the industry. *$2.95*
Annual
Circulation: 225,000

15153 Writer's Guide to Book Editors, Publishers and Literary Agents
Prima Publishing
3000 Lava Ridge Center
Roseville, CA 95661
916-787-7000
FAX: 916-787-7001 800-632-8676
sales@primapub.com
www.primapublishing.com
Offers information on more than 200 publishing houses and their editors. *$19.95*
370 pages Annual

15154 Writer's Handbook
Kalmbach Publishing Company
21027 Crossroads Circle
PO Box 1612
Waukesha, WI 53186-1612
262-796-8776
FAX: 262-796-1615 800-533-6644
A list of more than 3,000 markets for the sale of manuscripts, ads and awards. *$29.95*

Annual

15155 Writer's Market: Where and How to Sell What You Write
Writer's Market
1507 Dana Avenue
Cincinnati, OH 45207-1056
513-396-6160
FAX: 513-531-4082
Directory of services and supplies to the industry. *$29.95*
1000 pages Annual

15156 Writer's Northwest Handbook
Media Weavers, Blue Heron Publishing
24450 NW Hansen Road
Hillsboro, OR 97124

Over 3,000 markets for writers, including newspapers, magazines and book publishers in Northwestern United States and British Columbia, Canada. *$18.95*
232 pages Biennial

15157 Writers Conferences
Poets & Writers
72 Spring Street
New York, NY 10012-4019
212-317-7920
$7.50
50 pages Annual

15158 Writers Directory
St. James Press/Gale Research
27500 Drake Road
Farmington Hills, MI 48331
248-699-4253
FAX: 313-961-6741 800-877-GALE
Offers valuable information on over 15,000 living writers from the United States, United Kingdom, Canada and the British Commonwealth nations. *$125.00*
1400 pages Biennial

15159 Writers Guild Directory
Writers Guild of America, West
8955 Beverly Boulevard
West Hollywood, CA 90048-2456
323-512-2600
FAX: 323-782-4802
Bob Waters, Manager
Directory of services and supplies to the industry. *$17.50*
450 pages Annual

Industry Web Sites

15160 www.asja.org
American Society of Journalists and Authors

Association for journalists and authors.

15161 www.dramaguild.com
Dramatists Guild

Protects the rights of its international membership of playwrights, composers and lyricists. Supports fair royalty, maintenance of subsidiary rights, artistic control and ownership of copyright.

15162 www.freelancepubs.com
Freelance Editorial Association

Self-employed contractors, or consultants with expertise in editorial functions such as copyediting, researching, indexing and proofreading, writing, illustrating, editing, project managing, desktop publishing, and translating.

15163 www.greyhouse.com
Grey House Publishing

Selected Grey House directories in the fields of business, health and education are available online. Users can search our online databases by several different search criteria, such as product categories, geographic area, sales volume and much, much more. Full Grey House catalog and online ordering also available.

15164 www.ifwtwa.org
International Food, Wine and Travel Writers
Association

Staff and/or freelance writers in the food, wine and travel field. Also includes other media professionals and industry associate members in 28 countries worldwide.

15165 www.loc.gov/loc/cfbook/
Library of Congress

This organization strives to stimulate the consumer interest in books and reading.

15166 www.mysterywriters.org
Mystery Writers of America

Professional writers of crime and mystery stories and novels. Unpublished writers are affiliate members. MWA annually gives the Edagar Awards for excellence in the mystery geare.

15167 www.nationalwriters.com

Membership organization for writers.

15168 www.nfc.council.com
Newspaper Features Council

A forum for editors, writers, columnists, cartoonists and syndicates to exchange views and improve the content of newspapers.

15169 www.nfpw.org
National Federation of Press Women

Members are writers, editors and other communication professionals for newspapers, magazines, wire services, agencies and freelance.

15170 www.owaa.org
Outdoor Writers Association of America

A nonprofit, international organization representing over 2,000 professional outdoor communicators who report on diverse interests in the outdoors.

15171 www.the-efa.org
Editorial Freelancers Association

National nonprofit, professional organization of self-employed workers in the publishing and communications industries.

15172 www.wga.org
Writers Guild of America, West

An independent labor union representing writers in motion pictures, television and radio in the west.

15173 www.writersresearchgroup.com
Writers Research Group

Associations

15174 American Beverage Licensees
5101 River Road
Suite 108
Bethesda, MD 20816-1560
301-656-1494
FAX: 301-656-7539
nabr@nabronline.org
www.nabronline.org
Harry Wiles, Executive Director
Shawn Ross, Office Manager
Represents over 15,000 off-premise licensees in the open or license states and on-premise proprietors in markets across the nation. Offers members information on legislation and industry matters.
15000 Members Founded: 1933

15175 American Society for Enology and Viticulture
PO Box 1855
Davis, CA 95617-1855
530-753-3142
FAX: 530-753-3318
society@asev.org www.asev.org
Lyndie Boulton, Executive Director
Nonprofit scientific society of international professionals from wineries, vineyards, academic institutions and organizations.
2500 Members Founded: 1950

15176 American Society of Brewing Chemists
3340 Pilot Knob Road
Saint Paul, MN 55121-2055
651-454-7250
FAX: 651-454-0766 800-328-7560
asbc@scisoc.org www.asbcnet.org
Steven Nelson, VP
Susan Kohn, Contact
Scientific group of brewing chemists dealing with the chemistry and microbiology of brewing ingredients.
750 Members

15177 American Society of Enology
PO Box 1855
Davis, CA 95617-1855
530-753-3142
FAX: 530-753-3318
society@asev.org www.asev.org
Signe Zoller, President
Thomas Smith, First VP
Dr Robert Wample, Second VP
Dr Andrew Walker, Secretary/Treasurer
2200 Members Founded: 1950

15178 Association of Brewers
736 Pearl Street
Boulder, CO 80302
303-447-0816
FAX: 303-447-2825 888-822-6273
info@brewersassociation.org
www.beertown.org
Chris Black, Chairperson
John Bryant, Vice Chairperson
Charlie Papazian, President
A non-profit educational and trade organization for small and craft brewers. Its mission is to make quality brewing and beer knowledge accessible to all.
11000 Members Founded: 1978

15179 Association of Winery Supplies
21 Tamal Vista Boulevard
Suite 196
Corte Madera, CA 94925-1146
415-924-2640
John Warner, Executive Director
United States supplier of services and materials used in the winery industry.
34 Members Founded: 1983

15180 Beer Institute
122 C Street NW
Suite 750
Washington, DC 20001-2150
202-737-2337
FAX: 202-737-7004 800-379-2739
info@beerinstitute.org
www.beerinstitute.org
Jeff Becker, President
Art DeCelle, Executive VP/General Counsel
Joe Stanton, VP Government Affairs
Protects the market environment from unfair burdens imposed by government bodies. Represents members interest before Congress.
100 Members Founded: 1986

15181 Brewers' Association of America
736 Pearl Street
Boulder, CO 80302
303-447-0816
FAX: 303-447-2825 888-822-6273
tim@brewersassociation.org
www.breweradvocate.org
Charlie Papazian, President
Bob Pease, VP
To promote and protect American Craft Beer, American Craft Brewers and the Community of Brewing Enthusiasts.
150 Members Founded: 1941

15182 Concord Grape Association
5775 Peachtree Dunwoody Road NE
Suite G500
Atlanta, GA 30342-1542
FAX: 404-252-0774 cga@assnhq.com
Pam Chumley, President
Offers information and representation in the best interests and welfare of the Concord grape industry.
10 Members

15183 Distilled Spirits Council of the United States
1250 I Street NW
Suite 400
Washington, DC 20005-3998
202-628-3544
FAX: 202-682-8888 www.discus.org
Peter H Cressy, President/CEO
National trade association representing producers and marketers of liquor sold in the US.
32 Members Founded: 1973

15184 Distillers Feed Research Council
University of Louisville
Academy Building
Room 435
Louisville, KY 40292-0001
502-893-0323
FAX: 502-852-1574
Members are beverage and ethanol distillers.
6 Members Founded: 1945

15185 Distillery, Wine and Allied Workers' International Union
66 Grand Avenue
Englewood, NJ 07631-3506
201-894-8444
FAX: 201-569-9216
George J Orlando, President
Addresses the concerns of wine makers and fellow industry workers.
14M Members

15186 Home Wine and Beer Trade Association
PO Box 1373
Valrico, FL 33595
813-685-4261
FAX: 813-681-5625
dee@hwbta.org www.hwbta.org
Mark Alston, President
Steven Haynes, VP
Ray Ault, Secretary
Allison Babock, Treasurer
Dee Roberson, Executive Director
Manufacturers, wholesalers, retailers, authors and editors having a commercial interest in the beer and wine trade.
Founded: 1976

15187 Institute for Brewing Studies
736 Pearl Street
Boulder, CO 80302
303-447-0816
FAX: 303-447-2825 888-822-6273
info@brewersassociation.org
www.beertown.org
The professional brewing organization of the Association of Brewers.
Mailing list available for rent

15188 Italian Wine and Food Institute
Lincoln Building, 60 East 42nd Street
Suite 1341
New York, NY 10165
212-867-4111
FAX: 212-867-4114
iwfi@aol.com
www.italianwineandfoodinstitute.com
Lucio Caputo, President
Mario Bona, Executive VP
George Pavia, Secretary
Carlo Romairone, Treasurer
Eugenio Magnani, Directors
Members are producers, distributors and marketers of Italian wines and foods.
Founded: 1983

15189 National Alcohol Beverage Control Association
4216 King Street
Alexandria, VA 22302-1507
703-784-4201
FAX: 703-820-3551
James M Sgueo, Executive Director
Dixie Jamieson, Executive Assistant
Members include control jurisdictions, supplier members and industry trade associations.
175 Members Founded: 1938

15190 National Beer Wholesalers Association
1101 King Street
Suite 600
Alexandria, VA 22314-2944
703-739-0591
FAX: 703-683-8965
info@nbwa.org www.nbwa.org
David Rehr, President
Michelle Semones, Public Affairs Director
Trade association for beer wholesalers. Provides government and public affairs outreach as well as education and training for its wholesaler members.
2200 Members Founded: 1938

15191 National Wine Distribution Association
2701 E Street
Sacramento, CA 95816-3221
916-979-3051
FAX: 916-448-9115

GM Pucilowski, Executive Director

Dedicated to promoting the interests and education of smaller wine wholesalers, importers, wineries, and others who are involved in the wine distribution business.
285 Members Founded: 1978

15192 Wine Institute
425 Market Street
Suite 1000
San Francisco, CA 94105
415-512-0151
FAX: 415-442-0742
www.wineinstitute.org

Robert Koch, President
Nancy Light, Director
Steve Gross, State Relations
John De Luca, Manager

Organization that represents the wine and spirit industry to state and federal lawmaking bodies.
80 Members Founded: 1934

15193 Wine Spirits Wholesalers of America
805 15th Street NW
Suite 430
Washington, DC 20005
202-371-9792
FAX: 202-789-2405 www.wswa.org

Don Leebern III, Chairman
Juanita Duggan, President/CEO
Jim Rowland, Senior VP Government Affairs
Karen Gravois, Senior VP Communications
Rae Ann Bevington, VP Convention/Meetings/PR

National trade organization representing the wholesale branch of the wine and spirits industry.
450 Members Founded: 1943

15194 Wine and Spirits Shippers Association
11800 Sunrise Valley Drive
Suite 332
Reston, VA 20191-5396
703-602-2300
FAX: 703-860-2422
info@wssa.com www.wssa.com

Geoffrey Giovanetti, Director

Provides members, importers and exporters with efficient and economical ocean transportation and other logistic services.
460 Members Founded: 1976

15195 Wine and Spirits Wholesalers of America
805 15th Street NW
Washington, DC 20005
202-371-9792
FAX: 202-789-2405 www.wswa.org

J Smoke Wallin, Chairman
Don Leebern III, Vice Chairman
Juanita Duggan, Chief Executive Officer

This association is comprised of wholesale distributors of domestic and imported wine and distilled spirits.
450 Members Founded: 1943
Circulation: 1,000

Newsletters

15196 ASBC Newsletter
American Society of Brewing Chemists
3340 Pilot Knob Road
Saint Paul, MN 55121-2055
651-454-7250
FAX: 651-454-0766 800-328-7560
asbc@scisoc.org
http://www.asbcnet.org

Tim Kostelecky, President
Steven Nelson, VP
Karen Cummings, Director Publications
Joan A Raumschuh, Editor

Provides news items and technical reports on brewing and related matters. *$20.00*
Quarterly Founded: 1934

15197 Alcoholic Beverage Control: From the State Capitals
Wakeman Walworth
PO BOX 7376
Alexandria, VA 22307-7376
703-768-9600
FAX: 703-768-9690
newsletters@statecapitals.com
http://statecapitals.com/

Ellen Klein, Editor
Keyes Walworth, Publisher
Tommy Broyles, Manager

Reports on state-by-state liquor regulatory activities. Gives an accurate picture on how states are governing liquor advertising, liquor taxes, and bottle bills, Sunday sales laws, liquor shop liability, license regulation, drunken driving laws, legal drinking ages and other state endeavors affecting liquor. *$245.00*
4 pages Weekly
Printed in 1 color on matte stock
Computerized version available

15198 Beer Marketer's Insights Newsletter
Beer Marketer's Insights
PO Box 264
West Nyack, NY 10994
845-624-2337
FAX: 845-624-2340
http://www.beerinsights.com

Benj Steinman, President

Reports on the competitive battle among brewers for a share of the beer market. Analyzes recent legislation and factors that affect the industry. *$595.00*
23 issues a yea Founded: 1975

15199 Beer Statistics News
Beer Marketer's Insights
PO Box 264
West Nyack, NY 10994
845-624-2337
FAX: 845-624-2340
bmiexpress@aol.com
http://www.beerinsights.com

Benj Steinman, President
Eric Shephard, Executive Editor
Andy Leinicke, Circulation Manager

Supplies data for major brewers' shipments in 39 reporting states. *$450.00*
Monthly Founded: 1975

15200 Brewers Bulletin
PO Box 677
Thiensville, WI 53092
262-242-6105
FAX: 262-242-5133
bulletindigest@milwpc.com

Tom Volke, President/CEO

Brewing industry newspaper. *$53.00*
Monthly Founded: 1907
Circulation: 500

15201 Champagne Wines Information Bureau
KCSA
800 2nd Avenue Frnt 5
New York, NY 10017-4709
212-682-6300
FAX: 212-697-0910 800-642-4267
info@champagnes.com
www.champagnes.com

Jean-Louis Carbonnier, Editor

Representative of Comite Interprofessionnel duVinde Champagne, Epernay, France.
4 pages TriAnnual
Circulation: 10,000
Printed in 1 color on matte stock

15202 Impact International
M Shanken Communications
387 Park Avenue S
8th Floor
New York, NY 10016-8872
212-684-4224
FAX: 212-779-3383 800-848-7113
info@mshanken.com
http://www.mshanken.com

Marvin Shanken, Publisher/Editor/Chairman
Samantha Shanken, VP Market Development

Reports on the global alcoholic beverage market. *$595.00*
Annual+ Founded: 1972

15203 Italian Trade Commission
499 Park Avenue
New York, NY 10022-1240
212-980-1500
FAX: 212-758-1050
newyork@italtrade.com
www.italtrade.com/ice

Michelle Jones, Editor
Robert Luongo, Executive Director

Developments in the Italian wine industry and market, as well as reviews of imported wines from Italy.

15204 Kane's Beverage Week
Whitaker Newsletters
313 S Avenue
#340
Fanwood, NJ 07023-1364
908-889-6339
800-359-6049

Joel Whitaker, Publisher
Anne Bittner, Editor
Fred Rossi, Editor

News on marketing, economic and regulatory factors affecting the alcohol beverage industry. *$131.00*
6 pages Monthly

15205 Notiziario
Italian Wine and Food Institute
PO Box 789
New York, NY 10150
212-867-4111
FAX: 212-867-4114
iwfi@aol.com
http://www.italianwineandfoodinstitute.com

Lucio Caputo, President
Maria D Andrea, Editor
Eileen Parise, Associate Editor

Provides detailed information on the Italian gastronomy and wines. It distributes information materials and give press interviews for the American radio and television. It carries out an intense public relations program, participates in the most important local promotional initiatives and events and maintains contact with the American and Italian authorities in this sector. *$250.00*
Founded: 1983

15206 On Tap: Newsletter
WBR Publishing
PO Box 71
Clemson, SC 29633
864-654-2300
FAX: 864-654-5067
Steve Johnson, Publisher
North America breweries and microbreweries. *$.95*
20 pages Bi-Monthly
Circulation: 1000
Printed in 1 color on matte stock

15207 Spirited Living: Dave Steadman's Restaurant Scene
5301 Towne Woods Rd
Coram, NY 11727-2808
631-736-0436
FAX: 631-736-0436
spiritedliving@aol.com
Dave Steadman, Editor
Newsletter published Bi-Weekly except January, July, and August. *$75.00*

15208 US Beer Market
Business Trend Analysts/Industry Reports
2171 Jericho Turnpike
Suite 200
Commack, NY 11725-2937
631-462-5454
FAX: 631-462-1842 800-866-4648
sales@bta-ler.com
http://www.bta-ler.com
Charles J Ritchie, Executive VP
Donna Priani, Marketing Director
Profiles markets for premium, superpremium, popular and light beers. *$1495.00*
Computerized version available: Disk

15209 Uncorked
California Wine Club
2175 Goodyear Avenue
Suite 102
Ventura, CA 93006-3699
805-650-4330
FAX: 800-700-1599 800-777-4443
info@cawineclub.com
http://www.cawineclub.com
Bruce Boring, Proprietors
Judy Reynolds, Proprietors
Uncorked is an 8 page newsletter that describes the featured winery. It provides an upclose and personal look at a small 'boutique' California Winery.
Monthly Founded: 1990
Circulation: 10000

15210 Vinotizie Italian Wine Newsletter
Italian Trade Commission
33 East 67th Street
New York, NY 10021-5949
212-480-0300
FAX: 212-758-1050
newyork@newyork.ice.it
http://www.italtrade.com
Michelle Jones, Editor
Roberto Luongo, Executive Director
Giovanni Mafodda, Operations Manager
Aniello Musella, Manager
This newsletter discusses developments in the Italian wine industry and market, as well as reviews of imported wines from Italy.
Monthly Founded: 1998

15211 Wine Investor Buyers Guide
PGE Publications
1224 N Fairfax Avenue
Apartment 5
Los Angeles, CA 90046-5234
Paul Gillette, Publisher
JD Kronman, Editor
Reviews new releases of wines, recommends the best buys, predicts when wines will be at their peak and surveys markets for pricing trends. Accepts advertising. *$75.00*
10 pages Monthly

15212 World Beer Review
WBR Publishing
PO Box 71
Clemson, SC 29633-0071
864-654-2300
Steve Johnson, Publisher
Complete coverage of the beer and beermaking industry.

Magazines & Journals

15213 All About Beer
501-H Washington Street
Durham, NC 27701
919-530-8150
FAX: 919-530-8160 800-977-2337
editor@allaboutbeer.com
http://www.allaboutbeer.com
Daniel Bradford, Publisher
Julie Bradford, Editor
Natalie Abernethy, Circulation Manager
Quality beers, breweries and restaurants. *$19.99*
64 pages Founded: 1981

15214 Atlantic Control States Beverage Journal
Club & Tavern
3 12th Street
Wheeling, WV 26003-3276
304-232-7620
FAX: 304-233-1236
wvbevjournal@aol.com
Arnold Lazarus, Editor
A magazine for the alcoholic beverage industry. Serving bars, restaurants, clubs and industry personnel with West Virginia, Virginia, and North Carolina state editions. Includes states' liquor price lists.

15215 Bartender Magazine
Foley Publishing Corporation
PO Box 158
Liberty Corner, NJ 07938-158
908-766-6006
FAX: 908-766-6607 908-766-6607
Info@bartender.com
http://www.bartender.com
Raymond Foley, Publisher
Jaclyn Wilson Foley, Editor
Serves all full service drinking establishments. Including individual restaurants, hotels, motels, bars, taverns, lounges, and all other full service on premise licenses. Subscription price is $40 for Canada, and $55 for all other foriegn countries. *$30.00*
72 pages Monthly Founded: 1979
Circulation: 149044 149,044 names $125 per M.
Printed in 4 colors on glossy stock

15216 Beer Perspectives
National Beer Wholesalers Association
1101 King Street
Suite 600
Alexandria, VA 22314-2944
703-390-0591
FAX: 703-683-8965
info@nbwa.org http://www.nbwa.org
David Rehr, President
Erin Rutherford, Editor
Marcia S Jonas, Production Manager
Trade association for beer wholesalers. Provides government and public affairs outreach as well as education and training for its wholesaler members.
Founded: 1938

15217 Beverage Dynamics
Adams Business Media
304 Park Ave S
11th Floor
New York, NY 10010
646-542-2015
FAX: 212-590-2476
admin@adamsbusinessmedia.com
http://www.beveragenet.net
Richard Brandes, Editor
Marion Minor, President/CEO
Charles Forman, Publisher
Anthony Bongiovanni, Advertising Sales Director
James Fraser, Production Director
This trade magazine offers information on the alcoholic beverage business. *$35.00*

15218 Beverage Journal
Michigan Licensed Beverage Association
920 N Fairview
Lansing, MI 48912
517-374-9611
FAX: 517-374-1165 800-292-2896
info@mlba.org http://www.mlba.org
Jerry Smith, President
Cathy Pavick, Executive Director
Peter Broderick, Director of Communication
Offers information on the alcoholic beverage industry/retail sales *$52.00*
Monthly Founded: 1939
Printed in on glossy stock

15219 Beverage Network
Beverage Media Group
116 John Street
21st Floor
New York, NY 10038
212-713-3232
FAX: 212-571-4443 800-723-8372
info@bevmedia.com
http://www.bevmedia.com
B Gowen, Editor
Jason Glasser, CEO/President
S Paley, Circulation Manager *$99.00*
Monthly Founded: 1940
Circulation: 6000

15220 Beverage Retailer Magazine
Oxford Publishing
307 Jackson Avenue W
Oxford, MS 38655-2154
662-236-5510
FAX: 662-236-5541 800-247-3881
br@beverage-retailer.com
http://www.beverage-retailer.com

Brenda Owen, Editor
Ed Meek, Publisher
Stacy Clark, Production Manager
Jennifer Parsons, Marketing Director
Ruth Ann Wolfe, Circulation Director

A magazine covering the off premise market for retailers in the wine, beer and spirits business. *$30.00*
Founded: 1985
Circulation: 25000
Printed in 4 colors on glossy stock

15221 Cheers
Adams Business Media
17 High Street 2nd Floor
Norwalk, CT 06851
203-855-8499
FAX: 203-855-9446
rbrandes@adamsbevgroup.com
http://www.beveragenet.net

Richard Brandes, Editor
Jack Robertiello, Editor
Ernest Adams, Owner

Every issue is designed to help on-premise operators enhance the profitability of their beverage operations.
Founded: 1998

15222 Modern Brewery Age
Business Journals
50 Day Street
PO Box 5550
Norwalk, CT 06856-5550
203-853-6015
FAX: 203-853-8175
FayS@busjour.com
http://www.breweryage.com

Mac Brighton, Chairman/COO
Britton Jones, President/CEO
Peter V K Reid, Editor/Publisher
Arthur Heilman, Circulation Director
Diane Apicelli, Advertising Director

A magazine for the wholesale and brewing industry. *$95.00*
Founded: 1933

15223 Modern Brewery Age: Tabloid Edition
Business Journals
50 Day Street
PO Box #5550
Norwalk, CT 06856-5550
203-853-6015
FAX: 203-853-8175
http://www.breweryage.com

Peter VK Reid, Editor
Peter VK Reid, Publisher
Britton Jones, President/CEO
Diane Apicelli, Advertising Director
Mac Brighton, Chairman & COO

Brewery industry tabloid. *$95.00*
Weekly Founded: 1933

15224 Nightclub & Bar Magazine
Oxford Publishing
307 Jackson Avenue W
Oxford, MS 38655-2154
662-236-5510
FAX: 662-281-0104 800-247-3881
mitchell@op.oxpub.com
www.nightclub.com

Ed Meek, Production Manager
Mitchell Diggs, Managing Editor
Laura McCreary, Advertising Director
Jennifer Cummins, Production Manager

A monthly publication covering the nightclub and bar hospitality industry.
Monthly
Circulation: 30,000
Printed in 4 colors on glossy stock

15225 Southern Beverage Journal
14337 SW 119th Avenue
Miami, FL 33186-6006
305-233-7230
FAX: 305-252-2580
sobedjrnl@aol.com
www.bevnetwork.com

Wanda Rowe, Editor
William Slone, CEO/President
Sharon Mijares, Circulation Manager

A magazine for the alcoholic beverage industry. *$35.00*
Monthly Founded: 1944
Circulation: 29000

15226 Standard & Poor's Industry Surveys
Standard & Poor's Corporation
55 Water Street
New York, NY 10041
212-382-2000
800-221-5277

Terry McGraw, Chief Executive Officer

A two-volume book the examines the prospects for specific industries, including the beer and beverage industry. Also provides analyses of trends and problems, statistical tables and charts, and comparative company analyses. *$1475.00*

15227 StateWays
Adams Business Media
50 Washington Street
10th Floor
Norwalk, CT 06854
203-855-8499
FAX: 203-855-9446
www.beveragenet.net

Richard Brandes, Editor

Every issue addresses the subjects that are important to the Control State System.

15228 US Beer Market: Impact Databank Review and Forecast
M Shanken Communications
387 Park Avenue S
8th Floor
New York, NY 10016-8872
212-844-4224
FAX: 212-779-3383
ckull@mshanken.com

Christian Kull, Publisher
Samantha Shanken, Marketing Manager
$9.10

15229 US Liquor Industry
Business Trend Analysts/Industry Reports

2171 Jericho Turnpike
Suite 200
Commack, NY 11725-2900
631-462-5454
FAX: 631-462-1842
bta@li.net
www.businesstrendanalysts.com

Charles J Ritchie, Executive VP
Donna Priani, Marketing Director
Linda Sherman, Production Manager
Jennifer Wichert, Research Director

A survey summarizing the past, current and future markets and trends in the liquor industry. *$1195.00*
600 pages Founded: 1999
Computerized version available: Disk

15230 US Wine Market
Business Trend Analysts/Industry Reports

2171 Jericho Turnpike
Suite 200
Commack, NY 11725-2937
631-462-5454
FAX: 631-462-1842 800- 86- 464
sales@bta-ler.com
http://www.businesstrendanalysts.com

Charles J Ritchie, Executive VP
Donna Priani, Marketing Director

An analysis of the wine industry, domestic and imported. *$1995.00*
470 pages Founded: 1978
Circulation: 2004
Computerized version available: Disk

15231 Upfront
Wine and Spirits Wholesalers of America
805 15th Street NW
Suite 430
Washington, DC 20005-2273
202-371-9792
FAX: 202-789-2405
wswa@wswa.org
http://www.wswa.org

David Dickerson, Publisher/Editor
Juanita Duggan, President/CEO

This magazine offers information regarding government actions and news of interest to wholesale distributors of domestic and imported wine and distilled spirits.
Founded: 1943
Circulation: 1000

15232 Vineyard and Winery Management

Vineyard & Winery Services
PO Box 231
Watkins Glen, NY 14891-231
607-535-7133
FAX: 607-535-2998 800-535-5670
rleahy@vwm-online.com
http://vwm-online.com

Tom Loid, Executive Editor
Richard Leahy, Editor

To be the bottom line resource for growers and vintners; to keep our readers tuned and primed for profit. *$37.00*
100 pages Monthly Founded: 1975
Circulation: 4500
Printed in 4 colors on glossy stock

15233 Wine Advocate
Robert M Parker Jr
PO Box 311
Monkton, MD 21111
410-329-6477
FAX: 410-357-4504
wineadvocate@erobertparker.com
http://www.erobertparker.com

Robert M Parker Jr, Publisher/ Editor
Jacques Robinson, President

An independent magazine covering reviews of wine. *$60.00*
64 pages Founded: 1978
Circulation: 40000

15234 Wine and Spirits
Winestate Publications
1748 Market Street
San Francisco, CA 94102-4997
415-255-7736
FAX: 415-255-9659
mlkinney@wineandspiritsmagazine.com
http://www.wineandspiritsmagazine.com/

Joshua Greene, Editor/Publisher
Michael Kinney, Associate Publisher
Ray Isle, Managing Editor
W. Charles Squires, Circulation Director
Gilian Handelman, Marketing Manager/Education Directo

A consumer magazine for wine enthusiasts.
$26.00
70 pages Founded: 1987
Circulation: 75000
Printed in 4 colors on glossy stock

Trade Shows

15235 ASBC Annual Meeting
American Society of Brewing Chemists
3340 Pilot Knob Road
Saint Paul, MN 55121-2055
651-454-7250
FAX: 651-454-0766 800-328-7560
bford@scisoc.org
www.meeting.asbcnet.org

Betty Ford, Meetings Director
Sue Casey, Meetings Coordinator
Steven Nelson, VP

An opportunity to network, learn, build business relationships and hear first-hand the latest brewing science and related research. Contains exhibits, technical and keynote presentations and workshops.
$625.00
300 Attendees June/Non-Members Fee

15236 American Beverage Licensees Annual Convention & Trade Show
American Beverage Licensees
5101 River Road
Suite 108
Bethesda, MD 20816-1560
301-656-1494
FAX: 301-656-7539
nabr@nabronline.org
www.nabronline.org

Harry Wiles, Executive Director
Susan Day Pirieda, Office Manager

Annual show of 75 manufacturers, suppliers and distributors of alcoholic beverages.
700 Attendees March

15237 American Society for Enology and Viticulture
PO Box 1855
Davis, CA 95617-1855
530-753-3142
FAX: 530-753-3318

Lyndie Boulton, Executive Director

Three hundred booths displaying products and technology for the wine and grape industry.
2500 Attendees June Founded: 1950

15238 American Wine Society
3006 Latta Road
Rochester, NY 14612-3298
585-225-7613
FAX: 585-225-7613
angel910@aol.com
americanwinesociety.com

Angel E Nardone, Executive Director

12 booths.
600 Attendees November Founded: 1967

15239 Beer, Wine & Spirits Industry Trade Show
Indiana Association of Beverage
200 S Meridian Street
Suite 350
Indianapolis, IN 46225-3418
317-847-7580
FAX: 317-673-4210

Teresa Koch

Annual show of 125 exhibitors of alcohol beverage distillers brewers that are recognized primary sources in the state of Indiana as supplies for retailers.
2500 Attendees

15240 Craft Brewers Conference and Brew Expo America
Association of Brewers
736 Pearl Street
Boulder, CO 80302
303-447-0816
FAX: 303-447-2825 888-822-6273
info@brewersassociation.org
www.beertown.org

Nancy Johnson, Show Manager
Cindy Jones, Director Sales/Marketing
Charlie Papazian, President

1,200 Attendees April

15241 Great American Beer Festival
Association of Brewers
736 Pearl Street
Boulder, CO 80302
303-447-0816
FAX: 303-447-2825 888-822-6273
info@brewersassociation.org
www.beertown.org

Bob Pease, VP

September

15242 NABR Tasting & Display Event Annual Convention
American Beverage Licensees
5101 River Road
Suite 108
Bethesda, MD 20816-1560
301-656-1494
FAX: 301-656-7539
nabr@nabronlline.org
www.nabronline.org

Harry Wiles, Executive Director
Shawn Ross, Office Manager

Offers exhibits on spirits, beer and wine industry supplies, equipment, bar accessories and computers. The NABR Annual Convention is a gathering of alcohol beverage retailers and proprietors for networking and educational opportunities. An exclusive trade display and tasting event is held to promote brands and services of use to retailers and proprietors. There are 25-75 booths.

500+ Attendees March 15M names

15243 National Beer Wholesalers Association Convention and Trade Show
Corcoran Expositions
33 N Dearborn Street
Suite 505
Chicago, IL 60602-3103
312-541-0567
FAX: 312-541-0573 800-541-0359

Al Natker, Operations Manager

Biennial show of 166 manufacturers, suppliers and distributors of brewery software and hardware, trucking, beer cleaning equipment and related equipment, supplies and services.
3000 Attendees

15244 Wine Spirits Wholesalers of America
805 15th Street NW
Suite 430
Washington, DC 20005
202-371-9792
FAX: 202-789-2405 www.wswa.org

Don Leebern III, Chairman
Juanita Duggan, President/CEO
Rae Ann Bevington, VP Convention/Meeting/PR

Two hundred booths for suppliers of alcoholic beverages from around the world.

15245 Wine and Spirits Wholesalers of America Convention and Exposition
805 15th Street NW
Suite 430
Washington, DC 20005-2273
202-371-9792
FAX: 202-789-2405
wswa@wswa.org www.wswa.org

Juanita Duggan, Executive Director
Megan McIntire, Director Convention/Meetings
Karen Gravois, VP Public Relations/Communications

Three hundred exhibitors of producers of spirits, wine, beer, mixes, bottled water, freight routing/forwarding companies and point of sale product vendors.
2000 Attendees April

15246 Wineries Unlimited
Vineyard & Winery Services
PO Box 231
Watkins Glen, NY 14891
607-535-7133
FAX: 607-535-2998 800-535-5670

Richard Leahy, Show Manager
Bob Mignarri, Program Trade Show Sales

2000 Attendees March

Directories & Databases

15247 Beverage Marketing Directory
850 3rd Avenue
New York, NY 10022-6222
212-688-7640

Barclay Griffiths, Manager

Over 10,000 beer wholesalers, wine and spirits, and soft drink wholesalers and franchisers are profiled. *$705.00*
850 pages Annual

15248 Brewers Resource Directory
Association of Brewers
736 Pearl Street
Boulder, CO 80302
303-447-0816
FAX: 303-447-2825 888-822-6273
info@brewersassociation.org
www.beertown.org

Paul Gatza, Director
Ray Daniels, Editor
Charlie Papazian, President

Various categories of listees are included that have a direct relation to the beer and liquor industry.

Mailing list available for rent

15249 Contacts
National Alcohol Beverage Control Association
4216 King Street
Alexandria, VA 22302-1507
703-784-4201
FAX: 703-820-3551
James M Sgueo, Executive Director
Dixie Jamieson, Executive Assistant
Members include control jurisdictions, supplier members and industry trade associations.

15250 Directory & Products Guide
Vineyard & Winery Services
PO Box 2358
Windsor, CA 95492
707-836-6820
FAX: 707-836-6825 800-535-5670
Jennifer Merietti, Sales/Marketing Manager
A must have reference book that belongs on the desk of every wine professional. Whether it's tracking down a particular vendor, shopping for the best deal on oak barrels or searching for out-of-state winery contacts, the DPG is a powerhouse of information. Over 2,300 supplier listings and 2,700 winery/vineyard listings, it is a reliable resource that saves time and money. *$95.00*
450+ pages Annually

15251 Food & Beverage Market Place
Grey House Publishing
185 Millerton Road
PO Box 860
Millerton, NY 12546
518-890-0526
FAX: 518-789-0545 800-562-2139
books@greyhouse.com
www.foodmp.com
Leslie Mackenzie, Publisher
Richard Gottlieb, Editor
This information-packed 3-volume set is the most powerful buying and marketing guide for the US food and beverage industry. Includes thousands of industry freight and transportation listings. *$595.00*
6500 pages Annual

15252 Impact International Directory: Leading Spirits, Wine and Beer Companies
M Shanken Communications
387 Park Avenue S
8th Floor
New York, NY 10016-8872
212-684-4224
FAX: 212-684-5424
Marvin R Shanken, Editor
A directory offering information on the major players of the alcoholic beverage industry. *$295.00*

15253 Impact Yearbook: Directory of the US Wine, Spirits & Beer Industry
M Shanken Communications
387 Park Avenue S
8th Floor
New York, NY 10016-8872
212-684-4224
FAX: 212-684-5424
Marvin Shanken, Owner
A directory offering information on the top 40 American distributors and profiles of companies. *$170.00*
Annual

15254 Top 1,000 Beer Distributors
Beverage Marketing Corporation
850 3rd Avenue
New York, NY 10022-6222
212-688-7640
FAX: 212-826-1255
Michael Bellas, President
Richard Mack, VP Marketing *$595.00*
155 pages

15255 Top 300 Wineries
Beverage Marketing Corporation
850 3rd Avenue
New York, NY 10022-6222
212-688-7640
FAX: 212-826-1255
Michael Bellas, President
Richard Mack, VP Marketing
The top 300 wineries, ranked by gallonage capacity. *$695.00*
25 pages Annual

15256 U.S. Beverage Manufacturers and Filling Locations Category CD
Beverage Marketing Corporation
2670 Commercial Avenue
Mingo Junction, OH 43938
740-598-4133
FAX: 740-598-3977 800-332-6222
Andrew Standardi, Director Operations
Kathy Smurthwaite, Editor *$2203.00*
Annual

15257 U.S. Carbonated Soft Drink Operations Category CD
Beverage Marketing Corporation
2670 Commercial Avenue
Mingo Junction, OH 43938
740-598-4133
FAX: 740-598-3977 800-332-6222
Andrew Standardi, Director Operations
Kathy Smurthwaite, Editor *$2385.00*
Annual

15258 U.S. Non-Alcoholic Beverage Industry Category CD
Beverage Marketing Corporation
2670 Commercial Avenue
Mingo Junction, OH 43938
740-598-4133
FAX: 740-598-3977 800-332-6222
Andrew Standardi, Director Operations
Kathy Smurthwaite, Editor *$3969.00*
Annual

15259 U.S. Wine & Spirits Industry Category CD
Beverage Marketing Corporation
2670 Commercial Avenue
Mingo Junction, OH 43938
740-598-4133
FAX: 740-598-3977 800-332-6222
Andrew Standardi, Director Operations
Kathy Smurthwaite, Editor *$1661.00*
Annual

15260 US Beer Distributors: A Delivery Fleet Profile
Beverage Marketing Corporation
850 3rd Avenue
New York, NY 10022-6222
212-688-7640
FAX: 212-826-1255 800-275-4630
Over 3,200 beer distributors. *$895.00*

15261 US Beer Distributors: A Sales Profile
Beverage Marketing Corporation
850 3rd Avenue
New York, NY 10022-6222
212-688-7640
FAX: 212-826-1255 800-275-4630
Over 3,200 US beer distributors. *$895.00*
Annual

15262 US Wine & Spirits Distributors: A Sales Profile
Beverage Marketing Corporation
850 3rd Avenue
New York, NY 10022-6222
212-688-7640
FAX: 212-826-1255 800-275-4630
Over 1,350 US wine and spirits distributors. *$795.00*
Annual

15263 Vineyard & Winery Management Magazine
Vineyard & Winery Services
PO Box 2358
Windsor, CA 95492
707-836-6820
FAX: 707-836-6825 800-535-5670
Jennifer Merletti, Sales/Marketing Manager
A leading technical trade publication serving the North American Wine Industry and designed for today's serious wine business professional. *$37.00*
100+ pages Bi-Monthly Founded: 1975
Circulation: 6,000

15264 Wholesale Beer Association Executives of America Directory
Wholesale Beer Association Executives of America
2805 E Washington Avenue
Madison, WI 53704-5165
608-255-6464
FAX: 608-255-6466
7 pages Annual

15265 Wine & Spirits Industry Marketing
Jobson Publishing Corporation
100 Avenue of the Americas
9th Floor
New York, NY 10013-1678
212-274-7000
FAX: 212-431-0500
Nicolas Furlotte, Editor
List of about 300 wine and liquor firms including wineries, producers, distillers and importers. *$150.00*
Annual April

15266 Wine and Spirits Wholesalers: A Spirit Brand Profile
Beverage Marketing Corporation
850 3rd Avenue
New York, NY 10022-6222
212-688-7640
FAX: 212-826-1255
Michael Bellas, President
Richard Mack, VP Marketing
A who's who directory of wholesale services and supplies to the industry. *$795.00*
Annual

15267 Wine on Line
Wine on Line International
400 E 59th Street
Apartment 9F
New York, NY 10022-2344
212-755-4363
FAX: 212-755-7365

A database containing information including reviews about wines, production methods, serving advice, and more. Available on the Internet and worldwide web.
Daily

15268 **Wines and Vines Directory of the Wine Industry in North America Issue**
Hiaring Company
1800 Lincoln Avenue
San Rafael, CA 94901-1221
415-453-9700
FAX: 415-453-2517
geninfo@winesandvines.com
www.winesandvines.com
Dorthy Kubota-Cordery, Editor
Phil Hiaring, Publisher
Debbie Hennessy, Editor
Renee Skiadas, Circulation Direct
Chet Klingensmith, Owner

Annual guide offering listings of wineries and wine industry suppliers in the US, Canada and Mexico. *$85.00*
505 pages Annual
Circulation: 5000 1800 names $850 per M.

Industry Web Sites

15269 **www.beerinstitute.org**
Beer Institute

Protects the market environment from unfair burdens imposed by government bodies. Represents members interest before Congress.

15270 **www.beertown.org**
American Homebrewers Association

Devoted to the education of home brewed beer. Publishes the only magazine devoted exclusively to education, art and science of homebrewing. Services include: Beer Judge Certification Program, Sanctioned Competitions, World's Largest Homebrew Competition.

15271 **www.cawineclub.com**
California Wine Club

A wine of the month club that features only California's small boutique wineries. Each month members receive two bottles of award-winning wine.

15272 **www.greyhouse.com**
Grey House Publishing

Selected Grey House directories in the fields of business, health and education are available online. Users can search our online databases by several different search criteria, such as product categories, geographic area, sales volume and much, much more. Full Grey House catalog and online ordering also available.

15273 **www.nbwa.org**
National Beer Wholesalers Association

Research and development, quality control and ingredients.

15274 **www.scisoc.org/asbc**
American Society of Brewing Chemists

Annual scientific meeting for professionals in the brewing industry.

15275 **www.wineinstitute.org**
Wine Institute

Organization that represents the wine and spirit industry to state and federal lawmaking bodies.

15276 **www.wssa.com**
Wine and Spirits Shippers Association

Provides members, importers and exporters with efficient and economical ocean transportation and other logistic services.

Associations

15277 APA - The Engineered Wood Association
7011 S 19th
Tacoma, WA 98466
253-565-6600
FAX: 253-565-7265 www.apawood.org
Jonathan Martin, Chairman
David Rogoway, President
The mission of EWA is to advance technological and production innovations benefiting engineered wood product manufacturers and consumers through sponsorship of research and widespread industry information transfer. Trade association representing structural panel manufacturers in North America.

15278 American Fiberboard Association
853 North Quentin Road
Suite 317
Palatine, IL 60067
847-934-8394

afa@fiberboard.org
www.fiberboard.org
Bob Boyer, President
Rina McGuire, VP
Gary Keeling, Secretary/Treasurer
Louis E Wagner, Technical Director
The national trade organization of manufacturers of cellulose fiberboard products used for residential and commercial construction.
7 Members Founded: 1990

15279 American Forest Foundation
1111 19th Street NW
Suite 780
Washington, DC 20036-3603
202-463-2455
FAX: 202-463-2461
info@forestfoundation.org
www.affoundation.org
Laurence D Wiseman, President
Encourages the development of commerical forests and forestry products.
120 Members

15280 American Forest and Paper Association
1111 19th Street NW
Suite 800
Washington, DC 20036
202-463-2700
FAX: 202-463-2471
info@afandpa.org www.afandpa.org
Henson Moore, President
Susan Sherwood, Director Public Information
Represents member companies and related trade associations which grow, harvest and process wood and wood fiber, manufacture pulp, paper and paperboard products from both virgin and recovered fiber and produce solid wood products.
550 Members Founded: 1993

15281 American Forests
PO Box 2000
Washington, DC 20013-2000
202-955-4500
www.americanforests.org
Deborah Gangloff, Executive Director
Supports all those involved in tree planting and tree care equipment. Hosts annual trade show.

15282 American Hardwood Export Council
1111 19th Street NW
Suite 800
Washington, DC 20036
202-632-2700
FAX: 202-463-2787 www.ahec.org
Michael Snow, Executive Director
Andrew Roberts, Program Manager
Happy Whitlock, Program Manager
Henson Moore, President
Promotes the export of hardwood lumber to Europe.
38 Members Founded: 1989

15283 American Walnut Manufacturers Association
35 Village Court
PO Box 5046
Zionsville, IN 46077
317-873-8780
FAX: 317-873-8780
awmawalnut@cs.com
www.walnutassociation.com
Larry Frye, Owner
A national trade group representing manufacturers of walnut lumber, veneer, gunstock and dimensions.
8 Members Founded: 1912

15284 American Wood Chip Export Association
Stoel Rives
101 South Capitol Boulevard
Suite 1900
Boise, ID 83702
208-389-9000
FAX: 208-389-9040
mlmoody@stoel.com www.stoel.com
Mari Moody, Secretary
Researches and compiles data on the wood chip export association.
5 Members

15285 American Wood Preservers Association
100 Chase Park South
Suite 116
Birmingham, AL 35244-1851
205-889-9122
FAX: 205-733-4075
email@awpa.com www.awpa.com
Colin McCown, Executive Vice President
Jackie Ellis, Manager
Supports all those involved in the field of wood protection.
900 Members Founded: 1904

15286 Appalachian Hardwood Manufacturers
712 Lexington Avenue
Suite 202
High Point, NC 27261-0427
336-885-8315
FAX: 336-886-8865
www.appalacianwood.org
Mark Barford, President
Promotes the use of Appalachian hardwoods. Provides education and research programs.
154 Members Founded: 1926

15287 Association of Equipment Manufacturers
6737 West Washington Street
Suite 2400
Milwaukee, WI 53200
414-272-1170
FAX: 414-272-0943
aem@aem.org www.aem.org
Gerald Shaheen, Chairman
Representing manufacturers of architectural, construction, forestry, materials handling and liabilty equipment.

15288 Association of Millwork Distributors
10047 Robert Trent Jones Parkway
New Port Richey, FL 34655-4649
727-372-3665
FAX: 727-372-2879
mail@nsdja.com www.amdweb.com/
Rosalie Leone, Executive Director
Kim Cotterman, Director Membership/Marketing
William G Simon, Technology & Communications Manager
Recognized as the leader in representing wholesale millwork distribution companies for over 40 years.
1200 Members Founded: 1935

15289 Association of Woodworking & Furnishings Suppliers
5733 Rickenbacker Road
Commerce, CA 90040
323-838-9440
FAX: 323-838-9443 800-946-2937
awfsofc@aol.com www.awfs.org
Skip Hem, President
Joan Kemp, VP
Trade association for suppliers to the woodworking and furnishings industry. Services include three trade shows: Woodworking; Machinery and Supply Fair; Home and Commercial Furnishings.
425 Members Founded: 1979

15290 Capital Lumber Company
11 North 45th Avenue
Phoenix, AZ 85043-3902
602-381-0709

info@capital-lumber.com
www.capital-lumber.com
Van Vanderhoff, Division Manager
Steve Westfall, Sales Manager
Dedicated to being the leading district materials in the Western United States by providing unequaled service to customers, unequaled fairness with suppliers, the unequaled opportunity for a fulfilling career for each employee and a reasonable rate of return for its owners.

15291 Cedar Shake and Shingle Bureau
PO Box 1178
Sumas, WA 98295-1178
425-531-1323
FAX: 604-820-0266
info@cedarbureau.com
www.cedarbureau.org
Lynne Christensen, Director Operations
Barb Enns, Accountant
Dave Mooney, Cedar Quality Auditor
Nonprofite trade association representing manufacturer's, distributors, approved installers and service suppliers of Certilabel™ cedar shakes and shingles.
430 Members Founded: 1915

15292 Composite Panel Association
18922 Premiere Court
Gaithersburg, MD 20879-1574
301-670-0604
FAX: 301-840-1252
jfchlegel@cpamail.org

Thomas Julia, President

Represents Northern American Particle Board and Manufacturers' sister association, Composite Wood Council. Represents manufacturers and suppliers of Composite Wood Council.

232 Members Founded: 1960

15293 Fine Hardwood Veneer Association
American Walnut Manufacturers Association
260 S 1st Street
Suite 2
Zionsville, IN 46077
317-873-8780
FAX: 317-873-8788
FhvaAwmaWc@CompuServe.com
www.beveridge-audio.com

James Mathers, President
Larry R Frye, Executive Director

Represents the decorative veneer industry. Members are face veneer manufacturers, dealers, veneer custom cutters, rotary face and crossband manufacturers, hardwood industry suppliers, veneer salesman and veneer face plants.

15 Members Founded: 1933

15294 Forest Industries Telecommunications
1565 Oak Street
Eugene, OR 97401-2200
541-485-8441
FAX: 541-485-7556
license@landmobile.com
www.landmobile.com

KentonH Sturdevant, Executive VP

Organized to assist the forest industry in radio matters before the FCC.

600 Members Founded: 1947

15295 Forest Landowners Association
900 Circle 75 Parkway
Suite 205
Atlanta, GA 30339
404-325-2954
FAX: 404-325-2955 800-325-2954
info@forestlandowners.com
www.forestlandowners.com

Otis Ingram, President
Kirk Rodgers, Regional VP
C E Bush, Regional VP
Scott Jones, Executive Vice President

Proactive, progressive, grassroots organization of timberland owners - large and small - who operate more than 47 million acres of timberland in 17 southern and eastern states.

10500 Members Founded: 1941

15296 Forest Products Research Society
2801 Marshall Court
Madison, WI 53705-2295
608-231-1361
FAX: 608-231-2152
info@forestprod.org
www.forestprod.org

W Ramsay Smith, President
Carol Lewis, Executive VP
Arthur Brauner, VP

Researches products of American Forests.

Founded: 1947

15297 Forest Products Trucking Council
1025 Vermont Avenue NW
Suite 1020
Washington, DC 20005-3516
202-149-9250

Douglas Domenech, Secretary

An affiliate of the American Pulpwood Association.

50 Members

15298 Friends of the Trees
3117 NE, ML King Jr Boulevard
Portland, OR 97212
503-282-8846
www.friendsoftrees.org

Nicole D' Onofrio, President

Inspires community stewardship by bringing people together to plant and care for trees in urban and city environments.

Founded: 1989

15299 Hardwood Manufacturers Association
400 Penn Center Boulevard
Suite 530
Pittsburgh, PA 15235-5605
412-829-0770
FAX: 412-829-0844
www.hmamembers.org

Susan M Regan, Executive Vice President

Over 100 companies with over 150 locations in the US.

55 Members

15300 Hardwood Plywood & Veneer
PO Box 2789
Reston, VA 20190
703-435-2900
FAX: 703-435-2537
hpva@hpva.org www.hpva.org

Bill Altman, President
Gary Gramp, Technical Director
Curt Alt, Marketing Publications

Provides public relations, advertising, marketing, and technical services to members.

170 Members Founded: 1921

15301 Hardwood Utilization Consortium
USDA Forest Service
Southern Research Station
Blacksburg, VA 24061-0503
540-231-5341
FAX: 540-231-8868
paraman@vt.edu
www.consortium.forprod.vt.edu

Philip Araman

The role is to improve hardwood resource viability through better utilization, technology, markets, cooperative extension and education in the eastern United States.

15302 Hearth, Patio & Barbecue Association
1901 N Moore Street
Suite 600
Arlington, VA 22209
703-522-0086
FAX: 703-522-0548 www.hpba.org

Jack Goldman, President
Carter Keithley, Chief Executive Officer
Leslie Wheeler, Director Communications

2600 Members Founded: 1980

15303 Intermountain Forest Industry Association
3731 N Ramsey Road
Suite 110
Coeur D Alene, ID 83815-9037
208-667-4641
FAX: 208-664-0557 www.ifia.com

Joseph Hinson, Executive Director
Jim Riley, Manager

Seeks to provide a unified voice for the industry. Promotes a sustained timber yield. Monitors federal legislation.

30 Members Founded: 1986

15304 International Wood Products Association
4214 King Street West
Alexandria, VA 22302-1507
703-820-6696
FAX: 703-820-8550
info@iwpawood.org
www.iwpawood.org

Brent J McClendon, Executive VP/CAE
Annette Ferri, Member Services
Suzanne Morgan, Government Affairs

International trade association representing companies handling imported wood products of all types.

220 Members Founded: 1956

15305 Laminating Materials Association
116 Lawrence Street
Hillsdale, NJ 07642-2730
201-664-2700
FAX: 201-666-5665
infor@lma.org www.lma.org

George Carter, Executive Director

Nonprofit trade group representing all decorative overlays and edgebanding in North America. These products are applied to a composite wood substrate and used in the production of furniture, store fixtures, kitchen cabinets and more.

15306 Lumbermen's Credit Association
20 N Wacker Dr
Suite 1800
Chicago, IL 60606-2905
312-553-0943
FAX: 312-553-2149
www.lumbermenscredit.com

Steven Smith, President/Director
Elliott Smith, VP
Richard J Arde, Secretary/Treasurer

Assist credit managers and salesmen by providing listings and credit ratings of companies which deal in lumber and wood products. Also publishes a directory.

Founded: 1876

15307 Maple Flooring Manufacturers Association
60 Revere Drive
Suite 500
Northbrook, IL 60062-1591
847-480-9138
FAX: 847-480-9282
mfma@maplefloor.org
www.maplefloor.org

Kevin Hacke, Executive Director

International non-profit trade organization representing manufacturers of northern hard maple solid strip flooring along with flooring contractors, distributors and providers of instalation-related products and services. Maintains technical standards for product quality, grading, shipping and packaging, and quality central.

175 Members

15308 NOFMA: The Wood Flooring Manufacturers Association
22 North Front Street
Suite 660
Memphis, TN 38103
901-526-5016
FAX: 901-526-7022
info@nofma.org www.nofma.org
Timm Locke, Executive VP
Glen Miller, Director/Inspection Services

It's warmer with wood. Genuine hardwoods, plus one-of-a-kind beauty. You never get tired of solid hardware floors - provides the perfect setting.
27 Members Founded: 1908

15309 National Association of the Remodeling Ind ustry
780 Lee St
Suite 200
Des Plaines, IL 60016
847-298-9200
FAX: 847-298-9225 800-611-6274
info@nari.org www.nari.org
Purpose is to establish and maintain a firm commitment to developing and sustaining programs that expand and unite the remodeling industry; to ensure the industry's growth and security; to encourage ethical conduct, sound business practices and professionalism in the remodeling industry; and to present NARI as the recognized authority in the remodeling industry.

15310 National Frame Builders Association
4840 Bob Billings Parkway
Lawrence, KS 66049-3862
785-843-2444
FAX: 785-843-7555 800-557-6957
nfba@nfba.org www.nfba.org
John Fullerton, VP
Tom Knight, President
Kim Swartzendruber, Convention/Meetings Director
Scott McKinney, Accounting Manager
Sarah Lober, Marketing Manager
Building contractors, suppliers, design and code professionals and academic personnel specializing in the post frame construction industry.
Founded: 1971

15311 National Lumber & Building Material Dealers Association
900 2nd Street NE
Suite 305
Washington, DC 20002
202-547-2230
FAX: 202-547-7640 800-634-8645
Shawn Conrad, President
The mission of NLBMDA is to promote the success of America's lumber and building material dealers through advocacy, information, cooperation and innovation.

15312 National Wood Flooring Association
111 Chesterfield Industrial Boulevard
Chesterfield, MO 63005
636-199-9663
FAX: 636-519-9664 800-422-4556
info@nwfa.org www.woodfloors.org
Ed Korczak, President
Membership includes distributors, manufacturers, retailers and contractors. Association assists in advertising, education and developing standards and grade levels.
1990 Members Founded: 1985

15313 National Wood Tank Institute
PO Box 2755
Philadelphia, PA 19120-0755
215-329-9022
FAX: 215-329-1177
jackhillman@woodtank.com
www.woodtank.com
Harrison W Rippen, Secretary
Companies and individuals in the US and Canada involved in the manufacture of wood tanks, vats and pipes.

15314 National Wood Window and Door Association
1400 E Touhy Avenue
Suite 470
Des Plaines, IL 60018-3337
847-299-5200
FAX: 847-299-1286
nwwda@ais.net www.nwwda.org
Chris Simpson, Chairman
Jerry Mannigel, Vice Chairman Door Division
Dave Beeken, Vice Chairman Window Division
Linda Semling, Treasurer
Members are makers of standard building products such as doors, windows and frames.
140 Members Founded: 1926

15315 National Wooden Pallet & Container
329 S Patrick Street
Alexandria, VA 22314-3501
703-519-6104
FAX: 703-519-4720
pjsherry@nepapallet.com
www.nwpca.com
Patrick Sherry, VP
William E Biedenbach, President
David Eason, Secretary/Treasurer
Bruce N Scholnick, CEO
Represents manufacturers, recyclers and distributors of pallets, containers and reels.

575 Members Founded: 1947

15316 New England Kiln Drying Association
SUNY
College of Env Science and Forestry
1 Forestry Drive
Syracuse, NY 13210-2786
315-706-6600

wbsmith@esf.edu
www.kiln-direct.com
William Smith, Executive Director
Disseminates information on the dying of wood to the wood-using industry.
650 Members Founded: 1951

15317 North American Wholesale Lumber Association
3601 Algonquin Road
Suite 400
Rolling Meadows, IL 60008
847-870-7470
FAX: 847-870-0201
info@nawla.org www.nawla.org
Nicholas R Kent, President/CEO
Pamela A Baker, Director Meetings/Research
Benjamin A Stephens, Director Information
Supports the wholesale lumber industry. Publishes monthly NAWLA Bulletin that includes industry and association news, and produces the NAWLA Traders Market, an annual trade show bringing together over 2000 manufacturers and wholesale lumber traders at the premier event in the forest products industry. NAWLA also produces a variety of educational programs designed to enhance professionalism in the lumber industry.
600+ Members Founded: 1893

15318 Northeastern Loggers Association
3311 State Route 28
PO Box 69
Old Forge, NY 13420-0069
315-369-3078
FAX: 315-369-3736
nela@northernlogger.com
Joseph Phaneuf, Executive Director
Eric A Johnson, Editor
Works to improve the industry in the Northeast and educate the public about policies and products of the industry.
Founded: 1952

15319 Northern Woods Logging Association
PO Box 270
Jackman, ME 04945-0270

Provides members with a workers compensation protection program. Conducts on-site inspections and offers a first aid course and safety training program.
213 Members Founded: 1974

15320 Northwest Forestry Association
1500 SW 1st Avenue
Suite 700
Portland, OR 97201
503-229-9505
FAX: 503-222-3255
nfa/wiic@woodcom.seagull.com
www.batnet.com/woodcom/nfa
Tom Partin, President
Promotes forestry throughout the region to assure a permanent industry and stable economy. Works to keep informed on current changes affecting forest products.
70 Members Founded: 1987

15321 Northwestern Lumber Association
1405 Lilac Drive N
Suite 130
Minneapolis, MN 55422-4535
763-544-6822
FAX: 763-595-4060
gsmithnla@aol.com www.nlassn.org
Gary Smith, President
Retail lumber dealer in Iowa, Minnesota, North Dakota, and South Dakota.
1.5M Members Founded: 1890

15322 Pacific Logging Congress
PO Box 1281
Maple Valley, WA 98038
425-413-2808
FAX: 425-413-1359
pacificlogging@aol.com
www.pacificloggingcongress.com
Rikki Wellman, Executive Director
Ralph Torney, President
Ron Simon, Treasurer
Logging firms.
550 Members Founded: 1909

15323 Pacific Lumber Exporters Association
1260 NW Waterhouse Avenue
Suite 150
Beaverton, OR 97006-8114
503-439-6000
FAX: 503-439-6330
www.lumber-exporters.org
Vicki Onuliak, President
John Quast, VP
Provide forum to discuss trade issues and problems; promote member companies through governmental and other trade association channels.
35 Members Founded: 1923

15324 Pacific Lumber Inspection Bureau
33442 1st Way S
Suite 300
Federal Way, WA 98003
253-353-3344
FAX: 253-835-3371
info@plib.org www.plib.org
Greg Mobley, President
Ted Smith, VP
Jeff Fantozzi, Manager
Accredited for grading and grade stamping of softwood lumber. Issues certificates on domestic and export lumber shipments.
65 Members

15325 Pennsylvania Forest Products Association
545 W Chocolate Ave
Hershey, PA 17033
717-312-1244
FAX: 717-312-1335
hlma@hlma.org www.hlma.org
Represents the state's entire forest products industry, including foresters, loggers, sawmills, and value-added processors; maintains a full-time government affairs office and lobbyist; has been resposible for the passage of several pieces of legislation aimed at the protection and enhancement of our industry; responsible for the defeat and amendment of legislation threatning the viability of the forest of the forest products industry; & has been recognized as the voice for the forest industry

15326 Railway Tie Association
115 Commerce Drive
Suite C
Fayetteville, GA 30214-7335
770-460-5553
FAX: 770-460-5573
ties@rta.org www.rta.org
Jim Gauntt, Executive Director
Members include crosstie producers, sawmill owners, chemical manufacturers, wood preservation companies, railroad maintenance engineers, purchasing officials and others.
2500 Members Founded: 1919

15327 Redwood Inspection Service
405 Enfrente Road
Suite 200
Novato, CA 94949-7201
415-382-0662
FAX: 415-382-8531 888-225-7339
info@calredwood.org
www.calredwood.org
Christopher Grover, President
Pamela Allsebrook, Publicity Manager
Authorized by Department of Commerce to develop and supervise redwood lumber grading.
8 Members Founded: 1917

15328 Society of American Foresters
5400 Grosvenor Lane
Bethesda, MD 20814-2198
301-897-8720
FAX: 301-897-3690
safweb@safnet.org www.safnet.org
Michael T Goergen Jr, Executive VP/CEO
Barbara Weitzer, Assistant to the CEO and Council
Larry D Burner, Senior Director Finance
Supports all those involved with the forest industry. Publishes newsletter and hosts annual trade show.

15329 Society of Wood Science & Technology
One Gifford Pinchot Drive
Madison, WI 53726-2398
608-231-9347
FAX: 608-231-9592
vicki@swst.org www.swst.org
Douglas D Stokke, President
Paul M Smith, VP
Vicki L Herian, Executive Director
Promotes policies and procedures which assure the wise use of wood and wood-based products; assures high standards for professional performance of wood scientists and technologists; fosters educational programs at all levels of wood science and technology and further the quality of such programs; represents the profession in public policy development.
450 Members Founded: 1958

15330 Southeastern Lumber Manufacturers
671 Forest Parkway
PO Box 1788
Forest Park, GA 30298
404-361-1445
FAX: 404-361-5963 www.slma.org
Steve Rountree, President
Debbie Burns, VP
Represents membership in local, regional, and national problems that affect southeastern lumber industry. Conducts marketing and promotional activity.
350 Members Founded: 1962

15331 Southern Cypress Manufacturers Association
400 Penn Center Boulevard
Suite 530
Pittsburgh, PA 15235
877-607-7262
www.cypressinfo.org
Administrative support provided by the Hardwood Manufacturers Association.
19 Members Founded: 1905

15332 Southern Forest Products Association
2900 Indiana Avenue
Kenner, LA 70065
504-443-4464
FAX: 504-443-6612
mail@sfpa.org www.sfpa.org
Digges Morgan, President
Steven Bean, VP Marketing
265 Members Founded: 1915

15333 Southern Pine Inspection Bureau
4709 Scenic Highway
Pensacola, FL 32504-9018
850-434-2611
FAX: 850-433-5594
spib@spib.org www.spib.org
James Loy, President
Tom Jones, Executive Director
Develops grading standards for Southern pine lumber and provides an inspection service and grade marking systems.
Founded: 1940

15334 Structural Board Association
25 Valleywood Drive
Unit 27
Markham, L3R 5L9, ON
905-475-1100
FAX: 905-475-1101
webmaster@osbguide.com
www.osbguide.com
Members are manufacturers of structural panels.
Founded: 1978

15335 TOC Management Services
6825 SW Sandburg Street
Tigard, OR 97223-8083
503-620-1710
FAX: 503-620-3935 www.toc.org
Rodger Glos, President
Serves membership in the fields of labor, industrial, and employee relations. Provides counsel in wage and contract negotiations. Provides training and safety programs.
425 Members Founded: 1960

15336 Temperate Forest Foundation
14780 SW Osprey Dr
Suite 355
Beaverton, OR 97007-8070
503-579-6762
FAX: 503-579-0300
office@forestinfo.org
www.forestinfo.org
Robert M Owens, Chairman
Lee F Freeman, President & CEO
A tax-exempt, non-profit, public charity. Provides leadership by articulating the current realties, and a positive inspiring vision of the future. Helps people move toward the positive vision of living sustainably.
Founded: 1989

15337 Timber Products Manufacturers (TPM)
951 E 3rd Avenue
Spokane, WA 99202-2287
509-535-4646
FAX: 509-534-6106
tpm@tpmrs.com www.tpmrs.com
Greg McFarland, Immediate Past Chairman
Dick Molenda, Chairman
Charles Fox, President
Human resource and employee benefits association providing consulting services and quality products with an emphasis on integrity and value. Serves members throughout the Northwest and Intermountain area.
250 Members Founded: 1916

15338 Tree Care Industry Association
3 Perimeter Road
Unit 1
Manchester, NH 03103
603-314-5380
FAX: 603-314-5386
tcia@tcia.org www.tcia.org
Cynthia Mills, President
Peter Gerstenberger, Director Safety/Education
Supports all those involved with trees and tree care by offering education and training, community events, and publications.

2000 Members Founded: 1938
Mailing list available for rent 28000 names
$.11 per M.

15339 Truss Plate Institute
218 North Lee Street
Suite 312
Alexandria, VA 22314-2800
703-683-1010
www.tpinst.org

Charles Goehring, Managing Director

Develops design criteria, conducts statistical surveys, research and educational programs. Bestows awards.
300 Members Founded: 1961

15340 West Coast Lumber Inspection Bureau
PO Box 23145
Portland, OR 97281-3145
503-580-0289
FAX: 503-684-8928
info@wclib.org www.wclib.org

Bradley Shelley, Executive VP
Jim Kneaper, Manager/Operations
Jim West, Owner

Supervises manufacturing practices, grade stamping, and inspecting.
189 Members Founded: 1941

15341 Western Building Material Association
PO Box 1699
Olympia, WA 98507-1699
360-943-3054
FAX: 360-943-1219 www.wbma.org

Bruce Abel, President
Mike Hennick, VP
Jeff Swan, VP
Bob Perrin, National Director
Casey Voorhees, Executive Director

Regional trade association derving building material dealers throughout the states of Alaska, Idaho, Montana, Oregon and Washington and a federated association of the National Lumber and Building Material Dealers Association.
600 Members

15342 Western Forestry and Conservation
4033 SW Canyon Road
Portland, OR 97221
503-226-4562
FAX: 503-226-2515
richard@westernforestry.org
www.westernforestry.org

Mike Curran, President
Richard Zabel, Executive Director

Offers high-quality continuing education workshops and seminars for professional foresters throughout Oregon, Washington, Idaho, Montana, Northern California and British Columbia.
125 Members Founded: 1949

15343 Western Red Cedar Lumber Association
Po Box 952
Riverhead, NY 11901-2136
631-643-9725
FAX: 631-643-7252 800-266-1910
wrcla@wrcla.org www.wrcla.org

Peter Lang, General Manager
Edward Burke, Eastern Field Representative

Mission is to produce quality Western Red Cedar lumber products and support them with technical education and promotion.
Founded: 1954

15344 Western Wood Products Association
522 SW 5th Avenue
Portland, OR 97204-2122
503-224-3930
FAX: 503-224-3934
info@wwpa.org www.wwpa.org

Michael R O'Halloran, President
Tom Hanneman, VP/Director
Robert Bernhardt Jr, Director Information Services
Kevin CK Cheung, Director Technical Services
Kevin Binam, Director Economic Services

Represents lumber manufacturers in 12 Western states and Alaska. Provides lumber quality control, technical support, and business information to supporting mills.
135 Members Founded: 1964

15345 Window & Door Manufacturers Association
1400 East Touhy Avenue
Suite 470
Des Plaines, IL 60018
847-299-5200
FAX: 847-299-1286 800-223-2301
admin@wdma.com www.wdma.com

Jeffrey F Lowinski, Acting President

A trade association representing approximately 145 U.S. and Canadian manufacturers and suppliers of windows and doors for the domestic and export markiets.

15346 Wood Component Manufacturers Association
1000 Johnson Ferry Road
Suite A-130
Marietta, GA 30068-2194
770-565-6660
FAX: 770-565-6663
www.woodcomponents.org

Steve Lawser, Executive Director

Represents manufacturers of wood component products for urniture, cabinetry, building products, and decorative wood products.
Founded: 1929

15347 Wood Machinery Manufacturers of America
100 North 20th Street
4th Floor
Philadelphia, PA 19103-1443
215-564-3484
FAX: 215-963-9785
wmma@fernley.com www.wmma.org

Peter M Perez, President
Kenneth R Hutton, Executive VP
Bill Norton, Director Marketing/Information
Karen Boyle, Member Services
John Wood, Manager

Works to increase the productivity and profitability of US machinery and tooling manufacturers and the businesses that support them through advancement and awareness in the woodworking industry.
230 Members Founded: 1899

15348 Wood Machinery Maufacturers of America
1900 Arch Street
Philadelphia, PA 19103-1498
215-564-3484
FAX: 215-963-9785 www.wmma.org

Peter Perez, President
John Wood, Manager

WMMA has worked to increase the productivity and profitability of U.S. machinery and tooling manufacturers and the businesses that support them.

15349 Wood Moulding and Millwork Producers Assoc iation
507 First Street
Woodland, CA 95695
530-661-9591
FAX: 530-661-9586 800-550-7889
info@wmmpa.com www2.dcn.org

Craig Young, President
Tom Williams, Jr, VP

Promote quality products produced by its members, to develop sources of supply, to promote optimum use of raw materials to standardize products, and to increase the domestic and foreign usage of moulding and millwork products.

15350 Wood and Synthetic Flooring Institute
American Sports Builders Association
8480 Baltimore National Pike
Suite 307
Ellicott City, MD 21043
410-730-9595
FAX: 410-730-8833 888-501-2722
info@sportsbuilders.org
www.sportsbuilders.org

Gerry Wright, Chairman
Mark Brogan, Director

Wood flooring manufacturers and distributors.
50 Members

15351 Woodworking Machinery Industry Association
3313 Paper Mill Road
Suite 202
Phoenix, MD 21131
410-628-1970
FAX: 410-628-1972
bmiller@clemonsmgmt.com
www.wmia.org

Calvin K Clemons, Executive VP
Bill Miller, Chief Administrative Executive

Providing the North American wood products industry with technologically advanced woodworking systems available in the global market. A wide range of special programs provide industry awards, safety publications, scholarships and a host of other methods to support industry initiatives and address industry issues.
54 Members Founded: 1978

Newsletters

15352 American Wood Preservers Association Newsletter
American Wood Preservers Association
12100 Sunset Hills Road
Suite 130
Reston, VA 20190
703-204-0500
FAX: 703-204-4610 800-356-2974
info@awpa.org www.awpa.org

John Hall, Publisher

Reports on governmental issues and environmental news. *$7.50*
12 pages Monthly Founded: 1921

15353 Association Of Millwork Distributors Newsletter
Association Of Millwork Distributors
10047 Robert Trent Jones Parkway
New Port Richey, FL 34655-4649
727-372-3665
FAX: 727-372-2879 800-786-7274
mail@nsdja.com www.amdweb.com/
Rosalie Leone, Executive Director
Kim Cotterman, Director of Membership
Updates for wholesale millwork distribution companies.
Monthly Founded: 1964
Circulation: 1500
Printed in 2 colors on glossy stock

15354 Classified Exchange
Miller Publishing Corporation
1235 Sycamore View Road
Memphis, TN 38134
901-372-8280
FAX: 901-373-6180 800-844-1280
Pages and pages of bargains, several pages on raw material and service sources for everything from lumber to curved plywood, from dry kilns to sawmill equipment and boilers. Special liquidations and auctions offering everything from soup to nuts. *$65.00*
Monthly

15355 Forestry Source
Society of American Foresters
5400 Grosvenor Lane
Bethesda, MD 20814-2198
301-897-8720
FAX: 301-897-3690
safweb@safnet.org
http://www.safnet.org
Michael T Goergen Jr, Executive Vice-President and CEO
Delisa Barrons, Publications Project Manager
Joe Smith, Editor
A tabloid newsletter covering important information regarding critical issues in forestry research and technology, legislative updates and news about SAF programs and activities on a national and local level. *$45.00*
20 pages Monthly Founded: 1900
Printed in 4 colors on newsprint stock

15356 Import/Export Wood Purchasing News
Miller Publishing Corporation
1235 Sycamore View Road
Memphis, TN 38134
901-372-8280
FAX: 901-373-6180 800-844-1280
Read features about overseas buyers, U.S. factories buying imported forest products and North American exporters. Also carries forest products business trends on the domestic and international markets. *$75.00*
Bi-Monthly

15357 National Frame Builders Association Newsletter
National Frame Builders Association
4840 W 15th Street
Suite 1000
Lawrence, KS 66049-3862
785-843-2444
FAX: 785-843-7555 800-557-6957
nfba@postframe.org www.nfba.org
John Fullerton, VP
Published by the National Frame Builders Association.

15358 National Wooden Pallet & Container Association: Newsletter
National Wooden Pallet & Container Association
329 S Patric Street
Alexandria, VA 22314-3501
703-519-6104
FAX: 703-519-4720
palletcomm@aol.com
http://www.nwpca.com
Bruce N Scholnick, President
Pamela Wilson, Publisher
Kathy Conroy, Marketing Director
Newsletter published by The National Wooden Pallet and Container Association. *$2995.00*

15359 Softwood Forest Products Buyer
Miller Publishing Corporation
1235 Sycamore View Road
Memphis, TN 38134
901-372-8280
FAX: 901-373-6180 800-844-1280
Provides you with interesting feature articles on purchasing, inventory control, marketing, production, utilization and distribution of Softwood forest products such as lumber, plywood, moulding, etc. *$65.00*
Bi-Monthly

15360 The Tree Worker Newsletter
Tree Care Industry Association
3 Perimeter Road
Unit 1
Manchester, NH 03103
603-314-5380
FAX: 603-314-5386
tcia@treecareindustry.org
www.treecareindustry.org
Mark Garvin, Editor
Sachin Mohan, Advertising Editor

15361 Timberline
Bear Creek Lumber
Po Box 669
Winthrop, WA 98862
FAX: 509-997-2040 800-597-7191
customerservice@bearcreeklumber.com
www.bearcreeklumber.com
Features articles about the timber industry, the construction industry, how-to information, and it also lets folks know what's new at Bear Creek Lumber. *$15.00*
6000 pages

15362 Two-By-Four
Mountain States Lumber & Building Material Dealers
9034 E Easter Place
#103
Centennial, CO 80112
303-793-0859
FAX: 303-290-9137 800-365-0919
mslbmda@idcomm.com
www.mslbmda.org
Tom Stringham, President
Geri Adams, Executive VP

15363 Wood Machining News
Wood Machining Institute
PO Box 476
Berkeley, CA 94701
510-448-8363
FAX: 925-945-0947
szymani@woodmachining.com
http://www.woodmachining.com
Ryszard Szymani, Editor
Ryszard Szymani, Director
Information on the latest technological advances in the field of wood machining, including sawing, planning and sanding operations as well as the production of veneers and chips. *$72.00*
Fortnightly Founded: 1984
Circulation: 600

Magazines & Journals

15364 2 X 4
Editions CR
CP 1010
Victoriaville, PQ, CN, G6 P 8Y1
Claude Roy, Editor
News of the woodworking industry. *$34.00*
24 pages Monthly Founded: 1984

15365 American Forests
American Forests
734 15th Street NW
Suite 800
Washington, DC 20005
202-371-1944
FAX: 202-955-4588
mrobbins@amfor.org
http://www.americanforest.org
Michelle Robbins, Editor
Deborah Gangloff, Executive Director
Lydia Scalettar, Art Director
Jeff Olson, VP, Marketing and Devel
Updates on forest management and environmental policy, as well as news on the programs and policies of the American Forests organization. *$25.00*
Quarterly Founded: 1875
Circulation: 25000

15366 Building Material Dealer
National Lumbermans Publishing Corporation
1405 Lilac Drive N
Suite 131
Minneapolis, MN 55422-4528
763-544-6822
FAX: 612-595-4068 800-328-9125
bmr@bmrmag.com www.dealer.org
Gary Donnelly, Publisher
Content focuses on a mixture of regional and national news relating to governmental regulations, dealer and supplier news, meetings and seminars affecting the independent building retailer.
Monthly
Circulation: 24,647

15367 Crossties
Convey Communications Corporation
PO Box 2267
Gulf Shores, AL 36547-2267
251-968-5300
FAX: 251-968-4532
ties@rta.org http://www.rta.org
Talty O'Connor, President/CEO
Highlights new products, industry news, and personnel changes. *$35.00*
Founded: 1983
Circulation: 3000

15368 Crow's Forest Industry Journal
CC Crow Publications
PO Box 25749
Portland, OR 97298-749
503-417-7382
FAX: 503-646-9971
info@crows.com
http://www.crows.com

Frank J Vetorino, Publisher
Chad Crowe, President

Focuses on the condition of forests around the world. *$75.00*
Founded: 1921
Circulation: 100000

15369 Crow's Weekly Market Report
CC Crow Publications
PO Box 25749
Portland, OR 97298
503-417-7382
FAX: 503-646-9971
info@crows.com
http://www.crows.com

Frank J Vetorino, Publisher
Sam Sherrill, Editor
Chad Crowe, President

Tracks the wood and lumber industry, providing customers with accurate and timely pricing and analysis. *$285.00*
Weekly Founded: 1921
Circulation: 2000

15370 Custom Woodworking Business
Vance Publishing
PO Box 1400
Lincolnshire, IL 60069
847-342-2600
FAX: 847-634-4374 800-343-2016
industrialinfo@vancepublishing.com
http://www.iswonline.com

William C Vance, CEO
Helen Kuhl, Editor
Harry Urban, VP Publishing *$55.00*
Monthly Founded: 1937

15371 Design Solutions Magazine
Architectural Woodwork Institute
1952 Isaac Newton Square W
Reston, VA 20190-5001
703-733-0600
FAX: 703-733-0584
adsales@awinet.org
http://www.awinet.org

Judy Durham, Executive Vice President
Philip Duvic, Marketing Director
Kirsten Ingham, President

Featuring beautiful woodwork projects manufactured by members of the Architectural Woodwork Institute (AWI). Many other related publications, including woodworking quality standards used by woodwork manufacturers and design professionals. *$25.00*
Quarterly
Circulation: 27000

15372 Evergreen Magazine
Evergreen Foundations
5000 Cirrus Drive
#201
Medford, OR 97504-3102
541-770-4999
FAX: 406-837-1385
www.evergreenmagazine.com

James D Petersen, Publisher

Focuses on issues and events impacting forestry, forest communities, and the forest product industry. Includes profiles of industry leaders and advocates.
Bi-Monthly
Circulation: 100000

15373 Fine Woodworking
Taunton Press
63 South Main Street
PO Box 5506
Newtown, CT 06470-2355
203-270-6206
FAX: 203-270-3434 800-243-7252
fwads@taunton.com
http://www.taunton.com

James Chiavelli, Publisher
Richard West, Advertising Manager

Published since 1975, written by woodworkers for woodworkers regularly shows the finest work in wood being done today. *$34.95*
120 pages 7 Issues (1yr) Founded: 1980
Circulation: 250000
Mailing list available for rent 185M names
Printed in 4 colors on glossy stock

15374 Forest Industries
Miller Freeman Publications
600 Harrison Street
Suite 415
San Francisco, CA 94107-1391
415-905-2200
FAX: 415-905-2232

David Pease, Editor

Directed to foresters, loggers and manufacturers. *$55.00*
90 pages Monthly

15375 Forest Landowner Magazine
Forest Landowners Association
900 Circle 75 Pkwy Se
Ste 205
Atlanta, GA 30339-3075
404-325-2954
FAX: 404-325-2955 800-325-2954
info@forestlandowners.com
http://www.forestlandowners.com

Paige Cash, Editor
Joy Moore, Circulation Director
Scott Jones, CEO/President

Provides members with applied, practical and current forestry information written by the most experienced and successful forestry professionals. *$50.00*
Founded: 1941
Circulation: 9000

15376 Forest Products Journal
Forest Products Society
2801 Marshall Court
Madison, WI 53705-2295
608-231-1361
FAX: 608-231-2152
publications@forestprod.org
http://www.forestprod.org

Erin Bosch, Editor
Sheila Scafe, Circulation Manager
Susan Stamm, Publications Director
Ian de la Roche, President
Arthur Brauner, Vice President

Covers the latest research and technology from every branch of the forest products industry. *$155.00*
Founded: 1945

15377 Forests and People
Louisiana Forestry Association
PO Drawer 5067
Alexandria, LA 71307
318-443-2558
FAX: 318-443-1713
jtompkins@laforestry.com
http://www.laforestry.com

Janet Tompkins, Editor
Mike Merritt, President
Buck Vandersteen, Executive Director

Magazine *$250.00*
36 pages Quarterly Founded: 1947
Circulation: 5800
Printed in 4 colors on glossy stock

15378 Frame Building News
National Frame Builders Association
4840 W 15th Street
Suite 1000
Lawrence, KS 66049-3862
785-843-2444
FAX: 785-843-7555 800-557-6957
nfba@postframe.org www.nfba.org

John Fullerton, VP

The official publication of National Frame Builders Association.

15379 Journal of Forestry
Society of American Foresters
5400 Grosvenor Lane
Bethesda, MD 20814-2198
301-897-8720
FAX: 301-897-3690
safweb@safnet.org
http://www.safnet.org

William H Banzhaf, Publisher
Rebecca Staebler, Editor-in-Chief
Matthew Walls, Editor

For the forestry profession, both nationally and internationally. Delivers practical information to help forestry professionals meet the challenges of a rapidly changing and increasingly technical environment. *$85.00*
50 pages Founded: 1900
Circulation: 20000 18000 names $50 per M.
Printed in 4 colors on glossy stock

15380 Loggers' World
Loggers World Publications
4206 Jackson Highway
Chehalis, WA 98532-8425
360-262-3376
FAX: 360-266-3337 800-462-8283
logworld@aol.com
http://www.loggersworld.com

Susan E Crouse, General Manager
Michael P Crouse, Publisher
Finley Hays, Editor
Darin Burt, Writer

Accepts advertising. *$12.00*
56 pages Monthly Founded: 1966
Circulation: 16,000

15381 Logging & Sawmilling Journal
Po Box 86670
Vancouver, BC V7L-4L2
604-990-9970
FAX: 604-990-9971
stanhope@forestnet.com
www.forestnet.com

Rob Stanhope, Publisher
Lil Fawcus, Production Manager

15382 Logging Management
Baum International Media
203-2323 Boundary Road
Vancouver, Ca V5M 4
604-298-3005
FAX: 604-298-3966
editor.lm@bauminternational.com
http://www.bauminternational.com

Kevin Cook, Associate Publisher
Gunner Martin, Editor
Carol Lee, Circulation Manager

Logging equipment information for the United States and Canada.

Circulation: 23000

15383 Lumber Co-Operator
Northeastern Retail Lumber Association
585 N Greenbush Road
Rensselaer, NY 12144
518-861-1932
FAX: 518-286-1755 800-292-6752
jsacks@nrla.com http://www.nrla.org

Jeff Sacks, Publisher
Heidi Longton, Director Convention
James Ayotte, President
Rita Ferris, VP
Jeff Sacks, Editor

Includes the latest industry, legislative and regulatory news, as well as issues and trends that most influence the lumber and building materials business. Readers gain insight into the newest methods, management techniques, new product ideas, family owned business concerns and key industry issues. *$40.00*
100 pages Founded: 1894
Circulation: 5000

15384 Lumberman's Equipment Digest
PO Box 1146
Columbia, TN 38401
931-381-1638
FAX: 931-388-3564 800-477-7606
publisher@lumbermenonline.com
http://www.lumbermenonline.com

Brady Carr, Publisher
Tammy Coffman, Advertising Manager
$38.00
Monthly
Circulation: 35,000

15385 Modern Woodworking
3200 Rice Mine Road NE
Tuscaloosa, AL 35406

FAX: 205-391-2081 800-633-5953
bwisdom@randallpub.com
www.modernwoodworking.com

Brooke Wisdom, Executive Editor
W.W. Chip Wisdom, VP/Group Publisher

15386 National Hardwood Magazine
Miller Publishing Company
1235 Sycamore View Road
PO Box 34908
Memphis, TN 38184-908
901-372-8280
FAX: 901-373-6180 800-844-1280

Brady Buffalo, Editor
Wayne Miller, VP

A monthly journal serving the hardwood industry including sawmillls, distillation, lumber yards, wholesalers and buyers and woodworkers. *$45.00*
85 pages Monthly Founded: 1927
Circulation: 5000
Printed in 4 colors on glossy stock

15387 Northeastern Loggers Magazine
Northeastern Loggers Association
PO Box 69
Old Forge, NY 13420-69
315-369-3078
FAX: 315-369-3736
mona@loggertraining.com
http://www.loggertraining.com

Joseph Phaneuf, Executive Director
Eric A Johnson, Editor

A magazine published by Northeastern Loggers Association to improve the industry in the Northeast and educate the public about policies and products of the industry. *$18.00*
Monthly Founded: 1952
Circulation: 13000
Printed in 4 colors on glossy stock

15388 Northern Journal of Applied Forestry
Society of American Foresters
5400 Grosvenor Lane
Bethesda, MD 20814-2198
301-897-8720
FAX: 301-897-3690
safweb@safnet.org
http://www.safnet.org

Michael T Goergen Jr., Executive Vice-President/CEO
Joe Smith, Editor
Delisa Barrons, Publications Project Mana
Joe Smith, Editor

Covers new or improved management practices and applied research. *$85.00*
Founded: 1900

15389 Northern Logger & Timber Processor
Northeastern Loggers Association
3311 State Route 28
PO Box 69
Old Forge, NY 13420
315-369-3078
FAX: 315-369-3736 800-318-7561
nela@northernlogger.com
http://www.northernlogger.com

Nancy E Petrie, Circualtion Manager
Jack W Frost, Sr., President
Eric Johnson, Editor
Joseph Phaneuf, Executive Director

Trade publication servicing the forest products industry in the Northeast and lake states. *$12.00*
50 pages Monthly Founded: 1952
Circulation: 12000

15390 Pallet Enterprise
Industrial Reporting
10244 Timber Ridge Drive
Ashland, VA 23005
804-550-0323
FAX: 804-550-2181 800-805-0263
ed@ireporting.com
http://www.palletenterprise.com

Tim Cox, Editor
Chris Edwards, Production Manager
Edward C Brindley, Publisher
Scott Brindley, Marketing Director
Laura Seal, Circulation Manager

Written for those who manufacture, repair, sell or use wooden pallets and containers. Regular features include a market column, new products section and industry events. *$60.00*
104 pages Monthly Founded: 1981
Circulation: 15000 14000 names
Printed in 4 colors on glossy stock

15391 Panel World
Hatton-Brown Publishers
225 Hanrick Street(36104)
PO Box 2268
Montgomery, AL 36102-3317
334-834-1170
FAX: 334-834-4525
mail@hattonbrown.com
http://www.hattonbrown.com

Rich Donnell, Editor
Rhonda Thomas, Circulation Manager
Dan Shell, Managing Editor
Jennifer McCary, Associate Editor
Tonya Cooner, Associate Editor

For people who deal with production, sales, marketing, distribution, fabrication and utilization of veneer, plywood and other panel products. *$40.00*
Founded: 1948
Circulation: 12850 $145 per M.
Printed in 4 colors on matte stock

15392 Popular Woodworking
F And W Publications
4700 East Galbraith Road
Cincinnati, OH 45236
513-312-2222
www.fwpublications.com

Steve Shanesy, Publisher
Don Schroder, Ad Manager

Everything woodworkers need to develop their skills; in-depth tool reviews and tests, shop tips, finishing secrets, projects and more. *$28.00*
104 pages Monthly Founded: 1981
Circulation: 240151

15393 Rural Builder
Krause Publications
700 E State Street
Iola, WI 54990-2214
715-445-2214
FAX: 715-445-4087
info@krause.com www.krause.com

Steve Shanesy, Publisher
Don Schroder, Advertising Manager

15394 Society of American Foresters
5400 Grosvenor Lane
Bethesda, MD 20814-2198
301-897-8720
FAX: 301-897-3690
safeweb@safnet.org http://safnet.org

Michael T Goergen Jr, CEO
Joe Smith, Editor

Monthly newsletter for all those involved in forestry research and technology. Regular editorial features.
Founded: 1900

15395 Southern Loggin' Times
Hatton-Brown Publishers
225 Hanrick Street
Montgomery, AL 36104-3317
334-834-1170
FAX: 334-834-4525 800-669-5613
mail@hattonbrown.com
http://www.hattonbrown.com

Dave Ramsey, Publisher/CEO
Rich Donnell, Editor

Monitors the south's forest products industry. *$65.00*
Monthly Founded: 1948
Circulation: 13,408 13,408 names $145 per M.
Printed in 4 colors on glossy stock

15396 Southern Lumberman
Hatton-Brown Publishers
225 Hanrick Street
Montgomery, AL 36104-3317
334-834-1170
FAX: 334-834-4525
mail@hattonbrown.com
www.hattonbrown.com

Dave Ramsay, Publisher/CEO
Rich Donnell, Editor

Industry news for sawmill operators and dimension manufacturers. *$21.00*
60 pages Monthly
Circulation: 13500

15397 Southern Pine Inspection Bureau Magazine
Southern Pine Inspection Bureau
4709 Scenic Highway
Pensacola, FL 32504-9018
850-434-2611
FAX: 850-433-5594
spib@spib.org www.spib.org
James Loy, President
Tom Jones, Executive Director
Founded: 1940

15398 Timber Harvesting
Hatton-Brown Publishers
225 Hanrick Street (36104)
PO Box 2268
Montgomery, AL 36102-3317
334-834-1170
FAX: 334-834-4525 800-669-5613
mail@hattonbrown.com
http://www.hattonbrown.com
Dave Ramsey, Co-Publisher
D K Knight, Co-Publisher
Rich Donnell, Editor
News and methods reported that are of particular interest to loggers. *$40.00*
Monthly Founded: 1953
Circulation: 20130 20,130 names $145 per M.
Printed in 4 colors on matte stock

15399 Timber Processing
Hatton-Brown Publishers
225 Hanrick Street
PO Box 2268
Montgomery, AL 36102
334-834-1170
FAX: 334-834-4525 800-669-5613
rich@hattonbrown.com
http://www.hattonbrown.com
David H Ramsey, Co-Publisher
Rich Donnell, Editor-in-Chief
Dan Shell, Managing Editor
Timber Processing serves sawmill/chipmill operations; consultants in mill and processing operations; machinery manufacturers, dealers and distributors, others allied to the field. *$40.00*
44 pages Founded: 1948
Circulation: 20780
Printed in 4 colors on glossy stock

15400 Timber Producer
Timber Producers Association of WI and MI
6343 Highway 8 West
PO Box 1278
Rhinelander, WI 54501-1278
715-824-4938
FAX: 715-282-4941
timberpa@networth.net
www.timberpa.com
Nadine Bailey, Editor
Monthly
Circulation: 3500

15401 Timber West Journal
Po Box 610
300 Admiral Way, Suite 208
Edmonds, WA 98020-0610
425-778-3388
FAX: 425-771-3623 866-221-1017
timberwest@forestnet.com
www.forestnet.com/timberwest
Sheila Ringdahl, Publisher
Diane Mettler, Managing Editor
Packed with valuable and useful stories on successful mechanized harvesting and equipment, special editorial features, plus timely information on legislation, industry news, annual events, and people and products pertinent to America's largest forestry market.

15402 Timber West Magazine
Timber West Publications
300 Admiral Way Suite 208
PO Box 610
Edmonds, WA 98020-610
425-778-3388
FAX: 425-771-3623 866-221-1017
timberwest@forestnet.com
http://www.forestnet.com
Sheila Ringdahl, Publisher
Diane Mettler, Managing Editor
James Booth, Marketing
Reports on the logging and lumber industries of the western US. *$20.00*
48 pages Founded: 1975
Circulation: 10500
Printed in 4 colors on glossy stock

15403 Timberline
Industrial Reporting
10244 Timber Ridge Drive
Ashland, VA 23005
804-550-0323
FAX: 804-550-2181
editor@ireporting.com
http://www.ireporting.com
Ed Brindley Jr, Publisher
Tim Cox, Editor
Laura Seal, Circulation
Highlights sawmill, logging, and pallet interests including environmental issues, new machinery and technologies that impact the industry.
52 pages Monthly Founded: 1994
Circulation: 30000
Mailing list available for rent 28,000 names $250 per M.
Printed in 4 colors on newsprint stock

15404 Tree Care Industry
Tree Care Industry Association
3 Perimeter Road
Unit 1
Manchester, NH 03103
603-314-5380
FAX: 603-314-5386
TCIA@TreeCareIndustry.org
http://www.treecareindustry.org
Mark Garvin, Editor
Don Staruk, Managing Editor
Sachin Mohan, Advertising Contact
Cynthia Mills, President
On government legislation, municipal contracts, marketing and sales strategies, industry trends, current events and new products. *$30.00*
84 pages Monthly Founded: 1938
Circulation: 27502
Mailing list available for rent 28000 names $.11 per M.
Printed in 4 colors on glossy stock

15405 Tree Farmer Magazine
American Forest Foundation
1111 19th Street NW
Suite 780
Washington, DC 20036-3603
202-632-2455
FAX: 202-463-2461 888-889-4466
info@forestfoundation.org
http://www.treefarmsystem.org
Lawrence Wiseman, President
Practical information on a number of tree farming-related topics, including sustainable forestry, private landowners, professional forests, wildlife, recreation, as well as water and soil conservation.
Founded: 1982
Circulation: 20000

15406 Wood Digest
Cygnus Publishing
1233 Janesville Avenue
Fort Atkinson, WI 53538
920-563-6388
FAX: 920-563-1707 800-547-7377
Jay.Schneider@wooddigest.com
http://www.cygnuspub.com
Steve Ehle, Editor-in-Chief
John Anfderhaar, Associate Publisher
Paul Bowers, President
Jay Schneider, Publisher
Trade magazine, Accepts advertising.
64 pages Monthly Founded: 1965
Circulation: 51000

15407 Wood Finisher
7616 Banning Way
Inver Grove Heights, MN 55077-5819
Mitchell Kohansek, Editor
Wood finishing information. *$10.00*
20 pages Monthly Founded: 1981

15408 Wood and Fiber Science
Society of Wood Science & Technology
One Gifford Pinchot Drive
Madison, WI 53726-2398
608-231-9347
FAX: 608-231-9592
vicki@swst.org http://www.swst.org
Audrey Zink Sharp, President
Geza Lfju, Editor
Publishes papers with both professional and technical content. Original papers of professional concer, or based on research dealing with the science, processing, and manufacture of wood and composite products of wood or wood fiber origin are considered for publication. All papers are peer-reviewed and must be unpublished research not offered for publication elsewhere. *$250.00*
Quarterly Founded: 1958
Circulation: 950

15409 Wood and Wood Products
Vance Publishing
400 Knightsbridge Parkway
Lincolnshire, IL 60069-3628
847-634-2600
FAX: 847-634-4379
industrialinfo@vancepublishing.com
http://www.vancepublishing.com
Harry Urban, Publisher
Rich Christianson, Editorial Director
William C. Vance, President
For management and owners in the woodworking industry.
140 pages Monthly Founded: 1937
Circulation: 52521

15410 Woodshop News
Soundings Publications
10 Bokum Road
Essex, CT 06426
860-673-3200
FAX: 860-767-0645
info@woodshopnews.com
http://www.woodshopnews.com
Tod Riggio, Editor
Ian Bowen, Editorial Director
Brian Caldwell, Staff Writer
Peter Mitchel, Manager
News for and about people who work with wood. Trends, tips, solutions for the samll

to medium pro shop and serious amateur woodworker. *$21.95*
56 pages Monthly Founded: 1987
Printed in on newsprint stock

15411 World Wood Review
Widman Publishing
601 West Broadway
Suite 400
Vancouver, BC V5Z 4C2
604-675-6923
FAX: 604-675-6924
tlhaugen@widman.com
www.widman.com
The premier newsletter serving the global wood products industry, with news of trends and developments in the solid wood and panel manufacturing sector. *$55.00*
50 pages Monthly

Trade Shows

15412 American Forestry Association
PO Box 2000
Washington, DC 20013-2000
202-955-4500

Billl Tikkala, Show Manager
Deborah Gangloff, Executive Director
30 booths of tree planting and care equipment.
1M Attendees November

15413 Appalachian Hardwood Expo
Mercer County Technical Education Center
105 Old Bluefield Road
Princeton, WV 24740-8901
304-425-4583

Linda Cox
100 tables.
2M Attendees June

15414 Architectural Woodwork Institute Annual Convention
46179 Westlake Dr
Ste 120
Sterling, VA 20165-5874
571-323-3636
FAX: 571-323-3630 www.awinet.org
Kimberly Haynes, Director Meetings & Conventions
Seminar, workshop and woodwork products such as casework, fixtures and panelings, equipment and supplies.

15415 Forest Expo
Prince George Regional Forest Exhibition Society
850 River Road
Prince George, BC V2L-5S8
250-563-8833
FAX: 250-563-3697
info@forestexpo.bc.ca
www.forestexpo.bc.ca
Trudy Swaan, General Manager
Provides a showcase to display the latest in new technology, equipment, supplies and services, as well as educate the forest sector and the general public about the importance of our forests.

15416 Forest Products Machinery/Equipment
Southern Forest Products Association
2900 Indiana Avenue
Kenner, LA 70065
504-443-4464
FAX: 504-443-6612
mail@sfpa.org www.sfpa.org
Tami Kessler, Exposition Director
4,000 Attendees June, Biennial

15417 Frame Building Expo
National Frame Builders Association
4840 Bob Billings Parkway
Suite 1000
Lawrence, KS 66049
785-843-2444
FAX: 785-843-7555 800-557-6957
nfba@postframe.org www.nfba.org
John Fullerton, VP
Containing 200 booths.
2000+ Attendees February
Mailing list available for rent 2,000 names $50 per M.

15418 Hardwood Manufacturers Association
400 Penn Center Boulevard
Suite 530
Pittsburgh, PA 15235-5605
412-290-0770
FAX: 412-829-0844
Susan Regan, Executive VP
Offers 20 booths of sawmill and logging machinery and services.
300 Attendees March

15419 International Woodworking Machinery and Furniture Supply Fair: USA
Reed Exhibition Companies
1350 E Touhy Avenue
Des Plaines, IL 60018-3303
847-294-0300
FAX: 847-635-1571
Paul Pajor, National Marketing Manager
The largest woodworking machinery and furniture supply manufacturing exposition held in the Western Hemisphere. Exhibitors interface with North American furniture, cabinet, and woodworking manufacturers. One thousand booths.
37M Attendees August/Biennial

15420 Logging Congress Pacific
2300 SW 6th Avenue
Suite 200
Portland, OR 97201-4915

FAX: 503-612-0344
Al Wilson, Executive Director
50 booths.
800 Attendees September

15421 Lumbermen's Merchandising Conferences
137 W Wayne Avenue
Wayne, PA 19087-4018
610-293-7000
FAX: 215-293-7098
Jack Reznor, Show Manager
Anthony Decarlo, President
325 booths.
1.6M Attendees March

15422 MFMA Annual Conference
Maple Flooring Manufacturers Association

60 Revere Drive
Suite 500
Northbrook, IL 60062-1591
847-480-9138
FAX: 847-480-9282
mcarson@maplefloor.org
www.maplefloor.org
Madhuri Carson, Conference Manager
Containing 50 booths.
300 Attendees Annual/March

15423 National Wood Flooring Association Trade Show
16388 Westwoods Business Park
Ellisville, MO 63021-4522
636-519-9663
FAX: 636-391-6137 800-422-4556
natlwood@aol.com
www.woodfloors.org
Edward S Korczak, Executive Director
Membership includes distributors, manufacturers, retailers/contractors, etc. assists in advertising education and developmenting of standards and grade levels. Show will include 185 exhibitors with 280 booths featuring technical and business training and wood flooring products.
2000 Attendees April

15424 Northeastern Forest Products Equipment Expo
Northeastern Loggers Association
PO Box 69
Old Forge, NY 13420
315-369-3078
FAX: 315-369-3736
nela@northernlogger.com
nefpexpo.com
Joseph Phaneuf, Show Manager
201,000 square feet of products and services for the logging and forest industries. Containing 250 exhibitors.
6500 Attendees May

15425 Northeastern Retail Lumber Association
585 N Greenbush Road
Rensselaer, NY 12144
518-861-1932
FAX: 518-286-1755 800-292-6752
Jim Ayotte, President
John Brill, Executive VP
500 booths or more of builiding materials and education relating to the lumber and building industry.
8M Attendees January

15426 Northwestern Building Products Exposition
Northwestern Lumber Association
1405 Lilac Drive N
Suite 130
Minneapolis, MN 55422-4528
763-544-6822
FAX: 612-544-0820
P Siewert, Show Manager
Gary Smith, President
310 booths for retail lumber and building material dealers in Iowa, Minnesota, North Dakota, South Dakota and Wisconsin. Commodities products and services sold or used by retailers are displayed at this regional show.
3.8M Attendees February

15427 Pacific Logging Congress
Po Box 1281
Maple Valley, WA 98038
425-413-2808
FAX: 425-413-1359
pacificlogging@aol.com
www.pacificloggingcongress.org
Rikki Wellman, Executive Director
James Petersen, President
Mission is to fulfill the need to provide sound technical education about the forest industry.
Feb 22-24 Clatskanie

15428 Redwood Region Logging Conference California
PO Box 174
Garberville, CA 95542-0174
707-482-5033
FAX: 707-443-0151
Charles Benbow, Show Manager
100 booths of timber and forestry related products and services.
3M Attendees March

15429 Retail Lumbermen's Association Northeast
339 E Avenue
Rochester, NY 14604-2627
John Brill, Show Manager
681 booths of lumber and related services.
10M Attendees January

15430 Sawmill Logging Equipment Expo East Coast
220 E Williamsburg Road
PO Box 160
Sandston, VA 23150-0160
804-737-5625
FAX: 804-737-9437
info@exporichmond.com
www.exporichmond.com
Mike Washko, Expo Manager
Logging and forestry production and distribution.
12M Attendees May

15431 Southeastern Lumber Manufacturers Association
PO Box 1788
Forest Park, GA 30298-1788
404-361-1445
FAX: 404-361-5963
Steve Roundtree, President
50 booths.
350 Attendees July

15432 Southern Forestry Conference
Forest Landowners Association
4 Executive Park E NE
Suite 120
Atlanta, GA 30329-2212
404-325-2954
FAX: 404-325-2955 800-325-2954
Lisa Newsome, Manager
Stacie Lewis, Managing Editor
May Founded: 1941

15433 World of Wood Annual Convention
International Wood Products Association
4214 King Street
Alexandria, VA 22302
703-820-6696
FAX: 703-820-8550
info@iwpawood.org
www.iwpawood.org
Annette Ferri, Member Services
20-30 table-top displays.
250 Attendees March

Directories & Databases

15434 American Papermaker Mill and Personnel
Office of Paper Recycling
785 Fulton Industrial Boulevard
Suite 3
Atlanta, GA 30336
770-395-0606
Jerome Koncel, Editor
Offers a list of pulp, paper and paperboard mills. *$40.00*
Annual
Circulation: 28,000

15435 Cedar Shake and Shingle Bureau Membership Directory/Buyer's Guide
Cedar Shake & Shingle Bureau
PO Box 1178
Sumas, WA 98295-1178
425-531-1323
FAX: 604-820-0266
info@cedarbureau.com
www.cedarbureau.org
Lynne Christensen, Director Operations
About 102 member manufacturing mills in the Pacific Northwest and British Columbia, Canada; approximately 163 affiliated roofing applicators, builders, architects, remodelers and suppliers of related products and services. *$17.00*
SemiAnnual
Circulation: 450

15436 Dimension & Wood Components Buyer's Guide
Miller Publishing Corporation
1235 Sycamore View Road
Memphis, TN 38134
901-372-8280
FAX: 901-373-6180 800-844-1280
Instant access to manufacturers of furniture parts, mouldings, cabinet doors, stair parts, flooring, turnings, paneling, door parts, window parts, edge glued panels, etc. Gives the information on who to contact, firm name and address, phone number, fax number, number of employees, products manufactured, species of wood used, machining capabilities and marketing areas served. *$350.00*

15437 Forest Products Export Directory
Miller Publishing Corporation
1235 Sycamore View Road
Memphis, TN 38134
901-372-8280
FAX: 901-373-6180 800-844-1280
The only directory published listing all the major exporters of North American forest products. Edited to help the oversease buyer find reliable suppliers for the wide variety of Softwood and Hardwood forest products available in North America. *$175.00*

15438 Forest Products Research Society Membership Directory
2801 Marshall Court
Madison, WI 53705-2295
608-231-1361
FAX: 608-231-2152
info@forestprod.org
www.forestprod.org
Erin Bosch, Editor
Sheila Scafe, Circulation Manager
Arthur Brauner, Executive VP *$125.00*
1900 pages 10 Per Year Founded: 1947
Circulation: 3500

15439 Gebbie Press: All-In-One Media Directory
Po Box 1000
New Paltz, NY 12561
845-255-7560
FAX: 845-256-1239
www.gebbieinc.com
Mark Gebbie, Associate Editor
Founded: 1955

15440 Green Book's Hardwood Marketing Directory
Miller Publishing Corporation
1235 Sycamore View Road
Memphis, TN 38134
901-372-8280
FAX: 901-373-6180 800-844-1280
A sales booster that lists over 7,900 woodworking plants' Hardwood lumber and other Hardwood forest products purchasing needs. Gives up-to-date, documented facts on species, grades, thicknesses and quantities purchased by each plant annually in the U.S. and Canada. *$1200.00*

15441 Green Book's Softwood Marketing Directory
Miller Publishing Corporation
1235 Sycamore View Road
Memphis, TN 38134
901-372-8280
FAX: 901-373-6180 800-844-1280
Instant access to over 5,000 woodworking and industrial plants' Softwood lumber purchasing needs with complete, up-to-date, documented facts on species, grades, thicknesses, and quantities of Softwood lumber and other Softwood forest products bought regularly. *$900.00*

15442 Hardwood Manufacturers Association: Membership Directory
Hardwood Manufacturers Association
400 Penn Center Boulevard
Pittsburgh, PA 15235-5613
412-829-0770
FAX: 412-829-0844 800-373-9663
Susan Regan, Executive Vice President
Over 100 companies with over 160 locations in the US.
Annual December

15443 Hardwood Purchasing Handbook
Miller Publishing Corporation
1235 Sycamore View Road
Memphis, TN 38134
901-372-8280
FAX: 907-373-6180 800-844-1280
An easy-to-use digest size directory that has all the major Hardwood suppliers in the U.S.A. and Canada of Hardwood lumber, plywood, veneers, etc. Up-to-date sections describe Hardwood sawmills, wholesalers, distribution yards, etc. Complete mailing

addresses, phone numbers, fax numbers, email addresses, names of sales agents, main Hardwood species handled, specialty items listed and information on production facilities and shipping methods are given. *$175.00*

15444 Imported Wood Purchasing Guide
Miller Publishing Corporation
1235 Sycamore View Road
Memphis, TN 38134
901-372-8280
FAX: 901-373-6180 800-844-1280
A wide variety of imported suppliers of lumber, mouldings, veneers, wall paneling, furniture components, flooring, plywood, hardboard, doorskins, millwork, etc. *$175.00*

15445 Imported Wood: Guide To Applications, Sources and Trends
International Wood Products Association
4214 King Street
Alexandria, VA 22302-1507
703-820-6696
FAX: 703-820-8550
info@iwpawood.org
www.iwpawood.org
Brent J McCiendon CAE, Executive VP
Magazine featuring imported woods in applications, sustainable Forest Management issues and listing of IWPA members.
48 pages Annual Founded: 1956
Circulation: 15,000

15446 International Green Front Report
Friends of the Trees
PO Box 1064
Tonasket, WA 98855-1064
FAX: 509-485-2705
Michael Pilarski, Editor
Organizations and periodicals concerned with sustainable forestry and agriculture and related fields. *$7.00*
Irregular

15447 Lumbermen's Red Book
Lumbermens Credit Association
20 N Wacker Drive
Suite 1800
Chicago, IL 60606-2905
312-553-0943
FAX: 312-533-1842
www.lumbermanscredit.com
PD McLaughlin, Editor
Approximately 39,000 manufacturers and distributors of lumber and wood products in the US and Canada. *$1780.00*
SemiAnnual

15448 North American Forest Products Export Directory
International Wood Trade Publications
1235 Sycamore View Road
Memphis, TN 38134-7646
901-752-1246
FAX: 901-373-6180
Producers, exporters, agents, etc. of lumber, plywood, etc. in the US and Canada. *$150.00*
Annual August
Circulation: 10,000

15449 Northeastern Retail Lumber Association Buyer's Guide
585 N Greenbush Road
Rensselaer, NY 12144
518-861-1932
FAX: 518-286-1755 800-292-6752
Jim Ayotte, President
Offers information on over 2,000 retail dealers in lumber and forest products located in the Northeastern states of the US. *$ 125.00*
225 pages Annual

15450 Northwestern Lumber Association Dealer Reference Manual & Buyer's Guide
1405 Lilac Drive N
Suite 130
Minneapolis, MN 55422-4528
763-544-6822
FAX: 612-544-0820
Lori Kyllo, Editor
Gary Smith, President
A complete list of retail lumber yards along with manufacturers, wholesalers and distributors of lumber and building materials for Minnesota, Iowa, North Dakota and South Dakota. *$75.00*
175 pages Annual
Circulation: 2,000

15451 Random Lengths Big Book: Buyers' & Sellers' Directory of the Forest
Random Lengths Publications
PO Box 867
Eugene, OR 97440-0867
541-869-9925
800-874-7979
Dave Evans, Editor
Terri Richards, Editor
About 7,500 companies, consultants and associations involved in the softwood forest product industry in the US and Canada, including sawmills, treating plants, manufacturers of panels and specialty products, wholesalers and secondary manufacturers. *$188.00*
Annual February
Circulation: 2,200

15452 Rauch Guide to the US and Canadian Pulp & Paper Industry
Grey House Publishing
PO Box 860
Millerton, NY 12546
518-789-8700
FAX: 518-789-0545 800-562-2139
books@greyhouse.com
www.greyhouse.com
Leslie Mackenzie, Publisher
Richard Gottlieb, President
Approximately 507 manufacturers of pulp, paper and converted products. *$595.00*
Annual

15453 Timber Harvesting: Logger's Resource Guide
Hatton-Brown Publishers
225 Hanrick Street
Montgomery, AL 36104-3317
334-834-1170
FAX: 888-614-5255
mail@hattonbrown.com
www.hattonbrown.com
DK Knight, Publisher
Rich Donnell, Editor *$20.00*
88 pages Annually, January
Circulation: 20,179 1,086 names $145 per M.
Printed in on glossy stock : CD

15454 Where to Buy Hardwood Plywood, Veneer & Engineered Hardwood Flooring
Hardwood Plywood and Veneer Association
1825 Michael Faraday Drive
PO Box 2789
Reston, VA 20190-5350
703-435-2900
FAX: 703-435-2537
baltman@hpva.org www.hpva.org
ET Altman, President
Ketti Tyree, Editor *$5.00*
192 pages Annual Founded: 1921
Circulation: 5,000
Printed in 4 colors on glossy stock

15455 Wood & Wood Products: Laminating Users Guide Issue
Laminating Materials Association
116 Lawrence Street
Hillsdale, NJ 07642-2730
201-664-2700
FAX: 201-666-5665
gcarter@lma.org www.lma.org
George Carter, Editor
List of approximately 100 manufacturers and importers of decorative overlays, wood substrates, adhesives, laminating equipment and laminated products.
Annual June

15456 Wood Components Buyer's Guide
Wood Component Manufacturers Association
1000 Johnson Ferry Road
Suite A-130
Marietta, GA 30068-2114
770-565-6660
FAX: 770-565-6663
www.woodcomponents.org
Over 150 member manufacturers of wood components. *$5.00*
Annual Summer

15457 Wood Technology: Buyers' Guide Issue
Miller Freeman Publications
600 Harrison Street
Suite 400
San Francisco, CA 94107-1391
FAX: 415-905-2630 800-227-4675
David A Pease, Editorial Director
Companies supplying machinery, tools and other equipment to manufacturers of wood products worldwide.
Annual

15458 Wood and Wood Products: Laminating Users Guide
Laminating Materials Association
116 Lawrence Street
Hillsdale, NJ 07642-2730
201-664-2700
FAX: 201-666-5665 www.lma.org
George Carter, President
A list of over 100 manufacturers and importers of decorative materials, wood, adhesives and laminated products are reviewed in this directory.
Annual
Circulation: 64,000

15459 Wood and Wood Products: Red Book Issue
Vance Publishing
PO Box 1400
Lincolnshire, IL 60069-1400
847-634-2600

A list of over 4,000 manufacturers of machinery, equipment and supplies for industrial woodworking industries. *$40.00*
Annual
Circulation: 50,000

Industry Web Sites

15460 **www.afandpa.org**
American Forest and Paper Association

Represents member companies and related trade associations which grow, harvest and process wood and wood fiber, manufacture pulp, paper and paperboard products from both virgin and recovered fiber and produce solid wood products.

15461 **www.afma4u.org**
American Furniture Manufacturers Association

Provides a uniform voice in the furniture industry.

15462 **www.bearcreeklumber.com**
Bear Creek Lumber

Publishes a newsletter called the Timberline.

15463 **www.big-creek.com**
Big Creek

Produces a newspaper

15464 **www.calredwood.org**
California Redwood Association

Authorized by Department of Commerce to develop and supervise redwood lumber grading.

15465 **www.capital-lumber.com**
Capital Lumber Company

Dedicated to beinf the leading distributor of materials in the Western United States.

15466 **www.fiberboard.org**
American Fiberboard Association

The national trade organization of manufacturers of cellulosic fiberboard products used for residential and commercial construction.

15467 **www.forestinfo.org**
Temperate Forest Foundation

Source for information which is understandable, unbiased, fast, accurate, and available in a wide variety of formats.

15468 **www.forestnet.com**
Logging & Sawmilling Journal

A journal that provides information on logginf and sawmilling.

15469 **www.forestprod.org**
Forest Products Society

Focus is on the development and research of information for the wood industry.

15470 **www.fpl.fs.fed.us/swst**
Society of Wood Science & Technology

Promotes policies and procedures which assure the wise use of wood and wood-based products; assures high standards for professional performance of wood scientists and technologists; foster educational programs at all levels of wood science and technolgoy and further the quality of such programs; represents the profession in public policy development.

15471 **www.gebbieinc.com**
Gebbie Press

A directory with all information that is needed for the lumber industry.

15472 **www.greyhouse.com**
Grey House Publishing

Selected Grey House directories in the fields of business, health and education are available online. Users can search our online databases by several different search criteria, such as product categories, geographic area, sales volume and much, much more. Full Grey House catalog and online ordering also available.

15473 **www.hardboard.org**
American Hardboard Association

Represents major United States producers of hardwood.

15474 **www.hlma.org**
Pennsylvania Forest Products Association

Represents the state's entire forest products industry, including foresters, loggers, sawmills, and value-added processors.

15475 **www.iwpawood.org**
International Wood Products Association

International trade association representing companies handling imported wood products of all types.

15476 **www.lma.org**
Laminating Materials Association

Nonprofit trade group representing manufacturers and importers of decorative overlays, wood substrates, adhesives, laminating equipment and laminated products.

15477 **www.lumber.org**
North American Wholesale Lumber Association

NAWLA Bulletin is published monthly and includes industry and association news. The Association also produces the NAWLA Traders Market, an annual trade show bringing together over 2000 manufacturer and wholesale lumber traders at the premier event in the forest products industry. NAWLA also produces a variety of educational programs designed to enhance professionalism in the lumber industry.

15478 **www.maplefloor.org**
Maple Flooring Manufacturers Association

For manufacturers of northern hard maple solid strip flooring along with flooring contractors, distributors and providers of instalation-related products and services. Maintains technical standards for product quality, grading, shipping and packaging, and quality central.

15479 **www.millerpublishing.com**
Miller Publishing Corporation

Publishes many newspapers, magazines, and directories.

15480 **www.mslbmda.org**
Mountain States Lumber & Building Materials Dealer

15481 **www.nari.org**
National Association of the Remodeling Industry

Establishes and maintains a firm commitment to developing and sustaining programs that expand and unite the remodeling industry.

15482 **www.nlassn.org**
Northwestern Lumber Association

Retail lumber dealers in Iowa, Minnesota, North Dakota, and South Dakota.

15483 **www.nofma.org**
National Oak Flooring Manufacturers Association

Formulates and administers industry standards on hardwood floorings, inspection service, and semiannual Hardwood Flooring installation school.

15484 www.nsdja.com
National Sash and Door Jobbers Association

For wholesale millwork distribution companies.

15485 www.nwpca.com
National Wooden Pallet & Container Association

Represents wood and pallet container organizations.

15486 www.osbguide.com
Structural Board Association

Members are manufacturers of structural panels.

15487 www.pacificloggingcongress.org
Pacific Logging Congress

Fulfills the need to provide sound technical education about the forest industry.

15488 www.pbmdf.org
Composite Panel Association

For particle board manufacturers and suppliers.

15489 www.postframe.org
National Frame Builders Association

Building contractors, suppliers, design and code professionals and academic personnel specializing in the post frame construction industry.

15490 www.sfpa.org
Southern Forest Products Association

For lumber manufacturers across the mid-Atlantic and southern states as far west as Texas.

15491 www.spib.org
Southern Pine Inspection Bureau

Develops grading standards for Southern pine lumber and provides an inspection service and grade marking systems.

15492 www.swst.org
Society of Wood Science & Technology

Promotes policies and procedures which assure the wise use of wood and wood-based products; assures high standards for professional performance of wood scientists and technologists; foster educational programs at all levels of wood science and technology and further the quality of such programs; represents the profession in public policy development.

15493 www.toc.org
TOC Management Services

Serves membership in the fields of labor, industrial, and employee relations. Provides counsel in wage and contract negotiations. Provides training and safety programs.

15494 www.wdma.org
Window & Door Manufacturers Association

Trade association representing approximately 145 U.S. and Canadian manufacturers and suppliers of windows and doors for the domestic and export market.

15495 www.westernforestry.org
Western Forestry and Conservation Association

Offers high-quality continuing education workshops and seminars for professional foresters throughout Oregon, Washington, Idaho, Montana, Northern California and British Columbia.

15496 www.woodcomponents.org
Wood Component Manufacturers Association

Represents manufacturers of wood component products for urniture, cabinetry, building products, and decorative wood products.

15497 www.woodfloors.org
National Wood Flooring Association

For distributors, manufacturers, retailers, and contractors.

15498 www.woodtank.com
National Wood Tank Institute

Companies and individuals in the US and Canada involved in the manufacture of wood tanks, vats and pipes.

15499 www.wrcla.org
Western Red Cedar Lumber Association

Association of 26 quality producers of Western Red Cedar lumber products in Washington, Oregon, Canada.

15500 www.wwpa.org
Western Wood Products Association

Represents lumber manufacturers in 12 Western states and Alaska. Provides lumber quality control, technical support, and business information to supporting mills.

15501 www2.dcn.org/orgs/wmmpa.wm
Wood Moulding And Millwork Producers Association

Goal is to promote quality products produced by its members, to develop sources of supply, to promote optimum use of raw materials to standardize products, and to increase the domestic and foreign usage of moulding and millwork products.

Associations

15502 **American Gear Manufacturers Association**
500 Montgomery Street
Suite 350
Alexandria, VA 22314-2730
703-684-0211
FAX: 703-684-0242
webmaster@agma.org www.agma.org

Joe Franklin, President
Kurt Medert, VP/Admin Director
William Bradley, VP Technical Division
Jan Potter, VP/Membership

Manufacturers of gears and geared speed changers. Involved in writing industry standards.
400 Members Founded: 1916

15503 **American Machine Tool Distributors' Association**
1445 Research Boulevard
Suite 450
Rockville, MD 20850
301-738-1200
FAX: 301-738-9499 800-878-2683

John J Healy, CAE, President
Debbie Vieder, Director Education/Communications
Lisa Higgins, Membership Services Assistant
Karen Davenport, Finance Manager
Jean Bryant, Trade Show/Meeting Manager

Since 1925, the American Machine Tool Distributors' Association has been a major voice within the machine tool industry. The AMTDA represents independent distributors and worldwide builders of machine tools and related products used in the metalworking industry. The Association's mission is to provide marketers of manufacturing technology the essential services necessary to develop and perpetuate distribution businesses that make vital contributions to North American manufacturing.
400 Members Founded: 1925
Mailing list available for rent

15504 **American Mold Builders Association**
701 E Irving Park Road
#207
Roselle, IL 60172
630-980-7667
FAX: 630-980-9714
info@amba.org www.amba.org

Jeanette Bradley, Executive Director
Susan Hall, Member Services Manager
Olav L Bradley, Board of Director
Robert Earnhardt, Board of Directors

Promotes the development, welfare and expansion of businesses engaged in the manufacture of molds and related tooling.
$50.00
400 Members Annual Founded: 1973

15505 **American Society of Mechanical Engineers**
Three Park Avenue
New York, NY 10016-5990
212-917-7740
FAX: 973-882-1717 800-843-2763
infocentral@asme.org www.asme.org

Reginald I Vachon, President
Virgil R Carter, Executive Director
Harry Armen, President-Nominee

12000 Members Founded: 1880

15506 **American Textile Machinery Association**
201 Park Washington Court
Falls Church, VA 22046-4527
703-538-1789
FAX: 703-241-5603
info@atmanet.org www.atmanet.org

Joseph A Okey Jr, Chairman
Clay Tyeryar, President
Harry W Buzzerd, Jr, Management Counsel

ATMA's purpose is to advance the common interests of its members, improve business conditions within the US textile machinery industry from a global perspective and market the industry and members' machinery, parts and services.
Founded: 1933

15507 **Association for Computing Machinery**
1515 Broadway
New York, NY 10036
212-697-7440
800-342-6626

John White, Chief Executive Officer

A force in advancing the skills of information technology professionals and students worldwide.
Founded: 1947

15508 **Association of Machinery and Equipment**
315 S Patrick Street
Alexandria, VA 22314
703-836-7900
FAX: 703-836-9303 800-537-8629
amea@amea.org www.amea.org

Lorna Frazier-Lindsey, Director
Nathan Arnold, President

Members are appraisers of the metalworking industry.
284 Members Founded: 1983

15509 **Association of Vacuum Equipment Manufacturers International**
71 Pinon Hill Place NE
Albuquerque, NM 87122-1914
505-856-6924
FAX: 505-856-6716
aveminfo@avem.org www.avem.org

Walter Reimann, President

Promotes the interest of the vacuum science and technology industry participants through market analysis, educational seminars and as a forum for equipment manufactures.

15510 **Compressed Air and Gas Institutue**

1300 Sumner Avenue
Cleveland, OH 44115
216-241-7333
FAX: 216-241-0105
cagi@cagi.org www.cagi.org

John H Addington, Executive Vice President

A non-profit organization of companies which manufacture air and gas compressors, air or gas dryers, or pneumatic tools and machinery; products which have man applications in conswtruction, manufacturing, mining and the process and natural gas industries.
Founded: 1945

15511 **Contractors Pump Bureau**
6737 W. Washington Street
Suite 2400
Milwaukee, WI 53214-5647
414-272-0943
FAX: 414-272-1170

Walter D Anderson, Executive Director
Dennis Slater, President

The CPB promotes matters of mutual interest to contractor pump users, manufacturers and parts and component suppliers.
20 Members

15512 **Conveyor Equipment Manufacturers Associati on**
6724 Lone Oak Blvd
Naples, FL 34109
239-514-3441

bob@cemanet.org www.cemanet.org

Bob Reinfried, Executive Vice President

Considered to be the resource for conveyor safety dimensional and application standards. Actively promotes the capabilities of its members worldwide.

15513 **Crane Manufacturers Association of America**
8720 Red Oak Boulevard
Suite 201
Charlotte, NC 28217-3992
704-626-6706
FAX: 704-676-1199
jnofsinger@mhia.org
www.mhia.org/psc

Jeff Breitrick, President
F Hal Vandiver, Managing Director
Oddvar Norheim, VP
Cathy Moose, Executive Assistant
Victoria Wheeler, Director Member Services

Supports crane equipment manufacturers.
22 Members

15514 **Farm Equipment Manufacturers Association**
1000 Executive Parkway
St Louis, MO 63141-6369
314-878-2304
FAX: 314-878-1742
info@farmequip.org
www.farmequip.org

Vince Tomlonovic, President
Timothy Perkins, First VP
Jim Wessing, Second VP
Robert Schnell, Executive Vice President
Bob Atkinson, Treasurer

An information gathering and distributing organization for farm equipment manufacturers and suppliers.
340 Members

15515 **Fire Equipment Manufacturers' Association**
1300 Sumner Avenue
Cleveland, OH 44115-2851
216-241-7333
FAX: 216-241-0105
fema@taol.com www.taol\fema.com

John H Addington, Executive Director

Members are companies making devices that control or extinguish fires in residential or commercial buildings.
27 Members Founded: 1925

15516 Fluid Power Society
1930 E Marlton Pike
PO Box 1420
Cherry Hill, NJ 08003
856-296-6500
FAX: 856-424-9248 800-303-8520
paulprass@fps.org www.ifps.org

Paul Prass, Executive Director
Donna Pollander, Assistant Director
Sue Tesauro, Certification Manager
Adele Kayser, Public Relations Coordinator
Andrew Field, President

International organization for fluid power and motion control professionals.
2600 Members Founded: 1960

15517 Food Processing Suppliers Association
1451 Dolley Madison Blvd
Ste 200
McLean, VA 22101-3847
703-661-2600
FAX: 703-761-4334 www.fpmsa.org
A nonprofit trade association representing suppliers of machinery, equipment, supplies and services used to prepare the world's beverages and processed foods.
350+ Members

15518 Heat Exchange Insitutute
1300 Sumner Avenue
Cleveland, OH 44115-2851
216-241-7333
FAX: 216-241-0105
hei@heatexchange.org
www.heatexchange.org

John H Addington, Secretary/Treasurer

Members are manufacturers of heat exchange and/or vacuum apparatus such as steam jet ejectors, steam surface condensers, closed feedwater heaters, power plant heat exchangers and deaerators.

15519 Industrial Distribution Association
1277 Lenox Park Boulevard
Suite 275
Atlanta, GA 30319
404-266-3991
FAX: 404-266-8311 877-591-620
idainc@ida-assoc.org
www.ida-assoc.org

Jim Beckstein, President
Tom Berger, VP

Promotes the industry and the use of converting equipment. Conducts research and compiles statistics for wholesalers of industrial equipment.
650 Members Founded: 1988

15520 International Association of Diecutting and Diemaking
651 Terra Cotta Avenue
Suite 132
Crystal Lake, IL 60014
815-455-7519
FAX: 815-455-7510 800-828-4233
cccrouse@iadd.org www.ladd.org

Cynthia C Crouse, Chief Executive Officer
Jill May, Member Relations Coordinator

Members are firms involved in diemaking, diecutting and related equpment and supply areas.

15521 International Association of Machinists
9000 Machinists Place
Upper Marlboro, MD 20772-2687
301-967-4500
FAX: 301-967-4588
hgulley@iamaw.org www.iamaw.org

R Thomas Buffenbarger, International President
Lee Pearson, General VP
Warren L Mart, General Secretary-Treasurer
Dave Ritchie, General VP

Has an annual budget of approximately $101.3 million.
Founded: 1888

15522 Machinery Dealers National Association
315 S Patrick Street
Alexandria, VA 22314
703-836-9300
FAX: 703-836-9303 800-872-7807
office@mdna.org www.mdna.org

Mark Robinson, Executive Vice President

Represents dealers of used industrial equipment.
383 Members Founded: 1960

15523 Manufacturers Alliance/MAPI
1600 Wilson Boulevard
Suite 1100
Arlington, VA 22209
703-841-9000
FAX: 703-841-9514
cmackey@mapi.net www.mapi.net

Thomas J Duesterberg, President/CEO
David J Danjezek, VP/Admin/Corporate Sec
James F Engelhardt, Director Communications
Cameron L Mackey, Chief Marketing Officer
Peggy Morrissette, Director Public & Govern Affairs

A policy research organization whose members are companies drawn from the producers and users of capital goods and allied products. Includes leading companies in heavy industry, automotive, electronics, precision instruments, telecommunications, computers, office systems. aerospace, oil/gas, chemicals and similar high technology industries.

15524 Mechanical Power Transmission Association
6724 Lone Oak Boulevard
Naples, FL 34109-6834
239-514-3441
FAX: 239-514-3470
bob@mpta.org www.mpta.org

Robert A Reinfried, Executive Director

Formerly Multiple V-Belt and Mechanical Power Transmission Association.

15525 National Fluid Power Association
3333 North Mayfair Road
Suite 211
Milwaukee, WI 53222-3219
414-783-3362
FAX: 414-778-3361
nfpa@nfpa.com www.nfpa.com

Linda Western, Executive Director
Peter Alles, Director/Member Services/Develop
Karen Boehme, International Standards Manager
Sue Chase, Financial Director
Dawn Krueger, Memebership Manager

Members are companies which hav designed, manufactured and nationally marketed a fluid power component for a least two years in the US.

15526 National Tooling & Machining Association
9300 Livingston Road
Fort Washington, MD 20744-4905
301-486-6200
FAX: 301-248-7104 www.ntma.org

Matthew Coffey, Publishser
Sandra Bailey, Editor
Rob Akers, Manager

Members are makers of jigs, molds, tools, gages, dies and fixtures for companies doing precision machining. Supports the NTMA - Committee for A Strong Economy.

2800 Members Founded: 1943 2500 names

15527 North American Equipment Dealers Association
1195 Smizer Mill Road
Fenten, MO 63026-3480
636-349-5000
FAX: 636-349-5443
naeda@naeda.com www.naeda.com

Jim Meinhardt, President
Paul Kindinger, CEO
Robert Frazee, Second VP

Supports all those involved with retail equipment.
Founded: 1900

15528 Outdoor Power Equipment and Engine Service Association
37 Pratt Street
Essex, CT 06426
860-767-1770
FAX: 860-767-7932
info@oopeesa.com www.opeesa.com

Nancy Cueroni, Executive Director

Members are distributors of outdoor power equipment to retailers with a minimum of $1 million gross sales. Associate membership is available for suppliers and finance companies associated with the industry.

15529 Packaging Machinery Manufacturers Institute
4350 N Fairfax Drive
Suite 600
Arlington, VA 22203
703-243-8555
FAX: 703-243-8556
pmmiwebhelp@pmmi.org
www.pmmi.org, www.packexpo.com

Charles D Yuska, President
Joshua Caufield, Director/New Media
Matt Croson, Director/Member Services
Patricia Fee, VP/Meeting & Facilities
Jim Pittas, Director/Expositions

Trade association for manufacturers of packaging and packaging-related converting equipment. PMMI offers meetings, an inquiry service, statistics and surveys, and a business to business survey on its website. PMMI also offers several Pack Expos (packaging related tradeshows).

15530 Polycrystalline Products Association
11001 Dankaway North
Suite 1
St. Petersburg, FL 33716
727-577-5004
amee@csda.org
An industrial trade association of tool fabricators, machine tool builders, material suppliers, educators and users of polycrystalline products.
500 Members Founded: 1971

15531 Powder Actuated Tool Manufacturers Institute
1603 Boone's Lick Road
Saint Charles, MO 63301-2381
636-947-6610
FAX: 636-946-3336
info@patmi.org patmi.org
James A Borchers, Executive Director
Represents manufacturers of construction tools used to fasten to and into steel and concrete.
7 Members Founded: 1951

15532 Power Conversion Products Council International
4 Hollis Street
PO Box 378
Sherborn, MA 01770
508-979-5935
FAX: 508-651-3920
Elizabeth Bevington-Chambers, Executive Director
Members are manufacturers and suppliers to the wall plug-in transformer/transformer charger/converter industry. Sponsor two meetings each year covering business and engineering topics.
50 Members Founded: 1974

15533 Power Tool Institute
1300 Sumner Avenue
Cleveland, OH 44115-2851
216-241-7333
FAX: 216-241-0105
pti@powertoolinstitute.com
www.powertoolinstitute.com
Charles M Stockinger, Executive Manager
Trade association representing manufacturers of power tools.
12 Members Founded: 1937

15534 Power-Motion Technology Representative Association
PO Box 150229
Arlington, TX 76015
817-561-7272
FAX: 817-561-7275
info@ptra.org www.ptra.org
Pamela L Bess, Executive Director
To promote the science of power transmission/motion control engineering, to promote educational programs and activities and to promote representatives placed in the industry.

15535 Precision Machined Products Association
6700 West Snowville Road
Brecksville, OH 44141-3212
440-526-0300
FAX: 440-526-5803
webmaster@pmpa.org www.pmpa.org

Michael B Dufflin, Executive Vice President
Robert C Kiener, Director/Marketing
Bobbi Paul, Manager
Produces several educational opporunities for members, emphasizing quality assurance and emerging technologies. Sponsors the PMPA Political Action Committee.

15536 Robotic Industries Association
900 Victors Way
PO Box 3724
Ann Arbor, MI 48106
734-994-6088
FAX: 734-994-3338
ria@robotics.org
www.roboticsonline.com
Jeff Burnstein, Executive Director
Only trade group in North America specifically to serve the rototics industry.
Founded: 1974

15537 Service Dealers Association
PO Box 73796
Houston, TX 77273-3063
281-443-3063
FAX: 281-443-4859
Melinda Delgado, Executive Director
Represents dealers and distributors of power equipment.
690 Members Founded: 1986

15538 Service Specialists Association
4015 Marks Road
Apartment 2B
Medina, OH 44256-8316
330-725-7160
FAX: 330-722-5638 800-763-5717
Cara R Giebner, Executive VP
Members are persons, firms or corporations who have operated a full line heavy duty repair service shop for at least one year with sufficient inventory to service market area, having rebuilding department capable of making all necessary repairs.
140 Members Founded: 1981

15539 Society of Manufacturing Engineers
1 SME Drive
PO Box 930
Dearborn, MI 48121
313-271-1500
FAX: 313-271-2861 800-733-4763
service@sme.org www.sme.org
Nancy Berg, Executive Director
Serves its members and others in the international manufacturing community by identifying, evaluating and explaining the adoption and integration of emerging information technologies to create business value.
7000 Members Founded: 1932
Mailing list available for rent 77790 names $95 per M.

15540 Tooling Component Manufacturers Association
36505 Florida Avenue
Hemet, CA 92545-3534

FAX: 909-766-7443
Ray Fuhrer, Executive Secretary
Members are united primarily for the purpose of coordinating and standardizing sizes.
8 Members Founded: 1958

15541 Valve Manufacturers Association of America (VMA)
1050 17th Street Northwest
Suite 280
Washington, DC 20036
202-331-8105
FAX: 202-296-0378
info@vma.org or wsandler@vma.org
www.vma.org
William Sandler, President
Judy Tibbs, Associate Publisher
VMA represents the interests of nearly 100 U.S. and Canadian valve and actuator Manufacturers who account for approximately 80% of the total industrial valve shipments out of U.S. and Canadian facilities. The American valve industry supplies approximately 35% of worldwide valve demand. VMA member companies employ 20,000 men and women directly in supporting jobs. VMA is the only organization exclusively serving U.S. and Canadian manufacturers of industrial valves and actuators.
100 Members Founded: 1938

15542 Vibration Institute
6262 South Kingery Highway
Suite 212
Willowbrook, IL 60527
630-654-2254
FAX: 630-654-2271
vibinst@anet.com www.vibinst.org
Ronald L Eshleman, PhD, Director
Members are companies and individuals concerned with measuring and analyzing machinery vibration. Benefits of membership include subscription to Vibrations Magazine (published quarterly) and access to Around the Institute Newsletter. Dues vary depending on level of membership.
2500 Members Founded: 1972

15543 Wood Machinery Maufacturers of America
1900 Arch Street
Philadelphia, PA 19103-1498
215-564-3484
FAX: 215-963-9785 www.wmma.org
Peter Perez, President
John Wood, Manager
WMMA has worked to increase the productivity and profitability of U.S. machinery and tooling manufacturers and the businesses that support them.

Newsletters

15544 Association of Machinery and Equipment Appraisers - Newsletter

Association of Machinery and Equipment Appraisers
315 S Patrick Street
Alexandria, VA 22314-3501
703-836-7900
FAX: 703-836-9303 800-537-8629
amea@amea.org http://www.amea.org

Nathan J Arnold, President
Mary Flynn, Executive Director
Lorna Frazier-Lindsey, Director
Information about appraisers of the machinery equipment.
8 pages Founded: 1983
Circulation: 6800 282 names $100 per M.
Printed in 2 colors on matte stock

15545 CEMA Bulletin
Conveyor Equipment Manufacturers Association
6724 Lone Oak Boulevard
Naples, FL 34109
239-514-3441
FAX: 239-514-3470
cema@cemanet.org
http://www.cemanet.org
Robert A Reinfried, Executive VP
Association and conveyor industry news.
6 pages Founded: 1933
Circulation: 96

15546 Caster and Wheel Handbook
Youngs
55 Cherry Lane
Souderton, PA 18964-1550
215-723-4400
FAX: 800-544-3239 800-523-5454
custrep@youngscatalog.com
http://www.youngscatalog.com
Paul Tuckhorn, Marketing
Paul Young Jr, President
Technical news and information.
Monthly Founded: 1945

15547 Computer Aided Design Report
CAD/CAM Publishing
1010 Turquoise Street
Suite 320
San Diego, CA 92109-1268
619-379-9420
FAX: 858-488-6052
info@cadcamnet.com
http://www.cadcamnet.com
Albert Camilleri, Editor
Roopinder Tara, CEO
Uses of computers by engineers in the manufacturing trades. *$344.00*
Monthly Founded: 1977

15548 Computer Integrated Manufacture and Engineering
Lionheart Publishing
2555 Cumberland Parkway SE
Suite 299
Atlanta, GA 30339-3908
770-234-9360
FAX: 770-432-6969
Explores cutting edge developments in manufacturing systems operation management.

Circulation: 24,000

15549 High-Tech Materials Alert
John Wiley & Sons
111 River Street
Hoboken, NJ 07030-5774
201-748-6000
FAX: 201-748-6088 800-825-7550
subinfo@wiley.com
http://www.wiley.com
Kenneth A Kovaly, Publisher
Peter R Savage, Editorial Director
William J. Pesce, CEO
Harry Goldstein, Managing Editor
Details significant developments in high-performance materials ranging from alloys and metallic whiskers to ceramic and graphite fibers, their fabrication and industrial applications. *$1152.00*
Monthly Founded: 1807
Mailing list available for rent $180 per M.
Computerized version available

15550 Industrial Health & Hazards Update
InfoTeam
PO Box 15640
Plantation, FL 33318-5640
954-473-9560
FAX: 954-473-0544
infoteamma@aol.com
Merton Allen, Editor
Covers occupational safety, health, hazards, and disease, mitigatioin and control of hazardous situations; waste recycling and treaqtment; environmental pollution and control; product safety and liability; fires and explosions; plant and computer security,; air pollution; surface and ground water; wastewater; soil gases; combustion and incineration; earth warming; ozone layer depletion; electromagnetic radiation; toxic materials; and many other related topics.
Monthlyth
Computerized version available

15551 Innovators Digest
InfoTeam
PO Box 15640
Plantation, FL 33318-5640
954-473-9560
FAX: 954-473-0544
infoteamma@aol.com
Merton Allen, Editor
A multidisciplinary publication covering developments in science, engineering, products, markets, business development, manufacturing and other technological developments having industrial or commercial significance.
2 per month
Computerized version available

15552 Intelligent Manufacturing
Lionheart Publishing
506 Roswell Street
Suite 220
Marietta, GA 30060
770-431-0867
FAX: 770-432-6969
lpi@lionhrtpub.com
http://www.lionhrtpub.com
John Llewellyn, Publisher
David Blanchard, Editor
John Llewellyn, President
Provides expert solutions to manufacturing professionals covering production problems, developments in manufacturing systems. *$ 20.00*
Weekly Founded: 1987
Circulation: 1598

15553 Life Sciences & Biotechnology Update
InfoTeam
PO Box 15640
Plantation, FL 33318-5640
954-473-9560
FAX: 954-473-0544
infoteamma@aol.com
Merton Allen, Editor
Medical and biological technology; health and disease; genetics and genetic engineering; bodily fluids, bones, tissues and organs, cancer, medical diagnoisis and treatment; medical instrumentation and procedures; medical care systems; public health; mental health; child care; medical costs; research; and more.
Monthly
Computerized version available

15554 Machinery Outlook
Manfredi & Associates
20934 W Lakeview Parkway
Mundelein, IL 60060-9502
847-949-9080
FAX: 847-949-9910
info@manfredi.com
http://www.manfredi.com
Frank Manfredi, President
A newsletter about and for the construction and mining machinery industry. *$550.00*
14 pages Monthly Founded: 1984
Printed in 1 color on matte stock

15555 Machining Technology
Society of Manufacturing Engineers
One SME Drive
Dearborn, MI 48121-2408
313-271-1500
FAX: 313- 42- 340 800-733-4763
service@sme.org http://www.sme.org
Thomas Drozda, Publisher
Gene Korte, Editor
Covers all aspects of machining in manufacturing, milling, grinding, honing, etc. *$60.00*
8 pages Quarterly Founded: 1932
Circulation: 3770 Audited
Mailing list available for rent 77790 names $95 per M.
Printed in 2 colors on matte stock

15556 Manufacturing Technology
National Technical Information Service
SU 5285 Port Royal Road
Springfield, VA 22161-0001
703-874-4650
FAX: 703-487-4630
Covers CAD/CAM, robotics, robots, productivity, manufacturing, planning, processing and control, plant design and computer software.

15557 NTMA Record
Tooling
9300 Livingston Road
Fort Washington, MD 20744-4905
301-248-5071
FAX: 301-248-7104 800-248-6862
tom@ntma.org http://www.ntma.org
Rob Akers, Operations Director/ Publisher
Richard Wills, CEO
Thomas Garcia, Manager, Marketing/Meetin
Covers activities of 4,000 member companies of tool, die and precision machining industries. *$39.00*
16 pages Monthly Founded: 1943
Circulation: 2000

15558 Rotating Machinery: E-mail News & Analysis
Forecast International
22 Commerce Road
Newtown, CT 06470-1643
203-426-0800
FAX: 203-426-1964 www.forecast1.com

Kathy Bertrand, Production Manager
Monty Nebinger, Circulation Director
An electronic information/data service sourced from thousands of worldwide publications, in 15 languages. Provides concise summaries, news, trends and contract information with hyper-links to the source or a related website. Delivered 100 times a year. *$425.00*
2 week

15559 Wood Machining News
Wood Machining Institute
PO Box 476
Berkeley, CA 94701
510-448-8363
FAX: 925-945-0947
szymani@woodmachining.com
http://www.woodmachining.com

Ryszard Szymani, Director

Information on the latest technological advances in the field of wood machining, including sawing, planning and sanding operations as well as the production of veneers and chips and equipment associated with these operations. WMN also reports on new machinery, processes and software, cutting tools and machinery and worker safety. *$72.00*

38448 pages Founded: 1984
Circulation: 600

Magazines & Journals

15560 American Society of Mechanical Engineers
3 Park Avenue
21st Floor
New York, NY 10016-5990
212-917-7000
FAX: 212-591-7674 800-843-2763
infocentral@asme.org
http://www.asme.org

Terry E Shoup, President
John G Falcioni, Editor-in-Chief
Richard Feigel, International President

Monthly Founded: 1880

15561 American Tool, Die & Stamping News
Eagle Publications
42400 Grand River Avenue
Suite 103
Novi, MI 48375-2572
248-347-3487
FAX: 248-347-3492 800-783-3491
sales@ameritooldie.com
http://www.ameritooldie.com

Gail Dawson, Marketing Manager
Joan Oakley, Circulation Director
Art Brown, Owner

Applications, techniques, equipment and accessories of metal stamping, moldmaking, electric discharge machining; and new product information relating to the tool and die industry. Accepts advertising.

70 pages Founded: 1971
Circulation: 36000
Printed in 4 colors on glossy stock

15562 Compressed Air Magazine
Ingersoll Rand Company
200 Chestnut Ridge Road
Woodcliff, NJ 07677
201-573-0123
FAX: 201-573-3172 www.irco.com

Michele Zayle, Circulation Director
Thomas McAloon, Editor

A magazine of applied technology and industrial management for middle and upper level managers in diversified industries. *$15.00*

44 pages 8 per year
Circulation: 125,000
Printed in 4 colors on matte stock

15563 Contact
Furnas Electric Company
1000 McKee Street
Batavia, IL 60510-1682
630-879-6000
FAX: 630-879-0867

Steve Wilcox, Editor

Application of electric motor controls to electrically operated machinery and equipment.

Circulation: 4,000

15564 Diesel Progress: North American Edition
Diesel & Gas Turbine Publications
20855 Watertown Road
Suite 220
Waukesha, WI 53186
262-325-5000
FAX: 262-754-4175
mmcneely@dieselpub.com
http://www.dieselpub.com

Michael Osenga, Publisher
S Bollwahn, Circulation Manager
Robert Wilson, President

Geared towards readers interested in state-of-the-art systems technology. Features include new product listings, systems design, research and product testing as well as systems maintenance and rebuilding.

Monthly
Circulation: 26011

15565 EE-Evaluation Engineering
Nelson Publishing Inc
2500 Tamiami Trail North
Nokomis, FL 34275
941-966-9521
FAX: 941-966-2590
www.nelsonpub.com
Leading source of information for the electronics testing and evaluation market.
Founded: 1962

15566 Elevator World
Elevator World
PO Box 6507
356 Morgan Avenue
Mobile, AL 36660
251-479-4514
FAX: 251-479-7043 800-730-5093
editorial@elevator-world.com
http://www.elevator-world.com

Ricia Hendrick, President/Publisher/CEO
Robert S Caporale, Senior VP/Editor
Patricia Cartee, VP/Commercial Operations
T. Bruce MacKinnon, VP/Advertising Manager

International journal for those involved in short-range vertical transportation, including manufacturers, contractors, maintainers, consultants and inspectors. *$75.00*

170 pages Monthly Founded: 1953
Circulation: 7,000
Printed in 4 colors on glossy stock

15567 Equip-Mart
Story Communications
116 N Camp Street
Seguin, TX 78155
830-303-3328
FAX: 830-372-3011 800-864-1155

Tammy Reilly, Publisher

Largest industrial equipment magazine in North America. Received by manufacturig executives who purchase or sell industrial equipment, tools, supplies and accessories.

Monthly
Circulation: 108,000

15568 Gear Technology
Randall Publishing Company
PO Box 1426
Elk Grove Village, IL 60009
847-437-6604
FAX: 847-437-6618
people@geartechnology.com
http://www.geartechnology.com

Michael Goldstein, Publisher
William R Stott, Managing Editor
Dan Pels, Business Development Mana
Carol Tratar, Circulation Coordinator
Richard Goldstein, Vice President

Gear Technology offers technical articles from the top names in the industry; feature articles dealing with management and technology; top-notch tradeshow coverage; industry and products news.

Founded: 1934
Circulation: 13025
Printed in 4 colors on glossy stock

15569 High Performance Composites
Ray Publishing
4891 Independence Street
Suite 270
Wheat Ridge, CO 80033
303-467-1776
FAX: 303-467-1777
info@raypubs.com
www.compositeworld.com
Approach is technical, offering cutting-edge design, engineering, prototyping, and manufacturing solutions for aerospace and other traditional and emerging structural applications for advanced composites.

15570 Home Medical Equipment News
United Publications
106 Lafayette Street
PO Box 998
Yarmouth, ME 04096
207-846-0600
FAX: 207-846-0657
jgundersen@hmenews.com
http://www.hmenews.com

James G Taliaferro, CEO/President
Brenda Boothby, Circulation Director
Joline V Gilman, Production Director
Jim Sullivan, Editor
Rick Rector, Publisher

Serves home medical equipment providers.

Monthly Founded: 1995
Circulation: 17100

15571 Home Shop Machinist
Village Press
2779 Aero Park Drive
PO Box 968
Traverse City, MI 49685-968
231-946-3712
FAX: 231-946-3289 800-327-7377
info@villagepress.com
http://www.villagepress.com

Robert Goff, Publisher
Neil Knopf, Editor
Joe D. Rice, Editor in Chief

Articles on precision machining and metal working and how-to projects geared towards the amateur machinist and small commercial machine shops. *$25.00*

Circulation: 28000

15572 IEEE Transactions on Industry Applications
IEEE Operations Center
445 Hoes Lane
#3014
Piscataway, NJ 08854-1331
732-981-0060
FAX: 732-981-1721 http://www.ieee.org

Edward Rich, Editor
Johnathan Dahl, Marketing Manager

The development and applications of electrical systems, apparatus, devices and controls to the processes and equipment of industry and commerce. *$515.00*
Founded: 1980
Circulation: 5100

15573 InTech
ISA Services
67 Alexander Drive
PO Box 12277
Research Triangle Park, NC 27709
919-549-8411
FAX: 919-990-9434
info@isa.org http://www.isa.org

Greg Hale, Editor
Richard Simpson, Publisher

Covers the most recent developments in the instrumention, measurement and control market.
Monthly Founded: 1945
Circulation: 75000

15574 Industrial Machine Trader
Heartland Industrial Group
1003 Central Avenue
PO Box 1415
Fort Dodge, IA 50501
515-955-1600
FAX: 515-955-3753 800-203-9960
ads@industrialgroup.com
http://www.imtgetsresults.com/

Tony Smith, Publisher
Gele Mckinney, President
Angi Hesterman, Circulation Manager

Industrial machinery equipment, suppliers and manufacturers. *$67.85*
8 pages Weekly Founded: 1970
Circulation: 234000

15575 Industrial Market Place
Wineberg Publications
7842 Lincoln Avenue
Skokie, IL 60077
847-676-1900
FAX: 847-676-0063 800-323-1818
info@industrialmktpl.com
http://www.industrialmktpl.com

Joel Wineberg, President
Adrienne Gallender, Publisher

Advertising sales on new and used machinery and equipment. *$175.00*
Founded: 1951
Circulation: 100,000
Mailing list available for rent 120 names $70 per M.
Printed in 4 colors on glossy stock

15576 Journal of Engineering for Industry

American Society of Mechanical Engineers
3 Park Avenue
FLR.21
New York, NY 10016-5990
212-917-7000
FAX: 212-591-7674 800-843-2763
Infocentral@asme.org
http://www.asme.org
Covers interfaces of mechanical engineering. *$40.00*
Founded: 1880

15577 Locator Services
315 S Patrick Street
Alexandria, VA 22314-3501
703-836-9700
FAX: 703-836-7665 800-537-1446
sales@locatoronline.com
http://www.locatoronline.com

Terry J Pitman, Executive Publisher

Used metalworking equipment. *$38.00*
Monthly Founded: 1969
Circulation: 225000

15578 Machine Shop Guide
Worldwide Communications
401 Worthington Avenue
Harrison, NJ 07029-2039
973-977-7555
FAX: 253-872-7603
www.machineshopguide.com

Robert L Hatschek, Executive Editor
Frederick Mason, Editor

Information on manufacturing technology, new applications for manufacturing technology and new products. Focus is metal cutting machines and tooling.
10 per year Founded: 1996
Circulation: 102,893 $150 per M.
Printed in 4 colors on glossy stock

15579 Machinery Trader
Sandhills Publishing
120 W. Harvest Dr
Lincoln, NE 68521
402-792-2181
FAX: 402-479-2184 800-247-4898
feedback@machinerytrader.com
http://www.machinerytrader.com

Tom Peed, C.E.O.
Marva Wasser, Editor-in-Chief

Covering heavy equipment. *$59.00*
160 pages Weekly Founded: 1978
Circulation: 20000

15580 Managing Automation
Thomas Publishing Company
5 Penn Plaza
12th Floor
New York, NY 10001-1860
212-950-0500
FAX: 212-290-7335
businesslists@thomaspublishing.com
http://www.thomasbusinesslists.com

Don Ross, Circulation Director
Robert Malone, Editor
Heather L Mikisch, Publisher
Kim Vennard, Marketing Manager
David Brousell, Chief Executive Officer

Serves the needs of those managers and engineers responsible for the planning and implementation of factory automation at both the plant and enterprise levels.
Monthly Founded: 1898
Circulation: 100246

15581 Manufacturing Engineering
Society of Manufacturing Engineers
1 SME Drive
#930
Dearborn, MI 48121-2408
313-271-1500
FAX: 313-425-3401 800-733-4763
service@sme.org http://www.sme.org

Tom Drozda, Publisher/Advertising
John Coleman, Editor-in-Chief
Gene Nelson, President

Serves metalworking industry machining, forming, inspection, assembly and processing operations.
Monthly Founded: 1932
Circulation: 111966

15582 Modern Machine Shop
Gardner Publications
6915 Valley Avenue
Cincinnati, OH 45244-3029
513-527-8977
FAX: 513-527-8801 800-950-8020
mmsmkt@gardnerweb.com
http://www.mmsonline.com

Daniel C Luciano, Publisher
Mark D Albert, Editor-in-Chief
Richard Kline, President

Reaches metalworking plants of all sizes - from small job shops to giant aerospace and automotive plants. It is edited for those involved in metalworking operations, particularly those performed on machine tools. *$4.00*
Monthly Founded: 1928
Circulation: 107000
Mailing list available for rent 106M names
Printed in 4 colors on glossy stock

15583 Motion Control
ISA Services
PO Box 12277
Durham, NC 27709-2277
919-549-8411
FAX: 919-990-9434
sbatman@isa.org http://www.isa.org

Sam Batman, Editor
Richard Simpson, Publisher
Robert Renner, Executive Director

Information for those who design and maintain motion control systems. *$54.00*
56 pages Founded: 1945
Circulation: 41000
Printed in 4 colors on glossy stock

15584 Motion System Distributor
Penton Media
1300 E 9th Street
Cleveland, OH 44114-1503
216-696-7000
FAX: 216-696-1819
information@#penton.com
www.penton.com

Jack C Lyttle, Publisher

Provides selling and technical information to individuals and distributors specializing in power transmission, motion control and fluid products.

15585 OEM Worldwide
Cygnus Publishing
1233 Janesville Avenue
Watertown, WI 53538
920-563-6388
FAX: 920-563-1699
tjheinlein@cableinet.co.uk
http://www.oem-worldwide.com

Chad Elmore, Editor
Leslie Shalabi, Publisher
James S Rank, VP
Sue Cullen, Advertising Manager
Brett Apold, Production Manager

Designed to be a resource of operational and general productivity information for original equipment manufacturers in Europe, competing in the global marketplace. *$6.00*

Monthly Founded: 1984
Circulation: 16800

15586 Outdoor Power Equipment
1900 Arch Street
Philadelphia, PA 19103-1404
215-564-3484
FAX: 215-564-2175
assnhqt@netaxs.com

Julie S Burns, Executive Director

Members are distributors of outdoor power equipment to retailers with a minimum of $1 million gross sales. Associate members are suppliers and finance companies.
150 pages Founded: 1980

15587 Plant Engineering
Reed Business Information
360 Park Avenue South
New York, NY 10014
212-450-0067
FAX: 630-288-8686
http://www.reedbusiness.com

Tom Mehalko, Publisher
Richard L Dunn, Editor
Gerard Van de Aast, Director
Carel de Bos, Chief Information Officer
James Reed, Owner

The magazine for plant engineering professionals responsible for the maintenance, repair and operations of plant facilities, equipment and systems. *$3.00*

Circulation: 116700

15588 Processing Magazine
Grand View Media Group
Po Box 698
Birmingham, AL 35243

FAX: 205-408-3797 888-431-2877
webmaster@grandviewmedia.com
www.grandviewmedia.com
Leading source for up-to-date product and equipment solutions.

15589 Production Machining
Gardner Publications
6915 Valley Avenue
Cincinnati, OH 45244-3029
513-278-8977
FAX: 513-527-8801 800-950-8020
jjordan@gardnerweb.com
http://www.gardnerweb.com

Chris Koepfer, Editor-in-Chief
Leo Rakowski, Senior Editor
John Jordan, Assistant Editor
Lori Beckman, Production Manager
Walter Lowe, Owner

Monthly Founded: 1928
Circulation: 200000

15590 Pumps & Systems
Randall Publishing Company
1900 28th Avenue South
Suite 110
Birmingham, AL 35209
205-339-9120
http://www.pump-zone.com

Jane Alexander, Editor
George Lake, Associate Publisher
Scott Kidwell, Advertising Sales:
Tom Cory, Circulation
Robert Windle, Chief Executive Officer

Monthly Founded: 2002

15591 Sensors Magazine
Advanstar Communications
7500 Old Oak Boulevard
Cleveland, OH 44130-3369
440-243-8100
FAX: 440-826-2833
info@advanstar.com
www.sensormag.com /
www.advanstar.com

Barbara G Goode, Editor-in-Chief
Donna Pellerin George, Associate Editor
Joseph Loggia, CEO
Georgiann Decenzo, Director of Corporate marketing
Francis Heid, Vice President of Publishing Operat

Primary source among design and production engineers of information on sensor technologies and products, and topic integral to sensor-based systems and applications. Provides practical and in-depth yet accessible information on sensor operation, design, application, and implementation within systems. Covers the effective use of state-of-the-art resources and tools that enable readers to get the maximum benefit from their use of sensors.
Monthly Founded: 1984
Circulation: 75000

15592 Valve Magazine
Valve Manufacturers Association of America
1050 17th Street Northwest
Suite 280
Washington, DC 20036-5503
202-331-8105
FAX: 202-296-0378
info@vma.org or jtibbs@vma.org
www.valvemagazine.com

William Sandler, President
Judy Tibbs, Associate Publisher
Genilee Parente, Senior Editor

Promotion of significance and application of US and Canadian manufactured industrial valves and actuators.
Quarterly Founded: 1969
Circulation: 25000
Printed in 4 colors on glossy stock

15593 World Industrial Reporter
Keller International Publishing Corporation
150 Great Neck Road
Great Neck, NY 11021-3309
516-299-9722
FAX: 516-829-5414
info@kellerpubs.com
http://www.kellerpubs.com

Bryan DeLuca, Editor
Terry Beirne, Publisher
Jerry Keller, President

New equipment, machinery and techniques for the industry.
34 pages Monthly Founded: 1882
Circulation: 37107

Trade Shows

15594 Association of Machinery and Equipment Appraisers Annual Conference
315 S Patrick Street
Alexandria, VA 22314-3501
703-836-7900
FAX: 703-836-9303 800-537-8629
amea@amea.org www.amea.org

Lorna Lindsey, Manager

Exhibits of interest to machinery and equipment appraisers.
Founded: 1982

15595 FloorTek
American Fllorcovering Alliance
210 West Cuyler Street
Dalton, GA 30720
706-278-4101
FAX: 706-278-5323 800-288-4101
afa@americanfloor.org
www.floor-tek.com

Wanda J Ellis, Executive Director
Amanda Mullins, Executive Assistant

Only international flooring manufacturing tradeshoq dedicated to the production and materials industry.
Oct 23-25 Georgia

15596 Gear Expo
American Gear Manufacturers Association
500 Montgomery Street
Suite 350
Alexandria, VA 22314-1581
703-684-0211
FAX: 703-684-0242
info@gearexpo.com
www.gearexpo.com

Kurt Medert, VP

Biennial trade show held in October of the odd-numbered years. It is the only trade show devoted exclusively to the Gear Manufacturing process.
4.5M Attendees October Founded: 1987

15597 International Integrated Manufacturing
Reed Exhibition Companies
255 Washington Street
Newton, MA 02458-1637
617-584-4900
FAX: 617-630-2222

Elizabeth Hitchcock, International Sales

Expo and conference dedicated to the products and technology needed by engineering operations and management to automate and integrate manufacturing.
March

15598 International Manufacturing Technology Show
7901 Westpark Drive
Mc Lean, VA 22102-4206
703-893-2900
FAX: 703-893-1151
www.amtonline.org

John Byrd, President
Peter Eelman, VP Exhibitions

Manufacturing equipment trade show.
85M Attendees Biennial Founded: 1927

15599 International Woodworking Machinery and Furniture Supply Fair: USA
Reed Exhibition Companies
1350 E Touhy Avenue
Des Plaines, IL 60018-3303
847-294-0300
FAX: 847-635-1571

Paul Pajor, National Marketing Manager

The largest woodworking machinery and furniture supply manufacturing exposition held in the Western Hemisphere. Exhibitors interface with North American furniture, cabinet, and woodworking manufacturers. One thousand booths.
37M Attendees August/Biennial

15600 Job Shop Show: Midwest
Edward Publishing LLC
16 Waterbury Road
Prospect, CT 06712-1215
203-758-6658
FAX: 203-758-4476
www.jobshoptechnology.com

Jennifer Bryda, Production Manager
Christoper Davis, Manager
Gerald Schmidt, President

A source for forming, fabricating, shaping, and assemblies. The show is designed to attract the highest caliber engineers and buyers from product manufacturers. There will be 170 exhibitors and booths.
1500 Attendees

15601 Powder and Bulk Solids Conference and Exhibition
Reed Exhibition Companies
255 Washington Street
Newton, MA 02458-1637
617-584-4900
FAX: 617-630-2222

Elizabeth Hitchcock, International Sales

Equipment and technology for processing and handling of powder and bulk solids.
8.4M Attendees May

15602 South-Tec Machine Tool and Manufacturing Show
Society of Manufacturing Engineers
1 SME Drive
#930
Dearborn, MI 48128-2408
313-271-1500
FAX: 313-271-2861 www.sme.org

Philip Trimble, Executive Director/General Manager

A professional society dedicated to advancing scientific knowledge in the field of manufacturing and to applying its resources for researching, writing, publishing and disseminating information.
70M Attendees March Founded: 1932

Directories & Databases

15603 American Machine Tool Distributors' Association Directory
1445 Research Bowl
Suite 450
Rockville, MD 20852-1421
301-738-1200

Greg Safko, Editor
Ralph Nappi, President

Directory of services and supplies to the industry. *$60.00*
150 pages Annual

15604 American Machinist Buyers' Guide

Penton Media
1300 E 9th Street
Cleveland, OH 44114
216-696-7000
FAX: 216-696-1752
information@penton.com
www.penton.com

Tom Grasson, Editor
Pat Smith, Managing Editor

Guide to over manufacturers of products and services used by metalworking industries. *$6.00*
Annual
Circulation: 80,000
Printed in 4 colors on glossy stock

15605 American Mold Builders Association
PO Box 404
Medinah, IL 60157-0404
630-980-7667
FAX: 630-980-9714 www.amba.org

Jeanette Bradley, Editor

Directory of services and supplies to the industry. *$25.00*
50 pages Annual

15606 American Textile Machinery Association Official Directory
111 Park Place
Falls Church, VA 22046-4513
703-538-1789

Harry Buzzerd, Management Counsel

Offers information on over 100 member textile machinery and accessory manufacturers.
100 pages

15607 Directory of Machine Tools and Manufacturing
Association for Manufacturing Technology

7901 Westpark Drive
Mc Lean, VA 22102-4206
703-893-2900
FAX: 703-893-1151
Machine tools and related products built by members of the Association for Manufacturing Technology.
Annual

15608 Equip-Mart
116 N Camp Street
Seguin, TX 78155
830-303-3328
FAX: 830-372-3011 800-864-1155
Directory of available used metalworking equipment.
Weekly

15609 High-Performance Composites
Ray Publishing
4891 Independence
Suite 270
Wheat Ridge, CO 80033
303-467-1776
FAX: 303-467-1777
www.compositesworld.com

Judith Hazen, Publisher/Editor
Mike Mussleman, Managing Editor

60 pages Founded: 1993
Printed in 4 colors on glossy stock

15610 ISA Directory
Instrumentation, Systems,and Automation Society
PO Box 12277
Durham, NC 27709-2277
919-549-8411
FAX: 919-990-9434 www.isa.org
Premier guide to instrumentation, systems and automation

Printed in 4 colors

15611 Industrial Machine Trader
Heartland Industrial Group
1003 Central Avenue
PO Box 1415
Fort Dodge, IA 50501
515-955-1600
FAX: 515-955-3753 800-247-2000
igproduction@industrialgroup.com
www.industrialgroup.com

Denise McLellan, Editor

Printed directory of available used metalworking equipment.
Weekly

15612 Locator Services
315 S Patrick Street
Alexandria, VA 22314-3501
703-836-9700
FAX: 703-836-7665 800-537-1446
sales@locatoronline.com
www.locatoronline.com

Terry J Pitman, Executive Publisher

Printed directory of available used metalworking equipment.
Monthly
Circulation: 225,000

15613 Machine Design Product Locator
Penton Media
1300 E 9th Street
Cleveland, OH 44114
216-696-7000
FAX: 216-696-1752
information@penton.com
www.penton.com

Joe DiFranco, Publisher
Jane Cooper, Marketing Manager

Directory of services and supplies to the industry. *$35.00*
325 pages Annual
Circulation: 180,000
Printed in 4 colors on glossy stock

15614 Metalworking Machinery Mailer
Tade Publishing Group
29501 Greenfield Road
Suite 120
Southfield, MI 48076
248-552-8583
FAX: 248-552-0466 800-966-8233

Tom Lynch, Editor

Printed directory of available used metalworking equipment.
Monthly

15615 Motion Control Technical Reference and Buyers Guide
ISA Services
PO Box 12277
Durham, NC 27709-2277
919-549-8411
FAX: 919-990-9434 www.isa.org
The most comprehensive reference source for motion control market
Founded: 2000
Printed in 4 colors

15616 Multimedia Monograph Series
SIGDA Multimedia

pedram@seng.usc.edu
http://atrak.usc.edu/~sigda-mm/

Massoud Pedram, Program Director

Set of electronic media publications focusing on key talks/presentations given at various ACM sponsored conferences over the last few years.

15617 Orion Blue Book: Tools
Orion Research Corporation
14555 N Scottsdale Road
Suite 330
Scottsdale, AZ 85254-3487
480-951-1114
FAX: 480-951-1117 800-844-0759
orion@bluebook.com
www.bluebook.com
Roger Rohrs, Owner
List of manufacturers of tools.
Annual

15618 Surplus Record Machinery & Equipment Directory
Thomas Scanlan
20 N Wacker Drive
Chicago, IL 60606-2806
312-372-9077
FAX: 312-372-6537
surplus@surplusrecord.com
www.surplusrecord.com
Thomas Scanlan, Editor
Listing over 55,000 items of used/surplus machine tools, machinery, electrical apparatus, and capital equipment by more than 1200 suppliers worldwide. *$33.00*
736 pages Monthly Magazine Founded: 1924
Circulation: 150000

15619 Used Machinery Buyer's Guide
Machinery Dealers National Association
315 S Patrick Street
Alexandria, VA 22314-3501
703-836-9300
FAX: 703-836-9303 800-872-7807
office@mdna.org www.mdna.org
Mark Robinson, Executive VP
Over 400 dealers in used capital equipment.
Annual, September

Industry Web Sites

15620 www.amea.org
Association of Machinery and Equipment Appraisers

Members are appraisers of the metalworking industry.

15621 www.americanfloor.org
American Floorcovering Alliance

Promotes the industry's products and services to the world, and educates the members and others through seminars, press releases, and trade shows.

15622 www.cemanet.org
Conveyor Equipment Manufacturers Association

Continues to be considered the resource for conveyor safety dimensional and application standards.

15623 www.fpmsa.org (or www.iefp.org)
Food Processing Machinery & Supplies Association

List of exhibitors from IEFP (links included).

15624 www.greyhouse.com
Grey House Publishing

Selected Grey House directories in the fields of business, health and education are available online. Users can search our online databases by several different search criteria, such as product categories, geographic area, sales volume and much, much more. Full Grey House catalog and online ordering also available.

15625 www.mdna.org
Machinery Dealers National Association

Represents dealers of used industrial equipment.

15626 www.ntma.org
National Tooling and Machining Association

For makers of jigs, molds, tools, gages, dies and fixtures for companies doing precision machining.

15627 www.packexpo.com
Packaging Machinery Manufacturers Institute (PMMI)

For manufacturers of packaging and packaging-related converting equipment.

15628 www.pmpa.org
Precision Machined Products Association

Member companies are producers of high precision component products. Provides educational opportunities for members, emphasizing quality assurance and emerging technologies.

15629 www.polysort.com
Polysort.com

Includes materials, machinery and equipment, processors and industry services.

15630 www.taol\fema.com
Fire Equipment Manufacturers' Association

Members are companies making devices that control or extinguish fires in residential or commercial buildings.

15631 www.vma.org
Valve Manufacturers Association of America

Associations

15632 AAHC American Association of Healthcare
5938 N Drake Avenue
Chicago, IL 60659
773-662-2770
FAX: 773-463-3552 888-350-2242
info@aahc.net www.aahc.net
Douglas R Rich, Chairman
Linda Campbell, Executive Director
To serve as the preeminent credentialing, professional and practice development organization for the healthcare consulting profession; to advance the knowledge, quality and standards of practice for consulting to management in the healthcare industry; and to enhance the understanding and image of the healthcare consulting profession and member firms among its various publics.
Founded: 1949

15633 AFSM International
1342 Colonial Boulevard
Suite D-25
Fort Myers, FL 33907
239-275-7887
FAX: 239-275-0794 800-333-9786
jschoenewald@afsmi.org
www.afsmi.org
Tom Schlick, President
John Schoenewald, CEO
Ms Nancy Alm, VP/Americas
Henrik Moeller-Christensen, VP/Europe/Middle East/Africa
Edina Sobaleski, Director at Large
A global organization dedicated to furthering the knowledge, understanding, and career development of executives, managers and professionals in the high-technology service industry.
5000 Members Founded: 1975

15634 APICS: Association for Operations Management
5301 Shawnee Road
Alexandria, VA 22312-2317
703-354-8851
FAX: 703-354-8106 800-444-2742
service@apicshq.org www.apics.org
Nicholas M Testa, President
Douglas Kelly, Publisher
Joseph Shedlawski, Secretary/Treasurer
Michael T Walsh, Executive Vice President
Ronald K Althaus, VP/Membership/Chapter Development
Provides lifelong learning for lifetime success. APICS certification programs, training tools and networking opportunities increase workplace performance. The society supports 60,000 members in 20,000 manufacturing and service industry companies worldwide.
80000 Members Founded: 1957

15635 ARMA International
13725 West 109th Street
Suite 101
Lenexa, KS 66215
913-341-3808
FAX: 913-341-3742 800-422-2762
hq@arma.org www.arma.org
Peter Hermann, CAE, Executive Dir/CEO
Susan Avery, Senior Strategic Advisor
Jody Becker, Assoc Editor/Professional Resources
Diane Carlisle, Director Professional Resources
Melissa Ebert, Program Manager
A not-for-profit association and the leading authority on managing records and information - papers and electronic. Valuable resources such as: legislative and regulatory updates, standards and best practices, technology trends, live and web based education, marketplace news and analysis, book and video on managing, global network of records and information management professionals.
Founded: 1955

15636 Adizes Network International
2815 E Valley Road
Santa Barbara, CA 93108
805-565-2901
FAX: 805-565-0741
adizes@adizes.com www.adizes.com
philip Friedman, CEO/President
Dr Ichak Adizes, Professional Director
James Zukin, Senior Managing Director
Promotes Adizes management consulting as a profession. Facilitates discussion of ideas and conducts lectures and seminars.
115 Members Founded: 1981

15637 Agile Enterprises
John Wiley & Sons
111 River Street
Hoboken, NJ 07030
201-748-6000
FAX: 201-748-6088 800-825-7550
customer@wiley.com www.wiley.com
Peter B Wiley, Chairman
William J Pesce, President/CEO
Ellis Cousens, Executive VP/CFO
William J Arlington, Senior VP/Human Resources
Timothy B King, Sr VP/Planning/Development
Provides information to help executives manage their companies effectively.

15638 American Academy of Medical Administrators
701 Lee Street
Suite 600
Des Plaines, IL 60016-4516
847-759-8601
FAX: 847-759-8602
info@aameda.org www.aameda.org
James G Easter, Jr, Chairman
Janet L Jones, Board Chair - Elect
Renee S Schleicher, President/CEO
Nancy L Anderson, VP/Finance/Administration
Yon Yetzer, Director/Membership/Communications
Department heads and administrators in areas of hospital and health administration.
Founded: 1957

15639 American Association of Industrial
1625 Prince Street
Alexandria, VA 22314-2818
703-519-6200
FAX: 703-519-6299 888-968-1968
asis@asisonline.org
www.asisonline.org
Daniel J Consalvo, CPP, President
Michael J Stack, Executive Director
Dedicated to better management and the overall objective which is the formulation of broad management principles and strategies that will insure successful management and promote the principles of free, private and competitive enterprise with individual opportunity and freedom under a constitutional government.
Founded: 1955

15640 American Management Association
1601 Broadway
New York, NY 10019
212-586-8100
FAX: 212-903-8168 800-262-9699
Edward T Reilly, President/CEO
Membership-based management development organization. AMA provides valuable and practical action-oriented learning programs to people at all levels, in all industries, from companies and agencies of all sizes. More than 500,000 AMA customers and members a year learn new skills and behaviors, gain more confidence, advance their careers through a wide range of seminars, conferences and executive forums, as well as publications, research, print and online self-study courses.
20000 Members Founded: 1923

15641 American Marketing Association
311 S Wacker Drive
Suite 5800
Chicago, IL 60606
312-542-9000
FAX: 312-542-9001 800-262-1150
Dennis Dunlap, CEO
AMA is a resource providing relevant marketing information that experienced marketers can turn to.
38000 Members

15642 American Productivity and Quality Center
123 N Post Oak Lane
Suite 300
Houston, TX 77024-7718
713-681-4020
FAX: 713-681-8578 cflett@apqc.org
C Jackson Grayson Jr, Founder/Chairman
Carla O'Dell, President
Seeks to improve productivity and the quality of work life in the United States. Works with businesses, unions, academics and government agencies to improve productivity and quality.
300 Members Founded: 1977

15643 American Small Businesses Association
206 E College
Grapevine, TX 76034-2663
817-488-8770
FAX: 817-251-8578 800-801-2722
Bill Hill Sr, President
Wanda Johnson, Bookkeeper
Represents the interests of small businesses.
10M Members Founded: 1975

15644 American Society for Engineering
2801 Park Center Drive
A-1603
Alexandria, VA 22302
703-364-4606
FAX: 703-995-0691
asemexec@earthlink.net
www.asem.org
John Fari, President
Michael Neff, Executive Director
Harold A Kurstedt, President - Elect
Seeks to advance engineering management in theory and practice. Strives to promote professionalism and maintain high standards.
1M Members Founded: 1979

15645 American Society for the Advancement of Project Management
6547 North Academy #404
Colorado Springs, CO 80918
931-647-7373
FAX: 719-487-0637
info@asapm.org www.asapm.org
Stacy Goff, Representative
Standards and guidelines to define the work of project management personnel. Requirements to standardize the norms are collection, process and then institutionalization of the applied competence with acceptable protocols in managing the work for optimization of output. This includes the knowledge, experience and attitude of the manpower involved in the handling the assigned project.

15646 American Society of Association Executives
1575 I Street NW
Washington, DC 20005-1105
202-262-2723
FAX: 202-408-9634
John Graham, President
Elissa Matulis Myers, VP/Publisher
24.5M Members Founded: 1920
Mailing list available for rent 100M names

15647 Association For Strategic Planning
12021 Welshire Boulevard
Los Angeles, CA 90025
877-816-2080
www.strategicplus.org
Janice Laureen, Executive Director

15648 Association for Information Management Professionals
13725 W 109th Street
Suite 101
Lenexa, KS 66215
913-341-3808
FAX: 913-341-3742 800-422-2762
hq@arma.org www.arma.org
Peter Hermann, Executive Director/CEO
Susan Avery, Sr Strategic Advisor/Exec Office
Jody Becker, Associate Editor
Marilyn Bier, Deputy Exec Dir/Education
Diane Carlisle, Director Professional Resources
A nonprofit association serving information management professionals.
10000 Members

15649 Association for Systems Management
24587 Bagley Road
Cleveland, OH 44138
216-671-1919
FAX: 440-234-2930
Paula Winrod, Public Communication
Offers seminars and conferences in all phases of business systems and management.
5M Members Founded: 1947

15650 Association for Worksite Health Promotion
60 Revere Drive
Suite 500
Northbrook, IL 60062-1577
847-480-9574
FAX: 847-480-9282
awhp@awhp.org www.awhp.org
Joseph E Samson, Executive Director
Rachael Riggs, Conference Manager
Exists to advance the profession of worksite health promotion and the career development of its practitioners and to improve the performance of the programs they administer. Represents a variety of disciplines and worksites, for decision makers in the areas of health promotion/disease prevention and health care cost management.
3000 Members

15651 Association of Executive and Administrativ e Professionals
900 S Washington Street
Suite G13
Falls Church, VA 22046-4009
703-237-8616
FAX: 703-533-1153
headquarters@naesaa.com
www.naesaa.com or www.theaeap.com
Ruth Ludeman, Director
Has helped thousands of administrative and secretarial professionals grow in their chosen careers, and supported their efforts at becoming the best that they can be. Strives to provide its members with a pathway for setting and achieving accomplishments of all types and at all levels. Publishes a newsletter 11 times per year.
10000 Members 11 X'S Year Founded: 1975
Circulation: 10,000
Mailing list available for rent 12000 names $135 per M.

15652 Association of Investment Management Sales Executives
1320 19th street
Suite 300
Washington, DC 20036-1636
202-296-3560
FAX: 202-371-8977 800-343-5659
nkraich@erols.com www.simse.com
Norbert Kraich, Executive Director
Pam Svendsen, Director/Meetings/Membership
Provides marketing and sales educational programs for its members.
1400 Members Founded: 1977

15653 Association of Management
920 S Battlefield Boulevard
Suite 100
Chesapeake, VA 23322
757-482-2273
FAX: 757-482-0325
aomgt@inter-source.org
www.aom-iaom.org
Dr William Arthur Hamel, Co-Founder/President
Karin Klenke, CEO
Mansour Olawale Jumaa, Health Care Management
Formerly the Association of Human Resources Management and Organizational Behavior (HRMOB).
3.5M Members Founded: 1979

15654 Association of Management Consulting Firms
380 Lexington Avenue
Suite 1700
New York, NY 10168
212-551-7887
FAX: 212-551-7934
info@amcf.org www.amcf.org
Peter Brown, Vice Chair
Elizabeth A Kovacs, CEO
Alan Andolsen, President
Samantha Colon, Executive Administrator
Kathleen Fish, Director Programs
Seeks to unite management consulting firms in order to develop and improve professional standards and practice in the field. Offers information and referral services on management consultants.
65 Members Founded: 1929

15655 Association of Professional Energy
3916 W Oak Street
Suite D
Burbank, CA 91505
818-972-2159
FAX: 818-972-2863
buschre@earthlink.net www.apem.org
John Sykes, Communications
Mark Martinez, Chair/Chapter Development
Bernell Loveridge, Chair/Treasurer
Lynne Eichner Kelley, Chair/Membership
Members include individuals responsible for energy production, consumption or management decisions.
1.5M Members Founded: 1982

15656 Athletic Equipment Managers Association
460 Hunt Hill Road
Freeville, NY 13068
607-539-6300
FAX: 607-539-6340
Dale Strauf, President
Jon Falk, Executive Director
Dino Dennis, VP
Suzette Madej, Treasurer
Dorothy Cutting, Manager
Represents those who manage and maintain an interest in athletic equipment.
700+ Members Founded: 1974

15657 Automotive Trade Association Executives
8400 Westpark Drive
Mc Lean, VA 22102-3522
703-821-7072
FAX: 703-556-8581
Jennifer Lindsey, Executive Director
Promotes interests of executives of state and local auto dealers associations.
106 Members

15658 Awards and Recognition Association
4700 W Lake Avenue
Glenview, IL 60025
847-375-4800
FAX: 877-734-9380 800-344-2148
info@ara.org www.ara.org
Fran Carville, President
Donna Pollucci, Secretary/Treasurer
Membership organization of 4,000 companies dedicated to increasing the professionalism of recognition specialists and advancing the awards and engraving industry.

15659 Best Employers Association
2505 McCabe Way
Irvine, CA 92614
949-253-4080
FAX: 949-553-0883 800-237-8543
info@bestlife.com
www.besthealthplans.com
Steve Course, President
Jennifer Bolton, Sales Account Manager
Ramon Duran, Sales Account Manager
Cristina Rios, Sales Account Manager

Dorothy Sehramm, Salews Account Manager

Providing group medical, dental, long-term disability, vision and life insurance to employers.

Founded: 1970

15660 Center For Third World Organizing
1218 East 21st Street
Oakland, CA 94606
510-533-7583
FAX: 510-533-0923

Danielle Mahones, Executive Director
Jackie Byers, Program Director/Trainer

A national organization of books, periodicals and audiovisuals on transnational corporations and labor issues.

15661 Center for Breakthrough Thinking
PO Box 18012
Los Angeles, CA 90018
213-740-6415
FAX: 213-740-1120
info@breakthroughthinking.com
www.breakthroughthinking.com

Dr Gerald Nadler, President
Dr William Chandon, VP
Steven S Benson, VP/Development

Organized to promote and institutionalize the teaching and application of Breakthrough Thinking in universities, corporations and governments for solving problems, leveraging opportunities, and achieving change.

15 Members Founded: 1989

15662 Center for Creative Leadership
One Leadership Place
PO Box 26300
Greensboro, NC 27410-6300
336-887-7210
FAX: 336-282-3284
info@leaders.ccl.org www.ccl.org

Thomas K Hearn Jr, Chairman
John Alexander, President

An international, nonprofit educational institution devoted to behavioral science research, executive development and leadership education.

Founded: 1970

15663 Center for Management Effectiveness
15237 Sunset Boulevard
Pacific Palisades, CA 90272
310-454-2754
FAX: 310-459-9307
info@cmeinc.org www.cmeinc.org

Jerry Feist, President
Ron Smith, General Manager
Rob Wood, Publications Director
Sam Erdman, Manager Information Systems
Christie Randolph, Management Consultants

Conducts management training programs and publishes self-scoring inventories, trainer guides and workbooks on stress management, resolution of conflict, risk taking, decision making and building managerial skills.

Founded: 1981

15664 Center for Management Systems
PO Box 159
Akron, IA 51001-0159

FAX: 712-568-3427

Provides specialized education to improve management skills.

70M Members Founded: 1978

15665 Christian Management Association
635 Camino Be Los Mares
Suite 205
San Clemente, CA 92673-4090
949-487-0900
FAX: 949-487-0927
cma@cmaonline.org
www.cmaonline.org

John Pearson, President/CEO
Dick Bahruth, Senior Consultant
Sandy Huston, Member Services Manager
Joe Voorhies, Director Business Development
Charles S Blake, Director Finance

Designed to assist those involved in the management of Christian organizations.

3500+ Members Founded: 1976

15666 Club Managers Association of America
1733 King Street
Alexandria, VA 22314
703-739-9500
FAX: 703-739-0124
cmaa@cmaa.org www.cmaa.org

Jesse Thorpe, President
William Wagner, VP
Burton Ward, Secretary/Treasurer
Linda Carroll, Director
James B Singerling, Executive Committee

Supports the club management profession. Sponsors research, funds industry, education programs, provides financial assistance to educational institutes and awards scholarships to outstanding students interested in club management operations.

5M Members

15667 Data Processing Sciences Corporation
10810 Kenwood Road
Cincinnati, OH 45242
513-791-7100

info@dpsciences.com
www.dpsciences.com

Scott Nesbitt, CEO
Kurt Loock, President

DPS delivers solutions that simplify and manage technology for our clients so they can aggressively pursue their strategic business goals.

15668 Decision Sciences Institute
University Plaza
Atlanta, GA 30303
404-651-4000
FAX: 404-651-2804

Lee Krajewski, Publisher

Scientific quantitative, behavioral and computational approaches to decision making.

15669 Diversified Business Communications
121 Free Street
Portland, ME 04112-7437
207-842-5500
FAX: 207-842-5503
custserv@divcom.com
www.divbusiness.com

Nancy Hasselback, President/CEO
Brian Perkins, Executive VP/COO
Terry Baldwin, VP/CIO
Vicki Hennin, VP Marketing Communications
Tom Tomczyk, VP/Business Development

Has over 30 years of experience as trade magazine publishers and exhibition organizers. Provides exposition management services for associations and organizations seeking to expand domestically and overseas, as well as direct mail, internet, telemarketing campaigns and market research.

Founded: 1949

15670 Employers Group
1150 S Olive Street
Suite 2300
Los Angeles, CA 90015-2237
213-748-0421
FAX: 213-742-0301

William Dahlman, President

Aims to provide human resources management, management counseling and educational programs. Offers unemployment insurance services, and workers compensation programs.

3.9M Members

15671 Employers of America
PO Box 1874
Mason City, IA 50402-1874
641-424-3187
FAX: 641-424-3187 800-728-3187
employer@employerhelp.org
www.employerhelp.org

Jim Collison, President

Provides information and guidance to employers, managers and supervisors on Human Resources topics.

Founded: 1976

15672 Financial Management Association Internati
4202 East Fowler Avenue
BSN 3331
Tampa, FL 33620
813-974-2084
FAX: 813-974-3318 www.fma.org

Jennifer Conrad, President
William Megginson, VP/Financial Education
Ronald Watson, VP/Practitioner Service
Jack Rader, Executive Director

Global leader in developing and disseminating knowledge about financial decision making. Members include finance practitioners and academicians and students who are interested in the techniques and advances which define the field of finance.

Founded: 1970

15673 Floodplain Management Association
PO Box 712080
Santee, CA 92072-2080
619-204-4380
FAX: 619-749-9524 www.floodplain.org

Lovanka Todt, Manager

A nonprofit educational association established to promote the reduction of flood losses and to encourage the protection and enhancement of natural floodplain values through the use of effective wetland management strategies and engineering technologies.

Founded: 1990

15674 Freestanding Insert Council of North America
4700 West Lake Avenue
Glenview, IL 60025
847-375-4700
FAX: 888-828-1777
Mark Engle, Executive Officer

15675 Fulfillment Management Association
60 E 42nd Street
Suite 1166
New York, NY 10165
212-771-1530
FAX: 303-604-7840
thefurymonster@hotmail.com
www.fmanational.org
Nicole Bowman, President
Heather Holmes, VP
Corey Folta, Treasurer
Lynn Reinicke, Chairman
Deb Jackson, Contact
Educates, updates and maintains high standards of service in operations management and customer service. Sponsors four seminars per year. Members are direct mail fullfillment, marketing and circulation executives.
425 Members Founded: 1945

15676 IAHCSMM
213 W Institute Place
Suite 307
Chicago, IL 60610
312-440-0078
FAX: 312-440-9474 800-962-8274
mailbox@iahcsmm.com
www.iahcsmm.com
Don Gordon, President
Lisa Huber, Secretary/Treasurer
Betty Hanna, Executive Director
Ed Baker, SP/Manager
Lori Patterson, SP/Manager
Membership consists of persons serving in a technical, supervisory or management capacity in hospital central service departments responsible for the sterilization management and distribution of supplies.
9000 Members Founded: 1958 9000 names $250 per M.

15677 Industrial Asset Management Council
6625 The Corners Parkway
Suite 200
Norcross, GA 30092
770-325-3461
FAX: 770-263-8825 www.iamc.org
World's leading associates of industrial asset management and corporate real estate executives, their supplies and service providers and economic developers.
135 Members Founded: 1963

15678 Industry Coalition on Technology Transfer
1400 L Street NW
Suite 800
Washington, DC 20005
202-715-5700
Eric L Hirschhorn, Executive Secretary
Karen L Grubber, Deputy Executive Secretary
J Michael McGarry III, Counsel
Coalition of major high technology trade associations concerned with the US Government export controls. Monitors and addresses federal regulations on technology transfer.
10 Members Founded: 1983

15679 Information Resources Management Association
701 E Chocolate Avenue
Suite 200
Hershey, PA 17033
717-533-8879
FAX: 717-533-8661
member@irma-international.org
www.irma-international.org
Mehdi Khosrow-Pour, President
Muhammad Al-Khaldi, Executive Council
An international professional organization dedicated to advancing the concepts and practices of information resources management in modern organizations.

15680 Institute of Management Accountant
10 Paragon Drive
Montvale, NJ 07645-1718
201-739-9000
800-638-4427
Kathy Williams, Editor in Chief
Paul Sharman, President
A subunit of the Institute of Management Accountants, with a network of 3,000 controllers incorporating newsletters and seminars.
1.2M Members Founded: 1990

15681 Institute of Management Consultants - USA
2025 M Street NW
Suite 800
Washington, DC 20036
202-367-1134
FAX: 202-367-2134 800-221-2557
norm@ecksteinconsult.com
www.imcusa.org
Dr Baldwin H Tom, Chairman
Mark R Hoos, Vice Chair
Vito Tanzi, Vice Chair
Michael D Wheeler, Vice Chair
Gaylen Camera, Executive Director
IMC is the leading association representing management consultants in the United States, organized to establish consulting as a self-regulating profession, meriting public confidence and respect. Toward the achievement of this goal IMC awards the international appelation CMC for certified management consultants.

15682 Institute of Management and Administration
3 Park Avenue
30th Floor
New York, NY 10016
212-244-0360
FAX: 212-564-0465
subserve@ioma.com www.ioma.com
Joe Berman, President
Perry Patterson, VP
Brady Pickar, Director/Research
Assists members in management of corporate accounting to boost staff productivity, reduce operation costs, adopt new technology, take charge of their dealing with auditors and lenders and more.

15683 International Council for Small Business
Goerge Washington University
2201 G Street NW
Suite 315
Washington, DC 20052
202-944-0704
FAX: 202-994-4930
icsb@gwu.edu www.icsb.org
Colin Dunn, President
Zulma Quinones, President - Elect
Annette St Onge, VP/Finance/Control
Susan Dubby, Executive Director
Management development.
2000+ Members Founded: 1956

15684 International Council of Management Consulting Institutes
858 Longview Road
Burlingame, CA 94010-6974
650-342-2250
icmci@icmci.org www.icmci.org
Camera Gaylen, Executive Director
Michael Shays, Manager
John Roethle, Advisory Council
The global association of management consultants. The members of ICMCI are national institutes from around the world that certify professional management consultants. The ICMCI maintains an international code of professional conduct, an international uniform body of knowledge, and strict standards for certification and reciprocity between nations. It promotes professional development and networking between consultants and the highest standards of performance for clients.
39 Members Founded: 1987

15685 International Facility Management Associat
1 E Greenway Plaza
Suite 1100
Houston, TX 77046
713-623-4362
FAX: 713-623-6124
webmaster@ifma.org www.ifma.org
Joseph M Dawson, Chair
David Brady, President
Teena G Shouse, CFM/First VP
John McGee, Chief Operating Officer
Jeffrey M Woolf, Executive Director
To provide exceptional products, services, and opportunities that support and advance the facility management profession.

15686 International Personal Management Association
1617 Duke Street
Alexandria, VA 22314-3406
703-549-7100
FAX: 703-684-0948
ipma@ipma-hr.org www.ipma-hr.org
Neil E Reichenberg, Executive Director
Sima Hassassian, COO
Elizabeth Kirkland, Publications Manager
Shannon Adaway, Director Professional Development
Christina Cheappetta, Director Governmant Affairs
Human resource professionals, representing the interests of over 6,000 individual and 1,300 agency members, at the federal, state and local levels of government. Promotes excellence in human resource management through the ongoing development of professional and ethical standards, and through its publishing and educational training programs.

6M Members Founded: 1973

15687 Issues Management Association
1785 Massachusetts Avenue NW
Suite 501
Washington, DC 20036-2104
202-667-5244

Rebecca Klemm, President

Seeks to enhance members skills in organizational opportunities and in planning strategies to influence external events on international objectives.
400 Members Founded: 1982

15688 Latino American Management Association
PO Box 70561
Washington, DC 20024-0561
866-526-2123
FAX: 202-546-3807
lamausa@bellatlantic.net
www.lamausa.com

Steve Denhrgry, Manager

Promotes the interests of Hispanic and other minority-owned business firms through marketing and procurement information, education and training activities, publications, advocacy initiatives, outreach programs, and electronic bulletin board services.
2.5M Members Founded: 1972

15689 Life Office Management Association
2300 Windy Ridge Parkway
Suite 600
Atlanta, GA 30339-8443
770-951-1770
FAX: 770-984-0441 800-968-1738
marketing@loma.org www.loma.org

Thomas P Donaldson, President/CEO

Insurance worldwide association of insurance companies specializing in research and education.
1250 Members Founded: 1924

15690 Lippincott Mercer
499 Park Avenue
New York, NY 10022
212-521-0000
FAX: 212-308-8952 info@lm.mmc.com

Richard Wilke, Senior Partner

Image management.

15691 Medical Group Management Association
104 Inverness Ter E
Englewood, CO 80112-5313
303-799-1111
FAX: 303-643-4493 877-275-6462
sat@mgma.com www.mgma.com

William Jessee, Executive Director/CEO
Brenda Hull, Editor

The oldest and largest professional membership association dedicated to medical practice management. Serves their members by offering timely and relevant networking and educational opportunities that keep the members up-to-date on the practice management field.
18M Members Founded: 1926
Mailing list available for rent 1M names

15692 National Association Executive Club
1300 L Street NW
Suite 1050
Washington, DC 20005-4107
202-043-3001
FAX: 202-783-4410

Steven Fier, Secretary
Angela West, Manager

Provides networking services and facilities.

500 Members Founded: 1953

15693 National Association for the Self-Employed
PO Box 612067
DFW Airport, TX 75261
214-614-4990
800-232-6273

Robert Hughes, President

Goal is to promote small business growth through education and discounts earned through NASE negotiating power.
225M Members Founded: 1981

15694 National Association of Corporate Directors
2 Lafayette Centre
1133 21st Street NW/Suite 700
Washington, DC 20036
202-775-0509
FAX: 202-775-4857
info@nacdonline.org
www.nacdonline.org

Larry Gage, President/CEO
Peter R Gleason, COO/Director Research
Doreen Kelly Ruyak, VP/Marketing

A national non-profit membership organization dedicated exclusively to serving the corporate governance needs of corporate boards and individual board members.
15500 Members Founded: 1977

15695 National Association of Private Enterprise
4100 S Medford
Lufkin, TX 75901
817-244-4460
FAX: 817-332-4525 800-223-6273
Informative articles for small business owners.
12 Members Founded: 1984

15696 National Association of Service Managers
PO Box 250796
Milwaukee, WI 53225
414-466-6060
FAX: 414-466-0840 www.nasm.com

Ken Cook, Treasurer

Service manager association for professional development
100 Members Founded: 1955

15697 National Business Owners Association
1200 18th Street NW
Washington, DC 20036-2513
202-839-9000

Ed Bolen, President

A non-profit organization representing small business owners' interests and offers several money-saving services, valuable benefits and assistance.
4.5M Members Founded: 1986

15698 National Businesswomens Leadership Association
6901 Shawnee Mission Parkway
Shawnee Mission, KS 66202-4009
913-432-7755
FAX: 913-432-0824

Linda Truitt, President

Offers seminars and workshops on business related issues.
Founded: 1985

15699 National Businesswomens' Leadership
West 63rd Street
Shawnee Mission, KS 66202
913-432-7755
FAX: 913-432-0824 800-258-7546
cstserv@natsem.com
www.natsem.com

Diane Macpherson, Director
Fr Edward Kinerk, President
Mark Truitt, Chief Executive Officer

Offers seminars and workshops on business related issues.
Founded: 1986

15700 National Committee for Quality Assurance
2000 L Street NW
Suite 500
Washington, DC 20036-4918
202-556-6428
FAX: 202-955-3599 www.ncpanet.org

Margaret O'Kane, President

Independent, non profit organization dedicated to assessing and reporting on the quality of managed care plans.

15701 National Conference of Personal Managers
964 2nd Avenue
New York, NY 10022-6304
212-421-2670
FAX: 212-838-5105
webmaster@wwmgmt.com

Clinton Ford Billups Jr, National President
Jack Rollins, National First VP
Stanley Evans, National Second VP

A personal manager is engaged in the occupation of advising and counseling talent and personalities in the enternainment industry. personal managers have the expertis to find and develop new talent and create opportunities for those artists which they represent.

15702 National Contract Management Association
8260 Greensboro Drive
Suite 200
McLean, VA 22102
571-382-0082
FAX: 703-448-0939 800-344-8096
memberservices@ncmahq.org
www.ncmahq.org

Neal Couture, Executive Director

Concerned with various forms of contracting with federal, state and local government and industry.
20000 Members Founded: 1959

15703 National Employee Services and Recreation Association
Employee Services Management Association
568 Spring Road
Suite D
Elmhurst, IL 60126-3896
630-559-0020
FAX: 630-559-0025
esmahq@esmassn.org
www.esmassn.org

Pud Belek, President

Manufacturers and distributors offering products and services for employee discount programs and employee store merchandise to members.

15704 National Federation of Independent
150 W 20th Avenue
San Mateo, CA 94403
415-341-7441

Principal focus is on legislative relations and research.
60000 Members Founded: 1943

15705 National Institute of Business Management
1750 Old Meadow Road
McLean, VA 22102-4304
703-058-8000

Steve Sturm, President

Career guidance for managers and executives.

15706 National Institute of Management
PO Box 220193
Great Neck, NY 11022-0193
516-482-5683

Strives to improve standards through research and industry studies.
250 Members Founded: 1955

15707 National Management Association
2210 Arbor Boulevard
Dayton, OH 45439
937-940-0421

nma@nma1.org www.nma1.org

William T Mahaffey, Chairman
Wendell M Pichon, Vice Chairman
Daniel R Robertson, Chairman
Doug Shaw, Manager

Seeks to develop and recognize management as a profession and to promote the free enterprise system.
22000 Members Founded: 1925

15708 National Research Bureau
320 Valley Street
Burlington, IA 52601
319-752-5415
FAX: 319-752-3421
national@willinet.net

Diane Darnall, Owner

National organization focusing on practical tried and true selling techniques authored by selling professionals. Excellent for sales force training.
2 Members Founded: 1991

15709 National Small Business United
1156 15th Street NW
Suite 1100
Washington, DC 20005-1755
202-293-8830
FAX: 202-872-8543
nsbu@nsbu.org www.nsbu.org

Todd McCracken, President
David Mack, Government Affairs Manager
Molly Brogala, Government Affairs Manager

Merged with Small Business United in 1986 and sponsors and supports the NSBU Political Action Committee.

15710 National Training Systems Association
2111 Wilson Boulevard
Suite 400
Arlington, VA 22201
703-247-9471
FAX: 703-243-1659
prowe@ndia.org
www.trainingsystems.org

Fred L Lewis, President
Patrick Rowe, Director/Membership Services
Barbara McDaniel, Director/Conferences/Programs
Debbie Langelier, Director/Exhibits

Represents companies in the simulation and training and training support industry. Provides forums, market surveys, and business development information and other services to members.
944 Members Founded: 1988

15711 Newspaper Association Managers
New England Press Association
70 Washington Street
Salem, MA 01970-3518
978-744-8940
FAX: 978-744-0333

Bob New, Owner
Morley Piper, Executive Director

Executives of state, regional, national and international newspaper associations.
65 Members Founded: 1923

15712 Operations Management Society
5400 Bosque Boulevard
Waco, TX 76710-4414
254-752-6315
FAX: 254-776-3767

Helen Schneider Lemay, Executive Director

Members are senior management and deans of business schools in the field of operations management.

15713 Organization Development Institute
11234 Walnut Ridge Road
Chesterland, OH 44026-1240
440-729-9314
FAX: 440-729-9319
www.odinstitute.org

Dr. Donald W Cole RODC, President
Ted Nguyen, VP

Promotes the understanding of organization development and offers three categories of membership: professional consultant, regular and student. Offers the International Registry of O.D. Professionals and O.D. Handbook which lists names, addresses and E-mail addresses, publishes a monthly newsletter plus a quarterly journal of 100-150 pages. There are two conferences held every year, one in the USA and one International.
500 Members Founded: 1968 8000 names $200 per M.

15714 Paper Industry Management Association
4700 W Lake Avenue
Glenview, IL 60025-1485
847-375-6860
FAX: 877-527-5973
info@pimaweb.org
www.pimaweb.com

Ralph W Feck, President
Terry M Gallagher, Regional VP
Jim Weir, Executive VP/COO
Julie Weldon, Senior Manager
Patrick Andrus, Marketing Coordinator

Contributes to the strength of the international pulp and paper community by providing the means for our members to address relevant industry issues and to develop their management and leadership skills.
4500 Members Founded: 1919
Mailing list available for rent 4.6M names

15715 Product Development and Management
15000 Commerce Parkway
Suite C
Mount Laurel, NJ 08054
856-439-9052
FAX: 856-439-0525 800-232-5241
pdma@pdma.org www.pdma.org

Bob Brentin, President
Hansa Thota, President - Elect
Mark Atkins, VP/Marketing
Melissa Baldwin, Director
Tony DiBeneditto, Editor

Provides essential information to help foster new product development, giving an overview of the total product innovation process and presenting the latest advancements in product innovation. Also assists managers in innovating and producing products more effectively and efficiently.
Founded: 1976

15716 Professional Convention Management
2301 S Lake Shore Drive
Suite 1001
Chicago, IL 60616
312-423-7262
FAX: 312-423-7222 877-827-7262
administration@pcma.org
www.pcma.org

Gregg H Talley, Chairman
Leigh Wintz, Chairman - Elect
Deborah Sexton, President/CEO
Sharon D Delabarre, Secretary/Treasurer

Nonprofit, international association of professionals in the meeting industry whose mission is to deliver breakthrough education and promote the value of professional convention management.
Founded: 1957

15717 Professional Managers Association
PO Box 77235
Washington, DC 20013
202-440-0263
FAX: 202-874-1739
info@promanager.org
www.promanager.org

Tom Burger, National President
Shar Turner, National VP
Catherine Lunderville, National Treasurer
Joe Page, National Secretary

National membership asociation representing the interests of professional managers, management officials and non-bargaining unit employees in the federal government. Promote leadership and management excellence within the federal services.
10000 Members Founded: 1981

15718 Project Management Institute (PMI)
4 Campus Boulevard
Newtown Square, PA 19073-3299
610-356-4600
FAX: 610-356-4647
pmihq@pmi.org www.pmi.org
Louis J Mercken, Chairman
Iain Fraser, Vice Chair
Terrance G Warren, Secretary/Treasurer
Gregory Balistrero, CEO
Fosters recognition of the need for project management professionalism. Offers professional certification and bestows awards.
105M Members Founded: 1969
Mailing list available for rent

15719 Radiology Business Management Association
8001 Irvine Center Drive
Suite 1060
Irvine, CA 92618-3263
949-497-8864

info@rbma.org www.rbma.org
Sharon Urch, CEO
Cynthia G Waystack, President
Patrick L Epting, President - Elect
Daphne Brown, Marketing Director
Julie Pham, Membership/General Information
Promotes management education and study of practice economics, legislative issues and consumer trends.
1600 Members Founded: 1968

15720 SHRM Society for Human Resource Management
1800 Duke Street
Alexandria, VA 22314
703-548-3440
FAX: 703-535-6490 800-283-7476
bobgonz@us.ibm.com www.shrm.org
Johnny C Taylor, Chairman
Susan Meisenger, President/CEO
Robert O Gonzales, Secretary
Robb E Van Cleave, Treasurer
World's largest association devoted to human resource management. Serves the needs of the human resource management professional by providing the most essential and comprehensive set of resources available.
18500 Members Founded: 1948

15721 Section for Women in Public Administration
American Society for Public Administration
1120 G Street NW
Washington, DC 20005-3801
202-393-7878
FAX: 202-638-4952
www.cid,unomaha.edu/~wwwpa
Toni Samuel, Executive Director
Linda Lazer, Section Chair
Develops programs and projects which promote the full participation and recognition of women in all levels and areas of public service.
400 Members Founded: 1982
Mailing list available for rent 400 names

15722 Small Business Assistance Center
119 E Locust Lane
Kennett Square, Pa 19348
610-441-1720
FAX: 610-444-1724
inquire@sbacnetwork.org
www.sbacnetwork.org
Frank Farmer Jr, Executive Director
Provides information and assistance to small businesses. To train and consult entrepreneurs through information services, seminars and professional consultations.
Founded: 1988

15723 Society for Advancement of Management
Corpus Christi - College of Business
6300 Ocean Drive - FC 111
Corpus Christi, TX 78412
361-825-6045
FAX: 361-825-2725
moustafa@cob.tamucc.edu
www.cob.tamucc.edu/sam
Moustafa H Abdelsamad, President/CEO
Mervat Abdelsamad, VP Sales/Marketing
Sponsors conferences, study groups, seminars and special programs on economics, material handling, distribution, industrial relations and operating small business.
5000 Members Founded: 1912

15724 Strategic Management Association
19102 South Blackhawk Parkway
Unit 25
Mokena, IL 60448-4066
815-806-4908

slfmcb@telus.net
www.strategicleadershipforum.org
Chris Glatz, Executive Director/Administration
The international society for strategic management and planning. Presents awards, conducts seminars and foundation research.

6.5M Members Founded: 1985

15725 Support Services Alliance
107 Prospect Street
Schoharie, NY 12157-0130
518-295-7966
800-322-3920
membershipservices@ssamembers.com
www.ssainfo.com
Steven Cole, President
Multi-state membership organization that provides cost-savings services and legislative representation for small businesses and the self-employed. Also offers services to the memberships of more than 100 affiliated state, regional and national associations.
50 Members Founded: 1977

15726 Turnaround Management Association
100 S. Wacker Drive
Suite 850
Chicago, IL 60606
312-578-6900
FAX: 312-578-8336
ldelgadillo@turnaround.org
www.turnaround.org
Bill Skelly, President
Colin Cross, Chairman
Linda Delgadillo, Executive Director
The only international nonprofit association dedicated to corporate renewal and turnaround management. TMA's 7,300 members in 36 regional chapters comprise a professional community of turnaround practitioners, attorneys, accountants, investors, lenders, venture capitalists, appraiser, liquidators, executive recruiters and consultants. Three international conferences each year offer networking anf educational sessions on the latest trends and best practices in the restructuring field.
7300 Members Founded: 1988

15727 WACRA: World Association for Case Method Research & Application
23 Mackintosh Avenue
Needham, MA 02492-1218
781-444-8982
FAX: 781-444-1548
wacra@rcn.com www.wacra.org
Dr Hans E Klein, President/Executive Director
Dr Joelle Piffault, Director/Development/Membership
Dr Pavel Zufan, Director/Business/Economics
Dr Keith Martin, Director/Communications
Dr Pierre Mora, Director/Marketing
Members are professional and academicians with an interest in the use of the case method in teaching, training and planning. Interactive, innovative teaching and learning methods.
2000 Members Founded: 1984

15728 Women in Management
PO Box 1032
Dundee, IL 60118-9560
877-946-6285
FAX: 847-683-3751
nationalwim@aol.com
www.wimonline.org
Trish Peterser, President
K L Robertson, VP Membership
Sharon Nelson, VP Events
Sheila Mack, Treasurer
Karenn Schwartz, Awards Chairman
Aims to promote self-growth in management. Sponsors speakers and discussion groups.
1.7M Members Founded: 1976

15729 Young Presidents' Organization
451 Decker Drive
Suite 200
Irving, TX 75062-3954
972-650-4600
800-773-7976
David Martin, CEO
Les Ward, Manager
Members are corporate presidents under the age of fifty whose companies employ at least fifty employees.
8000 Members Founded: 1950

Newsletters

15730 American Academy of Medical Administration Executive Newsletter
701 Lee Street
Suite 600
Des Plaines, IL 60016-4516
847-759-8601
FAX: 847-759-8602
Thomas O'Donovan, Publisher
Renee Schleichar, Chief Executive Officer

Offers information and news to upper level administration of hospitals and medical institutions.

14 pages BiWeekly

15731 Best Practices Report
Management Roundtable
92 Crescent Street
Waltham, MA 02453
781-891-8080
FAX: 781-398-1889 800-338-2223
info@roundtable.com
www.managementroundtable.com

Alex Cooper, Publisher

A monthly newsletter on the best practices in product development. How to develop and deliver great products at the lowest cost in the shortest time.

15732 Better Supervision
Economics Press
12 Daniel Road
Fairfield, NJ 07004-2565
973-227-1224
FAX: 973-227-9742

Robert Guder, Publisher

Techniques for managing people successfully. *$1.00*

Circulation: 43,000

15733 Better Work Supervisor
Clement Communications
Concord Industrial Park
Concordville, PA 19331
610-459-4200
FAX: 610-459-0936
Offers important information, articles and news to upper level management. *$48.50*

15734 Blue Ribbon Service
Economics Press
12 Daniel Road
Fairfield, NJ 07004-2565
973-227-1224
FAX: 973-227-9742

Robert Guder, Publisher

Shows employees the importance of giving good customer service and methods of providing that service.

Circulation: 27,760

15735 Bridging the Gap
Section for Women in Public Administration
1120 G Street NW
Suite 700
Washington, DC 20005-3885
202-393-7878
FAX: 202-638-4952
info@aspanet.org
http://www.aspanet.org

Michelle Saint, Editor
Claire Felbinger, Chairman

Founded: 1939
Circulation: 400
Mailing list available for rent 400 names

15736 Bulletin to Management
Bureau of National Affairs
1231 25th Street NW
Washington, DC 20037-1197
202-452-4200
800-372-1033
customercare@bna.com
http://www.bna.com

Gregory C McCaffery, Publisher
Leslie Goldman, Managing Editor

Features summaries of current developments in human resource/personnel management and labor relations. Discusses real life job situations and provides policy guides on how companies have successfully handled employee related problems. Recurring features include statistics. *$317.00*
Weekly Founded: 1929

15737 Business Journal
Business Journals of North Carolina
120 W Morehead Street
Suite 200
Charlotte, NC 28202
704-472-2340
FAX: 704-973-1102 800-948-5323
charlotte@bizjournals.com
http://www.bizjournals.com/charlotte

Jeannie Falknor, Publisher
Robert Morris, Editor
David Harris, Managing Editor

72 pages Weekly
Printed in 4 colors on newsprint stock

15738 Business & Technology Briefings
Association for Entrepreneurial Growth
PO Box 875
Merrimack, NH 03054
603-429-1631
FAX: 603-424-8641 gouldnc@aol.com

Neil C Gould, Executive Director

For individuals and businesses in the finance and private capital markets as well as professionals who support business development and growth. Profiles businesses and technologies that will impact the 21st century.
15 pages Monthly

15739 Business Courier
101 W 7th Street
Cincinnati, OH 45202
513-621-6665
FAX: 513-621-2462 800-767-3263
cincinnati@bizjournals.com
http://www.bizjournals.com/cincinnati/

Richard Curtis, Senior Managing Editor
Doug Bolton, Publisher
Rob Daumeyer, Editor *$83.00*

Weekly Founded: 1947
Circulation: 11000

15740 Case Strategies
Cutter Information Corporation
37 Broadway
Suite 1
Arlington, MA 02474
781-648-8700
FAX: 781-648-1950 800-888-8939
service@cutter.com
http://www.cutter.com/

Paul Harman, Editor
Kim Leonard, Customer Service Director
Karen Coburn, CEO/President

Objective, timely information to help you successfully integrate CASE into your organization. *$387.00*
16 pages Monthly Founded: 1986

15741 Cash Flow Enhancement Report
Institute of Management & Administration
29 W 35th Street
5th Floor
New York, NY 10001-2221
212-244-0360
FAX: 212-564-0465

Tim Harris, Editor
Perry Patterson, Publisher

Focuses on business strategies for increasing liquidity. *$245.00*
16 pages Monthly

15742 Center for Creative Leadership Newsletter
Center for Creative Leadership
Attn: Client Services
PO Box 26300
Greensboro, NC 27438-6300
336-887-7210
FAX: 336-282-3284
info@leaders.ccl.org
http://www.ccl.org

Walter Ulmer Jr, Publisher
John Alexander, President

A newsletter featuring issues and observations on the behavioral science research and development field.
Monthly Founded: 1970
Circulation: 35000

15743 Chief Executive Officers Newsletter
Center for Entreprenuel Management
47 West Street
Suite 5C
New York, NY 10014-4606
212-633-0060
FAX: 212-633-0063
main@ceoclubs.org
http://www.ceoclubs.org/

Joseph Mancuso, Publisher
Christopher Jones, Office Manager

Unique management insights and sources for presidents of growing businesses. *$71.00*
Monthly Founded: 1978
Circulation: 40000

15744 Communications Insights
Comquest
112 Schubert Drive
Downingtown, PA 19335-3382
610-269-2100
FAX: 610-269-2275

Mark Schubert, Publisher

Tips and techniques for sucessful communication.

15745 Contractor's Business Management Report
Institute of Management & Administration
3 Park Avenue
30th Floor
New York, NY 10016-2299
212-244-0360
FAX: 212-564-0465
subserve@ioma.com
http://www.ioma.com

Donis Ford, Editor
Lee Rath, Publisher
William Allen, Managing Director
Brad Pickar, Director of Research and Advisory S

Shows you how to increase profitablity, maintain positive cash flow, find new projects in soft markets and more. Offers practical guidance on salary levels for management staff, construction bonds, purchasing equipment and more. *$269.00*
20 pages Monthly Founded: 1985

15746 Corporate EFT Report
Phillips Publishing
7811 Montrose Road
Suite 2
Potomac, MD 20854-3394
301-340-2100
FAX: 301-424-4297

Ellen Hamm, Publisher

Newsletter on business, EFT operations for corporate cash managers.

15747 Corporate Examiner
Interfaith Center on Corporate Response
Room 1842
475 Riverside Drive
New York, NY 10115
212-870-2295
FAX: 212-870-2023
info@iccr.org http://www.iccr.org
Timothy Smith, Publisher
Diane Bratcher, Editor
Analyzes corporate social responsibility issues and trends, reports corporate action news, reviews publications and media and presents the ideas and opinions of leaders of the corporate social responsibility movement. *$35.00*
8 pages Founded: 1981
Circulation: 1500 Audited Est. Pass-Along Circ: 5000
Printed in 1 color on matte stock

15748 Cost Controller
Siefer Consultants
PO Box 1384
Storm Lake, IA 50588-1384
712-732-7340
FAX: 712-732-7906
Dan Siefer, Publisher
Cost cutting techniques and ideas for business and industry. *$149.00*
8 pages Monthly

15749 Customer Communicator
Alexander Communications Group
28 W 25th Street
8th Floor
New York, NY 10010-1600
212-228-0246
FAX: 212-228-0376 800-232-4317
info@customerservicegroup.com
http://www.customerservicegroup.com
Margaret DeWitt, Publisher
Adam Reif, Marketing Manager
Laurence Alexander, Owner
Provides customer service representatives with the skills, techniques and motivation they need to be more productive. *$200.00*
Monthly Founded: 1990

15750 Customer Service Manager's Letter
Bureau of Business Practice
1185 Avenue of the Americas
New York, NY 10036
212-597-0333
FAX: 800-901-9075 800-638-8437
alicia.pierce@aspenpubl.com
www.bbpnews.com
Alicia Pierce, Operations
Laurence Alexander, Owner
Specially designed to show managers how to reduce their costs, their customer base, and maximize their employee capability. *$ 179.00*
8 pages 2 per year
Circulation: 5200

15751 Daily Report for Executives
Bureau of National Affairs
1231 25th Street NW
Washington, DC 20037-1197
202-452-4200
800-372-1033
customercare@bna.com
http://www.bna.com
Gregory C McCaffery, Publisher
Toby McIntosh, Managing Editor
A daily notification service covering legislative, regulatory, legal, tax and economic developments which affect both national and international businesses. *$9399.00*
Daily Founded: 1929

15752 Deal
Vicki King
105 Madison Avenue
New York, NY 10016
212-313-9200
FAX: 212-545-8442 888-667-3325
customerservice@thedeal.com
http://www.thedeal.com
Jeffery R Hartford, VP Circulation
Carol Parish, VP Marketing
Ed Paisley, Managing Editor
Vicki King, Publisher
Dedicated solely to reporting and analyzing all the aspects of the booming, high stakes world of the deeal economy. Areas of coverage include mergers and acquisitions, IPO's, private equity, venture capital and bankruptcies. Published in newsletter and on website. *$249.00*
26 pages

15753 Delphi Insight Series
Delphi Group
Ten Post Office Square
Suite 580
Boston, MA 02109-4603
617-247-1511
FAX: 617-247-4957 800-335-7440
client.services@delphigroup.com
http://www.delphigroup.com
Thomas Koulopoulos, President
Hadley Reynolds, Director Research
Mary Ann Kozlowski, Director Public Relations
Timely and insightful analysis and review of the markets, developments, and business cases for knowledge management, corporate portals and e-business solutions. Incorporates original Delphi research findings. Written for all management titles. Includes weekly email news update on relevant issues and access to DelphiWeb, an extensive online resource of product and market information. *$20000.00*
Daily

15754 Denver Business Journal
American City Business Journals
120 W Morehead Street
Suite 400
Charlotte, SC 28202
704-973-1000
FAX: 303-837-3535 800-486-3289
denver@bizjournals.com
http://www.bizjournals.com/denver
Scott Bemis, Publisher
Neil Westergaard, Editor *$86.00*
64 pages Monthly
Printed in 4 colors on newsprint stock

15755 Directorship
Directorship Search Group
8 Sound Shore Drive
Suite 250
Greenwich, CT 06830-7276
203-618-7000
FAX: 203-618-7007
editor@directorship.com
http://www.directorship.com
Russell Reynolds Jr, CEO/President
Barrett Stephens, VP
J.P. Donlon, Editor-in-Chief
Articles and news of interest to CEOs and directors of public companies, on every aspect of corporate governance. *$395.00*
12 pages Founded: 1975
Printed in 4 colors on glossy stock

15756 EAP Link
International Education Services and Publishing
1537 Franklin Street
#201-203
San Francisco, CA 94109-4571
415-239-4171
800-551-3005
Kendall Van Blarcom, Publisher
International news for human resource professionals. *$197.00*
8 pages Monthly

15757 Employee Assistance Program Management Letter
Health Resources Publishing
1913 Atlantic Avenue
Suite F4
Manasquan, NJ 08736
732-292-1100
FAX: 732-292-1111 888-843-6242
hrp@healthrespubs.com
http://www.healthrespubs.com
Bob Jenkins, President
Lisa Mansfield, Marketing Assistant
A monthly briefing on guidelines to help companies make decisions on managing their EAP programs. Contains information on what EAP's across the country are doing; help on policy issues dealing with and monitoring costs; framing coverages and limitations; and case histories. *$ 227.00*
Monthly Founded: 1978

15758 Enrollment Management Report
LRP Publications
747 Dresher Road Suite 500
PO Box 980
Horsham, PA 19044-980
215-840-0912
FAX: 215-784-9639 800-341-7874
custserve@lrp.com
http://www.lrp.com
Jay Margolis, Editor
Provides solutions and strategies for recruitment, admissions, retention and financial aid for higher-education institutions. Shows readers how to face the challenge of working across departmental lines to improve retention rates and how to respond to the upcoming surge in non-traditional students who apply. *$198.00*
Monthly Founded: 1977

15759 Executive Administrator
Seifer Consultants
525 Cayuga St
Storm Lake, IA 50588-2319
712-732-7340
FAX: 712-732-7906
John Siefer, Publisher
Management, job opportunities and news. *$70.00*
Monthly

15760 Executive Advantage
Briefings Publishing Group
1101 King Street
Suite 110
Alexandria, VA 22314
703-518-2343
FAX: 703-684-2136 800-888-2084
customerservice@briefings.com
http://www.briefings.com
Tina Ragland, Editorial Assistant
Lois Willingham, Marketing Manager
Deirdre Hackett, Executive Editor
William Dugan, Group Publisher
Michelle Cox, Publisher
A publication designed to help you learn the key interpersonal secrets to business suc-

cess through proper etiquette and protocol.
$147.00
8 pages Monthly Founded: 1981
Mailing list available for rent 6000 names
$125 per M.
Printed in 2 colors on matte stock

15761 Executive Edge
28 W 23rd Street
10th Floor
New York, NY 10010
212-367-4100
FAX: 212-367-4137

Rich Karlgaard, Publisher
David Hallerman, Editor

Covers quality customer service and marketing techniques.

15762 Executive Issues
Wharton School
255 S 38th Street
Philadelphia, PA 19104-3706
215-386-8300
FAX: 215-386-4304

Neil Neveras, Publisher

Discusses current business issues, business continuing information.

Circulation: 40000

15763 Executive Recruiter News
Kennedy Information
One Phoenix Mill Lane 5th Fl
Peterborough, NH 03458
603-924-1006
FAX: 603-924-4460 800-531-0007
support@kennedyinfo.com
http://www.kennedyinfo.com

Joseph McCool, Editor
William Allen, Managing Director

The authoritative voice of the recruiting industry, covering news, analysis, practice, advice, proprietary data and opinion. $ 229.00
8 pages Monthly Founded: 1980
Printed in 2 colors on matte stock

15764 Executive Report on Managed Care
Health Resources Publishing
1913 Atlantic Avenue
Suite F4
Manasquan, NJ 08736
732-292-1100
FAX: 732-292-1111 888-843-6242
info@themcic.com
http://www.themcic.com

Bob Jenkins, President/Managing Editor
Lisa Mansfield, Marketing Assistant

Bi-monthly report giving news of how major employers are implementing managed care programs. Helps companies prepare to evaluate and monitor various managed care proposals in terms of their cost effectiveness, quality and liability to the employer. *$497.00*
Weekly Founded: 1978

15765 Executive Report on Physician Organizations
Health Resources Publishing
1913 Atlantic Avenue
Suite F4
Manasquan, NJ 08736
732-292-1100
FAX: 732-292-1111 800-516-4343
info@themcic.com
http://www.themcic.com

Bob Jenkins, President/Managing Editor
Lisa Mansfield, Marketing Assistant
Caroline Pense, Editor

A bi-monthly newsletter published by Health Resources Publishing. *$197.00*
Monthly Founded: 1978
Circulation: 5000

15766 Executive Solutions
Dartnell Corporation
4660 N Ravenswood Avenue
Chicago, IL 60640-4510
773-907-9500
FAX: 561-622-2423 800-727-1227

Clark Fertridge, Publisher

Modern management techniques for executive training.

15767 Executive Wealth Advisory
National Institute of Business Management
1750 Old Meadow Road
Suite 302
McLean, VA 22102-4315
703-058-8000
FAX: 703-905-8042 800-543-2049
10 pages Monthly

15768 Federal Personnel Guide
LRP Publications
360 Hiatt Drive
Palm Beach Gardens, FL 33418
561-622-6520
FAX: 561-622-0757 800-341-7874
info@fedguide.com
http://www.fedguide.com

Daniel Gephart, Editorial Director

Annual almanac for US civilian federal personnel and training officers and individual federal and postal employees. An up-to-the-minute summary of rules and regulations affecting federal employees, including employment, pay and benefits.
$12.95
Founded: 1978 ISBN 1-881097-12-9
Circulation: 55000 39,000 names $110 per M. : PDF

15769 Global Environmental Change Report
Cutter Information Corporation
111 Eighth Avenue 7th Floor
New York, NY 10011-5552
212-771-0600
FAX: 212-771-0885
jrohaly@aspenpublishers.com
http://www.aspenpublishers.com

Wolters Kluwer, CEO
Richard Richard, Executive VP

An exclusive international service reporting on policy trends, industry actions and global environmental change. *$565.00*
8 pages Monthly

15770 HIPAA Bulletin for Management
Health Resources Publishing
1913 Atlantic Avenue
Suite F4
Manasquan, NJ 08736
732-292-1100
FAX: 732-292-1111 888-843-6242
hrp@healthrespubs.com
http://www.healthrespubs.com/

Bob Jenkins, President
Lisa Mansfield, Marketing Assistant

A monthly newsletter published by Health Resources Publishing. *$147.00*
Monthly Founded: 1978

15771 HR Briefings
Bureau of Business Practice
111 8th Avenue
New York, NY 10011
212-771-0733
FAX: 800-901-9075 800-243-1660
alicia.pierce@aspenbubl.com
http://www.aspenpublishers.com/

Alicia Pierce, President

Designed to help HR professionals become more effective on the job. It offers hands-on advice from other personnel managers who have experienced the kinds of problems facing readers. *$259.00*
8 pages Monthly Founded: 1925

15772 HR Weekly
SHRM/Society for Human Resource Management
1800 Duke Street
Alexandria, VA 22314
703-548-3440
FAX: 703-535-6490 800-283-7476
bobgonz@us.ibm.com www.shrm.org/

Johnny C Taylor, Chairman
Susan Meisinger, President/CEO
Robert O Gonzales, Secretary
Robb E Van Cleave, Treasurer

Weekly e-newsletter highlighting critical HR/Human Resourace issues.

15773 HR on Campus
LRP Publications
747 Dresher Road
PO Box 980
Horsham, PA 19044-980
215-784-0912
FAX: 215-784-9639 800-341-7874
custserve@lrp.com
http://www.lrp.com

Jay Margolis, Editor/publisher

Gives you the tools you need to solve your institution's human resource challenges. Provides pratical tips for handling real-life, day-to-day problems, along with the latest news and significant developments in higher education. *$165.00*
Monthly Founded: 1977

15774 HRmadeEasy
Employers of America
PO Box 1874
Mason City, IA 50402-1874
641-424-3187
FAX: 641-424-3187 800-728-3187
employer@employerhelp.org
http://www.employerhelp.org

Jim Collison, President

A weekly e-newsletter published by Employers of America. *$149.00*
Weekly Founded: 1976
Circulation: 600

15775 Helen Hecker
Twin Peaks Press
PO Box 129
Vancouver, WA 98666-129
360-694-2462
FAX: 360-696-3210
twinpeak@pacificer.com
http://www.pacificer.com

Victoria Nova, Production Manager

Publicity and marketing for small businesses, co-operative mailingsto ubmits, newspaper, tv - radio, and hundreds of mailing lists.
Founded: 1982

15776 Hiring the Best
Briefings Publishing Group
1101 King Street
Suite 110
Alexandria, VA 22314
703-548-3800
FAX: 703-684-2136 800-888-2084
customerservice@briefings.com
http://www.briefings.com

Deirdre Hackett, Editor
William G Dugan, Publisher
Tina Ragland, Editorial Assistant
Lois Willingham, Marketing Manager

A publication designed to help executives recruit, screen, and retain the best employees. *$697.00*

8 pages Monthly Founded: 1981
Circulation: 1300
Mailing list available for rent 6000 names $125 per M.
Printed in 2 colors on matte stock : online

15777 Human Resource Department Management Report
Institute of Management & Administration

29 W 35th Street
5th Floor
New York, NY 10001-2299
212-244-0360
FAX: 212-564-0465
subserve@ioma.com
http://www.ioma.com

Susan Patterson, Editor
Carlene Micheletto, President
David Foster, Executive Director

Shows HR department heads how to boost staff motivation and productivity, improve department automation, and cut costs while improving service. *$299.00*

Monthly

15778 Human Resources Management Reporter
Warren, Gorham & Lamont
395 Hudson Street
New York, NY 10014-3669
212-367-6300
FAX: 212-367-6718 800-742-3348

Eugene Simonoff, Publisher
Nancy Pratt, Editor
Rik Kopelan, President

For personnel practitioners.

Founded: 1935

15779 I/B/E/S Comments
Johnson Redbook Services
345 Hudson Street
15th Floor
New York, NY 10014-4502
212-649-2000
FAX: 212-541-4212

Joseph V Riccobono, Publisher
Edward Keon Jr, Editor

Encompasses three newsletters. US Comments: analyses of the major developments related to earnings per share expectations for US companies. International Comments: allows global investors to compare growth rates, changes in growth, price-to-earnings ratios and estimate revisions for 27 countries and the world as a whole. Canadian Review: offers quarterly analysis of the Canadian market. *$1000.00*

30 pages Daily
Circulation: 4000 Audited Est. Pass-Along Circ: 10000
Printed in 1 color on matte stock

15780 IOMA's Pay for Performance Report
Institute of Management & Administration

29 W 35th Street
5th Floor
New York, NY 10001-2299
212-244-0360
FAX: 212-564-0465
subserve@ioma.com www.ioma.com

Helps human resource and compensation executives improve their company's productivity through the use of variable pay and bonus programs for all types of employees.

15781 IOMA's Report on Managing Flexible Benefit Plans
Institute of Management & Administration

29 W 35th Street
5th Floor
New York, NY 10001-2221
212-244-0360
FAX: 212-564-0465
subserve@ioma.com www.ioma.com

Rebecca Morrow, Publisher
Lee Rath, Editor

Information to manage a firm's flex plan. *$245.00*

16 pages Monthly

15782 IT Services Business Report
Staffing Industry Analysts
881 Fremont Avenue
Suite A3
Los Altos, CA 94024-5637
650-948-9303
FAX: 650-948-9345 800-950-9496
info@sireport.com
http://www.sireport.com

Sona Sharma, Managing Editor
Peter Yessne, Chairman/Publisher
Ron Mester, President & CEO

Business news and industry trends analysis for professionals. *$297.00*

Monthly Founded: 1989

15783 Information Advisor
Information Advisory Services
330A S 1st Street W
Missoula, MT 59801-1853

Robert Berkman, Editor

Compares and evaluates business information services - print, online and CD-ROM. Covers international data, information quality, and new noteworthy products.

Monthly
Circulation: 700 Audited

15784 International Council for Small Business
3674 Lindell Boulevard
Saint Louis, MO 63108-3302
314-977-3896
FAX: 314-977-3627
icsb@slu.edu www.icsb.org

G Dale Meyer, President
Sharon Bower, Executive Administrator

Management development

Printed in 2 colors on glossy stock

15785 International Management Council
608 S 114th Street
Omaha, NE 68154-3153
402-330-6310
FAX: 402-330-7424 800-688-9622
imcoffice@msn.com
www.imc-ymca.org/join.html

Jodeen Sterba, National Administrator

Information on developing leadership and management skills through a network of shared experiences and education.

Printed in 2 colors on matte stock

15786 International Personnel Management Association Newsletter
1617 Duke Street
Alexandria, VA 22314-3406
703-549-7100
FAX: 703-684-0948
ipma@pma-hr.org
http://www.ipma-hr.org

Elezabeth Kirklan, Editor
Neil Reichenbert, Executive Director/CEO

Non-profit organization for agencies and individuals in public sector human resources. Numerous print and online resources available.

Monthly Founded: 1973 5000 names $105 per M.

15787 International Quality
Underwriters Laboratories
333 Pfingsten Road
Northbrook, IL 60062-2096
847-120-0136
FAX: 847-272-8129 888-503-5536
northbrook@us.ul.com
http://www.ul.com

Holly J Schubert, Publisher
Paul M Baker, Marketing

Free standards and other quality management topics.

Monthly Founded: 1894
Circulation: 18000

15788 Inventory Reduction Report
Institute of Management & Administration

29 W 35th Street
5th Floor
New York, NY 10001-2299
212-244-0360
FAX: 212-564-0465
subserve@ioma.com www.ioma.com

Mark Baven, Publisher
Perry Patterson, Editor

Focuses on reducing inventory costs, JIT methods and improving profitability. *$245.00*

16 pages Monthly

15789 Issues and Observations
Center for Creative Leadership & Jossay-Bass
350 Sansome Street
San Francisco, CA 94104-1304
415-334-4700
FAX: 800-605-2665 888-378-2537
info@leaders.ccl.org
http://www.ccl.org

John Alexander, President
Patricia Ohlott, Project Manager

Contains articles about leadership and management. *$99.00*

Quarterly Founded: 1970
Circulation: 3000

15790 Job Safety and Health
Bureau of National Affairs
1231 25th Street NW
Washington, DC 20037-1197
202-452-4200
800-372-1033
customercare@bna.net
http://www.bna.com
Gregory C McCaffery, Publisher
Stanley S Pond, Managing Editor
A biweekly review of workplace health and safety regulations, policies, practices and trends. *$898.00*
Founded: 1929

15791 Jots and Jolts
Economics Press
12 Daniel Road
Fairfield, NJ 07004-2565
973-227-1224
FAX: 973-227-9742
John Beckley, Publisher
Monthly planner for supervisors; includes information management theory. *$1.00*
Circulation: 32000

15792 Just-in-Time/Quick Response News
Phillips Publishing
9420 Key West Ave
Suite 2
Rockville, MD 20850-3394
301-279-4200
FAX: 301-309-3847 866-279-1930
Christopher Scotton, Publisher
Lane Cooper, Editor
Quality and productivity improvement strategies for world class manufacturers. *$397.00*
9 pages Monthly Founded: 1974

15793 Kennedy's Career Strategist
Career Strategies
1150 Wilmette Avenue
Wilmette, IL 60091-2603
847-251-1661
FAX: 847-251-5191 800-728-1709
mmkcareer@aol.com
http://www.moatskennedy.com/newsletter.html
Marilyn Moat Kennedy, Editor
Linda Mitchell, Production Manager
$65.00
Monthly Founded: 1986

15794 LAMA Newsletter/Washington Notes
Latin American Management Association
419 New Jersey Avenue SE
Washington, DC 20003-4046
202-546-3803
FAX: 202-546-3807
http://www.lamausa.com
Albert Jacques, Publisher
Stephen Denlinger, President/CEO
Covers national minority and small business issues. *$100.00*
10 pages Monthly Founded: 1972

15795 Laboratory Industry Report
Institute of Management & Administration
3 Park Avenue
30th Floor
New York, NY 10016-2299
212-244-0360
FAX: 212-564-0465
subserve@ioma.com
http://www.ioma.com/
Jondavid Klipp, Editor
David Foster, CEO/President
Covers major market trends, the latest news on strategic alliances and partnerships, how to deal with Medicare and new managed care mandates, how to redesign and restaff a clinical lab, news from Wall Street, the hottest growth areas for test revenues and even news on the latest technological advances in equipment and medical procedures. *$329.00*
Monthly
Circulation: 180,000

15796 Law Office Management & Administration Report
Institute of Management & Administration
29 W 35th Street
5th Floor
New York, NY 10001-2221
212-244-0360
FAX: 212-564-0465
subserve@ioma.com
http://www.ioma.com
Lisa Isom-Rodriguez, Editor
David Foster, Publisher
Provides information to efficiently manage law firms. *$299.00*
20 pages Monthly
Circulation: 180,000

15797 Leadership Strategies
Briefings Publishing Group
1101 King Street
Suite 110
Alexandria, VA 22314
703-548-3800
FAX: 703-684-2136 800-888-2084
dfrierson@briefings.com
http://www.briefings.com
Deirdre Hackett, Editor
Jacqueline Stonis, Production Manager
William G. Duggan, Group Publisher
Lois Willingham, Marketing Manager
A publication designed to sharpen your management and leadership abilities, improve your productivity, and accelerate your professional success. *$199.00*
8 pages Monthly Founded: 1981
Circulation: 8500
Mailing list available for rent 7000 names $125 per M.
Printed in 2 colors on matte stock

15798 Maintenance: Managers
Express Carriers Association
PO Box 4307
Bethlehem, PA 18018
610-740-5857
FAX: 610-740-3174 866-322-7447
eca@expresscarriers.com
www.expresscarriers.com
Cheryle Williamson, Executive Director
Focuses on current equipment management issues.

15799 Management Policies and Personnel Law
Business Research Publications
1533 H Street NW
Suite 200W
Washington, DC 20005-1005
202-364-6473
FAX: 202-466-3509 800-822-6338
Susan Sonnesyn-Brooks, Editor
Leading newsletter designed to give managers an inside view into the best run companies.
BiWeekly -

15800 Manager's Legal Bulletin
Alexander Hamilton Institute
70 Hilltop Road
Ramsey, NJ 07446-1119
201-825-3377
FAX: 201-825-8696 800-879-2441
custsvc@ahipubs.com
http://www.ahipubs.com
Fran Goggin, Circulation Director
Shows managers how to handle problems in the workplace without provoking lawsuits for illegal discrimination in hiring, firing, promotions, sexual harassment or discipline decisions. *$66.00*
4 pages Fortnightly Founded: 1909
Circulation: 20000 Audited
Mailing list available for rent 8M names $125 per M.
Printed in 2 colors on matte stock : Acrobat

15801 Managing Benefits Plans
Institute of Management & Administration
3 Park Avenue
30th Floor
New York, NY 10016-2299
212-244-0360
FAX: 212-564-0465
subserve@ioma.com
http://www.ioma.com
Rebecca Morrow, Editor
David Foster, CEO
Control costs and manage service providers, without sacrificing the quality of your benefits package. Contains suggestions for raising participation rates. *$271.95*
Monthly Founded: 1982

15802 Managing Customer Service
Institute of Management & Administration
29 W 35th Street
5th Floor
New York, NY 10001-2299
212-244-0360
FAX: 212-564-0465
subserve@ioma.com www.ioma.com
Boost the productivity, efficiency and visibility of your department, and keep it on the cutting edge.

15803 Managing Logistics
Institute of Management & Administration
29 W 35th Street
5th Floor
New York, NY 10001-2299
212-244-0360
FAX: 212-564-0465
subserve@ioma.com www.ioma.com
Covers new technologies and strategies, how to negotiate with outsourced service providers.

15804 Managing Training & Development
Institute of Management & Administration
29 W 35th Street
5th Floor
New York, NY 10001-2299
212-244-0360
FAX: 212-564-0465
subserve@ioma.com www.ioma.com
Covers all aspects of measuring, learning, development, getting employees trained for their jobs, and justifying the cost of training to upper management.

15805 Medical Group Management Update
Medical Group Management Association
104 Inverness Ter E
Englewood, CO 80112-5313
303-991-1111
FAX: 303-643-4427
Brenda Hull, Publisher
Eileen Barker, Editor
William Jessee, Manager
Monthly association newspaper offering up-to-the-minute articles on current legislation, practical management, health care trends, association activities and other timely subjects.
Monthly

15806 Object-Oriented Strategies
Cutter Information Corporation
37 Broadway
Suite 1
Arlington, MA 02474-5552
781-648-8700
FAX: 781-648-1950 800-888-8939
service@cutter.com
http://www.cutter.com
Paul Harman, Editor
Kim Leonard, Customer Service Director
Karen Coburn, CEO
Designed for managers and developers of object-oriented systems. *$495.00*
16 pages Monthly Founded: 1986

15807 Orlando Business Journal
Business Journals
315 E Robinson Street
Suite 250
Orlando, FL 32801-4323
407-649-8470
FAX: 407-420-1625 888-649-6254
orlando@bizjournals.com
http://www.bizjournals.com/orlando
Ann Sonntag, Publisher
Ken Cogburn, Editor
Cindy Barth, Managing Editor
Sue Ross, Ad Director
Alan Byrd, Director of Marketing/Circulation *$79.00*
64 pages Weekly Founded: 1995
Printed in 4 colors on newsprint stock

15808 PMI Today
Project Management Institute
4 Campus Boulevard
Newtown Square, PA 19073-3299
610-356-4600
FAX: 610-356-4647
customercare@pmi.org
http://www.pmi.org
Gregory Balestrero, CEO
Mark Langley, Managing Director
Louis Mercken, Chairman
Van Goldfisher, Editor
A monthly newsletter published by the Project Management Institute.
6 pages Monthly Founded: 1969
Circulation: 150000
Mailing list available for rent

15809 PSMJ Principal Strategies
PSMJ Resources
10 Midland Avenue
Newton, MA 02458-1000
617-965-0055
FAX: 617-965-5152 800-537-7765
info@psmj.com http://www.psmj.com
Frank Stasiowski, Production Manager
Offers management tactics and techniques for the design industry. *$195.00*
8 pages Monthly Founded: 1974
Mailing list available for rent $125 per M.
Printed in 2 colors on matte stock

15810 PSMJ Project Delivery
PSMJ Resources
10 Midland Avenue
Newton, MA 02458-1000
617-965-0055
FAX: 617-965-5152 800-537-7765
info@psmj.com www.psmj.com
Frank Stasiowski, Production Manager
Offers project management tactics and techniques to the design industry. *$196.00*
8 pages Monthly
Mailing list available for rent $125 per M.
Printed in 2 colors on matte stock

15811 Payroll Manager's Letter
Bureau of Business Practice
111 8th Avenue
7th Floor
New York, NY 10011
212-771-0600
800-638-8437
rfecustomer@aspenpubl.com
http://www.aspenpublishers.com
Marc Jennings, VP
Gerry Centrowitz, VP, Marketing and Commu
Contains concise, plain-English explanations of the latest federal payroll developments which helps companies comply with rapidly changing employment tax and minimum wage/overtime laws. *$235.00*
8 pages Founded: 1920
Circulation: 7000
Printed in 1 color on glossy stock

15812 Personal Report for the Administrative Professional
National Institute of Business Management

1750 Old Meadow Road
Suite 300
McLean, VA 22102-4315
703-058-8000
FAX: 703-905-8040 800-543-2049
customer@nibm.net
http://www.nibm.net
Heather Rice, Manager
Phil Ash, Marketing Director
Steve Sturm, President *$54.00*
10 pages Monthly Founded: 1937

15813 Pittsburgh Business Times
Pittsburgh Business Times
2313 E Carson Street
Suite 200
Pittsburgh, PA 15203
412-481-6397
FAX: 412-481-9956
pittsburgh@bizjournals.com
http://www.bizjournals.com/pittsburgh/
Christopher Davis, Managing Editor
Alan Robertson, Publisher *$98.00*
60 pages Weekly
Printed in 4 colors on newsprint stock

15814 Preventing Business Fraud
Institute of Management & Administration

29 W 35th Street
5th Floor
New York, NY 10001-2299
212-244-0360
FAX: 212-564-0465
subserve@ioma.com www.ioma.com
Stop corporate fraud before it happens. Get guidance on how to avoid supplier collusion and kickbacks, false invoicing, health insurance and workers' compensation fraud, payroll, petty cash and T and E overstatements, theft of equipment and materials and more.

15815 Professional Advisor
Int'l Society of Speakers, Authors & Consultants
PO Box 6432
Kingwood, TX 77325-6432
281-441-3558
FAX: 281-441-3538
Bernard Zick, Publisher
Includes information of the consulting industry. *$120.00*
10 pages Monthly

15816 Profit Line
Ernst and Young
3300 Gateway Drive
Pompano Beach, FL 33069-4841
954-979-0700
www.ey.com
Business information newsletter for entrepreneurs.

15817 Quality Assurance Bulletin
Bureau of Business Practice
1185 Avenue of the Americas
New York, NY 10036
212-597-0333
FAX: 800-901-9075 800-638-8437
alicia.pierce@aspenpubl.com
www.bbpnews.com
Alicia Pierce, Operations
Helps quality professionals improve the company's question-answer function. *$118.80*
8 pages 2 per year

15818 Real Estate & Leasing Report
Business Journals
120 W Morehead Street
Suite 400
Charlotte, SC 28202
704-347-2340
FAX: 704-973-1102
Jeannie Falknor, Publisher
Joanne Skoog, Editor *$70.00*
70 pages Weekly
Printed in 4 colors on newsprint stock

15819 Report on Salary Surveys
Institute of Management & Administration

3 park avenue
30 Floor
New York, NY 10016-2299
212-244-0360
FAX: 212-564-0465
subserve@ioma.com
http://www.ioma.com
Laime Vaitkus, Editor
David Froster, CEO
William Allen, Managing Director
Provides information on setting and managing compensation. The report analyzes data from major salary surveys released during the year by the biggest compensation survey companies, world at work, SHRM, state human resource societies and the big four accounting firms, to give readers an overview of those expensive, hard to manage services. *$269.00*
Monthly Founded: 1980

15820 **Rodenhauser Report**
Consulting Information Services
191 Washington Street
Keene, NH 03431
603-355-1560

info@consultinginfo.com
http://www.consultinginfo.com
Tom Rodenhauser, President
Rodenhauser Report is a monthly electronic briefing that forecasts consulting trends for senior management advisors and business executives.
Monthly Founded: 1998

15821 **Servicing Management**
LDJ Corporation
70 Edwin Avenue
PO Box 2180
Waterbury, CT 06708-2180
203-755-0158
FAX: 203-755-3480 800-325-6745
info@zeckin.com
http://www.sm-online.com/
Paul Zackin, Publisher
Michael Bates, Editor
June Han, Circulation Manager
Jeanette Laliberte, Subscriptions
Delivers news and how-to advice to executives and personnel in the servicing of mortgage loans nationwide. *$48.00*
Monthly Founded: 1969
Circulation: 18000

15822 **Small-Biz Growth**
Support Services Alliance
107 Prospect St
Schoharie, NY 12157
518-295-7966
FAX: 518-295-8556 800-322-3920
info@ssamembers.com
http://www.smallbizgrowth.com
Megan Thompson, Editor
Stephen Cole, President
Keeps SSA members and their employees up-to-date on developments affecting small-business communties. *$25.00*
Monthly Founded: 1977
Circulation: 17,000

15823 **Small-Business Strategies**
Page Group
PO Box 116
Dundee, IL 60118-0116
847-695-7887

Phillip Grisolia, Publisher
Contains practical ideas for use in successfully starting and profitably managing small businesses. Accepts advertising. *$95.00*
4 pages BiWeekly

15824 **Sound Thinking**
Jay Mitchell Associates
PO Box 1285
Fairfield, IA 52556-0022
641-472-4087
FAX: 641-472-2071
Jay Mitchell, Publisher
Notes and comments on the radio industry and related fields, specializing in an outside-in view. *$65.00*
2 pages Monthly

15825 **Source**
Rachel PR Services
1650 S Pacific Coast Highway
Suite 200C
Redondo Beach, CA 90277-5625

Janis Brett-Elspas, Editor
Jamie Steiner, Advertising/Sales
Annual reference guide for job hunters in advertising, public relations, marketing and journalism offering more than 2,000 resources for finding jobs at all levels in all 50 states. Listings includes job banks, job hotlines, executive recruiters, books/directories, trade publications, industry associations and more. *$39.00*
40 pages Annual
Circulation: 30,000 Audited
Printed in on matte stock

15826 **Southeastern Association Executive**

Special Edition Publishing
195 Wekiva Springs Road
Suite 300
Longwood, FL 32779
407-862-7737
FAX: 407-862-8102
specedpub@earthlink.net
http://www.specedpub.com
Albert R Sciuto, Publisher
Nichole Wunduke, Editor
Betty Harper, Director of Sales & Marke
Monthly news magazine serving associations meetings and hospitality executives in the southeast .
25 pages Monthly Founded: 1973
Circulation: 5200
Printed in 4 colors on glossy stock

15827 **Staffing Industry Report**
Staffing Industry Analysts
881 Fremont Avenue
Suite A3
Los Altos, CA 94024-5637
650-489-9303
FAX: 650-232-2360 800-950-9496
editor@sireport.com
http://www.staffingindustry.com
Peter Yessne, Publisher
Tim Murphy, Editor
Joyce Routson, Managing Editor
Greg Palmer, CEO
A twice monthly newsletter for temporary help, staff leasing and employment service companies. Industry information, company news, training and automation resource reviews, financial coverage, labor demand and supply analysis, key interviews. Association news, public company stock tables. SI Report sponsors an annual Staffing Industry Executive Forum in April. Emphasis is on business news. Includes advertising supplement. *$385.00*
Founded: 1989
Circulation: 3000 Audited Est. Pass-Along Circ: 6000
Mailing list available for rent 3500 names
Printed in 2 colors on matte stock

15828 **Success in Recruiting and Retaining**
National Institute of Business Management
1750 Old Meadow Road
Suite 302
McLean, VA 22102-4315
703-058-8000
FAX: 703-905-8042 800-543-2049
10 pages Monthly

15829 **Successful Self-Management**
Stahlka Associates
60 Westchester Road
Williamsville, NY 14221-5021
716-347-7070
FAX: 716-626-4188
wendystahlka@verizon.net
http://www.stahlkamarketing.com
Clayton A Stahlka, Production Manager
Wendy Stahlka, President
Mastering changes in yourself and your environment to be the best you can be with what you have. *$24.00*
5 pages Quarterly Founded: 1975
Circulation: 1800 Audited
Printed in 1 color on matte stock

15830 **Supplier Selection and Management Report**
Institute of Management & Administration
3 Park Avenue
30th Floor
New York, NY 10016-2221
212-244-0360
FAX: 212-564-0465
subserve@ioma.com
http://www.ioma.com
Mark Baven, Publisher
Joe Mazel, Editor
Focuses on supplier selection, partnering and management issues. *$289.00*
16 pages Monthly Founded: 1980
Circulation: 180,000

15831 **Travel Manager's Executive Briefing**
Health Resources Publishing
1913 Atlantic Avenue
Suite F4
Manasquan, NJ 08736
732-292-1100
FAX: 732-292-1111 888-843-6242
info@themcic.com
http://www.themcic.com
Bob Jenkins, President/Managing Editor
Judith Granholm, Marketing Assistant
A digest published twice a month that covers developments in the field of travel and expense cost control. Topics include discounts in air fare, car rentals, hotel bills, travel alternatives, phone savings, planning for meetings trends in government legislation affecting business travel costs, and case histories of companies that have successfully cut costs. Ideal for travel managers of corporations, small businesses and nonprofit organizations. *$447.00*
Founded: 1978

15832 **WACRA (The World Association For Case Method Research & Application)**
23 Mackintosh Avenue
Needham, MA 02492-1218
781-444-8982
FAX: 781-444-1548 800-523-6468
wacra@rcn.com
http://www.wacra.org
Hans E Klein, President/ Editor
Pierre Mora, Marketing Director
Newsletter published by WACRA. Interactive teaching, 23 books. Quarterly international journal for Case Method Research & Application. *$65.00*
Founded: 1984

15833 Wage-Hour Compliance Report
Institute of Management & Administration

29 W 35th Street
5th Floor
New York, NY 10001-2299
212-244-0360
FAX: 212-564-0465
subserve@ioma.com www.ioma.com
Covers white-collar exemptions, how to pay employees for rest and overtime periods, legal holidays, how to handle vacation, severance and negotiated termination pay rules, and give managers a concise rundown of new federal and state withholding and minimum wage changes, new rules, rates and requirements.

15834 What's Ahead in Personnel
Remy Publishing Company
350 W Hubbard Street
Suite 440
Chicago, IL 60610-6900
773-696-6760
FAX: 773-464-0166 800-542-6670
John Hickey, Editor
Contains information on current HR trends, legal issues and company practices.
SemiMonthly

15835 What's Working In Consulting
Kennedy Information
One Kennedy Place
Route 12 S
Fitzwilliam, NH 03447
603-585-3101
FAX: 603-585-6401
www.kennedyinfo.com
Alan Weiss, Editor
Provides practical guidance on improving consulting skills and managing a consulting practice. *$197.00*
Monthly

15836 Women in Business
Business Journal of Portland
851 SW 6th Avenue
Suite 500
Portland, OR 97204
503-274-8733
FAX: 503-227-2650 800-486-3289
portland@bizjournals.com
http://www.bizjournals.com/portland
Mike Consol, Publisher
Dan McMillan, Managing Editor
Rob Smith, Editor
George Vaughan, Advertising Director
Special supplement of The Business Journal that celebrates the achievements of women making a difference in the business world and community *$89.00*
36 pages
Printed in 4 colors on newsprint stock

15837 Work and Family Life
230 W 55th Street
Apartment 6B
New York, NY 10019-5212
212-557-3555
FAX: 212-557-6555
info@workfamily.com
http://www.workfamily.com
Kotie Thorndike, Circulation Director
Susan Ginsberg, Editor
Brian Torkkola, Director of Marketing and
Susan Seitel, President
Provides information and practical solutions to a wide range of family, job and health issues. Purpose is to help readers find pleasure and satisfaction in their many roles at work, at home, and in their communities. *$295.00*
Monthly Founded: 1984
Circulation: 50000
Printed in 4 colors on matte stock

15838 Working Smart
National Institute of Business Management

1750 Old Meadow Road
Suite 302
McLean, VA 22102-4315
703-058-8000
FAX: 703-905-8042 800-543-2055
customer@nibm.net
http://www.nibm.net
Philip Clark, Publisher
Morey Stettner, Editor
Phil Ash, Marketing Director
Ready, relevant and reliable advice for managers on workplace issues. *$48.00*
10 pages Monthly Founded: 1937
Printed in 2 colors on matte stock

Magazines & Journals

15839 AFSM: Professional Journal
Assoication for Services Management International
1342 Colonial Boulevard
Suite 25D
Fort Myers, FL 33907-1084
239-275-7887
FAX: 239-275-0794 800-333-9786
info@afsmi.org http://www.afsmi.org
Suzanne Tissier, Senior Editor
John Schoenewald, CEO
A journal aimed at management issues.
64 pages Monthly Founded: 1975

15840 APICS: The Performance Advantage
APICS Association for Operations Management
5301 Shawnee Road
Alexandria, VA 22312-2317
703-354-8851
FAX: 703-354-8106
editorial@apicshq.org www.apics.org
Doug Kelly, Editor
Jennifer Procter, Managing Editor
Beth Rennie, Senior Editor
Provides comprehensive articles on enterprise resources planning, supply chain management, e-business, materials management and production and inventory management. *$65.00*
64 pages 10/Year
Circulation: 66,000
Mailing list available for rent 40,000 names $100 per M.
Printed in 4 colors on glossy stock

15841 American Academy of Medical Administrators
701 Lee Street
Suite 600
Des Plaines, IL 60016
847-759-8601
FAX: 847-759-8602
info@aameda.org
http://www.aameda.org
Renee Schleicher, President/CEO
Holly Estal, Director Education
24 pages Quarterly Founded: 1957
Mailing list available for rent
Printed in 2 colors on glossy stock

15842 American Small Businesses Association
206 E College St
Ste 201
Grapevine, TX 76051-5381
817-488-8770
FAX: 817-251-8578 800-801-2722
Bill Will Sr, President
Wanda Johnson, Bookkeeper
Represents the interests of small businesses.

Printed in on glossy stock

15843 Association Management Magazine
American Society of Association Executives
1575 I Street NW
Suite 11
Washington, DC 20005-1103
202-626-2723
FAX: 202-371-8315 888-950-2723
service@asaenet.org
http://www.asaenet.org/
Karl Ely, CAE, Publisher
Keith C Skillman, Editor
Serves the field of trade business professional and philanthropic associations. *$30.00*
Monthly Founded: 1920
Circulation: 22507

15844 AzBusiness
Arizona Businss & Developement
2222 E Camelback Road
Suite 230
Phoenix, AZ 85016
602-748-2222
FAX: 602-650-0827 877-744-7516
editor@azbusinessmagazine.com
http://www.azbusinessmagazine.com
Michael Atkinson, President/CEO
David L Silver, Associate Publisher
Audrey Webb, VP Operations
Kerri Blumsack, Sales Director
Greg Sexton, Editor
Focuses on virtually every facet of the business community with ongoing departments such as Spotlight Small Business, Arizona Entrepreneur, Power of Attorney, Health Watch, High Tech, Market Report, Real Estate and Finance. *$30.00*
Bi-monthly Founded: 1985
Circulation: 22000
Printed in 4 colors on glossy stock

15845 Benchmarking: A Practitioner's Guide for Becoming & Staying the Best
Quality & Productivity Management Association
300 N Martingale Road
Suite 230
Schaumburg, IL 60173-2407

FAX: 847-619-3383
William Ginnodo, Publisher
Lesley Williams, Publications Manager
Promotes benchmarking as a technique for comparing processes, products or services with the world's best encouraging ways to do things faster, better, and less cost.

Management and common sense plus anecdotes and quotes. *$1.00*

Circulation: 266,000

15847 Building Operating Management
Trade Press Publishing Corporation
2100 W Florist Avenue
Milwaukee, WI 53209-3799
414-228-7701
FAX: 414-228-1134
scott.cunningham@tradepress.com
http://www.tradepress.com

Edward Sullivan, Editor
Bobbie Reid, Production Director
Scott Cunningham, Associate Publisher
Eric Muench, Director of Circulation
Robert J Wisniewski, President/CEO

Serves the field of facilities management, encompassing commercial building: office buildings, real estate/property management firms, developers, financial institutions, insurance companies, apartment complexes, civic/convention centers, including members of the Building Owners and Managers Association
Monthly Founded: 1943
Circulation: 70000

15848 Business Facilities
Group C Communications
44 Apple Street
Suite 3
Tinton Falls, NJ 07701
732-842-7433
FAX: 732-758-6634 800-524-0337
connie@groupc.com
http://www.businessfacilities.com

Edgar T Coene, Chairman
Ted Coene, Publisher
Karim Khan, Editor
Beth Sicignano, Marketing Manager
Connie Donatantonio, Circulation Manager

Magazine covering the fields of corporation expansion, economic development and real estate. *$30.00*
Monthly Founded: 1969
Circulation: 30309

15849 Business First
501 S 4th Street
Suite 130
Louisville, KY 40202
502-583-1731
FAX: 502-587-1703
louisville@bizjournals.com
http://www.bizjournals.com

Thomas Monahan, Publisher
Carol Brando Timmons, Editor
Judith Berzof, Associate Editor
Rebecca Ray, Assistant Editor *$83.00*
Monthly

15850 Business Week
McGraw Hill
1221 Avenue of the Americas
New York, NY 10020
212-512-2000
FAX: 614-759-3759
customer.service@mcgraw-hill.com
http://www.businessweek.com

Thane Peterson, Editor
Harold McGraw III, President
William Kupper Jr, Chief Executive Officer

Updates and forecasts for the business professional. *$4.95*
Weekly Founded: 1884

15851 C2M Consulting to Management
Journal of Management Consulting
858 Longview Road
Burlingame, CA 94010-6974
650-342-1954
FAX: 650-344-5005
c2m@c2m.com http://www.c2m.com

E Michael Shays, Publisher
Marsha Lewin, Chairman Editorial

The journal, which is read in over 60 countries, presents methods and processes for management consultants helping them to enlarge and perfect their skills and service to clients. *$80.00*
Quarterly Founded: 1981
Circulation: 5000

15852 CFO: the Magazine for Chief Financial Officers
CFO Publishing Corporation
253 Summer Street
Floor 3
Boston, MA 02210-1118
617-345-9700
FAX: 617-951-9306

David Laird, Publisher

Features insurance, cash management, taxes, benefits, accounting, buyers guide.

Circulation: 365,409

15853 COM-SAC, Computer Security, Audit & Control
Management Advisory Services & Publications
PO Box 81151
Wellesley Hills, MA 02481
781-235-2895
FAX: 781-235-5446
Info@masp.com
http://www.masp.com

N Lagos, Manager
JF Kuong, Editor

Presents tutorials and articles of current interest in computer security and audit, presents a comprehensive digest of all key articles and books published on the fields of computer security and control. *$98.00*
Quarterly Founded: 1973

15854 Central Penn Business Journal
Journal Publications
101 N 2nd Street
2nd Floor
Harrisburg, PA 17101-1600
717-236-4300
FAX: 717-909-6803
webmaster@journalpub.com
http://www.centralpennbusiness.com

David A Schankweiler, Publisher
Gary Nalbandian, CEO/President
Jason Klinger, Editor

Provides comprehensive news for the business community. *$64.95*
56 pages Weekly Founded: 1985
Circulation: 10,500

15855 Chain Leader
Raymond Herrmann
2000 Clearwater Drive
Oak Brook, IL 60523
630-288-8242
FAX: 630-288-8215
rherrmann@reedbusiness.com
http://www.chainleader.com

Mary Boltz Chapman, Editor-in-Chief
Maya Norris, Managing Editor
Ray Herrmann, Publisher

Targets senior management of chain restaurant companies.
Monthly Founded: 1960
Circulation: 17323

15856 Chief Executive
Chief Executive Group
110 Summit Avenue
Montvale, NJ 07645
201-930-5959
FAX: 201-930-5956
info@chiefexecutive.net
http://www.chiefexecutive.net

Carol Evans, Publisher
Robin Uhl, Circulation Manager
William J. Holstein, Editor-in-Chief
Edward M. Kopko, CEO/Chairman
Chris Chalk, Sales/Marketing Manager

A journal of strategy and analysis by and for chief executives.
75 pages Monthly Founded: 1976
Circulation: 42000

15857 Club Management Magazine
Finan Publishing Company
107 W Pacific
Saint Louis, MO 63119
314-961-6644
FAX: 314-961-4809
ddierkes@finan.com
http://www.club-mgmt.com

Thomas J Finan, Publisher/Editor
Dee Kaplan, Publisher
Dianne Dierkes, Circulation Manager

The resource for successful club operations. *$26.95*
3 Issues a year Founded: 1927
Mailing list available for rent 21,000 names
Printed in 4 colors on glossy stock

15858 Commitment Plus
Quality & Productivity Management Association
300 N Martingale Road
Suite 230
Schaumburg, IL 60173-2407

FAX: 847-619-3383

William Ginnodo, Editor/Author

This monthly newsletter is for managers who want to improve quality, productivity and service through people. It contains brief case studies, written primarily by QPMA staff, showing how operating managers, or their people, went about implementing improvements in their organizations' operating managers, and regularly reinforce the improvement message. This newsletter is free to members. *$95.00*
4 pages Monthly

15859 Competitive Intelligence Review
John Wiley & Sons
111 River Street
Hoboken, NJ 07030
201-748-6000
FAX: 201-748-6088 800-825-7550
customer@wiley.com
http://www.wiley.com

John Prescott, Publisher
William J Pesce, President/CEO

Collection and analysis of business information. *$68.95*
Quarterly Founded: 1807
Circulation: 3250

15860 Consulting Magazine
Kennedy Information
One Phoenix Mill Lane
5th Floor
Peterborough, NH 03458
603-924-1006
FAX: 603-924-4460 800-531-0007
bookstore@kennedyinfo.com
http://www.kennedyinfo.com
Jack Sweeney, Editor-in-Chief
Mina Landrisina, Managing Director
The only magazine written exclusively for management consultants, consulting is dedicated to fostering performance excellence and career success. Consulting serves the information needs of those responsible for shaping the business strategies of their clients. *$99.00*
Monthly Founded: 1970

15861 Contingency Planning & Management
Witter Publishing Corporation
20 Commerce Street
Flemington, NJ 08822
908-788-0343
FAX: 908-788-3782
CPMmagazine@WitterPublishing.com
http://www.witterpublishing.com
Bob Joudanin, Publisher
Paul Kirvan, Editor
Courtney Witter, Print Circulation/Subscriptions
Andrew Witter, President
Serves the fields of financial/banking, manufacturing industrial, transportation, utilities, telecommunications, health care, government, insurance and other allied fields. *$195.00*
Monthly Founded: 1987

15862 Contingency Planning & Recovery Journal
Management Advisory Services & Publications
PO Box 81151
Wellesley Hills, MA 02481
781-235-2895
FAX: 781-235-5446
Info@masp.com http://www.masp.com
N Lagos, Manager
JF Kuong, Editor
The only independent quarterly that is membership and subscriber supported. It presents current state of affairs in emergency preparedness, contingency planning and business resumption planning and business continuity. *$75.00*
The above price is for North America, $85.00 Overseas
16 pages Quarterly Founded: 1972
Printed in 2 colors

15863 Corporate Meetings & Incentives
Primedia
745 Fifth Avenue
New York, Ne 10151
212-745-0100
FAX: 212-745-0121
information@primedia.com
http://www.primedia.com
Barbara Scofidio, Editor
Melissa Fromento, Publisher
Kelly Conlin, CEO/President
Serves those involved in organizing business meetings, conventions, corporate travel agencies, and related fields. *$87.00*
Monthly Founded: 1980
Circulation: 32200
Printed in 4 colors

15864 Corporate Security
Strafford Publications
590 Dutch Valley Road NE
Atlanta, GA 30324-729
404-881-1141
FAX: 404-881-0074 800-926-7926
custserv@straffordpub.com
http://www.straffordpub.com
Richard M Ossoff, President
Joan McKenna, Editor
Marianne Mueller, Marketing
George Coleman, Manager
Intelligence briefing on the latest security developments, best practices, the most important trends and new technolgies. *$330.00*
23 pages Founded: 1984

15865 Cost Engineering Journal
AACE International
209 Prairie Avenue
Suite 100
Morgantown, WV 26501-5949
304-296-8444
FAX: 304-291-5728 800-858-3678
info@aacei.org http://www.aacei.org
Clive D Francis, President
Marvin Gelhausen, Editor
Jennie Amos, Marketing Manager
Cost engineering topics include latest news on estimation, cost control and management science. *$60.00*
Monthly Founded: 1956
Circulation: 5000
Mailing list available for rent

15866 Crain's New York Business
Crain Communications
711 3rd Avenue
New York, NY 10017
212-210-0100
FAX: 212-210-0465 888-909-9111
vcognard@crain.com
http://www.crainsnewyork.com
Vanessa Cognard, Marketing
Rance Crain, President
Crain's is the leading publication for exclusive coverage of business in New York. Crain's delivers a dynamic mix of breaking news, enlightening features and detailed analyses of events vital to the New York business community. It provides area business leaders with essential information they can't find in any other publication. CrainsNY.com gives our audience access to our resources 24/7, delivers news as it happens and offers fresh stories that do not appear in print. *$64.95*
Weekly
Circulation: 243000
Printed in 4 colors

15867 Customer Interaction Solutions
Technology Marketing Corporation
One Technology Plaza
Norwalk, CT 06854
203-852-6800
FAX: 203-853-2845 800-243-6002
tmc@tmcnet.com
http://www.tmcnet.com
Nadji Tehrani, CEO
Rich Tehrani, Editor-in-Chief
Dedicated to teleservices and e-services outsourcing, marketing and customer relationship management issues.
Monthly Founded: 1972

15868 Decision Sciences Journal
Decision Sciences Institute
35 Broad Street
Atlanta, GA 30303
404-651-4000
FAX: 404-651-2804
dsi@gsu.edu
http://www.decisionsciences.org
Gary L Ragatz, President
Julie Kendall, Treasurer
Carol J. Latta, Executive Director
Terrell G. Williams, Marketing Director
Vicki Smith-Daniels, Editor
Scientific quantitative, behavioral and computational approaches to decision making. *$100.00*
Quarterly Founded: 1968
Circulation: 5000

15869 Destination KC
Show-Me Publishing
306 E 12th Street
Suite 1014
Kansas City, MO 64106
816-358-8700
FAX: 814-474-1111
ingrams@unicom.net
Joe Sweeney, Editor-in-Chief
Kansas City's business relocation and information guide. *$36.00*
984 pages Monthly
Printed in 4 colors on glossy stock

15870 Direct
Primedia
9800 Metcalf Avenue
Overland Park, KS 66212
913-341-1300
FAX: 913-967-1898
sales@rmsreprints.com
http://www.directmag.com
Bryan Quinton, Editor
Charles Vietri, Managing Editor
Cheryll Richter, Marketing Manager
Andria Gennlauderslager, Circulation Manager
Serves the marketing and media industries.
Circulation: 46500
Printed in 4 colors

15871 Director
NFDA Publications
13625 Bishop's Drive
Brookfield, WI 53005-6607
262-789-1880
FAX: 262-789-6977 800-228-6332
nfda@nfda.org http://www.nfda.org
Christine Pepper, Chief Executive Officer
Chris Raymond, Editor
Benjamin Lund, Assistant Editor
Fay Spano, Director of Public Relations
The Director is specifically designed to inform and educate the funeral service professional in today's world. *$45.00*
114 pages Monthly Founded: 1882
Circulation: 14,761
Printed in 4 colors on glossy stock

15872 Discovery
Cooper Group
381 Park Avenue South 8th Floor
Suite 1100
New York, NY 10016-1775
212-696-2512
FAX: 212-696-2516
ihcooper@cooperdirect.com
http://www.thecoopergroup.com
Franklin Cooper, Editor
Harold Cooper, CEO

Focusing on critical management issues that drive growth, profitability and shareholder value. *$10.00*
Founded: 1984
Circulation: 1500

15873 Economist
PO Box 58524
Boulder, CO 80322-8524
303-945-1917
FAX: 303-604-7455 800-456-6086
usrights@economist.com
http://www.economist.com
Helen Alexander, Chief Executive Officer
Kate Cooke, Group Communications Manager
David Hanger, Publisher
The Economist is a news and business publication written for top business decision-makers and opinion leaders who need a wide range of information and views on world events. It explores the close links between domestic and international issues, business, finance, current affairs, science and technology.
160 pages Weekly Founded: 1843
Circulation: 1009759
Printed in 4 colors on glossy stock

15874 Executive Update
Greater Washington Society of Assn Executives
1300 Pennsylvania Avenue NW
Washington, DC 20004
202-048-8014
FAX: 202-326-0995
general@gwsae.org
http://www.gwsae.org
Liz Whittenmore, Publisher
Scott Briscoe, Editor
Theresa Magner, Director Advertising & Sp
Jam Armstrong, Circulation Manager
Susane Sarsati, CEO/President
Association news aimed at the executive level.
120 pages Monthly Founded: 1980
Circulation: 13300

15875 Expansion Management
Penton Media
1300 E 9th Street
Cleveland, OH 44114
216-696-7000
FAX: 216-696-1752
information@penton.com
http://www.expansionmanagement.com
Gorton Wood, Publisher
Bill King, Chief Editor
Jodi Svenson, Production Manager
Jodi Svenson, Circulation Manager
Mary Abood, Vice President
Employs charts, graphs and art to lead readers through well organized sections, such as regional reviews, state reports, industry news, case studies and international reports. Addresses the key issues that attract executives in companies that need facts on resource management.
Monthly Founded: 1986
Circulation: 45015

15876 Facilities Manager
Association of Physical Plant Administrators
1643 Prince Street
Alexandria, VA 22314-2818
703-684-1446
FAX: 703-549-2772
steve@appa.org http://www.appa.org
Steve Glazner, Editor
E. Lander Medlin, Executive VP
Betsy Colgan, Publications Manager
Offers information on the management of industrial plants. *$120.00*
64 pages Founded: 1914

15877 Financial Manager
Broadcast Cable Financial Management Association
550 Frontage Road Ste 3600
Northfield, IL 60093
847-960-0200
FAX: 847-716-7004
info@bcfm.com
http://www.bcfm.com
Joe Barlek, Chairman
Leslie Hartmann, Vice-Chairman
Edward Deichman, Treasurer
Mary Collins, President & CEO
Stewart Schley, Editor
A bi-monthly magazine published by the Broadcast Cable Financial Management Association. *$69.00*
36 pages Founded: 1961
Circulation: 300
Mailing list available for rent 1100 names $495 per M.

15878 Global IT Consulting Report
Kennedy Information
1 Kennedy Place
Route 12 S
Fitzwilliam, NH 03447
212-973-3855

Martin Zook, Editor
The business of information technology consulting, featuring news, analysis, benchmasking data and our exclusive Intelligence Briefing. *$895.00*
16 pages Monthly

15879 Golf Course Management
Golf Course Superintendents Association of America
1421 Research Park Drive
Lawrence, KS 66049-3858
785-841-2240
FAX: 785-841-2240 800-472-7878
infobox@gcsaa.org
http://www.gcsaa.org
Ed Hiscock, Editor-in-Chief
Lacy Stattelman, Marketing Specialist
Carla Sturgeon, Sales Coordinator
Steve Mona, Chief Executive Officer
Shelly Howard, Publications Coordinator

Golf Course Superintendent, economical, research and commercial interests concerned with golf course management and improvement. Provides information, education and representation for golf course managment profession. *$48.00*
Monthly Founded: 1926
Circulation: 40000

15880 HR Magazine
SHRM/Society for Human Resource Management
1800 Duke Street
Alexandria, VA 22314-3410
703-548-3440
FAX: 703-836-0367 800-283-7476
cpalazio@shrm.org www.shrm.org
Gary Rubin, Publisher
Leon Rubis, Editor
The world's leading HR resource, offering perspective and in-depth information to leading HR professionals for over 50 years. *$ 70.00*
Monthly Founded: 1956
Circulation: 197000

15881 Healthcare Financial Management
Healthcare Financial Management Association
2 Westbrook Corporate Center
Suite 700
Westchester, IL 60154-5700
708-319-9600
FAX: 708-531-0032 800-252-4362
taarya@hfma.org
http://www.hfma.org
Cheryl T Stachura, Publisher
Carole J Bolster, Editor
Richard l Clark, President
Gina Gina, Marketing Manager
Serves hospitals, medical clinics, nursing homes, extended care facilities, multi-hospital corporations, accounting, consulting firms, government, professional and academic institutions, consultants and others allied to the field. *$110.00*
94 pages Monthly Founded: 1946
Circulation: 32900
Printed in 4 colors on glossy stock

15882 High Technology Services Management
AFSM International
1342 Colonial Boulevard
Suite 25
Fort Myers, FL 33907-1084
239-275-7887
FAX: 239-275-0795
afsm@erols.com http://www.afsm.org

Suzanne Tissier, Senior Editor
Offers information aimed at the executive level of computer companies and high technology especially for customer service and customer support.
64 pages Monthly Founded: 1949
Circulation: 20000

15883 Industrial Management
Institute of Industrial Engineers
25 Technology Parkway S
Norcross, GA 30092-2928
770-417-1788
FAX: 770-263-8532
Charles Lopez, Publisher
Offers information and news to executives in the industrial industries.
32 pages Founded: 1962

15884 Information Strategy: Executives Journal
Auerbach Publications
535 5th Avenue
Room 806
New York, NY 10017-3610

FAX: 212-297-9176 800-737-8034
ckirkpatrick@crcpress.com
http://www.auerbach-publications.com
Christian Kirkpatrick, Publisher
Business computing for senior executives, helping them make strategic business decisions, manage departments and run computer applications that influence business performance.

Circulation: 5000

15885 Inside Supply Management
Institute for Supply Management
2055 E Centennial Circle
PO Box 22160
Tempe, AZ 85285-2160
480-752-6276
FAX: 480-752-7890 800-888-6276
custsvc@ism.ws http://www.ism.ws

Paul Novak, Chief Executive Officer
Kathy Braase, Sales Associate
Roberta Duffy, Editor

A publication for supply management professionals.
60 pages Monthly Founded: 1915
Printed in 4 colors on matte stock

15886 International Cemetery & Funeral Management
International Cemetery & Funeral Association
675 Hegenberger Road
Suite 230
Oakland, CA 94621-5434
510-633-9058
FAX: 510-633-9758
info@icf.org http://www.icf.org

Susan Loving, Managing Editor
Sheila Cephas, Product Development Coordinator
Leonard Rossi, President

Serves as the primary communication vehicle for ICFA news, membership activities, legislation, marketing and management, including the financial aspects of cemetery and funeral home operation. *$29.95*
64 pages
Circulation: 6000
Printed in 4 colors on glossy stock

15887 Journal of Corporate Renewal
Turnaround Management Association
100 South Wacker Drive
Suite 850
Chicago, IL 60606
312-577-7734
FAX: 312-578-8336
info@turnaround.org
www.turnaround.org

Lena Renteria, Manager

Devoted exclusively to professionals in the corporate renewal industry. Offers readers informative practice strategies and trends in the corporate renewal industry, current legal updates, economic perspectives and e-commerce developments. *$75.00*
Monthly
Circulation: 8000

15888 Journal of Operation Management
University of Missouri
10D Middlebush Hall
Columbia, MO 65211-1
573-882-2443
FAX: 573-882-0365
webeditor@missouri.edu

Ronald Ebert, Publisher

Publishes new thories concepts and models to advance current thought and practice to offer new directions for research. *$25.00*
Monthly
Circulation: 1200

15889 Journal of Product Innovation Management
Product Development and Management Association
15000 Commerce Parkway
Suite C
Mount Laurel, NJ 08054
317-783-9272
FAX: 856-439-0525 800-232-5261
pdma@pdma.org http://www.pdma.org

Thomas Hustad, Editor-in-Chief
Ken Kahn, VP Publications
Bob Brentin, President
C. Anthony Di Benedetto, Editor
Mark Adkins, VP Marketing

Provides essential information to help foster new product development, giving an overview of the total product innovation process and presenting the latest advancements in product innovation. Also assists managers in innovating and producing products more effectively and efficiently. Accepts advertising. *$125.00*
Founded: 1976

15890 Leadership
American Society of Association Executives
1575 I Street NW
Suite 11
Washington, DC 20005-1105
202-262-2723
FAX: 202-408-9634

Elissa Matulis Myers, Publisher
George Molfat, Advertising Director
Ann Mahoney, Editor
John Young, Production Director

For officers, board members and committee chairmen of trade associations and professional associations. Accepts advertising. *$ 5.00*
80 pages Annual
Circulation: 58,000

15891 Logistics Management & Distribution Report
Reed Business Information
225 Wyman Street
Waltham, MA 02451
617-643-3030
FAX: 781-734-8076
ecusack@reedbusiness.com
http://www.manufacturing.net

Stephen Moylan, President
Frank Quinn, Editorial Director

Logistics Management and Distribution Report is written for managers and professionals in charge of traffic, transportation, purchasing, inventory control, containerization and warehousing the functions of physical distribution and business logistics. Covers marketing and operating strategies, cost reduction opportunities and governmental regulation and law. *$99.90*
Monthly
Circulation: 83225

15892 Luxury Living
Business Journals
120 W Morehead Street
Suite 200
Charlotte, NC 28202
704-472-2340
FAX: 704-973-1102
charlotte@bizjournals.com
http://www.charlottebizjournals.com

Jeannie Falknor, Publisher
Robert Morrias, Editor
Megan Foley, Marketing Manager
Dale Moresield, Circulation Manager
$82.00
20 pages Quarterly
Printed in 4 colors on glossy stock

15893 MSI
Reed Business Information
2000 Clearwater Drive
Oak Brook, IL 60523
630-740-0825
FAX: 630-288-8764
corporatecommunications@reedbusines.com http://www.reedbusiness.com

Steve Rourke, Publisher
Kevin Parker, Editorial Director
Jim Casella, CEO
Nancy Bartels, Senior Editor
Eric Roth, Circulation Manager

Monthly Founded: 1977

15894 MWorld: Journal of the American Mangement Association
American Management Association
1601 Broadway
New York, NY 10019-7420
212-586-8100
FAX: 212-903-8181
fstone@amanet.org www.amanet.org

Larry Geiger, Publisher
Florence M Stone, Editor

Free quarterly mangement journal for American Management Association's executive and individual menbers.
48 pages Quarterly Founded: 2002
Circulation: 25,000 25,000 names $150 per M.
Printed in 2 colors on glossy stock

15895 Maintenance Technology
Applied Technology Publications
1300 S Grove Avenue
Suite 105
Barrington, IL 60010
847-382-8100
FAX: 847-304-8603
rcbaldwin@atpnetwork.com
http://www.mt-online.com

Tom Madding, Publisher
Robert C Baldwin, Editor
Susan Dahlberg, Managing Editor
Linda K. Fischer, Associate Editor
Nancy Williams, Production Manager

Maintanence Technology magazine serves the business and technical information needs of engineers, managers and supervisors responsible for the maintanence and reliability of plant equipment and facility systems.
62 pages Monthly Founded: 1998
Circulation: 50000
Printed in 4 colors on glossy stock

15896 Manage
National Management Association
2210 Arbor Boulevard
Dayton, OH 45439-1506
937-294-0421
FAX: 937-294-2374
nma@nma1.org http://www.nma1.org

Douglas Shaw, Publisher
Douglas Shaw, Editor
Steve Bailey, CEO

Association news for executives.
32 pages Quarterly Founded: 1925

15897 Management Consultants International
Kennedy Information
1 Kennedy Place
Route 12 S
Fitzwilliam, NH 03447
212-972-3855

News and busieness intelligence on management consulting worldwide. Monthly issues feature country by country surveys of local consulting firms. *$1122.00*
16 pages Monthly

15898 Medical Group Management Journal
104 Inverness Ter E
Englewood, CO 80112-5313
303-991-1111
FAX: 303-643-4427

Dennis Barnhardt APR, Communications Director
Eileen Barker, Advertising Director
William Jessee, Manager

Encompasses pertinent problems, questions and issues relating to group practice management.
Bi-Monthly

15899 New Mobility
PO Box 220
Horsham, PA 19044
215-675-9133
FAX: 215-675-9376
info@newmobility.com
http://www.newmobility.com

Tim Gilmer, Editor
Jean Dobbs, Editorial Director
Kim Montgomery, Circulation *$27.95*
Monthly

15900 Operations & Fulfillment
Primedia
11 River Bend Drive South
PO Box 4242
Stamford, CT 06907-242
203-589-9900
FAX: 203-358-5823 800-775-3777
schiger@primediabusiness.com
http://www.multichannelmerchant.com

Sherry Chiger, Editorial Director
Melisa Dowling, Executive Editor
Len Roberto, Circulation Manager
Kate Dimarco, Production Manager
Barry Litwin, VP Sales/Marketing

Provides executives information they can't get anywhere else and reach executives and managers with purchasing authority in all areas of operations management. Information on direct to customer fulfillment.. *$85.00*
Founded: 1984
Circulation: 40000

15901 Organization Development Institute
11234 Walnut Ridge Road
Chesterland, OH 44026-1299
440-729-7419
FAX: 440-729-9319
donwcole@aol.com
http://www.odinstitute.org

Dr. Donald W Cole, President
Jim Gustafson, Editor Journal

Promotes the understanding of organization development and offers three categories of membership: professional consultant, regular and student. Offers the International Registry of O.D. Professionals and O.D. Handbook which lists names, addresses and E-mail addresses, publishes a monthly newsletter plus a quarterly journal of 100-150 pages. There are two conferences held every year, one in the USA and one International. *$ 80.00*
Quarterly Founded: 1968 8000 names $200 per M.

15902 Organization Development Journal
OD Institute
11234 Walnut Ridge Road
Chesterland, OH 44026-1240
440-729-7419
FAX: 440-729-9319
dian@odinstitute.com
http://www.odinstitute.org/

Dr. Donald W Cole, Publisher
Dr. Donald W Cole, CEO/President
Jenny Maes, Editor

A journal published quarterly for human resource people, managers and organization development people. The most frequently cited OD/OB publication in the world. *$80.00*
100 pages Quarterly Founded: 1968
Circulation: 700
Mailing list available for rent 9M names
Printed in 1 color on newsprint stock

15903 PM Network
Project Management Institute
4 Campus Boulevard
Newtown Square, PA 19073-3299
610-355-1610
FAX: 610-356-4647
pmihq@pmi.org http://www.pmi.org

Gregory Balestrero, CEO
Louis J Mercken, Chair
Iain Fraser, Vice Chair
James McGeehan, Public Relations

A monthly magazine published by the Project Management Institute.
75 pages Monthly
Mailing list available for rent

15904 Print Solutions Magazine
Document Management Industries Association
433 E Monroe Avenue
Alexandria, VA 22301-1693
703-836-6232
FAX: 703-549-4966 800-336-4641
bholt@printsolutionsmag.com
http://www.printsolutionsmag.com/

Peter L Colaianni, Editor-in-Chief
Darin Painter, Managing Editor
Preeti Vasishtha, Assistant Editor
Andrew Brown, Assistant Editor

Source for marketing, management and product information.
Monthly Founded: 1962
Circulation: 42000
Printed in 4 colors on glossy stock

15905 Professional Journal
AFSM International
1342 Colonial Boulevard
Suite 25
Fort Meyers, FL 33907
239-275-7887
FAX: 239-275-0794
info@asfmi.org http://www.afsmi.org

John Schoenewald, CEO/Publisher
Suzanne Kaminski, Senior Editor
James Gaidry, Marketing manager

A magazine for executives, managers and professionals in the high-technology services industry. *$90.00*
114 pages Founded: 1975
Circulation: 7000
Printed in 4 colors on glossy stock

15906 Project Management Journal
Project Management Institute
4 Campus Boulevard
Newtown Square, PA 19073-3299
610-356-4600
FAX: 610-356-4647
pmipub@pmi.org http://www.pmi.org

Gregory Balestrero, CEO
Mark Langley, Managing Director
Gary Boyler, Publisher
Dan Goldfischer, Editor in Chief
Beverly Cook, Production Manager

A quarterly journal published by the Project Management Institute.
65 pages Quarterly
Mailing list available for rent

15907 Purchasing
Reed Business Information
275 Washington Street
Cahners Building
Newton, MA 02158
630-320-7000
FAX: 630-288-8686
http://www.purchasing.com

Kathy Doyle, Publisher
Lockie Montgomery, Production Manager
Anne Millen Porter, Business Manager
Paul Teague, Chief Editor.

About the purchasing professional in American industry.
Founded: 1920

15908 Quality Management Update
High Tech Publishing Company
PO Box 1275
Amherst, MA 01004-1275
413-534-4500
FAX: 413-256-6378

Philip T DiPeri, Editor

Provides senior executives with in-depth analysis and creative insights on the tools and techniques of Total Quality management. *$195.00*
Bi-Monthly

15909 Quality Progress
American Society for Quality
600 North Plankinton Avenue
Milwaukee, WI 53203-3005
414-272-8575
FAX: 414-272-1734 800-248-1946
help@asq.org http://www.asq.org

Paul E. Borawski, Executive Director
Christopher Bauman, Managing Director
Brian J. LeHouillier, Managing Director
$55.00
Monthly Founded: 1946

15910 Recruiting Trends
Kennedy Information
One Phoenix Mill Lane
5th Fl.
Peterborough, NH 03458
603-924-1006
FAX: 603-924-4460
support@kennedyinfo.com
http://www.kennedyinfo.com

Joseph McCool, Editor
Mina Landrisina, Managing Director

Provides strategies and tactics for creating and maintaining a competitive workforce. *$99.00*
8 pages Monthly Founded: 1970

15911 Retail Merchandiser
MacFadden Publishing
233 Park Avenue S
6th Floor
New York, NY 10003-1606
212-794-4800
FAX: 212-979-7431
info@retail-merchandiser.com
http://www.retail-merchandiser.com

Jeff Friedman, Publisher
Greg Masters, Managing Editor
Toni Riggio, Sales Coordinator
Anita M Wise, Production Manager

Serves those in management positions of mass retail and discount companies. *$99.00*

Monthly Founded: 1961
Circulation: 34,188

15912 Risk Management
Risk & Insurance Management Society
655 3rd Avenue
2nd Floor
New York, NY 10017
212-286-9292
FAX: 212-286-9716
cnelson@rims.org http://www.rims.org

Ted Donovan, Publisher
Bill Coffin, Editor-in-Chief
Jared Wade, Associate Editor
Callie Nelson, Circulation Manager
Todd Lockwood, Advertising Sales Manager *$64.00*

Monthly Founded: 1950
Circulation: 15000

15913 Shelby Report
Shelby Publishing Company
517 Green Street
Gainsville, GA 30501
770-534-8380
FAX: 770-535-0110
shelbpub@bellsouth.net
http://www.shelbypublishing.com

Roan Johnston, Publisher/President
Chuck Gilmer, Editor

Serving the grocery industry in Arizona, Arkansas, Colorado, Kansas, Louisana, Missouri, New Mexico, Oklahoma, and Texas, *$36.00*

Monthly Founded: 1966
Circulation: 25201

15914 Si Review
Staffing Industry Analysts
881 Fremont Avenue
Suite A3
Los Altos, CA 94024-5637
650-489-9303
FAX: 650-232-2360 800-950-9496
info@sireport.com
http://www.sireport.com

Jeff Reeder, Managing Editor
Theresa Daly, Production Manager
Ron Mester, CEO/President

Tools and techniques for staffing industry professionals. How-to's and survey articles for branch management, upper management, owners, and sales/service personnel in employment service companies. Display advertising included. *$99.00*

22 issues per y Founded: 1989
Printed in 4 colors on glossy stock

15915 South Florida Business Journal
American City Business Journals
120 W Morehead Street
Charlotte, NC 28202
704-973-1000
FAX: 704-973-1001 800-486-3289
southflorida@bizjournals.com
http://www.bizjournals.com

Robert Morris, Editor
Megan Foley, Marketing Director
David Harris, Managing Editor

Covers all aspects of business in South Florida. *$99.00*

Weekly

15916 St. Louis Business Journal
One Metropolitan Square
Suite 2170
Saint Louis, MO 63102
314-421-6200
FAX: 314-621-5031 800-486-3289
stlouis@bizjournals.com
http://www.amcity.com/stlouis

Patricia Miller, Editor
Bonnie Weinacht, Circulation Director

Covers the St. Louis business community. *$84.00*

Monthly

15917 Staffing Management
SHRM/Society for Human Resource Management
1800 Duke Street
Alexandria, VA 22314
703-548-3440
FAX: 703-836-0367 800-283-7476
cpalazio@shrm.org www.shrm.org

Gary Rubin, Publisher
Leon Rubis, Editor

Formerly known as Employment Management Today, this magazine provides information on the latest techniques and trends in recruiting and retaining your most important commodity: your employees. *$35.00*

56 pages Quarterly Founded: 1995
Circulation: 10000

15918 Supermarket News - Retail/Financial
Fairchild Publications
7 W 34th Street
New York, NY 10001
212-630-4000
FAX: 212-630-3675 800-204-4515
custserv@espcomp.com
http://www.supermarketnews.com

Dan Bagan, Publishing Director
David Orgel, Editor-in-Chief
Christina Veiders, Managing Editor
Joy Kulick, Marketing *$45.00*

Weekly Founded: 1892

15919 Supervision
National Research Bureau
320 Valley Street
Burlington, IA 52601
319-752-5415
FAX: 319-752-3421
national@willinet.net

Diane Darnall, Publisher
Teresa Levinson, Editor
Diane Darnall, CEO/President
Diane Darnall, Circulation Manager
Diane Darnall, Marketing Manager

Magazines for foremen, supervisors and office managers advising on how to cope with discipline, absenteeism, safety and productivity. *$68.00*

Monthly Founded: 1930
Circulation: 1200

15920 Supply Chain Management Review
Reed Business Information
225 Wyman Street
Waltham, MA 02451
617-643-3030
FAX: 781-734-8076
scmr@reedbusiness.com
http://www.scmr.com

Vince Cavaseno, Publisher
Frank Quinn, Chief Editor
Susan Lacefield, Associate Editor
Mary Ann Gajewski, Production Manager

Contains in-depth feature articles on various aspects of Supply Chain Management. SCM is the science of integrating the flow of goods and information from initial souring and purchasing, order processing and fulfillment, production planning and scheduling, inventory management, transportation, distribution and customer service. Each issue delivers in-depth feature articles from the thought leaders in the supply chain community. *$199.00*

Circulation: 12000

15921 Supply Chain Technology News
Penton Media
1300 E 9th Street
Cleveland, OH 44114
216-696-7000
FAX: 216-696-1752
information@penton.com
www.TOTALsupplychain.com
Focuses on the practical application of technology accross a broad range of supply chain functions.

15922 Tapping the Network Journal
Quality & Productivity Management Association
300 N Martingale Road
Suite 230
Schaumburg, IL 60173-2407
708-619-2909
FAX: 847-619-3383

William Ginnodo, Editor/Author

This quarterly publication is, By and For Organizational Change Agents. Most articles are written by QPMA members. Its purpose is to share - in a straightforward, factual and practical manner - what has been learned within the authors' organization during the course of a particular change effort. It is provided free to members, and made available to non-member subscribers.

15923 Training
50 S 9th Street
Minneapolis, MN 55402
612-333-0471
FAX: 612-333-6526
webeditor@hq.vnu.com
http://www.vnu.com

Rob van den Bergh, CEO
Rob Ruijter, CFO
AC Nielsen, Marketing

Founded: 1960

15924 Warehousing Management
Reed Business Information
360 Park Avenue South
New York, NY 10014
212-450-0067
FAX: 617-558-4327 800-550-0827
corporatecommunications@reedbusiness.com http://www.reedbusiness.com

Thomas A Esposito, Publisher
John R Johnson, Editor-in-Chief

James Reed, Owner
Jane Burgess, Marketing Director

Warehousing Management targets warehousing and distribution center operations managers with analysis, news, trends, equipment and events.

Founded: 1977
Circulation: 47185

15925 Workgroup Computing Report
Patricia Seybold Group
85 Devonshire Street
5th Floor
Boston, MA 02109-3504
617-742-5200
FAX: 617-742-1028
info@psgroup.com www.psgroup.com

Patricia Seybold, Publisher
Ronni Marshak, Editor-in-Chief

Provides information on implementing workflow, document management, groupware, and business process reengineering. *$440.00*
Monthly

15926 World
Economist
111 W 57th Street
The Economist Building
New York, NY 10019
212-541-5730
FAX: 212-541-9378
usrights@economist.com

Dudley Fishburn, Editor
David Hanger, Publisher

124 pages ISBN 0-862181-66-6
Printed in 4 colors on glossy stock

15927 Young Presidents' Organization - Magazine
Young Presidents' Organization
451 Decker Drive
Suite 200
Irving, TX 75062-3954
972-504-4600
FAX: 972-650-4777 www.ypo.org

Thomas Stauffer, Executive Director
Les Ward, Manager

BiAnnual
Circulation: 8000
Printed in on glossy stock

Trade Shows

15928 AACE International Annual Meeting & Exposition
AACE International
209 Prarie Avenue
Suite 100
Morgantown, WV 26507
304-296-8444
FAX: 304-291-5728 800-858-2678
info@aacei.org www.aacei.org

Clive D Francis, President
Philip D Larson, President - Elect
William E Kraus, VP/Administration
Robert B Brown, VP/Finance
Andy Dowd, Executive Director

Offers a unique opportunity to learn, network, and expand your professional horizons in a cost-effective manner. Our goal is to provide cost professionals with the knowledge necessary for survival in today's incredibly fast-changing marketplace. AACE's technical presentations, skills and knowledge track, exhibitors, transactions, certification program and special events combine to create an experience you can't afford to miss.

800 Attendees June 5000+ names $100 per M.

15929 AHRA Annual Meeting & Exposition
American Healthcare Radiology Administrators
490-B Boston Post Road
Suite 101
Sudbury, MA 01776
978-443-7591
FAX: 978-443-8046 800-334-2472
info@ahraonline.org
www.ahraonline.org

Sheila M Sferrella, Chair
Wanda M Casady, Vice Chair
Jay P Mazurowski, Secretary/Treasurer
Michael J Albertina, Director
Edward Cronin, Executive Director

A resource and catalyst for the development of professional leadership in imaging sciences. A driving force toward improving the healthcare environment. Containing 171 booths and 171 exhibits.

Mailing list available for rent 4000 names $250 per M.

15930 Administrative Assistants Executive Secretaries Seminar
PA Douglas & Associates
644 Strander Boulevard
#411
Seattle, WA 98188
206-244-6441
FAX: 780-444-8002
www.padouglas.com

Dr. Paul A Douglas MBA, PhD, CMC, Leader

To provide seminars, workshops and educational materials to individuals from the United States, Canada, and Europe. Includes an intensive three-day workshop for exploring and developing intellectual, organizational and interpersonal abilities.
$1795.00
Founded: 1975

15931 American Society of Association Executives Annual Meeting & Expo
American Society of Association Executives
The ASAE Building
1575 I Street NW
Washington, DC 20005
202-262-2723
FAX: 202-371-8315
asae@asae.asaenet.org
www.asaenet.org

John Graham, Executive Director

Professional service companies that specialize in providing management services for association on a fee-for-service basis. Exhibits related to managing associations.
Annual

15932 Association for Services Management
1342 Colonial Boulevard
Suite 25
Fort Myers, FL 33907-1084
239-275-7887
FAX: 239-275-0794 www.asm.org

John Schoenwald, CEO

Management convention and exposition.
Fall

15933 Association for Worksite Health Promotion Annual International Conference
60 Revere Drive
Suite 500
Northbrook, IL 60062-1577
847-480-9574
FAX: 847-480-9282
awhp@awhp.org www.awhp.org

Liz Freyn, Conference Manager

122 booths of information and supplies to promote and develop quality programs of health and fitness in business and industry. Seminar, workshop, conference, tours and luncheon.

950 Attendees Founded: 1974

15934 Circulation Managers Association International
11600 Sunrise Valley Drive
Reston, VA 20191-1412
703-506-1661

Joseph Forsee, Show Manager

100 booths exhibiting products such as newsracks, rubber products and software.

225 Attendees June

15935 Coaching and Teambuilding Skills for Managers and Supervisors
SkillPath Seminars
6900 Squibb Road
PO Box 2768
Mission, KS 66201-2768
913-623-3900
FAX: 913-362-4241 800-873-7545
enroll@skillpath.net
www.skillpath.com

One-day workshop to sharpen your leadership skills and boost your team's productivity. Various locations and dates.
$199.00

15936 Construction Specifications Institute Annual Show & Convention
99 Canal Center Plaza
Suite 300
Alexandria, VA 22314
703-684-0300
FAX: 703-684-8436 800-689-2900
csinet@csinet.org www.csinet.org

Lisa Derby, Events Senior Director
Jennifer Gorrie, Events & Awards Coordinator
Myra Ibrahimi, Events & Awards In-Training Coord.

Education sessions that focus on industry topics such as; Business and Professional Development, Design & Pre-Construction Activities, Facility Management, Formats & Documents, Legal, Public Facilities & Communities, Safety & Security, Specialty Construction, and Specifications.

6,000 Attendees Annual Founded: 1954

15937 EMA Annual Conference & Exposition
SHRM/Society for Human Resource Management
1800 Duke Street
Alexandria, VA 22314
703-548-3440
FAX: 703-535-6490 800-283-7476
bobgonz@us.ibm.com www.shrm.org/

Johnny C Taylor Jr, Chairman
Susan Meisinger, President/CEO
Robert O Gonzales, Secretary
Robb E Van Cleave, Treasurer

Conference devoted to employment management issues.
700 Attendees March/April

15938 Fundamentals of Personnel Law for Managers and Supervisors
Human Resources Council
6900 Squibb Road
PO Box 804441
Kansas City -4441

800-601-4636

Rose Miller, Trainer

One-day seminar covering the legal issues affecting everyday management of employees. Various locations and dates. *$199.00*

15939 Hartford Conference on Leadership Development & Teambuilding
SkillPath Seminars
6900 Squibb Road
PO Box 2768
Mission, KS 66201-2768
913-623-3900
FAX: 913-362-4241 800-873-7545
Conference teaches practical leadership skills thorough real-life examples, pratical methods and techniques. Suitable for managers, supervisors, team leaders and team members.

15940 IRMA Annual Conference
Information Resources Management Association
701 E Chocolate Avenue
Suite 200
Hershey, PA 17033
717-533-8879
FAX: 717-533-8661
member@irma-international.org
www.irma-international.org

Mehdi Khosrow-Pour, President
Muhammad Al-Khaldi, Executive Council

Managing modern organizations with information technology.
May

15941 Information Resources Management Journal
Information Resources Management Association
701 E Chocolate Avenue
Suite 200
Hershey, PA 17033
717-533-8879
FAX: 717-533-8861
members@irma-international.org
www.irma-international.org

Mehdi Khosrow-Pour, Editor

An applied research, refereed, international journal providing coverage of challenges, opportunities, problems, trends, and solutions encountered by both scholars and practitioners in the field of information technology management. *$95.00*
Quarterly

15942 New Jersey Accounting, Business & Technology Show
Flagg Management
353 Lexington Avenue
New York, NY 10016
212-286-0333
FAX: 212-286-0086
flaggmgmnt@msn.com
www.flaggmgmt.com

Russell Flagg, President

Human resources, personnel administration and training marketplace, HRMS, systems and services, 250 exhibits.
2000 Attendees Annual Founded: 1988

15943 Project Management for IT Professionals
CompuMaster
6900 Squibb Road
PO Box 2973
Mission, KS 66201-1373
913-362-3900
FAX: 913-432-4930 800-867-4340
compumaster@mcimail.com
www.compumaster.net

Casey Smith, Customer Service

A two-day workshop that will help you meet complex project deadlines and budgets. Held in various locations in November and December. Customization at your location available for groups of twenty or more. *$399.00*

15944 SSA Expo
Support Services Alliance
107 Prospect Street
PO Box 130
Schoharie, NY 12157-0130
518-295-7966
FAX: 518-295-8556 800-322-3920
info@ssamembers.com
www.ssainfo.com

Jim Gaw, VP

Believes small business are the economic backbone of America and could stregthen their economic position by forming a purchasing alliance. Programs and services include advocacy in the state legislature, group insurance programs, payroll and benefits administration, monthly newsletter magazine and membership help line
October

15945 SkillPath Seminars
6900 Sqibb Road
PO Box 2768
Mission, KS 66201-2768
913-623-3900
FAX: 913-362-4241 800-873-7545
enroll@skillpath.net
www.skillpath.com

Steve Nichols, Customer Care Representative
Robb Garr, President

Learn better skills in Administrative Assistance, Leadership, Software, Business Writing, Desktop Publishing, Customer Service, Coaching and Teambuilding, Conflict resolution, Management and conquering workplace negativity.

Directories & Databases

15946 ABI/INFORM
UMI/Data Courier
620 S 3rd Street
Suite 400
Louisville, KY 40202-2475

FAX: 502-589-5572 800-626-2823
This database contains more than 675,000 citations, appearing in over 900 international periodicals covering business and management related areas.
Bibliographic

15947 American Directory of Organized Labor
Gale Research
27500 Drake Road
Farmington Hills, MI 48331
248-699-4253
FAX: 248-699-8214 800-877-4253
galeord@gale.com www.gale.com

Gordon T Macomber, President
Dennis Stepaniak, Executive VP/CFO
Ray Lowrey, Executive VP/CTO
John Baines, Executive VP/Strategic Business Dev
Rich Foley, Executive VP/Sales/Marketing

Offers information on over 225 national and over 40,000 independent and local unions in the US. *$275.00*
1638 pages

15948 Analysis of Workers' Compensation Laws
Chamber of Commerce of the United States
1615 H Street NW
Washington, DC 20062-0001
202-659-6000

Offers a list of workers' compensation administrators. *$25.00*
Annual

15949 Association of Management Consulting Firms
AMCF
380 Lexington Avenue
Suite 1700
New York, NY 10168
212-551-7887
FAX: 212-551-7934
info@amcf.org www.amcf.org

Elizabeth A Kovacs, President/CEO
Kathleen Fish, Director Programs
Samantha Colon, Executive Administrator

About 50 management consulting firms that are members of ACME. *$50.00*
Biennial Founded: 1929

15950 Business Information Desk Reference: Where to Find Answers to Questions
Palgrave Macmillan
175 5th Avenue
New York, NY 10010
212-982-3900
FAX: 212-420-9314

Bruce McKenzie, President

Over 1,000 print material, online databases and federal agencies covering over 24 business areas are listed.

15951 Business Library
Dow Jones & Company
4300 North Route 1
South Brunswick, NJ 08852
609-520-4000

Covers all types of topics and subjects that are of interest to US business markets.
Full-text

15952 Business Opportunities Handbook
Enterprise Magazines
1020 N Broadway
Suite 111
Milwaukee, WI 53202-3157
414-272-9977
FAX: 414-272-9973
info@busop1.com www.busop1.com

Maria Lahm, Editor in Chief

Over 2,500 listings of franchises, dealers and distributors that offer business opportunities to individuals. *$5.99*

150 pages Quarterly

15953 Business Organizations, Agencies and Publications Directory

Gale Research
27500 Drake Road
Farmington Hills, MI 48331
248-699-4253
FAX: 248-699-8214 800-877-4253
galeord@gale.com www.gale.com

Gordon T Macomber, President
Dennis Stepaniak, Executive VP/CFO
Ray F Lowrey, Executive VP/CTO
Rich Foley, Executive VP/Sales/Management
Dennis Paupard, Executive VP/Editorial/Production

Over 30,000 organizations and publications of all kinds that are helpful to business are profiled. *$345.00*

1800 pages Biennial

15954 Career Guide: Dun's Employment Opportunities Directory

Dun & Bradstreet Information Service
3 Sylvan Way
Parsippany, NJ 07054-3805
973-455-0900
FAX: 973-605-6930

Offers information on more than 5,000 companies, leading employers of the United States, that provide career opportunities in sales, marketing and management. *$385.00*

2700 pages Annual

15955 Company Intelligence

Information Access Company
362 Lakeside Drive
Foster City, CA 94404-1171
650-378-5200
800-227-8431

Offers company news and financial information with an emphasis placed on hard-to-find privately held companies in the United States and worldwide.

Bibliographic

15956 Corporate Technology Database

One Source Information Services
300 Baker Avenue
Concord, MA 01742
978-318-4300
FAX: 978-318-4690 800-554-5501
sales@onesource.com
www.onesource.com

Yvonne Cekel, President
John Brewer, VP/Marketing
Philip Garlick, Sr VP/Global Sales
Brad Haigis, VP/Products
Beth Jacaruso, VP/Content

Offers profiles of over 45,000 public and private US corporations and operating units of large corporations that develop or manufacture some 100,000 high-technology products.

Directory

15957 Corporate Yellow Book

Leadership Directories
104 5th Avenue
New York, NY 10011-6901
212-627-4140
FAX: 212-645-0931
corporate@leadershipdirectories.com
www.leadershipdirectories.com

Vonessa Ruffin, Editor

Contact information for over 48,000 executives at over 1,000 companies and more than 9,000 board members and their outside affiliations. *$360.00*

1,400 pages Quarterly Founded: 1986
50,000 names $105 per M. : CD-Rom

15958 Directory of Business Information Resources

Grey House Publishing
185 Millerton Road
PO Box 860
Millerton, NY 12546
518-890-0526
FAX: 518-789-0545 800-562-2139
books@greyhouse.com
www.greyhouse.com

Leslie Mackenzie, Publisher
Richard Gottlieb, Editor

The source for contacts in over 98 business areas, from advertising and agriculture to utilities and wholesalers. This carefully researched volume details, for each business industry, the associations representing each industry, the newsletters that keep members current, the magazines and journals that are important to the trade, the top conventions and industry web sites that provide important marketing information. Includes contact names with phone, fax, website and e-mail information. *$250.00*

1,800 pages Annual

15959 Directory of Consultants and Translators for Engineered Materials

Materials Information
9639 Kinsman Road
Materials Park, OH 44073-0001
440-338-5151
FAX: 440-338-4634
www.asminternational.org

Stanley Theobald, Managing Director

Over 300 consultants and 170 translators in the field of composites and ceramics are profiled. *$76.00*

72 pages

15960 Directory of Executive Recruiters

Kennedy Information
One Phoenix Mill Lane
5th Floor
Peterboro, NH 03458
603-241-1006
FAX: 603-924-4460 800-531-0007

Lists over 8,900 offices of 5,678 executive search firms in the US, Canada and Mexico. Includes key data and contact info on each firm. Directory is indexed by recruiter specialities, function, industry, key principals, and geography. Corporate edition is specially designed for corporate buyers of search services and search providers. *$179.95*

1180 pages Annual ISBN 1-885922-81-7

15961 Directory of Management Consultants

Kennedy Information
1 Phoenix Mill Lane
5th Floor
Peterborough, NH 03458
603-924-1006
FAX: 603-924-4460 800-531-0007
bookstore@kennedyinfo.com
www.kennedyinfo.com

The premier directory of management consulting firms, published since 1979. The 10th edition profiles more than 2,400 firms in North America. Indexed by services, industries, geography, and key contacts. *$295.00*

850 pages Biennial Founded: 1919 ISBN 1-885922-69-8
Mailing list available for rent 7600 names $200 per M.

15962 Directory of Management Information Systems Faculty

Management Information Systems Research Center
355 Humphrey-271 9th Avenue S
Minneapolis, MN 55455
763-783-7496
FAX: 612-626-1316
jdegross@csom.umn.edu
www.webfoot.csom.umn.edu

Gordon B Davis, Editor
Janice I DeGross, Editor

College-level teachers of subjects related to management information systems and technology. *$25.00*

15963 Directory of Outplacement & Career Management Firms

Kennedy Information
One Phoenix Mill Lane
5th Floor
Peterborough, NH 03458
603-241-1006
FAX: 603-924-4460 800-531-0007

Profiles 365 firms in 1,351 offices worldwide and identifies 1,875 key principals. Includes key data on revenues, staff sizes, fees & expense policies, and contact information. Indexed by industry specialty, geography and individual outplacement professional. *$129.00*

606 pages ISBN 1-885922-65-5

15964 Directory of US Labor Organizations

BNA Books
1231 25th Street Nw
Washington, DC 20037-1164
202-452-4200
FAX: 202-452-4610 800-372-1033

Over 200 national unions and professional and state employees associations engaged in labor representation are profiled. *$55.00*

110 pages Annual

15965 Diversity in Corporate America

Hunt-Scanlon Corporation
700 Fairfield Avenue
Stamford, CT 06902
203-352-2920
FAX: 203-352-2930

James A Mueller, Founder
Scott Scanlon, Chief Executive Officer
Smooch S Reynolds, President
A David Brown, Managing Director
John D Delpino, Director - Executive Staffing

2,200 listings of executives responsible for managing corporate diversity in the US. *$179.00*

Biennial

15966 Employee Service Management: NESRA Buyers Directory

National Employee Services & Recreation Assn
568 Spring Road
Suite D
Elmhurst, IL 60126
630-559-0020
FAX: 630-559-0025
esmahq@esmassn.org
www.esmassn.org

Renee Mula, Editor

Includes a list of over 200 member manufacturers and distributors offering products and services for employee discount programs and employee store merchandise to members.
Annual

15967 Employment, Hours and Earnings
US Department Of Commerce
14 Constitutional Avenue NW
Washington, DC 20212-0001
202-821-1850

This database aimed at employees and management cover US employment, hours and earnings.

15968 Fortune Magazine
Time
1271 6th Avenue
16th Floor
New York, NY 10020
212-221-1212
800-274-6800
Bill Stephen, Manager
Information for non-business and business owners on how to start or manage your business. *$5.00*
Annual

15969 Fortune: Deals of the Year Issue
Time
1271 6th Avenue
16th Floor
New York, NY 10020-1300
212-221-1212
800-274-6800
Bill Stephen, Manager
Offers information on 50 of the largest United States corporate financial transactions, including mergers, acquisitions and leveraged buyouts. *$5.00*
Annual

15970 International Directory of Executive Recruiters
Kennedy Information
One Phonnix Mill Lane
5th Floor
Peterborough, NH 03458
603-241-1006
FAX: 603-924-4460 800-531-0007
A comprehensive source of worldwide executive recruiting firms and consultancies. List full contact information for search firms in 60 countries. Indexed by management function, industry, firm, and search firm principals. *$149.00*
800 pages ISBN 1-885922-53-1

15971 International Registry of OD Professional
Organization Development Institute
11234 Walnut Ridge Road
Chesterland, OH 44026-1240
440-729-7419
donwcole@aol.com
Dr. Donald W Cole RODC, President
A who's who directory of services and supplies to the industry. Includes: The OD Code of Ethics; a Statement on the Knowledge and Skill Necessary for Competence in O.D.; a listing of not just names and addresses, but the credential of all those registered with us; a list of all the OD organizations in the world and all the OD/OB academic programs in the world. *$25.00*
300 pages Annual

15972 Labor Arbitration Information System
LRP Publications
747 Dresher Road, Suite 500
PO Box 980
Horsham, PA 19044-0980
215-840-0912
FAX: 215-784-9639
custserve@lrp.com www.lrp.com
Sandy Johnson, Director/Manager
Comprehensive indexing system for arbitration awards available. The easy-to-use, one-stop indexing system covers all the major arbitration reporting services including AAA, BNA, and CCH. *$515.00*

.

Monthly Founded: 1977

15973 Management Contents
Gale Research
27500 Drake Road
Farmington Hills, MI 48331
248-699-4253
FAX: 248-699-8214 800-877-4253
galeord@gale.com
www.galegroup.com
Gordon T Macomber, President
Dennis Stepaniak, Executive VP/CFO
Ray F Lowrey, Executive VP/CTO
Rick Foley, Executive VP/Sales/Marketing
Dennis Paupard, Executive VP/Editorial/Production
Database offering information on business and management, including accounting, auditing, advertising and sales, banking, decision science, economics and employee benefits.
Bibliographic

15974 Meeting the Needs of Employees with Disabilities
Resources for Rehabilitation
22 Bonad Road
Winchester, MA 01890
781-368-9094
FAX: 781-368-9096 www.rfr.org
Offers various descriptions of organizations and products that assist those involved in the employment of people with disabilities. *$42.95*
Biennial

15975 National Directory of Managed Care Organzatons
Health Resources Publishing
1913 Atlantic Avenue
Suite F4
Manasquan, NJ 08736
732-292-1100
FAX: 732-292-1111 888-843-6242
info@themcic.com
www.themcic.com/www.healthresourceso nline.com
Bob Jenkins, President/Managing Editor
Lisa Mansfield, Marketing Assistant
Published by Health Resources Publishing. Available in print ($325), database ($1695) or CD-Rom ($695). *$325.00*

15976 SHRM Membership Directory Online
SHRM/Society for Human Resource Management
1800 Duke Street
Alexandria, VA 22314
703-548-3440
FAX: 703-535-6490 800-283-7476
bobgonz@us.ibm.com www.shrm.org
Johnny C Taylor Jr, Chairman
Susan Meisinger, President/CEO
Robert O Gonzales, Secretary
Robb E Van Cleave, Treasurer
An exclusive benefit for SHRM members, the SHRM Membership Directory Online is a searchable database catagorized by by name, title, company, company size, job function or location.

15977 Small Business Sourcebook
Gale Research
27500 Drake Road
Farmington Hills, MI 48331
248-699-4253
FAX: 248-699-8214 800-877-4253
galeord@gale.com www.gale.com
Gordon T Macomber, President
Dennis Stepaniak, Executive VP/CFO
Ray F Lowrey, Executive VP/CTO
Rich Foley, Executive VP/Sales/Marketing
Dennis Paupard, Executive VP/Editorial/Production
Comprehensive directory profiles more than 280 specific types of small businesses. *$235.00*
2900 pages 2 Volumes

15978 Small Business or Entrepreneurial Related Newsletter
Prosperity & Profits Unlimited
PO Box 416
Denver, CO 80201-0416
303-573-5564

A Doyle, Editor
A mini directory of listings for small businesses. *$19.95*
8 pages Every 2 Years Founded: 1990
Circulation: 2,500 Audited
Printed in 1 color on matte stock

15979 Staffing Industry Sourcebook
Staffing Industry Analysts
881 Fremont Avenue
Suite A3
Los Altos, CA 94024
650-948-9303
FAX: 650-948-9345 800-950-9496
info@sireport.com www.sireport.com
Joyce Routson, Mgr Editor/Staffing Industry Report
Jeff Reeder, Mgr Editor/SI Review
Sona Sharma, Mgr Editor/IT Serv Business Report
Linda Hubbard, Director of Marketing
Leslie Austin, Customer/Membership
Source Book, Facts and Figures for Market Research on the staffing industry. *$285.00*
451 pages BiAnnual ISBN 1-883814-10-3

15980 Transnational Corporations and Labor: A Directory of Resources
Third World Resources
1218 E 21st Street
Oakland, CA 94606
510-533-7583
FAX: 510-533-0923
Danielle Mahones, Executive Director
This directory is a source for books, periodicals and audiovisuals on transnational corporations and labor issues. *$14.95*
160 pages

15981 World Trade Resource Guide
Gale Research
27500 Drake Road
Farmington Hills, MI 48331
248-699-4253
FAX: 248-699-8214 800-877-4253
galeord@gale.com www.gale.com
Gordon T Macomber, President
Dennis Stepaniak, Executive VP/CFO
Ray F Lowrey, Executive VP/CTO
Rich Foley, Executive VP/Sales/Marketing
Dennis Paupard, Executive VP/Editorial/Production

Offers valuable information on companies, organizations and agencies involved in international trade in 80 countries. *$169.00*
891 pages

15982 Worldwide Franchise Directory
Gale Research
27500 Drake Road
Farmington Hills, MI 48331
248-699-4253
FAX: 248-699-8214 800-877-4253
galeord@gale.com www.gale.com
Gordon T Macomber, President
Dennis Stepaniak, Executive VP/CFO
Ray F Lowrey, Executive VP/CTO
Rich Foley, Executive VP/Sales/Marketing
Dennis Paupard, Executive VP/Editorial/Production

This valuable directory offers information for over 1,500 business franchises worldwide. *$129.50*
750 pages

Industry Web Sites

15983 www.aahc.net
AAHC American Association of Healthcare Consultant

15984 www.aaimnhta.com
American Association of Industrial Management

Dedicated to better management and the over-all objective which is the formulation of broad management principles and strategies that will insure sucessful management and promote the principles of free, private and competitive enterprise with individual opportunity and freedom under a constitutional government.

15985 www.aameda.org
American Academy of Medical Administrators

Department heads and administrators in areas of hospital and health administration.

15986 www.afsmi.org
AFSM International

A global organization dedicated to furthering the knowledge, understanding, and career development of executives, managers and professionals in the high-technology service industry.

15987 www.amanet.org
American Management Association

Offers a full range of business education and management development programs for indivudual and organizations in Europe, the Americas and Asia. Learn superior business skills and best management practices through a variety of seminars, conferences and special events.

15988 www.amcf.org
AMCF

Seeks to unite management consulting firms in order to develop and improve professional standards and practice in the field. Offers information and referral services on management consultants.

15989 www.americanassocofindmgmt.com
American Association of Industrial Management

Dedicated to better management and the formulation of broad management principles and strategies that will ensure sucessful management and promote the principles of free, private and competive enterprise with individual opportunity and freedom under a constitutional government.

15990 www.aom-iaom.org
Association of Management

Formerly the Association of Human Resources Management and Organizational Behavior.

15991 www.apics.org
APICS Association for Operations Management

The primary purpose of this specific industry group is to educate food and beverage manufacturers on effective marketing strategies, market trends and material management.

15992 www.aspanet.org
American Society for Public Administration

The nation's most respected society representing all forums in the public service arena. Advocate for greater effectiveness in government agents of goodwill and professionalism addressing key public service issues by promoting change at both the local and international levels, we can enhance the quality of lives worldwide.

15993 www.awhp.org
Association for Worksite Health Promotion

Exists to advance the profession of worksite health promotion and the career development of its practitioners and to improve the performance of the programs they administer. Represents a variety of disciplines and worksites, for decision-makers in the areas of health promotion/disease prevention and health-care cost management.

15994 www.besthealthplans.com
Best Employers Association

Market and administer medical and dental insurance for large and small groups. Specializes in group insurance and employee benefits.

15995 www.bizintell.com
Business Intelligence Association

Business to business research on a wide variety of industries. Specialize in primary and hard-to-find secondary information.

15996 www.cmaa.org
Club Managers Association of America

Professional association for managers of membership clubs. Members manage country, city, athletic, faculty, yacht, town and military clubs. Objectives to promote and advance friendly relations among persons connected with the management of clubs and other associations of similar character.

15997 www.cmaonline.org
The Christian Management Association

Designed to assist those involved in the management of Christian organizations.

15998 www.cmeinc.org
Center for Management Effectiveness

Conducts management training programs and publishes self-scoring inventories, trainer guides and workbooks on stress management, resolution of conflict, risk taking, decision making and building managerial skills.

15999 www.corptech.com
CORPTECH Information Services

Corporations and operating units of large corporations that develop or manufacture some 100,000 high-technology products.

16000 www.emsnetwork.com/cbt
Center for Breakthrough Thinking

Organized to promote and institutionalize the teaching and application of Breakthrough Thinking in universities, corporations and governments in solving problems, leveraging opportunities, and achieving change.

16001 www.expedia.com
Expedia.com

Internet travel service offers access to airlines, hotels, car rentals, vacation packages, cruises and corporate travel.

16002 www.greyhouse.com
Grey House Publishing

Selected Grey House directories in the fields of business, health and education are available online. Users can search our online databases by several different search criteria, such as product categories, geographic area, sales volume and much, much more. Full Grey House catalog and online ordering also available.

16003 www.iamc.org
Industrial Asset Management Council

Members are companies engaged in the management of two or more organizations on a professional client basis.

16004 www.icmci.org
ICMCI Intn'l Council of Mgnt Consulting Institutes

For national institutes from around the world that certify professional management consultants; promotes professional development and networking between consultants and the highest standards of performance for clients.

16005 www.icsa.com
International Customer Service Association

Dedicated to promoting the development and awareness of the customer service profession through networking, education and research.

16006 www.icsb.org
International Council for Small Business

Management development.

16007 www.imc-ymca.org/join.html
International Management Council

IMC provides individuals with opportunities for continually developing their leadership and management skills through a network of shared experiences and education.

16008 www.imcusa.org/
IMC-USA Institute of Management Consultants-USA

For management consultants in the United States, organized to establish consulting as a self-regulating profession, meriting public confidence and respect. Toward the achievement of this goal IMC awards the international appelation CMC for certified management consultants.

16009 www.ioma.com
Institute of Management & Administration

Organization helps to provides information and guidance to management teams for various businesses.

16010 www.ipma-hr.org
International/Public Management Assn For Human Res

Human resource professionals, representing the interests of over 6,000 individual and 1,300 agency members, at the federal, state and local levels of government. Promotes excellence in human resource management through the ongoing development of professional and ethical standards, and through its publishing and educational training programs.

16011 www.members.aol.com/odinst
Organization Development Institute

Promotes the understanding of organization development and offers three categories of membership: professional consultant, regular and student.

16012 www.mgma.com
Medical Group Management Association

The oldest and largest professional membership association dedicated to medical practice management. Serves their members by offering timely and relevant networking and educational opportunities that keep the members up-to-date on the practice management field.

16013 www.nacdonline.org
National Association of Corporate Directors

Fosters research, surveys, seminars and director for corporate. Maintains placement service.

16014 www.naesaa.com
National Association of Executive Secretaries and Administrative Assistants

Publishes a newsletter 11 times per year.

16015 www.nsha.biz
National Small Business United

Volunteer-led association. Primary mission is to advocate state and federal policies that are beneficial to small business, the state and the nation and to promote the growth of free enterprise.

16016 www.pmi.org
Project Management Institute

Fosters recognition of the need for project management professionalism. Offers professional certification and bestows awards.

16017 www.rbma.org
Radiology Business Management Association

Promotes management education and study of practice economics, legislative issues and consumer trends.

16018 www.shrm.org
Society for Human Resource Management

16019 www.shrm.org/ema
Society for Human Resources/Employment Mgt Assn

A national association comprised primarily of corporate human resource professionals responsible for hiring and staffing.

16020 www.ssainfo.com
Support Services Alliance

Multi-state membership organization that provides cost-savings services and legislative representation for small businesses and the self-employed. Also offers services to the memberships of more than 100 affiliated state, regional and national associations.

16021 www.wacra.org
World Assn for Case Method Research & Application

Members are professional and academicians with an interest in the use of the case method in teaching, training and planning. Interactive, innovative teaching and learning methods.

16022 www.ypo.org
Young Presidents' Organization

Members are corporate presidents under the age of fifty whose companies employ at least fifty employees.

Associations

16023 Adhesive & Sealant Council
7979 Old Georgetown Road
Suite 500
Bethesda, MD 20814
301-986-9700
FAX: 301-986-9795
membership@ascouncil.org
www.adhesives.org

Lawrence Sloan, President
Alan R Longstreet, Chairman

ASC provides a forum for "where the adhesives and sealants industry meets", serves as our industry's advocate before state and federal regulatory agencies, and strives to provide important and timely information to their members.
Founded: 1958

16024 Agile Manufacturing Benchmarking Consortium
4606 FM 1960 W
Suite #250
Houston, TX 77069
281-440-5044
FAX: 281-440-6677
www.ambcbenchmarking.org

Mark Czarnecki, Owner

AMBC is a focused group of manufacturing process improvement professionals that looks to identify the best practices surrounding manufacturing issues for the overall operations of the members.

16025 American Bearing Manufacturers Association
2025 M Street NW
Suite 800
Washington, DC 20036
202-367-1155
FAX: 202-367-2155
info.abma@smithbucklin.com
www.abma-dc.org

Richard Opatick, President/Secretary
Rock Baty, Chairman & CEO
Kyle Martin, Statistics Specialist
Brian Hess, Membership Coordinator

Promotes bearing standardization. Sponsors Bearing Technical Committee.
36 Members Founded: 1917

16026 American Brush Manufacturers Association
2111 Plum Street
Suite 274
Aurora, IL 60506-3268
630-631-5217
FAX: 630-897-9140
infoabma.org www.abma.org/

Kenneth L Rakusin, President
Barry D Harper, VP
David Parc, Executive Director

Trade association representing North American manufacturers of brooms, brushes, mops and rollers.
175 Members Founded: 1917

16027 American Edged Products Manufacturers Association
21165 Whitfield Place
#105
Potomac Falls, VA 20165
703-433-9281
FAX: 703-433-0369
info@aepma.org www.aepma.org

Alan Peppel, President
Brent Driscoll, VP

Serves the marketing and manufacturing of the cutlery industry.
23 Members

16028 American Pyrotechnics Association

PO Box 30438
Bethesda, MD 20824-0438
301-907-8181
FAX: 301-907-9148
ytimmons@americanpyro.com
www.americanpyro.com

Julie L Heckman, Executive Director
Gregg S Smith, Safety Program Manager

Members are importers, distributors, suppliers and manufacturers of fireworks.
Founded: 1948

16029 American Society for Testing & Materials:
100 Barr Harbor Drive
PO Box C700
West Conshohcken, PA 19428-2959
610-832-9585
FAX: 610-832-9555
lmorriss@astm.org www.astm.org

James Thomas, President
George Luciw, Director
Kathleen Kono, VP
Tim Brooke, Director

Nonprofit organization that provides a global forum for the development and publication of voluntary consensus standards for materials, products, systems and services. Members who represent 100 nations are producers, users, consumers and representatives of government and academia. In over 130 varied industry uses, ASTM standards serve as the basis for manufacturing, procurement and regulatory activities.
30000 Members Founded: 1898

16030 American Textile Machinery Association
201 Park Washington Court
Falls Church, VA 22046-4527
703-538-1789
FAX: 703-241-5603
info@atmanet.org www.atmanet.org

Clay D Tyeryar, President
Susan A Denston, Executive VP
Harry W Buzzerd, Jr, Management Counsel

ATMA's purpose is to advance the common interests of its members, improve business conditions within the US textile machinery industry from a global perspective and market the industry and members' machinery, parts and services.
Founded: 1933

16031 Association for Operations Management
5301 Shawnee Road
Alexandria, VA 22312-2317
703-354-8851
FAX: 703-354-8106
service@apicshq.org www.apics.org

Tom Krupka, President
Michael T Walsh, VP

200 booths of manufacturing companies, software/hardware, supplies and manufacturing equipment.
3.5M Members

16032 Association of Equipment Manufacturers
6737 W Washington St
Milwaukee, WI 53214-5647
414-272-0943
FAX: 414-272-1170 866-236-0442
info@aem.org www.aem.org

Charles Stamp, Chairman
Gerald Shaheen, Vice Chairman
Dennis Slater, President

Composed of manufacturers of screens and feeders used in aggregates, mining and industrial processing. Promotes and furthers the interests of members in safety, production, engineering, government relations and other industry matters.
8 Members Founded: 1959

16033 Contract Manufacturing & Packaging Association
1601 North Bond Street
Naperville, IL 60563
630-544-5053
FAX: 630-544-5055
info@contractpackaging.org
www.contractpackaging.org

John Mazelin, President
James Ellis, VP

To serve the growth of member companies by assisting in the establishment of productive links between buyers and member companies and by providing educational opportunities for member companies' executives to improve the efficiency and productivity of their operations.
72 Members Founded: 1992

16034 Conveyor Equipment Manufacturers Association (CEMA)
6724 Lone Oak Boulevard
Naples, FL 34109
239-514-3441
FAX: 239-514-3470
cema@cemanet.org www.cemanet.org

Tom Easterhouse, President
Fred Thimmel, VP
Robert Reinfried, Executive Director

Involved in writing industry standards, CEMA's purpose is to promote among its members and the industry standardization of design manufacture and application on a voluntary basis and in such manner as will not impede development of conveying machinery and component parts or lessen competition. CEMA sponsors an annual Engineering Conference allowing Member Company Engineers to meet and develop or improve CEMA Consensus Industry Standards and National Standards that affect the conveyor industry.
99 Members Founded: 1933

16035 Flexible Packaging Association
971 Corporate Boulevard
Suite 403
Linthicum, MD 21090
410-694-0800
FAX: 410-694-0900
mdonahue@flexpack.org
www.flexpack.org

Marla Donahue, President
Ram Singhal, Director Technology/Regulatory Dept

A trade association for converters and suppliers of flexible packaging materials and allied products for packaging, industrial and related end use markets.
Founded: 1950

16036 Grocery Manufacturers of America

2401 Pennsylvania Avenue NW
2nd Floor
Washington, DC 20037-3673
202-337-9400
FAX: 202-337-4508
info@gmabrands.com
www.gmabrands.com

C Manly Molpus, President/CEO
Mark W Baum, Executive VP

Manufacturers of food and nonfood products sold through the grocery trade. US sales are more than $500 billion, GMA members employ more than 2.5 million workers in the nation.

135 Members Founded: 1908

16037 Keep America Beautiful

1010 Washington Boulevard
Stamford, CT 06901
203-323-8987
FAX: 203-325-9199
info@m@kab.org www.kab.org

G Raymond Empson, President
Becky Lyons, VP
Sue Smith, Director Education/Training
Monica Spigelman, Director Communications

National, nonprofit, education organization whose corporate members include packagers, retailers, bottlers, and makers of chemical, steel, glass, paper and aluminum products.

Founded: 1953

16038 Manufacturers' Agents National Association

One Spectrum Pointe
Suite 150
Lake Forest, CA 92630
949-859-4040
FAX: 949-855-2973 877-626-2776
MANA@MANAonline.org
www.manaonline.org

Joseph Miller, President
Helen Degli-Angeli, VP

Association for independent agents and firms representing manufacturers and other businesses in specified territories on a commission basis, including consultants and associate member firms interested in the manufacturer/agency method of marketing.

Founded: 1947

16039 Material Handling Industry of America

8720 Red Oak Boulevard
Suite 201
Charlotte, NC 28217-3992
704-676-1190
FAX: 704-676-1199
jnofsinger@mhia.org www.mhia.org

John B Nofsinger, COO
F Hal Vandiver, Executive VP Business Development
Dr Richard E Ward, Executive VP

Industrial steel shelving is loaded by hand and generally stores materials that are small in size, with multiple parts stores on a given shelf separated by dividers, boxes and drawers.

400 Members Founded: 1945

16040 National Association of Display Industries

3595 Sheridan Street
Suite 200
Hollywood, FL 33021
954-893-7300
FAX: 954-893-7500
nadi@nadi-global.com
www.nadi-global.com

Klein Merriman, Executive Director
Robert Rosean, President, NADI
James Schubert, President, NASFM

A leading association for the visual merchandising profession. As visual merchandising has evolved over the years into playing an integral role in retail, NADI has always taken the lead in information and educating members. The association's already significant support for the visual design profession has grown with NADI's exclusive sponsorship of GlobalShop's Visual Merchandising Show and StoreXpo.

350 Members Founded: 1942

16041 National Association of Manufacturers

1331 Pennsylvania Avenue NW
Washington, DC 20004-1790
202-373-3000
FAX: 202-637-3182
manufacturing@nam.org
www.nam.org

John Angler, President
Jan Amundson, Senior VP/General Counsel
Michael Baroody, Executive VP Policy
Patrick Cleary, Senior VP Human Resources Policy

Enhances the competitiveness of manufacturers and improves American living standards by shaping a legislative and regulatory environment conductive to US economic growth and to increase understanding among policy makers; the media and the general public about the importance of manufacturing to America's economic strength.

14000 Members Founded: 1895

16042 National Automatic Merchandising Association

20 N Wacker Drive
Suite 3500
Chicago, IL 60606
312-346-0370
FAX: 312-704-4140
info@vending.org www.vending.org

Richard Geerdes, President/CEO
Dan Mathews, Senior VP/COO
Tom McMahon, Senior VP/Chief Counsel

Members are makers and operators of automatic vending equipment together. Provides members with products and services. Suppliers to the industry may also join as members. NAMA has two tradeshows per year showcasing any product or service directed to the vending operators. NAMA provides services to its members including legislative advocacy. Publishes a quarterly newsletter.

2600 Members Founded: 1936

16043 National Cotton Batting Institute

41 S Walnut Bend Road
Cordova, TN 38018
901-624-1200
FAX: 901-624-1200
info@natbat.com www.natbat.com

Alan Posners, President
Fred Middleton, Executive Secretary
Alan Posner, VP

Association representing members of the cotton batting industry.

27 Members Founded: 1954

16044 National Paint and Coatings Association

1500 Rhode Island Avenue NW
Washington, DC 20005-5597
202-462-6272
FAX: 202-462-8549
npca@paint.org www.paint.org/

Andrew Doyle, President
Thomas Graves, VP

Manufacturers of paints and industrial coatings and suppliers to the industry.

400+ Members Founded: 1886

16045 North American Punch Manufacturers Association

21 Turquoise Avenue
Naples, FL 34114
239-775-7245
FAX: 239-775-7245
bobjanmay@napma.org
www.napma.org

Robert E May, Executive Secretary

Principal program of NAPMA is the standardization of all punches, dies and retainers manufactured by the various member companies.

23 Members Founded: 1963

16046 P3 Partnershp In Print Production

276 Bowery
New York, NY 10012
212-334-2106
FAX: 212-431-5786
admin@P3-ny.org www.wip.org

Rosemary Sirico, President
Diane Pesce, VP

Promotes the interests of women in the production profession.

16047 Packaged Ice Association

PO Box 1199
Tampa, FL 33601
813-512-2783

jane@packagedice.com
www.packagedice.com

Manufacturers and distributors of ice and their suppliers.

150 Members Founded: 1917

16048 Pharmaceutical Research & Manufacturers of America

1100 Fifteenth Street NW
Washington, DC 20005
202-835-3400
FAX: 202-835-3414 www.phrma.org

Billy Tauzin Tadatka Yamada, Chairman
Peter B Corr, Vice Chairman

Represents the country's leading research based pharmaceutical and biotechnology companies, which are devoted to inventing medicines that allow patients to live longer, healthier and more productive lives.

16049 Pressure Vessel Manufacturers Association

8 S Michigan Avenue
Suite 1000
Chicago, IL 60603
312-456-5590
FAX: 312-580-0165
pyma@gss.net www.pvma.org/

James Getter, President
August L Sisco, Executive Director

Members are manufacturers of ASME code pressure vessels and suppliers, components and services to pressure vessel manfacturers.
31 Members Founded: 1975

16050 Production and Operations Management Society
Dept. of Management-Univ. of Baltimore
1420 N Charles Street
Baltimore, MD 21201-5720
410-837-4727
FAX: 410-837-5675
poms@eng,fiu.edu www.poms.org/
Kasra Ferdows, President
Sushil K Gupta, Executive Director
Members are professionals and academics with an interest in production and operations management.
1200 Members Founded: 1989

16051 Refractories Institute
650 Smithfield Street
Suite 1160
Pittsburgh, PA 15222
412-281-6787
FAX: 412-281-6881
www.refractoriesinstitute.org
Robert Crolius, President
National trade association for refractory manufacturers, suppliers of equipment and raw materials and installers of refractory products.
80 Members Founded: 1951

16052 Remanufacturing Institute
Po Box 48
Lewisburg, PA 17837
570-523-0992
FAX: 705-555-5555
rgiuntini@reman.org www.reman.org
Ron Giuntini, Executive Director
A coalition of associations and companies in the entire manufacturing industry. There are over 73,000 companies in this industry. Our goal is to unite them into a powerful organization.
11 Members Founded: 1997

16053 Retail Packaging Association
PO Box 17656
Covington, KY 41017
859-341-9623
FAX: 859-341-6211
info@retailpackaging.org
www.retailpackaging.org
Nancy Coons, Executive Director
Gina Breda, Marketing Director
RPA provides comprehensive educational and networking opportunities and has members representing all entities of retail packaging nationwide and abroad.
1000+ Members Founded: 1989

16054 Reusable Industrial Packaging Association
8401 Corporate Drive
Suite 450
Landover, MD 20785
301-577-3786
FAX: 301-577-6476
www.reusablepackaging.org
Paul Rankin, President
CL Pettit, VP
Founded: 1942

16055 Ultrasonic Industry Association
PO Box 2307
Dayton, OH 45401-2301
937-586-3725
FAX: 937-586-3699
uia@uia.meinet.com
www.ultrasonics.org
Foster Stulen, President
Mark Schafer, VP
Ron Stault, Treasurer
Janet Devine, Secretary
Improving processes, techniques and materials through the application of ultasonic technology.
70 Members Founded: 1956

16056 United Association of Manufacturers Representatives
PO Box 986
Dana Point, CA 92929
949-240-4966
FAX: 949-240-7001
info@uamr.com www.uamr.com/
Karen Mazzola, Executive Director
Benefits manufacturers and independent sales representatives and is a national marketing association.
3,000 Members Founded: 1965

16057 Waste Equipment Technology Association
4301 Connecticut Avenue NW
Suite 300
Washington, DC 20008-2304
202-244-4700
FAX: 202-966-4824
wastecinfo@WASTEC.org
www.wastec.org/
Bruce Parker, President/CEO
Gary Satterfield, Executive VP
Manufacturers of waste handling, collection and processing equipment.
Founded: 1972

16058 Web Sling Tiedown Association
2105 Laurel Bush Road
Suite 200
Bel Air, MD 21015
443-640-1070
FAX: 443-640-1031
wstda@ksgroup.org www.wstda.com
Becky Thiessen, President
Greg Crain, VP
Manufacturers of web slings which are used as hoists in various industrial lifting operations.
79 Members Founded: 1973

Newsletters

16059 Infocus Newsletter
319 SW Washington Street
Suite 710
Portland, OR 97204-2618
503-227-3393
FAX: 503-274-7667
tonya@bfma.org http://www.bfma.org

Lea Anne A Fuchs, President
Andy Palatka, Executive Director
Tonya Macalino, Adversiting and Sales
Infocus is a newsletter focused on industry topics and products. *$75.00*
Founded: 1960
Circulation: 1,100
Mailing list available for rent 1M names $200 per M.

16060 Innovators Digest
InfoTeam
PO Box 15640
Plantation, FL 33318-5640
954-473-9560
FAX: 954-473-0544
infoteamma@aol.com
Merton Allen, Editor
A multidisciplinary publication covering developments in science, engineering, products, markets, business development, manufacturing and other technological developments having industrial or commercial significance.
2 per year
Computerized version available

16061 Intelligent Manufacturing
Lionheart Publishing
2555 Cumberland Parkway SE
Suite 299
Atlanta, GA 30339-3908
770-234-9360
FAX: 770-432-6969
John Llewellyn, Publisher
David Blanchard, Editor
Provides expert solutions to manufacturing professionals covering production problems, developments in manufacturing systems. *$ 20.00*

Circulation: 1,598

16062 Manufacturing Technology
National Technical Information Service
S U 5285 Port Royal Road
Springfield, VA 22161-0001
703-874-4650
FAX: 703-487-4630
Covers CAD/CAM, robotics, robots, productivity, manufacturing, planning, processing and control, plant design and computer software.

16063 News & Views
American Mold Builders Association
701 E Irving Park Road
Suite 207
Roselle, IL 60172-2357
630-980-7667
FAX: 630-980-9714
info@amba.org http://www.amba.org
Jeanette Bradley, Executive Director
Peter Manship, President
Quarterly Founded: 1973
Circulation: 2000

16064 Noise Regulation Report
Business Publishers
8737 Colesville Road
Suite 1100
Silver Spring, MD 20910-3928
301-587-6300
FAX: 301-587-4530 800-274-6737
custserv@bpinews.com
www.bpinews.com
Leonard A Eiserer, Publisher
Exclusive coverage of airport, highway, occupational and open space noise, noise control and mitigation issues. *$511.00*
10 pages 12 per year
Printed in on matte stock : Newsletter

16065 Remanufacturing Industries Council International
RICI
4401 Fair Lakes Ct
Suite 210
Fairfax, VA 22033-3848

FAX: 703-968-2878
sparker@rici.org www.rici.org

Larry Rice, Chief Executive Officer

A coalition of associations and companies in the remanufacturing industry.
11 pages Founded: 1997
Circulation: 10,000

16066 Service Management
National Association of Service Management
PO Box 250796
Milwaukee, WI 53225
414-466-6060
FAX: 414-466-0840
http://www.nasm.com/

Don Buelow, Publisher
Caryn Anderson, Editor

Offers information on manufacturing and service companies.
40 pages Monthly

16067 Vision
Society of Manufacturing Engineers
1 SME Drive
PO Box 930
Dearborn, MI 48128
313-271-1500
FAX: 313-425-3417 800-733-4763
service@sme.org www.sme.org

Dianna Helka, Associate Editor

The newsletter highlights the latest developments in the machine vision industry including applications, techniques and methods. *$75.00*
Quarterly Founded: 1984
Circulation: 1,100 Audited

Magazines & Journals

16068 APICS: The Performance Advantage
APICS Association for Operations Management
5301 Shawnee Road
Alexandria, VA 22312-2317
703-548-8851
FAX: 703-354-8106
editorial@apicshq.org
http://www.apics.org

Doug Kelly, Editor
Jennifer Procter, Managing Editor
Jeffery Raynes, CEO

Provides comprehensive articles on enterprise resources planning, supply chain management, e-business, materials management and production and inventory management. *$65.00*
64 pages
Circulation: 66000
Mailing list available for rent 40,000 names $100 per M.
Printed in 4 colors on glossy stock

16069 Adhesives & Sealants
Business News Publishing Company
PO Box 400
Flossmoor, IL 60422
708-922-0761
FAX: 708-922-0762
mcphersont@bnpmedia.com
http://www.adhesivesmag.com

Susan Love, Publisher
Teresa Mc Pherson, Editor
Kari Rowe, Circulation Manager
Violeta Ivezaj, Senior Marketing Manager
$33.00
Monthly Founded: 1926
Circulation: 15000

16070 Adhesives Age
110 William Street
11th Floor
New York, NY 10038
212-621-4900
FAX: 212-621-4800
editorial.info@chemweek.com
http://www.adhesivesage.com/

Greg Valero, Editor-in-Chief
Lyn Tattum, Publisher
John Markovik, Sales/Marketing Manager

Adhesives Age provides readers with vital information: global industry coverage of the development, manufacture, and application of adhesives, sealants, and related products. *$75.00*
62 pages Weekly Founded: 1958
Circulation: 22994
Printed in 4 colors on glossy stock

16071 Advanced Materials & Processes
ASM International
9639 Kinsman Road
Materials Park, OH 44073-2
440-338-5151
FAX: 440-338-4634 800-336-5152
cust-srv@asminternational.org
http://www.asminternational.org

Margaret Hunt, Editor-in-Chief
Lana Shapowal, Marketing Manager
Joanne Miller, Production Manager
Tina Long, Circulation Manager
Vincent LeGendre, Publisher

Monthly Founded: 1977
Circulation: 32000

16072 American Cemetery
Kates-Boylston Publications
11300 Rockville Pike
Suite 1100
Rockville, MD 20852
800-500-4585
FAX: 301-287-2150 800-500-4585
AmericanFD@aol.com
http://www.kates-boylston.com

Adrian F Boylston, Publisher
Thomas Lorge, Publications Manager

Features articles on cemetery administration, maintenance, sales and public relations. Also includes coverage of conventions, new cemeteries and new building ideas. *$39.95*
Monthly
Circulation: 5800

16073 American Fastener Journal
Carol McGuire
27081 N 96th Way
Scottsdale, AZ 85262-8441
480-488-3500
FAX: 480-488-3247 877-760-3500
cmcguire@fastenerjournal.com
http://www.fastenerjournal.com

Carol McGuire, Publisher/Editor
Myra Brenneman, Circulation Manager

This journal for the fastener industry covers technical articles, inspections, quality assurance, materials applications, specifications and standards, as well as manufacturer, distributors and supplier profiles. *$45.00*
Founded: 1981
Circulation: 13000
Printed in 4 colors on glossy stock
Computerized version available

16074 American Funeral Director
Kates-Boylston Publications
11300 Rockville Pike
Suite 1100
Rockville, MD 20852
800-500-4585
FAX: 732-730-2515 800-500-4585
americanfd@aol.com
http://www.kates-boylston.com

Adrian F Boylston, Publisher

Articles on funeral home construction, finance, mortuary law, shipment of human remains by air transportation, sales and display methods, advertising and public relations, new equipment and other association activiies. Also includes personnel news about funeral directors and related supply firms. *$49.95*
Monthly Founded: 1918
Circulation: 12168

16075 Automatic Machining Magazine
Screw Machine Publishing Company
1066 Gravel Road
Webster, NY 14580
585-787-0820
FAX: 585-787-0868 800-610-6950

Donald E Wood, Publisher
Wayne A Wood, CEO
Linda Iobiondo, Circulation Manager

General industry news for professionals in the metal turning and cold forming fields. *$55.00*
142 pages Monthly Founded: 1939
Circulation: 13000 13000 names $75 per M.

Printed in 4 colors on glossy stock

16076 CNC West
Arnold Publications
14340 Bolsa Chica Avenue E
PO Box 100
Westminster, CA 92684-100
714-899-0733
FAX: 714-899-0738
larnold@cnc-west.com
http://www.cnc-west.com

Shawn Arnold, Publisher
Chuck Bush, Editor
Shawn Arnold, CEO/President
Shawn Arnold, Circulation Manager
Shawn Arnold, Marketing Manager

News and trends on western jobshops and manufacturers *$32.50*
Founded: 1981
Circulation: 22000 $85 per M.
Printed in 4 colors on glossy stock

16077 Card Manufacturing
International Card Manufacturing Association
PO Box 727
Princeton Junction, NJ 08550-727
609-799-4900
FAX: 609-799-7032
info@icma.com http://www.icma.com

Lynn McCullough, Association Manager
Jeffrey E Barnhart, Co-Founder/Executive Director

Advertiser supported trade magazine featuring industry news and features on all aspects of the plastic card production worldwide, and the news of the ICMA. *$75.00*

Circulation: 3000

16078 Coatings World
Rodman Publications
70 Hilltop Raod
Ramsey, NJ 07446
201-825-2552
FAX: 201-825-0553
coatingsales@rodpub.com
http://www.coatingsworld.com

Rodman J Zilenziger, President
Dale Pritchett, Publisher
Christine Canni Esposito, Editor
Mamata Chattopadhyay, Production Manager
Ellen Pfister, Circulation Manager

Coatings World is directed at industry personnel concerned with developing and manufacturing paints, coatings, adhesives and sealants. Feature articles and industry news are directed at chemists, formulators and all levels of management that must keep abreast of technical products and market developments. *$50.00*
136 pages Monthly Founded: 1996
Circulation: 17315
Printed in 4 colors on glossy stock

16079 Composites Fabrication
Composites Fabricators Association
1010 N Glebe Rd
Suite 450
Arlington, VA 22201
703-525-0511
FAX: 703-525-0743
info@acmanet.org
http://www.acmanet.org/

Missy Henriksen, Executive Director
Andy Rusnak, Editor
Roxanne Fraver, Marketing & Circulation
Sabeena Hickman, Deputy Director
Jessica Howard, Senior Sales Manager

Presents information on new technology, trends and techniques for manufacturers in the fiberglass and composites industry. *$41.00*
114 pages
Circulation: 8000
Printed in 4 colors on glossy stock

16080 Consumer Goods Technology
Edgell Communications
4 Middlebury Boulevard
Randolph, NJ 07869
973-252-0100
FAX: 973-252-9020
agaffney@edgellmail.com
http://www.consumergoods.com

Andrew Gaffney, Group Publisher
Steve Rosenstock, Publisher
Tim Clark, Editor-in-Chief
Alliston Ackerman, Assistant Editor

Provides case histories, technology overviews, new products and industry news to assist corporations and management in the consumer goods industry.
Monthly Founded: 1984
Circulation: 25000 25M names $155 per M.

16081 Contingency Planning & Management
Witter Publishing Corporation
20 Commerce Street
Flemington, NJ 08822
908-788-0343
FAX: 908-788-3782
info@witterpublishing.com
http://www.witterpublishing.com

Bob Joudanin, Publisher
Paul Kirvan, Editor In Chief
Courtney Writter, Circulation Manager
Andrew Witter, President

Serves the fields of financial/banking, manufacturing industrial, transportation, utilities, telecommunications, health care, government, insurance and other allied fields.
Monthly Founded: 1987

16082 Contract Management
National Contract Management Association
1912 Woodford Road
Vienna, VA 22182-3728
703-489-9231
FAX: 703-448-0939 800-344-8096
cm@ncmahq.org
http://www.ncmahq.org

Amy Miedema, Editor-in-Chief
Neal Couture, Executive Director

It covers the myriad aspects of government and commercial contract management. News and features provide information on such topics as procurement policy, on-the-job techniques, regulations, case law, ethics, contract administration, electronic commerce, international and small business matters, education and career development. *$75.00*
80 pages Monthly Founded: 1959
Circulation: 22000
Printed in 4 colors on glossy stock

16083 Control Design
Putman Media
555 W Pierce
#301
Itasca, IL 60143-2649
630-467-1300
FAX: 630-467-1124
lgoldberg@putman.net
http://www.putmanmedia.com

Keith Larson, Group Publisher
Joe Feeley, Editor-in-Chief/Publisher
Anetta Gauthier, Production Manager
Lori Goldberg, Operations Manager

Markets to the manufacturing facilities under the government's standard industry classification (SIC) code 35, which manufacture a broad range of products from turbines, conveyors and machine tools to food processing, printing presses and computers. *$96.00*
Founded: 1938
Circulation: 50,046 $125 per M.
Printed in 4 colors

16084 Design News
Reed Business Information
360 Park Avenue South
New York, NY 10010
212-450-0067
FAX: 617-558-4402
jogando@reedbusiness.com
http://www.designnews.com

Dan Hirsh, Publisher
Karen Auguston Field, Editor-in-Chief
James Reed, Owner

Informs professionals in the technology industry of all the latest in new product introductions in fields such as bearings, fastening/joining and new technology.

Circulation: 170000

16085 Distributor's Link
4297 Corporate Square N
Naples, FL 34104
239-643-2713
FAX: 941-643-5220 800-356-1639
leojcoar@linkmagazine.com
http://www.linkmagazine.com/

Leo J Coar, Publisher/Editor
Maryann Marzocchi, VP
Tracey Lumia, Advertising Sales

Information aimed at the fastener distributors nationwide. *$45.00*
Quarterly Founded: 1975
Circulation: 50000

16086 Edplay
Fahy-Williams Publishing
PO Box 1080
171 Reed St
Geneva, NY 14456-2137
315-789-0458
FAX: 315-789-4263 800-344-0559
kanderson@fwpi.com
http://www.fwpi.com

J Kevin Fahy, Publisher
Tina Manzer, Editorial Director
Bradley G. Gordner, Senior Editor
Mark Stash, Art Director
Kari Anderson, Associate Editor

Serves toy manufacturers and dealers. Offers product reviews, industry profiles, and reader surveys.
Founded: 1984
Circulation: 13000

16087 Fastener Technology International
Initial Publications
1867 West Market Street
Akron, OH 44313
330-864-2122
FAX: 330-864-5298
info@fastenertech.com
http://www.fastenertech.com

Michael McNulty, Editor

Contains articles on company profiles, new equipment, literature, products, fastener topics and patents. *$40.00*
Founded: 1981
Circulation: 13,000 13,000 names $55 per M.
Printed in 4 colors on glossy stock

16088 Fastening
Mike McGuire
293 Hopewell Drive
Powell, OH 43065-9350
614-848-3232
FAX: 614-848-5045 800-848-0304
mmcguire@mail.fastening.com
www.fastening.com

Mike McGuire, Publisher

In-depth and up-to-date information about fastening products, design/applications, people, companies, fastening industry events and specifications. *$30.00*
Quarterly Founded: 1995
Circulation: 28,000
Printed in 4 colors on glossy stock
Computerized version available

16089 **Forming & Fabricating**
Society of Manufacturing Engineers
1 SME Drive
Box 930
Dearborn, MI 48128-2408
313-271-1500
FAX: 313-271-2861
www.globalmfg.com

Arthur Klein, Editor-in-Chief

News and features regarding the forming and fabricating industry with the intention of improving process productivity and project quality. Special focus on technology and its applications in manufacturing.
Monthly
Circulation: 66616

16090 **Heat Treating Progress**
ASM International
9639 Kinsman Road
Materials Park, OH 44073-2
440-338-5151
FAX: 440-338-4634 800-336-5152
cust-srv@asminternational.org
http://www.asminternational.org

Dean Peters, Editor-in-Chief
Don Baxter, Managing Editor
Tina Long, Circulation Manager
Lana Shapowal, Marketing/Publications Manager
Vin LeGendre, Publisher

Founded: 1913

16091 **ITE Solutions**
Institute of Industrial Engineers
25 Technology Park
Norcross, GA 30092
770-449-0461
FAX: 770-263-8532
http://www.iienet.org

16092 **InTech**
Instrumentation, Systems,and Automation Society
67 Alexander Drive
Research Triangle Park, NC 27709
919-549-8411
FAX: 919-990-9434
info@isa.org http://www.isa.org

Richard Simpson, Publisher
Greg Hale, Editor
Rob Renner, Executive Officer
Chip Lee, Publication Director

Regular issue features include new product developments, new processes, research updates and general industry news. *$75.00*
Monthly Founded: 1945
Circulation: 67000

16093 **Industrial Equipment News**
Thomas Publishing Company
5 Penn Plz Ste 15
Manhattan, NY 10001
212-695-0500
FAX: 212-290-7206 800-733-1127
businesslists@thomaspublishing.com
http://www.thomaspublishing.com

Ciro Buttacavoli, Publisher
Joseph Rosta, Editor-in-Chief
Marie Urbanowicz, Marketing Manager

Serves the industrial field including manufacturing, mining, utilities, construction, transportation,governmental establishments, and educational services.
Monthly Founded: 1898

16094 **Industrial Maintenance & Plant Operation**
Reed Business Information
100 Enterprise Drive
Suite 600 Box 912
Rockaway, NJ 07866-912
973-920-7000
FAX: 973-920-7531
hpendrak@reedbusiness.com
http://www.impomag.com

Scott Sward, Publisher
Rick Carter, Editor-in-Chief
R Reed, Owner
Kyle Orr, Circulation Manager
Hank Pendrak, Marketing Director

Founded: 1975
Circulation: 100000

16095 **Industrial Market Place**
Wineberg Publications
7842 Lincoln Avenue
Skokie, IL 60077
847-676-1900
FAX: 847-676-0063 800-323-1818
info@industrialmktpl.com
http://www.industrialmktpl.com

Joel Wineberg, President
Adrienne Gallender, Publisher

Advertising sales on new and used machinery and equipment. *$175.00*
Founded: 1951
Circulation: 100000
Mailing list available for rent 120 names $70 per M.
Printed in 4 colors on glossy stock

16096 **International Cemetery & Funeral Management**
International Cemetery & Funeral Association
1895 Preston White Drive
Suite 220
Reston, VA 20191-5434
703-391-8400
FAX: 703-391-8416 800-645-7700
gen4@icfa.org http://www.icfa.org

Susan Loving, Managing Editor
Larry Stuart Jr, General Manager

Serves as the primary communication vehicle for ICFA news, membership activities, legislation, marketing and management, including the financial aspects of cemetery and funeral home operation. *$25.00*
64 pages Founded: 1887
Circulation: 6200
Printed in 4 colors on glossy stock

16097 **Job Shop Technology**
Edward Publishing
16 Waterbury Road
Prospect, CT 06712-1215
203-758-4474
FAX: 203-758-3427 800-317-0474

Mark W Shortt, Editor
Cindy Wilkinson, Circulation Director

Published to aid product manufacturers who outsource parts and manufacturing services. Specializes in manufacturing processes for the metals, plastics, rubber, and electronics industries, including virtually any outsourced manufacturing service.
Quarterly Founded: 1986
Circulation: 100,000
Mailing list available for rent 90875 names $125 per M.
Printed in 4 colors on glossy stock

16098 **Journal of Coatings Technology**
Federation of Societies for Coatings Technology
492 Norristown Road
Blue Bell, PA 19422-2350
610-940-0777
FAX: 610-940-0292
publications@coatingstech.org
www.coatingstech.org

Robert F Ziegler, Publisher
Patricia D Ziegler, Senior Editor

For the industrial and service organizations in paint and manufacturing plants, raw materials suppliers for coatings, printing inks and sealants. *$120.00*
Monthly

16099 **Journal of Process Control**
Butterworth Heinemann
313 Washington Street
Newton, MA 02458-1626
617-928-5460
FAX: 781-933-6333

JD Perkins, Editor
T McAvoy, Regional Editor

Covers the application of control theory, operations research, computer science and engineering principles to the solution of process control problems.

16100 **Journal of Quality Technology**
American Society for Quality
600 North Plankinton Avenue
Milwaukee, WI 53201-3005
414-272-8575
FAX: 414-272-1734 800-248-1946
help@asq.org http://www.asq.org

Danny Duhan, CEO/President
Debbie Phillips-Donaldson, Publisher
$45.00
Quarterly Founded: 1946
Circulation: 20000

16101 **Lubes-N-Greases**
LNG Publishing Company
6105 Arlington Boulevard
Suite G
Falls Church, VA 22044
703-536-0800
FAX: 703-536-0803 800-474-8654
gloria@lngpublishing.com
http://www.lngpublishing.com

Gloria Steinberg Briskin, Advertising Director
Nancy J. DeMarco, Publisher
Deborah Wessmiller, Circulation Manager
Tim Sullivan, Editor
Lisa Tocci, Managing Editor

The magazine of industry in motion.
64 pages Monthly Founded: 1995
Circulation: 16880

16102 **Maintenance Technology**
Applied Technology Publications
1300 S Grove Avenue
Suite 105
Barrington, IL 60010
847-382-8100
FAX: 847-304-8603
rcbaldwin@atpnetwork.com
http://www.mt-online.com

Tom Madding, Publisher
Robert C. Baldwin, Editor
Susan Dahlberg, Managing Editor

Maintanence Technology magazine serves the business and technical information needs of engineers, managers and supervisors responsible for the maintanence and reliability of plant equipment and facility systems.

Monthly
Circulation: 50000
Printed in 4 colors on glossy stock

16103 Managing Automation
Thomas Publishing Company
5 Penn Plaza
12th Floor
New York, NY 10001-1860
212-290-7341
FAX: 212-290-7206 800-733-1127
marketing@managingautomation.com
http://www.thomaspublishing.com

Heather L Mikisch, Publisher
Greg MacSweeney, Managing Editor
Kim Vennard, Senior Marketing Manager
Shawn Jacobs, Director of Sales
David Brousell, Chief Executive Officer

Serves the needs of those managers and engineers responsible for the planning and implementation of factory automation at both the plant and enterprise levels. *$60.00*

Monthly Founded: 1898
Circulation: 100246

16104 Manufacturers Mart
Philip G Cannon Jr
PO Box 310
Georgetown, MA 01833-0410
978-352-3320
FAX: 401-348-0797 800-835-0017
info@manufacturersmart.com
http://www.manufacturersmart.com

Phillip Cannon, Publisher
Linda Smith, Editor

Information and news on manufacturing companies with a regional focus in New England. New product articles, coverage of advances in technology, compliance issues, case studies, announcements and calendar events. Online version includes searchable index of products and services.
32 pages Monthly Founded: 1978
Circulation: 30000
Printed in 4 colors on newsprint stock
Computerized version available: online

16105 Manufacturing Engineering
Society of Manufacturing Engineers
1 SME Drive
PO Box 930
Dearborn, MI 48128-2408
313-271-1500
FAX: 313-425-3401 800-733-4763
magazines@sme.org
http://www.sme.org

Nancy Berg, Executive Director/General Manager
John Coleman, Editor-in-Chief
Karen Manardo, Director of Communication
Tom Drozda, Publisher/Advertising

Serves metalworking industry machining, forming, inspection, assembly and processing operations.
Monthly Founded: 1932
Circulation: 1,11,966

16106 Manufacturing News
Publishers & Producers
PO Box 36
Annandale, VA 22003
703-750-2664
FAX: 703-750-0064
editor@manufacturingnews.com
http://http://www.manufacturingnews.com

Richard McCormack, Publisher/Editor

Gives in-depth analysis of critical manufacturing trends, insightful interviews with top players in industry and government and up-to-the-minute business news about issues that directly affect your ability to compete and prosper and takes a look at software and hardware, sucessful manufacturers, and profound technological changes. *$495.00*
12 pages Fortnightly Founded: 1994
Circulation: 30,000
Printed in on matte stock

16107 Manufacturing Systems
2000 Clearwater Drive
Oak Brook, IL 60523-8809
630-288-8000
FAX: 630-320-7373
dgreenfield@reedbusiness.com
http://www.manufacturing.net

Michelle Palmer, Publisher
Mary Ann Brockway, Circulation Manager
David Greenfield, Editor

Information management for increased manufacturing productivity. *$6.00*
Monthly
Circulation: 114682

16108 Marketeer
1602 E Glen Avenue
Peoria, IL 61614-5451

VB Cook, Editor

New products for manufacturing. *$15.00*
16 pages Monthly Founded: 1952

16109 Marking Industry Magazine
Marking Devices Publishing Company
136 W Vallette
#6
Elmhurst, IL 60126-4377
630-832-5200
FAX: 630-832-5206
webmaster@markingdevices.com
http://www.markingdevices.com

David Hachmeister, Publisher/President/Editor

New products, processes and services, MDAI and other association news, shows and seminars, sales and management methods. *$54.00*
Monthly Founded: 1907
Circulation: 1300

16110 Material Handling Equipment Distributors Association
Data Key Communications
201 US Highway 45
Vernon Hills, IL 60061-2398
847-680-3500
FAX: 847-362-6989
connect@mheda.org
http://www.mheda.org

Loren Swakow, President
Elizabeth Richard, Editor/Executive VP
Kathy Carter, Marketing Manager

Updates on technology, association news and announcements, industrial perspectives and outlook and new product information. *$24.00*
Quarterly Founded: 1954
Circulation: 4000 $950 per M.

16111 Material Handling Network
Network Publishing
252 E. Washington Street
East Peoria, IL 61611-338
309-699-4431
FAX: 309-698-0801 800-447-6901
rcain@wcinet.com
http://www.mhnetwork.com

Andra Stephens, Editor
Bob Behrens, General Manager
Andra Stephens, Advertising/Sales

Monthly journal written for material handling distributors/dealers and people who sell racks, bins, conveyors, dock equipment, lift trucks, batteries, and pallet jacks - both power and non-power. *$65.00*
156 pages Monthly Founded: 1981
Circulation: 12058
Printed in 4 colors on n stock

16112 Material Handling Product News
Reed Business Information
225 Wyman Street
Waltham, MA 02451
617-643-3030
FAX: 781-734-8076
bmiller@reedbusiness.com
http://www.mhpn.com

Barbara Miller, Group Administrative Manager
Joseph Pagnotta, Editor-in-Chief
Joanna Schumann, Marketing Manager
Michael Holowchuck, Circulation Manager
Steve McCoy, Associate Publisher

Literature reviews, new product listings and new systems and services are featured regularly.
Monthly Founded: 1977

16113 Materials at High Temperatures
Butterworth Heinemann
313 Washington Street
Newton, MA 02458-1626
617-928-5460
FAX: 781-933-6333

T Suzuki, Co-Editor
TB Gibbons, Co-Editor

Serves the needs of those developing and using materials for high temperature applications in the power, chemical, engine, processing and furnace industries.

16114 Mid-America Commerce & Industry
2432 SW Pepperwood Road
Topeka, KS 66614-5293
785-272-5280
FAX: 785-272-3729
maci@maci-mag.com
http://www.maci-mag.com/

Colleen Lippe, Circulation
David Lippe, Managing Editor

Regional industrial magazine covering manufacturing in Missouri, Kansas, Nebraska, Oklahoma, Arizona and Iowa
$18.00
Monthly

16115 Midrange ERP
MFG Publishing
9 W Street
Beverly, MA 01915-2225
978-927-1419
FAX: 978-921-1255
editor@mfg-erp.com
http://www.mfg-erp.com

Deborah A Turbide, Publisher

Planning and scheduling issues, polices and procedures, as well as system improvements.
Founded: 1996
Circulation: 40000

16116 Modern Applications News
Nelson Publishing
2500 N Temiami Trail
Nakomis, FL 34275-3476
941-966-9521
FAX: 941-966-2590
nelpub@ix.netcom.com
http://www.nelsonpub.com

Larry Mahan, CEO/President
John Mullaly, Editor
Bob Olree, Publisher
Joan Southerland, Marketing
Wyanne Harwell, Circulation Manager

Information includes coverage of abrasives and grinding, automated handling and robotics, CAD/CAM, coatings and finishings, coolants, lubricants and filters, cutting tools, heat treating, ID marking, lasers, machining centers, and shop control software.
$127.00
Monthly Founded: 1962
Circulation: 80340

16117 NC Shop Owner
Penton Media
1300 E 9th Street
Cleveland, OH 44114
216-696-7000
FAX: 216-696-1752
information@penton.com
www.penton.com

Thomas Grasson, Editor

News of industry events, new product information, updates on manufacturing technology and a special technology focus section.
Semiannual
Circulation: 120,000

16118 National Association of Relay Manufacturers
2500 Wilson Boulevard
Arlington, VA 22201
703-907-8025
FAX: 703-875-8908
narm@ecaus.org
http://www.ecaus.org/narm

Jeffrey W. Boyce, Executive Director
Robert Willis, President

Electronical relay and associated switching devices. Engrs. Relay HB - 5th Edition - $60.00 plus $7.00 postage and handling; IRC Proceeding 2002 - $60.00 plus $7.00 postage and handling *$60.00*
Founded: 1947
Circulation: 1000

16119 New Equipment Digest
Penton Media
1300 E 9th Street
Cleveland, OH 44114-1503
216-696-7000
FAX: 216-696-1752
information@penton.com
http://www.newequipment.com

John Di Paola, VP
Robert F King, Editor
Sarah Hughes, Production Manager
Bobbie Macy, Circulation Manager
David B. Nussbaum, CEO

Serves the general industrial field which include manufacturing, processing, engineering services, construction, transportation, mining, public utilities, wholesale distributors, educational services, libraries, and governmental establishments.
Monthly Founded: 1892
Circulation: 206154

16120 Off-Highway Engineering
SAE
400 Commonwealth Drive
Warrendale, PA 15096-1
724-776-4841
FAX: 724-776-0790 877-606-7323
sohe@sae.org http://www.sae.org

Lawrence C Schneider, Publisher
J E Robertson, President

Off-Highway Engineering serves the international off highway design and manufacturing field which consists of producers of construction, lawn and garden, agricultural equipment, and industrial vehicles. Also served are makers of engines and parts and components and others allied to the field.
$70.00
66 pages Founded: 1905
Circulation: 16308
Printed in 4 colors on glossy stock

16121 Planning Guidebook
Reed Business Information
257 Washington Street
Newton, MA 02458
617-964-3030
FAX: 617-558-4700
corporatecommunications@reedbusiness.com http://www.reedbusiness.com

William Shordon, Editor
Jim Casella, CEO

Offers information and news on manufacturing companies.
Monthly Founded: 1946

16122 Plant
Rogers Media Publishing
777 Bay Street
Toronto, Ontario M5W1A
416-596-5729
FAX: 416-596-5552 www.plant.ca

Joe Terrett, Editor

PLANT serves manufacturing and processing industries in Canada. *$125.00*
18 per year Founded: 1941

16123 Plant Services
Putman Media
555 W Pierce Road
Suite 301
Itasca, IL 60143-2649
630-467-1300

hr@putman.net
http://www.putmanmedia.com

John Huff, Group Publisher
Gordon Weyemuller, Editor
John M Cappelletti, CEO

For maintenance and engineering managers responsible for keeping manufacturing plants running efficiently. *$3.00*
Founded: 1938
Circulation: 106500
Mailing list available for rent 10,000 names
Printed in 4 colors on glossy stock

16124 Plating and Surface Finishing
3660 Maguire Boulevard 3250
Orlando, FL 32803
407-281-6441
FAX: 407-281-6446
aesf@aesf.org http://www.aesf.org

Jon Bednerik CAE, Executive Director
Tom Urban, Advertising Manager
Donn Berry, Editor

AESF is an international society that advances the science of surface finishing to benefit industry and society through education information and social involvement, as well as those who provide services, supplies and support to the industry. *$125.00*
Monthly Founded: 1909
Circulation: 4000

16125 Powder Coating
OSC Publishing
1300 E 66th Street
Minneapolis, MN 55423-2642
612-866-2242
FAX: 612-866-1939

Richard R Cress, Publisher
Richard Link, Manager

Our information focuses on the application, pre-treatment, materials, materials handling, and curing processes. Also features case histories.
9 per year
Circulation: 23587

16126 Precision Manufacturing
Minnesota Precision Manufacturing Association
3131 Fernbrook Lane
Suite 111
plymouth, MN 55447
763-566-5696
FAX: 763-566-5780
http://www.mpma.com

Elizabeth Kuntz, Publications Manager
Garry Bultnick, Sales Manager
Charles Arnold, CEO/President
LuAnn Bartley, Executive Director

Publication for job shop owners, managers and engineers and industrial suppliers, distributors, OEM buyers and purchasing agents, manufacturing representatives and technical colleges.
Founded: 1958
Circulation: 7900
Printed in on glossy stock

16127 Process Cooling & Equipment
Business News Publishing Company
1050 IL Route 83
Suite 200
Bensenville, IL 48084-4900
630-616-0200
FAX: 630-694-4002
meaneys@bnpmedia.com
http://www.process-cooling.com

Doug Glenn, Publisher
Linda Becker, Editor
Sean Meaney, Sales Manager

Focuses on temperatures down through cryogenic levels in industrial processes and in equipment cooling.

16128 Process Heating
Business News Publishing Company
755 W Big Beaver Road
Suite 100
Troy, MI 48084-4900
248-362-3700
FAX: 248-362-0317
webmaster@bnp.com
http://www.process-heating.com

Linda Becker, Editor
Doug Glenn, Group Publisher
Anne Armel, Publisher
Beth McClelland, Production Manager

Covers heat processing at temperatures up to 1000 degrees F at end user and OEM plants in 9 industries.
Monthly Founded: 1926
Circulation: 25000

16129 Products Finishing
Gardner Publications
6915 Valley Avenue
Cincinnati, OH 45244-3029
513-278-8977
FAX: 513-527-8801 800-950-8020
narnold@gardnerweb.com
http://www.gardnerweb.com

Daniel C Luciano, Publisher
Matthew J Little, Editor
Nancy Eigel-Miller, Marketing Director
Nancy Arnold, Circulation Manager

Covers production, management, engineering, design, etc. in plants where metal and plastic products are eletroplated, anodized, painted, buffed, cleaned or otherwise finished. *$89.00*

Monthly Founded: 1928
Circulation: 42000
Printed in 4 colors on glossy stock

16130 Progressive Distributor
Pfingsten Publishing
730 Madison Avenue
Fort Atkinson, WI 53538
920-563-5225
FAX: 920-563-4269 800-932-7732
pmarkgraff@pfpublish.com
http://www.progressivedistributor.com

Rich Vurva, Editor

Sales and marketing magazines for top manager, salespeople and marketing executives in industrial and construction distribution firms.

Founded: 1996
Circulation: 24337
Printed in 4 colors on glossy stock

16131 Quality
Business News Publishing
1050 IL Route 83
Suite 200
Bensenville, IL 60106-1096
630-616-0200
FAX: 630-227-0204
williamst@bnpmedia.com
http://www.qualitymag.com

Rebecca Hennessy, Editor
Thomas A Williams, Publisher
Christopher Sheehy, Circulation Manager

Quality is a monthly business publication serving the quality assurance and process improvement needs of more than 80,000 North American manufacturing professionals. *$75.00*

74 pages Monthly Founded: 1962
Circulation: 64000
Printed in 4 colors on glossy stock

16132 Quality Observer: ICSS Journal
Quality University Press
3970 Chain Bridge Road
PO Box 1111
Fairfax, VA 22030-3316
703-691-9496

tqoedtr@erols.com
www.thequalityobserver.com

Johnson A Edosomwan, Editor

Case studies, interviews, international and national news and regular colums covering service in manufacturing, high-tech, government agencies and non-profit organizations. *$139.00*

50 pages 4 per year
Circulation: 15,000
Printed in 4 colors on glossy stock

16133 Quality Progress
American Society for Quality
600 North Plankinton Avenue
Milwaukee, WI 53203
414-272-8575
FAX: 414-272-1734 800-248-1946
help@asq.org
http://www.qualityprogress.asq.org/

John R Hackl, Editor
Daniel M Duhan, President
Susan E Daniels, Associate Editor

Contains highlights on the application of new management techniques, new equipment, developments in system design, and reviews the status of industry economic and financial trends fo both the manufacturing and service industries. *$80.00*

Monthly Founded: 1946
Circulation: 104000

16134 Scan Tech News
Reed Business Information
2000 Clearwater Drive
Oak Brook, IL 60523
630-740-0825
FAX: 630-320-8686 www.scantech.com

Peter M Boniface, Publisher

Updates in trends in ADC technology and standards, the latest news from leading industry events, and product developments that streamline the flow of essential information in industrial settings.

Monthly
Circulation: 82M

16135 Solid State Technology
PennWell Publishing Company
98 Spit Brook Road
Nashua, NH 03062-5737
603-891-0123
FAX: 603-891-0597
http://www.solid-state.com

Robert C Heavind, Editorial director
David Barach, Publisher

Serves firms involved in the manufacturing and testing of semi-conductor materials, equipment, device/circuits manufacturing and OEM manufacturing with in-house IC manufacturing facilities. *$213.00*

Monthly Founded: 1958

16136 Solid Surface
Cygnus Publishing
1233 Janesville Avenue
Fort Atkinson, WI 53538
920-636-6388
FAX: 920-568-2303 800-547-7377
paul.bowers@cygnuspub.com
http://www.solidsurface.com

Joanna Duggan, Publisher
Russ Lee, Editor
Paul Bowers, Group VP
Charlie Lillis, Content Licensing, Director Corpora

Solid surfaces link between fabricator, distributor, supplier, and manufacturer. It is dedicated to providing reliable and timely information, including updates on the latest fabrication trends and techniques, with a fresh perspective and a sense of humor. *$25.00*

Founded: 1966
Circulation: 4,500

16137 Springs Manufacturer Institute
Spring Manufacturers Institute
2001 Midwest Road
Suite 106
Oak Brook, IL 60523-1335
630-495-8588
FAX: 630-495-8595
info@smihq.org www.smihq.org

Ken Boyce, Chief Administrator Executive
Rita Schauer, Editor
Kim Kostecki, Member Services Coordinator
Pashun McNulty, Financial Admin Coordinator

Provides how-to and technical articles on inspection methods, design, finishes, manufacturing proccesses, materials and equipment, also contains financial and management articles on the interests of precision mechanical spring manufacturers.

130 pages Quarterly
Circulation: 12,000
Printed in 4 colors on glossy stock

16138 Supply Chain e-Business
Keller International Publishing Corporation
150 Great Neck Road
Great Neck, NY 11021
516-829-9722
FAX: 516-829-7265 www.glscs.com

Thomas A Foster, Editor-in-Chief
Russell W Goodman, Managing Editor
Jerry Keller, President

Offers a thorough analysis of on-line solutions designed to help corporations achieve greater supply-chain visiblity and real-time connections with suppliers and customers

Bi-Monthly
Circulation: 45M
Printed in 4 colors on glossy stock

16139 Target
Association for Manufacturing Excellence

380 W Palatine Road
Wheeling, IL 60090-5831
847-520-3282
FAX: 847-520-0163
info@ame.org http://www.ame.org

Robert W Hall, Editor-in-Chief

Contains coverage on educational events, opinion columns, a networking section and more, reflecting manufacturing competitiveness, and improvement concepts and activities for the members of the Association for Manufacturing Excellence and interested academia. *$125.00*

Quarterly Founded: 1985
Circulation: 5000

16140 US Industries Today
Postitive Publications
225 Madison Avenue
Morristown, NJ 07960
973-292-2600
FAX: 973-292-2696
corporate@usitoday.com
http://www.usitoday.com

Peter Mercer, Editor
Sabastian Fraser, CEO/President

Provides information on the latest developments across the whole range of the US manufacturing industry, covering stock market analysis, US business leaders, business profiles and industry sector reports, as well as new products and services. *$15.00*

Founded: 1998
Circulation: 65000

Trade Shows

16141 AES/EPA Conference/Exhibit: Environmental Control for Surface Finishing
American Electroplaters and Surface Finishers Soc.
3660 Maguire Boulevard
Suite 250
Orlando, FL 32803-3075
407-775-5406
FAX: 407-281-6446
exhibit@aesf.org www.aesf.org
Kathy Shumacher, Show Manager
One-hundred exhibitors of waste treatment, pollution control, surface finishing equipment and surfaces.
600 Attendees June

16142 AESF SUR/FIN Annual Technical Conference and Exhibit of Surface Finishers
American Electroplaters and Surface Finishers Soc.
3660 Maguire Boulevard
Suite 250
Orlando, FL 32803-3075
407-775-5406
FAX: 407-281-6446
exhibit@aesf.org www.aesf.org
More than 300 suppliers to the industry will attend.
June

16143 AESF Week - Society's Annual Winter Meeting
American Electroplaters and Surface Finishers Soc.
3660 Maguire Boulevard
Suite 250
Orlando, FL 32803-3075
407-775-5406
FAX: 407-281-6446
exhibit@aesf.org www.aesf.org
June

16144 ALMA Symposium
ALMA International
191 Clarksville Road
Princeton Junction, NJ 08550
609-799-8440
FAX: 609-799-7032
management@almainternational.org
www.alma.org
Steve Temme, President
Stu Lumsden, VP
Unlike other audio-related events, ALMA Symposia focuses exclusively on products, services and technical and business topics relevant to the loudspeaker industry. Invited speakers present technical papers to keep attendees abreast of the latest developments and expert panelists discuss the latest topics. Training programs are also offered. Exhibit hall features 30 industry professionals.
200 Attendees Annual

16145 AME Annual Conference
Association for Manufacturing Excellence
380 W Palatine Road
Suite 7
Wheeling, IL 60090-5863
847-520-3282
FAX: 847-520-0163
info@ame.org www.ame.org
Vivian Bartt, Manager
November Founded: 1985

16146 Adhesive and Sealant Council Convention
ASC
7979 Old Georgetown Road
Suite 500
Bethesda, MD 20814
301-986-9700
FAX: 301-986-9795
bob.willis@ascouncil.org
www.ascouncil.org
Larry Sloan, President
Mark Collatz, Director Government Relations
Serves as a leading marketplace for the exchange of information about products and services and interfacing among manufacturers, suppliers, and others in the industry.
October

16147 Annual Elevator Convention and Exposition
356 Morgan Avenue
PO Box 6507
Mobile, AL 36660
251-479-4514
FAX: 251-479-7043 800-730-5093
naec@mindspring.com
www.elevator-world.com
Ricia S Hendrick, President/Publisher
Robert Caporale, Senior VP and Editor
Annual

16148 Atlantic Design Engineering
Canon Communications
11444 W Olympic Boulevard
Suite 900
Los Angeles, CA 90064-1549
310-445-4200
FAX: 310-445-4299
exhibit@cancom.com
www.cancom.com/
Shannon Cleghorn, Customer & Media Coordinator
Erwin Laner, Promotional Manager
The Atlantic Design Engineering show serves the East Coast's design, process and manufacturing marketplace. Product classifications include Coatings & Finishes, composites, Computer Aided Design/Computer Aided Manufacturing, Electrical/Electronic, Electro Optical Components & Equipment, Engineered Safety Products, Engineering Management & Tools, Fasteners, Fluid Media, Fluid Power & Control and more. Held at the Jacob K. Javits Convention Center in New York, New York.
1319 Attendees June

16149 CleanRooms East
PennWell Conferences and Exhibitions
98 Spit Brook Road
Nashua, NH 03062-5723
603-891-0123
FAX: 603-891-9200
andrear@pennwell.com
www.cleanrooms.com
Andrea Rollins, Show Manager
Lisa Gowern, Registration Manager
Meg Villeure, Conference Manager
CleanRooms shows, the international forums exclusively serving the contamination control industry, couples exhibits with 100% technology-driver conference programs.
3000 Attendees March

16150 Close the Loop Technical Symposium
2001 Midwest Road
Suite 106
Oak Brook, IL 60523-1335
630-495-8588
FAX: 630-495-8595
info@smihq.org www.smihq.org
Symposium will highlight the latest technolgy and best practice solutions to difficult technical problems that are regularly experienced by the spring designer, spring user and manufacturing personel. *$370.00*

16151 Dollar Store Expo
Retail Dollar Store Association
11540 S Eastern Avenue
Suite 100
Henderson, NV 89052
702-893-9090
FAX: 702-893-9227 800-859-9247
info@bentleyintl.net
www.dollarstoreexpo.com
Kristina Mullen, Show Manager
Wendy Witherspoon, Manager
Four-hundred and fifty booths for products that retail for a dollar or less. Wholesalers, distributors, manufacturers, importers and representatives for surplus, jewelry, hair and beauty, automotive, food items, household goods, gifts, toys, party supplies, seasonal and closeouts.
2,500 Attendees June Founded: 2002

16152 Int'l Conference on Powder Injection Molding of Metals & Ceramics
Innovative Material Solutions
605 Severn Drive
State College, PA 16803
814-867-1140
FAX: 814-867-2813
info@imspowder.com
www.imspowder.com
March

16153 International Integrated Manufacturing Technology Trade Exhibition
Reed Exhibition Companies
383 Main Avenue
Norwalk, CT 06851
203-840-4800
FAX: 203-840-4801
inquiry@reedexpo.com
www.reedexpo.com/app/homepage
Elizabeth Hitchcock, International Sales
Expo and conference dedicated to the products and technology needed by engineering operations and management to automate and integrate manufacturing.
June

16154 International Manufacturing Technology Show
7901 Westpark Drive
Mc Lean, VA 22102-4206
703-893-2900
FAX: 703-827-5250 800-828-7469
Peter Eelman, VP Exhibitions
Michelle Edmonson, Exhibitions Operations Manager
Manufacturing equipment trade show.
85M Attendees Biennial Founded: 1927

16155 Lean Management and Solutions Conference
Institute of Industrial Engineers
3577 Parkway Lane
Suite 200
Norcross, GA 30092
770-490-0461
FAX: 770-441-3295 800-494-0460

Ed Williams, Chairman
Danny Pavan, Vice Chairman

The place to find the leaders in lean management and all the tools that you need for success.
300 Attendees September

16156 METALfab
532 Forest Parkway
Suite A
Forest Park, GA 30297-6137
404-363-4009
FAX: 404-366-1852
nommainfo@aol.com
www.nomma.org

Martha Pennington, Show Manager
Todd Daniel, Editor
Barbara Cook, Executive Director
Martha Pennington, Meetings Manager

Trade show sponsored by National Ornamental and Miscellaneous Metals Association.
1000 Attendees March

16157 Medical Design & Manufacturing East
Canon Family of Medical Design & Manufacturing Pub
11444 W Olympic Boulevard
Los Angeles, CA 90064
310-445-4200
FAX: 310-996-9499
register@cancom.com
www.mdmwest.com

Shannon Cleghorn, Customer & Media Coordinator
Erwin Laner, Promotional Manager

June

16158 Medical Design & Manufacturing Exhibition
Canon Communications
11444 W Olympic Boulevard
Los Angeles, CA 15494
310-445-4200
FAX: 310-996-9499
diane.o'conner@cancom.com
www.cancom.com

Shannon Cleghorn, Customer & Media Coordinator
Erwin Laner, Promotional Manager

Design, development, and manufacture of medical products, from high-volume, single-use disposables to next-generation diagnostic instruments and advanced imaging systems. Preview the latest advances in medical-grade materials, assembly components, electronics, machinery, software, systems, services, and more.
May

16159 Medical Design & Manufacturing West
Canon Family of Medical Design & Manufacturing
Publications
11444 W Olympic Boulevard
Los Angeles, CA 90064
310-445-4200
FAX: 310-996-9499
register@cancom.com
www.mdmwest.com

Shannon Cleghorn, Customer & Media Coordinator
Erwin Laner, Promotional Manager

February

16160 Medical Equipment Design & Technology Conference
Canon Communications
11444 W Olympic Boulevard
Los Angeles, CA 90064-1549
310-445-4200
FAX: 310-996-9499
feedback@cancom.com
www.cancom.com

Shannon Cleghorn, Customer & Media Coordinator
Erwin Laner, Promotional Manager

Design, development, and manufacture of medical products, from high-volume, single-use disposables to next-generation diagnostic instruments and advanced imaging systems. Preview the latest advances in medical-grade materials, assembly components, electronics, machinery, software, systems, services and more.
September

16161 Midwest Job Shop Show
Edward Publishing
16 Waterbury Road
Prospect, CT 06712-1215
203-758-4474
FAX: 203-758-4476
www.jobshoptechnology.com

Jennifer Bryda, Production Manager
Christoper Davis, Manager
Gerald Schmidt, President

A source for forming, fabricating, shaping, and assemblies. The show is designed to attract the highest caliber engineers and buyers from product manufacturers. There will be 170 exhibitors and booths.
1500 Attendees

16162 National Manufacturing Week
Reed Exhibition Companies
383 Main Street
Norwalk, CT 06851
203-840-4800
FAX: 203-840-4801
inquiry@reedexpo.com
www.reedexpo.com/app/homepage

Elizabeth Hitchcock, International Sales

The pre-eminent American forum for the display of industrial technology.
1.5M Attendees March

16163 National Plant Engineering and Facilities Management Show and Conference
Reed Exhibition Companies
383 Main Avenue
Norwalk, CT 06851
203-840-4800
FAX: 203-840-4801
inquiry@reedexpo.com
www.reedexpo.com/app/homepage
June

16164 Pacific Design Engineering
Canon Communications
11444 W Olympic Boulevard
Los Angeles, CA 90064
310-445-4200
FAX: 310-996-9499
feedback@cancom.com
www.cancom.com

Shannon Cleghorn, Customer & Media Coordinator
Erwin Laner, Promotional Manager

Serves the West Coast's dynamic design, process, and manufacturing marketplace. Product classifications include: Coatings and Finishes, Composites, Computer Aided Design/Computer Aided Manufacturing, Electrical/Electronic, Electrc Optical Compnents and Equipment, Engineered Safety Products, Engineering Management and Tools, Fasteners, Fluid Media, Fluid Power and Control.
January

16165 Powder and Bulk Solids Conference and Exhibition
Reed Exhibition Companies
383 Main Street
Norwalk, CT 06851
203-840-4800
FAX: 203-840-4801
inquiry@reedexpo.com
www.reedexpo.com/app/homepage

Elizabeth Hitchcock, International Sales

Equipment and technology for processing and handling of powder and bulk solids.
8.4M Attendees May

16166 South-Tec Machine Tool and Manufacturing Show
Society of Manufacturing Engineers
1 SME Drive
#930
Dearborn, MI 48121
313-271-1500
FAX: 313-425-3401 www.sme.org

Philip Trimble, Executive Director/General Manager

70M Attendees Founded: 1932

16167 Southern Job Shop Show
Edward Publishing
16 Waterbury Road
Prospect, CT 06712-1215
203-758-4474
FAX: 860-768-4475
www.jobshoptechnology.com

Mark W Shortt, Editor
Gerald Schmidt, President
Christopher Davis, Manager

The show is designed to attract the highest caliber engineers and buyers from your major DEM product manufacturers.
1500 Attendees March

16168 Spring World Expo
PO Box 1144
Highland Park, IL 60035
847-433-1335
FAX: 847-433-3769
info@casmi.org www.springworld.org

Gerald H Reese, Executive Director

4500 Attendees October

16169 Sumulation Solutions Conference
Institute of Industrial Engineers
3577 Parkway Lane
Suite 200
Norcross, GA 30092
770-490-0461
FAX: 770-441-3295 800-494-0460

Ed Williams, Chairman
Danny Pavan, Vice Chairman

Simulation techniques. Tools and software used in a wide range of industries and applications.
250 Attendees

Directories & Databases

16170 Agricultural & Industrial Manufacturers Membership Directory
Agricultural & Industrial Manufacturers Rep. Assn
7500 Flying Cloud Drive
Suite 900
Eden Prairie, MN 55344
952-253-6230
FAX: 952-835-4774 www.aimrareps.org
Michael J Kowalczyk, President
Ronald R Reed, VP *$25.00*
Annual October

16171 American Machine Tool Distributors Association
1445 Research Boulevard
Suite 450
Rockville, MD 20850-6113
301-738-1200
FAX: 301-738-9499 800-878-2683
Ralph Nappi, President
AMTDA will lead distributors of manufacturing technology by providing essential programs and services that help its members gain global recognition from customers and supplies as the preferred method of distribution. *$50.00*
8-12 pages Monthly Founded: 1924
Circulation: 3400

16172 Directory of Manufacturing Research Centers
Manufacturing Technology Information
10 W 35th Street
Chicago, IL 60616-3717
312-431-1442
FAX: 312-567-4736 800-421-0586
mtiac@iitri.org www.iitri.org
Paula Marggraf, Editor *$75.00*
Irregular

16173 Directory of Waste Equipment Manufacturers and Distributors
WASTEC Equipment Technology Association
4301 Connecticut Avenue NW
Suite 300
Washington, DC 20008-2304
202-244-4700
FAX: 202-966-4824 www.wastec.org
Ron McCracken, Chairman
Bruce Parker, President
Gary T Satterfield, Executive VP
Sandra Price, Director Member Services
About 250 member manufacturers of waste handling, collection and processing equipment. *$5.00*
Annual

16174 Rauch Guide to the US Rubber Industry
Grey House Publishing
PO Box 860
Millerton, NY 12546
518-789-8700
FAX: 518-789-0545 800-562-2139
books@greyhouse.com
www.greyhouse.com
Leslie Mackenzie, Publisher
Richard Gottlieb, President
Approximately 500 manufacturers of fabricated rubber products. *$595.00*
Annual

16175 Small Business Inovation Research
1000 Independence Avenue Sw
Washington, DC 20585-1207
202-571-1300
sbir-sttr@mailgw.er.doe.gov
www.er.doe.gov/
Lawrence Small, Chief Executive Officer
Annual

16176 Sound and Vibration: Buyer's Guide Issue
Acoustical Publications
PO Box 40416
27101 E. Oviatt Road
Bay Village, OH 44140-0416
440-835-0101
FAX: 440-835-9303
sv@mindspring.com
www.sandv.com.home/htm
Jack Mowry, Editor and Publisher
Scott J Lothes, Assistant Editor/Webmaster
This directory offers a list of manufacturers of products for noise and vibration control.
Monthly ISBN 0-038181-09-9
Circulation: 19,000
Mailing list available for rent 21M names
Printed in 4 colors on glossy stock

16177 Thomas Register of American Manufacturers
Thomas Publishing Company
5 Penn Plaza
12th Floor
New York, NY 10001-1860
212-290-7341
800-699-9822
LRigano@ThomasNet.com
www.thomasregisterdirectory.com
Ruth Hurd, Publisher
Linda M Rigano, Media Coordinator
Over 150,000 manufacturing firms are listed in more than 25 volumes of this directory set. Valuable information offered includes product headings, product line information, company profiles and more. *$270.80*
44000 pages Annual Founded: 1905

16178 Who Audits America
Data Financial Press
PO Box 668
Menlo Park, CA 94026-0668
650-321-4553
FAX: 650-321-4427
A who's who directory of services and supplies. *$133.00*
600 pages SemiAnnual

Industry Web Sites

16179 www.abrasiveengineering.com
Abrasive Grain Association

Members manufacture natural and artificial grains used in grinding wheels, coated abrasives etc.

16180 www.aesf.org
American Electroplaters and Surface Finishers Soc.

AESF is an international society that advances the science of surface finishing to benefit industry and society through education information and social involvement, as well as those who provide services, supplies and support to the industry.

16181 www.agma.org
American Gear Manufacturers Association

Manufacturers of gears and geared speed changers.

16182 www.ahma.org
American Hardware Manufacturers Association

Over 280 manufacturer representatives in the hardware industry.

16183 www.amba.org
American Mold Builders Association

Promotes the development, welfare, and expansion of businesses engaged in the manufacture of molds and related tooling.

16184 www.amtda.org
American Machine Tool Distributors Association

For distributors of manufacturing technology.

16185 www.ararental.org
American Rental Association

For rental business owners and equipment suppliers.

16186 www.arcat.com
National Association of Relay Manufacturers

NARM is a trade association for the electro-mechanical relay and associated switching devices industry. An affiliate of Electronic Industries Alliance.

16187 www.asphaltinstitute.org
Asphalt Institute

Conducts education, research, and engineering services related to asphalt products; conducts seminars and sells publications and videos on asphalt technology.

16188 www.awci.com/
American Watchmakers-Clockmakers Institute

Examines and certifies master watchmakers and clockmakers. Maintains a placement service. Conducts home study courses.

16189 **www.awci.org**
Association of the Wall and Ceiling Industries

Offers information on contractors, manufacturers, suppliers and organizations affiliated with the interior design, building and contracting community. Strives to provide services and undertake activities that enhance the members ability to operate a successful business.

16190 **www.bia.org**
Brick Industry Association

Supports the industry by rendering technical assistance to architects and designers, by providing marketing assistance to the industry, by monitoring and positively influencing governmental actions, by working to assure the long term availability of bricklayers and by providing other member services as appropriate.

16191 **www.cancentral.com**
Can Manufacturers Institute

Industry, environmental and consumer information.

16192 **www.carpet ushion.org**
Carpet Cushion Council

Encourages distribution and use of seperate carpet cushions. Works with regulatory agencies at the national, state and local levels.

16193 **www.cctiwdc.org/**
Composite Can & Tube Institute

Represents the composite can and tube industry.

16194 **www.cl2.com**
Chlorine Institute

Promotes safe handling of chlorine and caustic materials and sponsors awards.

16195 **www.cmit.edi.gatech.edu/**
Center for Manufacturing Information

Provides a non-instrusive environment in which manufacturers can objectively evaluate and compare the latest computer-based technologies.

16196 **www.cottonseed.com**
National Cottonseed Products Association

Services include the administration of trading rules and standards, a research program, information service center and product promotion of cotton seed food and feed products.

16197 **www.cti.org**
Cooling Technology

Seeks to improve technology, design and performance of water conservation apparatus. Provides inspection services and conducts research.

16198 **www.divbusiness.com**
Diversified Business Communications

Provides management services for associations and organizations seeking to expand domestically and overseas, as well as direct mail, internet, telemarketing campaigns and market research.

16199 **www.fluidcontrolsinstitute.org**
Fluid Controls Institute

Manufacturers of devices for fluid control, such as temperature and pressure regulators, strainers, gauges, control valves, solenoid valves, steam traps, etc.

16200 **www.fluidsealing.com**
Fluid Sealing Association

An international association of manufacturers of mechanical packings, sealing devices, gaskets, rubber expansion joints and allied products.

16201 **www.graphicsPor.org**
Graphics Products Association

Independent manufacturers and suppliers of paperboard packaging. Purposes are to futher development, use and sale of members product. Compiles statistics and bestows awards.

16202 **www.greyhouse.com**
Grey House Publishing

Selected Grey House directories in the fields of business, health and education are available online. Users can search our online databases by several different search criteria, such as product categories, geographic area, sales volume and much, much more. Full Grey House catalog and online ordering also available.

16203 **www.housewares.org**
National Housewares Manufacturers Association

Links to other associations.

16204 **www.iccsafe.org/**
International Code Council

Nonprofit membership association with more than 16,000 members who span the building community, from code enforcement officials to materials manufacturers. Dedicated to preserving the public health, safety and welfare in the built environment through the effective use and enforcement of model codes.

16205 **www.icea.net**
Insulated Cable Engineers Association

Professional organization dedicated to developing cable standards for the electric power, control and telecommunications industries. Ensures safe, economical and efficient cable systems utilizing proven state-of-the-art materials and concepts. ICEA documents are of interest to cable manufacturers, architects and engineers, utility and manufacturing plant personnel, telecommunication engineers, consultants and OEMs.

16206 **www.ifai.com**
Industrial Fabrics Association International

Provides many products, services and programs to industry members.

16207 **www.ilma.org**
Independent Lubricant Manufacturers Association

Independent blenders and compounders of lubricants.

16208 **www.iopp.org**
Institute of Packaging Professionals

Association for packing professionals.

16209 **www.ipc.org**
IPC-Association Connecting Electronics Industries

Works to develop standards in circuit board assembly equipment. Brings together all players in the electronic interconnection industry, including designers, board manufacturers, assembly companies, suppliers and original equipment manufacturers. Offers workshops, conferences, meetings and online communications.

16210 **www.isri.org**
Institute of Scrap Recycling Industries

Members include processors, brokers and consumers of scrap metal, rubber, paper, textiles, plastics and glass.

16211 **www.marinecanvas.com**
Marine Fabricators Association

Firms and individuals engaged in the design, construction, and installation of marine fabric products. Provides certification and product standards.

16212 www.mechanical.com
Mechanical.Com

Manufacturing industry database.

16213 www.mep.nist.gov
Manufacturing Extension Partnership

A nationwide network of more thatn 70 not-for-profit centers whose sole purpose is to provide small and medium-sized manufacturers with the help they need to succeed.

16214 www.mfgworld.com/index.html
Manufacturing World Online

Manufacturing news, software, industry reports and links.

16215 www.mhia.org/psc/PSC_Products_Racks.cfm
Rack Manufacturers Institute

Makers of steel industrial storage racks.

16216 www.naima.org
North American Insulation Manufacturers Assn

16217 www.nam.org
National Association of Manufacturers

Represents industry's views on national and international problems to government.

16218 www.naumd.com
National Association of Uniform Manufacturers

Promotes interests of manufacturers and distributors of uniforms and career wear.

16219 www.ncspa.org
National Corrugated Steel Pipe Association

NCSPA seeks to promote sound public policy relating to the use of corrugated steel drainage structures in private and public construction.

16220 www.nei.org
Nuclear Energy Institute

Members are of utilities, manufacturers of electrical generating equipment, researchers, architects, engineers, labor unions, and others interested in the generation of electricity by nuclear power.

16221 www.nomma.org
National Ornamental and Miscellaneous Metals
Association

Publishes the "Ornamental and Miscellaneous Metals Fabricator" magazine. Holds annual convention and trade show (METALfab). Membership dues: $275 fabricators, $250 local supplier, $325 regional supplier, $425 nationwide supplier.

16222 www.nwpca.org
National Wooden Pallet & Container Association

Represents manufacturers, recyclers and distributors of pallets, containers and reels.

16223 www.p3-ny.org/
Women in Production

Promotes the interests of women in the production profession.

16224 www.patmi.org
Powder Actuated Tool Manufacturers Institute

Represents manufacturers of construction tools used to fasten to and into steel and concrete.

16225 www.plma.com
Private Label Manufacturers Association (PLMA)

Online show information.

16226 www.powertoolinstitute.com/
Power Tool Institute

Trade association representing manufacturers of power tools.

16227 www.reman.org
Remanufacturing Institute International

A coalition of associations and companies in the entire manufacturing industry. There are over 73,000 companies in this industry. Our goal is to unite them into a powerful organization.

16228 www.sawingassociation.com/
North American Sawing Association

16229 www.smma.org
SMMA: Small Motors & Motion Association

Manufacturing trade association. Members include electric motor and motion control companies, as well as suppliers, users, and associated businesses such as consultants, universities and distributors.

16230 www.steeltubeinstitute.org
Steel Tube Institute of North America

Members produce steel tubes and pipes from carbon, stainless or alloy steel for applications ranging from large structural tubing to small redrawn tubing.

16231 www.sunglassassociation.com
Sunglass Association of America

A nonprofit trade association of manufacturers and import-wholesale sunglasses, sunglass parts, components, materials, and reading glasses.

16232 www.thomasnet.com/index.html
Thomas Register of American Manufacturers

Industrial buying guide of US and Canadian manufacturers.

16233 www.tileusa.com
Tile Council of America

Manufacturers and suppliers of ceramic wall and floor tiles.

16234 www.tpatube.org
Tube & Pipe Association International

TPA is an educational technology association serving the metal tube and pipe producing and fabricating industries.

16235 www.ttmanet.org
Truck Trailer Manufacturers Association

News of interest to trailer manufacturers and suppliers.

16236 www.vending.org
National Automatic Merchandising Association

For makers and operators of automatic vending equipment.

16237 www.westernroofing.net/
Roof Tile Institute

Manufacturers of clay and concrete roof tiles. Emphasis is on technical issues and codes that involve tile. Has annual budget of approximately $300,000 a year. Publications available to members.

Associations

16238 Academy of Marketing Science
PO Box 248012
Coral Gables, FL 33124-8012
305-284-6673
FAX: 305-284-3762
ams.sba@maimi.edu
www.ams-web.org

Dr. Harold W Berkman, Director
Sally Sultan, Coordinator

Fosters education professional standards in marketing science. Sponsers the AMS Foundation which provides grants for the advancement of teaching and research.
1500 Members Founded: 1971

16239 Advertising and Marketing International
1 City Center
Saint Louis, MO 63101-1883
314-589-3000
FAX: 314-436-0359
A worldwide network of cooperating, non-competitive advertising agencies in 45 cities which provides facilities and branch office services.

16240 American Chamber of Commerce Executives
4875 Eisenhower Avenue
Suite 250
Alexandria, VA 22304
703-998-0072
FAX: 703-212-9512
membership@acce.org www.acce.org

Mick Fleming, President
Brenda Luper, VP/CFO
1300+ Members Founded: 1914

16241 American Marketing Association
311 S Wacker Drive
Suite 5800
Chicago, IL 60606-6301
312-542-9000
FAX: 312-922-3763 800-262-1150
fvangorp@ama.org www.ama.org

Ronald E Keener, Publisher
Dr. Robert Lusch, Editor
Dennis Dunlap, Chief Executive Officer

Represents marketers and keeps members informed of trends in advertising. Fosters research, sponsors seminars and provides educational placement service.
44M Members Founded: 1947

16242 Assist International
90 John Street
Room 505
New York, NY 10038
212-244-2074
FAX: 212-725-3312
info@assist-intl.com
www.assist-intl.com
International trade promotion and consulting firm: mailing lists, seminars, conferences, international business expo.

16243 Association for Entrepreneurial Growth
PO Box 875
Merrimack, NH 03054
603-429-1631
FAX: 603-424-8641
gouldcapital@aol.com

Neil C Gould, Founding Sponsor
Ray F Chadwick, Founding Sponsor

Provides the business and entrepreneurial community with valuable information and networking capabilities to stimulate entrepreneurial and business growth.
700 Members Founded: 2000

16244 Association for Innovative Marketing
34 Summit Avenue
Sharon, MA 02067-2149
508-668-2575

Facilitates sharing of innovative ideas; bestows awards, maintains library and speaker bureau.
Founded: 1989

16245 Biomedical Marketing Association
10293 N Meridian Street
Suite 175
Indianapolis, IN 46290
317-816-1640
FAX: 317-816-1633 800-278-7886
info@bmaonline.org
www.bmaonline.org

Michael L Boner, President

Builds diagnostic industry leadership by providing market education, professional development and a forum for fellowship and the exchange of ideas.

16246 Bond Market Association
360 Madison Avenue
New York, NY 10017-7111
212-907-7510
FAX: 646-637-9126
www.bondmarkets.com

Micha Green, Owner

A trade association representing the largest securities marekts in the world. The association speaks for the bond industry, advocating its positions and representing its interests in New York; Washington, DC; London; Frankfurt; Brussels and Tokyo.

16247 Bureau of Salesmens' National Association
1801 Peachtree Road NE
Atlanta, GA 30309
404-870-7600

Trade association that offers consulting, seminars, conferences and networking to promote business growth.
10M Members Founded: 1945

16248 Business Marketing Association
400 N Michigan Avenue
15th Floor
Chicago, IL 60611

FAX: 312-822-0054 800-664-4BMA

Kirby Strickland, Chairman
Tom Stack, VP, Public Relations

Pre-eminent service organization for professionals in this vital industry.
Founded: 1922

16249 Cable & Telecommunications Association for Marketing
201 N Union Street
Suite 440
Alexandria, VA 22314
703-549-4200
FAX: 703-684-1167
info@ctam.com www.ctam.com

Char Beales, President
Daniel Cassidy, SVP Finance/Administration

CTAM is dedicated to the discipline and development of consumer marketing excellence in cable television, new media and telecommunications services.
5500 Members Founded: 1976

16250 Cherry Marketing Institute
PO Box 30285
Lansing, MI 48909-7785
517-731-1636
FAX: 517-669-3354
jbaker@cherrymkt.org
www.cherrymkt.org

Jane Baker, Marketing Director
Deborah Cherry, Manager

An organization providing cherry information and promoting material to food manufacturers, food service operators and others.
Founded: 1988

16251 Communications Roundtable
1250 24th Street NW
Suite 250
Washington, DC 20037
202-755-5180
FAX: 202-466-0544
www.roundtable.org

Michael Reichgut, Chairman
Shawn Dolley, Chief Executive Officer

Association of more than 20 public relations, marketing, graphics, advertising, training and other communications organizations with more than 12,000 professional members. The goals include furthering professionalism, cooperation between member organizations, career and employment support, and employer assistance.

16252 Construction Marketing Research Council C/O CMPA
4625 South Wendler Drive
Suite '111
Tempe, AZ 85282
602-431-1441
FAX: 602-431-0637 cmrc.net

Jim McMahon, Treasurer

Members are professionals in the construction products industry with responsiblities for their firms' corporate strategic planning and the conduct of marketing research activities. Membership is restricted to the highest level marketing research or planning professional within a company.
25 Members Founded: 1992

16253 Council for Marketing and Opinion
110 National Drive, 2nd Floor
Glastonbury, CT 06033
860-657-1881
FAX: 860-682-1010
info@cmor.org www.cmor.org

Donna Gillin, Director Of Operations

CMOR is a non-profit organization which works on behalf of the survey research industry, to improve respondent cooperation research & to promote positive legislation and prevent restrictive legislation which could impact the survey research industry.
160 Members

16254 Direct Marketing Association
1120 Avenue of the Americas
New York, NY 10036-6700
212-768-7277
FAX: 212-302-6714
customerservice@the-dma.org
www.the-dma.org

Leading global trade association of business and nonprofit organizations using and supporting direct marketing tools and techniques.
4800 Members Founded: 1917

16255 Distributive Education Clubs of America
1908 Association Drive
Reston, VA 20191-1594
703-860-5000
FAX: 703-860-4013
ed_davis@deca.org www.deca.org
Edward L Davis, PhD, Executive Director
Larry Lorenzi, Meeting Specialist
Members are students and educators concerned with distribution, marketing, merchandising and managment.

16256 Electronic Retailing Association
2000 N. 14th Street
Suite 300
Arlington, VA 22201
703-841-1751
FAX: 703-841-1860 800-987-6462
contact@retailing.org
www.retailing.org
Barbara Tulipane, President/CEO
For companies who use the power of electronics to sell goods and services to the public. The purpose of ERA is to foster growth, development and acceptance of the rapidly growing electronic retailing industry worldwide.
400 Members Founded: 1990

16257 Floral Marketing Association
1500 Casho Mill Road
PO Box 6036
Newark, DE 19714-6036
302-738-7100
FAX: 302-731-2409
pma@mail.pma.com www.pma.com
Stephen J Barnard, Chairman
Peter Goulet, Division Chairman Retail
Dave Murphy, Division Chairman Foodservice
Bryan E Silbermann, President
Serves the mass-market floral industry.
2400+ Members Founded: 1949

16258 Food Marketing Institute
655 15th Street NW
Washington, DC 20005
202-200-0600
FAX: 202-429-4519
fmi@fmi.org www.fmi.org
Tim Hammonds, Chief Executive Officer
Jack Block, VP
Members are food retailers and wholesalers.
2300 Members Founded: 1977

16259 Foodservice Sales & Marketing Association
c/o Grocery Manufacturers Association
2401 Pennsylvania Avenue
Second Floor
Washington, DC 20037
202-379-9400

info@fsmaonline.com
www.fsmaonline.com
Andy Wilson, Chair
Rick Abraham, Executive Director
Specializes in selling food and related products to retail companies.

Mailing list available for rent

16260 Graphic Arts Marketing Information Service
1421 Prince Street
Suite 230
Alexandria, VA 22314-2805
202-519-8136
FAX: 703-548-3227
jbland@printing.org www.printing.org

Jacqueline Bland, Executive Director
A section of Printing Industries of American that provides market research and statistics to its members. Research is member selected and directed.
72 Members Founded: 1966

16261 Healthcare Financial Management Association
2 Westbrook Corporate Center
Suite 700
Westchester, IL 60154-5700
708-531-9600
FAX: 708-531-0032 800-252-4362
Richard Clarke, President
Dave Neuendorf, VP
HFMA is a diverse, nonpartisan, professional organization that is committed to developing and promoting ethical, high-quality healthcare finance practices.

16262 Incentive Federation
5008 Castle Rock Way
Naples, FL 34112
239-775-7527
FAX: 239-775-7537
incentiveFed@aol.com
www.incentivecentral.org
Howard C Henry, Executive Director/CAE
Your portal to new ways of achieving business goals by capturing the power of your best customers and employees.
150 Members Founded: 1984

16263 Incentive Marketing Association
1801 North Mill Street
Suite R
Naperville, IL 60563
603-369-7780
FAX: 630-369-3773
karen@incentivemarketing.org
www.incentivemarketing.org
Karen Renk, Executive Director/CAE
Members are professional premium/incentive marketing executives.
650 Members Founded: 1998

16264 Information Resources Group
50495 Corporate Drive
Shelby Township, MI 48315-3132
248-360-4600

A national organization that offers over 1,000,000 MIS and corporate professionals at over 150,000 companies throughout the United States.

16265 Institute of Business Appraisers
PO Box 17410
Plantation, FL 33318
954-584-1144
FAX: 954-584-1184 800-299-4130
ibahq@go-iba.org www.go-iba.org
Michelle Miles, Executive Director
The oldest professional society devoted solely to the appraisal of closely-held businesses.
3,000 Members Founded: 1978

16266 International Newspaper Marketing Association
10300 N Central Expressway
Dallas, TX 75231-8621
214-373-9111
972-991-3151
Earl J Wilkinson, Executive Director
Individuals in marketing, circulation, research and public relations of newspapers.

16267 Legal Marketing Association
1926 Waukegan Road
Suite 1
Glenview, IL 60025
847-657-6717
FAX: 847-657-6819
www.legalmarketing.org
Joyce Paschall, Executive Director
LMA is a nonprofit organization dedicated to serving the needs and maintaining the professional standards of the men and women involved in marketing within the legal profession.
2700 Members Founded: 1986 2700 names $250 per M.

16268 Manufacturers Agents National Association
One Spectrum Pointe
Suite 150
Lake Forest, CA 92630
949-859-4040
FAX: 949-855-2973
mana@manaonline.org
www.manaonline.org
Helen Degliangel, VP
Joe Miller, Chief Executive Officer
Jerry Leteh, Manager
6600 Members Founded: 1947

16269 Manufacturers' Agents National Association
One Spectrum Point
Suite 150
Lake Forest, CA 92630
949-859-4040
FAX: 949-855-2973
mana@mana.online.org
www.manronline.org
Joseph W Miller, President
Jack Foster, Editor
National organization for manufacturer's agents and manufacturers who contract for the services of these representatives.
6600 Members Founded: 1947

16270 Marketing Agencies Association Worldwide
460 Summer Street
4th Floor
Stamford, CT 06901-2900
203-978-1590
FAX: 203-969-1499
vincentsottosanti@maaw.org
www.maaw.org
Keith McCrackeni, Executive Director
Joan Lombardo, Administrative Assistant
The Marketing Agencies Assocation Worldwide (MAA) is the only global organization dedicated solely to the CEOs, Presidents,Managing Directors and Principals of top marketing services agencies.
75 Members Founded: 1963

16271 Marketing Education Association
PO Box 27473
Tempe, AZ 85285-7473
602-750-6735

mea@nationalmea.org
www.nationalmea.org
Fosters the development and expansion of education for and about marketing as a descrete, clearly defined profession. Members are high school and postsecondary marketing educations as well as university-level teacher educations and collegiate marketing teacher education students.
Founded: 1982

16272 Marketing Research Association
110 National Dr
2nd Fl
Glastonbury, CT 06033-1212
860-682-1000
FAX: 860-682-1010
bluebook@mra-net.org
www.bluebook.org
Lisa Lockwood, Directories Manager
The Marketing Research Association's Blue Book Research Services Directory is the research industry number one reference source.

16273 Marketing Science Institute
1000 Massachusetts Avenue
Cambridge, MA 02138-5396
617-491-2060
FAX: 617-491-2065
msi@msi.org www.msi.org
Marni Zea Clippinger, COO
Leigh McAlister, Executive Director
Paul Root, CMO
Carolyn Caswell, Director Conferences
MSI publishes research done on a variety of marketing topics, including: E - Commerce, Metrics, Branding, New Products and Innovations, Communications and more. Individual papers and subscriptions are available. We accept proposals and papers for grant consideration.
65 Members Founded: 1961

16274 Mass Marketing Insurance Institute
14 W 3rd Street
Kansas City, MO 64105
816-221-7575
FAX: 816-561-7765
Kenneth R Bowman, Executive Director
Provides a forum for professionals engaged in marketing, sales and administration of employee benefits such as worksite marketing, payroll deduction and other mass marketed services.

16275 Materials Marketing Associates
136 South Keowee Street
Dayton, oh 45402
937-221-1024
FAX: 937-222-5794
email@mma4u.com
www.mma4u.com
Kim Fantaci, Executive Director
Members are chemical distributors representing manufacturers marketing chemical raw material specialties to makers of coatings, inks, pharmaceuticals, adhesives, cosmetics, plastics, soaps, detergents, etc.
19 Members Annual Meeting (February)
Founded: 1963

16276 Medical Marketing Association
575 Market St
Ste 2125
San Francisco, CA 94105-2870
415-644-4807
FAX: 415-927-5734 800-551-2173
sthomas@mmanet.org
www.mmanet.org
Sheri Thomas, Executive Director
Professional association comprises of over 1000 medical marketers from the pharmaceutical, device, diagnostic and marketing/advertising industries.

16277 Midwest Direct Marketing Association
4248 Park Glen Road
Minneapolis, MN 55416
952-928-4643
FAX: 952-929-1318
mdma@mdma.org www.mdma.org
Lavinia Johnson, President
Dean Sanberg, President
Lisa Ferrier, Executive Director
Ed Harrington, Manager
Advancing the professional and ethical practice of direct response marketing by members throughout the Upper Midwest. The MDMA seeks to accomplish this by sponsoring educational and professional networking events to share and encourage the best practices in telemarketing, direct mail and online marketing techniques and stategies.
600+ Members Founded: 1960

16278 Multi-Level Marketing International Association
119 Stanford Court
Irvine, CA 92612-1671
949-854-0484
FAX: 949-854-7687
info@mlmia.com www.mlmia.com
Doris Wood, President
Seeks to strengthen and improve the multi-level marketing industry in the United States and abroad. Members are companies which market their products and services directly to consumers through distributors, suppliers to the industry and distributors who interface with consumers.

Founded: 1985

16279 Multicultural Marketing Resources

101 5th Avenue
Suite 103
New York, NY 10003
212-242-3351
FAX: 212-691-5969
lisa@multicultural.com
www.multicultural.com
Lisa Skriloff, President/Founder
A public relations/marketing firm representing the nations' experts in targeting Hispanics, African Americans, and Asians.

8500 Members Founded: 1994

16280 NKH&W
600 Broadway
Kansas City, MO 64105-6410
816-842-8881
FAX: 816-842-1872
hr@nkhw.com www.nkhw.com
Pete Kovac, President/CEO
Gary McKenna, Management Supervisor
Brad Lang, Senior VP Client Services
Full service marketing communications agency. We give our clients integrated marketing communications programs by providing core advertising agency services combined with in-house market research, direct marketing, sales promotion and public relations capabilities.
93 Members Founded: 1981

16281 National Association of Collegiate
PO Box 16428
Cleveland, OH 44116-0428
440-892-4000
FAX: 440-892-4007
mdukov@nacda.com www.nacda.com

Bob Vecchione, Senior Associate
Executive Director
Mike Cleary, Executive Director
Members are public relations and marketing professionals in college and university athletic departments. Promotes standards and provides professional support.
500 Members Founded: 1990

16282 National Association of Display Industries
3595 Sheridan Street
Suite 200
Hollywood, FL 33021
954-893-7300
FAX: 954-893-7500
nadi@nadi-global.com
www.nadi-global.com
Klein Merriman, Executive Director
Robert Rosean, President, NADI
James Schubert, President, NASFM
A leading association for the visual merchandising profession. As visual merchandising has evolved over the years into playing an integral role in retail, NADI has always taken the lead in informing and educating members. The association's already significant support of the visual design profession has grown with NADI's exclusive sponsorship of GlobalShop's Visual Merchandising Show and StoreXpo.
Founded: 1942

16283 North American Agricultural Marketing
120 N Street
Room A270
Sacramento, CA 95814
902-424-8870
FAX: 916-445-2655
info@naamo.org www.naamo.org
Joe Gaines, President
Kelly Krug, First VP
Jim Duffy, Second VP
Linda MacDonald, Secretary/Treasurer
Members are state and provincial officials responsible for agricultural products marketing programs in the US, Canada and ultimately Mexico.
35 Members Founded: 1921

16284 PROMAX
9000 W Sunset Boulevard
Suite 900
Los Angeles, CA 90069
310-788-7600
FAX: 310-788-7616 www.promax.tv
Jim Chabin, CEO
Lee Hunt, Vice Chair/Treasurer
Michael Mischler, Secretary
International association of promotion and marketing, professionals in electronic media. Promotes the effectiveness of promotion and marketing within the industry and the academic community.

2400 Members Founded: 1952

16285 Photo Marketing Association International
3000 Picture Place
Jackson, MI 49201
517-788-8100
FAX: 517-788-8371
pma_information_central@pmai.org
www.pmai.org
Ted Fox, Executive Director
Bruce Aldrich, Senior Operation Officer
18000 Members Founded: 1930

16286 Private Label Manufacturers Association
369 Lexington Avenue
New York, NY 10017
212-723-3131
FAX: 212-983-1382
info@plma.com www.plma.com
Trade Association promoting the Private Label Industry.
2500 Members Founded: 1979

16287 Promotion Industry Council
1805 N Mill Street
Naperville, IL 60563-1275
630-369-7781
FAX: 630-369-3773
Manufacturers, distributors and users of promotion premiums. Increases understanding of incentives and the premium promotion process.
100 Members Founded: 1940

16288 Promotion Marketing Association of America
257 Park Avenue South
Suite 1102
New York, NY 10010
212-420-1100
FAX: 212-533-7622
pma@pmalink.org www.pmalink.org
Claire Rosenzweig, President
Linda A Goldstein, VP Government/Legal Affairs
H Pierce Pelouze, Treasurer
Mark L Barry, Secretary
Mission is to encourage the highest standards of excellence in promotion marketing. Represents member interests and promotes better understanding promotion in the marketing mix.
700 Members Founded: 1911

16289 Recognition Technologies Users Association
185 Devonshire Street
Boston, MA 02110-1421

FAX: 617-521-8675
Focuses on strategic marketing and planning in technology and industrial areas including technology commercialization. Also features articles on government programs and how to participate in them. International market and business development also are featured.

16290 Research Institute of America
395 Hudson Street
New York, NY 10014
212-676-6300

ria@thomson.com www.riahome.com
Peter Warwick, Chief Executive Officer
A national organization that focuses on marketing and sales intelligence for top level marketing executives.

16291 Sales and Marketing Executives International
PO Box 1390
Sumas, WA 98295-1390
312-893-0751

admin@smei.org www.smei.org
Willis Turner, President/CEO
Members are most commonly professionals in the fields of sales and marketing management, market research management, sales training, distribution management and other senior executives in small and medium businesses.
10000 Members Annual Meeting (Fall)

16292 Society for Marketing Professional Services (SMPS)
99 Canal Center Plaza
Suite 330
Alexandria, VA 22314-1588
703-549-6117
FAX: 703-549-2498 800-292-7677
info@smps.org www.smps.org
Ron Worth, CEO
Serving marketing and business development professionals employed by architectural, engineering and construction firms, SMPS provides education and networking opportunities tailored to build your bottom line.
5600 Members Founded: 1973
Mailing list available for rent 6000 names $200 per M.

16293 Society of Independent Gasoline Marketers
11495 Freedom Drive
Suite 215
Reston, VA 20190
703-750-0478
FAX: 703-709-7007
sigma@sigma.org www.sigma.org
Kenneth A Doyle, Executive VP
Thomas L Osborne, Director Communications
Lori Wolking, Director Meetings
Members are independent gasoline marketers.
270 Members Founded: 1958

16294 Specialty Equipment Market Association
PO Box 4910
Diamond Bar, CA 91765-0910
909-396-0289
FAX: 909-860-0184
sema@sema.org www.sema.org
Chris Kersting, President/CEO
Linda Czarkowski, VP Administration
Carl Sheffer, VP OEM Relations
Faith Barnese, VP Membership/Councils
Represents the automotive aftermarket industry with government agencies and trade and consumer groups.
5200 Members Founded: 1963

16295 Strategic Account Management Association
150 N Wacker Drive
Suite 2222
Chicago, IL 60606
312-251-3131
FAX: 312-251-3132
napolitano@strategicaccounts.org
www.strategicaccounts.org
Lisa Napolitano, President/CEO
Matt Fegley, Director Membership
Matthew Balthazor, Director Marketing/Communications
Melissa Olson, Director Education
The Strategic Account Management Association is a non-profit organization devoted to developing and promoting the concept of customer-supplier partnering. SAMA is dedicated to the professional and personal development of the executives charged with managing national, global, and strategic account relationships, and to elevating the status of the profession as a whole. SAMA provides literature, training and research into best practices in large, complex, global customer account management.
2000 Members Founded: 1964

16296 Trade Show Exhibitors Association
2301 S Lane Shore Drive
Suite 1005
Chicago, IL 60616
312-842-8732
FAX: 312-842-8744 tsea@tsea.org
Steve J Schuldenfrei, President
Members are companies using exhibits for marketing, advertising or public relations.
1800 Members Founded: 1966

16297 US International Trade Association
14 Street & Constitution Avenue NW
Washington, DC 20230
202-822-2867
FAX: 800-786-2329
David Aaron, Manager
Association for those interested in export opportunities for United States businesses.

16298 Writers Research Group LLC
PO Box 891568
Oklahoma City, OK 73159-1568
405-681-5074
FAX: 405-685-3390
info@writersresearchgroup.com
www.writersresearchgroup.com
Writers Research Group is a professional writing and research firm. Our knowledgeable employees gather, examine, edit, and compile data to your company's specifications. Our services include research, writing, directory listing updates and new entries, indexing, copyediting, proofreading, data entry, document markup and permissions negotiations.
Founded: 2000

Newsletters

16299 Advanced Selling Power
Thompson Group
6850 Austin Center Boulevard
Suite 100
Austin, TX 78731
512-418-8869
FAX: 512-418-1209
info@thompson-group.com
http://www.thompson-group.com
Terry E Thompson, Publisher
Valerie A Canaday, Editor
Carol Thompson, President
Provides sales tactics, strategies and ideas to sales professinals and entrepreneurs. Each issue helps salespeople learn how to put together presentations, develop openings that keep customers interested, use testimonials correctly and more. *$10.00*
Founded: 1993
Circulation: 1000

16300 Airline Financial News
Phillips Business Information
1201 Seven Locks Road
Suite 300
Potomac, MD 20854-2931
301-541-1400
FAX: 301-309-3847
slott@phillips.com
Grier Graham, Editor
Newsletter that provides the most timely financial reports and market analysis for the entire airline industry. *$695.00*
Weekly

16301 All Around the Town
Probe Research
3 Wing Drive
Suite 240
Cedar Knolls, NJ 07927-1000
973-285-1500
FAX: 973-285-1519
probe@proberesearch.com
www.proberesearch.com
Ethernet has become quite popular for LAN connectivity, but with the advent of higher - speed versions, it is also being used to interconnect metropolitan area networks and wide area networks. In this report, we will review the Gigabit Ethernet, and market drivers and take an in - depth look at what the former Bell operating companies (FRBOCs), relatively established CLECs and interexchange carriers are doing in the metro optical networking space.

16302 An Ethernet Protocol Odyssey
Probe Research
3 Wing Drive
Suite 240
Cedar Knolls, NJ 07927-1000
973-285-1500
FAX: 973-285-1519
probe@proberesearch.com
www.proberesearch.com
This bulletin describes the last mile access bottleneck, incumbent service providers' dilemma, how new entrant Ethernet service providers are offering lower cost services in the MAN using Ethernet protocol based optical networking services, evolution of the Ethernet protocol, applications that will be doplyed using Ethernet Services Market drivers, assessment of how service providers are competing in this new environment.

16303 Analytical Look at the Content Delivery Network Market
Probe Research
3 Wing Drive
Suite 240
Cedar Knolls, NJ 07927-1000
973-285-1500
FAX: 973-285-1519
probe@proberesearch.com
www.proberesearch.com
Examines CDN technologies, business models, major players and market trends. Forecast market revenues for each geographic region To 2006.

16304 Antin Marketing Letter
Alan Antin/Antin Marketing Group
19888 SW Monte Vista Dr
Suite 205
Beaverton, OR 97007
913-485-4535
FAX: 913-663-5552
AMG@commonsensemarketing.com
http://www.commonsensemarketing.com
Brad Antin, Editor
Alan Antin, Publisher
H. Brad Antin, President
How-to info on marketing for professionals and entrepreneurs (service businessess, retailers, wholesalers, professional practice). *$197.00*
Monthly

16305 Application Servers and Media Servers
Probe Research
3 Wing Drive
Suite 240
Cedar Knolls, NJ 07927-1000
973-285-1500
FAX: 973-285-1519
probe@proberesearch.com
www.proberesearch.com
This bulletin describes the market for both applications and media servers; examines key issues and provides a profile of selected players in various product categories.

16306 Art of Self Promotion
Ilise Benun/Creative Marketing and Management
PO Box 23
Hoboken, NJ 07030
201-653-0783
FAX: 201-222-2494 800-737-0783
ilise@marketing-mentor.com
http://www.artofselfpromotion.com
Lisa Cyr, Author
Ilise Benun, Marketing Manager
Nuts'n bolts for manageable marketing for small business owners and self employed professionals. *$100.80*
8 pages Quarterly Founded: 1995

16307 Association of Incentive Marketing News
Association of Incentive Marketing
1801 N Mill Street
Suite R
Naperville, IL 60563-3411
603-369-7780
FAX: 603-369-3773
ima@incentivemarketing.org
http://www.incentivemarketing.org
George Meredith, Editor
Cindy Mielke, President
Paul Spitzberg, Executive VP
Paul Cernohous, Director
Karen Renk, Executive Director
Articles cover promotion industry news and Association information and events.
Quarterly
Circulation: 300

16308 Auctioneer
National Auctioneers Association
8880 Ballentine
Overland Park, KS 66214
913-541-8084
FAX: 913-894-5281
wendy@auctioneers.org
http://auctions.auctioneers.org
Robert Shively, Chief Executive Officer
Wendy Dellinger, Advertising Manager
Steve Baska, Publications Editor
Ryan Putnam, Assistant Editor
Keeps members of the National Auctioneers Association informed of trends and legal issues related to auctioneering. Chronicles activities of the Association and its membership.
Monthly Founded: 1948
Circulation: 7000

16309 Automated and Self-Provisioning Servers
Probe Research
3 Wing Drive
Suite 240
Cedar Knolls, NJ 07927-1000
973-285-1500
FAX: 973-285-1519
probe@proberesearch.com
www.proberesearch.com
A look at service provider implementation of automated and self - provisioning software systems. An explanation of the causes of delay and QoS degradation in IP networks.

16310 BDA
BDA News
900 W Sunset Boulevard
Suite 900
Los Angeles, CA 90069
310-712-0040
FAX: 310-712-0039 http://www.bda.tv
Jill Masters, VP Member Services
Jim Chabin, President
Newsletter, awards annual, magazine and directory published by BDA for designers in the motion graphics industry. *$5.00*
Monthly
Circulation: 2000 1800 names
Printed in 4 colors on glossy stock

16311 Bandwidth Management: Driving Profitablity to the Botton Line
Probe Research
3 Wing Drive
Suite 240
Cedar Knolls, NJ 07927-1000
973-285-1500
FAX: 973-285-1519
probe@proberesearch.com
www.proberesearch.com
Provides an analysis of the type of issues that require Bandwidth Management solutions. Makes a comparison of the types of technical solutions implemented in different parts of the network and the major benefits of each solution. Also analyzes the trends seen in IP traffic and inter - relationship with bandwidth management.

16312 Bandwidth Minutes and IP Transport Markets Will Capacity Traders Succeed?
Probe Research
3 Wing Drive
Suite 240
Cedar Knolls, NJ 07927-1000
973-285-1500
FAX: 973-285-1519
probe@proberesearch.com
www.proberesearch.com
We look into capacity exchanges and determine how they add value, whter participants will find exchanges useful, what are the presequisites for a robust capacity market, what are the risk to telcos if they use exchanges, and what do the exchanges need to do in order to increase trading volume.

16313 Bandwidth Pricing Trends
Probe Research
3 Wing Drive
Suite 240
Cedar Knolls, NJ 07927-1000
973-285-1500
FAX: 973-285-1519
probe@proberesearch.com
www.proberesearch.com

Provides an analysis of the trends in capacity pricing and the expected effects on demand. It provides a view of the drivers that determine what the bandwidth cost will be on a particular route. Also looks at how these determinants have contributes to the level of price erosion each of the routes analyzed.

16314 Brandwidth Supply and Demand Analysis WIT IP Traffic Demand Update
Probe Research
3 Wing Drive
Suite 240
Cedar Knolls, NJ 07927-1000
973-285-1500
FAX: 973-285-1519
probe@proberesearch.com
www.proberesearch.com
Provides an analysis of the bandwidth supply and demand on number of interregional routes. Describes methodology of building up the bandwidth supply and demand picture on these routes. Analyzes what the supply and demand balance is on these routes. Concludes what the business ramifications are for ISPs and backbone providers, banks and vendors.

16315 Broadband Wireless
Probe Research
3 Wing Drive
Suite 240
Cedar Knolls, NJ 07927-1000
973-285-1500
FAX: 973-285-1519
probe@proberesearch.com
www.proberesearch.com
In this bulletin, we take a look into is going on with terrestrial fixed wireless last mile solutions in the MMDS, LMDS spectrums. LMDS is emerging as the next platform for CLECs. However, these CLECs will be entering the market at the end of a long line of competitors in many cities.

16316 Buisness IP Services in Brazil
Probe Research
3 Wing Drive
Suite 240
Cedar Knolls, NJ 07927-1000
973-285-1500
FAX: 973-285-1519
probe@proberesearch.com
www.proberesearch.com
Provides an overview of the business IP services market in Brazil; one of the most active IP markets in South America. Breakdown of Brazil companies. IT investment in B2B and networking applications. We discuss cable and ADSL broadband services and the e-government project. Profile of over 15 service providers.

16317 Bulletproof Marketing for Small Businesses
Kay Borden/Franklin-Sarrett Publishers
3761 Vinyard Trce NE
Marietta, GA 30062-5227
770-578-9410
FAX: 770-977-5495
Kay Borden, Editor
Publicity for small businesses, particularly producing news releases that get printed. *$15.00*
SemiAnnual Founded: 1994

16318 Business Venturing
Association for Entrepreneurial Growth
PO Box 875
Merrimack, NH 03054
603-429-1631
FAX: 603-424-5641
publisher@gouldreport.com
htpp://www.gouldreport.com
Betty Spence, Editor
Kathleen B Chadwick, Assistant Editor
Neil C. Gould, President/Founder
Paul F. Johnson, Managing Editor
Monique E. Fisher, Creative Director
Encourages entrepreneurial growth through acquiring or starting a business venture.
8 pages Quarterly Founded: 1985

16319 Business-2-Business Marketer
Business Marketing Association
400 N Michigan Avenue
15th floor
Chicago, IL 60611
312-822-0005
FAX: 312-822-0054 800-664-4262
bma@marketing.org
http://www.marketing.org
Rick Kean, Editor
William Marsteller, Marketing Director
Earl Barnes, Manager
Editorial covers all apsects of integrated marketing disciplines, including: sales management, trade show marketing, datbase and direct mail marketing, presentations, telemarketing, public relations, advertising and electronic marketing.
$150.00
16 pages Founded: 1922
Circulation: 4300
Printed in 4 colors on glossy stock : PDF

16320 Cable & Wireless
Probe Research
3 Wing Drive
Suite 240
Cedar Knolls, NJ 07927-1000
973-285-1500
FAX: 973-285-1519
probe@proberesearch.com
www.proberesearch.com
A look at cable & wireless IP infrastructure, how the company is operating it, and how it is managing services on its network.

16321 Cable Headed Equipment Markets Upstarts
Probe Research
3 Wing Drive
Suite 240
Cedar Knolls, NJ 07927-1000
973-285-1500
FAX: 973-285-1519
probe@proberesearch.com
www.proberesearch.com
This bulletin analyses the CMTS market and the role the equipment plays in the plans of the major cable operators to move towards the goal of full service operators. A market forecast is included and the major players profiled.

16322 Cambridge Reports Trends and Forecasts
Cambridge Reports
955 Massachusetts Avenue
Suite 80
Cambridge, MA 02139-3178
617-628-6100
FAX: 617-661-3575
Gene Pokorny, Publisher
Key changes in consumer and public opinions.

16323 Capital Spending Trends
Probe Research
3 Wing Drive
Suite 240
Cedar Knolls, NJ 07927-1000
973-285-1500
FAX: 973-285-1519
probe@proberesearch.com
www.proberesearch.com
Decline in telco capital spending is the cause of much of the pain felt in the industry. While many vendors are hoping for recovery during 2002, we fin that, with some bright spots, much of this optimism is misplaced. Vendors should start to prepare now for fuull - scale recovery in 2003, not 2002.

16324 Carrier Hotels: Telecom's Innkeepers
Probe Research
3 Wing Drive
Suite 240
Cedar Knolls, NJ 07927-1000
973-285-1500
FAX: 973-285-1519
probe@proberesearch.com
www.proberesearch.com
In this bulletin, we update the July 2000 Emerging Operators bulletin, which looked at the carrier hotel and collocation market. This market has changed in the past six month as providers have move from the build - out to the services phases and from promarily a real - estate business to more managerd service.

16325 Carrier Profiles: The Mature Carriers
Probe Research
3 Wing Drive
Suite 240
Cedar Knolls, NJ 07927-1000
973-285-1500
FAX: 973-285-1519
probe@proberesearch.com
www.proberesearch.com
In this bulletin, we focus on two areas. The first is the definition section in which we introduce the categories, explain the reasons behind the distinctions and give examples. We will also look at other categories used to classify carriers such as CLEC, ICP and whether or not these are meaningful. The second part of the bulletin profiles several carriers that have changed over time.

16326 Collegiate Trends
Strategic Marketing
550 N Maple Avenue
Ridgewood, NJ 07450-1632
201-612-8100
FAX: 201-612-1444
weil@studentmonitor.com
http://www.studentmonitor.com
Eric Weil, Editor/Publisher
Marketing and media trends for marketers targeting college students. *$95.00*
Quarterly Founded: 1987

16327 Colloquy
Frequency Marketing
1000 Summit Drive
Suite 200
Milford, OH 45150
513-248-2882
FAX: 513-248-9084
info@colloquy.com
http://www.colloquy.com

Michael T Capizzi, Executive Editor
Jill Z. McBride, Public Relations

Frequency Marketing, is the publisher of the COLLOQUY newsletter and COLLOQUY.com Web site, which are dedicated tot he discrimination of information about analysis of frequency marketing strategies and programs worldwide. COLLOQUY also provides educational and research services on a global basis to the loyalty marketing industry, and offers substantial news, research libraries and program archives to qualified subscribers at COLLOQUY.com.
Quarterly Founded: 1990
Circulation: 16,000+

16328 Comment on Intel Upstarts
Probe Research
3 Wing Drive
Suite 240
Cedar Knolls, NJ 07927-1000
973-285-1500
FAX: 973-285-1519
probe@proberesearch.com
www.proberesearch.com
This bulletin contains a commentary on Intel and its need to expand away from its traditional processor and related chip business. The main discussion examines the web server market and in particular the trends towards thin server appliance and reviews some of the major manufacturers. The recent troubles of Lucent are also reviewed and analyzed.

16329 Company Profile: TyCom
Probe Research
3 Wing Drive
Suite 240
Cedar Knolls, NJ 07927-1000
973-285-1500
FAX: 973-285-1519
probe@proberesearch.com
www.proberesearch.com
This bulletin looks at the development of the submarine cable market over the past three to four years, including how the market structure has changed. It then focuses on a numbner of aspects of the market including bandwidth supply and demand and trends in bandwidth pricing and how these are likely to develop over the next few years.

16330 Company Profile: UUNET Upstarts
Probe Research
3 Wing Drive
Suite 240
Cedar Knolls, NJ 07927-1000
973-285-1500
FAX: 973-285-1519
probe@proberesearch.com
www.proberesearch.com
Examines the UUNET network architecture, suppliers and products. Analyses how one of the largest and longest established providers of bandwith and service has performed over the past two years. How Worldcom's newly professed refocus on data services will impact UUNET's plans and development.

16331 Competitive Advantage
Competitive Advantage
PO Box 10828
Portland, OR 97296-0828
503-274-2953
FAX: 503-274-4349

Jim Moran, Publisher
Tonya Shrives, Promotional Director

Provides sales, marketing and management tools to make careers and companies more prosperous.

Circulation: 10,000

16332 Conference Board Management Briefing - Marketing
Conference Board
845 3rd Avenue
New York, NY 10022-6679
212-590-0900
FAX: 212-836-9740
http://www.conference-board.com

Frank Caropreso, Publisher
Richard Cavanagh, Chief Executive Officer

Trends and practices in marketing.
Monthly

16333 Consumer/SOHO IP Service
Probe Research
3 Wing Drive
Suite 240
Cedar Knolls, NJ 07927-1000
973-285-1500
FAX: 973-285-1519
probe@proberesearch.com
www.proberesearch.com
This is a companion piece to US ISPM, Vol.3, No. 9, 2001 that compares advertising and e-commerce business models presented in Vol.3, No.9. This report also briefly looks at leading online retailers' and traditional retailers' online business actions.

16334 Consumer/SOHO IP Service Part 1

Probe Research
3 Wing Drive
Suite 240
Cedar Knolls, NJ 07927-1000
973-285-1500
FAX: 973-285-1519
probe@proberesearch.com
www.proberesearch.com
Part 1 of two - part analysis of consumer/SOHO Internet service provider revenue; we identified the business models and revenue streams of the leading US consumer/SOHO ISPs, including revenues from access fees and advertising/e-commerce.

16335 Creative Marketing Newsletter
Association of Retail Marketing Services
10 Drs James Parker Boulevard
Suite 103
Red Bank, NJ 07701-1500
732-842-5070
FAX: 732-219-1938
info@goarms.com www.goarms.com

Gerri Hopkins, Executive Director
Lisa McCauley, Administrative Director

Retail promotion marketing newsletter for supermarkets, convenience stores, drug chains and suppliers of retail promotions.

Quarterly
Printed in 3 colors on matte stock

16336 Creative Selling
Bentley-Hall
120 Walton Street
Suite 201
Syracuse, NY 13202-1211
315-422-4488
FAX: 800-724-3881

Bob Popyk, Publisher
Kristen Simpson, Editor

Contains training material for sales managers and sales training managers. *$7.00*

Circulation: 6,500

16337 Current Global Carrier Market Environment, Global Carrier
Probe Research
3 Wing Drive
Suite 240
Cedar Knolls, NJ 07927-1000
973-285-1500
FAX: 973-285-1519
probe@proberesearch.com
www.proberesearch.com
Addresses a sweeping review of current strategic, business, economic, financial, network technology, network operations and service portfolio topics now at work in global and international carriage. Also includes a discussion of the potential risk assessment value of existing and future bandwidth trading and arbitrage exchanges.

16338 Current Thinking on Network Evolution and It's Laws
Probe Research
3 Wing Drive
Suite 240
Cedar Knolls, NJ 07927-1000
973-285-1500
FAX: 973-285-1519
probe@proberesearch.com
www.proberesearch.com
This issue focuses on three laws of network evolution used by new entrants and by vendors. These three laws seem to be justified when the stock market rewarded new entrants with enormous valuations simply based on technology and expensive business plans. Now that the stock market no longer rewards such ventures, an analysis of these three laws is warranted and what impact thay have had on the carrier business.

16339 Customers First
Dartnell Corporation
4660 N Ravenswood Avenue
Chicago, IL 60640-4510
773-907-9500
FAX: 773-561-3801

Clark Fetridge, Publisher
Jim Nawrocki, Editor

A practical periodical that provides employees with an organized plan of action for building and improving customer relations. *$ 62.00*

16340 Dartnell Sales and Marketing Executive Report
Dartnell Corporation
4660 N Ravenswood Avenue
Chicago, IL 60640-4510
773-907-9500
FAX: 773-907-0645 800-341-7874

Craig Scherer, Senior Partner *$168.00*
Monthly Founded: 1917

16341 Data Service: ISDN, Private Lines, Frame Relay and ATM
Probe Research
3 Wing Drive
Suite 240
Cedar Knolls, NJ 07927-1000
973-285-1500
FAX: 973-285-1519
probe@proberesearch.com
www.proberesearch.com
We survey and highlight four major data transport technologies detailing the technology's strengths, weakness, specific applications, and basic carrier strategies.

16342 Defining the M-Commerce Value Chain
Probe Research
3 Wing Drive
Suite 240
Cedar Knolls, NJ 07927-1000
973-285-1500
FAX: 973-285-1519
probe@proberesearch.com
www.proberesearch.com
Defines and unifies all participants in a mobile commerce transaction using the sentence Selecting, ordering and paying for items using a mobile device in a secure fashion. Examines the m-commerce business models selected carriers, ASPs and other vendors.

16343 Deflation and Its Implications: R&D Fundin g Slowdown, Networking Shocks
Probe Research
3 Wing Drive
Suite 240
Cedar Knolls, NJ 07927-1000
973-285-1500
FAX: 973-285-1519
probe@proberesearch.com
www.proberesearch.com
This issue covers the long-range impacts of shocks on the telecom systems of networks and the demographic changes facing the US. The US population is getting older as the baby boomers head towards retirement during this decade, forcing changes in national spedning on health care and retirement. This has big implications for the networking and IT industries as the over-55 polulation by 2010 will be almost as large as the under-20 population.

16344 Delaney Report
PRIMEDIA Intertec-Marketing & Professional Service
149 5th Avenue
#725
New York, NY 10010-6801
212-979-7881
FAX: 212-979-0691 tdrinfo@aol.com
Thomas Delaney, Editor
Provides information on personnel changes, trade literature and indsutry events for advertising, media, media, and public relations executives. Reports on global news and developments. *$74.00*

16345 Demand in Plain Sight
Probe Research
3 Wing Drive
Suite 240
Cedar Knolls, NJ 07927-1000
973-285-1500
FAX: 973-285-1519
probe@proberesearch.com
www.proberesearch.com
This is the introductory issue of NPNE and it contains the editorial point of view. Three fundamental drivers effect network evolution: technology, demand and competition and the ILECs in the US have been able to crush the competition and, therefore, are in a position to limit the impact of the technology drivers on their networks.

16346 Digital Subscriber Line Access Multiplexer Upstarts
Probe Research
3 Wing Drive
Suite 240
Cedar Knolls, NJ 07927-1000
973-285-1500
FAX: 973-285-1519
probe@proberesearch.com
www.proberesearch.com
This bulletin examines the major DSALM vendors and forecast the market for DSLAM ports and equipment revenue until 2006.

16347 Directory-Enabled Networking and Policy Servers
Probe Research
3 Wing Drive
Suite 240
Cedar Knolls, NJ 07927-1000
973-285-1500
FAX: 973-285-1519
probe@proberesearch.com
www.proberesearch.com
Examines directory - enabled networking and policy - based netwroking and how the two technologies will work together to manage networks and offer differentiated service.

16348 Does Silicon Have Any More Tricks?
Probe Research
3 Wing Drive
Suite 240
Cedar Knolls, NJ 07927-1000
973-285-1500
FAX: 973-285-1519
probe@proberesearch.com
www.proberesearch.com
This double issue contains a detailed analysis of the future of Moore's law and the prospects for its continued success. Critical issues are discussed, including the increasingly important problem of power consumption in chips. The discussion includes brief reviews of DNA and quantum computing.

16349 Don't Call Them Overbuilders: Competitors Serving the Residential Market
Probe Research
3 Wing Drive
Suite 240
Cedar Knolls, NJ 07927-1000
973-285-1500
FAX: 973-285-1519
probe@proberesearch.com
www.proberesearch.com
In this bulletin we discuss carriers whose business plans include the residential market.

16350 Downtown Promotion Reporter
Alexander Communications Group
28 W 25th Street
8th Floor
New York, NY 10010
212-228-0246
FAX: 212-228-0376 800-232-4317
info@downtowndevelopment.com
http://www.downtowndevelopment.com
Margaret DeWitt, Publisher
Nadine Harris, Marketing Manager
Laurence Alexander, Owner
Tested ideas for promotion, public relations, marketing, increasing business, participation, downtown image building, sales, and events. *$189.00*
Monthly Founded: 1954

16351 Drop Shippng News
Consolidated Marketing Services
PO Box 7838
New York, NY 10150
212-688-8797
FAX: 212-688-8797
nscheel@drop-shipping-news.com
http://www.drop-shipping-news.com
Nicholas T Scheel, Editor/Publisher
Covers all facets of Drop Shipping; source directory for 300,000 consumer products. Book 'Drop Shipping' marketing methods. *$25.00*
Monthly Founded: 1977

16352 Dynamic Selling
Economics Press
12 Daniel Road
Fairfield, NJ 07004-2565
973-227-1224
FAX: 973-227-9742
Covers sales issues and ways to improve sales.

16353 Edge Switching and Routing Upstarts
Probe Research
3 Wing Drive
Suite 240
Cedar Knolls, NJ 07927-1000
973-285-1500
FAX: 973-285-1519
probe@proberesearch.com
www.proberesearch.com
This bulletin comprises Probe's view of the edge routing and switching markets for service provider networks. It profiles the major players, reviews their market shares of 2000 abd the first six month of 2001. A global forecast for these markets is provided for the 2000 - 2006 time period, with the key issues highlighted.

16354 Effective Telephone Techniques
Dartnell Corporation
4660 N Ravenswood Avenue
Chicago, IL 60640-4510
773-907-9500
FAX: 773-561-3801
Clark Fetridge, Publisher
Kim Anderson, Editor
Training bulletin helps your team build profitable customer relations with every call. *$62.00*

16355 Emerging Intelligent Optical Platforms Switching Markets
Probe Research
3 Wing Drive
Suite 240
Cedar Knolls, NJ 07927-1000
973-285-1500
FAX: 973-285-1519
probe@proberesearch.com
www.proberesearch.com
Emerging Intelligent Optical Platforms go beyond high - speed transport, by typically incorporating the intelligence and functionality of additional network elements into one unit, such as DWDM, switching routing, and/or optical switch/cross - connect.

16356 Enhanced
Probe Research
3 Wing Drive
Suite 240
Cedar Knolls, NJ 07927-1000
973-285-1500
FAX: 973-285-1519
probe@proberesearch.com
www.proberesearch.com
This bulletin analyzed and forecast consumer/SOHO markets for enhanced communications services. The bulletin discusses market drivers, barriers and trends in the provisioning and update of VoP - enabled services such as messaging, call management, and other enhanced services.

16357 FRBOC Entry into Long Distance - III
Probe Research
3 Wing Drive
Suite 240
Cedar Knolls, NJ 07927-1000
973-285-1500
FAX: 973-285-1519
probe@proberesearch.com
www.proberesearch.com
In this bulletin, we update where each of the FRBOCs, including Qwest Communications stands in terms of testing, entry and marketing long distance and how the market entry fits into the rest of the carriers' strategies. Each of the FRBOCs is then profiled.

16358 FRBOC and CLEC Relations - A Regulatory Perspective
Probe Research
3 Wing Drive
Suite 240
Cedar Knolls, NJ 07927-1000
973-285-1500
FAX: 973-285-1519
probe@proberesearch.com
www.proberesearch.com
We take a look at some of the issues involved in interconnecting networks and network elements.

16359 Fiberoptics Market Intelligence
KMI Corporation
98 Spit Brook Road
Nashua, NH 03062-5737
603-891-9173
FAX: 603-891-9172
info@kmiresearch.com
http://www.kmiresearch.com
Richard Mack, VP/General Manager
David Janoff, President
Kurt A Ruderman, Analyst/Editor
Markets, technologies, strategic planning, issues, standards and competition in the fiber optics industry. *$595.00*
Fortnightly Founded: 1974

16360 Fixed Wireless Networks
Probe Research
3 Wing Drive
Suite 240
Cedar Knolls, NJ 07927-1000
973-285-1500
FAX: 973-285-1519
probe@proberesearch.com
www.proberesearch.com
In this bulletin, we take a look into what is going on with terrestrial fixed wireless las minute solutions in the MMDS, LMDS spectrums. Competition amongst fixed wireless carriers seem to be split by the two regulatory environments 3/4 licensed and unlicensed spectrum.

16361 Focusing on Fundamentals
Probe Research
3 Wing Drive
Suite 240
Cedar Knolls, NJ 07927-1000
973-285-1500
FAX: 973-285-1519
probe@proberesearch.com
www.proberesearch.com
This double issue contains a detailed analysis of the future of Moore's law and the prospects for its continued success. Critical issues are discussed, including the increasingly important problem of power consumption in chips. The discussion includes brief reviews of DNA and quantum computing.

16362 Fort Worth Business Press
3509 Hulen
Suite 201
Fort Worth, TX 76107
817-336-8300
FAX: 817-332-3038
bizpress@bizpress.net
http://www.fwbusinesspress.com
Deborah Connor, President
Mary Henslee, Marketing/Advertising Manager
Richard Connor, President/Publisher/Edito
Shevoyd Hamilton, Circulation Manager
Fort Worth Business Press is to accurately inform and assist customers and community by providing the highest-quality local business news and loyal customer service in a professional and creative manner. *$95.00*
Weekly Founded: 1988
Circulation: 10000

16363 Free ISP in Europe
Probe Research
3 Wing Drive
Suite 240
Cedar Knolls, NJ 07927-1000
973-285-1500
FAX: 973-285-1519
probe@proberesearch.com
www.proberesearch.com
This bulletin looks at the Free ISP market in Europe and is opportunity for survival. Free ISPs in Europe have depended on metered access fees for survival but with the spread of unmetered access the free ISPmarket will be marginalized as users turn to fixed fee access service.

16364 Frohlinger's Marketing Report
Marketing Strategist Communications
7 Coppel Drive
Tenafly, NJ 07670-2903
201-569-6088
FAX: 201-568-8538
Joseph Frohlinger, Editor/Publisher
Global marketing, advertising and media NL with emphasis on strategic and trend articles. *$200.00*
Bi-Monthly Founded: 1988

16365 Gateway Update: Part 1
Probe Research
3 Wing Drive
Suite 240
Cedar Knolls, NJ 07927-1000
973-285-1500
FAX: 973-285-1519
probe@proberesearch.com
www.proberesearch.com
This paper is the first of three part services covering the market for carrier - class Voice over Parket (VoP) gateways. For purposes of analysis, the market has been divided between gateways that provide functions equivalent toi tricking and those that substitute for traditional access methods. Part 1 provides a description of the trink gateway side including market forecast.

16366 Gateway Update: Part 2
Probe Research
3 Wing Drive
Suite 240
Cedar Knolls, NJ 07927-1000
973-285-1500
FAX: 973-285-1519
probe@proberesearch.com
www.proberesearch.com
This bulletin describes the various access gateway architecture approches, explores various issues associated with market acceptance and segments market based on network position and customer target.

16367 Global Consumer/SOHO Access Model
Probe Research
3 Wing Drive
Suite 240
Cedar Knolls, NJ 07927-1000
973-285-1500
FAX: 973-285-1519
probe@proberesearch.com
www.proberesearch.com
This bulletin forecast consumer/SOHO connections to the Internet by country, region and the world. Connections are counted and forecast and graphed by type of connection including analog, modem, ISDN, cable modem, xDSL and mobile wireless.

16368 Global Demographics and The Future of Networking
Probe Research
3 Wing Drive
Suite 240
Cedar Knolls, NJ 07927-1000
973-285-1500
FAX: 973-285-1519
probe@proberesearch.com
www.proberesearch.com
The population of numerous major countries in Europe, Asia and Latin America are all heading into a profound demographic shift in the coming decades. Aging populations force a re-allocation of resources to-

ward the elderly. Some couuntries like Japan, will become absolutely smaller and this will mean a diminishing of demand within the home market. All of this puts some limites to growwth on networks.

16369 Global IP Networks Update
Probe Research
3 Wing Drive
Suite 240
Cedar Knolls, NJ 07927-1000
973-285-1500
FAX: 973-285-1519
probe@proberesearch.com
www.proberesearch.com
This bulletin compares and contrasts global IP networks of service providers in terms of their facilities, technologies, products, services, strategies and financials. The issue includes profiles of five carriers. This is a year 2001 follow-up to a two-part bulletin series on global IP networks and service providers which was published last year.

16370 Global Optical Switch Market Upstarts
Probe Research
3 Wing Drive
Suite 240
Cedar Knolls, NJ 07927-1000
973-285-1500
FAX: 973-285-1519
probe@proberesearch.com
www.proberesearch.com
Discussion and analysis of optical switches, benefits of deployment, all - optical switch fabric developments, O - E - O vs O - O - O, core and edge users. Market sizing and forecast from 2001 - 2006. Vendor revenue market shares for first nine months of 2001.

16371 Global SONET, SDH and WDM Markets Switching Markets
Probe Research
3 Wing Drive
Suite 240
Cedar Knolls, NJ 07927-1000
973-285-1500
FAX: 973-285-1519
probe@proberesearch.com
www.proberesearch.com
Market sizing and forecast of the SONET, SDH and WDM markets. Separate break - outs and forecast for each segment. Also by region, North America vs Rest of the World.

16372 Global Service Provider Core Routing and Switching Markets
Probe Research
3 Wing Drive
Suite 240
Cedar Knolls, NJ 07927-1000
973-285-1500
FAX: 973-285-1519
probe@proberesearch.com
www.proberesearch.com
Market sizing and forcast of the core ATM/multiservice switching and core IP router markets from 1999 - 2006. Separate breakouts and forecast for each segment. Global forecast and by regions in North America, Europe, Asia/Pacific Rim, and Rest of the World. Discussion on market and technology trends. Company profiles of Lucent, Nortel, Alcatel, Cisco, Marconi, Juniper & Avici.

16373 Great Debate
Probe Research
3 Wing Drive
Suite 240
Cedar Knolls, NJ 07927-1000
973-285-1500
FAX: 973-285-1519
probe@proberesearch.com
www.proberesearch.com
In this bulletin we compare HPC - and IP - based telephony both in technical and business senses and then look at which operators are doing what.

16374 Growth Strategies
2118 Wilshire Boulevard
#826
Santa Monica, CA 90403-5784
310-718-8822
FAX: 310-828-0427
rogerselbert@aol.com
Dr. Roger Selbert, Production Manager/Editor/Publisher
A newsletter published twice a monthly since 1981 has been presciently reporting on economic, social, political, technological, demographic, lifestyle, consumer, business, management, workforce and marketing trends. *$146.00*
Monthly Founded: 1981
Printed in 2 colors on glossy stock

16375 Guerrilla Marketing International
Cascade Seaview Corporation
PO Box 1336
Mill Valley, CA 94942-1336
415-383-5426
FAX: 415-381-8361
William Shear, Publisher
Marketing insights, trends and tips for small business. *$59.00*
8 pages Bi-Monthly Founded: 1989
Printed in 1 color on glossy stock

16376 Have the FRBOCs Won the Residential Boradband Market?
Probe Research
3 Wing Drive
Suite 240
Cedar Knolls, NJ 07927-1000
973-285-1500
FAX: 973-285-1519
probe@proberesearch.com
www.proberesearch.com
In this bulletin we discuss broadband services for thr residential market and how the FRBOCs are responding to competition or lack thereof in this area.

16377 Health Product Marketing
PRS Group
6320 Fly Road
Suite 102
East Syracuse, NY 13057-9358
315-431-0511
FAX: 315-431-0200
custserv@prsgroup.com
http://www.prsgroup.com
Doris Walsh, Editor
Mary Walsh, President
Ben McTernan, Managing Editor
Patti Davis, Circulation Manager
Patty Redhead, Production Manager
Provides current information, analysis and ideas for strategic planning in the health industry.
Founded: 1979

16378 Healthcare PR & Marketing News
Phillips Business Information
1201 Seven Locks Road
Potomac, MD 20854-2931
301-354-1400
FAX: 301-309-3847 888-707-5814
trotman@phillips.com
http://www.prandmarketing.com
Matthew Schwartz, Editor
Diane Schwartz, Publisher
Amy Urban, Marketing Manager
Issues faced by health care executives in PR firms and hospitals. Regular features include industry surveys, case studies and executive profiles. *$397.00*
Founded: 1944

16379 Home Business Idea Possibility Newsletter
Prosperity & Profits Unlimited
PO Box 416
Denver, CO 80201-0416
303-573-5564
A Doyle, Editor
Possibilities for home businesses. *$7.50*
4 pages Annual Founded: 1996
Circulation: 1,000 Audited
Printed in 1 color on matte stock

16380 How Long Can Traffic Grow?
Probe Research
3 Wing Drive
Suite 240
Cedar Knolls, NJ 07927-1000
973-285-1500
FAX: 973-285-1519
probe@proberesearch.com
www.proberesearch.com
Carrier lack of agreement on standard metrics for traffic measurement allows for any interpretation of data, misleads investors and vendors. Optical networking's future depends on a more rational approach to traffic statistics. An assessment of the three drivers for optical networking are discussed.

16381 INFO Marketing Report
Towers Club Press
9170 NW 11th Avenue
Vancouver, WA 98665
360-574-3084
Jerry Buchanan, Editor
Focuses on marketing of HOW TO information in all its many forms: print, audio, video, public speaking, etc. *$69.95*
Monthly Founded: 1974

16382 IP Backbone
Probe Research
3 Wing Drive
Suite 240
Cedar Knolls, NJ 07927-1000
973-285-1500
FAX: 973-285-1519
probe@proberesearch.com
www.proberesearch.com
This bulletin examines the current development of the market for IP backbone services in China and profiles the four commercially licensed backbone providers.

16383 IP Services Market
Probe Research
3 Wing Drive
Suite 240
Cedar Knolls, NJ 07927-1000
973-285-1500
FAX: 973-285-1519
probe@proberesearch.com
www.proberesearch.com
This bulletin attempts to deconstruct and define the lexicon of IP services, segmenting and applying definitions. Network service sre separated from network applications, and both are separated again from business services and business application.

16384 IP VPN Services in Europe
Probe Research
3 Wing Drive
Suite 240
Cedar Knolls, NJ 07927-1000
973-285-1500
FAX: 973-285-1519
probe@proberesearch.com
www.proberesearch.com
This report analyzes the market for IP VPN services in Western Europe, looking at applications, service providers, market trends, segmentation, penetration, market sized and forecast.

16385 Imaging Market Forum
Technology Marketing Corporation
One Technology Plaza
Norwalk, CT 06854
203-852-6800
FAX: 203-853-2845 800-243-6002
John Vanden Brink, Publisher
Case studies and opinions.

16386 Independent ILECs: The Biggest of the Small
Probe Research
3 Wing Drive
Suite 240
Cedar Knolls, NJ 07927-1000
973-285-1500
FAX: 973-285-1519
probe@proberesearch.com
www.proberesearch.com
This bulletin discusses the environment in which the largest non - Bell local exchange carriers operate including related regulatory issues, then at specific carrier strategies and services, explaining how these carriers differ from the FRBOCs.

16387 Industry Forces: Changing Definitions of Carriers
Probe Research
3 Wing Drive
Suite 240
Cedar Knolls, NJ 07927-1000
973-285-1500
FAX: 973-285-1519
probe@proberesearch.com
www.proberesearch.com
In this bulletin, we update the July 2000 Emerging Operators bulletin, which looked at the carrier hotel and collocation market. This market has changed in the past six month as providers have move from the build - out to the services phases and from promarily a real - estate business to more managerd service.

16388 Infomercial Marketing Report
Steven Dworman and Associates
11533 Thurston Circle
Los Angeles, CA 90049-2426
310-472-6360

Steve Dworman, Editor/Publisher
Insider information on the infomercial industry. *$395.00*
Monthly

16389 Information Advisor
Information Today
143 Old Marlton Pike
Medford, NJ 08055-8750
609-654-6266
FAX: 609-654-4309
custserv@infotoday
www.infotoday.com
Robert Berkman, Editor
Provides comprehensive evlauation of research tools, timely and specific information you will use, new sources valuable to researchers and head to head analysis of the most popular information services. *$165.00*
Monthly

16390 Information Theory: Strategies and Fundame ntals
Probe Research
3 Wing Drive
Suite 240
Cedar Knolls, NJ 07927-1000
973-285-1500
FAX: 973-285-1519
probe@proberesearch.com
www.proberesearch.com
This bulletin covers the relationship between information theory and networking. Theorists have fallen behind in understanding the implications of theory for wireless and Internet networks.

16391 International Cyber Centers
Probe Research
3 Wing Drive
Suite 240
Cedar Knolls, NJ 07927-1000
973-285-1500
FAX: 973-285-1519
probe@proberesearch.com
www.proberesearch.com
Strategic positioning and product portfolios of major domestic and international carriers in collocation, Web hosting, applications hosting, e-commerce, IP-centric data, managed services and other value added offerings. Examines the global square footage race in building or upgrading what are variously known as Internet centers, data centers or cyber centers worldwide. Profiles of several key players are included in the bulletin issue.

16392 International Marketing Service Newsletter
IDG Communications
375 Cochituate Road
#9171
Framingham, MA 01701-4653

Frank Cutitta, Publisher
This newsletter concentrates on the overseas advertising and marketing industry.

16393 International Product Alert
Marketing Intelligence Service
6473D Route 64
Naples, NY 14512-9726
585-374-6326
FAX: 585-374-5217 800-836-5710
mi@productscan.com
http://www.productscan.com
Tom Vierhile, Editor
Reports product introductions from Europe, Asia and throughout the world. *$795.00*
Fortnightly Founded: 1983

16394 Internet Traffic Forecast to 2005
Probe Research
3 Wing Drive
Suite 240
Cedar Knolls, NJ 07927-1000
973-285-1500
FAX: 973-285-1519
probe@proberesearch.com
www.proberesearch.com
Provides analysis of the global demand for Internet bandwidth. The analysis focuses on peak traffic requirements, as the intent is to understand the capacity that service providers must prepare for. Several key assumptions drive the analysis, and probe will be continuosly updating both these assumptions and the forecasts that result.

16395 Introducing New Public Network Economics
Probe Research
3 Wing Drive
Suite 240
Cedar Knolls, NJ 07927-1000
973-285-1500
FAX: 973-285-1519
probe@proberesearch.com
www.proberesearch.com
This is the introductory issue of NPNE and it contains the editorial point of view. Three fundamental drivers effect network evolution: technology, demand and competition and the ILECs in the US have been able to crush the competition and, therefore, are in a position to limit the impact of the technology drivers on their networks.

16396 Introduction to the NGNS Service
Probe Research
3 Wing Drive
Suite 240
Cedar Knolls, NJ 07927-1000
973-285-1500
FAX: 973-285-1519
probe@proberesearch.com
www.proberesearch.com
Defines the IP provisioning software market and discusses major players in each segment. Brief discussion of denial - of - service attacks.

16397 Is SIP The Next Big Thing?
Probe Research
3 Wing Drive
Suite 240
Cedar Knolls, NJ 07927-1000
973-285-1500
FAX: 973-285-1519
probe@proberesearch.com
www.proberesearch.com
Discusses several vendors in the area of network performance management. Also includes a short discussion on SIP.

16398 Is Trend Destiny?
Probe Research
3 Wing Drive
Suite 240
Cedar Knolls, NJ 07927-1000
973-285-1500
FAX: 973-285-1519
probe@proberesearch.com
www.proberesearch.com
Carrier lack of agreement on standard metrics for traffic measurement allows for any interpretation of data, misleads investors and vendors. Optical networking's future depends on a more rational approach to traffic statistics. An assessment of the three drivers for optical networking are discussed.

16399 JonesReport
PO Box 50038
Indianapolis, IN 46250-7830
317-576-9889
FAX: 317-576-0441 800-878-9024
ctrmktg@jonesreport.com
http://www.jonesreport.com
William Willburn, Publisher/President
William Willburn, Editor
Lue Dyar, Circulation Manager
Monthly newsletter for shopping center marketing professionals. Free Resource Guide in September. Salary Survey results in December. Christmas planner issues in April. STEALable marketing ideas in every issue. Sample copies are available. *$145.00*
16 pages Monthly Founded: 1980
Circulation: 1000 Est. Pass-Along Circ: 3400
Mailing list available for rent 6M names $110 per M.
Printed in 2 colors on matte stock

16400 Large and Medium-Sized Enterprise Internet Access Market
Probe Research
3 Wing Drive
Suite 240
Cedar Knolls, NJ 07927-1000
973-285-1500
FAX: 973-285-1519
probe@proberesearch.com
www.proberesearch.com
This bulletin covers the US market for ISP services to large and medium - sized enterprises. Included are market forecasts segmented by access, speed and market share.

16401 Levin's Public Relations Report
Levin Public Relations & Marketing
147 Rockland Avenue
Larchmont, NY 10538
914-993-0900
FAX: 914-834-5919
levinpr@levinpr.com
www.levinpr.com
Don Levin, Publisher
Sylvia Moss, Editor
Strategies, tactics for the CEO, VP Sales and Marketing seeking new marketing/public relations effectiveness. *$29.00*
Quarterly Founded: 1978

16402 Licensing Journal
PO Box 1169
Stamford, CT 06904-1169
203-358-0848
Charles Grimes, Publisher
A publication directed to leaders in the Intellectual Property, Technology and Entertainment Communities. Accepts advertising. *$ 150.00*
23 pages Annual
Circulation: 1,000

16403 Licensing Letter
EPM Communications
160 Mercer Street
3rd Floor
New York, NY 10012-3208
212-941-0099
FAX: 212-941-1622 888-852-9467
info@epmcom.com
http://www.epmcom.com
Ira Mayer, Publisher
Marty Brochstein, Editorial Director/Executive Editor
Loretta Netzer, Circulation Manager
Contains features on licensed properties, market trends and survey analysis. *$467.00*
12 pages Founded: 1977

16404 Long Haul Market
Probe Research
3 Wing Drive
Suite 240
Cedar Knolls, NJ 07927-1000
973-285-1500
FAX: 973-285-1519
probe@proberesearch.com
www.proberesearch.com
In this report, we take a look into the long haul market space and discuss some of the reasons - supply, demand and the resulting prices - that have reversed these service providers fortunes so dramatically over the past year or so. We also discuss long haul product lines, new networking technology and provide a table comparing market participants for convenient reference.

16405 M-Commerce Security
Probe Research
3 Wing Drive
Suite 240
Cedar Knolls, NJ 07927-1000
973-285-1500
FAX: 973-285-1519
probe@proberesearch.com
www.proberesearch.com
In this bulletin, we examine the issue of security in the m-commerce transaction and the technologies that are appering to address it. We also create international m-commerce forecasts by region.

16406 MPLS in Service Provider Networks
Probe Research
3 Wing Drive
Suite 240
Cedar Knolls, NJ 07927-1000
973-285-1500
FAX: 973-285-1519
probe@proberesearch.com
www.proberesearch.com
Overview of current status of Multi - Protocol Label Switching implemantation in service provider networks, issues with progression of MPLS, service level agreement, discussion of implementation in four service level agreements, discussion of implementation in four service provider networks including examples of using MPLS for traffic engineering, and IP - VPNs.

16407 Mainly Marketing
Schoonmaker Associates
Drawer M
Coram, NY 11727
631-246-5466
WK Schoonmaker, Publisher
Marketing high technology products.

16408 Make It Happen
Action Marketing
3747 NE Sandy Boulevard
Portland, OR 97232-1840
503-287-8321
FAX: 503-282-2980
CE Colwell, Publisher
Marketing news for starting a business and marketing products.

16409 Market: Africa/Mid-East
PRS Group
6320 Fly Road
Suite 102
East Syracuse, NY 13057-9358
315-431-0511
FAX: 315-431-0200
prsgroup@prsgroup.com
http://www.prsgroup.com
Doris Walsh, Editor
Patti Davis, Circulation Manager
Mary Walsh, President
Ben McTernan, Managing Editor
Patty Redhead, Production Manager
Demographic and lifestyle information about consumers in Africa and the Middle East. *$397.00*
Monthly Founded: 1979

16410 Market: Asia Pacific
PRS Group
6320 Fly Road
Suite 102
East Syracuse, NY 13057-9358
315-431-0511
FAX: 315-431-0200
prsgroup@prsgroup.com
http://www.prsgroup.com
Doris L Walsh, Editor
Patti Davis, Circulation Manager
Mary Lou Walsh, President
Ben McTernan, Managing Editor
Patty Redhead, Production Manager
Population and lifestyle trend information about consumers in the Asia-Pacific region. *$397.00*
Monthly Founded: 1979
Circulation: 225 Audited
Printed in 2 colors on matte stock

16411 Market: Latin America
PRS Group
6320 Fly Road
Suite 102
East Syracuse, NY 13057-9358
315- 43- 051
FAX: 315-431-0200
prsgroup@prsgroup.com
http://www.prsgroup.com
Doris Walsh, Editor
Patti Davis, Circulation Manager
Mary Walsh, President
Ben McTernan, Managing Editor
Patty Redhead, Production Manager
Population and lifestyle trend information about consumers in the Latin America region.
Monthly Founded: 1979

16412 Marketing Communications Report
14629 SW 104 Street
#272
Miami, FL 33186-4929
305-595-0063
FAX: 305-595-0380
marketcomm@aol.com
Pete Silver, Editor
Highlights prevalent thoughts on successful marketing strategies and reviews new products.
Monthly

16413 Marketing Dynamics
Recognition Technologies Users Association
10 High Street
Suite 630
Boston, MA 02110-1605

FAX: 617-426-8911
Franklin Cooper, Publisher
Focuses on strategic marketing and planning in technology and industrial areas including technology commercialization. Also features articles on government programs and how to participate in them. International market and business development also are featured. *$120.00*
Bi-Monthly
Circulation: 5,000 Audited
Printed in 2 colors on glossy stock

16414 Marketing Insights
WPI Communications
55 Morris Avenue
Suite 312
Springfield, NJ 07081-1496
973-678-8700
FAX: 800-677-9742 800-323-4995
info@wpicomm.com
http://www.wpicomm.com/
Steven Klinghoffer, Publisher
Marilyn Lang, Circulation Manager
Founded: 1952

16415 Marketing Library Services
Information Today
143 Old Marlton Pike
Medford, NJ 08055-8750
609-654-6266
FAX: 609-654-4309
custserv@infotoday
www.infotoday.com
Thomas Hogan, Publisher/President
Lauree Padgett, Editorial Services Manager
Inge Coffey, Circulation Manager
Provides information professional in all types of libraries with specfic ideas for marketing their services. *$79.95*
Bi Monthly

16416 Marketing News
American Marketing Association
311 South Wacker Drive
Suite 5800
Chicago, IL 60606
312-542-9000
FAX: 312-542-9001 800-262-1150
info@ama.org http://www.ama.org
Jack Hollfeldar, Publisher
Lisa Keefe, Editor
Dennis Dunlap, Chief Executive Officer
Current articles on marketing and association activities. Newsletter free with membership. *$100.00*
33 pages
Circulation: 22000+
Printed in 4 colors on glossy stock

16417 Marketing Pulse
Unlimited Positive Communications
11 N Chestnut Street
New Paltz, NY 12561-1706
845-565-0615
FAX: 845-255-2231
Bill Harvey, Editor/Publisher
Focus on all aspects of new electronic media, advertising, entertainment, and marketing. *$300.00*
Monthly Founded: 1979

16418 Marketing Report
Progressive Business Publications
376 Technology Drive
Malvern, PA 19355-1315
610-695-8600
FAX: 610-651-2981 800-220-5000
customer_service@pbp.com
http://www.pbp.com
Julie Power, Editor
Christine Wheeler, Marketing Manager
$264.00
8 pages Founded: 1989

16419 Marketing Science Institute Newsletter
Marketing Science Institute
1000 Massachusetts Avenue
Cambridge, MA 02138-5316
617-491-2060
FAX: 617-491-2065
msi@msi.org http://www.msi.org
Susan Keane, Editor
Leana McAlister, CEO
Focuses on people and events of MSI.
Founded: 1968
Circulation: 8000

16420 Marketing Technology
Zhivago Marketing Partners
381 Seaside Drive
Jamestown, RI 2835
401-423-2400
FAX: 401-423-2700
kristin@zhivago.com
http://www.zhivago.com
Kristin Zhivago, Editor
Philip Zhivago, Publisher
Solutions to internal political problems encountered by high-tech marketers, critiques marketing campaigns, and discuss what's working. *$269.00*
Monthly Founded: 1970

16421 Marketscan International
Miller Freeman Publications
2655 Seely Avenue
San Jose, CA 95134
408-943-1234
FAX: 408-943-0513
Paul W Kelash, Editor/Publisher
PC and Networking news in Europe, Asia, and Latin America. *$395.00*
Monthly Founded: 1987

16422 Master Salesmanship
Clement Communications
10 LaCrue Avenue
PO Box 36
Concordville, PA 19331
610-459-4200
FAX: 610-459-4582 888-358-5858
coustmerservice@clement.com
http://www.clement.com
Andrew B Clancy, Managing Editor
George Clement, President
Newsletter for professional salespeople.
$156.00
Founded: 1919

16423 Meditation Software Market
Probe Research
3 Wing Drive
Suite 240
Cedar Knolls, NJ 07927-1000
973-285-1500
FAX: 973-285-1519
probe@proberesearch.com
www.proberesearch.com
Examines the mediation market, the major and niche players, functionality of the solutions, and service provider deployments.

16424 Meeting the Need of the Data Clan
Probe Research
3 Wing Drive
Suite 240
Cedar Knolls, NJ 07927-1000
973-285-1500
FAX: 973-285-1519
probe@proberesearch.com
www.proberesearch.com
In this bulletin we examine the budding metro optical service provider market and organize the players by business model.

16425 Migrating to IP VPN
Probe Research
3 Wing Drive
Suite 240
Cedar Knolls, NJ 07927-1000
973-285-1500
FAX: 973-285-1519
probe@proberesearch.com
www.proberesearch.com
This bulletin looks at the market and technology issues facing the enterprise end user in choosing or maintaining a Frame Relay or other traditional network service. The benefits and barriers of each approach are outlines with an effort to rationalized some of the less clear - cut decision factors.

16426 Minority Markets Alert
EPM Communications
160 Mercer Street
3rd Floor
New York, NY 10012-3212
212-941-0099
FAX: 212-941-1622 888-852-9467
Ira Mayer, Publisher
Ken Clark, Editor
Loretta Netzer, Circulation Manager
Research, trends and lifestyle coverage of minority markets. *$295.00*
Monthly Founded: 1988

16427 Mobility No Longer Just for the Elite
Probe Research
3 Wing Drive
Suite 240
Cedar Knolls, NJ 07927-1000
973-285-1500
FAX: 973-285-1519
probe@proberesearch.com
www.proberesearch.com
This US Competitive Markets bulletin looks at the five major wirelss networks: AT&T Wireless CIngular WIreless, Sprint PCS, Verizon Wireless and VoiceStream Communications. Each has its own approach to the market as well as services and technology they hope will make them the dominant carrier.

16428 Moore's Law in Networks, Once Again
Probe Research
3 Wing Drive
Suite 240
Cedar Knolls, NJ 07927-1000
973-285-1500
FAX: 973-285-1519
probe@proberesearch.com
www.proberesearch.com
This double issue contains a detailed analysis of the future of Moore's law and the prospects for its continued success. Critical issues are discussed, including the increasingly important problem of power consumption in chips. The discussion includes brief reviews of DNA and quantum computing.

16429 MyDMA Newsletter
Direct Marketing Association
1120 Avenue of the Americas
New York, NY 10036-6700
212-768-7277
FAX: 212-302-6714 www.the-dma.org
Provides you with information about DMA events, news, research and other direct marketing information.

16430 New Account Selling
Dartnell Corporation
4660 N Ravenswood Avenue
Chicago, IL 60640-4510
773-907-9500
FAX: 773-561-3801
Clark Fetridge, Publisher
Terry Breen, Editor
Timely and effective techniques for building sales and improving profits. Instructive series ideal for training new sales people and for increasing the productivity of your sales veterans. *$62.00*

16431 New Age Marketing Opportunities Newsletter
New Editions International
PO Box 2578
Sedona, AZ 86339-2578
928-282-9574
FAX: 928-282-9730 800-777-4751
newedit@sedona.net
www.newagemarket.com
Sophia Tarila PhD, Production Manager
Focuses on issues dealing with good marketing buys, resources and pertinent marketing programs dealing in the historic, visionary marketplace. *$24.00*
4 pages Bi-Monthly
Circulation: 450
Mailing list available for rent
Printed in 1 color on matte stock

16432 Next Genaration IAD for SOHO Markets
Probe Research
3 Wing Drive
Suite 240
Cedar Knolls, NJ 07927-1000
973-285-1500
FAX: 973-285-1519
probe@proberesearch.com
www.proberesearch.com
Examines the market for VoDSL - comapatible Integrated Access Devices (IAD) targeted toward SOHO customers. Identifies key issues associated with development, analyzes competitive dynamics and market requirements and reviews selected vendor products.

16433 NextGen Billing Software Market
Probe Research
3 Wing Drive
Suite 240
Cedar Knolls, NJ 07927-1000
973-285-1500
FAX: 973-285-1519
probe@proberesearch.com
www.proberesearch.com
Describes the market for the next generation billing solutions. Looks at architecture and implementation, and the major players. Forecast the market to 2005.

16434 North American Consumer/SOHO Internet Connectivity
Probe Research
3 Wing Drive
Suite 240
Cedar Knolls, NJ 07927-1000
973-285-1500
FAX: 973-285-1519
probe@proberesearch.com
www.proberesearch.com
This bulletin forecast consumer/SOHO connections to the Internet by country, region and the world. Connections are counted and forecast and graphed by type of connection including analog modem, ISDN, cable modem, DSL and mobile wireless.

16435 On-Premise Market
Probe Research
3 Wing Drive
Suite 240
Cedar Knolls, NJ 07927-1000
973-285-1500
FAX: 973-285-1519
probe@proberesearch.com
www.proberesearch.com
In this bulletin, we look at the multi - unit niche markets and examine the challenges and opportunities regarding a revised in - building service model which uses existing wire.

16436 Online Marketing Letter
Cyberware Media
1005 Terminal Way
Suite 110
Reno, NV 89502
808-874-0089
www.cyberware.com
Jonathan Mizel, Editor/Publisher
Reviews the marketing of products and services over commercial online services of the internet. *$195.00*
Quarterly Founded: 1993

16437 Online Marketplace
Jupiter Communications Company
627 Broadway
2nd Floor
New York, NY 10012-2612
212-338-8885
FAX: 212-780-6075
Adam Schoenfeld, Editor
Gene DeRose, Publisher
Interactive transaction. *$545.00*
Monthly

16438 Open Architecture in Edge Infrastructure Upstarts
Probe Research
3 Wing Drive
Suite 240
Cedar Knolls, NJ 07927-1000
973-285-1500
FAX: 973-285-1519
probe@proberesearch.com
www.proberesearch.com
Reviews the open service switch from EmergeCore, wich is intended as a multifunction platform based on open source principles for both hardware and software. We also review some of the key developments in Internet edge infraestructure.

16439 Optical Edge Part 1
Probe Research
3 Wing Drive
Suite 240
Cedar Knolls, NJ 07927-1000
973-285-1500
FAX: 973-285-1519
probe@proberesearch.com
www.proberesearch.com
Discussion of development of Ethernet as enterprise networking technology to Gigabit Ethernal and 10 Gigabit Ethernet, and their applications in metro area and wide area network technology. Technology and market drivers are discussed, standards efforts, and developments in the area of Risilent Packet Ring technology. Elements of metro optical Ethernet network are discussed.

16440 Optical Edge Part 2
Probe Research
3 Wing Drive
Suite 240
Cedar Knolls, NJ 07927-1000
973-285-1500
FAX: 973-285-1519
probe@proberesearch.com
www.proberesearch.com
Discussion of development of passive optical networking technology, both traditional ATM - based, (APONS) and newer Ethernet - based (EPON) platforms and growth of nascent market. Market drivers of passive optical netwroking and advantages of using passive vs avtive technology. FSAN - defined specifications for APONs. Early applications - T1 replacement for business; broadband access for new residential builds and MTUs/MDUs.

16441 Optical Technology Trends and Prospects: A Framework Approach
Probe Research
3 Wing Drive
Suite 240
Cedar Knolls, NJ 07927-1000
973-285-1500
FAX: 973-285-1519
probe@proberesearch.com
www.proberesearch.com
Carrier lack of agreement on standard metrics for traffic measurement allows for any interpretation of data, misleads investors and vendors. Optical networking's future depends on a more rational approach to traffic statistics. An assessment of the three drivers for optical networking are discussed.

16442 Optics Developments
Probe Research
3 Wing Drive
Suite 240
Cedar Knolls, NJ 07927-1000
973-285-1500
FAX: 973-285-1519
probe@proberesearch.com
www.proberesearch.com
Discussion of several technologies and products that are key to optical networking developments. Market and technology drivers include: distance, channel count; data rate per channel; paralell optics; high power; demand for Ethernet/Gigabit Ethernet services; cost of ownership; and integrated modules.

16443 Organized Executive
Briefings Publishing Group
1101 King Street
Suite 110
Alexandria, VA 22314
703-518-2343
FAX: 703-684-2136 800-722-9221
customerservice@briefings.com
http://www.briefings.com
Stephanie Winston, Editor-in-Chief
Lois Willingham, Production Manager
A publication designed to help busy people more effectively master their activities and time by applying advanced organizational strategies developed by Stephanie Winston. *$97.00*
8 pages Monthly Founded: 1981
Circulation: 30000
Mailing list available for rent 6000 names $125 per M.
Printed in 2 colors on matte stock

16444 Overcoming Objections
Dartnell Corporation
4660 N Ravenswood Avenue
Chicago, IL 60640-4510
773-907-9500
FAX: 773-561-3801
Clark Fetridge, Publisher
Christen Heide, Editor
Designed to give sales team practical responses to every objection they're likely to face and imparts proven techniques for turning every type of sales objection into a sales opportunity. *$62.00*

16445 Perspectives
1375 King Avenue
PO 12279
Columbus, OH 43212-2220
614-486-6708
FAX: 614-486-1819 800-448-0398
service@mark-ed.com
http://www.mark-ed.org
J Gleason, President
Information on education and marketing. Provides professional support and materials. Primary clients are schools, colleges and educational institutions. *$25.00*
Founded: 1971
Circulation: 7500 7500 names $80 per M.
Printed in 4 colors on matte stock

16446 Photo Marketing
Photo Marketing Association International
3000 Picture Pl
Jackson, MI 49201-8898
517-788-8100
FAX: 517-788-8371
pma_publications@pmai.com
http://www.photomarketing.com
Gary Pageau, Editor
Terri Cameron, Publisher
Ted Fox, Manager *$30.00*
Monthly Founded: 1980

16447 Population Shifts: A Powerful Force in Economics
Probe Research
3 Wing Drive
Suite 240
Cedar Knolls, NJ 07927-1000
973-285-1500
FAX: 973-285-1519
probe@proberesearch.com
www.proberesearch.com
The population of numerous major countries in Europe, Asia and Latin America are all heading into a profound demographic shift in the coming decades. Aging populations force a re-allocation of resources toward the elderly. Some couuntries like Japan, will become absolutely smaller and this will mean a diminishing of demand within the home market. All of this puts some limites to growwth on networks.

16448 Premium Marketing Club of New York
Association of Retail Marketing Services
10 Drs James Parker Boulevard
Suite 103
Red Bank, NJ 07701-1500
732-842-5070
FAX: 732-219-1938 www.goarms.com
Gerri Hopkins, Executive Director
Lisa McCauley, Administrative Director
Provides education and networking information.
10 per year Founded: 1930
Printed in 1 color

16449 Pricing Advisor
Pricing Advisor
3535 Roswell Road
Suite 59
Marietta, GA 30062
770-509-9933
FAX: 770-509-1963
info@pricingsociety.com
http://www.pricingsociety.com
Eric G Mitchell, Publisher/President
Michelle Darko, Editor
Sobem Nwoko, COO
Pricing strategy and tactics for marketing and corporate executives. *$400.00*
8 pages Monthly

16450 Pricing Models and Sofswitch
Probe Research
3 Wing Drive
Suite 240
Cedar Knolls, NJ 07927-1000
973-285-1500
FAX: 973-285-1519
probe@proberesearch.com
www.proberesearch.com
Examines some of the key competitives in the packet telephony call control space, and also provides insight into the challenges of pricing that face those who now hope to ship switches on a CR - ROM or other purely soft format. Problems with the definition of softswitch.

16451 Product Alert
Marketing Intelligence Service
6473D State Route 64
Naples, NY 14512-9726
585-374-6326
FAX: 585-374-5217 800-836-5710
mi@productscan.com
http://www.productscan.com
Christine Dengler, Marketing Manager
Tom Vierhile, CEO
Diane Beach, Editor
A twice-monthly briefing on new packaged goods introduced in North America. Featuring product pictures and descriptions with indexing provided in two convenient formats. Also available in a twice monthly, international version. *$795.00*

16452 Profiles On AT&T/BT/Concert, WorldCom, Spr int, Exodus/Global Crossing
Probe Research
3 Wing Drive
Suite 240
Cedar Knolls, NJ 07927-1000
973-285-1500
FAX: 973-285-1519
probe@proberesearch.com
www.proberesearch.com
Strategic positioning and product portfolios of major domestic and international carriers in collocation, Web hosting, applications hosting, e-commerce, IP-centric data, managed services and other value added offerings. Examines the global square footage race in building or upgrading what are variously known as Internet centers, data centers or cyber centers worldwide. Profiles of several key players are included in the bulletin issue.

16453 Profiles in Healthcare Marketing
Business Word
11211 E Arapahoe Road
Suite 101
Centennial, CO 80112-3851
303-290-8500
FAX: 303-290-9025 800-328-3211
customer.service@businessword.com
http://www.businessword.com/
Tom Rees, Editor
Donald Johnson, Publisher
Susan J. Alt, President
Richard J. Rhinehart, Circulation Manager
What's working in hospital/medical marketing. *$314.00*
Founded: 1985
Circulation: 500

16454 Profiles of Emerging Operators
Probe Research
3 Wing Drive
Suite 240
Cedar Knolls, NJ 07927-1000
973-285-1500
FAX: 973-285-1519
probe@proberesearch.com
www.proberesearch.com
Discusses overall telecom market, business and network conditions for emerging operators providing voice and data services in Western Europe, including bankruptcies. Segments are devoted to operators retrenching from Europe, building Pan-European networks, and concentrating on Southern Europe plus UK operators expanding into Europe. Numerous tables and profiles are included.

16455 Profiles of Intelligent Service Edge Upstarts
Probe Research
3 Wing Drive
Suite 240
Cedar Knolls, NJ 07927-1000
973-285-1500
FAX: 973-285-1519
probe@proberesearch.com
www.proberesearch.com
The environment for star - ups has never been so problematic. Lower capex and constrained VC funding fas forced many starups to the wall recovery. Profiled in the edge space. Some may be successful, others may not make it, some may be acquired; all are worthy of attention.

16456 Promos & Premiums
New World Media
PO Box 95
Newton Centre, MA 02156
781-483-8967
FAX: 617-367-9151
Jennifer Sawyer English, Editor/Publisher
Barbara Kalunian, Publisher
Informs consumers, collectors, dealers, and marketing executives about the best special offers available nationwide. *$19.95*
Monthly Founded: 1994

16457 Provisioning DSL Networks
Probe Research
3 Wing Drive
Suite 240
Cedar Knolls, NJ 07927-1000
973-285-1500
FAX: 973-285-1519
probe@proberesearch.com
www.proberesearch.com
Looks at the entire process, with technical and intercompany business issues discussed, of provisioning DSL, networks, and the problems that can occur along the way.

16458 Remote Access Server Upstarts
Probe Research
3 Wing Drive
Suite 240
Cedar Knolls, NJ 07927-1000
973-285-1500
FAX: 973-285-1519
probe@proberesearch.com
www.proberesearch.com
Analyzes the market for analog dial remote access servers and remote access concentrators. Typically, these systems allow service providers and enterprises to provision and manage dial - in access to their networks for remote subscribers.

16459 Research Alert
EPM Communications
160 Mercer Street
New York, NY 10012-3208
212-941-0099
FAX: 212-941-1622
info@cpmcom.com
http://www.epmcom.com
Ira Mayern, Publisher
Barbara Perrin, Editor
Analyzes research on consumer behavior and attitudes. *$389.00*
Fortnightly Founded: 1988

16460 Retrenchment Ahead?
Probe Research
3 Wing Drive
Suite 240
Cedar Knolls, NJ 07927-1000
973-285-1500
FAX: 973-285-1519
probe@proberesearch.com
www.proberesearch.com
With the collapse of the bull market and the apparent collapse of viable wireline competition, the ILECs must focus on the role of wireless as a major competitor. The new Bush administration appears to be pro-ILEC and this will translate into a series of reglatory initiatives that may in total favor the ILECs R&D agendas have to shift to support innovative solutions in the access domain and in mobile.

16461 Revisiting R&D
Probe Research
3 Wing Drive
Suite 240
Cedar Knolls, NJ 07927-1000
973-285-1500
FAX: 973-285-1519
probe@proberesearch.com
www.proberesearch.com
With the collapse of the bull market and the apparent collapse of viable wireline competition, the ILECs must focus on the role of wireless as a major competitor. The new Bush administration appears to be pro-ILEC and this will translate into a series of reglatory initiatives that may in total favor the ILECs R&D agendas have to shift to support innovative solutions in the access domain and in mobile.

16462 Roper's Public Pulse
Roper Starch Worldwide
29 W 35th Street
5th Floor
New York, NY 10001-2299
212-240-5300
FAX: 212-564-0465
dcrispell@roper.com www.roper.com/
Diane Crispell, Editor
Content includes the latest research on demographic trends, new insights from opinion research experts as to what Americans think, concise, brand-focused data, current consumer attitudes toward dozens of American themes, as well as news updates on special markets and brands. *$299.00*
Monthly
Circulation: 2000

16463 SBC
Probe Research
3 Wing Drive
Suite 240
Cedar Knolls, NJ 07927-1000
973-285-1500
FAX: 973-285-1519
probe@proberesearch.com
www.proberesearch.com
Discussion and analysis of ILEC/vendor market dynamics; case study of SBC's metro optical architecture; technology evolution; new services offered; incorporation of passive optical networking and metro DWDM rollouts; strategy going forward.

16464 SMS Drivers and Impediments in Europe Forecasts
Probe Research
3 Wing Drive
Suite 240
Cedar Knolls, NJ 07927-1000
973-285-1500
FAX: 973-285-1519
probe@proberesearch.com
www.proberesearch.com
With all the high expectations and poor results surrounding WAP, SMS has mushroomed into a significant business with far more traffic, users and revenues than the fledgling WAP - based offerings. SMS is a simple, narrowband application that has taken off considerably in certain key markets.

16465 Sales Bullet
Economics Press
12 Daniel Road
Fairfield, NJ 07004-2565
973-227-1224
FAX: 973-227-9742
Robert Guder, Editor
Diane Cody, Promotional Director
Covers the fundamental and subtleties of professional selling with methods, principles and ideas all salespoeple will find useful.

Circulation: 9,000

16466 Sales Manager's Bulletin
Bureau of Business Practice
1185 Avenue of the Americas
New York, NY 10036
212-597-0333
FAX: 800-901-9075 800-638-8437
alicia.pierce@aspenpubl.com
www.bbpnews.com
AliciaE Pierce, Operations
For front-line sales management. Focus on sales hiring, training, managing, motivation, results. Reports what people in sales management field are doing to produce measurable sales profits. *$9.00*

Circulation: 4,290

16467 Sales Productivity Review
Penoyer Communications
PO Box 2509
Santa Clara, CA 95055-2509
408-248-5458
FAX: 408-296-6917 800-248-5458
info@penoyer.com
http://www.penoyer.com
Flyn Penoyer, President
Edited for sales management with an editorial focus that will assist in improving sales productivity and effectiveness. *$5.00*
6 issues per ye

16468 Sales Promotion Monitor
Commerce Communications
418 N 3rd Street
Suite 303
Milwaukee, WI 55410-2444
414-225-9085
FAX: 414-225-9095
tom@com-broker.com
www.com-broker.com
K Sederberg, Publisher
Tom Millitzer, Contact
News and information concerning all aspects of sales promotion.

16469 Sales Rep's Advisor
Alexander Communications Group
28 W 25th Street
8th Floor
New York, NY 10010
212-228-0246
FAX: 212-228-0376 800-232-4317
info@repsadvisor.com
http://www.repsadvisor.com

Margaret DeWitt, Publisher
Bill Keenan, Editor
Adam Reis, Marketing
Laurence Alexander, Owner

For independent manufacturers sales representatives. Filled with concise advice and ideas for reducing costs and increasing profits. *$199.00*

Monthly Founded: 1954

16470 Sarah Stambler's E-Tactics Letter
E-Tactics
370 Central Park W
#210
New York, NY 10025-6517
212-222-1713
FAX: 212-678-6357
info@e-tactics.com
http://www.e-tactics.com

Sarah Stambler, Publisher/Editor/CEO
Shlomo Bar-Ayal, Circulation Manager

Publication devoted to the creative use of electronic alternative media in the design and implementation of customer driven marketing, research and publication strategies.

Founded: 1984
Circulation: 5000

16471 School Marketing Newsletter
School Market Research Institute
1721 Saybrook Road
PO Box 10
Haddam, CT 06438
860-345-8183
FAX: 860-345-3985 800-838-3444
school.market@snet.net
http://www.school-market.com

Bob Stimolo, Publisher
Lynn Stimolo, Creative Director

How to articles, trends, original research, interviews with experts on school marketing Pre-K - 12th. *$119.00*

12 pages Monthly Founded: 1980
Circulation: 500 Audited 500 names $100 per M.
Printed in 1 color on matte stock

16472 Selling Advantage
Progressive Business Publications
370 Technology Drive
Malvern, PA 19355-1315
610-695-8600
FAX: 610-647-8089 1 8-0 2-0 50
stomer_service@pbp.com
http://www.pbp.com

Edward Satell, Publisher
Phillip Ahr, Editor

Business-to-business sales advice to assist sales staff and sales managers. *$94.56*

Founded: 1989
Circulation: 60,000

16473 Selling To Kids
Phillips Publishing
PO Box 611130
Potomac, MD 20859-2931
301-208-6787
FAX: 301-340-1451
aduff@phillips.com
www.phillips.com/cgi/catalog/info?m2k

Angela Duff, Associate Publisher

Editorial offers news and practical advice on strategies in successful marketing. Includes information on market research, buying trends, and media opportunities and features news on conferences as well as a look at new products and services. *$495.00*

BiWeekly

16474 Selling to Seniors
CD Publications
8204 Fenton Street
Silver Spring, MD 20910
301-588-6380
FAX: 301-588-6385 800-666-6380
info@cdpublications.com
http://www.cdpublications.com

Mike Gerecht, Publisher
Jean Van Ryzin, Editor

Published as a subscriber driven newsletter targeting marketers and advertisers of products and services for the mature market. *$ 294.00*

Monthly Founded: 1961
Mailing list available for rent 2,000 names $160 per M.

16475 Service Level Agreements
Probe Research
3 Wing Drive
Suite 240
Cedar Knolls, NJ 07927-1000
973-285-1500
FAX: 973-285-1519
probe@proberesearch.com
www.proberesearch.com
Details service level agreements that are being offered by several major service providers, and examines many of the popular software solutions taht are being used in their networks. Also a briefly discusses XML, and its potential uses.

16476 Siedlecki on Marketing
Richard Siedlecki Business & Marketing
4767 Lake Forrest Drive NE
Atlanta, GA 30342-2539
770-436-8271
FAX: 403-303-9939

Richard Siedlecki, Editor

Tips, techniques, and insights on marketing. *$49.00*

6 pages BiWeekly
Circulation: 500 Audited
Printed in 1 color on matte stock

16477 Small and Medium Sized ISPs
Probe Research
3 Wing Drive
Suite 240
Cedar Knolls, NJ 07927-1000
973-285-1500
FAX: 973-285-1519
probe@proberesearch.com
www.proberesearch.com
Probe has been surveying small ISPs in the US for the past four years. In this issue, we share the observations we have made by tracking the Probe 50, 50 small/medium ISPs in the US in 2000, small ISPs grew their revenues at a rate of 6.5% This bullletin also includes a look at the slow - down in online advertising trends, as witnessed at the recent ADTECH trade show in Los Angeles.

16478 South American Telecom Markets
Probe Research
3 Wing Drive
Suite 240
Cedar Knolls, NJ 07927-1000
973-285-1500
FAX: 973-285-1519
probe@proberesearch.com
www.proberesearch.com
An examination of economic business and legal/regulatory conditions in the South American region and the affect on telecommunications, Internet and related carrier servcice providers, including the importance of undersea fiber optic cable routes.

16479 Special Issue: Terror Attacks and the Poss ible Impacts on US Carrier Networks
Probe Research
3 Wing Drive
Suite 240
Cedar Knolls, NJ 07927-1000
973-285-1500
FAX: 973-285-1519
probe@proberesearch.com
www.proberesearch.com
This bulletin discusses some of the impacts on the telecom industry due to the terror attacks of Septemeber 11th. A security framework is proposed and a series of underlying forces already at work in the economy are discussed as the foundations for understanding the impact of these attacks. A brief description of previous shocks to the telecom world is presented as well.

16480 Strategic Health Care Marketing
Health Care Communications
11 Heritage Lane
PO Box 594
Rye, NY 10580-594
914-967-6741
FAX: 914-967-3054
healthcomm@aol.com
http://www.strategichealthcare.com

Michele von Dambrowski, Editor/Publisher
Michele von Dambrowski, CEO

Business development and marketing startegies for health care executives. *$279.00*

12 pages Monthly Founded: 1984
Circulation: 1200
Printed in 2 colors on matte stock

16481 Structural Separation: Is Breaking Up Hard for the FRBOCs to Do?
Probe Research
3 Wing Drive
Suite 240
Cedar Knolls, NJ 07927-1000
973-285-1500
FAX: 973-285-1519
probe@proberesearch.com
www.proberesearch.com
In this bulletin, we discuss the issues surrounding the fights over whether the FRBOCs retail and wholesale operations should be split that are taking place in Pennsylvania and other states and assess whether functional and/or structural separation is necessary step in achieving local loop competition.

16482 Submarine Network Market Update
Probe Research
3 Wing Drive
Suite 240
Cedar Knolls, NJ 07927-1000
973-285-1500
FAX: 973-285-1519
probe@proberesearch.com
www.proberesearch.com
This bulletin looks at the development of the submarine cable market over the past three to four years, including how the market structure has changed. It then focuses on a numbner of aspects of the market including bandwidth supply and demand and trends in bandwidth pricing and how these are likely to develop over the next few years.

16483 Subscribe
PO Box 194
Bryn Mawr, PA 19010-0194

pageone1@aol.com
Lynn Kerrigan, Editor
Gail Jennings, Administration
A newsletter offering marketing ideas to help gain new subscribers and retain old ones. *$49.00*
Quarterly

16484 Successful Closing Techniques
Dartnell Corporation
4660 N Ravenswood Avenue
Chicago, IL 60640-4510
773-907-9500
FAX: 773-561-3801
Clark Fetridge, Publisher
Terry Breen, Editor
Fail-safe techniques for acquiring bigger sales and more frequent closings. *$62.00*

16485 Target Market News
Target Market News
228 S Wabash Avenue
Suite 210
Chicago, IL 60604-2308
312-408-1881
FAX: 312-408-1867
info@targetmarketnews.com
http://www.targetmarketnews.com
Ken Smikle, Publisher
Ken Smikle, CEO/President
Hallie Mummert, Editor
News and developments in the areas of black consumer marketing and black-oriented media. Accepts advertising. *$40.00*
12 pages Monthly Founded: 1988

16486 The INTRANETS Newsletter
Information Today
143 Old Marlton Pike
Medford, NJ 08055-8750
609-654-6266
FAX: 609-654-4309
custserv@infotoday
www.infotoday.com
Thomas Hogan, Publisher/President
Lauree Padgett, Editorial Services Manager
Inge Coffey, Circulation Manager
Covers strategies, tips, and tools required to help organizations develop, deploy, and manage intranest, extranets, portals, and other knowledge adnd information management initiatives. *$149.95*
Bi Monthly

16487 Traffic Applications Driving Demand
Probe Research
3 Wing Drive
Suite 240
Cedar Knolls, NJ 07927-1000
973-285-1500
FAX: 973-285-1519
probe@proberesearch.com
www.proberesearch.com
Focuses on which applications are currently driving traffic in IP service provider networks. Examines key trends, determine how they have changed and assess regional differences where possible. Is also focuses on how shifting user patterns, and changing access patterns are impacting application demand in the future.

16488 Transitor Radios
Probe Research
3 Wing Drive
Suite 240
Cedar Knolls, NJ 07927-1000
973-285-1500
FAX: 973-285-1519
probe@proberesearch.com
www.proberesearch.com
DoCoMo's $9.8 billion investment in AT&T wireless changed the US carrier's network ipgrade strategy and may improve revenues and subscriber counts as well. This bulletin explores assets and liabilities of both companies and uses four potential models to forecast revenues and subscribers for AT&T wireless in 2001 - 2006.

16489 Trends Journal
Trends Research Institute
PO Box 660
Rhinebeck, NY 12572-660
845-876-6700
FAX: 845-758-5252
joneill@trendsresearch.com
http://www.trendsresearch.com
Gerald Celente, Editor
Offers the inside track on trends affecting your business, your profession, your life. Forecasts on over 300 trend categories - consumer, social, economic, political, media, health, family, education, and other domestic and international trends. *$185.00*
Quarterly Founded: 1980
Printed in 2 colors on glossy stock

16490 US Web Hosting and Managed Services Market
Probe Research
3 Wing Drive
Suite 240
Cedar Knolls, NJ 07927-1000
973-285-1500
FAX: 973-285-1519
probe@proberesearch.com
www.proberesearch.com
This bulletin analyzes the US web hosting market. It includes market shares of the top 15 hosting service providers, US market size and growth forecast for the following three aggregated market segments and six web hosting market segments.

16491 US Wholesale Dial Access
Probe Research
3 Wing Drive
Suite 240
Cedar Knolls, NJ 07927-1000
973-285-1500
FAX: 973-285-1519
probe@proberesearch.com
www.proberesearch.com
Analyzes recent market trends in wholesale dial access in the US. Provides competitive analysis of selected market leaders and describes service offerings.

16492 Understanding ASPs
Probe Research
3 Wing Drive
Suite 240
Cedar Knolls, NJ 07927-1000
973-285-1500
FAX: 973-285-1519
probe@proberesearch.com
www.proberesearch.com
In this bulletin, we define the application service provider and describe how this business model fits into the current telecommunications landscape.

16493 Understanding the Velocity of Technology C hange and Carrier Networks
Probe Research
3 Wing Drive
Suite 240
Cedar Knolls, NJ 07927-1000
973-285-1500
FAX: 973-285-1519
probe@proberesearch.com
www.proberesearch.com
This double issue contains a detailed analysis of the future of Moore's law and the prospects for its continued success. Critical issues are discussed, including the increasingly important problem of power consumption in chips. The discussion includes brief reviews of DNA and quantum computing.

16494 Upline
MLM Publishing
106 W South Street
Charlottesvle, VA 22902-5039

FAX: 434-979-1602
John Milton Fogg, Editor
Randolph Byrd, Publisher
Distribution training for network (multilevel) marketers. *$69.00*
Monthly Founded: 1990

16495 Video Marketing Newsletter
Outback Group Productions
PO Box 872
Harrison, AR 72602-0872

FAX: 870-741-4727
Dan Reynolds, Editor/Publisher
Information, business opportunities, marketing tips, product reviews. For people interested in producing and marketing their own videos. *$185.00*
Monhtly Founded: 1989

16496 VoP on Channel Architectures
Probe Research
3 Wing Drive
Suite 240
Cedar Knolls, NJ 07927-1000
973-285-1500
FAX: 973-285-1519
probe@proberesearch.com
www.proberesearch.com
Examines the market, technology/standards for cable technology using VoIP architectures. Identifies key issues associated with development and deployment, analyzes the current state of emerging standards and provides a forecast of lines using cable infrastructures to provide packet telephony.

16497 Vop Basic Services
Probe Research
3 Wing Drive
Suite 240
Cedar Knolls, NJ 07927-1000
973-285-1500
FAX: 973-285-1519
probe@proberesearch.com
www.proberesearch.com
This bulletin presents the market and forecast for basic Voice over Packet services, expresses in traffic and service revenues. Local, domestic long distance and international traffic is included.

16498 What's Working in Sales Management
Progressive Business Publications
370 Technology Drive
Malvern, PA 19355-1315
610-695-8600
FAX: 610-647-8089 800-220-5000
Edward M Satell, Publisher
Richard Kern, Editor
Sales management news and issues. *$264.00*
Founded: 1989

16499 Wireless Advertising
Probe Research
3 Wing Drive
Suite 240
Cedar Knolls, NJ 07927-1000
973-285-1500
FAX: 973-285-1519
probe@proberesearch.com
www.proberesearch.com
In our first bulletin on wireless advertising, we focused on identifying metrics we could use to predict how a mature advertising industry would dictate the development of a nascent wireless equivalent. In this bulletin we take a closer look at the activities of some wireless advertising start - ups, looking at their technologies, market trials and user acceptance to date.

16500 Wireless Data in the Enterprise: Unchained from the Desktop
Probe Research
3 Wing Drive
Suite 240
Cedar Knolls, NJ 07927-1000
973-285-1500
FAX: 973-285-1519
probe@proberesearch.com
www.proberesearch.com
This bulletin will review the role of the enterprise customers in the development of business cases for wireless companies and forecast spending and subscribers for wireless revices. We focus much attention on field service support applications because these appear to be most pervasive.

16501 Wireless Games
Probe Research
3 Wing Drive
Suite 240
Cedar Knolls, NJ 07927-1000
973-285-1500
FAX: 973-285-1519
probe@proberesearch.com
www.proberesearch.com
This report examines the issues facing the deployment and adoption of wireless games by mobile carriers, including forecast of global subscriber numbers and possible revenue models.

16502 Wireless Internet
Probe Research
3 Wing Drive
Suite 240
Cedar Knolls, NJ 07927-1000
973-285-1500
FAX: 973-285-1519
probe@proberesearch.com
www.proberesearch.com
Identifies successful companies within three types of wireless portals: carrier - owned, independent and white label (wholesale).

16503 Wireless Internet Strategies
Probe Research
3 Wing Drive
Suite 240
Cedar Knolls, NJ 07927-1000
973-285-1500
FAX: 973-285-1519
probe@proberesearch.com
www.proberesearch.com
US wireless carriers are increasing their emphasis on offering wireless Internte services as a competitive advantage. This bulletin defines the types of services offered by voice - centric wireless carriers as well as data - only wireless carriers. Nextel is also identified as the US network that now provides 2.5G services in advance of neraly all other carriers in the world.

16504 Wireless PDA Operating Systems, Microsoft Enters Wirelss
Probe Research
3 Wing Drive
Suite 240
Cedar Knolls, NJ 07927-1000
973-285-1500
FAX: 973-285-1519
probe@proberesearch.com
www.proberesearch.com
Wireless Internet access devices will become more powerful and rely on open operating systems such as Microsoft Pocket PC and Palm OS. This bulletin forecast the global OS acceptance divided by region.

16505 Youth Markets Alert
EPM Communications
160 Mercer Street
3rd Floor
New York, NY 10012-3208
212-941-0099
FAX: 212-941-1622 888-852-9467
info@epmcom.com
http://www.epmcom.com
Ira Mayer, President & Publisher
Marty Brochstein, Editorial Director
Loretta Netzer, Circulation Manager
Research reports on trends in youth response to marketing techniques and buying. *$447.00*
Founded: 1988

Magazines & Journals

16506 ADCLIP
National Research Bureau
320 Valley Street
Burlington, IA 52601
319-752-5415
FAX: 319-752-3421
Diane Darnall, President
Nancy Heinzel, Circulation Manager
Individualized adclipping service providing market intelligence information on various retail operations. Includes full size, pages, market strategies, advertising promotion ideas, new store openings and more.

16507 Adage Global
Crain Communications
711 3rd Avenue
New York, NY 10017-111
212-100-0100
FAX: 212-210-0200
info@crain.com
http://www.crain.com
Paul Audino, Advertising Director
Scott Donaton, Editor
David Klein, Publisher
Philip Scarano, Circulation Director
Vanessa Reed, Marketing Director
Dedicated to being the world's essential advertising, marketing and media publication, with editors around the world, Adage covers topics of significance form Times Square to Taiwan. *$69.95*
Weekly Founded: 1943
Circulation: 57,800
Printed in 4 colors

16508 Advertising Age
Crain Communications
711 Third Avenue
New York, NY 10017-4036
212-210-0100
FAX: 212-210-0200
info@crain.com
http://www.crain.com
David Klein, VP Publishing/Editorial Director
Rance Crain, Editor-in-Chief
Jill Manee, VP/Publisher
Kerri Ross, marketing director
Phillip Scarano III, Circulation Director
Presents advertising methods for selling products and services, reports on effective communication tools and examines the use of audio/visual material, trade show exhibits, direct mail, catalogs and incentives. *$203.49*
Weekly Founded: 1916
Circulation: 59000

16509 Adweek
VNU Business Publications
770 Broadway
New York, NY 10003-9595
646-654-5100
FAX: 646-654-5886
bmcomm@vnuinc.com
http://www.vnubusinessmedia.com
Michael E Parker, Group Publisher
Rob Vanden Bergh, CEO

Adweek gives readers in the advertising community the global and national news they need, plus the local and metro news that no other advertising magazine can deliver. *$149.00*

80 pages Weekly Founded: 1964
Circulation: 27003
Printed in 4 colors on glossy stock

16510 Agency Sales Magazine
Manufacturers Agents National Association
PO Box 3467
Laguna Hills, CA 92654-3467
949-859-4040
FAX: 949-855-2973 877-626-2776
mana@manaonline.org
http://www.manaonline.org

Joseph Miller, Publisher
Jack Foster, Editor

For manufacturers agents and manufacturers who contract for the services of these representatives.

96 pages Monthly
Circulation: 50000
Printed in on glossy stock

16511 Agri Marketing Magazine
Doane Agricultural Services
11701 Borman Drive
Suite 300
Saint Louis, MO 63146-4193
314-569-2700
FAX: 314-569-1083
info@agrimarketing.com
http://www.doane.com

Judy Knoll, Advertising Sales Manager
Lynn Henderson, CEO/President
Rick Patton, VP Marketing
Bekah Reddick, Assistant Editor
William Schuermann, Editorial Director

Agri Marketing Magazine is the premier publication of the agriculture industry, reaching over 9,000 sales, marketing and advertising executives in the US and Canada. The Marketing Services Guide is published in December; it lists companies, advertising agencies, direct marketing, market research, print media, broadcast media, e-business and associations. *$40.00*

Founded: 1923
Circulation: 9000 9,227 names $105 per M.
Printed in on matte stock : Web

16512 American Demographics
Primedia
Customer Service
PO Box 2042
Marion, OH 43306-8142

FAX: 740-389-5574 800-529-7502
editors@marketingtools.com
www.demographics.com

Kerry J Smith, Publisher
Seema Nayyar, Editor

Coverage includes regional and national consumer trends, lifestyles, media preferences and purchasing behaviors. Regular features present case histories and in-depth demographic profiles. *$69.00*

Monthly
Circulation: 34,304

16513 B-to-B
Crain Communications
360 N Michigan Avenue
Chicago, IL 60601
312-649-5200
FAX: 312-649-5462
info@crain.com
http://www.btobonline.com

David Bernstein, Advertising Director
Bob Felsenthal, VP/Publisher
Tara Curran, Marketing Manager
Ricardo Moraga, Owner
Ellis Booker, Editor *$59.00*

Monthly Founded: 1916
Circulation: 45,000

16514 Brand Marketing
Fairchild Publications
7 W 34th Street
New York, NY 10001-8100
212-630-3880
FAX: 212-630-3768
faulr@fairchildpub.com
www.brandmarket.com

Richard Faul, Publisher
Mary Berner, President

Covers how manufactureres launch and build brands, and how they leverage brand equity in new ways using new techniques. These ways include partnerships with retailers via trade marketing and information technology and a variety of cost-reduction strategies such as everyday low pricing and efficient consumer response. *$90.00*

Monthly
Circulation: 18,543

16515 Brandweek
VNU Business Publications
770 Broadway
7th Floor
New York, NY 10003
646-654-5100
FAX: 646-654-5374 800-562-2706
info@brandweek.com
http://www.brandweek.com

Charlotte Erwin, Publisher
Karen Benezra, Editor
Mary Beth Johnston, VP

Brandweek is the only marketing magazine to offer saturation coverage of decision makers at America's SuperBrands — the 1,500 plus brands that spend over 90% of all measured national media dollars. This horizontal magazine covers product categories from automotive to travel. *$149.00*

60 pages Weekly
Circulation: 25784
Printed in 4 colors on glossy stock

16516 Broker News
Broker Publishing
PO Box 20287
Fountain Hills, AZ 85269-0287
480-816-1400
FAX: 480-836-7767 800-475-3565

Joanne Genualdi, Account Executive

Serving insurance producers and financial planners across the country. *$12.00*

32+ pages Bi-Monthly Founded: 1990

16517 Business Journal
120 W Morehead Street
Suite 200
Charlotte, NC 28202
704-472-2340
FAX: 704-973-1102 800-948-5323
charlotte@bizjournals.com
www.bizjournals.com/charlotte

Robert Morris, Editor
Megan Foley, Marketing Manager
Jeannie Falknor, Publisher

Provides marketing solutions and caring service. *$82.00*

Monthly

16518 CRM Magazine
Information Today
143 Old Marlton Pike
Medford, CT 08055-8750
609-654-6266
FAX: 609-654-4309 800-248-8466
custserv@infotoday.com
http://www.infotoday.com/

Alison Lowander, Managing Editor
Alexandra DeFelice, Senior Editor

Offers vital information that will help you benefit from the experience of others in the industry. *$23.95*

Mailing list available for rent 4M names
Printed in 4 colors on glossy stock

16519 Catalog Success
North American Publishing Company
401 N Broad St
Apt N
Philadelphia, PA 19108-1001
215-238-5300
FAX: 215-238-5457
phatch@napco.com
http://www.catalogsuccess.com

Donna Loyle, Editor-in-Chief
Matt Griffin, Associate Editor
Peggy Hatch, VP Group Publishing

Putting marketing management to the test.

Monthly Founded: 1999
Circulation: 20000
Printed in 4 colors

16520 Circulation Management
Primedia
9800 Metcalf Avenue
Overland Park, KS 66212
913-341-1300
FAX: 913-967-1898
www.primediabusiness.com

Cameron Bishop, President/CEO
Ron Wall, Chief Officer

Serves consumer/special interest and business/trade/association publications.

Monthly Founded: 1986
Printed in 4 colors

16521 Connect
Media-Mark
115 Sansome Street
#1224
San Francisco, CA 94104-3823
415-743-6220
FAX: 415-421-6225
connect@media-mark.com
www.media-mark.com

Art Garcia, Publisher

Features report on news-making agencies and corporate departments making news, as well as the people managing them, and rate/review PR services and products. Regular sections also report on international PR/marketing andmedia, women in marketing, investor relations, internet marketing, senior-level moves and promotions, account changes, trends, case studies and industry chatter.

Monthly
Circulation: 10M

16522 Consumer Goods Technology
Edgell Communications
4 Middlebury Boulevard
Randolph, NJ 07869
973-252-0100
FAX: 973-252-9020
cs@e-circ.net
http://www.edgellcommunications.com

Gabriele A. Edgell, Chairman & CEO
Joe Skorupa, Editor-in-Chief

Andrew Gaffney, Group Publisher
Gerald Ryerson, President

Consumer Goods Technology serves manufacturers of accessories, shoes, apparel, appliances, consumer electronics, office products, automotive aftermarket products, seasonal merchandise, transporters of consumer products, consultants and others allied to the field.

Monthly Founded: 1984
Circulation: 25035
Printed in 4 colors on glossy stock

16523 Currents
Council for Advancement & Support of Education
1307 New York Avenue NW
Suite 1000
Washington, DC 20005-4701
202-328-5900
FAX: 202-387-4973
eigeman@case.org
http://www.case.org

John Lippincott, President
Deborah Bongiorno, Editor in chief
Tracy Baird, Marketing
Anne Eigeman, Editor

Offers articles on integrated marketing, technology and other industry related information. *$115.00*
Monthly Founded: 1975

16524 Customer Interaction Solutions
Technology Marketing Corporation
One Technology Plaza
Norwalk, CT 06854
203-852-6800
FAX: 203-853-2845 800-243-6002
tmc@tmcnet.com
http://www.tmcnet.com

Rich Tehrani, President/Group Editor-in-chief
Tracey Schelmetic, Editorial Director

Dedicated to teleservices ans e-services outsoucing, marketing and customer relationship management issues.
Monthly
Circulation: 13400

16525 CyberDealer
Meister Publishing Company
37733 Euclid Avenue
Willoughby, OH 44094
440-942-2000
FAX: 440-942-0662 800-572-7740
Helps agricultural dealerships better manage their operations.
6 per year

16526 Daily Record
11 E Saratoga Street
Baltimore, MD 21202
410-752-3849
FAX: 410-332-0698
customer.service@mddailyrecord.com
http://www.mddailyrecord.com

Kris Eddings, CEO/President
Mark Chashir, Editor
Mark Chashir, Publisher
Susan Hoettner, Marketing
Kris Charddo, Circulation Manager
$190.00

Daily Founded: 1888
Circulation: 9000

16527 Dealerscope Merchandising
North American Publishing Company
1500 Spring Garden Street
Suite 1200
Philadelphia, PA 19130-4009
215-238-5300
FAX: 215-238-5094 800-818-8174
gclauser@napco.com
http://www.napco.com

Rhoda Dixon, Circulation Manager
Eric Schwartz, President
Grant Clauser, Editorial Director
David Dritsas, Editor-in-Chief
Sean Downey, Managing Editor

Offers news on the marketing of appliances and consumer electronics on a national and regional basis.
Monthly Founded: 1958
Circulation: 20000

16528 Direct
Primedia
249 W. 17th Street
New York, IL 10011
646-860-0340
FAX: 212-206-3622
cvietri@primediabusiness.com
http://www.primediabusiness.com

Jack Condon, Chief Operating Officer
Ray Schultz, Editorial Director
Charles Vietri, Managing Editor
Elizabeth O'Connor, Publisher

Magazine of direct marketing management. *$85.00*
Founded: 1989
Circulation: 46,527

16529 Direct Marketing Magazine
Hoke Communications
224 7th Street
Garden City, NY 11530-5771
516-746-6700
FAX: 516-294-8141 800-229-6700
dmmagazine@aol.com
http://www.directmarketingmag.com

Joseph D Gatti, Editor
Henry Reed Hoke, Publisher
Stuart W Boysen III, President

Covers all aspects of direct marketing including production, creative campaigns, telemarketing, interactive marketing, direct response, TV/radio, legal issues and more. Profiles professionals in the field and offers statistical information to the industry. *$52.00*
80 pages Monthly Founded: 1938

16530 Do-It-Yourself Retailing
5822 W 74th Street
Indianapolis, IN 46278-1787
317-297-1190
FAX: 317-328-4354
www.diyretailing.com

John Hammond, Executive Director

16531 Exhibitor Magazine

206 S Broadway
Suite 745
Rochester, MN 55904-6565
507-289-6556
FAX: 507-289-5253 888-235-6155

Lee Knight, Editor In Chief
John Pavek, VP of Publishing

Mission is to provide trade show marketing professionals with the tools and education to produce high-performance programs with measurable results. *$78.00*
Monthly

16532 Greenville Magazine
614 N Main St
Greenville, SC 29601-1612
864-271-1105
FAX: 864-271-1165
gmag@greenvillemagazine.com
www.greenvillemagazine.com

Gary Ault, Owner

Features content summary, web-only extras, advertiser links, and access to reader service forms and various contests and programs.
Monthly
Circulation: 10,002

16533 Journal of Marketing Research
American Marketing Association
311 S Wacker Drive
Suite 5800
Chicago, IL 60606-2266
312-542-9000
FAX: 312-542-9001 800-262-1150
info@ama.org http://www.ama.org

Jack Hollfelder, Publisher
Dick R. Wittink, Editor
Naveen Donthu, Marketing Manager

Examines philosophical, conceptual and technical aspects of marketing research and its applications. Written for academicians and practitioners who need to be current with the latest techniques, methods and applications of marketing research function. *$75.00*
Quarterly

16534 Journal of Nonprofit & Public Sector Marketing
Haworth Press
10 Alice Street
Binghamton, NY 13904-1580
607-722-5857
FAX: 607-722-1424 800-429-6784
getinfo@haworthpress.com
http://www.haworthpress.com

Walter W Wymer Jr, DBA, Editor
Bill Cohen, CEO/President
Centra Jones Sckels, Marketing Manager
Lauri Peagel, Circulation Manager
Bill Cohen, Publisher

Presents case studies and strategies for such diverse groups as governmental agencies, charitable organizations and institutions of higher education. *$48.00*
Quarterly Founded: 1976
Circulation: 500

16535 Journal of the Academy of Marketing Science
Sage Publications
2455 Teller Road
Thousand Oaks, CA 91320-2234
805-499-0721
FAX: 805-499-0871
reprint@sagepub.com
http://www.sagepub.com

George Zinkhan, Editor
Anita Cava, Marketing Director

Promotes research and the dissemination of research results through the study and improvement of marketing as an economic, ethical and social force. *$112.00*
112 pages Bi-annually Founded: 1965
Circulation: 1100

16536 KM World
Information Today
143 Old Marlton Pike
Medford, CT 08055-8750
609-654-6266
FAX: 609-654-4309 800-248-8466
custserv@infotoday.com
http://www.infotoday.com/

Hugh Mckellar, Editor in Chief
Sandra Haimila, Managing Editor
Andy Moore, Publisher

Serves the knowledge management industry by offering components and processes, including success stories, designed to improve business. *$23.95*

Mailing list available for rent 4M names
Printed in 4 colors on glossy stock

16537 License Magazine
Advanstar Communications
One Park Avenue
New York, NY 10016
212-797-7631
FAX: 212-951-6793 800-598-6008
info@advanstar.com
http://www.advanstar.com

Joyceann Cooney, Editor-in-Chief
Steven Ekstract, Publisher
Kerry C Gumas, CEO/President

Detailed coverage and research on the $177+ billion licensed consumer product business including: retail and merchandising trends; promotional partnerships; available and recently granted property licenses; research reports; and case studies on licensed consumer product categories based on publishing and art, entertainment, brands, sports, fashion, home decor, and interactive media properties *$59.00*
Monthly Founded: 1998
Circulation: 25000
Printed in 4 colors

16538 MC Magazine
ADWEEK
770 Broadway
7th Floor
New York, NY 10003
646-545-5220
FAX: 646-654-5886
publisher@adweek.com
http://www.adweek.com

Sidney Holt, Editor-in-Chief
Kathryn Dennis, Executive Editor
Michael E Parker, Group Publisher

Specifically written and edited for the highest ranking marketer at a given technology organization. Readers are directly responsible for corporate marketing and positioning. The magazine's content profiles marketing innovation in all areas of the technology industry including: telecommunications, Internet services, professional services, e-commerce, information technology, consumer electronics, networking, e-business and semiconductors.
Monthly

16539 MC Technology Marketing Intelligence
ASM Communications
770 Broadway
7th Floor
New York, NY 10003
646-654-5100
FAX: 646-654-5374
abrophy@adweek.com
www.brandweeek.com

Ami Brophy, Publisher

MC offers saturation coverage of marketing decision makers at the 1,000 high-tech companies. These companies account for 90% of all advertising and promotion spent on high-tech products and services. *$55.00*
100 pages Monthly
Circulation: 19,479
Printed in 4 colors on glossy stock

16540 Magnet Marketing & Sales
Graham Communications
40 Oval Road
Suite 2
Quincy, MA 02170-3813
617-328-0069
FAX: 617-471-1504 800-659-0069
info@graham.com
http://www.grahamcomm.com

John Graham, Publisher/President
Cynthia Cantrell, Editor
John Graham, CEO
Jonathan Bloom, Marketing manager

A marketing and sales newsletter. *$18.95*
9 pages Quarterly
Printed in 2 colors on matte stock

16541 Marketing
Mane/Marketing
13901 NE 175th Street
#M
Woodinville, WA 98072-8548
425-487-9111
FAX: 425-487-3158
coff@marketings.com

Larry Coffman, Publisher

Features important area events, industry projects, awards and executives of note. Highlights the latest information on marketing trends and pattern analysis. Free subscription.
Monthly
Circulation: 11M

16542 Marketing Health Services
American Marketing Association
311 S Wacker Drive
Suite 5800
Chicago, IL 60606-2266
312-542-9000
FAX: 312-542-9001 800-262-1150
info@ama.org
http://www.marketingpower.com

Kent Seltman, Editor
Richard Ballschmiede, Advertising Sales Director
Dennis Dunlap, CEO
Linda Zid, Managing Editor
Robert Marcano, Owner

Presents research on the issues affecting how health care organizations compete and are marketed. Provides in-depth analysis and knowledgeable insights on the delicate balance between the financial viability of health care systems and organizations and the quality of care. *$74.00*
Quarterly Founded: 1937
Circulation: 4500

16543 Marketing Management
American Marketing Association
311 S Wacker Drive
Suite 5800
Chicago, IL 60606-2266
312-542-9000
FAX: 312-542-9001 800-262-1150
info@amaorders.com
http://www.ama.org

Jack Hollfelder, Publisher
Mary Egan Leader, Managing Editor
Richard Ballschmiede, Advertising Sales Director
Shari Vass, President

Topics include benchmarking, experience engineering, mass customization, brand management, pricing, and new marketing concepts. Provides book reviews, case studies, marketing law insights, Web marketing updates, and marketing research tools. *$70.00*

16544 Marketing News
American Marketing Association
311 S Wacker Drive
Suite 5800
Chicago, IL 60606
312-542-9000
FAX: 312-542-9001 800-262-1150

Dennis Dunlap, Chief Executive Officer

Covers the most recent perspectives and innovations in marketing by focusing on the latest trends in strategy, technology and communications.
Biweekly

16545 Marketing Recreation Classes
Learning Resources Network
1554 Hayes Drive
Manhattan, KS 66502-5068
785-539-5376
FAX: 888-234-8633
http://www.lern.org/

William Draves, Editor

This magazine offers information on marketing and advertising trends.
8 pages Monthly Founded: 1980

16546 Marketing Research Magazine
American Marketing Association
311 South Wacker Drive
Suite 5800
Chicago, IL 60606
312-542-9000
FAX: 312-542-9001 800-262-1150
info@ama.org http://www.ama.org

Jack Hollfeldar, Publisher
Chuck Chakrapani, Editor
Jeanne Nemcek, Graphics Editor
Dennis Dunlap, CEO

Publication exclusively for marketing researchers. Explores methods and techniques as well as legal issues, ethical concerns and professional development. *$75.00*
Quarterly Founded: 1937
Circulation: 3800

16547 Marketing Research Review
High Tech Publishing Company
PO Box 1275
Amherst, MA 01004-1275
413-534-4500
FAX: 413-256-6378

Philip T DiPeri, Editor

Analyzes and evaluates commercially available marketing research and technology assessment reports. Assists readers to identify, appropriate and adapt commercially available reports to their own special and particular needs. *$265.00*
Monthly

16548 Marketing to Women
EPM Communications
160 Mercer Street
3rd Floor
New York, NY 10012
212-941-0099
FAX: 212-941-1622
http://www.epmcom.com/

Loretta Netzer, Circulation Manager
Lisa Finn, Editor
Ira Mayer, President/Publisher
Michele Jensen, VP Marketing
Riva Bennett, COO

Topics covers attitudes and buying behaviors of the female consumer, market segment demographics, gender gap and health issues, media preferences and the role of technology. *$357.00*
Monthly Founded: 1988

16549 Marketrac
Marketrac San Diego
1235 Hotel Circle S
#C
San Diego, CA 92108-3422

Gerald Schultz, Editor
Jim Lucich, Promotional Manager

Marketing communications: people, places, events, trends, new products, technology, public relations, advertising, broadcast, TV, radio, video production, promotions, market research, direct mail, trademark, copyright law, accounting, employee management printing, graphics, color separations, novelty promotions. *$15.00*

32 pages Monthly

16550 Mediaweek
ASM Communications
770 Broadway
7th Floor
New York, NY 10003
646-654-5100
FAX: 646-654-5374
info@mediaweek.com
http://www.mediaweek.com

Michael E Parker, Group Publisher

Mediaweek's highly targeted circulation covers media decision makers at the top 350 ad agencies in America, all top buying services and client media departments. *$149.00*

60 pages Weekly Founded: 1992
Circulation: 21208
Printed in 4 colors on glossy stock

16551 Multicultural Marketing Resources/Asian American Advertising Federation
101 5th Ave
Rm 10B
New York, NY 10003-1008
212-242-3351
FAX: 212-691-5969
pr@multicultural.com
http://www.multicultural.com

Lisa Skriloff, President

A public relations/marketing firm representing the nations experts in targeting Hispanics, African Americans, Asian Americans. We maintain a professional library with 700 cataloged resources for members to access. We publish Source Book of Multicultural Experts and free MMR Newsletter. *$125.00*

bimonthly Founded: 1994 ISSN suit-e
Circulation: 4000 8500 names $950 per M.

16552 NAPRA ReView
109 N Beach Road
PO Box 9
Eastsound, WA 98245-9
360-376-2001
FAX: 360-376-2704 800-367-1907
marilyn@marilynmcguire.com
http://www.napra.com

Erin Johnson, Advertising Sales
Marilyn McGuire, Editor
Marilyn McGuire, CEO/President

10 issues ayear Founded: 1986
Circulation: 180000

16553 POP Design
Hoyt Publishing
7400 Skokie Boulevard
Skokie, IL 60077
847-675-7400
FAX: 847-675-7494
info@instoremarketer.org
http://www.hoytpub.com/

Peter W Hoyt, President
William Schober, VP/Editorial Directo
Peter Breen, Managing Director
Harold Fischer, Publisher

Provides designers, builders and vendors of displays, signs and fixtures with current developments in materials, components, processes, systems and services used in production. Includes updates on products, industry literature, patents and legal matters affecting designers and manufacturers. *$59.00*

Circulation: 18000
Printed in 4 colors on glossy stock

16554 PROMAX
PROMAX
2029 Century Park E
Suite 555
Los Angeles, CA 90067-2906
310-788-7600
FAX: 310-788-7616 www.promax.tv

Jill Masters, VP Member Services
Jim Chabin, President

Magazine, newsletter and directory published by PROMAX for members only, promotion and marketing professionals in electronic media.

Annual Founded: 1952
Circulation: 2500 2400 names
Printed in 4 colors on glossy stock

16555 PSMJ Marketing Tactics
PSMJ Resources
10 Midland Avenue
Newton, MA 02458-1000
617-965-0055
FAX: 617-965-5152 800-537-7765
info@psmj.com http://www.psmj.com

Frank Stasiowski, Production Manager

Provides marketing tactics and techniques for the design industry. *$267.00*

8 pages Monthly Founded: 1975
Mailing list available for rent $125 per M.
Printed in 2 colors on matte stock

16556 Personal Selling Power
1140 International Parkway
PO Box 5467
Fredericksburg, VA 22406-467
540-752-7000
FAX: 540-752-7001 800-752-7355
generalinfo@sellingpower.com
http://www.sellingpower.com

John Nuzzi, VP / Associate Publisher
Laura Gschwandtner, Editor-in-Chief

Sales education/motivation magazine designed to train, educate, motivate salespeople. *$33.00*

140 pages 10 times a year
Printed in 4 colors on glossy stock

16557 Point of Purchase Magazine
1115 Northmeadow Parkway
Roswell, GA 30076
847-647-7987
FAX: 847-647-9566 800-241-9034
popmag@halldata.com
www.popmag.com

Murray Kasmenn, Publisher
Julie Andrews, Managing Editor

Addresses the industry perspective of the brand marketer and the retailer and focuses on retail trends, case studies, statistics and profitability. *$60.00*

9 per year
Circulation: 18,506

16558 Quirk's Marketing Research Review
Quirk Enterprises
4662 Slater Road
Eagan, MN 55122
952-224-1919
FAX: 952-224-1914
info@quirks.com
http://www.quirks.com

Tom Quirk, Publisher
Joe Rydholm, Editor
Evan Tweed, Associate Publisher
Dan Quirk, Marketing Manager

Emphasizes marketing research case histories and techniques used by researchers in a variety of industries, from consumer products to advertising, includes directories of research services and new products and features personnel announcements. *$70.00*

Founded: 1986
Circulation: 16013
Mailing list available for rent
Printed in 4 colors on glossy stock

16559 Recharger Magazine
Recharger Magazine
1050 E Flamingo Rd
Ste 237
Las Vegas, NV 89119-7479
702-505-9530
FAX: 702-873-9671 877-902-9759
info@rechargermag.com
http://www.rechargermag.com

Tom Enerson, Publisher
Amy Turner, Managing Editor

Information including articles that cover business and marketing, technical updates, association and industry news, and company profiles. Related features focus on the importance of recycling, government legislation, and product comparisons. *$45.00*

Monthly Founded: 1997
Circulation: 8000

16560 Research Alert
EPM Communications
160 Mercer Street
3rd Floor
New York, NY 10012-3212
212-941-0099
FAX: 212-941-1622 888-852-9467
info@epmcom.com
http://www.epmcom.com

Ira Mayer, Publisher
Alfred R Kahn, CEO
Barbara Perrin, Editor
Loretta Netzer, Circulation Manager

Analyzes research on consumer behavior and attitudes. *$295.00*

Founded: 1988

16561 Response TV
Advanstar Communications
201 Sandpointe Avenue
#600
Santa Ana, CA 92707-8700
714-513-8400
FAX: 714-513-8412 800-527-7008
jschember@advanstar.com
http://www.responsetv.com

John Yarring, Publisher
Thomas Haire, Editor
Joe Logia, CEO/President

Jodi Dressig, Circulation manager
Gina Cohen, Manager

Addresses industry concerns regarding regulatory issues, production, fulfillment and aftermarketing. Designed for direct marketers, product owners and related agencies. *$39.00*

Monthly Founded: 1993
Circulation: 21345

16562 Sales Executive
Sales Marketing Executives of Greater New York
13 E 37th Street
#8
New York, NY 10016-2821
212-685-3613
FAX: 212-725-3752

Edward Glanegan, Publisher
Patricia Israel, Editor

For sales executives in New York.

Circulation: 2,500

16563 Sales Upbeat
Economics Press
12 Daniel Road
Fairfield, NJ 07004-2565
973-227-1224
FAX: 973-227-9742

John Beckley, Publisher
Robert Guder, Editor

Sales methods and techniques, quotes and anecdotes about selling. *$2.00*

Circulation: 52,000

16564 Salesmanship
LRP Publications/Dartnell Corporation
747 Dresher Road
Suite 500, Po Box 980
Horshan, PA 19044-4510
215-840-0912
FAX: 215-784-9639 800-341-7874

Enhances training program with engaging and instructive reminders and shape-up tips that pay off in greater gains from sales force. *$62.00*

16565 Say Yes Marketing Script Presentations
Frieda Carrol Communications
PO Box 416
Denver, CO 80201-0416
303-575-5676

This reference contains marketing presentations for various kinds of businesses. *$52.95*

16566 Security Distributing & Marketing
Reed Business Information
1050 IL Route 83
Suite 200
Bensonville, IL 60106
630-616-0200
FAX: 630-227-0214 www.sdmmag.com

Bill Zalud, Editorial Director
Susan Whitehurst, Group Publisher

Security Distributing and Marketing serves security installing dealers, security installing dealers with central station equipment, central station services, access control system specialists and systems integrators. *$82.00*

104 pages 19 per year Founded: 1971
Circulation: 28,298
Printed in 4 colors on glossy stock

16567 Selling AS/400 Solutions
Duke Communications International
PO Box 3438
Loveland, CO 80593-3438
970-663-4700
FAX: 970-663-3285
pressreleases@sellingas400.com
www.sellingas400.com

Wayne Madden, Publisher/Editor-in-Chief

Practical advice for doing business each day as an AS/400 solution provider with information to improve sales, marketing services, and development.

Bi-Monthly
Circulation: 12,500

16568 Selling Magazine
Selling Magazine
477 Madison Avenue
New York, NY 10022-5802
212-751-0485
FAX: 212-224-3592

Marjorie Weiss, Publisher

Selling is targeted to business-to-business salespeople. *$5.00*

Circulation: 155162

16569 Senior Marketwatch
Campbell Associates
185 Martling Avenue
Tarrytown, NY 10591-4703
914-332-1177
FAX: 914-332-1177

Arnold Thiesfeldt, Publisher

Features research based on tastes, trends, and resources of the senior market, as a means for advertisers and marketers to target and focus their products. *$242.00*

12 pages Monthly Founded: 1997

16570 Southern California Marketing Media Communications Report
Southern California Marketing Media
5 Via Caseta
Rancho Santa Margarita, CA 92688-4947

949-713-3188
FAX: 714-713-3188
gklayman@pacbell.net

Gary Klayman, Publisher

Written to report on marketing strategies, techniques and new products for the Southern California area, includes various company, client and media updates, new trends, and guides to developing individualized marketing programs. *$15.00*

Monthly
Circulation: 3,000

16571 Subscription Marketing
Blue Dolphin Communications
526 Boston Post Road
Wayland, MA 01778-1833
978-358-5795
FAX: 508-358-5795
subs@bluedolphin.com
www.bluedolphin.com

Donald L Nicholas, Publisher

Offers trade strategies for maximizing product profitability. Provides perspective on success and failure stories. *$195.00*

Monthly

16572 Supermarket News
Fairchild Publications
750 3rd Ave
New York, NY 10017-2703
212-304-4274
FAX: 212-630-4201 800-204-4515
customerservice@fairchildpub.com
http://www.supermarketnews.com

Dan Bagan, Publishing Director
David Merrefield, Editorial Director
Mary Berner, CEO/President *$44.50*

40 pages Weekly Founded: 1892
Circulation: 36346

16573 Sys Admin
CMP Media
1601 W 23rd Street
Suite 200
Lawrence, KS 66046
785-838-3126
FAX: 785-841-2047 800-444-4881
webmaster@sysadminmag.com
http://www.sysadminmag.com

Amber Ankerhola, Editor-in-Chief
Trice Alford, Sales Manager
Edwin Rothrock, Publisher
Bob Cucciniello, Marketing Manager

SYS ADMIN serves the Unix and Linux system administration market. *$55.90*

100 pages Monthly Founded: 1992 27000 names $195 per M.
Printed in on glossy stock

16574 TODAY - The Journal of Work Process Improvement
Recognition Technologies Users Association
185 Devonshire Street
Suite 770
Boston, MA 02110-1407
617-426-1167
FAX: 617-521-8675
info@tawpi.org http://www.tawpi.org

Dan Bolita, Editor
Frank Moran, CEO/President
Jason Glass, VP Sales *$27.69*

Founded: 1997
Circulation: 5000 Audited
Printed in 2 colors on glossy stock

16575 Target Marketing
North American Publishing Company
410 N Broad Street
Philadelphia, PA 19108-1087
215-238-5300
FAX: 215-238-5270
editor.tm@napco.com
http://www.targetmarketingmag.com

Peggy Hatch, Publisher
Lisa Yorgey, Managing Editor
Ned Broski, CEO
Drew James, Sales Manager

Covers telemarketing, list rental, testing and management, circulation, catalogue and online/web marketing, and direct response advertising. *$65.00*

Monthly
Circulation: 42,000

16576 Telemarketing & Call Center Solutions
Technology Marketing Corporation
oneTechnology Plaza
Norwalk, CT 06854-1924
203-852-6800
FAX: 203-853-2845 800-243-6002
tmc@tmcnet.com
http://www.tmcnet.com

Nadji Tehrani, President
Linda Driscoll, Editor

First and only authoritative guide to effective and profitable marketing through business telecommunications. Provides information on technology and services releases, new techniques and management strategies. *$7.00*
24 times Founded: 1972
Circulation: 31419

16577 The DMA Quarterly Business Review
Direct Marketing Association
1120 Avenue of the Americas
New York, NY 10036-6700
212-768-7277
FAX: 212-302-6714 www.the-dma.org
Anne B Frankel, Editor
Peter A Johnson, Editor
Provides up-to-date economic performance indicators and business trends for the Direct and Interactive Marketing Industry. *$19.95*
Quarterly

16578 Velocity
Strategic Account Management Association
150 N Wacker Drive
Suite 2222
Chicago, IL 60606-1608
312-251-3131
FAX: 312-251-3132
http://www.strategicaccounts.org
Katherine Gotsick, Marketing Manager
Tom Johnson, Chairperson
Michelle Lapierre, Secretary
Lisa Napolitano, CEO/President
Velocity is a quarterly magazine dedicated to exploring the latest in trends, practices and research regarding customer-supplier relationship management. Sections of the magazine include: Technology, Best Practices, Global, Strategic Account Management Toolbox, Measurement, Customer Viewpoint, and Case Study. Distributed in both, hardcopy and electronic format. *$95.00*
52 pages Quarterly Founded: 1964
Circulation: 2000
Printed in 4 colors
Computerized version available: PDF

16579 Wireless for the Corporate User
Probe Research
3 Wing Drive
Suite 240
Cedar Knolls, NJ 07927-1000
973-285-1500
FAX: 973-285-1519
Jack Killion, Publisher
Edited for the corporate user/decision maker to keep abreast of the growth product and service offerings, the expanding uses and the technological, political and standardization issues of the wireless arena.
Circulation: 43000

16580 World Trade
BNP Media II, L.L.C.
2401 W Big Beaver Road
Suite 700
Troy, MI 48084-3333
248-362-3700
FAX: 248-362-0317
shistern@bnpmedia.com
www.worldtrademag.com
Neil Shister, Editorial Director
Lara L Sowinski, Managing Editor
$37.00
58 pages Monthly

16581 inMarketing
Direct Marketing Association
1120 Avenue of the Americas
New York, NY 10036-6700
212-768-7277
FAX: 212-302-6714
inMarketing@the-dma.org
www.the-dma.org/inmarketing/
Bill Pryor, Advertising
Provides DMA members with an opportunity to read articles from the best and the brightest practitioners in the industry.
Monthly

Trade Shows

16582 Annual Conference on Healthcare Marketing
Alliance for Healthcare Strategy & Marketing
11 S LaSalle Street
Suite 2300
Chicago, IL 60603
312-704-9700
FAX: 312-704-9709
www.alliancehlth.org/hlthmktg
Workshop and social events plus 50 exhibits of marketing communications, health care information lines, stategic planning and more.
600 Attendees Annual Founded: 1984

16583 Business Intelligence Conference
The Conference Board
845 Third Avenue
New York, NY 10022
212-339-0345
FAX: 212-836-9740
www.conference-board.org/intelligence.htm
Shows how you can utilize business intelligence in your own organization to enhance performace and drive results.
June, Chicago

16584 DM Days New York Conference and Expo
Direct Marketing Association
1120 Avenue of the Americas
New York, NY 10036-6700
212-790-1500
FAX: 212-302-7643
customerservice@the-dma.org
www.the-dma.org
Kevin Fox, Exhibits/Sponsorships
Paul McDonnough, Program Inquiries
Leaves you better equipped to make your integration seamless and transparent to your customer-and make them come back to you.
June

16585 DMB: Direct Marketing to Business Conference
Target Conference Corporation
11 Riverbend Drive S
Stamford, CT 06907-0949
203-358-9900
FAX: 203-358-5815
Ed Berkowitz
National conference for business to business direct marketers. 75 table tops
1000+ Attendees March
Mailing list available for rent

16586 Direct Marketing Association Annual Conference and Exhibition
1120 Avenue of Americas
New York, NY 10036-8002
212-768-7277
FAX: 212-398-6725
Anna Cheknis, Market Research Associate
John Greco Jr, Chief Executive Officer
3,500 exhibitors with 750 booths offering the newest products, information, resources and services for the direct marketing related industries.
10M Attendees October

16587 Direct Marketing Association Spring Conference and Exhibit
1120 Avenue of the Americas
14th Floor
New York, NY 10036-6713
212-768-7277
Jeffrey Wood, Conference Planning
John Greco Jr, Chief Executive Officer
130 booths of companies who are suppliers to direct marketers and solicit businesses and consumers.
2M Attendees March

16588 Direct Marketing Conference National Conference
DMB Miami
Fontainebleau Hilton Resort and Towers
Miami, FL 33152
203-358-3751
800-927-5007
Information on improving R.O.I. and stay ahead of the competition, create customer centric business, synthesize traditional marketing strategies with the internet.

16589 Exhibitor
Exhibitor Magazine
206 S Broadway
Suite 745
Rochester, MN 55904-6565
507-289-6556
FAX: 507-289-5253 888-235-6155
shaasis@aol.com
www.exhibitoronline.com
Sue Haasis, Conference Operations Manager
A top choice for serious education, hands-on training, new product launches, career networking, and special access to industry experts and thought leaders.
March 25-29 Las Vegas

16590 MDMA's Annual Direct Marketing Conference & Expo
Midwest Direct Marketing Association
4248 Park Glen Road
Minneapolis, MN 55416-4758
952-928-4643
FAX: 952-929-1318
mdma@mdma.org www.mdma.org
Amy Selheim, Executive Director
Containing 55 booths and 50 companies exhibiting.
450 Attendees April
Mailing list available for rent 1.1M+ names

16591 Marketing Education Conclave
Marketing Education Center
1375 King Avenue
Columbus, OH 43212-2220
614-486-6708
FAX: 614-486-1819 800-448-0398
service@mark-ed.com
www.mark-ed.com

Carmel Martin, Manager
Containing 20 booths and 15 exhibits.
500 Attendees June Founded: 1971

16592 Marketing Federation's Annual Conference on Strategic Marketing
Marketing Federation
109 58th Avenue
Saint Petersburg, FL 33706-2203
727-363-7805
FAX: 727-367-6545
Greg Stemm
Offers attendees information on how to boost attendance at their seminars, conferences and expositions.

16593 NCDM Conferences National Center for Database Marketing
Primedia Business Exhibitions
11 River Bend S
PO Box 4254
Stamford, CT 06907
203-358-9900
FAX: 203-358-5815
www.ncdmsummer.com or
www.ncdmwinter.com
Ed Berkowitz, Director Sales
A conference offering a highly qualified audience of database marketing decision-makers from all over the country, including a high concentration of marketers from the Midwest and West coast. Containing 210 booths and 100 exhibits.
2500 Attendees July/December

16594 National Center for Database Marketing Con ference & Exhibition
Direct Marketing Association
1120 Avenue of the Americas
New York, NY 10036-6700
203-358-3702
ed_berkowitz@primediabusiness.com
www.ncdmwinter.com or
www.ncdmsummer.com
Ed Berkowitz, Sales Director
Offers strategies and tactics for getting your message to the right consumers.

16595 National Hispanic Market Trade Show and Media Expo (Se Habla Espanol)
Hispanic Business
360 S Hope Avenue
Suite 300C
Santa Barbara, CA 93105-4031
805-563-1049
FAX: 805-687-4546
info@hispanstar.com
www.hispanstar.com
Luisa Donis, Corporate Communications
Annual show of 100 exhibitors of market/research, media, advertising, public relations, information services and recruitment.
1500 Attendees

16596 National Mail Order Merchandise Show
Expo Accessories
47 Main Avenue
Clifton, NJ 07014-1917
973-661-9681
Martin Deeks, Show Manager
300 booths.
5M Attendees January

16597 PROMO Live
Prism Business Media
PROMO Live
11 River Bend South
Stamford, CT 06907
508-743-0105
FAX: 508-759-4552 800-927-5007
registration@prism2b.com
www.thepromoevent.com
Kim Stolfi, Conference/Show Coordinator
Florence Torres, Conference Program Manager
Oct Chicago

16598 Photo Marketing Association International
3000 Picture Place
Jackson, MI 49201
517-788-8100
FAX: 517-788-8371
pma_education@pmai.org
www.pmai.org
Ted Fox, Executive Director
Mary Anne LaMarre, Operations Officer
Containing 3,230 booths and 645 exhibits. Promoting the growth of the photography industry through coorperation.
24M Attendees February

16599 Private Equity Analyst Conference
Dow Jones Financial Information Services
800 Harborside Financial Center
Plaza 2
Jersey City, NJ 07311
866-291-1800
The forum to meet the Heneral Partners, Institutional investment professionals and senior executives defining the industry landscape.
Sept New York

16600 Promo Expo
Promo Expo Sales
The Navy Pier
Chicago, IL 60606
FAX: 203-358-3751 800-927-5007
The largest conference and exhibition dedicated to the promotion marketing industry, and the one event where you can meet with over four thousand promotion marketing decision makers.
October

16601 Publishers Multinational Direct Conference
1501 3rd Avenue
New York, NY 10028-2101
212-734-7040
FAX: 212-986-3757
Alfred Goodloe, President
Offers publishers information and seminars on how to build sales and profits in foreign markets.
March

16602 Wall Street on Linux/Open Source
Flagg Management
353 Lexington Avenue
New York, NY 10016
212-286-0333
FAX: 212-286-0086
flaggmgmnt@msn.com
www.flaggmgmt.com
Russell Flagg, President
1000 Attendees February Founded: 2001

Directories & Databases

16603 ADWEEK Directory
ADWEEK
770 Broadway
7th Floor
New York, NY 10003
646-545-5220
FAX: 646-654-5351
publisher@adweek.com
www.adweek.com
Mitch Tebo, Directory Publisher
For anyone seeking agency-specific information. Over 29,000 personnel listings, more the 6,000 full service advertising agencies and networks, public relations firms, media buying services, recruitment entertainment marketing, yellow pages, health care, interactive, sports marketing, infomercials, direct marketing, creative design, marketing communications and research, consultancies and many more media related listings.

16604 Affluent Markets Alert
EPM Communications
488 E 18th Street
Brooklyn, NY 11226-6702
FAX: 718-469-7124
Offers complete coverage on affluent market trends containing complete contact and price information on books, monographs, journals and newspapers.
Full-text

16605 AmericanProfile
Donnelley Marketing Information Services
70 Seaview Avenue
#10250
Stamford, CT 06902-6036
203-259-9801
FAX: 203-553-7276 800-866-2255
Jeff Knebel, Marketing Manager
A database retrieval and reporting system that contains 1980 and 1990 census data, current year updates and 5-year projections of selected demographic characteristics and proprietary statistics.
Numeric

16606 Annual Directory of Marketing Information Companies
American Demographics
PO Box 4949
Stamford, CT 06907-0949
203-358-9900
Offers a list of firms offering demographic and research services, data retrieval and analysis, market evaluation and forecasting.
Annual
Circulation: 5,000

16607 Annual Mail Order Sales Directory & Mail Order 750 Report
Marketing Logistics
1460 Cloverdale Avenue
Highland Park, IL 60035-2817
847-831-1575
Arnold L Fishman, President
This comprehensive directory offers a list of mail order businesses reporting at least 5 million dollars in annual sales. The 750 report gives mail order companies, businesses

and mail order catalogs, 250 listings of each. *$1095.00*
Annual

16608 Boomer Report
FIND/SVP
625 6th Avenue
New York, NY 10011
212-645-4500
FAX: 212-645-7681 800-346-3787
With over 77 million baby boomers, this report carefully tracks news stories, market surveys, and interviews the experts to help you spot opportunities and position your products. *$195.00*
8 pages Monthly

16609 Bradford's Directory of Marketing Research Agencies & Consultants
Bradford's Directory of Marketing Research Agency
9991 Caitlin Center
Manassas, VA 20110-4282
703-614-4000

Thomas Bradford, Owner
Over 2,500 companies that are involved in management or market research are listed. *$90.00*
400 pages Biennial
Circulation: 5,000

16610 Business Marketing Association Membership Directory & Yellow Pages
Business Marketing Association
400 N Michigan Avenue
Suite 1510
Chicago, IL 60611
312-220-0005
FAX: 312-409-4262 800-664-4262
rkean@marketing.org
www.marketing.org
Offers information on over 4,500 member business communications professionals in the field of advertising, marketing communications and marketing. *$50.00*
Annual
Circulation: 7,500

16611 Catalog Connection
Holy B Pasiuk
PO Box 1427
Guilford, CT 06437-0527

Over 400 companies that supply catalogs of their merchandise to consumers and businesses are profiled in this directory.
55 pages Biennial

16612 Catalog Handbook
Enterprise Magazines
1020 N Broadway
Suite 111
Milwaukee, WI 53202-3157
414-272-9977
FAX: 414-272-9973
Maria Lahm, Editor
Betsy L Green, Publisher
Marsha Poulsen, Administrative Assistant
Offers information on companies that offer product catalogs. *$6.99*
106 pages Quarterly Founded: 1989
Circulation: 30,000

16613 Complete Directory of Mail Order Catalog Products
Sutton Family Communications & Publishing Company
155 Sutton Lane
Fordsville, KY 42343
270-740-0870

jlsutton@apex.net
www.fleamarketeer.net
Theresa Sutton, Editor
Lee Sutton, General Manager
Print-out from database of wholesalers, manufacturers, distributors, importers and close-out houses. Database is updated daily to guarantee the most current and up-to-date sources available. *$157.50*
100+ pages

16614 Directory Marketplace
Todd Publications
PO Box 635
Nyack, NY 10960-0635
845-358-6213
FAX: 845-358-1059 toddpub@aol.com
Barry Klein, Editor
Directories and Reference Books for business, education, and libraries; news of new directories. *$25.00*
Bi-Monthly Founded: 1987

16615 Directory of Franchising Organizations
Pilot Books
127 Sterling Avenue
PO Box 2102
Greenport, NY 11944
631-477-0978
FAX: 631-477-0978 800-797-4568
Over 1,300 current franchise opportunities in 45 categories. *$12.95*
Annual ISBN 0-875762-15-8

16616 Directory of Mail Order Catalogs
Grey House Publishing
185 Millerton Road
PO Box 860
Millerton, NY 12546
518-890-0526
FAX: 518-789-0545 800-562-2139
books@greyhouse.com
www.greyhouse.com
Leslie Mackenzie, Publisher
Richard Gottlieb, Editor
The premier source of information on the mail order catalog industry. Covers over 12,000 consumer and business catalog companies with 44 different product chapters from Animals to Toys and Games. *$350.00*
1600 pages Annual Founded: 1980 ISBN 1-592370-66-7

16617 Food & Beverage Market Place
Grey House Publishing
185 Millerton Road
PO Box 860
Millerton, NY 12546
518-890-0526
FAX: 518-789-0545 800-562-2139
books@greyhouse.com
www.foodmp.com
Leslie Mackenzie, Publisher
Richard Gottlieb, Editor
This information packed three-volume set is the most powerful buying and marketing guide for the US food and beverage industry. Includes thousands of industry freight and transportation listings. *$595.00*
6500 pages Annual

16618 GreenBook: Worldwide of Market Research Companies and Services
NY American Marketing Association
116 East 27th Street
6th Floor
New York, NY 10016-1799
212-687-3280
FAX: 212-202-7920 800-792-9202
info@greenbook.org
www.greenbook.org
Lucas Pospichal, Managing Director
Nancy Cardenas, Account Coordinator
Comprehensive listings of over 1,500 market research firms in the US and Canada. Listings in over 300 service categories and market industries. The most reliable reference resource for buyers of marketing research services. *$350.00*
880 pages Yearly Founded: 1962
Circulation: 4,500

16619 International Directory of Marketing Research Companies & Services
New York Chapter/American Marketing Association
310 Madison Avenue
New York, NY 10017-6009
212-986-1418

Offers more than 1,500 marketing research consultants and suppliers of marketing research data. *$105.00*
600 pages Annual
Circulation: 6,000

16620 International Network Marketing Reference Book & Resource Directory
MLM Group Publications
12 Rose Center
Norwood, MA 02062-2603

Offers valuable information on over 800 companies in the multi-level marketing industry. *$15.75*
85 pages

16621 Leadership Library on Internet and CD-ROM
Leadership Directories
104 5th Avenue
New York, NY 10011
212-627-4140
FAX: 212-645-0931
info@leadershipdirectories.com
www.leadershipdirectories.com
James M Petrie, Associate Publisher
David Hurvitz, Chief Executive Officer
Makes all 14 leadership directories available over the Internet and on CD-ROM in one integrated directory. They provide subscribers with complete contact information in one database. Subscription includes Internet access and four CD-ROM editions quarterly. *$3065.00*
Updated Daily Founded: 1999
Mailing list available for rent
Printed in A colors on B stock

16622 MDMA Membership and Resource Directory
Midwest Direct Marketing Association
4248 Park Glen Road
Minneapolis, MN 55416-4758
952-928-4643
FAX: 952-929-1318 mdma@mdma.org

Lavinia Johnson, President

400 pages April
Mailing list available for rent 1.1M+ names

16623 Mail Order Business Directory
B Klein Publishers
PO Box 8503
Coral Springs, FL 33075-8503

Bernard Klein, Editor

A listing of over 12,000 corporations in the US and 500 international firms doing business by mail order and catalogs. *$95.00*
400 pages Annual

16624 Mail Order Product Guide
Todd Publications
PO Box 635
Nyack, NY 10960-0635
845-358-6213
800-747-1086
A listing of over 1,500 manufacturers and importers to the mail order industry worldwide. *$50.00*
250 pages Triennial
Circulation: 5,000

16625 Marketing Guidebook
Trade Dimensions
45 Danbury Road
Wilton, CT 06897-4445
203-563-3000
FAX: 860-563-3131
info@tradedimensions.com
www.tradedimensions.com

Lynda Gutierrez, Managing Editor
Jane Sheulin, Editor

The 'blue book' sales and marketing professionals have depended on for 30 years. The directory details the supermarket industry from distribution standpoint, comprising over 800 profiles, organized into 52 market areas. Includes all grocery chains and wholesalers that do a minimum of $30 million in sales. Also includes food brokers, non-food distributors, and small wholesalers in each market. *$340.00*
Annual

16626 Marketing Made Easier: Directory of Mailing List Companies
Todd Publications
PO Box 635
Nyack, NY 10960-0635
845-358-6213
FAX: 845-358-3203 800-747-1056
toddpubQ@aol.com
toddpublications.com

Barry Klein, Editor

Over 1,100 companies that sell mailing lists and the type of lits they handle. *$55.00*
100 pages Biennial Founded: 1972 ISBN 0-915344-83-1
Circulation: 5,000
Mailing list available for rent 1,000 names $100 per M.
Printed in 2 colors
Computerized version available: Mac

16627 Marketing Tools Directory
American Demographics
PO Box 4949
Stamford, CT 06907-0949
203-358-9900
FAX: 607-273-3196 800-832-1486
List of firms offering demographic and research services, data retrieval, and analysis, market evaluation and forecasting media services.
Annual

16628 Marketing and Sales Career Directory
Gale Research
27500 Drake Road
Farmington Hills, MI 48331
248-699-4253
FAX: 248-699-8214 800-877-4253
galeord@gale.com www.gale.com
Over 300 companies and organizations that offer job opportunities and internships in the marketing industry are profiled. *$34.00*
340 pages

16629 Marketing on a Shoestring: Low-Cost Tips for Marketing Products & Services
John Wiley & Sons
111 River Street
Hoboken, NJ 07030
201-748-6000
FAX: 201-748-6088 800-825-7550
customer@wiley.com www.wiley.com
Business and professional associations that can assist individuals or companies in improving their marketing are profiled. *$14.95*
236 pages

16630 Mediaweek Directory
ADWEEK
770 Broadway
7th Floor
New York, NY 10003
646-545-5220
FAX: 646-654-5351
publisher@adweek.com
www.adweek.com

Mitch Tebo, Directory Publisher

Focuses on the most powerful segments covering 9,000 media companies from the top 100 media markets for radio, broadcast TV, cable TV and daily newspapers. Also includes the top 300 consumer magazines, the top 150 trade magazines, networks, syndicators, sales representatives, multi-media holding companies, trade associations and rating organizations.

16631 National Agri-Marketing Association
11020 King Street
Suite 205
Overland Park, KS 66210-1201
913-491-6500
FAX: 913-491-6502
agrimktg@nama.org www.nama.org

Eldon White, Chief Executive Officer
Dawn Foster, Contact

2500 pages Annual Spring Founded: 1956

16632 National Directory of Addresses and Telephone Numbers
Omnigraphics
2500 Penobscot Building
Detroit, MI 48226
313-961-1340

This new edition provides the most current names and addresses for businesses and services throughout the United States, arranged alphabetically and by business type. *$60.00*
1,500 pages Hardcover ISBN 0-780800-20-6

16633 National Trade and Professional Associations of the United States
Columbia Books
1212 New York Avenue NW
Suite 330
Washington, DC 20005-3987
202-641-1662
FAX: 202-898-0775 888-265-0600
info@columbiabooks.com
www.columbiabooks.com

Buck Downs, Senior Editor

Lists 7,600 national trade associations, professional societies and labor unions. Five convenient indexes enable you to look up associations by subject, budget, geographic area, acronym and executive director. Other features include: contract information, serial publications, upcoming convention schedule, membership/staff size, budget figures, and background information. *$99.00*
Annual Feburary 15,000 names $10 per M.

16634 New Marketing Opportunities
New Editions International
PO Box 2578
Sedona, AZ 86339-2578
928-282-9574
FAX: 928-282-9730 800-777-4751
newedit@sedona.net
www.newagemarket.com

Sophia Tarila, Author
Pat Bush, CEO

7,000 New Age and Metaphysical publishers, events, retailers, distributors, services, publications, reviewers, catalogers, media connections, internet connections, associations and other resources. *$139.95*
Annual ISBN 0-944773-18-4
Mailing list available for rent
Computerized version available: CD ROM

16635 Procter & Gamble Marketing Alumni Directory
Ward Howell International
300 S Wacker Drive
Suite 2940
Chicago, IL 60606-6703

Membership directory listings.
120 pages Annual

16636 Quirk's Marketing Research Review
Quirk Enterprises
PO Box 23536
Minneapolis, MN 55423-0536
952-854-5101
FAX: 612-854-8191 www.quirks.com

Thomas Quirk, Publisher
Evan Tweed, Associate Publisher
Joseph Rydholm, Editor

Publishing case histories and discussions of techniques which can be used by purchasers of research products and services. Also directories of research services. Accepts advertising. *$60.00*
64 pages 11 per year
Circulation: 15,500
Mailing list available for rent 15.5M names
Printed in 4 colors on glossy stock

16637 Research Alert
EPM Communications
160 Mercer Street
New York, NY 10012-3208
212-941-0099
FAX: 212-941-1622
Offers a list of companies that conduct marketing studies to analyze trends, lifestyles and prospective markets. *$369.00*

BiWeekly

16638 Shop-at-Home Directory
Belcaro Group
7100 E Belvue
Suite 305
Greenwood Village, CO 80111

Marc Braunstein, President

This valuable informational source offers information on over 400 companies that offer direct mail order sales. *$3.00*
60 pages SemiAnnual

16639 State and Regional Associations of the United States
Columbia Books
1212 New York Avenue NW
Suite 330
Washington, DC 20005-3987
202-641-1662
FAX: 202-898-0775 888-265-0600
info@columbiabooks.com
www.columbiabooks.com

Buck Downs, Senior Editor

Lists 7,200 of the largest and most significant state and regional trade and professional organizations in the US Look up associations by subject, budget, state, acronym, or chief executive. Also lists contract information, serial publications, upcoming convention schedule, membership/staff size, budget figures, and background information. *$79.00*
Annual March 10,000 names $10 per M.

Industry Web Sites

16640 www.adweek.com
Adweek

Leading decision makers in the advertising and marketing field go to Adweek.Com everyday for breaking news, insight, buzz, opinion, analysis, research and classifieds. The resources of all six regional editions of Adweek, as well as the national edition of Brandweek are combined with the knowledge of our online editors and the multimedia/interactive capabilities of the web to deliver vital information quickly and effectively to our target audience.

16641 www.ama.org
American Marketing Association

Represents marketers and keeps members informed of trends in advertising. Fosters research, sponsors seminars and provides educational placement service.

16642 www.apmaw.org
Assn of Promotion Marketing Agencies Worldwide

A trade association of sales promotion agencies with at least two years experience.

16643 www.assist-intl.com
Assist International

International trade promotion and consulting firm: mailing lists, seminars, conferences, international business expo.

16644 www.awmanet.org
American Wholesale Marketers Association

Government affairs, trade shows, publications, and products.

16645 www.cherrymkt.org
Cherry Marketing Institute

An organization providing cherry information and promoting material to food manufacturers, food service operators and others.

16646 www.fmi.org
Food Marketing Institute

Events, publications, industry and consumer information and media.

16647 www.greyhouse.com
Grey House Publishing

Selected Grey House directories in the fields of business, health and education are available online. Users can search our online databases by several different search criteria, such as product categories, geographic area, sales volume and much, much more. Full Grey House catalog and online ordering also available.

16648 www.inma.org
International Newspaper Marketing Association

Individuals in marketing, circulation, research and public relations of newspapers.

16649 www.manronline.org
Manufacturers Agents National Association

A national organization for manufacturer's agents and manufacturers who contract for the services of these representatives.

16650 www.mark-ed.org
Marketing Education Center

Committed to education for and about marketing. Provides professional support and training materials. Primary clients are schools, colleges, and educational institutions.

16651 www.marketing.org
Business Marketing Association

Pre-eminent service organization for professional's in this vital industry.

16652 www.mlmia.com
Multi-Level Marketing International Association

Seeks to strengthen and improve the multi-level marketing industry in the United States and abroad.

16653 www.msi.org
Marketing Science Institute

Seeks to improve marketing practice and education, conducts research.

16654 www.nacda.com
National Assn of Collegiate Marketing Admin.

Members are public relations and marketing professionals in college and university athletic departments. Promotes standards and provides professional support.

16655 www.pdma.org
Product Development and Management Association

International association serving those with a professional interest in improving the management of product innovation.

16656 www.pma.com
Produce Marketing Association

Products and services, issues and information, conventions and expos.

16657 www.pmc-ny.com
Premium Marketing Club of New York

Provides education and networking opportunities for members from all areas of the marketing field

16658 www.printing.org
Graphic Arts Marketing Information Service

A section of Printing Industries of American that provides market research and statistics to its members. Research is member selected and directed.

16659 www.promax.tv
PROMAX

International association of promotion and marketing, professionals in electronic media. Promotes the effectiveness of promotion and marketing within the industry and the academic community.

16660 www.retailing.com
Electronic Retailing Association

Members include infomercial producers, marketers, product developers, broadcasters and other industries serving the infomercial market.

16661 www.riahome
Research Institute of America

A national organization that focuses on marketing and sales intelligence for top level marketing executives.

16662 www.sigma.org
Society of Independent Gasoline Marketers

Members are independent gasoline marketers.

16663 www.smps.org
Society for Marketing Professional Services

Promotes new business development of architectural, engineering, planning, design and construction management firms.

16664 www.strategicaccounts.org
Strategic Account Management Association

Dedicated to the professional and personal development of the executives charged with managing national, global, and strategic account relationships, and to elevating the status of the profession as a whole.

16665 www.teleport.com
International Trade Resources

An overview of the steps required to market abroad. Updated guide to the web's best global business sites and more.

16666 www.the-dma.org
Direct Marketing Association

Leading global trade association of business and nonprofit organizations using and supporting direct marketing tools and techniques.

16667 www.tpnregister.com
TPN Register

Business to business marketplace.

International Trade Resources

16668 Albania Mission to the United Nations
320 E 79th Street
New York, NY 10021
212-249-2059

Geronimo Albano, Owner

16669 Austrian Trade Commission
500 N Michigan Avenue
Suite 1950
Chicago, IL 60611
312-644-5556

Peter Athanasiadis, Manager

16670 Barbados Trade Commission
800 2nd Avenue
2nd Floor
New York, NY 10017
212-867-8435

June Clark, Manager

16671 Belize Mission to the United Nations
800 2nd Avenue
Suite 400 G
New York, NY 10017
212-837-7482

Mohamed Latheef, Manager

16672 Botswana Embassy
1531 New Hampshire Avenue NW
Washington, DC 20036
202-244-4990

Lapolang Caesar Lekoa, President

16673 British Trade and Investment Office
845 3rd Avenue
9th Floor
New York, NY 10022
212-745-0495

16674 Bulgarian General Consulate
121 E 62nd Street
New York, NY 10021
212-935-4646

16675 Business Council for the United Nations
801 2nd Avenue
2nd Floor
New York, NY 10017
212-661-1772

16676 Chile Trade Commission
866 United Nations Plaza
Suite 603
New York, NY 10017
212-980-3366

Oscar Fuentes, Manager

16677 Colombia Government Trade Bureau
277 Park Avenue
47th Floor
New York, NY 10172
212-223-1120

16678 Consulate General of Bahrain
866 2nd Avenue
14th Floor
New York, NY 10017
212-236-6200

Jassim Buallay, Manager

16679 Consulate General of Belgium
235 Peachtree Street NE
N Tower, Suite 850
Atlanta, GA 30303
404-659-9611

Piet Morisse, Manager

16680 Consulate General of Bolivia
211 E 43rd Street
Suite 702
New York, NY 10017
212-599-6767
FAX: 212-687-0532
Jorge Heredia Cavero, Manager

16681 Consulate General of Brazil
1185 Avenue of the Americas
21st Floor
New York, NY 10036-2601
917-777-7777

Julio Cesar Gomes Dos Sant, Manager

16682 Consulate General of Costa Rica
80 Wall Street
Suite 718
New York, NY 10005
212-509-3066

Otto Barcas, Manager

16683 Consulate General of Germany
871 United Nations Plaza
New York, NY 10017
212-610-9700

Bernhard Von Der Planit, Manager

16684 Consulate General of Haiti
271 Madison Avenue
17th Floor
New York, NY 10016
212-697-9767

Marie Therese, Manager

16685 **Consulate General of Honduras**
80 Wall Street
Suite 415
New York, NY 10005
212-490-2722

16686 **Consulate General of India**
3 E 64th Street
New York, NY 10021
212-774-0600

16687 **Consulate General of Indonesia**
5 E 68th Street
New York, NY 10021
212-879-0600

16688 **Consulate General of Israel**
800 2nd Avenue
New York, NY 10017
212-499-5000

16689 **Consulate General of Kenya**
424 Madison Avenue
Suite 1401
New York, NY 10017
212-538-8191

Rolando Visconti, Manager

16690 **Consulate General of Lebanon**
9 E 76th Street
New York, NY 10021
212-744-7905

Hassan Saad, Manager

16691 **Consulate General of Lithuania**
420 5th Avenue
3rd Floor
New York, NY 10018
212-354-7840

Rimantas Morkvenas, Manager

16692 **Consulate General of Malta**
249 E 35th Street
New York, NY 10016
212-425-2345

16693 **Consulate General of Morocco**
1821 Jefferson Place NW
Washington, DC 20036
202-736-1000

Ramon Xilotl, Manager

16694 **Consulate General of Nicaragua**
820 2nd Avenue
Suite 802
New York, NY 10017
212-986-6562

Jose Flores, Manager

16695 **Consulate General of Nigeria**
828 2nd Avenue
New York, NY 10017
212-808-0301

16696 **Consulate General of Paraguay**
211 E 43rd Street
Suite 2101
New York, NY 10017
212-682-9441

Juan Baiardi, Manager

16697 **Consulate General of Peru**
215 Lexington Avenue
21st Floor
New York, NY 10016
212-481-7410

16698 **Consulate General of Qatar**
809 United Nations Plaza
4th Floor
New York, NY 10017
212-486-9335

16699 **Consulate General of Saudi Arabia**
866 United Nations Plaza
Suite 480
New York, NY 10017
212-980-3366

Abdulrahman Gdaia, Excellency

16700 **Consulate General of Slovenia**
600 3rd Avenue
24th Floor
New York, NY 10016
212-370-3007

Reimo Pettai, Manager

16701 **Consulate General of South Africa**
333 E 38th Street
9th Floor
New York, NY 10016
917-493-8950

16702 **Consulate General of St. Lucia**
800 2nd Avenue
9th Floor
New York, NY 10017
212-499-5000

Julian Hunte, Manager

16703 **Consulate General of Switzerland**
633 3rd Avenue
30th Floor
New York, NY 10017
212-599-5700

Raymond Loretan, Excellency

16704 **Consulate General of Trinidad & Tobago**
733 3rd Avenue
Suite 1716
New York, NY 10017-3204
212-682-7272

Hon Harold Robertson, Contact

16705 **Consulate General of Ukraine**
240 E 49th Street
New York, NY 10017
212-371-5690

16706 **Consulate General of Uruguay**
747 3rd Avenue
21st Floor
New York, NY 10017
212-935-9000

Basil Bryan, Manager

16707 **Consulate General of Venezuela**
7 E 51st Street
New York, NY 10022
212-826-1660

16708 **Consulate General of the Commonwealth of the Bahamas**
231 E 46th Street
2nd Floor
New York, NY 10017
212-717-5643

Hon Eldred E Bethel, Contact

16709 **Consulate General of the Dominican Republic**
1501 Broadway
4th Floor, Suite 410
New York, NY 10036
212-698-8899

16710 **Consulate General of the Netherlands**
1 Rockefeller Plaza
11th Floor
New York, NY 10020-2094
212-246-1429

Wanda Fleck, Manager

16711 **Consulate General of the Principality of Monaco**
565 5th Avenue
New York, NY 10017
212-286-0500

Magguy Maccario-Doyle, Manager

16712 **Consulate General of the Republic of Croatia**
369 Lexington Avenue
11th Floor
New York, NY 10017
212-972-2277

Abdul Seraj, Manager

16713 Consulate General of the Republic of Belarus
708 3rd Avenue
21st Floor
New York, NY 10017
212-682-5392

Sergei Kolos, Manager

16714 Consulate General of the Russian Federation
9 E 91st Street
New York, NY 10128
212-371-8222

16715 Consulate of Guyana
866 United Nations Plaza
New York, NY 10017
212-527-3215

Brentnold Evans, Manager

16716 Consulate of the Republic of Uzbekistan
866 United Nations Plaza
Suite 327-A
New York, NY 10017-7671
212-754-6178

16717 Cyprus Trade Commission
13 E 40th Street
New York, NY 10016
212-213-9100

Klio Demetriou, Manager

16718 Department of Trade- Government of Antigua & Barbuda
610 5th Avenue
Suite 311
New York, NY 10020
212-541-4117

16719 Ecuadorian Consulate
800 2nd Avenue
Suite 600
New York, NY 10017
212-808-0170

16720 Egyptian Consulate Economic & Commercial Office
45 Rockefeller Plaza
Suite 1507
New York, NY 10111
212-332-2570

Ayden Nour, Executive Director

16721 Embassy of Australia
1601 Massachusetts Avenue NW
Washington, DC 20036
202-797-3126

16722 Embassy of Benin
2124 Kalorama Road NW
Washington, DC 20008
202-232-6656

Cyrille Segbe Oguin, President

16723 Embassy of Cambodia
4500 16th Street NW
Washington, DC 20011
202-726-7742

Sereyath Ek, President

16724 Embassy of Estonia
2131 Massachusetts Avenue NW
Washington, DC 20008
202-880-0101

Kalaeikalev Stoicescu, Manager

16725 Embassy of Ethiopia Trade Affairs
3506 International Drive NW
Washington, DC 20008
202-364-1200

Kassahun Ayele, President

16726 Embassy of Finland
3301 Massachusetts Avenue NE
Washington, DC 20008
202-298-5800

Aukka Valtasaari, President

16727 Embassy of Georgia
1615 New Hampshire Avenue NW
Suite 300
Washington, DC 20009
202-387-2390

Levan Mikeladze, President

16728 Embassy of Jamaica (JAMPRO)
520 New Hampshire Avenue NW
Washington, DC 20036
202-452-0660

Gordon Shirley, President

16729 Embassy of Jordan
3504 International Drive NW
Washington, DC 20008
202-966-2664

Briggeneral Sariah, Chief Executive Officer

16730 Embassy of Mali
2130 R Street NW
Washington, DC 20009
202-322-2249

Abdoulaye Diop, President

16731 Embassy of Mongolia
2833 M Street NW
Washington, DC 20007
202-333-7117

Bold Ravdan, President

16732 Embassy of Panama
2862 McGill Terrace NW
Washington, DC 20008
202-387-6154

Francisco Morales, Manager

16733 Embassy of Tanzania
2139 R Street NW
Washington, DC 20008
202-939-6125

Andrew Mhando Daraja, President

16734 Embassy of Tunisia
1515 Massachusetts Avenue NW
Washington, DC 20005
202-862-1850

Mohamed Hachana, President

16735 Embassy of Uganda
5911 16th Street NW
Washington, DC 20011
202-726-7100

Edith Ssempala, President

16736 Embassy of Vietnam
1233 20th Street NW
Suite 400
Washington, DC 20036
202-861-0737

Nguyen Tam Chien, President

16737 Embassy of Zimbabwe
1608 New Hampshire Avenue NW
Washington, DC 20009
202-332-7100

16738 Embassy of the Lao People's Democratic Republic
2222 S Street NW
Washington, DC 20008
202-332-6416

Phanthong Phommahaxay, President

16739 Embassy of the People's Republic of China
2300 Connecticut Avenue NW
Washington, DC 20008
202-456-6764

Zhou Wenzhoung, President

16740 Embassy of the Republic of Angola
1615 M Street NW
Suite 900
Washington, DC 20036
202-785-1156

Josefina Pitra Diakite, President

16741 Embassy of the Republic of Latvia
4325 17th Street NW
Washington, DC 20011
202-726-8213

16742 Embassy of the Republic of Liberia
5201 Colorado Avenue NW
Washington, DC 20011
202-230-0437

Charles Minor, President

16743 Embassy of the Republic of Yemen
2600 Virginia Avenue NW
Suite 705
Washington, DC 20037
202-965-4760

Abdulwahab Al-Hajjri, President

16744 Embassy of the Republic of the Marshall Islands
2433 Massachusetts Avenue NW
Washington, DC 20008
202-234-5414

Banny DeBrum, President

16745 Fiji Mission to United Nations
630 3rd Avenue
7th Floor
New York, NY 10017
212-687-4130

Isikia Savua, Manager

16746 French Trade Commission
1 E Wacker Drive
Suite 3730
Chicago, IL 60601
312-661-1880

16747 Gambia Mission to the United Nations
800 2nd Avenue
Suite 400 F
New York, NY 10017
212-949-6640

B Jagne, Manager

16748 General Consulate of Luxembourg
17 Beekman Place
New York, NY 10022
212-888-6664

Georges Faber, Manager

16749 Gibraltar Information Bureau
1156 15th Street NW
Suite 1100
Washington, DC 20005
202-452-1108

Perry Stieglitz, Executive Director

16750 Greek Trade Commission
150 E 58th Street
17th Floor
New York, NY 10155
212-751-2404

Yannis Papadimitriou, Manager

16751 Grenada Mission (Consulate)
800 2nd Avenue
Suite 400 K
New York, NY 10017
212-599-0301

Lamuel Stanislaus, Manager

16752 Guatemala Trade Office
57 Park Avenue
New York, NY 10017
212-689-1014

Roberto Rosenberg, Manager

16753 Hong Kong Trade Development Council
219 E 46th Street
New York, NY 10017-2951
212-388-8941
FAX: 212-838-8941
mytdc@tdc.org.hk www.tdctrade.com

Louis Epstein, Press Officer
Promotes trade between the United States and Hong Kong.

16754 Hungarian Trade Commission
150 E 58th Street
33rd Floor
New York, NY 10155-3398
212-355-0240

16755 Icelandic Consulate General
800 3rd Avenue
New York, NY 10022
212-593-2700

16756 Irish Trade Board
345 Park Avenue
17th Floor
New York, NY 10154
212-180-0800

Jean McCluskey, Marketing Executive

16757 Italian Trade Commission
499 Park Avenue
New York, NY 10022-1240
212-980-1500
FAX: 212-758-1050
newyork@italtrade.com
www.italtrade.com/ice

Michelle Jones, Editor
Robert Luongo, Executive Director
Developments in the Italian wine industry and market, as well as reviews of imported wines from Italy.

16758 Japanese External Trade Organization
1221 Avenue of the Americas
42nd Floor
New York, NY 10020
212-997-0400

16759 Kazakhstan Mission to the United Nations
866 United Nations Plaza
Suite 586
New York, NY 10017
212-230-1900

16760 Korea Trade Promotion Center
460 Park Avenue
Room 402
New York, NY 10022
212-826-0900

Jae Woo, President

16761 Kyrgyzstan Mission to the United Nations
866 United Nations Plaza
Room 477
New York, NY 10017
212-486-4214

16762 Malaysia Trade Commission
313 E 43rd Street
3rd Floor
New York, NY 10017
212-986-6310

Mohamad Sadik Gany, Manager

16763 Mexico Trade Commission
757 3rd Ave
Ste 2400
New York, NY 10017-2042
212-826-2978

16764 Moldova Mission to the United Nations
573-577 3rd Avenue
15th Floor
New York, NY 10016
212-682-3523

16765 New Zealand Trade Development Board
780 3rd Avenue
Suite 1904
New York, NY 10017-2024
212-832-7420

16766 **Norwegian Trade Council**
800 3rd Avenue
23rd Floor
New York, NY 10022
212-421-9210

16767 **Pakistan Trade Commission**
12 E 65th Street
4th Floor
New York, NY 10021
212-879-5800

Abbas Zaidi, Manager

16768 **Permanent Mission of Bangladesh to the United Nations**
821 United Nations Plaza
8th Floor
New York, NY 10017
212-786-6300

16769 **Permanent Mission of Bhutan to the United Nations**
2 United Nations Plaza
27th Floor
New York, NY 10017
212-486-9191

Francesco Fulci, Manager

16770 **Permanent Mission of Ghana to the United Nations**
19 E 47th Street
New York, NY 10017
212-171-1670

16771 **Permanent Mission of Myanmar (Formerly Burma)**
10 E 77th Street
New York, NY 10021
212-986-6310

Janis Priedkalns, Manager

16772 **Permanent Mission of Saint Vincent & the Grenadines to the United Nations**
800 2nd Avenue
9th Floor
New York, NY 10017
212-599-0950
FAX: 212-599-1020
Margaret H Ferrari, Permanent Representative

16773 **Permanent Mission of the Czech Republic to the United Nations**
1109-1111 Madison Avenue
New York, NY 10028
212-288-0830

16774 **Permanent Mission of the Republic of Sudan to the United Nations**
655 3rd Avenue
Suite 500-10
New York, NY 10017
212-593-0999

Jenine Selson, Manager

16775 **Permanent Mission of the Republic of Armenia to the United Nations**
119 E 36th Street
New York, NY 10016
212-752-3370

Andrezej Towpik, Manager

16776 **Permanent Mission of the Solomon Islands to the United Nations**
800 2nd Avenue
Suite 400
New York, NY 10017
212-949-6640

B Jagne, Manager

16777 **Philippines Commercial Office**
556 5th Avenue
New York, NY 10036
212-764-1330

16778 **Poland Trade Commission**
675 3rd Avenue
19th Floor
New York, NY 10017
212-351-1713

Phyllis Poland, Owner

16779 **Portuguese Trade Commission**
590 5th Avenue
3rd Floor
New York, NY 10036
212-354-4610

16780 **Romanian Consulate General**
200 E 38th Street
New York, NY 10016
212-687-0180

Corina Suteu, Manager

16781 **Singapore Trade Commission**
55 E 59th Street
Suite 21-B
New York, NY 10022
212-421-2200

Kc Yeoh, Executive Director

16782 **Slovak Republic Mission to the United Nations**
866 United Nations Plaza
Suite 493
New York, NY 10017
212-980-1558

16783 **Swedish Trade Council**
150 N Michigan Avenue
Chicago, IL 60601
312-781-6222

Stefam Bergstrom, Manager

16784 **Syrian Arab Republic Embassy**
2215 Wyoming Avenue NW
Washington, DC 20008
202-232-6313

16785 **Taiwan Trade Center**
1 Penn Plaza
Suite 3410
New York, NY 10119
212-730-4466

16786 **Tajikistan Mission to the United Nations**
136 E 67th Street
New York, NY 10021
212-744-2196

Khamrokhon Zaripov, President

16787 **Thailand Trade Center- Consulate General of Thailand**
401 N Michigan Avenue
Suite 544
Chicago, IL 60611
312-467-0044
FAX: 312-467-1690 ttcc@wwa.com

16788 **Trade Commission of Denmark**
285 Peachtree Center Avenue NE
Suite 2102
Atlanta, GA 30303
404-588-1588

Henrik Bronner, Manager

16789 **Trade Commission of Spain**
500 N Michigan Avenue
Suite 1500
Chicago, IL 60611
312-644-1154

16790 **Turkish Trade Commission**
821 United Nations Plaza
4th Floor
New York, NY 10017
212-687-1530

16791 **Turkmenistan Mission to the United Nations**
866 United Nations Plaza
Suite 424
New York, NY 10017
212-486-8908

Aksoltan Ataeva, Manager

16792 **United Nations Mission to El Salvador**
46 Park Avenue
New York, NY 10016
212-759-9444

Antonio Montiero, Manager

Associations

16793 **AMT: Association for Manufacturing Technology**
7901 Westpark Drive
McLean, VA 22102-4206
703-893-2900
FAX: 703-893-1151
AMT@amtonline.org
www.amtonline.org
David J. Burns, Executive Director
Douglas K. Woods, First Vice Chairman
John Byrd, President
The Association for Manufacturing Technology represents and promotes the interests of American providers of manufacturing machinery and equipment. Its goal is to promote technological advancements and improvements in the design, manufacture, and sale of members' products in those markets and act as an industry advocate on trade matters to government and trade organizations throughout the world.
370 Members Founded: 1902

16794 **APMI International**
105 College Road E
Princeton, NJ 08540-6992
609-452-7700
FAX: 609-987-8523
apmi@mpif.org www.mpif.org/apmi
Christopher Adam, President
David L Schaefer, Director
Iver Anderson, Director
Jim Adams, Manager
Supports all those involved in the metal powder producing and consuming industries. Publishes monthly newsletter.
Founded: 1959

16795 **ASM International**
9639 Kinsman Road
Materials Park, OH 44073-0002
440-338-5151
FAX: 440-338-4634
cust-srv@asminternational.org
www.asminternational.org
Stanley Theobold, Managing Director
The society for materials engineers and scientists, a worldwide network dedicated to advancing industry, technology and applications of metals and materials.
40000 Members Founded: 1913

16796 **Aluminum Anodizers Council (AAC)**
1000 North Rand Road
Suite 214
Wauconda, IL 60084
847-526-2010
FAX: 847-526-3993
mail@aec.org www.anodizing.org/
Robert Peacock, Chairman
Thomas Hutch Jr, Vice Chairman
Gregory T Rajsky, President
Robin Greenslade, Director
Pat Alteriq, Administrative Assistant
The Aluminum Anodizers Council represents the interests of aluminum anodizers worldwide and is the principal trade organization for the anodizing industry in North America. It promotes the interests of its members through technical exchange, ongoing education, statistical data, market promotion, and industry representation.
155 Members Founded: 1950

16797 **Aluminum Association**
1525 Wilson Blvd
Ste 600
Arlington, VA 22209-2444
703-358-2960
FAX: 703-358-2961
J Stephen Larkin, President
Robin King, VP, Public Affairs
Members are manufacturers of aluminum mill products and producers of aluminum.
70 Members

16798 **American Electroplaters & Surface Finishers Society**
National Association for Surface Finishing
1155 Fifteenth Street, NW
Suite 500
Washington, DC 20005
202-457-8401
FAX: 202-530-0659
tkohler@nasf.org www.nasf.org
Tracey Kohler, Executive Director
John Flatley, Senior Advisor
AESF is an international, individual membership nonprofit society.
Founded: 1909

16799 **American Farriers Association**
4059 Iron Works Parkway #2
Suite 1
Lexington, KY 40511
859-233-7411
FAX: 859-231-7862
farriers@americanfarriers.org
www.americanfarriers.org
Craig Trnka, President
Bob Earle, VP
Bryan Quinsey, Executive Director
Founded: 1971

16800 **American Foundrymen's Society**
505 State Street
Des Plaines, IL 60016-2267
847-824-0181
FAX: 847-824-7848
David P Kanicki, Editor
A national organization designed to promote the technological advances in the industry.
Founded: 1938

16801 **American Foundrymens' Society**
1695 North Penny Lane
Schaumburg, IL 60173-4555
847-824-0181
FAX: 847-824-7848 800-537-4237
library@afsinc.org www.afsinc.org
Jerry Call, Executive VP
Ian Kay, VP
David Peterson, Membership Director
Trade association representing the interests of foundry workers across the nation. Offers publications, seminars and networking to promote business in the trade.
10000 Members Founded: 1896

16802 **American Institute of Mining, Metallurgical & Petroleum Engineers**
8307 Shaffer Parkway
Po Box 270728
Littleton, CO 80127-0013
303-948-4255
FAX: 303-948-4260
aime@aimehq.org www.aimeny.org
Rick Rolater, Executive Director
James R Jorden, President
Organized and operated exclusively to advance, record and disseminate significant knowledge of engineering and the arts and sciences involved in the production and use of minerals, metals, energy sources and materials for the benefits of humankind, both directly as AIME and through memeber societies.

16803 **American Iron & Steel Institute**
1140 Connecticut Avenue NW
Suite 705
Washington, DC 20036
202-452-7100
FAX: 202-463-6573
webmaster@steel.org www.steel.org
Andrew Sharkey III, President
David Bell, VP/CEO
Works with market development communications programs in automotive, construction and container markets.

16804 **American Welding Society**
550 NW 42nd Avenue
Suite 100
Miami, FL 33126-5699
305-443-9353
FAX: 305-443-7559 800-443-9353
Ray Shook, Executive Director
Andy Cullison, Publisher
Amy Nathan, Public Relations Manager
Involved in writing industry standards.
48000 Members Founded: 1919

16805 **American Wire Cloth Institute**
25 North Broadway
Tarrytown, NY 10591
914-332-0040
FAX: 914-332-1541
info@wireclothinstitute.org
www.wireclothinstitute.org
Richard C Byrne, Executive Director
Formerly the Industrial Wire Cloth Institute (1978)
Founded: 1933

16806 **American Zinc Association**
2025 M Street NW
Suite 800
Washington, DC 20036
202-571-1196
FAX: 202-367-2232
zincinfo@zinc.org www.zinc.org
George Vary, Executive Director
Joseph Spiciarich, Chairman
18 Members Founded: 1990

16807 **Artist-Blacksmiths Association of North America, Incorporated**
PO Box 816
Farmington, GA 30638-816
706-310-1030
FAX: 706-769-7147
abana@abana.org www.abana.org
Don Kemper, President
Clare Yellin, First VP
Dorothy Stiegler, Treasurer
Jerry Kagele, Secretary
For the professional and amateur blacksmith.
4500 Members Quarterly Founded: 1973
Circulation: 2 Mag.

16808 **Association for Iron & Steel Technology**
186 Thorn Hill Road
Warrendale, PA 15086-7528
724-776-6040
FAX: 724-776-1880
info@aist.org www.aist.org

Ronald E Ashburn, Executive Director
William A Albaugh, Membership Programs Manager
Nicholas Startitos, Controller

Information relating to the design and construction of equipment, machinery and plants for the production and processing of iron and steel.

9000 Members Founded: 2004

16809 Association for Manufacturing Technology
7901 Westpark Drive
McLean, VA 22102
703-893-2900
FAX: 703-893-1151
amt@mfgtech.org
www.motionnet.com
Supports all those involved in the US machine tool industry, including exports and imports. Involved in writing industry standards.

16810 Association of Battery Recyclers
PO Box 290286
Tampa, FL 33687
813-626-6151
FAX: 813-622-8388
joycemorales@aol.com
batteryrecyclers.com

Joyce Morales, Secretary/Treasurer

Investigates means and methods to achieve compliance with OSHA and EPA regulations impacting the secondary lead smelting industry.

Founded: 1976

16811 Association of Industrial Metallizers, Coaters and Laminators (AIMCAL)
201 Springs Street
Fort Mill, SC 29708
803-802-7820
FAX: 803-802-7821
aimcal@aimcal.org www.aimcal.org

Craig Sheppard, Executive Director

Nonprofit trade organization for makes of coated, laminated and metalized papers.

Founded: 1970

16812 Association of Steel Distributors
401 N Michigan Avenue
Chicago, IL 60611
312-644-6610
FAX: 312-527-6705
www.steeldistributors.org
ASD is a nonprofit organization, providing the steel distribution industry a forum for ideas exchange and market information.

16813 Association of Women in the Metal Industries
515 King Street
Suite 420
Alexandria, VA 22314-3137
703-739-8335
FAX: 703-684-6048
trideout@clarionmr.com
www.awmi.org

Haley Johnson, Executive Director
Tonya S Rideout, Director/Member Services

Fosters the professional growth of women in the metal industries.

16814 Cast Metals Institute
505 State Street
Des Plaines, IL 60016
847-824-0181
FAX: 847-824-7848 800-537-4237
Supports all those involved in the cast metal industry. Hosts annual trade show.

Founded: 1956

16815 Closure Manufacturers Association
PO Box 1358
Kilmarnock, VA 22482
804-435-9580
FAX: 804-435-2203
cmadc@rivnet.net www.cmadc.org

Darla Williamson, President

Conducts public relations for member companies and establishes idustry standards.

40 Members Founded: 1984

16816 Copper Development Association
260 Madison Avenue
New York, NY 10016
212-251-7200
FAX: 212-251-7234 800-232-3282
questions@cda.copper.org
www.copper.org

Andrew G Kireta Sr, President/CEO
Kenneth P Geremia, Manager Communications
Michels Harold, VP Casting/Technical Services
Arnold W Ray, VP Environmental Division
Lorraine Herzing Mills, VP/Finance/Administration

Seeks to expand the uses and applications of copper and copper products. Responsible for industry-wide market statistics and research.

75 Members Founded: 1963

16817 Copper and Brass Servicenter Association
994 Old Eagle School Road
Suite 1019
Wayne, PA 19087-1866
610-971-4850
FAX: 610-971-4859

Franklin Brownhill, Executive VP
Diane Lubraggen, Executive Assistant

Distriburors (servicenters) of fabricated copper and copper alloy products (sheet, plate, coil, rod bar, tube, etc) and their brass mill suppliers.

75 Members Founded: 1951

16818 Ductile Iron Pipe Research Association
245 Riverchase Parkway E
Suite O
Birmingham, AL 35244
205-402-8700
FAX: 205-402-8730 www.dipra.org

Troy F Stroud, President
Richard W Bonds, Technical Director

Established as the Cast Iron Pipe Publicity Bureau.

7 Members Founded: 1915

16819 Ductile Iron Society
28938 Lorain Road
Suite 202
North Olmsted, OH 44070
440-734-8040
FAX: 440-734-8182
jhall@ductile.org www.ductile.org

Alan Druschitz, President
Pete Guidi, VP
Hugh Kind, Treasurer
John V Hall, Executive Director

Supports all those involved with technical data and applications, production statistics, and profiles of foundries. Publishes magazine.

16820 Edison Welding Institute
1250 Arthur E Adams Drive
Columbus, OH 43221-3585
614-688-5000
FAX: 614-688-5001

Henry Cialone, President
Dr Karl Graff, Executive Director

Companies and organizations with an interest in new developments in welding equipment and technology.

16821 Electrical Manufacturing & Coil Winding Association
PO Box 278
Imperial Beach, CA 91933-0278
619-435-3629
FAX: 619-435-3639
cthurman@earthlink.net
www.emcw.org

Charles Thurman, Executive Director

Promotes welfare of the motor and coil industry. Offers courses and workshops.

400 Members Founded: 1973

16822 Fabricators and Manufacturers Association
Fabricators and Manufacturers Association

833 Featherstone Road
Rockford, IL 61107-6302
815-399-8700
FAX: 815-484-7700
info@fmanet.org www.fmanet.org

Gerald M Shankel, President/CEO
Kristen Darbys, Director/Membership
Paul Halberg, Director/Information Technology
Mark Hoper, Director/Expositions
Michael Long, Director/Education

FMA is an educational association serving the metal forming and fabricating industry. Technology areas include sheet metal fabricating, stamping, roll forming, coil processing, punching and plate structural fabricating.

1500 Members Founded: 1971

16823 Ferroalloys Association
900 2nd Street NE
Washington, DC 20002-3557
202-842-2888
FAX: 202-842-4840
www.scra.org/amc/tfa

Edward J Kinghorn Jr, President

Promotes the ferroalloy industry in the areas of technology, international trade, environment and health, safety and government relations.

19 Members Founded: 1971

16824 Garrett Metal Detectors
1881 West State Street
Garland, TX 75042-6797
972-494-6151
FAX: 972-494-1881 800-234-6151
sales@garrett.com www.garrett.com

Jim Dobrei, Director of Sales
Vaughn Garrett, Director Marketing/Communications

Global leader of walk-through, hand-held and ground search metal detection products and training for security and law enforcement.

4 Members Founded: 1964

16825 Global Platinum & Gold
8421 Top of the World Drive
Salt Lake City, UT 84121-6035
801-277-0744
FAX: 801-942-7045

16826 Gold Prospectors Association of America
43445 Business Park Drive
Temecula, CA 92590
951-994-4749
FAX: 909-699-4062
www.goldprospectors.org
Perry Massie, CEO
Tom Massie, Executive VP
Richard Dickson, COO/Counsel
GPAA is the largest recreational gold prospecting club. Owner of The Outdoor Channel, a cable TV channel featuring real outdoors for real people.
35M Members Founded: 1985

16827 Industrial Metal Containers Section of the Material Handling Institute
8720 Red Oak Boulevard
Suite 201
Charlotte, NC 28217-3996
704-676-1190
FAX: 704-676-1199
ahowie@mhia.org www.mhia.org
Allan M Howie, Director
Promotes the market and develops a code of ethics. Serves as liaison among members and other groups.
9 Members Founded: 1972

16828 Industrial Perforators Association
5157 Deerhurst Crescent Circle
Boca Raton, FL 33486
561-447-7511
iperf@iperf.org www.iperf.org
Delores Morris, Executive Secretary
Members are companies making perforated metal products.

16829 Innovative Material Solutions
225 Canterbury Drive
State College, PA 16803
814-867-1140
FAX: 814-867-2813
info@imspowder.com
www.imspowder.com/pim2002
Supports all those involved in research in the materials industry. Hosts annual trade show.

16830 Institute of Scrap Recycling Industries
1352 G Street
NW 1000
Washington, DC 20005
202-731-1770
FAX: 202-626-0900
dennywhite@scrap.org
www.scrap.org
Supports all those involved in the scrap processing and recycling industry. Publishes bi-monthly magazine.

16831 International Copper Association
260 Madison Avenue
16th Floor
New York, NY 10016
212-251-7240
FAX: 212-251-7245
Francis J Kane, President
Promoting the use of copper by communicating the unique attributes that make this sustainable element an essential contributor to the formation of life, to advances in science and technology, and to a higher standard of living worldwide.
Founded: 1989

16832 International Hard Anondizing
PO Box 579
Moorestown, NJ 08057-0579
856-234-0330
FAX: 856-727-9504
Denise.Downing@comcast.net
www.ihanodizing.com
Denise Downing, Executive Director
Formed by companies in the hard anodizing business to provide a forum for the exchange of technical information and to act as a clearing house for information about the industry.
Founded: 1989

16833 International Lead Zinc Research Organization
2525 Meridian Parkway
Durham, NC 27713-5243
919-361-4647
FAX: 919-361-1957
jhendric@ilzro.org www.ilzro.org
Stephen Wilkinson, President
Judith Hendrickson, Corporate Secretary
Members are miners, smelters and refiners of lead and zinc. Supports research and development of new uses for the metals and refinement existing uses. Has an annual budget of approximately $5.3 million.
77 Members Founded: 1958

16834 International Magnesium Association
1000 N Rand Road
Suite 214
Wauconda, IL 60084
847-526-2010
FAX: 847-526-3993
info@intlmag.org www.intlmag.org
Greg Patzer, Executive VP
Eileen Hoblit, Administrative Coordinator
IMA is to promote the use of the metal magnesium in material selection and encourage innovative applications of the versatile metal.
125 Members Founded: 1943

16835 International Precious Metals Institute
4400 Bayou Boulevard
Suite 18
Pensacola, FL 32503-1908
850-476-1156
FAX: 850-476-1548 www.ipmi.org
Kevin Beirner, President
Fred Saada, VP
Larry Manziek, Executive Director
International association of producers, refiners, fabricators, scientists, users, financial institutions, merchants, private and public sector groups and the general precious metals community created to provide a forum for the exchange of information and technology.
Founded: 1976

16836 International Thermal Spray Association
9639 Kinsman Road
Materials Park, OH 44073-0002
440-338-5151
FAX: 440-338-4634
ITSA@asminternational .org
www.thermalspray.org
Kathy M Dusa, Administrative Assistant
Strengthens the level of awareness in general industry and government on the increasing capabilities and advantages of thermal spray technology for surface engineering through business opportunities, technical support and a social network. Contributes to growth and education in the thermal spray industry.
55 Members Founded: 1948

16837 International Titanium Association
2655 West Midway
#300
Broomfield, CO 80020-3485
303-404-2221
FAX: 303-404-9111
ita@titanium.org www.titanium.org
Jennifer Simpson, Executive Director
Contact ITA for mailing list price. Visit website for a list of publications.
120 Members Founded: 1984 3000 names

16838 Lead Industries Association
13 Main Street
Sparta, NJ 07871
973-726-5323
FAX: 973-726-4484
miller@leadinfo.com
www.leadinfo.com
Jeffrey T Miller, Executive Director
Nonprofit trade association representing the lead industries in the US and abroad. It collects and distributes information about the users of lead products in industry, vehicles, radioactive waste disposal and noise barriers. Its services are availble, generally free of charge, to anyone interested in the uses of lead and lead products.

16839 Machinery Dealers National Association
315 S Patrick Street
Alexandria, VA 22314
703-369-9300
FAX: 703-836-9303 800-872-7807
office@mdna.org www.mdna.org
Mark Robinson, Executive Vice President
Supports manufacturers involved in metal working machine tools. Publishes annual directory.

16840 Magnet Distributors and Fabricators Association
8 S Michigan Avenue
Suite 1000
Chicago, IL 60603
312-541-2667
FAX: 312-580-0165 www.mdfa.org
August L Sisco, Executive Secretary
Distributors and magnetic materials and fabricators of magnetic components, plus suppliers to the distributor/fabricators.
31 Members Founded: 1991

16841 **Materials Properties Council**
PO Box 1942
New York, NY 10156
212-591-7693

mpc@forengineers.org
www.forengineers.org/mpc/
Martin Prager, PhD, Executive Director
An outgrowth of the ASTM-ASME Joint Committee on the effect of temperature on the properties of metals which was founded in 1925 to meet the apparent need for information on the subject in the construction of central power stations.
600 Members Founded: 1966

16842 **Metal Building Contractors and Erectors Association**
PO Box 117
West Milton, OH 45383-0117
937-698-4127
FAX: 937-698-6153
info@longmgt.com www.mbcea.org
Christopher Long, Executive Vice President
Founded as Metal Building Dealers, became Systems Builders Association in 1984 and assumed its current name in 2002.
235 Members Founded: 1968

16843 **Metal Building Manufacturers Association**
1300 Sumner Avenue
Cleveland, OH 44115-2851
216-241-7333
FAX: 216-241-0105
mbma@mbma.com www.mbma.com
Charles M Stockinger, General Manager
A trade association representing building systems manufacturers, roofing systems and manufacturers and suppliers to the industry.
56 Members

16844 **Metal Construction Association**
4700 West Lake Street
Glenview, IL 60025
847-375-4718
FAX: 877-665-2234
mengle@amctec.com
www.metalconstruction.org
Mark Engle, Executive Vice President
Julie Weldon, Senior Manager
Dedicated to promoting the use of metal in construction. Initiative include market development, educational programs, issue and product awareness compaigns and publication of technical guidelines and specifications manuals. Also monitors and confronts challenges affecting the industry such as code restructions.
100 Members Founded: 1983

16845 **Metal Findings Manufacturers**
30-R Houghton Street
Providence, RI 02904
401-861-4667
FAX: 401-861-0429
info@mfma.net www.mfma.net
John Augustyn, Executive Officer
Makers of metal parts and fittings used in the assembly of jewelry.
Founded: 1930

16846 **Metal Powder Industries Federation**
105 College Road E
Princeton, NJ 08540-6692
609-452-7700
FAX: 609-987-8523
info@mpif.org www.mpif.org
C James Trombino, Executive Director/CEO
David Schaefer, President
Promotes the science and industry of powder metallurgy through technical meetings, seminars, conferences and publications.
270 Members Founded: 1944

16847 **Metal Service Center Institute**
4201 Euclid Avenue
Suite 550
Rolling Meadows, IL 60008
847-405-3000
FAX: 847-486-3001
info@msci.org www.msci.org
Bob Weidner, President/CEO
Jonathan Kalkwarf, VP Finance/Administration
Rose Manfredini, VP Member Information Services
Chris Marti, VP Technology
375 Members Founded: 1907

16848 **Mineral Information Institute**
505 Violet Street
Golden, CO 80401
303-277-9190
FAX: 303-277-9198
mii@mii.org www.mii.org
Nelson Fugate, President
Jacqueline S Dorr, VP
Angie Simonton, Director Development
Supports all those involved in mineral and related industries. Publishes annual directory.

16849 **Minerals, Metals & Materials Society**
184 Thorn Hill Road
Warrendale, PA 15086-7514
724-769-9000
FAX: 724-776-3770 800-759-4867
tmsgeneral@tms.org www.tms.org
Alexander Scott, Executive Director
Nellie Luther, Professional Affairs Coordinator
Gail Miller, Executive Assistant
Supports all those devoted to exploring the many aspects of materials science and engineering. Publishes monthly magazine.
Founded: 1993

16850 **Mining and Metallurgical Society of**

476 Wilson Avenue
Novato, CA 94947
415-897-1380
FAX: 415-897-1380
info@mmsa.net www.mmsa.net
Alan K Burton, Business Manager
Mark leVier, President
Robert Schafer, VP
Kenneth Brunk, Treasurer
Concerned with the conservation of the nation's mineral resources and the best interest of the mining and metallurgical industries.
350 Members Founded: 1908

16851 **National Association for Surface Finishing**
1155 Fifteenth Street, NW
Suite 500
Washington, DC 20005
202-457-8404
FAX: 202-530-0659 www.nasf.org
Anthony Revier, President
The National Association for Surface Finishing is a trade association whose mission is to promote the advancement of the surface finishing industry worldwide.

16852 **National Association of Aluminum Developer s**
8550 Bryn Mawr
Suite 550
Chicago, IL 60631
773-867-1300
FAX: 773-867-8750
info@msci.org www.msci.org
Bob Weidner, President
Jonathan Kalkwarf, VP Finance/Administration
Rose Manfredini, VP Member Information Services
Chris Marti, VP Technology
Ann Zastrow, VP
NAAD is the trade association of North American service centers and principal suppliers engaged in marketing aluminum products.
400 Members Founded: 1914

16853 **National Blacksmiths and Welders**
PO Box 123
Arnold, NE 69120
308-848-2913

Dave Christen, President
Jim Lindquist, First Director
Gerry Westhoff, Second VP
James Holman, Executive Director
Blacksmiths, welders and manufacturing machine shops.
175 Members Founded: 1895

16854 **National Coil Coating Association**
1300 Summer Avenue
Cleveland, OH 44115
216-241-7333
FAX: 216-241-0105
www.coilcoating.org
NCCA is an established trade organization dedicated to the growth of coil coated products. They provide the coil coating service and are leading manufactures and suppliers of metal, coatings, chemicals and equipment.

16855 **National Institute for Metal Working Skills**
3251 Old Lee Highway
Suite 205
Fairfax, VA 22030
703-352-4971
FAX: 703-352-4991
www.nims-skills.org
Stephen Mandes, Executive Director
A nonprofit organization formed by metalworking trade associations, national labor organizations, a council of state governors, companies and educators to support the development of a skilled workforce for the metalworking industry.

16856 **National Mining Association**
101 Constitution Avenue, NW
Suite 500 E
Washington, DC 20001-2133
202-632-2654
FAX: 202-463-2666 www.nma.org
Connie Holmes, Executive Director
NMA is the voice of the American mining industry in Washington, DC. NMA is the only national trade organization that represents the interests of mining before Con-

gress, the Administration, federal agencies, the judiciary and the media.

16857 National Ornamental & Miscellaneous Metals
532 Forest Parkway
Suite A
Forest Park, GA 30297
404-363-4009
FAX: 404-366-1852
nommainfo@nomma.org
www.nomma.org
Curt Witter, President
Chris Connelly, VP/Treasurer
Supports all those involved in the ornamental and miscellaneous metal industry. Publishes bi-monthly magazine.
1000 Members Founded: 1959

16858 National Ornamental and Miscellaneous
1535 Pennsylvania Avenue
McDonough, GA 30253

FAX: 770-288-2006 888-516-8585
nommainfo@nomma.org
www.nomma.org
Barbara Cook, Executive Director
Liz Johnson, Administrative Assistant
Barbara Cook, Executive Director
The National Ornamental & Miscellaneous Metals Association serves its members and advances the industry through education and the promotion of a positive business environment.
900 Members Founded: 1958

16859 National Tooling & Machining Association
9300 Livingston Road
Fort Washington, MD 20744-4998
301-486-6200
800-248-6862
dick@ntma.org www.ntma.org
Dick Walker, Director Education
Rob Akers, Manager
Trade organization representing the precision custom manufacturing industry throughout the US. Has an active safety & education program.

16860 National Welding Supply Association Annual Convention
Fernley & Fernley
1900 Arch Street
Philadelphia, PA 19103-1498
215-564-3484
FAX: 215-564-2175 www.nwsa.com
GA Fernley, Director
1200 Members Founded: 1945

16861 Non-Ferrous Founder's Society
1480 Renaissance Drive
Suite 310
Park Ridge, IL 60068-1354
847-299-0950
FAX: 847-299-3598
staff@nffs.org www.nffs.org
James L Mallory CAE, Executive Director
Jerrod A Weaver, Quality Services Manager
Ryan J Moore, Member Services Manager
Manufacturers of bronze, brass and aluminum castings.
185 Members Founded: 1943

16862 North American Die Casting Association
9701 West Higgins Road
Suite 880
Rosemont, IL 60018-4721
847-537-8888
FAX: 847-292-3620
webmaster@diecasting.org
www.diecasting.org
Neal Shapiro, Affairs Committee Chairman
Supports all those involved in the die casting industry. Publishes bi-monthly magazine.
Founded: 1957

16863 Precious Metals Producers Group
Holland & Hart
1001 Pennsylvania Avenue NW
Washington, DC 20004-2505
202-876-6191
FAX: 202-737-8998

16864 Precision Metalforming Association
6363 Oak Tree Boulevard
Independence, OH 44131-2500
216-019-9667
FAX: 216-901-9190
pma@pma.org
www.metalforming.com
Nels Leutwiler, Chairman
Dennis J Keat, First Vice Chairman
Bernie Rosselli Jr, Second Vice Chairman/Treasurer
William Gaskin, President
Members include producers of metal stampings, spinnings, washers and precision sheet metal fabrications as well as suppliers of equipment, materials and services.
1300 Members Founded: 1913

16865 Resistance Welder Manufacturers
1900 Arch Street
Philadelphia, PA 19103-1498
215-564-3484
FAX: 215-564-2175
rwma@fernley.com www.rwma.org
David Beneteau, Chairman
Larry E Moss, President
Michael Simmons, VP
Strives to create widespread awareness and use of the various resistance welding processes and equipment, improve relations between individual manufacturers, foster higher ethical standards throughout the industry, develop industry standards to assist users of resistance welding equipment.
82 Members Founded: 1935

16866 Sheet Metal and Air Conditioning Contractors' National Association
4201 Lafayette Center Drive Chantilly
Chantilly, VA 20151-1209
703-803-2980
FAX: 703-803-3732
info@smacma.org www.smacna.org
John Sroka, Executive Vice President
SMACNA's mission is to provide products, services and representation to enhance members' businesses, markets and profitability.
Founded: 1943

16867 Silver Institute
1200 G Street NW
Suite 800
Washington, DC 20005
202-835-0185
FAX: 202-835-0155
info@silverinstitute.org
www.silverinstitute.org
Paul Bateman, Executive Director
International association of miners, refiners, fabricators and wholesalers of silver and silver products.

16868 Silver Users Association
11240 Waples Mill Road
Suite 200
Fairfax, VA 22030
703-934-0219
FAX: 703-359-7562 800-245-6999
silverusers@capitolonellc.com
www.silverusersassociation.org
Mike Merolla, President
John Gannon, VP
Represents the interests of corporations that make, sell and distribute products and services in which silver is an essential part. SUA membership includes representatives from the photographic, electronic, silverware and jewelry industries; producers of semi-fabricated and industrial products; and, mirror manufacturers.
30 Members Founded: 1947

16869 Society of American Silversmiths
PO Box 72839
Providence, RI 02907
401-461-6840
FAX: 401-461-6841
sas@silversmithing.com
www.silversmithing.com
Jeffrey Herman, Founder/Executive Director
Founded to preserve the art and history of handcrafted holloware and flatware plus provide support, networking and greater access to the market for its artisan members. Artisans are silversmiths both practicing and retired who now or used to smith as a livelihood. Educates the public as to the aesthetic and investment value of this art form and demystifies silversmithing techniques through its literature and national exhibits.
240 Members Founded: 1989

16870 Society of Manufacturing Engineers
1 SME Drive
PO Box 930
Dearborn, MI 48121
313-271-1500
FAX: 313-271-2861 800-733-4763
service@sme.org www.sme.org
Nancy Berg, Executive Director
Supports all those involved in the metalworking industry, specifically machining, forming, inspection, assembly and processing operations. Publishes magazine.
70M Members Founded: 1932

16871 Society of North American Goldsmiths
710 E Ogden Avenue
Suite 600
Naperville, IL 60563
630-369-2406
FAX: 630-369-2488
www.snagmetalsmith.org
Micki Lippe, President
Peggy Eng, Conferences

Promotes a favorable and enriching environment in which contemporary metalsmiths practice their art. One aspect of this process is educating the public about the quality and rich diversity within the field of metalsmithing. Exhibitions, public forums, lectures, and published documents are our primary methods of reaching out to the public. SNAG sponsors workshops, seminars, audio-visual services and an annual conference.
Founded: 1969

16872 Steel Deck Institute
PO Box 25
Fox River Grove, IL 60021-0025
847-458-4647
FAX: 847-458-4648
steve@sdi.org www.sdi.org
Steven A Roehrig, Managing Director
A non-profit association of steel deck producers and associate members furnishing products allied to steel deck use and construction.

16873 Steel Door Institute
30200 Detroit Road
Cleveland, OH 44145-1967
440-899-0010
FAX: 440-892-1404
Jeffery Wherry, Managing Director
Producers of all metal frames and doors for commercial, industrial and residential construction.

16874 Steel Founders Society of America
780 McArdle Drive
Unit G
Crystal Lake, IL 60014
815-455-8240
FAX: 815-455-8241
blairr@sfsa.org www.sfsa.org
Raymond W Monroe, Executive VP
Sandra Walker, Director of Administration
A technically oriented trade association serving the steel casting industry.
Founded: 1902

16875 Steel Manufacturers Association
1150 Connecticut Avenue NW
Washington, DC 20036
202-296-1515
FAX: 202-296-2506
stuart@steelnet.org www.steelnet.org
Phillip E Casey, Chairman
Thomas Danjczek, President
The majority of SMA members are minimills companies engaged in electric air furnace/continuous caster steel productions as well as hot and cold rolling of steel mill products. A growing number of integrated steel producers are also members.

16876 Steel Plate Fabricators Association
570 Oakwood Road
Lake Zurich, IL 60047
847-438-8265
FAX: 847-438-8766
info@steeltank.com www.spfa.org
Anne Kiefer, Director Of Administration
Wayne B. Geyer, President
J Michael Braden, VP
Jerry Stetzler, Treasurer
Protection of the environment and preservation of air and water quality are key concerns for the owners and operators of tanks, pressure vessels, specialty fabrications and piping systems.
Founded: 1933

16877 Steel Service Center Institute
4889 Neo Parkway
Cleveland, OH 44128
216-827-7816
FAX: 216-694-3940
info@ssci.org www.ssci.org
Thomas Conley, President
S Harbke, Director
570 Members Founded: 1909

16878 Steel Shipping Container Institute
1101 14th Street NW
Suite 2020
Washington, DC 20005-5601
202-408-1900
FAX: 202-408-1972
John McQuaid, Executive Director

16879 Steel Tank Institute
570 Oakwood Road
Lake Zurich, IL 60047-1585
847-438-8265
FAX: 847-438-8766
Wayne B Geyer, Executive VP
Conducts research and developes underground and above ground storage tank technologies and standards for the steel industry. Represents its members to congress and the executive branch.

16880 Steel Tube Institute of North America
8500 Station Street
Suite 270
Mentor, OH 44060-4970
440-974-6990
FAX: 440-974-6994
sti@apk.net
www.steeltubeinstitute.org
Timothy F Andrassy, Executive Director
Peggy Sams, Executive Assistant
Mary Gregel, Administrative Assistant
Members produce steel tubes and pipes from carbon, stainless or alloy steel, for applications ranging from large structural tubing to small redrawn tubing.
87 Members Founded: 1930

16881 Systems Builders Association
28 Lowry Drive
PO Box 117
West Milton, OH 45383
937-698-4127
FAX: 937-698-6153 www.arcat.com
Christopher Long, VP
Promotes the use of metal buildings and provides information on business practices, new markets and sales techniques. Offers scholarships and bestows awards.
650 Members Founded: 1968

16882 Tube Council of North America
1601 Northbond Street
Suite 101
Naperville, IL 60563
630-544-5050
FAX: 630-544-5055
info@tube.org www.tube.org
Patrick Farrey, Executive Secretary
Trade association to further the use of metal, laminate and plastic tubes. Sponsors competitions and bestows awards.
Founded: 1957

16883 Tube and Pipe Association International
833 Featherstone Road
Rockford, IL 61107
815-399-8700
FAX: 815-484-7700
info@tpatube.org www.tpatube.org
Gerald Shankel, President
Mike Hedges, VP Finance/CFO
TPA is an educational technology association serving the metal tube and pipe producing and fabricating industries. It is an affiliate association of the Fabricators and Manufacturers Association International.

16884 US Pipe and Foundry Company
PO Box 10406
Birmingham, AL 35202-0406
205-547-7254
FAX: 205-254-7494
David Mize, Plant Manager
Supports all those involved with the foundry industry. Publishes semi-monthly newsletter.
Founded: 1928

16885 United States Cutting Tool Institute
1300 Sunmer Ave
Cleveland, OH 44115-2851
216-241-7333
FAX: 216-241-0105
uscti@taol.com www.uscti.com
Charles Stockinger, Executive Director
USCTI was formed in 1988 by the merger of the Metal Cutting Tool Institute and the Cutting Tool Manufactures of America. USCTI represents more than two-thirds of the domestic cutting tool market.
Founded: 1988

16886 Welding Research Council
PO Box 201547
Shaker Heights, OH 44120
216-658-3847
FAX: 216-658-3854
mprager@forengineers.org
www.forengineers.org/wrc
Coordinates welding research.
Founded: 1935

16887 Wire Association International
1570 Boston Post Road
PO Box 578
Guilford, CT 06437-0578
203-453-2777
FAX: 203-453-8384 www.wirenet.org
Steven J Fetteroll, Executive Director
Phyilis Conon, Technical Information Director
Technical association serving the global wire and cable industry by providing educational materials, sponsoring trade shows and international technical conferences.
Founded: 1930 $150 per M.

Newsletters

16888 ASM News
ASM International
9639 Kinsman Road
Materials Park, OH 44073
440-338-5151
FAX: 440-338-4634 800-336-5152
cust-srv@asminternational.org
http://www.asminternational.org
Carla Sly, Managing Editor
Society and membership news.

Weekly Founded: 1913
Circulation: 38000

16889 Abrasive User's News Fax
Abrasive Engineering Society
144 Moore Street
Butler, PA 16001
724-282-6210
FAX: 724-234-2376
aes@abrasiveengineering.com
http://www.abrasiveengineering.com
Ted Giese, Manager *$50.00*
Founded: 1957

16890 Abrasive Users News Fax
Meadowlark Technical Services
144 Moore Road
Butler, PA 16001
724-282-6210
FAX: 724-234-2376
aes@abrasiveengineering.com
http://www.abrasivesmall.com
Ted Giese, Publisher
Newsletter from the Abrasive Engineering Society. *$50.00*
Founded: 1957
Circulation: 500

16891 American Iron and Steel Institute News
American Iron and Steel Institute
1140 Connecticut Ave
Suite 705
Washington, NW 20036-4704
202-452-7100
FAX: 202-463-6573
steelnews@steel.org
http://www.steel.org
Andrew Sharkey III, President/CEO
Dave James, Marketing
Publication of the nonprofit trade organization representing approximately 65 percent of steel companies in the US, Canada and Mexico.
Founded: 1855
Circulation: 6000

16892 American Metal Market
Michael G Botta
825 7th Avenue
New York, NY 10019-6014
212-887-8510
FAX: 212-887-8522
mbotta@chilton.net www.amm.com
Gloria T LaRue, Editor
Catalino Abrei, Owner
A daily newspaper of the metals industry covering news and pricing information for corporate, purchasing and manufacturing management.
Daily
Circulation: 10,500

16893 Association for Iron & Steel Technology
186 Thorn Hill Road
Warrendale, PA 15086-7511
724-776-6040
FAX: 724-776-1880
mailbag@iss.org www.iss.org
Ron Ashburn, Executive Director
Stacy Varmecky, Communications Supervisor
Monthly magazine for those involved with knowledge exchange in the global iron and steel industry. Regular editorial features.
9,000 pages Founded: 1974

16894 CBSA Capsules
Copper and Brass Servicenter Association

994 Old Eagle School Road
Suite 1019
Wayne, PA 19087
610-971-4850
FAX: 610-971-4859
info@cbsa.copper-brass.org
http://www.cbsa.copper-brass.org
R Franklin Brown Jr., Executive Vice President
Association and industry news. *$35.00*
6 pages Monthly Founded: 1951
Circulation: 200

16895 Cables Industry Analyst
CRU International
6305 Ivy Lane
Suite 422
Greenbelt, MD 20770-3538
301-418-8997
FAX: 301-441-9091
customerservice@cugroup.com
http://www.crugroup.com
Irv Adler, Editor
Written for managers and executives in the wire industry around the globe. Spotlights effective management techniques and superior administrative skills in the industry, profiles industry leaders, notes personnel movements and features general industry news. *$965.00*
12 pages Monthly

16896 Cahners Business Information
2000 Clearwater Drive
Oak Brook, IL 60523-8809
630-320-7000

El Hoeffer, Editor
Jeff Greisch, President
Edward Hale, Circulation Manager
Ferrous scrap prices for 17 cities. *$195.00*
Weekly
Circulation: 1,000 Audited
Computerized version available

16897 Futuretech
John Wiley & Sons
111 River Street
Hoboken, NJ 07030
201-748-6000
FAX: 201-748-6088 800-825-7550
subinfo@wiley.com www.wiley.com
Kenneth A Kovaly, Publisher
Gerry Gould, Editor
Edited for product development and technology transfer engineers. Intelligence service that deals with new technologies with demonstrated commercial appeal still in the early stages of development in leading corporate, academic and university labs. Contains analysis and exploitation information. *$1500.00*
24 pages Monthly
Mailing list available for rent $180 per M.

16898 IMA Weekly Updates
1000 N Rand Road
Suite 214
Wauconda, IL 60084
847-526-2010
FAX: 847-526-3993
ima@bellatlantic.net
http://www.intlmag.org
Greg Patzer, Executive Vice-President
Heidi Diederich, Administrative Coordinator
Develops international use and acceptance of magnesium metal and its alloys in all product forms. Members are organizations or individuals engaged in the production, manufacture or marketing of metallic magnesium or those supplying materials, equipment or consulting. *$ 90.00*
Weekly Founded: 1943
Circulation: 5000
Printed in 2 colors on glossy stock

16899 Magnesium News
International Magnesium Association
1000 N Rand Rd
Suite 214
Wauconda, IL 60084-3615
847-526-2010
FAX: 847-526-3993
ima@bellatlantic.net
http://www.intlmag.org
Kim Charovkine, Circulation Director
Greg Patzer, Executive Vice-President
Published nine times a year, reporting on IMA developments, membership news, and magnesium events worldwide. *$90.00*
Founded: 1943
Circulation: 500

16900 Metal Building Contractors and Erectors
MBCEA Network Newsletter
PO Box 117
West Milton, OH 45383-0117
937-698-4127
FAX: 937-698-6153
info@longmgt.com www.mbcea.org
Christopher Long, Executive Vice President
Annual Meetings/Winter

16901 Metal Construction Association
MCA Newsletter
4799 West Lake Street
Glenview, IL 60025
847-375-4718
FAX: 877-665-2234
mengle@amctec.com
www.metalconstruction.org
Mark Engle, Executive Vice President
Julie Weldon, Senior Manager
Dedicated to promoting the use of metal in construction. Initative include market development, educational programs, issue and product awareness campaigns, and publication of technical guidelines and specifications manuals.
100 pages Quartly Founded: 1983

16902 Metalworking Insiders' Report
6915 Valley Avenue
Cincinnati, OH 45244-3029
513-527-8977
FAX: 513-527-8801 800-950-8020
Joel Jablonowski, Editor
This report is issued 25 times per year. *$397.00*
Founded: 1928

16903 R&D Focus
International Lead Zinc Research Organization
2525 Meridian Parkway
PO Box 12036
Research Triangle Park, NC 27709-2036

919-361-4647
FAX: 919-361-1957
rputnam@ilzro.org
http://www.ilzro.org
Rob Putnam, Publisher
Doug Zabor, President
Reports on current research and development products in the metal industry.

Quarterly Founded: 1958
Circulation: 100

16904 Spraytime
9639 Kinsman Road
Materials Park, OH 44073-2
440-338-1950
FAX: 440-338-4634
spraytime@asminternational.org
http://www.asminternational.org

Kathy M Dusa, Managing Editor
Ellyn T. Vander Kaay, Journal Coordinator

Thermal Spray community newsletter presenting industry applications, commercial developments, research and industry news/press releases, as well as solutions and unique approaches for all thermal spray disciplines.
24 pages Quarterly Founded: 1992
Circulation: 3000

16905 Steel Industry Weekly Review
2 Uxbridge Road
Scarsdale, NY 10583-2725

Karl Keffer, Publisher

Offers industry news for steel workers.
$75.00
Monthly

16906 Titanium
International Titanium Association
2655 West Midway Blvd.
Suite 300
Broomfield, CO 80020-7186
303-404-2221
FAX: 303-404-9111 299-942-5371
jsimpson@titanium.org
http://www.titanium.org

Amy Fitzgerald, Editor
Jennifer Simpson, CEO

Quarterly Founded: 1960
Circulation: 5000

16907 US Piper
US Pipe and Foundry Company
PO Box 10406
James Canada
Birmingham, AL 35202-406
205-547-7254
FAX: 205-254-7494
http://www.uspipe.com

George Bogs, Publisher
Ray Torok, President
Walter Knollenberg, VP

Articles deal with advantages of using new products.
16 pages Founded: 1899
Circulation: 9000

16908 WRC Bulletin
Welding Research Council
3 Park Avenue
27th Floor
New York, NY 10016-5902
212-591-7956
FAX: 212-591-7183
www.forengineers.org/wrc

CR Felmley Jr, Publisher

Offers information and updates for the welding community. *$300.00*
Monthly
Circulation: 900

16909 Wiring Harness Manufacturers Association
3335 N Arlington Heights Road
Suite E
Arlington Heights, IL 60004
847-577-7200
FAX: 847-577-7276
whma@whma.org www.whma.org

Andrew Larsen, Executive Director

To provide the cooperative forum through which members companies can solve both their specific problems and also help resolve industry problems.
4 pages Quarterly
Circulation: 5,000

Magazines & Journals

16910 AISE Steel Technology
Association of Iron & Steel Engineers
186 Thorn Hill Road
Warrendale, PA 15086
724-776-6040
FAX: 724-776-1880
info@aist.org http://www.aise.org

Ronald Ashburn, Managing Director
Marge Baker, Editor
Gerry Kane, Sales Manager
Karen Hadley, Managing Editor
Janet McConnell, Production Editor

Information relating to the design and construction of equipment, machinery and plants for the production and processing of iron and steel. *$115.00*
Monthly Founded: 2004
Circulation: 8000

16911 APMI International
105 College Road E
Princeton, NJ 08540-6622
609-452-7700
FAX: 609-987-8523
apmi@mpif.org www.mpif.org

Christopher Adam, President
David L Schaefer, Director
Jim Adams, Manager

Monthly newsletter for all those involved the metal powder producing and consuming industries. Regular editorial features.
Founded: 1965

16912 Abrasives
PO Box 11
Byron Center, MI 49315
616-530-3220
FAX: 616-530-6466
abrasivesmag@comcast.net
http://www.abrasivesmagazine.com

Rose Trevino, Publisher/Editor

Covers research and development in the abrasives field including information about grinding and finishing applications. *$27.00*

Annual+
Circulation: 35000

16913 Advanced Materials & Processes
ASM International
9639 Kinsman Road
Materials Park, OH 44073-2
440-338-5151
FAX: 440-338-4634 800-336-5152
cust-srv@asminternational.org
http://www.asminternational.org

Margaret Hunt, Editor-in-Chief
Robert C Tucker Jr, President
Joanne Miller, Production Manager
Vin LeGendre, Publisher
Tina Long, Circulation Manager

Monthly Founded: 1913
Circulation: 32000

16914 American Machinist
Penton Media
1300 E 9th Street
Cleveland, OH 44114
216-696-7000
FAX: 216-626-1752
ameditor@penton.com
http://www.metalworking.penton.com

Thomas J. Grasson, Publisher / Editorial Director
Patricia L Smith, Executive Editor
Charles Bates, Senior Editor
Jim Benes, Associate Editor
Leslie Gordon, Associate Editor

Magazine of the manufacturing business. Plays an integral role in educating and informing our readers of the significant developments of manufacturing technology. The intent of every issue is to describe new metalworking technologies that help the readership speed production, cut costs, and stay competitive in the global market.
Monthly Founded: 1892
Circulation: 80000
Printed in 4 colors

16915 American Metal Market
Reed Business Information
345 Hudson Street
4th Floor
New York, NY 10014-4504
212-959-9550
FAX: 630-288-8686 www.amm.com

Michael Botta, Publisher
Gloria LaRue, Editor-in-Chief
Catalino Abrei, Owner

Thoroughly covers the metals industry, from production to distribution to recycling. American Metal Market is comprehensive, timely, reliable and invaluable daily newspaper for today's metal industry professionals. *$725.00*
16 pages Daily
Circulation: 10000
Printed in on glossy stock : web

16916 American Tool, Die & Stamping News
Eagle Publications
42400 Grand River Avenue
Suite 103
Novi, MI 48375-2572
248-473-3487
FAX: 248-347-3492 800-783-3491
sales@ameritooldie.com
http://www.ameritooldie.com

Gail Dawson, Marketing Manager
Joan Oakley, Circulation Director
Art Brown, Owner

Applications, techniques, equipment and accessories of metal stamping, moldmaking, electric discharge machining; and new product information relating to the tool and die industry. Accepts advertising.
70 pages Founded: 1971
Circulation: 36000
Printed in 5 colors on glossy stock

16917 Anvil Magazine
PO Box 1810
Georgetown, CA 95634-1810
530-333-2142
FAX: 530-333-2906 800-942-6845
anvil@anvilmag.com
http://www.anvilmag.com

Rob Edwards, Publisher
Timothy Sebastian, Editor-in-Chief
Jody Edwards, Circulation Manager

World-wide coverage of the blacksmithing and farrier trades. *$29.50*

Monthly Founded: 1980
Circulation: 5000

16918 Anvil's Ring
Artist-Blacksmiths' Association of North America
5821 Helias Drive
Jefferson, MO 65101-9316
573-395-3304
FAX: 573-395-3201

Jim McCarty, Editor

Covers such topics as architectural iron, decorative design, primitive artifacts, advice, and Association news. Also discusses supply sources, formal blacksmithing instruction and employment opportunities.

Monthly
Circulation: 4000

16919 Association of Iron and Steel Engineers Steel Technology
Three Gateway Center
Suite 1900
Pittsburgh, PA 15222-1004
412-281-6323
FAX: 412-281-6216 www.aise.org

Ronald E Ashburn, Publisher
Frank E Farmer, Executive Editor

AISE Steel Technology is the monthly technical journal of AISE. Highly authorative, it contains exclusive technical information relating to all phases of iron and steelmaking and finishing.

50+ pages Monthly
Printed in 4 colors

16920 Automatic Machining Magazine
Screw Machine Publishing Company
1066 Gravel Road
Suite 201
Webster, NY 14580
585-787-0820
FAX: 585-787-0868 800-610-6950
automach@rochester.rr.com
http://www.automachmag.com

Donald E Wood, Publisher
Wayne A Wood, Editorial Director

General industry news for professionals in the metal turning and cold forming fields. *$45.00*

142 pages Monthly Founded: 1941
Circulation: 13000 13000 names $75 per M.
Printed in 4 colors on glossy stock

16921 Casting World
Continental Communications
PO Box 1919
Bridgeport, CT 06601-1919
203-377-5566
FAX: 203-377-7230
contcon@compuserve.com

WW Troland, Editor

In-depth news on all aspects of ferrous and non-ferrous casting. *$99.00*

Quarterly
Circulation: 35000

16922 Coil World
CJL Publishing
8 High Point
Cedar Grove, NJ 07009
973-571-7155
FAX: 973-571-7102
philcola@optonline.net
http://www.coilworld.com

Philip E Colaiacovo, Editor-in-Chief/Publisher
Carl Hoffman, Circulation Manager
Shawn A Savage, Creative Director
A L Colaiacovo, Production/Advertising Svcs Manager

Offers articles on coil coating operations, fabricatiors, service centers, OEMs which use prepainted metals, new products, upcoming events, industry news, personnel announcements and committee updates.

Quarterly
Circulation: 10000

16923 Cutting Technology
Penton Media
1300 E. 9th St.
The Penton Media Building
Cleveland, OH 44114
216-696-7000
FAX: 216-696-1752
information@penton.com
http://www.metalworking.penton.com

David B Nussbaum, Chief Executive Officer
Patricia Smith, Executive Editor
Gil Apelis, Manager

Covers the full gamut of information essential to the success and productivity of those involved in metalcutting manufacturing. *$ 35.00*

Founded: 1892
Circulation: 40000
Printed in 4 colors

16924 Cutting Tool Engineering
CTE Publications
400 Skokie Boulevard
Suite 395
Northbrook, IL 60062-7903
847-498-9100
FAX: 847-559-4444 866-207-1450
alanr@jwr.com
http://www.ctemag.com

Don Nelson, Publisher
Alan Richter, Editor
John William Roberts, CEO

Cutting Tool Engineering serves manufacturing plants in the metal working industries. *$65.00*

72 pages Monthly Founded: 1955
Circulation: 34871
Printed in 4 colors on glossy stock

16925 Die Casting Engineer
North American Die Casting Association
241 Holbrook Dr
Suite 880
Wheeling, Il 60090-5809
847-279-0001
FAX: 847-279-0002
dce@diecasting.org
http://www.diecasting.org

Paul M Bralower, Editor
Daniel L Twarog, Publisher

News and technical information pertaining to the die casting industry. *$15.00*

Annual+ Founded: 1957
Printed in 4 colors on glossy stock

16926 Die Casting Management
C-K Publishing
PO Box 247
Wonder Lake, IL 60097-0247
815-728-0912
FAX: 815-728-0912
editor@diecastmgmt.com
www.diecastmgmt.com

Rob Crofts, Publisher

The main content focuses on profitable management, and includes articles on finance, marketing, technology, engineering, industry developments, and government legislation.

Bi-Monthly
Circulation: 4500

16927 Ductile Iron News
Ductile Iron Society
28938 Lorain Road
Suite 202
North Olmsted, OH 44070-4014
440-734-8040
FAX: 440-734-8182
jhall@ductile.org
http://www.ductile.org

Charlene Engel, Editor
John V Hall, Executive Director
William LeVan, President

The main material focuses on the technical data and applications, production statistics, and profiles of foundries. *$90.00*

Quarterly Founded: 1965
Circulation: 4500

16928 Engineering and Mining Journal
Mining Media
8751 East Hampden Avenue
Ste B1
Denver, CO 80231
303-283-0640
FAX: 303-283-0641
info@mining-media.com
http://www.e-mj.com

Peter Johnson, Publisher
Steve Fiscor, Editor-in-Chief
Russ Carter, Managing Editor
Gina Tverdak, Assistant Editor

Serves the field of mining including exploration, development, milling, smelting, refining of metals and nonmetallics. *$79.00*

Monthly Founded: 1866
Circulation: 10523
Printed in 4 colors on glossy stock

16929 Equip-Mart
116 N Camp Street
Seguin, TX 78155
830-303-3328
FAX: 830-372-3011 800-864-1155
story@storycomm.com
http://www.equip-mart.com

James Story, President
Tammy Reilly, Publisher
Kim Wiemann, Circulation Manager

Used metalworking equipment. *$50.00*

Monthly Founded: 1994
Circulation: 36000

16930 Fabricator
Croydon Group
833 Featherstone Road
Rockford, IL 61107
815-399-8700
FAX: 815-484-7700 866-879-9144
press_releases@thefabricator.com
http://www.thefabricator.com

Scot Stevens, Publisher
Dan Davis, Editor
Jerry Shankel, CEO

Jim Gorzek, Sales Manager
Kim Clothier, Circulation Manager

The Fabricator is North America's leading magazine for the metal forming and fabricating industry. Published monthly with more than 55,000 subscribers, it covers technology for the worldwide metal fabricating industry, including sheet metal punching, cutting, and bending; welding; coil processing; roll forming; material handling; laser cutting and welding; stamping; finishing; tube and pipe manufacturing; safety; automation; international technology trends; and more. *$75.00*

Monthly Founded: 1970
Circulation: 55000
Printed in 4 colors on glossy stock

16931 Finishers' Management
Publication Management
4350 Di Paolo Center
Glenview, IL 60025-5212
847-699-1700
FAX: 847-699-1703
www.finishers-management.com

David Friedman, Publisher
Kristy Judycki, Editor

Our publishing highlights include new product developments, equipment innovations, new production methods and reviews of current industry financial trends in the finishing industry. *$35.00*

50 pages 10 per year Founded: 1957
Circulation: 12000
Printed in 4 colors on glossy stock

16932 Forging
Penton Media
1300 E 9th Street
The Penton Media Building
Cleveland, OH 44114-1503
216-696-7000
FAX: 216-696-1752
forgeditor@penton.com
http://www.forgingmagazine.com

Dave Shanks, Publisher
Robert Brooks, Editor
Melody Berendt, Circulation

Dedicated to providing industrial part forgers with current market, product, process and equipment news and trend analysis. *$31.50*

62 pages Founded: 1990
Circulation: 5000
Printed in 4 colors on glossy stock

16933 Foundry Management & Technology
Penton Media
1300 E 9th Street
Cleveland, OH 44114-1503
216-696-7000
FAX: 216-696-7932
jwright@penton.com
http://www.foundrymag.com

Robert Brooks, Editor
Dave Shanks, Publisher
Melody Berendt, Circulation Manager

Received by management, production, engineering, research and technical professionals in the foundry industry. *$54.00*

70 pages Monthly
Printed in 4 colors on glossy stock

16934 Gases & Welding Distributor
Penton Media
1300 E 9th Street
Cleveland, OH 44114-1503
216-696-7000
FAX: 216-931-9524
infomation@penton.com
http://www.metalworking.penton.com

Thomas J Grasson, Publisher/Editorial Director
Patricia L Smith, Executive Editor
Charles Bates, Senior Editor
Jim Benes, Associate Editor
Melody Berendt, Circulation Manager

Marketing, management and technology magazine that aids distributors of welding supplies, industrial/medical/specialty gases, and safety products to sell more effectively to diverse markets. *$55.00*

74 pages six issues ayea
Printed in 4 colors

16935 Heat Treating Progress
ASM International
9639 Kinsman Road
Materials Park, OH 44073-2
440-338-5151
FAX: 440-338-4634 800-336-5152
cust-srv@asminternational.org
http://www.asminternational.com

Robert C Tucker Jr, President
Dean Peters, Editor-in-Chief
Lana Shapowal, Marketing Manager
Tina Long, Circulation Manager
Vin LeGendre, Publisher

Monthly Founded: 1913

16936 Industrial Paint & Powder
Reed Business Information
2000 Clearwater Drive
Oak Brook, IL 60523-8809
630-740-0825
FAX: 630-288-8686
www.ippmagazine.com

Jane Bailey, Editor

Coatings on manufacturing. *$55.00*

Monthly Founded: 1924
Circulation: 38000

16937 Industrial Product Bulletin
Gordon Publications
301 Gibraltar Drive
#650
Morris Plains, NJ 07950-3400
973-292-5100
FAX: 973-539-3476

Todd Baker, Publisher
Anita LaFond, Editor

Publication for executives and professionals in the process and metalworking industries. *$7.00*

Circulation: 200,050

16938 Inspection Trends
American Welding Society
550 N.W. LeJeune Road
Miami, FL 33126
305-443-9353
FAX: 305-443-7559 800-443-9353
info@aws.org http://www.aws.org/

Cassie Burrell, Associate Executive Director
Jeff Hufsey, Deputy Executive Director
Ray Shook, Executive Director
Kristin Campbell, Assistant Editor

Our information assists inspection personnel through information and reports on new technology and equipment, tips on inspection techniques and interpretation, as well as by giving examples of practical methodology. *$50.00*

Quarterly Founded: 1989
Circulation: 18000

16939 International Journal of Powder Metallurgy
American Powder Metallurgy Institute
105 College Road E
Princeton, NJ 08540-6622
609-452-7700
FAX: 609-987-8523
info@mpif.org http://www.mpif.org

Allan Lawley, Editor-in-Chief
C James Trombino, CEO

Covers metal powder producing and consuming industries. *$190.00*

4 pages Founded: 1959
Circulation: 3300

16940 Iron & Steel Technology
Association for Iron & Steel Technolgy
186 Thorn Hill Road
Warrendale, PA 15086-7528
724-776-6010
FAX: 724-776-1880
info@aist.org www.aist.org

Ronald E Ashburn, Executive Director
William A Albaugh, Technology Programs Manager
Stacy Varmecky, Membership Programs
Mark DiDiano, Finance And Administration

Advancing the technical development, production, processing and application of iron and steel. *$16.00*

Monthly
Circulation: 8,500

16941 JOM
Minerals, Metals & Materials Society
184 Thorn Hill Road
Warrendale, PA 15086-7528
724-776-9000
FAX: 724-776-3770 800-759-4867
tmsgeneral@tms.org
http://www.tms.org

Alexander Scott, Executive Director
James Robinson, Editor
Stephen Kendall, Publication Manager
Arlene Frances, Marketing

JOM is a technical journal devoted to exploring the many aspects of materials science and engineering. JOM reports scholarly work that explores the state of the art processing, fabrication, design, and application of metals, ceramics, plastics, composites, and other materials. In pursuing this goal, JOM strives to balance the interests of the laboratory and the marketplace by reporting academic, industrial, and government-sponsored work from around the world. *$131.00*

Monthly Founded: 1949
Circulation: 11000
Printed in 4 colors on glossy stock
Computerized version available: Internet

16942 Journal of Materials Engineering and Performance
9639 Kinsman Road
Materials Park, OH 44073-2
440-338-5151
FAX: 440-338-4634
cust-srv@asminternational.org
http://www.asm-intl.org

Ash Khare, President

Peer-reviewed journal which publishes contributions on all aspects of materials selection, design, characterization, processing and performance testing. The scope includes all materials used in engineering applications: those that typically result in components for larger systems. *$1184.00*

Founded: 1913
Circulation: 645

16943 Journal of Minerals, Metals & Materials Society
Minerals, Metals & Minerals Society
184 Thorn Hill Road
Warrendale, PA 15086-7511
724-776-9000
FAX: 724-776-3770
tmsgeneral@tms.org
http://www.tms.org

Alexander R Scott, Executive Director
Robert Makowski, Communications Director

To promote the global science and engineering profession's concerned with minerals, metals and materials. Founded in 1871. Publishes a monthly magazine. *$20.00*
Monthly Founded: 1880
Circulation: 10000

16944 Journal of Phase Equilibria
ASM International
9639 Kinsman Road
Materials Park, OH 44073-2
440-338-5151
FAX: 440-338-4634 800-336-5152
cust-srv@asminternational.org
http://www.asminternational.org

Gordon Geiger, President

Peer-reviewed journal which contains basic and applied research results, evaluated phase diagrams, a survey of current literature, and comments or other material pertinent to the previous three areas. The aim is to provide a broad spectrum of information concerning phase equilibria for the materials community. *$1716.00*
Annual+
Circulation: 305

16945 Journal of Thermal Spray Technology
ASM International
9639 Kinsman Road
Materials Park, OH 44073-2
440-338-5151
FAX: 440-338-4634
Cust-Srv@asminternational.org
http://www.asminternational.org

Robert Tucker, Jr, President

Peer-reviewed journal which publishes contributions on all aspects, fundamental and practical, of thermal spray science, including processes, feedstock manufacture, testing and characterization. As the primary vehicle for thermal spray information transfer, its mission is to synergize the rapidly advancing thermal spray industry and related industries by presenting research and development efforts leading to advancements in implementable engineering applications of the technology. *$1256.00*
Quarterly Founded: 1952
Circulation: 680

16946 Light Metal Age
Fellom Publishing Company
170 S Spruce Avenue
Suite 120
South San Francisco, CA 94080-4557
650-588-8832
FAX: 650-588-0901
lma@lightmetalage.com
http://www.lightmetalage.com

Ann Marie Fellom, Publisher *$45.00*

Monthly Founded: 1944
Circulation: 5000
Printed in 4 colors on glossy stock

16947 Locator Services
315 S Patrick Street
Alexandria, VA 22314-3501
703-836-9700
FAX: 703-836-7665 800-537-1446
webmaster@locatoronline.com
http://www.locatoronline.com

Terry J Pitman, Executive Publisher

Used metalworking equipment.
Monthly Founded: 1969
Circulation: 225000

16948 Machine Shop Guide
Worldwide Communications
401 Worthington Avenue
Harrison, NJ 07029-2039
973-497-7555
FAX: 973-497-7556

Robert L Hatschek, Executive Editor

Information on manufacturing technology, new applications for manufacturing technology and new products.

Circulation: 102893

16949 Manufacturers Showcase
Heartland Communications Group
1003 Central Avenue
Po Box 1052
Fort Dodge, IA 50501
515-955-1600
FAX: 515-955-3753 800-203-9960
ads@imtproduction.com
www.imtgetsresults.com

Natalie Fevold, Operations Manager
Sandy Simonson, Sales Manager

A magazine for new metalworking machinery, tooling and supplies.
Monthly

16950 Manufacturing Engineering
Society of Manufacturing Engineers
1 Sme Drive
PO Box 930
Dearborn, MI 48121
313-271-1500
FAX: 313-425-3401 800-733-4763
webmaster@sme.org
http://www.sme.org

Tom Drozda, Publisher
John Coleman, Editor-in-Chief
Gene Nelson, President

Serves metalworking industry machining, forming, inspection, assembly and processing operations.
Monthly Founded: 1932
Circulation: 111966

16951 Metal Architecture
Modern Trade Communications
7450 Skokie Boulevard
Suite 1
Skokie, IL 60077-3395
847-674-2200
FAX: 847-674-3676
shawnzuver@moderntrade.com
http://www.moderntrade.com

Sam Millnark, Publisher
Mark Wiebusch, Marketing & Operations
Shawn Zuver, Editorial & Production

Low-rise construction involving architects, engineers and specifiers.
Monthly
Circulation: 29513

16952 Metal Center News
Reed Business Information
2000 Clearwater Drive
Oak Brook, IL 60523
630-740-0825
FAX: 630-288-8686
www.metalcenternews.com
Reports on verious phases of metal center operations.

16953 Metal Finishing
Elsevier Science
655 Avenue of the Americas
New York, NY 10010-5107
212-989-5800
FAX: 212-633-3990
PressOffice@elsevier.com
http://www.elsevier.com

Doug Stivison, Publisher
Patti Ann Frost, Managing Editor
Susan Canalizo, Production Manager
Greg Valero, Manager

Finishes and finishing of metal products.
$87.00
Monthly Founded: 1903
Circulation: 19824

16954 Metal Finishing Guidebook Directory
Metal Finishing/Elsevier Science
360 Park Avenue South
New York, NY 10010-1710
212-895-5800
FAX: 212-633-3140
metalfinishing@elsevier.com
http://www.metalfinishing.com

Gregory A. Valero, Editor & Publisher
Patti Ann Frost, Managing Editor
Matthew Smaldon, Circulation Manager
$87.00

Founded: 1962

16955 Metal Finishing Magazine
Metal Finishing/Elsevier Science
360 Park Avenue South
New York, NY 10010-1710
212-895-5800
FAX: 212-633-3140
metalfinishing@elsevier.com
http://www.metalfinishing.com

Patti Ann Frost, Managing Editor
Gregory A Valero, Editor & Publisher
Ron Joseph, Organic Coatings Editor
Susan Canalizo-Baruch, Production Manager
Mathew Smaldon, Circulation Manager
$87.00

Monthly Founded: 1903
Circulation: 23000

16956 Metal Mecanica
Gardner Publications
901 poncedeleon blvd
sute 601
Coral Gables, FL 33134-3029
513-527-8977
FAX: 305-448-9942 800-950-8020
trivas@metalmecanica.com
http://www.metalmecanica.com

David Ash, President
Eduardo Tovar, Editor
Holgar Hilkinger, Circulation Manager
Alfredo Domador, Publisher

Founded: 1905
Circulation: 12157

16957 MetalForming
Precision Metalforming Association
6363 Oak Tree Boulevard
Independence, OH 44131-2500
216-019-9667
FAX: 216-901-9190
pma@pma.org
http://www.metalforming.com

Brad Kuvin, Editor
Kathy DeLollis, Publisher
William Gaskin, President
Daniel Ellashek, VP
Lou Kren, Senior Editor

Edited for decision makers in the precision metal forming industry. *$59.95*
100 pages Monthly Founded: 1967
Circulation: 60000 100 names $150 per M.
Printed in 4 colors on matte stock

16958 Metallurgical and Materials Transactions
Minerals, Metals & Materials Society
184 Thorn Hill Road
Warrendale, PA 15086-7528
724-776-9000
FAX: 724-776-3770
tmsgeneral@tms.org
http://www.tms.org

Robert Makowski, Publishing Director
$1467.00
13 issues

16959 Metallurgical and Materials Transactions A
Minerals, Metals & Materials Society
184 Thorn Hill Road
Warrendale, PA 15086-7528
724-776-9000
FAX: 724-776-3770
tmsgeneral@tms.org www.tms.org

Robert Makowski, Publishing Director
$1497.00
Monthly

16960 Metalsmith
Society of North American Goldsmiths
5009 Londonderry Drive
Tampa, FL 33647-1336
813-977-5326
FAX: 813-977-8462
metalsmitheditor@aol.com
http://www.snagmetalsmith.org

Suzanne Ramljak, Editor
Dana Singer, Executive Director
Ken Bova, President
Jean Savarese, Advertising Director

Information which explores new work in the jewelry, holloware, blacksmithing, and sculpture fields. Profiles of master metalsmiths are included. *$65.00*
Founded: 1969
Circulation: 13,500

16961 Metalworking Digest
Reed Business Information
100 Enterprice Drive
Suite 600
Rockaway, NJ 07866
973-920-7000
FAX: 973-920-7531
http://www.reedbusiness.com

Rich Stevancsecz, Editor
Joe May, Publisher
Cloin Ungaro, CEO/President
Steve Koppelman, Circulation Manager
R Reed, Owner

Monthly Founded: 1969
Circulation: 115000

16962 Metalworking Distributor
Penton Media
1300 E 9th Street
Cleveland, OH 44114
216-696-7000
FAX: 216-696-1752
information@penton.com
www.metalworking.penton.com

Joseph Fristik, Publisher
Thomas Grasson, Editor
Susan Cubranich, Production Manager

Publication exclusively devoted to distributors and wholesales in the metalworking industry to help improve marketing, management, and technology knowledge as well as provide information on new markets.
Quarterly
Circulation: 5,000
Printed in 4 colors

16963 Modern Applications News
Nelson Publishing
2500 Tamiami Trail North
Nakomis, FL 34275-3476
941-966-9521
FAX: 941-966-2590
subscriptions@nelsonpub.com
http://www.nelsonpub.com

Larry Olson, Editor

Information includes coverage of abrasives and grinding, automated handling and robotics, CAD/CAM, coatings and finishings, coolants, lubricants and filters, cutting tools, heat treating, ID marking, lasers, machining centers, and shop control software.
Monthly Founded: 1967
Circulation: 84000

16964 Modern Casting
American Foundrymen's Society
1695 North Penny Lane
Schaumburg, IL 60173-2267
847-824-0181
FAX: 847-824-7848 800-537-4237
circ@afsinc.org
http://www.moderncasting.com

Rolf Petersen, Publisher
Jerry Call, CEO/President
Kyle Bauer, Editor
Barbara Jackowski, Circulation Manager
Alfred Spada, Editer- in -chief

Designed to promote the technological advances in the industry. *$50.00*
Monthly Founded: 1896
Circulation: 19000

16965 Modern Machine Shop
Gardner Publications
6915 Valley Avenue
Cincinnati, OH 45244-3029
513-278-8977
FAX: 513-527-8801 800-950-8020
mmsmkt@gardnerweb.com
http://www.mmsonline.com

Daniel C Luciano, Publisher
Mark D Albert, Editor-in-Chief
Dianne Hight, Circulation Manager
Richard Kline, President

Reaches metalworking plants of all sizes - from small job shops to giant aerospace and automotive plants. It is edited for those involved in metalworking operations, particularly those performed on machine tools. *$89.00*
Monthly Founded: 1928
Circulation: 107000
Mailing list available for rent 106M names
Printed in 4 colors on glossy stock

16966 NACE International
NACE
1440 South
Creek Drive
Houston, TX 77084-4906
713-063-3400
FAX: 281-228-6300 800-797-6223
firstservice@nace.org
http://www.nace.org

Gretchen Jacobson, Publication director
Teri Elliott, Marketing Director
Amber Pappas, Executive Director
Neil Thompson, President *$98.00*
Monthly Founded: 1989

16967 National Ornamental and Miscellaneous Metals Association
532 Forest Parkway
Suite A
Forest Park, GA 30297-6137
404-363-4009
FAX: 404-366-1852
nommainfo@aol.com
http://www.nomma.org

Barbara Cook, Executive Director
Todd Daniel, Editor

Ornamental and Miscellaneous Metals Fabricator Magazine is a monthly publication for all those interested in ornamental and metallurgy industries.
Founded: 1958

16968 Occupational Hazards
Penton Media
1300 E 9th Street
Cleveland, OH 44114
216-696-7000
FAX: 216-696-1752
information@penton.com
http://www.penton.com

Penny McCullough, Editorial Assistant
Bob Marinez, Publisher
David B Nussbaum, CEO
Jennifer Daugherty, Communications Manager

Analysis of qualified recipients who have indicated that they recommend, select and/or buy the safety equipment, fire protection and other occupational health products.
65 pages Monthly Founded: 1892
Circulation: 65777
Printed in 4 colors on glossy stock

16969 Ornamental and Miscellaneous Metals Fabricator
National Ornamental & Miscellaneous Metals Assn
532 Forest Parkway
Suite A
Forest Park, GA 30297-6137
404-363-4009
FAX: 404-366-1852
nommainfo@nomma.org
http://www.nomma.org

Curt Witter, CEO/President
Todd Daniel, Editor

Magazine published by National Ornamental and Miscellaneous Metals Association. *$30.00*
Founded: 1958
Circulation: 10000

16970 Platt's Metals Week
McGraw Hill
3333 Walnut Street
Boulder, CO 80301
720-548-5000
FAX: 720-548-5701 800-752-8878
metals@platts.com
http://www.mcgraw-hill.com

Jackie Roche, Editor-in-Chief
Terry McGraw, CEO
Harry Sachinsis, President
Jackie Roche, Publisher

Extensive price listings in four currencies.
Weekly

16971 Powder Coating
OSC Publishing
1300 E 66th Street
Minneapolis, MN 55423-2642
612-866-2242
FAX: 612-866-1939

Richard R Cress, Publisher
Richard Link, Manager

Our information focuses on the application, pre-treatment, materials, materials handling, and curing processes. Also features case histories. *$95.00*
Monthly
Circulation: 23587

16972 Practical Welding Today
Fabricators and Manufacturers Association
833 Featherstone Road
Rockford, IL 61107-6302
815-399-8700
FAX: 815-484-7700
info@fmanet.org
http://www.fmanet.org

Gerald M Shankel, President/CEO
Michael Hedges, VP Finance/CFO
Scott Stevens, Publisher
Kim Clothier, Director of Circulation
Jim Gorzek, Marketing

Practical Welding Today is the only hands on, down-to-earth magazine with information that welders can use in the shop or out in the field. Published six times per year with more than 40,000 subcribers, it covers topics such as systems and equipment, safety, consumables, cutting and welding prep, welding inspection and more. In addition, Practical Welding Today has a regular lineup of application articles, welder profiles, product highlights and valuable buyers' guides.

Circulation: 40000
Printed in 4 colors on glossy stock

16973 Products Finishing
Gardner Publications
6915 Valley Avenue
Cincinnati, OH 45244-3029
513-527-8977
FAX: 513-231-2818
narnold@gardnerweb.com
http://www.pfonline.com

G Thomas Robison, Publisher
Beverly Graves, Editor
Melissa Skavlem, CEO

Covers production, management, engineering, design, etc. in plants where metal and plastic products are eletroplated, anodized, painted, buffed, cleaned or otherwise finished. *$89.00*
Monthly Founded: 1928
Circulation: 45552
Printed in 4 colors on glossy stock

16974 Projects in Metal
Village Press
2779 Aero Park Drive
PO Box 629
Traverse City, MI 49686-9101
231-463-3712
FAX: 231-946-3289
villagepre@aol.com
www.members.aol.com/vpshop/pim/htm

Robert Goff, Publisher

In each issue you will find plans for valuable tools and accessories, and challenging hobby projects. Every project is complete in one issue.
Bi-Monthly
Circulation: 15000

16975 Recycling Today
GIE Media
4012 Bridge Avenue
Cleveland, OH 44113-3320
216-961-4130
FAX: 216-961-0364 800-456-0707
btaylor@gie.net
http://www.recyclingtoday.com

Jim Keefe, Group Publisher
Brian Taylor, Editor
Richard Foster, CEO
Helen Duerr, Production Manager
Megan Ries, Advertising Coordinatior

Published for the secondary commodity processing/recycling market. *$30.00*
Monthly Founded: 1980

16976 SCRAP
Institute of Scrap Recycling Industries
1325 G Street NW
Suite 1000
Washington, DC 20005-3104
202-737-1770
FAX: 202-626-0900
kentkiser@scrap.org
http://www.scrap.org

Kent Kiser, Publisher
Ellen Ross, Production Director
Robert L Reid, Managing Editor
Valerie Hillyer, Circulation Associate
Robin Wiener, President

A bi-monthly magazine that covers all aspects of the international scrap recycling industry, including market trends, business management, personnel issues, equipment and technology, regulations and legislation, and more. *$36.00*
16 pages Founded: 1928
Circulation: 7400 6,432 names $125 per M.

16977 Secondary Marketing Executive
LDJ Corporation
PO Box 2330
Waterbury, CT 06722-2330
203-755-0158
FAX: 203-755-3480 800-325-6745

John Florian, Editorial Director
Linda Herrmann, Account Executive

Delivers news, analysis and how-to advice to people involved in the buying and selling of mortgage loans and servicing rights nationwide. *$48.00*
44 pages Monthly Founded: 1986
Circulation: 21,000

16978 Shop Owner
Penton Media
1300 E 9th Street
Cleveland, OH 44114-1503
216-696-7000
FAX: 216-931-9524
information@penton.com
http://www.metalworking.penton.com

Joseph Fristik, Publisher
Thomas J Grasson, Editorial Director
Charles Bates, Senior Editor
Melody Berendt, Circulation Manager
Janet Marioneaux, Administrative Assistant

Digest-sized publication covering information essential to the success of the small to medium manufacturing shop.
Quarterly Founded: 1998
Circulation: 120000
Printed in 4 colors

16979 Stamping Journal
Fabricators and Manufacturers Association
833 Featherstone Road
Rockford, IL 61107-6302
815-399-8700
FAX: 815-484-7700
info@fmanet.org
http://www.fmanet.org

Gerald Shankel, President/CEO
Michael Hedges, CFO
Scot Stevens, Publisher
Jim Gorzek, Sales Manager
Kim Clothier, Circulation Manager

Stamping Journal, the only North American magazine devoted exclusively to metal stamping, has been delivering the industry's latest techniques, news and ideas to subscribers worldwide for 13 years. Published six times per year, with more than 35,000 subscribers, Stamping Journal focuses on metal stamping technology including, tool and die, material handling, coil processing, stamping presses, press feeding, quick die change and more. *$65.00*
Monthly Founded: 1970
Circulation: 35000
Printed in 4 colors on glossy stock

16980 Tooling & Production
Adams Business Media
6001 Cochran Rd
Suite 104
Solon, OH 44139-1855
440-248-1125
FAX: 440-248-0187 800-638-5658
subscriptions@nelsonpub.com
http://www.toolingandproduction.com

Vern Nelson, Group Publisher
Jim Lorlancz, Editor-in-Chief

Our focus is on technology, its application, and the business and operation of metalworking manufacturing. Reports and news provide metalworking manufacturing solutions - leading edge product developments and application reports of new products.
100 pages Monthly Founded: 1934
Circulation: 70000
Printed in 4 colors on glossy stock

16981 Tube & Pipe Journal
Fabricators and Manufacturers Association
833 Featherstone Road
Rockford, IL 61107-6302
815-998-8700
FAX: 815-484-7701
info@fmanet.org
http://www.fmanet.org

Gerald Shankel, President/CEO
Michael Hedges, CFO

The Tube and Pipe Journal is North America's only magazine devoted exclusively to metal tube and pipe manufacturing. Published 8 times per year and with more than 30,000 subscribers, TPJ covers topics such as tube producing, bending and forming, cutting and sawing, welding, tooling, coil and material handling, and more. TPJ also provides expanded coverage of hydroforming technology in the Hydroforming Journal, a separate supplement published four time per year alongside TPJ. *$200.00*
Founded: 1970
Circulation: 30000
Printed in 4 colors on glossy stock

16982 **US Glass, Metal & Glazing**
Key Communications
PO Box 569
Garrisonville, VA 22463
540-577-7174
FAX: 540-720-5687
info@glass.com http://www.glass.com
Debra Levy, Publisher
Ellen Giard Chilcoat, Editor
Penny Stacey, Advertising Coordinator
Serves manufactures/fabricators, contract glaziers, distributors and wholesalers, retailors/dealers of glass/metal and or glass/metal products and other allied to the field.
Monthly Founded: 1995
Circulation: 15000
Printed in 4 colors on glossy stock

16983 **Welding Design & Fabrication**
Penton Media
The Penton Media Building
1300 E 9th Street
Cleveland, OH 44114
216-696-7000
FAX: 216-696-1752
information@penton.com
http://www.penton.com
Joseph Fristik, Publisher
Dean Peters, Editor
David Nussbaum, CEO
Reaches designers, engineers, managers, superviisors, and buyers in plants and field sites in the US and Canada who conduct welding and fabricating operations. Reports on processes and equipment, materials, safety, testing and inspection in the manufacturing of fabricated metal products, structural projects and equipment maintenance.
Monthly Founded: 1892
Circulation: 40000
Printed in 4 colors

16984 **Welding Innovation**
James F Lincoln Arc Welding Foundation
22801 Saint Clair Avenue
Cleveland, OH 44117-1199
216-481-4300
FAX: 216-486-1751
welding-innovation@lincolnelectric.
http://www.jflf.org/
Duane K Miller, Editor
Richard D Seif, Sales/Marketing Manager

Informative articles related to welding steel structures such as bridges and buildings, as well as notices of related conferences.
Founded: 1936
Circulation: 40000

16985 **Welding Journal**
American Welding Society
550 NW LeJeune Road
Miami, FL 33126-5699
305-443-9353
FAX: 305-443-7559 800-443-9353
info@aws.org http://www.aws.org
Ray Shook, Executive Director
Jefferey Weber, Publisher
Cecilia Barbier, Senior Coordinator Market
Our feature articles include new product listings, book reviews and the application of new operating procedures.
Monthly Founded: 1919
Circulation: 46000

16986 **Wire Rope News & Sling Technology**
Wire Rope News
PO Box 871
Clark, NJ 07066-871
908-486-3221
FAX: 732-396-4215
vsent@aol.com
http://www.wireropenews.com
Edward J Bluvias, Publisher
Conrad Miller, Editor
Wire Rope News & Sling Technology is edited for manufacturers and distributors of wire rope, chain, cordage, related hardware, and sling fabricators. Content includes technical articles, news, and reports describing the manufacture and use of wire rope in marine, construction, mining, aircraft and offshore drilling operations. Cordage, slings, chain and fittings are also covered. Editorial content contains articles about fabricating companies, new products and people in the news. *$20.00*
Founded: 1979
Circulation: 4400
Printed in 4 colors on glossy stock

Trade Shows

16987 **AFS/CMI Advanced Foundry Operations Conference**
American Foundrymen's Society
505 State Street
Des Plains, IL 60016-8399
847-824-0181
FAX: 847-824-7848 800-537-4237
March

16988 **ASM Heat Treating Society Conference and Heat Treat Show**
ASM International
9639 Kinsman Road
Materials Park, OH 44073-0002
440-385-5151
FAX: 440-338-4634 800-336-5152
asmexpos@asminternational.org
www.asminternational.org
Conference and 260 exhibits of heat treating equipment and supplies plus information of interest to metallurgists, manufacturing, research and design technical professionals.
4500 Attendees Bi-Annual Founded: 1974

16989 **ASM Materials Solutions Conference and Exposition**
ASM International
9639 Kinsman Road
Materials Park, OH 44073-0002
440-385-5151
FAX: 440-338-4634 800-336-5152
asmexpos@asminternational.org
www.asminternational.org
Annual event focusing on testing, analysis, characterization and research of materials such as engineered materials, high performance metals, powdered metals, metal forming, surface modification, welding and joining.
4,000 Attendees October

16990 **Advanced Productivity Conference and Expo- Cleveland**
Society of Manufacturing Engineers
1 SME Drive
PO Box 930
Dearborn, MI 48121-0930
313-271-1500
FAX: 313-271-2861 800-733-3976
radodan@sme.org www.sme.org
Dan Radomski, Show Manager
200 Exhibits of equipment, supplies and services for the tool and manufacturing engineering fields.
13800 Attendees Biennial Founded: 1984

16991 **American Foundrymen's Society Castings Congress and Cast Expo**
505 State St
Des Plaines, IL 60016-2267
847-824-0181
FAX: 847-824-7845
Kristy Glass, Show Manager
300 booths including technical papers and panel sessions for the metal casting industry.
12000 Attendees Annual

16992 **American Society Engineers: Design International**
Systems and Design Group
3 Park Avenue
Floor 27
New York, NY 10016-5902
212-903-4160

Fred Goldfarb, Program Manager
Virgil Carter, Chief Executive Officer
150 booths.
2.5M Attendees August

16993 **American Zinc Association**
1112 16th Street NW
Suite 240
Washington, DC 20036-4818
202-478-8200
FAX: 202-835-0155
zincinfo@zinc.org www.zinc.org
George Vary, Executive Director
David Adkins, Secretary
February

16994 **Annual International Titanium Conference**
International Titanium Association
1871 Folsom Street
Suite 200
Boulder, CO 80302-5714
303-443-7515
FAX: 303-443-4406
afitz@titanium.net www.titanium.org
Amy Fitzgerald, Manager
800 Attendees October Founded: 1984

16995 **Artist-Blacksmiths Association of North America Conference**
PO Box 206
Washington, MO 63090
636-390-2133
FAX: 636-390-2133 www.abasna.otg
Marcus Vickery, Conference Coordinator
Meeting and exhibitions, workshops, demonstrations and artistic metalwork for the professional and amateur blacksmith.
1000 Attendees Biennial

16996 **Association of Industrial Metallizers, Coaters and Laminators Conference**
201 Springs Street
Fort Mill, SC 29708
803-802-7820
FAX: 803-802-7821
aimcal@aimcal.org www.aimcal.org
Craig Sheppard, Executive Director
Displays relating to coaters and laminators, metallizers and producers of metallized film and or paper on continuous rolls, sup-

pliers of plastic films, papers and adhesives.
Annual Founded: 1970

16997 Cast Expo
Cast Metals Institute
505 State Street
Des Plaines, IL 60016
847-824-0181
FAX: 847-824-7848 800-537-4237
May

16998 FABTECH International
Fabricators and Manufacturers Association
833 Featherstone Road
Rockford, IL 61107-6302
815-399-8700
FAX: 815-399-7279
info@fmametalfab.org
www.fmametalfab.org
Mark Hoper, Manager
Kim Clothier, Circulation Director
A metal forming and fabricating equipment exposition and conference. Containing 900 booths and exhibits, with pavilions dedicated to stamping, tube, pipe and welding.
30M+ Attendees October

16999 FABTECH International AWS Welding Show
American Welding Society
550 NW 42nd Avenue
Miami, FL 33126-5699
305-443-9353
FAX: 305-443-7559 800-443-9353
Ray Shook, Executive Director
Jefferey Weber, Publisher
Amy Nathan, Public Relations Manager
350 booths of welding and allied industries held in conjunction with metal form.
Annual

17000 Furnaces North America
Metal Treating Institute
1550 Roberts Drive
Jacksonville, FL 32250
904-249-0448
FAX: 904-249-0459
scott@metaltreat.com
www.metaltreat.com
Scott Hardy, Show Manager
North America's Premier "Heat Treat Only" Event, Furnaces North America 2006, will be held September 27-28, 2006 at the brand new Reno Events Center in Reno, Nevada. FNA2006 is being designed with enhancements to interest everyone involved in the treatment of metal products.
1200 Attendees September Founded: 1995

17001 Int'l Conference on Powder Injection Molding of Metals and Ceramics
Innovative Material Solutions
225 Canterbury Drive
State College, PA 16803
814-867-1140
FAX: 814-867-2813
info@imspowder.com
www.imspowder.com/pim2002
March

17002 International Symposium for Testing and Failure Analysis
ASM International
9639 Kinsman Road
Materials Park, OH 44073-0002
440-385-5151
FAX: 440-338-4634
jdirosa@asminternational.org
Jan DiRosa, Expositions Sales
Annual event focusing on microelectronic and electronic device failure analysis, techniques, EOS/ESD testing and discretes aimed at failure analysis engineers and managers, technicians and new failure analysis engineers. Santa Clara Convention Center, Santa Clara, California.
1,100 Attendees November

17003 Iron & Steel Exposition
Association of Iron & Steel Engineers
3 Gateway Center
Suite 1900
Pittsburgh, PA 15222-1000
412-281-6323
FAX: 412-281-4657 www.aise.org
Ronald E Ashiurn, Managing Director
Includes technical sessions and exhibits of equipment, supplies and services for the metals producing industry.
25M Attendees

17004 METALFORM
Precision Metalforming Association
6363 Oak Tree Boulevard
Independence, OH 44131
216-901-8800
FAX: 216-901-9190
aprimiano@pma.org
www.metalform.com
Amy Primiano, Director Expositions
William Gaskin, President
A regional networking and educational event that brings buyers and sellers from metal stamping and fabricating markets together in a dynamic and interactive environment.
5,000 Attendees March

17005 Magnesium in Automotive
International Magnesium Association
1303 Vincent Place
Suite 1
Mc Lean, VA 22101-3615
703-442-8888
FAX: 703-821-1824 www.intlmag.org
Containing 12-15 exhibits.
250 Attendees

17006 Metalworking Machine Tool Expo
Marketing International Corporation
200 N Glebe Road
Suite 900
Arlington, VA 22203-3728
703-527-8000
FAX: 703-527-8006
Annual show of 100 machine tools suppliers.
8000 Attendees

17007 NFFS Summit Conference
Non-Ferrous Founders' Society
1480 Renaissance Drive
Suite 310
Park Ridge, IL 60068
847-299-0950
FAX: 847-299-3598
staff@nffs.org www.nffs.org
February

17008 National Ornamental and Miscellaneous Metals Association
532 Forest Parkway
Suite A
Forest Park, GA 30297-6137
404-363-4009
FAX: 404-366-1852
nommainfo@aol.com
www.nomma.org
Barbara Cook, Executive Director
Todd Daniel, Editor
Cyndi Smith, Office Manager
Martha Pennington, Meetings/Exposition Manager
This annual convention and trade show — METALfab — is for all those involved in the ornamental and metallury industries.
900 Attendees Founded: 1958

17009 TMS Annual Meeting Exhibition
Minerals, Metals & Materials Society
184 Thorn Hill Road
Warrendale, PA 15086
724-776-9000
FAX: 724-776-3770
mtgserv@tms.org www.tms.org
Cindy Wilson, Show Manager
Alexander Scott, Executive Director
International metals and materials exhibition. Production, processing, engineering and research. Held in Charlotte, North Carolina.
3,500 Attendees March

17010 WESTEC-Advanced Productivity Expo
Society of Manufacturing Engineers
1 SME Drive
PO Box 930
Dearborn, MI 48121-0930
313-271-1500
FAX: 313-271-2861 www.sme.org
Gary Mikola, Show Manager
600 booths displaying machine tools and metalworking products and services.
40M Attendees Annual

Directories & Databases

17011 Advanced Materials and Processes: Thermal Spray Buyer's Guide Issue
ASM International
9639 Kinsman Road
Materials Park, OH 44073-0002
440-338-5151
FAX: 440-338-4634
Directory of thermal spray coating products and services for the metalworking industry. *$10.00*

17012 Aluminum Association Aluminum Standards & Data
Aluminum Assocaition
900 19th Street NW
Washington, DC 20006-2105
202-862-5100

Contains the nominal composition and composition limits, typical mechanical and physical properties and tensile properties limits for US wrought aluminum alloys. Updated periodically.
Numeric

17013 DRI Steel Forecast
DRI/McGraw-Hill
24 Hartwell Avenue
Lexington, MA 02421-3158
781-863-5100

This comprehensive database offers over 500 quarterly and annual forecasts on production, shipment, and consumption of raw steel and steel products in the United States.

17014 Dun's Industrial Guide: Metalworking Directory
Dun & Bradstreet Information Service
3 Sylvan Way
Parsippany, NJ 07054-3805
973-455-0900
FAX: 973-605-6911 800-526-0651
Over 78,000 original equipment manufacturers, metal distributors, and machine tools/metalworking machinery distributors. *$775.00*
Annual

17015 EDM Today Yearbook
EDM Publications
230 W Parkway
Suite 3-1
Pompton Plains, NJ 07444-1065
973-831-1334
FAX: 973-831-1195
Jack Sebzda, Editor
Annual

17016 Economic Handbook of the Machine Tool Industry
AMT - The Association for Manufacturing Technology
7901 Westpark Drive
Mc Lean, VA 22102-4206
703-893-2900
FAX: 703-893-1151
amt@amtonline.org
www.amtonline.org
Pam Kachel, Public Relations Coordinator

Complete statistics for the US machine tool industry, including exports and imports. *$295.00*
Annual
Printed in 1 color on matte stock

17017 Equip-Mart
116 N Camp Street
Seguin, TX 78155
830-303-3328
FAX: 830-372-3011 800-864-1155
Directory of available used metalworking equipment.
Weekly

17018 Foundry Management & Technology: Where to Buy Directory Issue
Penton Publishing Company
216-696-7000
FAX: 216-696-1752
information@penton.com
www.penton.com
Dean Peters, Editor
Listing of about 1,700 manufacturers of foundry products. *$15.00*
Annual, September
Circulation: 22,000

17019 Industrial Laser Review: Buyers' Guide of Companies & Products
PennWell Publishing Company
10 Tara Boulevard
5th Floor
Nashua, NH 03062-2800
603-891-0123
FAX: 603-891-0574 www.ilr.com
David Belforte, Editor
Annual July

17020 Industrial Machine Trader
Heartland Industrial Group
1003 Central Avenue
PO Box 1415
Fort Dodge, IA 50501
515-955-1600
FAX: 515-955-3753 800-247-2000
igproduction@industrialgroup.com
www.industrialgroup.com
Denise McLellan, Editor
Printed directory of available used metalworking equipment.
Weekly

17021 International Lead and Zinc
WEFA Group
800 Baldwin Tower Boulevard
Eddystone, PA 19022-1368
610-490-4000
FAX: 610-490-2770
info@wefa.com www.wefa.com
This database contains quarterly and annual time series on lead and zinc.

17022 Iron and Manganese Ore Databook
Metal Bulletin
220 5th Avenue
New York, NY 10001-7708
212-136-6202
FAX: 212-213-6273 800-MET-L 25
John Bailey, Editor
Iron and manganese ore producers and traders worldwide. *$179.00*
Quadrennial

17023 Iron and Steel Works of the World
Metal Bulletin
220 5th Avenue
19th Floor
New York, NY 10001-7781
212-213-6202
FAX: 202-213-1870
www.metalbulleton.com
Henry Cooke, Editor
Lists over 1,500 major iron and steel plants worldwide. *$439.00*
730 pages

17024 Locator Services
315 S Patrick Street
Alexandria, VA 22314-3501
703-836-9700
FAX: 703-836-7665 800-537-1446
sales@locatoronline.com
www.locatoronline.com
Terry J Pitman, Executive Publisher
Printed directory of available used metalworking equipment.
Monthly
Circulation: 225,000

17025 Metal Bulletin's Prices and Data Book
Metal Bulletin
220 5th Avenue
19th Floor
New York, NY 10001-7781
212-213-6202
FAX: 212-213-1870
www.metalbulletin.com
A list of national and international associations and trading organizations concerned with iron, steel and nonferrous ores and metals. *$165.00*
Annual

17026 Metal Casting Industry Directory
Penton Media
1300 E 9th Street
Cleveland, OH 44114
216-696-7000
FAX: 216-696-1752
information@penton.com
www.penton.com
David Shanks, Publisher
Directory of services and supplies to the industry. *$425.00*
300 pages

17027 Metal Center New: Metal Distribution Directory
Reed Business Information
2000 Clearwater Drive
Oak Brook, IL 60523-8809
630-740-0825
FAX: 630-288-8686
www.metalcenternews.com
Timothy Triplett, Editor
Annual February

17028 Metal Center News: Metal Distribution Issue
Hitchcock Publishing Company
191 S Gary Avenue
Carol Stream, IL 60188-2095
630-690-5600

Joseph Marino, Editor
Offers a list of producers and industrial metals and metal products, manufacturers of metal processing and handling equipment. *$ 25.00*
Annual
Circulation: 14,000

17029 Metal Finishing: Guidebook Directory
Metal Finishing/Elsevier Science
650 Avenue of Americas
New York, NY 10011
212-633-5100
FAX: 212-633-5140
E.Nadel@Elsevier.com
www.metalfinishing.com
Eugene Nadel, Publisher
Annual January

17030 Metal Statistics
American Metal Market
350 Hudson Street
4th Floor
New York, NY 10014-4504
212-666-2420
FAX: 212-519-7522 800-662-4445
custserv@espcomp.com
www.amm.com
Gloria Larme, Editor-in-Chief
The statistical guide to North American metals. Hardcover $265.00, Softcover $185.00.

404 pages Annual Founded: 1908 ISBN 0-910094-01-2

17031 **Metal Statistics: Ferrous Edition**
American Metal Market
350 Hudson Street
4th Floor
New York, NY 10014-4504
212-662-2420
FAX: 818-487-4550 800-662-4445

Machael Botta, Publisher
Gloria LaRue, Editor-in-Chief

Statistics for North American metals, also Canadian and Mexican statistucs, International tables and graphs, International trade labor contractsand recycling and scrap alternatives. *$265.00*
Annual ISBN 0-910094-00-4

17032 **Metals Datafile**
Materials Information
ASM International
Materials Park, OH 44073
440-930-4888
FAX: 440-338-4634
This database contains designation and specification numbers for ferrous and non-ferrous metals and alloys.
Full-text

17033 **Metalworking Machinery Mailer**
Tade Publishing Group
29501 Greenfield Road
Suite 120
Southfield, MI 48076
248-552-8583
FAX: 248-552-0466 800-966-8233

Tom Lynch, Editor

Printed directory of available used metalworking equipment.
Monthly

17034 **Mineral and Energy Information**
Mineral Information Institute
505 Violet St
Golden, CO 80401-6714
303-277-9190
FAX: 303-277-9198
mii@mii.org www.mii.org
Profiles of associations, government agencies and special interest groups in North America that are sources of publications and products on mineral related subjects.
$15.00

17035 **Modern Machine Shop: CNC & Software Guide Software Issue**
Gardner Publications
6915 Valley Avenue
Cincinnati, OH 45244-3029
513-527-8977
FAX: 513-527-8801
www.gardnerweb.com

Thomas Beard, Editor
Richard Kline, President

Annual April

17036 **Parts Cleaning: Master Source Buyer's Guide**
Witter Publishing Corporation
84 Park Avenue
Suite 32
Flemington, NJ 08822-1172
908-788-0343
FAX: 908-788-3782
www.partscleaningweb.com

Andrew Witter, Owner

Annual July

17037 **Pipe and Tube Mills of the World with Global Technical Data**
Preston Publishing Company
6613 E 106th Street
Tulsa, OK 74133-7131
918-342-2356
FAX: 918-299-4795
preston@webzone.net
www.prestonpipe.com

Douglass P Yadon, CEO
LaSondra L O'Farrell, President

We also have a monthly trade journal The Preston Pipe and Tube Report. *$245.00*
842 pages BiAnnual Founded: 1995
Printed in 1 color on matte stock

17038 **Powder Metallurgy Buyers' Guide**
Metal Powder Industries Federation
105 College Road E
Princeton, NJ 08540-6692
609-527-7700
FAX: 609-987-8523
info@mpif.org www.mpif.org

JR Dale, VP Member & Industry Relations

Equipment suppliers are listed with information on their products and services, as well as their product catalogs.
Annual : On-Line

17039 **Powder Metallurgy Consultant's Directory**
Metal Powder Industries Federation
105 College Road E
Princeton, NJ 08540-6622
609-452-7700
FAX: 609-987-8523
info@mpif.prg www.mpif.org

JR Dale, Marketing/Technical Director

Focuses on 20 companies and individuals that provide consulting services to the powder metallurgy industry in the areas of technology, research and development and manufacturing. *$5.00*
Annual, Paperback : On-Line

17040 **Powder Metallurgy Suppliers Directory**
Metal Powder Industries Federation
105 College Road E
Princeton, NJ 08540-6622
609-452-7700
FAX: 609-987-8523
info@mpif.org www.mpif.org

JR Dale, VP Member & Industry Relations

Over 50 producers and suppliers of metal powder who belong to the Metal Powder Producers Association or Refractory Metals Association.
Paperback

17041 **Precision Cleaning: Master Source Buyer's Guide**
Witter Publishing Corporation
84 Park Avenue
Suite 32
Flemington, NJ 08822-1172
908-788-0343
FAX: 908-788-3782
www.precisioncleaningweb.com

Andrew Witter, Owner

Annual

17042 **Purchasing Magazine**
Reed Business Information
275 Washington Place
Newton, MA 02458-1630

FAX: 617-558-4327
www.manufacturing.net

About 1,800 metal producers, distributors, die casters, foundries, forgers, coil coaters and powder metals. *$15.00*
Annual

17043 **Reference Book for Metal Working Machinery**
Machinery Dealers National Association
1110 Spring Street
Silver Spring, MD 20910-4028
301-859-9496
FAX: 301-588-7830 800-872-7807
Nearly 1,000 metal working machine tool manufacturers; international coverage.
$75.00

17044 **Serial Number Reference Book**
Machinery Dealers National Association
315 S Patrick Street
Alexandria, VA 22314-3501
703-836-9300
FAX: 703-836-9303 800-872-7807
office@mdna.org www.mdna.org

Mark Robinson, Executive VP

Sourcebook for metalworking machinery has been designed to lead the reader as quickly as possible to the specific serial number/age information he is seeking.
$29.95
778 pages

17045 **Silver Refiners of the World and their Identifying Ingot Marks**
Silver Institute
1112 16th Street NW
Suite 240
Washington, DC 20036-4818
202-478-8200

Over 80 refiners in over 18 countries are profiled. *$33.00*
85 pages

17046 **Welding Design & Fabrication**
Penton Media
1300 E 9th Street
Cleveland, OH 44114
216-696-7000
FAX: 216-696-1752
information@penton.com
www.penton.com

Rosalie Brosilow, Editor

For owner operators and managers of professional welding shops.
Annual, December

Industry Web Sites

17047 **www.ace.org**
Aluminum Extruders Council

An international trade association representing aluminum extruders.

17048 **www.aimcal.org**
Association of Industrial Metallizers, Coaters
and Laminators

Packaging equipment.

17049 www.aisc.org
American Institute of Steel Construction

Nonprofit trade association and technical institute established to serve the structural steel industry in the US. Our purpose is to promote the use of structural steel through research activities, market development, education, codes and specifacations, technical assistance, quality certifacation and standardization.

17050 www.aise.org
Association of Iron & Steel Engineers

Production and processing of iron and steel.

17051 www.amea.org
Association of Machinery and Equipment Appraisers

Members are appraisers of the metalworking industry.

17052 www.asminternational.org

ASM International provides information and networking for metals and materials professionals through its website.

17053 www.aws.org
American Welding Society

17054 www.cbsa.copper-brass.org
Copper and Brass Servicenter Association

Distributors of fabricated copper and copperalloy products, Sheets,plate, coil, rod, bar, pipe, tubing, etc.

17055 www.cmadc.org
Closure Manufacturers Association

Conducts public relations for member companies and establishes idustry standards.

17056 www.coilcoaters.org
National Coil Coaters Association

17057 www.copper.org
Copper Development Association

Seeks to expand the uses and applications of copper and copper products. Responsible for industry-wide market statistics and research.

17058 www.emcw.org
Electrical Manufacturing & Coil Winding Assn

Promotes welfare of the motor and coil industry. Offers courses and workshops.

17059 www.fmametalfab.org
Fabricators and Manufacturers Association

FMA is an educational association serving the metal forming and fabricating industry. Technology areas include sheet metal fabrucating, stamping, roll forming, coil processing, punching, and plate structural fabricating.

17060 www.forengineers.org/wrc
Welding Research Council

Coordinates welding research.

17061 www.greyhouse.com
Grey House Publishing

Selected Grey House directories in the fields of business, health and education are available online. Users can search our online databases by several different search criteria, such as product categories, geographic area, sales volume and much, much more. Full Grey House catalog and online ordering also available.

17062 www.ilzro.org
International Lead Zinc Research Organization

For miners, smelters and refiners of lead and zinc. Supports research and developement of new uses for the metals and refinement existing uses.

17063 www.intlmag.org
International Magnesium Association

Develops international use and acceptance of magnesium metal and its alloys in all product forms. Members are organizations or individuals engaged in the production, manufacture or marketing of metallic magnesium or those supplying materials, equipment or consulting.

17064 www.ipmi.org
International Precious Metals Institute

Miners, refiners, producers and users of precious metals, as well as research scientists and mercantilists.

17065 www.iss.org
Iron & Steel Society

Seeks to be the premier professional and technical society serving its members and advancing knowledge exchange in the global iron and steel industry. Publishes a monthly magazine.

17066 www.mdna.org
Machinery Dealers National Association

17067 www.metalforming.com
Precision Metalforming Association

For producers of metal stampings, spinnings, washers and precision sheet metal fabrications as well as suppliers of equipment, materials and services.

17068 www.mfgtech.org
Association for Manufacturing Technology

17069 www.mhia.org
Material Handling Institute

Promotes the market and develops a code of ethics. Serves as liaison among members and other groups.

17070 www.mmsa.net
Mining and Metallurgical Society of America

A professional organization dedicated to increasing public awareness and understanding about mining and why mined materials are essential to modern society and human well being.

17071 www.mpif.org
Metal Powder Industries Federation

Promotes the science and industry of powder metallurgy through technical meetings, seminars, conferences, and publications.

17072 www.naad.org
National Association of Aluminum Distributors

NAAD is the trade association of North American service centers and principal suppliers engaged in marketing aluminum products.

17073 www.nffs.org
Non-Ferrous Founder's Society

Manufacturers of bronze, brass and aluminum castings.

17074 www.nwsa.com
Fernley & Fernley

17075 www.powdercoating.org
Powder Coating Institute

17076 www.scra.org/amc/tfa
Ferroalloys Association

Promotes the ferroalloy industry in the areas of technology, international trade, environment and health, safety and government relations.

17077 www.silversmithing.com
Society of American Silversmiths

Founded to preserve the art and history of handcrafted holloware and flatware plus provide support, networking and greater access to the market forsilversmiths. Educates the public as to the aesthetic and investment value of this art form.

17078 www.spfa.org
Steel Plate Fabricators Association

17079 www.ssci.org
Steel Service Center Institute

17080 www.steel.org
American Iron and Steel Institute

Works to protect interests of manufacturers in the steel industry.

17081 www.steeldi8stributors.org/asd
Association of Steel Distributors

Bestows Steel Distributor of The Year Award and the Presidents Award of Merit.

17082 www.steeltubeinstitute.org
Steel Tube Institute of North America

Members produce steel tubes and pipes from carbon, stainless or alloy steel, for applications ranging from large structural tubing to small redrawn tubing.

17083 www.taol.com/uscti
United States Cutting Tool Institute

For those in the domestic cutting tool market.

17084 www.thermalspray.org
International Thermal Spray Association

Strengthens the level of awareness in general industry and government on the increasing capabilities and advantages of thermal spray technology for surface engineering through business opportunities, technical support and a social network. Contributes to growth and education in the thermal spray industry.

17085 www.titanium.org
International Titanium Association

Contact ITA for mailing list price.

17086 www.uschamber.org/chamber/mall
Silver Users Association

Represents the interests of corporations that make, sell and distribute products and services in which silver is an essential part. SUA membership includes representatives from the photographic, electronic, silverware and jewelry industries; producers of semi-fabricated and industrial products; and, mirror manufacturers.

17087 www.wirenet.org
Wire Association International

Technical association serving the global wire and cable industry by providing educational materials, sponsoring trade shows and international technical conferences.

17088 www.zinc.org
American Zinc Association

Provides information on the zine industry and hosts international conference on zinc.

Associations

17089 Alabama Surface Mining Commission
PO Box 2390
Jasper, AL 35502
205-221-4130
FAX: 205-221-5077
nderocher@asmc.state.al.us
www.surface-mining.state.al.us
Randall Johnson, Director
Nick DeRoche, Permit Manager
Gary Heaton, Engineer
Bill Kitchens, Geologist
Doing its part to balance civilization's demands for natural resources and environmental conservation in the state of Alabama.
26 Members Founded: 1972

17090 Alaska Miners Association
3305 Arctic Boulevard
Suite 202
Anchorage, AK 99503
907-563-9229
FAX: 907-563-9225
ama@alaskaminers.org
www.alaskaminers.org
Steven Borell, Executive Director
Encourage and support responsible mineral production in Alaska.

17091 American Association for Crystal Growth
25 4th St
Somerville, NJ 08876-3205
908-575-0649
FAX: 908-575-0794
aacg@att.ent www.crystalgrowth.org
Anthony L Gentile, Executive Administrator
AACG is a nonprofit technical membership organization where the primary function is a organic conference in the fall of crystal growth and characterization. A newsletter is published 3 times per year and distributed to members.
600 Members Founded: 1968

17092 American Coal Ash Association
15200 E Girard Avenue
Suite 3050
Aurora, CO 80014
720-870-7897
FAX: 720-870-7889
info@acaa-usa.org www.acaa-usa.org
David C Goss, Executive Director
To advance the management and use of coal combustion products in ways that are technically sound, commercially competitive and environmentally safe.
75 Members Founded: 1967

17093 American Geological Institute
4220 King Street
Alexandria, VA 22302-1502
703-379-2480
FAX: 703-379-7563
agi@agiweb.org www.agiweb.org
Marcus Milling, Executive Director
John Rasanen, Marketing/Outreach
42 Members Founded: 1948

17094 American Institute of Mining, Metallurgical & Petroleum Engineers
Three Park Avenue
New York, NY 10016-5998
212-419-7676
FAX: 212-419-7671
aimeny@aimeny.org www.aimeny.org
Nellie E Guernsey, Executive Director
Organized and operated exclusively to advance, record and disseminate significant knowledge of engineering and the arts and sciences involved in the production and use of minerals, metals, energy sources and materials for the benefits of humankind, both directly as AIME and through memeber societies.

17095 American Institute of Professional Geologists
8703 Yates Drive
Suite 200
Westminster, CO 80234
303-412-6205
FAX: 303-253-9220
aipg@aipg.org www.aipg.org
William J Siok, Executive Director
Wendy Davidson, Assistant Director
Founded to certify the credentials of practicing geologists and to advocate on behalf of the profession.
Founded: 1963

17096 American Society for Surface Mining and Reclamation
American Society for Surface Mining & Reclamation
3134 Montevesta Road
Lexington, KY 40502-3548
859-351-2032
FAX: 859-335-6529
asmr@insidebb.com
www.ces.ca.uky.edu/assmr
Robert Darmody, President
Richard Bamhisel, Executive Secretary
Dissemination of technical information relating to the reclamation of lands disturbed by mineral extraction. Members yearly issue is paid out of proceeding. Membership dues $50 regular $10 students.
400 Members Founded: 1983

17097 American Society of Mining and Reclamation
3134 Montavesta Road
Lexington, KY 40502
859-335-6529
FAX: 859-335-6529
asmr@insightbb.com
www.ca.uky.edu//assmr
Richard I. Barnhisel, Executive Secretary
The American Society of Mining and Reclamation has programs and projects that recognize the multidisciplinary nature of land reclamation and provides opportunities for those with specialized interests, from ecology to wetlands, to organize workships, prepare special sessions for the National meetings, and publish handbooks and manuals.
Founded: 1973

17098 Arizona Mining Association
5150 N 16th Street
Suite B-134
Phoenix, AZ 85016-3900
602-266-4416
FAX: 602-230-8413
webmaster@azcu.org www.azcu.org
Sydney Hay, President
June Castelhano, Administrative Assistant
Recognizes the importance of educating Arizona's citizens about the critical role the mining industry plays not only in our state and nation, but also in the world.
Founded: 1965

17099 Asbestos Information Association North America
PMB 114
1235 Jefferson Davis Highway
Arlington, VA 22202-3283
703-560-2980
FAX: 703-560-2981
aiabjpiggj@aol.com
Bob L. Pigg, President
The Asbestos Information Association is the informations arm of U.S. and Canadian asbestos producers and asbestos products manufacturers and provides information on asbestos and health.
5 Members Founded: 1971

17100 Association for Mineral Exploration Britis h Columbia
889 West Pender Street
Suite 800
Vancouver, BC V6C-3B2
604-689-5271
FAX: 604-681-2363
info@amebc.ca www.amebc.ca
Dan Jepsen, President & CEO
Cassandra Hall, Director, Cmty Relations & Commun
Supports and promotes the mineral exploration community and related services by disseminating information to the public and governments, thereby assisting in the creation of wealth and jobs through sustainable minerla development.
5400 Members Founded: 1912

17101 Association of Bituminous Contractors
815 Connecticut Avenue, NW
Suite 620
Washington, DC 20006
202-785-4440
FAX: 202-331-8049
William H. Howe, Secretary/General Counsel
Members are general and independent contractors constructing coal mines and coal mine facilities and also bargains with the United Mine Workers.
150 Members Annual/March

17102 Association of Equipment Manufacturers
10 S Riverside Plaza
Suite 1220
Chicago, IL 60606-3710
312-321-1470
FAX: 312-321-1480 aem@aem.org
James Ebbinghaus, VP
Representing manufacturers of architectural, construction, forestry, materials handling and liabilty equipment.

17103 Bureau of Land Management
1800 C Street NW
Main Interior Building, Room 555
Washington, DC 20240-0001
202-343-5441
www.blm.gov
Ted Bingham
Robert C Bruce

35M Members Founded: 1968

17104 California Mining Association
1107 9th Street
Suite 705
Sacramento, CA 95814
916-447-1977
www.calmining.org

Adam Harper, Association Manager
Stephanie Pridmore, Association Administrator

Represents the breadth and depth of California's mining industry including producers of precious metals (such as gold and silver), industrial minerals (including borates, limestone, rare earth elements, clays, gypsum and tungsten) and rock, sand and gravel.

17105 Canadian Institute of Mining, Metallurgy and Petroleum
3400 de Maisonneuve Blvd W
Suite 855
Montreal, QC H3Z-3B8
514-939-2710
FAX: 514-939-2714
cim@cim.org www.cim.org

Russell E Hallbauer, CIM President
Jean Vavrek, CIM Executive Director

The leading technical society of professionals in the Canadian minerals, metals, materials and energy industries.
12000 Members Founded: 1898

17106 China Clay Producers Association
113 Arkwright Lndg
Macon, GA 31210-1364
478-571-1252
FAX: 478-757-1949
www.kaolin.com
info@georgiamining.org

Lee Lemke, Executive VP

The mission of the China Clay Producers Association is to promote the common business interest of producers of china clay and the development of coordinated policies which assure the industry will continue to provide jobs and contribute to the Georgia economy. In addition, objectives also include informing members of proposed legislations, regulatory actions and other matters affecting the kaolin industry; and to maintain the industry's strong community spirit.
Founded: 1978

17107 Colorado Mining Association
216 16th Street
Suite 1250
Denver, CO 80202
303-575-9199
FAX: 303-575-9194
colomine@coloradomining.org
www.coloradomining.org

Stuart A Sanderson, President
James T Cooper, Chairman

Composed of both small and large enterprises engaged in the exploration for, production and refining of, metals, coal, oil shale, and industrial minerals; firms that manufacture and distribute mining and mineral processing equipment and supplies; and other institutions providing services and supplies to the mineral industry.
Founded: 1876

17108 Copper Development Association
260 Madison Avenue
16th Floor
New York, NY 10016
212-517-7200
FAX: 212-251-7245 www.copper.org

Andrew Kireta, President

Promoting the use of copper by communicating the unique attributes that make this sustainable element an essential contributor to the formation of life, to advances in science and technology, and to a higher standard of living worldwide.
Founded: 1989

17109 Desert Research Institute
2215 Raggio Parkway
Reno, NV 89512
775-737-7315
FAX: 775-673-7421 www.dri.edu

Dr Stephen Wells, President

A nonprofit statewide division of the university and community college system of Nevada, DRI pursues a full-time program of basic and applied environmental research on a local, national, and international scale. DRI employees nearly 400 full and part-time staff scientists, technicians, and support personnel.
Founded: 1959

17110 Excavation Engineering Associates
1352 SW 175th Street
Seattle, WA 98166
206-248-7388
FAX: 206-244-7994
Underground excavation.

17111 Federal Mine Safety and Health Review Commission
601 New Jersey Avenue NW
Suite 9500
Washington, DC 20001-2021
202-653-5633
FAX: 202-434-9916
info@fmshrc.gov www.fmshrc.gov

Richard Baker, Executive Director

Independent adjudicative agency that provides administrative trial and apellate review of legal disputes arising under the Federal Mine Safety and Health Amendments Act of 1977 (mine act).

17112 Geological Society of America
3300 Penrose Place
Boulder, CO 80301-1806
303-447-2020
FAX: 303-357-1070 800-472-1988
gsa@geosociety.org
www.geosociety.org

Rob Van der Voo, President
William A Thomas, VP
Jack Hess, Manager

16000 Members Founded: 1888

17113 Gold Prospectors Association of America
PO Box 891509
Temecula, CA 92589
951-994-4749

info@goldprospectors.org
www.goldprospectors.org

Perry Massie, Chief Executive Officer

GPAA is the largest recreational gold prospecting club. Owner of The Outdoor Channel, a cable TV channel featuring real outdoors for real people.

17114 Idaho Mining Association
802 W Bannock Street
Suite 301
Boise, ID 83702
208-342-0031
FAX: 208-345-4210
ima@idahomining.org
www.idahomining.org

Charlie Ross, President
Jack Lyman, Executive VP

Founded to further the interests of Idaho's mining industry and minerals production. Mission is to act as the unified voice for its members to ensure the long-term health and well being of Idaho's mining industry.
Founded: 1903

17115 Lead Industries Association
13 Main Street
Sparta, NJ 07871
973-726-5323
FAX: 973-726-4484
miller@leadinfo.com
www.leadinfo.com
Nonprofit trade association representing the lead industries in the US and abroad. It collects and distributes information about the users of lead products in industry, vehicles, radioactive waste disposal and noise barriers. Its services are availble, generally free of charge, to anyone interested in the uses of lead and lead products.

17116 Lignite Energy Council
1016 East Owens Avenue, Suite 200
PO Box 2277
Bismarck, ND 58502-2277
701-258-7117
FAX: 701-258-2755
lec@lignite.com www.lignite.com

John Dwyer, President
Steve Van Dyke, Director of Communications
Jeff Burgess, Director Research & Development
Renee Walz, Director of Membership Services

Regional Trade Association - promotes policies and activities that maintain a viable lignite industry and enhance development of our regions' lignite resources.
300 Members Founded: 1974

17117 Mine Safety Institue Of America
319 Paintersville Road
Hunker, PA 15139
724-925-5150

sikora.lisa@dol.gov
www.miningorganizations.org/msia.htm

Frank Linkous, President
Ronnie Biggerstaff, VP

The objectives of the Mine Safety Institute of America is to provide successful educational programs, safer and healthier working conditions, more productivity in the mining industry, and support of good legislature pertaining to mining.
Founded: 1908

17118 Mine Safety and Health Administration
1100 Wilson Boulevard
Arlington, VA 22209-3939
202-693-9400
FAX: 202-693-9401 800-746-1553
webmasterold@msha.gov
www.msha.gov

David Dye, Executive Director

Administers the Federal Mine Safety and Health Act of 1977 (Mine Act) and enforces compliance with mandatory safety and health standards as a means to eliminate fatal accidents; to reduce the frequency and severity of nonfatal accidents, to minimize health hazards and to promote mineral processing operations in the US, regardless of size, employees, commodity mined or method of extraction.

17119 Mineral Information Institute
505 Violet Street
Golden, CO 80401
303-277-9190
FAX: 303-277-9198
mii@mii.org www.mii.org
Nelson Fugate, President
Jaqueline S Dorr, VP

Nonprofit organization dedicated to educating youth about the science of minerals and other natural resources and about their importance in our everyday lives.

17120 Mineral Insulation Manufacturers
44 Canal Center Plaza
Alexandria, VA 22314
703-684-0084
Oscar Mamaril, Manager

Trade association of North American manufacturers of fiberglass, rock wool, and slag wool insulation products.

17121 Mineral and Ecomnomics Management Society
Colorado School Of Mines
Golden, CO 49931
303-273-3150
FAX: 906-487-2944
www.minecon.com/index.html
Patricia Dillon, President

The Mineral and Economic Management Society is a not-for-profit organization that provides a professional forum for academic, industrial, private and government specialists interested in mineral economics and materials management.
200 Members Founded: 1991

17122 Minerals, Metals & Materials Society
184 Thorn Hill Road
Warrendale, PA 15086-7528
724-776-9000
FAX: 724-776-3770
tmsgeneral@tms.org www.tms.org
Dedicated to the development and dissemination of the scientific and engineering knowledge bases for materials-centered technologies.

17123 Mining Foundation of the Southwest
PO Box 42317
Tucson, AZ 85733
520-577-7519
FAX: 520-577-7073
mfsw@dakotacom.net
www.miningfoundationsw.org
William Dresher, President

Advances the science of mining and related industries by educating members and the public. Annual American Mining Hall of Fame First Saturday in December. A newsletter is published.
92 Members Founded: 1993

17124 Mining and Metallurgical Society of
476 Wilson Avenue
Novato, CA 94947-4236
415-897-1380
info@mmsa.net www.mmsa.net
Concerned with the conservation of the nation's mineral resources and the best interest of the mining and metallurgical industries.
340+ Members Founded: 1908

17125 National Association of State Land Reclamationists
Coal Research Center/Southern Illinois University
618-536-5521
FAX: 618-453-7346
aharrington@crc.siu.edu
www.crc.siu.edu/nasir.htm
Bruce Ragon, President
Dennis Baker, VP

The National Association of State and Land Reclamationists advocates the use of research, innovative technology and professional discourse to foster the restoration of lands and waters affected by mining related activities.
140 Members Founded: 1972

17126 National Lime Association
200 N Glebe Road
Arlington, VA 22203
703-243-5463
FAX: 703-243-5489
natlime@lime.org www.lime.org
Arlene Seeger, Executive Director
Lisa McFadden, Meetings

Trade association for US and Canadian manufacturers of high calcium quicklime, dolomitic quicklime and hydrated lime, collectively referred to as lime. NLA represents the interests of its members in Washington, provides input on standards and specifications for lime, and funds and manages research on current and new uses for lime.
63 Members Founded: 1902

17127 National Mining Association
101 Constitution Avenue NW
Suite 500 East
Washington, DC 20001-2133
202-463-2610
FAX: 202-463-2666
craulston@nma.org www.nma.org
Jack Gerard, President
Carol L Raulston, Senior VP
Connie Holmes, Executive Director

Membership within the National Mining Association includes corporations involved in all aspects of the mining industry including coal, metal and industrial mineral producers, mineral processors, equipment manufacturers, state associations, bulk transporters, engineering firms, consultants, financial institutions and other companies that supply goods and services to the mining industry.
325 Members Founded: 1995

17128 National Ocean Industries Association
1120 G Street NW
Suite 900
Washington, DC 20005
202-347-6900
noia@noia.org www.noia.org
Burt A Adams, President/CEO
George Boyadjieff, Chairman
Jon A Marshall, Vice Chairman
Dick Alario, President/COO
Tom Fry, President

National organization engaged in offshore construction, drilling and petroleum production, geophysical exploration, ship building and repair, deep-sea mining and related activities in the development and use of marine resources.
300 Members Founded: 1972

17129 National Ready Mixed Concrete Association
900 Spring Street
Silver Spring, MD 20910
301-871-1400
info@nrmca.org www.nrmca.org
Robert Garbini, President
Deana Angelastro, Executive Administrator

The mission of the National Ready Mixed Concrete Association is to provide exceptional value for our members by responsibly representing and serving the entire ready mixed concrete industry through leadership, promotion, education, and partnering to ensure ready mixed concrete is the building material of choice.
1200 Members Founded: 1930

17130 National Stone, Sand & Gravel Association
1605 King Street
Arlington, VA 22314
703-525-8788
FAX: 703-525-7782 800-342-1415
info@nssga.org www.nssga.org
Joy Wilson, Chief Executive Officer
Jane Spring, Executive Secretary

Represents the stone, sand and gravel — or aggregate — industries. Our members account for 90 percent of the crushed stone and 70 percent of the sand and gravel produced annually in the US.
25 Members Founded: 1916

17131 Nevada Mining Association
9210 Prototype Drive
Suite 200
Reno, NV 89521
775-829-2121
FAX: 775-852-2631
www.nevadamining.org
Russ Fields, President
Alexis Miller, Manager Govt Affairs & Public Rel

Represents all aspects of the mining industry. Provides representation for the broad mining industry in public outreach activities such as public relations, media relations, and community relations.

17132 Northwest Mining Association
10 N Post Street
Suite 220
Spokane, WA 99201-0772
509-624-1158
FAX: 509-633-1241
nwma@nwma.org www.nwma.org
Laura Skaer, Executive Director

Provides liaison between mining, industry and government. Offers short course on current technology.
2000 Members Founded: 1890

17133 Perlite Institute
4305 N 6th St
Ste A
Harrisburg, PA 17110-1650
717-238-9723
FAX: 717-238-9985
info@perlite.org www.perlite.org
Art Anderson, Standards Committee Chair
Bruce Schundler, Communications Chair
The Perlite Institute is an international association which establishes product standards and specifications, and which encourages the development of new product uses through research.
Founded: 1949

17134 Rocky Mountain Association of Geologists
820 16th Street
Suite 505
Denver, CO 80202
303-573-8621
FAX: 303-628-0546
rmagdenver@aol.com www.rmag.org
Donna Anderson, President
Mark Sonnenfeld, First VP
Jewel Wellborn, Second VP
Sandi Pillissier, Executive Director
2200 Members Founded: 1922

17135 Silver Institute
1200 G Street NW
Suite 800
Washington, DC 20005
202-835-0185
FAX: 202-835-0155
info@silverinstitute.org
www.silverinstitute.org
Paul Bateman, Executive Director
International association of miners, refiners, fabricators and wholesalers of silver and silver products.

17136 Silver Users Association
11240 Waples Mill Road
Suite #200
Fairfax, VA 22030
703-934-0219
FAX: 703-359-7562
silverusers@capitolonellc.com
www.silverusersassociation.org
Mike Merolla, President
John Gannon, VP
29 Members Founded: 1947

17137 Silver Valley Mining Association
Po Box 1286
Wallace, ID 83872
208-556-1621

info@silverminers.org
www.silverminers.org
Dedicated to promoting the Silver Valley of northern Idaho and its mining industry. Informs the public of the history and merits of the region, serving various beneficiary needs of the mining industry, and serving those who work in the industry and the investing public.

17138 Society for Mining, Metallurgy &
8307 Shaffer Pkwy
Littleton, CO 80127-4102
303-973-9550
FAX: 303-973-3845 800-763-3132
sme@smenet.org www.smenet.org
David Kanagy, Executive Director
Art Schweizer, President
Advances the worldwide mining and minerals community through information exchange and professional development.
13000 Members Founded: 1949

17139 Society of Economic Geologists
7811 Shaffer Parkway
Littleton, CO 80127
720-981-7882
FAX: 720-981-7874
seg@segweb.org www.segweb.org
Ross R Large, President
Virginia S Gillerman, VP
Brian G Hoal, Executive Director
International organization of individual members with interests in the field of economic geology. Membership includes representatives from the industry, academia and government institutions. Annual meetings, publications, field conferences and short courses ensure active communication of economic geology related concepts with the membership and the economic geology profession at large.
3400 Members Founded: 1920

17140 Society of Exploration Geophysicists
8801 South Yale
Tulsa, OK 74137-2740
918-497-5500
FAX: 918-497-5557
web@seg.org
www.seg.org/index.shtml
Terry K Young, President
Maria Angela Capello, VP
Yonghe Sun, Editor
Frank D Brown, Secretary/Treasurer
Mary Fleming, Executive Director
The Society of Exploration Geophysicists/SEG is a not-for-profit organization that promotes the science of geophysics and the education of applied geophysicists. SEG fosters the expert and ethical practice of geophysics in the exploration and development of natural resources, in characterizing the near surface, and in mitigating earth hazards.
25000 Members Founded: 1930

17141 Society of Mineral Analysts
PO Box 50085
Sparks, NV 89435-0085
562-467-8980
pbraun@sma-online.org
Patrick Brown, Director
The Society of Mineral Analysts is a non-profit organization, whose members are assayers, chemists, laboratory managers, geologists, suppliers and vendors both in and serving the mineral analysis industry.
250 Members Founded: 1986

17142 Solution Mining Research Institute

105 Apple Valley Circle
Clarks Summit, PA 18411
570-585-8092

smri@solutionmining.org
www.solutionmining.org
Jeff Hertzing, President
John Voigt, Executive Director
The Solution Mining Research Institute is a non-for-profit association interested in the production of salt brine and the utilization of the resulting caverns for the storage of oil, gas, chemicals, compressed air and waste; the solution mining of potash and soda ash are also of interest.
100 Members Founded: 1965

17143 Sorptive Minerals Institute
1155 Fifteenth Street NW
Suite 500
Washington, DC 20005
202-289-2760
FAX: 202-530-0659
lcoogan@navista.net
www.sorptive.org
Lee Coogan, Executive Director
The Sorptive Minerals Institute represents the absorbent clay industry and is a not-for-profit industry trade association that would serve as the marketing, promotion and research arm of the absorbent clay indsutry with the goal of enhancing long-range growth and profitability.
11 Members Founded: 1970

17144 State Mine Inspector
1700 West Washington Street
Suite 400
Phoenix, AZ 85007
602-542-5971

admin@mi.state.az.us
www.asmi.state.az.us
Greg Becken, Senior Deputy Mine Inspector
Tim Evans, Senior Deputy Mine Inspector
Hector Lovemore, Deputy Mine Inspector Reclamation
Douglas Martin, Executive Director
330 Members Founded: 1912

17145 Sulphur Institute
1140 Connecticut Avenue NW
Suite 612
Washington, DC 20036
202-331-9660
FAX: 202-293-2940
sulphur@sulphurinstitute.org
www.sulphurinstitute.org
Larry Mark, Chairman
Robert Morris, President
Founded: 1960

17146 US Geological Survey
12201 Sunrise Valley Drive
Reston, VA 20192
703-648-4000
FAX: 703-648-4888
dc_va@usgs.gov www.usgs.gov
Dr Charles G Groat, Director
Janet N Arneson, Staff Assistant
Robert E Doyle, Deputy Director
Joyce K Copeland, Secretary
Robert Bier, Executive Director
Founded: 1879

17147 United Mine Workers of America International Union
8315 Lee Highway
Fairfax, VA 22031
703-208-7200
FAX: 703-208-7227 www.umwa.org
Ceil Roberts, President
Dan Kane, Secretary/Treasurer
The United Mine Workers of America is an international union that works to fight for safe workplaces, good wages and benefits, and fair representation.
120M Members Founded: 1890

17148 Utah Mining Association
136 South Main
709
Salt Lake City, UT 84101
801-364-1874
FAX: 801-364-2640
www.utahmining.org
David Litvin, President
Ken May, Chairman
Provides its members with full-time professional industry representation before the State Legislature; various government regulatory agencies on the federal, state and local levels; other associations, and business and industry groups. Helps to promote and protect the mining industry.
Founded: 1915

17149 Vibrating Screen Manufacturers Association
6737 W. Washington Street
Suite 2400
Milwaukee, WI 53214-5647
414-272-0943
FAX: 414-272-1170 866-236-0442
Dennis Slater, President
Al Cervero, Senior VP
AEM is teh international trade and business development resource for companies that manufacture equipment, products andservices used worldwide in the construction, agricultural, minimg, forestry, and utility industries.
8 Members Founded: 1959

17150 Women in Mining National Organization
PO Box 260246
Lakewood, CO 80226-0246
303-298-1535

wim@womeninmining.org
www.womeninmining.org
Karen Jass, President
Susan Yadon, VP
Women in Mining is a nationwide organization composed of individuals employed in, associated with, or intersted in the mining industry.
600 Members Founded: 1972

17151 World Gold Council
444 Madison Avenue
New York, NY 10022
212-317-3800
FAX: 212-688-0410 www.gold.org
James Burton, CEO
Kelvin Williams, Executive Director
John Calnon, Manager
Organization formed and funded by the world's leading gold mining companies with the aim of stimulating and maximizing the demand for, and holding of gold by consumers, investors, industry and the official sector.
Founded: 1987

Newsletters

17152 Alaska Geology Survey News
Alaska Division of Geological Survey
3354 College Road
Fairbanks, AK 99709-3658
907-451-5000
FAX: 907-451-5050
dggsnews@dnr.state.ak.us
http://wwwdggs.dnr.state.ak.us/
Joni Robinson, Publication Technician
Alaska miners and earth scientists.
4 pages Monthly
Printed in on glossy stock

17153 Ash at Work
American Coal Ash Association
15200 E Girard Avenue
Suite 3050
Aurora, CO 80014
720-870-7897
FAX: 720-870-7889
info@acaa-usa.org
http://www.acaa-usa.org
David Goss, Director
Association news.

Printed in 4 colors on glossy stock

17154 Bulletin
Northwest Mining Association
10 N Post Street
Suite 220
Spokane, WA 99201-772
509-624-1158
FAX: 509-623-1241
nwma@nwma.com
http://www.nwma.org
Laura skaer, Executive Director
Mike Heywood, Marketing Director
Published every six weeks. 12-16 page newsletter covering issues relevant to the hardrock mining industry.
Founded: 1895
Circulation: 1500

17155 Coal Week International
McGraw Hill
PO Box 182604
Columbus, CO 43272
877-833-5524
FAX: 614-759-3749 800-752-8878
customer.service@mcgraw-hill.com
http://www.mcgraw-hill.com
John Slater, Publisher
Offers information and news to and of the mining industry in North America. *$467.00*

Monthly Founded: 1884

17156 Coaldat Productivity Report
Pasha Publications
1600 Wilson Boulevard
Suite 600
Arlington, VA 22209-2510
703-528-1244
FAX: 703-528-1253 800-424-2908
Harry Baisden, Group Publisher
Michael Hopps, Editor
Kathy Thorne, Circulatin Manager
Shows quarterly and year-to-date total coal production in tons, productivity in tons per miner per day, average number of employees for each mine, mining methods used, controlling company, mine location, district number, union affiliation and whether the mine is surface or underground. Both a controlling company and a state/country format are available. *$545.00*
60 pages Quarterly

17157 Control
Putman Media Company
555 W
Suite 301,Pierce Road
Itasca, IL 60143
630-467-1300
FAX: 630-467-1124
jcappelletti@putman.net
http://www.putmanpublishing.com
Keith Larson, Publisher/Editorial
Walter Boies, Circulation Manager
K Heitman, President
Designed for instrumentation and control systems professionals.
Fortnightly Founded: 1945
Circulation: 35000

17158 Legal Quarterly Digest of Mine Safety and Health Decisions
Legal Publication Services
888 Pittsford Mendon Center Road
Pittsford, NY 14534
585-582-3211
FAX: 585-582-2879
MineSafety@aol.com
http://www.minesafety.com
Ellen Smith, Owner/publisher
Melanie Aclander, Editor
Covers legal decisions on health and safety law in the mining industry. *$525.00*
100 pages Annual+ Founded: 1991

17159 Lignite Energy Council
1016 East Owens Avenue, Suite 200
PO Box 2277
Bismarck, ND 58502-2277
701-258-7117
FAX: 701-258-2755
lec@lignite.com www.lignite.com
John Dwyer, President
Steve Van Dyke, Director of Communications
Jeff Burgess, Director Research & Development
Renee Walz, Director Membership Services
Promotes policies and directs activities that maintain a viable lignite industry and enhance the development of our regions' lignite resources.
300 pages Founded: 1974
Circulation: 500

17160 Machinery Outlook
Manfredi & Associates
20934 W Lakeview Parkway
Mundelein, IL 60060-9502
847-949-9080
FAX: 847-949-9910
frank@manfredi.com
http://www.manfredi.com/
Frank Manfredi, Publisher
A newsletter about and for the construction and mining machinery industry. *$365.00*
14 pages Monthly Founded: 1984
Printed in 1 color on matte stock

17161 Mine Regulation Reporter
Pasha Publications
1600 Wilson Boulevard
Suite 600
Arlington, VA 22209-2509
703-528-1244
FAX: 703-528-1253 800-424-2908
Harry Baisden, Group Publisher
Michael Hopps, Editor
Kathy Thorne, Circulation Manager
The only biweekly newsletter and document service in the US for mine safety and environmental managers and attorneys. It covers mine safety, health and environmental regulations, legislation and court decisions that affect mine operations. *$785.00*
BiWeekly

17162 Mining Foundation of the Southwest
PO Box 42317
Tucson, AZ 85733
520-577-7519
FAX: 520-577-7073
mfsw@dakotacom.net
www.miningfoundationsw.org
William Dresher, President
Jean Austin, Office Manager
Advances the science of mining and related industries by educating members and the public. Annual Americna Mining Hall of Fame First Saturday in December.
90 pages Founded: 1973

17163 Mining and Metallurgical Society of America Newsletter
476 Wilson Avenue
Novato, CA 94947-4236
415-897-1380
FAX: 415-899-0262
info@mmsa.net http://www.mmsa.net
Alan K Burton, Executive Director
Society news and information for professionals in the mining industry.
6 pages Founded: 1908

17164 Utah Mining Association Newsletter
Utah Mining Association
136 South Main
#709
Salt Lake City, UT 84101
801-304-1874
FAX: 801-364-2640
www.utahmining.org/newsletter.htm
Provides updates on the mining industry.

Magazines & Journals

17165 CIM Magazine
Canadian Inst of Mining, Metallurgy & Petroleum
3400 de Maisonneuve Blvd W
Suite 855
Montreal, QC H3Z-3B8
514-939-2710
FAX: 514-939-2714 www.cim.org
Dawn Nelley, Publications
Provides important information on mine developments, new technologies, safety, HR, products and services, and business issues.
8x's a Year
Circulation: 11,289

17166 Coal
MacLean Hunter
29 N Wacker Drive
Floor 9
Chicago, IL 60606-3298
312-726-2802
FAX: 312-726-4103
Art Sanda, Editor
Elisabeth O'Grady, Executive Director
Articles cover maintenance and production of coal mines. *$62.50*
Monthly Founded: 1964
Circulation: 22,000

17167 Coal Age
Primedia
29 N Wacker Avenue
10th Floor
Chicago, IL 60606
312-726-2802
FAX: 312-726-2574
http://www.coalage.com
Peter Johnson, Publisher
Stever P Fiscor, Editor-in-Chief
Ben Fromenthal, Production Manager
Geared primarily toward professionals in the coal mining and processing industries. Coal Age focuses on news, with in-depth features on coal mining operations and changing technologies. *$49.00*
54 pages Monthly Founded: 1911
Circulation: 17900
Printed in 4 colors on glossy stock

17168 Coal Journal
PO Box 3068
Pikeville, KY 41502-3068
606-432-0206
FAX: 606-432-2162
Terry L May, Publisher
Information concentrating on government regulations, emerging technologies and trade literature, and analyzes governmental actions and their impact on the coal industry.
Quarterly
Circulation: 10000

17169 Coal People
Al Skinner Enterprises
PO Box 6247
Charleston, WV 25362-247
304-342-4129
FAX: 304-343-3124 800-235-5188
cpm@newwave.net
http://www.coalpeople.com
Al Skinner, Editor
Christina Karaum, Managing Editor
Beth Terranova, Sales Manager
Angela McNealy, Circulation Manager
Features special news and product sections for the coal industry. Home interest, historical pices, coal industry personalities. *$25.00*
60 pages 10 times ayear Founded: 1976
Circulation: 11500
Printed in 4 colors on glossy stock

17170 Engineering & Mining Journal
Primedia Publishing
330 N. Wabash Avenue
Suite 2300
Chicago, IL 60611
312-595-1080
FAX: 312-595-0295
info@mining-media.com
http://www.e-mj.com
Peter Johnson, Publisher
Steve Fiscor, Editor
Serves the field of mining including exploration, development, milling, smelting, refining of metals and nonmetallics
108 pages Monthly Founded: 1866
Circulation: 20589
Printed in 4 colors on glossy stock

17171 Geotimes
American Geological Institute
4220 King Street
Alexandria, VA 22302-1502
703-379-2480
FAX: 703-379-7563
agi@agiweb.org
http://www.agiweb.org
Marcus Milling, Executive Director
John Rasanen, Marketing Manager
John Rasanen, Circulation Manager
Lisa Pinsker, Editor
Marcus Milling, CEO/President
Nonprofit federation of 40 geoscientific and professional associations that represents more than 100,000 geologists, geophysicsts, and other earth scientists. AGI provides information services to geoscientists, serves as a voice of shared interests in our profession, plays a major role in strengthening geoscience education, and strives to increase public awareness of the vital role the geosciences play in society's use of resources and interaction with the environment. *$42.95*
40 pages Monthly Founded: 1948
Circulation: 100000

17172 Journal of Minerals, Metals & Materials Society
Minerals, Metals & Minerals Society
184 Thorn Hill Road
Warrendale, PA 15086-7514
724-776-9000
FAX: 724-776-3770 800-759-4867
tmsgeneral@tms.org
http://www.tms.org
Alexander R Scott, Executive Director
Robert Makowski, Director Communications
James J Robinson, Editor
Stephen Kendall, Publication Manager
Arlene Frances, Advertising Sales Representative
To promote the global science and engineering profession's concerned with minerals, metals and materials. Founded in 1871. Publishes a monthly magazine. *$131.00*
Monthly Founded: 1948
Circulation: 10000

17173 Mine Safety and Health News
Legal Publication Services
888 Pittsford Mendon Center Road
Pittsford, NY 14534
585-582-3211
FAX: 585-582-2879
MineSafety@aol.com
http://www.minesafety.com
Ellen Smith, Owner
Melanie Aclander, Editor *$525.00*
Founded: 1991

17174 Mine and Quarry Trader
Primedia
7355 N Woodland Drive
PO Box 603
Indianapolis, IN 46206
317-991-1350
FAX: 317-299-1356 800-827-7468
mine.quarry@intertec.com
http://www.mineandquarry.com
John Owen, Production Manager
Colleen Leath, Circulation Director
Kyle Agert, Publisher
Laura Larahaag, Marketing
Ellen Rolett, Manager
Equipment and services geared to the mining, aggregate and heavy construction industries. *$21.00*
76 pages Monthly Founded: 1976
Circulation: 34406 34406 names $115 per M.
Printed in 4 colors on matte stock

17175 Miners News
Miners News
9792 W Glen Ellyn Street
PO Box 4965
Boise, ID 83711

FAX: 208-658-4901 800-624-7212
minersnews@msn.com
http://www.minersnews.com
Gary White, Publisher
Shirley White, Public Relations
Information on mining history and provides insight into new technology and products used in mining. *$25.00*
Founded: 1985
Circulation: 6512

17176 Mines Magazine
Colorado School of Mines Alumni Association
1600 Arapahoe Street
PO Box 1410
Golden, CO 80402
303-733-3143
FAX: 303-273-3583 800-446-9488
magazine@mines.edu
http://www.oia.mines.edu
Maureen Keller, Editor
Anita Pariseau, CEO/President
Annette Clark, Manager
Our magazine chronicles the news of the Colorado School of Mines and its alumni. *$35.00*
Quarterly Founded: 1910
Circulation: 20000
Printed in 4 colors on glossy stock

17177 Mining Record
Mining Record Company
PO Box 1630
Castle Rock, CO 80104-6130
303-888-8871
FAX: 303-663-7823 800-441-4708
customerservice@miningrecord.com
http://www.miningrecord.com
Don E Howell, Editor
Dale Howell, Marketing
Has been in continuous publication for 115 years and is recognized as the industry's leading newspaper. Focuses on timely and credible news reporting on exploration, discovery, development, production, joint ventures, acquisitions, operating results, legislation, government reports and metals prices. Its readership is concentrated in the mining industry proper; mining companies and all individuals engaged in large or small mine production. *$45.00*
16 pages Monthly Founded: 1889
Circulation: 5100
Printed in on newsprint stock

17178 New Equipment Digest
Penton Media
1300 E 9th Street
Cleveland, OH 44114-1503
216-696-7000
FAX: 216-696-1752
information@penton.com
http://www.newequipment.com
David B Nussbaum, CEO
Jennifer Daugherty, Communications Manager
John DiPaola, Group Publisher
Robert F King, Editor
Bobbie Macy, Circulation Manager
Serves the general industrial field which includes manufacturing, processing, engineering services, construction, transportation, mining, public utilities, wholesale distributors, educational services, libraries, and governmental establishments. *$65.00*
Monthly Founded: 1892
Circulation: 206000

17179 North American Mining
Mining Media
1005 Terminal Way
#140
Reno, NV 89502-2179
775-323-1553
FAX: 775-323-1553
Dorothy Y Kosich, Editor
Information broken into departments which include environment, finance, government, management, new product news, profiles, safety issues and development technology updates.
Bi-Monthly
Circulation: 7000

17180 Northern Miner
Southam Magazine Group
950 Wadsworth Boulevard
Suite 308
Lakewood, CO 80215
303-607-0853
FAX: 303-607-0862 800-459-8314
northernminer2@northernminer.com
http://www.northernminer.com
John Cumming, Editor
Brian Warriner, Sales Representatives
News and information for the mining industry. *$89.00*
Weekly Founded: 1915
Printed in 4 colors on glossy stock

17181 Pay Dirt
Copper Queen Publishing Company
Copper Queen Plaza
PO Drawer 48
Bisbee, AZ 85603-48
520-432-2244
FAX: 520-432-2247
paydirt@thenver.com
Gary Dillard, Editor
Caryl Larkins, CEO
Frank Barco, Publisher
Gruce Rubin, Marketing
Keeps readers informed on current mining developments, changes in policies and decisions by state and federal agencies affecting mining. Accepts advertising. *$30.00*
34 pages Monthly Founded: 1938
Circulation: 2200

17182 Pit & Quarry Magazine
The Aggregates Authority
600 Superior Avenue East
Suite 1100
Cleveland, OH 44114
216-706-3700
FAX: 216-706-3710 800-669-1668
scarr@questex.com
www.pitandquarry.com
Sean Carr, Publisher
Exclusively for nonmetallic minerals producers.

17183 Silver Valley Mining Journal
414 Sixth Street
Wallace, ID 83873
208-556-1621

silverminers@usamedia.tv
www.silverminers.com
Provides information about silver mining.

17184 Skillings Mining Review
WestmorelandFlint
11 E Superior Street
Suite 514
Duluth, MN 55802
218-271-1552
FAX: 218-722-0134
hollyo@skillings.net
http://www.skillings.net
Harold Webster, Publisher/Editor
Ivan Hohnstadt, General Manager
Joseph A Carrabba, President
Holly Olson, Circulation Manager
Skillings Mining Review covers breaking news about mining companies and their suppliers, dynamics of the global marketplace, technical aspects of mining and processing, people in the industry and their contributions to it. Also production and shipping reports, and the latest news from coal and power industries. *$69.00*
28 pages Monthly Founded: 1912
Circulation: 1500
Printed in 4 colors on glossy stock

17185 United Mine Workers Journal
United Mine Workers of America
900 15th Street NW
Washington, DC 20005-2585
202-842-7200
FAX: 202-842-7227 www.wmwa.net
Doug Gibson, Editor
Information sent to members of the United Mine Workers of America, retirees, other labor unions, politicians and opinion makers in the United States and abroad. Reports on issues inside and outside the UMWA that are of interest to its members. Also contains features on politics, the arts, media and the culture of US workers.
Monthly
Circulation: 200000

17186 Valley Gazette
Hometown Publications
1000 Bridgeport Avenue
Shelton, CT 06484
203-926-2080
FAX: 203-926-2091
hometown@jctgroup.com
http://www.zwire.com
Regina Burkhart, CEO/President
Susane Hunter, Editor
Sharon Sakal, Circulation Manager
John Schneider, Marketing Manager
Weekly
Circulation: 12322

17187 World Dredging, Mining & Construction
Placer Corporation
PO Box 17479
Irvine, CA 92623-7479
949-474-1120
FAX: 949-863-9261
worlddredging@aol.com
http://www.worlddredging.com
MJ Richardson, Publisher
Steve Richardson, Editor
Robert Lindaur, Circulation Manager
International and national news for the dredging. *$40.00*
100 pages Monthly Founded: 1965
Circulation: 3400
Printed in 4 colors on glossy stock

17188 World Mining Equipment
13544 Eads Road
Prairieville, LA 70769
225-673-9400
FAX: 225-677-8277
info@mining-media.com
http://www.mining-media.com

Steve Fiscor, Editor in chief
Richard Johnson, Publisher *$29.95*

Monthly Founded: 1866
Circulation: 10,523

Trade Shows

17189 Alaska Miners Association
3305 Arctic Boulevard
Suite 202
Anchorage, AK 99503-4575
907-563-9229
FAX: 902-563-9225

Steven Borell, Executive Director

Forty booths supporting businesses of the mining industry and state and federal agencies involved with regulating the industry.
500 Attendees November

17190 American Conference on Crystal Growth and Epitaxy
American Association for Crystal Growth
25 4th Street
Somerville, NJ 08876
908-575-0649
FAX: 908-575-0794
aacg@att.net www.crystalgrowth.org

Laura Bonner, Executive Administrator

Conference registrants and crystallography professionals, scientists and engineers in crystal growth and epitaxy research, theory and manufacturing of crystal.
350+ Attendees July

17191 American Federation Mineralogical Society Rocky Mountain
816 Whipporwhill Sourt
Bartlesville, OK 74006
918-827-6405

T Alf, President

One hundred tables of gems, minerals and fossils for wholesale and retail dealers.
4M Attendees September

17192 American Gem & Mineral Suppliers Association
PO Box 741
Patton, CA 92369-0741
760-241-3191

Renata Williams, Executive Chairman

Ten booths.
100 Attendees February

17193 Arminera
Marketing International
200 N Glebe Road
Suite 900
Arlington, VA 22203
703-527-8000
FAX: 703-527-8006
micexpos@aol.com
Seminar, banquet and 400 exhibits of supplies, equipment and services for the mining industry.
8500 Attendees Biennial

17194 MIACON Construction, Mining & Waste Management Show
MIACON
2921 Coral Way
Miami, FL 33145-3053
305-441-2865
FAX: 305-529-9217 www.miacon.com

Michael Finocchiaro, President
Jose Garcia, VP
Justine Finocchiaro, Chief Operations

Annual show of 650 manufacturers, suppliers, distributors and exporters of equipment, machinery, supplies and services for the construction, mining and waste managment industries. There will be 600 booths.
10M Attendees December Founded: 1994

17195 MINExpo International
National Mining Association
101 Constitution Avenue NW
Suite 500 E
Washington, DC 20001-2133
202-632-2654
FAX: 202-463-2666 www.nma.org

Carol Raulston, Senior VP Communications
Connie Holmes, Executive Director

Quadrennial show of nearly 1300 exhibitors covering more than 588,000 square feet that showcases equipment, products and services for mining and processing coal, metals, industrial and agricultural minerals. Exhibitors include manufacturers of equipment, supliers of parts, consultants and providers of mining related services for exploration, mine development, production, processing/preparation, materials handling, environmental remediation, safety and much more.
30000 Attendees

17196 Mineral Exploration Roundup
Assn for Mineral Exploration British Columbia
604-689-4800
FAX: 604-682-5733
roundup@amebc.ca www.amebc.ca

Colleen Giroux Schmidt, Director, Conference/Special Events

Jan 29-Feb 1

17197 National Western Mining Conference
Colorado Mining Association
216 16th Street
Suite 1250
Denver, CO 80202
303-575-9199
FAX: 303-575-9194
colomine@coloradomining.org
www.coloradomining.org
Feb Denver

17198 National Western Mining Conference & Exhib ition
Colorado Mining Association
216 16th Street
Suite 1250
Denver, CO 80202-5161
303-575-9199
FAX: 303-575-9194
colomine@coloradomining.org
www.coloradomining.org

Stuart Sanderson, President

Annual show of 90 exhibitors of equipment and support services for the mining industry.
1000 Attendees

17199 Northwest Mining Association Annual Meeting and Exposition
Northwest Mining Association
10 N Post Street
Suite 220
Spokane, WA 99201
509-624-1158
FAX: 509-623-1241
nwma@nwma.com www.nwma.com

Pat Nelsen, Operations Director

Annual mining convention in the US. Containing 335 booths, 280 exhibits and more than 20 technical sessions. The second largest annual mining convention in the USA. Founded in 1895.
2.5M Attendees December

17200 Northwest Mining Association Convention
Northwest Mining Association
10 N Post St
Suite 220
Spokane, WA 99201
509-624-1158
FAX: 509-623-1241
pheywood@nwma.org
www.nwma.org

Pat Heywood, Exhibit Information

Dec 4-8 Nevada

17201 Randol Gold Forum
Randol International Limited
18301 W Colfax Avenue
#T1B
Golden, CO 80401-4834
303-526-7618
FAX: 303-271-0334

Hans Von Michaelis, President
Patti Hamilton, Sales Coordinator

Mining companies exposition.
350 Attendees September

17202 Rapid Excavation Tunneling Conference Expo
PO Box 625002
Littleton, CO 80162-5002
303-973-9550

DD Daley, Meeting Manager

75 booths.
1M Attendees June

17203 Society Mining Metallurgy Exploration
8307 Shaffer Parkway
Littleton, CO 80127-4102
303-973-9550
FAX: 303-973-3845 800-763-3132
sme@smenet.org www.smenet.org

Darlene D Daley, Meeting Manager

Five hundred booths for mining engineers, geologists and mineral industry professionals.
4M Attendees February

Directories & Databases

17204 Coal Data
National Coal Association
1130 17th Street NW
7th Floor
Washington, DC 20036-4677
202-463-2625

Offers important data on the 50 largest coal mines in the country. *$50.00*

17205 Coal Mine Directory
Primedia
29 N Wacker Drive
10th Floor
Chicago, IL 60606-3203
312-726-2802
FAX: 312-726-2574 800-621-9907

Art Sanda, Editor
Patricia L Yos, Editor

Over 2,000 coal mines are profiled that are based in the United States and Canada. *$149.00*
Annual January
Circulation: 700

17206 DRI Coal Forecast
DRI/McGraw-Hill
24 Hartwell Avenue
Lexington, MA 02421-3158
781-863-5100

Offers valuable information on the mining of coal by supply region and producing state; total coal by demand region; cost and demand by the consumer sector.

17207 Engineering and Mining Journal: Buying Directory Issue
Primedia
29 N Wacker Drive
10th Floor
Chicago, IL 60606
312-726-2802
FAX: 312-726-2574 800-621-9907

Robert Wyllie, Editor

List of manufacturers and suppliers of mining equipment. *$35.00*
Annual November
Circulation: 23,000

17208 Expanded Shale, Clay and Slate Institute Roster of Members
Expanded Shale, Clay and Slate Institute
2225 Murray Holladay Road
Suite 102
Salt Lake City, UT 84117-5385
801-272-7070
FAX: 801-272-3377
info@cscsi.org www.cscsi.org

John Ries, President
Robyn Rytting, Office Manager

About 15 producers by the rotary kiln method of lightweight aggregates of expanded shales, clays, and slates; international coverage.

17209 Geophysical Directory
Geophysical Directory
PO Box 130508
Houston, TX 77219-0508
713-291-1922
FAX: 713-529-3646 800-929-2462
info@geophysicaldirectory.com
www.geophysicaldirectory.com

Claudia LaCalli, Editor
Stewart Schafer, Owner

About 4,500 companies that provide geophysical equipment, supplies or services and mining and petroleum companies that use geophysical techniques. *$135.00*
400 pages Annual March Founded: 1946
Circulation: 2,000
Mailing list available for rent 2500 names
Printed in 4 colors on glossy stock

17210 Iron and Manganese Ore Databook
Metal Bulletin
220 5th Avenue
#Enus-19T
New York, NY 10001-7708
212-136-6202
FAX: 212-213-6273 800-MET-L 25

John Bailey, Editor

Iron and manganese ore producers and traders worldwide. *$179.00*
Quadrennial

17211 Keystone Coal Industry Manual
Primedia
29 N Wacker Drive
10th Floor
Chicago, IL 60611
312-726-2802
FAX: 312-726-2574 800-621-9907

Art Sanda, Editor
Patricia L Yos, Editor

Coal companies and mines, coke plants, coal preparation plants, domestic and export coal sales companies. *$260.00*
Annual January
Circulation: 1,400

17212 Landmen's Directory and Guidebook
American Association of Professional Landmen
4100 Fossil Creek Boulevard
Fort Worth, TX 76137-2723
817-847-7700
FAX: 817-847-7704
aapl@landman.org www.landman.org

Le'ann Callihan, Editor/Publications Department

About 7,500 member specialists in assembling or disposing of land or rights required for oil, gas, coal andmineral exploration and exploitation in the US and Canada. *$100.00*

Annual November
Circulation: 7,500

17213 Minerals Yearbook
US Geological Survey
1730 E Parham Road
Richmond, VA 23228
804-261-2600
FAX: 804-261-2659
dc_va@usgs.gov www.usgs.gov

Charles G Groats, Director

The Minerals Yearbook discusses the performance of the worldwide minerals and materials industry and provides background information to assist in interpreting that performance. Contents of the individual Minerals Yearbook volumes are, Volume I, Metals and Minerals, Volume II, Area Reports:Domestic, and Volume III, Area Reports: International.
200+ pages Annual Founded: 1935

17214 Mining Directory
Metal Bulletin
220 5th Avenue
10th Floor
New York, NY 10001-7708
212-213-6202
FAX: 212-213-6273 800-MET-L 25
72610.3721@compuserve.com
www.metbul.com/metbul/mbhome

Don Nelson, Editor

Offers valuable information on mines, mining equipment manufacturers, suppliers of equipment and services to the industry and industry consultants. *$158.00*

17215 Mining Engineering: SME Membership Directory
Society of Mining, Metallurgy & Exploration
8307 Shaffer Parkway
Littleton, CO 80127-4102
303-973-9550
FAX: 303-973-3845 www.smenet.org

Deborah Rich, Publisher
Tim O'Neil, Editor
Steve Kral, Senior Editor

A list of over 18,000 persons engaged in the location, exploration,treatment and marketing of all classes of minerals except petroleum. *$150.00*
Annual
Circulation: 20,000

17216 National Ocean Industries Association: Directory of Membership
National Ocean Industries Association
1120 G Street NW
Suite 900
Washington, DC 20005-3841
202-347-6900
FAX: 202-347-8650 www.noia.org

Frank K Stuntz, Editor
Tom Fry, President

Over 300 firms engaged in offshore construction, drilling and petroleum production, geophysical exploration, ship building and repair, deep-sea mining and related activities in the development and use of marine resources.
Annual

17217 Pit & Quarry: Reference Manual & Buyers' Guide Issue
Advanstar Communications
545 Boylston Street
Boston, MA 02116
617-514-4600
FAX: 617-267-6900
pitquar@en.com www.advanstar.com

Mark Kuhar, Editor

List of approximately 1,000 manufacturers and other suppliers of equipment, products and services to the nonmetallic mining and quarrying industry. *$25.00*
Annual, September
Circulation: 25,000

17218 Randol Buyer's Guide
Randol International Limited
18301 W Colfax Avenue
#T-2
Golden, CO 80401-4834
303-526-7618
FAX: 303-278-9229 800-726-3652

Hans Von Michaelis, Editor

Approximately 10,000 companies that offer equipment and services used in the mining industry. *$35.00*
Annual
Circulation: 10,000

17219 Randol Mining Directory
Randol International Limited
18301 W Colfax Avenue
#T1B
Golden, CO 80401-4834
303-526-7618
FAX: 303-271-0334

Hans Von Michaelis, President
Patti Hamilton, Sales Coordinator

The most comprehensive source of information on all mines in the USA. Used for systematic marketing to mines and exploration companies, statistical research and more, offering 10,000 industry contacts.

17220 **Rock Products: Buyer's Guide Issue**
Primedia
29 N Wacker Drive
10th Floor
Chicago, IL 60606
312-726-2802
FAX: 312-726-2574
www.primediabusiness.com
Rick Marley, Editor
Scot Bieda, Publisher
David Pistello, Classified
List of about 1,500 providers worldwide of equipment and services for the nonmetallic mineral mining and processing industry. *$ 100.00*
Annual November
Circulation: 23,000

17221 **Silver Refiners of the World and their Identifying Ingot Marks**
Silver Institute
1112 16th Street NW
Suite 240
Washington, DC 20036-4818
202-478-8200
Over 80 refiners in over 18 countries are profiled. *$33.00*
85 pages

17222 **Western Mining Directory**
Howell Publishing Company
PO Box 370510
Denver, CO 80237-0510
303-222-2419
FAX: 303-770-6796 800-441-4748
Dale Howell, Editor
Directory of mining companies and mines nationwide. *$49.00*
Founded: 1968
Circulation: 5,000

17223 **World Aluminum: A Metal Bulletin Databook**
Metal Bulletin
220 5th Avenue
19th Floor
New York, NY 10001-7781
212-213-6202
FAX: 212-213-1870
www.metalbulletin.com
Offers information on producers and traders of aluminum and aluminum alloys. *$247.00*
540 pages

17224 **World Mining Equipment**
Metal Bulletin
220 5th Avenue
New York, NY 10001
212-213-6202
FAX: 212-213-6619 www.wme.com
Mike Woof, Editor
Manufacturers of mining equipment. *$246.00*
66 pages
Circulation: 13M
Printed in 4 colors on glossy stock

Industry Web Sites

17225 **ca.uky.edu/assmr**
American Society of Mining and Reclamation

17226 **www.acaa-usa.org**
American Coal Ash Association
Promotes the beneficial use of coal cumbustion products.

17227 **www.aem.org**
Vibrating Screen Manufacturers Association

17228 **www.agiweb.org**
American Geological Institute
Provides information services to geoscientists, serves as a voice of shared interests in our profession.

17229 **www.aimeny.org**
American Institute of Mining & Petroleum Engineers
Organization was founded to further the arts and sciences employed to recover the earth's minerals and convert them to useful products.

17230 **www.aipg.org**
American Institute of Professional Geologists
Founded to certify the credentials of practicing geologists and to advocate on behalf of the profession.

17231 **www.alaskaminers.org**
Alaska Miners Association
Encourage and support responsible mineral production in Alaska.

17232 **www.amebc.ca**
Assn for Mineral Exploration British Columbia
Supports and promotes the mineral exploration community and related services by disseminating information to the public and governments, thereby assisting in the creation of wealth and jobs through sustainable mineral developement.

17233 **www.asmi.state.az.us**
State Mine Inspector

17234 **www.azcu.org**
Arizona Mining Association
Provides information about mining, specifically copper mining and the impact it has on our lives.

17235 **www.blm.org**
Bureau of Land Management

17236 **www.calmining.org**
California Mining Association
Represents the breadth and depth of California's mining industry.

17237 **www.ces.ca.uky.edu/assmr**
American Society for Surface Mining & Reclamation
Dissemination of Technical information relating to the reclamation of lands disturbed by mineral extraction. Members yearly issue is paid out of proceedings. Membership dues - $50/regular; $10/students.

17238 **www.chamberofmines.bc.ca**
BC & Yukon Chamber of Mines
A list of mines in the Unites States.

17239 **www.cim.org**
Canadian Inst of Mining, Metallurgy & Petroleum
Strives to be the association of choice for professionals in the minerals industries.

17240 **www.coloradomining.org**
Colorado Mining Association
Serves as a spokesman for the mining industry in Colorado.

17241 **www.copper.org**
Copper Development Association

17242 **www.crc.siu.edu/nasir.htm**
National Association of State Land Reclamationists

17243 **www.crystalgrowth.org**
American Association for Crystal Growth
For those interested in organic crystal growth.

17244 **www.dri.edu**
Desert Research Institute
Information on basic and applied environmental research on a local, national, and international scale. For scientists, technicians, and support personnel.

17245 www.fmshre.gov
Federal Mine Safety and Health Review Commission

17246 www.geosociety.org
Geological Society of America

17247 www.gold.org
World Gold Council

17248 www.goldprospecters.org
Gold Prospectors Association

17249 www.greyhouse.com
Grey House Publishing

Selected Grey House directories in the fields of business, health and education are available online. Users can search our online databases by several different search criteria, such as product categories, geographic area, sales volume and much, much more. Full Grey House catalog and online ordering also available.

17250 www.idahomining.org
Idaho Mining Association

Founded to further the interests of Idaho's mining industry and minerals production.

17251 www.kaolin.com
China Clay Producers Association

17252 www.leadinfo.com
Lead Industries Association

17253 www.lignite.com
Lignite Energy Council

Promotes policies and directs activities that maintain a viable lignite industry and enhance the development of our regions lignite resources.

17254 www.lime.org
National Lime Association

Trade association for US and Canadian manufacturers of high calcium quicklime, dolomitic quicklime and hydrated lime, collectively referred to as lime.

17255 www.minecon.com/index.html
Mineral Economics and Management Society

17256 www.miningfoundationsw.org
Mining Foundation of the Southwest

17257 www.miningorganizations.org/msia.htm
Mine Safety Institute of America

17258 www.miningusa.com
Mining Associations-National

A list of associations throughout the United States.

17259 www.mmsa.net
Mining and Metallurgical Society of America

A professional organization dedicated to increasing public awareness and understanding about mining and why mined materials are essential to modern society and human well being.

17260 www.msha.gov
Mine Safety and Health Administration

17261 www.naima.org
Mineral Insulation Manufacturers Association

Trade association of North American manufacturwers of fiberglass, rock wool, and slag wool insulation products.

17262 www.nevadamining.org
Nevada Mining Association

Represents all aspects of the mining industry in the state of Nevada.

17263 www.nma.org
National Mining Association

The only national trade organization represents the interests of mining before Congress, the Administration, federal agencies, the judiciary and the media.

17264 www.noia.org
National Ocean Industries Association

National organization engaged in offshore construction, drilling and petroleum production, geophysical exploration, ship building and repair.

17265 www.nssga.org
National Stone, Sand & Gravel Association

17266 www.nwma.org
Northwest Mining Association

Provides liaison between mining industry and government. Offers short course on current technology.

17267 www.perlite.org
Perlite Institute

17268 www.pitandquarry.com
The Aggregates Authority-Pit and Quarry

A magazine exclusively for nonmetallic minerals producers.

17269 www.rheology.org
Society of Rheology

17270 www.rmag.org
Rocky Mountain Association of Geologists

17271 www.seg.org
Society of Exploration Geophysicists

17272 www.segweb.org
Society of Economic Geologists

The society of economic geologists is an international organization of individual members with interest in the field of economic geology.

17273 www.silverinstitute.org
Silver Institute

17274 www.silverminers.org
Silver Valley Mining Association

dedicated to promoting the Silver Valley of northern Idaho and its mining industry.

17275 www.smenet.org
Society for Mining, Metallurgy & Exploration

Advances the worldwide mining and minerals community through information exchange and professional development.

17276 **www.solutionmining.org**
Solution Mining Research Institute

17277 **www.sorptive.org**
Sorptive Minerals Institute

17278 **www.sulphurinstitute.org**
Sulphur Institute

17279 **www.surface-mining.state.al.us**
Alabama Surface Mining Commission

Balance civilization's demands for natural resources and environmental conservation in the state of Alabama.

17280 **www.tmra.com**
Texas Mining & Reclamation Association

17281 **www.tms.org**
Minerals, Metals & Materials Society

Dedicated to the development and dissemination of the scientific and engineering knowledge bases for materials-centered technologies.

17282 **www.umwa.org**
United Mine Workers of America

17283 **www.usgs.gov**
US Geological Survey

17284 **www.utahmining.org**
Utah Mining Association

Provides members with full-time professional industry representation.

17285 **www.womeninmining.org**
Women in Mining

Associations

17286 Academy of Motion Picture Arts and Sciences
8949 Wilshire Boulevard
Beverly Hills, CA 90211-1972
310-247-3000
FAX: 310-859-9351 www.oscars.org
Sid Ganis, President
Bruce Davis, Executive Director
Andrew Horn, Controller
Thomas Thanangadan, Membership Administrator
Kim Tamny, Operations Manager
The Academy was founded to advance the arts and sciences of motion pictures; foster cooperation among creative leaders for cultural, educational and technological progress; recognize outstanding achievments; cooperate on technical research and improvement of methods and equipment; provide a common forum and meeting ground for various branches and crafts; represent the viewpoint of actual creators of the motion picture. Hosts annual Academy Awards.
6000 Members Founded: 1927

17287 Academy of Science Fiction Fantasy and Horror Films
334 West 54th Street
Los Angeles, CA 90037-3806
323-752-5811
FAX: 323-752-5811
rholguin@saturnawards.com
www.saturnawards.org
Robert Holguin, Head
Roger Fenton, VP
Jack B Delpit, Vice Chair
Michael Laster, Director Operations
Jeff Rector, Official Spokesperson
Culminated from the Count Dracula Society, the Academy hosts the annual Science Fiction Film Awards, called the Saturn Awards.
Founded: 1972

17288 American Cinema Editors
100 Universal City Plaza
Verna Fields Building 2282 Room 190
Universal City, CA 91608
818-777-2900
FAX: 818-733-5023
americancinema@earthlink.net
www.ace-filmeditors.org
Alan Heim, President
Michael Tronick, VP
Christopher Cooke, Secretary
Ed Abroms, Treasurer
A non-profit corporation committed to the encouragement of mutually-beneficial dialogue with other members of the motion picture industry and to educating the general public. Holds the annual ACE Eddie Awards honoring the nominees for the Film Editing Award given by the Academy of Motion Pictures Arts and Sciences.
Founded: 1951

17289 American Society of Cinematographers
1782 N Orange Drive
PO Box 2230
Hollywood, CA 90028
323-969-4333
FAX: 323-882-6391 800-448-0145
office@theasc.com www.theasc.com
Daryn Okadaan, President
Michael Negrin, Secretary
Victor J Kemper, Treasurer
The ASC is not a labor union or guild, but is an educational, cultural and professional organization. Membership is possible by invitation and is extended only to directors of photography with distinguished credits in the industry. Publishes 'American Cinematographer' magazine.
Founded: 1919

17290 Art Directors Guild
11969 Ventura Boulevard
Suite 200
Studio City, CA 91604
818-762-9995
FAX: 818-762-9997
lydia@artdirectors.org
www.artdirectors.org
Tom Walsh, President
Lisa Frazza, Secretary
Michael Baugh, Treasurer
Scott Roth, Executive Director
Alexandra Schaaf, Manager Membership Department
The creative talents that concieve and manage the background and settings for most films and television projects are members of the Art Directors Guild, Local 800. They and most other crafts of the entertainment industry are members of the International Alliance of Theatrical Stage Employees, Moving Picture Technicians, Artists and Allied Crafts of the United States, its Territories and Canada.
935 Members Founded: 1937

17291 Assistant Directors Training Program
14724 Ventura Boulevard
Suite 775
Sherman Oaks, CA 91403
818-386-2545
FAX: 818-386-2876
mail@trainingplan.org
www.trainingplan.org
Tom Joyner, Chair
Provides motion picture and television industry training as directed by the Alliance of Motion Picture and Television Producers and the Directors Guild of America.
Founded: 1965

17292 Association of Cinema and Video Laboratori es
Bev Wood C/O Deluxe Laboratories
1377 North Serrano Avenue
Hollywood, CA 90027
323-462-6171
FAX: 323-461-0608
beverly.wood@bydeluxe.com
www.acvl.org
Bev Wood, President
Chip Wilkenson, First VP
John Carlson, Second VP
Kevin Dillon, Treasurer
Bob Olson, Secretary
Provides opportunities for discussion and exchange of ideas in connection with administrative, technical and managerial problems in the motion picture and video industry. The Association is concerned with improvements in technical practices and procedures, public and industry relations, product specifications to vendors, the impact of current and impending governmental regulations, and any and all other areas of interest to the laboratory industry.
80 Members Founded: 1953

17293 Association of Talent Agents
9255 Sunset Boulevard
Suite 930
Los Angeles, CA 90069
310-274-0628
FAX: 310-274-5063
shellie@agentassociation.com
www.agentassociation.com
Sandy Bresler, President
Sheldon Sroloff, VP
Jim Gosnell, Secretary/Treasurer
Karen Stuart, Executive Director
Shellie Jetton, Administrative Director
A non-profit trade association representing talent agencies in the industry. ATA is the voice of unified talent and literary agencies. ATA agencies represent the vast majority of working artists, including actors, directors, writers, and other artists in film, stage, television, radio, commercial, literary work, and other entertainment enterprises.
Founded: 1937

17294 Casting Society of America
606 N Larchmont Boulevard
Los Angeles, CA 90004-1309
323-463-1925
FAX: 323-463-5753
info@castingsociety.com
www.castingsociety.com
Chemin S Bernard, President
CSA is the largest professional association of Casting Directors in the world. They work in all areas of entertainment in film, television and theatre. CSA continually seeks to expand their standing in the industry by providing information and opportunities that support is members.
500+ Members Founded: 1982

17295 Directors Guild of America
7920 Sunset Boulevard
Los Angeles, CA 90046
310-289-2000
FAX: 310-289-2029 800-421-4173
LDavis@dga.org www.dga.org
Michael Apted, President
Steven Soderbergh, National VP
Gilbert Cates, Secretary/Treasurer
The DGA represents Film and Television Directors, Unit Production Managers, First Assistant Directors, Second Assistant Directors, Technical Coordinators and Tape Associate Directors, Stage Managers and Production Assistants.

17296 Film Society of Lincoln Center
70 Lincoln Center Plaza
New York, NY 10023-6595
212-875-5610
FAX: 212-875-5636
marketing@filmlinc.com
www.filmlinc.com
Ann Tenenbaum, Chairman
Daniel H Stern, President
Wendy Keys, Secreatry
James Bouras, Treasurer
Claudia Bonn, Executive Director
Celebrates American and international cinema, recognizes and supports new filmmakers, and enhances awareness, accessibility and understanding of the art among a broad and diverse film going audience. The Film Society is best known for two international festivals - the New York Film Festival and the New Directors/New Films festival.
Founded: 1969

17297 Greek Americans in the Arts and Entertainment
1551 Midvale Avenue
Los Angeles, CA 90024-5501
310-477-7188
www.yasas.com
Follows the legacy of Greek-Americans in the arts and entertainment field.

17298 Historians Film Committee
Rural Route 3
Box 80
Cleveland, OK 74020-9515
918-243-7637
FAX: 918-243-5995
rollinspc@aol.com
www.filmandhistory.org
Peter C Rollins, Editor-in-Chief
The Committee exists to further the use of film sources in teaching and research, to disseminate information about film and film use to historians and other social scientists, to work for an effective system of film preservation so that scholars may have ready access to film archives, and to organize periodic conferences dealing with film.
Founded: 1970

17299 Hollywood Arts Council
PO Box 931056
Hollywood, CA 90093
323-462-2355
FAX: 323-465-9240
admin@hollywoodartscouncil.org
www.hollywoodartscouncil.org
Nyla Arslanian, President
Nancy J Brown, VP
Gary Borton, Treasurer
Andre Miripolsky, Secretary
Promotes, nurtures and supports the arts in Hollywood. Has served the community through advocacy, coalition building, free public arts events and after school programs.
450 Members Founded: 1978

17300 Independent Film & Television Alliance
10850 Wilshire Boulevard
9th Floor
Los Angeles, CA 90024-4321
310-446-1000
FAX: 310-446-1600
info@ ifta-online.org
www.ifta-online.org
Jean M Prewitt, President/CEO
Jonathan Wolfe, Executive VP/Managing Director
Michael Ryan, Chairman
Lew Horwitz, Vice Chairman Finance
A non-profit association whose mission is to provide the independent film and television industry with high-quality marketplace-oriented services and worldwide representation. The Alliance actively lobbies the United States and Eurpoean governments and the international organizations on measures that impact production and distribution.
Founded: 1980

17301 International Animated Film Society
2114 Burbank Boulevard
Burbank, CA 91506
818-842-8330
FAX: 818-842-5645
info@asifa-hollywood.org
www.asifa-hollywood.org
Antran Manoogian, President
A California nonprofit organization established to promote and encourage the art and craft of animation. They support and encourage animation education, supports the preservation and critical evaluation of animation history, recognize achievement of excellence in the art and field of animation, strive to increase the public awareness of animation, act as a liaison to encourage the free exchange of ideas within the animation community, as well as a variety of other goals.
350 Members Founded: 1974

17302 International Cinematographers Guild
7755 W Sunset Boulevard
Hollywood, CA 90046
323-876-0160
FAX: 323-876-6383
admin@camerguild.com
www.cameraguild.com
Steven Poster, President
Tom Weston, National VP
Paul V Ferrazzi, Secretary/Treasurer
Bruce C Doering, Executive Director
The International Cinematographers Guild welcomes camera professionals from across the United States and around the world.

17303 International Documentary Association
1201 W 5th Street
Suite M320
Los Angeles, CA 90017
213-534-3600
FAX: 213-534-3610
info@documentary.org
www.documentary.org
Sandra Ruch, Executive Director
Tracie Lewis, Program/Events Manager
Emily Moss, Fiscal Sponsorship Coordinator
Maria Arzola, Membership Coordinator
A nonprofit association founded to promote non-fiction film and video, to support the efforts of documentary film and video makers around the world, and to increase public appreciation and demand for the documentary. It provides a forum for documentary makers, their supporters and suppliers.
3000 Members Founded: 1982

17304 International Stunt Association
11331 Ventura Boulevard
Suite 100
Studio City, CA 91604
818-760-2072
FAX: 818-760-2217
info@isastunts.com
www.isastunts.com
Leading the industry in exciting action while holding safety above all else, ISA is a fraternal organization whose membership is by invitation only. It is comprised of the top stuntment, stunt coordinators and second unit directors that Hollywood has to offer and a safety record that is second to none.

17305 Motion Picture Association of America
15503 Ventura Boulevard
Eucine, CA 91436
818-995-6600
FAX: 818-382-1795 www.mpaa.org
Dan Glickman, President/CEO
Serves as the voice and advocate of the American motion picture, home video and television industries. The association advocates for strong protection of the creative works produced and distributed by the industry, fights copyright theft around the world, and provides leadership in meeting new and emerging industry challenges.
7 Members Founded: 1922

17306 Motion Picture Editors Guild
7715 Sunset Boulevard
Suite 200
Hollywood, CA 90046
323-876-4770
FAX: 323-876-0861 800-705-8700
webmester@editorsguild.com
www.editorsguild.com
Lisa Zeno Churgin, President
Carol Littleton, VP
Martin Levenstein, Second Vice Presdient
Diane Adler, Secretary
Rachel B Igel, Treasurer
A national labor organization representing freelance and staff post-production professionals. MPED negotiates new collective bargaining agreements and enfoces existing agreements with employers involved in post-production. They provide assistance for securing better conditions, including but not limted to financial, medical, safety and artistic concerns.
6000 Members Founded: 1937

17307 Motion Picture Pilots Association
7435 Valjean Avenue
Van Nuys, CA 91406
818-947-5454
moviepilots@cox.com
www.moviepilots.com
Cliff Fleming, Board Director
Dirk Vahle, Board Director
Steve Hinton, Board Director
Neil Looy, Board Director
Kevin LaRosa, Board Director
The MPPA promotes aviation safety and the interest of aviators working in the motion picture, television and entertainment industries; establishes, conducts and maintains such activities which promote higher aviation standards and better business methods as may assist in the advancement of aviation in the Entertainment Aviation Profession; cooperates with those government agencies, industry organizations, entities or association whose objective is the betterment or advancement of the industry.
Founded: 1997

17308 Producers Guild of America
8530 Wilshire Boulevard
Suite 450
Beverly Hills, CA 90211
310-358-9020
FAX: 310-358-9520
info@producersguild.org
www.producersguild.com
Marshall Herskovitz, President
Vance Van Paten, Executive Director
Grant Stoner, Director Membership
Courtney Cowan, Treasurer
Gale Ann Hurd, Secretary
The PGA represents, protects and promotes the interests of all members of the producing team by providing employment opportunities and health and welfare benefits for all members of the producing team; combating deceptive or uneraned credits within the producing team; and represent-

ing the interests of the entire producing team. The producing team consists of all those whose interdependency and support of each other are necessary for the creation of motion pictures and television programs.

500 Members Founded: 1950

17309 Society for Cinema Studies
640 Parrington Oval
Old Science Hall Room 302
Norman, OK 73019
405-325-8075
FAX: 405-325-7135 www.cmstudies.org

Stephen Prince, President
Eric Schaefer, Secretary
Amy Villarejo, Treasurer
Jane Dye, Administrative Coordinator

A professional organization of college and university educators, filmmakers, historians, critics, scholars, and others devoted to the study of the moving image. The gaols of SCMS are to promote all areas of media studies within universities and two- and four-year colleges; to encourage and reward excellence in scholarship and writing; to facilitate and improve the teaching of media studies as disciplines and to advance multi-cultural awareness and interaction.
1M Members Founded: 1959

17310 Society of Camera Operators
PO Box 2006
Toluca Lake, CA 91610
818-382-7070
FAX: 323-856-9155 info@soc.org

Dan Dodd, Advertising Director

Non-profit organization which advances the art and creative contribution of the operating cameraman in the Motion Picture and Television Industries.
Founded: 1978

17311 Society of Motion Picture & Television Eng ineers
3 Barker Ave
White Plains, NY 10601-1509
914-761-1100
FAX: 914-761-3115
smpte@smpte.org www.smpte.org

Edward P Hobson, President
Kimberly Maki, Executive Director
Sakky-Ann D'Amato, Director Operations
Carlos V Girod Jr, Director Engineering
David Juhren, Director Communications

The SMPTE is the leading technical society for the motion imaging industry. It was founded to advance theory and development in the motion imaging field. Today, it publishes ANSI-approved Standards, Recommended Practices, and Engineering Guidelines. SMPTE holds conferences and local Section meetings to bring people and ides together, allowing for useful interaction and information exchange.
100 Members Founded: 1916

17312 Stuntmen's Association of Motion Pictures
10660 Riverside Drive
2nd Floor, Suite E
Toluco Lake, CA 91602
818-766-4334
FAX: 818-766-5943
info@stuntmen.com
www.stuntmen.com

Steve Kelso, President
Kurt Lott, First VP
Alex Daniels, Second VP
Toby Holguin, Secretary
Harry Wowchuk, Treasurer

Seeks to improve working conditions for stuntmen. Encourages members to uphold high professional standards.
135 Members Founded: 1961

17313 Stuntwomen's Association of Motion Pictures
12457 Ventura Boulevard
Suite 208
Studio City, CA 91604-2411
818-762-0907
FAX: 818-762-9534 888-817-9267
stuntwomen@stuntwomen.com
www.stuntwomen.com

Jane Austin, President

A professional association for stuntwomen and stunt coordinators which seeks to uphold professional standards and improve working conditions.
Founded: 1967

17314 Sundance Institute
1835 Three Kings Drive
PO Box 684429
Park City, UT 84068
435-658-3456
FAX: 435-658-3457
Institute@sundance.org
www.sundance.org

Robert Redford, President
Kenneth Brecher, Executive Director
Geoffrey Gilmore, Director Sundance Film Festival
Brooke McAffee, Director Finance
Ellen Oh, Associate Director Marketing

Non-profit organization dedicated to the discovery and development of independent artists and audiences. The Institute seeks to discover, support, and inspire independent film and theatre artists from the United States and around the world, and to introduce audiences to their new work. The Institutes programs include the annual Sundance Film Festival, held in Park City, Utah each January.
Founded: 1981

17315 University Film and Video Association
UFVA Membership Office C/O Cheryl Jestis
University of Illinois Press
1325 South Oak Street
Champaign, IL 61820-6903
217-244-0626
FAX: 217-244-9910 866-244-0626

Karla Berry, President
Thomas Tomasulo, Executive VP
Beverly Seckinger, Secretary
Peter Bukalski, Treasurer
Cheryl Jestis, Membership Coordinator

Supports those interested in the fields of film and video production, history, criticism, and aesthetics. Provides training, education, and a quarterly magazine. *$75.00*

17316 Women in Film
8857 W Olympic Boulevard
Suite 201
Beverly Hills, CA 90211
310-657-5144
FAX: 310-657-5154
info@wif.org www.wif.org

Tichi Wilkerson-Kassel, Founder
CiCi Holloway, President
Glen Alpert, VP Membership
Nicole Katz, CFO
Gayle Nachlis, Executive Director

WIFs purpose is to empower, promote, nurture, and mentor women in the industry through a network of valuable contacts, events, and programs.
10000 Members Founded: 1974

Newsletters

17317 Film Advisory Board Monthly
Film Advisory Board
263 W Olive Ave
#377
Burbank, CA 91502
323-461-6541
FAX: 323-469-8541
www.filmadvisoryboard.org

Janet Stokes, President

Information and news on the entertainment industry.
Monthly Founded: 1975
Printed in 1 color on glossy stock

17318 Hollywood Arts Council
PO Box 931056
Hollywood, CA 90093
323-462-2355
FAX: 323-465-9240
bianca@hollywoodartcouncil.org
www.hollywoodartscouncil.org
Promotes, nurtures and supports the arts field in Hollywood. Newsletter is included with membership.
Founded: 1978
Printed in 4 colors on glossy stock

17319 Preview Family Movie & TV Review
Movie Morality Ministries
PO Box 407
Pomona, KS 66076-2561
785-255-4314
FAX: 785-255-4316 800-807-8071
preview@fni.com
www.reviewonline.org

Dave Haverty, President
Greg Shull, Editor
Susan Haverty, Desktop Publisher/Office Manager

Reviews current films and TV series from a Christian and family values perspective.
$34.00
Monthly
Printed in 2 colors on matte stock

Magazines & Journals

17320 American Cinematographer
American Society of Cinematographers
1782 North Orange Drive
PO Box 2230
Hollywood, CA 90078-2230
323-969-4333
FAX: 323-876-4973 800-448-0145
office@theasc.com www.theasc.com
Covers feature films, television, commerciais, music videos, digital video, new equipment, DVD and book releases and much more. An exploration and a reflection of today's cinematography. A publication of the American Society of Cinematographers. *$29.95*
Monthly Founded: 1919
Circulation: 42000

17321 Animation Magazine
Animation Magazine
30941 West Agoura Road
Suite 102
Westlake Village, CA 91361
818-991-2884
FAX: 818-991-3773
info@animationmagazine.net
www.animationmagazine.net

Ryan Ball, Editor

Promotes the art and business of animation and gives recognition to those animators and technicians who make the world of animation what it is today. *$50.00*

Monthly Founded: 1986
Circulation: 30000 $165 per M.
Printed in 4 colors on glossy stock

17322 Celebrity Service
8833 W Sunset Boulevard
Suite 401
Los Angeles, CA 90069-2171
213-883-3671
FAX: 310-652-9244

Robert Dean, Manager/Director

A listing of celebrities names and addresses. Publisher of the Celebrity Bulletin informing the entertainment and news industry of which celebrities are traveling to Hollywood and New York

Bi-Monthly

17323 Cineaste
Cineaste Magazine
243 Fifth Avenue
Suite 706
New York, NY 10016
212-366-5720
FAX: 212-366-5724
cineaste@cineaste.com
www.cineaste.com

Gary Crowdus, Editor-in-Chief
Cynthia Lucia, Editor
Richard Porton, Editor
Dan Georgakas, Consulting Editor
Vicki Robinson, Production Assistant

An internationally recognized independent film magazine. Features contributions from many of America's most articulate and outspoken writers, critics and scholars. Focussing on both the art and politics of the cinema. *$20.00*

Quarterly Founded: 1967
Circulation: 11000

17324 Cinefantastique
CFQ Media
PO Box 34425
Los Angeles, CA 90034-0425
310-204-0825
FAX: 310-204-5882
info@cfq.com www.cfq.com

Frederick Clarke, Editor

Provides coverage of genre entertainment. Each issue features in-depth coverage of sci-fi, fantasy and horror films, TV, DVDs, games, toys, books, comics and more. *$34.95*

Monthly
Circulation: 40,000

17325 Cinefex
79 Daily Drive
#309
Camarillo, CA 93010
805-383-0800
FAX: 805-383-0803
advertising@cinefex.com
www.cinefex.com
A quarterly magazine devoted to motion picture special effects. *$32.00*

180 pages Quarterly Founded: 1980
Circulation: 30000
Printed in 4 colors

17326 Cinema Journal
University of Texas Press
2100 Comal
PO Box 7819
Austin, TX 78713-7819
512-471-7233
FAX: 512-232-7178 800-252-3206
utpress@uts.cc.utexas.edu
www.utexas.edu/utpress
Sponsored by the Society for Cinema and Media Studies. The journal presents recent scholarship by SCMS members. It publishes essays on a wide variety of subjects from diverse methodological perspectives. A 'Professional Notes' section informs Society of Cinema and Media Studies readers about upcoming events, research opportunities, and the latest published research. Cinema Journal is a member of the CELJ, the Conference of Editors of Learned Journals. *$42.00*

144 pages Quarterly Founded: 1950
Circulation: 2800 2,000 names $125 per M.

Printed in on matte stock

17327 Cinematograph
San Francisco Cinematheque
145 Ninth Street
Suite 240
San Francisco, CA 94103-1430
415-552-1990
FAX: 415-552-2067
sfc@sfcinematheque.org
www.sfcinematheque.org
Supports risk-taking art, cutting edge artists and the boundless potential of creative expression. *$15.00*

Monthly Founded: 1961

17328 Daily Variety - Gotham Edition
Reed Business Information
5700 Wilshire Boulevard
Suite 120
Los Angeles, CA 90036-3659
323-857-6600
FAX: 323-857-0494
vtccustserv@cdsfulfillment.com
www.variety.com

Peter Bart, Editor-in-Chief
Timothy M Gray, Editor
Ted Johnson, Managing Editor
Kathy Lyford, Managing Editor
Phil Gallo, Associate Editor

Focus is on Broadway theater, network television headquarters, regional music business, and local film production. Explores the role of New York City in relation to the national and global entertainment industries. *$259.00*

Daily Founded: 1905

17329 Film & History
Historians Film Committee
Rural Route 3
Box 80
Cleveland, OK 74020-9515
918-243-7637
FAX: 918-243-5995
rollinspc@aol.com
www.h-net.org/~filmhis

Peter C Rollins, Director
Deborah Carmichael, Editor-in-Chief
Cynthia Miller, Associate Editor-in-Chief

An Interdisciplinary Journal of Film and Television Studies concerned with the impact of motion pictures on our society. Film and History focuses on how feature films and documentary films both represent and interpret history. Types of articles include: Analysis of individual films and/or television programs from a historical perspective, survey of documents related to the production of films, or analysis of history as explored through film. *$50.00*

Bi-annually Founded: 1970
Circulation: 1000

17330 Film & Video Magazine
110 William Street
11th Floor
New York, NY 10038
212-621-4900
FAX: 212-621-4635
www.studiodaily.com/filmandvideo

Bryant Frazer, Editor-in-Chief
Pete Putman, Senior Editor
Alison Johns, Editor-in-Chief
Scott Gentry, Group Publisher
Jarrett Cory, Classified Sales

Covers new ideas in creating entertainment by focusing on technique in the production and finishing of features, TV programming, music videos and commercials. No longer publishes print copies, magazine is 100% digital

Monthly Founded: 1983 36,000 names
Printed in 4 colors : online

17331 Film Journal International
VNU Business Media
770 Broadway
5th Floor
New York, NY 10003-9595
646-654-7680
FAX: 646-654-7694
filmjournal@espcomp.com
www.filmjournal.com

Michael Marchesano, President/CEO
Sid Holt, Editorial Director
Robert Sunshine, Publisher/Editor
Robin Klamfoth, Advertising Director
Kevin Lally, Executive Editor

A trade publication covering the motion picture industry, including theatrical exhibition, production, distribution, and allied activities. Articles report on US and international news, with features on current production, industry trends, theatre design, equipment, concessions, sound, digital cinema, screen advertising, and other industry-related news. Each issue also includes the Buying and Booking Guide, with comprehensive feature film reviews. *$65.00*

Monthly

17332 Film Threat
Film Threat International Headquarters
5042 Wilshire Boulevard
PMB 1500
Los Angeles, CA 90036

FAX: 310-274-7985
advertise@filmthreat.com
www.filmthreat.com

Mark Bell, Editor-in-Chief
Eric Campos, Senior Contributing Editor
Chris Gore, Founder/Publishjer

The print edition of Film Threat retired in 1997, but the legend has lived on as an internet journalism mainstay. FilmThreat.com delivers film reviews, film festival coverage, exclusive filmmaker interviews and original video content. *$10.50*

Bi-Monthly Founded: 1985
Circulation: 100,000

17333 Hollywood Reporter
5055 Wilshire Boulevard
Los Angeles, CA 90036-4396
323-525-2000
FAX: 323-525-2377 866-525-2150
subscriptions@hollywoodreporter.com
www.hollywoodreporter.com

John Kilcullen, Publisher
Howard Burns, Editorial Director
Cynthia Littleton, Editor
David Morgan, Managing Editor
Sharon Gifford, Information Marketing Director

Focuses on emerging new media and corporate finance. *$229.00*
Daily Founded: 1930
Circulation: 34770

17334 Hollywood Life
Movieline Magazine
10537 Santa Monica Boulevard
Suite 250
Los Angeles, CA 90025-4952
310-234-9501
FAX: 310-234-0332
hollywoodlife@pcspublink.com
www.hollywoodlife.net
Formerly called Movieline, an entertainment lifestyle featuring interviews with stars, directors and producers; as well as information on celebrity shopping, up and coming talent, soundtracks, electronics and fashion associated with hollywood style and trends. *$13.75*
Monthly Founded: 1989
Printed in 4 colors on glossy stock

17335 International Cinematographers Guild Magazine
7755 Sunset Boulevard
Suite 300
Hollywood, CA 90046
323-876-0160
FAX: 323-878-1180
info@icgmagazine.com
www.cameraguild.com

Gary Dunham, National President
John McCarthy, Marketing

Serves as the journal of 'how to' for film and digital techniques. It incorporates a wide range of editorial for specific job categories in relation to cinematography for Film/Hi-Def/Digital production and defines the tools and technology necessary for advancement in this field. The magazine is written for members of the International Cinematographers Guild, including cinematographers, camera operators, camera assistants, still photographers, publicists, film loaders, and others in the field. *$48.00*
Monthly Founded: 1929

17336 International Documentary Magazine
International Documentary Association
1201 West 5th Street
Suite M320
Los Angeles, CA 90017-1467
213-534-3600
FAX: 213-534-3610
info@documentary.org
www.documentary.org

Thomas White, Editor
Tamara Krinsky, Associate Editor
Jodi Pais Montgomery, Manager Advertising Sales
Maria Arzola, Membership Coordinator
Erik Bethke, Mutli Media Producer

Monthly publication of the International Documentary Association. The magazine features profiles of leading filmmakers and covers major international fim/video festivals with an emphasis on documentaries and distribution. Regular features include North American Cable and Broadcast Premieres, Events and Screenings, Short Takes (news items), Funding Sources, Call for Entries from Festivals and Competitions, Jobs and Opportunities, Member News, Fiscal Sponsorship and Classified Advertising.
Founded: 1982
Circulation: 8750
Printed in 4 colors on glossy stock

17337 Journal of Film and Video
University Film and Video Association
University of Illinois Press
1325 S Oak Street
Champaign, IL 61820
217-244-0626
FAX: 217-244-9910 866-244-0626
journals@uiuc.edu www.ufva.org

Stephen Tropiano, Editor
Cheryl Jestis, Membership

Focuses on scholarship in the fields of film and video production, history, criticism, and aesthetics. Topics include film and related media, education in these fields, and the function of film and video in society.
$40.00
Quarterly
Circulation: 1200

17338 Journal of Popular Film and Television
Heldref Publications
1319 Eighteenth Street NW
Suite 2
Washington, DC 20036-1802
202-296-6267
FAX: 202-296-5149 800-365-9753
subscribe@heldref.org
www.heldref.org

Michael Marsden, Co-Executive Editor
Gary Edgerton, Co-Executive Editor

Articles discuss networks, genres, series and audiences, as well as celebrity stars, directors and studios. Regular features include essays on the social and cultural background of films and television programs, filmographies, bibliographies, and commisioned book and video reviews.
$51.00
Quarterly Founded: 1956

17339 Keyframe Magazine
DMG Publishing
2756 N Green Valley Parkway
Suite 261
Henderson, NV 89014-2120
702-990-8656
FAX: 702-992-0471
info@dmgpublishing.com
www.hdri3d.com

Dariush Derakhshani, Editor-in-Chief
Cheri Madison, Managing Editor
Charles Edgin, Editorial Director
Alice Edgin, Executive Editor

In response to reader requests, Keyframe is adding to its LightWave and Photoshop tutorials and content additional bonus pages covering other tools used by digital artists. As Keyframe evolves into this larger, better magazine, its new title with be HDRI 3D.
$54.00
Founded: 1997
Circulation: 9000

17340 Millimeter Magazine
PO Box 2100
Skokie, IL 60076-7800
847-763-9504
FAX: 847-763-9682 866-505-7173
millimeter@pbinews.com
www.millimeter.com

Cynthia Wisehart, Editor

In a fast-changing and challenging industry, Millimeter anticipates the future. Its early coverage of important technology-driven trends such as 24p production, desktop post, and digital cinema has helped readers remain competitive and plan their business investments. Millimeter is an authoritative resource for professionals in production, postproduction, animation, streaming, and visual effects for motion pictures, television and commercials. *$70.00*
Monthly

17341 Movie Collectors World
Arena Publishing
PO BOX 309
Fraser, MI 48026
586-774-4311
FAX: 703-940-4566
mail@mcwonline.com
www.mcwonline.com

Brian Bukantis, Editor

Leading collector's publication for collectors of movie memorabilia, with an emphasis on collectible movie posters. Each issue is filled with ads from dealers and collectors all over the world. In any monthly issue, you will find movie posters common and rare - everything from the 'Golden Age' to today's blockbusters. *$36.00*
36-44 pages Monthly
Circulation: 6000

17342 Moviemaker
MovieMaker Magazine
121 Fulton Street
Fifth Floor
New York, NY 10038
212-766-4100
FAX: 212-766-4102
www.moviemaker.com

Timothy Rhys, Publisher/Editor-in-Chief
Jennifer M Wood, Editor
Phillip Williams, Editor at Large
Ian Bage, New Marketing Services

Movimaker is the world's most widely - read independent movie magazine that focuses on the art and business of making movies. Its editorial mix is a progressive mix of in depth interviews and criticism combined by practical techniques and advice on financing, distribution and production strategies. *$18.00*
Quarterly Founded: 1993
Circulation: 54000 $175 per M.

17343 Post
Advanstar Communications
545 Boylston Street
Boston, MA 02116
617-514-4600
FAX: 617-267-6900
bapar@advanstar.com
www.postmagazine.com

Randi Altman, Editor-in-Chief
Marc Loftus, Senior Editor
Ken McGorry, Consulting Editor

News and features emphasize innovation in equipment technology and creative technique for editing, graphics, and special effects. Covers all budget levels from desktop post to feature films.

130 pages Monthly Founded: 1986
Circulation: 31464

17344 Produced By
The Producers Guild of America
8530 Wilshire Boulevard
Suite 450
Beverly Hills, CA 90211
310-358-9020
FAX: 310-358-9520
info@producersguild.org
www.producersguild.com
Vance Van Petter, Ececutive Director
Audra Whaley, Director Operations
Kyle Katz, Director Member Benefits
Chris Greenr, Director Communications
Dan Dodd, Advertising
Provided as a benefit with membership to the Producers Guild of America.
Quarterly Founded: 1962
Circulation: 325

17345 Producer
Testa Communications
25 Willowdale Avenue
Port Washington, NY 11050-3779
516-767-2500
FAX: 516-767-9335
avvproducersguide.com
Randi Altman, Editor
Sande Seidman, Advertising Manager
Magazine aimed at producers, directors and creative people in the image and sound realms, with production stories on feature films, television, commercials, documentary, and corporate video projects. Accent is on the creative application of technology, following producers into the field and onto the studio set. *$15.00*
Bi-Monthly
Circulation: 18,300

17346 SMPTE Journal
Society of Motion Picture & Television Engineers
3 Barker Avenue
White Plains, NY 10601
914-761-1100
FAX: 914-761-3115
dpurrier@smpte.org www.smpte.org
Dianne Purrier, Managing Editor
Matthew Kurikose, Permissions/Advertising
Featuring industry-leading papers and standards, each month the Journal keeps its members on the cutting edge of the industry. Each issue provides the latest research and papers, ranging in style from technical, scientific, and tutorial, to applications/practices. Readers are kept up-to-date on events and meetings, the latest publications and brochures, and new products and developments. *$140.00*
Monthly Founded: 1916
Circulation: 10000
Printed in on glossy stock

17347 Script
Forum
5638 Sweet Air Road
Baldwin, MD 21013-9009
410-592-3466
FAX: 410-592-8062 888-245-2228
scriptmg@erols.com
www.scriptmag.com
Mark Madnick, Publisher
David Geatty, Founding Publisher
Shelly Mellot, Editor-in-Chief
Andrew Schneider, Managing Editor
Maureen Green, Editor
A leading source of information on the crage and business of writing for film and television. Each issues delivers informative articles on writing, developing and marketing screenplays and television scripts. Most articles are written by working writers. Additionally, development executives, agents, managers and entertainment attorneys contribute regularly. *$24.95*
Bi-Monthly
Circulation: 12000

17348 Starlog
1372 Broadway
2nd Floor
New York, NY 10018
212-689-2830
800-934-6788
rita@starloggroup.com
www.starlog.com
David McDonnel, Editor
Norman Jacobs, Founder
Information on science fiction happenings in the movies and television industries. *$56.97*
Monthly
Circulation: 350000

17349 Variety
Reed Business Information
5700 Wilshire Boulevard
Suite 120
Los Angeles, CA 90036-3659
323-857-6600
FAX: 323-857-0494 866-698-2743
VTCCustserv@cdsfulfillment.com
www.variety.com
Charles C Koones, Publisher
Peter Bart, Editor-in-Chief
Timothy Gray, Editor
Kathy Lyford, Managing Editor
Christopher Wessel, Circulation Director
Variety covers all aspects of film, television and cable, homevideo, music, new media and technolgy, theater and finance. Topics run from people, companies, products and performances, to development, financing, distribution, regulation and marketing. *$259.00*
Weekly Founded: 1905
Circulation: 35168

Trade Shows

17350 American Film Institute Festival: AFI Fest
American Film Institute
2021 N Western Avenue
Los Angeles, CA 90027-1657
323-856-7896
FAX: 323-856-9118 866-234-3378
festpublicity@AFI.com afifest.com
Jennifer Morgerman, Publicity Director
Stacey Leinson, Publicity Manager
Lagan Sebert, Publicity Coordinator
John Wildman, Filmmaker Press Liaison
Alison Deknatel, Director Communications
A 10-day event held each November, the festival features a rich slate of films from emerging filmmakers, nightly red-carpet gala premieres and global showcases of the latest work from the great film masters. AFI runs concurrently with the American Film Market. Together, AFT Fest and AFM provide the film industry with the only concurrent festival/market event in North America.
60000 Attendees November Founded: 1986

17351 International Cinema Equipment (ICECO) Showest
Magna-Tech Electronic Company
5600 NW 32nd Avenue
Miami, FL 33142
305-573-7339
FAX: 305-573-8101
www.iceco@iceco.com
www.showest.com
Steven H Krams, President
Dara Reusch, VP
Julio Urbay, VP International Sales/Marketing
Fancisco Blanco, VP Technical Services
Arturo Quintero, Architectural Design/Development
Annual convention for the Motion Picture industry. It is an international gathering devoted exclusively to the movie business. It is also the single largest international gathering of motion picture professionals and theatre owners in the world, with delegates from more than 50 countries in attendance each year.
March Founded: 1975

17352 International Cinema Equipment Company ICECO Show East
Magna-Tech Electronic Company
5600 NW 32nd Avenue
Miami, FL 33142
305-573-7339
FAX: 305-573-8101
iceco@aol.com www.iceco.com
Steven H Krams, President
Dara Reusch, VP
Julio Urbay, VP International Sales/Marketing
Francisco Blanco, VP/Technical Services
Arturo Quintero, Architectural Design & Development
This annual convention brings together over 1300 colleagues from the motion picture industry in the United States, Latin America and the Caribbean. The convention provides information on industry trends, screen films and product reels, state-of-the-art theatre equipment along with services and technologies vital to the industry.
1300 Attendees Founded: 1975

17353 Moondance Film Festival
970 9th Street
Boulder, CO 80302
303-545-0202

director@moondancefilmfestival.com
www.moondancefilmfestival.com
Elizabeth English, Festival Founder/Executive Director
Kyle/Erica Saylors, Festival Director/Event Coordinator
Karina Pyudik, Registration Coordinator
Douglis C Garvin, Special Events Coordinator
Roy Bodner, Publicist/Media Relations

The Festival's primary goal is to present films and scripts which have the power to raise awareness about vital social issues, educating writers and filmmakers, as well as festival audiences, and inspiring them to take positive action. The Festival's objective is to promote and encourage independent filmmakers, screenwriters and playwrights, and the best works in films, screenplays, stageplays, TV scripts, radioplays, film scores, lyrics, librettos, music videos, and short stories.
Annual

17354 **Sundance Film Festival**
Sundance Institute
1825 Three Kings Drive
PO Box 684426
Park City, UT 84068
801-328-3456
FAX: 801-575-5175
Institute@sundance.org
www.sundance.org
Robert Redford, Founder
Annual festival held in Park City, Utah as a US showcase for American and International independent film. The Institute is dedicated to the development of artists of independent vision and the exhibition of their new work. Since its inception, the Institute has grown into an internationally recognized resource for thousands of independent artists.
January Founded: 1981

Directories & Databases

17355 **Annual Index to Motion Picture Credits**
Academy of Motion Picture Arts and Sciences
8949 Wilshire Boulevard
Beverly Hills, CA 90211-1907
310-247-3000
FAX: 310-859-9619 www.oscars.org
The Index is closely tied to the annual Academy Awards presentation. As part of the Academy Awards process, the Academy of Motion Picture Arts and Sciences gathers credits for each film hoping to qualify for awards. These credits, compiled and verified by the film's producer or distributor, are the core of the Annual Index and IMPC database. In addition to personal credits, IMPC also records index production and releasing dates, MPAA ratings, running times, color, language, and more.
Annual Founded: 1934 ISBN 0-942102-37-1

17356 **Blu-Book Production Directory**
Hollywood Creative Directory
5055 Wilshire Boulevard
Los Angeles, CA 90036-4396
323-525-2369
FAX: 323-525-2398 800-815-0503
hcdcustomerservice@hcdonline.com
www.hcdonline.com
A comprehensive directory for professionals in the production and post-production industries. Provides current contact information needed to produce a film, TV program, commercial, or music video. The directory contains a special tabbed section on premier below-the-line craft professionals, along with selective credits, and has been expanded to include New York production facilities and services, making it one of the only bi-coastal resources of its kind.
$39.95
450 pages Annual ISBN 1-928936-44-X

17357 **Boxoffice: Buyers Directory Issue**
Boxoffice
PO Box 1634
Des Plains, IL 60019
212-627-7000
www.boxoffice.com
Peter Cane, Publisher
Joe Policy, CEO
Annlee Ellingson, Editor
Francesca Dinglasan, Senior Editor
Bob Vale, VP Advertising and Sales
Guide to equipment, supplies and services. Available to subscribers of Boxoffice Magazine. *$59.95*
Annual Founded: 1990

17358 **Boxoffice: Circuit Giants**
Boxoffice
PO Box 1634
Des Plains, IL 60019
212-627-7000
www.boxoffice.com
Peter Cane, Publisher
Joe Policy, CEO
Annlee Ellingson, Editor
Francesca Dinglasan, Senior Editor
Bob Vale, VP Advertising and Sales
Directory of the largest exhibition chains. Available to subscribers of Boxoffice magazine *$59.95*
Annual Founded: 1990

17359 **Boxoffice: Distributor Directory**
Boxoffice
PO Box 1634
Des Plains, IL 60019
212-627-7000
www.boxoffice.com
Peter Cane, Publisher
Joe Policy, CEO
Annlee Ellingson, Editor
Francesca Dinglasan, Senior Editor
Bob Vale, VP Advertising and Sales
Listings of studio and independent film suppliers. Available to subscribers of Boxoffice magazine *$59.95*
Annual Founded: 1990

17360 **Directors Guild of America Directory of Members**
Directors Guild of America
7920 W Sunset Boulevard
Los Angeles, CA 90046-3300
310-289-2000
FAX: 310-289-2029 800-421-4173
Jay D Roth, National Executive Director
Morgan Rumpf, Director Communications/Media Relat
Paul Zepp, Membership Administrator
Darrell L Hop, Editor DGA Monthly/Website
The DGA represents Film and Television Directors, Unit Production Managers, First Assistant Directors, Second Assistant Directors, Technical Coordinators and Tape Associate Directors, Stage Managers and Production Associates. The Directory is available in print and on-line *$ 25.00*
Annual

17361 **Editors Guild Directory**
Motion Picture Editors Guild
7715 Sunset Boulevard
Suite 200
Hollywood, CA 90046
323-876-4770
FAX: 323-876-0861 800-705-8700
mail@editorsguild.com
www.editorsguild.com
Ron Kutak, Executive Director
Tomm Carroll, Publications Director
Serena Kungr, Director Membership Services
Adriana Iglesias-Dietl, Membership Administrator
Tris Carpenter, Manager
An invaluable resource for producers, directors and post production professionals alike. It lists contact, credit, award and classification information for all of the Guild's active members at the time of publication, as well as a list of Oscar and Emmy winners for every year since the awards began. It also includes a retirees section. *$25.00*
Bi-Annual Founded: 1994

17362 **Fame Index**
Hollywood Madison Group
11684 Ventura Boulevard
#258
Studio City, CA 91604-2499
818-762-8008
FAX: 818-762-8089
holllywood-madison.com
Jonathan Holiff, Founder/President/CEO
Search over 10,000 celebrities from actors to athletes to find every performer who meets your needs. The Index has more than 250 searchable criteria including: age, sex, children, birthplace, genre, fees, ethnicity/heritage, biography, statistics, interests, hobbies, sports, personality attributes, charity affiliations, medical conditions, and endorsement histories. Contact information includes agent, manager, publicist, business manager, attorney, and personal assistant.
Founded: 1996

17363 **Film Journal: Distribution Guide Issue**
Film Journal International
770 Broadway
5th Floor
New York, NY 10003-9595
646-654-7680
FAX: 646-654-7694
www.filmjournal.com
Robert Sunshine, Publisher/Editor
Kevin Lally, Executive Editor
Rex Roberts, Associate Editor
Andrew Sunshine, Advertising Director
Katey Rich, Editorial Assistant
The International Distribution and subdistribution Guide supplements the regular monthly Buying and Booking Guide. It is designed to furnish ready reference information on the who, what, where and how of theatrical sales. It lists the names, addresses, personnel, telephone numbers and product of domestic and international distributors, both major and independent, along with similar information on regional exchanges together with national companies they handle.
Annual

17364 **Film Journal: Equipment Guide**
Film Journal International
770 Broadway
5th Floor
New York, NY 10003-9595
646-654-7680
FAX: 646-654-7694
www.filmjournal.com
Robert Sunshine, Publisher/Editor
Kevin Lally, Executive Editor
Robin Klamfoth, Advertising Director
Rex Roberts, Associate Editor
Katey Rich, Editorial Assistant
The Equipment, Concessions and Services Guide is designed to provide ready reference information on the theatrical equipment and concessions industry. It lists in detail the company names, addresses, telephone numbers, personnel, affiliations and products of equipment and concession manufacturers and service companies, along with similar information on US and foreign service dealers and suppliers, arranged in alphabetical order according to state or country.
Annual

17365 Film Journal: Exhibition Guide
Film Journal International
770 Broadway
5th Floor
New York, NY 10003-9595
646-654-7680
FAX: 646-654-7694
www.filmjournal.com
Robert Sunshine, Publisher/Editor
Kevin Lally, Executive Editor
Robin Klamfoth, Advertising Director
Rex Roberts, Associate Editor
Katey Rich, Editorial Assistant
The exhibition Guide is an alphabetical listing designed to provide ready reference information on the leading theatrical motion picture circuits. It lists in comprehensive detail such data as company names, addresses and phone numbers, total screens and new screens projected, division office locations, top personnel, recent circuit acquisitions, and a state-by-state breakdown of screens.
Annual

17366 Film Superlist: Motion Pictures in the Public Domain
Hollywood Film Archive
8391 Beverly Boulevard
#321
Los Angeles, CA 90048-2633
323-655-4968
Richard Baer, Director
Created by Walter E. Hurst and updated by Richard Baer. 1992-1994. Three volumes to date, covering 50,000 films from the years 1894-1939, 1940-1949 and 1950-1959.

17367 Grey House Performing Arts Directory
Grey House Publishing
185 Millerton Road
PO Box 860
Millerton, NY 12546
518-789-8700
FAX: 518-789-0545 800-562-2139
books@greyhouse.com
www.greyhouse.com
Leslie Mackenzie, Publisher
Richard Gottlieb, Editor
Laura Mars-Proietti, Editorial Director
Jessica Mooding, Director Marketing
The Grey House Performing Arts Directory is the most comprehensive resource covering the Performing Arts. This important directory provides current information on over 9,000 Dance Companies, Instrumental Music Programs, Opera Companies, Choral Groups, Theater Companies, Performing Arts Series and Performing Arts Facilities. *$185.00*
1500 pages Annual ISBN 1-592370-23-3

17368 Hollywood Creative Directory
VNU Business Media
5055 Wilshire Boulevard
Los Angeles, CA 90036-4396
323-525-2369
FAX: 323-525-2398 800-815-0503
hcdcustomerservice@hcdonline.com
www.hcdonline.com
Contact information for studios and networks, film and TV executives, production companies, independent producers, TV shows and staff, projects in development, production tracking and selected credits. Includes 11,000 producers and studio and network executives, more than 2,000 production companies, mobile content producers. Updated mid-January, end of May and end of September. *$64.95*
480 pages 3 per year ISBN 1-928936-50-4

17369 Hollywood Distribution Directory
Hollywood Creative Directory
5055 Wilshire Boulevard
Los Angeles, CA 90036-4396
323-525-2369
FAX: 323-525-2398 800-815-0503
hcdcustomerservice@hcdonline.com
www.hcdonline.com
Expanded listings include more entertainment finance companies and over 300 new domestic and international distributors, plus newly added information for mobile and internet distributors. The directory includes more than 2,000 companies, more than 10,000 names and job title information, domestic and international distributors, mobile/internet distributors, entertainment financing companies, TV syndicatoprs, network and cable channels, film festivals/markets and more.. Published every summer. *$59.95*
404 pages Annual ISBN 1-928936-52-0

17370 Hollywood Music Industry Directory
Hollywood Creative Directory
5055 Wilshire Boulevard
Los Angeles, CA 90036-4396
323-525-2369
FAX: 323-525-2398 800-815-0503
hcdcustomerservice@hcdonline.com
www.hcdonline.com
For aspiring musicians and professionals, this directory will assist in finding record executives, A&R staff, soundtrack personnel, music publishers, music supervisors and recording studios. Accurate and complete contact information including company name, job title, address, phone, fax, email, assistants' names, and web site. Every individual's name is indexed. *$39.95*
350 pages Annual ISBN 1-928936-45-8

17371 Hollywood Representation Directory
Hollywood Creative Directory
5055 Wilshire Boulevard
Los Angeles, CA 90036-4396
323-525-2369
FAX: 323-525-2398 800-815-0503
hcdcustomerservice@hcdonline.com
www.hcdonline.com
A complete, reliable and comprehensive reference book on Hollywood talent and literary agents and managers. In addition to talent agents and managers, the directory has been expanded to include separate tab sections an Entertainment Attorneys, Publicity Companies and Casting Directors. Released every Arpil and October. Includes over 2,000 companies, over 7,000 individuals, as well as addresses, staff and titles, e-mail addresses and web sites, phone and fax numbers. *$64.95*
440 pages Bi-Annual ISBN 1-928936-47-4
15000 names $599 per M.

17372 International Motion Picture Alamanc
Quigley Publishing Company
64 Wintergreen Lane
Groton, MA 01450
860-228-0247
FAX: 860-228-0157 800-231-8239
quigleypub@aol.com
www.quigleypublishing.com
William J Quigley, President/Publisher
Eileen Quigley, Editor
Contains over 400 pages of biographies and 500 pages of reference material. From 1928 to the present day, the complete set contains the biography of everyone who has ever been of importance to the Industry. Each edition includes thousands of company listings, credits for current films and films released in the prior ten years, statistics and awards and complete coverage of all aspects of the indiustry, including production, distribution and exhibition. *$175.00*
Annual

17373 International Television and Video Almanac
Quigley Publishing Company
64 Wintergreen Lane
Groton, MA 01450
860-228-0247
FAX: 860-228-0157 800-231-8239
quigleypub@aol.com
www.quigleypublishing.com
William J Quigley, President/Publisher
Eileen Quigley, Editor
Each edition contains over 400 pages of biographies and an additional 500 pages of reference material on television programs, broadcast, cable and satellie, production services, the video industry, statistics and awards. Included are detailed listings for thousands of companies, as well as coverage outside the United States. *$175.00*
Annual Founded: 1955

17374 Mini Reviews
Cineman Syndicate
31 Purchase Street
Suite 203
Rye, NY 10580-3013
914-967-5353
www.minireviews.com
John P McCarthy, Editor
An easy to read, easy to use guide for movie watchers updated weekly.
Weekly Founded: 2000

17375 Motion Picture TV and Theatre Directory
Motion Picture Enterprises
PO Box 276
Tarrytown, NY 10591-0276
212-245-0969
FAX: 212-245-0974
info@mpe.net www.mpe.net
Neal R Pilzer, Publisher
The Guide is mailed to members of 59 trade associations, unions and professional societies; decision-makers at advertising agencies, production companies, TV stations, and government agencies; faculty and students of nearly 200 film schools; and other prime purchasers of film and TV equipment and services nationwide. Companies are listed both by category and company name. Listings include company name, address and telephone number as well as fax numbers, e-mail addresses, and web site URLs. *$18.80*
335 pages Annual Founded: 1963
Circulation: 82500

17376 Movie World Almanac
Hollywood Film Archive
8391 Beverly Boulevard
#3E21
West Hollywood, CA 90048-2633
323-655-4968
Lists over 200 major American and foreign film distributors who handle old and contemporary films.

17377 Reel Directory
Lynetta Freeman
PO Box 1910
Boyes Hot Springs, CA 95416
415-531-9760
FAX: 707-581-1725
ivisual@aol.com
www.reeldirectory.com

Lynetta Freeman, Manager

Source for Film, Video and Multimedia in Northern California. *$25.00*
700 pages Annual Founded: 1979
Circulation: 5,000

17378 Studio Report: Film Development
Hollywood Creative Directory
5055 Wilshire Boulevard
Los Angeles, CA 90036-4396
323-525-2369
FAX: 323-525-2398 800-815-0503
hcdcustomerservice@hcdonline.com
www.hcdonline.com
The only directory of its kind, in print for the first time. A complete breakdown of film development project tracking. A-Z listings by title, spec screenplays sold, hot studio projects, cross-referenced by studio, production company and genre. The directory's main body consists of an alphabetical listing of all in-development projects that have achieved a forward-moving milestone some time in the last five months. Subsequent sections sort and cross-reference the information to highlight aspects *$19.95*
190 pages ISBN 1-928936-49-0

Industry Web Sites

17379 www.actioncutprint.com
Action-Cut-Print

Website for filmmakers. filmmaking resources, free ezine for directors, film and TV bookstore. The Director's Chair magazine by director Peter D. Marshall.

17380 www.artdirectors.org
Art Directors Guild

Conceive and manage the background and settings for most films and television projects.

17381 www.asatalent.com
ASA/Affordable Services

Entertainment services are brought to you as you need them and when you need them at the best price available. Security services, studio teachers, and medical services.

17382 www.castingsociety.com
Casting Society of America

An organization representing casting directors.

17383 www.discoverhollywood.com
Hollywood Arts Council

Promotes, nurtures and supports the arts field in Hollywood. Discover Hollywood on line.

17384 www.documentary.org
International Documentary Association

A nonprofit association founded to promote non-fiction film and video, to support the efforts of documentary film and video makers around the world, and to increase public appreciation and demand for the documentary.

17385 www.greyhouse.com
Grey House Publishing

Selected Grey House directories in the fields of business, health and education are available online. Users can search our online databases by several different search criteria, such as product categories, geographic area, sales volume and much, much more. Full Grey House catalog and online ordering also available.

17386 www.iqfilm.org
International Quorum of Film and Video Producers

Fosters the exchange of information and ideas. Seeks to raise professional standards. Disseminates information on new concepts and technology.

17387 www.millimeter.com
Millimeter Magazine

Authoritative resource for more than 33,000 qualified professionals in production, postproduction, animation, streaming and visual effects for motion pictures, television and commercials.

17388 www.mpaa.org
Motion Picture Association of America

Promotes high moral and artistic standards in motion picture production. Maintains Motion Picture Association Political Action Committee.

17389 www.nyfa.com
New York Film Academy

Educational institution devoted to providing focused filmmaking and acting instructions. Geared to offer an intensive, hands-on experience which gives students the opportunity to develop their creative skills to the fullest extent possible.

17390 www.oscars.org
Academy of Motion Picture Arts and Sciences

Current information on motion pictures, the arts and sciences, events and screenings.

17391 www.producersguild.com
Producers Guild of America

Members are producers of motion pictures and television shows mainly in the Los Angeles area.

17392 www.resumegenie.com

Motion Pictures job listings, salary information and job search tips.

17393 www.smpte.org
Society of Motion Picture & Television Engineers

Advances the practice and theory of engineering in television and film industry.

17394 www.stuntnet.com
International Stunt Association

Represents those involved in stunt work for the entertainment industry.

17395 www.stuntwomen.com
Stuntwomen's Association of Motion Pictures

A professional association for stuntwomen and stunt coordinators which seeks to uphold professional standards and improve working conditions.

17396 www.sundance.org
Sundance Institute

Nonprofit corporation dedicated to the support and development of emerging screenwriters and directors of vision. Hosts the Sundance Film Festival.

17397 www.wif.org
Women in Film

For global entertainment,communication and media industries. Focuses on contemporary issues facing women and provides an extensive network of valuable contacts, educational programs, scholars, film finishing funds, grants, community outreach, advocacy and practical services that promote, nurture and mentor women to achieve their highest potential.

Associations

17398 **American Historic Racing Motorcycle Association**
PO Box 1725
Goodlettsville, TN 37070
615-851-3674
FAX: 615-851-3678
davidlambert@ahrma.org
www.ahrma.org

David Lamberth, Executive Director
Matthew Benson, Communications Director

For individuals interested in vintage racing motorcycles.
5M Members Founded: 1989

17399 **American Motorcyclist Association**

13515 Yarmouth Drive
Pickerington, OH 43147
614-856-1900
FAX: 614-856-1920
tlindsay@ama-cycle.org
www.amadirectlink.com

Robert Rasor, President
Greg Harrison, Senior VP
Gary Sweet, VP
Scott Papenfus, Marketing Director
Tom Lindsay, Director Public Information

The association's purpose is to pursue, protect and promote the interests of motorcyclists, while serving the needs of its members.
270M Members Founded: 1924

17400 **Breakdown & Legal Assistance for Motorcycl ists**
5455 Wilshire Boulevard
Suite 1600
Los Angeles, CA 90036
323-321-1483
FAX: 818-377-6290 800-424-5377
russbrown@russbrown.com
www.russbrown.com

Russ Brown, President

A support group for motorcyclists. Offers roadside assistance for emergencies and breakdowns. Attorney referral service specializing in motorcycle accident cases. Brochures and guest speakers available upon request, also offers a twenty-four hour toll-free hotline.
800K Members

17401 **Harley Owners Group**
National H.O.G. Office
PO Box 453
Milwaukee, WI 53201

FAX: 414-343-4515 800-258-2464

James L Ziemer, President/CEO

Harley Davidson established the Harley Owners Group in response to a growing desire by Harley riders for an organized way to share their passion and show their pride.
60000 Members Founded: 1983

17402 **Motorcycle & Moped Industry Council**
716 Gordon Baker Road
Suite 100
North York, M2H 3B4, ON
416-491-4449
FAX: 416-491-1985 877-470-6642
info@mmic.ca www.mmic.ca

Robert Ramsay, President

National nonprofit trade association which represents the responsible interest of the major motorcycle distributors, as well as the manufacturers, distributors and the retail outlets of motorcycle-related products and services, and individual owners and riders of motorcycles in Canada.
140 Members Founded: 1971

17403 **Motorcycle Industry Council**
2 Jenner Street
Irvine, CA 92618-3806
949-727-4211
FAX: 949-727-3313
dkopf@mic.org www.mic.org

Robert Moffit, Chairman
Tim Buche, President
David Kopf, Manager

Nonprofit national trade association created to represent the motorcycle industry.
$25.00
300 Members Annual Founded: 1940

17404 **Motorcycle Riders Foundation**
236 Massachusetts Ave Ne
Ste 510
Washington, DC 20002-4972
202-546-0983
FAX: 202-546-0986 www.mrf.org

Karen Bolin, President
Kirk Willard, VP
Jeff Hennie, VP Government Relations
Deborah Butitta, Secretary
Sarah Muckenhoupt, Manager

MRF is the leading voice for the street rider in Washington, DC. The foundation is committed to less federal government involvement in daily lives.
Founded: 1987

17405 **Motorcycle Safety Foundation**
2 Jenner Street
Irvine, CA 92618-3806
949-727-3227
FAX: 949-727-4217 www.msf-usa.org

Carol Kington, VP

Founded by the five leading manufacturers and distributors of motorcycles for the purpose of public safety education.
7 Members Founded: 1973

17406 **Women in the Wind**
PO Box 8392
Toledo, OH 43605-0392

becky@womeninthewind.org
www.womeninthewind.org

Becky Brown, Founder/Treasurer
Gale Collins, President
Lauranne Bailey, VP
Peggy Zeeb, Secretary

Seeks to promote a positive image for women motorcyclists. Educates members on maintenance and safety.
1000 Members Founded: 1979

Newsletters

17407 **AHRMA Newsletter**
American Historic Racing Motorcycle Association
PO Box 882
Wausau, WI 54402-0882
715-842-9699
FAX: 715-842-9545 www.ahrma.org

Jeff Smith, Director
Matt Benson, Circulation Director

For individuals interested in vintage motorcycles. *$2.00*

Circulation: 5,000

17408 **MRF Reports**
Motorcycle Riders Foundation
PO Box 1808
Washington, DC 20013-1808
202-546-0983
FAX: 202-546-0986 www.mrf.org

Fred Rau, Editor

Bi-Monthly

Magazines & Journals

17409 **American Motorcyclist**
American Motorcyclist Association
13515 Yarmouth Drive
Pickerington, OH 43147
614-856-1900
FAX: 614-856-1920 800-262-5646
membership@ama-cycle.org
http://www.amadirectlink.com/

Greg Harrison, VP Communications
Bill Wood, Editor-in-Chief
Grant Parsons, Managing Editor
John Holliday, Circulation
Rob Rasor, President

Magazine covers every facet of motorcycling. Each monthly issue details the people, places and events - from road rallies to road races - that make up the American motorcycling experience.
$39.00
Monthly Founded: 1924
Circulation: 260000
Printed in 4 colors on glossy stock

17410 **Biker**
Paisano Publishers
PO Box 3075
Agoura Hills, CA 91376-3075
818-898-8740
FAX: 818-889-1252 800-962-985

Joe Teresi, Publisher
Dean Shawier, Editor

Events and charity events for the motorcycle enthusiast. *$15.00*
96 pages Founded: 1971

17411 **Cycle World**
Hachette Filipacchi Media US
1499 Monrovia Avenue
Newport Beach, CA 92663-2752
949-720-5300
FAX: 949-631-0651

Larry Little, Publisher
David Edwards, Editor-in-Chief

Publication for motorcycle enthusiasts.
$16.00
136 pages Monthly
Circulation: 325000 $22 per M.

17412 **Cycling USA**
United States Cycling Federation
1 Olympic Plaza
Colorado Springs, CO 80909
719-664-4730
FAX: 719-866-4628
web@usacycling.org
http://www.usacycling.org

Gerard Bisceglia, CEO
Sean Petty, Chief of Staff

Bike racing magazine. *$10.00*
24 pages Founded: 1920
Circulation: 3000

17413 Dealernews Magazine
Advanstar Communications
New York
New York, NY 10016-5778
212-951-6600
FAX: 212-951-6793 800-854-3112
info@advanstar.com
http://www.dealernews.com

Mike Vaughan, Publisher
Mary Slepicka, Associate Publisher/Editorial Direc
Arlo Redwine, Managing Editor

Written for and read by a qualified power sports dealer network and related industry associates. It features articles on merchandising, sales techniques and profiles of successful retailers. Industry trends and business conditions are monitored through exclusive industry research.
Monthly Founded: 1965
Circulation: 17535 1544 names $90 per M.
Printed in 4 colors on glossy stock

17414 Easyriders
Paisano Publishers
3547 Old Conejo Rd
Suite 106
Newbury Park, CA 91320
800-962-9857
FAX: 805-375-4591 800-825-7294
info@easyridersevents.com
http://easyridersevents.com

Joe Teresi, Publisher
Keith Ball, Editor
John Green, President

Motorcycle magazine. *$39.95*
136 pages Monthly Founded: 1971

17415 Motorcycle Dealer News
Edgell Communications
4500 Campus Drive
Suite 100
Santa Ana, CA 92705

FAX: 949-252-0499

Don Emde, Publisher

For dealers of power sports equipment and supplies. *$25.00*

17416 Motorcycle Industry Magazine
Industry Shopper Publishing
PO Box 160
Gardnerville, NV 89410-160
775-782-0222
FAX: 775-782-0266 800-576-4624
cycle@mimag.com
http://www.mimag.com

Rick Campbell, Publisher
Rick Campbell, Editor
Caroline Carr, Sales Manager

Provides information to the motorcycle and accessory dealer and or retailer on products, services, events and people aiming to maximize profitablity and growth, also includes personal watercraft vehicles, ATV's and snowmobiles.
Monthly Founded: 1976
Circulation: 14000
Printed in 4 colors on glossy stock

17417 Shootin the Breeze
Women in the Wind
PO Box 8392
Toledo, OH 43605-0392

becky@womeninthewind.org
www.womeninthewind.org

Becky Brown, Founder
Gale Collins, President
Lauranne Bailey, VP
Peggy Zeeb, Secretary

Available to all Women in the Wind members.
6x/year

17418 Statistical Annual
Motorcycle Industry Council
2 Jenner Street
Irvine, CA 92618-3806
949-727-4211
FAX: 949-727-3313
dkof@mic.org www.mic.org

Robert Moffitt, Chairman
Tim Buche, President
David Kopf, Manager

Provides a wealth of information on the industry. Many dealers and businesses investigating the industry find it useful business information tool. *$25.00*
25 pages Annual

17419 Upshift Magazine
Motorcycle & Moped Industry Council
716 Gordon Baker Road
Suite 100
North York, M2H 3B4, ON
416-491-4449
FAX: 416-491-1985 877-470-6642
upshift@mmic.ca www.mmic.ca

Steve Thornton, Producer

Features articles and information on motorcycles.
Quarterly

Trade Shows

17420 AMA Members Tour
American Motorcyclist Association
13515 Yarmouth Drive
Pickerington, OH 43147
614-856-1900
FAX: 614-856-1920
tlindsay@ama-cycle.org
www.amadirectlink.com

Will Stoner, Director Special Events

The goal is to spread awareness of the benefits of membership and the importance of the work of the AMA does in protecting all motorcyclists' right to ride.
Semi-Annual, June

17421 AMA Vintage Motorcycle Days
American Motorcyclist Association
13515 Yarmouth Drive
Pickerington, OH 43147
614-856-1900
FAX: 614-856-1920
tlindsay@ama-cycle.org
www.amadirectlink.com

Will Stoner, Director Special Events

Will benefit the Motorcycle Hall of Fame Museum and will feature an exhibit of classic motorcycles and memorabilia.
July

17422 Annual Meeting of the Minds
Motorcycle Riders Foundation
PO Box 1808
Washington, DC 20013-1808
202-546-0983
FAX: 202-546-0986 www.mrf.org

Carol Downs, Conference Director
Kathy Steinhauser, Assistant to Conference Director

Designed to educate and motivate those in the motorcyclists' rights community. These events are a great chance to meet other people who are as passionate about motorcyclists' rights as you are.
September

17423 Beast of the East
Motorcycle Riders Foundation
PO Box 1808
Washington, DC 20013-1808
202-546-0983
FAX: 202-546-0986 www.mrf.org

Carol Downs, Conference Director
Kathy Steinhauser, Assistant to Conference Director

Designed to educate and motivate those in the motorcyclists' rights community. These events are a great chance to meet other people who are as passionate about motorcyclists' rights as you are.
April

17424 Best of the West
Motorcycle Riders Foundation
PO Box 1808
Washington, DC 20013-1808
202-546-0983
FAX: 202-546-0986 www.mrf.org

Carol Downs, Conference Director
Kathy Steinhauser, Assistant to Conference Director

Designed to educate and motivate those in the motorcyclists' rights community. These events are a great chance to meet other people who are as passionate about motorcyclists' rights as you are.
June

17425 International Motorcycle Show
Advanstar Communications
201 E Sandpointe
Suite 600
Santa Ana, CA 92707
714-138-8400
FAX: 714-513-8481
identremont@advanstar.com
www.motorcycleshows.com

Jeff D'Entremont, Show Director
Leah Stevens, Event/Customer Relations Director

Exposition for motorcyclists and enthusiasts.

17426 Los Angeles Calendar Motorcycle Show
Breakdown & Legal Assistance for Motorcyclists
5455 Wilshire Boulevard
Suite 1600
Los Angeles, CA 90036
323-321-1483
FAX: 818-377-6290 800-424-5377
russbrown@russbrown.com
www.russbrown.com

Russ Brown, President

Biggest custom and performance streetbike event.
July

17427 Motocross American Reunion and Exhibit Grand Opening
American Motorcyclist Association
13515 Yarmouth Drive
Pickerington, OH 43147
614-856-1900
FAX: 614-856-1920
tlindsay@ama-cycling.org
www.amadirectlink.com

Will Stoner, Director Special Events

With a special Motocross Reunion, bringing together many of the racing and industry

legends who helped shape the history of America's first action sport.
July

17428 **Motorcycle and Parts**
Glahe International
PO Box 2460
Germantown, MD 20875-2460
301-515-0012
FAX: 301-515-0016
glahe@glahe.com www.glahe.com
Exhibits of motorcycle equipment, supplies and services.

17429 **Summer Nationals**
Women in the Wind
PO Box 8392
Toledo, OH 43605-0392

becky@womeninthewind.org
www.womeninthewind.org
Becky Brown, Founder/Treasurer
Gale Collins, President
Lauranne Bailey, VP
Peggy Zeeb, Secretary
July

Directories & Databases

17430 **MSF Guide to Motorcycling Excellence**
Motorcycle Safety Foundation
2 Jenner Street
Irvine, CA 92618-3806
949-727-3227
FAX: 949-727-4217 www.msf-usa.org
Nate Rauba, Editor
Covering the skills, knowledge and strategies for riding right. Subjects include: preparing yourself and your bike, developing street strategies, and advanced theory for experienced riders. *$24.95*
176 pages

17431 **Motorcycle Statistical Annual**
Motorcycle Industry Council
2 Jenner Street
Suite 150
Irvine, CA 92618-3806
949-727-4211
FAX: 949-727-3313
This industry-related directory offers statistical information on US motorcycle manufacturers and distributors, as well as national and state motorcycle associations.
$25.00
Annual

Industry Web Sites

17432 **www.ahrma.org**
American Historic Racing Motorcycle Association

For individuals interested in vintage racing motorcycles.

17433 **www.amadirectlink.com**
American Motorcyclist Association

Covers every facet of motorcycling: the people, places and events that make up the American motorcycling experience. In addition, this award winning website offers profiles of issues affecting everyone who rides, and provides tools that help motorcyclists communicate directly with legislators, business leaders and the news media.

17434 **www.greyhouse.com**
Grey House Publishing

Selected Grey House directories in the fields of business, health and education are available online. Users can search our online databases by several different search criteria, such as product categories, geographic area, sales volume and much, much more. Full Grey House catalog and online ordering also available.

17435 **www.mic.org**
Motorcycle Industry Council

Nonprofit national trade association created to represent the motorcycle industry.

17436 **www.mmic.ca**
Motorcycle & Moped Industry Council

National nonprofit trade association which represents the responsible interest of the major motorcycle distributors, as well as the manufacturers, distributors and the retail outlets of motorcycle related products and services, and individual owners and riders of motorcycles in Canada.

17437 **www.msf-usa.org**
Motorcycle Safety Foundation

Founded by the five leading manufacturers and distributors of motorcycles for the purpose of public safety education.

17438 **www.russbrown.com**
Breakdown & Legal Assistance for Motorcyclists

A support group for motorcyclists. Offers roadside assistance for emergencies and breakdowns. Attorney referral service specializing in motorcycle accident cases. Brochures and guest speakers available upon request, also offers a twenty-four hour toll-free hotline.

Associations

17439 Academy of Country Music
5500 Balboa Boulevard
Suite 200
Encino, CA 91316
818-788-8000
FAX: 818-788-0999
info@acmcountry.com
www.acmcountry.com

Gayle Holcomb, Chairman
David Young, Director Operations
Tiffany Moon, Secretary
Brandi Brammer, Project Manager
Tree Paine, Director Marketing

Involved in numerous events and activities promoting country music. Presents annual awards.
4M Members Founded: 1964

17440 Accordian Federation of North America
14126 E Rosencrans Boulevard
Santa Fe Springs, CA 90670
562-921-5058

afna@musician.org
www.afnafestival.org

Madeleine D'Ablaing, President
Debbie Gray, VP
Oakley Yale, Secretary
Prisscilla Martinez, Treasurer
Larryy Demian, Parliamentarian

Members are primarily teachers and music school owners with the primary purpose to encourage young people to pursue their music study. Holds festivals and competitions
75 Members Founded: 1972

17441 Accordion Teachers Guild
2312 West 71 Terrace
Prairie Village, KS 66208-3322
913-722-5625
www.accordions.com/atg

Joan C Sommers, President
Dee Langley, First VP
Stas Venglevski, Second VP
Joanna Arnold Darrow, Executive Secretary
Stanley Darrow, Historian

ATG members are accordian teachers and professionals committed to furthering the progress of the accordion by improving teaching standards, music and all phases of music education.
Founded: 1940

17442 American Choral Directors Association
545 Couch Drive
PO Box 2720
Oklahoma City, OK 73102
405-232-8161
FAX: 405-232-8162
acda@acdaonline.org
www.acdaonline.org

Gene Brooks, Executive Director
Michele Holt, President
Mitzi Groom, VP
Julie Morgan, Treasurer
Olga Funderburk, Secretary

Nonprofit music-education organization whose central purpose is to promote excellence in choral music through performance, composition, publication, research and teaching. In addition, ACDA strives to elevate choral music's position in American society through arts advocacy. Holds annual convention. *$90.00*
19500 Members Founded: 1959

17443 American College of Musicians
PO Box 1807
Austin, TX 78767
512-478-5775
FAX: 512-478-5843
ngpt@pianoguild.com
www.pianoguild.com

Richard Allison, President
Julia Kruger, VP

Provides student awards and teachers benefits.
Founded: 1929

17444 American Federation of Violin and Bow Make rs
1201 South Main Street
Mount Airy, MD 21771
301-607-9020
FAX: 301-607-9020
info@germainviolins.com
www.afvbm.com

Christopher Germain, President
David Van Zandt, Secretary
William Scott, Treasurer
Christopher Reuning, VP

Members are those with recognized professional abilities and experience in either making or repairing violins and bows. They are elected to the Federation and are entitled to all privileges and duties of membership. The Federation has designed programs to held develop the technical skills and knowledge of the membership through seminars and regular meeting events. The Federation sponsors exhibitions as a forum for makers,musicians and the general public.
$300.00
Founded: 1980

17445 American Guild of Music
PO Box 599
Warren, MI 48090
248-686-1975

agm@americanguild.org
www.americanguild.org

Barry Carr, President
Joanne Darby, Treasurer
Lorelei Eccleston Dart, First VP
Steve Petrunak, Second VP

The worls's oldest international music organization. Its membership is oipen to independent music teachers, music store owners and their teaching staffs, music publishers and instrument manufacturers and music students.
6000 Members

17446 American Guild of Musical Artists
1430 Broadway
14th Floor
New York, NY 10018
212-653-3688
FAX: 212-262-9088
agma@musicalartists.org
www.musicalartists.org

Linda Mays, President
Gerald Otte, First VP
Michael Geiger, Second VP
Mitchell Sendrowitz, Secretary
Lynn Lundgren, Treasurer

AGMA is a labor union. It negotiates collective bargaining agreements for its members that provide them with these vital benefits: guaranteed salaries; rehearsal and overtime pay; regulated work hours; vacation and sick pay; access to low-cost health benefits; good-faith resolution of disputes; and protection of their legal and contractual rights.
5.7M Members

17447 American Guild of Organists
475 Riverside Drive
Suite 1260
New York, NY 10115
212-870-2310
FAX: 212-870-2163
info@agohq.org www.agohq.org

Frederick Swann, President
Marcia Van Oyen, Director

Membership in the American Guild of Organists is primarily through local chapters, which hold regular meetings featuring performances, lectures, seminars, and discussions on a wide variety of topics. Many chapters also offer monthly newsletters, scholarship programs, musician placement services, and substitute referrals to employing institutions. Membership can also be without chapter affiliation.
20000 Members Founded: 1896

17448 American Harp Society
PO Box 38334
Los Angeles, CA 90038-0334
323-469-3050

kmoon@uclalumni.net
www.harpsociety.org

Kathleen Moon, Executive Secretary

Promotes and fosters the appreciation of the harp as a musical instrument, to encourage the composition of music for the harp and to improve the quality of performance of harpists. *$50.00*
3000 Members Founded: 1962

17449 American Music Therapy Association
8455 Colesville Road
Suite 1000
Silver Spring, MD 20910
301-589-3300
FAX: 301-589-5175
info@musictherapy.org
www.musictherapy.org

Dr Andrea Farbman, Executive Director
Michele Sornash, President

The mission of the American Music Therapy Association is to advance public awareness of the benefits of music therapy and increase access to quality music therapy services in a rapidly changing world.
3800 Members Founded: 1998

17450 American Musical Instrument Society
Guild Associates
389 Main Street
Suite 202
Malden, MA 02148
781-397-8870
FAX: 781-397-8887
amis@guildassoc.com www.amis.org

Kathryn Shanks Libin, President
Darcy Kuronen, VP
Marlowe Sigal, Treasurer
Carolyn Brant, Secretary

Promotes better understanding of all aspects of history, design, construction, restoration, and usage of musical instruments in all cultures and from all periods. The membership of AMIS includes collectors, historians, curators, performers, instrument makers, restorers, dealers, conservators, teachers, students, and many institutional members. *$45.00*
Founded: 1971

17451 American Musicological Society
6010 College Station
Brunswick, ME 04011-8451
207-798-4243
FAX: 877-679-7648 877-679-7648
ams@ams-net.org www.ams-net.org
Elaine Sisman, President
Robert Judd, Executive Director
Advances research in the various fields of music as a branch of learning and scholarship.
3600 Members Founded: 1934

17452 American Orff-Schulwerk Association
PO Box 391089
Cleveland, OH 44139-8089
440-543-5366
FAX: 440-543-2687
info@aosa.org www.aosa2.org
Cindi Wobig, Executive Director
Sue Mueller, President
JeElla Hug, VP
Suzette Swallow, Treasurer
Professional organization of music and movement educators dedicated to the creative teaching approach developed by Carl Orff and Gunild Keetman. *$70.00*

17453 American School Band Directors Association
227 N 1st Street
PO Box 696
Guttenberg, IA 52052-0696
563-252-2500
FAX: 563-252-2500
asbda@alpinecom.net
www.asbda.com
Edward S Cannava, PhD, President
August J Thoma, Secretary
Jeffrey T Phillips, Treasurer
Dennis Hanna, Office Manager
Nationwide organization dedicated to the support of professional and college band conductors. Membership by invitation only.
1200 Members Founded: 1952 1300 names

17454 American Society of Composers, Authors and Publishers
One Lincoln Plaza
New York, NY 10023-7129
212-621-6000
FAX: 212-724-9064
info@ascap.com www.ascap.com
Marilyn Bergman, President/Chairman
Arnold Broidon, Treasurer
Kathyr Spanberger, Secretary
John Lofrumento, Chief Executive Officer
Performing rights organization created and controlled by composers, songwriters and music publishers. Protects the rights of its members by licensing and distributing royalties for the non-dramatic public performances of their copyrighted works. An online newsletter is also available filled with the most up-to-date information about professional opportunities, legislative issues, member benefits and more.
26000 Members Founded: 1914

17455 American Society of Music Arrangers and Co mposers
PO Box 17840
Encino, CA 91416
818-994-4661
FAX: 818-994-6181
syd@theproperimageevents.com
www.asmac.org
John Clayton Jr, President
Duane L Tatro, VP
Ray Charles, VP
Fred Woessner, Treasurer
Scherr Lillico, Director
Professional society for arrangers, composers, orchestrators, and musicians. Monthly meetings with great speakers from the music industry.
500 Members Founded: 1938

17456 American String Teachers Association
4153 Chain Bridge Road
Fairfax, VA 22030
703-279-2113
FAX: 703-279-2114 www.astaweb.com
Mary Wagner, President
Michael Palumbo, Secretary
Donna Sizemore Hale, Executive Director
A membership committed to advancing string education and performance. Our members include teachers, faculty, performers, string industry representatives, students, and string enthusiasts. We are all passionately committed to the future of string education not only in our country but around the world.

17457 American Symphony Orchestra League
33 W 60th Street
5th Floor
New York, NY 10023-7905
212-262-5161
FAX: 212-262-5198
league@symphony.org
www.symphony.org
Lowell J Noteboom, Chair
Shirley McCrary, Secretary
Bruce E Clinton, Treasurer
Peter D Cummings, Vice Chair
Robert J Wagner, Vice Chair
Provides leadership and service to American orchestras while communicating to the public the value and importance of orchestras and the music they perform. The League links a national network of thousands of musicians, conductors, managers, board members, volunteers, staff members and business partners, providing a wealth of services, information, and educational opportunities to its members.
1000 Members Founded: 1942
Mailing list available for rent

17458 American Viola Society
14070 Proton Road
Suite 100
Dallas, TX 75244
972-233-9107
FAX: 972-490-4219
info@avsnationaloffice.org
www.americanviolasociety.org
Helen Callus, President
Madeleine Crouch, General Manager
An association for the promotion of viola performance and research. AVS membership is accompanied by two print issues of the Journal of the American Viola Society (JAVS) each year.
1000 Members

17459 Association of Concert Bands
6613 Cheryl Ann Drive
Independence, OH 44131-3718
FAX: 216-524-1897 800-726-8720
Allen Beck, President
Nada Vencl, Secretary
Mike Montgomery, CIO
Howard Habenicht, Treasurer
The purpose of ACB is to encourage and foster adult concert community, municipal, and civic bands and to promote the performance of the highest quality traditional and contemporary literature for band.
750 Members Founded: 1977

17460 Blues Foundation
49 Union Avenue
Memphis, TN 38103-3714
901-527-2583
FAX: 901-529-4030
jay@blues.org www.blues.org
Jay Sieleman, Executive Director
Paul Benjamin, President
Chip Eagle, VP
Chadd Webb, Treasurer
A nonprofit corporation which serves as the hub for the worldwide passion for Blues Music.
Founded: 1980

17461 Chamber Music America
305 7th Avenue
5th Floor
New York, NY 10001
212-242-2022
FAX: 212-242-7955
www.chamber-music.org
Susan Dadian, Program Director
Margaret M Lioi, CEO
Laura Sewell, Chair
Philip Ying, President
Charlotte Schroeder, Secretary
Promotes artistic excellence and economic stability within the profession and to ensure that chamber music is a vital part of American life. Their vision is that chamber music serve as a model of cooperation and collaboration, that audiences become more committed to supporting chamber music and the professionals who devote their lives to this art form, and that opportunities for the performance of chamber music increase in traditional concert venues and beyond.
Founded: 1977

17462 Chorus America
1156 15th Street NW
Suite 310
Washington, DC 20005
202-331-7577
FAX: 202-331-7599
service@chorusamerica.org
www.chorusamerica.org
Todd Estabrook, Chairman
Ann Meier Baker, President/CEO
Jane Colgrove, Director of Finance
Janet Sarbaugh, Secretary
Pete Dervan, Office Manager
Chorus America's mission is to strengthen choruses and increase appreciation of choral music so that more people are enriched by its beauty and power.
1600 Members Founded: 1977

17463 College Music Society
312 E Pine Street
Missoula, MT 59802
406-721-9616
FAX: 406-721-9419
cms@music.org www.music.org
Robby D Gunstream, Executive Director
C Tayloe Harding, Jr, President
Douglas Ovens, VP
David Brian Williams, Secretary
John J Deal, Treasurer
A consortium of college, conservatory, university and independent musicians and

scholars interested in all disciplines of music. Its mission is to promote music teaching and learning, musical creativity and expression, research and dialogue, and diversity and interdisciplinary interaction.
Founded: 1958

17464 Contemporary Record Society
724 Winchester Road
Broomall, PA 19008
610-544-5920
FAX: 915-808-4232
crsnews@verizon.net
http://mysite.verizon.net/vzeeewvp/contemporaryrecordsociety/
Caroline Hunt, Contact
Promotes both a fellowship in the musical arts between artists, composers and presenters and commercial recordingsa of participants in this endeavor. The intent of the Society is to advance the cause of music in the United States and throughout the world, promoting an association among its constituents. The scope of the Society's repertoire includes the musical masterworks of both well-known and relatively unknown composers of all periods. *$45.00*
Founded: 1981

17465 Country Music Association
One Music Circle S
Nashville, TN 37203
615-244-2840
FAX: 615-726-0314
www.cmaworld.com
Mike Dungan, Chairman
Clarence Spalding, President
CMA is dedicated to bringing the poetry and emotion of Country Music to the World. They will continue a tradition of leadership and professionalism, promotoing the music and recognizing excellence in all its forms. They foster a spirit of community and sharing, and respect and encourage creativity and the unique contributions of everyone. It is a place to have fun and celebrate success.
5000+ Members Founded: 1958

17466 Country Radio Broadcasters
819 18th Avenue S
Nashville, TN 37203
615-327-4487
FAX: 615-329-4492
news@crb.org www.crb.org
Ed Salamon, Executive Director
R J Curtis, President
Bill Mayne, VP
Carole Bowen, Secretary
Jeff Walker, Treasurer
A nonprofit eductional organization. It is the principal entity that brings Country radio together with the Country music industry for learning opportunities that promote growth.
Founded: 1969

17467 Creative Musicians Coalition
PO Box 6205
Peoria, IL 61601-6205
309-685-4843
FAX: 309-685-4879 800-882-4262
aimcmc@aol.com
www.creativemusicianscoalition.com
Ronald Wallace, Founder/President
An international organization dedicated to the advancement of new music and the success of independent musicians.
1000 Members Founded: 1984

17468 East-2-West Marketing & Promotion
559 Wanamaker Road
Jenkintown, PA 19046-2219
215-884-3308
FAX: 215-884-1083
Jackie Paul, President/CEO
Marketing and promotion.

Mailing list available for rent

17469 Folk Alliance
510 S Main
First Floor
Memphis, TN 38103-4488
901-221-1170
FAX: 901-522-1172
fa@folk.org www.folkalliance.org
Leslie Berman, President
Van Denn, VP
Alan Korolenko, Secretary
Mark Moss, Treasurer
The service association for the field, working on behalf of the folk music and dance industry year round. They offer a business directory of contacts for members, and a non-profit group exemption program for US-based organizations. *$70.00*
Founded: 1989

17470 Gospel Music Association
1205 Division Street
Nashville, TN 37203
615-242-0303
FAX: 615-254-9755
www.gospelmusic.org
John W Styll, President
Our mission is to expose, promote and celebrate the gospel through music. GMA serves as a voice for the Christian music community. It provides an atmosphere in which artists, industry leaders, retail stores, radio stations, concert promoters and local churches can coordinate their efforts for the purpose of benefitting the industry as a whole, while remaining true to the purpose of communicating the gospel message.
$85.00
5000 Members Founded: 1964

17471 Guitar Accessory and Marketing Association (GAMA)
Po Box 757
New York, NY 10033
212-795-3630
FAX: 212-795-3630
assnhdqs@earthlink.net
www.discoverguitar.com
Membership is comprised of guitar and guitar accessory manufacturers and various consumer magazines.

17472 Guitar Foundation of America
PO Box 4909
Garden Grove, CA 92842-4909

FAX: 877-570-3409 877-570-1651
info@guitarfoundation.org
www.guitarfoundation.org
Brian Head, President
Jill Winchell, Operations Manager
Martha Masters, Executive VP
Jeff Cogan, VP
Robert Lane, Vice President/Secretary
Provides its members the combined advantages of a guitar society, a library, a publisher, a continuing education resource, and an artis council. The GFA is a non-profit educational and literacy organization devoted to furthering the knowledge of and interest in the guitar and its music. *$40.00*
Founded: 1973

17473 International Association of Electronic Ke yboard Manufacturers
305 Maple Avenue
Wyncote, PA 19095-3228
617-747-2816
www.iaekm.org
An association that comprises the global manufacturers of electronic keyboards and affiliated software and publications.

17474 International Association of Jazz Educatio n
PO Box 724
Manhattan, KS 66505
785-776-8744
FAX: 785-776-6190
bill@iage.org www.iaje.org
Bill McFarlin, Executive Director
Chuck Owen, President
Ronald Carter, VP
Laura Johnson, Treasurer
Brian Coyle, Secretary
To ensure the continued development and growth of jazz through education and outreach. *$70.00*
8000 Members

17475 International Bluegrass Music Association
2 Music Circle South
Suite 100
Nashville, TN 37203
615-256-3222
FAX: 615-256-0450 888-438-4262
info@ibma.org www.ibma.org
Greg Cahill, President/Chairman
Stan Zdonik, Vice Chari/Associations
Peter D'Addario, Treasurer
Lee Michael Demsey, Secretary
Dan Hayes, Executive Director
IBMA works together for high standards of professionalism, a greater appreciation for our music, and the success of the worldwide bluegrass community.

17476 International Clarinet Association
PO Box 1310
Lyons, CO 80540-2650
801-867-4336
FAX: 212-457-6124
membership@clarinet.org
www.clarinet.org
Lee Livengood, President
Diane Barger, Treasurer
Kristina Belisle, Secretary
So Rhee, Executive Director
A community of clarinetists and clarinet enthusiasts that supports projects that will benefit clarinet performance; provides opportunities for the exchange of ideas, materials and information among its members; fosters the composition, publication, recording, and distribution of music for the clarinet; encourages the research and manufacture of a more definitive clarinet; and encourages and promotes the perfomance and teaching of a wide variety of repertoire for the clarinet.
4000 Members Founded: 1990

17477 International Horn Society
PO Box 630158
Lanai City, HI 96763-0158
808-565-7273
FAX: 808-565-7273
exec-secretary@hornsociety.org
www.hornsociety.org

Jeffrey Snedeker, President
Bruno Schneider, VP
Nancy Jordan Fako, Secretary/Treasurer
Heidi Vogal, Membership

An organization dedicated to performance, teaching, composition, research, and the preservation and promotion of the horn as a musical instrument. Members receive three issues of the journal, The Horn Call, every year. *$35.00*
3500 Members

17478 International Music Products Association NAMM
5790 Armada Drive
Carlsbad, CA 92008
760-438-8001
FAX: 760-438-7327 800-767-6266
info@namm.org www.namm.org
An association whose mission is to unify, lead and strengthn the international music products industry and increase active participation in music making.
9000 Members Founded: 1901

17479 International Piano Guild
808 Rio Grande Street
PO Box 1807
Austin, TX 78767
512-478-5775

ngpt@pianoguild.com
www.pianoguild.com
Richard Allison, President

A division of the American College of Musicians Professional society of piano teachers and music faculty members. Its primary function is to establish definite goals and awards for students of all levels, from the earliest beginner to the gifted prodigy. Its purpose is to encourage growth and enjoyment through the study of piano.
118m Members Founded: 1929

17480 International Polka Association
4608 S Archer Avenue
Chicago, IL 60632
773-254-7771
800-867-6552
ipa@internationalpolka.com
www.internationalpolka.com

Dave Ulczycki, President
Rick Rzeszutko, First VP
Fred Kenzierski, Second VP
Marlene Gill, Secretary
Linda Niewierowski, Treasurer

An educational and charitablt organization for the preservation, promulgation and advancement of polka music and; to promote, maintain and advance public interest in polka entertainment; to advance mutual interests and encourage greater cooperation among its members who are engaged in polka entertainment; and to encourage and pursue the study of polka music, dancing and traditional folklore. Responsible for the continued operation and growth of the Polka Music Hall of Fame and Museum. *$15.00*
8M Members Founded: 1968

17481 International Society of Folk Harpers and Craftsmen
1614 Pittman Drive
Missoula, Mt 59803
406-542-1976

harps@thorharp.com
www.folkharpsociety.org

Dave Woodworth, President
Chuck Wilson, First VP
Verlene Schermer, Second VP
Alice Williams, Secretary
Bette Virdrine, Treasurer

The mission of the ISFHC is: to promote the playing and enjoyment of the folk harp by all; to promote education, creation and development in the building of the folk harp; to increase awareness of professional folk harpers; and to increase public awareness of the music and joys of the folk harp. *$30.00*
Founded: 1985

17482 Keyboard Teachers Association Internationa l
361 Pin Oak Lane
Westbury, NY 11590-1941
516-333-3236
FAX: 516-997-9531

Dr. Albert DeVito, President

17483 Metropolitan Opera Guild
70 Lincoln Center Plaza
New York, NY 10023-6577
212-769-7000
FAX: 212-769-7002
info@metguild.org
www.metoperafamily.org/guild/
Seeks to encourage the appreciation of opera and to support the Metorpolitan Opera. The guild provides programs and services in many areas designed to further these goals. Publishes monthly magazine and organizes special events throughout the year that raised funds which reached over 780,000 students nationwide in 2002.
100M Members Founded: 1935

17484 Music Distributors Association
1026 Northwood Drive
Effingham, IL 62401
217-347-6699
FAX: 217-347-6699
geobev@consolidated.net
www.musicdistributors.org
International, nonprofit trade association representing and serving manufacturers, wholesalers, importers and exporters of musical instruments and accessories, sound reinforcement products and published music. *$675.00*
Founded: 1939

17485 Music Library Association
8551 Research Way
Suite 180
Middleton, WI 53562-3567
608-836-5825
FAX: 608-831-8200
mla@areditions.com
www.musiclibraryassoc.org

Bonna J Boettcher, President

Provides a forum for issues surrounding music, music in libraries, and music librarianship. *$90.00*
Founded: 1931

17486 Music Performance Fund
1501 Broadway
Suite 518
New York, NY 10036-5596
212-391-3950
FAX: 212-221-2604
info@Musicpf.org www.musicpf.org
A nonprofit public service organization headquartered in New York City. MPF is the world's largest sponsor of live, admission-free musical programs.
Founded: 1948

17487 Music Publishers Association
243 5th Avenue
Suite 236
New York, NY 10016
212-327-4044

mpa-admin@mpa.org www.mpa.org

Lauren Keiser, President
Lynn Sengstack, Treasurer
Kathleen Marsh, Secretary, Becretary

The MPA fosters communication among publishers, dealers, music educators, and all ultimate users of music. It is a nonprofit association which addresses itself to issues pertaining to every area of music publishing with an emphasis on the issues relevant to the publishers of print music for concert and educational purposes.
75 Members Founded: 1895

17488 Music Teachers National Association
441 Vine Street
Suite 505
Cincinnati, OH 45202-2811
513-421-1420
FAX: 513-421-2503 888-512-5278
mtnanet@mtna.org www.mtna.org

Gary L Ingle, Executive Director
Paul B Stewart, President
Martha Hilley, VP
Kathleen Rountree, Secretary/Treasurer

The mission of the MTNA is to advance the value of music study and music making to society and to support the professionalism of music teachers.
24000 Members Founded: 1876
Mailing list available for rent 23,000 names $85 per M.

17489 Music for All Foundation
16 Mount Bethel Road
Suite 202
Warren, NJ 07059-5604
908-542-9396
FAX: 908-542-9476
info@music-for-all.org
www.music-for-all.org
Committed to expanding the role of music and the arts in education, to heightening the public's appreciation of the value of music and arts education, and to creating a positive environment for the arts through societal changes.

17490 Musical Box Society International
MBSI Member Registration
PO Box 10196
Springfield, MO 65808-0196

FAX: 417-886-8839 www.mbsi.org
A nonprofit organization dedicated to the enjoyment, sstudy and preservation of all automatic musical instruments. Members receive the bimonthly scholarly journal, Mechanical Music, covering educational articles, relevant events, activities, news, information, and advertisements and the biennial, Directory of Members, Museums and Dealers. Hosts annual convention. *$55.00*
2.8M Members Founded: 1949

17491 Musicians Foundation
875 Sixth Avenue
Room 2303
New York, NY 10001
212-239-9137
FAX: 212-239-9138
info@musiciansfoundation.org
www.musiciansfoundation.org

Brent Williams, Executive Director

Representing interests on the condition and social welfare of professional musicians and their families. Provides emergency financial assistance to meet current living, medical and allied expenses.

17492 National Association for Music Education MENC
1806 Robert Fulton Drive
Reston, VA 20191
703-860-4000
FAX: 703-860-1531 800-336-3768
John J Mahlmann, Executive Director
Lynn Brinckmeyer, President
Mission is to advance music education by encouraging the study and making of music by all.

17493 National Association of Band Instrument Ma nufacturers
281 W 21st Street
5th Floor
New York, NY 10010-6906
212-924-9175
FAX: 212-675-3577
Jerome Hershman, Contact
A trade association of band instrument manufacturers, importers and distributors including accessories selling to the trade only.
34 Members Founded: 1920

17494 National Association of College Wind and P ercussion Instructors
Division of Fine Arts
Truman State University
Kirksville, MO 63501
660-785-4442
FAX: 660-785-7463
cmoore@fsu.edu www.nacwpi.org
Chris Moore, President
Michael Dean, VP
Richard K Weerts, Executive Secretary/Treasurer
A forum for communication within the profession of applied music on the college campus. The Association is composed of university, college, and conservatory teachers. *$35.00*
600 Members Founded: 1951

17495 National Association of Negro Musicians
11551 South Laflin Street
PO Box 43053
Chicago, IL 60643-5029
773-568-3818
FAX: 773-785-5388
nanm@nanm.org www.nanm.org
Roland M Carter, President
David Morrow, First VP
Serita Lattimore, Second VP
Ona B Campbell, Executive Secretary
Dan Long, Treasurer
Dedicated to the preservation, encouragement and advocacy of all genres of the music of African Americans. Holds a national convention in a different city eac year, offering a chance to participate in workshops, seminars, lectures and performances. NANM invites the professional artists, the educator, the student, the amateur, the lover of music to become a part of this organization's 'Pride in a Cultural Heritage.'
2.5M Members Founded: 1919

17496 National Association of Pastoral Musicians
962 Wayne Avenue
Suite 210
Silver Spring, MD 20910-4461
240-247-3000
FAX: 240-247-3001
npmsing@npm.org www.npm.org
Dr J Michaek McMahon, President
Kathleen Haley, Director Membership Services
Lowell Hickman, Office Manager/Executive Assistant
Joseph Lively, Comptroller
Fosters the art of musical liturgy. The members of NPM serve the Catholic Church in the United States as musicians, clergy, liturgists, and other leaders of prayer.
9000 Members Founded: 1976

17497 National Association of Professional Band Instrument Repair Technicians
2026 Eagle Road
PO Box 51
Normal, IL 61761
309-452-4257
FAX: 309-452-4825
napbirt@napbirt.org www.napbirt.org
Bill Mathews, President
A nonprofit international educational association dedicated to the advancement of the craft of band instrument repair. Their mission is to promote the highest possible standards of band instrument repair, restoration and maintenance by providing members with multi-level professional development by offering technical training, continuing education and the publication of their bi-monthky trade journal. *$95.00*
1300 Members Founded: 1976

17498 National Association of Recording Merchand isers
9 Eves Drive
Suite 120
Marlton, NJ 08053-3130
856-596-2221
FAX: 859-596-3268
donio@narm.com www.narm.com
Sue Peterson, Chair
Scott Wilson, Vice Chairman
Bob Schneider, Treasurer
Rachelle Friedman, Secretary
Jim Donio, President
A not-for-profit trade association that serves the music retailing community in the areas of networking, advocacy, information, education and promotion. Membership includes music and other entertainment retailers, wholesalers, distributorsm record labels, multimedia suppliers, and suppliers of related products and services, as well as individual professionals and educators in the music business field.
Founded: 1958

17499 National Association of Schools of Music
11250 Roger Bacon Drive
Suite 21
Reston, VA 20190-5248
703-437-0700
FAX: 703-437-6312
info@arts-accredit.org
www.arts-accredit.org
Daniel P Sher, President
Jo Ann Domb, VP
Mellesenah Y Morris, Treasurer
Mark Wait, Secretary
Samuel Hope, Executive Director
An organization of schools, conservatoris, colleges and universities. NASM provides information to potential students and parents, consultations, stastistical information, professional development and policy analysis. It is the national accrediting agency for music and music-related disciplines.
610 Members Founded: 1924

17500 National Association of Teachers of Singing
9957 Moorings Drive
Suite 401
Jacksonville, FL 32257
904-992-9101
FAX: 904-262-2587
info@nats.org www.nats.org
Scott McCoy, President
William Vessels, Executive Director
The largest association of teachers of singing in the world.
6000 Members Founded: 1944

17501 National Ballroom and Entertainment Associ ation
2799 Locust Road
Decorah, IA 52101-7600
563-382-3871

nbea@oneota.net www.nbea.com
John Matter, Executive Director
National nonprofit association which advocates that social dancing is a life-long activity that contributes to the physical, mantal, and social well-being of an individual. They believe that social dancing should be preserved for current and future generations and introduced to today's youth as an alternate form of social interaction.
450 Members Founded: 1947

17502 National Band Association
Membership Office
PO Box 25136
Baton Rouge, LA 70894
601-297-8168
FAX: 601-266-6185
info@nationalbandassociation.org
www.nationalbandassociation.org
Bobby Adams, President
Finley Hamilton, First VP
Mark Heidel, Second VP
Linda Moorehouse, Secretary/Treasurer
David Gregory, Advisor to the President
The purpose of the NBA to promote the musical and educational significance of bands and is dedicated to the attainment of a high level of excellence for bands and band music. It is open to anyone and everyone interested in bands, regardless of the length if his/her experience, type of position held, or the specific area at which he/she works. The membership roster includes men and women from every facet of the band world.
3M Members Founded: 1960

17503 National Federation of Music Clubs

1336 N Delaware Street
Indianapolis, IN 46202-2481
317-638-4402
FAX: 317-638-0503
info@nfmc-music.org
www.nfmc-music.org
Elizabeth Paris, President
Lana Bailey, First VP
Kay Hawthorne, Secretary
Barbara Hildebrand, Treasurer
Jennifer Keller, Administrative Manager
NFMC provides opportunities for musical study, performance and appreciation to

more than 200,000 senior, student and junior members in 6,500 music-related clubs and organizations nationwide. Members are professional and amateur musicians, vocalists, composers, dancers, performing artists, arts and music educators, music students, generous music patrons and benefactors, and music lovers of all ages.
170M Members Founded: 1898

17504 National Opera Association
PO Box 60869
Canyon, TX 79016-0869
806-651-2857
FAX: 806-651-2958 www.noa.org

Robert Hansen, Executive Director
JoElyn Wakefield-Wright, President
Carole Notestine, Secretary
Robert Thieme, Editor Opera Journal
Philip Hagemann, Treasurer

The NOA seeks to promote a greater appreciation of opera and music theatre, to enhance pedagogy and performing activities, and to increase performance opportunities by supporting projects that improve the scope and quality of opera. Members in the United States, Canada, Europe, Asia and Australia participate in a wide array of activities in support of this mission.
775 Members Founded: 1955

17505 Opera America
330 7th Ave
16th Floor
New York, NY 10001-5248
212-796-8620
FAX: 212-796-8631
frontdesk@operaamerica.org
www.operaam.org

Marc A Scorca, President/CEO
Charles MacKay, Chairman
David McIntosh, Treasurer
Susan Danis, Secretary
Rebecca Ackerman, Membership Manager

Opera America serves and strengthens the field of opera by providing a variety of informational, technical, and administrative resources to the greater opera community. Its fundamental mission is to promote opera as exciting and accessible to individuals from all walks of life.

17506 Organization of American Kodaly Educators
1612 29th Avenue South
Moorhead, MN 56560
218-227-6253
FAX: 218-227-6254
oakeoffice@oake.org www.oake.org

Brent Gault, President
Penny Whalen, VP
Paul Baumann, Secretary
Greg Williams, Treasurer
Joan Dahlin, Administrative Director

The purpose of this organization is to promote Zoltan Kodaly's concept of 'Music for Everyone' through the improvment of music education in schools.
Founded: 1973

17507 Pedal Steel Guitar Association
PO Box 20248
Floral Park, NY 11002-0248
516-616-9214
FAX: 516-616-9214
bobpsga@optonline.net
www.psga.org

Bob Maickel, President
John DeMaille, VP
Jeff De Maio, Treasurer
Darlene DeMaille, Secretary
Doug Mack, Newsletter Editor

A nonprofit organization whose primary purpose is to share information on playing the steel guitar and in particular the pedal steel guitar. Publishes the Pedal Steel Newsletter ten times per year
1540 Members Founded: 1973

17508 Percussive Arts Society
701 NW Ferris Avenue
Lawton, OK 73507-5442
580-353-1455
FAX: 580-353-1456
percarts@pas.org www.pas.org

Richard Holly, President
Steve Houghton, VP
Lisa Rogers, Secretary
Michael Balter, Treasurer
Michael Kenyon, Executive Director

A music service organization promoting percussion education, research, performance and appreciation throughout the world. Offers two print publications, the Percussive Arts Society International Headquarters/Museum and the annual Percussive Arts Society International Convention. *$85.00*
7000 Members Founded: 1961

17509 Piano Technicians Guild
4444 Forest Avenue
Kansas City, KS 66106
913-432-9975
FAX: 913-432-9986
ptg@ptg.org www.ptg.org

Barbara J Cassaday, Executive Director
Kent E Swafford, President
Allan Gilreath, Secretary/Treasurer
Kathy Maxwelly, Development Manager
Sandy Roady, Membership/Convention Manager

The world's premier source of expertise in piano service and technology. A non-profit trade association dedicated to promoting the highest possible standards of piano service.
4100 Members Founded: 1957 4000 names

17510 Retail Print Music Dealers Association
14070 Proton Road
Suite 100
Dallas, TX 75244
972-233-9107
FAX: 972-490-4219
office@printmusic.org
www.printmusic.org

Becky Lightfoot, President
Lori Supinie, VP/Secretary
Gayle Beackock, VP/Treasurer
Madeline Crouch, Executive Director

A professional trade organization founded to address the special needs and interests of the print music industry. RPMDA provides a common meeting ground for the congenial interchange of ideas among print music dealers; promotes ethical standards and policies in dealing with music publishers; promotes better dealer/publisher relations; serves the public and encourages music education; provides association-sponsored activities and publications that help its members prepare for future trends.
275 Members Founded: 1976

17511 Rhythm and Blues Foundation
100 S Broad Street
Suite 620
Philadelphia, PA 19110
215-568-1080
FAX: 215-561-1026
paden@rhythmblues.org
www.rhythm-n-blues.org

Kendall Minter, Chairman
Jim Fifield, Vice Chairman
Shawn Gee, Treasurer
David Nathan, Secretary
Patrica Wilson Aden, Executive Director

Nonprofit service organization dedicated to the historical and cultural preservation of Rhythm and Blues music. The Foundation provides financial support, medical assistance and edicational outreach through various grants and programs to support R&B amd Motown artists of the 40s, 50s, 60s and 70s.
Founded: 1988

17512 Society of Professional Audio Recording Se rvices
9 Music Square S
Suite 222
Nashville, TN 37203

FAX: 615-296-0386 800-771-7727
spars@spars.com www.spars.com

Karen Brinton, President
Eric W Johnson, Secretary
Andrew Kautz, Treasurer

SPARS is dedicated to excellence through innovation, education and communication.

200 Members Founded: 1979

17513 Songwriters Guild of America
209 10th Avenue South
Suite 534
Nashville, TN 37203
615-742-9945
FAX: 615-742-9948
nash@songwritersguild.com
www.songwritersguild.com

Rundi Ream, CEO

Provides agreements between songwriters, composers and publishers. The SGA will take 'such lawful actions as will advance, promote and benefit the profession.'
4000 Members Founded: 1931

17514 Sweet Adelines International
PO Box 470168
Tulsa, OK 74147-0168
918-622-1444
FAX: 918-665-0894 800-992-7464
admin@sweetadelineintl.org
www.sweetadelineintl.org

Donna Kerley, Dicector Finance/Administration
Kelly Kirchoff, Director Communications
Jane Hanson, Marketing/Membership Coordinator

A worldwide organization of women singers committed to advancing the musical art form of barbershop harmony through education and performances. Their motto is to 'Harmonize the World.'
27000 Members Founded: 1945

17515 World Piano Competition/AMSA
441 Vine Street
Suite 1030
Cincinnati, OH 45202-2908
513-421-5342
FAX: 513-421-2672
info@amsa-wpc.orgm
www.amsa-wpc.org

George Musekamp, Acting Chair
Gloria Ackerman, Founder/CEO
Stanley Aronoff, Event Chair
Leon Fleisher, President
William Selnick, Treasurer

Provides an continuum of services and role models to assist youth in need. Their task is to provide a venue of excitement and compassion to them to do their bast to prepare for the enormous challenge they face as they approach adulthood.

2.5M Members Founded: 1956

Newsletters

17516 American Guild Associate News Newsletter
American Guild of Music
PO Box 599
Warren, MI 48090-4905
248-686-1975
FAX: 630-968-0197
agm@americanguild.org
www.americanguild.org

Richard Chizmadia, Editor-in-Chief

Offers information and news for professionals in the music profession. *$25.00*

Quarterly Founded: 1901

17517 American Music Center Opportunity Update
American Music Center
30 W 26th Street
Suite 1001
New York, NY 10010-2011
212-366-5260
FAX: 212-366-5265
center@amc.net www.amc.net

A listing of composition competitions, calls for scores, workshops, and other opportunities delivered every month via e-mail to members of the American Music Center.

Monthly Founded: 1939

17518 American Musical Instrument Society Newsletter
270 Barret Road
Riverside, CA 92507
781-397-8870
FAX: 781-397-8887
amis@guildassoc.com www.amis.org

Barbara Gable, Editor

Official notices and news of the Society's activites; short articles and communications; recent acquisition lists from member institutions; news of members; and classified ads.

20 pages 3X Per Year Founded: 1971

17519 American Musicological Society Newsletter
University of Iowa
Arts Center Relations
300 Plaza Center One
Iowa City, IA 52242

FAX: 319-384-0024
peter-alexander@uiowa.edu
www.ams-net.org

Peter Alexander, Editor

The AMS Newsletter is published simiannually in February and August. The February Newsletter is mailed with the new Directory and Ballot each year. The August Newsletter is mailed with the Annual Meeting information and registration form each year.

Semi-Annually Founded: 1934

17520 American School Band Directors Association Newsletter
American School Band Directors Association
227 N 1st Street
PO Box 696
Guttenberg, IA 52052-0696
563-252-2500
FAX: 563-252-2500
asbda@comcast.net www.asbda.com

Ed Cannava, President
Bruce Fox, Editor
Denny Hanna, Office Manager

Reports and information for members of the ASBDA

Quarterly Founded: 1953
Printed in 2 colors on matte stock

17521 American Viola Society Newsletter
14070 Proton Roade
Suite 100
Dallas, TX 75244
972-233-9107

stemple@comcast.net
www.americanviolasociety.org

Sue Temple, Editor
Madelein Crouch, General Manager

A monthly e-newsletter. It contains announcements from the AVS, upcoming local chapter events, and other important items.

Monthly

17522 Banjo Newsletter
PO Box 3418
Annapolis, MD 21403-0418

800-759-7425
Bnl@annap,infi.net
www.banjonews.com
Newletter focusing on Bluegrass banjo music.

17523 Bluegrass Music Profiles
Bluegrass Publications
PO Box 850
Nicholasville, KY 40340-0850
859-333-6456

info@bluegrassmusicprofiles.com
www.bluegrassmusicprofiles.com
Information on Bluegrass music.

17524 Bluegrass Now
PO Box 2020
Rolla, MO 65402
573-341-7335

Bgn@fidnet.com
www.bluegrassnow.com
Information on Bluegrass music.

17525 Bluegrass Unlimited
PO Box 771
Warrenton, VA 20188-0771
540-349-8181
800-256-7427
info@bluegrassmusic.com
www.bluegrassmusic.com
Information on Bluegrass music.

17526 Brooklyn Institute for Studies in American Music
Brooklyn College
Institute for Studies in American Music
2900 Bedford Avenue
Brooklyn, NY 11210
718-951-5000

www.brooklyn.cuny.edu/bb/fac/american.htm
Music news and Academy activities.
Semi-Annual Founded: 1861

17527 Dirty Linen
PO Box 6660
Baltimore, MD 21239-6600
410-583-7973

office@dirtylinen.com
www.dirtylinen.com
Information on Bluegrass music.

17528 Early Keyboard Studies Newsletter
Westfield Center for Early Keyboard Studies
Westminster College
Box 154
New Wilmington, PA 16172

harrisea@westminster.edu
www.westfield.org

Elizabeth Harrison, Editor

E-newsletter providing information to professional keyboard musicians.

12 pages Monthly Founded: 1979

17529 Early Music Newsletter
New York Recorder Guild
145 W 93 Street
New York, NY 10025-7559
212-662-2946

mzumoff@nyc.rr.com
www.priceclan.com/nyrecorderguild/

Michael Zumoff, Executive Director

A publication of the New York Recorder Guild

10 pages Monthly

17530 Flatpicking Guitar
High View Publications
PO Box 51960
Pulaski, VA 24301
540-980-0338

Highview@flatpick.com
www.flatpick.com
Information on Bluegrass music and the Flatpick guitar.

17531 GMA Update
Gospel Music Association
1205 Division Street
Nashville, TN 37203-4011
615-242-0303
FAX: 615-254-9755
www.gospelmusic.org
GMA's industry e-newsletter available to any non-GMA member who wishes to receive it. Sent out once a month, GMA Update contains the latest news about the Christian music industry and valuable information about the GMA.
Monthly

17532 GMAil
Gospel Music Association
1205 Division Street
Nashville, TN 37203-4011
615-242-0303
FAX: 615-254-9755
www.gospelmusic.org
E-newsletter sent weekly to GMA members. Includes weekly music sales, charts, news, links to valuable resources, and information about upcoming GMA and industry events.
Weekly Founded: 1964

17533 Girl Groups Gazette
PO Box 69A04
Department HSND
West Hollywood, CA 90069-0066

Louis Wendruck, Editor/Publisher
For fans of girl groups and female singers of the 1960's and 70's including photos, discographies, records, t-shirts, postcards, and videos. *$20.00*
Quarterly Founded: 1988

17534 In the Groove
Michigan Antique Phonograph Society
60 Central Street
Battle Creek, MI 49017-3704
616-968-1299

ITG@michiganantiquephonographsociety.org
www.michiganantiquephonographsociety.org
Phil Stewart, Editor
Eileen Stewart, Editor
The Newsletter of the Michigan Antique Phonograph Society. Includes show, sales and auction announcements, MAPS chapter news, President's message, monthly feature articles, letters to the editor, and swap shop. *$25.00*
24 pages Monthly Founded: 1976

17535 International Bluegrass
IBMA
2 Music Circle South
Suite 100
Nashville, TN 37203
615-256-3222
888-438-4262
nancyc@ibma.org www.ibma.org
Information on Bluegrass music from the IBMA

17536 Marketing Through Music
Rolling Stone Magazine
1290 Sixth Avenue
2nd Floor
New York, NY 10104-0002
212-484-1616
FAX: 212-644-8982 800-283-1549
rollingstone@real.com
www.rollingstone.com
David M Rheins, Editor
A monthly newsletter geared for marketing, advertising and music exexecutives. It includes information on such matters as rock tours and musician endorsements, ad campaigns and rock contests. *$50.00*
Monthly Founded: 1967

17537 Music for the Love of It
67 Parkside Drive
Berkeley, CA 94705-2409
510-654-9134
FAX: 510-654-4656
tedrust@musicfortheloveofit.com
www.musicfortheloveofit.com
Edgar Rust, Publisher/Editor
Janet Telford, Co-Editor
A newsletter for people everywhere who love making music. Every issues brings new enthusiasm, new ideas and new opportunities for making music.
Bi-Monthly Founded: 1988
Printed in on matte stock

17538 National Music Museum Newsletter
National Music Museum
414 E Clark Street
Vermillion, SD 57069
605-677-5306
FAX: 605-677-6995
smm@usd.edu www.usd.edu/smm/
Andre P Larson, Publisher
Quarterly Newletter which includes feature articles written by the curatorial staff and lists recent acquisitions. Published in February, May, August and November. It is available with basic museum membership.
$35.00

Printed in 4 colors

17539 No Depression
908 Halcyon Avenue
Nashville, TN 37204
615-292-7084
www.nodepression.net
Information on Bluegrass music

17540 Notes a Tempo
West Virginia University
Division of Music
PO Box 6111
Morgantown, WV 26506-6111
304-293-4841

David Bess, Co-Editor
Becky Terry, Co-Editor
The official publication of the West Virginia Music Educators. Published Fall, Winter and Spring
20-32 pages 3 per year
Circulation: 1115

17541 Old Time Herald
PO Box 51812
Durham, NC 27717
919-402-8495

agerrard@mindspring.com
www.oldtimeherald.org
Information on Bluegrass music

17542 Pedal Steel Newsletter
Pedal Steel Guitar Association
PO Box 20248
Floral Park, NY 11002-0248
516-616-9214
FAX: 516-616-9214
bobpsga@optonline.net
www.psga.org
Doug Mack, Editor
Bob Maickel, President
Dedicated to the art of playing pedal steel guitar. Every issue contains tablature arrangements of songs for the steel guitar as well as coming events, record reviews, product reports and news concerning the instrument.
10 x Per Year Founded: 1973

17543 Percussion News
Percussive Arts Society
701 NW Ferris Avenue
Lawton, OK 73507-5442
580-353-1455
FAX: 580-353-1456
percarts@pas.org www.pas.org
Rick Mattingly, Editor
Hillary Henry, Art Director
Rich Holly, President
Newsletter devoted to membership activities. This colorful newsletter also features a Classified Advertising section. Percussion News is published in January, March, May, July, September and November.
6 Editions Per Year Founded: 1961
Mailing list available for rent

17544 Roots and Rhythm Newsletter
Roots and Rhythm
PO Box 837
El Cerrito, CA 94530
510-526-8373
FAX: 510-526-9001 888-766-8766
roots@toast.net
www.rootsandrhythm.com
Frank Scott, Owner
Nancy Scott-Noennig, Co-Owner
Lists, reviews and makes available for sale, recordings of blues, rhythm and blues, rockabilly, country, folk, ethnic, nostalgia and jazz music. Each newsletter reviews about 400 items and lists another 500 without reviews.
Bi-Monthly Founded: 1974
Circulation: 10000
Printed in 2 colors on newsprint stock

17545 Sing Out!
PO Box 5253
Bethlehem, PA 18015-5253
610-865-5366

info@singout.org www.singout.org
Information on Bluegrass music

17546 Tempo
Academy of Country Music
5500 Balboa Boulevard
Suite 200
Encino, CA 91316
818-788-8000
FAX: 818-788-0999
info@acmcountry.com
www.acmcountry.com
Devoted exclusively to the country music industry.
12 pages Quarterly Founded: 1964
Circulation: 4500

17547 Women in Bluegrass Newsletter
PO Box 2498
Winchester, VA 22604

Nmhentry@visuallink.com
www.murphymethod/com/womeninbluegrass.cfm
Information on women in bluegass music

Magazines & Journals

17548 AfterTouch: New Music Discoveries

Music Discovery Network
PO Box 6205
Peoria, IL 61601-6205
309-685-4843
FAX: 309-685-4878 800-882-4262
aimcmc@aol.com
www.musicdiscoveries.com

Ronald Wallace, Editor

A magazine for music lovers who would like to experience new sights and sounds and would like to keep their fingers on the pulse of the music industry.

Annual Founded: 1984
Circulation: 10,000
Printed in on glossy stock

17549 American Music

University of Illinois Press
Chicago Distribution Center
11030 South Langley Avenue
Chicago, IL 60628

FAX: 800-621-8476 800-621-2736
journals@uillinois.edu
www.press.uillinois.edu

Michael Hicks, Editor
Daniel Felsenfeld, Book Review Editor
Caroline Benser, Recording Review Editor
Jennifer DeLapp Brikett, Multimedia Review Editor
Jeff McArdle, Journals Marketing/Advertising Mgr

Publishes articles on American composers, performers, publishers, institutions, events, and the music industry as well as book and recording reviews, bibliographies, and discographies. *$45.00*

Quarterly Founded: 1981
Circulation: 1650
Mailing list available for rent 1,650 names $100 per M.
Printed in 2 colors on glossy stock

17550 American Music Teacher

Music Teachers National Association
MTNA National Headquarters
441 Vine Street, Suite 505
Cincinnati, OH 45202-2811
513-421-1420
FAX: 513-421-2503 888-512-5278
mtnanet@mtna.org www.mtna.org

Brian Shepard, Marketing Director
Gary L Ingle, Executive Director
Marcie Gerrietts Lindsey, Director of Publishing
Kristina Feldkamp, Assistant Editor

Provides articles, reviews and regular columns that inform, educate and challenge music teachers and foster excellence in the music teaching profession. *$30.00*

Founded: 1876
Circulation: 35000
Mailing list available for rent 24000 names $85 per M.
Printed in 4 colors on glossy stock

17551 American Organist

American Guild of Organists
475 Riverside Drive
Suite 1260
New York, NY 10115
212-870-2310
FAX: 212-870-2163 800-246-5115
info@agohq.org www.agohq.org

Most widely read journal devoted to organ and choral music in the world. Officialjournal of the American Guild of Organists, the Royal Canadian College of Organists, and the Associated Pipe Organ Builders of America. *$52.00*

Monthly Founded: 1967
Circulation: 24000

17552 American Viola Society Journal

American Viola Society
14070 Proton Road
Suite 100
Dallas, TX 75244
972-233-9107
FAX: 972-490-4219
info@avsnationaloffice.org
www.americanviolasociety.org

Matthew Dane, Editor
Madeleine Crouch, General Manager
Helen Callus, President
Kathryn Steely, Webmaster

Peer reviewed journal which promotes interest in the viola. *$42.00*

Annually Founded: 1984
Circulation: 1500

17553 BMI Musicworld

Broadcast Music
320 W 57th Street
New York, NY 10019-3790
212-586-2000
FAX: 212-245-8986 www.bmi.com

Del Bryant, President/CEO
John E Cody, COO/EVP

Performing rights organization. Articles of interest to the songwriting community.

Founded: 1985

17554 Billboard Magazine

Billboard Subscription
PO Box 15158
North Hollywood, CA 91615-5158
818-487-4582
800-562-2706
info@billboard.com
www.billboard.com

Scott McKenzie, Group Editorial Director
Tamara Conniff, Exec Editor & Associate Publisher

Packed with in-depth music and entertainment features including the latest in new media and digital music, global coverage, music and money, touring, new artists, radio news and retail reports. *$299.00*

Weekly

17555 CCM Magazine

Salem Publishing
104 Woodmont Boulevard
Suite 300
Nashville, TN 37205-2207
615-386-3011
FAX: 615-312-4266
info@ccmcom.com
www.ccmmagazine.com

The voice of Contemporary Christian Music. Each monthly issue features music news, exclusive interviews, and an in-depth look at the spiritual lives of today's leading Christian music artists. *$19.95*

Monthly Founded: 1978
Printed in 4 colors on glossy stock

17556 Callboard

Theatre Bay Area
870 Market Street
Suite 375
San Francisco, CA 94102-3002
415-430-1140
FAX: 415-430-1145
tba@theatrebayarea.org
www.theatrebayarea.org

Provides trade information for professionals in the Bay Area. The magazine contains the following departments: Letterbox, Inside the Industry, Community News, How Did They Do That, Keep An Eye On, Editors' Picks and Encore. *$65.00*

Monthly Founded: 1976
Printed in 2 colors on matte stock

17557 Chamber Music Magazine

Chamber Music America
305 7th Avenue
5th Floor
New York, NY 10001-6008
212-242-2022
FAX: 212-242-7955
egoldensohn@chamber-music.org
www.chamber-music.org

Ellen Goldensohn, Publication Director
Margaret M Lioi, CEO
Brenden O'Hanlon, Advertising Manager
Fred Cohn, Consulting Editor

The journal of the professional chamber music field. Its articles are aimed to professionals, amateurs, arts administrators, concert presenters, educators and music lovers. *$28.00*

Monthly Founded: 1977
Circulation: 10000

17558 Choral Journal

American Choral Directors Association
545 Couch Drive
PO BOX 2720
Oklahoma City, OK 73101-2720
405-232-8161
FAX: 405-232-8162
chojo@acdaonline.org
www.acdaonline.org

Carroll Gonzo, Editor
Gene Brooks, Executive Director
Nina Gilbert, Associate Editor
Ron Granger, Managing Editor

The official publication of the American Choral Directors Association. Articles that embrace both scholarly and practical approaches to understanding issues affecting choral directors and their craft. Prints reviews of octavos, compact discs, and books related to choral music. Members of the association teach choral music in public and private schools as well as in colleges and universities.

Founded: 1959
Circulation: 21,000
Mailing list available for rent 18500 names
Printed in 4 colors on glossy stock

17559 Clarinet Journal

International Clarinet Society
PO Box 5039
Wheaton, IL 60189-5039
630-665-3602
FAX: 630-665-3848
info@clarinet.org www.clarinet.org

James Gillespie, Editor
So Rhee, Executive Director

Contains articles in wide variety of areas written by performers and scholars. *$25.00*

Quarterly
Circulation: 3000

17560 Clavier
Instrumentalist Publishing Company
200 Northfield Road
Northfield, IL 60093-3390
847-446-5000
FAX: 847-446-6263 888-446-6888
James Rohner, Publisher
Judy Nelson, Editor
Provides new ideas and advice for piano teachers from leading educators. The focus of each issue is to offer practical advice for teachers. Articles include interviews with prominent performers, teachers and composers, the latest teaching methods, tributes to great artists of the past, and reviews of newly publshed music, educational software and videos. *$17.00*
10X Per Year Founded: 1965
Circulation: 16000

17561 Close Up Magazine
Country Music Association
One Music Circle S
Nashville, TN 37203
615-244-2840
FAX: 615-726-0314
international@cmaworld.com
www.cmaworld.com
Profiles of country music artists, various songwriters and industry news. Members of the Association receive the magazine as a benefit of their membership.
Founded: 1958
Circulation: 8000

17562 Country Weekly Magazine
American Media Inc
4950 Communications Ave
T-Rex Technology Center
Boca Raton, FL 33431
561-997-7733
FAX: 561-272-8411 www.cjr.org
Devoted to country music and entertainment. Packed with feature articles and photos of country music personalities, music and video reviews, tour dates and late breaking news from the world of country music. *$34.95*
Bi-Weekly

17563 DJ Times
Testa Communications
25 Willowdale Avenue
Port Washington, NY 11050-3779
516-767-2500
FAX: 516-767-9335 800-937-7678
testa@testa.com www.djtimes.com
Colorful tabloid magazine dedicated to professional mobile and club DJs. Specialized music sections, new product departments for sound and lighting, record reviews, business columns, informative entertainer profiles and more. *$19.40*
Monthly Founded: 1988
Circulation: 30000

17564 Diapason
Scranton Gillette Communications
3030 W Salt Creek Lane
Suite 201
Arlington Heights, IL 60005-0408
847-391-1045
FAX: 847-390-0408
jbutera@sgcmail.comom
www.thediapason.com
Jerome Butera, Publisher
Joyce Robinson, Associate Editor
Vicki Pierce, Subscriptions
An international journal dealing with organ, harpsichord, carillon and church music. *$35.00*
Monthly Founded: 1909

17565 Discoveries
700 East State Street
Ioal, WI 54990-0001
715-445-2214
FAX: 715-445-4087 800-258-0929
wayne.youngblood@fwpubs.com
www.discoveriesmag.com
Mark Willliams, Publisher
Wayne Youngblood, Editorial Director
Cathy Bernardy, Associate Editor
Todd Whitesel, Associate Editor
Trevor Lauber, Advertising Sales Manager
Keeps close watch on market trends for collectible records, CDs and memorabilia. The Market Watch pages serve to interpret the mass of information available online and break it down to the most useful data collectors need. Each monthly issue is full of personality and opinion, with many reviews to help you determine where to spend your money. Coverage includes rock 'n' roll, rhythm &Æblues, pop, doo-wop, classic jazz and country western recordings. *$28.00*
Monthly Founded: 1988
Circulation: 10,859

17566 Downbeat
102 N Haven Road
PO Box 906
Elmhurst, IL 60126
630-941-2030
FAX: 630-941-3210 800-554-7470
service@downbeat.com
www.downbeat.com
Kevin Maher, CEO
Monthly magazine includes such features as Readers Poll results, festival reviews, CD reviews, feature articles and more. *$29.95*
Monthly

17567 Electronic Musician
PRIMEDIA
6400 Hollis Street
Suite 12
Emeryville, CA 94608-1086
510-653-3307

emeditorial@prismb2b.com
www.emusician.com
Steve Oppenheimer, Editor-in-Chief
Joe Perry, Associate Publisher
Marie Briganti, List Manager
Magazine for musicians recording and producing music in a home or personal studio environment. They are a source of user-friendly technical information for musicans. Features include: Tech Page, ProFile, Working Musician, Sound Design Workshop, Making Tracks, Square One, Reviews, What's New, Master Class, Final Mix, and Editors Choice Awards. *$23.97*
Monthly Founded: 1986
Circulation: 61102

17568 Flute Talk
Instrumentalist Company
200 Northfield Road
Northfield, IL 60093-3390
847-446-5000
FAX: 847-446-6263 888-446-6888
fteditor@instrumentalistmagazine.com
www.instrumentalistmagazine.com
Flute Talk is written for professional flute players, teachers, and advanced students. Frequent topics include performance analyses of flute repertoire, current teaching techniques, piccolo articles, interviews with prominent performers and teachers, and reviews of new music, recordings, and books for flutists. *$13.00*
10 x Per Year Founded: 1981
Circulation: 12000

17569 Goldmine
700 E State Street
Iola, WI 54990
715-445-2214
FAX: 715-445-4087 800-258-0929
goldmine@krause.com
www.goldminemag.com
Jeff Pozorski, Publisher
Brian Earnest, Editorial Director
Peter Lindblad, Associate Editor
Tim Neely, Research Director
Trevor Lauber, Advertising Sales Manager
The world's largest marketplace for collectible records, CDs, and music memorabilia covering Rock N' Roll, Blues, Country, Folk, and Jazz. Large volumes of "For Sale" and "Wanted" ads are placed by collectors and dealers. Includes articles on recording stars of the past and present with discographies listing all known releases, a listing of upcoming record-and-CD-collector conventions, album reviews, hobby and music news, a collecting column, a letters section, and "Collector Mania" (Q&A). *$39.95*
Bi-Weekly Founded: 1974
Circulation: 17026

17570 Guitar One
Cherry Lane Magazines
6 E 32nd Street
11th Floor
New York, NY 10016-5422
212-561-3500
FAX: 212-251-0840 800-825-4942
guitarshop@worldnet.att.net
http://www.guitarmag.com
Brad Tolinski, Editorial Director
Jonathan Simpson-Bint, President
Holly Klingel, VP Circulation
Steve Aaron, Publishing Director
Greg Di Benedetto, Publisher
Information on everything from the guitar equipment evaluations to news on the latest trends and technological developments to special insider pieces covering the sound secrets of today's top players. *$24.95*
Monthly Founded: 1985
Circulation: 105,000

17571 Guitar Review
Albert Augustine Limited
151 W 26th Street
New York, NY 10001
917-661-0220
FAX: 917-661-0223
mail@guitarreview.com
www.guitarreview.com
Stephen Griesgraber, Editor
Eliot Fisk, Associate Editor
David Starobin, Associate Editor
Ian Gallagher, Music Editor
Matthew Hough, Circulation
Scholarly articles related to the classical guitar. *$28.00*
48 pages Quarterly Founded: 1946
Circulation: 4000

17572 Instrumentalist
Instrumentalist Company
200 Northfield Road
Northfield, IL 60093-3390
847-446-5000
FAX: 847-446-6263 888-446-6888
insteditor@instrumentalistmagazine.com
www.instrumentalistmagazine.com
A magazine school band and orchestra directors can depend on for practical information to use for then ensembles. The

articles written by veteran directors and performers cover a wide range of topics, including rehearsal techniques, conducting tips, programming ideas, instrument clinics, repertoire analyses, and much more. Monthly new music reviews guide directors to selecting the best music for their students. *$21.00*
Monthly Founded: 1945
Circulation: 16,000
Printed in 4 colors

17573 International Musician
American Federation of Musicians
1501 Broadway
Suite 600
New York, NY 10036-5503
212-869-1330
FAX: 212-764-6134
info@afm.org www.afm.org
Delivers the latest happenings in music. Focuses on the overall well-being of all musicians. Provides news pertaining to symphonic, rock, freelance, recording and touring musicians. IM features aricles on pressing issues sich as piracy, legislation, on-the-job struggles, and the effects of technology. *$25.00*
Monthly Founded: 1896
Circulation: 110000
Printed in on n stock

17574 Jazz Education Journal
International Association for Jazz Education
2803 Claflin Road
Manhattan, KS 66502
785-776-8744
FAX: 785-776-6190
karen@iage.org www.iaje.org
Leslie M Sabina, Editor
Karen Mayse, Advertising
Provides news and information in the field of jazz education. Contains information of today's top jazz artists, reviews, transcriptions, industry news, and articles on improvisation, teaching techniques, history, performance, composition, arranging and music business. *$23.95*
100 pages Founded: 1968
Circulation: 10,000
Printed in on glossy stock

17575 Journal of American Organbuilding
American Institute of Organ Builders
PO Box 130982
Houston, TX 77219
713-529-2212
FAX: 713-529-2212
editor@pipeorgan.org
www.pipeorgan.org
Jeffrey L Weiler, Editor
Features technical articles, product and book reviews, and a forum for the exchange of building and service information and techniqes. Subscriptions are provided free to AIO members, and are available to non-members for $24.00 per year. *$24.00*
Quarterly Founded: 1974
Mailing list available for rent 350 names $250 per M.
Printed in on glossy stock

17576 Journal of Music Theory
Yale University
Department of Music
PO Box 208310
New Haven, CT 06520-8310
203-432-2985
FAX: 203-432-2983
jmt.editor@yale.edu
www.yale.edu/jmt/
Ian Quinn, Editor
David Clampitt, Associate Editor
Richard Cohn, Associate Editor
Daniel Harrison, Associate Editor
Patrick McCreless, Associate Editor
Publishes peer-reviewed reseach in Music Theory. *$30.00*
Annual Founded: 1957

17577 Journal of Music Therapy
American Music Therapy Association
8455 Colesville Road
Suite 1000
Silver Spring, MD 20910
301-589-3300
FAX: 301-589-5175
info@musictherapy.org
www.musictherapy.org
Jayne Standley, Editor
Research in the area of music therapy and rehabilitation, a forum for authoratative articles of current music therapy research and theory, use of music in the behavioral sciences, book reviews, and guest editorials. *$120.00*
Quarterly Founded: 1998
Circulation: 6000 6 M names

17578 Journal of Research in Music Education
MENC Subscription Office
PO Box 1584
Birmingham, AL 35201

800-633-4931
menc@ebsco.com www.menc.org
Keeps members informed of the latest music education research. Offers a collection of reports that includes thorough analyses of theories and projects by respected music researchers. Issued four times yearly.
Quarterly Founded: 1907 3,000 names
Printed in on matte stock

17579 Journal of Singing
National Association of Teachers of Singing
9957 Moorings Drive
Suite 401
Jacksonville, FL 32257
904-992-9101
FAX: 904-262-2587 888-262-2065
info@nats.org www.nats.org
Richard Dale Sjoerdsma, PhD, Editor
Joan Adams, Advertising Manager
Provides current information regarding the teaching of singing as well as results of recent research in the field. The Journal serves as a historical record and a venue for teachers of singing and other scholars to share the resilts of their work in areas such as history, diction, voice science, medicine, and voice pedagogy. *$45.00*
5x times/year

17580 Journal of the American Musicological Soci ety
University of California Press, Journals Division
2000 Center Street Way
Suite 203
Berkeley, CA 94704-1223
510-643-7154
FAX: 510-642-9917
journals@ucpress.edu
www.ucpressjournals.com
Bruce Alan Brown, Editor
Louise Goldberg, Assistant Editor
Julie Cumming, Book Review Editor
The JAMS publishes scholarship from all fields of musical inquiry: from historical musicology, critical theory, music analysis, iconography and organology, to performance practice, aesthetics and hermeneutics, ethnomusicology, gender and sexuality, popular music and cultural studies. Each issue includes articles, book reviews, and communications. *$42.00*
Tri-Annual Founded: 1893
Circulation: 5000

17581 Jukebox Collector Magazine
2545 SE 60th Court
Pleasant Hill, IA 50327-5099
515-265-8324
FAX: 515-265-1980
JukeboxCollector@att.net
www.jukeboxmagazine.com
Rick Botts, Editor
Focuses on collectors of jukeboxes from the 40's, 50's, and 60's. There are approximately 150 jukeboxes for sale each month, along with show events information. Accepts advertising. *$33.00*
36 pages Monthly Founded: 1977
Circulation: 1800

17582 Live Sound International
169 Beulah Street
San Francisco, CA 94117
415-387-4009
FAX: 415-752-8144
amclean@livesoundint.com
www.livesoundint.com
Mark Herman, Publisher
Jeff MacKay, Editor
Mitch Gallagher, Associate Editor
Sara Elliott, Advertising
The editorial focus is performance audio and event sound. Contains audio production techniques, new products, equipment applications and associated commercial concerns. *$60.00*
Monthly
Circulation: 20,000
Printed in on glossy stock

17583 Mix
Prism Business Media
6400 Hollis Street
Suite 12
Emeryville, CA 94608-1086
510-653-3307
FAX: 510-653-5142 866-860-7087
mixeditorial@prismb2b.com
www.mixonline.com
George Petersen, Editorial Director
Erika Lopez, Associate Publisher
Tom Kenny, Editor
Dave Reik, Publisher
Christen Pocock, Marketing Director
Mix covers a wide range of topics including: recording, live sound and production, broadcast production, audio for film and video, and music technology. In addition, Mix includes coverage of facility design and construction, location recording, tape/disc manufacturing, education, and other topics of importanct to audio professionals. Distributed in 94 countries. *$35.97*

Monthly Founded: 1977
Circulation: 45244

17584 Modern Drummer
Modern Drummer Publications
12 Old Bridge Road
Cedar Grove, NJ 07009-1288
973-239-4140
FAX: 973-239-7139
mdinfo@moderndrummer.com
www.moderndrummer.com
Isabel Spagnardi, CFO
Tracy A Kearns, Associate Publisher

Bill Miller, Editor-in-Chief
Rick Van Horn, Senior Editor
Adam Budofsky, Managing Editor

Every issue of Modern Drummer includes interviews with the world's leading drummers, a full roster of columns on all facets of drumming, complete drum charts, solos and patterns performed by your favorite players, insightful reviews on the hottest new geat, the best in CDs, books, and DVDs for drummers, and giveaways worth thousands of dollars. *$29.97*

Monthly Founded: 1993
Circulation: 6000
Printed in 4 colors on glossy stock

17585 Music
102 N Haven Road
PO Box 906
Elmhurst, IL 60126-2932
630-941-2030
FAX: 630-941-3210
subscriptions@musicincmag.com
www.musicincmag.com

Zach Phillip, Editor
Kevin Maher, CEO
John Cahill, Eastern Advertising
Tom Burns, Western Advertising
Chris Maher, Classified Ads

Offered free to those involved in music products retailing. Delivers news you can use for the musical products industry. Geared toward store owners and managers in musical product retail and repair shops in the United States and Canada.

11 Per Year Founded: 1934
Circulation: 8,949

17586 Music & Sound Retailer
Testa Communications
25 Willowdale Avenue
Port Washington, NY 11050
516-767-2500
FAX: 516-767-9335 800-937-7678
testa@testa.com www.testa.com

Brian Berk, Editor

News magazine serving owners, managers and sales personnel in retail musical-instument and sound-product dealershops. The magazine's emphasis is on full-line and combo dealerships offering guitars, drums, electronic keyboards and digital pianos, recording and sound-reinforcement products, lighting, DJ equipment, software, print and accessories. Recurring features include 'MI Spy,' 'Top Ten,' 'Veddatorial,' 'Selling Points,' and editor's letter *$18.00*

Monthly Founded: 1985
Circulation: 11000

17587 Music Row
1231 17th Avenue S
PO Box 158542
Nashville, TN 37215-8542
615-321-3617
FAX: 615-329-0852
sales@musicrow.com
www.musicrow.com

David M Ross, CEO/President

Written for people who work in the music business. Contents include record reviews, current news items, timely interviews or discovering hot talent first. Music Row subscriptions include six print issues per year, daily Afternoon News updates via e-mail and @Musicrow reports every Tuesday, Thursday and Friday via e-mail. *$159.00*

Six Per Year Founded: 1981
Circulation: 14000
Printed in 4 colors on glossy stock

17588 Music Trades Magazine
Music Trades
80 W Street
Englewood, NJ 07631
201-871-1965
FAX: 201-871-0455 800-423-6530
music@musictrades.com
www.musictrades.com

Paul A Majeski, Publisher
Brian T Majeski, President/Editor
Richard T Watson, Managing Editor
Juanita Hampton, Circulation Manager

A blend of industry news, hard sales and marketing data, trend analysis and management tips in every issue. Target audience is retailers, distributors, and manufacturers of musical instruments, professional audio equipment and related products, worldwide. *$16.00*

Monthly Founded: 1890
Circulation: 7500

17589 Music and Sound Journal
912 Carlton Road
Tarpon Spring, FL 34689
727-938-0571

sound@masj.com www.masj.com

Don Kulak, Founder/Owner

Brings readers the future of sound today, with new music, experimental sound, cutting edge audio and acoustics and alternative media. MSJ is written for people who are discriminating about music, audio, and sound - people who want to improve their sonic environments on all levels, without having to study pages of data - people who want to more fully understand the profound impact sound has on every aspect of their daily lives.

Founded: 1988

17590 Musical Merchandise Review
21 Highland Circle
Suite One
Needham, MA 02494
781-453-9310
FAX: 781-453-9389 800-964-5150
mprescott@symphonypublishing.com
www.mmrmagazine.com

Lee Zapis, President
Sidney L Davis, Group Publisher
Richard E Kessel, Publisher/Advertising Sales
Maureen Johan, Classified Sales

Serves retailers of musical instruments, accessories, and related services as well as wholesalers, importers/exporters and manufacturers of related products. Its purpose is to communicate facts and ideas that will benefit musical merchandisers and their daily business operations as well as help them enhance their growth. Its editorial approach includes features on industry trends and innovations, new product promotion, in-store display techniques, financing, planning and dealer surveys. *$32.00*

Monthly Founded: 1879 $100 per M.
Printed in 4 colors

17591 New on the Charts
Music Business Reference
70 Laurel Place
New Rochelle, NY 10801-7105
914-632-3349
FAX: 914-633-7690
lenny@notc.com www.notc.com

Leonard Kalikow, Publisher/Editor

Circulation limited to professionals only, provides major signings, contracts and directories. *$365.00*

Monthly Founded: 1976
Circulation: 5,000

17592 Opera America Newsline
Opera America
330 7th Ave
16th Floor
New York, NY 10001-5248
212-796-8620
FAX: 212-796-8631
frontdesk@operaamerica.org
www.operaamerica.org

Provides company news from around the world, articles on issues affecting the field, professional opportunities, and updates on OPERA America programs and activities. Complimentary subscription with all membership levels, excluding stand-alone professional subscriptions.

10X Per Year Founded: 1970 : html

17593 Opera News
Metropolitan Opera Guild
70 Lincoln Center Plaza
New York, NY 10023
212-769-7000
FAX: 212-870-7695
info@metguild.org
www.metoperafamily.org

William C Morris, CEO/President

Monthly magazine that reports on opera around the world. Issues include reviews of commercial recordings and live performances, profiles of artists and articles by eminent writers on the music scene. *$29.95*

Monthly Founded: 1883
Circulation: 60000

17594 Percussive Notes
Percussive Arts Society
701 NW Ferris Avenue
Lawton, OK 73507-5442
580-353-1455
FAX: 580-353-1456
percarts@pas.org www.pas.org

Rick Mattingly, Editor
Hillary Henry, Managing Editor

The official journal of the Percussive Arts Society. Published in February, April, June, August, October and December, this magazine features a variety of articles and advertising aimed at professional and student percussionists. Regular sections are devoted to drumset, marching percussion, world percussion, symphonic percussion, technology, keyboard, health and wellness, research and reviews. *$85.00*

6 Times Per Year Founded: 1961
Circulation: 8000
Mailing list available for rent

17595 Piano Guild Notes
Piano Guild Publications
PO Box 1807
Austin, TX 78767-1807
512-478-5775
FAX: 512-478-5843
ngpt@pianoguild.com
www.pianoguild.com

Richard Allison, President

Music industry publication focusing on Piano Guild members and activities. *$16.00*

Quarterly Founded: 1929
Circulation: 11000
Printed in 2 colors

17596 Piano Technicians Journal
Piano Technicians Guild
4444 Forest Avenue
Kansas City, MO 66106
913-432-9975
FAX: 913-432-9986
ptg@ptg.org www.ptg.org
Monthly technical magazine covering all phases of working on pianos. Articles explore new tools, industry news and organizational issues. Feature articles range from setting up a repair shop to rebuilding techniques. *$104.50*
Monthly Founded: 1960 4,000 names
Printed in 4 colors on glossy stock

17597 Pitch Pipe
Sweet Adelines International
9110 S Toledo
PO Box 470168
Tulsa, OK 74137-0168
918-622-1444
FAX: 918-665-0894 800-992-7464
Joey@sweetadelineintl.org
www.sweetadelineintl.org
Pat LeVezu, President
Joey Mechell Stenner, Editor
Kelly Kirchhoff, Director Communications
Official publication of Sweet Adelines International, the world's largest singing performance and music education organization for women. The Pitch Pipe informs, educates and recognizes the members who have made the organization a success. The subscription price for members is included in the annual per capita fee. *$12.00*
Quarterly Founded: 1947
Circulation: 30,000
Mailing list available for rent 30M names
Printed in 4 colors on glossy stock

17598 Playback
American Society of Composers, Authors & Publisher
One Lincoln Plaza
New York, NY 10023
212-621-6000
FAX: 212-362-7328 800-952-7227
Playback@ascap.com www.ascap.com
Marilyn Bergman, President
Phil Crossland, Executive Editor
Jin Moon, Deputy Editor
Mike Barsky, Advertising
David Pollard, Design
The Society's magazine is loaded with full-color photos, features the latest news on ASCAP events, new member listings, legislative updates, feature articles on members, distribution info, upcoming workshops and showcases and much more. *$12.00*
Annual
Circulation: 100,000

17599 Pro Audio Review
IMAS Publishing
5827 Columbia Pike
Third Floor
Falls Church, VA 22041
703-998-7600
FAX: 703-998-2966
letters@proaudioreview.com
www.proaudioreview.com
John Gatski, Publisher/Executive Editor
Brett Moss, Managing Editor
Claudia Van Veen, Advertising
Reviews of the latest new equipment written by audio professionals in the field, from bench tests checking the specs, to new product announcements. *$24.95*
Monthly Founded: 1995
Circulation: 26000 30,000 names $145 per M.
Printed in 4 colors on glossy stock

17600 Pro Sound News
United Business Media
460 Park Avenue South
9th Floor
New York, NY 10016
212-378-0400
FAX: 212-378-2160
circulation@cmp.com
www.prosoundnews.com
Frank Wells, Senior Editor
Fred Goodman, Managing Editor
Margaret Sekelsky, Publisher
Tara Preston, Associate Publisher
Karen Godgart, Advertising Director
Provides timely and accurate news, industy analysis, features and technology updates to the expanded professional audio community. *$30.00*
Monthly
Circulation: 250003
Printed in 4 colors

17601 Replay Magazine
Replay Publishing
18757 Burbank Boulevard, #105
PO Box 7004
Tarzana, CA 91357-7004
818-776-2880
FAX: 818-776-2888
editor@replaymag.com
www.replaymag.com
Ed Adlum, Publisher
Monthly trade journal for the coin-operated amusement route, arcade, FEC and LBE owner. Its news and features are directed primarily at the American market, reporting developments of interest to manufacturers, distributors and operators of games and jukeboxes at locations ranging from single sites to family entertainment centers. *$65.00*
Monthly Founded: 1975
Circulation: 4000

17602 Rolling Stone Magazine
1290 Avenue of the Americas
New York, NY 10104-0298
212-484-1616

Covers pop culture, politics etc in a massive amount of music articles, interviews, news, reviews, photos, and sound clips.

17603 Sheet Music Magazine
PO Box 58629
Boulder, CO 80323
914-244-8500
FAX: 914-244-8560 800-759-3036
Ed Shanaphy, Publisher
Features actual reproduction of popular songs, both words and music, articles on various aspects of musical performance and interest for many types of musicians, and self improvement features for keyboard and fretter instrument players. A single year's subscription brings you at least 66 great songs best-loved standards and today's most lyrical hits. *$22.97*
Bi-Monthly
Circulation: 50,000

17604 Society News
Contemporary Record Society
724 Winchester Road
Broomall, PA 19008
610-544-5920
FAX: 915-808-4232
crsnews@verizon.net
http://mysite.verizon.net/vzeeewvp/contemporaryrecordsociety/id3.
Jack M Shusterman, Advertising
Offers opportunities to CRS consitituents, progress notes on its associates, various awards and performance possibilities. The Society News offers feature articles of renowned composers/performers and reviews of music, recordings and music books.
Founded: 1983
Mailing list available for rent $50 per M.

17605 Southwestern Musician
Texas Music Educators Association
7900 Centre Park
PO Box 140465
Austin, TX 78714-0465
512-452-0710
FAX: 512-451-9213 888-318-8632
rfloyd@tmea.org www.tmea.org
Robert Floyd, Executive Director
Karen Kneten, Communications Manager
Tesa Harding, Advertising/Exhibit Manager
Laura Kocian, Financial Manager
Maura Langan, Membership Assistant
The official magazine of the TMEA. Publsihed monthly August through May. Included with membership. A President's newsletter is published each June when necessary to provide an update on TMEA activities. The purposed of this publication is to serve the music educators of Texas as a means of communication or professional philosophy and action and to promote the field of music education within the state.
Founded: 1938
Circulation: 14000
Mailing list available for rent 10,000 names
Printed in 4 colors on glossy stock

17606 Symphony Magazine
American Symphony Orchestra League
33 W 60th Street
5th Floor
New York, NY 10023-7905
212-262-4051
FAX: 212-262-5198
editor@symphony.org
www.symphony.org
Rebecca Winzenried, Editor-in-Chief
Stephen Alter, Advertising Manager
Michael Rush, Production Manager
Bimonthly magazine of the American Symphony Orchestra League. Discusses issues critical to the orchestra community and communicates the value and importance of orchestras and the music they perform. Publishes articles on compelling issues and trends relevant to the entire orchestra field. Its readers include professional staff, musicians, and board members in the orchestra industry and related fields; orchestra patrons and volunteers; and music critics and arts and media professionals. *$22.00*
Bi-Monthly Founded: 1942
Circulation: 18000
Printed in 4 colors

17607 Symposium
312 E Pine Street
Missoula, MT 59802
406-721-9616
FAX: 406-721-9419 800-729-0235
cms@music.org www.music.org

Robby D Gunstream, Executive Director
Mary C Anno-Murk, Communications
Peter Park, Professional Activities
Julie L Johnson, Data Resources
Tod Trimble, Professional Development

Serves as a vehicle for the dissemination of information and ideas on music in higher education. The content of the publication highlights concerns of general interest and reflects the work of the Society in the areas of music represented on its Board of Directors.

One Per Year Founded: 1968
Circulation: 8000 38000 names $115 per M.
Printed in 1 color on matte stock

17608 Vibe

vbecustserv@cdsfulfillment.com
www.vibe.com

Mimi Valdez, Editor-In-Chief

Covers the trends, the events, and culture of the urban scene. Film, fashion and art to politics and music-pop, jazz, R&B, dance, hip hop, rap, house and more. *$11.95*
Monthly

Trade Shows

17609 American Choral Directors Association National Convention
American Choral Directors Association
545 Couch Drive
PO Box 2720
Oklahoma City, OK 73101-2720
405-232-8161
FAX: 405-232-8162
acda@acdaonline.org
www.acdaonline.org

Gene Brooks, Executive Director
Hilary Apfelstadt, Planning Committee
Galen Darrough, Planning Committee
Rebecca Reames, Planning Committee
Leane Defrancis, Membership

Features distinguished auditioned choirs and experienced clinicians, three tracks for the attendess, an exhibit hall, the ACDA Wall of Honor, and concessions which will be open in the exhibit hall throughout the convention.

20000 Attendees Biennial Founded: 1959

17610 American Guild of Organists, National Conference
475 Riverside Drive
Suite 1260
New York, NY 10115
212-870-2310
FAX: 212-870-2163
info@agohq.org www.agohq.org

James Thomashower, Executive Director
Jennifer Madden, Manager Membership
Harold Calhoun, Mgr Competitions

Over 20 exhibits and a workshop for professional, amatuer and student organists.
Biennial

17611 American Harp Society National Conference
PO Box 38334
Los Angeles, CA 90038-0334
323-469-3050
FAX: 323-469-3050
kmoon@uclalumni.net
www.harpsociety.org

Christa Grix, National Conference Chair
Lynne Aspnes, Conference Program Advisory Chair

Conference will explore the mind-body-music connection, the creative process, and the connection between creativity and learning. The conference will include multiple disciplines including educators, composers, performers, therapists and practioners.

300 Attendees Annual Founded: 1962

17612 American Institute of Organbuilders Annual Convention
American Institute of Organ Builders
PO Box 130982
Houston, TX 77219
713-529-2212
FAX: 713-529-2212
pipes@pipeorgan.org
http://convention.pipeorgan.org

Rene Marceau, Convention Committee Chairman

Annual convention includes supplier exhibits, technical lectures, sight-seeing tours, professional examinations, lectures and organ demonstrations.

October Founded: 1974
Mailing list available for rent 350 names $250 per M.

17613 American Music Therapy Conference
National Music Therapy Association
8445 Colesville Road
Suite 1000
Silver Spring, MD 20910
301-589-3300
FAX: 301-589-5175
www.musictherapy.org
Seminar and exhibits of publications, musical instruments, books, learning aids and recordings.
November

17614 American Musical Instrument Society
Guild Associates
389 Main Street
Suite 202
Malden, MA 02148
781-397-8870
FAX: 781-397-8887
amis@guildassoc.com www.amis.org

Susan Thompson, Program Co-Chair
Kathryn Libin, Program Co-Chair

A broad range of topics include the history, design, use, care and acoustics of musical instruments in all cultures and from all periods.
Annual

17615 American Musicological Society Annual Meeting
American Musicological Society
Bowdoin College
6010 College station
Brunswick, ME 04011-8451
207-798-4243
FAX: 877-679-7648 877-679-7648
ams@ams-net.org www.ams-net.org

Robert Judd, Executive Director

A society of professional musicologists and university educators. The annual meetings are held in the fall each year; 2007-Quebec; 2008- Nashville; 2009- Philadelphia. *$45.00*

2000 Attendees Annual Founded: 1948
Mailing list available for rent 3515 names $100 per M.

17616 American Orff-Schulwerk Association National Conference
American Orff-Schulwerk Association
PO Box 391089
Cleveland, OH 44139-8089
440-543-5366
FAX: 440-543-2687
info@aosa.org www.aosa2.org

Karen Medley, Conference Chair

One hundred exhibits of music, music books, software, insturments, and gifts in addition to National Conference of 2000+ music educators.

2400 Attendees November Founded: 1969

17617 American String Teachers Association National Convention
American String Teachers Association
4153 Chain Bridge Road
Fairfax, VA 22030
703-279-2113
FAX: 703-279-2114 www.astaweb.com

Beth Danner-Knight, Conference Services Deputy Director
Deanna Tompkins, Meetings & Events Manager

Recognizing the wealth of our rich traditions as well as offer members new horizons in teaching and performing strings.

2200 Attendees Annual/March $180 per M.

17618 American Symphony Orchestra League Nationa l Conference
33 W 60th Street
5th Floor
New York, NY 10023
212-262-5161
FAX: 212-262-5198
league@symphony.org
www.symphony.org

Stephen Alter, Advertising and Meetings Manager
Meghan Whitbeck, Advertising/Meetings Coordinator
Henry Fogel, President/CEO

Ninety booths incorporating all facets of classical music industries including industry suppliers, music publishers and computer technology.

1200 Attendees June

17619 Chorus America Annual Conference
910 17th Street NW
Washington, DC 20006
202-776-0215
FAX: 202-776-0224
service@chorusamerica.org
www.chorusamerica.org

Ann Meier Baker, President/CEO
Melanie Garrett, Membership Services Manager

This four day conference offers seminars, workshops, concerts, expert consultations and peer-group meetings in a friendly, dynamic environment.

500 Attendees June
Printed in 2 colors on matte stock

17620 College Music Society/Association for Tech nology in Music
College Music Society
312 E Pine Street
Missoula, MT 59802
406-721-9616
FAX: 406-721-9419
cms@music.org www.music.org

Robby D Gunstream, Executive Director
Peter Park, Professional Activities
Tod Trimble, Professional Development

Covers a broad array of topics such as advocacy, composition, cultural diversity, ethnomusicology, gender issues, music education, musicology, pedagogy, performance, music theory, teacher training, the latest technologies, and world music. Attendees includes adminstrators, publishers and music business personnel.
350 Attendees Annual Founded: 1958

17621 Country Radio Seminar
Country Radio Broadcasters
819 18th Avenue S
Nashville, TN 37203
615-327-4487
FAX: 615-329-4492
info@crb.org www.crb.org
Ed Salamon, Executive Director
Conference attendess include major radio groups and record labels as well as independents, Features include exhibits, seminars and shows.
2300 Attendees Annual Founded: 1969

17622 Folk Alliance Annual Meeting
Folk Alliance
510 South Main
1st Floor
Memphis, TN 38103
901-522-1170
FAX: 901-522-1172
fa@folk.org www.folkalliance.org
200+ artists, 4 nights of show cases, four days of feature concerts, exhibit hall parties, panels, workshops, clinics and much more all under one roof. *$650.00*
3000 Attendees

17623 Gospel Music Week
Gospel Music Association
1205 Division Street
Nashville, TN 37203-4011
615-242-0303
FAX: 615-242-9374
www.gospelmusic.org
Listen to new music as you experience over 100 eclectic performances throughout the week from today's top artists and tomorrow's hit-makers, invent new waysof enhancing your ministry through educational opportunities found in over 100 seminars and panels and through the sharing of your ideas with colleagues. Connect with your industry peers and friends at various networking opportunities including receptions, roundtables and more.
3,000 Attendees April Founded: 1964

17624 Gospel Music Workshop America
PO Box 34635
Detroit, MI 48208
313-898-6900
FAX: 313-898-4520
manager@gmwnational.org
www.gmwanational.org
Rev Albert L Jamison, Sr, Chair, Board of Directors
Sheila Smith, Director Operations
Mark Smith, Convention Manager
Conferences open with a highly spirited service including Sacraments, music from choirs within the GMWA, Psalmists and the preachedr 'Word." This is followed by lectures, speakers, preachers and over 100 courses offered during the week. Nightly musicals include chapter choirs and national recording artists. Midnight services are held which include music, preaching and various recordings by the Women's Division, Men's Division, Youth/Young Adult division and a service by Bishop Richard White.
16M Attendees August Founded: 1967

17625 Horns Over the Sea
Central Washington University Music Department
400 E University Way
Ellensburg, WA 98926-7458
509-963-1226
FAX: 509-963-1239
gross@music.ucsb.edu
www.hornsociety.org
Jeffrey Snedeker, President
Steven Gross, Conference Coordinator
Heidi Vogel, Membership Coordinator
Features renowned hornists, guest ensembles, recitals and master classes
450 Attendees August 3600 names $70 per M.

17626 International Association of Jazz Educators Conference
International Association of Jazz Education
PO Box 724
Manhattan, KS 66505
785-776-8744
FAX: 785-776-6190
info@iage.org www.iaje.org
Bill McFarlin, Executive Director
This four-day conference fatures a 75,000 square-food music industry exposition, commission premieres, technology presentations, research papers, award ceremonies, and performances by over 500 of the world's most respected professional jazz groups and musicians. *$375.00*
8000 Attendees Annual

17627 International Horn Competition of America
BGSU Continuing and Extended Education
14 College Park
Bowling Green, OH 43403-0200
509-963-1226
FAX: 509-963-1239
www.ihcamerica.org
Jeffrey Snedeker, President
Andrew Pelletier, Host
International competition specifically for the horn as a solo instrument.
450 Attendees July 3600 names $70 per M.

17628 International Steel Guitar Convention
College Music Society
9535 Midland Boulevard
Saint Louis, MO 63114-3314
314-427-7794
FAX: 314-427-0516
scotty@scottymusic.com
www.music.org
Dewitt Scott Sr, President
Mary Scott, Secretary
Sixty-five booths that provide entertainment from steel guitarists and various instruments including the bass guitar.
3M Attendees August

17629 Mid-South Horn Conference
Central Washington University Music Department
400 E University Way
Ellensburg, WA 98926-7458
509-963-1226
FAX: 509-963-1239
campbellel@umkc.edu
www.hornsociety.org
Jeffrey Snedeker, President
Ellen Campbell, Event Host
Heidi Vogel, Membership Coordinator
Features renowned hornists, guest ensembles, recitals and master classes
450 Attendees March 3600 names $70 per M.

17630 Midwest International Band & Orchestra Clinic
Midwest International Band & Orchestra Clinic
828 Davis Street
Suite 100
Evanston, IL 60201
847-424-4163
FAX: 847-424-5185
info@midwestclinic.org
www.midwestclinic.org
The purpose to the clinic is to raise the standards of music education, to develop new teaching techniqes, to examine, analyze, analyze and appraise literature dealing with music, demonstrations for the betterment of music education. 350 exhibitors, 565 booths, 30 concerts, and 50 instructional clinics. *$90.00*
12000 Attendees December

17631 Music Teachers National Association Convention
The Carew Tower
441 Vine Street
Suite 505
Cincinnati, OH 45202-2811
513-421-1420
FAX: 513-421-2503 888-512-5278
mtnanet@mtna.org www.mtna.org
Gary L Ingle, Executive Director
Atendees include independent music teachers, college faculty, students and parents from all over North America.
2500 Attendees Annual Founded: 1876
Mailing list available for rent 23000 names $85 per M.

17632 NAMM: International Music Products Association
5790 Armada Drive
Carlsbad, CA 92008-4608
760-438-8001
FAX: 760-438-7327 800-767-6266
tradeshow@namm.com
www.thenammshow.com
Joe Lamond, President
NAMM's trade shows are all about the experience. The experience of checking out the latest gear, of networking with other music product professionals, of attending free business-boosting classes. From the cook exhibits to the sizzling hot nightlife, music and music making always take center stage.
80000 Attendees January

17633 National Association for Music Education Conference
1806 Robert Fulton Drive
Reston, VA 20191-4348
703-860-4000
FAX: 703-860-1531 800-336-3768
John J Mahlmann, Executive Director
Margaret Jamborsky, Director Meetings/Conventions
Elizabeth Lasko, Director Public Relations/Marketing
Amanda Kidwell, Membership Director
To advance music education by encouraging the study and making of music by all.
5M Attendees April

17634 National Association of Pastoral Musicians Convention
National Association of Pastoral Musicians
962 Wayne Avenue
Suite 210
Silver Spring, MD 20910-4461
240-247-3000
FAX: 240-247-3001 www.npm.org
J Michael McMahon, President
Kathleen Haley, Membership Services Director
Paul H Colloton, Continuing Education Director
Lowell Hickman, Executive Assistant/Office Manager
200 workshop sessions, 5 major addresses, music education classes, clinics, new music showcases and exhibits, musical performances, prayer and songs, adult and children's choirs, handbells, youth gatherings, Liturgical Space Tour.
4000 Attendees July

17635 National Association of Recording Merchandising Trade Show
9 Eves Drive
Suite 120
Marlton, NJ 08053-3130
856-596-2221
FAX: 859-596-3268
still@narm.com www.narm.com
Jim Donio, President
Pat Daly, Meeting Planner
Evelyn Dichter, Membership Coordinatorsusan, VP Communications/Marketing
One-on-One meeting opportunities, welcome reception, keynote speakers, marketplace exhibits, live performances, forums, receptions and awards dinner
3M Attendees April/May

17636 National Opera Association Conference
National Opera Association
PO Box 60869
Canyon, TX 79016
806-651-2857
FAX: 806-651-2958
rhansen@mail.wtamu.edu
www.noa.org
Robert Hansen, Executive Director
Robert Thieme, Editor
Annual conference and exhibits of opera related equipment, supplies and services.
775 Attendees Annual Founded: 1954 1M names $75 per M.

17637 Northeast Horn Workshop
Central Washington University Music Department
400 E University Way
Ellensburg, WA 98926-7458
509-963-1226
FAX: 509-963-1239
rdodsonw@mansfield.edu
www.hornsociety.org
Jeffrey Snedeker, President
Rebecca Dodson, Workshop Host
Heidi Vogel, Membership Coordinator
Features renowned hornists, guest ensembles, recitals and master classes
450 Attendees February 3600 names $70 per M.

17638 Opera America Conference
Opera America
330 7th Ave
16th Floor
New York, NY 10001-5248
212-796-8620
FAX: 212-796-8631
www.operaamerica.org
Session topics include identifying ways to harness the power of the best new technologies, how to reach current and prospective audiences, how to gain support from donors, and how to enrich the lives of children and adults who are now downloading podcasts, reading blogs, and designing their own multimedia communications.
275 Attendees April

17639 Piano Technicians Guild Annual Convention
Piano Technicians Guild
4444 Forest Avenue
Kansas City, KS 66106
913-432-9975

ptg@ptg.org www.ptg.org
Come for the learning: find a hands-on class for your skill level; pick from sessions covering every type of piano service; squeeze in a mini-tech; prepare for the RPT exams; see the latest and greatest piano products.
1,000 Attendees June

17640 Sweet Adelines International Convention
Sweet Adelines International
PO Box 470168
Tulsa, OK 74147-0168
918-622-1444
FAX: 918-665-0894 800-992-7464
Kathy Hayes, Director Meetings/Corporate Service
Ruth Cameron, Meetings/Exhibits Coordinator
Jane Hanson, Marketing Coordinator
Connie Heyer, Membership Registrar
Kellye Kirchhoff, Director Communications
Heart-pounding chorus competitions, the rush and excitement of the quartet competition, education classes, shopping in the Harmony Bazaars and good times with old friends and new are all included in the International Convention.
8M Attendees October

17641 Winter Music Conference
3450 NE
12th Terrace
Fort Lauderdale, FL 33334
954-563-4444
FAX: 954-563-1599
info@wintermusicconference.com
www.wintermusicconference.com
Regarded as the singular networking event in the dance music industry, attracting professionals from over 60 different countries.

17642 World of Bluegrass
International Bluegrass Music Association

2 Music Circle South
Suite 100
Nashville, TN 37203
615-256-3222
FAX: 615-256-0450 888-438-4262
info@ibma.org www.ibma.org
Dan Hays, Executive Director
Nancy Cardwell, Special Projects Coordinator
Jill Snider, Member/Convention Services
Build relationships with event producers, record label reps, agents and managers, broadcasters, association leaders, educators, the media, instrument builders, artists and composers. Educational and networking events like seminars, facilitated discussions and workshops are the primary focus of the conference. Browse through 100+ booths in the Exhibit Hall. You will hear bluegrass music around the clock for seven days. The Highpoint of the Conference is the International Bluegrass Music Awards.
1,800 Attendees October

Directories & Databases

17643 American Music Center Directory
American Music Center
30 W 26th Street
Suite 1001
New York, NY 10010-2011
212-366-5260
FAX: 212-366-5265
center@amc.net www.amc.net
Joanne Cossa, CEO
Lyn Liston, Director New Music Information Svce
Peter Shavitz, Director Development
Lisa Taliano, Director Information Technology
Carlos Camposeco, Director Finance and Administration
Mailing lists include all United States members; all International and United States members; Composer Members in the United States; Members in the New York City Metropolitan area; and Members in the United States and Canada.

17644 American Society of Composers, Authors and Publishers
American Soc. of Composers, Authors & Publishers
1 Lincoln Plaza
New York, NY 10023-7129
212-621-6000
FAX: 212-724-9064
ACE@ascap.com www.ascap.com
Marilyn Bergman, President
Johnny Mandel, Writer Vice Chairman
Jay Morgenstern, Publisher Vice Chairman
Arnold Broido, Treasurer
Kathy Spanberger, Secretary
ASCAP created the dial-up ACE system as a useful tool for music professionals. An enhanced World Wide Web version of this database is now available. The database contains information on all compositions in the ASCAP repertory which have appeared in any of ASCAP's domestic surveys, including foreign compositions licensed by the ASCAP in the United States.
Annual Founded: 1993

17645 AudArena International Guide
Billboard Directories
PO Box 15158
North Hollywood, CA 91615
818-487-4582
800-562-2706
info@billboard.com
www.billboard.com/directories
Arkady Fridman, Inside Sales Manager

Complete data on over 4,400 venues worldwide, including Amphitheaters, Arenas, Stadiums, Sports Facilities, Concert Halls and New Constructions. Also includes complete listings of companies offering services to the touring industry in the Facilty Buyer's Guide. The guide features contact names, phone and fax numbers, e-mail and web site addresses, market population, facility capacities and staging configurations, and rental fees and ticketing rights. *$99.00*
325 pages Annual

17646 Billboard Subscriber File
Edith Roman Associates
One Blue Hill Plaza, 16th Floor
PO Box 1556
Pearl River, NY 10965-8556
845-620-9000
FAX: 845-620-9035 800-223-2194
john.logiudice@edithroman.com
www.edithroman.com

John LoGiudice, Postal List Info Contact
Wayne Nagrowski, E-Mail List Info Contact

Directory listees include booking agencies and agents, clubs, music publishers, promoters, radio stations, record labels, sound and lighting services, retailers, video, venues, wholesalers, equipment and manufacturing and general services.
Annual 80000 names $95 per M.

17647 Bluegrass Resource Directory
International Bluegrass Music Association
2 Music Circle South
Suite 100
Nashville, TN 37203
615-256-3222
FAX: 615-256-0450 888-438-4262
info@ibma.org www.ibma.org

Greg Cahikk, Chairman/President
Dan Hays, Executive Director
Nancy Cardwell, Special Projects Director
Jill Crabtree, Member Services
Tina Potter, Marketing/Public Relations Director

Member Directory can only be accessed by IBMA members. *$25.00*
88 pages Annual

17648 Gospel Music Industry Directory
Gospel Music Association
1205 Division Street
Nashville, TN 37203-4011
615-242-0303
FAX: 615-254-9755
GMAToday@aol.com
www.gospelmusic.org
Formerly called the Networking Guide, the GMA Music Industry Directory is a comprehensive listing of Christian and Gospel music artists, managers, booking agents, record companies, publishing companies and more. Active GMA Professional members get a copy of the directory free. Associate and Student GMA members can purchase one for a discounted rate.

17649 Grey House Performing Arts Directory
Grey House Publishing
185 Millerton Road
PO Box 860
Millerton, NY 12546
518-890-0526
FAX: 518-789-0545 800-562-2139
books@greyhouse.com
www.greyhouse.com

Leslie Mackenzie, Publisher
Richard Gottlieb, Editor

The most comprehensive resource covering the Performing Arts. This directory provides current information on over 9,000 Dance Companies, Instrumental Music Programs, Opera Companies, Choral Groups, Theater Companies, Performing Arts Series and Performing Arts Facilities. *$185.00*
1500 pages Annual ISBN 1-592370-23-3

17650 International Buyers Guide
Billboard Directories
PO Box 15158
North Hollywood, CA 91615
818-487-4582
800-562-2706
info@billboard.com
www.billboard.com/directories

Arkady Fridman, Inside Sales Manager

A must-have resource for doing business in the music industry, covers every aspect of the recording business worldwide. The latest edition includes contact information on: record labels, video and digital music companies, distributors and importers/exporters; music publishers and rights organizations - blank media manufacturers, pressing plants and services; manufacturers of jewel boxes and other packaging and equipment services; and suppliers of store fixtures, security and accessories. *$179.00*
340 pages Annual

17651 International Talent and Touring Guide
Billboard Directories
PO Box 15158
North Hollywood, CA 91615
818-487-4582
800-562-2706
info@billboard.com
www.billboard.com/directories

Arkady Fridman, Inside Sales Manager

A reference guide for anyone who books, promotes or manages talent. Features over 30,000 listings, including 12,900 artists, managers and agents worldwide, including the USA and Canada. The guide includes contact names, phone and fax numbers, e-mail and website addresses, artists and their record labels, managers and agents, tour services and merchandise, sound and lighting vendors, equipment and instrument rentals, limo rentals, security services, plus national promoters and their key personnel *$139.00*
242 pages Annual

17652 Keyboard Teachers Association International
Dr. Albert DeVito
361 Pin Oak Lane
Westbury, NY 11590-1941
516-333-3236
FAX: 516-997-9531

Albert DeVito, President

Music teachers and those related to keeping members updated as to activity going on in music world.
Quarterly Founded: 1963

17653 MLA Membership Handbook
Music Library Association
8551 Research Way
Suite 180
Middleton, WI 53562
608-836-5825
FAX: 608-831-8200
mla.areditions.com
www.musiclibraryassoc.org
A mailing list that is available for rental in a variety of formats. *$25.00*

17654 Music Library Association Membership Directory
Music Library Association
8551 Research Way
Suite 180
Middleton, WI 53562
608-836-9000
FAX: 608-831-8200
mla@areditions.com
www.musiclibraryassoc.org

Bonna Boettcher, President

The MLA mailing list is available for rental in a variety of formats. Members include music librarians, librarians who work with music as part of their responsibilities, composers and music scholars, and others interested in the program of the association.

17655 Musical America Directory
Musical America
400 Windsor Corporate Center
Suite 200
East Windsor, NJ 08520
609-371-7877
FAX: 609-371-7879 800-221-5488
info@musicalamerica.com
www.musicalamerica.com

Lynn Wall, Subscription Information
Bob Hudoba, Contact

Provides thousands of names, phone numbers, addresses, and Email and Web site addresses for manangers, orchestras, opera companies, festivals, presenters, venues and more around the world. *$125.00*

17656 Musician's Guide
Billboard Directories
PO Box 15158
North Hollywood, CA 91615
818-487-4582
800-562-2706
info@billboard.com
www.billboard.com/directories

Arkady Fridman, Inside Sales Manager

Everything the working musician needs to book gigs, contact record labels, find a manager, and locate tour services. The latest edition includes A & R Directory, Music Business Services, and City by City listings. *$15.95*
170 pages Annual

17657 National Opera Association Membership Directory
PO Box 60869
Canyon, TX 79016
806-651-2857
FAX: 806-651-2958
rhansen@mail.wtamu.edu
www.noa.org

Robert Hansen, Executive Director
JoElyn Wakefield Wright, President
Edith Kirkpatrick Vrenios, VP Resources
Philip Hageman, Treasurer
Carol Notestine, Recording Secretary

Members of the National Opera Association are entitled to receive the NOA Freelance Artists and Production Resources databases, the NOA membership directory, and access to the NOA e-mail listserve.
Annual

17658 **Orion Blue Book: Guitars and Musical Instruments**
Orion Research Corporation
14555 N Scottsdale Road
Suite 330
Scottsdale, AZ 85254-3487
480-951-1114
FAX: 480-951-1117
orion@orionbluebook.com
www.orionbluebook.com

Roger Rohrs, Owner

77,834 products listed; products listed from 1970s to present; over 450 manufacturers listed; 2 volumes - hardbound or on CD-ROM. Lists musical instruments from Accordians to Xylophones *$195.00*

Annual Founded: 1981

17659 **Orion Blue Book: Professional Sound**
Orion Research Corporation
14555 N Scottsdale Road
Suite 330
Scottsdale, AZ 85254-3487
480-951-1114
FAX: 480-951-1117 800-844-0759
orion@orionbluebook.com
www.orionbluebook.com

Roger Rohrs, Owner

Features over 48,964 products from the 1950's to present. Over 350 manufacturers listed. Comes in hardbound or on CD-ROM. Lists products from Cartridge Players to Wireless Microphone Systems. *$150.00*

970 pages Annual Founded: 1973

17660 **Orion Blue Book: Vintage Guitar**
Orion Research Corporation
14555 N Scottsdale Road
Suite 330
Scottsdale, AZ 85254-3487
480-951-1114
FAX: 480-951-1117 800-844-0759
orion@orionbluebook.com
www.orionbluebook.com

Roger Rohrs, Owner

Features more than 11,413 products from the 1800's to present. Over 30 manufacturers listed. Comes in hardbound or CD-ROM, Lists products from Banjos to Ukuleles. *$50.00*

Quarterly Founded: 1990

17661 **Record Retailing Directory**
Billboard Directories
PO Box 15158
North Hollywood, CA 91615
818-487-4582
800-562-2706
info@billboard.com
www.billboard.com/directories

Arkady Fridman, Inside Sales Manager

Over 5,500 listings covering the entire retailing community. Provides access to major chain headquarters and local outlets; complete coverage of independent retailers; hard-to-find audiobook retailers; and the booming world of online record retailing, plus store genre or specialization; executives, owners, buyers and planners; address, phone, fax, email and web. *$215.00*

Annual

17662 **Source Directory of Books, Records and Tapes**
Sutton's Super Marketplace
153 Sutton Lane
Fordsville, KY 42343
270-276-9880

mtsutton32@earthlink.net
www.pubdisco.com

Jerry Sutton, Owner/Founder

Publishers, recording studios, wholesalers, distributors, manifacturers and importers. Approximatley 450 records. Changes daily as updated. *$55.20*

17663 **Source Directory of Musical Instruments**
Sutton's Super Marketplace
153 Sutton Lane
Fordsville, KY 42343
270-276-9880

mtsutton32@earthlink.net
www.pubdisco.com

Jerry Sutton, Owner/Founder

Listings in directory include names, addresses, phone and fax numbers, and product descriptions from wholesale distributors, Importers, Manufacturers, Close-out houses and Liquidators. Updated daily. *$55.20*

Industry Web Sites

17664 **www.acdaonline.org**
American Choral Directors Association

Nonprofit music-education organization whose central purpose is to promote excellence in choral music through performance, composition, publication, research and teaching.

17665 **www.acmcountry.com**
Academy of Country Music

Involved in numerous events and activities promoting country music. Presents annual awards.

17666 **www.afm.org**
American Federation of Musicians of the United
States and Canada

Union representing over 100,000 professional musicians, performing in all genres of music.

17667 **www.afvbm.com**
American Federation of Violin and Bow Makers

Strives to elevate professional standards of craftmanship and ethical conduct among members. Helps members develop technical skills and knowledge.Research and study organization.

17668 **www.agohq.org**
American Guild of Organists

Promotes the organ in its historic and evolving roles and provides a forum for mutual support, inspiration, education and certification.

17669 **www.ascap.com**
American Society of Composers Authors & Publishers

Membership association of more than 260,000 US composers, song writers, lyricists and music publishers.

17670 **www.asmac.org**
American Society of Music Arrangers and Composers

Professional society for arrangers, composers, orchestrators, and musicians. Monthly meetings with great speakers from the music industry.

17671 **www.billboard.com**

The ultimate music industry research tool and information source. The Member Service database is state-of-the-art electronic information service, enabling users to efficiently access information from a variety of music industry databases via the World Wide Web.

17672 **www.chorusamerica.org**
Chorus America

National service for orchestral choruses, independent choruses and professional choruses.

17673 **www.clarinet.org**
International Clarinet Association

Seeks to focus attention on the importance of the clarinet and to foster communication of the fellowship between clarinetists.

17674 **www.cmaworld.com**
Country Music Association

Promotes and publicizes country music.

17675 **www.creativemusicalcoalition.com**
Creative Musician Coalition

A national organization that brings the world of new music to its readers. Includes in depth music reviews, informative artist interviews, interesting articles and feature columns, and valuable resource material.

17676 **www.flmusiced.org**
Florida Music Educators Association

Florida Music Educators Association and Florida School Music Association.

17677 **www.folkharpsociety.org**
International Society of Folk Harpers and Craftsmen

Conducts technical and artistic programs and promotes craft exchange.

17678 **www.gospelmusic.org**
Gospel Music Association

Dedicated to providing leadership, direction and unity for all facets of the gospel music industry. Through education, communication, information, promotion and recognition, the GMA is striving to help those involved in gospel music.

17679 **www.greyhouse.com**
Grey House Publishing

The Grey House Performing Arts Directory is the most comprehensive resource covering the Performing Arts. This important directory provides current information on over 9,000 Dance Companies, Instrumental Music Programs, Opera Companies, Choral Groups, Theater Companies, Performing Arts Series and Performing Arts Facilities.

17680 **www.guitarfoundation.org**
Guitar Foundation of America

Supports the serious studies of the guitar.

17681 **www.harpsociety.org**
American Harp Society

Improves the quality of the instrument and performance.

17682 **www.horndoggie.com/horn**
International Horn Society

A national organization that focuses on music industry news and information.

17683 **www.iaekm.org**
International Association of Electronic Keyboard
Manufacturers

Global manufacturers of electronic keyboards and affiliated software and publications.

17684 **www.ibma.org**
World of Bluegrass

IBMA: working together for high standards of professionalism, a greater appreciation for our music, and the success of the world-wide bluegrass community.

17685 **www.imeamusic.org**
Indiana Music Educators Association

Supports and advances music education in Indiana.

17686 **www.internationalpolka.com**
International Polka Association

Educational organization concerned with the preservation and advancement of polka music. Operates the Polka Music Hall of Fame and Museum, and presents the International Polka Fesitval every year during the complete first weekend of August.

17687 **www.metguild.org**
Metropolitan Opera Guild

Seeks to promote greater understanding and interest in opera.

17688 **www.mpa.org**
Music Publishers Association of the United States

Encourages understanding of the copyright laws and works to protect musical works against infringements and piracy.

17689 **www.mtna.org**
Music Teachers National Association

This is a nonprofit organization of independent and collegiate music teachers committed to furthering the art of music through teaching, performance, composition and scholarly research.

17690 **www.music.org**
College Music Society

The Society is a national service organization for college conservatory and university music teachers.

17691 **www.musicalartists.org**
American Guild of Musical Artists

Exclusive bargaining agent for all concert musical artists.

17692 **www.musicdistributors.org**
Music Distributor Association

A trade association of 160 manufactures, importers, wholesalers of musical instruments and accessories, domestic and international selling to the trade only

17693 **www.musiclibraryassoc.org**
Music Library Association

Promotes growth and establishment in the use of music libraries, musical instruments and musical literature.

17694 **www.nacwpi.org**
National Association of College Wind and Percussion Instructors

Teachers of wind and percussion instruments in American colleges and universities.

17695 **www.napbirt.org**
National Association of Professional Band Instrument Repair Technicians

Promotes technical integrity in the craft. Surveys tools and procedures to improve work quality. Makes available emergency repair of band instruments. Provides placement services.

17696 **www.narm.com**
National Association of Recording Merchandisers

Not-for-profit trade association that represents the retailers, wholesalers, and distributors of prerecorded music in the United States.

17697 **www.nbea.com**
National Ballroom and Entertainment Association

Provides exchange for owners and operators of ballrooms.

17698 **www.noa.org**
National Opera Association

To advance the appreciation, composition and production of opera.

17699 **www.npm.org**
National Association of Pastoral Musicians

Membership organization primarily composed of musicians, musician-liturgist, clergy, and other leaders of prayer devoted to serving the life and mission of the Church through fosterering the art of musical liturgy in Roman Catholic worshiping communities in the United States.

17700 **www.nyssma.org**
New York State School Music Association

Advocates and improves the education in music of all people in New York State.

17701 www.pas.org
Percussive Arts Society

Promotes drums and percussion through a viable network of performers, teachers, students, enthusiasts and sustaining members. Offers publications, a worldwide network of the World Percussion Network, the Percussive Arts Society International Headquarters/Museum and the annual Percussive Arts Society International Convention.

17702 www.pianoguild.com
International Piano Guild

A division of the American College of Musicians Professional society of piano teachers and music faculty members. Sponsers national examinations.

17703 www.printmusic.org
Retail Print Music Dealers Association

The voice of the print music industry.

17704 www.ptg.org
Piano Technicians Guild

Conducts technical institutes at conventions and seminars. Promotes public education in piano care. Bestows awards. Publishes monthly technical journal by subscriptions.

17705 www.spars.com
Society of Professional Audio Recording Services

Members are individuals, companies and studios connected with the professional recording industry.

17706 www.symphony.org
American Symphony Orchestra League

The national nonprofit service and educational organization dedicated to strengthening symphony and chamber orchestras. It provides artistic, organizational and financial leadership and service to orchestral conductors, managers, volunteers and staff.

17707 www.tmea.org
Texas Music Educators Association

Promoting excellence in music education.

Associations

17708 **BIFMA International**
2680 Horizon Drive SE
Suite A-1
Grand Rapids, MI 49546-7500
616-285-3963
FAX: 616-285-3765
email@bifma.org www.bifma.org
Thomas Reardon, Director
Thomas Reardon, Executive Director
Scott Schwinghammer, Treasurer
The voice of the office furniture industry, BIFMA members are manufacturers and suppliers of goods and services to the industry.
245 Members Founded: 1973

17709 **Graphic Arts Information Network**
200 Deer Run Road
Sewickley, PA 15143
412-741-6860
FAX: 412-741-2311 800-910-4283
piagtf@piagtf.org
www.gain.org/servlet/gateway/PIA
Michael Makin, President
Members are companies printing labels for food or consumer products.
40 Members

17710 **Independent Office Products & Furniture**
301 N Fairfax Street
Alexandria, VA 22314
703-549-9040
FAX: 703-683-7552
info@iopfda.org www.iopfda.org
Jim McGarry, President
Paul Miller, Director Government Affairs
Sheri Winter, Director Marketing
Mark Duros, Director Research/Technology
Association for independent office product and office furniture dealers. IOPFDA is comprised of the National Office Products Alliance (NOPA) and the Office Furniture Dealers Alliance (OFDA).
1500 Members Founded: 1904

17711 **Office Furniture Distribution Association**
739 Daniel Shaws Highway
D-16
Athol, MA 01331
978-249-0303
FAX: 978-249-5937
kmassoc@splusnet.com
www.theofda.org
75 Members Founded: 1923

17712 **Office Products Representatives**
3131 Elbee Road
Dayton, OH 45439
937-297-2250
FAX: 937-297-2254 800-447-1684
info@oprareps.org www.oprareps.org
Carol Hinton, Owner
100 Members Founded: 1974

17713 **Office Products Wholesalers Association**
5024 Campbell Boulevard
Baltimore, MD 21236
410-931-8100
FAX: 410-931-8111
opwa@clemonsmgmt.com
www.opwa.org
Members are chief executives of office product wholesalers and manufacturers.
165 Members Founded: 1995

17714 **Society for Service Professionals in Print ing**
433 E Monroe Avenue
Alexandria, VA 22301-1693
703-840-0044
FAX: 703-548-9137
ssppinfo@sspp.org www.sspp.org
Peter Colaianni, Executive Director
Marj Green, Director
Individual membership society dedicated to the needs of customer service professionals in the printing industry.
8 Members Founded: 1993

Newsletters

17715 **BTA Hotline Online**
Business Technology Association
12411 Wornall Road
Kansas City, MO 64145
816-941-3100
FAX: 816-941-2829 800-505-2821
info@bta.org http://www.bta.org
Bert Darling, Executive Director
Brent Hoskins, Editor
Robin Keller, Marketing Director
Current copier/printer and network systems industry news.
Founded: 1926

17716 **Digital Image Review**
Buyers Laboratory
20 Railroad Avenue
Hackensack, NJ 07601-3309
201-896-6439
FAX: 201-488-0461
info@buyerslab.com
http://www.buyerslab.com
Daria Hoffman, Managing Editor
Michael Danziger, CEO
Devoted to digital topics, all types of digital office products, industry news and trends, trade show, pricing changes and much more. *$305.00*
16 pages Monthly Founded: 1961

17717 **Executary**
National Association of Executive Secretaries
900 S Washington Street
Suite G13
Falls Church, VA 22046-4009
703-536-0735
FAX: 703-533-1153
headquarters@naesaa.com
http://www.naesaa.com
Ruth Ludeman, Director
This newsletter offers information pertinent to executive secretaries and administrative assistants in their business and personal lives. *$26.00*
8 pages Monthly Founded: 1975
Circulation: 5000
Mailing list available for rent 12000 names $135 per M.
Printed in 2 colors

17718 **Form & Document Industry Newsletter**
319 SW Washington Street
Suite 710
Portland, OR 97204-2618
503-227-3393
FAX: 503-274-7667
bfma@bfma.org http://www.bfma.org
Andy Palatka, Executive Director
Tonya Macalino, Editor
Tonya Macalino, Marketing
Industry newsletter containing educational articles and rules on the latest processes, techniques, and products in the form and document industry. Library rate is $35.00 per year. *$50.00*
38574 pages Founded: 1958
Circulation: 700
Mailing list available for rent 1000 names $400 per M.

17719 **Jot and Jolts**
Economics Press
12 Daniel Road
Fairfield, NJ 07004-2565
973-227-1224
FAX: 973-227-8360 800-526-2554
Monthly planner for supervisors to the office products industry. *$16.20*
26 pages Monthly
Printed in on glossy stock

17720 **MFP Report**
Bissett Communications
12844 Berkhamsted Street
Cerritos, CA 90703-7234
562-809-8917
FAX: 562-809-1627 http://
Brian R Bissett, Publisher
A newsletter providing information on manufacturers, suppliers, sellers, and managers of multifunction peripherals and connected office equipment of the latest MFP business, market and technology issues and their impact.
Monthly

17721 **Scanner**
Private Label Manufacturers Association (PLMA)
369 Lexington Avenue
3rd Floor
New York, NY 10017-6506
212-972-3131
FAX: 212-983-1382
info@plma.com http://www.plma.com
Thomas Prendergast, Editor
6 pages Quarterly
Circulation: 12000

Magazines & Journals

17722 **Better Buys for Business**
Progressive Business Publications
370 Technology Drive
Malvern, PA 19355
610-695-8600
FAX: 610-296-4967 800-247-2185
info@betterbuys.com
http://www.betterbuys.com
Jonathan Bees, Editor
Steve Hannaford, Editor
Ed Satell, President
Publishes 10 non-advertising buyer's guides for office equipment (copiers, printers, fax machines and scanners), with objective, unbiased information and evaluations. Each issue includes in-depth write-ups on all manufacturers and their models, easy to read specifications and price charts to compare models and Editor's Choice selections - awarded to the best machines in each product category *$149.00*
Founded: 1980
Circulation: 4,000 24,000 names $125 per

M.
Printed in 4 colors on matte stock : PDF

17723 Business Documents
North American Publishing Company
401 N Broad Street
Philadelphia, PA 19108-1001
215-238-5300
FAX: 215-238-5457 800-627-2689
tbay@napco.com
http://www.napco.com

Bill Drennan, Editor
Brian C Ludwick, Publisher

For professional buyers of forms, labels and electronic systems. Emphasizes internal and external design, production and management of business documents either as traditionally printed forms or electronically generated documents. *$24.00*
42 pages Monthly Founded: 1958
Printed in 2 colors on matte stock

17724 Business Forms, Labels & Systems
North American Publishing Company
401 N Broad Street
Philadelphia, PA 19108-1001
215-238-5300
FAX: 215-238-5457
webmaster@napco.com
http://www.napco.com/

Bill Drennan, Editorial Director
Judith Cavaliere, Publisher
Maggie DeWitt, Senior Editor
Cynthia Graham, Associate Editor
Jennifer Hans, Associate Editor

For independent manufacturers and distributors in the forms and systems industry. Emphasizes product applications, marketing and sales ideas and new technology. *$49.00*
Monthly Founded: 1958
Circulation: 12000
Printed in 4 colors on glossy stock

17725 Business Solutions
Corry Publishing
5539 Peach Street
Erie, PA 16506
814-380-0025
FAX: 814-864-2037 800-290-5460
editor@corrypub.com
http://www.corrypub.com

John Clifton, Group Publisher
Melinda Reed-Fadden, Circulation Manager
Dan Schell, Editor
Carrie Brocious, Marketing Director
Jim Roddy, General Manager

Informative magazine including analysis of technological and marketing developments.
Monthly Founded: 1980
Circulation: 43000

17726 Business Technology Association
12411 Wornall Road
Kansas City, MO 64145-1119
816-941-3100
FAX: 816-941-2829 800-505-2821
info@bta.org http://www.bta.org

Robin Keller, Publisher/Marketing Manager
Bert Derling, Editor/Executive Director

An international trade organization serving dealers, value added resellers, systems integrators, manufacturers and distributors in the network computing and office automation industries. The association provides educational programs, professional forums, discount services and other benefits designed to help members be more profitable and competitive. BTA members provide business solutions in local area networks, wide area networks, document management and a wide variety of office technologies. *$30.00*
Monthly Founded: 1927 ISSN 1092-9169
Circulation: 3500
Mailing list available for rent 1200 names

17727 Digital Information Network
Buyers Laboratory
20 Railroad Avenue
Hackensack, NJ 07601-3309
201-587-0828
FAX: 201-488-0461
info@buyerslab.com
www.buyerslab.com

Daria Hoffman, Managing Editor

A comprehensive test report service which provides test reports on all the office products BLI evaluates. Subscribers will also get a sixteen page monthly newsletter called Digital Imaging Review, and will recieve a copy of BLI's Multifunctional Specification Guide, Facsimile-Based Products, Copier-Based Products and the Printer Specification Guide, as well as updated specifications throughout the term of their subscription. *$755.00*

17728 Hard Copy Supplies Journal
Lyra Research
PO Box 9143
Newtonville, MA 02640-9143
617-454-2600
FAX: 617-454-2601
http://www.lyra.com

Charles LeCompte, Publisher
Frank Stefansson, CEO/President
Jim Forrest, Managing Editor
Jennifer Sprague, Marketing
Andre Rebelo, Marketing Manager

In-depth coverage of current innovations in marketing materials and media, including ink jet cartridges, toner, paper and film, and monitors the fast-moving corporate developments, such as lawsuits, mergers, distribution, tactics, and marketing campaigns. *$550.00*
Monthly Founded: 1991
Circulation: 2,000

17729 Mail:Journal of Communication Distribution
Excelsior Publications
One Millstone Road
Gold Key Box 2425
Milford, PA 18337
570-861-1969
FAX: 570-686-3495

Francis P Ruggiero, Publsher

Circulation: 43000

17730 Office Dealer
Quality Publishing
252 N. Main Street
Suite 200
Mount Airy, NC 27030-3810
336-783-0000
FAX: 336-783-0045
bcomer@os-od.com
http://www.os-od.com/

Richard Kunkel, Publisher
Simon DeGroot, Editorial Director
Bessie Comer, Sales/Advertising Coordin
Scott Cullen, Managing Editor
Debbie Hooker, Director of Publishing Services

Information including the latest industry news pertaining to resellers, plus office dealer conventions and other newsworthy events.

Circulation: 17020

17731 Office Solutions
Quality Publishing
252 N Main Street #200
PO Box 1028
Mount Airy, NC 27030-3810
336-783-0000
FAX: 336-783-0045
osod@os-od.com
http://www.os-od.com

Richard Kunkel, Publisher
Simon Degroot, Editorial Director
Debbey Hooker, Circulation Manager
Bill Middleton, Marketing Manager
Scott Cullen, Managing Editor

Information on state of the art, survey and overview of articles and product offerings. Emphasis on personal computing, software, telecommunications, personnel and financial management. *$36.00*
Founded: 2003
Circulation: 81250

17732 Office Systems Research Journal
SW Missouri Council of Governments
901 S National Avenue
Springfield, MO 65804
417-836-5000
FAX: 417-836-4146
dmm672F@smsu.edu
http://www.smsu.edu

Diane May, Executive Director

A journal offering research and news of the office supplies and products industry. *$35.00*

Circulation: 400

17733 Print Solutions Magazine
Document Management Industries Association
433 E Monroe Avenue
Alexandria, VA 22301-1693
703-836-6232
FAX: 703-549-4966
www.printsolutionsmag.com

Peter L Colaianni CAE, Editor-in-Chief

Source for marketing, management and product information. *$49.00*
276 pages Monthly
Printed in 4 colors on glossy stock

17734 Recharger Magazine
Recharger Magazine
1050 E Flamingo Rd
Ste 237
Las Vegas, NV 89119-7479
702-505-9530
FAX: 702-873-9671 877-902-9759
info@rechargermag.com
http://www.rechargermag.com

Phyllis Gurgevich, Publisher
Amy Turner, Managing Editor
Michael MacDonald, Graphics Director
Sara Feest, Sales Assistant
Monica Miceli, Associate Editor

Information including articles that cover business and marketing, technical updates, association and industry news, and company profiles. Related features focus on the importance of recycling, government legislation, and product comparisons. *$45.00*
Monthly
Circulation: 8000

Trade Shows

17735 ARMA Information and Image Technology Conference
Association of Records Managers & Administrators
13725 W. 109th Street
Suite 101
Lenexa, KS 66215
913-341-3808
FAX: 913-341-3742 800-422-2762
hq@arma.org www.arma.org/hq
Sarah G. Patt-Pronek, Trade Show Director
Peter Hermann, Chief Executive Officer
Conference, seminar, workshop, banquet, award ceremony and 250 exhibits of micrographics, optical disk, automated document storage and retrieval systems and more technology of interest to information professionals.
1700 Attendees Annual Founded: 1955

17736 American Business Women's Association Convention
9100 Ward Parkway
PO Box 8728
Kansas City, MO 64114
816-361-6621
FAX: 816-361-4991 800-228-0007
abwa@abwa.org www.abwa.org
Wendy Mabrey, Corporate Sponsorship Coordinator
Carolyn Elman, Executive Director
One-hundred exhibits of equipment, supplies and services for women in business, seminar and banquet.
2000 Attendees November

17737 American Society for Training & Development Conference & Exposition
American Society for Training & Development
1640 King Street
PO Box 1443
Alexandria, VA 22313-2043
703-683-8100
FAX: 703-683-8103
customercare@astd.org www.astd.org
Michael Neff, Executive Director
2000 Attendees

17738 Business Show
INPEX
217 9th Street
Pittsburgh, PA 15222-3506
412-881-1300
FAX: 412-288-4546 800-544-6739
info@inventionshow.com
www.inventionshow.com/
Annual show of 150 exhibits of office furniture, supplies and machines; computers; media; specialty items; financial services; printing services; security systems; entertainment; cellular phones and pagers; sinage; travel agencies; audio-visual equipment and car rental agencies.
5000 Attendees

17739 Business Technology Association
Business Technology Association
12411 Wornall Road
Kansas City, MO 64145-1119
816-941-3100
FAX: 816-941-2829
info@bta.org www.bta.org
Jeffrey Jehn, President
John Heiser, VP
Bert Darling, Executive Director
Founded: 1926
Mailing list available for rent 1200 names

17740 Document World/American Business Equipment and Computer Show
Key Productions
116 Murphy Road
Hartford, CT 06114-2121
860-247-8363

Eldred Codling, Show Manager
Features exhibits of computer software, hardware, supplies and services.
6M Attendees April

17741 National Stationery Show
George Little Management
10 Bank Street
White Plains, NY 10606-1954
914-486-6070
FAX: 914-948-6180 800-272-7469
Lori Robinson, VP
Kelly Bristol, Assistant Show Manager
George Little II, President
A show for greeting cards and social stationery, writing instruments and home office products, party ware and giftwrap, scrapbooking and craft supplies, albums, frames and much more.
14000 Attendees May

Directories & Databases

17742 Directory of Mail Order Catalogs
Grey House Publishing
185 Millerton Road
PO Box 860
Millerton, NY 12546
518-890-0526
FAX: 518-789-0545 800-562-2139
books@greyhouse.com
www.greyhouse.com
Leslie Mackenzie, Publisher
Richard Gottlieb, Editor
The premier source of information on the mail order catalog industry. Covers over 12,000 consumer and business catalog companies with 44 different product chapters including clothing and sportswear. *$350.00*

1600 pages Annual Founded: 1980 ISBN 1-592370-66-7

17743 Orion Blue Book: Copier
Orion Research Corporation
14555 N Scottsdale Road
Suite 330
Scottsdale, AZ 85254-3487
480-951-1114
FAX: 480-951-1117 800-844-0759
support@orionbluebook.com
www.orionbluebook.com/
Roger Rohrs, Editor
List of manufacturers of copiers and other office equipment. *$39.00*
Annual

Industry Web Sites

17744 www.americanpayroll.org
American Payroll Association

Association of payroll and human resource professionals. Website furthers information exchange and meeting announcements.

17745 www.bfma.org
Business Forms Management Association

For form systems professionals interested in the effective capture distribution and management of information in electronic and paper forms.

17746 www.bifma.org
Business and Institutional Furniture Manufacturers Association

The voice of the office furniture industry, BIFMA members are manufacturers and suppliers of goods and services to the industry.

17747 www.dmia.org
Document Management Industries Association

17748 www.greyhouse.com
Grey House Publishing

Selected Grey House directories in the fields of business, health and education are available online. Users can search our online databases by several different search criteria, such as product categories, geographic area, sales volume and much, much more. Full Grey House catalog and online ordering also available.

17749 www.iopfda.org
Independent Office Products & Furniture Dealers Association

Association for independent office product and office furniture dealers. IOPFDA is comprised of the National Office Products Alliance (NOPA) and the Office Furniture Dealers Alliance (OFDA).

17750 www.oprareps.org
Office Products Representatives Association

Provides programs and services that promote the role of the independant manufactures' representative in the various distribution channels within the entire office products industry.

17751 www.sspp.org
Society for Service Professionals in Printing

Individual membership society dedicated to the needs of customer service professionals in the printing industry.

17752 www.theofda.org
Office Furniture Distribution Association

Associations

17753 **American Forest & Paper Association**
1111 Nineteenth Street NW
Suite 800
Washington, DC 20036
202-463-2700
FAX: 202-462-2785 800-878-8878
info@afandpa.org www.afandpa.org

Charles Feghali, Chairman
Henson Moore, President

To provide significant value to member companies through outstanding performance in those areas that are key to members' success and where an association can be more effective than individual companies.
Founded: 1993

17754 **American Paper Machinery Association**
201 Park Washington Court
Falls Church, VA 22046-4513
703-538-1787
FAX: 703-241-5603
apmahq@aol.com
www.papermachinery.org

Clay D Tyeryar, Chief Administrative Executive
Judith O Buzzerd, Manager Meetings
Sharon Kelly, Coordinator Member Services

To promote the global common interests, image and business relations of the membership.
35 Members Founded: 1971

17755 **Association of Independent Corrugated Converters**
PO Box 25708
Alexandria, VA 22313
703-836-2422
FAX: 703-836-2795 877-836-2422
info@aiccbox.org www.aiccbox.org

A Steven Young, President
Zell Murphy, Director Operations
David Core, CAE, Director Education
Taryn Pyle, Director Meetings
Chris Richards, Webmaster/Systems Manager

Represents and protects, the business interests of the independent sector of the corrugated packaging industry. Dedicated to strengthening the independent's position in the marketplace through programs and publications that empower our members to compete successfully in a rapidly changing industry and an increasingly competitive and global business environment.
750 Members Founded: 1974

17756 **Fibre Box Association**
25 Northwest Point Blvd
Suite 510
Elk Grove VLG, IL 60007-1033
847-364-9600
FAX: 847-364-9639
fba@fibrebox.org www.fibrebox.org

Robert McIlvaine, Chairman
Daniel Pyne, First Vice Chairman
Bruce Benson, President

A non-profit association that represents and serves the corrugated industry. It also brings together the North American manufacturers to improve the overall well being of the industry and to provide an array of services that enable member companies to conduct their business more effectively , responsibly and efficiently.
170 Members Founded: 1940

17757 **Foodservice & Packaging Institute**
150 S Washington Street
Suite 204
Falls Church, VA 22046
703-538-2800
FAX: 703-538-2187
fpi@fpi.org www.fpi.org

John Burke, President
Elizabeth Phillips, Director,Member Services
Lynn Rosseth, Director Market Development

To promote the sanitation, safety, functional, economic, and environmental benefits of foodservice packaging products. Supports the environmentallyresponsible manufacture, distribution, use and disposal of these products.
25 Members Founded: 1933

17758 **International Corrugated Packaging Foundation**
113 SW Street
Alexandria, VA 22314
703-549-8580
FAX: 703-549-8670
info@icpfbox.org www.icpfbox.org

John L Kelley, Chairman
Michael D'Angelo, Vice Chairman
A Steven Young, Treasurer
Paul Vishny, Secretary

An industry led philantrophic organization dedicated to building a knowledgeable workforce for the corrugated packaging industry.
Founded: 1985

17759 **International Molded Pulp Environmental Packaging**
1425 W Mequon Road
Suite A
Mequon, WI 53092
262-241-0522
FAX: 262-241-3766
info@impepa.org www.impepa.org

Acts as an information center for the molded pulp industry with worldwide membership of users and manufacturers of molded pulp products as well as research and packaging companies.
Founded: 1996

17760 **National Council for Air and Stream Improvement**
PO Box 12868
New Bern, NC 28561-2868
252-637-4326
FAX: 252-637-7111
ryeske@ncasi.org www.ncasi.org

Ronald A Yeske, President
Dedra Barber, Business Manager
Pamela J Bruns, Communications Manager
Carol Dwyer, Executive Secretary
Cathy Emptage, Staff Accountant

Founded by the pulp and paper industry to serve the forest products industry as a center of excellence for providing technical information and scientific research needed to achieve the industry's environmental goals and principals.
Founded: 1943

17761 **National Paper Trade Association**
500 Bi-County Boulevard
Suite 200E
Farmingdale, NY 11735
631-777-2233
FAX: 631-777-2224 800-355-6782
webmaster@gonpta.com
www.gonpta.com

Michael E Kenneally, Chairman
Fred A Towler, First Vice Chairman
Steven A Barker, Second Vice Chairman
William Frohlich, President
George W Wurtz, Treasurer

Supports all those professionals in the paper, packaging and allied products distribution industries. Publishes monthly magazine.
2000 Members Founded: 1903

17762 **National Paperbox Association**
113 S West Street
3rd Floor
Alexandria, VA 22314
703-684-2212
FAX: 703-683-6920
npahq@paperbox.org
www.paperbox.org

Pete Reiber, Program Chairman
Scott Miller, Executive VP

Serves as the voice of the paperbox and packaging industry. Also represents the concerns of boxmaker nationally, internationally and at the local level through its Regional Divisions. Publishes bi-monthly magazine and holds an annual convention.
100 Members Founded: 1918

17763 **Paper Distribution Council**
National Paper Trade Association
111 Great Neck Road
Great Neck, NY 11021-5497
516-829-3070

Association for paper, packaging and applied products distribution channels.
52 Members Founded: 1968 ISSN 1092-8073

17764 **Paper Industry Management Association**
4700 W Lake Avenue
Glenview, IL 60025-1485
847-375-6860
FAX: 877-527-5973 877-527-5973
info@pimaweb.org
www.pimaweb.com

Jim Weir, Executive VP/COO
Julie Weldon, Senior Manager
Carol Waugh, Meetings Manager

Contributes to the strength of the international pulp and paper community by providing the means for our members to address relevant industry issues and to develop their management and leadership skills.
1200 Members Founded: 1919

17765 **Paper Shipping Sack Manufacturers Association**
520 E Oxford Street
Coopersburg, PA 18036
610-282-6845
FAX: 610-282-6921 www.pssma.com

Brent Dixon, President

Provides its member companies with programs and services which further the industry's objectives and in doing so promote and enhance the welfare of the industry.
45 Members Founded: 1933

17766 **Paperboard Packaging Council**
201 N Union Street
Suite 220
Alexandria, VA 22314
703-836-3300
FAX: 703-836-3290
paperboardpackaging@ppcnet.org
www.ppcnet.org

Jerome T Van De Water, President
James Brown, Director Business Services
Steve Smith, Operations Manager

Members are companies making folding cartons. Provides publications and instructional materials on the paper industry and recycling.
92 Members Founded: 1929

17767 **Technical Association of the Pulp & Paper Industry**
15 Technology Parkway South
Norcross, GA 30092
770-446-1400
FAX: 770-446-6947
memberconnection@tappi.org
www.tappi.org

Wayne H Gross, President
Mark R McCollister, VP

To engage the people and resources of our association in providing technically sound solutions to the workplace problems and opportunities that challenge our current and future members.
12000 Members Founded: 1915

17768 **United Paperworkers International Union**
100 Decatur Street SE
Atlanta, GA 30303-3202
404-651-2422
FAX: 404-651-4314
libdgg@langate.gsu.edu
www.library.gsu.edu

Mike Dees, President

Bestows awards and conducts training seminars.
Founded: 1972

Newsletters

17769 **Alkaline Paper Advocate**
Abbey Publishing
PO Box 18439
Munds Park, AZ 86017-.
928-286-1604
www.abbypublishing.com

Roland Dufault, Editor

Articles covering production and use of alkaline paper.

17770 **American Forest and Paper Association Report**
1111 19th Street NW
Suite 800
Washington, DC 20036-3611
202-463-2700
FAX: 202-463-2785 800-878-8878
info@afandpa.org
http://www.afandpa.org

Sharon Kneiss, Publisher
William Moore, CEO/President

Covers events of the paper, wood and forest industry. Distribution is limited to association members only. *$1200.00*
4 pages Weekly Founded: 1993

17771 **Conservatree Greenline**
Greenline Publications
PO Box 590780
San Francisco, CA 94159-780
415-386-8646
FAX: 415-391-7890
samia@greenlinepub.com
http://www.conservatree.com

Alan Davis, Founder/Publisher
Susan Kinsella, Editor

Reports on efforts and achievements by businesses on the environmental front. *$59.00*
Founded: 1976
Circulation: 25000

17772 **Essential Resources, LLC**
45 Park Place S
Suite 330
Morristown, NJ 07960
908-832-6979
FAX: 908-832-6970
essresou@na2k.net

Tim Friel

Newsletters for plastic, chemical, pharmaceutical, and packaging industries.
5-15 pages
Computerized version available: PC

17773 **Official Board Markets**
Advanstar Communications
2835 N Sheffield Ave
Ste 226
Chicago, IL 60657-9213
312-553-8922
FAX: 312-553-8929
marzoumanian@advanstar.com
http://www.packaging-online.com

Mark Arzoumanian, Editor-in-Chief
Esther Durkalski, Managing Editor

Covers the corrugated container and folding carton converting industries. *$180.00*
24 pages Weekly Founded: 1915
Circulation: 5900
Printed in on glossy stock

17774 **Seaboard Bulletin**
International Paper
PO Box 1200
Bucksport, ME 04416-1200
207-469-1700
FAX: 207-469-1705

David Bailey, President

Paper industry news.

Magazines & Journals

17775 **Asia Pacific PaperMaker**
Paper Industry Management Association
4700 West Lake Avenue
Glenview, IL 60025-1485
847-375-6860
FAX: 877-527-5973
info@pimaweb.org
http://www.pima-online.org

Jim Weir, Executive Vice President/CEO
Patrick Andrus, Marketing Coordinator
Patrick Filippelli, Sales Manager
Sarah Walsh, Administrative Assistant

Founded: 1919

17776 **Board Converting News**
NV Business Publishers Corporation
43 Main Street
Avon By The Sea, NJ 07717
732-502-0500
FAX: 732-502-9606
tvilardi@NVPublications.com
http://www.nvpublications.com

Tom Vilardi, President
Jim Curley, Editor-in-Chief
Robyn Smith, Executive Publisher
Gail Kalina, Production Manager
Dan Brunton, Marketing Manager

News for the corrugated box and folding carton industry along with box and carton transacted prices. *$180.00*
140 pages Weekly

17777 **Converting Magazine**
Reed Business Information
2000 Clearwater Drive
Oak Brook, IL 60523
630-740-0825
FAX: 630-288-8536
psaran@reedbusiness.com
http://www.convertingmagazine.com

Phil Saran, Publisher
Mark Spaulding, Editor-in-Chief
Steve Reiss, VP

Monthly
Circulation: 4000

17778 **Distribution Sales & Management**
National Paper Trade Association
500 B1 - County Boulevard
Suite 200E
Farmingdale, NY 11735-5402
631-777-2223
FAX: 631-777-2224
debra@goNPTA.com
www.goNPTA.com

Debra Ray, Editor
Bill Fronlinch, Publisher

The business magazine for the paper, packaging and allied products distribution channel. *$49.00*
48 pages Monthly Founded: 1959
Circulation: 17000
Printed in on matte stock

17779 **European PaperMaker**
Paper Industry Management Association
1699 Wall Street
Suite 212
Mount Prospect, IL 60056
847-699-1706
FAX: 847-956-0520
www.pima-online.org

17780 **International Paper Board Industry**
Brunton Publications & NV Public
43 Main Street
Avon By The Sea, NJ 07717-1051
732-502-0500
FAX: 732-502-9606
jcurley@NVPublications.com
http://www.nvpublications.com

Mike Brunton, Publisher
Jim Curley, Editor-in-Chief
Gail Kalina, Production Manager
Tom Vilardi, President
Dan Brunton, Marketing Manager

Information on corrugated paper and converting industry, encompassing news and production worldwide. *$60.00*
Monthly
Circulation: 10021

17781 Journal of Intelligent Materials and Structures
Technomic Publishing Company
PO Box 3535
Lancaster, PA 17601
717-291-5609
FAX: 717-295-4538 800-233-9936
aflannery@techpub.com
www.techpub.com

Amy Flannery, Marketing

Original papers, describing experimental or theoretical work on all aspects of intelligent materials, systems and structures research. The scope is generally inclusive. Papers related to the science and engineering of intelligent systems are featured, particularly biomimetrics, applied mathematics of phase transitions and material science, neural networks, structural dynamic control, and adaptive and sensing materials. *$ 995.00*

80 pages Monthly
Printed in 2 colors on matte stock : On-Line

17782 Latin American PaperMaker
Paper Industry Management Association
1699 Wall Street
Suite 212
Mount Prospect, IL 60056
847-956-0250
FAX: 847-956-0520
info@pima-online.org
http://www.pima-online.org

Ralph W. Feck, President
Jim Weir, COO/Executive VP
Patrick Andrus, Marketing Coordinator
Patrick Filippelli, Sales Manager
Sarah Walsh, Administrative Assistant

Founded: 1919

17783 Mill Trade Journal's Recycling Markets
NV Business Publishers Corporation
43 Main Street
Avon By The Sea, NJ 07717
732-502-0500
FAX: 732-502-9606 800-962-3001
advertising@NVPublications.com
http://www.nvpublications.com

Tom Vilardi, President
Roy Bradbrook, Editor
Jim Curley, Editor-in-Chief
Gail Kalina, Production Manager
Robyn Smith, Executive Publisher

Information on recycling mills paper stock, scrap metal and plastics brokers and dealers used by the municipal governments and private organizations as a basis for letting contracts. *$130.00*

Fortnightly Founded: 1984
Circulation: 3625
Printed in 2 colors on matte stock

17784 NPTA Distribution Sales & Management
111 Great Neck Road
Suite 418
Great Neck, NY 11021-5402
516-829-3070
FAX: 516-829-3074

17785 North American PaperMaker
Paper Industry Management Association
4700 West Lake Avenue
Glenview, IL 60025-1485
847-375-6860
FAX: 877-527-5973
info@pimaweb.org
http://www.pima-online.org

Jim Weir, Executive Vice President/COO
Pam Oddi, Administrative Assistant
Patrick Filippelli, Sales Manager
Patrick Andrus, Marketing Coordinator
Julie Weldon, Senior Manager

Founded: 1919

17786 Paper Age Magazine
O'Brien Publications
185 Lincoln Street
Suite 200B
Hingham, MA 02043
781-749-5255
FAX: 781-749-5896
info@paperage.com
http://www.paperage.com

Ken Patrick, Director-Editorial Development
John O'Brien, Managing Editor
Michael O'Brien, Publisher

For management and supervisory personnel of pulp, paper and paperboard mills. Tabloid-sized magazine covering the pulp, paper and converting industry, with a unique mix of timely and insightful coverage of corporate strategies, mill operations, technological innovations, industry issues, as well as analysis of the latest production and marketing trends. *$90.00*

Founded: 1884
Circulation: 36156

17787 Paper Industry Equipment Magazine
PO Box 5675
Montgomery, AL 36103
604-264-1158
FAX: 604-264-1367 888-224-6611
info@paperindustrymag.com
http://www.paperindustrymag.com

Tim Shaddick, Publisher
Peter N Williamson, Editor

Services and equipment for the pulp/paper industry. *$12.00*

32 pages Founded: 1984
Circulation: 1900 19,000+ names $100 per M.
Printed in 4 colors on glossy stock

17788 Paper Stock Report: News and Trends of the Paper Recycling Markets
McEntee Media Corporation
13727 Holland Road
Brook Park, OH 44142
216-362-7979
FAX: 216-362-6553
mcenteemedia@compuserve.com
www.recyle.cc

Ken McEntee, President

Covers news and trends of the scrap paper markets. *$115.00*

BiWeekly Founded: 1990

17789 Paper, Film & Foil Converter
PRIMEDIA
745 5th Avenue
New York, NY 10150
212-745-0100
FAX: 212-745-0121
information@primedia.com
www.primedia.com

Yolanda Simonsis, Editor/Associate Publisher
Claudia Hine, Managing Editor
Deborah Donberg, Associate Managing Editor
Nsenga Byrd Thompson, Associate Editor
Carrie Cleaveland, Assistant Editor

Recognizes experts and experienced staff that assist converters to become more effiecient and profitable in their manufacturing and business practices through newsworthy information on technology; marketing and management trends and products and services.

17790 Paper, Paperboard and Wood Pulp Monthly Statistical Summary
American Forest and Paper Association
1111 19th Street
Suite 800
Washington, DC 20036-2603
202-632-2700
FAX: 202-463-2785 800-345-6372
info@afandpa.org
http://www.afandpa.org

Ben Slatin, Editor
Henson Moore, President

For the pulp and paper industry. *$435.00*

Monthly Founded: 1878

17791 Pulp & Paper Report
3G Publishing
12814 Bullock Greenway Boulevard
Charlotte, NC 28277
704-321-9227

3Gpublishing@carolina.rr.com
www.pulpandpaperreport.com

Alfred Walden, Publisher
Greg Fales, Editor

Features recent prices, production, inventory, and shipment information, in addition to visual charts and graphs. Keyed toward professionals in the paperboard industry. *$325.00*

8 pages Bi-Monthly Founded: 1979
Printed in 2 colors

17792 Recycled Paper News
McEntee Media Corporation
9815 Hazelwood Avenue
Cleveland, OH 44149-2305
440-238-6603
FAX: 440-238-6712
info@recycle.cc http://www.recycle.cc

Ken McEntee, Publisher

Coverage of markets and environmental issues related to recycled paper and evironmentally friendly paper making process. *$235.00*

Monthly Founded: 1990

17793 Solutions! for People, Processes and Paper
TAPPI and PIMA
15 Technology Parkway S
Norcross, GA 30092
770-446-1400
FAX: 770-446-6947 800-332-8686

Randy Loeser, Publisher
Glen Ostle, Editor-In-Chief

17794 TAPPI Journal
Technical Association of the Pulp & Paper Industry
15 Technology Parkway South
Norcross, GA 30092
770-446-1400
FAX: 770-446-6947 800-332-8686
jbottiglieri@tappi.org www.tappi.org

Mary Beth O Cornell, Publishing Director
Janice Bottiglieri, Editor
Wayne H Gross, President

Serves domestic and international pulp, paper, paperboard, packaging and converting industries; manufacturers and suppliers of machinery, equipment, chemicals and other material. *$350.00*

130 pages Monthly Founded: 1915
Circulation: 40637
Printed in 4 colors on glossy stock

17795 Walden's Paper Report
Walden-Mott Corporation
225 N Franklin Turnpike
Ramsey, NJ 07446-1630
201-818-8630
FAX: 201-818-8720 888-292-5336
editorial@walden-mott.com
http://www.walden-mott.com

Charles Walden, Marketing Manager
Linda Colhen, Circulation Manager
Alfred Walden, CEO/President

Reports on company expansions and general financial notes on the manufacturers, as well as personnel changes and appointments. Concise review of news on the North American paper industry. *$240.00*
8 pages Founded: 1884
Circulation: 500

Trade Shows

17796 Annual Information Technology Conference
PIMA-Paper Industry Management Association
4700 West Lake Avenue
Glenview, IL 60025-1485
847-375-6860
FAX: 877-527-5973
info@pimaweb.org
www.pimaweb.org

Carol Waugh, Meetings Manager

Three-day conference to bring together IT and process control professionals from around the world to share their knowledge of information technology in the pulp and paper industry and to promote systems applications. The only IT conference planned for and by IT professionals.
500 Attendees Annual, April

17797 International Environmental Conference and Exhibit
Technical Association of the Pulp & Paper Industry
15 Technology Parkway South
Norcross, GA 30092
770-446-1400
FAX: 770-446-6947 800-332-8686
awellborn@tappi.org www.tappi.org

Amanda Wellborn, Conferences & Symposia
Charlene Bridges, Exhibit/Trade Fair Sales

Fifty booths; pulp and paper environmental control equipment and consultants.
500 Attendees May

17798 National Paper Trade Association Convention Expo
National Paper Trade Association
111 Great Neck Road
Suite 418
Great Neck, NY 11021-5497
516-829-3070
FAX: 516-829-3074
bill@goNPTA.com www.gonpta.com

William Frohlich, President

Annual convention of 135 manufacturers, suppliers and distributors of paper products, including packaging materials, health care disposables, industrial and retail packaging supplies, sanitary supplies and computer equipment.
3000 Attendees Annual September
Founded: 1903

17799 National Stationery Show
George Little Management
10 Bank Street
White Plains, NY 10606-1954
914-486-6070
FAX: 914-948-6180 800-272-7469

Lori Robinson, VP
Kelly Bristol, Assistant Show Manager
George Little II, President

A show for greeting cards and social stationery, writing instruments and home office products, party ware and giftwrap, scrapbooking and craft supplies, albums, frames and much more.
14000 Attendees May

17800 National Trade Association Paper Plastics Allied Products Exposition
National Paper Trade Association
111 Great Neck Road
Suite 418
Great Neck, NY 11021-5402
516-829-3070

bill@goNPTA.com www.gonpta.com

William Frohlich, President

Industrial and retail packaging, computer products and supplies and equipment. 30 booths.
7M Attendees October

17801 Paper Industry Management Association
4700 West Lake Avenue
Glenview, IL 60025-1485
847-375-6860
FAX: 877-527-5973
info@pimaweb.org
www.pimaweb.org

Jim Weir, Executive Vice President/COO
Carol Waugh, Meetings Manager

Thirty-five booths.
500 Attendees June

17802 Paper, Plastics and Allied Products Exposition
National Paper Trade Association
111 Great Neck Road
Suite 418
Great Neck, NY 11021-5497
516-829-3070
FAX: 516-829-3074
bil@goNPTA.com www.gonpta.com

William Frohlich, President

Annual show and exhibits of industrial papers, plastics and plastic products allied to the paper industry.
7000 Attendees

17803 Pulp and Paper
Glahe International
PO Box 2460
Germantown, MD 20875-2460
301-515-0012
FAX: 301-515-0016 glahe@glahe.com
Exhibits of equipment, supplies and services for the pulp and paper industries.

Directories & Databases

17804 Association of Independent Corrugated Converters
113 South West Street
3rd Floor
Alexandria, VA 22314
703-836-2422
FAX: 703-836-2795 877-836-2422
info@aiccbox.org www.aiccbox.org

A Steven Young, President

Offers information on more than 750 firms in the corrugated container industry, including corrugators, sheet plants, and suppliers of machinery. *$150.00*
375 pages Annual

17805 Directory of Corrugated Plants
Fibre Box Association
2850 Golf Road
Suite 412
Rolling Meadows, IL 60008
847-364-9600
FAX: 847-364-9639
shuske@fibrebox.org
www.fibrebox.org

Sharlene Huske

Lists companies and their related plant facilities that manufacture corrugated and solid fiber paperboard products in North America. *$200.00*

17806 Grade Finder's Competitive Grade Finder
Grade Finders
622 Exton Commons
Exton, PA 19341
610-524-7070
FAX: 610-524-8912
info@gradefinders.com
www.gradefinders.com

Mark A Subers, President
Phyllis Subers, Office Manager

List of about 5500 manufacturers and distributors of paper. Also lists 6,000 grades of paper competitive classification. *$60.00*
700 pages Annual April Founded: 1967
ISBN 0-929502-14-0
Circulation: 13,000 6,000 names $100 per M.
Printed in 1 color on matte stock : diskette

17807 Grade Finder's Paper Buyers Encyclopedia
Grade Finders
622 Exton Commons
Exton, PA 19341
610-524-7070
FAX: 610-524-8912
info@gradefinders.com
www.gradefinders.com

Mark Subers, President

A list of about 6,700 manufacturers, converters and suppliers to the paper industry. In addition, it lists over 4,000 grades of paper categorized into competitive classifications showing each grades rating, opacity, color availability, etc. Also contains an extensive how-to buy paper section. *$150.00*
530 pages Annual
Circulation: 7000

17808 National Institute of Packaging, Handling and Logistic Engineers
6902 Lyle Street
Lanham, MD 20706-3454
301-459-9105
FAX: 301-459-4925
niphle@erols.com www.niphle.org
Engineers, chemists and executives are profiled in this comprehensive directory aimed at the packaging and shipping industry. *$ 80.00*
84 pages Annual

17809 PIMA Buyers Guide
Paper Industry Management Association
4700 W Lake Avenue
Glenview, IL 60025-1485
847-375-6860
FAX: 877-527-5973
info@pimaweb.org www.pimaweb.org

Jospeh Agnew, Editor
Pam Oddi, Editorial Support
Directory aimed at the paper and pulp industry offering various information on manufacturers of chemicals and supplies used in the manufacturing of paper. *$120.00*
60 pages Annual
Circulation: 2,000
Printed in on matte stock

17810 Paperboard Packaging Resource Directory
Advanstar Communications
131 W 1st Street
Duluth, MN 55802
218-723-9180
FAX: 218-723-9146 800-598-6008
info@avanstar.com
www.container-directory.com
Ester Derolski, Editor
Francis Heid, VP
New annual Paperboard Packaging Resource Directory delivers thousands of suppliers to your every packaging need — corregated, folding carton, ridgid box, and much more. *$175.00*
250 pages Annual

17811 Rauch Guide to the US and Canadian Pulp & Paper Industry
Grey House Publishing
PO Box 860
Millerton, NY 12546
518-789-8700
FAX: 518-789-0545 800-562-2139
books@greyhouse.com
www.greyhouse.com
Leslie Mackenzie, Publisher
Richard Gottlieb, President
Approximately 507 manufacturers of pulp, paper and converted products. *$595.00*
Annual

17812 TAPPI Membership Directory and Company Guide
Technical Association of the Pulp & Paper Industry
15 Technology Parkway South
Norcross, GA 30092
770-446-1400
FAX: 770-446-6947 800-332-8686
ecompton@tappi.org www.tappi.org
Elizabeth Compton, Editor
Clare Reagan, Corporate Relations
About 35,000 member executives, managers, engineers, technologists and superintendents in the pulp, paper, packaging, converting, non-wovens and allied industries. *$140.00*
October

17813 Walden's ABC Guide and Paper Production Yearbook
Walden-Mott Corporation
225 N Franklin Turnpike
Ramsey, NJ 07446-1600
201-818-8630
FAX: 201-818-8720
www.walden-mott.com
Lee Rusenian, Owner
Offers a large list of manufacturers and suppliers of printing papers. *$117.50*
300 pages Annual January

Industry Web Sites

17814 www.afandpa.org
American Forest and Paper Association

Serves forest, paper, paperboard and wood products packaging industry

17815 www.fibrebox.org
Fibre Box Association

For national corrigated manufacturers.

17816 www.fpi.org
Foodservice & Packaging Institute

Manufacturers, suppliers and distributors of one-time use products used for food service, as well as packaging products made from paper, plastic, aluminum and other materials. Membership dues based on sales.

17817 www.gonpta.com
National Paper Trade Association

Association for paper, packaging and applied products distribution channel.

17818 www.greyhouse.com
Grey House Publishing

Selected Grey House directories in the fields of business, health and education are available online. Users can search our online databases by several different search criteria, such as product categories, geographic area, sales volume and much, much more. Full Grey House catalog and online ordering also available.

17819 www.tappi.org
Technical Association of the Pulp & Paper Industry

Associations

17820 Actors Equity Association
165 West 46th Street
New York, NY 10036
212-869-8530
FAX: 212-719-9815
www.actorsequity.org
Steve DiPaola, Executive Director
Mark Zimmerman, President
David Lotz, National Director of Communications
Mary Lou Westerfield, Natioanl Director Policy
Flora Stamatiades, National Director Organizing
A labor union that represents Actors and Stage Managers in the United States. Seeks to advance, promote and foster the art of live theatre as an essential component of our society. Negotiates wages and working conditions and provides a wide range of benefits, including health and pension plans.
45000 Members Founded: 1913

17821 American Alliance for Theatre and Educatio n
7475 Wisconsin Avenue
Suite 300A
Bethesda, MD 20814
301-951-7977
FAX: 301-968-0144
info@aate.com www.aate.com
Steve Barberio, President
The national voice for theatre and education, representing artists and educators serving young people in theatre and education. Its members play a vital role in advocating for the interests of children who benefit from theatre in their communities and classrooms. AATE embraces diversity and encourages inclusion of all races, social classes, ages, genders, religions, sexual orientatiosn, national organizations and abilities.
700 Members Founded: 1986

17822 American Association of Community Theatre
8402 BriarWood Circle
Lago Vista, TX 78645
512-267-0711
FAX: 512-267-0712 866-687-2228
info@aact.org www.aact.org
Julie Angelo, Executive Director
Mary Britt, President
William P Muchow, Executive VP
Frank Peot, Secretary
Gary Walker, Treasurer
The national voice of community theatre, representing the interests of its members and over 7,000 theatres across the US and with the armed services overseas. Its mission is to foster the encouragement and development of, and commitment to, the highest standards by community theatres, including standards of excellence for production, management, governance, community relations and service.
1800 Members Founded: 1986

17823 American Dance Therapy Association
10632 Little Patuxent Parkway
2000 Century Plaza, Suite 108
Columbia, MD 21044-3273
410-997-4040
FAX: 410-997-4048
info@adta.org www.adta.org
Robyn Flaum Cruz, President
Sharon Goodhill, VP
Patricia P Capello, Secretary
Meg Chang, Treasurer
Professional organization of dance movement therapists, with members both nationally and internationally; offers training, research findings, and a newsletter. Holds annual conference.
1.1M Members Founded: 1966

17824 American Disc Jockey Association
20118 N 67th Avenue
Suite 300-605
Glendale, AZ 85308

888-723-5776
The AJDA is an association of professional mobile entertainers. Their mission is to encourage success for its members through continuous eduction, camaraderie, and networking. They believe that through involvement in this professional organization, DJs achieve more as a group than they can individually. The American Disc Jockey Asssociationg is an organization of PROFESSIONAL disc jockeys.
3000 Members

17825 American Federation of Musicians of the United States and Canada
1501 Broadway
Suite 600
New York, NY 10036
212-869-1330
FAX: 212-764-6134
info@afm.org www.afm.org
Thomas F Lee, President
Linda Patterson, Executive Secreatry to President
AFM is an associatin of professional musicians united through their locals so that they can live and work in dignity; produce work that will be fulfilling and compensated fairly; have a meaningful voice in decisions that affect them; have the opportunity to develop their talents and skills; whose collective voice and power will be realized in a democratic and progressive union; and who oppose the forces of exploitation through their union solidarity.
10K Members Founded: 1896

17826 American Indian Registry for the Performing Arts
1717 N Highland
Suite 614
Los Angeles, CA 90028
213-962-6574

Organization of American Indian performers and technical personnel in the entertainment field.

17827 American Institute of Organbuilders
PO Box 130982
Houston, TX 77219
713-529-2212
FAX: 713-529-2212
pipes@pipeorgan.org
www.pipeorgan.org
Sponsors training seminars, quarterly journal and annual convention for pipe organ builders and service technicians.
385 Members Founded: 1974
Mailing list available for rent 350 names $250 per M.

17828 Associated Pipe Organ Builders of America
PO Box 155
Chicago Ridge, IL 60415

800-473-5270
A professional association of North American firms engaged in building traditional pipe organs. Members are a select group of organbuilders who have passed stringent memembership requirements which include commitment to principles regarding the use of electronic technology in organ building.
27 Members

17829 Association for Theatre in Higher Education
PO Box 1290
Boulder, CO 80306-1290
303-530-2167
FAX: 303-530-2168 888-284-3737
info@athe.org www.athe.org
Karen Berman, President
ATHE serves the interests of its diverse individual and organization members. Its vision is to advocate for the field of theatre and performance in higher education. It serves as an intellectual and artistic center for producing new knowledge about theatre and performance-related disciplines. cultivating vital alliances with other scholarly and creative disciplines, linking with professional and community-based theatres, and promoting access and equity.
1700 Members Founded: 1986

17830 Association of Arts Administration Educato rs
Bolz Center for Arts Administration
975 University Avenue
Madison, WI 53706
608-263-4161
FAX: 608-265-2735
ataylor@bus.wisc.edu
www.artsadministration.org
Andrew Taylor, President/Director
John McCann, VP
Phyllis Johnson, Treasurer
Stephen Boyle, Secretary
The Association of Administration Educators (AAAE) is an international organization incorporated as a nonprofit institution within the United States. Its mission is to represent college and university graduate and undergraduate programs in the arts administration, encompassing training in the management of visual, performing, literary, media, cultural and arts service organizations.
Founded: 1975

17831 Association of Hispanic Arts
PO Box 1169
El Barrio, NY 10029-0312
212-876-1242
FAX: 212-876-1285 888-876-1240
informacion@latinoarts.org
www.latinoarts.org
Nicholas L Arture, Executive Director
Julia L Gutierrez-Rivera, Program Officer/Arts Service Coord.
Crystal Chaparro, Office Assistant
Gregory Castro, Comptroller
Brenda L Jiminez, Board Chair
A nonprofit arts service organization serving the Latino arts and cultural community. AHA was established out of the need to create funding and presenting opportunities for individual Latino artists and cultural organizations whose contributions were unrecognized and whose efforts were

underserved by mainstream public and private institutions.
Founded: 1975

17832 Association of Performing Arts Presenters
1112 16th Street NW
Suite 400
Washington, DC 20036
202-833-2787
FAX: 202-833-1543 888-820-2787
info@artspresenters.org
www.artspresenters.org
Lisa Booth, Chair
Anita Scism, Treasurer
Sandra Gibson, President/CEO
Mark Kimble, VP Finance/Operations
Susan Noseworthy, Membership Manager
1
A national membership and advocacy organization dedicated to bringing performing artists and audiences together.
1600 Members Founded: 1957

17833 Broadcast Music Incorporated
320 W 57th Street
New York, NY 10019-3790
212-586-2000
FAX: 212-245-8986
webmaster@bmi.com www.bmi.com
Del Bryant, President/CEO
John E Cody, COO/Executive VP
American performing rights organization that represents approximately 300,000 songwriters, composers and music publishers in all genres of music. The nonprofit company collects license fees on behalf of those American creators it represents, as well as thousands of creators from around the world who chose BMI for representation in the US. These fees are then distributed as royalties to the writers, composers and copyright holders it represents.
300m Members Founded: 1939

17834 Chinese Music Society of North America
PO Box 5275
Woodridge, IL 60517-0275
630-910-1551
FAX: 630-910-1561
www.chinesemusic.net
Sin-Yan Shen, President
Kok-Koon Ng, VP
Yuan-Yuan Lee, Executive Director
Billie Jefferson, Artistic Administrator
Der-Tung Yuan, Membership
A national nonprofit organization founded to increase and diffuse the knowledge of Chinese music and performing arts. Today it has grown to become the national association of Chinese musicians and scholars and National and International organization specializing in Research and Educational Material in English concerning Music/Theater/Dance and Musical Instruments from China and Non-Western Cultures.
Founded: 1969

17835 Cincinnati Arts Association
650 Walnut Street
Cincinnati, OH 45202-2517
513-721-3344
FAX: 513-977-4150
info@cincinnatiarts.org
www.cincinnstiarts.org
Steve Loftin, President & Executive Director
Van Ackerman, Director Marketing/Public Relations
Oversees the programming and management of two of the Tri-state's finest performing arts venues-the Arnoff Center for the Arts and Music Hall- and is dedicated to supporting performing and visual arts.
Founded: 1992

17836 Classical Action
165 W 46th Street
Suite 1310
New York, NY 10036
212-997-7717
FAX: 212-997-7897
classicalaction@bcefa.org
www.classicalaction.org
Charles Hamlen, Founding Director
Janice Mayer, Associate Director
Chris Kenney, Projects Coordinator
Since 1993, Classical Action has provided a unified voice for all those within the performing arts community to help combat HIV/AIDS and the devastating effects of this epidemic.
3 Members Founded: 1988

17837 Conductors Guild
5300 Glenside Drive
Suite 2207
Richmond, VA 23228
804-553-1378
FAX: 804-553-1876
guild@conductorsguild.net
www.conductorsguild.org
Tonu Kalam, President
Earl Groner, VP
Lisa M White, Secretary
Lawrence J Fried, Treasurer
Amanda Burton, Executive Director
The Guild is concerned with the art and the crage of conducting, with practical problems encountered within the profession, with repertoire, and with the multiple roles that Music Directors must fulfillin orchestras, choruses, opera and ballet compandies, wind ensembles, bands, musical theater, and other instrumental and voal ensembles, whether these are professional or amateur, functioning independently or within the context of colleges, universities, and seconday or primary schools.
2000 Members Founded: 1975

17838 Congress on Research in Dance
SUNY College of Brockport
Department of Dance
350 New Campus Drive
Brockport, NY 14420-2939
585-395-2590
FAX: 585-395-5134
gcarlson@brockport.edu
www.cordance.org
Ray Miller, President
Julie Malnig, Chair, Editorial Board
A not-for-profit, interdisciplinary organization with an open, international membership. Its purposes are: to encourage research in all aspects of dance, including related fields; to foster the exchange of ideas, resources, and methodology, through publication, international and regional conferences and workshops; to promote the accessibility of research materials. *$35.00*
750 Members Founded: 1965
Mailing list available for rent

17839 Country Dance & Song Society
132 Main Street
PO Box 338
Haydenville, MA 01039-0338
413-268-7426
FAX: 413-268-7471
office@cdss.org www.cdss.org
Brad Foster, Executive/Artistic Director
Carol Compton, Financial Manager
Robin Hayden, Memberhsip Services Coordinator
A national organization dedicated to the preservation and promotion of English and Anglo-American traditional and historical folk dance, music and song. Composed of individual members and affiliate groups, it functions both as an international service bureau and as a facilitator in building and maintaining local and regional dance, music and song communities. It exists to meed needs for community-based activity, for active participation, and for sharing and keeping historical and folk
3400 Members Founded: 1915

17840 Dance Critics Association
Old Chelsea Station
PO Box 1882
New York, NY 10011
732-643-4008

contactus@dancecritics.org
www.dancecritics.org
Kena Herod, Co-Chair
Linda Traiger, Co-Chair
Encourages excellence in dance criticism through education, research and the exchange of ideas. Produces quarterly newsletter. *$ 50.00*
300 Members Founded: 1974

17841 Dance Educators of America
340 5th Ane
Pelham, NY 10803
914-636-3200
FAX: 914-636-5895 800-329-3868
dea@deadance.com
www.deadance.com
Vickie Sheer, Executive Director
Vic D'Amore, President
Dedicated to improving the quality and teaching abilities of its member teachers and enhancing their education of students, as well as furthering the professional and ethical standards in the performing arts and of dance in all its form. Membership is limited to qualified teachers. *$150.00*
1800 Members Founded: 1932

17842 Dance Films Association
48 W 21st Street
#907
New York, NY 10010
212-727-0764
FAX: 212-727-0764
info@dancefilms.org
www.dancefilmsassn.org
Deirdre Towers, Artistic Director
Latika Young, Education Director
Anna Brady Nuse, Festival Coordinator
Julian Barnett, Research/Development
Supports all those professionals in both the dance and the film community. Publishes bi-monthly magazine. *$50.00*
Founded: 1956

17843 Dance Masters of America
PO Box 610533
Bayside, NY 11361
718-254-4013
FAX: 718-225-4293
dmamann@aol.com
www.dma-national.org
Mimi Costa-White, National President
Robert Mann, National Executive Secretary
Charleen Locascio, National Treasurer
An international organization of dance educators who have been certified by test to teach whose main focus is advancing the art

of dance and improving the practice of its teaching.
2.5M Members Founded: 1884

17844 Dance USA
1111 16th Street NW
Suite 300
Washington, DC 20036-4830
202-833-1717
FAX: 202-833-2686
danceusa@danceusa.org
www.danceusa.org

Andrea Snyder, Executive Director
Bob Fogelgren, Deputy Director
Ann Norris, Director Membership/Communications
Monica Reid, Administration Manager
Anne Dunning, Chair

Provides a forum for the discussion of issues of concern to members and a support network for exchange of information; also bestows awards.
400 Members Founded: 1982

17845 Dramatists Guild of America
1501 Broadway
Suite 701
New York, NY 10036
212-398-9366
FAX: 212-944-0420
igor@dramaguild.com
www.dramatistsguild.com

Ralph Sevush, Esq, Executive Director
Rebecca Frank, Director Business Affairs
Joel Szulc, Managing Director
Tom Epstein, Director Membership Services
John Minore, Executive Assistant

The Guild was established for the purpose of aiding dramatists in protecting both the artistic and economic integrity of their work. The Guild believes that vibrant, vital and proactive theater is an essential element of the ongoing cultural debate which informs the citizens of a free society. The Guild believes that if such a theater is to survive, the unique, ideosyncratic voices of the men and women who write for it must be cultivated and protected.
6000 Members

17846 Educational Theatre Association
2343 Auburn Avenue
Cincinnati, OH 45219
513-421-3900
FAX: 513-421-7055
info@edta.org www.edta.org

Michael J Peitz, Executive Director

EdTA's mission is to make theatre a part of lifelong learning. The Association's major areas of effort - educational development, teacher training, and advocacy - serve to accomplish this mission by helping to improve the learning environment in the theatre arts.
4000 Members Founded: 1929

17847 Esperanza Performing Arts Association
Po Box 502591
San Diego, CA 92150
858-391-1311

info@esperanzaarts.org
http://esperanzaarts.org

Alan Cox, Executive Director
Adam Stout, Assistant Director

17848 Fritz and Lavinia Jensen Foundation
Foundation for the Carolinas
217 S Tryon Street
Charlotte, NC 28202
704-973-4500
FAX: 704-973-4599
info@jensenfoundation.org
www.jensenfoundation.org

Ann Todd, Competition Coordinator

Sponsors voice competitions supporting opera and other classical singers.

17849 Gina Bachauer International Piano Foundati on
138 W Broadway
Suite 220
Salt Lake City, UT 84101
801-297-4250
FAX: 801-521-9202
gina@bachauer.com
www.bachauer.com

Paul Pollei, Founder/Artistic Director
Kimi Kawashima, Manager
Linda Harrison, Secretary
James Woolley, Treasurer

The mission of the Foundation is to further the pianistic art, foster excellence in performance and teaching, develop opportunities for pianists beyond the scope of the organization and offer leadership in developing a musically-educated citizenry.
Founded: 1976

17850 Guild of American Luthiers
8222 S Park Avenue
Tacoma, WA 98408-5226
253-472-7853
FAX: 253-472-7853
orders@luth.org www.luth.org

Debra Olsen, Executive Director
Tim Olsen, Editor
Kurt Kendall, Membership

Manufacturers and repairs stringed instruments; offers quarterly journal and triennial meeting. *$45.00*
3000 Members Founded: 1972

17851 International Association of Piano Builders and Technicians
Piano Technicians Guild
4444 Forest Avenue
Kansas City, MO 66106
913-432-9975
FAX: 913-432-9986
ptg@ptg.org www.ptg.org

Kent T Swafford, President
Dale E Probst, VP
Allan L Gilreath, Secretary/Treasurer
Barbara Cassaday, Executive Director
Jason Hensley, Finance

A nonprofit organization serving piano tuners, technicians, and craftsman throughout the world, organized to promote the highest possible service and technical standards among piano tuners and technicians.

17852 International Association of Round Dance Teachers
176 S Cole Road
Boise, ID 83709-0932
208-377-1232
FAX: 208-377-1236 800-346-7522
roundalab@roundalab.org
www.roundalab.org

Gil & Judy Martin, General Chairman
Brent & Judy Moore, Vice Chairman
Chuck & Becky Jaworski, Marketing Membership

Supports all those involved in the field of square dancing. Publishes quarterly magazine.

17853 International Computer Music Association
1819 Polk Street
Suite 390
San Francisco, CA 94109

FAX: 734-878-3031
icma@umich.edu
www.computermusic.org
An international affiliation of individuals and institutions involved in the technical, creative and performance aspects of computer music. It serves composers, engineers, researchers and musicians who are interested in the integration of music and technology. *$63.52*
700 Members

17854 International Festivals & Events Associati on
2601 Eastover Terrace
Boise, ID 83706
208-433-0950
FAX: 208-433-9812
webmaster@ifea.com www.ifea.com

Derrick Fox, Chair
Robyn Nelson, Secretary
Steve Schmader, President/CEO
Kaye Campbell, Senior Vice President
Julie Parke, Director Operations

The most complete source of ideas, information and networking for festival and event professionals, worldwide, currently serving members in 40 countries on 5 continents.
2000+ Members Founded: 1956

17855 International Planned Music Association
5900 S Salina Street
Syracuse, NY 13205
315-469-7711
FAX: 315-469-8842 www.ipmanet.com

Roy Salgado, President
Steve Seiden, VP
Larry Zaiser, Secretary
Jon Baker, Treasurer

IPMA is a trade organization made up of providers of planned and programmed music services and key vendors. The Associatin exists to provide members with a common ground on which to share informatio about running exciting, profitable franchises and to provide associate members with opportunities to expand their sales in markets all over the world.
200 Members

17856 International Society for the Performing A rts
17 Purdy Avenue, Suite 200
PO Box 909
Rye, NY 10580
914-921-1550
FAX: 914-921-1593
info@ispa.org www.ispa.org

Martha H Jones, Chair
Willem Brans, Treasurer
Horacio Lecona, Secretary
Johann Zietsman, CEO
Lynne Caruso, Membership Manager

A nonprofit organization of executives and directors of concert and performance halls, festivals, performing companies, and artists competitions; government cultural officials; artists' managers; and other interested parties with a professional involvement in the performing arts around the world, and in every arts disciplie. The purpose of ISPA is to develop, nurture, energize and educate an international network of arts leaders and professionals who are dedicated to advancing its field.

600 Members Founded: 1949

17857 International Theatre Equipment Associatio n

770 Broadway
5th Floor
New York, NY 10003-9595
646-654-7680
FAX: 646-654-7694
info@itea.com www.itea.com

Robert Sunshine, Executive Director
Barry Ferrell, President
Jack Panzeca, VP
Joe DeMeo, Treasurer
Sarah Fuller, Secretary

Fosters and maintains professional, business and social relationships among its members within all segments of the motion picture industry. Bestows annual Teddy Award to manufacturer of the year and the annual Rodney Award to dealer of the year.

$375.00

180 Members Founded: 1971

17858 International Ticketing Association

330 W 38th Street
#605
New York, NY 10018
212-629-4036
FAX: 212-629-8532
info@intix.org www.intix.org

Karen Sullivan, Board Chair
Jeffrey Larris, President
Robert Reicher, Secretary
Karen Kowgois, Treasurer

Nonprofit trade and professional organization committed to the advancement of admission services as an industry and professions.

1200 Members Founded: 1979

17859 Jazz Education

3303 South Rice, Suite 107
PO Box 8031
Houston, TX 77288
713-397-7800
FAX: 715-839-8266
jazzed@jazzedcation.org
www.jazzeducation.org

Tracy Scott, Executive Director

Nonprofit music organization providing worthwhile educational activities for school-aged youth in the field of music. Includes many subjects not covered by school systems. Promotes appreciation and understanding of Jazz.

Founded: 1970

17860 League of American Theatres and Producers

226 W 47th Street
6th Floor
New York, NY 10036
212-764-1122
FAX: 212-944-8229
league@broadway.org
www.livebroadway.com

Charlotte St Martin, Executive Director
Colin Gibson, Director Finance
Jane Svendsen, Director Marketing
Ed Sandler, Director Membership Services

National trade association for the commercial theatre industry whose principal activity is negotiation of labor contracts and government relations.

400 Members Founded: 1930

17861 League of Historic American Theatres

334 N Charles Street
2nd Floor
Baltimore, MD 21201-4301
410-659-9533
FAX: 410-837-9664 877-627-0833
info@lhat.org www.lhat.org

Dulcie Grlmore, President
James A Boese, VP
Lance Olson, Treasurer
Harry Scanlan, Secretary
Fran Holden, Executive Director

An international nonprofit membership organization which serves as a network of people who appreciate the cultural and architectural heritage of historic theatres and who work locally and nationally to rehabilitate them to serve communities throughout North America and abroad.

500+ Members Founded: 1976

17862 Literary Managers and Dramaturgs of the Americas

PO Box 728
New York, NY 10014
212-561-0315

lmdanyc@hotmail.com www.lmda.org

Liz Engelman, Chair
Brian Quirt, President
Louise McKay, Administrative Director
Daniella Topol, Treasurer

The mission of the LMDA is to affirm the role of dramaturg, to expande the possibilities of the field to other media and institutions and to cultivate, develop and promote the function of dramaturgy and literary management.

500 Members

17863 Mid Atlantic Arts Foundation

201 N Charles Street
Suite 401
Baltimore, MD 21201
410-539-6656
FAX: 410-837-5517
info@midatlanticarts.org
www.midatlanticarts.org

Lisa Frigand, Chair
Anthony Gittens, Secretary
Alan W Cooper, Executive Director
Tom Gaeng, Director Operations
Bunky Market, Financial Officer

MAAF celebrates, promotes and supports the richness and diversity of the region's art resources and works to increase access to the arts and other cultures of the region and the world.

40000 Members Founded: 1979

Mailing list available for rent 30,000 names

17864 Music Distributors Association

1026 Northwood Drive
Effingham, IL 62401
217-347-6699
FAX: 217-347-6699
geobev@consolidated.net
www.musicdistributors.org

An international nonprofit trade association representing and serving manufacturers, wholesalers, importers and exporters of musical instruments and accessories, sound reinforcement products and published music.

$675.00

Founded: 1939

17865 National Association for Drama Therapy

15 Post Side Lane
Pittsford, NY 14534
585-381-5618
FAX: 585-383-1474
answers@nadt.org www.nadt.org

Barbara McKechnie, President
Kate Hurd, VP
Juliette Zaiser, Secretary
Red Rubenstein, Treasurer
Nancy Sondag, Membership

A nonprofit association which establishes and upholds high standards of professional competence and ethics among drama therapists; to develop criteria for training and registration; to sponsor publications and conferences; and to promote the profession of drama therapy through information and advocacy.

Founded: 1979

17866 National Association for Music Education

1806 Robert Fulton Drive
Reston, VA 20191
703-860-4000
FAX: 703-860-1531 800-336-3768

Lynn M Brinckmeyer, President

The mission of MENC is to advance music education by encouraging the study and making of music by all. MENC offers more than 100 books, videos and compact discs, as well as two general-interest magazines on music education and four more closely targeted journals.

Founded: 1907

Mailing list available for rent 60,000 names

17867 National Association of Theatre Owners

PO Box 77318
Washington, DC 20013-8318
202-962-0054
FAX: 202-962-0370
nato@natodc.com www.natoonline.org

Philip Harris III, Chairman
John Fithiann, President/CEO
Mark O'Meara, Secretary
Kurt Hall, Treasurer
Mary Ann Anderson, Executive Director

NATO represents more than 25,000 music screens in all 50 states, and additional cinemas in more than 40 countries. Membership includes a subscription to IN FOCUS a monthly magazine as well as THE ENCYLOPEDIA OF EXHIBITION published annually. Members also receive members-onlu update reports on legislation and technology developments, as well as distribution and marketing policies.

Founded: 1948

17868 National Costumers Association

121 N Bosart Avenue
Indianapolis, IN 46201-3729
317-351-1940
FAX: 317-351-1941 800-622-1321
office@costumers.org
www.costumers.org

Debbie Lyn Owens, President
Nancy Cox, First Vive President
Adrienne Anderson, Second VP
Jennifer Skarstedt, Secretary/Treasurer

The objectives on the NCA are to establish and maintain professional and ethical standards of business in the costume industry. They encourage and promote a greater and more diversified use of costumes in all fields of human activity. They provide trade information, cooperation and friendship

among its members together with a sound public relations policy.
400 Members Founded: 1923

17869 National Dance Association
1900 Association Drive
Reston, VA 20191-1598
703-476-3436
FAX: 703-476-9527 800-213-7193
nda@aahperd.org
www.aahperd.org/nda

Nancy Brooks Schmitz, President
Marcey E Siegel, VP Dance Education
Mary Ann Laverty, VP Dance Performance
Molly Snell, Vice Pricent Dance Science/Somatics

A nonprofit service organization dedicated to increasing knowledge, improving skills and encouraging sound professional practices in dance education while promoting and supporting creative and healthy lifestyles through high quality dance programs.
2000 Members Founded: 1932

17870 National Dance Education Organization
Department of Dance
4948 St Elmo Avenue
#301
Bethesda, MD 20814
301-657-2880
FAX: 301-657-2882
info@ndeo.org www.ndeo.org

Dale Schmid, MEd, President
Jane Bonbright, EdD, Executive Director
Doug Risner, PhD, Secretary
Mary Burns, Treasurer

A nonprofit organization dedicated to promoting standards of excellence in dance education by promoting standards of excellence in dance education by providing the dance artists and the dance educator a network of resources and support, a base for advocacy, and access to programs and projects that focus on the importance of dance in the human experience. *$95.00*
Founded: 1998

17871 National Endowment for the Arts
1100 Pennsylvania Avenue NW
Washington, DC 20506-0001
202-682-5400

webmgr@arts.endow.gov
www.arts.endow.gov

Dana Gioia, Chairman
Guilomar Barbi, Scheduler
Sarah Cook, Executive Assistant
Jon P Peede, Counselor to the Chairman
Sydney Smith, Administrative Specialist

The National Endowment for the Arts, an investment in America's living heritage, serves the public good by nurturing the expression of human creativity, supporting the cultivation of community spirit, and fostering the recognition and appreciation of the excellence and diversity of our nation's artistic accomplishments.

17872 National Music Publishers Association
101 Constitution Avenue NW
Suite 705 East
Washington, DC 20001
202-742-4375
FAX: 202-742-4377
pr@nmpa.org www.nmpa.org

David M Israelite, President/CEO
John Eastman, Director

The NMPA is committed to promoting and advancing the interests of music publishers and their songwriting partners. Their goal is to foster a business climate that allows its members to thrive creatively and financially.
800 Members Founded: 1917

17873 National Piano Manufcaturer Association
5960 W Parker Road
Suite 278 #233
Plano, TX 75093-7792
972-625-0110
FAX: 972-625-0110 www.pianonet.com

Piano industry trade association.
Founded: 1891

17874 National Piano Travelers Association
401 Sawkill Road
PO Box 2264
Kingston, NY 12401-2264
845-338-1464
FAX: 845-338-5751

Bob Smith, President

Buys and sells pianos.
110 Members

17875 New England Theatre Conference
215 Knob Hill Drive
Hamden, CT 06518
617-851-8535
FAX: 203-288-5938
mail@netconline.org
www.netconline.org

John Quinn, President
Jeffrey Watts, Executive VP
Charkes Emmons, VP Administration/Finance
David Frieze, VP Communication/Development
Ann Marie Shea, Secretary

Non-profit corporation, composed of individuals and organizations in the six-State region of New England, who are active and interested in the performing arts. The NETC promotes excellence in theatre for their region, and supports quality theatre and performance in all of its diversity.
500 Members Founded: 1952

17876 North American Performing Arts Managers an d Agents
459 Columbus Avenue
Suite 133
New York, NY 10024
212-799-5308

info@napama.org www.napama.org

Mark Baylin, President
Laura Colby, VP
Eleanor Oldham, VP
Barrie Steinberg, Secretary
Jennifer Morris, Treasurer

National not-for-profit trade association dedicated to promoting the professionalism of its members and the vitality of the performing arts. NAPAMA promotes the mutual advancement and the best interests of performing arts managers and agents; promotes open discourse among members and within the larger field; gives active consideration and expression of opinion on questions affecting the industry and develops and encourages ethical and sound business practices. *$150.00*
Founded: 1979

17877 Oratorio Society of New York
Carnegie Hall
881 7th Avenue, Suite 1204
New York, NY 10019-3321
212-247-4199

president@oratoriosocietyofny.org
www.oratoriosocietyofny.org

Ellen L Blair, Chairwoman
Richard A Pace, President
Marie Gangemi, Treasurer
Jay Jacobson, Secretary
Kent Tritle, Music Director

New York City's second oldest cultural organization. On December 25, 1874 the society began what has become an unbroken tradition of annual performances of Handel's 'Messiah" (at Carnegie Hall since its opening in 1891).
Founded: 1873

17878 Performing Arts Association
719 Edmond Street
St Joseph, MO 64501
816-279-1225

info@paastjo.org www.paastjo.org

David Waller, President
William Wright, VP

Mission is to provide a diverse selection of performing arts in the St Joseph area by presenting programs, which foster, increase and promote public knowledge and appreciation of music, theatre and dance and lectures on subjects of cultural interests.

17879 Performing Arts Medicine Association
Po Box 61228
Denver, CO 80206
303-632-9255

artsmed@comcast.net
www.artsmed.org

Mary Fletcher, Executive Director

Organization for physicians and other professionsl persons who are involved in treatment and/or research in the field of Performing Arts Medicine.
Founded: 1989

17880 Production Music Library Association
8551 Research Way
Suite 180
Middleton, WI 53562
608-836-5825
FAX: 608-831-8200
mla@areditions.com
www.musiclibraryassoc.org

Bonna Boettcher, President

Provides a forum for issues surrounding music, music in libraries, and music librarianship. Members include music librarians, librarians who work with music as part of their responsibilities, composers and music scholars, and others interested in the program of the association.
20 Members Founded: 1931

17881 Professional Women Singers Association
PO Box 884
New York, NY 10024
212-969-0590
FAX: 928-395-2560
info@womensingers.org
www.womensingers.org

Elissa Weiss, President
Allison Atteberry, First VP
Sarah Downs, Second VP
Ruth Ann Cunningham, Secretary
Mary Lou Zobel, Treasurer

Non-profit networking organization for professional women singers. The group sponsors concerts, master classes and seminars for both singers and the community at large.
40 Members Founded: 1982

17882 Screen Actors Guild
5757 Wilshire Boulevard
Los Angeles, CA 90036-3600
323-954-1600
www.sag.org

Alan Rosenberg, President
Kent McCord, First VP
Paul Christie, Second VP
Steve Fried, Third Vice President
Connie Stevens, Secretary/Treasurer

Labor union affiliated with AFL-CIO which represents actors in film, television and commercials. The Guild exists to enhance actors' working conditions, compensation and benefits and to be a powerful, unifed voice on behalf of artists' rights.
120M Members Founded: 1933

17883 Society of American Magicians
PO Box 510260
Saint Louis, MO 63151-0260
314-846-5659
FAX: 314-846-5659
rmblowers@aol.com
www.magicsam.com

Andy Dallas, President
Bruce Kalver, First VP
Mike Miller, Second VP
Chuck Lehr, Secretary
Mary Ann Blowers, Treasurer

Founded to promote and maintain harmonious fellowship among those interested in magic as an art, to improve ethics of the magical profession, and to foster, promote and improve the advancement of magical arts in the field of amusement and entertainment. Membership includes professional and amateur magicians, manufacturers of magical apparatus and collectors.
5.5M Members Founded: 1902

17884 Society of Stage Directors and Choreograph ers
1501 Broadway
Suite 1701
New York, NY 10036-5653
212-391-5204
FAX: 212-302-6195 800-541-5204
info@ssdc.org www.ssdc.org

Pamela Berlin, President
Sue Lawless, Secretary
Doug Hughes, Treasurer
Barbara Hauptman, Executive Director
Gretchen M Michelfeld, Membership Coordinator

An independent labor union representing directors and choreographers in American theatre.
1700 Members Founded: 1959

17885 Southern Arts Federation
1800 Peachtree Street NW
Suite 808
Atlanta, GA 30309
404-874-7244
FAX: 404-873-2148 www.southarts.org

Margaret Newman, Chair
Scott Shanklin-Peterson, Secretary
Richard Ranta, Treasurer
Gerri Combs, Executive Director
David Batley, Marketing/Communications Director

In partnership with nine state arts agencies: promotes and supports arts regionally, nationally and internationally; enhances the artistic excellence and professionalism of Southern Arts Organizations and artists; serves the diverse population of the south.
Founded: 1975

17886 Theatre Authority
6464 W Sunset Boulevard
Suite 590
Los Angeles, CA 90028-8008
323-462-5761

Presides over theatrical agencies and performing arts organizations.

17887 Theatre Bay Area
Theatre Bay Area
870 Market Street
Suite 375
San Francisco, CA 94102-3002
415-430-1140
FAX: 415-430-1145
tba@theatrebayarea.org
www.theatrebayarea.org

Brad Erickson, Executive Director
Dale Albrightk, Director Individual Services
Trevor Allen, Director Company Services
Rebecca Novik, Development Manager
Cara Chrisman, Director Ticketing Services

Theatre Bay Area's mission is to unite, strengthn and promote the theatre community in the San Francisco Bay Area, working on behalf of their conviction that the performing arts are an essential public good, critical to a healthy and truly democratic society, and invaluabel as a source of personal enrichment and growth.
3,000 Members Founded: 1976 $65 per M.

17888 Theatre Communications Group
520 8th Avenue
24th Floor
New York, NY 10018-4156
212-609-5900
FAX: 212-609-5901
tcg@tcg.org www.tcg.org

Gina Bolt, Interim Executive Director
Elizbeth Morrow Selfridge, Director Finance/Administration
Jennifer Cleary, Director of Membership
Leigh A Zona, Director Marketing
Martha Neighbors, Director of Development

The mission of the TCG is to strengthen, nurture and promote the professional not-for-profit American theatre. TCG believes that their diversity as a field is their greatest strength. They celebrate differences in aesthetic, culture, organizational structure, and geography. They believe that every theatre makes a contribution to the greater field as a whole, that every performance expands the artistic vocabulary for us all, and that we all benefit from one another's presence. *$39.95*
17000 Members Monthly Founded: 1961

17889 Theatre Development Fund
1501 Broadway
21st Floor
New York, NY 10036-5652
212-210-0013

info@tdf.org www.tdf.org
Not-for-profit service organization for the performing arts. TDF administers a wide range of audience development and financial assistance programs that encourage production of new plays and musicals and enable more New Yorkers and visitors to enjoy the riches and variety of the city's theatre, dance and music. *$25.00*
Founded: 1968

17890 Theatre Library Association
Shubert Archive 149 West 45th Street
New York, NY 10036

http://tla.library.unt.edu

Martha S LoManaco, President
Kenneth Schlesinger, VP
Nancy E Friedland, Secretary
Paul Newman, Treasurer

The Association supports librarians and archivists affiliated with theatre, dance, performance studies, popular entertainment, motion picture and broadcasting collections. TLA promotes professional best practices in acquistionm, organization, access and preservation of performing arts resources in libraries, archives, museums, private collections, and the digital environment.
500 Members Founded: 1937

17891 US Institute for Theatre Technology

6443 Ridings Road
Syracuse, NY 13206-1111
315-463-6463
FAX: 315-463-6525 800-938-7488
info@office.usitt.org www.usitt.org

Sylvia Hillyard Pannell, President
Patricia Dennis, Secretary
Lawrence J Hill, Treasurer
Barbara E R Lucas, Public Relations/Marketing
Michelle L Smith, Membership Manager

Association of design, production and technology professionals in the performing arts and entertainment industry whose mission is to promote the knowledge and skills of its members. International in scope, USITT draws its board of directors from across the US and Canada. Sponsors projects, programs, research, symposia, exhibits and annual conference. Disseminates information on aesthetic and technical developments.
3700 Members Founded: 1960

17892 United States Amateur Ballroom Dancers
Central Office
PO Box 152988
Cape Coral, FL 33915-2988

FAX: 239-573-0946 800-447-9047
central-office@usabda.org
www.usabda.org

Esther Freeman, National President
Stan Andrews, Senior VP
Daphna Locker, National Secretary
Leland Andrew, National Treasurer

Nonprofit organization working to promote ballroom dancing, both as a recreational activity and as a competitive sport.
23000 Members Founded: 1965

17893 Women in the Arts Foundation
C/O E Butler
32-35 30th Street
D24
Long Island City, NY 11106
212-941-0130

reginas@anny.org
www.anny.org/2/orgs/womeninarts/

Regina Stewart, Executive Director
Eric Butler, Executive Coordinator
Linda Butti, Executive Coordinator
Sari Menna, Financial Coordinator

WIA works to overcome discrimination against women artists. They provide information to help women function effectively as professional artists. WIA is open to all women interested in the arts.

150 Members Founded: 1971

Newsletters

17894 American Dance
Canal Street Station
PO Box 2001
New York, NY 10013
212-932-2789

info@americandanceguild.org
www.americandanceguild.org

Deborah Mauldin, President

Contains articles on member news, dance, and education.

4 per year Founded: 1956

17895 Artsearch
Theatre Communications Group
520 8th Avenue
24th Floor
New York, NY 10018-4156
212-609-5900
FAX: 212-609-5901
tcg@tcg.org www.tcg.org

Artsearch is divided into five main categories: Administration, Artistic, Production/Design, Career Development, and Education. *$ 75.00*

Bi-Monthly Founded: 1961
Printed in on newsprint stock

17896 Broadside
Theatre Library Association
C/O New York Public Library for Performing Arts
40 Lincoln Center Plaza
New York, NY 10023

http://tla.library.unt.edu

Nancy Friedland, Executive Secretary

Available only to members of the Theatre Library Association. Fosters creative and ethical use of performing arts materials to enhance research, live performance, and scholarly communication.

Monthly Founded: 1937

17897 Country Dance and Song Society News
Country Dance and Song Society
132 Main Street
PO Box 338
Haydenville, MA 01039-0338
413-268-7426
FAX: 413-268-7471
news@cdss.org www.cdss.org

Caroline Batson, Editor
Bradley Foster, Executive Director

A selection of articles, letters and poems. CDSS News is available as a benefit of membership in the Country Dance and Song Society.

Founded: 1915

17898 DNBulletin
151 W 30th Street
Suite 202
New York, NY 10001
212-564-0985
FAX: 212-216-9027
dnbinfo@dancenotation.org
www.dancenotation.org

Senta Driver, Editor

Dance news for consumers and professionals.

Founded: 1940
Printed in 2 colors on matte stock

17899 Dancedrill
3101 Poplarwood Court
Suite 310
Raleigh, NC 27604-1010
919-872-7888
FAX: 919-872-6888

Susan Wershing, Publisher
Kay Crawford, Editor

Publication informs members of dance drill teams and their directors.

4 per year

17900 Dramatists Guild Newsletter
Dramatists Guild of America
1501 Broadway
Suite 701
New York, NY 10036-3909
212-398-9366
FAX: 212-944-0420
www.dramaguild.com

Jeff Zadroga, Editor

Supplement to 'The Dramatist,' available only to Guild members, includes bi-monthly reports from New York and Los Angeles, advice from the Business Affairs Department, the latest information on submission and career development opportunities, and reminders of approaching deadlines.

17901 INTIX Bulletin
International Ticketing Association
330 W 38th Street
Suite 605
New York, NY 10018
212-629-4036
FAX: 212-629-8532
info@intix.org www.intix.org

E-bulletin provides news from the International Ticketing Association

Founded: 1980
Printed in 4 colors on glossy stock

17902 In Theater
Parker Publishing & Communications
1501 Broadway
#2605
New York, NY 10036-5601
212-869-6350
FAX: 212-719-4477 intheater@aol.com

Michael Parker, Publisher

Offers the reader a behind-the-scenes perspective of how a show is technically conceived, rehearsed and staged. Regular departments center on drama and musical reviews, listings of shows in major cities and columnist options. *$78.00*

Weekly
Circulation: 71,068

17903 Job Contact Bulletin
Southeastern Theatre Conference
1217 W Bessemer Avenue
PO Box 9868
Greensboro, NC 27429-0868
336-272-3645
FAX: 336-272-8810
arpil@setc.org www.setc.org

April J'C Marshall, Contact
April Marshall, Editor

On-line employment listing of Classified Ads for theatrical positions, auditions, and more.

Founded: 1949

17904 Performing Arts Insider
PAI C/O Total Theater
PO Box 62
Hewlett, NY 11557-0062
516-295-1511
800-536-0099
totalpost@totaltheater.com
www.totaltheater.com

A leading source of information about the perfoming arts in New York City and around the country. Each issue includes day-by-day calendar listings of shows on broadway, off and off-off broadway, plus dance, opera, cabaret and special events. Also includes comprehensive theatre guides, listing the author, director, cast, designers, synopsis, theater and box office details, as well as contact information for producers, press agents, general managers and casting directors. *$275.00*

Monthly+9 Mid-Month Updat Founded: 1944
Printed in on matte stock

17905 SETC News
Southeastern Theatre Conference
1217 W Bessemer Avenue
PO Box 9868
Greensboro, NC 27429
336-272-3645
FAX: 336-272-8810
deanna@setc.org.net www.setc.org

Deanna Thompson, Editor

Provides news and important information to members of the Southeaster Theatre Conference on upcoming SETC events, advocacy efforts, awards and competitions as well as items of special interest to the various divisions and interest areas. In addition, SETC News publishes news about people and organizations based in the Southeast.

Founded: 1949
Circulation: 4000

17906 Spotlight
American Association of Community Theatre
8402 Briar Wood Circle
Lago Vista, TX 78645-4118
512-267-0711
FAX: 512-267-0712 866-687-2228
info@aact.org www.aact.org

Julie Angelo, Executive Director
John Sullivan, President

News and updates on issues pertinent to community theatre. *$2.00*

24 pages Founded: 1958
Circulation: 2000
Mailing list available for rent 9,500 names $180 per M.
Printed in on matte stock

17907 **Technical Brief**
Yale School of Drama
222 York Street
PO Box 208244
New Haven, CT 06520
203-432-9664
FAX: 203-432-8332
bronislaw.sammler@yale.edu
www.technicalbrief.org

Ben Sammler, Editor
Dan Harvey, Editor

Produced for technical managers in theater. Written by professionals for professionals, its purpose is simple: communication. Technical Brief provides a dailogue between technical practitioners from the several performing arts who all share similar problems. *$15.00*
3 X Year Founded: 1924

17908 **Women in the Arts Bulletin**
Women in the Arts Foundation
32-35 30th Street
D24
Long Island City, NY 11106
212-941-0130

reginas@anny.org www.anny.org

Erin Butler, Editor
Regina Stewart, Executir Director
Sandra Cockerham, President

Gallery information and reviews. Women in the Arts Foundation works to overcome discrimination against women artists.
Monthly Founded: 1971

17909 **inLEAGUE**
League of Historic American Theatres
334 B Charles Street
2nd Floor
Baltimore, MD 21201
410-659-9533
FAX: 410-837-9664 877-627-0833
info@lhat.org www.lhat.org
Quarterly newsletter which reports news from historic theatre progects around the country and features articles on all facets of historic theatre restoration and operation. The newsletter solicits articles and information from the membership.
Quarterly Founded: 1976

Magazines & Journals

17910 **American Theatre Magazine**
Theatre Communications Group
520 Eighth Avenue
24th Floor
New York, NY 10018-4156
212-609-5900
FAX: 212-609-5902
custserve@tcg.org www.tcg.org

Jim O'Quinn, Editor in Chief
Sarah Hart, Managing Editor
Randy Gener, Senior Editor
Nicole Estvanik, Associate Editor
Cassandra Johnson, Play Editor

A vital repository of information for anyone and everyone concerned with contemporary theatre. Speaks to actors and directors, producers and artistic directors, teachers and students, designers and technicians, writers and dramaturges, theatre administrators, theatre lovers and more. Provides sophisticated insight and in-depth reporting that informs and inspires. A forum where artists talk about their work and reflect on the creative process itself and what it means to be an artist. *$39.95*
64 pages
Circulation: 17,000
Printed in 4 colors

17911 **Applause Magazine**
Denver Center for Performing Arts
1101 13th Street
Denver, CO 80204
303-893-4000
FAX: 303-575-0080 800-641-1222
A publication of the Denver Center Theatre Company and Dever Center Attractions
8-10 per year Founded: 1988
Printed in 4 colors on glossy stock

17912 **Asian Pacific American Journal**
Asian American Writers Workshop
16 W 32nd Street
Suite 10A
New York, NY 10001-3814
212-494-0061
FAX: 212-494-0062
desk@aaww.org www.aaww.org

Quang Bal, Executive Director
Jeannie L Wong, Adminstrative Director
Anjali Goyal, Programs Assistant
Jeffrey Lin, Designer
Hanya Yanagihara, Journal Editor

Features include short fiction, poems, essays, stage scripts, translations and artwork.
Semi-Annual Founded: 1992

17913 **Back Stage**
770 Broadway
4th Floor
New York, NY 10003
646-654-5700
FAX: 646-654-5744
advertising@backstage.com
www.backstage.com

Steve Elish, Publisher
Jamie Painter Young, Editor-in-Chief
Jenelle Riley, Film/TV Editor
Leonard Jacobs, Theatre Editor
Sherry Eaker, Editor-at-Large

Four print, four interactive and two face-to-face publications. Provides casting, news, articles and other resources for working actors, cingers, dancers and behind-the-scenes staff and crew. *$84.00*
Founded: 1960
Circulation: 30,000

17914 **Bomb Magazine**
New Art Publications
80 Hanson Place
Suite 703
New York, NY 11217-3233
718-636-9100
FAX: 212-431-5880 866-354-0334
info@bombsite.com
www.bombsite.com

Betsy Sussler, Publisher/Editor
Mary-Ann Monforton, Associate Publisher
Nell McClister, Senior Editor
Lucy Raven, Managing Editor
Paul W Morris, Director Marketing/Special Projects

Focuses on contemporary art, literature, theater, film, music. *$495.00*
Quarterly Founded: 1981
Circulation: 60,000
Printed in 4 colors on matte stock

17915 **Boxoffice**
PO Box 1634
Des Plaines, IL 60019
212-627-7000
FAX: 626-396-0248
editorial@boxoffice.com
www.boxoffice.com

Peter Cane, Publisher
Anlee Ellingson, Editor
Francesca Dinglasan, Senior Editor
Bob Vale, VP Advertising/Sales

Authoritative voice on The Business of Movies since before talkies. *$59.95*
Monthly Founded: 1920
Printed in on glossy stock

17916 **Callaloo**
Johns Hopkins University Press
2715 N Charles Street
Baltimore, MD 21218-4363
410-516-6900
FAX: 410-516-6968 800-537-5487

Charles H Rowell, Editor/Publisher
Kyle G Dargan, Managing Editor

Journal of African and African-American issues. Content includes original works by, and critical studies of, black writers worldwide. Offers a rich mixture of fiction, poetry, plays, critical essays, cultural studies, interviews, and visual art, as well as special thematic issues.
Quarterly Founded: 1976
Circulation: 2,500

17917 **Canadian Theatre Review**
University of Toronto Press
5201 Dufferin Street
Toronto, ON M3H-5T8
416-667-7777
FAX: 416-667-7881
journals@utpress.utoronto.ca
www.utpjournals.com

Anne Marie Corrigan, VP
Audrey Greenwood, Advertising/Marketing Coordinator

Provides critical analysis and innovative coverage of current developments in Canadian theatre. Advocates new issues and artists. Publishes at least one significant new playscript per issue. Each issue includes at least one complete playscript related to the issue theme, insightful articles, and informative reviews. *$40.00*
Quarterly Founded: 1974
Mailing list available for rent $250 per M.

17918 **Confrontation**
CW Post Campus English Department
Long Island University
720 Northern Boulevard
Brookville, NY 11548-1300
516-299-2720
FAX: 516-299-2735
confrontation@liu.edu
www.cwpost.liu/cwis/cwp/clas/english/confrontation
Brings new talent to light in the shadows cast by well-known authors. Each issue contains orignal work by famous and by lesser known writers. *$10.00*
Twice Yearly Founded: 1968

17919 **Contact Quarterly Journal of Dance and Improvisation**
Contact Collaborations
PO Box 603
Northampton, MA 01061
413-586-1181
FAX: 413-586-9055
info@contactquarterly.com
www.contactquarterly.com

Lisa Nelson, Co-Editor
Nancy Stark Smith, Co-Editor
Melinda Buckwalter, Associate Editor
Kristin Horrigan, Operations Manager/Advertising
Bill McCully, Development/Marketing

A journal of dance, improvisation, performance and contemporary movement arts. Presents materials that spring from the experience of doing. Encourages articulation and dialogue and stimulates activity and exploration within the field of movement and its performance. *$22.00*

BiAnnual Founded: 1975

17920 Cue Magazine
PO Box 2027
Burlingame, CA 94011-2027
415-348-8004
FAX: 650-348-7781
Devoted to the Northern California, Seattle and Portland commercial film, video and multimedia industries and locations that support production.
Monthly

17921 Dance Chronicle
Taylor & Francis Group
270 Madison Avenue
Floor 4
New York, NY 10016-0671
212-216-7800
FAX: 212-244-1563
www.routledge-ny.com

George Dorris, Co-Editor
Jack Anderson, Co-Editor
Edwin Bayrn, Associate Editor
Barbara Palfy, Associate Editor

Covers a wide variety of topics, including dance and music, theater, film, literature, painting and aesthetics. *$465.00*

TriAnnual

17922 Dance Magazine
110 William Street
23rd Floor
New York, NY 10038
646-459-4800
FAX: 646-459-4900
dancemag@dancemagazine.com
www.dancemagazine.com

Karla Johnson, Publisher
Wendy Perron, Editor-in-Chief
DeDe Pochos, Associate Publisher/Sales
Jessie Petrov, Publishing Manager

Provides entertaining, beautiful, up-to-date, in-the-know information for serious and aspiring dancers, dance teachers and professionals. *$34.95*

Monthly Founded: 1927
Circulation: 300,000
Printed in 4 colors on glossy stock

17923 Dance Research Journal
University of North Carolina at Greensboro
Deparment of Dance
323 HHP Building, PO Box 26170
Greensboro, NC 24702-6170
336-334-3266

drj@uncg.edu www.cordance.org

Ann Dils, Co-Editor
Jill Green, Co-Editor

Published twice a year by the Congress on Research in Dance, this journal carries scholarly articles, book reviews, lists of books and journals received, and reports of scholarly conferences, archives and other projects of interest to the field. *$65.00*

Bi-annually Founded: 1965
Mailing list available for rent 750+ names
$75 per M.

17924 Dance Spirit
McFadden Performing Arts Media
110 William Street
23rd Floor
New York, NY 10038
616-459-4800
FAX: 646-459-4900
www.dancespirit.com

Michael Weiskopf, President
Mary Evelyñ Holder, Associate Publisher

Provides training tips, advice from experts, exercises designed for dancers, combinations and competition news and results.
$16.95

10 Per Year Founded: 1980

17925 Dance Teacher Magazine
Macfadden Performing Arts Media
110 William Street
23rd Floor
New York, NY 10038
646-459-4800
FAX: 646-459-4900
www.dance-teacher.com

Karla Johnson, President
Jessie Petrov, Publishing Manager
Dede Pochos, Associate Publisher/Sales

A magazine for professional dance educators, senior students, and other professionals on practical information for the teacher and/or business owner, economic and historical issues related to the profession. Profiles of schools, methods and people who are leaving their marks on dance.
$24.95

Monthly Founded: 1979
Circulation: 60000
Printed in 4 colors

17926 Dance on Camera Journal
Dance Films Association
48 West 21st Street
Suite 907
New York, NY 10010-6806
212-727-0764
FAX: 212-727-0764
info@dancefilms.org
www.dancefilmsassn.org

Deirdre Towers, Artistic Director

Subjects range from reviews and essays, news items regarding dance films, festivals, opportunites, and issues facing artists

Bi-Monthly Founded: 1956

17927 Dance/USA Journal
Dance/USA
1156 15th Street NW
Suite 820
Washington, DC 20005
202-833-1717
FAX: 202-833-2686
danceusa@danceusa.org
www.danceusa.org

Andrea Snyder, Executive Director
Bob Fogelgren, Deputy Director
Monica Reid, Adminstration Director
Ann Norris, Director Membership/Communications
Vicki Kimble, Director Development

The journal features articles on issues of importance to the dance community; news stories relating to arts and dance; essays from leaders in the dance field; notes on changes, transitions and opportunties in the field; calendar of up coming events; and highlights of Dance/USA sponsored events. Subscription is free to members of Dance/USA. *$40.00*

28-36 pages Quarterly Founded: 1982
Printed in 2 colors on glossy stock

17928 Descant
50 Baldwin Street
PO Box 314 Station P
Toronto, ON M5S-2S8
416-593-2557
FAX: 416-593-9362
info@descant.on.ca
www.descant.on.ca

Karen Mulhallen, Editor-in-Chief
Mark Laliberte, Managing Editor
Mary Newberry, Project Manager
Stacey May Fowles, Circulation Manager
Pasha Malla, Director of Outreach

A quarterly journal publishing new and established contemporary writers and visual artists from Canada and around the world. Devoted to the discovery and development of new writers, and places their work in the company of celebrated writers. *$28.00*

Quarterly Founded: 1970
Circulation: 1200

17929 Drama Review
MIT Press
238 Main Street
Suite 500
Cambridge, MA 02142-1046
617-253-2864
FAX: 617-258-5028 800-207-8354
journals-info@mit.edu
www.mitpressjournals.org
TDR focuses on performances in their social, economic, and political conctexts. It emphasizes experimental, avant-garde, intercultural and interdisciplinary performance. TDR covers dance, theatre, performance art, visual art, popular entertainment, media, sports, rituals, and performance in politics and everyday life.
Quarterly Founded: 1955

17930 Dramatics
Educational Theatre Association
2343 Auburn Avenue
Cincinnati, OH 45219-2815
513-421-3900
FAX: 513-421-7077
info@edta.org www.edta.org

Kathleen Taylor, Advertising Manager

The Educational Theatre Association's magazine for theatre students and teacher. Published monthly nine times a year (September through May), the magazine contains practical articles on acting, directing, design, and other facets of theatre; profiles of working professionals that offer insights into theatre careers; new plays; book reviews; news about new productions in New York and other major theatre centers; and a monthly calendar of EdTA events. *$24.00*

9 Times per Year Founded: 1929
Circulation: 36500 $100 per M.
Printed in 4 colors

17931 Encore Performance Publishing
PO Box 95567
South Jordan, UT 84095-0567
801-282-8159

encoreplay@aol.com
www.encoreplay.com

Michael C Perry, President

Publishes a variety of publications for those professionals in the performing arts industry.

17932 **Gospel Today**
286 Highway 314
Suite C
Fayetteville, GA 30214
770-719-4825
FAX: 770-716-2660 800-472-6731
gospeltodaymag@aol.com
www.gospeltoday.com

Teresa Hairston, Publisher

The Voice of the Urban Christian Community. The publication focuses on the holistic Christian lifestyle including health, fashion, fitness, spirituality, music, entertainment and more. *$24.00*
8 Per Year Founded: 1989
Circulation: 250000 18,000 names $90 per M.
Printed in 4 colors on glossy stock

17933 **Hispanic Arts News**
Association of Hispanic Arts
161 East 106th Street
PO Box 1169
El Barrio, NY 10029
212-876-1242
FAX: 212-876-1285 888-876-1240
informacion@latinoarts.org
www.latinoarts.org
Features in depth articles on the local and national arts community, including artist profiles and a calendar of events.
9 Per Year
Mailing list available for rent 5000 names $80 per M.

17934 **JazzTimes**
8737 Colesville Road
9th Floor
Silver Spring, MD 20910-3921
301-588-4114
FAX: 301-588-5531 800-866-7664
JazzTimes contains extensive news coverage, award winning jazz journalism, hundreds of CD, Book and Video reviews, World class photography and award winning graphics, informative features and columns, special theme issues, special directories, readers poll and critic pics, and sound$weeps giveaways and prizes. *$23.95*

10 Issues per y Founded: 1980
Circulation: 86000

17935 **Journal of Arts Management, Law, Society**
Heldref Publishers
1319 18th Street NW
Washington, DC 20036-1802
202-296-6267
FAX: 202-296-5149 800-365-9753
subscribe@heldref.org
www.heldref.org
A resource for arts policymakters and analysts, sociologists, arts and cultural administrators, educators, trusteed, artists, lawyers, and citizens concerned with the performing, visual, and media arts as well as cultural affairs. Articles, commentaries, and reviews of publications address marketing, intellectual property, arts policy, arts law, governance, and cultural production and dissemination, from a variety of philosophical, disciplinary, and national and international perspectives. *$79.00*
Monthly Founded: 1956

17936 **Lighting Dimensions**
Primedia Business
249 W 17th Street
New York, NY 10011
212-716-8449
FAX: 212-514-3719 800-827-3322
Doug MacDonald, Group Publisher
David Johnson, Associate Publisher/Editorial
Marian Sandberg-Dierson, Editor
Mark Newman, Managing Editor

Trade publication for lighting professionals in film, theatre, television, concerts, clubs, themed environments, architecctural, commercial, and industrial lighting. Sponsors of the LDI Trade Show and the Broadway Lighting Master Classes. *$34.97*
12/year Founded: 1989
Circulation: 14,177

17937 **Mid-Atlantic Events Magazine**
1800 Byberry Road
Suite 901
Huntingdon Valley, PA 19006
215-947-8600
FAX: 215-947-8650 800-521-8588
editor@eventsmagazine.com
www.eventsmagazine.com

Jim Cohn, Publisher
Rich Kupka, Editor
Fred Cohn, VP Sales
Katie O'Connell, Director Sales/Marketing
Dana Kurtbek, Production

Focused on Hospitality in the Mid-Atlantic area. It assists the Associations, Corporations, Government, Group and Independent Meeting, Event and Travel Planners who are responsible for arranging Conventions, Trade Shows, Hotel Accommodations, Corporate/Group Travel, Meetings, Seminars, Conferences, Symposiums, Site Selections, Special Events, Banquets, Entertainment, Corporate Golf Outings and Golf Tournaments, Company Picnics, Team Building, Retreats, Board Meetings, Training & Development.
Founded: 1987
Circulation: 26000
Printed in 8 colors on glossy stock

17938 **National Squares**
National Square Dance Convention
C/O Gene and Connie Triplett
2760 Polo Club Boulevard
Matthews, NC 28105
704-847-1265

Richp27890@aol.com
www.nationalsquaredanceconvention.com

Dick/Linda Peterson, Editors
Gene/Connie Triplett, Circulation Managers
Dick/Linda Peterson, Public Relations

A national square dance magazine published by the National Executive Committee of the National Square Dance Convention. *$7.00*
Quarterly

17939 **New England Theatre Journal**
New England Theatre Conference
215 Knob Hill Drive
Hamden, CT 06518
617-851-8535
FAX: 203-288-5938
mail@netconline.org
www.netconline.org

Jim Quinn, President
David Frieze, VP Communications/Development
Stuart Hecht, Comm Chair/NETC Theatre Journal

Scholarly publication produced once per year. Includes book and theatre reviews, historical analyses, and other well-written articles by noted authors. Free to NETC members. Specifically designed to provide members, and others interested in live theatre arts, with the information and resources they need to enhance their careers, promote their groups, and sharpen their theatre skills. *$10.00*
Annual Founded: 1952 6000 names

17940 **Nouveau Magazine**
Barbara Tompkins
5933 Stoney Hill Road
New Hope, PA 18938-9602
215-794-5996
FAX: 215-794-8305
info@nouveaumagazine.com
www.nouveaumagazine.com

Barbara E Tompkins, Publisher

Features theater reviews.
Monthly Founded: 1981
Printed in 4 colors on glossy stock

17941 **OffBeat**
421 Frenchmen Street
Suite 200
New Orleans, LA 70116-2506
504-944-4300
FAX: 504-944-4306 877-944-4300
offbeat@offbeat.com
www.offbeat.com

Jan Ramsey, Publisher/Editor
Joseph L Irrera, Managing Editor
Bunny Matthews, Senior Editor
Michael Jastroch, Magazine Design/Production
Doug Jackson, Distribution Manager

Consumer-oriented music magazine focusing on New Orleans and Louisiana music. Regular columns on Cajun music, zydeco, traditional and contemporary jazz, brass band (Mardi Gras second-line music), New Orleans R & B, Louisiana and delta blues, Gospel, modern and roots rock and our internationally-appreciated culture and cusine. Information on music fairs and festivals in the region is given. *$29.00*
Monthly Founded: 1985 ISSN 1090-0810
Circulation: 50000 15000 names
Printed in 4 colors on newsprint stock

17942 **Performing Arts Insider Magazine**
PAI C/O Total Theater
PO Box 62
Hewlett, NY 11557-0062
516-295-1511

totalpost@totaltheater.com
http://hometown.aol.com/paipress/

David Lefkowitz, Publisher/Editor
Richmond Shepard, Publisher
Steven Fisch, Advertising Sales

Includes day-by-day calendar listings of shows on Broadway, Off and Off-Off Broadway, plus dance, opera, cabaret and special events. Also included are comprehensive theater guides, listing the author, director, cast, designers, synopsis, theater and box office details, as well as contact information for producers, press agents, general managers and casting directors. *$275.00*
Monthly+9 Updates Founded: 1944
Circulation: 2000

17943 **Playbill**
52 Vanderbilt Avenue
11th Floor
New York, NY 10017-3808
212-557-5757
FAX: 212-682-2932
agans@playbill.com
www.playbill.com

Andrew Gans, Editor

The exclusive magazine for Broadway and Off-Broadway theatregoers, providing the information necessary for the understanding and enjoyment of each show, including features articles and columns by and about theatre personalities, entertainment, travel, fashion, dining and other editorial pieces geared to the lifestyle of the upscale, active theatre attendee. Playbill also serves New York's three most prominent performing arts venues - the Metropolitan Opera House, Lincoln Center and Carnegie Hall
$24.00
Monthly Founded: 1884

17944 Plays: Drama Magazine for Young People
Plays Magazine
PO Box 600160
Newton, MA 02460
617-630-9100
FAX: 617-630-9101 800-630-5755
lpreston@playsmag.com
www.playsmag.com

Elizabeth Preston, Editor

Includes eight to ten royalty-free one-act plays, arranged by age level. Modern and traditional plays for the celebration of all important holidays and occasions. Adaptable to all cast sizes with easy to follow instructions for settings and costumes. A complete source of original plays and programs for school-age actors and audiences.
$39.00
7 X Per Year Founded: 1940
Circulation: 6000
Printed in on matte stock

17945 Pollstar
4697 W Jacquelyn Avenue
Fresno, CA 93722-6413
559-271-7900
FAX: 559-271-7979 800-344-7383
info@pollstar.com www.pollstar.com
Provides worldwide concert tour schedules, ticket sales results, music industry contact directories, trade news and unique specialized data services. POLLSTAR also maintains a large database of international concert tour information. Products and services include: weekly print and/or daily online delivery; music industry contact directories; tour histories; mailing labels; and data on disk. *$399.00*
Weekly Founded: 1981
Circulation: 20000

17946 Shakespeare Bulletin
University of North Carolina
Department of English
9201 University City Boulevard
Charlotte, NC 28223

sbeditor@email.uncc.edu
www.shakespeare-bulletin.org

Seymour Isenberg, Founding Editor
Andrew James Hartley, Editor
Jeremy Lopez, Theatre Review Editor
Genevieve Love, Book Review Editor
Kirk Melnikoff, Shakespeare on Film Editor

A peer-reviewed journal of performance and criticism and scholarship which provides commentary on Shakespeare and Renaissance drama through feature articles, thatre and film reviews, and book reviews. The journal is a member of the Conference of Editors of Learned Journals. *$ 35.00*
Quarterly Founded: 1982
Printed in on matte stock

17947 Show Music
Po Box A
East Haddam, CT 06423-0466
860-873-8664
FAX: 860-873-2329
rklink@goodspeed.org
www.showmusic.org

Ryan Klink, Managing Editor
Maz O Preeo, Editor-In-Chief

Internationally acclaimed by professionals and fans as the premier magazine covering musical theatre around the world. Show music combines insightful interviews and reviews of productions, recordings, videos and books. *$25.00*
80 pages Quarterly
Circulation: 5,000

17948 Sondheim Review
PO Box 11213
Chicago, IL 60611-0213
773-275-4254
FAX: 773-275-4254 800-584-1020
info@sondheimreview.com
www.sondheimreview.com
Dedicated to the work of the musical theater and Broadway's foremost composer and lyricist, Stephen Sondheim. Each issue containes news, interviews, upcoming productions in the area, puzzles and more.
$19.95
Quarterly Founded: 1994
Circulation: 40000 6,000 names $105 per M.
Printed in on glossy stock

17949 Southern Theatre
Southeastern Theatre Conference
1217 W Bessemer Avenue
PO Box 9868
Greensboro, NC 27429-868
336-272-3645
FAX: 336-272-8810
setc@setc.org www.setc.org

Elizabeth Baun, Executive Director
April J'Callahan Marshall, Professional Theatre Services Mgr
Hardy Koenig, Educational Services Manager

Spotlights people, places and organizations within the region that are paving new paths in theatre. Includes low-cost strategies for design success, tips on hot markets for playwrights, new books of special interest, innovative ideas for marketing theatre, inside track on new trends and some of the region's up-and-coming theatre stars. Subscription is free with SETC membership.
$18.75
Quarterly Founded: 1949
Circulation: 4000+

17950 Spectrum
110 S Jefferson Street
Dayton, OH 45402-3412
937-220-1600
FAX: 937-220-1642 800-247-1614
mservices@thinktv.org
www.thinktv.org
ThinkTV's monthly member magazine. Contains program listings for both ThinkTV 16 and ThinkTV14 as well as interesting feature stories, station news and more.
Weekly Founded: 1959
Circulation: 18000

17951 Stage Directions
Macfadden Performing Arts Media
110 William Street
23th Floor
New York, NY 10038
646-459-4800
FAX: 646-459-4900
sd@lifestylemedia.com
www.stagedirections.com

Iris Dorbian, Editor
Jessica Hodges, Advertising

Serves the strategic, practical and technical information needs of small theaters across the country. *$26.00*
Monthly Founded: 1988
Circulation: 7000

17952 Stage of the Art
American Alliance for Theatre and Education
7475 Wisconsin Avenue
Suite 300A
Bethesda, MD 20814
301-951-7977
FAX: 301-968-0144
info@aate.com.edu www.aate.com

David Young, Editor
JoBeth Gonzalez, Director Publications/Research

Published by the American Alliance for Theatre and Education. *$28.00*
Quarterly
Circulation: 1000
Mailing list available for rent 700 names $150 per M.

17953 Stagebill
Stagebill
144 E 44th Street
7th Floor
New York, NY 10017-4031
212-476-0640
FAX: 212-983-5976
bmattison@stagebill.com
www.avant-rus.com/stagebill

Gerry Byrne, CEO
Frederick W Becker III, Associate Publisher
John Istel, Editor-in-Chief
Robert Sandla, Executive Editor
Tricia Maher, Senior Managing Editor

Publisher of the program magazines for the leading, theaters, symphonies, dance companies and performing arts centers in the United States. A national performing arts magazine.
Monthly Founded: 1924

17954 Stages
Curtains
301 W 45th Street
Apartment 5A
New York, NY 10036-3825

FAX: 201-836-4107

Frank Scheck, Editor *$20.00*
Monthly
Circulation: 35,000

17955 TD & T: Theatre Design & Technology
US Institute for Theatre Technology
3001 Springcrest Drive
Louisville, KY 40241-2755
502-426-1211
FAX: 502-423-7467
info@oficce.usitt.org www.usitt.org

David Roger, Editor
Arnold Wengrow, Book Review Editor
Michelle Smith, Membership/Advertising

Manager
N Deborah Hazlett, Art Director

Published by United States Institute for Theatre Technology. Focuses on USITT's ten interest areas: architecture, costume design and technology, education, engineering, health and safety, lighting, management, scene design, sound design, and technical production.

Quarterly

17956 Teaching Theatre
Educational Theatre Association
2343 Auburn Avenue
Cincinnati, OH 45219
513-421-3900
FAX: 513-559-0012 www.edta.org

Educational Theatre Association's journal for theatre teachers. Includes articles on acting, directing, playwriting, technical theatre; profiles of outstanding educational theatre programs; pieces on curriculum design, assessment or teaching methodology; and reports on current trends or issues in the field, such as funding, standards, or certification. Subsciption are available only as a benefit of membership in the Educational Theatre Association. Libraries and other institutions may subscribe. *$34.00*

Quarterly

17957 Technical Brief
Yale School of Drama
222 York Street
PO Box 208244
New Haven, CT 06520
203-432-9664
FAX: 203-432-8332
bronislaw.sammler@yale.edu
www.technicalbrief.org

Ben Sammler, Co-Editor
Don Harvey, Co-Editor

Written by professionals for professionals, providing a dialogue between technical practitioners from the several performing arts. The succinct articles, complete with mechanical drawings, represent the best solutions to recurring technical problems. Published October, January and April. *$15.00*

3X Per Year Founded: 1924

17958 Theater Magazine
Yale School of Drama
222 York Street
PO Box 208244
New Haven, CT 06520
203-432-1568
FAX: 203-432-8336
theater.magazine@yale.edu
www.yale.edu/drama

Tom Sellar, Editor
Laraine Sammler, Business Manager
Alex Grennan, Director of Business/Comm

Periodicals, essays and articles of the Yale School of Drama. *$22.00*

Annual+ Founded: 1924
Circulation: 2500
Mailing list available for rent 1.5M names
Printed in 1 color on matte stock

17959 Theatre Bill
Jerome Press
332 Congress Street
2nd Floor
Boston, MA 02210-1217
617-423-3400
FAX: 617-423-7108

17960 Theatre Journal
Johns Hopkins University Press
2715 North Charles Street
Baltimore, MD 21218
410-516-6900
FAX: 410-516-6968 800-548-1784
wmb@press.jhu.edu
www.press.jhu.edu

Jean Graham-Jones, Editor
David Z Saltz, Co-Editor
Sonja Arsham Kuftinec, Performance Review Editor
James Peck, Book Review Editor
Bob Kowkabany, Managing Editor

One of the most authoritative and useful publications of theatre studies available today. Theatre Journal features social and historical studies, production reviews, and theoretical inquiries that analize dramatic texts and production. Official journal of the Association for Theatre in Higher Education. *$40.00*

Quarterly Founded: 1878
Circulation: 2492

17961 Theatre Symposium
Auburn University
Department of Theatre
211 Telfair Peet Theatre
Auburn, AL 36849
336-272-3645
FAX: 336-272-8810
phillm2@auburbn.edu www.setc.org

M Scott Phillips, Editor

An annual publication of works of scholarship resulting from a single topic meeting held on a southeastern university campus each year. Available to adult members only. A copublication of the Southeaster Theatre Conference and the University of Alabama Press.

17962 Theatre Topics
Johns Hopkins University Press
2715 North Charles Street
Baltimore, MD 21218
410-516-6900
FAX: 410-516-6968 800-548-1784
jonathc@bgsu.edu www.press.jhu.edu

Jonathan Chambers, Editor
Sandra G Shannon, Co-Editor
DeAnna Toten Beard, Book Review Editor
Elanore Lampners, Managing Editor
Beverley Pevitts, Founding Editor

Focuses on performance studies, dramaturgy, and theatre pedagogy. Concise and timely articles on a broad array of practical, performance-oriented subjects, with special attention to topics of current interest to the profession. Keeps readers informed of the latest developments on the stage and in the classroom. The official journal of the Association for Theatre in Higher Education. Published in March and September. *$32.00*

Semi-Annually Founded: 1878
Circulation: 1528

17963 Youth Theatre Journal
American Alliance for Theatre and Education
7475 Wisconsin Avenue
Suite 300A
Bethesda, MD 20814
301-951-7977
FAX: 301-968-0144
info@aate.com www.aate.com

Manon van de Water, Editor

Scholarly Journal of the American Alliance for Theatre and Education. A juried publication dedicated to advancing the study and practice of theatre and drama, with, for, and by people of all ages. It is concerned with all forms of scholarship of the highest quality that inform the fields of theatre for young audiences and drama/theatre education. *$25.00*

Annual
Circulation: 1000
Mailing list available for rent 700 names
$150 per M.

Trade Shows

17964 EXPO
Theatre Bay Area
870 Market Street
Suite 375
San Francisco, CA 94102-3002
415-430-1140
FAX: 415-430-1145
dale@theatrebayarea.org
www.theatrebayarea.org

Dale Albright, Director of Individual Services

Theatre Bay Area's EXPO is where attendees can meet those kinds of businesses that might offer services to the theatre community: theatre companies, actors, etc. There are also break-out sessions discussing issues of interest to the theatre community.

500+ Attendees May

17965 National Black Theatre Festival
610 Coliseum Drive
Suite 1
Winston-Salem, NC 27106
336-723-2266

nbtf@bellsouth.net www.nbtf.org

Patrice Toney, President

7/30-8/4 07'Winston-Salem

17966 National Square Dance Convention
PO Box 5790
Topeka, KS 66605-5790
317-635-4455
www.57nsdc.com
250 booths and 250 exhibitors.

20M+ Attendees June

17967 New England Theatre Conference
215 Knob Hill Drive
Hamden, CT 06518
617-851-8535
FAX: 203-288-5938
mail@netconline.org
www.netconline.org

Tara McCarthy, Executive Director

Promoting excellence in theatre, a conference of New England's oldest, largest regional theatre association.

800+ Attendees November Founded: 1952

17968 Performing Arts Facility Administrators Se minar
International Association of Assembly Managers
635 Fritz Drive
Suite 100
Coppell, TX 75019
972-906-7441
FAX: 972-906-7418 www.iaam.org

Annual

17969 **Prescott Park Arts Festival**
Po Box 4370
Portsmouth, NH 03802-4370
603-436-2848
FAX: 603-436-1034
info@prescottpark.org
www.artfest.org
Deborah Lielasus Tombleson, Executive Director
Russell Bolian, Festival Production Manager
Provide a financially accessible, quality multi-arts festival to a diverse audience.

17970 **Southeastern Theatre Conference**
1217 W Bessemer Avenue
PO Box 9868
Greensboro, NC 27429-0868
336-272-3645
FAX: 336-272-8810
setc@setc.org www.setc.org
David Thompson, President
Betsey Baun, Executive Director
Join over 4,000 Theatre Artists for education, exchanges, ideas, products, networking and great theatre. Convention activities include keynote speakers, auditions, guest speakers, festivals, design competition, commercial and educational expo exhibits, scholarship awards, social events and workshops.
4000+ Attendees March

17971 **US Institute for Theatre Technology Annual Conference & Stage Expo**
USITT
6433 Ridings Road
Suite 134
Syracuse, NY 13206
315-463-6434
FAX: 315-463-6525 800-398-3976
info@office.usitt.org www.usitt.org
The Conference offers over 175 sessions featuring design, technology, costume, sound, architecture, management, engineering, and production. The Stage Expo showcases businesses, products, services, and eductional opportunities in the performing arts and entertainment industry. With over 150 exhibitors, Stage Expo provides conference attendees with the opportunity to see the newest and best products and services on the market today. *$314.00*
3800 Attendees March

Directories & Databases

17972 **Academy Players Directory**
2210 W Olive Avenue
Suite 320
Burbank, CA 91506
310-247-3058
FAX: 310-550-5034
info@playersdirectory.com
www.playersdirectory.com
The Players Directory appeared in 1937 as the first reliable casting directory that listed both featured stars and extras. Today, more than 16,000 actors are included.
$75.00
Founded: 1937 : internet

17973 **American Association of Community Theatre Membership Directory**
8402 Briar Wood Circle
Lago Vista, TX 78645-4118
512-267-0711
FAX: 512-267-0712 866-687-2228
info@aact.org www.aact.org
Julie Angelo, Executive Director
Mary Britt, President
Carole Ries, VP Public Relations
Frank Peot, Secretary
Gary Walker, Treasurer
The database includes addresses for over 7,000 community theatre organizations in the USA: Only available to members.
Mailing list available for rent 10000 names $180 per M.

17974 **Americans for the Arts Field Directory**
Americans for the Arts
One E 53rd Street
6th Floor
New York, NY 10022
212-223-2787
FAX: 212-980-4857 www.artsusa.org
Suzanne Niemeyer, Editor
Robert L Lynch, President/CEO
Liz Bartolomeo, Public Relations/Marketing Coord
Chad Bauman, Director Print/Multimedia Commun
Graham Dunstan, Assoc Director Publication Sales
A must-have resource for anyone working in the arts and community development. The directory provides contact information for local, state, regional, and national arts service organizations-more than 4,000 entries broken down by state and region. Also includes contact information for professional consultants working in the nonprofit arts field. A great networking tool. *$35.00*
262 pages

17975 **Arts Presenters: Membership Directory**
1112 16th Street NW
Suite 400
Washington, DC 20036
202-833-2787
FAX: 202-833-1543 888-820-2787
help@artspresenters.org
http://www.artspresenters.org
Sandra Gibson, President/CEO
Alicia Anstead, Editor
Patrick Madden, Circulation Manager
An invaluable resource for keeping in touch with colleagues. Puts more than 1,450 presenters, service organizations, artists, management companies, consultants, and vendors at your fingertips. An excellent networking tool for everyone on your staff. *$129.00*
155 pages Annual+ Founded: 1957

17976 **Complete Catalogue of Plays**
Dramatists Play Service
440 Park Avenue S
New York, NY 10016-8050
212-683-8960
FAX: 212-213-1539
publications@dramatists.com
www.dramatists.com
Stephen Sultan, President
Rafael J Rivera, VP Finance/Administration
Michael Q Fellmeth, VP Publications/IT
Tamra Feifer, Director Operations
The Complete Catalogue is published in odd years and the Supplement of New Plays in even years. Both books are distributed, without charge, to current customers in the Fall of each year.
412 pages

17977 **Contemporary Theatre, Film and Television**
St. James Press/Thomson Gale
27500 Drake Road
Farmington Hills, MI 48331-3535
248-699-4253
FAX: 248-699-8035 800-877-4253
gale.galeord@thomson.com
www.gale.com
Peter M Gareffa, Managing Editor
Provides extensive biographical and career information on more than 11,000 professionals currently working in the entertainment industry, including performers, choreographers, directors, technicians, writers, composers, producers, executives, designers, critics and more. *$ 135.00*
843 pages

17978 **Costume Designers Guild Directory**
Costumer Designers Guild
4730 Woodman Avenue
Suite 430
Sherman Oaks, CA 91423-2400
818-905-1557
FAX: 818-905-1560
cdgia@earthlink.net
www.costumedesignersguild.com
Cheryl Downey, Executive Director
Deborah N Landis, President
Directory includes members' names, classification, and other statistical information.
Annual

17979 **Dance Annual Directory**
Dance Magazine
333 Seventh Avenue
11th Floor
New York, NY 10001
212-979-4937
FAX: 212-979-4817
emacel@dancemagazine.com
www.dancemagazine.com
Karla Johnson, President
Emily Macel, Editor
Karen Hildebrand, Editorial Director
Wendy Perron, Editor-in-Chief
Hanna Rubin, Managing Editor
Reach 300,000+ dancers, dance teachers, and dance professionals in the dance world.
$100.00
Annual

17980 **Dance Magazine College Guide**
Dance Magazine
110 William Street
23rd Floor
New York, NY 10038
646-459-4800
FAX: 212-979-4817
subscriptions@dancemagazine.com
www.dancemagazine.com
Karla Johnson, President
Karen Hildebrand, Editorial Director
Wendy Perron, Editor-in-Chief
Hanna Rubin, Managing Editor
Kate Lydon, Education Editor
With over 500+ listings, Dance Magazine College Guide is a comprehensive source for dance degree programs in higher education. Find application deadlines and audition dates. Get student perspectives and career advice. Online database offers the

ability to identify programs that match an individual's personal criteria for degree, type of dance, location, department size, tuition and more. *$29.95*
Annual

17981 Dance Magazine: Summer Dance Calendar Issue
Dance Magazine
33 W 60th Street
Floor 10
New York, NY 10023-7905
212-245-9050
800-331-1750
A list of dance workshops and special programs for students are listed. *$3.95*
Annual
Circulation: 100,000

17982 Dance/USA Annual Directory and List-Serv
Dance/USA
1111 16th Street NW
Suite 300
Washington, DC 20036
202-833-1717
FAX: 202-833-2686
danceusa@danceusa.org
www.danceusa.org
Andrea Snyder, Executive Director
Bob Fogelgren, Deputy Director
Ann Norris, Director Membership/Communications
John Munger, Research and Information
Vicki Kimble, Director Development
On-going list-servs keep many peer councils in touch throughout the year, by providing a quick and easy connection to peer counseling when members have an immediate question or problem. Information about dance companies, schools, presenters, service organizations and commercial suppliers is included in the annual copy of Dance Annual Directory.
Annual
Circulation: 400+

17983 Directory of Theatre Training Programs
Theatre Directories
2349 West Road
PO Box 159
Dorset, VT 05251
802-867-9333
FAX: 802-867-2297
info@theatredirectories.com
www.theatredirectories.com
Peg Lyons, Editor
PJ Tumielewicz, Editor
Profiles admissions, tuition, faculty, curriculum, facilities, productions and philosophy of training at 475 programs in the US, Canada and abroad: Colleges, Universities, Conservatories, Undergraduate and Graduate degrees. Includes Combined Auditions information. Indexed by degrees offered in each program. *$39.50*
ISBN 0-933919-61-1 580 names

17984 Dramatics College Theatre Directory
Educational Theatre Association
2343 Auburn Avenue
Cincinnati, OH 45219-2815
513-421-3900
FAX: 513-421-7077
info@edta.org www.edta.org
Lists more than 250 college, university, and conservatory theatre programs, offering a sketch of each based on information provided by the schools. The listings can be used to measure each school against one's own criteria for location, setting, courses of study, admission requirements, and cost. Find out which programs offer merit scholarships and grants and how those funds are awarded. Use the contact information to get in touch with the programs that seem to offer the best fit for your needs *$9.00*
Annual

17985 Dramatics Magazine: Summer Theatre Directory
Educational Theatre Association
2343 Auburn Avenue
Cincinnati, OH 45219-2815
513-421-3900
FAX: 513-421-7077
info@edta.org www.edta.org
Lists nearly 200 summer theatre programs and stock companies, offering a sketch of each based on factual information provided by the schools, camps, and theatre companies. The listings can be used to measure each program against one's own criteria for location, setting, housing, courses of study, admission requirements and fees. *$9.00*
Annual

17986 Dramatist's Sourcebook
Theatre Communications Group
520 8th Avenue
24th Floor
New York, NY 10018-4156
212-609-5900
FAX: 212-609-5901
tcg@tcg.org www.tcg.org
Teresa Eyring, Executive Director
Kelly Haydon, Database Manager
Jennifer Cleary, Director Membership
Terence Nemeth, Publisher
Kathy Sova, Editorial Director
Completely revised, with more than 900 opportunities for playwrights, translators, composers, lyricists, and librettists, as well as opportunities for screen, radio, and television writers. Thoroughly indexed, with a calendar of deadlines. The Sourcebook contains scrip-submission procedures for more than 350 theatres seeking new plays; guidelines for more than 150 prizes; and sections on agents, fellowships and residencies. *$22.95*
Annual Founded: 1980 ISBN 1-559362-94-4

17987 Dramatists Guild Annual Resource Directory
Dramatists Guild of America
1501 Broadway
Suite 701
New York, NY 10036
212-398-9366
FAX: 212-944-0420
www.dramaguild.com
John Weidman, President
The Resource Directory is an annual sourcebook available only to Guild members, sent automatically as one of the privileges of Guild members. It includes lists of conferences and festivals, contests, producers, publishers, agents and attorneys, fellowships and grants, and workshops throughout the US and the world.
Annual

17988 Encyclopedia of Exhibition
National Association of Theatre Owners
750 First Street N.E.
Washington, DC 20002
202-962-0054
FAX: 202-962-0370
nato@natodc.com www.natoonline.org
John Fithian, President
Mary Ann Anderson, VP/Executive Director
Mary dela Cruz, Advertising Director
An annual encyclopedia published by the National Association of Theatre Owners. *$100.00*
474 pages Annual Founded: 1948
Printed in on glossy stock

17989 Feedback Theatrebooks and Prospero Press
Feedback Theatrebooks & Prospero Press
PO Box 174
Brooklin, ME 04616
207-359-2781
FAX: 207-359-5532
Publishes theatre histories, cookbooks, directories, anthologies of plays, plays published before WWII, and format guidelines for playwrights.

17990 Grey House Performing Arts Directory
Grey House Publishing
185 Millerton Road
PO Box 860
Millerton, NY 12546
518-890-0526
FAX: 518-789-0545 800-562-2139
books@greyhouse.com
www.greyhouse.com
Leslie Mackenzie, Publisher
Richard Gottlieb, Editor
Laura Mars-Proietti, Editorial Director
Jessica Moody, Marketing Director
Karen Stevens, Production Manager
The Grey House Performing Arts Directory is the most comprehensive resource covering the Performing Arts. This important directory provides current information on over 9,000 Dance Companies, Instrumental Music Programs, Opera Companies, Choral Groups, Theater Companies, Performing Arts Series and Performing Arts Facilities. *$185.00*
1500 pages Annual ISBN 1-592370-23-3

17991 Money for Film and Video Artists
Americans for the Arts
One E 53rd Street
6th Floor
New York, NY 10022
212-223-2787
FAX: 212-980-4857 www.artsusa.org
Suzanne Niemeyer, Editor
Robert L Lynch, President/CEO
Liz Bartolomeo, Public Relations/Marketing Coord
Chad Bauman, Director Print/Multimedia Commun
Graham Dunstan, Assoc Director Publication Sales
A comprehensive resource guide to fellowships, grants, awards, low-cost facilities, emergency assistance programs, technical assistance, and support services. Entries include contact information; type of award and/or scope of service; eligibilty requirements; application procedures; deadlines and more. *$14.95*
317 pages ISBN 1-879903-09-1

17992 Money for International Exchange in the Arts
Americans for the Arts
One E 53rd Street
6th Floor
New York, NY 10022
212-223-2787
FAX: 212-980-4857 www.artsusa.org
Suzanne Niemeyer, Editor
Robert L Lynch, President/CEO

Liz Bartolomeo, Public Relations/Marketing Coord
Chad Bauman, Director Print/Multimedia Commun
Graham Dunstan, Assoc Director Publication Sales

This resource includes grants, fellowships and awards for travel and work abroad; support and technical assistance for international touring and exchange; international artists' residencies; programs that support artists' professional development, and more. Indexed by region, discipline and type of support. *$14.95*

122 pages ISBN 1-879903-01-6

17993 Money for Performing Artists
Americans for the Arts
One E 53rd Street
6th Floor
New York, NY 10022
212-223-2787
FAX: 212-980-4857 www.artsusa.org

Suzanne Niemeyer, Editor
Robert L Lynch, President/CEO
Liz Bartolomeo, Public Relations/Marketing Coord
Chad Bauman, Director Print/Multimedia Commun
Graham Dunstan, Assoc Director Publication Sales

Lists awards, grants, fellowships, competitions, auditions, workshops, and artists' colonies, as well as emergency and technical assistance programs. *$12.00*

240 pages Founded: 1991 ISBN 0-915400-96-0

17994 Money for Visual Arts
Americans for the Arts
One E 53rd Street
6th Floor
New York, NY 10022
212-223-2787
FAX: 212-980-4857 www.artsusa.org

Suzanne Niemeyer, Editor
Robert L Lynch, President/CEO
Liz Bartolomeo, Public Relations/Marketing Coord
Chad Bauman, Director Print/Multimedia Commun
Graham Dunstan, Assoc Director Publication Sales

A guide to grants, fellowships, awards, artist colonies, emergency and technical assistance, and support services. Entries include contact information; type of award and/or scope of service; eligibility requirements; application procedures; deadlines, and more. *$14.95*

340 pages

17995 Musical America International Directory of the Performing Arts
Commonwealth Business Media
400 Windsor Corporate Park
50 Millstone Road, Suite 200
East Windsor, NJ 08520
609-371-7700
FAX: 609-371-7879 800-221-5488
info@musicalamerica.com
www.musicalamerica.com

Lynn Wall, Subscriptions
Bob Hudoba, Listings

Features over 14,000 detailed listings of worldwide arts organizations, including key contact information such as name, address, phone, fax, Web site and E-mail addresses, budget category, type of event and seating capacity. In addition, through advertising, over 10,000 artists are indexed in the alphabetical and categorical indexes. Categories include artist managers, orchestras, opera companies, concert series, festivals, competitions, music schools and departments, record companies, and more.

Founded: 1898

17996 NYC/On Stage
Theatre Development Fund
1501 Broadway
21st Floor
New York, NY 10036-5652
212-221-0885

info@tdf.org www.tdf.org
Theater, dance, and music companies and performing arts centers in New York City.

17997 Opera America Membership Directory
Opera America
330 Seventh Avenue
16th Floor
New York, NY 10001
212-796-8620
FAX: 212-796-8631
frontdesk@operaamerica.org
www.operaamerica.org
Directory of Opera America's Company, Business, Library, and Affilliate Members, indexed alphabetically and geographically. Includes the Annual Report to Members, a description of Opera America's programs and services, and a list of individual members. *$25.00*

Annual

17998 Performing Arts Resources
Theatre Library Association
The New York Public Library for Performing Arts
40 Lincoln Center Plaza
New York, NY 10023
212-870-1630

nef4@columbia.edu
http://tla.library.unt.edu/

Nancy Friedland, Executive Secretary
Martha S LoManaco, President
Maryann Chach, Editor Membership Directory
Louis A Rachow, Historian
Paul Newman, Treasurer

Annual publication featuring articles on resource materials in the field of theatre, popular entertainment, film, television and radio, information on public and private collections, and essays on conservation and collection management of theatre arts materials. Also includes rare historical documents and out-of-print works that might otherwise be lost to theatre scholarship.

Annual

17999 Plays and Playwrights
International Society of Dramatists
1638 Euclid Avenue
Miami Beach, FL 33139-7744
305-882-1864

Offers valuable information on over 1,000 dramatists producing works in English. *$29.95*

200 pages Annual
Circulation: 10,000

18000 Regional Theatre Directory
Theatre Directories
2349 West Road
PO Box 159
Dorset, VT 05251
802-867-9333
FAX: 802-867-2297
info@theatredirectories.com
www.theatredirectories.com

Peg Lyons, Editor
PJ Tumielewicz, Editor

Profiles over 400 theatres including dinner theatres, equity and non-equity. Find out when/where auditions are held, when resumes shoul be sent, housing and transportation policy, and general description of company. If you want to find a job or an internship as an actor, designer, technician or staff in a professional regional or dinner theatre anywhere in the country, this directory can help you. *$29.50*

Annual Founded: 1984 ISBN 0-933919-63-8 400 names $180 per M.

18001 ShowBiz Bookkeeper
Theatre Directories
PO Box 159
Dorset, VT 05251
802-867-9333
FAX: 802-867-2297
info@theatredirectories.com
www.theatredirectories.com
The tax record-keeping system for professionals working in the arts. *$22.95*

18002 Stars in Your Eyes...Feet on the Ground
Theatre Directories
2349 West Road
PO Box 159
Dorset, VT 05251
802-867-9333
FAX: 802-867-2297
info@theatredirectories.com
www.theatredirectories.com

PJ Tumielewicz, Editor
Peg Lyons, Editor

For teens who want to act...Practical advice for young actors: learning how show business works; agents and managers; local cable shows and television commercials; auditioning for stage, student films and TV; choosing a school; dealing with rejection; parental support and more. Written by a 19-year old professional actress. *$16.95*

ISBN 0-933919-42-5

18003 Student's Guide to Playwriting Opportuniti es
Theatre Directories
2349 West Road
PO Box 159
Dorset, VT 05251
802-867-9333
FAX: 802-867-2297
info@theatredirectories.com
www.theatredirectories.com

Michael Write, Directory Editor
Christi Pyland, Directory Editor
PJ Tumielewicz, Theatre Directories, Inc Editor
Peg Lyons, Theatre Directories, Inc Editor

An essential tool for every high shool or college student with an interest in playwriting. Comprehensive listings of 79 academic programs and another 80 professional development programs geared for the young writer. New essays on the art, process and business of playwriting. *$23.95*

128 pages ISBN 0-933919-53-0

18004 Summer Theatre Directory
Theatre Directories
PO Box 159
Dorset, VT 05251
802-867-9333
FAX: 802-867-2297
info@theatredirectories.com
www.theatredirectories.com
Opportunities at over 350 summer theatres, theme parks, and summer training programs. *$29.50*

18005 Theatre Profiles
Theatre Communications Group
520 8th Avenue
24th Floor
New York, NY 10018-4156
212-609-5900
FAX: 212-609-5901
tcg@tcg.org www.tcg.org
Gigi Bolt, Interim Executive Director
Warren Nichols, Director Information Systems
Janelle Bernard, Customer Service/Circulation Mgr
Rebecca Marzalek-Kelly, Membership Coordinator
Phillip Matthews, Director Communications
A benefit available to TCG Member Theatres, listing in included in annual TCG Theatre Directory.
Annual

18006 Theatre Profiles Database
Theatre Communications Group
520 8th Avenue
24th Floor
New York, NY 10018-4156
212-609-5900
FAX: 212-609-5901
tcg@tcg.org www.tcg.org
Teresa Eyring, Executive Director
Kelly Haydon, Database Manager
Jennifer Cleary, Director Membership
Terence Nemeth, Publisher
Kathy Sova, Editorial Director
Online database of more than 400 theatre members in 47 states, 17,000 individual members, 100 Trustee Leadership Network members and a growing number of University, Funder and Business Affiliates.
Annual

18007 Whole Arts Directory
Midmarch Arts Press
300 Riverside Drive
Apartment 8A
New York, NY 10025
212-666-6990
FAX: 212-865-5510
info@midmarchpress.org
www.midmarchpress.org
Directory to arts resources, organiztions, museums, galleries, colonies, retreats, art therapy, information services, and much more. Highly useful material for all artists, students, organizations and institutions.
$12.95
175 pages Founded: 1987 ISBN 0-960247-67-x
Printed in on matte stock

Industry Web Sites

18008 www.aact.org
American Association of Community Theatre

Non-profit corporation fostering excellence in community theatre productions and governance through community theatre festivals, educational opportunity publications, network, resources, and website.

18009 www.aahperd.org/nda
National Dance Association

A nonprofit service organization dedicated to increasing knowledge, improving skills and encouraging sound professional practices in dance education while promoting and supporting creative and healthy lifestyles through high quality dance programs.

18010 www.aate.com
American Alliance for Theatre and Education

Members are artists, teachers and professionals who serve youth theatres and theatre educational programs.

18011 www.absolutewrite.com
Absolute Write

Advice for writers, including playwrights.

18012 www.actorsequity.org
Actors Equity Association

Labor union affiliated with AFL-CIO which represents actors in film, television and commercials.

18013 www.actorsite.com
Actor Site

Audition and other information.

18014 www.actorsource.com
Actorsource

Extensive information and resources for actors.

18015 www.actorstheatre.org
Actors Theatre of Louisville

Supports new playwrights. For information on entering a play, click Humana Festival.

18016 www.adta.org
American Dance Therapy Association

Founded in 1966; professional organization of dance movement therapists, with members both nationally and internationally; offers training, research findings, and a newsletter.

18017 www.aislesay.com
Aislesay

Internet magazine of stage reviews and opinions.

18018 www.americandanceguild.org
American Dance Guild

Non-profit membership organization; sponsors professional seminars, workshops, a student scholarship and other projects and institutes programs of national significance in the field of dance.

18019 www.americantheaterweb.com
American Theater Web

Find theaters, Broadway shows and musicals.

18020 www.answers4dancers.com
Answers for Dancers

Dance Magazine sponsors this site.

18021 www.artsmed.org
Performing Arts Medicine Association

Organization for physicians and professionals interested in the research of Performing Arts Medicine.

18022 www.artspresenters.org
Association of Performing Arts Presenters

Celebrates rich and diverse performing arts to the public.

18023 www.artstabilization.org
National Arts Strategies

Offers training and technical assistance to arts organizations.

18024 www.bachauer.com
Gina Bachauer International Piano Foundation

Produce a yearly piano international competition

18025 www.backstage.com
Backstage.com

Information for actors, casting calls, film reviews, auditions and acting jobs.

18026 www.backstagejobs.com
Theatre Design and Technical Jobs Page

Employment opportunities.

18027 www.backstageworld.com
Backstage World

Post your resume and search for design and technical job opportunities worldwide.

18028 www.bmi.com
BMI

Secures the rights of songwriters/composers. Collects license fees for the public performance of music and pays royalties to its copyright owners.

18029 www.catf.org
Contemporary American Theater Festival

Dedicated to providing and developing new American Theater.

18030 www.cincinnatiarts.org
Cincinnati Arts Association

Dedicated to supporting performing and visual arts.

18031 www.classicalaction.org
Classical Action

Provides a unified voice for all those within the performing arts community to help combat HIV/AIDS.

18032 www.conductorsguild.org
Conductors Guild

Dedicated to encouraging the highest standards in the art and profession of conducting. Founded in 1975.

18033 www.contactimprov.net
Contact Improv

Improvisation for dancers.

18034 www.costume-con.org
Costume Connections

Costume conferences.

18035 www.costume.org
International Costumers' Guild

An affiliation of amateur hobbyist and professional costumers.

18036 www.costumegallery.com
Costume Gallery

A central location on the web for fashion and costume since 1996.

18037 www.costumers.org
National Costumers Association

Seeks to establish and maintain professional and ethical standards of business in the costume industry.

18038 www.costumes.org
Costumer's Manifesto

Online book, information and links.

18039 www.costumesocietyamerica.com
Costume Society of America

Education, research, presentation and design.

18040 www.creativedir.com
Creative Directory Services

Diectory of suppliers for costumes, sets, special effects and stunts.

18041 www.criticaldance.com
Dance Critics Association

Critical dance forum and ballet dance magazine

18042 www.csulb.edu/~jvancamp/copyrigh.html
Csulb.edu

Copyrighting choreographic works.

18043 www.csusa.org/face/index.htm
Friends of Active Copyright Education

Playwrights should click on Words, then Copyright Basics.

18044 www.cyberdance.org
Cyber Dance

Collection of links to modern dance and classical ballet resources.

18045 www.danceart.com/edancing
Danceart.com

Ballet and dance art, features, chat and more.

18046 www.dancenotation.org
Dance Notation Bureau

Notation basics, Notated Theatrical Dances Catalogue and links.

18047 www.dancepages.com
Dance Pages.com

Offers resources to dance teachers.

18048 www.dancer.com/dance-links
Dance Links

Links to many dance sites.

18049 www.danceusa.org
Dance/USA

Provides a forum for the discussion of issues of concern to membersand a support network for exchange of information; also bestows awards.

18050 www.deadance.com
Dance Educators of America

Promotes the education of teachers in the performing arts.

18051 www.dma-national.org
Dance Masters of America

An organization of dance teachers.

18052 www.dramaguild.com
Dramatists Guild

Comprehensive organization that deals solely with Broadway and off-Broadway producers, off-off-Broadway groups, agents, theatres and sources of grants.

18053 www.dramaleague.org
Drama League

Seeks to strengthen American theatre through the nurturing of stage directors.

18054 www.dtw.org
Dance Theater Workshop

Identifies, presents and supports independent contemporary artists and dance companies to advance dance and live performances in New York and worldwide.

18055 www.edta.org
Educational Theater Association

Theater educators working to increase support for theater programs in the educational system.

18056 www.esperanzaarts.org
Esperanza Performing Arts Association

18057 www.etecnyc.net
Entertainment Technology Online

For employment in design and technical theatre, click on Classifieds. Also offers resources and buyers guides for theatrical lighting.

18058 www.gmn.com
Global Music Network

Go backstage, watch rehearsals, listen to performances of classical and jazz artists.

18059 www.goldmime.com
Goldston Mime Foundation: School for Mime

Holds summer seminars and workshops.

18060 www.harada-sound.com/sound/handbook
Kai's Sound Handbook

Information for sound designers.

18061 www.hawaii.edu
Association for Theatre in Higher Education

Promotes quality in theatre education.

18062 www.heniford.net/1234
Small Cast One-Act Guide Online

List of short plays.

18063 www.ifea.com
International Festivals and Events Association

Network for planning events and exchange programs; publishes quarterly magazine.

18064 www.intix.org
International Ticketing Association

Not-for-profit organizaiton whose purpose is to advance the success of the admission service industry and its members.

18065 www.ispa.org
International Society for the Performing Arts
Foundation

Supports international cooperation, facilitates networking and enhances professional dialogue.

18066 www.jensenfoundation.org
Fritz and Lavinia Jensen Foundation

Sponsors competitions.

18067 www.latinoarts.org
Association of Hispanic Arts

A multidisciplary organization which supports Hispanic arts organizations and individual artists with technical assistance. The organization facilitates projects and programs designed to foster the appreciation, growth, and well being of the Latino cultural community. It's quarter publication, AHA; Hispanic Arts News, features in depth articles on the local and national arts community, including artist profiles and a calendar of events.

18068 www.lib.colum.edu/costwais.html
Costume Image Database

Access costume images.

18069 www.light-link.com
Lightsearch.com

Lists of lighting equipment suppliers.

18070 www.livebroadway.com
League of American Theatres and Producers

National trade association for the commercial theatre industry whose principal activity is negotiation of labor contracts and government relations.

18071 www.lmda.org
Literary Managers and Dramaturgs of the Americas

Voluntary membership organization.

18072 www.luth.org
Guild of American Luthiers

Manufacturers and repairs stringed instruments; offers quarterly journal and triennial meeting.

18073 www.lycos.com
Lycos

Click Arts and Entertainment, then Dance, Theatre or Performing Arts.

18074 www.magicsam.com
Society of American Magicians

Founded to promote and maintain harmonious fellowship among those interested in magic as an art, to improve ethics of the magical profession, and to foster, promote and improve the advancement of magical arts in the field of amusement and entertainment. Membership includes professional and amateur magicians, manufacturers of magical apparatus and collectors.

18075 www.makeupmag.com
Make-Up Artist Magazine

Make-up artist magazine online.

18076 www.members.aol.com/thegoop/gaff.html
Gaff Tape Webring

Tech theatre.

18077 www.midatlanticarts.org
Mid Atlantic Arts Foundation

Provides leadership and support for artists and arts organizations in the Mid-Atlantic region and beyond.

18078 www.milieux.com/costume
Costume Source

Provides online sources for materials, costumes, accessories and books.

18079 www.mtishows.com
Music Theatre International

Scripts, cast recordings, study guides, production slides and other resources.

18080 www.musicalamerica.com
Musicalamerica.com

Late-breaking industry news, full search capabilities, immediate interaction between Presenter and Artist Manager/Artist.

18081 www.musicianshealth.com
Chiropractic Performing Arts Association

To educate amateur and professional entertainers, musicians and dancers about reaching optimum health potential through natural, drug-free, conservative chiropractic care.

18082 www.nadt.org
National Association for Drama Therapy

Promotes the profession of Drama Therapy.

18083 **www.namm.org**
NAMM-International Music Products Association

Offers professional development seminars; sells musical instruments and allied products.

18084 **www.napama.org**
North American Performing Arts Managers and Agents

A cooperative voice in a competitive business.

18085 **www.nbtf.org**
National Black Theatre Festival

18086 **www.netconline.org**
New England Theatre Conference

Non-profit educational corporation founded to develop, expand and assist theatre activity in community, educational and professional levels in New England. Holds annual auditions.

18087 **www.netsword.com/stagecombat.html**
Netsword

Lessons on stage combat.

18088 **www.newplaysforchildren.com**
New Plays Online

Plays for children and young adults.

18089 **www.nmpa.org**
National Music Publishers' Association

Publishes a quarterly newsletter and holds an annual meeting.

18090 **www.notam@2.no/icma**
International Computer Music Association

Supports the performance aspects of computer music; publishes newsletter and holds annual conferance.

18091 **www.ntcp.org**
Non-Traditional Casting Project

Promotes inclusive practices in television, theatre and film.

18092 **www.nyfa.org**
New York Foundation for the Arts

Employment openings in the arts.

18093 **www.nypl.org/reseach/lpa/lpa.html**
New York Public Library for the Performing Arts

Primary research collection.

18094 **www.nytimes.com**
New York Times on the Web

Arts and Theatre contains play reviews.

18095 **www.oobr.com**
Off-Off-Broadway Review

Lists information on off-off broadway shows such as: title of show, author, director, producing company, theatre, address, box-office phone number, dates and times, admission price and contact info.

18096 **www.opencasting.com**
Open Casting

Bulletin board containing auditions, crew calls, casting notices and links.

18097 **www.paastjo.org**
Performing Arts Association

Provides a diverse selection of performing arts.

18098 **www.pen.org**
PEN: American Center

Site of the international literary community organization.

18099 **www.performingarts.net**
Performing Arts Online

Dedicated to the perpetuation of quality performing arts.

18100 **www.pianonet.com**
Piano Manufacturers Association International

Manufacturers and suppliers of pianos and parts; holds annual trade show.

18101 **www.pipeorgan.org**
American Institute of Organ Builders

Sponsers training seminars, quarterly journal and annual convention for pipe organ builders and service technicians.

18102 **www.plasa.org**
Professional Lighting and Sound Association

Web site for PLASA, a leading trade body for Lighting and Sound Professionals.

18103 **www.playbill.com**
Playbill Online

Listings for Broadway and off Broadway theatre productions. Also guides for sites, including summer stock, national touring shows and regional theatres worldwide.

18104 **www.playwrights.org**
Playwrights Center of San Francisco

Playwrites directory.

18105 **www.playwrightshorizons.org**
Playwrights Horizon

At home page click arrow. On next page click working with PH. You will see Writing Submissions.

18106 **www.playwrightsproject.com**
Playwrights Project

Promotes literacy, creativity and communication skills in young people through drama-based activities.

18107 **www.press.jhu.edu/press/journals/paj**
Johns Hopkins University Press

A journal of performance and art.

18108 **www.press.jhu.edu/press/journals/tj**
Johns Hopkins University Press

Theatre Journal

18109 **www.press.jhu.edu/press/journals/tt**
Johns Hopkins University Press

Theatre Topics

18110 **www.proppeople.com**
Proppeople.com

Online home for props professionals.

18111 **www.renfaire.com/Language/index.html**
Renfaire.com

Lessons on proper Elizabethan accents.

18112 **www.rigging.net**
Rigger's Page

Technical information on stage rigging equipment.

18113 www.roundalab.org
Roundalab

A professional international society of individuals who teach round dancing at any phase.

18114 www.safd.org
Society of American Fight Directors

Promotes safety in directing staged combat and theatrical violence.

18115 www.sag.org
Screen Actors Guild

Labor union affiliated with AFL-CIO which represents actors in film, television and commercials.

18116 www.sapphireswan.com/dance
Dance Directory

Dance resources.

18117 www.setc.org
Southeastern Theatre Conference

Annual conventions include auditions.

18118 www.sfballet.org
San Francisco Ballet Association

Provides a repertoire of classical and contemporary ballet; to provide educational opportunities for professional dancers and choreographers; to excel in ballet, artistic direction and administration.

18119 www.southarts.org
Southern Arts Federation

Serves as the leadership voice to increase the regional, national and international awareness and prominence of Southern arts. Creates mechanisms and partnerships to expand local, regional, national and international markets for Southern arts.

18120 www.spolin.com
Spolin Center

Information on improvisational theatre.

18121 www.ssdc.org
Society of Stage Directors and Choreographers

An independent labor union representing directors and choreographers in American theatre.

18122 www.stage-directions.com
Stage Directions Magazine

The practical and technical side of theatrical operations.

18123 www.stageplays.com/markets.htm
Playwrights Noticeboard

Information on contests, publishing and production opportunities.

18124 www.stetson.edu/csata/thr_guid.html
McCoy's Guide to Theatre and Performance Studies

A brief guide to internet resources in theatre and performance studies put out by Stetson University.

18125 www.summertheater.com
Directory of Summer Theater in the United States

Search for summer theater opportunities by alphabetized listings or geographic region.

18126 www.talkinbroadway.com
Talkin' Broadway

Theatrical events and information on and off Broadway and other selected geographical locations.

18127 www.tcg.org
Theatre Communications Group

Supports alliances among playwrights, theatres and communities. Promotes not-for-profit theatre and offers resources to jobseekers. Offers financial support to designers and directors through its Career Development Program.

18128 www.tdf.org
Theatre Development Fund

Not-for-profit service organization. Provides support for every area of the dance, music and professional theatre field. Founded 1968.

18129 www.teleport.com/~bjscript/index.htm
Essays on the Craft of Dramatic Writing

Essays on writing a screenplay, play or novel.

18130 www.theatre-resource.com
Theatre Resource

Career and employment information.

18131 www.theatrebayarea.org
Theatre Bay Area

Serving more than 400 member theatre companies and 3,000 individual members in the San Francisco Bay Area and Northern California, Theatre Bay Area provides monthly classes, workshops, events, information and publications.

18132 www.theatrecrafts.com
Theatrecrafts.com

Practical information about technical theatre techniques for theatre folk at any level.

18133 www.theatrejobs.com
Theatrejobs.com

Online job placement. Festival listings, summer stock, assistantships, apprenticeships, fellowships and internships.

18134 www.theatrelibrary.org/links
Performing Arts Links

General resources including applied and interactive theatre, performing arts data service and art sites. Digital librarian includes glossary of technical theatre terms.

18135 www.theatrelibrary.org/links/index.html
Theatrelibrary.org

Master categories are Theatre, Dance, Cinema and Reviews.

18136 www.thecastingnetwork.com/webring.html
Casting Network.com

By and for actors.

18137 www.theplays.org
Electronic Literature Foundation

William Shakespeare's plays online.

18138 www.top20performingarts.com
Top 20 Performing Arts

Online directory for Perfoming Arts education.

18139 www.towson.edu/worldmusiccongresses
World Music Congresses

1997-2010 World Cello Congress' II-V, 2004 The First World Guitar Congress and 2008 World Guitar Congress II. Celebrations of music with international gatherings of the world's greatest musicians, composers, conductors, instrument manufacturers students, and music lovers from around the globe.

18140 www.unc.edu/depts/outdoor
Institute of Outdoor Drama

Summer jobs for all theatrical personnel.

18141 www.ups.edu/professionalorgs/dramaturgy
Dramaturgy Northwest

Relevant information for all dramaturgs.

18142 www.urta.com
University/Resident Theatre Association

Coalition of theatre training programs. Sponsors unified auditions.

18143 www.usabda.org
USA Dance

Non-profit organization working to promote ballroom dancing, both as a recreational activity and as a competetive sport.

18144 www.usitt.org
United States Institute for Theatre Technology

The association of design, production and technology professionals in the performing arts and entertainment industry whose mission is to promote the knowledge and skills of its members. International in scope, USITT draws its board of directors from across the US and Canada. Sponsors projects, programs, research, symposia, exhibits, and annual conference. Disseminates information on aesthetic and technical developments.

18145 www.variety.org
Variety

e-version of the show business newspaper.

18146 www.vcu.edu/artweb/playwriting
Playwriting Seminars

An opinionated web companion on the art and craft of playwriting for theatre and dance.

18147 www.vl-theatre.com
WWW Virtual Library

Links to theatre and drama resources. Updated daily.

18148 www.writersguild.com
Writers Guild of America

List of Agents and information on Mentor program.

18149 www.wwar.com
World Wide Arts Resources

Links to Theatre and Dance.

18150 www2.sundance.org
Sundance Institute

Information on the Sundance Theatre Laboratory summer workshop for directors, playwrights, choreographers, solo performers and composers. For information on submitting a play, click Theatre Program on home page.

Associations

18151 ADSC: The International Association of Foundation Drilling
Pacific Center 1
14180 Dallas Parkway
Suite 510
Dallas, TX 75254
214-343-2091
FAX: 214-343-2384
adsc@adsc-iafd.com
www.adsc-iafd.com

S Scott Litke, Executive Director
Marilyn Ellis, Business&Financial Administrator
Jan Hall, Director Meetings
Ted Ledgard, Admin Director

Seeks to advance technology in the drilled shaft, anchored geo-support and other related industries. Represents drilled shaft anchored geo-support and other related subcontractors, civil engineers and equipment manufacturing firms worldwide.
870 Members Founded: 1971

18152 American Association of Petroleum Geologists
PO Box 979
Tulsa, OK 74101-0979
918-584-2555
FAX: 918-560-2632
bulletin@aapg.org www.aapg.org

Rick Fritz, Executive Director

Supports those professionals involved in the field of geology as it relates to petroleum, natural gas, and other energy products. Publishes monthly journal of peer-reviewed articles.
30000 Members Founded: 1917
Mailing list available for rent

18153 American Association of Professional Landmen
4100 Fossil Creek Boulevard
Fort Worth, TX 76137
817-847-7700
FAX: 817-847-7704
info@infomine.com
www.infomine.com

Andy Robertson, Executive Chairman
Rod Young, CEO
Graham Baldwin, President
Robin Forte, Manager

Supports a four-year college curriculum developed by AAPL. Operates landmen certification programs. Maintains placement service.
7000 Members Founded: 1955

18154 American Gas Association
400 N Capitol Street NW
Suite 450
Washington, DC 20001
202-477-7337
FAX: 202-824-7115
khardardt@aga.org www.aga.org

Lawrence M Downes, Chairman
David N Parker, President/CEO
Kevin Hardardt, Administrator

Represents local energy utility companies that deliver natural gas to more than 56 million homes, businesses and industries throughout the United States.
195 Members

18155 American Independent Refiners Association
3315 Cummings Lane
Chevy Chase, MD 20815-3239
301-251-1537
FAX: 301-913-9041

Supports all those involved in the refining industry.

18156 American Institute of Mining Metallurgical & Petroleum Engineers
8307 Shaffer Parkway
P O Box 270728
Littleton, CO 80127-4012
303-948-4255
FAX: 303-948-4260
aime@aimehq.org www.aimehq.org

J Rick Rolater, Executive Director
L Michele Gottwald, Executive Assistant

AIME is and shall be a New York State Nonprofit Corporation organized and operated to advance and disseminate, through the programs of the Member Societies, knowledge of engineering and the arts and sciences involved in the production and use of minerals, metals, energy sources and materials for the benefit of humankind, and to represent AIME and the Member Societies within the larger engineering community.
90000 Members Founded: 1871

18157 American Petroleum Institute
1220 L Street NW
Suite 900
Washington, DC 20005-4070
202-682-8000
FAX: 202-682-8223 www.api.org

Red Cavaney, Executive Director

Seeks to maintain cooperation between government and industry, fosters foreign and domestic trade in American petroleum products, conducts research.
500 Members Founded: 1919

18158 American Public Gas Association
201 Massachusetts Avenue NE
Suite C-4
Washington, DC 20002
202-464-2742
FAX: 202-464-0246 800-927-4204
1willsdudich@apga.org www.apga.org

Bert Kalisch, President/CEO
David Schryver, Executive VP
David Schryver, VP Congressional Affairs
Robert Cave, Executive Director
Sheila Deringis, Business/Membership Manager

To be an advocate for public-owned natural gas distribution systems, educateand communicate with members to promote safety, awareness, performance and competitiveness.
592 Members Founded: 1961

18159 Association of Energy Service Companies
10200 Richmond Avenue
Suite 275
Houston, TX 77042
713-781-0758
FAX: 713-781-7542 800-672-0771
pjordan@aesc.net www.aesc.net

Kenny Jordan, Executive Director
Patty Jordan, Publisher/Sales Manager
Angla Fails, Administrative Manager

Professional trade association for well-site service contractors and businesses providing goods and services to well-site contractors. Develops and sells training and safety materials.
600 Members Founded: 1956

18160 Association of Oil Pipe Lines
1101 Vermont Avenue NW
Suite 604
Washington, DC 20005
202-408-7970
FAX: 202-408-7983
aopl@aopl.org www.aopl.org

Benjamin Cooper, Executive Director
Michele Joy, General Counsel
Raymond Paul, Director Public Affairs

Assembles statistics and other data relating to the pipeline industry for presentation to Congress, government departments, trade associations, and the public.
47 Members Founded: 1947

18161 Association of Petroleum Refiners
1899 L Street
Suite 1000
Washington, DC 20036-3896
202-457-0480
FAX: 202-457-0486
info@npra.org www.npradc.org

George Booth

Association that represents the petrochemical and refining industries, sponsors periodic conferences, and seeks to inform policymakers and the public. Issues include the recycling of used oils and other liquid wastes.
450 Members

18162 Coordinating Research Council
3650 Mansell Road
Suite 140
Alpharetta, GA 30022
678-795-0506
FAX: 678-795-0509
jantucker@crcao.com www.crcao.com

Tim Belian, Executive Director
Brent Bailey, Deputy Director
Renee Mamane, Controller
Beth Evans, Consultant

Coordinates research activities among petroleum and petroleum equipment and transportation industries.
1M Members Founded: 1942

18163 Council of Petroleum Accountants Societies
3900 East Mexico Avenue
Suite 602
Denver, CO 80210
303-300-1311
FAX: 303-300-3733 877-992-6727
NatlOfc@copas.org www.copas.org

Scott Hillman, Executive Director

Members are accountants involved in, or closely related to, the oil and gas industry. Also provides ethical standards for energy accountants and is the certification organization for the Accredited Petroleum Accountant program.
3200 Members Founded: 1961

18164 Crompton Corporation
One American Lane
Greenwich, CT 06831-2559

Produces specialty chemicals and equipment used in products from tires to textiles and paper to auto parts. Makes rubber chemicals and polymers, seed-treatment and crop-protection chemicals, additives for plastic and petroleum products, organosilicones used in fiberglass, and petroleum additives.

18165 Domestic Petroleum Council
101 Constitution Avenue NW
Suite 800
Washington, DC 20001-2133
202-742-4300

info@dcpusa.org www.dpcusa.org/
William F Whitsitt, President
To work constructively for sound energy, environmental and related public policies that encourage responsible exploration, development, and production of natural gas and crude oil to meet consumer needs and fuel our economy.
24 Members Founded: 1975

18166 Energy Security Council
5555 San Felipe Street
Suite 101
Houston, TX 77056
713-296-1893
FAX: 713-296-1895
info@energysecuritycouncil.org
www.energysecuritycouncil.org
John J Covert, Executive Director
Founded as Petroleum Industry Security Council and assumed its current name in 1999. Provides support to security professionals and business developers in the energy industry.
450 Members Founded: 1981

18167 Energy Telecommunications and Electrical Association
5005 Royal Lane
Suite 190
Irving, TX 75063
972-292-2918
888-503-8700
entelec@entelec.org www.entelec.org

Blain Siske, Executive Manager
Members are companies and corporations in the energy industries employing personnel having managerial, engineering or technical respnosibility in the electrical, electronics, communications and allied fields.
140 Members Founded: 1928

18168 Energy Traffic Association
3303 Main Street Corridor
Houston, TX 77002
713-528-2868
FAX: 713-464-0702
russell@energytraffic.org
www.energytraffic.org
Russell Powell, Executive Director
The members work in logistics or related company functions for shippers in the energy industry.
100 Members Founded: 1941

18169 Fiberglass Tank and Pipe Institute
11150 S Wilcrest Drive
Suite 101
Houston, TX 77099-4343
281-568-4100
FAX: 281-568-4500
sullycurra@aol.com
www.fiberglasstankandpipe.com
Sullivan D Curran, Executive Director
The fiberglass-reinforced, thermosetting, plastic tank and pipe manufacturing industry. Members are domestic manufacturers.
5 Members Founded: 1987

18170 Gas Research Machinery Council
3030 LBJ Freeway
Suite 1300
Dallas, TX 75234
972-620-4024
FAX: 972-620-8518
mshort@southerngas.org
www.gmrc.org
Marsha Short, VP
Members are companies in the natural gas, oil and petrochemical industries in mechanical and fluid systems design.
75 Members Founded: 1952

18171 Independent Liquid Terminals Association
1444 I Street NW
#400
Washington, DC 20005
202-842-9200
FAX: 202-326-8660
info@ilta.org www.ilta.org
E David Doane, President
Melinda Whitney, Director/Government Affairs
Supports all those bulk, liquid terminal owners/operators and establishments supplying equipment, goods and services to the bulk liquid terminaling industry. Publishes monthly newsletter.
Founded: 1974

18172 Independent Lubricant Manufacturers
400 N Columbus St
Ste 201
Alexandria, VA 22314-2264
703-684-5574
FAX: 703-836-8503
ilma@ilma.org www.ilma.org
Paul P Converso, President
James A Taglia, First VP
Celeste Powers, Executive Director
Glenn Boyle, Second VP
Dixon W Benz II, Executive Sales Manager
Independent blenders and compounders of lubricants.
Founded: 1948

18173 Independent Petroleum Association of America
1201 15th Street NW
Suite 300
Washington, DC 20005
202-857-4722
FAX: 202-857-4799 www.ipaa.org
Barry Russell, President
Teresa McCafferty, VP Administration/Chief of Staff
Lee Fuller, VP Government Relations
Tina Hamlin, VP Meetings
Fred Lawrence, VP Economics & International Affair
Members are small producers of oil and natural gas and their suppliers.
5500 Members Founded: 1929

18174 Independent Terminal Operators Association
1150 Connecticut Avenue NW
9th Floor
Washington, DC 20036-4129
202-828-4100
FAX: 202-828-4130 wbode@bode.com

William H Bode, Secretary & General Counsel
Represents indepedent petroleum distributors.
15 Members Founded: 1970

18175 Institute of Gas Technology
1700 S Mount Prospect Road
Des Plaines, IL 60018
847-680-0664
FAX: 847-768-0501
publicrelations@gastechnology.org
www.igt.org
Stanley S Borys, Executive VP/COO
Robert A Stokes, VP Research/Deployment Division
David C Carroll, VP Business Development Division
James E Dunne, VP Administration/CFO
Carol Worster, Manager
An independent, not-for-profit center for energy and environmental research, development, education and information. Main function is to perform sponsored and in-house research, development and demonstration, provide educational programs and services, and disseminate scientific and technical information.
Founded: 1941

18176 International Association of Drilling
10370 Richmond Avenue
Suite 760
Houston, TX 77042
713-292-1945
FAX: 713-292-1946
info@iadc.org www.iadc.org
Dr Lee Hunt, President
Ken Fischer, VP Operations
Brian Petty, Senior VP Government Affairs
Mike Killalea, VP Member Services
Alan Spackman, Director Offshore Technical Affairs
Conducts educational and training programs. Sponsors safety contest and bestows awards.
980 Members Founded: 1940

18177 International Association of Geophysical
2550 N Loop
W Suite 104
Houston, TX 77092
713-957-8080
FAX: 713-957-0008
iagc@iagc.org www.iagc.org
Chip Gill, President
Timothy Wells, Chairman
Companies involved in oil exploration.
203 Members Founded: 1971

18178 International Energy Credit Association
8325 Lantern View Lane
St John, IN 46373
219-365-7313
FAX: 219-365-0327
rraichle@ieca.net www.ieca.net
Robert Raichle, Executive Vice President

Members are credit and financial executives with companies whose product is a petroleum derivative.
800 Members Founded: 1923

18179 International Oil Scouts Association
PO Box 272949
Houston, TX 77277
512-472-8138

jyoung@newfld.com
www.oilscouts.org

Jim Young, President
David Martinez, VP
John Reedy, Treasurer
Bill Morris, Secretary

Compiles statistics on exploration and development wells in the United States. Offers professional development and scholarship programs. *$75.00*

175 Members Founded: 1924

18180 International Slurry Surfacing Association
3 Church Circle PMB 250
Annapolis, MD 21401
410-267-0023
FAX: 410-267-7546
krissoff@slurry.org www.slurry.org

Michael R Krissoff, Executive Director

A non profit association dedicated to the interests, education, and success of slurry surfacing professionals and corporations around the world.

200 Members Founded: 1963

18181 International Union of Petroleum and Industrial Workers
8131 E Rosecrans Avenue
Paramount, CA 90723
562-086-6187
FAX: 562-408-1073 800-624-5842

George R Beltz, International President
Pamela Parlow, Internat'l Secretary/Tresurer

5000 Members Founded: 1945

18182 Interstate Natural Gas Association of America
10 G Street NE
Suite 700
Washington, DC 20002
202-216-5900
FAX: 202-216-0870 www.ingaa.org

Donald F Santa Jr, President
Joan Dreskin, VP General Counsel/RA Secretary
Martin Edwards III, VP of Legislative Affairs
Terry D Boss, SVP/Safety/Environment/Tech Svcs

Trade association of natural gas pipelines in the United States, Canada, Mexico and Europe.

30 Members Founded: 1944

18183 Interstate Oil and Gas Compact Commission
PO Box 53127
Oklahoma City, OK 73152-3127
405-525-2556
FAX: 405-525-3592
iogcc@iogcc.state.ok.us
www.iogcc.oklaosf.state.ok.us

Christine Hansen, Executive Director
Alesha Leemaster, Manager Communications

The members are states that produce oil or gas; associate states support the conservation of America's energy resources. Also establishes rules andguidelines for the proper maintenance of wells.

700 Members Founded: 1935

18184 Liaison Committee of Cooperating Oil and Gas Association
1718 Columbus Road SW
PO Box 535
Granville, OH 13023-0535
740-587-0444
FAX: 740-587-0446
stewart@ooga.org
www.energyconnect.com/liason

Thomas E Stewart, Secretary/Treasurer

Established to facilitate communication among state and regional oil and gas associations.

25 Members Founded: 1957

18185 Mid-Continent Oil and Gas Association
801 North Blvd.
Baton Rouge,, LA 70802-2666

FAX: 202-638-5967 e-mail
info@lmoga.com

Wayne Gibbens, President

Oil and gas producers and royalty owners.

7.5M Members Founded: 1917

18186 NLGI
4635 Wyandotte Street
Suite 202
Kansas City, MO 64112-1542
816-931-9480
FAX: 816-753-5026
nlgi@nlgi.org www.nlgi.org

Chuck Hitchcock, General Manager
Kim Bott, Administrative Assistant

Members are companies that manufacture and market all types of lubricating greases, additive or equipment suppliers, and research and educational groups whose interests are primarily technical

280 Members Founded: 1933

18187 NORA: An Association of Responsible Recyclers
5965 Amber Ridge Road
Haymarket, VA 20169
703-753-4277
FAX: 703-753-2445
sparker@noranews.org
www.noranews.org

Scott D Parker, Executive Director

Members are companies that reprocess used antifreeze, wastewater, oil filters, chemicals and companies that provide products or services to the industry.

211 Members Founded: 1984

18188 National Association of Division Order Analysts
2805 Oak Trail Court
Suite 6312
Arlington, TX 76016
972-715-4489

nadoa_org@hotmail.com
www.nadoa.org

Lynn S McCord, Administrator

900 Members Founded: 1974

18189 National Association of Oil Heating Service Managers
PO Box 67
East Petersburg, PA 17520-0067
717-625-3076
FAX: 717-625-3077 888-552-0900
info@naohsm.org www.naohsm.org

David Bessette, President
Judy Garber, Executive Administrator

Members are oil heat service managers and small business owners. Also provides members with technical tapes, books and speakers to train thei employee technicians.

1400 Members Founded: 1952

18190 National Association of Royalty Owners
PO Box 21888
Oklahoma City, OK 73156-1888
405-286-9400
FAX: 405-286-9402 800-558-0557
naro@naro-us.org www.naro-us.org

James Stafford, President/COO
Margaret K Redwine, Chairman

Assists mineral and royalty owners in the effective management of their mineral properties. Provides information on tax, regulatory, and legislative matters. Conducts seminars and bestows awards.

5M Members Founded: 1980

18191 National Drilling Association
11001 Danka Way N
Suite 1
St. Petersburg, FL 33716
727-577-5006
FAX: 727-577-5012
info@nda4u.com www.nda4u.com

Patrick O'Brien, Executive Director
P Don Ulses, President
R Alan Garrard, Director
G Michael Tiani, Secretary/Treasurer

Supports national drilling contractors, and equipment drilling manufacturers. Publishes magazine.

250+ Members Founded: 1972

18192 National Ocean Industries Association
1120 G Street NW
Suite 900
Washington, DC 20005-3841
202-347-6900
FAX: 202-347-8650 www.noia.org

Tom Fry, President

Represents all facets of the domestic offshore and related industries. Member companies are dedicated to the development of offshore oil and natural gas for the continued growth and security of the US.

300 Members Founded: 1972

18193 National PetroChemical & Refiners Association
1899 L Street NW
Suite 1000
Washington, DC 20036-3810
202-457-0480
FAX: 202-457-0486 www.npra.org

Robert Slaughter, President

Members are petroleum, petrochemical and refining companies.

18194 National Petroleum Council
1625 K Street NW
Suite 600
Washington, DC 20006
202-393-6100
FAX: 202-331-8539
info@npc.org www.npc.org

Harry S Truman, President
Marshall Nichols, Executive Director

Self-supporting, federal advisory body to the Secretary of Eenergy established in 1946 at the request of President Truman.

175 Members Founded: 1946

18195 National Propane Gas Association
1150 17th Street NW
Suite 310
Washington, DC 20036
202-466-7200
FAX: 202-466-7205
info@npga.org www.npga.org

Richard Roldan, President/CEO
Brian Dunlapford, Chief Financial Officer

Members are producers and distributors of liquified petroleum gas and equipment manufacturers.

3500 Members Founded: 1931

18196 National Stripper Well Association

Equinox
1201 15th Street NW,
Suite 300
Washington, DC 20005
202-857-4722
FAX: 202-857-4799 www.ipaa.org

Lee O Fuller, President
Dan Naatz, VP

This operates under the Independent Petroleum Associatin of America, which is an informed voice for the exloration and production segment of the industry It provices economic and statistical information, and develops investment symposia and other opportunities for its memners.

300 Members Founded: 1934

18197 Natural Gas Supply Association

805 15th Street NW
Suite 510
Washington, DC 20005-2276
202-326-9300
FAX: 202-293-6558

Skip Horvath, President

An association for suppliers of natural gas, nationwide.

18198 Newport Associates

7400 E Orchard Road
Suite 320
Englewood, CO 80111-2528

FAX: 303-779-0908

Association for over 450 oil companies in over 20 world regions.

18199 Nuclear Energy Institute

1776 I Street NW
Suite 400
Washington, DC 20006-3708
202-739-8000
FAX: 202-785-4113 www.nei.org

Frank Bowman, President/CEO

Members are of utilities, manufacturers of electrical generating equipment, researchers, architects, engineers, labor unions, and others interested in the generation of electricity by nuclear power.

370 Members Founded: 1981

18200 Paper,Allied-Industrial,Chemical and Energy Workers International Union

3340 Perimeter Hill Drive
Nashville, TN 37211
615-834-8590
FAX: 615-731-6362
jhill@isdn.net www.paceunion.org

Jim Pannell, VP
Lynne Baker, Associate Director Communications
Joan Hill, Director Research & Education
Elaine Piper, Owner

Work to make life better for the workers and their families.

320M Members Founded: 1884

18201 Petroleum Equipment Institute

PO Box 2380
Tulsa, OK 74101-2380
918-494-9696
FAX: 918-491-9895
dooley@pei.org www.pei.org

Robert Renkes, Executive Director

Members are makers and distributors of equipment used in service stations, bulk plants and other petroleum marketing facilities.

1580 Members Founded: 1951
Mailing list available for rent 1600 names $275 per M.

18202 Petroleum Equipment Suppliers Association

9225 Katy Freeway
Suite 310
Houston, TX 77024-1510
713-932-0168
FAX: 713-932-0497

Sherry A Stephens, President

Members are makers of oil field production and drilling equipment, well site services and supplies.

350 Members Founded: 1982

18203 Petroleum Investor Relations Association

c/o Rowan Companies Inc
2800 Post Oak Road
Houston, TX 77056-6196
713-960-7575
FAX: 713-960-7560 www.pira.org

William Provine, President
Robert E Wright, Secretary/Treasurer

Represents investor communications professional in the peroleum and natural gas industry

100 Members Founded: 2000

18204 Petroleum Marketers Association

Petroleum Marketers Association of America
1901 Fort Myer Drive
Suite 1200
Arlington, VA 22209-1616
703-351-8000
FAX: 703-351-9160

Daniel Gilligan, President
Nancy Kniher, Director Member Service

Supports all those professional marketers in the petroleum industry. Publishes annual directory. *$50.00*

18205 Petroleum Technology Transfer Council

16010 Barkers Point Lane
Suite 220
, TX 77079
281-921-1720
FAX: 281-921-1723
hq@pttc.org www.pttc.org

Don Duttlinger, Executive Director
Brian Sim, Chairman
Gene Ames III, Secretary

Fosters the effective transfer of exploration and production technology to US petroleum producers through regional resource centers, workshops, websites, publications, etc.

Founded: 1993

18206 Pipeline Research Council International

1401wilson Boulevard
Suite 1101
Arlington, VA 22209
703-387-0190
FAX: 703-837-0192
gtenely@prci.com www.prci.com

George W Tenely Jr, President

Sponsors research on technical issues facing the natural gas transmission industry. Members are companies operating pipelnie systems.

24 Members Founded: 1952

18207 Rocky Mountain Oil and Gas Association

1900 Grant Street
Denver, CO 80203
303-860-0099
FAX: 303-860-0310

Jess D Cooper, General Manager
Linda Swain, Manager

A trade association, representing oil and gas industries.

600 Members Founded: 1920

18208 Service Station Dealers of America

801 N Fairfax Street
Suite 109
Alexandria, VA 22314-1757
703-684-5444
FAX: 703-548-0484

Melvin Sherbert, Executive Director

Service station operators.

Founded: 1947

18209 Society of Petroleum Engineers

PO Box 833836
Richardson, TX 75083-3836
972-529-9300
FAX: 972-952-9435
spedal@spe.org www.spe.org

Kate Baker, President
Peter Goode, VP Finance
Alex Neyin, Director Africa Region
Ali R Al-Jarwan, Director Middle East Region
Mark Rubin, Executive Director

Supports those professionals involved in the field of exploration, drilling, production, and reservoir management, as well as related manufacturing and service organizations. Publishes monthly magazine.

55000 Members Founded: 1957

18210 Society of Petroleum Evaluation Engineers

1001 McKinney
Suite 801
Houston, TX 77002
713-279-9991
FAX: 713-951-9659
bkspee@aol.com www.spee.org

B K Buongiorno, Executive Secretary
E Bernard Brauer, President
S Tim Smith, VP

Members are engineers specializing in the fields of petroleum and natural gas properties.

495 Members Founded: 1962

18211 Society of Petrophysicists and Well Log Analysts

8866 Gulf Freeway
Suite 320
Houston, TX 77002
713-947-8727
FAX: 713-947-7181
spwla@spwla.org www.spwla.org

Vicki J King, Executive Director

Provides information services to scientists in the petroleum and mineral industries, serves as a voice of shared interests in our profession, plays a major role in strengthening petrophysical education, and strives to increase the awareness of the role petrophysics has in the Oil and Gas Industry and the scientific community.

3300 Members Founded: 1959

18212 Society of Professional Well Log Analysts
8866 Gulf Freeway
Houston, TX 77017-6531
713-947-8727
FAX: 713-947-7181
vicki@spwla.org www.spwla.org

Vicki J King, Executive Director

Promotes the evaluation of formations, through well logging techniques, in order to locate gas, oil and other minerals.

2800 Members Founded: 1959

18213 Solution Mining Research Institute
105 Apple Valley Circle
Clarks Summit, PA 18411
570-585-8092
FAX: 570-585-8091
smri@solutionmining.org
www.solutionmining.org

John O Voigt, Executive Director
Carolyn L Diamond, Assistant Executive Director

Members are companies interested in the production of salt brine and sloution mining of potash and soda ash, as well as production of salt covers, used for storage of oi, gas, chemicals, compressed air and waste.

100 Members Founded: 1958

18214 Spill Control Association of America
8631 W Jefferson Avenue
Detroit, MI 48209-2691
313-245-5531
FAX: 313-849-1623
info@scaa-spill.org
www.scaa-spill.org

Marc K Shaye, Executive Director
David Usher, President
Ralph Bianchi, VP Manufacturers
Mark Miller, VP Contractors
Michael Sapala, Manager

Members are companies concerned with cleaning up spills of oil and hazardous products and manufacturers of specialized products for spill control.

Founded: 1973

18215 Tubular Exchanger Manufacturers Association
25 North Broadway
Tarrytown, NY 10591
914-332-0040
FAX: 914-332-1541
info@tema.org www.tema.org

Richard C Byrne, Secretary

Sets standards for the industry, known as TEMA Standards, which are sold to the chemical processing and petroleum refining industries

18 Members Founded: 1939

18216 Western Petroleum Marketers Association
4393 South Riverboat Road
Suite 380
Taylorsville, UT 84123-2593
801-263-9762
FAX: 801-262-9413
info@wpma.com www.wpma.com

Gene Inglesby, Executive Director
Mark Walker, President
Benny Hodges, President
Dennis Baird, VP

A trade association for oil jobbers.

Founded: 1953

18217 Western States Petroleum Association
1415 L Street
Suite 600
Sacramento, CA 95814
916-444-9981
FAX: 916-444-5745 www.wspa.org

Douglas F Henderson, President
Catherine Reheis-Boyd, COO
Steven Arita, Senior Environmental Coordinator
Barbara Chichester, Bookkeeper

Trade association that represents the full spectrum of those companies that refine, produce, transport, and market petroleum and petroleum products in six western states: Arizona, California, Oregon, Nevada, Hawaii and Washington.

35 Members Founded: 1907

Newsletters

18218 Alternative & Renewable Energy E-mail News & Analysis
Forecast International
22 Commerce Road
Newtown, CT 06470-1643
203-426-0800
FAX: 203-426-1964 www.forecast1.com

Kathy Bertrand, Production Manager
Monty Nebinger, Circulation Director

An electronic information/data service sourced from thousands of worldwide publications, in 15 languages. Provides concise summaries, news, trends and contract information with hyper-links to the source or a related website. Delivered 100 times a year. *$425.00*

2 per week

18219 Butane-Propane News
PO Box 660698
Arcadia, CA 91066-698
626-357-2168
FAX: 626-303-2854 800-214-4386
bpn@bpnews.com
http://www.bpnews.com

Natalie Peal, Publisher
Ann Rey, Editorial Director

Petroleum and propane industry news. *$32.00*

Monthly Founded: 1939 : web

18220 Clean-Coal/Synfuels Letter
McGraw Hill
PO Box 182604
Columbus, OH 43272
614-304-4000
FAX: 614-759-3749 877-833-5524
customer.service@mcgraw-hill.com
http://www.mcgraw-hill.com

John Higgins, Publisher

Provides worldwide coverage of the development of clean-coal technologies. *$840.00*

6 pages Monthly Founded: 1899

18221 Coal Outlook
Pasha Publications
1600 Wilson Boulevard
Suite 600
Arlington, VA 22209-2509
703-528-1244
FAX: 703-528-1253 800-424-2908

Harry Baisden, Group Publisher
Michael Hopps, Editor
Kathy Thorne, Circulation Manager

Primary strategic information source that keeps coal marketing executives and utilities up-to-date on who's getting coal contracts and at what price. *$795.00*

Weekly

18222 Coal Week International
McGraw Hill
2 Penn Plaza
25th floor
New York, NY 10121-2525
212-044-4097
FAX: 720-548-5701 800-752-8878
support@platts.com
http://www.platts.com

John Higgins, Publisher
David Stellfox, Editor
Harry Sachinis, CEO
Larry Barth, Marketing Manager

A market management intelligence service for executives concerned with world trade metallurgical and steam coal. *$987.00*

8 pages Weekly Founded: 1888

18223 Coal and Synfuels Technology
Pasha Publications
1600 Wilson Boulevard
Suite 600
Arlington, VA 22209-2510
703-528-1244
FAX: 703-528-1253 800-424-2908

Harry Baisden, Group Publisher
Michael Hopps, Editor

Reports on the US and international advances in clean coal technologies, synthetic fuels and clean air issues. *$790.00*

Weekly Founded: 1985

18224 Cold Water Oil Spills
Cutter Information Corporation
37 Broadway
Suite 1
Arlington, MA 02474-5552
781-648-8700
FAX: 781-648-1950 800-888-8939
service@cutter.com
http://www.cutter.com

Kim Leonard, Editor
Karen Coburn, President/CEO

Clean up and control of oil spills in cold and icy waters. *$175.00*

Founded: 1986

18225 Gas Daily
1200 G Street NW
#1000
Washington, DC 20005
202-383-2100
FAX: 202-383-2125 800-752-8878
support@platts.com
http://www.gasdaily.com

Mark Davidson, Publisher
Bill Loveless, Manager

Information on spot prices cash markets and regulatory developments for the natural gas industry. *$2255.00*

Daily

18226 Gas Storage Report
Pasha Publications
1600 Wilson Boulevard
#600
Arlington, VA 22209-2510
703-528-1244
FAX: 703-528-7821 180- 42- 290
gasstor@pasha.com
http://www.pasha.com

Jeff Pruzan, Editor

Detailed charts that list monthly storage activity of all interstate pipelines and covers all phases of the underground storage of natural gas. *$495.00*
Monthly

18227 Gasturbine-E-mail News & Analysis
Forecast International
22 Commerce Road
Newtown, CT 06470-1643
203-426-0800
FAX: 203-426-1964
www.forecast1.com

Kathy Bertrand, Production Manager
Monty Nebinger, Circulation Director

An electronic information/data service sourced from thousands of worldwide publications, in 15 languages. Provides concise summaries, news, trends and contract information with hyper-links to the source or a related website. Delivered 100 times a year. *$425.00*
2 per week

18228 Golob's Oil Pollution Bulletin
World Information Systems
PO Box 535
Cambridge, MA 02238-0535

FAX: 617-492-3312

Richard S Golob, Publisher
Roger B Wilson Jr, Editor

Provides news analysis on oil pollution prevention, control and cleanup. Covers oil spills worldwide, regulations, legislation and court decisions, technical reports, new equipment and products, contract opportunities and awards, and conference notices. *$335.00*
BiWeekly
Circulation: 20,000

18229 Gulf of Mexico Newsletter
Offshore Data Services
3200 Wilcrest Dr
Suite 170
Houston, TX 77042-1909
713-812-2713
FAX: 832-463-3100
editors@offshore-data.com
http://www.offshore-data.com

Brad Baethe, Publisher
Hannah Hartland, Sales Administrator

Aimed at the supply and service people of the off-shore oil and gas industry in the Gulf of Mexico, covers all significant industry news and events, and summarizes construction and field development activities. *$259.00*
Weekly Founded: 2002
Circulation: 2150

18230 Hart's Renewable Fuel News
Hart Evepy Publishing LP
1201 Seven Locks Road
#300
Potomac, MD 20854
301-354-2100
FAX: 301-424-7260
hartinfo@hartenergy.com
http://www.worldfuels.com

Rachel Gantz, Editor
Robert Gaph, Editorial Director

Refinery updates, oxygenation schemes, capital spending, strategic alliances and essential business intelligence on corporate moves. *$1495.00*
Weekly Founded: 1973

18231 ILMA Compoundings
Independent Lubricant Manufacturers Association
651 S Washington Street
Alexandria, VA 22314-4109
703-684-5574
FAX: 703-836-8503
ilma@ilma.org http://www.ilma.org

Carla mangone, Publisher
carla mangone, Editor
James A. Taglia, President

Focuses on legislative, regulatory, marketing and industry news of concern to independent blenders and compounders of high-quality lubricants. Accepts advertising. *$150.00*
20 pages Monthly Founded: 1948
Circulation: 1800

18232 Independent Liquid Terminals Association Newsletter
Independent Liquid Terminals Association
1444 I Street NW
Suite 400
Washington, DC 20005
202-842-9200
FAX: 202-326-8660
info@ilta.org http://www.ilta.org

E David Doane, President
E David Doane, Editor
Gwen Butler, Office Manager

Monthly publication detailing federal, state and local legislative and regulatory action, ILTA response and ILTA events. Geared specifically to bulk liquid terminal owners/operators and establishments supplying equipment, goods and services to the bulk liquid terminaling industry.
8 pages Monthly
Printed in 2 colors

18233 Institute of Gas Technology
1700 S Mount Prospect Road
Des Plaines, IL 60018-1804
847-680-0664
FAX: 847-768-0501
feingold@igt.org http://www.gti.org

Thomas L Fisher, Chairman
Leslie Penna, Membership
Carol Worster, Manager

Newsletter *$495.00*
Founded: 1945

18234 International Directory of Oil Spills and Control Products and Services
Cutter Information Corporation
37 Broadway
Arlington, MA 02474-5552
781-641-2886
FAX: 781-648-8707 800-964-5118

Kim Leonard, Publisher
Karen Coburn, President

Products and services listed by category. *$75.00*

18235 International Gas Technology Highlights
Institute of Gas Technology
1700 S Mount Prospect Road
Des Plains, IL 60018
847-680-0664
FAX: 847-768-0501
publicrelations@gastechnology.org
http://www.gastechnology.org

John F Riordon, CEO/President
Colleen Sen, Editor

A biweekly newsletter covering international developments in energy with a focus on natural gas. *$100.00*
4 pages Founded: 1946
Circulation: 1600 Audited Est. Pass-Along Circ: 6400
Printed in 2 colors on matte stock
Computerized version available

18236 International Oil News
William F Bland
709 Turmeric Lane
Durham, NC 27713-6666
919-544-1717
FAX: 919-544-1999
mbs@PetroChemical-News.com
http://www.petrochemical-news.com/pcn.htm

Susan B Kensil, Editor
Mollie B Sandor, Circulation Director

A weekly report of current news about all areas of the international petroleum industry, exploration, production, processing, transportation and marketing. *$857.00*
Weekly Founded: 1963

18237 International Summary and Review of Oil Spills
Cutter Information Corporation
37 Broadway
Suite 1
Arlington, MA 02474-5552
781-641-2886
FAX: 800-888-1816 800-964-5118
info@cutter.com www.cutter.com

Karen Fine Coburn, Publisher

International coverage of the gas and oil industry. *$100.00*
Monthly Founded: 1986

18238 LNG Observer
Institute of Gas Technology
1700 S Mount Prospect Road
Des Plaines, IL 60018-1800
847-768-0664
FAX: 847-768-0842 sen@igt.org

Colleen Taylor Sen, Editor

A bimonthly publication covering the worldwide liquefied natural gas industry, including political developments, technology, economics, statistics and interviews with industry leaders. *$395.00*
24 pages Bi-Monthly ISSN 1053-6949
Circulation: 2,000

18239 Leading Edge
Society of Exploration Geophysicists
PO Box 702740
Tulsa, OK 74170-2740
918-497-5500
FAX: 918-497-5557
subs@aip.org http://www.seg.org

Dean Clark, Editor
Gérard C Herman, Special Editor

A mix of earth sciences and geophysics, along with the latest exploration industry and Society news. *$105.00*
Monthly Founded: 1930
Circulation: 18000 17M names
Printed in 4 colors on glossy stock

18240 Lundberg Letter
Lundberg Survey
911 via alondra
PO Box 6002
Carmarillo, CA 93011
805-383-2400
FAX: 805-383-2424 800-660-4574
lsi@lundbergsurvey.com
http://www.lundbergsurvey.com
Trilby Lundberg, Publisher
News on the US gasoline and diesel market. Retail and wholesale prices, market shares, consumption, taxes, station populations and consumer trends. *$399.00*
Founded: 1950

18241 NGI's Daily Gas Price Index
Intelligence Press
PO Box 70587
Washington, DC 20024
202-583-2596
FAX: 202-318-0597 800-427-5747
subscriptions@intelligencepress.com
http://intelligencepress.com
Ellen Beswick, Publisher
Mike Nazzaro, CEO
Gas industry news, reports and statistics. *$1045.00*
Daily
Computerized version available

18242 National Association of Royalty Owners
12316 Andrews Drive
Suite B
Oklahoma City, OK 73120-5779
405-573-2972
FAX: 405-286-9402 800-558-0557
naro@naro-us.org
http://www.naro-us.org
Paul Covert, VP
Wana Box, President
David Guest, Manager
Newsletter for members. Also a book is available "Look Before You Lease". *$6.50*
Monthly Founded: 1980

18243 Natural Gas Intelligence/Gas Price Index
Intelligence Press
PO Box 70587
Washington, DC 20024
202-583-2596
FAX: 202-318-0597 800-427-5747
ellen@intelligencepress.com
http://www.intelligencepress.com
Ellen Beswick, Publisher
Statistics and research for the gas and petroleum industry. *$1195.00*
Weekly Founded: 1981
Computerized version available

18244 Natural Gas Week
Energy Intelligence Group
1401 New York Avenue NW
Suite 500
Washington, DC 20005-2150
202-935-5113
FAX: 202-662-0751
info@energyintel.com
http://www.energyintel.com
Tom Haywood, Acting Editor
Mike Sultan, Associate Editor
Thomas E. Wallin, President
Economics news covering the gas industry. *$1860.00*
20 pages Weekly Founded: 1985
Printed in 2 colors on matte stock

18245 News Fuel & Vehicles Report
Inside Washington Publishers
1225 South Clark Street
#1400
Arlington, VA 22202-4301
703-416-8500
FAX: 703-416-8543 800-424-9068
iwp@iwpnews.com
http://www.iwpnews.com
Roger Smith, Publisher
Latest news, research and reports on alternative fuels and vehicles development aimed toward the program managers, lobbyists, policy makers, and auto, oil and corn chemical industries. *$985.00*
Founded: 1980

18246 Ocean News & Technology
Technology Systems Corporation
PO Box 1096
Palm City, FL 34991-7174
772-221-7720
FAX: 772-221-7715
techsystems@sprintmail.com
http://www.ocean-news.com
Dan White, Editor
Sharon White, Circulation Manager
Magazine focusing on the major business areas of the ocean industry. News articles and technology developments are covered in areas including defense, offshore oil, diving, science, environment and marine. *$45.00*
Founded: 1981

18247 Offshore International Newsletter
Offshore Data Services
PO Box 19909
Houston, TX 77224-1909
713-781-7094
FAX: 713-781-9594
editors@offshore-data.com
http://www.offshore-data.com
Susanne Pagano, Editor
Thomas E Marsh, Publisher
News and information regrading the offshore oil and gas industry worldwide, while highlighting oil discoveries, licensing arrangements, contract awards, mergers and the market outlook. *$699.00*
Weekly Founded: 1973
Circulation: 750

18248 Offshore Rig Newsletter
Offshore Data Services
3200 Wilcrest Dr
Suite 170
Houston, TX 77042-1909
713-812-2713
FAX: 832-463-3100
editors@offhsore-data.com
http://www.offshore-data.com
Gavin Strachan, Editor
Barry Young, Marketing Director
Emerging markets, accidents, new technology, financing schemes, insurance trends, rig construction, moves, sales, and rates, labor problems, attrition, marketing strategies, and the corporate activities of drilling contractors. *$220.00*
Monthly Founded: 1973
Circulation: 900

18249 Oil & Gas Production-E-mail News & Analysis
Forecast International
22 Commerce Road
Newtown, CT 06470-1643
203-426-0800
FAX: 203-426-1964 www.forecast1.com
Kathy Bertrand, Production Manager
Monty Nebinger, Circulation Director
An electronic information/data service sourced from thousands of worldwide publications, in 15 languages. Provides concise summaries, news, trends and contract information with hyper-links to the source or a related website. Delivered 100 times a year. *$425.00*
2 per week

18250 Oil Daily
Energy Intelligence Group
1401 New York Avenue NW
Suite 500
Washington, DC 20005-2150
202-662-0700
FAX: 202-347-8089
info@energyintel.com
http://www.energyintel.com
Peter Kemp, Editor
Maria Otero, President
Magazine on the petroleum and oil industry, available on line. *$1880.00*
Daily Founded: 1951
Circulation: 60000

18251 Oil Express
United Communications Group
11300 Rockville Pike
Suite 1100
Rockville, MD 20852-3030
301-287-2700
FAX: 301-816-8945
webmaster@ucg.com
http://www.ucg.com
Brian Crotty, Publisher/President
Nancy Becker, Chief Marketing Officer
Information for gasoline marketers. *$447.00*
8 pages Monthly Founded: 1977

18252 Oil Spill Intelligence Report
Aspen Publishers
111 Eighth Avenue
7th Floor
New York, NY 10011-5552
212-771-0600
FAX: 212-771-0885 800-234-1660
newmediainfo@aspenpubl.com
http://www.aspenpublishers.com
Richard H Kravitz, Publisher
Gerry Centrowitz, Marketing/Communications Manager
Provides timely coverage of oil spills worldwide. *$695.00*
6 pages Weekly Founded: 1978

18253 Oil Spill United States Law Report
Aspen Publishers
37 Broadway
Arlington, MA 02474-5552
781-641-2886
FAX: 301-698-7100 800-234-1660
Paul Harman, Editor
Professionals who need to stay abreast of US federal and state regulations. *$7.67*
12 pages Monthly

18254 Oil, Gas and Petrochem Equipment
PennWell Publishing Company
1421 S Sheridan Road
Tulsa, OK 74112
918-353-3161
FAX: 918-831-9776 800-331-4463
jba@penwell.com
http://www.ogpe.com

Bill pryor, CEO/President
Tim L Tobeck, Group Publisher
J B Avants, Publisher & Editor

The petroleum industry's only all new products and services magazine. Each month it announces the newest developments in equipment, products, systems and services for drilling, production, refining, petrochemical manufacturing, pipeline/storage and gas processing. *$35.00*
Monthly Founded: 1955
Circulation: 32000
Mailing list available for rent 32,000 names
Printed in 4 colors on glossy stock

18255 PIW's Oil Market Intelligence
575 Broadway
New York, NY 10012-3230
212-573-3000
FAX: 212-941-5509
www.piw.pubs.com

Edward L Morse, Publisher
Jan Stuart, Editor
Jocelyn Strauber, Circulation Manager

Offers information on oil and gas stocks and bonds.
Monthly

18256 PTTC Network News
Petroleum Technology Transfer Council
16010 Barkers Point Lane
Suite 220
Houston, TX 77079
281-921-1720
FAX: 281-921-1723
hq@pttc.org http://www.pttc.org

Kristi Lovendahl, Webmaster/Newsletter Editor
Norma Gutierrez, Circulation Director
Donald Duttlinger, Executive Director

16 page newsletter with east to read summaries of new oil and natural gas technologies.
Quarterly Founded: 1994
Circulation: 17000

18257 PetroChemical News
William F Bland
PO Box 16666
Chapel Hill, NC 27516-6666
919-490-0700
FAX: 919-490-3002

Susan D Kensil, Editor

A fast, accurate report of significant world petrochemical developments. *$739.00*
4 pages Weekly

18258 Petroleum Intelligence Weekly
5 East 37th Street
5th Floor
New York, NY 10016-2807
212-532-1112
FAX: 212-532-4479
info@energyintel.com
http://www.energyintel.com

Thomas E Wallin, President
Peter Kemp, Editor
Raja W. Sidawi, Chairman
Sarah Miller, Editor-at-Large

News of the oil and gas industries worldwide. *$3340.00*
Weekly Founded: 1961

18259 Platt's Oilgram News
McGraw Hill
3333 Walnut Street
Boulder, CO 80301-2525
720-485-5000
FAX: 720-548-5701 800-752-8878
support@platts.com
http://www.platts.com

O Marashian, Publisher
James Keener, Marketing
Harry Sachinsis, President

News of the oil and gas industries worldwide.
Daily Founded: 1888

18260 Public Gas News
American Public Gas Association
201 Massachusetts Avenue NE
Suite C-4
Washington, DC 20002-5014
202-640-0240
FAX: 202-464-0246
website@apga.org
http://www.apga.org

Sheila Martel, Editor
Bert Kalisch, President
Bob Beauregard, Marketing

Written for public gas managers to keep them apprised of industry news. *$50.00*
Founded: 1961
Circulation: 1000
Printed in on matte stock

18261 Washington Report
Interstate Natural Gas Association of America
555 13th Street NW
Suite 300W
Washington, DC 20004-1109
202-378-8600
FAX: 202-626-3250

Cheryl W Hoffman, Publisher
Samuel Berger, Manager

Natural gas newsletter places a special emphasis on developments that affect the interstate pipeline industry. It covers Congress, the Federal Energy Regulatory Commission and other federal agencies, state and Canadian regulatory boards and company news.

18262 Weekly Propane Newsletter
Butane-Propane News
338 E Foothill Blvd.
Arcadia, CA 91006-2542
626-357-2168
FAX: 626-303-2854
bpn@bpnews.com
http://www.bpnews.com

Pete Ottman, Editor
Natalie Peal, Publisher
Kurt Ruhl, Marketing

Weekly updates and rates on the propane and gas industry. *$205.00*
8 pages Weekly Founded: 1939
Circulation: 2000 Audited
Printed in 1 color on matte stock
Computerized version available: e-mail

18263 Western Petroleum Marketers Association
4393 Riverboat Road
Suite 380
Taylorsville, UT 84123-2593
801-263-9762
FAX: 801-262-9413
info@wpma.com
http://www.wpma.com/

Linda Maloy, Publications Director
Sandra Peterson, Editor
Gene Inglesby, Executive Director
Dennis Baird, President

Accepts advertising.
Quarterly Founded: 1953

18264 World Gas Intelligence
575 Broadway
New York, NY 10012-3230
212-941-5500
FAX: 212-941-5509
www.piw.pubs.com

Edward L Morse, Publisher
Jocelyn Strauber, Circulation Director

International coverage of the oil and gas industry. *$985.00*
SemiMonthly
Mailing list available for rent

Magazines & Journals

18265 AAPG Bulletin
American Association of Petroleum Geologists
PO Box 979
Tulsa, OK 74101-979
918-584-2555
FAX: 918-560-2632
bulletin@aapg.org
http://www.aapg.org

Carol Christopher, Managing Editor
Rick Fritz, CEO/President
Larry Nations, Marketing

Peer reviewed articles that cover major extent and detailed geologic data. Information on petroleum, natural gas, and other energy products. *$305.00*
Monthly Founded: 1917
Circulation: 30000

18266 AAPG Explorer
American Association of Petroleum Geologists
1444 S Boulder Avenue
PO Box 979
Tulsa, OK 74101-979
918-584-2555
FAX: 918-560-2665 800-288-7636
postmaster@aapg.org
http://www.aapg.org

Patrick J F Gratton, President
Ernest A Mancini, Editor
Brenda Merideth, Advertising Sales Manage

News for explorationists of oil, gas and minerals as well as for geologists with environmental and water well concerns. *$50.00*
Monthly Founded: 1917 ISSN 0195-2986
Circulation: 30000
Printed in 4 colors on matte stock

18267 American Oil and Gas Reporter
National Publishers Group
PO Box 343
Derby, KS 67037
316-788-6271
FAX: 316-788-7568 800-847-8301
reporter@feist.com
http://www.fiest.com

Charlie Cookson, Publisher
Bill Campbell, Managing Editor

The American Oil & Gas Reporter serves the exploration, drilling and production segments of the oil and gas industry. *$65.07*

Monthly Founded: 1958
Circulation: 7384

18268 BIC - Business & Industry Connection
BIC Alliance
PO Box 40166
Baton Rouge, LA 70835-166
225-751-9996
FAX: 225-751-9993
bic@bicalliance.com
http://www.bicalliance.com

Jamie Craig, Editor
Earl Heard, CEO/President
Kathy Dugas, Administrator
Joe Storer, Manager

Information on oil and gas, refining, petrochemical, environmental, construction, engineering, pulp and paper, state agencies and municipalities business. *$45.00*

Circulation: 75000

18269 Bloomberg Natural Gas Report
Bloomberg Financial Markets
100 Business Park Drive
Princeton, NJ 08542-840
609-279-3000
FAX: 917-369-7000 800-395-9403
munis@bloomberg.com
http://www.bloomberg.com/energy

Michael Bloomberg, Publisher
Ronald Henkoff, Editor

News, interviews, and analysis of topics of importance to all levels of the natural gas market.

12 pages Weekly Founded: 1980
Circulation: 1700

18270 Butane-Propane News
Butane-Propane News
PO Box 660698
Arcadia, CA 91006
626-357-2168
FAX: 626-303-2854 800-214-4386
bpn@bpnews.com
http://www.bpnews.com

Natalie Peal, Publisher
Ann Rey, Editorial Director
Kurt Ruhl, Sales Manager

Petroleum and propane industry news. *$32.00*

56 pages Monthly Founded: 1939
Circulation: 16500
Printed in 4 colors on glossy stock : web

18271 Coal People
Al Skinner Enterprises
PO Box 6247
629 Virginia Street West
Charleston, WV 25362-247
304-342-4129
FAX: 304-343-3124 800-235-5188
cpm@newwave.net
http://www.coalpeople.com

Al Skinner, Publisher
Christina Karawan, Managing Editor
Beth Terranova, Sales Manager
Angela McNealy, Circulation Manager
C K Lane, Senior Vice President

Features special news and product sections for the coal industry. *$25.00*

60 pages Founded: 1976
Circulation: 11500
Printed in 4 colors on glossy stock

18272 Compressor Tech Two
Diesel & Gas Turbine Publications
20855 Watertown Road
Waukesha, WI 53186-1873
262-325-5000
FAX: 262-754-4175
slizdas@dieselpub.com
http://www.dieselpub.com

Phil Burnside, Editor-in-Chief
Brent Haight, Managing Editor
Kara Kane, Advertising Manager
Christa Johnson, Production Manager
Sheila Lizdas, Circulation Manager

Covers oil and gas exploration, drilling, oilfield contracting, gas and petrochemical pipeline and storage, as well as petrochemical, hydrocarbon and gas processing industries.

Circulation: 12000

18273 Diesel Progress: North American Edition
Diesel & Gas Turbine Publications
20855 Watertown Road
Suite 220
Waukesha, WI 53186-6386
262-325-5000
FAX: 262-754-4175 800-558-4322
mosenga@dieselpub.com
http://www.dieselpub.com

Michael Osenga, Publisher
Sheila Lizdas, Circulation Manager
Lynne Diefenbach, Advertising Manager
Christa Johnson, Production Manager

Geared towards readers interested in state-of-the-art systems technology. Features include new product listings, systems design, research amd product testing as well as systems maintenance and rebuilding.

Monthly Founded: 1969
Circulation: 26011

18274 Drill Bits
National Drilling Association
11001 Danka Way North
Suite 1
St Petersburg, FL 33716
727-577-5006
FAX: 727-577-5012
info@nda4u.com
http://www.nda4u.com/

Maryanne S Crews, Executive Director
Nancy Cooper, Editor

Formerly National Drilling Contractors Association; merged with Equipment Drilling Manufacturers Association and International Drilling Federation in 1995.

3 Issues per ye Founded: 1972

18275 Drilling Contractor
IADC
15810 Park Ten Place
Suite 222
Houston, TX 77084
281-578-7171
FAX: 281-578-0589
info@iadc.org
http://www.iadc.org/dcpi.htm

Mike Killalea, Publisher
Dr Lee Hunt, CEO/President
Mike Killalea, Editor

Information and news aimed at the oil and drilling industry. *$50.00*

40 pages Founded: 1994
Circulation: 28000
Printed in 4 colors

18276 Energy Markets
Hart Publications
4545 Post Oak Place
#210
Houston, TX 77027
713-993-9320
FAX: 713-840-8585

Linda K Rader, Editor
Robert C Jarvis, Publisher

Energy Markets serves the following energy industry business classifications: utilities, municipalities, consultants and financial services, regulators, and other companies allied to or supportive of the energy industry.

Monthly Founded: 1993
Circulation: 25,751

18277 Energy Network
Gulf Publishing Company
PO Box 2608
Houston, TX 77252-2608
713-529-4301
800-231-6275

Ray Cashman, Publisher

Edited for companies that sell products to the oil and gas industry.

18278 Fuel Oil News
Hunter Publishing Limited
833 W. Jackson Blvd
7th Floor
Chicago, IL 60607
312-846-4600
FAX: 312-846-4632
geoschultz@ewol.com
http://www.fueloilnews.com

Chris Traczek, Editor
Joanne Juda, Circulation Director
Kate Kenny, Publisher
Keith Reid, Senior Editor
Patricia McCartney, Associate Editor

For home heating oil retailers. *$28.00*

70 pages Monthly Founded: 1935
Circulation: 18000 18 M names
Printed in 4 colors on glossy stock

18279 Gas Turbine World
Pequot Publishing
PO Box 447
Southport, CT 36490
203-259-1812
FAX: 203-254-3431

Robert Farmer, Editor
Victor Debiasi, Publisher
Janes Janson, Marketing
Peg Walker, Circulation Manager

Serves the electric, utility and non-untility power generation, oil/gas production and processing industries. *$135.00*

Weekly Founded: 1979
Circulation: 11000

18280 Gas Utility Manager
James Informational Media
6301 Gaston Avenue
#541
Dallas, TX 75214-6204
214-827-4630
FAX: 847-391-9058
ruth@BetterRoads.com
http://www.betterroads.com

Mike Porcaro, Publisher
Mike Porcaro, CEO/President
Carole Spohr, Marketing Manager
Stacy Stiglic, Circulation Manager
Ruth Stidger, Editor

Federal and international regulations, new supply projects, research and development projects and gas industry news. *$95.00*

40 pages Annual+ Founded: 1931
Circulation: 40000

18281 Georgia Petroleum Marketer
Georgia Oilmen Association
1775 Spectrum Drive
Suite 100
Lawrenceville, GA 30043
770-995-7570
FAX: 770-995-9757
rlane@gaoilassoc.com
www.georgiaoilmenassoc.com
Roger T Lane, President/Editor
Mary R Franklin, Associate Editor
100 pages Annual
Circulation: 800

18282 Hart's E & P
Hart Publications
1616 S Voss Rd
Ste 1000
Houston, TX 77057-2641
713-993-9320
FAX: 713-840-8585
jfisher@hartenergy.com
http://www.eandpnet.com
Dana Griffin, Publisher
Joe Fisher, Editor
Rich Eichler, President
Technical approaches and improvements related to both offshore and land drilling and extraction of petroleum products, also new product information and personality profiles. *$59.00*
Monthly
Circulation: 25000

18283 Hart's Gas/LPG Markets
Hart Publications
6011 Executive Drive
#200
Rockville, MD 20852-3804
301-468-1039
FAX: 301-468-1039
hartinfo@phillips.cm
www.hartpub.com
Robert Gough, Editor
Financial reports on individual natural gas and liquid gasoline companies, their stock analysis, value and future mergers or acquisitions that may affect the pricing of gasoline or companies involved in the industry. *$1497.00*
Monthly

18284 Hart's Oil & Gas Interests
Hart Publications
6011 Executive Boulevard
#200
Rockville, MD 20852-3804
301-468-1039
FAX: 301-468-1039 www.hartpub.com
Brian Crotty, Group Publisher
Designed to keep readers abreast of developments and investment ideas in the petroleum and natural gas industry.
Monthly

18285 Hart's Oil & Gas Investor
Hart Publications
1616 S Voss Rd
Ste 1000
Houston, TX 77057-2641
713-993-9320
FAX: 713-840-8585 800-874-2544
ndarbonne@hartenergy.com
http://www.oilandgasinvestor.com
Bob Jarvis, Group Publisher
Leslie Haines, Editor-in-Chief
Nissa Darbonne, Executive Editor
Rich Eichler, President
Company performance, investment forecasts, economic outlooks, management strategy reports, focusing on the financial aspects of the petroleum and natural gas industry. *$297.00*
Monthly
Circulation: 5100
Printed in 4 colors

18286 Hart's World Refining
Hart Publications
4545 Post Oak Place
Suite 210
Houston, TX 77027-3105
713-993-9320
FAX: 713-840-8585 800-874-2544
David Coates, Publisher
Jeremy Grunt, Executive Editor
Terry Higgins, Executive Publisher
Robert Gough, Editorial Director
Rich Eichler, President
Covers projects, financing and market developments, along with feedstock and product supply, demand, pricing information, technical and regulatory events associated with the manufacture, supply, and use of transportation fuels refining technologies, business strategies and fuel policy legislation. *$149.00*
Founded: 1980
Circulation: 15,693

18287 Hydrocarbon Processing
Gulf Publishing Company
PO Box 2608
Houston, TX 77252-2608
713-529-4301
FAX: 713-520-4433
editorial@hydrocarbonprocessing.com
http://www.hydrocarbonprocessing.com
Mark Peters, Publisher
Les A Kane, Editor
Laura Kane, Advertising Manager
Concentrates on the problems facing management and technical personnel in the worldwide hydrocarbon processing industry. Accepts advertising. *$120.00*
Monthly Founded: 1916
Circulation: 30000
Printed in on glossy stock

18288 Journal of Geophysical Research
American Geophysical Union
2000 Florida Avenue NW
Washington, DC 20009-1277
202-462-6900
FAX: 202-328-0566 800-966-2481
webmaster@agu.org
http://www.agu.org
Paul Davis, Editor
John A Orcutt, President
Fred Spilhaus, Executive Director
There are five sections covering soid earth, oceans, atmosphere, planets, and space physics. *$20.00*
Monthly Founded: 1919
Circulation: 10,000

18289 Journal of Petroleum Technology
Society of Petroleum Engineers
222 Palisades Creek Drive
Richardson, TX 75080
972-529-9300
FAX: 972-952-9435 800-456-6863
jpt@spe.org http://www.spe.org
John Donnelly, Editor
Giovanni Paccaloni, President
Paul Thone, Senior Sales Manager
Journal of Petroleum Technology serves the field of exploration, drilling, production, and reservoir management as well as related manufacturing and service organizations.
98 pages Monthly Founded: 1949
Circulation: 51205
Printed in 4 colors on glossy stock

18290 LP/Gas
Advanstar Communications
131 W 1st Street
Duluth, MN 55802
218-723-9200
FAX: 218-723-9122
info@advanstar.com
http://www.advanstar.com
Patrick Hyland, Editor
Sean Carr, Publisher
Cerry Gumas, CEO
Kris Meyer, Circulation Manager
Brian Kanaba, National Sales Manager
The propane industry's premier information source. *$30.00*
36 pages Monthly
Circulation: 15320
Printed in 4 colors on glossy stock

18291 Landman
American Association of Professional Landmen
4100 Fossil Creek Boulevard
Fort Worth, TX 76137-2723
817-847-7700
FAX: 817-847-7704
aapl@landman.org
http://www.landman.org
Le'ann Callihan, Editor
Robin Forte, President
Accepts advertising. *$50.00*
76 pages Founded: 1955

18292 Lubricants World
4545 Post Oak Place
Suite 230
Houston, TX 77027
713-840-0378
FAX: 713-840-0379
Kathryn B Carnes, Editor

18293 NLGI Spokesman
National Lubricating Grease Institute
4635 Wyandotte Street
Kansas City, MO 64112
816-931-9480
FAX: 816-753-5026
nlgi@nlgi.org http://www.nlgi.org
Chuck Hitchcock, Editor
Kim Bott, Administrative Assistant
About 50% of technical or scientific information amied at the manufacturers, users and suppliers of lubricating grease. *$53.00*
Monthly Founded: 1933
Circulation: 2500

18294 National Petroleum News
Adams Business Media
833 W Jackson
7th Floor
Chicago, IL 60607
312-846-4600
FAX: 312-977-1042
webmaster@adamsbusinessmedia.com
http://www.adamsbusinessmedia.com
Darren Wright, Editor-in-Chief
Mark Adams, CEO
Kate Kenny, Publisher
joanne juda, circulation manager
Steve Lown, Marketing Manager
The leading news publication serving the petroleum marketing and convenience store/gasoline markets. NPN reaches top

executives and decision-makers in petroleum marketing firms, oil company marketing departments and convenience store chains. *$64.00*
90 pages Monthly
Circulation: 38000

18295 Natural Gas Fuels
RP Publishing
2696 S Colorado Blvd
Suite 595
Denver, CO 80222
303-863-0521
FAX: 303-863-1722
info@rppublishing.com
http://www.rppublishing.com
Frank Rowe, Publisher
Technological advances, marketing strategies, legislative activities, successful applications, and corporate and government initiatives to promote natural gas-powered vehicles
Founded: 1992
Circulation: 7000

18296 O&A Marketing News
KAL Publications
559 S Harbor Boulevard
Suite A
Anaheim, CA 92805-4525
714-563-9300
FAX: 714-563-9310
info@kalpub.com
http://www.kalpub.com
Kathy Laderman, Editor
Kathy Laderman, President
Kathy Laderman, Publisher
Jim Penn, Circulation Manager
Linda Squeo, Marketing Manager
Coverage of industry events and related shows for wholesale and retail marketers of gasoline, oil and automotive service replacement products in the thirteen Pacific-Western states. *$20.00*
Founded: 1966
Circulation: 7000

18297 Offshore
PennWell Publishing Company
1421 S Sheridan Road
Tulsa, OK 74112
918-835-3161
FAX: 918-831-9497 800-331-4463
Headquarters@PennWell.com
http://www.pennwell.com
John Royall, Group Publisher
Biol Chini, CEO
Tommie Grigg, Circulation Manager
Elbon Ball, Editor
Jayne Gilfinger, Marketing Manager
Offshore serves the international oil and gas industry in its marine/offshore operations. *$75.00*
186 pages Monthly Founded: 1910
Circulation: 40000
Printed in 4 colors on glossy stock

18298 Oil & Gas Journal
PennWell Publishing Company
1700 W Loop S
#1000
Houston, TX 77027-3006
713-621-8833
FAX: 713-963-6285
sales@pennwell.com
http://www.ogjonline.com
Tom T Terrell, Publisher
Tim Sullivant, Manager
Detailed interpreation and information of the world developments in the oil and gas industry *$79.00*
Weekly Founded: 1990
Circulation: 36090
Printed in 4 colors on glossy stock

18299 Oil Spill Contingency Planning: A Global Perspective
Aspen Publishers
37 Broadway
Arlington, MA 02474-5552
781-641-2886
FAX: 301-698-7100 800-234-1660
Kim Leonard, Editor
Wolters Kluwer, CEO/President
Richard H Kravitz, Publisher
Gerry Centrowitz, Marketing
Hands-on guidebook to contingency planning for oil spills. *$195.00*

18300 Oilheating
Industry Publications
3621 Hill Road
Parsippany, NJ 07054-1001
973-331-9545
FAX: 973-331-9547
info@oilheating.com
http://www.oilheating.com
Michael L San Giovanni, Editor
Donald J Farrell, Publisher
Addresses issues on dispatching and delivery efficiency, residential and commercial fuel oil use, as well as sales and services of oilfired equipment. *$42.00*
Monthly Founded: 1922
Circulation: 13280

18301 PetroMart Business
Virgo Publishing
3300 N Central Avenue, Suite 2500
PO Box 40079
Phoenix, AZ 85067-0079
480-990-1101
FAX: 480-675-8146
www.petromartbusiness.com
For owners and managers of gasoline stations.

18302 Petroleo International
Keller International Publishing Corporation
150 Great Neck Road
Great Neck, NY 11021-3309
516-829-9722
FAX: 516-829-5414
info@kellerpubs.com
http://www.kellerpubs.com
Victor Prieto, Editor
Sean Noble, Publisher
Steve Kann, Circulation Manager
Jerry Keller, President
Spanish language petroleum/petrochemical magazine.
100 pages Founded: 1943
Circulation: 10,314

18303 SPE Drilling & Completion
Society of Petroleum Engineers
PO Box 833836
Richardson, TX 75083-3836
972-529-9300
FAX: 972-952-9435 800-456-6863
spdal@spelink.spe.org
http://www.spe.org
Giovanni Paccaloni, President
Shashana Pearson, Editor
Mary Jane, Circulation Manager
Georgeann Bilich, Publisher
Technical papers selected for the drilling profession reviewed by peers on topics such as casing, instrumentation, bit technology, fluids, measurment, deviation control, telemetry, completion and well control. *$60.00*
Quarterly Founded: 1984
Circulation: 3588

18304 Sea Technology
Compass Publications
1501 Wilson Boulevard
Suite 1001
Arlington, VA 22209
703-524-3136
FAX: 703-841-0852
oceanbiz@sea-technology.com
http://www.sea-technology.com
C Amos Bussmann, Publisher
Michele Umansky, Assistant Editor
Worldwide information leader for marine business, science and engineering. Read in more than 100 countries by management, engineers, scientists and technical personnel working in industry, government and educational research institutions. Readers are involved with oceanographic research, fisheries management, offshore oil and gas exploration and production, and undersea defense including antisubmarine warfare, ocean mining and commercial diving.
Founded: 1963
Mailing list available for rent 20.5mil names
$40 per M.

18305 Society of Professional Well Log Analysts
8866 Gulf Freeway
Suite 320
Houston, TX 77017-6531
713-947-8727
FAX: 713-947-7181
info@spwla.org http://www.spwla.org
Vicki J King, Executive Director
John Quirein, President
Julian Singer, VP Publications *$105.00*
Annual+ Founded: 1959
Circulation: 2900

18306 Today's Refinery
Chemical Week Associates
888 7th Avenue
New York, NY 10106
212-621-4900
FAX: 212-621-4950
Editorials from industry leaders focusing on current problems facing the industry. Highlights on legistation, activity, government regulations,and reports on major industry meetings.
Monthly
Circulation: 10,000

18307 Utility & Pipeline Industries
WMO DannHausen Corporation
330 North Wabash
Suite 3201
Chicago, IL 60611
312-628-5870
FAX: 312-628-5878
wod@dannhausen.com
http://www.gasindustries.com
Bob Higgins, Publisher
Heidi Liddle, Production Manager
Karen Ebbesmeyer, Circulation Manager
Ruth W. Stidger, Editor-in-Chief
Cory Sekine Pettite, Managing Editor
Market to federal agencies, bureaus, government departments and toll authorities. Accepts advertising. *$20.00*
62 pages Monthly
Circulation: 10680

18308 **Washington Report**
National Ocean Industries Association
1120 G Street NW
Suite 900
Washington, DC 20005
202-347-6900
FAX: 202-347-8650
noia@noia.org www.noia.org
Thomas A Fry, III, President
Kim Harb, Director Government Affairs
Franki K Stuntz, Director Administration
Nolty J Thuriot, Director Congressional Affairs
Bi-Weekly

18309 **Well Servicing**
Workover Well Servicing Publications
10200 Richmond Avenue
Suite 275
Houston, TX 77042
713-781-0758
FAX: 713-781-7542 800-692-0771
Kenny Jordan, Executive DIrector
Polly Fisk, Editor
Patty Jordan, Circulation
New products listing and reviews, field reports, and information on companies in the industry. Written and edited for energy service company professionals, and oil & gas operations.
40 pages Founded: 1956
Circulation: 11000

18310 **World Oil**
Gulf Publishing Company
PO Box 2608
Houston, TX 77252-2608
713-529-4301
FAX: 713-520-4433
publications@gulfpub.com
http://www.worldoil.com
Ron Higgins, Associate Publisher
Perry A Fischer, Editor
John D Meador, President/CEO
Reaches the exploration, drilling, producing, and well servicing segments of the oil and gas industry. *$34.00*
100 pages Monthly Founded: 1916
Circulation: 36000
Printed in 4 colors on glossy stock

Trade Shows

18311 **ASME Asia: Petroleum, Gas Turbines, Ocean Engineering, Advanced Energy**
International Gas Turbine Institute
5775-B Glenridge Drive
Suite 370
Atlanta, GA 30328-5380
404-847-0072
FAX: 404-847-1051
igti@asme.org www.asme.org/igti
Scott J Moore CEM, Director/Conventions
Conference, reception, tours and 100 exhibits of engineering and energy technology.
1200 Attendees Biennial Founded: 1986

18312 **American Association of Petroleum Geologists Annual Convention/Expo**
American Association of Petroleum Geologists
PO Box 979
Tulsa, OK 74101-0979
918-584-2555
FAX: 918-560-2684 800-364-2274
convene@aapg.org www.aapg.org
Randa Reeder-Briggs, Annual Meeting Manager
Melissa Howerton, Annual Meeting Assistant
Steph Benton, Exhibit Manager
Rick Fritz, Executive Director
Exhibits of instrumentation, equipment, supplies, services and publications for petroleum geologists, geophysicists and engineers.
7000 Attendees Annual/April

18313 **American Petro Geologists Mediterranean Basins Conference**
PO Box 979
Tulsa, OK 74101-0979
918-584-2555
Sondra Biggs, Show Manager
75 booths.
1.5M Attendees

18314 **American School of Gas Measurement Technology Meeting**
PO Box 3991
Houston, TX 77253-3991
903-486-7875
FAX: 512-267-9243 www.asgmt.com
Seminar, workshop, and tours, plus 95 exhibits of gas measurement, equipment, supplies and services.
600 Attendees Annual Founded: 1927

18315 **Asia Pacific Improved Oil Recovery Conference**
Society of Petroleum Engineers-Texas
222 Palisades Creek Drive
PO Box 833836
Richardson, TX 75083-3836
972-952-9300
FAX: 972-952-9435 www.spe.org
Oil recovery exhibition.

18316 **Beaumont Industrial Petrochemical Trade Show**
Lobos Services
16016 Perkins Road
Baton Rouge, LA 70810-3631
225-751-5626
Debbie Balough, Show Manager
Informs local industry of the full array of industrial equipment for the chemical industries.
5M Attendees January

18317 **Circum-Pacific Council Energy Mineral Resources**
5100 Westheimer Road
Houston, TX 77056-5596
713-709-9071
FAX: 713-622-5360
Mary Stewart, Show Manager
Napoleon Carcamo, Owner
50 booths.
1.2M Attendees November

18318 **Eastern Oil and Gas Equipment Show**
Pennsylvania Oil and Gas Association
412 N 2nd Street
Harrisburg, PA 17101-1342
717-939-9551
Stephen Rhoads, Show Manager
175 booths displaying new technologies, products and services relating to the oil and gas industries.
1M Attendees June

18319 **Europe International Offshore Exchange**
222 Palisades Creek Drive
Richardson, TX 75080-2040
Donna Anderson, Show Manager
1,100 booths.
21M Attendees September

18320 **Landman**
American Association of Petroleum Landmen
4100 Fossil Creek Boulevard
Fort Worth, TX 76137-2723
817-847-7700
FAX: 817-847-7704
Carolyn Stephens, Editor
Le Ann Pembroke, Advertising Manager
50 booths.
1.5M Attendees June

18321 **Liquified Gas Association Southwest**
PO Box 9925
Austin, TX 78766-0925
FAX: 512-834-0758
Cheryl Tomanetz, Show Manager
125 booths.
1.8M Attendees September

18322 **Liquified Natural Gas**
Reed Exhibition Companies
255 Washington Street
Newton, MA 02458-1637
617-584-4900
FAX: 617-630-2222
Elizabeth Hitchcock, International Sales
Presentation for the liquefied natural gas industry.
2.5M Attendees May

18323 **Liquified Petroleum Gas Exposition Midwest**
4100 Country Club Drive
Jefferson City, MO 65109-0302
573-634-5345
FAX: 573-893-2623
Emma Krommel, Show Manager
100 booths of large transport and bobtail delivery trucks.
1M Attendees June

18324 **Midwest Petroleum & Convenience Tradeshow**
Illinois Petroleum Marketers Association
PO Box 12020
Springfield, IL 62791-2020
217-544-4609
FAX: 217-789-0222
Bill Fleischli, Executive VP, Managing Editor
Suppliers and manufacturers to petroleum marketing and convenience store trades, including pumps, computers, trucks, safety

devices, canopies, car washes and tank testing. 300 booths.
4M Attendees June

18325 National Petro Refiners Association Refinery Petrochemical Plant
1899 L Street NW
Suite 1000
Washington, DC 20036-3810
202-457-0480

Robert Dzuibañ, Show Manager
Robert Slaughter, President
A forum for the exchange of technical information and services to the petroleum industry.
1.3M Attendees May

18326 Offshore Technology Conference
PO Box 833868
Richardson, TX 75083-3868
972-952-9494

Alan Wegener, Show Manager
Consisting of a forum to disseminate technical information for the advancement of engineering.
30M Attendees May

18327 Oil & Energy Summit and Trade Show
Forum International
1101 Brickell Avenue
Suite 400
Miami, FL 33131-3143

FAX: 305-372-0071 800-926-2202
jforum@trianet.net
www.oil-energysummit.com
Jorge Palmero, President
Rafael Yiamonte, VP Marketing
A full week of petroleum and related products and industries. Includes an international trade show; a summit of secretaries of energy from the Americas and a series of interdisciplinary seminars dictated by the Energy Institute of the Americas and the Sarkeys Research Center. 750 booths.
20M Attendees September

18328 Petroleum Computer Conference
Society of Petroleum Engineers
222 Palisades Creek Drive
Richardson, TX 75080-2040
972-952-9300
FAX: 972-952-9435 www.spe.org
Annual show of 50 microcomputer manufacturers and suppliers who provide hardware and software to the petroleum industry.
650 Attendees

18329 Petroleum Equipment Institute (CONVEX) and Exhibits
Petroleum Equipment Institute
PO Box 2380
Tulsa, OK 74101-2380
918-494-9696
FAX: 918-491-9895
cdooley@pei.org www.pei.org
Connie Dooley, Administrative Director
Robert Renkes, Executive VP
Annual show of manufacturers of petroleum marketing equipment. There are 215 exhibiting companies with 675 booths.
4500 Attendees October Founded: 1951

18330 Society Petro Engineers Annual Meeting
PO Box 833836
Richardson, TX 75083-3836
972-952-9300
FAX: 972-952-9435
Lois Woods, Show Manager
Mark Rubin, Executive Director
Conference with exhibits of drilling and production equipment and materials.
10M Attendees September

18331 Society Petro Engineers Permian Basin Oil Gas Recovery Conference and Expo
PO Box 833836
Richardson, TX 75083-3836
972-952-9300

Susan Bell, Event Manager
70 booths.
400 Attendees March

18332 Society Petro Engineers Petroleum Computer Conference and Expo
PO Box 833836
Richardson, TX 75083-3836
972-952-9300

Georgie Cumiskey, Event Manager
30 booths of microcomputer hardware and software for the petroleum industry.
300 Attendees July

18333 Society Petro Engineers Production Operations Symposium
PO Box 833836
Richardson, TX 75083-3836
972-952-9300

Karen Rodgers, Event Manager
Mark Rubin, Executive Director
70 booths of oil and gas industry related products and services.
1M Attendees March

18334 Society Petro Engineers Rocky Mountain
PO Box 833836
Richardson, TX 75083-3836
972-952-9300

Georgie Cumiskey, Event Manager
60 booths.
300 Attendees April

18335 Society Petro Engineers Western Regional Meeting
PO Box 833836
Richardson, TX 75083-3836
972-952-9300

Lois Woods, Exchange Manager
Mark Rubin, Executive Director
65 booths.
700 Attendees May

18336 Society of Petro Engineers Eastern Regional Meeting
PO Box 833836
Richardson, TX 75083-3836
972-952-9300

Susan Bell, Event Manager
Mark Rubin, Executive Director
Offers a forum for the exchange of ideas between petroleum and gas engineers.
500 Attendees October

18337 Society of Petro Engineers Enhanced Oil Recovery Symposium and Exchange
PO Box 833836
Richardson, TX 75083-3836
972-952-9300

Georgie Cumiskey, Event Manager
Mark Rubin, Executive Director
100 booths.
1.6M Attendees April

18338 Southeast Petro Food Marketing Expo
7300 Glenwood Avenue
Raleigh, NC 27612
919-782-4411
FAX: 919-782-4414
ssvinson@ncpma.org www.sepetro.org

Sharon Vinson, Show Manager
550 booths and 400+ exhibitors serving the petroleum and convenience store industries in the southeast.
2,000 Attendees March

18339 Western Petroleum Marketers Convention & Convenience Store Expo
Western Petroleum Marketers Association
4393 South Riverboat Road
Suite 380
Taylorsville, UT 84123
801-263-9762
FAX: 801-262-9413 888-252-5550
judithw@wpma.com wpma.com
Judith White, Trade Show Coordinator
Gene Inglesby, Executive Director
430 booths.
5,000 Attendees February Founded: 1953

Directories & Databases

18340 APILIT
American Petroleum Institute
275 7th Avenue
9th Floor
New York, NY 10001-6708
212-989-9001
FAX: 212-366-4298
Over 500,000 citations are offered from 1978, to the literature related to the oil refining and petrochemical industries.
Bibliographic

18341 Africa-Middle East Petroleum Directory
PennWell Directories
1700 West Loop S
Suite 1000
Houston, TX 77027
713-621-8833
FAX: 281-499-6310 800-752-9764
susana@penwell.com
www.petroleumdirectories.com
Jonelle Moore, Editor
Tim Sullivant, Manager
A directory for: associations, government agencies, drilling, exploration and production of natural gas, petrochemicals, pipeline operators etc. *$125.00*
156 pages

18342 American Oil and Gas Reporter Directory
Domestic Petroleum Publishers
PO Box 343
Derby, KS 67037-0343
316-788-6271
FAX: 316-788-7568
reporter@wichita.fn.net

Bill Campbell, Editor
Charlie Cookson, Publisher

State oil and natural gas regulatory agencies. *$25.00*
Annual March
Circulation: 13,540

18343 American Oil and Gas Reporter: American Drilling Rig Directory Issues
National Publishers Group
PO Box 343
Derby, KS 67037-0343
316-788-6271
FAX: 316-788-7568
reporter@wichita.fn.net

Bill Campbell, Editor
Charlie Cookson, Publisher

List of contractors engaged in onshore drilling for petroleum and gas. *$25.00*
SemiAnnual
Circulation: 13,540

18344 American Oil and Gas Reporter: Directory of Crude Oil Purchasers Issue
Domestic Petroleum Publishers
PO Box 343
Derby, KS 67037-0343
316-788-6271
FAX: 316-788-7568
reporter@wichita.fn.net

Bill Campbell, Editor
Charlie Cookson, Publisher

List of companies buying crude oil in the US. *$25.00*
Annual July
Circulation: 13,540

18345 Armstrong Oil Directories
PO Box 9660
Amarillo, TX 79105-9660
806-457-9300

Alan Armstrong, Owner

Directory of services and supplies to the industry. *$53.50*
300 pages Annual

18346 Asia-Pacific Petroleum Directory
PennWell Directories
1700 W Loop S
Suite 1000
Houston, TX 77027-3007
713-621-8833
FAX: 281-499-6310 800-752-9764
susana@penwell.com
www.petroleumdirectories.com

Susan Anderson, Editor
Tim Sullivant, Manager

A directory for: suppliers, manufacturers, associations, government agencies, drilling, exploration and production of petroleum. *$95.00*

18347 Association of Energy Service Companies Directory
Association of Energy Service Companies

6060 N Central Expy
Dallas, TX 75206-5209
214-692-0771
FAX: 214-692-0162 800-692-0771

Patty Jordan, Publisher

About 750 energy service companies and industry suppliers.
Bi-Monthly
Circulation: 10,000

18348 Brown's Directory of North American and International Gas Companies
Advanstar Communications
131 W 1st Street
Duluth, MN 55802-2065
218-723-9200
FAX: 218-723-9122
info@advanstar.com
www.advanstar.com
Operating gas companies, brokers and refineries are listed in this comprehensive directory with worldwide coverage. *$265.00*

350 pages Annual
Circulation: 1,000

18349 Canadian Oil Industry Directory
PennWell Directories
1700 W Loop S
Suite 1000
Houston, TX 77027-3007
713-621-8833
FAX: 281-499-6310 800-752-9764
susana@penwell.com
www.petroleumdirectories.com

Susan Anderson, Editor
Tim Sullivant, Manager

A directory for: associations, government agencies, drilling contractors, engineering, construction, exploration, production, petrochemicals, pipeline operators, etc. *$135.00*

18350 Congress Legislative Directory
American Gas Association
1515 Wilson Boulevard
Suite 100
Arlington, VA 22209-2469
703-841-8400

Offers information on members of both houses of the United States Congress, federal government agencies relevant to the natural gas industry. *$10.00*
220 pages Annual

18351 Contracts for Field Projects & Supporting Research on Enhanced Oil Recovery
US Department of Energy
PO Box 1398
Bartlesville, OK 74005
918-336-0307
FAX: 918-337-4418

Herbert A Tiedemann, Editor

Energy Department technical project officers and contractors.
97 pages Quarterly Founded: 1997

18352 Crude Oil Analysis Data Bank
PO Box 2565
Bartlesville, OK 74005-2565
918-336-2400

Contains over 9,000 analyses, obtained from the Bureau of Mines, of worldwide crude oil deposits.
Full-text

18353 DRI International Oil
DRI/McGraw-Hill
24 Hartwell Avenue
Lexington, MA 02421-3158
781-863-5100

This statistical database offers country-specific information on oil and natural gas production, consumption, stocks and imports for members of the International Energy Agency.

18354 DRI Natural Gas Forecast
DRI/McGraw-Hill
24 Hartwell Avenue
Lexington, MA 02421-3158
781-863-5100

This time series database contains more than 600 annual forecasts of US oil and natural gas supply, prices and production costs. *$2500.00*
6 pages Founded: 1985
Computerized version available: email

18355 DRI Natural Gas Spot Prices
DRI/McGraw-Hill
24 Hartwell Avenue
Lexington, MA 02421-3158
781-863-5100

This time series covers weekly and monthly US natural gas spot prices for each major transaction point, including the wellhead, delivery to pipeline, and at the city-gate for local distribution.

18356 DRI World Oil Forecast
DRI/McGraw-Hill
24 Hartwell Avenue
Lexington, MA 02421-3158
781-863-5100

This comprehensive look at the oil industry includes information on worldwide crude oil production, supply stocks and consumption.

18357 DRI/Platt's Oil Prices
DRI/McGraw-Hill
24 Hartwell Avenue
Lexington, MA 02421-3158
781-863-5100

Database provides weekly, monthly and daily time series of worldwide petroleum product prices.

18358 Drilling & Well Servicing Contractors
Midwest Publishing Company
2230 E 49th Street, Suite E
PO Box 50350
Tulsa, OK 74105-8771
918-839-9999
FAX: 918-587-9349 800-829-2002
info@midwestpub.com
www.midwestpub.com

Will Hammack, Editor

Approximately 4,000 drilling and well servicing contractors, equipment suppliers, manufacturers and service companies.
$150.00

Annual, September

18359 Dwight's Offshore and Bid Data
Dwight's Energydata
1633 Firman Drive
Suite 100
Richardson, TX 75081-6790
972-783-8002
FAX: 972-783-0058 800-468-3381
This large database offers the most current information on bids, lease ownership data, and competitive intelligence data on the petroleum industry.
Numeric

18360 Fuel Oil News-Source Book Issue
Fuel Oil News
3496 E Lake Lansing Road
Suite 150
East Lansing, MI 48823-6223
517-337-4040

Offers a list of over 600 manufacturers and suppliers of oil handling, heating and delivering companies. *$10.00*
Annual
Circulation: 17,000

18361 GOA Membership Directory
Georgia Oilmen Association
1775 Spectrum Drive
Suite 100
Lawrenceville, GA 30043-5745
770-995-7570
FAX: 770-995-9757
mfranklin@gaoilassoc.com
www.georgiaoilmensassoc.com
Roger T Lane, President/Editor
Mary R Franklin, Associate Editor
Directory of active and associate members and other valuable information. *$250.00*
42 pages Monthly
Circulation: 1,300
Printed in on glossy stock

18362 Gas and Oil Equipment Directory
Underwriters Laboratories
333 Pfingsten Road
Northbrook, IL 60062-2096
847-120-0136
FAX: 847-272-0472
Jane Coen, Corporate Manager
Companies that have qualified to use the UL listing mark or classification marking on or in connection with products that have been found to be in compliance with UL's requirements. *$9.00*
Annual October

18363 Hart Energy Publishing
4545 Post Oak Place Drive
Suite 210
Houston, TX 77027-3105
713-993-9320
FAX: 713-840-8585 800-874-2544
Jeff Miller, Director Marketing
Matt Beltz, Marketing Associate
Rich Eichler, President
Hart Energy Publishing is the worldwide leader in energy industry publishing. With fiver energy magazines, E & P, Oil and Gas investors, Pipeline gas technology, energy markets and world refining. Hart Energy Publishing also has a range of newsletters and centers devoted to the downstream Energy industry.
15 pages Monthly

18364 Hart Publications
4545 Post Oak Place Drive
Houston, TX 77027-3105
713-993-9320
FAX: 713-840-8585 800-874-2544
Gina Acosta, Fulfillment
Rich Eichler, President
Directories, magazines and newsletters of the oil and gas industry
15 pages Annually

18365 International Oil Spill Control Directory
Cutter Information Corporation
37 Broadway
Arlington, MA 02474-5552
781-641-2886

Offers valuable information on more than 1,000 suppliers of more than 3,500 oil spill cleanup, prevention and control products and services. *$95.00*
225 pages Annual

18366 Marketers, Purchasers & Trading Companies
Midwest Publishing Company
PO Box 50350
Tulsa, OK 74150-0350
918-839-9999
FAX: 918-587-9349 800-829-2002
info@midwestdirectories.com
www.midwestdirectories.com
Will Hammack, Editor
Over 5,300 purchasers, marketers and traders of refined products, crude oil and natural gas. *$145.00*
Annual October ; Paperback

18367 McGraw-Hill GasWire
DRI/McGraw-Hill
24 Hartwell Avenue
Lexington, MA 02421-3158
781-863-5100

Contains news and analyses of the US natural gas market.
Full-text

18368 Member Directory and Oil & Gas Agencies
Interstate Oil and Gas Compact Commission
PO Box 53127
Oklahoma City, OK 73152-3127
405-525-3556
FAX: 405-525-3592 800-822-4015
iogcc@iogcc.state.ok.us
www.iogcc.state.ok.us
Christine Hansen, Executive Director
Alesha Leemaster, Communications Manager
About 600 state representatives to the commission from 29 oil and gas producing states and seven associate states and committee members from related industries and government agencies. *$11.00*
Annual

18369 NOIA Leaders
National Ocean Industries Association
1120 G Street NW
Suite 900
Washington, DC 20005
202-347-6900
FAX: 202-347-8650
noia@noia.org www.noia.org
Thomas A Fry, III, President
Kim Harb, Director Government Affairs
Franki K Stuntz, Director Administration
Nolty J Thuriot, Director Congressional Affairs
Annual

18370 National Petroleum News: Buyer's Guide Issue
2101 S Arlington Heights Road
Arlington Heights, IL 60005-4185
847-427-9512
FAX: 847-427-2041
Jim Bursch, Publisher
Don Smith, Editor
A comprehensive listing of products and services for the petroleum industry. *$30.00*
Annual
Circulation: 18,000

18371 National Petroleum News: Market Facts Issue
2101 S Arlington Heights Road
Arlington Heights, IL 60005-4185
847-427-9512
FAX: 847-427-2041
Jim Bursch, Publisher
Don Smith, Editor
Offers the industry's most up-to-date compilation of petroleum/convenience store facts, figures and trends. *$75.00*
Annual
Circulation: 18,000

18372 Natural Gas Industry Directory
PennWell Directories
1700 W Loop S
Suite 1000
Houston, TX 77027-3007
713-621-8833
FAX: 281-499-6310 800-752-9764
susana@penwell.com
www.petroleumdirectories.com
Susan Anderson, Editor
Tim Sullivant, Manager
Major divisions of the natural gas industry worldwide. *$165.00*

18373 Offshore Services and Equipment Directory
Greene Dot
11686 Jocatal Center
San Diego, CA 92127-1147
858-485-0189
FAX: 858-485-5139
Renee Garza, Editor
About 5,000 suppliers of equipment and services to the offshore petroleum exploration and production industry worldwide. *$235.00*
Annual May
Circulation: 4,000

18374 Oil and Gas Directory
Geophysical Directory
2200 Welch Avenue
Houston, TX 77019-0508
713-291-1922
FAX: 713-529-3646 800-929-2462
info@theoilandgasdirectory.com
www.theoilandgasdirectory.com
Claudia LaCalli, Manager
Valuable information is listed on over 5,000 companies worldwide that are involved in petroleum exploration and drilling. *$130.00*

700 pages Annual, October Founded: 1970
Circulation: 2,000

18375 Oil and Gas Field Code Master List
US Energy Information Administration
1000 Independence Avenue SW
#E1-231
Washington, DC 20585-0001
202-586-8800
FAX: 202-512-2168
Ingrid Springer, Editor
All identified oil and gas fields in the US.
$27.00
Annual December

18376 Permit Data On-Line
Petroleum Information Corporation
PO Box 2612
Denver, CO 80201-2612
303-595-7500
800-645-3282
Oil well drilling permits granted by regional governmental agencies.
Weekly

18377 PetroProcess HSE Directory
Atlantic Communications LLC
1635 W Alabama Street
Houston, TX 77006-4196
713-529-1616
FAX: 713-523-7804
info@oilonline.com
www.oilonline.com
James W Self, Publisher
Rob Garza, Director of Operations
$79.00
650 pages Annual Founded: 1990

18378 Petroleum Equipment Directory
Petroleum Equipment Institute
6514 E 69th Street
Tulsa, OK 74133-1729
918-494-9696
FAX: 918-491-9895
Robert Renkes, Executive Vice President
Member manufacturers, distributors and installers of petroleum marketing equipment worldwide are offered. *$50.00*
395 pages Annual
Circulation: 3,000

18379 Petroleum Marketers Association of America Directory
Petroleum Marketers Association of America
1901 Fort Myer Drive
Suite 500
Arlington, VA 22209-1616
703-351-8000
FAX: 703-351-9160 800-300-7622
Daniel Gilligan, President
Sarah Dodge, Director/Legislative Affairs
Patricia Murrey, Director/Administration
Holly Tuminello, VP
Izua Yang, Manager/Communications/Conferences
About 45 state and regional member associations. A national organization representing the nation's independent petroleum marketers. *$50.00*
Annual February
Circulation: 2,000

18380 Petroleum Marketing Management Buyers Guide
Graphic Concepts
1801 Rockville Pike
Suite 330
Rockville, MD 20852-1633
A list of suppliers of products, equipment and services to combination gas station owners and convenience stores.
Annual
Circulation: 20,000

18381 Petroleum Software Directory
PennWell Publishing Company
3050 Post Oak Boulevard
Suite 200
Houston, TX 77056-6570
713-219-9720
FAX: 713-963-6228 800-752-9764
More than 800 companies that produce over 1,800 micro-, mini- and mainframe computer software packages designed for petroleum industry applications. *$195.00*
Annual June
Circulation: 1,000

18382 Petroleum Supply Annual
Superintendent of Documents
PO Box 371954
Pittsburgh, PA 15250-7954
202-586-1361
Contains information on the supply and disposition of crude oil and petroleum products. Reflects data collected by the petroleum industry during 1998 through annual and monthly surveys, it is divided in to two volumes. The first volume contains three sections, Summary Statistics, Detailed Statistics, and Refinery Capacity, each with final annual data. Volume 1 cost is $17.00, volume 2 $51.00
175 pages Annual Founded: 1999
Computerized version available: pdf

18383 Pipeline & Gas Journal: Buyer's Guide Issue
Oildom Publishing Company of Texas
PO Box 941669
Houston, TX 77094-8669
281-558-6930
FAX: 281-558-7029
www.oildompublishing.com
Jeff Share, Editor
List of over 700 companies supplying products and services used in construction and operation of cross country pipeline and gas distribution systems. *$75.00*
May

18384 Pipeline & Gas Journal: Directory of Pipeline Operating Companies
Oildom Publishing Company of Texas
PO Box 941669
Houston, TX 77218-9368
281-558-6930
FAX: 281-558-7029
www.oildompublishing.com
Jeff Share, Editor
Oliver Klinger, Editor
List of companies operating oil and gas transmission pipelines worldwide. *$80.00*
September
Circulation: 27,000

18385 SPE: Annual Membership Directory
Society of Petroleum Engineers
PO Box 833836
Richardson, TX 75083-3836
972-952-9300
FAX: 972-952-9435 800-456-6863
Georgeann Bilich, Editor
List of 52,000 member petroleum engineers. *$150.00*
Annual May
Circulation: 5,000

18386 Supply, Distribution, Manufacturing and Service
Midwest Publishing Company
PO Box 50350
Tulsa, OK 74159
918-839-9999
FAX: 918-587-9349 800-829-2002
info@midwestdirectories.com
www.midwestdirectories.com
Will Hammack, Editor
8,000 oil well supply stores, service companies and equipment manufacturers.
$165.00
Annual, September Founded: 1943 : Paperback

18387 TULSA Database
Petroleum Abstracts
101 Harwell
Tulsa, OK 74104-3189
918-631-2297
FAX: 918-599-9361 800-247-8678
question@tured.pa.utulsa.edu
www.pa.utulsa.edu
Contains more than 700,000 citations, with abstracts, to the worldwide literature and patents on the exploration, development and production of petroleum resources.
Weekly Updates

18388 US Non-Utility Power Directory on CD-ROM
PennWell Publishing Company
PO Box 1260
Tulsa, OK 74101-1260
918-835-3161
FAX: 918-831-9555 800-752-9764
Gockel Delma, Sales
Offers a unique source of information to industry professionals including a listing of over 1,423 plant locations including project names, site addresses, plant types, fuels, installed capacity, power contract information, operating control systems, ownership and more. *$695.00*
Annual

18389 US Offshore Oil Company Contact List
Offshore Data Services
PO Box 19909
Houston, TX 77224-1909
713-781-7094
FAX: 713-781-9594
editors@offshore-data.com
Marie Sheffer, Editor
Linda Parino, Circulation Director
Approximately 265 oil companies with US offshore leases. *$135.00*
Annual ISSN 1058-5877
Circulation: 800
Mailing list available for rent
Computerized version available

18390 USA Oil Industry Directory
PennWell Publishing Company
3050 Post Oak Boulevard
Suite 200
Houston, TX 77056-6570
713-219-9720
FAX: 713-963-6228 800-752-9764
Laura Bell, Editor
Susan Anderson, Publisher
Over 3,600 independent oil producers, fund companies, petroleum marketing companies, crude oil brokers and integrated oil firms. *$165.00*
Annual October
Circulation: 5,000

18391 USA Oilfield Service, Supply and Manufacturers Directory
PennWell Publishing Company
3050 Post Oak Boulevard
Suite 200
Houston, TX 77056-6570
713-219-9720
FAX: 713-963-6228 800-752-9764
Guntis Moritis, Editor
About 3,600 companies that provide oil-field equipment, supplies and services to the oil industry. *$145.00*
Annual October
Circulation: 2,500

18392 West Coast Petroleum Industry Directory
Economic Insight
3004 SW 1st Avenue
Portland, OR 97201
503-222-2425
FAX: 503-242-2968
info@econ.com www.econ.com
Samuel A Van Vactor, President
Individuals and companies that refine, buy and sell oil and petroleum products are listed. *$85.00*
204 pages Quarterly

18393 World Oil-Marine Drilling Rigs
Gulf Publishing Company
3301 Allen Parkway
Houston, TX 77019-1896
713-294-4301
Offers inforamtion on over 600 mobile and self-contained drilling rigs including submersibles, drillships and barges. *$11.00*
Annual
Circulation: 30,000

Industry Web Sites

18394 www.aesc.net
Association of Energy Service Companies
Professional trade association for well-site service contractors and businesses providing goods and services to well-site contractors. Develops and sells training and safety materials.

18395 www.aopl.org
Association of Oil Pipe Lines
Assembles statistics and other data relating to the pipeline industry for presentation to Congress, government departments, trade associations, and the public.

18396 www.api.org
American Petroleum Institute
Seeks to maintain cooperation between government and industry, fosters foreign and domestic trade in American petroleum products, conducts research.

18397 www.bpnews.com
Butane-Propane News
Petroleum and propane industry news.

18398 www.greyhouse.com
Grey House Publishing
Selected Grey House directories in the fields of business, health and education are available online. Users can search our on-line databases by several different search criteria, such as product categories, geographic area, sales volume and much, much more. Full Grey House catalog and online ordering also available.

18399 www.iadc.org
International Association of Drilling Contractors
Conducts educational and training programs. Sponsors safety contest and bestows awards.

18400 www.igt.org
Institute of Gas Technology
An independent not-for-profit center for energy and environmental research, development; education and information. Main function is to perform sponsored and in-house research, development and demonstration, provide educational programs and services, and disseminate scientific and technical information.

18401 www.iosc.org
Oil Spill Conference
Strives to create a global colloquim for public, government and business ideas addressing all aspects of oil spills impacting the environment. International exchange of information and ideas dealing with spill prevention, planning, response and restoration processes, protocols and technology.

18402 www.liquidrecyclers.org
NORA, An Association of Responsible Recyclers
Members are companies that reprocess used antifreeze, wastewater, oil filters, chemicals and companies that provide products or services to the industry.

18403 www.naro-us.org
National Association of Royalty Owners
Assists mineral and royalty owners in the effective management of their mineral properties. Provides information on tax, regulatory, and legislative matters. Conducts seminars and bestows awards.

18404 www.noraoil.com
National Oil Recyclers Association
Members are companies that reprocess used oil into fuel oil or recycle antifreeze, wastewater, oil filters and companies that provide products or services to the industry.

18405 www.npc.org
National Petroleum Council
Self-supporting federal advisory body to the Secretary of Energy established in 1946 at the request of President Truman.

18406 www.npga.org
National Propane Gas Association
Members are producers and distributors of liquefied petroleum gas and equipment manufacturers.

18407 www.npradc.org
National PetroChemical & Refiners Association
Members are petroleum, petrochemical and refining companies.

18408 www.oilscouts.org
International Oil Scouts Association
Compiles statistics on exploration and development wells in the US. Offers professional development and scholarship programs.

18409 www.pei.org
Petroleum Equipment Institute
Members are makers and distributors of equipment used in service stations, bulk plants and other petroleum marketing facilities.

18410 www.pttc.org
Petroleum Technology Transfer Council
Fosters the effective transfer of exploration and production technology to US petroleum producers through regional resource centers, workshops, websites, publications, etc.

18411 www.spwla.org
Society of Professional Well Log Analysts
Promotes the evaluation of formations, through well logging techniques, in order to locate gas, oil and other minerals.

18412 www.wspa.org
Western States Petroleum Association
For companies that refine, produce, transport, and market petroleum and petroleum products in six western states: Arizona, California, Oregon, Nevada, Hawaii and Washington.

Associations

18413 ASPCA
424 E 92nd Street
New York, NY 10128-6804
212-876-7700
FAX: 212-876-0014
information@aspca.org
www.aspca.org
Ed Sayres, President
Society for the humane treatment of animals, established in 1866.
300+ Members Founded: 1866

18414 American Animal Hospital Association
12575 W Bayaud Avenue
Lakewood, CO 80228
303-986-2800
FAX: 303-986-1700
info@aahanet.org www.aahanet.org
John Albers, Executive Director
A group of hospitals and animal practitioners serving the industry.
33000 Members Founded: 1933

18415 American Boarding Kennels Association
1702 E Pikes Peak Avenue
Colorado Springs, CO 80909
719-667-1600
FAX: 719-667-0116
info@abka.com www.abka.com
James Krack, Executive Director
Seeks to upgrade the industry through educational programs and conventions. Promotes code of ethics and accreditation programs for kennel operators.
1500 Members Founded: 1977

18416 American Cat Fanciers Association
PO Box 1949
Nixa, MO 65714-1949
417-725-1530
FAX: 417-725-1533 www.acfacat.com
Carol Barbee, President
Judy Eastwood, First VP
Jeanne Osborne, Second VP
Connie Vandre, Executive Director
Central registry for cats. Sanctions shows, publishes a bimonthly newsletter, offers a yearbook and maintains pedigree records.
800 Members Founded: 1955

18417 American Farriers Association
4059 Iron Works Parkway
Suite 1
Lexington, KY 40511
859-233-7411
FAX: 859-231-7862
www.americanfarriers.org
Bryan Quinsey, Executive Director
To further the professional development of farriers, to provide leadership and resource for the benefit of the farrier industry, and to improve the welfare of the horse through continuing farrier education.
2.4M Members Founded: 1971

18418 American Humane Association
63 Inverness Drive E
Englewood, CO 80112
303-792-9900
FAX: 303-792-5333 800-227-4645
info@americanhumane.org
www.americanhumane.org
John Nobil, Chair/President
Marie Wheatley, Executive Director
Thomas P Howard, VP
Terrye Frisselle, Principal
Steven C Crosby, VP Corporate Communications
Protects children and animals from cruelty, neglect, abuse, and exploitation.
Founded: 1877

18419 American Kennel Club
260 Madison Avenue
New York, NY 10010-1603
212-696-8200
FAX: 212-696-8299
info@akc.org www.akc.org
Dennis B Sprung, President/CEO
James P Crowley, Executive Secretary
John Lyons, Chief Operations Officer
James T Steven, Chief Financial Officer
Charley Kneifel, Chief Information Officer
The prinicipal registry of pure-bred dogs in the United States. More ways to enjoy your dog.

18420 American Veterinary Medical Association
1931 N Meacham Road
Suite 100
Schaumburg, IL 60173-4364
847-036-6142
FAX: 847-925-1329 800-248-2862
sgranskog@avma.org www.avma.org
Sharon Curtis Granskog
Michael Walters, Director Communications Division
Dr. Gail Golab, Assistant Director
Publishes various journals and information for members. Acts as a clearinghouse for veterinarians.
67M Members Founded: 1863

18421 Animal Health Institute
1325 G Street NW
Suite 700
Washington, DC 20005
202-637-2440
FAX: 202-393-1667
rphillips@ahi.org www.ahi.org
Carolyn S Ayers, VP Administration/Finance
Alexander Mathews, President/CEO
Dr Richard A Carnevale, VP
Dr Kent McClure, General Counsel
Ron Phillips, VP Legislative/Public Affairs
Represents manufacturers of animal health care products.
30 Members Founded: 1960

18422 Animal Legal Defense Fund
170 E Cotati Ave
Cotati, CA 94931-4474
707-795-2533
FAX: 707-795-7280
info@aldf.org www.aldf.org
Joyce Tischler, Executive Director
Steve Ann Chambers, President
Stephen Wells, Director/Animal Law Program
Pamela Frasch, Director/Anti-Cruelty Division
Roger Brigham, Director/Communications
Information on animal protection, wildlife conservation and animal rights.
18 Members Founded: 1979

18423 Association of Pet Dog Trainers
150 Executive Center Drive
Box 35
Greenville, SC 29615
864-310-0764
800-738-3647
information@apdt.com
www.apdt.com
Richard Spencer, Executive Director
Pat Miller, President
Teoti Anderson, VP
Jackie Powell, Manager Operations
Enhancing the human/dog relationship by educating trainers, other animal professionals and the public and advocating dog friendly training.

18424 Delta Society
Interactions
875 124th Avenue NE
Suite 101
Bellevue, WA 98055-2297
425-226-7357
FAX: 425-235-1076 800-869-6898
info@deltasociety.org
www.deltasociety.org
Linda Hines, Executive Director
Lawrence J Norvell, President/CEO
Information on human-animal interactions. Service Dog Center provides information and advocacy for dogs trained to assist people with disabilities. Pet Partners Program trains volunteers, health professionals, animals for animal-assisted therapy and activities.
4.6M Members Founded: 1977

18425 Flint River Ranch
11205 Alpha Retta Highway
Suite H4
Roswell, GA 30076
678-905-5466
800-354-6858
LMK@healthfood4.com
www.healthfood4pets.com
Lisa M Kochenash, Manager/Distributor
J Flint, Owner
Provides super premium, all natural health food for your best friend. A natural diet is the best defense against chronic illness in pets. Our food containes no chemicals, preservatives, BHA, BHT, by products, ethoxyquin, propylene glycol, fillers, artificial colors or flavors.

18426 International Association of Pet Cemeteries & Crematories
5055 Route 11
PO Box 163
Ellenburg Depot, NY 12935
518-594-3000
FAX: 518-594-8801 800-952-5541
info@iaopc.com www.iaopc.com
Stephen Drown, Executive Director
Educates the public on pet burials and the disposal of sick and diseased animals to eliminate contamination of ground and water. Conducts workshops and research projects.
175 Members Founded: 1971

18427 International Professional Groomers
120 Turner Drive
Elk Grove Village, IL 60007-3214
847-758-1938
FAX: 847-758-8031 jkurpiel@aol.com
Judy Kurpiel, President

Represents the professional pet grooming industry, providing continuing education to members and public information on the proper care treatment. also publishes a quarterly newsletter.
500 Members Founded: 1988

18428 National Association of Professional Pet
15000 Commerce Parkway
Suite C
Mt. Laurel, NJ 08054
856-439-0324
FAX: 856-439-0525
napps@ahint.com www.petsitters.org
Jerry Wentz, President
Felicia Lembesis, Administrator Director
Rebecca Haines, Registration Coordinator
Kelly Calzarietta, Meetings/Exhibit Manager
Cathe Delaney, Membership Coordinator
Nonprofit organization dedicated to serving the needs of professional pet care providers. Promotes ethical standards and fosters cooperation among members in the pet care industry.
24 Members Founded: 1989

18429 National Congress of Animal Trainers
23675 W Chardon Road
Grayslake, IL 60030
847-546-0717
FAX: 847-546-3454
John F Cuneo, President
For trainers and breeders of rare animals.
300 Members

18430 National Dog Groomers Association of American
PO Box 101
Clark, PA 16113-0101
724-962-2711
FAX: 724-962-1919
Jeffrey Reynolds, Executive Director
To unite groomers through membership and offer optional certification testing throughout the United States.
2.4M Members

18431 National Humane Education Society
PO Box 340
Charles Town, WV 25414-340
304-725-0506
FAX: 304-725-1523
nhesinformation@nhes.org
www.nhes.org
Anna Briggs, Founder/VP
Cindy Taylor, Director
James Taylor, President
Virginia Dungan, Treasurer
Tina Fernandez, Secretary
Mission to foster a sentiment of kindness to animals.
400M+ Members Founded: 1948

18432 National Pigeon Association
PO Box 439
Newalla, OK 74857-439
405-386-6884

james4bird@aol.com
www.npausa.com
Frank Barrachina, President
Pat Avery, Secretary/Treasurer
James Avery, Secretary/Treasurer
Special information for members.
Founded: 1920

18433 National Taxidermists Association
108 Branch Drive
Slidell, LA 70461
866-662-9052
FAX: 985-641-9463
headquarters@nationaltaxidermists.com
www.nationaltaxidermists.com
Mark Wilson, President
Greg Crain, Executive Director
Bill Haynes, VP
Barb Lager, Secretary
Greg Crain, Executive Director
Preserving animals to their natural form.
2500 Members Founded: 1970

18434 PETCO Animal Supplies
9125 Rehco Road
San Diego, CA 92121
858-537-7845
FAX: 858-784-3489 888-824-7257
Walter Evans, Founder
Brian Devine, Chairman
James Myers, Chief Executive Officer
We put animals first. The Petco Foundation supports community organization and efforts that enhance the lives of companion animals.

18435 People for the Ethical Treatment of Animals
501 Front Street
Norfolk, VA 23510
757-622-7382
FAX: 757-622-0457
info@peta.org www.peta.org
Ingrid Newkirk, President
Opposes all forms of animal exploitation. Seeks to educate the public on what the group sees as the three major institutionalized cruelty issues: the exploitation and abuse of animals in experimentation, the manufacturing of fur apparel, and slaughtering for human consumption.
80000 Members Founded: 1980

18436 Pet Food Institute
2025 M Street NW
Suite 800
Washington, DC 20036-2412
202-367-1120
FAX: 202-367-2120
pfi@dc.sba.com
www.petfoodinstitute.org
Stephen Payne, VP Communications
Duane Ekedahl, Executive Director
Represents dog and cat food manufacturers. Supporting initiative to advance the quality of dog and cat food. Supporting research in pet nutrition and the important role of pets in our society. Promoting the overall care and well-being of pets.
100 Members Founded: 1958

18437 Pet Industry Distributors Association
2105 Laurel Bush Road
Suite 200
Bel Air, MD 21015
443-640-1060
FAX: 443-640-1031
pida@ksgroup.org www.pida.org
Blaine Phillips, President
Donald Fleming, First VP
Robert Merar, Second VP
Marci Hickey, Meetings/Membership Service
Amy Chetelat, Financial Manager
Represents wholesaler-distributors of pet products, providing training and education to members.
190 Members Founded: 1968

18438 Pet Industry Joint Advisory Council
1220 19th Street NW
Suite 400
Washington, DC 20036
202-452-1525
FAX: 202-293-4377 800-553-7387
info@pijac.org www.pijac.org
Nancy Knutson, Director Administration
N Marshall Meyers, Executive VP
Michael Maddox, Governmental Affairs
Howard Deardorff, Director Education/Research
Monitors federal and state regulations and legislation affecting industry. Sponsors research and educational projects including certification programs in veterinary care and husbandry for companion animals, in-store training videos, etc.
2M Members Founded: 1971

18439 Pet Lovers Association
PO Box 145
Joppa, MD 21085
410-679-0978

Elden Harrison, President
Advises pet owners of their responsibilities.

18440 Pet Pride
3350 South Robertson Boulevard
Los Angeles, CA 90034
310-836-5427
www.petpride.org
Ruth Argust, President
Public education programs for proper cat care.
50000 Members Founded: 1965

18441 Pet Sitters International
210 East King Street
King, NC 27021-9163
336-983-9222
FAX: 336-983-5266
info@petsit.com www.petsit.com
Kay Calzcmari, Operating Manager
Beth Stoltz, Membership Service Coordinator
John Long, Public Relations Coordinator
Amy Woodleaf, Manager/Membership
Patti Moran, President
Society of professional pet sitters. Membership provides valuable benefits - educational resources for those engaged in the pet-sitting industry. Also provides a forum to network with peers who share a common vision of excellence in at-home pet care.
2.5M Members Founded: 1994

18442 PetCenter.Com: Internet Animal Hospital PetFoodDirect.com
189 Main Street
Harleysville, PA 19438
215-513-1999
FAX: 215-513-7286 www.the petcenter.com
T J Dunn, Jr DVM, Director
Award winning virtual animal hospital for dog and cat love. Mission of providing dog and cat caretakers with a better understanding of the medical and surgical treatment of pets. Created by veterinarians under the direction of Dr T.J. Dunn, all articles are presented in non-medical terms, just as if the veterinarian was speaking to you personally in a real exam room. Associated with PetFoodDirect.com

18443 PetFoodDirect.com
189 Main Street
Harleysville, PA 19438
215-513-1999
FAX: 215-513-7286

Geoffrey Walker, CEO
Jon Roska, Jr, COO

Largest pure play entailer for premium pet food, supplies and accessories on the internet. Our customers can order from a huge selection of pet products, have access to value-added services, including information on pet healthcare and nutrition.
Founded: 1997

18444 Petgroomer.com
PO Box 2489
Yelm, WA 98597
360-446-5348
FAX: 360-446-5234
www.petgroomer.com
Where pet grooming is everything.

18445 Petmarket.com
PO Box 523
Laurel, DE 19956
302-875-7111
888-738-6758
info@petmarket.com
www.petmarket.com
Resource for dog breeders, groomers, trainers and other pet professional associations. We provide you many forums to find solutions to your pet problems.
Founded: 1969

18446 US Animal Health Association
8100 Three Chapt Road
Richmond, VA 23288
804-285-3210
FAX: 804-285-3367
usaha@usaha.org www.usaha.org

Dr Don Lein, President
Dr Bret Marsh, First VP
James Leafstedt, Second VP
Dr Don Hoenig, Third VP
Dr Jones Bryan, Treasurer

Science-based, non-profit, voluntary organization. Concerning disease eradication, animal health, emerging diseases, food safety, public health, animal welfare, and international trade.
1400 Members

18447 United Kennel Club
100 E Kilgore Road
Kalamazoo, MI 49002
269-343-9020
FAX: 269-343-7037
webmaster@ukcdogs.com
www.ukcdogs.com

Peggy Bickele, Manager

Responsible for dog pedigrees and transfer of ownership of pedigree dogs. Best registry of pure-bred dogs.
50 Members

18448 Western and English Sales Association
451 E 58th Avenue
Suite 4128
Denver, CO 80216
303-295-1040
FAX: 303-295-0941 800-295-1041
info@denver-wesa.com
www.denver-wesa.com

Toni High, Executive Director

Association members are from the Western and English tack and apparel industry.
1100 Members Founded: 1922

18449 World Society for the Protection of Animals
34 Deloss Street
Framingham, MA 01702
508-879-8350
FAX: 508-620-0786
wspa@wspausa.com
www.wspa.usa.org

Laura Simpson, USA Director
Peter Davies, Director General

International animal protection news reports. Lobbies for effective animal welfare laws and provides educational material.
12 Members

18450 World Wide Pet Supply Association
406 South First Avenue
Arcadia, CA 91006-3829
626-447-2222
FAX: 626-447-8350 800-999-7295

Rick Newman, President
Lewis M Sutton, CFO
Steve Segner, First VP
Russ Feller, Second Vice President
Doug Poindexter, Manager

A non-profit, membership-controlled trade association organized to represent its members and the interests of the companion animal and product industry. America's oldest pet industry trade association. Our mission is to promote responsible pet care worldwide.

Newsletters

18451 ASPCA Report
424 E 92nd Street
New York, NY 10128-6804
212-876-7700

napcc@aspca.org
http://www.aspca.com

Janice Borzendowski, Publisher
Ed Sayres, President

Pet care news, issues, features and reviews.

Weekly Founded: 1866

18452 Animals International
World Society for the Protection of Animals
34 Deloss Street
Framingham, MA 01702
508-879-8350
FAX: 508-620-0786
wspa@wspausa.com
http://www.wspa-international.org/

Laura Salter, USA Director
Susan Sherwin, Press Contact

International animal protection news reports. *$10.00*
12 pages Quarterly Founded: 1981

18453 Animals' Advocate
Animal Legal Defense Fund
170 E Cotati Ave
Cotati, CA 94931-4474
707-795-2533
FAX: 707-795-7280
info@aldf.org
www.aldf.org/action.htm

Joyce Tischler, Executive Director

A newsletter offering information on animal protection, wildlife conservation and animal rights.
4 pages Monthly

18454 Anthrozoos
Delta Society
875 124th Ave NE
Ste 101
Bellevue, WA 98005
425-226-7357
FAX: 425-235-1076
info@deltasociety.org
http://www.deltasociety.org/

Linda M Hines, Publisher
Robert T Franklin, Chairmain
Lawrence J. Norvell, CEO/President

Scientific journal on the interactions of people, animals and nature. *$40.00*
72 pages Quarterly Founded: 1977
Circulation: 800

18455 Association of Pet Dog Trainers Newsletter
150 Executive Center Drive
Box 35
Greenville, SC 29615
864-310-0764
FAX: 856-439-0525 800-738-3647
information@apdt.com
http://www.apdt.com

Richard Spencer, Executive Director
Pat Miller, President

Building better trainers through education.

Founded: 1993

18456 Cat Industry Newsletter
Good Communications
PO Box 10069
Austin, TX 78766-1069
512-454-9062
FAX: 512-454-3420 800-968-1738
ross@goodcommunications.com
www.petfoodnews.com

Ross Becker, Editor

Business newsletter for catfood, cat products and cat litter industries. Covers business news, marketing, new products in the pipeline, industry data. *$295.00*
6 pages Monthly Founded: 1992
Printed in on matte stock

18457 Dog Industry Newsletter
Good Communications
PO Box 10069
Austin, TX 78766-1069
512-454-9062
FAX: 512-454-3420 800-968-1738
ross@goodcommunications.com
www.petfoodnews.com

Ross Becker, Editor

Business newsletter for petfood,and pet products industries.Covers business news, marketing, new products in the pipeline, industry data. *$295.00*
10 pages Monthly Founded: 1990
Printed in on matte stock

18458 Humane News
Associated Humane Societies
124 Evergreen Avenue
Newark, NJ 07114-2133
973-824-7080
FAX: 973-824-2720
associatedhumane@aol.com
http://www.associatedhumanesocieties.or
g

Roseann Trezza, Editor
Lee Bernstein, Executive Director

News concerning animal welfare.

24 pages Monthly Founded: 1906
Circulation: 75000

18459 IPG Newsletter
International Professional Groomers
120 Turner Drive
Elk Grove Village, IL 60007-3214
847-758-1938
FAX: 847-758-8031 800-258-4765

Judy Kurpiel, President

A quarterly newsletter published by the International Professional Groomers.
6 pages Quarterly Founded: 1988
Circulation: 500

18460 International Pet Industry News
Good Communications
PO Box 10069
Austin, TX 78766-1069
512-454-9062
FAX: 512-454-3420 800-968-1738
help@googcommunications.com
www.petfoods.com

Ross Becker, Editor

Business newsletter for internatioal petfood, pet products industries. Covers business news, marketing, new products in the pipeline, industry data. *$295.00*
8 pages Monthly Founded: 1993
Printed in on matte stock

18461 K-9 Courier
PO Box 49
Jerico Springs, MO 64756

Monthly newsletter for breeders.
Monthly

18462 Pet Gazette
Gazette Publishing
1309 N Halifax Avenue
Daytona Beach, FL 32118-3658

www.geocities.com/Petsburgh/6860

Faith Senior, Publisher

Pictures, anaecdotes, cartoons and more for the pet industry. *$12.50*
24 pages Quarterly
Circulation: 300

18463 Pet Partners Newsletter
Delta Society
875 124th Ave
Suite 101
Bellevue, WA 98055
425-226-7357
FAX: 425-235-1076
info@deltasociety.org
http://www.deltasociety.org

Maureen Fredrickson, Editor
Lawrence Norvell, President

How-to newsletter for pet owners who volunteer in animal-assisted therapy and activity programs. *$6.00*
2 pages Monthly Founded: 1977
Circulation: 2500

18464 Pet Planet Newsletter
PO Box 150899
Denver, CO 80215-0899
303-986-2800
FAX: 303-986-1700
www.healthypet.com

John W Albers, Executive Director

A group of hospitals and animal practitioners serving the industry. *$60.00*
64 pages Bi-Monthly Founded: 1985
Circulation: 14,000
Printed in on glossy stock

18465 Pet Stuff
Pet Stuff
608 Tumbleweed Lane
Fall Brook, CA 92028-9446
760-728-9306
FAX: 760-728-9735 petstuff@cts.com

Robert Tanner, Publisher

A direct co-op mailing service to the pet industry. Accepts advertising.
BiWeekly

18466 Veterinary Industry Newsletter
Good Communications
PO Box 10069
Austin, TX 78766-1069
512-454-9062
FAX: 512-454-3420 800-968-1738
ross@goodcommunications.com
www.petfoodsnews.com

Ross Becker, Editor

Business newsletter for petfood, animal health and veterinary industries.Covers business news, marketing, new products in the pipeline, industry data. *$295.00*
10 pages Monthly Founded: 1993
Printed in 1 color on matte stock

18467 Watchbird
PO Box 56218
Phoenix, AZ 85079
602-484-0931
FAX: 602-484-0109
stat@wizard.net
http://www.afabirds.org/

Jerry Crowley, Executive VP
S Rosenbeltt, Circulation Director
Benny Gallaway, President

Journal on conservation, education, bird keeping and breeding.
Founded: 1974
Circulation: 6000

Magazines & Journals

18468 Animal Fair
7 Penn Plaza
11th Floor
New York, NY 10001
212-629-0392
FAX: 212-988-7486
editor@animalfair.com
http://www.animalfair.com

Wendy Diamond, Editorial Director
Wendy Diamond, CEO/President *$19.95*

Bi-annually Founded: 1999

18469 Aquarium Fish Magazine
Fancy Publications
PO Box 6050
Mission Viejo, CA 92690
949-855-8822
FAX: 949-855-3045
aquariumfish@fancypubs.com
http://www.animalnetwork.com
Devoted to pet stores and readers who keep freshwater and saltwater species of tropical fish. *$15.97*
Monthly Founded: 1905
Circulation: 49,700

18470 Bird Talk
Fancy Publications
3 Burroughs
Irvine, CA 92618
949-855-8822
FAX: 949-855-3045
ibt@bowtieinc.com
http://www.birdtalkmagazine.com

Edward Bauman, Editor

Pet news. *$13.99*
64 pages Monthly Founded: 1983

18471 BirdTimes
Pet Publishing
7-L Dundas Circle
Greensboro, NC 27407
336-292-4047
FAX: 336-292-4272
editorial@petpublishing.com
http://www.petpublishing.com

Mike Hammond, Publisher *$17.97*

Founded: 1992
Circulation: 50000 20000 names $100 per M.
Printed in 4 colors on glossy stock

18472 Bloodlines
United Kennel Club
100 E Kilgore Road
Kalamazoo, MI 49002
269-343-9020
FAX: 269-343-7037
hounds@ukcdogs.com
http://www.ukcdogs.com

Vickie Rander, Editor
Rosie Reeds, Advertising

A comprehensive publication covering breeding, showing and registering of animals. *$24.00*
Monthly Founded: 1898

18473 Cat Fancy Magazine
Fancy Publications
3 Burroughs
Irvine, CA 92618
949-855-8822
FAX: 949-855-3045
http://www.animalnetwork.com

Susan Logan, Editor
Sandy Meyer, Managing Editor

Offers information to cat owners and pet shop owners regarding cats. *$14.99*
Monthly Founded: 1965

18474 Cats & Kittens
Pet Publishing
7-L Dundas Circle
Greensboro, NC 27407
336-292-4047
FAX: 336-292-4272
cksubscriptions@petpublishing.com
http://www.petpublishing.com

Mike Hammond, Publisher
Rita Davis, Editor

Cat enthusiast magazine. *$19.97*
52 pages Founded: 1998
Circulation: 50000 40000 names $100 per M.
Printed in 4 colors on glossy stock

18475 Cats Magazine
PRIMEDIA Enthusiast Group
745 Fifth Avenue
Suite 1100
New York, NY 10151
212-745-0100
FAX: 212-745-0121
information@primedia.com
http://www.primedia.com

Mike Carney, Publisher
Doug Stange, Editor
Kelly P Conlin, CEO

For cat owners.

Founded: 1989

18476 Dog & Kennel
Pet Publishing
7-L Dundas Circle
Greensboro, NC 27407
336-292-4047
FAX: 336-292-4272
info@petpublishing.com
http://www.petpublishing.com

Mike Hammond, Publisher
Rita Davis, Editor

Dog enthusiast magazine. *$4.99*

64 pages Founded: 1996
Circulation: 50000 40000 names $100 per M.
Printed in 4 colors on glossy stock

18477 Dog Fancy Magazine
Fancy Publications
3 Burroughs
Irvine, CA 92618
949-855-8822
FAX: 949-855-3045 800-546-7730
bowtiepress@bowtieinc.com
http://www.animalnetwork.com

Susane Chney, Editor
Scott Montey, Publisher
Dock Style, CEO/President
Christy Chism, Circulation Manager
Steven Sapoher, Marketing Manager

A magazine covering the world of dogs. *$96.00*

Monthly

18478 Dog World Magazine
Charels A Tupta
3 Burroughs
Irvine, CA 92618
949-855-8822
FAX: 949-855-3045 800-361-8056
letters@dogworld.com
http://www.dogworldmag.com/

Charels A Tupta, Publisher
Donna Marcel, Editor

Written for the serious dog enthusiast, Dog World is the authority on dog care. Special editorial on behavior, nutrition, health care and training, plus thousands of classified and display listings in every issue. *$14.99*

132 pages Monthly Founded: 1916
Circulation: 64876 40,202 names $100 per M.

18479 Dogs USA
Fancy Publications
3 Burroughs
Irvine, CA 92618
949-855-8822
FAX: 949-855-3045
www.animalnetwork.com

Edward Bauman, Editor

Registration, breeding, pedigree news, bloodlines, etc. for dogs. *$5.95*

Annual

18480 Equestrian Retailer
Morris Communications
PO Box 7980
Colorado Springs, CO 80907-5339
719-633-5524
FAX: 719-633-1392
eqredit@westernahorseman.com
http://www.equestrianretailer.com

Rick Swan, Associate Publisher
Kathy Swan, Executive Editor
William S Morris, President
Karen Ficklin, Circulation Manager
Rob Fulkerson, General Manager

Serves to promote profitablity in the equine industry.

60 pages Founded: 1998
Circulation: 11000
Printed in 4 colors on matte stock

18481 Freshwater and Marine Aquarium Magazine
RC Modeler Corporation
144 W Sierra Madre Boulevard
Sierra Madre, CA 91024-2435
626-355-1476
FAX: 626-355-6415 800-523-1736
famamag@aol.com
http://www.mag-web.com

Don Dewey, Editor/Publisher
Patricia Crews, Assistant Editor

A magazine aimed at aquarium pertaining to fish and marine life, hobboyists. *$22.00*

200 pages Monthly Founded: 1978
Circulation: 65000
Printed in 4 colors on glossy stock

18482 Good Dog!
Good Dog!
PO Box 10069
Austin, TX 78766-1069
512-454-9062
FAX: 512-454-3420 800-968-1738
help@gooddogmagazine.com
http://www.gooddogmagazine.com

Judith Becker, Editor
Ross Becker, Publisher

Consumer magazine for dog owners. Nationally known for its test reports on dog food and products for dogs. Also publishes books on dog food, puppy selection and genetics. *$12.00*

36 pages Founded: 1988
Circulation: 40000 40000 names $100 per M.
Printed in 4 colors : website

18483 NAPPS Network
Association of Professional Pet Sitters
15000 Commerce Parkway
Suite C
Mt Laurel, NJ 08054
856-439-0324
FAX: 856-439-0525
napps@ahint.com
http://www.petsitters.org

Sally Liddick, Co-Director
Charlotte Reed, Editor/Publisher
Jerry Wentz, President

Official publication of the Association of Professional Pet Sitters.

Quarterly Founded: 1989
Circulation: 1500

18484 Pet Age Magazine
HH Backer Associates
200 S Michigan Avenue
Suite 840
Chicago, IL 60604-2455
312-663-4040
FAX: 312-663-5676
hhbacker@hhbacker.com
http://www.petage.com

Patty Backer, President/Publisher
Karen MacLeod, Editor in Chief
Mark Mitera, VP
Beth Morrissey, Production Coordinator
Cathy Foster, Senior Editor

Pet AGE helps pet/pet suppliers ratailers suceed in today competive marketplace. Editorial features emphasize progressive management and trends and issues. Accepts advertising. *$70.00*

80 pages Monthly Founded: 1965
Circulation: 23076 23,000 names $100 per M.
Printed in on glossy stock

18485 Pet Business Magazine
Pet Business
333 Seventh Avenue
11th Floor
New York, NY 10001-1645
212-979-4800
FAX: 646-674-0102
request@petbusiness.com
http://www.petbusiness.com

Rita Davis, Editor
Mike Burnette, Circulation Director
Craig M Rexford, Publisher
David Litwak, Editor In Chief
Nisa Cirulnick, Sales & Marketing Coordinator

Trade magazine for the pet industry. News, new products, animal care and legislative topics. Accepts advertising. *$49.97*

Founded: 1973
Circulation: 24,000
Mailing list available for rent 19.5M names
Printed in 4 colors on glossy stock

18486 Pet Product News Magazine
Fancy Publications
3 Burroughs
PO Box 6040
Irvine, CA 92618
949-855-8822
FAX: 949-855-3045
www.animalnetwork.com

Edward Bauman, Editor

Journal focusing on new products and other industry news.

18487 Petfood Industry
WATT Publishing Company
122 S Wesley Avenue
Mount Morris, IL 61054-1497
815-734-4171
FAX: 815-734-7727
olentine@wattmm.com
www.wattnet.com

Tim Phillips, Editor
Jennifer Kvanne, Associate Editor
Jeffery Swanson, Production Director
Clayton Schreiber, Publisher

Provides information to petfood industry professionals on the manufacturing and marketing of petfood products around the world. *$ 48.00*

46 pages Monthly Founded: 1959
Circulation: 9795 9,795 names $185 per M.

Printed in 4 colors on glossy stock

18488 World of Professional Pet Sitting
Pet Sitters International
201 East King Street
King, NC 27021-9163
336-983-9222
FAX: 336-983-5266
info@petsit.com
http://www.petsit.com

Patti Moran, President

Founded: 1985

Trade Shows

18489 America's Family Pet Expo
World Wide Pet Supply Association
406 S 1st Avenue
Arcadia, CA 91006-3829
626-447-2222
FAX: 626-447-8350 800-999-7295
info@wwpsa.com www.wwpsa.com
Rick Newman, President
Lewis M Sutton, CFO
Steve Segner, First VP
Russ Feller, Second Vice President
Dr. Robert Bray, Equine Outreach
Brings together all elements of the companion animal world and promotes responsible pet ownsership. Demonstrations, speakers, product exhibits, hobbyist shows, rides for the children, contests and more. 500 booths. April, Orange County, CA
80M Attendees April/September Founded: 1990

18490 American Animal Hospital Association Annual Meeting
American Animal Hospital Association
12575 W Bayaud Avenue
Lakewood, CO 80228
303-986-2800
FAX: 303-986-1700
donna.johnson@aahanet.org
www.aahanet.org
Donna Johnson, Exhibit Coordinator
Chuck Potter, Annual Meeting Manager
John Albers, Executive Director
250 scientific displays related to small animal veterinary care, computer software, marketing consulting services and pet care products.
3000 Attendees Annual Founded: 1933

18491 American Boarding Kennels Association Annual Convention & Trade Show
American Boarding Kennels Association
1702 E Pikes Peak Avenue
Colorado Springs, CO 80909
719-667-1600
FAX: 719-667-0116
info@abka.com www.abka.com
Kathryn Eddy, Show Manager
James Krack, Executive Director
Annual show and exhibit of pet industry products, including pet foods, supplements, retail supplies, construction materials, cages, computers and software. 60 booths.
300 Attendees October Founded: 1977

18492 American College of Veterinary Opthalmologists Confernce
2316 West Northern Avenue
Phoenix, AZ 85021
602-995-2871
FAX: 602-995-1770
www.maltesonly.com
Lisa Schultz, Practice Manager
Meeting and 30 exhibits of opthamology equipment and information.
400 Attendees Annual

18493 American College of Veterinary Surgeons - Veterinary Symposium
American College of Veterinary Surgeons
11 North Washington Street
Suite 720
Rockville, MD 20850
301-610-2000
FAX: 301-610-0371
acvs@acvs.org www.acvs.org
Ann T Loew, Executive Director
William B Henry, VP
Mark Markel, Chair
Marvin L Olmstead, ACVS President
Ann Loew, Executive Director
Over 150 exhibits featuring veterinary equipment, supplies and services.
1500 Attendees October 5-7 Founded: 1965
1500 names $375 per M.

18494 American Federation of Aviculture Convention
STAT Marketing
11240 Waples Mill Road
Suite 200
Fairfax, VA 22030
703-340-0164
FAX: 703-359-7562
info@statsmarketing.com
Sharon Rosenblatt Galler, President/Owner
Jerry Galler, VP/Operations
Annual convention of 60 exhibitors and 65 booths, that are manufacturers, suppliers, distributors and retailers of exotic birds and related products, including feed, seeds, cages, toys, vitamins and minerals.
750 Attendees Founded: 1974

18495 American Humane Association Annual Meeting and Training Conference
63 Inverness Drive E
Engelwood, CO 80112-5117
303-792-9900
FAX: 303-792-5333
www.americanhumane.org
Marie Wheatley, Executive Director
Over 50 exhibits of animal welfare equipment, including pet food, cages, trucks, id programs and veterinary services. Breakfast, luncheon, reception.
700 Attendees Annual Founded: 1982

18496 American Morgan Horse Association Grand National Show
3 Bostwick Road
PO Box 960
Shelburne, VT 05482-0960
802-985-4944
FAX: 802-985-8897
info@morganhorse.com
morganhorse.com
Raymond Gifford, Show Manager
Fred Braden, Executive Director
Offers you a way to enjoy your Morgan in a competitive setting, while enjoying the company of other Morgan exhibitors. 30 booths.
8M Attendees October

18497 American Paint Horse Association World Championship Horse Shows
PO Box 961023
Fort Worth, TX 76161-0023
817-834-2742
FAX: 817-834-3152
www.aphaworldshow.com
Carl Parker, President
Richard Cox, VP
Alice Singleton, Senior Committee Member
Ed Robert, Executive Secretary
A 14 day annual event that has become the proving ground for competitors striving to show that they ride or own the best American Paint Horses in the world. 100 booths.
5M Attendees July

18498 American Pet Products Manufacturers Association National Tradeshow
255 Glenville Road
Greenwich, CT 06831
203-532-0000
FAX: 203-532-0551 800-452-1225
andy@appma.org www.appma.org
Bob Vetere, COO/Managing Director
Jennifer Bilbao, Marketing/PR Administrator
Andrew Darmohraj, VP/Deputy Managing Director
Jamie Cavanaugh, Trade Show Coordinator
Edith Martingnetti, General Mgr/Exhibitor Registration
Breakfast, reception, and 1400 pet products manufacturers exhibits.
Annual Founded: 1959

18499 American Rabbit Breeders Association National Convention
8 Westport Court
Bloomington, IL 61704
309-664-7500
FAX: 309-664-0941
arbamail@aol.com arba.net
Glen Carr, Executive Director
Seminar, banquet, luncheon and 1500 rabbit breeders exhibits.
3000 Attendees Annual Founded: 1910

18500 American Veterinary Medical Association Annual Convention
American Veterinary Medical Association
1931 N Meacham Road
Suite 100
Schaumburg, IL 60173
847-036-6142
FAX: 847-925-1329
convention@avma.org www.avma.org
Dr Bonnie Beaver, President
David Little, Director
Seminar and 310 exhibits of products, materials, equipment, data, and services for veterinary medicine.
10000 Attendees Annual

18501 Annual Meeting & Leadership Conference
Private Label Manufacturers Association (PLMA)
369 Lexington Avenue
3rd Floor
New York, NY 10017
212-972-3131
FAX: 212-983-1382
info@plma.com www.plma.com
Discuss the state of the industry and opportunities for the future. It is your change to confer with other manufacturers as well as retailers and wholesalers.
Annual

18502 Annual Pet Industry Trade Show
World Wide Pet Supply Association
406 S 1st Avenue
Arcadia, CA 91006-3829
626-447-2222
FAX: 626-447-8350
info@wwpsa.com www.wwpsa.com
Doug Poindexter, Executive VP

A comprehensive collection of exhibits and educational events unparalleled in the industry.

18503 HH Backer Pet Industry Christmas Trade Show
HH Backer Associates
200 S Michigan Avenue
Suite 840
Chicago, IL 60604
312-663-4040
FAX: 312-663-5676
hhbacker@hhbacker.com
www.hhbacker.com

Patty Backer, President/Publisher
Karen Long MacLeod, Assoc Publisher/Editor in Chief
M Christopher Mitera, VP
Colette Fairchild, CMP, Trade Show Director
Julie Wichert, Show Manager

Containing 1000 plus booths and 550 plus exhibits consisting of pet supplies, products and services.
9M Attendees October Founded: 1967

18504 HH Backer Pet Industry Spring Trade Show
HH Backer Associates
200 S Michigan Avenue
Suite 840
Chicago, IL 60604
312-663-4040
FAX: 312-663-5676
hhbacker@hhbacker.com
www.hhbacker.com

Patty Backer, President/Publisher
Karen Long MacLeod, Assoc Publisher/Editor in Chief
M Christopher Mitera, VP
Collette Fairchild, CMP, Trade Show Director
Julie Wichert, Show Manager

Containing 1000 plus booths and 550 plus exhibits consisting of pet supplies, products and services.
10M Attendees April Founded: 1967

18505 NAPPS Annual Convention: National Associat ion of Professional Pet Sitters
17000 Commerce Parkway
Suite C
Mt. Laurel, NJ 08054
856-439-0324
FAX: 856-439-0525
napps@ahint.com www.petsitters.org

Felicia Lembesis, Administrative Director
Rebecca Haines, Registration Coordinator
Kelly Calzaretta, Meeting/Exhibit Manager
Cathe Delaney, Membership Coordinator

Exhibits, business sessions and networking opportunities. Provide tools and support to foster the success of members' businesses. To promote the value of pet sitting to the public and the advocate the welfare of animals.
September

18506 National Pet Products Controlled Marketing Conference
Controlled Marketing Conferences
PO Box 1771
Monument, CO 80132
719-488-0226
FAX: 719-488-8168 888-316-0226
info@nlgshow.com
www.nlgshow.com

Robert Mikulas, President
Chris Wolf, VP

This event is run in conjunction with the National Lawn and Garden Show.
3000 Attendees June

18507 National Pigeon Association
PO Box 439
Newalla, OK 74857-0439
405-386-6884
www.npausa.com

Frank Barrachina, President
Pat Avery, Secretary, Treasurer
James Avery, Secretary/Treasurer
Jerry McCalmon, Show Manager

Special information and exhibits about our members and the hobby of pigeon raising.
500 Attendees January Founded: 1920

18508 Pet Exposition Trade Show
Pet Industry Distributors Association
2105 Laurel Bush Road
Suite 200
Bel Air, MD 21015
443-640-1060
FAX: 443-640-1031
pida@ksgroup.org www.pida.org

Blaine Phillips, President
Donald Fleming, First Vice Presdent
Robert Merar, Second VP
Marci Hickey, Meetings/Membership Service
Amy Chetelat, Financial Manager

Containing 500 booths and 300 exhibits.
3000 Attendees March Founded: 1968

18509 Pet Food Institute Meeting and Trade Show
Pet Food Institute
2025 M Street NW
Washington, DC 20036
202-367-1120
FAX: 202-367-2120
pfi@dc.sbs.com
www.petfoodinstitute.org

Stephen Payne, Public Relations Manager
Duane Ekedahl, Executive Director

Annual exhibits of equipment, supplies and services for manufacturers of commercially prepared dry, semi-moist and canned pet foods.
250 Attendees October

18510 Petfood Forum
WATT Publishing Company
122 S Wesley Avenue
Mount Morris, IL 61054-1497
815-734-4171
FAX: 815-734-4201
olentine@wattmm.com
www.wattnet.com

Tim Phillips, Editor
Clay Schreiber, Publisher
James Watt, Owner

A technical trade show and symposium for the pet food industry including manufacturers, suppliers to the industry as well as other pet food professsionals. Containing 143 booths.
850 Attendees April Founded: 1993
Mailing list available for rent

18511 Quest for Excellence
Pet Sitters International
201 East King Street
King, NC 27021-9163
336-983-9222
FAX: 336-983-3755
info@petsit.com www.petsit.com

Kay Calzemari, Operating Manager
Beth Stoltz, Member Service Coordinator
Amy Woodleaf, Manager/Membership
John Long, Public Relations Coordinator
Dotty Shantz, Member Service

Containing 20+ exhibits.
250 Attendees September Founded: 1994

18512 Store Specific Merchandising & Marketing
770 Broadway
5th Floor
New York, NY 10003
646-654-7487
FAX: 646-654-7491
Nicole@eventsbynicole.com
www.store-specific.com

Nicole Bagdanov, Conference Director
Jill Mulitz, Registration Information

Executive conference focusing on the new consumer from a multi-channel view point. The year's conference will highlight: Hispanics, African-Americans, the working woman, teens and tweens.
300 Attendees April

18513 Super Zoo Annual WWPSA Pet Industry Trade Show
World Wide Pet Supply Association
406 S 1st Avenue
Arcadia, CA 91006-3829
626-447-2222
FAX: 626-447-8350
info@wwpsa.com www.wwpsa.com

Caryn Cohan-Bates, Manager

America's oldest pet industry trade show offering over 450 exhibitors with 850 booths. Seminars, workshops, grooming events and more are held for retailers and wholesalers.
9000 Attendees July Founded: 1951

18514 Superzoo
406 S 1st Avenue
Arcadia, CA 91006-3829
626-447-2222
FAX: 626-447-8350 800-999-7295
info@wwpsa.com www.wwpsa.com

Doug Poindexter, Executive VP

Sponsors consumer and trade shows for the pet industry. 900 booths.
10000 Attendees July Founded: 1951

18515 Tufts Animal Expo
Hynes Convention Center
900 Boylston Street
Boston, MA 02115
617-954-2000
FAX: 617-954-2125 800-845-8800
info@mccahome.com
www.mccahome.com
Animal care professionals addressed the social and medical impact pets have on human lives.
7000 Attendees October

18516 **World of Private Label International Trade Show**
Private Label Manufacturers Association (PLMA)
369 Lexington Avenue
3rd Floor
New York, NY 10017
212-972-3131
FAX: 212-983-1382
info@plma.com www.plma.com
This show has brought retailers together with manufacturers to help them find new products, make new contacts, and discover new ideas that will their private label programmers succeed and grow.

Directories & Databases

18517 **American Humane Association**
63 Inverness Drive E
Englewood, CO 80112-5117
303-792-9900
FAX: 303-792-5333 800-227-4645
Marie Wheatley, Executive Director
Animal protection agencies; Canadian and some other foreign agencies are available; national and individual state editions are available.

18518 **Directory of Animal Care and Control Agencies**
American Humane Association
63 Inverness Drive E
Englewood, CO 80112-5117
303-792-9900
FAX: 303-792-5333 800-227-4645
Marie Wheatley, Executive Director
Kay Clark, Membership Services
Over 6,000 animal protection agencies; Canadian and some other foreign agencies are available; national and individual state editions are available. *$75.00*

18519 **Market Research Report**
Animal Health Institute
1325 G Street NW
Suite 700
Washington, DC 20005-1304
202-637-2440
FAX: 202-393-1667 www.ahi.org
Alexander S Mathews, President/CEO
Dr Richard A Carnevale, VP Regulatory, Scientific, Int'l
Ron Phillips, VP/Legislative/Public Affairs
Sandra L Phelan, Director Regulatory Affairs
Carolyn S Ayers, VP Administration/Finance
An annual directory published by the Animal Health Institute. *$150.00*
50 pages Annual Founded: 1941

18520 **Pets/Animals Forum**
CompuServe Information Service
PO Box 60019
Tampa, FL 33660-0212
614-457-8600
800-848-8990
John Benn, Director
This database provides a forum for the discussion of typical house and exotic pets.
Bulletin Board

Industry Web Sites

18521 **www.aahanet.org**
American Animal Hospital Association
A group of hospitals and animal practitioners serving the industry.

18522 **www.abka.com**
American Boarding Kennels Association
Seeks to upgrade the industry through educational programs and conventions. Promotes code of ethics and accreditation programs for kennel operators.

18523 **www.ahi.org**
Animal Health Institute
Resource for you to learn more about how animals health products work, how they are used and their many benefits.

18524 **www.akc.org**
American Kennel Club
The principal registry of pure-bred dogs in the US.

18525 **www.allpets.com**
Dog.com
Best selection of dog supplies and prices, news and forum about dogs, health issues, grooming and the well-being for our four-legged friends.

18526 **www.apdt.com**
Association of Pet Dog Trainers
Official web site of the association. Includes members in the news, training events, industry news, trainer search engine, conference news and merchandise.

18527 **www.aspca.org**
ASPCA
Society for the humane treatment of animals, established in 1866.

18528 **www.avma.org**
American Veterinary Medical Association
Publishes various journals and information for members. Acts as a clearinghouse for veterinarians.

18529 **www.deltasociety.org**
Delta Society
Information on human-animal interactions. Service Dog Center provides information and advocacy for dogs trained to assist people with disabilities. Pet Partners Program trains volunteers, health professionals, animals for animal-assisted therapy and activities.

18530 **www.greyhouse.com**
Grey House Publishing
Selected Grey House directories in the fields of business, health and education are available online. Users can search our online databases by several different search criteria, such as product categories, geographic area, sales volume and much, much more. Full Grey House catalog and online ordering also available.

18531 **www.nhes.org**
National Humane Education Society
Fights for the prevention of cruelty to animals in any form. Fostering a sentiment of kindness since 1948.

18532 **www.npausa.com**
National Pigeon Association
Special information for members and for the hobby of pigeon raising.

18533 **www.peta.org**
People for the Ethical Treatment of Animals (PETA)
Opposes all forms of animal exploitation. Seeks to educate the public on what the group sees as the three major institutionalized cruelty issues: the exploitation and abuse of animals in experimentation, the manufacturing of fur apparel, and slaughtering for human consumption.

18534 **www.petfoodinstitute.org**
Pet Food Institute
Represents the manufacturer of 97% of all dog and cat food produced in the US. Dedicated to promoting the overall care and well-being of pets. Research in pet nutrition, proper feedings and pet care.

18535 **www.petpride.org**
Pet Pride
Operates a no kill free shelter for the lifetime of homeless cats.

18536 **www.petsit.com**
Pet Sitters International
Society of professional pet sitters. Membership provides valuable benefits - educational resources for those engaged in the pet-sitting industry. Also provides a forum to network with peers who share a common vision of excellence in at-home pet care.

18537 www.petsitters.org
National Association of Professional Pet Sitters

The only non-profit organization dedicated to serving the needs of professional pet care providers. Promotes ethical standards and fosters cooperation among members in the pet care industry.

18538 www.pida.org
Pet Industry Distributors Association

Represents wholesaler-distributors of pet products, providing training and education to members.

18539 www.pijac.org
Pet Industry Joint Advisory Council

Monitors federal and state regulations and legislation affecting the industry. Sponsors research and educational projects including certification programs in veterinary care and husbandry for companion animals, in-store training videos, etc.

18540 www.usaha.org
United States Animal Health Association

Science-based, non-profit, voluntary organization. Members are state and federal animal health officials, universities, veterinarians, livestock producers, research scientists, and extension services all to control livestock diseases in the US.

18541 www.wspa.americas.org
The Resource Center of the Americas

International animal protection news reports. Informs, educates and organizes economic justice and cross-cultural understanding in the Americas.

18542 www.wwpsa.com
World Wide Pet Supply Association

Seeks to advance the economic interests of members. Promotes responsible pet ownership. Sponsors consumer and trade shows for the pet industry.

Associations

18543 Advertising Photographers of America
27 West 20th Street
Suite 601
New York, NY 10011-3707
212-807-0399
FAX: 212-727-8120 800-817-2244
office@apany.com www.apany.com
Robert Ripps, Chairman
Joe Pritchard, Regional Director
Liz Steger, Secretary
Mike Breedlove, Program Administrator
A non-profit organization dedicated to our members. our goal is to establish, endorse and promote professsional practices, standards and ethics.
650 Members Founded: 1981

18544 American Photographic Artists Guild
568 Main Street
Wilbraham, MA 01095

katfalls@tdi.net www.apag.net
D John McCarthy, President
Joanie Ford, Historian/Merits/Degrees
Miles Andonov, Education
Lori Smith, Membership/Public Relations
Joanie Ford, Chairman
Encourages a better understanding between the photographer, the color artist and the retoucher. Conducts educational programs, sponsors competitions and bestows awards.

Founded: 1966

18545 American Society for Photobiology
PO Box 1897
Lawrence, KS 66044
785-843-1235
FAX: 785-843-1287 800-627-0629
phot@allenpress.com
www.photobiology.com
Linda Hardwick, Executive Secretary
Peter A Ensminger, Webmaster
Founded to further the scientific study of the effects of light on all living organisms.
1600 Members Founded: 1972

18546 American Society of Photogrammetry & Remote Sensing
5410 Grosvenor Lane
Suite 210
Bethesda, MD 20814-2160
301-493-0290
FAX: 301-493-0208
asprs@asprs.org www.asprs.org
James Plasker, Executive Director
Kimberly A Tiley, Assistant Executive Director
Jesse Winch, Program Manager
Membership society committed to advancing knowledge in the mapping sciences and promoting the responsible application of photogrammetry, remote sensing and related technologies.
128 Members

18547 American Society of Photographers

PO Box 1120
Caldwell, TX 77836
979-272-0900
FAX: 978-272-5201
dougbox@aol.com
www.asofp-online.com
Doug Box, Executive Director
Membership requirements include membership in Professional Photographers of America and either a Master of Photography, a Photographic Craftsmen, or a photographic specialist. Publishes a quarterly newsletter.
800 Members Founded: 1937

18548 American Society of Picture Professionals
117 South Saint Asaph Street
Alexandria, VA 22314
703-299-0219
FAX: 703-299-0219
cathy@aspp.com www.aspp.com
Cathy D Sachs, Executive Director
Eileen Flanagan, President
Linda Eger, VP
Holly Marshall, Treasurer
Members are image producers, stock photo agencies, and image users.Provides networking and educational opportunities in the image transaction industry.
800 Members Founded: 1966

18549 Antique and Amusement Photographers International
PO Box 150
Eureka Springs, AR 72632
479-253-8554
FAX: 479-253-8225
gail@oldtimephotos.org
www.oldtimephotos.org
Gail Pierce Larimer, Executive Director
Members are photography studies and photographers, primarliy in the US and Canada, specializing in costume photography and suppliers to the industry.
200 Members Founded: 1993

18550 Association of International Photography Art Dealers
1609 Connecticut Avenue NW
Suite 200
Washington, DC 20009
202-986-0105
FAX: 202-986-0448
AIPAD@aol.com
www.photoshow.com
Kathleen Ewing, Executive Director
Galleries and private dealers in fine photography who have been in business for at least three years.
125 Members Founded: 1979

18551 BioCommunications Association
220 Southwind Lane
Hillsborough, NC 27278
919-245-0906
FAX: 919-245-0906
BCAoffice@aol.com www.bca.org
Nancy Hurtgen, Manager, Central Office
Jim Fosse, President
Made up of professionals who create and use the highest quality images and presentations in visual communications media for teaching and documentation in the life sciences and medicine
450 Members Founded: 1931

18552 Center for Photography
59 Tinker Street
Woodstock, NY 12498
845-679-9957
FAX: 845-679-6337
info@cpw.org www.cpw.org
Kitty McCullough, President
Bob Wagner, VP
Dion Ogust, Secretary
Alan Siegel, Treasurer
Ariel Shanberg, Executive Director
Founded: 1977

18553 Council on Fine Art Photography
5613 Johnson Avenue
West Bethesda, MD 20817-3503
301-897-0083

Lowell Anson Kenyon, Executive Director
Members are fine art photographers employing silver processes.
50 Members Founded: 1982

18554 Evidence Photgraphers International Council
600 Main Street
Honesdale, PA 18431
570-253-5450
FAX: 570-253-5011 800-356-3742
epicheadquarters@verizon.net
www.epic-photo.org
Robert Jennings, Executive Director
A non profit educational and scientific organization with the primary purpose is the advancement of forensic photography/videography in civil evidence and law enforcement.
2000 Members Founded: 1968

18555 Independent Photo Imagers
405 Capitol Street
Suite 910
Charleston, WV 25301
304-720-6482
FAX: 304-720-6484
infor@ipiphoto.com
www.ipiphoto.com
Brent Bowyer, President
An association of independent photographers, who use various means of developing their pictures.
45 Members Founded: 1982

18556 International Fire Photographers Association
143 40th Street
New Orleans, LA 70124
504-482-9616
FAX: 504-486-4946
president@ifpaonline.com
www.ifpaonline.com
Chris E Mickal, President
Michael Heller, VP
Promote professionalism in all aspects of fire photography, specifically in the fields of fire, educational, and investigative photography and the recognition of all fire photography organizations as an important tool in the fire service and law enforcement
200 Members Founded: 1964

18557 International Graphic Arts Education Association
1899 Preston White Drive
Reston, VA 20191
703-758-0595
www.igaea.org
Darcy Harris, Contact
An association of educators in partnership with industry, dedicated to sharing theories, principles, techniques, and processes relating to graphic communications and imaging theory.
800 Members Founded: 1923

18558 International Imaging Industry Association
701 Westchester Avenue
Suite 317W
White Plains, NY 10604
914-285-4933
FAX: 914-285-4937
i3amembership@i3a.org www.i3a.org

Lisa Walker, President

Formerly (1997) National Association of Photographic Manufacturers and (2001) Photographic and Imaging Maufacturers Association. The Silver Council is a program sponsored by I3A that monitors environmental regulation of commercial silver use. Membership fee varies,based on annual sales.
81 Members Founded: 1946

18559 National Association of Photo Equipment Technicians
300 Picture Place
Jackson, MI 49201
517-788-8100
FAX: 517-788-8371
bcovey@pmai.org wwww.pmai.org

William Covey, Executive Liaison

Provides information on the photogrpahic industry to those engaged in the photographic repair.
250 Members Founded: 1973

18560 National Press Photographers Association
3200 Croasdaile Drive
Suite 306
Durham, NC 27705
919-383-7246
FAX: 919-383-7261 800-289-6772
info@nppa.org www.nppa.org

Greg Garneau, Executive Director
Karen Chen, Finance Director
Jim Haverkamp, Membership Director

Sponsors numerous, annual television and print media workshops. Conducts annual competition for news photos and television news film. Monthly magazine job information bank given to all members.
11M Members Founded: 1946

18561 National Reprographic Association

401 North Michigan Avenue
Chicago, IL 60611
312-245-1026
FAX: 312-527-6705 800-833-4742
info@irga.com www.irga.com

Steve Bova, Executive Director
Eric Johnson, Dir Convention/Exhibits

Membership consists of digital printing companies and reprographics equipment manufacturers and suppliers.
500 Members Founded: 1927

18562 North American Nature Photography Association
10200 W 44th Avenue
Suite 304
Wheat Ridge, CO 80033-2840
303-422-8527
FAX: 303-422-8894
info@nanpa.org www.nanpa.org

Jerry Bowman, Owner
Francine Butler, Executive Director
Ruth Gleason, Director Membership

Committed solely to serving the field of nature photography. Provides education, information develops standards and promotes nature photography as an art form and teaching medium.

18563 PERA
PO Box 77327
San Francisco, CA 94107-7327
415-620-0666
800-776-8616
info@peraonline.org
www.peraonline.org

Greg Myers, President
Kay Baker, VP
Lee Utterbach, Secretary

An association for production equipment rental personnel and organizations.
75 Members Founded: 1973

18564 Photo Chemical Machining Institute
38 Strawberry Lane
PO Box 739
East Dennis, MA 02641
508-385-0085
FAX: 508-385-0086
info@pcmi.org www.pcmi.org

Betty Berndt Brown, Executive Director

Members are companies producing metal products through photo chemical machining. In addition the Institute includes companies that service the PCM industry and supply its needs.
210 Members Founded: 1967

18565 Photo Imaging Manufacturers and Distributors Association
109 White Oak Lane
Suite 72F
Old Bridge, NJ 08857
732-679-3460
FAX: 732-679-2294
bclarkpmda@aol.com
www.takegreatpictures.com

Willard Clark, Executive Director

Founded as Photographic Merchandising and Distributing Association and became Photographic Manufacturers and Distributors Association before assuming its present name in 1999. Membership is $500/year for associate members and $1,000/year for voting members.
20000 Members Founded: 1939

18566 Photo Marketing Association International
3000 Picture Place
Jackson, MI 49201
517-788-8100
FAX: 517-788-8371 800-762-9287
pma_advertising@pmai.org
www.pmai.org

Jon Rousseau, Director Advertising Sales
Melissa Hempstone, Production Manager
Katrina Pfeifer, Production Coordinator
Beth A Duiser, Managing Editor
Ted Fox, Manager

A national organization of associations and manufacturers and suppliers of photographic equipment; also members of the National Association of Photo Equipment Technicians and of the Professional School Photographers of America.
18000 Members Founded: 1974

18567 Photographic Society of America
3000 United Founders Boulevard
Suite 103
Oklahoma City, OK 73112-3940
405-843-1437
FAX: 405-843-1438
hq@psa-photo.org
www.psa-photo.org

Richard Frieders, President
Fred Greene, Executive VP
Kara King, Operations Manager

Worldwide interactive organization for anyone interested in photography, professional or serious amateur. Offers a wide variety of activities, monthly magazine, photo and digital competitions, study groups via mail and Internet, how-to programs, an annal conference, and many other activites and services.

18568 Picture Agency Council of America

23046 Avenida De La Carlota
Suite 600
Laguna Hills, CA 92653
949-282-5065
FAX: 949-282-5066
execdirector@pacaoffice.org
www.stockindustry.org

Cathy Aron, Executive Director
Roger Ressmeyer, President

Trade association for stock picture companies in North America. Serves member agencies, their clients and their contributing photographers by promoting communication among photo agencies and other professional groups.
150 Members Founded: 1951

18569 PrintImage International
2250 East Devon Avenue
Suite 245
Des Plaines, IL 60601
847-298-8680
FAX: 847-298-8705 800-234-0040
info@printimage.org
www.printimage.org

Steven D Johnson, Executive Director

Furthers the business of quick printers, copy shops, and small format commercial printers. Also welcomes manufacturers and suppliers of equipment and consumables, trade publications, and consultants to the quick print industry.
1300 Members Founded: 1975

18570 Professional Photographers of America
229 Peachtree Street NE
Suite 2200
Atlanta, GA 30303
404-522-8600
FAX: 404-614-6400 800-786-6277
csc@ppa.com www.ppa.com

Steve Best, Chairman
Bob Lloyd, President
Dana Groves, Marketing Executive

Portrait, commercial, wedding, industrial and specialized photographers and photographic artists.
14000 Members Founded: 1880

18571 Professional Picture Framers Association
3000 Picture Place
Jackson, MI 49201
517-788-8100
FAX: 517-788-8371 800-762-9287
ppfa@ppfa.com www.ppfa.com

John Pruitt CPF, President
Fran Gray MCPF, VP

A trade association of manufacturers, wholesalers, print publishers, importers and retailers selling art, framing and related supplies.
3000 Members Founded: 1971

18572 Professional Travelogue Sponsors
El Camino College Foundation
16007 Crenshaw Boulevard
Torrance, CA 90506
310-323-3670
FAX: 310-715-7875
artstickets@elcamino.edu
www.centerforthearts.org

Thomas Fallow, President
Bruce Spain, Executive Director

Currently the largest documentary Travel Film Program Sponsor and Presenter.
55 Members Founded: 1967

18573 Professional Women Photographers

511 Avenue of the Americas
Suite 138
New York, NY 10011
212-867-7745

info@pwponline.org
www.pwponline.org

Fran Dickson, President
Gloria Waslyn, VP
Lenore Janis, President

To support and promote the work of women photographers through the sharing of ideas, resources and experience, to provide educational forums to engourage artistic growth and photographic development, and to stimulate public interst in and support for the art of photography
170 Members Founded: 1975

18574 SPIE-The International Society for Optical Engineering
1000 20th Street
PO Box 10
Bellingham, WA 98225-6705
360-676-3290
FAX: 360-647-1445 888-504-8171
spie@spie.org www.spie.org

Eugene G Arthurs, Executive Director
Dr Paul F McManamon, President

Members are scientists, engineers and companies interested in technology and applications of optical, electro-optical, fiber-optic, laser, and photonic systems.
14000 Members Founded: 1955

18575 Silver Users Association
11240 Waples Mill Road
Suite 200
Fairfax, VA 22030
703-934-0219
FAX: 703-359-7562
pmiller@mwcapitol.com
www.silverusersassociation.org

Paul A Miller, Executive Director

Represents manufacturers and distributors of products in which silver is an essential element. Works for the recognition of silver as a commodity and the removal of governmental regulations which retard its free exchange in commerce both foreign and domestic. Also helps provide a stable trading climate in the metal, it monitors the silver market to insure that silver information available to the industry and public is accurate.
28 Members Founded: 1947

18576 Society for Photographic Education

110 Art Building
Miami University
Oxford, OH 45056-2486
513-529-8328
FAX: 513-529-1532
speoffice@spenational.org
www.spenationsl.org

Jennifer Pearson Yamashiro, Executive Director

Members are college and university teachers of photography, photographers, museum curators and students of photography.
1600 Members Founded: 1963

18577 Society of American Travel Writers
1500 Sunday Drive
Suite 102
Raleigh, NC 27607
919-861-5586
FAX: 919-787-4916
satw@satw.org www.satw.org

Cathy Kerr, Executive Director
Emily Bartlett, Member Services

Photographers and 35 associate member representatives of airlines, hotels, resorts, tourist agencies and public relations firms.

18578 Society of Photographers and Artists Representatives (SPAR)
60 East 42nd Street
Suite 1166
New York, NY 10165
212-779-7464
FAX: 212-253-9996
info@spar.org www.spar.org

George Watson, President

The Society of Photographers and Artists Representatives (SPAR), encourages high standards of conduct from professional representatives across the country. It fosters an environment of shared information that includes the compilation, collection and distribution of equitable strategies and ethical guidelines concerning the effective marketing and sale of artists' work. Since it's founding in 1965, SPAR has sought to continuously improve the business of artist representation.
108 Members Founded: 1965

18579 University Photographers Association of America
SUNY Brockport
350 New Campus Drive
Brockport, NY 14420-2931
716-395-2133
FAX: 662-915-1298
jdusen@brockport.edu www.upaa.org

Jim Dusen, President
Dawn Van Hall, VP

Members are college and university photographers who are concerned with the application and practice of photography.
250 Members Founded: 1961

18580 Wedding & Portrait Photographers International
1312 Lincoln Boulevard
PO Box 2003
Santa Monica, CA 90406-2003

FAX: 310-395-9058
www.wppionline.com
Promotes high artistic and technical standards. Serves as a forum for an exchange of technical knowledge. Members are offered the opportunity to purchase special products and services.
2.8M Members Founded: 1973

18581 White House News Photographers Association
7119 Ben Franklin Station
Washington, DC 20044-7119
202-785-5230

info@whnpa.org www.whnpa.org

Susan Walsh, President
Doug Welsh, VP
Jeff Lawrence, Treasurer
Bob Pearson, Secretary

Volunteer association of professional photographers covering the Washington political venue. Activities include educational seminars, work with high school students and an annual awards contest. Our work is seen in newspapers, magazines, television and on the Internet.
500 Members

Newsletters

18582 American Society of Media Photgraphers Bulletin
Photo District News
150 North Second Street
Philadelphia, PA 19106
215-451-2767
FAX: 215-451-0880
info@asmp.org http://www.asmp.org

Holly Hughes, Editor
Jeffery Roberts, President

Member publication that addresses the news and preoccupations of the photography industry.
Quarterly Founded: 1944
Circulation: 5500

18583 Dance on Camera Journal
Dance Films Association
48 West 21st Street
Suite 907
New York, NY 10010-6806
212-727-0764
FAX: 212-727-0764
info@dancefilmsassn.org
http://www.dancefilmsassn.org

Deirdre Towers, Editor
Louise Spain, CEO

The only service organization in the world dedicated to both the dance and the film community. *$45.00*
Founded: 1956
Circulation: 350

18584 Future Image Report
Future Image
520 S El Camino Real
Suite 206A
San Mateo, CA 94402-1715
650-579-0493
FAX: 650-579-0566 800-749-3572
hbravo@futureimage.com
http://www.futureimage.com

Alexis J Gerard, Editor/Publisher
Paul Worthington, Managing Editor
Heidy Bravo, Circulaion Manager

News and analysis of technology and market developments in photo-digital imaging, for management-level industry professionals. *$ 500.00*
Founded: 1991

18585 Light Impressions Review
PO Box 940
Rochester, NY 14603-0940
716-271-8960

William Edwards, Publisher
Lance Speer, Director

Photography notes and news. *$15.00*
16 pages Monthly

18586 NTIS Alert- Photography & Recording Devices
National Technical Information Service
5285 Port Royal Road
US Department of Commerce
Springfield, VA 22161
703-874-4650
FAX: 703-605-6900
info@ntis.gov http://www.ntis.gov/
$140.00
Founded: 1955

18587 Photo Marketing
Photo Marketing Association International
3000 Picture Place
Jackson, MI 49201-8898
517-788-8100
FAX: 517-788-8371
gpageau@pmai.org
http://www.photomarketing.com

Gary Pageau, Publisher
Ted Fox, Executive Publisher

News of interest to the photo business on both a national and international basis. *$5.00*
4 pages Monthly Founded: 1925
Circulation: 12,141

18588 PhotoDaily
PhotoSource International
1910 35th Road
Pine Lake Farm
Osceola, WI 54020-5602
715-248-3800
FAX: 715-248-7394 800-624-0266
info@photosource.com
http://www.photosource.com

Rohn Engh, Director
Bruce Swenson, Production Manager
Jonna Zehma, Editor

Pairs photographers with the picture needs of magazine and book editors. *$330.00*
Daily Founded: 1976

18589 Photobulletin
PhotoSource International
Pine Lake Farm
1910 35th Avenue
Osceola, WI 54020-5602
715-483-3800
FAX: 715-248-7394 800-624-0266
info@photosource.com
http://www.photosource.com

Deb Koehler, Production Manager
Rohn Engh, Editor

Lists photographic needs of photobuyers buying in the top-notch markets.
Daily Founded: 1980
Printed in 1 color
Computerized version available

18590 Photofinishing News
Photofinishing News
219 Lafeyette Avenue
Westwood, NJ 07675-9049
201-819-2533

hans@photo-news.com
http://www.photo-news.com

Hans Kuhlman, Editor

Technical / marketing coverage of worldwide photography / photo-imaging industry, reviews of new products, tradeshows and market statistics. *$150.00*
12 pages Founded: 1970 ISSN 0889-2393

Printed in 1 color on matte stock

18591 Photograph Collector
140 East Richardson Avenue
Suite 301
Langhorne, PA 19047-2824
215-891-0214

info@photoreview.org
http://www.photoreview.org

Stephen Perloff, Editor

News and analysis for collectors, curators and dealers. Current coverage of the auction market, trends, discoveries, museums and trade shows. Accepts advertising. *$149.95*
8 pages Monthly Founded: 1980 ISSN 0271-0838
Printed in 1 color on matte stock

18592 Professional Photographers Association of New England
98 Windham Street
PO Box 316
Willimantic, CT 06226-316
203-488-2334
FAX: 860-423-9402 860-423-1402
info@ppane.com
http://www.ppane.com

Harvey Goldstein, Editor
Ruth Clegg, CEO/President

Founded: 1961
Circulation: 1000
Printed in on glossy stock

18593 SPE Newsletter
Society for Photographic Education
126 Peabody Hall
Miami University
Oxford, OH 45056-2486
513-529-8328
FAX: 513-529-9301
speoffice@spenational.org
www.spenational.org

Hannah Frieser, Newsletter/Web Editor
Jennifer Yamashiro, Executive Director
Kelly O'Malley, Circulation Manager

Educational newsletter offering information to persons studying photography. *$90.00*
6 pages Quarterly Founded: 1963
Circulation: 1800

Magazines & Journals

18594 Advanced Imaging
Cygnus Publishing
102 Wilmont Road
Suite 470
Deerfield, IL 60015-3601
847-405-0257

larry.adams@cygnusb2b.com
http://www.cygnusb2b.com

Dave Brambert, Group Publisher
Larry Adams, Editor-in-Chief
Richard Reiff, President
Hank Russell, Managing Editor

Contains information on professional photographic techniques and new approaches in all forms of media. *$60.00*
Monthly Founded: 1966
Circulation: 44009

18595 Afterimage
Visual Studies Workshop
31 Prince Street
Rochester, NY 14607-1405
585-442-8676
FAX: 585-442-1992
info@vsw.org
www.vsw.org/afterimage/index.html

Karen VanMeenen, Editor
Joanna Heatwole, Managing Editor

Geared toward media arts and photography artists, curators, academics, administrators and students. Features photography, independent film and video coverage, artist's books, alternative publishing and cultural studies issues. Also highlights conference and festival reports and scholarly feature articles. *$33.00*
Founded: 1980
Circulation: 10000

18596 American Photo
1633 Broadway
43rd Floor
New York, NY 10019
212-676-6000
FAX: 212-489-4217 800-274-4514
jiannello@hfmus.com
http://www.hfmus.com/

David Schonauer, Editor-in-Chief
Krissa Cavouras, Associate Editor
Richard Rabinowitz, Publisher

Profiles of professional photographers and other photographic topics. *$4.99*
6 Issues per year Founded: 1888
Circulation: 27,733

18597 Aperture
Aperture Foundation
547 West 27th Street
4th Floor
New York, NY 10001
212-505-5555
FAX: 212-598-4015 800-825-0061
info@aperture.org
http://www.aperture.org

Melissa Harris, Editor

Dedicates itself to celebrating the finest in creative photography. Through the periodicals exquisitely reproduced images, rivaling the quality of the photographers' original prints, subscribers experience a wealth of challenging, beautiful pictures on a series of significant topics. Accepts advertising. *$40.00*
80 pages Quarterly Founded: 1952

18598 History of Photography
Rutledge Publishing
325 Chestnut Street
8th Floor
Philadelphia, PA 19106-1598

800-354-1420

Graham Smith, Editor
Ann Haddrell, Advertising Manager

An international publication devoted to the history and criticism of the basic sematic unit of all modern media. *$396.00*
92 pages Annual+ Founded: 1977

18599 Imaging Business
Cygnus Business Media
3 Huntington Quadrangle
Ste 301N
Melville, NY 11747-4618
631-845-2700
FAX: 631-845-7109 800-308-6397
bill.schiffner@cygnuspub.com
http://www.labsonline.com

Bill Schiffner, Associate Publisher

Formerly called Photographic Processing. Covers photographic equipment, processing, suppliers and dealers. No longer in publication, but last six years of issues available in online archive. *$66.00*

Monthly Founded: 1936
Circulation: 21000
Printed in 4 colors

18600 News Photographer
National Press Photographers Association
3200 Croasdaile Drive
Suite 306
Durham, NC 27705
919-383-7246
FAX: 919-383-7261
magazine@nppa.org
http://www.nppa.org

Donald R Winslow, Editor
Robert Gould, President

Features articles, news and profiles about still and television news photography. *$38.00*

Monthly Founded: 1946
Circulation: 10500 9,500 names $50. per M.

Printed in 4 colors

18601 Outdoor Photographer
12121 Wilshire Boulevard
12th Floor
Los Angeles, CA 90025-1176
310-820-1500
FAX: 310-826-5008
editors@outdoorphotographer.com
http://www.wernerpublishing.com

Christopher Robinson, Managing Editor
Ibarionex Perello, Associate Editor
Steve Warner, Owner *$14.97*

Founded: 1965

18602 PCPhoto Magazine
Werner Publishing Corporation
12121 Willshire Blvd
12th Floor
Los Angeles, CA 90025

www.pcphotomag.com
Shows you how to enjy the exciting and affordable new world of computers and photography. Features step-by-step instructions, evaluations of the latest equipment, tips from the pros, and more! *$11.97*
9 Issues

18603 PHOTO Techniques
Preston Publications
6600 W Touhy Avenue
Niles, IL 60714
847-647-2900
FAX: 847-647-1155
jwhite@phototechmag.com
http://www.phototechmag.com

S Tinsley Preston III, Publisher
Joe White, Editor
Connie Turgon, Marketplace Advertising

PHOTO Techniques offers practical articles that help solve shooting, processing, lighting and printing problems. This is the one magazine that walks you step by step through new techniques. Every other issue contains a digital section. Departments you can rely on include; Master Printing Class, David Vestal's commentary, Photochemistry and more. There are valuable guides to cameras, papers, films, useful accessories and darkroom suppliers. *$27.99*

Founded: 1979
Mailing list available for rent 30,000 names $145 per M.

18604 Photo Business
VNU Business Media
770 Broadway
New York, NY 10003
646-654-5100
FAX: 646-654-5543
bmccomm@vnuinc.com
http://www.vnubusinessmedia.com

Holly S Hughes, Editor
Michael Marchesano, CEO/President
Jeffrey Roberts, Publisher
Audrey Numa, Circulation Manager
Chris O'Hara, Sales Director

Industry news for the photographic retailer. *$65.00*

52 pages Monthly Founded: 1956
Circulation: 26,162

18605 Photo District News
770 Broadway
7th floor
New York, NY 10003-8901
646-654-5780
FAX: 646-654-5813
jroberts@pdn-pix.com
http://www.pdn-pix.com

Holly S Hughes, Editor
Jeffrey Roberts, Group Publisher
Audrey Numa, Circulation manager
Danny Ryan, Production director

Intended to inform and educate its readers in all areas related to professional photography. *$65.00*

124 pages Monthly Founded: 1980

18606 Photo Insider
11 Vreeland Road
Florham Park, NJ 07932-1577
973-377-1003
FAX: 973-377-2679
editor@photoinsider.com
www.photoinsider.com

18607 Photo Lab Management
PLM Publishing
1312 Lincoln Boulevard
Santa Monica, CA 90401-1706
310-451-1344
FAX: 310-395-9058
info@plmpublishing.co.uk
www.plmpublishing.co.uk/home.htm

Claire F Irwin, Editor
Paula L McCulloch, Publishing Director
John DH Colley, Marketing Manager

Specifically for those who work in the photo lab business. Contains articles on personnel and technical information. *$15.00*

52 pages Monthly Founded: 1979

18608 Photo Marketing
Photo Marketing Association International
3000 Picture Place
Jackson, MI 49201
517-788-8100
FAX: 517-788-8371
PMA_Publications@pmai.org
http://www.photomarketing.com

Terri Cameron, Publisher
Beth A Duiser, Managing Editor
Melissa Hempstone, Production Manager
Jon Rousseau, Director Association Sales
Ted Fox, Manager

Directed to the marketing and advertising professionals, offers information on marketing photography nationally and internationally. *$50.00*

80 pages Monthly Founded: 1924
Circulation: 12141

18609 Photo Metro
1590 Golden Gate Avenue
San Francisco, CA 94115
415-243-9917
FAX: 415-243-9919
www.photometro.com

Henry Brimmer, Publisher

Image-oriented magazine dedicated to photography, features portfolios, interviews and book reviews. Accepts advertising. *$20.00*

32 pages Monthly Founded: 1982

18610 Photo Stock News
1910 35th Road
Pine Lake Farm
Osceola, WI 54020
715-248-3800
FAX: 715-248-7394
info@photosource.com
www.photosource.com

Ron Engh, Editor
Angela Dober, Managing Editor

Contains information of interest to freelance stock photographers, includes the latest industry trends and strategies. Regular issue features include Electronic Highway.

12 per year

18611 PhotoStockNotes
PhotoSource International
1910 35th Avenue
Pine Lake Farm
Osceola, WI 54020-5602
715-483-3800
FAX: 715-248-7394 800-624-0266
info@photosource.com
http://www.photosource.com

Rohn Engh, Editor
Angela Dober, Managing Editor

Trends in the editorial stock photo industry. *$36.00*

3 pages Monthly Founded: 1976 24,000 names $60 per M.

18612 Photography Quarterly
Center for Photography
59 Tinker Street
Woodstock, NY 12498-1236
845-679-9957
FAX: 845-679-6337
info@cpw.org http://www.cpw.org

Ariel Shamberg, CEO
Larry Lewis, Circulation Manager
Liz Glynn, Program Associate
Kate Menconeri, Program Director
Lawrence P Lewis, Operations Manager

Thematic issues include critical essays on contemporary photography, film and video; opportunities for artists; noted books and image portfolios by innovative contemporary photo based artists. *$25.00*

Quarterly Founded: 1977
Circulation: 2500 15000 names $70 per M.
Printed in 1 color on glossy stock

18613 Photoletter
PhotoSource International
1910 35th Avenue
Pine Lake Farm
Osceola, WI 54020-5602
715-483-3800
FAX: 715-248-3800 800-624-0266
info@photosource.com
www.photosource.com

Rohn Engh, Editor

A publication covering the world of photography. *$264.00*
4 pages Weekly 24,000 names $60 per M.

18614 Photopro Magazine
Patch Communications
5211 S Washington Avenue
Titusville, FL 32780-7315
321-268-5010
FAX: 321-267-1894

Christi Ashby, Publisher
Suzanne Odistro, Advertising Manager

A professional trade publication covering photography nationally and internationally. *$16.95*
80 pages Monthly Founded: 1990

18615 Picture Magazine
319 Lafayette Street
No 135
New York, NY 10012
212-352-2700
FAX: 212-352-2155
picmag@aol.com
www.picturemagazine.com

Brock Wylan, Pulisher
Katherine Nguyen, Associate Editor

Phot industry trade publication.

18616 Popular Photography
Hachette Filipacchi Magazines
1633 Broadway
43rd Floor
New York, NY 10019
212-767-6000
FAX: 212-767-5602 800-876-6636
popphoto@neodata.com
http://www.popularphotography.com

Jason Schneider, Editor
Tami Kelly, Internet Sales Manager

A publication offering information and updates to the photography world. *$12.00*
80 pages Monthly

18617 Popular Photography & Imaging American PHOTO Magazine
1633 Broadway
New York, NY 10019
212-767-6000
FAX: 212-767-5602
popphoto@hfnm.com
www.popphoto.com

Jeffrey Roberts, Publisher
Russell Brock, Associate Editor

Comprehensive coverage of the latest equipment, inspiring images by leading photographers, in-depth how-to articles and wuthoritative reports. Draws upon top professionals in the field to inform committed readers who are passionate about pictures.

18618 Premiere Magazine
1633 Broadway
New York, NY 10019
212-767-5400
FAX: 212-767-5450 www.premiere.com

Jessica Letkemann, Editor
Jennifer Cooper, Producer

A magazine for young adults, which focuses on the art and commerce of the film industry. Premiere's feature articles, profiles and monthly columns include original photgraphy, interviews with Hollywood's A-list and up-and-coming talent, studio heads and producers.

18619 Professional Photographer
PPA Publications
229 Peachtree Street NE
International Tower, Suite 2200
Atlanta, GA 30303-1608
404-522-8600
FAX: 404-614-6405 800-786-6277
ppa@bframe.com
http://www.ppmag.com

Cameron Bishopp, Senior Manager Publications
Jeff Kent, Senior Editor
Dana Groves, Marketing Executive

Business magazine for professional photographers. Delivers valuable articles packed with money making ideas to improve photography techniques and business skills. Accepts advertising. *$27.00*
80 pages Monthly Founded: 1910
Circulation: 30000

18620 Rangefinder
Rangefinder Publishing
PO Box 1703
1312 Lincoln Boulevard
Santa Monica, CA 90406-1787
310-451-8506
FAX: 310-395-9058
http://www.rangefindermag.com

Skip Cohen, President
Bill Hurter, Editor
Helen Svensson, Art Director
George Varanakis, Advertising Director
Bob Rose, Technical Editor

Dedicated to the advancement of the field of professional photography. *$18.00*
68 pages Monthly Founded: 1952
Circulation: 50500

18621 Select
Moser and Colby
841 Nineteenth Street
Miami Beach, FL 33139
305-299-9473
FAX: 305-532-6283
david.colby@select-magazine.com
http://www.selectonline.com

David Colby, Publisher/Editor

Geared toward creative decision makers and photographers, emphasis is placed on the imagination, favorite images and emotions induced by photos. Includes detailed photography location information. *$90.00*

Circulation: 8500

18622 Shutterbug
1419 Chaffee Drive
Suite #1
Titusville, FL 32780
321-269-3212
FAX: 321-267-7216
editorial@shutterbug.com
www.shutterbug.net

Russ Ellis, Publisher
Eileen Meister, Advertising Sales Manager
Josh Heitsenrether, Marketing Coordinator
George Schaub, Editor *$17.95*

Monthly Founded: 1989

18623 Studio Photography
Cygnus Business Media
3 Huntington Quadrangle
Suite 301N
Melville, NY 11747-3601
631-845-2700
FAX: 631-845-7109 800-308-6397
circulation@spdonline.com
www.imaginginfo.com/spd/

Liz Vickers, Group Publisher
Alice B Miller, Editor
Jackie Dandoy, Circulation Manager
Ashley Birkholz, Classified Sales
Barry Ancona, List Rental Manager

Formerly Studio Photography & Design. Showcases the hottest portrait, wedding, commercial, digital, and travel photographers every month. It is also supported by a selection of supplementary guides, tech tips, tutorials, and product round-ups.
Monthly Founded: 1936
Circulation: 50000

Trade Shows

18624 American Society of Photogrammetry & Remote Sensing Annual Conference
5410 Grosvenor Lane
Suite 210
Bethesda, MD 20814-2160
301-493-0290
FAX: 301-493-0208
asprs@asprs.org www.asprs.org

James Plasker, Executive Director
Kimberly A Tiley, Assistant Executive Director
Jesse Winch, Program Manager

Educational sessions and exhibits committed to advancing knowledge in the mapping sciences and promoting the responsible application of photogrammetry, remote sensing and related technologies.
Spring

18625 PMA Annual Convention and Trade Show
3000 Picture Place
Jackson, MI 49201
517-885-5980
FAX: 517-788-8371
pma_trade_exhibits@pmai.org
www.pmai.org

Rod Folland, Trade Exhibit Sevices Executive
Mary Anne LaMarre, Operations Officer
Ted Fox, Manager

Is a global forum for photo imaging industry education, networking and introductions of new products and technologies. Includes conferences and meetings of the Association of Professional Color Imagers, the Digital Imaging Marketing Association, the Photo Imaging Education Association, the Professional Picture Framers Association, the Professional Scrapbook Retailers Organization and the Professional School Photographers Association.
24M Attendees February/March

18626 Photohistory
Photographic Historical Society
PO Box 39563
Rochester, NY 14604-9563
585-461-4545

Triennial show and exhibits of cameras and photographic images.
October, Rochester

18627 Photovision
Glahe International
PO Box 2460
Germantown, MD 20875-2460
301-515-0012
FAX: 301-515-0016 glahe@glahe.com
Exhibits of photography equipment, supplies and services.

18628 Professional Photographer American Expo
Professional Photographers of America
229 Peachtree Street NE
International Tower, Suite 2200
Atlanta, GA 30303-1608
404-522-8600
FAX: 404-614-6401
Dana Groves, Advertising Director
Devoted to new technologies in the photography field. 300 booths.
5M Attendees July

18629 Professional Photographers Association
Professional Photographers Assoc. of New England
PO Box 316
Willimantic, CT 06226
860-423-1402
FAX: 860-423-9402
ppanerl@aol.com www.ppane.com
Roland L Laramie, Show Manager/Executive Director
1000 Attendees September Founded: 1860

Directories & Databases

18630 Complete Directory of Film & Photo Products
Sutton Family Communications & Publishing Company
155 Sutton Lane
Fordsville, KY 42343
270-740-0870

jlsutton@apex.net
www.fleamarketeer.net
Theresa Sutton, Publisher
Lee Sutton, Editor
Print-out from database of wholesalers, manufacturers, distributors, importers and close-out houses. Database is updated daily to guarantee the most current and up-to-date sources available. *$34.50*
100 pages

18631 Contemporary Photographers
St. James Press/Gale Research
27500 Drake Road
Farmington Hills, MI 48331
248-699-4253
FAX: 313-961-6741 800-877-GALE
Offers information on over 800 living photographers and deceased photographers from the recent past. *$145.00*
1100 pages

18632 Directory of Free Stock Photography
Infosource Publishing
10 E 39th Street
6th Floor
New York, NY 10016-0111
212-683-8905

Offers valuable information on federal, state and local governments which will provide photographs free of charge for commercial use. *$14.50*
150 pages Biennial

18633 Green Book: Directory of Natural History and General Stock Photography
AG Editions
41 Union Square W
Suite 525
New York, NY 10003
212-929-0959
FAX: 212-924-4796
info@agpix.com www.agpix.com
Ann Guifoyle, Editor
Sharon Powers, Manager
Over 400 photographers and photo agencies that provide stock photography. *$28.00*
368 pages Biennial Founded: 1986
Circulation: 6500

18634 Guide to Photography Workshops
Shaw Guides
625 Biltmore Way
Apartment 1406
Coral Gables, FL 33134-7539

Workshops are profiled that are aimed at amateurs and professionals, including photo tours, studio intensives and specialized instruction. *$19.95*
300 pages Biennial

18635 Hemingway's Glamour Photographer's Resource Directory

Looking Glass Photography
5975 Keller Road
Saint Louis, MO 63128-3359
314-849-8952

Buyers of glamour photography, including film and video producers are profiled. *$40.00*
200 pages Biennial
Circulation: 1,000

18636 Industrial Photography: Gold Book Issue
PTN Publishing Company
445 Broadhollow Road
Melville, NY 11747-3669
516-465-7684

Steve Shaw, Editor
A list of manufacturers of photographic equipment and supplies, motion picture laboratories, videotape production facilities, equipment rental services, custom developing services and photographic repair services. *$5.75*
Annual December
Circulation: 40,000

18637 Orion Blue Book: Camera
Orion Research Corporation
14555 N Scottsdale Road
Suite 330
Scottsdale, AZ 85254-3487
480-951-1114
FAX: 480-951-1117 800-844-0759
orion@bluebook.com
www.bluebook.com
Roger Rohrs, Owner
List of manufacturers of cameras.
Annual

18638 Photographer's Complete Guide to Exhibition & Sales Spaces
Consultant Press
163 Amsterdam Avenue
#201
New York, NY 10023-5001
212-685-9800

Directory of services and supplies to the industry. *$24.95*
280 pages

18639 Photographic Trade News: Master Buying Guide
Cygnus Business Media
445 Broad Hollow Road
Melville, NY 11747-3669
631-845-2700
FAX: 631-845-2723 www.cynuspub.com

Offers a list of manufacturers and distributors of photographic equipment and photography associations.
Annual

18640 Photography Forum
CompuServe Information Service
PO Box 20212
Columbus, OH 43220-0212
614-457-8600

Offers a forum for the discussion of photography on both the amateur and professional levels.
Bulletin Board

18641 Photography RoundTable
GE Information Services
401 N Washington Street
Rockville, MD 20850-1707
301-388-8284

Cathy Ge, Owner
Provides a forum for the exchange of photography tips and information.
Bulletin Board

18642 Who's Who in Photographic Management
Photo Marketing Association International
3000 Picture Place
Jackson, MI 49201-8898
517-788-8100
FAX: 517-788-8371 800-762-9287
Over 15,500 members of the association and manufacturers and suppliers of photographic equipment; also members of the National Association of Photo Equipment Technicians and of the Professional School Photographers of America. *$75.00*
Annual

Industry Web Sites

18643 **www.aspp.com**
American Society of Picture Professionals

Members are image producers, stock photo agencies, and image users.Provides networking and educational opportunities in the image transaction industry.

18644 **www.editorialphoto.com**
Editorial Photographers

Internet discussion forum on business issues with more than 3000 subscribers participating from over 30 countries around the globe. Via the forum photographers exchange information on business practices, copyright and contract concerns. Useful resources such as sample business forms, publisher contract reviews and more can be found here.

18645 **www.greyhouse.com**
Grey House Publishing

Selected Grey House directories in the fields of business, health and education are available online. Users can search our online databases by several different search criteria, such as product categories, geographic area, sales volume and much, much more. Full Grey House catalog and online ordering also available.

18646 **www.nppa.org**
National Press Photographers Association

Sponsors numerous annual television and print media workshops. Conducts annual competition for newsphotos and television newsfilm. Monthly magazine job information bank given to all members.

18647 **www.ppa.com**
Professional Photographers of America

Portrait, commercial, wedding, industrial and specialized photo- graphers and photographic artists.

18648 **www.stockindustry.org**
Picture Agency Council of America

The trade association for stock picture agencies in North America.

Associations

18649 Alliance for the Polyurethanes Industry
1300 Wilson Boulevard
Arlington, VA 22209
703-741-5103
FAX: 703-741-5655
api@plastics.org
www.polyurethane.org
Richard E Mericle, Executive Director
Neeva Candelori, Director Industry Affairs

API is composed of companies that supply polyurethane resins or chemicals used in polyurethane resins, manufacture polyurethanes, produce machinery used in the manufacture or processing polyurethane, or engage in the business of applying polyurethane products in end use applications. API consists of several groups that focus on critical industry issues such as product stewardship, recycling, communications.
80 Members Founded: 1977

18650 American Electroplaters and Surface Finish ers Society (AESF)
1155 Fifteenth Street NW
Suite 500
Washington, DC 20005
202-457-8401
FAX: 202-530-0659
info@aesf.org www.aesf.org/
Tracey Kohler, Executive Director
Alison Ashe, Membership/Education/Bookstore

The American Electroplaters and Surface Finishers Society, Inc. (AESF), is an international, individual-membership, non-profit professional society. Founded in 1909, the AESF has 78 Branches and more than 5,000 members, worldwide. The Society is regarded and respected as the foremost finishing authority in the world. Members include electroplaters and molders of plastics and suppliers of resin and chemicals.
60 Members

18651 American Institute of Physics
1 Physics Ellipse
College Park, MD 20740-3843
301-209-3100
FAX: 301-209-0843
aipinfo@aip.org www.aip.org
Marc Brodsky, Executive Director/CEO
Finnegan Robert, Journal Advertising/Exhibits Dtr
Darlene Walters, Senior VP
Wendy Marriott, Operations Director
Richard Baccante, Treasurer/CFO

Presents original research in high performance polymer science and technology. Primarily applications-driven, with a major focus on the molecular structure/processability/property relationship with regard to the specified applications.
1931 Members Founded: 1931

18652 American Plastics Council
1300 Wilson Boulevard
Arlington, VA 22209
703-253-0700
FAX: 703-741-6000 800-243-5790
Rodney Lowman, President
Judith Dunbar, Environmental/Technical Director
Tiffany Harrington, Director Communications

Major trade association for the US plastics industry. We demonstrate that plastics are a responsible choice and promote the countless ways that plastics make lives better, healthier and safer.
24 Members

18653 American Society for Plasticulture
526 Brittany Drive
State College, PA 16803
814-238-7045
FAX: 814-238-7051
info@plasticulture.org
www.plasticulture.org
Henry Taber, President
William Tietjen, Chairman
Patricia Heuser, Executive Director
Jodi Fleck-Arnold, VP

Promotes research, education and technology application for plastics used in agricultural and horticultural production systems. Hosts a congress every year or so; published proceedings of research presentations.
100 Members Founded: 1962

18654 Association of Industrial Metallizers, Coaters and Laminators (AIMCAL)
201 Springs Street
Fort Mill, SC 29715
803-802-7820
FAX: 803-802-7821
aimcal@aimcal.org www.aimcal.org
Craig Sheppard, Executive Director
Tracey Ingram, Administration Manager
Caleb Howe, Communications Manager
Norma Bryant, Office Manager

Nonprofit trade organization for makers of coated, laminated and metalized papers. AIMCAL serves as the global forum for the flexible metallizing, coating and laminating industry by providing resources, services and information. AIMCAL collects and distributes information to increase industry knowledge, while fostering an environment that builds relationships and a spirit of cooperation between member companies worldwide.
Founded: 1970

18655 Association of Postconsumer Plastic Recycl ers
1300 Wilson Blvd
Suite 800
Arlington, VA 22209

www.plasticsrecycling.org
Represents companies that acquire, reprocess and sell the output of more than 90 percent of the post-consumer plastic processing capacity in North America.

18656 Association of Rotational Molders International
2000 Spring Road
Suite 511
Oak Brook, IL 60523-1872
630-571-0611
FAX: 630-571-0616
www.rotomolding.org
Jeff Arnold, CEO/Executive Director
Michael Dorsey, President
Jeff Dunne, Treasurer/Secretary

Seeks to increase awareness of roto-molding, exchange technical information, provide education, and standardize production guidelines.
425 Members Founded: 1976

18657 Berkshire Plastics Network
100 North Street
Pittsfield, MA 01201
413-499-3367
FAX: 413-447-7210 800-438-9572
bpn@cbcc.bcwan.net
www.berkshireplastics.org
A consortium of more than 40 independent companies, representing virtually every discipline in the design and production of molds, components and plastic products.

18658 Composites Fabricators Association

1010 North Glebe Road
Suite 450
Arlington, VA 22201
703-525-0511
FAX: 703-525-0743
info@acmanet.org www.acmanet.org
Bill Kreysler, Executive Director
John Tickle, President
Randy Weghorst, VP
Leon Garoufalis, Secretary
John Schweitzer, Senior Director Government Affairs

Presents information on new technology, trends and techniques for manufacturers in the fiberglass and composites industry.

18659 Electrostatic Discharge Association
7900 Turin Road
Building 3
Rome, NY 13440-2069
315-339-6937
FAX: 315-339-6793
info@esda.org www.esda.org/
Kay Adams, President
Dave Swenson, Senior VP
Donn Bellmore, Treasurer
Michele McSwain, Secretary
Lisa Pimpinella, Operations Manager

Professional voluntary association dedicated to advancing the theory and practice of electrostatic discharge avoidance. Initial emphasis on the effects of ESD on electronic components has broadened to include textiles, plastics, web processing, explosives, clean rooms and graphic arts. Expands ESD awareness through educational programs, development of standards, tutorials, publications, local chapters, symposia and certification.
2000 Members Founded: 1982

18660 Film and Bag Federation
1667 K Street NW
Suite 1000
Washington, DC 20006-1620
202-964-4400
FAX: 202-296-7675
www.plasticbag.com
Donna Dempsey, Executive Director
Betsy Coleman, Assistant Director
Yvonne Wade, Assistant Manager
Jack Riopelle, Chairman
John Wilhite, Vice Chairman

Members are US and Canadian manufacturers of plastic retail bags. A business unite of the Society of the Plastics Industry, Inc. that actively promotes the growth of the plastic film and bag industry. FBF membership includes companies that are in the plastic bag segment of the industry as well as those in the film sector.
50 Members Founded: 1986

18661 IAPD/International Association of Plastics Distributors
4707 College Blvd
Suite 105
Leawood, KS 66211-1667
913-345-1005
FAX: 913-345-106
iapd@iapd.org www.iapd.org
Marc Lewis, Jr., President
Fred Schroeder, VP
Deborah Hamlin, Executive Director
Thomas L. Garrett, Treasurer
Brian Hense, Secretary
The International Association of Plastics Distributors, founded in 1956, is an international trade association comprised of companies engaged in the distribution and manufacture of plastics materials. Represented are materials in semi-finished stock shapes, such as sheet, rod, tube, pipe, valves, fittings, film and related products. Members' materials are produced and distributed for a wide variety of engineering and high performance applications.
Founded: 1956

18662 Materials Research Society
506 Keystone Drive
Warrendale, PA 15086-7573
724-793-3004
FAX: 724-779-8313
info@mrs.org www.mrs.org/
Peter F Green, President
John B Ballance, Executive Director
Michael Drive, Director Information Services
Robert H. Pachavis, Director Finance and Administration
The Materials Research Society is a not-for-profit organization which brings together scientists, engineers and research managers from industry, government, academia and research laboratories to share findings in the research and development of new materials of technological importance. The Materials Research Society promotes communication for the advancement of interdisciplinary materials research to improve the quality of life.
13000 Members Founded: 1973

18663 National Association for PET Container
PO Box 1327
Sonoma, CA 95476
707-996-4207
FAX: 707-935-1998
information@napcor.com
www.napcor.com
Dennis Sabourin, Executive Director
Mike Schedler, Technical Director
Kate Eagles, Communications Director, ²
National association for the PET plastic industry. Promotes the use of PET plastic packaging and facilitates the recycling of PET containers.
13 Members Bi-Monthly Founded: 1987

18664 National Certification In Plastics (NCP)
Society of the Plastics Industry
1667 K Street
Suite 1000
Washington, DC 20006
202-967-7243
FAX: 864-239-0549 888-627-3660
ncp@socplas.org
www.certifyme.org/?source=IDES.com
Barbara Darby, Manager Plastics Learning Network
Barry Eisenberg, Director Communications/Marketing
The National Certification in Plastics (NCP) program is a national, voluntary certification examination that tests plastics operations employees' skills and knowledge. The National Certification in Plastics exam tests the knowledge and skill level of plastics operations employees in one of the four major plastics processes - injection molding, extrusion, thermoforming or blow molding.The NCP program is sponsored by the Society of the Plastics Industry.

18665 National Plastics Center & Museum
210 Lancaster Street
Leominster, MA 01453
978-537-9529
FAX: 978-537-3220
info@plasticsmuseum.org
www.plasticsmuseum.org
David Hahn, President
Marjorie Weiner, Outreach Director
Marianne Zephir, Museum & Collections Director
Deborah Renzi, Visitor Services Manager

The National Plastics Center & Museum is a non-profit institution dedicated to preserving the past, addressing the present and promoting the future of plastics through public education and awareness. The educational staff has supported this mission throughout the years by conducting hands-on science programming for schools, organizations and the plastics community.

18666 Plastic Pipe and Fittings Association
800 Roosevelt Road
Building C, Suite 20
Glen Ellyn, IL 60137
630-858-6540
FAX: 630-790-3095
www.ppfahome.org/
Richard W. Church, Executive Director
The Plastic Pipe and Fittings Association (PPFA) is a national trade association comprised of member companies that manufacture plastic piping, fittings and solvent cements for plumbing and related applications, or supply raw materials, ingredients or machinery for the manufacturing process.
Founded: 1978

18667 Plastic Shipping Container Institute
1700 Pennsylvania Ave Nw
Ste 400
Washington, DC 20006-4707
202-498-8596
FAX: 202-331-8330
info@pscionline.org
www.pscionline.org/
David H. Baker, General Counsel/PSCI Contact
The Plastic Shipping Container Institute (PSCI) is an international organization of producers of plastic pails (rigid, plastic shipping containers). The Institute's mission is to promote the common interests of, and the general well being of, the plastic shipping container industry, including consideration of local, state and federal regulatory and legislative issues and international trade issues impacting customers, suppliers and consumers.
Founded: 1976

18668 Plastics Institute of America
600 Suffolk St
Ste 4
Lowell, MA 01854-3629
978-934-3130
FAX: 978-458-4141
info@plasticsinstitute.org
www.plasticsinstitute.org/
Aldo Crugnola, Executive Director
Manny Panos, Associate Director
The Plastics Institute of America is a not-for-profit educational and research organization dedicated to providing service to the plastics industries. We support, foster and guide plastics education and research at all levels to ensure the continued growth of the industry. Since our founding the Institute has held to this mission with ongoing educational programs and resources for skilled workers, professionals and industry executives.
Founded: 1961

18669 Plastics Learning Network
Society of the Plastics Industry
7 North Laurens Street
Greenville, SC 29601
864-239-2939
FAX: 864-239-0549
bdarby@socplas.org
www.plasticslearning.org/
Barbara Darby, Manager Plastics Learning Network
Barry Eisenberg, Director Communications/Marketing
Training opportunities are available for plastics employers and employees through the Plastics Learning Network (PLN) which is sponsored by the Society of the Plastics Industry's (SPI). Courses from qualified instructors are presented as on-site courses tailored to individual work schedules. Courses currently available are Operator Training in Injection Molding and Extrusion. Financial aid is available.
Founded: 2001

18670 Plastics Pipe Institute
1825 Connecticut Avenue NW
Suite 680
Washington, DC 20009
202-462-9607
FAX: 202-462-9779
info@plasticpipe.org
www.plasticpipe.org
Tony Radoszewski, Executive Director
Camille Rubeiz, Director Engineering
Stephen Boros, Technical Director
Mike Pluimer, Engineering Manager
Michael Byrne, President
Promotes the effective use of plastics piping systems; offers development assistance, reports and statistics, and educational programs.
131 Members Founded: 1950

18671 Plastics USA
1801 K Street NW
Suite 600K
Washington, DC 20006
202-745-5200
FAX: 202-296-7243
tradeshows@socplas.org
www.socplas.org/about/services/shows.htm
Adam Krumhansl, Trade Show Coordinator
Donald Duncan, President
Plastics USA, sponsored by The Society of the Plastics Industry/SPI, is held once ev-

ery three years. The three-day trade show and educational program, which is sponsored by the Society of Plastics Engineers, has proven to be an ideal business forum for the North American plastics industry. Last held in Chicago in 2001, Plastics USA attracted over 15,000 attendees and the show featured 435 exhibiting companies occupying 95,000 square feet of exhibit space.

12M Members

18672 Polymer Processing Institute
New Jersey Institute Of Technology
Guttenberg Information Technologies Center
University Heights, Suite 3901
Newark, NJ 07102-1982
973-596-3267
FAX: 973-642-4594
kshyun@polymers-ppi.org
www.polymers-ppi.org/

Kun Sup Hyun, Ph.D, President
Costos G. Gogos, Ph.D, Senior Advisor/President Emeritus
Mariann Pappagallo, Administrative Consultant
Niloufar Faridi, Ph.D, Research Consulting Engineer
David B. Todd, Senior Process Consultant

The Polymer Processing Institute is an independent research corporation headquartered at New Jersey Institute of Technology, Newark, New Jersey. Its mission is to assist industry by implementing the advanced knowledge in the field of polymer technology and related areas through sponsored research, development and education, and to disseminate information via technology transfer.

18673 Polystyrene Packaging Council (PSPC)
America Plastics Council
1300 Wilson Blvd
Arlington, VA 22209
703-741-5647
FAX: 703-741-5651
www.polystyrene.org/

Michael H. Levy, Senior Director
Annie F. Walton, Administrative Assistant

PSPC, a business unit of the American Plastics Council, is a nonprofit trade association dedicated to providing accurate information on the environmental impact of polystyrene packaging, including polystyrene recycling programs. PSPC's membership includes manufacturers of polystyrene resin, polystyrene foam and rigid food service packaging.

18674 Polyurethane Manufacturers Association
6737 West Washington Avenue
Suite 1420
Milwaukee, WI 53214
414-431-3094
FAX: 414-276-7704
info@pmahome.org
www.pmahome.org

Ken Neal, President
Corey D. Barge, VP
Nicholas Bitter, Treasurer
Donald P. Gallo, Legal Counsel

The Polyurethane Manufacturers Association is the trade association of the cast polyurethane elastomer industry, serving processors of polyurethane products, materials and equipment suppliers and independent agents. PMA exchanges and disseminates information on standards, materials, processes and technical matters, in addition to monitoring regulatory and legislative activity affecting the urethane industry.

80 Members Founded: 1971

18675 Society of Plastics Engineers
14 Fairfield Drive
PO Box 403
Brookfield, CT 06804
203-775-0471
FAX: 203-775-8490
info@4spe.org www.4spe.org

Gail R. Bristol, Managing Director
Roger M. Ferris, Editorial Director
Alice Blanco, Senior Associate Editor
Jeff Tremonte, Information Systems Manager
Susan Oderwald, Executive Director

The Society of Plastics Engineers/SPE was originally incorporated by the State of Michigan on January 6, 1942. SPE facilitates the communication amongst scientists and engineers engaged in the development, conversion and applications of plastics. As a leading professional society for the plastics industry, SPE is home to more than 20,000 plastics professionals in more than 70 countries around the world.

18676 Society of the Plastics Industry
1667 K Street NW
Suite 1000
Washington, DC 20006-1620
202-967-7243
FAX: 202-296-7005
feedback@socplas.org
www.plasticindustry.org

William R Carteaux, President
Walt Bishop, VP Trade Shows
Chris Brown, Senior Director Government Affairs
Tracy Cullen, VP Communications/Marketing

Trade association representing one of the largest manufacturing industries in the US. Members represent the entire plastics industry supply chain, including processors, machinery and equipment manufacturers and raw material suppliers. The US plastics industry employs 1.5 million workers and provides $304 billon in annual shipment.

1100 Members Founded: 1937

18677 Thermoforming Institute
2151 Michelson Drive
Suite 240
Irvine, CA 92612
949-261-6979
FAX: 949-261-6959
jbrandts@socplas.org
www.thermoforminginstitute.org

Jill Brandts, Executive Director
Paula Weis, Director Of Communications

A business unit of the Society of the Plastics Industry, Incorporated,the Thermoforming Institute is comprised of principal officers of companies or divisions significantly engaged in the manufacture of custom thermoformed products.

1200 Members Founded: 1937

Newsletters

18678 ACM Monthly
Composite Market Reports
PO Box 137
Gilbert, AZ 85299-0137
480-507-6882
FAX: 480-507-6986
info@compositemarketreports.com
www.compositemarketreports.com/

John R. White, Executive Director/CEO
Patricia Ryan, Operations/COO
Russell Harris, Director Financial Services
Wayne Graves, Director Information Systems
Brian Hebert, Marketing/Communications Manager

Reports on market and technology intelligence for materials suppliers.

18679 Additives for Polymers
Reed Elsevier Science Direct
9555 Springboro Pike
Miamisburg, OH 45342
937-865-6800
FAX: 937-865-1349
s.barrett@elsevier.com
www.elsevier.com

Guy Kitteringhem, Publisher
A Weawer, Editor
S. Barrett, Program Editor
Marike Westra, Director Corporate Relations
Ylann Schemm, Communications Executive

Each issue identifies and details relevant materials and products, new applications, new research and technical developments, newly issued US and British patents.

Monthly Founded: 1887
Printed in on matte stock

18680 Advanced Materials & Composites News
Composites Worldwide
991 C Lomas Santa Fe Drive
PMB469
Solana Beach, CA 92075-2141
858-755-1372
FAX: 858-755-5271
compositesnews@adelphia.net
http://www.compositesnews.com

Steve Loud, Editor
Susan Loud, Managing Editor

Focuses on the processes, applications markets, design, international activities and more related to composites and other advanced materials, particularly for civil engineering and construction, but for all markets and structural applications, including aerospace, transportation, and industrial. *$598.00*

Circulation: 1000

18681 Composite Industry Monthly
Composite Market Reports
PO Box 137
Gilbert, AZ 85299
480-507-6882
FAX: 480-507-6986
info@compositemarketreports.com
www.compositemarketreports.com

William Benjamin, Publisher
John R. White, Executive Director/CEO
Patricia Ryan, Operations/COO
Wayne Graves, Director Information

Systems
Russell Harris, Director Financial Services

Market and technology intelligence for users, prime and sub-contractors, universities, government and others. *$1495.00*

Monthly Founded: 1971
Circulation: 8177

18682 Modern Plastics Worldwide
Canon Communications
11444 West Olympic Blvd.
Suite 900
Los Angeles, CA 90064
310-445-4200
FAX: 310-445-4299
info@modplas.com
www.modplas.com/

Patrick Toensmeier, Editor
Kevin O'Grady, Publisher

Industry trends and developments. Accepts advertising. *$150.00*

125 pages Monthly

18683 POF Newsletter
Information Gatekeepers
320 Washington Street
Suite 302
Brighton, MA 02135
617-782-5033
FAX: 617-782-5735 800-323-1088
info@igigroup.com
http://www.igigroup.com

Paul Polishuk, President/CEO
Bev Wilson, Managing Editor
Will Ashley, IT Director/Media Manager

Covers recent developments in the plastic optical fiber industry. Also provides updates on components, systems, applications, standards and a calendar of related events. *$395.00*

Founded: 1977 20,000 names $150 per M. : e-mail

18684 Plastic Focus
Plastics Connection
PO Box 814
Amherst, MA 01004-0814
413-549-5020
FAX: 413-549-9955
www.trplastics.com

Michael L Berins, Publisher
Armando Honegger, CEO

Newsletter for buyers, sellers, and users of plastic. *$275.00*

Bi-Weekly

18685 Plastics Brief Newsletter
Plastic Marketing News Brief Market Search
2727 North Holland Sylvania Road
Suite A
Toledo, OH 43615-1800
419-535-7899
FAX: 419-535-1243

James Best, Publisher

For plastic sales and marketing executives. Covers new materials, new applications, market trends, price changes. *$249.00*

Monthly

18686 Plastics Machinery & Auxiliaries
Canon Communications
55 Madison Street
Suite 770
Denver, CO 80206
303-321-2322
FAX: 303-321-3552
msnyder@pma-magazine.com
www.pma-magazine.com/

Merle R. Snyder, Editor
Jamie Quanbeck, Online Editor
Heidi Hill, Managing Editor
Kate Hunley, Associate Editor

Plastics Machinery & Auxiliaries provides readers with a forum for learning about new products and services used in a wide range of plastics processes. Plastics Machinery & Auxiliaries is distributed free of charge to qualified professionals in the plastics processing industry, in the USA and Canada.

18687 Plastics Recycling Update
PO Box 42270
Portland, OR 97242-0270
503-233-1305
FAX: 503-233-1356
info@resource-recycling.com
www.resource-recycling.com/rr.html

Jerry Powell, Editor/Publisher
Rick Downing, Advertising Director
Andrew Santosusso Jr., Managing Editor
Mary Lynch, Assistant Publisher
Chad Powell, Director of Research

Resource Recycling is the journal of recycling and composting professionals. Each month, the latest information is provided about post-consumer waste recovery efforts including: collection system assessments; processing developments; markets analyses, and legislative and regulatory reviews. Additional features includes special commodity and regular departments on equipment, recycling and composting programs, association and state activities. *$58.00*

Monthly Founded: 1981
Printed in 2 colors : On-Line

18688 Plastics Week
Market Search
2727 North Holland Sylvania Road
Suite A
Toledo, OH 43615-1800
419-535-7899
FAX: 419-535-1243 800-537-9213

James R Best, Publisher
Linda Best, Production Manager
Jim Best, Editor
Jim Best, CEO

Weekly newletters on plastics. Focusing on strategies, markets, technology, recycling and environmental issues. *$480.00*

6 pages

18689 Polymer Blends, Alloys, and Interpenetrating Polymer Networks
Sage Publications
2455 Teller Road
Thousand Oaks, CA 91320
805-990-0721
FAX: 805-499-0871 800-818-7243
info@sagepub.com
www.sagepub.com

Sara Miller McCune, Founder/Publisher/Chairman
Blaise R. Simqu, President/CEO
David P McCune, Director

Survey and summary of the growing literature and patents in the promising area of plastics technology. Each issue provides new information on chemistry, properties and performance, testing, processing, and application. *$455.00*

40 pages Monthly
Printed in 2 colors on matte stock : On-Line

18690 Rubber and Plastics News
Crain Communications
1725 Merriman Road
Suite 300
Akron, OH 44313-5251
330-836-9180
FAX: 330-836-2831 800-678-9595
info@crain.com www.crain.com

Tony Eagan, Publisher
Edward Noga, Editor
Bruce Meyer, Managing Editor

Discusses production, research and development, management, sales and marketing. News about rubber industry. *$79.00*

24 pages Monthly Founded: 1916 ISSN 0300-6123
Circulation: 16500 15,ooo names
Printed in 4 colors on glossy stock

Magazines & Journals

18691 Advanced Composites Monthly
Composite Market Reports
PO Box 137
Gilbert, AZ 85299-0137
480-507-6882
FAX: 480-507-6986
info@compositemarketreports.com
www.compositemarketreports.com

William Benjamin, President/Editor
Chris Red, Market Research
Cher Benjamin, VP
Joe Benjamin, Office Manager

Provides information to personnel at all levels in the advanced composite manufacturing industry.

10 pages Monthly Founded: 1975

18692 Digest of Polymer Developments
STR-Specialized Technology Resources
10 Water Street
Enfield, CT 06082-8234
860-749-8371
FAX: 860-749-8234
strnet@strus.com www.strlab.com

Frank Duston, Editor

Covers domestic and international information on new plastics applications, potential growth and market performance, as well as current events in the plastics and allied chemicals industries. Contains a cumulative index by market and another by plastics materials for quick reference. *$625.00*

18693 GraFiber News
Composite Market Reports
PO Box 137
Gilbert, AZ 85299-0137
480-507-6882
FAX: 602-507-6986
info@compositemarketreports.com
www.compositemarketreports.com

William Benjamin, President/Publisher/Editor/CEO
Cher Benjamin, VP
Chris Red, Market Research
Joe Benjamin, Office Manager

Provides global coverage of the aerospace industry for advanced material suppliers. *$2556.25*

10 pages Monthly Founded: 1973
Printed in 4 colors on matte stock

18694 IAPD Magazine
International Association of Plastics Distributors
4707 College Boulevard
#105
Leawood, KS 66211-1667
913-345-1005
FAX: 913-345-1006
iapd@iapd.org www.iapd.org

Deborah Hamlin, Executive Director
Janet Thill, Director of Publications
Marc Lewis Jr, President
Sandra Tonkin, Meetings Director
Wendy Schantz, Marketing Manager

Information on the plastic industry with special emphasis on profitability and advances in technology. *$90.00*

68 pages Monthly Founded: 1956
Circulation: 10000
Printed in 4 colors on glossy stock

18695 Injection Molding Magazine
Canon Communications
55 Madison Street
Suite 770
Denver, CO 80206-5432
303-321-2322
FAX: 303-321-3552
cburke@immnet.com
www.immnet.com

Charles McCurdy, President/CEO
Kevin O'Grady, Publisher/VP/Sales & Marketing
Jeff Tade, Publications Production Manager
Willy Bruijns-Miller, VP Circulation

Custom and captive molding operations, product design, moldmaking, processing information, new materials and equipment, and management issues are the editorial focus. *$168.57*

Monthly Founded: 1999
Circulation: 37500

18696 Journal of Cellular Plastics
Sage Publications
2455 Teller Road
Thousand Oaks, CA 91320
805-990-0721
FAX: 805-499-0871 800-818-7243
journals@sagepub.com
www.sagepub.com

Sidney H Metzger, Editor

A permanent record for international achievements in the science, technology, and economics of cellular plastics. It has been a major source of information on this topic for 35 years. Each issue presents outstanding technical advances in chemistry, formulation, processing, testing, properties, performance, and applications. *$901.00*

96 pages Bi-Monthly
Printed in 2 colors on matte stock : On-Line

18697 Journal of Composite Materials
Sage Publications
2455 Teller Road
Thousand Oaks, CA 91320
805-990-0721
FAX: 805-499-0871 800-818-7243
journals@sagepub.com
www.sagepub.com

Amy Flannery, Marketing
Thomas Hahn, Editor

The leading medium for composite materials technology transfer. Featuring original studies from international material scientists, the journal seeks to emphasize practical applications with no compromise in technical integrity. *$4576.00*

96 pages Bi-Monthly Founded: 1965
Printed in 2 colors on matte stock : On-Line

18698 Journal of Elastomers and Plastics
Sage Publications
2455 Teller Road
Thousand Oaks, CA 91320
805-990-0721
FAX: 805-499-0871 800-818-7243
journals@sagepub.com
www.sagepub.com

H. Aglan, Editor
S. Qutubuddin, Editorial Board
N. Nakajima, Editorial Board
L.H. Lewandowski, Editorial Board
A.I. Isayev, Editorial Board

The latest contributions to the technology and properties of elastomers and related polymeric products. Major emphasis is placed on specialty and high performance elastomers. The journal regularly presents current information on the chemistry, processing, properties, and applications of recently developed and improved elastomeric materials. *$867.00*

96 pages Quarterly
Printed in 2 colors on matte stock : On-Line

18699 Journal of Materials Engineering and Performance
American Society for Metals
9639 Kinsman Road
Materials Park, OH 44073-0002
440-338-5151
FAX: 440-338-4634 800-336-5152
cust-srv@asminternational.org
www.asminternational.org

Mrityunjay Singh, Chairman
David E. Alman, Vice Chairman

Peer-reviewed journal which publishes contributions on all aspects of materials selection, design, characterization, processing and performance testing. The scope includes all materials used in engineering applications, those that typically result in components for larger systems. *$1492.00*

Monthly Founded: 1913
Circulation: 645

18700 Journal of Materials Processing
Elsevier ScienceDirect
360 Park Avenue
New York, NY 10010-1710
212-895-5800
FAX: 212-462-1974 888-437-4636
journals@sagepub.com
www.sagepub.com

M.S.J. Hashmi, Editor-in-Chief
J. Gunasekera, Regional Editor North America

Original papers developments in traditional and innovative processing technologies for metals, polymers, composites, ceramics, and specialty materials. The scope is international and interdisciplinary. *$5208.00*

96 pages 42 Issues Per Year
Printed in 2 colors on matte stock : On-Line

18701 Journal of Plastic Film & Sheeting
Sage Publications
2455 Teller Road
Thousand Oaks, CA 91320
805-990-0721
FAX: 805-499-0871 800-818-7243
journals@sagepub.com
www.sagepub.com

James P. Harrington, Editor
A. Ajji, Editorial Board
Raj Krishnaswamy, Editorial Board
Douglas E. Hirt, Editorial Board
Phillip T. DeLassus, Editorial Board

The Journal of Plastic Film and Sheeting improves communication concerning plastic film and sheeting with major emphasis on the propagation of knowledge which will serve to advance the science and technology of these products and thus better serve industry and the ultimate consumer. The journal reports on the wide variety of advances that are rapidly taking place in the technology of plastic film and sheeting. *$ 795.00*

88 pages Quarterly
Printed in 2 colors on matte stock : On-Line

18702 Journal of Polymer Science
John Wiley & Sons
111 River Street
Hoboken, NJ 07030
201-748-6000
FAX: 201-748-6088 www.wiley.com

Virgil Percec, Editor
Mitsvo Sawamoto, Editor

The Journal of Polymer Science provides a continuous forum for the dissemination of thoroughly peer-reviewed, fundamental, international research into the preparation and properties of macromolecules. Part A: Polymer Chemistry is devoted to studies in fundamental organic polymer chemistry and physical organic chemistry. Polymer Physics (Part B) details contemporary research on all aspects of polymer physics.

200 pages 48 Issues Per Year

18703 Journal of Reinforced Plastics and Composites
Sage Publications
2455 Teller Road
Thousand Oaks, CA 91320
805-990-0721
FAX: 805-499-0871 800-818-7243
journals@sagepub.com
www.sagepublications.com

George S. Springer, Editor
Christos C. Chamis, Editorial Board
Jonathan Gosse, Editorial Board
J.M. Whitney, Editorial Board
I. Verpoest, Editorial Board

The Journal of Reinforced Plastics and Composites presents research studies on a broad range of today's reinforced plastics and composites. The journal provides a permanent record of achievements in the science, technology, and economics of reinforced plastics and composites. Reports on special topics are regularly included such as recycling, environmental effects, novel materials, computer-aided design, predictive modelling, and composite materials. *$4509.00*

18 Times Per Year Founded: 1962

18704 Journal of Thermoplastic Composite Materials
Sage Publications
2455 Teller Road
Thousand Oaks, CA 91320
805-990-0721
FAX: 805-499-0871 800-818-7243
journals@sagepub.com
www.sagepub.com

J.W. Gillespie Jr., Editor
M.N. Ghasemi Jejhad, Associate Editor
Leif A. Carlsson, Editorial Board
Ranga Pitchumani, Editorial Board
Toan Vu-Khanh, Editorial Board

An international forum for the presentation of new advances in the technology of this class of materials. Emphasis is given to the fundamental areas of new material development and characterization, design, rheological behavior in short, discontinuous, and continuous fiber systems; process development, manufacturing science, matrix-fiber

interphase charaterization; short and long-term performance prediction; and engineering data base assistance for thermoplastic composites. *$1186.00*
96 pages Bi-Monthly
Printed in 2 colors on matte stock : On-Line

18705 Journal of Vinyl and Additive Technology
John Wiley & Sons
111 River Street
Hoboken, NJ 07030
201-486-6000
FAX: 201-748-8852
subinfo@wiley.com
www3.interscience.wiley.com/
William H. Starnes Jr., Editor
Elliot L. Weinberg, Associate Editor
James W. Summers, Associate Editor
Journal of Vinyl and Additive Technology is a peer-reviewed technical publication for new work in the fields of polymer modifiers and additives, vinyl polymers and selected review papers. Over half of all papers in JVAT are based on technology of additives and modifiers for all classes of polymers: thermoset polymers and both condensation and addition thermoplastics. Papers on vinyl technology include PVC additives. *$ 336.00*
Quarterly Founded: 1942
Circulation: 625

18706 Journal of Wide Bandgap Materials
Sage Publications
2455 Teller Road
Thousand Oaks, CA 91320
805-990-0721
FAX: 805-499-0871 800-818-7243
journals@sagepub.com
www.sagepub.com
Peter Gielisse, Editor
Shojiro Komatsu, Editorial Advisory Board
Boris V. Spitsyn, Editorial Advisory Board
The Journal of Wide Bandgap Materials is an international journal publishing original peer-reviewed papers on fundamental, experimental and theoretical developments in the science and engineering of wide bandgap materials. The Journal provides a broad-based forum for the publication and sharing of ongoing research and development efforts in the field of wide bandgap materials. *$245.00*
96 pages Quarterly
Printed in 2 colors on matte stock : On-Line

18707 Medical Plastics & Biomaterials
Canon Communications
11444 West Olympic Blvd.
Suite 900
Los Angeles, CA 90064
310-445-4200
FAX: 310-445-4299 800-243-9696
feedback@cancom.com
www.cancom.com
Kevin Quinn, Editor
Tonna Anuligo, Technical Editor
Kevin O'Grady, Group Publisher,
Bditorial Inquiries Manager
Technical information on the full range of plastics and biomaterials used in manufacturing and packaging medical products. *$59.00*
Monthly Founded: 1978
Circulation: 61200

18708 Modern Plastics
Canon Communications
11444 West Olympic Blvd.
Suite 900
Los Angeles, CA 90064
310-445-4200
FAX: 310-445-4299
info@modplas.com
www.modplas.com/
Patrick Toensmeier, Editor
Kevin O'Grady, Publisher
Serves companies utilizing plastics. Developments in resin technology, machinery/processing techniques and additive innovation. *$59.00*
Monthly Founded: 1978
Circulation: 50300

18709 Nonwovens World
MTS Publications
4100 South 7th Street
Kalamazoo, MI 49009-8461
269-375-1236
FAX: 269-375-6710
admin@marketingtechnologyservice.com
www.marketingtechnologyservice.com
James P Hanson, Director/Editor
Wayne C Carter, Advertising Sales Director
Elizabeth Hanson, News Editor
Cindy Costello, Circulation Manager
Mark A Bolyen, Business Editor
A journal for management.
Founded: 1986
Circulation: 53378

18710 PM/USA Green Sheet
Marketing Handbook
PO Box 243687
Boynton Beach, FL 33424-3687
561-732-5858
FAX: 561-732-2607
results@greensheetads.com
www.greensheetads.com
Lee Noe, Publisher/Editor
Bob Miller, Technical Director
For those responsible for manufacturing operations. *$45.00*
Monthly Founded: 1972

18711 Plastics Business News
Plastics Universe
2727 Holland Sylvania Road
Suite A
Toledo, OH 43615
419-535-7899
FAX: 419-535-1243
mberins@javanet.com
www.plasticx.com/pub/plast_11.html
Michael L. Berins, Publisher
A weekly newsletter published for the professionals in the plastic industry. Covers advances in materials and processes, pricing, new applications and markets, international competition, etc. *$327.00*
Weekly Founded: 1972

18712 Plastics Distributor and Fabricator Magazine
KLW Enterprises
PO Box 669
LaGrange, IL 60525-0669
708-470-0001
FAX: 708-588-1846
pdfm@plasticsmag.com
www.plasticsmag.com
David Whelan, Editor/Publisher
Riia O'Donnell, Associate Editor
Lynette Zeitler, Art Director
Contains industry and products news relevant to the manufacture, distribution and fabrication of plastic rod, sheet and tube.
Founded: 1983
Printed in 4 colors on glossy stock

18713 Plastics Engineering
Society of Plastics Engineers
14 Fairfield Drive
P O Box 403
Brookfield, CT 06804-0403
203-775-0471
FAX: 203-775-8490
info@4spe.org www.4spe.org
Roger M Ferris, Editor
Alyson Tabot, Editorial Assistant
Susan Oderwald, Executive Director
Gail R Bristol, Managing Director/Foundation
Edited for the technically oriented executives and engineers in the plastics industry. *$142.00*
Monthly Founded: 1942
Circulation: 36000

18714 Plastics Focus
Plastics Universe
2727 Holland Sylvania Road
Suite A
Toledo, OH 43615
419-535-7899
FAX: 419-535-1243
James Best, CEO
Bi-Monthly updates on new applicationsand markets for plastics, new polymers, alloys and blends as well as machinery, processing developments, and international competitions and opportunities. *$295.00*

18715 Plastics Hotline
Industry Marketing Solutions
809 Central Avenue
PO Box 893, 2nd Floor
Fort Dodge, IA 50501-1052
888-247-2006
FAX: 515-574-2237
steve@plasticshotline.com
www.plasticshotline.com
Steve Scanlan, Publisher
Jim Rykhus, List Marketing Specialist
Cara Jondle, Tradeshow & Marketing Manager
Jody Kirchoff, Operations
Plastics Hotline has been published since 1983. This weekly periodical continues to be the National Marketplace for Plastic Processors to buy and sell equipment, parts and services. *$69.00*
Weekly Founded: 1983

18716 Plastics Machining & Fabricating
Onsrud Cutter
800 Liberty Drive
Libertyville, IL 60048
847-362-1560
FAX: 847-362-5028
info@plasticsmachining.com
www.plasticsmachining.com
Harry Urban, Publisher
Plastics Molding & Fabricating is an online technical and management magazine dedicated to the secondary plastics processing industry. It is edited for qualified professionals whose operations include: machining, milling, fabricating, forming, bending, bonding, molding, printing and finishing of plastics. Editorial subjects include case studies, technology updates, trends & news and opinion pieces.

Bi-Monthly
Circulation: 15,015

18717 Plastics News
Crain Communications
1725 Merriman Road
Suite 300
Akron, OH 44313
330-836-9180
FAX: 330-836-2322 800-678-9595
editorial@plasticsnews.com
www.plasticsnews.com

Don Loepp, Editor
Robert S. Simmons, VP/Publications Director
Linda Whelan, Marketing Manager
Keith E. Crain, Chairman
Tony Eagan, Publisher

Plastics News is a weekly publication that serves executive and management personnel of firms in the plastics industry, which comprise independent custom plastics processors, design development and engineering firms, and others allied to the field. *$69.00*
32 pages Weekly Founded: 1989
Circulation: 60000
Printed in 4 colors on glossy stock

18718 Plastics Technology
Gardner Publications
6915 Valley Avenue
Cincinnati, OH 45244
513-278-8977
FAX: 513-527-8801 800-950-8020
cnorman@gardnerweb.com
www.gardnerweb.com

Matthew H. Naitove, Editor
Sherry Fuchs, Managing Editor
Theresa Basso, Production Editor
Joe Grande, Senior Editor
Mikell Knights, Senior Editor

A premier source of technical and business information for plastics processors, each issue reports on technological innovations and developments in the plastics processing market and reaches more than 47,000 processors who depend on authoritative coverage on applying new technology, evaluating products and practical manufacturing.
Monthly Founded: 1928
Circulation: 47559

18719 Polymer Engineering & Science
John Wiley & Sons
111 River Street
Hoboken, NJ 07030
201-486-6000
FAX: 201-748-8852
subinfo@wiley.com
www3.interscience.wiley.com/

Robert A Weiss, Editor
Alan J Lesser, Associate Editor
Laura Espinet, Journal Production
Kim Thompkins, Advertising/Media

Presents papers of fundamental significance to engineers and scientists interested in polmeric materials. *$545.00*
Monthly Founded: 1945
Circulation: 86000

Trade Shows

18720 ANTEC Society of Plastics Engineers Annual Technical Conference
Society of Plastics Engineering/SPE
SPE Event Management Department
14 Fairfield Drive, PO Box 403
Brookfield, CT 06804-0403
203-775-0471
FAX: 203-775-8490
antec@4spe.org www.4spe.org/conf

Lesley Kyle, Senior Event Manager
Maria Russo, ANTEC Exhibits Liaison
Elizabeth Mitchell, ANTEC Technical Program Coordinator

ANTEC (Annual Technical Conference) is sponsored by the Society of Plastics Engineers, and is the leading technical forum for providing cutting-edge technological issues and information pertinent to the needs of the plastics industry. Held only once a year, multiple peer-reviewed technical papers will be presented providing plastics professionals unique inside access to proprietary research and findings.
Annual/May

18721 Adhesive Sealant Council/ASC Fall & Spring Conventions
7979 Old Georgetown Road
Suite 500
Bethesda, MD 20814
301-986-9700
FAX: 301-986-9795
bob.willis@ascouncil.org
www.ascouncil.org/industry/conventions/index.cfm

Bob Willis, Senior Manager Conventions/Meetings
Joe Stevenson, ASC Director
Alan Longstreet, Board Chairman
Lawrence Sloan, President

ASC sponsors conventions and trade shows for the adhesive and sealant industry twice a year - in spring and fall. This is truly where the industry meets — bringing together personnel from large and small companies, both manufacturers and suppliers, academicians, and end-users. ASC conventions incorporate dynamic business- and technically-oriented educational programming and exhibits with social events to provide ample networking opportunities for attendees.
300 Attendees April/October

18722 Association of Industrial Metallizers, Coaters and Laminators Conference
201 Springs Street
Fort Mill, SC 29715
803-802-7820
FAX: 803-802-7821
aimcal@aimcal.org www.aimcal.org

Craig Sheppard, Executive Director
Caleb Howe, Communications Manager
Ed Cohen, Technical Consultant
Norma Bryant, Office Manager

Displays relating to coaters and laminators, metallizers and producers of metallized film and or paper on continuous rolls, suppliers of plastic films, papers and adhesives.

Annual Founded: 1970

18723 Health Pack Innovative Technology Conference
7500 Boone Aveune North
Minneapolis, MN 55428
763-372-2906
FAX: 762-493-6358
hjayson@theitc.com
www.healthpack.net

Heather Jayson, Show Coordinator
Steve Bunell, Operations Manager
Curtis Larson, Program Coordinator
John Spitzley, Program Co-Chairman
Angela Holty, Owner

Unique annual conference focuses exclusively on medical device packaging, bringing together medical device manufacturers, packaging materials suppliers and converters, contract packagers, test labs, and other service providers. Food and beverage functions served in the exhibition area provide repeated opportunities for networking between exhibitors, attendees, and conference speakers. Conference location in St. Petersburg, Florida, 20 booths.
100 Attendees March

18724 International Association of Plastics Distributors/IAPD Convention
4707 College Boulevard
Suite 105
Leawood, KS 66211-1667
913-345-1005
FAX: 913-345-1006
iapd@iapd.org www.iapd.prg

Deborah M Hamlin, Executive Director
Sandy Tonkin, Meetings Manager

IAPD is an international trade association comprised of companies engaged in the distribution and manufacture of plastics materials. The annual convention features numerous exhibits that represent a variety of materials in the plastics industry including semi-finished stock shapes, such as sheet, rod, tube, pipe, valves, fittings, film and related products. 76 booths.
450 Attendees September Founded: 1956
4000 names

18725 International Plastics Show
1801 K Street NW
Suite 1000
Washington, DC 20006
202-974-5200
FAX: 202-296-7005
tradeshows@socplas.org
www.socplas.org or www.npe.org

Ken Rietz, President
Brigid Hughes, Director Trade Show Promotions
Adam Krumhansl, Trade Show Coordinator

Containing 2,000 exhibits.
85M+ Attendees June

18726 National Agricultural Plastics Congress
American Society for Plasticulture
526 Brittany Drive
State College, PA 16803
814-238-7045
FAX: 814-238-7051
info@plasticulture.org
www.plasticulture.org

William Tietjen, Chairman Plastics Congress
Henry Taber, President
Jodi Fleck-Arnold, VP
Edward Carey, Secretary/Treasurer
Patricia Heuser, Executive Director

Plastic products used in agriculture. 15-25 booths.

150 Attendees March/November

18727 National Plastics Exposition
Society of The Plastics
1801 K Street NW
Suite 1000
Washington, DC 20006
202-974-5200
FAX: 202-296-7005
www.plasticsindustry.org/

Ken Rietz, President
Brigid Hughes, Director Trade Show Promotions
Adam Krumhansl, Trade Show Coordinator

This expo features exhibits of molded, extruded, fabricated, laminated and calendered plastics, raw materials, machinery and laboratory equipment for the industry.
75M Attendees June

18728 PLASTEC East Trade Show
Canon Communications
11444 West Olympic Boulevard
Los Angeles, CA 90064-1549
310-445-4200
FAX: 310-996-9499
register@cancom.com
www.plasteceast.com

Diane O'Connor, Trade Show Director
Shannon Cleghorn, Customer & Media Coordinator

Five co-located shows, 1,750 plastic exhibitors. The Trade Show takes place every 2 years, in odd years.
32000 Attendees

18729 PLASTEC West Trade Show
Canon Communications
11444 West Olympic Boulevard
Los Angeles, CA 90064
310-445-4200
FAX: 310-996-9499
register@cancom.com
www.plastecwest.com

Diane O'Connor, Trade Show Director
Jane Sullivan, Exhibit Contact

Five co-located shows, 3,000 exhibitors, trade show features plastics, packaging and manufacturing industries.
45000 Attendees January/February

18730 POLYCON
International Cast Polymer Association
5900 Harper Road
Suite 105
Solon, OH 44139-1935
440-349-3060
FAX: 440-498-9121 www.icpa-hq.org

Jeanne McCormack, Director Conferences & Meetings
Elizabeth Cookson, Mgr Conferences & Program Dvlpmt

The program includes three days of in-depth educational programming, exhibits, a product showcase, and more. Sponsored annually by the International Cast Polymer Association/ICPA, POLYCON is the largest convention and trade show for the cast polymer industry. Over 800 industry professionals attend the convention to network, attend educational sessions, and visit with over 70 exhibitors.
Annual

18731 Polyurethanes Technical Conference
Alliance for the Polyurethanes Industry
1300 Wilson Boulevard
Arlington, VA 22209
703-741-5103
FAX: 703-741-5655
api@plastics.org
www.polyurethane.org

Richard E Mericle, Executive Director
Kaye Robinson, Conference Planning Committee

Semi-annual trade show for the polyurethanes industry in North America. International technical conference and exposition will feature technical and industry issues sessions, poster session and exhibits.
September/October Founded: 1977

Directories & Databases

18732 American Mold Builders Association/AMBA Membership Directory
American Mold Builders Association
701 East Irving Park Road
Suite 207
Roselle, IL 60172
630-980-7667
FAX: 630-980-9714
info@amba.org www.amba.org or amba.org/adOppGrid.php

Jeanette Bradley, Editor

AMBA represents nearly 325 member companies comprised of approximately 9,000 employees and representing just over $2 billion in annual tooling sales. Members span 35 states with 12 chapter affiliations. AMBA member companies serve original equipment manufacturers in every industry including automotive, medical, electronics/electrical, toys, recreation and sporting goods, building and construction, lawn and garden, consumer, and industrial. Free to members and available to others for $50.00. *$50.00*
Annual Founded: 1973
Circulation: 2,200

18733 Handbook of Plastic Compounds, Elastomers and Resins
John Wiley & Sons
10475 Crosspoint Blvd
Indianapolis, IN 46256
317-723-3000
FAX: 800-597-3299 www.wiley.com/

Irene Ash, Editor
Michael Ash, Editor

Directory of services and supplies to the industry. A complete, accurate, and current data source on primary material tradename products for the rubber and plastic industries. This handbook gives short, easy-to-find information on over 15,000 chemical trademark products currently sold throughout the world. *$385.00*
ISBN 0-471188-30-1

18734 IAPD Membership Directory
International Association of Plastics Distributors
4707 College Boulevard
Suite 105
Leawood, KS 66211
913-345-1005
FAX: 913-345-1006
iapd@iapd.org www.iapd.org

Deborah M. Hamlin, Executive Director
Janet A. Thill, Director of Publications
Wendy Schantz, Marketing Manager
Sandra Tonkin, Meetings Manager

The IAPD Membership Directory lists almost 400 companies by membership category with their locations, phone and fax numbers, key personnel and plastic products. There is also a listing of companies by geographical location, as well as an alphabetical listing of individuals from the various companies. *$150.00*
Annual May

18735 Modern Plastics Encyclopedia
Canon Communications
11444 West Olympic Blvd.
Suite 900

310-445-3746
FAX: 310-445-4259 800-655-3330
feedback@cancom.com
www.cancombookstore.com/

Pat Toensmeier, Editor
Thomas Britton, Sales Director

An encyclopedia, materials and machinery reference book, buyers' guide, and trade name directory for the plastics industry. *$85.00*
800 pages Annual

18736 Modern Plastics Handbook
McGraw Hill Professional
1221 Avenue of the Americas
Suite C3A
New York, NY 10020-1095
212-512-3916
FAX: 212-512-6111
www.mcgraw-hill.com

Charles A. Harper, Editor

State-of-the-art guide to plastic product design, manufacture and application. Modern Plastics Handbook packs a wealth of up-to-date knowledge about plastics processes, forms and formulations, design, equipment, testing and recycling.
200 pages ISBN 0-070267-14-6

18737 Plastics Business News
Plastics Universe
2727 Holland Sylvania Road
Suite A
Toledo, OH 43615
419-535-7899
FAX: 419-535-1243
mberins@javanet.com
www.plasticx.com/pub/plast_11.html

Michael L. Berins, Publisher

Offers information on the plastics industry, forecasts, mergers, and new product developments. *$327.00*
Weekly Founded: 1972

18738 Plastics Compounding Redbook
Advanstar Communications
One Park Avenue
New York, NY 10016
212-797-7631
FAX: 212-951-6666
info@advanstar.com
www.advanstar.com

Joseph Loggia, Chief Executive Officer
David W. Montgomery, Chief Financial Officer
Rick Treese, VP/Chief Technology Officer
Georgiann Decenzo, VP/Marketing and Communications

List of suppliers — over 1,000 — of resin, additives, fillers and other materials compounding equipment and services to the plastic industry. *$150.00*

280 pages Annual
Circulation: 12,000

18739 Plastics Digest/PA Index
IHS/Information Handling Services
15 Inverness Way East
#6510
Englewood, CO 80112-5710
303-790-0600
FAX: 303-397-2400 800-525-7052

Charles Picasso, President/Chief Executive Officer
John Oechsle, Chief Information Officer

A list of over 200 manufacturers and suppliers of plastics materials are listed in this comprehensive directory. CD format only. *$768.00*

18740 Plastics Engineering Handbook of The Society of the Plastics Industry
Society of the Plastics Industry
1275 K Street NW
Suite 1000
Washington, DC 20005
202-967-7243
FAX: 202-296-7005 800-541-0736

William R. Carteaux, President
Barry Eisenberg, Director Communications/Marketing
Jim Maslend, Executive Director

Educational groups, associations, consultants and providers of technical data, literature and materials to the reinforced plastics industry. *$175.00*

18741 Plastics News Datebook Online
Crain Communications
1725 Merriman Road
Suite 300
Akron, OH 44313
330-836-9180
FAX: 330-836-2322 800-678-9595
editorial@plasticsnews.com
www.plasticsnews.com

Don Loepp, Editor
Robert S. Simmons, VP/Publications Director
Linda Whelan, Marketing Manager
Keith E. Crain, Chairman

Our online calendar of global plastics industry events is now a searchable database. Search by organizer, date, location, type of event or content. Click on the Datebook link at PlasticsNews.com.

Printed in 4 colors on glossy stock

18742 Plastics News Web Watch Directory

Crain Communications
1725 Merriman Road
Suite 300
Akron, OH 44313
330-836-9180
FAX: 330-836-2322 800-678-9595
editorial@plasticsnews.com
www.plasticsnews.com

Robert S Simmons, VP/Publications Director
Anthony Eagan, Publisher

Contains processors, primary equipment, auxiliary equipment, resin suppliers, compounders, recyclers, tooling and molds, design and prototyping, trade associations, industry services and more.
154 pages
Printed in 4 colors on glossy stock

18743 Rauch Guide to the US Adhesives & Sealants Industry
Grey House Publishing
PO Box 860
Millerton, NY 12546
518-789-8700
FAX: 518-789-0545 800-562-2139
books@greyhouse.com
www.greyhouse.com

Leslie Mackenzie, Publisher
Richard Gottlieb, President
Laura Mars-Proietti, Editorial Director
Jessica Moody, Marketing Director

Contains information providing data on industry economics, government regulations, technology, raw materials, products and markets in addition to industry activities, organizations and sources of information on trade shows, exhibits, professional associations and societies. Provides unique profiles of 781 suppliers. *$595.00*

18744 Rauch Guide to the US Plastics Industry
Grey House Publishing
PO Box 860
Millerton, NY 12546
518-789-8700
FAX: 518-789-0545 800-562-2139
books@greyhouse.com
www.greyhouse.com

Leslie Mackenzie, Publisher
Richard Gottlieb, President
Laura Mars-Proietti, Editorial Director
Jessica Moody, Marketing Director

Offers comprehensive data on the over $200 billion industry, the Guide is a highly valued industry resource covering the economics, processes, materials, sales and activities of more than 800 leading U.S. plastics producers. Additional features include a personnel index with 1,500 key industry executives and an enhanced company listing containing detailed information indicating subsidiary, division or parent information, Internet site addresses, E-mail addresses, and key contacts. *$595.00*

18745 Reference Guide to Polyurethane Processing
Polyurethane Manufacturers Association
6737 West Washington Avenue
Suite 1420
Milwaukee, WI 53202
414-431-3094
FAX: 414-276-7704
info@pmahome.org
www.pmahome.org

Ken Neal, President
Corey D. Barge, VP
Nicholas Bitter, Treasurer
Donald P. Gallo, Legal Counsel

Recently updated, this three-ring bound publication contains a wealth of information that has been presented in technical papers at PMA meetings over the years. General topics include: urethane chemistry; handling and storage; raw materials and additives; processing; toxicity; and applications. *$75.00*

18746 Who's Who in World Petrochemicals and Plastics
Reed Business Information
3730 Kirby Drive
Suite 1030
Houston, TX 77098
713-623-4627
FAX: 713-525-2659
sales.us@icis.com www.icis.com/

Jim Muttram, Publishing Director
Andy Soloman, Global Editorial Director
Chrissy Salisbury, Manager

More than 9,600 individuals from 3,700 petrochemical and plastic companies worldwide. *$276.00*
Annual November
Circulation: 1,500

18747 Worldwide Petrochemical Directory

PennWell Directories
1700 West Loop South
Suite 1000
Houston, TX 77027
713-218-8833
FAX: 713-621-6228 800-752-9764
billw@pennwell.com
www.pennwell.com

Bob Tippee, Editor
David Nakamura, Refining/Petrochemical Editor
Guntis Moritis, Production Editor
Tim Sullivant, Manager

2,980 operative petrochemical plants with 8,675 personnel in 4,320 locations are listed with their parent companies, plant locations, products produced, capacities, and current production volumes if available. Approximately 9,340 locations having 13,145 Email and 4,330 Website addresses are listed for engineering, construction, manufacturing, supply and service companies with a description of products and services provided. Included are 350 cross-references reflecting mergers and acquisitions. *$150.00*
Annual November
Circulation: 3,500

Industry Web Sites

18748 www.aimcal.org
Association of Industrial Metallizers, Coaters
and Laminators

Packaging equipment.

18749 www.americanmanufacturers.com
AmericanManufacturers.com

Product exchanges and electronic requests for quotes.

18750 www.apexq.com
American Plastics Exchange

Molders and extruders can review data sheets and bid for prime virgin resin.

18751 **www.ariba.com**
Ariba

Allows buyers and sellers to find trading partners and negotiate prices.

18752 **www.assettrade.com**
AssetTrade.com

Used equipment and machinery.

18753 **www.berkshireplastics.org**
Berkshire Plastics Network

Consortium of more than 40 independent companies, representing virtually every discipline in the design and production of molds, components and plastics products.

18754 **www.chematch.com**
CheMatch.com

Buyers and sellers exchange for plastic materials.

18755 **www.chemconnect.com**
ChemConnect

Buyers and sellers can find partners and negotiate price.

18756 **www.chemcross.com**
ChemCross

Online trading offered by Asian producers of plastics and chemicals.

18757 **www.commerxplasticsnet.com**
Commerx

Online training.

18758 **www.dovebid.com**
DoveBid

Bidding on used equipment, as well as capital assets.

18759 **www.e-resin.com**
e-Resin.com

Direct negotiation with suppliers for additives, materials and finished products.

18760 **www.efodia.com**
eFodia

Online purchasing of chemical processing, compounding and additives, other materials.

18761 **www.elastomersolutions.com**
ElastomerSolutions

Online trading for the elastomers industry.

18762 **www.ewinwin.com**
eWinWin

Associations, cooperatives, buyers and suppliers can employ an aggregation system for lower priced purchases.

18763 **www.freemarkets.com**
FreeMarkets

Reverse auction in which suppliers submit online bids for commodities, services, parts and materials.

18764 **www.getplastic.com**
GetPlastic.com

Materials designed for those who purchase resins.

18765 **www.greyhouse.com**
Grey House Publishing

Selected Grey House directories in the fields of business, health and education are available online. Users can search our online databases by several different search criteria, such as product categories, geographic area, sales volume and much, much more. Full Grey House catalog and online ordering also available.

18766 **www.i2i.com**
Industry to Industry

Buying and selling of plastics.

18767 **www.justforplastics.com**
Justforplastics.com

Marketplace for plastic services, tooling, equipment and products.

18768 **www.mfgconnect.com**
Mfgconnect.com

Exchange product development information and CAD files prior to bidding on contracts.

18769 **www.napcor.com**
National Association for Pet Container Resources

National trade association which promotes the recycling of pet con-tainers and the usage of pet plastic.

18770 **www.omnexus.com**
Omnexus Corporation

Trading in equipment, services, materials and tooling for central injection and blow molders.

18771 **www.onechem.com**
OneChem

Software applications and transactional storefront for global commercial transactions in plastics and chemicals.

18772 **www.packagingexchange.com**
PackagingExchange.Com

Storefront transactions and online auction for packaging products, equipment and materials.

18773 **www.packexpo.com**
Packexpo.com

Source for packaging materials, machinery, parts and services.

18774 **www.packtion.com**
Packtion Corporation

Informational tools and exchange opportunites for packaging services.

18775 **www.plasticlink.com**
PlasticLink.Com

Materials, equipment and products for thermoformers, extruders and semifinished shape processors.

18776 **www.plasticpipe.org**
Plastics Pipe Institute

Promotes the effective use of plastic piping systems.

18777 **www.plastics.org**
American Plastics Council

Gateway to plastics on the internet.

18778 **www.plasticsandchemicals.com**
Plasticsandchemicals.com

Bid-based marketplace.

18779 **www.plasticsbin.com**
NetVendor

Trading in scrap resin and surplus plastic inventory.

18780 www.plasticsindustry.org
Society of the Plastics Industry

The Society of the Plastics Industry is the trade association representing one of the largest manufacturing industries in the US. SPI's 1,500 members represent the entire plastics industry supply chain, including processors, machinery and equipment manufacturers and raw material suppliers. The US plastics industry employs 1.5 million workers and provides $304 billon in annual shipment.

18781 www.plasticsrecycling.org
AssociationOd Postconsumer Plastic Recyclers

Represents companies that acquire, reprocess and sell the output of more than 90 percent of the post-consumer plastic processing capacity in North America.

18782 www.plasticulture.com
American Society for Plasticulture

Promotes research, education, and technology application for plastics used in agricultural and horticultural production systems. Hosts a congress every year or so; published proceedings of research presentations.

18783 www.polymeradditives.com
PolymerAdditives.com

Purchase brand-name polymer additives online.

18784 www.polymersite.com
PolymerSite.com/PolySort

Exchange site for resins and compounds. Flexible negotiations in a sealed bid environment.

18785 www.polyurethane.org
Alliance for the Polyurethanes Industry

For companies that supply polyurethane resins or chemicals used in polyurethane resins, manufacture polyurethanes, produce machinery used in the manufacture or processing polyurethane, or engage in the business of applying polyurethane products in end use applications.

18786 www.primeadvantage.com
Prime Advantage Corporation

Buying consortium offers volume discounts on resins and components.

18787 www.sorcity.com
Sorcity.com

Reverse auction in which buyer files request for quote and supplier bids.

18788 www.supplierone.com
SupplierOne.com

Supply chain management and e-marketplace for manufactured components.

18789 www.thedock.com
The Dock Exchange

Buying and selling of equipment online.

18790 www.theplasticsexchange.com
ThePlasticsExchange.com

Trading in commodity prime resins.

18791 www.worldwideplastics.com
TheBuyersNet.com

Catalog of semifinished materials.

Associations

18792 American Society of Plumbing Engineers
8614 W. Catalpa
Suite 1007
Chicago, IL 60656-1116
773-693-2773
FAX: 773-695-9007
aspexdir@aol.com www.aspe.org

Norman Parks, VP
Julius A. Ballanco, P.E., President
Stanley Wolfson, Executive Director
Donald Turner, Finance/Administrative Manager
Patrick L. Whitworth, Secretary

The American Society of Plumbing Engineers (ASPE) is a professional organization dedicated to the advancement of the science of plumbing engineering, to the professional growth and advancement of its members and the health, welfare and safety of the public. The Society disseminates technical data and information, sponsors activities that facilitate interaction with fellow professionals, and, through research and education, expands the base of knowledge of the plumbing engineering industry.
7500 Members Founded: 1964

18793 American Society of Sanitary Engineering
901 Canterbury
Suite A
Westlake, OH 44145
440-835-3040
FAX: 440-835-3488
info@asse-plumbing.org
www.asse-plumbing.org

Shannon Corcoran, Executive Director
Sean Cleary, President
Craig Bing, Treasurer
Marianne Waickman, Qualifications Coordinator
Marla Gasser-Mogg, Advertising Manager

Members are from all segments of the plumbing industry, including contractors, engineers, inspectors, journeymen, apprentices and others who are involved in various segments of the industry. Provides information, an opportunity to exchange ideas, solve problems and offers a forum where all sides can express their views.
300 Members

18794 American Supply Association
222 Merchandise Mart Plaza
Suite 1400
Chicago, IL 60654
312-464-0090
FAX: 312-464-0091
info@asa.net www.asa.net

Dottie Ramsey, Chairman
George Conyngham, Jr., President
Colin Perry, Treasurer
Inge Calderon, Secretary

ASA is a not-for-profit national organization serving wholesale distributors and their suppliers in the plumbing, heating, cooling and industrial pipe, valves, and fittings industries. ASA provides a forum for trading partners from around the country to discuss critical issues facing them, and offers a menu of products and services uniquely geared to their needs.
800 Members Founded: 1969

18795 American Water Works Association
6666 W Quincy Ave
Denver, CO 80235
303-794-7711
FAX: 303-347-0804 800-926-7337

Jack W Hoffbuhr, Executive Director
Jon Runge, Communic/Marketing/Cust Serv Group

International nonprofit scientific and educational society dedicated to the improvement of water quality and supply.
57000 Members Founded: 1881

18796 International Association of Plumbing/IAPMO
5001 East Philadelphia Street
Ontario, CA 91761
909-472-4100
FAX: 909-472-4150
iapmo@iapmo.org www.iapmo.org

Christopher Salazar, President
Ron Rice, VP
Russ Chaney, Executive Director
Doug Fredericksen, Secretary
Jay Mundy, Treasurer

IAPMO began in 1926 as the Plumbing Inspectors Association of Los Angeles. Forty-two plumbing inspectors, banded together to bring about an improvement in the application of commonsense codification and application of ordinances based on scientific knowledge. Today the IAPMP has grown into one of the largest plumbing code writing associations in the world. IAPMO's bimonthly magazine features articles of interest to the plumbing industry, educational materials and information on code changes.

18797 International Association of Plumbing and Mechanical Officials

5001 E Philadelphia St
Ontario, CA 91761
909-472-4100
FAX: 909-472-4150 800-854-2766
iapmo@iapmo.org www.iapmo.org

GP Russ Chaney, Executive Director
Gaby Davis, Director of Operations

Commitment is to serve the plumbing and mechanical communities around the world.

Founded: 1926

18798 Manufacturers Standardization Society of the Valve and Fittings Industr/MSS
127 Park Street NE
Vienna, VA 22180-4602
703-281-6613
FAX: 703-281-6671
info@mss-hq.org www.mss-hq.com/

Robert O'Neill, Executive Director

The Manufacturers Standardization Society (MSS) of the Valve and Fittings Industry is a non-profit technical association organized for development and improvement of industry, national and international codes and standards for valves, valve actuators, valve modifications, pipe fittings, pipe hangers, flanges, and associated seals.
$1800.00
Founded: 1924

18799 Midwest Distributors Association (MWDA)
222 Merchandise Mart Plaza
Suite 1400
Chicago, IL 60654
312-464-0090
FAX: 312-464-0091
info@mwda.net www.mwda.net

Chris Murin, Executive Director Midwest Region
Dottie Ramsey, Chairman
George Conyngham, Jr., President
Colin Perry, Treasurer
Inge Calderon, Secretary

The mission of the MWDA is to professionally promote the improvement of the industry by providing quality programs, educational and training opportunities to improve operational efficiency and marketing effectiveness, and by facilitating the exchange of ideas and information throughout the distribution channel. The MWDA serves the states of Illinois, Iowa, Kansas, Minnesota, Missouri, Nebraska, North Dakota, South Dakota, Upper Michigan and Wisconsin.
110 Members Founded: 1942

18800 National Kitchen and Bath Association
687 Willow Grove Street
Hackettstown, NJ 07840
908-852-0033
FAX: 732-852-1695 800-843-6522
customerservice@nkba.org
www.nkba.org/

Allan S. Pattison, President
Sara Ann Busby, VP
Max G. Isley, Secretary
Suzie Williford, Treasurer
Larry Spangler, Chief Executive Officer

Protects the interests of members by fostering a better business climate. Awards certification. Conducts training schools and seminars.
30000 Members Founded: 1963

18801 North Central Wholesalers Association/NCWA
3271 Springcrest Drive
Hamilton, OH 45011
513-634-4600
FAX: 513-895-1739 800-537-6585
dan310@earthlink.net
www.asa.net/regional.asp or
www.asa4.org

Dan Schlosser, Exec. Director North Central Region
Dottie Ramsey, Chairman
George Conyngham, Jr., President
Colin Perry, Treasurer
Inge Calderon, Secretary

The NCWA serves wholesale distributors of plumbing, heating, cooling and piping products in Indiana, Michigan, Ohio, Western Pennsylvania and West Virginia, sponsoring educational conferences and offering networking opportunities. During the year NCWA offers its members seminars, workshops, newsletters, industry statistics, an annual regional convention and other traditional trade association programs.
Founded: 1973

18802 Pacific Southwest Distributors
7345 East Evans Road
Suite 704
Scottsdale, AZ 85260-3109
480-991-5703
FAX: 480-991-5704

Robert Bluth, Executive VP

Made up of distributors of heating, cooling and plumbing supplies.

18803 Plastic Pipe and Fittings Association
800 Roosevelt Road
Building C, Suite 20
Glen Ellyn, IL 60137
630-858-6540
FAX: 630-790-3095 www.ppfahome.org

Richard W Church, Executive Director

The Plastic Pipe and Fittings Association (PPFA) is a national trade association of member companies that manufacture plastic piping, fittings and solvent cements for plumbing and related applications, and supply raw materials, ingredients or machinery for the manufacturing process. The PPFA provides relevant information needed to properly design, specify and install plastic piping systems, promoting an understanding of the environmental impact and benefits of thermoplastic piping products.

78 Members Founded: 1978

18804 Plumbing Manufacturers Institute
1340 Remington Road
Suite A
Schaumburg, IL 60173
847-884-9764
FAX: 847-884-9775
pmiadmin@pmihome.org
www.pmihome.org/

Claude Theisen, President
Ken Martin, First VP
Rod Ward, Second VP
Bill Axeline, Treasurer
Barbara Higgens, Executive Director

The Plumbing Manufacturers Institute (PMI) is the trade association of plumbing products manufacturers. The Institute functions as a sounding board for its members, a source for industry and market information, and as a coordinating and decision-making body for dealing with industry issues. It is active in many arenas as it helps develop and maintain standards and codes, and works closely with government agencies at all levels - federal, state and local.

44 Members Founded: 1956

18805 Plumbing and Drainage Institute
800 Turnpike Street
Suite 300
North Andover, MA 01845
978-557-0720
FAX: 978-557-0721 800-589-8956
info@pdionline.org
www.pdionline.org

William Whitehead, Executive Director

An association of manufacturers of engineered plumbing products. Our members and licensees make products such as; flood drains, roof drains, sanitary floor drains, cleanouts, water hammer arresters, swimming pool drains, backwater valves, grease interceptors, fixture supports and other drainage specialties.

14 Members

18806 Plumbing and Mechanical Contractors Associ ation (PMCA)
8600 SW Street Helens Drive
Suite 200
Wilsonville, OR 97217
503-682-7919
FAX: 503-682-6241
www.pmcaoregon.com/

William Sikora, Executive Director

Founded: 1975

18807 Plumbing-Heating-Cooling Contractors National Association
180 South Washington Street
PO Box 6808
Falls Church, VA 22046
703-237-8100
FAX: 703-237-7442 800-533-7694
naphcc@naphcc.org
www.phccweb.org

Jim Stack, President
Jim Finley, VP
Thakur Persuad, Chief Financial Officer
Gerard J Kennedy Jr., Chief Operating Officer
Dwight L. Casey, Chief Executive Officer

An association for professional plumbing/heating/cooling contractors and member firms, that actively lobbies local, state and federal government, providing forums for networking and educational programs, and delivering the highest quality of products and services.

4000 Members Founded: 1883

18808 Southern Wholesalers Association
201 Seaboard Lane
Suite 106
PO Box 681966
Franklin, TN 37068-1966
615-771-3131
FAX: 615-771-3174
terry@southernwholesalers.org
www.southernwholesalers.org/

Terry Shafer, Executive VP
Pam Mrozinski, Administrative Assistant

The Southern Wholesalers Association is a regional association composed of leading Wholesalers of plumbing, heating, and cooling equipment and supplies; pipe, valves and fittings; and water systems throughout the southeast, as well as, Associate Member suppliers and reps to the phcp, pvf and water systems industry.

850 Members Founded: 1928

18809 Sweet Home Public Relations Marketing Support
200 East Randolph Street
Suite 5000
Chicago, IL 60601-6526
312-565-0044
FAX: 312-946-6100
questions@sweethomepr.com
www.sweethomepr.com

Kathy Parker, Director Public Relations
Kristi Grgeta, Marketing Coordinator

Specializes in products for the home including those within the plumbing industry. Services include media relations, product publicity, trade show support.

18810 Valve Manufacturers Association of America (VMA)
1050 17th Street Northwest
Suite 280
Washington, DC 20036
202-331-8105
FAX: 202-296-0378
info@vma.org or wsandler@vma.org
www.vma.org

William Sandler, President
Judy Tibbs, Associate Publisher/Editor-in-Chief
Sue Partyke, Advertising Director
Marc Pasternak, Special & Legislative Assistant

VMA represents the interests of nearly 100 U.S. and Canadian valve and actuator manufacturers who account for approximately 80% of the total industrial valve shipments out of U.S. and Canadian facilities. The American valve industry supplies approximately 35% of worldwide valve demand. VMA member companies employ 20,000 men and women directly in supporting jobs. VMA is the only organization exclusively serving U.S. and Canadian manufacturers of industrial valves and actuators.

100 Members Founded: 1938

18811 Western Suppliers Association
1777 Borel Place
Suite 102
San Mateo, CA 94402-3510
650-341-7222
FAX: 650-341-6408 800-752-8833

Don Robertson, President
Paul Davis, Executive Director
Debbie Wagner, Administrative Manager

A regional office that represents various wholesalers in the heating, plumbing and piping fields.

Newsletters

18812 Plumbing Systems & Design
8614 Catalpa Avenue
Suite 1007
Chicago, IL 60656-1116
773-693-2773
FAX: 773-695-9007
info@aspe.org http://www.aspe.org

Jill Dirksen, Managing/Technical Director
Tom Govedarica, Executive Publisher
Gretchen Pienta, Managing Editor
Tom Markusson, Engineered Plumbing Exposition Mgr.
Dave Ropinski, Graphic Design

Industry leading technical publication with ASPE news and features. Free to ASPE members and subscribers.

Monthly Founded: 1965
Circulation: 27000
Printed in on glossy stock

Magazines & Journals

18813 PM Engineer
Business News Publishing Company
1050 Illinois Route 83
Suite 200
Bensenville, IL 60106-1096
630-694-4006
FAX: 248-502-1023
privacy@BNPMedia.com
www.pmengineer.com

Scott Reimer, Publisher
Julius Ballanco, Editorial Director
Kelly Johnson, Managing Editor
George Zebrowski, Group Publisher
Jim Olsztynski, Consulting Editor

Provides technical sheets, manufacturer product brochures, news features and analysis of useful industry information on the engineering and design of plumbing, piping, hydronics, cooling/heating, and fire protection/sprinkler systems. Free to trade engineers.

80 pages
Circulation: 25000
Printed in 4 colors on glossy stock

18814 PM Plumbing & Mechanical
Business News Publishing Company
1050 Illinois Route 83
Suite 200
Bensenville, IL 60106-1096
630-694-4006
FAX: 630-694-4001
olsztynskij@bnpmedia.com
www.pmmag.com/

George Zebrowski, Publisher
Steve Smith, Editor
Jim Olsztynski, Editorial Director
Katie Rotella, Senior Editor
Stephanie Armstrong, Art Director

Serves plumbing, hydronic heating and mechanical contractors.
Monthly Founded: 1976
Circulation: 45091

18815 Plumbing Engineer
TMB Publishing
1838 Techny Court
Northrook, IL 60062-5474
847-641-1127
FAX: 864-564-1264
editor@plumbingengineer.com
www.plumbingengineer.com/

Mark Bruno, Chief Editor
Susan Ecker, Technical Editor
Marilyn Cunningham, Assistant Editor
Cate Brown, Production Manager
Yoshi Sekiguchi, Art Director

Offers news and updates to plumbing engineers and manufacturers. *$35.00*
Monthly Founded: 1973

18816 Plumbing Standards
American Society of Sanitary Engineering

901 Canterbury Road
Suite A
Westlake, OH 44145
440-835-3040
FAX: 440-835-3488
info@asse-plumbing.org
www.asse-plumbing.org

Shannon M Corcoran, Executive Director
Megan Bryant, Managing Editor
Joseph C. Zaffuto, Staff Engineer
Marla Gasser-Mog, Managing Director
Marianne Waickman, Professional Qualifications Manager

Topics include standards information, updates, water, wastewater, plumbing design guidelines, and technical information pertaining to the water industry. *$12.00*
Quarterly Founded: 1906
Circulation: 15000

18817 Reeves Journal
23421 South Pointe Drive
Suite 280
Laguna Hills, CA 92653
949-830-0881
FAX: 949-859-7845
hendersont@bnpmedia.com
www.reevesjournal.com

Ellyn Fishman, Publisher
Jack Sweet, Editor
Souzan Azar, Production Coordinator
Kati Larson, Sales Representative

Reeves Journal, one of the oldest publications in the plumbing industry, addresses the regional opportunities and challenges facing plumbing/heating/cooling-phc contractors, wholesalers and engineers in the 14 western United States, focusing on the products, issues, codes and regulations relevant to the phc industry.
Monthly Founded: 1926

18818 Supply House Times
American Supply Association
222 Merchandise Mart Plaza
Suite 1400
Chicago, IL 60654-1203
312-464-0090
FAX: 312-464-0091
info@asa.net www.asa.net

Inge Calderon, Executive VP

Articles on plumbing, heating, cooling, and piping products.
50 pages 6 per year
Circulation: 2,500
Mailing list available for rent 4,000 names
Printed in 4 colors on matte stock

18819 United Association Journal
United Associations of Journeymen
United Association Building
901 Massachusetts Avenue NW
Washington, DC 20001-4397
202-285-5071
FAX: 202-628-5024 www.ua.org/

Martin Maddaloni, President
Patrick Perno, General Secretary/Treasurer
Stephen F. Kelly, Assistant General President

On union issues, politics, economics, legislation, energy, environment and consumer affairs.
Monthly Founded: 1889
Circulation: 315000

18820 Valve Magazine
Valve Manufacturers Association of America
1050 17th Street NW
Suite 280
Washington, DC 20036
202-331-8105
FAX: 202-296-0378
info@vma.org www.vma.org or www.valvemagazine.com

William Sandler, President
Judy Tibbs, Editor-in-Chief
Chris Guy, Assistant Editor
Sue Partyke, Advertising

Promotion of significance and application of US and Canadian manufactured industrial valves and actuators. *$36.00*
Quarterly Founded: 1938
Circulation: 30000

Trade Shows

18821 ASPE Engineered Plumbing Exposition
National Trade Show Productions
313 South Patrick Street
Alexandria, VA 22314-1117
703-683-8500
FAX: 703-836-4486 800-687-7469
ntpinfo@ntpshow or info@aspe.org
www.ntpshow.com/ or www.aspe.org

Tom Murkusson, Senior Account Executive
Jenny Bogue, Operations/Director Customer Srvc

A biennial exhibits trade show for the plumbing and engineering industry, the Engineered Plumbing Exposition, sponsored by the American Society of Plumbing Engineers/ASPE, is a gathering of plumbing, engineering and design products, equipment and services. Everything from pipes to pumps to fixtures, from compressors to computers and consulting services, is on display to allow engineers and specifiers to view the newest and most innovative design materials available to them.
7000 Attendees Founded: 1964

18822 Kansas Sports, Boat and Travel Show
Industrial Expositions
1675 Larimer Street
Suite 700
Denver, CO 80202
303-892-6800
FAX: 303-892-6322 800-457-2434
dseymour@iei-expos.com
www.bigasalloutdoors.com

Jeff Haughton, President
Dianne Seymour, Expo Manager

Annual show produced by Industrial Expositions.
Annual

18823 Mid-Atlantic Plumbing Heating Cooling Expo
Reber-Friel Company
221 King Manor Drive
Suite A
King Of Prussia, PA 19406-2500
610-272-4020
FAX: 610-272-5190

Richard Retzback, Show Manager

350 booths featuring products and services used by the plumbing, heating and cooling industries.
4.3M Attendees November

18824 National Plumbing, Heating, Cooling and Piping Products Exposition
American Supply Association
222 Merchandise Mart Plaza
Suite 1400
Chicago, IL 60654
312-464-0090
FAX: 312-464-0091
info@asa.net www.asa.net/

Karen Weeks, Show Manager
Bob Higgason, Owner
George Conyngham Jr., President
Colin Perry, Treasurer
Inge Calderon, Secretary

Offers information and a forum for the exchange of ideas among plumbing, heating and cooling engineers.
11M Attendees

18825 Spring Septic System Conference
Granite State Designers & Installers Association
76 South State Street
Concord, NH 03301-3520
603-228-1231
FAX: 603-228-2118
clough@choiceonemail.com
www.gsdia.org

Walter Perry, Executive Director
Walter Perry, Executive Director
E. Clifford Trafton, Treasurer
Edwin Adriance, Secretary

Conference and trade show with 30 exhibitors and booths for septic system professionals and other allied industries.
400 Attendees March

Directories & Databases

18826 **Complete Directory of Plumbing Products**
Sutton Family Communications & Publishing Company
National Fleamarketeer
155 Sutton Lane
Fordsville, KY 42343
270-740-0870

jlsutton@apex.net
www.fleamarketeer.net

Theresa Sutton, Editor
Lee Sutton, General Manager

Print-out from database of wholesalers, manufacturers, distributors, importers and close-out houses. Database is updated daily to guarantee the most current and up-to-date sources available. *$55.20*
100+ pages

18827 **Directory of Custom Compounders**
Delphi Marketing Services
400 E 89th Street
Apartment 2J
New York, NY 10128-6728

Dr. Newman Giragosian, Editor

Offers information on manufacturers of custom mixtures of plastics and resins. *$295.00*
115 pages Annual

18828 **Directory of Listed Plumbing Products**
Int'l Assn of Plumbing & Mechanical Officials
5001 East Philadelphia Street
Ontario, CA 91761
909-472-4100
FAX: 909-472-4150
iapmo@iapmo.org
www.iapmo.org/iapmo/index.asp

Christopher Salazar, President
Ron Rice, VP
Jay Mundy, Treasurer
Doug Fredericksen, Secretary
Russ Chaney, Executive Director

Directory of products and supplies to the plumbing industry. *$93.00*
1300 pages Monthly

18829 **Plumbing Engineer: Product Directory Issue**
TMB Publishing
1838 Techny Court
Northrook, IL 60062-5474
847-641-1127
FAX: 864-564-1264
editor@plumbingengineer.com
www.plumbingengineer.com/

Mark Bruno, Chief Editor
Susan Ecker, Technical Editor
Marilyn Cunningham, Assistant Editor
Cate Brown, Production Manager
Yoshi Sekiguchi, Art Director

Over 400 plumbing products from approximately 250 manufacturers.
Annual January ISSN 0192-1711
Circulation: 2,6104

18830 **Who's Who in the Plumbing-Heating-Cooling Contracting Business**
Nat'l Assn of Plumbing-Heating-Cooling Contractors
180 South Washington Street
PO Box 6808
Falls Church, VA 22046-2900
703-237-8100
FAX: 703-237-7442 800-533-7694
naphcc@naphcc.org
www.phccweb.org

Julie Turner, Creative Production Director
Benjamin Harris, Director Publications

About 6,000 professional plumbing/heating/cooling contractors and member firms.
$75.00
Annual
Circulation: 15,000

Industry Web Sites

18831 **www.asa.net**
American Supply Association

For industry wholesale distributors and manufacturers.

18832 **www.aspe.org**
American Society of Plumbing Engineers

Seeks to resolve professional problems in plumbing engineering. Operates a certification program.

18833 **www.asse-plumbing.org**
American Society of Sanitary Engineering

Members are from all segments of the plumbing industry, including contractors, engineers, inspectors, journeymen, apprentices and others involved in the industry. Provides information, the opportunity to exchange ideas, solve problems and offers forum where all sides can express their views.

18834 **www.greyhouse.com**
Grey House Publishing

Selected Grey House directories in the fields of business, health and education are available online. Users can search our online databases by several different search criteria, such as product categories, geographic area, sales volume and much, much more. Full Grey House catalog and online ordering also available.

18835 **www.pdionline.org**
Plumbing and Drainage Institute

For manufacturers of engineered plumbing products, flood drains, roof drains, sanitary floor drains, cleanouts, water hammer arresters, swimming pool drains, backwater valves, grease interceptors, fixture supports, and other drainage specialties.

18836 **www.uboiler.com**
Uniform Boiler and Pressure Vessel Laws Society

Established to promote uniformity in rules, laws and regulations for boiler and pressure vessel safety based on the requirements of the American Society of Mechanical Engineers Boiler and Pressure Vessel Code and other related national standards.

18837 **www.vma.org**
Valve Manufacturers Association of America

Associations

18838 Amalgamated Printers Association
304 Mountain View Lane
Laurel, MT 59044-2047
406-928-4757

TWOEMPRESS@aol.com
www.apa-letterpress.org/

Ernie Blitzer, President
Dick Neihaus, VP
Howard Gelbert, Secretary/Treasurer
Rich Hopkins, Director
David Kent, Archivist

The Amalgamated Printers' Association was organized in 1958 as a hobby printers group so that members could improve their skills, expand their knowledge, and exchange samples of their letterpress work in addition to encouraging excellence of printing content, design, and techniques.
150 Members

18839 Assoc. Suppliers of Printing, Publishing & Converting Technologies
1899 Preston White Drive
Reston, VA 20191-4367
703-264-7200
FAX: 703-620-0994
npes@npes.org
www.npes.org/news/whatsnew.html

Ralph J. Nappi, President
William K. Smythe, VP
Douglas Sprei, Director Communications/Marketing
Mercedes Florio, International Exhibitions Manager
Steve Prejsner, Manager of Technology

The Association for Suppliers of Printing , Publishing and Converting Technologies is a trade association that represents manufacturers, importers and distributors of equipment, supplies, systems and software used in every printing, publishing and converting process from design to distribution. Virtually all industry products and processes are represented by the member companies, which range in size from under $1 million in annual sales revenue to more than $1 billion.
460 Members Founded: 1933

18840 Binding Industries of America
Printing Industry of Illinois
200 Deer Run Road
Sewickley, PA 15143
412-741-6860
FAX: 412-741-2311 800-910-4283
gain@piagatf.org www.gain.net/

Michael Makin, President/CEO
George Ryan, Executive VP/COO
Ned Herrick, Conference Manager
Connie Bibbee, VP/Finance and Administration
Nancy Campobello, Director Marketing

A trade association representing trade bindery and looseleaf manufacturers.
350 Members

18841 Book Manufacturers' Institute
Two Armand Beach Drive
Suite 1B
Palm Coast, FL 32137-2316
386-986-4552
FAX: 386-986-4553
info@bmibook.com
www.bmibook.com

Bruce W Smith, Executive Vice President

Since 1933, the Book Manufacturers' Institute, Inc. (BMI) has been the leading nationally recognized trade association of the book manufacturing industry. BMI member companies annually produce the great majority of books ordered by the U. S. book publishing industry. Today, BMI is a vital part of the industry, playing a leading role by providing an intra-industry communications link among book manufacturers, publishers, suppliers and governmental bodies.
90 Members

18842 Center for Book Arts
28 West 27th Street
3rd Floor
New York, NY 10001-6906
212-481-0295
FAX: 212-673-4635
info@centerforbookarts.org
www.centerforbookarts.org/newsite/

Richard Minsky, Chairman
Alexander Campos, Executive Director
Sarah Nicholls, Program Manager
Cindy Au-Kramer, Treasurer
Emily Shei Sadiq, Secretary

The Center for Book Arts is dedicated to preserving the traditional crafts of book-making, as well as exploring and encouraging contemporary interpretations of the book as an art object. Each year the Center offers three terms of courses, workshops and seminars taught by experienced book artists, and providing hands-on training in all aspects of traditional and contemporary bookmaking, including bookbinding, letterpress printing, papermaking, and other associated arts.

18843 Flexographic Technical Association

900 Marconi Avenue
Ronkonkoma, NY 11779-7212
631-737-6020
FAX: 631-737-6813
memberinfo@flexography.org
www.flexography.org/welcome.cfm

Mark Cisternino, President
John Anderson, Technical Director
Michael Schliesmann, Chairman
Kristin Kelly, Director Exhibits/Meetings

Is the leading technical society dedicated to the flexographic printing industry. Promoting, developing and maintaining the advancement of flexography is our prime directive with an emphasis on developing and maintaining standards of quality.
1800 Members Founded: 1958

18844 Foil Stamping and Embossing Association
2150 Southwest Westport Drive
Suite 101
Topeka, KS 66614
785-271-5816
FAX: 785-271-6404
fseamail@fsea.com www.fsea.com

Jeff Peterson, Executive Director
Eric J. Carter, Art Director & Webmaster
Kym Conis, Convention Coordinator
Tracey Gregg, Sales Director

A nonprofit international trade association of foil stampers, embossers, diecutters and industry suppliers working together for the enhancement of the industry.
325 Members
Mailing list available for rent 6000 names $80 per M.

18845 Graphic Communications International Union
1900 L Street Northwest
Washington, DC 20036-5002
202-462-1400
FAX: 202-721-0600
webmessenger@gciu.org
gciu.org/services.shtml

George Tedeschi, President
Robert Lacey, VP / Acting Secretary & Treasurer
Robert Lacey, Contracts & Research
Bonnie R. Lindsley, Information Systems
Herald Grandstaff, Media Director

The international union represents workers in the printing/publishing industry. Members range from desktop operators to paper handler.

18846 Gravure Association of America
1200A Scottsville Road
Rochester, NY 14624
585-436-2150
FAX: 585-436-7689
gaa@gaa.org www.gaa.org

Bill Martin, President/CEO
Laurard Wayland-Smith Hatch, Executive Director
Bruce Beyer, Technicl Director
Sofia Khatkin, Business Manager
Bill Sunter, Technical Director

Provides a forum for the exchange of specialized information through a network of GAA councils which address unique concerns and encourage the use of gravure. These councils include the Gravure Catalog and Insert Council, which brings together catalog and insert publishers as well as other direct marketers; and the Environmental Council, which acts as a liaison and source of information between the gravure industry and regulatory agencies.
200 Members Founded: 1947

18847 IPA
7200 France Avenue South
Suite 223
Edina, MN 55435-4300
952-896-1908
FAX: 952-896-0181 800-255-8141
info@ipa.org www.ipa.org

Steve Bonoff, President
Steven Bonnoff, Executive Director
David Schwak, Chairman
Roni Buczynski, Secretary/Treasurer
Donna McDevitt, Executive Assistant

IPA is a forum for peer networking and a vital source of business, technical and management resources for graphic solutions providers. It is where the industry's leading technical managers strengthen their graphics workflow competencies to create efficiencies and increased profitability. And it is where business leaders acquire tools and management skills for growing a profitable graphic solutions enterprise.
400 Members Founded: 1897

18848 International Association of Printing House Craftsmen (IAPHC)
7042 Brooklyn Boulevard
Minneapolis, MN 55429-1370
763-560-1620
FAX: 763-560-1350 800-466-4274

Kevin P. Keane, President/CEO
Bill Leahy, Chairman
Arthur Mole, Secretary/Treasurer
Cindy Johnson, VP Communications
Tim Vinson, Vice President Marketing

A voluntary graphic arts organization in which many people share their knowledge and their skill with one another. Open to anyone in any part of the graphic arts community who wish technical information.
8M Members Founded: 1919

18849 International Metal Decorators Association (IMDA)
9574 Deereco Rd
Timonium, MD 21093
410-252-5205
FAX: 410-628-8079
info@metaldecorators.org
www.nmda.org/contact.htm

Rick Clendenning, President
Neal Santangelo, VP

The purposes of the IMDA are to foster and encourage improvements and advances in the art of metal decorating and the industrial progress of the metal decorating trade by all lawful means and to stimulate the interest of the members of the Association in improvements in mechanical, technical and manufacturing phases of the metal decorating industry to the end that member concerns may be better informed as to developments in the industry and by the application of such knowledge.

18850 National Association for Printing Leadership (NAPL)
75 West Century Road
Paramus, NJ 07652-1408
201-634-9600
FAX: 201-634-0325 800-642-6275
info@napl.org www.napl.org

Joseph Truncale, President/CEO
Joan Davidson, Chairman
Stephen Johnson, Vice Chairman
Joan Kasper, Senior Director Corporate Planning

A not-for-profit national trade association serving companies in the $100 billion+ graphic communications industry. NAPL offers a comprehensive slate of business and building solutions that provides company leaders with the strategies, insights, and guidance they can use to make informed business decisions, minimize risk, anticipate change, and profitably grow their business.
2000 Members Founded: 1933

18851 National Association of Printing Ink Manufacturers
581 Main Street
Woodbridge, NJ 07095-1104
732-855-1525
FAX: 732-855-1838 www.napim.org

James E Coleman, Executive Director

Purpose is to represent the printing ink industry in the U.S.A. and to provide direction to management in the areas of environmental issues, business management, government regulations and regulatory compliance.

18852 PIA/GATF (PIA)Electronic Prepress Section
200 Deer Run Road
Sewickley, PA 15143
412-741-6860
FAX: 412-741-2311 800-910-4283
gain@piagatf.org www.piagatf.org

Eric Delzer, Chairman
Mary Garnett, VP/Executive Director
Nancy Campobello, Director Marketing
Michael Brickner, Network Manager
Connie Bibbee, VP Finance & Administration

The Printing Industries of America/Graphic Arts Technical Foundation (PIA/GATF), along with its affiliates, deliver products and services that enhance the growth, efficiency, and profitability of its members and the industry through: Advocacy, Education, Research, and Technical information. PIA/GATF serves the interests of more than 12,000 member companies and an industry with more than $16.1 billion in revenue and 1.2 million employees.

18853 Printing Brokerage Buyers Association
227 Royal Poinciana Way
PO Box 744
Suite 204
Palm Beach, FL 33480-0744
561-844-9834
FAX: 561-845-7130 866-586-9391
info@ pbbai.net www.pbbai.net

Vincent Mallardi, Chairman

Promotes business relationships among brokers, buying groups, manufacturers and related companies. Sets standards, codes and supplies information and referrals.

18854 Printing Industries of New England
5 Crystal Pond Road
Southborough, MA 01772-1758
508-804-4100
FAX: 508-804-4119 800-365-7463
webmaster@pine.org www.pine.org

Jim Tepper, President
Thomas Gardner, Chairman
Timothy Donohue, Secretary/Treasurer
Paul J. Marinelli, Chief Financial Officer
Richard Saltzberg, Vice Chairman

Serves more than 450 commercial printing and graphic communications companies throughout five New England states. Provides products and services on an ongoing basis to help member companies operate more profitably.
450 Members Founded: 1887

18855 Printing Industries of Northern California
665 3rd Street
Suite 500
San Francisco, CA 94107
415-950-0797
FAX: 800-824-1911 800-659-3363
info@pinc.org www.pinc.org

Dan Nelson, President
David Katz, VP
Gerry Bonetto, Government Affairs
Jim Frey, Executive VP
Laura Vargas, Member Programs Director

The Printing Industries of Northern California (PINC) is a non-profit trade association serving several industry segments in Northern California, primarily the print production and print buying segments.

18856 Printing Industry Association of the South
PO Box 290249
305 Plus Park Blvd
Nashville, TN 37229
615-366-1094
FAX: 615-366-4192
info@pias.org www.pias.org

Ed Chalifoux, President

The Printing Industry Association of the South (PIAS), a non-profit trade association, is dedicated to assisting the entire industry to continue to expand in the region and help the industry prosper across the seven-state region of Alabama, Arkansas, Kentucky, Louisiana, Mississippi, Tennessee and West Virginia.
520 Members

18857 Printing and Graphic Communications Associ ation
6411 Ivy Lane
Suite 700
Greenbelt, MD 20770

www.pgca.org

Serves the graphic communications community in the Washington, D.C. metropolitan area.
Founded: 1914

18858 Society for Service Professionals in Printing (SSPP)
Document Management Industries Association
433 East Monroe Avenue
Alexandria, VA 22301-1693
703-366-6232
FAX: 703-548-9137 877-777-7398
sspinfo@sspp.org www.sspp.org/

Peter Colainni, Executive Director
Marj Green, Director
Kevin Cooper, Billing Coordinator
Pam Decker, Webmaster

A national organization that focuses on rates, service and trends in the printing industry for consumers. SSPP provides information about both printing and customer service to its members through three monthly newsletters and special interest bulletins. SSPP sponsors the national Certification Examination for Printing Service Specialists (CPSS), which recognizes those printing service specialists who have attained a proscribed body of knowledge about both printing and customer service.
$150.00

18859 Specialty Graphic Imaging Association
10015 Main Street
Fairfax, VA 22031-3489
703-385-1335
FAX: 703-273-0456 888-385-3588
sgia@sgia.org www.sgia.org

Michael Robertson, President/CEO

Participants include corporations, institutions and individuals interested in screen printing. Conducts technical research and training workshops.
Founded: 1986

18860 Waterless Printing Association
Po Box 59800
Chicago, IL 60659

www.waterless.org

Dedicated to the informational and educational needs of its printer and sponsor members. Seeks to inform designers and print buyers about the many benefits the process offers.

Newsletters

18861 Business Printing Technologies Report
DMIA
433 East Monroe Avenue
Alexandria, VA 22301-1645
703-836-6232
FAX: 703-836-2241
dmia@dmia.org www.dmia.org

Timothy J Mehl, President
Peter L Colaianni, Executive VP
Brad Holt, VP Media/Publications
Robert O'Connell, Treasurer
Marj Green, VP Operations

Offers a complete overview of the printing industry.
Annual Founded: 1955
Circulation: 5600

18862 Economic Edge
National Association for Printing Leadership
75 West Century Road
Paramus, NJ 07652-1408
201-634-9600
FAX: 201-986-2976 800-642-6275
info@napl.org www.napl.org

Joseph P Truncale, President/CEO
Timothy Fischer, Chief Operating Officer
Richard S Papale, Director Publications
Cynthia Valentino, Director Marketing/Media Relations
Andrew D Paparozzi, Vice President & Chief Economist

Economic analysis of the graphic arts industry. *$150.00*
12 pages Quarterly Founded: 1933

18863 Footprints
Footprint Communications
4 Blacksmith Hollow
East Hampton, NY 11937
631-329-9972
FAX: 309-213-5733 800-962-5650
mike@footcom.com
www.footcom.com

Dick Vinocur, Publisher

A newsletter for the printing industry reporting news, management, marketing and financial data (including industry stock indexes), product introductions, personnel changes, association affairs and recent acquisitions and mergers. Footprints also reports on exhibits, shows, meetings and conferences in the graphic arts industry. *$327.00*
Fortnightly

18864 Graphic Arts Monthly Online
Reed Business Information
2000 Clearwater Drive
Oakbrook, IL 60523
630-740-0825
FAX: 630-288-8540 800-217-7874
psaran@reedbusiness.com
www.gammag.com/

Phil Saran, Publisher
Bill Esler, Editor-in-Chief
Lisa Cross, Web Site Editor
Stephanie Kauffman, Reprint Management Services

Graphic Arts Monthly Online is a subscriber-based Web portal for printing professionals and print buyers featuring current and archived news, research and business tools, online classifieds, used equipment marketplace and online training and education. *$159.00*
Monthly

18865 Graphic Communicator
Graphic Communications International Union
1900 L Street NW
Washington, DC 20036-5002
202-462-1400
FAX: 202-671-0641
webmessenger@gciu.org
www.gciu.org

Herald Grandstaff, Managing Editor
James Harff, President

Tabloid size newspaper for and about members of the GCIU. The international union represents workers in the printing/publishing industry. Members range from desktop operators to paper handler. *$12.00*
Founded: 1983
Circulation: 100000

18866 Printing News
Cygnus Publishing
3 Huntington Quadrangle
Suite 301N
Melville, NY 11747-3601
631-845-2700
FAX: 631-249-5774 800-308-6397
editor@printingnews.com
www.printingnews.com

David Kastriner, Publisher
Michael Zerner, Associate Publisher
David Lindsay, Editor-in-Chief
Rachel Frank, Editor

Includes timely news and information on a variety of subjects including technological breakthroughs, industry trends, marketing, finance, as well as industry leader and corporate profiles. *$39.95*
Weekly Founded: 1928
Circulation: 9000

18867 SGIA E-News
Specialty Graphic Imaging Association
10015 Main Street
Fairfax, VA 22031-3403
703-385-1335
FAX: 703-273-0456 888-385-3588
assist@sgia.org www.sgia.org

Michael E Robertson, President/CEO
Sondra Fey Benoudiz, VP Marketing

Provides members with access to information relative to industry trends and the latest news such as emerging markets, government regulations, and technological developments. *$149.00*
Bi-Monthly
Circulation: 3800
Printed in 2 colors on glossy stock

18868 Signature Service
Society for Service Professionals in Printing
433 East Monroe Avenue
Alexandria, VA 22301-1693
703-684-0044
FAX: 703-548-9137 877-777-7398
ssppinfo@sspp.org
http://www.sspp.org

Peter Colaianni, Executive Director
Marj Green, Director
Kevin Cooper, Billing Coordinator
Pam Decker, Webmaster

Newsletter covering rates, service and trends in the printing industry for consumers. *$115.00*
8 pages Monthly
Circulation: 2000

Magazines & Journals

18869 American InkMaker
Cygnus Publishing
1233 Janesville Avenue
Fort Atkinson, WI 53538
920-563-6388
FAX: 920-563-1699 800-547-7377
Rich.Reiff@CygnusPub.com
www.inkmakeronline.com

Rich Reiff, President
Robert Stange, Senior VP Marketing

Offers information to the professional ink manufacturer. The editorial content consists of contributed technical papers and nontechnical features about trends, technology and global happenings to help our readers to improve their profitability in addition to featuring a monthly interview with printers. *$46.00*
Founded: 1923
Circulation: 3800

18870 American Printer
PRIMEDIA Business
330 N Wabash
Suite 2300
Chicago, IL 60611
312-595-1080
FAX: 312-840-8455
apeditor@prismb2b.com
www.americanprinter.com

Katherine O'Brien, Editor
Michael P Koch, Senior Art Director
Denise Kapel, Managing Editor
Carrie Cleaveland, Assistant Editor
Jill Roth, Director Brand Development

Regular issue features include new products listings, new equipment technology and reports on system developments.
Monthly Founded: 1991
Circulation: 86037

18871 Awards & Engraving Magazine
National Business Media
2800 West Midway Boulevard
PO Box 1416
Broomfield, CO 80038-1416
303-469-0424
FAX: 303-469-5730 800-669-0424
dpomeroy@nbm.com
www.nbm.com/aemag

Steve Wieber, Editor
Dave Pomeroy, Publisher
Alan Farb, Staff Writer
Matt Peacock, Advertising Executive
Brandy Jamisosn-Neth, Trade Show Coordinator

Content includes a special focus, and regular articles on signage, the glass market, business management, people profiles, and advances in technology. *$38.00*
Monthly Founded: 1985

18872 Big Picture
ST Publications
407 Gilbert Avenue
Cinncinatti, OH 45202-2212
513-421-2050
FAX: 513-421-5144 800-925-1110
efritsch@stpubs.com
www.bigpicture.net

Gregg Sharpless, Editorial Department
Susan Patton, Advertising

Magazine devoted to the business and technology of large-format digital printing. *$42.00*

100 pages Monthly Founded: 1995
Circulation: 48000 48,000 names $200 per M.

18873 Dealer Communicator
Fichera Communications
441 South State Road 7
Suite 14
Margate, FL 33068-2823
954-971-4360
FAX: 954-971-4362 800-327-8999
omike@dealercommunicator.com
www.dealercommunicator.com

Orazio Fichera, Publisher/President
Particia Leavitt, VP

Provides national and international coverage for the graphic arts and printing industries. *$30.00*

32 pages Monthly Founded: 1982
Circulation: 13619
Printed in 4 colors on glossy stock

18874 Digital Graphics
National Business Media
2800 West Midway Boulevard
Suite 104
Broomfield, CO 80020
303-469-0424
FAX: 303-469-5730 800-669-0424
leddleman@nbm.com
www.nbm.com/digitalgraphics

Mary Tohill, Group Publisher
Christine Taraskiewicz, Advertising Executive
Robert H Wieber, CEO/President
Ken Mergentime, Executive Editor
Ethan Elliot, Associate Editor

Regular departments track public stock comapnies of interest to the industry, report on international graphics news and highlight recent technological advances.

64 pages Monthly Founded: 1985
Circulation: 18583 1,000 names $225 per M.
Printed in 4 colors

18875 Digital Output
Rockport Custom Publishing
100 Cummings Center
Ste 123G
Beverly, MA 01915
978-921-7850
www.digitaloutput.net

Tom Terteault, Owner
Lynn Weese, Account Executive

Provides case studies and trend updates, as well as discussing how and why companies integrate and coordinate their marketing strategies.

12 + 2 Buyers Guides

18876 Document Processing Technology
RB Publishing Company
2424 American Lane
PO Box 259906
Madison, WI 53725-9906
608-277-8785
FAX: 608-241-8666 800-536-1992
rbpub@rbpub.com
http://www.rbpub.com

Ron Brent, Publisher/President
Allison Lloyd, Managing Editor
Marll Thiede, Executive Editor/VP
Rachel Spahr, Circulation Manager
Tonjia Weber, Production Manager

Covers digital printing, publishing and distribution. Feature and special topic articles focus on industry trends, technology and strategies for high-volume document processors.

Monthly Founded: 1988
Circulation: 10000

18877 Electronic Publishing
PennWell Publishing Company
1421 South Sheridan Road
Tulsa, OK 74112-2880
918-835-3161
800-331-4463
Headquarters@PennWell.com
www.pennwell.com/ or
www.electronic-publishing.com

Keith Hevenor, Editor
Courtney E Howard, Managing Editor
Frank J Romano, Sr Contributing & Founding Editor
Nancy A Hitchcock, Senior Associate Editor

For those who communicate in print, including service bureaus, printers, prepress houses and desktop publishers, it provides latest products, news and related developments. *$59.00*

Monthly Founded: 1910
Circulation: 68441

18878 Flash Magazine
BlackLighting
252 Riddle Pond Road
West Topsham, VT 05086
800-252-2599
FAX: 802-439-6462 800-252-2599
salesBL@BlackLightning.com
www.flashweb.com

Walter Vose Jeffries, Publisher

Flash Magazine was started in 1989 and is all about desktop publishing, book-on-demand binding, inkjet & laser printinting, heat transfers and other topics of interest to the small time publisher and graphic artist. The Flash is filled with great how-to articles that will help you take care of your printer, do maintenance & repairs yourself, teach you about graphics, digital photography, scanning and laser etching glass and book-on-demand publishing, binding and so much more. *$20.00*

Monthly
Circulation: 112000

18879 Flexo Magazine
Flexographic Technical Association
900 Marconi Avenue
Ronkonkoma, NY 11779-7212
631-737-6020
FAX: 631-737-6813
membership@flexography.org
www.flexography.org

Robert Moran, Publisher
Jonna Jefferis, Editor
Christian Bonawandt, Associate Editor
Mark Cisternino, President

Trade publication for the flexographic printing industry. *$55.00*

Monthly
Circulation: 12,000
Printed in 4 colors on glossy stock

18880 Forms & Direct Mail Manufacturer's Marketplace
Bulls-Eye Communications
211 Champion Avenue
Webster, NY 14580
585-265-3045
waterford@waterfordweb.com

Marsha A Thompson, Editor

The resource magazine of business forms and direct mail printers. Spotlights news and products in the industry. *$49.00*

Bi-Monthly
Circulation: 4,870

18881 Graphic Communications World
Hayzlett & Associates
3313 South Western Avenue
Sioux Falls, SD 57106
605-355-5531
FAX: 605-275-2087
www.hayzlett.com/index.htm

Jeanette Clinkunbroomer, Editor
Jeff Hayzlett, Owner

Offers a comprehensive overview of the graphic arts and communications industry. *$347.00*

Monthly Founded: 1968

18882 Gravure
Gravure Association of America
1200A Scottsville Road
Rochester, NY 14624-5703
585-436-2150
FAX: 585-436-7689
lwshatch@gaa.org www.gaa.org

Laura Wayland-Smith Hatch, Editor
William Martin, President/CEO

Editorial coverage focuses on the technical developments in gravure printing, the financial performance of the industry and association member activities. *$67.00*

Founded: 1987
Circulation: 3500
Printed in 4 colors on matte stock

18883 High Volume Printing (HVP)
Innes Publishing Company
28100 North Ashley Circle
PO Box 7280
Libertyville, IL 60048
847-816-7900
FAX: 847-247-8855 800-247-3306
meinnes@innespub.com
www.innespub.com

Mary Ellen Innes, Publisher
Ray Roth, Editor
Barb Pettersen, Circulation Manager
Mary Ellin Innes, President
Judy Abbott, Administrative Assistant

HVP offers a strategic mix of management and production-oriented editorial content, and has consistently led in coverage of new technologies and regulatory issues. It focuses on the bottom-line realities involved in merging tomorrow's technologies with today's operating environment. Subjects include prepress, press, and postpress equipment and technology, sales and marketing management, training, regulatory issues and more.

Founded: 1982
Circulation: 39057

18884 IPA Bulletin
IPA: Association of Graphic Solutions Providers
7200 France Avenue South
Suite 223
Edina, MN 55435
952-961-1908
FAX: 708-596-5112 800-255-8141
bessie@ipa.org www.ipa.org

Bessie Halfacre, Editor
Becky Walroth, Editorial Assistant
Annette Wolfe, Editorial Assistant
Steven Bonoff, President

Association news offering information on prepress and graphic arts. *$20.00*

6 pages Founded: 1911
Circulation: 2,100
Printed in 4 colors on glossy stock

18885 In Plant Graphics
North American Publishing Company
1500 Spring Garden Street
Suite 1200
Philadelphia, PA 19130
215-238-5300
FAX: 215-238-5457
editor.ipg@napco.com
www.ipgonline.com

Bob Neubauer, Editor
Glen Reynolds, Publisher
Dorlissa Goodrich, Production Manager
Maggie Tajack, Advertising Promotion Manager
Brian Ludwig, Group Publisher

Articles include management advice, technical information, industry news and reader profiles. *$65.00*

60 pages Monthly Founded: 1996
Circulation: 20,000
Printed in 4 colors on glossy stock

18886 In Plant Printer
Innes Publishing Company
28100 North Ashley Circle
Suite 101
Libertyville, IL 60048
847-816-7900
FAX: 847-247-8855 800-247-3306
meinnes@innespub.com
www.innespub.com

Mary Ellin Innes, President
Jack Klasnic, Editor
Barbara Pettersen, Circulation Manager
Teri Saeed, Production Manager
Judy Abbott, Administrative Assistant

Serves printing, graphics and typesetting facilities located in business, industry, education, government, hospitals, associations, and nonprofit organizations. *$110.00*

70 pages Monthly Founded: 1977
Circulation: 247637
Printed in 4 colors on glossy stock

18887 Ink World
Rodman Publications
70 Hilltop Road
Ramsey, NJ 07446
201-825-2552
FAX: 201-825-0553
inksales@rodpub.com
www.inkworldmagazine.com

Rodman Zilenziger, President
David Savastano, Editor
Ellen Pfister, Circulation Manager
Donna Feiler, Advertising Sales
Dale Pritchett, Publisher

Covers the printing inks, coatings and allied industries.

64 pages Monthly Founded: 1994
Circulation: 6187
Printed in 4 colors on glossy stock

18888 Inside Finishing Magazine
Foil Stamping and Embossing Association

2150 Southwest Wesport Drive
Suite 101
Topeka, KS 66614
785-271-5816
FAX: 785-271-6404
fseamail@fsea.com www.fsea.com

Jeff Peterson, Executive Director
Tracey Gregg, Sales Director

A quarterly magazine published by the Foil Stamping and Embossing Association, Inside Finishing has a targeted circulation of 6,000 graphic finishing decision makers. These include trade finishers, folding carton companies, greeting card manufacturers, and commercial printers with finishing/bindery operations. It also includes a small percentage of graphic designers involved in the foil stamping and embossing industry, and, of course, industry suppliers to the graphic finishing industry.

56 pages 4 issues Founded: 1994 6000 names $80 per M.

18889 Instant and Small Commercial Printer ISCP
Innes Publishing Company
28100 North Ashley Circle
PO Box 7280
Libertyville, IL 60048-7280
847-816-7900
FAX: 847-247-8855 800-247-3306
daninnes@innespub.com
www.innespub.com

Dan Innes, Publisher
Linda Casey, Editor
Barb Pettersen, Circualtion MAnager
Mary Ellin Innes, President

ISCP magazine publishes "how-to" articles and case histories on printing and photocopy reproduction. Emphasis on desktop publishing and short-run digital technologies reflects the growth of this service in instant printing operations. Management stories are aimed at helping the publication's largely entrepreneurial audience grapple successfully with everyday problems and spot new opportunities for growth.

Monthly Founded: 1982
Circulation: 413671

18890 Label & Narrow Web Industry
Rodman Publications
70 Hilltop Road
Ramsey, NJ 07446
201-825-2552
FAX: 201-825-0553
label@rodpub.com
www.labelandnarrowweb.com

Kathleen Scully, Publisher
Rodman J Zilenziger Jr, President
Jack Kenny, Editor
Ellen Pfister, Circulation Manager
Cheryl Risi, Production Manager

Label and Narrow Web serves manufacturers of label and narrow web including labels, tags, tape, materials, substrates, machinery, and equipment and others allied to the field.

80 pages Founded: 1996
Circulation: 11000
Printed in 4 colors on glossy stock

18891 New England Printer and Publisher
5 Crystal Pond Road
Southborough, MA 01772-1758
508-044-4170
FAX: 508-804-4119 800-365-7463
jtepper04@pine.org www.pine.org

James J Tepper, President
John Scibelli, Editor
Brie Drummond, Production Manager

Trade magazine for printers and publishers. *$2.40*

48 pages Monthly Founded: 1938
Circulation: 4000
Printed in 4 colors on matte stock

18892 New Pages: Alternatives in Print and Media
New Pages Press
PO Box 1580
Bay City, MI 48706
989-671-0081
FAX: 313-743-2730
newpagesonline@hotmail.com
www.newpages.com

Casey Hill, Publisher
Denise Hill, Editor

News and information for bookstores and libraries. *$12.00*

64 pages Quarterly

18893 Newspapers & Technology
Conley Magazines
1623 Blake Street
Suite 250
Denver, CO 80202
303-575-9595
FAX: 303-575-9555
letters@newsandtech.com
www.newsandtech.com/

Mary Van Meter, Publisher
Chuck Moozakis, Editor-in-Chief
Tara McKeekin, Editor
Hays Goodman, Associate Editor/Webmaster

Newspapers & Technology is a monthly trade publication for newspaper publishers and department managers involved in applying and integrating technology. Written by industry experts, News & Tech provides regular coverage of the following departments: prepress, press, postpress and new media.

Circulation: 16,874

18894 PC Presentations Productions
Pisces Publishing Group
1400 South Nova Road
Suite 303
Daytona Beach, FL 32114-5851
203-877-1927
FAX: 203-877-1927
www.piscespub.com

Don Johnson, Editor/Publisher
Douglas Finlay, Managing Editor

PC Presentations Productions is a free online magazine intended for both the high-end professional and the student. Graphic and video tutorials for intermediate and advanced content producers are regular features as are HTML and Javascript tutorials and Website design tutorials intended for students and others wishing to add these skills.

Weekly

18895 Package Printing
North American Publishing Company
1500 Spring Garden Street
Suite 1200
Philadelphia, PA 19130
215-385-5300
FAX: 215-238-5429 800-627-2689
customerservice@napco.com
www.packageprinting.com

Tom Polischuk, Editor-in-Chief
Brian Ludwick, Publisher
Robert Margulies, Sales Manager
Megan Wolf, Assistant Editor
Sean Sams, Advertising Account Manager

Trade publication serving the business and technology needs of presidents and CEOs of flexible packaging, tag and label, folding rigid boxes and directing operations. *$99.50*

75 pages Monthly Founded: 1958
Circulation: 24000

18896 **Paper Magazine**
365 Broadway
6th Floor
New York, NY 10013
212-226-4405
FAX: 212-226-0062 800-829-9160
edit@papermag.com
www.papermag.com

Sharon Phair, Advertising & Marketing
Kim Hastreiter, Publisher
Alexis Swerdloff, Associate Editor
David Hershkovits, Editor
Carol Lee, Creative Director

PAPER Magazine focuses on the latest trends in pop culture, style, music and film, including information on New York art exhibits, club listings, literary events, movie reviews and shows. Includes night-life guide. *$9.97*
10 Issues Per Year Founded: 1984
Circulation: 90,000

18897 **Presstime**
Newspaper Association of America
1921 Gallows Road
Suite 600
Vienna, VA 22182-3900
703-902-1600
FAX: 703-917-0636
Su-Lin.Nichols@naa.org www.naa.org

Rebecca Albers, VP and Editor
Jeff Lemberg, Managing Editor
A S Berman, Associate Editor
Su-Lin Cheng Nichols, Senior VP Communications
Pamela Norman Higbie, Art Director

Serves Newspaper Association of America members and non-member executives and staffs, government officials, journalism schools and others allied to the field. *$175.00*
Monthly
Circulation: 17000
Printed in 4 colors on glossy stock

18898 **Print Business Register**
Cygnus Business Media
3 Huntington Quadrangle
Melville, NY 11747
631-845-2700
FAX: 631-249-5774
www.cygnusb2b.com

Michael Zerner, Publisher
Rachel Frank, Editor

Editorial material reports on mergers, acquisitions, reorganizations and major issues affecting the marketplace of the commercial printing industry.
Weekly
Circulation: 650

18899 **Print Magazine**
RC Publications
38 east 29th street, 3rd floor
New York, NY 10016
212-447-1430
FAX: 212-447-5231
info@printmag.com
www.printmag.com

Joel Toner, Publisher

Regular highlights include advertising and promotion design, corporate identity, design education and film/TV production. Also covered are creative trends and technological advances in photography, printing, web design, illustration, motion graphics and packaging. Includes profiles of visual artists, ad agencies and graphic design firms. *$37.00*
Monthly
Circulation: 54149

18900 **Print Solutions Magazine**
Document Management Industries Association
433 East Monroe Avenue
Alexandria, VA 22301-1693
703-366-6232
FAX: 703-549-4966 800-336-4641
editors@formmag.com
www.formmag.com

Peter L Colaianni CAE, Editor-in-Chief
Preeti Vasishtha, Assistant Editor
Lashell Stratton, Assistant Editor
Rebecca Trela, Assistant Editor

The independent's source for marketing, management and product information. *$49.00*
276 pages Monthly Founded: 1962
Circulation: 42000
Printed in 4 colors on glossy stock

18901 **Print on Demand Business**
Cygnus Business Media
3 Huntington Quadrangle
Suite 301N
Melville, NY 11747
631-845-2700
FAX: 631-845-2741
Bob@quickprinting.com
www.cygnusb2b.com/

Bob Hall, Executive Editor
Denise Gustavson, Managing Editor

Editorial includes a look at new products, industry news, updated technology, tips on the best equipment and a look ahead with an upcoming calendar of events.
Bi-Monthly

18902 **PrintImage Network**
PrintImage International
2250 East Devon Avenue
Suite 245
Des Plaines, IL 60018
847-298-8680
FAX: 847-298-8705
info@printimage.org
www.printimage.org

Keith Kemp, Chairman
Dale Aigner, Secretary/Treasurer
Steven D Johnson, President/CEO
Christina Vargas, VP
Steve Mills, Technology Director

Editorial content covers technological advances, product news, profiles on industry leaders, and club events.
Quarterly
Circulation: 4000

18903 **Printing Impressions**
North American Publishing Company
1500 Spring Garden Street
Suite 1200
Philadelphia, PA 19130
215-238-5300
FAX: 215-238-5217 800-627-2689
mmichelson@napco.com
www.napco.com

Mark T Michelson, Editor-in-Chief
Chris Bauer, Managing Editor
Tunisia Bey, Circulation Manager

Offers news, articles, updates, statistics, research reports and more for the printing industry including printers involved in commercial and newspaper printing and trades.
Weekly Founded: 1958
Circulation: 83035

18904 **Printing Industry Association of the South - Magazine**
Printing Industry Association of the South
305 Plus Park Blvd
Nashville, TN 37229-249
615-366-1094
FAX: 615-366-4192
info@pias.org http://www.pias.org

Ed Chalifoux, President
James Tepper, Board Member

Print industry information. Free with membership.
Monthly
Circulation: 5000
Printed in 4 colors on glossy stock

18905 **Printing Manager**
National Association of Printing Leadership
75 West Century Road
Paramus, NJ 07652-1408
201-634-9600
FAX: 201-634-0324 800-642-6275
Information@napl.org www.napl.org

Joseph P Truncale, President/CEO
Ron Mihills, Managing Director
Richard S Papale, Director of Publications

Provides current news for printing executives including the latest industry, marketing and management news.
40 pages Quarterly Founded: 1933
Circulation: 6000
Printed in 4 colors

18906 **Printing News Magazine**
Cygnus Business Media
3 Huntington Quadrangle
Suite 301N
Melville, NY 11747
631-845-2700
FAX: 631-249-5774
editor@printingnews.com
www.printingnews.com

David Kastriner, Publisher
Michael Zerner, Associate Publisher
David Lindsay, Editor-in-Chief
Rachel Frank, Editor

News and information on the graphic arts industry in New York, Connecticut, New Jersey and Pennsylvania. *$39.95*
44 pages Founded: 1937
Circulation: 7000

18907 **Printing News Online**
Cygnus Business Media
3 Huntingon Quadrangle
Suite 301N
Melville, NY 11747
631-845-2700
FAX: 631-249-5774 800-308-6397
editor@printingnews.com
www.printingnews.com

David Kastriner, Publisher
Michael Zerner, Associate Publisher
David Lindsay, Editor-in-Chief
Rachel Frank, Editor

Includes timely news and information on a variety of subjects including technological breakthroughs, industry trends, marketing, finance, as well as industry leader and corporate profiles.

18908 Publishing Executive
North American Publishing Company
1500 Spring Garden Street
Suite 1200
Philadelphia, PA 19130
215-238-5300
FAX: 215-238-5457
nskodzinski@napco.com
www.printmediamag.com/

Mark Hertzog, Group Publisher
Noelle Skodzinski, Editor-in-Chief
Matt Steinmetz, Associate Editor
Rhoda Dixon, Circulation Manager
Candas Carmen, Associate Publisher

Publishing Executive (formerly PrintMedia) delivers information to magazine publishers, associations, corporate publishers, advertising and marketing agencies.

Circulation: 17500

18909 Quick Printing
Cygnus Business Media
3 Huntington Quadrangle
Suite 301N
Melville, NY 11747-803
631-845-2700
FAX: 631-845-2741
Bob@quickprinting.com
www.quickprinting.com

Jann Levesque, Group Publisher
Kelley Holmes, Publisher
Bob Hall, Editor
Denise Gustavson, Managing Editor

Business journal for those in the printing business. *$66.00*
Monthly Founded: 1937
Circulation: 48000

18910 SGIA Journal
Speciality Graphic Imaging Association
10015 Main Street
Fairfax, VA 22031-3489
703-385-1335
FAX: 703-273-0456 888-385-3588
sgia@sgia.org www.sgia.org

Mike Robertson, Production Manager

Published quarterly in January, April, July and October.
Founded: 1948
Circulation: 14000

18911 Screen Printing
ST Publications
407 Gilbert Avenue
Cincinnati, OH 45202-2212
513-421-2050
FAX: 513-421-5144 800-925-1110
customer@stmediagroup.com
www.stmediagroup.com

Steve Duccilli, Publisher
Fred Frecska, Editor

This magazine includes screen printing: supplies, product news, industry news, reports, and management information for screen printers. *$39.00*
150 pages Monthly Founded: 1953
Circulation: 17000 17,000 names $200 per M.
Printed in 4 colors

18912 Signs of the Times & Screen Printing en Espanol
ST Publications
407 Gilbert Avenue
Cincinnati, OH 45202-2212
513-421-2050
FAX: 513-421-5144 800-925-1110
cristina.mella@stmediagroup.com
www.stmediagroup.com/index.php3?d=pubs&p=ssen

Steve Duccilli, Publisher
Nancy Bottoms, Associate Publisher
Cristina Mella, Customer Service (Spanish Speaking)

The publication covering the signmaking, screen printing and digital imaging industries for the Spanish-speaking visual communication markets. *$40.00*
100 pages Monthly Founded: 1995
Circulation: 17000

18913 Wide Format Imaging Magazine
Cygnus Publishing
3 Huntington Quadrangle
Suite 301 North
Melville, NY 11747
631-845-2700
FAX: 631-845-2741 800-308-6397
davis@wide-formatimaging.com
www.wide-formatimaging.com

David Nathenson, Publisher
Karen Lowry-Hall, Editor
Denise M Gustavson, Managing Editor/Web Editor
Charlie Lillis, Director Content Licensing
Katie Brennan, Vice President

Wide Format Imaginging Magazine provides information on new technologies, analysis of new products, business management tips, and profiles of significant people in the industry. The magazine is a monthly business publication serving 18,000 wide-format professionals. These mostly small business owners are responsible for wide- and large-format drawings, blueprints, soft signage, outdoor signage, posters, POP displays, digital fine art printmaking, and large trade show graphics. *$25.00*
Monthly

Trade Shows

18914 CMM International
Paperloop
212-268-4160
FAX: 212-268-4178
wparsley@paperloop.com
www.cmmshow.com
The premier converting and package printing event for thousands of professionals.
June4-7 Chicago Founded: 1978

18915 Graphic Arts
Graphic Arts Show Company
1899 Preston White Drive
Reston, VA 20197-4367
703-264-7200
FAX: 703-620-9187
info@gasc.org www.gasc.org

Chris Thiel, VP
Kelly Kilga, Director Operations
Regis Del Montagne, President

One of America's foremost regional prepress, printing, publishing, and converting trade shows. 300 booths, 70,000 square feet.
18000 Attendees March 47,000 names

18916 Graphics of the Americas
Printing Association of Florida
6275 Hazeltine National Drive
Orlando, FL 32822
407-240-8009
FAX: 407-240-8333
gain@piagatf.org www.pafgraf.org

Bill Maguire, Chairman
Larry Kudeviz, Treasurer
Rob Hasson, First Vice Chairman
Art Abbott, Second Vice Chairman

We are the second largest Graphic Arts and Converting show in America. We give you two vital markets, Southeast US and Latin America: Mexico, South America, Central America and the Caribbean. Our 28 year track record reflects our success with both exhibitors and show visitors.
20000 Attendees

18917 Gutenberg Festival
Graphic Arts Show Company
6275 Hazeltine National Drive
Orlanda, FL 32822
407-240-8009
FAX: 407-240-8333
info@gasc.org www.gasc.org

Kelly Kilga, Conference/Show Operations Director
Lilly Kinney, Conference Manager
Tina Scott, Exhibit Sales Director
Chrissie Hahn, Exhibit Sales Manager

The top printing event on the west coast and the only place to see live running equipment both traditional and digital.
15000 Attendees April

18918 Labelexpo America
Tarsus Group Plc

sales@labelexpo.com
www.labelexpo-americas.com
Label, printing, decoration, web printing and converting industry's largest expo.
Sept, Chicago

18919 National Association of Professional Print Buyers
15050 Northeast 20th Avenue
Suite A
North Miami, FL 33181-1123
305-956-9563

Vincent Mallardi, Executive Director

400 booths.
2.5M Attendees April Founded: 1969

18920 Non-Impact Printing Conference and Exhibit
IS&T-The Society for Imaging Science & Technology
7003 Kilworth Lane
Springfield, VA 22151-4008
703-642-9090
FAX: 703-642-9094
info@imaging.org www.imaging.org
Annual conference and exhibits of non-impact printing equipment, supplies and services, including printer components, printer consumables, paper and document handling devices and display units.
620 Attendees

18921 Print
Graphic Arts Show Company
1899 Preston White Drive
Reston, VA 20191-5435
703-264-7200
FAX: 703-620-9187
info@gasc.org www.gasc.org

Chris Thiel, VP
Jackie Wolfe, Director Operations

Showcase of printing, publishing and converting technologies. 1100 booths.
September

18922 Print & Converting Expo
Graphic Arts Show Company
1899 Preston White Drive
Reston, VA 20191-5435
703-264-7200
FAX: 703-620-9187
info@gasc.org www.gasc.org
Chris Thiel, VP
Kelly Kilga, Director Operations
David Poulos, Director Communications

This is the largest, most comprehensive event for the commercial, package printing and converting industry in the world in 2005. This huge international event held every four years offers you more running machinery under one roof than any other event anywhere.
70000 Attendees September/Annual
Founded: 1968
Mailing list available for rent

18923 Print Media Conference & Expo
c/o North American Publishing Company
1500 Spring Garden St, Suite 1200
Philadelphia, PA 19130-4094

FAX: 215-409-0100 888-627-2630
printmediaexpo@napco.com
www.pubxpo.com

18924 SGIA Technology Show
SGIA
10015 Main Street
Fairfax, VA 22031
703-385-1335
FAX: 703-273-0469 888-385-3588
convention@sgia.org www.sgia.org
Sylvia Hall, VP Conventions/Conferences
Michael Robertson, President

Technologies showcased include: embossing, printing, graphics, digital imaging, screen printing and embroidering.
14000 Attendees September Founded: 1948

18925 Vue/Point Conference
Graphic Arts Show Company
1189 Preston White Drive
Reston, VA 22091-4367
703-264-7200
FAX: 703-620-9187
info@gasc.org www.gasc.org
David Poulos, Conference Coordinator

Presents topics via panel discussions composed of printing professionals who are willing to share their experiences.

Directories & Databases

18926 Coldset Web Offset Directory
Printing Industries of America/Graphic Arts
Technical Foundation (PIA/GATF)
200 Deer Run Road
Sewickley, PA 15143
412-741-6860
FAX: 412-741-2311 800-910-4283
gain@piagatf.org www.gain.net
Tom Destree, Editor-in-Chief
Eric Delzer, Chairman
Michael Makin, President/CEO

Over 600 printing firms with more than 1,000 presses in the US, Puerto Rico and Canada are profiled. *$120.00*
BiAnnual

18927 Directory International Suppliers/Printing Publishing/Converting Technologies

Association for Suppliers of Printing, Publishing
& Converting Technologies
1899 Preston White Drive
Reston, VA 20191-4367
703-264-7200
FAX: 703-620-0994
npes@npes.org www.npes.org
Ralph J Nappi, President
Douglas Sprei, Director Marketing/Communications
Jesus A Romero, Database Manager
Steve Prejsner, Manager of Technology

An online, freely accessible, association database of NPES member companies and more than 500 products, searchable by product category, keyword or company name.
220 pages Biennial

18928 Heatset Web Offset Directory
Printing Industries of America/Graphic Arts
Technical Foundation (PIA/GATF)
200 Deer Run Road
Sewickley, PA 15143
412-741-6860
FAX: 412-741-2311
gain@piagatf.org www.gain.net/
Tom Destree, Editor-in-Chief
Eric Delzer, Chairman
Michael Makin, President/CEO

Offers information on nearly 500 heatset web printing firms in the United States, Puerto Rico and Canada including products produced. *$50.00*
110 pages BiAnnually

18929 In Plant Reproductions: Buyer's Guide Issu e
North American Publishing Company
401 N Broad Street
Philadelphia, PA 19108-1001
215-238-5300
FAX: 215-238-5457 800-627-2689
Bob Neubauer, Editor

Firms that manufacture or supply equipment, materials and services to printing facilities of firms or organizations, including art, paste-up and copy preparation, mailing systems, darkroom equipment, presses, paper, word processing, computerized composition and electronic publishing. *$35.00*
Annual December
Circulation: 41,000

18930 International Directory of Private Presses
Educators Research Service
2443 Fair Oaks Boulevard
Suite 316
Sacramento, CA 95825-7684

Offers valuable information on over 1,200 private presses and hobbyist printers worldwide. *$50.00*
300 pages Annual

18931 Print Image International
401 N Michigan Avenue
Suite 2100
Chicago, IL 60611-4245
312-268-8015
FAX: 312-321-6869 800-234-0640
John Giles, Editor
Steve Johnson, President

300 pages

18932 Rauch Guide to the US Ink Industry
Grey House Publishing
PO Box 860
Millerton, NY 12546
518-789-8700
FAX: 518-789-0545 800-562-2139
books@greyhouse.com
www.greyhouse.com
Leslie Mackenzie, Publisher
Richard Gottlieb, President

Approximately 287 manufacturers of ink.
$595.00
Annual

18933 Rauch Guide to the US and Canadian Pulp & Paper Industry
Grey House Publishing
PO Box 860
Millerton, NY 12546
518-789-8700
FAX: 518-789-0545 800-562-2139
books@greyhouse.com
www.greyhouse.com
Leslie Mackenzie, Publisher
Richard Gottlieb, President

Approximately 507 manufacturers of pulp, paper and converted products. *$595.00*
Annual

18934 Who's Who SGIA
Screenprinting and Graphic Imaging Assn Int'l
10015 Main Street
Fairfax, VA 22031-3403
703-385-1335
FAX: 703-273-0469
sgia@sgia.org www.sgia.org
Mike Robertson, Production Manager

Founded: 1948
Circulation: 3,800

Industry Web Sites

18935 www.fsea.com
Foil Stamping and Embossing Association

For companies engaged in the process of hot stamping or embossing in the graphics industry and companies that manufacture, distribute or provide services to the hot stamping/embossing industry.

18936 www.gaa.org
Gravure Association of America

Members are gravure printers, converters, suppliers and users.

18937 www.greyhouse.com
Grey House Publishing

Selected Grey House directories in the fields of business, health and education are available online. Users can search our online databases by several different search criteria, such as product categories, geographic area, sales volume and much, much more. Full Grey House catalog and online ordering also available.

18938 www.iaphc.org
International Assn of Printing House Craftsmen

A voluntary graphic arts organization in which many people share their knowledge and their skill with one another. Open to anyone in any part of the graphic arts community who wish technical information.

18939 www.ipa.org
International Prepress Association

Members produce pre-press material for the graphics industry.

18940 www.magazine.org
Magazine Publishers of America

Promotes magazines as an advertising medium. Provides information services and assistance to members in areas of circulation marketing.

18941 www.napim.org
National Association of Printing Ink Manufacturers

Purpose is to represent the printing ink industry in the U.S.A.

18942 www.napl.org
National Association for Printing Leadership

Promotes the interests in leadership for priniting professionals.

18943 www.npes.org
NPES-Association for Suppliers of Printing &
Publishing Technology

Members are manufacturers and distributors of graphic arts equipment, systems, software and supplies. Promotes marketing, safety and industry standards, international trade and government relations.

18944 www.pbbai.net
Printing Brokerage Buyers Assoc International

Promotes business relationships among brokers, buying groups, manufacturers and related companies. Sets standards and codes and supplies information and referrals.

18945 www.pgca.org
Printing and Graphic Communications Association

Serving the graphic communications community in the Washington, D.C. metropolitan area.

18946 www.pias.org
Printing Industry Association of the South

Represents the print industry.

18947 www.pinc.org
Print Buyers Association

For professionals in print buying.

18948 www.pine.org
Printing Institute of New England

18949 www.polymers.com
Polymers DotCom

18950 www.printing.org
Printing Industries of America (PIA)

The largest graphic arts organization founded over 100 years ago.

18951 www.teched.Vt.edu/gcc
Graphic Comm Central

Web portal for education in the graphic communications industry.

18952 www.waterless.org
Waterless Printing Association

Dedicated to the informational and educational needs of its printer and sponsor members.

Associations

18953 American Society of Health Care Marketing
1 N Franklin Street
Chicago, IL 60606-3421
773-327-1064
FAX: 312-422-4579

18954 Arthur W Page Society
32 Avenue of the Americas
Suite S638
New York, NY 10013
212-387-4259
FAX: 212-387-4028
admin@awpagesociety.com
www.awpagesociety.com
Thomas R Martin, President
Peter D Debreceny, VP
Valerie Di Maria, VP
Professional public relations organization with a single mission, to strengthen the management policy role of the chief public relations officer. Conducts seminars and conferences.
315 Members Founded: 1983

18955 Association of Women in Communications
780 Ritchie Highway
Suite 28-S
Severna Park, MD 21146
410-544-7442
FAX: 410-544-4640
emoy@womcom.org
www.womcom.org
Patricia Troy, Executive Director
Betsy Earley, Director Publications
Nancy Badertscher, Membership Director
Brenda Gracely, Public Relations Director

Professional organization that champions the advancement of women across all communications disciplines by recognizing excellence, promoting leadership and positioning its members at the forefront of the evolving communications era.
4600 Members Founded: 1909

18956 Automotive Public Relations Council
10 Laboratory Drive
PO Box 13966
Research Triangle Park, NC 27709
919-549-4800
FAX: 919-549-4824
hampshart@mema.org
www.aprc-online.org
Neal Zipser, Director
Jobie Dowd, Assistant Director
Provides a forum for information exchange among communication professionals with the automotive industry. Two conferences are held every year, topics are integrated marketing, communications and the automotive industry.
70 Members Founded: 1974

18957 Baptist Communicators Association

PO Box 270127
Nashville, TN 37227
615-329-7543

Mark Wingfield
PR and Journalism profesionals.
300 Members Founded: 1953

18958 Career Skills Press
Brody Communications
815 Greenwood Avenue
Suite 8
Jemkintown, PA 19046
215-886-1688
FAX: 215-886-1699 800-726-7936
brody@brodycommunications.com
www.brodycommunications.com
Marjorie Brody, President
Miryam S Roddy, Marketing Manager
Releases one to three new titles each calendar year in the business/self-help categories. Business communication skills books, self-help and career titles.
Founded: 1983

18959 Communications Roundtable
1250 24th Street NW
Suite 250
Washington, DC 20037
202-755-5180
FAX: 202-466-0544
www.roundtable.org
Michael Reichgut, Chairman
Shawn Dolley, Chief Executive Officer
Association of more than 20 public relations, marketing, graphics, advertising, training and other communications organizations with more than 12,000 professional members. The goals include furthering professionalism, cooperation between member organizations, career and employment support, and employer assistance.

18960 Consultants in Public Relations SA
4200 Massachusetts Avenue NW
Washington, DC 20016
202-244-2580
FAX: 202-224-2581
jreed94680@ad.com
John M Reed, Chairman
Founded: 1970

18961 Council of Communications Management
65 Enterprise
Aliso Viejo, CA 92656
866-463-6226
FAX: 949-330-7621
www.ccmconnection.com
Established more than 40 years ago as a forum for seasoned professionals to share best practices in organizational communications.

18962 Council of Public Relations Firms
317 Madison Avenue
Suite 2320
New York, NY 10017
877-773-4767
FAX: 877-773-2937
kcripps@prfirms.org www.prfirms.org

Kathy Cripps, President
Matt Shaw, VP
Kathy Cripps, President

18963 Institute for Public Relations
University of Florida
2096 Weimer Hall
PO Box 118400
Gainesville, FL 32611-8400
352-460-0372
FAX: 352-846-1122
prre@grove.utl.edu
www.instituteforpr.com
Peter D Debreceny, Co-Chair
W Ward White, Co-Chair
John W Felton, President/CEO
Improving the effectiveness of organizations by advancing the professional knowledge and practice of public relations through research and education.
Founded: 1956

18964 International Association of Business
One Hallidie Plaza
Suite 600
San Francisco, CA 94102
415-544-4700
FAX: 415-544-4747 800-776-4222
custserv@iabc.com www.iabc.com
Julie Griffiths, Chair
David C Kistle, Vice Chair
Janice J Thibodeau, Finance Director
Bish Mukherjee, District Director
International knowledge network for professionals engaged in strategic business communication management.
13500 Members Founded: 1982

18965 KSC Advertising & Public Relations
40 Sarasota Center Boulevard
Suite 107
Sarasota, FL 34240
941-906-1555
FAX: 941-906-1556
info@kscadvpr.com
www.kscadvpr.com
Christopher Carroll, APR, CPRC, Managing Partner
Cheray Keyes-Shima, APR, CPRC, Managing Partner
Jessica Hayes, APR, Account Executive
Chris Carroll, President
Full service advertising, public relations and marketing firm serving real estate developers, health care, automotive and manufacturers.
Founded: 1995

18966 LaBreche Murray Public Relations
500 Washington Avenue S
Suite 2020
Minneapolis, MN 55415
612-338-0901
FAX: 612-338-0921
jmurray@labrechemurray.com
www.labrechemurray.com
Beth LaBreche, Principal
Jerry Murray, Principal
Rich Sharp, Managing Director
Jacob Trippel, Director Finance/Technology
Beth LaBreche, President
Public relations agency.
11 Members Founded: 1990

18967 Library Public Relations Council
2565 Broadway
New York, NY 10025
212-456-6900

Eric Yaverbaum, Owner
Sherry O'Conna, President
Develops an awareness and understanding of the vital importance of public relations to library science. Bestows awards.

18968 National Association of Government Communicators
201 Park Washington Court
Falls Chruch, VA 22046-4527
703-538-1787
FAX: 703-241-5603
info@nagconline.org www.nagc.com
Elizabeth Armstrong, Executive Director
Dawn Shiley-Danzeisen, Communications Director
National nonprofit professional network of federal, state and local government employees who disseminate information within and outside government. Its members are editors, writers, graphic artisits, video professionals, broadcasters, photographers, information specialists and agency spokespeople.

18969 National Black Public Relations Society
6565 W Sunset Boulevard
Suite 301
Los Angeles, CA 90028-7208
323-466-8221
FAX: 323-856-9510
Wynona Redman, President
Formed to promote and expand the opportunities for minorities in public relations.
175 Members Founded: 1997

18970 National Communications Association
1765 N Street NW
Washington, DC 20036
202-464-4622
FAX: 202-464-4600 www.natcom.org
Roger Smitter, Executive Director
Nonprofit organization of researchers, educators, students, and practitioners, whose academic interests span all forms of human communication. Through its services, scholarly publications, resources, conferences and conventions, NCA works with its members to strengthen the profession and contribute to the greater good of the educational enterprise and society.
Founded: 1914

18971 National Council for Marketing and Public Relations
1809 74th Avenue
Greeley, CO 80634-3338
970-330-0771
FAX: 970-330-0769
bolson@ncmpr.org
Becky Olson, Executive Director
Communications specialist working with two year colleges in the media, government, publications and marketing fields. Bestows awards.
1600 Members Founded: 1974

18972 National Investor Relations Institute
8020 Towers Cresent Drive
Suite 250
Vienna, VA 22182
571-633-0532
FAX: 703-506-3571
lthompson@niri.org www.niri.org
Louis M Thompson Jr, President/CEO
Professional association of corporate officers and investor relations consultants responsible for communication among corporate management, the investing public and the financial community.
5000 Members Founded: 1969

18973 National School Public Relations Association
15948 Derwood Road
Rockville, MD 20855
301-519-0496
FAX: 301-519-0494
nspra@nspra.org www.nspra.org
Rich Bagin, Executive Director
Karen Kleinz, Associate Director
Tommy Jones, Business Services Manager
Andy Grunig, Manager Communications
Offers help to public relation directors and school administrators and others interested in further understanding of public schools. Maintains library.
2000 Members Founded: 1935

18974 North American Public Relations Network
245 5th Avenue
New York, NY 10016-8728
212-823-3155
FAX: 212-481-3071
Lori Lincoln, Executive Director
Conducts seminars and keeps members abreast of contemporary news in public relations.

18975 Public Affairs Council
2033 K Street NW
#700
Washington, DC 20006
202-872-1790
FAX: 202-835-8343 www.pac.org
Douglas Pinkham, President
Serves corporate and association members through a clearinghouse of information on how-to questions in conducting external affairs programs.
450 Members Founded: 1954

18976 Public Relations Society of America
33 Maiden Ln
Fl 11
New York, NY 10038-5149
212-601-1400
FAX: 212-995-0757 www.prsa.org
Catherine A Bolton, Executive Director/COO
Major professional association of public relations practitioners.
20000 Members Founded: 1948

18977 Rosalee Roberts Public Relations
4515 Eastridge Drive
Omaha, NE 68134-2555
402-493-9319
FAX: 402-445-0755
roberts@robertspr.com
www.robertspr.com
Rosalee A Roberts, President
Public relations and marketing communications, from specializing in crisis communications, product launches, media relations and media training.
2 Members Founded: 1998

18978 Sally Evans Public Relations
PO Box 56644
Houston, TX 77256
713-660-7990
FAX: 713-663-6542
sieapr@sboglobal.net
Sally I Evans APR, President
Founded: 1980

18979 Society of Consumer Affairs Professionals
801 N Fairfax Street
Suite 404
Alexandria, VA 22314
703-519-3700
FAX: 703-549-4886
socap@socap.org www.socap.org
Lou Garcia, President
Fosters business integrity with consumers. Conducts seminars and bestows awards.
2000 Members Founded: 1973

18980 Southern Public Relations Federation
3328 Culloden Way
Birmingham, AL 35242-3932

mfaulk@springhill.org
Jarrod Ravencraft, Central Chapter President
Donna Grant, President
Lea Ivey Stone, President
Jennifer Venditti, President
A regional professional association that represents public relations and informs them of new and current trends.
1200+ Members Founded: 1972

18981 Women Executives in Public Relations
PO Box 7657
New York, NY 10150-7657
212-859-7375
FAX: 212-859-7375
info@wepr.org www.wepr.org
Chris Pagano, President
Rachel Honig, VP
Lola Preiss, Secretary
Gilda Yolles Mintz, Treasurer
Supports career advancement of female practitioners and fosters the use of public relations to benefit the goals of business and society.
Founded: 1945

Newsletters

18982 Bulldog Reporter
InfoCom Group
5900 Hollis Street
Suite L
Emeryville, CA 94608-2008
510-653-3035
FAX: 510-596-9331 800-959-1059
bulldogrep@aol.com
http://www.infocomgroup.com
James Sinkinson, Publisher
Tim Gray, President
Emphasis on placement opportunities and media profiles, as well as personnel changes at media outlets throughout the US. *$599.00*
Fortnightly Founded: 1980
Circulation: 5000

18983 Contacts Newsletter
MerComm
500 Executive Boulevard
Ossinning, NY 10562
914-923-9400
FAX: 914-923-9484
contacts@mercommawards.com
http://www.mercommawards.com
Reni L Witt, Publisher
Nora Madonick, Editor
Essential and timely information for public relations, promotion and marketing profes-

sionals with regard to media placement of product or service information, press releases, and publicity materials. *$454.00*
Weekly Founded: 1970

18984 Contacts: Media Pipeline for PR People
Larimi Communications Association
500 Executive Blvd.
Ossining on Hudson, NY 10562-1114
914-923-9400
FAX: 914-923-9484
info@mercommawards.com
http://www.mercommawards.com/
Michael M Smith, Publisher
Madeleine Gillis, Editor
Provides pipeline of communications between what an editor needs and a public relations person can supply. *$287.00*
1 pages Weekly Founded: 1975
Printed in 1 color

18985 Downtown Promotion Reporter
Alexander Communications Group
28 W 25th Street
8th Floor
New York, NY 10010
212-228-0246
FAX: 212-228-0376 800-232-4317
info@downtowndevelopment.com
http://www.downtowndevelopment.com/
Margaret DeWitt, Publisher
Laurence Alexander, Owner
Tested ideas for promotion, public relations, marketing, increasing business, participation, downtown image building, sales, and events. *$189.00*
Monthly

18986 Healthcare PR & Marketing News
Phillips Business Information
1201 Seven Locks Road
Suite 300
Potomac, MD 20854-2931
301-354-1400
FAX: 301-340-1451
sbanik@phillips.com
Sharmi Banik, Editor
Kismet Toksu Gould, Publisher
Issues faced by health care executives in PR firms and hospitals. Regular features include industry surveys, case studies and executive profiles. *$397.00*
Bi-Monthly Founded: 1992

18987 High-Tech Hot Sheet
Hot Sheet Publishing
114 Sansome Street
Suite 1224
San Francisco, CA 94104
415-421-6225
FAX: 415-421-6225
Art Gracia, Editor/Publisher
Reporting updates and changes in staff, beat assignments, new publications, suspension of publishing in high-tech media. *$395.00*
Monthly Founded: 1987

18988 Holmes Report
Holmes Group
271 West 47th Street
Suite PHA
New York, NY 10036
212-333-2300
FAX: 212-333-2624
gdrury@holmesreport.com
http://www.holmesreport.com
Paul Holmes, President/CEO
Greg Drury, VP/COO
Source of information for public relations and corporate communications professionals. *$290.00*
Weekly Founded: 2001 ISBN 0-972364-50-1
Circulation: 15,000
Printed in 4 colors on glossy stock

18989 Interactive PR & Marketing News
Phillips Publishing
1201 Seven Locks Road
#300
Potomac, MD 20854-2931
301-354-1400
FAX: 301-424-8602
editor@interactivepr.com
www.phillips.com
Angela Duff, Publisher
Covers the latest trends and news on the World Wide Web and Internet markets and looks at their users. *$347.00*
23 per year
Circulation: 5M

18990 Interactive Public Relations
Ragan Communications
316 N Michigan Avenue
Suite 400
Chicago, IL 60601
312-604-4100
FAX: 312-960-4105 800-493-4867
sarahm@ragan.com
http://www.ragan.com
David Murray, Editor
Mark ragan, CEO
Kasia Chalko, Marketing Director
Includes targeted newsletters in the areas of employment communication, Web PR, organizational writing and editing, sales and marketing, media relations, motivational management, and investor relations. *$279.00*
Founded: 1970

18991 Jack O'Dwyer's Newsletter
JR O'Dwyer Company
271 Madison Avenue
New York, NY 10016-1001
212-791-1032
FAX: 212-683-2750
jack@odwyerpr.com
http://www.odwyerpr.com
Jack O'Dwyer, Editor-In-Chief
Fay Shapiro, Publisher
Eileen Kelly, Circulation Manager
Covers current happenings in both electronic and print media, including new PR products and accounts, PR campaigns, and books about public relations. *$295.00*
Weekly Founded: 1970

18992 Levin's Public Relations Report
Levin Public Relations & Marketing
147 Rockland Avenue
Larchmont, NY 10538-3254
914-834-5919
FAX: 914-834-5919
levinpr@levinpr.com
http://www.levinpr.com
Don Levin, Publisher
Sylvia Moss, Editor
Strategies, tactics for the CEO, VP Sales and Marketing seeking new marketing/public relations effectiveness. *$29.00*
Monthly Founded: 1984

18993 Media Relations Insider
InfoCom Group
5900 Hollis Street
Suite R2
Emeryville, CA 94608
510-533-3035
FAX: 510-959-9331 800-959-1059
tgray@infocomgroup.com
http://www.infocomgroup.com
James Sinkinson, Publisher
Tim Gray, VP
Eastern and Western editions give you media news and exclusive interviews with top business journalists in your region. *$399.00*
Monthly

18994 Media Relations Report
Ragan Communications
316 N Michigan
Suite 400
Chicago, IL 60601
312-604-4100
FAX: 312-960-4105 800-493-4867
cservice@ragan.com
http://www.ragan.com
Jim Ylisela, Editorial Director
Mark Ragan, CEO *$28.92*
Monthly Founded: 1975
Circulation: 1000
Mailing list available for rent
Printed in 2 colors on matte stock

18995 MediaQuest
MediaQuest Publishing
PO Box 9222
Boston, MA 02114-0996
617-536-5353
FAX: 617-367-9151
Barbara Kalunian, Editor/Publisher
Media placement becomes easier for PR professionals through behind the scenes interviews with leading journalists at top broadcast and print outlets. *$295.00*
Bi-Monthly Founded: 1990

18996 Memo to the President
American Association State Colleges & Universities
1307 New York Avenue NW
5th Floor
Washington, DC 20005
202-293-2450
FAX: 202-296-5819 800-542-2062
Constantine Curris, President
Susan M Chilcott, Editor *$100.00*
6 pages Monthly Founded: 1961
Circulation: 1200
Printed in 2 colors on matte stock

18997 O'Dwyers Washington Report
JR O'Dwyer Company
271 Madison Avenue
#600
New York, NY 10016
212-791-1032
FAX: 212-683-2750
jack@odwyerpr.com
http://www.odwyerpr.com
Jack O'Dwyer, Publisher
Kevin McCowley, Editor
Covers Washington public relations and public affairs lobbying news. *$95.00*
8 pages

18998 Opportunity
Career Skills Press/Brody Communications
815 Greenwood Avenue
Suite 8
Jemkintown, PA 19046
215-886-1688
FAX: 215-886-1699 800-726-7936
info@brodycommunications.com
http://www.brodycommunications.com

Marjorie Brody, President
Miryam S Raddy, Marketing Manager

Feature products published by Career Skills Press unit.

4 pages Quarterly Founded: 1983
Circulation: 10000
Printed in 4 colors on glossy stock

18999 PR Intelligence Report
Lawrence Ragan Communications
316 N Michigan
Suite 400
Chicago, IL 60601
312-604-4100
FAX: 312-960-4106
cservice@ragan.com
http://www.ragan.com

Christine Kent, Editor
Mark Regan, CEO

Digs below the surface to provide the details, insights and information you need to improve your career, make your next campaign a success, or avoid costly mistakes. *$279.00*

8 pages Founded: 1970
Circulation: 1000 $125 per M.
Printed in 2 colors on matte stock

19000 PR News
Phillips Business Information
4 Choke Cherry Rd
Fl 2
Rockville, MD 20850-4024
301-450-0035
FAX: 301-340-3169
dschwartz@pbimedia.com
http://www.prandmarketing.com

Matthew Schwartz, Editor
Diane Schwartz, Publisher

Briefing on the latest PR trends, what's working and what's not. We feature case studies of successful PR campaigns. *$697.00*

10 pages Weekly Founded: 1944

19001 PR Reporter
Lawrence Ragan Communications
316 N Michigan Avenue
Suite 400
Chicago, IL 60601
312-960-4100
FAX: 312-960-4105 800-493-4867
cservice@ragan.com
http://www.ragan.com

Kristen Lotz, Contact
Mark Ragan, President
Jim Ylisela, Group Publisher
Rebecca Anderson, Managing Editor

Weekly publication dedicated to the behavioral aspects of public relations, public affairs and communication strategies. Its quick read format keeps you up to date on the latest theories, research, public opinions, case studies and successful public relations techniques.

Weekly Founded: 1970

19002 PR Tactics
Public Relations Society of America
33 Maiden Lane
11th Floor
New York, NY 10038-5150
212-601-1400
FAX: 212-995-0757
hq@prsa.org http://www.prsa.org

Alison Statemen, Managing Editor
Gale Spreter, Maketing Manager *$75.00*

32 pages Monthly Founded: 1947
Circulation: 25000 $250 per M.
Printed in 4 colors on newsprint stock

19003 PR Watch
Center for Media and Democracy
520 University Avenue
Suite 227
Madison, WI 53703
608-260-9713
FAX: 608-260-9714
editor@prwatch.org
http://www.prwatch.org

Laura Miller, Editor
John Stauber, Executive Director
Sheldon Rampton, Research Director
Kristian Knutsen, Administrative Assistant

Investigates and exposes how the public relations industry and other professional propagandists manipulate public information, perceptions and opinion on behalf of governments and special interests.

Quarterly Founded: 1993

19004 PR Week
114 W 26th Street
3rd Floor
New York, NY 10001
646-638-6000
FAX: 646-638-6115
letters@prweek.com
www.prweek.com

Lisa Kirk, Publishing Director
Julia Hood, Editor-in-Chief

Cutting-edge newsletter of public relations.

Weekly

19005 Partyline: PR Media Newsletter Partyline Publishing
Party Line Publishing Company
35 Sutton Place
New York, NY 10022-2464
212-755-3487
FAX: 212-755-4859
byermon@ix.netcom.com
www.partylinepublishing.com

Morton Yarmon, Editor/Publisher

Weekly media placement newsletter with up-to-date new of the media for public relations executives in all aspects of business, hospitals, publishers and associations. *$200.00*

Weekly Founded: 1961
Circulation: 1,400

19006 Pro Motion
Beyond the Byte
PO Box 388
Fallston, MD 21047
410-877-3524
FAX: 410-877-7064 800-861-1235
elaisy@aol.com
http://www.pro-motionsnetwork.com

Emily Laisy, President

News of interest to Media Escort and publicists. *$12.00*

4 pages Quarterly Founded: 1985
Circulation: 325 Audited
Printed in 1 color on matte stock

19007 Public Relations Career Opportunities
CEO Update
1575 I Street NW
#1190
Washington, DC 20005-1105
202-408-7900
FAX: 202-408-7907

James Zaniello, Editor

Public relations and publis affairs job opportunities compensating $35,000 plus nationwide. *$217.00*

Bi-Monthly Founded: 1986

19008 Ragan's Interactive Public Relations
Lawrence Ragan Communications
316 N Michigan
Suite 400
Chicago, IL 60601
312-604-4100
FAX: 312-960-4106 800-878-5331
publicrelations@ragan.com
http://www.ragan.com

Mark Ragan, CEO
Jim Ylisela, Editor

Dedicated to helping PR people navigate cyberspace. *$269.00*

8 pages Monthly Founded: 1970
Circulation: 800 $125 per M.
Printed in 2 colors on matte stock

19009 Ragan's Media Relations Report
Lawrence Ragan Communications
316 N Michigan Avenue
Suite 400
Chicago, IL 60601
312-604-4100
FAX: 312-960-4105 800-493-4867
cservice@ragan.com
http://www.ragan.com

Mark Ragan Ragan, CEO
David Murray, Editor
Diane Tillman, Marketing Manager

Content focuses on personal changes, moves and additions in various media, including television, radio and print. Offers tips on angles to take, interviews top journalists on what type of information they prefer, and continuously updates contact numbers and addresses. *$ 317.00*

Monthly Founded: 1970 $125 per M.
Printed in 2 colors on matte stock

19010 West Coast PR Newsletter
West Coast MediaNet
5928 Lindley Avenue
Encino, CA 91316-1047
818-893-3449
FAX: 818-776-1930
darren@westcoastpr.com
www.westcoastprjobs.com

Darren Shuster, Publisher
Ken West, Manager

Delivers in-depth inteviews and features, new media contacts and personnel updates, tips from experts in various fields, and listings of new PR markets. Regular coverage includes media web site and book reviews, as well as how-to articles, all with a West Coast angle. *$75.00*

16 pages 12 issues
Circulation: 1M

Magazines & Journals

19011 ACH Marketing Handbook
NACHA: Electronic Payments Association

13665 Dulles Technology Drive
Suite 300
Herndon, VA 20171
703-561-1100
FAX: 703-787-0996
info@nacha.org http://www.nacha.org
Elliott McEntee, President/CEO
William B Nelson, Executive VP
Published by NACHA. *$40.00*
Annual+

19012 Communication World
Int'l Association of Business Communicators
One Hallidie Plaza
Suite 600
San Francisco, CA 94102-2842
415-544-4700
FAX: 415-544-4747 800-776-4222
service_centre@iabc.com
http://www.iabc.com
Julie Freeman, President
Joseph Ugalde, VP Marketing/Communications
Mari Pavia, Project Director
Association publication for members who are professionals in organizational communications and public relations. *$150.00*
6 issues per ye Founded: 1970

19013 Currents
Council for Advancement & Support of Education
1307 New York Avenue NW
Suite 1000
Washington, DC 20005-4726
202-285-5900
FAX: 202-387-4973
currents@case.org
http://www.case.org
Deborah Bangiorno, Editor
Donald Falkenstein, VP
Will Hayden, Production Coordinator
John Lippincott, President
Marla Misek, Senior Editor
Offers information on campus fund raising, public relations,and alumni administration. *$115.00*
Founded: 1974
Circulation: 15000

19014 International Public Relations Review
18 W Church Street
Saint Frederick, MD 31701
229-567-8074
FAX: 912-845-2991
John Reed, Publisher
Public relations international communications issues for senior level PR professionals. *$2.00*

Circulation: 1,300

19015 Jack O'Dwyer's Services Report
JR O'Dwyer Company
271 Madison Avenue
New York, NY 10016
212-791-1032
FAX: 212-683-2750
jack@odwyerpr.com
http://www.odwyerpr.com
Fay Shapiro, Publisher
Jack O'Dwyer, Editor
Eileen Kelly, Circulation Manager
Information on film, videotape, database and release distribution industries which serve public relations professionals. *$45.00*
Monthly Founded: 1980
Circulation: 4500

19016 Jack O'Dwyers Washington Report

JR O'Dwyer Company
271 Madison Avenue
Suite 600
New York, NY 10016
212-791-1032
FAX: 212-683-2750
jack@odwyerpr.com
http://www.odwyerpr.com
Jack O'Dwyer, Publisher *$60.00*
Weekly Founded: 1970

19017 Managing Media Relations in a Crisis
NACHA: Electronic Payments Association

13665 Dulles Technology Drive
#300
Herndon, VA 20171
703-561-1100
FAX: 703-787-0996
info@nacha.org www.nacha.org
Elliott McEntee, President/CEO
William B Nelson, Executive VP
Designed to assist your organization to develop, test and execute a crisis communication plan. With this guide, you will understand how to address issues, whom to call and in what order to alert them, which vendors you can count on to help and how to develop a means to track the crisis as it grows or abates.

19018 Public Relations Quarterly
Howard Penn Hudson
44 W Market Street
PO Box 311
Rhinebeck, NY 12572-311
845-876-2081
FAX: 845-876-2561 800-572-3451
prquarterly@aol.com
http://www.hudsonsdirectory.com
Howard Penn Hudson, Editor/Publisher
Elaine F Newman, Executive Editor
Berecah Sullivan, Circulation Manager
Nichole Latierre, Marketing Manager
Independent public relations magazine, now 48 years old, presenting articles and columns on the theory and process of public relations and communications. *$65.00*
Quarterly Founded: 1955
Printed in on matte stock

19019 Public Relations Review
Elsevier
6277 Seaharbor Drive
Orlando, FL 32887
877-839-7126
www.elsevier.com
Jan D Achenbach, Editor-In-Chief
Covers public relations, education, government, survey research, public policy, history and bibliographies. *$110.00*
12 issues
Circulation: 1M

19020 Public Relations Strategist
Public Relations Society of America
33 Irving Place
11th Floor
New York, NY 10038-2376
212-601-1400
FAX: 212-995-0757
http://www.prsa.comn
John Elasser, Editor-in-Chief
Catherine Bolton, Manager
With emphasis on the issues and trends affecting public relations management, it examines the changing concepts and challenges current practices with relevant, original and thought-provoking articles. *$100.00*
4 issues per ye Founded: 1947
Circulation: 20538

19021 Public Relations Tactics
Public Relations Society of America
33 Maiden Lane
11th Fl.
New York, NY 10038-2332
212-460-1400
FAX: 212-995-0757
hr@prsa.org http://www.prsa.org
John Elasser, Editor-in-Chief
Gale Spreter, Marketing Manager
Alison Stateman, Managing Editor
Catherine A Bolton, Executive Director
News, trends and how-to information for public relations people. *$75.00*
Monthly Founded: 1947
Circulation: 20538

19022 Reputation Management
Editorial Media & Marketing International
708 3rd Avenue
Frnt 2
New York, NY 10017-4201
212-687-5260

kingraham@prcentral.com
www.prcentral.com
Kara T Ingraham, Publisher/COO
Editorial focuses on finance, marketing, human resources, government and society. Highlights domestic and international corporate news presenting observations and perspectives vital to the industry. *$52.00*
Bi-Monthly Founded: 1995
Circulation: 12M

Trade Shows

19023 American Society of Health Care Marketing and Public Relations Trade Show
1 N Franklin Street
31st Floor
Chicago, IL 60606-3421
773-327-1064
FAX: 312-422-4579
Lauren Barnett, Executive Director
Sixty booths of communications, printing, computer equipment, public relations and fund raising consultants in the health care profession.
600 Attendees September

19024 National Hispanic Market Trade Show and Media Expo (Se Habla Espanol)
Hispanic Business
360 S Hope Avenue
Suite 300C
Santa Barbara, CA 93105-4031
805-563-1049
FAX: 805-687-4546
info@hispanstar.com
www.hispanstar.com
Luisa Donis, Corporate Communications
Annual show of 100 exhibitors of market/research, media, advertising, public relations, information services and recruitment.
1500 Attendees

19025 National School for Public Relations
1501 Lee Highway
Arlington, VA 22209-1109
703-312-7345

Mildred Wainger, Administration Services
Offers information and news for professionals in the field of public relations.
600 Attendees July

19026 Strategic Media Relations Conference
Ragan Communications
316 N Michigan Avenue
Chicago, IL 60601
312-960-4100
FAX: 312-960-4106 800-878-5331
cservice@ragan.com
www.raganinstitute.com
Showcase of best practices for winning top media coverage in a new era. Learn how peers have garnered more ink, managed crises, built their brands and gone global. Attend pre- and post-conference sessions that provide career-boosting skills in crisis survival, media training, online media relations, PR writing, persuasive communications, PR management, digital PR and pitching stories. *$895.00*
March

Directories & Databases

19027 ADWEEK Directory
ADWEEK
770 Broadway
7th Floor
New York, NY 10003
646-545-5220
FAX: 646-654-5351
publisher@adweek.com
www.adweek.com
Mitch Tebo, Directory Publisher
For anyone seeking agency-specific information. Over 29,000 personnel listings, more the 6,000 full service advertising agencies and networks, public relations firms, media buying services, recruitment entertainment marketing, yellow pages, health care, interactive, sports marketing, infomercials, direct marketing, creative design, marketing communications and research, consultancies and many more media related listings.

19028 Bacon's Newspaper & Magazine Directories
Bacon's Publishing Company
332 S Michigan Avenue
Chicago, IL 60604-4434
312-228-8239
FAX: 312-922-3127 800-621-0561
info@bacons.com www.bacons.com
Ruth McFarland, VP/Publisher
Stephen Newman, Chief Executive Officer
Two volume set listing all daily and community newspapers, magazines and newsletters, news service and syndicates, syndicated columists, complete editorial staff listings of each publication provided, covers US, Canada, Mexico,and Carribean *$350.00*
4,700 pages Annual Founded: 1951
Printed in 1 color on matte stock : internet

19029 Burrelle's Media Directory
Burrelle's Information Services
75 E Northfield Road
Livingston, NJ 07039-4501
973-992-6600
FAX: 973-992-7675 800-631-1160
Robert Waggoner, Chief Executive Officer
Approximately 60,000 media listings in North America. Listings cover newspapers, magazines (trades and consumer), broadcast, and internet outlets. *$795.00*
Annual

19030 Corporate Yellow Book
Leadership Directories
104 5th Avenue
New York, NY 10011-6901
212-627-4140
FAX: 212-645-0931
corporate@leadershipdirectories.com
www.leadershipdirectories.com
Vonessa Ruffin, Editor
Contact information for over 48,000 executives at over 1,000 companies and more than 9,000 board members and their outside affiliations. *$360.00*
1,400 pages Quarterly Founded: 1986
50,000 names $105 per M. : CD-Rom

19031 Leadership Library in Print
Leadership Directories
104 5th Avenue
New York, NY 10011
212-627-4140
FAX: 212-645-0931
info@leadershipdirectories.com
www.leadershipdirectories.com
James M Petrie, Associate Publisher
David Hurvitz, Chief Executive Officer
Complete set of all 14 leadership directories. Provides subscribers with complete contact information for the 400,000 individuals who constitute the institutional leadership of the US. *$2300.00*

Five directories quarterly, nine directories semiannually

Semiannually Founded: 1996
Computerized version available: CD-ROM

19032 PR News
Phillips Business Information
7811 Montrose Road
Potomac, MD 20854-3363
301-340-2100
FAX: 301-424-7261 www.phillips.com
Diane Schwartz, Publisher
Matthew Schwartz, Editor
This database offers information on public relations issues. *$597.00*
48 issues

19033 PR Newswire
150 E 58th Street
31st Floor
New York, NY 10155-0002
212-355-0090
FAX: 212-832-9406
This comprehensive database offers current news, financial news, earnings statements, mergers, acquisitions, proxy contests and general features pertaining to the public relations industry.
Directory

19034 Public Administration Career Directory
Gale Research
27500 Drake Road
Farmington Hills, MI 48331
248-699-4253
FAX: 313-961-6741 800-877-4253
galeord@gale.com www.gale.com
Career guidance resources directory. *$29.95*
300 pages Cloth

19035 Public Relations Tactics
Public Relations Society of America
33 Irving Place
New York, NY 10003-2332
212-601-1400
FAX: 212-995-0757
Adam Shell, Editor
List of products and services used by public relations professionals worldwide.
Annual June

19036 Public Relations Tactics: Register Issue/T he Blue Book
Public Relations Society of America
33 Irving Place
New York, NY 10003-2332
212-601-1400
FAX: 212-995-0757
Adam Shell, Editor
About 17,000 public relations practitioners in business government education etc., who are members. *$100.00*
Annual July

19037 Publicity at Your Finger Tips
Federal Systems
PO Box 298-L
Oliver Springs, TN 37840-0298
865-483-3579

Offers a comprehensive list of magazines, newspapers and other publications in the United States that provide publicity for businesses, churches and charitable organizations. *$24.95*

19038 Staffing Industry Supplier Directory and Buyers Guide
Staffing Industry Analysts
881 Fremont Avenue
Suite A3
Los Altos, CA 94024-5637
650-948-9303
FAX: 650-948-9345 800-950-9496
info@sireport.com www.sireport.com
Dianne Hodges, Product Manager
Complete listing of suppliers and products for temporary help, placement and recruiting firms in the staffing industry. *$89.50*
295 pages Annual ISBN 1-883814-11-1

Industry Web Sites

19039 **www.absolutelypr.com**
Absolutely Public Relations

Results-driven media relations - local, trade, national.

19040 **www.achieva.info**
ACHIEVA

19041 **www.aem.org**
Construction Equipment Advertisers and Public
Relations Council

A council of AEM that works to promote marketing, sales and advertising of construction equipment.

19042 **www.afgcan.org**
AFHCAN Project

19043 **www.aprc-online.org**
Automotive Public Relations Council

Provides a forum for information exchange among communication professionals with the automotive industry.

19044 **www.bloomgross.com**
Bloom Gross & Associates

Executive recruitment firm with corporate communications, public relations, marketing/branding/market research, and direct marketing/sales promotion practice areas.

19045 **www.case.org**
Council for the Advancement and Support of Ed.

Offers information on campus fund raising, public relations and alumni administration.

19046 **www.cof.org**
Council on Foundations

Non profit trade association for foundations

19047 **www.greyhouse.com**
Grey House Publishing

The Grey House Performing Arts Directory is the most comprehensive resource covering the Performing Arts. This important directory provides current information on over 9,000 Dance Companies, Instrumental Music Programs, Opera Companies, Choral Groups, Theater Companies, Performing Arts Series and Performing Arts Facilities.

19048 **www.iabc.com**
International Association of Business Communicators

An international association for members who are professionals in organizational communications and public relations. Accepts advertising.

19049 **www.instituteforpr.com**
Institute for Public Relations

To improve the effectiveness of organizations by advancing the professional knowledge and practice of public relations through research and education.

19050 **www.kscpublivrelations.com**
KSC Public Relations

Full-service advertising, public relations and marketing firm serving real estate developers, health care automotive, and manufacturers.

19051 **www.magnetcom.com**
Magnet - Communications

Public relations firm.

19052 **www.mediaaccessgroup.com**
Media Access Group

19053 **www.multiculturalmarketingresources.com**
Multicultural Marketing Resources Asian American
Advertising Federation

A public relations/marketing firm representing the nations experts in targeting Hispanics, African Americans and Asian Americans. We maintain a professional urban with 700 catalogued resources for members access and publish a source book for multicultural experts.

19054 **www.niri.org**
National Investor Relations Institute

Professional association of corporate officers and investors relations consultants.

19055 **www.petersgrouppr.com**
PetersGroup Public Relations

Provides a full range of marketing and public relations programs to national and international businesses. The agency works closely with technology clients ranging from Funded start-ups to Fortune 500 companies, to integrate the right mix of research, strategy, positioning and media to help customers meet their ongoing business and communication goals.

19056 **www.pinnacleww.com**
Pinnacle Worldwide

For independent public relations firms in major markets around the globe.

19057 **www.progressivepr.com**
PPR Communications

19058 **www.prpublishing.com**
Public Relations Publishing Company

Case studies, research and trends in public relations and information on issues of importance to PR professionals.

19059 **www.prsa.org**
Public Relations Society of America

A major professional association of public relations practitioners.

19060 **www.prweek.com**
PR Week

19061 **www.silveranvil.org**
Silver Anvil Resource Center

Online database of public relations campaigns.

19062 **www.washingtonpost.com**
Washington Post

19063 **www.wepr.org**
Women Executives in Public Relations

Provides a support network for women in public relations. Offers grants and scholarships for courses in public relations and for college students studying communications.

Associations

19064 Alliance of Area Business Publications
4929 Wilshire Boulevard
Suite 428
Los Angeles, CA 90010
323-937-5514
FAX: 323-937-0959
info@alliancebizpubs.com
www.bizpubs.com
C James Dowden, Executive Director
Dan Meyer, President
Represents metropolitan area and state wide business to business publications with conventions, newsletters, and other services.
80 Members Founded: 1979

19065 American Black Book Writers' Association
269 S. Beverly Drive Street 2600
Beverly Hills, CA 90212
310-306-4042
Will Gibson, President
Members include all African Americans who are involved with any aspects of the publishing industry.
4M Members

19066 American Book Producers Association
160 5th Avenue
New York, NY 10010
212-645-2368
FAX: 212-242-6799 800-209-4575
office@abpaonline.org
www.abpaonline.org
David Rubel, President
David Katz, Manager
Increases the book industry's awareness of members capabilities and exchanges information on improving business. Develops concepts for books and other publications.
Founded: 1980

19067 American Medical Publishers Association
122 Fox Rd
Media, PA 19063-4905
212-255-0200
FAX: 212-255-7007
bmeredith@publishers.org
www.pspcentral.org
Robin Bartlett, Director Marketing/Sales
Lisette Bralow, Editor-in-Chief
Greg Bussy, Director Marketing
Provides member forum for the exchange of current medical information, hosts continuing seminars, in addition to publishing a newsletter.
65 Members Founded: 1960

19068 American Society of Newspaper Editors
11609B Sunrise Valley Drive
Reston, VA 20191-1409
703-453-1122
FAX: 703-453-1133
asne@asne.org www.asne.org
Scott Bosley, Executive Director
Alison Wilcox, Asst Exec Dir/Meetings Coordinator
A membership organization for daily newspaper editors, people who serve the editorial needs of daily newspaper and certain distinguished individuals who have worked on behalf of editors through the years.
750 Members Founded: 1922

19069 Antiquarian Booksellers Association of Rare Book Dealers
20 W 44th Street
Fourth Floor
New York, NY 10036-6604
212-944-8291
FAX: 212-944-8293
inquiries@abaa.org www.abaa.org
John Crichton, President
Liane Wade, Executive Director
A trade association of rare book dealers.
480 Members Founded: 1949

19070 Associated Church Press
1410 Vernon Street
Stoughton, WI 53589-2248
608-877-0011
FAX: 608-877-0062
acpoffice@earthlink.net
www.associatedchurchpress.org
Mary Lynn Hendrickson, Executive Director
Aims to share ideas and concerns in religious publishing and to stimulate higher standards of religious journalism to exert a more positive influence.
240 Members Founded: 1916

19071 Associated Construction Publications
30 Technology Parkway S
Norcross, GA 30092-3627
770-417-4121
FAX: 800-930-3003 800-486-0014
Wayne Curtis, Publisher
Royce Morse, Production Director
Strives to assist the heavy construction industry with local and regional news on a nationwide basis.
14 Members Founded: 1938

19072 Association for Information and Image
1100 Wayne Avenue
Suite 1100
Silver Spring, MD 20910
301-587-8202
FAX: 301-587-2711 800-477-2446
aiim@aiim.org www.aiim.org
Don McMahan, Chairman Finance Committee
Martyn Christian, Chairman Awards Committee
Larry Wischerth, Chairman Nominating Committee
Don Post, Chairman Conference Planning
Members are users and manufacturers of equipment and supplies of the information and image industry.
10M Members Founded: 1943

19073 Association of American Publishers
71 5th Avenue
2nd Floor
New York, NY 10003-3004
212-255-0200
FAX: 212-255-7007
www.publishers.org
Patricia Schroeder, President/CEO
Thomas McKee, Executive VP
Kathryn Blough, VP
Principal trade association for the US book publishing industry members comprise most of the major commericial book publishers in the US, as well as smaller and medium sized houses, not-for-profit publishers, university presses and scholarly societies.
300 Members Founded: 1970

19074 Association of American University Presses
71 W 23rd Street
Suite 901
New York, NY 10010-4102
212-989-1010
FAX: 212-989-0275
SBeer@publishers.org
www.aaupnet.org
Peter Givler, Executive Director
Timothy Muench, Assistant Director
Members are university presses and a limited number of presses of non-degree-granting scholarly institutions.
125 Members Founded: 1937
Mailing list available for rent 2.2M names

19075 Association of Directory Publishers
116 Cass Street
PO Box 1929
Traverse City, MI 49685-1929
800-267-9002
FAX: 231-486-2182
hq@adp.org www.adp.org
Jim Hail, Chairman
Sieg Fischer, First Vice Chairman
The association is the communication link to the Telephone Directory industry. It provides a forum for the exchange of ideas and information among publishers of telephone, city and special interest directories and provides continuous training to assist in the enhancement of the publisher's operation.
240 Members Founded: 1898

19076 Association of Free Community Papers
1630 Miner Street
Suite 204 Box 1989
Idaho Springs, CO 80452
877-203-2327
FAX: 781-459-7770
info@afcp.org www.afcp.org
Craig McMullin, Executive Director
Offers national classified advertising placement services; conducts charitable programs, sponsors competition, compiles statistics.
250 Members Founded: 1951

19077 Audit Bureau of Circulation
900 N Meacham Road
Schaumburg, IL 60173-4968
847-605-0909
FAX: 847-605-0483
service@accessabc.com
www.accessabc.com
Robert Troutbeck, Chairman
Peter A Armour, Vice Chairman
Michael Lavery, Chief Executive Officer
Michael K Brown, Advertising Director
The world's largest circulation-auditing organization, ABC provides circulation data on 1,400+ newspapers and more than 1,100 periodicals to ABC-member publications, advertisers and advertising agencies.
4.1M+ Members Founded: 1914

19078 Book Industry Study Group
19 West 21st Street
Suite 905
New York, NY 10010
646-336-7141
FAX: 646-336-6214
info@bisg.org www.bisg.org
Joseph Gonnella, Chairman
Andrew Weber, Vice Chairman
Joseph Gonnella, Vice Chair
Promotes and supports research enabling various sectors of the industry to develop and expand their professional and business plans. Book Industry Study Group has various paperback publications.
210 Members Founded: 1976

19079 Book Manufacturers' Institute
2 Armand Beach Drive
Suite 1B
Palm Coast, FL 32137-2612
386-986-4552
FAX: 386-986-4553
info@bmibook.com
www.bmibook.com/
David N. Mead, President
William L. Lupton, VP
Bruce Smith, Executive VP
Trade association of the book manufacturing industry.
94 Members Founded: 1933

19080 Catholic Book Publishers Association
8404 Jamesport Drive
Rockford, IL 61108
815-332-3245
FAX: 815-332-3476
cbpa3@aol.com www.cbpa.org/
John D. Wright, President
Terry Wessels, Executive Director
To facilitate the exchange of information about Catholic book publishing and facilitate cooperation among members in editorial, business, marketing and publicity of Catholic books, audiocassettes, videocassettes and CD's.
180 Members Founded: 1987

19081 Catholic Press Association of the US and Canada
3555 Veterans Memorial Highway
Unit O
Ronkonkoma, NY 11779-7662
631-471-4730
FAX: 631-471-4804
rosep@catholicpress.org
www.catholicpress.org
Owen McGovern, Executive Director
Build and strengthen the value and worth of the Catholic Press by facilitating the professional, economic and spiritual growth of their members.
620 Members Founded: 1911

19082 Christian Science Publishing Society
1 Norway Street
Boston, MA 02115-3195
617-507-7929
FAX: 617-450-2031
gestert@csps.com
www.spirituality.com
Walter Jones, Executive Director
Paul Bermel, Manager
Maintains a research library. Sponsors daily and weekly radio and television news broadcasts throughout the world.

19083 Church Music Publishing Association
PO Box 158992
Nashville, TN 37215-8992
615-694-4561
FAX: 615-790-8847
www.cmpamusic.org/html/
Dale Matthews, President
Geoff Lorenz, VP
Bruce Church, Owner
Publishes music for Christian churches and schools.
46 Members Founded: 1926

19084 Columbia Scholastic Press Association
Columbia University
Columbia University Mail Code 5711
New York, NY 10027-6902
212-854-9400
FAX: 212-854-9401
cspa@columbia.edu
/www.columbia.edu/cu/cspa/
Edmund J. Sullivan, Director
International student press association composed of writing students, journalists and faculty advisers in schools and colleges through educational conferences, idea exchanges and recognition programs.
1850 Members Founded: 1925

19085 Comics Magazine Association of America
355 Lexington Avenue
New York, NY 10017-4261
212-297-2122
FAX: 212-370-9047 www.cmaa.com
Operates comics code authority - a self-regulation program for the industry to maintain high standards of decency and good taste.
12 Members Founded: 1954

19086 Copyright Society of the USA
352 Seventh Avenue
Suite 739
New York, NY 10001
212-354-6401
amy@csusa.org www.csusa.org
Barry Slotnick, President
Helene Blue, VP
Amy Nickerson, Manager
Established to foster interest in and advance the study of copyright law and rights in literature, music, art, theater, motion pictures and other forms of intellectual property.
600 Members Founded: 1953

19087 Council of Literary Magazines and Presses
154 Christopher Street
Suite 3C
New York, NY 10014-9110
212-741-9110
FAX: 212-741-9112
info@clmp.org www.clmp.org
Jeffrey Lependorf, Executive Director
Membership is open to any noncommercial literary magazine or press that publishes at least one or more books per year.
347 Members Founded: 1967

19088 Electronic Prepress Section Graphic Arts Technical Foundation
200 Deer Run Road
Sewickley, PA 15143
412-741-6860
FAX: 412-741-2311
piagatf@piagatf.org www.gain.net/
Michael Mikan, Executive Director
Nonprofit technical and educational organization serving the international graphics arts industry.
11300 Members Founded: 1871

19089 Engineering College Magazines Association
117 Pleasant Street SE
Minneapolis, MN 55414
612-626-7959
ecma@it.umn.edu www.ecmaweb.org
Paul Sorenson, Co-Chair
Sharon Kurtt, Co-Chair
Aims to promote improvement of engineering journalism, advertising and standardization of size and format of publications.
27 Members Founded: 1920

19090 Evangelical Christian Publishers
4816 S Ash Avenue
Suite 101
Tempe, AZ 85282
480-966-3998
FAX: 480-966-1944
info@ecpa.org www.ecpa.org
Mark Taylor, Chairman
Mark Kuyper, President/CEO
An international, not-for-profit, trade organization serving its industry by promoting excellence and professionalism, sharing relevant data, stimulating Christian fellowship, raising the effectiveness of member houses, and equipping them to meet the needs of the changing marketplace.
280 Members Founded: 1974

19091 Flexographic Technical Association Education & Training
900 Marconi Avenue
Ronkonkoma, NY 11779-7212
631-737-6020
FAX: 631-737-6813
membership@flexography.org
www.flexography.org
Mark Cisternino, President
Madeline Sanzano, Production Manager
Seeks to advance art and science of flexographic printing. Conducts educational seminars. Markets textbooks and audio-visual material for in plant training.
Founded: 1958

19092 Flexographic Technical Association Inc.
900 Marconi Avenue
Ronkonkoma, NY 11779-7212
631-737-6020
FAX: 631-737-6813
memberinfo@flexography.org
www.flexography.org/www.ftastore.com
Mark Cisternino, President
Rick Mix, Technical Director
Doreen Monteleone, Director Environmental Affairs
Lucille Sullivan, Membership Manager
To promote, develop and advance flexographic printing technology.
1500 Members Founded: 1958

19093 Guild of Book Workers
521 5th Avenue
17th Floor
New York, NY 10175-1799
212-285-5581
Margaret Johnson, Publisher
Karen Crisalli, President

To broaden public awareness of the hand book arts, to stimulate commissions of fine bindings, and to stress the need for sound book conservation and restoration.
900+ Members Founded: 1906

19094 Independent Free Papers of America
PO Box 69
Covington, OH 45318-0069
937-473-2028
800-441-4372
Deborah Phillips, President
Joe Green, VP
Carol Hoheisel, Director
Gary Rudy, Executive Director
Bestows awards and compiles statistics.
300 Members Founded: 1980

19095 International Digital Enterprise Alliance
100 Daingerfield Road
4th Floor
Alexandria, VA 22314
703-837-1070
FAX: 703-837-1072
info@idealliance.org
www.idealliance.org
Chuck Myers, Chair
Anne Marie Bushell, Vice Chair
David J. Steinhardt, President/CEO
Dan Minnick, Secretary/Treasurer
Enables publishers and other information-driven enterprisers to strategize, innovate, standardize and implement information technology solutions in an open and cooperative crops industry environment.
300+ Members Founded: 1966

19096 International Publishing Management
710 Regency Drive
Suite 6
Keaney, MO 64068
816-902-4762
FAX: 816-902-4766
ipmainfo@ipma.org www.ipma.org
Bruce Hunzeker, President
Carol Kraft, COO
The professional association for in-house corporate publishing professionals who work for eductional institurions, the government, and private industry.
Founded: 1964

19097 Jenkins Independent Publishers
400 W Front Street
Traverse City, MI 49684
231-330-0445
FAX: 231-933-0448 800-706-4636
Jerrold R. Jenkins, Chairman And CEO
Provides comprehensive marketing and custom book publishing services for independent and small press book publishers.
160 Members Founded: 1996

19098 Magazine Publishers of America
810 7th Avenue
24th Floor
New York, NY 10019
212-872-3700

mpa@magazine.org
www.magazine.org
Nina Link, President
Ellen Oppenheim, Executive VP/CMO
Howard Polskin, VP/Communications
Promotes magazines as an advertising medium. Provides information services and assistance to members in areas of circulation marketing.
240 Members Founded: 1919

19099 Music Publishers Association
711 3rd Avenue
New York, NY 10017-4014
212-274-4044
FAX: 646-487-6779
pr@nmpa.org www.nmpa.org
David M. Israelite, President/CEO
Martin Bandier, Chairman/CEO
An advocate for the protection of music copyrights.
800 Members Founded: 1919

19100 National Association of Desktop Publishers
462 Old Boston Road
Topsfield, MA 01983-1232
978-876-6855
800-874-4113
Barry Harrigan, Owner
Trade organization which serves the desk top publishing industry and offers information resources.
5M Members Founded: 1987

19101 National Association of Hispanic
529 14th Street NW
Suite 1085
Washington, DC 20045
202-240-0566
FAX: 212-662-7251 www.nahp.org
Eddie Mundo, Chairman
Luis Russi, Vice Chairman
Rex Nutting, Manager
Promotes the Hispanic print media as a valuable means of communication. Works to ensure that member publications are listed in National Media Directories.
200 Members Founded: 1982

19102 National Association of Independent Publishers
PO Box 430
Highland City, FL 33846-0430
863-648-4420

naip@aol.com
www.publishersreport.com
Betty A Lampe, Executive Director
Assists and educates small publishing companies. Conducts seminars on marketing strategies, target audience, and techniques of book distribution. Especially helpful for the beginning or self-publisher.
500 Members Founded: 1979

19103 National Association of Publishers' Representatives
25224 Brucefield Road
Cleveland, OH 44122

FAX: 216-831-8070 866-288-0354
bsgrep@aol.com
www.naprassoc.com/
Raymond Coppola, President
Everett Knapp III, Executive Director
Provides information for publishers' representatives selling advertising space.
250 Members Founded: 1950

19104 National Council for Research on Women
11 Hanover Square
20
New York, NY 10005-2819
212-785-7335
FAX: 212-785-7350
ncrw@ncrw.org www.ncrw.org
Mariam K. Chamberlain, President
Linda G. Basch, Executive Director
To generate and facilitate collaborative research, communication and cooperation exchange amoung member centers and affiliates.
3,000 Members Founded: 1981

19105 National Newspaper Association
PO Box 7540
Columbia, MO 65205-7540
573-882-5800
FAX: 573-884-5490 800-829-4662
LynnEdinger@nna.org www.nna.org
Brian Steffens, Executive Director
Lynn Edinger, Director
Membership/Marketing
Industry trade newspaper. Accepts advertising.
2600 Members Founded: 1885

19106 National Paper Trade Association Alliance
500 Bi-County Blvd.
Suite 200E
Farmingdale, NY 11735
631-777-2223
FAX: 631-777-2224 800-355-6782
gerri@goNPTA.com
www.gonpta.com
William Frohlich, President
Jack Vaccaro, VP
An Association for the paper, packaging, and supplies distribution industry.
2000 Members Founded: 1903

19107 Newsletter & Electronic Publishers Association (NEPA)
1501 Wilson Boulevard
Suite 509
Arlington, VA 22209-2431
703-527-2333
FAX: 703-841-0629 800-356-9302
nepa@newsletters.org
www.newsletters.org
Patti Wysocki, Executive Director
Harry Baisden, Director Publications
International trade association serving the interests of publishers of newsletters and specialized information services.
550 Members Founded: 1977
Mailing list available for rent $65 per M.

19108 PMA/Independent Book Publishers Association
627 Aviation Way
Manhattan Beach, CA 90266
310-189-9697
FAX: 310-374-3342
info@pma-online.org
www.pma-online.org/
Jan Nathan, Executive Director
Terry Nathan, Director
Lisa Kreb, Website Manager
Andrea Nathan, Newsletter Advertising
Susan Nicoletti, Marketing/Cooperative Catalogs
Provides cooperative marketing programs, education and advocacy within the publishing industry.
4000+ Members Founded: 1983

19109 Publishing Institute
2075 S University Boulevard
D114
Denver, CO 80210
303-871-2570
FAX: 303-871-2501
pi-info@du.edu www.du.edu/pi
Elizabeth A Geiser, Director
Jill Smith, Co-Director

A national organization that combines workshops in editing and marketing with lecture/teaching sessions conducted by leading experts from all areas of publishing.

Founded: 1975

19110 Small Publishers Association of North America (SPAN)
1618 West Colorado Avenue
Colorado Springs, CO 80904
719-475-1726
FAX: 719-471-2182
SPAN@spannet.org www.spannet.org
Scott Flora, Executive Director/Editor

A nonprofit trade association for independent presses and self-publishers who want to produce better books and market them successfully. SPAN offers a monthly newsletter with information-rich articles and great benefits.

1300 Members Founded: 1996

19111 Society for Collegiate Journalists
Virginia Inesleyan College
Norfolk, VA 23502-5599
757-455-3419
FAX: 757-461-5025
wjruehlmann@vwc.edu www.scj.us
Dr. William Ruehlmann, Executive
Shirley Shedd, Second VP

A collegiate journalism organization.

1200 Members Founded: 1975

19112 Society for Scholarly Publishing
10200 West 44th Avenue
Suite 304
Wheat Ridge, CO 80033-2840
303-422-3914
FAX: 303-422-8894
info@sspnet.org www.sspnet.org
Heather Joseph, President
Jerry Bowman, Executive Director

A group that represents scholarly publications, such as journals, university publications and magazines.

800 Members Founded: 1978

19113 Society of National Association Publications
8405 Greensboro Drive
#800
Mc Lean, VA 22102
703-506-3285
FAX: 703-506-3266
snapinfo@snaponline.org
www.snaponline.org
Peter Banks, President
Larry Price, VP
Larry Price, Treasurer

Develops standards for editorial and advertising content of association and professional society magazines.

1045 Members Founded: 1964

19114 Software & Information Industry Assocation
1090 Vermont Avenue NW
6th Floor
Washington, DC 20005-4095
202-289-7442
FAX: 202-289-7097
privacy@siia.net siia.net
Ken Wasch, President
Steve Manzo, Chairman

Members are microcomputer software firms. Services include data collection program, software protection, contracts reference disk, conferences and lobbying.

1200 Members Founded: 1984

19115 Time Warner Bookmark
Little, Brown Publishers
1271 Avenue of Americas
New York, NY 10020
212-522-8700
FAX: 212-522-2067 800-759-0190
cust.service@twbg.com
www.twbookmark.com
Lawrence J. Kirshbaum, CEO/Chairman
Jamie Raab, Senior VP

Publisher of hardcover and paperback books in a variety of categories including that of both fiction and nonfiction, as well as audiobooks.

Founded: 1970

19116 Western Publications Association
823 Rim Crest Drive
Westlake Village, CA 91361
805-495-1863
FAX: 805-497-1849 888-556-0756
wpa@wpa-online.org
www.wpa-online.org
Christopher Schulz, President
Brad Stauffer, VP
Jane Silbering, Executive Director

Represents magazine publishing companies and companies related to publishing industry, in the western United States.

200 Members Founded: 1954

19117 Women in Production
276 Bowery
New York, NY 10012
212-334-2106
FAX: 212-431-5786
admin@p3-ny.org www.p3-ny.org
Rosemary Sirico, President
Diane Pesce, VP

Nonprofit profesional and educational association whose mission is to facilitate career growth and education through peer support and the exchange of information.

500 Members Founded: 2003

19118 Women's National Book Association
FDR Station
PO Box 237
New York, NY 10150
212-208-4629
FAX: 212-208-4629
publicity@bookbuzz.com
www.wnba-books.org
Jill A Tardiff, President
Laurie Beckelman, VP
Susannah Greenburg, Public Relations

An organization of women and men in all occupations allied to the book industry.

800 Members Founded: 1917

19119 Yellow Pages Publishers Association
2 Connell Drive
First Floor
Berkeley Heights, NJ 07922-2747
908-286-2380
FAX: 908-286-0620
KimberlyEnik@ypassociation.org
www.ypassociation.org/
George Burnett, Chairman
Dennis Payne, Vice Chairman
Neg Norton, President

Trade association which represents the Yellow Pages industry. YPPA's publisher members collectively produce over 96 percent of all directories published in the United States and account for 99 percent of the revenues generated by Yellow Pages advertising.

340 Members Founded: 1975

Newsletters

19120 AAP Monthly Report
Association of American Publishers
71 5th Avenue
2nd Floor
New York, NY 10003-3004
212-255-0200
FAX: 212-255-7007
SBeer@publishers.org
http://www.publishers.org
Patricia Schroeder, President/CEO
Thomas McKee, Executive VP
Rene Alegria, Editor

A report offering information and news to the publishing community. *$800.00*

19121 American Book Producers-Newsletter
American Book Producers Association
160 5th Avenue
New York, NY 10010-7003
212-645-2368
FAX: 212-242-6799 800-209-4575
office@abpaonline.org
http://www.abpaonline.org
David Rubel, Publisher
Dan Tucker, Co-President
David Katz, Manager

Trade association of independent book producers in the United States and Canada.

6 pages Monthly Founded: 1980
Circulation: 2500
Printed in 2 colors on matte stock

19122 American Library Association Newsletter
50 East Huron Street
Chicago, IL 60611-2795
312-944-6780
FAX: 312-944-2641 1 8-0 5-5 24
subscriptions@ala.org
http://www.ala.org
Eileen Cooke, Publisher
Keith Michael Fiels, CEO

News and information on legislation concerning libraries, new publications and technology issues *$60.00*

Monthly Founded: 1876

19123 Ancillary Profits
Pronto Printer
21 Putnam Avenue
Port Chester, NY 10573-2750
914-937-3773

prontopc2@aol.com
www.shopinvyeny.com
Marlene Jensen, Publisher
Offers in-depth coverage of ancillary businesses profitable to periodical publishers. *$222.00*
8 pages Monthly

19124 Augsburg Fortress Book Newsletter
Augsburg Fortress
426 S 5th Street
Minneapolis, MN 55415
612-330-3300
FAX: 612-330-3455 800-328-4648
Roderick Olson, Publisher
Reviews of religious books.
12 pages

19125 Book Arts
Center for Book Arts
28 W 27th Street
New York, NY 10001
212-481-0295
FAX: 212-481-9853
info@centerforbookarts.org
www.centerforbookarts.org
Don Lindgren, Publisher
Rory Golden, Executive Director
Center news and activities.

19126 Book Industry Study Group Newsletter
Book Industry Study Group
19 West 21st Street
Suite 905
New York, NY 10010-7003
646-336-7141
FAX: 646-336-6214
info@bisg.org http://www.bisg.org
Kent Freeman, Director
Jeff Abraham, Executive Director
Angela Bole, Marketing & Communication
For members only.
4 pages Weekly Founded: 1976
Circulation: 350 : online

19127 Book Marketing Update
Open Horizons Publishing
PO Box 205
Fairfield, IA 52556
641-472-6130
FAX: 641-472-1560 800-796-6130
info@bookmarket.com
http://www.bookmarket.com
John Kremer, Editor
Robert Sanny, Advertising/Sales Manager
Marketing ideas and trends plus key contacts for authors, book publishers and others interested in selling more books. Accepts advertising. *$297.00*
16 pages Fortnightly Founded: 1982
Circulation: 1500
Printed in 2 colors on matte stock

19128 Book News
American Book Producers Association
160 Fifth Avenue
New York, NY 10010-7003
212-645-2368
FAX: 212-242-6799 800-209-4575
office@abpaonline.org
http://www.abpaonline.org
David Rubel, President
Bok Hee, Manager
Bill Raggio, Contact
Founded: 1980
Circulation: 100

19129 Bookwatch
Midwest Book Review
278 Orchard Drive
Oregon, WI 53575-1129
608-835-7937

mbr@execpc.com
http://www.midwestbookreview.com
James A Cox, Editor-in-Chief
Capsule reviews of recommended large and small press titles. Accepts advertising. *$16.00*
12 pages Monthly Founded: 1976
Circulation: 30,000

19130 Bookwoman
Women's National Book Association
2166 Broadway
#9-E
New York, NY 10024
212-208-4629
FAX: 212-208-4629
http://www.wnba-books.org
Ellen Myrick, Editor
Jill A. Tardiff, President
Tri-annual journal for members of the Women's National Book Association. Stories of interest for people in the world of books. Book review are includes, how-to information and chapter news from across the United States.
Quarterly Founded: 1917
Circulation: 1000

19131 Business Publisher
JK Publishing
PO Box 71020
Milwaukee, WI 53211-7120
414-466-2065
FAX: 414-964-0843
John Kenney, Publisher
Covers start-ups, mergers and acquisitions and the business publishing industry: including magazines, newsletters and other information delivery vehicles. Accepts advertising. *$395.00*
8 pages Monthly

19132 Christian Science Publishing Society - Newsletter
Christian Science Publishing Society
1 Norway Street
Boston, MA 02115-3105
617-507-7929
FAX: 617-450-2071
gestert@csps.com
http://www.spirituality.com
Paul Bermel, Manager
Anita Nilsen, Managing Publisher
$49.00
Monthly Founded: 1883

19133 Cole Papers
Cole Group
PO Box 719
Pacifica, CA 94044-719
650-557-9595
FAX: 650-557-9696
info@colegroup.com
http://www.colegroup.com
David M Cole, Publisher/Editor
Marge Wetmore, Circulation Manager
Covers technology of the publishing business - newspapers, magazines and information providers. *$167.00*
Weekly Founded: 1989

19134 DPFN
Directory & Database Publishers Forum & Network
PO Box 194
Nyack, NY 10960
845-358-8034
FAX: 212-877-4110
http://www.dpfn.com
Barry Lee, Membership Chairman
Contains events, seminar information, publishers story, industry snapshots, and news pertaining to the industry. Members are large and small directory publishers, vendors to the trade and consultants. Provides networking opportunities and exposure to industry experts through their meetings and workshops.
Founded: 1990
Printed in on matte stock

19135 Educational Marketer
Simba Information
60 Long Ridge Road
Suite 300
Stamford, CT 06902
203-325-8193
FAX: 203-325-8915
info@simbanet.com
http://www.simbanet.com/
Linda Kopp, Editorial Director
Paul Ringer, Marketing Manager
Michael Norris, Editor
John Fuller, Executive Editor
Anthony Carrick, Contributing Editor
Reports on the entire educational publishing spectrum from el-hi to College. It covers the complete range of print and electronic tools including software, and multimedia materials. It details mergers, acquisitions, financial reports, distribution, adoption and enrollment trends, legislative issues *$650.00*
8 pages Founded: 1989
Printed in 4 colors

19136 Exchange
Association of American University Presses
71 W 23rd Street
Suite 901
New York, NY 10010-4102
212-989-1010
FAX: 212-989-0275
aaupny@netcom.com
http://aaupnet.org/
Hollis Holmes, Publisher
Peter J Givler, Executive Director
Rachel Weiss, Marketing Manager
Reports on issues relevant to scholarly publishing. *$10.00*
16 pages Quarterly

19137 Footprints Newsletter
Evangelical Christian Publishers Association
4816 S Ash Avenueoad
Suite 101
Tempe, AZ 85282
480-966-3998
FAX: 480-966-1944
info@ecpa.org http://www.ecpa.org

Doug Ross, President
Kelly Gallagher, VP
Dave Bird, Marketing

An international, not-for-profit, trade organization serving its industry by promoting excellence and professionalism, sharing relevant data, stimulating Christian fellowship, raising the effectiveness of member houses, and equipping them to meet the needs of the changing marketplace.
Monthly
Circulation: 280

19138 Guild of Book Workers-Newsletter
Guild of Book Workers
521 5th Avenue
17th Floor
New York, NY 10175-1799
212-285-5581

bcallery@founder.com
http://palimpsest.stanford.edu/byorg/gbw

Margaret Johnson, Publisher
Bernadette Callery, Membership Secretary

Information for the book arts field.

Circulation: 800

19139 Hotline
Newsletter & Electronic Publishers Association
1501 Wilson Boulevard
Suite 509
Arlington, VA 22209-2431
703-527-2333
FAX: 703-841-0629 800-356-9302
nepa@newsletters.org
http://www.newsletters.org

Harry Baisden, Director Publication
Patti Wysocki, Executive Director

Furthers the professional and economic interests of members. Future plans include seminars, research and representing members before federal agencies. Available only to members.
Founded: 1977 3000 names $65 per M.
Printed in 1 color on matte stock

19140 Independent Publishers Trade Report
PO Box 176
Southport, CT 06490-176
860-669-5848
FAX: 203-332-7629

Henry Berry, Publisher

News and information for independent publishers, monthly column in the COSMEP Newsletter.

19141 Independent Small Press Review
WHW Publishing
930 Via Fruteria
Santa Barbara, CA 93110-2322

Offers a comprehensive look at the concerns and issues of the small business publisher.

19142 Lifelong Learning Market Report
Simba Information
60 Long Ridge Road
Suite 300
Stamford, CT 06902
203-325-8193
FAX: 203-325-8915
info@simbanet.com
http://www.simbanet.com

Linda Kopp, Editor
David Goddard, Senior Editor

News and analysis for content and service providers of corporate training and professional development materials. Includes news on merger and aczuisitions, industry financial performance and trends, product development and distribution. *$625.00*
Founded: 1989

19143 National Association of Professional Print Buyers
15050 NE 20th Avenue
Suite A
North Miami, FL 33181-1123
305-956-9563

Vincent Millardi, Publisher

Accepts advertising. *$315.00*
296 pages Monthly

19144 Newsletter on Newsletters
20 W Chestnut Street
Rhinebeck, NY 12572
845-876-5222
FAX: 845-876-4943
newsonnews@newsletterbiz.com
http://www.newsletterbiz.com

Paul Swift, Editor/Publisher

Graphics, editorial, promotions, management and reports on the entire newsletter industry. *$275.00*
Founded: 1970

19145 PMA Newsletter
Publishers Marketing Association
627 Aviation Way
Manhattan Beach, CA 90266-7107
310-372-2732
FAX: 310-374-3342
pmaonline@aol.com
http://www.pma-online.org

Jan Nathan, Editor
Terry Nathan, Director

Publishing law, copyrighting, marketing, business management all directed toward the independent book publishing community.
Monthly Founded: 1983
Circulation: 10000

19146 PMA/Independent Book Publishers Association Newsletter
PMA/Independent Book Publishers Association
627 Aviation Way
Manhattan Beach, CA 90266
310-189-9697
FAX: 310-374-3342
info@pma-online.org
www.pma-online.org/

Jan Nathan, CEO
Terry Nathan, Executive Director

Marketing opportunities and news for independent book publishers.
Founded: 1983 15M names $125 per M.

19147 Personal Composition Report
Graphic Dimensions
134 Caversham Woods
Pittsford, NY 14534-2834
585-381-3428

Michael Kleper, Publisher

Covers all aspects of electronic publishing and imaging including news, reviews and in-depth analysis. Begun in 1979 by Professor Michael Kleper of RIT, the newsletter has provided consistent, valuable information for its readers. *$100.00*
16 pages Annual
Printed in 1 color on matte stock

19148 Pleasures of Publishing
Columbia University
2960 Broadway
New York, NY 10027-6902
212-541-1754
FAX: 212-854-1754
mgm2015@columbia.edu
http://www.columbia.edu

Rebecca Sehrader, CEO
Mathew Martg, Marketing

Industry news.

19149 Professional Publishing Report
Simba Information
60 Long Ridge Road
Suite 300
Stamford, CT 06902
203-258-8193
FAX: 203-358-5825
info@simbanet.com
http://www.simbanet.com

Linda Kopp, Editor
Charlie Friscia, Marketing
John Fuller, Executive Editor

Newletter focuses on the $10 billion professional publishing industry. Features in-depth analysis of each of the four major professional publishing categories: scientific/technical, medical, legal and business. Provides revenue breakdowns by media and market, merger and acquisition news, and analysis of market trends. *$715.00*
Founded: 1989

19150 Publishers Monthly Domestic Sales
Association of American Publishers
50 F Street NW
Suite 400
Washington, DC 20001
202-347-3375
FAX: 202-347-3690
SBeer@publishers.org
http://www.publishers.org

Lily G Clark, Membership Director
Katie Blough, Editor
Patricia Schroeder, President

Sales charts, index and rates for the publishing community.
Monthly Founded: 1970 278 names

19151 Publishers Multinational Direct
Direct International
1501 Third Avenue
New York, NY 10028-2101
212-861-4188
FAX: 212-628-5070
directin@ix.netcom.com
http://www.publishersmultinational.com

Alfred Goodloe, Editor

National and international coverage of the publishing community including printing, prepress and direct marketing. *$195.00*
Monthly

19152 Publishers Report
National Association of Independent Publishers
PO Box 430
Highland City, FL 33846-430
863-648-4420
FAX: 836-648-4420
naip@aol.com
http://www.publishersreport.com

Betsy A Lampe, Publisher

Provides a clearinghouse of information on small/independent publishing for its members. Accepts advertising. Departments include: 'New Books, Audios & Videos,' It's a Date,' 'NAIP Book Review,' 'New Media Sources,' 'Wanted,' 'In the Know,' 'F41,' and various others helpful for new publishers and self-publishers. *$40.00*

8 pages
Circulation: 500
Printed in 2 colors on matte stock

19153 Publishers' Auxiliary
National Newspaper Association
1010 N Glebe Road
Suite 450
Arlington, VA 22201
703-658-8808
FAX: 703-907-7901
info@nna.org http://www.nna.org

Stan Schwartz, Managing Editor
Lynn Edinger, Marketing Manager

Providing personnel announcements, new technology, economic trends, and new publicaiton and distribution methods for executives in the newpaper industry. *$85.00*

Monthly Founded: 1885
Circulation: 8102

19154 Publishing Markets
Reed Business Information
275 Washington Street
Newton, MA 12058-1630
617-964-3030
FAX: 617-558-4327
www.reedbusiness.com

Deborah Selsky, Publisher
San Buchan, Editor

Economic and demographic trends that affect the book publishing market. *$129.00*

19155 Publishing Poynters
Para Publishing
PO Box 8206-240
Santa Barbara, CA 93118-8206
805-968-7277
FAX: 805-968-1379 800-727-2782
danpoynter@parapublishing.com
http://www.parapublishing.com

Dan Poynter, Editor
Becky Carbons, Production Manager

Nonfiction book publishing news and ideas: marketing, promotion and distribution. *$9.95*

20 pages Monthly Founded: 1969
Circulation: 16000
Printed in 1 color : online

19156 Report on Preschool Programs
Business Publishers
8737 Colesville Road
Suite 1100
Silver Spring, MD 20910-3928
301-587-6300
FAX: 304-587-4530 800-274-6737
custserv@bpinews.com
http://www.bpinews.com

Leonard A Eiserer, Publisher
Chuck Dervarics, Editor

The one source to turn to for timely, accurate coverage of important developments in Head Start, child care, health care, special education and much more. *$357.00*

8 pages Founded: 1963

19157 SPAN
Small Publishers Association of North America
1618 W Colorado Ave
Colorado Springs, CO 80904-4029
719-475-1726
FAX: 719-471-2182
span@spannet.org
http://www.spannet.org

Marilyn Ross, Editor
Cathy Bowman, Production Manager

Includes money-making articles and book industry information.

24 pages Monthly Founded: 1996
Circulation: 4000

19158 SPAN Internet Newsletter
Small Publishers Association of North America
1618 West Colorado Avenue
Colorado Springs, CO 80904
719-475-1726
FAX: 719-471-2182
span@spannet.org www.spannet.org

Marilyn Ross, Executive Director/Editor
Tom Ross, VP

The SPAN Internet Newsletter features timely and useful information on many aspects of writing and the publishing industry, including articles on book marketing and publicity in addition to providing links to industry related Websites.

Monthly Founded: 1996
Circulation: 4000

19159 Small Publisher Co-Op
Nigel Maxey
1521 SE Palm Court
PO Box 1620
Stuart, FL 34994-1620
772-287-8117

spcoop@hotmail.com
http://www.spco-op.com

Niyel Maxey, President/Editor
Kevin Hawken, Member Service Manager

This monthly newsletter offers a guide to publishing and marketing books, reports, periodicals, etc. *$15.00*

Circulation: 5900

19160 Span Connection
Small Publishers Association of North America
PO Box 1306
Buena Vista, CO 81211-1306
719-395-4790
FAX: 719-395-8374
span@spannet.org
http://www.spannet.org

Scoot Flora, Editor
Scoot Flora, CEO

Wide variety of news and information about small-scale and individual publishing. *$105.00*

Monthly Founded: 1996
Circulation: 4000

19161 Specialty Directory Publishing Market Forecast
Simba Information
60 Long Ridge Road
Suite 300
Stamford, CT 06902
203-325-8193
FAX: 203-325-8915
info@simbanet.com
http://www.simbanet.com

Megan St. John, VP
Linda Kopp, Editorial Director
John Fuller, Executive Editor

Complete market size, revenue and growth figures and forecasts including revenues driven by electronic products and exclusive reanking of leading publishers by revenue. *$495.00*

Anually Founded: 1989

19162 Yellow Pages & Directory Report
Simba Information
60 Long Ridge Road
Suite 300
Stamford, CT 06902
203-325-8193
FAX: 203-325-8915
simbainfo@simbanet.com
http://www.simbanet.com

Linda Kopp, Editor
Donna Devaul, Marketing Director
John Fuller, Executive Editor

The primary independent source of timely news and information on the yellow pages industry. This twice-monthly newsletter covers the activities of utility and independent yellow pages publishers, suppliers, certified marketing representatives, sales agents and yellow pages associations. YP&DR contains stories about mergers and acquisitions, expansion efforts, and new releases, financial results at top companies, new sales contracts and management changes. *$715.00*

Founded: 1989

Magazines & Journals

19163 AP Special Edition
Associated Press
450 Rockefeller Plaza
New York, NY 10001
212-621-1500
FAX: 212-621-1723
info@ap.org http://www.ap.org

Thomas Curly, CEO
Kathelene Carroll, Editor
Laure Morris, Marketing Manager

Monthly Founded: 1848
Circulation: 7000

19164 Book Dealers World
North American Bookdealers Exchange
PO Box 606
Cottage Grove, OR 97424
541-942-7455
FAX: 541-942-7455
bookdealersworld@bookmarketingprofit.com
http://www.bookmarketingprofits.com

Al Galasso, Editorial Director
Steve Sherman, Publisher

The book marketing magazine for independent publishers and mail order entrepreneurs. A publication of the North American Book Dealers Exchange, an international book marketing organization, specializing in cooperative opportunities at trade shows, in mail order, press releases and more. *$45.00*

32 pages Quarterly Founded: 1980
Circulation: 10000
Printed in on newsprint stock

19165 Book Promotion Hotline
Ad-Lib Publications
51 1/2 W Adam
PO Box 1102
Fairfield, IA 52556-3226
515-472-6617
FAX: 641-472-3186 800-669-0773

Marie Kiefer, Editor/Publisher

Provides media contacts and other marketing sources of interest to the publisher/marketing trade. *$150.00*

4 pages Weekly
Circulation: 1,000

19166 Booklist
American Library Association
50 E Huron Street
Chicago, IL 60611
312-944-6780
FAX: 312-440-9374 800-545-2433
blst@kable.com
http://www.ala.org/aasl

Sue Ellen Beauregard, Editor
Bill Ott, Editor/Publisher
Mary Ellen Quinn, Editor

The purpose of this guide is to provide information on materials worthy of consideration for purchase by small and medium sized public libraries. *$79.95*

Founded: 1876

19167 CBA Marketplace
9240 Explorer Drive
Colorado Springs, CO 80920-5001
719-265-9895
FAX: 719-272-3510 800-252-1950
info@cbaonline.org
http://www.cbaonline.org

Bill Anderson, President/CEO
Chris Childers, Chairman
Greg Thornton, Director of Publications

Resource for Christian retailers & suppliers. *$59.95*

Monthly
Circulation: 8000

19168 Christian Retailing
Strang Communications Company
600 Rinehart Road
Lake Mary, FL 32746-4868
407-333-0600
FAX: 407-333-7133
maqcustsvc@strang.com
http://www.christianretailing.com

Stephen Strang, President
Tircia Stafford, Circulation Director

A trade journal designed to inform Christian bookstore owners about books, music and gifts, videos, etc. Also it features topics to help retailers run a successful business. *$75.00*

72 pages Monthly Founded: 1975
Circulation: 10000

19169 Circulation Management
PRIMEDIA Intertec-Marketing & Professional Service
PO Box 4235
Stamford, CT 06907-0235
212-475-2212
FAX: 203-358-5823
cmedit@aol.com www.circman.com

Roberta Thomas, Publisher

Subscriptions, renewals, direct mail, list selection, circulation planning, data management, fulfillment and list management. *$ 39.00*

Monthly
Circulation: 10,000

19170 Collegiate Journalist
Society for Collegiate Journalists
1584 Wesleyan Drive
Virginia Wesleyan College
Virginia Beach, VA 23502-5599
757-455-3419
FAX: 757-461-5025
wjruehlmann@vwc.edu
http://www.scj.us

J D Tarpley, Publisher
William Ruehlmann, CEO/President
Adam Earnheardt, Editor

For editors of yearbooks, magazines and newspapers. *$5.00*

28 pages Monthly

19171 Complete Guide to Self-Publishing
Communication Creativity
425 Cedar
Buena Vista, CO 81211-0909
719-395-8659
FAX: 719-395-8374 800-331-8355

Marilyn Ross, Publisher
Matthew Sullivan, Editor

The most comprehensive resource available about the business of publishing. Offers everything you need to know to write, publish, promote and sell books. *$19.99*

521 pages ISBN 1-582970-91-2

19172 Desktop Publishers Journal
462 Boston Street
Topsfield, MA 01983

FAX: 800-492-1014
www.dtpjournal.com

Barry Harrigan, Contact

Offers a comprehensive array of news, analysis, features and reviews on the latest products and services on the market today. *$ 15.00*

12 issues

19173 E-Content
Information Today
143 Old Marlton Pike
Medford, CT 08055-8750
609-654-6266
FAX: 609-654-4309 800-248-8466
custserv@infotoday.com
http://www.infotoday.com/

Michelle Manafy, Editor
Jared Bernstein, Editorial Assistant

Delivers essential research, reporting, news and analysis of content related issues. It is essential reading for executive and professionals involved in content creation, management, acquisition, organization and distribution in both commercial and enterprise environments. *$115.00*

10 issues/yr
Mailing list available for rent 4M names
Printed in 4 colors on glossy stock

19174 Editor & Publisher
Editor & Publisher International Yearbook
11 W 19th Street
10th Floor
New York, NY 10011-4234
212-291-1259
FAX: 212-691-7287
www.mediainfo.com

Michael Parker, President

Covers all facets of the newspaper business today and is regarded as the bible of the newspaper industry. *$184.00*

46 issues Founded: 1884

19175 Editorial Eye
EEI Communications
66 Canal Center Plaza
Suite 200
Alexandria, VA 22314-5507
703-683-0683
FAX: 703-683-4915
info@eeicommunications.com
http://www.eeicom.com

Claire Kincaid, Publisher
Robin Cormier, VP
Candee Wilson, Director
Linda B. Jorgensen, , Editor

Offering information on written excellence, editorial information and communication skills for readers. *$125.00*

Monthly Founded: 1972

19176 Electronic Publishing
PennWell Publishing Company
10 Tara Boulevard
5th Floor
Nashua, NH 03062-2880
603-891-0123
FAX: 603-891-0539
genepri@pennwell.com
www.electronic-publishing.com

Gene Pritchard, Publisher

For those who communicate in print, including service bureaus, printers, prepress houses and desktop publishers, it provides latest products, news and related developments. *$45.00*

Monthly
Circulation: 68,441

19177 F&W Publications
1507 Dana Avenue
Cincinnati, OH 45207
513-396-6160
FAX: 513-531-1025
www.writersdigest.com

Jeff Lapin, President

Articles that reflect the current state of American freelance writing.

72 pages 8 per year Founded: 1930 ISBN 7-148602-50-8
Circulation: 85,000

19178 Folio: Magazine for Magazine Management
PRIMEDIA Intertec-Marketing & Professional Service
PO Box 4272
Stamford, CT 06907-272
203-358-9900
FAX: 203-358-5821 800-975-5536
tsilber@red7media.com
http://www.primediabusiness.com/

Barbara Love, Editor
Kerry Smith, President /CEO
Jennel Jordan, Director of Marketing
Tony Silber, Editor/ Publisher
Karen Putrimas, Director Advertising Sales Manager

Written for the people who run the nation's magazines. Offers authoritative intelligence on the magazine market to enable industry professionals to navigate the widening range of strategic options. Every issue delivers features on the people and technologies that are transforming the magazine business, along with useful columns and departments, thought-provoking analysis and tactical advice for building successful magazines. *$96.00*

Monthly Founded: 1971
Circulation: 11550

19179 ForeWord Magazine
ForeWord Magazine
129 Front Street
Traverse City, MI 49684
231-933-3699
FAX: 231-933-3899
support@forewordmagazine.net
http://www.forewordmagazine.com

Alex Moore, Managing Editor
Stacy Price, Director Advertising Sales
Victoria Sutherland, Owner *$40.00*

Monthly Founded: 1998
Circulation: 20000 5000 names $75 per M.
Printed in 4 colors on 6 stock

19180 Independent Publisher Magazine
Jenkins Group
1129 Woodmere Ave
Ste B
Traverse City, MI 49686-4275
231-933-0445
FAX: 231-933-0448 800-706-4636
info@bookpublishing.com
http://www.bookpublishing.com

Jerrold R Jenkins, President
Jim Barmes, Editor
Andrew Pargel, Marketing Manager

Trade journal for the independent publishing, community, university presses, librarians, bookstores and professionals. *$40.00*
Monthly Founded: 1988
Circulation: 8000
Mailing list available for rent 42M names
Printed in 4 colors on glossy stock

19181 Information Publishing: Business/ Professional Markets & Media
Simba Information
60 Long Ridge Rd Ste 300
Stamford, CT 06902-234
203-258-8193
FAX: 203-358-5824
simbainfo@simbanet.com
http://www.simbanet.com

Linda Kopp, Editor
Donna Devall, Marketing Director
Charlie Friscia, Director of Advertising S

Demonstrates how publishers are profiting from media. Discover the opportunities in newsletters, directories, books, magazines, journals and electronic information services. More than 300 pages of information and analysis, 100 tables and charts, financial and operating information on more than 50 key publishing companies, 16 principal information markets reviewed in-depth, with five year forecasts by market and by media. *$1995.00*
Founded: 1989

19182 Inside Edge
International Publishing Management Association
1205 W College Street
Liberty, MO 64068
816-781-1111
FAX: 660-781-2790
ipmainfo@ipma.org
http://www.ipma.org

Larry Aaron, Executive Director
Susan Murphy, Editor
Jack Welch, CEO

Offers information on the association's activities, industry trends, and corporate publishing facility profiles. *$50.00*
24 pages Monthly
Circulation: 1500
Mailing list available for rent 2M names

19183 KM World
Information Today
143 Old Marlton Pike
Medford, CT 08055-8750
609-654-6266
FAX: 609-654-4309 800-248-8466
custserv@infotoday.com
http://www.infotoday.com/

Hugh Mckellar, Editor in Chief
Sandra Haimila, Managing Editor
Andy Moore, Publisher

Serves the knowledge management industry by offering components and processes, including success stories, designed to improve business. *$23.95*

Mailing list available for rent 4M names
Printed in 4 colors on glossy stock

19184 Link-Up Digital
Information Today
143 Old Marlton Pike
Medford, CT 08055-8750
609-654-6266
FAX: 609-654-4309 800-248-8466
custserv@infotoday.com
http://www.infotoday.com/
A web-only product featuring articles, reviews and more for users and producers of electronic information products and services.

Mailing list available for rent 4M names
Printed in 4 colors on glossy stock

19185 MultiMedia & Internet @Schools
Information Today
143 Old Marlton Pike
Medford, CT 08055-8750
609-654-6266
FAX: 609-654-4309 800-248-8466
custserv@infotoday.com
http://www.infotoday.com/

David Hoffman, Editor

A practical guide for K-12 library media specialists, technology coordinators and other educators with information on how to get high-performance learning from technology-based school products, services and resources. *$39.95*
6 issues/yr
Mailing list available for rent 4M names
Printed in 4 colors on glossy stock

19186 New Age Publishing and Retailing Alliance Trade Journal
PO Box 9
Eastsound, WA 98245-0009
360-376-2702
FAX: 360-376-2704

Marilyn McGuire, Executive Director
Carole Scarfuto, Administrative Director

Covers the publishing and retailing trades.
Bi-Monthly
Circulation: 10,000

19187 NewsInc
PO Box 719
Pacifica, CA 94044-719
650-557-9595
FAX: 650-557-9696
news@newsinc.net
http://www.newsinc.net

David Cole, Publisher/Editor *$147.00*

Weekly Founded: 1989

19188 Newspapers & Technology
Conley Magazines
1623 Blake Street
Suite 250
Denver, CO 80202
303-575-9595
FAX: 303-575-9555
letters@newsandtech.com
www.newsandtech.com/

Mary Van Meter, Publisher
Chuck Moozakis, Editor-in-Chief
Tara McMeekin, Editor
Hays Goodman, Associate Editor/Webmaster

Newspapers & Technology is a monthly trade publication for newspaper publishers and department managers involved in applying and integrating technology. Written by industry experts, News & Tech provides regular coverage of the following departments: prepress, press, postpress and new media.

Circulation: 16,874

19189 ONLINE Magazine
Information Today
143 Old Marlton Pike
Medford, CT 08055-8750
609-654-6266
FAX: 609-654-4309 800-248-8466
custserv@infotoday.com
http://www.infotoday.com/

Thomas Hogan, Publisher
Marydee Ojala, Editor
Lauree Padgett, Editorial Services Manager

Written for information professionals and provides articles, product reviews, case studies, evaluation and informed opinion aobut selecting, using and managing electronic information products, plus industry and professional information about online database systems, CD-ROMs and the Internet. *$115.00*
6 issues/yr
Mailing list available for rent 4M names
Printed in 4 colors on glossy stock

19190 Poets & Writer's Magazine
Poets & Writers
72 Spring Street
New York, NY 10012-4019
212-317-7920

editor@pw.org http://www.pw.org

Daryln Brewer, Editor
Christine Cassidy, Marketing Director
William Hayes, Finance Executive

Interviews, essays, grants and awards, practical information for poets and writers. *$19.95*

Circulation: 60000

19191 Progressive Review
1312 18th Street NW
5th Floor
Washington, DC 20036
202-835-0770
FAX: 202-835-0779
news@prorev.com
http://www.prorev.com

Sam Smith, Editor

Monthly Founded: 1964

19192 Publish
462 Boston Street
Suite 310
Topsfield, MA 01983
978-887-6855
FAX: 978-887-9245

Barry Harrigan, Owner

19193 Publishers Weekly Magazine
Reed Business Information
360 Park Avenue South
New York, NY 10011-5330
212-450-0067
FAX: 630-288-8686 800-278-2991

Sara Nelson, Editor-in-Chief
Rob Goulding, Publishing Director
Wendy Wels, Marketing Director
James Reed, Owner
James Ficher, Circulation Manager

Highlights mechanical or possible financial problems and trends the book industry may face due to implementation of new technology. *$225.00*
Weekly Founded: 1874
Circulation: 27,000

19194 Publishing & Production Executive
Mark Hertzog
401 N Broad Street
Philadelphia, PA 19108
215-238-5300
FAX: 215-238-5457
www.ppe-online.com

Allison Schill Eckel, Managing Editor
Gretchen Kirby, Editor

Addresses technological trends and issues relevant to print production managers specializing in books, magazines, catalogs, agency or corporate communications.
12 per year
Circulation: 30,000

19195 Quill
PO Box 94080
Palatine, IL 60094-v
765-653-3333
765-653-4631

19196 Searcher: Magazine for the Database Profes sional
Information Today
143 Old Marlton Pike
Medford, CT 08055-8750
609-654-6266
FAX: 609-654-4309 800-248-8466
custserv@infotoday.com
http://www.infotoday.com/

Thomas Hogan, Publisher
Barbara Quint, Editor in Chief
Lauree Padgett, Copy Editor

Explores and deliberates on a comprehensive range of issues important to the professional database researcher. Combines evaluations of data content with discussions of delivery media. *$86.95*
10 issues/yr
Mailing list available for rent 4M names
Printed in 4 colors on glossy stock

19197 Student Press Review
Columbia University
2960 Broadway
New York, NY 10027
212-541-1754
FAX: 212-854-9401
cspa@columbia.edu
http://www.studentpressreview.com/

Edmund J Sullivan, Director
Helen F Smith, Editor
Edmund J Sullivan, Publisher

Reports and advises on high school and college student media. Offers how-to articles and features to improve student newspapers, magazines and yearbooks in schools, colleges, and universities.
Quarterly Founded: 1925
Circulation: 2200

19198 Volt Report on Directory Publishing
Volt Directory Marketing
1800 Byberry Road
Suite 800
Huntingdon Valley, PA 19006-3520

FAX: 215-938-5549 800-677-3839

Kathy Wolden, Editor

As the monitor of the directory publishing industry, the Morgan report provides news on the people, companies, products and opportunities shaping the industry today. Includes practical how-to guidance on key facets of the directory publishing process as well as strategic overviews. *$95.00*
12 pages Monthly

19199 Writer Magazine
21027 Crossroads Circle
PO Box 1612
Waukesha, WI 53187-1612
262-796-8776
FAX: 262-796-1615 800-533-6644

Sylvia Burack, Publisher
Elfrieda Abbe, Editor

Practical guide to instruct, inform, and inspire writers as they work toward the goal of publication. Writers of short stories, novels, poetry, plays or science fiction, readers will find straightforward advice, up-to-date market lists and tips on manuscript submission. *$ 29.00*
Monthly Founded: 1987
Circulation: 43000

19200 Writer's Digest
F&W Publications
4700 E. Galbraith Rd
Cincinnati, OH 45236
513-312-2222
FAX: 513-531-1843 800-258-0929
WritersDig@fwpubs.com
www.FWPublications.com

Bill Reed, President

Information and how to tips for freelance writers. *$19.96*
Monthly Founded: 1920

Trade Shows

19201 American Medical Publishers' Association Annual Meeting
122 Fox Rd
Media, PA 19063-4905
212-255-0200
FAX: 212-255-7007
AMPA@association-cba.org
www.pspcentral.org

Robin Barlett, Executive Director

Information provided to medical publishing field.
Annual Founded: 1960

19202 Annual Publisher's Multinational Direct Conference
Publisher's Multinational Direct
1501 3rd Avenue
New York, NY 10028-2101
212-861-4188
FAX: 212-628-5070
directin@ix.netcom.com
www.publishersmultinational.com

Alfred M. Goodloe, President

You'll learn from our panels of leading multinational experts: the steps to success-the mistakes to avoid; ways to find quality response lists abroad; winning tests in foreign markets; how to write copy that rings the bell with prospects in diverse markets; find out how to market successfully in Europe, Asia/Pacific, Latin America; how publishers meet the challenge of multinational direct marketing in three categories of publications.

19203 Association of American University Presses Conference
Association of American University Presses
71 W 23rd Street
Suite 901
New York, NY 10010-3264
212-989-1010
FAX: 212-989-0275
annualmeeting@aaupnet.org
www.aaup.uchicago.edu/aaup_home.html

Peter Givler, Executive Director
Timothy Muench, Assistant Director

Annual conference and exhibits of equipment, supplies and services for scholarly publishing divisions of colleges and universities.
125 Attendees Annual

19204 Association of Free Community Papers
1630 Miner Street
Suite 204, Box 1989
Idaho Springs, CO 80452
877-203-2327
FAX: 781-459-7770
info@afcp.org www.afcp.org

Craig Mullin, Executive Director

Exhibits for publishers of free circulation papers and shopping/advertising guides.
Annual Founded: 1951

19205 Book Expo America
Reed Exhibitions
383 Main Avenue
Norwalk, CT 06851
203-404-4800
800-840-5614
cmuller@reedexpo.com
www.bookexpoamerica.com

Courtney Muller, Event Manager
Cathy Glickstein, Registration

Sponsored by American Booksellers Association and Association of American Publishers. More than 2,000 exhibits, 500 authors, over 60 conference sessions as well as a special area for rights business, all the latest titles across genres, uncover hidden gems, network, and meet the industry contacts to put you instantly on top of what you need to know for your business and job.
May/June Founded: 2000

19206 Christian Booksellers Association
PO Box 62000
Colorado Springs, CO 80962-2000
719-265-9895
FAX: 719-272-3510 800-252-1950
info@cbaonline.org
www.cbaonline.org

Bill Anderson, President
Chris Childers, Chairman

Exhibition and sales of Christian oriented products to include categories of books and Bibles, music, framed art, jewelry, videos, clothing gifts, cards, stationary, children products, computer software, church supplies, curriculum and store supplies.

12M Attendees July

19207 Foio: Publishing Summit
Red 7 Media
33 South Main Street
South Norwalk, CT 06854
203-854-6730
FAX: 203-854-6735
mtownsley@red7media.com
www.foliosummit.com

Meredith Townsley, Event Coordinator
Kelly Koenig, Director Exhibit & Sponsorship Sale

About a comprehensive educational and networking experience.
Annual

19208 Folio Show
Red 7 Media
33 South Street
Norwalk, CT 06854
203-854-6730
FAX: 203-854-6735
azucchi@red7media.com
www.folioshow.com/

Kerry Smith, President
Amy B. Zucchi, Event Director

Biennial show and exhibits of publishing supplies, paper, printing equipment, color separators, fulfillment houses, lists and related equipment, supplies and services to the magazine and book publishing trades.
7,000 Attendees

19209 InfoCommerce
InfoCommerce Group Inc
2 Bala Plaza
Suite 300
Bala Cynwyd, PA 19004
610-649-1200
FAX: 610-471-0515
rchristensen@infocommercegroup.com
www.icgconferences.com

Roxanne Christensen, Dir Awards Conferences & Consulting

Convenes all kinds of publishers who are bound only by their ability and willingness to take risks.
Oct 10-12 Philadelphia

19210 LMP Awards Luncheon and Ceremony
Book PubWorld
PO Box 3867
Frederick, MD 21705-3867

Literary Market Place honors the best and the brightest in the publishing industry.
February

19211 National Directory Conference
InfoCommerce Group
2 Bala Plaza
Suite 300
Bala Cynwyd, PA 19004
610-649-1200
FAX: 610-645-5360 866-669-2889
rchristensen@commercegroup.com
www.infocommercegroupreport.com/

Roxanne Christensen, Marketing Manager

The key industry networking event for Reference Directory, Buying Guide and Yellow Pages publishers who come together to learn publishing techniques, make contacts, evaluate suppliers and make deals. 25 booths.
300 Attendees September Founded: 1995

19212 New England Booksellers Association Annual Trade Show
1770 Massachusetts Avenue
#332
Cambridge, MA 02140
617-576-3070
FAX: 617-576-3091 800-466-8711
rustyneba.org
www.newenglandbooks.org/

Allan Schmid, President
Dale Szczeblowski, VP

Offers the opportunity for publishers to get their products in the hands of the booksellers in an area with one of the highest concentrations of readers in the country. This traditional multi-media exhibition is the largest of the regional conference in bookseller attendance.
2M+ Attendees September/October

19213 Publishing Institute
Publishing Institute
2075 S University Boulevard
#D-114
Denver, CO 80210-4300
303-832-5280
FAX: 303-871-2501
pi-info@du.edu www.du.edu/pi

Elizabeth Geiser, Director

Combines workshops in editing and marketing with lecture/teaching sessions conducted by leading experts from all areas of publishing.
90 Attendees July-August

19214 Small Press Book Fair
Small Press Center
20 W 44th Street
New York, NY 10036-6604
212-764-7021
FAX: 212-354-5365
smallpress@aol.com
www.smallpress.org

Mary Bertschmann, Chair
Lloyd Jassin, Vice Chair
Mashala Solammi, Owner

One of the major book fairs for small press. Containing 100 booths and 100 exhibits.
2,500 Attendees March

19215 Writing Academy Seminar
Writing Academy
4010 Singleton Road
Rockford, IL 61114
815-877-9675

mailto.pattyk@wams.org
www.wams.org/indexhtm
Annual seminar and exhibits by Christian writers.

19216 Yellow Pages Publishers Association Convention
Yellow Pages Publishers Association
116 Cass Street
Traverse City, MI 49684

FAX: 231-486-2182 800-267-9002
hq@adp.org www.adp.org/

R. Lawrence Angove, President

Annual convention and exhibits of equipment, supplies and services for the publication of Yellow Pages telephone directories.

Directories & Databases

19217 Advertising and Publicity Resources for Scholarly Books
Association of American University Presses
71 W 23rd Street
Suite 901
New York, NY 10010-4102
212-989-1010
FAX: 212-989-0275
info@aaupent.org www.aaupnet.org

Peter Givler, Executive Director
Timothy Muench, Assistant Director

This comprehensive directory lists periodicals which accept advertising or review copies of scholarly publications. *$189.00*
425 pages

19218 Alternative Publications: A Guide to Directories and Other Sources
Mcfarland & Company
960 NC Nwy 88 W
Jefferson, NC 28640-0611
336-246-4460
FAX: 336-246-5018
info@mcfarlandpub.com
www.mcfarlandpub.com

Robert Franklin, President

Offers indexes and abstracts, review sources and bibliographies dealing with alternative publications. *$18.95*
96 pages

19219 American Book Producers Directory
American Book Producers Association
160 5th Avenue
New York, NY 10010-7003
212-645-2368
FAX: 212-242-6799 800-209-4575
abpahdq@abpaonline.org
www.abpaonline.org

David Rubel, President
David Katz, Manager

40 pages Founded: 1980
Circulation: 2,000
Printed in 2 colors on matte stock

19220 American Book Trade Directory
Information Today
143 Marlton Pike
Medford, NJ 08055-8750
609-654-6266
FAX: 609-654-4309
custserv@infotoday.com
www.infotoday.com

Thomas H Hogan, Publisher/President
John Bryans, Publisher/Editor-in-Chief Books
Lauree Padgett, Editorial Services Manager
Inge Coffey, Circulation Manager
Paat Palatucci, Assistant to the President

A US book trade community. Profiles 25,500 retail and antiquarian book dealers, plus 1,200 book and magazine wholesalers, distributors, and jobbers in all 50 states and US territories. *$299.00*
1800 pages ISBN 1-573872-12-1

19221 American Directory of Writer's Guidelines
Dustbooks
PO Box 100
Paradise, CA 95967-0100
530-877-6110
FAX: 530-877-0222 800-477-6110
directories@dustbooks.com
www.dustbooks.com
Brigitte M Phillips, Editor
Susan D Klassen, Editor
Doris Hall, Editor
These guidelines help writers target their submissions to the exact needs of the individual publisher. A compilation of information for freelancers from more than 1,500 magazine editors and book publishers. *$29.95*
752 pages ISBN 1-884956-40-8

19222 Association of American University Presses Directory
Association of American University Presses
71 W 23rd Street
Suite 901
New York, NY 10010-3264
212-989-1010
FAX: 212-989-0275
info@aaupnet.org
www.aaup.uchicago.edu/aaup_home.html
Peter Givler, Executive Director
Timothy Muench, Assistant Director
114 presses and affiliates worldwide. *$14.95*
Annual November

19223 Bacon's Calendar Directory
Bacon's Publishing Company
332 S Michigan Avenue
Chicago, IL 60604-4301
312-228-8239
FAX: 312-922-3127 800-621-0561
info@bacons.com www.bacons.com
Joseph Bernado, President/COO
Stephen Newman, CEO
Brian Birkholz, Sr. VP/CFO
Helps you match your story and products ideas with specific issues of publications containing upcoming related editorial features. *$350.00*
Annual
Printed in 1 color on matte stock : internet

19224 Bacon's Internet Media Directory
Bacon's Publishing Company
332 S Michigan Avenue
Chicago, IL 60604-4301
312-228-8239
FAX: 312-922-3127 800-621-0561
info@bacons.com www.bacons.com
Joseph Bernardo, President/COO
Stephen Newman, CEO
Brian Birkholz, Sr. VP/CFO
Information about online editors and media. *$300.00*
Annual
Printed in 1 color on matte stock : internet

19225 Bacon's Media Calendars
Bacon's Publishing Company
332 S Michigan Avenue
Chicago, IL 60604-4034
312-228-8239
FAX: 312-922-3127 800-521-0561
directories@bacons.com
www.bacons.com
Joseph Bernado, President/COO
Stephen Newman, CEO
Brian Birkholz, Sr. VP/CFO
Over 2,000 magazines and over 200 major daily newspapers editorial calendars for the upcoming year. *$350.00*
900 pages Annual

19226 Bacon's Newspaper & Magazine Directories
Bacon's Publishing Company
332 S Michigan Avenue
Chicago, IL 60604-4034
312-228-8239
FAX: 312-922-3127 800-621-0561
info@bacons.com www.bacons.com
Joseph Bernado, President/COO
Stephen Newman, CEO
Brian Birkholz, Sr. VP/CFO
Two volume set listing all daily and community newspapers, magazines and newsletters, news service and syndicates, syndicated columists, complete editorial staff listings of each publication provided, covers US, Canada, Mexico,and Carribean. *$350.00*
4,700 pages Annual Founded: 1951
Printed in 1 color on matte stock : internet

19227 Books and Periodicals Online
Literary Technology Alliance
264 Lexington Avenue
Room 4C
New York, NY 10016-4182
212-686-8816
FAX: 212-686-8776
info@booksandperiodicals.com
www.booksandperiodicals.com/
Nuchine Nobari MLS, MBA, Editor
BPO is an international directory of periodicals included in onlinedatabases. Arranged alphabetically, entries include Publication title, dates covered in each database, whether coverage is in Full text, Abstract, or Index, ISSN, and title changes. Online hosts and addresses for producers and vendors are given in separate list. Lists over 97,000 sources and includes an appendix of newspapers and their URL, in alphabetical and geographic order. *$399.00*
3400 pages 4 issues Founded: 1987 ISBN 0-963027-78-X
Circulation: 1400
Printed in 2 colors

19228 Business Info USA
InfoUSA
5711 S 86th Circle
Omaha, NE 68127-4146
402-934-4500
FAX: 402-331-5481 888-260-7943
karen.peters@infousa.com
www.directoriesusa.com
Vinod Gupta, Chief Executive Officer
Karen Peters, Account Executive
$2750.00
Monthly Founded: 1972
Circulation: 4000000

19229 Business Periodicals Index
HW Wilson Company
950 University Avenue
Bronx, NY 10452-4297
718-888-8405
FAX: 800-590-1617 800-367-6770
custserv@hwwilson.com
www.hwwilson.com
Designed for businesses, business schools and libraries, business periodicals index covers English-language business periodicals and trade journals. Users enjoy quick access to feature articles, product reviews, interviews, biographical sketches, corporate profiles, obituaries, surveys, book reviews, reports from associations, societies, trade shows and conferences, and more. The database also provides SIC codes for industries and names of corporations used as subject headings.

19230 Complete Directory of Large Print Books and Serials
RR Bowker
630 Central Avenue
New Providence, NJ 07974
908-286-1090
FAX: 908-219-0098 800-526-9537
info@bowker.com www.bowker.com
A D'Agostino, Marketing Director
Offers a list of over 125 publishers of more than 11,000 periodicals, books and paperbacks printed in at least 14-point type. *$ 180.00*
Annual

19231 Corporate Yellow Book
Leadership Directories
104 5th Avenue
New York, NY 10011-6901
212-627-4140
FAX: 212-645-0931
corporate@leadershipdirectories.com
www.leadershipdirectories.com
Vonessa Ruffin, Editor
Contact information for over 48,000 executives at over 1,000 companies and more than 9,000 board members and their outside affiliations. *$400.00*
1,400 pages Quarterly Founded: 1986
50,000 names $105 per M. : CD-Rom

19232 Directories in Print
Gale Research
27500 Drake Road
Farmington Hills, MI 48331
248-994-4253
FAX: 800-414-5043 800-877-4253
gale.salesassistance@thomson.com
www.gale.com
Offers more than 15,500 business and industrial directories, professional and scientific rosters and biographical directories published in the US. *$655.00*
2,200 pages

19233 Directory of Poetry Publishers
Dustbooks
PO Box 100
Paradise, CA 95967-0100
530-877-6110
FAX: 530-877-0222 800-477-6110
directories@dustbooks.com
www.dustbooks.com
Len Fulton, Editor
Over 2,100 magazines, small and commercial presses and university presses that accept poetry for publication. *$25.95*
300 pages Annual ISBN 0-916685-47-0
Circulation: 2,000

19234 Directory of Small Magazines Press Magazine Editors & Publishers
Dustbooks
PO Box 100
Paradise, CA 95967-0100
530-877-6110
FAX: 530-877-0222 800-477-6110
directories@dustbooks.com
www.dustbooks.com
Len Fulton, Editor
This directory contains more than 7,500 listings of editors and publishers in alphabetical order, along with their associated publishing companies, their addresses, phones, e-mail addresses and Web pages. Includes self publishers. *$25.95*

460 pages Annual Founded: 1967 ISBN 0-913218-28-6
Circulation: 1,000
Mailing list available for rent

19235 Editor & Publisher International Yearbook
Editor & Publisher Company
770 Broadway
New York, NY 10003-9595
212-291-1259
FAX: 646-654-5370 800-336-4380
editorandpublisher@espcomp.com
www.editorandpublisher.com

Sid Holt, Editor-in-Chief
Greg Mitchell, Editor
Michael Parker, President

Daily and Sunday newspapers in the US and Canada; weekly newspapers; foreign daily newspapers; special service newspapers; newspaper syndicates; news servides; journalism schools; foreign language and Black newspapers in the US; news, picture and press services; feature and news syndicates; comic and magazine services; advertising clubs; trade associations; clipping bureaus; house organs; journalism awards; manufacturers of equipment and supplies. *$230.00*
Annual March

19236 Editor & Publisher Market Guide
Editor & Publisher Company
770 Broadway
New York, NY 10003-9595
212-291-1259
FAX: 646-654-5370 800-336-4380
editorandpublisher@espcomp.com
www.editorandpublisher.com

Sid Holt, Editor-in-Chief
Greg Mitchell, Editor
Michael Parker, President

More than 1,700 newspaper markets in the US and Canada. *$100.00*
Annual November
Circulation: 4,500

19237 Editor & Publisher: Journalism Awards and Fellowships Directory Issue
Editor & Publisher Company
770 Broadway
New York, NY 10003-9595
212-291-1259
FAX: 646-654-5370 800-336-4380
editorandpublisher@espcomp.com
www.editorandpublisher.com

Sid Holt, Editor-in-Chief
Greg Mitchell, Editor
Michael Parker, President

Over 500 cash prizes, scholarships, fellowships and grants available to journalists and students for work on special subjects or in specific fields. *$4.00*
Annual December
Circulation: 28,500

19238 Grey House Publishing
185 Millerton Road
PO Box 860
Millerton, NY 12546
518-890-0526
FAX: 518-789-0545 800-562-2139
books@greyhouse.com
www.greyhouse.com

Leslie Mackenzie, Publisher
Richard Gottlieb, Editor

Publishes over 60 titles including reference directories in the areas of business, education, health and statistics and demographics, as well as educational encyclopedias and business handbooks. All titles offer detailed information in well-organized formats. Many titles available online.

19239 International Directory of Little Magazines & Small Presses
Dustbooks
PO Box 100
Paradise, CA 95967-0100
530-877-6110
FAX: 530-877-0222
directories@dustbooks.com
www.dustbooks.com

Len Fulton, Editor

Lists more than 4,000 book and magazine publishers of literary, avant garde, cutting-edge contemporary, left wing, right wing and radical chic fiction to non-fiction essays, reviews, artwork, music, satire, criticism, commentary, letters, parts of novels, longpoems, concrete art, collages, plays, news items and more. *$55.00*
Annual/Cloth ISBN 0-916685-49-7
Circulation: 1,000

19240 International Literary Market Place
Information Today
143 Old Marlton Pike
Medford, NJ 08055-8750
609-654-6266
FAX: 609-654-4309
custserv@infotoday.com
www.infotoday.com

Thomas H Hogan, Publisher/President
John Bryans, Publisher/Editor-in-Chief Books
Lauree Padgett, Editorial Services Manager
Inge Coffey, Circulation Manager

The directory of the international book publishing industry with 16,500 up to date profiles with book related concerns, including trade organizations, distributors, dealers, literary associations, trade publications, book trade events, and other resources conveniently organzied in a country by counrty format *$240.00*
1800 pages ISBN 1-573871-75-3

19241 Literary Market Place
Information Today
143 Old Marlton Pike
Medford, NJ 08055-8750
609-654-6266
FAX: 609-654-4309
custserv@infotoday.com
www.infotoday.com

Thomas H Hogan, Publisher/President
John Bryans, Publisher/Editor-in-Chief
Lauree Padgett, Editorial Services Manager
Inge Coffey, Circulation Manager

The ultimate insider's guide to US book publishing industry with over 14,000 listings in all.

19242 Livestock Publications Council Membership Directory
Livestock Publications
910 Currie Street
Fort Worth, TX 76107
817-336-1130
FAX: 817-232-4820
dianej@flash.net
www.livestockpublications.com
Offers information on over 100 US and Canadian LPC-member livestock magazines, newspapers and newsletters.
40 pages

19243 Magazines for Libraries
RR Bowker
630 Central Avenue
New Providence, NJ 07974
908-286-1090
FAX: 908-219-0098 800-526-9537
info@bowker.com www.bowker.com

A D'Agostino, Marketing Director

Provides detailed evaluations on more than 7,500 top-rated periodicals. *$170.00*
1,200 pages Triennial

19244 National Journal
National Journal
600 New Hampshire Avenue, NW
Washington, DC 20037
202-739-8400
FAX: 202-833-8069 800-207-8001
service@nationaljournal.com
www.nationaljournal.com

John Fox Sullivan, President/Publisher
Steve Hull, Senior VP
Timothy B Clark, VP

Publishes directories in the area of government.

19245 Newsletters in Print
Gale Research
27500 Drake Road
Farmington Hills, MI 48331
248-994-4253
FAX: 800-414-5043 800-877-4523
gale.salesassistance@thomson.com
www.gale.com
Offers over 12,000 periodicals in newsletter format issued on a regular basis by both commercial and noncommercial publishers. *$ 185.00*
1,600 pages Biennial

19246 Progressive Periodicals Directory
Progressive Education
PO Box 120574
Nashville, TN 37212-0574
615-367-1874

Craig T Canan, Editor

About 600 social-concerns periodicals. *$16.00*

19247 Publishers, Distributors, and Wholesalers of the United States
RR Bowker
630 Central Avenue
New Providence, NJ 07974
908-286-1090
FAX: 908-219-0098 800-526-9537
info@bowker.com www.bowker.com

A D'Agostino, Marketing Director

Directory of services and supplies to the industry. *$215.00*
2,544 pages Annual

19248 Publishing & Production Executive: Who's Who of Suppliers and Services
North American Publishing Company
401 N Broad Street
Philadelphia, PA 19108-1001
215-385-5300
FAX: 800-664-1533 800-777-8074
customerservice@napco.com
www.napco.com
Directory of services and supplies to the industry. *$35.00*

Circulation: 30,000

19249 Single Unit Supermarkets Operators
Chain Store Guide
3922 Coconut Palm Drive
Tampa, FL 33619-3506
813-276-6700
FAX: 813-627-6882 800-778-9794
info@csgis.com www.csgis.com
Chris Leedy, Advertising Sales
Shami Choon, Manager
Discover more than 7,100 single-unit supermarkets with annual sales topping $500,000 dollars. This comprehensive desktop reference makes it easy to reach our compiled list of 21,000 key executives and buyers, plus their primary wholesalers. *$335.00*
725 pages Annual

19250 Small Publishers Association of North America (SPAN)
PO Box 1306
Buena Vista, CO 81211-1306
719-395-4790
FAX: 719-395-8374
marilyn@spannet.org
www.spannet.org
Marilyn Ross, Executive Director/Editor
Tom Ross, VP
Cathy Bowman, Production Manager
Online resource for book publishing know-how. Works to advance the image and profits of self publishers and independent publishers through education and marketing opportunities.

19251 Something About the Author
Gale Research
27500 Drake Road
Farmington Hills, MI 48331
248-994-4253
FAX: 800-414-5043 800-877-4253
gale.salesassistance@thomson.com
www.gale.com
Authors and illustrators of children's books are the focus of this directory for the publishing industry. *$85.00*
Per Volume

19252 Standard Periodical Directory
Oxbridge Communications
186 5th Avenue
New York, NY 10010-4311
212-741-0231
FAX: 212-633-2938 800-955-0231
custserv@mediafinder.com
www.mediafinder.com
Patricia Hagood, Publisher
Cirulation, advertising and list rental info for more than 75,000 North American periodicals. *$1495.00*
2,326 pages Annual Founded: 1964 ISBN 1-891783-23-8
Circulation: 3,500
Printed in 4 colors

19253 Supermarket, Grocery & Convenience Store Chains
Lebhar-Friedman
425 Park Avenue
New York, NY 10022
212-756-5000
FAX: 813-627-6886
info@lf.com www.lf.com
J Roger Friedman, President
Directory of US and Canadian supermarket chains. *$335.00*

19254 Supermarket, Grocery & Convenience Stores
Chain Store Guide
3922 Coconut Palm Drive
Tampa, FL 33619-3506
813-276-6700
FAX: 813-627-6882 800-778-9794
info@csgis.com www.csgis.com
Chris Leedy, Advertising Sales
Shami Choon, Manager
Contains information on close to 3,400 U.S. and Canadian supermarket chains, each with at least $2 million in annual sales - one of the most profitable segments in this sector of the economy. The companies in this database operate over 41,000 individual supermarket, superstore, club store, gourmet supermarkets and combo-store units. A special convenience store section profiles 1,700 convenience store chains operating over 85,000 stores. *$335.00*
Annual 700 names

19255 Ulrich's International Periodicals Directory
RR Bowker
630 Central Avenue
New Providence, NJ 07974-1541
908-286-1090
FAX: 908-219-0098 800-526-9537
info@bowker.com www.bowker.com
A D'Agostino, Marketing Director
Offers over 165,000 regularly and irregularly issued periodicals published worldwide. *$459.95*
8,000 pages Annual

19256 Veterinary Economics
Veterinary Healthcare Communications
8033 Flint
Lenexa, KS 66214
913-492-4300
FAX: 913-492-4157 800-255-6864
vmpg@vetmedpub.com
www.vetmedpub.com
Daniel R. Verdon Chapman, Executive Director
Ray Click, VP/General Manager
Publishes two monthly magazines, a full drug list resource, and business books; conducts the Central Veterinary Conference trade show; rents its mail lists and does custom communication projects.
Monthly
Circulation: 52,000
Mailing list available for rent 48M+ names
Printed in 4 colors on matte stock

Industry Web Sites

19257 www.aaup.princetou.edu
Exchange

Reports on issues relevant to scholarly publishing.

19258 www.aaupnet.org/membership/directory
Association of American University Presses

Members are university presses and a limited number of presses of non-degree-granting scholarly institutions.

19259 www.abaa.org
Antiquarian Booksellers Association of America

A trade association of rare book dealers.

19260 www.abpaonline.org
American Book Producers Association

Increases the book industry's awareness of members capabilities and exchanges information on improving business. Develops concepts for books and other publications.

19261 www.accessabc.com
Audit Bureau of Circulations

The world's largest circulation-auditing organization, ABC provides circulation data on 1,400+ newspapers and more than 1,100 periodicals to ABC-member publications, advertisers and advertising agencies.

19262 www.ampaonline.org
American Medical Publishers' Association

Information provided to the medical publishing field.

19263 www.bisg.org
Book Industry Study Group

Promotes and supports research, enabling various sectors of the industry to develop and expand their professional and business plans. Book Industry Study Group has various paperback publications.

19264 www.bizpubs.org
Alliance of Area Business Publications

Represents metropolitan area and state-wide business to business publications with conventions, newsletters, and other services.

19265 www.bookbuilders.org
Bookbuilders West

A nonprofit organization that provides a forum for publishers and suppliers to share experiences via dinners, social events and educational seminars.

19266 www.bookmarketingprofits.com
North American Bookdealers Exchange

Independent publishers and mail order entrepreneurs. An international book marketing organization specializing in cooperative opportunities at trade shows, in mail order, press releases, and more.

19267 **www.bookpublishing.com**
Jenkins Independent Publishers

19268 **www.catholicpress.org**
Catholic Press Association of the US and Canada

19269 **www.clmp.org**
Council of Literary Magazines and Presses

Membership is open to any noncommercial literary magazine or press that publishes at least one or more books per year.

19270 **www.columbia.edu/eu/cspa**
Columbia Scholastic Press Association

International student press association composed of writing students, journalists and faculty advisers in schools and colleges through educational conferences, idea exchanges and recognition programs.

19271 **www.crain.com**
Crain Communications

19272 **www.du.edu/pi**
Publishing Institute

A national organization that combines workshops in editing and marketing with lecture/teaching sessions conducted by leading experts from all areas of publishing.

19273 **www.ecpa.org**
Evangelical Christian Publishers Association

Promotes excellence and professionalism, shares relevant data, and equips Christian publishers to meet the needs of the changing marketplace.

19274 **www.flexography.org**
Flexographic Technical Association

19275 **www.flexography.org/flexsys/index.cfm**
Flexographic Technical Assn Education & Training

Magazine publishing.

19276 **www.greyhouse.com**
Grey House Publishing

Selected Grey House directories in the fields of business, health and education are available online. Users can search our online databases by several different search criteria, such as product categories, geographic area, sales volume and much, much more. Full Grey House catalog and online ordering also available.

19277 **www.haworthpressinc.com**
Haworth Press

Independent publisher of academic and professional books and journals on a wide range of subjects focusing on contemporary issues. Haworth journals are edited by the leaders in their fields and are widely indexed and abstracted by the major services.

19278 **www.ipma.org**
International Publishing Management Association

The professional association for in-house corporate publishing professionals who work for educational institutions, governments and private industry.

19279 **www.newsletters.org**
Newsletter & Electronic Publishers Association

International trade association serving the interests of publishers of newsletters and specialized information services.

19280 **www.nmpa.org**
National Music Publishers' Association

19281 **www.p3-ny.org/**
Partnership in Print Production

Promotes the interests of women.

19282 **www.pacificpress.com**
Pacific Press Publishing Association

Promotes the interests of publishing, press, and media professionals.

19283 **www.papertrade.com**
National Paper Trade Association

19284 **www.publishers.org**
Association of American Publishers

Principal trade association for the US book publishing industry members comprise most of the major commerical book publishers in the US, as well as smaller and medium-sized houses, not-for-profit publishers, university presses, and scholarly societies.

19285 **www.publishersreport.com**
National Association of Independent Publishers

Assists and educates small publishing companies. Conducts seminars on marketing strategies, target audience, and techniques of book distribution. Especially helpful for the beginning or self-publisher.

19286 **www.snaponline.org**
Society of National Association Publications

Develops standards for editorial and advertising content of association and professional society magazines.

19287 **www.spannet.org**
Small Publishers Association of North America

For independent presses and self-publishers who want to produce better books and market them more successfully.

19288 **www.sspnet.org**
Society for Scholarly Publishing

A group that represents scholarly publications, such as journals, university publications and magazines.

19289 **www.theacp.org**
Associated Church Press

Aims to share ideas and concerns in religious publishing and to stimulate higher standards of religious journalism to exert a more positive influence.

19290 **www.thomson.com**
Thomson.Com

A shared Web service that provides critical tools for more than 35 publishers.

19291 **www.wpa-online.org**
Western Publications Association

Represents magazine publishing companies and companies related to publishing industry, in the western United States.

Associations

19292 Accredited Review Appraisers Council
ARAC
303 W Cypress Street
San Antonio, TX 78212

800-486-3676
Provides education and designation in appraisal and real estate review.

19293 American Association of Certified
3129 Perlett Drive
Cameron Park, CA 95682
530-676-0391
FAX: 530-676-0391 888-647-7564
aprslpro@frontiernet.net
www.appraisalpro.org
A national organization that offers designations to qualified appraisers, teaches courses on latest appraisal information and offers courses on home inspection.

19294 American College of Real Estate Lawyers
11300 Rockville Pike
Suite 903
Rockville, MD 20852
301-816-9811
FAX: 301-816-9786
webmaster@acrel.org www.acrel.org
Wayne S Hyatt, President
Philip M Horowitz, VP
Michael H Rubin, Treasurer
Mark F Mehlman, Secretary
Jill Pace, Executive Director
Members are CPAs working in the real estate field.

19295 American Congress on Surveying & Mapping
6 Montgomery Village Avenue
Suite 403
Gaithersburg, MD 20879
240-680-0765
FAX: 240-632-1321
info@acsm.net www.acsm.net
Curtis W Sumner, Executive Director
Ed McKay, President
Organization of professionals for networking and education in the topographical field.

5500 Members Annual Founded: 1942

19296 American Homeowners Foundation

6776 Little Falls Road
Arlington, VA 22213
703-536-7776
FAX: 703-536-7079
ahf@americanhomeowners.org
www.americanhomeowners.org
Bruce Itahn, President
A national consumer organization representing the nation's 75 million homeowners.
Founded: 1984

19297 American Industrial Real Estate
Pacific Financial Center
800 West 6 Th Street
Suite 800
Los Angeles, CA 90017
213-687-8777
FAX: 213-687-8616
jcruz@airea.com www.airea.com
Joy D'La Cruz, Chief Operations Officer
Tim Hayes, Executive Director
Encourages high professional standards. Has developed industrial multiple listing system and standard lease form. Publishes a quarterly newsletter.
1300+ Members Founded: 1960

19298 American Land Title Association
1828 L Street NW
Suite 705
Washington, DC 20036-5104
202-296-3671
FAX: 202-223-5843
lorri_ragan@alta.org www.alta.org
Jim Maher, Executive VP
Lorri Lee Ragan, Communications Director
Trade organization for title insurers, abstractors and agents.
1800 Members Founded: 1907
Mailing list available for rent 3000 names $500 per M.

19299 American Real Estate and Urban Economics
Po Box 9958
Richmond, VA 23228
866-273-8321
FAX: 866-273-8323
areuea@areuea.org www.areuea.org
Richard K Green, President
Frank E Nothaft, First VP
Addresses academic and commercial concerns in real estate and commercial economics.
1200 Members Founded: 1965

19300 American Rental Association
1900 19th Street
Moline, IL 61265
309-764-2475
FAX: 309-764-1533 800-334-2177
ara@ararental.org www.ararental.org
Allen Morehead, President
Benefits members (rental business owners and equipment suppliers) by promoting, representing and enhancing the rental industry, resulting in improved rental services to the public.
8600 Members Founded: 1955

19301 American Resort Development Association
1201 15th Street NW
Suite 400
Washington, DC 20005-2842
202-371-6700
FAX: 202-289-8544
webmaster@arda.org www.arda.org
Rob Dunn, VP Finance/Administration
Adrienne L Riley, Director Operations Center
Souri Jahanmir, Director Finance/Accounting
Rich Doherty, Senior General Ledger Accountant
Howard Nusbaum, President
International trade association composed of resort developers and resort industry suppliers.
1000 Members Founded: 1969

19302 American Society of Appraisers
555 Herndon Parkway
Suite 125
Herndon, VA 20170
703-478-2228
FAX: 703-742-8471 800-272-8258
asainfo@appraisers.org
www.appraisers.org
Ronald M Seaman, Chairman
Peter J Bruck, Vice Chairman
Jerry Larkins, Executive VP
Eugene Kaczkowski, President
Professional association of appraisers of all kinds.
6000 Members Founded: 1936

19303 American Society of Farm Managers and Rural Appraisers
950 South Cherry Street
Suite 508
Denver, CO 80246-2664
303-758-3513
FAX: 303-758-0190 www.asfmra.org
Douglas W Slothower, Executive VP
Nancy Hardiman, Director Education
Sally Quinn, Director Finances/Administration
Premier professional organization for professionals who provide management, consultation and valuation services on rural and agricultural assets. Provides members with the resources, information and leadership that enables them to provide valuable services to the agricultural community.
Founded: 1929

19304 Apartment Owners and Managers Association
65 Cherry Avenue
Watertown, CT 06795-2836

FAX: 860-274-2580
A national organization that presents the facts and information builder/developer/owners/manager members need to keep abreast of in the world of multi-family housing. Monthly issue will bring the reader timely insight on real estate, tax news, financing techniques, and effective management procedures, and keeps readers aware of the new developments in the condominium market.

19305 Building Owners and Managers Association
1201 New York Avenue NW
Suite 300
Washington, DC 20005
202-082-2662
FAX: 202-371-0181
info@boma.org www.boma.org/splash
Henry Chamberlain, President
Owners and managers of commercial office buildings.
7.5M Members

19306 Commercial Real Estate Women
655 15th Street NW
Washington, DC 20005
202-737-3262

Provides a forum for women who are involved in commercial real estate and wish to network as well as reap the benefits of their courses.
125 Members

19307 Commercial-Investment Real Estate Institute
430 N Michigan Avenue
Chicago, IL 60611-4002
312-270-0273

Steven F Pope, Executive VP
Functions as a professional association of real estate practitioners who have successfully completed its certification program or are striving toward it.

4M Members

19308 Community Associations Institute
225 Reinekers Lane
Suite 300
Alexandria, VA 22314
703-548-8600
FAX: 703-684-1581
caicentral@caionline.org
www.caionline.org
Paul Grucza, President
Tom Skiba, CEO
Composed of community and condominium associations managers, management companies and other business partners.
15000 Members Founded: 1973

19309 CoreNet Global
260 Peachtree Street
Suite 1500
Atlanta, GA 30303
404-589-3200
FAX: 404-589-3201
www.corenetglobal.org
Sean B Mccourt, Chairman
William F Concannon, President/CEO
Jeffrey L Elie, VP Real Estate/Facilities
Formerly NACORE International.

19310 Council of Real Estate Brokerage Managers
430 N Michigan Avenue
Chicago, IL 60611
312-298-8427
FAX: 312-329-8882
info@crs.com www.crs.com
William C Furst, President
Ginny Shipe, CEO
Tara Maric, VP Membership & Education
Katie Dwyer, Director Marketing/Communications
Lee Sheehan, Member Service Representative
Members are real estate firm owners and managers.
7000 Members Founded: 1968

19311 Council of Residential Specialists
430 N Michigan Avenue
3rd Floor
Chicago, IL 60611
312-214-4400
FAX: 312-329-8551
crshelp@crs.com www.crs.com
Nina Cottrell, CEO
Carol Raabe, VP Operations
Susan Karl, Director Finance
Seeks to establish cooperation among brokers engaged in buying, selling, trading and leasing of real estate.
40000 Members Founded: 1976

19312 Couselors of Real Estate
430 N Michigan Avenue
Chicago, IL 60611-4089
312-329-8427
FAX: 312-329-8881
info@cre.org www.cre.org
Mary Walker Fleischmann, President
Gloria Bowman, Director Marketing/Communications
Shea Shumpert, Manager Special Projects
Association members provide the public with expert, objective advice on property and land related matters. Individuals invited to join are awarded the CRE designation.
1200 Members Founded: 1953

19313 Employee Relocation Council
1717 Pennsylvania Avenue NW
Suite 800
Washington, DC 20006
202-857-0857
FAX: 202-659-8631
webmaster@erc.org www.erc.org
H Cris Collie, President
Beth Archibald, VP
Ruth M Davis, Secretary/Treasurer
A national organization that examines key issues affecting the relocation industry for the benefit of corporations, government agencies, and firms or individuals providing specific services to relocated employees and their families. Accepts advertising.
160 Members Founded: 1960

19314 Institute of Real Estate Management
430 N Michigan Avenue
3rd Floor
Chicago, IL 60611
312-296-6000
FAX: 312-329-8551
crshelp@crs.com www.crs.com
Gail Flagel, President
Ingrid Glancy, Financial VP
Randy Eagar, First VP
Russell Salzman, Chief Exceutive Officer
Awards property manager certificate to qualifying individuals and accreditates management organizations and management firms. Offers management courses.
40000 Members Founded: 1976

19315 International Council of Shopping Centers
1221 Avenue of the Americas
41st Floor
New York, NY 10020-1099
646-728-3800
FAX: 212-589-5555
icsc@icsc.org www.icsc.org
Gayle C Aertker, President
Michael Kercheval, CEO
Peter E Baccile, Managing Director
Fosters professional standards of performance in the development, construction, financing, leasing, management and operation of shopping centers throughout the world.
44000 Members Founded: 1957

19316 International Exchangers Association
PO Box L
Rancho Santa Fe, CA 92067-0560
973-496-5784
FAX: 973-496-5784
Works to standardize procedures and establish professional ethics.
3.2M Members Founded: 1978

19317 International Real Estate Federation
2000 N 15th Street
Suite 101
Arlington, VA 22201
703-240-0739
FAX: 703-991-6256
info@fiabci-usa.com
www.fiabci-usa.com
Thomas P Bennett, Executive Director
Bill Endsley, Business Development Specialist
Henry Chamberlain, CAE
Susan Newman, Manager
Encourages private ownership of real property and understanding of property rights and obligations.

19318 International Real Estate Institute
1224 North Nokomis NE
Alexandria, MN 56308
320-763-4648
FAX: 320-763-9290
irei@iami.org www.iami.org
Bale Ekdaho, Production Manager
Robert Johnson, Executive Director
An organization comprised of thousands of real estate professionals from over 98 countries around the world. Acts as a voting member of, and property advisor to, the United Nations. Members specialize in real estate and property management. Arranges and promotes international educational real estate seminars.
2000 Members Founded: 1975

19319 Mortgage Bankers Association of America
1919 Pennsylvania Avenue NW
Washington, DC 20006-3404
202-572-2700
800-793-6222
Robert M Couch, Chairman
Regina Lowrie, Vice Chairwoman
Dan Thoms, VP
Seeks to improve methods of originating, servicing and marketing loans.
2.8M Members Founded: 1914

19320 National Affordable Housing Management
400 N Columbus Street
Suite 203
Alexandria, VA 22314
703-683-8630
FAX: 703-683-8634 www.nahma.org
Kris C Cook, Executive Director
Daria Jakubowski, Deputy Director
Michelle Kitchen, Director Government Affairs
Trade association representing individuals involved in the management of affordable multifamily housing.
Founded: 1989

19321 National Apartment Association
201 N Union Street
Suite 200
Alexandria, VA 22314
703-518-6141
FAX: 703-518-6191
webmaster@naahq.org
www.naahq.org
Doug Culkin, Executive VP
Maureen Lambe, Senior VP
Karen Goggin, VP Governance
The largest organization dedicated solely to rental housing-serves 26,000 rental housing professionals representing 3.4 million apartments nationwide. NAA lobbies for the industry, provides education programs, publishes Units Magazine, and conducts an annual Education Conference and Trade Show.
25M Members Founded: 1939

19322 National Association of Counselors
NAC
303 W Cypress Street
San Antonio, TX 78212
210-262-2828
800-486-3676

Provides education leading to a designation for real estate and appraisal counseling services.

19323 National Association of Home Builders
1201 15th Street NW
Washington, DC 20005
202-220-0200
FAX: 202-266-8559 800-368-5242
info@nahb.com www.nahb.org

David F Wilson, President
David L Pressly Jr, First VP
Jerry Howard, Chief Executive Officer

Represents the building industry by serving its members and affiliated state and local builders associations.
22000 Members

19324 National Association of Housing Cooperatives
1707 H Street NW
Suite 201
Washington, DC 20006
202-737-0797
FAX: 703-549-5204

Barbara Meskunas, Chair
Bill Magee, President
Douglas Kleine, Executive Director

A nonprofit national federation of housing cooperatives, professionals, organizations and individuals promoting the interests of cooperative housing communities. Housing cooperatives are a form of multi family home ownership.
1000 Members Founded: 1960

19325 National Association of Master Appraisers
303 W Cypress Street
San Antonio, TX 78212-5512
210-271-0781
FAX: 210-225-8450 800-486-3676

Deborah J Deane, President
Teresa Y Peterson, Director Membership

Provides basic and advanced courses in techniques, management practices and marketing strategies. Offers designations in real estate appraisal MRA (Master Residential Appraisers), MFLA (Master Farm & Land Appraiser) and MSA (Master Senior Appraiser).

19326 National Association of Real Estate Technology
1875 Eye Street NW
Washington, DC 20006
202-628-1558
FAX: 202-739-9401
info@nareit.org www.nareit.com

Hamid R Moghadam, Chairman
David E Simon, First Vice Chairman
R Scot Sellers, Second Vice Chairman

19327 National Association of Real Estate Invest ment Trusts
1875 Eye Street NW
Washington, DC 20006-3403
202-739-9400
FAX: 202-785-8723 800-362-7348
info@nareit.org www.nareit.org

Steven A Wechsler, President
Sheldon M Groener, Senior VP Finance/Operations
Maura Browning, Marketing/Member Services

National trade association for publicly traded real estate companies. Members are real estate investment trusts and other businesses that own, operate and finance income-producing real estate, as well as those firms and individuals who advise, study and service these businesses.

19328 National Association of Real State
11755 Wishire Boulevard
Suite 1380
Los Angeles, CA 90025-1539
310-479-2219
www.nareim.org

Pamela J Herbst, Chairperson
Charles F Lydon Jr, Vice Chairman
Jerome J Claeys, Board of Directors
Charles L Davidson, Board of Directors
Thomas P Lydon, Board of Directors

Founded: 1990

19329 National Association of Realtors
430 N Michigan Avenue
Chicago, IL 60611-4002
312-645-7730
FAX: 312-329-8882
info@crs.com www.crs.com

Terrence McDermott, Chief Executive Officer
Sara Patterson, Director Communications

Promotes education, high professional standards and modern techniques of real estate work.
40000 Members Founded: 1976

19330 National Association of Residential Property Managers
184 Business Park Drive
Suite 200-P
Virginia Beach, VA 23462

FAX: 866-466-2776 800-782-3452
info@narpm.org www.narpm.org

Betty Fletcher, President

Provides education and publications for the single-family residential property manager.

19331 National Association of Review Appraisers and Mortgage Underwriters
8383 E Evans Road
Scottsdale, AZ 85260-3614
480-946-1066
FAX: 480-998-8022

Robert G Johnson, Executive Director
Fred Simon, Production Manager

Conducts educational seminars. Maintains library, speakers bureau and operates a placement service.
6.5M Members Founded: 1972

19332 National Council of Exchangors
PO Box 3658
Prescott, AZ 86302
928-771-2300
FAX: 928-771-2323
nb@infoville.com www.infoville.com

Thom Bohan, President

A non-profit association and is a nationwide network of real estate professionals who specilize in marketing real estate equities primarily through the medium of the real estate exchange. This network is comprised of local groups organized into regional chapters.
400 Members

19333 National Low Income Housing Coalition
727 15th St NW
6
Washington, DC 20005-2168
202-662-1530
FAX: 202-393-1973
info@nlihc.org www.nlihc.org

Sheila Crowley, President

A national nonprofit organization representing housing advocates, organizers, tenants and professionals in the housing field. The Coalition advocates, represents and educates for decent housing and neighborhoods for all low-income people. It works with Congress and the executive branch to obtain adequate Federal support for low-income housing and related programs.
Founded: 1975

19334 National Property Management Association
1102 Pinehurst Road
Oak Tree Center
Dunedin, FL 34698-5427
727-736-3788
FAX: 727-736-6707
HQ@nmpa.org www.npma.org

Bonnie Schlag, Executive Director
Felicia Johnson, Marketing Manager

Nonprofit professional association dedicated to the cost effective management of personal property and fixed assets.
3700 Members Founded: 1970

19335 National Real Estate Investors Association
525 W 5th Avenue
Covington, KY 41011
859-261-3335
FAX: 859-581-5993 888-762-7342
rebecca@nationalreia.com
www.nationalreia.com

Rebecca McLean, Executive Director

Coalition of trade associations serving real estate investors, landlords and owners. Provides education and product services for officers and members.
115 Members Founded: 1985

19336 National Residential Appraisers Institute
Registered Financial Planners Institute
2001 Cooper Foster Park Road
Amherst, OH 44001-1251
440-282-7176
FAX: 440-282-8027
info@repi.com
www.rfpi.com/wrai.htm

Ade J Schreiber, Executive Director

Promotes professionalism in the evaluation of residential real estate and requires demonstration appraisals and testing for professional certification.
451 Members Founded: 1977

19337 National Society of Environmental
303 W Cypress Street
San Antonio, TX 78212
210-252-2897
FAX: 210-225-8450 800-486-3676

Deborah Deane, President

Provides standards, education and a forum for real estate environmental site consultants. Provides a designation program for individuals doing environmental assessments and promotes education and further information about real estate environmental problems.

19338 Neighborhood Reinvestment Corporation
92 Argonaut
Suite 255
Aliso Viejo, CA 92656-3100
949-770-2000
FAX: 949-770-2157 800-808-3372
sales@federalregister.com
www.federalregister.com
Supplies training, grants, developmental assistance, and a range of other technical services designed to help the local partnerships achieve substantially self-reliant neighborhoods. The goal is to improve a neighborhood's housing and physical conditions, build a positive community image, and establish a healthy real estate market and a core of neighbors capable of managing the continued health of their neighborhood.
Founded: 1978

19339 Professional Certification Board
303 W Cypress Street
San Antonio, TX 78212
210-252-2897
800-486-3676
Deborah Deane, President
Provides education and board certificates for the real estate appraisal specialties of manufactured housing valuation, business valuation and litigation management.

19340 Professional Housing Management Association
154 Fort Evans Road NE
Leesburg, VA 20176
703-771-1888
FAX: 703-771-0299
mkcooper@earthlink.net
www.phma.com
Melissa Cooper, Office Manager
Members are federal government employees, civilian or military, who are directly involved in housing management or provides direct support to the field.
3,120 Members Founded: 1973

19341 Property Owners Association
1896 Morris Avenue
1250 Route 9 South
Howell, NJ 07731
732-780-1966
FAX: 732-780-1611
info@poanj.org www.poanj.org
Vincent Bove, President
Jeffrey Itzkowitz, VP
The Property Owners Association of New Jersey, Inc. brings together owners and operators of residential real estate, interested persons, and related industry personnel for educational and information sharing purposes.
550 Members Founded: 1949

19342 Real Estate Buyers Agent Council
430 N Michigan Avenue
Chicago, IL 60611
800-648-6224
800-648-6224
rebac@realtors.org www.realtor.org
Walter T McDonald, President
Larry Von Feldt, VP/Liaison to Gov Affairs
Pat Kaplan, VP Liaison to Committees
Represents professional real estate agents who act as buyers' agents.
40000 Members Founded: 1988

19343 Real Estate Capital Resources Association
1350 I Street NW
Washington, DC 20005-3305
202-663-3740
FAX: 202-371-0069
G David Fensterheim, Executive Director
G David Fensterheim, Executive Director

Represents firms that provide third party workout and capital recovery services in connection with distressed real estate and real estate related assets.
100 Members Founded: 1989

19344 Real Estate Educators Association
19 Mantua Road
Mt. Royal, NJ 08061
856-423-3215
FAX: 856-423-3420
info@reea.org www.reea.org
Eileen Taus, President
Individuals involved in training and education.
1,400 Members Founded: 1979

19345 Real Estate Information Providers Association
1420 16th Street NW
Washington, DC 20036-2218
202-298-8169
FAX: 202-332-2301
reipa@aol.com www.reipa.com
Randy Dyer, Executive Director
Supports professional information providers in the real estate industry.
Founded: 1995

19346 Real Estate Roundtable
1420 New York Avenue NW
Suite 1100
Washington, DC 20005-2122
202-639-8400
FAX: 202-639-8442
Christopher Nassetta, Chairman
Jeffrey D DeBoer, President/CEO
Daniel Neidich, Secretary
Michelle M Reid, Meetings Director/Executive Asst
Actively involves public and private real eastate owners, advisors, builders, investors, landers and managers on key tax, capitol and credit, environmental and tehcnology issues in Washington. Its members are senior principals fromevery spectrum on the commercial real estate industry and leaders of major national real estate trade associations.
230 Members Founded: 1969

19347 Realtors Land Institute
430 N Michigan Avenue
Chicago, IL 60611-4002
312-329-8440
FAX: 312-329-8633
Janet Branton, Executive Director
Jan Hope, Manager
Promotes competence and accredits members. Maintains educational programs for real estate brokers.
1.9M Members Founded: 1944

19348 Residential Sales Council
430 N Michigan Avenue
Chicago, IL 60611-4002
312-321-4400
FAX: 312-329-8882
info@crs.com www.crs.com
Sara Patterson, Director Communications
A council of the Realtors National Marketing Institute.
40000 Members Founded: 1976

19349 Society of Industrial and Office Realtors
700 11th Street NW
Washington, DC 20001-4507
202-737-1150
FAX: 202-737-8796
Pamela Hinton, Executive VP
Active members are brokers, consultants and appraisers.
1,800 Members Founded: 1941

19350 Women's Council of Realtors
430 N Michigan Avenue
Chicago, IL 60611-4002
312-329-8483
FAX: 312-329-8882
info@crs.com www.crs.com
Sara Patterson, Director Communications
Gary Krysler, Executive Director
Provides opportunities for women in real estate at the local, state and national level. Offers courses in leadership training and referral and relocation buisness.
40000 Members Founded: 1976

Newsletters

19351 AOMA Newsletter
Apartment Owners & Managers Assn of America
65 Cherry Avenue
Cherry Plaza
Watertown, CT 06795

FAX: 860-274-2580
Robert J McGough, Editor
Pietro
Each month the AOMA newsletter presents the facts and information builder/developer/owners/manager members need to keep abreast of in the world of Multi-Family housing. Every monthly issue will bring the reader timely insight on Real Estate, tax news, financing techniques, and effective management procedures, and keeps readers aware of the new developments in the condominium market.
$125.00
12 issues
Circulation: 6,200 Audited Est. Pass-Along Circ: 1000
Mailing list available for rent
Printed in 1 color

19352 ASFMRA News
Amer. Society of Farm Managers & Rural Appraisers
950 S Cherry Street
Suite 508
Denver, CO 80246-2664
303-758-3513
FAX: 303-758-0190
asfmra@agri-associations.org
http://www.asfmra.org
Cheryl L Cooley, Manager Communicatio
Thomas V. Boyer, President
Informs ASFMRA members of education, member, event, meeting and government issues. *$24.00*
Founded: 1929
Mailing list available for rent 2500 names $1M per M.

19353 Accredited Review Appraiser
Accredited Review Appraisers Council
303 W Cypress Street
San Antonio, TX 78212-5512
800-486-3676
FAX: 210-225-8450
rlp@lincoln-grad.org
http://arac.lincoln-grad.org
Deborah J Deane, Publisher
Rachel L Phelps, Marketing Manager
Offers information on appraisals and real estate reviews.
8 pages Quarterly Founded: 1987
Printed in 1 color on matte stock

19354 Advise and Counsel
National Association of Counselors
303 W Cypress Street
San Antonio, TX 78212-5512
210-271-0781
FAX: 956-225-8450 800-486-3676
Marvin T Deane, Publisher
Offers information on real estate and appriasal counseling services. *$45.00*
8 pages Quarterly
Circulation: 4000

19355 American Chapter News
American Chapter International Real Estate Assn
30700 Russell Ranch Road
Westlake Village, CA 91362
805-557-2300
FAX: 805-557-2680
http://www.realtors.com
Teresa Salmon, Publisher
International real estate news and information. *$110.00*
8 pages Monthly

19356 American Industrial Real Estate Association Newsletter
American Industrial Real Estate Association
700 S Flowers Street
Suite 600
Los Angeles, CA 90017
213-687-8777
FAX: 213-687-8616
rsurace@airea.com www.airea.com
Ron Surace, COO
6 pages Quarterly Founded: 1964
Printed in 3 colors on glossy stock

19357 American Society of Farm Managers and Rural Appraisers Newsletter
Amer. Society of Farm Managers & Rural Appraisers
950 S Cherry Street
Suite 508
Denver, CO 80246-2664
303-758-3513
FAX: 303-758-0190
asfmra@agri-associations.org
http://www.asfmra.org
Cheryl L Cooley, Manager Communications/ IT/PR
Hope S. Evans, Membership Coordinator
Provides professionals involved in rural property issues such as management and appraisal, with information on the industry as well as educational opportunities. Includes membership and information from the American Society of Farm Manager and Rural Appraisers. *$30.00*
Annual+ Founded: 1929
Mailing list available for rent 2500 names $1M per M.
Printed in 2 colors on glossy stock

19358 Andrews Report
Report Publications
9595 Whitney Drive
#100
Indianapolis, IN 46280
William Woburn, Publisher
For owners and operators of small shopping centers. *$147.00*
12 pages Monthly

19359 Apartment Management Newsletter
AMN Publishing
PO BOX 352
Massapequa, NY 11758
516-551-5343
amnpub@aol.com
http://amnpub.tripod.com/id4.html
Helene Mandelbaum, Editor
Vera West, Circulation Manager
News and information for apartment owners and managers, including tips and techniques for marketing, maintenance, personnel and compliance with national laws and requirements. *$6.00*
Founded: 2001

19360 Apartment Management Report
Apartment Owners & Managers Assn of America
65 Cherry Avenue
Cherry Plaza
Watertown, CT 06795-238
FAX: 860-274-2580
Robert J McGough, Editor
Janet Pietro, Circulation Manager
Researched and written for the owner/manager, overall property manager, and for the on site managers. Typical in depth subjects cover the nuts and bolts of every day management. Research reports on tenant renting strategies, model apartments, security, outside maintenance, how to avoid and handle tenant complaints, and more. *$72.85*
6 pages Monthly
Circulation: 6200 Audited Est. Pass-Along Circ: 1000
Mailing list available for rent 6000 names
Printed in 1 color

19361 Asset Watch
LDI Publishing
1401 16th Street NW
Washington, DC 20036-2201
202-232-2144
FAX: 202-232-4757
Steve Sullivan, Publisher
News and analysis of federal asset sales RDIC, LRTC, HUD, etc., contracting and resolutions. *$475.00*
6 pages 5 per year

19362 Asset-Backed Alert
Harrison Scott Publications
5 Marine View Plaza
Suite 301
Hoboken, NJ 07030-5795
201-659-1700
FAX: 201-659-4141 800-283-9363
info@hspnews.com
http://www.cmalert.com
Andrew Albert, Publisher
Thomas J Ferris, Editor
A weekly update on global securitization *$2297.00*
20 pages Weekly Founded: 1990
Circulation: 500 Audited Est. Pass-Along Circ: 1500
Mailing list available for rent 900 names $400 per M.
Printed in 1 color on matte stock
Computerized version available

19363 Bulletin
Property Management Association
7900 Wisconsin Avenue
Suite 305
Bethesda, MD 20814
301-657-9200
FAX: 301- 90- 932
pma@erols.com
http://www.pma-dc.org
Doris Topel, President
News and events surrounding the real estate industry. *$100.00*
24 pages Monthly

19364 Commercial Lease Law Insider
Brownstone Publishers
149 5th Avenue
16th Floor
New York, NY 10010-6801
212-473-8200
FAX: 212-473-8786
vendomecs@qualitycustomercare.com
http://www.brownstone.com
John M Striker Esq, Publisher
Nicole Lefton Esq, Editor
Commercial leasing strategies, techniques and insights with practical aids such as model lease clauses, checklists, do's and dont's, as well as coverage of new court decisions affecting commercial leases. Readership consists of commercial property owners, managers and real estate attorneys. *$337.00*
Monthly
Mailing list available for rent $110 per M.
Printed in 2 colors on matte stock

19365 Commercial Property News
Miller Freeman Publications
600 Harrison Street
Suite 400
San Francisco, CA 94107-1391
FAX: 415-905-2239
David Nussbaum, Publisher
Maxine Jaffe, Editor
Tabloid newspaper edited for commercial property professionals. *$4.00*
Circulation: 34,000

19366 Commercial Real Estate Digest
Vestal Communications
334 Humphrey Drive
Evergreen, CO 80439-9655
Robert Vestal, Publisher
Master copy newsletter allowing unlimited copy additions before subscriber prints and distributes to clients. *$495.00*
2 pages Quarterly

19367 Community Association Law Reporter
225 Reinekerf lane
V300
Alexandria, VA 22314-3426
703-548-8600
FAX: 703-684-1581
caidirect@caionline.org
http://www.caionline.org
Christ Durso, Editor
Tom Skiba, CE0

Information on legal cases and court decisions concerning condominum, cooperative and homeowner associations. *$208.00*

8 pages Monthly Founded: 1973 17,500 names $150 per M.

19368 Community Associations Institute News
225 Reinekers Lane
suite 300
Alexandria, VA 22314
703-548-8600
FAX: 703-684-1581
mingram@caionline.org
http://www.caionline.org

Christ Durso, Editor
Tom Skiba, CEO

Real estate news and reports.
Monthly Founded: 1973

19369 Community Management
225 Reinkerf Lane
V 300
Alexandria, VA 22314-3426
703-548-8600
FAX: 703-648-1581
acentral@ciaonline.org
http://www.ciaonline.org

Christ Durso, Editor
Tom Skiba, CEO

Bimonthly newsletter of news, strategies and trends written especially for managers of condominium and homeowner associations. This easy to read, award-winning newsletter comes packed with how-to information on such subjects as cutting expenses, complying with federal laws, working effectively with boards of directors, ensuring community safety and resolving disputes. It often features case studies of succcessful new approaches in community association management and operations. *$59.00*
8 pages Founded: 1973 17,500 names $150 per M.

19370 Daily Commerce
Daily Journal Corporation
915 E. First Street
Los Angeles, CA 90012-26
213-229-5300
FAX: 213-680-3682
Lisa_Churchhill@dailyjournal.com
http://www.dailyjournal.com

Gerald Salzman, Publisher
Ray Chagolla, Circulation Manager
Lisa Churchill, Editor

personnel announcements, datebook information, consumer news, and the internet, information on government foreclosers, default notices, lending reports and probate estate sales. *$237.00*
Monthly
Circulation: 10000

19371 Environmental Consultant
National Society of Environmental Consultants
303 W Cypress Street
San Antonio, TX 78212-5512
210-225-2897
FAX: 956-225-8450 800-486-3676

Deborah J Deane, Publisher/CEO

Offers information, articles and news of interest to real estate environmental site consultants. *$50.00*
16 pages Quarterly Founded: 1992
Circulation: 4000

19372 Housing Affairs Letter
CD Publications
8204 Fenton Street
Silver Spring, MD 20910
301-588-6380
FAX: 301-588-6385 800-666-6380
info@cdpublications.com
http://www.cdpublications.com

Mike Gerecht, Publisher
Tom Edwards, Editor

The latest news on housing activity nationwide, including private, public and subsidized housing, legislation and regulations. *$ 559.00*
Weekly Founded: 1961
Mailing list available for rent 2,000 names $160 per M. : On-Line

19373 Housing the Elderly Report
CD Publications
8204 Fenton Street
Silver Spring, MD 20910
301-588-0519
FAX: 301-588-6385 800-666-6380
hmr@cdpublications.com
http://www.cdpublications.com

Mike Gerecht, Publisher
Jeff Pines, Editor

News and advice for owners and managers of long-term care facilities on marketing and managing all types of elderly housing, with profiles of new senior housing projects, business reports and an exclusive annual salary survey. *$294.00*
Monthly Founded: 1961
Mailing list available for rent 2,000 names $160 per M.

19374 Inside IREM
Institute of Real Estate Management
430 N Michigan Avenue
Chicago, IL 60611-4002
312-296-6000
FAX: 312-329-8882
info@crs.com www.crs.com

Sara Patterson, Director Communications

Membership newsletter for members of the Institute of Real Estate Management. It includes news on IREM policies, programs and new products. Federal, state and local legislative developments affecting real estate and asset management are also reported.
40000 pages Founded: 1976

19375 Inspector
American Society of Home Inspectors
932 Lee Street
Suite 101
Des Plaines, IL 60016-3520
847-759-2820
FAX: 847-759-1620 800-248-2744
webmaster@ashi.org
http://www.ashi.org

Richard Clough, Executive Director
Paul Christensen, President

Newsletter for members of New England chapter of American Society of Home Inspectors. *$250.00*
Monthly Founded: 1976
Circulation: 6000

19376 International Real Estate Newsletter
1224 N Nokomis NE
Alexandria, MN 56308-5072
320-763-4648
FAX: 320-763-9290
iami@iami.org http://www.iami.org/

David Held, Production Manager
Robert Johnson, CEO

A compilation of international real estate information which is disseminated to the International Real Estate Institute's membership and to other subscribers. This publication also reviews the latest accomplishments of the Institute and those of its high quality professional members. *$29.50*
4 pages Monthly Founded: 1975
Printed in 1 color on newsprint stock

19377 Ledger Quarterly
Community Associations Institute
225 Reinekers Lane
Suite 300
Alexandria, VA 22314
703-548-8600
FAX: 703-836-6907
acentral@calonline.org
http://www.caionline.org

Chris Dursal, Editor
Mark Ingham, Marketing Manager

Quarterly newsletter of financial news for condominium, cooperative and homeowner associations. If you participate in any way in the financial management of an association, this eight-page newsletter is a resource you should have. It's absolutely vital for keeping up-to-date on trends in asssociation accounting practices, calculating the best strategies to minimize association taxes, and advising the board on investments. *$67.00*
Quarterly Founded: 1973
Circulation: 12000+ 17,500 names $150 per M.

19378 Mac News
Mid-Atlantic Council of Shopping Centers
8811 Colesville Road
Silver Spring, MD 20910-4343
301-890-1467

Tom Cohn, Publisher

News of the council. *$100.00*
20 pages Monthly

19379 Managing Housing Letter
CD Publications
8204 Fenton Street
Silver Spring, MD 20910
301-588-6380
FAX: 301-588-6385 800-666-6380
subscriptions@cdpublications.com
http://www.cdpublications.com

Mike Gerecht, Publisher
Charles Wisniowski, Editor

News and advice for owners, managers and professionals dealing with apartments and the real estate industry. *$269.00*
Monthly Founded: 1978
Mailing list available for rent 2,000 names $160 per M.

19380 Mobilehome Parks Report
Thomas P Kerr
3807 Pasadena Avenue
Suite 100
Sacramento, CA 95821-2880
916-971-0489
FAX: 916-971-1849 800-392-5180
tkerr@aol.com http://www.aol.com

Thomas P Kerr, Editor/Publisher

Reports on trends, issues, court decisions, legislation, financing and other matters of concern to owners and developers of manufactured housing communities. Valuable to attorneys and others who specialize in this segment of the Housing Industry. *$125.00*

8 pages Monthly Founded: 1998
Circulation: 350 Audited Est. Pass-Along Circ: 200
Printed in 1 color on matte stock

19381 National Association of Neighborhoods Newsletter
1300 Pennsylvania Avenue
NW Suite 700
Washington, DC 20004
202-332-7766
FAX: 202-332-2314
webmaster@nanworld.org
http://www.nanworld.org

C Y Doyd, Editor
Ricardo C Byrd, President

Offers news and information to the community real estate industry.

Quarterly Founded: 1975
Circulation: 10,000

19382 New England Real Estate Journal
East Coast Publications
PO Box 55
Accord, MA 02018
781-878-4540
FAX: 781-871-1853 800-654-4993
nerej@rejournal.com
http://www.rejournal.com

Tom Murray, Publisher
David Denelle, Editor

Business publication for the commercial-industrial-investment real estate industries. *$2.00*

Weekly Founded: 1961
Circulation: 13000
Printed in on newsprint stock

19383 Professional Apartment Management
Brownstone Publishers
149 5th Avenue
16th Floor
New York, NY 10010-6801
212-473-8200
FAX: 212-473-8786 800-643-8095
custserv@brownstone.com
http://www.brownstone.com

Mary Lopez, Production Manager
Michael Koplin, Circulation Director

Strategies, techniques and suggestions for attracting and retaining paying tenants, and avoiding legal disputes. Includes model language for leases, sample ads, plus coverage of legal issues, recent court decisions and the like. *$217.00*

Monthly Founded: 1972
Printed in 2 colors on matte stock

19384 Real Estate Alert
Harrison Scott Publications
5 Marine View Plaza
Suite 301
Hoboken, NJ 07030-5795
201-659-1700
FAX: 201-659-4141
info@hspnews.com
http://www.realert.com

Andrew Albert, Publisher/Editor
Andrew Albert, President

Contains information for real estate and financial professionals looking for opportunities to buy or manage assets. *$1397.00*

8 pages Weekly Founded: 1989
Circulation: 300+ 750 names $400 per M.
Printed in 4 colors : PDF

19385 Real Estate Asset Manager
Lincoln Graduate Center - Executive Offices
303 W Cypress Street
San Antonio, TX 78212-528
210-225-2897
FAX: 210-225-8450 800-531-5333
ms@lincoln-grad.org
http://www.lincoln-grad.org

Eddie Muhlenberg, President
Deborah Deanne, CEO
Rachel Phelps, Marketing Manager

Offers news and information on environmental concerns, real estate and appraisals.

8 pages

19386 Real Estate Brokers Insider
Alexander Communications Group
28 W 25th Street
8th Floor
New York, NY 10010
212-228-0246
FAX: 212-228-0376 800-232-4317
info@brokersinsider.com
http://www.brokersinsider.com/

Margaret DeWitt, Publisher
Nadine Harris, Marketing Manager
Laurence Alexander, Owner

Provides agency broker/owners with in depth information on how to run their businesses better. *$247.00*

8 pages Fortnightly Founded: 1978

19387 Real Estate Economics
AREUEA
PO Box 9958
Richmond, VA 23228-1148
866-273-8321
FAX: 877-273-8323
areuea@areuea.org
http://www.areuea.org

Susan Watcher, Publisher
Dennis R Capozza, President
David C. Ling, Editor

Discussions on topics such as housing prices, office markets, real estate valuation and appraisal. *$100.00*

Quarterly Founded: 1964

19388 Real Estate Investor's Monthly
John T Reed Publishing
342 Bryan Drive
Alamo, CA 94507-2858
925-820-6292
FAX: 925-820-1259
johnreed@johntreed.com
http://www.johntreed.com

John T Reed, Publisher

Information for owners who manage and own their own property, suggestions for increasing their investment returns. *$125.00*

8 pages Monthly Founded: 1980
Circulation: 500

19389 Tax Credit Advisor
1400 16th St Nw
Ste 420a
Washington, DC 20036-2216
202-391-1740
FAX: 202-265-4435
http://www.housingonline.com

Peter Bell, Publisher
Glenn Petherick, Editor

Monthly newsletter providing comprehensive coverage of all aspects of the federal low-income housing tax credit program, the primary incentive for low-income apartment development. Covers legislation, IRS rules, equity and debt programs, and market trends. *$269.00*

12 pages Monthly
Circulation: 750 Audited Est. Pass-Along Circ: 30

19390 Upward Directions
Community Associations Institute
1630 Duke Street
Alexandria, VA 22314-3426
703-488-8603
FAX: 703-836-6907
acentral@calonline.org
www.nbccam.orgg

NBBC-CAM's quarterly newsletter for the further education and professional development of CMCA Certificants. Program news, updates on state credentialing activities, legislation and regulation and continuing education opportunities make this newsletter required reading for Certified Managers of Community Associations (CMCA's. Everything you need to know to earn, maintain and optimize the benefits from manager certification from the National Board of Certification.

Quarterly 17,500 names $150 per M.

Magazines & Journals

19391 ALQ Real Estate Intelligence Report
Common Communications
PO Box 5702
Portsmouth, NH 03802-5702
800-299-9961
FAX: 603-436-5202 800-299-9961
IRexec@REintel.com
http://www.reintel.com

Pat Remick, Editor
Frank Cook, Publisher

A close examination of buyer agency movement, services rendered by brokerages, the impact of technology on real estate and success stories. *$200.00*

Quarterly Founded: 1989

19392 Affordable Housing Finance
Alexander & Edwards Publishing
111 Sutter Street
Suite 975
San Francisco, CA 94104-4547
415-315-1241
FAX: 415-315-1248 800-989-7255
ahf@housingfinance.com
http://www.housingfinance.com

Andre Shashaty, Publisher
Andre Shashaty, President
Susan Piel, Conference Director/Busin
Michael Premsrirat, Circulation Manager
Carol Yee, Office Manager

Offers practical information on obtaining debt and equality financing from federal, state, and local governments as well as private resources. In-depth coverage on the federal low-income housing tax credit program, tax-exempt bond financing, corporate tax credit investigation. *$119.00*

Monthly
Circulation: 9000

19393 Alliance
John W Yopp Publications
6540 Julian Rd.
Gainesville, GA 30506-5550
800-849-9677
FAX: 800-849-8418
info@jwyopp.com
http://www.jwyopp.com

Mary Y Cronley, Associate Pubisher/Editor
Natalie Gilmer, Accounts Manager

Articles provide news and information on topics of interest, including marketing and sales, pre-need campaigns and other operational topics.
Monthly Founded: 1919
Circulation: 8000

19394 Apartment Age Magazine
Apartment Association of Greater Los Angeles
621 S Westmoreland Avenue
West Los Angeles, CA 90005-3995
213-384-4131
FAX: 213-382-3970
aagla@aol.com http://www.aagla.org
Charles Isham, Publisher
Kevin Postema, Editor/Advertising Director
Larry Cannizzaro, President
Serving the interests of residential rental property owners. *$48.00*
80 pages Monthly
Circulation: 40000

19395 Apartment Finance Today Magazine
Alexander & Edwards Publishing
220 Sansome Street
11th Floor
San Francisco, CA 94104-2326
415-151-1241
FAX: 415-315-1248 800-989-7255
customerservice@housingfinance.com
http://www.housingfinance.com
Andre Shashaty, Editor/Publisher
Christine Serlin, Managing Editor
Cynthia Bartlett Hunter, Senior Editor
Michael Premsrirat, Circulation Manager
Brian Taussig, Production Coordinator
AFT serves the apartment finance industry including apartment building owners, building/constructing property managers, developers, financial services, government agencies, consulting services, asset managers, legal/accounting, institutional investment, suppliers, manufacturers and other allied to the field. *$29.00*
80 pages Founded: 1995
Circulation: 11784
Printed in 4 colors on glossy stock

19396 Apartment News
Arizona Multi-Housing Consulting Corporation
5110 N 44th Street
Suite L160
Phoenix, AZ 85018-2107
602-224-0135
FAX: 602-224-0657 800-316-6403
info@azama.org
http://www.azama.org
Terry Feinberg, President
Mitchell McBay, Marketing Manager
Erick Richard, Editor
Wayne Kaplan, Director of Community Relations
Marilyn Everroad, Events Manager
Articles on state and national government affairs, education, marketing, crime prevention, maintenance and legal issues relating to the Arizona multihousing industry. *$50.00*
Monthly Founded: 1964
Circulation: 2500
Printed in on glossy stock

19397 Area Development
Halcyon Business Publications
400 Post Avenue
Westbury, NY 11590-2267
516-338-0900
FAX: 516-338-0100
areadev@area-development.com
http://www.areadevelopment.com
Dennis Shea, Publisher/CEO
Geraldie Gambale, Editor
Gertrude Staudt, Circulation Manager
Focuses on the factors necessary for a successful corporate expansion or relocation, labor, taxes, incentives, quality of life, market access, and transportation. *$75.00*
Founded: 1970
Circulation: 45000

19398 Brownfield News
Brownfield News
5440 North Cumberland Avenue
Suite 155
Chicago, IL 60656
773-714-0407
FAX: 773-714-0989
bfnsub@brownfieldnews.com
http://www.brownfieldnews.com/
Robert Colangelo, Publisher
Rachel Sobel, Managing Editor
Ardis Mann, Circulation Manager
Mayalan Molina, Administrative Assistant
Louisa Chan, Head of Accounting
Industry watch of new products and services for the distressed property market. *$79.95*
Monthly Founded: 1999
Circulation: 15000

19399 Building Operating Management
Trade Press Publishing Corporation
2100 West Florist Avenue
Milwaukee, WI 53209-3799
414-228-7701
FAX: 414-228-1134
http://www.tradepress.com
Scott G Holverson, Regional Sales Manager
Edward Sullivan, Editor
Eric Muench, Director of Circulation
Bobbie Reid, Production Director
Robert Wisniewski, President/CEO
Serves the field of facilities management, encompassing commercial building: office buildings, real estate/property management firms, developers, financial institutions, insurance companies, apartment complexes, civic/convention centers, including members of the Building Owners and Managers Association
Monthly Founded: 1915
Circulation: 70000

19400 Business Facilities
Group C Communications
44 Apple Street Suite 3
Tinton Falls, NJ 07724
732-842-7433
FAX: 732-758-6634 800-524-0337
jsemple@groupc.com
http://www.facilitycity.com
Karim Khan, Editor-in-Chief
Jim Semple, National Sales Manager
Magazine covering the fields of corporation expansion, economic development and real estate. *$30.00*
Monthly Founded: 1968
Circulation: 43500

19401 Business Journal
120 W Morehead Street
Suite 200
Charlotte, NC 28202
704-347-2340
FAX: 704-973-1102 800-948-5323
charlotte@bizjournals.com
http://www.bizjournals.com/charlotte
Robert Morris, Editor
David Harris, Managing Editor
Kim Moser, Advertising Assistant
Megan Foley, Marketing Director
Jeannie Falknor, Publisher
Provides marketing solutions and caring service. *$82.00*
Daily

19402 CF Apartment Reporter
PO Box 480894
Denver, CO 80248-894
303-663-0606
FAX: 303-663-1616
ht@clayfil.com
http://www.clayfil.com
Peggy Berg, President *$199.00*
Quarterly Founded: 1984

19403 CF Industrial Reporter
Clayton-Fillmore
PO Box 480894
Denver, CO 80248-894
303-663-0606
FAX: 303-663-1616
nf@clayfil.com
http://www.clayfil.com
Howard Treibitz, Editor
Briefs of the markets broken down into specific cities, includes briefs of the economy and average manufacturing. *$189.00*
Monthly

19404 Commercial
Oakland Press
28 W Huron
Pontiac, MI 48342-2100
248-332-8181
FAX: 248-332-3003 248-332-1988
Robert Carr, Editor
A showcase of available commercial properties in the region. *$18.00*
Monthly
Circulation: 30,000

19405 Common Ground
Community Associations Institute
225 Reinekers Lane
Suite 300
Alexandria, VA 22314
703-548-8600
FAX: 703-836-6907
caidirect@caionline.org
http://www.caionline.org
Tom Sciba, CEO/President
Chris Durso, Editor
Chris Durso, Publisher
Marc Markingam, Marketing Manager
CAI's award-winning bimonthly magazine for condominium and homeowner associations, managers and other industry professionals. Would you like to learn how a Web site can help your community association? Or peruse tips on cutting your budget? Or find out about the New Urbanism and other community development trends? Stay informed and involved via features and departments on the legal, political mechanical, personal, and day-to-day realities of community association life. *$69.00*
Monthly Founded: 1978 17,500 names
$150 per M.

19406 Comparative Statistics of Industrial and Office Real Estate Markets
Society of Industrial & Office Realtors
1201 New York Ave
NW Suite 350
Washington, DC 20001-4507
202-449-8200
FAX: 202-449-8201
admin@sior.com http://www.sior.com
Linda Nasvaderani, Editor
Richard Hollander, Executive VP
Michelle Carmichael, Marketing/PR Manager
A comprehensive publication that summarizes the results of a nationwide survey of industrial and office real estate market activity. *$135.00*
300 pages Annual+
Circulation: 3000

19407 Condo Management
Papers
342 Hathaway Boulevard
Suite 26
New Bedford, MA 02740
978-524-1758
FAX: 508-993-2329 888-412-6636
info@condomgmt.com
http://www.condomgmt.com
Melanie L Lange, Publisher
Lisa Zimmerer, Marketing Manager
Ken Sheldon, Editorial Support
News and features on condominium management issues throughout these regions, regular features on financial services, product services and other related topics. *$50.00*
Circulation: 10000

19408 Connections
Women's Council of Realtors
430 N Michigan Avenue
Chicago, IL 60611-4002
312-329-8483
FAX: 312-329-3290 800-245-8512
publications@wcr.org www.wcr.org
Dianna Dearen, Editor
Gary Krysler, Executive VP
Top producers in the real estate industry share their strategies for success.
32 pages Founded: 1966
Circulation: 14000 14000 names
Printed in 4 colors on matte stock

19409 Cooperative Housing Journal
National Association of Housing Cooperatives
630 Eye Street NW
Washington, DC 20001-2719
202-893-3500
FAX: 202-289-8181
nahro@nahro.org
http://www.nahro.org
James M Inglis, President
Deniz Tunder, Director Publication
Articles of lasting value to leaders in cooperative housing. *$25.00*
Founded: 1933
Circulation: 3000

19410 Cooperator
Yale Robbins Publications
102 Madison Avenue
5th Floor
New York, NY 10016
212-890-0500
FAX: 212-545-0764
info@cooperator.com
http://www.cooperator.com
Matt Kovner, Publisher
Pam Liebman, CEO/President
Judith C Grover, Managing Editor
George Rubin, Circulation Manager
Ellen Levy, Advertising Manager
Articles covering management, maintenance business, finance, law, interior design and related topics. *$30.00*
Monthly Founded: 1985
Circulation: 75000
Printed in 4 colors

19411 Daily Record
11 East Saratoga Street
Baltimore, MD 21202
410-752-3849
FAX: 410-752-2894
customer.service@mddailyrecord.com
http://www.mddailyrecord.com
Christopher Eddings, Publisher/President
Suzanne Fischer-Huettner, VP Sales
Christopher J Chardo, Circulation Director
Mark R Cheshire, Editor-in-Chief
Jeffrey Raymond, Editor *$190.00*
Daily Founded: 1888

19412 Development
National Assn of Industrial & Office Properties
2201 Cooperative Way
3rd floor
Herndon, VA 20171
703-904-7100
FAX: 703-904-7942 800-666-6780
feedback@naiop.org
http://www.naiop.org
Thomas J Bisacquino, President
Shirley A Maloney, Publisher
Articles pertaining to industrial and office real estate - development, ownership, management, investment, financing, leasing, etc. *$65.00*
72 pages Quarterly Founded: 2000
Circulation: 14000
Printed in 4 colors on glossy stock

19413 Developments
American Resort Development Association
1220 L Street NW
Suite 500
Washington, DC 20005
202-371-6700
FAX: 202-289-8544
webmaster@arda.org
http://www.arda.org
Howard C Nusbaum, President/COO
Robert A Miller, Chairman
Sherry Eggers, Director of Sales & Marke
Jennifer Young, Editor
Jennifer Young, Publisher
Serves the timeshare industry.
Monthly Founded: 1978
Circulation: 1,000

19414 Entertainment Real Estate Report
Ecklein Communications
PO Box 5194
Novato, CA 94948-5194
415-883-1960
FAX: 415-883-9064
www.eci-global.com
John Ecklein, Publisher
Information to keep real estate executives up-to-date on people, projects, and events involved in the development of entertainment real estate. *$397.00*
12 issues

19415 Financial Freedom Report
2450 Fort Union Boulevard
Salt Lake City, UT 84121-3337
FAX: 801-944-4334
Carolyn Tice, Editor
An investor's information services company which specializes in home business start-up, analysis, acquisition and maintenance of real property. *$119.00*
72 pages 4 issues Founded: 1976

19416 First Tuesday
Realty Publications
PO Box 20069
Riverside, CA 92516-69
909-781-7300
FAX: 909-781-4721
Fred Crane, Publisher
Provides practical assistance to real estate professional. Includes legal and economic updates affecting the commercial and residential developments.
Monthly
Circulation: 5000

19417 Global Property Investor
Alexander & Edwards Publishing
220 Sansome Street
11th Floor
San Francisco, CA 94104-2326
415-151-1241
FAX: 415-249-1595 800-989-7255
Objective, independent journal covering commercial property investment and development trends with readership in Europe, Asia and North America.

19418 Hotel Journal
Stacey Horowitz
45 Research Way
Suite 106
East Setauket, NY 11733
631-246-9300
FAX: 631-246-9496
Info@hoteljournal.com
http://www.hoteljournal.com
Stacey Silver, Group Publisher
Stefani C O'Connor, Executive News Editor
Cathy Urell, Senior Desk Editor
Barbara Jordan, Production Manager
Hope Rosenzweig, Advertising Manager
$85.00
Monthly

19419 In Business
Business Information
2718 Dryden Drive
Madison, WI 53704
608-246-3599
FAX: 608-246-3597
jodyand@magnapubs.com
Jody Glynn Patrick, Publisher
Joseph Vanden Plas, Editor
The business magazine for the Greater Madison Market.
48 pages Monthly
Circulation: 15,000

19420 Ingram's
Show-Me Publishing
306 E 12th Street
Suite 1014
Kansas City, MO 64106
816-358-8700
FAX: 816-221-4610
ingrams@unicom.net
www.ingramsonline.com
Joe Sweeney, Editor-in-Chief

Kansas City's business magazine. *$36.00*
114 pages Monthly
Printed in 4 colors on glossy stock

19421 Institutional Real Estate Letter
Institutional Real Estate
1475 N Broadway
Suite 300
Walnut Creek, CA 94596-4641
925-933-4040
FAX: 925-934-4099
g.dohrmann@irei.com
http://www.irei.com

Geoffrey Dohrmann, Chairman/CEO
Sandy Terranova, VP Marketing
Steve Felix, Senior VP
Jessica Heidgerken, Editor
Michael Lester, Editorial Director

Information for pension, foundation and endowment fund investors in real estate. *$1495.00*
40 pages Monthly Founded: 1987 ISSN 1044-1662
Circulation: 1800

19422 International Real Estate Journal
International Real Estate Institute
1224 N Nokomis NE
Alexandria, MN 56308-5072
320-763-4648
FAX: 320-763-9290
irei@iami.org www.iami.org/irei.html

Roger Wood, Production Manager
James Held, Production Manager
Robert Johnson, CEO

A full color magazine dedicated to discussing and promoting real estate opportunities all over the world. The articles cover a wide array of international Real Estate topics and are written by top international professionals.
Monthly Founded: 1977
Circulation: 10,000

19423 Journal of Community Association Law
Community Associations Institute
225 reinekers lane
Suite 300
Alexandria, VA 22314-3426
703-548-8600
FAX: 703-836-6907
acentral@caionline.org
http://www.caionline.org

Tom Skiba, CEO
Debra Lewin, Publisher/Editor

This is the only scholarly journal that focuses on the highly specialized and rapidly changing field of community association law. This invaluable semi-annual not only reports on significant cases nationwide along with case notes, it also analyzes them and provides expert commentary keeping you up to date on important legal trends. *$165.00*
Founded: 1973
Circulation: 10000 17,500 names $150 per M.

19424 Journal of Housing
National Association of Housing & Redevelopment
630 Eye Street NW
Washington, DC 20001-3736
202-289-3500
FAX: 202-289-8181 nahro@nahro.org

Terence Cooper, Editor

Information on HUD programs, private partnerships, neighborhood development programs, community development and public housing. *$ 24.00*
Bi-Monthly
Circulation: 13,500

19425 Journal of Property Management
Institute of Real Estate Management
430 North Michigan Avenue
Chicago, IL 60611-4002
312-296-6000
FAX: 800-338-4736
custserv@irem.org
http://www.irem.org/

Sara Patterson, Director Communication
Russ Salzman, Publisher
Anthony W Smith, President

Features articles on management, leasing and development of all property types. *$69.95*
Founded: 1976
Circulation: 18000

19426 Journal of Real Estate Taxation
90 5th Avenue
10th Floor
New York, NY 10011-7629
212-807-2194
FAX: 212-337-4183

19427 MB News
Monument Builders of North America
401 N Michigan Avenue
Suite 2200
Chicago, IL 60611-4267

FAX: 312-673-6732 800-233-4472

Greg Patzer, Executive VP
Marty Kraslen, Manager

The Monument Builders of North America represent the leading retail, wholesale and manufacturing and supply firms of the monument industry. Articles promote public interest, knowledge and appreciation of memorialization. *$70.00*
12 issues
Circulation: 1400

19428 Midwest Real Estate News
The Law Bulletin Publishing Company
415 N State Street
Chicago, IL 60610
312-644-7800
FAX: 312-614-5076
dwalsh@lbpc.com
http://www.rejournals.com/

Mark Menzies, Publisher
Tricia Haddon, Associate Publisher
Bob Craig, Editor
Robert Carr, Associate editor

The Midwest's only commercial real estate source. *$60.00*
Monthly Founded: 1854
Circulation: 16914 16,914 names $150 per M.
Printed in 4 colors on glossy stock

19429 Mobility
Employee Relocation Council
1717 Pennsylvania Avenue NW
Suite 800
Washington, DC 20006-2900
202-857-0857
FAX: 202-659-8631
webmaster@erc.org
http://www.erc.org/

Jerry Holloman, Editor/Publisher
Richard McGuire, Manager
Frank Mauck, Managing Editor
H Cris Collie, President

Total relocation magazine, examines key issues affecting the relocation industry for the benefit of corporations, government agencies, and firms or individuals providing specific services to relocated employees and their families. Accepts advertising. *$48.00*
68 pages Monthly Founded: 1960
Circulation: 12500

19430 Mortgage and Real Estate Executives Report
PO Box 64833
Saint Paul, MN 55164-0833
212-929-7500
FAX: 212-367-6718 800-950-1205

19431 Multifamily Executive
MGI Publications
One Thomas Circle NW
Suite 600
Washington, DC 20005-7706
202-452-0800
FAX: 202-785-1974
arice@hanleywood.com
http://www.multifamilyexecutive.com

Ed McNeill, President
Stephanie Davis, Production Manager
Alison Rice, Editor
Nicola Pellegrini, Marketing
J Michael Boyle, Publisher

Software and technology innovations, legislation, property development, management and renovation topics. Subscription free to qualified individuals.
Monthly Founded: 1976
Circulation: 25000 25,000 names
Printed in 4 colors on glossy stock

19432 National Real Estate Investor
Primedia
5680 Greenwood Plaza Boulevard
Suite 100
Greenwood Village, CO 80111
303-741-2901
FAX: 720-489-3101
http://www.primediabusiness.com

Jerrold France, Publisher
Paula Stephens, Editor

Covers development, investment, financing and management of commercial real estate and its allied fields. Considered the leading real estate business periodical in the US. *$7.00*
Founded: 1939
Circulation: 33000

19433 National Relocation & Real Estate Magazine
Relocation Information Service
50 Water Street
South Norwalk, CT 06854-3061
203-852-4304
FAX: 203-852-7208
http://www.rismedia.com

John Featherston, Publisher
Steve Empey, CEO

Information on emerging trends and important issues affecting the various industries that are involved in relocating people and the home buying process. *$42.84*
Monthly Founded: 1985
Circulation: 34,500

19434 New Homes Guide
4902 Eisenhower Boulevard
Suite 216
Tampa, FL 33634
813-823-3535
FAX: 813-290-7380

Emily Boyd, Manager
Sharon Kirkbride, Contact

19435 Office & Industrial Properties
MGI Publications
301 Oxford Valley Road
#1301
Yardley, PA 19067-7706
215-321-5112
FAX: 215-321-5122
mgipubs@bellatlantic.com
Edward McNeill Jr, President/Editor-in-Chief
Contains business, technology, design and financial aspects concerning large private properties. *$36.00*
Bi-Monthly
Circulation: 15,000

19436 Office Buildings Magazine
Yale Robbins Publications
102 Madison Avenue
5 Floor
New York, NY 10016
212-890-0500
FAX: 212-545-0764 800-411-2229
info@mrofficespace.com
http://www.mrofficespace.com/
Yale Robbins, Publisher/CEO
Henry Robbins, Marketing
Debbie Estock, Editor
Dane Pedupo, Circulation
Offers information on appraising and betterment of the real estate community in major markets in the Northeast. *$675.00*
Annual+ Founded: 1982
Printed in 4 colors

19437 Pest Control
Questex Media
600 Superior Avenue E
Ste 1100
Cleveland, OH 44114
216-706-3700
FAX: 216-706-3711 800-669-1668
pestcon@questex.com
http://www.pestcontrolmag.com
Robert Krakoff, Chairman/CEO
Matt Waddell, Publisher
Matt Simoni, Sales Manager
Frank Andorka, Editorial Director
Serves the structural pest control industry.
Monthly Founded: 1933
Circulation: 21600
Printed in 4 colors on glossy stock

19438 Pest Control Technology
GIE Media
4012 Bridge Avenue
Cleveland, OH 44113
216-961-4130
FAX: 216-961-0364 800-456-0707
Dan Moreland, Publisher
Jodi Dorsch, Editor
Directed towards technological and educational advancement in the pest control industry. *$35.00*
76 pages Monthly Founded: 1972
Printed in 4 colors on glossy stock

19439 Plants, Sites & Parks
12350 NW 39th Street
Suite 101
Coral Springs, FL 33065
954-753-2660
FAX: 954-755-7048 800-753-2660
Kevin Castellani, Group Publisher
Steve Chaffin, Publisher/Editor-in-Chief
Lisa M Bouchey, Managing Editor
Industrial office and economic development, facility planning and site selection for manufacturing and service industries.
Circulation: 44,500

19440 Practical Real Estate Lawyer
American Law Institute
4025 Chestnut Street
Philadelphia, PA 19104-3099
215-431-1600
FAX: 215-243-1664
publications@ali-aba.org
http://www.ali-aba.org
Mark T Carroll, Editor
Julene Franki, Executive Director
Covers news and information regarding pending or proposed real estate law. Gives practical advice in relating to clients.
Founded: 1947
Circulation: 5000

19441 Professional Report
Society of Industrial & Office Realtors
1201 New York Avenue
NW, Suite. 350
Washington, DC 20005-4507
202-449-8200
FAX: 202-449-8201
admin@sior.com http://www.sior.com
Richard Hollander, Executive Vice President
Virginia Antevil, Executive Assistant
Steven Banovac, Administrative Assistant
Bill Stevenson, Marketing/PR Manager
Kevin J Crowley, President
Articles by industry experts focusing on new paradigm in the practice of commercial real estate. *$295.00*
Quarterly Founded: 1991
Circulation: 2,200

19442 RCI Timeshare Business
RCI
9998 N Michigan Road
Carmel, IN 46032
317-059-9584
FAX: 317-805-9507
alyssa.chase@rci.com
http://www.rci.com
Alyssa Chase, Editor
Katherine Jones, Publisher
David Tontius, CEO/President
Serves timeshare resorts/developers, hoteliers, operations and others allied to the field.
42 pages Monthly Founded: 1974
Circulation: 9000
Printed in 4 colors on glossy stock

19443 Real Estate Business
Realtors National Marketing Institute
430 N Michigan Avenue
#300
Chicago, IL 60611-4002
312-321-4400
FAX: 312-329-8882
spatterson@crs.com
http://www.crs.com
Sara Patterson, Editor-in-Chief
Eric Berkland, Marketing
Nina Cottrell, CEO
Information for real estate agents and brokers engaged in US residential sales activities. *$24.00*
64 pages Founded: 1976
Circulation: 48000

19444 Real Estate Executive
Sunshine Media
1540 E. Maryland Avenue
Phoenix, AZ 85014-1456
602-773-3103
FAX: 602-285-1485
info@sunshinemedia.com
http://www.sunshinemedia.com
Judith Tibbs, Editor-in-Chief
Jim Martin, CEO
Features stories on local real estate agencies, broker and outstanding sales agent, also real estate law, investment strategies, travel and liesure, sales and marketing trends. *$36.00*
Monthly Founded: 1982
Circulation: 3000

19445 Real Estate Finance Journal
West Group
1133 Broadway
New York, NY 10010
212-620-0870
FAX: 212-691-3604 800-950-1205
Terrence M Clauretie, Editor-in-Chief
Covers new trends and concepts in real estate investment, development, and asset management. *$305.00*
4 issues
Circulation: 2,000

19446 Real Estate Finance Today
Mortgage Bankers Association of America
1919 Pennsylvania Avenue NW
Washington, DC 20006-3438
202-557-2700
FAX: 202-721-0167 800-793-6222
Marshall Taylor, Director
Features inside news reports on events and trends affecting the residential and commercial mortgage markets.

19447 Real Estate Forum
Real Estate Media
520 8th Avenue
17th Floor
New York, NY 10018
212-929-6900
FAX: 212-929-7124
reforum@fulcoinc.com
http://www.reforum.com
Jonathan A Schein, Publisher
Cynthia J Hoffman, Editor
Alexa Fualkner, Production Manager
Margo Dobey, Marketing
Austin Malcolm, Circulation Manager
In depth analysis, market research studies and exclusive insights into corporate real estate. *$59.95*
Monthly Founded: 1940
Circulation: 35000

19448 Real Estate Review
Warren, Gorham & Lamont
395 Hudson Street
New York, NY 10014-3669
212-367-6300
FAX: 212-367-6718 800-742-3348
James Douglas, Editor-in-Chief
Information on financing, mortgage banking, investments, and related legal and tax issues, also covers US commercial, indiustrial and residential development.
Quarterly
Circulation: 5,500

19449 Real Property, Property and Trust Journal
American Bar Association
321 North Clark Street
Chicago, IL 60610-4497
312-988-5000
FAX: 312-988-6281
abajournal@abanet.org
http://www.abanet.org

Robert J Grey, President

Scholarly articles in the fields of estate planning, trust law and real property law. *$60.00*
Quarterly Founded: 1878

19450 Realtor Magazine
New York State Association of Realtors
430 N. Michigan Avenue
Suite 430
Chicago, IL 60611-4087
800-874-6500
FAX: 312-329-5978
narpubs@realtors.org
http://www.realtormag.com

Stacey Mancrieff, Editor
Frank Sibley, Senior VP/Publisher
Christina H Spira, Managing Editor
Wanda Clark, Publications Assistant
Pamela G Kabati, Vice President / Editorial Director

The business tool for real estate professionals. The New York Report is given after page 8. *$56.00*
70 pages Monthly Founded: 1908
Printed in 4 colors on glossy stock

19451 Rental Management
1900 19th Street
Moline, IL 61265-4179
309-764-2475
FAX: 309-764-1533 800-334-2177
ara@ararental.org
http://www.ararental.org

Chris Wehrman, Executive VP
Joe Lynch, Deputy Executive VP

A monthly magazine published by the American Rental Association
Monthly
Circulation: 18000

19452 Residential Specialist
430 N Michigan Avenue
Chicago, IL 60611-4002
312-321-4400
FAX: 312-329-8882
info@crs.com http://www.crs.com

Nina Cottrell, CEO/President
Eric Berkland, Director Marketing
Carol Raabe, VP
Carlee Londo, Marketing Manager
Richard Lawson, Director of Products

Published by the Council of Residential Specialists. *$29.95*
64 pages Founded: 1976
Circulation: 40000

19453 Site Selection
Conway Data
6625 Thocloners Parkway
Street 200
Norcross, GA 30092-2928
770-446-6996
FAX: 770-263-8825
http://www.sitenet.com

McKinley Conway, Publisher
Loura Lyne, President
Julie Clark, Circulation Manager
Rone Starne, Maketing Manager

Focus is on political, international and quality of life issues, also provides development groups, business parks, labor factors, relevant technology, real estate and finance information. *$90.00*
Monthly Founded: 1964
Circulation: 45000

19454 Timeshare Business
RCI
9998 N Michigan Road
Carmel, IN 46032
317-059-9584
FAX: 317-805-9507
alyssa.chase@rci.com
http://www.rciventures.com

Alyssa Chase, Editor
Nicole keller, Senior Associate Editor
Rita Corea, Circulation Manager

Magazine for resort developers, property managers, sales and marketing professionals, homeowners association boards, and other key personnel in the timeshare industry.
42 pages Monthly Founded: 1974
Circulation: 35000
Printed in 4 colors on 6 stock

19455 US Sites & Development
Vulcan Publications
PO Box 12846
Birmingham, AL 35202-2846
205-328-6198
www.vulcanpub.com

Val Carrier, Publisher

Includes tax laws, real estate trends, as well as labor and work force issues.
Monthly
Circulation: 12,000

19456 Unique Homes
327 Wall Street
Princeton, NJ 08540
609-688-1110
FAX: 609-688-0201 877-688-1110
krussell@uniquehomes.com
http://www.uniquehomes.com

Kathleen Carlin-Russell, Editor-in-Chief
Lauren Baier Kim, Managing Editor
Cheryl Jock, Production Manager
Robert Burke, Custom Publishing Manager *$24.97*

Founded: 1978
Circulation: 54,856

19457 Units
National Apartment Association Communications
201 N Union Street
#200
Alexandria, VA 22314-2642
703-518-6141
FAX: 703-518-6191
webmaster@naahq.org
http://www.naahq.org

Doug Culkin, Executive Vice President
John Bollinger, Sales Manager
Debbie Bilotta, Office Manager
David Slotwinski, Director of Information Technology
Nancy Dobberman, Chief Financial Officer

Information on national political, legal and economic significance to the members of the National Apartment Association and those involved in rental housing ownership. *$50.00*
80 pages Monthly
Circulation: 45161
Printed in on glossy stock

19458 Urban Land
Urban Land Institute
1025 Thomas Jefferson Street NW
Suite 500 West
Washington, DC 20007-5201
202-624-7000
FAX: 202-624-7140
ahart@uli.org http://www.uli.org

Rachelle Levitt, Publisher
Kristina Kessler, Editor in Chief
Karen Schaar, Managing Editor
Joan Campbell, Manager

Features trends and innovations in land use and real estate development practices, also brings practical research and expertise to the standards and conduct of land use planning and real estate development.
Monthly Founded: 1936
Circulation: 15000

19459 Vacation & Second Homes
3275 W Ina Road
Suite 110
Tucson, AZ 85741-2152
520-297-8200
FAX: 520-297-6219
www.homeplanners.com

19460 Vacation Industry Review
Interval International
6262 Sunset Drive
Miami, FL 33143-4843
305-661-1861
www.resortdeveloper.com

Matthew McDaniel, Editor
Alina Betancourt, Advertising Manager

Vacation Industry Review is a quarterly trade publication covering the global timeshare, fractional, vacation ownership resort industry. It discusses industry issues and trends and showcases new resort developments and key markets. It also covers products and services of interest to the industry, and the activities of prominent individuals and companies.
48/64 pages Quarterly Founded: 1984
Circulation: 28,000
Printed in 4 colors on glossy stock : web

19461 Vacation Ownership World
CHB Company
8701 Collins Ave Ph
Miami, Fl 33154
305-864-6083
FAX: 305-864-6085
resort@nas.com
http://www.vomagazine.com

Jon Paulisin, Publisher/President
Lou Skidmore, Editor
Howard White, Circulation Manager

News and feature stories, in depth analysis of the issues and trends affecting the industry of global timesharing. *$29.50*
Quarterly Founded: 1984
Circulation: 6500

19462 Valuation Insights & Perspectives
Appraisal Institute
550 W Van Buren Street
Suite 1000
Chicago, IL 60607
312-354-4100
FAX: 312-335-4474
web@appraisalinstitute.org
http://www.appraisalinstitute.org

Adam Webster, Managing Editor
Larisa Phillips, President

Offers a collection of high interest articles, and features industry and institute news section and columns on legal matters, tech-

nology, marketing and timely appraisal issues. *$48.00*
18 pages Quarterly Founded: 1996
Circulation: 82000
Printed in 4 colors on glossy stock

Trade Shows

19463 American Congress on Surveying & Mapping A nnual Conference
6 Montgomery Village Avenue
Suite 403
Gaithersburg, MD 20879
240-680-0765
FAX: 240-632-1321 www.acsm.net
Curt Sumner, Executive Director
One hundred and thirty exhibits of industry related equipment, supplies and services plus workshop and conference.
2000 Attendees Annual Founded: 1954

19464 American Land Tree Association Annual Convention
1828 L Street NW
Suite 705
Washington, DC 20036-5104
202-296-3671

James Maher, VP
1M Attendees October

19465 American Real Estate Society Annual Meeting
American Real Estate Society
Cleveland State University-BU327
Dept. Finance, Business College
Cleveland, OH 44114
216-687-4732
FAX: 216-687-9331
j.webb.csuohio.edu www.aresnet.org
James R Webb, Director/Development
Annual meeting and 10 exhibitors that are publishers, data providers, technical foundtions. Exhibits relate to decision-making within real estate finance, real estate market analysis, investment, valuation, development and other areas related to real estate.
300 Attendees April $250 per M.

19466 American Society of Appraisers International Appraisal Conference

555 Herdon Parkway
Suite 125
Herndon, VA 20170-5250
703-478-2228
FAX: 703-742-8741 800-272-8258
info@appraisers.org
www.appraisers.org
Jerry Larkins, Executive VP
Exhibits for professional appraisers.
Annual

19467 Apartment Association of Greater Dallas Annual Trade Show
4230 LBJ Freeway
Suite 140
Dallas, TX 75244
972-385-9091
FAX: 972-385-9412
pkelley@aagdallas.com
www.aagdallas.com
Paula Kelley CMP, Director of Events
Gerry Henigsman, Executive VP
Tours and 240 displays of industry related supplies and services.
3000 Attendees April Founded: 1963

19468 Apartment Association of Metro Denver Educational Expo and Trade Show
650 S Cherry Street
Suite 635
Denver, CO 80246
303-290-0403
FAX: 303-329-0403 info@aamdhg.org
Mark Williams, Executive Director
Seminar, reception and 142 exhibits of property management equipment, supplies, services and information.
1500 Attendees Annual

19469 BOMA Winter Business Meeting & Leadership Conference
Building Owners & Managers Association Int'l
1201 New York Avenue NW
Suite 300
Washington, DC 20005
202-408-2662
FAX: 202-371-0181
info@boma.org www.boma.org
Henry Chamberlain, President/CEO
Laura Best, Conference Director
Opportunity for business professionals to discuss problems, security, exchange ideas and share experience and knowledge.
January

19470 BUILDINGS-New York
Reed Exhibition Companies
383 Main Avenue
Norwalk, CT 06851-1543
203-840-4800
FAX: 203-840-9570
Annual show of 425 exhibitors of products and services for the building owner, developer, manager, co-ops and superintendents in the commercial and residential real estate market, including asbestos abatement, waterproofing, restoration, financial services, utilities, laundry equipment, cleaning services, computer software, elevators, heating and air conditioning, light safety/security, renovation and restoration.
9,000 Attendees

19471 Coldwell Bankers Annual National Show
27271 Las Ramblas
Mission Viejo, CA 92691-6386
949-673-3650
FAX: 973-496-5784
Sandra Deering, Manager
Seventy-five booths.
4.5M Attendees

19472 MIPIM
Reed Exhibition Companies
255 Washington Street
Newton, MA 02458-1637
617-584-4900
FAX: 617-630-2222
Elizabeth Hitchcock, International Sales
International property market conference.
4M Attendees March

19473 National Association of Realtors Meetings and Trade Show
430 N Michigan Avenue
Chicago, IL 60611-4087
312-645-7730
800-874-6500
infocentral@realtors.org
www.realtor.org
Karen Crafton, Convention Executive Secretary
Sue Gourley, Conventions VP
Terrence McDermott, Chief Executive Officer
Seminars and networking, plus updates in the industry. More than 200 exhibiting companies.
6500 Attendees May

19474 National Association of Realtors Trade Exposition
National Association of Realtors
430 N Michigan Avenue
Chicago, IL 60611-4002
312-645-7730
FAX: 312-329-8882
info@crs.com www.crs.com
Sara Patterson, Director Communications
Terrence McDermott, Chief Exceutive Officer
Spring show of 250 exhibitors of real estate industry equipment, supplies and services, including hardware and software, marketing programs, office products, mortgage and financial services and insurance.
40000 Attendees Founded: 1976

19475 Old House New House Home Show
630-515-1160

kp@corecomm.net
www.kennedyproductions.com
Beth Wall, Contact
Discover the latest innovations, seeing creative solutions and gathering the motivation to tackle home improvement projects.
Sept/Oct Illinois

19476 RCI Ventures Magazine
RCI
9998 N Michigan Road
Carmel, IN 46032
317-059-9584
FAX: 317-805-9507
alyssa.chase@rci.com
www.rciventures.com
Alyssa Chase, Editor
Nicole Keller, Senior Editor
Gathering of more than 4,000 of timesharing's best and brightest executives.
April
Circulation: 35000
Printed in 4 colors on 6 stock

19477 Real Show
Journal of Property Management
430 N Michigan Avenue
Chicago, IL 60611-4002
312-329-6064
FAX: 312-329-8882
info@crs.com www.crs.com
Sara Patterson, Director Communications
A trade show with 275 exhibitors and 450 booths, for professional owners and managers of investment residential and commercial property.
40000 Attendees Founded: 1976

19478 Realmart
National Association of Industrial & Office Prop.
Woodlyn Park-2201 Coop. Way
Herndon, VA 22071
703-267-6665
FAX: 703-904-7974 garvin@naiop.org
Annual show of 100 suppliers of companies catering to the commercial real estate industry.
1,000 Attendees

19479 **Realtors Conference & Expo**
National Association of Realtors
430 N Michigan Avenue
Chicago, IL 60611
312-457-7730
FAX: 312-329-8873 800-628-6338
coninfo@REALTORS.org
www.REALTOR.org/conference
Lisa Nicola, Director of Sales
20 K+ Attendees November

19480 **Trade Expo**
Professional Housing Management
PO Box 4251
Leesburg, VA 20177
703-327-6873
FAX: 703-327-4005 800-543-7188
phmainfo@earthlink.net
www.phma.com
Jon Moore, Director
Mona Pearson, Trade Expo Coordinator
At the expo there will be 230 booths with 150 exhibitors.
1,200 Attendees January

Directories & Databases

19481 **America's Top-Rated Cities**
Grey House Publishing
185 Millerton Road
PO Box 860
Millerton, NY 12546
518-890-0526
FAX: 518-789-0545 800-562-2139
books@greyhouse.com
www.greyhouse.com
Leslie Mackenzie, Publisher
David Garoogian, Editor
Provides current, comprehensive statistical information in one easy-to-use source on the 100 top cities that have been cited as the best for business and living in the US. Available as a four volume set or individual volumes (Southern, Western, Central and Eastern) *$195.00*
1700 pages ISBN 1-592370-38-1

19482 **America's Top-Rated Smaller Cities**
Grey House Publishing
185 Millerton Road
PO Box 860
Millerton, NY 12546
518-890-0526
FAX: 518-789-0545 800-562-2139
books@greyhouse.com
www.greyhouse.com
Leslie Mackenzie, Publisher
David Garoogian, Editor
Provides a current, comprehensive business and living profile of 100 smaller cities that have been cited as the best for business and living in the US. *$160.00*
1000 pages ISBN 1-592370-43-8

19483 **American Resort Development Association: Membership Directory**
American Resort Development Association
1201 15th Street NW
Suite 400
Washington, DC 20005
202-371-6700
FAX: 202-289-8544
Sheila Morris, Editor
Howard Nusbaum, President
Over 800 member firms in the resort development industry, including developers, finance companies, architectural firms, audiovisual companies, direct mail companies, rental and vacation exchange companies and law firms.
Annual Winter

19484 **American Society of Appraisers Directory**
American Society of Appraisers
555 Herndon Parkway
Suite 125
Herndon, VA 20170-5248
703-782-2228
FAX: 703-742-8471 800-272-8258
asainfo@appraisers.org
www.appraisers.org
Jerry F Larkins, Executive Director
Directory of association members who are accredited appraisers. *$12.50*
Circulation: 8,000

19485 **Buyers Broker Registry**
Who's Who in Creative Real Estate
PO Box 23275
Ventura, CA 93002-3275
Offers valuable information on over 650 real estate agents in the United States who have met performance requirements set by the publisher. *$25.00*
136 pages Annual

19486 **CRB/CRS Referral Directory**
Realtors National Marketing Institute
430 N Michigan Avenue
Suite 300
Chicago, IL 60611-4002
FAX: 312-329-8882
www.rscouncil.com
Gwen Voelker, Editor
Aimed at the real estate industry, this directory lists over 32,000 real estate brokerage managers and residential sales specialists. *$45.00*
776 pages Annual
Circulation: 32,000

19487 **CRE Member Directory**
Counselors of Real Estate
430 N Michigan Avenue
Chicago, IL 60611-4002
312-298-8427
FAX: 312-329-8881 www.cre.org
Mary Walker Fleischmann, Executive VP
Annual March

19488 **Commercial Investment Real Estate**
CCIM Institute
430 N Michigan Avenue
Chicago, IL 60611-4002
312-214-4460
FAX: 312-329-8882
magazine@ccim.com
www.crs.com/magazine
RJ Sirois, Publisher
Directory of services and supplies to the industry.
40000 pages Founded: 1976

19489 **Comparative Guide to American Suburbs**
Grey House Publishing
185 Millerton Road
PO Box 860
Millerton, NY 12546
518-890-0526
FAX: 518-789-0545 800-562-2139
books@greyhouse.com
www.greyhouse.com
Leslie Mackenzie, Publisher
David Garoogian, Editor
Covers statistics on the 2,000+ suburban communities surrounding the 50 largest metropolitan areas - their population characteristics, income levels, economy, school systems and important data on how they compare to one another. *$130.00*
1681 pages ISBN 1-930956-42-8

19490 **Crime in America's Top-Rated Cities**
Grey House Publishing
185 Millerton Road
PO Box 860
Millerton, NY 12546
518-890-0526
FAX: 518-789-0545 800-562-2139
books@greyhouse.com
www.greyhouse.com
Leslie Mackenzie, Publisher
David Garoogian, Editor
Details over twenty years of crime statistics in all major crime categories: violent crimes, property crimes and total crime. Conveniently arranged by city, it offers details that compare the number of crimes and crime rates for the city, suburbs and metro area with national crime trends for violent, property and total crimes. Statistics on anti-crime programs, crime risk, hate crimes, illegal drugs, law enforcement, correctional facilities, death penalty, laws and much more. *$155.00*
839 pages

19491 **Crittenden's Real Estate Buyers Directory**
Crittendon Research
250 Bel Marin Keys Boulevard
Novato, CA 94949-5727
415-382-2400
FAX: 415-382-2476 800-421-3483
John Goodwin, Editor/Publisher
Vitlario Laeson, Marketing Director
Pati Bess, Customer Service Director
A list of over 500 real estate buyers, including private institutional investors, banks, pension funds and real estate investment trusts.

19492 **Crittendon Directory of Real Estate Financing**
Crittendon Research
250 Bel Marin Keys Boulevard
Novato, CA 94949-5727
415-382-7790
FAX: 415-382-2476
Listing of over 400 major lenders, investors and joint ventures enagged in commercial and residential real estate financing and investing. *$387.00*
500 pages Semiannual

19493 **DAMAR Real Estate Information Service Online Database**
3550 W Temple Street
Los Angeles, CA 90004-3620
800-873-2627

This comprehensive database offers real estate information, with an emphasis on California.
Full-text

19494 Directory of 2,500 Active Real Estate Lenders
International Wealth Success
PO Box 186
Merrick, NY 11566-0186
516-766-5850
FAX: 516-766-5919 800-323-0548
admin@iwsmoney.com
www.iwsmoney.com
Tyler G Hicks, President
Lists 2,500 names and addresses of direct lenders or sources of information on possible lenders for real estate. *$25.00*
197 pages Annually Founded: 1985 ISBN 1-561503-37-1

19495 Directory of Accredited Real Property Appraisers
American Society of Appraisers
PO Box 17265
Washington, DC 20041-7265
202-337-0037
FAX: 202-742-8471 800-272-8258
Rebecca Ewing, Publication Manager
Approximately 1,700 urban, residential, rural, ad valorem and timberland appraisers; limited international coverage.
Annual January

19496 Directory of Professional Appraisal Services
American Society of Appraisers
PO Box 17265
Washington, DC 20041-7265
202-337-0037
FAX: 202-742-8471 800-272-8258
asainfo@apo.com www.appraisers.org
Rebecca Ewing, Publisher/Editor
Over 3,000 tested and accredited members appraisers of real and personal property, businesses, machinery and equipment are listed. *$10.00*
275 pages Annual
Circulation: 8,000

19497 Directory of Real Estate Development and Related Education Programs
Urban Land Institute
625 Indiana Avenue NW
Suite 400
Washington, DC 20004-2923
202-247-7116

Over 60 programs are profiled that are currently being offered at colleges and universities in the area of real estate. *$19.00*
132 pages Biennial

19498 ERC Directory of Real Estate Appraisers and Brokers
Employee Relocation Council
1720 N Street NW
Washington, DC 20036-2900
202-857-0857

Tina Lung, Editor *$35.00*
1,100 pages Annual

19499 European Investment in United States Real Estate
Mead Ventures
PO Box 44952
Phoenix, AZ 85064-4952

Investors, developers and brokers located in Europe are the focus of this valuable directory. *$195.00*
406 pages Annual

19500 Executive Guide to Specialists in Industrial and Office Real Estate
Society of Industrial & Office Realtors
777 14th Street NW
Suite 400
Washington, DC 20005
202-737-1150

Thousands of specialists are listed that are integrated with industrial real estate and related industries. *$60.00*
210 pages Annual

19501 FDIC: Investment Properties Publication
Federal Deposit Insurance Corporation
550 17th Street NW
Washington, DC 20429-0002
202-736-0000

Offers information on properties owned by the Federal Deposit Insurance Corporation, including land, commercial real estate, multifamily dwellings and hotels and motels.
200 pages Quarterly

19502 Finance, Insurance and Real Estate USA
Gale Research
27500 Drake Road
Farmington Hills, MI 48331
248-699-4253
FAX: 248-699-8214 800-877-4253
galeord@gale.com www.gale.com
Arsen J Darnay, Editor
Offers industry statistics, analyses and leading organizations in banking, finance, insurance, real estate and related industries. *$169.00*
Founded: 1994

19503 Guide to Real Estate and Mortgage Banking Software
Real Estate Solutions
2609 Klingle Road NW
Washington, DC 20008-1202
202-362-9854

Lists approximately 500 real estate and mortgage banking computer software, hardware and products. *$49.95*
640 pages Biennial

19504 Income & Cost for Organization & Servicing of 1-4 Unit Residential Loans
Mortgage Bankers Association of America

1919 Pennsylvania Avenue NW
Washington, DC 20006-3438
202-557-2700
FAX: 202-721-0167 800-793-6222
tiffany_rowan@mbaa.org
www.mbaa.org
Tiffany Rowan, Circulation Director
Annual report provides data and analysis on the income and expenses associated with the organization, warehousing, marketing and servicing or one-to-four-unit residential marketing loans.
80 pages $150 Member/$300 Non

19505 Japanese Investment in US Real Estate Review
Mead Ventures
PO Box 44952
Phoenix, AZ 85064-4952

FAX: 602-234-0076
This is a complete database listing documenting Japanese purchases of US golf courses, houses, office buildings and industrial properties.
Full-text

19506 Journal of the American Society of Farm Managers and Rural Appraisers
ASFMRA
950 S Cherry Street
Suite 508
Denver, CO 80246
303-758-3513
FAX: 303-758-0190
asfmra@agri-associations.org
www.asfmra.org
Cheryl L Cooley, Manager Communications/PR

Mailing list available for rent 2500 names $1M per M.

19507 Million Dollar Guide to Business and Real Estate Loan Sources
International Wealth Success
PO Box 186
Merrick, NY 11566-0186
516-766-5850
FAX: 516-766-5919 800-323-0548
admin@iwsmoney.com
www.iwsmoney.com
Tyler G Hicks, President
Lists hundreds of business and real estate lenders, giving their lending data in very brief form. *$25.00*
201 pages Annually Founded: 1990

19508 Monthly Resort Real Estate Property Index
MDR Telecom
4742 La Villa Marina
Unit A
Marina Del Rey, CA 90292-7086

Mario Collura, Editor
Offers information on resort timeshares and resort condominiums for rent or sale. *$10.00*
80 pages Monthly

19509 Mortgage Banking Performance Report
Mortgage Bankers Association of America

1919 Pennsylvania Avenue NW
Washington, DC 20006-3438
202-557-2700
FAX: 202-721-0167 800-793-6222
tiffany_rowan@mbaa.org
www.mbaa.org
Tiffany Rowan, Circulation Director
The report includes an annual summary, is a financial statement analysis of mortgage banking company performance.
80 pages $125 Member/$175 Non Founded: 1992

19510 Mortgage Banking Sourcebook
Mortgage Bankers Association of America
1919 Pennsylvania Avenue NW
Washington, DC 20006-3438
202-557-2700
FAX: 202-721-0167 800-793-6222
Comprehensive directory to federal and state government agencies, industry trade associations colleges and universities, and other organizations and sources of information on mortgage lending, Includes an entire network of industry contact complete with addresses, telephone and fax numbers and internet website addresses.
$40.00
144 pages Founded: 1997

19511 Mortgage Finance Database
Mortgage Bankers Association of America
1919 Pennsylvania Avenue NW
Washington, DC 20006-3438
202-557-2700
FAX: 202-721-0167 800-793-6222
Brian Carey, Circulation Director
This database contains the most comprehensive and up-to-date collection of mortgage-related variables currently available.

19512 National Association of Independent Fee Appraisers: Membership Directory
National Association of Independent Fee Appraisers
7501 Murdoch Avenue
Saint Louis, MO 63119-2810
314-645-7583
FAX: 314-781-2872
Donna Walters, Publications
Five thousand and five hundred independent real estate appraisers.
Annual January

19513 National Association of Master Appraisers Membership Directory
National Association of Master Appraisers
303 W Cypress Street
San Antonio, TX 78212-5512
210-271-0781
FAX: 361-225-8450 800-229-6262
Gary Deane, Editor
Approximately 3,500 real estate appraisers.
Annual January
Circulation: 3,500

19514 National Association of Real Estate Appraisers
1129 20th Street NW
Suite 705
Washington, DC 20036-3403
202-785-0453

Dallas Martin, President
A complete guide to the REIT industry with approximately 240 real estate investment trusts, and over 1,000 associate members listed. *$695.00*
600 pages Annual

19515 National Association of Real Estate Companies: Membership Directory

National Association of Real Estate Companies
216 W Jackson Blvd
Ste 625
Chicago, IL 60606-6945
312-220-0990
FAX: 410-992-6363
Jeff Harris, Editor
About 200 real estate development companies.
Quarterly

19516 National Directory of Exchange Groups
Creative Real Estate Magazine
PO Box L
Rancho Santa Fe, CA 92067-0560
858-756-1441
FAX: 818-156-1111
Lists over 125 professional real estate marketing groups practicing tax-deferred real estate exchanges. *$72.00*
48 pages Monthly ISSN 0194-7222
Circulation: 51,000 51M names

19517 National Real Estate Directory
Real Estate Publishing Company
322 W Rio Vista Ct
Tampa, FL 33604-6941
813-237-6267

Over 22,000 federal and state agencies, offices and departments related to the regulation of real estate, real estate associations and publications are listed. *$29.95*
110 pages Biennial

19518 National Real Estate Investor Sourcebook
Primedia
5680 Greenwood Plaza Boulevard
Suite 300
Greenwood Village, CO 80111
303-741-2901
FAX: 720-489-3101
www.primediabusiness.com
Barbara Katinsky, Editor
List of about 7,000 companies and individuals in 18 real estate fields. *$78.95*
Annual, September
Circulation: 33,000

19519 National Referral Roster
Candy Holub
615 5th Street SE
Cedar Rapids, IA 52401-2158
319-364-6167
FAX: 319-369-0029 800-553-8878
candy.holub@roster.com
www.roster.com
Candy Holub, Publisher
Mary Richeson, Business Developer
Joey Grim, Business Developer
Approximately 90,000 Real Estate offices nationwide. Provides an effective, comprehensive and easy-to-use tool for realtors to make successful referrals to other relators nationwide. *$95.00*
936 pages Annual Founded: 1923
Circulation: 18,000 80M names $110 per M.
Printed in 2 colors on newsprint stock

19520 National Toll-Free 800 Guide to Real Estate Publications and Publishers
Real Estate Publishing Company
4580 Brookside Road
Sacramento, CA 95682
530-677-3864

Directory of publications to the industry.
$15.95
82 pages Biennial

19521 Nelson's Directory of Institutional Real Estate
Nelson Publications
2500 Tamiami Trail N
Nokomis, FL 34275
941-966-9521
FAX: 941-966-2590
webmaster@nelsonpub.com
www.nelsonpub.com
A Verner Nelson, Owner
Marcia Boysen, Editor
Institutional investors who invest in real estate: investment managers, real estate service firms, insurance companies, plan sponsors, corporations and REIT's.
$335.00
Annual August

19522 One List Directory
MRH Associates
365 Willard Avenue
Suite 2K
Newington, CT 06111-2373

800-727-5478
Over 700 companies and 6,000 company divisions are involved as listees in this comprehensive directory. Included is a section of over 12,000 contact personnel in the real estate and construction industry.
$545.00
750 pages Annual

19523 Professional Relocation and Real Estate Services Directory
Relocation Information Service
113 Post Road E
2nd Floor
Westport, CT 06880-3410
203-256-1079
FAX: 203-227-3800
Offers over 6,000 real estate brokerage companies, appraisal firms, home inspectors and services companies. *$95.00*
800 pages Annual
Circulation: 35,000

19524 Profiles of America
Grey House Publishing
185 Millerton Road
PO Box 860
Millerton, NY 12546
518-890-0526
FAX: 518-789-0545 800-562-2139
books@greyhouse.com
www.greyhouse.com
Leslie Mackenzie, Publisher
Richard Gottlieb, Editor
This four volume set details over 40,000 places, from the biggest metropolis to the smallest unicorporated hamlet and provides statistical details and information on over 50 different topics including: geography, climate, population, economy, income, taxes, education, housing, health and environment, public safety, transportation, presidential election results and more.
$595.00
10058 pages ISBN 1-891482-80-7

19525 Real Estate & Land Use Regulation in Eastern and Central Europe
WorldTrade Executive
PO Box 761
Concord, MA 01742-0761
978-287-0301
FAX: 978-287-0302 www.wtexec.com
Alison French, Production Manager
Topics covered include: leasing in Russia: helpful hints for tenants; a guide to government agencies regulating development in Moscow and St. Petersburg; current law and practice for the Russian real estate market; the real estate lease in the Czech Republic; environmental considerations for acquisition of property in Hungary. *$135.00*

19526 Real Estate Applications Software Directory
Real Estate Center
Texas A and M University
College Station, TX 77843-0001
979-845-2031
FAX: 713-845-0460 800-244-2144
David S Jones, Senior Editor
Ted C Jones, Chief Economist
About 300 suppliers of several hundred software packages with applications related to the real estate industry. *$30.00*
Annual October

19527 Real Estate Books and Periodicals in Print
Real Estate Publishing Company
PO Box 41177
Sacramento, CA 95841-0177
530-677-3864
John Johnsich, Publisher
Over 400 publishers of real estate books and periodicals and their product lines are profiled in this directory. *$29.95*
256 pages Annual Founded: 1975 ISBN 0-914256-33-5

19528 Real Estate Data
DataQuick Information Systems
9171 Towne Centre Drive
San Diego, CA 92122-1234
858-973-3100
FAX: 858-455-6522 800-863-INFO
Steve Rosetta, Owner
More than 12 million developed and undeveloped real properties in California, Arizona, Nevada, Oregon and Washington.
Daily

19529 Real Estate RoundTable
GE Information Services
401 N Washington Street
Rockville, MD 20850-1707
301-388-8284
Cathy Ge, Owner
This database provides a forum for discussions between professional realtors and individuals interested in the buying and selling of residential and commercial property.
Bulletin Board

19530 Real Estate Software Directory and Catalog
Z-Law Software
PO Box 40602
Providence, RI 02940-0602
401-273-5588
FAX: 401-421-5334 800-526-5588
info@z-law.com www.z-law.com
Gary L Sherman, President
A comprehensive guide to real estate and mortgage banking software. Includes IBM and MAC applications for realtors, landlords, property managers, investors, developers, attorneys, contractors, appraisers, loan agents, and anyone in real estate.
SemiAnnual

19531 Timeshare Multiple Listing Service
MDR Telecom
11965 Venice Boulevard
Suite 204
Los Angeles, CA 90066-3954
323-539-9701
FAX: 310-915-7212 800-423-6377
triwest@att.net
www.triwest-timeshare.com
Mario A Collura, Production Manager
Mario A Collura, Author
Approximately 6,000 pieces of timeshare real estate in the US, Mexico, and Carribean. *$10.00*
60 pages Monthly Founded: 1984 ISBN 1-888176-11-3

19532 Timeshare Vacation Owners HIP Resort Directory
TRI Publishing
11965 Venice Boulevard
Suite 204
Los Angeles, CA 90066-3954
FAX: 310-915-7212 800-423-6377
triwest@att.net.com
www.triwest-timeshare.com
Mario A Collura, President
Viccie Mac, Managing Editor
This is the only combined resort directory for buyers, owners and industry professionals. Over 3,000 resorts. *$18.95*
111 pages Every 2 Years Founded: 1995 ISBN 1-888176-12-1

19533 US Real Estate Register
Barry
PO Box 551
Wilmington, MA 01887-0551
978-580-0440
John Barry, Manager
Offers information on real estate departments of large national companies, industrial organizations and chambers of commerce involved in real estate development. *$58.00*
575 pages Annual

19534 United National Real Estate Catalog
United National Real Estate
4700 Belleview Avenue
Kansas City, MO 64112-1315
816-561-1115
FAX: 816-231-5599 800-999-1020
James Marinovich
Offers information on several thousand farms, ranches and country estates. *$4.95*
200 pages Semiannual

19535 Who's Who in Luxury Real Estate
JBL
2110 Western Avenue
Seattle, WA 98121-2110
206-441-7900
FAX: 206-441-5297 800-488-4066
Approximately 500 international luxury real estate brokers. *$19.95*
Annual

Industry Web Sites

19536 www.aagdallas.com
Apartment Association of Greater Dallas

19537 www.airea.com
American Industrial Real Estate Association
Encourages high professional standards. Has developed industrial multiple listing system and standard lease form. Publishes a quarterly newsletter

19538 www.americanhomeowners.org
American Homeowners Foundation
Serves as an educational and research consumer group offering books, model contracts, special studies, home buying, selling,investing, building, financing and remodeling.

19539 www.appraisalinstitute.org
Appraisal Institute
Promotes a code of ethics and uniform standards of the real estate appraisal practice. Publishes periodicals, books and appraisal-related materials, and sponsors courses and seminars.

19540 www.appraisers.org
American Society of Appraisers
Professional association of appraisers of all kinds.

19541 www.areuea.org
American Real Estate and Urban Economics Assoc
Addresses academic and commercial concerns in real estate and commercial economics.

19542 www.asfmra.org
American Soc of Farm Managers and Rural Appraisers
Provides professionals involved in rural property issues such as management and appraisal, with information on the industry as well as educational opportunities. Includes membership and information from the American Society of Farm Manager and Rural Appraisers.

19543 www.commercialsources.com
The official commercial real state site of the National Association Of Realtors.

19544 www.crb.com
Council of Real Estate Brokerage Managers

Members are real estate firm owners and managers.

19545 www.cre.org
Couselors of Real Estate

Association members provide the public with expert, objective advice on property and land related matters. Individuals invited to join are awarded the CRE designation.

19546 www.erc.org
Employee Relocation Council

A national organization that examines key issues affecting the relocation industry for the benefit of corporations, government agencies, and firms or individuals providing specific services to relocated employees and their families. Accepts advertising.

19547 www.fiabci-usa.com
FIABCI-USA

Encourages private ownership of real property and understanding of property rights and obligations.

19548 www.greyhouse.com
Grey House Publishing

Selected Grey House directories in the fields of business, health and education are available online. Users can search our online databases by several different search criteria, such as product categories, geographic area, sales volume and much, much more. Full Grey House catalog and online ordering also available.

19549 www.homestore.com

Homestore.com's family of sites is the leading destination for the home and the real estate- related information on the Internet. Provides informatin on Finance and Insurance, Home Improvement, Decorating, Lawn and garden, Home Electronics amd more.

19550 www.iaia.org
International Association for Impact Assessment

IAIA provides a forum for the exchange of the ideas and experiences to stimulate innovation in assessing, managing and mitigating the consequences of development.

19551 www.icsc.org
International Council of Shopping Centers

Fosters professional standards of performance in the development, construction, financing, leasing, management and operation of shopping centers throughout the world.

19552 www.nahma.org
National Affordable Housing Management Association

Trade association representing companies and individuals involved in the management of affordable multifamily housing.

19553 www.npma.org
National Property Management Association

Represents asset management professionals and keeps members a breast of trends in asset accountability technologies. Sponsors seminars, training courses: certification program.

19554 www.realtor.com
National Association of Realtors

Seeks to establish cooperation among brokers engaged in buying, selling, trading and leasing for realestate.

19555 www.realtylocator.com
Realty Locator

Over 100,000 real estate links nationwide in 10,000 cities and towns in all 50 states.

19556 www.reea.org
Real Estate Educators Association

Individuals involved in training and education.

19557 www.reipa.com
Real Estate Information Providers Association

Supports professional information providers in the real estate industry.

19558 www.relibrary.com/index.html
Real Estate Library

Contains essential resources for buyers, sellers, home owners and real estate professionals.

19559 www.rfpi.com/wrai.htm
National Residential Appraisers Institute

Promotes professionalism in the evaluation of residential real estate and requires demonstration appraisals and testing for professional certification.

Associations

19560 **American Bakers Institute**
1350 I Street NW
Suite 1290
Washington, DC 20005-3305
202-789-0300
FAX: 202-898-1164
www.americanbakers.org
Paul C Abenante, President/CEO
Betty Johnson, President's Assistant
Association comprised of wholesale bakers.
300 Members

19561 **American Culinary Federation**
180 Center Place Way
Saint Augustine, FL 32095
904-824-4468
FAX: 904-825-4758 800-624-9458
acf@acfchefs.net www.acfchefs.org
Brent Frei, Director Marketing
Lisa Alessandro, PR Director
Michael Baskette, Executive Director
Member organization of professional chefs and cooks. Certifies chefs, accredits culinary programs and promotes culinary arts.
19000 Members Founded: 1929 19,000 names $150 per M.

19562 **American Culinary Federation: Chef & Child Foundation**
180 Center Place Way
Saint Augustine, FL 32095
904-824-4468
FAX: 904-825-4758 800-624-9458
acf@acfchefs.net www.acfchefs.org
Brent Frei, Director Marketing
Michael Baskette, Executive Director
Seeks to teach children proper nutrition and feed hungry children in the US.
20000 Members Founded: 1989

19563 **Chain Store Information Guide**
425 Park Avenue
New York, NY 10022
212-367-7450
www.ala.com
A national organization that serves the commercial and institutional food and lodging industry.
Founded: 1967

19564 **Cookware Manufacturers Association**
PO Box 531335
Birmingham, AL 35253-1335
205-823-3448
FAX: 205-823-3449
hrushing@usit.net www.cookware.org
Steve Fraser, President
Scott Meyer, VP
Represents manufacturers of cookware and bakeware in the US and Canada. Publishes consumer guide to cookware and engineering standards for industry.
21 Members Founded: 1920

19565 **Educational Foundation of the National Restaurant Association**
175 W Jackson Boulevard
Suite 1500
Chicago, IL 60604-2702
312-715-1010
800-765-2122
Daniel Gescheidle, Executive Director
Advances professional standards in the industry through education.
40 Members Founded: 1971

19566 **Foodservice Equipment Distributors Association**
223 W Jackson Boulevard
Chicago, IL 60606-6908
312-427-9605
FAX: 312-427-9607
Raymond W Herrick II, Executive Director
Dealers and distributors of foodservice equipment and supplies.
700 Members Founded: 1979

19567 **International Association of Culinary Professionals**
304 W Liberty Street
Suite 201
Louisville, KY 40202
502-587-7953
FAX: 502-589-3602 800-928-4227
iacp@hqtrs.com www.iacp.com
Kerry Edwards, Sr Member Services Representative
Trina Gribbins, Manager
A not for profit organization whose members represent virtually every profession in the culinary universe: teachers, cooking school owners, caterers, writers, chefs, media cooking personalities, editors, publishers, food stylists, food photographers, restauranteurs, leaders of major food corporations and vintners. Literally a who's who of the food world. Founded in 1978.

19568 **International Food Service Executives Association Headquarters**
2909 Surfwood Drive
Las Vegas, NV 89128-1282
702-838-8821
FAX: 702-838-8853
HQ@ifsea.com www.ifsea.com
Grant Thompson, Chairman of the Board
Edward Manley, President/COO
Provides education and community service to the foodservice industry.
3,000 Members Founded: 1901

19569 **James Beard Foundation**
167 W 12th Street
New York, NY 10011
212-675-4984
FAX: 212-645-1438 800-362-3273
info@jamesbeard.org
www.jamesbeard.org
Len Pickell, President
Caroline Stuart, VP
Anne Byrd, Treasurer
Arthur Abelman, Secretary
Matt Yust, Manager
Nonprofit organization dedicated to preserving the country's culinary heritage and fostering the appreciation and development of gastronomy by recognizing and promoting excellence in all aspects of the culinary arts.

19570 **Mobile Industrial Caterers' Association**
7300 Artesia Boulevard
Buena Park, CA 90621-1804
714-632-6800
FAX: 714-632-5405
Kelly Ramirez, Executive Director
Aids with problems common within the industry through exchange of ideas, advice on legal problems, safety standards and licensing regulations.
185 Members Founded: 1964

19571 **National Bar & Restaurant Management Association**
307 Jackson Avenue W
Oxford, MS 38655
662-236-5510
FAX: 662-236-5541 800-247-3881
jrobinson@oxpub.com
www.nightclub.com

19572 **National Council of Chain Restaurants: NCC**
325 7th Street NW
Suite 1100
Washington, DC 20004
202-626-8183
FAX: 202-626-8185 www.nccr.net
Terrie Dort, President
Scott Vinson, Senior Director
Division of the National Retail Federation, this organization is comprised of nearly 40 of the largest chain restaurant companies in the country. Since the 1960's NCCR has harnessed the power of the industry to advance sound public policy that represents the best interests of the industry.
Founded: 1965

19573 **National Restaurant Association**
1200 17th Street NW
Washington, DC 20036-3006
202-331-5900
FAX: 202-331-2429 800-424-5156
info@dineout.org www.restaurant.org
Steven C Anderson, President/CEO
Supports food service industry with programs in education, promotion and government relations.
43000 Members Founded: 1919

Newsletters

19574 **American Culinary Federation Newsletter**
180 Center Place Way
Saint Augustine, FL 32095
904-824-4468
FAX: 904-825-4758 800-624-9458
bfrei@acfchefs.net
http://www.acfchefs.org
Brent T Frei, Director Marketing
Edward G Leonard, President
Brent T. Frei, Marketing Manager
Kay Orde, Editor
Michael Baskette, Executive Director
The official membership newsletter of the American Culinary Federation.
Monthly Founded: 1929
Circulation: 21000
Printed in 2 colors on matte stock

19575 **CHRIE Communique**
Int'l Council on Hotel, Restaurant Institute Edu.
2810 North Parham Road
suite 230
Richmond, VA 23294-3006
804-747-4971
FAX: 804-346-5009
publications@chrie.org
http://www.chrie.org
Dale Gaddy, Publisher
Mike Zema, President
Kathy McCarty, Chief Executive Officer

Monthly newsletter offering information on industry, significant hospitality and tourism education job listings. *$65.00*
Monthly Founded: 1946
Circulation: 1800

19576 Cameron's Foodservice Marketing Reporter
Cameron's Publications
5423 Sheridan Drive
PO Box 676
Williamsville, NY 14231
519-586-8785
FAX: 519-586-8816
products@cameronpub.com
http://www.cameronpub.com
Nina T Cameron, Editor
Bob McClelland, Publisher
Peggy Kelly, Circulation Manager
Successful promotion and advertising case histories for the restaurant and hotel industry. *$197.00*
Fortnightly Founded: 1970 100.00 names

19577 Center of the Plate
American Culinary Federation
180 Center Place Way
Saint Augustine, FL 32095
904-824-4468
FAX: 904-825-4758 800-624-9458
acf@acfchefs.net
http://www.acfchefs.org
Brent Frei, Director Marketing
Edward Leonard, President
Official membership newsletter of the American Culinary Federation. *$50.00*
Monthly Founded: 1929
Circulation: 25000+

19578 Wine on Line Food and Wine Review
Enterprise Publishing
138 N 16th Street
Blair, NE 68008
402-426-2121
FAX: 402-426-2227
news@enterprisepub.com
http://www.enterprisepub.com
Mark Rhoades, Publisher
Dough Barber, Editor
Lynette Hansen, Marketing
Bill Smutko, Circulation Manager
Reviews, feature articles and information on all areas of food and wine, including restaurants, hotels, trains and airlines. Accepts advertising. *$36.00*
10 pages Founded: 1800
Circulation: 13150

Magazines & Journals

19579 Cheers
257 Park Avenue S
3rd Floor, Suite 303
New York, NY 10010
212-967-1551
FAX: 646-654-2099
John Eastman, Owner
Every issue is designed to help on-premise operators enhance the profitability of their beverage operations.

19580 Chef
Talcott Communications Corporation
20 N Wacker Drive
#1865
Chicago, IL 60606-2905
312-726-2410
FAX: 312-849-2174
chefmag@aol.com
http://www.talcott.com
Daniel von Rabenau, Publisher
Rob Benes, Senior Editor
Morgan Holzman, Contributing Editor
David Pizzimenti, Circulation Manager
Information on food production and presentation, includes chef profiles, trend studies, marketing information and restaurant profiles. *$32.00*
Monthly Founded: 1956
Circulation: 38769
Printed in 4 colors on glossy stock

19581 Coffee & Cuisine
Coffee Talk
1218 3rd Avenue
#1315
Seattle, WA 98101-3021
206-521-7247
FAX: 206-623-0446
http://www.coffeecuisine.com
Kerri Goodman, Publisher
Covers new products, personnel moves, industry news, how to articles, education, and techniques to increase sales growth for the coffee, cold beverage and foodservice industry. *$36.00*
Monthly
Circulation: 30000

19582 Cooking for Profit
CP Publishing
PO Box 267
Fond du Lac, WI 54936-267
920-923-3700
FAX: 920-923-6805
comments@cookingforprofit.com
http://www.cookingforprofit.com
Colleen Phalen, Editor-in-Chief
Paid subscription trade magazine targeted to foodservice owners, managers and chefs. Each month features current trends in food preparation with step-by-step recipes and photographs; effective management techniques; and the latest in foodservice equipment — all written by industry experts. Also features in-depth profiles of a successful foodservice operation. *$26.00*
28 pages Monthly Founded: 1932
Printed in 4 colors on glossy stock

19583 Cornell Hotel & Restaurant Administration Quarterly
Elsevier Science Publishing Company
537 Statler Hall
Ithaca, NY 14853-6902
607-255-9780
FAX: 607-254-2922
hosp_research@cornell.edu
http://www.hotelschool.cornell.edu
Dr. Michael Sturman, Editor
Glenn Withiam, Executive Editor
Nicole Roach, Marketing
A journal devoted to the development and exchange of management ideas for the hospitality industry. *$113.00*
Quarterly Founded: 1963
Circulation: 4500

19584 Culinary Trends
Culinary Trends Publications
6285 E Spring Street
#107
Long Beach, CA 90808-4000
310-496-2558
FAX: 310-421-8993
http://www.culinarytrends.com
Fred Mensigna, Publisher
Linda Mensinga, Editor
Information for food and beverage managers along with managers of hotels and restaurants. *$21.60*
Quarterly
Circulation: 10000

19585 El Restaurante Mexicano
Maiden Name Press
PO Box 2249
Oak Park, IL 60303
708-483-3200
FAX: 708-445-9477 800-407-5845
kfurore@restmex.com
http://www.restmex.com
Brenda Russell, Publisher
Kathleen Furore, Editor
A bilingual magazine featuring industry specific food news, features restaurant profiles and new product information for personnel of restaurants serving mexican/southwestern menu items nationwide. *$18.00*
Founded: 1997
Circulation: 27000

19586 FEDA News & Views
Foodservice Equipment Distributors Association
223 W Jackson Boulevard
#620
Chicago, IL 60606-6911
312-427-9605
FAX: 312-427-9607
feda@feda.com http://www.feda.com
Stacy Ward, Managing Editor
Ray Herrick, Executive VP
Adela Ramos, Advertising Manager
Bruce Gulbas, President
Focus is on sales, technology, new products and other areas of benefit to dealers, as well as industry trends and news. *$150.00*
Founded: 1933
Circulation: 1200

19587 Food & Beverage News
Food & Beverage News
1886 W Bay Drive
#E6
Largo, FL 33770-3017
727-585-7745
FAX: 727-585-7245 www.fbnews.com
Dennis J Regan, Publisher
News on the latest liquor law, new products, and government legislation. *$28.00*
Monthly
Circulation: 16,880

19588 Food Arts Magazine
M Shanken Communications
387 Park Avenue S
8th Floor
New York, NY 10016
212-684-4224
FAX: 212-684-5424
http://www.winespectator.com
Marvin Shanken, Editor
A magazine devoted to the restaurant industry. *$40.00*
Monthly Founded: 1988

19589 Foodservice Equipment & Supplies Specialist
Reed Business Information
1350 E Touhy Avenue
Des Plaines, IL 60018-3358
630-320-7000
FAX: 630-288-8686
www.reedbusiness.com

Mitchell Schechter, Editor-in-Chief
Niles Crum, Publisher

Magazine for professionals who specify, sell and distribute foodservice equipment, supplies and furnishings. *$69.95*

64+ pages Monthly Founded: 1947
Circulation: 27M
Printed in 4 colors on glossy stock : web site

19590 Foodservice Equipment Reports
Robin Ashton
2000 Clearwater Drive
Oak Brook, IL 60523-3358
630-288-8000
FAX: 630-288-8265 800-446-6551
webmaster@reedbusiness.com
http://www.reedbusiness.com

Josph Carbonara, Editor-in-Chief
Maureen Slocum, Publisher
Keithy Mcnamara, Marketing
katy Tucker, Circulation Manager
Jeff Greisph, CEO

Geared toward manufacturers of foodservice equipment and their agencies. *$106.90*

Monthly Founded: 1947
Circulation: 22719

19591 Fresh Cup Magazine
Fresh Cup Publishing Company
537 SE Ash Street Suite 300
PO Box 14827
Portland, OR 97293-827
503-236-2587
FAX: 503-236-3165 800-868-5866
jan@freshcup.com
http://www.freshcup.com

Julie Beals, Editor
Nicole Maas, Sales/Marketing Associate
Bill Berninger, Circulation Director
Ward Barbee, Publisher
Jan Gibson, Owner *$57.00*

68 pages Monthly Founded: 1992
Circulation: 14000
Printed in 4 colors on glossy stock : Website

19592 Gourmet News
United Publications
106 Lafayette Street
PO Box 1056
Yarmouth, ME 04096-1600
207-846-0600
FAX: 207-846-0657
info@gourmetnews.com
http://www.gourmetnews.com

Anna Wolfe, Editor
Rick Rector, Publisher
Mario Alves, Managing Editor
Brenda Boothby, Circulation Director
Joline V Gilman, Production Director

The business newspaper for the gourmet industry.

40 pages Monthly Founded: 1991
Circulation: 23381 223,000 names $100 per M.
Printed in 4 colors on glossy stock

19593 Journal of Restaurant & Foodservice Market ing
Haworth Press
10 Alice Street
Binghamton, NY 13904-1580
607-722-5857
FAX: 800-895-0582 800-429-6784
getinfo@hawothpress.com
http://www.haworthpress.com

David A Cranage, Editor
Bill Cohen, CEO/President
Sandra Jones Sickels, VP Marketing
Margaret Tatich, Sales & Publicity Manager

Information on foodservice operation practioners, academic scholars, and policy makers, also includes information on industry and research with summaries. *$65.00*

Quarterly Founded: 1978

19594 Midsouthwest Restaurant
3800 North Portland Avenue
Oklahoma City, OK 73112-2982
405-942-8181
FAX: 405-942-0541 800-375-8181

Jim Hopper, President/CEO
Shannon Moad, Editor
Debra Bailey, Deputy Director

Quarterly Founded: 1933
Circulation: 2500

19595 Nation's Restaurant News
Lebhar-Friedman Publications
425 Park Avenue
New York, NY 10022-3506
212-756-5000
FAX: 212-756-5215
info@lf.com http://www.lf.com

Alan Gould, Publisher
Michael Cardillo, VP Sales
Leslie Wolowitz, Advertising

Serves commercial and onsite food service and lodging establishments including restaurants, schools, universities, hospitals, nursing homes and other health and welfare facilities, hotels and motels with food service, government installations, clubs and other related firms. *$ 44.95*

Weekly Founded: 1925
Circulation: 85999
Mailing list available for rent 100,000 names $100 per M.
Printed in 4 colors on matte stock

19596 National Culinary Review
American Culinary Federation
180 Center Place Way
St Augustine, FL 32095
904-824-4468
FAX: 904-825-4758 800-624-9458
bfrei@acfchefs.net
http://www.acfchefs.org

Brent Frei, Director Marketing
Edward G Leonard, President
Michael Baskette, Executive Director

Accepts advertising. *$50.00*

Monthly Founded: 1929

19597 National Dipper
US Exposition Corporation
1841 Hicks Road
#C
Rolling Meadows, IL 60008-1215
847-202-4770
FAX: 847-202-4791
lynda@nationaldipper.com
http://www.nationaldipper.com

Lynda Utterback, Publisher

Information for retail ice cream and frozen yogurt owners and operators, includes changes and developments in the business. *$55.00*

Circulation: 17000
Printed in 4 colors on glossy stock

19598 Restaurant Digest
Panagos Publishing
3930 Knowles Avenue
#305
Kensington, MD 20895-2428
301-929-6200
FAX: 301-929-6550
http://www.foodservicedepot.com

Bruce Panagos, Publisher

Developments and news of interest to owners, managers, and operators of dining and entertainment establishments in the region. *$ 24.00*

Monthly
Circulation: 25000

19599 Restaurant Hospitality
Donohue/Meehan Publishing
1300 E. 9th Street
Cleveland, Oh 44114
216-696-7000
FAX: 216-696-1752
rheditor@penton.com
http://www.restaurant-hospitality.com

Michael Sanson, Editor-in-Chief
Jess Grossberg, Publisher
Gail Bellamy, Managing Editor
Sue Apple, Production Manager
Jeff Donohue CPA, Owner

Monthly Founded: 1892
Circulation: 117,721

19600 Restaurant Marketing
Oxford Publishing
307 W Jackson Avenue
Oxford, MS 38655
662-236-5510
FAX: 662-281-0104 800-247-3881
Bi-Monthly

19601 Restaurant Wine
Wine Profits
PO Box 222
Napa, CA 94559-222
707-224-4777
FAX: 707-224-6740
restwine@tastetour.com
http://www.restaurantwine.com

Ronn Wiegand, Publisher

Information on the marketing of wine in restaurants, hotels and clubs, wine and food pairing ideas and review of wines. *$99.00*

Monthly
Circulation: 3000
Printed in 2 colors on matte stock

19602 Restaurants & Institutions
Reed Business Information
2000 Clearwater Drive
Oak Brook, IL 60523
630-740-0825
FAX: 630-288-8215
jamie.popp@reedbusiness.com
http://www.rimag.com

Patricia B Dailey, Editor-in-Chief
Scott Hume, Managing Editor
Jeff Greisch, Publisher

Commercial and noncommercial foodservice establishments including restaurant, hotels, motels, fast-food chains,coffee shops, food stores with foodservice

Monthly Founded: 1937
Circulation: 155512
Printed in 4 colors on glossy stock

19603 Restaurants USA
National Restaurant Association
1200 17th Street NW
Washington, DC 20036-3006
202-331-5900
FAX: 202-997-3395 800-424-5156

Jennifer Batty, Editor
Sarah Hamaker, Managing Editor

A trade magazine offering information for restaurant owners and managers, including industry trends, operational pointers, management principles and association activities. *$125.00*

48 pages Monthly Founded: 1980
Circulation: 44000
Printed in 4 colors

19604 Restaurants, Resorts & Hotels
Publishing Group
PO Box 318
Trumbull, CT 06611-0318
860-279-0149
FAX: 203-254-7104

James Martone, Publisher

Information on new products, supplies, food and equipment for those executives and managers who have responsibility for the food. *$24.00*

Monthly
Circulation: 97,000

19605 Southeast Food Service News
5672 Peachtree Parkway
Suite E
Norcross, GA 30092
770-449-9800
FAX: 770-449-9802
http://www.sfsn.com

Elliott R Fischer, Marketing Director
John P Hayward, Account Executive
Ceil Jarrett, Production Manager
Mary Williams, Editor

Monthly Founded: 1977

19606 Southwest Food Service News
4011 W Plano Parkway
Suite 121
Plano, TX 75093-5620
972-431-1254
FAX: 770-457-3829
www.southwestfoodservice.com

19607 Total Food Service
282 Railroad Avenue
Greenwich, CT 06830-6308
203-661-9090
FAX: 203-661-9325

Fred Klashman, Owner

19608 Yankee Food Service
Griffin Publishing Company
201 Oak St
Suite A
Pembroke, MA 02359
781-294-4700
FAX: 781-829-0134 866-677-4700
lbassett@griffinpublishing.net
http://www.griffinpublishing.net

Kevin Griffin, President
Lynda Bassett, Editor
Henry Zacchini, Associate Publisher

Reports news and happenings of the food service industry in New England. *$47.00*

48 pages Monthly Founded: 1979
Circulation: 26110

Trade Shows

19609 American Culinary Federation Central Regional Conference
American Culinary Federation
10 San Bartola Drive
Saint Augustine, FL 32085
904-824-4468
FAX: 904-825-4758 800-624-9458
acf@acfchefs.net www.acfchefs.org

Brent Frei, Director Marketing
Michael Baskette, Executive Director

Culinary equipment, supplies and services. Seminars, workshops, cooking demos, more.

19610 American Culinary Federation National Convention
10 San Bartola Drive
Saint Augustine, FL 32086
904-824-4468
FAX: 904-825-4758 800-624-9458
acf@acfchefs.net www.acfchefs.org

Brent Frei, Director Marketing
Michael Baskette, Executive Director

200 booths of products and foodstuffs for the food service industry. Seminars, workshops, cooking demos, more.

19611 American Culinary Federation Northeast Regional Conference
American Culinary Federation
10 San Bartola Drive
Saint Augustine, FL 32086
904-824-4468
FAX: 904-825-4758 800-624-9458
acf@acfchefs.net www.acfchefs.org

Brent Frei, Director Marketing
Michael Baskette, Executive Director

Culinary equipment, supplies and services. Seminars, workshops, cooking demos, more.

19612 American Culinary Federation Southeast Regional Conference
American Culinary Federation
10 San Bartola Drive
Saint Augustine, FL 32086
904-824-4468
FAX: 904-825-4758 800-624-9458
acf@acfchefs.net www.acfchefs.org

Brent Frei, Director Marketing
Michael Baskette, Executive Director

Culinary equipment, supplies and services. Seminars, workshops, cooking demos, more.

19613 American Culinary Federation Western Regional Conference
American Culinary Federation
10 San Bartola Drive
Saint Augustine, FL 32086
904-824-4468
FAX: 904-825-4758 800-624-9458
acf@acfchefs.net www.acfchefs.org

Brent Frei, Director Marketing
Michael Baskette, Executive Director

Culinary equipment, supplies and services. Seminars, workshops, cooking demos, more.

19614 Annual Hotel, Motel and Restaurant Supply Show of the Southeast
Leisure Time Unlimited
708 Main Street
PO Box 332
Myrtle Beach, SC 29577
843-448-9483
FAX: 843-626-1513 800-261-5991
hmrss@sc.rr.com www.hmrsss.com

Brooke P Baker, Show Director

Trade show for the hospitality industry.

23000 Attendees January Founded: 1975

19615 Hospitality Food Service Expo Southeast and Atlanta International Wine
Reed Business Information
275 Washington Street
Boston, MA 02458
617-261-1166
FAX: 617-558-4327 www.cahners.com

Patrick Paleno, Show Manager
Barry Reed Jr, Manager

400 booths featuring educational seminars, culinary salon, and exhibits of products and services.

12M Attendees October

19616 National Restaurant Association: Restaurant, Hotel-Motel Show
1200 17th Street NW
Washington, DC 20036-3006
202-331-5900

Reed Hayes, Show Manager
Steven Anderson, President

1,800 booths for the food service industry exhibiting food and beverages.

105M Attendees May

19617 Oklahoma Restaurant Convention & Expo
Oklahoma Restaurant Association
3800 N Portland Avenue
Oklahoma City, OK 73112-2948
405-942-8181
FAX: 405-942-0541
lori@okrestaurants.com
www.okrestaurants.com

Debra Bailey, Operations Director

430 booths for restaurant owners and managers.

9M Attendees April Founded: 1938
Mailing list available for rent

19618 Year of Enchantment
Int'l Council on Hotel, Restaurant Institute Edu.
1200 17th Street NW
Washington, DC 20036-3006
202-467-6300

alliance@digex.net www.chrie.org

Susan Gould, Manager

Containing 70+ booths and 50+ exhibits.

750 Attendees August Founded: 1946

Directories & Databases

19619 Chain Restaurant Operators Directory
Chain Store Guide
3922 Coconut Palm Drive
Tampa, FL 33616
813-276-6700
FAX: 813-627-6882 800-972-9202
info@csgis.com www.csgis.com

Chris Leedy, Advertising Sales
Arthur Sciarrotta, Senior VP

Discover more than 5,600 listings and more than 26,000 unique personnel within the Restaurant Chain, Foodservice Management, and Hotel/Motel Operator markets in the U.S. and Canada. Each company must have at least $1 million in annual sales either system wide or industry and have two or more units/accounts. *$335.00*
Annual

19620 Culinary Collection Directory
International Association/Culinary Professionals
304 W Liberty Street
Suite 201
Louisville, KY 40202
502-587-7953
FAX: 502-589-3602 800-928-4227
iacp@hqtrs.com www.iacp.com

Kerry Edwards, Sr Member Services Representative
Trina Gribbins, Manager

Teachers, cooking school owners, caterers, writers, chefs, media cooking personalities, editors, publishers, food stylists, food photographers, restauranteurs, leaders of major food corporations and vintners. Literally a who's who of the food world.

19621 Food & Beverage Market Place
Grey House Publishing
185 Millerton Road
PO Box 860
Millerton, NY 12546
518-890-0526
FAX: 518-789-0545 800-562-2139
books@greyhouse.com
www.foodmp.com

Leslie Mackenzie, Publisher
Richard Gottlieb, Editor

This information packed three-volume set is the most powerful buying and marketing guide for the US food and beverage industry. Includes thousands of industry freight and transportation listings. *$595.00*
6500 pages Annual

19622 Getaways for Gourmets in the Northeast
Wood Pond Press
365 Ridgewood Road
W Hartford, CT 06107-3517
860-521-0389

Directory of services and supplies to the industry. *$14.95*
514 pages

19623 High Volume Independent Restaurants Database
Chain Store Guide
3922 Coconut Palm Drive
Tampa, FL 33616-3506
813-276-6700
FAX: 813-627-6882 800-778-9794
info@csgis.com www.csgis.com

Chris Leedy, Advertising Sales
Shami Choon, Manager

Covers this growing niche through its nearly 5,900 listings featuring casual dining, family restaurants and fine dining establishments. Plus, access to over 15,000 key personnel names puts you in contact with key decision makers. *$335.00*
1,000 pages Annual

19624 International Association of Culinary Professionals
304 W Liberty Street
Suite 201
Louisville, KY 40202
502-587-7953
FAX: 502-589-3602 800-928-4227
iacp@hqtrs.com www.iacp.com

Kerry Edwards, Sr Member Services Representative
Trina Gribbins, Manager

A not for profit organization whose members represent virtually every profession in the culinary universe: teachers, cooking school owners, caterers, writers, chefs, media cooking personalities, editors, publishers, food stylists, food photographers, restauranteurs, leaders of major food corporations and vintners. Literally a who's who of the food world. Founded in 1978.

19625 Restaurant Hospitality: Hospitality 500 Issue
Penton Media
1300 E 9th Street
Cleveland, OH 44114
216-696-7000
FAX: 216-696-1752
information@penton.com
www.penton.com

Michael P Keefe, Publisher

500 independent restaurants selected on basis of sales. *$25.00*
Annual, June
Circulation: 123,000

19626 Restaurants and Institutions: Annual 400 Issues
Reed Business Information
1350 E Touhy Avenue
Suite 200E
Des Plaines, IL 60018-3358
847-962-2200
FAX: 630-288-8686
www.reedbusiness.com

Roland Dietz, Chief Executive Officer
$25.00
Annual
Circulation: 16,000

19627 Zagat.Com Restaurant Guides
Zagat Survey
4 Columbus Circle
New York, NY 10019-1100
212-977-6000
FAX: 212-977-6488
customerservice@zagat.com
www.zagat.com

Tim Zagat, President

Zagat.com was launched in May of 1999 and contains the most trusted and authoritive dining information online for over 20,000 restaurants in twenty eight cities worldwide, with 17 more cities to be added shortly. Based in New York City, the Zagat survey was founded in 1979 by Tim and Nina Zagat.

Industry Web Sites

19628 www.acfchefs.org
American Culinary Federation

Member organization of professional chefs and cooks. Certifies chefs, accredits culinary programs and promotes culinary arts.

19629 www.chefcertification.com
American Culinary Federation

Offers the required courses for ACF certification online.

19630 www.chowbaby.com

This web site is search engine for restaurants.It makes finding the perfect eatery close to your home or travel destination. Online reservations, maps, menus and more. You can search by Internatinal Location, US Location, US Map, or Cuisine type.

19631 www.chrie.org
Int'l Council on Hotel, Restaurant Institute Edu.

To enhance professionalism at all levels of the hospitality and tourism industry through education and training.

19632 www.greyhouse.com
Grey House Publishing

Selected Grey House directories in the fields of business, health and education are available online. Users can search our online databases by several different search criteria, such as product categories, geographic area, sales volume and much, much more. Full Grey House catalog and online ordering also available.

19633 www.iacp.com
International Association of Culinary Professionals

A not for profit organization whose members represent virtually every profession in the culinary universe: teachers, cooking school owners, caterers, writers, chefs, media cooking personalities, editors, publishers, food stylists, food photographers, restauranteurs, leaders of major food corporations and vintners. Literally a who's who of the food world. Founded in 1978.

19634 www.ifsea.org
International Food Service Executives

Provides education and community service to the foodservice industry.

19635 www.restaurant.org
National Restaurant Association

Trends, government affairs, training, research, dining guides and links.

19636 www.therestaurantfinder.com

This search engine help to find restaurants by type or location.

Associations

19637 American Booksellers Association
200 White Plains Rd
Ste 675
Tarrytown, NY 10591-5805
914-591-2665
FAX: 914-591-2720 800-637-0037
info@bookweb.org www.bookweb.org

Avin Domnitz, CEO
Oren Teicher, COO

Trade organization pledge to protecting the well-being of book retailers and promoting the availability of books.
3,800 Members Founded: 1900

19638 American Collegiate Retailing Association
Loyola University/Department of Marketing
6363 Saint Charles Avenue
New Orleans, LA 70118-6195
504-865-2011
FAX: 504-865-3496

Dr. Michael Pearson, President

Organization of faculty from colleges with a background in retailing.
400 Members Founded: 1950

19639 Associated Surplus Dealers/Associated Merchandise Dealers
ASD/AMD Merchandise Group
2950 31st Street
Suite 100
Santa Monica, CA 90405-3037
310-396-6006
FAX: 310-399-2662 800-421-4511

Leading producer of trade shows and publications in the variety and general merchandise industry.
15000 Members Founded: 1961

19640 Association for Retail Technology
325 7th Street NW
Washington, DC 20004
202-626-8167
FAX: 202-737-2849
arts@nrf.com www.nrf.com

Subsidiary of the National Retail Federation, this is a retailer-driven membership organization dedicated to creating an international, barrier-free technology environment for retailers. ARTS was established to ensure that technology works to enhance a retailer's ability to develop store level business solutions and avoid situations that limit a retailer's ability to implement change while providing industry standards designed to provide greater value at lower costs.
175 Members Founded: 1993

19641 Association of Retail Marketing Services
10 Drs James Parker Boulevard
Suite 103
Red Bank, NJ 07701-1500
732-842-5070
FAX: 732-219-1938 866-231-6310
info@goarms.com www.goarms.com

Gerri Hopkins, Executive Director
Lisa McCauley, Administrative Director

Supports all those involved with the marketing of all aspects of the retail industry, manufacturing, distribution, representation.
100 Members Founded: 1957

19642 Black Retail Action Group
PO Box 1192
New York, NY 10185-1192
212-365-5300
FAX: 212-217-7096

Gloria Hartley, President
Jeffrey Block, Manager

500 Members Founded: 1976

19643 Bureau of Business Practice
1185 Avenue of the Americas
New York, NY 10036
212-597-0333
FAX: 800-901-9075 800-638-8437
alicia.pierce@aspenpubl.com
www.bbpnews.com

Alicia Pierce, Operations

Supports all those needing information on a specific business, or general business practice information.

19644 Christian Booksellers Association
PO Box 62000
Colorado Springs, CO 80962-2000
719-265-9895
FAX: 719-576-0795

Bill Anderson, President

Provides products and services to assist and support Christian retail stores.
3.4M Members Founded: 1950

19645 Educational Dealers and Suppliers Association
711 W 17th Street
Suite J5
Costa Mesa, CA 92627
949-645-9975

Supports all those involved with the dealing and supplying of retail educational products.

19646 Franchise Consultants International Association
5147 S Angela Road
Memphis, TN 38117-3454
901-368-3881
FAX: 901-368-1144
franmark@msn.com

William Richey, Executive Director

Seeks to coordinate effective and professional franchise consulting, serves as a clearinghouse and operates a library.
800 Members Founded: 1980

19647 Institute of Store Planners
25 N Broadway
Tarrytown, NY 10591
914-321-1806

adminisp@ispo.org www.ispo.org

Russell Sway, President
Kenneth Nisch, VP
Ronald Kline, Chairman
Richard Byrne, Manager

Provides a forum for debate and discussion by store design experts and retailers. Sponsors student design programs.
1300 Members Founded: 1961

19648 International Center for Companies of Food
3800 Moore Place
Alexandria, VA 22305-1219
703-549-4525

Provides management research on problems related to food distribution and serves as an international forum where food chain store executives can meet to exchange ideas and information.
500 Members

19649 International Council of Shopping Centers
665 5th Avenue
New York, NY 10022
646-283-3800
FAX: 212-486-0849

Michael Kercheval, Chief Executive Officer

Supports all those involved with any aspect of shopping centers.

19650 International Franchise Association

1501 K St NW
Ste 350
Washington, DC 20005-1412
202-628-8000
FAX: 202-628-0812 www.franchise.org

Matthew Shay, President
Debra Moss, VP Operations

Membership consists of companies franchising the distribution of goods or services.

19651 International Map Trade Association
2629 Manhattan Avenue
PMB 281
Hermosa Beach, CA 90254
310-376-7731
FAX: 310-376-7287
imta@maptrade.org
www.maptrade.org

Chris Knoebel, President
Sanford J Hill, Executive Director

Membership comprised of retail stores featuring maps, travel books, globes, and travel products, plus publishers and manufacturers producing these products. Publishes a monthly newsletter.
800 Members Founded: 1981

19652 Marine Retailers Association of America
PO Box 1127
Oak Park, IL 60304
708-763-9210
FAX: 708-763-9236
mraa@mraa.com www.mraa.com

Phil Keeter, President
Marge Eckenroad, Executive Administrator

Raising the standards of retailing within the industry. Promotes activities for the recreational boating industry and holds seminars to improve management.
2.5M Members Founded: 1971

19653 Museum Store Association
4100 E Mississippi Avenue
Suite 800
Denver, CO 80246-3055
303-504-9223
FAX: 303-504-9585
www.museumdistrict.com

Beverly Barsook, Executive Director
Stacey Woldt, Assitant Director Programs

2500 Members April, Annually Founded: 1955

19654 National Association General Merchandise Representatives
1037 Route 46 East
Suite C101
Clifton, NJ 07013
973-149-9211
FAX: 973-778-1030
frankp@performancesales.com
www.nagmr.org

Anthony Natoli, President
David Gosdin, VP

A professional association of consumer product brokers representing leading manufacturers to the drug, mass merchandise and food trade.

19655 National Association of Beverage Retailers
5101 River Road
Suite 108
Bethesda, MD 20816
301-656-1494
FAX: 301-656-7539
Supports all those involved with the retailing of beverages.

19656 National Association of Catalog Showroom
PO Box 736
Northport, NY 11768-0736
631-754-4364
FAX: 631-754-4364
Members are catalog showroom operators and catalog publishers & associate members are suppliers.
350 Members Founded: 1972

19657 National Association of Chain Drug Stores
413 N Lee Street
PO Box 1417-D49
Alexandria, VA 22313-1480
703-549-3001
FAX: 703-739-4869 www.nacds.org

Craig L Fuller, President/CEO
Mark Griffin, Chairman

Our chain pharmacy members operate one of the finest health care delivery infrastructures in the world. The NACDS membership base operates more than 31,000 retail community pharmacies. Additionally, NACDS membership includes nearly 1,400 suppliers of goods and services to chain community pharmacies.
105 Members Founded: 1933

19658 National Association of College Stores
528 E Lorain Street
Oberlin, OH 44074
440-757-7777
FAX: 440-775-4769 800-622-7498
webteam@nacs.com www.nacs.org

Roger L Delarco, Director
David K Holcomb, President
Ginny Dittmar, VP
Brian E Cartier, CEO
Len Jardine, Manager

Provides educational and support services and products to college stores. Promotes business methods and ethics. Conducts manager certification, educational services and research.
3.9M Members Founded: 1923

19659 National Association of Convenience Stores
1605 King Street
Alexandria, VA 22314-2726
703-684-3600
FAX: 703-836-4564
www.nacs.online.com

Carl Bayer, Co-Editor
Lindsay Hutter, Co-Editor
Kathy LeBeouf, Executive Director

Association supporting key industry trends and innovative practices of convenience store companies.
2.3M Members Founded: 1961

19660 National Association of Music Merchants
5790 Armada Drive
Carlsbad, CA 92008-4372
760-438-8001

Joe Lamond, President
Larry Linkin, Executive Director

Retailers of musical instruments.
3.6M Members

19661 National Association of Resale and Thrift
PO Box 80707
St Clair Shores, MI 48080
800-544-0751
FAX: 586-294-6776 800-544-0751
info@narts.org www.narts.org
A national trade association for owners and managers of resale thrift shops. Purpose is to provide educational networking to promote the industry.
950 Members Founded: 1984

19662 National Convenience Store Advisory Group
2063 Oak Street
Jacksonville, FL 32204
904-845-5989

jhowton@nag-net.com
www.nag-net.com

Joseph Howton, Executive Vice President

This association represents senior level management of retail companies organized to enhance buying power, merchandising programs and an exchange of ideas. Membership dues: Retail Average $300, Associations $350.
500 Members Founded: 1983

19663 National Grocers Association
1005 N Glebe Road
Suite 250
Arlington, VA 22201-5758
703-516-0700
FAX: 703-516-0115
info@NationalGrocers.org
www.nationalgrocers.org

Thomas Zachua, President/CEO

Works to advance understanding, trade, and cooperation in the food industry. Represents members interests before the government. Offers store planning, and engineering, training and advertising.
1.5M Members Founded: 1982

19664 National Ice Cream Retailers Association
1841 Hicks Road
Suite C
Rolling Meadows, IL 60008
847-934-0926
FAX: 847-202-4791
info@nicra.org www.nicyra.org

Lynda Utterback, Executive Director
Rick Davis, President
Rich Johnson, VP

Members are in retail frozen dessert businesses. Some offer food services either full of limited and some operate convenience stores. The common denominator is that all members offer frozen desserts for take home or on site consumption.
350 Members Founded: 1933

19665 National Pawnbroker Association
611 Dallas Drive, #109
PO Box 1040
Raonake, TX 76262
817-491-4554
FAX: 817-491-8770
info@nationalpawnbrokers.org
www.nationalpawnbrokers.org

Brian Smith, President
Bob Benedict, Manager

Nonprofits organization that supports all those involved with the retail pawnbrokers.

19666 National Research Bureau
320 Valley Street
Burlington, IA 52601
319-752-5415
FAX: 319-752-3421

Diane Darnall, President

Provides research and support for all those involved in the retailing industry.

19667 National Retail Federation
325 7th Street NW
Suite 1100
Washington, DC 20004-2808
202-783-7971
FAX: 202-737-2849 www.nrf.com

Tracy Mullin, President

Retail trade association with membership that comprises all retail formats and channels of distribution including department, specialty, discount, catalog, Internet and independent stores. NRF members represent an industry that encompasses more than 1.4 million US retail establishments which employ more than 23 million people — about one in five American workers — and registered 2002 sales of $3.6 trillion. NRF's international members operate stores in more than 50 nations.
55M Members Founded: 1990

19668 National Shoe Retailers Association
7150 Columbia Gateway Drive
Suite G
Columbia, MD 21046-1151
410-381-8282
FAX: 410-381-1167 800-673-8446
info@nsra.org www.nsra.org

Randy L Brown, Chairman
Phil Wright, Vice Chairman
Bill Boettge, President

Membership association for independent shoe ratailers. Provides busisness services such as credit-card processing and shipping at special low members only prices. Also provides educational and training programs, consulting and other services.
1400 Members Founded: 1912

19669 National Ski & Snowboard Retailers
1601 Feehanville Drive
Suite 300
Mount Prospect, IL 60056-6035
847-391-9825
FAX: 847-391-9827
info@nssra.com www.nssra.com
Thomas B Doyle, President
Brad Nelson, Chairman
Retail association providing ski shops with business-related services and representation.
200 Members Founded: 1987

19670 National Sporting Goods Association
1601 Feehanville Drive
Suite 300
Mount Prospect, IL 60056
847-296-6742
FAX: 847-391-9827
info@nsga.org www.nsga.org
Jim Faltinek, President/CEO
Sue Wenderski, VP
Membership/Administration
Rhonda Onuszko, Director Membership
Dan Kasen, Manager
Members consist of retailers, wholesalers, suppliers, sales agents and media. Sponsor of NSGA World Sports EXPO, held annually in Chicago, and the NSGA Management Conference. Has an annual budget of approximately $8 million.
2000+ Members Founded: 1929
Mailing list available for rent

19671 North American Equipment Dealers Association
1195 Smizer Mill Road
Fenton, MO 63026
636-349-5000
FAX: 636-349-5443
naeda@naeda.com www.naeda.com
Jim Meinhardt, President
Paul Kindinger, CEO
Supports all those involved with retail equipment.

19672 North American Retail Dealers Association
10 E 22nd Street
Suite 310
Lombard, IL 60148-6191
630-953-8950
FAX: 630-953-8957 800-621-0298
nardahdq@narda.com www.narda.com
Michael Corder, Chairman
Randy Whitehead, First Vice Chairman
Leon Barbachano, Second Vice Chairman
A national organization of association members, independent retailers selling and servicing major appliances, consumer electronics products, furniture and computers. Emphasis is placed on ideas that help readers become better, more profitable businesses. Articles are featured regularly on displays, salesmanship, financial analysis and service management.
1000 Members Founded: 1943

19673 Oriental Rug Importers Association of
100 Park Plaza Drive
Secaucus, NJ 07094
201-866-5054
FAX: 201-866-6169
oria@oria.org www.oria.org
Mikel Banilevi, President
Andrew Peykar, VP
Lucille Laufer, Executive Director
Membership is concentrated in the New York area.
Founded: 1958

19674 Point-of-Purchase Advertising Institute
66 N Van Brunt Street
Englewood, NJ 07631
201-568-2044
FAX: 973-894-0529
Supports all those involved with in-store promotional programs — and research on marketing and retail trends.

19675 Professional Audio-Video Retailers Association
10 E 22nd Street
Suite 310
Lombard, IL 60148-6191
630-268-1500
FAX: 630-953-8957 800-621-0298
Debra Smith, Executive Director
Supports owners and operators of independently owned, audio/video stores. Members includes manufacturers of high-end audio/video equipment.
204 Members Founded: 1979

19676 Professional Sales Association
2873 Daley Drive
Troy, MI 48083-1940
248-524-0606
An organization of manufacturers' representative firms which sell hardware, housewares, lawn and garden products and traffic appliances to the retail trade.
25 Members

19677 Retail Advertising & Marketing Association
325 7th Street NW
Suite 1100
Washington, DC 20004
202-626-8183
FAX: 202-661-3049 www.rama-nrf.org
Tom Holliday, President/CEO
Kelly Lamb, SVP
National association devoted exclusively to the needs of retail advertising and marketing professionals. Sponsors the annual Retail Advertising Conference.
2M Members Founded: 1952

19678 Retail Industry Leaders Association
1700 N Moore Street
Suite 2250
Arlington, VA 22209-1998
703-841-2300
FAX: 703-841-1184
www.retail-leaders.org
Sandy Kennedy, President
Rhett Asher, VP Retail Operations
Jennifer Adams, Marketing Coordinator
Hina Ansari, Database Manager
Retail Industry Leaders Association is a trade association of the lasgest and fastest growing companies in the retail industry, its members include over 400 retailers, product manufacturers, and service suppliers.
400+ Members Founded: 1976

19679 Retail Packaging Manufacturers Association
PO Box 17656
Covington, KY 41017-0656
859-341-9624
FAX: 859-341-9624
Vicki Miller, Executive Director
Founded: 1990

19680 Retail Systems Alert Group
377 Elliot Street Po Box 332
Newton Upper Falls, MA 02464
617-527-4626
FAX: 617-527-8102
info@retailsystems.com
www.retailsystems.com
Brian Kilcourse, President
Tom Friedman, Chairman
Retail Systems Alert Group has helped companies reach a highly qualified audience of Extened Retail Industry professionals through advertising, sponsorship, research, and exhibiting opportunities.

19681 Retail Tobacco Dealers of America
4 Bradley Park Ct
Ste 2H
Columbus, GA 31904-3637
706-494-1143
FAX: 706-494-1893
info@rtda.org www.rtda.org
Ira Fader Jr, Executive Director
Trade association of high quality tobacconists.
2,350 Members Founded: 1933

19682 Scuba Retailers Association
4 Florence Street
Somerville, MA 02145
617-623-7722
James Estabrook, Executive Director
Members are stores selling scuba and association underwater equipment.
500 Members Founded: 1989

19683 Small Business Association
2049 Birchcrest Dr
Charlotte, NC 28205-4913
704-536-3214
Jerry Stokes, Manager
Working with and providing web sites for the very small business.
120 Members Founded: 2000

19684 Vacuum Dealers Trade Association
2724 2nd Avenue
Des Moines, IA 50313
515-282-9101
FAX: 515-282-4483
mail@vdta.com www.vdta.com
Judy Patterson, Executive Director
Seeks to increase the independent vacuum cleaner and sewing machine dealer market share.
20,00 Members Founded: 1981

19685 Wine and Spirits Guild of America
1766 Dupont Avenue S
Minneapolis, MN 55403-3065
Promotes the exchange of information on merchandising, marketing and buying of wines and spirits.
40 Members Founded: 1948

19686 World Floor Covering Association
2211 E Howell Avenue
Anaheim, CA 92806-6009
714-978-6440

Christopher Davis, Chief Executive Officer
Offers an overview of the retail trade.

Newsletters

19687 American Collegiate Retailing Association Newsletter
Loyola University/Department of Marketing
6363 Saint Charles Avenue
New Orleans, LA 70118-6195
504-865-2011
FAX: 225-644-0700
jeiseman@loyno.edu
http://www.loyno.edu
Michael Pearson, Publisher
Kevin Wildes, CEO/President
Cynthia Tucker, Editor
Mary Degnan, Marketing Manager
Janice Long, Circulation Manager
Educational retailing news and information.
Quarterly Founded: 1923

19688 Campus Marketplace
National Association of College Stores
500 E Lorain Street
Oberlin, OH 44074-1294
440-775-7777
FAX: 440-775-4769 800-622-7498
info@nacs.org http://www.nacs.org
Cynthia D'Angelo, Publisher
Carrie Tompkins, Editor
Weekly newsletter covering college store industry: sales, trends, news, personnel and address changes for stores as well as vendors.
Monthly Founded: 1982
Circulation: 4000
Computerized version available

19689 For the President's Eyes Only
Bureau of Business Practice
1185 Avenue of the Americas
New York, NY 10036
212-597-0333
FAX: 800-901-9075 800-638-8437
alicia.pierce@aspenpubl.com
www.bbpnews.com
Alicia Pierce, Operations
Provides the latest information on areas of vital interest to the head of the company.
12 pages 2 per year

19690 Insider
Trade Dimensions
45 Danbury Road
Wilton, CT 06897-4445
203-563-3000
FAX: 203-563-3131
infog@tradedimensions.com
http://www.tradedimensions.com
Brain Thomas, Editor
Kristina Castle, Circulation Coordina
Shopping center weekly newsletter that profiles the latest retailer expansion plans, giving - in addition to the numbers of stores operated and planned, the areas targeted, and the type of locations sought - a thumbnail sketch of what makes the concept unique, and what the company specifically looks for in a site. *$299.00*
Weekly Founded: 1970

19691 International Map Trade Association
2629 Manhattan Avenue
PMB 281
Hermosa Beach, CA 90254-2447
310-376-7731
FAX: 310-376-7287
imta@maptrade.org
http://www.maptrade.org
Sandy Hill, Executive Director
Linda Hill, Editor
Membership comprised of retail stores featuring maps, travel books, globes, and travel products, plus publishers and manufacturers producing these products. Publishes a monthly newsletter *$60.00*
20 pages Monthly Founded: 1981
Printed in on matte stock

19692 Mouser Report
CAMCO
124 E Carolina Avenue
Crewe, VA 23930-1802
434-645-1993
FAX: 434-645-8232 800-448-8595
Charles Mouser, Publisher
Brend DeLuca, Circulation Director
Newsletter covers the latest trends in retail and advertising. *$96.00*
16 pages Monthly

19693 NRF-BTM Retail Executive Opinion Survey
National Retail Federation
325 7th Street NW
Suite 1100
Washinton, DC 20004
202-783-7971
FAX: 202-737-2849 www.nrf.com
Scott Krugman, Publisher
Tracy Mullin, President
Gathers the opinions of the industry's top executives on trends in merchandising, hiring, sales expectations, customer traffic and special seasonal related developments.

Monthly

19694 NRF/BIGresearch Consumer Intentions and Ac tions Survey
National Retail Federation
325 7th Street NW
Suite 1100
Washington, DC 20004
202-783-7971
FAX: 202-737-2849 1 8-0 6-3 46
Tracy Mullin, President/CEO
Scott Krugman, Publisher
Mader Richard, Executive Director
Michael Gatti, VP/Marketing
Index on consumer shopping behavior. The survey also gauges consumer spending during holidays.
Weekly

19695 NSSRA Newsletter
National Ski and Snowboard Retailers Association
1699 Wall Street
Mount Prospect, IL 60056-6213
847-228-8277
FAX: 847-439-0111
nsga1699@aol.com
Thomas Doyle, President
Offers information to retailers of skiing products and equipment.
Quarterly

19696 Newsletter
National Research Bureau
320 Valley Street
Burlington, IA 52601-0001
319-752-5415
FAX: 319-752-3421
Diane Darnall, Publisher
A newsletter is created for a company by combining a customized masthead with a four page, monthly issue of helpful information on a business field selected by the company.
4 pages Daily
Printed in 3 colors

19697 Retail CEO Insider
National Retail Federation
325 7th Street NW
Suite 1100
Washington, DC 20004
202-783-7971
FAX: 202-737-2849 www.nrf.com
Craig Shearman, Publisher
Two-page private news briefing for CEOs, chairpersons and presidents of National Retail Federation member companies. Provides concise, bullet-point coverage of issues facing the industry in the style of the Kiplinger Washington Letter, with a heavy emphasis on government affairs and public policy. Distributed to approximately 650 C-level executives.
Monthly

19698 Retail Sales Outlook
National Retail Federation
325 7th Street NW
Suite 1100
Washington, DC 20004
202-783-7971
FAX: 202-737-2849 www.nrf.com
Scott Krugman, Publisher
Economic analysis of the retail industry.
Quarterly

19699 Shopping Center Management Insider
Brownstone Publishers
149 5th Avenue
16th Floor
New York, NY 10010-6801
212-738-8200
FAX: 212-473-8786 1 8-0 5-9 36
custserv@brownstone.com
http://www.vendomegrp.com
Steven Gordon Esq, Editor
Tested management techniques, legal insights and how-to guidelines for running a shopping center or mall. Includes model notices to tenants, letters, agreements, rules, etc. *$297.00*
Monthly Founded: 1985
Printed in 2 colors on matte stock

19700 T-Shirt Business Info Mapping Newsletter
Prosperity & Profits Unlimited
PO Box 416
Denver, CO 80201-0416
303-575-5676

A Doyle, Editor
How-to T-shirt business and information.
$8.00
8 pages Annual Founded: 1989
Circulation: 1,450 Audited
Printed in 1 color on matte stock

Magazines & Journals

19701 Accessory Merchandising
Vance Publishing
400 Knightsbridge Parkway
Lincolnshire, IL 60069
847-634-2600
FAX: 847-634-4379
mreckling@vancepublishing.com
http://www.vancepublishing.com
Laura Van Zeyl, Editorial Director
Chandra Palermo, Editor
Michael R. Reckling, Group Publisher
Steven J. Kulikowski, Marketing Manager
Douglas Riemer, Circulation Director
Monthly
Circulation: 21000

19702 Army/Navy Store & Outdoor Merchandiser
445 Broad Hollow Road
Suite 21
Melville, NY 11747
631-845-2700
FAX: 631-845-2797 ansom@idt.net
Military surplus, workwear, casual apparel, camping, hunting and sporting goods, and outdoor clothing industries. *$25.00*
Monthly
Circulation: 12M

19703 Baby Shop
Spindle Publishing Company
4136 Library Road
#200
Pittsburgh, PA 15234-1300
412-531-9742
FAX: 412-531-2004
spindle@worldnet.att.net
http://www.spindlepub.com
Naresh Dewan, Publisher
Megan Bush, Managin Editor
Resource for independent juvenile product retailers with information on marketing and merchandising, retailing, training sales staff, and customer services.

19704 Barnard's Retail Trend Report
Barnard Enterprises
17 Kenneth Road
Upper Montclair, NJ 07043-2541
973-655-8888

kbarnard@retailtrends.com
http://www.retailtrends.com
Kurt Barnard, Publisher/Editor
Jim Adamson, CEO
Forecasts market trends in the retailing industry and on consumer spending. *$179.00*
10 pages Founded: 1984
Circulation: 1200
Printed in 2 colors on newsprint stock

19705 Casual Living
Reed Business Information
2000 Clearwater Drive
Oak Brook, IL 60523
630-740-0825
FAX: 630-320-8686
www.casualliving.com

19706 Chain Merchandiser
Merchandising Publications Company
PO Box 95C
Baker City, OR 97814-0095

FAX: 541-523-2063
Ruth Sanders, Business Manager
Henry Von Morpurgo, Editor/Publisher
A national service and promotion program incorporating Specialty Foods and Beverages and Deli-Dairy World. Devoted to improved merchandising methods at every level of the marketing and distributing processes - from the field and factory and warehouse to retail sales persons - to provide better customer values, lower costs and greater profits.

19707 Chain Store Age
Lebhar-Friedman
425 Park Avenue
New York, NY 10022-3506
212-756-5000
FAX: 212-756-5176 800-216-7117
info@lf.com http://www.lf.com
Murray Forester, Editor
John Rapuzzi, Group Publisher
Antonia Peterson, Desk Editor
J Roger Friedman, President
Offers a full overview of chain stores, including management, operation, construction and modernization, store equipment, real estate and advertising.
Monthly Founded: 1925
Circulation: 35551

19708 College Store
Executive Business Media
PO Box 1500
Westbury, NY 11590-0812
516-334-3030
FAX: 516-334-3059
info@nacs.org www.nacs.org
Cynthia D'Angelo, President
Ron Stevens, Editor
Covers the college bookstore market retail industry. *$40.00*
40 pages Bi-Monthly
Circulation: 6,800

19709 College Store Executive
Executive Business Media
825 Old Country Road
PO Box 1500
Westbury, NY 11590-812
516-334-3030
FAX: 516-334-3059
ebm-mail@ebmpubs.com
http://www.ebmpubs.com
Ken Baglino, Editor
Nancy Wilderwith, Advertising Manager
A merchandising and news magazine edited for those responsible for buying and merchandising products for college retail stores. *$ 35.00*
36 pages Founded: 1970
Circulation: 8547
Printed in 4 colors on glossy stock

19710 College Store Magazine
National Association of College Stores
500 E Lorain Street
Oberlin, OH 44074
440-775-7777
FAX: 440-775-4769 800-622-7498
thecollegestore@nacs.org
http://www.nacs.org/
Cynthia Angelo, Publisher
Keith Galestock, Editor
Tara Ellis, Associate Editor
Covers the college store industry's long term issues and trends, focusing on retailing, technology and serving campus communities. *$66.00*
Mailing list available for rent

19711 Convenience Store News
BMT Commodity Corporation
530 5th Avenue
24th Floor
New York, NY 10036-5101
212-302-4200
FAX: 212-302-0007 bmt@bmtny.com
Maureen Azzalo, Editor
A trade magazine offering information on convenience store marketing. *$60.00*
Monthly

19712 DSN Retailing Today
Lebhar-Friedman
425 Park Avenue
New York, NY 10022
212-756-5088
FAX: 212-756-5125 800-216-7117
info@lf.com
http://www.dsnretailingtoday.com
Kevin Kennedy, Publisher
Tim Craig, Editor-in-Chief
Tony Lisanti, Editorial Director
Roger Friedman, Chief Executive Officer
Leading international newspaper serving the growing mass market.
Monthly Founded: 1925
Circulation: 34000

19713 Dealerscope
North American Publishing Company
401 N Broad Street
Philadelphia, PA 19108
215-238-5300
FAX: 215-238-5346
sdowney@napco.com
http://www.dealerscope.com
Grant Clauser, Editorial Director
David Dritsas, Editor-in-Chief
Eric Schwartz, President/Publishing
Rhoda Dixon, Circulation Manager
Suzanne DeFruscio, Advertising Promotion Manager
Dedicated to delivering peer-based knowledge and experience, Dealerscope is the ultimate vehicle for presenting product and service solutions to the consumer.
Founded: 1958

19714 Display & Design Ideas
Shore Varrone
6255 Barfield Road
#200
Atlanta, GA 30328-4332
404-848-0077
FAX: 404-252-4436
dhope@svi-atl.com www.svi-atl.com
Doug Hope, Publisher
Steve Kaufman, Editor
Lee Pritcher, Owner
Product news and design solutions for those in the retail chain indusrty. *$60.00*
Monthly
Circulation: 18,039

19715 Do-It-Yourself Retailing
5822 W 74th Street
Indianapolis, IN 46278-1787
317-297-1190
FAX: 317-328-4354
vecchie@sbcglobal.net
http://www.diyretailing.com
Bill Lee, Marketing Manager
Kevin Hohman, Publisher
John Hammond, Executive Director
Monthly
Circulation: 44333

19716 Drug Store News
Lebhar-Friedman
425 Park Avenue
New York, NY 10022
212-756-5088
FAX: 212-756-5250
tlisanti@lf.com
http://www.drugstorenews.com

Lebhar Friedman, Publisher
Tony Lisanti, Editor

Publication consists of merchandising trends and pharmacy developments. Provides extensive coverage of every major segment of chain drug retailing and combination stores. *$189.00*

Weekly Founded: 1925
Circulation: 40000

19717 Edplay
Fahy-Williams Publishing
PO Box 1080
Geneva, NY 14456-2137
315-789-0458
FAX: 315-789-4263 800-344-0559
kanderson@fwpi.com
http://www.fwpi.com

J Kevin Fahy, Publisher
Tina Manzer, Editorial Director
Jason Hagerman, Advertising Account Repre
Bradley G Gordner, Senior Editor
Tricia King, Office Manager

Serves toy manufacturers and dealers. Offers product reviews, industry profiles, and reader surveys. *$22.00*

Quarterly
Circulation: 7684

19718 Flea Markets Magazine
FleaMarkets.com
PO Box 18646
Charlotte, NC 28218
704-536-3214
FAX: 704-536-3214
jstokes@jerrystokes.com
http://www.fleamarkets.com

Jerry Stokes, General Manager
Peggy Stokes, Editor

A quarterly magazine published by FleaMarkets.com. *$15.00*

Quarterly Founded: 1989
Circulation: 3000

19719 Gacs Today
Naylor Publications
PO Box 855
Snellville, GA 30078-855
770-736-9723
FAX: 770-736-9725
jtudor@gacs.com
http://www.gacs.com

Jim Tudor, CEO

Quarterly Founded: 1973
Circulation: 2500

19720 Garden Center Merchandising & Management
Branch-Smith Publishing
120 St. Louis Ave
Fort Worth, TX 76104-1286
817-882-4120
FAX: 817-882-4121 800-433-5612
pkuhl@branchsmith.com
http://www.greenbeam.com

Patrice Kuhl, Publisher
Terri Smith, Director Circulation
Carol Miller, Editor
Mike Branch, President

Monthly Founded: 1915
Circulation: 15143

19721 Garden Center Products & Supplies
Branch-Smith Publishing
120 St. Louise Avenue
Fort Worth, TX 76104
817-882-4120
FAX: 817-882-4121 800-433-5612

Yale Youngblood, Editor
Patrice Kuhl, Publisher/Sales Director
Mike Branch, President

Monthly Founded: 1910

19722 Hearth & Home
Village West Publishing
PO Box 1288
Laconia, NH 03247-2008
603-528-4285
FAX: 603-524-0643 800-258-3772
mailbox@villagewest.com
http://www.homehearth.com

Richard Wright, Editor
Jackie Avignone, Sales Manager

Information for retailers and others selling hearth products, patio furnishing, barbecues, spas, garden accessories, and other outdoor products. *$11.95*

Founded: 1980
Circulation: 18000

19723 Kitchenware News
United Publications
PO Box 1056
Yarmouth, ME 04096-2056
207-846-0600
FAX: 207-846-0657
btaliaferro@kitchenwares.com
www.kitchenwares.com

Brooke Taliaferro, President
Jim McNeil, Publisher

News and information on the latest products and equipment for the retail kitchenware industry. *$45.00*

Monthly
Circulation: 12,117

19724 License — Idea Marketplace for the Licens ing Industry
Advanstar Communications
545 Boylston Street
Boston, MA 02116
617-514-4600
FAX: 617-267-6900 800-331-5706
lic@advanstar.com
http://www.licensemag.com

James Mammarella, Editor-in-Chief
Kerry C Gumas, CEO/President

License serves the $175 million licensed merchandise community. Over half of the readers are retailers with the balance split among licensors, licensees, agents, manufacturers and consultants to the industry. Articles cover all aspects of licensing, from entertainment and fashion to sports, brands and logos. Editorial tracks the ever shifting dynamics of the marketplace. *$79.00*

Monthly Founded: 1998
Printed in 4 colors

19725 MMR/Mass Market Retailers
Racher Press
220 5th Avenue
New York, NY 10001-7798
212-213-6000
FAX: 212-725-4594
info@racherpress.com
http://www.massmarketretailers.com

Susan Schinitsky, Publisher
David Pinto, Editor
John Dioguardi, Director Sales/Marketing
Kevin Burke, Group Advertising Director
Pam Vandernoth, Circulation Director

News, analysis, trends, and events for drug, discount, and supermarket chain executives. *$185.00*

Founded: 1984
Circulation: 21645

19726 Magazine Retailer
MetaMedia
124 W 24th Street
#3-D
New York, NY 1011-1920
212-989-6978
FAX: 212-255-7143
magretail@aol.com

David Orlow, Publisher
Djalal Mohammadi, President

Merchandising tips, new tiles, publication changes, consumer purchasing trends, industry news and media impact on sales. *$19.00*

Quarterly
Circulation: 10,326

19727 Mass Market Retailer
Racher Press
220 5th Avenue
New York, NY 10001-7708
212-213-6000
FAX: 212-725-3961
info@racherpress.com
http://www.massmarketretailers.com

Susan Schinitsky, Publisher
David Pinto, Editor
Susan Schinitsky, CEO/President
John Dioguardi, Marketing
Pam Vandernoth, Circulation Manager

News and information on the drug store chain industry. *$35.00*

30 pages

19728 Military Market
Gannet Company
6883 Commercial Drive
Springfield, VA 22159
703-750-7400
FAX: 703-750-8603
rhynema@atpco.com
http://www.atpco.com

Roger Hyneman, Editor
David Craig, Managing Editor

Provides trade information, trends, and news for military commisionary and post/base exchange managers. *$84.00*

Monthly Founded: 1940
Circulation: 12000

19729 Museum Store Magazine
Museum Store Association
4100 E Mississippi Avenue
#800
Denver, CO 80246-3055
303-504-9223
FAX: 303-504-9585
membership@museumdistrict.com
http://www.museumdistrict.com

Shannon McNamara, Publisher
Amy Nicholas, Editor
Beverly Barsook, Executive Director
$34.00

Quarterly Founded: 1955
Circulation: 3000
Printed in 4 colors on glossy stock

19730 Museums & More Specialty Shops Product News
Museums & More Specialty Product News

PO Box 128
Sparta, Mi 49345-2122
616-887-9008
FAX: 616-887-2666
http://www.museumsandmore.com

Julie McCallum, Editor
Jon Kaufman, Publisher

Product highlights and marketing strategies for the owners and oporators of gift shops in museums and other public attractions. $ 35.00

Quarterly
Circulation: 28014

19731 NACS SCAN
National Association of Convenience Stores
1600 Duke Street
Alexandria, VA 22314-2726
703-684-3600
FAX: 703-836-4564
nacs@nacsonline.com
http://www.nacsonline.com

Jeff Lenard, Editor

A bi-monthly magazine offering information on key industry trends and innovative practices of convenience store companies. *$840.00*

Monthly Founded: 1961
Circulation: 3000

19732 NAEDA Equipment Dealer
NAEDA
1195 Smizer Mill Road
Fenton, MO 63026
636-349-5000
FAX: 636-349-5443
webmaster@naeda.com
www.naeda.com

Mike Kraemer, Managing Editor
Larry Krueger, Advertising Manager
$40.00

Monthly Founded: 1900
Circulation: 9,500
Printed in 4 colors on glossy stock

19733 NARDA Independent Retailer
North American Retail Dealers Association
10 E 22nd Street
Suite 310
Lombard, IL 60148-6191
630-953-8950
FAX: 630-953-8957 800-621-0298
tdrake@narda.com
http://www.narda.com

Tom Drake, CEO/President
Gennifer Michalek, Editor/Publisher/Circulation Manage

Emphasis is placed on ideas that help readers become better, more profitable businesses. Articles are featured regularly on displays, salesmanship, financial analysis and service management. *$78.00*

36 pages Monthly Founded: 1943
Circulation: 2000
Mailing list available for rent 2,000 names
Printed in 4 colors on glossy stock

19734 New Age Retailer
Continuity Publishing
2183 Alpine Way
Bellingham, WA 98226-8045
360-676-0789
FAX: 360-676-0932 800-463-9243
info@newageretailer.com
http://www.newageretailer.com

Molly Trimble, CEO
Ray Hemachandra, Editor-in-Chief
Laurel Leigh, Editor
Stephanie R Hager, Circulation Manager
Ellen Koolen, Production Manager

Provides information on new products and business to business trade magazine that supports store owners by providing independent product reviews, retail advice and coverage of the new age and spirtual lviing industry. *$85.00*

192 pages Founded: 1987
Circulation: 10000
Mailing list available for rent 6,000 names $150 per M.

19735 POP Design
Hoyt Publishing
7400 Skokie Boulevard
Skokie, IL 60077
847-675-7400
FAX: 847-675-7494
info@instoremarketer.org
http://www.popdesign.com

Peter W Hoyt, President
Harold Fischer, Publisher
Anne Clark, Managing Editor
Patricia McGuinness, Director of Circulation
Erin Kuhn, Director of Marketing

Provides designers, builders and vendors of displays, signs and fixtures with current developments in materials, components, processes, systems and services used in production. Includes updates on products, industry literature, patents and legal matters affecting designers and manufacturers. *$59.00*

Circulation: 18000
Printed in 4 colors on glossy stock

19736 POPAI News
Point-of-Purchase Advertising Institute
66 N Van Brunt Street
Englewood, NJ 07631-2737
201-568-2044
FAX: 973-894-0529
info@popai.com
http://www.popai.com

Marya Lupo, Executive Editor
Brian Flaherty, Sales Representative
Richard Blatt, CEO/President
Stephen Morant, Manager Production Services
Sean Simmons, General Manager

Provides the point-of-purchase industry with coverage of marketing and retail trends, with an emphasis on in-store promotional programs. Editorial offers coverage of marketing programs, display case histories, preview of new promotional campaigns, sales volume and trends. Accepts advertising. *$40.00*

Monthly Founded: 1940

19737 Pollution Engineering
Reed Business Information
2000 Clearwater Drive
Oak Brook, IL 60523
630-740-0825
FAX: 630-320-8686
greenr@bnpmedia.com
http://www.pollutionengineering.com

Douglas B Hebbard, Publisher
Erin Purananda, Marketing Manager
Seth Fisher, Products Editor

Serves the field of pollution control in manufacturing industries, utilities, consulting engineers and constructors. Also serves government agencies including administration of federal, state and local environmental programs.

Monthly Founded: 1977

19738 Retail Cost of Doing Business
American Floorcovering Association
2211 E Howell Avenue
Anaheim, CA 92806-6009
714-572-8370

Offers an overview of the retail trade.

Annual

19739 Retail Observer
Retail Observer
1442 Sierra Creek Way
San Jose, CA 95132-3618
408-272-8974
FAX: 408-272-3344 800-393-0509
info@retailobserver.com
http://www.retailobserver.com/

Chuck Edmonds, Publisher
Lee Boucher, Editor

Edited for owners, managers and retail sales personnel of appliance stores, home entertainment stores and kitchen and bath dealers.

Monthly
Circulation: 11750

19740 Retail Systems Alert
Retail Systems Alert Group
PO Box 332
Newton Upper Falls, MA 02464-02
617-527-4626
FAX: 617-527-8102
editor@retailsystems.com
www.retailsystems.com

Thomas H Friedman, Publisher

Provides updated information on automation news and trends, including decision systems, information systems implementation, in-store merchandise management, and case studies of retailers. *$295.00*

8 pages Monthly Founded: 1988

19741 Retail Systems Reseller
Edgell Communications
4 Middlebury Boulevard
Suite 107
Randolph, NJ 07869-1111
973-252-0100
FAX: 973-252-9020
mkachmar@edgellmail.com
http://www.edgellcommunications.com

Michael Kachmar, Publisher
Joseph S King, Editor-in-Chief
Gabriele A Edgell, CEO
Dan Ligorner, Director of Marketing

Offers information to retailers, dealers, systems integraters, VARs, VADs, etc., on retail technology for small to mid-size retailers.

19742 RetailTech
770 Broadway
New York, NY 10003-9595
646-654-7565
FAX: 646-654-7568 www.retailtech.com

19743 STORES Magazine
National Retail Federation
325 7th Street NW
Suite 1100
Washington, DC 20004
202-783-7971
FAX: 202-737-2849
pennw@nrf.com http://www.nrf.com

Rick Gallagher, Publisher
Tim Henderson, Editor-in-Chief
Elena Caiola, Circulation Manager
Susan Reda, Executive Director
Autor Erik, Vice President

Magazine of the National Retail Federation. Provides timely information of importance to senior retail headquarters executives. Every issue reports on trends in retail technology, credit and payment systems, logistics and supply chain and other vital store operations. *$120.00*

Monthly
Circulation: 35000

19744 SalesCoach/For Successful Retail Selling
JonesReport
PO Box 80209
Indianapolis, IN 46280-0209

FAX: 317-848-6953 800-878-9024
ctrmktg@jonesreport.com
www.jonesreport.com/report

Phil Stillerman, President/Publisher
Linda Lipp, Editor
Marsha Davis, Circulation Director

Provides tips on selling, management, display and includes promotional events/dates that retail store owners, managers and employees can use to further selling skills and services.

Printed in 2 colors on matte stock

19745 Succe$$ful $ource$
Sutton Family Communications & Publishing Company
155 Sutton Lane
Fordsville, KY 42343
270-740-0870

jlsutton@apex.net
http://www.fleamarketeer.net

Theresa Sutton, Publisher

The #1 trade magazine for multi-billion dollar flea market industry. *$5.00*

Founded: 1977
Circulation: 100000

19746 Supermarket News
Fairchild Publications
750 3rd Ave
New York, NY 10017-2703
212-304-4274
FAX: 212-630-4201 800-204-4515
customerservice@fairchildpub.com
http://www.supermarketnews.com

Mary Berner, CEO/President
David Merrefield, Editorial Director
Dan Bagan, Publishing Director
David Orgel, Editor-in-Chief *$44.50*

40 pages Weekly Founded: 1892
Circulation: 36346

19747 Today's Grocers
Florida Grocer Publications
PO Box 430760
S Miami, FL 33246
305-661-0792
FAX: 305-661-6720 800-440-3067

Jack Nobles, Publisher
Dennis Kane, Editor

Provides the latest food industry news and trends to Florida, Georgia, Alabama, Louisiana, Mississippi and the Carolinas. *$29.00*

24 pages Monthly Founded: 1956
Circulation: 19,000
Printed in on newsprint stock

Trade Shows

19748 ASD/AMD Houston Variety Merchandise Show
ASD/AMD Merchandise Group
2950 31st Street
Suite 100
Santa Monica, CA 90405
310-396-6006
FAX: 310-399-2662 800-421-4511

Julie Ichiba, Show Director

Our newest variety and general merchandise trade show offers buyers in the southwestern US and Mexico terrific product sourcing opportunities for all types of popular consumer goods.

12000 Attendees

19749 ASD/AMD Las Vegas Trade Show
ASD/AMD Merchandise Group
2950 31st Street
Suite 100
Santa Monica, CA 90405
310-396-6006
FAX: 310-399-2662 800-421-4511

Julie Ichiba, Show Director

The summer edition of the largest variety merchandise event in the US attracts over 50,000 buyers to Las Vegas. Tens of thousands of unique products in hundreds of popular consumer product categories are on display at this even

50000 Attendees August 14-18

19750 ASD/AMD's Atlantic City Variety Merchandise Show
ASD/AMD Merchandise Group
2950 31st Street
Suite 100
Santa Monica, CA 90405
310-396-6006
FAX: 310-399-2662 800-421-4511

Julie Ichiba, Show Director

Held in Atlantic City, New Jersey, this event is a popular destination for east coast retailers to make deals and place orders for variety and general merchandise in hundreds of popular consumer categories before the summer selling season begins.

10000 Attendees May

19751 ASD/AMD's Fall Variety Merchandise Show
ASD/AMD Merchandise Group
2950 31st Street
Suite 100
Santa Monica, CA 90405
310-396-6006
FAX: 310-399-2662 800-421-4511

Julie Ichiba, Show Director

The fall edition of the general merchandise event on the east coast takes place in New York City. It's the last opportunity of the year for retailers to place orders for goods before the busy holiday buying season.

12000 Attendees September

19752 ASD/AMD's Las Vegas Merchandise Expo
ASD/AMD Merchandise Group
2950 31st Street
Suite 100
Santa Monica, CA 90405
310-396-6006
FAX: 310-399-2662 800-421-4511

Julie Ichiba, Show Director

Held in Las Vegas, Nevada, this event is strategically timed for western US retailers to stock their shelves with quality, value-priced variety and general merchandise in between our larger Las Vegas Trade Shows in March and Agust.

5,000 Attendees June 5-7

19753 ASD/AMD's New York Variety Merchandise Show
ASD/AMD Merchandise Group
2950 31st Street
Suite 100
Santa Monica, CA 90405
310-396-6006
FAX: 310-399-2662 800-421-4511

Julie Ichiba, Show Director

Held in New York City, this event is the first opportunity of the New Year for variety and general merchandise retailers to stock their shelves after the holidays with popular, value-priced consumer goods in hundreds of product categories.

12500 Attendees January

19754 ASD/AMD's Orlando Variety Merchandise Show
ASD/AMD Merchandise Group
2950 31st Street
Suite 100
Santa Monica, CA 90405
310-396-6006
FAX: 310-399-2662 800-421-4511

Julie Ichiba, Show Director

Held in Orlando, Florida, this event is a popular destination for southeastern US retailers to make deals and place orders for variety and general merchandise in hundreds of popular consumer categories.

5,500 Attendees April

19755 Accent on Design
George Little Management
10 Bank Street
Suite 1200
White Plains, NY 10606-1954
914-486-6070
FAX: 914-948-2867 800-272-7469
elizabeth_murphy@glmshows.com
www.nyigf.com

Elizabeth Murphy, Manager
George Little II, President

370 booths of the latest and most innovative gift lines such as decorative accessories and home furnishings.

50M Attendees August Founded: 1984

19756 American Beverage Licensees Annual Convention & Trade Show
National Association of Beverage Retailers
5101 River Road
Suite 108
Bethesda, MD 20816-1560
301-656-1494
FAX: 301-656-7539
nabr@nabronline.org
www.nabronline.org

Harry Wiles, Executive Director
Shawn Ross, Office Manager

Annual show of 75 manufacturers, suppliers and distributors of alcoholic beverages.

1,000 Attendees

19757 **Associated Surplus Dealers/Associated Merchandise Dealers Trade Show**
ASD/AMD Merchandise Group
2950 31st Street
Suite 100
Santa Monica, CA 90405
310-255-4633
FAX: 310-399-3662 800-421-4511
Sam Bundy, Group President
Gifts, souvenirs and assorted merchandise for professional buyers.
15000 Attendees Annual/March

19758 **Book Expo America**
Reed Exhibitions
383 Main Avenue
Norwalk, CT 06851
203-404-4800
800-840-5614
cmuller@reedexpo.com
www.bookexpoamerica.com
Courtney Muller, Event Manager
Cathy Glickstein, Registration
Sponsored by American Booksellers Association and Association of American Publishers. More than 2,000 exhibits, 500 authors, over 60 conference sessions as well as a special area for rights business, all the latest titles across genres, uncover hidden gems, network, and meet the industry contacts to put you instantly on top of what you need to know for your business and job.
May/June Founded: 2000

19759 **CMM International: FLEX Expo**
Bruno Blenheim
Fort Lee Executive Park
Fort Lee, FL 07024
FAX: 201-346-1602 800-829-3976
Nick Helyer, President
Exhibits by franchisers and sellers to the franchise industry. 125 booths.
5M Attendees June

19760 **Customer Relationship Management Course: C RMretail**
National Retail Federation
325 7th Street NW
Suite 1100
Washington, DC 20004
202-783-7971
FAX: 202-737-2849
exhibit@nrf.com www.nrf.com
Michaal Tuttle, Director Exhibits
Cindy Shin, Director Sales
CRMretail is a cross-industry conference, bringing together retail business leaders and the leading technology companies, solutions providers, consultants and academicians in the field of customer relationship management. Annual CRMretail research conducted by Gartner Dataquest is also released at this conference.
200 Attendees Late Spring Founded: 1993

19761 **Green Profit's Retail Experience**
Green Profit Magazine
335 N River Street
Batavia, IL 60510
630-208-9080
FAX: 630-208-9350 888-888-0013
info@ballpublishing.com
www.ballpublishing.com/conferences
Michelle Mazza, Show Manager
Educational event and tradeshow dedicated exclusively to garden center retailing. Covers topics from store layout and design to merchandising strategies and business management. 20 booths
300 Attendees September Founded: 2006

19762 **International Council of Shopping Centers Fall Convention Trade & Exposition**
International Council of Shopping Centers
665 5th Avenue
#Enue-11T
New York, NY 10022-5305
646-283-3800
FAX: 212-486-0849
Michael Kercheval, Chief Executive Officer

19763 **International Franchise Association Expo**
1501 K St NW
Ste 350
Washington, DC 20005-1412
202-628-8000
FAX: 202-628-0812
Matthew Shay, President
Patricia Langfeld, VP
75 booths.
1M Attendees February

19764 **Internet Retailer Conference & Exhibition**
Internet Retailer
300 S Wacker Drive
Suite 602
Chicago, IL 60606
FAX: 312-362-9532
www.internetretailer.com
Learn the strategies, practices and tools to lift your site into e-retailing's second decade of growth. Network with your peers in the only show serving e-retailers from all merchant channels.
Annual

19765 **Logistics**
Retail Industry Leaders Association
1700 N Moore Street
Suite 2250
Arlington, VA 22209
703-841-2300
FAX: 703-841-1184
snodland@imra.org www.imra.org
Britt Wood, VP
Sean Nodland, Manager
This event brings together retailers, consumer product companies, and suppliers of goods and service logistics side of business
400 Attendees February

19766 **Loss Prevention Conference & Exhibition**
National Retail Federation
325 7th Street NW
Suite 1100
Washington, DC 20004
202-783-7971
FAX: 202-737-2849
exhibit@nrf.com www.nrf.com
Michaal Tuttle, Director Exhibits
Cindy Shin, Director Sales
Major conference for Loss Prevention, Internal Audit and Risk Management professionals in the retail industry.
1500 Attendees June Founded: 1993

19767 **Loss Prevention, Auditing & Safety Conference**
Retail Industry Leaders Association
1700 N Moore Street
Suite 2250
Arlington, VA 22209
703-841-2300
FAX: 703-841-1184
rhett.asher@retail-leaders.org
www.retail-leaders.org
Rhett Asher
Annual information exchange.
325 Attendees April

19768 **Marketing Conference**
International Mass Retail Association
1700 N Moore Street
Suite 2250
Arlington, VA 22209
703-841-2300
FAX: 703-841-1184 www.imra.org
Peter Kim, Owner

19769 **NACS Show Annual Meeting and Exposition**
National Association of Convenience Stores
1600 Duke Street
Alexandria, VA 22314
703-684-3600
FAX: 703-836-4564
nacs@nacs.com www.nacsshow.com
Jane Berzan, VP Events/Mktg/Supplier Relations
Sherry Romello, Director Meetings and Conventions
24000 Attendees October

19770 **National Lawn & Garden Controlled Marketing Conference**
Controlled Marketing Conferences
PO Box 1771
Monument, CO 80132
719-488-0226
FAX: 719-488-8168 888-316-0226
info@nlgshow.com www.nlgshow.com / www.marketingconferences.com
Robert Mikulas, President
Chris Wolf, VP
This year CMC events will be linked to the National Lawn ans Garden Show - The Expo Division. Don't miss out on the industries most important lawn and garden headlines event.
3000 Attendees June

19771 **National Retail Federation Annual Conferen ce and Expo**
National Retail Federation
325 7th Street NW
Suite 1100
Washington, DC 20004-2808
202-783-7971
FAX: 202-783-0581
exhibit@nrf.com www.nrf.com
Michaal Tuttle, Director Exhibits
Cindy Shin, Director Sales
Tracy Mullin, President
600 booths exhibiting the latest in retail technology, new developments in credit validation, security and materials handling.
12M Attendees January

19772 Retail Advertising Conference: RAC
Retail Advertising & Marketing International
325 7th Street NW
Suite 1100
Washington, DC 20004
202-626-8183
FAX: 202-737-2849 www.rama-nrf.org
Mike Gatti, VP Marketing
Definitive event for retail advertising and marketing professionals each year featuring the RAC Awards gala dinner and Retail Hall of Fame induction annually.
1000 Attendees February

19773 Retail Promotion Show
Association of Retail Marketing Services
10 Drs James Parker Boulevard
Suite 103
Red Bank, NJ 07701-1500
732-842-5070
FAX: 732-219-1938 866-331-6310
info@goarms.com www.goarms.com
Gerri Hopkins, Executive Director
Annual show of 65 manufacturers, suppliers, distributors and representatives of dinnerware, glassware, housewares, books, videos, games, sweepstakes, dolls and plush toys suppliers used as retail promotions.
1200 Attendees March, Annual

19774 Shop.org Annual Summit
Shop.org
325 7th Street NW
Suite 1100
Washington, DC 20004
202-626-8183
FAX: 202-626-8191 www.shop.org
Provides a unique opportunity for Internet and multi-channel retail industry leaders to exchange ideas, perspectives, opportunities and challenges in an intimate and comfortable setting. The Summit features dialogues with distinguished keynote speakers, provocative panels and debates on timely issues, and important original research.
600 Attendees September

19775 Shop.org Members' Forum
Shop.org
325 7th Street NW
Suite 1100
Washington, DC 20004
202-626-8183
FAX: 202-626-8191 www.shop.org
Attendees see presentations for an online holiday recap and new multichannel retail research sessions as well as roundtable discussions and other networking events.
350 Attendees January

19776 Southern Convenience Store & Petroleum Show
PO Box 855
Snellville, GA 30078
770-736-9723
FAX: 770-736-9725
jtudor@aol.com www.gacs.com
Jim Tudor, President
Contains 250 exhibits.
3,000 Attendees August 2005, October 2006
Founded: 2003

19777 Store Fixturing Show
Shore Varrone
6255 Barfield Road NE
Suite 200
Atlanta, GA 30328-4332
404-848-0077
FAX: 770-252-4436 800-241-9034
Russ Eisenhardt, VP Trade Shows
Lee Pritcher, Owner
The largest annual store design event in the world. The event also includes The Visual Merchandising Show, the Retail Operations & Construction Expo, the POPAI Expo and the Exhibit Ideas Show. 800 exhibitors in total.
15M Attendees April

19778 Store Operations & Human Resources Conference
International Mass Retail Association
1700 N Moore Street
Suite 2250
Arlington, VA 22209
703-841-2300
FAX: 703-841-1184 www.imra.org
This educational event provides attendees with an opportunity to learn from experts in their fields on the most pressing topics of the day

Directories & Databases

19779 Annual Trade Show Directory
Forum Publishing Company
383 E Main Street
Centerport, NY 11721-1538
631-754-5000
www.forum123.com
Martin Stevens, Editor
Over 1,800 merchandise trade shows throughout the United States and Canada.
$39.95
312 pages Annual

19780 Association of Retail Marketing Services Membership Directory
Association of Retail Marketing Services
10 Drs James Parker Boulevard
Suite 103
Red Bank, NJ 07701-1500
732-842-5070
FAX: 732-219-1938
info@goarms.com www.goarms.com
Gerri Hopkins, Executive Director
Lisa McCauley, Administrative Director
Membership directory. *$25.00*
Annual

19781 Directory of Convenience Stores
Trade Dimensions
45 Danbury Road
Wilton, CT 06897-4445
203-563-3000
FAX: 860-563-3131
info@tradedimensions.com
www.tradedimensions.com
Jennifer Gillbert, Editor
Lynda Guticulez, Managing Editor
The directory comprises nearly 1,500 detailed profiles on the companies you need to do business with - extensive dependable information on the grocery industry's most volatile segment. *$245.00*
Annual

19782 Directory of High Discount Merchandise Sources
B Klein Publishers
PO Box 6578
Delray Beach, FL 33482-6578
561-496-3316
FAX: 561-496-5546
Approximately 1,200 sources of products offered at high discounts. *$35.00*
Annual

19783 Directory of Mail Order Catalogs
Grey House Publishing
185 Millerton Road
PO Box 860
Millerton, NY 12546
518-890-0526
FAX: 518-789-0545 800-562-2139
books@greyhouse.com
www.greyhouse.com
Leslie Mackenzie, Publisher
Richard Gottlieb, Editor
The premier source of information on the mail order catalog industry. Covers over 12,000 consumer and business catalog companies with 44 different product chapters from Animals to Toys and Games.
$350.00
1600 pages Annual Founded: 1980 ISBN 1-592370-66-7

19784 Directory of Major Malls
PO Box 837
Nyack, NY 10960-0837
845-348-7000
FAX: 845-426-0802
Tama J Shor, Editor/Publisher
Murray Shor, Consulting Publisher
Contains 2865 listings with over 1800 leasing/site plans of major malls, with many showing the anchors, design layout, intersecting streets, peripheral land, and major highways.
ISBN 0-932599-13-3

19785 Directory of Mass Merchandisers
Trade Dimensions
45 Danbury Road
Wilton, CT 06897-4445
203-563-3000
FAX: 860-563-3131
info@tradedimensions.com
www.tradedimensions.com
Lynda Gutierrez, Managing Editor
Jennifer Gilbert, Editor
This directory defines this complex class of retail trade. Includes profiles of the chains and leading mass merchandisers by market area. Also includes HBC suppliers and store type breakdowns by state/region.
$245.00
Annual

19786 Discount & General Merchandising Stores
Chain Store Guide
3922 Coconut Palm Drive
Tampa, FL 33619
813-276-6700
FAX: 813-627-6882 800-972-9292
info@csgis.com www.csgis.com
Chris Leedy, Advertising Sales
Shami Choon, Manager
This database is an in-depth look at the mass-merchandising segment, bringing you access to more than 7,000 listings along with over 23,000 key personnel. This report includes targeted research from sectors such as Discount Department Stores, General Merchandise Stores, Dollar Stores, Automotive Aftermarket Retailers

and Computer & Consumer Electronics Chains. *$335.00*
720 pages Annual

19787 Discount Merchandiser
McFadden Publishing Company
233 Park Avenue S
6th Floor
New York, NY 10003-1663
212-794-4800
FAX: 323-979-7431
Steven Jacober, Editor
Profiles of the top 55 chains and list of top 85 discount merchandising companies. *$40.00*
Annual June

19788 Educational Dealers and Suppliers Association International Directory
711 W 17th Street
Suite J5
Costa Mesa, CA 92627-4348
949-645-9975
This directory lists international education dealers and suppliers.
Annual

19789 Fairchild's Retail Stores Financial Directory
Fairchild Publications
7 W 34th Street
New York, NY 10001-8100
212-630-3880
FAX: 212-630-3868 800-247-6622
Robert Benjamin, Research Editor
About 260 publicly held retail companies in the US and Canada. *$95.00*
Annual

19790 International Franchise Association - Franchise Opportunities Guide
1501 K St NW
Ste 350
Washington, DC 20005-1412
202-628-8000
FAX: 202-628-0812
John Reynolds, Editor
Matthew Shay, President
This directory lists over 3,000 companies offering franchises. *$21.00*
300 pages SemiAnnual

19791 Leading Chain Tenants Database
Chain Store Guide
3922 Coconut Palm Drive
Tampa, FL 33619
813-276-6700
FAX: 813-627-6882 800-778-9794
info@csgis.com www.csgis.com
Chris Leedy, Advertising Sales
Arthur Sciarrotta, Senior VP
Information on more than 8,600 retailers in the U.S. and Canada with over 32,000 personnel contacts. This database will lead you to new real estate prospects across a vast range of industries. Whether you are in real estate development, leasing or sales, the opportunities are endless. *$365.00*

19792 NAFTA Business Guide
WorldTrade Executive
PO Box 761
Concord, MA 01742-0761
978-287-0301
FAX: 978-287-0302 www.wtexec.com
Alison French, Production Manager
Sets out in clear language the issues that are most important in pursuing trade and investment objectives in North America, providing an insider's look into key business and cross-border issues involving the NAFTA member countries. *$185.00*

19793 NRB Shopping Center Directory
Trade Dimensions
45 Danbury Road
Wilton, CT 06897-4445
203-563-3000
FAX: 860-563-3131
info@nrbonline.com
www.nrbonline.com
Patricia Kelly, Managing Editor
Stephanie Strano, Circulation Director
The most comprehensive book on shopping centers available. Encompassing over 37,000 centers from neighborhood to super regional, the Directory is organized into four volumes: East, Midwest, South, West. A fifth volume is dedicated exclusively to the industry's top contacts, comprising the names and contact information for anyone who owns, leases, or manages three or more centers. *$325.00*
Annual

19794 Outlet Project Directory
Value Retail News
29399 US Highway 19 N
Suite 370
Clearwater, FL 33761-2138
727-781-7557
FAX: 727-536-4389 800-669-1020
Cher Russell-Street, Editor
Factory outlet projects. *$179.00*
SemiAnnual

19795 Outlet Retail Directory
Off-Price Specialists, Value Retail News
15950 Bay Vista Drive
Clearwater, FL 33760-3119
727-465-5522
Over 500 outlet retail chains are profiled.
280 pages Semiannual

19796 Phelon's Discount/Jobbing Trade
Phelon, Sheldon & Marsar
1364 Georgetowne Circle
Sarasota, FL 34232-2048
941-342-7990
FAX: 941-342-7994 800-234-8804
Joseph R Marsar Jr, Editor
Executives and buyers in the discount and mass merchandising stores and chains throughout USA, Canada and Mexico. *$175.00*
450 pages BiAnnual Founded: 1864 ISBN 0-942239-14-8
Circulation: 2,000
Printed in on matte stock

19797 Products & Services Directory
Value Retail News
29399 US Highway 19 N
Suite 370
Clearwater, FL 33761-2138
727-781-7557
FAX: 727-536-4389 800-669-1020
Cher Russell-Street, Editor
More than 2,000 service companies specializing in outlet or off-price retailing and development industries. *$49.00*
Annual

19798 Productscan Online
Marketing Intelligence Service
6473 Route 64
Naples, NY 14512
585-374-6326
FAX: 585-374-5217
mi@productscan.com
www.productscan.com
Daniel Smith, Marketing Director
Julie Fox, Finance Executive
This database is dedicated solely to new launches of consumer packaged goods. Includes label copy, in-depth reports on innovations, and product pictures capable of statistical analysis and manufacturer history reports. *$3995.00*

19799 Retail Industry Buying Guide: STORES Magaz ine
National Retail Federation
325 7th Street NW
Suite 1100
Washington, DC 20004
202-783-7971
FAX: 202-737-2849 www.nrf.com
Rick Gallagher, Publisher
Tim Henderson, Editor-in-Chief
Capital spending in the products and services that are imperitive to running a smooth and efficient retail operation were particularly hard hit in the past year. In the face of continued uncertainty, it's essential that retailers make informed decisions on how to best invest their limited capital to ensure a positive return on their investment. This directory is that source of information.
Monthly
Circulation: 35000

19800 Retail Tenant Directory
Trade Dimensions
45 Danbury Road
Wilton, CT 06897-4445
203-563-3000
FAX: 860-563-3131
info@tradedimensions.com
www.tradedimensions.com
Garrett Van Siclen, Publisher
Thomas Donato, Editor
Complete and accurate details for 5,000+ growing retailers that are looking for space. Holding company section lists corporate profiles for major parent companies which own two or more major retail chains in the US. Individual company profiles include retail classifications, total number of stores, operating names, sales volume, who to contact, extensive site selection criteria including demographic preferences, expansion plans, acquisitions, format changes and more. *$345.00*
1500 pages Annual ISBN 0-911790-29-2

19801 Sheldon's Major Stores & Chains
Phelon, Sheldon & Marsar
1364 Georgetowne Circle
Sarasota, FL 34232-2048
941-342-7990
FAX: 941-342-7994 800-234-8804
Joseph R Marsar Jr, Editor
Executives and buyers in the major stores and chains within the retail industry in USA, Canada & Mexico. *$200.00*
550 pages Annual Founded: 1864 ISBN 0-942239-22-9
Circulation: 2,000

19802 Shippers Guide to Department & Chain Stores Nationwide
Shippers Guides
PO Box 112
Duarte, CA 91009-0112
626-357-6430
FAX: 626-357-6366
Profiles over 1,000 department stores and chain stores and information about routing and freight movement. *$349.00*
350 pages Annual
Mailing list available for rent 1,000 names $299 per M.

19803 Shopping Center Directory
National Research Bureau
333 W Wacker Drive
Suite 900
Chicago, IL 60606-1284
312-346-3900

This large directory offers information on over 30,000 shopping centers in four regional volumes. *$225.00*
3,200 pages Annual

19804 Single Unit Supermarkets Operators
Chain Store Guide
3922 Coconut Palm Drive
Tampa, FL 33616-3506
813-276-6700
FAX: 813-627-6882 800-778-9794
info@csgis.com www.csgis.com
Chris Leedy, Advertising Sales
Shami Choon, Manager
Discover more than 7,100 single-unit supermarkets with annual sales topping $500,000 dollars. This comprehensive desktop reference makes it easy to reach our compiled list of 21,000 key executives and buyers, plus their primary wholesalers. *$335.00*
725 pages Annual

19805 Stores: Top 100 Retailers Issue
National Retail Federation
325 7th Street NW
Suite 1100
Washington, DC 20004-2808
202-783-7971
FAX: 202-737-2849
editor@nrf.com www.stores.org
Harrison Donnelly, Editor
Rick Gallagher, Editor
100 US retail companies having largest estimated sales during preceding year. *$75.00*
Annual July
Circulation: 35,000

19806 Supermarket News Retailers & Wholesalers Directory
Fairchild Publications
7 W 34th Street
New York, NY 10001-8100
212-630-3880
FAX: 212-630-3768 800-360-1700
Over 2,200 US and Canadian retailers, including supermarkets, discount department stores, membership clubs, drug stores, plus voluntary, cooperative and non-sponsoring wholesalers.

19807 Supermarket, Grocery & Convenience Stores
Chain Store Guide
3922 Coconut Palm Drive
Tampa, FL 33616-3506
813-276-6700
FAX: 813-627-6882 800-778-9794
info@csgis.com www.csgis.com
Chris Leedy, Advertising Sales
Shami Choon, Manager
Contains information on close to 3,400 U.S. and Canadian supermarket chains, each with at least $2 million in annual sales - one of the most profitable segments in this sector of the economy. The companies in this database operate over 41,000 individual supermarket, superstore, club store, gourmet supermarkets and combo-store units. A special convenience store section profiles 1,700 convenience store chains operating over 85,000 stores. *$335.00*
Annual 700 names

19808 Top Shopping Centers: Major Markets 1-50
National Research Bureau
333 W Wacker Drive
Suite 900
Chicago, IL 60606-1284
312-346-3900
$895.00

19809 US Trade Pages
Global Source
1511 K Street NW
Washington, DC 20005-1403

Kara Kent, Editor
These directories including a volume on Brazil, Chile, Canada, Mexico, Venezuela, and Argentina list trade associations and professional services that provide information on imports and exports between the US and the above listed companies. *$59.95*
6 Volumes

19810 World Federation of Direct Selling Associations Directory
1776 K Street NW
Washington, DC 20006-2304
202-194-4901

Industry Web Sites

19811 www.aamp.com
American Association of Meat Processors

The membership consists of small to medium sized meat, poultry and food businesses including: packers, processors, wholesalers, home food service businesses, retailers, deli and catering operators. AAMP is also affiliated with 34 state, regional and provincial organizations which represent meat and poultry businesses.

19812 www.bookweb.org
American Booksellers Association

Trade association for retail booksellers. Not for profit.

19813 www.fdi.org
International Center for Companies of Food Trade
and Industry/North America

Provides management research on problems related to food distribution and serves as an international forum where food chain store executives can meet to exchange ideas and information.

19814 www.fleamarkets.org
National Flea Market Association

Represents Flea Market and Swap Meet owners and managers and disseminates information to the general public and media regarding the flea market industry worldwide.

19815 www.goarms.com
Association of Retail Marketing Services

Approximately 60 retailers involved in the ARMS retail promotion show, held annually.

19816 www.greyhouse.com
Grey House Publishing

Selected Grey House directories in the fields of business, health and education are available online. Users can search our online databases by several different search criteria, such as product categories, geographic area, sales volume and much, much more. Full Grey House catalog and online ordering also available.

19817 www.ispo.org
Institute of Store Planners

Provides a forum for debate and discussion by store design experts and retailers. Sponsors student design programs.

19818 www.maptrade.org
International Map Trade Association

Membership comprised of retail stores featuring maps, travel books, globes, and travel products, plus publishers and manufacturers producing these products. Publishes a monthly newsletter

19819 www.mraa.com
Marine Retailers Association of America

Promotes activities for the recreational boating industry and holds seminars to improve management.

19820 www.nacs.org
National Association of College Stores

Provides educational and support services and products to college stores. Promotes business methods and ethics. Conducts manager certification, educational services and research.

19821 www.nag-net.com
Convenience Stores/Petroleum Marketers Association

This association represents senior level management of retail companies organized to enhance buying power, merchandising programs and an exchange of ideas. C-Stores/Petroleum Marketers membership dues: Retail Av. $300, Assoc. $500

19822 www.nagmr.org
National Association General Merchandise Repr

A professional association of consumer product brokers representing leading manufacturers to the retail trade.

19823 www.narda.com
North American Retail Dealers Association

A national organization of association members, independent retailers selling and servicing major appliances, consumer electronics products, furniture and computers. Emphasis is placed on ideas that help readers become better, more profitable businesses. Articles are featured regularly on displays, salesmanship, financial analysis and service management.

19824 www.nationalPawnbrokers.org
National Pawnbrokers Association

Nonprofits organization that supports all those involved with the retail pawnbrokers.

19825 www.nationalgrocers.org
National Grocers Association

Works to advance understanding, trade, and cooperation in the food industry. Represents members interests before the government. Offers store planning, and engineering, training and advertising.

19826 www.nicyra.org
National Ice Cream & Yogurt Retailers Association

Members are in retail frozen dessert businesses. Some offer food services either full of limited and some operate convenience stores. The common denominator is that all members offer frozen desserts for take-home or on-site consumption.

19827 www.nrf.com
National Retail Federation

Retail trade association with membership that comprises all retail formats and channels of distribution including department, specialty, discount, catalog, Internet and independent stores. NRF members represent an industry that encompasses more than 1.4 million US retail establishments which employ more than 23 million people — about one in five American workers — and registered 2002 sales of $3.6 trillion. NRF's international members operate stores in more than 50 nations.

19828 www.nsgachicagoshow.com
National Sporting Goods Association

Members consist of retailers, wholesalers, suppliers, sales agents and media. Sponsor of NSGA World Sports EXPO, held annually in Chicago, and the NSGA Management Conference. Has an annual budget of approximately $8 million.

19829 www.retailsystems.com
Retail Systems Alert Group

For retail and supply chain professionals. Access to community centers, newsletter information, and online ordering information is also available.

19830 www.rtda.org
Retail Tobacco Dealers of America

Trade association of high quality tobacconists.

19831 www.shop.org
Shop.org

Association for retailers online. It's where professional retailerscome together to garner the insight, knowledge and intellegence to make better decisions in the evolving world of the Internet and multi-channel retailing.

19832 www.smallbusinesslocator.com
Small Business Association

Providing information to mom and pop businesses.

Associations

19833 American Chemical Society: Rubber Division
PO Box 499
Akron, OH 44309-0499
330-972-7814
www.rubber.org
The Rubber Division of the American Chemical Society is a professional organization dedicated to providing educational programs, technical resources and other vital services for the people associated with rubber and affiliated industries.

19834 Engineering with Rubber: How to Design Rub ber Components
American Chemical Society: Rubber Division
PO Box 499
Akron, OH 44309-0499
330-972-7814
www.rubber.org
Teaches the beginning engineer the principles of rubber science and technology-what rubber is, how it behaves, and how to design simple engineering components.

19835 International Institute of Synthetic Rubber Producers
2077 S Gessner Road
Suite 133
Houston, TX 77063
713-783-7511
FAX: 713-783-7253
info@iisrp.com www.iisrp.com
James L McGraw, Managing Director/CEO
Dr K Leon Loh, Sr, Director Programs
International trade association for synthetic rubber producers to receive and benefit from statistical, environmental, and technical information in order to keep abreast of the world's market growth and events.
40 Members Founded: 1960

19836 North American Recycled Rubber Association
1621 Mcewen Drive
Unit 24
Whitby Ontario, CA L1N-9A5
905-433-7669
FAX: 905-433-0905
narra@oix.com wwwrecycle.net
Diane Sarracini, Contact
Created to bring together the various stakeholders affiliated with the recycled rubber industry.

19837 Polyurethane Foam Association
9724 Kingston Pike
Suite 503
Knoxville, TN 37922
865-690-4648
FAX: 865-690-4649
rluedeka@pfa.org www.pfa.org
The mission of the Polyurethane Foam Association (PFA) is to educate customers and other groups about flexible polyurethane foam (FPF) and to promote its use in manufactured and industrial products.
Founded: 1980

19838 Polyurethane Manufacturers Association
6737 W Washington Avenue
Suite 1420
Milwaukee, WI 53214
414-431-3094
FAX: 414-276-7704
info@pmahome.org
www.pmahome.org
Ken Neal, President, Board of Directors
Corey D Barge, VP, Board of Directors
The Polyurethane Manufacturers Association is the trade association of the cast polyurethane elastomer industry, serving processors of polyurethane products, materials and equipment suppliers and independent agents.

19839 Rubber Division, American Chemical Society
PO Box 499
Akron, OH 44309-0499
330-972-7814
FAX: 330-972-5269
crubber.org www.rubber.org
Tammy Sobleskie, Marketing/Meetings Manager
Sue Barr, Exhibition/Future Sites Manager
Rubber division of the American Chemical Society is a professional association dedicated to providing educational programs, technical resources and other vital services for the people associated with rubber and affiliated industries. Serves as a global resource for networking and partnerships with academics and industry.
3200 Members Founded: 1909

19840 Rubber Manufacturers Association
1400 K Street NW
Suite 900
Washington, DC 20005
202-682-4800
info@rma.org www.rma.org
Donald B Shea, President/CEO
RMA is the national trade association for the rubber products industry.
100 Members

19841 Rubber Pavements Association
1801 S Jentilly Lane
Suite A-2
Tempe, AZ 85281-5738
480-517-9944
FAX: 480-517-9959
www.rubberpavements.org
Doug Carlson, Executive Director
Guadalupe Dickerson, Office Manager
Dedicated to encouraging greater usage of high quality, cost effective asphalt pavements containing recycled tire rubber.

19842 Scrap Tire Management Council
1400 K Street NW
Suite 900
Washington, DC 20005
202-824-4800
FAX: 202-682-4854
info@rma.org oikos.com
Donald Shea, President
An advocacy organization sponsored by North American tire manufacturers created to identify and promote environmentally and economically sound markets for scrap tires.
Founded: 1990

19843 Single Ply Roofing Institute
77 Rumford Avenue
Suite 3B
Waltham, MA 02453
781-647-7026
FAX: 781-647-7222
info@spri.org www.spri.org
SPRI represents sheet membrane and related component suppliers in the commercial roofing industry.

19844 Society of the Plastics Industry
1667 K Street NW
Suite 1000
Washington, DC 20006
202-974-5200
202-296-7005
Represents the entire plastics industry in a manner that promotes development of the industry and enhances public understanding of its contributions while meeting the needs of society and providing value to members.

19845 Tire Industry Association
1532 Pointer Ridge Place
Suite G
Bowie, MD 20716-1883
301-430-7280
FAX: 301-430-7283 800-876-8372
info@tireindustry.org
www.tireindustry.org
Roy Littlefield, Executive VP
Sandra Martinez, Director Operations
Colleen Wood, Director of Marketing
TIA is an international association representing all segments of the tire industry, including those that manufacture, repair, recycle, sell, service or use new or retreaded tires, and also those suppliers or individuals who furnish equipment, material or services to the industry. TIA was formed by the July 2002 merger of the International Tire & Rubber Association (ITRA) and the Tire Association of North America (TANA).
4500 Members Founded: 2002

19846 Tire Retread Information Bureau
900 Weldon Grove
Pacific Grove, CA 93950
831-372-1917
FAX: 831-372-9210 888-473-8732
info@retread.org www.retread.org
Rachel Lewis, Website Manager
Our goal is to provide the motoring public (both in the private and public sectors) with the most up-to-date information about the economic and environmental benefits of tire retreading and tire repairing.

19847 Tread Rubber Manufacturers Group
Piper and Marbury
1200 19th Street NW
Washington, DC 20036-2430
202-614-4171
Works to improve tire retreading techniques and to safeguard the public interest in retreading.

Newsletters

19848 **Rubber Chemistry and Technology**
Rubber Division, American Chemical Society
PO Box 499
Akron, OH 44325-3801
330-972-7883
FAX: 330-972-5269
Lu Ann Blazeff, Publisher
Information on materials and equipment pertaining to the rubber industry. Accepts advertising. *$487.50*
5 Times per Year

19849 **Rubber and Plastics News**
Crain Communications
1725 Merriman Road
Suite 300
Akron, OH 44313-5283
330-836-9180
FAX: 330-836-2831 800-678-9595
editorials@rubbernews.com
http://www.rubbernews.com
Tony Eagan, Publisher
Edward Noga, Editor
Discusses production, research and development, management, sales and marketing. *$79.00*
24 pages Monthly Founded: 1971
Circulation: 16258
Printed in 4 colors on glossy stock

19850 **Worldwide Rubber Statistics**
Int'l Institute of Synthetic Rubber Producers
2077 S Gessner Road
Suite 133
Houston, TX 77063-1150
713-783-7511
FAX: 281-783-7253
jlmcgraw@iisrp.com
http://www.azom.com/
Britt Theismann, Editor
James McGraw, CEO
Guide to the synthetic and natural rubber industry, including Centrally Planned Economy Countries. *$1050.00*
Founded: 1960

Magazines & Journals

19851 **Global Tire News.com**
Rubber & Plastic News
1725 Merriman Road
Akron, OH 44313-5251
330-369-9180
FAX: 330-836-2831 330-836-9180
dsector@crain.com
www.rubbernews.com/
Edward Noga, Editor
Don Sector, Advertising Coordinator
Mike McNulty, Rubber & Plastics News Staff Writer
Brent Weaver, Classified Coordinator
Provides rubber industry information relative to tire manufacturers; top tire company managers; plant listings and other data. Subscription to annual publication includes access to Global Tire News.com. *$79.00*
Annual

19852 **Rubber World**
Lippincott & Peto
PO Box 5451
1867 W. Market St.
Akron, OH 44313-6901
330-864-2122
FAX: 330-864-5298
jhl@rubberworld.com
http://www.rubberworld.com
Job H Lippincott, Publisher
Dennis Kennelly, VP Sales
Don R Smith, Editor
Darlene Ballard, Director of Marketing Services
Jill Rohrer, Managing Editor
Provides complete technical coverage to the rubber industry. *$34.00*

Trade Shows

19853 **International Latex Conference**
Crain Communications
1725 Merriman Road
Suite 300
Akron, OH 44313-5283
330-836-9180
FAX: 330-836-1005
cstevens@crain.com
www.rubbernews.com
Twelve exhibitors with 12 booths.
July

19854 **International Tire Exhibition and Conference**
Crain Communications
1725 Merriman Road
Suite 300
Akron, OH 44313-5283
330-836-9180
FAX: 330-836-1005
cstevens@crain.com
www.rubbernews.com
One-hundred and thirty exhibitors with 110 booths.
September

19855 **Rubber Expo**
American Chemical Society-Rubber Division
PO Box 499
Akron, OH 44309-0499
330-972-7814
FAX: 330-972-5269 800-227-5558
help@acs.org www.chemistry.org
Sherri L Poorman, Exhibition Manager
Biennial show of 300 manufacturers and suppliers of equipment, supplies and services for the rubber industry, including machinery, chemicals, raw rubber, finished rubber products, quality control equipment and related equipment.
8,000 Attendees October, Cleveland

19856 **Rubber Mini Expo**
American Chemical Society-Rubber Division
PO Box 499
Akron, OH 44309-0499
330-972-7814
FAX: 330-972-5269
shbarr@rubber.org www.rubber.org
Sue Barr, Exposition & Future Sites Manager
Biennial show of 150 manufacturers, suppliers and custom services for the rubber industry, including machinery, chemicals, raw rubber, finished rubber products, quality control equipment and related equipment.
3000 Attendees October

19857 **Rubber and Plastics Industry Conference of the United Steelworkers of America**
5 Gateway Center
Pittsburgh, PA 15220
412-562-6971
FAX: 412-562-6963
John Sellers, Executive VP
90M Attendees Founded: 1935

Directories & Databases

19858 **Rauch Guide to the US Rubber Industry**
Grey House Publishing
PO Box 860
Millerton, NY 12546
518-789-8700
FAX: 518-789-0545 800-562-2139
books@greyhouse.com
www.greyhouse.com
Leslie Mackenzie, Publisher
Richard Gottlieb, President
Approximately 500 manufacturers of fabricated rubber products. *$595.00*
Annual

19859 **Rubber World Blue Book: Materials, Compounding and Machinery**
Lippincott & Peto
1867 W Market St
Akron, OH 44313-6901
330-864-2122
Job Lippincott, Owner
Over 850 suppliers of over 8,000 chemicals, materials and compounding ingredients for rubber manufacturers. *$103.00*
Annual
Circulation: 4,000

19860 **Rubber World: Custom Mixers Directory**
Lippincott & Peto
1867 W Market St
Akron, OH 44313-6901
330-864-2122
Job Lippincott, Owner
A list of rubber manufacturers providing custom mixes. *$3.00*
Annual

19861 **Rubber World: Machinery Suppliers Issue**
Lippincott & Peto
1867 W Market Street
Akron, OH 44313-6901
330-864-2122
Job Lippincott, Owner
Lists suppliers of used and rebuilt machinery and instrumentation and test equipment to the rubber industry. *$3.00*
Annual ISSN 0035-9572

19862 Rubber and Plastics News: Rubicana Issue
Crain Communications
1725 Merriman Road
Suite 300
Akron, OH 44313-5283
330-369-9180
800-678-9595

Tony Eagan, Publisher

A list of over 1,000 rubber product manufacturers and suppliers of equipment, services and materials. *$85.00*

Annual
Circulation: 15,000

Industry Web Sites

19863 www.greyhouse.com
Grey House Publishing

Selected Grey House directories in the fields of business, health and education are available online. Users can search our online databases by several different search criteria, such as product categories, geographic area, sales volume and much, much more. Full Grey House catalog and online ordering also available.

19864 www.iisrp.com
Int'l Institute of Synthetic Rubber Producers

For manufacturers of synthetic rubber.

19865 www.itra.com
International Tire and Rubber Association

Information on tire retreading and repairing, new tires, scrap tire reduction and removal equipment, rubber recycling technologies, recycled rubber products and allied services including brake equipment, wheel alignment, tire balancers, tire changers, service trucks, marketing/sales and management programs and computer systems.

19866 www.rma.org
Scrap Tire Management Council

For tire manufacturers marketers of scrap tires.

Associations

19867 AAA Foundation for Traffic Safety
14th Street NW
Suite 201
Washington, DC 20005
202-638-5944
FAX: 202-638-5943
info@aaafoundation.org
www.aaafoundation.org

Peter Kissinger, President/CEO
Fairley Mahlum, Communications Director

AAA Foundation for Traffic Safety is dedicated to saving lives and reducing injuries on the roads. It is a not-for-profit, publicly-supported charitable educational and research organization.

19868 Academy of Security Educators & Trainers
PO Box 802
Berryville, VA 22611
540-554-2540
FAX: 540-554-2558 www.asetcse.org

Dr Richard W Kobetz, Executive Director
William MacPhail, President

Non-profit organization of security professionals dedicated to exploring the large spectrum of issues confronting the security field. Meetings are held to discuss, design, develop, and exchange thoughts and ideas in an open forum. Awards the CST (certified security trainer) designation.

500 Members Founded: 1980

19869 Advanced Medical Technology Association: AdvaMed
701 Pennsylvania Avenue NW
Suite 800
Washington, DC 20004-2654
202-783-8700
FAX: 202-783-8750
info@AdvaMed.org
www.advamed.org

Stephen J Ubl, President/CEO
David Nexon, Senior Executive VP
Frank S Wilton, VP Membership

Dedicated to providing members with the advocacy, information, education and tangible solutions necessary for success in a world of increasingly complex medical regulations.

1300 Members

19870 Advocates for Highway and Auto Safety
750 1st Street NE
Suite 901
Washington, DC 20002
202-408-1711
FAX: 202-408-1699
advocates@saferoads.org
www.saferoads.org

Judith Lee Stone, President
Jacqueline Gillan, VP
Jeremy Gunderson, Administration Director

Advocates for Highway and Auto Safety is an alliance of consumer, health and safety groups and insurance companies and agents working together to make America's roads safer.

Founded: 1989

19871 Alarm Association of Florida
1802 N University Drive
Plantation, FL 33322-4115
954-748-7779
FAX: 954-748-4749 800-899-2099
bneely@fla-alarms.org
www.fla-alarms.org

Robert Neeley, Executive Director

A trade association for burglar and fire alarm contractors, as well as low voltage contractors.

19872 American Association for Aerosol Research
C/O Global Aersol Climatology
1330 Kemper Meadow Drive
Cincinnati, OH 45240
513-742-2227
FAX: 513-742-3355
info@aaaar.org www.aaar.org

Pratim Biswas, President
Spyros Pandis, VP Elect

Nonprofit professional organization for scientists and engineers who wish to promote and communicate technical advances in the field of aerosol research. fosters the exchange of information among members and with other disciplines through conferences, symposia, and publication of a professional journal, Aerosol and Science Technology.

1000 Members Founded: 1982

19873 American Association of Occupational Healt h Nurses
2920 Brandywine Road
Suite 100
Atlanta, GA 30341
770-455-7757
FAX: 770-455-7271
aaohn@aaohn.org www.aaohn.org

Ann Cox, Executive Director
Don Bollmer, Business Affairs Director
Bruce Lloyd, Communications/Marketing Director

AAOHN is a principal force in furthering the profession of occupational and environmental health nursing by providing education, resources, and advocacy.

Founded: 1942

19874 American Association of Poison Control Cen ters
3201 New Mexico Avenue
Suite 330
Washington, DC 20016
202-253-3333
800-222-1222
info@aapcc.org www.aapcc.org

Kathleen M Wruk, President
Toby Litovitz, Executive Director

Nonprofit nationwide organization of poison centers and others interested in the prevention and treatment of poisoning. Promotes the reduction of injury, illness and death from poisonings through public and professional education and scientific research. Promotes universal access to certified regional poison centers.

Founded: 1958

19875 American Bio-Recovery Association

PO Box 828
Ipswich, MA 01938

888-979-2272

James Monath, President

A nationwide non-profit association of crime and trauma scene recovery professionals who are dedicated to upholding the highest technical, ethical and educational guidelines of the biohazard remediation industry.

19876 American Biological Safety Association
1200 Allanson Road
Mundelein, IL 60060
847-949-1517
FAX: 847-566-4580
absa@absa.org www.absa.org

ABSA's goals are to provide a professional association that represents the interest and needs of practitioners of biological safety, and to providea forum for the continued and timely exchange of biosafety information.

Founded: 1984

19877 American Chemical Society
1155 16th Street NW
Washington, DC 20036
202-872-4600
FAX: 202-776-8258 800-227-5558
help@acs.org www.acs.org

E Ann Nalley, President
Madeleine Jacobs, Executive Director

Supports chemists and companies who work with chemicals and their by-products.

158 M Members Founded: 1876

19878 American College of Occupational & Environ mental Medicine
25 NW Point Boulevard
Suite 700
Elkgrove Village, IL 60007-1030
847-818-1800
FAX: 847-818-9266
acoeminfo@acoem.org
www.acoem.org

Barry Eisenberg, Executive Director
Marianne Dreger, Communications Director
Doris Konicki, Research & Development Director

Occupational and environmental medicine is devoted to the prevention and management of occupational and injury, illness and disability, and promotion of health and productivity of workers, thier families and communities.

6000 Members Founded: 1916

19879 American Conference of Governmental Indust rial Hygienists
1330 Kemper Meadow Drive
Cincinnati, OH 45240
513-742-2020
FAX: 513-742-3355
mail@acgih.org www.acgih.org

A Anthony Rizzuto, Executive Director
Robert D Soule, Chairman

A member-based organization and community of professionals that advances worker health and safety through education and the development and dissemination of scientific and technical knowledge.

Founded: 1938

19880 American Fire Safety Council
1909 K Street NW
Suite 400
Washington, DC 20006
202-419-3269
FAX: 202-955-6215
info@fire-safety.net
www.fire-safety.net

Mike Heimowitz, Program Manager

Improving fire safety through enhancement of fire codes and standards and promoting

responsible use of flame retardants and flame retardant products. AFSC was created to provide a stronger and broader voice on advocacy and safety issues.
Founded: 2003

19881 American Fire Sprinkler Association
9696 Skillman Street
Suite 300
Dallas, TX 75243-8264
214-349-5965
FAX: 214-343-8898
afsainfo@firesprinkler.org
www.sprinklernet.org
Steve Muncy, President
Janet Knowles, VP/Marketing & Communications
Nonprofit international association representing open shop fire sprinkler contractors, dedicated to the educational advancement of its members and promotion of the use of automatic sprinkler systems. Offers a convention and exhibition, correspondence course, monthly magazine and a monthly newsletter.
900 Members Founded: 1981

19882 American Gas Association
400 N Capitol Street NW
Suite 400
Washington, DC 20001
202-824-7000
FAX: 202-824-7115
ykorolevich@aga.org www.aga.org
David N Parker, President/CEO
Kevin Hardardt, Administration Director
Ysabel Korolevich, Membership Services
The American Gas Association advocates the interests of its members and their customers, and provides information and services promoting efficient demand and supply growth and operational excellence in the safe, reliable and efficient delivery of natural gas.
Founded: 1918

19883 American Industrial Hygiene Association
2700 Prosperity Avenue
Suite 250
Fairfax, VA 22031
703-849-8888
FAX: 703-207-3561
infonet@aiha.org www.aiha.org
Steven H Davis, Executive Director
Peter O'Neil, Assistant Executive Director
Lisa Junker, Communications Sr. Manager
AIHA promotes healthy and safe environments by advancing the science, principles, practice, and value of industrial hygiene and occupational and environmental health and safety.
12000 Members Founded: 1939

19884 American Insurance Association
1130 Connecticut Avenue NW
Suite 1000
Washington, DC 20036
202-828-7100
FAX: 202-293-1219
info@aiadc.org www.aiadc.org
Robert Vagley, President
A property, casualty insurance trade organization representing more than 40,000 insurers that write more than $120 billion in premiums each year. AIA member companies offer all types of property-casualty insurance, including personal and commercial auto insurance, commercial property and liability coverage for small businesses, worker's compensation, medical malpractice coverage, and product liability insurance.
40000 Members Founded: 1866

19885 American National Standards Institute (ANS I)
1819 L Street NW
6th Floor
Washington, DC 20036
202-293-8020
FAX: 202-293-9287
info@ansi.org www.ansi.org
Joe Bhatia, President/CEO
Frances Schrotter, Senior VP/COO
To enhance the global competition of business and quality of life by promoting and facilitating voluntary consensus standards and conformity assessment systems, and safeguarding their integrity.
1000 Members Founded: 1918

19886 American Polygraph Association
PO Box 8037
Chattanooga, TN 37414-0037
423-892-3992
FAX: 423-894-5435 800-272-8037
manager@polygraph.org
www.polygraph.org
Donald Krapohl, President
Robbie S Bennett, National Office Manager
The American Polygraph Association (APA) is the leading professional polygraph organization in the world.
3200 Members Founded: 1966
Mailing list available for rent $150 per M.

19887 American Public Health Association
800 I Street NW
Washington, DC 20001
202-777-2742
FAX: 202-777-2534
comments@apha.org www.apha.org
Dr Georges C Benjamin, Executive Director
Pat Mail, President
Influencing policies and setting priorities for over 125 years. Thoughout its history it has been in the forefront of numerous efforts to prevent disease and promote health.

19888 American Red Cross
2025 E Street NW
Washington, DC 20006
202-393-3685
FAX: 202-303-0044
info@usa.redcross.org
www.redcross.org
Jack McGuire, Interim President/CEO
The American Red Cross is where people moblilze to help their neighbors across the street, across the country and across the world, in emergencies. Each year, in communities large and small, victims of some 70,000 disasters turn to the nearly one million volunteers and 35,000 employees of the Red Cross.
31000 Members Founded: 1881

19889 American Safety & Health Institute
4148 Louis Avenue
Holiday, FL 34691
727-437-7560
800-682-5067
info@ashinstitute.org
www.ashinstitute.org
Frank Swiger, Manager
Nonprofit association of professional safety & health educators providing nationally recognized training programs through more than 5000 approved training centers across the US and in several foreign countries.
30000 Members Founded: 1996

19890 American Society for Industrial Security
1625 Prince Street
Alexandria, VA 22314-2818
703-519-6200
FAX: 703-519-6299
asis@asisonline.org
www.asisonline.org
Jeff M Spivey, President
Michael J Stack, Executive Director
ASIS International (ASIS) is the largest organization for security professionals, with more than 33,000 members worldwide. ASIS is dedicated to increasing the effectiveness and productivity of security professionals by developing educational programs and materials that address broad security interests, such as the ASIS Annual Seminar and Exhibits, as well as specific security topics.
33000 Members Founded: 1955

19891 American Society for Nondestructive Testin g
1711 Arlingate Lane
PO Box 28518
Columbus, OH 43228
614-274-6003
FAX: 614-274-6899 800-222-2768
kwie@asnt.org www.asnt.org
Wayne Holliday, Executive Director
Betsy Blazar, Marketing Director
Jim Houf, Technical Services
ASNT is the world's largest technical society for nondestructive tests (NDT) professionals.
10000 Members Founded: 1941

19892 American Society for Testing & Materials
100 Barr Harbor Drive
PO Box C-700
West Conshohocken, PA 19428-2959
610-832-9585
FAX: 610-832-3636
service@astm.org www.astm.org
James Thomas, President
Pat Picariello, Operations Director
Derek Franco, Customer Relations/Sales
A voluntary standards development organization for technical standards for materials, products, systems, and services. Known for high technical quality and market relevancy, ASTM International standards have an important role in the information infrastructure that guides design, manufacturing and trade in the global economy.
30000 Members Founded: 1898

19893 American Society of Crime Laboratory Direc tors (ASCLD)
139K Technology Drive
Garner, NC 27529
919-773-2044
FAX: 919-773-2602
president@ascld.org
www.ascld.org/index.htm

W Earl Wells, President
Jan L Johnson, Secretary
Harry A Fox III, Treasurer

The American Society of Crime Laboratory Directors (ASCLD) is a nonprofit professional society of crime laboratory directors and forensic science managers dedicated to providing excellence in forensic science through leadership and innovation.

19894 American Society of Criminology
1314 Kinnear Road
Columbus, OH 43212-1156
614-292-9207
FAX: 614-292-6767
asc41@infinet.com www.asc41.com

Michael Tonry, President
Chris Eskridge PhD, Executive Director
Doris MacKenzie, VP

The American Society of Criminology is an international organization concerned with criminology, embracing scholary, scientific and profesional knowledge concerning the etiology, prevention, control, and treatment of crime and delinquency.

19895 American Society of Mechanical Engineers
Three Park Avenue
New York, NY 10016-5990
212-591-7739
FAX: 212-591-7674 800-843-2763
infocentral@asme.org www.asme.org

Terry E Shoup, President
Virgil Carter, Chief Executive Officer
Warren R Leonard, Managing Director Governance
Leila Persaud, Coordinator Governance

Through its initiatives in education, advocacy and public policy, the ASME. Foundation impacts all aspects of the mechanical engineering community.

120 M Members Founded: 1880

19896 American Society of Safety Engineers
1800 E Oakton Street
Des Plaines, IL 60018
847-699-2929
FAX: 847-768-3434
customerservice@asse.org
www.asse.org

Fred Fortman, Executive Director
Kelly Fanella, Communications/Marketing Director
Michael Thompson, President

ASSE is a global organization that works to advance the technical, scientific, managerial and ethical knowledge and skills of occupational sarety, health and environmantal professionals, and is committed to protecting people, property and the environment.

30000 Members Founded: 1911

19897 American Traffic Safety Services Association
15 Riverside Parkway
Suite 100
Fredericksburg, VA 22406-1022
540-368-1701
FAX: 540-368-1717 800-272-8772

Joe Jeffrey, Traffic Services Director
Kurt Schuldt, Pavement Markings Director
David McKee, Director Membership/Tech Assistance

The American Traffic Safety Services Association, is an international trade association founded in 1969. It has has represented companies and individuals in the traffic control and roadway safety industry.

Founded: 1969

19898 American Welding Society
550 NW LeJeune Road
Miami, FL 33126
305-443-9353
800-443-9353
info@aws.org www.aws.org

Ray Shook, Executive Director
Frank Tarafa, Chief Financial Officer
Jeff Hufsey, Deputy Executive Director
Jack McLaughlin, Deputy Executive Director
Jason Friedman, Manager Member Services

The mission of the American Welding Society is to advance the science, technology and application of welding and allied joining and cutting processes, including brazing, soldering and thermal spraying.

50000 Members Founded: 1919

19899 Associated Locksmiths of America
3500 Easy Street
Dallas, TX 75247
214-819-9733
FAX: 214-827-1810 800-532-2562
aloa@aloa.org www.aloa.org

William Young, President
Charles Gibson, Secretary
Hoffman

ALOA is an international professional organization of highly qualified security professionals engaged in consulting, sales, installation and maintenance of locks, keys safes, premises security, access controls, alarms, and other security related endeavors.

10M Members Founded: 1956

19900 Association for Manufacturing Technology
7901 Westpark Drive
McLean, VA 22102-4206
703-893-2900
FAX: 703-893-1151 800-524-0475
amt@amtonline.org
www.amtonline.org

John B Byrd III, President
Diyana Hrzic, Membership Manager
Douglas K Woods, Second Vice Chairman
Richard P Bodine Jr, Director

Represents American providers of manufacturing machinery and equipment. Its goal is to promote technological advancements and improvements in the design, manufacture and sale of member's products in those markets and act as an industry advocate on trade organizations thoroughout the world.

Founded: 1902

19901 Association of Air Medical Services
526 King Street
Suite 415
Alexandria, VA 22314-3143
703-836-8732
FAX: 703-836-8920
information@aams.org www.aams.org

Dawn M Mancuso, Executive Director
Melissa Porter, Membership Manager
Blair Beggan, Communications/Marketing Manager

AAMS is built on the idea that representation from a variety of medical transport services and businesses can be brought together to share information, collectively resolve problems and provide leadership in the medical transport community.

581 Members Founded: 1980

19902 Association of Certified Fraud Examiners
716 West Avenue
Austin, TX 78701-2727
512-789-9070
FAX: 512-478-9297 800-245-3321
info@cfenet.com www.acfe.com

John T Wells, Founder/Chairman
Toby JF Bishop, President/CEO
Kathie Green Lawrence, VP
James D Ratley, Program Director
Scott Grossfeld, CFO

The mission of the Association of Certified Fraud Examiners is to reduce the incidence of fraud and white-collar crime and to assist its members in its dectection and prevention.

35000 Members Founded: 1988

19903 Association of Christian Investigators
2553 Jackson Keller
Suite 200
San Antonio, TX 78230
210-342-0509
FAX: 210-342-0731
kelmar@stic.net www.a-c-i.org

Kelly E Riddle, President

Provides a spirit-filled organization that promoste the investigative profession in a noncompetitive atmosphere. Provides an environment in which investigators can create meaningful and long-term relationships with other investigators outside the professional bonds.

500 Members

19904 Association of Contingency Planners
7044 S 13th Street
Oak Creek, WI 53154
414-768-8000
800-445-4227

Shirley Runnels, Director Membership Services
Paul L Striedl, Chairman/CEO
Dan Newton, Director Education
Jim Coleman, Director Public Relations
Scott Sherer, Manager

Nonprofit trade association dedicated to fostering continued professional growth and development in effective contingency and business resumption planning.

1700 Members Founded: 1983

19905 Association of Public Safety Communication s Officials-International
351 N Williamson Boulevard
Daytona Beach, FL 32114-1112
386-322-2500
FAX: 386-322-2501 888-272-6911
apco@apcointl.org www.apcointl.org

George Rice Jr, Executive Director
Tim Ryan, Deputy Executive Director/CFO

APCO International is the world's oldest and largest nonprofit professional organization dedicated to the enhancement of public safety communications.

16000 Members Founded: 1935

19906 Association of State Floodplain Managers
2809 Fish Hatchery Road
Madison, WI 53713
608-274-0123
FAX: 608-274-0696
asfpm@floods.org www.floods.org

Chad Berginnis, Chair
Pam Rogue, Vice Chair
Larry Larson, Executive Director
Bill Nechamen, Treasurer
Rhonda Montgomery, Secretary

It is the mission of the Association to mitigate the losses, costs and human suffering caused by flooding and to promote wise use of the natural and beneficial functions of floodplains.
6500 Members Founded: 1977

19907 Automatic Fire Alarm Association
PO Box 951807
Lake Mary, FL 32795-1807
407-833-9133
FAX: 407-833-9131
fire-alarm@afaa.org www.afaa.org

Thomas P Hammerberg, President/Executive Director
Michael B Baker, Training Director
Jeanne Hammerberg, Office Manager

Striving to be the foremost industry advocate organization dedicated to improving the quality, reliability and value of fire and life safety systems.
Founded: 1953

19908 Aviation Safety Institute
PO Box 690
Worthington, OH 43085
614-793-1619
110364.3550@compuserve.com

Edward H Wachs, President/Chair
Thomas Clevinger, VP/Treasurer

An aviation safety research center established in 1973. Studying the most overlooked, most important area of aviation safety.
Founded: 1973

19909 Board of Certified Safety Professionals
208 Burwash Avenue
Savoy, IL 61874-9571
217-359-9263
FAX: 217-359-0055
bcsp@bcsp.org www.bcsp.org

Roger Brauer Ph.D, Executive Director
Steven Schoolcraft, Examination Director
Mary Hosier, Operations Manager

Operating solely as a peer certification board with the purpose of certifying practitioners in the safety profession.
Founded: 1969

19910 Business Disaster Preparedness Council
Lee County Emergency Management
PO Box 398
Ft. Meyers, FL 33902-398
239-399-9779
FAX: 941-477-3636
board@leegov.com

Bob Lee, Owner

Public and private partnership whose goal it is to assist business in planning for and recovering from natural disasters and emergencies.
Founded: 1998

19911 Campus Safety Health & Environmental Management Association
National Safety Council
1121 Spring Lake Drive
Itasca, IL 60143
630-752-2213
FAX: 630-285-1315
lewissu@nsc.org www.cshema.org

Susan Lewis, Division Manager

CSHEMA leads by listening to its members, organizing their efforts,developing the leadership that researches communities effectively, and striving for excellence in everything its does.
936 Members Founded: 1954

19912 Canada Safety Council
1020 Thomas Spratt Place
Ottawa, Ontario
Canada, K1G 5L5
613-739-1535
FAX: 613-739-1566
canadasafetycouncil@safety-council.org
www.safety-council.org

Emile Therien, President
Ethel Archard, Manager Marketing
Judy Lavergne, Secretary
Peter Slivar, Manager Administrative Services
Jack Smith, General Manager Living Safety OH&S

The Canada Safety Counil is a national, non-government, charitable organization dedicated to safety. Mission is to lead in the national effort to reduce preventable deaths, injuries and economic loss in public and private places throughout Canada.
Founded: 1968

19913 Canadian Alarm & Security Association
610 Alden Road
Suite 100
Markham, L3R 9Z1, ON
905-513-0622
FAX: 905-513-0624 800-538-9919
staff@canasa.org www.canasa.org

Tracy Cannata, Executive Director
Roxanna Ali, Marketing/Communications Manager
Lynne Hewitson, Membership Services Manager
Patty Chen, Finance/Accounting Manager

A national non-profit organization dedicated to promoting the interests of its members and the safety and security of all Canadians.
Founded: 1977

19914 Center to Protect Workers' Rights
8484 Georgia Avenue
Suite 1000
Silver Spring, MD 20910
301-578-8500
FAX: 301-578-8572
cpwrwebsite@cpwr.com
www.cpwr.com

Pete Stafford, Executive Director
Jane Seegal, Director Communications Department
Michael McCann, Director Safety

CPWR is committed to preventing illness, injury, and death in the construction industry through its safety and health research.
Founded: 1990

19915 Central Station Alarm Association
440 Maple Avenue E
Suite 201
Vienna, VA 22180
703-242-4670
FAX: 703-242-4675
communications@csaaul.org
www.csaaul.org

John A Murphy, President
Stephen P Doyle, Executive VP
Celia Besore, Marketing/Communications Director

The Central Station Alarm Association (CSAA) is a trade association representing providers, users, bureaus, and other agencies.
Founded: 1950

19916 Commercial Vehicle Safety Alliance
1101 17th Street NW
Suite 803
Washington, DC 20036
202-775-1623
FAX: 202-775-1624
cvsahq@cvsa.org www.cvsa.org

Stephen F Campbell, Executive Director
Paul M Bomgardner, Administration Director

The Commercial Vehicle Safety Alliance (CVSA) is a nonprofit organization, established to promote an environment free of commercial vehicle accidents and incidents. Our mission is to promote commercial motor vehicle safty and security by providing leadership to enforcement, industry and policy makers.
540 Members Founded: 1980

19917 Computer Security Institute
600 Harrison Street
San Francisco, CA 94107
415-947-6320
FAX: 415-947-6023
csi@cmp.com www.gocsi.com

Jody Nurre, Sales Director
Mary Griffin, Membership Director

Computer Security Institute serves the needs of information security professionals through membership, educational events, security surveys and awareness tools.
Founded: 1974

19918 Consumer Data Industry Association
1090 Vermont Avenue NW
Suite 200
Washington, DC 20005-4905

FAX: 202-371-0134
bbyrnes@cdiaonline.org
www.cdiaonline.org

Stuart Pratt, President/CEO
Betty Byrnes, Member Services

The Consumer Data Industry Association is an international trade association, founded in 1906, that represents consumer information companies that provide fraud prevention and risk management products, credit and mortgage reports, tenant and employment screening services, check fraud and verification services, and collection services.
395 Members Founded: 1906

19919 Conveyor Equipment Manufacturers Association (CEMA)
6724 Lone Oak Boulevard
Naples, FL 34109-6834
239-514-3441
FAX: 239-514-3470
cema@cemanet.org www.cemanet.org

Tom Easterhouse, President
Fred Thimmel, VP
Robert Reinfried, Executive Director

Involved in writing industry standards, CEMA's purpose is to promote among its members and the industry standardization of design manufacture and application on a voluntary basis and in such manner as will not impede development of conveying machinery and component parts or lessen competition. A member of the Machinery and Allied Products Institute.
99 Members Founded: 1933

19920 Council of International Investigators
2150 N 107th Street
Suite 205
Seattle, WA 98133-9009
206-361-8869
FAX: 206-367-8777 888-759-8884
office@cii2.org www.cii2.org

Alan Marr, Executive Regional Director
Bertram S Falbaum, President

The Council of International Investigators was formed to encourage a greater association among owners and operators of investigation agencies while developing mutual trust and respect.
Founded: 1955

19921 Council on Certification of Health, Environmental & Technologists
208 Burwash Avenue
Savoy, IL 61874-9571
217-359-2686
FAX: 217-359-0055
cchest@cchest.org www.cchest.org

Roger L Brauer Phd, Executive Director
Adrian Hectog, President
Adrian Hertog, VP
Linda Sennett, Secretary/Treasurer

CCHEST is recognized as the leader in high-quality, third-party accredited health, safety, and environmental credentialing for technologists, technicians, supervisors, and workers.
3000 Members Founded: 1986

19922 Crime Prevention Coalition of America
1000 Connecticut Avenue NW
13th Floor
Washington, DC 20036
202-466-6272
FAX: 202-296-1356
webmaster@ncpc.org www.ncpc.org

Alfonso Lenhardt, President

Helps balance the definition of crime prevention as it related to property protection, surveillance, opportunity reduction, civic health, well-being, and quality-of-life approaches. It launched comprehensive neighborhood crime prevention strategies in crime-designated neighborhoods, including Community Responses to Drug Abuse, technical assistance to Weed & Seed communities, and Methamphetamine Summits across the country.
136+ Members Founded: 1977

19923 Crime Stoppers International
PO Box 614
Arlington, TX 76004-0614
817-451-9229
FAX: 817-446-1576 800-850-7574
mary@bcsp.org www.c-s-i.org

Mary Hosier, Operations Manager

An umbrella organization operated by a volunteer board of directors from Crime Stoppers programs worldwide that establishes guidelines to assure consistency. The aim of Crime Stoppers International is to establish local programs in countries around the world.

19924 Dangerous Goods Advisory Council
1100 H Street NW
Suite 740
Washington, DC 20005
202-289-4550
FAX: 202-289-4074
info@dgac.org www.dgac.org

Mike Morrissette, President
Frits Wybenga, Technical Director
Lisa Keyser, Communications Specialist

DGAC fulfills its mission by providing education, technical assistance and information to the private and public sectors. Members incude shippers in the chemical, petroleum, and pharmaceutical industries, manufacturers, carriers, container manufacturers and reconditioners, emergency/waste clean-up companies, trade associations, and others involved in the transport of dangerous goods.
Founded: 1978

19925 Electrical Safety Foundation International
1300 North 17th St.
Suite 1752
Rosslyn, VA 22209
703-841-3229
FAX: 703-841-3329
info@esfi.org
www.electrical-safety.org

Brett C Brenner, Company Contact

ESFI's mission is to advocate and improve electrical safety at work. ESFI is the premier electrical safety advocacy organization whose messages and programs contribute to the reduction of electrically related deaths, injuries and property loss.
Founded: 1994

19926 Environmental Information Association
6935 Wisconsin Avenue
Suite 306
Chevy Chase, MD 20814-6112
301-961-4999
FAX: 301-961-3094 888-343-4342
info@eia-usa.org www.eia-usa.org

Brent Kynoch, Managing Director
Kelly Rutt, Development/Communications Manager
B J Fungaroli, President

Nonprofit organization dedicated to providing environmental information to individuals, members and industry. Disseminates information on the abatement of asbestos and lead-based paint, indoor air quality, safety and health issues, analytical issues and environmental site assessments.

19927 False Alarm Reduction Association
10024 Vanderbilt Circle
Unit 4
Rockville, MD 20850
301-519-9237
FAX: 301-519-9508 www.faraonline.org

Brad Shipp, Executive Director

Primarily made up of persons employed by government and public safety agencies in charge of, or working in, False Alarm Reduction Units. The goal is to assist these individuals in reducing false alarms for their jurisdiction.
Founded: 1997

19928 Federal Law Enforcement Officers Association
PO Box 326
Lewisberry, PA 17339
717-938-2300
FAX: 717-932-2262
fleoa@fleoa.org www.fleoa.org

Art Gordon, National President
Jon Adler, National Executive VP

Founded by a group of concerned federal agents from Customs, the IRS, FBI and INS, its goal is to assure that legal assistance and representation are a phone call away.
24000 Members Founded: 1977

19929 Financial & Security Products Association (FSPA)
Plaza Ladera
5300 Sequoia Road NW, Suite 205
Albuquerque, NM 87120
505-839-7958
FAX: 505-839-0017 800-843-6082
info@fspal.com www.fspal.comm

John Vrabec, Executive Director
Elizabeth Vrabec, General Manager

Promotes growth of the security equipment industry. Professional business association representing companies involved in the manufacturing, selling, installing and servicing products sold primarily to financial institutions.
Founded: 1973

19930 Fire Apparatus Manufacturers' Association (FAMA)
PO Box 397
Lynnfield, MA 01940-0397
781-334-2911
FAX: 781-334-2911
info@fama.org www.fama.org

Tim Dean, President
Phil Turner, VP

A trade association organized in 1946. Members of FAMA are committed to enhancing the quality of the fire apparatus industry and emergency service community through the manufacture and sale of safe, efficient fire apparatus and equipment.
106 Members Founded: 1946

19931 Fire Equipment Manufacturers' Association
1300 Sumner Avenue
Cleveland, OH 44115-2851
216-241-7333
FAX: 216-241-0105
fema@taol.com
www.yourfirstdefense.com

John H Addington, Executive Director

The premier fire equipment manufacturers' association representing leading brands, and spanning dozens of products categories, related to fire protection.
27 Members Founded: 1925

19932 Fire Suppression Systems Association
5024 R Campbell Boulevard
Baltimore, MD 21236
410-931-8100
FAX: 410-931-8111
fssa@clemonsmgmt.com
www.fssa.net

Crista LeGrand, Executive Director
Cal Clemons, Managing Director
Brenda Martin, Association Coordinator

An organization of manufacturers, suppliers, and design-installers, dedicated to providing a higher level of fire protection. Members are specialists in protecting high value special hazardareas from fire.

Founded: 1982

19933 Flight Safety Foundation
601 Madison Street
Suite 300
Alexandria, VA 22314
703-739-6700
FAX: 703-739-6708
www.flightsafety.org

Stuart Matthews, President/CEO
Linda Crowley Horger, Support Services Manager
Robert H Vandel, Executive VP

Flight Safety Foundation is an independent, nonprofit, international organization engaged in research, auditing, education, advocacy and publishing to improve aviation safety. The Foundation's mission is to pursue the continuous improvement of global aviation safety and the prevention of accidents.

Founded: 1947

19934 Garrett Metal Detectors
1881 W State Street
Garland, TX 75042-6797
972-494-6151
FAX: 972-494-1881 800-234-6151
sales@garrett.com www.garrett.com

Jim Dobrei, Director of Sales
Vaughn Garrett, Director Marketing/Communications

Global leader of walk-through, hand-held and ground search metal detection products and training for security and law enforcement.

4 Members Founded: 1964

19935 Homeland Security Industries Association
666 11th Street NW
Suite 315
Washington, DC 20001
202-386-6471
FAX: 202-331-8191
info@hsianet.org www.hsianet.org

Brenda Boone, Owner

Nonprofit group providing a mechanism for government and the private sector to coordinate on a wide range of homeland security issues. Monitors legislation, regulations and hearings, provides training, and develops position papers reflecting industry concerns.

200+ Members Founded: 2002

19936 Industrial Health Foundation
2700 Prosperity Ave
Suite 250
Fairfax, VA 22031
412-363-6600
FAX: 412-363-6605 877-711-4443
admin@ihfincorp.com www.ihf.org
Industrial Health Foundation is one of the largest organizations serving the needs of occupational and environmental health professionals practicing industrial hygiene in industry, government, labor, academic institutions, and independent organizations.

Founded: 1935

19937 Institute for Health & Productivity

4435 Waterfront Drive
Suite 101
Glen Allen, VA 23060
804-527-1905
FAX: 804-747-5316
sean@ihpm.org www.ihpm.org

Sean Sullivan, President/CEO
W C Williams III, Senior VP
Joseph Leutzinger, President
Sloane Reed, Director Member Relations
Deborah Love, Director Publications

Nonprofit organization making employee health an investment in corporate success through enhanced workplace performance.

Founded: 1997

19938 Institute for Health & Productivity Manage ment
4435 Waterfront Drive
Suite 101
Glen Allen, VA 23060
804-747-9698
FAX: 804-747-5316
sean@ihpm.org www.ihpm.org

Sean Sullivan, President/CEO
WC Williams III, MD, Senior VP
Crystal Smith, VP Business Relations

Nonprofit organization making employee health an investment in corporate success through enhanced workplace performance.

Founded: 1997

19939 Insurance Institute for Highway Safety
1005 N Glebe Road
Suite 800
Arlington, VA 22201
703-247-1500
FAX: 703-247-1588
rrader@iihs.org www.iihs.org

Mike Menz, President
Russ Rader, Media Relations Director

The Insurance Institute for Highway Safety is a nonprofit research and communications organization funded by auto insurers.

19940 International Assn. of Professional Protec
5255 Stevens Creek Boulevard
Suite 308
Santa Clara, CA 95051
888-761-6803
FAX: 888-671-6803 888-671-6803
membership@iapps.org
www.iapps.org

Founded: 1990

19941 International Association for Computer Systems
6 Swarthmore Lane
Dix Hills, NY 11746
631-499-1616
FAX: 631-462-9178
iacssjalex@aol.com www.iacss.com

Robert J Wilk, President

Promotes the security of computer information systems. Certifies individuals as Computer Systems Security Professionals.

Founded: 1981

19942 International Association for Counterterro rism & Security Professionals
PO Box 10265
Arlington, VA 22210
201-461-5422

acsp@aol.com www.iacsp.com

Steven Fustero, Executive Director

Our goals include creating a center of information and educational services for those concerned about the challenges now facing all free societies, and promoting professional ethics in the counter terrorism field.

Founded: 1992

19943 International Association for Healthcare Security and Safety
PO Box 5038
Glendale Heights, IL 60139
888-353-0990
FAX: 630-871-9938 888-353-0990
info@iahss.org www.iahss.org

Jim Balija, Director
Thomas A Smith, President

Nonprofit professional organization of healthcare security and safety executives around the world. Works to improve and professionalize security and safety in healthcare facilities through the exchange of information and experiences among members. A magazine, newsletter and an annual meeting are benefits of membership.

1700 Members Founded: 1968 1700 names $200 per M.

19944 International Association for Identificati on
2535 Pilot Knob Road
Suite 117
Mendota Heights, MN 55120-1120
651-681-8566
FAX: 651-381-8443 www.theiai.org

Diana Castro, President
Joseph Polski, COO

This is a forum where forensic specialists worldwide can interact as a whole. The main focus of any forensic organization is training and research to ensure all specialists maintain the highest levels of integrity and professionalism in order to meet the constant challenges to our individual disciplines.

19945 International Association of Arson Investigators
12770 Boenker Road
Bridgeton, MO 63044
314-739-4224
FAX: 314-739-4219
awhitson@firearson.com
www.firearson.com

James Whitaker, Executive Director
Ashley Whitson, Membership Secretary/Receptionist

Fosters, supports and promotes fire and arson awareness through education and training.

19946 International Association of Black Professional Firefighters
1020 N Taylor Avenue
St. Louis, MO 63113
786-229-6914
FAX: 305-249-5230
iabpff@email.msn.com
www.iabpff.org

John Brewington, President

Promotes interracial progress throughout the fire service and encourages African American firefighters to seek elevated ranks. Offers an annual convention, education courses an an online resource page.
Founded: 1970

19947 International Association of Bomb Technicians and Investigators
PO Box 160
Goldvein, VA 22720-0160
540-752-4533
FAX: 540-752-2796
admin@iabti.org www.iabti.org

Ralph Way, Executive Director

The IABTI is an independent, non-profit, professional association formed for countering the criminal use of explosives. This is accomplished through the exchange of training, expertise and information among personnel employed in the fields of law enforcement, emergency services, the military, forensic science and other related fields.
Founded: 1973

19948 International Association of Campus Law Enforcement Administrators
342 N Main Street
West Hartford, CT 06117-2507
860-586-7517
FAX: 860-586-7550
info@iaclea.org www.iaclea.org

Peter J Berry, Chief Staff Officer
Lynn Sedlak, Membership/Administration Director

Advances public safety for educational institutions by providing educational resources, advocacy and professional development.
Founded: 1958

19949 International Association of Chiefs of Police
515 N Washington Street
Alexandria, VA 22314
703-836-6767
FAX: 703-836-4543 800-843-4227
information@theiacp.org
www.theiacp.org

Mary Ann Viverette, President
Daniel N Rosenblatt, Executive Director

The association's goals are to advance the science and art of police services; to develop and disseminate improved administrative. technical and opreration practices and promote their use in police work; to foster police cooperation and the exchange of information and experience among police administrators throughout the world; to bring about recruitment and training in the police profession of qualified person.
15000 Members Founded: 1893

19950 International Association of Crime Analysts
9218 Metcalf
PMB 364
Overland Park, KS 66212
919-940-3883

nfritz@du.edu www.iaca.net

Noah Fritz, Director
Christopher Bruce, VP Administration

The International Association of Crime Analysts was formed in 1990 to help crime analysts around the world improve their skills and make valuable contacts, to help law enforcement agencies make the best use of crime analysis, and to advocate for standards of performance and technique within the profession itself. This is accomplished through training, networking, and publications.
Founded: 1990

19951 International Association of Dive Rescue Specialists
201 N Link Lane
Fort Collins, CO 80524-2712
970-482-1562
FAX: 970-482-0896 800-423-7791
info@iadrs.org www.iadrs.org

Blades Robinson, Executive Director
Susan Watson, Operations Director

IADRS is dedicated to helping water rescue professionals stay informed about advances in training, equipment, and life saving techniques.
Founded: 1977

19952 International Association of Fire Chiefs
4025 Fair Ridge Drive
Suite 300
Fairfax, VA 22033-2868
703-273-0911
FAX: 703-273-9363
jashley@iafc.org www.iafc.org

Chief Bill Killen, President
Jennifer Ashley, Communications Director

Provides leadership to career and volunteer chief, chief fire officers and managers of emergency service organization throughout the inernational community through vision, information, education, services and representation to enhance their professionalsim and capabilities.
12000 Members

19953 International Association of Firefighters
1750 New York Avenue NW
Washington, DC 20006
202-737-8484
FAX: 202-737-8418
gburke@iaff.org www.iaff.org

Harold Schaitberger, President
George Burke, Spokesperson

Represents city and county firefighters and state and federal workers such as forestry firefighters and emergency medical workers at certain industrial facilities. Addressed are health and safety, labor relations, training, hazardous materials and burn injuries and education.
240k Members

19954 International Association of Home Safety
PO Box 2044
Erie, PA 16512-2044

Members include locksmiths, security consultants, alarm installers and others who promote the security of the residential market. Benefits of membership include special educational materials, certification programs, use of IAHSSP member logo in phone book listings, on business cards and in advertisements; special acess to restricted information areas on the Internet, and discounts offered on products offered by the use of IAHSSP.

19955 International Association of Personal
PO Box 266
Arlington Heights, IL 60006-266
847-870-8007
FAX: 847-870-8990
proproserv@aol.com www.iappa.org

Patrick Spoerry, Executive Director

Professional, nonprofit membership body open to military and civilian law enforcement personnel and people from the public and private sector who are engaged in the protection of royalty, presidential, state and diplomatic officials, government, military and corporate executives, personalities from the entertainment world and those involved in witness and prisoner protection.
Founded: 1989

19956 International Association of Professional Security Consultants
525 SW 5th Street
Suite A
Des Moines, IA 50309-4501
515-282-8192
FAX: 515-282-9117
iapsc@iapsc.org www.iapsc.org

Michael Perelman, President
Elliot Boxerbaum, VP

The International Association of Professional Security Consultants (IAPSC) is a widely recognized consulting association in the security industry. Its rigid membership requirements ensure that potential clients may select from the most elite group of professional, ethical and competent security consultants available to them.
Founded: 1984

19957 International Biometric Industry Associati on
1666 K Street, NW
Washington, DC 20006
202-293-8133
FAX: 202-872-1431
ibia@ibia.org www.ibia.org

Rebecca Dornbush, Information Officer
John Sedlars, Manager

IBIA provides strong and growing value to its members, expanding business opportunities for the industry, advocating government support for the useof biometrics in leading commercial and public-sector applications, and reporting on key issues of strategic importance to the membership.
Founded: 1998

19958 International Cargo Security Council
1255 23rd Street, NW
Suite 200
Washington, DC 20037-2209
202-452-1200
FAX: 202-833-3636
icsc@cargosecurity.com
www.cargosecurity.com

Joe M Baker Jr, Executive Director
Scott H Smith, Chairman

The International Cargo Security Council is an association of professionals active in intermodal transportation and supply chain security.
1200 Members

19959 International Centre for the Prevention of Crime
465 St-Jean Street
Suite 803
Montreal, QU H2Y-2R6
514-288-6731
FAX: 514-288-8763
cipc@crime-prevention-intl.org
www.crime-prevention-intl.org/english
Myriam Ezratty, Chair
Terrance Hunsley, Director General
The ICPC is an international forum for national government local authorities, public agencies, specialized institutions, and non-government organisations of exchange experience, consider emerging knowledge, and improve policies and programs in crime prevention and community safety. ICPC staff monitors developments, provides direct assistance to members, and contributes to public knowledge and understanding in the field.

19960 International Consumer Product Health & Sa fety Organization
PO Box 1785
Germantown, MD 20875-1785
301-528-0310
FAX: 301-601-3543
icphso@aol.com www.icphso.org
ICPHSO holds a unique position in its ability to attract the interest of a broad range of health and safety professionals and interested consumers, world-wide.
Founded: 1993

19961 International Fire Service Training Associ
930 N Willis
Stillwater, OK 74078
405-744-5723
FAX: 405-744-8204
customer.service@osufpp.org
www.ifsta.org
Michael Moore, Marketing
Nonprofit organization associated with Fire Protection Publications, a department of the College of Engineering, Architecture and Technology at Oklahoma State University.
Founded: 1934

19962 International Foundation for Protection Officers
PO Box 771329
Naples, FL 34107-1329
239-430-0534
FAX: 239-430-0533
sandi@ifpo.com www.ifpo.org
Sandi J Davies, Executive Director
Richard L Daniels, Secretary/Treasurer
Nonprofit organization for the purpose of facilitating the training and certification needs of protection officers and security supervisors from both the commercial and proprietary sectors.
Founded: 1988

19963 International High Technology Crime Invest igation Association
4021 Woodcreek Oaks Boulevard
Suite 156
Roseville, CA 95747
916-408-1751
FAX: 916-408-7543 www.htcia.org
Michael Menz, Public Relations Director
Carol Hutchings, Executive Secretary
Designed to encourage, promote, aid and effect the voluntary interchange of data, information, experience, ideas and knowledge about methods, processes, and techniques relating to investigations and security in advanced technologies.

19964 International Hologram Association
2149 West Cascade
Suite 106A
Hood River, OR 97031
514-490-7920
FAX: 541-386-1564
info@ihma.org www.ihma.org
Wilfried Schipper, Chairman
More than 60 of the worlds leading hologram manufacturers are members. Dedicated to promoting the interests of those quality hologram manufacturers worldwide and to helping our customers to achieve their security, packaging graphic and other objectives through the effective use of holography.
Founded: 1993

19965 International Locksmiths Association
PO Box 4188
Trenton, NJ 08610

866-745-5625
keys150@juno.com
www.ilanational.org
Bob Gress, Chairman
Don O'Shall, Co-Chairman
John Truempy, Co-Chairman
Thomas Negron, President
Members are locksmiths, carpenters and building engineers who are employed by colleges, universities, hospitals, companies and government facilities. Dedicated to the education of members and the benefit of our institutions.

19966 International Municipal Signal Association
165 E Union Street
PO Box 539
Newark, NY 14513-0539
315-331-2182
FAX: 315-331-8205 800-723-4672
info@imsasafety.org
www.imsasafety.org
Marilyn Lawrence, Executive Director/Publisher
Basic purpose of the organization is to keep its members and others in the profession, up-to-date on proper procedures of construction and maintenance of signal systems and informed on new products and equipment developments.
10000 Members Founded: 1896

19967 International Photoluminescent Safety
5050 Industrial Road
Farmingdale, NJ 07727
732-751-0100
FAX: 732-751-0508
usmsa@usmsa.org www.ipspc.org
Tom Thompson, Executive Director
A leader in the marine safety and implementation of the highest possible performance, manufacturing maintenance, service and training standards, for all lifesaving, survival and emergency rescue equipment.
131 Members Founded: 1986

19968 International Process Servers Association
217 Monroe Avenue #206
Suite 607
Rochester, NY 14618
585-232-8590
FAX: 585-546-3463
richard@processservers.com
www.processservers.com
Unifies process servers in the United States and throughout the world, as the single greatest resource for all process servers and private investigators.

19969 International Safety Equipment Association
1901 N Moore Street
Arlington, VA 22209
703-525-1695
FAX: 703-528-2148
info@safetyequipment.org
www.safetyequipment.org
Daniel K Shipp, President
Daniel I Glucksman, Public Affairs Director
Trade association in the US for companies that manufacture safety equipment. Member companies are world leaders in the design and manufacture of clothing and equipment used in factories, construction sites, hospitals and clinics, farms, schools, laboratories, and in the home — anywhere people are doing work. Our common goal is to protect the health and safety of people exposed to hazardous and potentially harmful environments.
Founded: 1933

19970 International Security Management Association
PO Box 623
Buffalo, IA 52728-0623
563-381-4008
FAX: 800-568-1894 800-368-1894
ISMA3@aol.com www.ismanet.com
Ken Wheatley, President
Susan W Pohlmann, Consulting Business Manager
David Saenz, Second VP
ISMA's mission is to provide and support an international forum of selected security executives whose combined expertise wil be utilized in a synergistic manner in developing, assimilating, sharing knowledge within security disciplines for the ultimate purpose of enhancing professional and business standards.
400 Members Founded: 1983

19971 International of Personal Protection Agent s
PO Box 266
Arlington Heights, IL 60006-0266
847-870-8007
FAX: 847-870-8990
proproserv@aol.com www.iappa.org
Patrick Spoerry, Executive Director
Professional, nonprofit membership body open to military and civilian law enforcement personnel and people from the public and private sector who are engaged in the protection of royalty, presidential, state and diplomatic officials, government, military and corporate executives, personalities from the entertainment world and those involved in witness and prisoner protection.

19972 Investigators of America
O Box 626
West Warwick, RI 2893

FAX: 401-615-0968 877-393-7792
mrdetectiveri1@wmconnect.com
www.investigatorsofamerica.com

Kelly Fromm, Director
David Zeldin, Director
Russell L Koogler, Director
Deborah Rose, Director

Investigators of America is a rapidly growing association comprised of elite private investigators, insurance adjusters, and expert witnesses across the United States with affiliates in other countries.

19973 Laser Institute of America
13501 Ingenuity Drive
Suite 128
Orlando, FL 32826
407-380-1553
FAX: 407-380-5588
lia@laserinstitute.org
www.laserinstitute.org

Peter Baker, Executive Director

The Laser Institute of America is the professional membership society dedicated to fostering lasers, laser applications and safety worldwide. Its mission is to foster lasers, laser applications, and laser safety worldwide. Serving the industrial, medical, research and government communities, LIA offers technical information and networking opportunities to laser users from around the globe.
1200 Members Founded: 1968

19974 Mine Safety and Health Administration
1100 Wilson Boulevard
21st Floor
Arlington, VA 22209-3939
202-693-9400
FAX: 202-693-9401 800-746-1553
webmaster@msha.gov www.msha.gov

Elaine L Chao, Secretary of Labor
Ruth D Knouse, Executive Secretariat Director
Karen Czarnecki, Director
David Dye, Executive Director
Jacqueline Halbig, Deputy Director

Mission is to enforce compliance with mandatory safety and health standards as a means to eliminate fatal accidents, reduce the frequency and severity of nonfatal accidents, minimnize health hazards, and to promote improved safety and health conditions in national mines.

19975 National Alarm Association of America
PO Box 3409
Dayton, OH 45401
937-461-2208
FAX: 937-461-4759 800-283-6285
info@naaa.org www.naaa.org

Gene Riddlebaugh, President
Grant Angell, Senior VP Associate Affairs

Mission is to advance the welfare of members through the free exchange, among members of ideas and the dissemination of information concerning trade practices, business conditions, technical developments, within the industry, and any related subject of concern to the security industry.
Founded: 1984

19976 National Association of Elevator Safety
6957 Littlerock Road SW
Suite A
Tirnwater, WA 98512
360-292-4968
FAX: 360-292-4973
info@naesai.org www.naesai.org

Richard A Atkinson, Executive Director
Raymond D Troiana, President
Harwood Woody Wright, VP
Marie McDonald, Treasurer
James D Lawrence, Secretary

Fosters and assists the promulgation of a standard safety code and interpretation thereof, for elevators and related equipment, and to engage in activities and establish programs to exchange and impart information of common interest to the membership and to develop the professional reputation of elevator safety authorities.
1300 Members Founded: 1966

19977 National Association of Fire Equipment Distributors
104 S Michigan Avenue
Suite 300
Chicago, IL 60603
312-263-8100
FAX: 312-263-8111
dharris@nafed.org www.nafed.org

Larry Angle, President
Danny Harris, Operations Executive Director

Mission is to improve the economic environment, business performance, and technical competence in the fire protection industry.
Founded: 1963

19978 National Association of Investigators &
2308 Donna Hill Court
Nashville, TN 37214
615-872-5401
www.npia.com

Provides educational material and equipment for the investigation industry.

19979 National Association of Legal Investigator s
908 21st Street
Sacramento, CA 95814-3118
303-757-3660
FAX: 303-825-2374
earmistead@coloradoinvestigators.com
www.nalionline.org

Tom Baird, National Director
Ellis Armistead, Assistant National Director

Membership in NAL is open to all professional legal investigators who are actively engaged in negligence investigations for plaintiff and/or criminal defense, and who are employed by investigative firms, law firms or public defender agencies.

19980 National Burglar & Fire Alarm Association
2300 Valley View Lane
Suite 230
Irving, TX 75062
214-260-5970
FAX: 214-260-5979 888-447-1689
MerlinG@alarm.org www.alarm.org

Merlin Guilbeau, Executive Director
Georgia Calaway, Communications/PR Director

A professional trade association with the purpose of representing, promoting and enhancing the growth and professional development of the electronic life safety, security, and integrated systems industry.
Founded: 1948

19981 National Classification Management Society
994 Old Eagle School Road
Suite 1019
Wayne, PA 19087-1866
610-971-4856
FAX: 610-971-4859
info@classmgmt.com
www.classmgmt.com

Sharon Tannahill, Executive Director

Advancing the practice of classification management in the disiplines of industrial security, information security, government designated unclassified information, and intellectual property, and to foster the highest qualities of security professionalism among its members.
1,300 Members Founded: 1964

19982 National Council of Investigation & Security
7501 Sparrows Point Boulevard
Baltimore, MD 21219-1927

FAX: 410-388-9746 800-445-8408
NCISS@verizon.net www.nciss.com

Carolyn Ward, Executive Director
Roy Bucklin, President

A cooperative of those companies and associations responsible for providing private security and investigation services to the legal profession, business community, government and the public.

19983 National Crime Justice Association
720 7th Street NW
3rd Floor
Washington, DC 20001
202-628-8550
FAX: 202-628-0080
info@ncja.org www.ncja.org

Cabell Cropper, Executive Director
Kay Chopard-Cohen, Deputy Executive Director

Promotes the development of justice systems in states, tribal nations, and units of local government that enhance public safety, and prevents and reduces the harmful effects of criminal and delinquent behavior on victims, individuals and communitie.

19984 National Defense Industrial Association
2111 Wilson Boulevard
Suite 400
Arlington, VA 22201
703-522-1820
FAX: 703-522-1885
info@ndia.org www.ndia.org

Lawrence Farrell Jr, President

A leading defense idustry association whose mission is to promote national security through a variety of means, including education, training and advocacy.
28100 Members Founded: 1997

19985 National Electrical Manufacturers
1300 North 17th Street
Suite 1752
Rosslyn, VA 22209
703-841-3200
FAX: 703-841-5900
webmaster@nema.org www.nema.org

Evan Gaddis, President
Timothy H Powers, Chairman

NEMA's mission is to promote the competitiveness of its member companies by providing quality services that will impact positively on standrds, government regulation and market economics.
400 Members Founded: 1926

19986 National Emergency Equipment Dealers Association
8521 Frost Way
Annandale, VA 22003
703-280-4622
FAX: 703-280-0942
KentonPl@aol.com www.needa.org

Kenton Pattie, Executive Director

Serves dealers who sell and service fire, rescue, and emergency rescue systems equipment and apparatus. Preserves and strengthens the free market system for dealers through advocacy, information and training. Assists dealers profitably deliver high quality products and support to the nation's emergency services.

19987 National Fire Protection Association
1 Batterymarch Park
Quincy, MA 02169-7471
617-770-3000
FAX: 617-770-0700
public_affairs@nfpa.org
www.nfpa.org

James Shannon, President/CEO

Mission is to reduce the world wide burden of fire and other hazards on the quality of life by providing and advocating consesus codes and standrds, research, training, and education. NFPA membership totals more than 79,000 individuals from around the world and more than 80 national trade and professional organization.
79000 Members Founded: 1896

19988 National Fire Sprinkler Association
PO Box 1000
Patterson, NY 12563
845-878-4200
FAX: 845-878-4215
info@nfsa.org www.nfsa.org

John A Viniello, President
Buddy Dewar, Regional Operations Director

The goal is to create a market for the widespread acceptance of competently installed automatic fire sprinkler systems in new and existing construction. Members are makers and installers of automatic fire sprinklers and related equipment.
Founded: 1905

19989 National Floor Safety Institute (NFSI)
PO Box 92607
Southlake, TX 76092
817-749-1700
FAX: 817-749-1702
info@nfsi.org www.nfsi.org

Laura Cooper, Manager, Membership Relations

Mission is to aid in the prevention of slip-and-fall accidents through education, training and recearch. The NFSI is led by a fifteen-member Board of Directors representing product manufacturers, insurance underwriters, trade associations, and independent consultants.
Founded: 1997

19990 National Institute for Occupational Safety & Health
1600 Cliton Road
Atlantaton, GA 30333
404-639-3311
FAX: 513-533-8573 800-311-3435
eidtechinfo@cdc.gov
www.cdc.gov/niosh/homepage.html

Linda Rosenstock, Executive Director
Hubert H Humphrey, Chief of Staff
Max Lum EdD, Assoc Director Health Commun.
John Howard MD, Director

To promote health and quality of life by preventing and controlling disease, injury, and disability.

19991 National Institute of Standards and Techno logy (NIST)
100 Bureau Drive
Stop 1070
Gaithersburg, MD 20899
301-975-6478

inquiries@nist.gov www.nist.gov

William A Jeffrey, Director
Hratch Semerjian, Deputy Director
Matthew Heyman, Chief of Staff
Thomas Klausing, Chief Financial Officer
Mary D Croggio, Manager

Promotes US innovation and industrial competitiveness by advancing measurement science, standards, and technology in ways that enhance economic security and improve quality of life. It's four cooperative programs are NIST Laboratories, Baldrige National Quality Program, Manufacturing Extension Partnership, and Advanced Technology Program.
Founded: 1901

19992 National Safety Council
1121 Spring Lake Drive
Itasca, IL 60143-3201
630-285-1121
FAX: 630-285-1315
customerservice@nsc.org
www.nsc.org

Alan C McMillan, President/CEO
Edward D Bullard, Chairman

Nonprofit, nongovernmental, international public service organization dedicated to protecting life and promoting health.
48000 Members Founded: 1913

19993 National Safety Management Society
PO Box 4460
Walnut Creek, CA 94596-0460

800-321-2910
nsmsinc@yahoo.com www.nsms.us

Roosevelt Smith, President
John H Bridges III, Director

Mission is to support managers and their employees in their responsibility to assure the safety of all employees.
Founded: 1966

19994 National Society of Professional Insurance Investigators
PO Box 88
Delaware, OH 43015-0088

FAX: 740-369-7155 888-677-4498
nspii@columbus.rr.com
www.nspii.com

Jack Morgan, President
Matthew J Smith, First VP
John R Yust, Secretary/Membership Chairman

A professional society for research and education.
590 Members Founded: 1983

19995 National Tooling & Machining Association
9300 Livingston Road
Fort Washington, MD 20744
301-486-6200
FAX: 301-248-7104 800-248-6862
dick@ntma.org www.ntma.org

Thomas Garcia, Business Development Director
Robert Akers, COO

Supports its members through education, training and resources.
2700 Members Founded: 1943

19996 National Youth Gang Center
PO Box 12729
Tallahassee, FL 32317
850-385-0600
FAX: 850-386-5356
nygc@iir.com www.iir.com

Keith G Burt, Advisory Board

19997 Nine Lives Associates
PO Box 802
Berryville, VA 22611-0802
540-554-2540
FAX: 540-554-2558
info@personalprotection.com
www.personalprotection.com

Dr Richard W Kobetz, Executive Director

A non-profit professional society whose members include academics, trainers, students, law enforcement and government officials, self-employed professionals, security officers, directors from major intenational corporations, security service organizations, and communications, energy, retail, chemicals, insurance, petroleum and utility companies.
2800 Members Founded: 1978

19998 Professional Investigators & Security Asso ciation
PO Box 1836
Vienna, VA 22180
703-818-0552
FAX: 703-818-0551
kbreenpi@yahoo.com
www.pisa.gen.va.us

Kenneth Breen, Membership Chair/Database
Shirley Moore, Meetings

PISA is recognized as the preeminent professional organization representing members of the Private Security Services.

19999 Professional Records & Information Servic es Management International: PRISM
131 US 70 West
Garner, NC 27529
919-771-0657
FAX: 919-771-0457 800-336-9793
staff@prismintl.org www.prismintl.org

Jim Booth, Executive Director

A nonprofit trade association for the commercial information management industry whose vision is to be the primary global resource for commercial information management outsourcing providers.

20000 SAFE Association
300 N Mill Street, Unit B
PO Box 130
Creswell, OR 97426
541-895-3012
FAX: 541-895-3014
safe@peak.org
www.safeassociation.com

Joel Albinowski, President
Christy Cornette, President-Elect

The SAFE Association is dedicated to the preservation of human life. It provides a common meeting ground for the sharing of problems, ideas and information.

20001 Safe & Vault Technicians Association
3500 Easy Street
Dallas, TX 75247-6416
214-819-9771
FAX: 214-819-9736 www.savta.org

Skip Eckert, President

Provides a host of benefits to help its members stay informed, solving day to day problems, and out-performing the competition. Has helped thousands of safe and vault techicians achiveve personal and professional success.
Founded: 1986

20002 Safety Equipment Distributors Association
2105 Laurel Bush Road
Suite 200
Bel Air, MD 21015
443-640-1065
FAX: 443-640-1086
jackie@ksgroup.org
www.safetycentral.org

Jackie King, Executive Director
Kaymie Thompson, Director Meetings/Membership
Richard Rivkin, President
Heidi Levitt, First VP
Larry Loizzo, Second VP

The Saftey Equipment Distributor's Association is the trade association comprised of companies that distribute safety equipmant and related products and services. Its member companies are leaders in the distribution of personal protective equipment to a broad spectrum of users, including general industry, construction, municipalities, utilities, schools and laboratories.
175 Members Founded: 1968

20003 Safety Glazing Certification Council
PO Box 730
Sackets Harbor, NY 13685
315-646-2234
FAX: 315-646-2297 www.sgcc.org

John C Kent, Administrative Staff
Christine Flitcroft, Administrative Staff

Nonprofit corporation that provides for the certifacation of safety glazing materials, comprised of safety glazing manufacturers and other parties concerned with public safety. SGCC is managed by a board of directors comprised of representatives from the safety glazing industry and the public interest sector.
105 Members Founded: 1971

20004 Scaffold Industry Association
PO Box 20574
Phoenix, AZ 85036-0574
602-257-1144
FAX: 602-257-1166
aimee@scaffold.org www.scaffold.org

Aimee Siems, Operations Manager
Nicki Santo, Development Director
Bill Breault, President

Nonprofit organization which promotes scaffold safety and education through its publications, conventions, tradeshows and training programs.

20005 Security Hardware Distributors Association
100 North 20th Street
4th Floor
Philadelphia, PA 19103-1443
215-564-3484
FAX: 215-564-2175
shda@fernley.com www.shda.org

Bill Silver, President
Trudie Rowello, Executive Director
Michael Mitkus, Director Member Services

Offers education and services to its members.
150 Members Founded: 1940

20006 Security Industry Association
635 Slaters Lane
Suite 110
Alexandria, VA 22314
703-683-2075
FAX: 703-683-2469 866-817-8888
info@siaonline.org www.siaonline.org

Richard Chace, Executive Director
Rand Price, Associate Executive Director
Donald Erickson, Government Relations Director

SIA is dedicated to promoting growth, advancement, and professionalism within the security industry. Its activities fall into four core concentrations: government relations, research & technology, education & training, and standards.
300 Members Founded: 1969

20007 Security on Campus
133 Ivy Laneson Road
Suite 200
King of Prussia, PA 19406-2101
610-768-9330
FAX: 610-768-0646 888-251-7959
soc@securityoncampus.org
www.securityoncampus.org

Catherine Bath, Executive Director
S Daniel Carter, Senior VP

A non-profit organization whose mission is to prevent violence, substance abuse and other crimes in college and university campus commumities across the United States, and to compassionately assist the vicitims of these crimes.
Founded: 1987

20008 Semiconductor Environmental Safety & Healt h Association
1313 Dolly Madison Boulevard
Suite 402
McLean, VA 22101
703-790-1745
FAX: 703-790-2672
sesha@burkinc.com
www.seshaonline.org

Bernie Frist, President
Brett J Burk, Executive Director

SESHA is the premier association serving the global semiconductor and associated technology industries by providing education and professional development.
1500 Members Founded: 1978

20009 Society for Occupational & Environmental H ealth
6728 Old Mclean Village Drive
McLean, VA 22101
703-556-9222
FAX: 703-556-8729
soeh@degnon.org www.soeh.org

George K Degnon, CAE, Executive Director
Connie Mackay, Associate Director

The Society plays a unique, integrating role by bringing together professionals in government, and academia. It reduces occupational and environmental hazards through the presentation of scientific data and the dynamic exchange of information across institutions and disciplines.
Founded: 1972

20010 Society of Fire Protection Engineers
7315 Wisconsin Avenue
Suite 620E
Bethesda, MD 20814
301-718-2910
FAX: 301-718-2242
sfpehqtrs@sfpe.org www.sfpe.org

David D Evans, Executive Director
Kathleen Almond, Chief Executive Officer
Arthur Cote, President

The purpose of the Society is to advance the science and practice of fire protection engineering and its allied fields, to maintain a high ethical standard among its members and to foster fire protection engineering education. It supports the development of the annual Professional Engineer licensing exam in fire protection and the grading of those exams under the auspices of the National Council of Examiners for Engineering and Surveying.
4500 Members Founded: 1950

20011 Southern Cotton Ginners Association
874 Cotton Gin Place
Memphis, TN 38106
901-947-3104
FAX: 901-947-3103
mary.stice@southerncottonginners.org
www.southerncottonginners.org

Curtis Stewart, President
Tim Price, Executive VP
Larry Davis, Safety Director
Mary Stice, Administrative Assistant

Serves its members by providing safety, training and regulatory representation. The organzation also sponsors certification programs and hosts the industry's leading trade show, The Mid-South Farm & Gin Show. Serving the five-state area of Arkansas,

Louisiana, Mississippi, Missouri, and Tennessee.

20012 System Safety Society
PO Box 70
Unionville, VA 22567-0070
540-854-8630
FAX: 540-854-4561
syssafe@ns.gemlink.com
www.system-safety.org
Russ Mitchell, Member Services Director
Larry Jones, President
John Livingston, Executive Secretary
The System Safety Society is a non-profit organization dedicated to supporting the safety professional in the application of system engineering and systems management to risk analysis. The Society is international in scope and draws members throughout the world.
4500 Members Founded: 1963

20013 Underwriters Laboratories
333 Pfingsten Road
Northbrook, IL 60062-2096
847-272-8800
FAX: 847-272-8129
northbrook@us.ul.com www.ul.com
Keith Williams, President/CEO
Fred Marcon, Chairman
Underwriters Labdoratories Inc. is an independent, not-for-profit product-safty testing and certification organization, that has been testing products for safety for more than a century.
Founded: 1894

20014 Veterans of Safety
Humphreys Building, Central Missouri State
Suite 323 C
Warrensburg, MO 64093
660-543-4281
Our mission is the promotion of safety, health, and environmental awareness by using and making available the lifetime experience of professionals thoughout the world.
Founded: 1941

20015 Western States Auto Theft Investigators
395 Second Street
Redwood, CA 92707
714-634-1385
webmaster@wsati.org www.wsati.org
Stephen Torres, President
Bud Hood, VP
A non-profit organization that is comprised of professionals representing law enforcement, rental car and insurance companies, and other individuals whose goal is to reduce vehicle theft.

20016 Women Investigators Association
PO Box 18305
Encino, CA 91416
800-603-3524
womeninvas@aol.com www.w-i-a.org
Debra J Burdette, Executive Director
Robinette Desrochers, VP/Membership Director
Offering education and training, certification, networking, group discounts and represents women in our industry to the media.

Newsletters

20017 ACP Sentinel
Association of Contingency Planners
7044 S 13th Street
Oak Creek, WI 53154
414-688-8000
800-445-4227
Membership@techenterprises.net
http://www.acp-international.com
Paul L. Striedl, CEO
Shirley Runnels, Membership
News and event information for national and local chapters dedicated to fostering continued professional growth and development in effective contingency and business planning. *$75.00*
Quarterly Founded: 1983

20018 American Society of Crime Laboratory Direc tors
139K Technology Drive
Garner, NC 27529
919-773-2044
FAX: 919-773-2602
info@nfstc.org http://www.ascld.org
William E Marbaker, President
Susan C Scholl, Membership
Contains useful information and news to maintain and improve communications among crime laboratory directors and their staff. *$ 100.00*
Quarterly Founded: 1973

20019 Councilor
Safety & Health Council of Northern New England
163 Manchester Street
Suite D
Concord, NH 03301
603-228-1401
FAX: 603-224-0998 800-834-6472
safety@shcnne.org
http://www.shcnne.org
Lyman Cousens, Executive Director
Covers current regulatory issues as well as health and safety information. Free to members.
16 pages Monthly Founded: 2004
Printed in 2 colors on matte stock

20020 Emergency Preparedness News
Business Publishers
2601 University Boulevard W
#200
Silver Spring, MD 20902
301-929-5700
FAX: 301-949-8844 800-274-6737
custserv@bpinews.com
http://www.bpinews.com
Adam P Goldstein, Publisher
Deborah Eby, Editor
Dedicated solely to disaster management: from securing pre-disaster mitigation and counter terrorism funds, to staying prepared for hurricanes, terrorist threats, fires, floods and other natural disasters. Only available online now. *$357.00*
Monthly

20021 FAMA Flyer
Fire Apparatus Manufactures Association
PO Box 397
Lynnfield, MA 01940-0397
781-334-2911
FAX: 781-334-2911
info@fama.org www.fama.org
Tim Dean, President
Phil Turner, VP
A newsletter that is written speciffically for Fire Apparatus Manufactures and Fire Associations across the United States.
3x/Yr
Circulation: 500

20022 Homeland Security & Defense
McGraw Hill
1200 G Street
Suite 922
Washington, DC 20005
202-383-2350
FAX: 202-383-2346
letters@aviationnow.com
http://www.aviationnow.com/avnow
Lee Ewing, Editor-in-Chief
Paul Hoversten, Managing Editor
Mark Lipowicz, Publisher
News items for defense and homeland security professionals. Available in print or electronically. *$595.00*
Weekly Founded: 1920

20023 Nine Lives Associates: Newsletter
PO Box 802
Berryville, VA 22611
540-554-2540
FAX: 540-554-2558
info@personalprotection.com
http://www.personalprotection.com
Dr. Richard Kobetz, Executive Director
Personal protection news and announcements for member graduates of Executive Protection Institute.
Founded: 1980

20024 Protection News
International Foundation for Protection Officers
PO Box 771329
Naples, FL 34107-1329
239-430-0534
FAX: 239-430-0533
sandi@ifpo.com http://www.ifpo.org
Sandi J Davies, Executive Director
Michael Stroberger, Secretary/Treasurer
Circulation to all IFPO members and candidates in associated programs. Publication is designed to keep professionals current on trends within the security industry and is full of valuable information and commentary pertinent to the enhancement of life, safety and property protection. *$18.00*
Quarterly Founded: 1988

20025 SAFE Journal
300 N Mill Street Unit B
PO Box 130
Creswell, OR 97426
541-895-3012
FAX: 541-895-3014
safe@peak.org
http://www.safeassociation.com
Joe Spinosa, President
Joel Albinowski, VP
A bi-annual journal published by the SAFE Association. *$30.00*
Founded: 1956
Circulation: 1000
Printed in 2 colors on matte stock

20026 SIA News
Security Industry Association
635 Slaters Lane
Suite 110
Alexandria, VA 22314-1177
703-683-2075
FAX: 703-683-2469
info@siaonline.org
http://www.siaonline.org

Richard Chace, Executive Director
Chris Kennedy, Manager Public Relations & Communic

Informs and educates members and prospective members of SIA activities, news, and information. Available online only.
2 X'S Monthly Founded: 1969

20027 Safety Compliance Letter
Bureau of Business Practice
111 Eight Avenue
New York, NY 10011

800-638-8437

Alicia Pierce, Publisher
Michele Rubin, Editor

Monitors and reports on the regulatory environment and provides subscribers with up-to-date information in a concise and easy-to-read format, with references and resources (including internet addresses) to get additional help on particular topics. *$289.00*
Monthly Founded: 1920 ISBN 9-900003-20-0

20028 Salt & Highway Deicing
Salt Institute
700 N Fairfax Street
Suite 600
Alexandria, VA 22314-2040
703-549-4648
FAX: 703-548-2194
info@saltinstitute.org
http://www.saltinstitute.org

Dick Hanneman, President
Tammy Goodwin, Administrative Director

A quarterly e-newsletter published by the Salt Institute.
Quarterly Founded: 1914
Circulation: 8000
Printed in on glossy stock

20029 Security Director's Report
Institute of Management & Administration

3 Park Avenue
30th Floor
New York, NY 10016-5902
212-244-0360
FAX: 212-564-0465
subserve@ioma.com
http://www.ioma.com

St Davis Foster, CEO
Garett Seivolb, Publisher

Helps security directors keep pace with the rapidly evolving world of corporate security. Provides alerts of critical news, important new security products, and up-to-date advice that is needed to know to effectively manage the security department. *$329.00*
Monthly Founded: 1980
Circulation: 100,000

20030 Society Update
American Society of Safety Engineers
1800 E Oakton Street
Des Plaines, IL 60018
847-699-2929
FAX: 847-768-3434
customerservice@asse.org
http://www.asse.org

Fred J Fortman, Executive Director

Membership benefit via e-mail with news, information on training, plus happenings in the 150 chapters throughout the US. *$60.00*

Founded: 1911

20031 Workplace Substance Abuse Advisor
LRP Publications
360 Hiatt Drive
Palm Beach Garden, FL 33418
561-622-6520
FAX: 561-622-2423 800-341-7874
custserve@lrp.com
http://www.lrp.com

Debbie Pelletier, Managing Editor

Current developments affecting how your workplace deals with alcohol and drug abusing employees. Comprehensive overview of all the areas you need to know to create and maintain an effective substance abuse program in your company. *$377.00*
2 X'S Month Founded: 1977

Magazines & Journals

20032 Access Control & Security Systems
PRIMEDIA Business Magazines & Media
9800 Metcalf Avenue
Overland Park, KS 66212
913-341-1300
FAX: 913-967-1898
prothman@primediabusiness.com
http://www.primediabusiness.com

Larry Anderson, Editor
Gregg Herring, Publisher
Paul Rothman, Associate Editor
Brenda Wiley, Advertising Production Manager
Marty McCallen, National Sales Manager

Product overview articles and columns cover topics on door entry, CCTV, operators and gates, sensors and perimeter security.
Monthly Founded: 1905
Circulation: 38000+

20033 American Industrial Hygiene Association Journal
American Industrial Hygiene Association
2700 Prosperity Avenue
Suite 250
Fairfax, VA 22031
703-849-8267
FAX: 703-207-3561
infonet@aiha.org http://www.aiha.org

Lisa Junker, Senior Editor
Donna M Doganiero, President
Dave Bentley, Marketing Manager
Sheila Brown,, Associate Editor
Steven H Davis, Executive Director

Essential source of information on occupational health and evironmental health and safety issues. Available in print and online.
780 pages Monthly Founded: 1982

20034 Business & Legal Reports
141 Mill Rock Road E
Old Saybrook, CT 06475-6011
203-180-0000
FAX: 860-510-7220 800-727-5257
service@blr.com www.blr.com

Kathy Long, VP Marketing
Peggy Carter-Ward, Editor-in-Chief

Provides essential tools for safety and environmental compliance and training needs.
32 pages

20035 Campus Safety Journal
Bricepac
12228 Venice Boulevard Suite 541
PO Box 66515
Los Angeles, CA 90066
310-390-5277
FAX: 310-390-4777
tnelson@campusjournal.com
http://www.campusjournal.com

Pat Restivo, Circualtion
John Horn, President

Provides a vehicle for communicating campus safety and security issues to all interested parties at the middle, secondary, college and university levels.
40 pages Monthly Founded: 1992
Circulation: 20000
Printed in 4 colors on glossy stock

20036 Compliance Magazine
Douglas Publications
2807 N Parham Road
Suite 200
Richmond, VA 23294
804-762-9600
FAX: 804-217-8999 888-246-8484
info@douglaspublications.com
www.compliancemag.com

Betty Hintch, Editor
Alan Douglas, President

News and product information relating to occupational safety, health and loss control issues. No charge to qualified subscribers. *$55.00*
Founded: 1985
Circulation: 65000

20037 Computer Fraud & Security
Elsevier Science
360 Park Avenue S
New York, NY 10010
212-989-5800
FAX: 212-633-3990 www.elsevier.com

S. Hilley, Editor

Provides practical, usable information to effectively manage and control computer and information security within commercial organizations.
Monthly Founded: 1979

20038 Computer Security Journal
Computer Security Institute
600 Harrison Street
San Francisco, CA 94107
415-947-6320
FAX: 415-947-6023
csi@cmp.com www.gocsi.com

Russell Kay, Publisher

Keeps you informed with comprehensive, practical articles, case studies, reviews and commentaries written by knowledgeable computer security professionals. *$224.00*
Quarterly Founded: 1974
Circulation: 3000

20039 Computers & Security
Elsevier Science
360 Park Avenue S
New York, NY 10010
212-989-5800
FAX: 212-633-3990
http://www.elsevier.com

N Dudley Gough, Managing Editor

Provides a blend of leading edge research and sound practical management advice.
Monthly Founded: 1997

20040 Corporate Security
Strafford Publications
590 Dutch Valley Road NE
Atlanta, GA 30324-0729
404-881-1141
FAX: 404-881-0074 800-926-7926
custserv@straffordpub.com
www.straffordpub.com

Richard Ossoff, President
George Coleman, Manager

Intelligence briefing on the latest security developments, best practices, the most important trends and new technolgies. *$330.00*
Bi-Monthly Founded: 1984

20041 EMS Product News
Cygnus Publishing
1233 Janesville Avenue
Fort Atkinson, WI 53538-0803
920-563-6388
FAX: 920-563-1699 800-547-7377
Ronnie.Garret@cygnuspub.com
www.publicsafety.com
/www.cygnusb2b.com

Scott Cravens, Publisher
Nancy Perry, Editor

Product information written with the emergency medical service professional in mind. *$53.00*
6 Issues
Circulation: 20000

20042 Emergency Medical Product News
Cygnus Business Media
1233 Janesville Avenue
Fort Atkinson, WI 53538

FAX: 920-563-1702 800-547-7377

Patrick Bernardo, Publisher
Ronnie Garrett, Editor in Chief

A bi-monthly tabloid-sized magazine showcasing new products in the Emergengy Medical Technician's scope of use.

20043 Emergency Medical Services
Cygnus Business Media
1233 Janesville Avenue
Fort Atkinson, WI 53538

scott.cravens@cygnusb2b.com
www.cygnusb2b.com

Scott Cravens, Publisher
Nancy Perry, Associate Publisher

A magazine designed for both career and volunteer EMS professionals. This magazine has been rated number one for editorial quality, reader interest and advertising pages.
Monthly

20044 Fire EMS
PennWell
1421 S Sheridan Road
Tulsa, OK 74112
918-353-3161
FAX: 973-251-5065 800-962-6484
dianef@pennwell.com
http://www.fireemsmag.com/

Jack Rogers, Managing Editor
Bobby Halton, Editor-in-Chief
Mike McEvoy, Editor

News, product information and feature articles of interest to paramedics. *$30.00*
Monthly
Printed in 4 colors on glossy stock

20045 Fire Engineering
PennWell
1421 S Sheridan Road
Tulsa, OK 74112
973-251-5040
FAX: 973-251-5065 800-962-6484
dianef@pennwell.com
http://fe.pennnet.com/

Jack Rogers, Managing Editor
Diane Feldman, Executive Editor
Bobby Halton, Editor-in-Chief

Provides education and training to the fire service through a hands-on, technically oriented editorial package. *$29.95*
106 pages Monthly
Circulation: 44824
Printed in 4 colors on glossy stock

20046 Fire Protection Engineering
Society of Fire Protection Engineers
7315 Wisconsin Avenue
Suite 620E
Bethesda, MD 20814
301-718-2910
FAX: 301-718-2242
sfpehqtrs@sfpe.org
http://www.sfpe.org

David D Evans, Executive Director
Rebecca Salzman, Membership Coordinator
Samuel Dannaway, President

Technical magazine advancing the science and practice of fire protection and its allied fields. *$145.00*
Quarterly Founded: 1950
Circulation: 4500

20047 Food Protection Trends
International Association for Food Protection
6200 Aurora Avenue
Suite 200W
Des Moines, IA 50322-2864
515-276-3344
FAX: 515-276-8655 800-369-6337
info@foodprotection.org
http://www.foodprotection.org

David W Tharp, Executive Director
Didi Loynachan, Administrative Assistant
Donna Bahun, Production Editor
Karla K Jordan, Order Processing
Dave Larson, Advertising Manager

Each issue contains refereed articles on applied research, applications of current technology and general interest subjects for food safety professionals. *$234.00*
Monthly Founded: 1911 ISSN 0362-028X
Circulation: 9,000
Mailing list available for rent 3000+ names $150 per M.
Printed in 4 colors on glossy stock

20048 ICT: Infection Control Today
Virgo Publishing
3300 N Central Avenue
Suite 300
Phoenix, AZ 85012
480-990-1101
FAX: 480-675-8154
asharman@vpico.com
www.infectioncontroltoday.com

Peggy Jackson, Publisher
Kelly Pyrek, Editor

Science-based articles for the general ward, operating room, sterile processing and environmental services departments of healthcare facilities, as well as for the public-health community. Articles are in-depth, comprehensively researched and explore important trends, legislative events, new guidelines and technologies impacting the areas of infection control, patient safety, occupational health, epidemiology, risk management and healthcare purchasing.
60 pages Monthly + Buyer's Guide
Founded: 1996
Circulation: 30000+
Mailing list available for rent 30000+ names $var per M.
Printed in 4 colors on glossy stock
Computerized version available: website

20049 Industrial Hygiene News
Rimbach Publishing
8650 Babcock Boulevard
Pittsburgh, PA 15237-5821
412-364-5366
FAX: 412-369-9720 800-245-3182
info@rimbach.com
http://www.rimbach.com

Raquel Rimbach, Managing Editor
Karen Galante, Circulation Manager

Articles, news and product information for professionals in Occupational Health and Industrial Hygiene.
Founded: 1978
Circulation: 60,111

20050 Industrial Safety & Hygiene News
Business News Publishing
2401 W Big Beaver Road
Suite 700
Troy, MI 48084
248-362-3700
FAX: 248-362-0317
ISHN@media.com
http://www.ishn.com

Dave Johnson, Editor
Randy Green, Publisher
Bill Noone, Managing Editor/Products Editor
Vince Miconi, Production Manager

Feature articles and product information for safety, health and environmental professionals. Free subscription to qualified professionals. *$58.00*
Monthly Founded: 1926

20051 International Municipal Signal Association Journal
165 E Union Street
PO Box 539
Newark, NY 14513-0539
315-331-2182
FAX: 315-331-8205 800-723-4672
Info@IMSAsafety.org
http://www.imsasafety.org

Marilyn Lawrence, Publisher & Executive Director
Sharon Earl, Editor

Information, education, and certification issues for public safety. *$50.00*
80 pages Founded: 1934
Circulation: 5500 8800+ names
Printed in 4 colors on glossy stock

20052 Journal of Fire Sciences
Sage Publications
2455 Teller Road
Thousand Oaks, CA 91320
805-499-0721
FAX: 805-583-2665 800-818-7243
journals@sagepub.com
www.sagepub.com

Gordon E Hartzell, Editor

Reporting new developments in related technology. Peer-reviewed articles by recognized specialists from around the world. In-depth articles provide new science based information useful in materials research and product development.
$1281.00

88 pages Bi-Monthly Founded: 1965
Printed in 2 colors on matte stock : On-Line

20053 Journal of Food Protection
International Association for Food Protection
6200 Aurora Avenue
Suite 200W
Des Moines, IA 50322-2864
515-276-3344
FAX: 515-276-8655 800-369-6337
info@foodprotection.org
http://www.foodprotection.org

Tamara P Ford, Administrative Editor
David W Tharp, Executive Director
Didi Sterling Loynachan, Administrative Assistant
Karla K. Jordan, Order Processing Head

Each issue contains scientific research and authoritative review articles reporting on a variety of topics in food science pertaining to food safety and quality. *$345.00*
Monthly Founded: 1937 ISSN 0362-028X
Circulation: 11,000
Printed in 4 colors on glossy stock

20054 Law and Order Magazine
Hendon Publications
130 Waukegan Road
Suite 202, 2nd Floor
Deerfield, IL 60015-4912
847-444-3300
FAX: 847-444-3333 800-843-9764
info@hendonpub.com
http://www.hendonpub.com

Pete Kingwill, Director, Advertising/Co-Owner
H Scott Kingwill, Director, Operations/Co-Owner

Latest news of interest to police and law enforcement professionals. New product and service information, available in print and online. *$24.95*
Monthly Founded: 1953
Circulation: 32304

20055 Materials Evaluation
American Society for Nondestructive Testing
1711 Arlingate Lane
PO Box 28518
Columbus, OH 43228-518
614-274-6003
FAX: 614-274-6899 800-222-2768
kwie@asnt.org http://www.asnt.org

Paul McIntire, Publication Manager
Betsy Blazar, Marketing Manager
Shelby Reeves, Owner

Research, reviews and information of nondestructive testing materials. Provides members and subscribers the latest news and technical information concerning this industry. *$10.00*
Monthly

20056 National Defense Magazine
National Defense Industrial Association
2111 Wilson Boulevard
Suite 400
Arlington, VA 22201
703-522-1820
FAX: 703-522-1885 703-247-9469
info@ndia.org www.ndia.org

Lawrence P Farrell, President
Sandra I Erwin, Editor
Sharon Foster, Circulation Manager

Places main focus on issues concerning the U.S. defense industry. Provides the trends in national security, including technology advancement, acquisition policy, critical industry sectors, and marketing are editorial staples. *$40.00*
Monthly Founded: 1946
Circulation: 30000

20057 National Fire Protection Association Newsl etter
1 Batterymarch Park
Quincy, MA 02169-7471
617-770-3000
FAX: 617-770-0700 800-344-3555
nfpajournal@nfpa.org www.nfpa.org

Kathleen Robinson, Editorial
James Shannon, CEO/President

Written for various fire safety professionals and covers major topics in fire protection and suppression. The Journal carries investigation reports written by NFPA specialists, special NFPA statistical studies on large-loss fires, multiple deaths, fire fighter deaths and injuries, and others annually and articles on fire protection advances, public education and information of interest to NFPA members.
Monthly Founded: 1896

20058 National Locksmith
National Publishing Company
1533 Burgundy Parkway
Streamwood, IL 60107-1861
630-371-1250
FAX: 630-837-1210
natllock@aol.com
http://www.thenationallocksmith.com

Marc Goldberg, Publisher
Greg Mango, Editor

New products, marketing, sales, merchandising, and the array of factors involved in successful locksmith enterprises and services. Informs professionals about the latest news and techniques in security. *$46.00*
Monthly Founded: 1983
Circulation: 17000

20059 Occupational Hazards
Penton Media
1300 E 9th Street
Cleveland, OH 44114
216-696-7000
FAX: 216-696-1752
information@penton.com
www.penton.com

Penny McCullough, Editorial Assistant
Bob Marinez, Publisher
Rob Howlett, Advertising Manager

Analysis of qualified recipients who have indicated that they recommend, select and/or buy the safety equipment, fire protection and other occupational health products. *$50.00*
65 pages Monthly Founded: 1892
Circulation: 71,000
Printed in 4 colors on glossy stock

20060 Oregon Investigator
PO Box 2705
Portland, OR 97208
866-584-8645

oali@oali.org www.oali.org

Ted J Tolliver, Executive Director
Patricia Vollbrect, President

Official journal of the organization setting a standard of excellence among investigators. Legislative issues and news of upcoming seminars.
Founded: 1983

20061 Pollution Equipment News
Rimbach Publishing
8650 Babcock Boulevard
Pittsburgh, PA 15237
412-364-5366
FAX: 412-369-9720 800-245-3182
info@rimbach.com www.rimbach.com

Raquel Rimbach, Managing Editor
Karen Galante, Circulation Manager

Product profiles for air, water, hazardous waste and wastewater concerns.
Bi-annually Founded: 1968
Circulation: 90267

20062 Process Safety Progress
John Wiley & Sons
1475 Crosspoint Boulevard
Indianapolis, IN 46256

FAX: 800-597-3299 877-762-2974

D A Crowl, Editor
Joseph F Louvar, Editor

Practical information for engineering professionals. Focuses on chemical and hydrocarbon safety, loss prevention and health. *$ 345.00*
Quarterly Founded: 1908

20063 Professional Safety
American Society of Safety Engineers
1800 E Oakton Street
Des Plaines, IL 60018
847-699-2929
FAX: 847-768-3434
customerservice@asse.org
http://www.asse.org/

Sue Trebswether, Editor
Tina Angley, Associate Editor
Fred Fortman, President
Janelle Ukleja, Editorial Assistant

Journal of the well known professional safety, health and environmental organization. Articles provide in-depth examination of health and safety concerns. *$60.00*
Monthly Founded: 1990

20064 Public Safety Communications/APCO Bulletin
Association of Public-Safety Comm Officials Int'l
351 N Williamson Boulevard
Daytona, FL 32114-1112
386-322-2500
FAX: 386-322-2501 888-272-6911
bulletin@apco911.com
http://www.apco911.org

Toni Edwards, Managing Editor
George S Rice, Jr, Executive Director

Newsletter dedicated to the enhancement of public safety communications and to serving its more than 15,000 members, the people who use public safety communications systems and services. subscription is a member benefit.
Monthly Founded: 1935
Circulation: 13000

20065 Quality Digest
QCI International
555 East Avenue
Chico, CA 95926
530-893-4095
FAX: 530-893-0395
qualitydigest@qualitydigest.com
www.qualitydigest.com

Michael Richman, Managing Editor
Dirk Dusharme, Technical Editor
Scott Papon, Publisher
April Johnson, Circulation Manager

Serves the field of quality-related activites in manufacturing, financial services, communications, utilities, transportation, government, military, retail, educational institutions, health care, consulting, aerospace, software, agricultural, forestry, fishing, mining, construction and other industries. Available in print and free online.
$59.00
Monthly Founded: 1981

20066 SC Magazine
Haymarket Media
161 Worcester Road
Suite 201
Framingham, MA 01701
508-879-9792
FAX: 508-879-2755
iarmstrong@westcoast.com
http://www.scmagazine.com

Illena Armstrong, Editor-in-Chief
Gil Torren, Sales Director
Sherry Oommen, Circulation Director

Covers all industries that use information security systems. Provides data on information security products, services, market trends and industry developments. *$60.00*
133 pages Monthly Founded: 1999
Circulation: 40,000
Printed in 4 colors

20067 Safe & Vault Technology
Safe & Vault Technicians Association
3500 Easy Street
Dallas, TX 75247
214-819-9771
FAX: 214-819-9736 www.savta.org

Ron Snively, President
Mike Oelert, Editor

Industry news, reviews, announcements and new products of paticular interest to readers. *$45.00*
Monthly Founded: 1986
Circulation: 3000

20068 Safety & Health
National Safety Council
1121 Spring Lake Drive
Itasca, IL 60143-3201
630-285-1121
FAX: 630-285-1315
info@nsc.org www.nsc.org

Bob Vavra, Editor
Melissa J Ruminski, Managing Editor
Suzanne Powills, Publisher

Coverage of safety news and changes, trade shows and training courses. *$58.50*
Monthly Founded: 1954

20069 Security Dealer
Cygnus Publishing
1233 Janesville Avenue
Fort Atkinson, WI 53538
920-563-6388
FAX: 920-563-1699 800-547-7377

Pete Harlick, Publisher
Susan Brady, Editor-in-Chief
Susan Whitehurst, Group Publisher

Trade publication for those in the electronic burglary and fire alarm system business. *$112.00*
Monthly Founded: 1966
Circulation: 25500

20070 Security Distributing and Marketing
Business News Publishing
1050 IL Route 83
Suite 200
Bensenville, IL 60106-1096
630-616-0200
FAX: 630-227-0214
zaludb@bnpmedia.com
http://www.sdmmag.com

Mark McCourt, Publisher
Laura Stepanek, Editor
Russ Gager, Senior Editor

Information source for the electronic security, life safety and home systems industries. Subscription free to professionals.
Monthly
Circulation: 28000

20071 Security Magazine
Business News Publishing
2401 W Big Beaver Road
Suite 700
Troy, MI 48084
248-893-3500
FAX: 630-227-0214
zalud@bnpmedia.com
www.securitymagazine.com

Bill Zalud, Editor
Mark McCourt, Publisher
Russ Gager, Senior Editor

Covers all types of businesses, including industrial manufacturing, service companies, institutions and government, as well as consulting, design, and integrator firms that specify security. News, columns and security product information. No charge to professionals.
Monthly Founded: 1964
Circulation: 40590
Printed in 4 colors on glossy stock

20072 Security Management
American Society for Industrial Security
1625 Prince Street
Alexandria, VA 22314-2818
703-519-6200
FAX: 703-519-6299 800-368-5685
sharowitz@asisonline.org
www.securitymanagement.com

Denny White, Publisher-in-Chief
Sherry Harowitz, Editor-in-Chief

Features, news and trends in the security world. In print and online. *$48.00*
Monthly Founded: 1955

20073 Security Products
Stevens Publishing Corporation
5151 Beltline Road
10th Floor
Dallas, TX 75254
972-687-6700
FAX: 972-687-6770
www.stevenspublishing.com or
www.secprodonline.com

Craig Stevens, CEO
Margaret Perry, Circulation Director
Russell Lindsay, Publisher
Ralph Jensen, Editor
Karina Sanchez, Managing Editor

Offers examples of security solutions set by such facilities as casinos and hospitals, and explores such issues as false alarm reduction and personnel training, it also highlights new technologies. *$75.00*
Monthly Founded: 1925
Circulation: 65000

20074 Security Sales & Integration
Bobit Publishing Company
3520 Challenger Street
Torrance, CA 90503
310-533-2400
FAX: 310-533-2502
info@securitysales.com
www.securitysales.com

Rodney Bosch, Senior Editor
Scott Goldfine, Editor-in-chief
Michael Zawinski, Publisher

News, feature articles, columnists and new products in the field ofelectronic security.
$15.00
Monthly

20075 Security and Privacy
IEEE Computer Society
10662 Los Vaqueros Drive
PO Box 3014
Los Alamitos, CA 90720-1314
714-821-8380
FAX: 714-821-4010 800-272-6657
help@computer.org
www.computer.org/security

Angela Burgess, Publisher
Kathy Clark-Fisher, Lead Editor
Georgann Carter, Circulation Manager
George Cybenko, Editor-in-Chief

Trans-border data flow issues, protocols, database management and security. Available online to members and in print to others. *$ 29.00*
6 Issues/Year Founded: 1979
Circulation: 1600

20076 Sound & Video Contractor
Primedia
PO Box 12914
Overland Park, KS 66282
913-341-1300
FAX: 913-967-1903
mjohnson@primediabusiness.com
www.svconline.com

Michael Goldman, Editor
Cynthia Wisehart, Editorial Director
Charissa Young, Associate Editor

Contains information on sound systems, video display, security, CCTV, home theater, and automation. Delivers in depth instruction and examples of successful installations, fundamental acoustical and video theory and news on new technologies affecting the systems contracting business.
$35.00
Monthly Founded: 1983
Circulation: 21000
Mailing list available for rent 20,500 names $110 per M.

20077 Standardization News
ASTM International
100 Barr Harbor Drive
PO Box C700
West Conshohocken, PA 19428-2959
610-329-9500
FAX: 610-832-9555
emcglinc@astm.org www.astm.org

Maryann Gorman, Editor-in-Chief

Feature articles deal with the development, use, and application of standards and related subjects. Feature and news articles report on research, testing and new activities of ASTM standards writing committees, as well as those of the domestic and global standards community. Also included are legal, regulatory, and international events impacting on the standards development process. *$18.00*
Monthly ISSN 0090-1210
Circulation: 35000

20078 Underground Focus
Planet Underground
411 South Evergreen
Manteno, IL 60950
815-468-7814
FAX: 815-468-7644
ufmagazine@underspace.com
www.theplanetunderground.com or
www.underspace.com
Ron Rosencrans, Founder
Amy Chmura, Editor
Documents the importance of careful excavation and helps them get the budgets to do the job. Powerfully dramatizes the need for underground damage prevention, excavation safety, and the hazards of not protecting the subsurface infrastructure. *$25.00*
46 pages Founded: 1986
Circulation: 21800
Printed in 4 colors on glossy stock

Trade Shows

20079 AAAR Annual Meeting
American Association for Areosol Research
15000 Commerce Parkway
Suite C
Mount Laurel, NJ 08054
877-777-6753
FAX: 856-439-0525
info@aaar.org www.aaar.org
Deanna Bright, Show Manager
Exibits related to aerosol research in areas including industrial process, air pollution, and industrial hygiene. Over 600 professionals attend.
600 Attendees Annual, September, Nevada

20080 ASFPM Annual Conference
Association of State Floodplain Managers
2809 Fish Hatchery Road
Suite 204
Madison, WI 53713
608-274-0123
FAX: 608-274-0696
asfpm@floods.org www.floods.org
Larry Larson, Executive Director
Becky Head, Member Services Coordinator
Focus on floodproofing techniques, materials, floodproofing and elevation contractors, current issues and programs, new federal tax impications and the various means of funding floodproofing projects. implications. Held June in Norfolk, VA.
Annual

20081 ASIS International
1625 Prince Street
Alexandria, VA 22314-2818
703-519-6200
FAX: 703-519-6299
asis@asisonline.org
www.asisonline.org
Shannon Burch, Exhibits Manager
Michael Stack, Executive Director
Exhibits related to loss prevention and security for public and private organizations. Held September 24-26, 2007 at the Las Vegas Convention Center in Las Vegas, Nevada.
September

20082 America's Fire & Security Expo
ROC Exhibitions
1963 University Lane
Lisle, IL 60532
630-271-8210
FAX: 630-271-8234
info@rocexhibitions.com
www.americassecurity.com
Jerry Carter, Marketing Director
Annual 3 day marketplace featuring state-of-the-art security products, systems and services. Over 50 free educational sessions. Emphasis on the markets of Latin America, the Caribbean and the Southeastern US.
July

20083 American Biological Safety Association Conference
1200 Allanson Road
Mundelein, IL 60060-3808
847-949-1517
FAX: 847-566-4580 847-566-4580
absa@covad.net www.absa.org
LouAnn Burnett, Chair
Exhibits of biological safety equipment, supplies and services. Held October at the Opryland Hotel in Nashville, Tennessee.
300 Attendees October

20084 American Fire Sprinkler Association Annual Convention & Exhibition
American Fire Sprinkler Association
9696 Skillman Street
Suite 300
Dallas, TX 75243-3200
214-349-5965
FAX: 214-343-8898
afsainfo@firesprinkler.org
www.sprinklernet.org
Steve Muncy, President
Lloyd Ivy, Director/Memebership
Marlene Garrett, Director/Sales/Meetings
120 exhibits of sprinkler heads, pipe, hangers, tools and other equipment. Seminar, workshop and tours. Held September in Phoenix, Arizona.
1000 Attendees September Founded: 1981

20085 American Industrial Hygiene Association Conference and Exposition
American Industrial Hygiene Association
2700 Prosperity Avenue
Suite 250
Fairfax, VA 22031
703-849-8888
FAX: 703-207-3561
infonet@aiha.org www.aiha.org
Caroline Lacey, Expo Manager
Carol Tobin, Director
Conference for occupational and environmental health and safety professionals around the globe. Held June in Philadelphia, Pennsylvania.
4,000 Attendees Annual

20086 American Society for Nondestructive Testing Conference

1711 Arlingate Lane
PO Box 28518
Columbus, OH 43228-0518
614-274-6003
FAX: 614-274-6899 800-222-2768
kwie@asnt.org www.asnt.org
Michael O'Toole, Senior Manager Conferences
Jacquie Giunta, Meeting Coordinator
Ruth Staat, Exhibit/Event Supervisor
Seminar, conference and 150 exhibits of nondestructive testing equipment, services, supplies and laboratory representatives. Holds a smaller conference in the spring. Held November in Las Vegas, Nevada.
3000 Attendees Fall

20087 American Society of Crime Laboratory Direc tors Annual Symposium
139 Technology Drive
Suite K
Garner, NC 27529-7970
919-773-2044
FAX: 919-773-2602
rkahn@ag.state.oh.us www.ascld.org
Bill Marbaker, President
Devoted to providing training in leadership and management techniques in the field of forensic science. Also offers membership the opportunity to network with other laboratory directors.
October

20088 American Society of Safety Engineers Profe ssional Development Conference
American Society of Safety Engineers
1800 E Oakton Street
Des Plaines, IL 60018-2187
847-699-2929
FAX: 847-768-3434
customerservice@asse.org
www.asse.org
Hall Erickson, Trade Show Director
Cindy Milner-Kornfeld, Conference & Meetings Coordinator
Stephanie Ronnie-Sanchez, Conference & Meetings Manager
Liza Visser, Conference & Meetings Coordinator
Annual conference and expo of 250 manufacturers and suppliers of safety equipment and health products. Held June
3500 Attendees June

20089 Applied Ergonomics Conference
Institute of Industrial Engineers
3577 Parkway Lane
Suite 200
Norcross, GA 30092
770-449-0461
FAX: 770-263-8532 800-494-0460
cs@iienet.org www.iienet.org/annual
Carol LeBlanc, Conference Manager
An exclusive event for ergonomists, engineers, and safety professionals. The conference focuses on how companies have successfully implemented programs that provide excellent return on their ergonomics investment. Held May Nashville, Tennessee.
800 Attendees March Founded: 1998

20090 Associated Locksmiths of America & Safe and Vault Tech Security Expo
Associated Locksmiths of America
3500 Easy Street
Dallas, TX 75247-6416
214-819-9733
800-532-2562
convention@aloa.org www.aloa.org
Karen Lyons, Conventions/Meetings
Kim Hammond, Exhibits/Sales
Features industry innovation, training, networking and education in the security world. Over 350 exhibitors with cash and carry merchandise. Held July, in Charlotte, North Carolina.

4000 Attendees July Founded: 1956

20091 BOMA Annual Convention
Building Owners & Managers Association Int'l
1201 New York Avenue NW
Suite 300
Washington, DC 20005
202-408-2662
FAX: 202-326-6377
info@boma.org www.boma.org

Henry Chamberlain, President/COO
Kurt R Padavano, Chairman & CEO

Opportunity for business professionals to discuss problems, security, exchange ideas and share experience and knowledge. Held July 21-24, 2007 at the Jacob K Javits Convention Center in New York City.
July

20092 Bomb Technicians & Investigators Annual Conference
PO Box 160
Goldvein, VA 22720-0160
540-752-4533
FAX: 540-752-2796
admin@iabti.org www.iabti.org

Ralph Way PhD, Executive Director

Speakers on the latest information on bomb and bio threats.Attendes are in the fields of law enforcement, fire and emergency services, the military, forensic science and other related fields.
Founded: 1973

20093 CSAA Electronic Security Forum & Exposition
Central Station Alarm Association
440 Maple Avenue E
Suite 201
Vienna, VA 22180
703-242-4670
FAX: 703-242-4675
meetings@csaaul.org www.csaaul.org

John McDonald, Meetings/Conferences

Exhibitors, speakers and workshops for the alarm and security professional. Held May
May

20094 California Alarm Association Winter Conven tion
3401 Pacific Avenue
Suite 1C
Marina del Rey, CA 90292
310-305-1277
FAX: 310-305-2077 800-437-7658
info@caaonline.org
www.caaonline.org

Jon Sargent, President
Jerry Lenander, Executive Director
George DeMarco, Southern VP
Ron Galippo, Secretary

Annual meeting of state trade association comprised of licensed alarm company operators and suppliers of products and services. Nearly 200 alarm companies and 50 suppliers are members. Alarm companies represent 70% of the electronic security industry in California. Held December in San Francisco, California.
December

20095 Campus Law Enforcement Administrators Annual Conference
342 N Main Street
Hartford, CT 06117-2507
860-586-7517
FAX: 860-586-7550
cewing@iaclea.org www.iaclea.org

Delores Stafford, President
Carol Ewing, Professional Development

Presentations on sucessful or new programs and current trends.
June

20096 Campus Safety Conference
Bricepac
12228 Venice Boulevard
PO Box 66515
Los Angeles, CA 90066
310-390-5277
FAX: 800-758-0935
swatson@bricepac.com
www.campusjournal.com

Sandra Watson, Conferences/Training

Training conference designed especially for campus safety professionals at both the secondary school and higher education levels. Features more than 13 seminars of critical importance to campus safety decision makers and staff. *$245.00*
2 Days/November

20097 Card Tech/Secur Tech: CTST Conference & Exhibition
SourceMedia
One State Street Plaza
27th Floor
New York, NY 10004
212-258-6093
FAX: 212-803-8515 800-803-3424
abconference@sourcemedia.com
www.ctst.com

Nicoal Crawford, Director of Operations
Nikole Tenbrink, Custom Events

250 booth exhibit hall, seminars, luncheons and keynote speakers in the advanced card and biometric technology field. Explores real world applications in several industries including financial services, goverment and security. Held May in San Francisco, California.
50000 Attendees April

20098 Chiefs of Police Annual Conference
International Association of Chiefs of Police
515 N Washington Street
Alexandria, VA 22314-2357
703-836-6767
FAX: 703-836-4543 800-843-4227
information@theiacp.org
www.theiacp.org

Dan Rosenblatt, Executive Director

Annual show of 550 manufacturers, suppliers and distributors of law enforcement equipment, supplies and services.

20099 Computer Security Conference & Expo
Computer Security Institute
600 Harrison Street
San Francisco, CA 94107
415-947-6320
FAX: 415-947-6023
csi@cmp.com www.gocsi.com

Jennifer Stevens, Conference Director

Annual event with over 150 educational sessions and exhibitor hall. Held October in Orlando, Florida.
November

20100 Contingency Planning & Management
WPC Expositions
84 Park Avenue
Flemington, NJ 08822
908-788-0343
FAX: 908-788-0316
blewis@witterpublishing.com
www.contingencyplanningexpo.com

Greg Sgroi, Events Director
Brad Lewis, Sales/Exhibits
Courtney Witter, Expo Manager

Serves the fields of financial/banking, manufacturing industrial, transportation, utilities, telecommunications, health care, government, security, assurance, insurance and other allied fields. Shows held in both the east and west coasts.
May/November Founded: 1996

20101 Counterterrorism & Security Professionals Annual Conference
PO Box 10265
Arlington, VA 22210
201-461-5422

acsp@aol.com www.iacsp.com

Steven Fustero, Executive Director

We believe that all elements of the world's societies must become better educated about the threats of terrorism as a first step toward developing innovative and effective countermeasures to combat these ongoing threats. A better informed society will result in a freer one.
May Founded: 1992

20102 Crime Analysts Annual Conference
9218 Metcalf
PMB 364
Overland Park, KS 66212
919-940-3883

nfritz@du.edu www.iaca.net

Noah Fritz, Director
Christopher Bruce, VP Administration

Annual themed conference helping crime analysts around the world improve their skills and make valuable contacts. Aids law enforcement agencies in making the best use of crime analysis and advocates for standards of performance and technique within the profession itself.
October Founded: 1990

20103 Disaster Response & Recovery Exposition NDMS Conference
J Spargo & Associates
11208 Waples Mill Road
Suite 112
Fairfax, VA 22030
703-631-6200
FAX: 703-654-6931 800-564-4220
drre@jspargo.com www.drrexpo.com

Nathan Wills, Account Manager

Held in conjunction with the NDMS Conference; it is an opportunity for local, State and Federal public health practitioners and policy makers to discover the latest equipment, technologies and services available.
2700 Attendees August

20104 Eastern Ergonomics Conference & Exposition
Continental Exhibitions
370 Lexington Avenue
New York, NY 10017
212-370-5005
FAX: 212-370-5699 800-222-2596
information@ergoexpo.com
www.ergoexpo.com
Lenore Kolb, Sales/Marketing
Walter Chamizon, President
Learn how to use ergonomics to increase productivity and safety at over 80 educational sessions. Try new products from over 100 companies, in over 2,000 square feet of floor space.
June

20105 Emergency Preparedness & Response Conferen ce & Exposition: READY
National Trade Productions
313 S Patrick Street
Alexandria, VA 22314
703-683-8500
FAX: 703-706-8234 800-687-7469
ready@ntpshow.com
www.readyinfousa.com
Janie Bridgeman, Sales Director
Maria Chaloux, Industry Relations
Annual symposium and trade show for personnel from federal, state and local agencies to learn about the latest emergency response equipment, technology, strategies and applications.
July

20106 Emergency Response Conference & Expo
PBI Media
1201 Seven Locks Road
Suite 300
Potomac, MD 20854
301-541-1400
FAX: 301-309-3847
rlewis@pbimedia.com
www.pbimedia.com
Robert Lewis, Conference Coordinator
Annual event for first responders and the companies who support them, working together on land, air and sea to save lives and property. Conference and exhibitors.
November

20107 Energy Security Expo
EJ Krause & Associates
6550 Rock Spring Drive
Suite 500
Bethesda, MD 20817-1126
301-493-5500
FAX: 301-493-5705
www.pipelinesecurity.com
Michael Rosenburg, Show Manager
Edward Krause, President
Intensive conference with workshops led by leading international experts from government and industry. Exhibit area featuring technologies, products and services for pipeline and energy infrastructure including oil, gas, electric grids, power plants and dams.
May

20108 GovSec
National Trade Productions
313 S Patrick Street
Alexandria, VA 22314
703-838-8500
FAX: 703-836-4486
www.govsecinfo.com
Denise Medved, General Manager
Provides a full spectrum of security solutions for federal, state, and local governments tasked with developing comprehensive strategies that address physical security, information security and cyber security needs. Educational programs held in conjunction with displays of a wide variety of security products and services designed specifically for government users.
Annual/May

20109 Government Convention on Emerging Technolo gies Partnerships for Homeland Sec.
National Conference Services
6440-C Dobbin Road
Columbia, MD 21045
301-596-8899
FAX: 301-596-6274 888-603-8899
mail@ncsievents.com
www.federalevents.com
Fredrick Martin, Director
Anne Slobodien, Registration
Forum for representatives from federal, state and local governments, along with the private sector to collaborate on and experiment with information technology that addresses mission needs critical to homeland security. Exhibits, workshops and simulation exercises.
January

20110 Homeland Security Expo & Conference
E-Gov Conferences
3141 Fairview Park Drive
Suite 777
Falls Church, VA 22042-4507
703-876-5060
FAX: 703-876-5059 800-746-0099
info@e-gov.com www.e-gov.com
Mike Smoyer, General Manager
Keynote presentations, conference sessions, plenary session and exhibition of solutions and technologies to enhance homeland security efforts.
November/December

20111 ISC Expo International Security Conference and Expo-Las Vegas
Reed Exhibition Companies
383 Main Avenue
Norwalk, CT 06851
203-840-4800
FAX: 203-840-9322
inquiry@isc.reedexpo.com
www.iscwest.com
Amie Cangelosi, Marketing Coordinator
Kara Buonanno, Marketing/Conference Manager
From around the globe, every relevant manufacturer, product, service and industry expert will be on hand for three days under one roof.
March/April

20112 ISC: International Security Conference & Expo
Reed Exhibitions
383 Main Avenue
Norwalk, CT 06851
203-840-4800
FAX: 203-840-9322
inquiry@isc.reedexpo.com
www.isceast.com
Amie Cangelosi, Marketing Coordinator
Kara Buonanno, Marketing/Conference Manager
From around the globe, relevant manufacturers, products, services and industry experts will be on hand under one roof.
November

20113 Inside ID: Identification Solutions Mega Show
Inside ID
8900 Saunders Lane
Bethesda, MD 20817
301-365-0186
FAX: 301-365-2519
info@insideid.com www.insideid.com
Ben Miller, President
Liz Wenchel, VP Conferences
Helps define and center the evolution of the emerging disipline of Identity Management. Education and displays of new products and technologies in identification. Facilitates the marketplace of buyers and sellers, provides a broad-based forum, and gathering place for standards groups and associations around the world.

20114 International Cargo Security Council
1400 I Street NW
Suite 1050
Washington, DC 20005-2209
202-821-1787
FAX: 410-956-0679
icsc@cargosecurity.com
www.cargosecurity.com
Joe Baker Jr, Executive Director
Ellen Parkereman, Meeting Director
Workshops and 60 booth exposition for cargo transportation and security professionals from the entire spectrum of cargo security: air, truck, rail maritime and intermodal.
450 Attendees Annual Founded: 1973

20115 International Consumer Product Health & Sa fety Organization Annual Meeting
PO Box 1785
Germantown, MD 20875-1785
301-601-3240
FAX: 301-601-3543
icphso@aol.com www.icphso.org
Dedicated to the health and safety issues related to consumer products manufactured and marketed in the global marketplace. Serving both health and safety professionals and consumers by sponsoring national and regional workshops. Annual meeting and training syposium.
March Founded: 1993

20116 National Council of Investigation & Securi ty Annual Conference
7501 Sparrows Point Boulevard
Baltimore, MD 21219-1927

FAX: 410-388-9746 800-445-8408
nciss@aol.com www.nciss.com
Carolyn Ward, Executive Director
State associations and firms providing contract security services and investigative services. Our cooperative effort includes a legislative watch and providing accurate information reguarding our profession.
March

20117 National Ergonomics Conference & Expositio n
Continental Exhibitions
370 Lexington Avenue
New York, NY 10017
212-370-5005
FAX: 212-370-5699 800-222-2596
lkolb@ergoexpo.com
www.ergoexpo.com

Lenore Kolb, Sales/Marketing
Walter Chamizon, President

Learn how to use ergonomics to increase productivity and safety at over 80 educational sessions. Try new products from over 100 companies, in over 2,000 square feet of floor space.

December

20118 National Fire Protection World Safety Conference & Exposition
National Fire Protection Association
1 Batterymarch Park
Quincy, MA 02669-9101
617-930-0100
FAX: 617-770-0700
public_affairs@nfpa.org
www.nfpa.org

James Shannon, President

Professional development, networking and hundreds of booths from key industry suppliers.

May

20119 National Safety Council Congress Expo
National Safety Council
1121 Spring Lake Drive
Itasca, IL 60143
630-775-2213
FAX: 630-285-0798 800-621-7619
customerservice@nsc.org
www.congress.nsc.org

Nancy Gavin, Expo Manager
Christine Paplaczyk, Exhibit Sales
Alan McMillan, Chief Executive Officer

Annual event for safety, health and the environment.

16000 Attendees September

20120 Police and Security Expo
PO Box 20068
Sarasota, FL 34276-0368
609-466-2111
FAX: 609-466-2675 800-323-1927
webmaster@police-security.com
www.police-security.com

Displaying goods, products and services for law enforcement and security professionals.

June

20121 Professional Security Consultants Annual Conference
525 SW 5th Street
Suite A
Des Moines, IA 50309-4501
515-282-8192
FAX: 515-282-9117
iapsc@iapsc.org www.iapsc.org

David G Aggleton, President
Robert A Schultheiss, VP
Dick Goodson, Executive Director

Seeks to enhance members knowledge through seminars, training programs, and educational materials. Works to foster public awareness of the security consulting industry.

April Founded: 1984

20122 Professional Security Alliance Conference & Exhibits
PSA Security Network
12011 N Tejon Street
Denver, CO 80234
303-520-0137
FAX: 303-252-1741
lisa@psasecurity.com
www.psasecurity.com

Lisa Speyer, Conference/Marketing
Shelley Binder, Customer/Vendor Service
Michelle Medina, Membership

For corporate management, salespeople, project managers and other technicians for PSA member companies. Educational sessions and pavillion featuring video surveillance, access control and biometrics.

20123 Rocky Mountain Health & Safety Conference
Colorado Safety Association
4730 Oakland Street
Suite 500
Denver, CO 80239
303-373-1937
FAX: 303-373-1955
melodye@coloradosafety.org
www.coloradosafety.org

Melodye Turek, President
Jan Harris, Finance Manager
Judy Sapp, Manager

Over 100 exhibitors of safety products, regulatory compliance updates and networking. Educational sessions are offered on various safety topics.

April Founded: 1968

20124 SAFE Association Annual Symposium
SAFE Association
PO Box 130
Creswell, OR 97426
541-895-3012
FAX: 541-895-3014
safe@peak.org
www.safeassociation.com

Jean Benton, Adminstrator

Presentation topics range from desert survival to the latest aircraft passenger egress aids, cockpit design, restraint systems, and school bus design to international symbols related to transportation and safety, and crew training. Attended by an international group of professionals who are there to share problems and solutions in the field of safety and survival.

800 Attendees September Founded: 1954

20125 Safetech
Safe & Vault Technicians Association
3003 Live Oak Street
Dallas, TX 75204-6128
214-199-9771
FAX: 214-827-1810 www.savta.org

Joanne Mims, Conventions/Meetings Manager

Annual symposium and trade show for professionals in the valuables protection industry.

March

20126 Securing New Ground
Securing New Ground
10100 Sherman Road
Chardon, OH 44024
440-286-4900
FAX: 440-286-9169
info@securingnewground.com
www.securingnewground.com

Dini Jones, Conference Coordinator
Rebecca Reed, Manager

Annual 2 day conference with influential people impacting the security industry. Learn about financing, new trends and opportunities for the security industry. Breakfast, lunch and reception included.

October

20127 Security Canada Trade Shows
Canadian Alarm & Security Association
610 Alden Road
Suite 100
Markam, ON L3R-9Z1
905-513-0622
FAX: 905-513-0624
hewitson@canasa.org
www.canasa.org

Tracy Cannata, Executive Director
Joyce Everton, Administrative Manager
Lynne Hewiston, Trade Show Manager

Offering four shows annually. Security Canada East is in April, Security Canada Atlantic is in September, Security Canada West is in June and Security Canada Central is in October. These gaterings offer professional development, information, networking and new products to dealers, distributors, manufacturers and monitoring companies across Canada.

Founded: 1977

20128 Sensors Expo & Conference
Advanstar Communications
1 Phoenix Mill Lane
Peterborough, NH 03458
603-924-5400
FAX: 603-924-5401
cwalters@advanstar.com
www.sensorsexpo.com

Cathy Walters, Show Director
Jeanne DuVal, Sales Manager

Informative, sensor related sessions, exhibits and special events for thousands of professionals who will help shape the future of sensing technology.

June

20129 Texas Association of Fire Educators Annual Instructors Conference
13492 Research Boulevard
Suite 120, PMB 262
Austin, TX 78750-2254

patclinton@tx-tafe.org
www.tx-tafe.org

Alan Storck, President
Tim Sendelbach, VP
Jim Lee, Secretary
Patricia Clinton, Treasurer

Annual gathering for state fire safety instructors to network and learn the latest in the industry.

January

20130 Texas Burglar & Fire Alarm Assn. Annual Me eting, Trade Show & Golf Classic
PO Box 59982
Dallas, TX 75229-1982
877-908-2322
FAX: 877-908-2522
president@tbfaa.org www.tbfaa.org

Rex Adams, President
JD Benfer, VP
Jan Wilson, Secretary
Malcolm Reed, Treasurer

Annual gathering of a large number of professional security and fire alarm companies that operate in the state of Texas.

October

20131 US Maritime Security Expo
EJ Krause & Associates
6550 Rock Spring Drive
Suite 500
Bethesda, MD 20817-1126
301-493-5500
FAX: 301-493-5705
field@ejkrause.com
www.maritimesecurityexpo.com

Lindsey Field, Show Manager
Edward Krause, President

Annual conference and exhibitor hall attended by those who protect ports, harbors, bridges, cargo containers, power plants, off shore oil rigs, railroads, cargo and passenger ships.
September

Directories & Databases

20132 American Society for Industrial Security: Annual Membership Directory
American Society for Industrial Security
1625 Prince Street
Alexandria, VA 22314-2818
703-519-6200
FAX: 703-519-6299 800-368-5685
asis@asisonline.org
www.asisonline.org

Keith Goins, Membership Manager
Michael Stack, Executive Director

25,000 member management specialists in the private and public sectors who formulate security policy and direct security programs to prevent terrorism, dcoument piracy. Available as a membership benefit only.

20133 BCSP Directory and International Registry of Certified Safety Professionals
Board of Certified Safety Professionals
208 Burwash Avenue
Savoy, IL 61874-9571
217-359-9263
FAX: 217-359-0055
bcsp@bcsp.org www.bcsp.org

Dr Roger Brauer, Executive Director
Heather Murphy, Marketing

Directory includes over 10,000 safety professionals holding the Certified Safety Professional (CSP) or Associate Safety Professional (ASP) designation. *$100.00*
Founded: 1969
Circulation: 10000 10,000 names $90 per M.
Printed in on matte stock : CD-Rom

20134 Business Insurance Directory of Safety Consultants & Rehabilitation Mgt.
Crain Communications
360 N Michigan Avenue
Chicago, IL 60601
312-495-5231
FAX: 312-280-3174

Martin J Ross, Publisher/Corporate VP
Ronnie Drachman, Director Communications

List of more than 150 employee safety consultants and over 70 employee rehabilitation management providers. *$4.00*
Annual
Circulation: 53,000

20135 Central Station Alarm Association Director y
440 Maple Avenue E
Suite 201
Vienna, VA 22180
703-242-4670
FAX: 703-242-4675
communications@csaaul.org
www.csaaul.org

Stephen P Doyle, Executive VP
Celia Besore, Director Marketing/Communications *$195.00*
94 pages Annual
Circulation: 1,000

20136 Computer Security Buyers Guide
Computer Security Institute
600 Harrison Street
San Francisco, CA 94107-1387
415-947-6320
FAX: 415-905-2218 800-227-4675
wwilson@infi.com www.gocsi.com/csi

Patrice Rapalus, Editor

About 650 suppliers and consultants of computer security products, including communications and network security, disaster recovery, media security, personnel security and security training. *$197.00*
Annual
Circulation: 4,500

20137 Directory of Mail Drop Addresses and Zip Codes
Fraud & Theft Information Bureau
PO Box 400
Boynton Beach, FL 33425
561-323-3653
FAX: 561-737-5800
sales@fraudandtheftinfo.com
www.fraudandtheftinfo.com

Larry Schwartz, Publisher/Editor
Pearl Say, Editor/VP

Identifies every one of the 35,000 mail drops used by credit card thieves to steel your merchandise. Thousands of credt card thieves use thse address, which sound like residential addresses, to hide their identity and true address while stealing from you with stolen credit card numbers. *$605.50*
Annual Founded: 1982 ISBN 0-914801-07-4

20138 Disaster Resource Guide
Disaster Resource Guide
PO Box 15243
Santa Ana, CA 92735

FAX: 714-558-8901
www.disaster-resource.com
Articles, business resources and product information for public and private emergency preparedness. Free of charge if subscriber is registered annually.
Annual

20139 Fire Protection Equipment Directory
Underwriters Laboratories
333 Pfingsten Road
Northbrook, IL 60062-2096
847-120-0136
FAX: 847-272-8129 www.ul.com

Shaquanda Debbs, Directory Sales

Companies that have qualified to use the UL listing mark or classification marking on or in connection with products that have been found to be in compliance with UL's requirements. *$35.00*
February

20140 Fire Resistance Directory
Underwriters Laboratories
3333 Pfingsten Road
Northbrook, IL 60062
847-120-0136
FAX: 847-272-8129
directories@us.ul.com www.ul.com

Shaquanda Debbs, Directory Sales

Companies that have qualified to use the UL listing mark or classification marking on or in connection with products that have been found to be in compliance with UL's requirements. 4 book set. *$110.00*
February

20141 Fire Retardant Chemicals Association: Membership Directory
Fire Retardant Chemicals Association
851 New Holland Avenue
Lancaster, PA 17601-5644
202-530-4590
FAX: 717-295-4538
frca@fireretardants.org
www.fireretardants.org
Approximately 35 member manufacturers and distributors of chemical fire retardants and related supplies.

20142 Fire Suppression Systems Association: Membership Directory
Fire Suppression Systems Association
5024 Campbell Boulevard
Suite R
Baltimore, MD 21236
410-931-2374
FAX: 410-931-8111 fssadhg@aol.com
Approximately 120 member companies that design, manufacture, distribute, install or repair and maintain fire suppression systems.
Annual

20143 Grey House Biometric Information Directory
Grey House Publishing
185 Millerton Road
PO Box 860
Millerton, NY 12546
518-890-0526
FAX: 518-789-0545 800-562-2139
books@greyhouse.com
www.greyhouse.com

Leslie Mackenzie, Publisher
Richard Gottlieb, Editor

The most comprehensive resource covering biometric technology. Contains hundreds of organizations providing biometric products and services. The directory encompasses emerging identification technology, such as fingerprint ID, facial recognition, key stroke scan, hand geometry, voice recognition, iris scan and many other methods. *$295.00*
360 pages Annual Founded: 2005

20144 Grey House Homeland Security Directory
Grey House Publishing
185 Millerton Road
PO Box 860
Millerton, NY 12546
518-890-0526
FAX: 518-789-0545 800-562-2139
books@greyhouse.com
www.greyhouse.com

Leslie Mackenzie, Publisher
Richard Gottlieb, Editor

Features the latest contact information for government and private organizations involved with Homeland Security along with the latest product information. The directory provides detailed profiles of nearly 2,000 Federal & State Organizations & Agencies and over 3,000 Officials and Key Executives involved with Homeland Security. *$195.00*

800 pages Annual ISBN 1-592370-56-X

20145 Grey House Safety & Security Directory

Grey House Publishing
185 Millerton Road
PO Box 860
Millerton, NY 12546
518-890-0526
FAX: 518-789-0545 800-562-2139
books@greyhouse.com
www.greyhouse.com

Leslie Mackenzie, Publisher
Richard Gottlieb, Editor

Two-volume guide to the safety and security industry, including articles, checklists, OSHA regulations and product listings. The 16 chapters focus on creating and maintaing a safe and secure enviroment, and deal specifically with hazardous materials, noise and vibration, workplace preparation and maintenance, electrical and lighting safety, fire and rescue and more. Accepts advertising. *$225.00*

1500 pages Annual ISBN 1-592370-67-5

20146 Grey House Transportation Security Directory

Grey House Publishing
185 Millerton Road
PO Box 860
Millerton, NY 12546
518-890-0526
FAX: 518-789-0545 800-562-2139
books@greyhouse.com
www.greyhouse.com

Leslie Mackenzie, Publisher
David Garoogian, Editor

Information on everything from Regulatory Authorities to Security Equipment, this top-flight database brings together the relevant information necessary for creating and maintaining a security plan for a wide range of transportation facilities. *$195.00*

800 pages Founded: 2004 ISBN 1-592370-75-6

20147 Kodex Security Equipment/Systems Database

Security Defense Systems
139 Chestnut Street
#626
Nutley, NJ 07110-2311
973-235-0606
FAX: 973-235-0132 800-325-6339

More than 32,000 manufacturers and distributors worldwide of home and office security equipment and systems. *$295.00*

Biennial

20148 Material Safety Data Sheet Reference

C&P Press
302 5th Avenue
5th Floor
New York, NY 10001
212-326-6760
FAX: 646-733-6010
cpp@cppress.com www.cppress.com

Regulatory and product safety requirements. Contains full text MSDS's for products listed in the Crop Protection Reference plus additional safety information such as DOT shipping information, SARA Title III regulations, Hazardous Chemical inventory reporting information plus much more. Available in print, database, continually updated electronic version or CD-ROM.

20149 NFPA Journal: Buyers' Guide

National Fire Protection Association
1 Batterymarch Park
Quincy, MA 02169-7454
617-793-0100
FAX: 617-770-0700 800-344-3555
awandell@nfpa.org www.nfpa.org

Dorinda Tergason, Editor
A Wandell, Marketing
Jim Shannon, President

List of manufacturers and consultants of fire protection, fire safety and fire service products. *$30.00*

February
Circulation: 95,000

20150 National Directory of Fire Chiefs & EMS Administrators

National Public Safety Information Bureau
2173 Church Street, Suite 201
PO Box 365
Stevens Point, WI 54481-0365
715-345-2772
FAX: 715-345-7288 800-647-7579
info@safetysource.com
www.safetysource.com

Laura Gross, Data Aquisition Manager
Steve Cywinski, Publisher

Vital contact resource for busy professionals. Contact nearly every fire and emergency department in the US, nearly 35,000 departments. *$129.00*

June Founded: 1964
Circulation: 10000 33M names

20151 National Directory of Law Enforcement Administrators

National Public Safety Information Bureau
2173 Church Street, Suite 201
PO Box 365
Stevens Point, WI 54481-0365
715-345-2772
FAX: 715-345-7288 800-647-7579
info@safetysource.com
www.safetysource.com

Laura Gross, Data Aquisition Manager
Steve Cywinski, Publisher

Listing of police departments, sheriffs, criminal prosecutors, state law enforcement, criminal investigation and homeland security agencies. *$129.00*

June Founded: 1964 ISBN 1-880245-22-1
Circulation: 10000 33M names

20152 National Work Zone Safety Information Clea ringhouse

Texas Transportation Institute
TAMU 3135
College Station, TX 77843-3135

888-447-5556
workzone@tamu.edu
www.wzsafety.tamu.edu

Cooperative partnership between the American Road and Transportation Builders Association and the Texas Transportation Institute. Offers information traffic accidents and crashes, equipment and technology, legislation, research projects and training.

20153 Occupational Safety & Health Database

American Industrial Hygiene Association
2700 Prosperity Avenue
Suite 250
Fairfax, VA 22031
703-849-8267
FAX: 703-207-3561
infonet@aiha.org www.aiha.org

Steven Davis, Executive Director
Wanda Barbour, Manager Customer Service

Web accessible database with over 22,000 original abstracts covering virtually all aspects of the occupational safety and health field. Records contain original abstracts as well as complete bibliographic information. Documents represented are from sources dating back to the early 1970s as well as important articles from earlier literature. *$240.00*

Individual Subscription

20154 Security Industry Sourcebook

PRIMEDIA Business Magazines & Media

9800 Metcalf Avenue
Overland Park, KS 66212
913-341-1300
FAX: 913-967-1898
landerson@primediabusiness.com
www.primediabusiness.com

Larry Anderson, Editor

Listings of over 600 manufacturers and distributors of security and safety products.

Annual
Circulation: 28,400

20155 Society of Fire Protection Engineers: Membership Roster

Society of Fire Protection Engineers
7315 Wisconsin Avenue
Suite 1225W
Bethesda, MD 20814
301-718-2910
FAX: 301-781-2242

Pamela A Powell, Editor
Kathleen Almond, Chief Executive Officer

Annual February

Industry Web Sites

20156 www.abih.org

American Board of Industrial Hygiene

Information on credentials for Certified Industrial Hygienist status.

20157 www.afaa.org

Automatic Fire Alarm Association

Members are made up of manufacturers, installers and others interested in fire alarm and detection equipment. Seminars are conducted on a national basis.

20158 www.allbounty.com

North American Recovery Network

Worldwide portal for agents of collateral repossesion and bail bonds. Chats, forums and industry news.

20159 www.aloa.org
Associated Locksmiths of America

News and event information for the locksmith industry. Maintains referral service and offers insurance and bonding programs.

20160 www.alw.nih.gov/Security/security
Center for Information Technology

Computer security information and links.

20161 www.apco911.org
Association of Public-Safety Communications Officials International

Dedicated to the enhancement of public safety communications and to serving its more than 15,000 members, the people who use public safety communications systems and services.

20162 www.asisonline.org
American Society for Industrial Security

Organization which features ideas and practices for business and industrial security managers.

20163 www.asse.org
American Society of Safety Engineers

Information for members on upcoming meetings, training and local chapters.

20164 www.bioxs.com
Bio XS

Biometrics newsletter updated weekly. Features company profiles and new products.

20165 www.buildershardware.com
Builders Hardware Manufacturers Association

Code & life safety regulation information concerning locks and builders hardware.

20166 www.businesssecuritytips.com
Security Industry Association

Provides businesses with technology specific information and helps business owners and managers understand how available technology can be be better utilized.

20167 www.ccohs.ca
Canadian Centre for Occupational Safety & Health

Information on safety and industrial health topics in Canada.

20168 www.cdc.gov/niosh/homepage.html
National Institute for Occupational Safety/Health

Information on chemical safety, emergency response, injuries, construction, mining, agriculture concerns, respirators and much more.

20169 www.cert.org
Carnegie Mellon Software Engineering Institute

News, statistics and helpful articles relating to computer security.

20170 www.chemsafety.gov
US Chemical Safety & Hazard Investigation Board

Investigative reports of chemical safety incidents and an archive of completed investigations and recommondations made to regulators.

20171 www.cisecurity.org
Center for Internet Security

Helps organizations around the world effectively manage the risks related to internet security.

20172 www.csrc.nist.gov
National Institute of Standards & Technology

Information, links and white papers from the Information Technology Laboratory, the Computer Security Division and the Computer Security Resource Center.

20173 www.disaster-resource.com
Disaster Resource Guide

News, articles, business resources and product highlights for security and business managers as well as contingency planners who are in charge of emergency business recovery.

20174 www.eia-usa.org
Environmental Information Association

Nonprofit organization dedicated to providing environmental information to individuals, members and the industry. Disseminates information on the abatement of asbestos and lead-based paint, indoor air quality, safety and health issues, analytical issues and environmental site assessments.

20175 www.findbiometrics.com
Topickz

Showcases new technologies in biometric security and provides links to companies providing them.

20176 www.firefighting.com
National Fire Protection Association

News and editorial items of interest to fire fighters.

20177 www.first.org
Forum of Incident Response and Security Teams

Brings together a variety of computer security incident response teams from government, commercial and academic organizations. This site encourages cooperation in incident prevention, rapid reaction to incidents and to promote information sharing.

20178 www.fraud.org
National Consumers League

Your source for Internet and telemarketing fraud information.

20179 www.fraudandtheftinfo.com
Fraud and Theft Information Bureau

Provides problem solving, crime prevention, money saving manuals and fraud blocker databases.

20180 www.fssa.net
Fire Suppression Systems Association

Association news and events for designers, suppliers and installers of special hazard fire suppression equipment, gases and detectors.

20181 www.ginetwork.com
Global Investigators Network

Worldwide internet based organization for private investigators.

20182 www.gocsi.org
Computer Security Institute

Information on computer and network security.

20183 www.greyhouse.com
Grey House Publishing

Selected Grey House directories in the fields of business, health and education are available online. Users can search our online databases by several different search criteria, such as product categories, geographic area, sales volume and much, much more. Full Grey House catalog and online ordering also available.

20184 www.highwaysafety.org
Insurance Institute for Highway Safety

Vehicle safety news and statistics from traffic and motor vehicle safety organization supported by auto insurers.

20185 www.infoguys.com
Spyville

Process servers associations, articles and certification information, forensic experts and a searchable database for private investigators or those seeking to hire one.

20186 www.infosecuritymag.techtarget.com
Tech Target

Online information technology magazine.

20187 www.intsi.org
International Security Industry Organization

Dedicated to improving effcient communication to all stakeholders in the security industries and provides them with the necessary information to be more effective in their daily tasks.

20188 www.investigativeprofessionals.com
Investigative Professionals

Consult with a professional investigator, accomplish a people locator search, do a background check, conduct your own investigation or get information on becoming a private investigator.

20189 www.issa.org
Information Systems Security Association

International computer system information from an organization of security professionals and practitioners.

20190 www.museum-security.org
Museum Security Network

Free internet service and mailing list for museum security professionals, curators, librarians, registrar and specialized police.

20191 www.naaa.org
National Alarm Association of America

Alarm dealers association offers training, tips, an online newsletter and other member benefits.

20192 www.ndia.org
National Defense Industrial Association

To provide legal and ethical forum for the interchange of ideas between the government and industry to resolve industrial problems of joint concern.

20193 www.net-security.org
Help Net Security

Daily updated security related site.

20194 www.nnsa.doe.gov
National Nuclear Security Administration

Increasing public awareness of nuclear security and current energy issues. Links to website of supporting offices.

20195 www.nsi.org
National Security Institute

Features industry and product news, computer alerts, travel advisories, a calender of events, a directory of products and services and access to a virtual security library.

20196 www.ope.ed.gov/security
Campus Security Statistics

Direct link to reported criminal offenses for over 6000 colleges and universities in the US. If you are considering a college in a large urban city, a small liberal arts college, a specialized college or a community college you can find their security statistics here.

20197 www.osh.net
Workcare

Links to health and safety news. Offers online newslettter free to subscribers.

20198 www.osha.gov
Occupational Safety & Health Administration

Regulations and standards for worker safety in the US. Also included are a searchable database of recent safety violation citations, electronic safety lessons for many industries, a spot where workers can report safety concerns, safety tipsheets and a section for Spanish speaking workers.

20199 www.osha.gov/dop/nacosh.html
Nat'l Advisory Comm. on Occupational Safety/Health

News releases, federal register notices, reports, meeting agendas and contact information for the 12 members representing management, labor, occupational health and safety and the public. This group advises the secretaries of labor and health and human services on occupational safety and health programs and policies.

20200 www.pavnet.org
Partnership Against Violence Network

Virtual library of information about violence and youth-at-risk, representing data from seven different Federal agencies.

20201 www.personalprotection.com
Nine Lives Associates

Information on programs which emphasize personal survival skills and techniques for the protection of others. Information on training and list of protective agents and consultants.

20202 www.picoffeshop.com
PI Coffee Shop

Articles and a national forum of interest to private investigators.

20203 www.pimall.com
PI Mall

Information for private investigator contacts, products, training and services.

20204 www.processservers.com
International Process Servers Association

Resource for process servers and private investigators. Message board and searchable database by zipcode to locate a local process server.

20205 www.ready.gov
US Government

Updates and information on how the Department of Homeland Security is working to keep America safe.

20206 www.rims.org
Risk & Insurance Management Society

Information on worker's compensation, enterprise risk, risk management and financing, corporate governance and risk management.

20207 www.rmsecgroup.com
Risk Management Security Group

Addresses general aviation and cargo security concerns, training for professional transportation personnel, provides threat vulnerability assessments and literature.

20208 www.safeassociation.com
SAFE Association

Website of the nonprofit organization dedicated to the preservation of human life. It provides a common meeting ground for the sharing of problems, ideas and information.

20209 www.saferoads.org
Advocates for Highway and Auto Safety

Information on road safety issues, federal programs, polls, reports and helpful links for consumers, safety and law enforcement agencies, insurance agents and organizations.

20210 www.safetycentral.org
Safety Equipment Distributors Association

Represents wholesale-distributors of safety equipment and works to enhance and improve distribution through excellence in communications, training, education and services.

20211 www.safetyhealthmanager.org
National Safety Management Society

A professional society dedicated to the advancement of new concepts of accident prevention and loss control, promoting safety management.

20212 www.safetysmart.com
Bongarde Holdings

Safety education products and information.

20213 www.safetysource.com
National Public Safety Information Bureau

News, events, web guide and public safety shopping for professionals in corrections, EMS, fire and police departments.

20214 www.securityfocus.com
Symantec

Offers a forum for objective reporting by security experts on the latest computer security threats and prevention.

20215 www.securitysales.com
Security Sales & Integration

Breaking news of electronic security concerns and articles from the current issue of Security Sales & Integration.

20216 www.siaonline.org
Security Industry Association

Promotes growth, expansion and professionalism within the security industry. Online newsletter has the daily top ten headlines in security.

20217 www.stats.bls.gov
Bureau of Labor Statistics

Data on workplace injuries, illnesses and fatalities.

20218 www.terrorismcentral.com
Terrorism Central

Responding to the need for a single, trusted source of information about terrorism and related security issues, this central information repository comprises original and secondary sources spanning decades of research.

20219 www.ul.com/auth/tca
Underwriters Laboratories

Code Authority — online newsletter for the code community.

20220 www.vpppa.org
Voluntary Protection Program Participant's Assoc.

Information on the Occupational Safety and Health Administration's Voluntary Protection Participant program for companies.

20221 www.whitehouse.gov/homeland
Whitehouse

Updates of Homeland Security department and staff activities, list of state homeland security officers and contact information.

20222 www1.blr.com
Business & Legal Reports

Provides essential tools for safety and environmental compliance and training needs.

Associations

20223 American Apparel & Footwear Association
1601 N Kent Street
Suite 1200
Arlington, VA 22209
703-241-1864
FAX: 703-522-6741 800-520-2262
slapetina@apparelandfootwear.org
www.apparelandfootwear.org

Edward C Emma, Chairman
Kevin Burke, President/CEO
Marti Rust, Executive Administrator

National trade association representing apparel, footwear and other sewn products companies and their suppliers. Our mission is to promote and enhance our members competitiveness, productivity and profitability in the global market.
Founded: 1960

20224 Association of Footwear Distributors
110-114 N George Street
York, PA 17401-1106

FAX: 717-845-9789

Dan Peterman Jr, Executive Director

Major distributors of footwear.
13 Members Founded: 1956

20225 Fashion Footwear Association of New York
1414 Avenue of the Americas
Suite 203
New York, NY 10019
212-751-6422
FAX: 212-751-6404
info@ffany.org www.ffany.org

Joseph C Moore, President & CEO
Shelley Berquist, VP Operations

Representing footwear manufacturers globally. Mission is to promote ans assist the common business interests of our members, who include over 300 footwear manufacturers, representing over 800 fashion footear brands.

20226 Footwear Distributors and Retailers of America
1319 F Street NW
Suite 700
Washington, DC 20004-1121
202-737-5660
FAX: 202-638-2615

Peter Mangione, Executive Director

Trade association for footwear distributors and volume retailers.
70 Members Founded: 1944

20227 National Shoe Retailers Association (NSRA)
7150 Columbia Gateway Drive
Suite G
Columbia, MD 21046-1151
410-381-8282
FAX: 410-381-1167
info@nsra.org www.nsra.org

Phil Wright, Chairman
Ed Habre, Vice Chairman

Trade organization representing independent shoe retailers. Provides independent shoe retailers with solid, practical workplace benefits that enable them to operate their business more profitably and successfully.
Founded: 1912

20228 Pedorthic Footwear Association
7150 Columbia Gateway Drive
Suite G
Columbia, MD 21046
410-381-7278
FAX: 410-381-1167 800-673-8447
info@pedorthics.org
www.pedorthics.org

Brian Laguna, Executive Director
Nancy Hultquist, Director Communications

Membership organization for individuals and companies involved in the design, manufacture, modification and fit of therapeutic footwear. Provides educational programs, publications, legislative monitoring, marketing materials, professional liason and business operations services. *$55.00*
2000 Members Founded: 1958

20229 Sporting Goods Manufacturers Association
1150 17th Street NW
Suite 850
Washington, DC 20036-1604
202-775-1762
FAX: 202-296-7462
info@sgma.com www.sgma.com

Andrea Cernich, Communications Director
Tom Cove, President

Our purpose is to support our member companies and promote a healthy environment for the sporting goods industry. SGMA enhances industry vitality and fosters sports, fitness and active lifestyle participation.
1000 Members Founded: 1906

20230 Two Ten Footwear Foundation
1466 Main Street
Waltham, MA 02451
781-736-1500
FAX: 781-736-1555 800-FIN-D210

Peggy Kim Meill, President
Laura Woodward, Director of Special Events

Mission is to take action and create change for those in need. Built upon a foundation of caring, serving our community through social services and educational programs.

Newsletters

20231 Footwear News
Fairchild Publications
750 3rd Ave
Fl 7
New York, NY 10017-2700
212-304-4274
800-360-1700
atmore@fairchildpub.com
http://www.fairchildpub.com/

Jay Spaleta, Publisher
Katie Abel, Editor

Weekly publication covering the international footwear industry's fashion trends, news developments, finances and market data. *$ 72.00*
Weekly Founded: 1892
Circulation: 17892

20232 WSA Today
Show Dailies International
460 Richmond Street West
Suite 701
Toronto, ON 90049-5103
416-730-8488
FAX: 416-730-1878 800-360-3234

Rich DiGiacomo, Publisher
Robin Ingle, Chairman/CEO

Features products and industry news, conference information and interviews. Published daily during the semiannual Western Shoe Show.
Founded: 1946

Magazines & Journals

20233 Current Pedorthics
Pedorthic Footwear Association
7150 Columbia Gateway Drive
Suite G
Columbia, MD 21046-1151
410-381-7278
FAX: 410-381-1167 800-673-8447
info@pedothrics.org
http://www.pedorthics.org

Mike Forgrave, President
Nancy Hultquist, Editor
Bill Boettge, CEO
Nancy Hultquist, Circulation Manager
Rancho Cordova, Marketting Manager

Covers pedorthics; the design, manufacture, modification and fit of shoes and foot orthoses to alleviate foot problems caused by disease, overuse or injury. *$35.00*
44 pages Quarterly Founded: 1958
Circulation: 5000

20234 Footwear Market Guide
307 West 38th Street
Suite 1005
New York, NY 10018
212-398-5505
FAX: 212-398-5504
customercare@infomat.com
www.infomat.com
Provides a broad industry overview, including key press, manufacturing and sales contacts in one superb, value-prived package. *$ 165.00*

20235 National Shoe Retailers Magazine
7150 Columbia Gateway Drive
Suite G
Columbia, MD 21046-1151
410-381-8282
FAX: 410-381-1167 800-673-8446
info@nsra.org www.nsra.org

Nancy Hultquist, Director Communications
Bill Boettge, President

Provides businesses information such as credit-card processing and shipping at special features for the industry.
36 pages Founded: 1912
Printed in 2 colors on glossy stock

20236 Pedorthic Footwear Magazine
7150 Columbia Gateway Drive
Suite G
Columbia, MD 21046-1151
410-381-7278
FAX: 410-381-1167 800-673-8447
info@pedorthics.org
http://www.pedorthics.org

Brian Lagana, Executive Director
Nancy Hultquist, Director Communications

Kalin Wilburn, Sales Coordinator
Mike Forgrave, President
Amy Bloom, Membership Manager

Provides educational articles, marketing materials and professional information. *$55.00*

44 pages Founded: 1958
Circulation: 5000 15,000 names $150 per M.
Printed in 2 colors on glossy stock

20237 Runner's World
Runner's World Magazine Company
135 N 6th Street
Emmaus, PA 18098
610-967-5171
FAX: 610-967-8883 800-845-8050
rwforums@rodale.com
http://www.runnersworld.com

Andrew R Hersam, Publisher
David Willey, Editor
Steven Pleshette Murphy, CEO/President
Charles DeLana, Marketing
Richard Alleger, Circulation Manager

A magazine dedicated to the lifestyle fitness activity of running. Aims to inform, advise, educate and motivate runners of all ages and abilities. *$21.00*

Monthly Founded: 1966
Circulation: 530511
Mailing list available for rent 370,000 names

Printed in on glossy stock

20238 Shoe Retailing Today
National Shoe Retailers Association
7150 Columbia Gateway Drive
Suite G
Columbia, MD 21046-1151
410-381-8282
FAX: 410-381-1167 800-673-8446
info@nsra.org http://www.nsra.org

Bill Boettge, Managing Director
Nancy Hultquist, Editor

Offers information to independent shoe retailers across the country. *$35.00*

Founded: 1912
Circulation: 4000

20239 Shoestats
Footwear Industries of America
1420 K Street NW
Suite 600
Washington, DC 20005-2505
202-789-1420
FAX: 202-789-7257
info@fia.org
http://www.shoeinfonet.com

Fawn K Evenson, President

Complete statistical coverage of the footwear industry. *$40.00*

210 pages Bi-annually

Trade Shows

20240 American Apparel & Footwear Association An nual Meeting
1601 N Kent Street
Suite 1200
Arlington, VA 22209
703-241-1864
FAX: 847-522-6741 800-520-2262
alengels@apparelandfootwear.org
www.apparelandfootwear.org

Kevin Burke, President/CEO
Joan McNeal, Membership
Ann Engles, Meeting Coordinator

International event for the sewn products industries. Bringing together top level executives in an exclusive yet personable forum, you'll have the opportunity to share ideas, exchange information and cultivate new opportunities in today's global marketplace.

180 Attendees Founded: 1969

20241 Annual Symposium
Pedorthic Footwear Association
7150 Columbia Gateway Drive
Columbia, MD 21046-2972

FAX: 410-381-1167 800-673-8447

Jeanne Williams, Manager

The Annual Symposium is a combination education event and trade show expo. Containing 100+ booths and exhibits.

600+ Attendees November Founded: 1958
$75 per M.

20242 Global Leather
Footwear Industries of America- Division of AAFA
1601 N Kent Street
Suite 1200
Arlington, VA 22205
703-524-1864
FAX: 703-522-6741 800-520-2262
info@fia.org www.fia.org

Showcases the best in new leather materials and components for the footwear leather, needle and allied trades of North America. Brings together hundreds of exhibitors from the major sourcing cities around the world, showcasing thousands of products.

1500 Attendees February/August

20243 Metropolitan Shoe Show New York
50 W 34th Street
Apartment 8A6
New York, NY 10001-3057
212-564-1069

Mary Stanton, Show Manager

225 booths.

2M Attendees March/September

20244 Northwest Show Travelers Buying Show Market
2720 W 43rd Street
Minneapolis, MN 55410-1643
612-920-5005

Dona Merchant, Show Manager

100 booths of shoe retailers and specialty store personnel from Minnesota, Iowa, North Dakota, Maryland and South Dakota.

1.5M Attendees January

20245 Pedorthic Footwear Association Annual Symposium
Pedorthic Footwear Association
7150 Columbia Gateway Drive
Suite G
Columbia, MD 21046-1170
410-381-7278
FAX: 410-381-1167
info@pedorthics.org
www.pedorthics.org

Jeanne Williams, Show Manager
Brian Lagana, Executive Director
Nancy Hultquist, Director Communications

One hundred fifty booths plus educational sessions regarding the design, manufacture or modification and fit of shoes and foot orthoses to alleviate foot problems caused by disease, congenital condition, overuse or injury.

1000 Attendees November 2200 names $75 per M.

20246 University of Shoe Retailing Conference
National Shoe Retailers Association

www.nsra.org

Rob Kaufman, Conference Chairman
Tricia Keane, Conference Co-Chair

July, Las Vegas

20247 World Shoe Associates: Shoe Show
15821 Ventura Blvd
Ste 415
Encino, CA 91436-2974
818-799-9400
FAX: 949-851-8523
info@wsashow.com
www.wsashow.com

Chris Aiken, Show Manager

One million square feet of exhibition space. Features thousands of footwear styles, accesories, handbags and foot care products.

12M Attendees August/February

Directories & Databases

20248 American Shoemaking
Shoe Trades Publishing Company
61 Massachusetts Avenue
PO Box 1530
East Arlington, MA 02174-8160
781-648-8160
FAX: 781-646-9832
info@shoetrades.com
www.shoetrades.com

John J Moynihan, Publisher

Brings the shoe manufacturer the news he needs to know. *$55.00*

30 pages Monthly

20249 Business Performance Report
National Shoe Retailers Association

800-673-8446
info@nsra.org www.nsra.org

Comprehensive, in-depth, financial account of retail shoe stores. Benchmark for retailers to compare their own operations.

20250 Complete Directory of Socks & Shoes
Sutton Family Communications & Publishing Company
155 Sutton Lane
Fordsville, KY 42343
270-740-0870

jlsutton@apex.net
www.fleamarketeer.net

Theresa Sutton, Editor
Lee Sutton, General Manager

Print-out from database of wholesalers, manufacturers, distributors, importers and close-out houses. Database is updated daily to guarantee the most current and up-to-date sources available. *$44.50*

100+ pages

20251 Financial Performance Profile of Public Consumer Products Manufacturers
Kurt Salmon Associates
1355 Peachtree Street NE
Suite 900
Atlanta, GA 30309-3257
404-892-0321
FAX: 404-898-9590

William Pace, Chief Executive Officer

About 23 publicly held footwear manufacturers.
Annual June

20252 Footwear Distributors and Retailers of America: Membership Directory
Footwear Distributors and Retailers of America
1319 F Street NW
Washington, DC 20004-1106
202-628-1838
FAX: 202-638-2615

Peter Mangione, President

About 65 American footwear importers and retailers.

20253 Shoe Factory Buyer's Guide
Shoe Trades Publishing Company
323 Cornelia Street
Suite 274
Plattsburgh, NY 12901
514-457-8787
FAX: 514-457-5832
sfbg@shoetrades.com
www.shoetrades.com

George McLeash, Publisher

Over 750 suppliers and their representatives to the shoe manufacturing industries in the US and Canada. *$59.00*
Annual
Circulation: 1,000

Industry Web Sites

20254 www.apparelandfootwear.org
American Apparel & Footwear Association

National trade association representing apparel, footwear and other sewn products companies and their suppliers. Our mission is to promote and enhance our members competitiveness, productivity and profitability in the global market.

20255 www.greyhouse.com
Grey House Publishing

Selected Grey House directories in the fields of business, health and education are available online. Users can search our online databases by several different search criteria, such as product categories, geographic area, sales volume and much, much more. Full Grey House catalog and online ordering also available.

20256 www.sgma.com
Sporting Goods Manufacturers Association

For manufacturers, producers, and distributers of sports apparel, athletic footwear, fitness,and sporting goods equipment.

20257 www.ssia.info
Shoe Service Institute of America

Shop to shop chat room, links and listings of manufacturers and wholesalers plus shoe care tips.

Associations

20258 ADMA Annual Meeting
Alaskan Dog Mushers Association
PO Box 70662
Fairbanks, AK 99707-0662
907-457-6874
FAX: 907-479-3516
adma@sleddog.org www.sleddog.org
Jonnelle Roos, Executive Director
Shannon Erhart, President
Alaskan Dog Mushers Association annual meeting

20259 ATP Tour
201 ATP Tour Boulevard
Ponte Vedra Beach, FL 32082
904-856-6400
FAX: 904-285-5966 800-527-4811
Mark Miles, CEO
Patrice Dominguez, Tournament Representative
Laurent Delanney, SVP Sales/Marketing
Operates the official tennis computer ranking system. Administers entry system for international tennis circuit and tennis system. Membership restricted to male, touring, professional tennis players.
Founded: 1972

20260 Adventure Cycling Association
150 East Pine Street
PO Box 8308
Missoula, MT 59802
406-721-1776
FAX: 406-721-8754 800-755-2453
info@adventurecycling.org
www.adventurecycling.org
Jim Sayer, Executive Director
Guy Barel, Tours Manager
Julie Emnett, Associate Development Director
Teri Maloughney, Sales/Marketing Director
Their mission is to inspire people of all ages to travel by bicycle for fitness, fun and self-discovery. A non-profit organization, it is a resource offering many programs for cyclists, including a national network of bicycle touring routes and organized trips.
42000 Members Founded: 1973

20261 Aerobics and Fitness Association of America
15250 Ventura Boulevard
Suite 200
Sherman Oaks, CA 91403-3297
818-905-0040
FAX: 818-990-5468 877-968-7263
contactafaa@afaa.com www.afaa.com
Linda Pfeffer, President
Association for the education, certification and training of exercise instructors; information resource center for consumers.
Founded: 1983

20262 Amateur Athletic Union of the United States
1910 Hotel Plaza Boulevard
PO Box 22409
Lake Buena Vista, FL 32830
407-934-7200
FAX: 407-828-4710 www.aausports.org
Bobby Dodd, President/CEO
Michael Killpack, Director Sports
Rachel D'Orazio, Director Marketing/Websites
John Hodges, Director Sponsorship
Amy Racicot, Director Finance
The AAU hosts the Junior Olympic Games, 30 youth sports programs, 25 adult sports programs, awards over 200,000 championship medals annually, partnered with Walt Disney World to host events at Disney's Wide World of Sports Complex, and presents an annual James E. Sullivan memorial award.
500M Members Founded: 1888

20263 Amateur Softball Association
2536 Greenacre Avenue
Anaheim, CA 92801
717-952-9311

info@afasoftball.com
www.afasoftball.com
Terry Fullmer, Director
Ron Gossmer, Director
Represents those individuals engaged in amateur softball.
250M Members

20264 American Academy of Podiatric Sports Medicine
109 Greenwich Drive
Walkersville, MD 21793

FAX: 301-962-3850 888-854-3338
info@aapsm.org www.aapsm.org
Rita Yates, Executive Director
Serves to advance the understanding, prevention and management of lower extremity sports and fitness injuries. They believe that providing such knowledge to the profession and the public will optimize enjoyment and safe participation in sports and fitness activities. They accomplish this mission through professional education, scientific research, public awareness and membership support.
800 Members Founded: 1970
Mailing list available for rent 600 names $125 per M.

20265 American Alliance for Health, Physical Education, Recreation and Dance
1900 Association Drive
Reston, VA 20191-1598
703-476-3400
FAX: 703-476-9527 800-213-7193
messagecenter@aahperd.org
www.aahperd.org
Jerry E Landwer, President
Michael G Davis, CEO
Organization of professionals supporting and assisting those involved in physical education, leisure, fitness, dance, health promotion and education and all specialties related to having a healthy lifestyle.
25000 Members Founded: 1885

20266 American Amateur Baseball Congress
100 West Broadway
Farmington, NM 87401
505-327-3120
FAX: 505-327-3132
aabc@aabc.us.net www.aabc.us
Mike Diamond, President
Richard Neely, Executive VP
Provides profressive and continuous organized competition for sub teens through adults.bers.
250M Members Founded: 1935

20267 American Baseball Coaches Association
108 S University Avenue
Suite 3
Mount Pleasant, MI 48858-2327
989-775-3300
FAX: 989-775-3600
abca@abca.org www.abca.org
Irish O'Reilly, President
Bill Holowaty, First VP
Kent Shelley, Second VP
Steve Smith, Third VP
Dave Keilitz, Executive Director
Association of Baseball Coaches in the United States.
5M Members Founded: 1945

20268 American Camp Association
5000 State Road 67 N
Martinsville, IN 46151-7902
765-342-8456
FAX: 765-342-2065 800-428-2267
pr@acacamps.org www.acacamps.org
Ann Sheets, President
Peg Smith, Executive Director
Formerly known as the American Camping Association, is a community of camp professionals who have joined together to share their knowledge and experience and to ensure the quality of camp programs.
6700 Members Founded: 1910
Mailing list available for rent

20269 American Canoe Association
7432 Alban Station Boulevard
Suite B-232
Springfield, VA 22150
703-451-0141
FAX: 703-451-2245
aca@americancanoe.org
www.acanet.org
Pamela Dillon, Executive Director
Gerald Babao, Director Recreation Outreach
Judy Rodriguez, Membership Coordinator

A nationwide not for profit organization that is in service to the broader paddling public by providing education on matters related to paddling, supporting stewardship of the paddling environment, and enabling programs and events to support paddlesport recreation. *$18.00*
50000 Members 6 Per Year Founded: 1880
Circulation: 35000 40000 names $90 per M.

20270 American College of Sports Medicine
401 W Michigan Street
Indianapolis, IN 46202-3233
317-347-7817
FAX: 317-634-7817
publicinfo@acsm.org www.acsm.org
Carl Foster, President
James Whitehead, Executive Director
The ACSM promotes and integrates scientific research, education, and practical applications of sports medicine and exercise science to maintain and enhance physical performance, fitness, health, and quality of life.
20000 Members Founded: 1954 ISSN 0195-9131

20271 American Council on Exercise
4851 Paramount Drive
San Diego, CA 92123
858-279-8064
FAX: 858-279-8064 800-825-3636

Scott Goudeseune, Chief Operating Officer
Al Mirnezam, Chief Financial Officer

A nonprofit organization committed to enriching quality of life through safe and effective physical activity. ACE protects all segments of society against ineffective fitness products, programs and trends through its ongoing public education, outreach and research. ACE further protects the public by setting certification and continuing education standards for fitness professionals.

Founded: 1985

20272 American Greyhound Track Operators Association
1100 N Wickham Road
Melbourne, FL 32935-8941
321-259-9800
FAX: 321-259-3437

Patrick E Winters, Executive Director
Patrick Biddix, General Manager

Trade association representing the interest of and providing services to greyhound racetrack owners and operators via government advocacy, information sharing, annual conference and trade shows.

35 Members Founded: 1946

20273 American Orthopaedic Society for Sports Medicine
6300 N River Road
Suite 500
Rosemont, IL 60018-'
847-292-4900
FAX: 847-292-4905 877-321-3500
aossm@aossm.org
www.sportsmed.org

William A Grana MD, President
Bernard R Bach Jr MD, VP
Bruce Reider MD, Journal Editor
Irvin E Bomberger, Executive Director
Camille Petrick, Manager

A national organization of orthopaedic surgeons specializing in sports medicine, including national and international sports medicine leaders.

2000 Members Founded: 1972

20274 American Recreation Coalition
1225 New York Avenue NW
Suite 450
Washington, DC 20005-6405
202-682-9530
FAX: 202-662-7424

Derrick Crandall, President
Catherine Ahern, VP

Triennial exhibits relating to the responsible use of US aquatic resources, including issues such as wetlands conservation, boating safety, sportfish research and enhancement and boating access improvements.

100+ Members Founded: 1979

20275 American Running Association
4405 East-West Highway
Suite 405
Bethesda, MD 20814
301-913-9517
FAX: 301-913-9520 800-776-2732
run@americanrunning.org
www.americanrunning.org

Sam Pettway, President
Geoff Hollister, VP
Ed Farris, Logistics Manager
David Watt, Executive Director

A nonprofit organization dedicated to encouraging all people from youth to adults to improve their health and fitness by walking and running, and maintaining an active and healthy lifestyle.

13000 Members Founded: 1968

20276 American Society of Golf Course Architects
125 N Executive Drive
Suite 106
Brookfield, WI 53005
262-786-5960
FAX: 262-786-5919
info@asgca.org www.asgca.org

Greg Muirhead, President
Chad Ritterbusch, Manager

A non-profit organization comprised of leading golf course designers in North America. ASGCA is actively involved in many issues realted to the game of golf, including responsible environmental designs.

130 Members Founded: 1946

20277 American Spa and Health Resort
PO Box 585
Lake Forest, IL 60045
847-234-8851
FAX: 847-295-7790

Melanie Ruehle, Contact

Seeks to establish and maintain high standards of quality in US health spas.

Founded: 1982

20278 Aquatic Exercise Association
PO Box 1609
Nokomis, FL 34274-1609
941-486-8600
FAX: 941-486-8820 888-232-9283
aea@ix.netcom.com
www.aeawave.com

Julie See, President
Angie Proctor, Executive Director
Dan Nelson, Administration/Database Management
Kim Huff, Corporate Relations/Events & Promos

A not-for-profit educational organization dedicated to the growth and development of the aquatic fitness industry and the safety of the public served.

6,000 Members Founded: 1984
Mailing list available for rent 85,000 names

20279 Archery Range and Retailers Organization
156 N Main Street
Suite D
Oregon, WI 53575
608-835-9060
FAX: 608-835-9360 800-234-7499
webmaster@up-north.com
www.archeryretailers.com

John Larsen Sr, President
Martin Stubstad, VP
Ervin Wagner, Treasurer
Ron Pelkey, Director
Lynn Stiklestad, Administrative Director

A national organization of porfessional full time archery ranges and pro shops.

140 Members Founded: 1970

20280 Archery Trade Association
860 E 4500 South
Suite 310
Salt Lake City, UT 84107
801-261-2380
FAX: 801-261-2389 866-266-2776
info@archerytrade.org
www.archerytrade.org

Jay McAninch, President/CEO
Denise Parker, VP/Director Marketing
Kelly A Kelly, Operations Manager
Cindy Brophy, Manager Tradeshow
Bryan Roe, Membership Services

Formerly the Archery Manufacturers and Merchants Organization, provides the core funding and direction for two foundations critical to the future of archery and bowhunting.

Founded: 2003

20281 Association of Diving Contractors International
5206 FM 1960 West
Suite 202
Houston, TX 77069
281-893-8388
FAX: 281-893-5118
rroberts@adc-int.org www.adc-int.org

Ross Saxon, Executive Director
Barbara Treadway, Administrative Manager
Rebecca Roberts, Communications Administrator
Suzie Foster, Administrative Assistant

The Association of Diving Contractors International, Inc. was founded in 1968 by a small group of diving companies. Their goal was to create a non-profit organization to cultivate and promote the art and science of commercial diving, establish uniform safe standards for commercial divers, and encourage industry-wide observance of these standards.

500 Members

20282 Athletic Equipment Managers Association
460 Hunt Hill Road
Freeville, NY 13068
607-539-6300
FAX: 607-539-6340
dec13@cornell.edu www.aema1.com

Jon Falk, Executive Director
Mike Royster, Associate Executive Director
Dale Strauf, President
Dino Dennis, VP
Dorothy Cutting, Manager

The purpose of the AEMA is to promote, advance, and improve the Equipment Managers Profession in all of its many phases.

700 Members Founded: 1974

20283 Billiard and Bowling Institute of America
PO Box 6363
West Palm Beach, FL 33405
561-835-0077
FAX: 561-659-1824
bbia@billiardandbowling.org
www.billiardandbowling.org

John Carzo, President
Henry Hayes, VP
Lori Tessmar, Convention Chairman

A not-for-profit association formed to service the billiard and bowling industries. The BBIA network is uniquely structured to open channels of communication between manufacturers and distributors in order to assist and improve members' business operations. BBIA provides an innovative forum for billiard and bowling businesses to share ideas, gain information, gather feedback and explore the dynamics of the product pipeline between manufacturer and end user.

150 Members Founded: 1940

20284 Bowling Proprietors' Association of America
PO Box 5802
Arlington, TX 76005-5802
817-649-5105
FAX: 817-633-2940 800-343-1329
answer@bpaa.com www.bpaamax.com

Vladmir Wapensky, Executive Director

Supports the Bowling Proprietors' Association of American Political Action Committee.
3.6M Members Founded: 1932

20285 Cross Country Ski Areas Association
259 Bolton Road
Winchester, NH 03470
603-239-4341
FAX: 603-239-6387 877-779-2754
ccsaa@xcski.org www.xcski.org

Chris Frado, President

A non-profit organization representing member ski service providers. The association's purpose is to promote the growth and improve the quality of cross country ski operations in North America. *$25.00*
350 Members Quarterly Founded: 1977
Circulation: 350

20286 Football Writers Association of America (FWAA)
18652 Vista Del Sol Lane
Dallas, TX 75287-4021
972-713-6198

tigerfwaa@aol.com
www.sportswriters.net/fwaa

Dennis Todd, President

Established to improve working conditions in college press boxes.
900 Members Founded: 1941
Mailing list available for rent 800 names $50 per M.

20287 Golf Superintendents Association of

1421 Research Park Drive
Lawrence, KS 66049-3859
785-841-2240
FAX: 785-832-4455 800-472-7878
infobox@gcsaa.org www.gcsaa.org

Sean A Hoolehan, President
Rickey D Heine, VP
Mark D Kuhns, Director
Stephen F Mona, CEO

Provides education programs in formal settings and at home through videotapes and correspondence courses. Administers professional certification programs, publishes magazines and multiple newsletters, conducts and supports research, provides scholarship opportunities, offers employment assistance and career development support, promotes the image of the golf course superintendent through cable TV program 'Par For The Course' and other vehicles. Provides leadership in governmental issues.
22000 Members Founded: 1920

20288 Harness Tracks of America
4640 East Sunrise
Suite 200
Tucson, AZ 85718
520-529-2525
FAX: 520-529-3235
info@harnesstracks.com
www.harnesstracks.com

Stanley F Bergstein, Executive Vice President
Jessica Carner, Editorial Coordinator

Mission is to help members obtain their economic objectives by promoting live racing, enhancing and preserving the integrity and image of the sport, and providing information to members and the general public about the sport and the significant economic impact of the industry.
60 Members

20289 Ice Skating Institute
17120 N Dallas Parkway
Suite 140
Dallas, TX 75248-1187
972-735-8800
FAX: 972-735-8815
isi@skateisi.org www.skateisi.org

Peter Martell, Executive Director
Emily Silva, Marketing/Communications Director

Industry trade association dedicated to providing leadership, education and services to the ice skating industry.
64500 Members Founded: 1959

20290 International Professional Rodeo
2304 Exchange Avenue - Stockyards
Oklahoma City, OK 73108
405-235-6540
FAX: 405-235-6577
info@iprarodio.com
www.iprarodeo.com

Butch Stewart, Chief Field Representative

Governing body for professional rodeo. 500 rodeos across USA and Canada, $5 million prize money per year, 5 million fans.
3500 Members Founded: 1960

20291 International Sports Heritage Association
PO Box 3093
Ponte Vedra Beach, FL 32004-3093
904-955-0126
FAX: 904-810-5305
info@sportsheritage.org
www.sportsheritage.org

Karen Bednarski, Executive Director

Effective January 1, 2006, the International Association of Sports Museums and Halls of Fames changed its name to the International Sports Heritage Association. The change represents a renewed vision for the association, now in its 35th year. ISHA's membership includes 120 sports heritage organizations from five continents.
140+ Members Founded: 1971

20292 Lacrosse Foundation and Hall of Fame
113 W University Parkway
Baltimore, MD 21210-3301
410-357-7392
FAX: 410-366-6735
info@uslacrosse.org
www.uslacrosse.org

Steve Stenersen, Executive Director
Jody Martin, Men's Division Director
Ann Kitt Carpenetti, Women's Division Director
Glen Schorr, Managing Director Marketing

The national governing body of men's and women's lacrosse. Their mission is to ensure a unifed and responsive organization that develops and promotes the sport by providing services to its members and programs to inspire participation, while preserving the integrity of the game.
182 T Members Founded: 1998

20293 Ladies Professional Golf Association
100 International Golf Drive
Daytona Beach, FL 32124-1092
386-274-6200
FAX: 386-274-1099 www.lpga.com

Liz Ausman, Chief Strategic Officer
Karen Durkin, EVP/Chief Marketing Officer
Christopher Higgs, Senior VP/COO
Ken Wooten, VP Finance
Ty Votaw, Manager

The LPGA is a non-profit organization involved in every facet of golf. In addition to staging the LPGA Tour, the LPGA is also committed to advancing women, youth and the sport of golf through expanding the programs of the LPGA Teaching and Club Professional Division, as well as increasing contributions of the organization and its tournaments to charity.
Founded: 1950

20294 League of American Bicyclists
1612 K Street NW
Suite 800
Washington, DC 20006
202-822-1333
FAX: 410-539-3496
bikeleague@bikeleague.org
www.bikeleague.org

Andy Clarke, Executive Director
Mike Mackin, Director Membership

Founded in 1880, the League is the only national membership organization of bicyclists in the United States. The League works to promote and encourage bicycling for recreation and transportation, and to protect and defend the rights of bicyclists through advocacy and education.
Founded: 1880

20295 National Aeronautic Association
1737 King Street
Suite 220
Alexandria, VA 22314
703-527-0226
FAX: 703-527-0229 800-644-9777
naa@naa.aero www.naa-usa.org

David L Ivey, President
Shannon Chambers, Director Membership/Marketing

A non-profit association dedicated to the advancement of the art, sport and science of aviation in the United States. The official record-keeper for United States aviation.
3000 Members Founded: 1922

20296 National Amateur Baseball Association
PO Box 705
Bowie, MD 20715
301-625-5005
FAX: 301-352-0214
nabf1914@aol.com www.nabf.com

Dino Costanzo, President
Ronald MacLeod, First VP
David E Jerome, Second VP
Greg Reddington, Third VP
Charles Blackburn Jr, Executive Director

The oldest continually operated national basesball organization in the country.
10M Members Founded: 1914

20297 National Archery Association (USA Archery)
1 Olympic Plaza
Colorado Springs, CO 80909
719-866-4576
FAX: 719-632-4733
info@usarchery.org
www.usarchery.org

Bradely Camp, Executive Director
Cynthia Jackson, Executive Assistant
Kathleen Frazier, Finance/Membership
Mary Beth Vorwerk, Media/Public Relations
KiSik Lee, National Head Coach

Formed to develop and promote the sport of archery. Recognized by the US Olympic committee as the national governing body for the olympic sport of archery. The NAA selects and trains mens and womens archery teams to represent the US in international, pan american and olympic competitions.
Founded: 1879

20298 National Association for Girls and Women in Sports
1900 Association Drive
Reston, VA 20191-1502
703-476-3410
FAX: 703-476-4566
nagws@aahpend.org
www.aahperd.org/nagws

Lynda Ransdell, President
Sharon Shields, Representative/Board of Governors
Charlene Burgeson, Executive Director
Sonja Lilienthal, VP Marketing

A non-profit organization serving the needs of teachers, coaches and participants of sports programs for girls and women.
4000 Members Founded: 1999

20299 National Association for Sport and Physical Education
1900 Association Drive
Reston, VA 20191-1598
703-763-3410
FAX: 703-476-9527
naspe@aahperd.org
www.aahperd.org/naspe

Charlene R Burgeson, Executive Director
Michael Ochsey, Director Government Relations
Paula K Kun, Director Communications
De Raynes, Program Manager Physical Education
Diana Snyder, Marketing Manager

A nonprofit professional organization comprised of individuals engaged in the study of human movement and the delivery of sport and physical activity programs. NASPE develops and supports quality sport and physical activity programs that promote healthy behaviors and individual well-being.
20000 Members Founded: 1938

20300 National Association of Basketball Coaches
1111 Main
Suite 1000
Kansas City, MO 64105-2136
816-878-6222
FAX: 816-878-6223 www.nabc.com

James Haney, Executive Director
Reggie Minton, Deputy Executive Director
Kevin Henderson, Associate Executive Director
Dottie Yearout, Director Membership
Jenna Wright, Convention Manager

Promotes the advancement and opportunities for coaches and teachers in the sport of basketball.
5M Members Founded: 1927

20301 National Association of Collegiate Directors of Athletics
PO Box 16428
Cleveland, OH 44116
440-892-4000
FAX: 440-892-4007 www.nacda.com

Michael Cleary, Executive Director
Bob Vecchione, Senior Associate Executive Director
Brian Horning, Membership Coordinator

Professional association for college atheltics directors, assistants and conference administrators. Provides educational opportunities and serves as a vehicle for networking and the exchange of information to others in the college sports profession.
1.5M Members

20302 National Association of Professional Baseball Leagues
201 Bayshore Drive SE
Box A
Saint Petersburg, FL 33731
727-822-6937
FAX: 727-821-5819

Mike Moore, President
RJ Sparks, Promotional Director

Two hundred and seventy booths.
2.5M Members

20303 National Association of Sporting Goods Wholesalers
POÆBox 881525
772-621-7162
FAX: 772-264-3233
nasgw@nasgw.org www.nasgw.org

Wayne Smith, President
Richard Lipsey, Chairman

Serves as a liaison with other sporting goods associations. The NASGW is the organizer and sponsor of the industry's annual meeting/expo event.
400 Members Founded: 1953

20304 National Association of Sports Officials
2017 Lathrop Avenue
Racine, WI 53405
262-632-5448
FAX: 262-632-5460
naso@naso.org www.naso.org

Barry Mano, President
Marc Ratner, Chair
Anita Ortega, Vice Chair
Henry Zaborniak, Treasurer

Nonprofit 501(c)(3), educational association providing individual benefits such as training materials, liability and assault protection insurance and more to sports officials of all sports and every level.
16000 Members Founded: 1980

20305 National Athletic Trainers Association
2952 Stemmons Freeway
Dallas, TX 75247
214-637-6282
FAX: 214-637-2206
ebd@nata.org www.nata.org

Eve Becker-Doyle, Executive Director
Teresa Foster Welch, Assistant Executive Director
Karen Peterson, Manager Executive Operations
Ellen Satlof, Public Relations Manager
Cynthia Nadel, Marketing Coordinator

Association for professionals in athletic training.
28000 Members Founded: 1950

20306 National Basketball Trainers Association
1201 Peachtree Street NE
400 Colony Square Suite 1750
Atlanta, GA 30361
404-875-4000
FAX: 404-892-8560
rmallernee@mallernee-branch.com
www.nbata.com

Tim Walsh, Chairman

A satelite of the National Athletic Trainers Association. Members are athletic trainers in the NBA.

20307 National Bicycle Dealers Association
777 W 19th Street
Suite O
Costa Mesa, CA 92627
949-722-6909
FAX: 949-722-1747
info@nbda.com www.nbda.com

Fred Clements, Executive Director
Mike Baker, Marketing/Communications Director

The mission of the NBDA is to inspire and serve the specialty bicycle retailer through communicating the value and needs of the specialty bicycle retailer, enhancing the specialty bicycle retailer's profitability, and promoting the passion for cycling. The NBDA is a non-profit association promoting the interests of every specialty bicycle retailer in the United States.
2M Members Founded: 1946

20308 National Cutting Horse Association
260 Bailey AvenueS
Fort Worth, TX 76116-1862
817-244-6188
FAX: 817-244-2015
www.nchacutting.com

Mike Mowery, President
Bob Mayfield, VP
Jeff Hooper, Executive Director

Members are individuals and organizations interested in the development of superior horses and the refinement of the cutting horse competition.
Founded: 1946

20309 National Golf Car Manufacturers
2 Ravinia Drive
Suite 1200
Atlanta, GA 30346
770-394-7200
FAX: 770-454-0138
somersf@abanet.org

Fred L Somers Jr, General Counsel/Secretary

Non-profit national trade association comprised of the leading golf car and personal transport vehicle manufacturers. NGCMA sponsors the development and maintenance of ANSI sanctioned standards to establish safety specifications for the design and operation of golf cars and PTVs driven by electric motors and internal combustion engines for golf cars.

20310 National Golf Foundation
1150 S US Highway One
Suite 401
Jupiter, FL 33477
561-744-6006
FAX: 561-744-6107 888-275-4643
general@ngf.org www.ngf.org

Mark King, Chairman
Jim Connor, Vice Chairman
Joseph Beditz, President/CEO

Provides market research and serves as an information clearinghouse for the industry. Conducts seminars for golf teachers, coaches and professionals. Conducts golf course development feasibility studies for developers.
6000 Members Founded: 1936

20311 National Hockey League
1251 Avenue of the Americas
Floor 47
New York, NY 10020
212-789-2000
FAX: 212-789-2020 www.nhl.com

Gary Bettman, Manager

Based in Canada and the United States.

20312 National Junior College Athletic Association
1755 Telstar Drive
Suite 103
Colorado Springs, CO 80920
719-590-9788
FAX: 719-590-7324
wbaker@njcaa.org www.njcaa.org

George Killian, Executive Director
Mary Ellen Leicht, Associate Executive Director
Amy Tagliareni, Director Sports Information/Media

The purpose of the NJCAA is to promote and foster junior college athletics on intersectional and national levels so that results will be consistent with the total educational program of its members.
510 Members Founded: 1938 2500 names $150 per M.

20313 National Recreation & Park Association
22377 Belmont Ridge Road
Ashburn, VA 20148-4150
703-584-4635
FAX: 703-858-0794
info@nrpa.org www.nrpa.org

Ronald Lehman, Chairman of the Board
Steven M Neu, President
John A Thorner, Executive Director

Advancing parks, recreation and environmental conservation efforts that enhance the quality of life for all people.

20314 National Rifle Association of America
11250 Waples Mill Road
Fairfax, VA 22030
703-671-1400
FAX: 703-267-3970
membership@nrahq.org
www.nrahq.org

Oldest sportsmen's organization in the US. Maintains the NRA Political Victory Fund and supports the Institute for Legislative Action. Has an annual budget over $140 million.
4 Members Founded: 1871

20315 National Sporting Goods Association
1601 Feehanville Drive
Suite 300
Mount Prospect, IL 60056
847-296-6742
FAX: 847-391-9827 800-815-5422
info@nsga.org www.nsga.org

Ron Kruse, Chairman
Jim Faltinek, President/CEO
Dan Kasen, Manager

Association of retailers, manufacturers and suppliers of sports equipment, footwear, and apparel.
2000+ Members Founded: 1927

20316 National Youth Sports Coaches Association
Courthouse Annex, 725 Maple
Hillsboro, MO 63050-0100
636-797-5334
FAX: 636-797-5084
nysca@nays.org www.nays.org

Represents coaches involved in youth athletics.
Founded: 1981

20317 Pop Warner Little Scholars
586 Middletown Boulevard
Suite C-100
Langhorne, PA 19047
215-752-2691
FAX: 215-752-2879
webmaster@popwarner.com
www.popwarner.com

Jon Butler, Executive Director
Mary Fitzgerald, COO
Lisa Moroski, National Cheer/Dance Commissioner

A national youth football and cheerleading organization that provides assistance to its various chapters.
400M Members Founded: 1929

20318 Professional Association of Diving
30151 Tomas Street
Rancho Santa Margarita, CA 92688-2125

949-858-7234
FAX: 949-858-7264 800-729-7234
webmaster@padi.com www.padi.com

Brian Cronin, Chief Executive Officer

Certifies scuba diving instructors. Provides education/training materials and retail support to its members.
67M Members Founded: 1966

20319 Professional Association of Volleyball Officials
PO Box 780
Oxford, KS 67119

FAX: 620-455-3800 888-791-2074
pavo@pavo.org www.pavo.org

Marcia Alterman, Executive Director
Joan Powell, President
Crystal Lewis, Board Delegate
Ben Jordan, Director Examinations
Karen Gee, Director Finance

The Professional Association of Volleyball Officials is dedicated to improving the quality of volleyball officiating for all rules codes and skill levels. PAVO strives to increase the number of competent officials through education and mentoring and promotes involvement in the governing bodies of other volleyball officiating groups.
2M Members

20320 Professional Baseball Athletic Trainers Society
1201 Peachtree Street NE
Suite 1750
Atlanta, GA 30361-6304
404-875-4000
FAX: 410-730-2219
questions@pbats.com www.pbats.com

Jamie Reed, President
Jim Carroll, Director Public Relations

Serve as an educational resource for the Major League and Minor League baseball athletic trainers. Serves its members by providing for the continued education of the athletic trainer as it relates to the profession, helping improve his understanding of sports medicine so as to better promote the health of his constituency - professional baseball players.
60 Members Founded: 1983

20321 Professional Bowlers Association
719 2nd Avenue
Suite 701
Seattle, WA 98104
206-332-9688
FAX: 206-332-9722
info@pba.com www.pba.com

Chris Peters, Chairman
Fred Schreyer, President/CEO
Steve Miller, Board Member
Lisa Gil, VP Brand Communications

Acts on behalf of professional bowlers.
3800 Members Founded: 1958

20322 Professional Football Athletic Trainer
1201 Peachtree Street NE
Suite 1750
Atlanta, GA 30361-6304
404-875-4000
FAX: 404-892-8560 www.pfats.com

Rollin E Mallernee II, General Counsel

Professional association whose members are the athletic trainers of the NFL. They provide, lead and manage helathcare for the NFL athletes, club employees and members of the NFL community. Dedicated to insuring the highest quality health care is practiced. Guided by the profesional integrity and ethical standards of its members and by the unity they share.
650 Members Founded: 1982

20323 Professional Golfers Association
100 Avenue of the Champions
Palm Beach Gardens, FL 33418
561-624-8400
FAX: 561-624-8452
webmaster@pga.com www.pga.com

Roger Warren, President
Joe Steranka, CEO

The world's largest working sports organization comprised of more than 25,000 men and women PGA professionals to promote the game of golf to everyone, and to promote its members as leaders in the golf industry.
28000 Members Founded: 1916

20324 Professional Skaters Association
3006 Allegro Park SW
Rochester, MN 55902
507-281-5122
FAX: 507-281-5491
office@skatepsa.com
www.skatepsa.com

Robbie Kaine, President
Kelley Morris, First VP
Jackie Brenner, Third VP
Carole Shulman, Executive Director

An international organization responsible for the education of skating coaches. Membership is offered to coaches in every discipline and at all levels, as well as to performing professionals, judges, eligible skaters and friends or patrons of the sport of figure skating.
6000 Members Founded: 1938

20325 Roller Skating Association
6905 Corporate Drive
Indianapolis, IN 46278
317-347-2626
FAX: 317-347-2636
rsa@rollerskating.com
www.rollerskating.org

Dan Brown, President
Joe Champa, VP
Robin Brown, Executive Director

A trade association representing skating center owners and operators; teachers, coaches and judges of roller skating; and manufacturers and suppliers of roller skating equipment.
1100 Members Founded: 1937

20326 Society for American Baseball Research
812 Huron Road
Suite 719
Cleveland, OH 44115
216-575-0500
FAX: 216-575-0502
info@sabr.org www.sabr.org

John Zajc, Executive Director
Dick Beverage, President
Ryan Chamberlain, Membership Services

Foisters the study of baseball past and present and provides an outlet for educational, historical and research information about the game.
6700 Members Founded: 1971
Mailing list available for rent 25000 names $85 per M.

20327 Society of Recreation Executives
PO Box 520
Gonzalez, FL 32560-0520
850-937-8354

Works to provide a perspective on needs, trends and changes within the industry. Informs, trains and instructs members in industry principles and practices and consulting services for recreation, leisure and travel businesses.
8300 Members Founded: 1983

20328 Sporting Arms and Ammunition Manufacturers Institute
11 Mile Hill Road
Newtown, CT 06470-2359
203-426-4358
FAX: 203-426-1087 www.saami.org

Doug Painter, President
Robert T Delfay, Executive Director

SAAMI is an association of the nation's leading manufacturers of sporting firearms, ammunition, and components.
Founded: 1926

20329 Sporting Goods Agents Association (SGAA)
PO Box 998
Morton Grove, IL 60053
847-296-3670
FAX: 847-827-0196
sgaa998@aol.com
www.sgaaonline.org

Skip Nipper, President
Lois Halinton, Chief Operating Officer

International trade association of independent and established sporting goods agents.
500 Members Founded: 1934 500 names $200 per M.

20330 Sporting Goods Manufacturers Association
1150 17th Street NW
8th Floor
Washington, DC 20036-1604
202-775-1762
FAX: 202-296-7462
info@sgma.com www.sgma.com

Tom Cove, President/CEO
Gregg Hartley, VP
Andrea Cernich, Director Communications
Chris Strong, Director Business Development
Kalinda Mathis, Director Marketing

SGMA is the trade association of North American manufacturers, producers, and distributers of sports apparel, athletic footwear, fitness, and sporting goods equipment. SGMA represents and supports its members through programs and strategies for sports participation, market intelligence, and public policy.
1000 Members Founded: 1906

20331 Sports Turf Managers Association
805 New Hampshire
Suite E
Lawrence, KS 66044
785-432-2549
FAX: 800-366-0391 800-323-3875

Mike Trigg, President
Kim Heck, CEO

Grounds care for golf and athletic fields.
2500 Members Founded: 1981

20332 Sportsplex Operators and Developers
Westgate Station
PO Box 24263
Rochester, NY 14624-0263
585-426-2215
FAX: 585-247-3112
info@sportsplexoperators.com
www.sportsplexoperators.com

Bob Papich, President
Don Aselin, Executive Director

SODA was formed to meet the needs of the private concerns, public agencies, and other organizations that own or maintain sports complex facilities.
300 Members Founded: 1981

20333 Tennis Industry Association
117 Executive Center
PO Box 7845
Hilton Head Island, SC 29928
843-686-3036
FAX: 843-686-3078
info@tennisindustry.org
www.tennisindustry.org

Jim Baugh, President
Jolyn DeBoer, Executive Director
Chris Mireles, National Coordinator

Trade association for tennis industry. Represents the business interests of its members and promotes recreational tennis.
Founded: 1974

20334 US Field Hockey Association
1 Olympic Plaza
Colorado Springs, CO 80909
719-866-4567
FAX: 719-632-0979
usfha@usfieldhockey.com
www.usfieldhockey.com

Sheila Walker, Executive Director
Laura Bolin, Member Services Coordinator

Represents field hockey, professional and amateur sports.
14000 Members $30 Adults/$25 Juniors Founded: 1928

20335 US Handball Association
2333 N Tucson Boulevard
Tucson, AZ 85716
520-795-0434
FAX: 520-795-0465 800-289-8742
handball@ushandball.org
www.ushandball.org

Mike Sttelen, President
Vern Roberts, Executive Director

Organization that runs all the tournaments for the professional and amateur players. Home of the Handball Hall of Fame.
75 pp Members

20336 US Olympic Committee
1 Olympic Plaza
Colorado Springs, CO 80909
719-632-5551

media@usoc.org
www.usolympicteam.com

Jim Sherr, Chief Executive Officer

The national committee for the US handles the preparation of the US Olympic, Paralympic and Pan American Games teams.

20337 US Professional Tennis Association
3535 Briarpark Drive
Suite One
Houston, TX 77042
713-978-7782
FAX: 713-978-7780 800-877-8248
uspta@uspta.com www.uspta.com

Tim Heckler, CEO
Rich Fanning, Director Operations
Shawna Riley, Director Communications
Rick Bostrom, Sports Marketing Coordinator

A nonprofit association for professional tennis teachers.
14000 Members Founded: 1927

20338 US Raquetball Association
AARA National Office
1685 W Uintah Street
Colorado Springs, CO 80904-2906
719-635-5396
FAX: 719-635-0685
racquetball@usra.org www.usra.org

Randy Stafford, President
Jan Stelma, VP
Jim Hiser, Executive Director
Kevin Joyce, Director Membership
Melody Weiss, Director Finance

A nonprofit corporation designed to promote the development of competitive and recreational racquetball in the United States. The association offers a 'competitive license' membership for a one year term at $30.00 annually. A lifetime membership is also offered.
40M Members 6 Per Year Founded: 1968
Circulation: 25,000

20339 US Ski & Snowboard Association
1500 Kearns Boulevard
PO Box 100
Park City, UT 84060
435-649-9090
FAX: 435-649-3613
info@ussa.org www.usskiteam.com

Bill Marolt, President/CEO
Bill Gorton, COO
Mark Lampe, CFO
Ted Morris, VP Sales/Marketing

The national governing body for Olympic skiing and snowboarding.
30000 Members Founded: 1904

20340 US Soccer Federation
1801 S Prairie Avenue
Chicago, IL 60616
312-808-1300
FAX: 312-808-1301
centercircle@ussoccer.org
www.ussoccer.com

Sunil Gulati, President
Daniel T Flynn, CEO

The governing body of soccer in all its form in the United States. US Soccer has helped chart the course for the sport in the USA for 90 years.
Founded: 1913

20341 US Speedskating
PO Box 450639
Westlake, OH 44145
440-899-0128
FAX: 440-899-0109
kmorquard@usspeedskating.org
www.usspeedskating.org

Katie Marquard, Executive Director
Thomas McLean, Managing Director Marketing
Melissa Scott, Director Media/Public Relations

Devoted to speedskating and its participants on the national and international levels.
2000 Members Founded: 1966

20342 US Squash Racquet Association
23 Cynwyd Road
PO Box 1216
Bala Cynwyd, PA 19004
610-667-4006
FAX: 610-667-6539
office@us-squash.org
www.us-squash.org

Kevin Klipstein, CEO
Vijay Chitnis, Director Junior Development

The USSRA is the national governing body for the sport of squash racquets in the United States. A nonprofit, service organization whose primary function is that of management and maintenance of all squash related activities for a growing membership- driven organization.
8000 Members Founded: 1907

20343 US Synchronized Swimming
201 S Capitol Avenue
Suite 901
Indianapolis, IN 46225
317-237-5700
FAX: 317-237-5705
webmaster@usasynchro.org
www.usasynchro.org

Terry Harper, Executive Director
Taylor Paine, Media Relations Director
Laura Lacursia, National Team Director
Laura Mase, Education Manager
Stephanie Crocker, Membership Manager

Dedicated to the promotion of synchronized swimming. Sanctions and governs all synchronized swimming in the US and selects and trains National and Olympic Teams to represent the US in international competitions.

20344 US Track and Field
One RCA Dome
Suite 140
Indianapolis, IN 46225
317-261-0500
FAX: 317-261-0513 www.usatf.org

Bill Roe, President
Craig Masback, CEO

The national governing body for track and field, long-distance running and race walking in the United States.
100 T Members

20345 US Volleyball Association
PO Box 1461
Los Gatos, CA 95031

volleyballorg@hotmail.com
www.volleyball.org
Promotes volleyball in the US trains the USA men's and women's teams promotes beach and grassroots volleyball in the United States.
140M Members Founded: 1928

20346 USA Gymnastics
Pan Am Plaza, 201 S Capitol Avenue
Suite 300
Indianapolis, IN 46225
317-237-5050
FAX: 317-237-5069 800-345-4719
rebound@usa-gymnastics.org
www.usa-gymnastics.org

Ron Froehlich, Chairman
Steve Penny, President
Kathy Feldmann, VP Member Services
Kelly Feilke, Senior Director Marketing
Connie Israel, Director Events

The sole national governing body for the sport of gymnastics in the United States. USA Gymnastics creates, organizes and conducts clinics, training camps, team competitions and other aspects of athlete, coach and official selection and development.
13000 Members Founded: 1963

20347 USA Hockey
1775 Bob Johnson Drive
Colorado Springs, CO 80906
719-576-8724
FAX: 719-538-1160
usah@usahockey.org
www.usahockey.com

Ron DeGregoria, President
Dave Fischer, Director Media/Public Relations
Dave Oregean, Executive Director

Promotes the sport of hockey. USA Hockey is the national governing body for the sport of ice hockey in the US. *$39.95*
60000 Members 10X Year Founded: 1936

20348 USA Roller Sports
PO Box 6579
Lincoln, NE 68506
402-483-7551
FAX: 402-483-1465
www.usarollersports.org

George Kolibaba, Chairman/President
David Adamy, VP

The national governing body for all amateur skating sports including artistic, roller, and speed skating.
15K Members Founded: 1937

20349 USA Swimming
One Olympic Plaza
Colorado Springs, CO 80909
719-866-4578
www.usaswimming.org

Chuck Wielgus, Executive Director
Amanda Bryant, Director Corporate Marketing
Mike Unger, Chief Operating Officer
Jim Harvey, Managing Director Financial Affairs

Devoted to the sport of swimming and its enjoyment nationwide. Governing body for the sport of swimming.
290M Members Founded: 1844

20350 USA Table Tennis
1 Olympic Plaza
Colorado Springs, CO 80909
719-866-4583
FAX: 719-632-6071
usatt@usatt.org www.usatt.org

Doru Gheorghe, Executive Director

Dedicated to the promotion of the sport of table tennis and sponsors the US team. Membership dues are $40 per year for adults and $20 for those 17 years old and under.
8000+ Members Founded: 1933

20351 USA Water Ski Association
1251 Holy Cow Road
Polk City, FL 33868
863-324-4341
FAX: 863-325-8259
usawaterski@usawaterski.org
www.usawaterski.org

Steve McDermeit, Executive Director
Scott Atkinson, Director Communications
Steve Upp, Director Marketing
Sandy Hardee, Manager Membership Services
Bobie Razor, Manager

The national governing body for organized water skiing in the United States. A member of the International Water Ski Federation (World Governing Body), the Pan American Sports Association and the United States Olympic Committee.
37500 Members Founded: 1939

20352 USA Weightlifting
1 Olympic Plaza
Colorado Springs, CO 80909
719-784-4508
FAX: 719-866-4781
usaw@usaweightlifting.org
www.usaweightlifting.org

Wesley Barnett, Executive Director
Juliet Moore, Membership Services

USA Weightlifting is the National Governing Body (NGB) for the Olympic sport of weightlifting in the United States. USA weightlifting is a member of the United States Olympic Committee and a member of the International Weightlifting Federation. As the NGB, USA Weightlifting is responsible for conducting Olympic weightlifting programs throughout the country. The organization conducts a variety of programs that will ultimately develop Olympic, World Championship and Pan American Games' winners. *$20.00*
4000 Members Quarterly Founded: 1981
Circulation: 4500

20353 United States Amateur Boxing
1 Olympic Plaza
Colorado Springs, CO 80909
719-664-4730
FAX: 719-632-3426
media@usoc.org www.usolimplc.com

Bill Meartz, President
Joe Smith, VP
Jose Rodriguez, Executive Director
Julie Goldsticker, Director Media/Public Relations

The national governing body for Olympic-style boxing. It is responsible for the administration, development and promotion of Olympic-style boxing in the United State.
7000 Members

20354 United States Bowling Congress
5301 S 76th Street
Greendale, WI 53129
414-216-6400
FAX: 414-421-8560 800-514-2695
abcpr@bowinginc.com
www.bowl.com

Roger Dalkin, CEO
Jack Mordini, COO
Roseann Kuhn, Chief Tournament Officer
Tim Payne, Chief Information Officer
Kevin Dornberger, Director, Team USA

Established in 2005 as the organization to serve amateur adult and youth bowlers of the United States. It resulted from the merger of the American Bowling Congress, Young American Bowling Alliance and USA Bowling. USBC is the national governing body for bowling as recognized by the United States Olympic Committee.
3 M Members Founded: 2005

20355 United States Fencing Association
1 Olympic Plaza
Colorado Springs, CO 80909-5774
719-664-4730
FAX: 719-632-5737
info@usfencing.org
www.usfencing.org

Nancy Anderson, President
Jose Rodriguez, Executive Director
Bent Findlay, Media Coordinator

National Governing Body for the sport of fencing in the United States. Their mission is to develop fencers to achieve international success and to administer and promote the sport in the USA.
9M Members Founded: 1891

20356 United States Golf Association
PO Box 708
Far Hills, NJ 07931
908-234-2300
FAX: 908-234-9687
mediarelations@usga.org
www.usga.org

Walter W Driver Jr, President
James E Reinhart, VP
David Fay, Executive Director

An association of member clubs and courses. Conducts the US Open and Women's Open Championships, the Walker and Curtis Cup matches and ten national amateur championships.
7.5M Members Founded: 1894

20357 United States Harness Writers Association
POÆBox 1314
Mechanicsburg, PA 17055
717-766-3219

ushwa@paonline.com
www.ustrotting.com/absolutenm

Gordon Waterstone, President
Judy Davis-Wilson, First VP
Debbie Little, Second VP

Members are media members who cover the sport of harness racing.
300 Members Founded: 1947

20358 United States Parachute Association
1440 Duke Street
Alexandria, VA 22314
703-836-3495
FAX: 703-836-2843 800-371-8772
uspa@uspa.org www.uspa.org

Christopher Needels, Executive Director

A not-for-profit membership association dedicated to the promotion of safe skydiving and the support of those who enjoy it. Sponsors Instructor Rating Program to train and certify instructors, jump masters and examiners.
34000 Members Founded: 1946

20359 United States Racquet Stringers
330 Main Street
Vista, CA 92084
760-536-1177
FAX: 760-536-1171
usra@racquettech.com
www.usrsa.com

David Bone, Executive Director
Dianne Pray, Membership Coordinator
Crawford Lindsey, Editor/Webmaster
Kristine Thom, Production Manager

Educates constituencies to better understand, service, perform with, and enjoy the technological wonders known as racquests, strings, balls, courts, shoes, and stringing machines.
7000 Members Founded: 1975

20360 United States Trotting Association
750 Michigan Avenue
Columbus, OH 43215
614-242-2291
FAX: 614-228-1385 877-800-8782
stats@ustrotting.com
www.ustrotting.com

F. Phillip Langley, President
Joseph A Faraldo, Chairman
Eric M Sharbaugh, Executive VP

The USTA licenses owners, trainers, drivers and officials; formulates the rules of racing; maintains and disseminates racing information and records; serves as the registry for the Standardbred breed; endeavors to ensure the integrity of harness racing; insists on the humane treatment of Standardbreds; and promotes the sport of harness racing and the Standardbred breed.

Founded: 1939

20361 United States Water Fitness Association
PO Box 3279
Boynton Beach, FL 33424-3279
561-732-9908
FAX: 561-732-0950
info@uswfa.org www.uswfa.com

John R Spannuth, President/CEO

Nonprofit educational organization that promotes aquatics throughout the US and other countries. Publishes the National Aquatics Newsletter, names the 100 top programs and aquatics in the country, by state and in 25+ categories. Conducts a wide variety of national aquatics certifications including Water Fitness Instructors (primary and masters), aquatic directors, coordinators of water fitness programs. Conducts annual international aquatics conference.
Founded: 1988

20362 Western Toy & Hobby Representatives Association
9397 Reserve Drive
Corona, CA 92883
951-277-1598
FAX: 951-277-1599
info@wthra.com www.wthra.com

Phylis St John, Show Director

A nonprofit association organization. For the last 40 years we have produced and promoted the Western States Toy & Hobby Show.
Founded: 1961

20363 Women's Sports Foundation
Eisenhower Park
East Meadow, NY 11554
516-542-4700
FAX: 516-542-4716 800-227-3988
info@womenssportsfoundation.org
www.womenssportsfoundation.org

Billie Jean King, Founder
Donna Lopiano, Chief Executive Officer
Allison Sawyer, Senior Communications Coordinator

Disseminates information as well as encourages girls and women in sports and physical activity. Organization offers free access to quarterly electronic newsletter, Women's Sports Experience, that provides general updates on the world of girls'and women's sports as well as the Foundation's work.
4000 Members Founded: 1974
Circulation: 15000

20364 YMCA of the USA
101 N Wacker Drive
Chicago, IL 60606
312-770-0031
800-872-9622

Kenneth Gladish, Chief Executive Officer

Provides national and state branch divisions.
20.1M Members

Newsletters

20365 AAPSM Newsletter
American Academy of Podiatric Sports Medicine
109 Greenwich Drive
Walkersville, MD 21793-9121
334-448-2391
FAX: 301-845-9888 888-854-3338
info@aapsm.org www.aapsm.org

Stephen m Pribut, President
David M Davidson, Director
Rita J. Yates, Executive Director

A quarterly newsletter published by the American Academy of Podiatric Sports Medicine.
12 pages Quarterly Founded: 1970
Circulation: 700

Mailing list available for rent 600 names $125 per M.

20366 Behind the Seams
National Amateur Baseball Federation
PO Box 705
Bowie, MD 20715
301-625-5005
FAX: 301-352-0214
NABF1914@aol.com www.nabf.com
J Patrick Eaken, Editor
Charles M Blackburn, Executive Director
The official newsletter of the National Amateur Baseball Federation. Sent to NABF league members.
Quarterly Founded: 1914

20367 Hunting Report for Big Game Hunters
Oxpecker Enterprises
9300 S Dadeland Boulevard
Suite 605
Miami, FL 33156-2721
305-670-1361
FAX: 305-716-1376 800-272-5656
Subscriptions@HuntingReport.com
www.huntingreport.com
Don Causey, President/Publisher
Nick Titus, Production Manager
Provides information on hunting opportunities and conditions in the US, Africa and other parts of the world. *$60.00*
Monthly Founded: 1980

20368 Hunting Report: Birdshooters and Water
Oxpecker Enterprises
9300 S Dadeland Boulevard
Suite 605
Miami, FL 33156-2721
305-670-1361
FAX: 954-370-1376
subscriptions@huntingreport.com
www.huntingreport.com
Don Causey, Publisher
Serving the Sportsman who travels. *$45.00*
14 pages Monthly
Circulation: 1850
Printed in 2 colors on matte stock

20369 Leader Board
Golf Course Superintendents Association of America
1421 Research Park Drive
Lawrence, KS 66049-3859
785-841-2240
FAX: 785-832-4433 800-472-7878
infobox@gcsaa.org www.gcsaa.org
Jeff Bollig, Director Communications
Melissa Householder, Communications Coordinator
Ed Hiscock, Editor-In-Chief
Bi-monthly newsletter for golf facility decision makers, including superintendents and their employers, presenting timely and useful informaiton about golf course management in a quick easy-to-read format.
Monthly Founded: 1926
Circulation: 40000

20370 Media Sports Business
Kagan Research
One Lower Ragsdale Drive
Building One Suite 130
Monterey, CA 93940
831-624-1536
FAX: 831-625-3225 800-307-2529
info@kagan.com
http://www.kagan.com
George Niesen, Editor
Tom Johnson, Marketing Manager
Statistics of a different kind. How much media pay to carry sports events, the impact of media on pro sports franchises, and more. Scores big with major league and media players. Three month trial available. *$945.00*
Monthly Founded: 1969

20371 NSGA Sporting Goods Alert
1601 Feehanville Drive
Suite 300
Mount Prospect, IL 60056
847-296-6742
FAX: 847-391-9827
info@nsga.org www.nsga.org
Ron Kruse, Chairman
James L Faltinek, President/CEO
Dan Kasen, Manager
News and rule changes affecting team dealers. Newsletter is free to members.
Founded: 1936
Circulation: 1000

20372 Newsline
Golf Course Superintendents Association of America
1421 Research Park Drive
Lawrence, KS 66049-3859
785-841-2240
FAX: 785-832-4433 800-472-7878
infobox@gcsaa.org www.gcsaa.org
Terry Ostmeyer, Senior Staff Writer
Membership newsletter highlighting programs and services, and featuring news about the association, its members, the golf course management profession and industry.
Founded: 1926

20373 Sport Scene
North American Youth Sport Institute
4985 Oak Garden Drive
PO Box 957
Kernersville, NC 27285
336-784-4926
FAX: 336-784-5546 800-767-4916
jack@naysi.com www.naysi.com
Jack Hutslar, Publisher/Editor
News, features, tips, reviews, statistics, and summaries for people who work with tots, children and teens in fitness, recreation, education, sport and health with the focus on management, resources latest coaching and teaching methods, do's and dont's, safety, program ideas, legal issues, and training programs for leaders. Goal is to provide current information to improve learning while making activities more safe and positive so children can have more fun. *$16.00*
6X/yr Founded: 1979 ISSN 0270-1812

20374 Team Marketing Report
Team Marketing Report
1653 North Wells St
Suite 2F
Chicago, IL 60614-3962
312-280-2311
FAX: 312-280-2322 888-616-1867
info@teammarketing.com
www.teammarketing.com
Becky Vallett, Executive Editor
Information on rates, ticket prices, and consumer attitudes, new ideas to help increase sales and exposure through the sports market. *$195.00*
Monthly Founded: 1988

20375 Winning Edge Newsletter
520 Dix Road
Suite C
Jefferson City, MO 65109
573-635-1660
FAX: 573-635-8233
hq@somo.org www.somo.org
Mark Musso, President
Mandi Steward Mueller, Public Relations Coordinator
Diannah White, Chief Communications Officer
Publication produced for the athletes, volunteers and supports of the Special Olympics.
Quarterly Founded: 1983

Magazines & Journals

20376 ADDvantage
US Professional Tennis Association
3535 Briarpark Drive
Suite 1
Houston, TX 77042-5245
713-978-7782
FAX: 713-978-7780 800-877-8248
uspta@uspta.org www.uspta.com
Shawna Riley, Editor
Kim Forrester, Managing Editor
A monthly magazine published by the US Professional Tennis Association. Available through membership only.
36 pages Monthly Founded: 1927
Circulation: 13,000
Printed in 4 colors on glossy stock

20377 AKWA Magazine
Aquatic Exercise Association
201 Tamiami Trail
PO Box 1609
Nokomis, FL 34274-1609
941-486-8600
FAX: 941-486-8820 888-232-9283
register@aeawave.com
www.aeawave.com
Angie Nelson, Executive Director
Julie See, President
Kim Huff, Director of Marketing
The aqautics fitness industry's leading magazine. Brings professionals the most up to date and innovative ideas in programming, management, safety and nutrition for group exercise and personal training in the pool. Available to AEA members with their $65.00 membership.
Founded: 1987
Circulation: 6000
Mailing list available for rent 90M names
Printed in 4 colors on glossy stock

20378 American Bicyclist Magazine
League of American Bicyclists
1612 K Street NW
Suite 800
Washington, DC 20006-2802
202-822-1333
FAX: 202-822-1334
elizabeth@bikeleague.org
www.bikeleague.org
Elizabeth Preston, Editor
Andy Clark, Executive Director
Contains cycling stories; how-to articles; health; legal and safety columns; legislative updates, fitness, cycling technique and travel. *$35.00*
Quarterly Founded: 1880
Circulation: 40000
Printed in 4 colors on glossy stock

20379 American Firearms Industry
AFI Communications
2400 E Las Olas Boulevard
#397
Fort Lauderdale, FL 33301
954-467-9994
FAX: 954-463-2501
webmaster@amfire.com
www.amfire.com

Andrew Molchan, Editor
Alexandra Molchan, Circulation Manager
Kathleen Molchan, Sales Manager

A business-to-business trade magazine containing articles and information centered on the retailing of firearms and shooting products. Areas covered are: handguns, revolvers, pistols, rifles, shotguns, ammunition, rifle scopes, reloading, holsters, hunting accessories, gun parts, cutlery, knives, archery, bows, crossbows, camping, camouflage, black powder, smokeless powder, binoculars, safes, gunlocks, air guns, used gun news and political news and views relatingto firearms and the industry. *$18.00*
Monthly Founded: 1973
Circulation: 34 80M names

20380 American Fitness
Aerobics and Fitness Association of America
15250 Ventura Boulevard
Suite 200
Sherman Oaks, CA 91403
818-905-0040
FAX: 818-990-5468 877-968-7263
contactafaa@afaa.com www.afaa.com

Linda Pfeffer, President
Roscoe K Fawcett Jr, Publisher

The official publication of the Aerobics and Fitness Association of America. Known for reporting health-related fitness research, current trends, advances in equipment and training applications. *$27.00*
Bi-annually Founded: 1983
Circulation: 100,000

20381 American Hunter
National Rifle Association
11250 Waples Mill Road
Fiarfax, VA 22030
703-671-1400
877-672-2000

Mark A Keefe IV, Editor

American Hunter offers expertise on how and where to hunt all types of North American game and encourages readers to take advantage of the rich opportunities and to pass along the tradition to the next generation.

20382 American Quarter Horse Journal
American Quarter Horse Association
1600 Quarter Horse Drive
PO Box 200
Amarillo, TX 79104
806-764-4888
FAX: 806-349-6400 www.aqha.com

Bill Brewer, Executive VP
Jim Jennings, Publisher

Industry magazine for Quarter Horse breeders, farm managers and owners. *$25.00*
550 pages Monthly Founded: 1948
Circulation: 66575 $23 per M.
Printed in 4 colors on glossy stock

20383 American Rifleman
National Rifle Association
11250 Waples Mill Road
Fairfax, VA 22030
703-267-1000
FAX: 703-267-3971 800-672-3888

Mark Keefe IV, Editor-In-Chief

Premier magazine for shooting and firearms enthusiasts. Coverage is devoted to rifles, shotguns, handguns, ammunition, reloading, optics and shooting accessories. *$35.00*
Monthly Founded: 1975
Circulation: 100000

20384 Americas 1st Freedom
National Rifle Association
11250 Waples Mill Road
Fairfax, VA 22030
703-671-1400
877-672-2000
NRA's pure news magazine. Its mission is to deliver professional, compelling, accurate, timely and hard-hitting journalism that tells the truth about the threats to our Second Amendment rights. Subscription complementary with membership in NRA. Otherwise $9.95

20385 Aquatic Therapy and Fitness Research
Aquatic Exercise Association
201 Tamiami Trail South
Suite 3
Nokomis, FL 34275
941-486-8600
FAX: 941-486-8820 888-232-9283
info@aeawave.com
www.aeawave.com

Angie Proctor, Executive Director
Julie See, President

Journal. Peer-reviewed publication providing documentated opinions of industry leaders. A multidisciplinary publication, each issue includes two focus areas. Subscription included with AEA membership. *$65.00*
Monthly Founded: 1984
Circulation: 6000

20386 Aquatics International
Leisure Publications
3923 W 6th Street
Los Angeles, CA 90020-4244
323-644-4801
FAX: 323-964-4842 888-269-8410
aquaticsintl@earthlink.com
www.aquaticsintl.com
Articles of interest to colleges and schools; municipal, county and state pool facilities; hotels, resorts and country clubs; fitness clubs; rehab centers; YMCAs; military facilities; and waterparks. *$30.00*
11X/Yr
Circulation: 30000

20387 Arabian Horse World
1316 Tamson Drive
Suite 101
Cambria, CA 93428
805-771-2300
FAX: 805-927-6522 800-955-9423
info@ahwmagazine.com
www.ahwmagazine.com

Denise P Hearst, Publisher

Our philosophy at Arabian Horse World is to promote the Arabian - through education and entertainment - to new levels of appreciation and usefullness. Show results and breeding farms are featured. *$40.00*
Monthly Founded: 1990
Circulation: 15000
Printed in 4 colors on glossy stock

20388 Archery Business Magazine
Grand View Media Group
14505 21st Ave N
Ste 202
Plymouth, MN 55447
763-473-5800
FAX: 763-473-5801 800-766-0039
pbrady@affinitygroup.com
www.bowhuntingworld.com

Steve Schiffman, Publisher
Mark Melotik, Editor
Patty Brady, Advertising
Steven Hedlund, President

Controlled circulation trade magazine covering the business side of bowhunting and archery: trade news, industry statistics, marketing and product trends, new product research and development, tips for better business management and effective training.
Monthly Founded: 1975
Circulation: 11000+

20389 Arrow Trade Magazine
3479 409th Avenue NW
Braham, MN 55006
320-963-3473
FAX: 320-396-3473 888-796-2083
atrade@ecenet.com
www.fieldandstream.com

Tim Dehn, Publisher
Matt Granger, Advertising

A business magazine published for retailers, distributors, sales representatives and manufacturers of bowhunting equipment and camouflage clothing.
Founded: 1997

20390 Athletic Management
MAG
2488 N Triphammer Road
Ithaca, NY 14850
607-257-6970
FAX: 607-257-7328
info@athleticbid.com
www.momentummedia.com

Mark Goldberg, President
Eleanor Frankel, Editor

Free to college athletic administrators and high school athletic directors in the US and Canada. The editorial mission of Athletic Management is to help Athletic Directors enhance their operations, to share new ideas, and cover pertinent news topics. Feature stories and regular sections address the various facets of managing an athletic department. *$25.00*
Weekly Founded: 1988
Circulation: 30200
Printed in 4 colors on glossy stock

20391 Bass Times
ESPN
334-272-9530

customerservice@bassmaster.com
http://sports.espn.go.com/outdoors/bassmaster
Bass Times is packed with news and information for serious bass fishermen. The perfect compliment to Bassmaster Magazine. *$12.00*
Monthly

20392 Bassmaster
ESPN
334-272-9530

advertising@basmaster.com
http://sports.espn.go.com/bassmaster
Bassmaster Magazine monthly.
Monthly

20393 Black's Buyers Directory
PO Box 2029
Red Bank, NJ 07701
732-224-8700
FAX: 732-741-2827 800-224-9464
ms-blacks@attglobal.net
www.fieldandstream.com

James F Black Jr, Publisher
Lois Re, Editor
Christopher Pluck, Owner

The complete buyer's guide to equipment. A one-stop source of information on anything and everything that's archery/bowhunting.
Founded: 2001

20394 Bowlers Journal International
Luby Publishing Company
122 S Michigan Avenue
Suite 1506
Chicago, IL 60603-'
312-341-1110
FAX: 312-341-1469
email@bowlersjournal.com
www.bowlersjournal.com

Mike Panozzo, Publisher
Mason King, Editor

Information geared toward all levels of industry personnel. Regular issue features include new products listings, tournament reviews, personality profiles and proprietor workshops. *$24.00*
Monthly Founded: 1913
Circulation: 22319

20395 Bowling Center Management
Bowling Proprietors Association of America
122 S Michigan Avenue
Suite 1506
Chicago, IL 60603-6107
312-341-1110
FAX: 312-341-1180
bowlctrman@aol.com
www.bcmmag.com

Mike Panozzo, Publisher
Bob Nieman, Editor
Emily Kupper, Circulation Director

Information designed for bowling center owners to help them in the operation and management of their centers. *$60.00*
Monthly Founded: 1995
Circulation: 5000

20396 Camping Magazine
American Camp Association
5000 State Road 67 North
Martinsville, IN 46151-7902
765-342-8456
FAX: 765-342-2065 800-428-2267
pr@acacamps.org www.acacamps.org

Peg Smith, Executive Director
Kim Bruno, Communication/Development Head
Terrie Nicodemus, Manager

The official publication of the American Camp Association. Experts in the camp field contribute informative articles and essays on current advances in camp management, staffing and human resources, programming, risk management, special populations and diversity, health and wellness, and more. *$24.95*
Founded: 1920
Mailing list available for rent

20397 Coaching Management
MAG
2488 N Triphammer Road
Ithaca, NY 14850-5220
607-257-6970
FAX: 607-257-7328
info@athleticbid.com
www.momentummedia.com

Mark Goldberg, Publisher/CEO
Eleanor Frankel, Editor

Information including team equipment, apparel, injury prevention, conditioning, as well as field, stadium and court maintenance and improvement. Primary feature articles cover a wide range of coaching tools and techniques.
Bi-annually Founded: 1988
Circulation: 20556

20398 Cross Country Skier
PO Box 550
Cable, WI 54821
715-798-5500
800-827-0607
info@crosscountryskier.com
www.crosscountryskier.com

Ron Bergin, Owner

The journal of nordic skiing - destinations, news, training and technique, waxing, competition, equipment and new products, and great features on all facets of the sport of cross country skiing.

20399 Deer & Deer Hunting
Krause Publications
700 East State Street
Iola, WI 54990-1
715-445-2214
FAX: 715-445-4087 800-258-0929
info@krause.com www.krause.com

Hugh McAloon, Publisher

Edited for serious, year-round whitetail hunting enthusiasts and focuses on hunting techniques, deer biology and behavior, deer management, habitat requirements, the natural history of deer, and hunting ethics. Contains how-to articles designed to help hunters be successful. Regular columns and departments include book reviews, "Deer Browse" (unusual observations by hunters), new products, an editor's column, letters from readers, "Deer Behavior," "Can You Outsmart This Deer?" and Q&A. *$19.99*
Founded: 1977
Circulation: 212500

20400 Fantasy Sports
Krause Publications
700 E State Street
Iola, WI 54990-0001
715-445-2214
FAX: 715-445-4087 800-258-0929
fb@krause.com
www.fantasysportsmag.com

Tom Kessenich, Editor
Greg Ambrosius, Editor

The essential manual for those who participate in Rotisserie and other fantasy sports leagues. Reports extensive statistics to help "managers" in making personnel moves. Also includes recommendations on who to draft or trade. The April and May issues focus on baseball. The August and September issues focus on football. An up-to-the-minute, online version is also available fo a small fee at www.fantasysportsmag.com *$9.97*
132 pages 4 Per Year Founded: 1989
Circulation: 78,767

20401 Fishermen's News
Philip's Publishing Group
2201 W Commodore Way
Seattle, WA 98199-1298
206-284-8285
FAX: 206-284-0391 800-258-8609
circulation@rhppublishing.com
www.fishermensnews.com

Peter Philips, Publisher
Lisa Albers, Managing Editor
Bill Forslund, Advertising Manager
Maggie Cheung, Circulation Manager
Sharon Adjiri, Production Manager

In addition to important fisheries news, every month they bring readers important information and lessons on Safety, entertaining pieces about commercial fishing history, a commercial listing of fishing vessels and equipment in their classified section, updated information on seafood market trends and important notices about all the meetings and conferences occurring on the West Coast. *$21.00*
Monthly Founded: 1945
Circulation: 14,933
Printed in 4 colors on newsprint stock

20402 Fishing Tackle Retailer
ESPN Productions
5845 Carmichael Road
Montgomery, AL 36117-2329
407-566-2277
FAX: 334-279-7148
customerservice@bassmaster.com
www.bassmaster.com

Clem Dippel, Publisher
Scott Wall, Advertising Sales

Information to inform and instruct America's fishing tackle retailers, merchandisers, and distributors on merchandise and sales techniques used to sell fishing tackle. *$4.00*
11X/yr Founded: 1980
Circulation: 17720
Printed in 4 colors

20403 Free Hunters
National Rifle Association
11250 Waples Mill Road
Fairfax, VA 22030
703-671-1400
877-672-2000

A separate magazine and lobbying department of the NRA. Its mission is to consolidate and strengthen American hunter's political power through a visible advocacy group that preserves the sport, expands seasons, opens lands and celebrates the culture of hunting. Subscription complementary with membership in NRA. Otherwise $9.95

20404 Funworld
International Association of Amusement Parks
1448 Duke Street
Alexandria, VA 22314-3403
703-836-4800
FAX: 703-836-4801
iaapa@iaapa.org www.iaapa.org

Charlie Bray, President/CEO
Susan Mosedale, Executive VP

Funworld Magazine is a service for IAAPA members and provides discussion and illustrative examinations of the amusement and attractions industry form members to stay current and connected. The magazine contains features that analyze various aspects of the amusement business including safety, thrill rides, financial issues, event coverage and profiles of member and nonmember facilities from around the world. *$45.00*

Circulation: 8,500

20405 Golf Business
National Golf Course Owners Association

291 Seven Farms Drive
Charleston, SC 29492
843-881-9956
FAX: 843-856-3288 800-933-4262
golfbusiness@ngcoa.org
www.golfbusinessmagazine.com

Rodney Foushee, Managing Editor
Joe Rice, Publisher
Frank Santangelo, Manager

The official publication of the National Golf Course Owners Association. The editorial content is designed to promote the exchange of information and ideas among course owners and senior industry executives to improve the profitability of their operations. Golf Business is dedicated to serving the entire interest of the golf course operation. *$35.00*
Monthly Founded: 1971
Circulation: 20000
Printed in 4 colors on glossy stock

20406 Golf Course Management
Golf Course Superintendents Association of America
1421 Research Park Drive
Lawrence, KS 66049-3858
785-841-2240
FAX: 785-832-4433 800-472-7878
ehiscock@gcsaa.org www.gcsaa.org

Ed Hiscock, Editor-In-Chief
Scott Hollistor, Editor
Bunny Smith, Managing Editor
Mark Gabrick, Sr Manager Corp Sales/Marketing

Official monthly magazine of Golf Course Superintendents Association of America and golf course management industry's leading professional journal. Includes scientific, technical and practical management articles. *$60.00*
Monthly Founded: 1932
Circulation: 40,000

20407 Golf Course News
4012 Bridge Avenue
Cleveland, OH 44113
216-961-4130
FAX: 216-961-0364
www.golfcoursenews.com

Kevin Gilbride, Publisher
John Walsh, Editor
Richard Foster, CEO
Chris Foster, President/COO
Doug Adams, Director Marketing

Focuses on course maintenance and management, new course openings, and awards and promotions. New products related to the industry and environment and government issues. *$45.00*

Circulation: 30000

20408 Golf Inc Magazine
Cypress Manazines
250 Bei Marin Key Boulevard, #A
PO Box 1150
Novato, CA 94949-5727
415-382-2400
FAX: 415-382-2416 800-436-6149
mikeb@cypressmagazines.com
www.cyspressmagazines.com

Jack Crittenden, President
Kim Boalick, Advertising
Mindy Heral, Marketing
Jim Dunlap, Editor-in-Chief

Provides news, success stories and benchmark data for all aspects of the golf course industry - including development, operations, marketing, retail, turf, sales and driving range. *$65.00*
Monthly
Circulation: 15000

20409 Golf Range Times
Forecast Golf Group
5206 Market Road
Suite 103
Richmond, VA 23230
804-379-5760
FAX: 804-378-5780
info@forecastgolf.com
www.forecastgolf.com

James E Turner, Publisher/Editor
Betty Jo Bass, Advertising Manager

Information on Golf Range industry changes and closings, new ranges, and development information and services. *$49.95*
Monthly Founded: 1990
Circulation: 6000

20410 Golfdom
Questex Medica Group
PO Bo 5057
Brentwood, TN 37024
615-377-3322
FAX: 615-377-3322 866-344-1315
questex@sunbeltfs.com
www.golfdom.com

Patrick Jones, Publisher
Larry Aylward, Editor

Publication is written for golf course architects, superintendents, management companies, owners, developers, consultants and others in the industry with an interest in golf course design, construction, remodeling and related business and management topics. Subscription is free to Golf course superintendents, owners and managers. Individuals who are not qualified as superintendents, owners and managers can subscribe at the current subscription rate. *$30.00*
Founded: 1927
Circulation: 3000

20411 Government Recreation & Fitness
Executive Business Media
825 Old Country Road
PO Box 1500
Westbury, NY 11590
516-334-3030
FAX: 516-334-3059
ebm-mail@ebmpubs.com
www.ebmpubs.com

Murry Greenwald, Publisher
Paul Ragnoz, Managing Editor

Government Recreation and Fitness reaches recreation and fitness professionals in every department and agency of the federal government, goes directly to the people who purchase your products, and covers both appropriated and nonappropriated fund budgets. Subscription is free to managers and operators of fitness centers and recreation facilities at US military bases, federal agencies and offices as well as procurement agents for these facilities and others allied to the field *$35.00*
15 issues per year Founded: 1994
Circulation: 9974
Printed in 4 colors on glossy stock

20412 Hockey Business News
Straight Line Communications
12327 Santa Monica Boulevard
#202
Los Angeles, CA 90025-2552
310-207-9916
FAX: 310-442-6663 hbn@artnet.net

Mark Brown, Publisher

Features articles on ice hockey news and events, Canadian and international news, industry trends and forecasts and new products. *$60.00*
9 per year
Circulation: 5,000

20413 Horseman's Journal
National Horsemen's Administration Corporation
4063 Iron Works Parkway
B-2
Lexington, KY 40511
859-259-0451
FAX: 859-259-0452 866-245-1711
racing@hpba.org www.hbpa.org

Richard E Glover, Editor
Sandy Erreguin, Advertising Director

Official magazine of the National Horsemen's Benevolent and Protective Association. Designed to give owners and trainers of racehorses information helpful for the running of their horse related businesses.
56 pages Founded: 1942
Circulation: 32,000
Printed in 4 colors on glossy stock

20414 ISI EDGE
Ice Skating Institute
17120 N Dallas Parkway
Suite 140
Dallas, TX 75248-1187
972-735-8800
FAX: 972-735-8815
isi@skateisi.org www.skateisi.org

Peter Martell, Executive Director
Lori Fairchild, Editor
Emily Silva, Marketing Manager

Professional journal for the ice skating industry. Focuses on the needs and interests of the industry's managers, skating and hockey directors, instructors, and builders/suppliers.
Bi-Monthly Founded: 1959
Circulation: 50000
Printed in on matte stock

20415 Inside Archery
2960 N Academy Boulevard
Suite 101
Colorado Springs, CO 80917
719-495-9999
FAX: 719-495-8899
info@insidearchery.com
www.fieldandstream.com

Bill Krenz, President/Editor
Sherry Krenz, VP/Publisher

The Archery Industry Authority
Founded: 1997

20416 International Bowling Industry
13245 Riverside Drive
Suite 501
Sherman Oaks, CA 91423
818-789-2695
FAX: 818-789-2812
info@bowlingindustry.com
www.bowlingindustry.com

Scott Frager, Publisher & Editor
Nick West, Associate Publisher
Fred Groh, Managing Editor
Patty Heath, Office Manager

Information on customer services, new products, industry trends, new concepts in management and marketing techniques, and employee motivation. *$32.00*

Monthly
Circulation: 10,205

20417 Master Skier
PO Box 187
Escabana, MI 49829
906-789-1139

mskier@chartermi.net
www.masterskier.com
Journal dedicated to the skiing industry. Delivered to 51,000 readers in 19 countries.

20418 Medicine and Science in Sports and Exercise
American College of Sports Medicine
401 W Michigan Street
PO Box 1440
Indianapolis, IN 46206
317-347-7817
FAX: 317-634-7817
msse@acsm.org www.acsm.org

Kent B Pandolf, Editor-in-Chief

Scientific research, education, and practical applications of sports medicine and exercise science to maintain and enhance physical performance, fitness, health and quality of life. *$300.00*

Monthly Founded: 1968
Circulation: 14842
Printed in 4 colors on matte stock

20419 NRA InSights
National Rifle Association
11250 Waples Mill Road
Fairfax, VA 22030
703-671-1400
877-672-2000
NRAs official publication for its Junior members. Designed to motivate its readers to participate in all aspects of the shooting sports. Features personality profiles on top junior shooters, hunting stories, how-to pieces, program announcements, product surveys, safety features and educational information about firearms. Subscription included in membership dues.

20420 Online Magazine
Information Today
143 Old Marlton Pike
Medford, NJ 08055-8750
609-654-6266
FAX: 609-654-4309 800-300-9868
custserv@infotoday.com
www.infotoday.com

Marydee Ojala, Editor
Thomas H Hogan, President/Publisher
John Brokenshire, Chief Financial Officer
Tom Hogan, Jr, VP Marketing

Online is written for information professionals and provides articles, product reviews, case studies, evaluation and informed opinion about selecting, using and managing electronic information products, plus industry and professional information about onlline database systems. *$ 115.00*

Monthly Founded: 1976

20421 Outdoors Magazine
Elk Publishing
531 Main Street
Colchester, VT 05446
802-792-2013
FAX: 802-879-2015 800-499-0447
info@outdoorsmagazine.net
www.outdoorsmagazine.net

James Ehlers, Editor
Mark Fludgate, Publisher

A monthly publication covering hunting, fishing and wildlife issues in Vermont, New York, Maine, Massachusetts and Connecticut. *$ 18.95*

Monthly Founded: 1996
Circulation: 10000
Printed in 4 colors on matte stock

20422 PGA TOUR Partners Magazine
North American Media Group
12301 Whitewater Drive
Suite 260
Minnetonka, MN 55343
952-936-9333
FAX: 952-936-9169 800-688-7611
NAMGhq@namginc.com
www.namginc.com

Seth Hoyt, Publisher

An exclusive, members-only publication filled with tips and techniques that can be used to improve your game, from the first tee to the 18th green.

Bi-Monthly Founded: 1978
Circulation: 1.3 m

20423 Paddler
Paddle Sport Publishing
PO Box 775450
Steamboat Springs, CO 80477-5450
970-879-1450
FAX: 970-870-1404 888-774-7554
circulation@paddlermagazine.com
http://www.paddlermagazine.com

Eugene Buchanan, Publisher/Editor
Tom Bie, Managing Editor

Each issues is filled with stories on places to paddle, skill enhancement, gear reviews, environmental issues, industry updats and profiles of leading paddlers. *$18.00*

Monthly
Circulation: 5527
Printed in 4 colors on glossy stock

20424 Parachutist
United States Parachute Association
1440 Duke Street
Alexandria, VA 22314-3403
703-836-3495
FAX: 703-836-2843 866-585-4590
uspa@uspa.org www.uspa.org

Christopher Needels, Executive Director
Glenn Bangs, President

Safe skydiving and the support of those who enjoy it. Subscription included in membership to USPA. *$4.50*

Monthly Founded: 1957
Circulation: 36000
Printed in 4 colors on glossy stock

20425 Pool and Spa News
Leisure Publications
3923 W 6th Street
Los Angeles, CA 90020-4244
323-644-4801
FAX: 323-801-4986 888-269-8410
poolspanews@hanleywood.com
www.poolspanews.com

Dick Coleman, Publisher
Erika Taylor, Editor
Steve Schlange, Marketing Manager

Pool and Spa News goals are: to furnish information to help pool and spa professionals function better in their businesses; to showcase products that can be sold or used in the industry; to help make their business life easier and more rewarding. *$16.50*

Semi-Monthly Founded: 1960

20426 Powersports Business
Ehlert Publishing Group
6420 Sycamore Lane North
Suite 100
Maple Grove, MN 55369
763-383-4400
FAX: 763-383-4499 800-848-6247
customerservice@powersportsbusiness.com www.powersportsbusiness.com

Joe Delmont, Editor
Guido Ebert, Managing Editor
Steven Hedlund, President

Gives dealers, distributors, and manufacturers timely business news and analysis every three weeks.

Weekly Founded: 1969
Circulation: 18000

20427 Pro Football Weekly
302 Saunders Road
Suite 100
Riverwoods, IL 60015-5514
847-940-1100
FAX: 847-940-1108 800-331-7529
editors@pfwmedia.com
www.profootballweekly.com

Ron Pollack, Editor-in-chief
Hub Arkush, President

Seeks to bring the best coverage in the NFL to its readers. *$49.95*

Weekly Founded: 1967

20428 Professional Skater
Professional Skaters Association
3006 Allegro Park SW
Rochester, MN 55902
507-281-5122
FAX: 507-281-5491
office@skatepsa.com
www.skatepsa.com

Carole Shulman, Executive Director

A bi-monthly magazine published by the Professional Skater Association. *$19.95*

40 pages Bi-Monthly Founded: 1984 $300 per M.

20429 QUAD Off-Road Magazine
Transworld Publishing
353 Airport Road
Oceanside, CA 92054
760-722-7777
FAX: 760-722-0653
jasonyoung@twsnet.com
www.neodata.com

Jason Young, Publication Contact

Quad off-road magazine delivers all things ATV: Breathtaking photography, tons of practical tips, the hottest nwe products, Quad comparison tests, ARV adventure stories, and much more. *$9.97*

Monthly

20430 Quarter Horse Racing Journal
American Quarter Horse Association
1600 Quarter Horse Drive
Amarillo, TX 79104
806-764-4888
www.aqha.com
News and races, health and management, business and industry, winner's circle, the handicapper, horse health, quarter paths, sports medicine, finish line and others are featured articles.

Monthly

20431 Racquetball Magazine
USA Racquetball
1685 W Uintah Street
Colorado Springs, CO 80904-2906
719-635-5396
FAX: 719-635-0685
rjohn@usra.org www.racqmag.com

Jim Hiser, Executive Director
Kevin Joyce, Director Membership
Melody Weiss, Director Finance
Heather Fender, Executive Assistant/Event Coord

Geared toward a readership of informed, active enthusiasts who seek entertainment, instruction and accurate reporting of events. Available by subscription through the US Racquetball Association National Office. *$20.00*
64 pages Bi-Monthly Founded: 1990
Circulation: 16,000
Printed in 4 colors on glossy stock

20432 Recreational Ice Skating
Ice Skating Institute
17120 N Dallas Parkway
Suite 140
Dallas, TX 75248
972-735-8800
FAX: 972-735-8815 www.skateisi.org
Quarterly magazine distributed to ISI individual skater members, skating coaches, and rinks and pro shops worldwide. Written for and about ice skating enthusiasts and focuses on promotoing ice skating as a recreation and sport.
Quarterly

20433 Referee
National Association of Sports Officials
2017 Lathrop Avenue
Racine, WI 53405
262-325-5448
FAX: 262-632-5460 800-733-6100
questions@referee.com
http://www.naso.org

Barry Mano, President

Monthly magazine published by the National Association of Sports Officials. Containes interviews, feature articles, late-breaking news, personality profiles, investigative reports, health, legal and tax tips, and a wide range of technical information for many sports. *$44.95*
80 pages Monthly Founded: 1976
Circulation: 77000
Printed in 4 colors on glossy stock

20434 Ride BMX
Transworld Magazines
353 Airport Road
Oceanside, CA 92054
760-722-7777
FAX: 760-722-0653
jasonyoung@twsnet.com
www.neodata.com

Jason Young, Publication Contact

Publication with information for BMX riders. *$15.97*
Monthly

20435 Rodale's Scuba Diving
Krause Publications
700 E State Street
Iola, WI 54990-0001
715-445-2214
FAX: 715-445-4087 800-666-0016
edit@scubadiving.com
www.scubadiving.com
Edited to provide information about the practice of diving, dive travel opportunities, the marine environment, the reader's health and safety and the dive equipment on which they depend. Travel editorial focuses on both domestic and international dive travel and equipment editorial offers readers comparative product reviews. *$16.97*
11 Per Year Founded: 1992
Circulation: 187,059

20436 Shooting Illustrated
National Rifle Association
11250 Waples Mill Road
Fairfax, VA 22030
703-671-1400
877-672-2000
Comprehensive, tiemly and all-inclusive. In its pages you will find the best gun writers in the world, assembled to bring you the latest information on rifles, pistols or shotguns. From handloading to gunsmithing to highpower competition; from varmint rifles to rifles for the world's biggest game; from competition pistols to heavy field revolvers. *$9.95*

20437 Shooting Industry
12345 World Trade Drive
San Diego, CA 92128-3102
858-674-4898
FAX: 619-297-5353 858-605-0254
subs@shootingindustry.com
www.shootingindustry.com

Russ Thurman, Editor
Brian Friesen, Sales Manager

A trade publication covering the hunting and shooting industries. This publication is available to select dealers and select police personnel only. Dealers must have a current Federal Firearms License and no less than two additional credentials. Police personnel must have a letter from their Police Chief or Range Officer requesting a subscription (on department letterhead). *$25.00*
Monthly Founded: 1955

20438 Shooting Sports Retailer
SSR Communications
255 West 36th Street
Suite 1202
New York, NY 10018-7901
212-840-0660
FAX: 212-944-1884
www.shootingsportsretailer.com

Bruce Karaban, Publisher

Features articles on shooting sports equipment, sales techniques, new products, sales aids, and potential problems for the wholesale seller of shooting equipment.
Monthly Founded: 1980
Circulation: 17463

20439 Shooting Sports USA
National Rifle Association
11250 Waples Mill Road
Fairfax, VA 22030
703-671-1400
877-672-2000
Information for the competitive shooter, from smallbore to high power, air action pistol and everything in between. *$9.95*

20440 Single Shot Rifle Journal
American Single Shot Rifle Association
PO Box 1162
Niles, MI 49120
269-687-9550

journaleditor@assra.com
www.assra.com

Gary Staup, President
John Merz, VP
D. Wayne Stiles, Editor

The official magazine of The American Single Shot Rifle Association. Susbscription is included with membership in the ASSRA. *$ 35.00*
60 pages Bi-Monthly Founded: 1948
Circulation: 2400
Printed in on matte stock

20441 Ski Area Management
Beardsley Publishing Corporation
45 Main Street North
PO Box 644
Woodbury, CT 06798
203-263-0888
FAX: 203-266-0452
news@saminfo.com
www.saminfo.com

Jennifer Rowan, Publisher
Olivia Rowan, Marketing/Associate Publisher
Donna Jacobs, V.P./Administration
Rick Kahl, Editor
Ann Hasper, Senior Editor

SAM magazine is the professional trade publication for the mountain resort market. It is a bi-monthly, all-paid publication. *$ 48.00*
Monthly Founded: 1962
Circulation: 3992
Printed in 4 colors on glossy stock

20442 Ski Magazine
929 Pearl Street
#200
Boulder, CO 80302
303-448-7600
FAX: 303-442-6321 800-678-0817
subsvcs@ski.customersvc.com
www.skimag.com

Kendall Hamilton, Editor-In-Chief
Greg Ditrinco, Executive Editor
Kim Beekman, Managing Editor
Samantha Berman, Senior Editor

Includes information on travel, gear, instruction, snow reports, mountain cams, and gift shops. *$11.00*
8X/year

20443 SkiTrax Magazine
317 Adelaide Street
Suite 703 West
Toronto, Canada M5V1P9, ON
416-977-2100
FAX: 416-977-9200
skitrax@passport.ca www.skitrax.com

North America's premier nordic publication is the official magazine of the USSA and CCC and offers the broadest coverage of nordic skiing available. Coverage includes comprehensive Annual North American Buyer's Guide; local touring centers and exotic backcountry hide-a-ways; complete North American and international competition coverage; regular tips on products; training, technique, telemark, masters, and waxing; extensive calendar of events; plus much more.

20444 Soccer Journal
National Soccer Coaches Association of America
6700 Squibb Road
Suite 215
Mission, KS 66202
913-362-1747
FAX: 913-362-3439 800-458-0678
info@nscca.com www.nscaa.com

The official publication of the National Soccer Coaches of America. Produced exclusively for soccer coaches. Each issue contains technical and tactical articles, news and updates on important events, thoughts from opinion leaders in the sport and features on the interesting people and issues of the game. Subscription included in NSCAA membership. *$50.00*

8X/Year Founded: 1941
Circulation: 18000

20445 Speedway Illustrated
Speedway Illustrated
107 Elm St
Salisbury, MA 01952
978-465-9099
FAX: 978-465-9033 888-837-3684
editorial@speedwayillustrated.com
www.speedwayillustrated.com

Dave Ferrato, Director Advertising/Marketing
Steve Chryssos, Advertising Manager
Lynne Henry, Advertising Sales
Dick Berggren, Owner

They'll show you how to build and race your own car, and take you inside at NASCAR's hottest teams and stars. *$19.94*

Monthly Founded: 2000
Circulation: 150000

20446 Sporting Goods Business
VNU Business Publications
2900 Veterans Hwy
Bristol, PA 19007-1606
847-763-9050
FAX: 847-763-9037
www.sportinggoodsbusiness.com

Michael Marchesano, President
Derek Irwin, Chief Financial Officer
Sid Holt, Editorial Director

Covers information on all facets of sporting goods, including industry news, sales volume analysis, market events coverage, and other statistics, also covers store operation, merchandising, pricing, promotion, cost control, and sales training. *$75.00*

Monthly
Circulation: 27,374

20447 Sporting Goods Dealer
VNU Publications
PO Box 1184
Skokie, IL 60076-8194
847-763-9050
FAX: 847-763-9037
info@sgdealer.com www.sgdealer.com

Michael Marchesano, President/CEO
Sid Holt, Editorial Director
Derek Irwin, Chief Financial Officer

Sporting Goods Dealer offers reporting on industry insiders, new products, and merchandising trends affecting team dealers and retailers that service schools, colleges, and pro and local teams. *$75.00*

Founded: 1905
Circulation: 10000

20448 Sporting News
Sporting News Publishing Company
PO Vox 51570
Boulder, CO 80322-1510
314-997-7111
FAX: 314-993-7798 800-777-6785

Pete Spina, Publisher
Kathy Kinkeade, VP

A comprehensive publication covering sporting goods manufacturers, retailers, wholesalers and distributors. *$15.97*

Bi-Monthly

20449 Sports Illustrated
Time Life Building
New York, NY 10020-1393
212-229-9797
FAX: 212-467-4049
cnnsi@cnnsi.com www.cnnsi.com

Ann Moore, Chief Executive Officer

Magazine dedicated to the world of sports. *$39.95*

56 Issues/Year

20450 Sports Illustrated for Kids
Sports Illustrated
Time & Life Building
New York, NY 10020-1393
212-221-1212
212-467-4049

Paul Fichtenbaum, Managing Editor
Dave Watt, Publisher

Great action photos, easy-to-read stories about star athletes, helpful instructional tips from the pros, humor, comics and activities. *$24.95*

Monthly

20451 SportsTravel
Schneider Publishing Company
11835 W Olympic Boulevard
Suite 1265
Los Angeles, CA 90064
310-577-3700
FAX: 310-577-3715 877-577-3700
info@schneiderpublishing.com
www.sportstravelmagazine.com

Timothy Schneider, Publisher/Editor
Nathan Price, Managing Editor
Ann Shepphird, Executive Editor
Rachel Carr, Assistant Editor

SportsTravel magazine is the event organizer's guide to successfully creating and staging sports events. SportsTravel provides information on sports destinations and venues, transportation and accommodations, bidding for events, sponsorships, and marketing. SportsTravel facilitates relationships among sports governing bodies, host destinations, sponsors, and suppliers. *$48.00*

Founded: 1997
Circulation: 14,000
Printed in 4 colors on glossy stock

20452 Sportsbusiness Journal
American City Business Journals
112 West Morehead Street
Suite 310
Charlotte, NC 28202
704-731-1000
FAX: 704-973-1401
rweiss@sportsbusinessjournal.com
www.sportsbusinessjournal.com

Richard Weiss, Publisher
Abraham Madkour, Executive Editor
Ross Nethery, Managing Editor
Ray Shaw, Manager

Provides important news information for sports industry franchises, corporations, advertising, media and regulatory agencies, professional sports firms on salaries, liscensing, team updates, marketing and promotion with an emphasis on both popular and small sports. *$ 239.00*

49X/Year Founded: 1998
Circulation: 17,000

20453 Squash Magazine
23 Cynwyd Road
PO Box 1216
Bala Cynwyd, PA 19004-5216
610-667-4006
FAX: 610-667-6539 www.us-squash.org

Craig W Brand, Executive Director
Keith Klipstein, Executive Director

Articles on the sport of squash racquets in the United States. *$35.00*

10 per year

20454 Synchro Swimming USA
United States Synchronized Swimming
201 S Capitol Avenue
Suite 901
Indianapolis, IN 46225
317-237-5700
www.usasynchro.org

Terry Harper, Executive Director

Here's your chance to stay up-to-date with the latest news, results and happenings in the synchro world by subscribing to Synchro Swimming USA magazine. Printed quarterly. *$20.00*

Quarterly

20455 TEE Time Magazine
PO Box 225
Whitman, MA 02382
781-447-2299
FAX: 781-447-7773
www.teetime-mag.com

Mary Porter, Editor
Karen Christoforo, Sales

The Mid-Atlantics region's most comprehensive golf magazine. Each issue includes golf instruction, profiles of Mid-Atlantic personalities, course reviews and more. *$12.95*

64 pages

20456 Training & Conditioning
MAG
2488 N Triphammer Road
Ithaca, NY 14850-5220
607-257-6970
FAX: 607-257-7328
info@athleticbid.com
www.momentummedia.com

Articles on injury protection and treatment, rehabilitation, strength and speed training, as well as cardiovascular equipment for competitive athletes.

BiMonthly
Circulation: 27,400

20457 Transworld Motocross
Transworld Publications
353 Airport Road
Oceanside, CA 92054
760-722-7777
FAX: 760-722-0653
jasonyoung@twsnet.com
www.neodata.com

Jason Young, Publications Contact
Al Crolius, Manager

Magazine designed for the motocross enthusiast. *$16.97*

Monthly

20458 Transworld Skateboarding Business

Transworld Business Subscriptions
353 Airport Road
Oceanside, CA 92054-1203
760-722-7777
FAX: 760-722-0653 850-682-7644
subsvcs@skate.cusomtersvc.com
www.twsbiz.com

Larry Balma, Publisher
Brad McDonald, Manager

Geared toward skateboard retailers, apparel chain buyers, and manufacturers of skateboard products, includes new product information, industry news, and technical innovations. *$16.97*

Monthly
Circulation: 14500

20459 Transworld Snowboarding
Transworld Business
353 Airport Road
Oceanside, CA 92054-1203
760-722-7777
FAX: 760-722-0653 850-682-7644
twsnowbiz@aol.com
www.twsnow.com
Larry Balma, Publisher
Brad McDonald, Manager
Articles on industry news, retailer surveys, new products, and technical studies. *$14.97*
9/Year
Circulation: 20000

20460 Transworld Surf
Transworld Publishing
353 Airport Road
Oceanside, CA 92054
760-722-7777
FAX: 760-722-0653
jasonyoung@twsnet.com
www.neodata.com
Jason Young, Publications Contact
Brad McDonald, Manager
Magazine for surfing enthusiasts. *$12.00*
Monthly

20461 Trapper & Predator
Krause Publications
700 E State Street
Iola, WI 54990-0001
715-445-2214
FAX: 715-445-4087 www.krause.com
Hugh McAloon, Publisher
Paul Wait, Editor
Contains news, in-depth features, and how-to tips on trapping, the art of predator calling, and animal damage control. Contributors include the top names in the business. Regular columns and departments include "The Fur Shed," "Let's Swap Ideas," "Q&A," and news from state trapping associations nationwide. *$18.95*
10 Per Year Founded: 1975
Circulation: 38,260

20462 Turkey & Turkey Hunting
Krause Publications
700 East State Street
Iola, WI 54990-0001
715-445-2214
FAX: 715-445-4087 www.krause.com
Hugh McAloon, Publisher
Edited for serious, technical, year-round, gun and bow turkey hunters. Features emphasize success and enjoyment of the sport. Articles focus on hunting, scouting, turkey behavior and biology, hunting ethics, new equipment, methodologies, turkey management, and current research. Columns include "Tree Call," "Mail Pouch," "Turkey Biology," a Q&A column, "Hunter's Library," "Turkey Gear," and "Last Call." *$15.95*
6 Per Year Founded: 1991
Circulation: 68,962

20463 USA Table Tennis
One Olympic Plaza
Colorado Springs, CO 80909-5746
719-578-4583
FAX: 719-632-6071
watts@usatt.org www.usatt.org
Teodor Gheonghe, Executive Director
Sheri Soder Pittman, President
A bi-monthly magazine dedicated to the promotion of table tennis. Complementary with membership to USA Table Tennis. *$40.00*
Monthly Founded: 1933
Circulation: 9000
Printed in 4 colors on matte stock

20464 Velobusiness
Inside Communications
1830 N 55th Street
Boulder, CO 80301-2700
303-440-0601
FAX: 303-444-6788
Felix Magowen, President
Trends in the market, new product develoment updates and spot news reports, also includes testing and performance evaluations, as well as marketing, merchandising and sales techniques. *$35.00*
Monthly
Circulation: 10,560

20465 Woman's Outlook
National Rifle Association
11250 Waples Mill Road
Fiarfax, VA 22030
703-671-1400
877-672-2000
Created especially for women. Covers topics from personal protection and home security to general firearms safety and recreation. Subscription complimentary with membership in NRA. Otherwise $9.95

20466 Woodall's Campground Management
Woodall Publishing Company
2575 Vista Del Mar Drive
Ventura, CA 93001
805-672-2001
FAX: 847-362-8776 877-680-6155
info@woodallpub.com
www.woodalls.com
Barbara Leonard, Editor
Kristopher Bunker, Editor
Terry Thompson, Advertising
Michael Schneider, Chief Executive Officer
Information for campground owners and managers, provides methods of management and industry trends along with reports from independent and franchise campgrounds, public parks and state associations. *$24.95*
Monthly Founded: 1935
Circulation: 10,000

Trade Shows

20467 AACCA Spirit Coaches Conference
American Association of Cheerleading Coaches
6745 Lenox Center Court
Suite 318
Memphis, TN 38115
FAX: 901-251-5851 800-533-6583
Monti Hillis, President
Jeffrey Webb, Chief Executive Officer
Terri Johnson, Contact
The official NFHS Sprit Coaches Education Program. *$100.00*
Annual/April Founded: 1988

20468 AAU Annual Convention
AAU National Headquarters
1910 Hotel Plaza Boulevard
PO Box 22409
Lake Buena Vista, FL 32830
407-934-7200
FAX: 407-934-7242
pam@aausports.org
www.aausports.org
Pam Marshall, Convention Contact
John Hodges, Exhibitor Information
Bobby Dodd, President/CEO
National Convention of the Amateur Athletic Union.

20469 ASA Sportfishing Summit
American Sportfishing Association
225 Reinekers Lane
Suite 420
Alexandria, VA 22314
703-519-9691
FAX: 703-519-1872
info@asafishing.org
www.asafishing.org
Gordon Robertson, VP
More than 125 sportfishing industry leaders representing 65 companies and organizations and Europe. The summis is the association's annual membership meeting and provides the Board of Directors, committees, members and ASA's partners the best opportunity for networking and strategic planning. Three days.

20470 Action Sports Retailer Trade Exhibit West Fall and Spring
ASR Trade Expo
31910 Del Obispo
Suite 200
San Juan Capistrano, CA 92675
949-226-5744
FAX: 949-226-5659 www.asrbiz.com
Tina Middleton, Marketing Director
Lisha Steinkoenig, Registration Coordinator
Megan Lara, Expo Coordinator
Provides the ultimate showcase of the action sports and youth lifestyle market by attracting the world's largest and most powerful brands and buyers representing such diverse markets as surf, skate, swim, snow, footwear and fashion.
10M Attendees September/February

20471 Allegheny Sport, Travel and Outdoor Show
Expositions
PO Box 550
Edgewater Branch
Cleveland, OH 44107-0550
216-529-1300
FAX: 216-529-0311 800-600-0307
Chris Fassnacht, Show Producer
Dedicated to hunting, shiftin and camping. Features hundreds of state-of-the-art exhibitors, dozens of live demonstrations, and a top notch line-up of seminar experts. *$7.95*
Annual Founded: 1985

20472 Amateur Softball Association of America
2801 NE 50th Street
Oklahoma City, OK 73111
405-424-5266
FAX: 405-424-3855
bplummer@softball.org
www.asasoftball.com

Bill Plummer III, Hall of Fame/Trade Show Manager
Ron Radigonda, Executive Director

Annual meeting of the Amateur Softball Association.

1000+ Attendees Annual/November Founded: 1933

20473 American Alliance for Health, Phys Ed, Rec reation & Dance Conference & Expo
American Alliance for Hlth. Phys. Edu. Rec. Dance
1900 Association Drive
Reston, VA 20191-1599
703-476-3400
FAX: 703-476-9527 800-213-7193
conv@aahperd.org www.aahperd.org

Harve Horowitz, Show Manager
Michael Davis, Manager

Two hundred and eighty exhibits concerning physical education, sporting goods, supplies, equipment, service and organization representatives.

7000 Attendees Annual/April

20474 American Baseball Coaches Association Convention
108 S University Avenue
Suite 3
Mount Pleasant, MI 48858-2327
989-775-3300
FAX: 989-775-3600
abca@abca.org www.abca.org

Dave Keilitz, Executive Director

The annual convention features four days of non-stop baseball including approximately 30 clinic speakers; over 250 exhibitors displaying state-of-the-art baseball gear, equipment, and services; meetings of collegiate, high school and youth league divisions; Honors Luncheon, Hall of Fame/Coach of the Year Banquet, and International Coaches Reception. *$800.00*

4185 Attendees Annual Founded: 1945

20475 American Bowling Congress Annual Convention
United States Bowling Congress
5301 South 76th Street
Greendale, WI 53129
414-216-6400
FAX: 414-421-8560 800-514-2695
bowlinfo@bowl.com www.bowl.com

Annual conference of the United States Bowling Congress whose mission is to ensure the integrity and protect the future of the sport by providing programs and services and enhancing the bowling experience.

20476 American Camp Association Conference & Exhibits
American Camp Association
5000 State Road 67 N
Martinsville, IN 46151-7902
765-342-8456
FAX: 765-342-2065 800-428-2267

One hundred and forty to one hundred and fifty booths of arts and crafts, computer software, sporting goods, waterfront equipment and more plus a seminar and workshop.

1,200 Attendees Annual Founded: 1943

20477 American College of Sports Medicine Annual Meeting
401 W Michigan Street
Indianapolis, IN 46202
317-347-7817
FAX: 317-634-7817
acsm@acsm.org www.acsm.org

James R Whitehead, Executive VP

One hundred and eighty-five exhibits of sports equipment, publications, supplies and services, conference and banquet. CME credits available for a nominal fee at time of registration. *$425.00*

5000 Attendees Annual Founded: 1954

20478 American Football Coaches Association Convention
American Football Coaches Association
100 Legends Lane
Waco, TX 76706
254-754-9900

info@acfa.com www.afca.com

Grant Teaff, Executive Director

120 booths of equipment, supplies and services relevant to the game of football. Three-day event includees coaching clinic, awards luncheon and Coach of the Year dinner.

6000 Attendees Annual/January Founded: 1921

20479 American Greyhound Track Operators Association
Palm Beach Kennel Club
1111 North Congress Avenue
West Palm Beach, FL 33409
561-688-5799
FAX: 801-754-2404 www.agtoa.com

Richard Winning, President
Dennis Bicsak, Managing Coordinator

A forum for all those affiliated with the sport to exchange ideas and to develop new techniques for the improvement and growth of the greyhound industry.

400 Attendees Annual/March

20480 American Hockey Coaches Association Convention
American Hockey Coaches Association
7 Concord Street
Gloucester, MA 01930
781-245-4177
FAX: 781-245-2492
www.ahcahockey.com

Joe Bertagna, Executive Director
George Gwozdecky, President
Kevin Sneddon, VP/Convention Planning

70 exhibits of ice hockey equipment and supplies plus worksop and banquet.

500 Attendees Annual/April Founded: 1960

20481 American Orthopaedic Society for Sports Medicine Annual Meeting
American Orthopaedic Society for Sports Medicine
6300 N River Road
Suite 500
Rosemont, IL 60018-4229
847-292-4900
FAX: 847-292-4905 877-321-3500
aossm@aossm.org www.sportsmed.org

Michelle Schaffer, Exhibits Coordinator
Camille Petrick, Manager

130 exhibits of equipment supplies and services for sports medicine and related fields. Banquet and tours available. *$375.00*

1,500 Attendees June/July Founded: 1972
1750 names $500 per M.

20482 American Swimming Coaches Association
5101 NW 21st Avenue
Suite 200
Fort Lauderdale, FL 33309
954-563-4930
FAX: 954-563-9813 800-356-2722

John Leonard, Executive Director
Lori Klatt, Marketing

Annual convention

1.5M Attendees September

20483 American Youth Soccer Organization
12501 S Isis Avenue
Hawthorne, CA 90250
310-643-6455
FAX: 310-643-5310 800-872-2976

Rick Smith, Executive Director

The AYSO annual general meeting is your opportunity to represent your region, area or section on a national level.

800 Attendees Annual

20484 Archery Trade Show
Archery Trade Association
860 E 4500 Southrkway, Suite 1
Suite 310
Salt Lake City, UT 84107
801-261-2380
FAX: 801-261-2389 866-266-2776
info@archerytrade.org
www.archerytrade.org

Jay McAnich, President/CEO
Denise Parker, VP/Director Marketing
Cindy Brophy, Manager Tradeshow/Membership Svces

Formerly the Archery Manufacturers and Merchants Organization (AMO), the ATA provides the core funding and direction critical to the future of archery and bowhunting. The trade show features 499 exhibitors cover 155,500 square feet.

8000 Attendees Annual

20485 Athletic Equipment Managers Association Convention
723 Keil Ct
Bowling Green, OH 43402-2235

www.aemal.com

Sporting goods equipment manufacturers.

300 Attendees June

20486 Bowling Proprieters Association of America International Bowl Expo
615 Six Flags Drive
PO Box 5802
Arlington, TX 76011-6347
817-649-5105
FAX: 817-633-2940 888-649-5585

Lee Ann Norton, Director Meetings/Events

The bowling industry's premier event. Brings together thousands of bowling industry professionals in one place. You can find the latest trends, bowling-related products and services, marketing ideas, profit center opportunities, and tools to help you spread the excitement of bowling throughout your communities. Trade show showcases the latest products and services from more than 300 companies in over 900 exhibit booths.

5000 Attendees June

20487 CMAA Annual Conference
Club Managers Association of America
1733 King Street
Alexandria, VA 22314
703-739-9500
FAX: 703-739-0124
cmaa@cmaa.org www.smaa.org

Jim Singerling, Executive Vice President

Club Managers Association of America Annual World Conference. This International Conference brings together club industry professionals from around the world for five days of challenging education, entertaining social events and an industry trade show.

20488 Cedar Rapids Boat, Sports and Travel Show
Iowa Show Productions
PO Box 2460
Waterloo, IA 50704-2460
319-232-0218
FAX: 319-235-8932
info@iowashows.com
www.iowashows.com

John Bunge, Show Manager

See a huge display of boats including fishing boats, family runabouts, ski boats, pontoons, and performance boats. Light-weight campers, fifth wheels, and motorhomes will all be on display. Fishing camps, fly-ins, outposts, family resorts, Lake Michigan sportfishing, canoe outfitters, big game outfitters, tourism associations, campgrounds, fishing tackle, archery equipment, targets, decoys, calls, golf cars, all terrain vehicles, motorcycles and much more.
Annual/January

20489 Colorado RV Adventure Travel Show
Industrial Expositions
1675 Larimer, Suite 700
PO Box 480084
Denver, CO 80248-0084
303-892-6800
FAX: 303-892-6322 800-457-2434
info@iei-expos.com
www.bigasalloutdoors.com

Jeff Haughton, President
Dianne Seymour, Expo Manager

Recreational vehicles, accessories and travel.
18000 Attendees Annual/January Founded: 1990

20490 Colorado RV, Sports, Boat and Travel Show
Industrial Expositions
1675 Larimer Street
Suite 700
Denver, CO 80202
303-892-6800
FAX: 303-892-6322 800-457-2434
dseymour@iei-expos.com
www.bigasalloutdoors.com

Jeff Haughton, President
Dianne Seymour, Expo Manager

Annual trade show of recreational vehicles, sports, boats and travel.

20491 Crescent Ski Council
PO Box 17944
Greenville, SC 29606-8944
864-229-7488
FAX: 864-235-2504
www.crescentskicouncil.org

Michelle Shuford, Contact

Exhibits of snow ski resorts and related lodging services. 50 booths.
500 Attendees April

20492 DEMA/Diving Equipment & Marketing Association Trade Show
3750 Convoy Street
Suite 310
San Diego, CA 92111-3741
858-616-6408
FAX: 858-616-6495 800-862-3483
info@dema.org www.dema.org

Christine Von Steiger, Exhibit Space Sales
Tom Markusson, Sponsorship Sales
Tom Ingram, Executive Director

Annual trade show produced by the Diving Equipment & Marketing Association.
10M Attendees Annual

20493 Duluth Boat, Sports and Travel Show
Shamrock Productions
14550 Granada Drive
Apple Valley, MN 55124
952-431-9630
FAX: 952-431-9633
info@shamrockprod.com
www.shamrockprod.com

Randy Schauer, President/CEO

Boats, sports and travel equipment, supplies and services.
Annual/February

20494 Eastern Fishing and Outdoor Exposition
International Sport Show Producers Association
PO Box 4720
Portsmouth, NH 03802-4720
603-431-4315
FAX: 603-431-1971
info@sportshows.com
www.sportshows.com

Paul Fuller, President

Over 450 exhibitors representing the entire world of fishing and hunting. *$10.00*
45k Attendees Annual/February Founded: 1996

20495 Eastern Iowa Sportshow
Iowa Show Productions
PO Box 2460
Waterloo, IA 50704
319-232-0218
FAX: 319-235-8932
info@iowashows.com
www.iowashows.com

See a huge display of fishing boats, family sport boats, personal watercraft, pontoons, tent campers, travel trailers, fifth wheels, vans, and motorhomes. Plus boat accessories, truck toppers, motorcycles, ATVs, fishing camps, fly-ins, outposts, Lake Erie Walleye charters, family resorts, Lake Michigan sportfishing, houseboat rentals, Golf vacations, canoe outfitters, big game outfitters, tourism associations, campgrounds, camping gear, fishing tackle, archery equipment, targets, decoys, calls.
$6.00

20496 Fall RV & Van Show
O'Loughlin Trade Shows
PO Box 80750
Portland, OR 97280-1750
503-246-8291
FAX: 503-246-1066
otssport@earthlink.net
www.oloughlintradeshows.com

Peter O'Loughlin, Show Manager

Portland, OR. Recreational vehicles and vans *$7.00*
September

20497 Fly Fishing Show - Denver
854 Opossum Lake Road
Carlisle, PA 17013
717-243-6733
FAX: 717-243-8603 800-420-7582
flyfishingshow@aol.com
www.flyfishingshow.com

Barry Serviente, Executive Director

Annual fly fishing show.

20498 Football Officials Association Southwest Convention
Dallas Football Officials Association
2005 Fairmeadow
Richardson, TX 75080
972-235-9110
FAX: 972-235-7675
dfoasecretary@aol.com
www.dfoa.com

David Tucker, Registration
Mike Woodard, President

Texas Association of Sports Officials annual convention.
1.8M Attendees Annual

20499 Fred Hall's Western Fishing Tackle & Boat Show: Delmar
Fred Hall & Associates
PO Box 2925
Camarillo, CA 93011
805-389-3339
FAX: 805-389-1219

Bart Hall, Show Manager

Featuring all forms of outdoor recreation including boats, fishing tackle, adventure travel and recreational vehicles.
300000 names $150 per M.

20500 Golf Course Superintendents Association of America
GCSAA
1421 Research Park Drive
Lawrence, KS 66049-3858
785-841-2240
FAX: 785-832-4455 800-472-7878

Julia Ozark, Sr Trade Show Manager
Caroline Gollier, Trade Show Project Manager
Scotti Corley, Meeting/Trade Show Coordinator
Kelly Jo Springirth, Director Exhibit Services
Steve Mona, Chief Executive Officer

Trade show designed for the owners/operators of golf facilities and the professional members of the golf course and club management industries. The event combines education, networking and solutions for golf course superintendents, owners/operators, general managers, chief operating officers, architects and builders.
25M Attendees February

20501 Grand Center Boat Show
Show Span
2121 Celebration Drive NE
Grand Rapids, MI 49525
616-447-2860
FAX: 616-447-2861 800-328-6550
events@showspan.com
www.showspan.com

Carolyn Alt, Manager

Held at the Grand Center in Grand Rapids, Michigan. Every kind of boat under the sun. Over 400 boats. *$9.00*
82000 Attendees February

20502 Great Lakes Athletic Trainers
1200 McHenry Avenue
Crystal Lake, IL 60014-7495
815-455-3860
FAX: 815-477-6907 www.glata.org
Mark Schauer, Co Coordinator
Kevin Gerlach, Co Coordinator
Annual meeting and symposium.
1M Attendees March

20503 Greater Cincinnati Golf Show
North Coast Golf Productions
PO Box 372
Twinsburg, OH 44087-0372
330-963-6963
FAX: 330-487-0352 800-939-0040
consumer@northcoastgolfshows.com
www.northboastgolfshows.com
America's favorite consumer golf show.

20504 ICAST American Sportfishing Association Expo
225 Reinekers Lane
Suite 420
Alexandria, VA 22314
703-519-9691
FAX: 703-519-1872
info@asafishing.org
www.asafishing.org
Gordon Robertson, VP
View new products, vote for Best in Show at the New Product Showcase, free education and training seminars addressing sales, operations and business needs.
12500 Attendees Annual Founded: 1933

20505 Ice Skating Institute
17120 Dallas Parkway
Suite 140
Dallas, TX 75248-1140
972-735-8800
FAX: 972-735-8815
isi@skateisi.com www.skateisi.com
Peter Martell, Executive Director
The industry's leading trade show where you're sure to find the technical information, products and suppliers you need to run your business every day. Who should attend: Arena owners and managers; Hockey and figure skating coaches and instructors; Ice arena programming directors; Operations personnel; builders and suppliers to the industry.
Annual/May

20506 International Billiard and Home Recreation Expo
Billiard Congress of America
4345 Beverly Street
Suite D
Colorado Springs, CO 80918
719-264-8300
FAX: 719-264-0900 www.bca-pool.com
Stephen Ducoff, Executive Director
Carolyn Lewis, Director Trade Services
Amy Long, Director Marketing
Linda Mojer, Director Communications
Kathy Simmons, Member Services Administrator
This show hosts nearly 300 companies in 1400 booths, featuring every product line in the home recreation industry, from billiard and game tables, cues and cue accessories, cloth, balls and apparel, to spas, bowling, darts, foosball, art, home furnishings, novelty items, outdoor living, books, publications, video games, coin-op, pinball, jukeboxes, gaming and much more.
Founded: 1984

20507 International Pool & Spa Expo
PO Box 612128
Dallas, TX 75261-2128
972-536-6350
FAX: 972-536-6364 888-869-8522
Tina Brinkley, Operations Coordinator
Kathy Ruff, Operations Manager
Tracy Beaulieu, Conference Manager
Vila Snider, Registration Manager
Donna Bellantone, Assoc Show Director
Latest trends, newest products, and innovative ways to increase sales and add profits to your business.
16M Attendees November

20508 Iowa Boat and Vacation Show
Iowa Show Productions
PO Box 2460
Waterloo, IA 50704
319-232-0218
FAX: 319-235-8932
info@iowashows.com
www.iowashows.com
Family runabouts, fishing boats, cabin cruisers, cuddies, powerboats, waterski boats, personal watercraft, jet boats, bass boats, walleye boats, deck boats, pontoons, fish/ski boats, marine accessories, motorhomes, boat docks, lifts, covers, propellers, waterskis, boat repair, motors, tourism destinations, vacations, fishing camps, fishing tackle and more!

20509 Kentucky Golf Show
All American Exhibitions
PO Box 610
Fishers, IN 46038
317-231-1533
FAX: 317-578-3015
johnvalant@allamericanexpositions.com
www.golfexpos.com
Meet other avid golfers, participate in free clinics and competitions, mingle with PGA pros, see golf related emerging technologies, get information on golf resorts, try out custom clubs, and more.
January

20510 La Crosse Boat, Sports and Travel Show
Shamrock Productions
14550 Granada Drive
Apple Valley, MN 55124
952-431-9630
FAX: 952-431-9633
info@shamrockprod.com
www.shamrockprod.com
Randy Schauer, President/CEO
Boats, sports and travel equipment, supplies and services.
February

20511 Let's Play Hockey International Expo
Let's Play Hockey
2721 East 42nd Street
Minneapolis, MN 55406
612-729-0023
FAX: 612-729-0259
letsplay@letsplayhockey.com
www.letsplayhockey.com
Doug Johnson, Contact
Hockey Industry Trade Show. Five days of events. Seminars, races, tournaments, awards banquet, expo demo day, Hall of Fame display, buying group meetings and more.
Founded: 1999

20512 Lincoln Boat, Sport and Travel Show
Egan Enterprises
PO Box 5465
Lincoln, NE 68505-5465
402-466-8102
FAX: 402-467-5630
www.nebraskasportshow.com
Pat Egan, Contact Person
Equipment and supplies for the outdoor life.
Annual

20513 Minneapolis Snowmobile/Powesports Show
Affinity Group
Convention Center Downtown
Minneapolis, MN
952-943-2002
FAX: 952-943-2001 www.agievents.com
Come to see the latest model ATVs, snowmobiles and everything related to american motorcycles. Shop and compare dozens of dealers and hundreds of products at one time in one place.

20514 NASC Sports Event Symposium
9916 Carver Road
Suite 100
Cincinnati, OH 45242
513-281-3888
FAX: 513-281-1765
info@nascsymposium.com
www.nascsymposium.com
Don Schumacher, Executive Director
Beth Hecquet, Director Membership Services
National Association of Sports Commissions. Representing almost 400 organizations. Attendees are provided with new ideas, practical tips and the hottest trends.
500 Attendees

20515 NCAA Annual Convention
317-917-6222
FAX: 317-917-6888
feedback@ncaasports.com
www.ncaasports.com
Trade show and convention
January

20516 NSAA National Convention and Trade Show
National Ski Areas Association
133 S Van Gordon Street
Suite 300
Lakewood, CO 80228
303-987-1111
FAX: 303-986-2345
nsaa@nsaa.org www.nsaa.org
Michael Berry, President
Keri Hone, Director Events/Projects
Tom Moore, Director Conventions/Meetings
Kate Powers, Director Member Services
Amy Steele, Director Sponsorships
Annual convention of the National Ski Areas Association

20517 NSGA: National Sporting Goods Association World Sports Exposition
National Sporting Goods Association
1601 Feehanville Drive
Suite 300
Mount Prospect, IL 60056
847-966-6742
FAX: 847-391-9827 800-815-5422
Ron Kruse, Chairman
Jim Sadek, President
Dan Kasen, Manager
Annual Management Conference and Team Dealer Summit *$960.00*
85000 Attendees Annual/May Founded: 1929

20518 National Association of Basketball Coaches
1111 Main St
Ste 1000
Kansas City, MO 64105-2136
816-878-6222
FAX: 816-878-6223
www.nabc.cstv.com
James Haney, Executive Director
Kevin Henderson, Expo Show Manager
Annual convention and approximately 150 booths offering services and resources for Basketball Coaches. *$160.00*
3M Attendees March/April

20519 National Institute for Golf Management
National Golf Foundation
1150 South US Highway One
Suite 401
Jupiter, FL 33477
561-744-6006
FAX: 561-744-6107 888-275-4643
general@ngf.org www.ngf.org
Annual golf institute sponsored by the National Golf Foundation.
Annual

20520 National Intramural Recreational Sports Association
4185 SW Research Way
Corvallis, OR 97333-1067
541-766-8211
FAX: 541-766-8284
nirsa@morsa.org www.nirsa.org
Kent Blumenthal, Executive Director
This show provides an annual marketplace for athletic and recreational equipment, supplies and services.
1.6M Attendees Annual/April

20521 National Recreation & Park Association's Conference & Exposition
National Recreation & Park Association
22377 Belmont Ridge Road
Ashburn, VA 20148-4150
703-584-4635
FAX: 703-858-0794 800-626-6772
expo@nrpa.org www.nrpa.org
Provides targeted learning opportunities specifically for parks and recreation directors, supervisors and managers, community center directors, recreation programmers, natural resources personnel, therapeutic recreation specialists, citizen advocates and students.
4000 Attendees

20522 National Soccer Coaches Association of America
6700 Squibb Road
Suite 215
Mission, KS 66202-3252
913-362-1747
FAX: 913-362-3439 800-458-0676
Cari McFarland, Show Manager
Jim Sheldon, Executive Director
Every coach who attends will find something new to add to their soccer reperoire. The trade show consists of more than 200 companies. Attendees can examine the latest soccer-related technology and equipment.
9000 Attendees Annual/January

20523 National Trappers Association Sports Show
648 S Main Street
Oregon, WI 53575-3201
608-884-8205

info@nationaltrappers.com
www.nationaltrappers.com
Jim Buell, President
Chris Flynn, VP
Kraig Kaatz, General Organizer
300 booths including outdoor sports supplies and dealers.
6M Attendees Annual/August

20524 New York National Boat Show
National Marine Manufacturers Association
200 East Randolp Drive
Suite 1500
Chicago, IL 60601
312-466-6262
www.boatshows.com
Thomas Dammrich, President
Carl Blackwell, VP Marketing/Communications
Mark Adams, VP NMMA Sportshows
Amy Murray, Event Marketing Director
Annual boat show held at Jacob Javitz Convention Center in New York
January

20525 North American Society for Sport Management Conference
North American Society for Sport Management
Slippery Rock University
West Gym 014
Slippery Rock, PA 16057
724-738-4812
FAX: 724-738-4858
nassm@sru.edu www.nassm.com
North American Society for Sport Management annual convention and trade show.

20526 Northwest Sportshow
General Sports Shows
3539 Hennepin Avenue
Minneapolis, MN 55408-3830
612-827-5833
FAX: 612-827-1424 800-777-4766
David Perkins, President
Public show offering the finest presentation of outdoor recreation and marine products and services.
205M Attendees March

20527 Omaha Boat, Sports and Travel Show
Cox/Johnson Corporation
2116 Mullen Drive
Omaha, NE 68124
402-581-1088
FAX: 402-393-3360
Dick Johnson, President
Sporting goods, boats and supplies plus travel information.
Annual Founded: 1948

20528 Outdoorama Family Sport and Travel Show
Michigan United Conservation Clubs
2101 Wood Street
PO Box 30235
Lansing, MI 48912-3785
517-371-1041
FAX: 517-371-1505 800-777-6720
membership@mucc.org
www.mucc.org
Sam Washington, Executive Director
Kelly Snyder, Event/Fundraising Assistant
Evan Steiner, Events/Fundraising Specialist
Michigan's favorite outdoor show featuring over 200,000 square feet of exhibit space dedicated to the latest in fishing and hunting equipment, fishing and power boats, recreational vehicles, outdoor gear and vacationing destinations throughout North America. Four-hundred plus booths.

42000 Attendees February Founded: 1974

20529 PTR International Symposium
Professional Tennis Registry
PO Box 4739
Hilton Head Island, SC 29938
843-785-7244
FAX: 843-686-2033 800-421-6289
ptr@ptrtennis.org www.ptrtennis.org
Symposium of professional tennis teachers and coaches. PTR has excellent relationships and partnerships with industry leaders such as the USTA, Tennis Industry Association, the ITF and many National Tennis Federations.

20530 Professional Golfers Association Merchandise Show
Reed Exhibitions
383 Main Avenue
Norwalk, CT 06851
203-404-4800
FAX: 203-840-9628 800-840-5628
inquiry@pga.reedexpo.com
www.pgamerchandiseshow.com
Kara Codio, Marketing/Conference Manager
Sherry Major, Media Relations Manager
Jay Andronaco, Event Marketing Manager
The PGA Merchandise Show provides a snap-shot of the industry as a whole and access to products and services that pertain to every aspect of the game. It is the focal point for new product introductions, professional development programs, business meetings and more.
30M Attendees January

20531 Professional Golfers Association Golf Show
Sydney Convention and Exhibition Centre
Darling Harbour
Sydney
Australia NSW 2000

www.pgaexpo.com
International PGA Golf Show. 2006 Show held in Australia
50000 Attendees Annual

20532 Quad City Boat, RV and Vacation Show
Iowa Show Productions
PO Box 2460
Waterloo, IA 50704
319-232-0218
FAX: 319-235-8932
info@iowashows.com
www.iowashows.com
Canoes, Kayaks, personal watercraft, fishing boats, jet boats, family sport boats, high performance, waterski boats, bass boats, walleye boats, pontoons, deck boats, fish/ski boats, cuddy cabins, cruisers, the latests in tent campers, expandables, light-weight trailers, fifth wheels and motor homes. Exhibits on resorts and fishing camps, canoe outfitters, Canadian camps, fly-ins, golf, Lake Michigan & Lake Erie Fishing Charters and more. *$5.00*

20533 RSA Convention and Trade Show
6905 Corporate Drive
Indianapolis, IN 46278
317-347-2626
FAX: 317-347-2636
admin@rollerskating.org
www.rollerskating.org
Robin Brown, Executive Director
Roller Skating Association International. Annual Convention and Trade show.
annual

20534 Rocky Mountain Snowmobile Expo
Industrial Expositions
1675 Larimer Street
Suite 700
Denver, CO 80202
303-892-6800
FAX: 303-892-6322 800-457-2434
dseymour@iei-expos.com
www.bigasalloutdoors.com
Jeff Haughton, President
Diane Seymour, Expo Manager
Large display of snowmobiles and accessories, meet performance experts, resorts and lodges, winter clothing, ice fishing, winter travel destinations, snowmobile adventure theatre, avalanche awareness, swap meet and more.

20535 SHOT Show: Shooting Hunting Outdoor Trade Show
Reed Exhibition Companies
383 Main Avenue
Norwalk, CT 06851
203-404-4800
FAX: 203-840-9628 800-840-5628
Worldwide annual gathering that unites manufacturer and retailer and all other industry stakeholders to trade, source and learn about the latest products, innovations and trends in the shooting sports industry.
15M Attendees January

20536 SIA Snowsports Trade Show
SnowSports Industries America
8377-b Greensboro Drive
McLean, VA 22102-3587
703-556-9020
FAX: 703-821-8276
siamail@thesnowtrade.org
www.thesnowtrade.org
Mary DeOrnellas, Trade Show/Membership Svce Coord
Debbie Brown Des Roches, Director Trade Show
David Ingemie, President
Bob Orbacz, Director Finance
From fashion to skis and snowboards to Nordic, snowshoes, outdoor and basic essentials, the SIA SnowSports Trade Show previews the entire winter sports market.
18M Attendees Annual/January

20537 Saltwater Fishing Expo
Eastern Fishing and Outdoor Exposition
PO Box 4720
Portsmouth, NH 03802
603-431-4315
FAX: 603-431-1971
wqww.sportshows.com
The Saltwater Fishing Expo is expecting over 300 exhibitors representing the entire spectrum of saltwater sportfishing. There will be dozens of seminars throughout the three days of the show, which will be presented by experts who are at the top of their game. *$10.00*

20538 San Mateo Inernational Sportsmen's Expo
International Sportsmen's Exposition
PO Box 2569
Vancouver, WA 98668-2569
360-693-3700
FAX: 360-693-3352 800-545-6100
Brian Layng, President/CEO
Rick Flattum, Director Operations
Heidi Crannell, Marketing Coordinator
Bruce Tarbet, Sponsorship/Advertising
Brent Layng, Sales Manager
Fishing, hunting, outdoor sports and destination travel show. Connect with new dealers and network with other exhibitors.

20539 Ski Dazzle Ski Show and Snowboard Expo: Chicago
Ski Dazzle
807 Laguna Canyon Road
Laguna Beach, CA 92651
949-497-4977
FAX: 949-497-4123
snowdog@skidazzle.com
www.skidazzle.com
Judy Gray, Owner
Jim Foster, Owner
Hundreds of local, national and international exhibitors including over 85 resorts, ski and snowboard retailers, manufacturers, a huge ski and snowboard sale, and lots of surprises. Over 250 exhibit booths showcasing core companies of skiing and snowboarding.

20540 Ski Dazzle: The Los Angeles Ski Show & Snowboard Expo
807 Laguna Canyon Road
Laguna Beach, CA 92651-1839
949-497-4977
FAX: 949-497-4123
snowdog@skidazzle.com
www.skidazzle.com
Judy Gray, Co-Owner
Jim Foster, Owner
Consumer ski show and snowboard expo at the Los Angeles Convention Center offering 350 ski and snowboard related exhibits. Excellent sponsor and promotional opportunities for 18-49 demographic audience.
90000 Attendees November 16-19

20541 Soaring Society of America Annual Convention
Soaring Society of America
5425 West Jack Gomez Boulevard
Hobbs, NM 88241
505-392-1177
FAX: 505-392-8154
feedback@ssa.org www.ssa.org
C Wright, Executive Director
Annual convetion of the Soaring Society of America.

20542 Sporting Goods Manufacturers Markets
1150 17th Street NW
8th Floor
Washington, DC 20036-1604
202-775-1762
FAX: 202-296-7462
info@sgma.com www.sgma.com
Tom Cove, President/CEO
Gregg Harrlety, VP
Kalinda Mathis, Director Marketing
Retailers, distributors, wholesalers, importers/exporters and other buyers of sports related products come for 10,000 exhibits of sports apparel, footwear, accessories and e-commerce products and services.
80000 Attendees Spring/Fall

20543 Sports Licensing & Entertainment Marketplace Tailgate Picnic Show
Showproco, LLC
1450 NE 123rd Street
North Miami, FL 33161
305-893-8771
FAX: 305-893-8783 800-327-3736
showpoco@csnipicom
www.showproco.com
Ann Keusch, Show Director
Hardy Katz, Show Director
A show dedicated to sports licensed apparel & products with participation from major sports licensors and their licensees. In conjunction will be the Tailgate & Picnic Show, which will bring together all of the products sports fans want to buy. Attendees will represent everything from sporting goods stores to fan shops, grocery to gift shops, drug stores to convenience stores and more.

November 9-11

20544 Strictly Sail Pacific
Jack London Square
Oakland, CA

FAX: 401-847-2044 800-817-7245
info@sailamerica.com
www.strictlysail.com
Cynthia Goss, Contact
Annual Boat Show. A mix of boats and gear, seminars and special events. It will feature over 300 exhibitors from 25 states and over 90 seminars.

20545 Surf Expo
Surf Expo Offices
990 Hammond Drive
Suite 325
Atlanta, GA 30328
678-817-7970
FAX: 404-220-3030 www.surfexpo.com

Where manufacturers and retailers in the boardsports, and swim and resort industries have come together in a business-first buying and selling environment.
8M Attendees Twice Annually

20546 Tacoma Dome Boat Show
O'Loughlin Trade Shows
PO Box 110849
Tacoma, WA 98411-0849
253-756-2121
FAX: 253-756-6898
www.oloughlintradeshows.com

Bob O'Loughlin, Manager

Whether you area a seasoned captain or a first time buyer, everything you need for a perfect voyage in under one roof. Over 8 acres of boats, booth after booth of marine electronics, water sports accessories, motors, trailers, brokerages, and resort harbors.

20547 Tacoma Fall RV Show
O'Loughlin Trade Shows
PO Box 110849
Tacoma, WA 98411-0849
253-756-2121
FAX: 253-756-6898
www.oloughlintradeshows.com

Bob O'Loughlin, Manager

The perfect opportunity to make a deal on a closeout current model year RV or preview and purchase the new models straight from the factory. Booth after booth of the latest after market accessories, newest RV lifestyle products and services all under one roof.

20548 US Gymnastics Federation
US Gymnastics Congress
Pam American Plaza
201 South Capitol, Suite 300
Indianapolis, IN 46225
317-237-5050
FAX: 317-692-5212

Steve Penny, President

Three days of eduction with over 135 sessions offered. Lectures given by recognized top people in the field. Sessions on coaching, judging, business, preschool, recreational, sports science, fitness, Group Gymnastics and cheerleading. The Trade Show exhibit hall will feature 200 booths of products and information from over 85 different Industry Member vendors. *$235.00*
2M Attendees Annual

20549 USA Track and Field Annual Meeting
One RCA Dome
Suite 140
Indianapolis, IN 46225
317-261-0500
FAX: 317-261-0481
membership@usatf.org
www.usatf.org

Jill Geer, Public Relations

Annual meeting of the USA Track and Field organization.
Annual

20550 Underwater Intervention
5206 FM 1960 West
Suite 202
Houston, TX 77069
281-893-8539
FAX: 281-893-5118 800-316-2188
rroberts@adc-int.org
www.underwaterintervention.com/

Rebecca Roberts, Show Manager
Roff Saxon, Executive Director

Conference covering all aspects of underwater operations. Next trade show is scheduled for 2007 with 200+ booths, sponsored by both the Marine Technology Society and the Association of Diving Contractors International.
2500 Attendees Founded: 1991

20551 WBCA National Convention
Women's Basketball Coaches Association

4646 Lawrenceville Highway
Lilburn, GA 30047
770-279-8027
FAX: 770-279-8473
wbca@wbca.org www.wbca.org

Beth Bass, CEO
Shannon Reynolds, COO
Seana Peck, Manager Marketing
Stephanie S Baron, Director Events
Dorinda Schremmer, Director
Membership/Convention Svce

Women's Basketball Coaches Association national convention. Held annually.

20552 Water Ski and Wakeboard Expo
1251 Holy Cow Road
Polk City, FL 33868
863-324-4341
FAX: 863-325-8529
usawaterski@usawaterski.org
www.usawaterski.org
Annual event of the USA Water Ski Organization.
Annual

20553 Western States Toy and Hobby Show
Western Toy and Hobby Representative Association
9397 Reserve Drive
Corona, CA 92883
951-277-1598
FAX: 951-277-1599
info@wthra.com www.wthra.com

Phylis St. John, Contact

If it's for kids, it's here. Show is for trade members only, not open to the public.
3000 Attendees March

20554 World Fishing and Outdoor Exposition
Eastern Fishing and Outdoor Exposition
PO Box 4720
Portsmouth, NH 03802-4720
603-431-4315
FAX: 603-431-1971
info@sportshows.com
www.sportshows.com
You'll find the entire world of fishing and hunting and much more. *$10.00*
Annual Founded: 1978

20555 World Fly Fishing Expo
Eastern Fishing and Outdoor Exposition
PO Box 4720
Portsmouth, NH 03802-4720
603-431-4315
FAX: 603-431-1971
info@sportshows.com
www.sportshows.com

This expo has all the major manufacturers of fly rods and reels, fly fishing accessories, fly tying materials, guides and lodges.
$10.00
Annual

Directories & Databases

20556 Amusement Park Guide
Globe Pequot Press
246 Goose Lane
Suite 200
Guilford, CT 06437-0480
203-458-4500

The complete guide to the amusement parks in the United States and Canada gives the latest details about new rides at each park, with a special focus on roller coasters. *$14.95*
ISBN 0-762725-37-0

20557 Athlete and Celebrity Address Directory/Autograph Hunter's Guide
Global Sports Productions
1223 Broadway
Suite 101
Santa Monica, CA 90404
310-454-9480
FAX: 310-454-6590
globalnw@earthlink.net
www.sportsbooksempire.com

Ed Kobak, President
Greg Andrews, VP Operations

Complete source of athlete and sports personality addresses from baseball, basketball, football, hockey, golf, tennis, soccer, boxing and autosports. Also included are television, movie and other celebrities' addresses. *$29.95*
198 pages Annual Founded: 2005 ISBN 0-966796-17-9

20558 Baseball Bluebook
8373 N Cedar Hills Lane
Fair Grove, MD 65648
417-833-6550
FAX: 417-833-9911
dj@baseballbluebook.com
www.baseballbluebook.com
Directory of baseball club personnel at all levels of play. Spiral bound directory contains Major Leagues, Minor Leagues and Independent League Personnel, contact information and schedules *$55.00*
500 pages Annual Founded: 1909

20559 Complete Directory of Fishing Tackle
Sutton Family Communications & Publishing Company
155 Sutton Lane
Fordsville, KY 42343
270-740-0870

jlsutton@apex.net
www.fleamarketeer.net

Jerry Sutton, Contact

Listings in directory include names, addresses, phone and fax numbers, and product descriptions from wholesale distributors, Importers, Manufacturers, Close-out houses and liquidators. *$72.20*
100+ pages

20560 Complete Directory of Outdoor Products
Sutton Family Communications & Publishing Company
155 Sutton Lane
Fordsville, KY 42343
270-740-0870

jlsutton@apex.net
www.fleamarketeer.net

Jerry Sutton, Manager

Print-out from database of wholesalers, manufacturers, distributors, importers and close-out houses. Database is updated daily to guarantee the most current and up-to-date sources available. *$95.20*
100+ pages

20561 Complete Directory of Sporting Goods
Sutton Family Communications & Publishing Company
155 Sutton Lane
Fordsville, KY 42343
270-740-0870

jlsutton@apex.net
www.fleamarketeer.net

Jerry Sutton, Manager

Print-out from database of wholesalers, manufacturers, distributors, importers and close-out houses. Database is updated daily to guarantee the most current and up-to-date sources available. *$139.00*
100+ pages

20562 Computer Sports World
675 Grier Drive
Las Vegas, NV 89119-3738
702-735-0101
FAX: 702-294-1322 800-321-5562
Statistical information on all aspects of the sports industry.
Full-text Founded: 1983

20563 Encyclopedia of Sports Business Contacts
Global Sports Productions
1223 Broadway
Suite 101
Santa Monica, CA 90404
310-454-9480
FAX: 310-454-6590
globalnw@earthlink.net
www.sportsbooksempire.com

Ed Kobak, President

This huge book covers the business side of sports with addresses, telephone and fax numbers, emails, websites and entire contact personnel from sports organizations, teams, leagues, publications, lawyers and agents, corporate sponsors, sports marketing and management firms and others. *$79.95*
600 pages Annual Founded: 2005

20564 Golf Traveler
Affinity Group
64 Inverness Drive E
Englewood, CO 80112-5114
303-282-2267
FAX: 877-439-1586 www.golfcard.com
Golf courses and affiliated resorts are listed. *$2.50*
88 pages BiMonthly
Circulation: 75,000

20565 International Sports Directory
Global Sports Productions
1223 Broadway
Suite 101
Santa Monica, CA 90404
310-454-9480
FAX: 310-454-6590
globalnw@earthlink.net
www.sportsbooksempire.com

Ed Kobak, President

This all-in-one directory covers the entire world of sports from A to Z. Included are addresses, e-mails, websites, telephone and fax numbers and contact personnel from sports organizations, clubs, teams and publications. The most comprehensive sports directory available, covering both national and international listings. *$29.95*
500 pages Annual Founded: 1980 ISBN 1-891655-02-7

20566 Motor Sports Forum
Racing Information Systems
2314 Harriman Lane
Unit A
Redondo Beach, CA 90278-4426

racing@motorsportsforum.com
www.motorsportsforum.com

Michael F Hollander, Editor-in-Chief
Bab Karambelas, Senior Editor

This database contains information on auto racing in the United States and Canada.
Bulletin Board

20567 News/Retrieval Sports Report
Dow Jones & Company
1 World Financial Center
200 Liberty Street
New York, NY 10281
212-416-2000
FAX: 212-416-4348 www.dj.com
Offers information on sports news stories and statistics from United Press International.
Full-text

20568 Orion Blue Book: Guns and Scopes
Orion Research Corporation
14555 N Scottsdale Road
Suite 330
Scottsdale, AZ 85254-3487
480-951-1114
FAX: 480-951-1117 800-844-0759

Roger Rohrs, Owner

List of manufacturers of guns. Current issue contains 18,543 products. Lists products from 1800's to present. Over 300 manufacturers listed. *$45.00*
480 pages Annual Founded: 1992

20569 Parks Directory of the United States
Omnigraphics
615 Griswold Street
Detroit, MI 48226
313-961-1340
FAX: 313-961-1383 800-234-1340
editorial@omnigraphics.com
www.omnigraphics.com

Darren L Smith, Editor

Covers nearly 5,000 national and state parks, and other designated recreational, scenic, and historic areas in the United States and Canada. It provides up-to-date contact and descriptive information for every national and state park in the U.S. *$185.00*
1,100 pages Biennial ISBN 0-780806-63-8

20570 Q&A Booklets
Sporting Goods Agents Association
PO Box 998
Morton Grove, IL 60053
847-296-3670
FAX: 847-827-0196
sgaa998@aol.com
www.sgaaonline.org

Skip Nipper, President
Lois Halinton, Chief Operating Officer

Sporting Goods Agents Association booklets for manufacturers and agents. Answers questions such as: Why should I use an independent agent rather than hire my own salespeople? What are the most important aspects to examine when I interview an agency? What are independent sporting goods agents and what do they do? What factors should be considered when forming a territory to cover. And more. *$15.00*

20571 Recreation Facilities Products & Services
Sutton Family Communications & Publishing Company
155 Sutton Lane
Fordsville, KY 42343
270-740-0870

jlsutton@apex.net
www.fleamarketeer.net

Jerry Sutton, Manager

Print-out from database of wholesalers, manufacturers, distributors, importers and close-out houses. Database is updated daily to guarantee the most current and up-to-date sources available. Accepts advertising. *$97.20*
100+ pages

20572 Recreational Sports Directory
National Intramural Recreational Sports Assn
4185 SW Research Way
Corvallis, OR 97333-1067
541-766-8211
FAX: 541-766-8284
nirsa@nirsa.org www.nirsa.org
Directory of services and supplies to the industry. *$20.00*
400 pages Annual
Circulation: 1,500

20573 Sporting News Baseball Guide
Sporting News Publishing Company
10176 Corporate Square Drive
Suite 200
Saint Louis, MO 63132-2924
314-997-7111
FAX: 314-993-7798
www.sportingnews.com

Jim Nuckols, Chief Executive Officer

A list of National and American League and their affiliate minor leagues. *$12.95*
Annual

20574 Sporting News Football Register
Sporting News Publishing Company
10176 Corporate Square Drive
Suite 200
Saint Louis, MO 63132-2924
314-997-7111
FAX: 314-993-7798
www.sportingnews.com

Jim Nuckols, Chief Executive Officer

Directory of services and supplies to the industry. *$12.95*
430 pages Annual

20575 Sports Address Bible and Almanac

Global Sports Productions
1223 Broadway
Suite 101
Santa Monica, CA 90404
310-454-9480
FAX: 310-454-6590
globalnw@earthlink.net
www.sportsbooksempire.com

Ed Kobak, President
Greg Andrews, VP Operations

Over 7,500 sports listings from professional, semi-pro, Olympic and amateur, collegiate and interscholastic sports organizations, leagues, teams, halls of fame, media outlets and more. *$34.95*

505 pages Biennial Founded: 1998 ISBN 1-891655-11-6

20576 Sports Market Place

Grey House Publishing
185 Millerton Road
Millerton, NY 12546-1135
518-890-0526
FAX: 518-789-0545 800-562-2139
books@greyhouse.com
www.sportsmarketplace.com

Leslie Mackenzie, Publisher
Richard Gottlieb, Editor

Provides organizations' contact information with detailed descriptions including: key contacts, physical, mailing, email and web addresses plus phone and fax numbers. *$225.00*

1800 pages Annual ISBN 1-592370-77-2

20577 Sports RoundTable

GE Information Services
401 N Washington Street
Rockville, MD 20850-1707
301-388-8284

Cathy Ge, Owner

This database provides coverage of major professional, amateur and collegiate sports including football, basketball, baseball, and hockey.

Full-text

20578 SportsAlert

Comtex Scientific Corporation
911 Hope Street
#4838
Stamford, CT 06907-2318

FAX: 203-358-0236
www.sportsalert.net

This database contains sports news and statistics providing real-time coverage of US and international professional, collegiate and amateur athletic events.

Full-text

20579 Tennis-Places to Play: Camps and Clinics Issue

Golf Digest Tennis NY Times Magazine Group
5520 Park Avenue
Trumbull, CT 06611-3400
203-373-7000
FAX: 203-371-2162

Directory of services and supplies to the industry. *$2.50*

Annual
Circulation: 800,000

Industry Web Sites

20580 www.aahperd.org
American Alliance for Hlth, Phys. Edu. Rec. Dance

20581 www.aahperd.org/uawgs
National Association for Girls and Women in Sports

A non-profit organization serving the needs of teachers, coaches and participants of sports programs for girls and women.

20582 www.aapsm.org
American Academy of Podiatric Sports Medicine

The American Academy of Podiatric Sports Medicine was founded in San Francisco by a group of podiatric sports physicians who had the insight to realize the need for a podiatric sports medicine association devoted to the treatment of athletic injuries. Today the AAPSM has over 500 members.

20583 www.aausports.org
Amateur Athletic Union of the United States

20584 www.abca.org
American Baseball Coaches Association

Formerly called the American Association of College Baseball Coaches.

20585 www.aca-camps.org
American Camping Association

Educational programs. Legislative monitoring, child and youth development.

20586 www.acanet.org
American Canoe Association

Promotes the sport of canoeing and its safety, recreational and conservation

20587 www.acsm.org
American College of Sports Medicine

The ACSM promotes and integrates scientific research, education, and practical applications of sports medicine and exercise science to maintain and enhance physical performance, fitness, health, and quality of life.

20588 www.adventurecycling.org
Adventure Cycling Association

Developes road and mountain bike routes, runs bike tours and eventsand also acts as information resource for bicyclists planning trips.

20589 www.aeawave.com
Aquatic Exercise Association

Covers topics relating to aquatic fitness and therapy including industry trends, research, programs, exercises and products.

20590 www.afaa.com
Aerobics and Fitness Association of America

Association for the education, certification and training of exercise instructors; information resource center for consumers.

20591 www.athleticclubs.com
Athletic Net

Click on links to find fitness, sports medicine, general health and wellness, government sites, directories, nutrition and newsgroups.

20592 www.bikeleague.org
League of American Bicyclists

Founded in 1880, the League is the only national membership organization of bicyclists in the United States. The League works to promote and encourage bicycling for recreation and transportation, and to protect and defend the rights of bicyclists through advocacy and education.

20593 www.greyhouse.com
Grey House Publishing

Selected Grey House directories in the fields of business, health and education are available online. Users can search our online databases by several different search criteria, such as product categories, geographic area, sales volume and much, much more. Full Grey House catalog and online ordering also available.

20594 www.iasv.net
International Academy of Sports Vision

Promotes education, research and development of sports visions. Publishes Sportsvision Magazine and annual scientific journal. Mission is to prevent eye injuries and imprrove visual performance in sports.

20595 www.instituteofdiving.com
Institute of Diving

Membership includes sports, commercial and military divers with the purpose being to operate the Museum of Man in the Sea, publish a newsletter, provide a technical library, offer an information exchange, and promote programs and projects for the improvement of knowledge about the underwater world.

20596 www.iprarodeo.com
International Professional Rodeo Association

Governing body for professional rodeo. 500 rodeos across USA and Canada, $5 million prize money per year, 5 million fans.

20597 www.lpga.com
Ladies Professional Golf Association

For women and youth golfers.

20598 www.naa-usa.org
National Aeronautic Association

Members include aerospace corporations, aero clubs, affiliates and major national sporting aviation organizations.

20599 www.nabc.com
National Association of Basketball Coaches

Promotes the advancement and opportunities for coaches and teachers in the sport of basketball.

20600 www.nabf.com
National Amateur Baseball Association

Promotes amateur baseball and the industry in general.

20601 www.naso.org
National Association of Sports Officials

Not-for-profit 501(c)(3) educational association providing individual benefits such as training materials, liability and assault protection insurance and more to sports officials of all sports and every level.

20602 www.nauticalworld.com
Nautical World

Dedicated to bringing all related web sites within easy access to watersports enthusiasts. This search engine has been designed to locate advertiser's information within Nautical World but will also offer access to other watersport related web sites as well. Offers sections on marine electronics and hardware, sailing, boats, dock supplies, fishing accessories, diving accessories, industry news, watersports, weather forecasting and more.

20603 www.nays.org
National Youth Sports Coaches Association

Represents coaches involved in youth athletics.

20604 www.nflalumni.org
National Football League Alumni

Provides a forum for those individuals retired from the NFL but still playing an active role.

20605 www.ngf.org
National Golf Foundation

Provides market research and serves as an information clearinghouse for the industry. Conducts seminars for golf teachers, coaches and professionals. Conducts golf course development feasibility studies for developers.

20606 www.njcaa.org
National Junior College Athletic Association

NJCAA members are two year institutions recognized by the American Association of Community and Junior Colleges.

20607 www.nra.org
National Rifle Association

Oldest sportsmen's organization in the US. Maintains the NRA Political Victory Fund and supports the Institute for Legislative Action.

20608 www.nsga.org
National Sporting Goods Association

Association of retailers, manufacturers and suppliers of sports equipment, footwear, and apparel.

20609 www.nsgachicagoshow.com
Athletic Goods Team Distributors

Strives to keep athletic team dealers informed of rule changes that affect equipment sales.

20610 www.pga.com
Professional Golfers Association of America

The world's largest working sports organization comprised of more than 25,000 men and women PGA professionals to promote the game of golf to everyone, and to promote its members as leaders in the golf industry.

20611 www.popwarner.com
Pop Warner Little Scholars

A national youth football and cheerleading organization that provides assistance to its various chapters.

20612 www.r-sports.com
Sporting Goods Agents Association

International trade association of independent and established sporting goods agents.

20613 www.restaurantreport.com/top100
Resturant Report On-Line

Includes top 100 food sites, feature stories, newsletters, buyer's guide, marketplace, hospitality jobs.

20614 www.rollerskating.com
Roller Skating Association

Exists for private businessmen and women engaged in the enterprise of roller skating.

20615 www.sabr.org
Society for American Baseball Research

Membership association whose purpose is to facilitate and disseminate baseball research.

20616 www.sgma.com
Sporting Goods Manufacturers Association

For manufacturers, producers, and distributors of sports apparel, athletic footwear, fitness, and sporting goods equipment.

20617 www.skateisi.org
Ice Skating Institute

Industry trade association dedicated to providing leadership, education and services to the ice skating industry.

20618 www.sportsmarketplce.com
Grey House Publishing

Provides organizations' contact information with detailed descriptions including: key contacts, physical, mailing, email and web addresses plus phone and fax numbers.

20619 www.sportsmed.org
American Orthopaedic Society for Sports Medicine

Promotes the prevention, recognition and orthopedic treatment of sports injuries.

20620 www.sportsplexoperators.com
Sportsplex Operators and Developers of Association

SODA was formed to meet the needs of the private concerns, public agencies, and other organizations that own or maintain sports complex facilities.

20621 www.usa-swimming.org
USA Swimming

Devoted to the sport of swimming and its enjoyment nationwide.

20622 www.usahockey.com
USA Hockey

Promotes the sport of hockey.

20623 www.usarchery.org
National Archery Association

Supports archers while aiming to advance the sport of archery in the US. Monthly newsletter, Nock-Nock, provides communication among the NAA office, NAA clubs, state associations and the individual members of the NAA. Provides members with news and tournament results ranging from the local and state level to international competition.

20624 www.usatt.org
USA Table Tennis

Dedicated to the promotion of the sport of table tennis and sponsors the US team. Membership dues are $30 per year for adults and $20 for those 18 years old and under.

20625 www.usawaterski.org
USA Water Ski Association

Encourages interest in the sport as well as training and safety.

20626 www.usaweightlifting.org
USA Weightlifting

USA Weightlifting is the National Governing Body (NGB) for the Olympic sport of weightlifting in the United States. USA weightlifting is a member of the United States Olympic Committee and a member of the International Weightlifting Federation. As the NGB, USA Weightlifting is responsible for conducting Olympic weightlifting programs throughout the country. The organization conducts a variety of programs that will ultimately develop Olympic, World Championship and Pan American Games' winners.

20627 www.usfencing.org
United States Fencing Association

Promotes the sport of fencing in the US.

20628 www.usfieldhockey.com
US Field Hockey Association

Represents field hockey, professional and amateur sports.

20629 www.ushandball.org
US Handball Association

Organization that runs all the tournaments for the professional and amateur players. Home of the Handball Hall of Fame.

20630 www.usoc.org
US Olympic Committee

The national committee for the US. Handles the preparation of the US Olympic, Paralympic and Pan American Games teams.

20631 www.usolimplc.com
United States Amateur Boxing

Promotes the sport of boxing nationwide.

20632 www.uspa.org
United States Parachute Association

A not-for-profit membership association dedicated to the promotion of safe skydiving and the support of those who enjoy it. Sponsors Instructor Rating Program to train and certify instructors, jump masters and examiners.

20633 www.usra.org
US Raquetball Association

A nonprofit corporation designed to promote the development of competitive and recreational racquetball in the United States. The association offers a 'competitive license' membership for a one year term at $15.00 annually, or at discounted longer term rates. A lifetime membership is also offered. A 'Club Recreational Membership' program is offered for an annual fee of $150.00 with a reduced AARA recreational membership available to club members for $3.00 per player.

20634 www.usskiteam.com, www.ussnowboardteam.com
US Ski & Snowboard Association

Association for skiing and snowboarding nationwide.

20635 www.usspeedskating.org
US Speedskating

Devoted to speedskating and its participants on the national and international levels.

20636 www.uswfa.com
United States Water Fitness Association

Nonprofit educational organization that promotes aquatics throughout the United States and other countries. Publishes the National Aquatics Newsletter, names the 100 top US water fitness programs and program 5 aquatics in the country, by state and in 25+ categories. Conducts a wide variety of national aquatics certifications including Water Fitness Instructors (primary and masters), aquatic directors, coordinators of water fitness programs. Conducts annual international aquatics conference.

20637 www.volleyball.org
US Volleyball Association

Promotes volleyball in the US trains the USA men's and women's teams promotes beach and grassroots volleyball in the United States.

20638 www.voyager.net/aabc
American Amateur Baseball Congress

Provides administrative services for amateur baseball youth through adults. 250,000 members.

20639 www.ymca.net
YMCA of the USA

Provides national and state branch divisions.

Associations

20640 Allied Stone Industries
PO Box 288145
Chicago, IL 60628-8145
773-928-4800
FAX: 773-928-4129

John Van Etten, Secretary

Quarries, fabricators and dealers in stone and concrete.
55 Members

20641 American Concrete Institute
PO Box 9094
Farmington Hills, MI 48333
248-483-3700
FAX: 248-848-3801 www.cement.org

William Tolley, Executive Vice President

ACI is a scientific and educational society representing the interests of concrete users concerned with the design, construction, or maintenance of concrete structures. Conventions and meetings, monthly periodicals and special publications; chapter activities; and technical committees all provide a forum for concrete interests to discuss problems relating to concrete.

20642 American Concrete Pavement Association
5420 Old Orchard Road
Skokie, IL 60077
847-966-2272
FAX: 847-966-9970

Jerry Voigt, President

ACPA is committed to promoting the quality and superiority of concrete pavements. It leads and assists its members in market development, technical expertise, design innovation, research, and public relations. ACPA's membership includes contractors, cement companies, material suppliers, equipment manufacturers and suppliers, ready mix producers, allied associations, bonding and insurance companies, consulting firms, and interested individuals.

20643 American Concrete Pipe Association
222 W Las Colinas Boulevard
Suite 641
Irving, TX 75039-5423
972-506-7216
FAX: 972-506-7682

Matt Childs, President

ACPA is the technical, educational, and promotional voice of the concrete pipe industry. Members are manufacturers of concrete pipe for highway culverts, sewers, drainage, and irrigation, and supporters of extending the concrete pipe industry.

20644 American Natural Soda Ash Corporation
15 Riverside Avenue
2nd Floor
Westport, CT 06880
203-226-9056
FAX: 203-227-1484
dms@ansac.com www.ansac.com

Donna McSwain-Santos, Marketing

ANSAC markets, sells and distributes high quality soda ash to over 40 countries around the world.
Founded: 1984

20645 American Society of Concrete Contractors
2025 S Brentwood Boulevard
St Louis, MO 63144
314-962-0210
FAX: 314-968-4367

Bev Garnant, Executive Director

ASCC seeks to continually advance the qualifications of concrete constructors and encourage greater interaction between designer and constructor. Publishes the Contactor's Guide to Quality Concrete Construction jointly with ACI. Issues Safety Alerts, Safety Bulletins, and a Safety Manual as well as a troubleshooting newsletter, management reports, and a members bulletin.

20646 Concrete Employers Association
900 Spring Street
Silver Spring, MD 20910-4015
301-587-1400
FAX: 301-585-4219

Raymond Wisniewski Jr, Executive Secretary

Concrete plant manufacturers.

20647 Concrete Foundationas Association
PO Box 204
Mount Vernon, IA 52314
319-895-6940
FAX: 319-895-8830

Ed Sauter, Executive Director

Members are residential foundation contractors and their suppliers. The association produces promotional, marketing and technical materials for members' potential customers; provides its members with newsletters, industry publications, and seminar and trade show opportunities; develops specifications, technical information, and safety programs; and represents its members on national code bodies.

20648 Concrete Promotion Council of Northern Cal ifornia
4021 Woodcreek Oaks Blvd
#156-205
Roseville, CA 95747

888-633-0393
info@cpcnc.org www.cpcnc.org

Bill Albanese, President
Robert E Wallace, Executive Director

A member of the Pacific Southwest Concrete Alliance and is composed of companies from all parts of the Northern Californian concrete industry including ready mix suppliers, cement producers, admixture manufacturers, concrete contractors as well as members of the public and private design committees.

20649 Concrete Reinforcing Steel Institute

933 N Plum Grove Road
Schaumburg, IL 60173-4758
847-517-1200
FAX: 847-517-1206
brisser@crsi.org www.crsi.org

Robert J Risser Jr, President
John Healy, Chief Executive Officer
Sue O'Sullivan, Controller

Conducts research and provides technical information on reinforced concrete design and construction practices.
1600 Members Founded: 1924

20650 Concrete Sawing and Drilling Association
11001 Danka Way North
Suite 1
St. Petersburg, FL 33716
727-577-5004
FAX: 727-577-5012
info@csda.org www.csda.org

Patrick O'Brien, Executive Director

CSDA is a nonprofit association of contractors and manufacturers from the concrete construction and renovation industry. Its mission is to promote the selection of professional sawing and drilling contractors and their methods. Concrete cutting with diamond tools offers the industry many benefits.
300 Members Founded: 1972

20651 Expanded Shale Clay and Slate Institute
2225 Murray Holladay Road
Suite 102
Salt Lake City, UT 84117
801-272-7070
FAX: 801-272-3377
info@escsi.org www.escsi.org

John Ries, President

Sponsors research at engineering schools, educational seminars and develops industry standards.
Founded: 1908

20652 Flexicore Manufacturers Association
7941 New Carlisle Pike
Huber Heights, OH 45424
937-879-5775
FAX: 937-879-0826 www.flexicore.com
Strives to protect industry from trade abuses and develop good business practices and quality of product.
11 Members Founded: 1952

20653 Indiana Limestone Institute of America
400 Stone City Bank Building
Bedford, IN 47421
812-275-4426
FAX: 812-279-8682
jim@iliai.com www.iliai.com

Jim Owens, Executive Director

The trade association which represents quarries and fabricators of Indiana Limestone, as well as associate members who supply goods or services to the industry, ILIA's charte is to eductate and promote
90 Members Founded: 1928

20654 International Cast Polymer Alliance
435 N Michigan Avenue
Chicago, IL 60611-4084

FAX: 312-644-8557
icpa-info@icpa-hq.org
www.icpa-hq.org

Debbie Cannon, President
Jeanne McCormack, Director Conferences/Meetings
Shaine Anderson, Director Membership/Marketing
Andy Rusnak, Editor/Director Communications

Formerly known as the Cultured Marble Institute, is a nonprofit organization representing over 300 members including manufacturers, suppliers, fabricators, and installers of cultured marble, cultured granite, cultured onyx, and solid surface kitchen and bath products.

20655 Marble Institute of America
28901 Clemens Road
Suite 100
Cleveland, OH 44145
440-250-9222
FAX: 440-250-9223
psabel@aol.com
www.marble-institute.com

Garis F Distelhorst, Executive Vice President
Helen Distelhorst, Director Meetings/Special Events
Cathy Mayer, Director Membership

The Marble Institute of America (MIA) is the authoritative source of information on standards of natural stone workmanship and practice and the suitable application of natural stone products.
1600 Members Founded: 1907

20656 Masonry Society
3970 Broadway
Suite 201-D
Boulder, CO 80304
303-939-9700
FAX: 303-541-9215
info@masonrysociety.org
www.masonrysociety.org

Phil Samblanet, Executive Director

The Masonry Society is an international gathering of people interested in the art and science of masonry. It is a professional, technical, and educational association dedicated to the advancement of knowledge on masonry. TMSÆmembers are design engineers, architects, builders, researchers, educators, building officials, materials suppliers, manufacturers, and others who want to contribute to and benefit from the global pool of knowledge on masonry.

20657 National Concrete Burial Vault Association
195 Wekiva Springs Road
Suite 200
Longwood, FL 32779-2552
407-788-1996
FAX: 407-774-6751 www.ncbva.org

Darren Baxter, President
Thomas A Monahan, Executive Director
Jan Monahan, Director Publications
Heather Jones, Convention/Event Planning

A voluntary nonprofit organization of concrete burial vault manufacturers throughtout the United States and Canada. The purpose of the organization is to provide a unified voice for the concrete burial vault industry regardless of product affiliation, brand recognition or location.
350 Members Founded: 1930

20658 National Concrete Masonry Association
13750 Sunrise Valley Drive
Herndon, VA 20171-3499
703-713-1900
FAX: 703-713-1910
ncma@ncma.org www.ncma.org

Mark Hogen, President

The national trade association representing the concrete masonry industry. The association is involved in a broad range of technical, research, marketing, government relations and community activities.
Founded: 1918

20659 National Lime Association
200 N Glebe Road
Suite 800
Arlington, VA 22203-3728
703-243-5463
FAX: 703-243-5489
natlime@lime.org www.lime.org

Arlene Seeger, Executive Director
Lisa McFadden, Meetings

Trade association for US and Canadian manufacturers of high calcium quicklime, dolomitic quicklime and hydrated lime, collectively referred to as lime. NLA represents the interests of its members in Washington, provides input on standards and specifacations for lime, and funds and manages research on current and new uses for lime.
Founded: 1902

20660 National Precast Concrete Association
National Precast Concrete Association
10333 N Meridian Street
Suite 272
Indianapolis, IN 46290-1074
317-571-9500
FAX: 317-571-0041 800-366-7731
npca@precast.org www.precast.org

Ty Gable, President
Danielle Bowman, Director Meetings/Conventions
Lacinda Hobbs, Member Services
Claudia Hunter, Director Finance/Human Resources
Ron Hyinck, Managing Editor

An international trade organization, NPCA represents manufacturers of plant produced precast concrete products and companies that provide the equipment, supplies and services to make these products. NPCA also provides technical information throught 13 product committees, which consist of members who concentrate on specific product lines within the precast industry.
900 Members Founded: 1965

20661 National Ready Mixed Concrete Association
900 Spring Street
Silver Spring, MD 20910
301-587-1400
FAX: 301-585-4219

Robert Garbini, COO

NRMCA represents its membership of ready mixed concrete producrs in market development, technical research, engineering advances, government relations, and regulatory issues. In addition to conducting educational seminars, workshops, conferences and trade shows, NRMCA disseminates a wide variety of publications for its members, ranging from Congressional digests and promotion pointers to driver education.

20662 Ornamental Concrete Producers Association
502 Kay Avenue SE
Bemidji, MN 56601
218-751-1982
FAX: 218-751-2186
delpreus@paulbunyan.net
www.ornamentalconcrete.org

Del Preuss, Executive Director

An international nonprofit educational association comprised of producers and suppliers. *$50.00*
500 Members Founded: 1991

20663 Portland Cement Association
5420 Old Orchard Road
Skokie, IL 60077
847-966-6200
FAX: 847-966-8389
info@cement.org www.cement.org

John P Gleason Jr, President
George Barney, Senior VP Marketing

The Portland Cement Association represents cement companies in the United States and Canada. It conducts market development, engineering, research, education, and public affairs programs.
Founded: 1916

20664 Post-Tensioning Institute
8601 North Black Canyon Highway
Suite 103
Phoenix, AZ 85021
602-870-7540
FAX: 602-870-7541
info@post-tensioning.org
www.post-tensioning.org

Theodore L Neff, Executive Director
Russell Price, President
Douglas J Schlegel, VP

Provides research, technical development, marketing and promotional activities for companies engaged in post-tensioned prestressed construction. Members include fabricators and manufacturers.
900 Members Founded: 1976

20665 Refractories Institute
650 Smithfield Street
Suite 1160
Pittsburgh, PA 15222-3907
412-281-6787
FAX: 412-281-6881
www.refractoriesinstitute.org

Robert Crolius, President

A trade association which promotes the interests of the refractories industry. TRI has a long tradition of providing support and services to manufacturers of refractory materials and products and suppliers of raw materials, equipment, and services to the refractories industry.
80 Members Founded: 1951

20666 Specialty Minerals
Minerals Technology
The Chrysler Building
405 Lexington Avenue
New York, NY 10174-1901
212-781-1800
FAX: 610-882-8726 800-801-1031
smi.productinfo@specialtyminerals.com
www.mineralstech.com

Paul R Saueracker, President/CEO

A subsidiary of Minerals Technology, Inc., a resource and technology based organization that develops and produces performance-enhancing minerals, mineral-based and synthetic mineral products for the paper, steel, polymer, healthcare and other manufacturing industries on a worldwide basis.

20667 Tilt-Up Concrete Association
PO Box 204
Mount Vernon, IA 52314
319-895-6911
FAX: 319-895-8830

Ed Sauter, Executive Director

TCA members include contractors, suppliers, architects, and engineers dedicated to the advancement of quality tilt-up concrete construction. Activities include a national promotional program, information clearinghouse, educational seminars, referral service, achievement awards program, development of codes and standards, and a quarterly magazine.

Newsletters

20668 Refractory News
Refractories Institute
630 Smithfield Street
Suite 1160
Pittsburgh, PA 15222-3907
412-281-6787
FAX: 412-281-6881
triassn@aol.com
http://www.refractoriesinstitute.org

Flo Story, Editor

A monthly newsletter featuring timely industry news, information on federal regulations, member updates, announcements on seminars, and the latest refractory information and statistics. *$24.00*

4 pages Monthly Founded: 1951
Circulation: 700
Printed in 2 colors on matte stock

Magazines & Journals

20669 ACI Materials Journal
38800 Country Club Drive
Farmington Hills, MI 48331
248-848-3751
FAX: 248-848-3701
journals.manuscripts@concrete.org
www.concrete.org

Jamie McMann, Editorial & Production Department

Includes; properties of materials used in concrete; research on materials and concrete; properties, use, and handling of concrete; and related ACI standards and committee reports.

20670 ACI Structural Journal
38800 Country Club Drive
Farmington Hills, MI 48331
248-848-3800
FAX: 248-848-3801
bkstore@concrete.org
www.concrete.org

Jamie McMann, Editorial & Production Department

Includes; structural design and analysis of concrete elements and structures; research related to concrete elements and structures; design and analysis theory; and related ACI standards and committee reports.

20671 Cement Americas
Primedia
29 N Wacker Drive
10th Floor
Chicago, IL 60606
312-726-2802
FAX: 312-726-2574
www.cementamericas.com

Steven Prokopy, Editor

Cement Americas provides comprehensive coverage of the North and South American cement markets from raw materials extraction to delivery and transportation to the end user. Production-oriented articles focus on areas where the market activity is at its greatest. Coverage of new ideas, technological improvements, industry trends, and views from leading figures in the cement industry ensure that Cement Americas remains the cement industry journal of the Americas.

Printed in 4 colors on glossy stock

20672 Concrete InFocus
Naylor Publications
5950 NW 1st Place
Gainesville, FL 32607

FAX: 352-331-3525 800-369-6220
chodges@naylor.com
www.naylor.com

Christopher Hodges, Pulisher

Magazine that's mailed to 5,000+ industry personnel.

20673 Concrete Masonry Designs
NCMA
13750 Sunrise Valley Drive
Herndon, VA 20171-4662
703-713-1900
FAX: 703-713-1910
ncma@ncma.org www.ncma.org

Brooke Berthelsen, Editor
Jerry Harke, Publisher

Highlights concrete masonry applications, best practice tips, specifications and details. Also showcases concrete masonry landscape products. *$1.00*

Monthly Founded: 1918
Circulation: 25000
Printed in 4 colors on glossy stock

20674 Concrete Producer
Hanley Wood
426 S Westgate
Addison, IL 60101
630-543-0870
FAX: 847-564-9287
ryelton@hanleywood.com
www.theconcreteproducer.com

Richard Yelton, Editor-in-Chief
Tom Bagsarian, Managing Editor
Chari O'Rourke, Circulation Manager

Written for decision-making professionals who buy and specify materials, plant equipment, accessories, trucks, and related products used in the major concrete-producing market segments. Each issue offers money saving operational tips, management advice, new products and technology, and solutions to complex concrete-production questions.

20675 Contemporary Stone & Tile Design
Business News Publishing Company
299 Market Street
Suite 320
Saddle Brook, NJ 07663
201-845-5035
FAX: 201-291-9002
cstd@bnp.com
http://www.stoneworld.com

Alex Backrach, Publisher
Michael Reis, Editor

Promotes the benefits of natural stone and ceramic tile to a readership of architects, interior designers, specifiers and consumers. Practical tips and commentary on stone and tile design are included, featuring interviews with architects and designers from the world's leading firms. *$125.00*

Quarterly Founded: 1987
Circulation: 21000

20676 MC
National Precast Concrete Association
10333 N Meridian Street
Suite 272
Indianapolis, IN 46290
317-571-9500
FAX: 317-571-0041 800-366-7731
rhyink@precast.org www.precast.org

Ron Hyink, Editor
Brenda Ibitz, Manager Advertising

MC magazine features detailed articles about the latest industry technologies and developments, perspectives on current industry events, profiles on leading precast concrete companies and case studies of various manufactured concrete applications.

Bi-Monthly

20677 Masonry Construction
Hanley Wood
426 S Westgate
Addison, IL 60101
630-543-0870
FAX: 847-564-9287
ryelton@hanleywood.com
www.masonryconstruction.com

Richard Yelton, Editor-in-Chief
Ron Holzhauer, Deputy Editor
Kari Moosman, Associate Editor
Ted Worthington, Managing Editor
Chari O'Rourke, Circulation Manager

Masonry Construction brings together the complex and fragmented components of the masonry industry—contractors, general contractors, architects, engineers, and producers—providing technical advice, innovative methods and materials, state-of-the-art projects, and essential product information.

20678 Precast Solutions
National Precast Concrete Association
10333 N Meridian Street
Suite 272
Indianapolis, IN 46290
317-571-9500
FAX: 317-571-0041 800-366-7731
gsnapper@precast.org
www.precast.org

Greg Snapper, Editor
Kim Wilson, Manager Marketing/Communications
Brenda Ibitz, Advertising
Ty Gable, President

Designed to educate specifiers about the uses and benefits of precast concrete. Showcases construction projects that rely on precast concrete products for successful completion. The goal of the magazine is to increase the use of precast concrete by specifiers and provide a marketing tool for members.

Quarterly

20679 Professional Builder
Reed Business Information
8878 Barrons Boulevard
Highlands Ranch, CO 80129-2345
303-704-4000
FAX: 303-470-4280 800-446-6551
subsmail@reedbusiness.com
www.reedbusiness.com

Heather McCune, Editor

The magazine for professionals within the residential building industry. Articles cover industry news, company profiles, market reports, construction technology and merchandising information needed to successfully complete each job.

Monthly Founded: 1977

20680 Rock Products
Primedia
29 N Wacker Drive
10th Floor
Chicago, IL 60606
312-726-2802
FAX: 312-726-2574
rmarkley@primediabusiness.com
www.rockproducts.com
Rick Markley, Editor
Scott Bieda, Publisher
The aggregate industry's journal of applied technology.
Monthly Founded: 1905

20681 Stone World
BNP Media
210 Route 4 East
Suite 311
Paramus, NJ 07652
201-291-9001
FAX: 201-291-9002
inof@stoneworld.com
www.stoneworld.com
Alex Bachrach, Publisher
Michael Reis, Editor
Janelle Minghine, Advertising Manager
Information on stone use in architecture and interior design as well as stone production, distribution, installation, and maintenance. With technical information, high quality architectural photography and in-depth international industry coverage. Designed for and read by the top buyers and makers who specify, quarry, fabricate, export, import, distribute, design, sell and install stone and stone-related equipment and supplies.
21000 pages Monthly Founded: 1984
Circulation: 18000

Trade Shows

20682 Composites and Polycon Convention
American Composites Manufacturers Association
1010 North Glebe Road
Suite 450
Arlington, VA 22201
703-525-0511
FAX: 703-525-0743
info@acmanet.org www.icpashow.org
Three-day convention. Attendees will have the opportunity to choose from 100 presentations, live demonstrations and technical papers. Covering every level of expertise from beginer to advanced, industry experts will address dozens of subject areas in the most striking detail, from technical to production to regulatory to management and more.
Annual

20683 MCX
National Precast Concrete Association
10333 N Meridian Street
Suite 272
Indianapolis, IN 46290-1074
317-571-9500
FAX: 317-571-0041 800-366-7731
npca@precast.org www.precast.org
Danielle Bowman, Director Meetings/Conventions
Trade show for the precast concrete industry, containing 300 booths and 300 exhibits.
3,500 Attendees February

20684 Manufactured Concrete Products Exposition
National Concrete Masonry Association
13750 Sunrise Valley Drive
Herndon, VA 20171-3499
703-713-1900
FAX: 703-713-1910
ncma@ncma.org www.ncma.org
The Manufactured Concrete Products Exposition is brought to you by a partnership between the National Concrete Masonry Association, the Interlocking Concrete Paving Institute and the American Concrete Pipe Association.
Annual

20685 National Concrete Burial Vault Association Convention
NCBVA
195 Wekiva Springs Road
Suite 200
Longwood, FL 32779
407-788-1996
FAX: 407-774-6751 www.ncbva.org
Thomas A Monahan, Executive Director
Heather Jones, Conventions/Event Planning
Convention held annually. Includes awards banquet, installation of officers and more.
Annual

20686 POLYCON
International Cast Polymer Alliance
1010 North Glebe Road
Suite 450
Arlington, VA 22201
703-525-0320
FAX: 703-525-0743
icpa@cfa-hq.org www.icpa-hq.org
Sabeena Hickman, Managing Director
Annual convention of the American Composites Manufacturers Association.
820 Attendees Annual/February

20687 PTI Technical Conference and Exhibition
Post-Tensioning Institute
8601 North Black Canyon Highway
Suite 103
Phoenix, AZ 85021
602-870-7540
FAX: 602-870-7541
info@post-tensioning.org
www.post-tensioning.org
Ted Neff, Executive Director
Earn CEUs, attend technical sessions, awards events, exhibits, and ask-the-expert forum. *$475.00*
May

20688 Stone Expo
Hanley Wood Exhibitions
8600 Freeport Parkway
Suite 200
Irving, TX 75063
972-366-6300
FAX: 972-536-6301 866-490-3097
lrobidoux@hanleywood.com
www.stonexpo.com
Lisa Robidoux, Marketing Manager
Importers, finishers, wholesalers, fabricators, quarriers and exporters of stone for both interior and exterior application as well as suppliers of machines, tools and services.
3000+ Attendees Annual Founded: 1989

20689 World of Concrete Exposition
Post Tensioning Institute
8601 North Black Canyon Highway
Suite 103
Phoenix, AZ 85021
602-870-7540
FAX: 602-870-7541
info@post-tensioning.org
www.post-tensioning.org
Seminars, exhibits and trade shows. Sponsored by the Post-Tensioning Institute.
36M Attendees January/Febuary

Directories & Databases

20690 Dimension Stone Design Manual
Marble Institute of America
2801 Clemens Road
Suite 100
Cleveland, OH 44145
440-250-9222
FAX: 440-250-9223
www.marble-institute.com
An authoritative source for guidelines on using natural stone in architectural designs. Contents include sections on granite, marble, limestone, serpentine, travertine, quartz-based stone and slate with product descriptions and technical data; general installation guidelines; guidelines and typical detailing for horizontal surfaces, vertical surfaces, wet areas, furniture and countertops; maintenance of exterior/ interior stone installations; and a glossary of terms relating to dimension stone. *$90.00*
350 pages

20691 Dimension Stones of the World: Book of Color Plates
Marble Institute of America
28901 Clemens Road
Suite 100
Cleveland, OH 44145
440-250-9222
FAX: 440-250-9223
www.marble-institute.com
This set contains over 600 full color reproductions of granites, limestones, marbles, onyx, quartz based stone, slate and travertine. On the reverse side of each page are the ASTM test values for absorbption, density, compressive strength, hardness and flexural strength. Also listed for each stone are primary name, country of origin, quarry location, geological age, color range, recommended usage and available sizes. *$330.00*

20692 Online MCP
38800 Country Club Drive
Farmington Hills, MI 48331
248-848-3800
FAX: 248-848-3801
bkstore@concrete.org
www.concrete.org
Contains all of the ACI documents you need to answer your questions about code requirements, specifications, tolerance, concrete proportions, construction methods, evaluations of test results, and many more topics.

20693 Stone World Annual Buyer's Guide

Stone World Magazine
210 Route 4 East
Suite 311
Paramus, NJ 90001
201-291-9001
FAX: 201-291-2002
info@stoneworld.com
www.stoneworld.com

Alex Bachrach, Publisher
Michael Reis, Senior Editor/Associate Publisher

Comprised of six sections covering: stone suppliers, fraricating equipment and suppliers, installation and stone care materials and supplies, associations, services, trade shows and organizers. *$6.00*
Annual
Circulation: 22,000

Industry Web Sites

20694 www.crsi.org
Concrete Reinforcing Steel Institute

Conducts research and provides technical information on reinforced concrete design and construction practices.

20695 www.greyhouse.com
Grey House Publishing

Selected Grey House directories in the fields of business, health and education are available online. Users can search our online databases by several different search criteria, such as product categories, geographic area, sales volume and much, much more. Full Grey House catalog and online ordering also available.

20696 www.icri.org
International Concrete Repair Institute

To improve the quality of repair, restoration, and protection of concrete and other structures.

20697 www.marble-institute.com
Marble Institute of America

Importers, finishers, wholesalers, fabricators, quarriers and exporters of stone for both interior and exterior application as well as suppliers of machines, tools and services.

20698 www.post-tensioning.org
Post-Tensioning Institute

Provides research, technical development, marketing and promotional activities for companies engaged in post-tensioned prestressed construction. Members include fabricators and manufacturers.

20699 www.precast.org
National Precast Concrete Association

Associations

20700 APL Logistics
1111 Broadway
Oakland, CA 94607
510-272-8000
FAX: 510-272-7011
www.apllogistics.com
Mike Zampa, Director Corporate Communications
Designs and operates global supply chains that deliver products to everywhere you need them. Innovative end-to-end solutions usse data connectivity for greater visibility and control.

20701 American Radio Relay League
225 Main Street
Newington, CT 06111
860-594-0200
FAX: 860-594-0259 888-277-5289
membership@arrl.org www.arrl.org
Allen Pitts, Media Relations
Joel Harrison, President
David Sumner, CEO
Barry Shelley, CFO
Harold Kramer, COO
National membership association for amateur radio operators.
170m Members Founded: 1890

20702 Antenna Measurement Techniques Association
6065 Roswell Road
Atlanta, GA 30328
770-864-3488
FAX: 770-864-3491
president@amta.org www.amta.org
Lawrence L Mandeville, President
Jeff Kemp, Technical Coordinator
Janet Nichols ONeil, Meeting Coordinator
Nonprofit professional organization open to individuals with an interest in antenna measurements. Areas of interest include: measurement facilities, unique or innovative measurement techniques, test instrumentation and systems, RCS measurements, compact range design and evaluation, near-field techniques and their applications, and the practical aspects of measurement problems and their solutions.
400 Members Founded: 1979

20703 Armed Forces Communications and Electronics Association
AFCEA International Headquarters
4400 Fair Lakes Court
Fairfax, VA 22033-3899
703-631-6100
FAX: 703-631-6169 800-336-4583
service@afcea.org www.afcea.org
VADM Herb Brown, President/CEO
A non-profit international association dedicated to supporting global security by providing an ethical environment that encourages a close cooperative relationship among civil government agencies, the military and industry. *$35.00*
31000 Members Founded: 1946

20704 Association for Local Telecommunications Services
900 17th Street, NW
Suite 400
Washington, DC 20006
202-296-6650
FAX: 202-296-7585
membership@alts.org www.alts.org
COMPTEL is the leading industry accociation representing communications service providers and their supplier partners.

20705 Association of Public-Safety Communication s Officials-International, Inc
351 N Williamson Blvd
Daytona Beach, FL 32114-1112
386-322-2500
FAX: 386-322-2501 888-272-6911
apco@apco911.org www.apcointl.org
George S Rice, Jr, Executive Director
Tim Ryan, Chief Financial Officer
Courtney McCarron, Communications Affairs Director
A not-for-profit professional organization dedicated to the enhancement of public safety communications. Exists to serve the people who manage, operate, maintain, and supply the communications systems used to safeguard the lives and property of citizens everywhere.
16000 Members Founded: 1935

20706 Association of Teleservices International
12 Academy Avenue
Atkinston, NH 03811

FAX: 603-362-9486 866-896-2874
admin@atsi.org www.atsi.org
Lori Jenkins, President
Promotes fair competition through appropriate regulation and legislation; provides research and development provides support services and educational opportunities to address challenges in operating environments; in encourages and maintains the high standards of ethics and service.
800+ Members Founded: 1942

20707 Broadcast Designers' Association International
145 W 45th Street
Room 1100
New York, NY 10036-4008
212-376-6222
FAX: 212-376-6202
Association for manufacturers or suppliers of broadcast design equipment, supplies and services.

20708 Carnegie Mellon University: Information Networking Institute
Electrical & Computer Engineering Department
4616 Henry Street
Pittsburgh, PA 15213
412-268-7195
FAX: 412-268-7196
ini@cmu.edu www.ini.cmu.edu
Dena Haritos Tsamitis, Director
Lynn Carroll, Assistant Director Program Develop
Andrew Pueschel, Project Manager/Events/Marketing
Chriss Swaney, Director Public Relations
Sean O'Leary, Manager
The Information Networking Institute was established by Carnegie Mellon as the nation's first research and education center devoted to Information Networking.
Founded: 1989

20709 Cellular Telecommunications Industry
CTIA
1400 16th Street NW
Suite 600
Washington, DC 20036
202-785-0081
FAX: 202-785-0721 www.ctia.org
Michael Altschul, Senior VP/General Counsel
Steve Largent, President
Rob Mesirow, VP Operations
John Walls, VP Public Affairs
Bonnie Knight, Director Membership
An international organization representing all sectors of wireless communications. As a nonprofit membership organization, they represent service providers, manufacturers, wireless data and Internet companies and other contributors to the wireless universe.
Founded: 1984

20710 Direct Marketing Association
1120 Avenue of the Americas
New York, NY 10036-6700
212-768-7277
FAX: 212-302-6714
customerservice@the-dma.org
www.the-dma.org
Francesco C Leboffe, President
Jonah Gitlitz, Senior VP
Anna Cheknis, Market Research Associate
John Greco Jr, Chief Executive Officer
For businesses interested in direct, database and interactive global marketing, with about 4,700 member companies from the US and 53 foreign nations on six continents. Members include catalog companies, direct mailers, teleservices firms, Internet marketers and other at-distance marketers from every consumer and business-to-business segment, both commercial and nonprofit as well as companies that provide supplies and services to marketers.
3.5M Members Founded: 1917

20711 Electronics Retailing Association
2000 North 14th Street
Suite 300
Arlington, VA 22201
703-841-1751
FAX: 703-841-1860 800-987-6462
contact@retailing.org
www.retailing.org
Dan Danielson, Chairman
Barbara Tulipane, President/CEO
For companies who use the power of electronics to sell goods and services to the public. The purpose of ERA is to foster the growth, development and acceptance of the rapidly growing electronic retailing industry worldwide.
400+ Members Founded: 1991

20712 Enterprise Wireless Alliance
Enterprise Wireless Alliance
8484 Westpark Drive
Suite 630
McLean, VA 22102
703-528-5115
FAX: 703-524-1074 800-482-8282
Mark E Crosby, President
Donald J Vasek, Executive Director
Julie Amann, CFO
Andre F Cote, Chief Technology Officer

Membership is made up of operators on the 220MHz, 450 MHz, 800 MHz and 900 MHz bands, as well as product and service providers for the industry. Many members are exploring other areas of the mobile telecommunications industry — digital SMR, Personal Communications Services, data communications, mobile satellite, cable telephony and international wireless interests. AMTA is working with its members and with government to insure that these areas can be pursued succsessfully.
400 Members Founded: 1985

20713 Insulated Cable Engineers Association
PO Box 1568
Carrollton, GA 30112
770-300-0369
FAX: 303-397-2740
info@icea.net www.icea.net
Professional organization dedicated to developing cable standards for the electric power, control and telecommunications industries. Ensures safe, economical and efficient cable systems utilizing proven, state-of-the-art materials and concepts. ICEA documents are of interest to cable manufacturers, architects and engineers, utility and manufacturing plant personnel, telecommunication engineers, consultants and OEMs.
Founded: 1925

20714 Kagan Research
One Lower Ragsdale
Building One Suite 130
Monterey, CA 93940
831-241-1536
FAX: 831-624-1536 800-307-2529
info@kagan.com www.kagan.com
Sandie Borthwick, Executive Director
Provides knowledge, insight and industry perspectives, anticipates trends, projects revenues, tracks financing and values the debt and equity of hundreds of privately held and publicly traded media and communications companies.
Founded: 1969

20715 National Exchange Carrier Association
80 S Jefferson Road
Whippany, NJ 07981-1009
973-848-8000
FAX: 973-884-8469
webmastr@neca.org www.neca.org
William Hegmann, President/CEO
Peter A Dunbar, VP/CFO
James W Frame, VP Operations
Regina McNeil, VP/General Counsel/Corp Secretary
NECA administer's the FCCs access charge plan. They file access charge tariffs with the FCC, collect and validate cost and revenue data, ensure compliance with FCC rules, distribute revenues from access charges among pool members, process FCC regulatory fees, and offer training and education on a wide variety of telecom topics.
1500 Members Founded: 1983

20716 National Telephone Cooperative Association
4121 Wilson Boulevard
Suite 1000
Arlington, VA 22203
703-351-2000
FAX: 703-351-2001
contact@ntca.org www.ntca.org
Michael E Brunner, Executive VP
Non-profit association offering a wide array of member services including a government affairs program; expert legal and industry representation; a broad range of educational services; a comprehensive assortment of regular and special publications and public relations programs; and a well-rounded complement of national and regional meetings.
560+ Members Founded: 1954 547 names $495 per M.

20717 Organization for the Promotion and Adv. of Small Telecommunications
21 Dupont Circle NW
Washington, DC 20036-1109
202-833-2775
FAX: 202-659-4619
John N Rose, Executive VP
Martha Silver, Editor
Protects the interests of small, rural, independent commercial telephone companies and cooperatives that have less than 50,000 access lines.
650 Members Founded: 1963

20718 Personal Communications Industry
500 Montgomery Street
Suite 700
Alexandria, VA 22314
703-390-0300
FAX: 703-836-1608 800-759-0300
webmaster@pcia.com www.pcia.com
Jay Kitchen, President
Represents companies that develop, own, manage and operate towers, commercial rooftops and other facilities for the provision of all types of wireless, broadcasting and telecommunication services. PCIA is dedicated to advancing an understanding of the benefits of wireless services and required infrastructure to local and federal government officials and communities at large.
3000 Members Founded: 1949

20719 Power and Communication Contractors
103 Oronoco Street
Suite 200
Alexandria, VA 22314
703-212-7734
FAX: 703-548-3733 800-542-7222
info@pccaweb.org www.pccaweb.org
Greg Johnson, Co-President
Steve Spears, Co-President
Herbert Fluharty, First VP
Luke Spalj, Second Vice President
Tim Wagner, Manager
Contractors and suppliers specializing in electric and telephone power line and cable television construction.
300 Members Founded: 1945

20720 Society of Cable Telecommunications Engineers
140 Philips Road
Exton, PA 19341-1318
610-363-6888
FAX: 610-363-5898 800-542-5040
scte@scte.org www.scte.org
John Clark, President/CEO
Patricia Zelenka, VP Finance
Heather Gosciniak, Coordinator Marketing/Communication
Joe Madagan, Manager Publications
JoAnn Pushcarovich, Director Membership Support
A nonprofit, professional organization committed to advancing the careers of cable telecommunications professionals and serving their industry through excellence in professional development, information and standards.
15000 Members Founded: 1969

20721 Society of Satellite Professionals
New York Information Technology Center

55 Broad Street
14th floor
New York, NY 10004
212-809-5199
FAX: 212-825-0075
rbell@sspi.org www.sspi.org
Robert Bell, Executive Director
Louis Zacharilla, Director Development
Tamara Bond, Membership Director
Carol McKibben, Publications Editor
A nonprofit association that serves people working in the satellite industry in countries arount the world. Professional development society of the global satellite industry.

1000 Members Founded: 1983

20722 Society of Telecommunications Consultants
13275 State Highway 89
PO Box 70
Old Station, CA 96071
530-335-7313
FAX: 530-335-7360 800-782-7670
Cathy Cimaglia, Administration Manager
Wendy Rubes, Membership/Trade
The STC is an international organization of independent telecommunications and information technology consultants who serve clients in business and government.
250 Members Founded: 1976
Mailing list available for rent 250 names $250 per M.

20723 Telecom Pioneers
930 15th Street
12th Floor
Denver, CO 80202
303-571-1200
FAX: 303-572-0520 800-872-5995
info@telecompioneers.org
www.telecompioneers.com
Mary T Manning, Chairman Board
Marty Lee, President
Formerly known as the Telephone Pioneers of America, TelecomPioneers is comprised of nearly 620,000 current and retired telecommunications employees who have joined together to make their communities better places in which to live and work
Founded: 1911

20724 Telework Coalition
204 E Street NE
Washington, DC 20002
732-329-2266
www.telcoa.org
Enabling virtual, mobile and distributed work through education, technology and legislation.

20725 United Communications Group
11300 Rockville Pike
Suite 1100
Rockville, MD 20852-3030
301-287-2700
FAX: 301-816-8945 800-509-5062
webmaster@ucg.com www.ucg.com
A portfolio of highly focused business and professional publishing companies providing guidance, information, analysis, data

and solutions to over two million clients worldwide.
Founded: 1977

20726 United States Telecom Association
607 14th Street NW
Suite 400
Washington, DC 20005
202-326-7300
FAX: 202-326-7333
membership@ustelecom.org
www.ustelecom.org

Walter B McCormick Jr, President/CEO
Allison Remsen, Media Relations

Trade association representing service providers and suppliers for the telecom industry.
1200 Members

Newsletters

20727 Broadband
IGI Group
320 Washington Street
Suite 302
Brighton, MA 02135
617-782-5033
FAX: 617-782-5735 800-323-1088
info@igigroup.com
www.igigroup.com

Paul Polishuk, President/CEO
Hui Pan, Conference Director
Bev Wilson, Managing Editor
Will Ashley, IT Director/Media Manager

The Broadband Newsletter covers such subjects as: growth in broadband access such as ADSL, cable modems, satellite and fixed wireless; spending plans of the telcos and MSOs for broadband access; important applications that will drive the market; and growth of the internet based on fast internet access. *$695.00*
Monthly Founded: 1977
Circulation: 1500

20728 Broadband Advertising
Kagan World Media
One Lower Ragsdale Drive
Building One, Suite 130
Monterey, CA 93940-8746
831-624-1536
FAX: 831-625-3225 800-307-2529
info@kagan.com www.kagan.com

George Niesen, Editor
Tom Johnson, Marketing Manager

Provides critical information about how and where advertising sales will intersect across all broadband platforms. Includes data and analysis previously published in Internet Advertising and Cable TV advertising *$1095.00*
Monthly Founded: 1969

20729 Broadband Technology
Kagan World Media
One Lower Ragsdale Drive
Building One Suite 130
Monterey, CA 93940
831-624-1536
FAX: 831-625-3225 800-307-2529
info@kagan.com www.kagan.com

George Niesen, Editor
Tom Johnson, Marketing Manager
Michael Schroeder, Manager

Incisive, thorough reports on deployments of bundled services, high-spped data, digital video and telephony. Analyzes and projects growth of set-top boxes, modems, switches, routers and other infrastructure. Provides data and stats on services offered and plant construction by cable, DSL, satellite, wireless and wired phone providers. *$1045.00*
Monthly Founded: 1969

20730 Broadcast Investor
Kagan World Media
One Lower Ragsdale Drive Suite 130
Building One
Monterey, CA 93940
831-624-1536
FAX: 831-625-3225 800-307-2529
info@kagan.com www.kagan.com

George Niesen, Editor
Tom Johnson, Marketing Manager

The market's most comprehensive sourve of current and historical data on valuations, deals and finance. Trends, forecasts, data. *$1295.00*
Monthly Founded: 1969

20731 CBQ-Communication Booknotes Quarterly
Lawrence Erlbaum Associates
10 Industrial Avenue
Mahwah, NJ 07430
201-258-2200
FAX: 201-760-3735
journals@erlbaum.com
www.leaonline.com/loi/cbq

Christopher Sterling, Editor
James K Bracken, Assistant Editor

Descriptive reviews of new publications and websites. *$350.00*
Quarterly Founded: 1969

20732 Cable Program Investor
Kagan World Media
One Lower Ragsdale Drive
Building One, Suite 130
Monterey, CA 93940
831-624-1536
FAX: 831-625-3225 800-307-2529
info@kagan.com www.kagan.com

George Niesen, Editor
Tom Johnson, Marketing Manager

Provides exclusive data and analysis, deal benchmarks and balance sheet assessments. It covers home shopping networks, programming trends, multichannel penetration by platform and ratings data. *$1045.00*
Monthly Founded: 1969

20733 Cable TV Investor
Kagan World Media
One Lower Ragsdale
Building One,Suite 130
Monterey, CA 93940-8746
831-241-1536
FAX: 831-624-1536 800-307-2529
info@kagan.com www.kagan.com

George Niesen, Editor
Tom Johnson, Marketing Manager

Provides information on the data, the deals, the valuation metrics, the distillation of information into intelligence. The information you want and need to remain competitive *$1295.00*
Monthly Founded: 1969

20734 Cable TV Law Reporter
Kagan World Media
One Lower Ragsdale Drive
Building One Suite 130
Monterey, CA 93940-8746
831-624-1536
FAX: 831-625-3225 800-307-2529
info@kagan.com www.kagan.com

George Niesen, Editor
Tom Johnson, Marketing Manager

The quintessential library of cable court cases, arbitrations, legal precedents. Labeled and catalogued for easy reference. Required reading for attorneys, government regulators and top executives. Three month trial available. *$995.00*
Monthly Founded: 1969

20735 Communication
National Technical Information Service
5285 Port Royal Road
Springfield, VA 22161-0001
703-874-4650
FAX: 703-487-4630

Covers common carrier and satellite communications, information theory, graphics, policies, regulations, studies, radio and television.

20736 Communications Daily
Warren Publishing
2115 Ward Court NW
Washington, DC 20037-1209
202-729-9200
FAX: 202-318-8350 800-771-9202
info@warren-news.com
www.warren-news.com

Albert Warren, Publisher
Paul Warren, President
Daniel Warren, Vice Chairment/Executive Editor
R Michael Feazel, Managing Editor
Gina Storr, Director Sales/Marketing

Daily publication for the entire telecommunications indusrty.
Daily Founded: 1945
Circulation: 70000+

20737 Fiber Optic Sensors and Systems
IGI Group
320 Washington Street
Suite 302
Brighton, MA 02135
617-782-5033
FAX: 617-782-5735 800-323-1088
info@igigroup.com
www.igigroup.com

Paul Polishuk, CEO
Hui Pan, Conference Director
Bev Wilson, Managing Editor

Covers procurements, contract awards, requests for qualifications and proposals, reports on market studies, patents filed and awarded, new product announcements, new technology, market forecasts, reviews of important contracts, important conferences and trade shows, and Japanese and European developments. *$695.00*
Monthly Founded: 1977 20,000 names
$150 per M. : pdf

20738 Fiber Optics News
Phillips Business Information
1201 Seven Locks Road
Potomac, MD 20854-2931
301-354-1400
FAX: 301-340-0542

Ellen Hamm, Publisher
Mark Mikolas, Editor

Fiber optics in the telecommunications fields. *$37.00*

20739 Fiber Optics Weekly Update
IGI Group
320 Washington Street
Suite 302
Brighton, MA 02135
617-782-5033
FAX: 617-782-5735 800-323-1088
info@igigroup.com
www.igigroup.com
Paul Polishuk, CEO
Hui Pan, Conference Director
Bev Wilson, Managing Editor
Covers procurements, new contracts, company buyouts, new products, important publications, latest news, planned projects, financial reports, market forecasts, conference and trade show reviews, joint ventures, contract awards, impact of technology, and international developments. *$695.00*
Weekly Founded: 1977

20740 Fiber Optics and Communications
IGI Group
320 Washington Street
Suite 302
Brighton, MA 02135
617-782-5033
FAX: 617-783-5735 800-323-1088
editor@igigroup.com
www.igigroup.com
Paul Polishuk, Publisher
Hui Pan, Conference Director
Bev Wilson, Managing Editor
Fiber optics is spreading rapidly into all major high and low tech fields. This newsletter helps relieve the pressure on busy executives by reviewing over 300 sources on a regular basis and providing only the most relevant information. *$695.00*
Monthly Founded: 1977 : pdf

20741 Fixed Wireless
IGI Group
320 Washington Street
Suite 302
Brighton, MA 02135
617-782-5033
FAX: 617-782-5735 800-323-1088
editor@igigroup.com
www.igigroup.com
Paul Polishuk, CEO
Hui Pan, Conference Director
Bev Wilson, Managing Editor
Tracks technological breakthroughs, network developments, market trends, contacts and examines who the players are in this re-emerging market. *$695.00*
Monthly Founded: 1977

20742 Home Networks
IGI Group
320 Washington Street
Suite 302
Brighton, MA 02135
617-782-5033
FAX: 617-782-5735 800-323-1088
info@igigroup.com
www.igigroup.com
Paul Polishuk, Publisher/CEO
Hui Pan, Conference Director
Bev Wilson, Managing Editor
The market for home networks is driven by the 15 million homes with two or more PCs requiring interconnection and new housing units being built for tomorrow's home network environment. This newsletter keeps you connected to this rapidly developing arena of opportunities. *$ 695.00*
Monthly Founded: 1977

20743 Industry Pulse
Telecommunications Industry Association
2500 Wilson Boulevard
Arlington, VA 22201-3834
703-907-7700
FAX: 703-907-7727
tia@tiaonline.org www.tiaonline.org
Sharon Grace, Editor
Matt Flanigan, President
Monthly Founded: 1988
Circulation: 6000

20744 Interactive TV Strategies
Phillips Business Information
9420 Key West Ave
Rockville, MD 20850
301-279-4200
FAX: 301-340-0542 866-279-1930
information@phillips.com
http://www.phillips.com/
Thomas Phillips, Chairman
Thomas Burne, Executive VP
John Coyle, President
John Farley, Corporate Vice President
Interactive video and data networks.
Founded: 1974

20745 Interval
Society of Cable Telecommunications Engineers
140 Philips Road
Exton, PA 19341-1318
610-363-6888
FAX: 610-363-5898 800-542-5040
scte@scte.org www.scte.org
Serving the members of SCTE, Interval highlights the events of the Society and it's Chapters. *$40.00*
Founded: 1969
Circulation: 15000

20746 Kagan Media Money
Kagan World Media
One Lower Ragsdale Drive
Building One, Suite 130
Monterey, CA 93940-8746
831-624-1536
FAX: 831-625-3225 800-307-2529
info@kagan.com www.kagan.com
George Niesen, Editor
Tom Johnson, Marketing Manager
Sandie Borthwick, Executive Director
Designed to continually focus on the essential trends and hottest topics. Each issue is jammed with leading media indicators, media merger and acquisition data, handy benchmarks and reference charts and the most thought-provoking and insightful analysis. *$1245.00*
48 issues per y Founded: 1969

20747 LAN Newsletter
IGI Group
320 Washington Street
Suite 302
Brighton, MA 02135
617-782-5033
FAX: 617-782-5735 800-323-1088
editor@igigroup.com
www.igigroup.com
Paul Polishuk, President/CEO
Hui Pan, Conference Director
Bev Wilson, Managing Editor
Provides information on new developments and products in the LAN-local area network-industry. Discusses both foreign and domestic markets, including new LAN purchases and installation and management changes. *$695.00*
Monthly Founded: 1977
Circulation: 12000

20748 LAN Product News
Worldwide Videotex
Po Box 3273
Boynton Beach, FL 33424
561-738-2276

markedit@juno.com
www.wvpubs.com
Provides news and information on the computer Local Area Network (LAN) industry. Covers new hardware and software products, as well as research and development.
$25.00
Monthly

20749 MIC/TECH Data Communications
1111 Marlkress Road
Cherry Hill, NJ 08003-2334
856-489-4310
FAX: 856-424-1999 800-678-4642
Lawrence Feidelman, Publisher
Michael Smith, Editor
Carol Bell, Advertising/Sales
Complete performance and pricing of modems, multiplexus, networks and processing. *$920.00*
Daily
Computerized version available

20750 Microcell Report
150 E 2nd Street
New York, NY 10009-8400

FAX: 212-366-9798 800-883-8989
Roger Newell, Publisher
A monthly report on personal communication services including advanced digital mobile telephone applications. Covers regulatory, technical and communication aspects of PCS which includes wireless LANS and PBX. *$397.00*
10 pages Monthly

20751 Microwave News
155 East 77th Street
Suite 3D
New York, NY 10021-1799
212-517-2800
FAX: 212-734-0316
info@microwavenews.com
http://www.microwavenews.com
Louis Slesin, Publisher/Editor
Issues relating to non-ionizing radiation.
$325.00
6 issues per ye Founded: 1981

20752 Modem Users News
Worldwide Videotex
Po Box 3273
Boynton Beach, FL 33424
561-738-2276

markedit@juno.com
www.wvpubs.com
Provides the latest news and information on software, hardware, supplies and services for individuals and companies who communicate via modems in computer and/or facsimile applications. Contains detailed information, prices, and evaluations of products ranging from protable laptop PC and fax boards, to a wide range of accessible services. *$25.00*
Monthly

20753 Newsletter
United Communications Group
11300 Rockville Pike
#1100
Rockville, MD 20852-3012
301-816-8950
FAX: 301-816-8945
ccmi@ucg.com www.ucg.com
Sean Oberle, Publisher
Editorial content provides hands-on advice on how to improve their services and reduce their overall operating expenses. *$379.00*
BiMonthly

20754 North American Telecom Newswatch
United Communications Group
11300 Rockville Pike
#1100
Rockville, MD 20852-3012
301-287-2700
FAX: 301-816-8945
webmaster@ucg.com
http://www.ucg.com
Betty Lehnus, Publisher
Glynn Willet, President
The news that impacts daily business operations, including equipment updates, regulation issues, long distance and internet useage, and wireless financials.
Founded: 1977

20755 Online Newsletter
Information Intelligence
PO Box 31098
Phoenix, AZ 85046-1098
602-996-2283
info@infointelligence.com
www.infointelligence.com
Richard Huleatt, Publisher/Editor
Covers all on-line services, suppliers, vendors, CD-ROM data bases, microcomputers and associated equipment. *$6.25*
9 pages 10 per year Founded: 1980
Printed in on newsprint stock

20756 Optical Networks and WDM
IGI Group
320 Washington Street
Suite 302
Brighton, MA 02135
617-782-5033
FAX: 617-782-5735 800-323-1088
info@igigroup.com
www.igigroup.com
Paul Polishuk, CEO
Hui Pan, Conference Director
Bev Wilson, Managing Editor
The WDM newsletter provides worldwide coverage of technology, markets and applications. Covers such subjects as: WDM systems, MAN applications, Gigabit networks, ATM, financials reports, premise wiring, optical amplifiers, optical networks, new products, network management, standards, optical cross connects, frame relay, competitive analysis, manufacturers strategies, optical access, regulations, tariffs, technology, broadband services, WANs, market forecasts, BOC strategies and more. *$695.00*
Monthly Founded: 1977 20,000 names
$150 per M.

20757 Photonics Components/Subsystems
IGI group
320 Washington Street
Suite 302
Brighton, MA 02135
617-782-5033
FAX: 617-782-5735 800-323-1088
info@igigroup.com
www.igigroup.com
Paul Polishuk, Publisher
Hui Pan, Conference Director
Bev Wilson, Managing Editor
Provides worldwide coverage of technology, markets, and applications. Some subjects covered include: market forecasts, product comparisons, new products, contract awards, new technologies, start-up funding, customer requirements, standards, industry trends, photonics automation, systems developments, licensing, competitive assessments, mergers and acquisitions, and pricing trends. *$695.00*
Monthly Founded: 1977

20758 Plastic Optical Fiber (POF)
IGI Group
320 Washington Street
Suite 302
Brighton, MA 02135
617-782-5033
FAX: 617-782-5735 800-323-1088
editor@igigroup.com
www.igigroup.com
Paul Polishuk, CEO
Hui Pan, Conference Director
Bev Wilson, Managing Editor
Some of the subjects covered are: applications, products, imaging, patents, technology, market research, suppliers, publications, standards, sensors, cost analyses, mergers, audio systems, lighting/illuminations, medical acquisitions, medical, market opportunities, contracts awarded, automotive, licensing opportunities, RFPs, component costs, investments and signs. *$395.00*
6 issues per yr Founded: 1977 : e-mail

20759 SCTE Interval
Society of Cable Telecommunications Engineers
140 Philips Road
Exton, PA 19341-1318
610-363-6888
FAX: 610-363-5898 800-542-5040
scte@scte.org www.scte.org
John Clark, CEO
Joe Madagan, Manager Publications
SCTE's monthly newsletter keeps members abreast of association events, activities and member accomplishments. *$40.00*
Circulation: 15,000

20760 Satellite News
Phillips Publishing
7811 Montrose Road
Suite 2
Potomac, MD 20854-3394
301-340-2100
FAX: 301-659-5927
Ellen Hamm, Publisher
Satellite telecommunications.
Monthly

20761 Society of Telecommunications Consultants Newsletter
Society of Telecommunications Consultants
13275 State Highway 89
PO Box 70
Old Station, CA 96071
530-335-7313
FAX: 530-335-7360 800-782-7670
stchdq@stcconsultants.org
http://www.stcconsultants.org
Cathy Cimaglia, Administrative Manager
Wendy Rubio, Membership Coordinator
Joseph M. Webb, President
A newsletter for update and informational purposes.
Quarterly Founded: 1976
Circulation: 500 250 names $250 per M.
Printed in 2 colors

20762 State & Local Communications Report
BRP Publications
1333 H Street NW
Suite 100 E
Washington, DC 20005-4746
202-312-6060
FAX: 202-842-3047 800-822-6338
Lynn Stanton, Editor
Victoria Mason, Publisher
Premier biweekly news service covering state and local communications issues. The in-depth reporting includes regular coverage of such timely topics as legislation and regulation, new state regulatory activities and important business and industry developments in the areas of telephone, data and enhanced services. *$599.00*
8 pages BiWeekly

20763 State Telephone Regulation Report
Telecom Publishing Group
1101 King Street
Suite 444
Alexandria, VA 22314-2944
703-683-4100
FAX: 703-739-6490 800-327-7205
Chris Vestal, Publisher
Herbert Kirchoff, Editor
Analysis of state telecommunications legislation. *$535.00*
12 pages BiWeekly
Printed in 2 colors on matte stock

20764 Submarine Fiber Optic Communications Systems
IGI Group
320 Washington Street
Suite 302
Brighton, MA 02135
617-782-5033
FAX: 617-782-5735 800-323-1088
editor@igigroup.com
www.igigroup.com
Paul Polishuk, Publisher
Hui Pan, Conference Director
Bev Wilson, Managing Editor
Provides a monthly market intelligence report on new developments in markets, technology and applications. Of special interest will be developments in optical amplifier technology, solutions, Wavelength Division Multiplexing and how these are having an impact on the Submarine Fiber Optic business *$695.00*
Monthly Founded: 1977 : pdf

20765 TR Wireless News
BRP Publications
1333 H Street NW
Suite 100 E
Washington, DC 20005-4707
202-312-6060
FAX: 202-842-3047 800-822-6338

Victoria Mason, Publisher
Andrew Kreig, President

Montiors regulatory, technological and market developments in the rapidly expanding wireless communications industry. It covers new services, corporate activity, and licensing and specturm allocation in the areas of personal communication services. *$597.00*
BiWeekly

20766 TV Program Investor
Kagan World Media
One Lower Ragsdale Drive
Building One, Suite 130
Monterey, CA 93940-8746
831-624-1536
FAX: 831-625-3225 800-307-2529
info@kagan.com www.kagan.com

John Mansell, Editor
Tom Johnson, Marketing Manager

More than just a newsletter, practically a seminar on how much programs cost and what they are worth. Exclusive spreadsheets with estimates of what goes between the commercials. Three month trial available. *$895.00*
Monthly Founded: 1969

20767 Telco Competition Report
BRP Publications
1333 H Street NW
Suite 100 E
Washington, DC 20005-4746
202-312-6060
FAX: 202-842-3047 800-822-6338

Victoria Mason, Publisher
Brian Hammond, Editor

Provides important information on events and issues surrounding the $90 billion local exchange markets. Each issues covers the continuing regulatory, financial, strategic and technological ramifications of local exchange competition, including the second and third-tier cities being targeted by competitions and strategies for success. *$596.00*
20 pages BiWeekly

20768 Tele-Service News
Worldwide Videotex
Po Box 3273
Boynton Beach, FL 33424
561-738-2276

markedit@juno.com
www.wvpubs.com
Provides news and information on the telephone industry. Covers services, products, research and development and business plans of RBOCs (Regional Bell Operating Companies), long distance carriers, and independent vendors. *$25.00*
Monthly

20769 Telecom Daily Lead from US Telecom Association
SmartBrief
1401 H Street
N.W, Suite 600
Washington, DC 20005
202-326-7300
FAX: 202-326-7333
webmaster@smartbrief.com
http://www.dailylead.com/usta

Portia Krebs, VP Communications
Jason Ross, Lead Editor
Eric Hoffman, Sales Account Director

Free daily newsbriefing, delivered by e-mail, that covers the telecom industry's top news stories.
Daily
Circulation: 11000

20770 Telecom Outlook
Market Intelligence Research Company
2525 Charleston Road
Mountain View, CA 94043-1626

Wyman Bravard, Publisher

Reports on the telecommunications industry.
Monthly

20771 Telecom Standards
IGI Group
320 Washington Street
Suite 302
Brighton, MA 02135
617-782-5033
FAX: 617-782-5735 800-323-1088
editor@igigroup.com
www.igigroup.com

Paul Polishuk, President/CEO
Hui Pan, Conference Director
Bev Wilson, Managing Editor

Provides coverage of standards activities around the world, schedules of standards meetings, the availablity of standards, and how to obtain standards, minutes of standards meetings and drafts of standards. *$695.00*
Monthly Founded: 1977

20772 Telecommunications Mergers and Acquisitions
IGI group
320 Washington Street
Suite 302
Brighton, MA 02135
617-782-5033
FAX: 617-782-5735 800-323-1088
editor@igigroup.com
www.igigroup.com

Paul Polishuk, President/CEO
Hui Pan, Conference Director
Bev Wilson, Managing Editor

Covers worldwide developments in the telecommunications mergers and acquisitions. In addition to reporting to these activities, the newsletter analyzes potential merger and acquisition candidates, summarizes in an easy-to-read form trends by different companies and industry requirements. *$695.00*
Monthly Founded: 1977

20773 Telecommunications Reports International
BRP Publications
111 Eighth Avenue
7th Floor
New York, NY 10011-4707
212-771-0600
FAX: 212-771-0885 800-234-1660
jrohaly@aspenpublishers.com
http://www.aspenpublishers.com

Andrew Jacobson, Publisher
George Brandon, Editor
Jim Monahan, President
Richard H Kravitz, Execitive VP

International telecom policy and trade issues, global services, satellites, tariffs and financial developments. *$1789.00*
24 issues per y

20774 Telemarketing Update
Prosperity & Profits Unlimited
PO Box 416
Denver, CO 80201-0416
303-573-5564

AC Doyle, Publisher

Telemarketing script presentation suggestions and ideas. *$200.00*
8 pages Annual
Circulation: 2,000
Printed in on matte stock

20775 Telemarketing Update-Catering Service Business Script Presentations
Prosperity & Profits Unlimited
PO Box 416
Denver, CO 80201-0416
303-573-5564

A Doyle, Editor

Catering service telemarketing script presentations. *$19.95*
10 pages Irregular Founded: 1990
Circulation: 2,100 Audited
Printed in 1 color on matte stock

20776 VoiceNews
Stoneridge Technical Services
PO Box 1891
Rockville, MD 20849-1891
301-424-0114
FAX: 301-424-8971

William Creitz, Publisher/Editor

Covers voice technology for telecommunications and office automation: voice messaging, voice response, speech recognition, speech synthesis. *$25.00*

20777 Why Not An Answering Service?
Prosperity & Profits Unlimited
PO Box 416
Denver, CO 80201-0416
303-573-5564

A Doyle, Editor

Offers information and ideas on telephone answering service possibilities. *$29.95*
73 pages Every Five Years Founded: 1989
Circulation: 5,000
Printed in on matte stock

20778 Wireless Market Stats
Kagan World Media
1 Lower Ragsdale Drive
Building One Suite 130
Monterey, CA 93940-8746
831-624-1536
FAX: 831-625-3225 800-307-2529
info@kagan.com www.kagan.com

George Niesen, Editor
Tom Johnson, Marketing Manager

In-depth analysis of metropolitan and rural cellular market efficiency, plus operating statistics, private deal market data, economic and demographic data for narrowband and broadband PCS, ESMR, paging and more. *$1095.00*
Monthly Founded: 1969

20779 Wireless Satellite and Broadcasting

IGI Group
320 Washington Street
Suite 302
Brighton, MA 02135
617-782-5033
FAX: 617-782-5735 800-323-1088
editor@igigroup.com
www.igigroup.com

Paul Polishuk, Publisher
Hui Pan, Conference Director
Bev Wilson, Managing Editor

Subjects covered include: market opportunities, technology, international developments, regulation/policy, standards, applications, procurements, PCN, market forecasts, new products, mergers/acquisitions, joint ventures and more. *$695.00*
Monthly Founded: 1977 : pdf

20780 Wireless Telecom Investor
Kagan World Media
One Lower Ragsdale Drive
Building One, Suite 130
Monterey, CA 93940-8746
831-624-1536
FAX: 831-625-3225 800-307-2529
info@kagan.com www.kagan.com

George Niesen, Editor
Tom Johnson, Marketing Manager

Exclusive analysis of private and public values of wireless telecommunications companies, including cellular telephone, ESMR and PCS. Exclusive databases of subscribers, market penetrations, market potential, industry growth. Catching super-fast growth in a capsule. *$1095.00*
Monthly Founded: 1969

20781 Wireless Week
Chilton Company
600 S Cherry Street
Suite 400
Denver, CO 80246-1706
303-393-7449
FAX: 303-399-2034

Tom Brooksher, Publisher
Judith Lockwood, Editor

Covers the wireless telecommunications industry.

Circulation: 32,000

20782 Worldwide Videotex Update
Worldwide Videotex
Po Box 3273
Boynton Beach, FL 33424
561-738-2276

markedit@juno.com
www.wvpubs.com
Reports news and information on videotex, The Internet, online services, electronic mail, satellite communications and television related technologies, such as teleconferencing and teletext. *$25.00*
Monthly

20783 XDSL
IGI Group
320 Washington Street
Suite 302
Boston, MA 02135
617-782-5033
FAX: 617-782-5735 800-323-1088
bmark@igigroup.com
www.igigroup.com

Paul Polishuk, President/CEO
Hui Panb, Conference Director
Bev Wilson, Managing Editor

Subjects covered include: field trials, applicatins, competition ffrom cable and satellite, new products, Telco plans, fiber optics, market forecasts, techology developments, wireless, major player strategies, cable modems, ISDN and more. *$695.00*
Monthly Founded: 1977 : pdf

Magazines & Journals

20784 ACUTA Journal of Communications Technology in Higher Education
ACUTA
152 W Zandale Drive
Suite 200
Lexington, KY 40503-2486
859-278-3338
FAX: 859-278-3268
pscott@acuta.org
http://www.acuta.org

Pat Scott, Editor
Tamara Closs, President
Jerry A Simmer, Director

Journal is distributed to telecom, information management professionals at colleges and universities, along with industry professionals with products and services for the higher education vertical market. *$80.00*
48 pages Quarterly Founded: 1997
Circulation: 2320
Mailing list available for rent 2,300 names
Printed in 4 colors on matte stock

20785 America's Network
Questex Media Group
201 E Sandpointe Avenue
Suite 600
Santa Ana, CA 92707-8700
714-513-8400
FAX: 714-513-8481 800-854-3112
psemple@advanstar.com
www.americasnetwork.com

Paul Semple, Publisher
Bill Pettit, National Sales Director

Independent reporting and business analysis of telecommunications technologies for today's public network. *$100.00*
Monthly
Circulation: 60,006

20786 Audiotex Update
Worldwide Videotex
PO Box 3273
Boynton Beach, FL 33424-3273
561-738-2276

markedit@juno.com
www.wvpubs.com

Mark E Wright, Editor

Provides the latest news and infromation about the audiotex industry, including voice processing information, products, services, as well as research and development. *$165.00*
Monthly Founded: 1981

20787 Business Communications Review
BCR Enterprises
999 Oakmont Plaza Drive
Suite 100
Westmont, IL 60559-1381
630-986-1432
FAX: 630-323-5324 800-227-1234
info@bcr.com www.bcr.com

Fred Knight, Publisher

Offers a complete package of the latest information for persons associated with the communications industry. *$45.00*
80 pages Monthly Founded: 1971

20788 CTI the Authority on Computer, Internet, & Network Telephony
Technology Marketing Corporation
One Technology Plaza
Norwalk, CT 06854
203-852-6800
FAX: 203-853-2845 800-243-6002
ctipress@tmcnet.com
http://www.tmcnet.com

Richard Tehrani, Group Publisher
Nadji Tehrani, CEO/President
Greg Galitzine, Editorial Director
Anthony Graffeo, National Advertising Sales Manager

Provides tutorials, application stories, and new product listings and reviews, as well as service information. Emphasizes furthering the development, implementation and use of CTI technology.
Monthly Founded: 1998
Circulation: 50256

20789 Cabling Business
Cabling Publications
12035 Shiloh Road
Suite 350
Dallas, TX 75228-1591
214-328-1717
FAX: 214-319-6077
russell@cablingbusiness.com
www.cablingbusiness.com

Russell Paulov, Editor-in-Chief
Christy Sheeran, Business Manager
Rita Paulov, Senior Sales Associate
David Deal, Webmaster
Margaret Patterson, Managing Editor

New product information, troubleshooting hints, and information on installation and repair.
Monthly
Circulation: 24070

20790 Cabling Installation & Maintenance
PennWell Publishing Company
PennWell
1421 S Sheridan Road
Tulsa, OK 74112
603-891-0123
FAX: 603-891-0587
patrick@pennwell.com
www.omeda.com/cgi-win/

Patrick McLaughlin, Chief Editor
Steve Smith, Executive Editor

Emphasizes the problem solving aspects of cable installation in telecommunications, data, and video systems.
Monthly Founded: 1993
Circulation: 23604

20791 Call Center Magazine
Miller Freeman Publications
11 Est 19th Street
3rd Floor
New York, NY 10011
212-600-3000
FAX: 212-691-1191
msteiger@cmp.com
www.callcentermagazine.com

Keith Dawson, Editor
Max Steiger, Sales Manager

Dedicated to providing in-depth and unbiased product and strategic information for call center executives.
Monthly
Circulation: 32904

20792 Communication Theory
International Communication Association
U de Montreal, Department de Communication
CP 6128 Succursale Centre-Ville
Montreal, QB H3C-3J7

communicationtheory@umontreal.ca.
www.icahdq.org
Francois Cooren, Editor
Publishes research articles, theoretical essays, and reviews on topics of broad theoretical interest from across the range of communication studies. Recognizes that approaches to theory develpment and explication are diverse.

20793 Communication Yearbook
International Communication Association
Ohio University, School of Communication Study
210 Lasher Hall
Athens, OH 45701
740-593-9167

beck@ohio.edu www.icahdq.org
Dr Christina S. Beck, Editor
Features state-of-the discipline literature reviews of communication research. Highlights reviews of research exploring communication concepts that span traditional 'division' divides, issues of central importance to the accomplishment of communication in a variety of contexts and for diverse communicators throughout the world.

20794 Communications Billing Report
Telecommunications Reports International
1333 H Street NW
#100-E
Washington, DC 20005-4707
202-842-3022
FAX: 202-842-1875 www.tr.com
Victoria Mason, Editor-in-Chief
Content provides hard-to-find facts on such issues as developing internet electronic payment systems, keeping on top of new outsourcing opportunities, enhancing customer care and back office functions and making the most of new software developments. *$765.00*
BiWeekly

20795 Communications Crossroads
United States Telecom Association
1401 H Street NW
Suite 600
Washington, DC 20005
202-326-7300
FAX: 202-326-7339
editor@usta.org www.usta.org
Walter B McCormick Jr, President/CEO
Dedicated to the success stories, investment opportunities and industry events that herald the future of small and rural carriers. *$60.00*
Founded: 2006
Circulation: 3500

20796 Global Telephony
Primedia
330 N Wabash Avenua
Suite 2300
Chicago, IL 60611
312-595-1080
FAX: 312-595-0295
www.primediabusiness.com
Larry Lannon, Publisher
Carol Wilson, Editor
Telephony delivers timely and intelligent coverage of the news, technologies and business strategies driving the industry.
24/Yr
Circulation: 63,500

20797 Handbooks of Communication Series
International Communication Association
Dept of Comm, University of Colorado at Boulder
270 UCB
Boulder, CO 80309-0270
303-492-6498
FAX: 303-492-8411
robert.craig@colorado.edu
www.icahdq.org
Robert T Craig, Editor
Linda Bathgate, Senior Editor
Handbooks that serve as benchmark summaries of current communication scholarship and will set the agenda for future theory and research in the communication discipline. Series will consider content areas in communication research, methodological approches to communication research, and theoretical lenses for scholarship in communication.

20798 Human Communication Research
International Communication Association
Dept of Communication Arts & Science,234 Sparks
Pennsylvania State University
University Park, PA 16802
814-865-3461
FAX: 814-863-7986
jpd16@psu.edu www.icahdq.org
James P Dillard, Editor
Presents empirical work in any area of human communication. Advances the understanding of human symbolic processes, so there is a strong emphasis on theory-driven research, the development of new theoretical models in communication, and the development of innovative methods for observing and measuring communication behavior.
Quarterly

20799 ICA Communique
International Communications Association

1730 Rhode Island Avenue NW
Suite 300
Washington, DC 20036
202-530-9855
FAX: 202-530-9851
icahdq@icahdq.org www.icahdq.org
Angela Gallagher, Editor
Michael Haley, Executive Director
Association news. *$135.00*
10/Year Founded: 1950

20800 IEEE Communications Magazine
Institute of Electrical & Electronics Engineers
3 Park Avenue
17th FLR
New York, NY 10016-5902
212-705-8900
FAX: 212-705-8999
publications@comsoc.org
www.comsoc.org
Joseph Milizzo, Assistant Publisher
Eric Levine, Associate Publisher
Roch Glitho, Editor-in-Chief
Written in tutorial applications-driven style by the industry's leading experts. IEEE Communications Magazine delivers usable information on the latest international coverage of current issues and advances in key areas. *$20.00*
Monthly
Circulation: 43832

20801 IEEE Network
IEEE Operations Center
445 Hoes Lane
#3014
Piscataway, NJ 08855-0459
732-981-0060
FAX: 732-981-0225
publications@comsoc.org
www.cosmoc.org
Thomas Plevyak, Publisher
The magazine of Global Internetworking provides the most current information for communications professionals involved with the interconnection of computing systems.
Bi-Monthly

20802 Intele-Card News
Quality Publishing
523 N Sam Houston Parkway E
Suite 300
Houston, TX 77060
281-272-2744
FAX: 281-847-5752 800-792-6397
info@intelecard.com
www.intelecard.com
Theresa Ward, Editor-in-Chief
Jo Ann Davy, Managing Editor
Laurette Veres, Owner
Reports on news and events impacting the business of telephone cards, identifies significant trends and profiles industry newsmakers.
Monthly Founded: 1995
Circulation: 12000

20803 Journal of Communication
International Communication Association
Department of Communication-101
Burton Hall
University of Oklahoma
Norman, OK 73019
405-325-9503

joc@ou.edu www.icahdq.org
Michael Pfau, Editor
A general forum for communication scholarship and publishes articles and book reviews examining a broad range of issues in communication theory and research. Publishes the best available scholarship on all aspects of communication.

20804 Journal of Computer-Mediated Communication
International Communication Association

FAX: 812-855-6166
jcmc@indiana.edu
http://jcmc.indiana.edu
Susan C Herring, Editor
Well-based journal that publishes scholarship on computer-mediated communication. Publishes most empirical research making use of social science methods, which should be presented according to the accepted standards for each method.

20805 Lightwave
PennWell Publishing Company
1421 S Sheridan Road
Tulsa, OK 74112
918-835-3161
FAX: 603-891-0574 800-331-4463
stephenh@pennwell.com
www.light-wave.com

Stephen M Hardy, Editorial Director
Carrie Meadows, Managing Editor
Meghan Fuller, Senior News Editor
Matt Vincent, Associate Editor/Web Editor

An international journal of fiber optics that covers all applications of the technology in telecommunications, data communications, broadcast and cable TV and specialized military applications. *$137.00*
224 pages Monthly Founded: 1910
Printed in 4 colors on matte stock

20806 Locating, Testing and Repairing
Stober Research and Communications
PO Box 517
McHenry, IL 60051
815-385-6123
FAX: 815-385-7151 www.ltrmag.com

L Jack Stober, Publisher

Information on copper and fiber optic sets available for telecommunication applications, as well as listings of companies and categories of this equipment. Regular departments contain fault locating and test equipment tips, a new product showcase and a look at new industry literature. *$100.00*
Quarterly Founded: 1998
Circulation: 27355

20807 Mobile Communication Business
Phillips Business Information
7811 Montrose Road
Suite 2
Potomac, MD 20854-3394
301-340-2100
FAX: 301-659-5927 www.phillips.com

Don Steele, Editor

Offers information and the latest technological advances in telecommunications.
Monthly Founded: 1985

20808 Multimedia Telecommunication News
Stoneridge Technical Services
PO Box 1891
Rockville, MD 20849-1891
301-424-0114
FAX: 301-424-8971
www.stoneridgetech.com

William W Creitz, Editor

Focuses on new products, applications, technological developments, markets and company activites.
Monthly

20809 NTCA Exchange
National Telephone Cooperative Association
4121 Wilson Boulevard
Suite 1000
Arlington, VA 22203-1617
703-351-2000
FAX: 703-351-2001 www.ntca.org

Jennifer Mayne, Managing Editor

Bi-monthly newsletter examining association and member news, including profiles, business tips and member updates. *$15.00*
Bi-Monthly Founded: 1980
Circulation: 5100

20810 Network Magazine
CMP Media
600 Community Drive
Manhasset, NY 11030
516-562-5000
FAX: 516-562-7013 866-880-8219
cmp@cmp.com www.cmp.com

Art Wittmann, Editor
Paula McGinlinchey, Publisher

Network Magazine serves communications carriers, communications service providers including interexchange/PTT's/long distance carriers, business services (non-computer) and other industry organizations. *$175.00*
162 pages Monthly Founded: 1986
Circulation: 125000
Printed in 4 colors on matte stock

20811 Networks Update
Worldwide Videotex
Po Box 3273
Boynton Beach, FL 33424
561-738-2276

markedit@juno.com
www.wvpubs.com

Provides the latest news and information about the computer network industry. This includes national, international, public, private, and military network products, services, companies, marketing strategies, and research and development. *$25.00*
Monthly

20812 Opastco Roundtable
OPASTCO
21 Dupont Circle NW
Suite 700
Washington, DC 20036-1544
202-659-5990
FAX: 202-659-4619
roundtable@opastco.org
www.opastco.org

Martha Silver, Editor
John Rose, President

Provides practical, how-to information that small local exchange carriers can use in their day-to-day operations, as well as plain English explanations of industry issues and technologies.
BiMonthly

20813 Outside Plant
Practical Communications
220 N Smith St
Ste 228
Palatine, IL 60067-2488
847-202-4683
FAX: 847-639-9542
sharon@ospmag.com
www.ospmag.com

Sharon Stober, VP/Editorial Director
Karen Adolphson, Managing Editor
Mary Beth Koelling, Executive Director Sales/Marketing

Magazine for telecom outside plant professionals. Reaches ASP engineers, planners, managers and technicians in Bell and independent phone companies. *$30.00*
100 pages Monthly Founded: 1983
Circulation: 25000

20814 Pen Computing Magazine
Pen Computing Publishing Office
120 Bethpage Road
Suite 300
Hicksville, NY 11801
516-433-8725
FAX: 516-433-8724
cb@pencomputing.com
www.pencomputing.com

Howard Borgen, Publisher
Lisa Krebs, VP Advertising
Wayne Laslo, Advertising Manager
Conrad H Blickenstorfer, Editor-in-Chief
David MacNeill, Executive Editor

Bi-Monthly print journal of pen-based and mobile computing. Hardware and software reviews, expert opinions, feature articles, case studies, how-to, industry news, technical primers and more. *$18.00*
Bi-Monthly Founded: 1993
Circulation: 79515

20815 Phone Plus International
Virgo Publishing
3300 N Central Avenue
Suite 2500
Phoenix, AZ 85012-79
480-990-1101
FAX: 480-990-0819
cs@vpico.com www.vpico.com

Mike Saxby, Group Publisher
Khali Henderson, Group Editor, Telecom Division
Margie Beall, Traffic Coordinator
Kyle Blair, Marketing/Communications Manager

Premier magazine for VoIP, data, wireless, internet and content solutions for the channel. *$80.00*
Monthly
Circulation: 20000

20816 QST
American Radio Relay League
225 Main Street
Newington, CT 06111-1494
860-594-0200
FAX: 860-594-0259 888-277-5289
webmaster@arrl.org www.arrl.org

David Sumner, CEO
Allen Pitts, Media Relations

Geared at the IRF and amatuer radio operators industry, provides information on communications theory and technical advances in design and construction. The official journal of the American Radio Relay League. *$24.00*
Monthly Founded: 1915
Circulation: 7000

20817 RCR Wireless News
Crain Communications
1746 Cole Blvd
Suite 150
Golden, CO 80401
303-733-2500
FAX: 303-733-9941 888-909-9111
subs@crain.com www.rcrnews.com

John Sudmeier, Publisher/VP
Tracy Ford, Associate Publisher/Editor
Dan Meyer, Managing Editor
Mary Pemberton, Advertising Director
Pete Racelis, President

News and analysis of the wireless communications industry. *$69.00*
Weekly Founded: 1981
Circulation: 65000 $190 per M.
Printed in on matte stock

20818 Satellite Business News
Satellite Business News
1990 M Street NW
Suite 510
Washington, DC 20036-3102
202-785-0505
FAX: 202-785-9291
general.mail@satbiznews.com
www.satbiznews.com

Bob Scherman, Publisher
Jeffrey Williams, Managing Editor
Charlie Ergen, CEO/President

Up-to-date news on satellite television industry, upcoming events, and new technology for the industry. *$44.75*
Bi-annually Founded: 1983
Circulation: 565700

20819 Satellite News
Phillips Business Information
9420 Key West Ave
Rockville, MD 20850-43
301-279-4200
FAX: 301-424-2709 866-279-1930
information@phillips.com
http://www.phillips.com
Beth McNamara, Publisher
Robert Phillips, CEO
Information on satellite launches, companies rebounding from losses, blows to competitors and regulatory issues.
Weekly Founded: 1974
Circulation: 18000

20820 Satellite Week
Warren Publishing
2115 Ward Court NW
Washington, DC 20037
202-872-9200
FAX: 202-318-8350 800-771-9202
info@warren-news.com
www.warren-news.com
Albert Warren, Chairman, Editor, Publisher
Paul Warren, President, Executive Publisher
Daniel Warren, Vice Chairman, Executive Editor
R Michael Feazel, Managing Editor
The definitive weekly source for fast-breaking, international news on space communications policy, regularion, technology and business. Offers up-to-date, comprehensive reports on new technologies, notices of international advances, details about regulation and deregularion, satellite marketplace intelligence, news of DBS developments, and continuous coverage of what industry leaders are doing and saying.
Weekly Founded: 1945

20821 Sound & Communications
Testa Communications
25 Willowdale Avenue
Port Washington, NY 11050-3779
516-767-2500
FAX: 516-767-9335 800-937-7678
testa@testa.com
www.testacommunications.com
Vincent P Testa, President
David A. Silverman, Editor
Covers sound, display, security and multimedia systems, also theory and applications.
Monthly Founded: 1955
Circulation: 22500

20822 Sound & Video Contractor
Primedia
PO Box 12914
Overland Park, KS 66282
913-341-1300
FAX: 913-967-1903
mjohnson@premediabusiness.com
www.svconline.com
Mark Johnson, Editor
Trevor Boyer, Associate Editor
Trevor Boyer, Associate Editor
Contains information on sound systems, video display, security, CCTV, home theater, and automation. Delivers in depth instruction and examples of successful installations, fundamental acoustical and video theory and news on new technologies eaffecting the systems contracting business. *$35.00*
Monthly Founded: 1983
Circulation: 21,000
Mailing list available for rent 20,500 names $110 per M.

20823 Sys Admin
CMP Media
1601 W 23rd Street
Suite 200
Lawrence, KS 66046
785-838-3126
FAX: 785-841-2047
aankerholz@cmp.com
www.sysadminmag.com
Amber Ankerhola, Editor-in-Chief
SYS ADMIN serves the Unix and Linux system administration market. *$39.00*
100 pages Monthly Founded: 1992 27000 names $195 per M.
Printed in on glossy stock

20824 TELEconference Magazine
Applied Business Telecommunications
201 Sandpoint Ave
Suite 600
Santa Ana, CA 92707-8700
714-513-8400
FAX: 714-513-8680 800-854-3112
Keith Gallagher, Publisher
Paul DeVeaux, Editor
Devoted to the field of teleconferencing and contains in-depth articles to provide updates on audio/graphic and video teleconferencing applications, trends and developments. *$10.00*
Founded: 1992
Circulation: 15000

20825 Telecommunications
Horizon House Publications
685 Canton Street
Norwood, MA 02062-2608
781-769-9750
FAX: 781-762-9071
editorial@telecommagazine.com
www.telecommagazine.com
David B Egan, Group Publisher
Robert Bass, Production Manager
Bob Wallace, Editor
Charles A Ayotte, CEO/President
William Harrison, Manager
Communication technology and market developments for users, service providers and manufacturers worldwide.
Monthly Founded: 1960
Circulation: 80854

20826 Telephone IP News
Worldwide Videotex
Po Box 3273
Boynton Beach, FL 33424
561-738-2276

markedit@juno.com
www.wvpubs.com
Provides news and information concerning the information provider (IP) industry for telephone services and two-way paging and wireless information services. Reports on new products available to providers and monitors public service commission rulings as they aplly to information services. *$25.00*
Monthly

20827 Telephony
Telephony Division
One IBM Plaza
Suite 2300
Chicago, IL 10151
312-595-1080
FAX: 312-595-0296
telephony@prismb2b.com
http://www.primedia.com
Mark Hickey, Publisher
Dan O'Shea, Editor-in-Chief
Kim Brower, Marketing Manager
Written for professionals involved in management, construction, maintenance and marketing of modern telecommunication systems. Focus is on new, technical advances, filed applications and management techniques. *$3.00*
Weekly Founded: 1989
Circulation: 59000

20828 Wire Journal International
Wire Association International
1570 Boston Post Road
PO Box 578
Guilford, CT 06437
203-453-2777
FAX: 203-453-8384
mmarselli@wirenet.org
www.wirenet.org
Brian A Bouvier, President
Steven J Fetteroll, Executive Director
Mark A Marselli, Editor-in-Chief
Janice E Swindells, Director of Marketing Services
Robert J Xeller, Director Sales
The leading technical publication for the wire and cable industry. Written for executives, engineers, technical and sales professionals, and purchasing agents engaged in the manufacture of ferrous and nonferrous wire and cable; electrical wire and cable; fiber optic cable; and formed and fabricated wire products.
Monthly Founded: 1930
Circulation: 13434
Printed in 4 colors on glossy stock

20829 Worldwide Telecom
Worldwide Videotex
Po Box 3273
Boynton Beach, FL 33424
561-738-2276

markedit@juno.com
www.wvpubs.com
Provides the latest news and information on international telecommunication products, services, and contracts. The emphasis is on U.S. telecommunications companies doing business in foreign markets and on products with a potential market overseas. *$25.00*
Monthly

20830 XCHANGE
Virgo Publishing
3300 N Central Avenue Suite 2500
PO Box 40079
Phoenix, AZ 85067-79
480-990-1101
FAX: 480-675-8181
cs@vpico.com www.xchangemag.com
Mike Saxby, Group Publisher
Paula Bernier, Editor-in-Chief
Megan McCoy, Managing Editor
Tara Seals, Associate Editor
Kyle Blair, Marketing/Communications
Strategic window on developments of vital concern to facilities-based providers in the competitive local exchange marketplace.
Annual+ Founded: 1996
Circulation: 35,003

20831 Yellow Pages Industry Sourcebook
SIMBA Information
60 Long Ridge Road
Suite 300
Stamford, CT 06902
203-258-8193
FAX: 203-325-8915
info@simbanet.com
www.simbanet.com
Linda Kopp, Editorial Director
Kathy Mickey, Managing Editor
Lists key officers, revenues, leading books, major accounts, sales offices and suppliers for more than 1500 firms involved in yellow pages publishing. *$99.00*

Trade Shows

20832 AFCEA TechNet Asia-Pacific
Armed Forces Communications and Electronics Assn
4400 Fair Lakes Court
Fairfax, VA 22033
703-631-6200
FAX: 703-654-6931 800-564-4220
technet@jspargo.com www.afcea.org
Paul doCarmo, Assistant Director/Exhibit Sales
Connie Shaw, Exhibit Sales Account Manager
Military, government and industry communications and electronics professionals gather to see exhibits of communications and electronics equipment, supplies and services.
2000 Attendees November/Annual
Founded: 1985

20833 AFCEA Technical Committee Tech Forum TechNet International
AFCEA Headquarters
4400 Fair Lakes Court
Fairfax, VA 22033-3899
703-631-6100
FAX: 703-631-6169 800-336-4583
service@afcea.org www.afcea.org
Herbert Browne, President
One of the nation's largest C4I conventions and expositions and features numerous professional development opportunities and tremendous networking opportunies.

20834 AFCEA/USNI West Conference & Exposition
Armed Forces Communications and Electronics Assn
4400 Fair Lakes Court
Fairfax, VA 22033
703-631-6200
FAX: 703-654-6931 800-564-4220
west@jspargo.org www.afcea.org
Paul doCarmo, Assistant Director/Exhibit Sales
Connie Shaw, Exhibit Sales Account Manager
Over 350 of the industry's most recognized defense and technology organizations showcase their technology products and services to top decision-makers from the US Pacific Fleet, Naval Station San Diego, Space & Warfare Command, Naval Base Coronado, Camp Pendleton Marine Corps Base and many other west coast military and government facilities.
6000 Attendees January/Annual Founded: 1980

20835 AIIM Annual Conference and Expo
Association for Information and Image Management
1100 Wayne Avenue
Suite 1100
Silver Spring, MD 20910-5603
301-587-8202
FAX: 301-587-2711 888-552-4346
aiim@aiim.org www.aiimexpo.com
Kim Gallozzi, Event Contact
John Mancini, President
The leading industry event for Enterprise Content and Document Management, which encompasses the technologies and strategies used to capture, manage, share, and store documents and digital content.
April

20836 Antenna Measurement Techniques Association Show
6065 Roswell Road
Suite 2252
Atlanta, GA 30328
770-864-3488
FAX: 770-864-3491 www.amta.org
Janet O'Neil, Contact
Antenna test equipment, supplies and services for government, private and institutional laboratories involved in design and development.

20837 Association for Communications Technology Professionals in Higher Education
ACUTA
152 W Zandale Drive
Suite 200
Lexington, KY 40503-2486
859-278-3338
FAX: 859-278-3268
kbowman@acuta.org www.acuta.org
Kellie Bowman, Registration
Jeri Semer, Executive Director
Annual conference and exhibits of educational telecommunications equipment, supplies and services. Containing 95 booths.
600 Attendees Annual Founded: 1971

20838 Association of Teleservices International Conference
ATSI
12 Academy Avenue
Atkinson, NH 03811
FAX: 603-362-9486 866-896-2874
admin@atsi.org www.atsi.org
Lori Jenkins, President
Marcy Hewlett, Convention Chair
Exhibits of interest to telephone answering and voice message providers. *$575.00*
800+ Attendees Founded: 1942

20839 Cable-Tec Expo
Society of Cable Telecommunications Engineers
140 Philips Road
Exton, PA 19341-1318
610-524-1725
FAX: 610-363-5898 800-542-5040
info@scte.org http://expo.scte.org
Heather Gosciniak, Director
The Society's Cable-Tec Expo is the premier industry hardware exhibition that also offers an engineering conference, workshops and meetings. Expo contains more than 500 booths and 400 exhibits. *$525.00*
12M Attendees Annual

20840 Call Center Conference and Exposition
CMP Media
11 West 19th Street
New York, NY 10011
FAX: 212-600-3080 888-428-3976
CCEventInfo@cmp.com
www.cmpevents.com
Joni Mitchell, Marketing Manager
Joy Cerequas, Director Events
125 booths, plus conference covering all applications of new technologies and services in call processing, transaction processing and telemarketing. *$1595.00*
2.5M Attendees February

20841 GLOBALCOMM
Telecommunications Industry Association
2500 Wilson Boulevard
Suite 300
Arlington, VA 22201-3834
703-907-7700
FAX: 703-907-7727
mwaters@tiaonline.org
www.tiaonline.org
Matthew J Flanigan, President
Mary Piper Waters, Manager Meetings/Special Events
Annual conference and exhibits of telecommunications equipment and services.

20842 IEEE Communications Expo IEEE Globecom
J Spargo & Associates
11208 Waples Mill Road
Suite 112
Fairfax, VA 22030
703-631-6200
FAX: 703-654-6931 800-564-4220
ieee@jspargo.com www.ieee.org
Connie Shaw, Exhibit Sales Account Manager
In addition to targeting IEEE Communications Society members, also draws companies from Silicon Valley, Northern California, and the Pacific Rim, who manufacture or distribute products or services to support wireless technologies, optical networking, the Internet, or the telecom marketplace.
2000 Attendees November

20843 International Wireless Communication Expo
6300 S Syracuse Way
Suite 650
Englewood, CO 80111-6726
303-904-0407
rugianskis@prismb2b.com
www.iwceexpo.com
Rita Ugianskis, Group Show Director
Laura Magliola, Marketing Manager
The one place where all industries and communications professionals come together to share thoughts and ideas on wireless communications technologies.
6.5M Attendees March

20844 NATOA Annual Conference
Nat'l Assn of Telecommunication Officer & Advisors
1800 Diagonal Road
Suite 495
Alexandria, VA 22314
703-519-8035
FAX: 703-519-8036
info@natoa.org www.natoa.org
Elizabeth Beaty, Executive Director
Jennifer Harman, Manager Operations
Containing 30 booths featuring telecommunications equipment and supplies. Cable operators and local governments. Educational sessions topics include technology, competitive markets, programming, and cable franchise administration.
700 Attendees September

20845 NEAX 2400 IMS Users Group
455 St Andrews Road
Columbia, SC 29221-0886
803-798-4800
www.necusergroup.com
Carlisle Reames, Contact
15 booths of educational sessions for NEC 2400 DBX systems users.
350 Attendees April

20846 Public-Safety Communication Officials International Conference & Expo
351 N Williamson Boulevard
Daytona Beach, FL 32114-1112
386-322-2500
FAX: 386-322-2501 888-272-6911
apco@apco911.org www.apco911.org
George S Rice, Executive Director
Barbara Myers, Conference/Meeting Services
Banquet, breakfast and 200 exhibitors of radio, computer, and supporting equipment companies.
6000 Attendees Annual Founded: 1935

20847 TechNet North 2006
AFCEA Canada & AFCEA International
102 Centrepointe Drive
Ottawa, ON K2G-6B1
613-786-2619
FAX: 613-230-1554
kevin@expocorpinc.com
www.technetnorth.com
Kevin d'Entremont, Exhibit Director
Rick Tachuk, Marketing & Communications Director
Delivers an inovative professional development conference and a major trade exhibition focused on the latest C4ISR solutions, products and technologies for the North American defense and security sectors.

20848 Telecom
1401 H Street NW
Suite 600
Washington, DC 20005-2164
202-547-2680
FAX: 202-326-7333 www.usta.org
Walter B McCormick Jr, President/CEO
Conference and exhibition offers a variety of educational sessions, special interest seminars and keynote speakers. The show features an estimated 160 exhibitors.
1300 Attendees Annual

20849 Utilities Telecommunications Council Annual Conference and Exhibition
Utilities Telecommunications Council
1140 Connecticut Avenue NW
Washington, DC 20036-4001
202-872-0030
FAX: 202-872-1331
William Moroney, President
Annual conference and exhibits of telecommunications equipment and services.
1,000 Attendees

20850 Wire Expo
Wire Association International
1570 Boston Post Road
PO Box 578
Guilford, CT 06437-0578
203-453-2777
FAX: 203-453-8384 www.wirenet.org
Livia Jacobs, Manager Convention/Events
Wire Expo provides you with ready-made opportunities—including meeting with more than 450 suppliers on the show floor. You'll gain manufacturing and technical information by attending short courses and listening to some of the 75+ paper that will be presented at WCTS. Social events also provide oppertunities to make conections with other professionals in the wire industry.
4000 Attendees May/June Founded: 1930

Directories & Databases

20851 Audiotex Directory
ADBG Publishing
PO Box 25929
Los Angeles, CA 90025-0929
310-914-9000
FAX: 310-479-0654
Larry Podell, Editor
Over 1,200 product and service suppliers in the voice processing fax, and audiotex fields, including hardware, software, vendors, telephone companies, service bureaus, audio programmers, and consultants
$50.00
Annual

20852 Bacon's Internet Media Directory
Bacon's Publishing Company
332 S Michigan Avenue
Chicago, IL 60604-4434
312-228-8239
FAX: 312-922-3127 866-639-5087
info@bacons.com www.bacons.com
Steve Newman, CEO
Joe Bernardo, COO
Brian Birkholz, CFO
Peter Granat, Sr VP/Marketing
Information about online editors and media.
$300.00
Annual Founded: 1932
Printed in 1 color on matte stock : internet

20853 Bacon's Radio/TV/Cable Directory
Bacon's Publishing Company
332 S Michigan Avenue
Chicago, IL 60604-4434
312-228-8239
FAX: 312-922-3127 866-639-5087
info@bacons.com www.bacons.com
Steve Newman, CEO
Joe Bernard, COO
Ruth McFarland, Sr VP/Publisher
Includes expanded listings for television and radio stations in major markets.
$350.00
Annual
Printed in 1 color on matte stock : internet

20854 Communication News: Network Access Directory
Nelson Publishing
250 Tamiami Trail N
Nokomis, FL 34275-3482
941-966-9521
FAX: 941-966-2590
Curt Harler, Editor *$7.00*
Annual, June
Circulation: 71,000

20855 Communications News: Broadband Directory
Nelson Publishing
2504 Tamiami Trail N
Nokomis, FL 34275-3482
941-966-9521
FAX: 941-966-2590
Curt Harler, Editor *$7.00*
Annual, December
Circulation: 71,000

20856 Communications News: PBX/CTI Directory
Nelson Publishing
2504 Tamiami Trail N
Nokomis, FL 34275-3482
941-966-9521
FAX: 941-966-2590
Curt Harler, Editor *$7.00*
Annual, April
Circulation: 71,000

20857 Communications News: Test Directory
Nelson Publishing
2504 Tamiami Trail N
Nokomis, FL 34275-3482
941-669-9521
FAX: 941-966-2590
Curt Harler, Editor *$7.00*
Annual, February
Circulation: 71,000

20858 Communications News: Video/ Audioconferencing Directory
Nelson Publishing
2504 Tamiami Trail N
Nokomis, FL 34275-3482
941-966-9521
FAX: 941-966-2590
Curt Harler, Editor *$7.00*
Annual, October
Circulation: 71,000

20859 Communications News: Wireless Directory
Nelson Publishing
2504 Tamiami Trail N
Nokomis, FL 34275-3482
941-966-9521
FAX: 941-966-2590
Curt Harler, Editor *$7.00*
Annual, August
Circulation: 71,000

20860 Complete Directory of Telephones & Accessories
Sutton Family Communications & Publishing Company
155 Sutton Lane
Fordsville, KY 42343
270-740-0870

jlsutton@apex.net
www.fleamarketeer.net

Theresa Sutton, Editor
Lee Sutton, General Manager

Print-out from database of wholesalers, manufacturers, distributors, importers and close-out houses. Database is updated daily to guarantee the most current and up-to-date sources available. *$55.20*
100+ pages

20861 Corporate Yellow Book
Leadership Directories
104 5th Avenue
New York, NY 10011-6901
212-627-4140
FAX: 212-645-0931
info@leadershipdirectories.com
www.leadershipdirectories.com

Vonessa Ruffins, Editor

Contact information for over 48,000 executives at over 1,000 companies and more than 9,000 board members and their outside affiliations. *$420.00*
1,400 pages Quarterly Founded: 1986
50,000 names $105 per M. : CD-Rom

20862 Directory of Communications Professionals
National Assn of Regulatory Utility Commissioners
1101 Vermont Avenue
Suite 200
Washington, DC 20044-0684
202-898-2200
FAX: 202-898-2213

Offers information on consultants and other professionals active in regulated telecommunications. *$33.00*
240 pages Annual

20863 International Fiber Optics Yellow Pages
Information Gatekeepers
214 Harvard Avenue
Suite 200
Allston, MA 02134-4641
617-232-3111
FAX: 617-734-8562 800-323-1088
webmaster@igigroup.com
www.fiberopticsyp.com

Will Ashley, Contact

The most extensive Fiber Optics reference volume available anywhere. This directory is still the world's only source book devoted exclusively to Fiber Optics. *$89.95*
Annual Founded: 1977 5000 names $150 per M. : e-mail

20864 LATA Directory
Center for Communications Management
11300 Rockville Pike
Suite 1100
Rockville, MD 20852-3012
301-816-8950
FAX: 301-287-2445

Offers information on local access transport areas by states. *$195.00*
220 pages Annual

20865 Local Calling Area Directory
Center for Communications Management
11300 Rockville Pike
Suite 1100
Rockville, MD 20852-3012
301-816-8950
FAX: 301-287-2445

Offers area codes and their zones or exchanges in cities of 100,000 or more in population. *$795.00*
1,050 pages Annual

20866 Lynx Global Telecom Database
Lynx Technologies
710 Route 46 East
PO Box 368
Little Falls, NJ 07424-0368
973-256-7200
FAX: 973-882-3583
msalerno@lynxtech.com
www.lynxtech.com

Kathleen Elsayed, Production Manager
Mike Salerno, Circulation Director

350 telecommunications carriers services in approximately 200 countries, territories and other political divisions.

20867 Network Management Guidelines and Contact Directory
Network Operations Forum
1200 G Street NW
Washington, DC 20005-3814
202-347-1228
FAX: 202-393-5453

Over 25 telecommunications companies.

20868 North American Telecommunications Association - Sourcebook
2000 M Street NW
Suite 550
Washington, DC 20036-3307
202-161-1724

Paul Werth, Owner

Offers a wide array of information on manufacturers and suppliers of non-utility telephone terminal equipment. *$53.00*
208 pages

20869 Outside Plant: Directory of Outside Plant Contractors Issue
Practical Communications
PO Box 183
Cary, IL 60013-0183
847-639-2200
FAX: 847-639-7598

John Saxtan, Editor

Offers a list of over 800 contractors in the telecommunications industry that specialize in outside plant projects. *$30.00*
Annual
Circulation: 20,000

20870 Phillips Satellite Industry Directory
Phillips Business Information
1201 Seven Locks Road
Potomac, MD 20854-2931
301-354-1400
FAX: 301-309-9473 800-777-5006

Minica Kenny, Editor
Don Pazour, Chief Executive Officer

Over 6,000 contacts and more than 3,800 hardware and technical service companies, transponder brokers and resellers, consultants, communications attorneys, publishers, uplinks and downlinks, video conference suppliers, related trade associations, government agencies and satellite telecommunications carriers. *$257.00*
Annual January

20871 Phillips Who's Who in Electronic Commerce
Phillips Business Information
1201 Seven Locks Road
Potomac, MD 20854-2931
301-354-1400
FAX: 301-309-9473 800-777-5006

Jennifer O Newman, Editor
Don Pazour, Chief Executive Officer

Service providers, value-added banks and networks, software vendors, associations, user groups, consultants, business and technical services for electronic commerce industry. *$199.00*
Annual

20872 Pocket Guides to the Internet: Terminal Connections
Information Today
143 Old Marlton Pike
Medford, NJ 08055-8750
609-654-6266
FAX: 609-654-4309

George Hartnell, Editor
Mark Veijkov, Editor

Unix/VMS systems and other basic terminal applications and telecommunications programs. *$9.95*

20873 Q-TEL 1000
United Communications Group
11300 Rockville Pike
Suite 1100
Rockville, MD 20852-3030
301-816-8950
800-526-5307

This database offers information on telecommunications charges.
Full-text

20874 RCR Publications
RCR Publications
1746 Cole Boulevard
Suite 150
Golden, CO 80401
303-733-2500
FAX: 303-733-9941 800-678-9696
mbush@crain.com www.rcrnews.com

Melodye Bush, Database Coordinator

Offers a wide variety of information on cellular and personal communications industries. Includes detailed information on carriers and vendors around the world. *$950.00*
Annual Founded: 1991
Computerized version available: 3.5 floppy

20875 RCR's Cellular Database
RCR Publications
1746 Cole Boulevard
Suite 150
Golden, CO 80401
303-733-2500
FAX: 303-733-9941 800-678-9696
mbush@crain.com www.rcrnews.com

Melodye Bush, Database Coordinator

Offers a wide variety of information on cellular communications industry. Includes detailed information on cellular carriers and vendors. *$300.00*
Annual Founded: 1991
Computerized version available: 3.5 floppy

20876 **RCR's PCS Database**
RCR Publications
1746 Cole Boulevard
Suite 150
Golden, CO 80401
303-733-2500
FAX: 303-733-9941 800-678-9696
mbush@crain.com www.rcrnews.com
Melodye Bush, Database Coordinator
Offers a wide variety of information on the personal communications industry. Includes detailed information on PCS carriers and vendors. *$300.00*
Annual Founded: 1991
Computerized version available: 3.5 floppy

20877 **Satellite Industry Directory**
Phillips Business Information
1201 Seven Locks Road
Suite 300
Potomac, MD 20854-2931
301-354-1400
FAX: 301-309-9473
Monica Kenny, Editor
Profiles operational and planned satellite systems, equipment and service providers, satellite brokers, uplinkers/downlinkers and more. *$247.00*
750 pages Annual

20878 **Sbusiness**
AFSM International
1342 Colonial Boulevard
Suite 25
Fort Myers, FL 33907
239-275-7887
FAX: 239-275-0794
service@afsmi.org www.afsmi.org
Suzanne Kaminski, Publisher/Editor
James Gaidry, VP Marketing
The professional journal for customer service and support managers. *$60.00*
100 pages Bi-Monthly Founded: 1975
Circulation: 10000

20879 **TCP/IP for the Internet**
Mecklermedia Corporation
20 Ketchum Street
Westport, CT 06880-5908
203-341-2806
FAX: 203-454-5840
Marshall Breeding, Editor
Standard network protocol for data transmission over the global internet - products and packages for Unix, DOS, Windows and Macintosh platforms. *$24.95*

20880 **Telecommunications Directory**
Gale Research
27500 Drake Road
Farmington Hills, MI 48331
248-699-4253
FAX: 248-699-8214 800-877-4253
galeord@gale.com www.gale.com
Offers valuable information on over 2,500 national and international voice and data communications networks, electronic mail services and teleconferencing facilities. *$325.00*
1,100 pages Biennial

20881 **Telecommunications Export Guide**
North American Telecommunications Association
2000 M Street NW
Suite 550
Washington, DC 20036-3307
202-161-1724
Paul Werth, Owner
Offers a list of over 135 foreign telecommunications agencies, and federal and state government agencies concerned with exports in the United States. *$103.00*

20882 **Telemarketing and Call Center Solutions Buyer's Guide and Directory Issue**
Technology Marketing Corporation
1 Technology Plaza
Norwalk, CT 06854
203-852-6800
FAX: 203-853-2845 800-243-6002
Linda Driscoll, Editor
Over 1100 domestic and foreign suppliers of equipment products and services to the telecommunications/telemarketing industry. *$ 25.00*
Annual December

20883 **Telephone Industry Directory**
Phillips Business Information
1201 Seven Locks Road
Suite 300
Potomac, MD 20854-2931
301-354-1400
FAX: 301-349-9473
Jennifer Newman, Assistant Managing Editor
Offers valuable information on over 4,800 manufacturers, distributors and suppliers to the telecommunications industry. *$249.00*
750 pages Annual

20884 **Voice Mail Reference Manual and Buyer's Guide**
Robins Press
2675 Henry Hudson Parkway W
Apartment 6J
Bronx, NY 10463-7741
718-548-7245
FAX: 718-548-7237 800-238-7130
robinspr@ix.netcom.com
www.mmdimensions.com/telstore
Marc Robins, Publisher
Offers information on over 60 suppliers of about 90 voice mail systems and service bureaus. *$65.00*
384 pages Annual
Mailing list available for rent 10M names
Printed in 2 colors on matte stock

20885 **Voice Processing Printed Circuit Cards: A Sourcebook of Suppliers & Products**
Robins Press
2675 Henry Hudson Parkway W
Apartment 6J
Bronx, NY 10463-7741
718-548-7245
Offers a list of over 50 vendors of voice processing circuit cards and related technology worldwide. *$150.00*
Annual

20886 **Voice Response Reference Manual & Buyer's Guide**
Robins Press
PO Box 630204
Bronx, NY 10463-0802
718-543-3364
FAX: 718-548-7237 800-238-7130
robinspr@ix.netcom.com
www.mmdimensions.com/telstore
Marc Robins, Publisher
Over 50 manufacturers and suppliers of over 65 voice response systems are listed. *$85.00*
325 pages Annual
Mailing list available for rent 10M names
Printed in 2 colors on matte stock

20887 **World Satellite Almanac**
Phillips Business Information
1201 Seven Locks Road
Suite 300
Potomac, MD 20854-2931
301-354-1400
FAX: 301-340-1520
Monica Kenny, Editor
All commercial satellite systems and operators are profiled. *$247.00*
700 pages Annual

20888 **World Telecommunications Tariff Directory**
Lynx Technologies
PO Box 368
Little Falls, NJ 07424-0368
973-256-7200
A comprehensive directory of over 1,200 Local Exchange Carriers and other telecom companies make up this directory. Inlcudes a detailed index for easy cross-referencing by company name, contacts, titles, geographical region, services provided, email and more. *$699.00*
9,000 pages

Industry Web Sites

20889 **www.adweek.com**
ADWEEK
Leading decision makers in the advertising and marketing field go to Adweek.Com every day for breaking news, insight, buzz, opinion, analysis, research and classifieds. The resources of all six regional editions of Adweek, as well as the national edition of Brandweek are combined with the knowledge of our online editors and the multimedia-interactive capabilities of the web to deliver vital information quickly and effectively to our target audience.

20890 **www.alts.org**
Association of Local Telecommunications Services
Represents state and local telecommunications offices.

20891 **www.amtausa.org**
American Mobile Telecommunications Association
Membership is made up of operators in the 220 MHz, 450 MHz, 800 MHz and 900 MHz bands, as well as product and service providers for the industry. Many members are exploring other areas of the mobile telecommunications industry — digital SMR, Personal Communications Services, data communications, mobile satellite, cable telephony and international wireless interests. AMTA is working with its members and with government to insure that those areas can be pursued successfully.

20892 www.arrl.org
American Radio Relay League

National membership association for amateur radio operators.

20893 www.atis.org
Alliance for Telecommunications Industry Solutions

Membership organization that provides the tools necessary for the industry to identify standards, guidelines and operating procedures that make the interoperability of existing and emerging telecommunications proiducts and services possible.

20894 www.atsi.org
Association of Telemessaging Services International

Promotes fair competition through appropriate regulation and legislation; provides research and development provides support services and educational opportunities to address challenges in operating environments; in encourages and maintains the high standards of ethics and service.

20895 www.floridapsc.com
Telecommunications Cooperative Network

Offers group purchasing discounts on long-distance telephone services, equipment counseling, and analysis of communications needs.

20896 www.greyhouse.com
Grey House Publishing

Selected Grey House directories in the fields of business, health and education are available online. Users can search our online databases by several different search criteria, such as product categories, geographic area, sales volume and much, much more. Full Grey House catalog and online ordering also available.

20897 www.icea.net
Insulated Cable Engineers Association

Professional organization dedicated to developing cable standards for the electric power, control and telecommunications industries. Ensures safe, economical and efficient cable systems utilizing proven state-of-the-art materials and concepts. ICEA documents are of interest to cable manufacturers, architects and engineers, utility and manufacturing plant personnel, telecommunication engineers, consultants and OEMs.

20898 www.igigroup.com
Information Gatekeepers

Provides worldwide coverage of wireless LAN's, LAN interconnection, wireless in-building and major applications such as point-of-sales, portable computer interconnections and remote data collection.

20899 www.imc.org
Internet Email Consortium

Information about IMC and its members, all the internet email standards and more.

20900 www.isoc.org
Internet Society

International, professional membership organization focusing on standards, education and policy issues.

20901 www.kagan.com
Wireless/Private Cable Investor

The original bible of the wireless cable, multipoint distribution pay TV industry. Published continuously since 1972, this newsletter is the window on cable competition. Three month trial available.

20902 www.ntca.org
National Telephone Cooperative Association

Represents both cooperative and commercial, independent rural phone companies.

20903 www.scte.org
Society of Cable Telecommunications Engineers

For people engaged in engineering, construction, installation, manufacture, technical direction, management, regulation, or administration of broad band communications technologies.

20904 www.steconsulting.org
Society of Telecommunications Consultants

The Society of Telecommunications Consultants is aprofessional association of Independent telecommunications consultants who provide expert, non based councel to business industry service organizations and government, worldwide. It serves its constituency by providing educational business and networking opportunities and by negotiating tangible and intangible benefits. The STC also serves as a resource, connecting end users to consultants to business, educational and promotrional opportunities.

20905 www.telecommagazine.com
Telecommunications Industry Association

This magazine reports on carrier class and wide area communications technologies for service providers and their corporate network customers worldwide. Coverage includes technology, product, market and application information for serious communications professionals, interexchange, cellular/wireless/satellite carriers, cable companies as well as commercial users and government agencies in the communications industry.

20906 www.telecommute.org
Telecommuting Advisory Council

A comprehensive monthly digest of news about employer-sponsored telecommuting programs for employers working at home or elsewhere off-site. Contains case studies, international news, technology updates, legal and regulatory news, and managerial topics.

20907 www.usta.org
United States Telecom Association

Broad based association for the local exchange carrier industry worldwide.

Associations

20908 Acrylic Council
1285 Avenue of the Americas
35th Floor
New York, NY 10019
212-397-4600
FAX: 212-554-4042
info@fabriclink.com
www.fabriclink.com

Lynn Misiak, Executive Director

A business league created to provide products in facilities maintained in the US. Educates the retailer and consumer of the benefits of acrylic fiber.

20909 Amalgamated Clothing and Textile Workers Union
1710 Broadway
New York, NY 10019-5254
212-255-9655

Jack Sheinkman, President
William Towne, Manager

Sponsors and supports the Political Action Committee in this field.
249M Members Founded: 1976

20910 American Association of Textile Chemists
PO Box 12215
Research Triangle Park, NC 27709
919-549-8141
FAX: 919-549-8933 800-360-5380
jonesb@aatcc.org www.aatcc.org

John Y Daniels, Executive Director
Pat Watkins, Accounting Manager
Alda Blanton, Business Services Manager
Marie Daniel, Accounts Receivable

20911 American Cotton Growers
PO Box 430
Sheffield, TX 79339
806-385-6401
FAX: 806-385-5155

20912 American Fiber, Textile and Apparel
1801 K Street NW
Washington, DC 20006-1301
202-862-0500
FAX: 202-862-0570
Promotes pride in American products by educating consumers and retailers on the high quality of US goods.
21 Members Founded: 1965

20913 American Flock Association
6 Beacon Street
Suite 1125
Boston, MA 02108
617-542-8220
FAX: 617-542-2199
info@flocking.org www.flocking.org

Barrett F Ripley, Executive Director

Fosters the use of flocked products. Strives to improve and advance flocking technology.
60 Members Founded: 1985

20914 American Home Sewing & Craft Association
PO Box 1312
Monroeville, PA 15146
212-714-1633
FAX: 412-372-5953
info@sewing.org www.sewing.org

20915 American Sheep Industry Association
9785 Maroon Circle
Suite 360
Englewood, CO 80112
303-771-3500
FAX: 303-771-8200
info@sheepusa.org www.sheepusa.org

Paul Frischknecht, President
Peter Orwick, Executive Director
Rita Kourlis Samuelson, Wool Marketing Director

A federation of state associations dedicated to the welfare and profitability of the sheep industry. *$25.00*
Monthly
Circulation: Mbrshp

20916 American Textile Machinery Association
201 Park Washington Court
Falls Church, VA 22046
703-538-1789

webmaster@atmanet.org
www.atmanet.org

Harry Buzzard Jr, Management Counsel
Susan A Denston, Executive VP
Clay D Tyeryar, President

Our purpose is to improve business conditions within the textile machinery industry of the United States within a global context; to encourage the use of the products of the industry; and to protect, promote, foster and advance the common interests of the members as manufacturers and distributors of textile machinery and parts and machinery accessory to textile machinery on a worldwide basis.
1.5M Members Founded: 1933

20917 American Textile Machinery Association: ATMA
201 Park Washington Court
Falls Church, VA 22046-4527
703-538-1789
FAX: 703-241-5603
info@atmanet.org www.atmanet.org

Clay D Tyeryar, President
Susan A Denston, Executive VP
Harry W Buzzard Jr, Management Counsel

US professional trade association devoted solely to the advancement of manufacturers of textile machinery, parts and accesories. Headquartered in the Washington, DC area, ATMA represents one of the nation's largest basic industries and it's purpose is to advance the common interests of its members, improve business conditions within the US textile machinery industry from a global perspective and market the industry and members' machinery, parts and services.
1.5M Members Founded: 1933

20918 American Textile Manufacturers Institute
1801 K Street NW
Suite 900
Washington, DC 20006-1301
202-457-6610
FAX: 202-862-0537

Carlos Moore, Executive Director

Operates a public relations program for the industry, government and textile market program and a statistical and economic information service.
Founded: 1949

20919 American Wool Council
9785 Maroon Circle
Suite 360
Englewood, CO 80112
303-771-3500
FAX: 303-771-8200
info@sheepusa.org www.sheepusa.org

Paul Frischknecht, President
Peter Orwick, Executive Director
Rita Kourlis Samuelson, Wool Marketing Director

Promotes the use of wool and wool products.

20920 American Yarn Spinners Association
PO Box 99
Gastonia, NC 28053
704-824-3522
FAX: 704-824-0630 www.aysa.org

Michael Hubbard, Executive Director

Provides full service to the sales yarn industry.
100 Members Founded: 1967

20921 Association of Knitted Fabrics
575 Lexington Avenue
19th Floor
New York, NY 10022
212-495-1784

Manufacturers of knitted cotton and wool products.
6 Members Founded: 1935

20922 Association of Specialists in Cleaning and Restoration
10830 Guilford Road
Annapolis Junction, MD 20701-1120
410-880-4896
FAX: 301-604-4713

Marty Berry, Editor
Founded: 1958

20923 Carpet & Rug Institute: West
2648 E Workman Avenue
#513
West Covina, CA 91791
626-152-2016
FAX: 626-967-7819
www.carpet-rug.com

Terri Caputo, Manager

20924 Cotton Council International
1521 New Hampshire Avenue NW
Washington, DC 20036
202-745-7805
FAX: 202-483-4040
cottonuse@cotton.org

20925 Craft Yarn Council of America
2500 Lowell Road
Ranjo, NC 28054
704-824-7838
FAX: 704-824-0630

20926 Crafted with Pride in USA Council
PO Box 65326
Washington, DC 20035
202-775-0658
FAX: 202-819-4493
cwp@craftedwithpride.org
www.craftedwithpride.org

Bob Swift, Executive Director

Strengthens the competitive position of the US textile, apparel and home furnishings industry by increasing consumer demand, and

reinforcing the current positive attitude of made in the USA apparel and home furnishings.
508 Members Founded: 1984

20927 Durene Association of America
PO Box 66
Gastonia, NC 28053-0066
704-651-1651
FAX: 704-824-0638
Russell Duren, Owner
Develops and uses tests to determine quality. Licenses manufacturers to use Durene identification on products.
4 Members Founded: 1929

20928 Elastic Fabric Manufacturers Council of
230 Congress Street
Boston, MA 02110
617-542-8220
FAX: 617-542-2199
textilenta@aol.com
www.textilenta.org
Provides exchange and management services, trade promotions, statistical programs and information bulletins.
32 Members Founded: 1915

20929 Electrostatic Discharge Association
7900 Turin Road
Building 3
Rome, NY 13440-2069
315-339-6937
FAX: 315-339-6793
info@esda.org www.esda.org/
Kay Adams, President
Dave Swenson, Senior VP
Donn Bellmore, Treasurer
Michele McSwain, Secretary
Lisa Pimpinella, Operations Manager
Professional voluntary association dedicated to advancing the theory and practice of electrostatic discharge avoidance. Initial emphasis on the effects of ESD on electronic components has broadened to include textiles, plastics, web processing, explosives, clean rooms and graphic arts. Expands ESD awareness through educational programs, development of standards, tutorials, publications, local chapters, symposia and certification.
Founded: 1982

20930 GTMA: Association of Georgia's Textile, Carpet & Consumer Products Mfg.
50 Hurt Plaza
Suite 985
Atlanta, GA 30303
404-688-0555
FAX: 404-584-0720
G Bowen III, President

20931 Hard Fibers Association
120 Genesee Street
Suite 601
Auburn, NY 13021-3603
315-520-0871
FAX: 315-255-3292
John Hurd, President
Importers and distributors of sisal, abaca and other hard fibers.

20932 Home Sewing Association
PO Box 1312
Monroeville, PA 15146
412-725-5950
FAX: 412-372-5953
info@sewing.org www.sewing.org
Joyce Perhac, Manager
Represents most facets of the home sewing industry. National trade association for independent sewing machine dealers and distributors.
1.5M Members Founded: 1912

20933 INDA Association of Nonwoven Fabrics
1200 Crescent Green, Suite 100
PO Box 1288
Cary, NC 27511
919-233-1210
FAX: 919-233-1282 www.inda.org
Rory Holmes, President
Annette Balint, Director Finance
Ian Butler, Director Market Research/Stats
INDA is a trade assocation for the nonwoven industry. Our mission is to promote the profitability on nonwoven fabrics.
Founded: 1968

20934 Industrial Fabrics Association International
1801 W County Road B
Roseville, MN 55413-4061
651-222-2508
FAX: 651-631-9334 800-225-4324
generalinfo@ifai.com www.ifai.com
Mary Hennessy, Publisher
Sarah Hylendy, Advertising Editor
Stephen Warner, Chief Executive Officer
Association of geosynthetics, fabricators, installers, equipment manufacturers, suppliers, testing firms, consultants and educators who produce textiles, nets, mats, grids and other products. Industrial Fabrics Association International is the industry's first source for technical fabric resources and information.
2000 Members Founded: 1912

20935 Institute of Textile Technology
North Carolina State University
2401 Research Drive
Box 8301
Raleigh, NC 27695-8301
919-513-7704
FAX: 919-882-9410
wgoneal@itt.edu www.itt.edu
W Gilbert O'Neal, President
George Edmunds, VP
A graduate school supported in part by member companies. Publishes the Textile Technology Digest.

20936 International Silk Association
PO Box 907
Englewood Cliffs, NJ 07632
201-568-4920
William Rattermann, President
Members are silk converters and importers.
25 Members Founded: 1950

20937 International Society of Industrial Fabric
1801 County Road B W
Roseville, MN 55113-2851
651-631-9334
FAX: 651-222-2508 800-898-3905
generalinfo@ifai.com www.ifai.com
Stephen M. Warner, President
Scott C. Campbell, Vice Chairman
A not-for profit trade association whose more than 2,000 member companies represent the international specialty fabrics marketplace. Members range in size from one-person shops to multinational corporations; member products span the entire spectrum of the specialty fabrics industry from fiber and fabric suppliers to manufacturers of end products, equipment and hardware.
350 Members

20938 International Textile & Apparel Association
PO Box 1360
Monument, CO 80132-1360
719-488-3716
itaaoffice@cs.com
www.itaaonline.org
Sandra S Hutton, Executive Director
Professional association for 1,000 college professors of clothing and textile studies.
Founded: 1944 950 names $80 per M.

20939 Knitted Textile Association
386 Park Avenue South
Suite 901
New York, NY 10016-8804
212-689-3807
FAX: 212-889-6160 info@ktausa.org
The KTA is an active participant in the International Mechinery and Equipment exhibition that takes place in Textile Hall in Greenville, South Carolina and highlights the latest in knitting and related dying and finishing equipment.

20940 Knitting Guild of America
1100-H Brandywine Blvd
Zanesville, OH 43701-7303
740-452-4541
FAX: 740-452-2552
tkga@tkga.com www.tkga.com
Penny Sitler, Executive Director
50 booths.
500+ Members

20941 Narrow Fabrics Institute
1801 County Road BW
Roseville, MN 55113
651-222-2508
FAX: 651-631-9334
nfi@ifai.com www.narrowfabrics.org
Karen Musech, Managing Director
Bruce Harris, President
Conducts research programs and compiles statistics.
38 Members Founded: 1956

20942 National Cotton Batting Institute
41 S Walnut Bend Road
Cordova, TN 38018
901-624-1200
FAX: 901-624-1200
info@natbat.com www.natbat.com
Alan Posners, President
Fred Middleton, Executive Secretary
Alan Posner, VP
Association representing members of the cotton batting industry.

27 Members Founded: 1954

20943 National Council for Textile Education
Georgia Institute of Technology
School of Textile and Fiber
Atlanta, GA 30332-0001
404-894-2000
FAX: 404-894-8780
Members are administrators of college textile departments whose curriculum comprise science-based programs with substantial laboratory and plant experience.

20944 National Knitwear & Sportswear Association
386 Park Avenue South
Suite 514
New York, NY 10016
212-683-7520
FAX: 212-532-0766
nksa@pop.interport.net
Seth Bodner, Director
Peter Woodsworth, Events Coordinator
Represents U.S. manufacturers and contractors, designing studios and related business engaged in the production of knitted sportswear and knitted products of all types.

20945 Northern Textile Association
6 Beacon Street
Suite 1125
Boston, MA 02108
617-237-7001
FAX: 617-542-2199
info@nationaltextile.org
www.nationaltextile.org
Textile manufacturing trade association.
200 Members Founded: 1951

20946 Schiffi Lace & Embroidery Manufacturers Association
22 Industrial Ave
Fairview, NJ 07022
201-943-7757
FAX: 201-943-7793
info@schiffli.org www.schiffli.org
Larry Squiccimari, President
Vincent Mesiano, VP
Crafted lace, and embroidery that adorns lingerie and dresses t towels, sheets, curtains, tablecloths, patches, logos and much more.

20947 Secondary Materials and Recycled Textiles
7910 Woodmont Avenue
Suite 1130
Bethesda, MD 20814
301-544-4684
FAX: 301-656-1079
smartasn@erols.com
www.smartasn.org
Sandy Schneider, Manager
Members are manufacturers and distributors of industrial wiping cloths, used clothing, mill ends, remnants and recycled textiles.
285 Members Founded: 1932

20948 Shippers of Recycled Textiles
7910 Woodmont Avenue
Bethesda, MD 20814
301-070-0001
FAX: 301-656-1079
smartasn@erols.com
www.smartasn.org
Borton Shapiro, Owner
75 Members Founded: 1988

20949 Southern Textile Association
PO Box 66
Gastonia, NC 28053
704-824-3522
FAX: 704-824-0630
www.southerntextile.org
Larry W Oates, Chairman
Lee Thomas, President
Russell W Mims, Jr, First VP
Represents the textile and clothing industry in the South.
Founded: 1908

20950 Surface Design Association
PO Box 360
Sebastopol, CA 95473-0360
707-829-3110
FAX: 707-829-3285
surfacedesign@mail.com
www.surfacedesign.org
Jason Pollen, President
Aims to stimulate, promote and improve education in the area of surface design, to encourage the surface designer as an individual artist and to provide a forum for exchange of ideas through conferences and publications.
Founded: 1977
Mailing list available for rent $75 per M.

20951 TRI/Princeton
PO Box 625
Princeton, NJ 08542
609-924-3150
FAX: 609-683-7836
info@triprinceton.org
www.triprinceton.org
Dr Gail R Eaton, President
Thomas C Pickel, CFO
Yash K Kamath, Research Director
Provides advanced research and education in polymers, fibers, films, personal care and porous materials.
40 Members Founded: 1930

20952 Textile Care Allied Trades Association
271 Route 46W
Suite D203
Fairfield, NJ 07004
973-441-1790

tcata@ix.netcom.com www.tcata.org
David Cotter, Executive Director
Represents the interests of distributors and manufacturers of equipment and supplies for the cleaning industry.

20953 Textile Rental Services Association
1800 Diagonal Road
Suite 200
Alexandria, VA 22314
703-519-0029
FAX: 703-519-0026
trsa@trsa.org www.trsa.org
Roger Cocivera, President/CEO
Covers the uniform, linen supply, health care and dust control service markets.

Newsletters

20954 Embroidery News
Schiffi Lace & Embroidery Manufacturers Assn
596 Anderson Avenue
Suite 203
Cliffside Park, NJ 07010-1831
201-943-7757
FAX: 201-943-7793
Leonard Seiler, Editor
Eugene Schrouzol, Publisher
Newsletter for the embroidery industry.
BiMonthly
Circulation: 500

20955 Marine Textiles
RCM Enterprises
12 Oaks Center #922
Wayzata, MN 55391

800-451-9278
Mara Sidney, Publisher
Jim Penningroth, Editor
Serves firms in the boating market who use fabrics and furnishings. Accepts advertising. *$28.00*

Magazines & Journals

20956 AATCC Review
American Assn. of Textile Chemists and Colorists
PO Box 12215
Research Triangle Park, NC 27709-2215
919-549-8141
FAX: 919-549-8933 888-830-4989
satters@aatcc.org
http://www.aatcc.org
Sherri Satterwhite, Publications Director
Maria Thiry, Features Editor
John Y Daniels, Executive Director
Jennifer Hall, Circulation Manager
Robert Lattie, President
Covers all aspects of design, dyeing, printing, finishing, and testing as they relate to textile manufacturing, including fibers, fabrics of all types, garments, carpets, home textiles, and industrial products.
Monthly Founded: 1997
Printed in 4 colors on glossy stock

20957 Cleaning and Restoration
Assn of Specialists in Cleaning & Restoration
8229 Cloverleaf Dr
Suite 460
Millersville, MD 21108
410-299-9900
FAX: 410-729-3603 800-272-7012
alhwrite@erols.com
http://www.ascr.org
Patricia Harman, Editor-in-Chief
Tony Greenfield, General Sales Mgr
Amy Shipley, Account Executive
Association news. *$69.00*
Monthly Founded: 1947

20958 Fabric Architecture
Industrial Fabrics Association International
1801 County Road B W
Roseville, MN 55113
651-222-2508
FAX: 651-631-9334 800-225-4324
generalinfo@ifai.com
http://www.ifai.com

Mary Hennessey, Publisher
Bruce Wright, Editor
Stephen B Duerk, Chairman
Steve Warner, President
Beth L Hungiville, Managing Director

This magazine strives to inform architects, designers, landscape architects, engineers and other specifiers about architectural fabric structures, the fibers and fabrics used to make them, their design possibilities, their construction, and issues regarding their applicability and acceptance. Fabric Architecture showcases industrial-fabric applications to 13,000+ architects. Featured works include awnings, canopies, flags, banners, tension structures and other end products. *$43.00*

Founded: 1988
Circulation: 13,000 $250 per M.
Printed in 4 colors on glossy stock

20959 Fabrics Architecture
Industrial Fabrics Association International
1801 County Road B W
Roseville, MN 55113
651-222-2508
FAX: 651-631-9334 800-225-4324
generalinfo@ifai.com
http://www.ifai.com

Mary Hennessey, Publisher
Bruce Wright, Editor
Beth L Hungiville, Managing Director:
Steve Warner, President
Stephen B Duerk, Chairman

This magazine strives to inform architects, designers, landscape architects, engineers and other specifiers about architectural fabric structures, the fibers and fabrics used to make them, their design possibilities, their construction, and issues regarding their applicability and acceptance. Fabric Architecture showcases indutrial-fabric applications to 13,000+ architects. Featured works include awnings, canopies, flags, banners, tension structures and other end products. *$43.00*

Founded: 1988
Circulation: 13,000 $250 per M.
Printed in 4 colors on glossy stock

20960 Geotechnical Fabrics Report
Industrial Fabrics Association International
1801 County Road B W
Roseville, MN 55113
651-222-2508
FAX: 651-631-9334 800-225-4324
generalinfo@ifai.com
http://www.ifai.com

Mary Hennessey, Publisher
James Dankert, Managing Editor
Stephen B Duerk, Chairman
Steve Warner, President
Beth L Hungiville, Managing Director

Peer reviewed technical journal for civil engineers using geosynthetics in road construction, errosion control, hazardous waste, drainage, containment and reinforcement. *$49.00*

Founded: 1988
Circulation: 16,000 $250 per M.
Printed in 4 colors on glossy stock

20961 Home Textiles Today
Reed Business Information
360 Park Avenue South
New York, NY 10010
212-450-0067
FAX: 646-746-7300 800-446-6551
corporatecommunications@reedbusiness.com http://www.reedbusiness.com

Jennifer Negley, Editor-in-Chief
Mark Fraser, Publisher
Tad Smith, Owner

Textile industry news, reports, research and summaries for the professional.

Founded: 1979
Circulation: 8000

20962 IFAI'S Marine Fabricator
Industrial Fabrics Association International
1801 County Road B W
Roseville, MN 55113-4052
651-222-2508
FAX: 651-631-9334 800-225-4324
generalinfo@ifai.com
http://www.ifai.com

Frank McGinty, Publisher
George K Ochs, Chairman
Jeffrey W Kirk, Vice Chairman
Stephen M Warner, PRESIDENT
Scott C Campbell, Vice Chairman

Publication contains articles designed for beginning to intermediate level fabricators, advanced techniques and technology, profiles, business tips, industry news, new products and publications, and showcases of fabricators' craftmanship.

Quarterly Founded: 1964
Circulation: 5000

20963 Impressions Magazine
Miller Freeman Publications
13760 Noel Road
Suite 500
Dallas, TX 75240-7336
972-239-3060
FAX: 972-419-7825 800-527-0207

Carl Piazza, Publisher
Laura Gonz, Editor

Covers the textile screen printing imprinted sportswear retailing, and commercial embroidery industry. Accepts advertising. *$ 36.00*

250 pages Annual

20964 Industrial Fabric Products Review
Industrial Fabrics Association International
1801 County Road B W
Roseville, MN 55113
651-222-2508
FAX: 651-631-9334 800-225-4324
generalinfo@ifai.com
http://www.ifai.com

Mary Hennessey, Publisher
Mary Conner, Managing Editor
Galynn Nordstrom, Editorial Director
Sarah Hyland, Advertising Director
Stephen Warner, Chief Executive Officer

Published monthly, this magazine provides timely reports on emerging and traditional end markets for products made of industrial fabrics; new technical developments in fiber, fabrics, and treatments; general interest articles on growth-oriented products and companies; profiles on industry members; and the latest information on equipment. *$69.00*

Monthly Founded: 1915
Circulation: 10,000 $250 per M.
Printed in 4 colors on glossy stock

20965 Journal of Industrial Textiles
851 New Holland Avenue
Suite 3535
Lancaster, PA 17604
717-291-5609
FAX: 717-295-4538 800-233-9936

20966 Marine Fabricator
Industrial Fabrics Association International
1801 County Road B W
Roseville, MN 55413-4061
651-222-2508
FAX: 651-631-9334 800-225-4324
generalinfo@ifai.com
http://www.marinecanvas.com

Mary Hennessey, Publisher
Melissa Kaudy, Editor
Galynn Nordstrom, Editorial Director
Sarah Hyland, Advertising Director
Mary J Moore, Circulation Manager

Written to educate and inform marine aftermarket fabricators of textile components such as tops, covers and interiors. Features include Marine Fabricators Association news, beginning and advanced cut-and-sew articles, photo showcases, fabricator profiles, business tips and solutions and more. *$35.00*

Quarterly Founded: 1995
Circulation: 5,000 $250 per M.
Printed in 4 colors on glossy stock

20967 Nonwovens Industry
Rodman Publications
70 Hilltop Road
Ramsey, NJ 07446-2522
201-825-2552
FAX: 201-855-0553
nonwovens@rodpub.com
http://www.nonwovens-industry.com

Rodman Zilenziger, Publisher
Ellen Noonan, Editor

Written for nonwoven roll goods producers, converters and end-use manufacturers.

70 pages Monthly Founded: 1970
Circulation: 11000

20968 Nonwovens World
MTS Publications
4100 S 7th Street
Kalamazoo, MI 49009-8461
269-375-1236
FAX: 269-375-6710
admin@marketingtechnologyservice.com
http://www.marketingtechnologyservice.com

James P Hanson, Editor
Cindy Costello, Circulation Manager
Wayne C Carter, Advertising Sales Directo

Covers new products, as well as production and marketing strategies.

Founded: 1986
Circulation: 10384

20969 Surface Design Journal
P. O. Box 360
Sebastopol, CA 95473-360
707-829-3110
FAX: 707-829-3285
surfacedesign@mail.com
www.surfacedesign.org

Patricia Malarcher, Editor
Jason Pollen, President
Joy Stocksdale, Advertising Manager

Professional organization of more than 2,000 textile artists, designers for industry, and academicians. *$8.00*

52 pages Quarterly Founded: 1977
Circulation: 6000

20970 Textile Chemist and Colorist
American Assn of Textile Chemists & Colorists
PO Box 12215
Research Triangle Park, NC 27709
919-549-8141
FAX: 919-549-8933 888-830-4989
quantem@aatcc.org
http://www.aatcc.org

John Y Daniels, Executive Director
Susan H Keesee Jr, Editor
Sherri Satterwhite, Publisher
Jennifer Hall, Circulation Manager
Chris Shaw, Advertising Sales

The world's largest technical and scientific society devoted to the advancement of textile chemistry. The membership and staff also produce publications, test methods and quality control aids and offer professional development programs. *$40.00*
Monthly Founded: 1997
Circulation: 10500

20971 Textile Research Journal
TRI Princeton
PO Box 625
Princeton, NJ 08542
609-924-3150
FAX: 609-683-7836
www.triprinceton.com

Dr. Gail R Eaton, President

Provides advanced research and education in polymers, fibers, films, personel care and porous materials.
Monthly Founded: 1930

Trade Shows

20972 American Association Textile Chemists & Colorists International Conference
PO Box 12215
Research Triangle Park, NC 27709-2215
919-549-8141
FAX: 919-549-8933 800-360-5380
chrietb@aatc.org www.aatc.org

B Chrietzberg, Advertising Manager
John Daniels, Manager

120 booths of colorants and chemical finishes for textile and related industries.
2000 Attendees October

20973 American Home Sewing & Craft Association Sewing & Craft Show: AHSCA
American Home Sewing and Craft Association
1350 Broadway
Suite 1601
New York, NY 10018
212-714-1633
FAX: 212-714-1655
info@sewing.org www.sewing.org
200 exhibits of fabric, notions, patterns, sewing and knitting machines, crafts and trimmings. Attended by professionals from major chain stores, independent retailers, wholesalers and manufacturers.
3000 Attendees Semiannual

20974 American Textile Machinery Exhibition International
Textile Hall Corporation
PO Box 5823
Greenville, SC 29606
864-331-2277
FAX: 864-331-2282
atmei@textilehall.com

Butler Mullins, Director

Exhibition of machinery, supplies and services required for manufacture of yarn and fiber, for the weaving, knitting and dying/printing/finishing processes, for manufacture of non-wovens and for plant maintenance.
10000 Attendees September

20975 Apparel Printing and Embroidery Expo
Primedia
9800 Metcalf Avenue
Overland Park, KS 66212
913-341-1300
FAX: 913-967-1898
www.primediabusiness.com

Joanie Forsythe, Sales Manager

Semi-annual show of 200 manufacturers, suppliers and distributors of commercial screen printing and embroidery equipment and supplies, computer graphic systems and softgoods such as T-shirts, sweats, jackets and caps.
3000 Attendees

20976 Apparel Show of the Americas
Bobbin Publishing/Miller Freeman
PO Box 279
Euless, TX 76039
817-215-1600
FAX: 817-215-1666 800-693-1363
bobbin.expoinfo@mfi.com
wwwmfi.com

Betty Webb, Trade Show Director

Conference, seminar and 329 exhibits of equipment, fabrics, accessories and services for sewn products and apparel.
5790 Attendees Annual Founded: 1992

20977 Geosynthetics
Industrial Fabrics Association International

1801 County Road B W
Roseville, MN 55113
651-222-2508
FAX: 651-631-9334
confmgmt@ifai.com
www.ifaiexpo.info

Susan Larson, VP Conference Management

Conference dedicated to advancing the use of geosynthetic material in civil engineering and environmental applications.
February

20978 IFAI Expo
Industrial Fabrics Association International

1801 County Road B W
Roseville, MN 55113
651-222-2508
FAX: 651-631-9334
confmgmt@ifai.com
www.ifaiexpo.info

Jennifer Thompson, Director Conference Management

8500 Attendees October Founded: 1912

20979 International Fashion and Boutique Shows
100 Wells Avenue
#9103
Newton, MA 02459-3210
617-731-8316

Samuel Starr, Show Manager

1,800 booths.
30M Attendees January

20980 International Fastener Exposition
PEMCO
383 Main Avenue
Norwalk, CT 06851-1543
203-840-7700
FAX: 630-260-0395

Barbara Silverman, VP, Show Manager
Laura Rezek, Advertising

450 booths developed specifically for the fastener manufacturing and precision formed parts industry.
4.8M Attendees March

20981 International Hosiery Exposition
200 N Sharon Amity Road
Charlotte, NC 28211-3004
704-365-0913

Jennette Ennis, Director Show

225 booths.
10M Attendees May

Directories & Databases

20982 ATI's Textile Red Book: America's Textile Industries
Billian Publishing Company
2100 Powers Ferry Road
Suite 300
Atlanta, GA 30339-5014
770-955-5656
FAX: 770-952-0669 800-533-8484
redbook@billian.com
www.billian.com/redbook

Joyce Metzer, Editor
Dave Ramsays, Database Sales
Douglas Billian, Owner

Comprehensive reference guide for the textile industry. Includes over 6,000 mills in the US, Canada and Mexico. In addition to providing the complete contact information for the plant, each listing gives key personnel, products produced, fibers processed and mill equipment used. *$160.00*
Annual

20983 America's Textiles International
Billian Publishing Company
2100 Powers Ferry Road
Suite 300
Atlanta, GA 30339-5014
770-955-5656
FAX: 770-952-0669 www.atimeg.com

Jay Perkins, Publisher
James Borneman, Editor
Douglas Billian, Owner

Annual directory provides the complete contact information - including Web sites and e-mail addresses for over 2,400 equipment, technology and service providers to the textile industry.
Annual Founded: 1887
Circulation: 32,000

20984 American Wool Industry White Pages
American Sheep Industry Association
9785 Maroon Circle
Suite 360
Englewood, CO 80112
303-771-3500
FAX: 303-771-8200
info@sheepusa.org
www.sheepusa.org

Paul Frischknecht, President
Peter Orwick, Executive Director
Rita Kourlis Samuelson, Wool Marketing Director

Wool and wool product services, warehouses, pools, buyers, processors, sources of pelts and suppliers.

20985 Davison's Textile Blue Book
Davison Publishing Company
PO Box 1289
Concord, NC 28026-1289
704-785-8700
FAX: 704-785-8701 800-328-4766
sales@davisonbluebook.com
www.davisonbluebook.com

Carol Nealy, Advertising Manager

5,400 mills, dryers, finishers, in the United States, Canada, and Mexico. *$165.00*
800 pages Annual Founded: 1866 ISBN 0-875150-69-1 $160 per M.

20986 Fairchild's Textile & Apparel Financial Directory
Fairchild Publications
7 W 34th Street
New York, NY 10001-8100
212-630-3880
FAX: 212-630-3868 800-247-6622

Robert Benjamin, Editor

Over 180 publicly owned textile and apparel corporations are profiled. *$185.00*
Annual

20987 Interior Textiles Fabric Resource Directory
Wool Bureau/Atlanta Merchandise Mart
240 Peachtree Street NW
Suite 6F11
Atlanta, GA 30303-1361
404-577-4320

Approximately 108 manufacturers and suppliers of wool and wool blend upholsteries, wallcoverings and draperies.
45 pages

20988 International Textile & Apparel Association Membership Directory

PO Box 1360
Monument, CO 80132-1360
719-488-3716

itaaoffice@cs.com
www.itaaonline.org

Sandra S Hutton, Executive Director

Professional association for 1,000 college professors of clothing and textile studies.
8-12 pages 6 per year Founded: 1944 Circulation: Members 950 names $80 per M.

20989 Knitted Textile Association: Official Resource Guide and Fact Book
Knitted Textile Association
386 Park Avenue
New York, NY 10016-8804
212-545-9014
FAX: 212-889-6160

Peter Adelman, Editor

A list of over 150 member manufacturers, suppliers and distributors of knitted fabric products and services. *$10.00*
Annual

20990 Knitting Times: Buyers' Guide Issue
National Knitwear & Sportswear Association
386 Park Avenue S
New York, NY 10016-8804
212-545-9014
FAX: 212-532-0766

Dawne G Shink, Editor

List of about 4,500 suppliers and manufacturers of chemicals, contract, management and computer services, cutting room equipment, dyeing, finishing and printing equipment, knitted and woven fabrics, fibers and yarn, interfacing, pressing and steaming, knitting, sewing and trimming equipment, materials handling and plant control services. *$25.00*
Annual, September
Circulation: 10,000

20991 LDB Interior Textiles Buyers' Guide
EW Williams Publications
342 Madison Avenue
Room 1901
New York, NY 10173-1999
212-697-1122
FAX: 212-661-1713 ldb342@aol.com

Renee Bennett, Editor-in-Chief
Aleksandra Kazimierska, Directory Manager
Janys Kuznier, Circulation Director

Over 2,000 manufacturers, importers and suppliers of home fashions products and services, decorative fabric converters and alternative window coverings, fabricators, manufacturer's representatives and others allied to the home fashions trade. *$40.00*
Annual June
Circulation: 12,000

20992 Narrow Fabrics Institute: Buyer's Guide
Narrow Fabrics Institute
345 Cedar Street
Suite 800
Saint Paul, MN 55101-1004

FAX: 651-222-8215 800-225-4324

Approximately 34 producers of narrow fabrics for use in automotive medical, lifting, environmental safety, recreational, military, air cargo, trucks, and other fields, requiring industrial fabrics.
Annual fall

20993 Textile Chemist and Colorist Buyers Guide
PO Box 12215
Research Triangle Park, NC 27709-2215

919-549-8141
FAX: 919-549-8933

Over 500 dye, pigments, machinery and equipment manufacturers are profiled.
ISSN 0040-4900

20994 Textile Technology Digest
2551 Ivy Road
Charlottesville, VA 22903
434-296-5511
FAX: 434-296-2957 www.itt.edu

Offers abstracts to worldwide literature from more than 1,300 sources annually such as proceedings, trade literature and other sources collected by the institutes library. The CD-ROM quarterly is available for $1,710 plus shipping. Network licenses begin at $500 for up to 10 simultaneous users. *$545.00*
Monthly Founded: 1944

20995 Wool Source List
Kairalla Agency
27 Raymond Street
Manchester, MA 01944-1614

Eleanor Kairalla, Executive Director

Conducts trade and consumer polls on woolen apparel.
360 pages Founded: 1939

Industry Web Sites

20996 www.aatcc.org
American Association of Textile Chemists &
Colorists

20997 www.atmanet.org
American Textile Machinery Association

Advances the common interests of its members, works to improve business conditions within the US textile machinery industry from a global perspective and markets the industry and members' machinery, parts and services.

20998 www.carpet-rug.com
Carpet & Rug Institute

20999 www.cottoninc.com
Cotton

21000 www.fibersource.com
American Fiber Manufacturers Association

Trade association for US companies that manufacture synthetic and cellulostic fibers. The industry employs 30,000 people and produces over 9 billion pounds of fiber in the US. The association maintains close ties to other manufactured fiber trade associations worldwide.

21001 www.flocking.org
American Flock Association

Fosters the use of flocked products. Strives to improve and advance flocking technology.

21002 www.greyhouse.com
Grey House Publishing

Selected Grey House directories in the fields of business, health and education are available online. Users can search our online databases by several different search criteria, such as product categories, geographic area, sales volume and much, much more. Full Grey House catalog and online ordering also available.

21003 www.ifai.com
Industrial Fabrics Association International

Association of geosynthetics, fabricators, installers, equipment manufacturers, suppliers, testing firms, consultants, and educators, who produce textiles, nets, mats, grids, and other products. Industrial Fabrics Association International is the industry's first source for technical fabric resources and information.

21004 www.inda.org
INDA Association of Nonwoven Fabrics Industries

21005 www.itt.edu
Institute of Textile Technology

A graduate school supported in part by member companies. Publishes the Textile Technology Digest.

21006 www.sewing.org
Home Sewing Association

Represents most facets of the home sewing industry. National trade association for independent sewing machine dealers and distributors.

21007 www.sleepproducts.org
International Sleep Products Association

Maintains a strong organization to influence government actions, inform and educate the membership and act on industry issues to enhance the growth,profitability and stature of the sleep products industry. Provides members with information and services to manage their business more effectively and efficiently. Publishes a magazine devoted exclusively to the mattress industry, BEDtimes covers a broad range of issue and news important to the industry.

21008 www.smartasn.org
Shippers of Recycled Textiles

21009 www.textilenta.org
Northern Textile Association

Textile manufacturing trade association.

21010 www.triprinceton.org
TRI Princeton

TRI/Princeton provides advanced research and education in polymers, fibers, films, personel care, and porous materials.

Associations

21011 American Wholesale Marketers Association
2750 Prosperity Avenue
Suite 530
Fairfax, VA 22031
703-208-3358
FAX: 703-573-5738 800-482-2962
jenniferm@awmanet.org
www.awmanet.org

Jennifer Moulton, VP Marketing/Industry Affairs

An organization supporting the confectionery, tobacco and allied products industries through programs and services. Members include wholesale distributor, manufacturers and other allieds to the industry.
1000 Members Founded: 1942

21012 Association of Dark Leaf Tobacco Dealers
Po Box 638
Springfield, TN 37172-0638
615-384-9576
FAX: 615-384-6461
h.krozel@hailcotton.com
www.hailcotton.com
An affiliate of Burley and Dark Leaf Tobacco Export Association.
Founded: 1902

21013 Bright Belt Warehouse Association
PO Box 120004
Raleigh, NC 27605
919-828-8988
FAX: 919-821-2092
donaf@clemson.edu
www.clemson.edu/peedeerec/Tobacco/BBWA.htm
Association of flue-cured tobacco warehousemen.

21014 Burley Stabilization Corporation
PO Box 6447
Knoxville, TN 37914
865-259-9381
FAX: 865-525-9381
burleytobacco@aol.com
www.burleystabilization.com

George Marks, President
Joe K Thomas III, VP
Charlie C Finch, Managing Director

Association of Burley tobacco warehouses in Kentucky, Tennessee, Ohio, Missouri, Indiana, Virginia, West Virginia and North Carolina.

21015 Burley Tobacco Growers Cooperative Association
620 South Broadway
Lexington, KY 40508
859-252-3561
FAX: 859-231-9804
stephanie@burleytobacco.com
www.burleytobacco.com

Henry West, President
Eddie Warren, VP
Danny McKinney, Chief Executive Officer
Stephanie Harlow, Graphic Design Artist
Daniel Green, Comptroller

Burley and Dark Leaf tobacco growers' trade association.

21016 Cigar Association of America
1707 H Street NW
Suite 800
Washington, DC 20006-3919
202-223-8204
FAX: 202-833-0379

Norman F Sharp, President

Consists of cigar manufacturers, importers and major industry suppliers. Provides government relations and statistical services to the industry and promotes the image of the cigar.
60 Members Founded: 1937

21017 Eastern Dark-Fired Tobacco
1109 South Main Street
Springfield, TN 37172-0517
615-384-4543
FAX: 615-384-4545

Dan S Borthick, President

Association of North Central Tennessee and South Central Kentucky growers that produce Type 22 Dark fire-cured and Type 35 Dark air-cured (one sucker) tobacco.

21018 Flue-Cured Tobacco Cooperative
1304 Annapolis Drive
Raleigh, NC 27608
919-821-4560
FAX: 919-821-4564
arnoldh3151@ipass.net
www.ustobaccofarmer.com

Ken Bopp, Treasurer
L Arnold Hamm, CEO/General Manager
Jimmy Barefoot, Assistant General Manager

Marketing cooperative which administers price support and provides %100 US flue-cured tobacco direct to purchasers.
Founded: 1946

21019 Friends of Tobacco
14611 Godrich Drive NW
Gig Harbor, WA 98329
253-857-8934
FAX: 253-857-0143
fot@fujipub.com fujipub.com/fot

Gary Corbett, President

Nonprofit organization promoting the economic importance of tobacco and freedom of choice in using tobacco products.
16000 Members Founded: 1991

21020 Retail Tobacco Dealers of America
4 Bradley Park Court
Suite 2H
Columbus, GA 31904-3637
706-494-1143
FAX: 706-494-1893
info@rtda.org www.rtda.org

Joe Rowe, Executive Director

Represents and assists retail tobacconists.

21021 Specialty Tobacco Council
204 Northgate Park Drive
Winston-Salem, NC 27106
336-759-0391
FAX: 336-759-0965
hcroemer@bellsouth.net
specialtytobacco.org

Henry C Roemer III, Executive Director

Represents manufacturers and importers of specialty tobacco products.
Founded: 1984

21022 Tobacco Associates
1725 K Street NW
Suite 512
Washington, DC 20006
202-828-9144
FAX: 202-828-9149
taw@tobaccoassociates.org
www.tobaccoassociatesinc.org

Kirk Wayne, President

Represents US flue-cured tobacco producers in export, promotion and market development.
Founded: 1947

21023 Tobacco Association Of The United States
3716 National Drive
Suite 114
Raleigh, NC 27612
919-782-5151
FAX: 919-781-0915

Tommy Bunn, Executive VP

Promotes market for US leaf tobacco.
100 Members Founded: 1900

21024 Tobacco Growers Association of North Carolina
3901 Barrett Drive
Suite 202
Raleigh, NC 27619
919-781-2307
FAX: 919-781-0066 www.tganc.com

Sam Crews, President
Graham Boyd, Executive VP

Commodity association for North Carolina tobacco growers.
10000 Members Founded: 1981

21025 Tobacco Merchants Association
PO Box 8019
Princeton, NJ 08543-8019
609-275-4900
FAX: 609-275-8379
tma@tma.org www.tma.org

Farrell Delman, President

Tobacco trade association and source of current information on the tobacco industry.
170 Members Founded: 1915

Newsletters

21026 Tobacco Barometer
Tobacco Merchants Association of the United States
PO Box 8019
Princeton, NJ 08543-8019
609-275-4900
FAX: 609-275-8379
tma@tma.org http://www.tma.org

Mark Schoenseld, Editor
Roberta Crosdy, Marketing Manager
Mark Schoenseld, Publisher

Tobacco industry news.
Monthly Founded: 1915

21027 Tobacco Products Litigation Reporter
TPLR
PO Box 1162
Back Bay Annex
Boston, MA 02117-1162
617-373-2026
FAX: 617-437-3672
info@tplr.com http://www.tplr.com/

Richard Daynard, Publisher
Lissy Friedman, Publication Director
Mark Gottlieb, Legal Editor

Tobacco industry news. *$995.00*
8 issues per year Founded: 1975

21028 Tobacco on Trial
Tobacco Products Liability Project
102 The Fenway
Cushing Hall, Suite 117
Boston, MA 02115-5098
617-373-2026
FAX: 617-373-3672
http://www.tobacco-on-trial.com

Richard A Daynard, Publisher
Susan L Frank, Editor
Mark Gottlieb, Executive Director
Richard A Daynard, President

Tobacco industry news. *$95.00*
Founded: 1979

Magazines & Journals

21029 American Wholesale Marketers Association
1128 16th Street NW
Washington, DC 20036-4808
202-463-2124
FAX: 202-467-0559 800-482-2962
robertp@awmanet.org
www.awmanet.org

Robert Pignato, VP Marketing/Industry Affairs

Information on candy, chewing gum, tobacco, HBC, general merchandise, snack foods and related items.

Printed in 4 colors on glossy stock

21030 Smokeshop
Lockwood Trade Journal
26 Broadway
Floor 9M
New York, NY 10004
212-697-7053
FAX: 212-827-0945 800-766-2633
sales@smokeshopmag.com
http://www.smokeshopmag.com

Robert Lockwood, Publisher
Edward Hoyt III, Editor
Bob Olesen, Advertising Sales Manager

Retail tobacco dealer's prevailing source for industry news designed to help readers operate their business more successfully. *$ 24.00*
Founded: 1970

21031 Tobacco International
Lockwood Trade Journal
130 W 42nd Street
Suite 1050
New York, NY 10036-7804
212-697-7053
FAX: 212-827-0945
www.tobaccointernational.com

George Lockwood, Publisher

This trade publication offers information and news on the importing and exporting of tobacco. *$25.00*
Monthly

21032 Tobacco Reporter
SpecComm International
3000 Highwoods Boulevard
Suite 300
Raleigh, NC 27604-1029
919-878-0540
FAX: 919-876-8531
sales@tobaccoreporter.com
www.tobaccoreporter.com *$36.00*

21033 Tobacco Retailer
Adams Business Media
833 W Jackson Blvd
7th Floor
Chicago, IL 60607
312-846-4600
FAX: 312-846-4634
info@greenindustry.com
http://www.tobaccoretailer.com

Kate Kenny, Publisher
Steve Brackett, Group Publisher
Mark Adams, President
Joanne Juda, Circulation
John Kmitta, Editor

Monthly Founded: 1998
Circulation: 7125

21034 Tobacco Science
2016 Fanning Bridge Road
Fletcher, NC 28732
828-684-3562
FAX: 828-684-8715
pam_puryear@ncsu.edu
www.tobaccoscience.com

Dr David Shew, Editor
Pam Puryear, Managing Editor

Scientific journal containing technical reports on tobacco and tobacco smoke.

21035 Tobacconist
SpecComm International
3000 Highwoods Boulevard
Suite 300
Raleigh, NC 27604-1029
919-872-5040
FAX: 919-876-6531
mjackson@speccomm.com
www.tobacconistmagazine.com

Dayton Matlick, Publisher
Ed O'Connor, Advertising/Sales Manager
Dayton Matlick, Editor
Dayton Matlick, CEO

A business publication for retail tobacconists in the United States that includes information ranging from critical issues to new products and business advice. *$28.00*
Quarterly

Trade Shows

21036 AWMA Expo
American Wholesale Marketers Association
1128 16th Street NW
Washington, DC 20036-4808
202-463-2124
FAX: 202-467-0559 800-642-2962
robertp@awmanet.org
www.awmanet.org

Robert Pignato, VP Marketing/Industry Affairs

Annual show of 4500 manufacturers and suppliers of confectionery, tobacco, snack foods, juice, novelties and related products.

21037 Retail Tobacco Dealers of America Trade Show
4 Bradley Park Court
Suite 2H
Columbus, GA 31904-3637
706-494-1143
FAX: 706-494-1893
rtda@msn.com www.rtda.org

Ira Fader Jr, Show Manager

Trade show for premium tobacco products. Not open to the public. For the benefit of association members only. Containing 950 booths and 6,400 exhibits.
5,500 Attendees July

Directories & Databases

21038 Tobacco Barometer: Cigarettes and Cigars/ Smoking, Chewing and Snuff
Tobacco Merchants Association of the United States
231 Clarkville Road
Princeton, NJ 08543
609-275-4900
FAX: 609-275-8379
These two databases offers information on every aspect of the tobacco industry.
Full-text

21039 Tobacco Reporter's Global Tobacco Industry Guide
SpecComm International
3000 Highwoods Boulevard
Suite 300
Raleigh, NC 27604-1029
919-878-0540
FAX: 919-876-8531
sales@tobaccoreporter.com

Noel Morris, Publisher
Taco Tuinstra, Managing Editor

Directory of tobacco suppliers, leaf dealers, processors, manufacturers, brokers, marketing boards and associations. *$78.00*
Annual

Industry Web Sites

21040 www.awmanet.org
American Wholesale Marketers Association

A trade association representing corporations in the wholesale tobacco industries.

21041 www.buycheapcigarettes.com

We offer discount cigarettes and tobacco products. Cigarettes and tobacco products are for consumer use only. Minimum order is 3 Cartons.

21042 www.freedomnet.org/tobacco.html
Pipe Tobacco Council

Consists of manufacturers and importers of smoking tobacco in the United States. Provides government relations and statistical services to the industry.

21043 www.greyhouse.com
Grey House Publishing

Selected Grey House directories in the fields of business, health and education are available online. Users can search our online databases by several different search criteria, such as product categories, geographic area, sales volume and much, much more. Full Grey House catalog and online ordering also available.

21044 www.paylesscigarettes.com

Sells dicount cigarettes and tobacco products.

21045 www.taxfreetobacco.com

Sells dicount cigarettess.

21046 www.thetobaccoshop.com

Offers discount cigarettes and tobacco products.

21047 www.tobaccoassociatesinc.org

Website of the association representing US flue-cured tobacco producers.

21048 www.ustobaccofarmer.com

Information of interest to tobacco farmers.

Associations

21049 AIT Worldwide Logistics
701 N Rohlwing Road
Itasca, IL 60143
630-766-8300
800-669-4248
info@aitworldwide.com
www.aitworldwide.com
Daniel Lisowski, Founder
Steven Leturno, Founder
Provide customers with the inovative high-tech support and customization that enhances every shipment. Tailors the technology to the systems of each individual customer.

21050 Advanced Transit Association
9019 Hamilton Drive
Fairfax, VA 22031-3075
703-591-8328
www.advancedtransit.org
Tom Richert, Chairman
Catherine G Burke, President
Bob Dunning, VP
Jerry Kieffer, Manager
Supports the transportation association.
100 Members

21051 Affiliated Warehouse Companies, Inc.
PO Box 295
Hazlet, NJ 07730-0295
732-739-2323
FAX: 732-739-4154
sales@awco.com www.awco.com
Jim McBride, President
120 Members Founded: 1953
Mailing list available for rent 12000 names

21052 Air Courier Conference of America
Express Delivery & Logistics Association
6309 Beachway Dr
Falls Church, VA 22044-1510
703-998-7121
FAX: 703-998-7123
jmorris@aircour.org www.aircour.org
Keith Storey, President
George Trapp, VP
Air courier and air package delivery companies.

21053 Air Transport Association of America
1301 Pennsylvania Avenue NW
Suite 1100
Washington, DC 20004-1707
202-626-4000
ata@airlines.org www.airlines.org
Gilbert F Viets, Chairman
Dave Wing, Executive VP/CFO
Jim Hlavacek, Vice Chairman
Robert A Abel, Director
James May, President
Represents US scheduled airlines in domestic and international passenger and cargo operations.
Founded: 1936

21054 American Association of Railroad Superintendents
PO Box 456
Tinley Park, IL 60477
708-342-0210
FAX: 708-342-0257
aars@railroadsuperintendent.org
www.railroadsuperintendent.org
Robert M Denny, President
Patricia A Weissmann, Administrative Manager
Operating department officers of railroads.
500 Members Founded: 1881

21055 American Automobile Association
1000 AAA Drive
Heathrow, FL 32746-5062
407-444-7966

21056 American Bus Association
700 13th Street NW
Suite 575
Washington, DC 20005-5923
202-842-1645
FAX: 202-842-0850
abainfo@buses.org www.buses.org
Peter J Pantuso, President/CEO
Charles Zelle, Chairman
Ronald L Eyre, Vice Chairman
Trade association for the North American bus industry.
3307 Members Founded: 1926

21057 American Commodity and Shipping
1385 Iris Drive
Conyers, GA 30208
770-460-8920
FAX: 770-929-3201

21058 American Moving and Storage Association
1611 Duke Street
Alexandria, VA 22314-3406
703-683-7410
FAX: 703-683-7527 www.moving.org
Joseph Harrison, President
Acts as a clearinghouse for information on the moving and transporation industries.
3500 Members Founded: 1936

21059 American Public Transit Association
1666 K Street NW
Suite 1100
Washington, DC 20006
202-964-4800
www.apta.com
George F Dixon III, President Board of Trustees
Richard A White, General Manager/CEO
Karol Popkin, Chief Executive Officer
Maintains biographical archives and operates a placement service.
15M Members Founded: 1974

21060 American Railroads Association
50 F Street NW
Washington, DC 20001-1564
202-392-2334
www.aar.org
Edward R Hamberger, President/CEO
Jeff Marsh, VP Finance/Administration
Stephanie A Kilfeather, Director Meeting Services
Mark McRoberts, Director Budget Planning
Joyce Koeneman, Manager
Founded: 1934

21061 American Railway Bridge and Building
8201 Corporate Drive
Suite 1125
Landover, IL 20785
301-459-3200
FAX: 301-459-8077 www.arema.org
Dr Charles Emely, Executive Director
Vickie Fisher, Director Finance
Beth Caruso, Director Administration
Stacy Wright, Director Committees/Tech Services
Janice Clements, Director Membership
Fosters concern for design, construction and maintenance of bridges, buildings, water service facilities and other railway structures.
Founded: 1891

21062 American Railway Development Association
PO Box 44369
Eden Prairie, MN 55344-4369
952-828-9750
FAX: 952-828-9751
gil@amrailder.org
www.amraildevelop.org
E Gilbert Tyckoson, Jr, Executive Director
Members are marketing, real estate and industrial development officers of railroads. Objectives are to foster the industrial, real estate, natural resources and market development activities of North American railroads and throught the advancement of ideas and education of its members further promote the effectiveness of railway development and related work.
200 Members Founded: 1906

21063 American Road and Transportation Builders
1219 28th St NW
Washington, DC 20007-3362
202-289-4434
artbadc@aol.com www.artba.org
Dave Bauer, VP Government Relations
Alison Black, Research Economist
Randy Freedman, VP Business/Legal Affairs
Peter Ruane, President
Offers information and resources for members associated with the transporation building industry.
Founded: 1902

21064 American Short Line Railroad Association
50 F Street NW
Suite 7020
Washington, DC 20001-1536
202-628-4500
FAX: 202-628-6430
aslrra@aslrra.org www.aslrra.org
Richard F Timmons, President
Stephen M Sullivan, Executive Director Administration
Monitors and reports legislative and regulatory activities.
750 Members Founded: 1913

21065 American Space Transportation Association
General Dynamics
1801 Alexander Bell Drive
Reston, VA 20191-4400
703-548-2723
FAX: 703-295-6222 800-548-2723

The successor organization to the Ad Hoc Industry Group promoting the development of commercial space transportation in the United States.
25 Members

21066 American Underground Space Association
511 11th Avenue S
Suite 248
Minneapolis, MN 55415-1500
612-825-8933
FAX: 612-339-3207
Susan R Nelson, Executive Director
700 Members Founded: 1976

21067 American Waterways Operators
801 N Quincy Street
Suite 200
Arlington, VA 22203
703-841-9300
FAX: 703-841-0389
www.americanwaterways.com
Thomas A Allegretti, President
Anne Davis Burns, VP/Public Affairs
Members include domestic carriers transporting commodities by water, shipyards, terminals and affiliated, business.
375 Members

21068 Association for Commuter Transportation
1444 "I" Street NW
Suite 700
Washington, DC 20005
202-393-3497

info@actweb.org www.actweb.org
Chris Simmons, President
Kris Fransen, VP
ACT provides you with the resources of an international organization and the support of a regional affiliate of experienced Transportation Demand Management professionals.
810 Members Founded: 1991

21069 Association of Air Medical Services

526 King Street
Suite 415
Alexandria, VA 22314-3143
703-836-8732
FAX: 703-836-8920
information@aams.org www.aams.org

D Gregory Powell MD, President
Shirley Scholz, VP
Dawn Mancuso, Executive Director
Voluntary nonprofit organization, encourages and supports its members in maintaining a standard of performance reflecting safe operations and efficient, high quality patient care. Built on the idea that representation from a variety of medical transport services and businesses can be brought together to share information, collectively resolve problems and provide leadership in the medical transport community.
350 names $250 per M.

21070 Association of American Railroads
50 F Street NW
Washington, DC 20001-1564
202-392-2334
FAX: 202-639-2286
pubsrvcs@aar.org www.aar.org
Edward R Hamberger, President/CEO
Peggy Wilhide, VP Communications
Joyce Koeneman, Manager
Presently serves a joint agency of its individual railroad members to ensure an efficient nationwide rail system.
80 Members Founded: 1934

21071 Association of Railway Museums
PO Box 370
Tujunga, CA 91043-0370
818-951-9151
FAX: 818-951-9151
www.railway.museums.org
Ellen Fishburn, Secretary
Paul Hamond, President
The association of railway museums is for the preservation of railway equipment, artifacts and history.
125 Members Founded: 1961

21072 BAX Global
440 Exchange
Irvine, CA 92602
602-458-6200
888-671-6953
Joseph L Carnes, President
Jay Arnold, VP Human Resources & Administration
Specializes in managing the movement of heavyweight packages and cargo of all shapes and sizes.

21073 Brotherhood of Locomotive Engineers
1370 Ontario Street, Mezzanine
Cleveland, OH 44113-1702
216-241-2630
FAX: 216-861-0932
policy@ble.org www.ble.org
Don Hahs, Chief Executive Officer

21074 Brotherhood of Railroad Signalmen
917 Shenandoah Shores Road
Front Royal, VA 22630-6418
540-622-6522
FAX: 540-622-6532
kelly@brs.org www.brs.org
Kelly Haley, Communications Director
National organization representing the men and women who install and maintain signal systems for most of the nation's railroads.

21075 C.H. Robinson Worldwide Inc
8100 Mitchell Road
Eden Praire, MN 55344
952-937-8500
www.chrobinson.com
John Wiehoff, President & CEO
Provides multimodal transportation solutions throughout the world. Transports freight door to door, and delivers customized logistics solutions for clients of all sizes.
Founded: 1905

21076 Committee for Better Transit
38 W Cliff Street
Somerville, NJ 08876

An organization on urban transportation and related subjects.

21077 Crowley Maritime Corporation
155 Grand Avenue
Oakland, CA 94612
510-251-7500
FAX: 510-251-7788 800-CRO-WLEY
Thomas B Crowley Jr, Chairman, President & CEO
William A Pennella, Vice Chairman & Executive VP
Provides diversified transportation services in domestic and international markets by means of four operating lines of business: Liner services, Logistics, Marine services and Petroleum services.
Founded: 1972

21078 Driving School Association of America
11 W Pomona Boulevard
Monterey Park, CA 91754

FAX: 626-722-0485

21079 Expediting Management Association
931-823-1122
FAX: 877-524-5218
Larry Phipps, President
The Expediting Management Association, Inc. will maintain a certification program for it's memebers giving them the opportunity to achieve recognition from their peers in the association and industry.
200 Members Founded: 1972

21080 Express Carriers Association
PO Box 4376
Allentown, PA 18105-4376
866-322-7447
FAX: 866-322-3299
eca@expresscarriers.com
www.expresscarriers.com
Brad Westrom, President
Bruce Birtwell, First VP
Richard Ziemba, Second VP
The missio of the ECA is to develop business between carriers, shippers and vendors of products and services to the transportation industry.

21081 FedEx Freight
942 South Shady Grove Road
Memphis, TN 38120
901-369-3600
800-435-7949
Frederick W Smith, President & CEO
T Michael Glenn, Executive VP Market Dev & Corp Comm
Mission is to produce superior financial returns for shareowners by providing high value-added supply chain, transportation, business and related informationservices through focused operating companies.

21082 Fleet Management Institute (NAFA)
100 Wood Avenue S
Suite 310
Iselin, NJ 08830
732-494-8100
FAX: 732-494-6789
info@nafa.org www.nafa.org
Patricia Murtaugh, Assistant Executive Director
Joanne Marsh, Manager

21083 High Speed Grand Transportation
1010 Massachusetts Avenue NW
Washington, DC 20001
202-789-8107
www.hsgt.org

21084 Highway Users Federation for Safety and
PO Box 6285
Olympia, WA 98507-1904
253-376-8492

Diane Steed, President

The Highway Users Federation (WHUF) is an association concerned ith increasing capacity and safter on Highways.

21085 Institute of Transportation Engineering
1099 14th Street, NW
Suite 300 West
Washington, DC 20005-2729
202-289-022
FAX: 202-289-7722 www.ite.org

Thomas W Brahms, Executive Director

The Institute of Transportation Engineers is an internatioonal educational and scientific association of transportation professionals who are reponsible for meeting mobility and safety needs.

16000 Members Monthly Founded: 1930
Circulation: 18,000

21086 Institute of Transportation Engineers
1099 14th Street NW
Suite 300 W
Washington, DC 20005-3438
202-289-0222
FAX: 202-289-7722
ite_staff@ite.org www.ite.org

Richard T Romer, International President
Thomas Brahms, Executive Director/CEO

16000 Members Founded: 1930

21087 Intermodal Association of North America
11785 Beltsville Dr
Ste 1100
Beltsville, MD 20705-4049
301-982-3400
FAX: 301-982-4815
iana@intermodal.org
www.intermodal.org

Joanne F Casey, President/CEO
Thomas J Malloy, VP
Constance M Sheffield, VP Administration/Programs
Anne Beatty, Director Finance/Systems
Debbie Sasko, Director

Members are motor, rail and water transportation companies. Promotes the benefits and growth of the intermodal freight transportation.

600 Members

21088 International Association of Structural Movers
PO Box 2637
Lexington, SC 29071-2637
803-951-9304
FAX: 803-951-9314
gbrymer@alltel.net www.iasm.org

N Eugene Brymer, Staff Executive

Members are movers of heavy structural products, trusses, houses, machinery and masonry structures.

385 Members Founded: 1982

21089 International Brotherhood of Teamsters
25 Louisiana Avenue NW
Washington, DC 20001
202-246-6800
FAX: 202-624-8137 www.teamster.org

James Hoffa, President
Fred Gegare, VP
Carl E Haynes, VP
Thomas R O'Donnell, VP
Ralph J Taurone, VP

Affiliated with the AFL-CIO.

1.3MM Members Founded: 1954

21090 International Council of Cruise Lines
1211 Connecticut Avenue NW
Suite 800
Washington, DC 20036-2703
202-628-8000
FAX: 202-296-1676 www.iccl.org

John T Estes, President

A trade association representing about 90% of the North American oceangoing, overnight major cruise line companies.

7 Members Founded: 1990

21091 International Furniture Transportation and Logistics Council
PO Box 889
Gardner, MA 01440-0889
978-632-1913
FAX: 978-630-2917
jsears@iftlc.org www.iftlc.org

Raynard F Bohman Jr, Managing Director

Members are furniture manufacturers, retrilers, carriers, wholesalers and warehouses of allied products.

300 Members

21092 International Marine Transit Association
34 Otis Hill Road
Hingham, MA 02043
781-749-0078
FAX: 781-749-0078 terryboots@cs.com

Membership includes ferry operators, naval architects, manufacturers, suppliers, and others in the ferry industry around the world.

400 Members Founded: 1976

21093 International Safe Transit Association
1400 Abbott Road
Suite 160
East Lansing, MI 48823-1900
517-333-3437
FAX: 517-333-3813 888-367-4782
ista@ista.org www.ista.org

Edward Church, Executive Director
Meredith Young, Director Of Member Services

Members are shippers, carriers, manufacturers, packagers, package designers and testing laboratories, included in transport packaging.

750 Members Founded: 1948
Mailing list available for rent 4000 names $500 per M.

21094 International Taxicab, Limousine & Paratransit Association
3849 Farragut Avenue
Kensington, MD 20895-2004
301-946-5700
FAX: 301-946-4641
info@tlpa.org www.tlpa.org

Alfred LaGrasse, Executive VP

Members include owners of taxicab, limousine, airport shuttle, paratranist and nonemergency medical transportation fleets.

1107 Members Founded: 1917
Mailing list available for rent 5000 names $100 per M.

21095 Interstate Trucking Association
Express Carriers Association
PO Box 4307
Bethlehem, PA 18018
610-740-5857
FAX: 610-740-3174 866-322-7447
eca@expresscarriers.com
www.expresscarriers.com

Cheryle Williamson, Executive Director

Organization of newly enacted state legislation regulations having direct impact on vehicle operations, fuel taxes, registration size and weight.

21096 Landstar Global Logistics
13410 Sutton Park Drive S
Jacksonville, FL 32224

800-872-9400
corpcomm@landstar.com
www.landstar.com

Jim M Handoush, President

Mission is to be the leading non-asset based provider of transportation capacity delivering safe, sepcialized transportation services to customers worldwide utilizing a network of agents, third-party capacity owners and employees.

21097 Mid-West Truckers Association
2727 N Dirksen Parkway
Springfield, IL 62702
217-525-0310
FAX: 217-525-0342
info@mid-westtruckers.com
www.mid-westtruckers.com

Don Schaefer, Executive VP

Serves trucking industry by lobbying on their behalf, assisting with registration, license plate procurement and group insurance programs. Conducts educational programs, has own self-funded workers compensation insurance program. Trade association represents truck owners in 14 states.

2700 Members Founded: 1962

21098 Motor Transport Management Group
3251 Beacon Road
West Sacramento, CA 95691-3475
916-373-3630
FAX: 916-852-5707

21099 National Air Carrier Association
1000 Wilson Boulevard
Suite 1700
Arlington, VA 22209
703-358-8060
FAX: 703-358-8070 www.naca.cc

Ronald N Priddy, President
Hollis L Harris, Board Chairman

George Paul, Director Technical Services
Paul H Doell, Director Government Affairs

7 Members Founded: 1963

21100 National Air Transportation Association
4226 King Street
Alexandria, VA 22302
703-845-9000
FAX: 703-845-8176
cstroud@nata-online.org
www.nata.aero

James K Coyne, President
Greg Arnold, Chairman
Jeffrey Brown, Treasurer
Beth Haskins, Vice Chairman

Aviation company.

1800 Members Founded: 1940

21101 National Association of Freight
PO Box 21418
Albuquerque, NM 87154-1418
505-844-8443

21102 National Association of Rail Shippers
50 F Street NW
Room 6400
Washington, DC 20001-1530
202-824-6800

nars@onramp.net
www.rampages.onramp.net/~nars/

Martha Kappel, Executive Director
Laurie Battaglia, Publisher

Strives to provide a sound transporation system. Bestows annual Award of Excellence.

2M Members Founded: 1937

21103 National Association of Railroad
900 2nd Street NE
Washington, DC 20002
202-408-8362
FAX: 202-408-8287
narp@narprail.org www.narprail.org

Ross Capon, Executive Director

Seeks to increase public awareness of rail passenger service and its benefits. Works for a national transportation policy.

12M Members Founded: 1967

21104 National Business Travel Association
110 N Royal Street
4th Floor
Alexandria, VA 22314
703-684-0836
FAX: 703-684-0263
info@nbta.org www.nbta.org

Bill Connors, Executive Director/COO
Amy Weist, Director
Daphne Bryant, Foundation Director
Hank Roeder, Senior Director
Kristi Long, Director

Offers over 1,300 corporate travel managers and allied members in the United States and Canada.

2400 Members Founded: 1968

21105 National Child Transport Association
Hall of States
444 N Capitol Street NW
Washington, DC 20001-1512
202-083-3860

Lonnie Hall, Manager

Thirty booths.

1.2M Members

21106 National Customs Brokers and Forwarders
1200 18th Street NW
#901
Washington, DC 20036
202-466-0222
FAX: 202-466-0226
staff@ncbfaa.org www.ncbfaa.org

Federico C Zuniga, President
Peter H Powell Sr, Chairman
Mary Jo Muoio, VP
Barbara Reilly, Executive Vice President
John Hyatt, Secretary

Learn about new business leads, stay on top of Customs Service and other agency regulations that will impact your operations and provide invaluable professional development resources for your employees.

600+ Members

21107 National Defense Transportation Association
50 S Pickett Street
Suite 220
Alexandria, VA 22304-7296
703-751-5011
FAX: 703-823-8761
info@ndtahq.com www.ndtahq.com

LTG Kenneth Wykle, USA (Ret), President

Intended as a liasion between government and private transportation officials.

7800 Members Founded: 1944

21108 National Highway Carriers
PO Box 6099
Buffalo Grove, IL 60089
847-634-0606
FAX: 847-634-1026
nhcdg@aol.com
www.national-highway.com

Founded: 1942

21109 National Industrial Transportation League
1700 N Moore Street
Suite 1900
Arlington, VA 22209
703-524-5011
FAX: 703-524-5017
info@nitl.org www.nitl.org

Thomas F Pellington, Chairman
Michael J Barr, First Vice Chairman
John Ficker, President
Peter Gatti, Executive VP

Annual show of 250 exhibitors of computer services software and innovations for transportation operations.

600 Members Founded: 1907

21110 National Institute of Certified Moving
1611 Duke Street
Alexandria, VA 22314
703-683-7410
FAX: 703-683-7527 800-538-6672

Michael Clark, Manager

Awards the certified moving consultant designation to those who have passed an exam testing their liability.

Founded: 1974

21111 National Institute of Packaging, Handling and Logistic Engineers
6902 Lyle Street
Lanham, MD 20706-3454
301-459-9105
FAX: 301-459-4925

Barbara Johnson, Editor

A national organization of over 700 engineers, chemists, consultants, and executives.

21112 National Parking Association
1112 16th Street NW
Suite 300
Washington, DC 20036
202-296-4336
FAX: 202-331-8523 800-647-7275
info@npapark.org www.npapark.org

Martin L Stein, Executive Director
Logan Hunter-Thompson, Director Communications
Patricia Langfield, Director Marketing/Business

Proudly serving the nation's parking industry since 1951. Our members are comprised of parking professionals in both the public and private sectors from across the country and around the world. NPA members are private operators, parking consultants, colleges and universities, municipalities, parking authorities, hospitals and medical centers and industry vendors.

1200 Members Founded: 1951
Mailing list available for rent

21113 National School Transportation Association
113 S West St
Ste 400
Alexandria, VA 22314-2851
703-684-3200
FAX: 703-684-3212 800-222-6782
info@yellowbuses.com
www.yellowbuses.org

Dale Krapf, President
Jeffrey Kulick, Executive Director

Strives to provide safe transportation, foster safety, and an atmosphere conducive to private enterprise.

3M Members Founded: 1964

21114 National Small Shipments Traffic
758 Quail Run
Waconia, MN 55387
952-442-8850
FAX: 952-442-8850
brian@nasstrac.org www.nasstrac.org

Terri Ferraro, Chairperson
Randy Schaeffer, President
Matt Ehlinger, First VP
Shawn O'Sullivan, Second VP

Members are truck, air, rail and sea shippers of freight weighing less than 10,000 pounds.

250 Members Founded: 1952

21115 National Waterways Conference
4650 Washington Blvd.
#608
Arlington, VA 22201
703-243-4090
FAX: 703-243-4155
webmaster@waterways.org
www.waterways.org

Worth Hager, President

An umbrella group of shippers, barge lines and local port authorities working to promote a better understanding of the public value of the American waterways system.

350 Members Founded: 1960

21116 National/International Safe Transit Association
205 N Michigan Avenue
Suite 1900
Chicago, IL 60601-5923
312-946-4000
FAX: 773-645-9770

21117 Natural Gas Vehicles for America
400 N. Capitol St. NW
Washington, DC 20001
202-824-7366
FAX: 202-824-7087
rkolodziej@ngvamerica.org
www.ngvc.org

Richard R Kolodziej, President

Members are organizations with an interest in encouraging the development of natural gas powered vehicles.

250 Members Founded: 1988

21118 North American Shippers Association
PO Box 249
Rahway, NJ 07065-0249
201-460-4800
FAX: 540-586-0207

Case Pieterman, Executive Director

Members are shippers of wine and alcoholic beverages.

430 Members Founded: 1987

21119 Railway Supply Institute
29 W 140 Butterfield Road, Street 103-A
Warrenville, IL 60555
630-393-0106
FAX: 630-393-0108
rsupplya@aol.com www.rsiweb.org

Thomas D Simpson, Executive Director
Nicole B Brewin, Assistant VP

The railway equipment and supply industry.

300 Members Founded: 1909

21120 Railway Systems Suppliers
9304 News LaGrange Road, Street 200
Louisville, KY 40242
502-327-7774
FAX: 502-327-0541
rssi@rssi.org www.rssi.org

Donald F Remaley, Executive Director
Robert P DeMarco, Chairman/President
James A Huntley, Executive VP
James R Higginbottom, First VP

A trade association serving the communication and signal segment of the rail transportation industry. Manages an annual trade show.

230 Members Founded: 1966

21121 Regional Airline Association
2025 M Street NW
Washington, DC 20036
202-367-1170
FAX: 202-367-2170
raa@dc.sba.com www.raa.org

Deborah C McElroy, President
Scott W Foose, VP
David Lotterer, VP Technical Services
Erica Thomas, Membership Coordinator
Faye Malarkey, VP Legislative Affairs

Membership consists of more than 70 airlines and 350 associate members that provide goods and services.

300 Members Founded: 1975

21122 Roadmasters and Maintenance of Way Association of America
18154 Harwood Avenue
Cary Building
Homewood, IL 60430-2128
708-799-4650

Pat Weissman, Executive Director

Railroad executives concerned with track and roadway management.

2.1M Members

21123 Shippers National Freight Claim Council
120 Main Street
Huntington, NY 11743-6906
631-270-0100

Joyce Grandy, Administrative Assistant

21124 Shippers Oil Field Traffic Association
907 Kiowa Drive E
Gainesville, TX 76240-9575
940-668-7735
FAX: 940-668-7212

50 Members Founded: 1941

21125 Society of Automotive Engineers
400 Commonwealth Drive
Warrendale, PA 15096-0001
724-772-8548
FAX: 724-776-9765 877-606-7323
customerservice@sae.org www.sae.org

Jack Lewis, Automotive HQ Manager
Jane Lewis, Automotive HQ Special Events
Patti Kreh, Meetings/Exhibits Manager

Offers automotive engineers the technical information and expertise used in building, maintaining and operating self propelled vehicles for use on land, sea, air or space.

21126 Space Transportation Association
4305 Underwood Street
University Park, MD 20782
703-855-3917

rich@spacetransportation.us
www.spacetransportation.us

Richard Coleman, President
Ty McCoy, Chairman

Represents the interests of organizations which intend to develop, build, operate and use space transportation vehicles and systems in order to provide reliable, economical, safe and routine access to space for public and private entities.

20 Members Founded: 1990

21127 Taxicab, Limousine & Paratransit Association
3849 Farragut Avenue
Kensington, MD 20895-2004
301-946-5700
FAX: 301-946-4641
info@tlpa.com www.ttpa.org

Alfred La Gasse III, Executive Vice President

6,000 names $100 per M.

21128 Transport Workers Union of America
80 W End Avenue
New York, NY 10023-6399
212-873-6000
FAX: 212-721-1431 www.tww.org

James S Gannon, Editor

Chartered by the Congress of Industrial Organizations.

110M Members Founded: 1934 ISSN 0039-8659

21129 Transportation Clubs International
PO Box 1072
Glen Alpine, NC 28628
253-858-8627

Members are individuals in all phases of transportation, traffic management and physical distribution.

10M Members

21130 Transportation Institute
5201 Auth Way
Camp Springs, MD 20746
301-423-3335
FAX: 301-423-0634
info@trans-inst.org
www.trans-inst.org

James L Henry, President
Jerome K Welsch Jr, COO
Thomas B Crowley Jr, COO
Robert E Johnston, Executive VP
Mark Tabbutt, President

Members are US flag shipping, towing and dredging companies.

100 Members Founded: 1967

21131 Transportation Intermediaries Association
3601 Eisenhower Avenue
Suite 110
Alexandria, VA 22304
703-317-2140
FAX: 703-329-1898
info@tianet.org www.tianet.org

Robert A Voltmann, Executive Director/CEO
Kelly Scott, Contact

Education and policy organization for North American transportation intermediaries. TIA is the only national association representing the interests of all third party transportation service providers. The members of TIA include logistics management firms, property brokers, perishable commodities brokers, freight forwarders, intermodal marketers, ocean and air forwarders, and NVOCC's.

700 Members Founded: 1977

21132 Transportation Research Board
2101 Constitution Avenue NW
Washington, DC 20418-0007
202-342-2933
FAX: 202-334-2519
TABSales@nas.edu
www.nationalacademies.org/trb

21133 Transportation Research Forum
Po Box 5074
Fargo, ND 58105
701-231-7766
FAX: 701-231-1945 www.trforum.org

Anthony Pagano, President
John Wells, Executive President

An independent organization of transportation professionals.

680 Members Founded: 1950

21134 Truck Renting and Leasing Corporation
PO Box 1518
Bellvue, WA 98004-1808

FAX: 425-468-8211 800-426-1420

J Michael Payne, Executive VP

A multi-national technology company, NRLC monitors legislation and other issues affecting the truck/trailer leasing and rental industry. It also manufacturers heavy-duty, on-and-off-road trucks worldwide.

275 Members Founded: 1978

21135 Truck Trailer Manufacturers Association
1020 Princess Street
Alexandria, VA 22314-2247
703-549-3010
FAX: 703-549-3014
ttma@erols.com www.ttmanet.org

Richard Bowling, President

News of interest to trailer manufacturers and suppliers.

21136 United Bus Owners of America
1300 L Street NW
Suite 1050
Washington, DC 20005-4107

Wayne J Smith, Executive Director

Serves the bus industry, with particular emphasis on group travel and tourism.

800 Members

21137 United States Telecom Association
607 14th Street NW
Suite 400
Washington, DC 20005
202-326-7300
FAX: 202-326-7333
membership@ustelecom.org
www.ustelecom.org

Walter McKormick, President
Francis X Frantz, Chairman of the Board

Trade association representing service provides and suppliers for the telecom industry. *$699.00*

21138 Wine and Spirits Shippers Association
11800 Sunrise Valley Drive
Reston, VA 20191
703-860-2300
FAX: 703-860-2422
info@wssa.com www.wssa.com

V James Andretta, Chairman
Derek H Anderson, President
Howard Jacobs, VP
Geoffrey Giovanetti, Executive Director

Provides members with services that allow for the efficient and economical transportation of alcoholic beverages.

320 Members Founded: 1976

21139 Women's Transportation Seminar: National
808 17th Street NW
Suite 200
Washington, DC 20006-3910
202-964-4340

Helen Hall, Executive Director
Kelly Gallagher, Manager

Strives to advance the knowledge and training of transportation professionals. Offers seminars on career planning and management skills.

2.5M Members Founded: 1977

21140 Womens Transportation Seminar
1701 K St NW
Ste 800
Washington, DC 20006-1504
202-955-5085
FAX: 202-955-5088
wts@wtsinternational.org
www.wtsinternational.org

Debra Baskett, Director
Mary Jane O'Meara, National President
Afsaneh Sunnie, National VP
Robin Malacrea, National Secretary
Kelly Gallagher, Manager

3500 Members Founded: 1977

21141 World Organization of Dredging
PO Box 5797
Vancouver, WA 98668
360-750-0209
FAX: 360-750-1445
weda@juno.com www.woda.org

Lawrence M Patella, Executive Director
B A Wheeler, Vice Chairman
G L Hartman, Director

Develops professionalism in individuals involved in the dredging industry.

2700 Members Founded: 1981

Newsletters

21142 Advanced Transit News
Advanced Transit Association
PO Box 162
Palo Alto, CA 94302
800-779-0544
FAX: 800-779-0544 800-779-0544
jpaskry@davinciglobal.com
http://www.advancedtransit.org

Catherine G. Burke, President
Bob Dunning, VP
Lawrence Fabian, Publisher

Offers information on the American transit system.

100 pages Quarterly Founded: 1953
Printed in 1 color on matte stock

21143 Center for Microcomputers in Transportation
512 Weil Hall
PO Box 116585
Gainesville, FL 32611
352-392-7575
FAX: 352-389-2324 800-226-1013
mctrans@ce.ufl.edu
www.mctrans.ce.ufl.edu
Founded: 1986

21144 Dual News
Driving School Association of America
11 W Pomona Boulevard
Monterey Park, CA 91754

FAX: 626-722-0485

George Hensel, Publisher

Association news for student driving instructors and educational personnel.

BiWeekly
Circulation: 5,000

21145 Fleet Street
Greenwich Consulting
15821 Fetlock Lane
Chino Hills, CA 91709
909-606-2271
FAX: 909-597-7759

Karen Edward, Publisher

Consulting newsletter geared toward Distribution and Fleet Management Executives - Provides transportation managers with cost-cutting methodogies.

Circulation: 15500

21146 HazMat Transport News
Business Publishers
8737 Colesville Road
Suite 1100
Silver Spring, MD 20910-3925
301-876-6300
FAX: 301-587-4530 800-274-6737
bpinews@bpinews.com
http://www.bpinews.com

Leonard A Eiserer, Publisher
Beth Early, Operations Director

Regulatory and legislative development affecting hazardous materials transportation. In-depth coverage on research and special programs administration, hazmat regulation programs and enforcement actions. *$447.00*

Founded: 1963

21147 Inside DOT and Transportation Week
King of Communications Group
1325 G St. NW
Suite 1003
Washington, DC 20005-1601
202-638-4260
FAX: 202-662-9744 800-926-5464
webmaster@kingpublishing.com
http://www.kingpublishing.com

Llewellyn King, Publisher
Dave Ahearn, Editor
Wenita Lhill-waddell, Marketing

Offers information to persons working in the transportation profession. *$1300.00*

12 pages Daily Founded: 1973
Printed in 1 color on newsprint stock
Computerized version available: Fax

21148 Interstate Information Report
Express Carriers Association
PO Box 4376
Allentown, PA 18105-4376
610-740-5857
FAX: 610-740-3174 866-322-7447
eca@expresscarriers.com
http://www.expresscarriers.com

Cheryle Williamson, Executive Director

Compilation of newly enacted state legislation regulations having direct impact on vehicle operations, fuel taxes, registration size and weight.

21149 McTrans
Center for Microcomputers in Transportation
512 Weil Hall
PO Box 116585
Gainesville, FL 32611
352-392-7575
FAX: 352-389-2324 800-226-1013
mctrans@ce.ufl.edu
www.mctrans.ce.ufl.edu

CE Wallace, Publisher

Information about microcomputer software and resources in transportation.

Founded: 1986
Circulation: 8,000

21150 Notes from Underground
Committee for Better Transit
PO Box 3106
Long Island City, NY 11103-0106
718-728-0091
alpha.fdu.edu/~dobrow/transit.htm

Stephen Dobrow, President

Notes on urban transportation and related subjects.
Monthly

21151 **Proclaim**
Slesia Companies
619 Broad Creek Drive
Fort Washington, MD 20744-5800
301-292-1970
FAX: 301-292-1787
Dale Anderson, Publisher
Covers transportation freight claims.
Monthly

21152 **Rail & Mass Transit Systems: E-mail News**
Forecast International
22 Commerce Road
Newtown, CT 06470-1643
203-426-0800
FAX: 203-426-1964 800-451-4975
consulting@forecast1.com
http://www.forecast1.com
Kathy Bertrand, Production Manager
Monty Nebinger, Circulation Director
An electronic information/data service sourced from thousands of worldwide publications, in 15 languages. Provides concise summaries, news, trends and contract information with hyper-links to the source or a related website. Delivered 100 times a year. *$265.00*
Founded: 1973

21153 **Rider's Digest**
Metropolitan Atlanta Road Transit
2424 Piedmont Road NE
Atlanta, GA 30324-3311
404-848-5000
FAX: 404-848-5098
Judith Welsberg, Publisher
Public transportation news.
Monthly

21154 **Roads, Highways & Bridges: E-mail News**
Forecast International
22 Commerce Road
Newtown, CT 06470-1643
203-426-0800
FAX: 203-426-1964 800-451-4975
info@forecast1.com
http://www.forecast1.com
Kathy Bertrand, Production Manager
Monty Nebinger, Circulation Director
An electronic information/data service sourced from thousands of worldwide publications, in 15 languages. Provides concise summaries, news, trends and contract information with hyper-links to the source or a related website. Delivered 100 tomes a year. *$425.00*
Founded: 1973

21155 **Ships & Maritime Facilities: E-mail News**
Forecast International
22 Commerce Road
Newtown, CT 06470-1643
203-426-0800
FAX: 203-426-1964 800-451-4975
info@forecast1.com
http://www.forecast1.com
Kathy Bertrand, Production Manager
Monty Nebinger, Circulation Director
An electronic information/data service sourced from thousands of worldwide publications, in 15 languages. Provides concise summaries, news, trends and contract information with hyper-links to the source or a related website. Delivered 100 times a year.
$425.00
Founded: 1973

21156 **TransitPulse**
Trans 21
PO Box 249
Boston, MA 02122-0002
617-825-9687
FAX: 617-482-7417
Lawrence J Fabin, Publisher
Newsletters and faxed advisory service on worldwide developments in Automated People Movers. *$75.00*
4 pages BiMonthly
Circulation: 500 Audited Est. Pass-Along Circ: 1000
Printed in 1 color on matte stock
Computerized version available: Fax

21157 **Transport Workers Union of America**
1700 Broadway
New York, NY 10019
212-259-4900
FAX: 212-265-4537
mailbox@twu.org http://www.twu.org
Mike O'Brien, International President
Chartered by the Congress of Industrial Organizations.
Monthly Founded: 1934 ISSN 0039-8659

21158 **Transportation Intermediaries Association**
3601 Eisenhower Avenue
Suite 110
Alexandria, VA 22304
703-317-2140
FAX: 703-329-1898
info@tianet.org www.tianet.org
Robert A Voltmann, Executive Director/CEO
Kelly Scott, Contact
Education and policy organization for North American transportation intermediaries. TIA is the only national association representing the interests of all third party transportation service providers. The members of TIA include logistics management firms, property brokers, perishable commodities brokers, freight forwarders, intermodal marketers, ocean and air forwarders, and NVOCC's.
700 pages Monthly Founded: 1977

21159 **US Rail News**
Business Publishers
8737 Colesville Road
10th floor
Silver Spring, MD 20910-3928
301-587-6300
FAX: 301-587-4530 800-274-6737
custserv@bpinews.com
http://www.bpinews.com
Leonard A Eiserer, Publisher/President
Andy Arnold, Editor
Reports on the trends, legislation, regulations, acquisitions, business opportunities and technological developments that directly affect the rail industry. *$437.00*
25 issues per y Founded: 1963

21160 **Urban Transport News**
Business Publishers
8737 Colesville Road
Suite 1100
Silver Spring, MD 20910-3928
301-876-6300
FAX: 301-587-4530 800-274-6737
custserv@bpinews.com
http://www.bpinews.com
Leonard A Eiserer, Publisher
Beth Early, Operations Director
Comprehensive briefings on trends, regulations, legislation, business and technological developments in the mass transit area. *$ 437.00*
Founded: 1963

Magazines & Journals

21161 **Air Medical Journal**
526 King Street
Suite 415
Alexandria, VA 22314-3143
703-836-8732
FAX: 703-836-8920 800-525-3712
information@aams.org
http://www.aams.org
Renee Hollerem, Editor
Dawn M Mancuso, Executive Director
An association of health care entities operating helicopter transport services. Magazine is published, price included in membership.
375 pages Founded: 1980 375 names $300 per M.
Printed in on glossy stock

21162 **American Journal of Transportation**
Fleur de Lis Publishing
1354 Hancock Street
Suite 300
Quincy, MA 02169
617-328-5005
FAX: 617-328-5999 800-599-6358
ajot@ajot.com http://www.ajot.com/
George Lauriat, Editor
Ann Radwan, Associate Editor
William Bourbon, Publisher
Bob Kirk, Production Manager
Newspaper serving the shipping, trucking, air freight and railroad industries in the US and Canada. *$98.00*
Weekly Founded: 1994
Circulation: 8115
Printed in on newsprint stock

21163 **American Mover**
American Movers Conference
1611 Duke Street
Alexandria, VA 22314-3406
703-683-7410
FAX: 703-683-7527
info@moving.org
http://www.promover.org
David Sparkman, Editor
Joseph M Harrison, President
Michael S Shaffer, Chairman
Norma Gyovai, Advertising Manager
Carol Laird, Production Manager
This publication covers the moving and storage industry. *$60.00*
24 pages Monthly Founded: 1958
Circulation: 3700

21164 **American Shipper**
Howard Publications
300 W Adams Street Suite 600
PO Box 4728
Jacksonville, FL 32201-4728
904-355-2601
FAX: 904-791-8836 800-874-6422
nbarry@shippers.com
http://www.americanshipper.com
Nancy Barry, Production Manager
Hayes Howard, Publisher
Kerry Cowart, Circulation Manager
James Blaeser, Sales Associate

Provides those involved in domestic and global supply chain management with news and information of a strategic nature, useful in the formation of logistics polices and partnerships. *$36.00*
104 pages Monthly Founded: 1951
Circulation: 13705
Printed in 4 colors on glossy stock

21165 American Trucker
Primedia
7355 Woodland Drive
Indianapolis, IN 46278-1769
317-991-1350
FAX: 317-299-1356 800-827-7468
atmarketing@primediabusiness.com
http://www.trucker.com
Dallas Nauert, Production Manager
Diana Starks, Circulation Director
A trade publication featuring new and used trucks, trailors,parts and services for the heavy duty trucking industry. *$21.00*
Monthly Founded: 1975
Circulation: 930338 930338 names $115 per M.
Printed in 4 colors on matte stock

21166 Analysis of Class I Railroads
Association of American Railroads
50 F Street NW
Floor 3
Washington, DC 20001-1564
202-392-2334
FAX: 202-639-5546 877-999-8824
Kelly Donley, Marketing
Tom White, Editor
Edward Hamberger, CEO/President
Joyce Koeneman, Manager
Offers information on the railroad travel industry. *$250.00*
Founded: 1934

21167 Atlantic Northeast Rails & Ports
162 main street
Yarmouth, ME 04096
207-846-3549
FAX: 603-215-4482
chop@atlanticnortheast.com
http://www.atlanticnortheast.com
Chop Hardenbergh, CEO/President
$375.00
Monthly Founded: 1994
Circulation: 300

21168 Better Roads
WMO DannHausen Corporation
PO Box 558
Park Ridge, IL 60068
847-696-2391
FAX: 847-696-3445
wod@dannhausen.com
Wm O Dannhausen, Publisher
Market to federal agencies, bureaus, government departments, states, counties township road and city public works. *$26.96*
Monthly Founded: 1769
Circulation: 38406

21169 Brotherhood of Locomotive Engineers
1370 Ontario Street, Mezzanine
Cleveland, OH 44113-1702
216-241-2630
FAX: 216-241-6516
policy@ble.org www.ble.org
Don M Hahs, National President
John Bentley, Editor

21170 Bus Conversions Magazine
MAK Publishing
7246 Garden Grove Boulevard
Westminster, CA 92683
714-799-0062
FAX: 714-799-0042
editor@busconversions.com
http://www.busconversions.com
Michael A Kadletz, Publisher
Rikki Gee, Publication Manager
how-to, full color, monthly magazine that includes photos, floor plans, helpful hints and guides for buying, selling, selecting, and converting a bus to an RV or executive entertainer's coach. Features pages of classified ads and valuable info on maintaining, operating and updating your coach. *$38.00*
72 pages Founded: 1992
Circulation: 8000
Printed in 4 colors on glossy stock

21171 Bus Ride
Friendship Publications
4742 N 24th St
Suite 340
Phoenix, AZ 85016-4884
602-265-7600
FAX: 602-277-7588 800-541-2670
steve@busride.com
http://www.busride.com
Steve Kane, Publisher/Editor-in-Chief
Wayne Bryan, Editor
Donna Arnseth, Circulation Administrator
Maria Jolly, Assistant Editor
Valerie Valtierra, Production Director
Bus industry trade journal with articles about bus companies, training agencies and manufacturers and suppliers to the bus industry. *$39.00*
120 pages Monthly Founded: 1965
Circulation: 16000
Printed in 4 colors on glossy stock

21172 Chief Logistics Officer
Penton Media
1300 E 9th Street
Cleveland, OH 44114
216-696-7000
FAX: 216-696-1752
information@penton.com
www.tdmagazine.com
Tony D'Avino, Publisher
Perry A Trunick, Editor
Pam Hardy, Marketing Manager
Maryann Jovorek, Production Manager
Magazine for supply chain leaders, supplement to Transportation and Distribution. *$50.00*
48 pages Quarterly Founded: 1960
Circulation: 12M
Printed in 4 colors on glossy stock

21173 Classic Trains
James Folcum
21027 Crossroads Circle
Waukesha, WI 53187
262-796-8776
FAX: 262-796-1615
http://www.classictrain.com
Rob McGornigal, Editor
Mike Yuhaf, Advertising Manager
Publication features stories on antique and old trains.

21174 Commercial Carrier Journal
Chilton Company
3200 Rice Mine Road NE
Tuscaloosa, AL 35406
800-633-5953
FAX: 610-964-4647
prichards@randallpub.com
http://www.ccjmagazine.com
Chip Magner, Publisher
F Michael Reilly, CEO
Catherine J Randall, Chairman
Avery Vise, Editorial Director
Paul Richards, Editor
For fleet management.
Monthly Founded: 1934
Circulation: 101176

21175 Contingency Planning & Management
Witter Publishing Corporation
20 Commerce Street
Flemington, NJ 08822
908-788-0343
FAX: 908-788-3782
CPMmagazine@WitterPublishing.com
http://www.witterpublishing.com
Steve Biggers, Publisher
Andy Hagg, Editor
Bob Joudanin, Publisher
Mike Viscel, Production Manager
Courtney Witter, Print/Subscription Manager
Serves the fields of financial/banking, manufacturing industrial, transportation, utilities, telecommunications, health care, government, insurance and other allied fields.
Monthly Founded: 1996
Circulation: 62,000

21176 Contracting for Transportation & Logistics Services
120 Main Street
Huntington, NY 11743-6906
631-270-0100
FAX: 516-549-8962
tcpc@transportlaw.com
www.transportlaw.com
William J Augello, Executive Director
Published by the Transportation Consumer Protection Council. *$48.00*
Founded: 2001

21177 Corporate Procedures for Shipping & Receiving
120 Main Street
Huntington, NY 11743-6906
631-270-0100
FAX: 516-549-8962
tcpc@transportlaw.com
www.transportlaw.com
William J Augello, Executive Director
Published by the Transportation Consumer Protection Council. *$95.00*
Founded: 1998

21178 Defense Transportation Journal
National Defense Transportation Association
50 S Pickett Street
Suite 220
Alexandria, VA 22304-7296
703-751-5011
FAX: 703-823-8761
info@ndtahq.com www.ndtahq.com
Kenneth Wykle, President
Col Denny Edwards, VP Marketing
Don Perkins, Advertising Manager
Karen Schmitt, Editor

A bi-monthly journal published by the National Defense Transportation Association. *$35.00*
Founded: 1947
Circulation: 8000

21179 Destinations
American Bus Association
700 13th Street NW
Suite 575
Washington, DC 20005-2681
202-842-1645
FAX: 202-842-0850 800-283-2877
abainfo@buses.org
http://www.buses.org

Michael Hayes, Publisher
Judi Bredemeier, Editor
Patric Scully, Circulation Manager
Peter Pantuso, CEO

Motorcoach travel across North America and Association news. *$25.00*
80 pages Monthly Founded: 1926
Circulation: 6000 3200 names
Printed in 4 colors on glossy stock

21180 Digest
American Bus Association
700 13th Street NW
Suite 575
Washington, DC 20005-5932
202-842-1645
FAX: 202-842-0850 800-283-2877
abainfo@buses.org
http://www.buses.org

Beth Wenger, Senior Writer
Peter J Pantuso, President/CEO
Chrystal Farmer, Marketing and Sales Mana
Michael Hayes, Publisher
Judi Bredemeier, Editor

Legislation news. *$150.00*
Founded: 1996
Circulation: 3200 3200 names
Printed in 2 colors on matte stock

21181 Doing Business Under the New Transportation Law
120 Main Street
Huntington, NY 11743-6906
631-270-0100
FAX: 516-549-8962
tcpc@transportlaw.com
www.transportlaw.com

William J Augello, Executive Director

Published by the Transportation Consumer Protection Council. Provides information on the Negotiated Rates Act of 1993. *$20.00*
Founded: 1993

21182 Fleet Equipment Magazine
Maple Publishing Company
3550 Embassy Parkway
Akron, OH 44333-8318
330-670-1234
FAX: 330-670-0874
tgelinas@truklink.com
http://www.truklink.com

Tom Gelinas, Editor
Bill Babcox, President
Robert Dorn, Publisher
Kelly McAleese, Ad Services Manager
Lindsey Fritz, Circulation Manager

Edited for fleet equipment managers of truck fleets. *$82.00*
Monthly Founded: 1974
Circulation: 61,571

21183 Freight Claims Prevention in Plain English
120 Main Street
Huntington, NY 11743-6906
631-270-0100
FAX: 516-549-8962
tcpc@transportlaw.com
www.transportlaw.com

William J Augello, Executive Director

Published by the Transportation Consumer Protection Council. *$25.00*

21184 Freight Claims in Plain English
120 Main Street
Huntington, NY 11743-6906
631-270-0100
FAX: 516-549-8962
tcpc@transportlaw.com
www.transportlaw.com

William J Augello, Executive Director

Published by the Transportation Consumer Protection Council. *$100.00*
Founded: 1995

21185 Freight Claims: Filing & Recovery
120 Main Street
Huntington, NY 11743-6906
631-270-0100
FAX: 516-549-8962
tcpc@transportlaw.com
www.transportlaw.com

William J Augello, Executive Director

Published by the Transportation Consumer Protection Council. *$48.00*
Founded: 2001

21186 Go-West Magazine
Motor Transport Management Group
3251 Beacon Road
West Sacramento, CA 95691-3475
916-373-3630
FAX: 916-852-5707

Jim Beach, Editor

Complete overview of the transportation industry.
Monthly

21187 Guide to Transportation After the Sunsetting of the ICC
120 Main Street
Huntington, NY 11743-6906
631-270-0100
FAX: 516-549-8962
tcpc@transportlaw.com
www.transportlaw.com

William J Augello, Executive Director

Published by the Transportation Consumer Protection Council. *$75.00*
Founded: 1997

21188 Heavy Duty Trucking
Newport Communications
38 Executive Park
Suite 300
Irvine, CA 92614-6755
949-261-1636
FAX: 949-261-2904
editorial@truckinginfo.com
http://www.truckinginfo.com

Deborah Whistler, Editorial Director
Dug Condra, President
Susan Patterson, Marketing
Marty Mc Collan, Publisher
Susan Condra, Circulation Mnager

National business magazine for managers of medium and heavy duty truck fleets, and manufacturers and dealers of those trucks and the components used to build them. *$65.00*
Monthly Founded: 1922
Circulation: 90000
Printed in 4 colors on glossy stock

21189 Hemispheres
Pace Communications
1301 Carolina Street
Suite 100
Greensboro, NC 27401-1022
336-378-6065
FAX: 336-273-2864 800-346-1336

Randy Johnson, Editor
Bonnie Mceov Hunter, CEO/President

Children's magazine for US airline fliers.
Monthly Founded: 1973
Circulation: 60000

21190 How To Select A Public Warehouse As Your Third Party Provider
Affiliated Warehouse Companies
PO Box 295
Hazlet, NJ 07730-0295
732-739-2323
FAX: 732-739-4154
sales@awco.com www.awco.com

Jim McBride, President

This is free and available upon request.

21191 How to Read Tariffs to Avoid Surprises
120 Main Street
Huntington, NY 11743-6906
631-270-0100
FAX: 516-549-8962
tcpc@transportlaw.com
www.transportlaw.com

William J Augello, Executive Director

Published by the Transportation Consumer Protection Council. *$20.00*
Founded: 2001

21192 ITE Journal
Institute of Transportation Engineers
1099 14th Street NW
Suite 300 West
Washington, DC 20005-3438
202-289-0222
FAX: 202-289-7722
ite_staff@ite.org http://www.ite.org

Marianne E Saglam, Marketing
Shannon Gore Peters, Editor
Christina Denekas, Circulation Manager
Richard T Romer, International President
Thomas Brahms, Executive Director/CEO

Provides timely news and information on subjects of interest to professionals responsible for traffic engineering, transportation planning, ITS, transit, safety, demand management, education etc. *$100.00*
300 pages Monthly Founded: 1930
Circulation: 7500

21193 Inbound Logistics Magazine
Thomas Publishing Company
5 Penn Plaza
New York, NY 10001-1810
212-950-0500
FAX: 212-629-1565
inboundlogistics@greyhouse.com
http://www.inboundlogistics.com

Keith Biondo, Publisher
Felecia Stratton, Editor
Carolyn Smolin, Circulation Manager
Robert Malone, Executive Editor

Accepts advertising.
Monthly Founded: 1981
Circulation: 55050 55000 names

21194 Institute of Transportation Engineering Journal
1099 14th Street
NW, Suite 300 West
Washington, DC 20005-3438
202-289-0222
FAX: 202-289-7722
ite_staff@ite.org http://www.ite.org

Richard T Romer, International President
Thomas Brahms, Executive Director/CEO
Christina Denekas, Marketing Manager
Marianne E Saglam, Communications & Marketing Senior
Clare James, Editor

Dedicated to the transportation engineering field. A journal is published for members only. *$65.00*
Monthly Founded: 1930
Circulation: 17000

21195 Lifting & Transportation International
7249 Dorset Avenue
Saint Louis, MO 63130
314-863-8979
FAX: 314-863-8786
adwyer@douglaspublications.com

Eugene Brymer, Publisher
Andrew Dwyer, Editor

Covers trucking overdimensional loads, heavy crane, and ridging work. *$8.00*

21196 Locomotive Engineers Journal
Brotherhood of Locomotive Engineers
1370 Ontario Street
Standard Building
Cleveland, OH 44113-1702
216-241-2630
FAX: 216-861-0932
execstaff@ble.org http://www.ble.org

John Bentley Jr., Editor
Kathleen Policy, Associate Editor
Don M Hahs, President

Designed to meet the information needs of professional engineers throughout North America, also for railroad enthusiasts. *$10.00*
Quarterly Founded: 1863
Circulation: 54000

21197 Logistics Management & Distribution Report
Reed Business Information
225 Wyman Street
Waltham, MA 02451
617-643-3030
FAX: 781-734-8076 800-662-7776
lm@reedbusiness.com
http://www.lmdr.com

Thomas A Esposito, Publisher
Peter Bradley, Editor-in-Chief

Logistics Management and Distribution Report is written for managers and professionals in charge of traffic, transportation, purchasing, inventory control, containerization and warehousing the functions of physical distribution and business logistics. Covers marketing and operating strategies, cost reduction opportunities and governmental regulation and law.
Monthly Founded: 1977
Circulation: 30,000

21198 Marine Digest & Transportation News
Marine Publishing
1710 South Norman Street
Seattle, WA 98144-1234
206-709-1840
FAX: 206-324-8939
marinedigest@marinedigest.com
http://www.marinedigest.com

Peter Hurme, Publisher/Senior Editor
Gary Greenewald, Circulation Manager
Tom Henning, Sales/Marketing Manager
M Daigle, Owner

Serves the maritime shipping community primarily in the western United States. Updates on new products, suppliers, legislation and insurance are featured. *$28.00*
Monthly Founded: 1922
Circulation: 7200

21199 Mass Transit Magazine
Cygnus Publishing
1233 Janesville Avenue
Fort Atkinson, WI 53538
920-563-6388
FAX: 920-563-1699
www.masstransitmag.com/www.cygnusb2b.com

Lori Lundquist, Editor
Carie Grall, Associate Publisher
Paul Bowers, Group VP
Debbie Dumke, Circulation Manager
Deb Krause, National Accounts Manager
$120.00
Monthly Founded: 1966

21200 Movers News
New York State Movers & Warehousemen's Association
125 Maiden Lane
11th Floor
New York, NY 10038
212-635-0510
FAX: 212-635-0511
nymovers@msn.com
www.movernet.com/nysmwa

David Blake, Editor
John Palisand, President

Association news. *$24.00*
BiMonthly Founded: 1937

21201 National Bus Trader
National Bus Trader
9698 W Judson Road
Polo, IL 61064-9015
815-946-2341
FAX: 815-946-2347
ndt@busmag.com
http://www.busmag.com

Larry Placino, Editor
Larry Placino, CEO

Equipment magazine for over-the-road and integral buses in the United States and Canada. *$25.00*
Monthly Founded: 1977
Circulation: 7000
Printed in on glossy stock

21202 New Electric Railway Journal
Cityrail
6305 N Kenmore, #1
Chicago, IL 60660-1601
773-764-5785
FAX: 773-764-7551
www.mcs.net/~cityrail

Richard Kunz, Editor-in-Chief

Emphasizes on maximum taxpayer benefit from public moneys used to support rail transit while looking objectively at the developments in the transportation field. *$27.50*
Quarterly
Circulation: 5,000

21203 New Equipment Digest
Penton Media
1300 East 9th Street
Cleveland, OH 44114-1503
216-696-7000
FAX: 216-696-1752
information@penton.com
http://www.newequipment.com

Steven Bush, Administrative Editor
Tom Sockel, Associate Editor
Robert King, Editor
Sarah Hughes, Production Manager
Bobbie Macy, Circulation Manager

Serves the general industrial field which includes manufacturing, processing, engineering services, construction, transportation, mining, public utilities, wholesale distributors, educational services, libraries and governmental establishments.
Monthly Founded: 1936
Circulation: 206154

21204 P&D Magazine
Motor Transport Management Group
3251 Beacon Road
West Sacramento, CA 95691-3475
916-373-3630
FAX: 916-852-5707

Robert L Titus, Publisher

Edited for the needs of pick up and delivery. *$5.00*
Circulation: 33,571

21205 PC-Trans
University of Kansas
2011 Learned Hall
Lawrence, KS 66044-7526
785-864-2700
FAX: 785-864-5655 http://www.ku.edu

Lisa Harris, Editor
Mehrdad Givechi, Manager
Alice Kuo, Advertising
Pat Weaver, Director

Software reviews and miscellaneous computer information for transportation professionals.
Founded: 1872
Circulation: 13000

21206 Progressive Railroading
Trade Press Publishing Corporation
PO Box 694
Milwaukee, WI 53201-694
414-271-5011
FAX: 414-228-1134
http://www.facilities.com

Steve Bolte, Publisher
Pat Foran, Editor
Tim Rowe, Marketing
Wendy Melnick, Production Manager
Robert J Wisniewski, CEO

Feature includes management techniques, purchasing developments, engineering innovations and general industry news. *$55.00*
Monthly Founded: 1994
Circulation: 25,207

21207 Protecting Shippers' Interests
120 Main Street
Huntington, NY 11743-6906
631-270-0100
FAX: 516-549-8962
tcpc@transportlaw.com
www.transportlaw.com

William J Augello, Executive Director

Published by the Transportation Consumer Protection Council. *$75.00*
Founded: 1997

21208 RV Business
TL Enterprises
3601 Calle Tecate
Camarillo, CA 93012-5056
805-987-1800
FAX: 805-389-0484
tlecs@magserv.com
http://www.rvbusiness.com
Katherine Sharma, Editor
Denielle Sternburg, Business Manager
Sherman Goldenberg, Publisher
Reports on various aspects of the recreational vehicle industry, including forecasting trends, new technologies, marketing and business concepts. *$12.00*
Monthly

21209 Rail News Update
Association of American Railroads
50 F Street NW
Floor 3
Washington, DC 20001-1564
202-392-2334
FAX: 202-639-5546
Publishes pertinent new in the railroad industry especially covering Washington news. Covers Department of Transportation and Interstate Commerce activities.
BiWeekly

21210 Railroad Facts
Association of American Railroads
50 F Street NW
Floor 3
Washington, DC 20001-1564
202-392-2334
FAX: 202-639-5546
pubsrvcs@aar.org http://www.aar.org
Kelly Donley, Marketing
Tom White, Editor
Edward R Hamberger, CEO/President
Offers statistical information and research reports on railroad travel. *$15.00*
Annual+ Founded: 1934

21211 Railroad Ten-Year Trends
Association of American Railroads
50 F Street NW
Floor 3
Washington, DC 20001-1564
202-392-2334
FAX: 202-639-5546
pubsrvcs@aar.org http://www.aar.org
Edward R. Hamberger, President
Tom White, Director, Editorial Services
Peggy Wilhide, VP Communications
Kelly Donley, Director Marketing
Offers historical facts and perspectives on America's railroad industry. *$100.00*
Annual+ Founded: 1934

21212 Refrigerated Transporter
Primedia
9800 Metcalf Avenue
Overland Park, KS 66212
913-341-1300
FAX: 913-967-1898 800-441-0294

21213 School Bus Fleet
Bobit Publishing Company
3520 Challenger Street
Torrance, CA 90503
310-533-2400
FAX: 310-376-9043
http://www.bobit.com
Jody Bush, Editor
Cliff Henke, Editor
Ty Bobit, Chief Executive Officer
A magazine that serves the field of pupil transportation, to public and private schools and to independent contract operators transporting students. *$42.00*
Monthly Founded: 1961
Circulation: 24000

21214 Shippers' Domestic Truck Bill of Lading & Common Carrier Rate Agreement Kit
120 Main Street
Huntington, NY 11743-6906
631-549-8988
FAX: 631-549-8962
tcpc@transportlaw.com
http://www.transportlaw.com
William J Augello, Executive Director
Dan Bolzenius, President
Published by the Transportation Consumer Protection Council. *$50.00*
Monthly Founded: 1974

21215 Signalman's Journal
Brotherhood of Railroad Signalmen
601 W Golf Road
Box U
Mount Prospect, IL 60056-4276
847-439-3732
FAX: 847-439-3743
signalman@brs.org http://www.brs.org
W Dan Pickett, President
Walter A Barrows, Treasurer
Information concerning railroad signaling devices, equipment and apparatus, also includes current events and items pertaining to railroad signalmen.
40 pages Quarterly Founded: 1901
Circulation: 10700
Printed in 4 colors on glossy stock

21216 Southern Motor Cargo
477 S Shady Grove Road
Memphis, TN 38120-2512
901-346-5943
FAX: 901-276-5400
Wallace Witmer Jr, Editor
Offers information on shipping. *$30.00*
66 pages Monthly Founded: 1945

21217 Speedlines
High Speed Grand Transportation Association
1010 Massachusetts Avenue NW, #110
Washington, DC 20001-5402
202-789-8107
FAX: 212-789-8109
mindspring@hsgt.org www.hsgt.org
Mark Dysart, Editor
Exclusively devoted to the High Speed Ground Transportation Association covering broad policy debates, state activity reports, federal developments and technological papers.
Quarterly
Circulation: 3,200

21218 Structural Mover
International Association of Structural Movers
PO Box 2637
Lexington, SC 29071-2637
803-951-9304
FAX: 803-951-9314
gbrymer@alltel.net www.iasm.org
N Eugene Brymer, Staff Executive
A magazine written specifically for members of the International Association of Structural Movers. Subcription to quarterly magazine included in price of membership to IASM.
Quarterly
Circulation: 500

21219 Teamster Magazine
International Brotherhood of Teamsters
25 Louisiana Avenue NW
Washington, DC 20001-2130
202-624-6800
FAX: 202-624-8970
communications@teamster.org
http://www.teamster.org
James P Hoffa, General President
Per Bernstein, Editor-in-Chief
Affiliated with the AFL-CIO. Magazine is published for members only of 30 pages. *$12.00*
Founded: 1903
Circulation: 1.4 mill

21220 Traffic Management
Reed Business Information
275 Washington Street
Newton, MA 02458-1637
617-964-3030
FAX: 617-630-3730
webmaster@reedbusiness.com
http://www.reedbusiness.com
Mitch MacDonald, Editor
Ron Bondlow, Publisher
Robert Reed, Owner
Accepts advertising.
100 pages Monthly Founded: 1982
Circulation: 73000

21221 Traffic World
Journal of Commerce
33 Washington Street
13th Floor
Newark, NJ 07102
973-848-7000
FAX: 973-848-7068 800-255-1341
bill_cassidy@trafficworld.com
http://www.trafficworld.com
William B Cassidy, Managuing Editor
Discusses all facets of the transportation industry. Also online at www.joc.com. *$174.00*
Weekly Founded: 1907

21222 Trailer/Body Builders
Tunnell Publications
PO Box 66010
Houston, TX 77266
713-523-8124
FAX: 713-523-8384 800-880-0368
wtunnell@primediabusiness.com
http://advertisers.trailer-bodybuilders.com
Paul Schenck, Editor
Ray Anderson, Publisher
Bruce Sauer, Editorial Director
Wanda Tunnell, Advertising Director
Diana Smith, Advertising Sales
Serves the truck trailer and truck body manufacturing industry. Accepts advertising. *$38.00*
Monthly

21223 Transport Fleet News
Transport Publishing
1962 N Bissell Street
#3
Chicago, IL 60614-5015
773-058-8540
Lillana Rogala, Publisher

Industry news and product for fleet supervisors.

Circulation: 10,500

21224 Transportation & Distribution
Penton Media
1300 E 9th Street
Cleveland, OH 44114-1503
216-696-7000
FAX: 216-696-2737
editor@logisticstoday.com
http://www.logisticstoday.com

Perry Trunick, Executive Editor
Antoinette Sanchez-Perkins, Circulation Manager
Newt Barret, Publisher
Dave Blanchard, Editor
David Nussbaum, CEO

Serves the information needs of logistics professionals, identifying trends and providing expert views on strategic, management and operational subjects affecting logistics. Accepts advertising. *$60.00*
78 pages Monthly Founded: 1960
Circulation: 85000
Printed in 4 colors on glossy stock

21225 Transportation & Logistics: Q&A in Plain English Book 3
120 Main Street
Huntington, NY 11743-6906
631-270-0100
FAX: 516-549-8962
tcpc@transportlaw.com
www.transportlaw.com

William J Augello, Executive Director

Published by the Transportation Consumer Protection Council. *$60.00*
Founded: 2003

21226 Transportation & Logistics: Q&A in Plain English Book 2
120 Main Street
Huntington, NY 11743-6906
631-270-0100
FAX: 516-549-8962
tcpc@transportlaw.com
www.transportlaw.com

William J Augello, Executive Director

Published by the Transportation Consumer Protection Council. *$50.00*
Founded: 2001

21227 Transportation & Logistics: Q&A in Plain English Book 1
120 Main Street
Huntington, NY 11743-6906
631-549-8984
FAX: 631-549-8962
tcpc@transportlaw.com
http://www.transportlaw.com

William Augello, Executive Director
George Carl Pezold, General Counsel
Stephen Beyer, Associate Editor

Published by the Transportation Consumer Protection Council. *$50.00*
Founded: 2001

21228 Transportation Insurance in Plain English
120 Main Street
Huntington, NY 11743-6906
631-549-8984
FAX: 631-549-8962
tcpc@transportlaw.com
http://www.transportlaw.com

William Augello, Executive Director
George Pezold, General Counsel
Stephen Beyer, Associate Editor

Published by the Transportation Consumer Protection Council. *$15.00*
Founded: 1985

21229 Transportation Leader
Taxicab, Limousine & Paratransit Association
3849 Farragut Avenue
Kensington, MD 20895-2004
301-946-5700
FAX: 301-946-4641
info@tlpa.com www.ttpa.org

Irene Kiebuzinski, Editor
Julia Lynch, Marketing Director

Leading resource for news and information on issues, trends, and people in the private, for-hire passenger transportation industry. Provides readers with an array of features, articles, and columns that include information on managing a transportation company, industry trends, driver's tips, an industry calendar of events, coverage of TLPA events, and advertisements from the industry's leading suppliers. *$4.00*
48 pages Founded: 1920
Circulation: 5900 6,000 names $100 per M.

Printed in 4 colors on glossy stock

21230 Trucker's Connection
Megan Cullingford
5960 Crooked Creek Road
Suite 15
Norcross, GA 30092
770-416-0927
FAX: 770-416-1734
dan@truckersconnection.com
http://www.truckersconnection.com

Dan Barnhill, Editor
Reid Ramsay, Production Manager
Megan Cullingford, General Manager
David Guthrie, Advertising Sales

Published for the use of long haul, over-the-road truck drivers, owner operators, small trucking company fleet owners, safety and recruiting of personnel for trucking companies in the US and Canada.
Monthly Founded: 1986
Circulation: 16,5,000
Printed in 4 colors on glossy stock

Trade Shows

21231 AAR Annual Convention and Exhibit
Railway Systems Suppliers
10507 Timberwood Circle
Suite 208
Louisville, KY 40223-5313
502-327-7774
FAX: 502-327-0541
rssi@rssi.org www.rssi.org
Railroad signal and communication equipment displays, annual meeting & banquet.
Annual Founded: 1960

21232 American Bus Marketplace
1015 15th Street NW
Washington, DC 20005-2605
202-842-9100
FAX: 202-842-0850 800-283-2877

Katie Robbins

Sales and marketing event for the North American group travel industry. 350 booths.
2M Attendees December

21233 American Car Rental Association Convention
11250 Roger Bacon Drive
#8
Reston, VA 20190
703-787-7718
FAX: 703-435-4390
ghogan@drohanmgmnt.com
www.acra.org

Gwendolyn Hogan

One hundred exhibits of cars, vans, buses, computers, equipment and services for car rental company owners and officers. Conference, reception and dinner.
600 Attendees Annual Founded: 1978

21234 American Public Transportation Association Annual Meeting & Expo
American Public Transit Association
1666 K Street NW
Suite 1100
Washington, DC 20006
202-496-4800
FAX: 202-496-4324
rbattle@apta.com www.apta.com

Renee Battle, Director Meetings/Conferences
Karol Popkin, Chief Executive Officer

Seminar, workshop, conference, luncheon, banquet, tours and 650 exhibits for the planning designing and finance & operation of public transportation.
15000 Attendees October 2008/2011
Founded: 1981

21235 American Railroads Association Communication and Signal Division
50 F Street NW
Washington, DC 20001-1530
202-392-2334

William Peters, Show Manager
Joyce Koeneman, Manager

Transportation equipment and services.
1.5M Attendees

21236 Association for Commuter Transportation Convention
808 17th Street NW
Suite 200
Washington, DC 20006-3910
202-393-3497

acthq@aol.com tmi.cob.fsu.edu/act

Elizabeth Stutts, President
Kenneth M Sufka, Executive Director
Shamus Misek, VP

Thirty booths.
300 Attendees September

21237 Association of Railway Museums Convention
Association of Railway Museums
PO Box 370
Tujunga, CA 91043-0370
818-951-9151
FAX: 818-951-9151
railwaymuseums.org

Paul Hammond, President ARM

Annual show and exhibits for the preservation of railway equipment, artifacts and history. Seminar, tours, banquet and dinner.
125 Attendees October Founded: 1961

21238 Biodiesel Investor Conference
Platts
24 Hartwell Avenue
Lexington, MA 02421
781-860-6100
866-355-2930
registration@platts.com
www.platts.com
June Houston

21239 Fleet Management Institute (NAFA) Convention
100 Wood Avenue S
Suite 310
Iselin, NJ 08830
732-494-8100
FAX: 732-494-6789
info@nafa.org www.nafa.org
Patricia Murtaugh, Assistant Executive Director
Joanne Marsh, Manager
Fleet management education and automobile parts and services, as well as maintenance for business and public service vehicles. 250 booths
2M Attendees April/May

21240 Institute of Transportation Engineers Annual Meeting
Institute of Transportation Engineers
525 School Street SW
Suite 410
Washington, DC 20024-2729
202-548-8050
FAX: 202-863-5486 www.ite.org
Marianne Wool, Manager
Shannon Gore Peters, Editor
Annual meeting of 100 exhibitors of transportation equipment, supplies and services.
2,000 Attendees Las Vegas

21241 International Association of Structural Movers Annual Convention
PO Box 600
Oakton, VA 22124
703-648-3225
FAX: 703-648-0387
gbrymer@cox.net www.iasm.org
Containing 20 booths and 15 exhibits.

21242 International Public Transit Expo
Pemco/Professional Expo Management Company
191 S Gary Avenue
Carol Stream, IL 60188-2092
630-690-5600
FAX: 203-840-9662
Barbara Silverman, VP
The world's largest transit industry event offering a chance for top transit officials to meet with manufacturers from around the world.
16M Attendees October

21243 International Truck and Bus Expo
Society of Automotive Engineers
400 Commonwealth Drive
Warrendale, PA 15096-0001
724-772-8548
FAX: 724-776-0790 www.sae.org

21244 Link
R&D Associates
16607 Blanco Road
Suite 305
San Antonio, TX 78232-1940
210-682-4302
FAX: 830-493-8036
David Dee, Editor
Articles of interest to the food, food packaging, food processing and foodservice industry. 50 booths.
300 Attendees Spring/Fall

21245 NPA
National Parking Association
1112 16th Street NW
Suite 300
Washington, DC 20036
202-296-4336
FAX: 202-331-8523 800-647-PARK
info@npapark.org www.npapark.org
Herb Anderson, VP Advertising & Exposition
Oct Washington

21246 National Private Truck Council Management/ Education Conference
National Private Truck Council
66 Canal Center Plaza
Alexandria, VA 22314-1591
703-683-1300
FAX: 703-683-1217
Gary Petty, Chief Executive Officer
Annual conference and exhibits of equipment, supplies and services for processors, shippers, distributors and retailers who operate their own truck fleets to advance their primary nontransportation business enterprises.

21247 North American Truck Show
North American Expositions Company
33 Rutherford Avenue
Boston, MA 02129-3795
617-242-6092
FAX: 617-242-1817 800-225-1577
Gregory Soughlin, Show Manager
Six hundred booths.
25M Attendees May

21248 Shippers National Freight Claim Council
120 Main Street
Huntington, NY 11743-6906
631-270-0100
Joyce Grandy, Administrative Assistant
Programs and information for the freight claim industry. 24 booths.
300 Attendees March

21249 TransComp Exhibition
National Industrial Transportation League
1700 N Moore Street
Suite 1900
Arlington, VA 22209-1931
703-524-5011
FAX: 703-524-5017
info@nitl.org www.nitl.org
Ellie Gilanshah, VP Finance and Membership
3000 Attendees November Founded: 1907

21250 Transportation Intermediaries Annual Conve ntion & Trade Show
Transportation Intermediaries Association
3601 Eisenhower Avenue
Suite 110
Alexandria, VA 22304
703-317-2140
FAX: 703-329-1898
info@tianet.org www.tianet.org
Robert Voltmann, President
Nancy King, Contact
Education and policy organization for North American transportation intermediaries. TIA is the only national association representing the interests of all third party transportation service providers. The members of TIA include logistics management firms, property brokers, perishable commodities brokers, freight forwarders, intermodal marketers, ocean and air forwarders, and NVOCC's.
700 Attendees Founded: 1977

21251 Women's Transportation Seminar
Women's Transportation Seminar
1 Walnut Street
Boston, MA 02108-3616
617-367-3273
FAX: 617-227-6783
Annual seminar and exhibits of transportation equipment, supplies and services.

Directories & Databases

21252 AAA Bridge and Ferry Directory
American Automobile Association
1000 AAA Drive
Heathrow, FL 32746-5062
407-444-7966
Melanie Fuller, Highway Infoformation Coordinator
Offers information on over 500 toll facilities in the US, Canada and Mexico that enable automobiles and passengers to complete toll non-highway portions of their journey. *$12.50*
103 pages Annual

21253 Affiliated Warehouse Companies Directory
Affiliated Warehouse Companies
PO Box 295
Hazlet, NJ 07730-0295
732-739-2323
FAX: 732-739-4154
sales@awco.com www.awco.com
Jim McBride, President
Patrick McBride, VP
Third party logistics and public warehousing, marketing and sales company.
Founded: 1953
Mailing list available for rent $100 per M.
Printed in 4 colors

21254 Air CargoWorld & Traffic World
Knight-Ridder Financial
75 Wall Street
Floor 23
New York, NY 10005-2833
212-429-2307
FAX: 212-372-7148
Offers valuable information on cash, futures and options markets.
Numeric

21255 Airline, Ship & Catering: Onboard Service Buyer's Guide & Directory
International Publishing Company of America
664 La Villa Drive
Miami Springs, FL 33166-6095
305-887-1700
FAX: 305-885-1923
Offers information on over 6,000 airlines, railroads, ship lines and termianl restaurants. *$125.00*

Annual
Circulation: 6,000

21256 American Public Transit Association Member ship Directory
American Public Transit Association
1666 K Street NW
Sutie 1100
Washington, DC 20005-6141
202-496-4800
FAX: 202-496-4324 www.apta.com
William Millar, President
Karol Popkin, Chief Executive Officer
A who's who directory of services and supplies.
400 pages Founded: 1882

21257 American Road and Transportation Builders Assoc.-Transportation Directory
American Road and Transportation Builders Assn
1219 28th St NW
Washington, DC 20007-3362
202-289-4434
FAX: 202-289-4435
Jacque McDowell, Editor
Noelle C Sotack, Managing Editor
Peter Ruane, President
Over 5,000 administrative engineers and officials in federal, state and county transportation agencies. Includes officials from state departments of transportation, highways and aeronautics, metropolitan planning organizations and equivalent federal officials, plus federal officials concerned with railroads and urban mass transit. *$40.00*
Annual March

21258 American Shortline Railway Guide
Kalmbach Publishing Company
21027 Crossroads Cir
Waukesha, WI 53186-4055
262-796-8776
FAX: 262-796-1615
Directory of services and supplies to the industry. *$18.95*
320 pages

21259 Bus Garage Index
Friendship Publications
PO Box 1472
Spokane, WA 99210-1472
FAX: 509-325-0405 800-541-2670
Bruce Sankey, President
Leslie Maris, VP Marketing
Linda Metler, Production Manager
Offers information on over 900 garages and service centers in the United States and Canada offering services to buses on charter service and tours. *$28.00*
140 pages
Circulation: 3,000
Mailing list available for rent 14M names
Printed in 4 colors on glossy stock

21260 Bus Industry Directory
Friendship Publications
PO Box 1472
Spokane, WA 99210-1472
FAX: 509-325-0405 800-541-2670
Bruce Sankey, President/Publisher
Leslie Maris, VP Marketing
A comprehensive list of over 4,500 intercity and charter bus companies and local transit authorities in the United States and Canada. *$78.00*
500 pages Annual
Mailing list available for rent 14M names
Printed in 4 colors on glossy stock

21261 Carrier Routing Director
Transportation Technical Services
500 Lafayette Boulevard
Fredericksburg, VA 22401-6070
540-899-9872
FAX: 888-665-9887 800-666-4887
truckinpo@ttstruck.com
www.ttstrucks.com
Thomas R Fugee, Executive VP
Two thousand six hundred top common and contract carriers, toll-free faxes, states served + Canadian provinces and Mexico, equipment types, commodities. *$145.00*
Annual Founded: 1992 26 M names

21262 DRI Transportation Detail
DRI/McGraw-Hill
24 Hartwell Avenue
Lexington, MA 02421-3158
781-863-5100
This time series contains annual and quarterly data describing aspects of the transportation industry.

21263 Defense Transportation Journal NDTA Almanac
National Defense Transportation Association
50 S Pickett Street
Suite 220
Alexandria, VA 22304-7296
703-751-5011
FAX: 703-823-8761
info@ndtahq.com www.nadtahq.com
Lt. Kenneth Wykle, President
An annual directory published by the National Defense Transportation Association. *$35.00*
89 pages Annual
Circulation: 8000

21264 Directory of Shippers
Transportation Technical Services
500 Lafayette Boulevard
Fredericksburg, VA 22401-6070
540-899-9872
FAX: 888-665-9887 800-666-4887
truckinpo@ttstruck.com
www.ttstrucks.com
Thomas R Fugee, Executive VP
Compilateion of 14,000 logistics executives. Key information on 13,500 companies, phone, fax-e-mail, addresses, SIC's, revenue. Great marketing sales and research tool. *$170.00*
Annual Founded: 1992 26 M names

21265 Directory of Transportation Professionals
National Assn of Regulatory Utility Commissioners
PO Box 684
Washington, DC 20044-0684
202-898-2200
Offers valuable information on over 100 regulated transportation firms and professionals. *$20.00*
150 pages Annual

21266 Directory of Truck Dealers
Transportation Technical Services
500 Lafayette Boulevard
Fredericksburg, VA 22401-6070
540-899-9872
FAX: 888-665-9887 800-666-4887
truckinpo@ttstruck.com
www.ttstrucks.com
Thomas R Fugee, Executive VP
Unique, extensive list of 2,700 of the nation's kmid-size/heavy truck dealers. Address, brands sold, serviced, keky contacts, phone and fax. *$95.00*
Annual Founded: 1992 26 M names

21267 Foreign Flag Merchant Ships Owned by US Parent Companies
US Department of Transportation
400 7th Street SW
Room 8117
Washington, DC 20590-0001
202-366-4000
Directory of services and supplies to the industry.
20 pages SemiAnnual

21268 Greenwood's Guide to Great Lakes Shipping
Freshwater Press
1700 E 13th Street
Suite 3-R
Cleveland, OH 44114-3213
216-241-0373
FAX: 216-781-6344
mdillselakeboats.com
www.lakeboats.com
Michael Dills, VP/General Manager
Offers companies that ship water-carried commodities and service firms on the Great Lakes Seaway systems. Details of vessels, dock facilities, shipyards, etc. *$71.00*
650 pages Annual Founded: 1960
Circulation: 2,500
Printed in on glossy stock

21269 Grey House Biometric Information Directory
Grey House Publishing
185 Millerton Road
Millerton, NY 12546
518-890-0526
FAX: 518-789-0545 800-562-2139
books@greyhouse.com
www.greyhouse.com
Leslie Mackenzie, Publisher
Richard Gottlieb, Editor
The most comprehensive resource covering biometric technology. Contains hundreds of organizations providing biometric products and services. The directory encompasses emerging identification technology, such as fingerprint ID, facial recognition, key stroke scan, hand geometry, voice recognition, iris scan and many other methods. *$295.00*
360 pages Annual Founded: 2005

21270 Grey House Transportation Security Directory
Grey House Publishing
185 Millerton Road
PO Box 860
Millerton, NY 12546
518-890-0526
FAX: 518-789-0545 800-562-2139
books@greyhouse.com
www.greyhouse.com
Leslie Mackenzie, Publisher
David Garoogian, Editor

Information on everything from Regulatory Authorities to Security Equipment, this top-flight database brings together the relevant information necessary for creating and maintaining a security plan for a wide range of transportation facilities. *$195.00*

800 pages Founded: 2004 ISBN 1-592370-75-6

21271 High-Performance Composites
Ray Publishing
4891 Independence
Suite 270
Wheat Ridge, CO 80033
303-467-1776
FAX: 303-467-1777
www.compositesworld.com

Judith Hazen, Publisher/Editor
Mike Mussleman, Managing Editor

60 pages Founded: 1993
Printed in 4 colors on glossy stock

21272 Inland River Guide
Waterways Journal
319 N 4th Street
Suite 650
Saint Louis, MO 63102-1994
314-241-7354
FAX: 314-241-4207
info@waterwaysjournal.net
www.waterwaysjournal.net

Nelson Spencer Jr., Publisher
John S Shoulberg, Editor/Associate Publisher
Ed Rahe, Advertising Sales

The only directory published specifically for the benefit of the companies doing business along the inland and intracoastal waterways. It contains vital information about companies servicing all industry segments. *$65.00*

600+ pages Annual Founded: 1972
Circulation: 3,000

21273 Inland River Record
Waterways Journal
319 N 4th Street
Suite 650
Saint Louis, MO 63102-1994
314-241-7354
FAX: 314-241-4207
hnspencer@waterwaysjournal.net
www.waterwaysjournal.net

Nelson Spencer, Publisher
John S Shoulberg, Editor/Associate Publisher

Lists in detail more than 3,500 commercial towboats and tugs, U.S. engineer vessels and Coast Guard vessels navigating the Mississippi and Ohio, their tributaries and the Gulf Intracoastal Waterway. *$37.50*

475 pages Annual
Circulation: 3,000

21274 Leonard's Guide National Third Party Logistics Directory
GR Leonard & Company
49 E Huntington Drive
Arcadia, CA 91006-3210
626-574-1800
800-574-5250

David Augustine, Editor
David Ercolani, President

Approximately 2,000 transportation brokers and third party logistics firms and brokerages in the US and Canada. *$75.00*

Annual Spring

21275 Light List
United States Coast Guard
2100 2nd Street SW
Washington, DC 20593-0002
202-488-8157
FAX: 202-366-5063

Offers information to the shipping industry in the form of lights. This comprehensive directory offers a list of lights, fog signals, daybeacons, radiobeacons and LORAN stations operated or authorized by the US Coast Guard. Various volumes are offered. *$25.00*

200+ pages Volumes

21276 Mass Transit: Consultants Issue
Cygnus Publishing
1233 Janesville Avenue
Fort Atkinson, WI 53538-2738
920-563-6388
FAX: 920-563-1702
www.cygnuspub.com

Rich Reiff, President of Publishing

Offers listings of over 300 urban transportation architects, designers, engineers and other specialists serving the urban transportation industry.

BiMonthly

21277 Mexican Motor Carrier Directory
Transportation Technical Services
500 Lafayette Boulevard
Fredericksburg, VA 22401-6070
540-899-9872
FAX: 888-665-9887 800-666-4887
truckinpo@ttstruck.com
www.ttstrucks.com

Thomas R Fugee, Executive VP

Unique, extensive and key information on 500 Mexican carriers. *$145.00*

Annual 26 M names

21278 Motor Carrier Industry in Transition
Transportation Technical Services
500 Lafayette Boulevard
Fredericksburg, VA 22401-6070
540-899-9872
FAX: 888-665-9887 800-666-4887
truckinpo@ttstruck.com
www.ttstrucks.com

Thomas R Fugee, Executive VP

For-hire trends in charts/analysis, revenue growth, operating expenses, vehicles, labor, and more. *$95.00*

Annual Founded: 1992 26 M names

21279 NARUC Compilation of Transportation Regulatory Policy
National Assn of Regulatory Utility Commissioners
PO Box 684
Washington, DC 20044-0684
202-898-2200

Offers a list of over 100 regulatory agencies in the United States and Canada for the transportation industry. *$33.00*

21280 National Customs Brokers and Forwarders Association of America
National Customs Brokers & Forwarders Association
1200 18th Street NW
#901
Washington, DC 20036
202-466-0222
FAX: 202-466-0226
staff@ncbfaa.org www.ncbfaa.org

Greg Pitkoff, Editor
Barbara Reilly, Executive VP

About 600 customs brokers, international air cargo agents, and freight forwarders in the United States. *$24.00*

Annual

21281 National Highway Carriers Directory
National Highway Carriers Directory
PO Box 6099
Buffalo Grove, IL 60089-6099
847-634-0606
FAX: 847-634-1026
nhcdg@aol.com
www.national-highway.com

Pam W Ferreira, President/Editor

Offers information on over 700 motor carriers, LTL carriers, truckload companies, warehousing companies, transportation brokers, freight forwarders, Canadian carriers, over 250,000 points and terminals for LTL carriers, refrigerated carries, and more. Now also on CD-ROM: $399.00 with free book. *$195.00*

1,400 pages Spring & Fall Founded: 1948
5000 names
Printed in 2 colors on newsprint stock

21282 National Industrial Transportation League Reference Manual
National Industrial Transportation League
1700 N Moore Street
Suite 1900
Arlington, VA 22209-1931
703-524-5011
FAX: 703-524-5017 info@nitl.org

Edward M Emmett, Editor
John Ficker, President

SemiAnnual

21283 National Institute of Packaging, Handling and Logistic Engineers
Forbes Printing
6902 Lyle Street
Lanham, MD 20706-3454
301-459-9105
FAX: 301-459-4925 www.niphle.org

James Russell, Executive Director

Over 700 engineers, chemists, consultants, and executives. *$100.00*

Annual Fall Founded: 1956

21284 National Motor Carrier Directory
Transportation Technical Services
500 Lafayette Boulevard
Fredericksburg, VA 22401-6070
540-899-9872
FAX: 888-665-9887 800-666-4887
truckinpo@ttstruck.com
www.ttstrucks.com

Thomas R Fugee, Executive VP

CEO, fleet size, toll-free/fax number, revenue, SCAC, trailer type, TK or LTL, trucks plus tractors owned and leased and more. *$ 395.00*

1982 pages Annual Founded: 1992 26 M names

21285 Official Railway Guide: North American Freight Service Edition
Commonwealth Business Media
400 Windsor Corporate Center
50 Millstone Road, Suite 200
East Windsor, NJ 08520-1415
609-371-7703
FAX: 609-371-7830 800-221-5488
customerservice@cbizmedia.com
www.cbizmedia.com

Kathy Keeney, Publisher

Directory of services and supplies to the industry. *$245.00*
BiMonthly

21286 Pacific Shipper's Transportation Services Directory
PRIMEDIA Information
10 Lake Drive
Hightstown, NJ 08520-5321
609-371-7700
800-224-5488

Amy Middlebrook, Editor
John Capers III, Publisher
John Murphy, Circulation Director

Offers valuable information on coastal transportation operations and support services on the Pacific Coast. *$202.00*
730 pages Annual $150 per M.
Printed in 4 colors on newsprint stock

21287 Private Fleet Directory
Transportation Technical Services
500 Lafayette Boulevard
Fredericksburg, VA 22401-6070
540-899-9872
FAX: 888-665-9887 800-666-4887
truckinpo@ttstruck.com
www.ttstrucks.com

Thomas R Fugee, Executive VP

Over 26,000 private fleets in the US that transport their own freight (Wal-Mart, Ace Hardware, Toys R Us). *$295.00*
1,900 pages Annual July Founded: 1992
26 M names

21288 Railway Age: Railroad Financial Desk Book Issue
Simmons-Boardman Publishing Corporation
345 Hudson Street
New York, NY 10014-4502
212-337-9300
FAX: 212-633-1863
sbrailgroup@sbpub.com
www.railwayage.com

Tony Kruglinski, Financial Editor

Directory of institutions and individuals involved in railroad finance, including banks, arrangers, operating lessors, consultants, accountants and attorneys. *$6.00*
Annual
Printed in 4 colors

21289 Railway Line Clearances
Commonwealth Business Media
10 Lake Drive
Hightstown, NJ 08520-5321
609-371-7703
FAX: 609-371-7830 800-224-5488

Alan Glass, Chairman/CEO
Susan Murray, Publisher
Kathy Keeney, Associate Publisher

This directory offers weight limitations, heights and widths of clearances for railroads in North America and Canada, parts of the United States, clearance contacts and AAR rules and regulation. *$200.00*
Annual
Printed in 2 colors on matte stock

21290 Railway Track and Structures: Railroad Track Contractors Directory
Simmons-Boardman Publishing Corporation
175 W Jackson Boulevard
Suite A1927
Chicago, IL 60604-2601
312-830-0130

A directory that offers over 300 companies that specialize in track construction, maintenance and equipment maintenance for railways in the United States and Canada. *$3.00*
Annual
Circulation: 10,000

21291 Refrigerated Transporter: Warehouse Directory Issue
Tunnell Publications
PO Box 66010
Houston, TX 77266
713-523-8124
FAX: 713-523-8384

Gary Macklin, Editor

Listing of approximately 265 refrigerated warehouses in the US and Canada.

21292 Survey of State Travel Offices
United States Travel Data Center
1100 New York Avenue NW
Washington, DC 20005-3934
202-326-7300
FAX: 202-408-1255

Patrick Thompson, Editor

State and territorial government agencies responsible for travel and travel promotion in their states. *$475.00*
Annual March

21293 Transportation Management Association Directory
Association for Commuter Transportation
1518 K Street NW
Suite 503
Washington, DC 20005-1203
202-393-3497

Over 50 established transportation management associations in the United States are the focus of this comprehensive directory.
123 pages
Circulation: 400

21294 Transportation Research Board Directory
Transportation Research Board
2101 Constitution Avenue NW
Washington, DC 20418-0007
202-342-2933
FAX: 202-334-2519
TABSales@nas.edu
www.nationalacademies.org/trb
Directory lists organizations and committee members with an interest in transportation. Individual affiliate information is no longer available in print or in electronic format.
Annual

21295 USTA Industry Directory
United States Telecom Association
1401 H Street NW
Suite 600
Washington, DC 20005-2164
202-326-7300
FAX: 202-326-7333 www.usta.org
Comprehensive directory of over 1200 local exchange carriers and other telecom companies make up this directory. Includes a detailed index for easy cross-referencing by company name, contacts, titles, geographical region, services provided, e-mail and more. USTA's directory is your gateway to the telecom industry. *$699.00*
Annual

21296 WESTLAW Transportation Library
West Publishing Company
610 Opperman Drive
Eagan, MN 55123-1340
651-687-7327
www.westgroup.com
This database offers information on US transportation laws.
Full-text

Industry Web Sites

21297 www.apta.com
American Public Transit Association

Maintains biographical archives and operates a placement service.

21298 www.ar.org
Association of American Railroads

Seeks to advance knowledge of scientific and economic location, construction, maintenance and operation of railroad.

21299 www.buses.org
American Bus Association

Trade association for the North American bus industry.

21300 www.expedia.com
Expedia.com

Internet travel service offers access to airlines, hotels, car rentals, vacation packages, cruises and corporate travel.

21301 www.expresscarriers.com
Interstate Trucking Association

Organization of newly enacted state legislation regulations having direct impact on vehicle operations, fuel taxes, registration size and weight.

21302 www.gams.org
Association of Air Medical Services

An association of health care entities operating helicopter transport services.

21303 www.greyhouse.com
Grey House Publishing

Selected Grey House directories in the fields of business, health and education are available online. Users can search our online databases by several different search criteria, such as product categories, geographic area, sales volume and much, much more. Full Grey House catalog and online ordering also available.

21304 www.hotwire.com
Hotwire.com

Internet travel service offering discounts on flights, hotels, car rentals, packages and cruises.

21305 www.iasm.org
International Association of Structural Movers

Members are movers of heavy structural products, trusses, houses and machinery and masonry structures.

21306 www.iccl.org
Internhational Council of Cruise Lines

For North American oceangoing, overnight major cruise line companies.

21307 www.intermodal.org
Intermodal Association of North America

Members are motor, rail and water transportation companies. Promotes the benefits and growth of intermodal freight transportation.

21308 www.ista.org
International Safe Transit Association

Members are shippers, carriers, manufacturers, packagers, package designers and testing laboratories, included in transport packaging.

21309 www.ite.org
Institute for Transportation Engineering

Dedicated to the transportation engineering field.

21310 www.narprail.org
National Association of Railroad Passengers

Seeks to increase public awareness of rail passenger service and its benefits. Works for a national transportation policy.

21311 www.nbta.org
National Business Travel Association

Offers over 1,300 corporate travel managers and allied members in the United States and Canada.

21312 www.nitl.org
National Industrial Transportation League

Annual show of 250 exhibitors of computer services software and innovations for transportation operations.

21313 www.npapark.org
National Parking Association

For operators of public and private parking facilities, including government, hospitals, colleges, universities and others.

21314 www.raa.org
Regional Airline Association

Membership consists of more than 70 airlines, plus 350 Associate members provide goods and services.

21315 www.railway.museums.org
Association of Railway Museums

The association of railway museums is for the preservation of railway equipment, artifacts and history.

21316 www.rampages.onramp.net/~nars/
National Association of Rail Shippers

Strives to provide a sound transporation system. Bestows annual Award of Excellence.

21317 www.rpi.org
Railway Progress Institute

The railway equipment and supply industry.

21318 www.rssi.org
Railway Systems Suppliers

A trade association serving the communication and signal segment of the rail transportation industry. Manages an annual trade show.

21319 www.scooltrans.com
National School Transportation Association

Strives to provide safe transportation, foster safety, and an atmosphere conducive to private enterprise.

21320 www.teamster.org
International Brotherhood of Teamsters

Affiliated with the AFL-CIO.

21321 www.terry.org
International Marine Transit Association

Membership includes ferry operators, naval architects, manufacturers, suppliers, and others in the terry industry around the world.

21322 www.tianet.org
Transportation Intermediaries Association

For North American transportation intermediaries including logistics management firms, property brokers, perishable commodities brokers, freight forwarders, intermodal marketers, ocean and air forwarders.

21323 www.travel.yahoo.com
Yahoo.com

Internet travel service providing access to flights, hotels, car rentals, vacation packages and cruises.

21324 www.travelocity.com
Sabre Holdings

Travel service offering consumers access to hundreds of airlines and thousands of hotels, as well as cruise, last-minute and vacation packages and best-in-class car rental companies.

21325 www.tww.org
Transport Workers Union of America

Chartered by the Congress of Industrial Organizations.

21326 www.waterways.org
National Waterways Conference

For shippers, barge lines and local port authorities working to promote a better understanding of the public value of the American waterways system.

21327 www.woda.org
World Organization of Dredging Associations

Develops professionalism in individuals involved in the dredging industry.

Associations

21328 Airport Operators Council International
1215 Geneva 15-Airport
PO Box 16, DC 20036-2463
412- 71-7888
FAX: 412-717-8585 aci@aero
Mission is to safeguard members interests and their influence on the global airport industry. Its goal is to support the world's airports and promote professional excellence and operations.

21329 American Bus Association
700 13th Street NW
Suite 575
Washington, DC 20005
202-842-1645
FAX: 202-842-0850 www.buses.org
Peter J Pantuso, President/CEO
Clyde J Hart Jr, VP Government Affairs
William F Mahorney, Director Safety Programs
Ginger D Croce, Director Marketing/Membership
Lynn Brewer, VP Meetings/Education
Trade association for the North American bus industry.
2300 Members Founded: 1926

21330 American Council of Highway Advertisers
PO Box 809
North Beach, MD 20714
301-386-3330

21331 American Society of Travel Agents (ASTA)
1101 King Street
Suite 200
Alexandria, VA 22314
703-739-2782
FAX: 703-684-8319
Richard C Knodt, Executive VP
Bill Maloney, Manager
Promotes and encourages travel among people of all nations. Serves as an information resource for the travel industry.
21M Members Founded: 1931

21332 Association of Corporate Travel Executives
570 Springfield Avenue
Summit, NJ 07901-4501
908-273-3000
FAX: 908-273-2343
Robert Graze, Executive Director
Provides a forum for the discussion of ideas and information related to the corporate travel industry. Conducts educational programs and conferences.
700 Members Founded: 1988

21333 Association of Group Travel Executives
AH Light Company
424 Madison Avenue
New York, NY 10017
212-486-4300
FAX: 212-755-2135
Arnold H Light, President
Affiliated with the Travel Industry Association of America.
675 Members

21334 Association of Retail Travel Agents
4320 North Miller Road
Scottsdale, AZ 85251
FAX: 615-985-0600 800-969-6069
info@artonline.com
www.artaonline.com
Nancy Linares, Board of Director
Promotes the interests of retail travel agents through representation on industry councils and testimony before Congress. Conducts joint marketing and educational programs.
2800 Members Founded: 1963

21335 Association of Travel Marketing Executives
20 North Avenue
Suite 4
Larchmont, NY 10538
914-834-2144
FAX: 914-834-2143
admin@atme.org www.atme.org
Kristin Zern, Executive Director

21336 Association of Travel Marketing Executives
20 North Avenue
Stuite 4
Larchmont, NY 10538
914-834-2144
FAX: 914-834-2143
admin@atme.org www.atme.org
Kristin Zern, Executive Director
Travel and tourism reports.

21337 Caribbean Hotel Association
1000 Ponce de Leon Avenue
5th Floor
San Juan, PR 00907-1682
787-725-9139
FAX: 787-725-9180
www.cha.chahotels.com
Peter Odle, President
Bertha Parle, Chairwoman
Mission is to optimize the full potential of the Caribbean hotel and tourism industry by serving member needs and building partnerships. It's a LLC registered in the Cayman Islands, with offices in San Juan, Puerto Rico and Miami, FL.

21338 Greater Independent Association of National Travel Services
915 Broadway
New York, NY 10010-7108
212-270-0001
FAX: 212-260-1227
Desiree Gruber, Owner
Susan Shapiro, Executive Director
Aims to establish a travel industry marketing cooperative. Holds regional workshops and seminars.
1.8M Members Founded: 1968

21339 Hospitality Sales & Marketing Association International
1201 Greensboro Drive
Suite 300
McLean, VA 22102
703-610-9024
FAX: 703-610-9005
bgilbert@hsmai.org www.hsmai.org
Robert A Gilbert CHME, President/CEO
Mary Hanger, Manager/Programs
To provide resources to sales and marketing professionals at all levels of thier career in travel, hospitality and tourism.
7000 Members Founded: 1927 7000 names

21340 International Association of Convention and Visitor Bureaus
2025 M Street
Suite 500
Washington, DC 20036
202-296-7888
FAX: 202-296-7889
info@iacvb.org www.iacvb.org
Michael D Gehrisch, President/CEO
Promotes sound professional practices in the solicitation and servicing of meetings and conventions. Members represent travel/tourism related businesses. Publications include an electronic newsletter and online directory.
Founded: 1914
Mailing list available for rent 1200 names $400 per M.

21341 International Association of Travel
PO Box D
Hurleyville, NY 12747
845-434-7777
Promotes accurate reporting on fields of aviation, travel, tourism and airports.
50+ Members Founded: 1988

21342 International Family Recreation
PO Box 520
Gonzalez, FL 32560-0520
850-937-8354
FAX: 800-477-7992
nrvockws@spydee.net
Introduction to the recreation and leisure lifestyle and benefits. Fun fest activities and events.
8300 Members Founded: 1983

21343 National Association of Business Travel Agents
1233 20th Street NW #505
Washington, DC 20036-1418
202-463-6223
FAX: 202-463-6239 nabe@nade.com
Susan Doolittle, Executive Director
NABE is an association of professionals who have an interest in business economics and who want to use the latest economic data and trends to enhance their ability to make sound business decisions.
1.6M Members Founded: 1980

21344 National Association of RV Parks and Campgrounds
113 Park Avenue
Falls Church, VA 22046
703-241-8801
FAX: 703-241-1004
info@arvc.org www.arvc.org
Linda Profaizer, President
Cyndy Robinson, Executive Assistant
The association actively protects the best interests of its members on a federal level and provides awareness and assistance against government legislation & regulations at all levels(national, state and local).
3,200 Members Founded: 1966
Mailing list available for rent 3,200 names

21345 National Bed & Breakfast Association
148 E Rocks Rd
Norwalk, CT 06851-1723
FAX: 203-847-0469 www.nbba.com

Phyllis Featherston, Executive Director
Innkeepers of bed and breakfast lodgings.
2000 Members Founded: 1980

21346 National Motorcoach Network
10527C Braddock Road
Fairfax, VA 22032-2236
703-250-7897
FAX: 703-503-5922 800-469-0062
smk@motorcoach.com
www.motorcoach.com/byways
Founded: 1983

21347 National Tour Association
546 E Main Street
Lexington, KY 40508
859-226-4444
FAX: 859-226-4414 800-682-8886
questions@NTA.travel
www.NTA.travel
Hank Phillips, CTP, President
The National Tour Association is an organization of nearly 4,000 international tourism professionals focused on the development, promotion and increased use of tour operators packaged travel.
3800 Members Founded: 1951
Mailing list available for rent $500 per M.

21348 Passenger Vessel Association
901 N Pitt St
Ste 100
Alexandria, VA 22314-1549
703-518-5005
FAX: 703-518-5151 800-807-8360
Thomas A Allegretti, President/CEO
Anne Davis Burns, VP Public Affairs
Lee H Hill, CFO/Senior VP
Jennifer Kelly Carpenter, Senior VP Government Affairs
John Groundwater, Executive Director
Represents operators of tours, excursions, ferries, charter vessels, dinner boats and other small passenger vessels.
375 Members Founded: 1944

21349 Receptive Services Association
17000 Commerce Parkway
Suite C
Mt. Laurel, NJ 08054
856-439-0500
FAX: 856-439-0525
rsa@ahint.com www.rsana.com
Peter Dorner, Chairman
Suzi Steiger Kavanaugh, President
Adam Rogers, VP
Rick Guzman, Treasurer
Helping receptive operators serve international tour companies through partnerships with North American suppliers.
570 Members

21350 Recreational Vehicle Industry Association
1896 Preston White Drive
PO Box 2999
Reston, VA 20195-0995
703-206-6003
www.rvia.org
David Humphreys, President

21351 Society of American Travel Writers
4101 Lake Boone Trl
Suite 201
Raleigh, NC 27607-7506
919-518-1919
FAX: 919-787-4916
Nancy Belcher, Editor
Photographers and 35 associate member representatives of airlines, hotels, resorts, tourist agencies and public relations firms.

21352 Society of Incentive and Travel Executives
401 North Michigan Avenue
Chicago, IL 60611
312-321-5148
FAX: 312-527-6783
Brenda_Anderson@site-intl.org
www.site-intl.org
Brenda Anderson, CEO
Allison Summers, Director of Operations
An individual membership society covering 70 countries. Members are corporate users, airlines, Tourist Boards, cruise lines, destination management companies, consultants, hotels/resorts, travel agents, incentive travel houses and publications.
2,200 Members Founded: 1973

21353 Travel Industry Association of America
1100 New York Avenue NW
Suite 450 W
Washington, DC 20005
202-408-8422
FAX: 202-408-1255 www.tia.org
Judith Harris, Membership Director
Roger Dow, Chief Executive Officer
Members are hotels, airlines and travel agencies interested in promoting increased travel to and within the US.
2100 Members Founded: 1941 2700 names $450 per M.

21354 Travel and Tourism Research Association
546 E Main Street
Lexington, KY 40508-2342
859-226-4355
FAX: 859-226-4355
lisalcarey@aol.com www.ttra.com

21355 VFP International Workcamps
Volunteers for Peace
1034 Tiffany Road
Belmont, VT 05730
802-259-2759
FAX: 802-259-2922
vfp@vfp.org www.vfp.org
Peter Coldwell, Director
A Vermont nonprofit membership organization promoting over 3000 international workcamps in 100 countries. Workcamps are an affordable way to travel, live and work abroad.
3000 Members Founded: 1982

Newsletters

21356 AAA World
2040 Market Street
Philadelphia, PA 19103
215-851-0291
FAX: 215-851-0297 800-763-9900
letters@aaaworld.com
http://www.aaaworld.com
Allen EeWalle, CEO
Sandy Kaden, Circulation Manager
Promotes travel destinations, gives advice on traveling and helpful automobile information. *$71.00*
Founded: 1900
Circulation: 2.1 mill

21357 Business Travel Management
Coastal Communications Corporation
488 Madison Avenue
New York, NY 10022-5702
212-691-1000
FAX: 212-888-8008
http://www.corporate-inc-travel.com
Michael Billing, Publisher
Created for the travel manager and planner. Covers policy-making as well as hands-on operations within the business travel marketplace. *$75.00*
Monthly

21358 Caribbean Reporter
Caribbean Hotel Association
18 Calle Marseilles
San Juan, PR 907-1682
787-725-2901
FAX: 787-725-9180
jdohrmann@caribbeanhotels.org
http://www.chahotels.com
Beverly Telemague, Publisher
Membership news. *$4.99*
Monthly Founded: 1959

21359 Craighead's Country Reports
Craighead Publications
397 Post Road
PO Box 1006
Darien, CT 06820-1006
203-655-1007
FAX: 203-655-0018
scraighead@craighead.com
http://www.craighead.com
Scott Craighead, President
Reports on more than 80 countries focusing on living and working conditions for international business travelers and employees who relocate abroad on business assignments. *$95.00*
50 pages Founded: 1977

21360 Cruise Industry News
Nissel-Lie Communications
441 Lexington Avenue
Room 1209A
New York, NY 10017-3910
212-986-1025
FAX: 212-986-1033
info2@cruiseindustrynews.com
http://www.cruiseindustrynews.com
Oivind Mathisen, Editor
Angela Reale Mathisen, Publisher
The newsletter covers industry news and developments, including the financial performance of the cruise lines, and is published 22 times a year. *$575.00*
Annual+ Founded: 1988
Circulation: 50000

21361 Entree Travel Newsletter
Entree Publishing
PO Box 5148
Santa Barbara, CA 93150-5148
805-969-5848
FAX: 805-969-5849
wtomicki@aol.com
http://www.entreenews.com
William Tomicki, Editor/Publisher
Travel, fashion and beauty ideas, sports and photography, wines and restaurants reviews new literature, music and film of interest to the travel and food enthusiast. *$75.00*
Monthly
Circulation: 8000 8000 names $450 per M.
Printed in 1 color on matte stock

21362 IACVB e-News
Int'l Association of Convention & Visitor Bureaus
2025 M Street
Suite 500
Washington, DC 20036
202-296-7888
FAX: 202-296-7889
info@iacvb.org http://www.iacvb.org
Michael D Gehrisch, President/CEO
Kristen Clemens, Editor
An electronic newsletter published by the International Association of Convention and Visitor Bureaus. Available with membership.
Weekly Founded: 1914
Circulation: 1300
Mailing list available for rent 1200 names
$400 per M.

21363 National Tour Association Newsletter
546 East Main Street
Lexington, KY 40508-3071
859-226-4444
FAX: 859-226-4404 800-682-8886
questions@ntastaff.com
http://www.ntaonline.com
Hank Phillips, Executive Director
Lisa Seumon, Senior VP
The National Tour Association is an organization of nearly 4,000 North American tourism professionals focused on the development, promotion and increased use of tour operators packaged travel. *$36.00*
100 pages Monthly Founded: 1998
Circulation: 5000 3,800 names

21364 Nationwide Intelligence Travel Alert Bulletin
Nationwide Intelligence
PO Box 1922
Saginaw, MI 48605-1922
989-793-0123
FAX: 989-793-8830
info@nationwideintelligence.com
http://www.nationwideintelligence
David Opperman, Publisher
David Opperman, Editor
For the corporate traveler or travel planner.
$95.00
Founded: 1987
Circulation: 30000

21365 Ocean and Cruise News
PO Box 329
Northport, NY 11768
203-329-2787
FAX: 203-329-2767
news@wocls.org
http://www.wocls.org/
Tom Cassidy, VP
Geroge Devol, President
Complete news on cruises. *$30.00*
Monthly Founded: 1980
Circulation: 7000

21366 Travel Industry Association of America Newsletter
Travel Industry Association of America
1100 New York Avenue NW
Suite 450 W
Washington, DC 20005-3934
202-408-8422
FAX: 202-408-1255
feedback@tia.org http://www.tia.org
Judith Harris, Membership Director
C Betsi, Marketing Manager
Kathy Keefe, Editor
Roger Dow, Chief Executive Officer
Travel information. *$1350.00*
Monthly Founded: 1941
Circulation: 3500
Printed in 3 colors on glossy stock

21367 Travel Management Newsletter
Reed Travel Group
500 Plaza Drive
Secaucus, NJ 07094-3685
201-021-1960
FAX: 202-902-2053
tmdaily@compuserve.com
www.tmdaily.com
Steve Bailey, Publisher
Discusses the news and views of the travel professional. *$735.00*
Weekly

21368 Travel Manager's Executive Briefing
Health Resources Publishing
1913 Atlantic Avenue
Suite F4
Manasquan, NJ 08736
732-292-1100
FAX: 732-292-1111 800-516-4343
info@themcic.com
http://www.themcic.com/www.healthresources
Bob Jenkins, President
Lisa Mansfield, Marketing Assistant
Read by travel managers of major corporations, Fortune 500 companies and corporate travel agencies twice a month to get up to the minute developments in the important field of travel and expense cost control. *$447.00*
$150 per M.

21369 Travel Weekly
500 Plaza Drive
Secaucus, NJ 07094-3685
201-902-1696
FAX: 201-902-2053
William D Scott, Publisher
Industry news, articles and stories on the travel industry. *$26.00*
BiWeekly

21370 Travel and Tourism Executive Report
10200 W 44th Avenue
Suite 304
Wheat Ridge, CO 80033-2840
303-463-2887
Francine Butler, Executive Director
Established as the Travel Research Association as the result of a merger.
750 pages

21371 Travelwriter Marketletter
PO Box 1782
Springfield, VA 22151
208-988-7672
FAX: 208-988-7672
mimi@travelwriterml.com
http://www.travelwriterml.com
Mimi Backhausen, Editor & Publisher
A monthly newsletter for travel writers and travel photographers. It's mainly about marketing travel articles, photography and travel books; also describes free trips for professional travel writers. *$75.00*
10 pages Monthly
Circulation: 1000

Magazines & Journals

21372 ABC Preferred Flight Planner: Europe- Middle East-Africa
ABC Corporate Services/Reed Travel Group
500 Plaza Drive
Secaucus, NJ 07094-3619
201-678-8775
FAX: 201-902-2053
www.infotec-travel.com
Luis Murcia, Owner
Offers information on properties and locations of interest to corporate business travelers.
250 pages SemiAnnual
Circulation: 65,000

21373 ASTA Agency Management
Miller Freeman Publications
2655 Seely Avenue
San Jose, CA 95134
408-943-1234
FAX: 408-943-0513
Mary Pat Sullivan, Publisher
Provides concise and useful information on trends in the industry and practical ideas regrading the profitable administration of travel agencies. *$36.00*
Monthly
Circulation: 35,182

21374 ASU Travel Guide
448 Ignacio Boulevard
Suite 333
San Rafael, CA 94949-5539
415-898-9500
FAX: 415-898-9501 866-459-0300
info@asutravelguide.com
http://www.asutravelguide.com
Christopher Gil, Managing Editor
Hank Sousa, VP
Provides information concerning worldwide travel destinations and other locales of interest to travelers and the bargains and discounts available to airline employees.
352 pages Quarterly Founded: 1971
Circulation: 700000
Printed in 4 colors on glossy stock

21375 Adjourn
National Association of Business Travel Agents
110 N Royal Street
4th Floor
Alexandria, VA 22314
703-684-0836
FAX: 703-684-0263
info@nbta.org http://www.nbta.org
Stuart Faber, Editor-in-Chief
Bill Connors, Executive Director
Tanya Racz, President
Colette Skeen, Manager, Exhibits & Advertising
Hank Roeder, Vice President
Provides accurate evalulations of cities, hotels, restaurants, airlines, and other travel products and services. *$47.50*

21376 Bank Travel Management
Group Travel Leader
401 W Main Street
#222
Lexington, KY 40507-1630
859-253-0455
FAX: 859-253-0499
info@grouptravelleader.com
http://www.banktravelmanagement.com
Mac Lacy, CEO/President/Publisher
Herb Starrow, Editor
Regular sections include: The Banker's Box, managing your senior program, and marketing your trips, with special features on personal travel accounts, trends in travel and banking clubs. *$20.00*
Monthly Founded: 1994
Circulation: 4000

21377 Best Read Guide Smokey Mountains
PO Box 6328
Sevierville, TN 37864-6328
865-908-4368
FAX: 865-908-4371
contact@bestreadguidesmokymountains.com
http://www.smokymountainsbestreadguide.com
Michael Smith, Publisher
Monthly Founded: 1976

21378 Bus Tours Magazine
National Bus Trader
9698 W Judson Road
Polo, IL 61064-9015
815-946-2341
FAX: 815-946-2347
nbt@busmag.com
http://www.busmag.com/
Larry Plachno, Editor and Publisher
Shaye Hall, Assistant Editor
Nancy Ann Plachno, Business Manager
Focuses on the operations, arrangements and marketing techniques used to plan these excursions as well as what's new in the industry. *$10.00*
Monthly Founded: 1979
Circulation: 7,200

21379 Business Travel Management
Coastal Communications Corporation
488 Madison Avenue
New York, NY 10022-5772
212-691-1000
FAX: 212-888-8008
Michael Billing, Publisher
Created for the travel manager and planner. Covers policy-making as well as hands-on operations within the business travel marketplace. *$75.00*
BiMonthly

21380 Byways
National Motorcoach Network
PO Box 1088
Mt Jackson, VA 22842
540-773-3323
FAX: 540-477-3858
nmn@motorcoach.com
http://www.motorcoach.com/byways
Stephen M Kirchner, Publisher/Editor
Includes riverboat gambling updates and special reports on the top 50 motorcoach destinations.
48 pages Founded: 1983
Circulation: 5000

21381 City Visitor
Travelhost
10701 N Stemmons Freeway
Dallas, TX 75220-2419
972-556-0541
FAX: 972-432-8729
http://www.travelhost.com
James Beuger, Editor
James Buerger, Publisher
James Buerger, Chairman
Travelhost is an in room publisher edited for the business and vacation traveler, with news features and general information relating to travel, recreation, business, new products and services and leisure activities. *$33.00*
Monthly Founded: 1967

21382 Classic Shoreline Times
2830 Long Hill Road
Suite 32
Guilford, CT 06437
203-453-2711
FAX: 203-453-4152 800-922-7065
Barbara Douglas, Editor
Erik Hesselberg, Managing Editor
A newspaper that is published twice a week on Wednesdays and Saturdays.

21383 Conde Nast Traveler Business Extra
4 Times Square
14th Floor
New York, NY 10036
212-880-0800
FAX: 212-286-2190
ecotourism@condenast.com
Brook Wilkinson, Executive Assistant Editor
Charles Townsend, Chief Executive Officer
Relates to gathering information for tourism.

21384 Corporate and Incentive Travel
Coastal Communications Corporation
2650 N Military Trail
Suite 250
Boca Raton, FL 33431-6390
561-890-0600
FAX: 561-989-9509
Harvey Grotsky, Publisher
Edited for corporate and meeting planners incentive travel executives and travel agents who are responsible for specifying accomodations, site selection and transportation. *$5.00*
Circulation: 60,082

21385 Country Discoveries
5400 S 60th Street
Greendale, WI 53129-1404
414-423-0100
FAX: 414-423-8463 800-344-6913
Focuses on backwoods travel in both the United States and Canada. *$14.98*
Founded: 1965

21386 Courier
National Tour Association
546 E Main Street
Lexington, KY 40508
859-226-4444
FAX: 859-226-4424 800-682-8886
courier@ntastaff.com www.nta.travel
Frances Figart, Editor
Lisa Simon, Publisher
Hank Philips, CEO/President
Karla Bimardo, Circulation Manager
Sara Morton, Public Relations Specialist
Courier Magazine helps readers to meet their responsibilities involved with their jobs. *$36.00*
110 pages Monthly Founded: 1955
Circulation: 6000
Printed in 4 colors on glossy stock

21387 Creative Business Traveler
High Tech Publishing Company
PO Box 1275
Amherst, MA 01004-1275
413-534-4500
FAX: 413-256-6378
Philip T DiPeri, Editor
Provides advice and timely information for people who want richer and more diversified business travel experiences. *$88.00*
Monthly

21388 Cruise & Vacation Views
Orban Communications
60 E 42nd Street
Suite 905
New York, NY 10165
cvvoffice@aol.com
Michael Brown, Publisher/Editor
Includes ideas and information on promotion and sales oppertunities, market trends, guides on training and support, and vacation reviews. *$48.00*
BiMonthly
Circulation: 32,000

21389 Cruise Industry News - Annual
Nissel-Lie Communications
441 Lexington Avenue
Room 1209A
New York, NY 10017-3910
212-986-1025
FAX: 212-986-1033
info2@cruiseindustrynews.com
http://www.cruiseindustrynews.com
Oivind Mathisen, Editor/Co-Publisher
Angela Mathisen, Advertising Manager/Co-Publisher
Johanna Marmon, Associate Editor
Wayne D. Schneiderman, Assistant Editor
The only book of its kind, and often rated "the most comprehensive information source on the industry" by cruise line executives. *$575.00*
Annual+ Founded: 1988

21390 Cruise Industry News Quarterly Magazine
Nissel-Lie Communications
441 Lexington Avenue
Room 1209A
New York, NY 10017-3910
212-986-1025
FAX: 212-986-1033
info2@cruiseindustrynews.com
http://www.cruiseindustrynews.com
Oivind Mathisen, Editor
Angela Mathisen, Advertising Manager
Johanna Marmon, Associate Editor
Wayne D. Schneiderman, Assistant Editor
The magazine covers all aspects of cruise operations, shipbuilding, new ships, cruise companies, ship reviews, onboard services, food and beverage, and ports and destinations. *$495.00*
Quarterly Founded: 1991
Circulation: 50000
Printed in 4 colors

21391 Cruise Trade
Travel Trade Publications
15 W 44th Street
New York, NY 10036-6611
212-730-6600
FAX: 212-730-7137
info@traveltrade.com
http://www.traveltrade.com
Joel M Abeis, CEO/President
Patricia J Collins, Editor-in-Chief
Provides travel agent owners and managers with industry news and analysis. *$10.00*
Monthly Founded: 1929
Circulation: 45000

21392 Digital Travel
Jupiter Communications Company
475 Park Avenue South
4th Floor
New York, NY 10016
212-389-2000
FAX: 212-725-4640 800-481-1212
info@jupitermedia.com
http://www.jup.com
Eva Papoutsakis, Editor
Marla Kammer, Managing Editor
Alan M Meckler, CEO
Editorial includes the latest information and technology in agencies, airlines, lodging, ticketing, mapping, Web advertising, transaction processing, revenue models, demographics, and full-service sites. *$595.00*
Monthly

21393 Family Motor Coaching Magazine
Family Motor Coach Association
8291 Clough Pike
Cincinnati, OH 45244-2756
513-474-3622
FAX: 513-388-5286 800-543-3622
jyeatts@fmca.com www.fmca.com
Jerry Yeatts, Convention Director
Ranita Jones, Sales Manager
Don Eversman, Executive Director
$3.99
Monthly
Circulation: 140000

21394 Frequent Flyer Magazine
2000 Clearwater Drive
Oak Brook, IL 60523
630-574-6000
FAX: 630-574-6565 800-342-5674

21395 Going on Faith
Group Traveler Leader
401 W Main Street
Suite 222
Lexington, KY 40507-1227
859-253-0455
FAX: 859-253-0499 888-253-0455
circmanager@grouptravelleader.com
http://www.grouptravelleader.com
Mac Lacy, Publisher
Brian Jewell, Editor
The national travel newspaper for churches, synagogues and Religious organizations. *$20.00*
Monthly Founded: 1991
Circulation: 5500

21396 Group Travel Leader
Group Travel Leader
301 E High St
Lexington, KY 40507-1509
859-253-0455
FAX: 859-253-0503
maclacy@grouptravelleader.com
http://www.grouptravelleader.com
Herbert Sparrow, Editor
Mac Lacy, CEO/President
Mac Lacy, Publisher
Kally Tyner, Marketing Manager
Supplies the senior travel planner with new destinations, unique points of interest and historical venues for their group, club or organization. *$39.00*
Monthly Founded: 1991
Circulation: 30000

21397 Hospitality Sales and Marketing Associatio n International
1201 Greensboro Drive
Suite 300
McLean, VA 22102
703-610-9024
FAX: 703-610-9005
bgilbert@hsmai.org
http://www.hsmai.org
Robert A Gilbert, President/CEO
To provide resources to sales and marketing professionals at all levels of thier career in travel, hospitality and tourism. *$ 65.00*
7000 pages Quarterly Founded: 1927
Circulation: 10000 7000 names

21398 Inside Flyer
Flight Plan
1930 Frequent Flyer Point
Colorado Springs, CO 80915
719-597-8889
FAX: 719-597-6855 800-767-8896
editor@insideflyer.com
http://www.insideflyer.com/
Randy Petersen, Editor/publ/CEO
Karen Heldt, Advertising Coordina/mark
Jeff Johnstone, Managing Editor
Leading publication of information for and about frequent traveler programs. *$45.00*
Monthly Founded: 1986
Mailing list available for rent
Printed in 4 colors on matte stock

21399 Jax Fax Travel Marketing
52 W Main St.
Milford, CT 06460
203-301-0255
FAX: 203-301-0250
jaxfaxnews@aol.com
http://www.jaxfax.com
Doug Cooke, Publisher
Marc Spac, Publishing Director
Theresa Scanlon, Editor
Marjorie Vincent, Circulation Manager
Peter Badeau, Associate Publisher
Monthly travel trade magazine featuring destination information and listings of discounted airfares and tour packages. *$15.00*
Monthly Founded: 1973
Circulation: 25000 28000 names $85 per M.
Printed in 4 colors on glossy stock

21400 Le Guide
201 Jefferson Street
Lafayette, LA 70501-7009
337-237-3560
FAX: 337-233-7484

21401 Leisure Travel News
Miller Freeman Publications
One Penn Plaza
10th Floor
New York, NY 10119-0099
212-615-2635
FAX: 212-279-3951 www.ttgweb.com
Mary Pat Sullivan, Publisher
Includes regular columns and departments covering retail travel agent activities, tour management, packages and group travel programs, supplier news, cruise lines, and coverage of specific destinations throughout the world with particular appeal to leisure/vacation travel. *$ 95.00*
Circulation: 55,215

21402 Marco Polo
1299 Bayshore Bouleveard
Suite B
Oldsmar, FL 34698-4246
727-735-9455
FAX: 727-735-9534

21403 Mexico Today
2009 S 10th Street
McAllen, TX 78503-5405
956-686-0711
FAX: 956-686-0732 800-222-0158
info@sanbornsinsurance.com
www.sanbornsinsurance.com
Pete Castillo, Marketing Director
Quarterly
Circulation: 5000
Printed in 4 colors on glossy stock

21404 Mid-Atlantic Group Tour Magazine
Shoreline Creations
PO Box 638
Yarmouth Port, MA 02675-638
508-398-0400
FAX: 616-393-0085 1 8-0 7-7 34
travel@grouptour.com
http://www.grouptour.com
Carl Wassink, Publisher
Carol Smith, Editor
Katie Weller, Circulation Manager
Jamie Cannon, Marketing Manager
Ruth Wassink, Vice President
Material looks at the latest offerings in tour travel including restaurants,theater, shopping, hotels, festivals, and events and activities.
Quarterly Founded: 1980
Circulation: 10000

21405 Midwest Traveler
12901 N Forty Drive
Saint Louis, MO 63141
314-523-6981
FAX: 314-523-6982 800-222-7623
Mike Right, Editor *$3.00*
Founded: 1902
Circulation: 45000

21406 Mobility
1717 Pennsylvania Avenue NW
8th Floor
Washington, DC 20006
202-293-7744
FAX: 202-659-8631
www.erc.org/MOBILITY_Online

21407 NTA Courier
546 E Main Street
Lexington, KY 40508-2342
859-226-4444
FAX: 859-226-4404 800-682-8886
questions@ntastaff.com
http://www.ntaonline.com
Frances Figart, Editor
Ann Thomas, CEO/President
Monthly
Circulation: 6000

21408 New England Tour Magazine
Shoreline Creations
PO Box 638
Yarmouth Port, MA 02675-638
508-398-0400
FAX: 508-398-4703 1 8-0 7-7 34
travel@grouptour.com
http://www.grouptour.com

Carol Smith, Editor
Carl Wassink, President
Katie Weller, Circulation Manager
Jamie Cannon, Marketing
Ruth Wassink, Executive Vice President

Promotes and covers the attractions, lodging, dining, events and other highlights of popular and less-famous travel destinations in the region.

Quarterly Founded: 1925
Circulation: 10000

21409 Onboard Services
International Publishing Company of America
664 La Villa Drive
Miami, FL 33166-6095
305-887-1700
FAX: 305-885-1923 800-525-2015
onboard@ipca.com
http://www.onboard-services.com

Alexander C Morton, Publisher
George Hulcher, Contributing Editor

Keeps airline, cruise ships, railroad, and terminal concessions management and purchasing departments up-to-date on all phases of passenger services. *$25.00*

24 pages Founded: 1968
Printed in 4 colors on glossy stock

21410 Outbound Traveler
Travel Review Publishing
PO Box 484
Marblehead, MA 01945-0484
781-631-1690
FAX: 781-631-0203
74777.1302@compuserve.com
www.outboundtrav.com

Carmi Zona-Paris, Publisher

Contents incude illustrated destination pieces, proactive marketing ideas, PATA cruise information for Asia and the South Pacific, all-inclusive resort coverage, and the latest on car rentals, rail excursions and related international services and products. *$20.00*

BiMonthly
Circulation: 32,000

21411 Outdoor Hospitality
8605 Westwood Center Drive
Ite201
Vienna, VA 22182-2240
703-932-2342
FAX: 703-734-3004
arvc@erols.com
www.gocampingamerica.com

Chandana Karmarkar, Manager

Outdoor hospitality serves the RV parks and campground industry. Its focus is on improving business practice offering new ideas and highlight personalities and parks at the leading edge of the outdoor hospitality industry.

Founded: 1966
Mailing list available for rent 3,200 names

21412 Ozark Mountain Visitor
200 Industrial Park Drive
Hollister, MO 65672-5327
417-334-3161
FAX: 417-335-3933

21413 Pacific Asia Travel News
Americas Publishing Company
3657 Harriet Road
Victoria, Can, BC V8Z-3T1
250-260-1883
FAX: 250-953-5250

Malcolm Scott, Publisher

Issues include a news datline with features on travel trends and outlooks, a special destination focus,and updates from the Pacific Asia Travel Association. *$30.00*

BiMonthly
Circulation: 24,000

21414 Practical Gourmet
Linick Group
7 Putter Lane
PO Box 102
Middle Island, NY 11953
631-924-3888
FAX: 631-924-3890
linickgrp@att.net
http://www.lgroup.addr.com

Gaylen Andrews, Publisher/Editor
Roger Dextor, Production
Barbara Deal, Marketing Manager

The focus of this publication is light, healthy gourmet dining; includes reports on wine tastings, food festivals, contests, celebrations, cooking schools and other events. *$48.00*

36 pages Monthly Founded: 1975
Circulation: 210,000 Controlled
Mailing list available for rent 210 M names $110 per M.
Printed in 4 colors on glossy stock
Computerized version available

21415 Recommend
Worth International Communication Corp
PO Box 171070
Hialeah, FL 33017-1070
305-828-0123
FAX: 305-826-6950 800-447-0123

Laurel A Herman, Publisher
Lorri Robbins, National Director

Contains colorful information on worldwide destinations, resorts, hotels, transportation and tour operators, as well as marketing angles to help travel agents sell travel. *$48.00*

Monthly Founded: 1967
Circulation: 60000
Printed in on glossy stock

21416 Runzheimer Reports on Travel Management
Runzheimer Park
Rochester, WI 53167-9999
262-712-2200
FAX: 262-971-2254 800-558-1702

Rex Runzheimer, President

21417 Sea Mass Traveler
PO Box 3189
Newport, RI 02840-0322
401-848-2922

21418 Shipboard Cruiser
Beach Investments
PO Box 1643
Orlando, FL 32802-1643
407-422-6095
FAX: 407-422-3608
sbcruiser@aol.com
http://www.shipboardcruiser.com

Phil R Beach, Publisher/Editor

Emphasizes new boats, cruise package offers and travel resources. For consumers who are vacation cruisers. *$49.00*

12 pages Monthly Founded: 1993
Printed in 3 colors on matte stock

21419 Southwest Airlines Spirit
4333 American Carter
MD 5374
Fort Worth, TX 75261
817-931-2579
FAX: 817-931-5782
marketing@spiritmag.com
http://www.spiritmag.com

Laura Wilson, Marketing Manager
Ross McCammon, Editor
Julie Wood, Production Manager
Susan Hicks, Publisher

Monthly Founded: 1971
Circulation: 400088

21420 Specialty Travel Index
PO Box 458
San Anselmo, CA 94979
415-594-4900
FAX: 415-455-1648 888-624-4030
info@specialtytravel.com
http://www.specialtytravel.com

Karin Kinsey, Art Director
Stean Hansen, Circulation Manager
Andy Alpine, Marketing Manager
Risa Weinreb, Editor
Judith Alpine, Advertising Manager

Directory/magazine of adventure and specialty travel. *$10.00*

Founded: 1980
Circulation: 32000
Printed in 4 colors on glossy stock

21421 SportsTravel
Schneider Publishing Company
11835 W Olympic Boulevard
Suite 1265
Los Angeles, CA 90064
310-577-3700
FAX: 310-577-3715
info@schneiderpublishing.com
http://www.schneiderpublishing.com

Timothy Schneider, Publisher/Editor
Nathan Price, Managing Editor
Lisa Furfine, Publisher
Chad Starbuck, Marketing Manager

Includes articles on travel training, sports law, event spotlights, and vital information on sites, hotels, transportation, trade shows and upcomiong events for team travel planners and event organizers. *$48.00*

Monthly Founded: 1997
Circulation: 1400 $175 per M.
Printed in on glossy stock

21422 Sun Valley Magazine
12 E. Bullion St
Suite B
Hailey, ID 83333-697
208-788-0770
FAX: 208-788-3881
sales@sunvalleymag.com
http://www.sunvalleymag.com

Laurie S Wall, Publisher *$15.00*

Quarterly
Circulation: 15000

21423 Sundancer's West
1108 Meadowview Drive
Euless, TX 76039
817-545-5265
FAX: 817-571-6481
gwat/@swbell.net
www.sundancerswest.com

Gerry Watkins,
Webmaster/Editor/Photographer

21424 Tourism Development Report
Ecklein Communications
PO Box 5194
Ignacio, CA 94948-5194
415-883-1960
FAX: 415-883-9064
editorial@eci-global.com
www.eci-global.com
John Ecklein, Publisher
Covers the latest national and internationalindustry news, trends and developments for resorts, transit systems and hotels, and a calendar of events. *$377.00*
Monthly

21425 Travel & Leisure
1120 Avenue of the Americas
10th Floor
New York, NY 10036
212-382-5600
FAX: 212-382-5878 800-888-8728
Yossi Langer, Editor
Nancy Novogrod, Editor-in-Chief
Antonia LoPresti, Senior Marketing Manager
Ed Kelly, CEO/President *$19.95*
Monthly
Circulation: 950000

21426 Travel & Leisure Golf
American Express Publishing Corporation

1120 Avenue of the Americas
New York, NY 10036
212-382-5600
FAX: 212-768-1568 800-947-7961
john.c.rodenburg@aexp.com
http://www.travelandleisure.com
Nancy Novogrod, Editor
Antonia LoPresti, Senior Marketing Manager
Maura Smale, Project Manager
John Rodenburg, Publisher
Rashmi George, Advertising Coordinator
$19.95
Monthly
Circulation: 950000

21427 Travel Agent International
Universal Media
801 2nd Avenue
12th Floor
New York, NY 10017-4706
212-986-5100
FAX: 212-983-2548 taiedit@aol.com
Richard P Friese, Publisher
Provides profiles on resorts and attractions for each given season. *$250.00*
10 per year
Circulation: 19,100

21428 Travel Counselor
Miller Freeman Publications
600 Harrison Street
San Francisco, CA 94107-1387
415-905-2200
FAX: 415-905-2234
Joanne N Nelson, Publisher
Contains business information and analysis apporiate to the retail agency profession

7 per year
Circulation: 28,000

21429 Travel Exclusives
520 SW 6th Avenue
Suite 1030
Portland, OR 97204
503-802-4624
FAX: 503-802-4625 800-572-4624

21430 Travel Trade News Edition
Travel Trade Publications
15 W 44th Street
New York, NY 10036-6611
212-730-6600
FAX: 212-730-7020
travelcat@aol.com
http://www.traveltrade.com
Lenore Lewis Abels, Editor
Joel M Abels, Publisher
Provides pertinent information and newsin the industry, along with sales reference information. *$10.00*
Weekly Founded: 1995
Circulation: 41237

21431 Travel Trends
Meredith Corporation
125 Park Avenue
New York, NY 10017-5529
212-513-3710
FAX: 212-551-7161
Peter Mason, Publisher/Editor
Information on the trends of the travel industry.
Quarterly
Circulation: 5,000

21432 Travel World
East - West News Bureau
531 Main Street
#902
El Segundo, CA 90254
310-836-8712
FAX: 310-836-8769
www.eastwestnews.org
Elizabeth Barnes, Executive Director

21433 Travel World News
Travel Industry Network
50 Washington Street
South Norwalk, CT 06854
203-853-4955
FAX: 203-866-1153
editor@travelworldnews.com
http://www.travelworldnews.com
Charles Gatt Jr, Publisher
Peter Gatt, Associate Publisher
Provides extensive features on tourist destinations, travel deals, coverage of conventions, new products and personnel notices and changes. *$25.00*
Monthly Founded: 1988
Circulation: 22000

21434 Travel, Food & Wine
Punch-In-Syndicate
400 E 59th Street
Floor 9
New York, NY 10022-2342
212-755-4363

punchin@usa.net www.punchin.com
J Walman, Editor
A magazine featuring articles and reviews on travel, food and wine, columns on airlines, hotels, cruise ships, railroads, resorts, restaurants, and spas. Also theater reviews, cinema, radio and all forms of entertainment. *$300.00*
Monthly

21435 Travelhost Magazine
10701 N Stemmons Freeway
Dallas, TX 75220-2419
972-556-0541
FAX: 972-432-8729
travelhost@dc.rr.com
http://www.travelhost.com/
James E Buerger, Chairman/Publisher
David B Portener, Associate Publisher
Monthly Founded: 1967
Circulation: 60000

21436 Trip
2424 N Davidson Stret
Suite 106 B
Charlotte, NC 28205
704-376-7800
FAX: 704-376-7802
mag@charlottetrip.com
http://www.charlottetrip.com
Marie Margaret, CEO/President/Publisher
Dana Jorden, Editor
Jenifer Krupa, Marketing Manager
Angie Jones, Circulation Manager
$18.00
Monthly Founded: 1990
Circulation: 35000

21437 V/A
600 SW Market Street
Portland, OR 97201-5218
503-220-8262
FAX: 503-222-6756 800-452-1643

21438 Vermont Green Mountain Guide
44 Country Road
North Springfield, VT 05150-9738
802-886-3333

Cindy Thiel, Owner

Trade Shows

21439 Adventure Travel and Outdoor Show
McRand International
1 Westminster Place
Suite 300
Lake Forest, IL 60045-1867

FAX: 847-295-4419
Richard Dux, VP
Sue Wildman, VP
Exhibits by tour operators, outfitters and others geared toward soft and hard adventure travel vacations and outdoor activities.
15M Attendees January

21440 American Society of Travel Agents Conferen ce
1101 King Street
Alexandria, VA 22314-2944
703-739-2782
FAX: 703-684-8319
Chris Vranas, VP
Gathering of travel agents, airlines, hotels and tour operators that provides the opportunity to view and discuss new products, services and trends in the industry. 700 booths.
6M Attendees November

21441 American Travel Market Exhibition Company
Reed Exhibition Companies
383 Main Avenue
Norwalk, CT 06851-1543
203-840-4800
FAX: 203-840-9628
inquiry@atm.reedexpo.com
www.reedexpo.com

Gregg Vautrin, Chief Executive Officer

The national event for all US travel buyers, including tour operators, travel agents, corporate travel buyers and meeting/conference planners. One of a global series of Travel Market events.
September

21442 Annual American and Canadian Sport, Travel and Outdoor Show
Expositions
Edgewater Branch
PO Box 550
Cleveland, OH 44107-0550
216-529-1300
FAX: 216-529-0311
975 exhibits of hunting and fishing equipment, travel services, boats, recreational vehicles and related equipment, supplies and services.
300k Attendees Annual Founded: 1935

21443 Annual Boat, Vacation and Outdoor Show
Showtime Productions
PO Box 4372
Rockford, IL 61110
815-877-8043
FAX: 815-877-9037
brenda@showtimeproduction.net
showtimeproduction.net

Duane Nichols, President
Brenda Rotoco, Event Coordinator

Boat, travel, outdoor equipment, supplies, and services plus demonstrations.
28000 Attendees February Founded: 1970

21444 Annual Capital Sport Fishing, Travel and Outdoor Show
International Sport Show Producers Association
PO Box 4720
Portsmouth, NH 03802-4720
603-431-4315
FAX: 603-431-1971
info@sportshows.com
www.sportshows.com

Paul Fuller, President

Over 350 exhibits of sports, fishing, recreation and travel equipment, supplies and services.
45k Attendees Annual Founded: 1996

21445 Arabian Travel Market
Reed Exhibition Companies
383 Main Avenue
PO Box 6059
Norwalk, CT 06851
203-840-4800
FAX: 203-840-9628
Three hundred exhibitors with travel related information, supplies and services.
5915 Attendees Annual

21446 Corporate and Incentive Travel
488 Madison Avenue
New York, NY 10022-5702
212-753-5511
FAX: 212-888-6388
Corporate travel forum.

21447 Destinations Showcase
Intl. Association of Convention/Visitors Bureaus
2025 M Street
Suite 500
Washington, DC 20036
202-296-7888
FAX: 202-296-7889
info@iacvb.org www.iacvb.org

Michael D Gehrisch, President/CEO

Containing 80-100 exhibits.
575 Attendees Founded: 1914
Mailing list available for rent 1200+ names $400 per M.

21448 Discover America International Pow Wow
Travel Industry Association of America
1100 New York Avenue NW
Suite 450
Washington, DC 20005-3934
202-408-8422
FAX: 202-408-1255
agoldfin@tia.org www.tia.org

Alison Goldfind, Marketing Manager

Annual show of 1050 suppliers of travel products and services.
5,600 Attendees

21449 Euro Travel Forum
Reed Exhibition Companies
255 Washington Street
Newton, MA 02458-1637
617-584-4900
FAX: 617-630-2222

Elizabeth Hitchcock, International Sales

A mobile, multi-product and multi-destination travel trade exhibition bringing travel products from all over the world into direct contact with travel agents and travel buyers from the leisure, business and incentive products industries.
27M Attendees April

21450 Family Motor Coach Association Convention
8291 Clough Pike
Cincinnati, OH 45244-2756
513-474-3622
FAX: 513-388-5286 800-543-3622
jyeatts@fmca.com www.fmca.com

Jerry Yeatts, Convention Director
Ranita Jones, Sales Manager
Shawna Grubbs, Sales Assistant

Convention for Motorhome enthusiasts. Includes hundreds of motorhome displays, supplier displays and component displays.
15M Attendees Mar/Apr/July/Aug Founded: 1963

21451 Heartland Travel Showcase
Hart Productions
3307 Clifton Avenue
Suite 4
Cincinnati, OH 45220-2065
513-281-0022
FAX: 513-281-3322
hart@hartproductions.com
www.hartproductions.com
Annual show and exhibits of information from 10 midwest states and the province of Ontario on travel destinations, attractions, accomodations, activities and restaurants.
February

21452 Incentive Travel and Meeting Executives Show
Hall-Erickson
98 E Naperville Road
Westmont, IL 60559-1559
630-963-9185
FAX: 630-434-1216 800-752-6312
moti@heiexpo.com
www.motivationshow.com

Nancy A Petitti, Show Director

20M Attendees October Founded: 1972

21453 La Crosse Boat, Sports and Travel Show
Shamrock Productions
14550 Granada Drive
Apple Valley, MN 55124
952-431-9630
FAX: 952-431-9633
info@shamrockprod.com
www.shamrockprod.com

Randy Schauer, President/CEO

Boats, sports and travel equipment, supplies and services.
February

21454 Motivation Show
Hall-Erickson
98 E Naperville Road
Westmont, IL 60559-1559
630-963-9185
FAX: 630-434-1216 800-752-6312
moti@heiexpo.com
www.motivationshow.com

Nancy A Petitti, Exhibit Show Manager

25M Attendees September Founded: 1929

21455 National Camping Industry Expo
8605 Westwood Center Drive
#Ite201
Vienna, VA 22182-2240
703-932-2342
FAX: 703-734-3004
arvc@erols.com
www.gocampingamerica.com

Rick Carbo, Manager
Chandana Karmarkar, Manager

National camping industry expo, only trade expo for RVÆparks and campground oweners/operators. Containing 120 booths and 100 exhibitors.
850+ Attendees November Founded: 1966
Mailing list available for rent 3,200 names

21456 Recreational Vehicle Industry Association National RV Trade Show
1896 Preston White Drive
Reston, VA 20191-4325
703-206-6003

David Humphreys, President
Mary Hutya, VP

Six hundred and thirty booths.
10M Attendees November

21457 Seatrade Cruise Convention
Miller Freeman Publications
13760 Noel Road
Suite 500
Dallas, TX 75240

FAX: 214-419-8855 800-527-0207

21458 Sport Travel Outdoor Show
Expositions
PO Box 550
Cleveland, OH 44107-0550
216-529-1300
FAX: 330-529-0311

Judy Fassnacht, Show Manager

475 booths of products and services related to the outdoor travel industry.

93M Attendees February

21459 Sports Travel and Adventure
Show Productions
800 Roosevelt Road
Suite 407
Glen Ellyn, IL 60137-5839
630-694-4611
FAX: 630-790-0209

Sandra Lewis, Show Manager

Two hundred and fifty six booths geared toward outdoor enthusiasts.

15M Attendees February

21460 Travel Industry Association American Pow Wow Marketing
1100 New York Avenue NW
Suite 450W
Washington, DC 20005
202-408-8422

Sue Elms, Show Manager
Roger Dow, Chief Executive Officer

Seven hundred booths where providers of US travel products promote these products.

3M Attendees April

21461 Travel and Tourism Research Association Show
546 E Main Street
Lexington, KY 40508-2342
859-226-4355
FAX: 859-226-4355
lisalcarey@aol.com www.ttra.com

Twenty booths exhibiting information of interest to members of the Tourism Research Association.

400 Attendees June

21462 TravelAge Tradeshows
1775 Broadway
Floor 19
New York, NY 10019-1903
212-246-7671
FAX: 212-237-3007

Nancy Montella, Show Manager

Four hundred booths of educational and business-oriented tradeshow that provides a vehicle for various people within the travel industry to meet and exchange information on products, services and trends.

2.5M Attendees March

21463 World Travel Market
Reed Exhibition Companies
255 Washington Street
Newton, MA 02458-1637
617-584-4900
FAX: 617-630-2222

Elizabeth Hitchcock, International Sales

Premium travel show.

43M Attendees November

Directories & Databases

21464 ABC Cruise and Ferry Guide
Reed Travel Group
Church Street
Hertfordshire, England, LU 5 4HB

Offers information on international shipping companies operating passenger services and cruises.

320 pages Quarterly ISSN 0001-0480

21465 ABC Guide to International Travel
Reed Travel Group
Church Street
Hertfordshire, England, LU 5 4HB

Offers a list of foreign consulates in London, England that offer travel information to tourists.

Quarterly

21466 Access Travel: Airports
Airport Operators Council International
1220 19th Street NW
Suite 200
Washington, DC 20036-2463
202-293-8500
FAX: 202-331-1362

Information is given on over 500 airports worldwide that offer handicapped facilities.

50 pages

21467 Airport Hotel Directory
3255 Wilshire Boulevard
Suite 1514
Los Angeles, CA 90010-1418
213-739-1956

Restaurants and hotels are listed that are a close proximity to major airports. *$12.00*

170 pages

21468 American Bus Association's Motorcoach Marketer
American Bus Association
1100 New York Avenue NW
Suite 1050
Washington, DC 20005-3934
202-982-2703

This directory is a complete guide of the intercity bus and travel industry offering over 2,000 hotels and sightseeing services.

400 pages Annual

21469 American Society of Travel Agents Membership Directory
1101 King Street
Alexandria, VA 22314-2944
703-739-2782

Bill Maloney, Manager

Travel agents that represent over 17,000 agencies in the United States, Canada and overseas are the focus of this comprehensive directory. *$125.00*

600 pages Annual

21470 CMP Publications Travel File
CMP Publications
600 Community Drive
Manhasset, NY 11030-3847
516-625-5000
FAX: 516-562-5718

This large database covers the travel industry, with emphasis on news for travel agents and business travelers.

Full-text

21471 Club Metro
Metro Online
PO Box 6849
New York, NY 10128-0017
212-794-2664

This database contains information on travel, entertainment, and metropolitan services.

Bulletin Board

21472 Condo Vacations: the Complete Guide
Lanier Publishing International
PO Box 20429
Oakland, CA 94620-0429

Condominiums that are available for vacation rentals are listed. *$14.95*

320 pages Annual

21473 Cruise Industry News Annual
Nissel-Lie Communications
441 Lexington Avenue
Room 1209A
New York, NY 10017-3910
212-661-7613
FAX: 212-986-1033
www.cruiseindustrynews.com

Oivind Mathisen, Editor

This book presents the entire worldwide cruise industry from news ships on order to supply/demand scenarios; plus reports on relevant issues, financial results, newbuilding and second-hand ship values, shipbuilding, new technology and on board services; plus exclusive reports on each sailing region, and a comprehensive directory of all cruisde lines, shipyards, ports and other suppliers. *$450.00*

300 pages Annual

21474 Environmental Vacations: Volunteer Projects to Save the Planet
John Muir Publications
PO Box 613
Santa Fe, NM 87504-0613
505-466-6360
FAX: 505-988-1680

Information is given on vacations that provide opportunities to assist environmental projects. *$16.95*

250 pages

21475 Federal Travel Directory
Office of Federal Supply & Services
4 Crystal Mall Building
Washington, DC 20406-0001
202-564-2480

A list of airlines is offered in this directory that are under contract to the federal government. *$77.00*

Monthly

21476 Ford's Travel Guides
Ford's Travel Guides
19448 Londelius Street
Northridge, CA 91324-3511
818-987-1413

Offers valuable information on cruise ships and their planned cruises for one year ahead. *$14.95*

200 pages Quarterly
Circulation: 5,000

21477 Foster Travel Publishing Website
Foster Travel Publishing
PO Box 5715
Berkeley, CA 94705-0715
510-549-2202
FAX: 510-549-1131
lee@fostertravel.com
www.fostertravel.com

Lee Foster, Owner

award winning travel writing and photography on 200 worldwide locations, presented to the consumer and to the content

buyer on the web or in print looking for travel writing or travel photography.
Full-text

21478 Free US Tourist Attractions
Pilot Books
127 Sterling Avenue
PO Box 2102
Greenport, NY 11944
631-477-0978
FAX: 631-477-0978 800-797-4568
A directory of free family entertainment in every state of the union. *$12.95*
ISBN 0-875762-04-2

21479 Historic Landmarks of Black America
Gale Research
27500 Drake Road
Farmington Hills, MI 48331
248-699-4253
FAX: 248-699-8214 800-877-4253
galeord@gale.com www.gale.com
Major sites where black history has been made. *$39.95*
375 pages

21480 International Workcamp Directory
Volunteers for Peace
1034 Tiffany Road
Belmont, VT 05730
802-259-2759
FAX: 802-259-2922
vfp@vfp.org www.vfp.org
Peter Coldwell, Director
An annual booklet listing over 2400 opportunities for meaningful travel throughout Western and Easter Europe, Russia, Africa, Asia, Australia and Latin America. 2-3 week programs are $200 including room and board. *$20.00*
289 pages Annual Founded: 1982 ISBN 0-945617-20-8
Circulation: 2,000
Printed in 4 colors

21481 National Bed and Breakfast Association Gui de
National Bed & Breakfast Association
PO Box 332
Norwalk, CT 06852-0332
203-847-6196
FAX: 203-847-0469 www.nbba.com
Phyllis Featherston, Executive Director
$17.95
600 pages Every 2-3 Years Founded: 1982
ISBN 0-961129-86-7
Printed in 2 colors on matte stock

21482 OAG Business Travel Planner
Official Airline Guide
2000 Clearwater Drive
Oak Brook, IL 60523-8809
630-574-6000
FAX: 630-574-6565
Directory of services and supplies to the industry. *$142.00*
1,100 pages Quarterly ISSN 0894-1726
Circulation: 65,000

21483 OAG Mobile
Reed Travel Group
2000 Clearwater Drive
Oak Brook, IL 60523-8809
630-740-0825
FAX: 630-574-6070 800-323-4000
info@oag.com www.oag.com
OAG mobile offers wireless access to up-to-date travel information via wireless web-enabled phones and personal digital assistants (PDAs). The overall vision of OAG mobile is to empower the frequent traveler to fully manage their arrangements while out of the office using the OAG travel application, via the mobile device of their choice. OAG Mobile offers wireless device users access to the most comprehensive and independent flight schedule information available, for over 800 airlines. *$25.00*

21484 OAG Worldwide Cruise & Shipline Guide
Official Airline Guide
2000 Clearwater Drive
Oak Brook, IL 60523-8809
630-574-6000
FAX: 630-574-6565
Offers information on steamship companies that offer cruises and scheduled port-to-port and ferry services. *$99.00*
300 pages Quarterly
Circulation: 5,000

21485 Office of Federal Supply and Services
4 Crystal Mall Building
Washington, DC 20406-0001
202-564-2480
A list of airlines is offered in this directory that are under contract to the federal government. *$77.00*

21486 Official Bus Guide
Russell's Guides
834 3rd Avenue SE
Cedar Rapids, IA 52403-2408
319-364-6138
FAX: 319-364-4853
A list of 475 intercity bus companies in the United States, Canada and Mexico. *$9.90*
Monthly
Circulation: 14,000

21487 Official Handbook of Travel Brochures
Vacation Publications
1502 Augusta Drive
Suite 415
Houston, TX 77057-2484
713-974-6903
16 pages Quarterly
Circulation: 38,000

21488 Official Tour Directory
Thomas Publishing Company
5 Penn Plaza
New York, NY 10001
212-950-0500
www.vacationpackager.com
David Juman, Editor
Approximately 2,200 tour operators offering tours and vacation packages to over 500 worldwide destinations and 200 special interests and activities. *$48.00*
SemiAnnual
Circulation: 36,000

21489 Real Guides
Farmers Trip & Travel
PO Box 473
Mount Morris, IL 61054-0473
FAX: 815-734-1223
A series of guidebooks that list sites, attractions and events in a city or country. *$8.00*
300 pages Per Edition

21490 Reed's Travel Group's Travel Agent Database
Reed Travel Group
2000 Clearwater Drive
Oak Brook, IL 60523-8809
630-740-0825
FAX: 630-574-6360
Kenneth Ritter, Editor
Jeff Greisch, President
About 65,000 wholesale, retail and cooperative travel agencies worldwide, including tour operators. *$270.00*

21491 Society of American Travel Writers: Member ship Directory
Society of American Travel Writers
4101 Lake Boone Trail
Suite 201
Raleigh, NC 27607-7506
FAX: 919-787-4916
Sarah Haw, Member Services
About 550 newspaper and magazine travel editors, writers, columnists, photo journalists and broadcasters in the US and Canada. *$ 95.00*
Annual February

21492 Thomas Cook Airports Guide Europe
Thomas Cook
Unit 11, Coningsby Road
Peterborough, England, PE 3 85B
Offers valuable information on over 75 public airports in Europe.
255 pages Biennial

21493 Thomas Cook Airports Guide International
Thomas Cook
Unit 11, Coningsby Road
Peterborough, England, PE 3 85B
Offers valuable information on over 90 airport facilities outside of the United Kingdom.
255 pages Biennial

21494 Tours.com
490 Post Street
Suite 1701-A
San Francisco, CA 94102
415-677-0961
FAX: 415-332-7980
info@tours.com www.tours.com
Maria Polk, President/CEO/Co-Founder
Karin Wacaster, Public Relations
Marijo Douglass, Finance Executive
Home of the Worldwide Directory of Tours and Vacation Packages.
Founded: 1995

21495 Travel Agent: Focus 500 Directory Issue
Universal Media
801 2nd Avenue
New York, NY 10017-4706
212-986-5100
FAX: 212-338-9445
Lists of attractions, restaurants, convention and visitor bureaus, hotel chains and management companies, cruise lines, state tourism offices, travel trade associations, tourist railways.
Annual October
Circulation: 50,000

21496 Travel Editors: US Consumer & Inflight Magazines
Rocky Point Press
4830 Ranchito Avenue
Sherman Oaks, CA 91423-1927

FAX: 818-763-4818
Listings of travel editors of US consumer and inflight magazines.
Annual

21497 Travel Forum
CompuServe Information Service
PO Box 20212
Columbus, OH 43220-0212
614-457-8600

This database contains information on travel and related topics of interest, including travel planning.
Bulletin Board

21498 Travel Industry Association of America: Tr avel Media Directory
Travel Industry Association of America
1100 New York Avenue NW
Suite 405W
Washington, DC 20005-6130
202-408-8422
FAX: 202-408-1255
Thomas Berrigan, Editor
Roger Dow, Chief Executive Officer
Travel editors of major newspapers, magazines and broadcast outlets. *$40.00*
Annual
Circulation: 3,000

21499 Travel Industry Personnel Directory
Fairchild Publications
7 W 34th Street
New York, NY 10001-8100
212-630-3880

Marsheela Evans, Senior Editor
Air and steamship lines, tour operators, bus lines, hotel representatives, foreign and domestic railroads, foreign and domestic tourist information offices, travel trade associations, etc. *$30.00*
Annual April

21500 Travel Insider's Guide to Alternative Accommodations
Travel Insider
PO Box 14
Streamwood, IL 60107-0014
206-338-3381
FAX: 206-338-3381
John E Sullivan, Editor
Over 400 sources for alternative accommodations worldwide, such as farmhouses, castles, universities and country inns. *$9.95*
Annual October

21501 Travel Photo Source Book
Society of American Travel Writers
4101 Lake Boone Trail
Suite 201
Raleigh, NC 27607-7506

FAX: 919-787-4916
Nancy Belcher, Editor
Nearly 100 member photographers and 35 associate member representatives of airlines, hotels, resorts, tourist agencies and public relations firms.
Biennial

21502 Travel Tips USA
Renaissance Publications
7819 Barkwood Drive
Worthington, OH 43085-5803
614-777-1227

Amusement parks, attractions and festivals are among some of the categories listed in this travel directory. *$17.95*
320 pages

21503 Travel and Hospitality Career Directory
Gale Research
27500 Drake Road
Farmington Hills, MI 48331
248-699-4253
FAX: 248-699-8214 800-877-4253
galeord@gale.com www.gale.com
Bradley J Morgan, Editor
Over 400 airlines, cruise lines, hotels, motels, resorts, major attractions, meeting planning firms, convention facilities, visitors' bureaus, tourist boards and travel agencies offering careers in the travel industry. *$34.00*

21504 Travel and Tourism Research Association: M embership Directory
Travel and Tourism Research Association

546 E Main Street
Lexington, KY 40508-2342
859-226-4355
FAX: 859-226-4355
lisalcarey@aol.com
Lisa Carey, Executive Director
Over 750 state and local tourism bureaus and other federal and provincial government agencies, airlines, media, hotels, university bureaus of business research and other university departments and research and consulting firms concerned with travel research, marketing and promotion. *$50.00*
Annual June

21505 Travel, Leisure and Entertainment News Med ia
Larriston Communications
PO Box 20229
New York, NY 10025-1518
212-864-0150
FAX: 212-662-8103
Sheila Gordon, Editor
Over 350 travel and leisure magazines and daily newspapers with circulations of over 50,000 that have special leisure or entertainment sections. *$89.00*
Annual May

21506 Traveler's Hotline Directory
Forte Travel Lodge
1960 Harbor Island Drive
San Diego, CA 92101-1013
858-879-9596
FAX: 619-293-0694 800-578-7878
Dorothy DuBois, Editor
Approximately 12,000 travel services such as air couriers, auto rental agencies, campgrounds, resorts, hotels, spas, travel groups and airlines that offer toll-free domestic or international telephone numbers. *$15.95*

21507 Travelers Information RoundTable

GE Information Services
401 N Washington Street
Rockville, MD 20850-1707
301-388-8284

Cathy Ge, Owner
Provides a forum enabling users to share information on a range of travel topics.
Bulletin Board

21508 West Coast Travel
Foster Travel Publishing
PO Box 5715
Berkeley, CA 94705-0715
510-549-2202
FAX: 510-549-1131
lee@fostertravel.com
www.fostertravel.com
This database offers information for travelers and tourists on approximately 150 locations in the western United States, Canada and Mexico.
Full-text

21509 Worldspan TravelShopper
WORLDSPAN
300 Galleria Parkway
Atlanta, GA 30339
770-637-7400
FAX: 770-563-7004
www.worldspan.com
Rakesh Gangwal, Chief Executive Officer
This database offers travel information, including 5 million domestic and international flights for every airline in the world for more than 100,000 cities.
Directory

Industry Web Sites

21510 www.biztravel.com
Biztravel.com

Internet travel service offering discounts on flights, hotels, car rentals, packages and cruises.

21511 www.expedia.com
Expedia.com

Internet travel service offers access to airlines, hotels, car rentals, vacation packages, cruises and corporate travel.

21512 www.gocampingamerica.com
National Association of RV Parks and Campgrounds

Nat ARVC serves the business and legislative needs of more than 3,200 member RV parks and campgrounds.

21513 www.goworldnet.com/cgi-bin
Worldnet USA

States and their hotels, theaters and museums.

21514 www.greyhouse.com
Grey House Publishing

Selected Grey House directories in the fields of business, health and education are available online. Users can search our online databases by several different search criteria, such as product categories, geographic area, sales volume and much, much more. Full Grey House catalog and online ordering also available.

21515 www.hotwire.com
Hotwire.com

Internet travel service offering discounts on flights, hotels, car rentals, packages and cruises.

21516 www.hsmai.org
Hospitality Sales and Marketing Association

To provide resources to sales and marketing professionals at all levels of thier career in travel, hospitality, and tourism.

21517 www.iacvb.org
International Association of Convention and
Visitor Bureaus

Promotes sound professional practices in the solicitation and servicing of meetings and conventions. Members represent travel/tourism-related businesses. Publications include a electronic newsletter and on-line directory.

21518 www.info.now.com/site
Society of Incentive and Travel Executives

An individual membership society covering 70 countries. Members are corporate users, airlines, Tourist Boards, cruise lines, destination management companies, consultants, hotels/resorts, travel agents, incentive travel houses and publications.

21519 www.nbba.com
National Bed & Breakfast Association

Innkeepers of bed and breakfast lodgings.

21520 www.ntaonline.com
National Tour Association

For North American tourism professionals focused on the development, promotion and increased use of tour operators packaged travel.

21521 www.orbitz.com
Orbitz.com

Internet travel service offering discounts on flights, hotels, car rentals, packages and cruises.

21522 www.rsana.com
Receptive Services Association

Helping receptive operators serve international tour companies through partnerships with North American suppliers.

21523 www.tia.org
Travel Industry Association of America

For hotels, airlines and travel agencies interested in promoting increased travel to and within the US

21524 www.travel.com
Travel.com

Internet travel service providing access to flights, hotels, car rentals, vacation packages and cruises.

21525 www.travel.lycos.com
Lycos.com

Internet travel service offering discounts on flights, hotels, car rentals, packages and cruises.

21526 www.travel.yahoo.com
Yahoo.com

Internet travel service providing access to flights, hotels, car rentals, vacation packages and cruises.

21527 www.travelocity.com
Sabre Holdings

Travel service offering consumers access to hundreds of airlines and thousands of hotels, as well as cruise, last-minute and vacation packages and best-in-class car rental companies.

21528 www.waveconcepts.com/arta
Association of Retail Travel Agents

Promotes the interests of retail travel agents through representation on industry councils and testimony before Congress. Conducts joint marketing and educational programs.

Associations

21529 ABF Freight Systems
3801 Old Greenwood Road
Fort Smith, AR 72903
800-610-5544
FAX: 800-599-2810 877-ABF-0000
abfinfocenter@abf.com www.abf.com

Robert Davidson, President & CEO
Shannon Lively, Vive President of Transportation

Concentrates on national and regional transportation of general commodities freight, involving primarily LTL shipments. Mission is to provide reliable transportation services in a responsible manner to meet customers' unique needs.

21530 American Towman Network
246 3rd Avenue
Westwood, NJ 07675-2106
201-722-3000
FAX: 201-722-3010
towcrazy@wrecker.com
www.towman.com

21531 American Trucking Association
2200 Mill Road
Alexandria, VA 22314-4677
703-838-1700
FAX: 703-838-8884
www.truckline.com

Bill Graves, President

21532 Carrier Information Exchange
Box 51105
New Berlin, WI 53151
262-786-5500
FAX: 262-786-3881

21533 Council of Fleet Specialists
315 Delaware Street
Kansas City, MO 64105-1256
816-421-2600
FAX: 816-421-0515

UJ Reese, Executive VP

Members are distributors of parts and services for heavy-duty trucks.
210 Members Founded: 1967

21534 Driver Employee Council of America
1001 G Street NW
Suite 500-W
Washington, DC 20001-4545
202-344-4268
FAX: 202-434-4646
Members are companies leasing truck drivers to private carriers.
43 Members Founded: 1992

21535 Express Carriers Association
PO Box 4376
Allentown, PA 18105-4376
866-322-7447
FAX: 866-322-3299
eca@expresscarriers.com
www.expresscarriers.com

Cheryle Williamson, Executive Director

The mission of the ECA is to develop business between carriers, shippers and vendors of products and services to the transportation industry.

21536 Heavy Duty Representatives Association
4015 Marks Road
Apartment 2B
Medina, OH 44256-8316
330-725-7160
FAX: 330-725-7160

Cara R Giebner, Editor

Independent sales agencies which sell heavy-duty components to the trucking and aftermarket industries.

21537 Independent Truck Owner-Operators
PO Box 621
Stoughton, MA 02072-0621

Trade association for business and human resources equipment financing.

21538 Light Truck Assessory Alliance
SEMA
Po Box 4910
Diamond Bar, CA 91765-0910
909-396-0289

info@sema.org www.sema.org

Todd Yeoman, Chairman
Ron DiVincenzo, Chair-Elect

A national organization with 150 manufacturers of truck caps and light truck accessories.

21539 Mid-West Truckers Association
2727 N Dirksen Parkway
Springfield, IL 62702
217-525-0310
FAX: 217-525-0342
info@mid-westtruckers.com
www.mid-westtruckers.com

Don Schaefer, President

2700 Members Founded: 1962

21540 Munitions Carriers
PO Box 1446
Fairfax, VA 22030-1446
703-273-8144
FAX: 703-273-8147
Transporters of munitions and explosive materials.

21541 NATSO
1199 N Fairfax Street
Suite 801
Alexandria, VA 22314
703-549-2100
FAX: 703-684-4525 888-ASK-NATS
headquarters@natso.com
www.natso.com

Sharon L Corigliano, Executive Director
Lisa J Mullings, President/CEO
Linda Van Arsdale, Director Government Affairs
Theresa M Spinola, Director Public Affairs
Kimberly A Roberts, Director Finance

NATSO is the professional association of America's $42 billion travel plaza and truckstop industry. NATSO represents the industry on legislative and regulatory matters; serves as the offical source of information on the diverse travel plaza and truckstop industry; provides education to its members; conducts an annual convention and trade show; and supports efforts to generally improve the business climate in which its members operate.
1100 Members Founded: 1990

21542 National Automobile Dealers Association
8400 Westpark Drive
McLean, VA 22102
703-821-7000
FAX: 703-821-7234
nadainfo@nada.org www.nada.org

Charley R Smith, Chairman
Jack Kain, Vice Chairman
Phillip D Brady, President

Manufacturers, suppliers and distributors of products and services designed to control dealership expenses, help merchandising or improve profitability.
19700 Members Founded: 1917

21543 National Food Distributors Association
120 Wall Street
27th Floor
New York, NY 10005
212-482-6440
FAX: 212-482-6459
www.specialtyfoods.org
An organization comprised of independent store-to-door service distributors and suppliers of specialty food items.
2100 Members Founded: 1952

21544 National Motor Freight Traffic Association
1001 North Fairfax
Suite 600
Alexandria, VA 22314
703-838-1810
FAX: 703-683-1094 866-411-6632

Bill Pugh, Executive Director
Amanda Sisk, Assistant Ex. Director
Lynn Clayton, Director
Brad Westrom, President

Members are regulated motor common carriers of general frieght.

21545 National Private Truck Council
2200 Mill Road
Suite 350
Alexandria, VA 22314
703-683-1300
FAX: 703-683-1217
webmaster@nptc.org www.nptc.org

Gary F Petty, President/CEO
Patti Burke, Director Conference
Bob Inderbitzen, Director Safety/Compliance
Richard LaRoche, Director Membership
George Mundell, Senior VP

Distributors, shippers, processors, jobbers and manufacturers who transport their own goods and are owners of their own truck fleets. Sponsors national safety contests, safety seminars, management workshops, fleet management certification.
500 Members Founded: 1939

21546 National Tank Truck Carriers
Express Carriers Association
PO Box 4307
Bethlehem, PA 18018
610-740-5857
FAX: 610-740-3174 866-322-7447
eca@expresscarriers.com
www.expresscarriers.com

Dave Anderson, Director
Tim Bergin, Director
Lynn Clayton, Director
Brad Westrom, President

Conducts research, promotes federal standards of construction, design, use and operation of tank trucks.
Founded: 1939

21547 National Truck Equipment Association
37400 Hills Tech Drive
Farmington Hills, MI 48331-3414
248-489-7090
FAX: 248-489-8590 800-441-6832
info@ntea.com www.ntea.com
Robert S Green, President
Jim Carney, Executive Director
Sheree Campbell, Executive Assistant
NTEA currently represents nearly 1,600 small to mid sized companies that manufacture, distribute, install, buy, sell and repair commercial trucks, truck bodies, truck equipment, trailers and accessories. The major commercial truck chassis manufacturers also belong to the NTEA as associate members.
1600 Members Founded: 1964 1600 names $400 per M.

21548 National Truck Leasing System
1 S 450 Summit Avenue
Oakbrook Terrace, IL 60181
630-538-8878
FAX: 630-953-0040
www.nationalease.com
John Grainger, President
Members are independent truck leasing companies.
Founded: 1944

21549 National Trucking Industrial Relations
908 King Street
Alexandria, VA 22314-3067
703-836-5506
Trucking executives and lawyers concerned with personnel and labor relations issues.
128 Members Founded: 1987

21550 Owner Operator Independent Drivers
1 NW Ooida Drive
Grain Valley, MO 64029
816-295-5791
800-444-5791
ooida_info@ooida.com
www.ooida.com
James Johnston, President
National association for owner-operators, professional drivers and small fleet owners. Lobbies federal and state government and advises on all legislation affecting the trucking industry. Provides insurance, financial products and business services.
95000 Members Monthly Founded: 1973
Circulation: 200000

21551 Owner Operators of America
PO Box 582
Orchard Park, NY 14127-0582
Merchants providing goods and services to truck drivers, operators and owners. Seeks to protect the status, interests and image of truck drivers. Offers discounts on fuel, tires, food, repairs, parts and insurance. Provides tax filing assistance. Sponsors trade shows, conferences and public relations programs.
250 Members Founded: 1982

21552 Professional Truck Driver Institute
Express Carriers Association
2200 Mill Road
Alexandria, VA 22314
703-381-1960
FAX: 703-836-6610 866-322-7447
Robert Hirsch, President
Richard Clemente, Program Director
Marlene Dakita, Certification Coordinator
The nation's foremost advocate of optimum standards and professionalism for entry level truck driver training.
60 Members Founded: 1986

21553 Professional Trucking Services Association
United Truckers Service
1385 Iris Drive
Conyers, GA 30208
770-226-6200
FAX: 770-929-3201
Members are service bureaus which assist trucking companies in obtaining licensing and permits.
52 Members Founded: 1984

21554 Regional and Distribution Carriers
2200 Mill Road
Alexandria, VA 22314-4654
703-381-1960
FAX: 703-836-6870
Clifford Harvison, President
Members are 'for-hire motor common carriers of general freight in packaged lots.'
150 Members Founded: 1943

21555 Regular Common Carrier
211 N Union Street
Alexandria, VA 22314-2643
703-838-1990
FAX: 703-739-3105
The only national organization created solely to serve the needs to less-than-truckload highway common carriers of general commodity freight.
200 Members Founded: 1939

21556 Specialized Carriers and Rigging
2750 Prosperity Avenue
Fairfax, VA 22031-4312
703-698-0291
FAX: 703-698-0297 www.scranet.org
Joel M Dandrea, Executive VP
Douglas Ball, VP
Phyllis L Cockerham, Director
Kim Enderle, Manager Meetings
Sharon Follin, Director Information Services
Members are carriers, crane and rigging operators and millwrights engaged in the transport of heavy goods.
1100 Members Founded: 1959

21557 Transportation Loss Claim and Security
120 Main Street
Huntington, NY 11743-6906
631-270-0100
FAX: 516-549-8962
A nonprofit trade association dedicated to the prevention of freight loss, damage and delay, the promulgation of reasonable liability rules, laws and claim policies.
660 Members Founded: 1973

21558 Truck Frame and Axle Repair Association
3741 Enterprise Drive SW
Rochester, MN 55902-0122
FAX: 507-529-0380 800-232-8272
w.g.reich@att.net
www.taraassociation.com
Dudley Powell, President
Bill Hinchdiffe, VP
For operators and owners of heavy duty truck repair facilities, fleet managers, truckers and insurance damage appraisers.
110 Members Founded: 1966

21559 Truck Trailer Manufacturers Association
1020 Princess Street
Alexandria, VA 22314-2247
703-549-3010
FAX: 703-549-3014
ttma@erols.com www.ttmanet.org
Lynn Wiles, Editor
Richard Bowling, President
A national organization of truck and tank trailer manufacturers and 120 suppliers to the industry.
Founded: 1941

21560 Truck and Heavy Equipment Claims Council
1128 Burgundy Lane
Ballwin, MO 63011-4108
Bill Ketchelmeier, Executive Officer
Repair and manufacturing facilities, insurance companies and adjusters concerned with insuring of heavy equipment and trucks. Promotes safety.
45 Members Founded: 1961

21561 Truckload Carriers Association
2200 Mill Road
Alexandria, VA 22314-4654
703-838-1960
FAX: 703-836-6610
tca@truckload.org www.truckload.org
Kristie Kehoe, Director Communications
Clifford Harvison, President
For truckload carriers executives.
: website

21562 Used Truck Association
7355 N Woodland Drive
Indianapolis, IN 46278
FAX: 317-299-1356 800-827-7468
jfaulkner@primediabusiness.com
www.uta.org
Eddie Walker, President
Justin Faulkner, Secretary
Used truck manufacturers and dealerships.
300 Members Founded: 1988

Newsletters

21563 American Trucker
PRIMEDIA Intertec-Technology & Transportation
9800 Metcalf
Overland Park, KS 66282
913-411-1300
FAX: 317-299-1356 800-827-7468
amtrucker@trucker.com
http://www.trucker.com

Kyle Eggert, Publisher
Coleen Liatch, Supervisor

Information for those interested in the truck industry. Contains articles on new and used trucks, supplies, equipment, financing, pricing, and other truck related services. *$21.00*
Monthly Founded: 1926
Circulation: 600000

21564 Diesels-E-mail News & Analysis
Forecast International
22 Commerce Road
Newtown, CT 06470-1643
203-426-0800
FAX: 203-426-1964
www.forecast1.com

Kathy Bertrand, Production Manager
Monty Nebinger, Circulation Director

An electronic information/data service sourced from thousands of worldwide publications, in 15 languages. Provides concise summaries, news, trends and contract information with hyper-links to the source or a related website. Delivered 100 times a year. *$425.00*

21565 Owner Operator News
PO Box 582
Orchard Park, NY 14127-0582

FAX: 716-941-5582

Charles DeVaul, Publisher

Trucking news and information.
Monthly

21566 Truck Equipment News
National Truck Equipment Association
37400 Hills Tech Drive
Farmington Hills, MI 48331-3414
248-489-7090
FAX: 248-489-8590 800-441-6832
info@ntea.com http://www.ntea.com

Laura Heinrich, Communications Manager
Jim Carney, Executive Director

Covers NTEA and member/industry activities, business management issues, technical topics, excise tax applications, sales/marketing managment topics, legislative and regulatory news, monthly new truck retail sales figures, NTEA/industry events calender, and other current topics of interest to industry members. *$72.00*
150 pages Monthly Founded: 1964
Circulation: 1600

21567 Trucker Publications
Trucker Publications
PO Box 3413
Little Rock, AR 72203-3413
501-666-0500
FAX: 501-666-0700
roadnews@thetrucker.com
www.thetrucker.com

Ray Wittenberg, Publisher

Up to date, comprehensive coverage of news affecting both drivers and management, including regulatory issues, road conditions, fuel, and current trends in technology. *$21.50*
BiWeekly
Circulation: 27,500

21568 Truckload Carriers Report
Truckload Carriers Association
2200 Mill Road
Alexandria, VA 22314-4654
703-838-1960
FAX: 703-836-6610
tca@truckload.org
http://www.truckload.org

Kristie Kehoe, Director Communications
Lance Craig, Chairman
Clifford Harvison, President

A newsletter for truckload carriers executives. Free to association members.
8 pages Weekly Founded: 1938
Circulation: 1600 : website

21569 Trucks-E-Mail News & Analysis
Forecast International
22 Commerce Road
Newtown, CT 06470-1643
203-426-0800
FAX: 203-426-1964 800-451-4975
info@forecast1.com
http://www.forecast1.com

Kathy Bertrand, Production Manager
Monty Nebinger, Circulation Director

An electronic information/data service sourced from thousands of worldwide publications, in 15 different languages. Provides concise summaries, news, trends and contract information with hyperlinks to the source or related website. Delivered 100 times a year. *$425.00*
Monthly Founded: 1973

Magazines & Journals

21570 Commercial Carrier Journal
Reed Business Information
2000 Clearwater Drive
Oak Brook, IL 60523-0001
630-740-0825
FAX: 630-288-8686
www.reedbusiness.com

Gerald F Standler, Editor

For executives who manage, operate and maintain United States utility and specialty fleets. *$45.00*
Monthly

21571 Diesel Equipment Superintendent
Business Journals
50 Day Street
Norwalk, CT 06854-3100
203-853-6015
FAX: 203-852-8175

James Jones, Editor

Maintenance management in areas of selection, of heavy duty trucks and trailers. *$25.00*
100 pages Monthly Founded: 1923

21572 Fastline Productions
PO Box 248
Buckner, KY 40010-248
502-222-0146
FAX: 502-222-0615 800-626-6409
helpdesk@fastline.com
http://www.fastlinepub.com

William Howard, Editor
Crysten Minzenberger, Marketing Director
Gail Olszewski, Owner

Nationwide and regional picture buying guides for the trucking industry.
Founded: 1978
Circulation: 4900

21573 Fleet Owner Magazine
Primedia
11 River Bend Drive South
PO Box 4949
Stamford, CT 06907-949
203-358-9900
FAX: 203-358-5811
frcs@pbsub.com
http://www.primediabusiness.com

Paul B Kisseberth, Publisher
Jim Mele, Editor-in-Chief

Monthly business magazine serving executives and managers in commercial trucking fleets. *$40.00*
Monthly Founded: 1928

21574 Keep on Truckin' News
Mid-West Truckers Association
2727 N Dirksen Parkway
Springfield, IL 62702-1407
217-525-0310
FAX: 217-525-0342
info@mid-westtruckers.com
http://www.mid-westtruckers.com

Don Schaefer, Publisher

For members of Mid-West Association.
64 pages Monthly Founded: 1964
Circulation: 4000
Printed in 4 colors on glossy stock

21575 Land Line Magazine
PO Box 1000
Grain Valley, MO 64029-712
816-229-5791
FAX: 816-443-2227 800-444-5791
info@landlinemag.com
http://www.landlinemag.com

Todd Spencer, Editor-in-Chief
Sandi Soendker, Publisher
Jim Johnson, CEO/President
Mike Schermoly, Marketing
Pam Perry, Circulation Manager

Edited for the owner/operator and independent trucker and small fleet operator who drive heavy duty trucks.
13 pages Monthly Founded: 1973
Circulation: 200000+
Printed in 4 colors on glossy stock

21576 Lifting & Transportation International
2895 Chad Drive
Eugene, Or 97408
800-493-2295
FAX: 541-342-3307
adwyer@douglaspublications.com
http://www.liftandtransport.com/

Eugene Brymer, Publisher
Andrew Dwyer, Editor
Jason Pierce, VP

Covers trucking overdimensional loads, heavy crane, and ridging work. *$110.00*
Founded: 1958

21577 Light & Medium Truck
TT Publishing
2200 Mill Road
Alexandria, VA 22314-4654
703-838-1770
FAX: 703-548-3662
bharmon@trucking.org
http://www.ttnews.com

Bruce Harmon, Managing Editor
Debra Devine, Production Coordinator
Stanford Erickson, Associate Publisher
Scott Smith, Circulation Manager
Paul Rosenthal, Marketing Manager

Provides information for day to day management of a company using light to medium duty trucks, such as equipment

safety, alternative fuels, maintenance and government regulations.
Monthly Founded: 1945
Circulation: 50509

21578 Mid-West Truck Trader
Heartland Communications
15400 Knoll #500
Dallas, TX 75248

FAX: 515-574-2213 800-247-2000

Bruce Foval, Editor

Trucking industry news and views. *$59.00*
56 pages Monthly Founded: 1976

21579 Milk & Liquid Food Transporter
Brady Company
N 80 W
12878 Fond du Lac Avenue
Menomonee Falls, WI 53051-4474
262-255-0100
FAX: 262-255-3388
lmittag@bradyco.co

Linda Mittag, Publisher

Information for owners, operators and managers of companies that haul milk or other liquid foods in sanitary or food grade tankers. Publication covers maintenance, association news, state of the industry, business management, and activities of independent haulers. *$12.00*
Monthly
Circulation: 4,100

21580 Modern Bulk Transporter
Tunnell Publications
PO Box 66010
Houston, TX 77266
713-523-8124
FAX: 713-523-8384

Charles Wilson, Editor
Robin Anderson, Advertising Director

Serves the truck industry that transports petroleum and petroleum products. Accepts advertising. *$25.00*
Monthly

21581 Mover Magazine
Virgo Publishing
3300 N Central Avenue, Suite 2500
PO Box 40079
Phoenix, AZ 85067-0079
480-990-1101
FAX: 480-675-8146
Moving and storage industry.

21582 NATSO Truckers News
Newport Communications
PO Box W
Newport Beach, CA 92658-8910
949-261-1636
FAX: 949-261-2904
www.heavytruck.com

W Dewey Clower, Publisher

Provides industry news, legislation affecting drivers, product developments, and on road service. *$20.00*
Monthly
Circulation: 182,716

21583 Newport's Road Star
Newport Communications
38 Executive Park
Suite 300
Irvine, CA 92614-6755
949-261-1636
FAX: 949-261-2904 800-233-1911
ssturgess@truckinginfo.com
http://www.truckinginfo.com

Maria Barnett, Production Manager
Faye Solem, Circulation Manager
Steve Sturgess, Editor
Doug Condra, President

Monthly magazine for professional long-distance tractor-trailer drivers, who either own their own trucks or drive for trucking companies.
Monthly Founded: 1898
Circulation: 153000

21584 Oklahoma Motor Carrier
Okalhoma Trucking Association
7201 N. Classen Blvd
Suite 106
Oklahoma City, OK 73116-620
405-843-9488
FAX: 405-843-7310 800-368-9576
advertise@oktrucking.org
http://www.oktrucking.org

Dan Case, Executive Director
Craig Schneithorst, Chairman

Official publication of Associated Motor Carriers of Oklahoma, the state trade association for the trucking industry.
30 pages Quarterly Founded: 1932
Circulation: 3000
Printed in 4 colors

21585 Over the Road
Ramp Publishing Group
PO Box 549
Roswell, GA 30077
770-587-0311
FAX: 770-642-8874 www.ramppub.com

Marvin Shefsky, Publisher

Information for professsional truck drivers, owners, operators, and fleet drivers on current events, industry news, driver profiles, and employment opportunities. *$30.00*
Monthly
Circulation: 116624

21586 Overdrive Magazine
Randall Publishing Company
3200 Rice Mine Road
Tuscaloosa, AL 35406-3187
205-539-9396
FAX: 205-349-3765 800-633-5953
editors@overdriveonline.com
http://www.randallpub.com

Michael Reilly, CEO/President
Brad Holthaus, Publisher
Linda Longton, Editor

For the owner/operator and small fleet operator. *$30.00*
Monthly Founded: 1934
Circulation: 104753
Printed in 4 colors on glossy stock

21587 Owner Operator
Reed Business Information
200 Clearwater Drive
Oak Brook, IL 60523
630-740-0825
FAX: 630-320-8686

Gregory S Sheremet, Publisher

For independent truckers and small fleet owners.
Monthly

21588 Pro Trucker
Ramp Publishing Group
PO Box 549
Roswell, GA 30077-549
770-587-0311
FAX: 770-642-8874 800-878-0311
sales@otrprotrucker.com
http://www.otrprotrucker.com

Greg McClendon, Sales Manager
Marvin Shefsky, Publisher

Professional truck drivers, owners, operators, and fleet drivers, information on interviews, industry news, employment information, distribution locations and leasing options for the professional drivers.

Monthly Founded: 1981
Circulation: 116000

21589 Refrigerated Transporter
Tunnell Publications
4200 S Shepherd Drive
Suite 200
Houston, TX 77098
713-523-8124
FAX: 713-523-8384
http://www.refrigeratedtrans.com

Raymond Anderson, Publisher
Gary Macklin, Editor-in-Chief

Serves transportation and distribution companies concerned with the handling of temperature controlled commodities. Accepts advertising. Free to qualified subscribers.
$45.00
103 pages Monthly
Printed in 4 colors on glossy stock

21590 Road King
Hammock Publishing
3322 W End Avenue
#700
Nashville, TN 37203-1073
615-385-9745
FAX: 615-386-9349
roadking@hammock.com
www.roadking.com

Adele Rowan, Publisher

Focuses on trucking lifestyles, achievements and interests. Offers articles on equipment and driver success. *$15.00*
BiMonthly
Circulation: 222,590

21591 Successful Dealer
Kona Communications
707 Lake Cook Road
Deerfield, IL 60015
847-498-3180
FAX: 847-498-3197 800-767-5662
truckbooks@konacommunications.com
http://www.konacommunications.com

Denise Rondini, Editorial Director
James D Moss, Publisher
James D Moss, President
Tom Cory, Circulation Manager
John S Dickson, National Sales Manager

Edited for the dealer organization covering dealerships, selling and servicing medium to heavy-duty trucks, trailers and construction equipment. Accepts advertising.
$50.00
52 pages bi-monthly Founded: 1918
Circulation: 23000 23,000 names $120 per M.
Printed in g colors on 4 stock

21592 Trailer/Body Builders
Tunnell Publications
PO Box 66010
Houston, TX 77266
713-523-8124
FAX: 713-523-8384 800-880-0368

Bruce Sauer, Editor
Ray Anderson, Group Publisher
Taylor Motsinger, Circulation Manager

Serves the truck trailer and truck body manufacturing industry. Accepts advertising.
$25.00
Monthly Founded: 1960
Circulation: 15500

21593 Transport Topics
Express Carriers Association
PO Box 4307
Bethlehem, PA 18018
610-740-5857
FAX: 610-740-3174 866-322-7447
eca@expresscarriers.com
www.expresscarriers.com

Cheryle Williamson, Executive Director

Trucking industry news, features and analysis.

21594 Transportation Equipment News
Vulcan Publications
PO Box 55886
Birmingham, AL 35255
205-328-6198
FAX: 205-987-2882
www.vulcanpub.com

Ian Greenspan, Publisher

Extensive coverage of government regulations, recruiting and training issues as well as buying and leasing, maintenance and industry trade shows.
Monthly
Circulation: 20,000

21595 Truck Accessory News
Bobit Publishing
3520 Chalanger St
Torrance, CA 90503
310-533-2400
FAX: 310-533-2504 http://www.

Jonathen Lamas, Editor
Travis Weeks, Publisher
Jerry Martin, Circulation Manager
Aver J Bobit, CEO/President

Provides information on product and merchandise trends, covers industry news on retail activities, and interviews top executives and buyers. *$37.00*
Monthly Founded: 1961
Circulation: 10000

21596 Trucker's Connection
Megan Cullingford
5960 Crooked Creek Road
Suite 15
Norcross, GA 30092
770-416-0927
FAX: 770-416-1734
dan@truckersconnection.com
http://www.truckersconnection.com

David Guthrie, Advertising Sales
Dan Barnhill, Editor
Megan Cullingford, General Manager
Reid Ramsay, Production Manager
Jamie Adcock, Advertising Sales

Published for the use of long haul, over-the-road truck drivers, owner operators, small trucking company fleet owners, safety and recruiting of personnel for trucking companies in the US and Canada.
Monthly Founded: 1986
Circulation: 165000
Printed in 4 colors on glossy stock

21597 Truckin'
McMullen Argus Publishing
2400 E Katella Avenue
11th Floor
Anaheim, CA 92806-6832
714-939-2559
FAX: 714-978-6390
info@primedia.com
http://www.primediaautomotive.com

Steve Parr, CEO
Susan Brocett, Marketing Manager
Brad Christopher, Publisher
Steve Warner, Editor
Jerome Dziechiasz, Sales Manager

Provides information on testing new trucks, reviewing accessories and truckin' activities. *$24.95*
Monthly
Circulation: 180000

21598 Trucking Technology
167 Cherry Street
Suite 430
Milford, CT 06460-3466
203-882-9485

Trade Shows

21599 American Truck Dealers Convention and Equipment Exposition
National Automobile Dealers Association
8400 Westpark Drive
Mc Lean, VA 22102-3522
703-217-7000
FAX: 703-821-7075
gheimes@nanda.org www.nada.org

Gary Heimes

Annual show of 100 manufacturers, suppliers and distributors of products and services designed to control dealership expenses, help merchandising or improve profitability.
2,500 Attendees Founded: 1963

21600 American Trucking Association Management Conference and Exhibition
American Trucking Association
2200 Mill Road
Alexandria, VA 22314-4677
703-838-1700
FAX: 703-838-5720 800-282-5463
trucking@cais.com www.cais.com/ata

Bill Graves, President

Annual show of 168 exhibitors of equipment, supplies and services related to the trucking industry.
1,500 Attendees Annual Founded: 1984

21601 ECA Shipper: Carrier Marketplace
Express Carriers Association
PO Box 4376
Allentown, PA 18105-4376

FAX: 866-322-3299 866-322-7447
eca@expresscarriers.com
www.expresscarriers.com

Cheryle Williamson, Executive Director

Premier business to business event featuring one on one interviews between shippers, carriers and vendors of products/services to the transportation industry.
300+ Attendees April Founded: 1997

21602 International Truck and Bus Expo
Society of Automotive Engineers
400 Commonwealth Drive
Warrendale, PA 15096-0001
724-772-8548
FAX: 724-776-0790 www.sae.org

21603 Light Truck Accessory Expo
Truck Cap and Accessory Association
6564 Loisdale Court
Suite 430
Springfield, VA 22150-1812
703-822-0707
FAX: 703-922-7806 800-283-8242

Kendra Moore, Director Meetings/Marketing

Annual show of 150 manufacturers of truck caps and light truck accessories.
2,500 Attendees

21604 Midwest Truck Show
Mid-West Truckers Association
2727 North Dirksen Parkway
Springfield, IL 62702
217-525-0310
FAX: 217-525-0342
truckers@iname.com
www.mid-westtruckers.com

Don Schaefer, Executive VP
Jeanne Campo, Show Manager

Annual show and exhibits of trucks, trailers, financing information, computers, insurance information and related equipment, supplies and services. Containing 200 booths and 150 exhibitors.
6,000 Attendees February

21605 Munitions Carriers Conference
PO Box 1446
Fairfax, VA 22030-1446

FAX: 703-273-8147

Jerry Turner, Managing Director

Transporters of munitions and explosive materials.
16 Attendees Founded: 1952

21606 Regional and Distribution Carriers Confere nce
2200 Mill Road
Suite 640
Alexandria, VA 22314-4654
703-387-7978
FAX: 703-836-6870

AD Gearner Jr, Managing Director

Members are 'for-hire motor common carriers of general freight in packaged lots.'
150 Attendees Founded: 1943

21607 Regular Common Carrier Conference
211 N Union Street
Suite 102
Alexandria, VA 22314-2643
703-838-1990
FAX: 703-739-3105

James C Harkins, Executive Director

The only national organization created solely to serve the needs to less-than-truckload highway common carriers of general commodity freight.
200 Attendees Founded: 1939

21608 Truck Show Las Vegas
Independent Trade Show Management
1155 Chess Drive
Suite 102
Foster City, CA 94404-1117
650-349-4876
FAX: 650-349-5169 800-227-5992
rsherrard@truckshow.com
www.truckshow.com

Sue K Fena, Sr. Show Coordinator
Roger Sherrard, President

The premier commercial truck and equipment show in the USA. Containing 2,500 booths and 350 exhibits, also offers semi-

nars and workshops on current topics in the trucking industry.
20M Attendees June Founded: 1961
Mailing list available for rent

21609 Truckerfest
Newport Communications
38 Executive Park
Suite 300
Irvine, CA 92614-6755
949-261-1636
FAX: 949-261-2904 800-233-1911
bfarquhar@truckinginfo.com
www.truckerfest.com
Bud Farquhar, Show Manager
BJ Iverson, Events Coordinator
Trucker appreciation event at Alamo Travel Plaza, Reno, NV. Truck Parade, trucker games, music, free dinners, truck beauty contest, and fireworks. Containing 75 booths and 60 exhibits.
10M Attendees August

21610 Trucking Show Mid-America
3038 Breckenridge Lane
Suite 101
Louisville, KY 40220-2195

Timothy Young, Show Manager
Four hundred and fifty booths displaying the latest in trucking.
35M Attendees March

21611 Work Truck Show
National Truck Equipment Association
37400 Hills Tech Drive
Farmington Hills, MI 48331-3414
248-489-7090
FAX: 248-489-8590 800-441-6832
info@ntea.com www.ntea.com
Steve Carey, Show Manager
Annual business to business event designed to bring together distributors, upfitters, manufacturers, buyers and users of work trucks in all industries including delivery, government, construction and landscaping.

7,000 Attendees March

Directories & Databases

21612 Fleet Owner-Specs and Buyers' Directory Issue
Primedia
9800 Metcalf Avenue
Overland Park, KS 66212
913-341-1300
FAX: 913-967-1898
www.primediabusiness.com
Jack Dwyer, Editor
Tom Moore, Editor
Lists of manufacturers of equipment and materials used in the operation, management and maintenance of truck and bus fleets. *$5.00*
Annual October
Circulation: 100,250

21613 Heavy Duty Representatives Profile Directory
Heavy Duty Representatives Association
4015 Marks Road
Apartment 2
Medina, OH 44256-8316
330-725-7160
800-763-5717
Cara R Giebner, Editor
About 60 independent sales agencies which sell heavy-duty components to the trucking and aftermarket industries.
Annual January

21614 Heavy Duty Trucking: CFS Buyers Guide
Newport Communications Div.-HIC Corporation
38 Executive Park
Suite 300
Irvine, CA 92614-6755
949-261-1636
FAX: 949-261-2904
Doug Condra, Publisher
Five hundred Council of Fleet Specialists member manufacturers and wholesalers specializing in heavy-duty truck parts and repairs. *$45.00*
Annual January
Circulation: 98,502

21615 NTEA Membership Roster & Product Directory
National Truck Equipment Association
37400 Hills Tech Drive
Farmington Hills, MI 48331-3414
248-489-7090
FAX: 248-489-8590 800-441-6832
info@ntea.com www.ntea.com
Jim Carney, Executive Director
Mike Frizzell, President
Over 1,600 manufacturers and distributors of commerical trucks, bodies, trailers and related equipment. Information includes: product info, membership category, affiliate membership, join date, address, phone and fax numbers, e-mail address, website address. *$50.00*
Annual Founded: 1964

21616 National Private Truck Council: Official Membership Directory
2200 Mill Road
Suite 350
Alexandria, VA 22314
703-683-1300
FAX: 703-683-1217 www.nptc.org
Gary Petty, President/CEO
Richard LaRoche, Director Membership
The only organization that represents the interests and concerns of private fleets — companies that use in-house or dedicated truck fleets to support distribution of their products. The directory includes members listed by: company, individual and industry. Both private fleet and supplier members are listed. *$145.00*
100 pages Annual
Printed in 4 colors on glossy stock

21617 National Tank Truck Carrier Directory
Express Carriers Association
PO Box 4307
Bethlehem, PA 18018
610-740-5857
FAX: 610-740-3174 866-322-7447
eca@expresscarriers.com
www.expresscarriers.com
Cheryle Williamson, Executive Director
A who's who directory of services and supplies to the industry.

21618 Transportation Security Directory & Handbook
Grey House Publishing
185 Millerton Road
PO Box 860
Millerton, NY 12546
518-789-8700
FAX: 518-789-0545 800-562-2139
books@greyhouse.com
www.greyhouse.com
Richard Gottlieb, President
Leslie Mackenzie, Publisher
Provides information on everything from Regulatory Authorities to Security Enforcement, this top-flight directory brings together the relevant information necessary for creating and maintaining a security plan for a wide range of transportation facilities.
$195.00
900 pages Bi-Annual

21619 Truck Trailer Manufacturers Association: Membership Directory
Truck Trailer Manufacturers Association
1020 Princess Street
Alexandria, VA 22314-2247
703-549-3010
FAX: 703-549-3014 www.ttmanet.org
Lynn Wiles, Editor
Richard Bowling, President
About 100 truck and tank trailer manufacturers and 120 suppliers to the industry.
$135.00
Annual

21620 Trucksource: Sources of Trucking Industry Information
Express Carriers Association
PO Box 4307
Bethlehem, PA 18018
610-740-5857
FAX: 610-740-3174 866-322-7447
eca@expresscarriers.com
www.expresscarriers.com
Cheryle Williamson, Executive Director
Features over 1,000 sources of information on the trucking industry, including industry reports, videos, periodicals and databases about the motor carrier industry.

21621 Vocational Equipment Directory for GMC Truck Dealers
Verbiest Publishing Company
1155 Henrietta Street
Birmingham, MI 48009-1906

Directory of services and supplies to the industry. *$25.00*
200 pages Annual
Circulation: 6,000

Industry Web Sites

21622 www.expresscarriers.com
National Tank Truck Carriers

Conducts research, promotes federal standards of construction, design, use and operation of tank trucks.

21623 www.greyhouse.com
Grey House Publishing

Selected Grey House directories in the fields of business, health and education are available online. Users can search our online databases by several different search criteria, such as product categories, geographic area, sales volume and much, much more. Full Grey House catalog and online ordering also available.

21624 www.natso.com
NATSO

NATSO is the professional association of America's $42 billion travel plaza and truckstop industry. NATSO represents the industry on legislative and regulatory matters; serves as the offical source of information on the diverse travel plaza and truckstop industry; provides education to its members; conducts an annual convention and trade show; and supports efforts to generally improve the business climate in which its members operate.

21625 www.nptc.org
National Private Truck Council

Distributors, shippers, processors, jobbers and manufacturers who transport their own goods and are owners of their own truck fleets.

21626 www.ntea.com
National Truck Equipment Association

For small to mid-sized companies that manufacture, distribute, install, sell and repair commercial trucks, truck bodies, truck equipmnt, trailers and accessories.

21627 www.ooida.com
Owner Operator Independent Drivers Association

For owner-operators, professional drivers and small fleet onwers.

21628 www.ptdi.org
Professional Truck Driver Institute

Advocate of optimum standands and professionalism for entry-level truck driver training.

21629 www.scranet.org
Specialized Carriers and Rigging Association

Members are carriers, crane and rigging operators and millwrights engaged in the transport of heavy goods.

21630 www.specialtyfoods.org
National Food Distributors Association

An organization comprised of independent store-to-door service distributors and suppliers of specialty food items.

21631 www.truckline.com
American Trucking Association

21632 www.ttmanet.org
Truck Trailer Manufacturers Association

A national organization of truck and tank trailer manufacturers and 120 suppliers to the industry.

Associations

21633 Action Committee for Rural Electrification
4301 Wilson Boulevard
Arlington, VA 22203-1867
703-243-2245
FAX: 703-907-5515
Political action committee that advocates support for rural electrification.
18M Members Founded: 1967

21634 American Gas Association
400 N Capitol Street NW
Washington, DC 20001
202-477-7337
FAX: 202-824-7115
David Parker, Director

21635 American Nuclear Society
555 N Kensington Avenue
La Grange Park, IL 60526-5535
708-352-6611
FAX: 708-352-6464 800-NUC-NEWS
advertising@ans.org
www.ans.org/advertising
Harry Bradley, Executive Director
For personnel involved in nuclear power operation and development. Coverage includes power, plant operations and maintenance, fuel cycle, legislation, international employment and more.
Founded: 1954 $210 per M.

21636 American Public Energy Agency
1111 O Street
Suite 203
Lincoln, NE 68508
FAX: 402-742-0022 800-476-3749
Roger W Mock, President/CEO
Denise Barnhill, Executive Assistant
Purpose is to provide energy acquisition and energy-related services for its members and other public agencies, and to assist such agencies in acquiring stable energy supplies, reducing energy costs through group purchases, and developing enhanced energy acquisition mechanisms.

21637 American Public Gas Association
11094D Lee Highway
Suite 102
Fairfax, VA 22030-5014
703-352-3890
info@apga.org www.apga.org
Robert Cave, Executive Director
Association of municipal gas systems.
560 Members

21638 American Public Power Association
2301 M Street NW
Floor 3
Washington, DC 20037-1427
202-467-2900
FAX: 202-467-2910
Barbara Opicka, Marketing Assistant
Alan Richardson, President/CEO
50 booths.
1.3M Members

21639 American Public Works Association
2345 Grand Blvd
Ste 700
Kansas City, MO 64108-2625
816-472-6100
FAX: 816-472-1610 800-848-2792
apwa@apwa.net www.apwa.net
Martin Manning, President
Kaye Sullivan, Chief Executive Officer
International educational and professional association of public agencies, private sector companies, and individuals dedicated to providing high quality public works goods and services. APWA provides a forum in which public works professionals competency, increase the performance of their agencies and companies, and bring important public works-related topics to public attention in local, state, and federal areas. Mailing list for members only.
26M Members Founded: 1936

21640 American Solar Energy Society
2400 Central Avenue
Sutie A
Boulder, CO 80301-2843
303-443-3130
FAX: 303-443-3212
ases@ases.org www.ases.org
Regina Johnson, Editor
Individuals and professionals working in the field of solar energy and conservation.

21641 American Water Works Association
6666 W Quincy Avenue
Denver, CO 80235-3098
303-794-7711
www.awwa.org
Jack W Hoffbuhr, Executive Director
The professional society of North American drinking water experts. Develop standards and support research programs in waterworks design, construction, operation, and management. Conducts in-service training schools and offers placement service.
56M Members

21642 Association of Regulatory Utility Commissioners
PO Box 684
Washington, DC 20044-0684
202-898-2200
A a non-profit organization founded in 1889. Its members include the governmental agencies that regulate the activities of telecommunications, engergy, and water utilities.

21643 Automatic Meter Reading Association
60 Revere Drive
Suite 500
Northbrook, IL 60062
847-480-9628
FAX: 847-480-9282 888-612-2672
amra@amra-intl.org
www.amra-intl.org
Joyce Paschall, Executive Director
John Waxman, Manager
Founded: 1986

21644 Edison Electric Institute
701 Pennsylvania Avenue NW
3rd Floor
Washington, DC 20004-2696
202-085-5995
www.eei.org
Thomas Kuhn, President
David Owens, Director
Advocates public policy, expands market opportunities and provides strategic business information for the shareholder-owned electric utility industry.
180 Members Founded: 1930

21645 Electric Power Research Institute
3412 Hillview Avenue
Palo Alto, CA 94304
650-552-2354
www.epri.com
Richard L Rudman, Executive VP/COO
Eugene W Zeltmann, Chairman
Kurt E Yeager, President/CEO
Judith Mills, Manager
Nonprofit energy research consortium for the benefit of utility members, their customers and society. Mission is to provide science and technology-based solutions of indispensable value to our global energy customers by managing a far-reaching program of scientific research, technology development and product implementation.
660 Members Founded: 1973

21646 Electric Power Supply Association
1401 New York Avenue NW
11th Floor
Washington, DC 20005
202-628-8200
FAX: 202-789-7201 www.epsa.org
Lynne H Church, Director

21647 Energy Engineering
Association of Energy Engineers
4025 Pleasantdale Road
Suite 420
Atlanta, GA 30340
770-447-5083
FAX: 770-446-3969
webmaster@aeecenter.org
www.aeecenter.org
Wayne Turner, Editor-in-Chief
Albert Thumann, Executive Director
Engineering solutions to cost efficiency problems and mechanical contractors who design, specify, install, maintain, and purchase non-residential heating, ventilating, air conditioning and refrigeration equipment and components.

21648 Energy Information Administration
National Energy Information Center
El 30, 1000 Independence Avenue SW
Washington, DC 20585
202-586-8800
FAX: 202-586-8534
infoctr@eia.doe.gov www.eia.doe.gov
John Weiner, Executive Director
Government agency that provides statistical energy data, information and referral assistance to the government and private sectors, academia and the public. NEIC also provides Government Printing Office ordering information. Single copies of blank data collection forms, directories and EIA press releases are free of charge to all users. Ordering information on EIA machine readable files available through the National

Technical Information Service and the Government Printing Office.
Founded: 1977

21649 Gas Research Institute
1700 S Mount Prospect Road
Des Plaines, IL 60018-1804
847-768-0500
FAX: 847-768-0500
businessdevelopmentinfo@gastechnology.or www.gri.org
John Riordan, President/CEO

21650 Institute of Industrial Engineers
25 Technology Park/Atlanta
Norcross, GA 30092
770-449-0461
770-263-8532
Dedicated to supporting engineers involved in all industrial applications.

21651 Institute of Public Utilities
240 Nisbet Center
Michigan State University
East Lansing, MI 48823
517-355-1876
FAX: 517-355-1854
www.bus.msu.edu/ipu
Janice A Beecher, Director
Research and training center at Michigan State University. Program focuses on regulation and management of energy, telecommunications and water companies.

21652 Insulated Cable Engineers Association
PO Box 1568
Carrollton, GA 30112
770-830-0369
www.icea.net
Professional organization dedicated to developing cable standards for the electric power, control and telecommunications industries. Ensures safe, economical and efficient cable systems utilizing proven state-of-the-art materials and concepts. ICEA documents are of interest to cable manufacturers, architects and engineers, utility and manufacturing plant personnel, telecommunication engineers, consultants and OEMs.
Founded: 1925

21653 International Gas Turbine Institute
5775-B Glenridge Drive
Suite 370
Atlanta, GA 30328-5380
404-847-0072
FAX: 404-847-1051
igti@asme.org www.asme.org/igti
Michael Ireland, Executive Director
Founded: 1986

21654 International Right of Way Association
13650 Gramercy Pl
Gardena, CA 90249-2453
310-323-0112
FAX: 310-538-1471
Raymond H Rosenberg, Executive VP
Members are responsible for acquiring land over which to run utility lines, pipelines and roads.
9,444 Members Founded: 1934

21655 International Union of Operating Engineers
1125 17th Street NW
Washington, DC 20036-4707
202-429-9100
FAX: 202-778-2688
iuce@access.digex.net www.iuce.org
N Budd Coutts, General Secretary
Frank Hanley, President
Founded: 1902

21656 Municipal Waste Management Association
1620 I Street NW
Floor NW-4
Washington, DC 20006-4005
202-293-7330
FAX: 202-293-2352
David Gatton, Managing Director
Concerned with the processing of municipal solid waste for the production of recyclable materials, heat, and energy. Members are local government organizations; associate members are from the private sector.
200 Members Founded: 1982

21657 National Association of Energy Service Companies
1615 M Street NW
Suite 800
Washington, DC 20036
202-822-0950
FAX: 202-822-0955 www.naesco.org/
Terry E Singer, Director

21658 National Association of Regulatory Utility Commissioners (NARUC)
1101 Vermont Avenue NW, Suite 200
PO Box 200005
Washington, DC 20005
202-898-2200
FAX: 202-898-2213 www.naruc.org
Charles Gray, Director
A national organization that offers valuable information on over 150 consultants and other professionals active in regulated water, sewer and related industries.

21659 National Association of State Energy Officials
1414 Prince Street
Suite 200
Alexandria, VA 22314
703-299-8800
FAX: 703-299-6208 www.naseo.org/
Diane S Shea, Executive Director
The only non-profit organization that represents the Governor-designated energy officials from each state and territory. The organization was established to improve the effectiveness and quality of state energy programs and policies, provide policy input and analysis of federal energy issues and be a repository of information on energy issues of concern to the states.
56 Members Founded: 1986

21660 National Association of State Utility
8380 Colesville Road
Suite 101
Silver Spring, MD 20910
301-589-6313
FAX: 301-589-6380
nasuca@nasuca.org www.nasuca.org
Charles A Acquard, Executive Director
Nicole Haslup, Assistant to the Director
Members are state appointed individuals that represent rate-payers in their state.
44 Members Founded: 1979

21661 National Energy Marketers Association
3333 K Street NW
Suite 110
Washington, DC 20007
202-333-3288
FAX: 202-333-3266
info@energymarketers.com
www.energymarketers.com
Craig Goodman, President

21662 National Hydropower Association
1 Massachusetts Avenue NW
Suite 850
Washington, DC 20001
202-682-1700
FAX: 202-682-7478
help@hydro.org www.hydro.org
Linda Church Ciocci, Executive Director
Mark R Stover, Director Government Affairs
Stephanie Knox, Manager Finance/Administration
Jeff Leahey, Asst. Manager of Regulatory Affairs
Diane C Lear, Consultant Marketing
Provides regulatory and legislative advocacy for hydropower industry. Members include public and private utilities, developers, equipment manufacturers, engineering and design firms, environmental and hydro liscensing consultants, and legal and financial firms. Membership dues: $1,000 - $18,000.
140 Members Founded: 1983

21663 National Rural Electric Cooperative Association
4301 Wilson Boulevard
Arlington, VA 22203-1860
703-907-5500
FAX: 703-907-5514
Glenn L English, CEO
Membership consists of cooperative systems, public power and public utility districts. Annual budget of approximately $94 million. Sponsors and supports the Action for Rural Electrification Political Action Committee.
1000 Members Founded: 1942

21664 North American Electric Reliability
116-390 Village Boulevard
Princeton, NJ 08540-5731
609-452-8060
FAX: 609-452-9550
webmaster@nerc.com www.nerc.com
Michehl R Gent, President/CEO
David R Nevius, Senior VP
Donald M Benjamin, VP
David N Cook, VP/General Counsel
Ora L Klein, Manager/Administrative Services
Principal organization for coordinating and promoting North America's electrical supplies, demands and reliability issues.
11 Members Founded: 1968

21665 Northwest Public Power Association
9817 NE 54th Street
Vancouver, WA 98662
360-254-0109
FAX: 360-254-5731
nwppa@nwppa.org www.nwppa.org

Terry Holzer, President
Bob Speckman, First VP
Dave Pflugrath, Secretary/Treasurer
Will Lutgen, Executive Director
Debbie Kuraspediani, Director Communications

A international training organization for electric utilities in 10 western states and 4 western Canadian provinces. *$75.00*

200 Members Monthly/Annunal Founded: 1940

21666 Platts UDI
1200 G Street NW
Suite 1000
Washington, DC 20005
202-832-2250
FAX: 202-942-8789
udi@platts.com
www.platts.com/udidata

Charlotte Wright, Manager

Publisher of directories for world-wide electric power industry.

21667 Power Transmission Distributors Association
230 W Monroe Street
Suite 1410
Chicago, IL 60606-4703
312-516-2100
FAX: 312-516-2101
ptda@ptda.org www.ptda.org

Mary Sue Lyon, Executive VP
Brenda Holt, Director Membership Services
Stephanie A Kaplan, Director Marketing
Beth Silas, Manager Meetings/Finance
Justine Haka, Communications Specialist

Members are industrial power transmission/motion control distributor firms representing locations throughout North America and several other countries and manufacturing firms.

Founded: 1960

21668 US Energy Information Administration
Energy Information Administration, EI 30
1000 Independence Avenue SW
Washington, DC 20585
202-868-8800

wmaster@eia.doe.gov
www.eia.doe.gov

John Weiner, Director
Stephen F Durbin, Director Resource Management

21669 United States Telephone Association

607 14th St Nw
Ste 400
Washington, DC 20005-2051
202-267-7300
FAX: 202-326-7333
aremsen@usta.org www.usta.org

Walter B McCormick Jr, President/CEO
Brian Strom, Chairman
Regina Hopper, Executive VP
Tom Amontree, Senior VP

21670 Water Environment Federation
601 Wythe Street
Alexandria, VA 22314-1994
703-684-2400
FAX: 703-684-2492 www.wef.org

William Bertera, Executive Director

Newsletters

21671 Clearing Up
Energy NewsData
PO Box 900928
Seattle, WA 98109-9228
206-285-4848
FAX: 206-281-8035
newsdata@newsdata.com
http://www.newsdata.com

Steve Ernst, Managing Editor
Daniel Sackett, Circulation Director

Covers energy policy, resource development, public utility and energy litigation and energy marketing financing in the Pacific Northwestern United States and Western Canada. *$1199.00*

14 pages Weekly Founded: 1982
Printed in 1 color on matte stock
Computerized version available

21672 Electric Utility Week
McGraw Hill
PO Box 182604
Columbus, OH 43272
614-304-4000
FAX: 614-759-3749 800-752-8878
customer.service@mcgraw-hill.com
http://www.mcgraw-hill.com

Dan Tanz, Chief Editor
Paul Carlsen, Senior Editor
Harold McGraw, III, President

Provides news of significant developments affecting the electric utility industry focusing on state and federal regulation, management and bulk power markets. Publishes charts of prices utilities pay for fuels. *$2165.00*

Weekly Founded: 1909

21673 Energy Daily
King Publishing Group
1325 g street nw
suite 1003
Washington, DC 2005-1601
202-638-4260
FAX: 202-662-9740 800-926-5464
kingcom@kingpublishing.com
http://www.kingpublishing.com

george lobsenz, Publisher
George Lobsenz, Editor

Information regarding energy use, supply and demand, power and heat generation, energy sources, conversion and storage, and energy and fuel conversion processes. *$1900.00*

Daily Founded: 1974

21674 Energy Report
Pasha Publications
1616 N. Fort Meyer Dr
Suite 1000
Arlington, VA 22209-2510
703-528-1244
FAX: 703-528-1253 800-424-2908

Harry Baisden, Group Publisher
Barry Cassell, Editor

Coverage includes comprehensive policies and issues affecting oil, natural gas, electricity, cogeneration, power markets, nuclear energy, taxation, global warming and energy business opportunities. *$872.00*

20 pages Weekly Founded: 1978

21675 HydroWorld Alert
HCI Publications
410 Archibald Street
Kansas City, MO 64111-3000
816-931-1311
FAX: 816-931-2015
info@hcipub.com
http://www.hcipub.com

Gary Perlman, Director
Leslie Eden, Publisher

Bi-weekly fax report on international hydroelectric project developments, business trends, and news relevant to organizations seeking business developments. *$635.00*

Weekly Founded: 1970

21676 Hydrowire
HCI Publications
410 Archibald Street
Kansas City, MO 64111-3000
816-931-1311
FAX: 816-931-2015
hci@aol.com http://www.hcipub.com

Leslie Eden, Publisher/President

Concise, bi-weekly report on major news in the hydroelectric industry. Includes timely listings of licensing for hydroelectric power projects. Also covers news and business opportunities in the North American hydroelectric industry. *$425.00*

Founded: 1994
Circulation: 500

21677 IE News: Utilities
Institute of Industrial Engineers
3577 Parkway Lane
Suite 200
Norcross, GA 30092-2928
770-490-0461
FAX: 770-441-3295 800-494-0460
jmilczarski@iienet.org
http://www.iienet.org

Nancy Burks, Publisher
Joan Milczarski, Director of Marketing

Association news.

4 pages Quarterly Founded: 1948
Circulation: 400

21678 Inside Energy
Platts, McGraw Hill Companies
1200 G Street NW
Suite 1000
Washington, DC 20005-3845
202-832-2250
FAX: 202-383-2025 800-752-8878
support@platts.com
http://www.platts.com

Bill Loveless, Editor
Georgia Safos, Circulation Director

Covers the Department of Energy including energy, science/technology, and environmental management programs as well as energy programs at the Interior Department. *$1810.00*

16 pages Weekly Founded: 1888

21679 NARUC Bulletin
Nat'l Assn of Regulatory Utility Commissioners
1101 Vermont Avenue NW
Suite 200
Washington, DC 20005
202-898-2200
FAX: 202-898-2213
admin@naruc.org
http://www.naruc.org

Charles D Gray, Editor
Charles Gray, Executive Director
Jaclyn Wintle, Publications Coordinator
Diane Munns, President

A quasi-governmental nonprofit corporation composed of governmental agencies engaged in the regulation of public utilities and carriers. Its primary mission is to serve the consumer interest by seeking to improve the quality and effectiveness of public regulation in America. *$110.00*
16 pages Weekly Founded: 1889
Circulation: 2000
Mailing list available for rent
Printed in 1 color on matte stock

21680 National Association of Regulatory Utility Commissioners Newsletter
1101 Vermont Avenue NW
Suite 200
Washington, DC 20005
202-898-2200
FAX: 202-898-2213
admin@naruc.org
http://www.naruc.org
Charles Gray, Director
Jaclyn Wintle, Media Relations/Publications Coordi
Judi Sord, Circulation Manager
A national organization that offers valuable information on over 150 consultants and other professionals active in regulated water, sewer and related industries. *$125.00*
Founded: 1889
Circulation: 1800

21681 Northeast Power Report
McGraw Hill
3333 Walnut Street
Boulder, CO 80301
720-485-5000
FAX: 720-548-5701 800-752-8878
Ron Dionne, Publisher
Covers issues affecting utility and non-utility generations. *$745.00*
16 pages BiWeekly

21682 Nuclear Waste News
Business Publishers
8737 Colesville Road
Suite 1100
Silver Spring, MD 20910-3928
301-587-6300
FAX: 301-587-4530 800-274-6737
custserv@bpinews.com
http://www.bpinews.com
Leonard A Eiserer, Publisher
Kathleen Harrow, Circulation Manager
Worldwide coverage of the nuclear waste management industry including waste generation, packaging, transport, processing and disposal. *$697.00*
10 pages 25 issues Founded: 1963
Mailing list available for rent
Printed in 2 colors on matte stock : Newsletter

21683 NuclearFuel
McGraw Hill
3333 Walnut Street
Boulder, CO 80301
720-485-5000
FAX: 720-548-5701 800-752-8878
Michael Knapik, Editor
An information service on the nuclear fuel cycle.
14 pages

21684 Nucleonics Week
McGraw Hill
3333 Walnut Street
Boulder, CO 80301
720-485-5000
FAX: 720-548-5701 800-752-8878
support@platts.com
http://www.platts.com
Margaret Ryan, Editor
Covers all aspects of commercial nuclear power. *$2265.00*
12 pages Monthly Founded: 1888

21685 Public Gas News
American Public Gas Association
11094D Lee Highway
Suite 102
Fairfax, VA 22030-5014
703-352-3890

info@apga.org www.apga.org
Sheila Martel, Editor
Robert Cave, Executive Director
Written for public gas managers to keep them apprised of industry news. *$50.00*

Circulation: 1000
Printed in 2 colors

21686 Public Utilities
State Capitals Newsletters
PO Box 7376
Alexandria, VA 22307-7376
703-768-9600
FAX: 703-768-9690
legistate@statecapitals.com
statecapitals.com *$345.00*
Weekly

21687 Public Utilities: From the State Capitals
Wakeman Walworth
300 N Washington Street
Suite 204
Alexandria, VA 22314-2530
703-689-9600
FAX: 703-549-1372
Keyes Walworth, Publisher
Covers state regulations of all forms of public utilities across the nation. It reports on new rate structures, allowable profit margins, special taxes, consumer relations, environmental legislation, nuclear plant regulations, deregulation programs and programs for low-income customers. *$235.00*
4 pages Weekly
Printed in 1 color on matte stock
Computerized version available

21688 Utility Environment Report
McGraw Hill
3333 Walnut Street
Boulder, CO 80301-2515
720-485-5000
FAX: 212-904-2723 800-424-2908
webmaster@mcgraw-hill.com
http://www.mcgraw-hill.com
Rob Ingraham, Publisher
Harold McGraw, III, President
Steven H. Weiss, VP
Covers news on the environmental concerns of the utility and independent power industries. *$695.00*
18 pages Founded: 1899

21689 Utility Reporter: Fuels, Energy and Power
InfoTeam
PO Box 15640
Plantation, FL 33318-5640
954-473-9560
FAX: 954-473-0544
infoteamma@aol.com
Randy M Allen CPA, Editor
Focuses on activities involving: power generation, combustion, delivery and transmission; alternative energy devices and systems; heat transfer, storage and utilization; and myriad of related topics. *$289.00*
20 pages Monthly ISSN 0890-2984
Printed in 1 color on matte stock
Computerized version available

Magazines & Journals

21690 APWA Reporter
American Public Works Association
2345 Grand Boulevard
Suite 500
Kansas City, MO 64108-2641
816-472-6100
FAX: 816-472-1610
apwa@apwa.net
http://www.apwa.net/reporter
Kevin Clark, Editor
David Dancy, Director Marketing
Kaye Sullivan, Chief Executive Officer
Circulation to entire membership of American Public Works Association. *$100.00*
Monthly Founded: 1937 ISSN 0092-4873
Circulation: 25000
Mailing list available for rent

21691 Alternative Energy
PWG
205 S Beverly Drive
#208
Beverly Hills, CA 90212-3827
310-273-3486
FAX: 310-858-8272
Irwin Stambler, Publisher
Ahmad Taleban, President
Reports on future economic and technological trends. *$95.00*
12 pages Monthly
Printed in 2 colors on matte stock

21692 Alternative Energy Retailer
Zackin Publications
PO Box 2180
Waterbury, CT 06722-2180
203-755-0158
FAX: 203-755-3480 800-325-6745
info@aer-online.com
http://www.aer-online.com
Paul Zackin, Publisher
Michael Griffin, Editor
Arlene Sorrentino, Production Coordinator
Jeanette Laliberte, Marketing Manager
June Han, Subscription Manager
Covers solid fuel burning, marketing, technology, and sales.
Monthly
Circulation: 14,000

21693 American Public Works Association

2345 Grand Blvd
Ste 700
Kansas City, MO 64108-2625
816-472-6100
FAX: 816-472-1610 800-848-2792
apwa@apwa.net www.apwa.net

Martin Manning, President
Kaye Sullivan, Chief Executive Officer

International educational and professional association of public agencies, private sector companies, and individuals dedicated to providing high quality public works goods and services. APWA provides a forum in which public works professionals competency, increase the performance of their agencies and companies, and bring important public works-related topics to public attention in local, state, and federal areas. Mailing list for members only. *$100.00*

40 pages Monthly Founded: 1937

21694 American Water Works Association Journal

6666 W Quincy Avenue
Denver, CO 80235-3098
303-794-7711
FAX: 303-794-7310
journal@awwa.org www.awwa.org

Marcia Lacey, Editor
Jack Hoffbuhr, Chief Executive Officer

Journal of the professional society of North American drinking water experts. Dues cover subscription for members. *$120.00*

152 pages Monthly

21695 Bulletin

NW Public Power Association
9817 NE 54th Street
Vancouver, WA 98662-6064
360-254-0109
FAX: 360-254-5731
nwppa@nwppa.org
http://www.nwppa.org

Debbie Kuraspediana, Editor
Will Lutgen, Executive Director

Readership consists of directors, chairmen and managers of electric utilities in the ten Western States and four Canadian provinces. Provides news and events of the public power industry in the Pacific Northwest Region. *$32.00*

32 pages
Circulation: 6200
Printed in 4 colors

21696 Chief Engineer

Chief Engineers Association of Chicagoland
15503 S 70th Street
Orland Park, IL 60462-5105
708-633-1400
FAX: 708-633-7008

Ernest K Wulff, Editor

Covers building maintenance issues, laws and rulings relative to chief engineers, as well as mechanical and general HVAC equipment.

Monthly Founded: 1935
Circulation: 2000
Mailing list available for rent 2K names

21697 Cogeneration Monthly Letter

Cogeneration Publications Company
509 Tennessee Avenue
Alexandria, VA 22305-1336
703-683-1868
FAX: 703-683-1878
www.powermarketers.com

Scott Spiewak, Publisher

Discusses new technology and legislation governing power generating facilities. Includes listings of planned projects.

5 per year
Circulation: 5000

21698 Diesel & Gas Turbine Worldwide

Diesel & Gas Turbine Publications
20855 Watertown Rd
Suite 220
Waukesha, WI 53186-6266
262-325-5000
FAX: 262-754-4175 800-558-4322
slizdas@dieselpub.com
http://www.dieselpub.com

Sheila Lizdas, Circualtion Manager
Mark McNeely, Editor
Lynne Diefenbach, Advertising Manager
Christa Johnson, Production Manager
Robert Wilson, President

Focuses on the design, production, installation, operation, and maintenance of engines in the global marine, power generation, oil and gas, or railroad industries.

bi-Monthly Founded: 1969
Circulation: 20100

21699 Diesel Progress: International Edition

Diesel & Gas Turbine Publications
20855 Watertown Road
Suite 220
Waukesha, WI 53186-6286
262-325-5000
FAX: 262-754-4175
mosenga@dieselpub.com
http://www.dieselpub.com

Michael Osenga, Publisher
Sue Bollwahn, Circulation Manager
Robert Wilson, President
Michael J Brezonick, Editor-in-Chief
Katie M Evans, Sales Manager

Focuses on new products and technology that serves engineering, marketing, service and equipment, purchasing, administrative, and others allied to the field.

Founded: 1945
Circulation: 10273

21700 Electric Light & Power

Technical Publishing
1350 E Touhy Avenue
#5080
Des Plaines, IL 60018-3303
847-635-8800
FAX: 847-299-8622

Wayne Beaty, Editor

Offers articles on the electric utility industry. *$38.00*

84 pages Monthly Founded: 1922

21701 Electric Perspectives

Edison Electric Institute
701 Pennsylvania Avenue N.W
Washington, DC 20004-2696
202-085-5995
FAX: 202-508-5759 800-344-5453
ep@eei.org http://www.eei.org

Eric Blume, Editor
William Mambert, Advertising Director
Lavonne Rose, Circulation Manager
Bill Bickel, Production Manager
Bill Mambert, Marketing Manager

The magazine for management in America's investor-owned electric utilities. Covers all areas of utility operations and concerns, providing detailed analyses and farsighted commentary on how issues and trends are shaping the industry today and the future impact. *$50.00*

Monthly Founded: 1981
Circulation: 20000
Printed in 4 colors on glossy stock

21702 Energy Efficiency Journal

NAESCO
1615 M Street NW
#800
Washington, DC 20036-3219
202-822-0950
FAX: 202-822-0955

Terry E Singer, Executive Editor
Nina Lockhart, Senior Program Manager
Donald Gilligan, President
Wallace Duncan, Counsel

Targets energy service companies, electric and gas utilities amd other energy providers. Highlights industry news and features energy conservation.

Quarterly
Circulation: 200

21703 Energy Manager

Primedia
9800 Metcalf Avenue
Overland Park, KS 66212-2901
913-341-1300
FAX: 913-967-1898
www.primediabusiness.com

Subjects include energy management systems, HVAC, automated building systems, plant and facilities control, and negotiating supplier contracts. Features include legislative news from Washington, analysis of rare updates, relevant news from around the world and new product reviews.

5 per year Founded: 1998
Circulation: 50,000

21704 Energy Today

Trend Publishing
954 National Press Building
Washington, DC 20045-1901
202-628-8827
FAX: 202-393-1732

Arthur Kranish, Editor

Includes news and analysis, new regulatory and technical developments, grant and contract opprtunities, investigative reports, and market studies.

Monthly

21705 Energy User News

Business News Publishing Company
755 W Big Beaver Road
Suite 1000
Troy, MI 48084
248-362-3700
FAX: 248-362-0317 smithn@bnp.com

Nikki Smith, Marketing Manager

21706 Energy and Housing Report

Alan L Frank Associates
9124 Bradford Road
Silverspring, MD 20901-4918
703-866-4397
FAX: 301-565-3298
http://homeenergy.org

Mary James, Publisher
Iain Walker, Executive Editor
Cass Duggan, Circulation Manager
Carol A. Markell, Marketing Manager
Alan Meier, President

Research in consumption with the goal of increasing energy conservation at the residential level. Follows trends in consumption and the effects of conservation efforts on energy use.

Founded: 1994

21707 Energy in the News
New York Mercantile Exchange
One N End Avenue
New York, NY 10282-1102
212-299-2000
FAX: 212-301-4700
marketing@nymex.com
www.nymex.com

James Conmy, Editor

Covers market fundamentals, trading strategies and market conditions. Provides information that keeps future commision merchants, industry executives, options and cash market traders up-to-date with trends affecting the energy industry.
Quarterly
Circulation: 35000

21708 Gas Turbine World
Pequot Publishing
PO Box 447
Southport, CT 06490-447
203-259-1812
FAX: 203-259-0532
http://www.business-magazines.com

Victor Debiasi, Publisher

Focuses on implementing policy, specification, design, maintenance, and modernization of the systems and equipment of electric power generation. *$135.00*
Monthly
Circulation: 10000

21709 Generation Week
Pasha Publications
1600 Wilson Boulevard
#600
Arlington, VA 22209-2509
703-528-1244
FAX: 703-816-7821 800-424-2908
coalsyn@pasha.com www.pasha.com

Tod Sedgwick, Publisher

On new technology and innovative operation of power plants.
Weekly

21710 HRW: Hydro Review Worldwide
HCI Publications
410 Archibald Street
Kansas City, MO 64111-3000
816-931-1311
FAX: 816-931-2015
hci@aol.com http://www.hcipub.com

Leslie Eden, Owner
Marla Barness, Editor
Bob Merrigan, Marketing

Magazine serving information needs of people associated with hydro throughout the world. Managing and improving plant operations, solving problems, financing and essential business news are covered extensively. *$44.00*
Founded: 1982
Circulation: 4673

21711 Hart's Energy Markets
Hart Publications
4545 Post Oak Place
#210
Houston, TX 77027-3105
713-993-9320
FAX: 713-840-0983
dgriffin@hartenergy.com
http://www.energy-markets.com

Dana Griffin Smith, Publisher
Joe Fisher, Editor
Richard Eichler, President

Keeps readers abreast of trends and opportunities in the marketplace. Covers such topics as electricity deregulation, gas unbundling, rebundling of services, nuclear and renewable energy, technological developments and regulatory issues.
Monthly Founded: 1973
Circulation: 14000

21712 Home Power
PO Box 520
Ashland, OR 97520-18
541-512-0201
FAX: 530-475-0836 800-707-6585
info@homepower.com
http://www.homepower.com

Karen Perez, Publisher
Joe Schwartz, Manager

Covers photovoltaics, wind turbinesm solar heating, methane, batteries, inverters, water pumping, electric vehicles, controls, and instruments. Examines the design and installation of balanced renewable energy systems in the home, while also reviewing products ranging from solar pumps to refrgieraters. *$22.50*
Founded: 1987
Circulation: 19200

21713 Hydro Review
HCI Publications
410 Archibald Street
Kansas City, MO 64111-3000
816-931-1311
FAX: 816-931-2015
info@hcipub.com
http://www.hcipub.com

Leslie Eden, Publisher/Editor

Magazine providing in-depth coverage of the North American hydroelectric industry. Rehab, redevelopment, dam safety and the environment are explored. *$65.00*
Founded: 1980
Circulation: 500

21714 Independent Energy
PennWell Publishing Company
1421 S Sheridan Road
Tulsa, OK 74112-6619
918-835-3161
FAX: 918-831-9834
www.pennwell.com

Richard Baker, Publisher

Focuses on analysis and views aimed at doing business more successfully. Reports important market information, trends and equipment adcances affecting power project development, financing, construction, operation and management.
Monthly
Circulation: 10962

21715 International Operating Engineer
International Union of Operating Engineers
1125 17th Street NW
Washington, DC 20036-4707
202-429-9100
FAX: 202-778-2688
iuce@access.digex.net
http://www.iuoe.org

N Budd Coutts, General Secretary

Contains news and information on the union and its members as well as general business news about the industry as a whole.
bi-monthly Founded: 1896
Circulation: 400000

21716 New Equipment Digest
Penton Media
1300 East 9th Street
Cleveland, OH 44114-1503
216-696-7000
FAX: 216-696-1752
information@penton.com
http://www.newequipment.com

Steven Bush, Administrative Editor
Tom Sockel, Associate Editor
Robert King, Editor
Sarah Hughes, Production Manager
Bobbie Macy, Circulation Manager

Serves the general industrial field which includes manufacturing, processing, engineering services, construction, transportation, mining, public utilities, wholesale distributors, educational services, libraries and governmental establishments.
Monthly Founded: 1936

21717 Northeast Sun
NE Sustainable Energy Association
50 Miles Street
Greenfield, MA 01301-3212
413-774-6051
FAX: 413-774-6053
nesea@nesea.org
http://www.nesea.org

Tom Thompson, Publisher
Nancy Hazard, Executive Director

Addresses the current issues of solar energy and natural gas power. Also provides an exchange of ideas for those seeking other environmentally sound energy sources.
Monthly Founded: 1974
Circulation: 5000

21718 Northwest Public Power Bulletin
Northwest Public Power Association
9817 NE 54th Street
Vancouver, WA 98662-6064
360-254-0109
FAX: 360-254-5731
nwppa@nwppa.org
http://www.nwppa.org

Will Lutgen, Executive Director
Nelson Holmberg, Associate Editor
Debbie Kuraspediani, Director Communications

Trade publication for consumer-owned electric utilities managers, directors, commissioners and management staff. *$25.00*
28 pages Monthly Founded: 1947
Circulation: 6000

21719 Nuclear News
American Nuclear Society
555 N Kensington Avenue
La Grange Park, IL 60526-5535
708-352-6611
FAX: 708-352-0499
advertising@ans.org
http://www.ans.org/advertising

Jeff Mosses, Advertising Sales Manager
Harry Bradley, Executive Director
Sarah Wells, Editor
Gloria Nawrocki, Marketing Manager
Mike Diekman, Information Department Head

For personnel involved in nuclear power operation and development. Coverage includes power, plant operations and maintenance, fuel cycle, legislation, international employment and more. *$290.00*
Monthly Founded: 1954
Circulation: 12000 $210 per M.
Printed in on glossy stock

21720 Nuclear Plant Journal
EQES
799 Roosevelt Road
Building 6, #208
Glen Ellyn, IL 60137-5908
630-858-6161
FAX: 630-858-8787
npj@goinfo.com
http://www.npjonline.com

Newal K Agnihotri, Publisher/Editor

Nuclear Plant Journal includes technicap papers, informative articles and departments aimed at developing better methods, systems, products and services in the nuclear power industry. The Journal is compiled through the research efforts of professional engineers who are specialists in their respective fields.
Founded: 1983
Circulation: 14000 20017 names $100 per M.
Printed in on glossy stock

21721 Power Engineering International
PennWell Publishing Company
1421 S. Sheridan Road
Tulsa, OK 74112-1260
918-835-3161
FAX: 918-831-9834 800-331-4463
Headquarters@PennWell.com
http://www.pennwell.com
Kent Hudson, Group Publisher
Candice Doctor, Regional Sales Manager
Rick Huntzicker, National Sales Manager
Junior Isles, Publisher & Editorial Director
Rafael A Junquera, Editor
A variety of topics including plant design, operations, management and applications. New products are also reviewed.
Monthly Founded: 1910
Circulation: 34000

21722 Private Power Executive
Pequot Publishing
PO Box 447
Southport, CT 06490-0447
203-259-1812
FAX: 203-259-0532
Victor de Biasi, Publisher
Written for cogeoerators and developers involved in planning, design, financing, installation and operation of cogeneration plants for industrial, municipal, hospitals, and commercial district heating and cooling.
BiMonthly
Circulation: ll,500

21723 Public Power Magazine
American Public Power Association
2301 M Street NW
Suite 300
Washington, DC 20037-1484
202-467-2900
FAX: 202-467-2910
mrufe@appanet.org
http://www.appanet.org
J Labella, Editor
Michael L Kurtz, President
The only national magazine published especially for policymaking and managerial personnel of local publically owned electric systems. Public Power keeps readers abreast of policy developments, managerial techniques, new technologies, research and development and legislative issues. Subscription, $50.00 *$10.00*
72 pages Founded: 1942
Circulation: 11100

21724 Public Utilities Fortnightly
Public Utilities Reports
8229 Boone Boulevard
Suite 400
Vienna, VA 22182-2623
703-847-7720
FAX: 703-847-0683 800-368-5001
pur@pur.com http://www.pur.com/
Bruce W Radford, President/CEO
Christy Cochran, Circulation Manager
Joseph Paparello, Production Manager
Richard Stavros, Executive Editor
Philip Cross, Vice President/Legal Publisher *$169.00*
Monthly Founded: 1929
Circulation: 4000

21725 Public Utility Weekly
Public Utilities Reports
8229 Boone Boulevard
#401
Vienna, VA 22182-2623
703-847-7720
FAX: 703-847-0683 800-368-5001
info@pur.com http://www.pur.com
Bruce Radford, Editor-in-Chief
Richard Stavros, Executive Editor
Joseph Paparello, Marketing Manager
Phillip Cross, Legal Publisher
Designed to serve as a communication forum for the utility industry covering state commission rulings and federal regulatory issues. *$459.00*
Weekly Founded: 1915

21726 Solar Energy
Elsevier Science
655 Avenue of the Americas
PO Box 945
New York, NY 10010-945
212-989-5800
FAX: 212-633-3680
usinfo-f@elseview.com
http://www.elsevier.com
John A Duffie, Editor
D Yogi Goswami, Editor-in-Chief
Paul Spencer, Publisher *$2425.00*
Monthly Founded: 1954

21727 Solar Today
American Solar Energy Society
2400 Central Avenue
Suite A
Boulder, CO 80301-2843
303-443-3130
FAX: 303-443-3212
ases@ases.org http://www.ases.org
Brad Collins, President
Regina Johnson, Editor
Donald S Serfass, Advertising Sales
Provides information, case histories and reviews of a variety of renewable energy technologies, including solar, wind, biomass and geothermal. *$29.00*
90 pages Founded: 1987
Circulation: 7000

21728 Transmission & Distribution World
Primedia
9800 Metcalf Avenue
Overland Park, KS 66212
913-341-1300
FAX: 913-967-1898 800-441-0294
rbush@primediabusiness.com
http://www.tdworld.com
Dennis Triola, Publisher
Rick Bush, Editor
Monthly Founded: 1996
Circulation: 49000

21729 Turbomachinery International
Business Journals
PO Box 5550
Norwalk, CT 06856-5550
203-853-6015
FAX: 203-852-8175
Skip Ruch, Publisher
Includes updates of new approaches to energy conservation, new equipment listings and business/financial news.
BiMonthly
Circulation: 12000

21730 Utilities Law Review
John Wiley & Sons
Office A10 Spinners Court
55 West End
Witney, Ox OX8 6
199-370-6183
FAX: 199-370-9410 800-825-7550
enquiries@lawtextpub.demon.co.uk
http://www.lawtext.com/
Nicholas Gingell, Publisher
Cosmo Graham, Editor
William J Pesce, CEO/President
Charlotte Villiers, Assistant Editor
Peter Crowther, Current Survey Editor
Edited by a team of specialist UK and European lawyers, it is the leading journal in this fast-changing field. Providing detailed coverage of electricity, gas, telecommunications, transport, water and broadcasting. *$4920.00*
Bi-Monthly Founded: 1807
Circulation: 250

21731 Utility & Telephone Fleets
Practical Communications
482 Holly Ave
Saint Paul, MN 55102
651-91 -997
FAX: 651-224-2347
cbirkland@truklink.com
http://www.utfleets.com/
Judith F Chance, Group Publisher
Mike Domke, Publisher
Carol Birkland, Editor
Tom Gelinas, Editorial Director
The equipment, accessory and information resource for fleet professionals.
Founded: 1980
Circulation: 18,000

21732 Utility Automation
PennWell Publishing Company
1421 S Sheridan
PO Box 1260
Tulsa, OK 74112
918-835-3161
FAX: 918-831-9497
ua@pennwell.com
http://www.utility-automation.com
Shirley Wilson, Marketing Manager
Steven M Brown, Editor
Michael Grossman, Publisher
Robert F Biolchini, CEO/President
Janet Orteon, Circulation Manager
Innovative energy solutions. *$74.00*
50 pages Founded: 1996
Circulation: 32200

21733 Utility Automation International
PennWell Publishing Company
1421 S Sheridan Road
Tulsa, OK 74112
918-835-3161
FAX: 918-831-9875 800-331-4463
headquarters@pennwell.com
http://www.pennwell.com
S Henry Sacks, Publisher
Tina Jackson, Circulation Manager
Doug Pryor, Editor
Brad Dillman, Marketing
Founded: 1910
Circulation: 24002

21734 Utility Business
PRIMEDIA Intertec-Technology & Transportation
9800 Metcalf Avenue
Overland Park, KS 66212-2216
913-341-1300
FAX: 785-987-1905
barry-lecerf@intertec.com

Barry LeCerf, Publisher

Editorial emphasis is on providing the reader with solutions and commentary for identifying and developing company assets, realizing the impact technology has on the business, and responding to the evolving demands of the marketplace.

8 per year
Circulation: 50,000

21735 Utility Contractor
4301 N Fairfax Drive
Suite 360
Arlington, VA 22203
703-358-9300
FAX: 703-358-9307
utilitycontractor@nuca.com
http://www.nuca.com

Paula Ketter, Editor
Cheryl Yoder, President
Bill Hillman, CEO
Susan Williams, Senior Editor
Joyce Donkor, Marketing Manager

Serves the underground utility construction industry, including contractors, manufacturers, suppliers, engineering firms, municipal/public/private utilities, and others allied to the field.

Monthly Founded: 1963
Circulation: 59329

21736 Utility Executive
Water Environment Federation
601 Wythe Street
Alexandria, VA 22314-1994
703-842-2400
FAX: 703-684-2492 800-666-0206
csc@wef.org http://www.wef.org

Matthew Rowan, Publisher
Jack Benson, Marketing Manager
William Bertera, Executive Director

Editorial focuses on issues such as continuous improvement, privatization, financial and risk management, as well as benchmarking and leadership. Problem solving strategies are included for everything from wastewater treatment efficiency to negotiation contracts and proposal evaluations, and address relevant, current issues facing utility managers today. *$33.00*

Monthly Founded: 1928

21737 Utility Fleet Management
TT Publishing
2200 Mill Road
Alexandria, VA 22314-1994
703-838-1770
FAX: 703-838-6259
76432.1234@compuserve.com
www.ttnews.com

Bob Raft, Publisher

Focuses on fleet management issues and new equipment. *$25.00*

Monthly
Circulation: 15,000

21738 Western Energy
Magellan
100 N Brand, #302
PO Box 4185
Glendale, CA 91222-0185
818-440-0411
FAX: 818-241-6356

Robin Nichols, Publisher
Joe Milani, Owner

Contains technical features designed to inform and educate workers and technicians in the energy production field.

BiMonthly
Circulation: 5,058

Trade Shows

21739 AMRA Symposium
Automatic Meter Reading Association
60 Revere Drive
Suite 500
Northbrook, IL 60062
847-480-9628
FAX: 847-480-9282 888-612-2672
amra@amra-intl.org
www.amra-intl.org

Joyce Paschall, Executive Director

Gas, water and electric utilities, telephone companies and installation companies equipment and supplies for meter reading.

1600 Attendees Annual Founded: 1986

21740 APWA International Public Works Congress & Expo
American Public Works Association
2345 Grand Boulevard
Suite 700
Kansas City, MO 64108-2641
816-472-6100
FAX: 816-472-1610
dpriddy@apwa.net www.apwa.net

Dana Priddy, Meetings Director
Kaye Sullivan, Chief Executive Officer

Offers the benefit of a variety of educational sessions, depth of the exhibit program and endless opportunities for networking. The latest cutting-edge technologies, managerial techniques and regulatory trends designed to keep you focused on the right solutions at the right time.

6500 Attendees Annual/September
Founded: 1894

21741 ASME Asia: Petroleum, Gas Turbines, Ocean Engineering, Advanced Energy
International Gas Turbine Institute
5775-B Glenridge Drive
Suite 370
Atlanta, GA 30328-5380
404-847-0072
FAX: 404-847-1051
igti@asme.org www.asme.org/igti

Scott J Moore CEM, Director/Conventions

Conference, reception, tours and 100 exhibits of engineering and energy technology.

1200 Attendees Biennial Founded: 1986

21742 American Public Power Association of Engineers Operations Workshop
2301 M Street NW
Floor 3
Washington, DC 20037-1427
202-467-2900

Barbara Opicka, Marketing Assistant
Alan Richardson, President/CEO

50 booths.

1.3M Attendees February/March

21743 Buscon East/West
Conference Management Company
200 Connecticut Avenue
Norwalk, CT 06854-1940
203-866-4400

David Caplin, Show Manager

Principal industry event for systems builders and electronics engineers.

5M Attendees

21744 Northwest Public Power Engineering & Operations Show
9817 NE 54th Street
Vancouver, WA 98662-6064
360-254-0109
FAX: 360-254-5731
nwppa@nwppa.org www.nwppa.org

Tracy Harness, Manager
Debbie Kuraspediani, Director Communications

This annual trade show is for engineering and operations personnel of public power utilities. Containing 152 booths.

900 Attendees May

Directories & Databases

21745 DRI Utility Cost Forecasting
DRI/McGraw-Hill
24 Hartwell Avenue
Lexington, MA 02421-3158
781-863-5100

This large database covers the US public utility industry, including cost inputs for pumps, gas compressors, steam pipes and gas and electric meters.

Numeric

21746 Directory of Electric Power Producers and Distributors
McGraw Hill
Two Penn Plaza
5th Floor
New York, NY 10121
212-044-4097
FAX: 212-904-2723
www.mhenergy.com

Offers information on over 3,500 investor-owned, municipal, rural cooperative and government electric utility systems in the United States and Canada. *$395.00*

1,200 pages Annual

21747 Directory of Electric Utility Company Libraries in the United States
Library Services Committee/Edison Electric Inst
701 Pennsylvania Avenue NW
Washington, DC 20004-2608
202-347-2693

Over 90 investor-owned electric utility company libraries throughout the country are profiled. *$10.00*

149 pages Annual

21748 Directory of Energy Professionals
Assn of Regulatory Utility Commissioners
PO Box 684
Washington, DC 20044-0684
202-898-2200

Offers information on consultants and other professionals active in regulated energy utility industries. *$44.00*

450 pages Annual

21749 Directory of Publicly Owned Natural Gas Systems
American Public Gas Association
11094D Lee Highway
Suite 102
Fairfax, VA 22030-5014
703-352-3890
FAX: 703-352-1271
info@apga.org www.apga.org
Bob Cave, President
A listing of all publicly owned natural gas systems in the US. *$50.00*
80 pages Annual
Circulation: 1,000
Printed in on matte stock

21750 Electric Utility Cost Forecast
WEFA Group
800 Baldwin Tower Boulevard
Eddystone, PA 19022-1368
610-490-4000
FAX: 610-490-2770
info@wefa.com www.wefa.com
Mary Novak
This time series covers prices, construction and operating costs pertinent to the electric utilities industry.

21751 Electric Utility Industry
Midwest Publishing Company
PO Box 4468
Tulsa, OK 74159
918-839-9999
FAX: 918-587-9349 800-829-2002
info@midwestdirectories.com
www.midwestdirectories.com
Will Hammack, Editor
Approximately 6,000 utility companies, contractors, engineering firms, equipment manufacturers and supply companies. *$155.00*
Annual February Founded: 1943 : Paperback

21752 Financial Statistics of Major Investor-Owned Electric Utilities
US Energy Information Administration
1000 Independence Avenue SW
Washington, DC 20585-0001
202-586-4848
Offers data from over 180 major investor-owned electric utilities in the United States. *$33.00*
Annual

21753 Gas Industry Training Directory
American Gas Association
1515 Wilson Boulevard
Suite 100
Arlington, VA 22209-2469
703-841-8400
FAX: 703-841-8406
David F Sullivan, Industry Training
Over 600 programs are available in this directory from gas transmission and distribution companies, manufacturers of gas-fired equipment, consultants, etc., and from gas associations.
Annual February

21754 Guide to Hydropower Mechanical Design
HCI Publications
410 Archibald Street
Kansas City, MO 64111-3000
816-931-1311
FAX: 816-931-2015 hci@aol.com
Leslie Eden, Publisher
Developed by the Hydropower Technical Committee of the American Society of Mechanical Engineers. A ready reference for individuals who design hydropower facilities and producers and distributors of electricity. *$125.00*
Circulation: 4673

21755 Handy-Whitman Index of Public Utility Construction Costs
Whitman, Requardt and Associates
801 S Caroline Street
Baltimore, MD 21231
443-241-1521
FAX: 410-243-5716 www.wrallp.com
This database covers indexes of building costs for construction of public utilities in the United States.

21756 International Directory of Electric Power Producers and Distributors
McGraw Hill
1200 G Street NW
Suite 250
Washington, DC 20005-3843
202-383-2350
FAX: 212-904-2723
www.mhenergy.com
Offers valuable information on over 3,000 power generating and distribution systems in over 200 countries overseas. *$345.00*

21757 International Directory of Nuclear Utilities
Nuexco
950 17th Street
Suite 2500
Denver, CO 80202-2825
303-534-3100
This comprehensive directory offers information on over 120 utilities in 30 countries that operate nuclear plants with a capacity of at least 100 megawatts. *$220.00*
264 pages Annual

21758 Inventory of Power Plants in the United States
US Energy Information Administration
1000 Independence Avenue SW
Washington, DC 20585-0001
202-586-4848
Information is given on existing and projected and jointly-owned power plants within electric utility systems. *$23.00*
393 pages Annual

21759 LEXIS Public Utilities Law Library
Mead Data Central
9443 Springboro Pike
Dayton, OH 45401
FAX: 518-487-3584 888-223-6337
Andrew Prozes, Chief Executive Officer
This database contains information on public utilities-related case decisions from all state supreme courts and most state appellate courts.
Full-text

21760 Northwest Electric Utility Directory
Northwest Public Power Association
9817 NE 54th Street
#4576
Vancouver, WA 98662-6064
360-254-0109
FAX: 360-254-5731
Don Noel, Communications Director
Randy Shipley, Project Manager
Scott Thorp, Owner
Annual directory for electric utilities in 10 western states and 4 western Canadian provinces.
Annually

21761 PUR Analysis of Investor-Owned Electric & Gas Utilities
Public Utilities Reports
2111 Wilson Boulevard
Suite 200
Arlington, VA 22201-3001
Covers over 200 investor-owned electric and gas operating and holding companies. *$395.00*
Annual

21762 Pipeline & Utilities Construction: Contrac tors Issue
Oildom Publishing Company of Texas
PO Box 219368
Houston, TX 77218-9368
281-558-6930
Offers a comprehensive list of over 5,000 individual contracting firms concerned with the construction of oil and gas pipelines, water and sewer lines and gas distribution systems. *$80.00*
Annual
Circulation: 25,000

21763 Power Engineering
PennWell Publishing Company
1421 S Sheridan Road
Tulsa, OK 74112-6600
918-353-3161
FAX: 918-831-9834 800-331-4463
Carlotta Smith, Editor
List of manufacturers and suppliers of products and services to the power plant and utility engineering industries. *$10.00*
Annual, September

21764 Public Power Directory of Local Publicly Owned Electric Utilities
American Public Power Association
2301 M Street NW
Suite 300
Washington, DC 20037-1484
202-467-2900
FAX: 202-467-2910
Alan Richardson, President/CEO
Larry S Hobert, Executive Director
$90.00
Annual
Circulation: 13,000

21765 Rural Electrification: Directory Issue
National Rural Electric Cooperative Association
4301 Wilson Boulevard
Arlington, VA 22203-1867
703-907-5500
FAX: 703-907-5531
Frank K Gallant, Editor
Over 1,000 electric cooperatives.

Annual July
Circulation: 35,000

21766 UDI Who's Who at Electric Power Plants
Utility Data Institute
1200 G Street NW
Suite 250
Washington, DC 20005-3843
202-428-8788

Offers valuable information on over 6,000 key personnel at over 1,200 electriuc utility plants. *$195.00*
Annual

21767 US Electric Utility Industry Software Directory
PennWell Publishing Company
PO Box 1260
Tulsa, OK 74101-1260
918-835-3161
FAX: 918-831-9555 800-752-9764
Wayne Beaty, Editor
Steve Hall, Advertising/Sales
An amazing reference directory offering information on over 400 programs in 75 applications categories covering all aspects of the electric power industry. *$175.00*
140 pages Annual

21768 United States Telephone Association Phonefacts
900 19th Street NW
Suite 800
Washington, DC 20006-2105
202-229-9444

Nels Olson, Executive Director
This list of over 150 of the largest telephone companies reporting to USTA. *$3.00*
Annual

Industry Web Sites

21769 www.aeecenter.org
Association of Energy Engineers

Source of information on the field of energy efficiency, utility deregulation, plant engineering, facility management and environmental compliance. Membership includes more than 8,000 professionals and certification programs. Offers seminars, conferences, job listings and certification programs.

21770 www.apea.org
American Public Energy Agency

Purpose is to provide energy acquisition and management services for public agencies.

21771 www.apga.org
American Public Gas Association

Association of municipal gas systems.

21772 www.apwa.net
American Public Works Association

For public agencies, private sector companies, and individuals dedicated to providing high quality public works goods and services.

21773 www.awwa.org
American Water Works Association

The professional society of North American drinking water experts. Develop standards and support research programs in waterworks design, construction, operation, and management. Conducts in-service training schools and offers placement service.

21774 www.bus.msu.edu/ipu
Institute of Public Utilities

Research and training center at Michigan State University. Program focuses on regulation and management of energy, telecommunications and water companies.

21775 www.eei.org
Edison Electric Institute

Advocates public policy, expands market opportunities and provides strategic business information for the shareholder-owned electric utility industry. Find out more about EEI's members, upcoming meetings, career opportunities and products and services.

21776 www.eia.doe.gov/
Energy Information Administration

21777 www.electricity-online.com
Electricity-Online

21778 www.electricity-online.com/
Electricity Journal and Daily

21779 www.energycentral.com
Energy Central

21780 www.energymarketers.com
National Energy Marketers Association

21781 www.energyonline.com
EnergyOnLine

21782 www.energysearch.com
EPRI Energysearch

Provides fast, accurate search results on global energy topics, and science and technolgoy R&D for the electricity industy.

21783 www.energyusernews.com
Energy User News Magazine

21784 www.epri.com
Electric Power Research Institute

Nonprofit organization providing science and technology-based solutions to its global energy customers. Manages a far-reaching program of research, technology development and product implementation.

21785 www.epsa.org
Electric Power Supply Association

21786 www.greyhouse.com
Grey House Publishing

Selected Grey House directories in the fields of business, health and education are available online. Users can search our online databases by several different search criteria, such as product categories, geographic area, sales volume and much, much more. Full Grey House catalog and online ordering also available.

21787 www.gri.org
Gas Research Institute

21788 www.hydro.org
National Hydropower Association

For public and private utilities, developers, equipment manufacturers, engineering and design firms, environmental and hydro liscensing consultants, and legal and financial firms. Membership dues: $1,000 - $18,000.

21789 www.icea.net
Insulated Cable Engineers Association

Professional organization dedicated to developing cable standards for the electric power, control and telecommunications industries. Ensures safe, economical and efficient cable systems utilizing proven state-of-the-art materials and concepts. ICEA documents are of interest to cable manufacturers, architects and engineers, utility and manufacturing plant personnel, telecommunication engineers, consultants and OEMs.

21790 www.mcgraw-hill.com
McGraw Hill

Provides news of significant developments affecting the electric utility industry focusing on state and federal regulation, management and bulk power markets.

21791 www.naesco.org
National Association of Energy Service Companies

21792 www.naruc.org
National Association of Regulatory Utility Commissioners

A national organization that offers valuable information on over 150 consultants and other professionals active in regulated water, sewer and related industries.

21793 www.naseo.org
National Association of State Energy Officials

21794 www.nerc.com
North American Electric Reliability Council

Voluntary organization promoting bulk electric system reliability and security.

21795 www.nreca.org
Action Committee for Rural Electrification

Political action committee that advocates support for rural electrification.

21796 www.oilonline.com
OilOnLine

21797 www.platts.com
Electrical World

The latest trends in utility engineering and IT, equipment and services, best business practices and critical industry thinking. For managers, engineers and technicians who plan, design, build, maintain and upgrade electric T&D systems around the world.

21798 www.ptda.org
Power Transmission Distributors Association

Members are power transmission/motion control distributor throughout manufacturing firms.

21799 www.publicworks.com
Public Works Online

For professionals in the public works industry.

21800 www.wateronline.com
Water Online

Associations

21801 1394 Trade Association
1560 East Southlake Boulevard
Suite 242
Southlake, TX 76092
817-416-2200
FAX: 817-416-2256
jsnider@1394ta.org www.1394ta.org
James Snider, Executive Director
A trade association devoted to IEEE 1394 communications product furtherance.

21802 Adult Video Association
8033 Sunset Boulevard
PMB 851
Los Angeles, CA 90046-5323
323-436-0060
FAX: 818-501-7502
bmargold@aol.com
William Margold, Director
Trade association primarily concerned with opposing legislative initiatives to restrict the sale of sexually explicit film and video.
400 Members Founded: 1987

21803 Alarm Association of Florida
1802 North University Drive
Plantation, FL 33322-4115
954-748-7779
FAX: 954-748-4749 800-899-2099
bneely@fla-alarms.org
www.fla-alarms.org
Bob Neely, Executive Director
A trade association for burglar and fire alarm contractors, as well as low voltage contractors.

21804 American Society of Interior Designers (ASID)
608 Massachusetts Avenue NE
Washington, DC 20002-6006
202-546-3480
FAX: 202-546-3240
asid@asid.org www.asid.org
Michael Alin, Executive Director
An association for interior designers and home A/V system designers.

21805 Association of Visual Communicators
8130 La Mesa Boulevard
#406
La Mesa, CA 91941-6437
619-427-7524
Philip Shuey, Executive Director
Sponsors seminars and competitions. Presents CINDY awards annually for 16mm films, videotapes, 35mm filmstrips, and video disc production.
500 Members Founded: 1957

21806 BICSI
8610 Hidden River Parkway
Tampa, FL 33637-1000
813-979-1991
FAX: 813-971-4311 800-242-7405
ayocum@bicsi.org www.bicsi.org
Aurora Yocum, Special Projects Coordinator
Donna Dunn, Executive Director
BICSI members include cabling contractors, manufacturers, systems integrators and other telecom professionals.

21807 Bay Area Video Coalition
2727 Mariposa Street
2nd Floor
San Francisco, CA 94110
415-861-3282
FAX: 415-861-4316
bavc@bavc.org www.bavc.org
Jennifer Gilomaen, Communications Manager
Sabrina Jacobs, Enrollment Counselor
Rina Ayuyang, Marketing/Web Associate
Judy Holme Agnew, Executive Director
Jeremy O'Neal, Associate Director
A national organization for independent video producers and artists. Advanced, noncomercial, media arts center dedicated to providing access to media, education and technology.
Founded: 1976

21808 Central Station Alarm Association
440 Maple Avenue East
Suite 201
Vienna, VA 22180
703-242-4670
FAX: 703-242-4675
communications@csaaul.org
www.csaaul.org
Stephen P Doyle, Executive VP
Celia Besore, Director Marketing
John A Murphy, President
Trade association representing providers, users, bureaus and other agencies of UL-listed and or FM Approved Central Station protection services.
Founded: 1950

21809 CompTIA
1815 South Myers Road
Suite 300
Oakbrook Terrace, IL 60181
630-678-8300
FAX: 630-268-1384 www.comptia.org
Laurel Chivari, VP Communications/Marketing
An IT trade association whose goal is to provide a unified voice, global advocacy, and leadership, and to advance industry growth through standards professional competence, education, and business solutions.

21810 Consumer Electronics Association (CEA)
2500 Wilson Boulevard
Arlington, VA 22201
703-907-7600
FAX: 703-907-7675 866-858-1555
gshapiro@ce.org www.ce.org
Gary Shapiro, President/CEO
An association for the furtherance of consumer electronics.

21811 Continental Automated Buildings Association (CABA)
1200 Montreal Road
Building M-20
Ottawa, Canada K1A 0R6, ON
caba@caba.org www.caba.org
Bob Becker, VP/GM
An association for the furtherance of automated buildings.

21812 Copper Development Association (CDA)
260 Madison Avenue
New York, NY 10016
212-251-7200
FAX: 212-251-7234 800-232-3282
questions@cda.copper.org
www.copper.org
Andrew Kireta Sr, President/CEO
An association devoted to furthering the use of copper, which is commonly found in film.

21813 Custom Electronic Design & Installation Association (CEDIA)
7150 Winton Drive
Suite 300
Indianappolis, IN 46268
317-328-4336
FAX: 317-280-8527 800-669-5329
jantcliff@cedia.org www.cedia.org
Jamie Antcliff, Media Contact
Andy Willcox, President
Sharon Gorup, CAE

21814 Independent Professional Representatives Organization (IPRO)
34157 West 9 Mile Road
Farmington Hills, MI 48335
248-474-0522
800-420-4268
ray@avreps.org www.avreps.org
Raymond Wright, Executive Director
Represents independent A/V professionals.

21815 International Society of Videographers
PO Box 296
Sparkill, NY 10976-0296
859-624-5429
Exchanges information on technologies, techniques, and equipment, sponsors Hall of Fame and an international convention.
Founded: 1981

21816 National Systems Contractors Association (NSCA)
625 1st Street SE
Suite 420
Cedar Rapids, IA 52401
319-366-6722
FAX: 319-366-4164 800-446-6722
mabernathy@nsca.org www.nsca.org
Mike Abernathy, Business Development Manager
Deb Gaskill, Expo Coordinator
Chuck Wilson, Executive Director
Helps connect systems contractors with information they need to know.

21817 Production Equipment Rental Association
PO Box 77327
San Francisco, CA 94107-7327
415-552-2094
Greg Meyers, President
Promotes the professional aspects of the film and videotape equipment industry. Maintains a speakers bureau and bestows awards.
75 Members Founded: 1973

21818 Professional Audio-Video Retailers Association
10 E 22nd Street
Suite 301
Lombard, IL 60148-6191
630-268-1500
FAX: 630-953-8957 800-621-0298
webmaster@paralink.org
www.paralink.org

Rosemary Wenstrom

An organization formed to assist the owners and operators of independently owned, high-end audio/video stores to work toward the mutually compatible goal of providing services to members which would be unattainable by retailers working separately.
204 Members

21819 Recording Industry Association of America
1330 Connecticut Avenue NW
Washington, DC 20036
202-775-0101
FAX: 202-775-7257 www.riaa.com

Jason S Berman, Chairman

Nonprofit trade association representing the US sound recording industry. Member companies create, manufacture and market approximately 90 percent of all legitimate recordings produced and sold in the US.
70 Members Founded: 1952

21820 Security Industry Association
635 Slaters Lane
Suite 110
Alexandria, VA 22314
703-683-2075
FAX: 703-683-2469
info@siaonline.org www.siaonline.org

Richard Chace, Executive Director
Cindy Haimowitz, Associate Director Sales
Leigh A McGuire, Director Marketing
Stephanie Smith, Director Finance

Full service, international trade association promoting growth, expansion and professionalism within the security industry.
300 Members Founded: 1969

21821 Society of Camera Operators
PO Box 2006
Toluca Lake, CA 91610
323-856-9100
FAX: 323-856-9155
info@soc.org www.soc.org

Dan Dodd, Advertising Director

Non-profit organization representing camera operators, camera assistants, DPs and other crew members worldwide. Also helps to advance the art and contribution of the operating cameraman in the Motion Picture and Television industries.
Founded: 1978

21822 Special Interests
590 Knox Run Road
PO Box 193
Lanse, PA 16849-0193
814-345-6845
FAX: 814-345-5566 800-735-6997

Vera A Lockey, Owner

Sales of occupational safety and health videos and dvd's, training videos and dvd's workplace safety.
Founded: 1997

21823 Telecommunications Industry Association (TIA)
2500 Wilson Boulevard
Suite 300
Arlington, VA 22201
703-077-7700
FAX: 703-907-7727
tia@tiaonline.org www.tiaonline.org

Matthew J Flanigan, President

TIA reprensts information and communications technology suppliers serving the global marketplace.

21824 Video Software Dealers Association
16530 Ventura Boulevard
Suite 400
Encino, CA 91436
818-385-1500
FAX: 818-385-0567 800-955-8732
servicecenter@vsda.org www.vsda.org

Crossan Andersen, President
Carrie Dieterich, VP Marketing
Mark Fisher, VP Membership/Strategic Initiatives
Sean Bersell, VP Public Affairs
Nancy Gordon, iDEA Manager Ops & Special Projects

Nonprofit international trade association with a membership exceeding 4,500 member companies, representing more than 25,000 locations. Members include retailers, as well as manufacturers, distributors and related businesses that constitute the home video industry. Acts as a spokesperson for home video industry both internally and legislatively.
4.5M Members Founded: 1981

Newsletters

21825 Consumer Multimedia Report
Warren Publishing
2115 Ward Court NW
Washington, DC 20037-1209
202-872-9200
FAX: 212-889-5097 800-771-9202
info@warren-news.com
www.warren-news.com

Albert Warren, Publisher/Editor
Daniel Warren, Vice Chairman/Executive Editor
Paul Warren, President/Executive Publisher

Emphasizes on emerging technologies, marketing strategies, and industry events and news. *$462.00*
BiWeekly

21826 DVD: Laser Disc Newsletter
PO Box 420
East Rockaway, NY 11518-420
516-594-9304
FAX: 516-594-9307
doug@dvdlaser.com
www.dvdlaser.com

Douglas Pratt, Publisher

A consumer guide to DVD's with news, reviews, ads and more. *$47.50*
24 pages Monthly Founded: 1984
Circulation: 5000 Audited
Mailing list available for rent 5000 names $100 per M.

21827 PRC News
Corbell Publishing Company
11500 West Olympic Boulevard
Suite 400
West Los Angeles, CA 90064
213-834-4559
FAX: 310-258-8096
info@corbell.com www.corbell.com

Maureen Healy, Publisher
Joseph Daneshrad, Circulation Manager

A weekly newsletter for the home video industry. Covers pre-recorded video statistics, people, calendar, etc. *$577.00*
8 pages Monthly Founded: 1988
Circulation: 2000 Audited Est. Pass-Along Circ: 3000
Mailing list available for rent 7000 names $75 per M.
Printed in on newsprint stock
Computerized version available

21828 Video Business
Reed Business Information
2000 Clearwater Drive
Oak Brook, IL 60523
630-740-0825
FAX: 630-288-8390
kevin.davis@reedbusiness.com
http://www.videobusiness.com

Kevin L J Davis, Publisher
Paul Sweeting, Editor-at-Large
Charles Tanner, Circulation Manager

Publication includes the retail marketplace, probes business trends and issues, reviews new and upcoming video titles, and contains information and advice for running a successful retail business, and charts top video titles. *$70.00*
Weekly Founded: 1983
Circulation: 47807

21829 Video Investor
Kagan Research
1 Lower Ragsdale Drive
Building One Suite 130
Monterey, CA 93940
831-624-1536
FAX: 831-625-3225 800-307-2529
info@kagan.com www.kagan.com

George Niesen, Editor
Tom Johnson, Marketing Manager

Authoritative look inside the business of renting and selling video cassettes. Exclusive estimates of retail and wholesale transactions and inventories. Tracking movies into the home. Three month trial is available. *$795.00*
Monthly

Magazines & Journals

21830 AudioVideo International
Dempa Publications
275 Madison Avenue
New York, NY 10016-1101
212-682-3755
FAX: 212-682-2730
http://www.dempa.net/

Harry Iguchi, General Manager

Articles cover systems of home entertainment. *$48.00*
100 pages Quarterly Founded: 1950

21831 CE Pro
EH Publishing
111 Speen Street
Suite 200
Framingham, MA 01701-2000
508-201-1515
FAX: 508-663-1599
ehpubinc@ionet.net www.hapro.com
Ken Moyes, Publisher
Jason Knott, Editor
Provides timely, top quality business, industry and product information, technical how-to articles, product comparisons, dealer profiles and marketing and management tips.
Monthly
Circulation: 30,000

21832 CVC Report
Creative Video Consulting
PO Box 5195
Saratoga Springs, NY 12866-8038
212-533-9870
FAX: 212-473-3772 cvcreort@aol.com
Mitchell Rowen, Publisher
Information for music video programming and production fields, contains charts, reviews, play lists, industry dialogue and news. *$225.00*
BiMonthly
Circulation: 800

21833 Digital Content Producer
Prism Business Media
9800 Metcalf Avenue
Overland Park, KS 66212-2216
913-341-1300
FAX: 913-967-1905
subs@prismb2b.com
www.digitalcontentproducer.com
Scott Schwadron, Publisher
Cynthia Wisehart, Editoral Director
Kerby Asplund, Marketing
Laury Reeves, Circulation Manager
Features new product listings, updates on state of the art technology applied to new production techniques, and business industry news. *$70.00*
Monthly Founded: 1975
Circulation: 50000

21834 Markee
HJK Publications
366 E Graves Avenue
Suite D
Orange City, FL 32763
386-774-8881
FAX: 386-774-8908
markee@markeemag.com
http://www.markeemag.com/
Janet Karcher, Publisher
Jonathan T Hutchinson, Editor-In-Chief
Shirley Boone, Circulation
For the Southeast and Southwest film industry. *$24.00*
Monthly Founded: 1986
Circulation: 12200

21835 Media & Methods Magazine
American Society of Educators
502 Woodside Ave
Narberth, PA 19072-2335
610-664-1345

info@media-methods.com
www.media-methods.com
Michele Sokoloff, Publisher
Christine Weiser, Editor
Melissa Eulas, Subscription Department
Caliann Mitoulis, VP of Sales
Derek Carnegie, Production Manager
Media & Methods is the leading education magazine that provides information on how to integrate technology effectively into the K-12 curriculum. A pragmatic and hands-on magazine that teachers value and cherish. The perfect publication to assist classroom teachers, librarians, administrators, technology coordinators, media specialists, principals and department chairpeople. *$33.50*
45 pages Monthly Founded: 1964
Circulation: 50000
Mailing list available for rent 8000 names $140 per M.
Printed in 4 colors on glossy stock

21836 PRC News
Corbell Publishing Company
11500 W. Olympic Blvd
Suite 400
West Los Angeles, CA 90064
213-834-4559
FAX: 310-312-4551
info@corbell.com
http://www.corbell.com
Maureen A Healy, Publisher
Contains information on pre-recorded videos, software, hardware and blank cassettes, includes industry news, pricing and distribution updates, and reviews videos soon to be released. *$577.00*
8 pages Monthly Founded: 1988
Circulation: 2000 $150 per M.
Printed in 1 color

21837 Prosound News
United Entertainment Media
460 Park Avenue South
9th Floor
New York, NY 10016
212-378-0400
FAX: 212-378-2160
circulation@cmpinformation.com
www.prosoundnews.com
Frank Wells, Editor
Margaret Sekelsky, Associate Publisher
Tara Preston, National Sales Manager
Keefe Tony, Executive Director
Monthly
Circulation: 25500

21838 Sound & Video Contractor
Primedia
9800 Metcalf Avenue
Overland Park, KS 66212
913-341-1300
FAX: 913-967-1898 866-505-7173
svcs@pbsub.com www.svconline.com

Mark Johnson, Editor
Maria Arnone, Publisher
Kelly Conlin, CEO
Lori Reeves, Circulation Manager
Kiby Asplund, Marketing Manager
Contains information on sound systems, video display, security, CCTV, home theater, and automation. Delivers in depth instruction and examples of successful installations, fundamental acoustical and video theory and news on new technologies eaffecting the systems contracting business. *$35.00*
Monthly Founded: 1895
Circulation: 21000
Mailing list available for rent 20,500 names $110 per M.

21839 Television Broadcast
Miller Freeman Publications
460 Park Avenue S
9th Floor
New York, NY 10016
212-378-0400
FAX: 212-378-2160
tvbcast@psn.com
www.TVBroadcast.com
Paul G Gallo, Publisher
Michael Grotticelli, Editor
Television Broadcast primarily serves TV stations including commercial, public, educational, religious military TV stations or networks; teleproduction facilities including production, post-production, tape duplication, effects, audio production or independent program producer.
Monthly Founded: 1978
Circulation: 30,374
Printed in 4 colors on glossy stock

21840 Video & Entertainment
Fairchild Publications
7 W 34th Street
New York, NY 10001
212-630-3880
FAX: 212-630-4201 800-204-4515

21841 Video Age International
216 East 75th Street
Suite PW
New York, NY 10021
212-288-3933
FAX: 212-734-9033
sales@videoageinternational.com
www.videoageinternational.com
Dom Serafini, Publisher
Offers information on program sales and distribution of videocassettes, discs and allied media. *$30.00*
7x/Year
Circulation: 12000

21842 Video Librarian
Video Librarian
8705 Honeycomb Court NW
Seabeck, WA 98380
360-309-9345
FAX: 360-830-9346 800-692-2270
vidlib@videolibrarian.com
www.videolibrarian.com
Randy Pitman, Publisher/Editor
Anne Williams, Marketing Director
Jazza Williams, Associate Editor
Offers video reviews and news for public, school, academic and special libraries. *$64.00*
56 pages Founded: 1986
Circulation: 2000

21843 Video Store Magazine
201 Sandpointe Avenue
Suite 600
Santa Ana, CA 92707-8700
714-386-6700
FAX: 714-513-8402 800-854-3112
selliott@advanstar.com
http://www.homemediaretailing.com
Thomas Arnold, Editor
Don Rosenberg, Publisher
Susan Elliott, Publications Coordinator
Steven J. Apple, Director, Business Development
Renee Rosado, Online Manager
Offers market research and buying information for industry people. *$48.00*
Weekly
Circulation: 44257

Trade Shows

21844 **International Society of Videographers**
PO Box 296
Sparkill, NY 10976-0296
859-624-5429
FAX: 845-359-8527

Steve Jambeck, Executive Director

Exchanges information on technologies, techniques, and equipment, sponsors Hall of Fame and an international convention.
Founded: 1981

Directories & Databases

21845 **AV Market Place**
RR Bowker
630 Central Avenue
New Providence, NJ 07974
908-286-1090
FAX: 908-464-3553 800-521-8110

Karen Hallard, Editor

Over 7,000 producers and distributors of audiovisual materials, including production companies, production services and manufacturers and dealers handling equipment and supplies. Also includes awards and festivals, associations, film and TV commercials, periodicals and reference books. *$157.50*
Annual January

21846 **Orion Blue Book: Computer**
Orion Research Corporation
14555 N Scottsdale Road
Suite 330
Scottsdale, AZ 85254-3487
480-951-1114

Roger Rohrs, Owner

A list of manufacturers of data processing hardware and products for the computer industry. *$200.00*
Annual

21847 **Orion Blue Book: Video and Television**
Orion Research Corporation
14555 N Scottsdale Road
Suite 330
Scottsdale, AZ 85254-3487
480-951-1114
FAX: 480-951-1117 800-844-0759
orion@bluebook.com
www.bluebook.com

Roger Rohrs, Editor

List of more than 450 manufacturers of video and television products such as cameras, recorders, disc players, projectors, extenders, microphones, mixers, processors and color monitors. *$144.00*
Annual January

21848 **Video Networks**
Bay Area Video Coalition
1111 17th Street
San Francisco, CA 94107-2406
415-613-3282
FAX: 415-861-4316 www.bavc.com
List of over 100 film festivals for independent video producers and artisits. *$3.00*
Annual

21849 **Video Source Book**
Gale Research
27500 Drake Road
Farmington Hills, MI 48331
248-699-4253
FAX: 248-699-8214 800-877-4253
galeord@gale.com www.gale.com
Offers various videos covering approximately 130,000 programs available from more than 2,500 producers and distributors.
$260.00
3,000 pages Annual

21850 **Videomaker Magazine**
Videomaker
1350 East 9th Street
PO Box 4591
Chico, CA 95927-4591
530-891-8410
FAX: 530-891-8443
smuratore@videomaker.com
www.videomaker.com

Stephen Muratore, Editor-in-Chief
Jennifer O'Rourke, Managing Editor

Information about the world of camcorders, computers, tools and techniques for making video in a way that is timely, applicable, pertinent, engaging and understandable. Each month we teach production techniques, explain technology and include no less than two informative buyer's guides of products central to video. In addition, we are committed to objective analysis of videomaking products so our audience can rely on us for unbiased reporting. *$3.99*
Monthly
Circulation: 90,000
Printed in 4 colors on glossy stock

Industry Web Sites

21851 **www.1394ta.org**
1394 Trade Association

21852 **www.asid.org**
American Society of Interior Designers (ASID)

21853 **www.avreps.org**
Independent Professional Representatives Org

21854 **www.bavc.org**
Bay Area Video Collection

21855 **www.bicsi.org**
BICSI

21856 **www.caba.org**
Continental Automated Buildings Association (CABA)

21857 **www.ce.org**
Consumer Electronics Association (CEA)

21858 **www.cedia.org**
Custom Electronic Design & Installation Associatio

21859 **www.comptia.org**
CompTIA

21860 **www.copper.org**
Copper Development Association (CDA)

21861 **www.csaaul.org**
Central Station Alarm Association

21862 **www.fla-alarms.org**
Alarm Association of Florida

21863 **www.greyhouse.com**
Grey House Publishing

Selected Grey House directories in the fields of business, health and education are available online. Users can search our online databases by several different search criteria, such as product categories, geographic area, sales volume and much, much more. Full Grey House catalog and online ordering also available.

21864 **www.nsca.org**
National Systems Contractors Association (NSCA)

21865 **www.paralink.org**
Professional Audio-Video Retailers Association

21866 **www.riaa.org**
Recording Industry Association of America

21867 **www.siaonline.org**
Security Industry Association

21868 **www.soc.org**
Society of Camera Operators

21869 www.tiaonline.org
Telecommunications Industry Association (TIA)

21870 www.vsda.org
Video Software Dealers Association

Associations

21871 Affiliated Warehouse Companies
PO Box 295
Hazlet, NJ 07730-0295
732-739-2323
FAX: 732-739-4154
sales@awco.com www.awco.com

Jim McBride, President
Patrick McBride, VP

Assists public warehouse users to gather rates and data, provides information on warehousing and distribution at no charge or obligation for over 100 public warehouse clients in the US, Canada and Mexico.
120 Members Founded: 1953
Mailing list available for rent 10000 names

21872 Allied Distribution
4839 Sherburn Road
PO Box 607
Eagle River, WI 54521
715-479-3530
FAX: 715-479-3551
info@warehousenetwork.com
www.warehousenetwork.com

Ernest Brunswick, President
Cyd Brunswick, Customer Service Manager

A sales and marketing association representing public warehouses and distribution centers in the United States.
75 Members Founded: 1929

21873 American Chain of Warehouses
156 Flamingo Drive
Beecher, IL 60401
708-946-9792
FAX: 708-946-9793
bjurus@acwi.org www.acwi.org

Paul Delp, Warehouse Director
William L Jurus, VP Sales/Marketing

Sales and marketing company representing public warehouses.
50 Members Founded: 1911

21874 Automotive Warehouse Distributors
7101 West Street
Suite 1300
Bethesda, MD 20814
301-654-6664
FAX: 301-654-3299
info@awda.org www.awda.org

Kathleen Shetz, CEO
Rich White, VP

Promotes interests of warehouse distributors of auto parts and supplies.
450 Members Founded: 1947

21875 Burley Auction Warehouse Association
620 S Broadway
Suite 201
Lexington, KY 40508-3150
859-255-4504
FAX: 859-255-4534

Denny Wilson, Managing Director

Members are warehouse companies selling burley tobacco at auction in eight burley-producing states.
225 Members

21876 Engine Service Association
1900 Arch Street
Philadelphia, PA 19103-1404
215-564-3484
FAX: 215-564-2175

William L Robinson, Executive Director

Members are central warehouse distributors of internal combustion engines.
60 Members

21877 Independent Liquid Terminals Association
1444 I Street NW
#400
Washington, DC 20005
202-842-9200
FAX: 202-326-8660
info@ilta.org www.ilta.org

E David Doane, President
Melinda Whitney, Director/Government Relations

We represent bulk liquid terminal companies that store commercial liquids in aboveground storage tanks (ASTs) and transfer products to and from oceangoing tank ships, tank barges, pipelines, tank trucks and tank rail cars.
400 Members Founded: 1974

21878 International Association of Refrigerated Warehouses
1500 King Street
Suite 201
Alexandria, VA 22314
703-373-4300
FAX: 730-373-4301
email@iarw.org www.iarw.org

J William Hudson, President/CEO
Benjamin Milk, VP/Secretary
Lorien Onderdonk, Member Srvcs/Comm Coordinator
Corey Rosenbusch, Business Development Director

Trade association of public refrigerated warehouses storing of all types of perishable products.
900 Members Founded: 1891

21879 International Warehouse Logistics Association
2800 River Road
Suite 260
Des Plaines, IL 60018
847-813-4699
FAX: 847-813-0115
email@iwla.com www.iwla.com

Joel Hoiland, President/CEO
Nathan Noy, Gov't Affairs/Legal Services
Scott Brewster, Membership/Partnership
Carrie Gremer, Marketing/Communications

The unified voice of the global logistics outsourcing industry, representing third party warehousing, transportation and logistics service providers. Our member companies provide the most timely and cost-effective global logistics solutions for their customers and are committed to protecting the free flow of products across international borders.
500 Members Founded: 1997

21880 Internationl Warehouse Logistics Association
International Warehouse Logistics Association
2800 S. River Road
Suite 260
Des Plains, IL 60018-5764
847-813-4699
FAX: 847-813-0115 www.iwlz.com

Carrie Gremer, Contact

Trade association of public warehouses.
500+ Members

21881 RCS Limited
1301 Commerce Street
Birmingham, AL 35217
205-841-9955
FAX: 205-841-2106 888-833-1970
skipBurch@rcands.com
www.rcands.com
Design and build contractor for cold storage warehouses.

21882 Refrigeration Research and Education
World Food Logistics Organization
1500 King Street
Suite 201
Alexandria, VA 22314
703-373-4300
FAX: 703-373-4301
email@larw.org www.larw.org

J William Hudson, President/CEO
Benjamin Milk, VP Secretary
Susan Shores, Director Administration

Sponsors graduate-level scientific research in the refrigeration of perishable commodities. Offers annual training institute for public refrigerated warehouse personnel.
1M Members Founded: 1943

21883 Self Storage Association
1900 North Beauregard Street
Suite 110
Alexandria, VA 22311
703-575-8000
FAX: 703-575-8901 888-735-3784
ssa@selfstorage.org
www.selfstorage.org

Michael T Scanlon Jr, President/CEO
Timothy J Dietz, VP Communications/Gov't Relations
Martha Morrison, CMP, VP Meetings/Trade Shows

Self-storage facility owners/operators and suppliers to the industry.
6000 Members Founded: 1975

Newsletters

21884 AUA News
American Underground Space Association

3001 Hennepin Avenue So.
Suite D202
Minneapolis, MN 55408
212-465-5541
FAX: 212-631-3787
underground@auca.org
www.auaonline.org

Thomas O'Neil, President
Elaine Gray, Editor

Offers the latest news on underground space construction development and use in North America. Includes information on infrastructures. *$107.00*
Quarterly
Circulation: 1000
Printed in 4 colors on glossy stock

21885 Affiliated Warehouse Companies Newsletter
Affiliated Warehouse Companies
PO Box 295
Hazlet, NJ 07730-0295
732-739-2323
FAX: 732-739-4154
sales@awco.com www.awco.com

Jim McBride, Publisher
Patrick McBride, VP

Assists public warehouse users to gather rates and data, provides information on warehousing and distribution at no charge or obligation for over 100 public warehouse clients in the US, Canada, Mexico and Puerto Rico.

Mailing list available for rent 9000 names

21886 Distribution Center Management
Alexander Communications Group
28 W 25th Street
8th Floor
New York, NY 10003-1600
212-280-0246
FAX: 212-228-0376 800-232-4317
info@distributiongroup.com
www.distributiongroup.com

Larry Alexander, President
Margaret Dewitt, Publisher/Marketing Manager

Provides practical strategies and industry news to help distribution center and warehouse professionals improve distribution center efficiency. *$199.00*

8 pages Monthly Founded: 1985 ISSN 0894-7651

Magazines & Journals

21887 Inside Self Storage
Virgo Publishing
3300 N Central Avenue Suite 2500
PO Box 40079
Phoenix, AZ 85067-79
480-990-1101
FAX: 486-675-8146
cs@vpico.com
www.insideselfstorage.com

Troy Bix, Publisher
Teri L Lanza, Editor

For moving and storage professionals. *$95.00*

Monthly
Circulation: 20000

21888 Logistics Management & Distribution Report
Reed Business Information
225 Wyman Street
Waltham, MA 02451-1637
617-643-3030
FAX: 781-734-8076
fquinn@reedbusiness.com
www.lmdr.com

Kevin McPherson, Publisher
Mike Levin, Group Editor-in-Chief
Frank Quinn, Editorial Director
Michael Levans, Chief Editor
Stephen Moylan, President,Divisions

Logistics Management and Distribution Report is written for managers and professionals in charge of traffic, transportation, purchasing, inventory control, containerization and warehousing the functions of physical distribution and business logistics. Covers marketing and operating strategies, cost reduction opportunities and governmental regulation and law. *$99.90*

Monthly Founded: 1977
Circulation: 68000

21889 Mini-Storage Messenger
MiniCo
2531 W Dunlap Avenue
Phoenix, AZ 85021
602-701-1711
FAX: 602-678-3511 800-824-6864
publishing@minico.com
www.ministoragemessenger.com

Sherri Acord, Circulation Manager
Denise Nunez, Director Publishing
Hardy Good, Manager

As the industry's first trade journal, the mini-storage messenger has become the leading trade magazine for anyone involved in self-storage. This magazine covers rental rates, marketing trends, and finance. *$59.95*

89 pages Monthly Founded: 1979
Printed in 4 colors on glossy stock

21890 Mover Magazine
Virgo Publishing
3300 N Central Avenue, Suite 2500
PO Box 40079
Phoenix, AZ 85067-0079
480-990-1101
FAX: 480-675-8146
For the moving and storage professional.

21891 Refrigerated Transporter
Primedia
9800 Metcalf Avenue
Overland Park, KS 66212
913-341-1300
FAX: 913-967-1898 800-441-0294

Kathleen Schmatz, Group Publisher
Ray Anderson, Group Editor

Monthly Founded: 1898
Circulation: 15000

21892 Storage
West World Productions
420 N Camden Drive
Beverly Hills, CA 90210-4507
310-432-7100
FAX: 310-246-1405
sinan@kanatsiz.com www.wwpi.com

Christine Chudnow, Editor
Yuri Spiro, CEO/Executive Publisher
Laura Klein, Production Manager

Storage is the unique storage-intensive magazine supplement to Computer Technology Review. It is recognized as the bible of the entire storage industry. *$10.00*

72 pages Quarterly Founded: 1981
Circulation: 72000 72,000 names $185 per M.
Printed in 4 colors on glossy stock : html

21893 Warehousing Management
Reed Business Information
225 Wyman Street
Waltham, MA 02451
617-643-3030
FAX: 610-205-1185
www.reedbusiness.com

Jim Casella, CEO
John R Johnson, Editor

Warehousing Management targets warehousing and distribution center operations managers with analysis, news, trends, equipment and events.

Circulation: 47185

Trade Shows

21894 Eastpack
Reed Exhibition Companies
255 Wyman Streett
Waltham, MA 02451
781-734-8761
FAX: 781-734-8042

Elizabeth Hitchcock, International Sales

275 booths.
7.5M Attendees March

21895 Household Goods Forwarders Association
5904 Richman Avenue
Suite 304
Alexandria, VA 22303-4691
703-684-3780

Belvian Carpinton, Show Manager
Terry Head, President

20 tables.
1M Attendees September

21896 Independent Liquid Terminals Assoc. Annual Operating Conference & Trade Show
Independent Liquid Terminals Association
1444 I Street NW
Suite 400
Washington, DC 20005
202-842-9200
FAX: 202-326-8660
info@ilta.org www.ilta.org

E. David Doane, President
Melinda Whitney, Director/Government Affairs

Two-hundred and two booths of products including goods and services designed for the construction and operation of bulk liquid storage terminals. Includes international companies.
2,700 Attendees June

21897 International Transportation and Logistics Exhibition and Conference
ILT
1300 Higgins Road
Suite 111
Park Ridge, IL 60068-5764
847-292-1891
FAX: 847-823-3901
logistx@aol.com
www.warehouselogistics.org

Marge Whalen, Director of Sales
Regan Williams, Trade Show Coordinator

Annual conference and trade show focusing on public warehousing, distribution, transportation, logistics and systems. Containing 200 exhibits.
3,000 Attendees June

21898 NORPACK
Northern American Expositions Company

33 Rutherford Avenue
Charlestown, MA 02129
617-242-6092
FAX: 617-242-1817 800-225-1577
naexpo@hotmail.com
http://naexpo.com
The Northeast's premier trade show for packaging, material handeling, warehouse automation, shipping/receiving, storage and bottling.

4500 Attendees

21899 Northwest Material Handling & Packaging Show
Professional Trade Shows-Division of Penton Media
47817 Fremont Boulevard
Fremont, CA 94538
510-651-6698
FAX: 510-354-3159 proshows.com
5,000 Attendees May

21900 Pack Expo
Pakaging Machinery Manufacturers Institute
4350 N Fairfax Drive
Suite 600
Arlington, VA 22203
703-243-8555
888-275-7664
pmmi@pmmi.org www.packexpo.com
Matt Crossn, Communications Director
Sara Kryder, Assistant Communications
Informational meeting and exposition held by the Packaging Machinery Manufacturers Institute.
15000 Attendees

21901 Warehousing, Technology & Distribution Show
Industrial Shows of America
164 Lake Front Drive
Hunt Valley, MD 21030-2215
410-771-1445
FAX: 410-771-1158 800-638-6396
This show will feature hands-on workshops for the practical applications of new technologies, safety issues and more all designed to improve productivity and cut losses in today's competitive market.
1500 Attendees April

Directories & Databases

21902 Affiliated Warehouse Companies Database of Public Warehouse Users
Affiliated Warehouse Companies
PO Box 295
Hazlet, NJ 07730-0295
732-739-2323
FAX: 732-739-4154
sales@awco.com www.awco.com
Jim McBride, President
Patrick McBride, VP
In excess of 9,000 listings of individuals and companies that use public warehousing, products produced and services required.

Mailing list available for rent

21903 American Chain of Warehouses Directory
20500 S La Grange Road
Frankfort, IL 60423-1356
815-469-7882
FAX: 815-469-2941
Donald R Greenland, Executive VP
Public warehouse listings in the United States are profiled.
50 pages Annual

21904 American Public Warehouse Register
Reed Business Information
2 Brandywine Way
Sicklerville, NJ 08081-0750
856-728-9745
FAX: 630-288-8686
www.reedbusiness.com
Laura Masapollo, National Sales Director
Laura MasaPollo, National Sales Director
Worldwide listings of dry, refrigerated, contract and HazMat Public Warehouses Annual. *$50.00*

21905 Associated Warehouses Directory of Services
PO Box 471
Cedar Knolls, NJ 07927-0471
973-539-1277
FAX: 973-538-0944
richards@aol.com
www.awilogistics.com
Mark Richards, Editor
Barbara Brown, Circulation Director
A who's who directory of services to the industry.
100 pages Annual

21906 Directory of Bulk Liquid Terminal and Storage Facilities
ITLA
1133 15th Street NW
Sutie 650
Washington, DC 20005
202-659-2301
FAX: 202-466-4166
info@ilta.org www.ilta.org
John Prokop, President
EB Calvert, Director Administration
Locates over 480 bulk liquid terminal/storage facilities. Lists key personnel, addresses, telephone numbers. Lists products handled-petroleum products, crude oil, chemicals, animal fats and oils, vegetable oils, molasses, spirits, etc. Lists storage tanks, modes served, pipeline connections. Other services and capabilities-canning, barreling, bleaching, blending, weighing, warehousing, etc. Subc. available for Directory and Newsletter *$95.00*
300 pages Annual

21907 Food & Beverage Market Place
Grey House Publishing
185 Millerton Road
PO Box 860
Millerton, NY 12546
518-890-0526
FAX: 518-789-0545 800-562-2139
books@greyhouse.com
www.foodmp.com
Leslie Mackenzie, Publisher
Richard Gottlieb, Editor
This information-packed 3-volume set is the most powerful buying and marketing guide for the US food and beverage industry. Includes thousands of industry freight and transportation listings. *$595.00*
6500 pages Annual

21908 Independent Liquid Terminals Association
1444 I Street NW
Suite 400
Washington, DC 20005
202-842-9200
FAX: 202-326-8660
info@ilta.org www.ilta.org
E David Doane, President
Melinda Whitney, Director/Government Affairs
A 285 page directory, listing 577 for hire, marketing, throughput, and pipeline bulk liquid storage terminals. *$95.00*
285 pages Founded: 1975

21909 International Directory of Public Refrigerated Warehouses
1500 King Street
Suite 201
Alexandria, VA 22314
703-373-4300
FAX: 703-373-4301
email@iwra.org www.iarw.org
J William Hudson, President/CEO
Offers information on more than 950 member warehouses in 32 countries and on companies supplying products and services to the refrigerated warehouse industry. *$150.00*
232 pages Annual
Circulation: 6,000

21910 International Warehouse Logistics Directory
1300 Higgins Road
Suite 111
Park Ridge, IL 60068-5764
847-292-1891
FAX: 847-292-1896
bstephens@warehouselogistics.org
www.warehouselogistics.org
Joel Hoiland, President/CEO
Ben Stephens, Public Relations/Media Coordinator
The membership directory is published annually in January in book and CD-ROM form.
Annually

21911 National Refrigeration Contractors Association
National Refrigeration Contrtactors
1900 Arch Street
Philadelphia, PA 19103-1404
215-564-3484
FAX: 215-963-9785
Elizabeth Barnett, Editor
About 100 member refrigeration contracting companies
Annual

21912 Transportation & Distribution Magazine's Integrated Warehousing/Storage
Penton Media
1300 E 9th Street
Cleveland, OH 44114
216-696-7000
FAX: 216-696-1752
information@penton.com
www.penton.com
Dave Madonia, Publisher
Carrie Doidze, Marketing Manager
Lists over 1,200 manufacturers of products related to the warehousing and distribution industries.
Annual
Circulation: 71,000
Printed in 4 colors on glossy stock

21913 Warehouses Licensed Under US Warehouse Act
Farm Service Agency-US Dept. of Agriculture
PO Box 2415
Washington, DC 20013-2415

FAX: 202-690-0014

Agricultural warehouses voluntarily licensed under the US Warehouse Act governing public storage facilities.
Annual

21914 Warehousing Distribution Directory
PRIMEDIA Information
10 Lake Drive
Hightstown, NJ 08520-5321
609-371-7700
FAX: 609-371-7819 800-224-5488

Amy Middlebrook, Editor
John Capers III, Publisher

List of about 800 warehousing and consolidation companies and firms offering trucking, trailer on flatcar, container on flatcar and piggyback carrier services. *$55.00*
250 pages SemiAnnual Founded: 1949
Circulation: 10,000 $150 per M.
Printed in 4 colors on glossy stock

Industry Web Sites

21915 www.awco.com
Affiliated Warehouse Companies

Assists public warehouse users to gather rates and data, provides information on warehousing and distribution at no charge or obligation for over 100 public warehouse clients in the US, Canada, Mexico, Europe and Southeast Asia.

21916 www.greyhouse.com
Grey House Publishing

Selected Grey House directories in the fields of business, health and education are available online. Users can search our online databases by several different search criteria, such as product categories, geographic area, sales volume and much, much more. Full Grey House catalog and online ordering also available.

21917 www.larw.org
Refrigeration Research and Education Foundation

Sponsors graduate-level scientific research on the refrigeration of perishable commodities. Offers annual training institute for public refrigerated warehouse personnel.

21918 www.warehouselogistics.org
International Warehouse Logistics Association

For third-party warehousing and related logistics services throughout the world. Collectively, the Association's members ship over 3 trillion pounds annually in North America.

Associations

21919 American Recreation Coalition
1225 New York Avenue NW
Suite 450
Washington, DC 20005
202-682-9530
FAX: 202-682-9529
arc@funoutdoors.com
www.funoutdoors.com

Derrick Crandall, President
Catherine Ahern, VP
Dorothy Shea, Communications

A non-profit Washington based federation that provides a unified voice for recreation interests to conserve their full and active participation in government policy making on issues such as public land management. ARC works to build public-private partnerships to enhance and protect outdoor recreation opportunities and resources.
100+ Members Founded: 1979

21920 American Society of Irrigation Consultants
125 Paradise Lane
PO Box 426
Rochester, MA 02770
508-763-8140
FAX: 508-763-8102
NormanB@asic.org www.asic.or

Norman F Bartlett, Executive Director
Kathleen A Bartlett, Executive Secretary
Luke Frank, Advertising Director

Promotes education skills on data exchange landscape irrigation. Members are irrigation consultants, suppliers, and manufacturers.
Founded: 1970

21921 American Water Works Association
6666 W Quincy Avenue
Denver, CO 80235
303-794-7711
FAX: 303-347-0804 800-926-7337

Andrew Richardson, President
Jack W Hoffbuhr, Executive Director

The professional society of North American drinking water experts. Develops standards and support research programs in waterworks design, construction, operation, and management. Conducts in-service training schools and offers placement service.
57000 Members Founded: 1881

21922 Ground Water Protection Council
13308 N MacArthur Boulevard
Oklahoma City, OK 73142
405-516-4972
FAX: 405-516-4973
dan@gwpc.org www.gwpc.org

Mike Paque, Executive Director
Ben Grunewald, Associate Director
Paul Jehn, Technical Director
Dan Yates, Member Servicess Coordinator

State ground water and underground injection control agencies whose mission is to promote the protection and conservation of ground water resources for all beneficial uses, recognizing ground water as a component of the ecosystem.
1.75M Members Founded: 1983

21923 Irrigation Association
6540 Arlington Boulevard
Falls Church, VA 22042-6638
703-536-7080
FAX: 703-536-7019
webmaster@irrigation.org
www.irrigation.org

Deborah Hamlin, Executive Director
John Roberts, President
Beth Casteel, Communications Manager
Michael Hemsley, Membership Manager

Members are manufacturers of irrigation systems, with the goal to promote efficient and effective water management and to be the voice of the irrigation industry worldwide.
1.2M Members Founded: 1949

21924 National Drilling Association
11001 Danka Way N
Suite 1
St. Petersburg, FL 33716
727-577-5006
FAX: 727-577-5012 800-445-8629
info@nda4u.com www.nda4u.com

Larry Gibel, President
Michael Tiani, Secretary/Treasurer
Patrick O'Brien, Executive Director
R Allan Garrard, VP

An association of contractors, manufacturers and affiliated members from the the drilling industry representing the geotechnical, environmental and mineral exploration sectors of this industry.
254 Members Founded: 1972

21925 National Institute for Water Resources
University of Massachusetts
Blaisdell House
Amherst, MA 01003
413-545-0111
FAX: 413-545-2304
godfrey@tei.umass.edu
www.umsu.edu/niwr/

Paul Godfrey, Executive Secretary

Offers information on water resource directions across the nation.
54 Members Founded: 1974

21926 National Onsite Wastewater Recycling
PO Box 1270
Edgewater, MD 21037
410-798-1697
FAX: 410-798-5741 800-966-2942
webmaster@nowra.org
www.nowra.org

Jerry Stonebridge, President
Brian McQuestion, Secretary/Treasurer
Linda Hanifin Bonner, Ph.D, Executive Director

Dedicated solely to educating and representing members within the onsite and decentralized industry. And also to provide leadership and promote the onsite waste water treatment and recycling through education, training, communication and quality tools to support excellence in performance.
3500 Members Founded: 1991

21927 National Rural Water Association
2915 S 13 Street
Duncan, OK 73533
580-252-0629
FAX: 580-255-4476
info@nrwa.org www.nrwa.org

Bobby Scott, CEO

Dedicated to the preservation, as well as the protection of water and other natural resources.
615 Members

21928 National Water Resources Association
3800 Fairfax Drive
Suite 4
Arlington, VA 22203
703-524-1544
FAX: 703-524-1548
nwra@nwra.org www.nwra.org

Norman Semanko, President
Thomas Donnelly, VP

Dedicated to the wise management and use of the nation's water and land resources.
5M+ Members Founded: 1932

21929 Soil and Water Conservation Society
945 SW Ankeny Road
Ankeny, IA 50023-9723
515-289-2331
FAX: 515-289-1227 800-847-7645
webmaster@swcs.org www.swcs.org

Craig A Cox, Executive Director

Promotes erosion control and water quality. Publishes scholarly journal and practical magazine, and conducts an annual conference and trade show.
7000 Members Founded: 1945

21930 Submersible Waste Water Pump Association
1866 Sheridan Road
Suite 201
High Park, IL 60035-2545
847-681-1868
FAX: 847-681-1869
swpaexdir@tds.net www.swpa.org

Charles Stolberg, Executive Director

Represents and serves the manufacturers of submersible pumps for the municipal and industrial wasterwater applications. Manufacturers of components and accessory items for those products and companies providing services to users of those products.
Founded: 1976

21931 Water Environment Federation
601 Wythe Street
Alexandria, VA 22314-1994
703-842-2400
FAX: 703-684-2492 800-666-0206

Phyllis Eastman, Managing Director
Dianne Crilley, Manager
Teresa Evans Hunter, Manager
William Bertera, Executive Director

A technical and educational organization with members from varied disciplines who work toward the vision of preservation and enhancement of the global water environment.
79 Members Founded: 1928

21932 Water Quality Association
4151 Naperville Road
Lisle, IL 60532-1088
630-505-0160
FAX: 630-505-9637
info@mail.wqa.org www.wqa.org

Peter J Censky, Executive Director
Margit Fotre, Membership/Marketing Director
Laurie Metanchuk, Communications Manager

An international, nonprofit trade association representing retail/dealers and manufacturer/suppliers in the point of use/entry water quality improvement industry. Membership benefits and services include technical and scientific information, educational seminars and home correspon-

dence course books, professional certification and discount services.
2.5M Members Founded: 1974

21933 Water and Wastewater Equipment Manufacturers Association
PO Box 17402
Washington, DC 20041
202-184-4123
FAX: 703-444-1779
info@wwema.org www.wwema.org
Dawn C Kristof, President
Represents the interests of companies that manufacture the products that are sold to the portable water and wastewater treatment industries. Also informs, educates and provides leadership on the issues which affect the worldwide water and wastewater equipment industry.
80 Members Founded: 1908

21934 WaterJet Technology Association
906 Olive Street
Suite 1200
Saint Louis, MO 63101-1434
314-241-1445
FAX: 314-241-1449
wjta@wjta.org www.wjta.org
George A Savanick PhD, Editor
Members research for new findings in waterjet technology.
Founded: 1983

Newsletters

21935 Drinking Water and Backflow Prevention
SFA Enterprises
11166 Huron Street
Unit 29
Northglenn, CO 80234-3330
303-510-0979
FAX: 303-452-9776 888-367-3927
backflow@dwbp-online.com
www.dwbp-online.com
Stuart Asay, Publisher
Accepts advertising. *$38.00*
24 pages Monthly

21936 Jet News
WaterJet Technology Association
906 Olive Street
Suite 1200
Saint Louis, MO 63101-1434
314-241-1445
FAX: 314-241-1449
wjta@wjta.org http://www.wjta.org
George A Savanick, Editor
Includes research and new findings in waterjet technology. Members only
Monthly Founded: 1983
Circulation: 1000
Printed in 2 colors on matte stock

21937 National Association of Regulatory Utility Commisioners
1101 Vermont Avenue NW
Suite 200
Washington, DC 20005
202-898-2200
FAX: 202-898-2213
admin@naruc.org www.naruc.org
Charles Gray, Executive Director
Diane Munns, President
A national organization that offers valuable information on over 150 consultants and other professionals active in regulated water, sewer and related industries.
Monthly Founded: 1889
Circulation: 1800

21938 National Water Line
National Water Resources Association
3800 Fairfax Drive
Suite 4
Arlington, VA 22203-1703
703-524-1544
FAX: 703-524-1548
nrwa@nrwa.org www.nwra.org
Bridget O'Grady, Publisher
Thomas Donnelly, VP
Association news and information.
Monthly

21939 US Water News
230 Main Street
Halstead, KS 67056-1913
316-835-2222
FAX: 316-835-2223 800-251-0046
Inquiries@uswaternews.com
www.uswaternews.com
Thomas Bell, Publisher
Mary DeSana, Editor
Reports news of current events in water resources from across the nation. Accepts advertising. *$59.00*
24 pages Monthly

21940 Water Newsletter
Water Information Center
1099 18th Street
#2100
Denver, CO 80202-1939
303-972-1200
FAX: 303-294-1239
http://www.gmgw.com
Lee Phipps, Editor
Contents include water supply and waste disposal information, and presents articles on conservation/usage. *$127.00*
Monthly Founded: 1959

Magazines & Journals

21941 APWA Reporter
American Public Works Association
2345 Grand Boulevard
Suite 500
Kansas City, MO 64108-2625
816-472-6100
FAX: 816-472-1610 800-848-2792
apwa@apwa.net
www.apwa.net/reporter
Kevin Clark, Editor
Kaye Sullivan, Deputy Executive Director/COO
Connie Hartline, Publications Manager
Lillie Plowman, Publications/Premiums Marketing Mgr
Christine Robinson, Marketing/Publications Coordinator
Circulation to entire membership of American Public Works Association. *$100.00*
Monthly Founded: 1937 ISSN 0092-4873
Circulation: 34000
Mailing list available for rent

21942 Bottled Water Reporter
International Bottled Water Association
1700 Diagonal Road
Suite 650
Alexandria, VA 22314
703-683-5213
FAX: 703-683-4074 800-928-3711
ibwainfo@bottledwater.org
www.bottledwater.org
Cathleen Howard, Publisher/Editor
Provides a vital source of information to bottlers and agencies, consultanats and engineers. Also contains statistical data, marketing and managemant tips and profiles of bottled water operations and supplier companies. *$50.00*
Founded: 1958
Circulation: 3000

21943 Cleaner Times
Advantage Publishing Company
1000 Nix Road
Little Rock, AR 72211
501-280-9111
FAX: 501-280-9233 800-525-7038
gpuls@adpub.com www.adpub.com
Charlene Yarbrough, Publisher
Gerry Puls, Circulation
Chuck Prieur, Sales Manager
Application, information, and productivity for persons engaged in the manufacturing, distribution, or the use of high pressure water systems and accessories. The emphasis is on safety, regulatory, which affect the industry as well as cleaning applications. *$18.00*
72 pages Monthly Founded: 1989
Circulation: 10000
Printed in 4 colors on glossy stock

21944 Cleanwater Report
Business Publishers
8737 Colesville Road
Suite 1100
Silver Spring, MD 20910-3928
301-587-6300
FAX: 301-587-4530 800-274-6737
bpinews@bpinews.com
http://www.bpinews.com
Adam Goldstien, Publisher
Beth Early, Operations Director
Lewis Harris, Editor
Margery Wyna, Marketing
Pat Maness, Circulation Manager
Tracks legislation, regulation, litigation and technological innovations affecting the waterworks industry. *$387.00*
Founded: 1963

21945 Clearwaters
New York Water Environment Association
525 Plum Street
Suite 102
Syracuse, NY 13204
315-422-7811
FAX: 315-422-3851
rdh@nywea.org www.nywea.org
Lois Hickey, Editor
Patricia Cerro-Reehil, Executive Director

Contains information on pollution control legislation, regulation, and compliance. *$25.00*
Quarterly Founded: 1929
Circulation: 3000

21946 Drill Bits
National Drilling Association
11001 Danka Way North
Suite 1
St Petersburg, FL 33716
727-577-5006
FAX: 727-577-5012 800-445-8629
info@nda4u.com www.nda4u.com

R Alan Garrard, Director-at-Large
Nancy Cooper, Editor
P Don Ulses, President
Patrick O'Brien, Executive Director
G Michael Tiani, Secretary/Treasurer

Magazine of the formerly National Drilling Contractors Association, which merged with Equipment Drilling Manufacturers Association and International Drilling Federation in 1995. Advertising available.

2x/Year Founded: 1972
Circulation: 210

21947 Ground Water
National Ground Water Association
601 Dempsey Road
Westerville, OH 43081-8978
614-898-7791
FAX: 614-898-7786 800-551-7379
customerservice@ngwa.org
www.ngwa.org

Dr. Mary Anderson, Editor-in-Chief
Thad Plumley, Publications Director
Shelby Fleck, Advertising
Cindi Taylor, Advertising
Kevin McKray, Executive Director

Focuses on ground water hydrogeology as a science. *$395.00*

160 pages Founded: 1963
Circulation: 15000 10000 names
Printed in 1 color

21948 Ground Water Monitoring and Remediation
National Ground Water Association
601 Dempsey Road
Westerville, OH 43081-8978
614-987-7791
FAX: 614-898-7786 800-551-7379
ngwa@ngwa.org www.ngwa.org

Paul C Johnson, Editor
Thad Plumley, Publications Director
Kevin McKray, Executive Director

Contains peer-reviewed papers, product and equipment news, EPA updates, industry news, and a mix of original columns authored by industry leaders. *$195.00*

Quarterly Founded: 1981
Circulation: 15201

21949 Industrial Wastewater
Water Environment Federation
601 Wythe Street
Alexandria, VA 22314-1994
703-842-2400
FAX: 703-684-2492 www.wef.org

Kelley N Lubovich, Editor

Provides the information on the practical application of science and technology in the management of water dischages, air emmissions, ground water and soil remediation to the industrial personnel, consultants and other involved in all aspects of management, treatment and disposal of industrial wastewater. *$129.00*

Bi-Monthly Founded: 1928
Circulation: 35500

21950 Journal American Water Works Association
American Water Works Association
6666 W Quincy Avenue
Denver, CO 80235
303-794-7711
FAX: 303-794-7310 800-926-7337
custsvc@awwa.org
http://www.awwa.org

Anne Serrano, Manager Editor
Monica Baruth, Editor
Sandra Lankenau, Circulation Manager
Jane Johnson, Advertising Manager
Katie McCain, President

Information and updates on the water supply business. *$185.00*

124 pages Monthly Founded: 1881
Circulation: 40000
Printed in 4 colors on glossy stock

21951 Journal of the American Water Resources Association
PO Box 1623
Middleburg, VA 20118-1626
540-687-8390
FAX: 540-687-8395 540-687-8390
info@awra.org www.awra.org

Kenneth J Lanfear, Editor
Charlene E Young, Publications Production Director
Billy Journell, Manager

Annual directory offering information on all water resources, technologies, systems and services for the water resources industry. *$205.00*

Bi-Monthly Founded: 1964

21952 Landscape & Irrigation
Adams Business Media
250 S Wacker Drive
Chicago, IL 60606
773-932-2774
FAX: 312-846-4638
http://www.adamsbusinessmedia.com

21953 National Driller
Business News Publishing Company
755 W Big Beaver Road
Suite 1000
Troy, MI 48084
248-362-3700
FAX: 248-362-0317
www.bnpmedia.com

Linda Moffat, Pubilsher
Greg Ettling, Editor
Lisa Schroeder, Managing Editor
Paulette Beall, Production Director
Dean Laramore, Advertising Sales Manager

Provides feature articles, timely and valuable industry information, newly developed products and technologies, and quality marketing and business management advice.

Monthly

21954 Operations Forum
Water Environment Federation
601 Wythe Street
Alexandria, VA 22314-1994
703-842-2400
FAX: 703-684-2492 800-666-0206
officers@wef.org http://www.wef.org

Matt Rowan, Publisher
William J Bertera, Executive Director
Lynn Orphan, President

The emphasis is on process control, plant operations, collection systems and industry news. *$4995.00*

Monthly Founded: 1928
Circulation: 17005

21955 Rural Water Magazine
National Rural Water Association
2915 S 13th Street
Duncan, OK 73533
580-252-0629
FAX: 580-255-4476
info@nrwa.org www.nrwa.org

Wendy Quarles, Editor

Targeted at the operators and board members of rural and small municipal water and wastewater utilities.

56 pages Quarterly Founded: 1979
Circulation: 22800

21956 US Water News
US Water News
230 Main Street
Halstead, KS 67056-1913
316-835-2222
FAX: 316-835-2223 800-251-0046
Inquiries@uswaternews.com
http://www.uswaternews.com

Tom Bell, President/Publisher

Reports news of current events from across the nation in themunicipal and industrial water and wastewater segments of the water industry. *$59.00*

28 pages Monthly Founded: 1984
Circulation: 20000 18,000 names $100 per M.
Printed in on n stock

21957 Water Conditioning and Purification Magazine
Publicom
2800 E Fort Lowell Road
Tucson, AZ 85716
520-323-6144
FAX: 520-323-7412
info@wcponline.com
www.wcponline.com

Kurt C Peterson, Publisher/Eastern Advertising Exec
Sharon M Peterson, President/Owner
Karen R Smith, Executive Editor
Margo Goldbaum, Circulation Services
Denise M Roberts, Assistant Editor

Comprehensive magazine for all aspects of the water quality improvement industry. Accepts advertising. *$49.00*

100 pages Founded: 1959
Circulation: 20000
Mailing list available for rent 1000 names $250 per M.
Printed in 4 colors on glossy stock

21958 Water Environment & Technology
Water Environment Federation
601 Wythe Street
Alexandria, VA 22314-1994
703-842-2400
FAX: 703-684-2492 800-666-0206
csc@wef.org www.wef.org

Melissa Jackson, Editor
Margaret Richards, Editorial Assistant
Tracy Hardwick, Publication Services Manager
Glenn Reinhardt, Foundation Executive Director

Covers a wide range of water quality and municipal wastewater treatment issues, from the design, engineering, and management of domestic wastewater treatment plants to watershed management and wet weather issues. *$178.00*

Monthly Founded: 1928
Circulation: 27304

21959 Water Environment Federation
601 Wythe Street
Alexandria, VA 22314-1994
703-842-2400
FAX: 703-684-2492 1 8-0 6-6 02
webfeedback@wef.org
http://www.wef.org

William Bertera, Executive Director
J Read, President
Mohamed Dahab, VP
Keith Radick, Plant Operations and Maintenance
David James, Publications Committee

Magazine published monthly for 41,000 members *$19.00*
Founded: 1928

21960 Water Environment Research
Water Environment Federation
601 Wythe Street
Alexandria, VA 22314-1994
703-684-2400
FAX: 703-684-2492
officers@wef.org www.wef.org

William J Bertera, Executive Director
J Michael Read, President
Tom Wolfe, Advertising
Glenn Reinhardt, Foundation Executive Director

Research journal reviewed by peers and covering the effects of water pollution and the technology and advances ued for it's control. *$158.00*
Founded: 1928
Circulation: 9000

21961 Water Resources Research
American Geophysical Union
2000 Florida Avenue NW
Washington, DC 20009-1231
202-462-6900
FAX: 202-328-0566 800-966-2481
service@kosmos.agu.org
http://www.agu.org

Scott W Tyler, Editor
Nina Cristini, Marketing Manager
Karne Blaususs, Circulation Manager
John Orcutt, President
A. F. Spilhaus Jr., Executive Director

Presents articles on the social, natural, and physical sciences, with emphasis on geochemistry, hydrology, and groundwater transfer technology. *$1200.00*
Monthly Founded: 1919
Circulation: 4700

21962 Water Technology
National Trade Publications
13 Century Hill Drive
Latham, NY 12110
518-783-1281
FAX: 518-783-1386
asavino@ntpinc.com
www.waternet.com

Humphrey S Tyler, President
Abdul Rehman, Account Executive
Mike Hilts, Publisher
Tom Williams, Senior Editor
Katie Bain, Marketing Manager

Serves the POU/POE water treatment industry. Accepts advertising. *$39.00*
48 pages Monthly Founded: 1981
Circulation: 21000
Mailing list available for rent 20000 names $125 per M.
Printed in 4 colors on glossy stock

21963 Water Well Journal
Ground Water Publishing Company
601 Dempsey Road
Westerville, OH 43081-8978
614-898-7791
FAX: 614-898-7786 800-551-7379

Thad Plumley, Publications Director/Editor
Jennifer Strawn, Associate Editor
Joanne Grant, Manager

A complete publication of the water supply industry. Covers technical issues related to drilling and pump installation, rig maintenance, business management and professional development, well rehabilitation, water treatment and more. *$95.00*
84 pages Monthly Founded: 1948

21964 WaterWorld
PennNet
1421 S Sheridan Road
Tulsa, OK 74112
918-831-9143
FAX: 918-831-9415 www.pennnet.com

James Laughlin, Editor/Associate Publisher

Gives information about products and services, technology, applications, legislation and regulations to help the water industry pros successfully plan, design, operate and maintain their systems.
Monthly Founded: 1985

21965 World Wastes: the Independent Voice
Communication Channels
6151 Powers Ferry Road NW
Atlanta, GA 30339-2959
770-953-4805
FAX: 770-618-0348

Bill Wolpin, Editor
Jerrold France, President Argus Business

Reaches individuals and firms engaged in the removal and disposal of solid wastes. *$48.00*
Monthly
Circulation: 36,000

Trade Shows

21966 American Society of Irrigation Consultants Conference
PO Box 426
Byron, CA 94514-0426
925-516-1124
FAX: 925-516-1301

Wanda M Sarsfield, Secretary

Irrigation design equipment, supplies, services and seminar.
Annual Founded: 1970

21967 American Water Resources Conference
American Water Resources Association
4 West Federal Street
PO Box 1626
Middleburg, VA 20118-1626
540-687-8390
FAX: 540-687-8395
info@awra.org www.awra.org

Terry Meyer, Marketing Coordinator
Ken Reid, Executive VP

Show of water resources science and technology.
Annual, November Founded: 1964

21968 American Water Works Association Annual Conference and Exhibition
6666 W Quincy Avenue
Denver, CO 80235
303-794-7711
FAX: 303-794-7310 800-926-7337

Kristine A Taylor, Show Manager
Jack Hoffbuhr, Chief Exceutive Officer

With more than 500 exhibitors, who are a source of knowledge and information for water professionals who work to improve the supply and quality of water in North America and beyond
12000 Attendees Annual, June Founded: 1881

21969 Chartmaker
American Recreation Coalition
1225 New York Avenue NW
Suite 450
Washington, DC 20005-6405
202-829-9530
FAX: 202-662-7424

Derrick Crandall, President

Triennial exhibits relating to the responsible use of US aquatic resources, including issues such as wetlands conservation, boating safety, sportfish research and enhancement and boating access improvements.

21970 Computers in the Water Industry: The Computer Conference
American Water Works Association
6666 W Quincy Avenue
Denver, CO 80235
303-794-7711
FAX: 303-347-0804

21971 Info Management Conference
American Water Works Association
6666 W Quincy Avenue
Denver, CO 80235
303-794-7711
FAX: 303-347-0804

21972 Irrigation Association Annual Meeting
6260 Willow Oaks Corporate Drive
#120
Fairfax, VA 22031
703-573-3551
FAX: 800-937-8477

Bob Sears, Executive VP

Four hundred and twenty five booths of the newest in irrigation equipment for the agricultural industry.
3.5M Attendees November

21973 National Ground Water Association Annual Convention and Exposition
National Ground Water Association
601 Dempsey Road
Westerville, OH 43081
614-987-7791
FAX: 614-898-7786 800-551-7379
ngwa@ngwa.org www.ngwa.org

Bob Masters, Conference Coordinator
Greg Phelps, Meeting Planner/Expositions Dir
Kevin McKray, Executive Director

Annual show of 4600 manufacturers, suppliers, distributors, consultants and scientists, and contractors/pump installers.
5,100 Attendees December

21974 National Rural Water Association
2915 S 13th Street
Duncan, OK 73533
580-252-0629
FAX: 580-255-4476
info@nrwa.org www.nrwa.org
Larissa M Wood, Publications Coordinator
100 booths; 300 exhibitors.
1.5M Attendees September

21975 National Water Resources Association Annual Conference
National Water Resources Association
3800 Fairfax Drive
Suite 4
Arlington, VA 22203
703-524-1544
FAX: 703-524-1548
nwra@nwra.org www.nwra.org
Norman Semanko, President
Thomas Donnelly, VP
Annual conference and exhibits relating to the development, control, conservation and utilization of water resources in the reclamation states.
700 Attendees November

21976 North American Lake Management Society International Symposium
North American Lake Management Society
4513 Vernon Boulevard, Suite 103
PO Box 5443
Madison, WI 53705-0443
608-233-2836
FAX: 608-233-3186
nalms@nalms.org www.nalms.org
Carol Winge, Manager
Annual symposium and exhibits related to lake ecology and management.

21977 Water Environment Federation
Water Environment Federation
601 Wythe Street
Alexandria, VA 22314-1994
703-684-2400
FAX: 703-684-2175
Bill Bertera, Executive Director
Annual show of 650 manufacturers, suppliers and distributors of water treatment equipment, supplies and services.
14M Attendees October, Chicago

21978 Water Quality Association Convention
Water Quality Association
4151 Naperville Road
Suite 100
Lisle, IL 60532-1088
630-505-0160
FAX: 630-505-9637
info@wqa.org www.wqa.org
Peter J Censky, Executive Director
Jeannine Collins, CMP, Convention/Meetings Manager
Annual convention and exhibits of water treatment equipment and related articles.
4,300 Attendees

Directories & Databases

21979 American Water Works Association: Buyers' Guide Issue
American Water Works Association
6666 W Quincy Avenue
Denver, CO 80235
303-794-7711
FAX: 303-794-7310 800-926-7337
Sandra Mandell, Editor
Jack Hoffbuhr, Chief Exceutive Officer
Member suppliers and distributors of water supply products and services, contractors for water supply projects and engineering consultants.
Annual November
Circulation: 80,000

21980 Directory of Water/Sewer and Related Industries Professionals
National Assn of Regulatory Utility Commissioners
1101 Vermont Avenue, NW
Suite 200
Washington, DC 20005
202-898-2200
FAX: 202-898-2213
admin@naruc.org www.naruc.org
Offers valuable information on over 150 consultants and other professionals active in regulated water, sewer and related industries. *$25.00*
195 pages Annual

21981 Ground Water Age: Directory of Manufacture rs
National Trade Publications
13 Century Hill Drive
Latham, NY 12110-2197
518-831-1281
FAX: 518-783-1386
Roslyn Scheib Dahl, Editor
List of over 150 companies that provide products and services to the ground water industry. *$30.00*
Annual December
Circulation: 13,448

21982 Ground Water Monitoring & Remediation: Buy ers Guide Issue
Ground Water Publishing Company
601 Dempsey Road
Westerville, OH 43081-8978
614-882-8179
FAX: 614-898-7786 800-332-2104
Paul C Johnson, Editor
Thad Plumley, Publications Director
Kevin McKray, Executive Director
List of companies that provide products used in the ground water monitoring and remediation industry. *$15.00*
Annual Founded: 1981
Circulation: 12,382

21983 Ground Water Monitoring Review: Consultant & Contract Directory
National Ground Water Association
601 Dempsey Road
Westerville, OH 43081-8978
614-898-7791
FAX: 614-898-7786 800-332-2104
Anita Stanley, Editor
Shelby Fleck, Advertising Manager
Kevin McCray, Executive Director
About 400 consultant and contracting firms engaged in ground water monitoring projects. *$200.00*
Annual
Circulation: 17,000

21984 Ground Water On-Line
National Ground Water Association
601 Dempsey Road
Westerville, OH 43081-8978
614-898-7791
FAX: 614-898-7786 800-554-7379
ngwa@ngwa.org www.ngwa.org
Kevin McCray, Executive Director
Database offers information on more than 90,000 ground water literature citations, which includes information like key words, abstracts, chemical compounds, biological factors, geographic locations, aquifer names, authors, titles, publication source names and a lot more.
Bibliographic

21985 Validated Water Treatment Equipment Directory
Water Quality Association
4151 Naperville Road
Suite 100
Lisle, IL 60532-3696
630-505-0160
FAX: 630-505-9637
Over 700 water treatment products tested by the Water Quality Association and their manufacturers are listed. *$6.00*
SemiAnnual

21986 WATERNET
American Water Works Association
6666 W Quincy Avenue
Denver, CO 80235-3098
303-794-7711
FAX: 303-794-7310
This database contains more than 23,000 citations, with abstracts, to literature on water quality, water utility management, analytical procedures fro water quality testing.
Bibliographic

21987 Water Technology: Directory of Manufacturers and Suppliers Issue
National Trade Publications
13 Century Hill Drive
Latham, NY 12110-2197
518-783-1281
FAX: 518-783-1386 www.ntpmedia.com
Mark Wilson, Editor
List of about 250 manufacturers, distributors and other suppliers of water conditioning and treatment products. *$21.00*
Annual December
Circulation: 17,213

21988 Water Treatability
National Ground Water Information Center
6375 Riverside Drive
Dublin, OH 43017-5045
614-717-2770
FAX: 614-761-3446
Offers information on treatment technologies for the removal of various containments from water supplies.
Full-text

21989 Water Well Journal: Buyer's Guide Issue
National Ground Water Association
601 Dempsey Road
Westerville, OH 43081-8978
614-898-7791
FAX: 614-898-7786 800-332-2104
Tamara Moore, Editor
Shelby Fleck, Advertising Manager

List of manufacturers, suppliers and manufacturers' representativess for equipment, machinery and other products for the water well industry. *$6.00*
Annual January
Circulation: 26,000

Industry Web Sites

21990 **www.greyhouse.com**
Grey House Publishing

Selected Grey House directories in the fields of business, health and education are available online. Users can search our online databases by several different search criteria, such as product categories, geographic area, sales volume and much, much more. Full Grey House catalog and online ordering also available.

21991 **www.gwpc.org**
Ground Water Protection Council

Provides a forum for dicussing ground water, watershed and community wallhead protection and underground injection practices. Conducts seminars and workshops on these subjects.

21992 **www.nda4u.com**
National Drilling Association

Formerly National Drilling Contractors Association; merged with Equipment Drilling Manufacturers Association and Internatioal Drilling Federation in 1995.

21993 **www.swcs.org**
Soil and Water Conservation Society

Promotes erosion control and water quality. Publishes scholarly journal and practical magazine. Conducts annual conference and trade show

21994 **www.umsu.edu/niwr/**
National Institute for Water Resources

Offers information on water resource directions across the nation.

21995 **www.wef.org**
Water Environment Federation

A not-for-profit technical and educational organization, consisting of regional association comprised of air quality professionals concerned with all types of air pollution.

21996 **www.wjta.org**
WaterJet Technology Association

Members research for new findings in waterjet technology.

21997 **www.wqa.org**
Water Quality Association

For retail/dealers and manufacturer/suppliers in the point of use/entry water quality improvement industry.

Associations

21998 American Association of Meat Processors
PO Box 269
Elizabethtown, PA 17022-0269
717-367-1168
FAX: 717-367-9096
info@aamp.com www.aamp.com
Steve Krut, Executive Director
Jay Wenther PhD, Assistant Executive Director
Membership consists of small to medium-sized meat, poultry and food businesses including slaughter, processors, wholesalers, home food service businesses, deli and catering operators and suppliers to the industry. AAMP is affliated with 34 state, regional and provincial organizations which represent meat and poultry businesses
1700 Members Founded: 1939

21999 American Machine Tool Distributors Association
1445 Research Boulevard
Suite 450
Rockville, MD 20850
301-738-1200
FAX: 301-738-9499
klaramay@amtda.org www.amtda.org
Ralph Nappi, President
Debbie Vieder, Director Education
Gary Schiffres, Director Membership
Lisa Higgins, Member Relations Coordinator
AMTDA will lead distributors of manufacturing technology by providing essential programs and services that help its members gain global recognition from customers and suppliers as the preferred channel of distribution.
300 Members Founded: 1925

22000 American Nursery & Landscape Association
1000 Vermont Avenue NW
Suite 300
Washington, DC 20005-4914
202-789-2900
FAX: 202-789-1893 www.anla.org
The American Nursery and Landscape Association serves firms who grow, sell or use plants. ANLA advocates the industry's interests before government and provides its members with unique business knowledge essential to long-term growth and profitability.
2200 Members Founded: 1876

22001 American Wholesale Marketers Association
2750 Prosperity Avenue
Suite 530
Fairfax, VA 22031

FAX: 703-573-5738 800-482-2962
info@awmanet.org www.awmanet.org
Scott Ramminger, President
Anne Holloway, Director Government Affairs
Robert Pignato, VP Marketing/Industry Affairs
Jill Kosko, Director Research
Jennifer Moulton, Manager Administration
An organization supporting the confectionery, tobacco and allied products industries through programs and services.
1000 Members Founded: 1942

22002 Automotive Service Industry Association
4600 E West Highway
Suite 300
Bethesda, MD 20004
301-654-6664
FAX: 301-654-3299
aaia@aftermarket.org
www.aftermarket.org
Kathleen Schmatz, President/CEO
Al Gasper, President Emeritus
Association members are involved in the motor vehicle replacement parts industry.
4400 Members Founded: 1959

22003 Copper and Brass Servicenter Association
994 Old Eagle School Road
Suite 1019
Wayne, PA 19087
610-971-4850
FAX: 610-971-4859
info@cbsa.copper-brass.org
www.cbsa.copper-brass.org
Franklin Brown, Executive VP
Diana Lubragge, Executive Assistant
Distributors (servicenters) of fabricated copper and copper alloy products (sheet, plate, coil, rod, bar tube, etc) and their brass mill suppliers.
78 Members Founded: 1951

22004 Farm Equipment Wholesalers Association
611 Southgate Avenue, Suite A
PO Box 1347
Iowa City, IA 52244-1347
319-354-5156
FAX: 319-354-5157
info@fewa.org www.fewa.org
Brad Stout, President
Chris Ford, First VP
Patricia Collins, VP
International trade association of wholesale/distributors of agricultural equipment and related products.
190 Members Founded: 1945

22005 Financial & Security Products Association
Plaza Ladera, 5300 Sequoia NW
Suite 205
Albuquerque, NM 87120
505-839-7958
FAX: 505-839-0017 800-843-6082
nibesa@nibesa.com www.nibesa.com
Tom Sands, President
Pat Hughes, VP
Association of financial security equipment nationwide. Annual convention and showcase and monthly newsletter.
244 Members Founded: 1973

22006 Fliud Power Distributors Association
PO Box 1420
Cherry Hill, NJ 08034-54
856-424-8988
FAX: 856-424-9248
info@fpda.org www.fpda.org
Paul Prass, Managing Director
Kathy DeMarco, Executive Director
Donna Pollander, Director Operations
Membership is composed of distributors and manufacturers of hydraulic and pneumatic equipment.
475 Members Founded: 1974

22007 Food Industry Suppliers Association
1207 Sunset Drive
Greensboro, NC 27408-7215
336-274-6311
FAX: 336-691-1839
stella@fisanet.org/ www.fisanet.org/
Jeffrey Hennessey, President
Stella Jones, Executive Director
Member's are distributors and suppliers to the food processing industry.
245 Members Founded: 1968

22008 Foodservice Equipment Distributors Association
2250 Point Blvd
Ste 200
Elgin, IL 60123-7887
224-293-6500
FAX: 224-293-6505
feda@feda.com www.feda.com
Raymond Herrick, Executive Director
Bruce Gulbas, VP
Jim Hanson, Treasurer
Marc Fuchs, Chairman
Kimberley Gill-Rimsza, Secretary
Dealers and distributors of foodservice equipment and supplies.
300 Members Founded: 1933

22009 International Foodservice Distributors Association
201 Park Washington Court
Falls Church, VA 22046-4519
703-532-9400

sbarrett@ifdaonline.org
www.ifdaonline.org
Mark S Allen, President/CEO
J Michael Roach, Chairman
Provides educational, research and governmental services to wholesale grocers servicing independent retail grocers and foodservice distributors.
135 Members Founded: 2003

22010 International Sanitary Supply Association
7373 N Lincoln Avenue
Lincolnwood, IL 60712-1799
847-821-1012
FAX: 847-982-1012 800-225-4772
info@issa.com www.issa.com
Mattie Chinks, President
Bobby Cohens, VP
John Garfinkel, Executive Director
Manufacturers, distributors, wholesalers, representatives and publishers engaged in the manufacture and/or distribution of cleaning and maintenance products.
4700 Members Founded: 1923

22011 Jewelry Industry Distributors Association
701 Enterprise Drive
Harrison, OH 45030
513-367-2357
FAX: 513-367-1414
info@jida.info www.jida.info
Larry Goldberg, President
Bill Nagle, First VP
Harvey Cobrin, Second VP
Sallie Goldwyn, Director
A list of over 130 member firms and their suppliers.
Founded: 1946

22012 Metals Service Center Institute
4201 Euclid Avenue
Rolling Meadows, IL 60008
847-485-3000
FAX: 847-485-3001
info@msci.org www.msci.org/

Bob Weidner, President
Jonathan Kalkwarf, VP Finance & Administration

MSCI is a trade association that supports and represents the elements of the metals value chain, including metals producers, distributors and processors.
350 Members Founded: 1907

22013 Music Distributors Association
13610 92nd Street
Alto, MI 49302
616-765-9912
FAX: 616-765-3479
gplummer@iserv.net
www.musicdistributors.org

Glenda Plummer, Executive Director

International, nonprofit trade association representing and serving manufacturers, wholesalers, importers and exporters of musical instruments and accessories, sound reinforcement products and published music.
250 Members Founded: 1939

22014 National Association of Sporting Goods Wholesalers
PO Box 881525
Port St Lucie, FL 34988-1525
772-621-7162
FAX: 772-264-3233
wsmith@nasgw.org www.nasgw.org

Wayne Smith, President
Richard Lipsey, Chairman

Compiles data on business operations.
325 Members Founded: 1954

22015 National Beer Wholesalers Association
1101 King Street
Alexandria, VA 22314-2944
703-390-0591
FAX: 703-683-8965
info@nbwa.org www.nbwa.org

David K Rehr, President
Craig Purser, VP
Laurie Knight, Director Government Affairs
Susan Hilaski, Manager Technology

Trade association for beer wholesalers. Provides government and public affairs outreach as well as education and training for its wholesaler members.
2200 Members Founded: 1938

22016 National Electronics Service Dealers
3608 Pershing Avenue
Fort Worth, TX 76107-4527
817-921-9061
FAX: 817-921-3741 800-797-9197
webmaster@nesda.com
www.nesda.com

Brian Gibson, President
Don Cressin, VP

Provides educational assistance in electronic training to public schools, compiles statistics, offers certification programs and apprenticeships. Functions as trade association for the electronics service industry.

22017 National Fastener Distributors Association
401 N Michigan Avenue
Suite 2200
Chicago, IL 60611
312-527-6671
FAX: 312-673-6740
nfda@nfda-fastener.org
www.nfda-fastener.org

Bryn Tuttle-Stock, President
Joel Roseman, VP

Develops new uses for fasteners, offers training and educational programs.
250 Members Founded: 1968

22018 National Frozen & Refrigerated Foods Association
4755 Linglestown Road
Suite 300
Harrisburg, PA 17112-8526
717-657-8601
FAX: 717-657-9862
info@nfraweb.org www.nfraweb.org

Nevin Montgomery, President/CEO
H V Skip Shaw, Jr, Executive VP/COO

NFRA is a non-profit trade association representing all segments of the frozen and refrigerated foods industry. Headquartered in Harrisburg, PA, NFRA is also the sponsor of March National Frozen Food Month, June Dairy Month and October Frozen & Refrigerated Foods Festival.
450 Members Founded: 1945

22019 National Kitchen and Bath Association
687 Willow Grove Street
Hackettstown, NJ 07840
908-520-0033
FAX: 908-852-1695
feedback@nkba.org www.nkba.org

Larry Spangler, Chief Executive Director
Lili Corman, Director Professional Programs
Jill Levy, Director Membership
Bill Schankel, Director Marketing
Harry Smith, Director Finance

Protects the interests of members by fostering a better business climate. Awards certification. Conducts training schools and seminars.
25000 Members Founded: 1963

22020 National Poultry and Food Distributors Association
958 McEver Road Ext
Unit B-8
Gainesville, GA 30504
770-535-9901
FAX: 770-535-7385 877-845-1545
info@npfda.org www.npfda.org

Keith Mennella, President
CC Hill, VP
Kristin McWhorter, Executive Director

A nationwide association that serves the needs of the poultry and food distribution and processing industries. Provides member services, cost cutting benefits and networking opportunities. Sponsors Poultry Suppliers Showcase every January in Atlanta.
220 Members Founded: 1967

22021 North American Meat Processors Association
1910 Association Drive
Reston, VA 20191-1545
703-758-1900
FAX: 703-758-8001 800-368-3043
info@namp.com www.namp.com

Joseph A Miller, Executive VP
Sabrina Moore, Accounting/Meetings Manager
Ann Rasor, Director Scientific Affairs
Jane Jacobs, Communications Director

Represents processors and distributors of meat, poultry, seafood and game to the food-service industry.
400 Members Founded: 1942

22022 North American Wholesale Lumber Association
3601 Algonquin Road
Suite 400
Rolling Meadows, IL 60008-3144
847-870-7470
FAX: 847-870-0201 800-527-8258
nawla@lumber.org www.lumber.org

Nicholas Kent, President/CEO
Ben Stephens, Director/Information
Pam Baker, Meetings Director
Shannon Sabres, Manager Membership/Communication

Not-for-profit trade association founded in 1893 dedicated to serving the unique needs of lumber and building distributors and manufacturers. NAWLA provides numerous networking events and educational programs, including the highly successful annual Traders Market. Membership dues based on annual sales revenue.
630 Members Founded: 1893

22023 Optical Laboratories Association
11096-B Lee Highway
Suite 102
Fairfax, VA 22030-5014
703-359-2830
FAX: 703-359-2834 800-477-5652
ola@ola-labs.org www.ola-labs.org

Bob Dziuban, Executive Director

Independent ophthalmic laboratories and supply houses that manufacture prescription eye glasses.
337 Members Founded: 1894

22024 Outdoor Power Equipment Aftermarket Association
1726 M Street NW
Suite 1101
Washington, DC 20036-4502
202-528-8278
FAX: 202-833-1577
opeaa@opeaa.org www.opeaa.org

Jack Woodruff, President
William S Bergman, Executive VP
Bob Titterington, VP
Laura James, Director/Membership Services
Linda Brownlee, Executive Director

Businessmen dedicated to promoting the use of aftermarket parts in outdoor power equipment, as well as trade in the industry.
85 Members Founded: 1986

22025 Pet Industry Distributors Association
2105 Laurel Bush Road
Suite 200
Bel Air, MD 21015
443-640-1060
FAX: 443-640-1031
pida@ksgroup.org www.pida.org

Blaine Phillips, President
Donald Fleming, First VP
Robert Merar, Second VP
Roger Johannigman, Secretary/Treasurer
George Baker, Director

Represents wholesaler-distributors of pet products, providing training and education to members.

190 Members Founded: 1968

22026 Petroleum Equipment Institute
PO Box 2380
Tulsa, OK 74101-2380
918-494-9696
FAX: 918-491-9895
info@pei.org www.pei.org
Robert N Renkes, Executive VP
Carletta Denison, Membership Coordinator
Sondra Sutton, Accounting
Members are makers and distributors of equipment used in service stations, bulk plants and other petroleum marketing facilities.
1600+ Members Founded: 1951
Mailing list available for rent 1600 names $275 per M.

22027 Petroleum Equipment Suppliers Association
9225 Katy Freeway
Suite 310
Houston, TX 77024-1510
713-932-0168
FAX: 713-932-0497
Sherry A Stephens, President
Galen Cobb, VP
Members are makers of oil field production and drilling equipment, well site services and supplies.
200 Members Founded: 1933

22028 Post Card & Souvenir Distributors Association
2105 Laurel Bush Road
Suite 200
Bel Air, MD 21015
443-640-1055
FAX: 443-640-1031
steve@ksgroup.org
www.postcardcentral.org/
Companies distributing local view scenic post cards and souvenirs in North America and the Caribbean.
110 Members Founded: 1973

22029 Power Transmission Distributors Association
250 South Wacker Drive
Suite 300
Chicago, IL 60606-5840
312-876-9461
FAX: 312-876-9490
ptda@ptda.org www.ptda.org
John R Neal, President
Mary Sue Lyon, Executive VP
Stephanie A Kaplan, Director Marketing
Beth Silas, Manager Meetings/Finance
Members are power transmission/motion control distributors throughout manufacturing firms.
485 Members Founded: 1960

22030 Quality Bakers of America Cooperative
1055 Parsippany Boulevard
Suite 201
Parsippany, NJ 07054
973-263-6970
FAX: 973-263-0937
info@qba.com www.qba.com
Norman Trapp, Executive VP
Members are independent wholesale bakeries and their suppliers.
35 Members Founded: 1922

22031 Safety Equipment Distributors Association
2105 Laurel Bush Road
Bel Air, MD 21015
443-640-1065
FAX: 443-640-1031
jackie@ksgroup.org
www.safetycentral.org
Richard Rivkin, President
Heidi Levitt, First VP
Larry Loizzo, Second VP
Steve King, Executive Director
Jackie King, Meetings/Member Services
Trade association comprised of companies that distribute safety equipment & related products and services.
300 Members Founded: 1968

22032 The NPTA Alliance
NPTA Alliance 500 Bi-County Boulevard
Suite 200E
Farmingdale, NY 11735
631-777-2223
FAX: 631-777-2224 800-355-6782
webmaster@gonpta.com
www.gonpta.com
William Frohlich, President
Michael E Keneally, Chairman
Gerrie J D'Aversa, Membership Coordinator
Wholesale distributors of printing and industrial paper.
2000 Members Founded: 1903

22033 United Product Formulators and Distributor
2034 Beaver Ruin Road
Norcross, GA 30071-3380
770-417-1418
FAX: 770-417-1419
Valera B Jessee, Executive Director
Members are firms which are directly involved in formulating and distributing products or equipment to the pest control industry.

22034 Wine/Spirits Wholesalers of America
805 15th Street NW
Suite 430
Washington, DC 20005
202-371-9792
FAX: 202-789-2405
Juanita Duggan, President/CEO
Johnny Aaron, Senior VP
Two hundred booths for suppliers of alcoholic beverages from around the world.
3M Members

Newsletters

22035 Creative Marketing Newsletter
Association of Retail Marketing Services
10 DRS james parker BLVD
suite 103
Red Bank, NJ 07701-2003
732-842-5070
FAX: 732-219-1938
info@goarms.com
http://www.goarms.com
Gerri Hopkins, Executive Director
Lisa McCauley, Administrative Director
Retail promotion marketing newsletter for supermarkets, convenience stores, drug chains and suppliers of retail promotions.
Quarterly Founded: 1957
Printed in 3 colors on matte stock

22036 Cutting Edge
Outdoor Power Equipment Aftermarket
1726 M Street NW
Washington, DC 20036-4502
202-775-8605
FAX: 202-833-1577
wsb@opeaa.org www.opeaa.org
William S Bergman, Executive VP
Jack Woodruff, President
Businessmen dedicated to promoting the use of aftermarket parts in outdoor power equipment, as well as trade in the industry.
$ 25.00
Quarterly Founded: 1986

22037 Emerging Business
Master Security Company
PO Box 6661
Roanoke, VA 24017-0661

FAX: 540-982-8407
Debra Napier, Publisher
Provides summary on articles of interest to small business owners, consultants corner, highlights services available pertaining to alternative financing of growing businesses.
6 pages Quarterly

22038 Insider
MacLean Hunter
4 Stamford Forum
Stamford, CT 06901-3253

FAX: 203-325-8423
Vanessa Grey, Publisher
Adrienne Toth, Editor
A shopping center industry newsweekly. Each issue contains critical information concerning retailer news, new development items, agent announcements and new tenant listings. *$250.00*
6 pages Monthly

22039 M&E Appraiser
American Society of Appraisers
555 Herndon Parkway
Sutie 125
Herndon, VA 20170-5248
703-782-2228
FAX: 703-742-8471 800-272-8258
asainfo@apo.com
http://www.appraisers.org
Jerry F Larkins, Executive Vice President
Jackie Montalvo, Editor
J Michael Clarkson, Publisher
Machinery and equipment appraisal information. Accepts advertising. *$45.00*
48 pages Quarterly Founded: 1936

22040 NAW Report
National Association of Wholesalers & Distributors
1725 K Street NW
Washington, DC 20006-1401
202-872-0885

Phillip Jaffa, Publisher
Peter Cook, Executive Director
Dirk VanDongen, Contact
Information on regulation, industry research and programs for distributors and wholesalers.

22041 NSPI News
National Spa and Pool Institute
2111 Eisenhower Avenue
Alexandria, VA 22314
703-838-0083
FAX: 703-549-0493 800-323-3996
MemberServices@TheAPSP.org
http://www.theapsp.org
Barbara Brady, Editor
Jack Cregol, CEO

22042 National Wholesaler Association
251 W Renner Road
#102
Richardson, TX 75080-1318

FAX: 972-470-0134
Don Akerman, Publisher
Offers products, new or old, marketing, distribution expertise, customer analysis, positioning, advertising, promotion planning. Accepts advertising.
Quarterly

22043 North American Wholesale Lumber Association Bulletin
North American Wholesale Lumber Association
3601 Algonquin Road
Suite 400
Rolling Meadows, IL 60008-3144
847-870-7470
FAX: 847-870-0201 800-527-8258
info@lumber.org
http://www.nawla.org
Nicholas R. Kent, President/CEO, Editor
Newsletter published by North American Wholesale Lumber Association.
Monthly Founded: 1892

22044 Petroleum Equipment Suppliers Association
9225 Katy Freeway
Suite 310
Houston, TX 77024-1586
713-932-0168
FAX: 713-932-0497
Sherry A Stephens, President
Oil field production and drilling equipment, well site services and supplies.
8-12 pages 8 per year
Circulation: 1,000
Printed in on glossy stock

22045 Winning in Washington-NAW Annual Report
National Association of Wholesalers & Distributors
1725 K Street NW
Washington, DC 20006-1401
202-872-0885

Philip Jaffa, Publisher
Activities of the National Association of Wholesalers and Distributors.

Magazines & Journals

22046 AFI
AFI Communications
2455 E Sunrise Boulevard
Suite 916
Fort Lauderdale, FL 33304-3112

FAX: 954-561-4129
Andrew Molchan, President
Bob Lesmeister, Managing Editor
Edited for professional firearm retailers. Editorial emphasis is on new products, new industry and new sales programs for distributors and retailers. Also covers management level trends for manufacturers and wholesalers. Other features include New Products, Archery, Andy's Industry Insights and more.

Circulation: 23,930

22047 American Wholesale Marketers Association
2750 Prosperity Avenue
Suite 530
Fairfax, VA 22031
703-208-3358
FAX: 703-208-5738 800-482-2962
robertp@awmanet.org
http://www.awmanet.org
Robert Pignato, VP Marketing
Traci Carneal, Editor-in-Chief
Joan Fay, Associate Publisher
Scott Ramminger, CEO/President
Information on candy, chewing gum, tobacco, HBC, general merchandise, snack foods and related items.

Printed in 4 colors on glossy stock

22048 Beer Perspectives
National Beer Wholesalers Association
1101 King Street
Suite 600
Alexandria, VA 22314-2944
703-390-0591
FAX: 703-683-8965
info@nbwa.org http://www.nbwa.org
David Rehr, President
Michelle Semones, Public Affairs Director
Trade association for beer wholesalers. Provides government and public affairs outreach as well as education and training for its wholesaler members.
2200 pages Founded: 1938

22049 Convenience Store News
BMT Commodity Corporation
530 5th Avenue
24th Floor
New York, NY 10036-5101
212-302-4200
FAX: 212-302-0007
info@BMTNY.com
http://www.bmtny.com/
Maureen Azzalo, Editor
A trade magazine offering information on convenience store marketing. *$60.00*
Monthly Founded: 1922

22050 Distributor's Link
4297 Corporate Square
Naples, FL 34104
239-643-2713
FAX: 239-643-5220 800-356-1639
leojcoar@linkmagazine.com
http://www.linkmagazine.com
Leo J Coar, Publisher/Editor
Maryann Marzocchi, VP
Tracey Lumia, Advertising Sales
Greg Brown, President/CEO
Michael T Wrenn, Marketing Manager
Information aimed at the fastener distributors nationwide. *$45.00*
300 pages Quarterly Founded: 1975
Circulation: 50000

22051 Employment Guide
Bureau of National Affairs
1231 25th Street NW
Washington, DC 20037-1197
202-452-4200
800-372-1033
customercare@bna.com
http://www.bna.com
Gregory C McCaffery, Publisher
Gail Moorstein, Managing Editor
An easy-to-read, practical reference guide to a broad range of employment topics, designed for the small to medium sized organization. *$745.00*
Founded: 1929

22052 Licensing Book
Adventure Publishing Group
1107 Broadway
Suite 1204
New York, NY 10010-1512
212-575-4510
FAX: 212-575-4521
akinner@licensingbook.com
http://www.adventurepub.com
Judy Basis, Publisher
Mathew C Scheiner, Editor-in-Chief
Owen Shorts, Owner
Licensing in successful retailing, licensed product merchandising in various aspects. *$48.00*
40 pages Monthly Founded: 1983

22053 Licensing International
WFC
3000 Hadley Road
South Plainfield, NJ 07080-1183
908-684-4747
FAX: 732-769-1711
info@wfcinc.com www.wfcinc.com
Howard Wainer, Publisher
Kimberly Calabrese, Production Manager

Business merchandising magazine serving the licensing industry at all levels. Publishes whole foods magazine. *$70.00*
64 pages Monthly
Circulation: 14,933

22054 Material Handling Wholesaler
Specialty Publications International
801 Bluff Street
PO Box 725
Dubuque, IA 52004-725
563-557-4495
FAX: 563-557-4499 877-638-6190
circulation@mhwmag.com
http://www.mhwmag.com
Dean Millius, General Manager
Cathy Murphy, Editor
Sharon Dague, Account Executive
Cathy Murphy, Contributing Editor
Published for used and new material handling equipment dealers, parts suppliers, manufacturers reps, repair shops, and brokers includes articles on issues, conventions, products and people that impact the industry. *$31.00*
Monthly Founded: 1979
Circulation: 27000
Printed in 4 colors on newsprint stock

22055 NSPI Business Owners Journal
National Spa and Pool Institute
2111 Eisenhower Avenue
Alexandria, VA 22314-4679
703-838-0083
FAX: 703-549-0493 800-323-3996
ksuzuki@nspi.org www.nspi.org
Ken Suzuki, Editor

A resource service offered by the national spa and pool inst. published four times a year. Contains concise, pertinent and useful information of critical importance to business owners.throughout the year, this journal delivers information that is easily applied to a business, including more than 100 action alerts and ideas,and 25 to 30 how-to articles, advisories and reports. Covers such topics as ways to cash flows; ways to save and defer taxes; how to sell and buy a business.

Founded: 1956

22056 New Equipment Digest
Penton Media
1300 East 9th Street
Cleveland, OH 44114
216-696-7000
FAX: 216-696-1752
information@penton.com
http://www.newequipment.com

John DiPaola, VP
Dave Madonia, Associate Publisher/eMedia General
Robert F King, Editor
Garnetta Russell, Ad Services Manager
Bobbie Macy, Circulation Manager

Serves the general industrial field which includes manufacturing, processing, engineering services, construction, transportation, mining, public utilities, wholesale distributors, educational services, libraries and governmental establishments.

Monthly Founded: 1936
Circulation: 206164

22057 Plumbing Engineer
TMB Publishing
1838 Techny Court
Northbrook, IL 60062-5474
847-564-1127
FAX: 847-564-1264
tmbpubs@earthlink.net
http://www.plumbingengineer.com

Mark Bruno, Chief Editor
Cate Brown, Production Manager
Tom M Brown, Jr, Publisher

Over 400 plumbing products from approximately 250 manufacturers.

Monthly Founded: 1973
Circulation: 26104 5000 names
Printed in 4 colors

22058 Supply House Times
Reed Business Information
1050 IL Route 83
Suite 200
Bensenville, IL 60106
630-616-0200
FAX: 630-288-8686 800-323-4958
leniusp@bnpmedia.com
http://www.supplyht.com

Patricia Lenius, Managing Editor
Scott Franz, Publisher
Kevin Hackney, Marketing Coordinator
Ashley Anderson, Associate Editor
George Zebrowski, Group Publisher

For plumbing, heating, air conditioning and piping wholesalers *$92.00*

62 pages Monthly Founded: 1958
Printed in 4 colors on glossy stock

Trade Shows

22059 AWMA Real Deal Expo
American Wholesale Marketers Association
2750 Prosperity Avenue
Suite 530
Fairfax, VA 22031
703-208-3358
FAX: 703-573-5738 800-482-2962
info@awmanet.org
www.realdealexpo.com

Scott Ramminger, President/CEO
Robert Pignato, VP Marketing/Industry Affairs

Annual show of 4500 manufacturers and suppliers of confectionery, tobacco, snack foods, juice, novelties and technology and allieds to the industry.

March

22060 American Nursery & Landscape Association Convention
American Nursery & Landscape Association
1000 Vermont Avenue NW
Suite 300
Washington, DC 20005-3922
202-789-2900
FAX: 202-789-1893 www.anla.org

Peter Orum, President
Robert J Dolibois, Executive Director

Serves firms who grow, sell or use plants. ANLA advocates the industry's interests before government and provides its members with unique business knowledge essential to long-term growth and profitability.

July

22061 FEWA's Industry Showcase
Farm Equipment Wholesalers Association
PO Box 1347
Iowa City, IA 52244
319-354-5156
FAX: 319-354-5157
info@fewa.org www.fewa.org

Patricia A Collins, Executive VP
Jane Hotz, Office Manager

Annual convention and 130 exhibits of equipment, supplies and services for independent wholesalers of shortline and specialty farm equipment, light industrial tractors, lawn and garden tractors, turf care equipment, estate and park maintenance equipment and power vehicles for outdoor recreation and sports.

800 Attendees November

22062 International Pool & Spa Expo
National Spa and Pool Institute
2111 Eisenhower Avenue
Alexandria, VA 22314
703-838-0083
FAX: 703-549-0493
jcergol@nspi.org
wwww.poolandspaexpo.com

Rick McConnel, Senior Show Director
Donna Bellatone, Senior Show Manager

The International Pool & Spa Expo is a trade show for the pool, spa and backyard living industry that provides current market updates, info on cutting edge technology and trends.

15M Attendees November

22063 NARM Annual Convention
National Association of Recording Merchandisers
9 Eves Drive
Suite 120
Marlton, NJ 08053-3138
856-596-2221
FAX: 856-596-3268
still@narm.com www.narm.com

Linda M Still, Director Meetings/Conventions
James Donio, President

Containing 39 booths. Featuring AFIM.

2,100 Attendees March

22064 Pet Exposition Trade Show
Pet Industry Distributors Association
2105 Laurel Bush Road
Suite 200
Bel Air, MC 21015
443-640-1060
FAX: 443-640-1031
pida@ksgroup.org www.pida.com

Blaine Phillips, President
Donald Fleming, VP

Containing 500 booths and 300 exhibits.

3,000 Attendees March Founded: 1968

22065 Post Card & Souvenir Distributors Assocation Trade Show
Post Card & Souvenir Distributors Association
2105 Laurel Bush Road
Suite 200
Bel Air, MD 21015
443-640-1055
FAX: 443-640-1031
marci@ksgroup.org
www.postcardcentral.org

Maria Linton, Manager

Containing 110 booths and 80 exhibits.

175 Attendees September Founded: 1973

22066 Read Deal Expo Convention
American Wholesale Marketers Association
1128 16th Street NW
Washington, DC 20036-4808
202-463-2124
FAX: 202-467-0559 800-482-2962
robertp@awmanet.org
www.awmanet.org

Robert Pignato, VP Marketing/Industry Affairs

The AWMA Real Deal Expo and Convention is the country's oldest and largest show for distributors of confections, snacks and convenience products. The AWMA is the only national trade association working on behalf of the convenience products distribution market. AWMA members also include companies and individuals from across the distribution channel, retailers, brokers, manufacturers and others allied to the industry.

February

Directories & Databases

22067 A-Z Wholesale Source Directory
Sutton Family Communications & Publishing Company
155 Sutton Lane
Fordsville, KY 42343
270-740-0870

jlsutton@apex.net
www.fleamarketeer.net

Theresa Sutton, Editor
Lee Sutton, General Manager

Print-out from database of wholesalers, manufacturers, distributors, importers and close-out houses. Database is updated daily to guarantee the most current and up-to-date sources available. *$550.00*

1M pages

22068 American Warehouse Association and Canadian Association of Warehousing

Association For Logistics Outsourcing
2800 South River Road
Suite 260
Chicago, IL 60018-6003
847-813-4699
FAX: 847-813-0115
email@iwla.com www.iwla.com

Joel Hioland, President
Alex Glan, VP/CEO

Nearly 700 warehouse firms with over 2,000 locations specializing in storage, distribution, and third party logistics.

22069 American Wholesalers and Distributors Directory

Gale Research
27500 Drake Road
Farmington Hills, MI 48331
248-699-4253
FAX: 248-699-8214 800-877-4253
galeord@gale.com www.gale.com

Over 25,000 wholesalers and distributors of consumer products in the US are profiled. *$290.00*

1,715 pages Annual

22070 Complete Directory of Close-outs and Super-buys

Sutton Family Communications & Publishing Company
155 Sutton Lane
Fordsville, KY 42343
270-740-0870

jlsutton@apex.net
www.fleamarketeer.net

Theresa Sutton, Editor
Lee Sutton, General Manager

Print-out from database of wholesalers, manufacturers, distributors, importers and close-out houses. Database is updated daily to guarantee the most current and up-to-date sources available. *$67.50*

100+ pages

22071 Complete Directory of General Flea Market Merchandise

Sutton Family Communications & Publishing Company
155 Sutton Lane
Fordsville, KY 42343
270-740-0870

jlsutton@apex.net
www.fleamarketeer.net

Theresa Sutton, Editor
Lee Sutton, General Manager

Print-out from database of wholesalers, manufacturers, distributors, importers and close-out houses. Database is updated daily to guarantee the most current and up-to-date sources available. *$289.00*

100+ pages

22072 Complete Directory of High Profit Items

Sutton Family Communications & Publishing Company
155 Sutton Lane
Fordsville, KY 42343
270-740-0870

jlsutton@apex.net
www.fleamarketeer.net

Theresa Sutton, Editor
Lee Sutton, General Manager

Print-out from database of wholesalers, manufacturers, distributors, importers and close-out houses. Database is updated daily to guarantee the most current and up-to-date sources available. *$189.00*

100+ pages

22073 Complete Directory of Importers

Sutton Family Communications & Publishing Company
155 Sutton Lane
Fordsville, KY 42343
270-740-0870

jlsutton@apex.net
www.fleamarketeer.net

Theresa Sutton, Editor
Lee Sutton, General Manager

Print-out from database of wholesalers, manufacturers, distributors, importers and close-out houses. Database is updated daily to guarantee the most current and up-to-date sources available. *$109.00*

100+ pages

22074 Complete Directory of Low-Price Merchandise

Sutton Family Communications & Publishing Company
155 Sutton Lane
Fordsville, KY 42343
270-740-0870

jlsutton@apex.net
www.fleamarketeer.net

Theresa Sutton, Editor
Lee Sutton, General Manager

Print-out from database of wholesalers, manufacturers, distributors, importers and close-out houses. Database is updated daily to guarantee the most current and up-to-date sources available. *$72.20*

100+ pages

22075 Complete Directory of Promotional Products

Sutton Family Communications & Publishing Company
155 Sutton Lane
Fordsville, KY 42343
270-740-0870

jlsutton@apex.net
www.fleamarketeer.net

Theresa Sutton, Editor
Lee Sutton, General Manager

Print-out from database of wholesalers, manufacturers, distributors, importers and close-out houses. Database is updated daily to guarantee the most current and up-to-date sources available. *$139.00*

100+ pages

22076 Complete Directory of Stationery Items

Sutton Family Communications & Publishing Company
155 Sutton Lane
Fordsville, KY 42343
270-740-0870

jlsutton@apex.net
www.fleamarketeer.net

Theresa Sutton, Editor
Lee Sutton, General Manager

Print-out from database of wholesalers, manufacturers, distributors, importers and close-out houses. Database is updated daily to guarantee the most current and up-to-date sources available. *$55.20*

100+ pages

22077 Complete Directory of Tabletop Items

Sutton Family Communications & Publishing Company
155 Sutton Lane
Fordsville, KY 42343
270-740-0870

jlsutton@apex.net
www.fleamarketeer.net

Theresa Sutton, Editor
Lee Sutton, General Manager

Print-out from database of wholesalers, manufacturers, distributors, importers and close-out houses. Database is updated daily to guarantee the most current and up-to-date sources available. *$55.20*

100+ pages

22078 Complete Directory of Unusual Items & Fads

Sutton Family Communications & Publishing Company
155 Sutton Lane
Fordsville, KY 42343
270-740-0870

jlsutton@apex.net
www.fleamarketeer.net

Theresa Sutton, Editor
Lee Sutton, General Manager

Print-out from database of wholesalers, manufacturers, distributors, importers and close-out houses. Database is updated daily to guarantee the most current and up-to-date sources available. *$139.00*

100+ pages

22079 Complete Directory of Wholesale Bargains

Sutton Family Communications & Publishing Company
155 Sutton Lane
Fordsville, KY 42343
270-740-0870

jlsutton@apex.net
www.fleamarketeer.net

Theresa Sutton, Editor
Lee Sutton, General Manager

Print-out from database of wholesalers, manufacturers, distributors, importers and close-out houses. Database is updated daily to guarantee the most current and up-to-date sources available. *$92.70*

100+ pages

22080 FEWA Membership Directory
Farm Equipment Wholesalers Association
611 Southgate Avenue, Suite A
PO Box 1347
Iowa City, IA 52244-1347
319-354-5156
FAX: 319-354-5157
info@fewa.org www.fewa.org
Patricia A Collins, Executive VP/Editor
Jane Hotz, Editorial Assistant
Annual directory of FEWA members, includes address, phone, fax, web, e-mail, territory covered (with map) product descriptions, key personnel descriptive paragraph. *$50.00*

22081 Food & Beverage Market Place
Grey House Publishing
185 Millerton Road
PO Box 860
Millerton, NY 12546
518-890-0526
FAX: 518-789-0545 800-562-2139
books@greyhouse.com
www.foodmp.com
Leslie Mackenzie, Publisher
Richard Gottlieb, Editor
This information packed three-volume set is the most powerful buying and marketing guide for the US food and beverage industry. Includes thousands of industry and transportation listings. *$595.00*
6500 pages Annual

22082 Global Logistics & Supply Chain Strategies
Keller International Publishing Corporation
150 Great Neck Road
Great Neck, NY 11021
516-299-9722
FAX: 516-829-5414
jmurph@starpower.net www.glscs.com
Jerry Keller, President
Brad Berger, Group President/Publisher
Russell Goodman, Editor-in-Chief
Serves manufacturing, wholesale/retail trade, third party logistics, freight fowarding and transportation/warehousing firms. *$ 55.00*
96 pages 11 per year Founded: 1997
Circulation: 40M
Printed in 4 colors on glossy stock

22083 Membership Directory/Buyer's Guide
Naylor Publications
5950 NW 1st Place
Gainesville, FL 32607-3138
352-321-1252
FAX: 352-331-3525 800-369-6220
chodges@naylor.com
www.naylor.com
Jim Donio, Editorr
Provider of integrated communications and image-building solutions for associations.
Circulation: 1,200

22084 Outlet Project Directory
Off-Price Specialists, Value Retail News
29399 US Highway 19 North
Suite 370
Clearwater, FL 33761-2137
727-781-7557
FAX: 727-781-9717
vrn@icsc.org
www.valueretailnews.com/
Linda Humphers, Editor-In-Chief
Tom Kirwan, Senior Editor
Offers valuable information on factory outlet projects. *$225.00*
200 pages Semiannual

22085 Plumbing Engineer: Product Directory Issue
TMB Publishing
1838 Techny Ct
Northbrook, IL 60062-5474
847-564-1127
FAX: 847-564-1264
tmbpubs@earthlink.net
www.plumbingengineer.com
Tom M Brown, Publisher
Cate Brown, Production Manager
Over 400 plumbing products from approximately 250 manufacturers.
Annual January ISSN 0192-1711
Circulation: 2,6104

22086 Processors and Wholesale Dealers of Fishery Products in the US
US National Marine Fisheries Service
1315 East West Highway
9th Floor
Silver Spring, MD 20910
301-134-4000
FAX: 301-713-4137
nmfs.webmaster@noaa.gov
www.nmfs.noaa.gov/
William T Hogarth, Director
Rebecca Lent, Deputy Assistant Administrator
Offers information on over 4,000 producers and wholesale dealers of fish and fishery products. *$55.00*
436 pages

22087 Sheldon's Major Stores & Chains
Phelon, Sheldon & Marsar
1364 Georgetowne Circle
Sarasota, FL 34232-2048
941-342-7990
FAX: 941-342-7994 800-234-8804
Joseph R Marsar Jr, Editor
Approximately 3,000 retailing stores, chain headquarters; including: department stores, department store chains, women's stores, women's chains, men's, children's and teens chains, furniture & home furnishing chains, shoe chains, sporting goods chains, post exchanges, gift & jewelry chains, cosmetic chains & college book stores. All for USA, Mexico and Canada. Special section on resident buying offices. *$200.00*
550 pages 2 issues Founded: 1864 ISBN 0-942239-18-0
Circulation: 3,000
Printed in on matte stock : cd rom

22088 Shippers Guide to Department & Chain Stores Nationwide
Shippers Guides
PO Box 112
Duarte, CA 91009-0112
626-357-6430
Profiles over 1,000 department stores and chain stores and their traffic managers in the United States. *$349.00*
350 pages Annual
Circulation: 2,000

22089 Who's Who
Association of Pool & Spa Professionals
2111 Eisenhower Avenue
Alexandria, VA 22314-4679
703-838-0083
FAX: 703-549-0493
MemberServices@TheASAP.org
www.theasap.org/
Jack Cergol, Chief Staff Executive
Marianne Kiernan, Executive Secretary
Trade association for pool, spa and hot tub industry. Annual Convention for trade.
Founded: 1956

22090 Wholesale Grocers
Chain Store Guide
3922 Coconut Palm Drive
Tampa, FL 33616-3506
813-276-6700
FAX: 813-627-6882 800-778-9794
info@csgis.com www.csgis.com
Chris Leedy, Advertising Sales
Shami Choon, Manager
We have uncovered the facts on more than 1,900 grocery suppliers in the U.S. and Canada in this database. This targeted database allows you to reach food wholesalers, cooperatives and voluntary group wholesalers, non-sponsoring wholesalers, and cash and carry operators who serve grocery, convenience, discount and drug stores. You will also find information regarding company headquarters, divisions, branches, and over 11,000 key executives and buyers. *$335.00*
Annual 700 names

22091 Wholesaler
TMB Publishing
1838 Techny Ct
Northbrook, IL 60062-5474
847-564-1127
FAX: 847-564-1264
jaschweizr@aol.com
www.thewholesaler.com
Tom M Brown Jr, Publisher
Ranks 100 leading wholesalers of plumbing, heating, air conditioning, refrigeration equipment and industrial pipe, valves and fittings. *$25.00*
Annual July
Circulation: 30,000

22092 Wholesaler-Wholesaling 100 Issue
TMB Publishing
1884 Techny Ct
Northbrook, IL 60062-5474
847-564-1127
FAX: 847-564-1264
www.thewholesaler.com
Tom M Brown Jr, Publisher
Offer information on over 100 leading wholesalers of plumbing-heating equipment and supplies. *$25.00*
Circulation: 25,000

Industry Web Sites

22093 www.aamp.com
American Association of Meat Processors
For small to medium sized meat, poultry and food businesses including: packers, processors, wholesalers, home food service businesses, retailers, deli and catering operators.

22094 **www.anla.org**
American Nursery & Landscape Association

The American Nursery and Landscape Association serves firms who grow, sell or use plants. ANLA advocates the industry's interests before government and provides its members with unique business knowledge essential to long-term growth and profitability.

22095 **www.awmanet.org**
American Wholesale Marketers Association

An organization supporting the confectionery, tobacco and allied products industries through programs and services.

22096 **www.fewa.org**
Farm Equipment Wholesalers Association

International trade association of whole-sale/distributors of agricultural equipment and related products.

22097 **www.fpda.org**
Fluid Power Distributors Association

Membership is composed of distributors and manufacturers of hydraulic and pneumatic equipment.

22098 **www.gmdc.org**
General Merchandise Distributors Council

International trade association representing pharmacy products to the mass market retail industry.

22099 **www.greyhouse.com**
Grey House Publishing

Selected Grey House directories in the fields of business, health and education are available online. Users can search our online databases by several different search criteria, such as product categories, geographic area, sales volume and much, much more. Full Grey House catalog and online ordering also available.

22100 **www.issa.com**
International Sanitary Supply Association

Manufacturers, distributors, wholesalers, representatives and publishers engaged in the manufacture and/or distribution of cleaning and maintenance products.

22101 **www.lumber.org**
North American Wholesale Lumber Association

For lumber and building distributors and manufacturers.

22102 **www.msci.org/**
Metal Service Center Institute (MSCI)

MSCI is the trade association that supports and represents most elements of the metals value chain, including metals producers, distributors, and processors.

22103 **www.narm.com**
National Association of Recording Merchandisers

Represents the retailers and suppliers of recorded entertainment as well as many suppliers of ancillary products.

22104 **www.nbwa.org**
National Beer Wholesalers Association

Research and development, quality control and ingredients.

22105 **www.nesda.com**
National Electronics Service Dealers Association

Provides educational assistance in electronic training to public schools, compiles statistics, offers certification programs and apprenticeships. Functions as trade association for the electronics service industry.

22106 **www.nfraweb.org**
National Frozen & Refrigerated Foods Association

NFRA is a non profit trade association comprised of 650 member companies representing all segments of the frozen and refrigerated foods industry. NFRA has been serving the frozen food industry since 1945 and just recently in 2001 began serving the refrigerated foods industry. The mission of NFRA is to promote the sales and consumption of frozen and refrigerated foods through: education, training, research, sales planning and menu development and providing a forum for industry dialogue.

22107 **www.npfda.org**
National Poultry & Food Distributors Association

For poultry and food distribution and processing industries. Provides member services, cost cutting benefits and networking opportunities.

22108 **www.pida.com**
Pet Industry Distributors Association

Represents wholesaler-distributors of pet products, providing training and education to members.

22109 **www.ptda.org**
Power Transmission Distributors Association

Members are power transmission/motion control distributor throughout manufacturing firms.

22110 **www.safetycentral.org**
Safety Equipment Distributors Association

Represents wholesale-distributors of safety equipment and works to enhance and improve distribution through excellence in communications, training, education and services.

22111 **www.ssia.info**
Shoe Service Institute of America

Shop to shop chat room, links and listings of manufacturers and wholesalers plus shoe care tips.

A

B

C

E

F

G

H

J

K

L

M

N

O

P

Q

R

S

T

U

V

X

Y

Z

w

B

C

D

F

G

K

L

M

P

Q

R

T

V

W

X

Grey House Publishing
Business Directories

Nations of the World, 2007 A Political, Economic and Business Handbook

This completely revised edition covers all the nations of the world in an easy-to-use, single volume. Each nation is profiled in a single chapter that includes Key Facts, Political & Economic Issues, a Country Profile and Business Information. In this fast-changing world, it is extremely important to make sure that the most up-to-date information is included in your reference collection. This edition is just the answer. Each of the 200+ country chapters have been carefully reviewed by a political expert to make sure that the text reflects the most current information on Politics, Travel Advisories, Economics and more. You'll find such vital information as a Country Map, Population Characteristics, Inflation, Agricultural Production, Foreign Debt, Political History, Foreign Policy, Regional Insecurity, Economics, Trade & Tourism, Historical Profile, Political Systems, Ethnicity, Languages, Media, Climate, Hotels, Chambers of Commerce, Banking, Travel Information and more. Five Regional Chapters follow the main text and include a Regional Map, an Introductory Article, Key Indicators and Currencies for the Region. As an added bonus, an all-inclusive CD-ROM is available as a companion to the printed text. Noted for its sophisticated, up-to-date and reliable compilation of political, economic and business information, this brand new edition will be an important acquisition to any public, academic or special library reference collection.

"A useful addition to both general reference collections and business collections." –RUSQ

1,700 pages; Print Version Only Softcover ISBN 1-59237-177-9, $155.00

The Directory of Venture Capital & Private Equity Firms, 2007

This edition has been extensively updated and broadly expanded to offer direct access to over 2,800 Domestic and International Venture Capital Firms, including address, phone & fax numbers, e-mail addresses and web sites for both primary and branch locations. Entries include details on the firm's Mission Statement, Industry Group Preferences, Geographic Preferences, Average and Minimum Investments and Investment Criteria. You'll also find details that are available nowhere else, including the Firm's Portfolio Companies and extensive information on each of the firm's Managing Partners, such as Education, Professional Background and Directorships held, along with the Partner's E-mail Address. *The Directory of Venture Capital & Private Equity Firms* offers five important indexes: Geographic Index, Executive Name Index, Portfolio Company Index, Industry Preference Index and College & University Index. With its comprehensive coverage and detailed, extensive information on each company, *The Directory of Venture Capital & Private Equity Firms* is an important addition to any finance collection.

"The sheer number of listings, the descriptive information provided and the outstanding indexing make this directory a better value than its principal competitor, Pratt's Guide to Venture Capital Sources. Recommended for business collections in large public, academic and business libraries." –Choice

1,300 pages; Softcover ISBN 1-59237-176-0, $565.00/$450.00 Library ◆ Online Database (includes a free copy of the directory) $889.00

The Grey House Performing Arts Directory, 2007

The Grey House Performing Arts Directory is the most comprehensive resource covering the Performing Arts. This important directory provides current information on over 8,500 Dance Companies, Instrumental Music Programs, Opera Companies, Choral Groups, Theater Companies, Performing Arts Series and Performing Arts Facilities. Plus, this edition now contains a brand new section on Artist Management Groups. In addition to mailing address, phone & fax numbers, e-mail addresses and web sites, dozens of other fields of available information include mission statement, key contacts, facilities, seating capacity, season, attendance and more. This directory also provides an important Information Resources section that covers hundreds of Performing Arts Associations, Magazines, Newsletters, Trade Shows, Directories, Databases and Industry Web Sites. Five indexes provide immediate access to this wealth of information: Entry Name, Executive Name, Performance Facilities, Geographic and Information Resources. *The Grey House Performing Arts Directory* pulls together thousands of Performing Arts Organizations, Facilities and Information Resources into an easy-to-use source – this kind of comprehensiveness and extensive detail is not available in any resource on the market place today.

"Immensely useful and user-friendly … recommended for public, academic and certain special library reference collections." –Booklist

1,500 pages; Softcover ISBN 1-59237-138-8, $185.00 ◆ Online Database $335.00

To preview any of our Directories Risk-Free for 30 days, call (800) 562-2139 or fax to (518) 789-0556

The Directory of Mail Order Catalogs, 2007

Published since 1981, the *Directory of Mail Order Catalogs* is the premier source of information on the mail order catalog industry. It is the source that business professionals and librarians have come to rely on for the thousands of catalog companies in the US. New for 2007, The Directory of Mail Order Catalogs has been combined with its companion volume, *The Directory of Business to Business Catalogs,* to offer all 13,000 catalog companies in one easy-to-use volume. Section I: Consumer Catalogs, covers over 9,000 consumer catalog companies in 44 different product chapters from Animals to Toys & Games. Section II: Business to Business Catalogs, details 5,000 business catalogs, everything from computers to laboratory supplies, building construction and much more. Listings contain detailed contact information including mailing address, phone & fax numbers, web sites, e-mail addresses and key contacts along with important business details such as product descriptions, employee size, years in business, sales volume, catalog size, number of catalogs mailed and more. Three indexes are included for easy access to information: Catalog & Company Name Index, Geographic Index and Product Index. *The Directory of Mail Order Catalogs,* now with its expanded business to business catalogs, is the largest and most comprehensive resource covering this billion-dollar industry. It is the standard in its field. This important resource is a useful tool for entrepreneurs searching for catalogs to pick up their product, vendors looking to expand their customer base in the catalog industry, market researchers, small businesses investigating new supply vendors, along with the library patron who is exploring the available catalogs in their areas of interest.

"This is a godsend for those looking for information." –Reference Book Review

1,700 pages; Softcover ISBN 1-59237-156-6 $350.00/$250.00 Library ▯ Online Database (includes a free copy of the directory) $495.00

Sports Market Place Directory, 2007

For over 20 years, this comprehensive, up-to-date directory has offered direct access to the Who, What, When & Where of the Sports Industry. With over 20,000 updates and enhancements, the *Sports Market Place Directory* is the most detailed, comprehensive and current sports business reference source available. In 1,800 information-packed pages, *Sports Market Place Directory* profiles contact information and key executives for: Single Sport Organizations, Professional Leagues, Multi-Sport Organizations, Disabled Sports, High School & Youth Sports, Military Sports, Olympic Organizations, Media, Sponsors, Sponsorship & Marketing Event Agencies, Event & Meeting Calendars, Professional Services, College Sports, Manufacturers & Retailers, Facilities and much more. *The Sports Market Place Directory* provides organization's contact information with detailed descriptions including: Key Contacts, physical, mailing, email and web addresses plus phone and fax numbers. Plus, nine important indexes make sure that you can find the information you're looking for quickly and easily: Entry Index, Single Sport Index, Media Index, Sponsor Index, Agency Index, Manufacturers Index, Brand Name Index, Facilities Index and Executive/Geographic Index. For over twenty years, *The Sports Market Place Directory* has assisted thousands of individuals in their pursuit of a career in the sports industry. Why not use "THE SOURCE" that top recruiters, headhunters and career placement centers use to find information on or about sports organizations and key hiring contacts.

1,800 pages; Softcover ISBN 1-59237-189-2, $225.00 ▯ Online Database $479.00

Food and Beverage Market Place, 2007

Food and Beverage Market Place is bigger and better than ever with thousands of new companies, thousands of updates to existing companies and two revised and enhanced product category indexes. This comprehensive directory profiles over 18,000 Food & Beverage Manufacturers, 12,000 Equipment & Supply Companies, 2,200 Transportation & Warehouse Companies, 2,000 Brokers & Wholesalers, 8,000 Importers & Exporters, 900 Industry Resources and hundreds of Mail Order Catalogs. Listings include detailed Contact Information, Sales Volumes, Key Contacts, Brand & Product Information, Packaging Details and much more. *Thomas Food and Beverage Market Place* is available as a three-volume printed set, a subscription-based Online Database via the Internet, on CD-ROM, as well as mailing lists and a licensable database.

"An essential purchase for those in the food industry but will also be useful in public libraries where needed. Much of the information will be difficult and time consuming to locate without this handy three-volume ready-reference source." –ARBA

8,500 pages, 3 Volume Set; Softcover ISBN 1-59237-152-3, $595.00 ▯ Online Database $795.00 ▯ Online Database & 3 Volume Set Combo, $995.00

To preview any of our Directories Risk-Free for 30 days, call (800) 562-2139 or fax to (518) 789-0556

The Grey House Homeland Security Directory, 2007

This updated edition features the latest contact information for government and private organizations involved with Homeland Security along with the latest product information and provides detailed profiles of nearly 1,000 Federal & State Organizations & Agencies and over 3,000 Officials and Key Executives involved with Homeland Security. These listings are incredibly detailed and include Mailing Address, Phone & Fax Numbers, Email Addresses & Web Sites, a complete Description of the Agency and a complete list of the Officials and Key Executives associated with the Agency. Next, *The Grey House Homeland Security Directory* provides the go-to source for Homeland Security Products & Services. This section features over 2,000 Companies that provide Consulting, Products or Services. With this Buyer's Guide at their fingertips, users can locate suppliers of everything from Training Materials to Access Controls, from Perimeter Security to BioTerrorism Countermeasures and everything in between – complete with contact information and product descriptions. A handy Product Locator Index is provided to quickly and easily locate suppliers of a particular product. Lastly, an Information Resources Section provides immediate access to contact information for hundreds of Associations, Newsletters, Magazines, Trade Shows, Databases and Directories that focus on Homeland Security. This comprehensive, information-packed resource will be a welcome tool for any company or agency that is in need of Homeland Security information and will be a necessary acquisition for the reference collection of all public libraries and large school districts.

"Compiles this information in one place and is discerning in content. A useful purchase for public and academic libraries." –Booklist

800 pages; Softcover ISBN 1-59237-151-5, $195.00 ▯ Online Database (includes a free copy of the directory) $385.00

The Grey House Transportation Security Directory & Handbook

This brand new title is the only reference of its kind that brings together current data on Transportation Security. With information on everything from Regulatory Authorities to Security Equipment, this top-flight database brings together the relevant information necessary for creating and maintaining a security plan for a wide range of transportation facilities. With this current, comprehensive directory at the ready you'll have immediate access to: Regulatory Authorities & Legislation; Information Resources; Sample Security Plans & Checklists; Contact Data for Major Airports, Seaports, Railroads, Trucking Companies and Oil Pipelines; Security Service Providers; Recommended Equipment & Product Information and more. Using the *Grey House Transportation Security Directory & Handbook*, managers will be able to quickly and easily assess their current security plans; develop contacts to create and maintain new security procedures; and source the products and services necessary to adequately maintain a secure environment. This valuable resource is a must for all Security Managers at Airports, Seaports, Railroads, Trucking Companies and Oil Pipelines.

800 pages; Softcover ISBN 1-59237-075-6, $195

The Grey House Safety & Security Directory, 2007

The Grey House Safety & Security Directory is the most comprehensive reference tool and buyer's guide for the safety and security industry. Arranged by safety topic, each chapter begins with OSHA regulations for the topic, followed by Training Articles written by top professionals in the field and Self-Inspection Checklists. Next, each topic contains Buyer's Guide sections that feature related products and services. Topics include Administration, Insurance, Loss Control & Consulting, Protective Equipment & Apparel, Noise & Vibration, Facilities Monitoring & Maintenance, Employee Health Maintenance & Ergonomics, Retail Food Services, Machine Guards, Process Guidelines & Tool Handling, Ordinary Materials Handling, Hazardous Materials Handling, Workplace Preparation & Maintenance, Electrical Lighting & Safety, Fire & Rescue and Security. The Buyer's Guide sections are carefully indexed within each topic area to ensure that you can find the supplies needed to meet OSHA's regulations. Six important indexes make finding information and product manufacturers quick and easy: Geographical Index of Manufacturers and Distributors, Company Profile Index, Brand Name Index, Product Index, Index of Web Sites and Index of Advertisers. This comprehensive, up-to-date reference will provide every tool necessary to make sure a business is in compliance with OSHA regulations and locate the products and services needed to meet those regulations.

"Presents industrial safety information for engineers, plant managers, risk managers, and construction site supervisors..." –Choice

1,500 pages, 2 Volume Set; Softcover ISBN 1-59237-160-4, $225.00

The Grey House Biometric Information Directory

The Biometric Information Directory is the only comprehensive source for current biometric industry information. This 2006 edition is the first published by Grey House. With 100% updated information, this latest edition offers a complete, current look, in both print and online form, of biometric companies and products – one of the fastest growing industries in today's economy. Detailed profiles of manufacturers of the latest biometric technology, including Finger, Voice, Face, Hand, Signature, Iris, Vein and Palm Identification systems. Data on the companies include key executives, company size and a detailed, indexed description of their product line. Plus, the Directory also includes valuable business resources, and current editorial make this edition the easiest way for the business community and consumers alike to access the largest, most current compilation of biometric industry information available on the market today. The new edition boasts increased numbers of companies, contact names and company data, with over 700 manufacturers and service providers. Information in the directory includes: Editorial on Advancements in Biometrics; Profiles of 700+ companies listed with contact information; Organizations, Trade & Educational Associations, Publications, Conferences, Trade Shows and Expositions Worldwide; Web Site Index; Biometric & Vendors Services Index by Types of Biometrics; and a Glossary of Biometric Terms. This resource will be an important source for anyone who is considering the use of a biometric product, investing in the development of biometric technology, support existing marketing and sales efforts and will be an important acquisition for the business reference collection for large public and business libraries.

800 pages; Softcover ISBN 1-59237-121-3, $225

The Rauch Guide to the US Adhesives & Sealants, Cosmetics & Toiletries, Ink, Paint, Plastics, Pulp & Paper and Rubber Industries

The Rauch Guides are known worldwide for their comprehensive marketing information. Acquired by Grey House Publishing in 2005, new updated and revised editions will be published throughout 2005 and 2006. Each Guide provides market facts and figures in a highly organized format, ideal for today's busy personnel, serving as ready-references for top executives as well as the industry newcomer. *The Rauch Guides* save time and money by organizing widely scattered information and providing estimates for important business decisions, some of which are available nowhere else. Each Guide is organized into several information-packed chapters. After a brief introduction, the ECONOMICS section provides data on industry shipments; long-term growth and forecasts; prices; company performance; employment, expenditures, and productivity; transportation and geographical patterns; packaging; foreign trade; and government regulations. Next, TECHNOLOGY & RAW MATERIALS provide market, technical, and raw material information for chemicals, equipment and related materials, including market size and leading suppliers, prices, end uses, and trends. PRODUCTS & MARKETS provide information for each major industry product, including market size and historical trends, leading suppliers, five-year forecasts, industry structure, and major end uses. For easy access, each *Guide* contains a chapter on INDUSTRY ACTIVITIES, ORGANIZATIONS & SOURCES OF INFORMATION with detailed information on meetings, exhibits, and trade shows, sources of statistical information, trade associations, technical and professional societies, and trade and technical periodicals. Next, the COMPANY DIRECTORY profiles major industry companies, both public and private. Generally several hundred companies are analyzed. Information includes complete contact information, web address, estimated total and domestic sales, product description, and recent mergers and acquisitions. Each Guide also contains several APPENDICES that provide a cross-reference of suppliers, subsidiaries and divisions. The Rauch Guides will prove to be an invaluable source of market information, company data, trends and forecasts that anyone in these fast-paced industries.

The Rauch Guide to the U.S. Paint Industry Softcover ISBN 1-59237-127-2 $595 ♦ The Rauch Guide to the U.S. Plastics Industry Softcover ISBN 1-59237-128-0 $595 ♦ The Rauch Guide to the U.S. Adhesives and Sealants Industry Softcover ISBN 1-59237-129-9 $595 ♦ The Rauch Guide to the U.S. Ink Industry Softcover ISBN 1-59237-126-4 $595 ♦ The Rauch Guide to the U.S. Rubber Industry Softcover ISBN 1-59237-130-2 $595 ♦ The Rauch Guide to the U.S. Pulp and Paper Industry Softcover ISBN 1-59237-131-0 $595 ♦ The Rauch Guide to the U.S. Cosmetic and Toiletries Industry Softcover ISBN 1-59237-132-9 $895

New York State Directory, 2006/07

The New York State Directory, published annually since 1983, is a comprehensive and easy-to-use guide to accessing public officials and private sector organizations and individuals who influence public policy in the state of New York. *The New York State Directory* includes important information on all New York state legislators and congressional representatives, including biographies and key committee assignments. It also includes staff rosters for all branches of New York state government and for federal agencies and departments that impact the state policy process. Following the state government section are 25 chapters covering policy areas from agriculture through veterans' affairs. Each chapter identifies the state, local and federal agencies and officials that formulate or implement policy. In addition, each chapter contains a roster of private sector experts and advocates who influence the policy process. The directory also offers appendices that include statewide party officials; chambers of commerce; lobbying organizations; public and private universities and colleges; television, radio and print media; and local government agencies and officials.

New York State Directory - 800 pages; Softcover ISBN 1-59237-145-0; $145.00
New York State Directory with Profiles of New York – 2 volumes; 1,600 pages; Softcover ISBN 1-59237-162-0; $225

Profiles of New York ♦ Profiles of Florida ♦ Profiles of Texas ♦ Profiles of Illinois ♦ Profiles of Michigan ♦ Profiles of Ohio ♦ Profiles of New Jersey ♦ Profiles of Massachusetts ♦ Profiles of Pennsylvania ♦ Profiles of Wisconsin ♦ Profiles of Connecticut ♦ Profiles of Indiana ♦ Profiles of North Carolina ♦ Profiles of Virginia

Packed with over 50 pieces of data that make up a complete, user-friendly profile of each state, these directories go even further by then pulling selected data and providing it in ranking list form for even easier comparisons between the 100 largest towns and cities! The careful layout gives the user an easy-to-read snapshot of every single place and county in the state, from the biggest metropolis to the smallest unincorporated hamlet. The richness of each place or county profile is astounding in its depth, from history to weather, all packed in an easy-to-navigate, compact format. No need for piles of multiple sources with this volume on your desk. Here is a look at just a few of the data sets you'll find in each profile: History, Geography, Climate, Population, Vital Statistics, Economy, Income, Taxes, Education, Housing, Health & Environment, Public Safety, Newspapers, Transportation, Presidential Election Results, Information Contacts and Chambers of Commerce. As an added bonus, there is a section on Selected Statistics, where data from the 100 largest towns and cities is arranged into easy-to-use charts. Each of 22 different data points has its own two-page spread with the cities listed in alpha order so researchers can easily compare and rank cities. A remarkable compilation that offers overviews and insights into each corner of the state, *Profiles of New York*, *Profiles of Florida* and *Profiles of Texas* go beyond Census statistics, beyond metro area coverage, beyond the 100 best places to live. Drawn from official census information, other government statistics and original research, you will have at your fingertips data that's available nowhere else in one single source. Data will be published on additional states in 2006 and 2007.

Each Profiles of… title ranges from 400-800 pages, priced at $149.00 each

Research Services Directory: Commercial & Corporate Research Centers

This Ninth Edition provides access to well over 8,000 independent Commercial Research Firms, Corporate Research Centers and Laboratories offering contract services for hands-on, basic or applied research. *Research Services Directory* covers the thousands of types of research companies, including Biotechnology & Pharmaceutical Developers, Consumer Product Research, Defense Contractors, Electronics & Software Engineers, Think Tanks, Forensic Investigators, Independent Commercial Laboratories, Information Brokers, Market & Survey Research Companies, Medical Diagnostic Facilities, Product Research & Development Firms and more. Each entry provides the company's name, mailing address, phone & fax numbers, key contacts, web site, e-mail address, as well as a company description and research and technical fields served. Four indexes provide immediate access to this wealth of information: Research Firms Index, Geographic Index, Personnel Name Index and Subject Index.

"An important source for organizations in need of information about laboratories, individuals and other facilities." –ARBA

1,400 pages; Softcover ISBN 1-59237-003-9, $395.00 ▯ Online Database (includes a free copy of the directory) $850.00

International Business and Trade Directories

Completely updated, the Third Edition of *International Business and Trade Directories* now contains more than 10,000 entries, over 2,000 more than the last edition, making this directory the most comprehensive resource of the worlds business and trade directories. Entries include content descriptions, price, publisher's name and address, web site and e-mail addresses, phone and fax numbers and editorial staff. Organized by industry group, and then by region, this resource puts over 10,000 industry-specific business and trade directories at the reader's fingertips. Three indexes are included for quick access to information: Geographic Index, Publisher Index and Title Index. Public, college and corporate libraries, as well as individuals and corporations seeking critical market information will want to add this directory to their marketing collection.

"Reasonably priced for a work of this type, this directory should appeal to larger academic, public and corporate libraries with an international focus." –Library Journal

1,800 pages; Softcover ISBN 1-930956-63-0, $225.00 ▯ Online Database (includes a free copy of the directory) $450.00

To preview any of our Directories Risk-Free for 30 days, call (800) 562-2139 or fax to (518) 789-0556

Grey House Publishing Canada
Canadian Information Resources

Canadian Almanac & Directory, 2007

The Canadian Almanac & Directory contains ten directories in one – giving you all the facts and figures you will ever need about Canada. No other single source provides users with the quality and depth of up-to-date information for all types of research. This national directory and guide gives you access to statistics, images and over 45,000 names and addresses for everything from Airlines to Zoos - updated every year. It's Ten Directories in One! Each section is a directory in itself, providing robust information on business and finance, communications, government, associations, arts and culture (museums, zoos, libraries, etc.), health, transportation, law, education, and more. Government information includes federal, provincial and territorial - and includes an easy-to-use quick index to find key information. A separate municipal government section includes every municipality in Canada, with full profiles of Canada's largest urban centers. A complete legal directory lists judges and judicial officials, court locations and law firms across the country. A wealth of general information, the Canadian Almanac & Directory also includes national statistics on population, employment, imports and exports, and more. National awards and honors are presented, along with forms of address, Commonwealth information and full color photos of Canadian symbols. Postal information, weights, measures, distances and other useful charts are also incorporated. Complete almanac information includes perpetual calendars, five-year holiday planners and astronomical information. Published continuously for 160 years, The Canadian Almanac & Directory is the best single reference source for business executives, managers and assistants; government and public affairs executives; lawyers; marketing, sales and advertising executives; researchers, editors and journalists.

Hardcover ISBN 978-1-89502-149-3; 1,600 pages; $315.00

Associations Canada, 2007

The Most Powerful Fact-Finder to Business, Trade, Professional and Consumer Organizations
Associations Canada covers Canadian organizations and international groups including industry, commercial and professional associations, registered charities, special interest and common interest organizations. This annually revised compendium provides detailed listings and abstracts for nearly 20,000 regional, national and international organizations. This popular volume provides the most comprehensive picture of Canada's non-profit sector. Detailed listings enable users to identify an organization's budget, founding date, scope of activity, licensing body, sources of funding, executive information, full address and complete contact information, just to name a few. Powerful indexes help researchers find information quickly and easily. The following indexes are included: subject, acronym, geographic, budget, executive name, conferences & conventions, mailing list, defunct and unreachable associations and registered charitable organizations. In addition to annual spending of over $1 billion on transportation and conventions alone, Canadian associations account for many millions more in pursuit of membership interests. Associations Canada provides complete access to this highly lucrative market. Associations Canada is a strong source of prospects for sales and marketing executives, tourism and convention officials, researchers, government officials - anyone who wants to locate non-profit interest groups and trade associations.

Hardcover ISBN 978-1-59237-219-5; 1,600 pages; $315.00

Financial Services Canada, 2006/07

Financial Services Canada is the only master file of current contacts and information that serves the needs of the entire financial services industry in Canada. With over 18,000 organizations and hard-to-find business information, Financial Services Canada is the most up-to-date source for names and contact numbers of industry professionals, senior executives, portfolio managers, financial advisors, agency bureaucrats and elected representatives. Financial Services Canada incorporates the latest changes in the industry to provide you with the most current details on each company, including: name, title, organization, telephone and fax numbers, e-mail and web addresses. Financial Services Canada also includes private company listings never before compiled, government agencies, association and consultant services - to ensure that you'll never miss a client or a contact. Current listings include: banks and branches, non-depository institutions, stock exchanges and brokers, investment management firms, insurance companies, major accounting and law firms, government agencies and financial associations. Powerful indexes assist researchers with locating the vital financial information they need. The following indexes are included: alphabetic, geographic, executive name, corporate web site/e-mail, government quick reference and subject. Financial Services Canada is a valuable resource for financial executives, bankers, financial planners, sales and marketing professionals, lawyers and chartered accountants, government officials, investment dealers, journalists, librarians and reference specialists.

900 pages; Hardcover ISBN 978-1-89502-145-5 $315.00

To preview any of our Directories Risk-Free for 30 days, call (800) 562-2139 or fax to (518) 789-0556

Grey House Publishing Canada
Canadian Information Resources

Directory of Libraries in Canada, 2007/08

The Directory of Libraries in Canada brings together almost 7,000 listings including libraries and their branches, information resource centers, archives and library associations and learning centers. The directory offers complete and comprehensive information on Canadian libraries, resource centers, business information centers, professional associations, regional library systems, archives, library schools and library technical programs. The Directory of Libraries in Canada includes important features of each library and service, including library information; personnel details, including contact names and e-mail addresses; collection information; services available to users; acquisitions budgets; and computers and automated systems. Useful information on each library's electronic access is also included, such as Internet browser, connectivity and public Internet/CD-ROM/subscription database access. The directory also provides powerful indexes for subject, location, personal name and Web site/e-mail to assist researchers with locating the crucial information they need. The Directory of Libraries in Canada is a vital reference tool for publishers, advocacy groups, students, research institutions, computer hardware suppliers, and other diverse groups that provide products and services to this unique market.

850 pages; Hardcover ISBN 978-1-59237-222-5; $315.00

Canadian Environmental Directory, 2007/08

The Canadian Environmental Directory is Canada's most complete and only national listing of environmental associations and organizations, government regulators and purchasing groups, product and service companies, special libraries, and more! The extensive Products and Services section provides detailed listings enabling users to identify the company name, address, phone, fax, e-mail, Web address, firm type, contact names (and titles), product and service information, affiliations, trade information, branch and affiliate data. The Government section gives you all the contact information you need at every government level – federal, provincial and municipal. We also include descriptions of current environmental initiatives, programs and agreements, names of environment-related acts administered by each ministry or department PLUS information and tips on who to contact and how to sell to governments in Canada. The Associations section provides complete contact information and a brief description of activities. Included are Canadian environmental organizations and international groups including industry, commercial and professional associations, registered charities, special interest and common interest organizations. All the Information you need about the Canadian environmental industry: directory of products and services, special libraries and resource, conferences, seminars and tradeshows, chronology of environmental events, law firms and major Canadian companies, The Canadian Environmental Directory is ideal for business, government, engineers and anyone conducting research on the environment.

Hardcover ISBN 978-1-59237-218-8; 900 pages; $315.00

To preview any of our Directories Risk-Free for 30 days, call (800) 562-2139 or fax to (518) 789-0556

Grey House Publishing
General Reference Titles

The Value of a Dollar 1600-1859, The Colonial Era to The Civil War

Following the format of the widely acclaimed, *The Value of a Dollar, 1860-2004, The Value of a Dollar 1600-1859, The Colonial Era to The Civil War* records the actual prices of thousands of items that consumers purchased from the Colonial Era to the Civil War. Our editorial department had been flooded with requests from users of our Value of a Dollar for the same type of information, just from an earlier time period. This new volume is just the answer – with pricing data from 1600 to 1859. Arranged into five-year chapters, each 5-year chapter includes a Historical Snapshot, Consumer Expenditures, Investments, Selected Income, Income/Standard Jobs, Food Basket, Standard Prices and Miscellany. There is also a section on Trends. This informative section charts the change in price over time and provides added detail on the reasons prices changed within the time period, including industry developments, changes in consumer attitudes and important historical facts. This fascinating survey will serve a wide range of research needs and will be useful in all high school, public and academic library reference collections.

600 pages; Hardcover ISBN 1-59237-094-2, $135.00

The Value of a Dollar 1860-2004, Third Edition

A guide to practical economy, *The Value of a Dollar* records the actual prices of thousands of items that consumers purchased from the Civil War to the present, along with facts about investment options and income opportunities. This brand new Third Edition boasts a brand new addition to each five-year chapter, a section on Trends. This informative section charts the change in price over time and provides added detail on the reasons prices changed within the time period, including industry developments, changes in consumer attitudes and important historical facts. Plus, a brand new chapter for 2000-2004 has been added. Each 5-year chapter includes a Historical Snapshot, Consumer Expenditures, Investments, Selected Income, Income/Standard Jobs, Food Basket, Standard Prices and Miscellany. This interesting and useful publication will be widely used in any reference collection.

"Recommended for high school, college and public libraries." –ARBA

600 pages; Hardcover ISBN 1-59237-074-8, $135.00

Working Americans 1880-1999
Volume I: The Working Class, Volume II: The Middle Class, Volume III: The Upper Class

Each of the volumes in the *Working Americans 1880-1999* series focuses on a particular class of Americans, The Working Class, The Middle Class and The Upper Class over the last 120 years. Chapters in each volume focus on one decade and profile three to five families. Family Profiles include real data on Income & Job Descriptions, Selected Prices of the Times, Annual Income, Annual Budgets, Family Finances, Life at Work, Life at Home, Life in the Community, Working Conditions, Cost of Living, Amusements and much more. Each chapter also contains an Economic Profile with Average Wages of other Professions, a selection of Typical Pricing, Key Events & Inventions, News Profiles, Articles from Local Media and Illustrations. The *Working Americans* series captures the lifestyles of each of the classes from the last twelve decades, covers a vast array of occupations and ethnic backgrounds and travels the entire nation. These interesting and useful compilations of portraits of the American Working, Middle and Upper Classes during the last 120 years will be an important addition to any high school, public or academic library reference collection.

"These interesting, unique compilations of economic and social facts, figures and graphs will support multiple research needs. They will engage and enlighten patrons in high school, public and academic library collections." –Booklist

Volume I: The Working Class ◆ 558 pages; Hardcover ISBN 1-891482-81-5, $145.00 ◆ Volume II: The Middle Class ◆ 591 pages; Hardcover ISBN 1-891482-72-6; $145.00 ◆ Volume III: The Upper Class ◆ 567 pages; Hardcover ISBN 1-930956-38-X, $145.00

Working Americans 1880-1999 Volume IV: Their Children

This Fourth Volume in the highly successful *Working Americans 1880-1999* series focuses on American children, decade by decade from 1880 to 1999. This interesting and useful volume introduces the reader to three children in each decade, one from each of the Working, Middle and Upper classes. Like the first three volumes in the series, the individual profiles are created from interviews, diaries, statistical studies, biographies and news reports. Profiles cover a broad range of ethnic backgrounds, geographic area and lifestyles – everything from an orphan in Memphis in 1882, following the Yellow Fever epidemic of 1878 to an eleven-year-old nephew of a beer baron and owner of the New York Yankees in New York City in 1921. Chapters also contain important supplementary materials including News Features as well as information on everything from Schools to Parks, Infectious Diseases to Childhood Fears along with Entertainment, Family Life and much more to provide an informative overview of the lifestyles of children from each decade. This interesting account of what life was like for Children in the Working, Middle and Upper Classes will be a welcome addition to the reference collection of any high school, public or academic library.

600 pages; Hardcover ISBN 1-930956-35-5, $145.00

Working Americans 1880-2003 Volume V: Americans At War

Working Americans 1880-2003 Volume V: Americans At War is divided into 11 chapters, each covering a decade from 1880-2003 and examines the lives of Americans during the time of war, including declared conflicts, one-time military actions, protests, and preparations for war. Each decade includes several personal profiles, whether on the battlefield or on the homefront, that tell the stories of civilians, soldiers, and officers during the decade. The profiles examine: Life at Home; Life at Work; and Life in the Community. Each decade also includes an Economic Profile with statistical comparisons, a Historical Snapshot, News Profiles, local News Articles, and Illustrations that provide a solid historical background to the decade being examined. Profiles range widely not only geographically, but also emotionally, from that of a girl whose leg was torn off in a blast during WWI, to the boredom of being stationed in the Dakotas as the Indian Wars were drawing to a close. As in previous volumes of the *Working Americans* series, information is presented in narrative form, but hard facts and real-life situations back up each story. The basis of the profiles come from diaries, private print books, personal interviews, family histories, estate documents and magazine articles. For easy reference, *Working Americans 1880-2003 Volume V: Americans At War* includes an in-depth Subject Index. The *Working Americans* series has become an important reference for public libraries, academic libraries and high school libraries. This fifth volume will be a welcome addition to all of these types of reference collections.

600 pages; Hardcover ISBN 1-59237-024-1; $145.00
Five Volume Set (Volumes I-V), Hardcover ISBN 1-59237-034-9, $675.00

Working Americans 1880-2005 Volume VI: Women at Work

Unlike any other volume in the *Working Americans* series, this Sixth Volume, is the first to focus on a particular gender of Americans. *Volume VI: Women at Work*, traces what life was like for working women from the 1860's to the present time. Beginning with the life of a maid in 1890 and a store clerk in 1900 and ending with the life and times of the modern working women, this text captures the struggle, strengths and changing perception of the American woman at work. Each chapter focuses on one decade and profiles three to five women with real data on Income & Job Descriptions, Selected Prices of the Times, Annual Income, Annual Budgets, Family Finances, Life at Work, Life at Home, Life in the Community, Working Conditions, Cost of Living, Amusements and much more. For even broader access to the events, economics and attitude towards women throughout the past 130 years, each chapter is supplemented with News Profiles, Articles from Local Media, Illustrations, Economic Profiles, Typical Pricing, Key Events, Inventions and more. This important volume illustrates what life was like for working women over time and allows the reader to develop an understanding of the changing role of women at work. These interesting and useful compilations of portraits of women at work will be an important addition to any high school, public or academic library reference collection.

600 pages; Hardcover ISBN 1-59237-063-2; $145.00

Working Americans 1880-2005 Volume VII: Social Movements

The newest addition to the widely-successful *Working Americans* series, *Volume VII: Social Movements* explores how Americans sought and fought for change from the 1880s to the present time. Following the format of previous volumes in the Working Americans series, the text examines the lives of 34 individuals who have worked — often behind the scenes — to bring about change. Issues include topics as diverse as the Anti-smoking movement of 1901 to efforts by Native Americans to reassert their long lost rights. Along the way, the book will profile individuals brave enough to demand suffrage for Kansas women in 1912 or demand an end to lynching during a March on Washington in 1923. Each profile is enriched with real data on Income & Job Descriptions, Selected Prices of the Times, Annual Incomes & Budgets, Life at Work, Life at Home, Life in the Community, along with News Features, Key Events, and Illustrations. The depth of information contained in each profile allow the user to explore the private, financial and public lives of these subjects, deepening our understanding of how calls for change took place in our society. A must-purchase for the reference collections of high school libraries, public libraries and academic libraries.

600 pages; Hardcover ISBN 1-59237-101-9; $145.00
Seven Volume Set (Volumes I-VII), Hardcover ISBN 1-59237-133-7, $945.00

The Encyclopedia of Warrior Peoples & Fighting Groups

Many military groups throughout the world have excelled in their craft either by fortuitous circumstances, outstanding leadership, or intense training. This new second edition of The Encyclopedia of Warrior Peoples and Fighting Groups explores the origins and leadership of these outstanding combat forces, chronicles their conquests and accomplishments, examines the circumstances surrounding their decline or disbanding, and assesses their influence on the groups and methods of warfare that followed. This edition has been completely updated with information through 2005 and contains over 20 new entries. Readers will encounter ferocious tribes, charismatic leaders, and daring militias, from ancient times to the present, including Amazons, Buffalo Soldiers, Green Berets, Iron Brigade, Kamikazes, Peoples of the Sea, Polish Winged Hussars, Sacred Band of Thebes, Teutonic Knights, and Texas Rangers. With over 100 alphabetical entries, numerous cross-references and illustrations, a comprehensive bibliography, and index, the Encyclopedia of Warrior Peoples and Fighting Groups is a valuable resource for readers seeking insight into the bold history of distinguished fighting forces.

"This work is especially useful for high school students, undergraduates, and general readers with an interest in military history." –Library Journal

Pub. Date: May 2006; Hardcover ISBN 1-59237-116-7; $135.00

The Encyclopedia of Invasions & Conquests, From the Ancient Times to the Present

Throughout history, invasions and conquests have played a remarkable role in shaping our world and defining our boundaries, both physically and culturally. This second edition of the popular Encyclopedia of Invasions & Conquests, a comprehensive guide to over 150 invasions, conquests, battles and occupations from ancient times to the present, takes readers on a journey that includes the Roman conquest of Britain, the Portuguese colonization of Brazil, and the Iraqi invasion of Kuwait, to name a few. New articles will explore the late 20th and 21st centuries, with a specific focus on recent conflicts in Afghanistan, Kuwait, Iraq, Yugoslavia, Grenada and Chechnya. Categories of entries include countries, invasions and conquests, and individuals. In addition to covering the military aspects of invasions and conquests, entries cover some of the political, economic, and cultural aspects, for example, the effects of a conquest on the invade country's political and monetary system and in its language and religion. The entries on leaders – among them Sargon, Alexander the Great, William the Conqueror, and Adolf Hitler – deal with the people who sought to gain control, expand power, or exert religious or political influence over others through military means. Revised and updated for this second edition, entries are arranged alphabetically within historical periods. Each chapter provides a map to help readers locate key areas and geographical features, and bibliographical references appear at the end of each entry. Other useful features include cross-references, a cumulative bibliography and a comprehensive subject index. This authoritative, well-organized, lucidly written volume will prove invaluable for a variety of readers, including high school students, military historians, members of the armed forces, history buffs and hobbyists.

"Engaging writing, sensible organization, nice illustrations, interesting and obscure facts, and useful maps make this book a pleasure to read." –ARBA

Pub. Date: March 2006; Hardcover ISBN 1-59237-114-0; $135.00

Encyclopedia of Prisoners of War & Internment

This authoritative second edition provides a valuable overview of the history of prisoners of war and interned civilians, from earliest times to the present. Written by an international team of experts in the field of POW studies, this fascinating and thought-provoking volume includes entries on a wide range of subjects including the Crusades, Plains Indian Warfare, concentration camps, the two world wars, and famous POWs throughout history, as well as atrocities, escapes, and much more. Written in a clear and easily understandable style, this informative reference details over 350 entries, 30% larger than the first edition, that survey the history of prisoners of war and interned civilians from the earliest times to the present, with emphasis on the 19th and 20th centuries. Medical conditions, international law, exchanges of prisoners, organizations working on behalf of POWs, and trials associated with the treatment of captives are just some of the themes explored. Entries range from the Ardeatine Caves Massacre to Kurt Vonnegut. Entries are arranged alphabetically, plus illustrations and maps are provided for easy reference. The text also includes an introduction, bibliography, appendix of selected documents, and end-of-entry reading suggestions. This one-of-a-kind reference will be a helpful addition to the reference collections of all public libraries, high schools, and university libraries and will prove invaluable to historians and military enthusiasts.

"Thorough and detailed yet accessible to the lay reader. Of special interest to subject specialists and historians; recommended for public and academic libraries." - Library Journal

Pub. Date: March 2006; Hardcover ISBN 1-59237-120-5; $135.00

The Religious Right, A Reference Handbook

Timely and unbiased, this third edition updates and expands its examination of the religious right and its influence on our government, citizens, society, and politics. From the fight to outlaw the teaching of Darwin's theory of evolution to the struggle to outlaw abortion, the religious right is continually exerting an influence on public policy. This text explores the influence of religion on legislation and society, while examining the alignment of the religious right with the political right. A historical survey of the movement highlights the shift to "hands-on" approach to politics and the struggle to present a unified front. The coverage offers a critical historical survey of the religious right movement, focusing on its increased involvement in the political arena, attempts to forge coalitions, and notable successes and failures. The text offers complete coverage of biographies of the men and women who have advanced the cause and an up to date chronology illuminate the movement's goals, including their accomplishments and failures. This edition offers an extensive update to all sections along with several brand new entries. Two new sections complement this third edition, a chapter on legal issues and court decisions and a chapter on demographic statistics and electoral patterns. To aid in further research, The Religious Right, offers an entire section of annotated listings of print and non-print resources, as well as of organizations affiliated with the religious right, and those opposing it. Comprehensive in its scope, this work offers easy-to-read, pertinent information for those seeking to understand the religious right and its evolving role in American society. A must for libraries of all sizes, university religion departments, activists, high schools and for those interested in the evolving role of the religious right.

" Recommended for all public and academic libraries." - Library Journal

Pub. Date: November 2006; Hardcover ISBN 1-59237-113-2; $135.00

To preview any of our Directories Risk-Free for 30 days, call (800) 562-2139 or fax to (518) 789-0556

From Suffrage to the Senate, America's Political Women

From Suffrage to the Senate is a comprehensive and valuable compendium of biographies of leading women in U.S. politics, past and present, and an examination of the wide range of women's movements. Up to date through 2006, this dynamically illustrated reference work explores American women's path to political power and social equality from the struggle for the right to vote and the abolition of slavery to the first African American woman in the U.S. Senate and beyond. This new edition includes over 150 new entries and a brand new section on trends and demographics of women in politics. The in-depth coverage also traces the political heritage of the abolition, labor, suffrage, temperance, and reproductive rights movements. The alphabetically arranged entries include biographies of every woman from across the political spectrum who has served in the U.S. House and Senate, along with women in the Judiciary and the U.S. Cabinet and, new to this edition, biographies of activists and political consultants. Bibliographical references follow each entry. For easy reference, a handy chronology is provided detailing 150 years of women's history. This up-to-date reference will be a must-purchase for women's studies departments, high schools and public libraries and will be a handy resource for those researching the key players in women's politics, past and present.

"An engaging tool that would be useful in high school, public, and academic libraries looking for an overview of the political history of women in the US." –Booklist

Pub. Date: October 2006; Two Volume Set; Hardcover ISBN 1-59237-117-5; $195.00

An African Biographical Dictionary

This landmark second edition is the only biographical dictionary to bring together, in one volume, cultural, social and political leaders – both historical and contemporary – of the sub-Saharan region. Over 800 biographical sketches of prominent Africans, as well as foreigners who have affected the continent's history, are featured, 150 more than the previous edition. The wide spectrum of leaders includes religious figures, writers, politicians, scientists, entertainers, sports personalities and more. Access to these fascinating individuals is provided in a user-friendly format. The biographies are arranged alphabetically, cross-referenced and indexed. Entries include the country or countries in which the person was significant and the commonly accepted dates of birth and death. Each biographical sketch is chronologically written; entries for cultural personalities add an evaluation of their work. This information is followed by a selection of references often found in university and public libraries, including autobiographies and principal biographical works. Appendixes list each individual by country and by field of accomplishment – rulers, musicians, explorers, missionaries, businessmen, physicists – nearly thirty categories in all. Another convenient appendix lists heads of state since independence by country. Up-to-date and representative of African societies as a whole, An African Biographical Dictionary provides a wealth of vital information for students of African culture and is an indispensable reference guide for anyone interested in African affairs.

"An unquestionable convenience to have these concise, informative biographies gathered into one source, indexed, and analyzed by appendixes listing entrants by nation and occupational field." –Wilson Library Bulletin

Pub. Date: July 2006; Hardcover ISBN 1-59237-112-4; $125.00

American Environmental Leaders, From Colonial Times to the Present

A comprehensive and diverse award winning collection of biographies of the most important figures in American environmentalism. Few subjects arouse the passions the way the environment does. How will we feed an ever-increasing population and how can that food be made safe for consumption? Who decides how land is developed? How can environmental policies be made fair for everyone, including multiethnic groups, women, children, and the poor? American Environmental Leaders presents more than 350 biographies of men and women who have devoted their lives to studying, debating, and organizing these and other controversial issues over the last 200 years. In addition to the scientists who have analyzed how human actions affect nature, we are introduced to poets, landscape architects, presidents, painters, activists, even sanitation engineers, and others who have forever altered how we think about the environment. The easy to use A–Z format provides instant access to these fascinating individuals, and frequent cross references indicate others with whom individuals worked (and sometimes clashed). End of entry references provide users with a starting point for further research.

"Highly recommended for high school, academic, and public libraries needing environmental biographical information." –Library Journal/Starred Review

Two Volume Set; Hardcover ISBN 1-57607-385-8 $175.00

World Cultural Leaders of the Twentieth Century

An expansive two volume set that covers 450 worldwide cultural icons, World Cultural Leaders of the Twentieth Century includes each person's works, achievements, and professional careers in a thorough essay. Who was the originator of the term "documentary"? Which poet married the daughter of the famed novelist Thomas Mann in order to help her escape Nazi Germany? Which British writer served as an agent in Russia against the Bolsheviks before the 1917 revolution? These and many more questions are answered in this illuminating text. A handy two volume set that makes it easy to look up 450 worldwide cultural icons: novelists, poets, playwrights, painters, sculptors, architects, dancers, choreographers, actors, directors, filmmakers, singers, composers, and musicians. World Cultural Leaders of the Twentieth Century provides entries (many of them illustrated) covering the person's works, achievements, and professional career in a thorough essay and offers interesting facts and statistics. Entries are fully cross-referenced so that readers can learn how various individuals influenced others. A thorough general index completes the coverage.

"Fills a need for handy, concise information on a wide array of international cultural figures."-ARBA

Two Volume Set; Hardcover ISBN 1-57607-038-7 $175.00

To preview any of our Directories Risk-Free for 30 days, call (800) 562-2139 or fax to (518) 789-0556

Universal Reference Publications
Statistical & Demographic Reference Books

America's Top-Rated Cities, 2007

America's Top-Rated Cities provides current, comprehensive statistical information and other essential data in one easy-to-use source on the 100 "top" cities that have been cited as the best for business and living in the U.S. This handbook allows readers to see, at a glance, a concise social, business, economic, demographic and environmental profile of each city, including brief evaluative comments. In addition to detailed data on Cost of Living, Finances, Real Estate, Education, Major Employers, Media, Crime and Climate, city reports now include Housing Vacancies, Tax Audits, Bankruptcy, Presidential Election Results and more. This outstanding source of information will be widely used in any reference collection.

"The only source of its kind that brings together all of this information into one easy-to-use source. It will be beneficial to many business and public libraries." –ARBA

2,500 pages, 4 Volume Set; Softcover ISBN 1-59237-184-1, $195.00

America's Top-Rated Smaller Cities, 2006/07

A perfect companion to *America's Top-Rated Cities, America's Top-Rated Smaller Cities* provides current, comprehensive business and living profiles of smaller cities (population 25,000-99,999) that have been cited as the best for business and living in the United States. Sixty cities make up this 2004 edition of *America's Top-Rated Smaller Cities,* all are top-ranked by Population Growth, Median Income, Unemployment Rate and Crime Rate. City reports reflect the most current data available on a wide-range of statistics, including Employment & Earnings, Household Income, Unemployment Rate, Population Characteristics, Taxes, Cost of Living, Education, Health Care, Public Safety, Recreation, Media, Air & Water Quality and much more. Plus, each city report contains a Background of the City, and an Overview of the State Finances. *America's Top-Rated Smaller Cities* offers a reliable, one-stop source for statistical data that, before now, could only be found scattered in hundreds of sources. This volume is designed for a wide range of readers: individuals considering relocating a residence or business; professionals considering expanding their business or changing careers; general and market researchers; real estate consultants; human resource personnel; urban planners and investors.

"Provides current, comprehensive statistical information in one easy-to-use source... Recommended for public and academic libraries and specialized collections." –Library Journal

1,100 pages; Softcover ISBN 1-59237-135-3, $160.00

Profiles of America: Facts, Figures & Statistics for Every Populated Place in the United States

Profiles of America is the only source that pulls together, in one place, statistical, historical and descriptive information about every place in the United States in an easy-to-use format. This award winning reference set, now in its second edition, compiles statistics and data from over 20 different sources – the latest census information has been included along with more than nine brand new statistical topics. This Four-Volume Set details over 40,000 places, from the biggest metropolis to the smallest unincorporated hamlet, and provides statistical details and information on over 50 different topics including Geography, Climate, Population, Vital Statistics, Economy, Income, Taxes, Education, Housing, Health & Environment, Public Safety, Newspapers, Transportation, Presidential Election Results and Information Contacts or Chambers of Commerce. Profiles are arranged, for ease-of-use, by state and then by county. Each county begins with a County-Wide Overview and is followed by information for each Community in that particular county. The Community Profiles within the county are arranged alphabetically. *Profiles of America* is a virtual snapshot of America at your fingertips and a unique compilation of information that will be widely used in any reference collection.

A Library Journal Best Reference Book "An outstanding compilation." –Library Journal

10,000 pages; Four Volume Set; Softcover ISBN 1-891482-80-7, $595.00

The Comparative Guide to American Suburbs, 2007

The Comparative Guide to American Suburbs is a one-stop source for Statistics on the 2,000+ suburban communities surrounding the 50 largest metropolitan areas – their population characteristics, income levels, economy, school system and important data on how they compare to one another. Organized into 50 Metropolitan Area chapters, each chapter contains an overview of the Metropolitan Area, a detailed Map followed by a comprehensive Statistical Profile of each Suburban Community, including Contact Information, Physical Characteristics, Population Characteristics, Income, Economy, Unemployment Rate, Cost of Living, Education, Chambers of Commerce and more. Next, statistical data is sorted into Ranking Tables that rank the suburbs by twenty different criteria, including Population, Per Capita Income, Unemployment Rate, Crime Rate, Cost of Living and more. *The Comparative Guide to American Suburbs* is the best source for locating data on suburbs. Those looking to relocate, as well as those doing preliminary market research, will find this an invaluable timesaving resource.

"Public and academic libraries will find this compilation useful... The work draws together figures from many sources and will be especially helpful for job relocation decisions." – Booklist

1,700 pages; Softcover ISBN 1-59237-180-9, $130.00

To preview any of our Directories Risk-Free for 30 days, call (800) 562-2139 or fax to (518) 789-0556

Crime in America's Top-Rated Cities

This volume includes over 20 years of crime statistics in all major crime categories: violent crimes, property crimes and total crime. *Crime in America's Top-Rated Cities* is conveniently arranged by city and covers 76 top-rated cities. *Crime in America's Top-Rated Cities* offers details that compare the number of crimes and crime rates for the city, suburbs and metro area along with national crime trends for violent, property and total crimes. Also, this handbook contains important information and statistics on Anti-Crime Programs, Crime Risk, Hate Crimes, Illegal Drugs, Law Enforcement, Correctional Facilities, Death Penalty Laws and much more. A much-needed resource for people who are relocating, business professionals, general researchers, the press, law enforcement officials and students of criminal justice.

"Data is easy to access and will save hours of searching." –Global Enforcement Review

832 pages; Softcover ISBN 1-891482-84-X, $155.00

The Asian Databook: Statistics for all US Counties & Cities with Over 10,000 Population

This is the first-ever resource that compiles statistics and rankings on the US Asian population. *The Asian Databook* presents over 20 statistical data points for each city and county, arranged alphabetically by state, then alphabetically by place name. Data reported for each place includes Population, Languages Spoken at Home, Foreign-Born, Educational Attainment, Income Figures, Poverty Status, Homeownership, Home Values & Rent, and more. Next, in the Rankings Section, the top 75 places are listed for each data element. These easy-to-access ranking tables allow the user to quickly determine trends and population characteristics. This kind of comparative data can not be found elsewhere, in print or on the web, in a format that's as easy-to-use or more concise. A useful resource for those searching for demographics data, career search and relocation information and also for market research. With data ranging from Ancestry to Education, *The Asian Databook* presents a useful compilation of information that will be a much-needed resource in the reference collection of any public or academic library along with the marketing collection of any company whose primary focus in on the Asian population.

1,000 pages; Softcover ISBN 1-59237-044-6 $150.00

The Hispanic Databook: Statistics for all US Counties & Cities with Over 10,000 Population

Previously published by Toucan Valley Publications, this second edition has been completely updated with figures from the latest census and has been broadly expanded to include dozens of new data elements and a brand new Rankings section. The Hispanic population in the United States has increased over 42% in the last 10 years and accounts for 12.5% of the total US population. For ease-of-use, *The Hispanic Databook* presents over 20 statistical data points for each city and county, arranged alphabetically by state, then alphabetically by place name. Data reported for each place includes Population, Languages Spoken at Home, Foreign-Born, Educational Attainment, Income Figures, Poverty Status, Homeownership, Home Values & Rent, and more. Next, in the Rankings Section, the top 75 places are listed for each data element. These easy-to-access ranking tables allow the user to quickly determine trends and population characteristics. This kind of comparative data can not be found elsewhere, in print or on the web, in a format that's as easy-to-use or more concise. A useful resource for those searching for demographics data, career search and relocation information and also for market research. With data ranging from Ancestry to Education, *The Hispanic Databook* presents a useful compilation of information that will be a much-needed resource in the reference collection of any public or academic library along with the marketing collection of any company whose primary focus in on the Hispanic population.

"This accurate, clearly presented volume of selected Hispanic demographics is recommended for large public libraries and research collections."-Library Journal

1,000 pages; Softcover ISBN 1-59237-008-X, $150.00

The American Tally: Statistics & Comparative Rankings for U.S. Cities with Populations over 10,000

This important statistical handbook compiles, all in one place, comparative statistics on all U.S. cities and towns with a 10,000+ population. *The American Tally* provides statistical details on over 4,000 cities and towns and profiles how they compare with one another in Population Characteristics, Education, Language & Immigration, Income & Employment and Housing. Each section begins with an alphabetical listing of cities by state, allowing for quick access to both the statistics and relative rankings of any city. Next, the highest and lowest cities are listed in each statistic. These important, informative lists provide quick reference to which cities are at both extremes of the spectrum for each statistic. Unlike any other reference, *The American Tally* provides quick, easy access to comparative statistics – a must-have for any reference collection.

"A solid library reference." -Bookwatch

500 pages; Softcover ISBN 1-930956-29-0, $125.00

Ancestry in America: A Comparative Guide to Over 200 Ethnic Backgrounds

This brand new reference work pulls together thousands of comparative statistics on the Ethnic Backgrounds of all populated places in the United States with populations over 10,000. Never before has this kind of information been reported in a single volume. Section One, Statistics by Place, is made up of a list of over 200 ancestry and race categories arranged alphabetically by each of the 5,000 different places with populations over 10,000. The population number of the ancestry group in that city or town is provided along with the percent that group represents of the total population. This informative city-by-city section allows the user to quickly and easily explore the ethnic makeup of all major population bases in the United States. Section Two, Comparative Rankings, contains three tables for each ethnicity and race. In the first table, the top 150 populated places are ranked by population number for that particular ancestry group, regardless of population. In the second table, the top 150 populated places are ranked by the percent of the total population for that ancestry group. In the third table, those top 150 populated places with 10,000 population are ranked by population number for each ancestry group. These easy-to-navigate tables allow users to see ancestry population patterns and make city-by-city comparisons as well. Plus, as an added bonus with the purchase of *Ancestry in America*, a free companion CD-ROM is available that lists statistics and rankings for all of the 35,000 populated places in the United States. This brand new, information-packed resource will serve a wide-range or research requests for demographics, population characteristics, relocation information and much more. *Ancestry in America: A Comparative Guide to Over 200 Ethnic Backgrounds* will be an important acquisition to all reference collections.

"This compilation will serve a wide range of research requests for population characteristics ... it offers much more detail than other sources." –Booklist

1,500 pages; Softcover ISBN 1-59237-029-2, $225.00

The Environmental Resource Handbook, 2007/08

The Environmental Resource Handbook is the most up-to-date and comprehensive source for Environmental Resources and Statistics. Section I: Resources provides detailed contact information for thousands of information sources, including Associations & Organizations, Awards & Honors, Conferences, Foundations & Grants, Environmental Health, Government Agencies, National Parks & Wildlife Refuges, Publications, Research Centers, Educational Programs, Green Product Catalogs, Consultants and much more. Section II: Statistics, provides statistics and rankings on hundreds of important topics, including Children's Environmental Index, Municipal Finances, Toxic Chemicals, Recycling, Climate, Air & Water Quality and more. This kind of up-to-date environmental data, all in one place, is not available anywhere else on the market place today. This vast compilation of resources and statistics is a must-have for all public and academic libraries as well as any organization with a primary focus on the environment.

"...the intrinsic value of the information make it worth consideration by libraries with environmental collections and environmentally concerned users." –Booklist

1,000 pages; Softcover ISBN 1-59237-195-7, $155.00 ◆ Online Database $300.00

Weather America, A Thirty-Year Summary of Statistical Weather Data and Rankings

This valuable resource provides extensive climatological data for over 4,000 National and Cooperative Weather Stations throughout the United States. *Weather America* begins with a new Major Storms section that details major storm events of the nation and a National Rankings section that details rankings for several data elements, such as Maximum Temperature and Precipitation. The main body of *Weather America* is organized into 50 state sections. Each section provides a Data Table on each Weather Station, organized alphabetically, that provides statistics on Maximum and Minimum Temperatures, Precipitation, Snowfall, Extreme Temperatures, Foggy Days, Humidity and more. State sections contain two brand new features in this edition – a City Index and a narrative Description of the climatic conditions of the state. Each section also includes a revised Map of the State that includes not only weather stations, but cities and towns.

"Best Reference Book of the Year." –Library Journal

2,013 pages; Softcover ISBN 1-891482-29-7, $175.00

Older Americans Information Directory, 2006/07

Completely updated for 2006/07, this sixth edition has been completely revised and now contains 1,000 new listings, over 8,000 updates to existing listings and over 3,000 brand new e-mail addresses and web sites. You'll find important resources for Older Americans including National, Regional, State & Local Organizations, Government Agencies, Research Centers, Libraries & Information Centers, Legal Resources, Discount Travel Information, Continuing Education Programs, Disability Aids & Assistive Devices, Health, Print Media and Electronic Media. Three indexes: Entry Index, Subject Index and Geographic Index make it easy to find just the right source of information. This comprehensive guide to resources for Older Americans will be a welcome addition to any reference collection.

"Highly recommended for academic, public, health science and consumer libraries…" –Choice

1,200 pages; Softcover ISBN 1-59237-136-1, $165.00 ◆ Online Database $215.00 ◆ Online Database & Directory Combo $300.00

The Complete Directory for Pediatric Disorders, 2007

This important directory provides parents and caregivers with information about Pediatric Conditions, Disorders, Diseases and Disabilities, including Blood Disorders, Bone & Spinal Disorders, Brain Defects & Abnormalities, Chromosomal Disorders, Congenital Heart Defects, Movement Disorders, Neuromuscular Disorders and Pediatric Tumors & Cancers. This carefully written directory offers: understandable Descriptions of 15 major bodily systems; Descriptions of more than 200 Disorders and a Resources Section, detailing National Agencies & Associations, State Associations, Online Services, Libraries & Resource Centers, Research Centers, Support Groups & Hotlines, Camps, Books and Periodicals. This resource will provide immediate access to information crucial to families and caregivers when coping with children's illnesses.

"Recommended for public and consumer health libraries." –Library Journal

1,200 pages; Softcover ISBN 1-59237-150-7 $165.00 ◆ Online Database $215.00 ◆ Online Database & Directory Combo $300.00

The Directory of Drug & Alcohol Residential Rehabilitation Facilities

This brand new directory is the first-ever resource to bring together, all in one place, data on the thousands of drug and alcohol residential rehabilitation facilities in the United States. *The Directory of Drug & Alcohol Residential Rehabilitation Facilities* covers over 1,000 facilities, with detailed contact information for each one, including mailing address, phone and fax numbers, email addresses and web sites, mission statement, type of treatment programs, cost, average length of stay, numbers of residents and counselors, accreditation, insurance plans accepted, type of environment, religious affiliation, education components and much more. It also contains a helpful chapter on General Resources that provides contact information for Associations, Print & Electronic Media, Support Groups and Conferences. Multiple indexes allow the user to pinpoint the facilities that meet very specific criteria. This time-saving tool is what so many counselors, parents and medical professionals have been asking for. *The Directory of Drug & Alcohol Residential Rehabilitation Facilities* will be a helpful tool in locating the right source for treatment for a wide range of individuals. This comprehensive directory will be an important acquisition for all reference collections: public and academic libraries, case managers, social workers, state agencies and many more.

"This is an excellent, much needed directory that fills an important gap…" –Booklist

300 pages; Softcover ISBN 1-59237-031-4, $135.00

Sedgwick Press
Education Directories

The Comparative Guide to American Elementary & Secondary Schools, 2007

The only guide of its kind, this award winning compilation offers a snapshot profile of every public school district in the United States serving 1,500 or more students – more than 5,900 districts are covered. Organized alphabetically by district within state, each chapter begins with a Statistical Overview of the state. Each district listing includes contact information (name, address, phone number and web site) plus Grades Served, the Numbers of Students and Teachers and the Number of Regular, Special Education, Alternative and Vocational Schools in the district along with statistics on Student/Classroom Teacher Ratios, Drop Out Rates, Ethnicity, the Numbers of Librarians and Guidance Counselors and District Expenditures per student. As an added bonus, *The Comparative Guide to American Elementary and Secondary Schools* provides important ranking tables, both by state and nationally, for each data element. For easy navigation through this wealth of information, this handbook contains a useful City Index that lists all districts that operate schools within a city. These important comparative statistics are necessary for anyone considering relocation or doing comparative research on their own district and would be a perfect acquisition for any public library or school district library.

"This straightforward guide is an easy way to find general information. Valuable for academic and large public library collections." –ARBA

2,400 pages; Softcover ISBN 1-59237-223-6, $125.00

Educators Resource Directory, 2007/08

Educators Resource Directory is a comprehensive resource that provides the educational professional with thousands of resources and statistical data for professional development. This directory saves hours of research time by providing immediate access to Associations & Organizations, Conferences & Trade Shows, Educational Research Centers, Employment Opportunities & Teaching Abroad, School Library Services, Scholarships, Financial Resources, Professional Consultants, Computer Software & Testing Resources and much more. Plus, this comprehensive directory also includes a section on Statistics and Rankings with over 100 tables, including statistics on Average Teacher Salaries, SAT/ACT scores, Revenues & Expenditures and more. These important statistics will allow the user to see how their school rates among others, make relocation decisions and so much more. For quick access to information, this directory contains four indexes: Entry & Publisher Index, Geographic Index, a Subject & Grade Index and Web Sites Index. *Educators Resource Directory* will be a well-used addition to the reference collection of any school district, education department or public library.

"Recommended for all collections that serve elementary and secondary school professionals." –Choice

1,000 pages; Softcover ISBN 1-59237-179-5, $145.00 ◆ Online Database $195.00 ◆ Online Database & Directory Combo $280.00